From the Library of:
Baldwin Local
History Collection

106TH EDITION

Photograph by Karsh of Ottawa, 1985, © Camera Press, London

HM The Queen

BURKE'S PEERAGE & BARONETAGE

106TH EDITION

EDITOR-IN-CHIEF
CHARLES MOSLEY

VOLUME I
ABDY–LANGRISHE

To 'This royal throne of kings, this scepter'd isle'

Morris Genealogical Books SA
owners of
Burke's Peerage (Genealogical Books) Ltd

Published by
Burke's Peerage (Genealogical Books) Ltd
7 rue du Bugnon
1299 Crans
Switzerland

Tel: +4122 776 5109
Fax: +4122 776 0889
Editorial email: CMosley@compuserve.com

ISBN 2-940085-02-1

While the publisher makes every effort possible to publish full and correct information in these volumes, sometimes errors of omission or substance may occur. For this the publisher is most regretful, but hereby must disclaim any liability.

Distributed by
Morris Genealogical Books SA
c/o RotoVision SA
Sheridan House
112–116 Western Road
Hove BN3 1DD
UK

Tel: (+44) 1273 716026
Fax: (+44) 1273 727269
email: brianm@rotovision.com

Published for libraries worldwide by
Fitzroy Dearborn Publishers

919 North Michigan Avenue
Chicago
Illinois 60611
USA

Tel: (+1) 312 587 0131
Fax: (+1) 312 587 1049

310 Regent Street
London
W1R 5AJ
England

Tel: (+44) 171 636 6627
Fax: (+44) 171 636 6982

ISBN 1-57958-083-1

Burke's logo designed by Clive Spring, Brighton, England
Technical support, design, layout and preparation by Bookcraft Ltd, Stroud, England
Production by Provision Pte Ltd, Singapore
Printed and bound in Hong Kong

Publisher's Preface

Brian Morris

This 106th edition of *Burke's Peerage & Baronetage* is the first since 1970, that is, for 29 years. Indeed in purely editorial terms the gap is more like 30 years. In the pre-computer era of the late 1960s it was necessary to finish the editorial process much further in advance of publication, too soon to include many members of peerage or baronetage families born about then. In genealogical terms that amounts to roughly two 'lost' generations. The newly born children of 1970 have now grown up and begotten their own children. With the publication of the 106th edition it is possible to include them. Perhaps up to half the living persons in *Burke's Peerage & Baronetage* have never featured in it before.

The new edition is the result of five years' unremitting toil by a full-time editorial team of eleven. They have been supplemented by seven outside researchers, copy editors and proofreaders, who in turn have been backed up by the services of distinguished consultants in such specialised fields as Celtic family history, heraldry and peerage law. Still further information has been obtained through the goodwill, diligence and generosity with their time of members of the two and a half thousand or so families who feature in *Burke's Peerage & Baronetage* and to whom we have sent proofs of their entries.

Sir Bernard Burke, one of the former editors of *Burke's Peerage & Baronetage*, was in addition the author of a book entitled the *Vicissitudes of Families*. The historic reference book he gave his name to has undergone its own vicissitudes. In 1980 there was an incomplete reissue of the 105th edition. Since the mid-1980s its authority and prestige have been exploited for crudely commercial ends by persons displaying minimal concern for scholarship or indeed serious genealogical publishing generally. It cannot be stated too emphatically that such persons have nothing whatever to do directly with this publication, *Burke's Peerage & Baronetage*.

Since the purchase by Morris Genealogical Books SA in 1989 of Burke's Peerage (Genealogical Books) Ltd (the copyright holder of *Burke's Peerage & Baronetage*), both I as publisher and the Editor-in-Chief, Charles Mosley, have been dedicated to restoring the good name and scholarly content of this cornerstone of British publishing. Though it is a reference work, indeed a major one, *Burke's Peerage & Baronetage* is much more. It amounts to a narrative of the leading families in these islands and shows how they have played a formative role in shaping the civilisation of the entire English-speaking world. In that context it complements *American Presidential Families*, the other major work published by Morris Genealogical Books, which traces the remarkable number of links between the first families of the United States and those in *Burke's Peerage & Baronetage*.

The 106th edition contains many innovations and improvements. The following are particularly worth noting:

- The larger format and change of typeface to enhance legibility and ease of use.
- The inclusion of many more titles following the proliferation of life peers, continuing additions to the hereditary peerage and baronetage, however small, and historic titles brought out of abeyance or dormancy.
- The inclusion of many more collateral branches, particularly where they are related to other families in *Burke's Peerage & Baronetage*. We now include for the first time since their titles became extinct figures of national importance such as Pitt the Elder, Pitt the Younger and Lord Palmerston.
- Details of political and court appointments of peers and baronets, both living and dead.
- An index of living people which extends to over 200 pages and includes some 100,000 names.
- A description and history of leading family seats.
- An account of previous creations of identically named titles. As this work covers over 1,000 years of history, many titles have been created several times and cross-references in other articles to a given title do not necessarily signify the present one. Where such is the case it is now made clear.
- The inclusion of nearly 30,000 addresses of living people, together with their correct form of written address.
- Translations of family mottoes.
- The inclusion of much new and revised Celtic genealogy.
- Thorough consultation of advances in scholarship over the last century, and correction of many past errors.

As with any work, particularly of this magnitude, inaccuracies and omissions may occur. The *Burke's Peerage & Baronetage* editorial staff are only human; so too are our correspondents, who sometimes compose letters containing genealogical information that is illegible, exaggerated or internally inconsistent. We have even at times received contradictory information from different members of the same family. Unfortunately, the urgency of meeting our editorial schedule has not always permitted us to clarify matters. We fully intend to correct any such errors in future editions, and our readers are cordially invited to inform us of any changes or additions which should be incorporated.

Acknowledgements

The publisher wishes to thank all those people whose dedication and hard work have made this 106th edition possible: Charles Mosley, Editor-in-Chief, whose knowledge of the subject and attention to detail are equal to none; Lt-Cdr Peter Hinton MBE, Maj James Johnston and Roger Powell, senior editors; Tricia Badham, Sandra Banbury, Mary Banks, Carol Glover, Anne Griffiths, Helen Major, Bawn O'Beirne-Ranelagh, Debbie Postlethwaite and Judy Robson, junior editors and researchers; the outside experts Sir Crispin Agnew of Lochnaw, Rothesay Herald of Arms; Max Craven, of the Derbyshire Record Office; Frederick Hogarth; Cecil Humphery-Smith, of the Institute of Heraldic and Genealogical Studies; Sir Malcolm Innes of Edingight, Lord Lyon King of Arms; Charles Lysaght; Kenneth Nicholls, Statutory Lecturer, University College Cork; Len Nicol and Ted Sparrow of Fileset, who put the text of the 105th edition of *Burke's Peerage and Baronetage* into computer files; Dr Michael Siddons, Wales Herald Extraordinary; the staff of the House of Lords Library; Mr P C Thompson of the King's School, Worcester; Peter Townend, former editor of *Burke's Peerage & Baronetage*; and Thomas Woodcock, Norroy and Ulster King of Arms.

Thanks also to Bookcraft Ltd, who have made the production of such a massive work technically possible: John Button who, as project manager, oversaw each stage of the process; Katy Elphinstone who redrew the coats of arms; Caroline Sheldrick who undertook the bulk of the indexing; Jessica Standing and Kim Wilkins who organised the mailing of proofs; Mary Barton, Jessica Bale and Philippa Morgan who were responsible for incorporating thousands of additions and amendments; and Posy Gosling, for final proofreading.

CONTENTS

VOLUME I

The following list includes courtesy titles (for a definition of which *see* Glossary). Not all such titles are currently in use, but they have been so historically and could be again. They are shown here in upper and lower case with a cross-reference (e.g. Aberdour, Lord, *see* MORTON) to the substantive title. Since all title holders are listed here they do not appear in the Index as well, unless they are mentioned in an entirely different article through a connection by marriage.

VOLUME II

INTRODUCTION

CHARLES MOSLEY

In 1826 John Burke (1786–1848), of a minor landed gentry family from Co Tipperary, Ireland, published the first edition of the reference book that was to become famous as *Burke's Peerage & Baronetage*. The full, even prolix, title then was *A general and Heraldic Dictionary of the Peerage and Baronetage of the United Kingdom for MDCCCXXVI. Exhibiting, under strict alphabetical arrangement, The Present State of those exalted Ranks, with their Armorial Bearings, Mottoes etc., And deducing the Lineage of each House from the Founder of its Honors* [sic]. *With an Appendix, comprising the Prelates, the Surnames of Peers, Titles by courtesy of their eldest sons, Names of Heirs Presumptive, etc. etc.*

Other reference books on the nobility already existed, among them *Debrett's*, which survives to this day. But they tended to arrange each family according to whatever position its head enjoyed in the Table of Precedence, and specifically, if the family dealt with had a peerage, according to whether the title was a creation in the Peerage of England, Scotland, Ireland, Great Britain or the United Kingdom. A taxonomy like that presupposed in the reader encyclopaedic knowledge of the date of a title's creation and its precise rank, to say nothing of which constituent polity that creation had been in out of the five that had eventually coalesced to form the United Kingdom. In practice even Garter King of Arms or a Regius Professor of History would have had difficulty finding his way around such books.

Burke's Peerage & Baronetage was therefore revolutionary, or, to use a modern expression, 'user-friendly', despite the obsequious treatment of its subject matter which is already evident in the original title quoted above and which was *de rigueur* for all such books then. Its success was swift, not just because it arranged material sensibly but because it sketched the history of the families as far back as possible, often well before the conferring of the extant title — and sometimes further back than was strictly warrantable according to historical evidence.

It also started the arrangement of the founder of a branch of a family on the left-hand margin and the indentation of successive generations (the founder's descendants, in other words) a set space to the right. By and large it now became possible to trace fairly remote family connections without having to spread a huge sheet of paper on a surface the size of a billiard table. That layout was something of a house speciality and has remained one ever since, making it much easier to read than rival publications. Further innovations included placing illustrations of coats of arms at the top of a family's entry, as happened from the 4th edition of 1833 onwards.

John Burke continued as sole editor till the 9th edition in 1847, when for the first time his younger son John Bernard Burke featured on the title page as co-editor. A single further co-edition followed the next year, after which the sole editor was John Bernard (or J Bernard then Bernard as he began to call himself, particularly from 1854, when as Ulster King of Arms, that is to say a senior herald, he was knighted).

The early editions came out at roughly two-year intervals. From 1840 to 1917 inclusive (and again from 1923 to 1940) *Burke's Peerage & Baronetage* was an annual. Although Sir Bernard died in 1892 his name was kept on the title page, doubtless for commercial reasons, till 1899 and inserted again for the 1906–17 editions, at first with the rider 'edited by his sons' then with the names of Sir Henry, his eldest son, or Ashworth P, his fourth son, as co-editors. There was some justification for this since much of the florid narrative dealing with the early histories of the various families was Sir Bernard's and remained in print (and unrevised) long after his death.

But it was also a pity, less on stylistic grounds than on those of scholarship. Sir Bernard had a tendency to treat family legend as historical fact — an unjustifiable attitude in any reference book editor but doubly so in someone who was Ulster King of Arms. And many such legends were not even of great antiquity. Like other supposedly immemorial traditions, they had actually been invented by the Victorians. Sir Bernard's eldest son Sir Henry had a more distinguished career in official terms, reaching the top of the herald's tree as Garter King of Arms, but he published less than his father and was only featured as co-editor of two editions, the 1897 and 1898 ones. It is possible that had he been involved for longer the pruning of fantasy from what was supposed to be a work of non-fiction would have occurred earlier. As it was, only the savage philippics of J Horace Round from the 1890s onwards, following the researches of serious historians like Maitland, Stubbs and Tout, resulted in *Burke's Peerage & Baronetage* attaining anything like comprehensive veracity, and even then it was somewhat belatedly.

What were called new editions had throughout the 19th century often consisted of a previous edition plus an appendix. The great problem with a work the size, complexity and tendency to obsolescence of *Burke's Peerage & Baronetage* was to amend old material, add new material, typeset it all over again and re-index it without incurring unsustainable costs. What is impressive about the 19th- and early 20th-century editions is nevertheless the sheer amount of detail they contain for an era lacking computer technology. Some of them even have hand-coloured plates of coats of arms. To include those today would push the price of a copy into the thousands of pounds.

The Burke connection was broken in 1919 with the death unmarried of Ashworth, for although Sir Henry did not die till 1930 he had long ceased to be involved with the most famous of the family reference books. Nevertheless the prestige of the work as *Burke's Peerage & Baronetage* was by now well established and the title has continued to be so called to the present day. The 1921 edition was brought out under the editorship of Mr A Winton Thorpe; the next one, in 1923, under that of Mr Alfred T Butler, Sir Henry Burke's secretary. From 1927 to 1934 Butler and a Miss E M Swinhoe were listed as co-editors. She continued as sole editor of the 1935, 1936 and 1937 issues, following which a Mr Smallshaw took over, though his name is not mentioned on the title page of the 1938, 1939 or 1940 editions. The last of these was little more than a set of corrigenda to the 1939 one anyway. During World War II the late Baron de Spon, member of a family of minor nobility originating in Mainz, in the German Rhineland, acted as caretaker editor, keeping up genealogical records, although he never in fact presided over a new edition. Baron de Spon only died in late 1998. For the 1949, 1953, 1956 and 1959 editions Mr Leslie G Pine was in editorial charge and for the 1963, 1967 and 1970 ones Mr Peter Townend, who has also given help with this edition.

By the early 20th century there were really only two names synonymous with works on the titled families of the British Isles: Burke's and Debrett's. The commercial potential of owning such trade titles began to have some attraction, though perhaps less so than the social cachet. A Mr Mallaby-Deeley (*see* 1959 edn DEELEY, Bt) was among the proprietors of *Burke's Peerage & Baronetage* at one stage, following which a US-owned publishing imprint called Shaw's Reference Series acquired control, then the Mercury House Group and later still the Holdway Group. The last of these companies, represented by Mr Jeremy Norman (*see* NORMAN, Bt), who was Chairman and Managing Director of Burke's Peerage Ltd from 1974 to 1984, in 1973 bought the rights to the Burke's series of publications, which included such titles as *Burke's Landed Gentry*. Hugh Montgomery-Massingberd (*see* RIPLEY, Bt), as he then was (he has subsequently dropped the 'Montgomery-'), was installed as Executive Editor then Editorial Director and an ambitious publishing programme embarked upon. No new edition of *Burke's Peerage & Baronetage* appeared, it is true, but some extremely useful works on the genealogies of the British and other royal families were brought out, as were works on country houses in the British Isles and an updating of the *Landed Gentry of Ireland* renamed *Irish Family Records*.

Sadly, the programme was never brought to fruition. Rights to the Burke's series went different ways. Those to *Burke's Peerage & Baronetage*, what would now be called the 'flagship' publication, vested in a company called Burke's Peerage (Genealogical Books) Ltd and were acquired by Baron Frederick van Pallandt, who is better known as the 'Frederick' of the 1960s singing duo Nina and Frederick and who was murdered in Thailand a few years ago. From him it passed into the hands of a Mr Joseph Goldberg, who in 1980 brought out a second impression of the 1970 edition, that is to say a straightforward reprinting without any updating whatsoever. In 1989 ownership was acquired by Mr Brian Morris, who was already a publisher. He remains the proprietor and has brought out the present 106th edition, which is a thorough updating and widespread revision of the 1970 edition, not just a second printing.

A wholly separate company called The Burke's Partnership or some other permutation of the Burke's name, which owned rights to most of the other titles, was acquired out of receivership by people associated with the former company, by now defunct. The new owners issued numerous press releases but to this day have not brought out a new edition of even one of the old titles. It was not the first time *Burke's Peerage & Baronetage* and a title originally associated with it had been owned separately. In the 1920s J Maundy Gregory, who touted peerages and baronetcies to war profiteers on behalf of Lloyd George, held rights to *Burke's Landed Gentry*, though not *Burke's Peerage & Baronetage* itself. It should by now be clear that it is important to make a distinction between *Burke's Peerage & Baronetage*, the actual publication, and whatever may issue forth from the offices of whoever owns 'Burke's Peerage'.

Mention has already been made of *Debrett's Peerage*, and since there is a widespread tendency in the public to confuse it with *Burke's Peerage & Baronetage*, some account of the differences may prove useful. *Debrett's* divides up its material, putting the peers in one section and the baronets in another. *Burke's Peerage & Baronetage* lists peers and baronets together alphabetically. If there is a peerage and baronetcy with the same name, Chichester for example, the peer is listed before the baronet since he is of higher rank. If there is more than one baronet with the same name, for example Clark, *Debretts* lists them in order of their date of creation but *Burke's Peerage & Baronetage* lists them in alphabetical order of the place of domicile of the first holder of the title. Clark of Dunlambert, for instance, comes before Clark of Melville Crescent.

Baronets do not in fact have an official territorial designation in the way peers do, but since JAMES I's pledge to limit their numbers was abandoned from quite soon after the institution of the order it has long been found useful to be able to distinguish between them, the existence of more than one with the same name occurring from very early on in the history of the Baronetage. Where a peer has a territorial qualifying phrase as part of his full title, for example 'Lord Wilson of Tillyorn', the former Governor of Hong Kong elevated to the House of Lords and so designated to distinguish him from the Lord Wilson who is a hereditary peer, we place him after all other Wilsons whether a peer or baronet provided their titles are Wilson only. The distinguishing marks in such cases are that the peer with a territorial qualifying phrase as part of his full title is printed all in capital letters, whereas the baronets with the same name but different places of origin have the latter in capital letters and small ones. Accordingly the order goes WILSON, Baron; WILSON, Bt, of Airdrie; WILSON, Bt, of Carbeth; WILSON, Bt, of Eshton Hall; WILSON OF TILLYORN.

Unlike *Debrett's*, *Burke's Peerage & Baronetage* is primarily a history of the families it features rather than a publication that concentrates on the current title-holders. Both publications used to alphabetise multiple-barrelled names under the initial letter of the last barrel rather than of the first one on the grounds that the last barrel represented the original family, onto which was grafted the names of other families marrying into it and perhaps bringing with them estates or other forms of wealth. *Burke's Peerage & Baronetage* has now ceased this quaint custom, not just because it confused the general reader but because it was not even invariably justified by the history of the family in question. *Debrett's* lists the names of holders of minor courtesy titles between its peerage section and the baronetage one (whereas the major ones — direct heirs of earls, marquesses and dukes — it lists with cross references in the main pages). The list indicates which peerage articles they appear in. The new edition of *Burke's Peerage & Baronetage* contains an index of living persons featured in its pages, whether holders of courtesy titles or not, and including members of baronetage families as well as of peerage ones. Lastly, the *Burke's Peerage & Baronetage* method of indenting successive generations, already mentioned in the brief history given above, is very different from *Debrett's* layout, where successive generations stemming from a common ancestor are gathered in a single paragraph and as far as the eye of the reader is concerned are differentiated as to their relationship one to another chiefly by long or short dashes.

Enquiries from the public evincing yet further confusion suggest that a further distinction needs to be made here between *Burke's Peerage & Baronetage* and *Who's Who*. The latter covers only living people whereas *Burke's Peerage & Baronetage*'s concentration on family history means that it includes people who lived up to a thousand years ago. People are only selected for an entry in *Who's Who* if they have attained some personal as opposed to family distinction. Nevertheless, a remarkable selection of celebrities in their own right feature in *Burke's Peerage & Baronetage* too, for instance the jockey turned race horse-trainer Luca Cumani (PLUNKET), the novelist Mary Wesley (SWINFEN) and the singer Roger Whitaker (INCHIQUIN). *Who's Who* is primarily autobiographical in that the people it features draft their entries themselves. *Burke's Peerage & Baronetage* carries out its own research on the people it features as well as asking them to supply information directly.

So much for *Burke's Peerage & Baronetage* itself and the history of it over the last 172 years. What of developments in its subject matter, that is to say the history of the families that hold titles of honour and the titles themselves? Here it is instructive to compare the situation when the last edition came out with that now, when the present edition is published.

In 1970 inflation was in its infancy, losses at Lloyd's were well in the future and British overseas possessions or bases were still extensive. The consequences of the first two have been fully covered in numerous books of social and economic history. As regards their immediate effect on *Burke's Peerage & Baronetage* families it is sufficient here to say that the diminution in the number of family seats since 1970 has been very noticeable. The consequences of the diminution in British overseas commitments since 1970, although also fully covered in purely geopolitical terms, has had one very interesting sociological sequel which has not been covered at all.

It is nothing less than the enormous drop in what one might broadly call long-term upper-class involvement in the armed forces, the severing of a connection which till the last 15 years or so had persisted for centuries, as a glance at a typical *Burke's Peerage & Baronetage* family entry for any prior period will testify. As recently as the early 1980s announcements of promotions in the Army and Navy were essential regular reading for editors of reference works such as *Burke's Peerage & Baronetage* because so many members of the families featured had sons (and very occasionally daughters) in those services. That is now no longer the case, although any sensible editor does of course still keep an eye on promotions.

The reasons are probably not just the shrinking of Britain's world role but the need for members of previously comfortably-off families to find more lucrative employment than fighting. The change is not just sociological. It is symbolic, even atavistic. The oldest families in *Burke's Peerage & Baronetage*, and implicitly the peerage as an institution, were originally supportive of the early-medieval kings as a fighting caste. Success in the battlefield remained a sure route to ennoblement long after the tenure of land by military service had become obsolete. Until the late 19th century many families who might until then have had no title but who were of ancient lineage (*see* for example MARLBOROUGH, WELLINGTON and the section on the Viscountcy of Wolseley in WOLSELEY of Mount Wolseley) became the recipients of hereditary honours because of a single member's military record.

The most obvious alternative career since the attrition of the armed services is finance. It would probably be fair to say that *Burke's Peerage & Baronetage* families have a disproportionate number of members involved in that field compared with other British Isles families. But there has also been a noticeable drift into the media. Employment in that field is sometimes extremely lucrative, but for the most part is not. One can therefore only hazard a guess that it is popular because it offers the sort of prospects for fame, perhaps even glory, that a military career used to do. Some of the media people in *Burke's Peerage & Baronetage*, like Lords Deedes and Rees-Mogg (*qqv*) and Bamber Gascoigne (O'NEILL, B), have been involved for decades. Others, like Richard Attenborough (*qv*) or Melvyn Bragg (*see* ADDENDA), have only been ennobled at all because they were media personalities in the first place. But the majority are people who have entered media-related professions over a period extending back to the 1970s. And their family connections presumably have nothing to do with their prominence in it.

They include The Hon Dominic Lawson, Editor of the *Sunday Telegraph* (LAWSON OF BLABY), Charles Moore, Editor of the *Daily Telegraph* (MOORE of Hancox), Ferdinand Mount, Editor of the *Times Literary Supplement* (MOUNT), and among former editors, freelances or staffers Simon Blow (TOLLEMACHE, Baron), Craig Brown (BETHELL), Cressida Connolly (CRAIGAVON), Nigel Dempster (QUEENSBERRY), A A Gill (CRAIGAVON), Julian Havilland (FERGUSSON), Richard Ingrams (REID of Ellon), Henry Porter (HERTFORD) and Miranda Seymour (HERTFORD). Among the family of PAGET of Cranmore Hall the media kinship pattern approximates to a dynasty within a dynasty. The novelist Will Self is married to the sister of the actress Anna Chancellor who appeared in *Four Weddings and a Funeral*. Her uncle the columnist Alexander Chancellor is father-in-law of Auberon Waugh's son Alexander and brother-in-law of the late John Wells, the satirist. On a smaller scale there is the family connection between Alan Rusbridger, editor of the *Guardian*, and his nephew-in-law Ian Aitken, that newspaper's political editor till 1990 and still a columnist on it (MACKIE OF BENSHIE).

Mention of Anna Chancellor is a reminder that actors and actresses have long been connected with peerage and baronetage families — film directors too, though on a much more modest scale. Most of the links have arisen through marriage — Robert Donat (WISEMAN), Shirley Anne Field (BUTE), Michael Gough (LEON), Jamie Leigh Curtis (HADEN-GUEST), Miles Malleson (ANNESLEY), David Niven (ROLLO), Fiona Richmond (MONTGOMERY), Diana Rigg (HERON-MAXWELL) — but not all. Maria Aitken (BEAVERBROOK), Jane Asher (SAINT GERMANS), Rupert Everett (VYVYAN), Ralph Fiennes (SAYE AND SELE) and Dennis Price (PRICE) are 'natives' in that they have been born into the relevant families.

Acting and the media have ceased to be unrespectable in all except the stuffiest families. With illegitimacy it is less easy to be certain. It has increased enormously over the last three decades. To omit illegitimate children from *Burke's Peerage & Baronetage* would not make sense, partly because a number of titles have been specifically created for bastards (and not just royal ones), a fact former editions have been announcing for some decades now, but chiefly because in certain circumstances an illegitimate child can be brought back into remainder (*see* Glossary) to a title by the subsequent marriage of his or her parents (*see* Thomas Woodcock article). Indeed if one were to hush up such episodes altogether one would have to commit the ultimate folly of cutting out the entire royal lineage since it stems from WILLIAM I (THE CONQUEROR), himself the product of a dalliance unsolemnised by the Church between a tanner's daughter and a reigning duke. Moreover, some states in Australia or Canada accord full civil rights to children born out of wedlock, and though this would seem not to include the right to inherit a title of honour if the limitation of that honour is to 'issue lawfully begotten', as the usual wording has it, there has yet to be a test case.

The other contrast between 1970 and 1998 occurs with hereditary honours. In 1970 it looked as if all future peerages would be for life only, at any rate as far as anybody was concerned other than members of the royal family. Although the last such had been conferred only six years earlier, in 1964, a socialist government had been in power ever since, Harold Wilson had announced that his administration would confer no more of them and the spirit of the 1960s generally was unsympathetic to such a supposedly archaic institution. In the late 1990s the position is by no means so clear.

There have been four hereditary creations for commoners since 1970: the Earldom of Stockton in 1984, the Viscountcies of Whitelaw and Tonypandy in 1983 and the Thatcher baronetcy in 1991, all conferred with limitation to heirs male of the body of the grantee. True, only the first and last of these look likely to survive. And even back in 1983 neither Lords Tonypandy nor Whitelaw looked likely to beget sons. But their peerages were still hereditary ones. Life peerages of higher rank than that of baron had been conferred in the past, for instance the Marquessate and then Dukedom conferred on the 9th Earl of Oxford (*see* SAINT ALBANS, D), though it is not clear that Oxford sat in Parliament under such titles as opposed to doing so in right of his earldom. But remedial legislation could have taken care of any such problems, just as it had when setting up the modern life peerage system in 1958.

The Viscountcy of Tonypandy expired in 1997 with its grantee. That of Whitelaw looks likely to expire with its grantee since he has only daughters. It may here be observed that the limitation to heirs male of the body of the grantee only was a curiously restrictive one given that (a) a peerage creation as recent as Mountbatten of Burma in 1947 had been conferred with a limitation that included the grantee's actual daughters as well as any sons he might have; (b) the spirit of the 1980s was much more sensitive to feminist sentiment than it was inimical to inherited assets so that to overlook Lord Whitelaw's daughters was courting criticism in that quarter; and (c) the Prime Minister at the time was a woman.

But the crucial aspect of these creations is that they have set, or perhaps it would be more accurate to say have revived, a precedent. Lord Tonypandy was a prominent Speaker of the House of Commons. Future Speakers of equal distinction may reasonably feel it is their right to bespeak a hereditary viscountcy too, just as they would have done earlier in the 20th century (*see* for example DUNROSSIL) or in the 19th century when it was a more regular prize for someone of such eminence (*see* for instance the section on the Viscountcy of Canterbury in the article RUTLAND, D).

Lord Whitelaw had been his party's Chief Whip then one of its elders and was by 1983 a loyal lieutenant to its current leader. In state as opposed to party terms he had held several very senior Cabinet posts. But as with Lord Tonypandy there is no reason to suppose someone equally distinguished may not arise in future political life, in which case he or she could cite Lord Whitelaw's precedent as an argument for being ennobled on equally exalted and extended terms. It is not a unique precedent, but it is much more recent than the viscountcies which only 20 to 30 years earlier in the 20th century went by custom to former ministers of Cabinet rank (*see* for example the articles BLAKENHAM, BOYD OF MERTON, CHANDOS, ECCLES, HEAD, INGLEBY, MILLS, MONCKTON OF BRENCHLEY, STUART OF FINDHORN and TENBY), a custom which had fallen into disuse after the early 1960s.

Lastly and most significantly, Harold Macmillan resuscitated in 1984 the convention that a former Prime Minister is entitled to an Earldom. Attlee, Macmillan's predecessor as Prime Minister by only six years, and a socialist, had taken one. Churchill had presumably been offered one — indeed as we know from the memoirs of Sir Jock Colville (*see* COLVILLE OF CULROSS, V) had been offered a dukedom — but had turned it down. Eden had been given one in 1961; Macmillan's immediate successor Sir Alec Douglas-Home had had an earldom already, which he had renounced but which was to be taken up by his successor on his death (*see* HOME, E). Sir Edward Heath was (and is) still in the House of Commons so the matter had not yet arisen, or not publicly. Even the two Labour Prime Ministers after Macmillan had both taken peerages, though they were life baronies.

The prospects for future hereditary creations looked good, then. Enthusiasts for that system may have been disheartened when in 1992, a couple of years after her resignation, Lady Thatcher (as she was by then) took only a life barony. But her husband had been created a baronet the year before, so even that rank was seen to be extant and as a general principle the convention of settling a specifically *hereditary* title on the family of an ex-Prime Minister had been perpetuated. In precedent terms it may come to pass that husbands of other female Prime Ministers are deemed to have a right to a baronetcy. Then again, the next female Prime Minister may prove less self-effacing than Lady Thatcher and on retiring argue that she is entitled to become a (presumably hereditary) countess in her own right. The feminist movement, which is every bit as strong in the late 1990s as it was in the early 1980s, has not addressed this particular issue, but it would be strange if it acquiesced in a woman's being treated as less deserving than a man.

With the departure of Mrs Thatcher from the premiership the modest revival of hereditary titles was suspended. In the six and a half years in office of her successor over 150 life peers were made but no hereditary ones. That was not a particularly large number compared with the past. The Macmillan and Home administrations had been responsible for 65, but they had also recommended 48 hereditary peerages. Harold Wilson had been responsible for 141 between 1964 and 1970 and he and James Callaghan between them for another 139 in the years 1974 to 1979. That establishes the all-time record, since modern life peerages were introduced, for a period of government by a single party where the change of prime minister (if any) is mid-term, of 280 in 131 months, or about one a fortnight on average. Edward Heath had confined himself to 46 in his three and a half years as Prime Minister between June 1970 and February 1974. Mrs Thatcher had been responsible for more than 150 too, but over a longer period than her immediate successor.

Despite the 18 years of Conservative power from 1979 to 1997, the fairly generous creation of life peers was not a one-sided party-political policy. Opposition supporters had frequently been ennobled, whichever party was in power, ever since the modern life peerage was introduced in 1958, and continued so to be even when Mrs Thatcher was Prime Minister. After the 1997 election the new Labour Prime Minister made 68 in his first eight months alone. It is true that some of these were resignation honours 'inherited' from his Conservative predecessor, but then that is equally true of previous Prime Ministers so that in the long run the number of creations for any administration balances out. A further 39 had been created by late summer 1998.

The upshot is that the House of Lords has for over 30 years become substantially fuller of prime ministerial nominees than is generally recognised — even before the withdrawal of voting and sitting rights of hereditaries which became imminent following the Labour victory of 1997. What saves the life element from being the repository of nominations by the Prime Minister in power is that a substantial minority come from previous Prime Ministers and potential future ones, that is to say, the leaders of the other principal parties, though until Tony Blair promised to renounce it the sitting Prime Minister had a power of veto. Moreover, once ennobled, life peers have a habit of defying their original party's dictates. In practice, therefore, it seems unlikely that the principle of House of Lords independence could ever come under serious threat, even if nominations were wholly to replace selection by birth. Just as this edition was going to press it was in fact reported that a substantial membership of a reformed House of Lords would be by election. Even that could raise problems, for instance in making it harder to select Government ministers from purely appointive members, as the life peers are now. After all, they would not have been chosen directly by the people. Democratic legitimacy would rest with the elective members, rather as it is thought to do now with life peers in contrast to the hereditary element.

It is not our policy at *Burke's Peerage & Baronetage* to comment on the party political aspects of the impending deprivation of hereditary peers' sitting and voting rights in the House of Lords. But it is a subject of legitimate non-party political comment. First, serious historians now broadly agree that an early writ of summons to the council of the realm which evolved into the Upper House of Parliament was probably issued to a man for his life time only. The hereditary nature of the composition of the House of Lords developed later. Accordingly it could be argued that a return to temporary membership only, perhaps for the rest of the appointee's life, perhaps not even for that long, is a return to the original concept of the institution rather than a radical innovation. Second, there are two specialised points that need clarification and which have not yet been discussed publicly, namely what machinery there will be, once the hereditary peerage as a body is no longer summoned to Parliament, for (a) terminating the abeyance or dormancy (*see* Thomas Woodcock's essay and GLOSSARY for respective definitions) of a peerage and (b) deciding who is the rightful heir to a title in the case of a disputed succession.

This sort of problem arises right down to the present time. The abeyance in the Barony of Grey (of Codnor) in the English Peerage was terminated in 1989. The dormancies in the Scottish Viscountcy of Oxfuird and Scottish Lordship of Parliament of Borthwick were both resolved in 1986; that in the Baronetcy of St John-Mildmay in 1997. The machinery for coping with Scottish titles is the Lord Lyon Court. It will not be affected by the proposed changes in the composition of the House of Lords and should continue to be capable of deciding any future problem involving titles in the Scottish peerage, for example the dormancy in the Earldom of Breadalbane and Holland, which occurred in 1995 on the death without issue of its 10th holder. The Baronetage has its official roll, maintained by the Home Office, and it was under that body's aegis that the dormancy in the St John-Mildmay baronetcy was terminated recently, as the claimant had satisfied the criteria for inclusion on that roll.

The abeyance in the Barony of Grey (of Codnor) is a different matter. It was terminated following a recommendation to the Crown by the House of Lords Privileges Committee followed in turn by the issue of a writ of summons to Parliament to the man who had established his claim. How, if at all, would that abeyance be terminated in future? Another old title in the Peerage of England, the Barony of Audley, fell into abeyance on the death in mid-1997 of the 25th Lord, who left three daughters and coheiresses. Considerable official time and energy have in the past been spent resolving the question of who if anyone is entitled to succeed to such titles. Can it be guaranteed in future? If not, can some adequate machinery be substituted for the old one?

The impending deprivation of hereditary peers of sitting and voting rights in the House of Lords may end the conferring of hereditary titles, even given the rebirth of 1983–91. But not necessarily. Who in the 1960s could have foreseen that rebirth? The very change reveals the evanescence of received wisdom. The distant past does too. In the first Elizabethan Era peerage creations dried up, dukedoms being entirely wiped out. The Stuarts were generous with new titles, not least dukedoms, and invented an entirely new order, the baronets. A similar change could recur.

The expulsion from the Upper House of holders of hereditary peers actually weakens the case against creating more. Choosing legislators by birth may now be indefensible but once hereditary peerages are purely prestigious honours, carrying no undemocratic privileges, much as baronetcies have always been, making new ones grows as harmless as that early-1990s act of prestidigitation by which Denis Thatcher became Sir Denis Thatcher, Bt.

There is no proposal to abolish hereditary posts such as the Earl Marshal, Lord Great Chamberlain or Lord High Constable of Scotland, which are purely ceremonial offices. Clearly successive Dukes of Norfolk, Marquesses of Cholmondeley (in alternate reigns) and Earls of Erroll are still thought worthy to help run the state. Moreover inherited commercial power is not up for abolition. If it were, the Government would curb mighty dynasts like Rupert Murdoch and his heirs presumptive Lachlan and Elizabeth. Such power is much more formidable than the right to sit in a mere revising chamber. And the Government has specifically said that the hereditary monarchy is not under threat, because it does not legislate, being the picturesque rather than the efficient machinery of the Constitution. But if hereditary pageantry is acceptable in the head of state, then it is surely so in the apparatus surrounding the head of state, chief among which are families from whom royalty selects spouses (*see* BUCCLEUCH and QUEENSBERRY, DACRE, HAREWOOD, HARRINGTON, POWERSCOURT, SNOWDON, SPENCER, STRATHMORE AND KINGHORNE, WORSLEY) and courtiers (*see* AIRD, DACRE, NEWTON, B, WEMYSS and MARCH, WIGRAM, B, etc).

Hereditary peers without sitting and voting rights in the House of Lords will wield no more political power than the monarchy. Perhaps less. But they will presumably enjoy the same social prestige as they do now. The sort of person who reveres titles has never made any distinction between peers with House of Lords seats and those without. Prestige is both ineradicable and, luckily, harmless; hereditary titles are at worst harmless too and at best useful. They provide a counter-attraction to the unadulterated celebrity worship found in purely meritocratic societies. The consumer has more choice: he can look up to someone other than television presenters, weather forecasters, pop musicians, actors, athletes and chefs. In an age when the celebrity has to appear increasingly flamboyant to get attention the hereditary title-holder, whose distinction is non-material, performs an important service by presenting the case for that very British quality, understatement.

When a former politician goes into the City to make money it is expected that he will be allowed to leave any fortune he makes to his children. Why should he not, if sufficiently distinguished, be allowed to perpetuate the memory of his career in his descendants through a title — as was once the case? Why should not some of the millionaires who now get given only life peerages, so that their heirs may learn to administer the family fortunes with the same eye towards a suitably opulent style of living allied to restrained taste and qualified by a sense of what is due the country in public service that at its best characterised the hereditary peerage, however recent the individual creation, in the 19th and 20th centuries? Some heirs squander inherited wealth and dishonour a great name. They may make more news, but they are less plentiful than those who behave responsibly. The peerage thus predominantly infused with great riches might become again what it originally was, representative of the most economically powerful in the land.

The body of legislating peers could then revert to something like the French Ancien Régime *noblesse de robe*, a body of worthy men and women of public affairs: academics, doctors, educationists, judges, middle and upper management, social workers, still-active politicians. The equivalent of the *noblesse d'epée* would be the golden but officially apolitical caste of hereditaries. Each group has its appeal, the former to the classical, Apollonian outlook, the latter to the romantic, Dionysiac one.

PRECEDENCE

CHARLES MOSLEY

Precedence concerns itself with such matters as the order in which people go in to dinner, leave the dinner table, march in procession (though here people usually move in reverse order of precedence, the least to the fore, the most important to the rear), are announced at gatherings or are listed in an official description of some ceremonial function. But there are various tables of precedence: social, official, political, local, ecclesiastical, legal, military.

The Dictum of Kenilworth of 1266 seems to contain the oldest official ruling on the subject. In 1399 there followed the Order of all Estates of Nobles and Gentry of England. For HENRY VI's coronation in 1429 the Constable of England, John Duke of Bedford (*see* BEDFORD, D, preliminary remarks), promulgated a similar decree called the Order of all States of Worship and Gentry of England. Similar instruments followed in 1466/7 and some time between 1487 and 1495. The most authoritative statement on precedence so far was the order for 'the placynge of Lordes and Ladyes' called the 'Precedence of Great Estates in their owne degrees' of 1520. In 1539 the House of Lords Precedence Act was passed, settling the pecking order of the Great Officers of State and peers. Although HENRY VIII was thus the first sovereign to use Parliament to settle the matter, he declared he was merely confirming the law of precedence. He did, however, announce in the Bill's preamble that it was entirely within the royal prerogative to 'give such honour, reputation, and placing to his Councillors and others his subjects as should be seeming to THE KING'S Most excellent wisdom'. Thus in 1532, when HENRY had made ANNE BOLEYN Marchioness of Pembroke in her own right, he had according to his own interpretation not been exceeding his powers in giving her precedence above every other marchioness.

A similar law of 1547 listed the dignity of archbishop and bishop below the titles of duke and baron respectively, whereas nowadays the two archbishops and all bishops of the Church of England rank above dukes and barons respectively. Whatever might be claimed in the 16th century, precedence is subject to custom as well as the royal prerogative, although it is occasionally clarified by royal ordinances. For instance, the positions in the local table of precedence of the Lord Lieutenant of the County and the High Sheriff are fixed by both usage and royal warrant. And there have been cases since HENRY VIII where an attempt by a sovereign to introduce modifications was resisted. The invention of baronets in JAMES I's reign, for instance, touched off a three-day dispute in the presence of the King between legal representatives of barons' and viscounts' younger sons on the one hand and of members of the new order on the other as to which group should take precedence. JAMES finally settled the matter in favour of the viscounts' and barons' younger sons in 1612. When QUEEN VICTORIA tried to procure the PRINCE CONSORT a higher precedence than the aristocracy thought suitable there was a peers' revolt led by the 1st Duke of Wellington (*qv*).

Precedence has its anomalies. In the case of hereditary titles it is only to be expected that children and even grandchildren of peers and baronets are given places in the tables of precedence. But children of persons given non-hereditary titles, such as knights, also qualify. Yet children of office-holders are ignored, even of the Archbishop of Canterbury, until he is made a peer, which in the case of the Archbishop usually happens when he retires, so that a child of the highest ranking non-royal personage in the realm is nowhere while his or her father is actually in office, but slips in at a high position once the father retires, just as the latter is re-entering the Table of Precedence at a much lower level.

Children derive their precedence from their father not their mother unless she is a peeress in her own right or one of the senior members of the Royal Family such as PRINCESS MARGARET or THE PRINCESS ROYAL. Women have their own table of precedence. The process whereby the constituent realms came to be knit in a whole is reflected in separate tables of precedence for England, Scotland and Northern Ireland. Because of the delicate situation in the latter province there is no discrimination in precedence terms favouring certain members of the Protestant hierarchy or an official connected with it in the way there is in England with the Church of England Bishops and north of the border with the Lord High Commissioner to sessions of the General Assembly of the Church of Scotland. At very high levels the two sexes mingle to a certain extent, so that a combined Table of Precedence is given here.

1 The Sovereign.
2 The Duke of Edinburgh. A royal warrant of 15 September 1952 decreed that he should take precedence immediately after his wife and Sovereign 'except where otherwise provided by Act of Parliament'. In the Parliament Roll he is positioned as the most junior of the dukes in the peerage of the United Kingdom inasmuch as his dukedom was only created in 1947. This reflects the provisions of Henry VIII's act of 1539.
3 The Queen Mother.
4 The Prince of Wales, or the eldest son of the Sovereign if not yet created Prince of Wales.
5 The Princess of Wales, where such exists.
6 The Duke of York.
7 The Duchess of York, where a current, undivorced wife of the Duke of York exists.
8 Prince Edward.
9 The Princess Royal. (Cdr Tim Laurence derives no official position in the table of precedence from his wife, but in practice if he were attending a function with her he would be assigned a precedence commensurate with hers.)
10 The grandsons of the Sovereign, in order of age if born of the same two parents, and according to their position in line to the Throne generally. Thus Prince William would take precedence of:
11 Prince Harry.
12 Princess Beatrice of York.
13 Princess Eugenie of York.
14 Peter Phillips.
15 Zara Phillips.
16 Princess Margaret.
17 The Sovereign's uncles, where such exist.
18 The Sovereign's uncles' wives, now represented only by

Princess Alice, Duchess of Gloucester.

19 Viscount Linley, as the Sovereign's nephew.

20 Viscountess Linley.

21 Lady Sarah Chatto, as the Sovereign's niece.

22 Samuel Chatto, as the Sovereign's great-nephew.

23 The Duke of Gloucester.

24 The Duchess of Gloucester.

25 The Duke of Kent. Future Dukes of Gloucester and Kent of the present creations, *i.e.*, the present Earls of Ulster and St Andrews respectively, together with their eldest male children, where such exist, and the latter's eldest male children and so on, will have precedence above the other non-royal Dukes but beneath the two Archbishops and the Great Officers of State, in accordance with the precedent of 1439. The position of the Earl of St Andrews in the Table of Precedence is not affected by his having married a Roman Catholic, even though his right to the Throne is. So also with Prince Michael of Kent.

26 The Duchess of Kent.

27 Prince Michael of Kent. In the orders of precedence of 1479 and *c* 1490 the younger sons of Dukes of the Blood Royal were placed below the eldest sons of Marquesses and above the younger sons of Marquesses respectively. In 1840, when PRINCE GEORGE OF CAMBRIDGE had become 21 and was within a few years of succeeding his father ADOLPHUS (GEORGE III's 7th son) as DUKE OF CAMBRIDGE, he was assigned precedence before the Archbishop of Canterbury and after all the other members of the Royal Family covered by HENRY VIII's Act of 1539.

28 Princess Michael of Kent.

29 Princess Alexandra.

The table of precedence continues (for men):

30 Archbishop of Canterbury.

31 Lord Chancellor.

32 Archbishop of York.

33 The Prime Minister (Royal Warrant of 2 December 1905).

34 Commonwealth Prime Ministers, if visiting the UK, in seniority of appointment.

35 Lord High Treasurer (office in commission since 1714).

36 Lord President of the Council.

37 Speaker of the House of Commons (Order in Council of 30 May 1919, but the present Speaker is a woman, Betty Boothroyd, so features in the table of precedence for women).

38 Lord Privy Seal.

39 Ambassadors of foreign countries and High Commissioners of Commonwealth countries in London according to the date of their arrival to take up official duties. A Royal Warrant of 24 December 1948 provided that if a minister of the Crown of a Commonwealth country is visiting the UK he is accorded precedence just above the High Commissioner of his country. Nowadays several countries retain Commonwealth membership but have no ministers of the Crown because they are republics — India, for instance, or Zimbabwe. But courtesy would dictate that a visiting Indian cabinet minister, say, should take precedence over his country's High Commissioner resident in London. Moreover, visiting cabinet ministers of foreign countries not in the Commonwealth are accorded precedence above their country's Ambassador in the UK.

40 Lord Great Chamberlain if a Duke and in actual performance of his duty, or when in attendance on the person of the Sovereign for the time being or when introducing a peer into the House of Lords. No Lord Great Chamberlain has been a Duke since 1779, however, after which the hereditary post descended to coheirs. The representatives (in practice, senior descendants) of these take it in turn to perform the office in successive reigns. Since 1990 the post has been held by the Marquess of Cholmondeley (*qv*), who accordingly ranks at the head of the Marquesses rather than at the head of the Dukes. Moreover, he holds the post of Lord Great Chamberlain strictly speaking as a deputy, but is styled and given precedence as if he were a full Lord Great Chamberlain.

41 Lord High Constable. This post is only recreated for a day at a time on the occasion of a new Sovereign's coronation.

42 Earl Marshal if a Duke (which he always has been since 1672, the post of Earl Marshal being hereditary in the family of the Duke of Norfolk (*qv*), who has precedence of all the other Dukes anyway as premier Duke of England).

43 Lord High Admiral if a Duke. The office has been in commission since 1828, when the future WILLIAM IV held it while still Duke of Clarence.

44 Lord Steward of the Household if a Duke. If of lower rank in the peerage at the head of his fellow holders of that rank.

45 Lord Chamberlain if a Duke. If of lower rank in the peerage at the head of his fellow holders of that rank.

46 Master of the Horse if a Duke (Royal Warrant of 2 December 1905). If of lower rank in the peerage then by Royal Warrant of 6 May 1907 next after the Lord Chamberlain.

47 Dukes in the peerage of England ranked among themselves according to the date of creation or any precedence assigned them different from the date of creation of their title. (*See* individual cases; the same applies to other ranks of the peerage.)

48 Dukes in the peerage of Scotland (23rd article of Act of Union 1707).

49 Dukes in the peerage of Great Britain.

50 Dukes in the peerage of Ireland created before the Union of British and Irish parliaments in 1801.

51 Dukes in the peerages of the United Kingdom or Ireland created since the Union of 1801.

52 Eldest son of Dukes of the Blood Royal if not a brother, uncle, grandson or nephew of the reigning sovereign.

53 Ministers representing foreign states as diplomats and other very distinguished foreigners. Formerly very few countries appointed Ambassadors — usually only the great powers. Accordingly, most representatives of foreign countries held a lower rank of Minister. Nowadays virtually every country appoints an Ambassador. The category 'other very distinguished foreigners' would tend to comprise only senior politicians visiting the UK, who would rank among themselves according to the date of their appointment.

54 Marquesses in the peerage of England.

55 Marquesses in the peerage of Scotland.

56 Marquesses in the peerage of Great Britain.

57 Marquesses in the peerage of Ireland created before the Union of 1801.

58 Marquesses in the peerages of the United Kingdom or Ireland created since the Union.

59 Dukes' eldest sons according to the same order as dukes themselves.

60 Earls in the peerage of England.

61 Earls in the peerage of Scotland.

62 Earls in the peerage of Great Britain.

63 Earls in the peerage of Ireland created before the Union of 1801.
64 Earls in the peerages of the United Kingdom and of Ireland created since the Union.
65 Younger sons of Dukes of the Blood Royal.
66 Marquesses' eldest sons.
67 Dukes' younger sons.
68 Viscounts in the peerage of England.
69 Viscounts in the peerage of Scotland.
70 Viscounts in the peerage of Great Britain.
71 Viscounts in the peerage of Ireland created before the Union of 1801.
72 Viscounts in the peerages of the United Kingdom or Ireland created since the Union.
73 Earls' eldest sons and the eldest sons of peeresses in their own right who are Countesses.
74 Marquesses' younger sons (this category includes Lord Frederick Windsor, Prince Michael of Kent's son, who was assigned the rank and style following his birth).
75 The Bishop of London.
76 The Bishop of Durham.
77 The Bishop of Winchester.
78 Other Church of England Diocesan Bishops with seats in the House of Lords in order of seniority of confirmation of election.
79 Church of England Diocesan Bishops without seats in the House of Lords in same order as 78.
80 Church of England Suffragan Bishops in same order as 78.
81 Retired Church of England Bishops in order of original date of confirmation of election (a retired Bishop is still in valid Holy Orders and remains a Bishop).
82 Secretaries of State if of the rank of Baron.
83 Barons in the peerage of England.
84 Lords of Parliament in the peerage of Scotland.
85 Barons in the peerage of Great Britain.
86 Barons in the peerage of Ireland.
87 Barons in the peerages of the United Kingdom or Ireland created since the Union of 1801. Life peers, who these days are always of baronial rank, are included here, as also are Lords of Appeal in Ordinary, who these days are made life peers too. They rank among themselves according to the date of the peerage's creation or the date of appointment as a Lord of Appeal in Ordinary.
88 Treasurer of the Household.
89 Comptroller of the Household.
90 Master of the Horse if not a peer.
91 Vice-Chamberlain of the Household.
92 Secretaries of State if not of the rank of Baron. Among themselves they rank according to the seniority of their appointment.
93 Viscounts' eldest sons.
94 Earls' younger sons, and younger sons of peeresses in their own right who are Countesses.
95 Barons/Scottish Lords of Parliament's eldest sons and eldest sons of hereditary peeresses in their own right who hold baronies or Scottish lordships of Parliament. Life Barons'/Baronesses' eldest sons do not have precedence here because they cannot inherit their father's/mother's peerages.
96 Knights of the Garter.
97 Knights of the Thistle.
98 Knights of St Patrick. No new knights of this order have been admitted since the late Duke of Gloucester was created a KP in 1934, 12 years after the founding of the Irish Free State in 1922, but the order is still in existence.
99 Privy Counsellors according to date of appointment.
100 Chancellor of the Order of the Garter if not a peer (decree of the chapter of the Order of the Garter 23 April 1629). Since 1837 the chancellorship has been held with the Bishopric of Oxford, however.
101 Chancellor of the Exchequer.
102 Chancellor of the Duchy of Lancaster.
103 Lord Chief Justice.
104 Master of the Rolls.
105 President of the Family Division of the High Court of Justice (Administration of Justice Act of 1920).
106 Lord Justices of Appeal by seniority of appointment (statute of 1851, when the Court of Appeal in Chancery was created). In practice they tend to be Privy Counsellors and often life peers as well.
107 High Court Judges by seniority of appointment. These days High Court Judges are knighted as Knights Bachelor.
108 Viscounts' younger sons.
109 Barons'/Scottish Lords of Parliament's younger sons, and all sons of Lords of Appeal in Ordinary, all sons of life peers and all sons of life peeresses.
110 Baronets by seniority of creation.
111 Knights Grand Cross of the Order of the Bath. Honorary GCBs do not have precedence in the UK under this qualification because they do not receive the accolade.
112 Knights Grand Commander of the Order of the Star of India (statute of the Order of 19 April 1866) (GCSIs).
113 Knights Grand Cross of the Order of St Michael and St George (GCMGs).
114 Knights Grand Commander of the Order of the Indian Empire (statute of the Order of 1 June 1887) (GCIEs).
115 Knights Grand Cross of the Royal Victorian Order (GCVOs).
116 Knights Grand Cross of the Order of the British Empire (GBEs).
117 Knights Commander of the Order of the Bath (KCBs).
118 Knights Commander of the Order of the Star of India (KCSIs).
119 Knights Commander of the Order of St Michael and St George (KCMGs).
120 Knights Commander of the Order of the Indian Empire (KCIEs).
121 Knights Commander of the Royal Victorian Order (KCVOs).
122 Knights Commander of the Order of the British Empire (KBEs).
123 Knights Bachelor.
124 Circuit Judges in the following order: (a) Vice-Chancellor of the County Palatine of Lancaster; (b) Circuit Judges who just prior to 1 January 1972 were Official Referees to the Supreme Court, in order of appointment as between themselves; (c) The Recorder of London; (d) The Recorder of Liverpool or of Manchester according to whichever has seniority of appointment; (e) The Common Serjeant; (f) Circuit Judges who just prior to 1 January 1972 were (i) Additional Judges of the Criminal Court, or (ii) Assistant Judges of the Mayor's and City of London Court, or (iii) County Court Judges, or (iv) Full-time Chairmen or Deputy Chairmen of Courts of Quarter Sessions for Greater London, Cheshire, Durham, Kent and Lancashire, or (v) other Circuit Judges; all by seniority of appointment.
125 Companions of the Order of the Bath (CBs).
126 Companions of the Order of the Star of India (CSIs).
127 Companions of the Order of St Michael and St George (CMGs).

128 Companions of the Order of the Indian Empire (CIEs).
129 Commanders of the Royal Victorian Order (CVOs).
130 Commanders of the Order of the British Empire (CBEs).
131 Companions of the Distinguished Service Order (DSOs).
132 Lieutenants of the Royal Victorian Order (LVOs).
133 Officers of the Order of the British Empire (OBEs).
134 Companions of the Imperial Service Order (ISOs).
135 Eldest sons of younger sons of hereditary peers or hereditary peeresses in their own right and eldest sons of their heirs male (usually, of course, their eldest sons) among themselves according to the precedence enjoyed by their fathers (Ordinance of the Earl Marshal's Court 18 March 1615).
136 Baronets' eldest sons.
137 Eldest sons of Knights of the Garter.
138 Eldest sons of Knights of the Thistle.
139 Eldest sons of Knights of St Patrick. For the last few generations before new members of the Order ceased to be created every Knight of St Patrick was a peer, so any eldest son still alive would take higher precedence since he would have inherited his father's peerage.
140 Eldest sons of Knights Grand Cross of the Order of the Bath.
141 Eldest sons of Knights Grand Commander of the Star of India.
142 Eldest sons of Knights Grand Cross of the Order of St Michael and St George.
143 Eldest sons of Knights Grand Commander of the Order of the Indian Empire.
144 Eldest sons of Knights Grand Cross of the Royal Victorian Order.
145 Eldest sons of Knights Grand Cross of the Order of the British Empire.
146 Eldest sons of Knights Commander of the Order of the Bath.
147 Eldest sons of Knights Commander of the Order of the Star of India.
148 Eldest sons of Knights Commander of the Order of St Michael and St George.
149 Eldest sons of Knights Commander of the Order of the Indian Empire.
150 Eldest sons of Knights Commander of the Royal Victorian Order.
151 Eldest sons of Knights Commander of the Order of the British Empire.
152 Eldest sons of Knights Bachelor.
153 Members of the Royal Victorian Order (MVOs).
154 Members of the Order of the British Empire (MBEs).
155 Baronets' younger sons.
156 Younger sons of Knights of the Garter.
157 Younger sons of Knights of the Thistle.
158 Younger sons of Knights of St Patrick.
159 Younger sons of Knights Grand Cross of the Order of the Bath.
160 Younger sons of Knights Grand Commander of the Star of India.
161 Younger sons of Knights Grand Cross of the Order of St Michael and St George.
162 Younger sons of Knights Grand Commander of the Order of the Indian Empire.
163 Younger sons of Knights Grand Cross of the Royal Victorian Order.
164 Younger sons of Knights Grand Cross of the Order of the British Empire.
165 Younger sons of Knights Commander of the Order of the Bath.
166 Younger sons of Knights Commander of the Order of the Star of India.
167 Younger sons of Knights Commander of the Order of St Michael and St George.
168 Younger sons of Knights Commander of the Order of the Indian Empire.
169 Younger sons of Knights Commander of the Royal Victorian Order.
170 Younger sons of Knights Commander of the Order of the British Empire.
171 Younger sons of Knights Bachelor.

Precedence in England and Wales for Ladies

Dowagers (*see* Glossary) take precedence of the wife of the present holder of the title. Although wives of men whose precedence derives from their official position have no precedence as a result, wherever possible they are given the precedence of their husbands. Husbands of women of high official position are not accorded any particular precedence.

In one respect females are treated more favourably than males as regards precedence. The 'Precedence of Great Estates in their Own Degrees' of 1520 states that a man's daughters all have the same rank as their eldest brother would have among men in the lifetime of their father. That would seem to be reflected in the way all Earls' daughters take the style Lady before their first names, whereas an Earl's younger son takes the inferior courtesy title Honourable. Women also retain the precedence they contract when they marry even if later divorced, though they do not keep it on remarrying. A daughter of a peer who disclaims his title for life keeps her precedence as a peer's daughter.

Note that the majority of the members of the Royal Family have been dealt with already.

---

1 Betty Boothroyd as Speaker of the House of Commons.
2 Duchesses in same order as Dukes.
3 The Countess of St Andrews as wife of the eldest son of a Duke of the Blood Royal.
4 Lady Davina Windsor, as a daughter of a Duke (Gloucester) of the Blood Royal.
5 Lady Rose Windsor (younger daughter of the Duke of Gloucester).
6 Lady Helen Taylor (daughter of the Duke of Kent).
7 Marchionesses in same order as Marquesses.
8 Wives of Dukes' eldest sons.
9 Dukes' daughters not married to peers.
10 Countesses in same order as Earls.
11 Wives of Marquesses' eldest sons.
12 Marquesses' daughters not married to peers (this category includes Lady Ella Windsor, Prince Michael of Kent's daughter, who was assigned the rank and style following her birth)

13 Wives of younger sons of Dukes.
14 Viscountesses in same order as Viscounts.
15 Wives of eldest sons of Earls or of Countesses in their own right.
16 Earls' daughters not married to peers.
17 Wives of Marquesses' younger sons.
18 Baronesses in the peerage of England.
19 Wives of Lords of Parliament or female holders of Lordships of Parliament in the peerage of Scotland.
20 Other Baronesses in the same order as Barons. Life peeresses, who are these days always of baronial rank, are included here.
21 Secretaries of State.
22 Wives of Viscounts' eldest sons.
23 Viscounts' daughters not married to peers.
24 Wives of younger sons of Earls or of Countesses in their own right.
25 Wives of eldest sons of Barons or of Scottish Lords of Parliament or of female holders of Scottish Lordships of Parliament.
26 Daughters of (a) Barons, (b) Baronesses in their own right; (c) Lords of Parliament in the peerage of Scotland; (d) Female holders of Lordships of Parliament in the peerage of Scotland; (e) Lords of Appeal in Ordinary; (f) Life Peers; (g) Life Peeresses, provided such daughters are not married to peers.
27 Wives of Knights of the Garter.
28 Wives of Knights of the Thistle.
29 Wives of Knights of St Patrick.
30 Privy Counsellors.
31 High Court Judges.
32 Wives of Viscounts' younger sons.
33 Wives of younger sons of (a) Barons; (b) Baronesses in their own right; (c) Lords of Parliament in the peerage of Scotland; (d) Female holders of Lordships of Parliament in the peerage of Scotland and wives of sons of (i) Lords of Appeal in Ordinary; (ii) Life Peers; (iii) Life Peeresses.
34 Wives of Baronets.
35 Dames Grand Cross of the Order of the Bath (GCBs).
36 Dames Grand Cross of the Order of St Michael and St George (GCMGs).
37 Dames Grand Cross of the Royal Victorian Order (GCVOs).
38 Dames Grand Cross of the Order of the British Empire (GBEs).
39 Wives of Knights Grand Cross of the Order of the Bath.
40 Wives of Knights Grand Commander of the Order of the Star of India.
41 Wives of Knights Grand Cross of the Order of St Michael and St George.
42 Wives of Knights Grand Commander of the Order of the Indian Empire.
43 Wives of Knights Grand Cross of the Royal Victorian Order.
44 Wives of Knights Grand Cross of the Order of the British Empire.
45 Dames Commander of the Order of the Bath (DCBs).
46 Dames Commander of the Order of St Michael and St George (DCMGs).
47 Dames Commander of the Royal Victorian Order (DCVOs).
48 Dames Commander of the Order of the British Empire (DBEs).
49 Wives of Knights Commander of the Order of the Bath.
50 Wives of Knights Commander of the Order of the Star of India.
51 Wives of Knights Commander of the Order of St Michael and St George.
52 Wives of Knights Commander of the Order of the Indian Empire.
53 Wives of Knights Commander of the Royal Victorian Order.
54 Wives of Knights Commander of the Order of the British Empire.
55 Wives of Knights Bachelor
56 Companions of the Order of the Bath.
57 Companions of the Order of St Michael and St George.
58 Commanders of the Royal Victorian Order.
59 Commanders of the Order of the British Empire.
60 Wives of Companions of the Order of the Bath.
61 Wives of Companions of the Order of the Star of India.
62 Wives of Companions of the Order of St Michael and St George.
63 Wives of Companions of the Order of the Indian Empire.
64 Wives of Commanders of the Royal Victorian Order.
65 Wives of Commanders of the Order of the British Empire.
66 Wives of Companions of the Distinguished Service Order.
67 Lieutenants of the Royal Victorian Order.
68 Officers of the Order of the British Empire.
69 Wives of Lieutenants of the Royal Victorian Order.
70 Wives of Officers of the Order of the British Empire.
71 Companions of the Imperial Service Order.
72 Wives of Companions of the Imperial Service Order.
73 Wives of the eldest sons of (a) the male heirs of peers or hereditary peeresses in their own right, (b) younger sons of peers or hereditary peeresses in their own right.
74 Daughters of (a) the male heirs of peers or hereditary peeresses in their own right; (b) the younger sons of peers or hereditary peeresses in their own right.
75 Wives of the eldest sons of Baronets.
76 Daughters of Baronets.
77 Wives of Knights' eldest sons.
78 Knights' daughters.
79 Members of the Royal Victorian Order.
80 Members of the Order of the British Empire.
81 Wives of Members of the Royal Victorian Order.
82 Wives of Members of the Order of the British Empire.
83 Wives of Baronets' younger sons.
84 Wives of Knights' younger sons.

LOCAL PRECEDENCE

1 At local functions generally, the Lord Lieutenant of the county should take precedence of everybody else since he represents the Sovereign, unless there are also specific representatives of the Queen present, such as an equerry at a memorial service. It is possible that specific representatives of the Duke of Edinburgh and the Queen Mother might take precedence of the Lord Lieutenant also. Should the Vice-Lieutenant be acting for the Lord Lieutenant he would take his superior's precedence. Next to the Lord Lieutenant comes:
2 The High Sheriff of the county in question.
3 The local Mayor or Lord Mayor. But if either of these is acting as the host at a municipal function, a reception, say, he takes precedence of everybody else.
4 The Chairman of the County Council.
5 The Deputy Mayor.
6 The local MP. This is by courtesy only since MPs have no precedence as such.
7 The local Aldermen, ranked among themselves by seniority of office.
8 The local Councillors.
9 Justices of the Peace.
10 The Clerk of the County Council.
11 The Town Clerk.
12 The Chief Constable.
13 The County or Borough Engineer.

PRECEDENCE IN SCOTLAND

1 The Sovereign.
2 The Duke of Edinburgh.
3 Lord High Commissioner to the General Assembly of the Church of Scotland when it is in session.
4 Duke of Rothesay (title held by the Prince of Wales).

The rest of the royal family are as for precedence in England.

5 Lords Lieutenant of counties during their terms of office and within the county and Lord Provosts of cities (who are Lords Lieutenant of counties of cities *ex-officio*), subject to the same conditions as Lords Lieutenant.
6 Sheriffs Principal during their terms of office and only when within the boundaries of their counties, cities or sheriffdoms.
7 The Lord Chancellor.
8 The Moderator of the General Assembly of the Church of Scotland during his term of office.
9 The Prime Minister.
10 The Secretary of State for Scotland as Keeper of the Great Seal of Scotland if a peer.
11 The Keeper of the Privy Seal of Scotland if a peer.
12 The Earl of Erroll as Hereditary High Constable of Scotland.
13 The Duke of Argyll as Hereditary Master of the Household in Scotland.

The rest as in England, till:

14 Dukes' younger sons.
15 The Secretary of State for Scotland as Keeper of the Great Seal of Scotland if not a peer.
16 The Keeper of the Privy Seal of Scotland if not a peer.
17 Lord Justice-General.
18 Lord Clerk Register.
19 Lord Advocate.
20 Lord Justice-Clerk.
21 Viscounts, as in England.

Then as in England generally, till:

22 Privy Counsellors.
23 Senators of the College of Justice (Lords of Session), including the Chairman of the Scottish Land Court.
24 Viscounts' younger sons, as in England.

Then as in England generally, till:

25 Knights Commander of the Order of the British Empire.
26 Solicitor-General for Scotland.
27 Lyon King of Arms.
28 Sheriffs Principal other than when within their own counties.
29 Knights Bachelor.
30 Sheriffs.
31 Companions of the Order of the Bath, then as in England.

Precedence of Ladies in Scotland is as in England except that the current Lord High Commissioner to the General Assembly of the Church of Scotland, if a woman, comes after the Queen, and wives of Senators of the College of Justice, otherwise known as Lords of Session, rank with wives of Knights Bachelor.

PRECEDENCE IN NORTHERN IRELAND

The Royal Family as in England, then:

1 Lords Lieutenant of counties and Lieutenants of Belfast and Londonderry under the same conditions governing their counterparts in Scotland.

2 High Sheriffs of counties according to the same conditions as just noted.

3 The Primates and Archbishops of Ireland, whether Catholic or Protestant, or the Moderator of the General Assembly of the Presbyterian Church, ranked between themselves according to the seniority of their consecration or translation if Archbishops and the date of election if the Moderator.

4 The Lord Mayor of Belfast and the Mayors of boroughs in Northern Ireland, but as in England the Mayors take precedence next to the Royal Family if within their city halls' precincts.

5 Recorders of boroughs in Northern Ireland during civic functions in their boroughs.

6 The High Sheriffs of Belfast and Londonderry under the same conditions as with Recorders.

Then precedence as in England until the most junior of the younger sons of Marquesses, who is followed by:

7 Bishops of the Church of Ireland and Roman Catholic Bishops according to seniority of consecration.

Then as in England until the most junior of the Barons, who is followed by:

8 The Lord Chief Justice of Northern Ireland.

Then as in England till the most junior of the Privy Counsellors, who is followed by:

9 The Senior Naval Officer in charge in Northern Ireland waters, the General Officer Commanding Northern Ireland and the Air Officer Commanding Northern Ireland, amongst themselves according to Queen's regulations.

10 Attorney-General.

11 Lords Justices of Appeal in Northern Ireland.

12 High Court Judges in Northern Ireland.

13 Recorders of boroughs in Northern Ireland if within their cities but when they are not at civic functions.

14 High Sheriffs of Belfast and Londonderry if within their cities but when they are not at civic functions.

Then as with England until the most junior of the Knights Bachelor, who is followed by:

15 The Town Clerk, City Chamberlain of Belfast and District Clerks of Northern Ireland inside the bounds of their jurisdiction.

16 County Court Judges in Northern Ireland and Recorders of boroughs when outside these boroughs.
As with England until the most junior of the younger sons of Knights, who is followed by:

17 The Head of the Northern Ireland Civil Service.

18 The Permanent Secretary to the Department of Finance and Personnel.

19 The Permanent Secretary to the Department of Education for Northern Ireland.

20 The Permanent Secretary to the Department of Agriculture for Northern Ireland.

21 The Permanent Secretary to the Department of the Environment (Northern Ireland).

22 The Permanent Secretary to the Department of Economic Development.

23 The Permanent Secretary to the Department of Health and Social Services.

24 The Clerk of the Northern Ireland Assembly (who is still in office despite the Northern Ireland Assembly's dissolution).

25 The Comptroller and Auditor General for Northern Ireland.

26 The Legislative Draftsman of Northern Ireland.

27 The Crown Solicitor for Northern Ireland.

28 Queen's Counsel of Northern Ireland.

29 The Chief Constable of the RUC.

The Irish Peers and the House of Lords — The Final Chapter

Charles Lysaght
of Lincoln's Inn and Kings' Inns, Dublin, Barrister-at-Law

The right of the Irish peers to be represented in the House of Lords was part of the unfinished business of Ireland left behind when the Irish Free State was established in 1922, reflecting the fact that the arrangements then made were regarded by all sides as an interim settlement. Most of these peers were descended from peers of the old Kingdom of Ireland which became part of the United Kingdom of Great Britain and Ireland created by the Act of Union of 1800. That Act provided that the peers of Ireland should elect 28 of their number (to be called Irish representative peers) to sit for life on the part of Ireland in the House of Lords of the new United Kingdom. Vacancies were filled by elections on the death of a representative peer. Meanwhile, during the course of the 19th century, some further Irish peerages were created although the kingdom of which they were peers no longer existed; the last creation was that of George Nathaniel Curzon (not in fact an Irishman, even by domicile) upon being made Viceroy of India in 1898 — in this way he was able to clothe himself in the appropriate dignity for his office while not depriving himself of the possibility of returning to politics as a member of the House of Commons. But most Irishmen who were ennobled between 1800 and 1922 became peers of the United Kingdom. For the sake of completeness it should also be noted that a small number of Irish peerages were conferred both before and after the Union on other persons with no connection with Ireland whom for one reason or another it was desired to ennoble without giving them the right to sit in the House of Lords.

In 1922 by virtue of the Anglo-Irish Treaty of 6 December 1921, which was given effect by the Irish Free State (Agreement) Act, 1921, the greater part of Ireland ceased to be part of the United Kingdom and was granted dominion status under the title of the Irish Free State. That legislation allowed the Parliament of Northern Ireland created by the Government of Ireland Act 1920 to resolve that Northern Ireland would not become part of the Irish Free State. It duly did so and as a consequence remained in the United Kingdom.

None of the legislation under which Northern Ireland and the Irish Free State were established contained any provision relating to the position of the Irish peers nor were they mentioned in the debates in Parliament on these measures. However, the legislation abolished offices such as Lord Chancellor of Ireland and Clerk of the Crown in Ireland who were charged by the Act of Union and other legislation to carry out certain duties in connection with the election of Irish representative peers. In 1925 the Government was advised by its Attorney General Sir Douglas Hogg that this evinced an intention to terminate the right of the Irish peers to elect representative peers to fill vacancies as they arose. Although Lord Oranmore and Browne had obtained an opinion from two leading members of the Bar, F H Maugham, the future Lord Chancellor, and Wilfred Greene, the future Master of the Rolls, that the right of the Irish peers to elect representative peers had survived and was unassailable, the matter was not pressed. The existing Irish representative peers continued to be summoned to sit in the House of Lords until the last survivor, the Earl of Kilmorey, died in 1961. It may be that they feared that if they pressed the question of their right to fill vacancies in their number, the right of the existing peers to go on sitting would be challenged. Around the time of Lord Kilmorey's death an Irish Peers Association was founded by Lord Dunboyne. It was representative of the 145 peers of Ireland about half of whom also held peerages of Great Britain or of the United Kingdom and were in that capacity entitled to sit in the House of Lords.

As well as holding a number of glittering social gatherings the Association campaigned for the restoration of the right of the Irish peers to be represented in the House of Lords. This claim was considered by the Joint Committee on House of Lords Reform which reported in 1962 expressing themselves as 'not in favour of the revival of any form of representation for the peerage of Ireland in the House of Lords.' The Peerage Act 1963 gave all peers of Scotland a right to sit in the House of Lords instead of requiring them to elect certain of their number for each session of Parliament as had been the situation since the Union with Scotland in 1707. But no similar measure was introduced for the peers of Ireland. An amendment moved in the House of Lords to restore the previous rights of the Irish peers was defeated by 90 votes to eight.

In 1965 a number of Irish peers led by the Earl of Antrim petitioned the House of Lords for the recognition of their right to elect 28 representative peers to sit in the House of Lords. The matter was referred to the Committee for Privileges, a mixed body of lay peers and law lords. It conducted hearings over several days before stating its conclusion that the provisions of the Union with Ireland Act 1800, by virtue of which 28 Irish representative peers were elected by the peers of Ireland to sit in the House of Lords had ceased to be effective on the passage of the Irish Free State (Agreement) Act 1922 and the establishment of the Irish Free State.

Lord Reid, a law lord, delivered the opinion with which most of the members of the Committee expressed their agreement. He rejected the argument made on behalf of the petitioners that as the Irish representative peers represented the peers of Ireland and not Ireland itself, any change in the status of Ireland was irrelevant to their rights. It was, he pointed out, stated in the Act of Union that Irish representative peers were to be elected to sit 'on the part of Ireland . . .'; as a result of the creation of the Irish Free State consisting of the 26 counties of Southern Ireland, Ireland as a whole no longer existed politically. Lord Reid expressed himself unable to see how there could be an election to represent something which no longer existed politically. 'A statutory provision,' he concluded, 'is impliedly repealed if a later enactment brings to an end a state of things the continuance of which is essential for its operation.' Lord Dilhorne, the former Lord Chancellor, delivered an opinion that was substantially similar to that of Lord Reid.

The other major opinion in the case was delivered by Lord Wilberforce, another law lord. He expressed doubts that 'an Act of such constitutional significance as the Union with Ireland Act could be repealed by implication or obsolescence, all the more when the effects are claimed to result from the later legislation which could have brought them about by express enactment.' He pointed out that the abolition of the office of Lord Chancellor and other offices designated by the Union with Ireland Act to perform acts in connection with the election of Irish representative peers made it impossible to follow the procedures laid down in the Union with Ireland Act for their election. 'The mode whereby alone the presence of the Irish peers in your Lordships' House could be brought about was', he concluded, 'removed in 1922 and could only be restored by fresh legislation.' Lord Reid, for his part, was clearly not convinced by Lord Wilberforce's reasoning that the removal of the machinery of election could abrogate the rights of the Irish peers as he stated that if he could have held that the Irish representative peers were representatives of the Irish peerage he would not have found it possible to say that any right of the Irish peerage to be represented in the House of Lords had lapsed or been repealed.

The conclusions of the Committee for Privileges were endorsed by resolution of the House of Lords in 1966. But the opinions delivered in the Committee were criticised both in the House of Lords and by other lawyers. The fact that Lord Reid and Lord Wilberforce both rejected the other's reasons for rejecting the petition did not inspire confidence in the conclusion. Suggestions were made that the law was used as a cloak for a decision of a nakedly political nature. There were undoubtedly reasons that might be categorised as political rather than legal for rejecting the petition. At the time the Peerage Act 1963 was enacted a clear decision of policy had been taken to exclude the Irish peers entirely from the House of Lords. Although as a matter of law it was not relevant, the fact that the Irish peers had done nothing to assert their rights for over 40 years during which these rights were denied cannot have won them much sympathy. It was possible that if another category of hereditary peers were added to the House of Lords, critics of the hereditary principle might have renewed their attacks on it. In so far as it involved representation of Ireland in the Parliament of the United Kingdom, the restoration of the rights of the Irish peers could have provoked tiresome protests from the Irish Government. While none of these considerations was mentioned by the Committee for Privileges or would have been proper for consideration by it, they formed a background against which there would have been an inclination to favour an interpretation of the law which resulted in the rejection of the petition. Lawyers proceed in this kind of way more often than they admit. It is often expressed by saying that they have had regard to the merits of the case rather than the strict letter of the law. But when this is done, it leaves behind an impression that the law has not been applied objectively.

A highly unsatisfactory aspect of the proceedings was that the issue was decided without consideration of the relevance of the continued existence of part of Ireland now called Northern Ireland in the United Kingdom and of the related argument that the Irish representative peers might be elected to sit on the part of Northern Ireland. This was the basis on which F H Maugham and Wilfred Greene had advised that the rights of the Irish peers had not been abrogated by the creation of the Irish Free State outside the United Kingdom. The reason it was not put forward, which had never been publicly explained, was that leading counsel for the petitioning Irish peers was convinced that the members of the Committee for Privileges were with him on what he considered was his best argument and did not want to alienate them by introducing another point. In this case the crude wisdom of the common law advocate that you should stick to your best point served his clients badly — if only because the best point was not made. If it had been accepted that the Irish peers sat on the part of Northern Ireland, the difficulties raised in Lord Wilberforce's opinion about the machinery for election would have dissolved as there were successors in Northern Ireland for all the officers and offices charged in the Act of Union and subsequent legislation to take steps in connection with the election of Irish representative peers.

It was possible that another group of Irish peers who had not been party to the earlier petition would have presented a further petition and resisted the application of the precedent in the earlier case on the basis that a relevant argument had not been considered. To prevent this happening the Government included the provisions of the Act of Union relating to the Irish peers among the measures to be repealed in the Statute Law Repeals Bill 1971. As a rule Statute Law Repeals bills confine themselves to obsolete provisions which are never likely to be invoked in any future case. An Irish peer who sat in the House of Lords by virtue of having a United Kingdom peerage, Viscount Massereene and Ferrard, protested against the abrogation of the rights of Irish peers 'in the midst of this little ragbag of a Bill taken on the afternoon of Gold Cup in the midst of Ascot Week.' He pointed out that 'by some extraordinary oversight', which he was pleased to describe as typically Irish, the argument accepted by F H Maugham and Wilfred Greene in favour of the right of the Irish peers had not been put at the hearing of the earlier petition. He was supported by the Earl of Cork and Orrery, a British as well as an Irish peer, and Lord Moyne, a United Kingdom peer and a member of the Guinness family with a residence in Ireland. The Lord Chancellor Lord Hailsham opposed the motion proposed by Lord Masserene to remove the provisions about the Irish peers from the Statute Law Repeals Bill. He displayed an imperfect knowledge of the legal literature critical of the opinion of the Committee for Privileges on the 1965 petition when he remarked that he did not know anybody who had subsequently agreed with the opinion expressed by Maugham and Greene in 1924. He quoted with relish from the advice given by his father Sir Douglas Hogg to the Government in answer to the Maugham-Greene opinion. The opinion focused on the fact that Northern Ireland remained in the United Kingdom because of the right given to her to vote herself out of the Irish Free State under the Anglo-Irish Treaty and concluded that this right did not give her a right to be represented in the House of Lords. Suffice to state that it was a line of reasoning never subsequently advanced against the claims of the Irish peers. Sir Douglas Hogg's opinion did not address the Maugham-Greene argument that in the absence of an express provision Northern Ireland should succeed to the rights of Ireland as a whole. When the matter was put to a vote, Lord Masserene's amendment was defeated by 100 votes to 12. Out of over 70 Irish peers who were entitled to sit in the House of Lords and who would have been entitled to vote in an election for Irish representative peers only six bothered to attend to take part in the division and one of these, Lord Carrington, a member of the Government, voted against the amendment.

It might fairly have been assumed that this would have brought the issue of the Irish peers to an end. However, in 1991 Andrew Turek, a solicitor in the Treasury Solicitor's Department, published an article in a personal capacity in the *Cambridge Law Journal* entitled 'The Irish Peerage: A Modest Proposal'. It was his contention that if, as Lord Reid had argued, the right of the Irish peers to elect representatives to sit on the part of Ireland lapsed because the Irish Free State came into existence, so logically should the right of the existing representative peers to sit. He invoked the doctrine of barony by writ, 'the masterpiece of Lord Coke's fertile imagination', the effect of which is that any person who is not entitled to receive a writ of summons to the House of Lords does so and takes his seat in obedience thereto, he becomes a baron by writ, that is to say there is created in that person an hereditary peerage in the degree of baron descendible to the heirs general of his body.

Acting on the basis of the arguments put forward in this article, Lord Farnham, the 12th holder of the Barony of Farnham in the peerage of Ireland, petitioned to be permitted to sit as heir to his grandfather who, he argued, had been created a baron by writ because he had sat as an Irish representative peer after the creation of the Irish Free State. The matter was referred to the Committee for Privileges, which heard arguments on 21 and 22 March 1995. The Attorney General Sir Nicholas Lyell appeared for the Government and declared that after very careful analysis and consideration the Crown's position was not one of opposition to the principle that a writ, even if passed by mistake, will, if followed by a sitting in pursuance to it, create a barony in fee. The opposition of the Attorney General to the petition was therefore concentrated on the contention in it that the Irish representative peers had not been entitled to receive a writ of summons after the Irish Free State came into existence. He pointed out that the Irish representative peers were elected to sit for life on the part of Ireland and argued that the right of those already elected to sit for life was not affected just because there had been an implied repeal of the right to elect further representative peers. The Committee accepted this argument. Opinions were delivered by Lord Keith of Kinkel and Lord Jauncey of Tullichettle, both Scottish law lords. They emphasised that the Irish representative peers had been elected for life and declined to give the statement in the same sentence that they sat on the part of Ireland precedence over the statement that they sat for life. Lord Jauncey justified this approach because he could not believe that in 1800 it was contemplated that there would ever be a time when Ireland did not exist as a political entity as the Act of Union was stated to be 'for ever'. He said it was inconceivable that so important a constitutional right should have been removed from the Irish representative peers by implication when there was every opportunity to achieve the result by express provision.

The arguments made in the opinions delivered in the Committee of Privileges on Lord Farnham's petition, while not totally unsupportable, are less than compelling. If, as was the basis of the opinion of the majority of the Committee on the Earl of Antrim's petition, Ireland had been deprived of its right of representation by the creation of the Irish Free State, it was anomalous that those representative peers sitting on the part of Ireland should continue to sit in the Parliament of the United Kingdom. It was peculiar to have interpreted a provision in the Act of Union of 1800 on the basis that those drafting it expected the Union to last for ever when applying it to circumstances where it had not so lasted but had been substantially amended by the creation of the Irish Free State. It was productive of inconsistency to invoke the general principle that the constitution of Parliament may not be changed by implied repeal when that principle had been disregarded in relation to the very same provision in order to dismiss the Irish peers' petition. It is clear that Lord Jauncey of Tullichettle was not happy with the reasoning of Lord Reid in the earlier case with which the majority of the committee who heard that petition had agreed. This must reinforce misgivings already expressed about the outcome of the Irish peers' petition and the feeling that the Irish peers did not get a fair crack of the whip on that occasion.

In his petition Lord Farnham faced the difficulty that his invocation of the ancient doctrine of barony by writ had little appeal on the merits. The idea that a person who receives a writ of summons to the House of Lords as a result of a mistake should *ipso facto* be created a hereditary peer is repugnant to common sense. It was predictable that the Committee for Privileges would seek an interpretation of the law that would enable it to reject the petition if this could be found. That they were able to decide the case on the basis of the right of the existing Irish representative peers to sit in the House of Lords after 1922 enabled them to avoid much more difficult and complicated issues of peerage law on which the Attorney General was not prepared to contest Lord Farnham's petition. As a result, the engaging argument also made by Mr Turek that certain life peeresses have become hereditary peeresses because they received writs of summons in error between 1957 and 1963 remains open. Women no less than the Irish are a section of the population who feel they have been put upon in the past. With this argument and proposals that have been made in the House of Lords to alter the devolution of peerages so that they descend to the eldest child rather than the eldest male child, they seem set to take over the mantle of the Irish in challenging the composition of the House of Lords.

Different Forms of Inheritance of Titles of Honour and Lord Archer's Proposed Change in the Descent of the Crown

Thomas Woodcock
LVO, BA (Dunelm), LLB (Cantab), FSA,
Norroy and Ulster King of Arms

On 31 July 1997 a bill was proposed which, if it had become law, would have removed any distinction between the sexes in determining the succession to the Crown. Lord Archer of Weston-super-Mare, better known as the fiction writer Jeffrey Archer, was its sponsor. It read '1. (1) In determining the line of succession to the Crown and to all the rights, privileges and dignities belonging thereto no account shall be taken of gender, notwithstanding any custom or rule of law to the contrary. (2) This section does not affect any succession to the Crown before the date on which this Act was passed.'

During the second reading debate on 27 February 1998 Lord Williams of Mostyn, the Parliamentary Under-Secretary of State for The Home Office, stated that the Government did not think that a private peer's bill was an appropriate vehicle for so important a change and that a major constitutional measure of this sort ought properly to be the subject of a Government bill. He pointed out that under the Statute of Westminster 1931 before any alteration in the law touching the succession to the throne can take effect the assent of all those countries of which Her Majesty is Queen is required. The motion for the second reading was consequently withdrawn with the prospect of a future Government bill governing succession to the Throne on which it was stated that the only issue on which a decision has been taken is of equality of treatment for men and women in relation to succession to the Throne.

The possible consequences of such a change in the law were touched on in the debate. Lord Archer said 'Some of Your Lordships have put to me the thin edge (*sic*) of the wedge argument; namely, that if the bill became law, hereditary Peers would be next in line . . . I would not wish to be accused of avoiding the issue so I shall say only that if it is good enough for the Royal Family, I do not see why it should not be good enough for the rest of us.' Lord Simon of Glaisdale supported Lord Archer although he disagreed on the thin end of the wedge argument saying that 'the British Constitution is full of wedges which the good sense of the Community refrains from driving home.' However he did say that 'The reason for the present rules of Royal succession are long past. They reflect the rules by which real property — that is, land — descended before the reforms of 1925. Those rules in turn depended on the feudal law . . . The French took over the rule of the Salem (*sic*, Salian is intended, Salem being a place mentioned in Genesis 14 as the seat of the Kingdom of Melchizedek) Franks whereby the Crown could not merely not descend to women but could not descend through a woman. It was because our system was different that the English Kings maintained their claim to the French Crown throughout the Middle Ages. The Salem (*sic* for Salic) rule or anything like it was never applied in this country. On the contrary, a woman might inherit but she was postponed in her inheritance to her male siblings. When one looks at it like that, that is surely even more derogatory to the female sex than a total exclusion because it is invidious. One is bound to ask in these days — and as the Noble Lord said so resonantly — why should a woman be postponed in her moral right to her male siblings?'. Lord Simon's views expose the arbitrary nature of succession. One could equally ask why a younger child should be postponed in his or her moral right to an elder sibling. Lord Archer's bill was replacing one arbitrary system of succession with another. The present system has the benefit of having been established for centuries. In the future public opinion may favour youngest sons rather than equal rights for women. Succession by youngest sons is not as improbable as it may sound. There was such a form of customary tenure of land in England known as Borough English where a man was succeeded by his youngest son. There are many other forms of succession such as tanistry in which under ancient Irish and Gaelic law succession was conferred by election amongst the surviving kinsmen.

If the bill had become law the immediate consequence would have been that the Princess Royal would rank before the Duke of York in line to the throne. The long-term effect is best assessed by examining what would have happened if it had been the law in the past. The succession to the throne would have been unchanged back to 1910, but Queen Victoria, who died in January 1901, would have been succeeded by her eldest child the Princess Royal, who died in August 1901, when the latter's son, the German Emperor and King of Prussia, William II would have become King of the United Kingdom in preference to his uncle Edward VII. If any daughter of a British Sovereign marries someone of her own rank, who succeeds to the Crown of another country, there will be a greater chance that her child will also ascend the British throne if she ranks before younger brothers. This is not satisfactory. When James VI of Scotland inherited the English Crown in 1603 he became the Sovereign of two halves of the same island. It might be that if the Kaiser had become King, presumably as William V, in 1901 there would have been no World War I, but his accession would have been very unpopular and might have led to civil war. When the descent of the Crown was last altered, by The Act of Succession of 1701, there followed two uprisings, in 1715 and 1745, in support of the Old Pretender, the son of James II, who would otherwise have been King. The Act of Succession vests the succession in such heirs of the body of Princess Sophia (mother of George I) as are Protestants. Under The Princess of Sophia Naturalisation Act 1705 all Protestants lineally descended from her were British subjects till that Act was repealed by the British Nationality Act 1948. This Act did not affect those who were already British subjects as established in the case of Attorney-General and Prince Ernest Augustus of Hanover (1957). The Kaiser was therefore a British subject and his great-grand-daughter, Princess Felicitas (born 1934), would now be The Queen provided she is a

Protestant and if her father's renunciation of rights as a first born son in 1933 had no legal effect in England.

Before the Act of Succession the title to the Crown of England was governed at common law by the same rules of descent as applied to land except that in the case of females the title passed to the eldest daughter alone and as with peerage titles one had to be the heir of the first holder of the title not just the most recent. Accordingly the doctrine of the half blood did not apply. A half brother would therefore take precedence over a whole sister. The descent of a title of honour depends on the wording of the document, if any, creating that title. This simple principle is complicated by a number of factors, of which the first is that whilst most titles originate in Charters or Letters Patent from the Crown not all do so. A second is that whilst it is for the Crown to determine what the limitations of the descent of a title shall be the power of the Crown is not absolute and some limitations have been held to be invalid. There is also more than one relevant legal system and a form of descent possible for a Scottish title of honour may not be possible for an English one. The principal non-Royal titles of honour are peerages, of which there are five degrees Duke, Marquess, Earl, Viscount and Baron or, in Scotland, Lord not Baron; the last created before the Union with England on 1 May 1707. An Englishman might be created a Scottish peer, for example Sir Thomas Fairfax was created Lord Fairfax of Cameron in the Peerage of Scotland in 1627. Similarly an English peerage must have been created before 1 May 1707. Those peerages created between 1707 and 1800 were either Peerages of Great Britain or Peerages of Ireland. The latter are considered to have existed since shortly after the Treaty of Windsor in 1175 when Ireland became subject to the British Crown. After the Union of the British and Irish Parliaments on 2 July 1800 peerages of the Kingdom of Ireland were still created and other peerages subsequently created were classed as Peerages of the United Kingdom. The last Irish Peerage, the Barony of Curzon of Kedleston, was created in 1898. A member of the House of Commons, such as Lord Curzon, could continue to sit if given an Irish Peerage unless elected a Representative Peer. The means of electing Irish representative peers lapsed following the Irish Free State Act 1922 and the last surviving Representative Peer, the 4th Earl of Kilmorey, died in 1961. His great-nephew, the 6th Earl, sat in the House of Commons as Richard Needham from 1979 till 1997. Baronetcies are a hereditary dignity below the rank of peerage. In England they were first created in 1611, in Ireland in 1618 and in Scotland where they were associated with the Plantation of Nova Scotia in 1625.

In England legal judgements from the early 17th century onwards have established that a writ of summons to a properly constituted Parliament and a subsequent sitting in Parliament created a barony by writ. There is a legal presumption that baronies by writ are limited to the heirs of the body of the person originally summoned. This means that the title can only be inherited by a descendant of the first holder. Under English law daughters rank equally and as a peerage is impartible, that is it cannot be divided, where the holder of an English barony by writ dies leaving more than one daughter but no son the title falls into abeyance between those daughters or other female heirs descended from the first holder of the title, such as sisters or nieces who lack a brother. An abeyance ends when either there is a single heir because there are surviving descendants of only one female coheir and that coheir's share has not itself been sub-divided or because the Crown has decided to terminate the abeyance in favour of one of the coheirs. In practice till 1927 peerages were brought out of abeyance when one of the coheirs petitioned the Crown to terminate the abeyance in their favour. The Crown was not obliged to do so and there was considerable expense for the petitioner as all the lines of coheirs had to be proved.

Case law established that a petitioner need neither be the senior coheir, as the eldest daughter and her heir might be considered, nor represent the largest fraction. Examples of two baronies held to have been created by writ of summons in the 13th century are those of de Ros and de Clifford. Both have been in abeyance on three occasions. Abeyances often lasted for many hundreds of years. The Baronies of Camoys, Fauconberg, Cromwell, Strabolgi and Grey of Codnor were all in abeyance for over 400 years, the longest abeyance being 547 years in the case of Strabolgi. In 1927 the King accepted the recommendation of a Select Committee of the House of Lords that peerages should not be brought out of abeyance after more than one hundred years of abeyance or where the claimant represented less than one third of the dignity unless that claimant was either a child of the most recent holder of the title or descended from that person's parent. Subsequent Sovereigns have not altered the policy adopted by King George V. The Barony of Grey of Codnor, which became abeyant in 1496 and was called out of abeyance in 1989, escaped this restriction as the claim had been submitted in 1926 before the new restrictions came into existence. The Baronies of Botetourt and Herbert, which fell into abeyance on the death of the 10th Duke of Beaufort in 1984, are baronies by writ, which could be brought out of abeyance, as also, till the year 2005, could the Barony of Butler of Moore Park, which became abeyant on the death of the 7th and last Earl Cowper in 1905.

Irish Baronies were never created by writ of summons to Parliament. The earliest known patent of creation of an Irish Barony is that of Lord Trimleston in 1462. He was one of three Earls and 12 other Irish Peers summoned to Greenwich by Henry VII in 1489. Only one of the other 12, Viscount Gormanston, had a patent and the remaining ten were considered Barons by prescription and the descent of their titles has always been to the heirs male of the body of the presumed grantee. The Baronies of Kingsale and Dunsany are surviving early Irish baronies of this type.

In England a peerage cannot be created with a limitation unknown to the common law. In England a grant to 'heirs male for ever' although allowed in the 1831 claim to the Earldom of Devon was not allowed in 1869 following the claim to the Earldom of Wiltes granted in 1397 to William Scrope and his heirs male for ever (*sibi et heredibus suis masculis imperpetuum*). A footnote in *The Complete Peerage* (Volume XII/2, pages 731–2m) states that the decision in the Devon case is now generally admitted to have been a mistake. Edward Courtenay was created Earl of Devon in 1553 with a remainder to his heirs male for ever and the Earldom was successfully claimed by a descendant of his great-great-great-great-grandfather's younger brother. This means that in England the Crown cannot give a title of honour a form of descent unknown to non-peerage law, for instance a settlement of property to heirs male for ever would be void. In contrast Scottish peerages were often granted to heirs male whatsoever. The Earldom of Home had such a limitation when created in 1605. On the death in 1633 of the 2nd Earl the title passed to a descendant of the 1st Earl's great-grandfather's younger brother, the ancestor of all the subsequent Earls of Home.

Under English law the surrender of a peerage to the Crown is invalid unless confirmed by Act of Parliament. This was established by Viscount Purbeck's case in 1678. Lord Purbeck had attempted to dispossess his son by surrendering his title to the Crown and having it regranted with a limitation excluding his son. This was held to be invalid although the son did not succeed as the House of Lords held that though born in wedlock he was illegitimate. He was the son of his mother but not of her husband, Lord Purbeck. In contrast under the law in Scotland a title could be surrendered. In 1706 the Duke of Queensberry surrendered his Dukedom and most of his other titles to the Crown and they were regranted to him and his heirs of entail succeeding to the Queensberry estates, but excluding his eldest son, an idiot. As a result on the death of the 4th Duke of Queensberry in 1810 the Dukedom passed to the Duke of Buccleuch as heir to the entail and the Marquessate of Queensberry which had been created in 1682 with a remainder to heirs male whatsoever, and which had not been specifically surrendered in 1706, passed to Sir Charles

Douglas, 5th Bt, a descendant of an uncle of the 1st Marquess and Duke of Queensberry. A case in the Court of the Lord Lyon in 1973 concerning the succession to the Marquessate of Queensberry established that a child legitimated in Scotland by the subsequent marriage of his or her parents can succeed to a title in the peerage of Scotland whereas a child similarly situated cannot succeed to any other class of peerage. The 1973 decision has the unsatisfactory consequence that a peer of Scotland might have a number of illegitimate children by different mothers or fathers and then choose an heir by marrying the other parent of that child.

Although Lord Purbeck was unable to deprive his son of his right to succeed to an existing title by surrendering it to the Crown, English law does recognise as possible a limitation to a younger son. For instance the grant of the Dukedom of Somerset in 1547 to Edward Seymour with remainder to his heirs male by his second wife failing which with remainder to his heirs male by his first wife was valid. It was not till 1750 on the extinction of the male line of the second wife that his senior descendants inherited the Dukedom. A peerage with a shifting provision is not however valid as far as the shifting provision is concerned since a dignity cannot be removed upon the occurrence of a collateral event. This was held in the Buckhurst peerage case of 1876. The Barony of Buckhurst had been granted to Countess De La Warr in 1864 with remainder to her second and younger sons and the heirs male of their bodies with a proviso that if any future Lord Buckhurst should succeed to the Earldom of De La Warr the Barony of Buckhurst should shift as if that person was dead without male issue. In 1870 her second son succeeded her, but when in 1873 he succeeded his elder brother as 7th Earl De La Warr the Barony of Buckhurst did not shift over to the next brother.

The potentially more complicated descent of Scottish than English peerages can be seen in the Earldom of Selkirk. This was granted in 1646 to a younger son of the 1st Marquess of Douglas, Lord William Douglas, who subsequently married the Duchess of Hamilton in her own right. In 1688 Lord Selkirk resigned the Earldom, which was regranted in favour of his second and younger named sons and failing their male issue to his other heirs male. This meant initially the descendants of his eldest son, who succeeded as Duke of Hamilton and there was a proviso that if any of the younger sons or their heirs succeeded to the Dukedom of Hamilton then the Earldom of Selkirk should descend to the immediately younger brother of him who succeeded to the Dukedom of Hamilton. In 1885 the male issue of all the younger sons became extinct and the Earldom passed to the heir male of the 1st Earl, namely to the 12th Duke of Hamilton. The proviso then took effect and his younger brother became 7th Earl of Selkirk. Lord Selkirk died in 1886 and as he had no son and there were no more younger brothers his elder brother the 12th Duke of Hamilton became 8th Earl of Selkirk as there was no clause prohibiting his succession if he had no younger brother. On the 12th Duke's death in 1895 he was succeeded by a distant cousin who had no younger brother so the titles remained together till the 13th Duke's death in 1940. The 13th Duke had four sons of whom the eldest became 14th Duke and the second as immediate younger brother of the Duke of Hamilton became 10th Earl of Selkirk. The 14th Duke of Hamilton died in 1973 leaving five sons of whom the eldest succeeded him as 15th Duke, and the 10th Earl of Selkirk died without issue in November 1994. Lord Selkirk's heir was the 15th Duke and as the Duke had an immediate younger brother Lord James Douglas-Hamilton, MP, the latter became 11th Earl of Selkirk. Under the provisions of The Peerage Act 1963 the 11th Earl disclaimed his peerage for life so that he could retain his seat in the House of Commons. Although the succession appears to be comparatively straightforward printed sources such as *Debrett's Peerage* (1995) assumed that the heir presumptive to the Earldom was Alasdair Douglas-Hamilton the son of the 10th Earl of Selkirk's deceased younger brother and had the 10th Earl of Selkirk predeceased his elder brother the 14th Duke the peerage would have passed to Alasdair Douglas-Hamilton. In Scots law there is a *jus repræsentationis*, that is to say a right of representation whereby a son or grandson may stand in place of his deceased father or grandfather so the fact that the 10th Earl's younger brother predeceased him would have been irrelevant.

The Earldom of Breadalbane is a Scottish peerage created in 1681, which has a wider limitation than heirs male, since in the event of there being no heirs male the remainder is to the heirs whatsoever of the 1st Earl. The heirs male of the body of the 1st Earl became extinct on the death in 1782 of his grandson the 3rd Earl. The Earldom then passed to John Campbell, a descendant of an uncle of the 1st Earl. If there is no Campbell male heir of the present 10th Earl the remainder to heirs whatsoever would bring the title back to descendants of the 3rd Earl's only daughter Jemima, Baroness Lucas of Crudwell and Marchioness Grey in her own right, and thus to the present Lord Lucas of Crudwell. The Barony of Lucas has an unusual remainder for an English title. It was conferred on a woman in 1663 with remainder to her heirs male by her husband with remainder to heirs female without division. This means that an elder sister ranks before a younger as would be the case in a Scottish peerage capable of passing through the female line. When the Countess of Loudoun, who was also Baroness Botreaux, Stanley and Hastings, died in 1960 leaving five daughters she was succeeded in the Scottish Earldom by the eldest but the English baronies by writ fell into abeyance between all five daughters.

Any study of the medieval peerage involves reconciling historical fact and subsequent legal interpretation. Many men subsequently held to have been barons by writ may only have been known as knights. Similarly most early peerage grants were in fee simple, *fee* meaning an inheritance and *simple* that it was descendible to heirs generally not necessarily only heirs of the body. However, when applied to peerages fee simple does not seem to be interpreted as it would be with land. In the Earldom of Oxford case in 1626 Lord Chief Justice Crewe recognised that an earldom in fee simple might exist but reinterpreted this original concept of fee simple saying that 'tenant in fee simple of an honour takes it by Act of Parliament in tail to the males' in other words defining fee simple as an inheritance that was to descend to heirs male of the body of the first holder of the title only. Peerage law becomes much simpler with the advent of letters patent of creation, which in the case of baronies began with the Barony of Beauchamp of Kidderminster in 1387 limited to the heirs male of the body of the grantee. There are many later baronies by writ but they became less frequent.

After the Union of England and Scotland in 1707 the normal limitation was to the heirs male of the body of the first holder of the title. Exceptions arose where men had both influence and no male heirs and particularly in the case of military and naval heroes. In 1706 the Duke of Marlborough obtained an Act of Parliament, which extended the limitations of the Dukedom to each of his daughters and the heirs male of their bodies, failing which to all his issue. Consequently as long as there is a legitimate descendant of the 1st Duke of Marlborough there will be a holder of the Dukedom. Since 1733 the Dukes of Marlborough have been descendants in the male line of the 1st Duke's second daughter Anne and her husband Charles Spencer, Earl of Sunderland. Extended limitations for national heroes can be seen in the cases of Nelson and Kitchener. In 1801, three months after he was created a Viscount, Horatio Nelson was granted a Barony of Nelson with a special remainder failing heirs male of his body to his father, the Reverend Edmund Nelson, who died in 1802 and the heirs male of his body failing whom to the heirs male of the body of his two sisters. In 1805 Horatio Nelson's brother William was created an Earl with limitations similar to those of 1801 and the Earldom passed in 1835 to Nelson's nephew Thomas Bolton, who changed his name to Nelson. In 1902 Lord Kitchener of Khartoum, who had been created a Baron in 1898, was created a Viscount with a special remainder failing male issue to each of his daughters and their male issue failing which to his brothers and their male issue. He was created an Earl in 1914 with the same remainders and as he died unmarried he was succeeded by his brother.

The special consideration given to military heroes can be seen in the baronetcy given in 1858 to Henry Marshman Havelock, VC, subsequently Lieutenant-General Sir Henry Marshman Havelock-Allan, VC, GCB, with special remainder to the other male issue of his father Sir Henry Havelock, KCB, the hero of Lucknow, who died two days before a baronetcy was conferred on him in 1857. In contrast nothing was done for 20 years when Sir Dudley Ryder, Chief Justice of the Court of King's Bench, died the day after a warrant to raise him to the peerage was signed in 1756. His son Nathaniel, who was a Whig MP for Tiverton from 1756–1776, had to wait till 1776 before being raised to the peerage as Baron Harrowby.

The limitations of baronets' patents can be as unusual as those of peers. In 1674 Richard Onslow was created a baronet in reversion after the death of his father-in-law Sir Thomas Foote without male issue with the precedency of his father-in-law's baronetcy created in 1660. Sir Thomas Foote eventually died aged 96 in 1687, when his son-in-law Sir Richard Onslow became a baronet. There are examples where remainders in patents are to strangers in blood. In 1641 James (Ogilvy) Earl of Findlater in Scotland resigned his peerages to the Crown and was regranted them with remainder to his son-in-law Sir Patrick Ogilvy and the heirs male of his body. The surrender and regrant possible with Scottish titles, but not with English ones, can have the unhappy consequence that the heir under the earlier patent is dispossessed. For example in 1704 Sir Humphrey Colquhoun of Luss, 5th Bt, resigned his baronetcy to the Crown and obtained a new grant, or *novodamus* (we give anew) as such new grants are known. The original 1625 grant had been to heirs male whatsoever of the 1st Baronet. Under the *novodamus* the title retained the precedence of 1625 and went to the heirs male of the body of Sir Humphrey, failing whom to his son-in-law James Grant and the heirs male of his body by Sir Humphrey's daughter Anne. On Sir Humphrey's death in 1718 he was succeeded by his son-in-law, who took the surname of Colquhoun. In 1719 Sir James Colquhoun, 6th Bt. as he then was, succeeded his elder brother in the estate of Grant and once more changed his name becoming Sir James Grant of Grant, 6th Bt. The 5th Baronet's first cousin John Colquhoun, who would have succeeded to the baronetcy but for the *novodamus*, received nothing.

The Act of Succession 1701 was passed for political reasons. Lord Archer's bill sought to alter the succession to the Crown for no better reason than political correctness. There has been a similar attempt to alter the succession to peerages. In 1992 a bill was introduced in the House of Lords, again by a Life Peer, which stated that 'On a petition from the holder of a hereditary peerage Her Majesty shall have power to amend the letters patent creating that peerage to permit that peerage to descend to the eldest child of the body lawfully begotten, whether male or female'. Fortunately this bill never became law as every peer whose eldest child was a daughter would be faced with the choice of effectively disinheriting either that daughter or his son. If a peer only had a daughter and no son it would be difficult for him to resist the claim of his daughter against the heir under the original patent. The personal opinions of the holder of a title should not be relevant just as the personal views of a Constitutional Monarch as to the descent of the Crown should not be. Any further legislation on altering the devolution of peerages would apparently have Lord Archer's support in view of his statement that 'if it is good enough for the Royal Family I do not see why it should not be good enough for the rest of us.' Before one seeks to destroy any system one should first understand it. On a simple level much of the present appearance of the most beautiful and internationally regarded parts of the British Isles is the result of inheritance of property by strict settlement and peerage trusts. Estate villages in single ownership are usually the most attractive. They cannot all be transferred to the National Trust or similar bodies. Legislation which altered the devolution of peerages would destroy many expectant rights and the chief beneficiaries would be lawyers. If one follows Lord Simon's argument, is it not derogatory to the female sex that children take their surnames from their fathers? Historically anyone's most certain ancestry is their mother's mother's mother as before the days of test tube babies and in the absence of fraud the maternity of a child has always been a question of fact whereas the paternity was a question of presumption. The law relating to the peerage and titles of honour has developed in Britain over many centuries and continues to do so. The Life Peerages Act 1958 enabled the Crown to confer baronies for life on men and women which give the holder a seat in the House of Lords. Before this there were a number of medieval life peerages and the Duchess of Kendal was created a Duchess for life in 1719. They did not however have a seat in the House of Lords. Any new legislation should neither disregard history nor alter the lines of succession whether for the Crown or for titles of honour. If Lord Archer's bill had been law in 1900 the Kaiser would have reigned in the United Kingdom from 1901 till his death in 1941. If the Crown and peerage titles did not follow their individual and historic forms of devolution the dignity and standing of both would be lessened. Hereditary peerages would pass from family to family and seldom if ever go extinct. Lord Archer's bill addressed what he saw as a modish evil. It disregarded the basic human instinct to be succeeded by one's son seen throughout history and in both monarchies and regimes as diverse as those of Kim Il-sung and his son Kim Jong-il in North Korea and the Duvaliers in Haiti. Of course it is only people who are in such positions of supreme power who are able to achieve it. In a few years' time it may be considered politically expedient to give younger children a chance to succeed to a title at the expense of their elder siblings. What would Lord Archer then propose?

Any system of succession must be arbitrary and attempts to replace one arbitrary form of descent with another should be opposed. The only result is to reduce the standing of the institution subjected to this change whether it is the Crown or the peerage. There is a natural wish that an historic title should be perpetuated by changing the rules governing its descent but this should be resisted. No one has expressed this more lucidly than Lord Chief Justice Crewe in the Earldom of Oxford case when he closed his opening speech with the following words 'This great honour, this high and noble dignity hath continued ever since in the remarkable surname of De Vere, by so many ages, descents and generations, as no other kingdom can produce such a peer in one and the self same name and title. I find in all this length of time, but two attainders of this noble family, and those in stormy and tempestuous times, when the government was unsettled, and the kingdom in competition. I have laboured to make a covenant with myself, that affection may not press upon judgment, for I suppose there is not many that hath any apprehension of gentry or nobleness, but his affection stands to the continuance of so noble a name and house, and would take hold of a twig or a twine thread to uphold it. And yet, time hath his revolutions; there must be a period and an end to all things temporal — *finis rerum* — an end of names and dignities and whatever is terrene, and why not of De Vere? For where is Bohun? Where is Mowbray? Where is Mortimer? Nay, which is more and most of all, where is Plantagenet? They are entombed in the urns and sepulchres of mortality! And yet let the name and dignity of De Vere stand so long as it pleaseth God.'

Reader's Guide

Indentation and Enumeration

The traditional *Burke's Peerage & Baronetage* arrangement of showing successive generations by indenting each one a further space to the right has been adhered to. In previous editions the first generation was marked in bold arabic numerals and the second one in regular arabic numerals. It was then found that the distinction between the two sorts was not visible enough. Accordingly the present edition has regular arabic numerals for the first generation followed by arabic numerals in brackets for the second one. Thereafter the 1a, 1b, 1c, formula is followed for successive generations exactly as in past editions, thus:

GEORGE VI; had issue:
1 ELIZABETH II etc
2 Margaret; *m* 1st Earl of Snowdon and has:
(1) David etc
(1) Sarah; *m* Daniel Chatto and has:
1a Samuel

Plus Signs and Asterisks

All living people, except former spouses deprived by divorce of continued membership of the family under discussion, are marked with either a plus sign (+, in previous editions a diamond) or an asterisk. Those with a plus sign are usually in remainder (*see* Glossary for definition) to the main title whose holder's family is the subject of the article. Sometimes such persons are only in remainder to a subsidiary title, such as a baronetcy conferred before the peerage came into existence. In that case the situation is explained, usually in biographical details concerning the ancestor from whom their branch of the family descends. Living people marked with an asterisk are not in remainder to any of the titles being dealt with. (In the following example the 'titles being dealt with' should be regarded as those appertaining to the Crown or Heir Apparent, for the Earl of St Andrews *is* in remainder to his father's Dukedom of Kent, though not to the Crown and its associated titles; unfortunately no other sufficiently well-known example exists.) Thus:

GEORGE V; had, with other issue:
1 EDWARD VIII etc
2 GEORGE VI
3 GEORGE, 1st DUKE OF KENT; had issue:
(1) +EDWARD etc, 2nd DUKE OF KENT; *m* etc and has:
1a *GEORGE etc, *Earl of St Andrews*; *m* 1988 *Sylvana Tomaselli [since he married a Catholic he is no longer in line to the throne, though his children are] and has:
1b +Edward, *Lord Downpatrick*
1b +Marina-Charlotte
2b +Sophia

The current holder of a title, whether appearing in the **Lineage** section or at the head of the entire article, is not given either a + or a * sign as he (or she) cannot be in remainder to his/her own title yet at the same time can hardly be said to be *not* in remainder.

Males and Females, Order of Listing

Because the majority of hereditary titles can descend only to males, sons continue to be listed before daughters. For a historical overview of how this situation arose, for all that it is nowadays considered indefensible by apostles of sexual equality, *see* in particular the Thomas Woodcock article. Where fathers-in-law are mentioned as being 'of' a place this should be taken to refer to the domicile at the time of his child's marriage (unless he is a Scottish chieftan or laird, when no comma will be found between his surname and his territorial designation). The purpose here is to facilitate further genealogical research. Where two people are each a member of a family in *Burke's Peerage & Baronetage* their children are usually listed in one article only, and a cross-reference to them is given in the other article. The choice of the family in which to list the children is dictated by which title those children are in remainder to, if any.

Cadet Lines

In previous editions the second and subsequent marriages of a founder of a cadet (junior) line of a family were unidentified by either a numeral or a name, *i.e.*, the narrative continued, sometimes after more than a page of descendants of the progenitor by his first wife, 'He *m* 2ndly etc'. It was thus not clear who 'He' was. The new system continues the numeral — 1, (2), 3a or whatever — plus '(cont.)' to indicate continuity.

Dating

Dates between the beginning of January and the end of March for years before the mid-18th century are often given in the form 1594/5. That is because until the English calendar reform of the years 1750–53 the year was calculated as beginning in spring, as it still does where the tax year is concerned, and the drastically out-of-synchronisation Julian Calendar was still in force. Unfortunately it has not always been possible to ascertain which side of a single date the overlap occurred, *i.e.*, whether, when one comes across an event said to have taken place in February 1546, that means 1545/6 or 1546/7.

The position is complicated by the fact that in the Catholic countries of Europe a major revision of the Calendar was undertaken as far back as 1582 by POPE GREGORY XIII, hence the modern calendar being called the Gregorian one. But the Protestant countries, out of reluctance to countenance a system of Romish origins, took longer to accept it. And even in Catholic Europe not all countries followed suit immediately. The territories under the Spanish Crown, that is to say Spain proper and southern Italy, also Portugal, converted their calendars in March 1582, along with Rome and the papal states. France delayed until nine months later, the Catholic states of Germany (roughly southern and southwestern Germany) until the next year. The Protestant states of Germany only changed over in 1700. Scotland was a century and a half in advance of England, adopting 1 January as New Year's Day from 1600. Thus for not much under two centuries (and right up till the Revolution in the case of Russia) what were called Old Style and New Style dating systems existed side by side. They were at various times 10 or 11 days apart.

Typography of Titles

Extant titles are in bold type except for generations in which they were held *de jure* (by right, as opposed to being officially recognised) when they are in regular capitals, thus:

1d THEOPHILUS HENRY HASTINGS, *de jure* 11th EARL OF HUNTINGDON according to the decision of the Ho Lords 1819 which recognised his nephew as Earl; etc
2d George; *d* 6 Feb 1802, having had, with two er sons:
1e Francis; *b* 1770; *d* 1776
2e Henry; *b* 1774; *d* 1796
3e Ferdinando; *b* 1776; *d* 1801
4e HANS FRANCIS, **12th Earl**

Extinct, dormant or abeyant titles (*see* respectively Glossary and Thomas Woodcock article for definitions) held by cadet branches of the family which is the subject of the article are always printed in regular capitals, however many generations they may have been extant in their time, for example:

4e HANS FRANCIS, **12th Earl**
3d Ferdinando; *d* in his 14th year
2a Walter Hastings; Mil Kt Windsor; *d* 1672
3a Sir RICHARD HASTINGS, 1st and last Bt; *dsp* 1666/8, when the btcy expired

Where a female member of the family dealt with marries a peer or baronet his title is in initial capital letters then lower case:

FRANCIS HASTINGS, **16th Earl of Huntingdon**; *m* 1st and had:
1 *Moorea; *m* 1st 22 June 1957 (*divorce* 1966), as his 2nd w, Woodrow Wyatt, later Baron Wyatt of Weeford (*d* 7 Dec 1997) etc

Heads of state, including Popes and OLIVER CROMWELL, are in capitals, as are heirs to a title, whether apparent (*e.g.*, an eldest son) or presumptive (*e.g.*, a childless title-holder's next younger brother, who may subsequently be displaced on the title-holder's begetting a son). When the holder of a baronetcy who is the subject of the article is created a peer, or when a holder of a lesser peerage is promoted to a higher one, his lesser titles should be taken to have survived but to have been submerged in his chief title, thus:

Sir GERARD's bro,
Sir Joshua Vanneck, 2nd Bt, and **1st Baron Huntingfield of Heveningham Hall**; had issue:
1 JOSHUA VANNECK, **2nd Baron Huntingfield of Heveningham Hall**
2 Gerard etc

In some cases a title of higher rank was held in the past by the predecessor of the present peer but this has become extinct. In cross-references in other articles to such cases it has been found easiest for the general reader to mention the title by which the current peer is known because that is the name of the article itself. It may nonetheless have been of lower rank than the title, now extinct, which the peer of former times would ultimately have held. Thus in the article CHICHESTER, E, the cross-reference against the husband of Catherine, daughter of The Rt Hon Henry Pelham, is to the 9th Earl of Lincoln, a title which still exists, rather than to the 2nd Duke of Newcastle-under-Line [*sic*], a title which does not. Where a specific title has expired but others continued, the text says so.

It may be objected (and indeed has been already by one correspondent writing in to our editorial offices) that a personage is always referred to by the highest title he achieves in his lifetime. That is not the case, however. The 18th-century Prime Minister Lord North is usually so known, rather than as Earl of Guilford. The early 19th-century statesman Lord Castlereagh succeeded in the last year of his life to the Marquessate of Londonderry (*qv*) but virtually no serious history book calls him anything other than Castlereagh.

Abbreviations

To save space, certain abbreviated forms have been used which refer to specific cases although they could have other applications. For example, Newcastle the city (the context will always make it plain when this rather than the dukedom is being referred to) should be taken as referring to Newcastle-upon-Tyne and Legion of Honour (or Legn Hon) to the French order of that name. Where one of the other geographical Newcastles is meant, *e.g.*, -under-Lyme, or the Belgian Legion of Honour, the text says so.

Subsidiary Titles

Where a peer holds more than one title the chief of them is listed first in capital letters and the others follow. Some, with two or more peerages of the same rank, may nevertheless use fewer than the total. The Duke of Richmond and Gordon, for instance, is also Duke of Lennox (as well as holder of a French dukedom) but chooses to be known by his first two dukedoms only. Others hold nearly identically worded titles, in which case the version preferred by the peer or the senior of the two (*see* for example ROSSMORE) is placed first in capital letters. A distinction is drawn in the headings of, and cross- references to, articles between a multiple title which is in fact a single such (for example ABERDEEN AND TEMAIR, that being the full designation of the Marquessate) and one that is not, for example BUCCLEUCH and QUEENSBERRY, which consists of two separate dukedoms. In the first case the AND is upper case; in the second, lower case.

Title-Holders' Preferences

The holder's preference as to title when he holds two or more of the same rank may vary from generation to generation. Thus Lord Stanley of Alderley, who is also Lord Sheffield (*i.e.*, he posseses two baronies of equal rank), chooses to be known principally as the former. But his predecessor in the titles preferred to be known principally as Lord Sheffield.

Other peers who prefer to use only one of their titles, although possessing another of equal rank, include Lord Egremont and Lord Oaksey, hence the listing of them in *Burke's Peerage & Baronetage* as 'EGREMONT, LECONFIELD and', and 'OAKSEY, TREVETHIN and', a wording which on the face of it may appear eccentric as flouting alphabetical order but which is faithful to the personal taste of the individual who is the principal subject of the article.

Nomenclature of Titles

It will be noticed that the full recital of a peer's title is not necessarily the same as the version on the heading or the version the peer in question chooses to be known by. For example, the former of the two earldoms held by the Earl of Cork and Orrery was in the original letters patent of 1620 drafted in the form 'Earl of the County of Corke'. The final 'e' of 'Corke' was subsequently dropped and the version used today is 'Earl of Cork'. In 1620 the distinction between a county and a town, even a county town, was still significant in a title of honour. An earldom, for instance, that took its name from a county was more prestigious than one that took its name from a town or other entity, this being a dim memory of the early Middle Ages when an earl was necessarily earl of a county only. Today the distinction has become meaningless.

The initial paragraph of any given article, that is to say the recital of all the current peer's titles, gives the full wording of them in the version that appears to have been used in the drawing up of the original letters patent or writ of summons (*see* Glossary). Even here obvious errors abound, some dating back to the drawing up of the original document. Examples survive of preternaturally garbled Anglo-Norman French or dog Latin, to say nothing of abbreviations which may have had a perfectly clear meaning in the house style of the medieval chancellery but which have had to be patiently construed since. Accordingly the occasional modification to the original has been ventured upon by subsequent transcribers.

Similar considerations apply to mottoes. It has been our intention to provide a translation that makes sense. This is not always possible, for example because the motto has become garbled over the centuries, or was composed by a person with an imperfect grasp of the language it is in. It is not even clear that every motto was actually composed by an individual as opposed to evolving through a process of family tradition passed down orally from generation to generation. Thus the interpretation of many mottoes must remain a matter of debate.

As to the wording of the title, the version given is that which as far as can be ascertained is the one preferred by the peer or peeress for everyday use; this is reflected in the wording of the heading. (The recital of a peer's names in round brackets after the listing of the peerages in bold sometimes takes the form 'Sir

John Smith Bt' if he possesses a baronetcy as well; it is thus always the form of wording he would be known by if he possessed no peerage or were to renounce his present ones.)

Correct Form of Epistolary Address

The use of square brackets for every living person in *Burke's Peerage & Baronetage* for whom we have an address allows any reader to write to the person featured without fear of committing a solecism. The letters after a person's name in square brackets are confined to decorations or appointments emanating from the Crown. Academic and professional qualifications have been excluded from the square brackets because they are strictly speaking of institutional rather than national provenance. They do feature in the subject's career details, however.

Family Names and Individual Style of Address

The surname of the peer as given inside round brackets following the recital of all his titles is presumed to be that of other members of the family in the male line unless stated otherwise. Where another version has been adopted (usually the original surname with another surname grafted on to it to make a 'double-barrelled' one) it is spelled out in capital letters in the case of the founder of the specific branch of the family and its adoption by all his descendants is then to be presumed. Where a title or major descent of a family is through a female line, the presumed change of surname on the marriage of an heiress is marked by giving her forenames in capitals and her maiden name in lower case, but her husband (or rather the husband through whom she transmits the relevant descent if she marries more than once) is treated the other way round.

In practice things may well be more complex. Examples are the article DENBIGH and DESMOND, where one branch of the family have for at least two centuries spelled their surnames Fielding whereas the main branch prefers Feilding, although the exact moment at which this divergence took place is impossible to pinpoint. Then again, in the enormous family of the Barons ASHTOWN, although one branch predominantly uses the surname Chenevix-Trench or Chenevix Trench (for variations in use of hyphens *see* the next paragraph), not all that branch's members do. In still other families the original surname may be extended by the regular but never quite formalised addition of one of the 'family' forenames (*e.g.*, Price and Rose Price or Beresford and De la Poer Beresford).

In previous generations major changes of surname tended to be officially recorded, either by the granting of royal licences or, latterly, the use of deed poll. Stress is laid upon the phrases 'tended' and 'tends'. Pontificating about trends in family history for periods before the last century and a half, when some degree of homogeneity began to occur, is extremely rash. The knitting of different ethnic groups with different customs into a single nation state took place over eons. Indeed the entity called the United Kingdom only dates from 1800. Standardised spelling, particularly of names, is even more recent. In older editions of *Burke's Peerage & Baronetage* forenames were hyphenated ('Mary-Alice', 'Charles-Edward') and the 'Mac-/Mc' prefix in the case of Scottish or Irish families called, say, MacGregor or McCarthy, was elided to 'M'Gregor' or 'M'Carthy'. They are not now. Accordingly the sort of notion that is sometimes advanced, *e.g.*, in the case of the Fielding/Feilding example quoted above, *viz.*, that the change from 'ei' to 'ie' came about because Henry Fielding the novelist was the first member of the family sufficiently educated to be able to spell, misses the point. It presupposes in 18th-century England (a) a conscious desire to match a family name (Feilding/Fielding) to a common noun (field); (b) standardised spelling of that common noun; (c) a steady and widespread awareness of the difference between the 'ie' and 'ei' versions in the first place, whereas many documents that survive from that era, even those drafted by educated persons, may contain two different spellings of the same word indifferently juxtaposed within a single paragraph.

Today change of nomenclature tends to be more casual, at any rate in its manner as opposed to its motivation. A look at the motivation behind such changes throws light on why there are such variations. It may be part of a process of enhanced political consciousness, the classic example being the evolution of 'Anthony Wedgwood Benn' to 'Tony Benn'. Some women who retain their maiden names following marriage do so from a sense of burgeoning feminism, others from a wish to maintain a professional identity formed earlier in life.

Among forms of address we have been asked to insert in square brackets along with an address for a woman are 'The Hon Ms. —' and in the case of a peer's daughter divorced from a French Count and now domiciled in Monaco 'The Hon Mme Jane Binks', where 'Jane' was her forename and 'Binks' her maiden name. These examples, though less unorthodox than they may seem on first appearance ('The Honourable Mr Binks', for instance, was perfectly *en règle* during the Regency), are cited to demonstrate how the doctrine of 'empowerment' motivates people to impose their own private code of correct form on the pre-existing one.

The change of nomenclature is neither one-way nor simultaneous along all fronts, to use a military term. Members of a peerage family may use several versions of their name, one for the workplace, another for social life. Being christened Lyulph Ydwallo Odin Nestor Egbert Lyonel Toedmag Hugh Saxon Esa Cromwell Orma Nevill Dysart Plantagenet Tollemache-Tollemache would today be a definite career handicap. A hundred years ago such mannerist strings of vocables were more widely accepted. Even in social life it is not unknown for people to use several aliases, depending on the social stratum of their companions of the moment. Nor is the development recent. HENRY V, whether in his Prince Hal phase or as King on the eve of Agincourt, is a classic example of what one might call the Haroun al-Raschid syndrome. Incognitos were much used by QUEEN VICTORIA and EDWARD VII when travelling as private individuals. The DUKE OF EDINBURGH in our own day has changed his name several times throughout a long and distinguished career.

Where a baronet changes his name the two (or more) versions are printed in regular (*i.e.* non-bold) capital letters, though the recital of the actual title (*e.g.*, **5th Bt**) remains in bold. For example:

Sir SIGMUND NEUMANN later NEWMAN (deed poll 9 March 1936), **1st Bt**

Some children take their mother's surname (such cases include the aforesaid DUKE OF EDINBURGH's children). Others, born out of wedlock, take their biological father's surname, even if their mother has married someone else. Still other children, born in wedlock, may take the surname of a subsequent husband of their mother's (the best known case of this is Bill Clinton, born William Jefferson Blythe). In all these cases that surname is shown in capital letters after their forenames.

The problems connected with changes of nomenclature mentioned above are not confined to surnames. The Earl of Rosse, for instance, is known by those Irish neighbours and friends fortunate enough to be on first name terms with him as Brendan (his fourth of five such) but by his English relatives as William (his first of five such).

The hyphenation of surnames is equally hard to give a definitive ruling on. Its presence or absence can arouse strong contending passions in members of a single family. In some cases, Leslie(-)Melville for instance, the family name of the Earls of Leven and Melville, earlier generations appear to have favoured the hyphen, latter ones by and large not. But in the case of at least one other Scottish family two brothers use different versions at this very moment, one hyphenated and the other not, and each, together with his adherents among his other relatives, insists that his is the 'correct' version.

GLOSSARY

This glossary is designed to help readers understand terms used in *Burke's Peerage & Baronetage*. It does not purport to have wider application, for instance to general or specialist law, so that terms such as **writ** are dealt with only insofar as they refer to titles of honour, nor to foreign countries, so that **impeachment**, for instance, is not discussed in its US context. Words in **bold** type occurring in any given article have an entry of their own, for which *see*, especially since observations on one topic frequently have reference to one or more of the others.

abeyance: *see* Thomas Woodcock article.

attainder: in **peerage** (1) matters, a primarily political means, now obsolete, of enforcing the sovereign's punitive will in a manner which bypassed the usual judicial system. Being political, the vehicle was parliamentary, hence the phrase 'Bill' and (if the Bill was passed) 'Act' of attainder. The practice was formally introduced in England in 1459, although similar operations involving the stripping of an overmighty subject of his lands and/or titles had of course been carried out by Kings for many centuries previously. Attainder was abolished in 1879, although the last Act of Attainder had been passed many years earlier, against Lord Edward FitzGerald (*see* LEINSTER, D) following his participation in the 1798 Uprising in Ireland.

Attainder was an especially favourite method of the Tudor monarchs for eliminating possible rivals for the throne (whether actual or potential) while incurring the least possible risk of an acquittal. For instance, the rules of evidence admissible in an ordinary law court were either restricted to whatever might lead to a conviction or suspended altogether. An attainted person was said to be corrupted in blood, whereby neither he nor his descendants could ordinarily inherit either a title of honour or property. If the attainted person was already the holder of the title or property these were forfeited.

Attainders could be and were reversed, sometimes as much as several centuries later, but as with the imposition of the attainder itself only by an Act of Parliament. Individuals, even if by now deceased, who had in the meantime descended from an attainted person holding a **peerage** (1) dignity such that they would have subsequently inherited that dignity had it not been for the attainder were sometimes retrospectively restored. But sometimes only the living person who would at the moment of the passing of the Act of Restoration have been entitled to the dignity was restored (and of course from then on that person's successors in the title). It depended on the wording of the Act of Parliament.

baron: holder of lowest rank of dignity, called a barony, in the **peerage** (2) of England, Great Britain, Ireland or United Kingdom (but almost never of Scotland, for which *see* **lord**). A related term is the now obsolescent 'baronage', meaning either the collective noun for the order of barons or a reference book dealing with them.

In early medieval society in England a baron was a man who held land directly from a sovereign. The sovereign was not necessarily the king. He might be a Count Palatine, for instance the Earl of Chester, or a Palatine Bishop, for instance that of Durham (*see* VERNON, B. for an example of a holder of baronial rank in such circumstances), both of whom at that time wielded massively devolved powers because of the important positions of their domains on the borders with Wales and Scotland respectively. But on a national scale barons comprised not just the body of men who were later to become barons in the sense of holders of a **peerage** (1) title of that rank but also every **earl**, or strictly speaking every such **earl** as held land directly from the King (which in practice amounted to all of them), for an **earl** at that time was primarily an official rather than a nobleman who possessed a personal dignity with a certain rank in the **peerage**.

The term baron later came to be applied to the more important magnates, that is to say those who were issued by the Crown with a **writ of summons** to the councils of the realm that developed into Parliament, specifically its Upper House. Since the heirs of such magnates tended to be of similar substance the practice grew up fitfully of repeating a **writ of summons** to a man's son, grandson and so on, though this was not invariably done and the consensus of scholarly opinion nowadays is that the creation of a specifically hereditary **peerage** (1) was not intended by the issue in early times of such a **writ**.

The wording of a **writ** was predominantly to a *dominus*, or **lord** in Latin. That is how the custom arose of addressing or referring to all peers below the rank of **duke**, but particularly those of baronial rank, as 'Lord Blank' (or in print as 'The Lord Blank' or 'The Rt Hon The Lord Blank' in ascending degrees of formality), hence also the *Burke's Peerage & Baronetage* policy of putting the word 'Baron' in parentheses in such cases. Indeed to refer in the third person to any baron in the **peerage** (2) of England, Great Britain, Ireland, Scotland or the United Kingdom as 'Baron Blank' rather than 'Lord Blank' is a solecism, though most female holders of a barony (but not Scottish lordships of Parliament) seem to prefer to be both addressed and referred to in the third person as 'Baroness Blank', while holders of a barony in foreign nobilities should invariably be addressed and referred to as 'Baron Blank'.

From the late 14th century a baron might also be so created by **letters patent**, that is to say by the King's express wish. His qualification for the rank of baron did not now depend on the extent of his lands or the degree of sovereignty wielded by the person he held them from, only by his favour with the monarch. Later, **letters patent** took over almost entirely from **writs of summons** as a mode of creating titles. From roughly the 18th century on, the monarch tended to be supplanted as chief mover in the award of baronies, indeed all titles of honour, by politicians, principally the prime minister, though the monarch could and did protest in private (but often to no avail) at what he or she considered unsuitable choices. The monarch retained the right of nominating his or her own choice of persons for ennoblement but this was sparingly exercised. Nevertheless the official 'fount of honour' remains the Crown.

A baron's wife should be referred to in print as 'Lady Blank', 'The Lady Blank' or 'The Rt Hon The Lady Blank' in ascending order of formality and a baron's divorced wife as 'Jane Lady Blank'. A baron's children are addressed on an envelope as 'The Hon [short for 'Honourable' and sometimes still, if in rather old fashioned style, only partly shortened to Hon.ble] Adam/Eve Binks' (where Binks is the name of the family holding the barony of, *e.g.*, Blank). They have no special form of address in direct speech. A baron would normally be addressed to his face as 'Lord Blank', his wife, whether current or divorced, and widow as 'Lady Blank'. Some peers and peeresses do not use the prefix Rt Hon on the grounds that it more properly belongs to Privy Counsellors: Lady Grimthorpe is one such among wives of barons. The form of second person address 'My Lord'/'My Lady', formerly in use even by those who felt themselves the social equal (or even the social superior) of the holder of the barony or his wife/former wife/widow, would now tend to be used only by domestic servants (if any), estate workers (if any), tenants (if any) and tradesmen in a small way of business.

In Ireland the term barony could have three meanings: (1) a title of honour; (2) an administrative unit of territory, smaller than a county, roughly equivalent to a hundred in England; (3) a feudal status involving the administration of local law courts and imposition of certain dues. The last of these was roughly equivalent to the original meaning attached to barons in early medieval England in that they usually appertained to land holdings held 'in chief'; in short, other, lesser holdings, were held from them. A feudal barony might be, but was not necessarily, co-terminous with an administrative one. A few feudal baronies developed into peerages of Parliament, notably Delvin (*see* WESTMEATH, E), and thus, confusingly, became baronies in the sense of (1). The rest tended to be used in an increasingly honorific sense, though they were not passed on when the territorial holdings with which they had once been associated changed ownership. The market in Irish baronies that has grown up in the late-20th century appears therefore to rest on a confusion over the three meanings of the term.

In Scotland the term baron means broadly a holder of a feudal territorial entity. He had originally to hold his territorial barony directly of the Crown and to have been at some point, either *ab initio* or by the later erecting of his lands into a barony, endowed with jurisdictional powers in civil and criminal cases. As in England a distinction developed between lesser barons and greater ones. Unlike in England this was codified in a law, passed in 1428. The greater baron continued to attend Parliament and developed into the holder of a peerage called a **lord** of Parliament. This came about since barony was a type of land tenure; a large agglomeration of lands held *in baroniam* could result in the holder being recognised as of higher rank, that is to say a **lord** of Parliament, and on a still more extensive scale as an **earl**. A very few lordships of Parliament have been created in the Scottish **peerage** involving the wording 'baron' and it has sometimes been argued that the Barony of Renfrew which is one of the PRINCE OF WALES's Scottish titles is one such by virtue of a law of 1469 settling it on the eldest son of the King of Scots or by virtue of the union of English and Scottish crowns in 1603. Another school argues that it is fundamentally a territorial designation, still subsidiary to the Dukedom of Rothesay.

Barons of the Exchequer were judges who presided in certain types of revenue litigation. They were abolished in 1875.

baronet: holder of a hereditary title of honour called a baronetcy. This title is unique to the kingdoms of the British Isles that since the 17th century have at different times merged to form the United Kingdom. The collective name for baronets is baronetage, though this can also mean a reference book listing holders of baronetcies (*e.g., Burke's Peerage & Baronetage*). The order of baronets was invented by JAMES I to raise money. Nominally this was for the upkeep of military forces in Ireland, hence the badge of the Red Hand of Ulster featuring as a baronet's device (except in the case of Nova Scotia creations (*see* below), where the saltire (*see* Heraldic Glossary) of Ulster was used instead). At the same time the Red Hand is not invariably shown in a baronet's coat of arms. It was made clear at the time that no order should henceforth be called into existence that was of equal or higher degree than the baronetage yet beneath the lowest rank of peerage.

Many baronets have subsequently been created peers, but the order is wholly distinct from both the knightage (*see* **knight**) and the **peerage** (2) as can be shown by the fact that the 1st and last Lord Barrett of Newburgh was made a baronet after being created a peer. Baronets were originally given the right to be knighted, which would make no sense if they were merely, as is sometimes wrongly asserted, hereditary knights. They also once had the right to have their eldest sons knighted on the latter attaining their majority, a privilege which was bestowed by JAMES I in 1616 after candidates dried up following his ruling that baronets' precedence should be lower than that of barons' younger sons but which was rescinded by GEORGE IV in 1827.

Nevertheless as late as 1842 Sir Richard Broun, 8th Bt (*qv*), who did not succeed to his father's baronetcy till 1844, started calling himself Sir Richard Broun on the grounds that the right of a baronet's heir apparent to be knighted had not lapsed, though the Lord Chancellor of the day had declined to bring him before QUEEN VICTORIA to be dubbed when he had petitioned for the honour back in 1836. Broun had two years previous even to that occasion tried to get the order to which his father belonged granted certain privileges, among them the right of all baronets to wear a neck badge, one that had been extended back in 1629, but to Nova Scotia baronets only. Although Broun has been widely ridiculed (by no one more than Disraeli, who put him in *Sybil* as the absurd Sir Vavasour Firebrace), his campaign was not wholly unsuccessful. In 1854 Sir John Kingston James, who was to succeed his father as 2nd Baronet 15 years later (*see* 1970 edn JAMES, Bt), was knighted, specifically as a baronet's eldest son. In 1874, Ludlow, eldest son of Sir James Cotter, 4th Bt (*qv*), was knighted on coming of age. (He predeceased his father by 20 years, dying unmarried in 1882.) But when in 1895 Claude, the eldest son of Sir Claude de Crespigny, 4th Bt (*see* 1949 edn), petitioned to be knighted he was turned down. Lastly, in 1929 Broun won his most significant, if posthumous, victory when all baronets were accorded their own neck badge.

The baronetage of England dates from 22 May 1611, that of Ireland from the following 30 September, that of Nova Scotia or Scotland (so called in the former case because the moneys raised were supposed to go towards establishing the colony of Nova Scotia in North America and applicants received a land grant there; the grants were stopped in 1638) from 28 May 1625, that of Great Britain following the Union of English and Scottish Parliaments in 1707 and that of the United Kingdom following the Union of Parliaments of Great Britain and Ireland in 1801. Nearly all baronetcies are heritable by and through males only. The exceptions are a handful in the baronetage of Nova Scotia, for example the one held (but not used) by the Labour MP Tam Dalyell (*qv*). There is no mechanism for formally renouncing a baronetcy in the way there is for a **peerage** (1).

In the 19th century the custom grew up of conferring baronetcies on distinguished men who were deemed by Victorian convention not quite worthy of a peerage, usually because of their calling rather than because of lack of wealth. Engineers were one group frequently so honoured. The other chief group was members of the medical profession, whereas lawyers, who were also members of a profession, tended to be honoured, where they were honoured at all, with peerages. It also became the custom to confer a baronetcy on Lord Mayors of London. The last person so honoured was Sir Ralph Perring in 1963.

An Official Roll of the Baronetage is kept up by the Home Office. Anyone who wishes to be officially recognised as a baronet must prove his succession, as with peers. A royal warrant of 8 February 1910 decreed that no person should be received as a baronet or addressed or mentioned by that title in any civil or military commission, letters patent or any other official document unless his name figured on the Official Roll. But in practice it may take years for a claim to be recognised, even supposing a claim is pursued. Yet the potential new baronet may not even wish to take up the title, either through a reluctance to incur expenditure or through lack of interest. Accordingly, most books of reference, including *Burke's Peerage & Baronetage*, treat the successor, where clearly indicated, as having established his claim. For example, by the end of 1995 no claim had been made regarding the baronetcy of FitzGerald of Geraldine Place, although the most recent officially recognised holder of the title, the 2nd baronet, had died 38 years previously. Meanwhile his second but eldest surviving son and non-official successor as 3rd baronet had died in 1988. Yet the line of inheritance was perfectly obvious. It was just that both the putative 3rd and 4th baronets were Catholic priests. They were also probably citizens of the Republic of Ireland and may well have deemed it inappropriate to make a claim. They nonetheless appeared as holders of the baronetcy in books of reference. Where the succession is not obvious the baronetcy may have fallen into a state of **dormancy**.

The Standing Council of the Baronetage, founded as the Honourable Society of the Baronetage in 1898 to protest against the declaration granting sons of life peers superior precedence the year before but renamed in 1903, promotes the interests of the order, in particular by helping claimants.

A baronet is addressed on an envelope as 'Sir John Blank, Bart [or 'Bt', both forms being short for Baronet]', his wife as 'Lady Blank'. The prefix 'Sir' (also used for a **knight**) derives from the Latin comparative adjective *senior, i.e.*, older or of higher rank. A baronetess, *i.e.*, the female holder of a baronetcy, is addressed on an envelope as 'Dame Anne Blank, Btess'. The form of address in direct speech to a baronet called Sir John Blank is 'Sir John', to his wife 'Lady Blank' and to a baronetess called Dame Anne Blank 'Dame Anne'. Husbands of baronetesses and children of baronets or baronetesses have no special form of address.

Blue, Admiral (of) the: forerunner of modern Rear-Admiral; a commanding officer of one of three squadrons, the other two being the Red and White, into which the Royal Naval fleets were divided under a system in force between the 17th and 19th centuries. The Admiral of the Red was the senior and commanded from the centre of the Fleet. The Admiral of the White commanded from in front and that of the Blue from the rear.

courtesy title: strictly speaking any honorific prefix, whether 'Hon', 'Lady' etc, extended by custom to the near relative of a peer. (For such lesser prefixes, *see* the individual articles **baron, duke, earl, marquess, viscount**.) It is here proposed to concentrate on the major ones. Many a holder of a **peerage** (1), especially if of senior rank such as an **earl**, **marquess** or **duke**, has more than one title. He usually 'lends' one of his lesser titles to his eldest son and sometimes one to the latter's eldest son as well. Thus the eldest surviving son and heir of the Duke of Marlborough (*qv*) is called Marquess of Blandford and the latter's son is called Earl of Sunderland, the two titles being among the Duke's lesser substantive ones. Such 'loans' are called courtesy titles since their bearers are not substantive peers but only commoners in a relationship of expectancy to their father's (or grandfather's) genuine peerages, and although they may be addressed as titled personages it is by courtesy. The lesser title so 'lent' may not necessarily exist, or if it does may not necessarily be one of the substantive peer's actual titles, for example the Barony of Clinton on past occasions in the case of the Earldom of Lincoln, though at present the eldest son of the latter does not use it precisely because it is not a title held by the immediate family. Again, on the death of the 10th Earl of Huntingdon (*qv*) in 1789 his subsidiary titles passed to his sister but the Earldom passed to a cousin, who became 11th Earl. The 12th Earl's eldest son was known by courtesy as Lord Hastings till he succeeded to the Earldom, even though neither of the two Baronies of that name were held by his branch of the family. And his son, the future 14th Earl, was known by courtesy as Viscount Hastings although that title had not only never been held by the family at all but had never even existed. It is customary to refer in writing to a courtesy **marquess**, **earl** or **viscount**, **baron** or **lord**, as 'Marquess of Blandford', 'Earl of Sunderland', etc, without the preceding definite article ('The'). In the body of *Burke's Peerage & Baronetage* courtesy titles are printed in italics.

custos rotulorum: a Latin phrase meaning 'keeper of the rolls' and referring to an honorific post, often associated with the Lord Lieutenancy of a county.

decreet: Scottish term meaning judgment in a court of law.

dormancy: state of suspension of a title of honour. A **peerage** (1) or baronetcy is said to be dormant when it has not yet been established who the current holder is, if any. The process of establishing the rightful holder of the title may take centuries, depending on the vigour and wealth of interested parties. Unlike **abeyance**, with which it is often confused (*see* Thomas Woodcock article), there is no time limit on the process whereby dormancies may be terminated.

dowager: theoretically any widow possessed of a dower, or life interest in part of her deceased husband's property, but by extension and in modern practice the widow of (1) a **baron**; (2) a **baronet**; (3) a **duke**; (4) an **earl**; (5) a **marquess** or (6) a **viscount**. If the new holder of the title has not married and there are no other widows of previous title holders in the family, the widow's style of address does not change from what it was when her husband was alive. But since hereditary titles may pass through several hands over a relatively short period, for instance during a war, there may be more than one dowager associated with that title at any one time. The senior dowager, *i.e.*, the one who has first become a dowager, is addressed or referred to as (1) 'The Dowager Lady Blank'/'The Rt Hon The Dowager Lady Blank'/'Jane Lady Blank'/'The Rt Hon Jane Lady Blank'; (2) 'Dowager Lady Blank' [note the absence of any definite article]/'Jane Lady Blank'; (3) 'The Dowager Duchess of Blank'/'Her Grace The Dowager Duchess of Blank'/'Jane Duchess of Blank'/'Her Grace Jane Duchess of Blank'; (4) 'The Dowager Countess (of) Blank'/'The Rt Hon The Dowager Countess (of) Blank'/'Jane Countess (of) Blank'/'The Rt Hon Jane Countess (of) Blank'; (5) 'The Dowager Marchioness (of) Blank'/'The Most Hon The Dowager Marchioness (of) Blank'/'Jane Marchioness (of) Blank'/'The Most Hon Jane Marchioness (of) Blank'; and (6) 'The Dowager Viscountess (of) Blank'/'The Rt Hon The Dowager Viscountess (of) Blank'/'Jane Viscountess (of) Blank'/'The Rt Hon Jane Viscountess (of) Blank'. Junior dowagers may only use the form featuring their forename. The use of 'Rt Hon' etc is in each case the more formal version.

The state of dowagerhood is taken to imply that the current holder of the title following the dowager's bereavement will, if he has not already done so, take to himself a wife and that the latter will become the 'reigning' baroness, baronet's wife, duchess etc. For that reason it makes no sense to speak of the widow of a **knight** or **life peer** as 'dowager' since on the knight's or life peer's death the title becomes extinct. The earliest use of the word in conjunction with a specific title appears to have been for CATHERINE OF ARAGON on her surviving her first husband ARTHUR, when she was called 'Princess Dowager' till she married her brother-in-law the future HENRY VIII. At that time, owing to low life expectancy, a dowager was often a young woman, even a girl. It was only in later centuries, when life expectancy rose substantially, that its association with advanced age began. In modern times that association has caused many widows of peers or of baronets to reject the style of address 'Dowager' and adhere to 'Jane Lady Blank' etc instead.

duke: holder of highest rank of dignity in **peerage** (2), called a dukedom. The female equivalent is duchess. The word derives from the Latin *dux*, a military leader or general under the Roman Empire as early as the 2nd century AD who was usually appointed to command troops in a specific campaign. In later centuries he tended to be put in charge of a border region as the equivalent of the modern General Officer Commanding. Similar officials existed in the Merovingian and Carolingian Empires of a few hundred years later. As royal power declined in the 10th century dukes acquired more independence. Meanwhile a class of non-official military leaders developed and where they managed to establish themselves as independent sovereign rulers they kept the title duke as opposed to king. The Dukes of Normandy constitute the example most relevant to English history.

It is often said that the title duke was unknown in England till it was conferred on the Black Prince in 1337, but Kings from WILLIAM I (THE CONQUEROR) down to EDWARD III from the moment of his accession styled themselves Duke of Normandy, Duke of the Normans or Duke of Aquitaine as well as being known by their regal titles. Sixty years later RICHARD II made up for lost time, as it were, when he created five dukedoms in a single day. This is still the record for peerage creations combining both profusion and eminence of rank. He had already created a life dukedom, that of Ireland, conferring it on his close friend the 9th Earl of Oxford (*see* SAINT ALBANS). In Scotland the first dukedom, that of Rothesay (*see* ROYAL FAMILY, section PRINCE OF WALES), was created in 1398.

Those on whom dukedoms were conferred were always close blood relatives of the sovereign till the 16th century, and even then the first wholly non-royal creation, Charles Brandon, made Duke of Suffolk in 1514, was HENRY VIII's brother-in-law. By the latter half of ELIZABETH I's reign a series of Acts of **attainder** had totally eliminated dukedoms from the English peerage. The order revived in the 17th and 18th centuries and during the latter period there were at one time 50 extant, though held by only 40 persons, more than has ever been the case since. Dukedoms by now had tended to become the crowning glory for very rich noblemen who controlled several seats in the House of Commons. Two notable exceptions were those of Marlborough and Wellington, awarded for military success and therefore closer in spirit to the original purpose of a *dux* or duke.

Among those who are reliably reported to have refused dukedoms are the 3rd Marquess of Lansdowne (*qv*), Disraeli (*see* 1881 edn BEACONSFIELD, E), following his diplomatic triumph at the Congress of Berlin, and Sir Winston Churchill (*see* MARLBOROUGH) on his retirement from the premiership in 1955. On the last occasion Buckingham Palace is said to have declared to Sir Jock Colville (*see* COLVILLE OF CULROSS), Churchill's Principal Private Secretary, that no dukedoms would ever again be conferred on non-royals but that the offer would be made to Churchill on the understanding that he was certain to turn it down.

A duke is addressed or referred to formally as 'Your/His Grace' and addressed less formally as 'Duke'. For his eldest son's style of address *see* **courtesy title**. His younger sons and all daughters are referred to as '(The) Lord John Manners/(The) Lady Diana Manners' (*see* **earl** for discussion of the definite article before 'Lord'/'Lady'). A duchess is addressed or referred to formally as 'Your/Her Grace' but a duke's divorced wife should not be, though the late Margaret Duchess of Argyll (the correct way of referring to a divorced wife of a duke) campaigned doggedly to retain the prefix.

A related expression, the Dukeries, describes an area of Nottinghamshire rich in estates or mansions that have historically belonged to dukes: Clumber House (Dukes of Newcastle; *see* LINCOLN, E), Thoresby House (Dukes of Kingston; *see* KINGSTON, preliminary remarks, also 1953 edn MANVERS, E), Welbeck Abbey (Dukes of Portland; *see* PORTLAND, E), Worksop Manor (Dukes of Norfolk; *qv*).

earl: holder of third highest rank of dignity in the **peerage** (2), called an earldom. The word derives from the Norse *jarl* or *earl* (*see* also CAITHNESS) via the Anglo-Saxon *eorl* and is the sole **peerage** (2) rank not to have a latinate etymology. For a discussion of earls in the immediate pre-Conquest era and for two or three centuries afterwards, both in England and Scotland, *see* in particular the articles BUCHAN, NORTHUMBERLAND, RUTLAND and WINCHESTER. *See* also **baron**. The earl in the first few centuries after the Conquest, being still chiefly an official, was granted the 'third penny', or a slice of the revenue accruing from fees for cases brought in the county court of the shire over which he presided. From the later Middle Ages (*see* section on earlier creations of Earldom of March in WEMYSS and MARCH) the practice grew up of creating earldoms named after non-county entities, sometimes even families, *e.g.*, Earl Ferrers or Earl Fortescue (note that in such cases the 'of' is omitted).

An earl is referred to on paper or addressed on an envelope as 'The Earl (of) Blank' or 'The Rt Hon The Earl (of) Blank' in ascending order of formality, though a few such, notably the Earl of Mar and Kellie and the Earl of Scarbrough (*qqv*), prefer not to be addressed as 'The Rt Hon' at all on the grounds that the prefix more properly belongs to Privy Counsellors. In a social context 'Lord Blank' rather than 'The Earl (of) Blank' is considered preferable, though if the precise rank of the person referred to needs to be indicated the latter is the only way out. When addressing an earl in the second person 'Lord Blank' will suffice.

An earl's wife is called a countess, reflecting his notional equivalence in rank to the continental count. The same rules of address apply to her as to him, the word 'Countess' being substituted for 'Earl', and where divorced wives of earls are concerned the form of address is as with the divorced wives of a **baron** except that the words 'Countess (of)' replace 'Lady'. For an earl's eldest son *see* **courtesy title**. An earl's younger son(s) is/are addressed as for a baron's son. An earl's daughter is addressed as 'Lady Jane Binks', where 'Jane' is her forename and 'Binks' her surname, whether maiden or married. The practice has revived in recent years of adding a 'The' to 'Lady' when referring to her in the third person (also to 'Lord' where he is a duke's or marquess's younger son). It emanates from Court Circles but is deprecated by some members of the College of Arms. This is on the understandable grounds that it not only encroaches on the definite article which more properly pertains to a full peer but also implicitly places in an inferior position not just the eldest son and heir of an **earl**, **marquess** or **duke** since he has no 'The' to his **courtesy title** but a Prince or Princess who is not a child of the sovereign since they too are not accorded a 'The'. But the practice may well commend itself inasmuch as it presumbly has the sanction of the Crown.

Earldoms have for the last 200 years been traditionally granted to former Prime Ministers, though neither exclusively nor invariably so.

extinct: state of demise of title, when all possible heirs under the terms of the **remainder** with which it was originally granted have died out. *See* also **abeyant** and **dormant**.

heir of entail/tailzie: he (or she) who inherits under the terms of an entail.

heir general: senior descendant of original grantee of title regardless of sex, whether of the heir himself/herself or the line by which he/she is so placed in relationship to the grantee.

heir male: he who may inherit a title or titles by virtue of being the senior male-line kinsman of the grantee.

heir male and of provision: in Scottish law, he who inherits as heir male general, that is, not just a direct descendant but the descendant of a brother or ascendant, such as an uncle, great-uncle or cousin (provided the relationship is through the male line).

heir male of the body: as immediately above, but directly descended from the original grantee.

ilk: Scottish term meaning 'of the same name'. Hence a Chief called 'MacQuern of that Ilk' is identical with 'MacQuern of MacQuern'.

impeachment: prosecution before House of Lords as judges, House of Commons being the accuser. Unlike **attainder** it follows judicial rules. Thus the defence can call witnesses. On the other hand sentencing does not necessarily follow a verdict of guilty but only if the House of Commons favours it. The latter body can thereby in effect also pardon the defendant. The earliest impeachment known was that of the 3rd/4th Lord (Baron) Latimer (of Corby) in 1376 (*see* LATYMER), whose association with JOHN OF GAUNT had made him unpopular, and was a milestone in the rising power of the House of Commons, as was the frequent use of impeachment in the 17th century. The last impeachment was that of the 1st Viscount Melville (*qv*) of Melville in 1806.

knight: person who holds a title of honour called a knighthood, almost invariably conferred for the grantee's lifetime only. (Holders of three hereditary knighthoods of feudal origin have long existed in Ireland: the Knight of Glin, or the Black Knight (*see* WAKEFIELD), the Knight of Kerry, or the Green Knight (*see* FitzGERALD, Bt, of Valencia), and the White Knight, a member of the FitzGibbon family, among whom a claimant to the title apparently exists athough it has been **dormant** for many years.) A knight is usually referred to in the third person as 'Sir John Smith', where John is his sole or preferred forename and Smith his surname. A somewhat more familiar variant (and one which can be used in direct speech as well) is 'Sir John'. The hereditary Knights already mentioned are not so addressed or referred to. The Knight of Glin is addressed formerly in the second person as 'Knight' (his wife as 'Madam FitzGerald') and colloquially referred to in the third person as 'The Knight'. The Knight of Kerry, being a **baronet**, is addressed in the same way as with other members of that order. The title of White Knight, being dormant, has no form of address, though should the claimant be successful the Knight of Glin's form of address as 'The Knight' would presumably have to be modified since it would not be clear which of the two was being referred to. Honorary knighthoods awarded to foreign nationals, such as Bob Geldof or various former US Presidents, do not carry with them the right of the grantee to be called 'Sir', nor do knighthoods awarded to those in holy orders. The wife of a knight is addressed as 'Lady Smith' (*not* 'Lady Jane Smith' unless the daughter of a **duke**, **earl** or **marquess**). If her husband falls into one of the categories just mentioned as not being called 'Sir' she remains 'Mrs' (or 'Ms').

The style 'Sir Smith' is considered a solecism, though not uncommon among people whose first language is other than English, the error probably arising from a literal translation of the form Chevalier plus a surname, as in the Chevalier St George or the Chevalier Bayard. The French word *chevalier*, as also *ritter* (cognate with 'rider') in German, suggests an equestrian origin for knights, and certainly the class of *equites* (literally 'horsemen') in Ancient Rome, who ranked just below senators, are usually translated as 'knights'. Moreover Sir Richard Broun in his propagandising on behalf of the privileges he held were possessed by **baronets** spoke of them as *equites aurati* ('gilded knights'), presumably on the grounds of their similar form of address ('Sir John Smith'), even though a **baronet** is not a knight. The Anglo-Saxon word *cnight* from which the term is derived meant originally a youth or subordinate fighting man, however, and later a confidential servant. The Anglo-Saxons did not fight on horseback, so that the knighting of his infant grandson ATHELSTAN by KING ALFRED in the 890s, apparently the earliest known instance of its kind in England, should probably be seen as a primarily religious ceremony. The ritual nature of investiture with knighthood, now obsolete, should not be overlooked. The keeping of a vigil on the eve of admission to knighthood persisted for some centuries, as did a cleansing ceremony by bathing, hence ultimately the Order of the Bath. As late as the 19th century the writer Thomas Love Peacock attacked the award of a knighthood, which he insisted was still an exclusively Christian institution, on a Parsee and two members of the Jewish faith.

But in England from the Norman Conquest knighthood was predominantly military in character. The **baron** would grant some of his lands as a knight's fee to a subtenant who in return had to serve on campaign under his feudal superior, though only for a fixed term. At that time the dubbing of a knight, that is to say the brief resting of the sword on the shoulder of the person so honoured, could be carried out by the feudal superior. The knighting of men, particularly on military service, by commanding officers persisted for many centuries and was the origin of the term knight banneret, where the grantee's pennon was clipped as a mark of distinction. Meanwhile, as the system of land tenure by military service became increasingly replaced by money payments, the holder of a knight's fee increasingly failed to get himself knighted. As early as 1247 it was decreed that all freeholders with an annual income of 40 shillings (roughly £50,000 in late-1990s terms) should present themselves for dubbing as knights. Meanwhile those who did get themselves knighted tended more and more to make of it a species of coming-of-age rite of passage. And so evolved the landless knight, the precursor of the knight bachelor.

A knight in recent times has held his title in one of several chivalric orders, *e.g.*, the Garter, Thistle, St Patrick, Bath, Star of India, St Michael and St George, Indian Empire, Royal Victorian Order or Order of the British Empire, or as a knight bachelor (for the ramifications of all of which *see* the essay on Precedence). Since nowadays a knight can only have been created such in his own lifetime and of his own volition it would be absurd for the possibility of renunciation to exist. In earlier centuries, when persons of sufficient distinction were sometimes fined for refusing to take up knighthood (the possession of which imposed in turn various obligations), it was a different matter.

lady: general honorific designation for wife of a **lord** (of which word it is the female version), **baronet** or **knight**. Alternatively the substantive title of the female holder of (1) a Scottish lordship of Parliament, (2) **barony**. Also used as an honorific prefix before the forename and surname of the daughter of a **duke**, **marquess** or **earl** (*see* also **courtesy title**).

letters patent: official documents, so called from their being 'patent', that is to say open or unsealed, issued under the Great Seal and containing various pronouncements by the sovereign. Increasingly since the late 14th century the means of creating a **peer** or **baronet**.

life peer: member of the House of Lords appointed to it for the rest of his/her natural life. Life peerages were conferred as early as the 14th century, and in several different ranks of the **peerage** (2), but for the most part, especially when on women (usually royal mistresses), did not carry the right to a seat in the legislature. From 1958 on that situation has changed and life membership of the House of Lords has since then been the principal condition under which additions to it are made. A life peer nowadays is invariably of the rank of **baron**.

limitation: *see* **remainder**.

lord: a general term denoting a dignity. It may be hereditary, in which case it is specifically applied to a lord of Parliament in the **peerage** (2) of Scotland and colloquially or loosely to a male who holds the title of **baron**, **earl**, **marquess** or **viscount**, either substantively or as a **courtesy title**. (A **duke** is not usually so referred to, although it might be argued that inasmuch as he has usually been a member of the House of Lords he is a lord by virtue of his being a duke.) It may be appointive and for the grantee's life only or a fixed term, such as is the case with a **life peer**, law lord (a high-ranking appellate judge) or bishop with a seat in the House of Lords. Not every lord, even one with a seat in the House of Lords, is a **peer**. Bishops, for instance, are spiritual lords. On the other hand every **peer** is a lord. The Lord Advocate and Lord Chancellor are high-ranking politically appointed lawyers. The Lord Chamberlain, Lord High Almoner, Lord High Commissioner to the General Assembly of the Church of Scotland, Lord Steward and some Lords-in-Waiting are Court appointments. The Lord Chancellor, Lord President of the Council and Lord Privy Seal are senior Government ministers. The Lord Great Chamberlain is the holder of a hereditary ceremonial post concerned with the sovereign's attendance at Parliament and great state occasions such as the lying in state of a recently deceased sovereign and the coronation of the new one. The post is shared in alternate reigns by the Marquess of Cholmondeley (*qv*), the present incumbent, and representatives of the Marquess of Lincolnshire (*see* CARRINGTON) and Earl of Ancaster (*see* WILLOUGHBY DE ERESBY). The Lord High Constable and Lord High Steward hold ceremonial offices nowadays filled only for the single day of a coronation. The Lord High Constable of Scotland holds a hereditary post passed down with the Earldom of Erroll (*qv*). Politically appointed Lords-in-Waiting are Government whips. A lord of the manor was previously a person with certain powers of jurisdiction and the right to collect feudal dues in the administrative unit called a manor but is now often little more than the possessor of some documents relating to a place name and at the most a few residual minor property rights, though confusion in the popular mind between the various categories of lord has lent the term in recent years a factitious importance and encouraged the commercial exchange of such documents.

marquess/marquis: holder of second highest rank of dignity in **peerage** (2), called a marquessate. The term is said to derive from the term march, a border area, whose custodian was of high rank as early as Carolingian times. The first marquess in the English peerage was created in 1385 (*see* SAINT ALBANS, **Lineage (of de Vere)**). The spelling marquis is preferred by some holders of that title, usually Scottish and in particular the Duke of Roxburghe (*qv*). In such cases it is said to recall the historic links between Scotland and France, the French word for marquess being of course *marquis*.

As with an **earl**, a marquess's title may derive from a place name, in which case it carries an 'of', or be a personal one, such as 'Conyngham', in which case it does not. A marquess is addressed or referred to as 'The Marquess (of) Blank' or 'The Most Hon The Marquess (of) Blank' in ascending order of formality. His wife is addressed or referred to as 'The Marchioness (of) Blank' or 'The Most Hon The Marchioness (of) Blank'. For his eldest son and heir *see* **courtesy title**. His younger sons and all daughters are addressed as for those of a **duke**. Marquessates were often awarded to Viceroys of India.

peerage: (1) a type of title of honour; (2) a collective term for persons, called peers, who possess certain titles of honour; (3) a reference work listing persons holding one or more (1) who make up (2). Where (1) is concerned, the reader should bear in mind that not all titles of honour are peerages (*see* for instance **baronet** and **knight**). Those that are comprise the ranks of **duke**, **marquess**, **earl**, **viscount** and **baron** in that order of descending relative seniority.

The term peerage derives from the Latin word for equal (*par*) and to the extent that all peers with seats in the House of Lords have tended to be summoned to it irrespective of their relative rank, importance or wealth, the term still has some relevance. But not every holder of a peerage (1) is summoned to the House of Lords. Minors are not, for instance, nor are Irish peers (for the complex reasons why in the latter case, *see* Charles Lysaght essay). Between 1707 and 1963 Scottish peers elected representatives from among themselves to sit in the House of Lords, hence the term 'rep S peer' in individual family articles in the main body of this work. As this work was going to press it seemed likely that most holders of a hereditary peerage (1) would shortly cease to be allowed to sit and vote in the House of Lords.

The institution of a peerage (2) as a body of notional equals, sometimes even the equal of the King in the extent of land they held, existed in mainland Europe long before the development of the House of Lords offshore. Under CHARLEMAGNE in the 9th century and in Flanders and France some two or three centuries later bodies of great nobles existed to whom historians have given the name peerage (2). In Scotland an early form of national peerage (2) is said by some scholars to have existed in the shape of the *mormaers* (*see* BUCHAN, preliminary remarks). But the main ones in the British Isles have historically been those of (a) England, which existed from early times till the Union of English and Scottish Parliaments in 1707; (b) Scotland, which ditto, (c) Ireland, which existed from the Middle Ages for the most part till the Union of Parliaments of Great Britain and Ireland in 1801 but to which further additions were made afterwards (*see* Charles Lysaght essay); (d) Great Britain, which existed from the above-mentioned Union of English and Scottish Parliaments till the 1801 Union, also above-mentioned; and (e) the United Kingdom, in which nearly every creation since 1801 has been made.

Someone possessing a title in the peerage (2) of England is not necessarily an Englishman by birth as opposed to a Scot, Irishman etc. Nor has he even necessarily always been English by birth as opposed to naturalisation. The same goes for the other national categories of peer. Piers de Gaveston, a Gascon, was created Earl of Cornwall in the peerage of England in 1308. The Duke of Schomberg, so created in the Irish peerage in 1689, was born at Heidelberg of a German father and an English mother. He could have been created a Duke in the peerage of England, indeed was naturalised as an Englishman a few weeks before his ennoblement. The peerage of England comprises all peers created by sovereigns of England up to 1707. From 1603 to 1707 sovereigns of England and sovereigns of Scotland were the same person, though the kingdoms themselves were still separate, and continued to create titles in the peerages of both kingdoms. The peerage of Scotland comprises all peers created by Kings or Queens of Scots up to 1707. Again, not all such grantees were necessarily Scottish. The Viscountcy of Falkland, for instance, now the oldest in the Scottish peerage (2), was originally conferred on an Englishman.

For a discussion of the principal examples of peerage (3), *see* the Introduction.

Red, Admiral (of) the: forerunner of modern Admiral; *see* also **Blue, Admiral (of) the**

regality: in Scotland, jurisdiction over an area of landed estate granted by the Crown or the landed estate over which the jurisdiction was so granted.

remainder: terms under which a hereditary title of honour may be transmitted, thus anyone in remainder to a title is a potential inheritor of it. An alternative expression is **limitation**. For an exhaustive account of the various kinds of remainder *see* Thomas Woodcock essay.

retour: in Scotland, a jury's decision as to who is the rightful heir.

sasine: the holding of land, originally by virtue of having been presented with constituent elements of that land, *viz*, earth and stone.

viscount: holder of the second lowest rank of **peerage** (1), called a viscounty or viscountcy. The word derives from the Latin *vice-comes*, or deputy to a *comes* (early equivalent of count), and in the British Isles was in early times used to refer to the Sheriff of a county, the **earl** (Anglo-Saxon equivalent of a count) of that county being then its chief administrative officer, appointed by the Crown. The Latin term *vicecomitatu*, meaning a sheriffdom, was used in Scottish legal documents until quite recently. Viscount only began to be used as a peerage honour in the 15th century, and is in fact the most recent addition to the ranks of the **peerage** (2). The first viscountcy was conferred in February 1439/40 on the 6th Lord (Baron) Beaumont (*see* BEAUMONT, Bt), who thus became Viscount Beaumont. Unlike viscounts in the English peerage, those in the Scottish peerage, the first of whom was Fentoun, so created in 1606, were known as 'Viscount of Blank', even where 'Blank' was a family name rather than a place. The only one still to use this form would appear to be the Viscount of Arbuthnott. For observations on the level of distinction considered as meriting a viscountcy in the 19th and 20th centuries *see* the appropriate passage in the Introduction. *Mutatis mutandis*, a viscount, his wife, widow and children are addressed or referred to as for a **baron**.

White, Admiral of the: forerunner of modern Vice-Admiral; *see* also **Blue, Admiral (of) the**

writ/writ of summons: instrument for calling an individual to the councils of the realm that developed into Parliament and later to the Upper House of Parliament itself. From the early 16th century the issuing of writs of summons as a means of creating peers declined, being replaced increasingly by **letters patent**. It is still used for accelerated promotions, however, that is to say the method of calling up the heir to a peerage by the name of one of his father's subsidiary titles. The most recent such instance was the case of Lord Cecil of Essendon, formerly (and colloquially still) known as Viscount Cranborne, eldest son and heir of the Marquess of Salisbury (*qv*). Occasionally as late as the 17th century a writ of summons was issued to a peer's eldest son calling him up to the House of Lords in the name of a **barony** his father did not in fact possess. Such a case was that of Strange (*qv*) in 1628. It became a doctrine, as decided in a legal judgment of 1736, that such 'mistaken' writs had the effect of creating a fresh peerage.

HERALDIC GLOSSARY

Heraldry evolved in 12th-century Western Europe, probably in response to the growing difficulty of recognising men in armour as that armour became heavier and more enveloping. At Hastings, when a rumour spread among the Normans that WILLIAM I (THE CONQUEROR) had been killed, he had only to tilt his helmet back as he rode among them for all to see that he was alive. Two hundred years later such a feat would have required considerable exertion and the help of a squire. Knights could by now only distinguish one another by devices on their shields or on the surcoats worn over their armour. Noblemen's devices were used by their followers as badges on their own shields and coats, and in the feudal army men were accustomed to muster under the banner of their lord, which was marked with his coat of arms. Crests, which were also distinguishing marks, came later.

Heraldic devices became hereditary as first the son then the more remote descendants of the original feudal lord retained the original device so as to guide their followers in battle. The devices outlived the use of armour, however, and by the 17th century were being widely used in non-military ways. By now the granting and use of coats of arms in England had come under the supervision of a body of heralds called the College of Arms, which had been set up under royal authority in 1483. In Scotland the Lyon Office, later Lord Lyon Office, supervised the use of arms.

It is probable that arms were not originally granted by anyone, but were assumed by various person as and when they pleased. Thus from time to time two or more people might be using the same device. In the Scrope-Grosvenor case in the late 14th century, when Lord Scrope challenged the right of Sir Robert Grosvenor to use the same coat of arms that he did himself, the duplication was accidental. Indeed a third person mentioned as using those arms was a Cornish knight called Carminow.

This celebrated case was only finally settled by the King himself, who found for Scrope. By now the Crown was assuming jurisdiction over the use of arms. A century later this had become firmly established, and since then it has been heraldic law that arms can only be borne in accordance with the rules made by the heralds under royal authority. Unfortunately, the forum for prosecuting illicit assumptions of arms in England, the Court of Chivalry, is obsolescent, despite a brief revival in the early 1950s. In Scotland the Court of the Lord Lyon has more teeth and still enforces laws against the irregular or illicit assumption of arms.

Note: for the convenience of the ordinary reader the word 'colour' in definitions is almost always to be understood as having its everyday meaning rather than the restricted one it has in heraldic language, where it is only one of three basic types of **tincture**. On the very few occasions it is used in this specialised sense it is set in **bold** type, as are all other terms given their own entry.

abased or **abaisé** used of an **ordinary** borne below its usual position
abatement one of the nine marks of degradation of coat armour
accollé (*see* **gorged**)
accosted side by side
accrued grown to maturity
achievement a fully **marshall**ed coat of arms
acorned bearing acorns
addorsed placed back to back, used especially of wings lying close to a creature's back
affrontée full-faced
Agnus Dei a lamb bearing a cross with a halo round its head
aislé winged
alant or **aland** a mastiff with short ears
allerion an eagle without beak or feet
ambulant (*see* **passant**)
amethyst a semi-precious stone, formerly used to express **purpure**
ancient a small flag on the stern of a ship
ancred or **anchored** used of cross whose four tips resemble anchor flukes
annulet a ring
antique crown (*see* **eastern crown**)
appaumé a hand open, with fingers and thumb at full length
argent (arg.) the **metal** silver, shown as white in heraldic illustration
armed used to describe all birds of prey whose talons and beaks are coloured differently from their bodies, also quadrupeds so variegated
arraché (*see* **erased**)
arrondie rounded
assis (*see* **sejant**)
attired applied to the horns of animals of the deer species instead of **armed**
attires the horns of a buck
azure (az.) blue
badge decorative device identifying a family, often borne by retainers, *e.g.*, on livery. It is not strictly speaking part of a heraldic **achievement** and is therefore not included in the illustrations of arms in this book. Indeed it is only included in this glossary at all because of popular misapprehension as to its status. (For a similar misapprehension *see* also **crest**)
baillond used of a lion holding a staff in its mouth
banded encircled with a band or riband
bar a horizontal division occupying one fifth of the shield
barbed (from the French word *barbe*) the leaves surrounding a full-blown rose are called barbs, hence the phrase 'a rose gu. barbed etc'
barnacles instruments used by farriers to curb horses
baron and femme, per the **impalement** of the arms of husband and wife
bars gemel two **bars** or **barrulets** placed parallel to each other, 'gemel' deriving from the Italian *gemelli*, twins
barrulet diminutive of **bar**
barry/barruly used of a **field** or **charge** divided by horizontal lines
base the lower part of a shield
basilisk a monster, like a **wyvern** or **cockatrice** but with a dragon's head at the end of its tail
basnet/basinet a helmet
baton (from the French *baston*, a staff or cudgel) a shape like a truncheon, generally a mark of bastardy. Unlike a **bend** it is **couped**, or cut short of the shield's edges
battled arrondie denotes that a battlement is rounded at the top
battled-imbattled one battlement on another
beaked (*see* **armed**)
bearing applicable to any single **charge** or heraldic device
beaver (*see* **visor**)
bend a division of a shield formed by two diagonal lines from the **dexter chief** to the **sinister base**
bendlet half-size diminutive of **bend**
bend sinister a **bend** issuing from the **sinister chief**
bendy used of a **field** or **charge** divided diagonally into four or more even-numbered parts
bezant a Byzantine gold coin, represented as a round flat piece of gold without impress
bezanté **semée** of **bezants**
billets rectangles
billeté **semée** of **billets**
bird-bolt a small blunt-headed arrow
blazon rules under which coats of arms are drawn up; also, as a verb, to describe a coat of arms in correct heraldic language

bordure a uniform edge to a shield, occupying one fifth of the **field**

botonnée used of a cross whose tips resemble **trefoils**

bouget (*see* **water-bouget**)

bowed embowed or arched

braced (*see* **interlaced**)

breys (*see* **barnacles**)

brimsey a gad-fly

brassarts/ brassets armour for the elbows and arms

burgonet a steel cap worn in battle

cabossed/ caboshed used of a full-faced animal head cut off just above the neck

cabrée, effray or **salient** used of a horse rising on its hind legs

cadency used of younger sons or descent from a junior branch of the family

caduceus a wand with two snakes entwined round it

caltrap, galtrap or **chevaltrap** an iron weapon used to wound horses' hooves, its spikes being positioned so that however it lies on the ground one will always point upwards

Calvary or **passion cross** a cross with three steps

canting arms arms which include a punning allusion to the name of the bearer

canton corner division occupying one third of the **chief**

cartouche an oval, formerly used to show armorials of Popes and other clerics

cap of maintenance or **dignity**, or **chapeau** headgear of crimson velvet **doubled** ermine

caparison the trappings of a warhorse

carbuncle (*see* **escarbuncle**)

casque a helmet

castle shown in heraldry as two towers at either end of a wall, the latter embattled and with a gateway

cat-a-mountain a wild cat, always drawn **guardant**

celestial crown an **eastern** or **antique crown** with a star on each point

cercellée (*see* **recercellée**)

chain-shot bullets linked by a chain

chamber piece a short piece of artillery without a gun carriage (*see* **mortar**)

chapeau (*see* **cap of maintenance**)

chaplet a garland of flowers and leaves

charge a figure or device on a shield

charged used of a **field** or **ordinaries** with a device on them

chaussé shod

chequy or **checky** used of a **field** covered with small squares of alternate **tinctures**

chevron a division of a shield shaped like the lower half of a **saltire** and occupying one third or one fifth of the area, according to whether it is charged or not

chevronel half-size diminutive of **chevron**

chief the upper third of a shield

chimera a monster with a woman's face, a lion's mane and legs, a goat's body and a dragon's tail

cinquefoil a five-petalled flower

civic wreath or **crown** a garland of oak leaves and acorns

clarion or **claricord** a rest for a lance

clenched used of a closed hand

closet diminutive of **bar**

cockatrice a monster with a bird's wings and legs and a snake's tail

colour in its specialised heraldic meaning, one of three types of **tincture**

combatant fighting or **rampant** face to face

compony and **compony counter-compony** used of an **ordinary** made up of one (**compony**) or two (**counter-compony**) rows of alternate squares of **metals** and **colours**

confronté facing each other

conjoined joined together

conjoined in lure used of two wings joined together, their tips downwards

contourné used of an animal facing to the **sinister**

corbie a raven

corded an **ordinary** or **charge** bound with cords

cotised or **cottised** (in French a *bande diminuée qui cotoye un autre bande*) a diminutive of the **bend**, a quarter of its breadth and one half of the width of the **bendlet**, generally borne in couples with a **bend** or **charge** between them. Two together are termed **cotises**, but when one is on each side of the **fess** or **bend** they are usually termed a **bend** or **fess** cotised

couchant used of an animal lying down

couché used of a shield suspended by one corner from a belt

counter-changed used of a **field** divided by a **bend** or other **ordinary** in which the **charges** in each section are of the **colour** or **metal** of the **field** of the other section

counter-embowed bent with the elbow to the **sinister** or bent in a reverse direction

counterflory a **tressure flory** in which the alternate **fleurs-de-lys** are reversed

counter-potent one of the heraldic **furs** in which the heads of the T-shaped sections are juxtaposed (*see* **potent**)

counter-vair differs from **vair** in that the rows of shields are arranged **base** against **base** and point against point

couped term used when the head or limb of an animal or any other **charge** is cut off by an even line

couple-close a diminutive of the **chevron** and often borne with it as the **cotise** is borne with the **bend**; it contains a quarter of the **chevron** and is always borne in pairs

courant running

coward used of an animal when drawn with its tail between its legs

cramp a piece of iron turned up at each end, usually borne in pairs

crampet, crampit, chape or **batterolle** the steel mounting at the bottom of a scabbard

crenellée (*see* **embattled**)

crescent differs from the **increscent** and the **decrescent** in having its horns turned towards the **chief** of the shield

crest heraldic device originally borne on top of a helmet, particularly in tournaments, but latterly used to decorate signet rings, cutlery, plate, crockery etc. as a mark of ownership by a family. Frequently misused nowadays to mean **achievement**, or the entire coat of arms rather than just a part of it.

crined used to describe the beard or hair when different in colour from the body

cronel the iron head of a tilting-spear

crozier the staff of a prelate

crusily used when the **field** or **charge** is strewn with crosses

cubit arm an arm with the hand attached, **couped** at the elbow

cuisses armour covering the thighs and knees

dancettée (in French *danché* and *dentellé*) is applied to lines whose teeth or indents are larger and wider than those of a line **indented**

debruised used when an **ordinary** or **subordinary** is placed over an animal or **charge** (*see* **surmounted**)

dechaussé (*see* **dismembered**)

decked used when the feathers of a bird are trimmed at the edges with a small line of a different colour from the rest of the body

decrescent a half moon, having the horns towards the **sinister**

defamed without a tail

degreed or **degraded** having degrees or steps at the end

dejected anything thrown down, *e.g.* 'a **garb** dejected.'

delve or **delf** one of the nine marks of **abatement**, resembling a square clod of earth

demi half, the top half being understood when no other is mentioned

despectant used of animals looking downwards

developed unfurled, as in flying colours

dexter the right-hand side of a shield viewed from the position of the person holding it

dimidiated divided in two equal parts

disclosed, expanded or **expansed** an alternative to **displayed**, used of tame birds

dismembered used of a **charge** cut into pieces, which are set a small distance apart but preserve the original form

displayed a bird of prey with its wings expanded

disponed arranged

distilling letting blood

dormant sleeping; differs from **couchant** in that the head is lowered

doubled with the lining turned up around the edge

double-queued having two tails

drapeau a flag

drawing-iron an instrument used by wire-drawers

ducal coronet or **crest coronet** a coronet composed of four leaves of equal height above the rim

duciper a **cap of maintenance**

eastern crown the crown worn by Jewish kings

eft (*see* **newt**)

eightfoil or **huitfoil** an eight-petalled flower

elevated used of birds' wings when open and upright

embattled or **imbattled** used of buildings having battlements

embowed bent or bowed

embrued having drops of blood upon or falling from it
enaluron eight birds placed in the border
endorse a quarter-size diminutive of the **pale**
endorsed (*see* **addorsed**)
enfield a monster with a fox's head, an elephant's chest, a horse's mane, an eagle's forelegs, a greyhound's body and hind legs and a lion's tail
enfiled pierced by the blade of a weapon
Englishman's head used in Welsh **blazons** to mark feats in the struggle against the English
engould used of a **charge** whose ends enter an animal's mouth
engrailed a scalloped partition line with the spikes outwards
enhanced an **ordinary** placed higher than its usual position
enmanche (*see* **manche**)
ensigned a **charge** with another above it
entoyre a border charged with eight inanimate **charges**
enurney a border charged with eight animals
environné surrounded
enwrapped folded round
epaulier armour for the shoulders
equipped used of a horse with all its trappings
eradicated uprooted, as of trees or plants
erased torn from the body, with jagged edges
erect upright
ermine (erm.) white **fur** with black spots
ermines black **fur** with white spots
erminois gold **fur** with black spots
escallop-shell a pilgrim's badge
escarbuncle a precious stone, shown as eight sceptres issuing from a central **annulet**
escutcheon of pretence the shield on which a man bears his wife's arms if she is an heiress. It is borne in the centre of his own shield and is usually of the same shape
esquierre a bearing similar to the gyron (see **gyronny**), but extending across the whole shield
estoile a star, usually of six wavy points; when an estoile has more than six points they are alternately straight and wavy
evett or **lizard** a small animal like a crocodile, usually shown **vert**, used in the arms of some Irish families
expanded or **expansed** displayed
falchion a broadsword
fan the instrument by which chaff is blown away
feathered used of arrows whose flights are a different colour from the shafts; also called **flighted**
fer-de-moline the iron fixed in the centre of a millstone, holding it up and guiding its motion; also called a **millrind**, **inkmoline** or **inke-de-moline**
fer-de-fourchette used of a cross or **saltire** whose tips end with a forked iron
femau or **fermaile** a belt buckle
fess a division of a shield formed by two lines drawn horizontally and occupying one third of it
fess point the centre of the shield
fesswise placed like a fess
feuil-de-scie a **pale** or **fess** indented on one side with teeth like the edge of a saw
field the entire surface of the shield upon which the **charges** or **bearings** are depicted
figured used of a **charge** shown with a human face, such as the sun
file (*see* **label**)
fillet a diminutive of the **chief**
fimbriated bordered or hemmed with a different colour
firme used of a cross **patée** extending to both sides of a shield
fireball a grenade with flames issuing from the top
fire beacon (*see* **beacon**)
fitchée pointed at the end
flanches or **flaunches** divisions on both sides of a shield formed by the segment of a circle drawn from the **chief** to the **base**
fleur-de-lys the flower of the lily, having three leaves instead of nature's five
flexed bent or bowed
flory, fleury, flurty or **floretty** flowered with **fleurs-de-lys**
flotant floating
flouretté the same as **fleury**
flower of the flag the same as **fleur-de-lys**
foliated leaved
fountain a **roundle barry wavy** of six **arg.** and **az.**
fourchée forked at the end
fracted broken
fraise a strawberry leaf
fresnée used of an animal rearing on its hind legs
fret a **saltire** and a **mascle** interlaced
fretty a **field** covered with **conjoined frets**
fructed bearing fruit
fur a pattern, constituting part of an achievement, based on the appearance of animal pelts; *see* for example **ermine** and **vair**.
furnant emitting smoke
furnished used of a horse when caparisoned, or of a stag to refer to its **attires**
fusil an elongated lozenge
fusilly covered with **fusils**
gad-bee a dun fly
gads plates of steel or iron
galley (*see* **lymphad**)
galtrap (*see* **caltrap**)
gamb (from the French *jambe*) the foreleg of an animal; when **couped** or **erased** near the middle joint it is only a paw
garb a sheaf of any kind of grain; when other than wheat the kind must be stated
gardant (*see* **guardant**)
gardebras the elbow-piece of a suit of armour
garde-visure a vizor
garnished decorated
gaze applied to a beast of the chase when looking full front. *See* **guardant** for other animals in this posture
gemel (*see* **bars gemel**)
genet a small animal like a fox
gillyflower, July flower a blood-red carnation
giron (*see* **gyronny**)
givers (*see* **guiuré**)
gliding used of snakes when moving **fessways**
glory a series of rays issuing from a **charge** or **ordinary**
gobony (*see* **company**)
golpe a purple **roundle**
gonfannon a banner
gordian knot double **annulets** linked to each other and to one in the centre **gyronny**
gore or **gusset** two curved lines, one from the **sinister chief** point the other from the **base** middle point, meeting in an acute angle at the **fess** point
gorge or **gurge** a **water-bouget**
gorged encircled round the throat
gorges a whirlpool
gorget armour for the chest
goutte a drop
gouttée (*see* **guttée**)
gradient used of a tortoise when shown walking
greave armour for the legs
grice a young wild boar
grieces steps on which crosses may be placed (*see* **Calvary**)
griffin or **gryphon** a monster with the upper half an eagle and the lower half a lion
griffin-male a **griffin** without wings but with large ears
grittic used of a **field** made up equally of **metal** and **colour**
guardant full-faced; *see* also **gaze**
guidon or **pennon** a flag
guiuré, givers, or **gringolé** (from *guivris*, viper) used of **charges** which end in serpent's heads
gules (gu.) red
gun shot or **gun stone** a black **roundle**
guttée or **gutty** (from the Latin *gutta*, drop) sprinkled with drops (*gouttes*)
guttée d'eau sprinkled with water
guttée de larmes sprinkled with tears
guttée de poix sprinkled with pitch
guttée de sang sprinkled with blood
guttée d'huile or **guttée d'olive** sprinkled with drops of green oil
guttée d'or sprinkled with gold
guttée reversed inverted drops
guze a red **roundle**
gyronny the division of a shield by cross and **saltire** in six to twelve even-numbered parts
habergeon a short coat of mail without sleeves
habited clothed; the same as **vested**
halbert a pole-axe
halcyon a kingfisher

half-spear a spear with a short handle

harpy a mythical bird with a woman's face, neck and breasts, and a vulture's body and legs

harpoon a salmon or eel-spear

hart a stag more than seven years old

harvest-fly a butterfly

hatchment (corruption of **achievement**) the coat of arms of a dead person, put up on the front of the house then taken and displayed in the local church

hauberk a twisted coat of mail

hauriant or **haurient** used of a fish when upright, as if putting its head above water to take in air

haussé or **enhanced** used of a **chevron** or **fess** when higher than its usual position

hawk's jesses leather thongs fastening the bells attached to a hawk's legs

hawk's lure a falconer's decoy of two wings joined with their tips downwards and fastened to a line and ring

hay-fork (*see* **shake-fork**)

heads usually have their posture stated: **affrontée** when in profile, **guardant** when full-faced and **regardant** when looking backwards; 'head' on its own implies in profile

healme or **casque** a helmet

hem break or **hackle** an instrument for bruising hemp

herison a hedgehog

hill or **hillock** used when only one hill is intended; if more than one the correct term is hillocks or molehills

hilted used of the handle of a sword

hind a female stag, generally **blazon**ed **trippant**

hirondelle a swallow

honourable ordinaries used of nine basic heraldic charges: **chief**, **fess**, **pale**, **bend**, **bend sinister**, **bar**, cross, **saltire** and **chevron**

hooded used of a human face when the head-dress is of a different colour from the face; or of a bird of prey when it has a hood over its head

hoofed used to describe the colour of the hooves of an animal when different from the colour of the animal itself; cloven-footed animals are said to be **unguled**

horned used to describe the colour of the horns of an animal when different from the colour of the animal itself (*see* **attired**)

huit-foil (*see* **eightfoil**)

humet or **humetté** used of an **ordinary** when its tips do not reach the sides of the shield

hunting-horn, **cornet** or **buglehorn** a semicircular horn; when the belt is of another colour it is called **stringed** of that colour

hurst a group of trees

hurt a blue **roundle**

hurtée or **hurty** **semée** of **hurts**

hydra a many-headed dragon

imbattled (*see* **embattled**)

imbowed (*see* **embowed**)

imbrued or **imbued** (*see* **embrued**)

impalement/impaling two coats of arms side by side on the same shield

incensed or **incensan** used of angry animals with fire issuing from their mouths and ears

increment or **increscent** used when a crescent is shown with the horns towards the **dexter**

indented a serrated line, like **dancettée** but with smaller notches

Indian or **Assyrian goat** a goat with bent horns and ears like those of a **talbot**

indorsed or **endorsed** (*see* **addorsed**)

inescutcheon a small shield borne as a **charge** on another, usually indicating marriage with an heir or co-heir

inflamed burning in flames

infula a tiara

ink moline (*see* **fer-de-moline**)

in lure two wings joined with the tips downward

in pride used of a peacock or turkey cock with its tail spread out

in splendour the sun surrounded by rays

inter between

interlaced linked together

invected like **engrailed** but with the spikes pointing inwards

invexed arched

iron ring a tool used by wire-drawers

issuant rising or coming out of; when an animal is **blazon**ed as such only the upper half is shown

jamb or **jambe** (*see* **gamb**)

jellop or **jowlop** a cock's comb

jessant shooting forth as vegetables spring forth; half the **charge** only is depicted when **blazon**ed jessant

jessant-de-lys a **fleur-de-lys** in a leopard's mouth

jesses the leather thongs that fasten the bells to the legs of a hawk

joinant (*see* **conjoined**)

jupon a surcoat

knowed (*see* **nowed**)

label or **lambel** a piece of silk or linen with three pendants, usually used as a mark of **cadency**

lambrequin (*see* **mantle**)

langued used when an animal's tongue is of a different colour from its body

lattice, tirlace, trellée a trellis whose pieces are nailed together at the crossings

laurel an emblem of victory and triumph

laver a cutter or ploughshare

legged or **membered** used when the legs of an animal or bird are of a different colour from its body

leopard French heralds used to call the lion **passant guardant** a leopard, and the royal lions of England were at one time so **blazon**ed

leopard's faces a phrase used when no part of the neck appears and the posture is full-faced; when **erased** or **couped** at the neck in profile the word 'head' is used instead

lever a cormorant

leveret a young hare

lined the inside lining of a piece of clothing when differently coloured from the outside; also used of chains and ropes fixed to the collars of animals

lioncel or **lionel** a young lion

lion dragon a monster with the upper half a lion and the lower half a dragon

Lion of England sometimes used for a lion **rampant guardant**

lion poisson or **sea lion** a monster resembling a lion in the upper half and a fish in the lower, with webbed feet

listen the scroll or ribbon on which the motto is inscribed

lodged used of beasts of the chase when lying on the ground

lopped or **snagged** cut so as to show the thickness

lozenge a diamond-shaped **charge**

lozengy covered with **lozenges**

lucy or **luce** a pike (fish)

luna the moon

lure or **leure** (*see* **hawk's lure**)

lymphad or **galley** a ship with one mast and many oars

maiden's head the head and neck of a woman **couped** below the breast, the head wreathed with roses and crowned with an **eastern crown**

mail protective clothing made of small close rings, linked together as if woven and shown as being like fish scales

mailed clothed in mail

main a hand

maintenance (*see* **cap of maintenance**)

manche or **maunche** a sleeve with long hanging ends

maned used of an animal when the mane is of a different colour from the body

mantelle or **chappe** used when the two upper angles to the **field** are cut off by two lines issuing from the middle **chief** point to either side of the shield, forming two triangles of a different colour from the field, as if a mantle were thrown over it and the ends drawn back

man-tiger a monster with a lion's body, the head and face of an old man and horns like an ox

mantle or **lambrequin** the cloak on which achievements are painted

mantlings ornamented foliage-work for adorning helmets in painting armorial **bearings**

marined used of any monster with the lower body like a fish

marine wolf a seal

marshal to arrange **charges**, **ordinaries** etc in correct order on a coat of arms

martlet or **merion** a mythical bird shaped like a martin with feathers in place of its legs, the mark of a fourth son

mascle a hollowed-out **lozenge**

masculy covered with **mascles**

masoned, masony or **maçonné** used when the **field**, **charge** or **crest** is divided like a wall by lines of a given colour

membered (*see* **legged**)

meslé mingled

metal one of the basic types of **tincture** or colour used in heraldry: white and yellow, for instance, are described not as themselves but as **argent** and **or** (silver and gold)

millpick an instrument used by millers and millwrights to dress millstones

millrind (*see* **fer-de-moline**)

modilion, cotoose or **scroll** — the foliage ornament of a pillar

mooted or **moulted** (*see* **eradicated**)

morion — a steel cap or helmet prevalent particularly in the 16th century, its upper half curving downwards, its edges curving upwards

morné or **mortné** — (French 'stillborn') a lion **rampant** without tongue, teeth or claws

morse — a sea-lion

mort — a skull, usually placed on the **hatchment** of the last of a family

mortier — a cap of state

mound — (French *monde*, Latin *mundus*, the world) a globe encircled with a horizontal band of diamonds and other precious stones, from the upper edge of which springs a similarly studded semicircular band, and having on the top a cross; the mound forms part of the regalia of an emperor or king

mount — when the bottom or **base** of the shield is represented as a **field**, and curved

mourned — blunted

mullet — the rowel of a spur, in English heraldry with five straight points and in French heraldry with six

mullet pierced — a **mullet** with a hole in the centre, allowing the colour on which it is borne to appear through it

muraillé — walled

mural crown — a circle of gold, crenellated like a battlement

murrey — blood-coloured

muschetors or **mushetours** — the black tail of the **ermine**, but without the three spots used to depict **ermine**

naiant or **natant** — swimming, used of fish when drawn horizontally

naissant — rising or coming out of

narcissus — a flower of six petals, each resembling a **cinquefoil**

naval crown — a crown composed of ships' sterns and sails arranged alternately

nebulée or **nebuly** — a line of partition like a dove-tail joint with the corners rounded

nerved — used of leaves and plants whose veins are a different colour from the rest

nislée or **nyllée** — slender, narrow or reduced almost to nothing

nowed — tied in a knot

ogress (*see* **pellet**)

ombré — shadowed

ondé (*see* **undée**)

opinicus — a winged monster with a lion's body, an eagle's head and neck and a short tail like a camel's

oppressed (*see* **debruised**)

or — the **metal** gold, shown as yellow in heraldic illustration

orange — a tawny **roundle**

organ rest (*see* **rest**)

orle — a diminutive of the **bordure** but not attached to the outside of the shield; charges so arranged are in orle

orlé — bordered

over all — when a **charge** or **ordinary** is placed over other **bearings**; **surmounted**, **debruised** and **oppressed** are similar terms

overt — used of bird's wings when open

pale — a band placed vertically in the middle of a shield

pall or **paile** — an archiepiscopal vestment of white lamb's wool, formed in heraldry by half a **pale** issuing from the **base** meeting in the **fess** point half a **saltire** issuing from the **dexter** and **sinister chief** to form a letter Y

pallet — a diminution of the **pale**

palisado — a crown composed of palisade-shaped points

palisse — a division of the **field** in the form of **piles** reaching from top to bottom, representing the palisades before a fortification

paly — divided into an equal number of pieces of alternate colours by perpendicular partition lines; the number of divisions must be specified: paly of six, of eight, etc

paly-bendy — **pales** cut by diagonal partition lines

palmer's staff — (French *bourdon*) a pilgrim's staff

papilone — a field divided into variegated specks like those on a butterfly, but ranged like the scales of a fish

park pales — palings depicted close to each other, with pointed tops

pascuant or **pasquant** — used of animals when grazing

Paschal or **Holy Lamb** — a lamb **passant arg.** carrying the banner of St George

passant — used of an animal in a walking position

passant guardant — used of an animal walking with its head full-face

Passion Cross (*see* **Calvary Cross**)

passant reguardant — walking, but looking back

passant repassant — used when animals are shown walking past each other in opposite directions

Pater Noster or **Nostré** — a cross composed of beads

pa(t)té — (French *patte*, paw) splayed towards the end, as a paw is

pattes — paws

pavement — depicted like masonry

pavilion — an oblong tent with a projecting entrance

pean — a **fur** with gold spots on a black ground

peel — a tool used for drawing bread from the oven

pegasus — a horse with wings

pelican — always shown pecking her breast so that it bleeds; when feeding her young in this manner she is said to be 'in her piety'

pellet or **ogress** — a black **roundle**

pelletty or **pellettée** — **semée** of **pellets**

penner and ink horn — a case for holding pens and ink

pennon — a pointed or swallow-tailed flag

permoncel or **pencil** — a small streamer or flag

penny-yard — a small coin

per — used to show how a shield, **ordinary** or **charge** is divided by any of the partition lines, as per **bend**, per **pale** etc

petronel — a pistol

pheon — the head of a dart or arrow

pierced — used when an **ordinary** or **charge** is perforated; the shape should be specified — square, round etc

piety (*see* **pelican**)

pile — a wedge issuing from the **chief** and tapering towards the **base**

pilgrim's scrip — a wallet or pouch

plate — a silver or white **roundle**

playing tables — backgammon tables

plenitude — a full moon

plié — used of a bird when its wings are folded

ployé — bowed and bent

plummet — a plumb line

poing — a closed hand

pomme — a green **roundle** (plural **pomels**)

popinjay — a small green parrot with red beak and legs

portant — used of a cross that is not erect but placed across the shield as if being carried on the shoulder

posé (*see* **statant**)

pot — a steel hat

potent — a crutch; also a **fur** composed of crutch- or T-shaped divisions

potenté — a line of division formed by crutch-shaped figures

pouldron — armour for the shoulder

pounce — the talons of a bird of prey

powdered — *see* **semeé**

pride (*see* **in pride**)

proper/ppr. — used of objects when shown in their natural colours

purfled, trimmed or **garnished** — used of the studs and rims of armour when they are a different colour from the armour itself

purflew or **purfled** — used of a border of **fur** shaped like **vair**; when of one row it is termed purflewed, when of two, counter-purflewed

purpure — purple

python — a winged serpent

quarterly — used of a shield divided into four equal sections by vertical and horizontal lines

quatrefoil — a four-leaved grass

queue — tail

queue-fourchée (*see* **double queued**)

quintain — a tilting post

quise, à la — at the thigh (French *à la cuisse*)

radiant, rayonned, rayonnant, rayoneé — used to express any **ordinary** or **charge** edged with glittering rays, like the sun

raguly — like **embattled**, but with the protuberances set obliquely

ramé — a French term for branched or **attired**

rampant — used of an animal standing on its hind legs

rampant sejant — used of a lion when sitting with the forelegs raised

rangé — arranged in order

raping — used of animals devouring their prey

razed (*see* **erased**)

rays — when round the sun they are 16 in number, when round an estoile nine; they are shown alternately straight and wavy

rearing — used of a horse when standing on the hind legs with the forelegs raised

rebated — when the point of a weapon or part of a cross is broken off

reboundant — used of a lion's tail when it forms the letter 'S' with the point outwards

rebus — used of an **achievement** whose **charge**s allude to the name of the bearer, *e.g.* castles for Castleton

recercellée — used of a cross whose ends are slightly forked and curled back

reclinant — bending backwards

reflexed or **reflected** — curved or turned round, as the chain from the collar of a beast thrown over its back

regardant — looking behind or backwards

reindeer — in heraldry, a stag with double **attires**

remora — a snake

removed — implies that the **ordinary** has fallen or become removed from its proper position

rencontre (*see* **cabossed**)

renverse — when anything is set with its head downwards or contrary to its natural way or turned upside down

rere mouse — a bat

respectant or **respecting** — used of animals when placed face to face

reserved — contrary to the usual position

rests, clarions or **clavichords** — the rest for a lance; by some authorities called musical instruments, they bear a resemblance to a fluted bracket

retorted — used of snakes when intertwined

reversed — turned upside down

riband or **ribbon** — an eighth part of a **bend**, of which it is a diminutive

rising — used of birds when preparing to take flight

rompu or **rompé** — broken

rose — always represented as full-blown with the petals expanded, **seeded** in the middle, and backed by five green barbs or leaves. When a heraldic rose is red it must be **blazon**ed **gu.** not **ppr.**; a rose is termed '**barbed** and **seeded** ppr.' when the barbs are green and the seeds yellow

roundels/ roundles — round **charges**, flat when of **metal** and spherical when of **colour**; they change their names according to their **tinctures** (*see* under individual names)

rousant — the same as **rising**

rustre — a **lozenge** pierced; similar to a **mascle** but with a round instead of a diamond-shaped hole

sable (sa.) — black

sacre or **saker** — a falcon with a grey head, blue feet and legs and a dark brown back; also a small cannon

sagittarius — a creature half man and half horse shooting with a bow and arrow

salamander — a mythical animal whose natural habitat is fire; it is shown green, surrounded with flames

salient — the posture of an animal leaping on its prey

salmon spear — the same as a **harpoon**

saltant — used of a squirrel, cat, weasel, rat etc when springing forward

saltire — an 'X'-shaped cross

saltirewise — in the position of a **saltire**

sanglier — a wild boar

sanguine — blood-coloured (*see* also **murrey**)

sanglant — bloody, torn off or erased

sarcellée — cut through in the middle

satyr — a creature with a lion's tail, the ears and horns of an antelope and the face of a man

scallop — a type of shell

scarpe — a diminutive of the **bend sinister**, representing a shoulder-belt or officer's scarf

scintillant — sparkling

scrip (*see* **pilgrim's scrip**)

sea dog — a creature like a **talbot** but with a beaver's tail, a scalloped fin down the back from head to tail, scaled body, legs and tail and webbed feet

sea lion — a monster with a lion's body and a fish's tail

sea pie — a dark brown water fowl with a red head and white neck and wings

seax — a scimitar with a semi-circular notch on the back of the blade

seeded — used of the seeds of roses, lilies etc when of a different colour from the flower itself

segreant — used of the **griffin** when erect with wings **addorsed**

sejant or **segeant** — sitting

sejant addorsed — used when two animals are sitting back to back

semée — used when a **field**, **crest** or **supporter** is scattered with minor **charges**, e.g. **crescents**, **mullets** or **fleurs-de-lys**; *see* also **powdered**

seraph's head — a child's head between three pairs of wings, two in **chief**, two in **fess** and two in **base**

sexfoil — a grass or flower with six leaves, in form like a **cinquefoil**

shack-bolt — a fetter put on the wrists or ankles of prisoners

shafted — used to denote that a spear-head has a handle

shake-fork — like the **pall**, but not touching the edges of the shield, and with a point at each end like the **pile**

shambrough — a ship

shapewined — in a curved line

sheaf (*see* **garb**)

side — a portion of the shield cut off by a perpendicular line

single — the tail of a deer

sinister — the left side of the shield (*see* **dexter**)

sinister chief — the left side of the chief

sinople — green

siren or **syren** — a mermaid

skean — a short sword or dagger

slashed — sleeves of garments cut open lengthways, the gashes filled in with puffing of another colour

slay, slea or **reed** — an instrument used by weavers

slipped — having a stalk, shown as torn from the original stem

spancelled or **fettered** — used of a horse that has the fore and hind legs fettered by fetter locks fastened to the end of a stick

spear-head imbrued — with the point bloody

speed, at — used of a stag when running

sperver — a tent

sphinx — a monster with a lion's body, the wings of an eagle and the head and breasts of a woman

spindle (*see* **fusil**) — a spade

splendour — a term for the sun when represented with a human face and emitting rays

sruttle — a winnowing fan or basket

starved (*see* **estoile**) — stripped of leaves, etc

statant — standing

staves — walking sticks used by pilgrims

subordinaries — class of **charges** next in importance to the **honourable ordinaries** (*qv*), comprising the **canton**, **inescutcheon**, **gyron**, **orle**, **tressure**, **lozenge**, **mascle**, **rustre**, **fusil**, **fret**, **flanch**, **bordure**, **pile**, **label**, **billet** and **flasque**

subverted — reversed, turned upside down

sufflue — rest or clarion

super charge — one figure **charged** or borne upon another

supporters — figures placed on either side of a shield

surcoat — a loose, light coat worn over armour

surgeant — rising

surmounted — where one **charge** is placed over another

surtout or **sur-le-tout** — used of a small shield placed on the centre of a larger one

syke (*see* **fountain**)

tabard — the surcoat embroidered with the Sovereign's arms and worn by heralds

talbot — a hunting dog with thick snout and hanging ears

targant, torgant or **torqued** — bending and rebending like the letter 'S'

target — a round buckler or shield

tasces or **tasses** — armour which covers the thighs

tau — a cross with no upper vertical arm

tenne or **tawney** — orange

terras — the representation of a piece of ground at the bottom of the **base**, generally shown green

tiara or **triple crown** — a cap or helmet of golden cloth, from which hang two pendants, embroidered and fringed at the ends, **semée** of crosses of gold. The cap is enclosed by three marquess's coronets and on the top is a mound of gold with a cross of the same material

tiercé — used when the shield is divided into three equal parts of different colours

timbre — signifies the helmet when placed over the arms in a complete **achievement**

tincture — colour in heraldic illustration; there are three basic types: colours (all unpatterned colours that are not **metals**), **metals** (such as **argent** or **or**) and **furs**

tirret — manacles or handcuffs

toison d'or — a golden fleece, or the Holy Lamb

torqued — wreathed

torse — the wreath on which the crest is placed

torteau — a red **roundle**

tortillé — **nowed** or **wreathed**

tourné (*see* **reguardant**)

tower — triple-towered; when the word 'tower' is used in **blazon** without any further description it should be shown without the three small turrets rising from the battlements

transmuted — counterchanged

transpierced — pierced through

traversed — turned to the **sinister** side of the shield

treflée — used of a cross whose arms end in three semicircles, each representing the **trefoil**; a **bend** treflée has **trefoils** issuing from the side

trefoil — a three-leaved grass

treille or **trellise** latticed; differs from **fretty** in that the pieces do not interlace under and over but cross over each other and are nailed at the joints

tressure the half-size diminutive of the **orle**

tressure flory a **tressure** having **fleurs-de-lys** placed at intervals round it

tressure flory counter-flory a **tressure flory** in which the alternate **fleurs-de-lys** point to the centre of the **field**

trian aspect showing three-quarters of the body

tricorporate when the bodies of three animals are shown issuing from the **dexter**, **sinister** and **base** points of the shield, meeting joined to one head in the centre

trien three

trippant used of beasts of the chase as **passant** is to beasts of prey, shown with one foot up as if trotting; counter-trippant is when two beasts are tripping past each other in opposite directions

triumphal crown or **garland** composed of laurel

trononée or **demembrée** used of cross or other **bearing** which is dismembered but so arranged that the pieces retain the original form of the bearing

true lovers' knot a double knot made with two bows on each side, interlacing each other and with two ends: snakes are sometimes twisted in this form

umbraced (*see* **vambraced**)

umbrated or **adumbrated** shadowed

undée, ondée or **undy** wavy

unguled used of animals' hooves when they are coloured differently from the body

urchin a hedgehog

uriant used of a fish when shown with the head downwards and the tail erect

urvant or **urved** turned or bowed upwards

vair or **vaire** a **fur** shown as rows of small shields, alternately reversed

vallary crown a gold circlet surmounted by flat, pointed strips

vambrace armour for the arm

vambraced used when the arm is completely covered with armour

vamplate a gauntlet

vamplet a broad pan of steel attached to the lower part of a tilting-spear to protect the hand

vannet the **escallop** when shown without the ears

verblée a hunting-horn edged with **metal** of a different colour

verdoy a border charged with eight flowers, leaves or fruit, *e.g.* 'a **border gu.**, verdoy of oak leaves or'

vert green

verted or **reverted** same as **flexed** or **reflexed**

verules or **ferrals** several rings, one within another, with the same centre

vested clothed

vigilant used of a cat when watching for prey

vol two wings of an eagle displayed and **conjoined**

volant flying

voided used of a **charge** with the middle cut out so that the **field** is seen through it

voiders a diminutive of **flanch**

vorant or **engoulant** devouring

vulned wounded so that blood appears

wallet (*see* **pilgrim's scrip**)

watching (*see* **vigilant**)

water bouget a vessel to carry water

wavy (*see* **undée**) a line of partition formed like waves

weare, weir or **dam** in **fess**, is made with stakes and osier twigs interwoven as a fence against water

welt or **edge** a narrow border to an **ordinary** or **charge**

wings conjoined wings expanded, elevated and united at the bottom (*see* **lure**)

woodman wild man or savage

wound a purple **roundle** (*see* **golpe**)

wreath a garland or chaplet; the wreath upon which the **crest** is usually borne is composed of two bands of silk twisted together

wyvern a monster with the wings and upper part of a dragon and the lower part of a snake

ABBREVIATIONS

A

AA	Anti-aircraft; Automobile Association; Architectural Association; Augustinians of the Assumption
AAA	Amateur Athletics Association; American Accounting Association
AAAC	Australian Army Air Corps
AAAL	American Academy of Arts and Letters
AAAS	American Association for the Advancement of Science
AAC	Army Air Corps
AACCA	Associate, Association of Certified and Corporate Accountants
AACE	Association for Adult and Continuing Education
AADip	Architectural Association Diploma
A&AEE	Aeroplane and Armament Experimental Establishment
AAF	Auxiliary Air Force
AAFCE	Allied Air Forces in Central Europe
AAG	Assistant Adjutant-General
AAI	Associate, Chartered Auctioneers' and Estate Agents' Institute
AAIL	American Academy and Institute of Arts and Letters
AAM	Association of Assistant Mistresses in Secondary Schools
AAMC	Australian Army Medical Corps
AA&QMG	Assistant Adjutant and Quartermaster-General
AAPS	Aquatic and Atmospheric Physical Sciences
AAS	American Astronomical Society
AASA	Associate, Australian Society of Accountants
AASC	Australian Army Service Corps
AATSE	Australian Academy of Technological Sciences and Engineering
AAUQ	Associate in Accountancy, University of Queensland
AB	Bachelor of Arts (US); able-bodied seaman
ABA	Amateur Boxing Association; Antiquarian Booksellers' Association; American Bar Association
ABC	Australian Broadcasting Commission; American Broadcasting Companies; Amateur Boxing Club; Associate, Birmingham Conservatoire
ABCA	Army Bureau of Current Affairs
ABCC	Association of British Chambers of Commerce
ABCFM	American Board of Commissioners for Foreign Missions
ABI	Association of British Insurers
ABIA	Associate, Bankers' Institute of Australasia
ABINZ	Associate, Bankers' Institute of New Zealand
ABIS	Association of Burglary Insurance Surveyors
ABM	Advisory Board of Ministry
ABNM	American Board of Nuclear Medicine
Abp/Archbp	Archbishop
ABP	Associated British Ports
ABPsS	Associate, British Psychological Society
ABRC	Advisory Board for the Research Councils
ABS	Associate, Building Societies' Institute
ABSA	Association for Business Sponsorship of the Arts
ABSI	Associate, Boot and Shoe Institution
ABSM	Associate, Birmingham and Midland Institute School of Music
ABTA	Association of British Travel Agents
ABTAPL	Association of British Theological and Philosophical Libraries
AC	Companion, Order of Australia; *Ante Christum* (before Christ)
ACA	Associate, Institute of Chartered Accountants
Acad	Academy
ACARD	Advisory Council for Applied Research and Development
ACAS	Advisory, Conciliation and Arbitration Service; Assistant Chief of the Air Staff
ACBSI	Associate, Chartered Building Societies Institute
ACC	Association of County Councils; Anglican Consultative Council
ACCA	Associate, Chartered Association of Certified Accountants
ACCEL	American College of Cardiology Extended Learning
ACCM	Advisory Council for the Church's Ministry
ACCS	Associate, Corporation of Secretaries (formerly of Certified Secretaries)
ACDP	Australian Committee of Directors and Principals
A/Cdre	Air Commodore
ACDS	Assistant Chief of Defence Staff
ACE	Association of Consulting Engineers; Member, Association of Conference Executives
ACF	Army Cadet Force
ACFA	Army Cadet Force Association
ACFAS	Association Canadienne-Française pour l'Avancement des Sciences
ACFHE	Association of Colleges for Further and Higher Education
ACG	Assistant Chaplain-General
ACGI	Associate, City and Guilds of London Institute
ACGS	Assistant Chief of the General Staff
ACIArb	Associate, Chartered Institute of Arbitrators
ACIB	Associate, Chartered Institute of Bankers
ACII	Associate, Chartered Insurance Institute
ACIS	Associate, Institute of Chartered Secretaries and Administrators (formerly Chartered Institute of Secretaries)
ACIT	Associate, Chartered Institute of Transport
ACLS	American Council of Learned Societies
ACM	Association of Computing Machinery
ACMA	Associate, Chartered Institute of Management Accountants (formerly Institute of Cost and Management Accountants)
ACNS	Assistant Chief of Naval Staff
ACommA	Associate, Society of Commercial Accountants
ACORD	Advisory Committee on Research and Development
ACOS	Assistant Chief of Staff
ACOST	Advisory Council on Science and Technology
ACP	Association of Clinical Pathologists; Associate, College of Preceptors; African/Caribbean/Pacific
ACPO	Association of Chief Police Officers
ACRE	Action with Rural Communities in England
ACS	American Chemical Society; Additional Curates Society
ACSEA	Allied Command South East Asia
ACSM	Associate, Camborne School of Mines
ACT	Australian Capital Territory; Australian College of Theology; Associate, College of Technology; Association of Corporate Treasurers
Actg	Acting
ACTT	Association of Cinematograph, Television and Allied Technicians
ACTU	Australian Council of Trade Unions
ACU	Association of Commonwealth Universities
ACWA	Associate, Institute of Cost and Works Accountants
AD	Dame of the Order of Australia: *Anno Domini* (in the year of the Lord); Air Defence
ADAS	Agricultural Development and Advisory Service
ADB	Asian Development Bank; Associate of the Drama Board (Education)
ADB/F	African Development Bank/Fund
ADC	Aide-de-Camp
ADC(P)	Personal Aide-de-Camp to The Sovereign
ADCM	Archbishop of Canterbury's Diploma in Church Music
AD Corps	Army Dental Corps
Addl	Additional
ADEME	Assistant Director Electrical and Mechanical Engineering
ADFManc	Art and Design Fellow, Manchester
ADFW	Assistant Director of Fortifications and Works
ADGB	Air Defence of Great Britain
ADGMS	Assistant Director-General of Medical Services
ADH	Assistant Director of Hygiene
Adj	Adjutant
ADJAG	Assistant Deputy Judge Advocate General
ADK	Order of Ahli Darjah Kinabalu
ADM	Advanced Diploma in Midwifery
Admin	Administration
Adml	Admiral
Admlty	Admiralty
ADMS	Assistant Director of Medical Services
ADOS	Assistant Director of Ordnance Services
ADP	Automatic Data Processing
ADPA	Associate Diploma of Public Administration

ADS&T	Assistant Director of Supplies and Transport
ADVS	Assistant Director of Veterinary Services
advsr/y	adviser/advisory
ADWE&M	Assistant Director of Works, Electrical and Mechanical
AE	Air Efficiency Award
AEA	Atomic Energy Authority; Air Efficiency Award
AEAF	Allied Expeditionary Air Force
AEC	Agriculture Executive Council; Army Educational Corps; Atomic Energy Commission
AECMA	Association Européenne des Constructeurs de Matériel Aérospatial
AEE	Atomic Energy Establishment
AEEU	Amalgamated Engineering and Electrical Union
AEF	Amalgamated Union of Engineering and Foundry Workers; American Expeditionary Forces
AEGIS	Aid for the Elderly in Government Institutions
AEI	Associated Electrical Industries
AEM	Air Efficiency Medal
AER	Army Emergency Reserve
AERE	Atomic Energy Research Establishment (Harwell)
AEU	Amalgamated Engineering Union
AFA	Amateur Football Alliance
AFAIAA	Associate Fellow, American Institute of Aeronautics and Astronautics
AFASIC	Association for All Speech Impaired Children
AFB	Air Force Base
AFBPsS	Associate Fellow, British Psychological Society
AFC	Air Force Cross; Association Football Club
AfC	Association for Colleges
AFCAI	Associate Fellow, Canadian Aeronautical Institute
AFCEA	Armed Forces Communications and Electronics Association
AFCENT	Allied Forces in Central Europe
AFD	Doctor of Fine Arts (US)
AFDS	Air Fighting Development Squadron
AFF	Agriculture, Fisheries and Food (*see* also MAFF)
Affrs	Affairs
AFHQ	Allied Force Headquarters
AFI	American Film Institute
AFIA	Associate, Federal Institute of Accountants (Australia)
AFIAP	Artiste, Fédération Internationale de l'Art Photographique
AFIAS	Associate Fellow, Institute of Aeronautical Sciences (US)
AFICD	Associate Fellow, Institute of Civil Defence
AFIMA	Associate Fellow, Institute of Mathematics and its Applications
AFM	Air Force Medal
AFNORTH	Allied Forces in Northern Europe
AFOM	Associate, Faculty of Occupational Medicine
AFRAeS	Associate Fellow, Royal Aeronautical Society
AFRC	Agricultural and Food Research Council
AFV	Armoured Fighting Vehicles
Ag	Agricultural
AG	Attorney-General
AGAC	American Guild of Authors and Composers
AGARD	Advisory Group for Aerospace Research and Development
AGC	Adjutant General's Corps
AGH	Australian General Hospital
AGI	Artistes Graphiques Internationaux; Associate, Institute of Certificated Grocers
AGR	Advanced Gas-cooled Reactor
AGRA	Army Group Royal Artillery; Association of Genealogists and Record Agents
AGSM	Associate, Guildhall School of Music and Drama; Australian Graduate School of Management
Agy	Agency
AHA	Area Health Authority; American Hospitals Association; Associate, Institute of Health Service Administrators
AHA(T)	Area Health Authority (Teaching)
AHQ	Army Headquarters
AHSM	Associate, Institute of Health Services Management
AH-WC	Associate, Heriot-Watt College, Edinburgh
AIA	Associate, Institute of Actuaries; American Institute of Architects; Association of International Artists
AIAA	American Institute of Aeronautics and Astronautics
AIAgrE	Associate, Institution of Agricultural Engineers
AIAL	Associate Member, International Institute of Arts and Letters
AIArb	Associate, Institute of Arbitrators
AIAS	Associate, Incorporated Association of Architects and Surveyors
AIB	Associate, Institute of Bankers
AIBD	Associate, Institute of British Decorators
AIBP	Associate, Institute of British Photographers
AIBScot	Associate, Institute of Bankers in Scotland
AIC	Agricultural Improvement Council; Associate, Institute of Chemistry
AICA	Associate Member, Commonwealth Institute of Accountants; Association Internationale des Critiques d'Art
AICC	All-India Congress Committee
AICE	Associate, Institution of Civil Engineers
AIChE	American Institute of Chemical Engineers
AICPA	American Institute of Certified Public Accountants
AICS	Associate, Institute of Chartered Shipbrokers
AICTA	Associate, Imperial College of Tropical Agriculture
AIDS	Acquired Immune Deficiency Syndrome
AIE	Associate, Institute of Education
AIEE	Associate, Institution of Electrical Engineers
AIF	Australian Imperial Forces
AIFireE	Associate, Institution of Fire Engineers
AIG	Adjutant-Inspector-General
AIH	Associate, Institute of Housing
AIHort	Associate, Institute of Horticulture
AIIA	Associate, Insurance Institute of America; Associate, Indian Institute of Architects
AIIMR	Associate, Institute of Investment Management and Research
AIInfSc	Associate, Institute of Information Scientists
AIIRA	Associate, International Industrial Relations Association
AIL	Associate, Institute of Linguists
AILA	Associate, Institute of Landscape Architects
AILocoE	Associate, Institute of Locomotive Engineers
AIM	Associate, Institution of Metallurgists; Australian Institute of Management
AIMarE	Associate, Institute of Marine Engineers
AIMC	Associate, Institute of Management Consultants
AIME	American Institute of Mechanical Engineers
AIMgt	Associate, Institute of Management
AIMSW	Associate, Institute of Medical Social Work
AInstM	Associate Member, Institute of Marketing
AInstP	Associate, Institute of Physics
AInstPI	Associate, Institute of Patentees and Inventors
AIP	Association of Independent Producers
AIPR	Associate, Institute of Public Relations
AIProdE	Associate, Institution of Production Engineers
AIQS	Associate Member, Institute of Quantity Surveyors
AIRTE	Associate, Institute of Road Transport Engineers
AIRTO	Association of Independent Research and Technology Organizations
AIS	Associate, Institute of Statisticians
AISA	Associate, Incorporated Secretaries' Association
AIStructE	Associate, Institution of Structural Engineers
AITI	Associate, Institute of Translators and Interpreters
AITP	Associate, Institute of Town Planners, India
AJAG	Assistant Judge Advocate General
AJEX	Association of Jewish Ex-Service Men and Women
AK	Knight, Order of Australia; Alaska
AKC	Associate, King's College London
AL	Alabama
ALA	Associate, Library Association; Association of London Authorities
ALAA	Associate, Library Association of Australia
ALAI	Associate, Library Association of Ireland
ALAM	Associate, London Academy of Music and Dramatic Art
ALCD	Associate, London College of Divinity
ALCM	Associate, London College of Music
ALCS	Authors Lending and Copyright Society
ALFSEA	Allied Land Forces South-East Asia
ALI	Argyll Light Infantry; Associate, Landscape Institute
ALICE	Autistic and Language Impaired Children's Education
ALLC	Association for Literary and Linguistic Computing
ALP	Australian Labor Party
ALPSP	Association of Learned and Professional Society Publishers
ALS	Associate, Linnean Society
ALVA	Association of Leading Visitor Attractions
AM	Albert Medal; Member, Order of Australia; Master of Arts (US); Alpes Maritimes
AMA	Association of Metropolitan Authorities; Assistant Masters Association; Associate, Museums Association; Australian Medical Association
AMARC	Associated Marine and Related Charities
Amb	Ambassador
AMBDA	Associate Member, British Dyslexia Association
AMBIM	Associate Member, British Institute of Management
AMBritIRE	Associate Member, British Institution of Radio Engineers
AMC	Association of Municipal Corporations
AMCST	Associate, Manchester College of Science and Technology
AMCT	Associate, Manchester College of Technology

AME	Association of Municipal Engineers
AMEME	Association of Mining Electrical and Mechanical Engineers
AMet	Associate of Metallurgy
AMF	Australian Military Forces
AMGOT	Allied Military Government of Occupied Territory
AMIAE	Associate Member, Institution of Automobile Engineers
AMIAgrE	Associate Member, Institution of Agricultural Engineers
AMIBF	Associate Member, Institute of British Foundrymen
AMICE	Associate Member, Institution of Civil Engineers
AMIChemE	Associate Member, Institution of Chemical Engineers
AMIE(Aust)	Associate Member, Institution of Engineers, Australia
AMIE(Ind)	Associate Member, Institution of Engineers, India
AMIED	Associate Member, Institution of Engineering Designers
AMIEE	Associate Member, Institution of Electrical Engineers
AMIERE	Associate Member, Institution of Electronic and Radio Engineers
AMIH	Associate Member, Institute of Housing
AMIMechE	Associate Member, Institution of Mechanical Engineers
AMIMinE	Associate Member, Institution of Mining Engineers
AMIMM	Associate Member, Institution of Mining and Metallurgy
AMInstBE	Associate Member, Institution of British Engineers
AMInstCE	Associate Member, Institution of Civil Engineers
AmInstEE	American Institute of Electrical Engineers
AMInstR	Associate Member, Institute of Refrigeration
AMInstT	Associate Member, Institute of Transport
AMInstTA	Associate Member, Institute of Traffic Administration
AMINucE	Associate Member, Institution of Nuclear Engineers
AMIRSE	Associate Member, Institute of Railway Signalling Engineers
AMIStructE	Associate Member, Institution of Structural Engineers
AMMA	Assistant Masters and Mistresses Association
AMN	Ahli Mangku Negara (Malaysia)
AMNZIE	Associate Member New Zealand Institute of Engineers
AMP	Advanced Management Program; Air Member for Personnel
AMRC	Association of Medical Research Charities
AMRINA	Associate Member, Royal Institution of Naval Architects
AMS	Assistant Military Secretary; Army Medical Services
AMSO	Air Member for Supply and Organisation
AMTE	Admiralty Marine Technology Establishment
AMTRI	Advanced Manufacturing Technology Research Institute
ANA	Associate National Academician (US)
ANAF	Arab Non-Arab Friendship
ANC	African National Congress
ANECInst	Associate, NE Coast Institution of Engineers and Shipbuilders
ANGAU	Australian New Guinea Administrative Unit
Anon	Anonymously
ANU	Australian National University
ANZAAS	Australian and New Zealand Association for the Advancement of Science
Anzac	Australian and New Zealand Army Corps
AO	Officer, Order of Australia; Air Officer
AOA	Air Officer in charge of Administration
AOC	Air Officer Commanding
AOC-in-C	Air Officer Commanding-in-Chief
AOD	Army Ordnance Department
AOER	Army Officers Emergency Reserve
APA	American Psychiatric Association
APACS	Association of Payment and Clearing Systems
APCK	Association for Promoting Christian Knowledge, Church of Ireland
APD	Army Pay Department
APEX	Association of Professional, Executive, Clerical and Computer Staff
APHA	American Public Health Association
APIS	Army Photographic Intelligence Service
APM	Assistant Provost Marshal
APMI	Associate, Pensions Management Institute
apptd	appointed
APR	Accredited Public Relations Practitioner
APS	Aborigines Protection Society; American Physical Society
APsSI	Associate, Psychological Society of Ireland
APSW	Association of Psychiatric Social Workers
APT&C	Administrative, Professional, Technical and Clerical
APTC	Army Physical Training Corps
AQ	Administration and Quartering
AQG/AQMG	Assistant Quartermaster-General
AR	Associated Rediffusion (Television); Arkansas
ARA	Associate, Royal Academy
ARACI	Associate, Royal Australian Chemical Institute
ARAD	Associate, Royal Academy of Dancing
ARAeS	Associate, Royal Aeronautical Society
ARAgS	Associate, Royal Agricultural Societies (*i.e.*, of England, Scotland and Wales)
ARAIA	Associate, Royal Australian Institute of Architects
ARAM	Associate, Royal Academy of Music
ARAS	Associate, Royal Astronomical Society
ARBA	Associate, Royal Society of British Artists
ARBC	Associate, Royal British Colonial Society of Artists
ARBS	Associate, Royal Society of British Sculptors
ARC	Architects' Registration Council; Agricultural Research Council; Aeronautical Research Council
ARCA	Associate, Royal College of Art; Associate, Royal Canadian Academy
ARCamA	Associate, Royal Cambrian Academy of Art
ARCE	Academical Rank of Civil Engineer
ARCIC	Anglican-Roman Catholic International Commission
ARCM	Associate, Royal College of Music
ARCO	Associate, Royal College of Organists
ARCO(CHM)	Associate, Royal College of Organists with Diploma in Choir Training
ARCPsych	Associate Member, Royal College of Psychiatrists
ARCS	Associate, Royal College of Science
ARCST	Associate, Royal College of Science and Technology (Glasgow)
ARCUK	Architects' Registration Council of the United Kingdom
ARCVS	Associate, Royal College of Veterinary Surgeons
ARE	Associate, Royal Society of Painter-Printmakers (formerly of Painter-Etchers and Engravers); Arab Republic of Egypt; Admiralty Research Establishment
AREINZ	Associate, Real Estate Institute, New Zealand
ARELS	Association of Recognised English Language Schools
ARIAS	Associate, Royal Incorporation of Architects in Scotland
ARIBA	Associate, Royal Institute of British Architects
ARIC	Associate, Royal Institute of Chemistry
ARICS	Professional Associate, Royal Institution of Chartered Surveyors
ARINA	Associate, Royal Institution of Naval Architects
ARLT	Association for the Reform of Latin Teaching
ARMS	Associate, Royal Society of Miniature Painters
ARP	Air Raid Precautions
ARPS	Associate, Royal Photographic Society
ARR	Association of Radiation Research
ARRC	Associate, Royal Red Cross
ARSA	Associate, Royal Scottish Academy
ARSC	Association of Recorded Sound Collections
ARSCM	Associate, Royal School of Church Music
ARSM	Associate, Royal School of Mines
ARTC	Associate, Royal Technical College (Glasgow)
ARVIA	Associate, Royal Victoria Institute of Architects
ARWA	Associate, Royal West of England Academy
ARWS	Associate, Royal Society of Painters in Water-Colours
ASA	Associate Member, Society of Actuaries; Associate of Society of Actuaries (US); Australian Society of Accountants; Army Sailing Association; Advertising Standards Authority
ASAA	Associate, Society of Incorporated Accountants and Auditors
ASAI	Associate, Society of Architectural Illustrators
ASAM	Associate, Society of Art Masters
ASBAH	Association for Spina Bifida and Hydrocephalus
ASC	Administrative Staff College, Henley; Army Service Corps
ASCA	Associate, Society of Company and Commercial Accountants
ASCAB	Armed Services Consultant Approval Board
ASCAP	American Society of Composers, Authors and Publishers
ASCE	American Society of Civil Engineers
ASCHB	Association for Study of Conservation of Historic Buildings
AScW	Association of Scientific Workers
ASD	Armament Supply Department
ASE	Amalgamated Society of Engineers; Association for Science Education
ASEAN	Association of South East Asian Nations
ASEE	American Society for Engineering Education
ASH	Action on Smoking and Health
ASIA(Ed)	Associate, Society of Industrial Artists (Education)
ASIAD	Associate, Society of Industrial Artists and Designers
ASLE	American Society of Lubrication Engineers
ASLEF	Associated Society of Locomotive Engineers and Firemen
ASLIB/Aslib	Association for Information Management (formerly Association of Special Libraries and Information Bureaux)
ASM	Association of Senior Members
ASME	American Society of Mechanical Engineers; Association for the Study of Medical Education
ASO	Air Staff Officer
ASSC	Accounting Standards Steering Committee

ASSET Association of Supervisory Staffs, Executives and Technicians
Assist Assistant
Assoc Association
AssocISI Associate, Iron and Steel Institute
AssocMCT Associateship of Manchester College of Technology
AssocMIAeE Associate Member, Institution of Aeronautical Engineers
AssocRINA Associate, Royal Institution of Naval Architects
AssocSc Associate in Science
Assur Assurance
ASTA Association of Short Circuit Testing Authorities
ASTC Administrative Service Training Course
ASTMS Association of Scientific, Technical and Managerial Staffs
AS&TS of SA Associated Scientific and Technical Societies of South Africa
ASVU Army Security Vetting Unit
ASWDU Air Sea Warfare Development Unit
ASWE Admiralty Surface Weapons Establishment
ATA Air Transport Auxiliary
ATAE Association of Tutors in Adult Education
ATAF Allied Tactical Air Force
ATC Air Training Corps; Art Teacher's Certificate
ATCDE Association of Teachers in Colleges and Departments of Education
ATCL Associate, Trinity College of Music, London
ATD Art Teacher's Diploma
ATI Associate, Textile Institute
ATL Association of Teachers and Lecturers
ATO Ammunition Technical Officer
ATPL (A)or(H) Airline Transport Pilot's Licence (Aeroplanes), or (Helicopters)
ATS Auxiliary Territorial Service
attd attached
ATTI Association of Teachers in Technical Institutions
ATV Association TeleVision
AUA American Urological Association
AUCAS Association of University Clinical Academic Staff
AUEW Amalgamated Union of Engineering Workers
AUS Army of the United States
AUT Association of University Teachers
Aux Auxiliary
AVCC Australian Vice-Chancellors' Committee
AVCM Associate, Victoria College of Music
AVD Army Veterinary Department
Ave Avenue
AVLA Audio Visual Language Association
AVR Army Volunteer Reserve
AWA Anglian Water Authority
AWAS Australian Womens' Army Service
AWO Association of Water Officers
AWRE Atomic Weapons Research Establishment
AZ Arizona

B

b born
B Baron
BA Bachelor of Arts; British Airways
BAA British Airports Authority
BAAB British Amateur Athletic Board
BAAL British Association for Applied Linguistics
BAAS British Association for the Advancement of Science
BAB British Airways Board
BAC British Aircraft Corporation
BACM British Association of Colliery Management
BACUP British Association of Cancer United Patients
BAe British Aerospace
BAED Bachelor of Arts in Environmental Design
BAFO British Air Forces of Occupation
BAFPA British Association of Fitness Promotion Agencies
BAFTA British Academy of Film and Television Arts
BAG Business Art Galleries
BAgrSc Bachelor of Agricultural Science
BAI *Baccalarius in Arte Ingeniaria* (Bachelor of Engineering)
BAIE British Association of Industrial Editors
BALPA British Air Line Pilots' Association
BAO Bachelor of Art of Obstetrics
BAOMS British Association of Oral and Maxillo-Facial Surgeons
BAOR British Army of the Rhine (formerly on the Rhine)
BAOS British Association of Oral Surgeons
BAppSc(MT) Bachelor of Applied Science (Medical Technology)
bapt baptised
BARB Broadcasters' Audience Research Board
BARC British Automobile Racing Club
BArch Bachelor of Architecture
BAS Bachelor in Agricultural Science
BASc Bachelor of Applied Science
BASCA British Academy of Songwriters, Composers and Authors
BASEEFA British Approvals Service for Electrical Equipment in Flammable Atmospheres
BASW British Association of Social Workers
BBA British Bankers' Association; Bachelor of Business Administration
BBB of C British Boxing Board of Control
BBC British Broadcasting Corporation
BB&CIRly Bombay, Baroda and Central India Railway
BBFC British Board of Film Classification
BBM Bintang Bakti Masharakat (Public Service Star) (Singapore)
BBS Bachelor of Business Studies
BBSRC Biotechnology and Biosciences Research Council
BC Before Christ; British Columbia; Borough Council
BCAR British Civil Airworthiness Requirements
BCC British Council of Churches
BCE Bachelor of Civil Engineering; Before the Christian Era
BCh/BChir Bachelor of Surgery
BChD Bachelor of Dental Surgery
BCIA British Clothing Industries Association
BCL Bachelor of Civil Law
BCMF Bible Churchmen's Missionary Society
BCMF British Ceramic Manufacturers' Federation
BCOF British Commonwealth Occupation Force
BCom/BComm Bachelor of Commerce
BComSc Bachelor of Commercial Science
BCPC British Crop Protection Council
BCS Bengal Civil Service; British Computer Society
BCSA British Constructional Steelwork Association
BCURA British Coal Utilization Research Association
BCYC British Corinthian Yacht Club
BD Bachelor of Divinity
Bd Board
BDA British Dental Association; British Deaf Association; British Dyslexia Association
Bdcasting Broadcasting
Bde Brigade
BDQ Bachelor of Divinity Qualifying
Bdrs Borderers
BDS Bachelor of Dental Surgery
BDSc Bachelor of Dental Science
BE Bachelor of Engineering; British Element
BE&A Bachelor of Engineering and Architecture (Malta)
BEA British East Africa; British European Airways; British Epilepsy Association
BEAMA Federation of British Electrotechnical and Allied Manufacturers' Associations (formerly British Electrical and Allied Manufacturers' Association)
BEAS British Educational Administration Society
BEc Bachelor of Economics
BEC Business Education Council
BECTU Broadcasting, Entertainment, Cinematograph and Theatre Union
BEd Bachelor of Education
Beds Bedfordshire
BEE Bachelor of Electrical Engineering
BEF British Expeditionary Force; British Equestrian Federation
BEM British Empire Medal
BEMAS British Education Management and Administration Society
BEME Brigade Electrical and Mechanical Engineer
BEng Bachelor of Engineering
BEO Base Engineer Officer
Berks Berkshire
BESO British Executive Service Overseas
BEVA British Equine Veterinary Association
B&FBS British and Foreign Bible Society
BFI British Film Institute
BFMIRA British Food Manufacturing Industries Research Association

BFPO	British Forces Post Office
BFSS	British Field Sports Society
BFWG	British Federation of Women Graduates
BGS	Brigadier General Staff
BHA	British Hospitality Association
BHF	British Heart Foundation
BHL	Bachelor of Hebrew Letters
BHRA	British Hydromechanics Research Association
BHRCA	British Hotels, Restaurants and Caterers' Association
BHS	British Horse Society
BIBA	British Insurance Brokers' Association
BIBRA	British Industrial Biological Research Association
BICC	British Insulated Callender's Cables
BICERA	British Internal Combustion Engine Research Association
BICERI	British Internal Combustion Engine Research Institute
BICSc	British Institute of Cleaning Science
BIEC	British Invisible Exports Council
BIEE	British Institute of Energy Economics
BIF	British Industries Fair
BIFU	Banking Insurance and Finance Union
BIIBA	British Insurance and Investment Brokers' Association
BIM	British Institute of Management
BIR	British Institute of Radiology
BIS	Bank for International Settlements
BISF	British Iron and Steel Federation
BISFA	British Industrial and Scientific Film Association
BISPA	British Independent Steel Producers Association
BISRA	British Iron and Steel Research Association
BJ	Bachelor of Journalism
BJSM	British Joint Services Mission
BKSTS	British Kinematograph, Sound and Television Society
BL	Bachelor of Law; British Library
BLA	British Liberation Army
Bldg Soc	Building Society
BLDSA	British Long Distance Swimming Association
BLE	Brotherhood of Locomotive Engineers; Bachelor of Land Economy
BLegS	Bachelor of Legal Studies
BLESMA	British Limbless Ex-Servicemen's Association
BLitt	Bachelor of Letters
Blvd	Boulevard
BM	British Museum; Bachelor of Medicine; British Monomark
BMA	British Medical Association
BMedSci	Bachelor of Medical Science
BMEO	British Middle East Office
BMet	Bachelor of Metallurgy
BMEWS	Ballistic Missile Early Warning System
BMG	British Military Government
BMH	British Military Hospital
BMilSc	Bachelor of Military Science
BMJ	British Medical Journal
BMM	British Military Mission
BMR	Bureau of Mineral Resources
BMRA	Brigade Major Royal Artillery
Bn	Battalion
BNAF	British North Africa Force
BNC	Brasenose College (Oxford)
BNEC	British National Export Council
BNF	British National Formulary
BNFL	British Nuclear Fuels Ltd
BNOC	British National Oil Corporation; British National Opera Company
BNP	Banque Nationale de Paris
BNSc	Bachelor of Nursing Science
BNSC	British National Space Centre
BOAC	British Overseas Airways Corporation
BomCS	Bombay Civil Service
BOT	Board of Trade
BOTB	British Overseas Trade Board
BOU	British Ornithologists' Union
Bp	Bishop
BPA	British Paediatric Association
BPG	Broadcasting Press Guild
BPharm	Bachelor of Pharmacy
BPIF	British Printing Industries Federation
BPMF	British Postgraduate Medical Federation
BPsS	British Psychological Society
Br/br	British; Branch; branch
BR	British Rail
BRA	British Rheumatism and Arthritis Association
BRB	British Railways Board
BRC(S)	British Red Cross Society
BRE	Building Research Establishment
Brig	Brigadier
Brig-Gen	Brigadier-General
BritIRE	British Institution of Radio Engineers
BRNC	Britannia Royal Naval College
bro	brother
BRS	British Road Services
BRurSc	Bachelor of Rural Science
BS	Bachelor of Surgery; Bachelor of Science; British Standard
BSA	Bachelor of Scientific Agriculture; Birmingham Small Arms; Building Societies' Association
BSAA	British South American Airways
BSAP	British South Africa Police
BSAS	British Society of Animal Science
BSc	Bachelor of Science
BSC	British Steel Corporation; Bengal Staff Corps
BScA, BScAgr	Bachelor of Science in Agriculture
BSc(Dent)	Bachelor of Science in Dentistry
BSc(Est Man)	Bachelor of Science in Estate Management
BScN/BSN	Bachelor of Science in Nursing
BScSoc/BSocSc	Bachelor of Social Sciences
BSE	Bachelor of Science in Engineering (US)
BSES	British Schools Exploring Society
BSF	British Salonica Force
BSFA	British Science Fiction Association
BSI	British Standards Institution
BSIA	British Security Industry Association
BSJA	British Show Jumping Association
BSME	Bachelor of Science in Mechanical Engineering; British Society of Magazine Editors
BSNS	Bachelor of Naval Science
BSRA	British Ship Research Association
BSS	Bachelor of Science (Social Science)
BST	Bachelor of Sacred Theology
BSurv	Bachelor of Surveying
BT	Bachelor of Teaching; British Telecommunications
Bt	Baronet
BTA	British Tourist Authority (formerly British Travel Association)
BTC	British Transport Commission
BTCV	British Trust for Conservation Volunteers
BTDB	British Transport Docks Board
BTEC	Business and Technology (formerly Technician) Education Council
BTh	Bachelor of Theology
BTP	Bachelor of Town Planning
Btss	Baronetess
BUAS	British Universities Association of Slavists
Bucks	Buckinghamshire
BUGB	Baptist Union of Great Britain
BUPA	British United Provident Association
bur	buried
BURA	British Urban Regeneration Association
BV	Besloten Vennootschap
BVA	British Veterinary Association
BVetMed	Bachelor of Veterinary Medicine
BVI	British Virgin Islands
BVM	Blessed Virgin Mary
BVMS	Bachelor of Veterinary Medicine and Surgery
BVSc	Bachelor of Veterinary Science
BWI	British West Indies
BWM	British War Medal

C

c	*circa* ('around', of dates)
C	Conservative
CA	County Alderman; Chartered Accountant (Scotland and Canada); California
CAA	Civil Aviation Authority
CAABU	Council for the Advancement of Arab and British Understanding
CAAV	(Member of) Central Association of Agricultural Valuers
CAB	Citizens' Advice Bureau; Centre for Agricultural and Biosciences (formerly Commonwealth Agricultural Bureau)
CACTM	Central Advisory Council of Training for the Ministry
CAER	Conservative Action for Electoral Reform
CAFOD	Catholic Fund for Overseas Development
CALE	Canadian Army Liaison Executive
Calif	California
CAM	Communications, Advertising and Marketing
Cambs	Cambridgeshire
CAMC	Canadian Army Medical Corps
CAMRA	Campaign for Real Ale
CAMS	Certificate of Advanced Musical Study
CAMW	Central Association for Mental Welfare
Cantab	*Cantabrigiensis* (of Cambridge)
Cantuar	*Cantuariensis* (of Canterbury)
Capt	Captain
CARD	Campaign against Racial Discrimination
Cards	Cardiganshire
CARE	Cottage and Rural Enterprises
CARICOM	Caribbean Community
CARIFTA	Caribbean Free Trade Area
Carmarths	Carmarthenshire
CAS	Chief of the Air Staff
CASI	Canadian Aeronautics and Space Institute
CAT	College of Advanced Technology; Countryside Around Towns
CATE	Council for the Accreditation of Teacher Education
Cav	Cavalry
CAWU	Clerical and Administrative Workers' Union
CB	Companion, Order of the Bath; County Borough
CBC	County Borough Council
CBCO	Central Board for Conscientious Objectors
CBE	Commander, Order of the British Empire
CBI	Confederation of British Industry
CBIM	Companion, British Institute of Management
CBiol	Chartered Biologist
CBNS	Commander British Navy Staff
CBS	Columbia Broadcasting System; Confraternity of the Blessed Sacrament
CBSA	Clay Bird Shooting Association
CBSJ	Chartered Building Societies Institute
CBSO	City of Birmingham Symphony Orchestra
CC	Companion, Order of Canada; City Council; County Council(lor); Cricket Club; Cycling Club; County Court
CCAB	Consultative Committee of Accountancy Bodies
CCAHC	Central Council for Agricultural and Horticultural Co-operation
CCBE	Commission Consultative des Barreaux de la Communauté Européenne
CCBI	Council of Churches for Britain and Ireland
CCC	Corpus Christi College; Central Criminal Court; County Cricket Club
CCE	Chartered Civil Engineer
CCF	Combined Cadet Force
CCFM	Combined Cadet Forces Medal
CCG	Control Commission Germany
CCH	Cacique's Crown of Honour, Order of Service of Guyana
CChem	Chartered Chemist
CCHMS	Central Committee for Hospital Medical Services
CCIA	Commission of Churches on International Affairs
CCIS	Command Control Information System
CCJ	Council of Christians and Jews
CCPR	Central Council of Physical Recreation
CCRA	Commander Corps of Royal Artillery
CCRE	Commander Corps of Royal Engineers
CCREME	Commander Corps of Royal Electrical and Mechanical Engineers
CCRSigs	Commander Corps of Royal Signals
CCS	Casualty Clearing Station; Ceylon Civil Service; Countryside Commission for Scotland
CCSU	Council of Civil Service Unions
CCTA	Commission de Coopération Technique pour l'Afrique
CCTS	Combat Crew Training Squadron
CD	Canadian Forces Decoration; Commander, Order of Distinction (Jamaica); Civil Defence
CDA	Co-operative Development Agency
CDEE	Chemical Defence Experimental Establishment
CDipAF	Certified Diploma in Accounting and Finance
Cdr	Commander
CDRA	Committee of Directors of Research Associations
Cdre	Commodore
CDS	Chief of the Defence Staff
CDU	Christlich-Demokratische Union
CE	Civil Engineer
C of E	Church of England
CEA	Central Electricity Authority
CEC	Commission of the European Communities
CECD	Confédération Européenne du Commerce de Détail
CECG	Consumers in European Community Group
CEDEP	Centre Européen d'Education Permanente
CEE	Communauté Economique Européen
CEED	Centre for Economic and Environmental Development
CEF	Canadian Expeditionary Force
CEFIC	Conseil Européen des Fédérations de l'Industrie Chimique
CEGB	Central Electricity Generating Board
CEI	Council of Engineering Institutions
CEIR	Corporation for Economic and Industrial Research
CEM	Council of European Municipalities
CEMA	Council for the Encouragement of Music and Arts
CEMR	Council of European Municipalities and Regions
CEMS	Church of England Men's Society
CEN	Comité Européen de Normalisation
CENELEC	European Committee for Electrotechnical Standardization
CEng	Chartered Engineer
Centl	Central
Cento	Central Treaty Organisation
CEO	Chief Executive Officer
CEPT	Conférence Européenne des Postes et des Télécommunications
CERL	Central Electricity Research Laboratories
CERN	Organisation (formerly Centre) Européenne pour la Recherche Nucléaire
Cert	Certificate
CERT	Charities Effectiveness Review Trust
CertCPE	Certificate in Clinical Pastoral Education
Cert Ed	Certificate of Education
CertITP	Certificate of International Teachers' Program (Harvard)
CEST	Centre for Exploitation of Science and Technology
CET	Council for Educational Technology
CETS	Church of England Temperance Society
CF	Chaplain to the Forces; Companion, Order of Fiji
CFA	Canadian Field Artillery
CFE	Central Fighter Establishment; College of Further Education
CFM	Cadet Forces Medal
CFR	Commander, Order of the Federal Republic of Nigeria
CFS	Central Flying School
C&G	City and Guilds of London Institute
CGA	Community of the Glorious Ascension; Country Gentlemen's Association
CGeol	Chartered Geologist
CGH	Order of the Golden Heart of Kenya (1st class)
CGIA	Insignia Award of City and Guilds of London Institute
CGLI	City and Guilds of London Institute
CGM	Conspicuous Gallantry Medal
CGRM	Commandant-General Royal Marines
CGS	Chief of the General Staff
Ch/ch	Chief/chief; Church
CH	Companion of Honour
CHAR	Campaign for the Homeless and Rootless
ChB	Bachelor of Surgery (Chirurgy)
CHB	Companion of Honour of Barbados
CHC	Community Health Council
Ch Ch	Christ Church
CHE	Campaign for Homosexual Equality
ChLJ	Chaplain, Order of St Lazarus of Jerusalem
Chllr	Chancellor
chm	chairman/chairwoman
ChM	Master of Surgery
CHM	Chevalier of Honour and Merit (Haiti)

CHN Community of the Holy Name
CHSC Central Health Services Council
ChStJ Chaplain, Most Venerable Order of the Hospital of St John of Jerusalem
CI Imperial Order of the Crown of India; Channel Islands
CIA Chemical Industries Association; Central Intelligence Agency
CIAD Central Institute of Art and Design
CIAgrE Companion, Institution of Agricultural Engineers
CIAL Corresponding Member, International Institute of Arts and Letters
CIArb Chartered Institute of Arbitrators
CIB Chartered Institute of Bankers
CIBS Chartered Institution of Building Services
CIBSE Chartered Institution of Building Services Engineers
CIC Chemical Institute of Canada
CICB Criminal Injuries Compensation Board
CICHE Committee for International Co-operation in Higher Education
CICI Confederation of Information Communication Industries
CID Criminal Investigation Department
CIDEC Conseil International pour le Développement du Cuivre
CIE Companion, Order of the Indian Empire; Confédération Internationale des Etudiants
CIFRS Comité International de la Rayonne et des Fibres Synthétiques
CIGasE Companion, Institution of Gas Engineers
CIGRE Conférence Internationale des Grands Réseaux Electriques
CIGS Chief of the Imperial General Staff
CIIA Canadian Institute of International Affairs
CIL *Corpus inscriptionum latinarum* (body of Latin writings)
CIM China Inland Mission
CIMA Chartered Institute of Management Accountants
CIMarE Companion, Institute of Marine Engineers
CIMEMME Companion, Institution of Mining Electrical and Mining Mechanical Engineers
CIMgt Companion, Institute of Management
CIMGTechE Companion, Institution of Mechanical and General Technician Engineers
C-in-C Commander-in-Chief
CINCHAN Allied Commander-in-Chief Channel
CIOB Chartered Institute of Building
CIPD Companion, Institute of Personnel and Development
CIPFA Chartered Institute of Public Finance and Accountancy
CIPL Comité International Permanent des Linguistes
CIPM Companion, Institute of Personnel Management
CIR Commission on Industrial Relations
CIRES Co-operative Institute for Research in Environmental Sciences
CIRIA Construction Industry Research and Information Association
CIRP Collège Internationale pour Recherche et Production
CIS Institute of Chartered Secretaries and Administrators (formerly Chartered Institute of Secretaries); Command Control Communications and Information Systems; Commonwealth of Independent States
CISAC Confédération Internationale des Sociétés d'Auteurs et Compositeurs; Centre for International Security and Arms Control
CIT Chartered Institute of Transport; California Institute of Technology
CITB Construction Industry Training Board
CIU Club and Institute Union
CIV City Imperial Volunteers
Civ Civil
CJ Chief Justice
CJC Companions of Jesus Christ
CJM Congregation of Jesus and Mary (Eudist Fathers)
Cl Class; Close
CL Commander, Order of Leopold
CLA Country Landowners' Association
CIEx Companion, Institute of Export
CLIC Cancer and Leukemia in Children
CLIP Common Law Institute of Intellectual Property
CLit Companion of Literature (Royal Society of Literature Award)
CLJ Commander, Order of St Lazarus of Jerusalem
CLP Constituency Labour Party
CLRAE Congress (formerly Conference) of Local and Regional Authorities of Europe
CLY City of London Yeomanry
CM Member, Order of Canada; Congregation of the Mission (Vincentians); Master in Surgery; Certificated Master; Canadian Militia
CMA Canadian Medical Association; Cost and Management Accountant (NZ)
CMAC Catholic Marriage Advisory Council
CMath Chartered Mathematician
CMB Central Midwives' Board
CMC Certified Management Consultant
Cmd Command (*e.g.*, Southern Command)
cmded commanded
cmdg commanding
Cmdt Commandant
CMet Chartered Meteorologist
CMF Commonwealth Military Forces; Central Mediterranean Force
CMG Companion, Order of St Michael and St George
CMLJ Commander of Merit, Order of St Lazarus of Jerusalem
CMO Chief Medical Officer
CMP Corps of Military Police
CMS Church Missionary Society
CMS Church Mission (formerly Church Missionary) Society; Certificate in Management Studies
CMT Chaconia Medal of Trinidad
CMZS Corresponding Member, Zoological Society
CNAA Council for National Academic Awards
Cncl Council
Cncllr Councillor
CND Campaign for Nuclear Disarmament
CNI Companion, Nautical Institute
CNIM Commander, Order of Military Merit (Canada)
CNO Chief of Naval Operations
CNR Canadian National Railways
CNRS Centre National de la Recherche Scientifique
Co County; Company
c/o care of
CO Commanding Officer; Commonwealth Office (after Aug 1966); Colonial Office (before Aug 1966): Conscientious Objector; Colorado
CODEST Committee for the Development of European Science and Technology
COHSE Confederation of Health Service Employees
COI Central Office of Information
CoID Council of Industrial Design (now Design Council)
Col Colonel
Coll College; Collegiate
Colo Colorado
COMEC Council of the Military Education Committees of the Universities of the UK
COMET Committee for Middle East Trade
Commn Commission
commnd commissioned
Commr Commissioner
CompAMEME Companion, Association of Mining Electrical and Mechanical Engineers
CompICE Companion, Institution of Civil Engineers
CompIEE Companion, Institution of Electrical Engineers
CompIERE Companion, Institution of Electronic and Radio Engineers
CompIGasE Companion, Institution of Gas Engineers
CompIWES Companion, Institution of Water Engineers and Scientists
ComplMechE Companion, Institution of Mechanical Engineers
CompOR Companion, Operational Research Society
CompTI Companion of the Textile Institute
CON Commander, Order of the Niger
Conf Conference
Conn Connecticut
Const Constitutional
Co-op Co-operative
COPA Comité des Organisations Professionels Agricoles de la CEE
COPEC Conference of Politics, Economics and Christianity
COPUS Committee on the Public Understanding of Science
Corp Corporation
Corresp Memb Corresponding Member
COS Chief of Staff; Charity Organization Society
COSA Colliery Officials and Staffs Association
CoSIRA Council for Small Industries in Rural Areas
COSLA Convention of Scottish Local Authorities
COSPAR Committee on Space Research
COSSAC Chief of Staff to Supreme Allied Commander
COTC Canadian Officers' Training Corps
CP Central Provinces; Cape Province; Congregation of the Passion; Communist Party
CPA Commonwealth Parliamentary Association; Chartered Patent Agent; Certified Public Accountant (Canada)
CPAG Child Poverty Action Group
CPAS Church Pastoral Aid Society

CPC Conservative Political Centre
CPCH College of Paediatrics and Child Health
CPEng Chartered Professional Engineer (of Institution of Engineers of Australia)
CPFA Member or Associate, Chartered Institute of Public Finance and Accountancy
CPhys Chartered Physicist
CPL Chief Personnel and Logistics
Cpl Corporal
CPM Colonial Police Medal
CPR Canadian Pacific Railway
CPRE Council for the Protection of Rural England
CPRS Central Policy Review Staff
CPRW Campaign for the Protection of Rural Wales
CPS Crown Prosecution Service
CPSA Civil and Public Services Association; Church of the Province of South Africa
CPSU Communist Party of the Soviet Union
CPsychol Chartered Psychologist
CPU Commonwealth Press Union
CQSW Certificate of Qualification in Social Work
cr created/creation
CR Community of the Resurrection
CRA Commander, Royal Artillery
CRAC Careers Research and Advisory Centre
CRAeS Companion, Royal Aeronautical Society
CRAG Clinical Resources and Audit Group
CRASC Commander, Royal Army Service Corps
CRC Cancer Research Campaign; Community Relations Council
CRCP(C) Certificant, Royal College of Physicians of Canada
CRE Commander, Royal Engineers; Commission for Racial Equality; Commercial Relations and Exports
CREME Commander, Royal Electrical and Mechanical Engineers
Cres Crescent
CRMP Corps of Royal Military Police
CRNCM Companion, Royal Northern College of Music
CRO Commonwealth Relations Office
CS Civil Service; Clerk to the Signet
CSA Confederate States of America; Child Support Agency
CSAB Civil Service Appeal Board
CSB Bachelor of Christian Science
CSC Conspicuous Service Cross; Congregation of the Holy Cross
CSCA Civil Service Clerical Association
CSCE Conference on Security and Co-operation in Europe
CSD Civil Service Department; Co-operative Secretaries Diploma; Chartered Society of Designers
CSDE Central Servicing Development Establishment
CSEU Confederation of Shipbuilding and Engineering Unions
CSG Companion, Order of the Star of Ghana; Company of the Servants of God
CSI Companion, Order of the Star of India
CSIR Commonwealth Council for Scientific and Industrial Research
CSIRO Commonwealth Scientific and Industrial Research Organization (Australia)
CSM Company Sergeant-Major
CSO Chief Scientific Officer; Chief Signal Officer; Chief Staff Officer; Central Statistical Office
CSP Chartered Society of Physiotherapists; Civil Service of Pakistan
CSS Companion, Star of Sarawak; Council for Science and Society
CSSB Civil Service Selection Board
CSSR Congregation of the Most Holy Redeemer (Redemptorist Order)
Cstat Chartered Statistician
CSTI Council of Science and Technology Institutes
CStJ Commander, Most Venerable Order of the Hospital of St John of Jerusalem
CSU Christlich-Soziale Union in Bayern
CSV Community Service Volunteers
CSW Certificate in Social Work
CT Connecticut
Ct Court
CTA Chaplain Territorial Army
CTB College of Teachers of the Blind
CTC Cyclists' Touring Club; Commando Training Centre; City Training College
Ctee Committee
CText Chartered Textile Technologist
CTR(Harwell) Controlled Thermonuclear Research
CU Cambridge University
CUAC Cambridge University Athletic Club
CUAFC Cambridge University Association Football Club
CUBC Cambridge University Boat Club
CUCC Cambridge University Cricket Club
CUF Common University Fund
CUHC Cambridge University Hockey Club
CUMS Cambridge University Musical Society
CUNY City University of New York
CUP Cambridge University Press
CURUFC Cambridge University Rugby Union Football Club
cv *curriculum vitae*
CV Cross of Valour (Canada)
CVCP Committee of Vice-Chancellors and Principals of the Universities of the United Kingdom
CVO Commander, Royal Victorian Order
CVS Council for Voluntary Service
CVSNA Council of Voluntary Service National Association
CWA Crime Writers Association
CWGC Commonwealth War Graves Commission
Cwlth Commonwealth
CWS Co-operative Wholesale Society
CWU Communication Workers Union

D

d died
D Duke
DA Dame of St Andrew, Order of Barbados; Diploma in Anaesthesia; Diploma in Art
DAAG Deputy Assistant Adjutant-General
DAA&QMG Deputy Assistant Adjutant and Quartermaster-General
DAC Development Assistance Committee; Diocesan Advisory Committee
DACG Deputy Assistant Chaplain-General
DAD Deputy Assistant Director
D&AD Designers and Art Directors Association
DAdmin Doctor of Administration
DADMS Deputy Assistant Director of Medical Services
DADOS Deputy Assistant Director of Ordnance Services
DADQ Deputy Assistant Director of Quartering
DADST Deputy Assistant Director of Supplies and Transport
DAEd Diploma in Art Education
DAG Deputy Adjutant-General
DAgr Doctor of Agriculture
DAgrFor Doctor of Agriculture and Forestry
DAMS Deputy Assistant Military Secretary
DAppSc Doctor of Applied Science
DA&QMG Deputy Adjutant and Quartermaster-General
DArch Doctor of Architecture
DArt(s) Doctor of Art(s)
das died on active service
DASc Doctor in Agricultural Sciences
DATA Draughtsmen's and Allied Technicians' Association
DATEC Art and Design Committee, Technician Education Council
dau daughter
DBA Doctor of Business Administration
DBE Dame Commander, Order of the British Empire
DC District Commissioner; District Council; District of Columbia
DCAe Diploma of College of Aeronautics
DCAS Deputy Chief of the Air Staff
DCB Dame Commander, Order of the Bath
DCC Diploma of Chelsea College
DCCH Diploma in Community Child Health
DCDS Deputy Chief of Defence Staff
DCE Diploma of a College of Education
DCG Deputy Chaplain-General
DCGRM Department of the Commandant General Royal Marines
DCGS Deputy Chief of the General Staff
DCH Diploma in Child Health
DCh Doctor of Surgery
DCIGS Deputy Chief of the Imperial General Staff
DCL Doctor of Civil Law

DCLI Duke of Cornwall's Light Infantry
DCLJ Dame Commander, Order of St Lazarus of Jerusalem
DCM Distinguished Conduct Medal
DCMG Dame Commander, Order of St Michael and St George
DCMHE Diploma of Contents and Methods in Health Education
DCnL Doctor of Canon Law
DCO Duke of Cambridge's Own
DComm Doctor of Commerce
DCP Diploma in Clinical Pathology; Diploma in Conservation of Paintings
DCS Deputy Chief of Staff; Doctor of Commercial Sciences
DCSO Deputy Chief Scientific Officer
DCT Doctor of Christian Theology
DCVO Dame Commander, Royal Victorian Order
DD Doctor of Divinity
DDes Doctor of Design
DDGAMS Deputy Director General, Army Medical Services
DDH Diploma in Dental Health
DDL Deputy Director of Labour
DDME Deputy Director of Mechanical Engineering
DDMI Deputy Director of Military Intelligence
DDMO Deputy Director of Military Operations
DDMS Deputy Director of Medical Services
DDMT Deputy Director of Military Training
DDNI Deputy Director of Naval Intelligence
DDO Diploma in Dental Orthopaedics
DDPH Diploma in Dental Public Health
DDPR Deputy Director of Public Relations
DDPS Deputy Director of Personal Services
DDR Deutsche Demokratische Republik
DDRA Deputy Director Royal Artillery
DDS Doctor of Dental Surgery; Director of Dental Services
DDSc Doctor of Dental Science
DDSD Deputy Director Staff Duties
DDSM Defense Distinguished Service Medal
DDST Deputy Director of Supplies and Transport
DDWE&M Deputy Director of Works, Electrical and Mechanical
DE Doctor of Engineering; Delaware
DEA Department of Economic Affairs
decd deceased
DEconSc Doctor of Economic Science
DEd Doctor of Education
Def Defence
Deleg Delegate
Delegn Delegation
DEME Directorate of Electrical and Mechanical Engineering
DEMS Defensively Equipped Merchant Ships
DenD Docteur en Droit
DEng Doctor of Engineering
DenM Docteur en Médicine
DEOVR Duke of Edinburgh's Own Volunteer Rifles
Dep/dep Deputy/deputy
DEP Department of Employment and Productivity; European Progressive Democrats
Dept/Deptl Department/Departmental
DERA Defence Evaluation and Research Agency
Derbys Derbyshire
DèS/DèsSc Docteur ès sciences
DES Department of Education and Science
DèsL Docteur ès lettres
DesRCA Designer of the Royal College of Art
Devpt Development
DFA Doctor of Fine Arts
DFAS Decorative and Fine Art Society
DFC Distinguished Flying Cross
DFE Department for Education
DFEE Department for Education and Employment
DFH Diploma of Faraday House
DFLS Day Fighter Leaders' School
DFM Distinguished Flying Medal
DG Director General
DGAA Distressed Gentlefolks Aid Association
DGAMS Director-General Army Medical Services
DGEME Director General Electrical and Mechanical Engineering
DGLP(A) Director General Logistic Policy (Army)
DGMS Director-General of Medical Services
DGMT Director-General of Military Training
DGMW Director-General of Military Works
DGNPS Director-General of Naval Personal Services
DGP Director-General of Personnel
DGPS Director-General of Personal Services
DGS Diploma in Graduate Studies
DGStJ Dame of Grace, Order of St John of Jerusalem
DGU Doctor of Griffith University
DH Doctor of Humanities
DHA District Health Authority
Dhc *Doctor honoris causa*
DHEW Department of Health Education and Welfare (US)
DHL Doctor of Humane Letters; Doctor of Hebrew Literature
DHM Dean Hole Medal
DHMSA Diploma in the History of Medicine (Society of Apothecaries)
DHQ District Headquarters
DHSS Department of Health and Social Security
DHum Doctor of Humanities
DHumLit Doctor of Humane Letters
DIAS Dublin Institute of Advanced Sciences
DIC Diploma of the Imperial College
DICTA Diploma of Imperial College of Tropical Agriculture
DIG Deputy Inspector-General
DIH Diploma in Industrial Health
DIMP Daijah Indera Mahkota Pahang
DIntLaw Diploma in International Law
Dip Diploma; Diplomatic
DipAA Diploma in Applied Art
DipAD Diploma in Art and Design
DipAe Diploma in Aeronautics
DipArch Diploma in Architecture
DipASE Diploma in Advanced Study of Education, College of Preceptors
DipAvMed Diploma of Aviation Medicine, Royal College of Physicians
DipBA Diploma in Business Administration
DipBS Diploma in Fine Art, Byam Shaw School
DipCAM Diploma in Communications, Advertising and Marketing of CAM Foundation
DipCC Diploma of the Central College
DipCD Diploma in Civic Design
DipCE Diploma in Civil Engineering
DipEcon Diploma in Economics
DipEd Diploma in Education
DipEE Diploma in Electrical Engineenng
DipEI Diploma in Electronics
DipESL Diploma in English as a Second Language
DipEth Diploma in Ethnology
DipFD Diploma in Funeral Directing
DipFE Diploma in Further Education
DipFM Diploma in Forensic Medicine
DipGSM Diploma in Music, Guildhall School of Music and Drama
DipHA Diploma in Hospital Administration
DipHSM Diploma in Health Services Management
DipHum Diploma in Humanities
DipLA Diploma in Landscape Architecture
DipLib Diploma of Librarianship
DipM Diploma in Marketing
DipN Diploma in Nursing
DipNEC Diploma of Northampton Engineering College
DipPA Diploma of Practitioners in Advertising
DipPSA Diploma in Public Service Administration
DipREM Diploma in Rural Estate Management
DipSMS Diploma in School Management Studies
DipSoc Diploma in Sociology
DipTA Diploma in Tropical Agriculture
DipT&CP Diploma in Town and Country Planning
DipTh Diploma in Theology
DipTMHA Diploma in Training and Further Education of Mentally Handicapped Adults
DipTP Diploma in Town Planning
DipTPT Diploma in Theory and Practice of Teaching
Dir/dir Director/director
DIS Diploma in Industrial Studies
Dist District
DistTP Distinction in Town Planning
DIur Doctor of Law
div divorced
Div Division
Div Test Divinity Testimonium (of Trinity College, Dublin)
Divnl Division(al)
DJAG Deputy Judge Advocate General
DJPD Dato Jasa Purba Di-Raja Negeri Sembilan (Malaysia)
DJStJ Dame of Justice, Order of St John of Jerusalem
DJur *Doctor Juris* (Doctor of Law)
DK Most Esteemed Family Order (Brunei)
DL Deputy Lieutenant

DLC Diploma of Loughborough College
DLES Doctor of Letters in Economic Studies
DLI Durham Light Infantry
DLit/DLitt Doctor of Literature; Doctor of Letters
DLittS Doctor of Sacred Letters
DLJ Dame of Grace, Order of St Lazarus of Jerusalem
DLO Diploma in Laryngology and Otology
DM Doctor of Medicine
DMA Diploma in Municipal Administration
DMD Doctor of Medical Dentistry (Australia)
DME Director of Mechanical Engineering
DMet Doctor of Metallurgy
DMI Director of Military Intelligence
DMin Doctor of Ministry
DMiss Doctor of Missiology
DMJ Diploma in Medical Jurisprudence
DMJ(Path) Diploma in Medical Jurisprudence (Pathology)
DMLJ Dame of Merit, Order of St Lazarus of Jerusalem
DMO Director of Military Operations
DMR Diploma in Medical Radiology
DMRD Diploma in Medical Radiological Diagnosis
DMRE Diploma in Medical Radiology and Electrology
DMRT Diploma in Medical Radio-Therapy
DMS Director of Medical Services; Decoration for Meritorious Service (South Africa); Diploma in Management Studies
DMSc Doctor of Medical Science
DMSSB Direct Mail Services Standards Board
DMT Director of Military Training
DMus Doctor of Music
DMW Dame, St Michael of the Wing (Portugal)
DN Diploma in Nursing
DNB Dictionary of National Biography
DNE Director of Naval Equipment
DNH Department of National Heritage
DNI Director of Naval Intelligence
DO Diploma in Ophthalmology; Diploma in Osteopathy
DOAE Defence Operational Analysis Establishment
DObstRCOG Diploma of Royal College of Obstetricians and Gynaecologists
DOC District Officer Commanding
DocEng Doctor of Engineering
DoE Department of the Environment
DoH Department of Health
DoI Department of Industry
DOL Doctor of Oriental Learning
Dom *Dominus* (Lord)
DOMS Diploma in Ophthalmic Medicine and Surgery
DOR Director of Operational Requirements
DOrthRCS Diploma in Orthodontics, Royal College of Surgeons
DOS Director of Ordnance Services; Doctor of Ocular Science
DP Data Processing
DPA Diploma in Public Administration; Discharged Prisoners' Aid; Doctor of Public Administration
DPD Diploma in Public Dentistry
DPEc Doctor of Political Economy
DPed Doctor of Pedagogy
DPh/DPhil Doctor of Philosophy
DPH Diploma in Public Health
DPharm Doctor of Pharmacy
DPhilMed Diploma in Philosophy of Medicine
DPhysMed Diploma in Physical Medicine
DPLG Diplômé par le Gouvernement
DPM Diploma in Psychological Medicine
DPMS Dato Paduka Mahkota Selangor (Malaysia)
DPP Director of Public Prosecutions
DPR Director of Public Relations
DPS Director of Postal Services; Director of Personal Services; Doctor of Public Service
DPSA Diploma in Public and Social Administration
DPSE Diploma in Professional Studies in Education
DPsych Doctor of Psychology
DQMG Deputy Quartermaster-General
Dr Doctor
Dr ing Doctor of Engineering
Dr jur Doctor of Laws
Dr rer nat Doctor of Natural Science
Dr rer pol Doctor of Political Science
DRA Defence Research Agency
DRAC Director Royal Armoured Corps
DrArch Doctor of Architecture
DRC Diploma of Royal College of Science and Technology, Glasgow
DRCOG Diploma of Royal College of Obstetricians and Gynaecologists
DRD Diploma in Restorative Dentistry
DrŒcPol *Doctor Œconomiæ Politiæ* (Doctor of Political Economy)
DRS Diploma in Religious Studies
DRSAMD Diploma of the Royal Scottish Academy of Music and Drama
DS Directing Staff; Doctor of Science
DSA Diploma in Social Administration
DSAC Defence Scientific Advisory Council
DSAO Diplomatic Service Administration Office
DSc (SocSci) Doctor of Science in Social Science
DSC Distinguished Service Cross
DSc Doctor of Science
DScA Docteur en sciences agricoles
DSCHE Diploma of the Scottish Council for Health Education
DScMil Doctor of Military Science
DSD Director Staff Duties
DSF Director Special Forces
DSIR Department of Scientific and Industrial Research
DSL Doctor of Sacred Letters
DSLJ Dato Seri Laila Jasa (Brunei)
DSM Distinguished Service Medal
DSNB Dato Setia Negara Brunei
DSNS Dato Setia Negeri Sembilan (Malaysia)
DSO Distinguished Service Order
DSocSc Doctor of Social Science
dsp *decessit sine prole* (died without issue)
dspl *decessit sine prole legitima* (died without legitimate issue)
dspm *decessit sine prole mascula* (died without male issue)
dspml *decessit sine prole mascula legitima* (died without legitimate male issue)
dspms *decessit sine prole mascula superstite* (died without surviving male issue)
dsps *decessit sine prole superstite* (died without surviving issue)
DSP Director of Selection of Personnel; Docteur en sciences politiques (Montreal)
Dss Deaconess
DSS Department of Social Security; Doctor of Sacred Scripture
DSSc Doctor of Social Science
DST Director of Supplies and Transport
DStJ Dame of Grace, Most Venerable Order of the Hospital of St John of Jerusalem; Dame of Justice, Most Venerable Order of the Hospital of St John of Jerusalem
DTA Diploma in Tropical Agriculture
DTD Dekoratie voor Trouwe Dienst (Decoration for Devoted Service)
DTech Doctor of Technology
DTh/DTheol Doctor of Theology
DTH Diploma in Tropical Hygiene
DThPT Diploma in Theory and Practice of Teaching
DTI Department of Trade and Industry
DTM&H Diploma in Tropical Medicine and Hygiene
DU/DUniv Honorary Doctor of the University
Dunelm *Dunelmensis* (of Durham)
DUP Democratic Unionist Party; Docteur de l'Université de Paris
DVA Diploma of Veterinary Anaesthesia
Dve Drive
DVH Diploma in Veterinary Hygiene
DVLA Driver and Vehicle Licensing Authority
DVLC Driver and Vehicle Licensing Centre
DVM Doctor of Veterinary Medicine
DVMS/DVM&S Doctor of Veterinary Medicine and Surgery
dvm *decessit vita matris* (died in the lifetime of the mother)
dvp *decessit vita patris* (died in the lifetime of the father)
DVR Diploma in Veterinary Radiology
DVSc Doctor of Veterinary Science
DVSM Diploma in Veterinary State Medicine

E

E	East; Earl; England, used usually of titles of honour created in the peerage or baronetage of England
EAA	Edinburgh Architectural Association
EACR	European Association for Cancer Research
EAGA	Energy Action Grants Agency
EAHY	European Architectural Heritage Year
EAP	East Africa Protectorate
EAW	Electrical Association for Women
EBC	English Benedictine Congregation
Ebor	*Eboracensis* (of York)
EBRD	European Bank for Reconstruction and Development
EBU	European Broadcasting Union
Ec	Economic
EC	Etoile de Courage (Canada); European Community; European Commission; Emergency Commission
ECA	Economic Co-operation Administration; Economic Commission for Africa
ECAFE	Economic Commission for Asia and the Far East
ECCTIS	Education Courses and Credit Transfer Information Systems
ECE	Economic Commission for Europe
ECGD	Export Credits Guarantee Department
ECLA	Economic Commission for Latin America
ECLAC	United Nations Economic Commission for Latin America and the Caribbean
ECOVAST	European Council for the Village and Small Town
ECSC	European Coal and Steel Community
ECU	English Church Union
ed	edited; editor
ED	Efficiency Decoration; Doctor of Engineering (US); European Democrat
EdB	Bachelor of Education
EDC	Economic Development Committee
EdD	Doctor of Education
EDF	European Development Fund
EDG	European Democratic Group; Employment Department Group
Edin	Edinburgh
edn	edition
EDP	Executive Development Programme
EdS	Specialist in Education
edtl	editorial
educ	educated
Educn	Education
EEC	European Economic Community
EEF	Engineering Employers' Federation; Egyptian Expeditionary Force
EEIBA	Electrical and Electronic Industries Benevolent Association
EETPU	Electrical Electronic Telecommunication & Plumbing Union
EETS	Early English Text Society
EFCE	European Federation of Chemical Engineering
EFTA	European Free Trade Association
eh	ehrenhalber (honorary)
EI	East Indian; East Indies
EIA	Engineering Industries Association
EIB	European Investment Bank
EICS	East India Company's Service
EIS	Educational Institute of Scotland
EISCAT	European Incoherent Scatter Association
EIU	Economist Intelligence Unit
ELBS	English Language Book Society
ELSE	European Life Science Editors
ELT	English Language Teaching
EM	Edward Medal
EMBL	European Molecular Biology Laboratory
EMBO	European Molecular Biology Organisation
EMP	Electro Magnetic Pulse; Executive Management Program Diploma
EMS	Emergency Medical Service
Engr/engr	engineer
Engrg	Engineering
ENO	English National Opera
ENSA	Entertainments National Service Association
ENT	Ear Nose and Throat
EO	Executive Officer
EOC	Equal Opportunities Commission
EOPH	Examined Officer of Public Health
EORTC	European Organisation for Research on Treatment of Cancer
EP	European Parliament
EPP	European People's Party
EPSRC	Engineering and Physical Sciences Research Council
ER	East Riding; Eastern Region (British Railways)
er	elder
ERA	Electrical Research Association
ERC	Electronics Research Council
ERD	Emergency Reserve Decoration (Army)
ESA	European Space Agency
ESCAP	Economic and Social Commission for Asia and the Pacific
ESF	European Science Foundation
ESL	English as a Second Language
Esq	Esquire
ESRC	Economic and Social Research Council; Electricity Supply Research Council
ESRO	European Space Research Organization
est	eldest
ESTA	European Sciences and Technology Assembly
Estab/s	Establishment/s
ESU	English-Speaking Union
ETA	Engineering Training Authority
ETH	Eidgenössische Technische Hochschule
ETUC	European Trade Union Confederation
ETUCE	European Trade Union Committee for Education
EU	European Union
EUDISED	European Documentation and Information Service for Education
Euratom	European Atomic Energy Community
EurBiol	European Biologist
EurChem	European Chemist
EurIng	European Engineer
EUROM	European Federation for Optics and Precision Mechanics
EUW	European Union of Women
eV	eingetragener Verein
exec	executive
Expdn(y)	Expedition(ary)
Extrdy	Extraordinary

F

f	father
FA	Football Association
FAA	Fellow, Australian Academy of Science; Fleet Air Arm
FAAAI	Fellow, American Association for Artificial Intelligence
FAAAS	Fellow, American Association for the Advancement of Science
FAAO	Fellow, American Academy of Optometry
FAAP	Fellow, American Academy of Pediatrics
FAARM	Fellow, American Academy of Reproductive Medicine
FAAV	Fellow, Association of Agricultural Valuers
FAAVCT	Fellow, American Academy of Veterinary and Comparative Toxicology
FABE	Fellow, Association of Building Engineers
FACC	Fellow, American College of Cardiology
FACCA	Fellow, Association of Certified and Corporate Accountants
FACCP	Fellow, American College of Chest Physicians
FACD	Fellow, American College of Dentistry
FACDS	Fellow, Australian College of Dental Surgeons
FACE	Fellow, Australian College of Education
FACerS	Fellow, American Ceramic Society
FACHSE	Fellow, Australian College of Health Service Executives
FACI	Fellow, Australian Chemical Institute
FACMA	Fellow, Australian College of Medical Administrators
FACMG	Fellow, American College of Medicinal Genetics
FACOG	Fellow, American College of Obstetricians and Gynaecologists
FACOM	Fellow, Australian College of Occupational Medicine
FACP	Fellow, American College of Physicians
FACR	Fellow, American College of Radiology
FACRM	Fellow, Australian College of Rehabilitation Medicine

FACS	Fellow, American College of Surgeons
FACVT	Fellow, American College of Veterinary Toxicology
FADM	Fellow, Academy of Dental Materials
FADO	Fellow, Association of Dispensing Opticians
FAeSI	Fellow, Aeronautical Society of India
FAFPHM	Fellow, Australian Faculty of Public Health Medicine
FAGO	Fellowship in Australia in Obstetrics and Gynaecology
FAGS	Fellow, American Geographical Society
FAHA	Fellow, Australian Academy of the Humanities
FAI	Fellow, Chartered Auctioneers' and Estate Agents' Institute; Fédération Aéronautique Internationale
FAIA	Fellow, American Institute of Architects
FAIAA	Fellow, American Institute of Aeronautics and Astronautics
FAIAS	Fellow, Australian Institute of Agricultural Science
FAIB	Fellow, Australian Institute of Bankers
FAIBiol	Fellow, Australian Institute of Biology
FAICD	Fellow, Australian Institute of Company Directors
FAIE	Fellow, Australian Institute of Energy
FAIEx	Fellow, Australian Institute of Export
FAIFST	Fellow, Australian Institute of Food Science and Technology
FAII	Fellow, Australian Insurance Institute
FAIM	Fellow, Australian Institute of Management
FAIP	Fellow, Australian Institute of Physics
FAMA	Fellow, Australian Medical Association
FAMI	Fellow, Australian Marketing Institute
FAmNucSoc	Fellow, American Nuclear Society
FAMS	Fellow, Ancient Monuments Society
FANY	First Aid Nursing Yeomanry
FANZCA	Fellow, Australian and New Zealand College of Anaesthetists
FANZCP	Fellow, Australian and New Zealand College of Psychiatrists
FAO	Food and Agriculture Organization of the United Nations
FAOrthA	Fellow, Australian Orthopaedic Association
FAPA	Fellow, American Psychiatric Association
FAPHA	Fellow, American Public Health Association
FAPI	Fellow, Australian Planning Institute
FAPM	Fellow, Association of Project Managers
FAPS	Fellow, American Phytopathological Society
FArborA	Fellow, Aboricultural Association
FARE	Federation of Alcoholic Rehabilitation Establishments
FARELF	Far East Land Forces
FAS	Fellow, Antiquarian Society; Fellow, Nigerian Academy of Science; Funding Agency for Schools
FASA	Fellow, Australian Society of Accountants
FASCE	Fellow, American Society of Civil Engineers
fase	fascicule
FASI	Fellow, Architects' and Surveyors' Institute
FASME	Fellow, American Society of Mechanical Engineers
FASPOG	Fellow, Australian Society for Psychosomatic Obstetrics and Gynaecology
FASSA	Fellow, Academy of the Social Sciences in Australia
FAusIMM	Fellow, Australasian Institute of Mining and Metallurgy
FAustCOG	Fellow, Australian College of Obstetricians and Gynaecologists
FBA	Fellow, British Academy; Federation of British Artists
FBCartS	Fellow, British Cartographic Society
FBCO	Fellow, British College of Optometrists (formerly of Ophthalmic Opticians (Optometrists))
FBCS	Fellow, British Computer Society
FBEC(S)	Fellow, Business Education Council (Scotland)
FBES	Fellow, Biological Engineering Society
FBHA	Fellow, British Hospitality Association
FBHI	Fellow, British Horological Institute; Fellow, British Horticultural Institute
FBHS	Fellow, British Horse Society
FBI	Federation of British Industries; Federal Bureau of Investigation
FBIA	Fellow, Bankers' Institute of Australasia
FBIAT	Fellow, British Institute of Architectural Technicians
FBIBA	Fellow, British Insurance Brokers' Association
FBID	Fellow, British Institute of Interior Design
FBIIBA	Fellow, British Insurance and Investment Brokers' Association
FBIM	Fellow, British Institute of Management
FBINZ	Fellow, Bankers' Institute of New Zealand
FBIPP	Fellow, British Institute of Professional Photography
FBIRA	Fellow, British Institute of Regulatory Affairs
FBIS	Fellow, British Interplanetary Society
FBKS	Fellow, British Kinematograph Society
FBKSTS	Fellow, British Kinematograph, Sound and Television Society
FBOA	Fellow, British Optical Association
FBOU	Fellow, British Ornithologists' Union
FBPICS	Fellow, British Production and Inventory Control Society
FBPsS	Fellow, British Psychological Society
FBritIRE	Fellow, British Institution of Radio Engineers (later FIERE)
FBS	Fellow, Building Societies Institute (later FCBSI)
FBSI	Fellow, Boot and Shoe Institution
FBSM	Fellow, Birmingham School of Music
FC	Football Club
FCA	Fellow, Institute of Chartered Accountants; Fellow, Institute of Chartered Accountants in Australia; Fellow, New Zealand Society of Accountants; Federation of Canadian Artists
FCAI	Fellow, New Zealand Institute of Cost Accountants; Fellow, Canadian Aeronautical Institute
FCAM	Fellow, CAM Foundation
FCAnaes	Fellow, College of Anaesthetists
FCASI	Fellow, Canadian Aeronautics and Space Institute
FCBSI	Fellow, Chartered Building Societies Institute
FCCA	Fellow, Chartered Association of Certified Accountants
FCCEA	Fellow, Commonwealth Council for Educational Administration
FCCS	Fellow, Corporation of Secretaries (formerly of Certified Secretaries)
FCCT	Fellow, Canadian College of Teachers
FCEC	Federation of Civil Engineering Contractors
FCFI	Fellow, Clothing and Footwear Institute
FCGI	Fellow, City and Guilds of London Institute
FCGP	Fellow, College of General Practitioners
FCH	Fellow, Coopers Hill College
FChS	Fellow, Society of Chiropodists
FCI	Fellow, Institute of Commerce
FCIA	Fellow, Corporation of Insurance Agents
FCIArb	Fellow, Chartered Institute of Arbitrators
FCIB	Fellow, Corporation of Insurance Brokers; Fellow, Chartered Institute of Bankers
FCIBS	Fellow, Chartered Institution of Building Services; Fellow, Chartered Institute of Bankers in Scotland
FCIBSE	Fellow, Chartered Institution of Building Services Engineers
FCIC	Fellow, Chemical Institute of Canada (formerly Canadian Institute of Chemistry)
FCIEH	Fellow, Chartered Institute of Environmental Health
FCIH	Fellow, Chartered Institute of Housing
FCII	Fellow, Chartered Insurance Institute
FCIJ	Fellow, Chartered Institute of Journalists
FCILA	Fellow, Chartered Institute of Loss Adjusters
FCIM	Fellow, Chartered Institute of Marketing; Fellow, Institute of Corporate Managers (Australia)
FCIOB	Fellow, Chartered Institute of Building
FCIPA	Fellow, Chartered Institute of Patent Agents
FCIPS	Fellow, Chartered Institute of Purchasing and Supply
FCIS	Fellow, Institute of Chartered Secretaries and Administrators (formerly Chartered Institute of Secretaries)
FCISA	Fellow, Chartered Institute of Secretaries and Administrators (Australia)
FCIT	Fellow, Chartered Institute of Transport
FCIWEM	Fellow, Chartered Institution of Water and Environmental Management
FCM	Faculty of Community Medicine
FCMA	Fellow, Chartered Institute of Management Accountants (formerly Institute of Cost and Management Accountants)
FCMSA	Fellow, College of Medicine of South Africa
FCNA	Fellow, College of Nursing, Australia
FCO	Foreign and Commonwealth Office
FCOG(SA)	Fellow, South African College of Obstetrics and Gynaecology
FCollH	Fellow, College of Handicraft
FCollP	Fellow, College of Preceptors
FCommA	Fellow, Society of Commercial Accountants
FCOphth	Fellow, College of Ophthalmologists
FCOptom	Fellow, College of Optometrists
FCP	Fellow, College of Preceptors
FCP(SoAf)	Fellow, College of Physicians, South Africa
FCPA	Fellow, Australian Society of Certified Practising Accountants; Fellow, Canadian Psychological Association
FCPath	Fellow, College of Pathologists
FCPCH	Fellow, College of Paediatrics and Child Health
FCPS	Fellow, College of Physicians and Surgeons
FCPS (Pak)	Fellow, College of Physicians and Surgeons of Pakistan
FCPSO(SoAf)	Fellow, College of Physicians and Surgeons and Obstetricians, South Africa
FCRA	Fellow, College of Radiologists of Australia
FCS	Federation of Conservative Students
FCS/FChemSoc	Fellow, Chemical Society

FCSD	Fellow, Chartered Society of Designers
FCSHK	Fellow, College of Surgeons of Hong Kong
FCSLT	Fellow, College of Speech and Language Therapists
FCSP	Fellow, Chartered Society of Physiotherapy
FCSSA	Fellow, College of Surgeons, South Africa
FCSSL	Fellow, College of Surgeons of Sri Lanka
FCST	Fellow, College of Speech Therapists
FCT	Federal Capital Territory; Fellow, Association of Corporate Treasurers
FCTB	Fellow, College of Teachers of the Blind
FCU	Fighter Control Unit
FCWA	Fellow, Institute of Costs and Works Accountants
FDA	Association of First Division Civil Servants
FDF	Food and Drink Federation
FDI	Fédération Dentaire Internationale
FDP	Freie Demokratische Partei
FDS	Fellow in Dental Surgery
FDSRCPSGlas	Fellow in Dental Surgery, Royal College of Physicians and Surgeons of Glasgow
FDSRCS	Fellow in Dental Surgery, Royal College of Surgeons of England
FDSRCSE	Fellow in Dental Surgery, Royal College of Surgeons of Edinburgh
FE	Far East
FEAF	Far East Air Force
FEANI	Fédération Européenne d'Associations Nationales d'Ingénieurs
FEBS	Federation of European Biochemical Societies
FECI	Fellow, Institute of Employment Consultants
Fedn	Federation
FEE	Fédération des Expertes Comptables Européens
FEEC/FEFCE	Further Education Funding Council for England
FEF	Far East Fleet
FEI	Fédération Equestre Internationale
FEIDCT	Fellow, Educational Institute of Design Craft and Technology
FEIS	Fellow, Educational Institute of Scotland
FELCO	Federation of English Language Course Opportunities
Fell	Fellow
FEng	Fellow, Royal Academy (formerly Fellowship) of Engineering
FES	Fellow, Entomological Society; Fellow, Ethnological Society
FESC	Fellow, European Society of Cardiology
FF	Fianna Fáil; Field Force
FFA	Fellow, Faculty of Actuaries (in Scotland); Fellow, Institute of Financial Accountants
FFA(SA)	Fellow, Faculty of Anaesthetists (South Africa)
FFAEM	Fellow, Faculty of Accident and Emergency Medicine
FFARACS	Fellow, Faculty of Anaesthetists, Royal Australasian College of Surgeons
FFARCS	Fellow, Faculty of Anaesthetists, Royal College of Surgeons of England
FFARCSI	Fellow, Faculty of Anaesthetists, Royal College of Surgeons in Ireland
FFAS	Fellow, Faculty of Architects and Surveyors, London
FFB	Fellow, Faculty of Building
FFCM	Fellow, Faculty of Community Medicine
FFCMI	Fellow, Faculty of Community Medicine of Ireland
FFDRCSI	Fellow, Faculty of Dentistry, Royal College of Surgeons in Ireland
FFF	Free French Forces
FFFP	Fellow, Faculty of Family Planning of the Royal College of Obstetricians and Gynaecologists
FFHC	Freedom from Hunger Campaign
FFHom	Fellow, Faculty of Homoeopathy
FFI	French Forces of the Interior; Finance for Industry
FFOM	Fellow, Faculty of Occupational Medicine
FFOMI	Fellow, Faculty of Occupational Medicine of Ireland
FFPath, RCPI	Fellow, Faculty of Pathologists of the Royal College of Physicians of Ireland
FFPHM	Fellow, Faculty of Public Health Medicine
FFPHMI	Fellow, Faculty of Public Health Medicine of Ireland
FFPM	Fellow, Faculty of Pharmaceutical Medicine
FFPS	Fauna and Flora Preservation Society
FFR	Fellow, Faculty of Radiologists
FG	Fine Gael
FGA	Fellow, Gemmological Association
FGCL	Fellow, Goldsmiths' College, London
FGCM	Fellow, Guild of Church Musicians
FGDS	Fédération de la Gauche Démocratique et Socialiste
FGGE	Fellow, Guild of Glass Engineers
FGI	Fellow, Institute of Certificated Grocers
F and GP	Finance and General Purposes
FGS	Fellow, Geological Society
FGSM	Fellow, Guildhall School of Music and Drama
FGSM(MT)	Fellow, Guildhall School of Music and Drama (Music Therapy)
FHA	Fellow, Institute of Health Service Administrators (formerly Hospital Administrators)
FHAS	Fellow, Highland and Agricultural Society of Scotland
FHCIMA	Fellow, Hotel Catering and Institutional Management Association
FHFS	Fellow, Human Factors Society
FHKIE	Fellow, Hong Kong Institution of Engineers
FHMAAAS	Foreign Honorary Member, American Academy of Arts and Sciences
FHS	Fellow, Heraldry Society; Forces Help Society and Lord Roberts Workshops
FHSA	Family Health Services Authority
FHSM	Fellow, Institute of Health Services Management
FH-WC	Fellow, Heriot-Watt College (now University), Edinburgh
FIA	Fellow, Institute of Actuaries
FIAA	Fellow, Institute of Actuaries of Australia
FIAA&S	Fellow, Incorporated Association of Architects and Surveyors
FIAAS	Fellow, Institute of Australian Agricultural Science
FIAgrE	Fellow, Institution of Agricultural Engineers
FIAgrM	Fellow, Institute of Agricultural Management
FIAI	Fellow, Institute of Industrial and Commercial Accountants
FIAL	Fellow, International Institute of Arts and Letters
FIAM	Fellow, International Academy of Management
FIAP	Fellow, Institution of Analysts and Programmers
FIArb	Fellow, Institute of Arbitrators
FIArbA	Fellow, Institute of Arbitrators of Australia
FIAS	Fellow, Institute of Aeronautical Sciences (US)
FIASc	Fellow, Indian Academy of Sciences
FIAWS	Fellow, International Academy of Wood Sciences
FIB	Fellow, Institute of Bankers
FIBA	Fellow, Institute of Business Administration, Australia
FIBD	Fellow, Institute of British Decorators
FIBiol	Fellow, Institute of Biology
FIBiotech	Fellow, Institute for Biotechnical Studies
FIBMS	Fellow, Institute of Biomedical Sciences
FIBP	Fellow, Institute of British Photographers
FIBScot	Fellow, Institute of Bankers in Scotland
FIC	Fellow, Institute of Chemistry; Fellow, Imperial College, London
FICA	Fellow, Commonwealth Institute of Accountants; Fellow, Institute of Chartered Accountants in England and Wales
FICAI	Fellow, Institute of Chartered Accountants in Ireland
FICD	Fellow, Institute of Civil Defence; Fellow, Indian College of Dentists; Fellow, International College of Dentists
FICDDS	Fellow, Institute of Civil Defence and Disaster Studies
FICE	Fellow, Institution of Civil Engineers
FICeram	Fellow, Institute of Ceramics
FICFM	Fellow, Institute of Charity Fundraising Managers
FICFor	Fellow, Institute of Chartered Foresters
FIChemE	Fellow, Institution of Chemical Engineers
FICI	Fellow, Institute of Chemistry of Ireland; Fellow, International Colonial Institute
FICM	Fellow, Institute of Credit Management
FICMA	Fellow, Institute of Cost and Management Accountants
FICorrST	Fellow, Institution of Corrosion Science and Technology
FICS	Fellow, Institute of Chartered Shipbrokers; Fellow, International College of Surgeons
FICT	Fellow, Institute of Concrete Technologists
FICW	Fellow, Institute of Clerks of Works of Great Britain
FIDA	Fellow, Institute of Directors, Australia
FIDCA	Fellow, Industrial Design Council of Australia
FIDE	Fédération Internationale des Echecs; Fellow, Institute of Design Engineers; Fédération Internationale pour le Droit Européen
FIDEM	Fédération Internationale de la Médaille
FIEAust	Fellow, Institution of Engineers, Australia
FIEC	Fellow, Institute of Employment Consultants
FIED	Fellow, Institution of Engineering Designers
FIEE	Fellow, Institution of Electrical Engineers
FIEEE	Fellow, Institute of Electrical and Electronics Engineers (NY)
FIEHK	Fellow, Institution of Engineering, Hong Kong
FIEI	Fellow, Institution of Engineering Inspection; Fellow, Institution of Engineers of Ireland
FIEIE	Fellow, Institution of Electronics and Electrical Incorporated Engineers
FIEJ	Fédération Internationale des Editeurs de Journaux et Publications
FIElecIE	Fellow, Institution of Electronic Incorporated Engineers
FIERE	Fellow, Institution of Electronic and Radio Engineers

FIES Fellow, Illuminating Engineering Society; Fellow, Institution of Engineers and Shipbuilders, Scotland
FIET Fédération Internationale des Employés, Techniciens et Cadres
FIEx Fellow, Institute of Export
FIExpE Fellow, Institute of Explosives Engineers
FIFA Fédération Internationale de Football Association
FIFF Fellow, Institute of Freight Forwarders
FIFireE Fellow, Institution of Fire Engineers
FIFM Fellow, Institute of Fisheries Management
FIFor Fellow, Institute of Foresters
FIFST Fellow, Institute of Food Science and Technology
FIGasE Fellow, Institution of Gas Engineers
FIGCM Fellow, Incorporated Guild of Church Musicians
FIGD Fellow, Institute of Grocery Distribution
FIGO International Federation of Gynaecology and Obstetrics
FIH Fellow, Institute of Housing; Fellow, Institute of the Horse
FIHE Fellow, Institute of Health Education
FIHM Fellow, Institute of Housing Managers
FIHort Fellow, Institute of Horticulture
FIHospE Fellow, Institute of Hospital Engineering
FIHT Fellow, Institution of Highways and Transportation
FIHVE Fellow, Institution of Heating and Ventilating Engineers
FIIA Fellow, Institute of Industrial Administration; Fellow, Institute of Internal Auditors
FIIB Fellow, International Institute of Biotechnology
FIIC Fellow, International Institute for Conservation of Historic and Artistic Works
FIIDA Fellow, International Interior Design Association
FIIM Fellow, Institution of Industrial Managers
FIInfSc Fellow, Institute of Information Scientists
FIInst Fellow, Imperial Institute
FIIP Fellow, Institute of Incorporated Photographers
FIIPC Fellow, India International Photographic Council
FIIPE Fellow, Indian Institution of Production Engineers
Fil Hed Filosofie Hedersdoktor
FIL Fellow, Institute of Linguists
FILA Fellow, Institute of Landscape Architects
FILDM Fellow, Institute of Logistics and Distribution Management
FilDr Doctor of Philosophy
FILLM Fédération Internationale des Langues et Littératures Modernes
FIllumES Fellow, Illuminating Engineering Society
FILog Fellow, Institute of Logistics
FIM Fellow, Institute of Materials (formerly Institution of Metallurgists, then Institute of Metals)
FIMA Fellow, Institute of Mathematics and its Applications
FIMarE Fellow, Institute of Marine Engineers
FIMatM Fellow, Institute of Materials Management
FIMBRA Financial Intermediaries, Managers and Brokers Regulatory Association
FIMC Fellow, Institute of Management Consultants
FIMCB Fellow, International Management Centre from Buckingham
FIMechE Fellow, Institution of Mechanical Engineers
FIMfgE Fellow, Institution of Manufacturing Engineers
FIMFT Fellow, Institute of Maxillo-facial Technology
FIMgt Fellow, Institute of Management
FIMGTechE Fellow, Institution of Mechanical and General Technician Engineers
FIMH Fellow, Institute of Materials Handling (later FIMatM); Fellow Institute of Military History
FIMI Fellow, Institute of the Motor Industry
FIMinE Fellow, Institution of Mining Engineers
FIMIT Fellow, Institute of Musical Instrument Technology
FIMLS Fellow, Institute of Medical Laboratory Sciences
FIMLT Fellow, Institute of Medical Laboratory Technology (later FIMLS)
FIMM Fellow, Institution of Mining and Metallurgy
FIMMA Fellow, Institute of Metals and Materials Australasia
FIMS Fellow, Institute of Mathematical Statistics
FIMT Fellow, Institute of the Motor Trade
FIMTA Fellow, Institute of Municipal Treasurers and Accountants
FIMunE Fellow, Institution of Municipal Engineers
Fin/fin Financial/financial
FIN Fellow, Institute of Navigation
FINA Fédération Internationale de Natation Amateur
FInstAM Fellow, Institute of Administrative Management
FInstArb(NZ) Fellow, Institute of Arbitrators of New Zealand
FInstB Fellow, Institution of Buyers
FInstBiol Fellow, Institute of Biology
FInstD Fellow, Institute of Directors
FInstE Fellow, Institute of Energy
FInstEnvSci Fellow, Institute of Environmental Sciences
FInstF Fellow, Institute of Fuel
FInstFF Fellow, Institute of Freight Forwarders Ltd
FInstHE Fellow, Institution of Highways Engineers
FInstLEx Fellow, Institute of Legal Executives
FInstM Fellow, Institute of Meat; Fellow, Institute of Marketing
FInstMC Fellow, Institute of Measurement and Control
FInstMet Fellow, Institute of Metals
FInstMSM Fellow, Institute of Marketing and Sales Management
FInstNDT Fellow, Institute of Non-Destructive Testing
FInstP Fellow, Institute of Physics
FInstPet Fellow, Institute of Petroleum
FInstPI Fellow, Institute of Patentees and Inventors
FInstPS Fellow, Institute of Purchasing and Supply
FInstSM Fellow, Institute of Sales Management
FInstSMM Fellow, Institute of Sales and Marketing Management
FInstW Fellow, Institute of Welding
FINucE Fellow, Institution of Nuclear Engineers
FIOA Fellow, Institute of Acoustics
FIOB Fellow, Institute of Building
FIOH Fellow, Institute of Occupational Hygiene
FIOM Fellow, Institute of Office Management
FIOP Fellow, Institute of Printing
FIOSH Fellow, Institute of Occupational Safety and Health
FIP Fellow, Australian Institute of Petroleum
FIPA Fellow, Institute of Practitioners in Advertising
FIPD Fellow, Institute of Personnel and Development
FIPDM Fellow, Institute of Physical Distribution Management (later FILDM)
FIPEMB Fellow, Institution of Physics and Engineering in Medicine and Biology
FIPENZ Fellow, Institution of Professional Engineers, New Zealand
FIPG Fellow, Institute of Professional Goldsmiths
FIPHE Fellow, Institution of Public Health Engineers
FIPlantE Fellow, Institute of Plant Engineers
FIPM Fellow, Institute of Personnel Management
FIPR Fellow, Institute of Public Relations
FIProdE Fellow, Institution of Production Engineers
FIQ Fellow, Institute of Quarrying
FIQA Fellow, Institute of Quality Assurance
FIQS Fellow, Institute of Quantity Surveyors
FIRA Furniture Industry Research Association
FIRA(Ind) Fellow, Institute of Railway Auditors and Accountants (India)
FIRE(Aust) Fellow, Institution of Radio Engineers (Australia)
FIREE(Aust) Fellow, Institution of Radio and Electronics Engineers (Australia)
FIRI Fellow, Institution of the Rubber Industry (later FPRI)
FIRM Fellow, Institute of Risk Management
FIRSE Fellow, Institute of Railway Signalling Engineers
FIRTE Fellow, Institute of Road Transport Engineers
FIS Fellow, Institute of Statisticians
FISA Fellow, Incorporated Secretaries' Association; Fédération Internationale des Sociétés d'Aviron
FISE Fellow, Institution of Sales Engineers; Fellow, Institution of Sanitary Engineers
FISITA Fédération Internationale des Sociétés d'Ingénieurs des Techniques de l'Automobile
FISM Fellow, Institute of Supervisory Managers
FISOB Fellow, Incorporated Society of Organ Builders
FISP Fédération Internationale des Sociétés de Philosophie
FIST Fellow, Institute of Science Technology
FISTC Fellow, Institute of Scientific and Tochnical Communicators
FISTD Fellow, Imperial Society of Teachers of Dancing
FIStructE Fellow, Institution of Structural Engineers
FISW Fellow, Institute of Social Work
FITD Fellow, Institute of Training and Development
FITE Fellow, Institution of Electrical and Electronics Technician Engineers
FIW Fellow, Welding Institute
FIWE Fellow, Institution of Water Engineers
FIWEM Fellow, Institution of Water and Environmental Management
FIWES Fellow, Institution of Water Engineers and Scientists
FIWM Fellow, Institution of Works Managers
FIWPC Fellow, Institute of Water Pollution Control
FIWSc Fellow, Institute of Wood Science
FIWSP Fellow, Institute of Work Study Practitioners
FJIE Fellow, Junior Institution of Engineers
FJL Fellow, Institute of Journalists
FKC Fellow, King's College London
FKCHMS Fellow, King's College Hospital Medical School

fl *floruit* (flourished)
FL/Fla Florida
FLA Fellow, Library Association
FLAI Fellow, Library Association of Ireland
FLAS Fellow, Chartered Land Agents' Society
FLCM Fellow, London College of Music
FLHS Fellow, London Historical Society
FLI Fellow, Landscape Institute
FLIA Fellow, Life Insurance Association
FLS Fellow, Linnean Society
Flt Flight
F/Lt Flight Lieutenant
FM Field-Marshal
FMA Fellow, Museums Association
FMAAT Fellow Member, Association of Accounting Technicians
FMANZ Fellow, Medical Association of New Zealand
FMES Fellow, Minerals Engineering Society
FMF Fiji Military Forces
FMI Foundation for Manufacturing and Industry
FMS Federated Malay States; Fellow, Medical Society; Fellow, Institute of Management Services
FMSA Fellow, Mineralogical Society of America
FNA Fellow, Indian National Science Academy
FNAEA Fellow, National Association of Estate Agents
FNCO Fleet Naval Constructor Officer
Fndn Foundation
fndr founder
FNECInst Fellow, North East Coast Institution of Engineers and Shipbuilders
FNI Fellow, Nautical Institute; Fellow, National Institute of Sciences in India
FNIA Fellow, Nigerian Institute of Architects
FNM Free National Movement
FNZEI Fellow, New Zealand Educational Institute
FNZIA Fellow, New Zealand Institute of Architects
FNZIAS Fellow, New Zealand Institute of Agricultural Science
FNZIC Fellow, New Zealand Institute of Chemistry
FNZIE Fellow, New Zealand Institution of Engineers
FNZIM Fellow, New Zealand Institute of Management
FNZPsS Fellow, New Zealand Psychological Society
FO Foreign Office; Field Officer; Flying Officer
F/O Flying Officer
FODA Fellow, Overseas Doctors' Association
FODC Franciscan Order of the Divine Compassion
FOIC Flag Officer in charge
FOMI Faculty of Occupational Medicine of Ireland
FONA Flag Officer, Naval Aviation
FONAC Flag Officer Naval Air Command
For Foreign
FOR Fellowship of Operational Research
For Affrs Foreign Affairs
FOREST Freedom Organisation for the Right to Enjoy Smoking Tobacco
FOX Futures and Options Exchange
FPA Family Planning Association
FPC Family Practitioner Committee
FPEA Fellow, Physical Education Association
FPHM Faculty of Public Health Medicine
FPhS Fellow, Philosophical Society of England
FPhysS Fellow, Physical Society
FPI Fellow, Plastics Institute (later FPRI)
FPIA Fellow, Plastics Institute of Australia
FPMI Fellow, Pensions Management Institute
FPRI Fellow, Plastics and Rubber Institute
FPS Fellow, Pharmaceutical Society; Fauna Preservation Society
FRA Fellow, Royal Academy
FRACDS Fellow, Royal Australian College of Dental Surgeons
FRACGP Fellow, Royal Australian College of General Practitioners
FRACI Fellow, Royal Australian Chemical Institute
FRACMA Fellow, Royal Australian College of Medical Administrators
FRACO Fellow, Royal Australian College of Ophthalmologists
FRACOG Fellow, Royal Australian College of Obstetricians and Gynaecologists
FRACP Fellow, Royal Australasian College of Physicians
FRACR Fellow, Royal Australasian College of Radiologists
FRACS Fellow, Royal Australasian College of Surgeons
FRAD Fellow, Royal Academy of Dancing
FRAeS Fellow, Royal Aeronautical Society
FRAgS Fellow, Royal Agricultural Societies (of England, Scotland and Wales)
FRAHS Fellow, Royal Australian Historical Society
FRAI Fellow, Royal Anthropological Institute of Great Britain and Ireland
FRAIA Fellow, Royal Australian Institute of Architects
FRAIB Fellow, Royal Australian Institute of Building
FRAIC Fellow, Royal Architectural Institute of Canada
FRAIPA Fellow, Royal Australian Institute of Public Administration
FRAM Fellow, Royal Academy of Music
FRAME Fund for the Replacement of Animals in Medical Experiments
FRANZCP Fellow, Royal Australian and New Zealand College of Psychiatrists
FRAPI Fellow, Royal Australian Planning Institute
FRAS Fellow, Royal Astronomical Society; Fellow, Royal Asiatic Society
FRASB Fellow, Royal Asiatic Society of Bengal
FRASE Fellow, Royal Agricultural Society of England
FRAstS Fellow, Royal Astronomical Society
FRBS Fellow, Royal Society of British Sculptors; Fellow, Royal Botanic Society
FRCA Fellow, Royal College of Art; Fellow, Royal College of Anaesthetists
FRCCO Fellow, Royal Canadian College of Organists
FRCD(Can) Fellow, Royal College of Dentists of Canada
FRCGP Fellow, Royal College of General Practitioners
FRCM Fellow, Royal College of Music
FRCN Fellow, Royal College of Nursing
FRCO Fellow, Royal College of Organists
FRCO(CHM) Fellow, Royal College of Organists with Diploma in Choir Training
FRCOG Fellow, Royal College of Obstetricians and Gynaecologists
FRCOphth Fellow, Royal College of Ophthalmologists
FRCP Fellow, Royal College of Physicians, London
FRCPA Fellow, Royal College of Pathologists of Australasia
FRCPath Fellow, Royal College of Pathologists
FRCP(C) Fellow, Royal College of Physicians of Canada
FRCPE/FRCPEd Fellow, Royal College of Physicians, Edinburgh
FRCPI Fellow, Royal College of Physicians of Ireland
FRCP&S (Canada) Fellow, Royal College of Physicians and Surgeons of Canada
FRCPsych Fellow, Royal College of Psychiatrists
FRCR Fellow, Royal College of Radiologists
FRCS Fellow, Royal College of Surgeons of England
FRCSCan Fellow, Royal College of Surgeons of Canada
FRCSE/FRCSEd Fellow, Royal College of Surgeons of Edinburgh
FRCSGlas Fellow, Royal College of Physicians and Surgeons of Glasgow
FRCSI Fellow, Royal College of Surgeons in Ireland
FRCSoc Fellow, Royal Commonwealth Society
FRCUS Fellow, Royal College of University Surgeons (Denmark)
FRCVS Fellow, Royal College of Veterinary Surgeons
FREconS Fellow, Royal Economic Society
FREI Fellow, Real Estate Institute (Australia)
FRES Fellow, Royal Entomological Society of London
FRFPSG Fellow, Royal Faculty of Physicians and Surgeons, Glasgow
FRG Federal Republic of Germany
FRGS Fellow, Royal Geographical Society
FRGSA Fellow, Royal Geographical Society of Australasia
FRHistS Fellow, Royal Historical Society
FRHS Fellow, Royal Horticultural Society
FRHSV Fellow, Royal Historical Society of Victoria
FRIAS Fellow, Royal Incorporation of Architects of Scotland; Royal Institute for the Advancement of Science
FRIBA Fellow, Royal Institute of British Architects
FRIC Fellow, Royal Institute of Chemistry
FRICS Fellow, Royal Institution of Chartered Surveyors
FRIH Fellow, Royal Institute of Horticulture (NZ)
FRIN Fellow, Royal Institute of Navigation
FRINA Fellow, Royal Institution of Naval Architects
FRIPA Fellow, Royal Institute of Public Administration
FRIPHH Fellow, Royal Institute of Public Health and Hygiene
FRMCM Fellow, Royal Manchester College of Music
FRMedSoc Fellow, Royal Medical Society
FRMetS Fellow, Royal Meteorological Society
FRMIA Fellow, Retail Management Institute of Australia
FRMS Fellow, Royal Microscopical Society
FRNCM Fellow, Royal Northern College of Music
FRNS Fellow, Royal Numismatic Society
FRPharmS Fellow, Royal Pharmaceutical Society
FRPS Fellow, Royal Photographic Society
FRPSL Fellow, Royal Philatelic Society, London
FRS Fellow, Royal Society
FRS(Can) Fellow, Royal Society of Canada (also a Fellow of the Royal Society of Chemistry)

FRSA Fellow, Royal Society of Arts
FRSAI Fellow, Royal Society of Antiquaries of Ireland
FRSAMD Fellow, Royal Scottish Academy of Music and Drama
FRSanI Fellow, Royal Sanitary Institute
FRSC Fellow, Royal Society of Canada; Fellow, Royal Society of Chemistry
FRSC (UK) Fellow, Royal Society of Chemistry (used when a person is also a Fellow of the Royal Society of Canada)
FRSCM Hon Fellow, Royal School of Church Music
FRSE Fellow, Royal Society of Edinburgh
FRSGS Fellow, Royal Scottish Geographical Society
FRSH Fellow, Royal Society for the Promotion of Health
FRSL Fellow, Royal Society of Literature
FRSM/FRSocMed Fellow, Royal Society of Medicine
FRSNZ Fellow, Royal Society of New Zealand
FRSSAf Fellow, Royal Society of South Africa
FRST Fellow, Royal Society of Teachers
FRSTM&H Fellow, Royal Society of Tropical Medicine and Hygiene
FRTPI Fellow, Royal Town Planning Institute
FRTS Fellow, Royal Television Society
FRVA Fellow, Rating and Valuation Association
FRVC Fellow, Royal Veterinary College
FRVIA Fellow, Royal Victorian Institute of Architects
FRZSScot Fellow, Royal Zoological Society of Scotland
FS Field Security
FSA Fellow, Society of Arts; Fellow, Society of Antiquaries
FSAA Fellow, Society of Incorporated Accountants and Auditors
FSAE Fellow, Society of Automotive Engineers; Fellow, Society of Art Education
FSAI Fellow, Society of Architectural Illustrators
FSAIEE Fellow, South African Institute of Electrical Engineers
FSAM Fellow, Society of Art Masters
FSArc Fellow, Society of Architects (merged with RIBA 1952)
FSaRS Fellow, Safety and Reliability Society
FSAScot Fellow, Society of Antiquaries of Scotland
FSASM Fellow, South Australian School of Mines
FSBI Fellow, Savings Banks Institute
fsc Foreign Staff College
FSCA Fellow, Society of Company and Commercial Accountants
FScotvec Fellow, Scottish Vocational Education Council
FSCRE Fellow, Scottish Council for Research in Education
FSDC Fellow, Society of Dyers and Colourists
FSE Fellow, Society of Engineers
FSG Fellow, Society of Genealogists
FSGT Fellow, Society of Glass Technology
FSI Fellow, Chartered Surveyors' Institution; Fellow, Securities Institute
FSIA Fellow, Securities Institute of Australia
FSIAD Fellow, Society of Industrial Artists and Designers
FSLAET Fellow, Society of Licensed Aircraft Engineers and Technologists
FSLCOG Fellow, Sri Lankan College of Obstetrics and Gynaecology
FSLTC Fellow, Society of Leather Technologists and Chemists
FSMA Fellow, Incorporated Sales Managers' Association (later FInstMSM, then FInstM)
FSMC Freeman of the Spectacle-Makers' Company
FSME Fellow, Society of Manufacturing Engineers
FSMPTE Fellow, Society of Motion Picture and Television Engineers (US)
FSNAD Fellow, Society of Numismatic Artists and Designers
FSNAME Fellow, American Society of Naval Architects and Marine Engineers
FSRHE Fellow, Society for Research into Higher Education
FSRP Fellow, Society for Radiological Protection
FSS Fellow, Royal Statistical Society
FSTD Fellow, Society of Typographic Designers
FSVA Fellow, Incorporated Society of Valuers and Auctioneers
FT *Financial Times*
FTAT Furniture, Timber and Allied Trades Union
FTC Flying Training Command, Full Technological Certificate, City and Guilds of London Institute
FTCD Fellow, Trinity College, Dublin
FTCL Fellow, Trinity College of Music, London
FTI Fellow, Textile Institute
FTII Fellow, Chartered Institute (formerly Incorporated Institute, then Institute) of Taxation
FTMA Fellow, Telecommunications Managers Association
FTP Fellow, Thames Polytechnic
FTS Fellow, Australian Academy of Technological Sciences and Engineering; Flying Training School; Fellow, Tourism Society
FTSC Fellow, Tonic Sol-fa College
FTSE Fellow, Australian Academy of Technological Sciences and Engineering
FUCUA Federation of University Conservative and Unionist Associations
FUMDS Fellow, United Medical and Dental Schools
FUMIST Fellow, University of Manchester Institute of Science and Technology
Fus Fusiliers
FVRDE Fighting Vehicles Research and Development Establishment
FWAAS Fellow, World Academy of Arts and Sciences
FWACP Fellow, West African College of Physicians
FWCMD Fellow, Welsh College of Music and Drama
FWeldI Fellow, Welding Institute
FWSOM Fellow, Institute of Practitioners in Work Study, Organisation and Method
FZS Fellow, Zoological Society
FZSScot Fellow, Zoological Society of Scotland

G

GA Geologists' Association; Gaelic Athletic (Club); Georgia
GAI Guild of Architectural Ironmongers
GAP Gap Activity Projects
GAPAN Guild of Air Pilots and Air Navigators
GATT General Agreement on Tariffs and Trade
GB Great Britain, used chiefly of creations of titles of honour of
GBA Governing Bodies Association
GBE Knight or Dame Grand Cross, Order of the British Empire
GBGSA Governing Bodies of Girls' Schools Association (formerly Association of Governing Bodies of Girls' Public Schools)
GBSM Graduate, Birmingham and Midland Institute School of Music
GC George Cross
G/Capt Group Captain
GCB Knight/Dame Grand Cross of the Order of the Bath
GCBS General Council of British Shipping
GCFR Grand Commander, Order of the Federal Republic of Nigeria
GCH Knight Grand Cross, Hanoverian Order
GCHQ Government Communications Headquarters
GCIE Knight Grand Commander, Order of the Indian Empire
GCLJ Grand Cross, St Lazarus of Jerusalem
GCLM Grand Commander, Order of the Legion of Merit of Rhodesia
GCM Gold Crown of Merit (Barbados)
GCMG Knight or Dame Grand Cross, Order of St Michael and St George
GCON Grand Cross, Order of the Niger
GCSE General Certificate of Secondary Education
GCSG Knight Grand Cross, Order of St Gregory the Great
GCSI Knight Grand Commander of the Order of the Star of India
GCSJ Knight Grand Cross of Justice, Order of St John of Jerusalem (Knights Hospitaller)
GCSL Grand Cross, Order of St Lucia
GCStJ Bailiff or Dame Grand Cross, Most Venerable Order of the Hospital of St John of Jerusalem
GCVO Knight or Dame Grand Cross, Royal Victorian Order
gdau grand-daughter
Gd(s) Guard(s)
GDBA Guide Dogs for the Blind Association
GDC General Dental Council
Gdn(s) Garden(s)
GDR German Democratic Republic
Gen General
GER Great Eastern Railway
Ges Gesellschaft
gf grandfather
GFD Geophysical Fluid Dynamics
GFS Girls' Friendly Society
ggdau great-grand-daughter
ggf great-grandfather
gggf great-great-grandfather
ggggf great-great-great-grandfather
gggggf great-great-great-great-grandfather, etc
gggs great-great-grandson, etc
ggmother great-grandmother

ggs great-grandson
GGSM Graduate in Music, Guildhall School of Music and Drama
GHQ General Headquarters
Gib Gibraltar
GIMechE Graduate, Institution of Mechanical Engineers
GL Grand Lodge
GLAA Greater London Arts Association
GLAB Greater London Arts Board
GLC Greater London Council
Glos Gloucestershire
GM George Medal; Grand Medal (Ghana)
GMB (Union for) General, Municipal, Boilermakers
GMBATU General, Municipal, Boilermakers and Allied Trades Union
GmbH Gesellschaft mit beschränkter Haftung
GMC General Medical Council; Guild of Memorial Craftsmen; General Management Course (Henley)
GMIE Grand Master, Order of the Indian Empire
GMSI Grand Master, Order of the Star of India
GMWU General and Municipal Workers' Union
gn great-nephew/-niece
GNC General Nursing Council
Gns Guineas
GOC General Officer Commanding
GOC-in-C General Officer Commanding-in-Chief
GOE General Ordination Examination
Govr Governor
Govt Government
Gp/gp Group/group
GP General Practitioner; Grand Prix
GPDST Girls' Public Day School Trust
GPMU Graphical, Paper and Media Union
GPO General Post Office
GQG Grand Quartier Général
Gr Greek
GR General Reconaissance
Gren Grenadier
GRSM Graduate, Royal Schools of Music
gs grandson
GS General Staff; Grammar School
GSA Girls' Schools Association
GSM General Service Medal; (Member of) Guildhall School of Music and Drama
GSMD Guildhall School of Music and Drama
GSO General Staff Officer
Gt Great
GTCL Graduate, Trinity College of Music
GTS General Theological Seminary (New York)
GUI Golfing Union of Ireland
GWR Great Western Railway

H

HA Historical Association; Health Authority
HAA Heavy Anti-Aircraft
HAC Honourable Artillery Company
HACAS Housing Association Consultancy and Advisory Service
Hants Hampshire
HARCVS Honorary Associate, Royal College of Veterinary Surgeons
Harv Harvard
HAT Housing Action Trust
HBM His/Her Britannic Majesty (Majesty's); Humming Bird Gold Medal (Trinidad)
HC High Commissioner
H of C House of Commons
HCEG Honourable Company of Edinburgh Golfers
HCF Honorary Chaplain to the Forces
HCIMA Hotel, Catering and Institutional Management Association
HCO Higher Clerical Officer
HCSC Higher Command and Staff Course
HDA Hawkesbury Diploma in Agriculture (Australia)
HDD Higher Dental Diploma
HDFA Higher Diploma in Fine Art
HDipEd Higher Diploma in Education
HE His/Her Excellency; His Eminence
HEA Health Education Authority
HEC Ecole des Hautes Etudes Commerciales; Higher Education Corporation
HEFCE Higher Education Funding Council for England
HEFCW Higher Education Funding Council for Wales
HEH His/Her Exalted Highness
HEIC Honourable East India Company
HEICS Honourable East India Company's Service
HEO Higher Executive Officer
HEQC Higher Education Quality Council
Herefs Herefordshire
Herts Hertfordshire
HF Home Fleet
HFARA Honorary Foreign Associate, Royal Academy
HFEA Human Fertilisation and Embryology Authority
HFRA Honorary Foreign Member, Royal Academy
HG Home Guard
HGTAC Home Grown Timber Advisory Committee
HH His/Her Highness; His Holiness; Member, Hesketh Hubbard Art Society
HHA Historic Houses Association
HHD Doctor of Humanities (US)
HI Hawaii
Highrs Highlanders
HIH His/Her Imperial Highness
HIllH His/Her Illustrious Highness
HIM His/Her Imperial Majesty
HJ Hilal-e-Jurat (Pakistan)
HKIA Hong Kong Institute of Architects
HKIPM Hung Kong Institute of Personnel Management
HLD Doctor of Humane Letters
Hldgs Holdings
HLI Highland Light Infantry
HM His/Her Majesty
HMA Head Masters' Association
HMAS His/Her Majesty's Australian Ship
HMC Headmasters' and Headmistresses' (formerly Headmasters') Conference; Hospital Management Committee
HMCIC His/Her Majesty's Chief Inspector of Constabulary
HMCS His/Her Majesty's Canadian Ship
HMHS His/Her Majesty's Hospital Ship
HMI His/Her Majesty's Inspector
HMIED Honorary Member, Institute of Engineering Designers
HMMTB His/Her Majesty's Motor Torpedo Boat
HMNZS His/Her Majesty's New Zealand Ship
HMOCS His/Her Majesty's Overseas Civil Service
HMS His/Her Majesty's Ship
HMSO His/Her Majesty's Stationery Office
HNC Higher National Certificate
HND Higher National Diploma
Ho House
Ho Lds House of Lords
Hon Honourable; Honorary
Hons Honours
Hosp Hospital
HPk Hilal-e-Pakistan
HQ Headquarters
HQA Hilali-Quaid-i-Azam (Pakistan)
HRCA Honorary Royal Cambrian Academician
HRE Holy Roman Empire
HRGI Honorary Member, The Royal Glasgow Institute of the Fine Arts
HRH His/Her Royal Highness
HRHA Honorary Member, Royal Hibernian Academy
HRI Honorary Member, Royal Institute of Painters in Water Colours
HROI Honorary Member, Royal Institute of Oil Painters
HRSA Honorary Member, Royal Scottish Academy
HRSW Honorary Member, Royal Scottish Water Colour Society
HS High School
HSC Health and Safety Commission
HSE Health and Safety Executive
HSH His/Her Serene Highness
Hts Heights
Hum Humanity, Humanities (Classics)
Hunts Huntingdonshire
Hus Hussars
husb husband
HVCert Health Visitor's Certificate
Hy Heavy

I

I	Island; Ireland, used chiefly of creations of titles of honour of; 'The First' in a sequence of I, II, III etc
IA	Indian Army; Iowa
IAAF	International Amateur Athletic Federation
IAC	Indian Armoured Corps; Institute of Amateur Cinematographers
IACP	International Association of Chiefs of Police
IACR	Institute of Arable Crops Research
IADB	Inter American Development Bank
IADR	International Association for Dental Research
IAEA	International Atomic Energy Agency
IAF	Indian Air Force; Indian Auxiliary Force
IAHM	Incorporated Association of Headmasters
IAM	Institute of Advanced Motorists; Institute of Aviation Medicine
IAMAS	International Association of Meteorology and Atmospheric Sciences
IAMC	Indian Army Medical Corps
IAMTACT	Institute of Advanced Machine Tool and Control Technology
IAO	Incorporated Association of Organists
IAOC	Indian Army Ordnance Corps
IAPS	Incorporated Association of Preparatory Schools
IAPSO	International Association for the Physical Sciences of the Oceans
IARO	Indian Army Reserve of Officers
IAS	Indian Administrative Service; Institute for Advanced Studies; International Academy of Science
IASC	International Arctic Science Committee
IASS	International Association for Scandinavian Studies
IATA	International Air Transport Association
IATUL	International Association of Technological University Libraries
IAU	International Astronomical Union
IAWPRC	International Association on Water Pollution Research and or Control
ibid	*ibidem* (in the same place)
IBA	Independent Broadcasting Authority; International Bar Association
IBCA	International Braille Chess Association
IBG	Institute of British Geographers
IBRD	International Bank for Reconstruction and Development (World Bank)
IBRO	International Bank Research Organisation; International Brain Research Organisation
IBTE	Institution of British Telecommunications Engineers
i/c	in charge; in command
ICA	Institute of Contemporary Arts; Institute of Chartered Accountants in England and Wales
ICAA	Invalid Children's Aid Association
ICAEW	Institute of Chartered Accountants in England and Wales
ICAI	Institute of Chartered Accountants in Ireland
ICAO	International Civil Aviation Organization
ICBP	International Council for Bird Preservation
ICBS	Irish Christian Brothers' School
ICC	International Chamber of Commerce
ICCA	International Council for Commercial Arbitration
ICCROM	International Centre for Conservation at Rome
ICD	*Iuris Canonici Doctor* (Doctor of Canon Law); Independence Commemorative Decoration (Rhodesia)
ICE	Institution of Civil Engineers
ICED	International Council for Educational Development
ICEF	International Federation of Chemical, Energy and General Workers' Unions
ICES	International Council for the Exploration of the Sea
ICF	International Federation of Chemical and General Workers' Unions
ICFC	Industrial and Commercial Finance Corporation
ICFTU	International Confederation of Free Trade Unions
ICHCA	International Cargo Handling Co-ordination Association
IChemE	Institution of Chemical Engineers
ICI	Imperial Chemical Industries
ICJ	International Commission of Jurists
ICL	International Computers Ltd
ICM	International Confederation of Midwives
ICMA	Institute of Cost and Management Accountants
ICME	International Commission for Mathematical Education
ICOM	International Council of Museums
ICOMOS	International Council of Monuments and Sites
ICorrST	Institution of Corrosion Science and Technology
ICPO	International Criminal Police Organization (Interpol)
ICRC	International Committee of the Red Cross
ICRF	Imperial Cancer Research Fund
ICS	Indian Civil Service
ICSA	Institute of Chartered Secretaries and Administrators
ICSD	International Council for Scientific Development
ICSID	International Council of Societies of Industrial Design; International Centre for Settlement of Investment Disputes
ICSS	International Committee for the Sociology of Sport
ICSTIS	Independent Committee for Supervision of Telephone Information Services
ICSTM	Imperial College of Science, Technology and Medicine, London
ICSU	International Council of Scientific Unions
ICT	International Computers and Tabulators Ltd
ID	Independence Decoration (Rhodesia); Idaho
IDA	International Development Association
IDB	Internal Drainage Board; Industrial Development Board
idc	completed a course at, or served for a year on the Staff of, the Imperial Defence College
IDC	Imperial Defence College; Inter-Diocesan Certificate
IDRC	International Development Research Centre
IDS	Institute of Development Studies; Industry Department for Scotland
IEA	Institute of Economic Affairs
IEC	International Electrotechnical Commission
IEE	Institution of Electrical Engineers
IEEE	Institute of Electrical and Electronics Engineers (NY)
IEEIE	Institution of Electrical and Electronics Incorporated Engineers
IEETE	Institution of Electrical and Electronics Technician Engineers
IEI	Institution of Engineers of Ireland
IEIE	Institution of Electronics and Electrical Incorporated Engineers
IEME	Inspectorate of Electrical and Mechanical Engineering
IEng	Incorporated Engineer
IERE	Institution of Electronic and Radio Engineers
IES	Indian Educational Service; Institution of Engineers and Shipbuilders in Scotland; International Electron Paramagnetic Resonance Society
IExpE	Institute of Explosives Engineers
IFAC	International Federation of Automatic Control
IFAD	International Fund for Agricultural Development (UNO)
IFAW	International Fund for Animal Welfare
IFBWW	International Federation of Building Woodworkers
IFC	International Finance Corporation
IFIAS	International Federation of Institutes of Advanced Study
IFIP	International Federation for Information Processing
IFL	International Friendship League
IFLA	International Federation of Library Associations
IFORS	International Federation of Operational Research Societies
IFPI	International Federation of the Phonographic Industry
IFRA	World Press Research Association
IFS	Irish Free State; Indian Forest Service
IG	Instructor in Gunnery
IGasE	Institution of Gas Engineers
IGPP	Institute of Geophysics and Planetary Physics
IGS	Independent Grammar School
IGU	International Geographical Union; International Gas Union
IHA	Institute of Health Service Administrators
IHospE	Institute of Hospital Engineering
IHSM	Institute of Health Services Management
IHVE	Institution of Heating and Ventilating Engineers (later CIBS)
IILS	International Institute for Labour Studies
IIM	Institution of Industrial Managers
IIMR	Institute of Investment Management and Research
IIMT	International Institute for the Management of Technology
IInfSc	Institute of Information Scientists
IIS	International Institute of Sociology
IISI	International Iron and Steel Institute
IISS	International Institute of Strategic Studies
IIT	Indian Institute of Technology
IL/Ill	Illinois
ILA	International Law Association
ILEA	Inner London Education Authority
ILEC	Inner London Education Committee
IIExE	Institution of Incorporated Executive Engineers

ILO	International Labour Office; International Labour Organisation
ILP	Independent Labour Party
ILR	Independent Local Radio; International Labour Review
IM	Individual Merit
IMO	International Maritime Organization
IMA	International Music Association; Institute of Mathematics and its Applications
IMCB	International Management Centre from Buckingham
IMCO	Inter-Governmental Maritime Consultative Organization
IME	Institute of Medical Ethics
IMEA	Incorporated Municipal Electrical Association
IMechE	Institution of Mechanical Engineers
IMechIE	Institution of Mechanical Incorporated Engineers
IMEDE	Institut pour l'Etude des Méthodes de Direction de l'Entreprise
IMF	International Monetary Fund
IMGTechE	Institution of Mechanical and General Technician Engineers
IMinE	Institution of Mining Engineers
IMM	Institution of Mining and Metallurgy
IMMLEP	Immunology of Leprosy
IMMTS	Indian Mercantile Marine Training Ship
Imp	Imperial
IMRO	Investment Management Regulatory Organisation
IMS	Indian Medical Service; Institute of Management Services; International Military Staff
IMTA	Institute of Municipal Treasurers and Accountants
IMU	International Mathematical Union
IMunE	Institution of Municipal Engineers (now amalgamated with Institution of Civil Engineers)
IN	Indian Navy; Indiana
INASFMH	International Sports Association for People with Mental Handicap
Inc	Incorporated
INCA	International Newspaper Colour Association
Incog	Incognito
Ind	Independent
Industs	Industries
Inf	Infantry; Information
INFORM	Information Network Focus on New Religious Movements
INSA	Indian National Science Academy
INSEA	International Society for Education through Art
INSEAD/Insead	Institut Européen d'Administration des Affaires
Inspr	Inspector
Inst	Institute; Institution
InstBE	Institution of British Engineers
Instr	Instructor
InstSMM	Institute of Sales and Marketing Management
InstT	Institute of Transport
insur	insurance
Internat	International
Intell	Intelligence
INTELSAT	International Telecommunications Satellite Organisation
IOB	Institute of Banking
IOC	International Olympic Committee; Intergovernmental Oceanographic Commission
IOCD	International Organisation for Chemical Science in Development
IOD	Institute of Directors
IODE	Imperial Order of the Daughters of the Empire
IOGT	International Order of Good Templars
IoM	Isle of Man
IOM	Indian Order of Merit
IOOF	Independent Order of Odd-fellows
IOP	Institute of Painters in Oil Colours
IOTA	(Fellow of) Institute of Transport Administration
IoW	Isle of Wight
IPA	International Publishers' Association
IPCS	Institution of Professional Civil Servants
IPFA	Member or Associate, Chartered Institute of Public Finance and Accountancy
IPHE	Institution of Public Health Engineers
IPI	International Press Institute; Institute of Patentees and Inventors
IPlantE	Institution of Plant Engineers
IPM	Institute of Personnel Management
IPPA	Independent Programme Producers' Association; International Planned Parenthood Federation
IPPR	Institute for Public Policy Research
IPPS	Institute of Physics and The Physical Society
IProdE	Institution of Production Engineers
IPS	Indian Police Service; Indian Political Service; Institute of Purchasing and Supply
IPU	Inter-Parliamentary Union
IRA	Irish Republican Army
IRAD	Institute for Research on Animal Diseases
IRC	Industrial Reorganization Corporation; Interdisciplinary Research Centre
IRCAM	Institute for Research and Co-ordination in Acoustics and Music
IRCert	Industrial Relations Certificate
IREE(Aust)	Institution of Radio and Electronics Engineers (Australia)
IRI	Institution of the Rubber Industry
IRO	International Refugee Organization
IRPA	International Radiation Protection Association
IRRV	(Fellow/Member of) Institute of Revenues, Rating and Valuation
IRTE	Institute of Road Transport Engineers
Is	Island(s)
IS	International Society of Sculptors, Painters and Gravers
ISBA	Incorporated Society of British Advertisers
ISC	Imperial Service College, Haileybury; Indian Staff Corps
ISCM	International Society for Contemporary Music
ISCO	Independent Schools Careers Organisation
ISE	Indian Service of Engineers
ISI	International Statistical Institute
ISIS	Independent Schools Information Service
ISJC	Independent Schools Joint Council
ISM	Incorporated Society of Musicians
ISMAR	International Society of Magnetic Resonance
ISME	International Society for Musical Education
ISMRC	Inter-Services Metallurgical Research Council
ISO	Imperial Service Order; International Organization for Standardization
ISSA	International Social Security Association
ISSTIP	International Society for Study of Tension in Performance
ISTC	Iron and Steel Trades Confederation; Institute of Scientific and Technical Communicators
ISTD	Imperial Society of Teachers of Dancing
IStructE	Institution of Structural Engineers
It/Ital	Italian
IT	Information Technology; Indian Territory (US)
ITA	Independent Television Authority (later IBA)
ITAB	Information Technology Advisory Board
ITB	Industry Training Board
ITC	International Trade Centre; Independent Television Commission
ITCA	Independent Television Association (formerly Independent Television Companies Association Ltd)
ITDG	Intermediate Technology Development Group
ITEME	Institution of Technician Engineers in Mechanical Engineering
ITF	International Transport Workers' Federation
ITN	Independent Television News
ITO	International Trade Organization
ITU	International Telecommunication Union
ITV	Independent Television
ITVA	International Television Association
IUA	International Union of Architects
IUB	International Union of Biochemistry
IUBMB	International Union of Biochemistry and Molecular Biology
IUC	Inter-University Council for Higher Education Overseas
IUCN	World Conservation Union (formerly International Union for the Conservation of Nature and Natural Resources)
IUCW	International Union for Child Welfare
IUGS	International Union of Geological Sciences
IUHPS	International Union of the History and Philosophy of Science
IULA	International Union of Local Authorities
IUP	Association of Independent Unionist Peers
IUPAC	International Union of Pure and Applied Chemistry
IUPAP	International Union of Pure and Applied Physics
IUPC	Inter-University and Polytechnic Council for Higher Education Overseas
IUPS	International Union of Physiological Sciences
IUTAM	International Union of Theoretical and Applied Mechanics
IVF	In-vitro Fertilisation
IVS	International Voluntary Service
IWA	Inland Waterways Association
IWEM	Institution of Water and Environmental Management
IWES	Institution of Water Engineers and Scientists (later IWEM)
IWGC	Imperial War Graves Commission
IWM	Institution of Works Managers
IWO	Institution of Water Officers

IWPC Institute of Water Pollution Control (later IWEM)
IWS International Wool Secretariat
IWSA International Water Supply Association
IWSOM Institute of Practitioners in Work Study Organisation and Methods
IWSP Institute of Work Study Practitioners
IY Imperial Yeomanry
IYRU International Yacht Racing Union
IZ I Zingari

J

JA Judge Advocate
JACT Joint Association of Classical Teachers
JAG Judge Advocate General
Jas James
JCB *Juris Canonici* (or *Civilis*) *Baccalaureus* (Bachelor of Canon (or Civil) Law)
JCD *Juris Canonici* (or *Civilis*) Doctor (Doctor of Canon (or Civil) Law)
JCI Junior Chamber International
JCL *Juris Canonici* (or *Civilis*) *Licentiatus* (Licentiate in Canon (or Civil) Law)
JCO Joint Consultative Organisation
JCR Junior Common Room
JCS Journal of the Chemical Society
JD Doctor of Jurisprudence
JDipMA Joint Diploma in Management Accounting Services
JG Junior Grade
JInstE Junior Institution of Engineers
jl(s) journal(s)
JMB Joint Matriculation Board
JMN Johan Mangku Negara (Malaysia)
JMOTS Joint Maritime Operational Training Staff
jnlst journalist
Jno/Joh John
JP Justice of the Peace
Jr Junior
jsc qualified at a Junior Staff Course, or the equivalent, 1942–46
JSD Doctor of Juristic Science
jsdc completed a course at Joint Service Defence College
JSDC Joint Service Defence College
JSLS Joint Services Liaison Staff
JSM Johan Setia Mahkota (Malaysia)
JSPS Japan Society for the Promotion of Science
jssc completed a course at Joint Services Staff College
JSSC Joint Services Staff College
jt/jtly joint, jointly
JUD *Juris Utriusque Doctor* (Doctor of Both Laws (Canon and Civil))
JWS/jws Joint Warfare Staff

K

k killed
ka killed in action
KA Knight of St Andrew, Order of Barbados
Kans Kansas
KAR King's African Rifles
kas killed on active service
KB Knight of the Bath; Knight Bachelor; Knight Banneret
KBE Knight Commander, Order of the British Empire
KC King's Counsel
KCB Knight Commander, Order of the Bath
KCC Commander, Order of the Crown, Belgium and Congo Free State
KCH King's College Hospital; Knight Commander, Hanoverian Order
KCHS Knight Commander, Order of the Holy Sepulchre
KCIE Knight Commander, Order of the Indian Empire
KCL King's College London
KCLJ Knight Commander, Order of St Lazarus of Jerusalem
KCMG Knight Commander, Order of St Michael and St George
KCSA Knight Commander, Military Order of the Collar of St Agatha of Paternò
KCSG Knight Commander, Order of St Gregory the Great
KCSHS Knight Commander with Star, Order of the Holy Sepulchre
KCSI Knight Commander, Order of the Star of India
KCSJ/KCStJ Knight Commander, Order of St John of Jerusalem (Knights Hospitaller)
KCSS Knight Commander, Order of St Silvester
KCVO Knight Commander, Royal Victorian Order
KCVSA King's Commendation for Valuable Services in the Air
KDG King's Dragoon Guards
KEH King Edward's Horse
KEO King Edward's Own
KG Knight, Order of the Garter
KGCSS Knight Grand Cross, Order of St Silvester
KGO King George's Own
KGStJ Knight of Grace, Order of St John of Jerusalem
KH Knight, Hanoverian Order
KHC Honorary Chaplain to the King
KHDS Honorary Dental Surgeon to the King
KHNS Honorary Nursing Sister to the King
KHP Honorary Physician to the King
KHS Honorary Surgeon to the King; Knight, Order of the Holy Sepulchre
K-i-H Kaisar-i-Hind
KJStJ Knight of Justice, Order of St John of Jerusalem
KLJ Knight, Order of St Lazarus of Jerusalem
KM Knight of Malta
KORR King's Own Royal Regiment
KOSB King's Own Scottish Borderers
KOYLI King's Own Yorkshire Light Infantry
KP Knight, Order of St Patrick
KPM King's Police Medal
KRH King's Royal Hussars
KRRC King's Royal Rifle Corps
KS King's Scholar; Kansas
KSC Knight of St Columba
KSG Knight, Order of St Gregory the Great
KSJ Knight, Order of St John of Jerusalem (Knights Hospitaller)
KSLI King's Shropshire Light Infantry
KSS Knight, Order of St Silvester
KStJ Knight, Most Venerable Order of the Hospital of St John of Jerusalem
KStJ(A) Associate Knight of Justice, Most Venerable Order of the Hospital of St John of Jerusalem
Kt Knight
KT Knight, Order of the Thistle
ktd knighted
KY Kentucky

L

L (Scottish) Lord of Parliament
LA Los Angeles; Library Association; Literate in Arts; Liverpool Academy; Louisiana
LAA Light Anti-Aircraft
Lab Labour
LAC London Athletic Club
LACSAB Local Authorities Conditions of Service Advisory Board
LAE London Association of Engineers
LAMDA London Academy of Music and Dramatic Art
LAMSAC Local Authorities' Management Services and Computer Committee
LAMTPI Legal Associate Member, Town Planning Institute

Lancs	Lancashire
LAPADA	London and Provincial Antique Dealers' Association
LARSP	Language Assessment, Remediation and Screening Procedure
LAUTRO	Life Assurance and Unit Trust Regulatory Organisation
LBC	London Broadcasting Company; London Borough Council
LBHI	Licentiate, British Horological Institute
LC	Cross of Leo
L of C	Library of Congress; Lines of Communication
LCAD	London Certificate in Art and Design (University of London)
LCC	London County Council (later GLC)
LCh	Licentiate in Surgery
LCJ	Lord Chief Justice
LCL	Licentiate of Canon Law
LCP	Licentiate, College of Preceptors
LCSP	London and Counties Society of Physiologists
LCST	Licentiate, College of Speech Therapists
LD	Liberal and Democratic; Licentiate in Divinity
Ld	Lord (*e.g.*, of the Manor)
LDDC	London Docklands Development Corporation
LDiv	Licentiate in Divinity
Ld Lt	Lord-Lieutenant
Ldr	Leader
LDS	Licentiate in Dental Surgery
LDV	Local Defence Volunteers
Ldy	Lady (*e.g.*, -in-Waiting)
LEA	Local Education Authority
LEDU	Local Enterprise Development Unit
Legn Hon	Legion of Honour
Leics	Leicestershire
LEP	Local Ecumenical Project
LEPRA	British Leprosy Relief Association
LèsL	Licencié ès Lettres
LG	Lady Companion, Order of the Garter
LGSM	Licentiate, Guildhall School of Music and Drama
LGStJ	Lady of Grace, Order of St John of Jerusalem
LGTB	Local Government Training Board
LH	Light Horse
LHD	*Literarum Humaniorum Doctor* (Doctor of Literature)
LHSM	Licentiate, Institute of Health Services Management
LI	Light Infantry; Long Island
Lib	Liberal
Lib Dem	Liberal Democrat
LIBA	Lloyd's Insurance Brokers' Association
LIBER	Ligue des Bibliothèques Européennes de Recherche
Lic	Licence
LicMed	Licentiate in Medicine
LIFFE	London International Financial Futures and Options Exchange
Lincs	Lincolnshire
LIOB	Licentiate, Institute of Building
Lit	Literature; Literary
Lit Hum	*Literae Humaniores* (Classics)
Lit	Literary
LittD	Doctor of Literature; Doctor of Letters
LJ	Lord Justice
LJStJ	Lady of Justice, Order of St John of Jerusalem
LLA	Lady Literate in Arts
LLB	Bachelor of Laws
LLC	Limited Liability Company
LLCM	Licentiate, London College of Music
LLD	Doctor of Laws
LLL	Licentiate in Laws
LLM	Master of Laws
LM	Licentiate in Midwifery
LMBC	Lady Margaret Boat Club
LMC	Local Medical Committee
LMCC	Licentiate, Medical Council of Canada
LMed	Licentiate in Medicine
LMH	Lady Margaret Hall, Oxford
LMR	London Midland Region (BR)
LMRTPI	Legal Member, Royal Town Planning Institute
LMS	London, Midland and Scottish Railway; London Missionary Society
LMSR	London Midland and Scottish Railway
LMSSA	Licentiate in Medicine and Surgery, Society of Apothecaries
LNat	Liberal National
LNER	London and North Eastern Railway
LNWR	London and North West Railway
LOB	Location of Offices Bureau
LP	Life Peer; Limited Partnership
LPh	Licentiate in Philosophy
LPO	London Philharmonic Orchestra
LPTB	London Passenger Transport Board
LRAD	Licentiate, Royal Academy of Dancing
LRAM	Licentiate, Royal Academy of Music
LRB	London Rifle Brigade
LRCP	Licentiate, Royal College of Physicians, London
LRCPE	Licentiate, Royal College of Physicians, Edinburgh
LRCPI	Licentiate, Royal College of Physicians of Ireland
LRCPSGlas	Licentiate, Royal College of Physicians and Surgeons of Glasgow
LRCS	Licentiate, Royal College of Surgeons of England
LRCSE	Licentiate, Royal College of Surgeons, Edinburgh
LRCSI	Licentiate, Royal College of Surgeons in Ireland
LRFPS(G)	Licentiate, Royal Faculty of Physicians and Surgeons, Glasgow
LRIBA	Licentiate, Royal Institute of British Architects
LRPS	Licentiate, Royal Photographic Society
LRSM	Licentiate, Royal Schools of Music
LRT	London Regional Transport
LSA	Licentiate, Society of Apothecaries; Licence in Agricultural Sciences
LSE	London School of Economics and Political Science
LSHTM	London School of Hygiene and Tropical Medicine
LSO	London Symphony Orchestra
LSWR	London and South-Western Railway
Lt	Lieutenant
LT	London Transport; Licentiate in Teaching
LTA	Lawn Tennis Association
LTB	London Transport Board
Lt-Cdr	Lieutenant-Commander
LTCL	Licentiate, Trinity College of Music, London
Lt-Col	Lieutenant-Colonel
Ltcy	Lieutenancy
Ltd	Limited
LTE	London Transport Executive
Lt-Gen	Lieutenant-General
LTh	Licentiate in Theology
LUOTC	London University Officers' Training Corps
LVO	Lieutenant, Royal Victorian Order (formerly MVO (Fourth Class))
LWT	London Weekend Television

M

m	married
M	Marquess; Middle; Monsieur
MA	Master of Arts; Military Assistant; Massachusetts
M&A	Mergers and Acquisitions
MAA	Manufacturers' Agents Association of Great Britain
MAAF	Mediterranean Allied Air Forces
MAAT	Member, Association of Accounting Technicians
MACE	Member, Australian College of Education; Member, Association of Conference Executives
MACI	Member, American Concrete Institute
MACM	Member, Association of Computing Machines
MACS	Member, American Chemical Society
MADO	Member, Association of Dispensing Opticians
MAE	Member, Academia Europaea
MAEE	Marine Aircraft Experimental Establishment
MAF	Ministry of Agriculture and Fisheries
MAFF	Ministry of Agriculture, Fisheries and Food
MAHL	Master of Arts in Hebrew Letters
MAI	*Magister in Arte Ingeniaria* (Master of Engineering)
MAIAA	Member, American Institute of Aeronautics and Astronautics
MAICE	Member, American Institute of Consulting Engineers
MAIChE	Member, American Institute of Chemical Engineers
Maj	Major
Maj-Gen	Major-General
MALD	Master of Arts in Law and Diplomacy
Man	Manitoba
MAO	Master of Obstetric Art
MAOT	Member, Association of Occupational Therapists
MAOU	Member, American Ornithologists' Union

MAP	Ministry of Aircraft Production
MAPsS	Member, Australian Psychological Society
MARAC	Member, Australasian Register of Agricultural Consultants
MArch	Master of Architecture
MASAE	Member, American Society of Agricultural Engineers
MASc	Master of Applied Science
MASC	Member, Australian Society of Calligraphers
MASCE	Member, American Society of Civil Engineers
MASME	Member, American Society of Mechanical Engineers
Mass	Massachusetts
MAT	Master of Arts and Teaching (US)
Math	Mathematics; Mathematical
MATh	Master of Arts in Theology
MATSA	Managerial Administrative Technical Staff Association
MAusIMM	Member, Australasian Institute of Mining and Metallurgy
MB	Medal of Bravery (Canada); Bachelor of Medicine
MBA	Master of Business Administration
MBASW	Member, British Association of Social Workers
MBC	Metropolitan/Municipal Borough Council
MBCS	Member, British Computer Society
MBE	Member, Order of the British Empire
MBES	Member, Biological Engineering Society
MBFR	Mutual and Balanced Force Reductions (negotiations)
MBHI	Member, British Horological Institute
MBIFD	Member, British Institute of Funeral Directors
MBIM	Member, British Institute of Management
MBKS	Member, British Kinematograph Society
MBKSTS	Member, British Kinematograph, Sound and Television Society
MBOU	Member, British Ornithologists' Union
MBPICS	Member, British Production and Inventory Control Society
MBritIRE	Member, British Institution of Radio Engineers
MBS	Member, Building Societies Institute
MBSc	Master of Business Science
MC	Military Cross; Missionaries of Charity
MCAM	Member, CAM Foundation
MCB	Master in Clinical Biochemistry
MCBSI	Member, Chartered Building Societies Institute
MCC	Marylebone Cricket Club; Metropolitan County Council
MCCDRCS	Member in Clinical Community Dentistry, Royal College of Surgeons
MCD	Master of Civic Design
MCE	Master of Civil Engineering
MCFP	Member, College of Family Physicians (Canada)
MCGI	Member, City and Guilds of London Institute
MCh/MChir	Master of Surgery
MChE	Master of Chemical Engineering
MChemA	Master in Chemical Analysis
MChOrth	Master of Orthopaedic Surgery
MCIBS	Member, Chartered Institution of Building Services
MCIBSE	Member, Chartered Institution of Building Services Engineers
MCIH	Member, Chartered Institute of Housing
MCIM	Member, Chartered Institute of Marketing
MCIOB	Member, Chartered Institute of Building
M.CIRP	Member, International Institution for Production Engineering Research
MCIS	Member, Institute of Chartered Secretaries and Administrators
MCIT	Member, Chartered Institute of Transport
MCIWEM	Member, Chartered Institution of Water and Environmental Management
MCL	Master in Civil Law
MCMES	Member, Civil and Mechanical Engineers' Society
MCom	Master of Commerce
MConsE	Member, Association of Consulting Engineers
MConsEl	Member, Association of Consulting Engineers of Ireland
MCOphth	Member, College of Ophthalmologists
MCP	Member of Colonial Parliament; Master of City Planning (US)
MCPA	Member, College of Pathologists of Australia
MCPath	Member, College of Pathologists
MCPP	Member, College of Pharmacy Practice
MCPS	Member, College of Physicians and Surgeons
MCS	Madras Civil Service; Malayan Civil Service
MCSD	Member, Chartered Society of Designers
MCSEE	Member, Canadian Society of Electrical Engineers
MCSP	Member, Chartered Society of Physiotherapy
MCST	Member, College of Speech Therapists
MCT	Member, Association of Corporate Treasurers
md	managing director
MD	Doctor of Medicine; Military District; Maryland
MDC	Metropolitan District Council
MDes	Master of Design
MDiv	Master of Divinity
MDS	Master of Dental Surgery
MDSc	Master of Dental Science
ME	Mining Engineer; Middle East; Master of Engineering; Maine
MEAF	Middle East Air Force
MEc	Master of Economics
MEC	Member of Executive Council; Middle East Command
MECAS	Middle East Centre for Arab Studies
Mech	Mechanics; Mechanical
MECI	Member, Institute of Employment Consultants
Med	Medical
MEd	Master of Education
Med	Medical
MEF	Middle East Force
MEIC	Member, Engineering Institute of Canada
MELF	Middle East Land Forces
Memb/memb	Member/member
Meml	Memorial
Mencap	Royal Society for Mentally Handicapped Children and Adults
MEng	Master of Engineering
MEO	Marine Engineering Officer
MEP	Member of the European Parliament
MESc	Master of Engineering Science
MetR	Metropolitan Railway
Metsoc	Metals Society
MEXE	Military Engineering Experimental Establishment
MF	Master of Forestry
MFA	Master of Fine Arts
MFC	Mastership in Food Control
MFCM	Member, Faculty of Community Medicine
MFGB	Miners' Federation of Great Britain
MFH	Master of Foxhounds
MFHom	Member, Faculty of Homeopathy
MFOM	Member, Faculty of Occupational Medicine
MFPaed	Member, Faculty of Paediatrics, Royal College of Physicians of Ireland
MFPHM	Member, Faculty of Public Health Medicine
mfr	manufacturer
MG	Machine Gun
MGA	Major General in charge of Administration
MGC	Machine Gun Corps
MGDSRCS	Member in General Dental Surgery, Royal College of Surgeons
MGGS	Major-General, General Staff
MGI	Member, Institute of Certificated Grocers
MGM	Metro-Goldwyn-Mayer
MGO	Master General of the Ordnance; Master of Gynaecology and Obstetrics
Mgr	Monsignor
MHA	Member of House of Assembly
MHCIMA	Member, Hotel Catering and Institutional Management Association
MHK	Member of the House of Keys
MHort(RHS)	Master of Horticulture, Royal Horticultural Society
MHR	Member of the House of Representatives
MHRA	Modern Humanities Research Association
MHRF	Mental Health Research Fund
MHSM	Member, Institute of Health Services Management
MI	Military Intelligence; Michigan
MIAeE	Member, Institute of Aeronautical Engineers
MIAgrE	Member, Institution of Agricultural Engineers
MIAM	Member, Institute of Administrative Management
MIAS	Member, Institute of Aeronautical Science (US)
MIBC	Member, Institute of Business Counsellors
MIBF	Member, Institute of British Foundrymen
MIBiol	Member, Institute of Biology
MIBritE	Member, Institution of British Engineers
MIB(Scot)	Member, Institute of Bankers in Scotland
MICE	Member, Institution of Civil Engineers
MICEI	Member, Institution of Civil Engineers of Ireland
MICFor	Member, Institute of Chartered Foresters
Mich	Michigan
MIChemE	Member, Institution of Chemical Engineers
MICM	Member, Institute of Credit Management
MICorrST	Member, Institution of Corrosion Science and Technology
MICS	Member, Institute of Chartered Shipbrokers
Middx	Middlesex
MIDI	Member, Institute of Design of Ireland

MIDPM	Member, Institute of Data Processing Management
MIE	Member Institution of Engineers
MIE(Aust)	Member, Institution of Engineers, Australia
MIE(Ind)	Member, Institution of Engineers, India
MIED	Member, Institution of Engineering Designers
MIEE	Member, Institution of Electrical Engineers
MIEEE	Member, Institute of Electrical and Electronics Engineers (NY)
MIEEM	Member, Institute of Ecology and Environmental Management
MIEI	Member, Institution of Engineering Inspection
MIEIE	Member, Institution of Electronics and Electrical Incorporated Engineers
MIEMgt	Member, Institute of Environmental Management
MIEnvSc	Member, Institute of Environmental Science
MIERE	Member, Institution of Electronic and Radio Engineers
MIES	Member, Institution of Engineers and Shipbuilders, Scotland
MIET	Member, Institute of Engineers and Technicians
MIExpE	Member, Institute of Explosives Engineers
MIFA	Member, Institute of Field Archaeologists
MIFF	Member, Institute of Freight Forwarders
MIFireE	Member, Institution of Fire Engineers
MIFM	Member, Institute of Fisheries Management
MIFor	Member, Institute of Foresters
MIGasE	Member, Institution of Gas Engineers
MIGeol	Member, Institution of Geologists
MIH	Member, Institute of Housing
MIHM	Member, Institute of Housing Managers (later MIH)
MIHort	Member, Institute of Horticulture
MIHT	Member, Institution of Highways and Transportation
MIHVE	Member, Institution of Heating and Ventilating Engineers (later MCIBS)
MIIA	Member, Institute of Industrial Administration (later FBIM)
MIIM	Member, Institution of Industrial Managers
MIInfSc	Member, Institute of Information Sciences
Mil	Military; Militia
MIL	Member, Institute of Linguists
MILGA	Member, Institute of Local Government Administrators
MILocoE	Member, Institution of Locomotive Engineers
MILog	Member, Institute of Logistics
MIM	Member, Institute of Metals (formerly Institution of Metallurgists)
MIMarE	Member, Institute of Marine Engineers
MIMC	Member, Institute of Management Consultants
MIMechE	Member, Institution of Mechanical Engineers
MIMEMME	Member, Institution of Mining Electrical and Mining Mechanical Engineers
MIMgt	Member, Institute of Management
MIMGTechE	Member, Institution of Mechanical and General Technician Engineers
MIMI	Member, Institute of the Motor Industry
MIMinE	Member, Institution of Mining Engineers
MIMM	Member, Institution of Mining and Metallurgy
MIMunE	Member, Institution of Municipal Engineers
Min	Minister; Ministry
MIN	Member, Institute of Navigation
Minn	Minnesota
MInstAM	Member, Institute of Administrative Management
MInstBE	Member, Institution of British Engineers
MInstCE	Member, Institution of Civil Engineers
MInstD	Member, Institute of Directors
MInstE	Member, Institute of Energy
MInstEnvSci	Member, Institute of Environmental Sciences
MInstF	Member, Institute of Fuel
MInstHE	Member, Institution of Highway Engineers
MInstM	Member, Institute of Marketing
MInstMC	Member, Institute of Measurement and Control
MInstME	Member, Institution of Mining Engineers
MInstMet	Member, Institute of Metals
MInstP	Member, Institute of Physics
MInstPet	Member, Institute of Petroleum
MInstPI	Member, Institute of Patentees and Inventors
MInstPkg	Member, Institute of Packaging
MInstPS	Member. Institute of Purchasing and Supply
MInstR	Member, Institute of Refrigeration
MInstRA	Member, Institute of Registered Architects
MInstT	Member, Institute of Transport
MInstTM	Member, Institute of Travel Managers in Industry and Commerce
MInstW	Member, Institute of Welding
MInstWM	Member, Institute of Wastes Management
MINucE	Member, Institution of Nuclear Engineers
MIOA	Member, Institute of Acoustics
MIOB	Member, Institute of Building
MIOM	Member, Institute of Office Management
MIOSH	Member, Institution of Occupational Safety and Health
MIPA	Member, Institute of Practitioners in Advertising
MIPD	Member, Institute of Personnel and Development
MIPlantE	Member, Institution of Plant Engineers
MIPM	Member, Institute of Personnel Management
MIPR	Member, Institute of Public Relations
MIProdE	Member, Institution of Production Engineers
MIQ	Member, Institute of Quarrying
MIQA	Member, Institute of Quality Assurance
MIRE	Member, Institution of Radio Engineers (later MIERE)
MIREE(Aust)	Member, Institution of Radio and Electronics Engineers (Australia)
MIRO	Mineral Industry Research Organisation
MIRT	Member, Institute of Reprographic Technicians
MIRTE	Member, Institute of Road Transport Engineers
MIS	Member, Institute of Statisticians
MIS(India)	Member, Institution of Surveyors of India
MISI	Member, Iron and Steel Institute (later part of Metals Society)
MIStructE	Member, Institution of Structural Engineers
MIT	Massachusetts Institute of Technology
MITA	Member, Industrial Transport Association
MITD	Member, Institute of Training and Development
MITE	Member, Institution of Electrical and Electronics Technician Engineers
MITI	Member, Institute of Translation and Interpreting
MITT	Member, Institute of Travel and Tourism
MIWE	Member, Institution of Water Engineers
MIWEM	Member, Institution of Water and Environmental Management
MIWES	Member, Institution of Water Engineers and Scientists
MIWM	Member, Institution of Works Managers
MIWPC	Member, Institute of Water Pollution Control
MIWSP	Member, Institute of Work Study Practitioners
MJA	Medical Journalists Association
MJI	Member, Institute of Journalists
MJIE	Member, Junior Institution of Engineers
MJS	Member, Japan Society
MJur	*Magister Juris* (Master of Law)
ML	Licentiate in Medicine; Master of Laws
MLA	Member of Legislative Assembly; Modern Language Association; Master in Landscape Architecture
MLC	Member of Legislative Council
MLCOM	Member, London College of Osteopathic Medicine
MIEx	Member, Institute of Export
MLitt	Master of Letters
Mlle	Mademoiselle
MLM	Member, Order of the Legion of Merit (Rhodesia)
MLO	Military Liaison Officer
MLR	Modern Language Review
MM	Military Medal; Merchant Marine
MMA	Metropolitan Museum of Art
MMB	Milk Marketing Board
MMD	Movement for Multi-Party Democracy
Mme	Madame
MME	Master of Mining Engineering
MMechE	Master of Mechanical Engineering
MMet	Master of Metallurgy
MMGI	Member, Mining, Geological and Metallurgical Institute of India
MMin	Master of Ministry
MMM	Member, Order of Military Merit (Canada)
MMS	Member, Institute of Management Services
MMSA	Master of Midwifery, Society of Apothecaries
MN	Merchant Navy; Minnesota
MNAS	Member, National Academy of Sciences (US)
MND	Motor Neurone Disease
MNECInst	Member, North East Coast Institution of Engineers and Shipbuilders
MNI	Member, Nautical Institute
MNSE	Member, Nigerian Society of Engineers
MNZIS	Member, New Zealand Institute of Surveyors
MNZPI	Member, New Zealand Planning Institute
MO	Medical Officer; Military Operations; Missouri
MOD	Ministry of Defence
Mods	Moderations (Oxford)
MOF	Ministry of Food
MOH	Medical Officer(s) of Health
MOI	Ministry of Information

MOMI	Museum of the Moving Image
Mon	Monmouthshire
MOP	Ministry of Power
MOrthRCS	Member in Orthodontics, Royal College of Surgeons
MoS	Ministry of Supply
Most Rev	Most Reverend
MoT	Ministry of Transport
MOV	Member, Order of Volta (Ghana)
MP	Member of Parliament
MPA	Master of Public Administration; Member, Parliamentary Assembly, Northern Ireland
MPBW	Ministry of Public Building and Works
MPH	Master of Public Health
MPIA	Master of Public and International Affairs
MPMI	Member, Property Management Institute
MPO	Management and Personnel Office
MPP	Member, Provincial Parliament
MPRISA	Member, Public Relations Institute of South Africa
MPS	Member, Pharmaceutical Society
MR	Master of the Rolls; Municipal Reform
MRAC	Member, Royal Agricultural College
MRACP	Member, Royal Australasian College of Physicians
MRACS	Member, Royal Australasian College of Surgeons
MRAeS	Member, Royal Aeronautical Society
MRAIC	Member, Royal Architectural Institute of Canada
MRAS	Member, Royal Asiatic Society
MRC-LMB	Medical Research Council Laboratory of Molecular Biology
MRC	Medical Research Council
MRCA	Multi-Role Combat Aircraft
MRCGP	Member, Royal College of General Practitioners
MRCOG	Member, Royal College of Obstetricians and Gynaecologists
MRCOphth	Member, Royal College of Ophthalmologists
MRCP	Member, Royal College of Physicians, London
MRCPA	Member, Royal College of Pathologists of Australia
MRCPath	Member, Royal College of Pathologists
MRCPE	Member, Royal College of Physicians, Edinburgh
MRCPGlas	Member, Royal College of Physicians and Surgeons of Glasgow
MRCPI	Member, Royal College of Physicians of Ireland
MRCPsych	Member, Royal College of Psychiatrists
MRCS	Member, Royal College of Surgeons of England
MRCSE	Member, Royal College of Surgeons of Edinburgh
MRCSI	Member, Royal College of Surgeons in Ireland
MRCVS	Member, Royal College of Veterinary Surgeons
MRE	Master of Religious Education
MRES/MREmpS	Member, Royal Empire Society
MRHS	Member, Royal Horticultural Society
MRI	Member, Royal Institution
MRIA	Member, Royal Irish Academy
MRIAI	Member, Royal Institute of the Architects of Ireland
MRIC	Member, Royal Institute of Chemistry
MRIN	Member, Royal Institute of Navigation
MRINA	Member, Royal Institution of Naval Architects
MRO	Member, Register of Osteopaths
MRPharmS	Member, Royal Pharmaceutical Society
MRSanI	Member, Royal Sanitary Institute
MRSC	Member, Royal Society of Chemistry
MRSH	Member, Royal Society for the Promotion of Health
MRSL	Member, Order of the Republic of Sierra Leone
MRSM	Member, Royal Society of Medicine
MRST	Member, Royal Society of Teachers
MRTPI	Member, Royal Town Planning Institute
MRurSc	Master of Rural Science
MRUSI	Member, Royal United Service Institution
MRVA	Member, Rating and Valuation Association
MS, MSS	Manuscript, Manuscripts
MS	Master of Surgery; Master of Science (US); Mississippi
MSA	Master of Science, Agriculture (US); Mineralogical Society of America
MSAAIE	Member, Southern African Association of Industrial Editors
MSAE	Member, Society of Automotive Engineeers (US)
MSAICE	Member, South African Institution of Civil Engineers
MSAInstMM	Member, South African Institute of Mining and Metallurgy
MSAutE	Member, Society of Automobile Engineers
MSC	Manpower Services Commission; Missionaries of the Sacred Heart; Madras Staff Corps
MSc	Master of Science
MSD	Meritorious Service Decoration (Fiji)
MSE	Master of Science in Engineering (US)
MScD	Master of Dental Science
MSF	(Union for) Manufacturing, Science, Finance
MSH	Master of Stag Hounds
MSI	Member, Securities Institute
MSIAD	Member, Society of Industrial Artists and Designers
MSINZ	Member, Surveyors' Institute of New Zealand
MSIT	Member, Society of Instrument Technology
MSM	Meritorious Service Medal; Madras Sappers and Miners
MSN	Master of Science in Nursing
MSocIS	Member, Société des Ingénieurs et Scientifiques de France
MSocSc	Master of Social Sciences
MSocWork	Master of Social Work
MSR	Member, Society of Radiographers
MS&R	Merchant Shipbuilding and Repairs
MSW	Master, Social Work/Welfare
MSt	Master of Studies
MSTD	Member, Society of Typographic Designers
MT	Mechanical Transport; Montana
Mt	Mount, Mountain
MTA	Music Trades Association
MTAI	Member, Institute of Travel Agents
MTB	Motor Torpedo Boat
MTCA	Ministry of Transport and Civil Aviation
MTD	Midwife Teachers' Diploma
MTech	Master of Technology
MTEFL	Master in the Teaching of English as a Foreign or Second Language
MTh	Master of Theology
MTIA	Metal Trades Industry Association
MTIRA	Machine Tool Industry Research Association
MTPI	Member, Town Planning Institute
MTS	Master of Theological Studies
MUniv	Honorary Master of the University
MusB	Bachelor of Music
MusD	Doctor of Music
MusM	Master of Music
MV	Merchant Vessel; Motor Vessel (naval)
MVEE	Military Vehicles and Engineering Establishment
MVO	Member, Royal Victorian Order
MVSc	Master of Veterinary Science
MW	Master of Wine
MWA	Mystery Writers of America
MWeldI	Member, Welding Institute
MWSOM	Member, Institute of Practitioners in Work Study Organisation and Methods

N

n	nephew/niece
N	Nationalist; Navigating Duties; North
NA	National Academician (America)
NAACP	National Association for the Advancement of Colored People
NAAFI	Navy, Army and Air Force Institutes
NAAS	National Agricultural Advisory Service
NAB	National Advisory Body for Public Sector Higher Education
NABC	National Association of Boys' Clubs
NAC	National Agriculture Centre
NACAB	National Association of Citizens' Advice Bureaux
NACCB	National Accreditation Council for Certification Bodies
NACETT	National Advisory Council for Education and Training Targets
NACF	National Art-Collections Fund
NACRO	National Association for the Care and Resettlement of Offenders
NADFAS	National Association of Decorative and Fine Arts Societies
NAE	National Academy of Engineering
NAEW	Nato Airborn Early Warning
NAHA	National Association of Health Authorities
NAHAT	National Association of Health Authorities and Trusts
NALGO/Nalgo	National and Local Government Officers' Association
NAMAS	National Measurement and Accreditation Service
NAMCW	National Association for Maternal and Child Welfare
NAMH	MIND (National Association for Mental Health)
NAMMA	NATO MRCA Management Agency
NAPAG	National Academies Policy Advisory Group
NAPT	National Association for the Prevention of Tuberculosis

NARM National Association of Recording Merchandisers (US)
NAS/UWT National Association of Schoolmasters/Union of Women Teachers
NAS National Academy of Sciences
NASA National Aeronautics and Space Administration (US)
NASDIM National Association of Security Dealers and Investment Managers (later FIMBRA)
Nat/l National
Nat Sci Natural Sciences
NATCS National Air Traffic Control Services
NATFHE National Association of Teachers in Further and Higher Education (combining ATCDE and ATTI)
Natl Natural
NATLAS National Testing Laboratory Accreditation Scheme
NATO North Atlantic Treaty Organisation
NATS National Air Traffic Services
NATSOPA National Society of Operative Printers, Graphical and Media Personnel (formerly of Operative Printers and Assistants)
NAYC Youth Clubs UK (formerly National Association of Youth Clubs)
NB New Brunswick; Nebraska
NBA North British Academy
NBC National Book Council (later NBL); National Broadcasting Company (US)
NBL National Book League
NBPI National Board for Prices and Incomes
NC National Certificate; North Carolina
NCA National Certificate of Agriculture
NCARB National Council of Architectural Registration Boards
NCB National Coal Board
NCC National Computing Centre; Nature Conservancy Council; National Consumer Council
NCCE Nature Conservancy Council for England (English Nature)
NCCI National Committee for Commonwealth Immigrants
NCCL National Council for Civil Liberties
NCD National Capital District, Papua New Guinea
NCDAD National Council for Diplomas in Art and Design
NCEA National Council for Educational Awards
NCET National Council for Educational Technology
NCH National Children's Homes
NCLC National Council of Labour Colleges
NCOPF National Council for One Parent Families
NCSE National Council for Special Education
NCSS National Council of Social Service
NCTA National Community Television Association (US)
NCTJ National Council for the Training of Journalists
NCU National Cyclists' Union
NCVCCO National Council of Voluntary Child Care Organisations
NCVO National Council for Voluntary Organisations
NCVQ National Council for Vocational Qualifications
ND North Dakota
NDA National Diploma in Agriculture
NDD National Diploma in Dairying; National Diploma in Design
NDH National Diploma in Horticulture
NDIC National Defence Industries Council
NDP New Democratic Party
NDTA National Defense Transportation Association (US)
NE North-east
NEAB Northern Examinations and Assessment Board
NEAC New English Art Club
NEAF Near East Air Force
NEARELF Near East Land Forces
NEB National Enterprise Board
NEBSS National Examinations Board for Supervisory Studies
NEC National Executive Committee
NECCTA National Education Closed Circuit Television Association
NECInst North East Coast Institution of Engineers and Shipbuilders
NEDC National Economic Development Council; North East Development Council
NEDO National Economic Development Office
NEH National Endowment for the Humanities
NEL National Engineering Laboratory
NERC Natural Environment Research Council
NFC National Freight Consortium (formerly Corporation, then Company)
NFCG National Federation of Consumer Groups
NFER National Foundation for Educational Research
NFHA National Federation of Housing Associations
NFMS National Federation of Music Societies
NFS National Fire Service
NFSH National Federation of Spiritual Healers
NFT National Film Theatre
NFU National Farmers' Union
NFWI National Federation of Women's Institutes
NGO Non-Governmental Organisation(s)
NGTE National Gas Turbine Establishment
NH New Hampshire
NHBC National House-Building Council
NHS National Health Service
NI Northern Ireland; Native Infantry
NIAB National Institute of Agricultural Botany
NIACRO Northern Ireland Association for the Care and Resettlement of Offenders
NIAE National Institute of Agricultural Engineering
NIAID National Institute of Allergy and Infectious Diseases
NICEC National Institute for Careers Education and Counselling
NICG Nationalised Industries Chairmen's Group
NICS Northern Ireland Civil Service
NID Naval Intelligence Division; National Institute for the Deaf; Northern Ireland District; National Institute of Design (India)
NIESR National Institute of Economic and Social Research
NIH National Institutes of Health (US)
NIHCA Northern Ireland Hotels and Caterers Association
NII Nuclear Installations Inspectorate
NILP Northern Ireland Labour Party
NIMR National Institute for Medical Research
NISTRO Northern Ireland Science and Technology Regional Organisation
NJ New Jersey
NLCS North London Collegiate School
NLF National Liberal Federation
NLYL National League of Young Liberals
NM New Mexico
NMR Nuclear Magnetic Resonance
NNMA Nigerian National Merit Award
NNOM Nigerian National Order of Merit
Northants Northamptonshire
NOTB National Ophthalmic Treatment Board
Notts Nottinghamshire
NP Notary Public
NPA Newspaper Publishers' Association
NPFA National Playing Fields Association
NPk Nishan-e-Pakistan
NPL National Physical Laboratory
nr near
NR North Riding
NRA National Rifle Association; National Recovery Administration (US); National Rivers Authority
NRAO National Radio Astronomy Observatory
NRCC National Research Council of Canada
NRD National Registered Designer
NRDC National Research Development Corporation
NRPB National Radiological Protection Board
NRR Northern Rhodesia Regiment
ns Graduate of Royal Naval Staff College, Greenwich
NS Nova Scotia, *i.e.*, Scotland, where creations of Baronets are concerned; New Style in the Calendar (in Great Britain since 1750–53); National Society; National Service
NSA National Skating Association
NSAIV Distinguished Order of Shaheed Ali (Maldives)
NSF National Science Foundation (US)
NSM Non-Stipendiary Minister
NSMHC National Society for Mentally Handicapped Children
NSPCC National Society for the Prevention of Cruelty to Children
NSQT National Society for Quality through Teamwork
NSRA National Small-bore Rifle Association
N/SSF Novice, Society of St Francis
NSTC Nova Scotia Technical College
NSW New South Wales
NT New Testament; Northern Territory (Australia); National Theatre; National Trust
NTDA National Trade Development Association
NT&SA National Trust and Savings Association
NTUC National Trades Union Congress
NUAAW National Union of Agricultural and Allied Workers
NUBE National Union of Bank Employees
NUFLAT National Union of Footwear Leather and Allied Trades
NUGMW National Union of General and Municipal Workers (later GMBATU)
NUHKW National Union of Hosiery and Knitwear Workers
NUI National University of Ireland
NUJ National Union of Journalists
NUJMB Northern Universities Joint Matriculation Board
NUKFAT National Union of Knitwear, Footwear and Apparel Trades
NUM National Union of Mineworkers

NUMAST National Union of Marine, Aviation and Shipping Transport Officers
NUPE National Union of Public Employees
NUR National Union of Railwaymen
NUS National Union of Students
NUT National Union of Teachers
NUTG National Union of Townswomen's Guilds
NUTN National Union of Trained Nurses
NUU New University of Ulster
NV Nevada
NVQ National Vocational Qualification
NW North-west
NWC National Water Council
NWF North West Frontier
NWFP North-West Frontier Province
NWP North-Western Province
NWT North-Western Territories
NY New York
NYC New York City
NYO National Youth Orchestra
NZ New Zealand
NZEF New Zealand Expeditionary Force
NZIA New Zealand Institute of Architects
NZRSA New Zealand Retired Services Association

O

O Ohio (USA)
OA Officier d'Académie
OAM Medal of the Order of Australia
OAS Organization of American States; On Active Service
OASC Officer Aircrew Selection Centre
OAU Organisation for African Unity
OB Order of Barbados
OBC Order of British Columbia
OBE Officer, Order of the British Empire
OBI Order of British India
OC Officer Commanding; Order of Canada (equivalent to former award SM)
OCA Old Comrades Association
OCC Order of the Caribbean Community
OCDS Overseas College of Defence Studies (Canada)
OCF Officiating Chaplain to the Forces
OCS Officer Candidates School
OCSS Oxford and Cambridge Shakespeare Society
OCTU Officer Cadet Training Unit
OCU Operational Conversion Unit
OD Officer, Order of Distinction (Jamaica)
ODA Overseas Development Administration
ODI Overseas Development Institute
ODM Ministry of Overseas Development
ODSM Order of Diplomatic Service Merit (Lesotho)
OE Order of Excellence (Guyana)
O & E Operations and Engineers (US)
OEA Old Etonian Association; Overseas Education Association
OECD Organization for Economic Co-operation and Development
OED Oxford English Dictionary
OEEC Organization for European Economic Co-operation
OF Order of the Founder, Salvation Army
OFEMA Office Française d'Exportation de Matériel Aéronautique
OFFER Office of Electricity Regulation
Offr Officer
OFM Order of Friars Minor (Franciscans)
OFMCap Order of Friars Minor Capuchin (Franciscans)
OFMConv Order of Friars Minor Conventual (Franciscans)
OFR Order of the Federal Republic of Nigeria
OFS Orange Free State
OFSTED Office for Standards in Education
OFT Office of Fair Trading
Oftel Office of Telecommunications
OGS Oratory of the Good Shepherd
OH Ohio
OHMS On His/Her Majesty's Service
O i/c Officer in charge
OJ Order of Jamaica
OK Oklahoma
OL Officer, Order of Leopold; Order of the Leopard (Lesotho)
OLJ Officer, Order of St Lazarus of Jerusalem
OLM Officer, Legion of Merit (Rhodesia)
OM Order of Merit
O & M organisation and method
OMCS Office of the Minister for the Civil Service
OMI Oblate of Mary Immaculate
OMM Officer, Order of Military Merit (Canada)
ON Order of the Nation (Jamaica)
OND Ordinary National Diploma
Ont Ontario
ONZ Order of New Zealand
O & O Oriental and Occidental Steamship Co.
OON Officer, Order of the Niger
OOnt Order of Ontario
OP *Ordinis Praedicatorum* (of the Order of Preachers (Dominican)); Observation Post
op(s) operation(s)
Opcon Operational Control
OPCS Office of Population Censuses and Surveys
Oppn Opposition
OPSS Office of Public Service and Science
OQ Officer, National Order of Quebec
OR Order of Rorima (Guyana); Operational Research; Oregon
ORC Orange River Colony
ORGALIME Organisme de Liaison des Industries Métalliques Européennes
ORL Otorhinolaryngology
ORS Operational Research Society
ORSA Operations Research Society of America
ORSL Order of the Republic of Sierra Leone
ORT Organization for Rehabilitation through Training
ORTF Office de la Radiodiffusion et Télévision Française
OSA Order of St Augustine (Augustinian); Ontario Society of Artists
OSB Order of St Benedict (Benedictine)
osc Graduate of Overseas Staff College
OSCE Organisation for Security and Co-operation in Europe
OSFC Franciscan (Capuchin) Order
O/Sig Ordinary Signalman
OSNC Orient Steam Navigation Co.
OSRD Office of Scientific Research and Development
OSS Office of Strategic Services
OST Office of Science and Technology
OStJ (Officer of the) Order of St John of Jerusalem
OStJ Officer, Most Venerable Order of the Hospital of St John of Jerusalem
OSUK Ophthalmological Society of the United Kingdom
OT Old Testament
OTC Officers' Training Corps
OTL Officer, Order of Toussaint L'Ouverture (Haiti)
OTU Operational Training Unit
OTWSA Ou-Testamentiese Werkgemeenskap in Suider-Afrika
OU Open University
OUAC Oxford University Athletic Club
OUAFC Oxford University Association Football Club
OUBC Oxford University Boat Club
OUCC Oxford University Cricket Club
OUDS Oxford University Dramatic Society
OUP Oxford University Press; Official Unionist Party
OURC Oxford University Rifle Club
OURFC Oxford University Rugby Football Club
OURT Order of the United Republic of Tanzania
Oxon Oxfordshire; *Oxoniensis* (of Oxford)

P

p	page
pa	*per annum* (a year)
PA	Pakistan Army; Personal Assistant; Pennsylvania
PAA	President, Australian Academy of Science
pac	passed the final examination of the Advanced Class, The Military College of Science
PACE	Protestant and Catholic Encounter
PAg	Professional Agronomist
PAO	Prince Albert's Own
Parl(y)	Parliament(ary)
PASI	Professional Associate, Chartered Surveyors' Institution
PBMA	President of the British Medical Association
PBS	Public Broadcasting Service
PC	Privy Council/Counsellor; Police Constable; Perpetual Curate; Peace Commissioner (Ireland); Progressive Conservative (Canada)
PCC	Parochial Church Council
PCE/PGCE	Postgraduate Certificate of Education
PCEF	Polytechnic and Colleges Employers' Forum
PCFC	Polytechnics and Colleges Funding Council
PCL	Polytechnic of Central London
PCMO	Principal Colonial Medical Officer
PdD	Doctor of Pedagogy (US)
Pde	Parade
PDG	Président Directeur Général
PDR	People's Democratic Republic
PDRA	post doctoral research assistant
PDSA	People's Dispensary for Sick Animals
PDTC	Professional Dancer's Training Course Diploma
PE	Procurement Executive
PEI	Prince Edward Island
Pembs	Pembrokeshire
PEN	Poets, Playwrights, Editors, Essayists, Novelists (Club)
PEng	Registered Professional Engineer (Canada); Member, Society of Professional Engineers
Penn	Pennsylvania
PEP	Political and Economic Planning
PER	Professional and Executive Recruitment
Perm	Permanent
PEST	Pressure for Economic and Social Toryism
PETRAS	Polytechnic Educational Technology Resources Advisory Service
PF	Procurator-Fiscal
PFA	Professional Footballers' Association
pfc	Graduate of RAF Flying College
PFE	Program for Executives
PGA	Professional Golfers' Association
PH	Presidential Order of Honour (Botswana)
PHAB	Physically Handicapped and Able-Bodied
PhB	Bachelor of Philosophy
PhC	Pharmaceutical Chemist
PhD	Doctor of Philosophy
Phil	Philology, Philological; Philosophy, Philosophical
PhL	Licentiate of Philosophy
PHLS	Public Health Laboratory Service
PhM	Master of Philosophy (USA)
PhmB	Bachelor of Pharmacy
Phys	Physical
PIA	Personal Investment Authority
PIARC	Permanent International Association of Road Congresses
PIB	Prices and Incomes Board (later NBPI)
PICAO	Provisional International Civil Aviation Organization
PIRA	Paper Industries Research Association
PITCOM	Parliamentary Information Technology Committee
PJG	Pingat Jasa Gemilang (Singapore)
PJK	Pingkat Jasa Kebaktian (Malaysia)
Pk	Park
Pl	Place; Plural
PLA	Port of London Authority
PLC/plc	public limited company
Plen	Plenipotentiary
PLI	President, Landscape Institute
PLP	Parliamentary Labour Party; Progressive Liberal Party (Bahamas)
PLR	Public Lending Right
PM	Prime Minister
PMA	Personal Military Assistant
PMC	Personnel Management Centre
PMD	Program for Management Development
PMG	Postmaster-General
PMN	Panglima Mangku Negara (Malaysia)
PMO	Principal Medical Officer
PMRAFNS	Princess Mary's Royal Air Force Nursing Service
PMS	Presidential Order of Meritorious Service (Botswana); President, Miniature Society
PNBS	Panglima Negara Bintang Sarawak
Pncpl	Principal
PNEU	Parents' National Educational Union
PNG	Papua New Guinea
PNP	People's National Party
PO	Post Office
P/O	Pilot Officer
P&O	Peninsular and Oriental Steamship Company
POB	Presidential Order of Botswana
Poly	Polytechnic
POMEF	Political Office Middle East Force
Pop	Population
POUNC	Post Office Users' National Council
POW	Prisoner of War; Prince of Wales's
pp	pages
PP	Parish Priest; Past President
PPA	Periodical Publishers Association
PPARC	Particle Physics and Astronomy Research Council
PPCLI	Princess Patricia's Canadian Light Infantry
PPDF	Parti Populaire pour la Démocratie Française
PPE	Philosophy, Politics and Economics
PPInstHE	Past President, Institution of Highway Engineers
PPIStructE	Past President, Institution of Structural Engineers
PPITB	Printing and Publishing Industry Training Board
PPP	Private Patients Plan
PPRA	Past President, Royal Academy
PPRBA	Past President, Royal Society of British Artists
PPRBS	Past President, Royal Society of British Sculptors
PPRE	Past President, Royal Society of Painter-Printmakers (formerly of Painter-Etchers and Engravers)
PPRIBA	Past President, Royal Institute of British Architects
PPROI	Past President, Royal Institute of Oil Painters
PPRP	Past President, Royal Society of Portrait Painters
PPRTPI	Past President, Royal Town Planning Institute
PPRWA	Past President, Royal Watercolour Association
PPS	Parliamentary Private Secretary
PPSIAD	Past President, Society of Industrial Artists and Designers
PQ	Province of Quebec
PR	Public Relations; Parti républicain
PRA	President, Royal Academy
PRAS	President, Royal Agricultural Society
PRBA	President, Royal Society of British Artists
PRBS	President, Royal Society of British Sculptors
PRCS	President, Royal College of Surgeons
PRE	President, Royal Society of Painter-Printmakers (formerly of Painter-Etchers and Engravers)
Preb	Prebendary
PrEng	Professional Engineer
Pres	President
PRHA	President, Royal Hibernian Academy
PRI	President, Royal Institute of Painters in Water Colours; Plastics and Rubber Institute
PRIA	President, Royal Irish Academy
PRIAS	President, Royal Incorporation of Architects in Scotland
PRISA	Public Relations Institute of South Africa
Priv	Private
pro tem	*pro tempore* (for the time being)
PRO NED	Promotion of Non-Executive Directors
PRO	Public Relations Officer, Public Records Office
Proc	Proctor; Proceedings
Prof	Professor; Professional
PROI	President, Royal Institute of Oil Painters
PRORM	Pay and Records Office, Royal Marines
Prov	Provost, Provincial
Prox	*Proximo* (next)
Prox acc	*Proxime accessit* (next in order of merit to the winner)
PRS	President, Royal Society; Performing Right Society Ltd
PRSA	President, Royal Scottish Academy
PRSE	President, Royal Society of Edinburgh
PRSH	President, Royal Society for the Promotion of Health
PRSM	President, Royal Society of Medicine

PRSW President, Royal Scottish Water Colour Society
PRUAA President, Royal Ulster Academy of Arts
PRWA President, Royal West of England Academy
PRWS President, Royal Society of Painters in Water Colours
ps passed School of Instruction (of Officers)
PS Pastel Society; Paddle Steamer
psa Graduate of RAF Staff College
PSA Property Services Agency; Petty Sessions Area
psc Graduate of Staff College
PSD Petty Sessional Division; Social Democratic Party (Portugal)
PSGB Pharmaceutical Society of Great Britain
PSI Policy Studies Institute
PSIAD President, Society of Industrial Artists and Designers
psm Certificate of Royal Military School of Music
PSM Panglima Setia Mahkota (Malaysia)
PSMA President, Society of Marine Artists
PSNC Pacific Steam Navigation Company
PSO Principal Scientific Officer; Personal Staff Officer
PSOE Partido Socialista Obrero Español
PSSC Personal Social Services Council
PTA Passenger Transport Authority; Parent-Teacher Association
PTE Passenger Transport Executive
Pte Private
ptnr partner
ptsc passed Technical Staff College
Pty Proprietary (used of Australian and some other countries' businesses)
Publicns Publications
PUP People's United Party
PVSM Pararn Vishishc Seva Medal (India)
PWD Public Works Department
PWE Political Welfare Executive
PWO Prince of Wales's Own
PWR Pressurized Water Reactor
PYBT Prince's Youth Business Trust

Q

Q Queen
QAIMNS Queen Alexandra's Imperial Military Nursing Service
QALAS Qualified Associate, Chartered Land Agents' Society
QARANC Queen Alexandra's Royal Army Nursing Corps
QARNNS Queen Alexandra's Royal Naval Nursing Service
QBD Queen's Bench Division
QC Queen's Counsel
QCVSA Queen's Commendation for Valuable Service in the Air
QEH Queen Elizabeth Hall
QEO Queen Elizabeth's Own
QFSM Queen's Fire Service Medal for Distinguished Service
QGM Queen's Gallantry Medal
QHC Honorary Chaplain to the Queen
QHDS Honorary Dental Surgeon to the Queen
QHNS Honorary Nursing Sister to the Queen
QHP Honorary Physician to the Queen
QHS Honorary Surgeon to the Queen
Qld Queensland
Qly Quarterly
QMAAC Queen Mary's Army Auxiliary Corps
QMC Queen Mary College, London
QMG Quartermaster-General
QMW Queen Mary and Westfield College, London
QO Qualified Officer; Queen's Own
QOOH Queen's Own Oxfordshire Hussars
Q(ops) Quartering (operations)
QOY Queen's Own Yeomanry
QPM Queen's Police Medal
Qr Quarter
QRIH Queen's Royal Irish Hussars
QRV Qualified Valuer, Real Estate Institute of New South Wales
QS Quarter Sessions; Quantity Surveying
qs RAF graduates of the Military or Naval Staff College
QSM Queen's Service Medal (NZ)
QSO Queen's Service Order (NZ)
QUB Queen's University, Belfast
qv *quod vide* (which see)
QWI Qualified Weapons Instructor

R

(R) Reserve
RA Royal Academician; Royal (Regiment of) Artillery
RAA Regional Arts Association; Royal Australian Artillery
RAAF Royal Australian Air Force
RAAMC Royal Australian Army Medical Corps
RABI Royal Agricultural Benevolent Institution
RAC Royal Automobile Club; Royal Agricultural College; Royal Armoured Corps
RACDS Royal Australian College of Dental Surgeons
RACGP Royal Australian College of General Practitioners
RAChD Royal Army Chaplains' Department
RACI Royal Australian Chemical Institute
RACO Royal Australian College of Ophthalmologists
RACOG Royal Australian College of Obstetricians and Gynaecologists
RACP Royal Australasian College of Physicians
RACS Royal Australasian College of Surgeons; Royal Arsenal Co-operative Society
RADA Royal Academy of Dramatic Art
RADAR Royal Association for Disability and Rehabilitation
RADC Royal Army Dental Corps
R-Adml Rear Admiral
RADIUS Religious Drama Society of Great Britain
RAE Royal Australian Engineers; Royal Aerospace Establishment (formerly Royal Aircraft Establishment)
RAEC Royal Army Educational Corps
RAeS Royal Aeronautical Society
RAF Royal Air Force
RAFA Royal Air Force Association
RAFO Reserve of Air Force Officers
RAFRO Royal Air Force Reserve of Officers
RAFVR Royal Air Force Volunteer Reserve
RAI Royal Anthropological Institute of Great Britain and Ireland; Radio Audizioni Italiane
RAIA Royal Australian Institute of Architects
RAIC Royal Architectural Institute of Canada
RAM (Member of) Royal Academy of Music
RAMC Royal Army Medical Corps
RAN Royal Australian Navy
RANR Royal Australian Naval Reserve
RANVR Royal Australian Naval Volunteer Reserve
RAOC Royal Army Ordnance Corps
RAPC Royal Army Pay Corps
RARDE Royal Armament Research and Development Establishment
RARO Regular Army Reserve of Officers
RAS Royal Astronomical Society; Royal Asiatic Society; Recruitment and Assessment Services
RASC Royal Army Service Corps
RASE Royal Agricultural Society of England
RAuxAF Royal Auxiliary Air Force
RAVC Royal Army Veterinary Corps
RB Rifle Brigade
RBA Member, Royal Society of British Artists
RBC Royal British Colonial Society of Artists
RBK&C Royal Borough of Kensington and Chelsea
RBL Royal British Legion
RBS Royal Society of British Sculptors
RBSA (Member of) Royal Birmingham Society of Artists
RBY Royal Bucks Yeomanry
RC Roman Catholic
RCA Member, Royal Canadian Academy of Arts; Royal College of Art; (Member of) Royal Cambrian Academy
RCAC Royal Canadian Armoured Corps
RCAF Royal Canadian Air Force
RCamA Member, Royal Cambrian Academy
RCAS Royal Central Asian Society
RCDS Royal College of Defence Studies

RCEME Royal Canadian Electrical and Mechanical Engineers
RCGP Royal College of General Practitioners
RCHA Royal Canadian Horse Artillery
RCHM Royal Commission on Historical Monuments
RCM (Member of) Royal College of Music
RCN Royal Canadian Navy; Royal College of Nursing
RCNC Royal Corps of Naval Constructors
RCNR Royal Canadian Naval Reserve
RCNVR Royal Canadian Naval Volunteer Reserve
RCO Royal College of Organists
RCOG Royal College of Obstetricians and Gynaecologists
RCP Royal College of Physicians, London
RCPath Royal College of Pathologists
RCPE/RCPEd Royal College of Physicians, Edinburgh
RCPI Royal College of Physicians of Ireland
RCPSG Royal College of Physicians and Surgeons of Glasgow
RCPsych Royal College of Psychiatrists
RCR Royal College of Radiologists
RCS Royal College of Surgeons of England; Royal Corps of Signals; Royal College of Science
RCSE/RCSEd Royal College of Surgeons of Edinburgh
RCSI Royal College of Surgeons in Ireland
RCT Royal Corps of Transport
RCVS Royal College of Veterinary Science; Royal College of Veterinary Surgeons
Rd Road
RD Rural Dean; Royal Naval and Royal Marine Forces Reserve Decoration
R&D Research and Development
RDA Royal Defence Academy
RDC Rural District Council
RDF Royal Dublin Fusiliers
RDI Royal Designer for Industry (Royal Society of Arts)
RDS Royal Dublin Society
RE Royal Engineers; Fellow, Royal Society of Painter-Printmakers (formerly of Painter-Etchers and Engravers); Religious Education
REACH Retired Executives Action Clearing House
recd received
REconS Royal Economic Society
Regnl Regional
Regt Regiment
rels relations
REME Royal Electrical and Mechanical Engineers
Renfrews Renfrewshire
REngDes Registered Engineering Designer
REOWS Royal Engineers Officers' Widows' Society
Rep/rep Representative/representative
REPC Regional Economic Planning Council
RERO Royal Engineers Reserve of Officers
Res Resigned; Reserve; Resident; Research
RES Royal Empire Society
ret retired
RETI Association of Traditional Industrial Regions
Rev Reverend; Review
RFA Royal Field Artillery; Royal Fleet Auxiliary
RFC Royal Flying Corps; Rugby Football Club
RFD Reserve Force Decoration
RFH Royal Festival Hall
RFN Registered Fever Nurse
RFPS(G) Royal Faculty of Physicians and Surgeons, Glasgow
RFR Rassemblement des Français pour la République
RFU Rugby Football Union
RGA Royal Garrison Artillery
RGI Royal Glasgow Institute of the Fine Arts
RGJ Royal Green Jackets
RGN Registered General Nurse
RGS Royal Geographical Society
RGSA Royal Geographical Society of Australasia
RHA Royal Hibernian Academy; Royal Horse Artillery; Regional Health Authority
RHAS Royal Highland and Agricultural Society of Scotland
RHB Regional Hospital Board
RHBNC Royal Holloway and Bedford New College, London
RHC Royal Holloway College, London
RHF Royal Highland Fusiliers
RHG Royal Horse Guards
RHistS Royal Historical Society
RHQ Regional Headquarters
RHR Royal Highland Regiment
RHS Royal Horticultural Society; Royal Humane Society
RHV Royal Health Visitor
RI (Member of) Royal Institute of Painters in Water Colours; Rhode Island
RIA Royal Irish Academy
RIAI Royal Institute of the Architects of Ireland
RIAM Royal Irish Academy of Music
RIAMC Royal Indian Army Medical Corps
RIAS Royal Incorporation of Architects in Scotland
RIASC Royal Indian Army Service Corps
RIBA (Member of) Royal Institute of British Architects
RIBI Rotary International in Great Britain and Ireland
RIC Royal Irish Constabulary; Royal Institute of Chemistry
RICS Royal Institution of Chartered Surveyors
RIE Royal Indian Engineering (College)
RIF Royal Inniskilling Fusiliers
RIIA Royal Institute of International Affairs
RILEM Réunion internationale des laboratoires d'essais et de recherches sur les matériaux et les constructions
RIM Royal Indian Marines
RIN Royal Indian Navy
RINA Royal Institution of Naval Architects
RINVR Royal Indian Naval Volunteer Reserve
RIPA Royal Institute of Public Administration
RIPH&H Royal Institute of Public Health and Hygiene
RIrF Royal Irish Fusiliers
RLC Royal Logistic Corps
Rlrd(s) Railroad(s)
RLSS Royal Life Saving Society
Rlwy Railway
RM Royal Marines; Resident Magistrate; Registered Midwife
RMA Royal Marine Artillery; Royal Military Academy, Sandhurst
RMB Rural Mail Base
RMC Royal Military College
RMC Royal Military College Sandhurst
RMCM (Member of) Royal Manchester College of Music
RMCS Royal Military College of Science
RMedSoc Royal Medical Society, Edinburgh
RMetS Royal Meteorological Society
RMFVR Royal Marine Forces Volunteer Reserve
RMIT Royal Melbourne Institute of Technology
RMLI Royal Marine Light Infantry
RMN Registered Mental Nurse
RMO Resident Medical Officer(s)
RMP Royal Military Police
RMPA Royal Medico-Psychological Association
RMS Royal Microscopical Society; Royal Mail Steamer; Royal Society of Miniature Painters
RMT Rail, Maritime and Transport Union
RN Royal Navy; Royal Naval; Registered Nurse
RNAS Royal Naval Air Service
RNAY Royal Naval Aircraft Yard
RNC Royal Naval College
RNCM (Member of) Royal Northern College of Music
RND Royal Naval Division
RNEC Royal Naval Engineering College
RNIB Royal National Institute for the Blind
RNID Royal National Institute for Deaf People (formerly Royal National Institute for the Deaf)
RNLI Royal National Lifeboat Institution
RNLO Royal Naval Liaison Officer
RNR Royal Naval Reserve
RNS Royal Numismatic Society
RNSA Royal Naval Sailing Association
RNSC Royal Naval Staff College
RNT Registered Nurse Tutor; Royal National Theatre
RNTNEH Royal National Throat, Nose and Ear Hospital
RNVR Royal Naval Volunteer Reserve
RNVSR Royal Naval Volunteer Supplementary Reserve
RNXS Royal Naval Auxiliary Service
RNZAC Royal New Zealand Armoured Corps
RNZAF Royal New Zealand Air Force
RNZIR Royal New Zealand Infantry Regiment
RNZN Royal New Zealand Navy
RNZNVR Royal New Zealand Naval Volunteer Reserve
R of O Reserve of Officers
ROC Royal Observer Corps
ROF Royal Ordnance Factories
ROI Member, Royal Institute of Oil Painters
RoSPA Royal Society for the Prevention of Accidents
Roy Royal
RP Member, Royal Society of Portrait Painters
RPC Royal Pioneer Corps
RPE Rocket Propulsion Establishment

RPMS Royal Postgraduate Medical School
RPO Royal Philharmonic Orchestra
RPR Rassemblement pour la République
RPS Royal Photographic Society
RPSGB Royal Pharmaceutical Society of Great Britain
RRC Royal Red Cross
RRE Royal Radar Establishment
RRF Royal Regiment of Fusiliers
RRS Royal Research Ship
RSA Royal Scottish Academician; Royal Society of Arts; Republic of South Africa
RSAA Royal Society for Asian Affairs
RSAF Royal Small Arms Factory
RSAI Royal Society of Antiquaries of Ireland
RSAMD Royal Scottish Academy of Music and Drama
RSanI Royal Sanitary Institute
RSAS Royal Surgical Aid Society
RSC Royal Society of Canada; Royal Society of Chemistry; Royal Shakespeare Company
RSCM Royal School of Church Music
RSCN Registered Sick Children's Nurse
RSE Royal Society of Edinburgh
RSF Royal Scots Fusiliers
RSFSR Russian Soviet Federated Socialist Republic
RSGS Royal Scottish Geographical Society
RSH Royal Society for the Promotion of Health
RSL Royal Society of Literature; Returned Services League of Australia
RSM/RSocMed Royal Society of Medicine
RSM Royal School of Mines
RSMA Royal Society of Marine Artists
RSME Royal School of Military Engineering
RSMHCA Royal Society for Mentally Handicapped Children and Adults
RSNC Royal Society for Nature Conservation
RSO Rural Sub-Office; Railway Sub-Office; Resident Surgical Officer
RSPB Royal Society for Protection of Birds
RSPCA Royal Society for Prevention of Cruelty to Animals
RSPP Royal Society of Portrait Painters
RSRE Royal Signals and Radar Establishment
RSSAf Royal Society of South Africa
RSSAILA Returned Sailors, Soldiers and Airmen's Imperial League of Australia
RSSPCC Royal Scottish Society for Prevention of Cruelty to Children
RSTM&H Royal Society of Tropical Medicine and Hygiene
RSUA Royal Society of Ulster Architects
RSV Revised Standard Version
RSW Member, Royal Scottish Society of Painters in Water Colours
Rt Hon Right Honourable
Rt Rev Right Reverend
RTC Royal Transport Corps
RTE Radio Telefis Eireann
RTL Radio-Télévision Luxembourg
RTO Railway Transport Officer
RTPI Royal Town Planning Institute
RTR Royal Tank Regiment
RTS Religious Tract Society; Royal Toxophilite Society; Royal Television Society
RTYC Royal Thames Yacht Club
RU Rugby Union
RUC Royal Ulster Constabulary
RUI Royal University of Ireland
RUKBA Royal United Kingdom Beneficent Association
RUR Royal Ulster Regiment
RURAL Society for the Responsible Use of Resources in Agriculture and on the Land
RUSI Royal United Services Institute for Defence Studies (formerly Royal United Service Institution)
RVC Royal Veterinary College
RWA/RWEA (Member of) Royal West of England Academy
RWAFF Royal West African Frontier Force
RWF Royal Welch Fusiliers
RWS (Member of) Royal Society of Painters in Water Colours
RYA Royal Yachting Association
RYS Royal Yacht Squadron
RZSScot Royal Zoological Society of Scotland

S

s son
s succeeded
S Saint; Scotland (of creation in peerage of); South
(S) (in Navy) Paymaster; Scotland
SA South Australia; South Africa; Société Anonyme
SAAF South African Air Force
SABC South African Broadcasting Corporation
sac qualified at small arms technical long course
SAC Scientific Advisory Committee
SACEUR Supreme Allied Commander Europe
SACIF Sociedad Anónima Commercial Industrial Financiera
SACLANT Supreme Allied Commander Atlantic
SACRO Scottish Association for the Care and Resettlement of Offenders
SACSEA Supreme Allied Command, SE Asia
SA de CV Sociedad Anónima de Capital Variable
SADF Sudanese Auxiliary Defence Force
SADG Société des Architectes Diplômés par le Gouvernement
SAE Society of Automobile Engineers (US)
SAInstMM South African Institute of Mining and Metallurgy
Salop Shropshire
SAMC South African Medical Corps
SARL Société à Responsabilité Limitée
Sarum Salisbury
SAS Special Air Service
Sask Saskatchewan
SASO Senior Air Staff Officer
SAT Senior Member, Association of Accounting Technicians
SATB Soprano, Alto, Tenor, Bass
SATRO Science and Technology Regional Organisation
SB Bachelor of Science (US)
SBAA Sovereign Base Areas Administration
SBAC Society of British Aerospace Companies (formerly Society of British Aircraft Constructors)
SBS Special Boat Service
SBStJ Serving Brother, Most Venerable Order of the Hospital of St John of Jerusalem
SC Senior Counsel (Eire and some other countries' equivalent to QC)
SC Star of Courage (Canada); Senior Counsel; South Carolina
sc student at the Staff College
SCA Society of Catholic Apostolate (Pallottine Fathers); Société en Commandité par Actions
SCAA School Curriculum and Assessment Authority
SCAO Senior Civil Affairs Officer
SCAPA Society for Checking the Abuses of Public Advertising
SCAR Scientific Committee for Antarctic Research
ScD Doctor of Science
SCDC Schools Curriculum Development Committee
SCF Senior Chaplain to the Forces; Save the Children Fund
Sch School
SCI Society of Chemical Industry
SCIS Scottish Council of Independent Schools
SCL Student in Civil Law
SCM State Certified Midwife; Student Christian Movement
SCONUL Standing Conference of National and University Libraries
Scot Scotland; Scottish
ScotBIC Scottish Business in the Community
SCOTMEG Scottish Management Efficiency Group
SCOTVEC Scottish Vocational Education Council
SD Staff Duties; South Dakota
SDA Social Democratic Alliance; Scottish Diploma in Agriculture; Scottish Development Agency
SDB Salesian of Don Bosco
SDF Sudan Defence Force; Social Democratic Federation
SDI Strategic Defence Initiative
SDLP Social Democratic and Labour Party
SDP Social Democratic Party
SE South East
SEAC South-East Asia Command
SEALF South-East Asia Land Forces
SEATO South-East Asia Treaty Organization
Sec Secretary
SEC Security Exchange Commission
SED Scottish Education Department

SEE	Society of Environmental Engineers
SEFI	European Society for Engineering Education
SEN	State Enrolled Nurse
SEPM	Society of Economic Palaeontologists and Mineralogists
SERC	Science and Engineering Research Council
SERT	Society of Electronic and Radio Technicians
Serv(s)	Service(s)
SESO	Senior Equipment Staff Officer
SFA	Securities and Futures Authority
SFInstE	Senior Fellow, Institute of Energy
SFInstF	Senior Fellow, Institute of Fuel
SFTA	Society of Film and Television Arts
SFTCD	Senior Fellow, Trinity College Dublin
SGA	Member, Society of Graphic Art
SGBI	Schoolmistresses' and Governesses' Benevolent Institution
Sgt	Sergeant
SHA	Secondary Heads Association; Special Health Authority
SHAC	London Housing Aid Centre
SHAEF	Supreme Headquarters, Allied Expeditionary Force
SHAPE	Supreme Headquarters, Allied Powers, Europe
SHEFC	Scottish Higher Education Funding Council
SHHD	Scottish Home and Health Department
SH&MA	Scottish Horse and Motormen's Association
SIAD	Society of Industrial Artists and Designers
SIAM	Society of Industrial and Applied Mathematics (US)
SIB	Shipbuilding Industry Board; Securities and Investments Board
SICAV	Société d'Investissement à Capital Variable
SICOT	Société Internationale de Chirurgie Orthopédique et de Traumatologie
SID	Society for International Development
SIESO	Society of Industrial and Emergency Services Officers
SIMA	Scientific Instrument Manufacturers' Association of Great Britain
SIME	Security Intelligence Middle East
SIMG	Societas Internationalis Medicinae Generalis
SinDrs	Doctor of Chinese
SIROT	Société Internationale pour Recherche en Orthopédie et Traumatologie
sis	sister
SIS	Secret Intelligence Service
SITA	Société Internationale de Télécommunications Aéronautiques
SITPRO	Simpler Trade Procedures Board (formerly Simplification of International Trade Procedures)
SJ	Society of Jesus (Jesuits)
SJAB	St John Ambulance Brigade
SJD	Doctor of Juristic Science
SJJ	Setia Jubli Perak Tuanku Ja'afar
SKGB	Ski Club of Great Britain
SL	Serjeant-at-Law; Sociedad Limitada
SLA	Special Libraries Association
SLAC	Stanford Linear Accelerator Centre
SLAET	Society of Licensed Aircraft Engineers and Technologists
SLAS	Society for Latin-American Studies
SLD	Social and Liberal Democrats
S/Ldr	Squadron Leader
SLG	Community of Sisters of the Love of God
SLP	Scottish Labour Party
slr	solicitor
SM	Medal of Service (Canada); Master of Science; Officer qualified for Submarine Duties
SMA	Society of Marine Artists
SMB	Setia Mahkota Brunei
SME	School of Military Engineering
SMHO	Sovereign Military Hospitaller Order (Malta)
SMIEE	Senior Member, Institute of Electrical and Electronics Engineers (New York)
SMIRE	Senior Member, Institute of Radio Engineers (New York)
SMMT	Society of Motor Manufacturers and Traders Ltd
SMN	Seri Maharaja Mangku Negara (Malaysia)
SMO	Senior Medical Officer; Sovereign Military Order
SMP	Senior Managers' Program
SMPTE	Society of Motion Picture and Television Engineers (US)
SMRTB	Ship and Marine Requirements Technology Board
SNAME	Society of Naval Architects and Marine Engineers (US)
SNCF	Société Nationale des Chemins de Fer Français
SND	Sisters of Notre Dame
SNH	Scottish Natural Heritage
SNP	Scottish National Party
SNR	Society for Nautical Research
SNTS	Society for New Testament Studies
SO	Staff Officer; Scientific Officer; Symphony Orchestra
SOAS	School of Oriental and African Studies
Soc	Society
SocCE(France)	Société des Ingénieurs Civils de France
Soc & Lib Dem	Social and Liberal Democrats
SODEPAX	Committee on Society, Development and Peace
SOE	Special Operations Executive
SOGAT	Society of Graphical and Allied Trades
SOLACE	Society of Local Authority Chief Executives
SOLT	Society of London Theatre
Som	Somerset
SOM	Society of Occupational Medicine
SOSc	Society of Ordained Scientists
SOTS	Society for Old Testament Study
Sov	Sovereign
sowc	Senior Officers' War Course
sp	*sine prole* (without issue)
SP	Self-Propelled (Anti-Tank Regiment)
SpA	Società per Azioni
SPAB	Society for the Protection of Ancient Buildings
SPARKS	Sport Aiding Medical Research for Children
SPCA	Society for the Prevention of Cruelty to Animals
SPCK	Society for Promoting Christian Knowledge
SPCM	Dadah Seri Paduka Cura Si Manja Kim (Malaysia)
SPD	Salisbury Plain District; Sozialdemokratische Partei Deutschlands
SPDK	Seri Panglima Darjal Kinabalu
SPG	Society for the Propagation of the Gospel
SPk	Sitara-e-Pakistan
SPMB	Seri Paduka Makhota Brunei
SPMK	Darjah Kebasaran Seri Paduka Mahkota Kelantan (Malaysia)
SPMO	Senior Principal Medical Officer
SPNC	Society for the Promotion of Nature Conservation
SPNM	Society for the Promotion of New Music
SPR	Society for Psychical Research
SPRC	Society for Prevention and Relief of Cancer
sprl	société de personnes à responsabilité limitée
SPSO	Senior Principal Scientific Officer
SPTL	Society of Public Teachers of Law
SPUC	Society for the Protection of the Unborn Child
Sq	Square
sq	staff qualified
SQA	Sitara-i-Quaid-i-Azam (Pakistan)
Sqdn	Squadron
Sr	Señor
Sr/sr	senior
SR	Special Reserve; Southern Railway; Southern Region (BR)
SRC	Science Research Council; Students' Representative Council
SRCh	State Registered Chiropodist
SRHE	Society for Research into Higher Education
SRIS	Science Reference Information Service
SRN	State Registered Nurse
SRNA	Shipbuilders and Repairers National Association
SRO	Supplementary Reserve of Officers; Self-Regulatory Organisation
SRP	State Registered Physiotherapist
SRY	Sherwood Rangers Yeomanry
SS	Saints; Straits Settlements; Steamship
SSA	Society of Scottish Artists
SSAC	Social Security Advisory Committee
SSAFA/SS&AFA	Soldiers', Sailors' and Airmen's Families Association
SSBN	Nuclear Submarine, Ballistic
SSC	Solicitor before Supreme Court (Scotland); Sculptors Society of Canada; Societas Sanctae Crucis (Society of the Holy Cross); Short Service Commission
SSEB	South of Scotland Electricity Board
SSEES	School of Slavonic and East European Studies
SSF	Society of St Francis
SSJE	Society of St John the Evangelist
SSM	Society of the Sacred Mission; Seri Setia Mahkota (Malaysia)
SSO	Senior Supply Officer; Senior Scientific Officer
SSR	Soviet Socialist Republic
SSRC	Social Science Research Council
SSSI	Site of Special Scientific Interest
SSStJ	Serving Sister, Most Venerable Order of the Hospital of St John of Jerusalem
St	Street; Saint
STA	Sail Training Association
Staffs	Staffordshire

STB *Sacrae Theologiae Baccalaureus* (Bachelor of Sacred Theology)
STC Senior Training Corps
STD *Sacrae Theologiae Doctor* (Doctor of Sacred Theology)
STh Scholar in Theology
Stip Stipend; Stipendiary
STL *Sacrae Theologiae Lector* (Reader or a Professor of Sacred Theology)
STM *Sacrae Theologiae Magister* (Master of Sacred Theology)
STP *Sacrae Theologiae Professor* (Professor of Divinity, old form of DD)
STRIVE Society for Preservation of Rural Industries and Village Enterprises
STSO Senior Technical Staff Officer
STV Scottish Television
Sub-Lt Sub-Lieutenant
SUNY State University of New York
Supp Res Supplementary Reserve (of Officers)
Supt Superintendent
Surgn Surgeon
surv surviving
SW South-west
SWET Society of West End Theatre
SWIA Society of Wildlife Artists
SWPA South West Pacific Area
SWRB Sadler's Wells Royal Ballet

T

T Telephone; Territorial
T/ Temporary rank, *e.g.*,T/Capt (Temporary Captain)
T&AFA Territorial and Auxiliary Forces Association
T&AVR Territorial and Army Volunteer Reserve
TA Telegraphic Address; Territorial Army
TAA Territorial Army Association
TAF Tactical Air Force
TANS Territorial Army Nursing Service
TANU Tanganyika African National Union
TAR Territorial Army Reserve
TARO Territorial Army Reserve of Officers
TAS Torpedo and Anti Submarine Course
TASS Technical, Administrative and Supervisory Section of AUEW
TAVRA/TA&VRA Territorial Auxiliary and Volunteer Reserve Association
Tbnl Tribunal
TC Order of the Trinity Cross (Trinidad and Tobago)
TCCB Test and County Cricket Board
TCD Trinity College, Dublin (University of Dublin, Trinity College)
TCF Temporary Chaplain to the Forces
TCPA Town and Country Planning Association
TD Territorial Decoration; Territorial Efficiency Decoration; Efficiency Decoration (T&AVR) (from April 1967); Teachta Dala (Member of the Dáil, Eire)
TDD Tubercular Diseases Diploma
TE Technical Engineer
TEAC Technical Educational Advisory Council
TEC Technician Education Council; Training and Enterprise Council
Tech Technical
TEFL Teaching English as a Foreign Language
TEFLA Teaching English as a Foreign Language to Adults
TEM Territorial Efficiency Medal
TEMA Telecommunication Engineering and Manufacturing Association
temp in the time of; temporary
TEng(CEI) Technician Engineer
Tenn Tennessee
TeolD Doctor of Theology
TES *Times Educational Supplement*
TESL Teaching English as a Second Language
TESOL Teaching English to Speakers of Other Languages
TET Teacher of Electrotherapy
Tex Texas
TF Territorial Force
TFA Territorial Forces Association
TFR Territorial Force Reserve
TFTS Tactical Fighter Training Squadron
TGEW Timber Growers England and Wales Ltd
TGO Timber Growers' Organisation
TGWU Transport and General Workers' Union
ThD Doctor of Theology
THED Transvaal Higher Education Diploma
THELEP Therapy of Leprosy
THES *Times Higher Education Supplement*
ThL Theological Licentiate
ThSchol Scholar in Theology
TIMS The Institute of Management Sciences
TLS *Times Literary Supplement*
TM Their Majesties
TMMG Teacher of Massage and Medical Gymnastics
TN Tennessee
TNC Theatres National Committee
TOSD Tertiary Order of St Dominic
TP Transvaal Province
TPI Town Planning Institute
Tport Transport
Trans/trans Translation; Translated
Transf Transferred
TRC Thames Rowing Club
TRE Telecommunications Research Establishment (later RRE)
Treas Treasurer
Trg Training
TRH Their Royal Highnesses
TRIC Television and Radio Industries Club
Trin Trinity
TRRL Transport and Road Research Laboratory
TS Training Ship
TSB Trustee Savings Bank
tsc passed a Territorial Army Course in Staff Duties
TSD Tertiary of St Dominic
TSSA Transport Salaried Staffs' Association
Tst Trust
Tstee/tstee Trustee/trustee
TUC Trades Union Congress
TULV Trade Unions for a Labour Victory
TUS Trade Union Side
TV Television
TVEI Technical and Vocational Education Initiative
TWA Thames Water Authority
TX Texas
TYC Thames Yacht Club

U

U Unionist; University
UACE Universities Association for Continuing Education
UAE United Arab Emirates
UAR United Arab Republic
UAU Universities Athletic Union
UBC University of British Columbia
UBI Understanding British Industry
UC University College
UCAS Universities and Colleges Admissions Service
UCCA Universities Central Council on Admissions
UCCF Universities and Colleges Christian Fellowship of Evangelical Unions
UCE University of Central England
UCET Universities Council for Education of Teachers
UCH University College Hospital (London)
UCL University College London (University)
UCLA University of California at Los Angeles
UCLES University of Cambridge Local Examinations Syndicate
UCMSM University College and Middlesex School of Medicine
UCNS Universities' Council for Non-academic Staff
UCNW University College of North Wales

UCRN	University College of Rhodesia and Nyasaland
UCS	University College School
UCSD	University of California at San Diego
UCW	University College of Wales; Union of Communication Workers
UDC	Urban District Council; Urban Development Corporation
UDF	Union Defence Force; Union Démocratique Française
UDR	Ulster Defence Regiment; Union Démocrates pour la Vème République
UDSR	Union Démocratique et Socialiste de la Résistance
UE	United Empire Loyalist (Canada)
UEA	University of East Anglia
UED	University Education Diploma
UEFA	Union of European Football Associations
UF	United Free Church
UFAW	Universities Federation for Animal Welfare
UFC	Universities' Funding Council
UGC	University Grants Committee (later UFC)
UIAA	Union Internationale des Associations d'Alpinisme
UICC	Union Internationale contre le Cancer
UIE	Union Internationale des Etudiants
UISPP	Union Internationale des Sciences Préhistoriques et Protohistoriques
UITP	International Union of Public Transport
UJD	*Utriusque Juris Doctor* (Doctor of both Laws, Doctor of Canon and Civil Law)
UK	United Kingdom of Great Britain and Ireland 1801–1922; United Kingdom of Great Britain and Northern Ireland 1922–; used chiefly of peerage and baronetage creations of
UKAC	United Kingdom Automation Council
UKAEA	United Kingdom Atomic Energy Authority
UKCC	United Kingdom Central Council for Nursing, Midwifery and Health Visiting
UKCIS	United Kingdom Chemical Information Service
UKERNA	United Kingdom Education and Research Networking Association
UKIAS	United Kingdom Immigrants' Advisory Service
UKISC	United Kingdom Industrial Space Committee
UKLF	United Kingdom Land Forces
UKMF(L)	United Kingdom Military Forces (Land)
UKMIS	United Kingdom Mission
UKOOA	United Kingdom Offshore Operators Association
UKPIA	United Kingdom Petroleum Industry Association Ltd
UKSC	United Kingdom Support Command
UKSLS	United Kingdom Services Liaison Staff
ULCI	Union of Lancashire and Cheshire Institutes
ULPS	Union of Liberal and Progressive Synagogues
UMDS	United Medical and Dental Schools
UMIST	University of Manchester Institute of Science and Technology
UN	United Nations
UNA	United Nations Association
unc	uncle
UNCAST	United Nations Conference on the Applications of Science and Technology
UNCIO	United Nations Conference on International Organisation
UNCITRAL	United Nations Commission on International Trade Law
UNCSTD	United Nations Conference on Science and Technology for Development
UNCTAD/Unctad	United Nations Commission for Trade and Development
UNDP	United Nations Development Programme
UNDRO	United Nations Disaster Relief Organisation
UNECA	United Nations Economic Commission for Asia
UNEP	United Nations Environment Programme
UNESCO/Unesco	United Nations Educational, Scientific and Cultural Organisation
UNFAO	United Nations Food and Agriculture Organisation
UNFICYP	United Nations Force in Cyprus
UNHCR	United Nations High Commissioner for Refugees
UNICE	Union des Industries de la Communauté Européenne
UNICEF/Unicef	United Nations Children's Fund (formerly United Nations International Children's Emergency Fund)
UNIDO	United Nations Industrial Development Organisation
UNIDROIT	Institut International pour l'Unification du Droit Privé
UNIFEM	United Nations Development Fund for Women
UNIFIL	United Nations Interim Force in Lebanon
UNIPEDE	Union Internationale des Producteurs et Distributeurs d'Energie Electrique
UNISIST	Universal System for Information in Science and Technology
UNITAR	United Nations Institute of Training and Research
Univ	University College (Oxford)
unm	unmarried
UNO	United Nations Organization
UNRRA	United Nations Relief and Rehabilitation Administration
UNRWA	United Nations Relief and Works Agency
UNSCOB	United Nations Special Commission on the Balkans
UP	United Provinces; Uttar Pradesh; United Presbyterian
UPGC	University and Polytechnic Grants Committee
UPNI	Unionist Party of Northern Ireland
UPU	Universal Postal Union
UPUP	Ulster Popular Unionist Party
URC	United Reformed Church
URSI	Union Radio-Scientifique Internationale
US(A)	United States (of America)
USAAF	United States Army Air Force
USAF	United States Air Force
USAID	United States Agency for International Development
USAR	United States Army Reserve
USC	University of Southern California
USDAW	Union of Shop Distributive and Allied Workers
U-Sec	Under Secretary
USM	Unlisted Securities Market
USMA	United States Military Academy
USMC	United States Marine Corps
USN	United States Navy
USNR	United States Naval Reserve
USPG	United Society for the Propagation of the Gospel
USPHS	United States Public Health Service
USPS	United States Postal Service
USR	Universities' Statistical Record
USS	United States Ship
USSR	Union of Soviet Socialist Republics
USVI	United States Virgin Islands
UT	Utah
UTC	University Training Corps
Utd	United
UU	Ulster Unionist
UUUC	United Ulster Unionist Coalition
UUUP	United Ulster Unionist Party
UWCC	University of Wales College of Cardiff
UWE	University of the West of England
UWIST	University of Wales Institute of Science and Technology
UWT	Union of Women Teachers

V

v	*versus* (against)
V	Five (Roman numerals); Version; Vicar; Viscount; Vice
V-	Vice-
VA	Lady, Royal Order of Victoria and Albert
VA/Va	Virginia
V&A	Victoria and Albert Museum
VAD	Voluntary Aid Detachment
VAT	Value Added Tax
VC	Victoria Cross; Voluntary Controlled
VCAS	Vice-Chief of the Air Staff
VCDS	Vice-Chief of the Defence Staff
VCGS	Vice-Chief of the General Staff
VCNS	Vice-Chief of the Naval Staff
VD	Royal Naval Volunteer Reserve Officers' Decoration (later VRD); Volunteer Officers' Decoration; Victorian Decoration
VDC	Volunteer Defence Corps
Ven	Venerable
Vet	Veterinary
VG	Vicar-General
VHS	Honorary Surgeon to Viceroy of India
VIC	Victoria Institute of Colleges
vm	*vita matris* (in the lifetime of the mother)
VM	Victory Medal
VMH	Victoria Medal of Honour (Royal Horticultural Society)
Vol	Volume; Volunteer
Voly	Voluntary
vp	*vita patris* (in the lifetime of the father)

VPP	Volunteer Political Party
VPRP	Vice-President, Royal Society of Portrait Painters
VPRS	Vice-President, Royal Society
VQMG	Vice-Quartermaster-General
VR	*Victoria Regina* (Queen Victoria); Volunteer Reserve
VRD	Royal Naval Volunteer Reserve Officers' Decoration
VSO	Voluntary Service Overseas
VT/Vt	Vermont
VUP	Vanguard Unionist Party

W

w	wife
W	West
WA	Western Australia; Washington
WAAF	Women's Auxiliary Air Force (later WRAF)
WAOS	Welsh Agricultural Organisations Society
Warwicks	Warwickshire
Wash	Washington State
WCC	World Council of Churches
W/Cdr	Wing Commander
WCMD	Welsh College of Music and Drama
WDA	Welsh Development Agency
WEA	Workers' Educational Association; Royal West of England Academy
WES/PNEU	Worldwide Education Service of Parents' National Educational Union
WEU	Western European Union
WFSW	World Federation of Scientific Workers
WFTU	World Federation of Trade Unions
WhF	Whitworth Fellow
WHO	World Health Organization
WhSch	Whitworth Scholar
WI	West Indies; Women's Institute; Wisconsin
Wilts	Wiltshire
WIPO	World Intellectual Property Organization
Wis	Wisconsin
WJEC	Welsh Joint Education Committee
WLA	Women's Land Army
WLD	Women Liberal Democrats
WLF	Women's Liberal Federation
Wm	William
WMO	World Meteorological Organization
WNO	Welsh National Opera
WO	War Office; Warrant Officer
Worcs	Worcestershire
WOSB	War Office Selection Board
WR	West Riding; Western Region (British Railways)
WRAC	Women's Royal Army Corps
WRAF	Women's Royal Air Force
WRANS	Women's Royal Australian Naval Service
WRNS	Women's Royal Naval Service
WRVS	Women's Royal Voluntary Service
WS	Writer to the Signet
WSAVA	World Small Animal Veterinary Association
WSPA	World Society for the Protection of Animals
WSPU	Women's Social and Political Union
WUS	World University Service
WV	West Virginia
WVS	Women's Voluntary Services
WW	World War
WWF	World Wide Fund for Nature (formerly World Wildlife Fund)
WY	Wyoming

X

X	Ten (Roman numerals)

Y

YC	Young Conservative; Yeomanry Cavalry
YCNAC	Young Conservatives National Advisory Committee
Yeo	Yeomanry
YES	Youth Enterprise Scheme
YHA	Youth Hostels Association
YMCA	Young Men's Christian Association
YOI	Young Offenders Institute
Yorks	Yorkshire
YPTES	Young People's Trust for Endangered Species
yr	younger
yrs	years
yst	youngest
YTS	Youth Training Scheme
YVFF	Young Volunteer Force Foundation
YWCA	Young Women's Christian Association

Z

ZANU	Zimbabwe African National Union
ZAPU	Zimbabwe African People's Union

SURNAMES OF PEERAGE FAMILIES

Where the surname and title are identical, or where the latter is no more than an elaboration of the former (*e.g.* 'Jenkins' and 'Jenkins of Hillhead'), it has been thought unnecessary to include it in this listing. Surnames given are those in use by one or more male-line branches of the family holding the peerage, and are subject to minor variations, such as the inclusion or exclusion of a hyphen, among individual members of that family.

(I) IN ALPHABETICAL ORDER OF PEERAGE

ABERCONWAY . . . McLaren
ABERCORN . . . Hamilton
ABERDARE . . . Bruce
ABERDEEN AND TEMAIR . . . Gordon
ABERGAVENNY . . . Nevill
ABINGER . . . Scarlett
ACTON . . . Lyon-Dalberg-Acton
ADDINGTON . . . Hubbard
AILESBURY . . . Brudenell-Bruce
AILSA . . . Kennedy
AIRLIE . . . Ogilvy
ALANBROOKE . . . Brooke
ALBEMARLE . . . Keppel
ALDENHAM and HUNSDON OF HUNSDON . . . Gibbs
ALDINGTON . . . Low
ALLENDALE . . . Beaumont
ALTRINCHAM . . . Grigg
ALVINGHAM . . . Yerburgh
AMHERST OF HACKNEY . . . Cecil
AMPTHILL . . . Russell
AMWELL . . . Montague
ANGLESEY . . . Paget
ANNALY . . . White
ANNANDALE AND HARTFELL . . . Hope(-)Johnstone, Johnstone
ANTRIM . . . McDonnell
ARGYLL . . . Campbell
ARRAN . . . Gore
ASHBOURNE . . . Gibson
ASHBROOK . . . Flower
ASHBURTON . . . Baring
ASHCOMBE . . . Cubitt
ASHTOWN . . . Chenevix(-)Trench, Trench
ATHOLL . . . Murray
AUCKLAND . . . Eden
AVEBURY . . . Lubbock
AYLESFORD . . . Finch-Knightley
BALFOUR OF BURLEIGH . . . Bruce
BANGOR . . . Ward
BARNARD . . . Vane
BASING . . . Sclater-Booth
BATH . . . Thynn, Thynne
BEARSTED . . . Samuel
BEAUFORT . . . Somerset
BEAVERBROOK . . . Aitken
BEDFORD . . . Russell
BELHAVEN AND STENTON . . . Hamilton
BELLWIN . . . Bellow
BELMORE . . . Lowry-Corry
BELPER . . . Strutt
BELSTEAD . . . Ganzoni
BERKELEY . . . Gueterbock
BERNERS . . . Kirkham, Pollock
BESSBOROUGH . . . Ponsonby
BICESTER . . . Smith
BIDDULPH . . . Biddulph, Maitland-Biddulph
BLAKENHAM . . . Hare
BLEDISLOE . . . Bathurst
BOLINGBROKE and SAINT JOHN . . . St John
BOLTON . . . Orde-Powlett
BOSTON . . . Irby
BOYD OF MERTON . . . Lennox-Boyd
BOYNE . . . Hamilton-Russell
BRABAZON OF TARA . . . Moore-Brabazon
BRABOURNE . . . Knatchbull
BRADFORD . . . Bridgeman
BRAYBROOKE . . . Neville
BRAYE . . . Aubrey-Fletcher
BRENTFORD . . . Joynson-Hicks
BRIDPORT . . . Hood
BRISTOL . . . Hervey
BROCKET . . . Nall-Cain
BROOKEBOROUGH . . . Brooke
BROUGHAM AND VAUX . . . Brougham
BROUGHSHANE . . . Davison
BROWNLOW . . . Cust
BRUNTISFIELD . . . Warrender
BUCCLEUCH AND QUEENSBERRY . . . Montagu(-)Douglas(-)Scott
BUCHAN . . . Erskine
BUCKINGHAMSHIRE . . . Hobart-Hampden
BURGH . . . Leith
BURNHAM . . . Lawson
BURTON . . . Baillie
BUTE . . . Crichton-Stuart
BUXTON OF ALSA . . . Buxton
CAITHNESS . . . Sinclair
CALDECOTE . . . Inskip
CALEDON . . . Alexander
CALVERLEY . . . Muff
CAMDEN . . . Pratt
CAMOYS . . . Stonor
CAMROSE . . . Berry
CARBERY . . . Evans-Freke
CAREW . . . Conolly-Carew
CARLISLE . . . Howard
CARNARVON . . . Herbert
CARNOCK . . . Nicolson
CARRICK . . . Butler
CARRINGTON . . . Carington
CASTLE STEWART . . . Stuart
CASTLEMAINE . . . Handcock
CAVAN . . . Lambart
CAWDOR . . . Campbell
CHALFONT . . . Gwynne Jones
CHANDOS . . . Lyttelton
CHARLEMONT . . . Caulfeild
CHELMSFORD . . . Thesiger
CHESHAM . . . Cavendish
CHICHESTER . . . Pelham
CHILSTON . . . Akers-Douglas
CHURCHILL . . . Spencer
CHURSTON . . . Yarde-Buller
CLANCARTY . . . Le Poer Trench
CLANMORRIS . . . Bingham
CLANWILLIAM . . . Meade
CLARENDON . . . Villiers
CLEDWYN OF PENRHOS . . . Hughes
CLINTON . . . Fane, Fane Trefusis
CLITHEROE . . . Assheton
CLWYD . . . Roberts
CLYDESMUIR . . . Colville
COBBOLD . . . Lytton Cobbold
COBHAM . . . Lyttelton
COLERAINE . . . Law
COLGRAIN . . . Campbell
COLWYN . . . Smith
COLYTON . . . Hopkinson
COMBERMERE . . . Stapleton-Cotton
CONGLETON . . . Parnell
CORK and ORRERY . . . Boyle
COTTENHAM . . . Pepys
COTTESLOE . . . Fremantle
COURTOWN . . . Stopford, Stopford-Sackville
COWDRAY . . . Pearson
COWLEY . . . Wellesley
CRAIGAVON . . . Craig
CRAIGMYLE . . . Shaw
CRANBROOK . . . Gathorne-Hardy
CRANWORTH . . . Gurdon
CRATHORNE . . . Dugdale
CRAWFORD and BALCARRES . . . Lindsay
CRAWSHAW . . . Brooks
CRICKHOWELL . . . Edwards
CROHAM . . . Allen
CROMARTIE . . . Mackenzie
CROMER . . . Baring
CROMWELL . . . Bewicke-Copley
CULLEN OF ASHBOURNE . . . Cokayne
DACRE . . . Douglas-Home
DACRE OF GLANTON . . . Trevor-Roper
DALHOUSIE . . . Ramsay
DARCY DE KNAYTH . . . Ingrams
DARESBURY . . . Greenall
DARNLEY . . . Bligh
DARTMOUTH . . . Legge
DARWEN . . . Davies
DAVENTRY . . . FitzRoy-Newdegate
DEAN OF THORNTON-LE-FYLDE . . . McDowall
DECIES . . . Beresford, De la Poer Beresford, Horsley-Beresford
DE CLIFFORD . . . Russell
DE FREYNE . . . French
DELAMERE . . . Cholmondeley
DE LA WARR . . . Sackville
DE L'ISLE . . . Sidney
DE MAULEY . . . Ponsonby
DENBIGH and DESMOND . . . Feilding, Fielding
DENHAM . . . Bowyer
DERAMORE . . . De Yarburgh-Bateson
DE RAMSEY . . . Fellowes
DERBY . . . Stanley
DE ROS . . . Maxwell
DERWENT . . . Vanden-Bempde-Johnstone
DE SAUMAREZ . . . Saumarez
DE VESCI . . . Vesey
DEVON . . . Courtenay
DEVONPORT . . . Kearley
DEVONSHIRE . . . Cavendish
DILHORNE . . . Manningham-Buller
DONEGALL . . . Chichester
DONERAILE . . . St Leger
DONOUGHMORE . . . Hely-Hutchinson
DOWNE . . . Dawnay
DOWNSHIRE . . . Hill
DROGHEDA . . . Moore
DUCIE . . . Moreton
DUDLEY, Baroness . . . Hamilton, Wallace
DUDLEY, Earl of . . . Ward
DUFFERIN AND CLANEBOYE . . . Blackwood
DULVERTON . . . Wills
DUNALLEY . . . Prittie
DUNBOYNE . . . Butler
DUNDEE . . . Scrymgeour, Scrymgeour(-)Wedderburn
DUNDONALD . . . Cochrane
DUNLEATH . . . Mulholland
DUNMORE . . . Murray
DUNRAVEN AND MOUNT-EARL . . . Wyndham-Quin
DUNROSSIL . . . Morrison
DUNSANY . . . Plunkett
DURHAM . . . Lambton
DYNEVOR . . . Rhys
DYSART . . . Grant of Rothiemurchus, Greaves,Tollemache
EBURY . . . Grosvenor
EDINBURGH . . . Mountbatten
EFFINGHAM . . . Howard

Title	Surname
EGLINTON and WINTON	Montgomerie
EGMONT	Perceval
EGREMONT, LECONFIELD and	Wyndham
ELDON	Scott
ELGIN and KINCARDINE	Bruce
ELIBANK	Erskine-Murray
ELLENBOROUGH	Law
ELY	Tottenham
ENNISKILLEN	Cole
ERNE	Crichton
ERROLL	Hay
ESHER	Brett
ESSEX	Capell
EXETER	Cecil, Joicey-Cecil
EXMOUTH	Pellew
FAIRHAVEN	Broughton
FALKLAND	Cary
FALMOUTH	Boscawen
FANSHAWE OF RICHMOND	Royle
FARINGDON	Henderson
FARNHAM	Maxwell
FERMOY	Burke-Roche, Roche
FERRERS	Shirley
FEVERSHAM	Duncombe, Duncombe-Anderson
FIFE	Carnegie
FITZWALTER	Plumptre
FORESTER	Weld(-)Forester
FORRES	Williamson
FORTEVIOT	Dewar
GAINFORD	Pease
GAINSBOROUGH	Noel
GALLOWAY	Stewart
GALWAY	Monckton, Monckton-Arundell
GARVAGH	Canning
GERAINT	Howells
GISBOROUGH	Chaloner
GLADWYN	Jebb
GLANUSK	Bailey
GLASGOW	Boyle
GLENAMARA	Short
GLENARTHUR	Arthur
GLENCONNER	Tennant
GLENDEVON	Hope
GLENDYNE	Nivison
GLENTORAN	Dixon
GLOUCESTER	Windsor
GORELL	Barnes
GORMANSTON	Preston
GORT	Vereker
GOSFORD	Acheson
GOWRIE	Hore-Ruthven
GRAFTON	FitzRoy
GRANARD	Forbes
GRANTCHESTER	Suenson-Taylor
GRANTLEY	Norton
GRANVILLE	Leveson-Gower
GRAY	Campbell-Gray
GREY (of Codnor)	Cornwall-Legh
GRIMTHORPE	Beckett
GUILFORD	North
HADDINGTON	Baillie-Hamilton
HAILSHAM OF ST MARYLEBONE	Hogg
HALIFAX	Meynell, Wood
HALSBURY	Giffard
HAMBLEDEN	Smith
HAMILTON and BRANDON	Douglas-Hamilton
HAMPDEN	Brand
HAMPTON	Pakington
HANNINGFIELD	White
HANWORTH	Pollock
HARBERTON	Pomeroy
HARDWICKE	Yorke
HAREWOOD	Lascelles
HARLECH	Ormsby-Gore
HARRINGTON	Stanhope
HARROWBY	Dudley-Ryder, Ryder
HARTWELL	Berry
HASTINGS	Astley
HATHERTON	Littleton
HAWARDEN	Maude
HAYTER	Chubb
HEADFORT	Taylour
HEMINGFORD	Herbert
HEMPHILL	Martyn-Hemphill
HENLEY	Eden
HENNIKER	Henniker-Major
HEREFORD	Devereux
HERRIES OF TERREGLES	Cowdrey
HERTFORD	Seymour
HESKETH	Fermor-Hesketh
HEYTESBURY	Holmes à Court
HILL	Clegg-Hill
HINDLIP	Allsopp
HOLDERNESS	Wood
HOLLENDEN	Hope-Morley
HOLM PATRICK	Hamilton
HOME	Douglas-Home
HOTHFIELD	Tufton
HOWARD DE WALDEN	Scott-Ellis
HOWE	Curzon-Howe-Herrick, Curzon-Howe, Curzon, Penn-Curzon
HOWICK OF GLENDALE	Baring
HUNTINGDON	Hastings, Hastings-Bass
HUNTINGFIELD	Vanneck
HUNTLY	Gordon
HYLTON	Jolliffe
IDDESLEIGH	Northcote
ILCHESTER	Fox-Strangways
INCHCAPE	Mackay
INCHIQUIN	O'Brien
INCHYRA	Hoyer(-)Millar, Millar
INGLEBY	Peake
INGLEWOOD	Fletcher-Vane
INGROW	Taylor
INVERFORTH	Weir
IVEAGH	Guinness
JAMES OF HOLLAND PARK	James, White
JERSEY	Child(-)Villiers
KELVEDON	Channon
KEMSLEY	Berry
KENILWORTH	Siddeley
KENNET	Young
KENSINGTON	Edwardes
KENSWOOD	Whitfield
KENT	Windsor
KENYON	Kenyon, Tyrell-Kenyon
KILBRACKEN	Godley
KILLANIN	Morris
KILLEARN	Lampson
KILMAINE	Browne
KILMARNOCK	Boyd
KILMOREY	Needham
KIMBERLEY	Wodehouse
KINGSALE	De Courcy
KINGSDOWN	Leigh-Pemberton
KINGSTON	King-Tenison
KINLOSS	Freeman-Grenville
KINNOULL	Hay
KINROSS	Balfour
KINTORE	Keith
KIRKHILL	Smith
KNUTSFORD	Holland-Hibbert
LANESBOROUGH	Butler
LANGFORD	Rowley-Conwy
LANSDOWNE	FitzMaurice, Mercer-Nairne, Mercer-Nairne-Petty-FitzMaurice, Petty-FitzMaurice
LATYMER	Money-Coutts
LAUDERDALE	Heriot-Maitland, Maitland, Maitland-Heriot, Maitland-Makgill-Crichton, Makgill-Crichton-Maitland
LEICESTER	Coke
LEIGHTON OF ST MELLONS	Seager
LEINSTER	FitzGerald
LEVEN AND MELVILLE	Leslie Melville
LEVERHULME	Lever
LICHFIELD	Anson
LIFFORD	Hewitt
LILFORD	Powys
LIMERICK	Pery
LINCOLN	Fiennes-Clinton
LINDSAY	Lindesay-Bethune
LINDSEY and ABINGDON	Bertie
LINLITHGOW	Hope
LISBURNE	Vaughan
LISLE	Lysaght
LISTOWEL	Hare
LIVERPOOL	Foljambe
LLOYD GEORGE OF DWYFOR	Lloyd George
LOCKWOOD	Hall
LONDESBOROUGH	Denison
LONDONDERRY	Vane-Tempest-Stewart
LONGFORD	Pakenham
LONSDALE	Lowther
LOTHIAN	Kerr
LOUDOUN	Abney-Hastings
LOUTH	Plunkett
LOVAT	Fraser
LOVELACE	King
LUCAN	Bingham
LUCAS OF CRUDWELL	Palmer
LUKE	Lawson(-)Johnston
LYVEDEN	Vernon
MACCLESFIELD	Parker, Parker-Bowles
MALMESBURY	Harris
MALVERN	Huggins
MANCHESTER	Montagu
MANSFIELD and MANSFIELD	Murray
MANTON	Watson
MAR	Of Mar
MAR and KELLIE	Erskine
MARCHAMLEY	Whiteley
MARCHWOOD	Penny
MARGADALE	Morrison
MARLBOROUGH	Churchill, Spencer-Churchill
MARLESFORD	Schreiber
MARTONMERE	Robinson
MASSEREENE and FERRARD	Johnston, Skeffington, Vere Laurie, Willis
MAYO	Bourke
MEATH	Brabazon
MELCHETT	Mond
MELVILLE	Dundas
MERRIVALE	Duke
MERSEY	Bigham
MERTHYR	Lewis
MEXBOROUGH	Savile
MIDDLETON	Willoughby
MIDLETON	Brodrick
MILFORD	Philipps
MILFORD HAVEN	Mountbatten
MILVERTON	Richards
MINTO	Elliot-Murray-Kynynmound
MONK BRETTON	Dodson
MONKSWELL	Collier
MONTAGU OF BEAULIEU	Douglas-Scott-Montagu
MONTEAGLE OF BRANDON	Spring Rice
MONTROSE	Graham
MORAN	Wilson
MORAY	Stuart
MORLEY	Parker
MORTON	Douglas
MOSTYN	Lloyd-Mostyn, Mostyn
MOTTISTONE	Seely
MOUNTBATTEN OF BURMA	Knatchbull
MOUNT EDGCUMBE	Edgcumbe
MOUNTEVANS	Evans
MOUNTGARRET	Butler
MOWBRAY, SEGRAVE and STOURTON	Stourton
MOYNE	Guinness
MOYOLA	Chichester-Clark
MUNSTER	Fitz(-)Clarence
MUSKERRY	Deane
NAIRNE	Bigham
NAPIER and ETTRICK	Napier
NASEBY	Morris
NETHERTHORPE	Turner
NEWBOROUGH	Wynn
NEWBURGH	Rospigliosi
NEWTON	Legh
NORBURY	Graham-Toler
NORFOLK	Fitzalan(-)Howard, Howard, Howard-Sneyd
NORMANBY	Phipps
NORMANTON	Agar
NORTHAMPTON	Compton
NORTHBOURNE	James
NORTHBROOK	Baring
NORTHESK	Carnegie
NORTHFIELD	Chapman
NORTHUMBERLAND	Heber-Percy, Percy
NORTON	Adderley
NORWICH	Cooper
NUNBURNHOLME	Wilson
OAKSEY, TREVETHIN and	Lawrence
O'CATHAIN	Bishop

Title	Surname
OGMORE	Rees-Williams
O'HAGAN	Strachey
ORANMORE AND BROWNE	Browne
ORKNEY	Fitz-Maurice, St John
OXFORD AND ASQUITH	Asquith
OXFUIRD	Makgill
PARMOOR	Cripps
PEMBROKE and MONTGOMERY	Herbert
PENDER	Denison-Pender
PENRHYN	Douglas-Pennant
PERTH	Drummond
PLYMOUTH	Windsor-Clive
POLTIMORE	Bampfylde
POLWARTH	Hepburne-Scott
PORTARLINGTON	Dawson-Damer
PORTLAND	Bentinck
PORTSMOUTH	Wallop
POWERSCOURT	Wingfield, Wingfield-Stratford, Wingfield-Stratford-Johnstone
POWIS	Herbert
QUEENSBERRY	Douglas
RADNOR	Pleydell-Bouverie
RAGLAN	Somerset
RANFURLY	Knox
RANKEILLOUR	Hope
RATHCAVAN	O'Neill
RATHCREEDAN	Norton
RATHDONNELL	McClintock-Bunbury
RAVENSDALE	Mosley
RAVENSWORTH	Liddell
RAYLEIGH	Strutt
READING	Rufus(-)Isaacs
REAY	Mackay
REDESDALE	Freeman-Mitford, Mitford
RENDLESHAM	Thellusson
RENNELL	Rodd
REVELSTOKE	Baring
RICHMOND and GORDON	Gordon(-)Lennox
RIVERDALE	Balfour
ROBOROUGH	Lopes
ROCHDALE	Kemp
ROCHESTER	Lamb
ROCKLEY	Cecil
RODEN	Jocelyn
ROMNEY	Bullock-Marsham, Field-Marsham, Marsham, Morris-Marsham
ROSEBERY	Primrose
ROSSE	Parsons
ROSSLYN	St Clair-Erskine
ROSSMORE	Westenra
ROTHERMERE	Harmsworth
ROTHERWICK	Cayzer
ROTHES	Leslie
ROWALLAN	Corbett
ROXBURGHE	Innes-Ker
ROYAL FAMILY	Mountbatten-Windsor, Windsor
RUGBY	Maffey
RUSSELL-JOHNSTON	Johnston
RUTLAND	Manners, Manners-Sutton
RYDER OF WARSAW	Cheshire
SACKVILLE	Sackville-West
SAINT ALBANS	Beauclerk
SAINT ALDWYN	Hicks-Beach
SAINT DAVIDS	Philipps
SAINT GERMANS	Eliot
SAINT HELENS	Hughes-Young
ST JOHN OF FAWSLEY	St John-Stevas
SAINT LEVAN	St Aubyn
SAINT OSWALD	Winn
SAINT VINCENT	Jervis, Parker-Jervis
SALISBURY	Cecil, Gascoyne-Cecil
SALTOUN	Fraser
SANDFORD	Edmondson
SANDHURST	Mansfield
SANDWICH	Montagu
SANDYS	Hill
SAVILE	Lumley-Savile
SAYE AND SELE	Fiennes
SCARBROUGH	Lumley
SCARSDALE	Curzon
SEAFIELD	Ogilvie-Grant
SELBORNE	Palmer
SELBY	Gully
SELKIRK	Douglas-Hamilton
SELKIRK OF DOUGLAS	Douglas-Hamilton
SELSDON	Mitchell-Thomson
SHAFTESBURY	Ashley-Cooper
SHANNON	Boyle
SHARPLES	Swan
SHERFIELD	Makins
SHREWSBURY and WATERFORD	Chetwynd-Talbot, Talbot, Talbot-Ponsonby
SHUTTLEWORTH	Kay-Shuttleworth
SIDMOUTH	Addington
SILSOE	Eve, Trustram Eve
SINCLAIR	St Clair
SKELMERSDALE	Bootle-Wilbraham
SLIGO	Browne
SNOWDON	Armstrong-Jones
SOMERLEYTON	Crossley
SOMERS	Cocks, Somers-Cocks
SOMERSET	Seymour
SOULBURY	Ramsbotham
SOUTHAMPTON	FitzRoy
STAFFORD	FitzHerbert
STAIR	Dalrymple
STANSGATE	Benn, Wedgwood Benn
STEWARTBY	Stewart
STOCKTON	Macmillan
STRABOLGI	Kenworthy
STRADBROKE	Rous
STRAFFORD	Byng
STRANGE	Drummond of Megginch
STRATHALMOND	Fraser
STRATHCARRON	Macpherson
STRATHCLYDE	Galbraith
STRATHCONA AND MOUNT ROYAL	Howard
STRATHEDEN and CAMPBELL	Campbell
STRATHMORE AND KINGHORNE	Bowes(-)Lyon
STRATHSPEY	Grant of Grant
SUDELEY	Hanbury-Tracy
SUFFIELD	Harbord-Hamond
SUFFOLK and BERKSHIRE	Howard
SUTHERLAND, Countess of	Janson
SUTHERLAND, Duke of	Egerton, Leveson-Gower
SWANSEA	Vivian
SWAYTHLING	Montagu
SWINFEN	Eady
SWINTON	Cunliffe-Lister
SYSONBY	Ponsonby
TALBOT OF MALAHIDE	Arundell, Talbot
TANKERVILLE	Bennet
TANLAW	Mackay
TEMPLE OF STOWE	Gore-Langton, Temple-Gore-Langton
TENBY	Lloyd George
TERRINGTON	Woodhouse
TEVIOT	Kerr
TEYNHAM	Roper-Curzon
THURLOW	Hovell-Thurlow-Cumming-Bruce
THURSO	Sinclair
TORPHICHEN	Sandilands
TORRINGTON	Byng
TREVOR	Hill-Trevor
TRIMLESTOWN	Barnewall
TRUMPINGTON	Barker
TWEEDDALE	Hay
TWEEDSMUIR	Buchan
ULLSWATER	Lowther
VALENTIA	Annesley
VAUX OF HARROWDEN	Gilbey
VENTRY	Daubeny De Moleyns
VERULAM	Grimston
WAKEHURST	Loder
WALSINGHAM	De Grey
WARDINGTON	Pease
WARWICK, BROOKE and	Greville
WATERFORD	Beresford, De la Poer Beresford
WATERPARK	Cavendish
WAVERLEY	Anderson
WELLINGTON	Wellesley
WEMYSS and MARCH	Charteris
WESTBURY	Bethell
WESTMEATH	Nugent
WESTMINSTER	Grosvenor
WESTMORLAND	Fane
WHADDON	Page
WHARNCLIFFE	Montagu(-)Stuart(-)Wortley
WHARTON	Robertson
WILLOUGHBY DE BROKE	Verney
WILLOUGHBY DE ERESBY	Heathcote-Drummond-Willoughby
WILTON	Egerton
WIMBORNE	Guest
WINCHESTER	Paulet
WINCHILSEA and NOTTINGHAM	Finch(-)Hatton
WINDLESHAM	Hennessy
WINTERTON	Turnour
WOLVERTON	Glyn
WOOLTON	Marquis
WRAXALL	Gibbs
WRENBURY	Buckley
WYFOLD	Hermon-Hodge
WYNFORD	Best
YARBOROUGH	Pelham
ZETLAND	Dundas
ZOUCHE	Frankland

(II) In Alphabetical Order of Surname

Surname	Title
Abney-Hastings	LOUDOUN
Acheson	GOSFORD
Adderley	NORTON
Addington	SIDMOUTH
Agar	NORMANTON
Akers-Douglas	CHILSTON
Aitken	BEAVERBROOK
Alexander	CALEDON
Allen	CROHAM
Allsopp	HINDLIP
Anderson	WAVERLEY
Annesley	VALENTIA
Anson	LICHFIELD
Armstrong-Jones	SNOWDON
Arthur	GLENARTHUR
Arundell	TALBOT OF MALAHIDE
Ashley-Cooper	SHAFTESBURY
Asquith	OXFORD AND ASQUITH
Assheton	CLITHEROE
Astley	HASTINGS
Aubrey-Fletcher	BRAYE
Bailey	GLANUSK
Baillie-Hamilton	HADDINGTON
Baillie	BURTON
Balfour	KINROSS, RIVERDALE
Bampfylde	POLTIMORE
Baring	ASHBURTON, CROMER, HOWICK OF GLENDALE, NORTHBROOK, REVELSTOKE
Barker	TRUMPINGTON
Barnes	GORELL
Barnewall	TRIMLESTOWN
Bathurst	BLEDISLOE
Beauclerk	SAINT ALBANS
Beaumont	ALLENDALE
Beckett	GRIMTHORPE
Bellow	BELLWIN
Benn	STANSGATE
Bennet	TANKERVILLE
Bentinck	PORTLAND
Beresford	DECIES, WATERFORD
Berry	CAMROSE, HARTWELL, KEMSLEY
Bertie	LINDSEY and ABINGDON
Best	WYNFORD
Bethell	WESTBURY
Bewicke-Copley	CROMWELL

Johnston . . . MASSEREENE and FERRARD, RUSSELL-JOHNSTON
Johnstone . . . ANNANDALE AND HARTFELL
Joicey-Cecil . . . EXETER
Jolliffe . . . HYLTON
Joynson-Hicks . . . BRENTFORD
Kay-Shuttleworth . . . SHUTTLEWORTH
Kearley . . . DEVONPORT
Keith . . . KINTORE
Kemp . . . ROCHDALE
Kennedy . . . AILSA
Kenworthy . . . STRABOLGI
Keppel . . . ALBEMARLE
Kerr . . . LOTHIAN, TEVIOT
King . . . LOVELACE
King-Tenison . . . KINGSTON
Kirkham . . . BERNERS
Knatchbull . . . BRABOURNE, MOUNTBATTEN OF BURMA
Knox . . . RANFURLY
Lamb . . . ROCHESTER
Lambart . . . CAVAN
Lambton . . . DURHAM
Lampson . . . KILLEARN
Lascelles . . . HAREWOOD
Law . . . COLERAINE, ELLENBOROUGH
Lawrence . . . OAKSEY, TREVETHIN and
Lawson . . . BURNHAM
Lawson(-)Johnston . . . LUKE
Le Poer Trench . . . CLANCARTY
Legge . . . DARTMOUTH
Legh . . . NEWTON
Leigh-Pemberton . . . KINGSDOWN
Leith . . . BURGH
Lennox-Boyd . . . BOYD OF MERTON
Leslie . . . ROTHES
Leslie Melville . . . LEVEN and MELVILLE
Lever . . . LEVERHULME
Leveson-Gower . . . GRANVILLE, SUTHERLAND, Duke of
Lewis . . . MERTHYR
Liddell . . . RAVENSWORTH
Lindsay . . . CRAWFORD AND LINDSAY
Lindesay-Bethune . . . LINDSAY
Littleton . . . HATHERTON
Lloyd George . . . LLOYD GEORGE OF DWYFOR, TENBY
Lloyd-Mostyn . . . MOSTYN
Loder . . . WAKEHURST
Lopes . . . ROBOROUGH
Low . . . ALDINGTON
Lowry-Corry . . . BELMORE
Lowther . . . LONSDALE, ULLSWATER
Lubbock . . . AVEBURY
Lumley . . . SCARBROUGH
Lumley-Savile . . . SAVILE
Lyon-Dalberg-Acton . . . ACTON
Lysaght . . . LISLE
Lyttelton . . . CHANDOS, COBHAM
Lytton Cobbold . . . COBBOLD
Mackay . . . INCHCAPE, REAY, TANLAW
Mackenzie . . . CROMARTIE
Macmillan . . . STOCKTON
Macpherson . . . STRATHCARRON
Maffey . . . RUGBY
Maitland . . . LAUDERDALE
Maitland-Biddulph . . . BIDDULPH
Maitland-Heriot . . . LAUDERDALE
Maitland-Makgill-Crichton . . . LAUDERDALE
Makgill . . . OXFUIRD
Makgill-Crichton-Maitland . . . LAUDERDALE
Makins . . . SHERFIELD
Manners . . . RUTLAND
Manners-Sutton . . . RUTLAND
Manningham-Buller . . . DILHORNE
Mansfield . . . SANDHURST
Marquis . . . WOOLTON
Marsham . . . ROMNEY
Martyn-Hemphill . . . HEMPHILL
Maude . . . HAWARDEN
Maxwell . . . DE ROS, FARNHAM
McClintock-Bunbury . . . RATHDONNELL
McDonnell . . . ANTRIM
McDowell . . . DEAN OF THORNTON-LE-FYLDE
McLaren . . . ABERCONWAY
Meade . . . CLANWILLIAM
Mercer-Nairne . . . LANSDOWNE
Mercer-Nairne-Petty-FitzMaurice . . . LANSDOWNE
Meynell . . . HALIFAX
Millar . . . INCHYRA
Mitchell-Thomson . . . SELSDON
Mitford . . . REDESDALE
Monckton . . . GALWAY
Monckton-Arundell . . . GALWAY
Mond . . . MELCHETT
Money-Coutts . . . LATYMER
Montagu . . . AMWELL, MANCHESTER, SANDWICH, SWAYTHLING
Montagu(-)Douglas(-)Scott . . . BUCCLEUCH and QUEENSBERRY
Montagu(-)Stuart(-)Wortley . . . WHARNCLIFFE
Montgomerie . . . EGLINTON and WINTON
Moore-Brabazon . . . BRABAZON OF TARA
Moore . . . DROGHEDA
Moreton . . . DUCIE
Morris . . . KILLANIN, NASEBY
Morris-Marsham . . . ROMNEY
Morrison . . . DUNROSSIL, MARGADALE
Mosley . . . RAVENSDALE
Mountbatten-Windsor . . . ROYAL FAMILY
Mountbatten . . . EDINBURGH, MILFORD HAVEN
Muff . . . CALVERLEY
Mulholland . . . DUNLEATH
Murray . . . ATHOLL, DUNMORE, MANSFIELD AND MANSFIELD
Nall-Cain . . . BROCKET
Napier . . . NAPIER and ETTRICK
Needham . . . KILMOREY
Nevill . . . ABERGAVENNY
Neville . . . BRAYBROOKE
Nicolson . . . CARNOCK
Nivison . . . GLENDYNE
Noel . . . GAINSBOROUGH
North . . . GUILFORD
Northcote . . . IDDESLEIGH
Norton . . . GRANTLEY, RATHCREEDAN
Nugent . . . WESTMEATH
O'Brien . . . INCHIQUIN
Of Mar . . . MAR
Ogilvie-Grant . . . SEAFIELD
Ogilvy . . . AIRLIE
O'Neill . . . RATHCAVAN
Orde-Powlett . . . BOLTON
Ormsby-Gore . . . HARLECH
Page . . . WHADDON
Paget . . . ANGLESEY
Pakenham . . . LONGFORD
Pakington . . . HAMPTON
Palmer . . . LUCAS OF CRUDWELL, SELBORNE
Parker . . . MACCLESFIELD, MORLEY
Parker-Bowles . . . MACCLESFIELD
Parker-Jervis . . . SAINT VINCENT
Parnell . . . CONGLETON
Parsons . . . ROSSE
Paulet . . . WINCHESTER
Peake . . . INGLEBY
Pearson . . . COWDRAY
Pease . . . GAINFORD, WARDINGTON
Pelham . . . CHICHESTER, YARBOROUGH
Pellew . . . EXMOUTH
Penn-Curzon . . . HOWE
Penny . . . MARCHWOOD
Pepys . . . COTTENHAM
Perceval . . . EGMONT
Percy . . . NORTHUMBERLAND
Pery . . . LIMERICK
Petty-FitzMaurice . . . LANSDOWNE
Philipps . . . MILFORD, SAINT DAVIDS
Phipps . . . NORMANBY
Pleydell-Bouverie . . . RADNOR
Plumptre . . . FitzWALTER
Plunkett . . . DUNSANY, LOUTH
Pollock . . . BERNERS, HANWORTH
Pomeroy . . . HARBERTON
Ponsonby . . . BESSBOROUGH, DE MAULEY, SYSONBY
Powys . . . LILFORD
Pratt . . . CAMDEN
Preston . . . GORMANSTON
Primrose . . . ROSEBERY
Prittie . . . DUNALLEY
Ramsay . . . DALHOUSIE
Ramsbotham . . . SOULBURY
Rees-Williams . . . OGMORE
Rhys . . . DYNEVOR
Richards . . . MILVERTON
Roberts . . . CLWYD
Robertson . . . WHARTON
Robinson . . . MARTONMERE
Roche . . . FERMOY
Rodd . . . RENNELL
Roper-Curzon . . . TEYNHAM
Rospigliosi . . . NEWBURGH
Rous . . . STRADBROKE
Rowley-Conwy . . . LANGFORD
Royle . . . FANSHAWE OF RICHMOND
Rufus(-)Isaacs . . . READING
Russell . . . AMPTHILL, BEDFORD, DE CLIFFORD
Ryder . . . HARROWBY
Sackville . . . DE LA WARR
Sackville-West . . . SACKVILLE
St Aubyn . . . SAINT LEVAN
St Clair . . . SINCLAIR
St Clair Erskine . . . ROSSLYN
St John . . . BOLINGBROKE and SAINT JOHN, ORKNEY
St John-Stevas . . . ST JOHN OF FAWSLEY
St Leger . . . DONERAILE
Samuel . . . BEARSTED
Sandilands . . . TORPHICHEN
Saumarez . . . DE SAUMAREZ
Savile . . . MEXBOROUGH
Scarlett . . . ABINGER
Schreiber . . . MARLESFORD
Sclater-Booth . . . BASING
Scott . . . ELDON
Scott-Ellis . . . HOWARD DE WALDEN
Scrymgeour . . . DUNDEE
Scrymgeour-Wedderburn . . . DUNDEE
Seager . . . LEIGHTON OF ST MELLONS
Seely . . . MOTTISTONE
Seymour . . . HERTFORD, SOMERSET
Shaw . . . CRAIGMYLE
Shirley . . . FERRERS
Short . . . GLENAMARA
Siddeley . . . KENILWORTH
Sidney . . . DE L'ISLE
Sinclair . . . CAITHNESS, THURSO
Skeffington . . . MASSEREENE and FERRARD
Smith . . . BICESTER, COLWYN, HAMBLEDEN, KIRKHILL
Somers-Cocks . . . SOMERS
Somerset . . . BEAUFORT, RAGLAN
Spencer . . . CHURCHILL
Spencer-Churchill . . . MARLBOROUGH
Spring Rice . . . MONTEAGLE OF BRANDON
Stanhope . . . HARRINGTON
Stanley . . . DERBY
Stapleton-Cotton . . . COMBERMERE
Stewart . . . GALLOWAY, STEWARTBY
Stonor . . . CAMOYS
Stopford . . . COURTOWN
Stopford-Sackville . . . COURTOWN
Stourton . . . MOWBRAY, SEGRAVE and STOURTON
Strachey . . . O'HAGAN, TALBOT OF MALAHIDE
Strutt . . . BELPER, RAYLEIGH
Stuart . . . CASTLE STEWART, MORAY
Suenson-Taylor . . . GRANTCHESTER
Swan . . . SHARPLES
Talbot . . . SHREWSBURY and WATERFORD, TALBOT OF MALAHIDE
Talbot-Ponsonby . . . SHREWSBURY and WATERFORD
Taylor . . . INGROW
Taylour . . . HEADFORT
Temple-Gore-Langton . . . TEMPLE OF STOWE
Tennant . . . GLENCONNER
Thellusson . . . RENDLESHAM
Thesiger . . . CHELMSFORD
Thynn . . . BATH
Thynne . . . BATH
Tollemache . . . DYSART
Tottenham . . . ELY
Trench . . . ASHTOWN
Trevor-Roper . . . DACRE OF GLANTON
Trustram Eve . . . SILSOE
Tufton . . . HOTHFIELD
Turner . . . NETHERTHORPE
Turnour . . . WINTERTON
Tyrell-Kenyon . . . KENYON

Vanden-Bempde-Johnstone . . . . . DERWENT
Vane . . . . BARNARD
Vane-Tempest-Stewart . . . . LONDONDERRY
Vanneck . . . . HUNTINGFIELD
Vaughan . . . . LISBURNE
Vere Laurie . . . MASSEREENE and FERRARD
Vereker . . . . GORT
Verney . . . . . . WILLOUGHBY DE BROKE
Vernon . . . . LYVEDEN
Vesey . . . . DE VESCI
Villiers . . . . CLARENDON
Vivian . . . . SWANSEA
Wallace . . . . DUDLEY, Baroness
Wallop . . . . PORTSMOUTH
Ward . . . . BANGOR, DUDLEY
Warrender . . . . BRUNTISFIELD
Watson . . . . MANTON
Wedgwood Benn . . . . STANSGATE
Weir . . . . INVERFORTH
Weld(-)Forester . . . . FORESTER
Wellesley . . . . . . COWLEY, WELLINGTON
Westenra . . . . ROSSMORE
White . . . . . . ANNALY, HANNINGFIELD
JAMES OF HOLLAND PARK
Whiteley . . . . MARCHAMLEY
Whitfield . . . . KENSWOOD
Williamson . . . . FORRES
Willis . . . . . MASSEREENE and FERRARD
Willoughby . . . . MIDDLETON
Wills . . . . DULVERTON
Wilson . . . . . MORAN, NUNBURNHOLME
Windsor . . . . ROYAL FAMILY
(EDINBURGH, GLOUCESTER, KENT, WALES)
Windsor-Clive . . . . PLYMOUTH
Wingfield . . . . POWERSCOURT
Wingfield-Stratford . . . . . POWERSCOURT
Wingfield-Stratford-Johnstone . . . . POWERSCOURT
Winn . . . . SAINT OSWALD
Wodehouse . . . . KIMBERLEY
Wood . . . . HALIFAX, HOLDERNESS
Woodhouse . . . . TERRINGTON
Wyndham . . . EGREMONT, LECONFIELD and
Wyndham-Quin . . . . . . DUNRAVEN AND MOUNT-EARL
Wynn . . . . NEWBOROUGH
Yarde-Buller . . . . CHURSTON
Yerburgh . . . . ALVINGHAM
Yorke . . . . HARDWICKE
Young . . . . KENNET

THE ROYAL FAMILY

Note: The Order of Succession to the Crown is: (1) The Prince of Wales, (2) Prince William, (3) Prince Harry, (4) The Duke of York, (5) Princess Beatrice, (6) Princess Eugenie, (7) Prince Edward, (8) The Princess Royal, (9) Peter Phillips, (10) Zara Phillips, (11) Princess Margaret, (12) Viscount Linley, (13) Lady Sarah Chatto, (14) Samuel Chatto, (15) The Duke of Gloucester, (16) Earl of Ulster, (17) Lady Davina Windsor, (18) Lady Rose Windsor, (19) The Duke of Kent, (20) Lord Downpatrick, (21) Lady Marina-Charlotte Windsor, (22) Lady Amelia Windsor, (23) Lord Nicholas Windsor, (24) Lady Helen Taylor, (25) Columbus Taylor, (26) Cassius Taylor, (27) Lord Frederick Windsor, (28) Lady Ella Windsor, (29) Princess Alexandra, (30) James Ogilvy, (31) Alexander Ogilvy, (32) Flora Ogilvy, (33) Mrs Marina Mowatt, (34) Christian Mowatt, (35) Zenouska Mowatt.

Prince Michael of Kent is excluded as having married a Catholic, so too the Earl of St Andrews, though not their children. (The Duchess of Kent's conversion to Catholicism, being post-nuptial, has not affected her husband's right of succession.) But note that both Prince Michael and the Earl of St Andrews are in remainder to the Dukedom of Kent and its associated titles.

The Order of Succession therefore does not include all members of the Royal Family. As well as the persons already mentioned above as being excluded, neither the Queen Mother nor the Duke of Edinburgh features in it — at any rate not so high up. Accordingly the members of the Royal Family given separate entries in this section are arranged in a slightly different order which combines nearness to the throne and possession of a title of honour. It is as follows: (1) The Queen, (2) The Queen Mother, (3) The Duke of Edinburgh, (4) The Prince of Wales, (5) The Duke of York, (6) Prince Edward, (7) The Princess Royal, (8) The Duke of Gloucester, (9) The Duke of Kent.

Shortage of space has made it impracticable to list all the organisations of which royal personages are patrons (650 for the Queen, 350 for the Duke of Edinburgh, 55 for Princess Margaret, 60 for the Duke of York, 20 for Prince Edward, 140 for the Princess Royal, 70 for the Duke of Gloucester and 80 for the Duke of Kent). Instead a selection has been made of those with which the royal personage in question is most prominently associated through frequent mentions in the Court Circular.

HM THE QUEEN

Crown: A circle of gold, issuing therefrom four crosses patées and four fleurs-de-lys arranged alternately, from the crosses patées arise two golden arches ornamented with pearls, crossing at the top under a mound also gold, the whole enriched with precious stones. The cap is of crimson velvet, doubled ermine. **Royal Arms:** Quarterly, 1st and 4th, gules three lions passant guardant in pale or (for ENGLAND); 2nd, or a lion rampant within a double tressure flory counterflory gules (for SCOTLAND); 3rd, azure a harp or stringed argent (for IRELAND), the whole encircled with the Garter. **Crests:** 1. Upon the royal helmet the Royal crown proper, thereon statant guardant or a lion imperially crowned also proper (for ENGLAND), 2. On the Crown proper a lion sejant affronté gules crowned or, holding in the dexter paw a sword and in the sinister a sceptre erect also proper (for SCOTLAND), 3. On a wreath or and azure a tower triple- towered of the first, from the portal a hart springing argent, attired and hoofed gold (for IRELAND). **Supporters:** Dexter, a lion rampant guardant or, crowned as the crest; sinister, a unicorn argent, armed, crined and unguled or, gorged with a coronet composed of crosses patées and fleurs-de-lys, a chain affixed thereto, passing between the forelegs and reflexed over the back of the last. **Motto:** *Dieu et mon droit* ('God and my right'). **Badges:** 1. The red and white rose united, slipped and leaved proper (for ENGLAND), 2. A thistle, slipped and leaved proper (for SCOTLAND), 3. A shamrock leaf slipped vert, also a harp or stringed argent (for IRELAND), 4. The Rose of England, the Thistle of Scotland and the Shamrock of Ireland engrafted on the same stem proper, and an escutcheon charged as the Union Flag (for THE UNITED KINGDOM) (all the foregoing ensigned with the Royal Crown), 5. Upon a mount vert a dragon passant, wings elevated gules, and (Augmented Badge) within a circular riband argent fimbriated or, bearing the motto *'Y Ddraig goch Ddyry Cychwyn'* in letters vert and ensigned with a representation of the Crown proper, an escutcheon per fess argent and vert, thereon the Red Dragon passant (for WALES), 6. On a mount vert the Round Tower of Windsor Castle argent, mason sable, flying thereon the Royal Standard, the whole within two branches of oak fructed or and ensigned with the Royal Crown (for the Royal House of WINDSOR). In Scotland the Royal Arms depict the Lion of Scotland in the 1st and 4th quarters (as on the Great Seal of Scotland, Scottish official publications and the tabards of the Scottish Officers of Arms).

ELIZABETH II (styled till 26 March 1953 'By the Grace of God, of Great Britain, Ireland, and of the British Dominions beyond the Seas, Queen, Defender of the Faith' and thereafter [exclusive to the United Kingdom; other Commonwealth countries of which HM is sovereign use different forms] 'By the Grace of God, of the United Kingdom of Great Britain and Northern Ireland, and of her other Realms and Territories, Queen, Head of the Commonwealth, Defender of the Faith') (Elizabeth Alexandra Mary Windsor) [Her Majesty The Queen, Buckingham Palace, London SW1A 1AA; Windsor Castle, Berks SL4 1NJ; Balmoral Castle, Aberdeenshire AB35 5TB; Sandringham House, Norfolk PE35 6EN]; *b* 17 Bruton Street, London W1, 21 April 1926; *s f* 6 February 1952, proclaimed Queen 8 February 1952, crowned Westminster Abbey 2 June 1953; declared in Council 9 April 1952 that She and her children shall be styled and known as the House and Family of Windsor and 8 Feb 1960 that Her descendants other than those enjoying the style, title or attribute of HRH and the titular dignity of Prince or Princess and female descendants who marry and their descendants shall bear the name Mountbatten-Windsor; Ld High Adml UK; Col-in-Ch: Blues and Royals (RHG and 1st Dragoons), Calgary Highrs, Canadian Forces Mil Engrs Branch, Life Gds, Roy Scots Dragoon Gds (Carabiniers and Greys), Queen's Roy Lancers, Roy Tank Regt, RE, Gren Gds (Col 1942–52), Coldstream Gds, Scots Gds, Irish Gds, Welsh Gds, Roy Welch Fusiliers, Queen's Lancs Regt, Argyll and Sutherland Highrs (Princess Louise's), RGJ, Adj-Gen Corps, Roy Mercian and Lancastrian Yeo, Corps of RMP, King's Own Calgary Regt, Roy 22e Regt, Govr-Gen's Foot Gds, Canadian Gren Gds, Le Régiment de la Chaudière, Roy New Brunswick Regt, 48th Highrs of Canada, Argyll and Sutherland Highrs of Canada (Princess Louise's), Roy Australian Engrs, Royal Australian Inf Corps, Roy Australian Army Ordnance Corps, Roy Australian Army Nursing Corps, Roy NZ Engrs, Roy NZ Inf Regt, Roy NZ Army Ordnance Corps, Malawi Rifles, Roy Malta Artillery; Capt-Gen: RA, HAC, CCF, Roy Canadian Artillery, Roy Regt Australian Artillery, Roy NZ Artillery, Roy NZ Armoured Corps; Air-C-in-C: RAuxAF, RAF Regt, ROC, RCAFAux, Australian Citizen Air Force, Territorial Air Force NZ; Hon Air Cdre RAF Marham; Cmdt-in-C RAF Coll Cranwell; Hon Commr RCMP; Master Merchant Navy and Fishing Fleets; Head CD Corps; Sovereign all British Orders Knighthood, OM, Roy Order Victoria and Albert, Order Crown India, Order CH, DSO, ISO and OC; Sovereign Head: OStJ, OA, Queen's Serv Order NZ; Patron: BRC (and Pres), Grey Coat Hsp Westminster Tercentenary 1998, Guy's Hosp, Leonard Cheshire Fndn, RHS, Roy Norfolk Veterans' Assoc, St Loye's Coll Fndn Exeter, Scout Assoc, Shaftesbury Homes and 'Arethusa', SPCK, WRVS, YHA; Freeman Drapers' Co; Hon BMus Lond 1946, FRS 1947, Hon DCL Oxon 1948, Hon LLD: Edin, London 1951, Hon MusD Wales 1949, Hon FRCS and FRCOG 1951, Freedom: Drapers' Co, Roy Borough Windsor 1947, Burgess: Roy Burgh Stirling, Cities of London 1948, Cardiff 1948, Edinburgh and Belfast 1949; 1947: Memb Imp Order Crown India, LG, DGStJ, Order Elephant Denmark; 1948: Grand Cordon Order El Kemal Egypt, Grand Cross Or Cordon Legn Hon; Order Ojaswi Rajanya Nepal 1949; Grand Cross Order Netherlands Lion 1950; 1953: Order Seraphim Sweden, Gold Collar Order Manuel Amador Guerrero Panama, Chain Order El-Hussein Ibn Ali Jordan; 1954: Grand Collar Order Idris I Libya, Chain and Collar Order Seal Solomon Ethiopia; 1955: Grand Cross with Chain St Olav Norway, Grand Sash and Cross Three Orders of Christ, Aviz and Santiago Portugal; Grand Order Hashimi with Chain Iraq 1956; 1958: Chev with Grand Cross and Grand Cordon Order Merit Italy, Special Grand Cross with Star Order Merit Fedl Republic Germany; 1960: Grand Cross with Diamonds Order Peruvian Sun, Nishan-i-Pakistan, Grand Collar Order Liberator General San Martin Argentina, Order Roy House Chakri Thailand; 1961: Mahendra Chain Nepal, Grand Collar Order Independence Tunisia, Collar Order White Rose Finland, Grand Cross Nat Order Senegal, Grand Cordon Order Knighthood Pioneers Liberia, Grand Cross Nat Order Ivory Coast; 1962: Collar and Grand Cordon Order Chrysanthemum Japan, Grand Band Order Star Africa Liberia; 1963: Grand Cross Ordre de la Valeur Camerounaise, Grand Cordon Order Leopold Belgium, Grand Cross Order Redeemer Greece, Grand Cross with Chain Order Falcon Iceland; Chain of Honour Sudan 1964; Grand Collar Order Merit Chile 1965; Grand Cordon Austrian Order Merit 1966; Grand Collar Order Southern Cross Brazil 1968; 1969: Grand Cdr National Order The Niger Nigeria, Order Al Nahayyan 1st Cl Abu Dhabi, Grand Cross Equatorial Star Gabon; Order Supreme Sun Afghanistan 1971; 1972: Order Golden Lion House of Nassau Luxembourg, Order Gt Yugoslav Star, Darjah Utama Seri Mahkota Negara Malaysia, Order Temasek Singapore, Most Esteemed Family Order 1st Cl Darjah Kerabat Yan Amat Di-Homali Darjah Pertama Brunei, Distinguished Order Ghaazi Maldive Islands, Order Golden Heart Kenya; 1973: Grand Collar Nat Order Aztec Eagle Mexico, Grand Cordon Nat Order Leopard Zaire; 1974: Star Indonesia 1st Cl, Grand Cdr Order Republic Gambia; 1975: Chain Order Seraphim Sweden, Collar Order Nile Egypt; 1978: Order Star Socialist Republic Romania 1st Cl, Gt Collar Order S Tiago da Espada Portugal; 1979: Necklace Mubarak Al Kabir Kuwait, Order Khalifa Necklace Bahrain, Collar Order King Abdul Aziz Saudi Arabia, Collar Independence Qatar, Order Oman 1st Cl, Order Lion Malawi 1st Cl, Presidential Order Botswana, Collar Grand Cordon Order Knighthood Pioneers Liberia; 1980: Grand Cordon Order Republic Tunisia, Collier de la Classe Exceptionelle Order El Mohammedi Morocco; 1982: Order Al Said Oman, Order Solomon Islands 1st Cl; Sash and Badge Order Qeladet El Hussein Ibn Ali Jordan 1984; 1985: Award of Honour Dominica, Trinity Cross Medal Order of Trinity (TC) (Gold) Trinidad and Tobago; 1986: Collar Order of Carlos III Spain, Grand Order Mungunghwa Republic of Korea; Order Golden Fleece Spain 1988, 1989: Grand Star Nigeria, Chain of UAE; 1991: Grand Ribbon Order Merit Poland, Grand Cross Order Merit Hungary; 1992: Roy Family Order Sultan Brunei, Silver Jubilee Medal Brunei; 1993: Grand Collar Order Boyaca Colombia and Great Collar Military Order Tower and Sword S Africa; 1995: Order Mubarak al Kabeer Kuwait, Order Good Hope 1st Cl and Grand Cross (gold) S Africa; 1996: Order White Eagle Poland, Order White Lion Czech Republic; Order Merit Order of Grand Cross Peru 1998; *m* Westminster Abbey 20 Nov 1947 her cousin *HRH PRINCE PHILIP MOUNTBATTEN previously BATTENBERG (*see* EDINBURGH, D), s of HRH PRINCE ANDREW OF GREECE by Lady (Victoria) Alice Elizabeth Julia Marie Mountbatten, er dau of 1st Marquess of Milford Haven (*qv*), and has issue (who by letters patent 22 Oct 1948 take the style 'HRH' and titular dignity of Prince/Princess):

1 +CHARLES PHILIP ARTHUR GEORGE WINDSOR, PRINCE OF WALES (*qv*)

2 +ANDREW ALBERT CHRISTIAN EDWARD WINDSOR, 1st DUKE OF YORK (*qv*)

3 +EDWARD ANTONY RICHARD LOUIS (THE PRINCE EDWARD; *qv*)

1 +ANNE ELIZABETH ALICE LOUISE Windsor, THE PRINCESS ROYAL (*qv*)

Lineage of the House of Windsor: For lineage of earlier Houses, *see* previous edns.

GEORGE V 'By the Grace of God, of Great Britain, Ireland, and of the British Dominions beyond the Seas, King, Defender of the Faith, Emperor of India', GEORGE FREDERICK ERNEST ALBERT (probably) WIPPER (but possibly WETTIN) later WINDSOR (to which changed 1917 on the advice of officials, the dominant influence among whom was Lord (1st and last Baron) Stamfordham (*see* 1931 edn), despite the existence of (a) the Earldom of Windsor as one of the subsidiary titles of the Marquess of Bute (*qv*) and (b) the Viscountcy of Windsor and (c) Barony of Windsor, both subsidiary titles of the Earls of Plymouth (*qv*), whose family name had been Windsor till 1833, after which it became Windsor-Clive), previously of the House of Saxe-Coburg-Gotha but from 1917 of the House of Windsor, KG (1884), KT (1893), KP (1897), GCMG (1901, Grand Master 1905), GCSI (1905), GCIE (1905), GCVO (1897), ISO (1893), PC (GB 1894, I 1897), Roy Victorian Chain 1902; *b* Marlborough House, Pall Mall, London SW1, 3 June 1865 (*bapt* Windsor Castle 7 July 1865); *s* f 6 May 1910; RN: Cadet 1877, Midshipman 1880, Sub-Lt 1884, Lt 1885, Cdr 1891, Capt 1893, R-Adml 1901, V-Adml 1903, Adml 1907, Adml of the Fleet 1910, Adml Danish and Swedish Navies; Gen 1902, FM 1910, Personal ADC to TM QUEEN VICTORIA 1887–1901 and EDWARD VII 1901–10, Col-in-Ch: RM, Life Gds, RHG, 1st Roy Dragoons, 10th Roy Hus, Roy Regt Artillery, RE, Gren Gds, Coldstream Gds, Scots Gds, Irish Gds, Welsh Gds, King's Own Roy Regt, King's Regt, Roy Fus, Norfolk Regt, Roy Welch Fus, Black Watch, KRRC, Queen's Own Cameron Highrs, Roy Irish Fus, RTC, OTC, Duke of Lancaster's Own Yeo, Norfolk Yeo, Suffolk Yeo, 108th Field Bde, 8th Bn Hants Regt, Manchester Regt, W African Frontier Force, KAR, RFC and RAF (Ch RAF 1919) and (in the IA) Skinner's Horse, 8th King George's Own Light Cav, 18th King Edward's Own Cav, 5th King Edward's Own Probyn's Horse, 19th King George's Own Lancers, 21st King George's Own Centl India Horse, 1st Sappers and Miners, 11th Sikh Regt, 1st Madras Pioneers, 4th Bombay Grens, 10th Baluch Regt, 1st Gurkha Rifles, 2nd Gurkha Rifles, Capt-Gen and Hon Col HAC, Hon Col 3rd Bn W Yorks Regt, Roy Canadian Dragoons, 43rd Canadian Inf, Roy Malta Artillery, 8th (Zamora) Inf Regt Spain, Hon Memb HAC Massachusetts, FM Japanese Army; Bailiff Grand Cross OStJ, Kt: Golden Fleece Spain, St Andrew Russia, Elephant Denmark, Annunziata and Savoy Italy; Hon LLD: Cantab 1894, Melbourne, Sydney, Adelaide, McGill, Laval, Toronto and Queen's Coll Kingston (Ontario) 1901, U of Wales 1902, London 1903, Glasgow 1907, Hon DCL Oxon 1897, DLitt Sheffield 1909, Chllr Cape U 1901 and U of Wales 1902, Bencher Lincoln's Inn 1892 (Treas 1903), Er Bro Trin Ho, Ld Warden Cinque Ports and Constable Dover Castle 1905–07, Hon FRCS, Patron RCM and RAM, Ranger Windsor Gt Pk 1917; *m* Chapel Royal St James's Palace 6 July 1893 his cousin HSH PRINCESS (VICTORIA) MARY (MAY) AUGUSTA LOUISA OLGA PAULINE CLAUDINE AGNES, KG (*d* 1953), only dau of HH THE DUKE OF TECK, GCB, GCVO, by HRH PRINCESS MARY ADELAIDE WILHELMINA ELIZABETH, yr dau of HRH 1st DUKE OF CAMBRIDGE (s of GEORGE III), and *d* Sandringham 20 Jan 1936, having had:

1 **EDWARD VIII** (styled the same as his f), EDWARD (ALBERT CHRISTIAN GEORGE ANDREW PATRICK) DAVID WINDSOR, 20 Jan–10 Dec 1936 (when abdicated), 1st and last DUKE OF WINDSOR, so *cr* 8 March 1937, KG (1910), KT (1922), KP (1927), GCB (1936), GCSI (1921), GCIE (1921), GCVO (1920), MC (1916), PC (UK 1920, Canada 1927), Roy Victorian Chain 1921; *b* White Lodge, Richmond Park, Surrey 23 June 1894; *educ* RNCs Osborne and Dartmouth and Magdalen Coll Oxford; RN: Midshipman 1911, Lt 1913, Capt 1919, Adml of the Fleet 1936; Army: joined 1st Bn Gren Gds Aug 1914, served WW I Flanders and Italy, ADC to C-in-C BEF 16 Nov 1914, Lt 18 Nov 1914, Capt 10 March 1916, Staff Capt, DAQMG and GSO(2) 14th Army Corps 1916, Hon Col 4th and 5th Bns Cheshire Regt, 5th Bn Devonshire Regt and 16th Bn London Regt 1917, T/Maj 1918, Personal ADC to his f 1919–36, Col 1919, Col Welsh Gds, FM 1936, Gen Japanese Army, RAF: Gp Capt 1922, Marshal 1936, Hon Air Cdre-in-Ch RAuxAF 1932–36; Grand Master Orders St Michael and St George and Br Empire 1917–36, Chm Roy Patriotic Fund 1916, KJStJ 1917 (Bailiff Grand Cross 1926 and Prior Wales), High Steward: Windsor 1918 and Plymouth 1919, Govr and Pres Bart's Hosp, Govr Wellington Coll, Pres King Edward's Hosp Fund London, King Edward VII Hosp Fund for Offrs and RNLI, Grand Pres League Mercy, Er Bro Trin Ho, barrister and Bencher Middle Temple 1919, Chllr: U Wales 1920, Cape Town U 1925, Hon Pres Roy Statistical Soc 1921, Sr Grand Warden Utd Grand Lodge Freemasons 1922, Provincial Grand Master Surrey 1924, Grand Supt Roy Arch Masonry Surrey 1930, Pres Br Empire Exhibn 1924 and BA 1926, Tstee Br Museum and Nat Gallery, Patron Roy Africa Soc, Master Merchant Navy and Fishing Fleets 1928–36, Ch Boy Scouts Wales, Hon LLD: Edinburgh, Toronto, Alberta and Queen's U Kingston (Ontario) 1919, Melbourne 1920, Cantab and Calcutta 1921, St Andrews and Hong Kong 1922, Witwatersrand 1925, Hon DCL Oxon, DSc and Hon MCom London, DLitt Benares 1921, Hon FRCP Edin and FRCS, FRS, Hon MICE and FRIBA, Order Golden Fleece Spain and Grand Cross Legn Hon 1912, Order Elephant Denmark and Grand Cross St Olav Norway 1914, Order Annunziata Italy and Croix de Guerre 1915, Orders St George Russia 1916 and Michael the Brave Romania 1918, War Merit Cross Italy 1919, Grand Cordon Mohamed Ali Egypt 1922, Collar Order Carol of Romania 1924, Chilean Order Merit 1st Cl 1925, Grand Collar Chilean Order Merit and Grand Cross Condor Andes 1931; *m* Château de Candé, Monts, France, 3 June 1937 (Bessie) Wallis (*d* Paris 24 April 1986, *bur* Frogmore), only dau of Teakle Wallis Warfield, of Baltimore, Md., and formerly w of (a) Earl Winfield Spencer and (b) Ernest Aldrich Simpson, and *dsp* Paris 28 May 1972 (*bur* Frogmore), when the Dukedom expired

2 **GEORGE VI** (styled the same as his f till 22 June 1948, when the title 'Emperor of India' dropped), ALBERT (BERTIE) FREDERICK ARTHUR GEORGE WINDSOR, KG (1916), KT (1923), KP (1936), GCMG (1926), GCVO (1921), PC (1925), Roy Victorian Chain 1927; *b* Sandringham 14 Dec 1895; *s* bro 10 Dec 1936; crowned 12 May 1937; *educ* RNCs Osborne and Dartmouth; RN: Midshipman 1913, Actg Lt 1916 (served WW I, present Battle of Jutland 1916 (despatches)), Lt 1918, Cdr 1920, Capt 1925, V-Adml and Adml 1936, Adml of the Fleet 11 Dec 1936, Adml Sea Corps and Roy Canadian Sea Cadets, Hon Adml Danish Navy; Gen 1936, FM 11 Dec 1936, Personal ADC to his f 1919–36 and er bro 1936, Capt-Gen: RM, RAC and HAC; Col-in-Ch: Life Gds, RHG, 1st Roy Dragoons, RSG, 11th Hus, RTR, RRA, RE, Gren, Coldstream, Scots, Irish and Welsh Gds, Roy Norfolk Regt, Somerset LI, E Yorks Regt, Roy Welch Fus, Roy Berks Regt, KRRC, Queen's Own Cameron Highrs, Roy Malta Artillery, RAOC, Leics Yeo, Duke of Lancaster's Own Yeo, Trg Corps, ACF, (in Canadian Army) 7th Reconnaissance Regt, 17th Duke of York's Roy Canadian Hus, Roy Canadian Artillery, Corps of Roy Canadian Engrs, Roy 22e Regt, Roy Hamilton LI, Cameron Highrs of Ottawa, Winnipeg Grens, Govr-Gen's Foot Gds, Canadian Gren Gds, Roy Canadian Army Cadets, Australian Inf, RNZAC, RNZA, Auckland Regt, 1st Roy Natal Carbineers, 2nd Roy Natal Carbineers, Imp Light Horse, Kaffrarian Rifles, Transvaal Scottish, (in IA) 16th Light Cav, 1st Punjab Regt, 13th Frontier Force Rifles, also Ceylon Def Force, KAR, Roy Rhodesia Regt, N Rhodesia Regt, Roy W Africa Frontier Force, Hon Col: 4th/5th Bn Cameron Highrs (TA), Gen Danish Army, Hon Cmdg Gen Nepalese Army; RAF: Capt and Staff Offr 1918, S/Ldr 1919, W/Cdr 1920, G/Capt 1921, AM and ACM 1936, Marshal RAF 11 Dec 1936, Air Cdre-in-Ch ATC and RAF Regt; Hon LLD: Cantab 1922, Belfast 1924, Brisbane, Melbourne and Adelaide 1927, Glasgow 1932; DCL Oxon 1928, Protector U of Wales 1937, Hon MICE, Hon FRIBA, FRS, Bencher Inner Temple 1917 (Treas 1949), Master Merchant Navy and Fishing Fleets 1937, High Steward Windsor 1936, Ranger Windsor Gt Pk and Er Bro Trin Ho 1937, Provincial Grand Master Middx 1924–36, Past Grand Master England 1937, Grand Master Mason Scotland 1936; *m* Westminster Abbey 26 April 1923 *Lady Elizabeth Angela Marguerite Bowes-Lyon, LG (1936), LT (1937), GCVO (1937), CI (1931), GBE (1927), Roy Victorian Chain (1937) (*see* QUEEN ELIZABETH THE QUEEN MOTHER), yst dau of 14th Earl of Stathmore and Kinghorne (*qv*), and *d* Sandringham 6 Feb 1952 (*bur* Windsor), leaving:

(1) **ELIZABETH II**

(2) +Margaret Rose, CI (1947), GCVO (1953), Roy Victorian Chain (1990) [HRH The Princess Margaret Countess of Snowdon CI GCVO, Kensington Palace, London W8 4PU]; *b* Glamis Castle, Angus, 21 Aug 1930; Col-in-Ch: Light Dragoons, Roy Highland Fus (Princess Margaret's Own Glasgow and Ayrshire Regt), Princess Louise Fus, Highland Fus of Canada, QARANC; Dep Col-in-Ch Roy Anglian Regt; Hon Air Cdre RAF Coningsby; Pres: Scottish Children's League, Victoria League, Roy Nat Inst Blind, Roy Ballet, NSPCC, Roy Scottish Soc for Prevention Cruelty Children, Friends of the Elderly, Invalid Children's Aid Nationwide (Chm Cncl), English Folk Dance and Song Soc, Horder Centre for Arthritis, Guide Assoc; Hon Pres: Br Museum Devpt Tst, Jt-Pres Lowland Bde Club; Patron-in-Ch English Harbour Repair Fund; Patron: Assoc Anaesthetists GB and NI, Clarence House Restoration Fund, Friends of the Iveagh Bequest Kenwood, Light Infantry Club, London Lighthouse, Mustique Educnl Tst, Purine Research Lab, QARANC Assoc, Barristers' Benevolent Assoc, Bristol Roy Soc for the Blind, Guilds British and Internat Sailors' Soc, Ladies' Guild, Friends of Southwark Cathedral, Friends of St John's, Mary Hare GS for the Deaf, Nat Pony Soc, Princess Margaret Rose Hosp Edinburgh, Services Sound and Vision Corp, RCN, Nat Cncl Nurses UK, Princess Margaret Cancer Hosp Toronto, The Mathilda and Terence Kennedy Inst of Rheumatology, St Margaret's Chapel Guild Edinburgh Castle, Youth Clubs Scotland, Scottish Community Drama Assoc, Suffolk Regimental Assoc, Union of Schs for Social Serv, Architects' Benevolent Soc, Tenovus (Inst of Cancer Research), Migraine Tst, Zebra Tst, St Pancras Housing Assoc in Camden, Roy Caledonian Ball 1956–; Grand Pres St John Ambulance, Br Legn Womens' Section; Hon Memb: AA, Hallé Concerts Soc, Heart Disease and Diabetes Research Tst, Northern Ballet Theatre, Pottery and Glass Trades Benevolent Inst, Scottish

Ballet, Roy Anglian Regtl Assoc, Sealyham Terrier Breeders' Assoc; Hon Memb and Patron Grand Antiquity Assoc Glasgow; Freeman: City London 1966, Haberdashers' Co 1966, Roy Borough Queensferry 1972; Hon Life Memb Century House Assoc (Br Columbia) and RAF Club; Hon Fell Roy Photographic Soc; CStJ; Grand Cross Order Netherlands Lion 1948; Order Brilliant Star Zanzibar 1st Cl 1956, Grand Cross Order Crown Belgium 1960, Order Crown Lion and Spear Toro Kingdom (Uganda) 1965, Order Precious Crown 1st Cl Japan 1971, Grand Cross Order Merit 1st Cl Fedl Republic Germany; Hon DMus London 1957; Hon LLD Cantab 1958; Hon DLitt Keele 1962; Hon LLD U of BC 1958; Hon FRIBA 1953; Hon FRSM 1957, Hon FRCS England 1963, Hon FRCOG 1966; Hon Life FZS; Master Bench Lincoln's Inn (Treas 1967); *m* Westminster Abbey 6 May 1960 (*divorce* 5 July 1978) 1st Earl of Snowdon (*qv*) and has:

1a +David Albert Charles, *Viscount Linley* [Viscount Linley, David Linley Furniture Ltd, 60 Pimlico Rd, London SW1W 8LP]; *b* Clarence House 3 Nov 1961 (HM THE QUEEN stood sponsor); *educ* Bedales and John Makepiece Sch for Craftsmen in wood, Beaminster, Dorset; furniture designer, chm David Linley Furniture Ltd 1985– and David Linley Co 1985–, Commr and memb bd management Roy Commission for 1851 Exhibition 1998–, author: *Classical Furniture* (1993), *Extraordinary Furniture* (1993); *m* 8 Oct 1993 *Hon Serena Alleyne Stanhope, only dau of Charles Henry Leicester, Viscount Petersham (*see* HARRINGTON, E)

1a +Sarah Frances Elizabeth; *b* 1 May 1964; *educ* Bedales and Roy Acad Sch; *m* 14 July 1994 *Daniel Chatto, yr s of Thomas and Rosalind Chatto, and has:

1b +Samuel David Benedict; *b* 28 July 1996

3 HENRY WILLIAM FREDERICK ALBERT WINDSOR, **1st Duke of Gloucester**, so *cr* 31 March 1928, as also BARON CULLODEN and EARL OF ULSTER (all UK), KG (1921), KT (1933), KP (1934), GMB (1942), GCMG (1935), GCVO (1922), PC (1925), Roy Victorian Chain 1932; *b* York Cottage, Sandringham, 31 March 1900; *educ* Eton, RMC Sandhurst and Trin Coll Cambridge; joined KRRC 1920, tfd 10th Roy Hus (ret as Maj-Gen 1937), Hon Col Cambridge U OTC 1934, Col-in-Ch Glos Regt 1935, 10th Roy Hus, Roy Inniskilling Fus, Gordon Highrs, Australian Light Horse and Natal Mtd Rifles 1937, Col Scots Gds 1937, Hon Col Ceylon Planters Rifle Corps and Ceylon LI 1937, barrister and Bencher Gray's Inn 1926, Personal ADC to his f 1929–36, Govr and C-in-C Australia 1944–47, Pres: Victoria Hosp for Children 1936, Christ's Hosp, Bart's Hosp, Nat Assoc Boys' Clubs, NRA, Roy Humane Soc, Imp War Museum, Imp War Graves Commn, RVC, AVM RAF and Hon Capt RNVR 1937, Hon LLD Cantab 1930, Adelaide, Melbourne and Sydney 1934, High Steward King's Lynn and Windsor, Bailiff Grand Cross OStJ, Grand Pres League Mercy, Chm Cncl BRCS and King George's Jubilee Tst; *m* Buckingham Palace 6 Nov 1935 *Lady Alice Christabel Montagu-Douglas-Scott, GCB, CI, GCVO, GBE, GCStJ [HRH Princess Alice Duchess of Gloucester GCB CI GCVO GBE, Kensington Palace, London W8 4PU], 3rd dau of 7th Duke of Buccleuch and (9th Duke of) Queensberry (*qv*), and *d* Barnwell Manor, Northants, 10 June 1974, having had:

(1) William Henry Andrew Frederick; *b* 18 Dec 1941; *educ* Eton; *d* unm (*k* plane crash) 28 Aug 1972

(2) RICHARD ALEXANDER WALTER GEORGE, **2nd and present Duke of Gloucester**

4 GEORGE EDWARD ALEXANDER EDMUND WINDSOR, **1st Duke of Kent**, so *cr* 12 Oct 1934, as also BARON DOWNPATRICK and EARL OF ST ANDREWS (all UK), KG (1923), KT (1935), GCMG (1934), GCVO (1924), PC (1937), Roy Victorian Chain 1936; *b* Sandringham 20 Dec 1902; RN: Lt 1926, Cdr 1934, Capt 1937, Personal ADC to his f, Col and Gp Capt RAF 1937, Maj-Gen, R-Adml, Hon Air Cdre No 500 (County of Kent) (Bomber) Sqdn RAuxAF 1938, Pres: London UCH 1928, St George's Hosp and NSPCC 1935, RCM and Br Sch Rome 1936, Overseas League 1937, Roy Commn for Exhibn of 1851; Hon Freeman: Cardiff 1932, Edinburgh, barrister and Bencher Lincoln's Inn 1932, Col-in-Ch Queen's Own Roy W Kent Regt and 1st City Regt Grahamstown 1935, Roy Fus 1937, Ld HC to Gen Assembly Ch Scotland, Chllr U of Wales 1937, Bailiff Grand Cross OStJ, Kt Order Chrysanthemum Japan, Grand Crosses Order Merit and Condor of the Andes Chile, Hon LLD Edinburgh 1929, Sheffield 1930, St Andrews 1936, Hon DCL Durham 1935, Fell and Memb Cncl King's Coll London, Patron *The Complete Peerage*; *m* Westminster Abbey 29 Nov 1934 HRH PRINCESS MARINA, CI (1937), GCVO, GBE (1937), DGStJ (*d* Kensington Palace 27 Aug 1968), yst dau of HRH PRINCE NICHOLAS OF GREECE AND DENMARK, and was *kas* in a plane crash 25 Aug 1942, leaving:

(1) EDWARD GEORGE NICHOLAS PAUL PATRICK WINDSOR, **2nd and present Duke of Kent**

(2) *Michael George Charles Franklin, KCVO [His Royal Highness Prince Michael of Kent KCVO, Kensington Palace, London W8 4PU; Nether Lypiatt Manor, Stroud, Glos GL6 7LS]; *b* Coppins, Iver, Bucks, 4 July 1942; *educ* Eton and RMA Sandhurst; commnd 11th Hus (PAO); Cdre RNR; memb HAC; Grand Master Lodge of Mark Master Masons; Cwlth Pres: Roy Life Saving Soc; Pres: RAC, Inst Motor Industry, SSAFA, Medical Commn Accident Prevention, Dogs' Home Battersea, Roy Patriotic Fund Corp, Nat Eye Research Centre, Kennel Club, Inst Road Safety Offrs, Soc Genealogists; Patron: Museum Army Flying, Veteran Car Club GB, Thames Rowing Club, Popular Flying Assoc, David Shepherd Conservation Fund, Carriage Fndn, Brooklands Museum Tst Appeal, Bermuda Maritime Museum; Fndr Prince Michael Road Safety Award Scheme; Fell: Inst Motor Industry, Roy Aeronautical Soc; Tstee Nat Motor Museum; Chm Advsy Bd House of Windsor; Hon Liveryman: Clothworkers', Leathersellers', Scientific Instrument Makers', Coachmakers' and Coach Harness Makers' Cos; *m* Vienna 30 June 1978 *Marie-Christine Agnes Hedwig Ida, Patron Soc Women Artists, dau of Baron Günther Hubertus von Reibnitz and formerly w of Thomas Troubridge (*see* TROUBRIDGE, Bt), and has:

1a +Frederick Michael David Louis; *b* St Mary's Hosp Paddington 6 April 1979

1a +(Gabri)Ella Marina Alexandra Ophelia; *b* St Mary's Hosp Paddington 23 April 1981

(1) +Alexandra Helen Elizabeth Olga Christabel, GCVO (1960) [HRH Princess Alexandra The Hon Lady Ogilvy GCVO, Thatched House Lodge, Richmond Park, Surrey TW10 5HP]; *b* 3 Belgrave Square 25 Dec 1936; Chllr Lancaster U 1964–; Col-in-Ch: Queen's Own Rifles Canada 1960–, 17th/21st Lancers 1969–93, King's Own Roy Border Regt 1977–, Canadian Scottish Regt (Princess Mary's) 1977–; Dep Col-in-Ch: The Light Infantry 1968–, Queen's Roy Lancers 1993–; Dep Roy Hon Col King's Own Yorks Yeo (LI) 1996–; Dep Hon Col Roy Yeo 1975–; Hon Cmdt-Gen: Roy Hong Kong Police Force 1969–97, Roy Hong Kong Aux Police Force 1969–97; Hon Fell: Roy Faculty Physicians and Surgns Glasgow 1960 (Roy Coll Glasgow 1962–), Faculty of Anaesthetists (Roy Coll Anaesthetists 1992–), Roy Coll Surgns England 1967–, Roy Coll Obstetricians and Gynaecologists 1969–; Hon Freedom City Lancaster 1987; Patron: Anchor, CARE, Cystic Fibrosis Tst, ENO, Fairbridge, Florence Nightingale Fndn, Guide Dogs for the Blind Assoc, MIND, PDSA, Princess Mary's RAF Nursing Serv 1966– (also Air Ch Cmdt), QARNNS, Queen Victoria Seamen's Rest, Ruskin Fndn, St Christopher's Hospice; Pres: Alexandra Rose Day, Br Sch Rome, Children's Country Holidays Fund, Friends of the V&A, Queen Alexandra's House Assoc, Roy Humane Soc, Roy Star and Garter Home for Disabled Sailors, Soldiers and Airmen, Sight Savers Internat, WWF for Nature UK; Dep-Pres BRC; Hon LLD: Qld U Australia 1959, Hong Kong 1961, Mauritius 1974; *m* Westminster Abbey 24 April 1963 *Hon Sir Angus James Bruce Ogilvy, KCVO, and has issue (*see* AIRLIE, E)

5 John Charles Francis; *b* York Cottage 12 July 1905; *d* there unm 18 Jan 1919

1 (Victoria Alexandra Alice) Mary, GBE (1927); *b* York Cottage 25 April 1897; Col-in-Ch Roy Scots 1918, DGStJ, Ldy Grand Pres League Mercy, Cmdt in Ch BRC, Freedom Edinburgh 1930, Hon LLD Leeds and Sheffield, DCL Oxon; *m* Westminster Abbey 28 Feb 1922 6th Earl of Harewood (*qv*) and *d* 28 March 1965, leaving issue

Seats:

1. Buckingham Palace

The site of Buckingham Palace was originally the Mulberry Garden, so called from an early attempt to breed silk worms in St James's Park. In 1633 the 1st Earl of Norwich (*see* GORING) erected adjacent to it a country residence, known as Goring House after his only peerage title at the time. It was destroyed by fire in 1675, but for the previous 10 years had been rented by the 1st Earl of Arlington, whose replacement of it, built in 1677, was called Arlington House. On Arlington's death the property passed to his son-in-law, the 1st Duke of Grafton (*qv*), who as one of CHARLES II's bastards may be said to have been its first occupant with royal connections. Part of the site had been Crown land all along and was accordingly held on lease even when the rest was sold as a freehold. The divided ownership, inconvenient for subsequent non-royal occupants, ended when the house and grounds were wholly acquired by GEORGE III in 1761 (*see* also NORMANBY, section **Earldom of Mulgrave and Marquessate of Normanby**).

Meanwhile the place was taken over from 1698 by the 1st Duke of the County of Buckingham and of Normanby (*see* SHEFFIELD, Bt). He tore down the 1677 building and put up a larger and more splendid mansion apparently to designs by William Talman, formerly WILLIAM III's Comptroller of the Works. The site was shifted northwards and the main entrance was arranged to debouch directly onto the Mall. The layout consisted of a rectangular central block flanked by twin curved colonnaded wings ending in two-storey pavilions. The former survives to this day as part of the west front looking out over the gardens.

To extend his new house GEORGE III employed Sir William Chambers, who between 1762 and 1764 enlarged the wings either side of the main block. On the south side an octagon was added. With three other large rooms it was filled with GEORGE III's enormous library. Towards the end of his reign Buckingham House was inhabited chiefly by QUEEN CHARLOTTE, who as the leading royal female hosted drawing-rooms and receptions there while enjoying an augmented Civil List. It was a further stage in the process whereby the building developed into the principal royal residence.

On CHARLOTTE's death in 1818 the PRINCE REGENT, soon to be GEORGE IV, decided to move there from Carlton House. Buckingham House became a testimony in its decorative features to Britain's triumph over NAPOLEON. For instance the Marble Arch (moved in 1850 to the top of Park Lane), which was incorporated into the eastern side where the main entrance was to be, was inspired by the Arch of Constantine in Rome. A display of heroic statuary along the top of the elevation facing the Mall further emphasised the nation's world ascendancy. The neo-classical style chosen, though typically French, accorded with the personal tastes of the new King, who with his circle of cronies contributed numerous ideas and modifications to the overall scheme drawn up by his pet architect John Nash.

From this it was but a step to GEORGE's declaring that his newly refurbished residence should become the chief seat of the Head of State, indeed a palace. The rechristening occurred in 1826, when Nash had already for a year and a half been designing the original, essentially domestic, improvements. The plans were therefore enlarged. The budget had originally been funded at £150,000 (some £4,725,000 in late-1990s terms) but by 1828 costs had soared to just under £300,000 (some £12m in late-1990s terms) and by the next year to just under £500,000 (over £21m in late-1990s terms). After GEORGE's death in 1830 Nash got the blame, though he did his best to shift culpability onto his late master's multitudinous changes of plan in mid-project. He was dismissed in 1831.

His replacement was the less distinguished and less expensive Edward Blore, who needed a mere £100,000 (some £4,150,000 in late-1990s terms) to complete the work. At least much of Buckingham Palace's contents already existed, the greater part coming from the now demolished Carlton House and the rest from Windsor, though even so a further £55,000 (nearly £2,300,000 in late-1990s terms) of public money was earmarked for this aspect of the project. WILLIAM IV, like many subsequent members of his family, chafed at the thought of living in Buckingham Palace. He tried to persuade the Government to take it off his hands, first as a barracks and then as a replacement for the Houses of Parliament after they had burnt down in late 1834.

It was QUEEN VICTORIA who formally made Buckingham Palace the principal town seat of the sovereign and till PRINCE ALBERT's death in 1861 it was the scene of numerous balls, concerts, banquets, investitures and receptions. Her philoprogenitive habits, as well as her social ones, necessitated the building's further enlargement. Blore was again called in and from the mid-1840s on linked up the two wings reaching forwards to the Mall from the main block to form an enclosed courtyard. Thomas Cubitt (*see* ASHCOMBE) was the contractor. The cost was £106,000 (some £4,225,000 in late-1990s terms) and was offset by the sale of Brighton Pavilion for just under £100,000, though its contents and fittings were used to embellish Blore's new interiors. In the 1850s a massive ballroom was added on the southwest side of the Palace to designs by James Pennethorne, who had once studied under Nash.

On EDWARD VII's accession the Palace was remodelled by Frank Verity, who worked in the sham neo-classical idiom best exemplified by the Ritz. His principal contribution at Buckingham Palace was the Ballroom, particularly the miniature proscenium over the royal thrones (Verity's speciality hitherto had been theatre interiors). In 1913 Sir Aston Webb altered the east front of the Palace, giving it essentially the appearance it wears today. Minor bomb damage in World War II, chiefly to the private chapel installed by QUEEN VICTORIA on the southwest flank, gave the opportunity to erect the Queen's Gallery, where items from the Royal Collection are on public display. The state rooms were thrown open to the public in 1993.

2. Windsor Castle, Berks

The site of Windsor had been a royal possession even before the Conquest. WILLIAM I the year after Hastings chose the chalk hill which at that point overlooks the Thames Valley on which to build a motte, or mound, consisting of earth reinforced with wood, with two baileys, or enclosed courtyards, either side. One account has it that this was intended as no more than a hunting box. Early-Norman Windsor was more probably one of a number of defending fortresses put up round London, from which it lay a long day's march. A little later, seemingly under HENRY I, Windsor was strengthened by being remodelled as a single keep on the summit. No more than 15 feet high, it was of the type called 'shell', that is, a stone wall circumscribing the motte. It was in HENRY II's reign that a more durable castle, one predominantly in stone, first took shape, when the Round Tower, still the climax of the whole gigantic edifice today, was first erected as a 35-foot high inner defence surrounded by the earlier shell-keep wall. HENRY III made further additions, notably the Great Hall, which dates from the mid-1220s, the Great Kitchen of 1259 and the small chapel which till the completion of St George's Chapel was where the Garter Knights' services took place.

St George's Chapel was founded by EDWARD III though the building itself dates chiefly from EDWARD IV's reign nearly a century later. EDWARD III also constructed the Norman Gate and St George's Hall. His extensions to Windsor as a whole focused on the enclosed space east of the Round Tower called the Upper Ward, the higher of the two great open areas within the half-mile-long curtain wall. They are said to have cost £50,000 (well over £12m in late-1990s terms). Towards the end of his reign the Bishop of Winchester, William of Wykeham, oversaw the construction of more buildings east of the Round Tower, notably the one called after him the Winchester Tower. HENRY VIII added the northwest entrance from the town of Windsor through which the public is admitted.

Further substantial changes were carried out by CHARLES II, who used the architect Hugh May to refurbish the Upper Ward and Antonio Verrio and Grinling Gibbons to provide him with painted ceilings and wood carving respectively in the State Apartments, though these were destroyed by Sir Jeffry Wyatville to make way for his own embellishments in GEORGE IV's time. The latter is responsible for the latest large-scale remodelling to date: Wyatville raised the level of the Round Tower by a further 30 feet and crenellated, machicolated and buttressed it. Such adornments made strengthening of the core necessary. A programme of repairs from the mid-1980s eventually took in the whole of the Upper Ward and led indirectly to the disastrous 15-hour long fire of 1992, when a spotlight in the Private Chapel in contact with a curtain heated it to ignition point and caused the destruction of historic architecture and fabric at a rate which has been calculated as not far short of £40,000 a minute. An earlier fire in 1853 had led to restoration work by Anthony Salvin, notably of the Prince of Wales Tower. The repairs to the 1992 conflagration, which were broadly in the spirit of the original without being slavishly so, were more or less finished by the fifth anniversary of the catastrophe. They cost just under £37m, substantially more than EDWARD III had laid out admittedly, but from a far deeper public purse, for his expenditure had represented well over one and a half times a single year's government revenue.

Other interior rooms include the Waterloo Chamber, originally an inner courtyard which was roofed over in 1831, where the annual banquet celebrating Wellington's victory over NAPOLEON in 1815 was instituted every 18 June by GEORGE IV. The Sovereign's private dwelling quarters lie on the east and south flanks of the Upper Ward.

3. Holyrood House, Edinburgh

Holyrood is named after the piece of the true Cross ('rood') left DAVID I King of Scots (reigned 1124–53) by his mother ST MARGARET, a granddaughter of the English King EDMUND (IRONSIDE). But it was at first an Augustinian abbey and only started to become a royal palace in the early 16th century. The James IV Tower, occupied by MARY QUEEN OF SCOTS, was where her secretary David Rizzio was murdered. Holyrood was thoroughly rebuilt by CHARLES II in the 1670s to the designs of Sir William Bruce, 1st Bt, of the 1668 creation (*see* ELGIN and KINCARDINE). It was occupied by the Young Pretender during the '45 and (this time with official permission) by the future CHARLES X OF FRANCE during the French Revolution and again after his deposition in 1830. HM THE QUEEN is briefly in residence there early each summer.

4. Sandringham House, Norfolk

One of the PRINCE CONSORT's last actions before his death in late 1861 was to set in action the buying of the 7,000-acre Sandringham estate in Norfolk, using surplus funds accumulated from his thrifty management of the Duchy of Cornwall estates ever since marrying QUEEN VICTORIA. (He nearly quintupled its income, from £11,000 a year [under £450,000 p.a. in late-1990s terms] to £50,000 a year [something over £2m p.a. in late-1990s terms].) The place had belonged to a family called Cobbe (*see* WALPOLE, B) between the early 16th century and JAMES II's reign, being then sold to another family called Hoste, from whom it was inherited by yet a third family called Henley. In 1836 it was bought from the latter owners by John Motteux, an eccentric bachelor with a passion for fruit tree cultivation, who left it to Charles Cowper, a younger son of the 5th Earl Cowper (*see* LUCAS OF CRUDWELL, B). Cowper was also nephew to Lord Melbourne and became a stepson to Lord Palmerston (*see* TEMPLE OF STOWE, E) so that the property could well have been known to the Royal Family by reason of its owner's close association with two of QUEEN VICTORIA's most distinguished Prime Ministers. The house at this point was a late-18th-century building facing east-west, with two principal floors surmounted by an attic storey. Cowper can have had no immediate plans to sell since he commissioned Samuel Sanders Teulon, an architect who worked extensively elsewhere in East Anglia, to embellish the east front with a porch and add a conservatory. Later he married his mistress, Lady Harriet d'Orsay, Count Alfred d'Orsay's widow, and was obliged by the stuffy attitude of his Norfolk neighbours to leave the county.

Though it was the PRINCE CONSORT's flair for business that had made the purchase possible, the intended beneficiary was the then PRINCE OF WALES, later EDWARD VII. Sandringham must already have been quite large since it had seven bays on the west front, including a bay window in the centre, and one of five bays augmented by wings either side on the east front — substantially larger, for instance, than Highgrove, which has been found perfectly adequate by the current PRINCE OF WALES (*qv*). But it proved far too small for the future EDWARD VII, whose expansive habits included not just the personal ones of *gourmandise* but a social life that involved hosting large-scale house parties. On taking possession he therefore demolished everything bar the conservatory, which he had converted to a billiard room, and commissioned A J Humbert to erect a very large mansion in brick enlivened with dressings of Ketton stone in vaguely Tudor Revival style. The rebuilding considerably embarrassed the PRINCE OF WALES's finances. The new house was completed in 1871, though a ballroom was added in 1883 and, following a fire in 1891, a two-storey section was capped by a third, both projects to the designs of Sir Robert Edis. Thus enlarged, Sandringham was said to have about as many rooms as there are days in the year and in the 1970s was partly demolished to give a more manageable house of something like two-thirds that number.

In the 20th century it has tended to be the favourite home not of the Heir Apparent but of the Sovereign himself, whether GEORGE V or GEORGE VI, both of whom died there. Doubtless much of its attraction is the shooting, developed by EDWARD VII into one of the finest for pheasant in all England, but so too has its relative tranquillity as first Buckingham Palace then, in the present reign, Windsor have become too stifled by the spread of Greater London and increasingly subject to nuisances such as overflying aircraft.

5. Balmoral Castle, Aberdeenshire

Balmoral is largely the work of the PRINCE CONSORT himself, working, albeit loosely, in the idiom that became famous as Scottish Baronial (though Balmoral is a generation later than the pioneering work in that idiom) with the help of William Smith, an Aberdonian architect little known outside the district, his very obscurity allowing his employer to impose his own ideas. The estate, currently of some 30,000 acres, had once belonged to the GORDONs of Deeside, then to the FARQUHARSONs and finally to the Earls of Fife (*see* FIFE, D), from the 4th of whom the PRINCE CONSORT bought it in 1852. The new house was finished by 1856. It became the favourite northern haunt of QUEEN VICTORIA, and is still a favourite with the Royal Family, particularly the PRINCE OF WALES, who use it mostly during the late summer/early autumn break.

HM QUEEN ELIZABETH THE QUEEN MOTHER

Arms: The Royal Arms impaling quarterly 1st and 4th the arms of Bowes-Lyon (*i.e.*, 1st and 4th argent a lion rampant azure, armed and langued gules, within a double tressure flory-counterflory of the second (for LYON); 2nd and 3rd, ermine three bows, strings palewise proper (for BOWES)). **Supporters:** Dexter, that of the Sovereign; sinister, a lion per fess or and gules (one of the supporters of the Earls of Strathmore and Kinghorne).

QUEEN ELIZABETH THE QUEEN MOTHER (Lady Elizabeth Angela Marguerite Bowes-Lyon, LG (1936), LT (1937), GCVO (1937), CI (1931), GBE (1927), Roy Victorian Chain (1937)) [Her Majesty Queen Elizabeth The Queen Mother LG LT GCVO CI GBE, Clarence House, St James's, London SW1A 1BA; Royal Lodge, Windsor Great Park, Berks; Birkhall, Ballater, Aberdeenshire; Castle of Mey, Caithness]; *b* London 4 Aug 1900; Col-in-Ch: 1st Queen's Dragoon Gds, Queen's Roy Hus (Queen's Own and Roy Irish), 9th/12th Roy Lancers (Prince of Wales's), King's Regt, Roy Anglian Regt, Light Inf, Black Watch (Roy Highland Regt), RAMC, Black Watch (Roy Highland Regt) of Canada, Toronto Scottish Regt, CFMS, RAAMC, RNZAMC, Hon Col: Roy Yeo, London Scottish (Gordon Highrs TA), Cmdt-in-Ch: WRNS, RAF Centl Flying Sch, WRAF, Nursing Corps, Divs St John Ambulance Bde, Hon Freeman: Barbers', Butchers', Grocers', Merchant Taylors', Musicians and Shipwrights' Cos, Hon Memb Lloyd's, Pres: BRCS 1937–52 (Dep Pres 1952–), Nat Tst, Roy Highland and Ag Soc 1963–64, Patron WRAC Assoc, Hon LLD: Queen's U Belfast 1924, St Andrews 1929, Glasgow 1932, Edinburgh 1937, Cape Town 1947, Cantab 1948, Manchester 1951, Leeds 1954, Columbia NY 1954, Melbourne 1958, Liverpool 1958, Auckland 1966, Halifax NS 1967, Dundee 1967, Hon DCL Oxon 1931, Hon DLitt: London 1937, W Indies 1965, Hon LittD Keele 1965, Hon DMus Sheffield 1966, Chllr: London U 1955–81, Dundee U 1967, Hon Fell: London 1977, KCL 1978, Hon FRCOG 1949, Hon FRCS 1950, Hon FRCP Edin 1953, FRCP 1962, Bencher Middle Temple 1944 (Treas 1949), FRS, Grand Cross Orders: Legn Hon, Lion Netherlands, Crown Romania, St Olga and St Sophia Greece, St Sava Serbia, Lernor Ala Afghanistan, Sun Peru, Independence Republic Tunisia, Ojaswi Rajanya Nepal; French Red Cross Medal; Norwegian War Cross, Freedom City: Glasgow 1927, Burghs Stirling and Dunfermline 1928, Perth 1935, Edinburgh 1936, Burgh of Inverness 1953, London 1953, Dundee 1954, King's Lynn 1954, Burghs of Forfar, Musselburgh and Wick 1956, Aberdeen 1959, St Albans 1961; RSA Gold Albert Medal 1952; Grand Master Roy Victorian Order 1937; GCStJ; Pres U Coll Rhodesia and Nyasaland 1957–70; Ld Warden and Adml Cinque Ports and Constable Dover Castle Sept 1978; *m* Westminster Abbey 26 April 1923 **HM GEORGE VI** (*see* above) and has issue

HRH THE DUKE OF EDINBURGH

Arms: Quarterly; 1st, or, semée of hearts gules, three lions passant in pale azure ducally crowned of the first; 2nd, azure a cross argent; 3rd, argent two pallets sable; 4th argent, upon a rock proper a castle triple towered sable, masoned argent, windows, port, turret caps and vanes gules. **Crest:** A plume of five ostrich feathers alternately sable and argent issuant from a ducal coronet or. **Supporters:** Dexter, a representation of Heracles girt about the loins with a lion skin, crowned with a chaplet of oak leaves and holding in the dexter hand a club proper; sinister, a lion, queue fourchée, ducally crowned or and gorged with a naval coronet azure. **Coronet:** A coronet composed of crosses-patées and fleurs-de-lys alternately or. **Motto:** God is my help. **Creations:** B., E. and D. (UK) 19 Nov 1947.

THE 1ST DUKE OF EDINBURGH, EARL OF MERIONETH and **BARON GREENWICH**, of Greenwich, Co London (Philip Battenberg later (28 Feb 1947, when also naturalised a Br subject, renouncing his right of succession to Crowns of Denmark and Greece) Mountbatten, KG (1947), OM (1968), GBE (1953), AC, QSO, PC (UK 1951 Canada 1957)) [HRH The Prince Philip Duke of Edinburgh KG KT OM GBE AC QSO, Buckingham Palace, London SW1 1AA; Windsor Castle, Berks SL4 1NJ; Balmoral Castle, Aberdeenshire AB35 5TB; Sandringham House, Norfolk PE35 6EN]; *b* Mon Repos, Corfu, 10 June 1921; *educ* Cheam Sch, Salem (Baden), Gordonstoun and RNC Dartmouth; WW II: Med Fleet, Home Waters, Br Pacific Fleet (despatches); 1947, granted title, style and attribute of Royal Highness 1947 and style and titular dignity of Prince of UK 1957, ktd 1952, granted by warrant 18 Sept 1952 precedence next to HM THE QUEEN except where otherwise provided by Act of Parliament; Grand Master and 1st or Principal Kt Order Br Empire 1953, Personal ADC to HM GEORGE VI 1948; Adml of the Fleet: RAN, RNZN; Marshal: RAF, RAAF, RNZAF; FM: Australian Mil Forces, NZ Army; Capt-Gen RM; Dep Col-in-Ch Queen's Roy Hus (Queen's Own and Roy Irish); Col-in-Ch: Roy Glos Berks and Wilts Regt, Highrs (Seaforth, Gordons and Camerons), Intell Corps, Army Cadet Force, Roy Canadian Regt, Seaforth Highs Canada, Roy Canadian Army Cadets, Roy Australian Electrical and Mechanical Engrs, Australian Cadet Corps, Corps RNZ Electrical and Mechanical Engrs; Col Gren Gds; Hon Col: Edinburgh U OTC, Heriot-Watt U OTC, Trinidad and Tobago Regt; Air Cdre-in-Ch Air Training Corps; Air Cdre: Air Sqdn 1983–, Roy Canadian Air Cadets; Hon Air Cdre RAF Kinloss; Cmdt-in-Ch and Extra Master Merchant Navy; Ranger Windsor Gt Pk 1952–; Ld High Steward Plymouth 1960–; Chllr: Edinburgh 1952–, Cambridge 1976– and Salford Us 1967–90; Grand Master Guild Air Pilots and Air Navigators; Grand Pres: Br Cwlth Ex-Servs League; Visitor: Upper Canada Coll 1955–, Manchester Coll Sci and Tech 1957–, Churchill Coll Cambridge 1959–; Life Govr King's Coll London 1954–; Master Bench Inner Temple 1954–; Er Bro Trin Ho 1952– (Master 1969–); Hon Bro Hull Trin House 1956–; Roy Govr Charterhouse 1953–; Pres in Ch: Br Racing Drivers' Club 1952–92; Pres: Assoc for Schs' Sci, Engrg and Tech, Roy Nat Playing Fields Assoc 1949–84, Br Amateur Athletic Bd 1952–, Cwlth Games Fedn 1955–90, Br Sportsman's Club 1958–, Central Cncl Physical Recreation 1951–, City and Guilds London Inst 1961–, ESU 1952–, Guinea Pig Club 1960–, Gds Polo Club 1955–, Nat Playing Fields Assoc, Roy Ag Soc Cwlth 1958–, Roy Commn for Exhibition of 1851 1965–, Roy Household Cricket Club 1953–, Roy Merchant Navy Sch 1952–, Roy Mint Advsy Ctee design seals, coins and medals 1952–, RSA 1952– (and Hon Fell), World Wild Life Fund 1961–82, World Wild Life Internat (later World Wide Fund for Nature-Internat) 1981 (late Pres Emeritus), Fedn Equestre Internat 1964–84, Maritime Tst 1969–, Bath and West and Southern Counties Soc 1981, Roy Windsor Horse Show 1991–94, Westminster Windsor Abbey Tst, Park Equestrian Club 1982–, Naval and Military Club; Grand Pres Br Cwlth Ex-Services League 1974; Tstee: L St George's House Cncl; V-Pres Soc Friends St George's and Descendants Kts of Garter 1948–; Patron: Air League, Assoc for Schs' Sci, Engrg and Tech, Br Driving Soc, Br Gliding Assoc, Br Sch Athens to 1998, Cambridge Soc, Cornwall RFU, Gallipoli Assoc, London Fedn Clubs for Young People, Lord's Taverners (and Twelfth Man), Outward Bound Tst, Shakespeare Globe Tst, VSO; Hon Fell Inst Marine Engrs; Hon Memb King's Lynn Rotary Club; Hon Life Memb Roy Assoc Br Dairy Farmers; FRS 1951; Perm Fell Inst Petroleum 1963–; Hon Fell Roy Soc Canada 1957–, Australian Acad Sci 1962–, Roy Zoological Soc Scotland 1963–, Zoological Soc London; Tstee: Nat Maritime Museum Greenwich 1948–, Roy Ag Soc England 1957–; Patron: Ghana Acad Sciences 1961– (Hon Pres 1959–61, first Hon Fell 1961), Gresham's Coll, Roy Inst Navigation, Lord's Taverners (Pres Cncl 1960–61, Twelfth Man 1961–), Charities Aid Fndn, Inst Chemical Engrs; Patron and Tstee Duke of Edinburgh's Award; Liveryman and Assist Shipwrights' Co (Prime Warden 1954, Perm Master 1956–); Freeman and Liveryman: Fishmongers' Co (Prime Warden 1961, 4th Warden 1962–63), Mercers' Co; Adml Master Mariners' Co; Grand Master Guild Air Pilots and Air Navigators; Guild Bro: Glasgow, Craft Rank Qua Hammermen, Trades Ho Glasgow; Adml: Roy Yacht Sqdn 1953–, Ho Lds Yacht Club, Roy Motor Yacht Club, RN Sailing Assoc, Roy Southern Yacht Club, Bar Yacht Club, Roy Dart Yacht Club, Roy Gibraltar Yacht Club, Roy Yacht Club Victoria Australia; Cdre-in-Ch: Sandringham Yacht Club Victoria 1980–, Great Navy State of Nebraska, USA; Freedom City: London 1948, Greenwich 1948, Edinburgh 1948, Belfast 1949, Cardiff 1954, Glasgow 1955, Melbourne 1956, Dar-es-Salaam 1961, Nairobi 1963, Guadalajara 1964, Acapulco 1964, Bridgetown (Barbados) 1964, Los Angeles 1966; Hon Citizen: Montevideo 1962, Chicago 1966; Hon LLD: Wales 1949, London 1951, Karachi 1959, Malta 1964, California 1966; Hon DCL: Durham 1951, Oxford 1964; Hon DSc: Delhi 1959, Reading 1957, Salford 1967, Southampton 1967, Victoria U, BC, 1969; Hon LLD W Ontario U 1983; Hon Degree Jordan U 1984; Hon Degree Engrg Lima 1962; Hon FRCP London 1952; Hon FRCSE; Hon FRCS England; Hon Fell Univ Coll Oxford 1953; Greek War Cross 1939–45; Atlantic, Africa, Burma (with Pacific rosette) and Italy Stars; War Medal 1939–45 (with Oak Leaf); Croix de Guerre with Palm; Grand Cross Redeemer, Phoenix and George I (with swords) Greece, Order St George and St Constantine (with swords, 4th Cl) Greece, Kt Order Elephant Denmark 1947, Grand Cross Order St Charles Monaco 1951, Order St Olav Norway 1952, Order Manuel Amador Guerrero Panama 1953, Order Seraphim Sweden 1954, Chain Queen of Shoba Ethiopia 1954, Grand Cross Order Tower and Sword Portugal 1955, Order King Faisal I Iraq 1956, Order Legn Hon 1957, Kt Grand Cross Order Merit Italy 1958, Grand Cross Order Lion Netherlands 1958, Order Merit Fedl German Republic 1st Cl 1958, Order Ojaswi Rajanya Nepal 1960, Kt Grand Band Star Africa Liberia 1961, Grand Cross Order San Martin Argentina 1962, Grand Cross Order Condor Bolivia 1962, Grand Cross Nat Order Southern Cross Brazil 1962, Chain Chilean Order Merit 1962, Grand Gross Extraordinary Order Boyaca Colombia 1962, Grand Cross Nat Order Merit Ecuador 1962, Nat Order Merit Paraguay 1962, Gr Cross Order Sun with Brilliants Peru 1962, Grand Cordon Order Leopold Belgium 1963, Order Brilliant Star Zanzibar 1st Cl 1963, Decoration Republic Sudan 1st Cl 1964, Grand Cross Order Icelandic Falcon 1964, Collar Aztec Eagle Mexico 1964, Star and Riband Order Nahdah Jordan 1966, Decoration of Honour for Servs to Republic Austria, Grand Cordon 1966, Grand Cdr Order Maritime Merit San Francisco Port Authority 1968, Order White Rose Finland 1969, Order Superior Sun Afghanistan 1971, Grand Cordon Supreme Order Chrysanthemum Japan 1971, Most Esteemed Family Order Brunei 1972, Chev Grand Cross Order Golden Lion Luxembourg 1972, Memb Distinguished Order Izzuddin Maldives 1972, Hon Memb Darjah Utama Temasek Singapore 1972, Grand Cross Yugoslav Star 1972, Grand Cordon Nat Order Leopard Zaire 1973, Grand Collar Nat Order Infante Dom Henrique Portugal 1973, Cdr Order Golden Ark Netherlands 1979, 1st Cl Mil Order Oman 1979, Collar Order Independence Qatar 1979, 1st Cl Order Muhammadi Morocco 1980, Companion Queen's Serv Order NZ 1981, Canadian Forces Decoration 1982, Grand Cross Carlos III Spain 1986, Companion Order Australia 1988, Grand Ribbon Order Merit Poland 1991, King George VI Coronation Medal 1937, Queen Elizabeth II Coronation Medal 1953, Commemoration Medal NZ 1990, Sultan of Brunei Silver Jubilee Medal 1992, George Cross 50th Anniversary Medal Malta 1992; *m* 20 Nov 1947 ***HM ELIZABETH II** (*qv*) and has issue

Edinburgh, previous creations: In 1726 PRINCE FREDERICK, the eldest son of the future GEORGE II, had conferred on him among other titles the Dukedom of Edenburgh [*sic*]. On his predeceasing his father (who by now had ascended the throne) in March 1750/1 this particular title passed to his eldest son the future GEORGE III, although the ones traditionally associated with the Heir Apparent reverted to the Crown (*see* PRINCE OF WALES, subsections on the titles of Prince of Wales, Duke of Cornwall and Earl of Chester, also the Scottish titles of the Heir Apparent). When GEORGE III became King the Dukedom merged with the Crown. The title was revived, more conventionally spelled this time and in tandem with a Dukedom of Gloucester, for GEORGE III's younger brother in 1764 but expired on the death without issue of the 2nd Duke, the grantee's only son, in 1834. In 1866 a Dukedom of Edinburgh was conferred on PRINCE ALFRED, QUEEN VICTORIA's second son. Having turned down the offer of the Crown of Greece four years earlier and having had the offer of the Crown of Spain turned down on his behalf by his mother and her ministers two years after his elevation to the peerage, he succeeded his uncle ERNEST II as reigning DUKE OF SAXE COBURG AND GOTHA in 1893 but died without surviving male issue in 1900, when his peerage titles expired.

Greenwich, previous creations: *See* ARGYLL, D.

Lineage: *See* MILFORD HAVEN, M.

HRH THE PRINCE OF WALES

Arms: The Royal Arms, differenced by a label of three points argent, in the centre an escutcheon of the arms of the Principality of Wales, *viz.*, quarterly or and gules four lions passant guardant counterchanged, ensigned by the coronet of the Heir Apparent, the whole encircled with the Garter.
Crest: The Royal Crest, differenced with a label of three points argent but with the coronets of the Heir Apparent.
Supporters: The Royal supporters differenced by a like coronet and label. **Badges:** 1 Dexter, a plume of three ostrich feathers argent enfiled by a coronet composed of fleurs-de-lys and crosses-patées or alternately, with the motto *Ich Dien* ('I serve'), 2 sinister, a representation of the Royal Badge of Wales, *viz.*, on a mount vert a dragon passant gules, differenced as in the crest with a label of three points argent; between the badges the shield of the arms of the Duchy of Cornwall, *viz.*, sable fifteen bezants or, ensigned by the coronet of the Heir Apparent.
Personal Flag in Wales: Quarterly or and gules, four lions passant guardant counterchanged, over all an inescutcheon vert charged with the coronet of the Heir Apparent.
Scottish banner: Quarterly, 1st and 4th, or a fess chequy azure and argent (for the Great Steward of Scotland); 2nd and 3rd, argent a lymphad sable flagged gules (for the Lord of the Isles), overall on an inescutcheon or a lion rampant gules armed and langued azure within a royal tressure gules, the inescutcheon charged overall at the honour point with a label of three points azure (for the Duke of Rothesay). **Creations:** Prince of Wales and Earl of Chester 26 July 1958 (invested 1 July 1969) (the other titles became his automatically at his mother's accession).

THE PRINCE OF WALES, DUKE OF CORNWALL, DUKE OF ROTHESAY, EARL OF CHESTER, EARL OF CARRICK, BARON OF RENFREW, LORD OF THE ISLES, GREAT STEWARD OF SCOTLAND (Charles Philip Arthur George Windsor, KG (1958, invested and installed 1968), KT (1977), GCB (1975), AK (1981), QSO (1983), PC (1977)) [HRH The Prince of Wales KG KT GCB PC, Highgrove House, Doughton, nr Tetbury, Glos GL8 8TN; St James's Palace, London SW1A 1BS]; *b* Buckingham Palace 14 Nov 1948; *educ* Cheam School, Gordonstoun, Geelong GS Australia, Trin Coll Cambridge (MA, Hon Fell 1988) and U Coll Wales Aberystwyth; Personal ADC to HM 1973–, ktd 1977, Capt RN 1988 (ret), Col-in-Ch: Roy Regt Wales (24th/41st Foot) 1969–, Cheshire Regt 1977–, Lord Strathcona's Horse (Roy Canadian) Regt 1977–, Para Regt 1977–, Roy Australian Armoured Corps 1977–, Roy Gurkha Rifles 1977–, Roy Regt Canada 1977–, Air Reserve Gp Air Cmd Canada 1977–, Roy Winnipeg Rifles 1977–, Papua New Guinea 2nd Bn Roy Pacific Islands Regt 1984–, Roy Canadian Dragoons 1985–, Army Air Corps 1992–, Roy Dragoon Gds 1992–; Dep Col-in-Ch Highrs 1994–; Col Welsh Gds 1975–; Gp Capt RAF 1988–; Hon Air Cdre: RAF Brawdy 1977–92, RAF Valley 1993–; Air Cdre-in-Ch RNZAF 1977–; Pres: Bach Choir 1976–, Br Horse Soc 1997–, Business in the Community, Disability Ptnrship, Fndn for Integrated Medicine, King's Fund, Mary Rose Tst, Phoenix Tst, Prince of Wales Business Leaders Forum 1990–, Prince of Wales's Inst Architecture 1992–, Prince's Tst Bd 1977–, Prince's Scottish Youth Business Tst 1986–, Prince's Tst 1976–, Prince's Youth Business Tst, Roy Acad Tst 1993–, Roy Ag Soc of England 1990–91, Roy Coll GPs 1991–92, Roy Jubilee Tst 1977–, Roy Shakespeare Co 1991–, Scottish Business in the Community, Soc Friends of St George's and Descendants of KGs 1975–, Utd World Colleges 1978–93, Wetlands Tst 1979–, Wildfowl Tst, Prince's Tst Vols; Adml Roy Thames Yacht Club 1986–; High Steward Roy Borough Windsor and Maidenhead 1975–; Patron: Abbeyfield 1979–, African Medical and Research Fndn, Age Concern England, Almshouse Assoc, Ancient Monuments Soc 1990–, Assoc for Business Sponsorship of the Arts 1988–, Bath Internat Music Festival, BBC Nat Orchestra Wales, Bristol Roy Hosp for Sick Children 1996–, Br Sch Athens 1997–, Civic Tst 1985–, English Chamber Orchestra and Music Soc, Gloucester Cathedral 900-Year Fund, Gurkha Welfare Tst, Henry Doubleday Research Assoc, Macmillan Cancer Relief, Nat Gallery Tst 1993–, Music in Country Churches, Oxford Centre for Islamic Studies, Phoenix House, Roy Opera, Roy Soc Nature Conservation 1977–, Roy TV Soc 1997–, Scottish Civic Tst, Scottish Wildlife Tst, Tradescant Tst, Welsh Nat Opera, Yorkshire Dales Millennium Tst; V-Patron Br Cncl 1984–; V-Pres Nat Tst; Chllr: U of Wales 1976–; Chm: Cambridge Cwlth Tst, Roy Collection Tst 1993–; Coronation Medal 1953, Queen's Silver Jubilee Medal 1977, Great Master Order Bath 1975, Extra Companion Queen's Service Order NZ 1983, Grand Cross White Rose Finland 1969, Grand Cordon Supreme Order Chrysanthemum Japan 1971, Grand Cross House of Orange Netherlands 1972, Grand Cross Order Oak Crown Luxembourg 1972, Kt Order Elephant Denmark 1974, Grand Cross Order Ojasvi Rajanya Nepal 1975, Kt Order Seraphim Sweden 1975, Grand Cross Order Southern Cross Brazil 1978; Grand Cross Collar Republic of Egypt 1981, Grand Cross Order Orange Nassau Netherlands 1982, Grand Cross Order St Olav Norway 1978, Offr Order Star Ghana 1977, Grand Cross Legn Hon 1984, Grand Cross Order Carlos III Spain, Nepal Coronation Medal 1975, Grand Cross Khalifiyyeh Order Bahrain, Grand Cross Order Lion Malawi, Grand Cross Order Merit Saudi Arabia, Papua New Guinea Independence Medal 1975, Fijian Independence Medal 1970, NZ Commemorative Medal 1990, Order Merit Qatar 1986, Order Mubarak the Gt Kuwait 1993; Freedom: Cardiff 1969, Roy Borough New Windsor 1970, Cities of London 1971, Chester 1973, Canterbury 1978, Portsmouth 1979, Lancaster 1993, Swansea 1994; Liveryman: Farmers' Co 1980, Pewterers' Co 1982, Fruiterers' Co 1989, Fishmongers' Co 1971, Gardeners' Co 1987, Carpenters' Co 1992; Freeman: Drapers' Co 1971, Shipwrights' Co 1978, Goldsmiths' Co; Hon Memb: Master Mariners' Co 1977 (Master 1988–90) and Bar Gray's Inn 1974 (Hon Bencher 1975); Bencher Middle Temple 1988; Hon DCL Oxon 1983, Durham 1998; *m* 29 July 1981 at St Paul's Cathedral London (*divorce* 28 Aug 1996) Lady Diana Frances Spencer (*d* in a car crash 31 Aug 1997), yst dau of 8th Earl Spencer (*qv*), and has:

1 +WILLIAM ARTHUR PHILIP LOUIS; *b* St Mary's Hosp Paddington 21 June 1982; *educ* Ludgrove and Eton

2 +Henry (Harry) Charles Albert David; *b* St Mary's Hosp Paddington 15 Sept 1984; *educ* Ludgrove and Eton

Prince of Wales (and Earldom of Chester), previous holders of title of: The dignity of Prince of Wales, though exclusive since 1301 (when it was instituted) to the Heir Apparent of the Sovereign, is not automatically conferred. Moreover, as will be seen, its possessor by no means always inherits the Crown.

The first such, EDWARD of Caernarvon, later EDWARD II, was so created 7 Feb 1301, just under three months before his 17th birthday. On succeeding his father as King in 1307, the title merged with the Crown. This has been the pattern ever since where the title is extant at all. Yet the next holder was not EDWARD II's own first-born son, the future EDWARD III, even though he was at least 16 at the time of his father's deposition, but EDWARD III's own eldest boy, EDWARD of Woodstock, better known as the Black Prince, created PRINCE OF WALES in 1343, when he was not quite 13. EDWARD II's failure to create his own successor PRINCE OF WALES is perhaps due to the turbulence of his reign in its closing stages, perhaps also to the novelty of the title.

The Black Prince predeceased his father, dying a year before him in June 1376. For his son, however, the future RICHARD II, the title had to be created anew, not inherited. The creation in question occurred in November 1376, eight months before RICHARD succeeded his grandfather as King. RICHARD II died childless, so for the time being the question of whether to create his first-born male PRINCE OF WALES did not arise.

HENRY IV's first-born son, the future HENRY V, was made at the age of 12 PRINCE OF WALES. This was in 1399, some two weeks after his father's usurping the throne from RICHARD II. HENRY V died when his own son, the future HENRY VI, was only nine months old, so the failure to create him PRINCE OF WALES is perhaps understandable. On the other hand HENRY VI's son, EDWARD of Westminster, who predeceased his father in 1471, was made PRINCE OF WALES in March 1454, when at the most not even 18 months old. And EDWARD IV's elder son, another EDWARD of Westminster (better known as one of the two Princes in the Tower) was made PRINCE OF WALES when not quite nine months old. Perhaps the uncertainty of dynastic survival during the Wars of the Roses prompted Kings to confer the princely title on their heirs as early as possible. If so, it would seem that in earlier generations the succession appeared too secure for the matter to be seen as urgent. Or perhaps the crisis of the moment had arisen so swiftly that it found earlier Sovereigns as unready as ETHELRED is misunderstood to have been by those who do not know that his sobriquet means 'lacking in advice'.

In fact 11 out of the 21 recorded royal personages known as or styled PRINCEs OF WALES have not, or not yet, ascended the throne. For instance, RICHARD III's only son, EDWARD of Middleham, was created PRINCE OF WALES in August 1483 but predeceased his father aged ten, dying less than eight months later. HENRY VII's eldest son ARTHUR, also made PRINCE OF WALES, died seven years before his father at the age of 16. JAMES I's eldest son HENRY did likewise aged 18. CHARLES I had a first-born son called CHARLES JAMES who died the day of his birth, 13 May 1629, but was interred under the title of 'Prince of Wales' even though he was never formally so created. JAMES II's only surviving son JAMES FRANCIS EDWARD, styled 'Prince of Wales' in an official publication within a month of his birth in June 1688, and the latter's elder son, also styled 'Prince of Wales' (by his adherents), otherwise known as The Old and Young Pretender respectively, were never acknowledged as having rights to the Crown at all following JAMES II's deemed vacating of it late in 1688 and the former was attainted by the English Parliament in March 1701/2, when all his honours were forfeited. GEORGE II's eldest son FREDERICK is another case of a PRINCE OF WALES predeceasing his father (his son, the future GEORGE III, having to be created PRINCE OF WALES anew a month after FREDERICK's death in spring 1751).

The first holder of an Earldom of Chester was one Gherbod, a native of Flanders who was granted a few years after the Conquest a substantial part of the former province of Mercia along with Chester itself, the whole being designated a County Palatine, that is, a county whose Earl had a large measure of devolved power. Earl Gherbod soon went back to the Continent, never to return. The Earldom of Chester was next conferred, in 1071, on Hugh d'Avranches, subsequently Vicomte d'Avranches, in Normandy, but better known as Hugh *Lupus* ('Wolf', for his rapacity) and as far as his family background went a grandson of Herleve/Harlotte, mother of WILLIAM I (THE CONQUEROR), to whom he was thus half-nephew. His son, Richard, succeeded him in the Earldom and married a cousin, Maud, granddaughter of WILLIAM I, but was drowned in the wreck of the White Ship in 1120, leaving no legitimate children. The Earldom was next conferred on Hugh *Lupus*'s nephew through his sister Margaret, one Ranulph, Vicomte de Bayeux. The Earldom remained with the latter's descendants till the death without issue in 1232 of his great-grandson Ranulph (also known as Earl of Lincoln; *qv*, preliminary remarks). Ranulph's sister's son John le Scot, Earl of Huntingdon and on his father's side nephew of WILLIAM THE LION KING OF SCOTS, was the next person to be invested with the Earldom of Chester but died, also without issue, five years later in 1237.

The Earldom of Chester had therefore already been held for over 150 years by family connections, however remote, of the reigning dynasty. From 1254 it has been held always by an eldest or eldest surviving son of the Sovereign, with the single exception of a period of less than eight months between Christmas Eve 1264 and the Battle of Evesham in early August the following year, when it was extorted from HENRY III by Simon de Montfort (*see* LEICESTER, E, preliminary remarks). The early holders (the future EDWARD I, his first-born son ALPHONSO, his second-born son the future EDWARD II, the future EDWARD III and the Black Prince) were created Earls of Chester independently of the title of Prince of Wales, although in EDWARD II's case the two dignities happened to be conferred the same day. From 1398, by an Act of Parliament which though repealed in the following reign has in practice been observed ever since, the Earldom of Chester has been treated as a principality and conferred with that of Wales.

Cornwall, previous titles under name of: Shadowy dignities which may possibly have involved the name Cornwall or a variation thereof include Earldoms supposedly held by (a) Brient de Bretagne (a Breton, as his name suggests) shortly after the Conquest, (b) Robert de Mortain, a half-brother of WILLIAM I (THE CONQUEROR), and his son and successor William de Mortain between the Conquest and 1106, (c) Alan de Bretagne (another Breton; *see* also RICHMOND and GORDON, D, preliminary remarks) between 1140 and 1146, (d) Baldwin de Reviers, Earl also of Devon (*qv*, preliminary remarks), (e) JOHN, fifth son of HENRY II, and (f) Henry, an illegitimate son of the first apparently authentic Earl of Cornwall, Reynold de Dunstanville, so created *c* 1141 and himself an illegitimate son, but of more august paternity, his father being HENRY I. (A Barony of Corn(e)wall(e) created according to later doctrine by writ of summons in 1433 was held by (Sir?) John Cornewalle till 1443, when on his death without legitimate issue any Barony/-ies he may have held, including the much more substantive ones of Fanhope and Milbroke, which were undoubtedly conferred on him, expired.)

Reynold de Dunstanville's Earldom passed back to the Crown when in 1175 he died without having had any legitimate sons. It was revived for RICHARD, KING JOHN's second son (*see* also GREY, B), in 1227, only to expire with the life of Edmund, its second holder and the grantee's fifth son, in 1300. Only two further creations of an Earldom (as opposed to Dukedom) of Cornwall were made, the first in favour of Piers Gaveston, EDWARD II's favourite, in 1307 and, following the former's murder five years later by a lynch mob of nobles jealous of his influence over the King, in 1328 on EDWARD II's own flesh and blood, namely his second son JOHN of Eltham. The latter died childless in 1336, killed apparently by his elder brother EDWARD III. Thereafter all creations involving the County of Cornwall have been in the shape of Dukedoms and have been held exclusively by the eldest son, eldest surviving son or on one occasion grandson (the future RICHARD II) of the Sovereign. The first such, indeed the first Dukedom created in England ever, was in March 1336/7, conferred on the Black Prince. On his predeceasing his father EDWARD III it reverted to the Crown, being recreated anew five and a half months later for the Black Prince's son, the future RICHARD II. From 1421 (but backdated to 1337) it has been held that the eldest son and heir of a reigning Sovereign becomes Duke of Cornwall at birth. When in 1502 the Heir Apparent ARTHUR, HENRY VII's eldest son, predeceased his parent as Sovereign, having a younger brother but no children, the Dukedom was treated as passing automatically to the next heir (the future HENRY VIII) rather than reverting to the Crown. But when FREDERICK PRINCE OF WALES (and DUKE OF CORNWALL) predeceased his father GEORGE II in March 1750/1 the Dukedom was deemed to have reverted to the Crown (along of course with the title of Prince of Wales). It may be assumed that if an Heir Presumptive who is not a child of the Sovereign ascends the throne, as happened with JAMES I in 1603, his (or her) eldest son and heir (in 1603 this was HENRY, later known as HENRY PRINCE OF WALES) automatically becomes Duke of Cornwall.

Scottish titles (Dukedom of Rothesay, Earldom of Carrick, Barony of Renfrew, Lordship of the Isles and Great Stewardship of Scotland) held by the Heir Apparent: These titles are held under the terms of an Act of the Scottish Parliament of 27 Nov 1469 by the first-born 'Prince' (interpreted as meaning son, even though the word 'Prince' then could apply to either sex) of the Kings (to be interpreted as including Queens) of Scots. Since the union of English and Scottish Crowns in 1603 (more precisely the death in 1613 of HENRY PRINCE OF WALES, CHARLES I's elder brother) the limitation of the Scottish titles of the Heir Apparent has been treated as identical to that of the Dukedom of Cornwall. The Dukedom of Rothesay was first conferred in 1398 on DAVID STEWART, first-born son and Heir Apparent of ROBERT III KING OF SCOTS. On DAVID's dying without issue in his father's lifetime the titles reverted to the Crown. His younger brother JAMES was granted in 1404 the entire parcel of territory which went with the post of Steward of Scotland and since this included Rothesay, the lands that appertained to the Earldom of Carrick and the (then presumably territorial) Barony of Renfrew and since at that time such honours were inextricably bound up with the holding of land rather than personal to the title-holder, as is nowadays the case, he is deemed to have become Duke of Rothesay, Earl of Carrick and Baron Renfrew, also Lord of Kyle (though this last honour does not now feature in the recital of the Heir Apparent's dignities). When JAMES succeeded as JAMES I his peerages merged in the Crown.

For the way in which the Earldom of Carrick in the Peerage of Scotland became a royal title *see* the preliminary remarks to the article CARRICK, E (*i.e.*, the title of that name in the Peerage of Ireland). There is also in existence a Life Peerage of Renfrew of Kaimsthorn (*qv*), whose holder was between 1986 and 1997 Master of Jesus College Cambridge, PRINCE EDWARD's alma mater. For the way the Lordship of the Isles came to be vested in the Royal House of Scotland *see* BOSVILLE MACDONALD, Bt. For the early evolution of the post of Great Steward of Scotland *see* MORAY, E.

Seat: Highgrove House, Doughton, Glos. Highgrove was originally the property of a family of Huguenot extraction called Paul. They were cousins of a family of Baronets of the same name (*see* 1970 edn PAUL, Bt, of Rodborough) who had a marriage connection with the Earls of Strathmore and Kinghorne (*qv*), hence remotely with the present owner, the PRINCE OF WALES, himself, and back in the 17th century with a member of OLIVER CROMWELL's Council of State.

Highgrove was built by an unknown architect in the late 1790s. The estate itself came to the family through the marriage in 1771 of Josiah Paul TIPPETTS later PAUL (his mother's family name, which he adopted under the terms of the will of his uncle, her brother) with Mary Clark, whose father Robert was the local squire. They sold it on in 1860 to Lt-Col Edward John STRACEY later STRACEY-CLITHEROW (*see* STRACEY, Bt), who in turn sold it some four years later to a barrister called William Hamilton Yatman.

Yatman seems to have insufficiently insured his property and a fire in 1893 forced him to part with it since he apparently could not afford the repairs. The new owner was Arthur Charles Mitchell (*see* SAINT ALDWYN, E), who carried out restoration work to the designs of John Hart, of Bristol. It was probably then that the bow windows on the garden front were added. Mitchell's second wife continued living as a widow at Highgrove till the close of World War II, following which the estate was acquired by Lt-Col Gwyn Morgan-Jones, son-in-law of the 1st and last Baron Buckland (*see* HARTWELL, B). In 1965 the Colonel and his wife sold Highgrove to Maurice Macmillan, son of the former Prime Minister (*see* STOCKTON, E), for allegedly £89,000 (not much under £800,000 in late-1990s terms). The Macmillans demolished a wing the next year (since restored by the PRINCE OF WALES in Cotswold vernacular style) but even then the house had four reception rooms, nine bedrooms, six bathrooms, a nursery wing and servants' quarters, or so the particulars boasted when it was put up for sale in 1980. It changed hands for a sum said to have been between three-quarters of a million and a million pounds (close to £4m in late-1990s terms) but has been constantly renovated and improved ever since. The estate (technically owned, along with the house, by the Duchy of Cornwall) amounted to some 350 acres in 1980 but has been virtually trebled in size since.

Highgrove originally consisted of a rectangular layout, the main front having three storeys of five bays each. There was a portico supported by columns at ground-floor level and above it the type of window called Venetian, that is, curvilinear as to the top (whereas the rest of the windows were, and still are, rectilinear). Pilasters ran up outside the top two floors to a cornice underneath a low parapet at roof level. During the PRINCE OF WALES's occupancy the parapet has been replaced by a balustrade in Bath stone which rises considerably higher, the globular finials at the corners by urns, the pilasters by new versions topped off with Ionic capitals and a triangular pediment superimposed with an oculus at its centre. The old Venetian window was at some point lowered and made rectangular, like the others, though its louvred shutters emphasise its primacy. The portico is now weather-proof, having been sealed and glazed. The estate has been developed on organic farming lines and modest commercial schemes started which involve the sale of such items as bread made from stone-ground wholemeal flour. The gardens also have been transformed to present a more naturalistic appearance, the absence of chemical pesticides encouraging the reappearance of wild flowers and insects.

HRH The Duke of York

Arms: The Royal Arms differenced by a label of three points argent, charged on the centre point with an anchor azure. **Crest:** On a coronet of crosses and fleurs-de-lys a lion statant guardant or, crowned with a like coronet and differenced by a label as in the Arms. **Supporters:** As with the Royal Arms differenced by a like coronet and label. **Creations:** B., E. and D. (all UK) 1986.

THE 1ST DUKE OF YORK, EARL OF INVERNESS and **BARON KILLYLEAGH** (Andrew Albert Christian Edward Windsor, CVO (1979)) [HRH The Duke of York CVO ADC, Buckingham Palace, London SW1 1AA]; *b* Buckingham Palace 19 Feb 1960; *educ* Gordonstoun, (Govr) Lakefield Coll Ontario (now Tstee) and RNC Dartmouth; RN: joined as Midshipman 1979, helicopter pilot HMS *Invincible* S Atlantic Campaign 1982, Personal ADC to his mother 1984–, sr pilot 815 Sqdn HMS *Osprey* at Portland 1994, MOD 1996, Lt-Cdr 1992, psc Dec 1992, Adml Sea Cadet Corps 1992–, cmded *HMS Cottesmore* 1993–94, with 702 Sqdn 1994–95, sr pilot 815 Sqdn 1995–96, MOD 1997–; Col-in-Ch: Canadian Airborne Regt 1991–93, Roy Irish Regt 1992–, Staffs Regt (Prince of Wales's) 1989–, Roy New Zealand Army Logistic Regt 1997–, Queen's York Rangers 1997–; Freedom City York 1987; Cdre Roy Thames Yacht Club, Freeman Shipwrights' Co, Er Bro Corp Trin Ho, Patron: Army Museums Ogilvy Tst, Army Offrs' Golfing Soc, Aycliffe Centre for Young People, Badminton Assoc of England, JBr Deaf Assoc, BSES Expdns, Children North East, Children's Fndn, City Ballet of London, Cwlth Golfing Soc, Co Antrim Yacht Club, Contemporary Dance Tst, Defeating Deafness, Falklands Conservation, Fight for Sight, Fire Serv Sports and Athletics Assoc, Fleet Air Arm Museum, Friends of Lakefield Coll Sch, Friends of the Staffs Regt (POW's), Golf Fndn, Greenwich Hosp, Jubilee Sailing Tst, Killyleagh Yacht Club, Lucifer Golfing Soc, Opera North, Round Square, Roy Artillery Golfing Soc, Roy Belfast Golf Club, Roy Blackheath Golf Club, Roy Coll Ophthalmologists, Roy Cwlth Soc for Deaf, Roy Co Down Golf Club, Roy Free Hampstead NHS Tst, Roy Jersey Golf Club, Roy Liverpool Golf Club, Roy Montrose Golf Club, RN Golf Assoc, RN Golfing Soc, Roy Perth Golfing Soc, Roy Portrush Golf Club, Roy St David's Golf Club, Roy Victoria Yacht Club, Roy W Norfolk Golf Club, Sail Trg Assoc, SS Great Britain Project, Swordfish Heritage Tst, Understanding Industry, Welsh Badminton Union, Weston Spirit, York Minster Fund, Yorks Business Conf, Young Electronic Designer Awards; Pres Roy Household Golf Club and Faldo Jr Series, Tstee Nat Maritime Museum, Outward Bound Tst, Visitor Roy Hosp Sch; author: *Photographs* (1985); *m* Westminster Abbey 23 July 1986 (*divorce* 1996) Sarah Margaret, 2nd dau of Brig Ronald Ivor Ferguson (*see* DACRE, B, and POWERSCOURT, V), and has:

1 +Beatrice Elizabeth Mary; *b* Portland Hosp London 8 Aug 1988

2 +Eugenie Victoria Helena; *b* Portland Hosp 23 March 1990

York, previous creations: Unless one counts William de Aumale, briefly Earl of Yorkshire from late August 1138, it may be said that York as a title has only ever existed as a Dukedom and has invariably been conferred on an immediate member of the Royal family, usually the Sovereign's next to eldest son. The first Duke of York was EDMUND of Langley, EDWARD III's 4th surviving son and founder of the House of York. His great-grandson EDWARD, 4th DUKE OF YORK of this, the 1385 creation, became EDWARD IV, when his titles merged in the Crown. The next creation (in 1474) was in favour of RICHARD, EDWARD IV's younger son and one of the Princes in the Tower, with whose death it expired. HENRY, later HENRY VIII, was created DUKE OF YORK in 1494 when his elder brother ARTHUR was still alive but as with EDWARD IV the title merged with the Crown on his coming to the throne. So too with CHARLES I, who had been created DUKE OF YORK in January 1604/5, when his elder brother HENRY was still alive; and again in the case of JAMES II.

The pattern was disarranged slightly when GEORGE I created his youngest brother ERNEST AUGUSTUS not DUKE OF YORK but DUKE OF YORK AND ALBANY, and in 1716, when he had already come to the throne, rather than when he was merely expected to. 'Albany' referred to the Scottish territory north of the Firths of Clyde and Forth and was a title traditionally given to second sons of the Kings of Scots. It was doubtless now added to 'York' to conciliate feelings north of the Border, where the Jacobite Uprising had occurred the year before. The Old Pretender, who had been directly involved in the 1715 Uprising, nevertheless reverted to the form 'Duke of York' only when he conferred the titular peerage of that name on Henry, his younger son, around the time of the boy's birth in 1724/5. The dual form DUKE OF YORK AND ALBANY was resuscitated by GEORGE II in 1760, six months before his own death, when he conferred that title on his eldest son's second son EDWARD AUGUSTUS, the future GEORGE III's next younger brother. The title expired seven years later when the grantee died unmarried.

GEORGE III followed his grandfather's example, creating the second in line to the throne (and his second son) DUKE OF YORK AND ALBANY in 1784. The latter was always known as DUKE OF YORK, however. He was a competent but not outstanding general, the rhyme about him marching his men up and down a hill giving an inadequate curriculum vitae, and was promoted Commander-in-Chief, as which he tightened up discipline and improved the professionalism of the officer corps, notably by founding what later became the Staff College and the Royal Military College Sandhurst. His love of good order did not extend to money matters, however, and his career was destroyed by the revelation that his former mistress Mary Anne Clarke had been trafficking in promotions. (She was an ancestress of the novelist Daphne Du Maurier, though apparently not by HRH.) The next DUKE OF YORK, so created in 1892, was the present holder's great-grandfather GEORGE V, whose titles on his ascending the throne merged in the Crown, as was the case also when GEORGE VI succeeded in 1936, he having been created DUKE OF YORK in 1920.

Inverness, previous creations: For the Duchy of Inverness conferred in 1840 on Lady Cecilia Underwood, *see* ARRAN, E. For the Viscountcy of Inverness created in 1684 *see* HUNTLY, M. Both GEORGE V and GEORGE VI had as a subsidiary title when still DUKE OF YORK an Earldom of Inverness. For the titular Earldom and Dukedom of Inverness conferred by the titular James III *see* KINNOULL, E.

Killyleagh, constituent title in other peerage creation: *See* DUFFERIN AND CLANEBOYE, B.

HRH The Prince Edward

Arms: The Royal Arms, differenced by a label of three points, charged on the 2nd point with a rose barbed and seeded proper.

THE PRINCE EDWARD (Edward Antony Richard Louis Windsor, CVO (1989)) [HRH The Prince Edward CVO, Buckingham Palace, London SW1A 1AA]; *b* Buckingham Palace 10 March 1964; *educ* Gordonstoun and Jesus Coll Cambridge; 2nd Lt RM 1983–87; Chm Duke of Edinburgh's Award Special Projects Gp 1986–96 and Internat Cncl Duke of Edinburgh's Award Internat Assoc 1993–; Patron: Auckland Performing Arts Educn Tst (renamed UNITEC Institute of Technology 1991), Cambridge Youth Theatre (renamed Classworks Theatre Tst 1985), City of Birmingham Symphony Orchestra and Chorus 1991–, Roy Exchange Theatre Co 1991–, Friends of Wanganui Opera House 1990–, Globe Theatre Saskatchewan 1992–, Haddo House Hall Arts Tst 1987–, London Mozart Players 1990–, Nat Youth Orchestra Scotland 1987–, Nat Youth Theatre GB 1987–, Ocean Youth Club 1990–, Scottish Badminton Union 1990–, Roy Tournament 1986–; Pres: Children's Film Unit 1992–, Cwlth Games Fedn 1990–, Lord's Taverners 1993–94, Nat Youth Music Theatre 1987–; Tstee: Duke of Edinburgh's Award 1988–, Duke of Edinburgh's Award Internat Fndn 1988–

HRH The Princess Royal

Arms: The Royal Arms, differenced by a label of three points, charged on the 1st and 3rd points with a cross and on the 2nd with a heart. **Creation:** 13 June 1987.

THE PRINCESS ROYAL (Anne Elizabeth Alice Louise Windsor, KG (1994), GCVO (1974)) [HRH The Princess Royal KG CCVO QSO, Buckingham Palace, London SW1A 1AA; Gatcombe Park, Minchinhampton, Glos GL6 9AT]; *b* Clarence House 15 Aug 1950; *educ* Benenden; Ch-Cmdt WRNS; Chllr London U 1981–; Cmdt-in-Ch: Women's Tport Serv, St John Ambulance and Nursing Cadets; Col-in-Ch: Canadian Forces Communications and Electronics Branch, 8th Canadian Hussars (Princess Louise's), 14th/20th King's Hussars, King's Roy Hus, Grey and Simcoe Foresters Militia, Roy Australian Corps Signals, Roy Corps Signals,

Roy Logistic Corps, Roy Newfoundland Regt, Roy NZ Corps of Signals , Roy NZ Nursing Corps, Roy Regina Rifles, Roy Scots (Roy Regt), Worcs and Sherwood Foresters Regt (29th/45th Foot), Gold Stick Blues and Royals 1998–; Fell King's Coll London, FICE, FISMM, FRSGS; Freedom City London 1976; Freeman: Falkirk Dist, Fishmongers' Co; Hon Air Cdre: RAF Lyneham, London U Air Sqdn; Hon Col OTC London U Contingent; life memb Roy Br Legn Women's Section; Hon Freeman: Farmers' Co and Loriners' Co, Yeoman in Saddlers' Co; Hon life memb RNVR Officers' Assoc; Hon Liveryman Farriers' Co; Hon Memb: Br Equine Veterinary Assoc, Nat Osteoporosis Soc; Hon Pres: Chartered Inst Tport, Roy Caledonian Hunt; Jt Pres Lowland Bde Club; Internat Humanitarian Award Variety Club 1987; Master Carmen's Co; memb: Internat Olympic Ctee 1988–, Lloyd's 1989; Past Master Woolmen's Co; Past Pres: Chartered Inst Tport; Patron: Amateur Jockeys Assoc GB, Animal Diseases Research Assoc, Army and Roy Artillery Hunter Trials, Assoc Combined Youth Clubs, Australian Veterinary Assoc, Basic Skills Agency, Benenden Ball, Br Exec Serv Overseas, Br Nutrition Fndn, Br Olympic Medical Tst, Br Quality Fndn, Br Sch Osteopathy, Br-US Sports Assoc, Butler Tst, Canadian Communications and Electronic Branch Inst, Canadian Therapeutic Riding Assoc, Canal Museum Tst, Centl Scotland Countryside Tst, Citizens Advice Scotland, Coll Occupnl Therapists, Concert Global Challenge, Cornwall '98, Cranfield Tst, Devpt Tst (for mentally handicapped), Dunn Nutrition Centre, English Lacrosse Assoc, Farms for City Children, Flying Scot Club, Friends of Hosp for Tropical Diseases, Glos and N Avon Fedn Young Farmers' Clubs, Glos Rugby Union, Home Farm Tst, Hearing Dogs for the Deaf, Home Farm Tst Devpt Tst, Hong Kong Save The Children Fund Corporate Fund Raising Ctee, Intensive Care Soc, Inst Logistics, Internat Health Exchange, Jersey Wildlife Preservation Tst, Liverpool Sch Tropical Medicine, Minchinhampton Centre for the Elderly, Moredun Fndn, Nat Assoc CAB, Nat Assoc Prison Visitors, Nat Assoc Victim Support Schemes, Nat Autistic Soc, Nat Coaching Fndn, Nat Union Townswomen's Guilds, NI Prison Serv Centl Benevolent Fund, Northern Lighthouse Bd, Quarry Bank Mill Tst, Riding for the Disabled Assoc (Australia), Roy Coll Anaesthetists, Roy Coll Paediatrics and Child Health, Roy Corinthian Yacht Club, Roy Corps Signals Inst, Roy Dick Sch Veterinary Studies, Roy LymingtonYacht Club, Roy Port Moresby Soc for Prevention Cruelty Animals, Roy Scots Club, Roy Signals Assoc, Roy Tournament, Sailability, Scottish Assoc Young Farmers' Clubs, Scottish Business Achievement Award Tst, Scottish Fiddle Orchestra, Scottish Field Studies Assoc, Scottish Inst Sports Medicine and Sports Sci, Scottish Nat Fatstock Club, Scottish Rugby Union, SENSE (Nat Deaf-Blind and Rubella Assoc), Shire Horse Soc, Six Circle Club, Spinal Injuries Assoc, Splash Ball, Suffolk Horse Soc, Textile Conservn Centre, Townswomen's Guilds, Transaid, UK Antarctic Heritage Tst, UK Sailing Acad, Ulster Sports and Recreation Tst, Victim Support Scotland, Westminster and London Horse Show, Wooden Spoon Soc, World Breeding Fedn for Sport Horses, World Student Debating Championships 1999, Year of Sport, Youth Sail Trg Tst; Pres: Animal Health Tst, BAFTA, Br Horse Soc 1998–, Br Knitting and Clothing Export Cncl, Br Olympic Assoc, CNAA, ILPH, Internat Riders' Scholarships Awards Panel, Missions to Seamen, Nat Riding Week, Patrons Crime Concern, Princess Royal Tst for Carers, RedR (Engrs for Disaster Relief), Riding for the Disabled Assoc, Roy Sch for Daughters of Offrs of RN and RM (Haslemere), Roy Yachting Assoc, Rural Housing Tst, Save the Children Fund, Scottish Chamber Commerce, Shipwrecked Fishermen and Mariners' Roy Benevolent Soc, Windsor Horse Trials, Working Clumber Spaniel Soc, WRNS Benevolent Tst; Roy Bencher Inner Temple 1990; Visitor: Felixstowe Coll, St Mary's Cathedral (Edinburgh) Workshop; V-Patron: British Show Jumping Assoc, Memorial to the Women of World War II, WRNS Assoc; V-Pres: Nat Fedn Young Farmers' Clubs, RGS, Roy Bath and W County Show, Soc of Friends of St George's and Descendants of Knights of the Garter, Southern Counties Show; FRS 1987, FRCVS 1986, Hon FRCS 1986, Hon FIEE 1987, Hon FRCP 1990; *m* 1st Westminster Abbey 14 Nov 1973 (*divorce* 1992), as his 1st w, Capt Mark Anthony Peter Phillips, CVO, late ADC(P) (*m* 2nd 1 Feb 1997 Sandy, dau of James Pflueger, of Honolulu, Hawaii), only s of Maj Peter William Garside Phillips, MC, late 1st King's Dragoon Gds, and has:

1 +Peter Mark Andrew; *b* St Mary's Hosp Paddington 15 Nov 1977; *educ* Gordonstoun

1 +Zara Anne Elizabeth; *b* St Mary's Hosp Paddington 15 May 1981

THE PRINCESS ROYAL *m* 2nd Crathie Church, Aberdeenshire, 12 Dec 1992 *Cdr Timothy James Hamilton Laurence, MVO (1989), RN, yr s of Cdr Guy Stewart Laurence, RN, by Barbara Alison Symonds

Princess Royal, previous holders: The style is exclusive to the eldest or sole daughter of the Sovereign. It is for life only and there can never be more than one Princess Royal at a time, so that the dignity is conferred only if the previous Princess Royal has died. The mode of conferring is by declaration. The earliest daughter of an English or Scottish sovereign to be so styled was CHARLES I's daughter MARY, mother of WILLIAM III. The first daughter of a sovereign of Britain (*i.e.*, following the Union of English and Scottish Parliaments of 1707) to be so styled was ANNE, GEORGE II's child, who lived from 1709 to 1759. She married William IV Prince of Orange and their grandson WILLIAM I became first sovereign of the modern Kingdom of The Netherlands in 1815. His great-great-great granddaughter is the current QUEEN BEATRIX. The style Princess Royal was subsequently conferred on (a) GEORGE III's eldest daughter CHARLOTTE AUGUSTA MATILDA, who married FREDERICK I, KING OF WURTTEMBERG; (b) QUEEN VICTORIA's eldest daughter, VICTORIA ADELAIDE MARY LOUISA, who married the German Emperor FREDERICK III and was mother of the last Kaiser, WILLIAM II; (c) EDWARD VII's eldest daughter, LOUISE VICTORIA ALEXANDRA DAGMAR, who married the 1st Duke of Fife (*qv*); and (d) GEORGE V's only daughter, (VICTORIA ALEXANDRA ALICE) MARY, who married the 6th Earl of Harewood (*qv*).

Seat: Gatcombe Park, Minchinhampton, Glos. An earlier manor house adjoining Minchinhampton Church was replaced in the early 1740s by the present structure, possibly to the designs of Francis Franklin, a native of Chalford in the Stroud valley and the master mason employed on the project. His patron was Edward Sheppard, from a family of prosperous Cotswold clothiers who had bought the property in 1651 from the 1st Earl of Plymouth (*qv*) of the 1682 creation. The latter's family name, oddly enough, was Windsor (*see* PLYMOUTH, E).

Internal plasterwork after Adam dates from the mid-18th century. Some 70 years later the estate was bought by David Ricardo, the father of political economy in Britain. He called in Disraeli's cousin George Basevi to extend wings either side of the two-storey-over-basement ashlar-clad main block. This, with its moulded cornice and balustraded parapet climaxing in a triangular break-front pediment over a Venetian window, was extended slightly forward at ground level with a portico, again topped with a balustrade, resting on four doric columns. The two wings are single-storey, with bow-windows, that on the left as one faces the house greatly extended in its turn by a conservatory added in 1829.

Just before World War II Col Henry Ricardo sold Gatcombe to Samuel Courtauld, a member of the textile family, from whom it was inherited in 1947 by R A Butler, his son-in-law, later Lord Butler of Saffron Walden (*see* 1970 edn). The latter sold it to HM THE QUEEN in 1976 for a reported £500,000 (well over £2m in late-1990s terms).

HRH THE DUKE OF GLOUCESTER

Arms: The Royal Arms, differenced by a label [labels assigned a sovereign's grandchild (bar the est s of a Prince of Wales) are hereditary (roy warrant 24 Feb 1975)] of five points argent, the centre and two outer points charged with a cross gules, and the inner points with a lion passant guardant. **Crest:** On a coronet composed of four crosses-patées alternated with four strawberry leaves, a lion statant guardant or, crowned with the like coronet, and differenced with the label as in the Arms.

Supporters: The Royal Supporters, differenced with the like coronet and label.

THE 2ND DUKE OF GLOUCESTER, EARL OF ULSTER and **BARON CULLODEN** (RICHARD ALEXANDER WALTER GEORGE WINDSOR, KG, GCVO (1974)) [HRH The Duke of Gloucester KG GCVO, Kensington Palace, W8 4PU]; *b* Northampton 26 Aug 1944; *s* f 1974; *educ* Eton and Magdalene Coll Cambridge (MA, DipArch); RIBA, FSA, KStJ; Commr English Heritage, Memb St George's Chapel Advsy Ctee; Pres: Inst Advanced Motorists 1971–, Cancer Research Campaign 1973–, London Soc, Nat Assoc Boys Clubs' 1974–, Public Monuments and Sculpture Assoc 1998–, St Bartholomew's Hosp 1975–, Soc Architect Artists, Br Consultants Bureau 1978–; V-Pres: Br Leprosy Relief Assoc 1971–; Patron: Appeal to replace organ in Chapel Royal Tower London, ASH 1974–, Br-Mexican Soc, Habitat for Humanity Great Britain, Inst of Advanced Motorists, Internat Cncl on Monuments and Sites, London Choral Soc, Japan Soc, Nuffield Farming Scholarships Tst, Peterborough Cathedral Tst, Richard III Society 1980–, Roy Pioneer Corps Assoc, Soc Engineers 1974–, Samsung Br Legion Korean Scholarship Scheme 1998 , Severn Valley Railway, Silver Jubilee Walkway Tst 1978–,Victorian Soc 1976–; Ranger Epping Forest 1975–; Queen's Tstee Br Museum 1973–; FRSA 1976, Dep Col-in-Ch: Roy Glos, Berks and Wilts Regt 1994–, Roy Logistic Corps 1993–, Hon Air Cdre RAF Odiham, Hon Col Roy Mon RE (Militia) 1977, Cdre Roy Ulster Yacht Club 1974–, Govr Building Centre Tst 1991–, Hon Life Memb Friends of All Saints Brixworth 1991–, Grand Prior OStJ 1975–, Liveryman Vintners' Co, Tstee Br Museum, Hon Freeman Grocers' Co; Hon Freeman and Liveryman Goldsmiths' Co, Grand Cross Order St Olav Norway; *m* Barnwell Parish Church 8 July 1972 *Birgitte Eva, GCVO (1989), DStJ, Dep Col-in-Ch Adj Gen's Corps, Col-in-Ch: Roy Australian Army Educn Corps 1977–, Roy NZ Army Educn Corps 1985–; Cmdt-in-Ch St John's Ambulance Wales; Patron: Bobath Cymru, Enham Tst, BLISS (Baby Life Support Systems), Counsel and Care (Advice and Help for Older People), Fedn Army Wives, Friends of Institut Français, Nat Asthma Campaign, Notting Hill Housing Tst, Parkinson's Disease Soc, Assoc Spina Bifida and Hydrocephalus, Scottish Opera, St Peter's Research Tst, Cheltenham Internat Music Festival, Bobath Centre and Fndn for Study Infant Deaths; Ch Patron Women Caring Tst (for Children of Northern Ireland); Pres: London Regns WRVS, Roy Alexander and Albert Sch, Roy Sch Needlework, Civ Serv Sports Cncl, Roy Sch Bath; V-Patron The Queen's Club), yr dau of Asger Preben Wissing Henriksen, lawyer, of Odense, Denmark, by his 1st w Vivian, dau of Waldemar Oswald van Deurs, whose name his gdau assumed, and has:

1 +ALEXANDER PATRICK GREGERS RICHARD, *Earl of Ulster*; *b* St Mary's Hosp Paddington 24 Oct 1974

1 +Davina Elizabeth Alice Benedikte; *b* St Mary's Hosp Paddington 19 Nov 1977

2 +Rose Victoria Birgitte Louise; *b* St Mary's Hosp Paddington 1 March 1980

Gloucester, previous creations: Pre-Conquest Earldoms of Gloucester, but embracing a much wider territory than the county currently centred on that city, were held possibly by Brictric, son of Algar, *alias* Brictric Meaw, and more certainly by Swein, eldest son of Godwin Earl of Kent and elder brother of HAROLD, the last Saxon King of England. For the medieval blurring of any distinction between the county town (*e.g.*, Gloucester) and county (*e.g.*, Gloucestershire) when conferring earldoms which were nevertheless intended to make their possessor governor of an entire county, *see* principally WINCHESTER, M, preliminary remarks.

After the Conquest it is possible that the Earldom of Gloucester was held by (a) William FitzEustace, perhaps son of Eustace II Count of Boulogne, and (b) Robert FitzHamon, Sieur de Creully in the Calvados region of Normandy, allegedly grandson of Hamo *Dentatus* ('The Toothy', *i.e.*, probably buck-toothed).

An undoubted Earl of Gloucester, perhaps the first authentic one, at any rate after the Conquest, is Robert FitzHamon's son-in-law, another Robert, who was an illegitimate son of HENRY I and was so created in 1122. The Earldom passed to his eldest son, William FitzRobert, and from him to JOHN, later KING JOHN and husband from 1189 to 1199 (when he divorced her) of Isabel, the youngest of William FitzRobert's three daughters. On JOHN's coming to the throne the title did not merge in the Crown for it was not his in his own right but in right of his wife.

Isabel's situation now became that of a great heiress, for whoever she married next would gain the Earldom. JOHN prevented her taking a second husband at all for the time being, however, and exchanged the Earldom of Gloucester with Aumarie de Montfort, son of William FitzRobert's eldest daughter Mabel, for the *comté* of Evreux, which he then used as a dowry to secure the marriage of his niece Blanche with the King of France's son. Aumarie died childless and Isabel, who towards the end of JOHN's reign married as her second husband Geoffrey de Mandeville, Earl of Essex and in right of his new wife now Earl of Gloucester too, died childless after marrying in the autumn of 1217 yet a third husband, Hubert de Burgh, Earl of Kent.

The latter seems not to have been recognised as Earl of Gloucester as well as of Kent, despite his wife's undoubted possession of the former Earldom by the time of their marriage. But then she died only a few days later and her sister Amice, by now the only one of William FitzRobert's daughters still living, seems to have been recognised as Countess of Gloucester till her own death some seven and a half years later. On the other hand Amice's son Gilbert de Clare, Earl of Hertford or of Clare (usually called the latter), was apparently acknowledged as Earl of Gloucester in addition to his other dignity from as soon as the month after his aunt Isabel's death back in 1217. For the subsequent history of the de Clare-held Earldom of Gloucester *see* HERTFORD, M, preliminary remarks.

The 7th and last de Clare Earl of Gloucester married Joan of Acre, second daughter of EDWARD I, and a son-in-law of theirs, the 1st Lord (Baron) Audley (*qv*, 1970 edn) was created Earl of Gloucester in March 1336/7. On his death without sons the Earldom expired. The title had now for three hundred years been largely conferred on those with close ties of blood to the King and held by descendants who had from time to time reinforced those ties by marriages with close relatives of susbsequent Kings. From then on, with the exception of the short-lived Earldom of Gloucester of 1397–99 (*see* FALMOUTH, V), the title of GLOUCESTER was conferred as a Dukedom, and on immediate members of the Royal Family: (a) THOMAS of Woodstock, EDWARD III's youngest son; (b) HUMPHREY of Lancaster, HENRY IV's youngest son; (c) RICHARD PLANTAGENET, later RICHARD III, younger brother of EDWARD IV; (d) PRINCE HENRY, CHARLES I's youngest son; (e) PRINCE WILLIAM HENRY, GEORGE III's younger brother (whose title was DUKE OF GLOUCESTER AND EDINBURGH; *see* EDINBURGH, D, above); (f) the present creation. Only one of these creations other than the present one lasted more than a generation, the exception being the combined Dukedom of Gloucester and Edinburgh.

The only son of QUEEN ANNE to live beyond infancy, PRINCE WILLIAM, was declared by his uncle, the then King, WILLIAM III, to be Duke of Gloucester at his birth in 1689, but no formal documentation for such a creation exists. The same is true of PRINCE FREDERICK, GEORGE II's Heir Apparent and father of GEORGE III.

Ulster, previous creations: An Earldom of Ulster was held by Hugh de Lacy between 1205 and 1242 and expired with him on the latter date. In 1264 the Earldom was revived for Walter de Burgh, thought to have been great-nephew of Hubert de Burgh, the Earl of Kent mentioned above. Through his mother he seems to have been great-nephew of the previous Earl of Ulster, Hugh de Lacy. On the death of Walter's great-grandson William de Burgh, 3rd Earl of Ulster of the 1264 creation, the title apparently became held by the latter's sole daughter Elizabeth. She married EDWARD III's second surviving son LIONEL, DUKE OF CLARENCE, who also became known in right of his wife as EARL OF ULSTER. Their daughter Philippa, apparently Countess of Ulster in her own right, as her mother had been, married Edmund de Mortimer, 3rd Earl of March, who as with his father-in-law was in addition known as Earl of Ulster, again in right of his wife. The Earldom of Ulster was drawn back into the Royal Family when Philippa's granddaughter Anne married her cousin Richard Earl of Cambridge (grandson of EDWARD III) and gave birth to Richard, 3rd Duke of York, also 6th Earl of March and 8th Earl of Ulster. The latter's son became EDWARD IV, when the Earldom of Ulster merged with the Crown. Ever since then the Earldom of Ulster has only ever been created as a junior appendage to the Dukedom of York (as in the case of the future JAMES II) or the Dukedom of York and Albany (*see* YORK, DUKE OF, previous creations, above), apart from in 1866, when it was one of the subsidiary titles created along with the Dukedom of Edinburgh (*qv*, previous creations).

Culloden, previous creation: A Barony of Culloden was conferred in 1801 along with the Dukedom of Cambridge on PRINCE ADOLPHUS FREDERICK, GEORGE III's seventh son, and expired with it on the death in 1904 of the grantee's son, the 2nd DUKE, who was uncle of QUEEN MARY, GEORGE V's wife.

HRH THE DUKE OF KENT

Arms: The Royal Arms differenced by a label of five points argent, the points charged with an anchor azure and a cross gules alternately. **Crest:** On a coronet of four crosses-patées alternated with four strawberry leaves a lion statant guardant or, crowned with the like coronet and differenced with a label as in the Arms. **Supporters:** The Royal Supporters differenced with the like coronet and label.

THE 2ND DUKE OF KENT, EARL OF ST ANDREWS and **BARON DOWNPATRICK** (EDWARD GEORGE NICHOLAS PAUL PATRICK WINDSOR, KG (1985), GCMG (1967), GCVO (1960)) [His Royal Highness The Duke of Kent KG GCMG GCVO, Wren House, Palace Green, London W8 4PY]; *b* 3 Belgrave Sq, London SW1, 9 Oct 1935; *s* f 1942; *educ* Eton, Switzerland and RMA Sandhurst; Col-in-Ch: Roy Regt Fus, Devonshire and Dorset Regt, Lorne Scots Regt (Canada); Col Scots Gds; Personal ADC to HM THE QUEEN 1966–, GSO(2) E Cmd RMA Sandhurst 1968–70; commissioned C Sqdn RSG 1970–71; ret as Lt-Col 1976 (Dep Col-in-Chief 1993–); Maj-Gen 1983, FM 1993; Hon Air Cdre RAF Leuchars 1993, Hon AVM; Grand Master Utd Grand Lodge Freemasons England, Grand Master Order St Michael and St George 1967–; Pres: AA, All England Lawn Tennis and Croquet Club, Edexcel Fndn, Wellington Coll 1969–, Cavalry and Gds Club, Chest Heart and Stroke Assoc, Cwlth War Graves Commn 1970–, Engrg Cncl, FA, Henley Soc 1994–, Imp War Museum, RAF Benevolent Fund, RNLI, Roy Armouries Devpt Tst, Roy Masonic Benevolent Inst, Roy Choral Soc, Roy Institution of Gr Britain, RUSI, Scout Assoc 1975–, Wimbledon All England Lawn Tennis and Croquet Club; Pres in Ch: Br Racing Drivers' Club, Hon Liveryman Clothworkers' Co, Hon Pres: RGS, V-Chm Br Overseas Trade Bd 1976–; Chm Duke of Edinburgh's Cwlth Study Conf (UK Fund); Patron: Anglo-German Assoc 1994–, Assoc of Men of Kent and Kentish Men, Combined Cavalry Old Comrades Assoc, Hanover Band, Help Poland Fund (Northern) 1994–, Leukaemia Research Fund, Stoke Mandeville Hosp Aylesbury, Trin Coll Music, Tree Cncl, Chllr Surrey U 1977–; Hon DCL Durham 1961, Hon FRAerS 1993, Hon Freeman Clothworkers' Co, Freeman Mercers' Co, Hon Liveryman: Salters' Co, Engrs' Co; Hon Freedom City Georgetown Guyana 1966; Orders St George, St Constantine Greece 1st Cl, Tri Shakti Patta Nepal 1st Cl, Grand Band Star Africa Liberia, Grand Cross Al-Nahda Jordan; *m* York Minster 8 June 1961 *Katharine Lucy Mary, GCVO, Dep Col-in-Ch: Adj Gen's Corps 1992–, Roy Dragoon Gds, Roy Logistic Corps, Pres Action Research 1993–, Pres Age Concern England 1993–, Patron: ENABLE and SCOPE, Br

Arts Festival Year 1995 1993–, Dyson Perrins Museum Appeal 1993–, Nat Fedn Music Socs 1993–, Ripon Coll Cuddesdon 1993–, Hon Memb: Roy Philharmonic Soc 1992, Musicians' Co 1993, only dau of Sir William Arthington Worsley, 4th Bt (*qv*), and has:

1 *GEORGE PHILIP NICHOLAS, *Earl of St Andrews*; *b* Coppins, Iver, Bucks, 26 June 1962; *educ* Eton and Downing Coll Cambridge; attd FCO 1987–88, Christie's Books and MSS Dept 1996–, Tstee GB-Sasakawa Fndn 1995–, Patron: Assoc for Internat Cancer Research 1995– and Princess Margarita of Romania Tst 1997–; *m* Leith 9 Jan 1988 *Sylvana Palma, dau of Maximilian Karl Tomaselli and formerly w of John Paul Jones, and has:

(1) +Edward Edmund Maximilian George, *Lord Downpatrick*; *b* St Mary's Hosp Paddington 2 Dec 1988

(1) +Marina-Charlotte Alexandra Katharine Helen; *b* Cambridge 30 Sept 1992

(2) +Amelia Sophia Theodora Mary Margaret; *b* Cambridge 24 Aug 1995

2 +Nicholas Charles Edward Jonathan; *b* King's Coll Hosp London 25 July 1970

1 +Helen Marina Lucy; *b* Coppins 28 April 1964; *m* St George's Chapel Windsor Castle 18 July 1992 *Timothy Verner Taylor, est s of Cdr Michael Verner Taylor, RN, and has:

(1) +Columbus George Donald; *b* 6 Aug 1994

(2) +Cassius Edward; *b* 26 Dec 1996

Kent, previous creations: Odo Bishop of Bayeux, the celebrated half-brother of WILLIAM I (THE CONQUEROR) through Herleve/Harlotte, was made Earl of Kent shortly after Hastings. He was deprived of the dignity many years later after rebelling against WILLIAM II and on his death the Earldom expired in any case. It was revived in February 1226/7 for Hubert de Burgh (for whom *see* against **Gloucester, previous creations** above). Although Hubert had sons living at his death the Earldom expired with him. It was again revived, this time for EDMUND of Woodstock, EDWARD I's youngest son, in 1321. For the subsequent history of this creation *see* WAKE, Bt. For the Earldom of Kent of the 1461 creation *see* ABERGAVENNY, M. For the Earldom of Kent of the 1465 creation *see* GREY, B. For the Marquessate and Dukedom of Kent created in 1706 and 1710 respectively, *see* LUCAS OF CRUDWELL, B. The first royal Dukedom of Kent was conferred on PRINCE EDWARD, GEORGE III's fourth son and the father of QUEEN VICTORIA. It expired with his death in 1820. VICTORIA's second son the DUKE OF EDINBURGH, so created in 1866, was given as one of his subsidiary titles an Earldom of Kent.

St Andrews, previous creations: WILLIAM IV before ascending the throne was made DUKE OF CLARENCE and ST ANDREWS, though usually known by the first half of the title only. On his succeeding his elder brother GEORGE IV, the Dukedom merged with the Crown. For other titles incorporating the place name St Andrews *see* STRATHEDEN and CAMPBELL, B, and 1939 edn PLAYFAIR, B.

ABDY

Arms: Or two chevronels between three trefoils slipped sable.
Crest: An eagle's head couped proper, beaked azure.
Motto: *Tenax et fidelis* ('Tenacious and faithful').
Creation: Bt. (UK) 8 Jan 1850.

SIR VALENTINE ROBERT DUFF ABDY, 6TH BT, of Albyns, Essex [Sir Valentine Abdy Bt, Hadsley House, Lefebvre St, St Peter Port, Guernsey, CI; 13 Villa Molitor, 75016 Paris, France]; *b* 11 Sept 1937; *s f* 1976; *educ* Eton; European Rep (1983–95) and memb Nat Bd (1995–) Smithsonian Inst Washington DC, Administrator Musée des Arts Decoratifs Paris, Special Advsr Internat Fund Promotion of Culture UNESCO 1991–; *m* 1971 (*divorce* 1982) Mathilde Marie Alexe Christianne (*m* 2nd Edouard Etienne Alphonse de Rothschild; *see* ROTHSCHILD, B), dau of Etienne Coche de la Ferté, and has issue:

1 +ROBERT ETIENNE ERIC; *b* 22 Feb 1978

Lineage: ANTHONY ABDY, of St Dionis Backchurch, London; *bapt* 18 Oct 1579; Alderman, Sheriff 1630/1, dir HEICS 1617 and dep govr 1639; *m* 14 Aug 1610 Abigail, dau of Sir Thomas Campbell, Ld Mayor London 1609–10, and *d* 10 Sept 1640, having had issue:

1 Sir THOMAS, 1st Bt
2 Anthony; *bapt* 16 March 1615; *bur* 16 Jan 1621/2
3 Sir ROBERT ABDY, 1st Bt (E), so *cr* 9 June 1660, of Albyns, Essex; *bapt* 23 Jan 1616; *m* Catherine (*d* 1662), dau of Sir John Gayer, of London, and *d* 1670, having had issue:
(1) Sir JOHN ABDY, 2nd Bt, of Albyns; *b c* 1643; *educ* Trin Coll Cambridge and Middle Temple; *m* 1687 Jane, only dau of George Nicholas, yst s of Sir Edward Nicholas, Sec of State to CHARLES I and CHARLES II, and *d* 1691, having had issue:
1a Sir ROBERT ABDY, 3rd Bt, of Albyns; *bapt* 8 April 1688; *educ* Trin Coll Oxford; FSA, MP Essex 1727–48; *m* 5 July 1711 Theodosia, dau and heir of George Bramston, LLD, and *d* 27 Aug 1748, having had issue:
1b Sir JOHN ABDY, 4th Bt, of Albyns; *b c* 1714; *educ* Trin Coll Oxford and Middle Temple; MP Essex 1748–59; *d* unm 1 April 1759, when the baronetcy *cr* 9 June 1660 expired
2b Robert; *b c* 1715; *educ* Trin Coll Oxford; *d* unm Dec 1735
1b Jane; *d* young
2b Theodosia; *m* (licence 14 March 1752) her 3rd cousin Rev Stotherd Abdy (*see* below) and *dsp* 1758
1a Anne
2a Jane; *bapt* 19 March 1690; *m* 18 Feb 1732 Rev Edward Crank, MA, rector Halford, Bucks
(2) Anthony; *bapt* 16 Aug 1653
(3) Robert; *bapt* 29 April 1656
(4) Roger; *bapt* 7 July 1657
(5) Charles; *bapt* 17 March 1658
(6) Edward; *bapt* 16 Sept 1660; *educ* St John's Coll Oxford and Magdalene Coll Cambridge (BA 1681/2, MA 1685); rector Salcot Virley, Essex, 1689–90 and Theydon Garnon, Essex, 1684–1701; *d* 1701
(7) Roger; *bapt* 1 July 1662
(1) Catherine; *bapt* 29 July 1645
(2) Mary; *bapt* 27 Sept 1647
(3) Sara; *bapt* 5 June 1649; *m* (licence 24 Nov 1669) Robert Pennington, of Chigwell, Essex
(4) Elizabeth; *bapt* 5 Sept 1650
(5) Abigail; *bapt* 7 Nov 1651
4 Sir JOHN ABDY, 1st and last Bt (E), so *cr* 22 June 1660, of Moores, Salcot, Essex; *bapt* 4 June 1617; *dsp* 1662, when the baronetcy *cr* 22 June 1660 expired
5 Nicholas; *bapt* 30 Aug 1618
6 Roger; *bapt* 9 May 1620
1 Alice; *bapt* 2 June 1611; *m* 19 Nov 1635 Sir John Bramston, KB
2 Abigail; *bapt* 21 Feb 1622
3 Sarah; *bapt* 18 Oct 1624

ANTHONY ABDY's est s,

Sir THOMAS ABDY, 1st Bt (E), so *cr* 7 July 1641, of Felix Hall, Essex; *bapt* 18 May 1612; *educ* Trin Coll Cambridge and Lincoln's Inn; *m* 1st 1 Feb 1637/8 Mary (*d* 6 April 1645), dau and coheir of Lucas Corsellis, of London, and had issue:

1 James; *bapt* 1 Jan 1638/9; *d* young
1 Rachel; *bapt* 25 May 1640; *m* (licence 20 June 1679) Philip Gurdon, of Assington, Suffolk
2 Abigail; *m* Sir Mark Guyon

Sir THOMAS *m* 2nd 16 Jan 1646/7 Anne (*d* 19 June 1679), dau and coheir of Sir Thomas Soame, Alderman London, and *d* 14 Jan 1685/6, having had further issue:

2 Sir ANTHONY, 2nd Bt
3 Thomas; *dsp* 1697
4 William; *dsp* 1682
3 Joanna; *bapt* 28 June 1654; *dsp* 1710
4 Alice; *bapt* 30 June 1661; *m* William Stane, of Folyetts Hall, Essex
5 Anne; *dsp* 1682
6 Mary; *m* Wentworth Garneys, of Boyland Hall, Norfolk
7 Judith; *d* young
8 Sarah; *d* young

Sir THOMAS's est surv s,

Sir ANTHONY ABDY, 2nd Bt; *bapt* 4 July 1655; *educ* Trin Coll Cambridge; *m* 9 June 1682 Mary (*d* 18 Aug 1744), dau and heiress of Rev Richard Milward, canon Windsor, and *d* 2 April 1704, having had issue:

1 Thomas; *d* young
2 Sir ANTHONY THOMAS ABDY, 3rd Bt; *bapt* 5 Oct 1688; *educ* Trin Coll Cambridge; *m* 1st Mary (*dsp* 1718), dau and heir of Hugh Gifford, of Colchester; *m* 2nd 1720 Charlotte (*d* 17 Feb 1731), dau and coheir of Sir Thomas Barnardiston, 3rd Bt, of Ketton, Suffolk (*cr* 1663; *extinct* 1750), and by her had issue:
(1) Charlotte Maria; *bapt* 11 June 1723; *m* John Williams, of Tendring, Suffolk
(2) Elizabeth; *m* Thomas Reeves
2 (cont.) Sir ANTHONY *m* 3rd Anne (*dsp* 21 Sept 1745), dau and heir of Thomas Williams, of Tendring Hall, Suffolk, and *d* 11 June 1733
3 WILLIAM (Sir), 4th Bt
4 Charles; *bapt* 27 May 1693
5 Richard; *bapt* 21 Sept 1694
1 Joanna; *bapt* 12 Aug 1686; *d* unm 1 Oct 1765
2 Elizabeth; *bapt* 30 Sept 1687
3 Rachel; *bapt* 22 Jan 1690
4 Alice; *bapt* 8 Sept 1695
5 Margaret; *bapt* 7 Jan 1696; *d* unm 7 Oct 1779
6 Martha; *bapt* 15 Jan 1700; *d* unm 31 Jan/1 Feb 1780
7 Mary

The 3rd Bt's yr bro,

Sir WILLIAM ABDY, 4th Bt, of Chobham Place, Surrey; *bapt* 1 Sept 1689; *m* (licence 13 May 1714) Mary (*d* 6 April 1743), only dau and heir of Philip Stotherd, of Terling, Essex, and *d* 18 Jan 1749/50, having had issue:

1 Sir ANTHONY THOMAS ABDY, 5th Bt, KC (1765); *b c* 1720; *educ* Felsted and St John's Coll Cambridge; barrister 1744, MP Knaresborough 1763–75; *m* 13 Aug 1747 Catherine (*d* 1792), dau and coheir of William Hamilton, of Chancery Lane, London, and *dsp* 7 April 1775
2 Stotherd (Rev); *b c* 1728; MA, Archdeacon Essex 1771–73 and Preb St Paul's 1771; *m* 1st (licence 14 March 1752) his 3rd cousin Theodosia (*dsp* 1758), dau of Sir Robert Abdy, 3rd Bt, of Albyns; *m* 2nd (licence 31 July 1759) Harriot, dau of Peyton Altham, of Mark Hall, Essex, and *dsp* 5 April 1773
3 Sir WILLIAM ABDY, 6th Bt; *b c* 1732; Capt RN; *m* 4 Jan 1776 Mary (*d* 4 March 1829), dau of James Brebner Gordon, of Moore Place, Herts, and *d* 21 July 1803, having had issue:
(1) Sir WILLIAM ABDY, 7th and last Bt of the 1641 *cr*; *b c* 1779; *educ* Eton 1791–93 and Ch Ch Oxford; Capt RN, Lt S Essex Militia 1798, 2nd Lt Southwark Volunteers 1807, MP Malmesbury 1817–18; *m* 3 July 1806 (*divorce* 1816) Anne Wellesley (*m* 2nd William Cavendish-Bentinck; *see* PORTLAND, E), illegitimate dau of 1st and last Marquess Wellesley (*see* WELLINGTON, D), and *dspl* 16 April 1868, when the baronetcy expired
(1) Catherine Mary; *bapt* 27 Dec 1776; *m* Capt Thomas Fellowes, RN
(2) Charlotte Anne; *bapt* 27 March 1783; *m* 1 Dec 1808 Charles Caldwell
(3) Harriet; *bapt* 20 July 1786; *m* 4 Dec 1817 George Caldwell, for whom *see* further below
1 Charlotte Elizabeth; *m* 11 April 1752 Thomas Rutherforth, DD, Regius Prof Divinity Cambridge (*d* 5 Oct 1771), and had issue:
(1) THOMAS (Rev), for whom *see* further below
2 Ann Hester; *bapt* 3 Jan 1734

The 7th Bt's 1st cousin,

Rev THOMAS ABDY RUTHERFORTH later ABDY (roy licence 3 June 1775 on succeeding to the estates of his uncle, Sir ANTONY ABDY, 5th Bt, and his gf's 3rd cousin Sir JOHN ABDY, 4th Bt, of Albyns, of the 1660 *cr*); *b* 5 Dec 1755; took the name and arms of ABDY in lieu of RUTHERFORTH; *m* 13 Jan 1778 Mary (*d* 8 Dec 1820), dau of James Hayes, of Holyport, Berks, Bencher Middle Temple, and *d* 14 Oct 1798, having had issue:

1 John Rutherforth Abdy Hatch, of Albyns, Essex; *b c* 1779; High Sheriff Essex 1809; *m* 17 July 1800 Caroline Elizabeth (*d* 5 May 1838), est dau of James Hatch, of Clayberry Hall, Essex, and *dsp* 1 April 1840
2 Anthony; Capt RN; *m* 1808 Grace, illegitimate dau of Adml Sir Thomas Rich, 5th and last Bt, of Sonning (*cr* 1661; *extinct* 1803), and *d* 9 June 1838, leaving issue:
(1) THOMAS NEVILLE (Sir), **1st Bt**, of the 1850 *cr*, for whom *see* further below
3 Charles Boyd (Rev), JP (Essex); Rector Theydon Garnon 1812–43; *d* unm 20 Aug 1843

4 James Nicholas; Lt Col HEICS; *m* Georgina Charlotte, dau of Thomas King, of Eltham, Kent, and *d* 1855, having had issue
5 Edward Strutt; *b c* 1790; *educ* Jesus Coll Cambridge (BA 1813, MA 1817); author: *Journal of a Residence and Tour in the United States of North America, from April 1833 to Oct 1834 etc*; *d* unm 12 Oct 1846
1 Charlotte Ann; *d* unm
2 Maria Henrietta; *m* James Sykes, of Arundel St, London
3 Margaret; *d* young
4 Mary; *m* Rev James Williams, of Matherne, Monmouth
5 Caroline; *m* Henry Middleton, of Wanborough, Wilts

Capt ANTHONY ABDY's only s,

Sir Thomas Neville Abdy, 1st Bt, JP, DL; *b* 21 Dec 1810; *educ* Winchester, St John's Coll Cambridge (BA 1833) and Middle Temple; MP Lyme Regis 1847–52, *cr* 8 Jan 1850 a Baronet (UK), High Sheriff Essex 1875; *m* 19 Oct 1841 Hariot (*d* 8 July 1877), 2nd dau of Rowland Alston, of Pishiobury, Herts, and *d* 20 July 1877, having had issue:

1 **Sir William Neville Abdy, 2nd Bt**, JP (Essex); *b* 18 June 1844; High Sheriff 1884; *m* 1st 10 July 1883 Marie Theresa (*d* 17 Sept 1902), dau of — Petritzka, of Prague; *m* 2nd 6 Dec 1902 (*divorce* 1905) Eliza Sarah, dau of Oscar William Beech; *m* 3rd 16 Feb 1909, as her 2nd husb, Florence (*m* 3rd 7 Jan 1913 Maurice Grant, of Slings Malton, Yorks, and *d* 3 Feb 1922), dau of Lehmann Louis Cohn and widow of Gen George Palmer Robinson, and *dsp* 9 Aug 1910

2 **Sir Anthony Charles Sykes Abdy, 3rd Bt**; *b* 19 Sept 1848; Capt 2nd Life Gds, served Egyptian campaign 1882, Mily Attaché Vienna 1885; *m* 11 Nov 1886 Hon Alexandrina Victoria Macdonald (*d* 4 March 1953), yst dau of 4th Baron Macdonald (*qv*), and *d* 17 May 1921, leaving issue:

(1) Grace Lilian; *b* 22 Sept 1887; *m* 6 Dec 1917 8th Earl of Lanesborough (*qv*) and had issue
(2) Violet; *b* 4 Jan 1892; *m* 5 Jan 1925 Hugh Godsal (*d* 11 May 1936), er s of Edward Hugh Godsal, of Ruscombe Down, Twyford, and *d* 22 Aug 1957, having had issue
(3) Constance Mary; *b* 4 June 1895; *m* 1 Nov 1941 Harold Frederic Andorsen, OBE, BA, barrister, only s of Harald Andorsen, Kt 1st Class Order of St Olaf

3 Robert John; *bapt* 12 Dec 1850; served 4th Dragoon Gds
4 HENRY BEADON (Sir), **4th Bt**, for whom *see* further below
1 Grace Emma Townshend; *bapt* 6 July 1846; *m* 19 March 1872 Lord Albert Leveson-Gower (*d* 23 Dec 1874), Capt 2nd Life Gds (*see* SUTHERLAND, D), and *d* Dec 1923, having had issue

The 3rd Bt's yr bro,

Sir Henry Beadon Abdy, 4th Bt; *b* 13 July 1853; *m* 22 March 1891 Anna Adele Coronna (*d* 21 March 1920) and *d* 1 Dec 1921, having had issue:

1 William Neville; *b* 10 Feb 1895; *d* 4 Nov 1911
2 Sir ROBERT HENRY EDWARD, **5th Bt**
1 Gladys Erica; *b* 23 May 1892; *m* 3 July 1919 Col Patrick Campbell Anderson DSO, MC (*d* 12 Feb 1965), Res of Offrs Seaforth Highrs, s of Duncan Sinclair Anderson

The 4th Bt's 2nd s,

Sir Robert Henry Edward Abdy, 5th Bt; *b* 11 Sept 1896; *educ* Charterhouse and RMC Sandhurst; Lt 15th/19th King's Hus (Res of Offrs) 1915–18; *m* 1st 23 June 1923 (*divorce* 1928) Iya (*d* Jan 1993), dau of George De Gay, dramatic author, of St Petersburg, and formerly w of Gerrit Jongeyans; *m* 2nd 10 Feb 1930 (*divorce* 1962) Lady (Helen) Diana Bridgeman (*d* 7 May 1967), est dau of 5th Earl of Bradford (*qv*); *m* 3rd 5 Sept 1962 (*divorce* 1973) Jane, dau of Dr John Noble, and *d* 16 Nov 1976, leaving issue:

1 Sir VALENTINE ROBERT DUFF ABDY, **6th and present Bt**

ABERCONWAY

Arms: Or two chevronels invected gules, between two shepherd's crooks in chief and in base a castle triple towered sable, masoned argent, flags, windows and portcullis of the second.
Supporters: On either side a wyvern argent, wings erect gules, each supporting a banner or charged with a horse-shoe sable.
Crest: A representation of the Virgin Mary with the dexter arm uplifted vested azure, holding in the sinister arm the child Jesus.
Motto: *Bi' se mac na Cromaig* ('I am a son of the Church').
Creations: B. (UK) 21 June 1911, Bt. (UK) 8 Aug 1902.

THE 3RD BARON ABERCONWAY, of Bodnant, Co Denbigh, and a **Baronet** (Sir Charles Melville McLaren, Bt, JP (Denbighshire 1946)) [The Rt Hon The Lord Aberconway JP, Bodnant, Taly-y-Cafn, Colwyn Bay, N Wales LL28 5RE; 25 Egerton Terrace, London SW3 2DP; 40 Lowndes St, London SW1]; *b* 16 April 1913; *s* f 1953; *educ* Eton and New Coll Oxford (BA 1937); barrister Middle Temple 1937, 2nd Lt RA 1940, High Sheriff Denbighshire 1950, dir: Nat Westminster Bank 1953–83 and Westland Aircraft 1947–85 (dep chm 1979–84), pres: Roy Horticultural Soc 1961–84 (pres emeritus thereafter) and John Brown and Co 1978–1985 (chm 1953–78), chm Sheepbridge Engrg 1961–79 and English China Clays 1963–84, dep-chm Sun Alliance and London Insur 1976–85, Commr-Gen Internat Garden Festival Liverpool 1984; *m* 1st 6 Dec 1941 (*divorce* 1949) Deirdre, yst dau of John Knewstub, and has:

1 +(HENRY) CHARLES; *b* 26 May 1948; *educ* Eton and Sussex U (BA); *m* Aug 1981 Sally Ann (*divorce* 19–), yr dau of Capt Charles Nugent Lentaigne, DSO, RN (ret), of Hawkley Place, Hawkley, Liss, Hants, and formerly w of Philip Charles Bidwell, and has:

(1) +Charles Stephen; *b* 27 Dec 1984
(1) *Emily Rose; *b* 4 March 1982

1 *Julia Harriet [The Hon Mrs Ridley, c/o UPI, Rome, Italy]; *b* 22 Sept 1942; *educ* Grenoble U; *m* 1969 *Capt Charles Walter Hayes Ridley, MC, Reconnaissance Corps, and has issue:

(1) *Caspar Charles; *b* 1977
(1) *Emma Jane; *b* 1970
(2) *Harriet Deirdre; *b* 1971

2 *Caroline Mary [The Hon Mrs Howard, Forest House, Barbados Hill, Tintern, Gwent NP4 6SX]; *b* 24 Oct 1944; *educ* Imperial Coll London (BSc, PhD, DIC, FLS); botanist; *m* 1st 8 Feb 1962 (*divorce*) Raimund Guernsey Sargent, yr s of Winthrop Sargent III, of Beverly Farms, Mass, USA, and has issue:

(1) *Dominic Fitzwilliam; *b* 30 Aug 1963; *educ* Blundell's and Trin Coll Cambridge
(2) *Orlando Gorham; *b* 4 Nov 1964; *educ* Blundell's and Sussex U

2 (cont.) The Hon Mrs Caroline Sargent *m* 2nd 1978 (*divorce* 19–) Graham Charles Steele, BSc, PhD; *m* 3rd 19– *William Howard

The 3rd BARON *m* 2nd 15 Oct 1949 *Ann Lindsay, only dau of Alexander Lindsay Aymer, of New York, and formerly w of Robert Lee Bullard III (*see* ONSLOW, E), and has further issue:

2 +Michael Duncan [The Hon Michael McLaren, 27 Phillimore Gdns, London W8 7QG]; *b* 29 Nov 1958; *educ* Eton and Christ's Coll Cambridge (BA 1980); barrister Middle Temple 1981; *m* 25 May 1985 *Caroline Jane, er dau of Air Ch Marshal Sir John Stacey, KCB, CBE, of Winchester, and has:

(1) +Angus John Melville; *b* 21 Oct 1987
(2) +Hamish Charles Duncan; *b* 23 Nov 1993
(1) *Iona Ann Mariel; *b* 20 Feb 1991

Lineage: JOHN McLAREN, of Glenorchy, Argyllshire; *m* Catherine McLellan and had issue:

DUNCAN McLAREN, JP, DL, of Newington House, Edinburgh; *b* 12 Jan 1800; Ld Provost Edinburgh 1851–54, MP Edinburgh 1865–81; *m* 1st 7 July 1829 Grant (*d* 23 April 1833), dau of William Aitken, of Haddington, and had issue:

1 John, DL (Edinburgh); *b* 17 Aug 1831; MP Wigtown 1880 and Edinburgh 1881, Ld Advocate 1880–81, Judge Court of Session as LORD McLAREN, Hon LLD Edinburgh, Glasgow and Abderdeen Us; *m* 14 Dec 1868 Ottilie Augusta (*d*

18 April 1914), dau of Herman Leopold Schwabe, of Glasgow, and *d* 6 April 1910, having had issue:

(1) Duncan Bright; *b* 21 March 1874; *educ* Trin Coll Cambridge (BA); Sec Br Public Sch Club Victoria, BC, with CS BC; *m* 14 Feb 1906 Ethel (*d*), est dau of Watkin Davies, of Broom House, Hold Whittington, Chesterfield, Derbys, and *dsp* 15 Dec 1934

(2) Ludovic; *b* 20 Oct 1877; *d* 18 Oct 1898

(1) Katharine; *m* 1 March 1893 her cousin Frederick Scott Oliver (*d* 3 June 1934), of Edgerston, Jedburgh, s of John Scott Oliver, and *d* 25 April 1966 aged 96, leaving issue

(2) Esther Joanna Marie; *m* 29 April 1899 Alan Blackburn (*d c* 1920), yst s of Prof Hugh Blackburn, of Roshven, and *d* 28 Oct 1950, leaving issue

(3) Ottilie Helen, OBE; ARBS; *m* 11 April 1905 Dr William Wallace (*d* 16 Dec 1940), er s of Dr Wallace, of Greenock, and *d* 17 Oct 1947

1 Grant; *m* 14 April 1868 John Millar (*dsp* 26 Jan 1873), of Sherdale

DUNCAN McLAREN *m* 2nd 1836 Christina Gordon (*d* 1 Nov 1841), dau of William Renton, of Edinburgh, and by her had further issue:

2 Duncan; *b* 1840; *m* 10 Feb 1881 Eliza, dau of John Struthers, of Edinburgh, and *dsp*

2 Katharine; *m* John Scott Oliver and *d* 15 Oct 1869, leaving issue (*see* above)

3 Agnes; MD Montpellier, France; *d* unm 18 April 1913

DUNCAN McLAREN *m* 3rd 6 July 1848 Priscilla (*d* 5 Nov 1906), dau of Jacob Bright, of Green Bank, Rochdale, Lancs, and sis of John Bright, PC, MP, the celebrated 19th-century reformer and radical, and *d* 26 April 1886, having by her had issue:

3 CHARLES BENJAMIN BRIGHT, **1st Baron**

4 Walter Stowe Bright; *b* 17 April 1853; MP (Lib) Crewe 1886–95 and 1910–12; *m* 18 April 1883 Eva (*d* 16 Aug 1921), yst dau of William Muller, of Valparaiso, Chile, and Hillside, Shenley, Herts, and *d* 29 June 1912

4 Helen Priscilla, MBE; *b* 28 Oct 1851; *m* 25 May 1877 Andrea Carlo Francisco Rabagliati (*d* 7 Dec 1930), MA, FRCSE, of Whinbrac, Ben Rhydding, Yorks, and *d* 3 Jan 1934, leaving issue

DUNCAN McLAREN's 3rd s,

Sir Charles Benjamin Bright McLaren, 1st Bt, and **1st Baron Aberconway**, PC (1908), QC (1897), JP (Denbigh, Flint, Middx and Surrey); *b* 12 May 1850; *educ* Edinburgh (MA), Bonn and Heidelberg Us; barrister Lincoln's Inn 1874, MP (Lib) Stafford 1880–86 and Bosworth, Leics, 1892–1910, chm: Metropolitan Rlwy Co, Tredegar Iron and Coal Co, John Brown and Co and Sheepbridge Coal and Iron Co, also Br Iron Trade Assoc 1909 and Inst Naval Architects, a fndr Nat Lib Club, *cr* 8 Aug 1902 a Baronet and 21 June 1911 BARON ABERCONWAY, of Bodnant, Co Denbigh (both UK), Order Sacred Treasure Japan, 3rd Class Takova of Serbia and Redeemer Greece, author: *Our Basic Industries*; *m* 6 March 1877 Laura Elizabeth, CBE (1918), DGStJ (*d* 4 Jan 1933), only dau of Henry Davis Pochin, JP, DL, of Bodnant, Denbigh, MP Stafford, by Agnes, dau of George Gretton Heap, and *d* 23 Jan 1934, leaving issue:

1 HENRY DUNCAN, **2nd Baron**

2 Francis Walter Stafford, JP (Denbigh); *b* 16 June 1886; *educ* Eton and Balliol Coll Oxford; MP (Lib) Spalding 1910–17, PPS to Colonial Sec 1910–15, Lt RNVR and RFC 1916; *m* 20 July 1911 Barbara GBE (1953, OBE 1943), DStJ (*m* 2nd 14 June 1922 Lt-Gen 1st Baron Freyberg (*qv*), and *d* 24 Sept 1973), dau of Col Sir Herbert Jekyll, KCMG, RE, and was *kas* 30 Aug 1917, leaving issue:

(1) Martin John; *b* 11 Jan 1914; *educ* New Coll Oxford (BA 1936, MA 1941) and Harvard; Maj Gren Gds WWII, Pncpl Home Office 1945–47, barrister Middle Temple 1948, MP (C) Bristol NW 1959–66 and 1970–74, Assist Govt Whip 1961–63, a Ld Commr Treasury 1963–64, dir Archway Investment and Scientific and Electronic Industries Tst, Polish Silver Cross of Merit; *m* 18 Sept 1943 *Nancy [Mrs Martin McLaren, 30 Smith Sq, London SW1], dau of Gordon Ralston, of Toronto, Canada, by his w Nita Josephine, yst dau of Henry William Radcliff Tisdall, and *d* 27 July 1979, leaving issue:

1a +Richard Francis (Rev); *b* 9 Nov 1946; *educ* Eton and Mansfield Coll Oxford; curate Elthery

2a Francis Andrew; *b* 5 Aug 1949; *d* as the result of an accident 2 Sept 1960

3a Patrick Andrew; *b* 27 Sept 1963; *educ* Eton and Harvard; *d* unm 14 Dec 1990

(2) Guy Lewis Ian; *b* 8 Nov 1915; *educ* Eton and Univ Coll Oxford (BA 1938); Hon Maj Coldstream Gds WW II, resigned commn 1949, dir: Clive Lester 1961–78 and Trans-Ocean Servs and Brazilian Hardwoods 1968–78, chm Nairn France SA; *m* 16 May 1946 Maryse (*d* 22 June 1987), only child of Dr Alfred Jubin and Mme Jean Delorme, of Les Antets, Chalet A Gobet, Lausanne, Switzerland, and *d* 18 Aug 1978, leaving issue:

1a +Michael [Michael McLaren Esq, 1 bis rue du Printemps, 78230 Le Pecq, France]; *b* 26 Oct 1947; *educ* Eton and St Andrews U; *m* 27 May 1993 *Sally Anne, dau of James Firth Reid, of Lowry Bay, NZ, and has:

1b +James Alexander Michael; *b* 31 May 1994

1b *Sophie Annabel Mary; *b* 9 July 1997

1a *Mary Caroline [Mrs Nicholas Durlacher, Archendines, Chapel Rd, Fordham, Colchester, Essex]; *b* 9 Oct 1951; *m* 13 Oct 1971 *Nicholas John Durlacher, er s of Jack Durlacher, of Whitefriars, Sevenoaks, Kent, and has:

1b *David Michael; *b* 1976

1 Elsie Dorothea; *m* 28 April 1904 Col Sir Edward Alexander James Johnson-Ferguson, 2nd Bt (*qv*), and *d* 15 May 1973, leaving issue

2 Florence Priscilla, CBE (1917), JP (London); served WWI (1914 star with bar, two medals, despatches), Tstee Imperial War Museum; *m* 8 May 1907 Sir Henry Norman, 1st Bt (*qv*), and *d* 1 March 1964, leaving issue

The 1st BARON ABERCONWAY's only surv s,

HENRY DUNCAN McLAREN, **2nd Baron Aberconway**, CBE, JP (Denbigh); *b* 16 April 1879; *educ* Eton and Balliol Coll Oxford (MA); barrister Lincoln's Inn 1903, MP (Lib) W Staffs 1906–10, Bosworth 1910–22, PPS to Pres BOT 1906–08, Chllr Exchequer 1908–10, dir: Palmers Shipbuilding and Iron, Nat Provincial Bank, London Assur and Bolckow and Vaughan & Co, chm: John Brown Ltd, Tredegar Iron and Coal, Yorkshire Amalgamated Collieries, Sheepbridge Coal and Iron, English Clays Loverin Pochin & Co, chm Quarter Sessions, pres Roy Horticultural Soc 1931–53, Hon: ARIBA, LLD U Wales 1949; *m* 19 July 1910 Christabel Mary Melville (*d* 7 Aug 1974), yr dau of Sir Melville Leslie Macnaghten, CB (*see* MACNAGHTEN, Bt), and *d* 23 May 1953, leaving issue:

1 CHARLES MELVILLE McLAREN, **3rd and present Baron Aberconway**

2 John Francis; *b* 19 June 1919; *educ* Eton; S/Ldr RAF WWII, barrister Inner Temple 1946, High Sheriff Denbigh 1952; *m* 3 April 1940 *Lady Rose Mary Primrose Paget [The Lady Rose McLaren, Old Bodnod, Eglwysbach, Colwyn Bay LL28 3AT], 4th dau of 6th Marquess of Anglesey (*qv*)I, and *d* 23 March 1953, leaving issue:

(1) *Victoria Mary Caroline [Mrs Jonathan Taylor, 42 Addison Rd, London W14]; *b* 23 May 1945; *m* 4 Oct 1966 *Jonathan Jeremy Kirwan Taylor, BA, barrister, yst s of Sir Charles Stuart Taylor, TD, DL, MP, of Ratton Wood, Willington, Eastbourne, Sussex (*see* GRANTCHESTER, B), and has issue

(2) *Harriet Diana Christabel [Mrs Hugh Geddes, 20 Gatcombe Rd, London N19]; *b* 18 Jan 1949; *m* 27 Jan 1972 *Hugh John Reay Geddes, only child of Hon John Reay Campbell Geddes, TD, of 15 Merrick Sq, London SE1 (*see* GEDDES, B), and has issue

3 +Christopher Melville [The Hon Christopher McLaren, 31 Upper Addison Gdns, London W14 8AJ]; *b* 15 April 1934; *educ* Eton and King's Coll Cambridge (BA 1955, MA); barrister Inner Temple 1961, chm Govrs and Chllr South Bank U 1992–; Hon Treas ESU 1996–; *m* 31 Oct 1973 *Jane Elizabeth, est dau of James Matthew Barrie, of Highgate Village, London N6, and formerly w of — Field, and has:

(1) +Robert Melville; *b* 28 Sept 1974; *educ* Eton

(1) *Lara Jane Christabel; *b* 1 June 1976

1 Elizabeth Mary; *b* 31 May 1911; *m* 9 June 1938 Kenneth Ralph Malcolm (Peter) Carlisle (*d* 1983), est s of Kenneth Methven Carlisle, of Wyken Hall, Stanton, Bury St Edmunds, and *d* 4 Dec 1991, leaving:

(1) *Kenneth Melville; *b* 25 March 1941; *educ* Harrow and Magdalen Coll Oxford

(1) *Christabel Mary; *b* 1 March 1939; *m* 12 Jan 1965 *Sir James Andrew Watson, 5th Bt (*qv*), and has issue

(2) *Katharine Jane; *b* 25 March 1941

(3) *Barbara Ann; *b* 21 Jan 1951

2 *Anne Laura Dorinthea, DBE (1993) [Dr Anne McLaren DBE, Flat 1, 40 Ainger Rd, London NW3 3AT]; *b* 26 April 1927; *educ* LMH Oxford (MA, DPhil 1952); with Inst of Animal Genetics, Edinburgh U then dir MRC Mammalian Devpt Unit London, FRS 1975, FRCOG 1986, V-Pres and For Sec Roy Soc 1992–, Pncpl Research Assoc Wellcome/Cancer Research Campaign Inst, Research Fell King's Coll Cambridge 1992–, pres British Assoc for the Advancement of Science 1993–94; *m* 6 Oct 1952 (*divorce* 1959) Donald Michie (DPhil), est s of James Kilgour Michie, of 42 Great Cumberland Place, London W1, and Gunsite, Aldeburgh, Suffolk, and has issue:

(1) *Jonathan Mark [Jonathan Michie Esq, 19 Porson Rd, Cambridge CB2 9BD]; *b* 25 March 1957; *m* twice and has issue

(1) *Susan Fiona Dorinthea; *b* 19 June 1955; *m* 1981 *Andrew Philip Drummond-Murray and has issue (*see* PERTH, E)

(2) *Caroline Ruth; *b* 1 Aug 1959

ABERCORN

Arms: Quarterly, 1st and 4th, gules three cinquefoils pierced ermine (for HAMILTON); 2nd and 3rd, argent, a ship with sails furled and oars in action sable (for ARRAN), in the point of honour and over all an escutcheon azure, charged with three fleurs-de-lys or, and surmounted by a French ducal coronet (for CHATELLERAULT). **Crest:** Out of a ducal coronet or an oak tree proper, fructed and penetrated transversely in the main stem by a frame-saw proper, the blade inscribed with the word 'Through', the frame gold. **Supporters:** Two antelopes argent, armed, unguled, ducally gorged and chained or. **Mottoes:** 'Through' and *Sola nobilitas virtus* ('The only nobility is virtue'). **Creations:** D. (France) 8 Feb 1548/9, L. (S) 29 July 1587, (S) 5 April 1603, (S) 10 July 1606, B. (I) 8 May 1617 and (I) 2 Sept 1701, Bt. (I) *c* 1660, V. (I) 2 Sept 1701 and (GB) 8 Aug 1786, E. (S) 10 July 1606, M. (GB) 15 Oct 1790 and (I) 10 Aug 1868, D. (I) 10 Aug 1868.

THE 5TH DUKE OF ABERCORN, Marquess of Abercorn, Marquess of Hamilton, Earl of Abercorn, Viscount Strabane, Viscount Hamilton, Lord Paisley, Lord Aberbrothick, Lord Abercorn, Lord Hamilton, Lord Mountcastle, Lord Kilpatrick, Lord Hamilton, Baron Strabane, Baron Mountcashell and a **Baronet**, also **Duke of Châtellerault** (Sir James Hamilton, Bt) [His Grace The Duke of Abercorn, Barons Court, Omagh, Co Tyrone, N Ireland BT78 4EZ; 10 Little Chester St, London SW1]; *b* 4 July 1934; *s f* 1979; heir male of the House of Hamilton; *educ* Eton and RAC Cirencester; Lt Gren Gds; MP (UU) Fermanagh and S Tyrone 1964–70; DL Co Tyrone, High Sheriff 1970, Ld-Lt 1987–; Pres Bldg Socs Assoc 1986–92 and RUKBA 1979–, chm Laganside Devpt Corp 1989–96 and Templeton Investment Management 1985–; Hon LLB Queen's U Belfast 1997; Patron Roy Ulster Ag Soc 1990–96, Tstee Winston Churchill Meml Tst 1991–; *m* 20 Oct 1966 *Hamilton, Alexandra Anastasia, est dau of Lt-Col Harold Pedro Joseph Phillips, Coldstream Gds, FRGS, of Checkendon, Reading (*see* 1970 edn WERNHER, Bt), and has:

1 +JAMES HAROLD CHARLES, *Marquess of Hamilton*; *b* 19 Aug 1969 (HRH THE PRINCE OF WALES stood sponsor); *educ* Harrow; Page of Honour to HM THE QUEEN 1982–84

2 +Nicholas Edward Claud; *b* 8 July 1979; *educ* Harrow

1 *Sophia Alexandra; *b* 8 June 1973; *educ* St Mary's Wantage; model to 1996

Lineage: GILBERT de HAMILTON (*see* also STRATHCLYDE, B); had:

WALTER Fitz GILBERT, 1st of Cadzow; witness to a charter to Paisley Abbey 10 Jan 1294/5, named in the Homage Roll 28 Aug 1296, granted by ROBERT I (THE BRUCE) Dalserf 3 March 1314/5 and afterwards Cadzow, which became the chief lordship and seat of the Hamilton family, also Kinneil 28 July 1323; *m* 1st—Helen; *m* 2nd Mary, dau of Sir Adam Gordon, feudal Ld of Gordon, by whom he had issue:

1 DAVID Fitz WALTER Fitz GILBERT, for whom *see* further below

2 John Fitz WALTER; ancestor of the Hamiltons of Innerwick and the Earls of Haddington (*qv*)

WALTER Fitz GILBERT's er s,

Sir DAVID Fitz WALTER Fitz GILBERT, 2nd of Cadzow; fought Battles of Halidon Hill 1333 and Durham 1346 (where captured by English), benefactor diocese of Glasgow 1361, one of the leading Scottish nobles who consented to the settlement of the Crown on ROBERT II 1371; *m* Margaret, dau of William, 7th Earl of Ross, and *d* 1374, having had issue:

1 DAVID HAMILTON, for whom *see* further below

2 Sir John, of Fingaltoun; ancestor of the HAMILTONs of Preston (*see* STIRLING-HAMILTON, Bt)

3 Walter; ancestor of the HAMILTONs of Cambuskeith, Ayrshire

Sir DAVID Fitz WALTER Fitz GILBERT HAMILTON's est s,

Sir DAVID HAMILTON, 3rd of Cadzow; had grants from ROBERT II 1375 and 1378; *m* Janet/Joan/Jonetta, dau of Sir William Keith, of Galston, and *d* by 14 May 1392, leaving an est s:

Sir JOHN HAMILTON, 4th of Cadzow; witnessed a charter 14 May 1392; *m* Jacoba/Janet, dau of Sir James Douglas of Dalkeith, and had, with possibly a dau (Elizabeth, *m* by 1400 Alexander Fraser, 1st of Philorth; *see* SALTOUN, L), an est s:

Sir JAMES HAMILTON, 5th of Cadzow; a hostage for the ransom of JAMES I from the English 1424 and 1426; *m c* 20 Oct 1422 Janet, dau of Sir Alexander Livingston, of Callendar, and *d* by May 1441, having had issue:

1 JAMES HAMILTON, 1st LORD HAMILTON

2 Alexander; had issue (*see* HAMILTON Bt, of Silvertonhill)

3 John; had a charter of Whitecamp and Kirkhope 14 June 1449 and *d* by 23 Oct 1455, leaving issue:

(1) William

(2) Robert

4 Gavin; Provost collegiate church of Bothwell; ancestor of the HAMILTONs of Orbieston (*see* HAMILTON OF DALZELL, B); had an illegitimate s:

(1) Thomas

Sir JAMES HAMILTON, 5th of Cadzow's est s,

Sir JAMES HAMILTON, 6th of Cadzow, 1st LORD HAMILTON (S), so *cr* by roy charter 28 June 1445; at first joined the Douglas revolt of 1455 against JAMES II, later went over to the King's side and helped suppress it, Sheriff Lanarks 1 July 1455, had a new charter of all his lands and baronies 23 Oct 1455; *m* 1st (dispensation 2 Feb 1440/1) Lady Eupheme Graham (*d* by 1 Nov 1468), est dau of Sir Patrick Graham (*see* MONTROSE, D) and Eupheme, Countess of Strathearn in her own right, and widow of 5th Earl of Douglas (*see* QUEENSBURY, M), and had issue:

1 Elizabeth; *m* 1459 (*divorce* by 1485) David Lindsay, 5th Earl of Crawford, afterwards Duke of Montrose (*see* CRAWFORD and BALCARRES, E); *m* 2nd (*divorce* by 1508) John Forrester of Niddrie and *d* in or after 1516

The 1st LORD HAMILTON *m* 2nd *c* 25 April 1476 PRINCESS MARY, est dau of JAMES II and previously w of Thomas Boyd, Earl of Arran (*see* KILMARNOCK, B), and *d* 16 Nov 1479, having by her had issue:

1 JAMES HAMILTON, 2nd LORD HAMILTON and 1st EARL OF ARRAN, for whom *see* further below

2 Elizabeth; *m* April 1494, as his 2nd w, Matthew Stuart, 11th Earl of Lennox (*see* MORAY, E), and *d* in or after April 1531

The 1st LORD HAMILTON's only s,

JAMES HAMILTON, 2nd LORD HAMILTON and 1st EARL OF ARRAN, PC (S); *b c* 1475; obtained a charter of the lands and earldom of Arran to himself and his heirs male in failure of which they were to revert to the Crown 11 Aug 1503, Adml Scotland 1513, Lt-Gen Kingdom of Scotland, Warden Marches, one of the Lds of the Regency 1517, obtained the lordship of Bothwell on the forfeiture of the Earl of Angus; *m* 1st (charter 28 April 1490; *divorce* 16 Nov 1504 on grounds of her previous marriage to Thomas Hay of Hoprew (living 20 June 1491, *i.e.*, at the time of the marriage, though believed dead at the time), s of 1st Lord Hay of Yester (*see* TWEEDDALE, M), further *divorce* 11 March 1509/10) Elizabeth (*d* 1544), dau of 2nd Lord Home (*see* HOME, E); *m* 2nd (charter 23 Nov 1516) Janet (*d c* 1522), dau of Sir David Beaton of Creich, Fifeshire (Comptroller Scotland *temp* JAMES VI), and widow of Sir Robert Livingston of Easter Wemyss, and *d* by 22 July 1529, having had at least one illegitimate child (Elizabeth, *m c* 1543 Robert, Master of Sempill; *see* SEMPILL, L) and leaving legitimate issue by his 2nd w

The 1st EARL OF ARRAN's est legitimate s,

JAMES HAMILTON, 2nd EARL OF ARRAN; Regent of Scotland 1542–54, declared Heir Presumptive to the Crown 13 March 1542/3, Guardian to MARY QUEEN OF SCOTS and Govr of the Realm during latter's minority, Order of St Michael France 1548, *cr* by HENRY II OF FRANCE 8 Feb 1548/9 DUKE OF CHATELLERAULT, in Poitou, with a pension, to win his consent to the match between MARY QUEEN OF SCOTS and the DAUPHIN OF FRANCE; *m c* 23 Sept 1532 Lady Margaret Douglas, est dau of 3rd Earl of Morton (*qv*), and *d* 22 Jan 1574/5, leaving, with a dau (Barbara, *m* 1st Alexander, Lord Gordon (*see* HUNTLY, M), and 2nd 4th Lord Fleming and had issue; *see* LAUDERDALE, E) a 5th s:

CLAUD HAMILTON, **1st Lord Paisley**, Co Renfrew (S), so *cr* 29 July 1587; *b c* 1542; Lay Abbot Paisley 1553; cmded the vanguard for MARY QUEEN OF SCOTS Battle of Langside 1568 (having previously helped her escape from Lochleven), subsequently outlawed and estates forfeited, but restored for loyalty to JAMES VI 1572/3 though again subject to forfeiture for activities in MARY's cause 1579, barony of Paisley restored to him 1585, though he continued plotting for MARY's release; *m* 1 Aug 1574 Margaret (*d* by 18 Feb 1616), dau of 5th Lord Seton (*see* EGLINTON and WINTON, E), and *d* by 3 May 1621, leaving, with a yr s (Sir John, whose widow Johanna *m* 4th Lord Sempill; *qv*) a 2nd s:

JAMES HAMILTON, **2nd Lord Paisley** and **1st Earl of Abercorn**, PC (S), MP (S) Linlithgow 1597, Gent of Bedchamber to JAMES VI, granted office of Sheriff Linlithgowshire for him and his heirs male 1600; *cr*: 5 April 1603 LORD ABERCORN, Co Linlithgow (S), and 10 July 1606 EARL OF ABERCORN, LORD PAISLEY, HAMILTON, MOUNTCASTELL and KILPATRICK (all S); *m* Marion (*d* 20 Aug 1632), dau of 6th Lord Boyd (*see* KILMARNOCK, B), and *dvp* 23 March 1617/8, leaving, with other issue:

1 JAMES HAMILTON, **2nd Earl of Abercorn**; *s* his cousin 2nd Duke of Hamilton (*qv*) as heir male of the House of Hamilton, *cr* 8 May 1617 LORD HAMILTON, BARON OF STRABANE, Co Tyrone (I) with remainder to the heirs male of the body of his f, an honour transferred to his next bro Claud 11 Nov 1633 following his (James's) resignation, a resignation itself following James's succession to his f's and gf's peerages; *m c* 1632 Catharine (*d* 17 Sept 1637), dau and heiress of 1st Baron Clifton (of Leighton Bromswold), and widow of 3rd Duke of Lennox (*see* MORAY, E), and *d c* 1670, having had issue (with two er sons who *dvp*):

(1) GEORGE HAMILTON, **3rd Earl of Abercorn**; *b c* 1636; *d* unm Padua by 1683

2 CLAUD HAMILTON, **2nd Lord Hamilton, Baron of Strabane**; *s* to the family's Irish estates on the resignation of his bro and was *cr* (effectively a recognition) 14 Aug 1634 LORD HAMILTON, BARON OF STRABANE, Co Tyrone (I), with the precedence of the former patent 8 May 1617 (*see* below); *m* 28 Nov 1632 Lady Jean Gordon (*m* 2nd after 1641 Sir Phelim O'Neill; *see* O'NEILL, B), dau of 1st Marquess of Huntly (*qv*), and *d* 14 June 1638, having by her had, with other issue:

(1) JAMES HAMILTON, **3rd Lord Hamilton, Baron of Strabane**; *b* 1633; *d* unm 16 June 1655

(1) GEORGE HAMILTON, **4th Lord Hamilton, Baron of Strabane**; *m* 1659 Elizabeth, dau of Christopher Fagan, of Feltrim, Co Dublin, and *d* 14 April 1668, leaving issue, with two daus (one of whom *m* Sir John Browne, 3rd Bt; *see* KILMAINE, B):

1a CLAUD HAMILTON, **5th Lord Hamilton, Baron of Strabane** and **4th Earl of Abercorn**, PC (I); *bapt* 13 Sept 1659; Ld of the Bedchamber to JAMES II whom he accompanied to France after the Battle of the Boyne 1 July 1690, outlawed 11 May 1691 and his Irish peerages and estates confiscated, cmded a Jacobite Regt Battle of Aughrim, Ireland, 12 July 1691; *ka* soon after in an engagement with a Dutch man-of-war nr Brest, whilst returning to France

2a CHARLES HAMILTON, **5th Earl of Abercorn**; restored to the title and estates 24 May 1692; *m* Catharine (*d* 24 May 1723), dau and heir of James, Lord Paisley, est s of James, 2nd Earl of Abercorn, and widow of William Lenthall, of Burford Priory, Oxford; *dsps* June 1701

(1) Catherine; *m* 1st 1647 her cousin James Hamilton, er bro of 1st Viscount Boyne (*qv*); *m* 2nd Owen Wynne; *m* 3rd John Bingham, of Castlebar, Co Mayo

3 **Sir George Hamilton, 1st Bt**, of Donalong, Co Tyrone, and Nenagh, Co Tipperary; *cr c* 1660 a Baronet (NS); *m* (contract 2 June 1629) Mary (*d* Aug 1680), 3rd dau of Thomas Butler, Viscount Thurles (*see* ORMONDE, M), and sis of 1st Duke of Ormonde, and *d* 1679, leaving, with other issue:

(1) James; Col in serv of CHARLES II and Groom of the Bedchamber; *m* 1661 Elizabeth (*d* 1709), dau of 1st Baron Colepeper of Thoresway (*extinct* 1725), and *dvp* of a wound recd in a naval engagement with the Dutch 6 June 1673, leaving, with other issue:

1a JAMES HAMILTON, **6th Earl of Abercorn**, PC (I); did not take the title of Bt on gf's death, took part in defence of Londonderry during Siege by JAMES II, MP (I) Tyrone 1692 and 1695, *cr* 2 Sept 1701 BARON MOUNTCASHELL, Co Tyrone, and VISCOUNT STRABANE (both I); *m c* 24 Jan 1683/4 Elizabeth (*d* 19 March 1754), dau and heiress of Sir Robert Reading, 1st and last Bt, of Dublin; *d* 28 Nov 1734, having had, with other issue:

1b JAMES, **7th Earl**

2a William, of Chilston Pk, Kent (*see* HAMILTON, Bt, of Trebinshun)

(2) George (Sir); Count Hamilton in France and Maréchal du Camp; *m* 1665 Frances ('La Belle Jenyns', who *m* 2nd 1679, as his 2nd w, 1st Duke of Tyrconnell *see* TALBOT OF MALAHIDE, B), and *d* 9 March 1730), est dau and coheir of Richard Jenyns, of Sandridge, Herts, and sis of Sarah, Duchess of Marlborough (*see* MARLBOROUGH, D), and *d* 1676, having had three daus (including Frances, *m* 1st 1687 8th Viscount Dillon (*qv*) of Costello-Gallen, *m* 2nd *c* 1714 Patrick Bellew; *see* BELLEW, B)

(3) Anthony, Count Hamilton; Lt-Gen French serv; author: *Mémoires de Gramont*; *d* 20 April 1719 aged 74

(1) Elizabeth; *m* Philibert, Count de Gramont, and had issue (*see* STAFFORD, B)

1 Anne; *m c* 1611 5th Lord Semphill (*qv*)

The 6th EARL OF ABERCORN's est s,

JAMES HAMILTON, **7th Earl of Abercorn**, PC (E and I) ; *b* 22 March 1685/6; FRS; *m* (licence 26 March 1711) Anne (*d* 7 Aug 1776), est dau of Col John Plumer, of Blakesware, Herts; *d* 11 Jan 1744, having had, with other issue:

1 JAMES HAMILTON, **8th Earl of Abercorn**; *b* 22 Oct 1712; Rep Peer Scotland 1761–86, *cr* 8 Aug 1786 VISCOUNT HAMILTON (GB), with remainder in default of male issue to his n John James Hamilton; *d* unm 9 Oct 1789

2 John; Capt RN; *m* 13 Oct 1749 Harriet (*d* 1 Feb 1769), illegitimate dau of James Craggs, PC, and widow of Richard Eliot, (*see* ST GERMANS, E), and was drowned off Portsmouth 18 Dec 1755, leaving issue:

(1) JOHN JAMES, **1st Marquess**

(1) Anne; *d* unm 4 Nov 1764

3 George (Rev); *b* 11 Aug 1718; Canon Windsor; *m* Elizabeth (*d* 1800), dau of Lt-Gen Richard Onslow, Govr Plymouth (*see* ONSLOW, E); *d* 26 Nov 1787, having had one s and eight daus (including Elizabeth, *m* Glynn Belasyse-Wynn; *see* NEWBOROUGH, B)

The 8th EARL OF ABERCORN's n,

JOHN JAMES HAMILTON, **9th Earl** and **1st Marquess of Abercorn** (I), so *cr* 15 Oct 1790, KG (1805), PC (I 1794); *b* posthumously July 1756; *m* 1st 20 June 1777 Catherine (*d* 13 Sept 1791), dau of Sir Joseph Copley, 1st Bt, of Sprotborough, Yorks, and had issue:

1 James, *Viscount Hamilton*; *b* 7 Oct 1786; *m* 25 Nov 1809 Harriet (*m* 2nd 8 July 1815 4th Earl of Aberdeen (*see* ABERDEEN AND TEMAIR, M); *d* 26 Aug 1833), dau of Hon John Douglas (*see* MORTON, E); *dvp* 27 May 1814, leaving issue:

(1) JAMES, **2nd Marquess** and **1st Duke of Abercorn**, for whom *see* further below

(2) Claud, PC; *b* 27 July 1813; MP Co Tyrone 1835–37 and 1839–74; V-Chamberlain Household 1866–68; *m* 7 Aug 1844 Lady Elizabeth Emma Proby (ld 24 June 1900), 2nd dau of 3rd Earl of Carysfort (*extinct* 1909), and *d* 3 June 1884, leaving issue:

1a Douglas James HAMILTON later PROBY (roy licence 1904), JP (Hunts and Northants), DL (Hunts and Co Wicklow), of Elton Hall, Peterborough; *b* 23 Sept 1856; *educ* Ch Ch Oxford (MA); High Sheriff Cambs and Hunts 1923, OStJ, Lt-Col and Brevet Col Irish Gds and cmded Regtl Dist 1914–17, MP Saffron Walden 1910; *m* 6 July 1882 Lady Margaret Frances Hely-Hutchinson (*d* 2 March 1937), dau of 4th Earl of Donoughmore (*qv*); *d* 18 Nov 1931 leaving issue:

1b Granville, JP, DL, of Elton Hall; *b* 13 Sept 1883; *educ* Eton and Trin Coll Oxford (MA); Capt Beds Yeo; CC Hunts: CCllr, High Sheriff 1935, Chm QS 1941, Ld-Lt 1945; Clerk Ho of Lds, barrister Inner Temple 1920, FSA, FRHistS, Silver Jubilee 1935 and Coronation 1937 medals; *d* unm 9 March 1947

2b Claud Richard; *b* 26 April 1885; Cadet RN; *d* 18 Feb 1901

3b Sir RICHARD GEORGE PROBY, 1st Bt (*qv*)

4b Jocelyn Campbell Patrick; *b* 3 March 1900; *educ* Eton and Magdalen Coll Oxford (BA 1921, BLitt 1924, MA 1926); barrister Inner Temple 1923, graduate of Kirksville Coll of Osteopathy and Surgery, Missouri, USA, history lecturer Toronto U; *m* 1st 16 Aug 1930 Elizabeth Angelique (*d* 26 Jan 1962), est dau of William Archibald Hastings Kerr, of Toronto, and adopted:

*Allen Patrick [Allen Proby Esq, Bollabradda, Inch, Gorey, Co Wexford, Ireland]; *b* 30 Oct 1942; *educ* Lancing; *m* 21 July 1969 *Gloria Florence, dau of William Robert Hughes, of Inch

*Miranda Ruth [Mrs Roger Brown, 31 Portman Avenue, London SW14]; *b* 20 May 1937; *m* 30 April 1967 *Roger Arthur Martin Brown, only s of Hugh Brown, of Buenos Aires, Argentina

4b (cont.) Jocelyn Proby *m* 2nd 3 Jan 1969 *Katherine, er dau of Lt-Col Hugh Simpson, RA, of Penrith, Cumberland, and widow of Brig John Henry Edward, 6th Baron de Robeck, CBE, RA

1b Betty Alice Adeline; *b* 17 May 1889; *m* 27 April 1920 Lt-Col Sir Henry Charles Lowry Corry, MC (*d* 23 Dec 1973), er s of Col Henry William Lowry Corry, JP, DL, and had issue (*see* BELMORE, E)

1a Louisa Charlotte; *m* 29 Feb 1876 John Tyndall, LLD, DCL, FRS (*d* 4 Dec 1893), s of John Tyndall, of Leighlin Bridge, Co Carlow; *d* 18 Aug 1940

2a Emma Frances; *d* 2 Jan 1924

3a Mary Stuart; *m* 2 Oct 1878 2nd Baron Tollemache (*d* 17 Dec 1904) (*qv*); *d* 6 Jan 1939

(1) Harriet; *m* 15 May 1836 Adml William Alexander Baillie Hamilton, 3rd s of Ven Charles Baillie, Archdeacon of Cleveland (*d* 1 Oct 1881), and *d* 19 March 1884 leaving issue (*see* HADDINGTON, E)

2 Claud; *b* 1 Nov 1787; *d* 1808

1 Harriet Margaret; *d* 30 April 1803

2 Katharine Elizabeth; *m* 28 July 1805 4th Earl of Aberdeen (*d* 14 Dec 1860) (*qv*); *d* 20 Feb 1812 leaving issue who *d* unm

3 Maria; *d* unm 21 Jan 1814

The **1st Marquess** *m* 2nd 4 March 1792 (*divorce* 1799) his cousin Cecil, dau of Rev Hon George Hamilton (*see* above), and by her had issue:

4 Cecil Frances; *m* 16 Feb 1816 4th Earl of Wicklow (*d* 22 March 1869); *d* 7 July 1860 leaving issue

The **1st Marquess** *m* 3rd 3 April 1800 Lady Anne Jane Gore (*dsp* 8 May 1827), dau of 2nd Earl of Arran (*qv*) and widow of Henry Hatton, of Clonard, and *d* 27 Jan 1818, having had illegitimately by Frances Hawkins:

3 Arthur Fitz-James; *b* 1799

His gs,

JAMES HAMILTON, **2nd Marquess** and **1st Duke of Abercorn**, KG, PC, DCL, LLD; *b* 21 Jan 1811; Ld-Lt Ireland 1866–68 and 1874–6, Groom Stole to HRH THE PRINCE CONSORT, Lt and Custos Rotulorum Co Donegal, Col Donegal Militia, Maj-Gen Roy Co of Archers; a Govr Harrow Sch, Chllr Roy U of Ireland, *cr* 10 Aug 1868 DUKE OF ABERCORN and MARQUESS OF HAMILTON (both I), served heir male of the body of the 1st Duke of Chatellerault by the Sheriff of Chancery in Scotland 13 Jan 1862 and, as heir male of the 1st Duke, asserted his hereditary right to the original title of Duke of Chatellerault of 1549, the descent of French dukedoms having been declared by edict of KING LOUIS XIV 1711 to be to heirs 'descendus de male en males'; *m* 25 Oct 1832 Lady Louisa Jane Russell, VA (*d* 31 March 1905), 2nd dau of 6th Duke of Bedford (*qv*), and *d* 31 Oct 1885 having had issue:

1 JAMES, **2nd Duke**

2 Claud John, PC (1917); *b* 20 Feb 1843; *educ* Harrow; Capt Gren Gds, Hon Col 5th Bn Roy Inniskilling Fus; High Steward Borough of Gt Yarmouth and of Harwich, MP Londonderry 1865–68, King's Lynn 1869–80, Liverpool 1880–88, and S Kensington 1910–18, a Ld of the Treas 1868, ADC to HM QUEEN VICTORIA 1887–97, KJStJ; *m* 20 July 1878 Carolina (*d* 21 Sept 1911), dau of Edward Sacheverell Chandos Pole, of Radborne Hall, Derby; *d* 26 Jan 1925 leaving issue:

(1) Gilbert Claud, CMG (1919), DSO (1915); *b* 21 April 1879; Col Gren Gds, S African War 1899–1902 (despatches, two medals, eight clasps) and WW I (despatches twice); *m* 1st 16 May 1911 Enid Awa (*d* 19 April 1916), dau of Charles Elgar, of Fernside, Featherston, New Zealand; *m* 2nd 29 Nov 1916 Mary (*d* 8 Jan 1961), dau of Joseph Allan Blair, of New York, USA, and formerly w of Gould Brokaw; *dsp* 30 March 1943

(1) Ida Hamilton; *b* 23 July 1883; *m* 24 April 1909 (*divorce* 1923) Hugh Duncombe Flower (*d* 9 Dec 1950), 2nd s of Arthur Flower; *d* Nov 1970 leaving issue:

1a Peter Hugh; *b* 30 Jan 1910; *educ* Harrow; Lt-Col Coldstream Gds, WW II (despatches), ADC to High Commr Egypt 1934–36, Assist Mily Attaché Greece 1956–57 and France 1957–59; *m* 26 April 1937 *Lydia Josephine, yr dau of Maj Geoffrey Edward Huth, JP, of Marlborough, Wilts, and *d* 3 May 1993, leaving:

1b *Charles Hugh; *b* 26 Oct 1941; *educ* Harrow and Ch Ch Oxford (BA 1963); *m* 24 Sept 1960 *Harriet, sis of Baroness Nicholson of Winterbourne (*qv*)

1b *Venetia [Lady Hugh Smith, The Old Rectory, Grendon Underwood, Bucks HP18 0SY]; *b* 21 April 1939; *m* 22 July 1964 *Sir Andrew Colin Hugh- Smith, chm London Stock Exchange 1988–94, er s of Lt-Cdr Colin Edward Hugh Smith, RN, of Underwood, Bucks, and has:

1c *David Hugh; *b* 12 Feb 1967; *m* 1995 *Maresa-Clare, dau of Peter Moloney, of Liverpool

2c *Peter; *b* 31 March 1969; *m* 1994 *Kate Elisabeth, dau of Peter John Lyons Gray; and has

1d *Piers Henry; *b* 12 June 1995

1d *Zara Lily; *b* 25 Feb 1997

3 George Francis, GCSI (1903), PC (1878), JP Middx and Westminster; *b* 17 Dec 1845; *educ* Harrow; Lt Rifle Bde and Coldstream Gds; MP Middx 1868–85, Ealing 1885–1906, Under-Sec of State India 1874–78, V-Pres Ctee Cncl on Educn 1878–80, First Ld Admlty 1885–86 and 1886–92, Chm London Sch Bd 1894–95, Sec of State India 1895–1903; DCL Oxford and Hon LLD Glasgow, Capt Deal Castle 1899–1923, Mayor Deal 1909; *m* 28 Nov 1871 Lady Maud Caroline Lascelles, CI (*d* 14 April 1938), dau of 3rd Earl of Harewood (*qv*), and *d* 22 Sept 1927, leaving issue:

(1) Ronald James, OBE (1919); *b* 26 Sept 1872; First Sec Dip Serv; WW I (wounded), Order Crown Belgium; *m* 10 Feb 1915 Florence Marguerite (Sarah Brooke) (*d* 5 Aug 1959), only dau of Maj John Hanna by Emilie Sarah, dau of Rev Charles Darby Reade, JP, and *d* 22 Jan 1958, leaving:

1a *Maud Sarah [Mrs Maud Czernin, 50 Hartismere Road, London SW6]; *b* 4 April 1917; *m* 4 Nov 1939 (*divorce* 1947) S/Ldr Count Manfred Maria Edmund Ralph Beckett Czernin, DSO, MC, DFC, RAF (*d* 6 Oct 1962), yst s of Count Otto Czernin (*see* GRIMTHORPE, B), and has issue:

1b *(Manfred) Nicholas; *b* 12 Oct 1942; *educ* Harrow; *m* 1st 1970 (*divorce* 1982) Danielle Alligier and has issue:

1c *Nicholas; *b* 1962

1c *Sarah Moon; *b* 1970

1b (cont.) Nicholas Czernin *m* 2nd 1987 *Orapin Champanich, of Bangkok, and has further issue:

1c *Pawau Beckett; *b* 1989

1b *Carolyn Lucille [Mrs Charles Peploe, 54 Liberton Brae, Edinburgh EH16 6TF]; *b* 9 May 1941; *m* 9 July 1966 *Charles Norman George Peploe, yr s of Capt Charles Peploe, RN, of White Lodge, Gullane, East Lothian, and has issue:

1c *Manfred Crispin David; *b* 1969

2c *Fergus Charles Nicholas; *b* 22 Aug 1970

(2) Anthony George; *b* 17 Dec 1874; WW I as Maj E Kent Regt; *d* 11 July 1936

(3) Robert Cecil; *b* 31 Jan 1882; V-Adml WW I; *m* 30 May 1911 Edith Maud (*d* 8 July 1967), 2nd dau of Algernon Herbert Paley, barrister, of Henley-on-Thames; *dsp* 31 July 1947

4 Ronald Douglas; *b* 17 March 1849; *d* Nov 1867

5 Cosmo; *b* and *d* 16 April 1853

6 Frederick Spencer; *b* 13 Oct 1856; 2nd Sec Dip Serv 1877–84, MP SW Manchester 1885–86 and N Tyrone 1892–95; author: *Vanished Pomps of Yesterday*, *The Days Before Yesterday* and *Here, There and Everywhere*; *d* unm 11 Aug 1928

7 Ernest William; *b* 5 Sept 1858; *educ* Harrow and RMC; Capt (ret) 11th Hus; MP N Tyrone 1885–92; *m* 2 June 1891 Pamela (*d* 11 May 1931), dau of Capt Frederic Augustus Campbell (*see* CAMPBELL, Bt); *d* 14 Dec 1939 having had issue:

(1) Guy Ernest Frederic; *b* 11 Nov 1894; *d* unm 23 Nov 1914

(2) John George Peter; *b* 15 Oct 1900; *educ* Harrow; *m* 25 May 1932 Alexandra Christine (*d* 10 Aug 1963), dau of William Egerton, of Kimberley, S Africa, and formerly w of Alexander Lodewyk Bennink-Jassonius; *dsp* 17 June 1967

(1) Mary Brenda; *b* 28 March 1897; *m* 22 April 1922 Lt-Col Prince Alphonse de Chimay, TD, Scots Gds (*d* 1 Oct 1973), only s of Prince Alphonse de Chimay, Count de Caraman, and had issue:

1a *(Pamela Therese) Louise; *b* 18 Nov 1932; *m* 10 July 1956 8th Marquess of Hertford (*qv*) and has issue

(2) Jean Barbara; *b* 6 Sept 1898; *m* 8 June 1921 (*divorce* 1944) Sir John William Buchanan-Jardine, 3rd Bt (*d* 5 Nov 1969) (*qv*), and had issue

1 Harriet Georgiana Louisa; *m* 10 April 1855 2nd Earl of Lichfield (*d* 7 Jan 1892) (*qv*); *d* 23 April 1913 leaving issue

2 Beatrix Frances; *m* 23 May 1854 2nd Earl of Durham (*d* 27 Nov 1879) (*qv*); *d* 21 Jan 1871 leaving issue

3 Louisa Jane, VA, Mistress of the Robes to TM QUEEN VICTORIA 1885–92 and 1895–1901 and QUEEN ALEXANDRA 1901–12; *m* 22 Nov 1859 6th Duke of Buccleuch (*d* 5 Nov 1914) (*qv*); *d* 17 March 1912 leaving issue

4 Katherine Elizabeth; *m* 26 Oct 1858 4th Earl of Mount Edgcumbe (*d* 25 Sept 1917) (*qv*); *d* 3 Sept 1874 leaving issue

5 Georgiana Susan; *m* 16 March 1882 5th Earl Winterton (*d* 5 Sept 1907) (*qv*), and *d* 23 March 1913 leaving issue

6 Albertha Frances Anne; *m* 8 Nov 1869 (*divorce* on her petition 1883) 8th Duke of Marlborough (*qv*) and *d* 7 Jan 1932, having had issue

7 Maud Evelyn, CI, GBE, VA, CH, DGStJ, Ldy of the Bedchamber to HM QUEEN ALEXANDRA 1905–09, Extra Ldy of the Bedchamber 1910–25; *m* 8 Nov 1869 5th Marquess of Lansdowne (*qv*) and *d* 21 Oct 1932 leaving issue

The 1st DUKE OF ABERCORN's est s,

JAMES HAMILTON, **2nd Duke of Abercorn**, KG, PC, CB; *b* 24 Aug 1838; *educ* Ch Ch Oxford (MA); Hon Col N Irish Horse and of the 5th Bn Roy Inniskilling Fus; MP 1860–80; Lt and Custos Rotulorum Co Donegal, Ensign Roy Co of Archers 1908–12; Ld of the Bedchamber to HM EDWARD VII when PRINCE OF WALES 1866–86, Groom Stole 1886–1901; Special Envoy Denmark, Sweden, and Norway, Russia, Germany and Saxony to announce accession of HM EDWARD VII 1901; High Constable Ireland Coronation of HM GEORGE V; *m* 7 Jan 1869 Lady Mary Anna Curzon (*d* 10 May 1929), 4th dau of 1st Earl Howe (*qv*), and *d* 3 Jan 1913 having had issue:

1 JAMES ALBERT EDWARD, **3rd Duke**

2 Claud Penn Alexander; *b* and *d* 18 Oct 1871

3 Charlie; *b* and *d* 10 April 1874

4 Claud Francis; *b* 25 Oct, *d* 25 Dec 1878

5 (Arthur) John ; *b* 20 Aug 1883; Capt Irish Gds, Dep-Master of the Household 1913–14; *ka* 6 Nov 1914

6 A son; *b* and *d* 31 Oct 1886

7 Claud Nigel, GCVO (1949), CMG (1920), DSO (1914); *b* 10 Nov 1889; *educ* Wellington; Capt Gren Gds, WW I (despatches), re-employed WW II 1939–42; Equerry-in-Ordinary to HRH THE PRINCE OF WALES 1919, Dep Master HM's Household 1921, Extra Equerry 1922–24, Equerry-in-Ordinary to HM GEORGE V 1924–36, Comptroller, Treas and Extra Equerry to HM QUEEN MARY 1936–53, Extra Equerry to HM THE QUEEN 1953–75; *m* 11 July 1933 Violet Ruby (*d* 1984), dau of James Ashton, of London, and formerly w of Lt-Cdr Keith Newall, RN, and *dsp* 22 Aug 1975

1 Alexandra Phyllis (HM QUEEN ALEXANDRA stood sponsor); *b* 23 Jan 1876; *d* unm, lost at sea 10 Oct 1918

2 Gladys Mary; *b* 10 Dec 1880; *m* 14 Jan 1902 7th Earl of Wicklow (*d* 11 Oct 1946; *see* 1970 edn) and *d* 12 March 1917, leaving issue

The 2nd DUKE OF ABERCORN's est s,

JAMES ALBERT EDWARD HAMILTON, **3rd Duke of Abercorn**, KG (1928), KP (1922), PC (GB 1945, NI 1922); *b* 30 Nov 1869 (HM EDWARD VII stood sponsor); Capt 1st Life Gds and Maj N Irish Horse, Hon Col 9th AA Regt 1939; MP Londonderry City 1900–13; Treas Household 1903–05; HM's Lt Co Tyrone; DL Co Donegal; Govr N Ireland 1922–45; KGStJ; one of the four Peers bearing the Canopy Coronation 1937, Roy Victorian Chain 1945, Hon LLD Queen's U Belfast 1928; *m* 1 Nov 1894 Lady Rosalind Cecilia Caroline Bingham, DBE, Hon LLD Queen's U Belfast (*d* 18 Jan 1958), only dau of 4th Earl of Lucan (*qv*); *d* 12 Sept 1953 having had issue:

1 JAMES EDWARD, **4th Duke**

2 Claud David; *b* 13 Feb 1907; *educ* Eton and Ch Ch Oxford (BA 1929); barrister Inner Temple 1930; Capt Irish Gds WW II; *m* 21 Feb 1946 Genesta Mary (*d* 20 Dec 1990), only dau of Cuthbert Eden Heath, OBE, of Anstie Grange, Holmwood, Surrey, and formerly w of (a) Arthur McNeill Farquhar and (b) Capt Edward Caswell Long, and *dsp* 15 Feb 1968

1 Mary Cecilia Rhodesia; *b* 21 Jan 1896; *m* 1st 24 May 1917 (*divorce* 1930) Capt Robert Orlando Rodolph Kenyon-Slaney, Gren Gds (*d* 14 Jan 1965), only s of Rt Hon William Slaney Kenyon-Slaney, PC, JP, DL, of Hatton Grange, Shropshire, and had issue (*see* KENYON, B); *m* 2nd 26 Nov 1930 Sir John Little Gilmour, 2nd Bt (*d* 13 Feb 1977), and *d* 5 Sept 1984, having had further issue (*see* GILMOUR OF CRAIGMILLAR, B)

2 Cynthia Elinor Beatrix, DCVO (1953), OBE (1943); *b* 16 Aug 1897; Ldy of the Bedchamber to HM QUEEN ELIZABETH (later HM QUEEN ELIZABETH THE QUEEN MOTHER) 1937–72; *m* 26 Feb 1919 7th Earl Spencer (*d* 9 June 1975) (*qv*); *d* 4 Dec 1972 leaving issue

3 Katherine, DCVO (1961); *b* 25 Feb 1900; Woman of the Bedchamber to HM QUEEN MARY 1927–30, (Extra Woman of the Bedchamber 1930–53), Woman of the Bedchamber to HM QUEEN ELIZABETH (later HM QUEEN ELIZABETH THE QUEEN MOTHER) 1937–60, Extra Woman of the Bedchamber 1960–85; *m* 6 Aug 1930 Lt-Col Sir Reginald Henry Seymour, KCVO (*d* 2 Oct 1938), 2nd s of George Evelyn Seymour, and *d* 28 April 1985, leaving issue (*see* HERTFORD, M)

The 3rd DUKE OF ABERCORN's er s,

JAMES EDWARD HAMILTON, **4th Duke of Abercorn**; *b* 29 Feb 1904 (HM EDWARD VII stood sponsor); *educ* Eton; Capt (RARO) Gren Gds, Hon Col 5th Bn Roy Inniskilling Fus (TA) 1963; HM Lt Co Tyrone 1950 and 1975, High Sheriff 1946, CC (1946) Co Tyrone, Memb Senate Govt of N Ireland 1949, Chm Tstees Ulster Museum 1962, Pres Roy Forestry Soc of England, Wales and N Ireland 1964–66; *m* 9 Feb 1928 Lady Mary Kathleen Crichton, DCVO (1969) (*d* 2 Feb 1990), Mistress of the Robes to HM QUEEN ELIZABETH THE QUEEN MOTHER 1964–90, sis of 5th Earl of Erne (*qv*), and *d* 4 June 1979, leaving:

1 JAMES HAMILTON, **5th and present Duke of Abercorn**

2 +(Claud) Anthony, JP (1991) DL (Co Fermanagh 1978) [The Lord Anthony Hamilton JP DL, Killyreagh, Tamlaght, Enniskillen, Co Fermanagh]; *b* 8 July 1939; *educ* Eton; Lt Irish Gds 1957–60; *m* 7 April 1982 *Catherine Janet, est dau of Sir (James) Dennis Compton Faulkner, CBE, of Ringhaddy House, Killinchy, Co Down, and has:

(1) +Alexander James; *b* 8 June 1987

(1) *Anna Kathleen; *b* 23 Aug 1983

1 *Moyra Kathleen, CVO (1963) [The Lady Moyra Campbell CVO, Hollybrook House, Randalstown, Co Antrim]; *b* 22 July 1930; a Train Bearer to HM THE QUEEN Coronation 1953, T/Ldy-in-Waiting to HRH PRINCESS ALEXANDRA 1954–64, Ldy-in-Waiting 1964–66, Extra Ldy-in-Waiting 1966–69; *m* 12 Nov 1966 *Cdr Peter Colin Drummond Campbell, LVO, RN, est s of Maj-Gen Sir (Alexander) Douglas Campbell, KBE, CB, DSO, MC, of Green Bough Cottage, Shipley, Horsham, Sussex, and has:

(1) *Rory Gerald Peter; *b* 9 Aug 1967 (HRH PRINCESS ALEXANDRA stood sponsor); *educ* Harrow and Trin Coll Cambridge

(2) *Michael James Douglas; *b* 3 Nov 1970 (HRH PRINCE MICHAEL OF KENT stood sponsor); *educ* Harrow and Trin Coll Cambridge

Seat: Barons Court, Newtownstewart, Co Tyrone, Northern Ireland. Despite the galaxy of distinguished architects who have worked on it, Barons Court is externally speaking a bit of a disappointment. Its garden front, where originally the main entrance was sited, looks somewhat slablike and too long for its height of only two storeys. True, the facade is relieved by having the seven-bay central block jut far forward from the wings, which are of four bays each. But the central pediment here rises insufficiently high above its supporting masonry and is placed too close to the tops of the twelve-pane windows of the upper storey. Moreover, ungainly chimney stacks dominate the skyline.

On the present entrance side the vast port-cochère dominates the rest of the facade, more so than ever following the truncation of the main block by Sir Albert Richardson just after the War and the sweeping away of a redundant eastwards-facing service wing by Raymond Erith in the early 1970s. But Barons Court's glories are predominantly internal, and the port-cochère does at least shelter the visitor sufficiently to justify conversion of the original entrance hall, on what is now the garden side, to a long gallery. This, in plan if not execution, is the achievement of Sir John Soane, who was called in by the **1st Marquess** in 1791. It has a magnificent plaster ceiling supported by Corinthian columns (the ones are Ionic). They divide up the length much as, though less solidly, the original walls of the three rooms did.

The Ionic order is brought into play again in the rotunda, which is covered by a dome the height of the entire house and now serves as a dining-room. It was formerly a billards-room, whereas what was once the dining-room is now used for general family recreation. Also circular is the library ceiling. The Corinthian order returns in the pilasters adorning other rooms, such as the family one just mentioned, while coffering, which is used in both the rotunda ceiling (octagonally) and the staircase hall (in rectangles), is a recurrent decorative motif.

Soane, despite his great influence on the way the house developed, was not the original architect. That distinction belongs to George Steuart, a Scot who later worked on Attingham Hall, Shropshire, and who was employed throughout nearly the entire 1780s by the **8th Earl**, uncle of Soane's patron the **1st Marquess**. Soane's work did not last long, falling victim to a fire in 1796, and it was nearly forty years before work was resumed by the father-and-son team of Sir Richard and William Vitruvius Morrison. There is some uncertainty as to which of the two was originally commissioned to inspect the house, the weight of informed opinion inclining to William Vitruvius. Sir Richard is known to have outlived his son and therefore must have completed the plans whichever of them was first involved. In modern times David Hicks has contributed heavily to the decor.

ABERCROMBY

Arms: Quarterly, 1st and 4th, argent a chevron gules between three boar's heads erased azure, langued of the second; 2nd and 3rd: grand quarters, 1st and 4th argent, a lion passant guardant gules, crowned with an Imperial crown; 2nd and 3rd argent, three popinjays vert, beaked and membered gules. **Crest:** A falcon rising belled proper. **Supporters:** Two greyhounds argent, collared gules. **Motto:** (above the crest) *Petit alta* ('He seeks the heights') and Mercy is my desire. **Creation:** Bt. (NS) 20 Feb 1636.

SIR IAN GEORGE ABERCROMBY, 10TH BT, of Birkenbog, Co Banff, DL (Banffshire) [Sir Ian Abercromby Bt DL, Casa 456, Calle 23c, Guadalmina Alta, Marbella, (Malaga), Spain]; *b* 30 June 1925; *s* kinsman 1972; *educ* Lancing and

Bloxham; *m* 1st 24 June 1950 (*divorce* 1957) Joyce Beryl, only dau of Leonard Griffiths, of Sheraton House, Spencers Wood, Berks; *m* 2nd 17 July 1959 (*divorce*) Fanny Mary ('Mollie') Udale, only dau of Dr Graham Udale-Smith, of Tenerife, and adopted:

1 *Maria Amelia [Mrs Wellesley Wallace, Whitecroft, W Clandon, Surrey]; *b* 10 Jan 1955; *m* 1988 *Wellesley Theodore Octavius Wallace, s of Dr Caleb Paul Wallace, of W Clandon, and has:

(1) *James Abercromby Octavius; *b* 1989

(1) *Lucy Maria Diana; *b* 1991

Sir IAN *m* 3rd 1976 *Diana Marjorie, dau of Horace Geoffrey Cockell, of Ditton House, Oxley Wood, Herts, and widow of Capt Ian Charles Palliser Galloway, Seaforth Highrs, of Blervie, Forres, Morayshire

Lineage: HUMPHREY ABERCROMBY, of Pitmedden; living 1457; had:

ALEXANDER ABERCROMBY; *d* by 26 Aug 1484; had:

ALEXANDER ABERCROMBY; *m* Marjory Mowat and *d* by 2 May 1505, leaving:

GEORGE ABERCROMBY, of Pitmedden, whose lands were by charter 18 Feb 1512/3 erected into a barony; *m* 1st Christina Barclay and had issue; *m* 2nd *c* 29 Oct 1533 Margaret Gordon, of Over and Nether Clune, Banff (*m* 2nd 24 April 1553 Alexander Cumming of Altyre) and by his 1st w had:

JAMES ABERCROMBY, of Pitmedden; put in possession *vp* by charter 13 July 1527; *m* 1st Marjory Hay; *m* 2nd after 9 July 1540 Elizabeth, dau of Gilbert Gray, of Schives, and by his 1st w had, with an er s (William, living 14 May 1544):

ALEXANDER ABERCROMBY, of Pitmedden; had a charter of his lands 19 April 1550; *m* Elizabeth, dau of Alexander Leslie of Pitcaple, and had, with a yr s (John, living 29 April 1582):

ALEXANDER ABERCROMBY, of Towie and later Pitmedden; *d* by 9 Dec 1586/7, having had:

ALEXANDER ABERCROMBY, of Pitmedden; *m* Margaret, dau of William Leslie of Balquhain, and was murdered 12 March 1593, having had an est s:

JAMES ABERCROMBY of Birkenbog; had:

ALEXANDER ABERCROMBY, of Birkenbog; Grand Falconer Scotland to CHARLES I; *m* 1602 Elizabeth, dau of — Bethune/Beaton of Balfour, and had, with two yr s (John, of Glassaugh; Walter, of Brakenhills) and two daus:

Sir Alexander Abercromby, 1st Bt (NS), so *cr* 20 Feb 1635/6, with remainder to heirs male whatsoever, of Birkenbog; *b c* 1603; MP (S Parl) Banffshire 1640–41, 1643, 1646–47, 1648 and 1661–63; covenanter (opponent of anglicising tendencies in ecclesiastical matters) against CHARLES I; *m* 1st Jean, dau of Sir Thomas Urquhart of Cromarty, and had:

1 Alexander; *d* young

1 Christian; *m* James Fraser of Tyrie (*see* SALTOUN, L)

2 Marie; *m* 1662 Sir George Gordon of Edinglassie and left issue

3 Violet; *m* 1st 1664 John Kinnaird and had issue; *m* 2nd 1670 Robert Grant of Dalveg and Dunlugas and had further issue

Sir Alexander *m* 2nd Jean, dau of — Sutherland, of Kinminity, and had further issue:

4 Agnes; *b* 1663; *m* Robert Bisset of Lessendrum

Sir Alexander *m* 3rd 22 Aug 1668 Elizabeth (*m* 2nd Col Patrick Ogilvie of Lonmay and Inchmartine; *see* SEAFIELD, E), dau of Sir James Baird of Auchmedden, and had:

2 Sir JAMES, **2nd Bt**

3 Alexander, of Tullibody; *b* 1675; advocate; MP (S Parl) Clackmannan 1703–07; *m* 1699 Mary Duff and was ancestor of the Barons Abercromby (*see* 1924 edn)

4 Patrick; *m* —, dau of Col Sempill, and had two sons

5 Elizabeth; *d* unm

Sir ALEXANDER's est surv sons,

Sir James Abercromby, 2nd Bt; *b* 1668; MP (S Parl) Banffshire 1694; *m* 1690 Mary (*d* 1742), dau of Arthur Gordon of Straloch, and *d* 20 Sept 1734, having had, with four est sons (Alexander, *bapt* 6 Dec 1692, Lt Army, *dvp & sp*; James, *bapt* 13 Dec 1693, *d* young; Robert, *bapt* 3 May 1695, *d* young; Lewis, *bapt* 19 Aug 1697, *d* young), four yst sons (Arthur; *bapt* 30 Nov 1707, HEICS, *dsp* 1761; William, *bapt* 29 May 1710, *dsp* Holland 1739; John, *bapt* 11 Oct 1711, *dsp* Russia; James, *bapt* 21 July 1713, *dsp* Russia) and five daus (Elizabeth, *bapt* 7 July 1696; Mary, *bapt* Nov 1698; Anna, *bapt* 19 June 1700, *m* George Stewart of Tannochy; Jean, *bapt* 24 Nov 1701; Isabell, *bapt* 11 April 1703, *m* James Dunbar of Kincorth):

1 ROBERT ABERCROMBY (Sir), **3rd Bt**

2 George; settled in Mexico; *m* 1746 in Mexico — (*d* 1754), dau of John Ingleby, and *d* Dec 1776, having had:

(1) Alexander; monk; *b* 1747

(2) John; Capt Spanish Army; *b* 1752; living 1779

(3) Robert; *b* 1753; *d* 1763

(1) Mary Luisa; *b* 1748

The 2nd Bt's 5th s,

Sir Robert Abercromby, 3rd Bt; *m* 17 July 1739 his 1st cousin Helen, dau of Alexander Abercromby of Tullibody (*see* above), and *d* 11 March 1787, having had, with two er sons (*d* young) and four daus:

Sir George Abercromby, 4th Bt; *bapt* 7 Nov 1750; advocate 1773, Sheriff Elginshire and Nairnshire 1783, Clerk admission Notars 1807; *m* 1778 Hon Jane Ogilvie, est dau and ultimate heiress of 7th Lord Banff (*cr* 1642, *ext* 1803), and *d* 18 July 1831, having had, with other issue (including a dau Grace, *m* 1823 Joseph Murray of Ayton; *see* MURRAY, Bt, of Ochtertyre):

Sir Robert Abercromby, 5th Bt, DL (Kirkcudbrightshire and Banffshire); *b* 4 Feb 1784; MP Banff 1812–18; *m* 22 Oct 1816 Elizabeth Stephenson (*d* 28 Dec 1863), only child of Samuel Douglas of Netherlaw, and *d* 6 July 1855, having had, with eight daus:

1 GEORGE SAMUEL ABERCROMBY (Sir), **6th Bt**

2 Samuel Douglas; *b* 1825; 42nd Highrs; *d* 16 May 1847

3 Robert; *b* 2 Aug 1833; Army Offr; *ka* The Alma 20 Sept 1854

4 David James; *b* 25 April 1837; *educ* Trin Coll Cambridge (BA); Capt Roy Aberdeenshire Highland Militia 1864–69; *m* 25 Oct 1877 Beatrice Jane Temple (*d* 25 Feb 1909), est dau of Rev Henry Temple Frere, and *d* 9 March 1918, having had issue:

(1) Robert Ogilvie; *b* 9 Sept 1881; *educ* Eton; Maj RFC and Gordon Highrs Boer War 1899–1902, WWs I (wounded) and II CD 1939, RA 1940–42 and ROF 1942–45; *m* 1st 14 July 1921 Gladys Vivian (*d* May 1931), dau of Henry Willock Boileau and widow of Capt Charles Colwyn Rolph, Leics Regt, and had issue:

1a Sir IAN GEORGE ABERCROMBY, **10th and present Bt**

(1) (cont.) Robert Abercromby *m* 2nd 19 May 1936 Monica Margaret, 5th dau of Joseph Monteith, JP, DL, and *d* 11 May 1964

(2) Aubrey Frere; *b* 4 Sept 1889; *d* 15 March 1937

(3) Temple Henry; *b* 30 March 1891; *d* 6 April 1891

(1) Elsie Douglas; *m* 9 July 1902 Maj William Orr Campbell, MC, JP (*d* 18 Jan 1967), s of William Henry Campbell, and *d* 10 Feb 1961, having had issue

The 5th Bt's est son,

Sir George Samuel Abercromby, 6th Bt; *b* 22 May 1824; *m* 12 June 1849 Hon Agnes Georgina Browne (*d* 27 June 1898), dau of 3rd Baron Kilmaine (*qv*), and *d* 15 Nov 1872, having had:

1 **Sir Robert John Abercromby, 7th Bt**, DL (Banffshire and Aberdeen); *b* 14 June 1850; *educ* Eton; V-Lt Banffshire; *m* 26 June 1883 Florence Anita Eyre, CBE (*m* 2nd 10 June 1899 2nd Earl of Northbrook (*see* NORTHBROOK, B); *d* 4 Dec 1946), only dau of Eyre Coote, of West Park, Hants (*see* COOTE, Bt), and *d* 24 July 1895, having had issue:

(1) **Sir George William Abercromby, 8th Bt**, DSO (1917), JP (Banffshire 1930–61), DL (1928); *b* 18 March 1886; *educ* Eton; Lt-Col and brevet-Col cmdg 6th Bn Gordon Highrs (TA), 8th Service Bn and Cadet Bn Black Watch (Roy Highrs), Lt Scots Gds and Spec Res, ADC to GOC-in-C Ireland, Hon Col 6th Bn Gordon Highrs 1931, served WW I (despatches); Ld Lt Banffshire 1946–64; *m* 17 Jan 1935 Eleanor, only dau of Sir Arthur Robert Anderson, CIE, CBE, of Roffey Place, Horsham, Sussex, and *dsp* 9 Sept 1964

(2) **Sir Robert Alexander Abercromby, 9th Bt**, MC, DL (Banffshire); *b* posthumously 15 Aug 1895; *educ* Eton and RMC Sandhurst; Maj Scots Gds WWs I (wounded, despatches) and II, V-Lt Banffshire 1965; *m* 1st 12 June 1923 Hon Diamond Hardinge (*d* 11 Jan 1927), only dau of 1st Baron Hardinge of Penshurst (*qv*); *m* 2nd 31 Oct 1929 Pamela (*d* following an accident 5 Oct 1944), only dau of John Chadwick Lomax; *m* 3rd 20 Feb 1951 Elizabeth (*d* 20 July 1971), only dau of Maj William James Corcoran, of Co Meath, and formerly w of Walter Woollard Lawrence, and *dsp* 19 Oct 1972

(1) Nina; *b* 28 Feb 1885; *m* 22 Feb 1910 Capt Horace Leonard Kemble, MVO, JP, DL, Scots Gds, of Laggan, Scaniport, Inverness-shire (*d* 27 Dec 1966), only s of Col Horace William Kemble, Cameron Highrs, of Knock, Isle of Skye, and *d* 30 Oct 1933, having had issue

(2) Myrtle Vere; *b* 1 June 1890; *m* 17 Feb 1913 Reginald Henry Macaulay Abel Smith (*d* 12 March 1964), er surv s of Reginald Abel Smith, of Goldings, Herts, and *dsp* 18 April 1920

2 George Cosmo; *b* 31 March 1854; Capt Scots Gds, Maj 3rd Bn Gordon Highrs; *d* unm 13 Oct 1930

3 Cavendish Douglas; *b* 23 March 1858; *d* unm 20 Dec 1941

4 Douglas Charles; *b* 1 Nov 1860; *m* 27 Feb 1886 Helen Louisa Hodgson, OStJ (*d* 1 Feb 1933), dau of William Powell Murray and sis of Keith William Murray (*see* below), and *d* 15 June 1915, having had issue:

(1) Keith Douglas; *b* 2 Feb 1887; *educ* Haileybury; S/Ldr RAF WW II; *m* 1st 9 Sept 1913 Eva Winifred (*d* 25 Sept 1930), only dau of Harry Millward Wright, and had:

1a *Joan Eileen Abercromby [Mrs James Robertson, 36 Marlborough Pl, London NW8 OPD]; *b* 20 Jan 1919; *m* 1st 25 Sept 1939 (*divorce* 1948) Alan James Butler Aldridge, yr s of Gerald Butler Aldridge, and has issue:

1b *Gail Susan Eva; *b* 4 March 1946; *m* 1974 *Raymond Henry Cornish and has issue:

1c *Belinda Mary Eva; *b* 1975

2c *Peta Eleanor; *b* 1986

1a (cont.) Mrs Joan Aldridge *m* 2nd 3 Aug 1948 Richard Lloyd Joseph Wills, CBE, MC (*d* 25 Sept 1969), yst s of Charles Percy Wills; *m* 3rd 1972 *Maj-Gen James Alexander Rowland Robertson, CB, CBE, DSO and bar, DL, er s of Col James Robertson, CMG, CIE, CBE, IMS

(1) (cont.) Keith Abercromby *m* 2nd 23 Dec 1939 Hilda Brocket (*d* 1985), dau of Alan Sandys, barrister, and formerly w of Guy Lemon, and *d* 30 Sept 1968

(2) Ralph Frank; *b* 27 Aug 1893; lost in the *Lusitania* 7 May 1915

(1) Nora Maude; *b* 22 April 1888; *m* 21 Dec 1912 Lt-Col James Ochoncar Forbes, 3rd Gordon Highrs, of Corse, Aberdeenshire (*d* 25 July 1945), only surv child of Hon James Ochoncar Forbes of Corse, and *d* 17 Oct 1958, having had issue (*see* SEMPILL, L)

(2) Sybil Helen; *b* 16 Jan 1890; *m* 27 July 1915 Capt Henry Winton Seton, 9th Gurkhas, yst s of Col Alexander David Seton, of Mounie Castle, Aberdeenshire, and had issue:

1a *Margaret Helen; *b* 30 May 1916; *m* 15 Aug 1940 Col Rolland Padraig Stewart Erskine-Tulloch, CBE, Northants Regt, s of Capt Denis Rolland Diarmid Stewart Erskine-Tulloch, and has:

1b *Elspeth Jane; *b* 7 Feb 1948

2b *Charlotte Lucy; *b* 27 May 1958

1 Elizabeth Agnes; *m* 1 June 1882 Henry Alexander Farquhar-Spottiswood (*d* 10 Aug 1925), of Muiresk, Aberdeenshire, and *d* 15 June1929, having had issue

2 Grace Amelia; *m* 28 Dec 1887 Keith William Murray (*see* above), Portcullis Pursuivant of Arms (*d* 11 Jan 1922), s of William Powell Murray, barrister, Registrar High Court Bankruptcy, by Georgina Charlotte Daysh, only dau of Cdr Hon Arthur Richard Turnour, RN (*see* WINTERTON, E), and *d* 11 Jan 1932, having had issue

ABERDARE

Arms: Or a saltire gules, on a chief of the last a martlet of the field. **Crest:** A cubit arm in armour in bend, the hand holding a sceptre in bend sinister proper. **Supporters:** Dexter, a lion argent collared or, pendant therefrom an escutcheon of the arms of Knight, *viz.*, paly of six argent and azure, on a canton of the last a spur with rowel downwards leathered or; sinister, a lion azure, collared or, pendant therefrom an escutcheon of the arms of Bruce (*see* above). **Mottoes:** Above the crest, *Fuimus* ('We have been'); under the arms, *Ofner na ofno angau* ('Let him be feared who fears not death'). **Creation:** B. (UK) 23 Aug 1873.

THE 4TH BARON ABERDARE OF DUFFRYN, Co Glamorgan (Sir Morys George Lyndhurst Bruce, KBE (Civil 1984), PC (1974), DL (Dyfed 1985)) [The Rt Hon The Lord Aberdare KBE PC DL, 32 Elthiron Rd, London SW6 4BW]; *b* 16 June 1919; *s f* 1957; *educ* Winchester and New Coll Oxford (MA); Capt Welsh Gds WW II (HQ 12 Corps 1944, GSO3 Main HQ 21 Army Gp 1945, GSO2 HQ 30 Corps Dist 1946), with: J Arthur Rank Organisation 1947–49 and BBC 1949–56, V-Pres Br Cwlth and Empire Games Cardiff 1958, DL Glam 1966–80, Min of State DHSS 1970–74, Min without Portfolio 1974, Chm Ctees Ho of Lds 1976–92, Dep Speaker Ho of Lds, Prior for Wales OStJ 1958–88, Bailiff GCStJ 1974, pres: Welsh Nat Cncl YMCAs, London Welsh Assoc, Kidney Research Unit Wales Fndn, Tennis and Rackets Assoc, chm: Metlife (UK) 1968–92, Albany Life Assur 1975–92, Football Tst 1979–97, Educn Ctee St David's Theatre Tst, Youth Work Ctee YMCA and Assoc Br Chambers Commerce, non-exec dir Albany Life 1975–, Hon LLD Wales 1985, author: *The Story of Tennis* (1959) and *Willis Faber Book of Tennis and Rackets* (1980); *m* 1 June 1946 *Maud Helen Sarah, only dau of Sir John Lindsay Dashwood, 10th Bt, CVO, of West Wycombe Park (*qv*), and has issue:

1+ALASTAIR JOHN LYNDHURST [The Hon Alastair Bruce, 16 Beverley Rd, London SW13 OLX]; *b* 2 May 1947; *educ* Eton and Ch Ch Oxford; *m* 6 May 1971 *Elizabeth Mary Culbert, dau of John Frederick Foulkes, of St Leonards-on-Sea, Sussex, and has issue:

(1) +Hector Morys Napier; *b* 25 July 1974; *educ* Eton

(1) *Sarah Katherine Mary; *b* 18 April 1976

2 +James Henry Morys [The Hon James Bruce, 1 St Peter's Sq, London W6 9AB]; *b* 28 Dec 1948; *educ* Eton; *m* 1st 16 July 1977 (*divorce* 19–) Grace, dau of Allen Jao Wu, and has issue:

(1) *Antonia Katherine Sarah; *b* 12 Jan 1979

2 (cont.) The Hon James Bruce *m* 2nd 4 April 1991 *Lucinda Jane, only dau of Richard Temple West, and has further issue:

(1) +Robert Algernon Copley; *b* 10 May 1994

(2) +Algernon Morys Lyndhurst; *b* 29 May 1997

(2) *Augusta Jane Sophia; *b* 8 April 1992

3 +(Henry) Adam Francis [The Hon Adam Bruce, St Davids Court, Merdrim, SA33 5QF]; *b* 5 Feb 1961; *educ* Eton and Trin Coll Oxford; slr 1988, serving bro OStJ 1990; *m* 30 May 1992 *Victoria Gillian, yr dau of Maj Ivor Basil Ramsden, MBE (*see* SAINT DAVIDS, V), and has:

(1) +Angus; *b* 6 March 1997

4 +Charles Benjamin [The Hon Charles Bruce, Summerdale, Greenway Lane, Bath BA2 4LJ]; *b* 29 May 1965; *educ* Eton; chartered accountant; *m* 7 April 1990 *Anna, dau of Bo Brannerydh, of Gävle, Sweden

Lineage:

JAMES BRUCE; probably illegitimate s of an established Scottish family; *b* 1670; joined Merchant Navy but later; served RN; *m* margaret Holloway and *d* 1 Nov 1727 aboard HMS *BEDFORD*, leaving an er s:

WILLIAM BRUCE; *b* 1705; served RN, navy agent, banker, High Sheriff Glam, acquired Duffryn estate in what is now Mid Glam, some 6 mi east of Neath; *m* 1st Jane, dau of Gabriel Lewis, of Lllanishen House, Glam; *m* 2nd Mary, sis of Richard Turbervill(e), of Ewenny Abbey, leaving issue by his 1st w (with two s and another dau, all of whom *d* unm):

Margaret BRUCE; *m* 29 Aug 1779 John KNIGHT (*d* 15 Oct 1799), of Llanblethian, only s of James Knight, and *d* 20 May 1809, leaving an est s:

JOHN BRUCE KNIGHT later BRUCE later still BRUCE-PRYCE, of Duffryn, Glamorgan, JP, DL; *b* 23 July 1784; took 1805 the name BRUCE on inheriting his unc's Duffryn estate and added PRYCE July 1837 on inheriting from his cousin Hon Mrs Booth Grey the estates of Duffryn St Nicholas and Monknash, though his children kept the name BRUCE without adding PRYCE; *m* 1st 5 May 1807 Sarah (*d* 2 Nov 1842), 2nd dau of Rev Hugh Williams Austin, rector St Peter's Barbados, and had issue, with an er s, three yr sons and seven daus:

1 HENRY AUSTIN BRUCE, **1st Baron Aberdare of Duffryn**

JOHN BRUCE KNIGHT BRUCE-PRYCE *m* 2nd 30 Nov 1844 Alicia Grant, dau of William Bushby, of Gt Cumberland Place, London W, and *d* 19 Oct 1872

JOHN BRUCE-PRYCE's 2nd s,

HENRY AUSTIN BRUCE, **1st Baron Aberdare of Duffryn**, Co Glamorgan (UK), so *cr* 23 Aug 1873, GCB (1885), PC (1864), JP, DL (Glamorgan 1847); *b* 16 April 1815; barrister Lincoln's Inn 1837, MP (Lib) Merthy Tydfil 1852–68 and Renfrew 1869–73, Under Sec Home Office 1862–64, V-Pres Cncl Educn 1864–66, Home Sec 1868–73, Ld Pres Cncl 1873–74, FRS 1876, Hon DCL Oxford 1880, Pres RGS 1880–84 and 1885–86; *m* 1st 6 Jan 1846 Annabella (*d* 28 July 1852), only dau of Richard Beadon, of Clifton, by Annabella A'Court, sis of 1st Baron Heytesbury (*qv*), and had issue:

1 HENRY CAMPBELL BRUCE, **2nd Baron**

1 Margaret Cecilia; *m* 16 Sept 1869 Douglas Close Richmond, CB, MA (*d* 3 April 1930), s of Rev Henry Sylvester Richmond, MA, rector Wyck Rissington, Glos, and *d* 10 April 1978, leaving issue

2 Rachel Mary; *m* 10 Sept 1872 Augustus George Vernon-Harcourt, of St Clare, Ryde, IOW (*d* Aug 1919), s of Adml Frederick Edward Vernon-Harcourt, and *d* 24 June 1927, leaving issue (*see* VERNON, B)

3 Jessie Frances; *m* 3 Sept 1878 Rev John William Wynne-Jones, MA, rector Llantrisant, Anglesey (*d* 28 Oct 1928), s of John Wynne-Jones, JP, DL, of Treiorwerth, Bodedern, Holyhead, Anglesey, Archdeacon Bangor 1863–86, and *d* 22 June 1940, leaving issue

The 1st **Baron** *m* 2nd 17 Aug 1854 Norah Creina Blanche (*d* 27 April 1897), yst dau of Lt-Gen Sir William Napier, KCB, by Caroline Amelia, 2nd dau of Gen Hon Henry Edward Fox (*see* ILCHESTER, E), and *d* 25 Feb 1895, having had further issue:

2 William Napier, CB (1905), CH (1935); *b* 15 Jan 1858; *educ* Harrow and Balliol Coll Oxford; barrister, 2nd Sec Bd Educn, Pro-Chllr U of Wales 1928–34, Hon LLD U Wales; *m* 5 Aug 1882 Emily (*d* 15 Dec 1937), dau of Gen Sir William Montagu Scott MacMurdo, GCB, and *d* 20 March 1936, leaving issue:

(1) William Fox, DSO (1918), MC, TD; *b* 7 Aug 1883; *educ* New Coll Oxford (BA); Lt-Col and Brevet-Col Roy Signals (TA) WWI (despatches thrice), Maj Roy Signals WWII, Dep Ch Inspector Fisheries Min Ag and Fish, Bronze Medal Roy Humane Soc; *m* 7 Dec 1921 Sybil (*d* 2 March 1954), dau of Maj Alfred Owen Lyon and widow of Maj Francis Maxwell Chenevix Trench, RA (*see* ASHTOWN, B), and *d* 19–

(1) Susan Norah; *b* 7 Nov 1884; *d* unm 2 Feb 1970

3 Charles Granville, CB (1918), MVO (1903); *b* 7 April 1866; served: Burma 1889, Hazara Expdn 1891, Miranzai Expdn 1891 (despatches), Waziristan 1894–95, Tirah 1897–98 (despatches thrice), and WW I 1914 Egypt (despatches) and Gallipoli (wounded, brevet, despatches), cmded N Waziristan Field Force 1917 (despatches), Afghanistan 1919, Brevet-Col IA, Hon Brig-Gen 1920, Col 5th Gurkha Rifles 1931, headed Mt Everest Expdns 1922 and 1924, Hon LLD Edinburgh, Hon DSc Oxford and Wales, Hon DCL St Andrews U, Gill Memorialist RGS 1915, Founder's Medal 1925; *m* 12 Sept 1894 Finetta Madelina Julia, MBE (*d* 16 June 1932), 3rd dau of Col Sir Edward Fitzgerald Campbell, 2nd Bt (*qv*), and *d* 12 July 1939

4 Caroline Louisa; *d* unm 3 Feb 1915

5 Sarah Napier; *m* 17 Aug 1888 Montague Johnstone Muir-Mackenzie (*d* 18 April 1919), s of Sir John William Pitt Muir-Mackenzie, 2nd Bt, of Delvine (*qv*), and *d* 21 Dec 19 31, leaving issue

6 Norah Creina Blanche; *m* 4 Jan 1883 Henry Arthur Whately (*d* 2 May 1957 aged 102), s of Canon William Joseph Whately, rector Rise, Hull, and *d* 26 May 1886, leaving issue

7 Isabel Ellen; *m* 12 July 1887 Champion Branfill Russell (*d* 8 Sept 1945 aged 85), s of Champion Russell, of Stubbers, Essex, and *d* 13 Feb 1934, leaving issue

8 Elizabeth Fox; *m* 9 April 1896 Percy Ewing Matheson, MBE, MA, of 3 Brookside, Headington, Oxford, Fell New Coll Oxford (*d* 11 May 1946), s of Rev James Matheson, BA, of Nottingham, and *d* 14 Jan 1935

9 Pamela Georgiana; *d* unm 30 Oct 1931

10 Alice Moore; MA, Hon Fell Somerville Coll Oxford; *d* unm 4 Nov 1951

The 1st BARON's est s,

HENRY CAMPBELL BRUCE, **2nd Baron Aberdare of Duffryn**, JP; *b* 19 June 1851; *educ* Rugby and Berlin; Hon Col 5th Bn Welsh Regt, Lt-Col 3rd Vol Bn, pres U Coll S Wales and Nat Museum Wales, V-Lt Glam; *m* 10 Feb 1880 Constance Mary (*d* 8 Feb 1932), only dau of Hamilton Beckett (*see* GRIMTHORPE, B), by his w Hon Sophia Clarence Copley, 2nd dau of 1st and last Baron Lyndhurst, and *d* 20 Feb 1929, having had issue:

1 Henry Lyndhurst; *b* 25 May 1881; Capt 3rd Bn Roy Scots; *m* 11 Oct 1906 Camilla Antoinetta (*d* 28 June 1971), a 'Gibson girl' at the Gaiety Theatre (*m* 2nd 9 Aug 1917 Brig John Meredyth Jones Evans, CBE, MC, Roy Welch Fus, and *d* 28 June 1971), dau of Reynold Clifford, and was *ka* 14 Dec 1914, having had issue:

(1) Margaret; *b* 13 Aug, *d* 18 Aug 1909

2 CLARENCE NAPIER, **3rd Baron**

3 John Hamilton, CBE (1950), JP, DL (Glamorgan); *b* 14 June 1889; *educ* Winchester and New Coll Oxford; Lt Glam Yeo; KStJ, pncpl sec Priory Wales; *m* 3 May 1923 Cynthia Juliet, DStJ (*d* 1977), dau of Julian Grant Duff, and *d* 8 April 1964, leaving issue:

(1) +David Hamilton Grant Duff [David Bruce Esq, Anker Far East, Dongwon Bldg, Rm 603, 128–27 Dangjoo-Dong, Jongro-Gu, Seoul, Korea]; *b* 18 Sept 1933; *educ* Winchester and New Coll Oxford; served Coldstream Gds 1952–54, subsequently with Gulf Oil; *m* 17 Dec 1960 (*divorce* 1965) Diana Rosemary, only dau of Douglas Sinclair Miller, CBE, of Nairobi, Kenya

(1) *Daphne Juliet [Baroness Ando, Corso Vittorio Emanuele II 252, Rome, Italy; Flat 3, 33 Caledonia Place, Clifton, Bristol]; *b* 19 March 1928; *m* 7 March 1953 *Baron Carlo Giuseppe Ando, s of Commendatore Giuseppe Ando, of Messina, Sicily, by his w Emanuela, Baronness di Gotto, and has issue:

1a *Alexander Francis Carlo; *b* 4 Oct 1955; *m* 11 July 1982 *Lorenya Raponi and has issue:

1b *Edward Carlo George; *b* 13 Dec 1987

1b *Victoria Emanuela Eleanora; *b* 1988

2a *Roderick David Clarence; *b* 9 May 1960

(2) Gillian Constance; *b* 16 Feb 1930; *d* unm 22 March 1949

4 Victor Austin; *b* 8 April 1897; *educ* Wye Ag Coll; 2nd Lt RM WW I; *m* 1st 16 Feb 1926 (*divorce* 1941) Mildred Mary, aviatrix, racing driver and speed-boat pilot (*d* 1990), dau of Laurence Joseph Petre (*see* PETRE, B); *m* 2nd 19 June 1941 *Margaret (Peggy) Charlotte [The Hon Mrs Victor Bruce, Cranmore, 1 Frog Grove Lane, Wood St Village, Guildford, Surrey], yr dau of Ernest Alfred Beechey, of The Old Vicarage, Hilgay, Norfolk, and *d* 1978, leaving issue:

(1) +Colin Michael Lyndhurst [Colin Bruce Esq, 1 Frog Grove Lane, Wood Street Green, Guildford, Surrey]; *b* 5 July 1944; *educ* Ripley Court Sch Surrey and Rose Hill Sch, Wotton-under-Edge, Glos

(1) *(Margaret) Jill [Mrs Jill Hope, Browes Close, Mickleton, nr Barnard Castle, Co Durham]; *b* 2 Jan 1943; *m* 2 May 1970 (*divorce* 1994) Thomas Richard Hope and has:

1a *Christopher Victor John; *b* 19 May 1977

1a *Louise Margaret; *b* 20 Jan 1971

2a *Karen Anne [Mrs Sean Jackson, 53 Leckworth Gdns, Middleton-in-Teesdale]; *b* 21 July 1972; *m* *Sean Jackson

(2) *Wendy Elizabeth [Mrs Richard Grimmond, Inholms Farm, Wood Street Green, Guildford, Surrey]; *b* 16 May 1948; *m* 1966 *Richard Keith Grimmond and has issue:

1a *Michael Richard; *b* 1971

2a *David Matthew; *b* 1984

1a *Nicola Jane; *b* 1966; *m* 19- *—

2a *Caroline Anne; *b* Sept 1967; *m* 19- *—

5 Robert; *b* 1 Oct, *d* 22 Oct 1898

1 Margaret Cecilia; *b* 28 Oct 1882; *m* 21 July 1904 5th Earl of Bradford (*qv*) and *d* 16 April 1949, leaving issue

2 Violet; *b* 8 Nov, *d* 10 Nov 1887

3 Eva Isabel Marian, DBE (1955), JP (Bucks); *b* 17 June 1892; Hon LLD Edinburgh 1957, Chevalier Legion of Honour; *m* 1st 26 April 1911 (*divorce* 1922) 3rd Baron Belper (*qv*) and had issue; *m* 2nd 24 June 1924 6th Earl of Rosebery (*qv*) and *d* 29 Jan 1987, having had further issue

4 (Constance) Pamela Alice, OBE (1944), JP (1934); *b* 14 June 1895; memb Dorset CC 1943–52, CA Dorset 1957, Sr Cmdt ATS Dorset 1938–40, Ch Cdr 1940–44, pres Dorset Branch BRCS 1964–78; *m* 1 July 1919 11th Baron Digby (*qv*) and *d* 15 March 1978, leaving issue

The 2nd BARON's est surv s,

CLARENCE NAPIER BRUCE, **3rd Baron Aberdare of Duffryn**, GBE (1954, CBE 1949); *b* 2 Aug 1885; *educ* Winchester and New Coll Oxford (BA); barrister Inner Temple 1911, Capt Glamorgan Yeo, T/Lt 2nd Life Gds, HQ 61st Div and Gds MG Regt WW I, Capt 1919, Hon Col 77 (subsequently 282) (Welsh) Heavy AA Brigade RA (TA) 1930–52, Maj 11th Bn Surrey Home Gd WW II; Internat Olympic Ctee Exec 1931–51, memb: Miners' Welfare Commn 1931–46, Nat Youth Ctee Bd Educn 1939–42, Jt Ctee OStJ and BRCS, Int Olympic Ctee (memb exec 1931–51), Nat Tst and Standing Conf Nat Voly Youth Organisns, Queen's Inst of District Nursing 1944, Internat Congress Physical Educn Recreation and Rehabilitation 1947, Organising Ctee Olympic Games London 1948, Exec Centl Ctee Physical Recreation and BRCS 1948 and Sports and Games Ctee, Standing Ctee Nat Parks, Academic Advsy Cncl FO (German Section) 1949 and ITA 1954–56, chm: Nat Advsy Cncl Physical Trg and Recreation 1936–39, Nat Assoc Boys' Clubs, Br Sportsman's Club, Lansdowne Club, Fortnightly Review Ltd 1938–55 and Internat Congress Physical Educn 1948, pres: Welsh Nat Sch Medicine, U of Wales, Br POWs (Books and Games Funds) 1941–46, Five Million Club (children's playgrounds) 1942–51, New Coll Soc 1952053, KStJ, memb Jt Ctee OStJ, Prior of Priory for Wales OStJ 1948, hon adviser J Arthur Rank Organisation on Children's Cinema Clubs 1948, Hon LLD Wales 1953, rackets: amateur champion 1922 and 1931, 10 times doubles champion, USA: doubles champion 1928 and 1930, Canada: singles champion 1928 and 1930 and doubles champion 1930, Br Isles open champion 1931, tennis: USA: amateur champion 1930, Br Isles: amateur champion 1932 and 1938, author: *First Steps to Rackets* (with E B Noel, 1926) and (ed) *Rackets, Squash Rackets, Tennis, Fives and Badminton* (1933); *m* 1st 12 Dec 1912 Margaret ('Betty') Bethune (*d* 8 Feb 1950), only dau of Adam Black, and had issue:

1 MORYS GEORGE LYNDHURST BRUCE, **4th and present Baron Aberdare of Duffryn**

2 +Nigel Henry Clarence [The Hon Nigel Bruce, Maitland Lodge, 21 The Causeway, Edinburgh EH15 3QA]; *b* 17 June 1921; *educ* Winchester, New Coll Oxford (MA) and Edinburgh U (Dip Soc Study 1962, MSc (Social Sciences) 1968); Capt Welsh Gds WWII, For Serv 1946–61; *m* 1 Sept 1964 Catherine Marion (*d* 19–), dau of Thomas Wolfe, and has:

(1) +Thomas; *b* 7 June 1965; *educ* Portobello High Sch and Edinburgh U

(1) *Sarah; *b* 24 Feb 1967

1 *Rosalind Louise Balfour [The Hon Mrs Heywood, 1 Elm Park Rd, London SW3 6BD]; *b* 11 Nov 1923; served WRNS WW II 1943–46; *m* 25 Sept 1956 *Benjamin Coote Heywood, MA, late RN, er s of Col Henry Frank Heywood, MC, of 3 The Drive, London SW20, and has issue:

(1) *Annabel Jane Louise; *b* 18 Oct 1958

(2) *Olivia Sarah Rosalind; *b* 1 Feb 1961

2 *Gwyneth Margaret [The Hon Mrs Andrew, Hams Barton, Chudleigh, Devon TQ13 0DL]; *b* 3 July 1928; *m* 3 July 1952 *Robert McCheyne Andrew, For Serv, s of Robert Charles Andrew, of Hoylake, Cheshire, and has:

(1) *Robert Hugh Clarence; *b* 4 Sept 1954; *educ* Winchester; *m* and has issue

(1) *Caroline Margaret; *b* 16 Dec 1956; *m* and has issue

(2) Jennifer Anne Louise; *b* 26 Aug 1960; *d* 1984

The 3rd **Baron** *m* 2nd 12 Sept 1957 Griselda Harriet Violet Finetta Georgina (*d* 1980), only dau of Dudley Francis Amelius Hervey, CMG, JP (*see* BRISTOL, M), and was *k* in a motor accident in Yugoslavia 4 Oct 1957

ABERDEEN AND TEMAIR

Arms: Azure, three boar's heads couped or, armed proper, langued gules, within a double tressure flowered counterflowered interchangeably with thistles, roses and fleur-de-lys of the second. **Crest:** Two arms holding a bow and arrow straight upwards in a shooting posture and at full draught, all proper. **Supporters:** Dexter, an earl in his robes; sinister, a doctor of law in his robes, both proper. **Motto:** *Fortuna sequatur* ('Let fortune follow').

Creations: Bt. (NS) 13 Aug 1642; L. (Haddo, Methlick, Tarves, and Kellie), V. (Formartine), E. (Aberdeen) (all S) 30 Nov 1682, V. (Gordon) (UK) 1 June 1814, E. (Haddo) and M (both UK) 4 Jan 1916.

THE 6TH MARQUESS OF ABERDEEN AND TEMAIR, Cos Aberdeen, Meath and Argyll, **Earl of Aberdeen**, **Earl of Haddo**, Co Aberdeen, **Viscount Formartine**, **Viscount Gordon**, of Aberdeen, **Lord Haddo, Methlick, Tarves, and Kellie** and a **Baronet** (Sir Alastair Ninian John Gordon, Bt) [The Most Hon The Marquess of Aberdeen and Temair, Quicks Green, Ashampstead, Berks RG8 8SN]; *b* 20 July 1920; *s* bro 1984; *educ* Harrow; WW II as Capt Scots Gds; memb: Assoc Internationale des Critiques d'Art and Bach Choir 1939–82, author: *A Slight Touch of Safari* (1952); *m* 24 Feb 1950 *Anne, est dau of Lt-Col Gerald Barry, MC (*see* BARRY, Bt), and has issue:

1 +ALEXANDER GEORGE, *Earl of Haddo*, DL (Aberdeenshire 1998) [Earl of Haddo, DL, House of Formartine, Methlick, Ellon, Aberdeenshire AB41 0EQ]; *b* 31 March 1955; *educ* Harrow; *m* 30 May 1981 *Joanna Clodagh, est dau of Maj Ian George Henry Houldsworth, TD, JP, DL, of Dallas Lodge, Forres, Moray, and has issue:

(1) +George Ian Alastair, *Viscount Formartine*; *b* 4 May 1983; *educ* Harrow

(2) +Sam Dudley; *b* 25 Oct 1985

(3) +Charles David; *b* 4 June 1990

(1) *Anna Katharine; *b* 2 Sept 1988

1 *Emma Cecile [The Lady Emma Foale, 25 Bristol Gdns, London W9]; *b* 26 May 1953; *m* 6 Sept 1980 *Dr Rodney Foale, est s of Maurice Spencer Foale, of Melbourne, Australia, and has:

(1) *Archie Alexander; *b* 17 Sept 1984

(2) *Jamie; *b* 1 April 1986

2 *Sophia Katherine; *b* 20 July 1960

Lineage: JOCK GORDON, of Scurdargue; living 1418, was s (by a handfast marriage) of Sir John Gordon of Strathbogie (*d c* 1395) and first cousin of Elizabeth Gordon (who inherited Strathbogie, *m* Sir Alexander Seton and was ancestor of the Marquesses of Huntly (*qv*)); had, with two er sons:

JAMES GORDON; *m* Canea Harper, half-portioner of Methlic; had:

PATRICK GORDON of Methlic and Haddo; *k* Battle of Brechin 18 May 1452, leaving, with at least one dau (Agnes, *m* as his 1st w Alexander Seton of Meldrum; *see* SETON Bt, of Pitmedden):

JAMES GORDON, of Methlic and Kelly; acquired Haddo from William Foularton 22 June 1469 and had, with a 3rd s (Alexander, Bp Aberdeen), an est s:

JAMES GORDON, of Methlic and Haddo; obtained charters under the Great Seal from JAMES III 1481, JAMES IV 1505 and JAMES V 1514; *d* 1531, having had an est s:

GEORGE GORDON; *dvp*, leaving:

JAMES GORDON; rallied to the defence of the young PRINCE JAMES (later JAMES VI of Scotland and I of England) towards the end of the effective reign of MARY QUEEN OF SCOTS 1567; joined the 4th Earl of Huntly (MARY's Lt in the North) and remained loyal to the Queen; obtained roy charters of several other lands and baronies; *m* Marjory, dau of Sir Thomas Menzies, of Pitfoddels, Comptroller of Scotland, and *d* 1582, having had, with other issue:

PATRICK GORDON; *m* Agnes, dau of Alexander Frazer, of Muchal, and *dvp*, leaving:

JAMES GORDON, of Methlic and Haddo; *m c* 25 July 1582 Jean, dau of William, Lord Keith, and *d* Nov 1623, having had:

GEORGE GORDON; *m* Margaret, dau of Sir Alexander Bannerman of Elsick, and *dvp* Oct 1610, leaving, with at least one dau (Jean, *m* Sir John Forbes of Waterton), an only s:

Sir John Gordon, 1st Bt (NS), so *cr* 13 Aug 1642, for his distinguished conduct at the Battle of Turriff, being 2nd in command of forces raised against the Covenanters 1630 and defender of the House of Kellie against them, though forced to surrender and imprisoned in St Giles's Cathedral, Edinburgh, where his cell was a recess in the wall which became known as Haddo's Hole (a plate on the wall today marks the spot); subsequently executed at the Cross of Edinburgh 19 July 1644 (the first Royalist to be executed by a judicial sentence), his estates being sequestrated till the Restoration; *m* 1630 Mary, dau of William Forbes of Tolquhoun, and had, with other issue (including a dau Janet, *m* Sir Walter Innes, 2nd Bt of Balvenie; *qv*):

1 **Sir John Gordon, 2nd Bt**, of Haddo; *m* Mary, only dau of 1st Lord Forbes, of Pitsligo; *d* 1665, having had an only child:

(1) Jean; *m c* 19 Dec 1676 Sir James Gordon, 5th Bt, of Lesmoir

2 **Sir George Gordon, 3rd Bt**, of Haddo, and **1st Earl of Aberdeen**; *b* 3 Oct 1637; Senator Coll of Justice 1680, Pres Session 1681, Ld High Chllr Scotland 1682–84, *cr* 30 Nov 1682 LORD HADDO, METHLICK, TARVES and KELLIE, VISCOUNT OF FORMARTINE and EARL OF ABERDEEN (all S); *m* 1671 Anne (*bur* 19 July 1707), dau and heir of George Lockhart of Torbrecks; *d* 20 April 1720, having had, with other issue (including Martha, *m* John Uday of that Ilk and had issue (*see* LOVAT, L); and Mary, *m* 13th Lord Saltoun (*qv*) of Abernethy):

(1) WILLIAM GORDON, **2nd Earl of Aberdeen**; *bapt* 22 Dec 1679; rep S peer 1721–27; *m* 1st 1708 Lady Mary Leslie (*bur* 29 Jan 1710), only dau of 5th Earl of Leven and (2nd of) Melville, and had issue:

1a Ann; *m* 5th Earl of Dumfries (*dsps* 27 July 1768; *see* BUTE, M) and *d* 15 April 1755

(1) (cont.) The **2nd Earl** *m* 2nd 25 April 1716 Lady Susan Murray (*d* 22 June 1725), dau of 1st Duke of Atholl (*qv*), and by her had issue:

1a GEORGE, **3rd Earl**

2a Catherine; *m* 1st 3 Sept 1741 3rd Duke of Gordon (*d* 5 Aug 1752) and had issue (*see* HUNTLY, M); *m* 2nd March 1756 Staats Long Morris, Col 61st Foot, MP Elgin, and *d* 10 Dec 1799

(1) (cont.) The **2nd Earl** *m* 3rd 9 Dec 1729 Lady Anne Gordon (*d* 26 June 1791), dau of 2nd Duke of Gordon; *d* 30 March 1746, having by her had, with other issue:

2a William; Gen; *d* unm 25 May 1816

3a Cosmo; Col

4a Alexander; *b* 1739; Ld of Session as LORD ROCKVILLE 1788; *m* 26 July 1769 Anne, dau of William Duff of Crombie and widow of (a) 5th Earl of Dumfries (*see* BUTE, M) and (b) 4th Earl of Stair (*qv*), and *d* 13 March 1792, leaving, with other issue:

1b Charles; *b* 27 April 1770; *m* and had issue

2b William; *b* 8 April 1772; *s* maternal unc Sir James Duff as 2nd Bt (*see* DUFF GORDON, Bt)

The 2nd EARL's est s,

GEORGE GORDON, **3rd Earl of Aberdeen**; *b* 19 June 1722; rep peer for Scotland 1747–61 and 1774–90; *m* Catharine Elizabeth (*d* 15 March 1817), dau of Oswald Hanson, of Wakefield, Yorks, and *d* 30 Aug 1801, having had with, other issue:

George, *Lord Haddo*; *b* 28 Jan 1764; *m* 18 June 1782 Charlotte (*d* 8 Oct 1795), yst dau of William Baird, of Newbyth, and *dvp* 2 Oct 1791, leaving with other issue:

GEORGE HAMILTON GORDON later HAMILTON-GORDON (roy licence 13 Nov 1818), **4th Earl of Aberdeen**, KG (1855), KT (1808), PC (1814); *b* 28 Jan 1784; *educ* Harrow and St John's Coll Cambridge (MA); FRS, FSA, FHS, rep S peer 1806–14, Min Plen Vienna, *cr* 1 June 1814 VISCOUNT GORDON OF ABERDEEN (UK), Grand Cross St Stephen of Austria 1815, For Sec 1828–30 and 1841–46, PM 1852–55, Ld-Lt and Sheriff-Pncpl Aberdeen, Ranger Greenwich Pk and Chllr King's Coll Aberdeen; *m* 1st 28 July 1805 Lady Catherine Elizabeth Hamilton (*d* 29 Feb 1812), est surv dau of 1st Marquess of Abercorn (*see* ABERCORN, D), and had a s who *d* an infant and three daus who all *dvp* unm; *m* 2nd 8 July 1815 Harriet (*d* 26 Aug 1833), dau of Hon John Douglas (*see* MORTON, E) and widow of James, Viscount Hamilton (*see* ABERCORN, D) and *d* 14 Dec 1860, having had:

1 GEORGE JOHN JAMES, **5th Earl**

2 Alexander (Sir), KCB; *b* 11 Dec 1817; Gen, MP Aberdeenshire 1875–85, Kt Legion of Honour and the Medjidie, Hon Equerry to HM QUEEN VICTORIA, Col 1st Bn Prince of Wales's Leinster Regt; *m* 9 Dec 1852 Caroline Emilia Mary, VA (*d* 29 Jan 1909), dau of Sir John Herschel, 1st Bt, and *d* 19 May 1890, leaving:

(1) Alexander (Sir), KCB (1918); *b* 6 July 1859; *educ* Winchester; Lt-Gen late RA, Afghan Campaign 1880, S African War 1899–1901 (despatches three times and Brevet Lt-Col) and WW I (despatches), Dir Mil Ops India 1910–14, GOC Aldershot 1914–16, GOC Army Corps BEF 1916–18, Col Cmdt RA 1919, Grand Offr Crown of Belgium, Legion of Honour and Croix de Guerre Belgium; *m* 15 Oct 1888 Isabel (*d* 25 May 1947), 2nd dau of Maj-Gen George Newmarch, late RE; *d* 13 Feb 1939, having had issue:

1a Robert Alexander; *b* 11 April, *d* 29 April 1893

2a Alan Herschel; *b* 7 March 1898; *educ* Winchester and RMA Woolwich; Lt RHA 1917; Dip Serv 1921, Consul Porto Alegre; GSO War Off (Maj) 1940; returned to For Serv 1945; *m* 7 July 1933 *Deenya Kovachevska, dau of Dimitri Kovachevsky, of Sofia, Bulgaria

1a Eileen Muriel; *b* 17 July 1889; *m* 1st 5 Dec 1912 Capt Peter Benson Maxwell, E Yorks Regt (*d* 24 Sept 1914 of wounds recd in action France), yst s of Sir William Edward Maxwell, KCMG, and had issue:

1b *Joan; *b* 28 Sept 1913; *m* 22 June 1936 A/Cdre John Newall Tomes, CBE, RAF, s of Brig Clement Thurstan Tomes, CBE, DSO, MC, Roy Warwicks Regt, of Minson's Common, Charmouth, Dorset, and has had issue:

1c *Ian Maxwell; *b* 8 Jan 1940; *educ* Davisville Sch, Toronto, Canada, Roy GS High Wycombe and RMA Sandhurst; Capt Roy Fus; *m* 16 Aug 1968 *Verena, dau of Anton Meyer, of 263 Rychenbergstrasse, Winterthur, Switzerland

2c Patrick Thurstan; *b* 7 Aug 1941; *educ* Davisville Sch, Toronto, Canada, Roy GS High Wycombe and RMA Sandhurst; *k* 19 March 1963

3c *Simon Christopher [Simon Tomes Esq, 7 Shawfield St, London SW3]; *b* 15 Feb 1944; *educ* Davisville Sch, Toronto, Roy GS High Wycombe and Leeds U (LLB 1967)

1a (cont.) Mrs Peter Maxwell *m* 2nd 23 Jan 1919 Claude Pemberton Wilkinson Lloyd, MA, Indian Educnl Serv (*d* 8 Oct 1966), s of Rev Pemberton Lloyd, vicar Ancaster, Lincs, and had further issue:

2b *Sheila Rosemary; *b* 19 April 1922; *m* 7 Jan 1950 Alan Chapman Lloyd Browne, AMICE, AMIMechE, AMIPE, s of Col William Lloyd Browne, RA, and has issue:

1c *Christopher St John; *b* 21 Oct 1950; *educ* Winchester

(2) Francis Henry; *b* 19 March 1861; *d* 11 May 1885

(3) William Reginald; *b* 28 Nov 1864; 1st WI Regt; *d* unm 12 Jan 1890

(4) Ernest Arthur; *b* 27 June 1866; temp Capt RE, Quartermaster and Hon Maj 14th Bn London Regt, S Africa 1900 (despatches, DCM) and WW I; *d* 9 Dec 1920

(5) George Herschel; *b* 16 May 1872; Capt TAR, Capt Scottish Horse Yeo; *m* 29 July 1918 *Mary Elizabeth, only dau of Samuel John Benwell, of Coolacorara, Co Offaly, Ireland; *d* 15 May 1939

(1) Victoria Alberta Alexandrina; *m* 25 April 1876 Victor Alexander Ernest Garth Marshall (*d* 27 Dec 1928), of Monk Coniston, Lancs; *d* 16 Oct 1936 leaving issue

(2) Caroline Augusta; *m* 14 Feb 1885 Arthur John Lewis Gordon, CMG (*d* 13 Aug 1918), of Ellon, Aberdeenshire; *d* 30 Nov 1937, leaving issue

(3) Louisa; *d* unm 11 Oct 1929

(4) Kathleen Isabella; *d* unm 6 Jan 1930

3 Douglas (Rev); *b* 13 March 1824; MA Cambridge; Hon Chaplain to HM EDWARD VII, formerly Chaplain in Ordinary to HM QUEEN VICTORIA, canon Salisbury; *m* 15 July 1851 Lady Ellen Susan Anne Douglas (*d* 22 Jan 1914), dau of 16th Earl of Morton (*qv*); *d* 6 Dec 1901 leaving issue:

(1) Douglas George, OBE (1920); *b* 17 Aug 1852; JP (London); *m* 1st 7 June 1877 Edith Anne (*d* 11 July 1929), 2nd dau of Rev Walter Trevelyan Bullock, MA, JP, of Faulkbourn Hall, Essex; *m* 2nd 31 July 1929 Annie Amelia (*d* 28 Jan 1965), dau of William James Arkcoll; *d* 24 April 1938 having had issue by his 1st w:

1a Douglas Walter; *b* 18 March 1878; Cdr RN; *m* 20 June 1903 Emilie (who *m* 2nd 14 Oct 1915 Cdr Arthur Evans, RN (*d* 16 June 1947), s of Rev Arthur Evans, rector Snelston, Derbys, and *d* 18 Sept 1952), er dau of Leonard James Maton, of Grosvenor Lodge, Wimbledon, Surrey; *d* 20 Jan 1914

2a Sholto; *b* 13 Sept 1879; *d* unm 25 Jan 1911

3a Hugh, OBE (1919); *b* 14 June 1883; Cdr RN; *m* 1st 1 Sept 1912 (*divorce* 1924) Violet Blanche, dau of S Stanbury, of Plymouth; *m* 2nd 14 Sept 1925 Katharine, dau of Thomas Edward May, MA, of Southsea; *dsp* 8 May 1960

1a Edith Hilda; *b* 23 July 1881; *m* 12 Dec 1906 Sir Richard Fitzgerald Glyn, 8th Bt, DSO, JP, DL (*d* 23 March 1960) (*see* GLYN, Bt, of Ewell and Gaunts), and *d* 10 June 1957, leaving issue

2a Rosamund; *b* 17 May 1885; *d* unm 11 April 1961

3a Esmée Veronica; *b* 19 July 1900

(2) George William; *b* 15 June 1854; Dir Public Works, Orange River Colony; *d* unm 31 Dec 1906

(3) William Hugh; *b* 1 Oct 1855; clerk Ho of Lds; *m* 6 Aug 1890 Florence Evelyn (*d* 15 May 1947), dau of Col Thomas Edward Vickers, CB, of Timsbury Manor, Romsey; *d* 25 June 1936

(1) Catharine Ellen; *d* unm 21 Feb 1913

(2) Ellen Louisa; *d* unm 25 July 1942

4 ARTHUR HAMILTON-GORDON, **1st Baron Stanmore**, of Great Stanmore, Middx (UK), so *cr* 21 Aug 1893, GCMG (1878, KCMG 1871, CMG 1859), JP and DL (Cos Aberdeen and Berks); *b* 26 Nov 1829; MA Cambridge; Lt-Col 2nd Aberdeen RV; MP Beverley 1854–57, Lt-Govr New Brunswick 1861–66, Govr and C-in-C Trinidad 1866–70, Mauritius 1871–74, Fiji 1875–80, NZ 1880–82, HC and Consul-Gen W Pacific 187783, Govr Ceylon 1883–90, KJStJ, Hon DCL Oxford; *m* 24 Sept 1865 Rachel Emily (*d* 26 Jan 1889), dau of Sir John George Shaw-Lefevre, KCB; *d* 30 Jan 1912 leaving issue:

(1) GEORGE ARTHUR MAURICE HAMILTON-GORDON, **2nd and last Baron Stanmore**, PC 1932, KCVO 1930 (CVO 1922); *b* 3 Jan 1871; *educ* Winchester and Trin Coll Cambridge (BA 1892); Capt 3rd Bn Hampshire Regt; Ld-in-Waiting 1914–22, Dep Speaker Ho Lds 1916; KJStJ and Sec Gen that Order 1921–22, Treas St Bartholomew's Hosp 1921–37, Ch Lib Whip Lds 1923–44, Chm Ctees and Dep Speaker Ho Lds 1944–46; *d* unm 13 April 1957, when the Barony expired

(1) Rachel Nevil; *b* 13 July 1869; *d* unm 22 Oct 1947

1 Frances; *d* unm 20 April 1834

The 4th EARL's est s,

GEORGE JOHN JAMES HAMILTON-GORDON, **5th Earl of Aberdeen**; *b* 28 Sept 1816; *m* 5 Nov 1840 Mary (*d* 3 April 1900), 2nd dau of George Baillie of Mellerstain and Jerviswoode and sis of 10th Earl of Haddington (*qv*); *d* 22 March 1864 having had issue:

1 GEORGE HAMILTON-GORDON, **6th Earl of Aberdeen**; *b* 10 Dec 1841; accidentally drowned on a voyage from Boston to Melbourne 27 Jan 1870; *d* unm

2 James Henry; *b* 11 Oct 1845; *d* unm 12 Feb 1868

3 JOHN CAMPBELL, **7th Earl** and **1st Marquess**

1 Mary; *m* 30 Jan 1863 8th Lord Polwarth (*qv*); *d* 13 Feb 1914 leaving issue

2 Harriet; *m* 7 May 1870 William Alexander Lindsay, CVO, KC, Clarenceux King of Arms (*d* 13 Sept 1926), est s of Colin Lindsay, JP, of Deer Park, Honiton, Devon, and *d* 15 Feb 1942 leaving issue (*see* CRAWFORD and BALCARRES, E)

3 Katherine Eliza; *m* 21 Nov 1876 6th Lord Balfour of Burleigh (*qv*); *d* 28 Feb 1931 leaving issue

The 6th EARL's only surv bro,

JOHN CAMPBELL HAMILTON-GORDON, **7th Earl** and **1st Marquess of Aberdeen and Temair**, KT (1906), PC (1886), GCMG (1895), GCVO (1911), JP (Aberdeenshire), DL (Aberdeen City); *b* 3 Aug 1847; MA U Coll Oxford (Hon Fell March 1932); Ld-Lt and Pres TA Assoc Aberdeen, a V-Pres Roy Empire Soc, Capt Roy Co of Archers, Hon Col 1st Highland Bde RFA; LLD Aberdeen, St Andrews, Queen's (Ontario), Toronto, McGill (Montreal), Ottawa, Laval, Princeton and Harvard Us, Hon DCL Oxford and Bishop's Coll, Lennoxville, Ld Rector St Andrews U 1913–16, HM's High Commr Gen Assembly Church of Scotland 1881–85 and 1915, Ld-Lt Ireland Feb-Aug 1886 and 1905–15, Govr-Gen Canada 1898, bore Standard of Canada Coronation 1911, Icr 4 Jan 1916 MARQUESS OF ABERDEEN AND TEMAIR, Cos Aberdeen, Meath and Argyll, and EARL OF HADDO, Co Aberdeen (both UK); *m* 7 Nov 1877 Hon Ishbel Maria Marjoribanks, GBE, LLD, Legn of Honour, Pres Int Cncl Women 1893–1936, Freedom of Edinburgh (*d* 18 April 1939), yst dau of 1st Baron Tweedmouth (*extinct* 1935); *d* 7 March 1934 having had issue:

1 GEORGE GORDON, **2nd Marquess of Aberdeen and Temair**, OBE (1920), JP, DL (Aberdeen City); *b* 20 Jan 1879; *educ* Harrow, St Andrews U and Balliol Coll Oxford; Ld-Lt and Pres TA Assoc Aberdeen 1934–59, CC (Aberdeen 1945) (Chm Educn Ctee 1950–56), CC London (Peckham) 1910–25, Alderman 1925–31, CC West Fulham 1931–34, V-Pres Nat Cncl YMCA, V-Pres Met U YMCA, Pres Bd Hon Dirs Alliance of Honour 1942–51, rep LCC Met Water Bd 1913–46 and Crystal Palace Tstees 1914–24 and 1926–51, Gov Body Regent St Polytechnic 1920–65, Chm Cncl Charity Organisation Soc 1934–37 and 1938–39; KStJ 1949, Prior Scottish Priory OStJ 1951–57, Hon LLD Aberdeen U 1954; *m* 1st 6 Aug 1906 Mary Florence (*dsp* 5 Jan 1937), dau of Joseph Clixby, of Owmby Cliff, Lincs, and widow of Edward Shepherd Cockayne, of Sheffield; *m* 2nd 21 Dec 1940 Sheila (*d* 12 March 1949), dau of Lt-Col John Foster Forbes of Rothiemay and widow of Capt James William Guy Innes, CBE, RN (*see* INNES, Bt), and *dsp* 6 Jan 1965

2 DUDLEY GLADSTONE GORDON, **3rd Marquess**

3 Archibald Ian; *b* 3 Oct 1884; *d* unm 16 Dec 1909

1 Marjorie Adeline, DBE (1917), DGStJ; *b* 7 Dec 1880; *m* 12 July 1904 1st Baron Pentland (*d* 11 Jan 1925) (*extinct* 1984); *d* 26 July 1970 leaving issue

2 Dorothea Mary; *b* 12 March, *d* 25 Nov 1882

The 2nd Marquess's bro,

DUDLEY GLADSTONE GORDON, **3rd Marquess of Aberdeen and Temair**, DSO (1917); *b* 6 May 1883; *educ* Harrow; Lt-Col 9th Serv Bn Gordon Highrs WW I (despatches), cmded 8/10th Bn Gordon Highrs 1917–19; staff J and E Hall Ltd (engrs, Dartford) 1907 (dir 1910), chm Hadfields Ltd (Sheffield), Pres Br Engrs Assoc 1936–39, pres Br Assoc Refrigeration 1926–29, memb Exec Ctee Fedn Br Industries, chm Dartford UDC 1923–24, pres: Fedn Br Industries 1940–43, Inst Mechanical Engrs 1947–48, Allied Circle, Br Iron Steel Research Assoc, Engrg Section Br Assoc Advancement of Science 1953, LLD Aberdeen, pres Bach Choir, chm The Jacques Orchestra 1953, govr Harrow Sch 1950 (dep chm), Gold Staff Offr Coronations 1911 and 1937; *m* 1st 25 April 1907 Cecile Elizabeth (*d* 17 Sept 1948), est dau of George James Drummond, of Swaylands Ho, Penshurst, Kent (*see* PERTH, E), and had issue:

1 DAVID GEORGE IAN ALEXANDER GORDON, **4th Marquess of Aberdeen and Temair**, CBE (1963), JP (Aberdeenshire 1955), DL (Aberdeenshire 1949); *b* 21 Jan 1908; *educ* Harrow and Balliol Coll Oxford (BA 1930, MA 1968); Maj 5th/7th Bn Gordon Highrs WW II (despatches); Gold Staff Offr Coronation 1937, KStJ (1964), CC (Aberdeenshire 1950), Ld-Lt Aberdeenshire 1973 (V-Lt 1959–1974), memb Roy Co of Archers 1955, FLAS, Convener Scottish Landowners' Fedn 1962–66 (v-pres 1967), chm Aberdeen T&AFA 1962–68, pres: Roy Scottish Benevolent Ag Instn 1967 and Experiment in Int Living 1965, dir Northern Area Clydesdale Bank Ltd 1968; *m* 29 April 1939 *(Beatrice Mary) June, DGStJ (1977), CBE (1989), DL (Aberdeenshire 1971), FRCM (1966), Hon LLD Aberdeen U (1968) [The Most Hon June Marchioness of Aberdeen and Temair MBE DL, Haddo House, Aberdeen], only dau of Arthur Paul Boissier, Headmaster Harrow 1939–42; *d* 13 Sept 1974, having adopted:

*Andrew David [Andrew Gordon Esq, Laverockbrae, Old Meldrum, Aberdeenshire AB51 0DA]); *b* 6 March 1950; *educ* Harrow and LSE (BSc 1973); *m* 1982 *Lucy Mary Frances, est dau of Canon WJ Milligan, of London SW9, and has:

1a *William David; *b* 1988

1a *Rosie Kate Jessamine; *b* 1986

2a *Rachel Mary Ishbel; *b* 1991

*James Drummond [James Gordon Esq, Drummond House, 62 Manor Rd, Worthing, W Sussex]; *b* 11 April 1953; *educ* Harrow; *m* 1985 *Marilyn, yr dau of A F Sim, of Sompting, Lancing, W Sussex

*Mary Katharine [Mrs Simon Welfare, Den of Keithfield, Tarves, Ellon, Aberdeenshire]; *b* 30 May 1946; *m* 3 Aug 1968 *Simon Piers Welfare, television reporter, 2nd s of Kenneth William Welfare, of The Old Doctor's Ho, Stradbroke, Suffolk, and has issue:

1a *Toby William David; *b* 29 March 1973

1a *Hannah Mary; *b* 30 Sept 1969

2a *Alice Emily Ishbel; *b* 6 Sept 1971

*Sarah Caroline [Mrs Eric Money, Scot's Float, Star Lock, Playden, nr Rye, E Sussex TN31 7PH]; *b* 25 March 1948; *m* 1st 31 May 1969 (*divorce* 1992) Patrick John Raleigh Scott, er s of Robert S G Scott, of The Hermitage, Peasmarsh, E Sussex, and has issue:

1a *Edward Gilbert Raleigh; *b* 1971

2a *Oliver Dickon Robert; *b* 1972

3a *Simon Gordon Thomas; *b* 1977

4a *Sasha Adam Quintus; *b* 1979

5a *Jody Timothy Fingal; *b* 1981

1a *Georgiana Morag June; *b* 1974

(cont.) Mrs Sarah Scott *m* 2nd 1993 *Eric Norman Money, artist, only s of G E Money, of N Mimms, Herts and adopted:

*Silas Gabriel Uther Money; *b* 1982

2 ARCHIBALD VICTOR DUDLEY GORDON, **5th Marquess of Aberdeen and Temair**; *b* 9 July 1913 (HM QUEEN MARY stood sponsor); *educ* Harrow; Gold Staff Offr Coronation of HM GEORGE VI 1937, Assist to Sec CPRE 1936–40, BBC Monitoring Serv 1940, BBC Radio Talks Dept 1946–72, producer: *The Week in Westminster* and party political and election broadcasts (Radio) 1946–66, Head Talks and Documentaries (Radio) 1967–72; *d* unm 1984

3 Michael James Andrew; *b* 22 May 1918; *educ* Harrow; Capt Scots Gds (SR), WW II; *ka* Italy 8 Oct 1943

4 ALASTAIR NINIAN JOHN GORDON, **6th and present Marquess of Aberdeen and Temair**

1 Jessamine Cecile Marjorie; *b* 14 Aug 1910; Co Dir BRCS 1968, chm: Co Fedn SWRI 1963–69 and Co Music Ctee 1962–95, Co-Pres Save the Children Fund 1957–95; *m* 2 Nov 1937 (Stanley George) Michael St John Harmsworth, DL (*d* 8 Aug 1981), and *d* 14 Dec 1994, leaving issue (*see* ROTHERMERE, V)

The **3rd Marquess** *m* 2nd 17 June 1949 Margaret Gladys (*d* 22 Nov 1990), RRC, JP, Chm E Grinstead UDC 1960–61, only dau of Lt-Col Reginald George Munn, CMG, of Turley Cottage, E Grinstead, W Sussex; *d* 16 April 1972

ABERGAVENNY

Arms: Gules a saltire argent, charged with a rose of the field, barbed and seeded proper. **Crest:** Out of a ducal coronet or a bull's head proper, charged with a rose gules. **Supporters:** On either side a bull argent, pied sable, armed, unguled, collared and chained or, the latter terminating in a staple or. **Badges:** Dexter, a rose gules, barbed and seeded proper; sinister, a portcullis or.
Motto: *Ne vile velis* ('Wish not wickedly').
The saltire in the Nevill family arms derives from the seal of Robert fitz Maldred, who flourished in the early 13th century. The bull featuring in the crest and supporters commemorates the Bulmers, who in turn acquired the device, along with Brancepeth Castle, by inheritance from the Norman family of du Hommet.
Creations: B. (E) 5 Sept 1450, V. (GB) 17 May 1784, E. (GB) 17 May 1784 and (UK) 14 Jan 1876, M. (UK) 14 Jan 1876.

THE 5TH MARQUESS OF ABERGAVENNY, Co Monmouth, **Earl of Abergavenny**, Co Monmouth, **Earl of Lewes**, Sussex, **Viscount Nevill**, of Birling, Kent, and **Lord** (Baron) **Abergavenny** (Sir John Henry Guy Nevill, KG (1974), OBE (1945), JP (Sussex 1948)) [The Most Hon The Marquess of Abergavenny KG OBE JP, Eridge Park, Tunbridge Wells, E Sussex TN3 9JT; Flat 2, 46 Pont St, London SW1 0AD]; *b* 8 Nov 1914; s f 1954; *educ* Eton and Trin Coll Cambridge; Life Gds 1936–46 including WW II (despatches), ret as Lt-Col 1946, Hon Col Kent and Co London Yeo 1948–62, memb: Nat Hunt Ctee 1942 (sr steward 1953 and 1963), E Sussex CC 1947–54 (CA 1954–62), E Sussex Ag Ctee 1948–52 and Jockey Club 1952, tstee Ascot Authority 1953– and HM's Rep Ascot 1972–82, E Sussex: DL 1955, V-Lt 1970–74 and Ld Lt 1974–89, dir: Massey-Ferguson Hldgs 1955–85, Lloyds Bank 1962–85, Lloyds Bank UK Management 1962–85 and Whitbread Investment, chm: Lloyds Bank SE Rgnl Bd 1962–85, Br Equestrian Promotions and Nuffield Nursing Home Management, pres: Roy Assoc Br Dairy Farmers 1955 and 1963, Hunters' Improvement Soc 1959, Assoc of Ag 1961–63, Roy Ag Soc England 1967 (dep pres 1968 and 1972) and Br Horse Soc 1970–71, v-chm Turf Bd 1967–68, Chllr Order of the Garter 1977–94, KStJ 1976 (pres Cncl OStJ Sussex 1975), Hon LLD Sussex U 1986; *m* 4 Jan 1938 *(Mary) Patricia, DCVO (1981, CVO 1971), Ldy of Bedchamber to HM THE QUEEN 1966–87, Extra Ldy of Bedchamber 1960–66 and 1987–, 4th dau of Lt-Col John Fenwick Harrison, JP, RHG, of King's Walden Bury, Hitchin, Herts, by his w Hon Margery Levy-Lawson, dau of 3rd Baron Burnham (*qv*), and has had issue:

1 Henry John Montagu, *Earl of Lewes*; *b* 2 Feb 1948; *educ* Eton; Page of Honour to HM THE QUEEN 1962–64; *d* 2 April 1965

1 *Anne Patricia [The Lady Anne Whiteley, Dalmar House, Culworth, nr Banbury, Oxon OX17 2BD]; *b* 25 Oct 1938; *m* 16 July 1971 Capt Martin Frank Whiteley (*d* 17 March 1984), s of Brig John Percival Whiteley, OBE, MP, of Dalmar House, Culworth, Oxon, and has issue:

(1) *Camilla Mary; *b* 19 May 1972

(2) *Davina Marian Beatrice; *b* 17 Nov 1973

(3) *Lucinda Jane; *b* 12 May 1978

2 *Vivienne Margaret [The Lady Vivienne Lillingston, Mount Coote, Kilmallock, Co Limerick, Ireland]; *b* 15 Feb 1941; *m* 12 July 1962 *Alan Lillingston, only s of Capt Luke Theodore Lillingston, of Ulverscroft, Leics, and has issue:

(1) *Luke; *b* 21 May 1963; *educ* Eton and RAC Cirencester

(2) *Andrew Harry; *b* 2 Feb 1972; *educ* Eton

(1) *Georgina Patricia [Mrs Michael Bell, Fitzroy House, Black Bear Lane, Newmarket, Suffolk]; *b* 24 March 1965; *m* 1988 *Michael L W Bell, yr s of Capt Brian Bell, of Todenham Manor, Moreton-in-Marsh, Glos, and has issue:

1a *Alexander Luke Wentworth; *b* 1990

2a *Nicholas Stewart Wentworth; *b* 1997

1a *Amy Kitty Wentworth; *b* 1991

(2) *Sophie Susan; *b* 5 Nov 1967

3 Jane Elizabeth; *b* 7 April 1944; *d* 16 Oct 1946

4 *Rose [The Lady Rose Clowes, Freemantle Farmhouse, Oakley, nr Tadley, Hants]; *b* 15 July 1950; *m* 8 March 1990 *George Mark Somerset Clowes, s of Archibald Somerset Clowes, of Ashlands, Billesdon, Leics, and has:

(1) *Toby Harry Somerset; *b* 24 Nov 1990

(2) *Lucy Elizabeth; *b* 23 May 1992

Barony of (A)Bergavenny: It has sometimes been asserted that this title is held by tenure, that is, by virtue of possessing under the feudal system or its successor system(s) of property ownership Abergavenny Castle and the lands that have gone immediately with it. (Such lands are to be distinguished from those granted with Abergavenny Castle to a tenant but subsequently regranted by him to subtenants). This would have meant that whoever had the castle had the Barony, whatever his name (*see* below for the various holders of the castle). Certainly before 1392, when the first writ of summons to Parliament to 'Willelmo Beauchamp de Bergeveny [*sic*]' created according to later doctrine a specifically Parliamentary Barony of Bergavenny or Beauchamp de Bergavenny, the Barony of (A)Bergavenny was a feudal one, which necessarily involved tenure. After 1392 the position is less clear. Most authorities would nowadays probably argue that the Barony was not one by tenure. The matter is complicated by the fact that the original grantee's son was never in possession of the castle at Abergavenny and was not called to Parliament as Lord (Baron) Bergavenny. These two circumstances might combine to give negative reasons for thinking the Barony was regarded as one by tenure. On the other hand at that date a writ of summons to Parliament to one man was not necessarily repeated to his son and successor. Moreover, the closing years of HENRY V's reign and the opening ones of HENRY VI's were an era of confusion, especially with regard to writs of summons to Parliament.

It is only when this background is taken into consideration that one can put some kind of interpretation on the unusual sequence of events whereby Sir Edward Nevill(e) was summoned to Parliament as Lord (Baron) Bergavenny or Nevill de Bergavenny after his wife's death. Although she would have been regarded by later doctrine as Baroness Bergavenny or Beauchamp de Bergavenny in her own right, that would not have been the case in the 15th century. Moreover, although men were often summoned to Parliament in right of their wives by titles which those wives' fathers had held where the wives in question were sole heirs of the previous title-holder, in this case Sir Edward Nevill(e)'s wife had been dead over two years by the time he was summoned. And since the doctrine that there could be such a person as a baroness in her own right only evolved later, it seems most reasonable to regard the summons of 1450 to Sir Edward Nevill(e) as constituting a new peerage creation.

For whereas Nevill(e)'s wife's paternal ancestors may have been regarded as in some sense lords of Parliament by virtue of possessing the castle and demesne lands of Abergavenny, Neville(e) was called to Parliament as a peer under what was in effect a more modern writ of summons to him personally (Ii.e., one that passed to the descendants and heirs of the baron in question whether they held Abergavenny Castle or not). As it happens Sir Edward Nevill(e) *did* also possess the castle and demesne lands of Abergavenny, though for a short while and not at the time of his summons to Parliament. It may be that his association generally with these lands and the castle through his wife gave rise to the designation 'Lord Bergavenny' or 'Lord Nevill de Bergavenny'.

The Barony created in 1450 would by subsequent doctrine have been regarded as heritable by an heir general, such as a sole heiress. But this doctrine did not become a hard and fast rule till the late 17th century. So after Feb 1586/7, when the 4th Baron Bergavenny left a sole heiress, Mary Nevill(e), she did not inherit. Instead, following considerable vacillation by the House of Lords, the Crown decided that the heir male was entitled to inherit, not the heir general. It might seem as if the Crown did this because the Barony was thought to be one by tenure, and indeed the heir male Edward Nevill(e) already held the castle and demesne lands of Abergavenny. Moreover the precedence (*i.e.*, notional date of first summons to Parliament) assigned the Barony of Bergavenny on 25 May 1604 was 1295, when the first Baron Bergavenny, whether by tenure or not, was summoned to Parliament. Meanwhile the Crown terminated the Barony of Despenser in favour of Mary Nevill(e) as compensation for its refusal to recognise her as heir to her father's Barony of Bergavenny. The effect on the Barony of Bergavenny was to make it heritable by heirs male only thereafter. (The form Abergavenny rather than Bergavenny was first used as early as the 16th century but only became the usual one from the early 18th century. Similarly the modern spelling Nevill rather than Neville has been adopted for members of the family born after 1800.)

The heir male in 1604 was granted the Barony as if his branch of the Nevill(e)s had had a right to it from the moment of the 3rd Baron's death. Thus although the 5th Baron was never summoned to or sat in Parliament he is *ex post facto* referred to as 5th Baron.

The name Abergavenny derives from the Welsh *Aber*, meaning 'mouth' of a river and *Gafenni*, denoting where the river of that name joins the Usk. The name is sometimes pronounced 'Abergenny' and this version has been preferred by the family who hold the Marquessate.

WILLIAM II 'Rufus' granted the lordship of 'Over Gwent', which included a castle at the mouth of the Genny where it joins the Usk, probably some time after 1088 to one Hamelin de Ballon, so called from his having been born at Ballon, in Maine. Subsequent holders of Over Gwent or Abergavenny included the 1st and 2nd Earls of Hereford of the 1141 *cr* (*see* HEREFORD, V) and the 2nd Earl's four younger brothers, for all of whom a shadowy family connection with Hamelin de Ballon has been claimed, though this is very hard, if not impossible, to sustain.

By 1165 one Walter de Beauchamp commanded the garrison at Abergavenny and his brother Hugh de Beauchamp seems to have succeeded him in the possession of that place. From *c* 1173 to 1230 successive fathers, sons and younger brothers called de Briouze were feudal lords of Abergavenny. William de Briouze, the first of them, who derived his name from his lordship of Briouze in Normandy, married the sister and coheir of the 2nd Earl of Hereford mentioned above, which seems to account for his coming into possession of a lordship in that part of the Welsh marches. Eve, the daughter of the youngest de Briouze brother, married *c* 1238 William de Cauntelo.Their son George held Abergavenny for some 18 years but died without issue. His heirs were his sister Mil(l)icent, who married as her second husband Eon La Zouche and with him was the ancestor of the Lords (Barons) Zouche (of Haryngworth) (*qv*), and his nephew by another sister, Joan.

Abergavenny, which of course was only one of William de Cauntelo's possessions, passed to Joan's son the 1st Lord (Baron) Hastings (*qv*) and afterwards to his son, the 2nd Lord (Baron) Hastings. The 2nd Lord (Baron) Hastings's son, the 3rd Lord, was *cr* Earl of Pembroke (*see* PEMBROKE and MONTGOMERY, E, preliminary remarks) in 1339, but his grandson the 3rd Earl died when still a minor and possession of Abergavenny passed to William Beauchamp.

This William was first cousin once-removed to the 3rd Earl of Pembroke (of the 1339 *cr*) through his mother Katharine Mortimer, sister of Agnes Mortimer who had married the 1st Earl of Pembroke of the 1339 *cr*. It has been asserted that there was no connection between him and the Walter de Beauchamp or Hugh de Beauchamp who had been in possession of Abergavenny over 200 years earlier. On the other hand it has been suggested that Walter and Hugh were sons of Walter de Beauchamp of Elmley, Worcs, and brothers of William de Beauchamp, Sheriff of Hereford 1160–69. Now the William Beauchamp who came into possession of Abergavenny in 1389 was fourth son of Thomas Beauchamp, 11th Earl of Warwick of the 1088 *cr* (*see* WARWICK, BROOK and, E, preliminary remarks), who descended from William de Beauchamp, of Elmley, Worcs, who flourished in the early 13th century. Some blood connection between the two lots of Beauchamps may therefore have existed.

Sir WILLIAM BEAUCHAMP, 1st LORD (Baron) BERGAVENNY, KG (1375 or 1376) (*see* above); *b c* 1330–40; served Hundred Years War, Capt Calais 1383, called to Parliament by writ 23 July 1392 as LORD (Baron) BERGAVENNY or BEAUCHAMP DE BERGAVENNY (E), Justiciary S Wales and Govr Pembroke 1399, entailed 20 Feb 1395/6 Abergavenny Castle on himself and his w and their male issue with remainder to his bro Thomas, *de facto* 12th Earl of Warwick, and the latter's heirs male in perpetuity; *m* Lady Joan Fitz Alan (*b* 1375; *d* 14 Nov 1435), dau of 11th/4th Earl of Arundel (*see* NORFOLK, D), and *d* 8 May 1411, leaving issue (with a dau Joan, *m* as his 1st w 4th Earl of Ormonde, *see* MOUNTGARRET, V):

Sir RICHARD BEAUCHAMP, *de jure* 2nd(?) LORD (Baron) BERGAVENNY or BEAUCHAMP DE BERGAVENNY and 1st and last EARL OF WORCESTER, KB (1413); *b* by 1397; Jt Warden Welsh Marches 1415, Capt lancers and archers Normandy 1418, *cr* Feb 1420/1 EARL OF WORCESTER (E); *m* 27 July 1411 Lady Isabel Le Despenser (*b* posthumously 26 July 1400; on her bro Richard's death became according to later doctrine BARONESS BURGHERSH in her own right; *m* 2nd *c* 26 Nov 1423, as his 2nd w, her late husb's cousin Richard Beauchamp, 13th Earl of Warwick, who *s* Nov 1435 to Abergavenny Castle and its demesne lands as male heir under the entail drawn up Feb 1395/6; she *d* 27 Dec 1439), dau of 1st and last Earl of Gloucester of the 1397 *cr* (*see* WESTMORLAND, E, and FALMOUTH, V), and *dspm* 18 March 1421/2 of wounds recd at Siege of Meaux (successfully concluded against the French by HENRY V 10 May 1422), whereupon the earldom of Worcester became extinct or reverted to the Crown (with in effect the same result), while the barony of Bergavenny or Beauchamp de Bergavenny, unless looked on as one by tenure, passed according to later doctrine to his only dau:

ELIZABETH Beauchamp, according to later doctrine BARONESS BERGAVENNY or BEAUCHAMP DE BERGAVENNY in her own right; *b* 16 Sept 1415; *m* by 18 Oct 1424 Edward NEVILL(E) (*see* below), 11th and yst s of 1st Earl of Westmorland of the 1397 *cr*, and *d* 18 June 1448, having had issue

Lineage of Nevill: The name is said to derive from Neuville in Normandy, near the modern St Valéry-en-Caux on the coast roughly halfway between Dieppe and Fécamp. Yet the family who adopted the Nevill(e) name after marrying a Nevill(e) heiress in the early 13th century were still older and grander than any 11th-century Norman adventurers. Thus the Marquesses of Abergavenny, though possessing an unbroken male line ancestry as Nevill(e)s from the reign of HENRY III, something that is very rare in modern England, possess a still more ancient one going back to the 8th-century King of Dalriada in Scotland in the shape of the line of Anglo-Scottish thanes and mormaers who held sway on the English-Scottish borders long before the original Nevill(e)s even arrived in England.

The Nevill(e)s were for a time in the 14th and 15th centuries the most powerful house in England. In the person of Richard Nevill(e), 16th and 1st Earl of Warwick (the 'Kingmaker'), a member of the family even disposed of the crown. And through the marriage of one of the Kingmaker's daughters with a Plantagenet his great-grandchildren, who bore the surname Pole, had a better legal right to the throne than the Tudors. They were accordingly regarded by HENRY VIII as one of the most serious dynastic threats to his ascendancy.

The 'Kingmaker's' grandfather the 1st Earl of Westmorland settled about half the original Nevill(e) estates on the children of his second marriage, whereas the subsequent Earls of Westmorland were the product of his first. It thus came about that the 2nd–6th Earls of Westmorland were actually less well-endowed territorially than their ancestors who had been mere barons. The pre-eminence of that branch of the family represented by the Earls of Salisbury/Warwick, who stemmed from the 1st Earl of Westmorland's second marriage, was made correspondingly easier.

The 1st Earl of Westmorland had a multiplicity of children: nine by his first wife, fourteen by his second. Of his 23 in all, four were peers, three were duchesses and another four daughters the wives of lesser peers; moreover of those three duchesses one was mother of two kings. Between 1450 and 1455 no fewer than 13 members of the family had seats in the House of Lords. This very fecundity, like that of EDWARD III, engendered quarrels.There was rivalry between the two branches of the family, which grew from a dispute about family estates into a difference as to dynastic loyalties. It thus served as an overture to the Wars of the Roses, one which was made even more ominous by a dispute between the Nevill(e)s, represented by the 1st Marquess of Montagu, and the Percys (*see* NORTHUMBERLAND, D).

This Nevill(e)-Percy rivalry dominated not just the North but all England. The Nevill(e)s' power was largely broken by the failure of the Rebellion of the Northern Earls in 1569, however, and unlike the Percys they hardly recovered until the 20th century, during which they have been conspicuous as courtiers.

GILBERT (I) de NEVILL(E); held in the year 1086 carucates (a carucate was an area of land that could be cultivated by an eight-ox plough-team throughout a single year) at Walcot, Lincs, and Yawthorpe, together with others in that part of England by 1115–18; kinship is plausible but has not been proved with:

GEOFFREY (I) de NEVILL(E); held Walcot 1146; was probably f of two bros:

1 GILBERT (II), for whom *see* further below

2 Alan (I); co-fndr with his bro of Tupholme Abbey or Priory, Lincs, 1156–66, Judge Court of Exchequer 1165, Justice of the forest in all England 1165–77, excommunicated by St Thomas à Becket 1166 for supporting HENRY II in his insistence that the clergy were subject to the ordinary law; *d* 1177/8, leaving issue:

(1) Alan (II); assist Justice of the Forest 1169–(?)90; *m* Juliane — (living 1189/90); *d* 1190

(2) Geoffrey (II); Chamberlain to KING JOHN 1207, Sheriff Yorks 1214, Seneschal Poitou 1215–19; *d* Oct 1225 or Jan-March 1225/6, leaving issue:

1a John (I); *d* by 1253, leaving issue:

1b Geoffrey (III); *m* Helewise or Hawise (*d* in or after 1275), dau of William de Montagu, and *dsp* by 15 Aug 1267

2a Geoffrey (IV); Keeper Pickering Forest in reign of KING JOHN; *m* by 1226 Mabel (*d* by 1253), dau and heir of William de la Mare, and *d* just before 31 July 1249, leaving issue:

1b Hugh (Sir); *m* as her 1st husb Margaret (she *m* 2nd Hugh de Myton and *d* in or after 1289), dau of Thomas de Furnival, and *d* by 1275, leaving issue:

1c Geoffrey (V); *d* 1316, leaving:

1d Philip de NEVILL(E); *dsp* 1345

3a Alan (III)

(3) Thomas

(4) Ives de; *d* by 1191

(5) Ralph; *m* — Rafin, dau of Bertram Rafin, living in STEPHEN's reign (Bertram's paternal aunt *m* Simon fitz William and with him was ancestor of the Lords (Barons) Kyme (*see* also AMERICAN PRESIDENTIAL FAMILIES, 1994, Morris Genealogical Books SA pp. 41)), and had issue:

1a Hugh (I); allegedly memb of RICHARD I's household when young, joined RICHARD in 3rd Crusade 1190 and participated Siege of Jaffa 1192, Keeper Marlborough Castle 1194 and afterwards Benfield, Ludgershall, Porchester, Rockingham, Rodbaston, St Briavel's, Sauvey, Southampton, Stratton and Warwick Castles, ch of the itinerant justices of the forest by 1199, Sheriff Essex and Herts 1198–99 and 1202–03 and Lincs 1227, (Chief?) Forester (of all England?) for life 1203, Treasurer by 27 Jan 1208/9, Keeper seaports between Cornwall and Hants 1213, memb of JOHN's entourage at the signing of Magna Carta at Runnymede 1215 but later surrendered Marlborough to LOUIS VIII of France when latter invaded England at behest of the barons ranged against JOHN, Ch Justice and Keeper of the Forest 1224; *m* 1st by 30 April 1200 Joan (*d* in or after Dec 1224), dau and heir of Henry de Cornhill; *m* 2nd by April 1230 Beatrice (*m* 3rd Hugh de Playz and *d* by Dec 1245), dau of Stephen de Turnham and widow of Ralph de Fay, and *d* by 21 July 1234, leaving by his 1st w:

1b John (II); Ch Forester and Justice of the entire royal forest throughout England 1235; *m* Hawise, dau of Sir Robert de Courtenay, of Okehampton, Devon (*see* DEVON, E), and *d* just before 8 June 1246, leaving issue:

1c Hugh (II); not yet of age in 1246 but had attained his majority by Feb 1256, captured by the future EDWARD I at Siege of Kenilworth 1265–6, having previously sided with Simon de Montfort and his fellow barons against HENRY III, pardoned 1266; *m c* Aug 1254(?) Beatrice, dau of Robert de Brewes, and *dsp* by 5 Oct 1269

2c John (III); also captured during Siege of Kenilworth, roy pardon 1266, Constable Tower of London 1272–73; *m* 1st(?) —; *m* 2nd(?) Margaret — and *d* by 20 May 1282, leaving issue:

1d HUGH de NEVILL(E), 1st LORD (Baron) NEVILLE (of Essex) (E), so *cr* (according to later doctrine) by writ of summons to Parl 19 Dec 1311; *b* 23 Aug 1276; served Scottish Wars of EDWARD I and EDWARD II 1300–19, ktd 1300; *m* 1st *c* 1290 Eleanor, dau of Thomas de Weyland, Ch Justice Common Pleas; *m* 2nd *c* 1309 Ida FitzWalter (*d* 7 Nov 1361), dau of 1st Lord (Baron) FitzWalter (*qv*) by his 2nd w Alianore and widow of 1st and last Lord (Baron) Warde, and *d* by 27 May 1335, leaving by his 1st w:

1e JOHN de NEVILL(E), 2nd LORD (Baron) NEVILLE (of Essex); *b c* 1299; served Crécy campaign in Hundred Years war 1346–47; *m* 1st (*annulled* 15 June 1345) Margaret, dau of 1st and last Lord (Baron) Warde, and had issue; *m* 2nd Alice (*d* 14 May 1344), widow of Thomas de Nerford, and *dspm* 25 July 1358, when any peerage that may have been *cr* by the writ of 1311 probably fell into abeyance

2e Hugh (III); served with his er bro in the Crécy campaign; *d* in or after 1356, leaving:

1f John (IV); joined religious order of Hosp of St John of Jerusalem Aug 1357

3e Edmund; living 1334; took holy orders

2b Herbert; held 1242/3 the manor of Arnold, Notts, which he acquired through his f; *m* and *dsp* by April 1257

1b Agnes

2a Roger; s his er bro Hugh as Keeper Rockingham Castle 1213, Sheriff Northants 1215, surveyor of the forest

3a Adam; excommunicated by St Hugh of Lincoln after marrying the putative dau and heir (aged 4) of Thomas de Saleby

4a Thomas

5a William

1a Alice; *m* Piers de Athelakeston (*d* in KING JOHN's reign), Keeper of the Forest Leics and Rutland, and had:

1b — de Athelakeston; had:

1c Piers de ATHELAKESTON later NEVILL(E); took his granmother's name

The er bro,

GILBERT (II) de NEVILL(E); witnessed various charters between 1142 and 1163, held various lands that GILBERT (I) had had, which again suggests kinship; *d* by 1169, leaving:

1 Geoffrey (VI); had attained his majority by 1161, a justice in Yorks 1184; *m* by Michaelmas 1176 Emma (*d* by 1208), only dau and ultimately heir of Bertram de Bulmer, feudal lord of Brancepeth, Co Durham, and widow of Geoffrey de Valoignes, and *d* by Michaelmas 1193, leaving:

(1) Henry; one of the barons of the North who KING JOHN demanded 1216 should pledge him loyalty; *m* Alice — and *dsp* 1227

(1) Isabel; *m* 1st Robert Fitz Maldred (*d* between 1242 and 1248) and had issue (*see* below); *m* 2nd Gilbert de Brakenberg and *d* by May 1254

2 William

3 Walter

The line of Maldred: MALDRED, bro of DUNCAN I 'The Gracious', KING OF STRATHCLYDE 1018–34 and KING OF SCOTS 1034–40 (for MALDRED's previous ancestry and a discussion as to what extent this may derive from EOCHU MUGMEDON, HIGH KING OF IRELAND in the mid-4th century AD, *see* AMERICAN PRESIDENTIAL FAMILIES, pp. 40–41 and 45–46, Morris Genealogical Books SA, 1994); feudal Ld Allerdale; *m* Ealdgyth or Aldgyth, dau of Uchtred, Ughtred or Uhtred Earl of Northumberland or Northumbria by his 3rd w Elgiva or Ælgifu, dau of ETHELRED II 'The Unready' KING OF ENGLAND 979–1013 and 1014–16, and was probably *k* in battle 1045 when trying to avenge his bro's murder by MACBETH, leaving issue:

1 Gospatric, Earl of Northumberland 1067–72 (*see* DUNBAR, Bt, of Mochrum; NORTHUMBERLAND, D, preliminary remarks; and AMERICAN PRESIDENTIAL FAMILIES, pp. 46–97)

MALDRED and his w probably also had issue:

2 Maldred; received *c* 1084 the vill (township or manor) of Winlaton, now in Tyne and Wear, from the Bp of Durham in exchange for part of the vill of Newton Katton; had issue:

(1) Uchtred fitz Maldred; a great Northern magnate whose life and death are recorded in the Durham *Liber Vitae*; *d* by 1128/9, leaving issue:

1a Dolfin fitz Uchtred; feudal lord of Raby, Co Durham; probably a tenant in chief of both the Kings of England and Scotland since he is recorded as reserving his homage to them direct by 1131, when granted all Staindrop and Staindropshire (an administrative unit centred on Staindrop but later incorporated into Co Durham), including the township of Raby, by the Prior of Durham; *d* leaving issue:

1b MALDRED, for whom *see* further below

2b Patrick fitz Dolfin

DOLFIN Fitz UCHTRED's er s,

MALDRED Fitz DOLFIN; feudal Ld Raby; *m* —, dau of John de Stuteville, of Long Lawford, Warwicks, yr s of Robert (II) de Stuteville, Sheriff of Northumberland, and *d* by 1183, leaving, with other issue:

ROBERT Fitz MALDRED; came of age 1195; feudal Ld Raby, Commr to collect an aid (irregular tax) in Northumberland 1230, served in HENRY III's campaign against Welsh Aug 1241; *m* Isabel, dau of Geoffrey (VI) de Nevill(e) (*see* above), whereby he became also feudal lord of Brancepeth, Co Durham, and *d* 25 June 1242–26 May 1248, leaving issue:

GEOFFREY Fitz ROBERT or Fitz ROBERT Fitz MALDRED, later (VII) de NEVILL(E); took his mother's family name because of the vast estates she had brought with her, notably Brancepeth and Sheriff-Hutton, now in N Yorks, together with land in Lincs; *m* Joan, possibly coheir of John de Monmouth, and *d* by Michaelmas 1242, leaving issue:

1 ROBERT

2 Geoffrey (VIII); fought for HENRY III at Battle of Lewes against Simon de Montfort 1264, Govr Scarborough Castle 1270, Ch Justice: pleas of forests beyond Trent 1270 and pleas of the forest in Cumberland, Northumberland, Notts and Yorks 1270, called for mily serv against the Welsh 1277, 1282 and 1283; *m* by 1267 Margaret (*d c* Feb 1318/9), dau and heir of John de Longvillers or Lungvillers, through whom he acquired Hornby Castle, Lancs, and *d* a short while before 26 March 1285, leaving issue:

(1) John (V); *b* 10 Aug 1269; feudal lord of Hornby; *m* Pernel — (*d* between Sept 1346 and June 1349) and *d* by April 1309, leaving issue:

1a John (Sir), JP (N and W Ridings Yorks 1326); *b* 30 Nov 1299 or 1300; memb household of Thomas, 1st Earl of Lancaster of the 1267 *cr* (gs of HENRY III), called to the Gt Cncl 1324 and for mil service Guienne 1325 and against the Scots 1335, ktd 1326; *dsp* a short while before 1 Dec 1355

(2) Geoffrey (IX)

(3) Robert (I) (Sir); fought in Scotland 1296, defeated Scots raiders 1303, called for mil service in Scotland 1312 and 1324 and to Gt Cncl 1324; had issue:

1a Robert (II) (Sir), JP (W R Yorks 1344 and 1346); feudal lord of Hornby, summoned to the Gt Cncl at Westminster 1342, ktd 1344, fought at Crécy 1346, was at the Siege of Calais (successfully conducted by EDWARD III 1346–47); *m* 1st Joan, dau and heir of Henry de Atherton; *m* 2nd Elizabeth, dau of Thomas de St Laurence and widow of Sir Roger de Kirkeby, of Horton Kirby, Kent, and *d c* July 1373, leaving by his 1st w, with five other sons (John, Giles, Thomas, William and Geoffrey, but not necessarily in that order):

1b Robert (III) (Sir); feudal lord of Hornby, MP Yorks 1377, Sheriff Yorks 1378–79, memb Black Prince's household, served Battle of Poitiers 1356; *m c* 1344 Margaret de la Pole, sis of 1st Earl of Suffolk of the 1385 *cr*, and *d* 4 April 1413, having had, with two daus (Margaret; *m* Sir William Haryngton; Joan; *m* — Langton):

1c Thomas (Sir); *dvp* before 1387, leaving a dau and heiress:

1d Margaret; *b c* 1384; *m* by 15 Feb 1403/4 Thomas Beaufort (*b c* Jan 1377; *dsps* 27 Dec 1427), 1st and last Duke of Exeter of the 1416 *cr* and yst of the three originally illegitimate (but legitimated 1396) sons of John of Gaunt (4th s of EDWARD III) by his 3rd w Katherine Swynford, and *d* before her husb

(4) Edmund

(5) William

(1) Margaret; *m* Sir Robert de Northmilford and had issue:

1a John; *dsp*

3 John; priest, held living of Badsworth

GEOFFREY (VII) de NEVILL(E)'s er s,

ROBERT (I) de NEVILL(E); feudal lord of Raby and Brancepeth, campaigned against Welsh 1257, Sheriff Northumberland Jan-Nov 1258, Keeper: Bamburgh, Newcastle(-upon-Tyne), Norham and Werk Castles 1258, also Scarborough Castle 1277, Justice of the forests beyond the Trent 1261 and Ch Justice of the same 1265, Cdr HENRY III's forces beyond the Trent, Capt for the defence of Yorks and Sheriff Yorks 1263, Commr to hear pleas of disinherited persons 1267–68, Ch assessor of the fifteenth (a tax) in Northumberland and Westmorland 1275; *m* 1st —; *m* 2nd by 13 April 1273 Ida (she *m* 3rd by 8 May 1285 John FitzMarmaduke, of Horden and Ravensholm, Co Durham, and *d* on or after 18 May 1315), widow of Sir Roger Bertram, of Mitford, Northumberland, and *d* just before 20 Aug 1282, leaving issue by his 1st w:

1 ROBERT (II)

2 John

ROBERT (I) de NEVILL(E)'s er s,

ROBERT (II) de NEVILL(E); *m c* 1260 Mary (*d* by 11 April 1320), est dau and co-heiress of Ralf fitz Randolf or Ranulf (probably a descendant of the Counts of Brittany), of Middleham, now in N Yorks, whereby he acquired the lordship of Middleham together with extensive holdings elsewhere in Yorks, as well as some in Norfolk, and *dvp* 1271, leaving issue:

1 RANDOLPH or RANULF, 1st LORD (Baron) NEVILLE (of Raby), for whom *see* further below

2 Ralph, clerk; living 1321

3 Robert, clerk; living 1321

ROBERT (II) de NEVILL(E)'s est s,

RANDOLPH or RANULF de NEVILL(E), 1st LORD (Baron) NEVILLE (of Raby) (E), so *cr* (according to later doctrine) by writ of summons to Parl 24 June 1295; *b* 18 Oct 1262; found guilty 1313 of incest with his dau Lady de Faucomberge; *m* 1st Eupheme, dau of 1st Lord (Baron) FitzRoger of the 1295 *cr*; *m* 2nd Margery, dau of John de Thweng, and *d* a little while after 18 April 1331, having had issue by his 1st w (but none by his 2nd):

1 Robert ('The Peacock of the North'); captured by the Scots at their victory of Bannockburn 24 June 1314; *m c* 1315/6 Ellen — and *dvp* & *sp* June 1319, being *k* by Sir James Douglas (known as 'the Good', but also, especially by the English, as the 'Black Douglas' from his dark complexion) outside the walls of Berwick in single combat, a contest arranged in revenge for the killing by Nevill(e) and his bros the previous Dec of Richard FitzMarmaduke

2 RALPH, 2nd LORD

3 Alexander (Sir); taken prisoner by the Scots with his er bro Ralph and yr bro John on the occasion of his est bro's death 1319; their ransoming cost their father a crippling sum; *d* 15 March 1366/7

4 John; imprisoned at York 1322, probably because he was one of those opposed to EDWARD II, pardoned late 1322 for his complicity in the killing of Richard FitzMarmaduke; *k* 1333 at Battle of Halidon Hill (English victory over Scots)

5 Thomas; Preb St Patrick's Dublin, Archdeacon Durham 1340

1 Anastasia; *m* Sir Walter de Faucomberge, er s of 2nd Lord (Baron) Faucomberge (*see* YARBOROUGH, E)

2 Mary

3 Ida

4 Eupheme

The 1st LORD (Baron) NEVILL(E) (of Raby)'s 2nd s,

RALPH de NEVILL(E), 2nd LORD (Baron) NEVILLE (of Raby); *b c* 1291; *educ* Oxford; Constable Warkworth Castle 1322, Steward of the Household 1331–37, Keeper Forest beyond Trent 1332 (appointed for life 1336), Warden Scottish Marches 1334, Keeper Bamburgh Castle 1335 for life, memb Cncl of Prince Edward as Keeper of the Realm 1338 and 1340, participated in English sieges of Dunbar 1338 and relief of Perth when besieged by Scots 1339, jt cdr in repelling Scots invasion of Westmorland 1345 as well as perennially involved in warfare and negotiations with Scots generally, also in diplomatic negotiations on the Continent, commr of the peace Cumberland, Northumberland, Westmorland and Yorks 1343, Dep Sheriff Westmorland 1345, cmded 1st Div at victory over Scots of Nevill(e)'s Cross nr Durham 1346 where DAVID II KING OF SCOTS was captured by English; *m* (licence 14 Jan 1326/7) Alice (*d* 12 Jan 1373/4), dau of 1st and last Lord (Baron) Audley (of Stratton Audley) of the 1321 *cr* and widow of 1st Lord (Baron) Greystoke of the 1321 *cr*, and *d* 5 Aug 1367, having had issue:

1 JOHN, 3rd LORD

2 Alexander; Preb York 1361, Archdeacon Durham 1369–71, Archbp York 1374–88, titular Bp St Andrews (nominated 1388 by POPE URBAN IV but papal authority in this matter not recognised by Scots), close adherent of RICHARD II, advising him not to give in to demands for less partisan rule, found guilty of treason by Parl 1388 when RICHARD temporised with the Lords Appellant (nobles opposed to him) by sacrificing his closest adherents; *d* in exile 16 May 1392 at Louvain, where he ministered as a parish priest

3 Robert; *dsp* post 1345

4 Ralph of Cundall, N Yorks; living 1345; ancestor of the Nevills of Thornton Bridge

5 William (Sir); Adml of the Fleet from the Thames northwards 1372, Kt of RICHARD II's Chamber 1383, Constable Nottingham Castle 1383, jt commr to treat for peace with France and Scotland 1383, a friend of John Wyclif and the Lollard movement, joined Lords Appellant 1388–89 and was thus opposed to his er bro the Archbp; *m* Elizabeth — and *d* in or after 1389

1 Eufeme or Eupheme; *m* 1st April 1343 4th Lord (Baron) Clifford (*see* DE CLIFFORD, B); *m* 2nd Reynold Lucy, s of 2nd Lord (Baron) Lucy of the 1321 *cr*; *m* 3rd Sir Walter de Heselarton and *d* Oct-Nov 1393

2 Katherine; *m* 2nd Lord (Baron) Dacre (*qv*)

3 Margaret; *m* 1st 3rd Lord (Baron) Ros (of Helmsley) (*see* DE ROS, B); *m* 2nd 12 July 1358 1st and last Earl of Northumberland of the 1377 *cr* (*see* NORTHUMBERLAND, D) and *d* 11, 12 or 13 May 1372

4 Isabel; *m* Hugh Fitz Henry (*dsp* & *vp* by 21 Sept 1349), er bro of 2nd Lord (Baron) FitzHugh of the 1321 *cr*

5 Eleanor; *m* Sir Geoffrey le Scrope (*dsp* & *vp*, being *k* at the Siege of the Castle of Piskre, Lithuania, 1362 while campaigning with the Teutonic Kts against heathen), est s of 1st Lord (Baron) Scrope (of Masham) of the 1350 *cr*; in widowhood became Abbess of the Minories, London

6 Elizabeth; nun of the Minories, London

The 2nd LORD (Baron) NEVILLE (of Raby)'s est s,

JOHN de NEVILL(E), 3rd LORD (Baron) NEVILLE (of Raby), KG (1369); *b c* 1330; Capt in Div cmded by his f at Nevill(e)'s Cross 1346, ktd *c* April 1360, Jt Amb to France 1368, Adml of the North 1370, jt commr to treat with Genoa 1370, Steward King's Household 1372–81, Keeper Bamburgh Castle 1377 for life and Fronsac Castle in France 1378, Seneschal Gascony 1378, Jt Warden Marches 1377, 1381/2 and 1382/3, Warden E March 1381 and 1385/6, jt commr to negotiate peace with Scots 1383 and March 1386/7; *m* 1st Maud, dau of 2nd Lord (Baron) Percy (*see* NORTHUMBERLAND, D), and had, with other issue:

1 RALPH, 4th LORD (Baron) NEVILLE (of Raby) and 1st EARL OF WESTMORLAND of the 1397 *cr*, for whom *see* further below

2 THOMAS de NEVILL(E), regarded as (5th) LORD (Baron) FURNIVALL(E) in right of his w, though called to Parl by writ 20 Aug 1383 as NEVILL OF HALUMSHIRE [*sic*]; agreed in Parl to clandestine incarceration of RICHARD II 23 Oct 1399, Keeper Annandale and Constable Lochmaben Castle in W Scottish Marches 23 Oct 1399, Keeper Alnwick, Berwick and Warkworth Castles 1403, memb gt cncl of HENRY IV 1404, Jt War Treasurer 1404–06, Treasurer of England July-Nov 1406; *m* 1st by 1 July 1379 Joan de Furnevalle, BARONESS FURNIVALL(E) in her own right according to later doctrine (*b c* 1369), dau and heir of 5th Lord (Baron) Furnivalle (*see* PETRE, B) of the 1295 *cr*, and had issue:

(1) MAUD de Nevill(e), BARONESS FURNIVALL(E) in her own right according to later doctrine; *b c* 1392; *m* by 12 March 1406/7, as his 1st w, 1st Earl of Shropshire or Shrewsbury (*see* SHREWSBURY and WATERFORD, E), who, however, before his *cr* as Earl in 1442 was called to Parl 26 Oct 1409 as LORD De FURNYVALL or De HALOMSHIRE [*sic*] in right of his w, and *d c* 1423, having had issue (*see* PETRE, B)

2 (cont.) The (6th) LORD (Baron) FURNIVALL(E)/NEVILL OF HALUMSHIRE *m* 2nd by 4 July 1401 Ankaret, dau and eventual heir of 1st Lord (Baron) Strange or Lestrange of the 1360 *cr* (*see* ST DAVIDS, V) and widow of Lord (Baron) Talbot (of Blackmere) (*see* SHREWSBURY and WATERFORD, E), and *dspm* 14 March 1406/7

1 Elizabeth; nun of the Minories, London

2 Alice; *m* by 24 June 1380 3rd Lord (Baron) Deincourt of the Feb 1298/9 *cr* and *d* 20 June 1433

3 Maud; *m* Sir William le Scrope (*d* Spain 1367)

4 Eleanor; *m* 1st and last Lord (Baron) Lumley of the 1384 *cr* (*see* SCARBROUGH, E) and *d* in or after 1441

The 3rd LORD (Baron) NEVILL(E) *m* 2nd by 9 Oct 1381 Elizabeth Latimer, BARONESS LATIMER (of Corby) in her own right according to later doctrine (*m* 2nd, as his 3rd w, 4th Lord (Baron) Willoughby de Eresby (*qv*) and *d* 5 Nov 1395), dau and heiress of 4th Lord (Baron) Latimer (of Corby) of the Feb 1298/9 *cr*, and *d* 17 Oct 1388, leaving further issue:

3 JOHN de NEVILL(E), 6th LORD (Baron) LATIMER (of Corby); *b* 1382; settled most of his lands on his Nevill(e) half-bro Ld Westmorland to the exclusion of his full sister's s, even though many of these lands came to him through his mother; *m* by 24 July 1406 (*divorce* because of his impotence) Maud de Clifford (*m* 2nd *c* 1414 1st Earl of Cambridge of the 1414 *cr* (gs of EDWARD III) and *dsp* 26 Aug 1446), dau of 6th Lord (Baron) Clifford (*see* DE CLIFFORD, B), and *dsp* 10 Dec 1430

5 Elizabeth; *m* Sir Thomas Willoughby and left issue (*see* WILLOUGHBY DE BROKE, B)

The 3rd LORD (Baron) NEVILLE (of Raby)'s est s,

RALPH de NEVILL(E), 1st EARL OF WESTMORLAND (E), so *cr* 29 Sept 1397, KG (*c* 1403), PC (1399); *b c* 1364; ktd 1380, Jt Keeper castle and city of Carlisle 1385, Jt Warden W March 1385/6 and 1389, Keeper Forest beyond Trent 1389–1425, Constable Tower of London 21 Sept-30 Oct 1397, promoted Earl for loyalty to RICHARD II when the latter struck back at the Lds Appellant who in 1387 had engineered convictions for treason against RICHARD's friends (the Earl had no estates in Westmorland, but it was the nearest county geographically to those where he did hold land, the names of these counties being already embodied in titles bestowed on other families; in any case he was now granted the honour (territorial unit) of Penrith); he nevertheless was among the earliest nobles to side with his bro-in-law the banished Duke of Hereford (later HENRY IV) after the latter returned to England July 1399 and played a leading role in the deposition of RICHARD II; Ch Commr to perform duties of Constable of England 1391, Marshal of England 1399–1412/3, Keeper Roxburgh Castle March 1401/2–08, Warden: Berwick and E March 1403, Carlisle and W March (the latter following his suppression of a revolt by 1st and last Earl of Northumberland of the 1377 *cr*, who had previously held the post (*see* NORTHUMBERLAND, D)) 1403–14, Memb Cncl of Regency 1415 and 1422 during HENRY V's absence abroad and for minority of HENRY VI respectively; *m* 1st by 1370 Lady Margaret de Stafford (*d* 9 June 1396), dau of 2nd Earl of Stafford of the March 1350/1 *cr* (*see* STAFFORD, B), and by her had:

1 John; *b c* 1387; Keeper Roxburgh Castle 1408–11, Warden West March towards Scotland 1414–20, accompanied HENRY V to France and took part in the sieges of Caen (1418) and Rouen (1418/9), Capt town and castle of Verneuil France 1417, Keeper Warren of St John Argences Bailiwick of Caen 1419; *m c* 29 Aug 1394 Elizabeth de Holand (*d* 4 Jan 1422/3), dau and eventual co-heiress of 2nd Earl of Kent of the 1360 *cr*, and *dvp c* 20 May 1420, leaving issue:

(1) RALPH NEVILL(E), 2nd EARL OF WESTMORLAND; *b* 17 or 22 Sept 1406/7; ktd 19 May 1426 in the Parl at Leicester by the infant HENRY VI, Commr to keep the truce with Scotland 1426, 1430 and 1437/8, commr of array in the N and Capt in the Marches towards Scotland 1436, commr of array in the N to resist the rebellion 1459 of his unc-by-marriage (*see* below) Richard 3rd Duke of York (ggs of EDWARD III and the Yorkist claimant to the throne till his death 1460) and to oppose the Scots and HENRY VI 1461; *m* 1st between 7 May and 30 Aug 1426 Elizabeth (*d* 26 Oct 1437), dau of Sir Henry ('Harry Hotspur') Percy, s of 1st and last Earl of Northumberland of the 1377 *cr* (*see* NORTHUMBERLAND, D) and widow of 7th Lord (Baron) Clifford (*see* DE CLIFFORD, B); *m* 2nd *c* Feb 1441/2 Margaret (*dsps* before 1461), dau and heiress of Sir Reynold de Cobham, and *d* 3 Nov 1484, having had issue by his 1st w:

1a John (Sir); ktd before 1 Dec 1449; *m* before 18 Feb 1440/1 Lady Anne Holand (she *m* 2nd before 5 Sept 1452 her unc-in-law Sir John Neville, 1st Lord (Baron) Neville of the 1459 *cr* (*see* immediately below); *m* 3rd 9th and last Earl of Douglas; *see* QUEENSBERRY, M), dau of 1st Duke of Exeter of the Jan 1443/4 *cr*, and *dsp* & *vp* just before 16 March 1449/50

(2) JOHN NEVILL(E), 1st LORD (Baron) NEVILLE of the 1459 *cr*; *b c* 1410; called to Parl by writ 20 Nov 1459 as LORD (Baron) NEVILLE (E), Constable Middleham and Sheriff Hutton Castles, Lancastrian in Wars of Roses, fought yr branch of Nevill(e)s (issue of his gf's 2nd w) for the Yorks estates his gf had held; *m* between March 1450/1 and 27 July 1454 his n's widow Anne Holand (*see* above) and was *k* Battle of Towton (Yorkist victory) 29 March 1461 and attainted 4 Nov 1461, though this was reversed 6 Oct 1472, leaving issue:

1a RALPH NEVILL(E), 2nd LORD (Baron) NEVILLE and 3rd EARL OF WESTMORLAND, KB (1475); *b* 1456; *s* f as 2nd LORD (Baron) NEVILLE of the 1459 *cr* on f's attainder being reversed 1472 and unc as 3rd EARL OF WESTMORLAND 1484; commr to keep truce with Scotland 1484, a cdr in army assembled to wage war on Scots 1497; *m* before 20 Feb 1472/3 Isabel, dau of Roger Booth, of Sawley, Derbys and allegedly n of Laurence Booth, ArchbpYork, and *d* 6 Feb 1498/9, having had issue:

1b Ralph, *Lord Neville*; commr to negotiate marriage of HENRY VII's dau Margaret with JAMES IV of Scotland 1495 and 1496, keeper truce with Scotland 1497; *m* 1st Mary (*b* 19 Jan 1469/70; *dsp c* 25 Dec 1489), dau of William Paston by his w Lady Anne Beaufort, dau of 1st Duke of Somerset (himself ggs of EDWARD III through John of Gaunt) of the 1448 *cr*; *m* 2nd Edith (*m* 2nd 1st and last Lord (Baron) Darcy of the 1509 *cr* and *d* 22 Aug 1529), dau of Sir William Sandys, of the Vyne, Sherborne St John, Hants, and sis of 1st Lord (Baron) Sandys of the 1529 *cr* (*see* SANDYS, B, preliminary remarks) and *dvp* 1498, having had by his 2nd w, with an er s (*d* young):

1c RALPH NEVILL(E), 4th EARL OF WESTMORLAND, KG (1525), PC (1525); *b* 21 Feb 1497/8; ktd 1523, Ch Commr to negotiate with Scots 1525, Dep Capt Berwick and V-Warden E and Middle Marches 1525–26, a judge at trial of ANNE BOLEYN 1536, Memb Cncl of N Jan 1536/7; *m* before June 1520 Lady Catherine Stafford (*d* 14 May 1555), 2nd dau of 3rd and last Duke of Buckingham of the 1444 *cr*, and *d* 24 April 1549, having had issue, with nine other children:

1d HENRY NEVILL(E), 5th EARL OF WESTMORLAND, KG (1552), PC (Feb 1550/1); *b* 1524/5; ktd 1544, Memb Cncl of N 1549, Ld Lt Bishopric of Durham 1552, one of the 26 peers who 16 June 1553 agreed to settle crown on LADY JANE GREY but swiftly declared for MARY, Capt-Gen Horse in N 1557, Lt Gen of the N 1558; *m* 1st 3 July 1536 Lady Anne Manners, dau of 1st Earl of Rutland (*see* RUTLAND, D); *m* 2nd Jane (*d* before Dec 1558), dau of Sir Roger Cholmley; *m* 3rd before 21 June 1560 his sis-in-law Margaret (*bur* 2 April 1570), dau of Sir R Cholmley and widow of Sir Henry Gascoigne, and *d* 10 Feb 1563/4, having had issue by his 1st w:

1e CHARLES NEVILL(E), 6th and last EARL OF WESTMORLAND of the 1397 *cr*; *b* between 18 Aug 1542 and 28 Aug 1543; commr musters (local defence levies) Co Durham 1569, Memb Cncl of N, conspired (being urged to rebellion it is said by his unc Christopher Nevill(e) (*see* below)) with 1st Earl of Northumberland of the 1557 *cr* (*see* NORTHUMBERLAND, D) in the Northern Rebellion Nov 1569, for which he was attainted 1571 (Raby Castle, the ancient seat of the Nevill(e)s, being taken into the possession of the Crown till its purchase by Sir Harry Vane (*see* BARNARD, B) *c* 1645); fled overseas, Col of a regt under the Spanish flag of Englishmen in exile from ELIZABETH I's regime 1580, Capt of all English troops under Duke of Parma (one of his unc PHILIP II of Spain's generals) 1583; *m* 1563/4 Lady Jane Howard (*bur* 30 June 1593), sis of 4th Duke of Norfolk (*qv*), and *dspms* 16 Nov 1601, when all his titles had already been forfeited, having had issue, with an only s (*d* young):

1f Catherine; *m* Sir Thomas Grey, of Chillingham, Northumberland (*see* GREY, E)

2f Eleanor; *d* unm

3f Margaret; *m* Sir Nicholas Pudsey, of Yorks

4f Anne; *m* David Ingleby, unc of Sir William Ingleby, 1st Bt of the 1642 *cr*

2d Christopher, of Kirkbymoorside, N Yorks; attainted as a ringleader Northern Rebellion 1569 in which he captured Hartlepool, fled to Low Countries, where pensioned by PHILIP II of Spain; *m* Ann(i)e, dau of John Fulthorpe, of Hipswell, N Yorks, and widow of Francis Wandisford, and *dsp* in exile

3d Cuthbert; a ringleader 1569; *d* in Low Countries a pensioner of Spain

1d Dorothy; *m* 3 July 1536, as his 1st w, 16th Earl of Oxford (*see* ST ALBANS, D) and *dspm* between 17 Dec 1545 and 27 June 1547

2d Mary; *m* Sir Thomas Danby

3d Margaret; *m* 3 July 1536, as his 1st w, 2nd Earl of Rutland and *d* 13 Oct 1559, leaving issue (*see* RUTLAND, D)

4d Elizabeth; *m* as his 1st w 4th Lord (Baron) Dacre of Gillesland (*see* DACRE, B) and *dsp*

5d Eleanor; *m* Brian Stapleton, of Carlton (*see* NORFOLK, D)

6d Anne; *m c* 1553 Sir Fulke Greville and had issue (*see* WARWICK, E)

(3) Thomas (Sir); *m* Elizabeth, dau of 5th Lord (Baron) Beaumont (*see* NORFOLK, D), and had:

1a Humphrey (Sir), of Brancepeth; *b* 1439?; Lancastrian, attainted Nov 1461 but pardoned and ktd 1463/4, attainted again Jan 1465, captured and executed in EDWARD IV's presence at York 29 Sept 1469, having had:

1b Arthur, of Scole Acle, Weardale, Co Durham; *d c* 1502, leaving issue:

1c Ralph, of Scole Acle and Coveshouses, Weardale; f of:

1d —; f of:

1e Ralph; *d* 1615, leaving issue:

1f Anne

2c Lancelot; *m* Anne, dau of Rowland Tempest, of Holmeside, Co Durham

2a Charles; executed with his brother 1469

2 Ralph (Sir), of Oversley, Warwicks; *m* Mary (*b c* 1379), yr dau and co-heir of Robert de Ferrers (called to Parl 1375 as LORD (Baron) LE BOTILLER in right of his w Elizabeth, who according to later doctrine would have been Baroness Le Botiller in her own right, being dau and heir of 3rd Lord (Baron) Le Botiller of the March 1307/8 *cr*), and had:

(1) John; *m* Elizabeth, dau and heiress of Robert Newmarch, and had:

1a Joan; *m* Sir William Gascoigne and had issue

1 Mathilda or Maud; *m* before 6 Aug 1400 5th Lord (Baron) Mauley (*dspm* 6 Sept 1415; *see* DE MAULEY, B) and *d* Oct 1438

2 Philippa or Philippe; *m* 6th Lord (Baron) Dacre (*qv*) and *d* between 8 July 1453 and 5 Jan 1457/8

3 Alice; *m* 1st Sir Thomas Grey, of Heton, Co Durham (*see* GREY, E, and TANKERVILLE, E); *m* 2nd Sir Gilbert Lancaster

4 Elizabeth; nun in the Minories, London

5 Anne; *m* before 3 Feb 1412/3 Sir Gilbert de Umfreville, of Kyme, Lincs

6 Margaret; *m* 1st before 31 Dec 1413 3rd Lord (Baron) Scrope (of Bolton) (*d* 29 Aug 1420); *m* 2nd before 5 Nov 1427 William Cressoner, of Sudbury, Suffolk, and *d* between 4 March 1463/4 and 3 March 1464/5, leaving issue by her 1st husb

7 Anastasia

The 1st EARL OF WESTMORLAND *m* 2nd before 29 Nov 1396 Joan Beaufort (*d* 13 Nov 1440), dau of John of Gaunt and gdau of EDWARD III and widow of Sir Robert Ferrers, and *d* 21 Oct 1425, leaving further issue:

3 RICHARD NEVILL(E), 1st or 5th EARL OF SALISBURY, KG (1436/8), PC (437); *b* 1400; ktd 1420, Warden W March Scotland 1420–34, Warden E and W Marches 1434–35, Jt Keeper W March 1453, Keeper Forest beyond Trent 1424, Constable of England at HENRY VI's coronation 1429, Constable Pontefract Castle 1432, commr to negotiate peace with France in Hundred Years War 1436, Justice Forest Beyond Trent 1443, Govr Barnard Castle 1446, Chllr of England 1454, Keeper Porchester Castle 1454, leading Yorkist in early years of Wars of the Roses, fought at Battles of St Albans (Yorkist victory) 1455 and Blore Heath, Staffs, (Yorkist victory) 1459, attainted Nov 1459 and pardoned 7 Oct 1460, Ld Gt Chamberlain for life 29 Oct 1460; *m* before Feb 1420/1 Alice Montagu (*b c* 1406; *d* 1462), COUNTESS OF SALISBURY in her own right and only dau and heiress of 4th Earl of Salisbury of the March 1336/7 *cr* (who *d* 3 Nov 1428, whereupon his s-in-law RICHARD NEVILL(E) seems to have been acknowledged as EARL OF SALISBURY) by his 1st w, and was beheaded 31 Dec 1460 the day after the Battle of Wakefield (Lancastrian victory), having had issue:

(1) RICHARD NEVILL(E), 1st or 16th EARL OF WARWICK ('THE KING-MAKER') and 2nd or 6th EARL OF SALISBURY (in which latter title he *s* his mother 1462), also self-styled LORD (Baron) BERGAVENNY in right of his w, he being in *de facto* possession of the castle and honor (feudal territorial unit) of Abergavenny (for the significance of this *see* above against **Barony of (A)Bergavenny**), KG (1460), PC (before 6 Dec 1453); *b* 22 Nov 1428; ktd before 6 Aug 1445, Jt Warden Carlisle and W Marches towards Scotland 1446 and 1453, *s* in right of his wife (following her n Anne's death 3 Jan 1448/9) to the major part of the vast Warwick estates, including, as well as Abergavenny already mentioned, Barnard (Castle), Cardiff, Elmley, Neath, Warwick and Worcester Castles, also the feudal lordship of Glamorgan; confirmed 23 July 1449 as EARL OF WARWICK (E), with remainder to his w's heirs with the precedence of Premier Earl enjoyed by her ancestors as Earls of Warwick; he later exchanged the aforementioned patent of confirmation for *cr* 2 March 1449/50 as EARL OF WARWICK and (his wife Anne as) COUNTESS OF WARWICK, each for life, though with remainder after both their deaths to Anne's heirs of the body, with further remainder, should she have *dsp*, to Anne's est half-sis Margaret Countess of Shrewsbury (*see* SHREWSBURY and WATERFORD, E) and the heirs male of her body, failing which remainder to the heirs general of her body, failing which remainder to the heirs of her f the late Earl of Warwick; Hereditary Sheriff Worcs 1450–70, confirmed as Hereditary Chamberlain of Exchequer in right of his w 1450, Yorkist cdr at victoy of St Albans 1455, Capt Calais 1455, naval cdr in maritime actions against Spaniards and Hanseatic merchants (from the north German coast) 1458 and 1459, attainted with other Yorkist leaders 20 Nov 1459 but pardoned Oct 1460 after he led Yorkists to victory over Lancastrians at Battle of Northampton 10 July 1460 and obtained custody of HENRY VI, Govr Channel Islands 1460, Ld Gt Chamberlain Jan 1460/1and again May 1461 for life, cdr Yorkist army defeated by Lancastrians at 2nd Battle of St Albans Feb 1460/1, cdr central block Yorkist army at victory over Lancastrians of Towton March 1461, Constable Dover Castle and Ld Warden Cinque Ports 1461 for life, Warden E and W Marches towards Scotland July 1461, Ld High Steward England Dec 1461, Adml of England 1462; envoy to negotiate at various times with Brittany, Burgundy, France and Scotland; put down Lancastrian

rising in North under his relative Sir Humphrey Nevill(e) (*see* above) 1469; having switched support from EDWARD IV to HENRY VI early 1470 he proclaimed HENRY king Sept-Oct 1470; Jt Lt of the Realm Nov 1470, Adml England, Ireland and Aquitaine Jan 1470/1; *m* 1434 Anne Beauchamp (*b c* Sept 1426; *d c* 20 Sept 1492), sis and eventual heiress of 1st and last Duke of Warwick of the 1444 *cr*, and dau of 15th Earl of Warwick, and *dspm*, being *k* 14 April 1471 at Battle of Barnet, whereupon the earldom of Salisbury reverted to the Crown while the earldom of Warwick remained vested in his w according to the dual grant of 1450 (although a separate earldom of Warwick was conferred 1472 on her s-in-law by patent), leaving issue:

1a Isabel; *b* 5 Sept 1451; *m* 11 July 1469 GEORGE PLANTAGENET, DUKE OF CLARENCE, KG (*b* 21 Oct 1449; initially joined his f-in-law Warwick in the attempt to restore HENRY VI and depose his bro EDWARD IV but deserted the former for the latter at the Battle of Barnet and helped defeat Warwick; *cr* 25 March 1471/2 EARL OF WARWICK and EARL OF SALISBURY as a consequence of his marriage; found guilty of high treason and attainted 8 Feb 1477/8, whereupon all his titles were forfeited, and then executed by being drowned in a butt of malmsey wine in the Tower of London 18 Feb 1477/8), and *d* 22 Dec 1476, having had, with other issue (*d* young):

1b EDWARD PLANTAGENET (the last legitimate male Plantagenet), styled EARL OF WARWICK on EDWARD IV's orders from the time of his christening (EDWARD IV being his godfather as well as unc), *s* his maternal grandmother as 2nd/17th EARL OF WARWICK (of the 1450 dual grant and the original 1088 *cr*) by 20 Sept 1492; *b* 21 or 25 Feb 1474/5; imprisoned in the Tower of London by HENRY VII 1485, impersonated 1487 by Lambert Simnel; found guilty 21 Nov 1499 of high treason and *dsp*, being executed by beheading 28 Nov 1499, whereupon his honours were forfeited (they were also subject to posthumous attainder Jan 1503/4, this attainder being in its turn reversed 1513 so that his sis Margaret could have restored to her the title Countess of Salisbury)

1b MARGARET Plantagenet (the last Plantagenet to survive), declared by Parl COUNTESS OF SALISBURY in her own right 1513; *b* Aug 1473; Ldy of the Chamber to CATHERINE OF ARAGON 1509, Governess to PRINCESS MARY (later QUEEN MARY) 1520–33; *m* between 1491 and 1494 (probably 1491) Sir Richard POLE, KG, s of Sir Geoffrey Pole by Edith St John (*see* SAINT JOHN OF BLETSO, B), and was imprisoned in the Tower of London between 20 March and 20 May 1539, attainted 12 May 1539 (whereupon her honours were forfeited) and executed by beheading 28 May 1541, having had issue:

1c HENRY POLE, 1st and last LORD (Baron) MONTAGU of the putative 1514 *cr*, JP (Dorset, Hants, Somerset and Sussex 1530–38); *b c* 1492; ktd 1513, from 12 Oct 1514, or just before it, was called (which by something like a consensus among modern historians is taken to constitute a new *cr*) LORD (Baron) MONTAGU (E), Steward of manors belonging to Tewkesbury Abbey 1526; *m* by May 1520 his maternal grandmother's 2nd cousin Jane Nevill(e), dau of 4th Lord (Baron) Bergavenny (*see* below), and, after being imprisoned in the Tower of London 4 Nov 1538, attainted (whereupon all his honours were forfeited) and declared guilty of treason 2 Dec 1538 and was executed by beheading 9 Jan 1538/9, having had issue:

1d Henry; imprisoned in the Tower from an early age and *dsp* there some time after Sept 1542

1d Catherine; restored in blood (*i.e.*, her f's attainder reversed as regards ability to inherit honours) by the Parl of 1554–55; *m* 25 June 1532 2nd Earl of Huntingdon (*qv*; *see* also LOUDOUN, E) and *d* 23 Sept 1576, having had issue

2d Winifred; *m* 1st Sir Thomas Hastings (*dsp*), yr bro of her sister's husb; *m* 2nd, as his 2nd w, Sir Thomas Barrington, of Barrington Hall, Essex, and had issue, with another s and a dau:

1e Sir FRANCIS BARRINGTON, 1st Bt, so *cr* 29 June 1611 (*see* SIMEON, Bt)

2c Geoffrey (Sir); *b* 1502(?); ktd 1529; *m* by 9 July 1528 Constance (*d* on or after 12 Aug 1570), er dau and coheir of Sir Edmund Pakenham (*see* LONGFORD, E), of Lordington, Sussex; imprisoned in the Tower 29 Aug 1538, pleaded guilty at his trial for treason 4 Dec 1538 but pardoned 4 Jan 1538/9, fled abroad 1541 following his mother's execution and only returned to England after MARY came to the throne 1553; *d* Nov 1558 (a few days before his bro the Cardinal), having had issue, with three other s (one of whom was called Thomas) and six daus (two of whom *m* and one of whom was a nun):

1d Arthur; *b* 1531; conspired, sometimes with his yr bro Edmund, to advance his own or MARY QUEEN OF SCOTS' claims to the throne of England; arrested with Edmund Oct 1562, found guilty, again with Edmund, of treason 26 Feb 1562/3 and imprisoned in the Tower of London; *d* there between Jan and 12 Aug 1570(?), having *m* between 15 Sept 1562 and 27 Jan 1563 Mary (*d* by 16 Nov 1570), dau of Sir Richard Holland, of Denton, Lancs, by his w Eleanor (whose 1st husb had been the 1st Earl of Northumberland of the 1557 *cr* (*see* NORTHUMBERLAND, D))

2d Thomas, of W Stoke and Lordington, Sussex; *m* Mary (*m* 3rd Francis Cotton and was *bur* 27 March 1576), widow of John Lewes, and *d* between 12 Aug and 22 Nov 1570

3d Edmund; *b* 1541; *d* imprisoned in the Tower of London by 12 Aug 1570

4d Geoffrey, of Lordington; *b* 1546; *educ* Winchester; *m* by 1573 Catherine Dutton (*d* in or after 1608) and *d* Antwerp by 9 March 1590/1, leaving issue, with five daus (two of whom *m* but only one of whom had issue, while another was a nun):

1e Arthur; *b c* 1575; *educ* Rome at Palazzo Farnese with the s of Alessandro Farnese Duke of Parma (*see* above); Ld of the Manor of Walderton, Sussex, and memb household Cardinal Odoardo Farnese; *d* unm, being assassinated Rome 23 June 1605

2e Geoffrey, of Lordington; *b c* 1577; *educ* seminaries at Douai and Eu and English Coll Rome; *d* unm, being assassinated Rome just before 7 Jan 1619, when the male line descendants of Margaret Countess of Salisbury became *extinct*

5d Henry POLE; living 1570

3c Arthur (Sir); Ld of the Manor of Broadhurst, Sussex, Gent of Bedchamber to HENRY VIII 1518 and Esq of the Body 1520, ktd 1523; *m* by 24 Oct 1522 Jane/Joan (*m* 3rd Sir William Barentyne, of Gt Haseley, Oxon, and *d* by 12 March 1562/3), dau of Sir Roger Lewkenor, of Trotton, Sussex, and widow of Sir Christopher Pickering, and *d* just after 10 May 1527, having had a s (*dvp* unm) and two daus (both of whom *m*)

4c Reginald; *b* March 1500; *educ* the Charterhouse, Sheen, and Magdalen Coll Oxford (BA 1515); Dean Wimborne Minster, Preb Salisbury, Dean Exeter 1527, Vicar Piddletown, Dorset, 1532–35, Cardinal Dec 1536, Papal Legate to England Feb 1536/7 and again 1553–57, attainted *in absentia* 1539 (attainder reversed 1554), appointed by POPE PAUL III Abbot of Gavello or Canalnuovo 1549, Archbp Canterbury 1555, ordained priest 20 March 1555/6, Chllr Cambridge and Oxford Us 1555/6 and 1556 respectively; *dsp* 17 Nov 1558

1c Ursula; *m* 16(?) Feb 1518/9 1st Baron Stafford of the 1547 *cr* and *d* 12 Aug 1570, having had issue at least 13 children (*see* STAFFORD, B)

2a Anne; *b* 11 June 1456; *m*(?) 1st(? There has been some doubt as to whether the marriage took place) Aug 1470 EDWARD PRINCE OF WALES (*dsp* & *vp*, being *k* at or in cold blood just after the Battle of Tewkesbury (Yorkist victory) 4 May 1471), only s of HENRY VI; *m* 2nd(?) 12 July 1472 RICHARD PLANTAGENET, DUKE OF GLOUCESTER, proclaimed king as RICHARD III 26 June 1483 (*b* 2 Oct 1452; crowned with Anne 6 July 1483; defeated by HENRY VII and *k* Battle of Bosworth (the last engagement of the Wars of the Roses) 22 Aug 1485), and *d* 16 March 1485, having had issue:

1b EDWARD PLANTAGENET, PRINCE OF WALES; *dvp* 9 April 1484

(2) Thomas (Sir); ktd 1449; *m* Aug 1453 Maud (she *m* 3rd by 20 March 1462/3 Sir Gervase Clifton and *dsp* 30 Aug 1497), er dau of Sir Richard Stanhope (*see* HARRINGTON, E, also 1967 edn, CHESTERFIELD and STANHOPE, E) and widow of 6th Lord (Baron) Willoughby de Eresby (*qv*), and was *k* 30 Dec 1460 Battle of Wakefield

(3) John NEVILL(E), 1st MARQUESS OF MONTAGU, KG (1460), PC (Jan 1460/1), JP (Co Durham 1463 and many other counties both before and after); *b c* 1431; ktd 1449, took part in Yorkist victory of Blore Heath 1459 but was nevertheless captured by the Lancastrians, attainted 20 Nov 1459, attainder reversed and he freed following Yorkist victory of Northampton 10 July 1460, Chamberlain to HENRY VI late 1460, again captured by Lancastrians 2nd Battle of St Albans 17 Feb 1460/1, called to Parl by writ 23 May 1461 as LORD (Baron) MONTAGU (E), Ch Steward bishopric of Durham 1463, Warden E March 1463–July 1470 and Oct 1470–71, defeated Lancastrians at Hedgeley Moor, Northumberland, 25 April 1464 (this victory allowed him to make a truce with the Scots for 15 years which denied Lancastrians a refuge north of the Border) and at Hexham 15 May 1464 (the final destruction of Lancastrians in the North at that stage of the Wars of the Roses), *cr* as a reward 27 May 1464 EARL OF NORTHUMBERLAND (E) but forced to renounce this 25 March 1470 when Henry Percy (whose family both before and after customarily held the earldom of Northumberland; *see* NORTHUMBERLAND, D) swore fealty to EDWARD IV and was *cr* 25 March 1470 MARQUESS OF MONTAGU (E) in compensation (though without an estate for the title's support, which with such matters as his being relieved of the wardenship of the eastern March so irked him that he conspired with his bro Warwick and others to restore HENRY VI), Sheriff Northumberland 1466, Lt in the North 1470; *m* 25 April 1457 Elizabeth or Isabel (she *m* 2nd 25 April 1472 Sir William Norreys and *d* 20 May 1476), dau and coheir of Sir Edmund Ingaldesthorpe by Joan Tiptoft (*d* 20 May 1476), sis and eventual heiress of 1st Earl of Worcester of the 1449 *cr*, and was *k* 14 April 1471 at the Battle of Barnet, having had issue:

1a GEORGE NEVIL(E), 2nd and last MARQUESS OF MONTAGU and 1st and last DUKE OF BEDFORD of the Jan 1469/70 *cr*; *b c* 1461; *cr* 5 Jan 1469/70 DUKE OF BEDFORD (E) because about to *m* Elizabeth, est dau of EDWARD IV, but deprived of all his peerages (*viz.*, the Dukedom of Bedford, Marquessate of Montagu and Barony of Montagu) by Parl March 1477/8 on the grounds that he lacked the means to support those dignities (whereupon they became *extinct*); *d* unm 4 May 1483

1a Anne; *m* Sir William Stonor (*see* CAMOYS, B) and *d* by 1486, having had issue

2a Elizabeth; *b c* 1464; *m* 1st before 1477 6th Lord (Baron) Scrope (of Masham) (*b c* 1459; *dspm* 23 April 1493) and had issue a dau; *m* 2nd *c* Oct 1494, as his 2nd w, Sir Henry Wentworth and *dsps* Sept 1517

3a Margaret; *b* 1466; *m* 1st(?) Thomas Horne; *m* 1st/2nd Sir John Mortimer (ld by 12 Nov 1504); *m* 2nd/3rd by 7 Feb 1506/7 (*annulled* by London Archidiaconal Court *c* 1507 and by Papal Bull 12 May 1528), as his 2nd w of some four, 1st Duke of Suffolk of the Feb 1513/4 *cr*; *m* 3rd/4th *c* Feb 1521/2 Robert Downes and *d* 31 Jan 1527/8

4a Lucy; *m* 1st Sir Thomas Fitzwilliam and had, with other issue:

1b Thomas; *m* and was *k* Battle of Flodden (English victory over Scots) 1513, leaving issue (with a s who *d* young):

1c Alice; *m* as his 1st w Sir James Foljambe and had issue (*see* LIVERPOOL, E)

2c Margaret; *m* Godfrey Foljambe

2b WILLIAM FITZWILLIAM, 1st and last EARL OF SOUTHAMPTON (E) so *cr* 18 Oct 1537, KG (1526), PC (by April 1522); *b c* 1490; Gent Usher at HENRY VII's funeral 1509, Cupbearer to HENRY VIII 1509, Esq of the Body 1513, Kt of the Body, Master of the Harriers Feb 1512/3, V-Adml of England 1520 and 1522–23, Amb to France Feb 1520/1–Jan 1521/2, Treasurer Household 1525–37, MP Surrey 1529–36, Chllr Duchy Lancaster 1529–42, High Steward Oxford U 1532–42, High Adml England 1536–40, Ch Steward of his 2nd cousin Margaret Countess of Salisbury's possessions after her attainder 1539, Ld Privy Seal 1540–42, Lt and Capt Gen towards the N 1542; *m* Nov 1513 Mabel Clifford (Gentlewoman to CATHERINE OF ARAGON; *d* 1550), sis of 1st Earl of Cumberland (*see* DE CLIFFORD, B) and *dspl* 15 Oct 1542, whereupon the Earldom expired

4a (cont.) Lady Fitzwilliam *m* 2nd Sir Anthony Browne, Standard-Bearer of England, gf by her of 1st Viscount Montagu of the 1554 *cr*

5a Isabella; *m* Sir William Hodleston, 3rd s of Sir John Hodleston, Ld of Millom, Cumberland

(4) George; *b* 1432 or 1433; *educ* Balliol Coll Oxford(?) (BA 1450, MA 1452); Preb York 1446, Chllr Oxford U 1453–57, Archdeacon Northampton, Preb Lincoln and canon and Preb Ripon 1454, ordained 21 Dec 1454, Bp Exeter 1458, Archdeacon Carlisle by May 1463, Ld Chllr 1460–67 and 1470, Archbp York 1464, Abbot Westminster 1475; *d* 8 June 1476

(1) Joan; *m* after 17 Aug 1438 16th/9th Earl of Arundel (*see* NORFOLK, D) and *d* just before 9 Sept 1462, having had issue

(2) Cicely; Sheriff Worcs 1449; *m* 1434 (the same year her bro 'the King-maker' *m* Beauchamp's sis Anne; *see* above) Henry de Beauchamp, 14th Earl and subsequently 1st and last Duke of Warwick of the 1444 *cr* (*dspm* 11 June 1446) and had issue a dau; *m* 2nd *c* 3 April 1449 1st and last Earl of Worcester of the 1449 *cr* and *d* 28 July 1450

(3) Alice; *m* 5th Lord (Baron) Fitzhugh of the 1321 *cr* and *d* on or after 22 Nov 1503, having had issue (*see* DACRE, B)

(4) Eleanor; *m* after 10 May 1457, as his 1st w, 1st Earl of Derby (*qv*) and *d* by Nov 1482, having had issue

(5) Katherine; *m* 1st by 1458 William Bonville, 6th Lord (Baron) Harington of the 1326 *cr* (*dspm*, being *k* Battle of Wakefield 31 Dec 1460) and had issue a dau and heir (*m* 1st and last Earl of Wiltshire of the Jan 1509/10 *cr*; *see* STAFFORD, B); *m* 2nd by 6 Feb 1461/2 1st Lord (Baron) Hastings (of Hastings) (*see* HUNTINGDON, E) and *d* just before 22 Nov 1503, having had further issue

(6) Margaret; *m* as his 1st w 13th Earl of Oxford (*see* SAINT ALBANS, D) and *d* after 20 Nov 1506

4 Henry; *dsp* young

5 Thomas; *dsp* young

6 Cuthbert; *dsp* young

7 Robert; *b* 1404; *educ* Oxford (MA); Preb: Eldon Co Durham 1413, Grindall 1414, Laughton (York) 1416 and Lincoln 1423, Provost Beverley *c* 1421, Bp: Salisbury 1427 and Durham 1438; *dspl*(?) 8 or 9 July 1457

8 WILLIAM NEVILL(E), 1st and last EARL OF KENT (E), so *cr* 1 Nov 1461, KG (1440); ktd 1426, called to Parl by writ of summons 3 Aug 1429 as Sir WILLIAM NEVILL(E) and 26 May 1455 in right of his w as LORD (Baron) FAUCOMBERGE or FAUCONBERGE (E), Capt-Gen in the Marches of the Chartrain (France) 1439, Keeper Roxburgh Castle 1444 (Jt Keeper 1451/2), Jt Keeper Windsor Castle 1455–58, led the advance detachment of the Yorkist army Battles of Northampton 10 July 1460 and Towton 29 March 1461, Adml of England 1462; *m* by 28 April 1422, as her 1st husb, Joan, according to later doctrine BARONESS FAUCOMBERGE in her own right, and *dspml* 9 Jan 1462/3, when the Earldom of Kent expired, having had three daus (*see* YARBOROUGH, E) and an illegitimate s (together with others):

(1) Thomas FAUCONBRIDGE, alias the 'Bastard of Fauconberg'; irregular naval cdr, ally of his cousin Warwick the 'Kingmaker' in the shifting alliances fashioned by the latter throughout the Wars of the Roses, descended on London May 1471 in an unsuccessful bid to restore HENRY VI; beheaded 22 Sept 1471

9 John; *dsp* young

10 GEORGE NEVILL(E), 1st (?) LORD (Baron) LATIMER/LATYMER (E), so *cr* 25 Feb 1431/2, PC (1439), JP (Cumberland 1437); ktd 1426, *s* 1430 to his paternal half-unc JOHN NEVILL(E) 6th LORD (Baron) LATIMER (of Corby)'s estates (*see* above); *m c* Feb 1436/7, as her 1st husb, Lady Elizabeth Beauchamp (*b c* 1417; *m* 2nd, as his 2nd w, Thomas Wake (*see* WAKE, Bt) and *d* by 2 Oct 1480), dau of 13th Earl of Warwick, and *d* 30 or 31 Dec 1469, having had issue (*see* LATYMER, B)

11 EDWARD NEVILL(E), **1st Lord** (Baron) **Bergavenny**, for whom *see* further below

8 Joan; nun Minories, London

9 Katharine or Katherine; *m* 1st 2nd Duke of Norfolk of the 1397 *cr* (*see* MOWBRAY, SEGRAVE and STOURTON, B); *m* 2nd before 27 Jan 1441/2 Sir Thomas Strangways; *m* 3rd after 1442, as his 2nd w, 1st Viscount Beaumont (*see* BEAUMONT, Bt); *m* 4th just after 1464 Sir John Woodville, bro of ELIZABETH, QUEEN CONSORT of EDWARD IV

10 Alianore/Eleanor; *m* 1st after 23 May 1412 Richard le Despenser (*dsp* 7 Oct 1414 aged 14), only s of 1st and last Earl of Gloucester of the 1397 *cr* (*see* FALMOUTH, V) by his w Constance, dau of Edmund Plantagenet, Duke of York, 5th s of EDWARD III; *m* 2nd a short while after Oct 1414 1st Earl of Northumberland of the 1415/6 *cr* (*see* NORTHUMBERLAND, D), and had issue

11 Anne; *m* 1st by 18 Oct 1424 1st Duke of Buckingham of the 1444 *cr* (*ka* 10 July 1460) and had issue (*see* STAFFORD, B); *m* 2nd by 25 Nov 1467, as his 2nd w, 1st Lord (Baron) Mountjoy (*d* 1 Aug 1474; *see* BLOUNT, Bt) and *d* 20 Sept 1480, having had no issue by her 2nd husb

12 Cecily; *b* 3 May 1415; *m* by 18 Oct 1424 Richard Plantagenet, 3rd Duke of York, KG (*k* 30 Dec 1460 at the Battle of Wakefield), gs of Edmund of Langley, 1st Duke of York of the 1385 *cr* and 5th s of EDWARD III, and *d* 31 May 1495, having had, with other issue (*see* 1967 edn THE ROYAL LINEAGE):

(1) EDWARD IV

(2) GEORGE PLANTAGENET, DUKE OF CLARENCE; *m* Isabel Nevill(e), dau of 1st or 16th Earl of Warwick (the 'Kingmaker'; *see* above)

(3) RICHARD III

The 1st EARL OF WESTMORLAND's yst s,

EDWARD NEVILL(E), **1st Lord** (Baron) **Bergavenny** or **Neville de Bergavenny (E)**, so *cr* by writ of summons 5 Sept 1450 ; granted licence by HENRY VI to take possession of the lands of Abergavenny but in possession of the castle at Abergavenny for only a short while; *m* 1st by 18 Oct 1424 Elizabeth Beauchamp, according to later doctrine BARONESS BERGAVENNY or BEAUCHAMP DE BERGAVENNY in her own right (*see* above), and had:

1 Richard; *dvp*

2 GEORGE, **2nd Lord**

1 Alice; *m* Sir Thomas Grey

2 Catherine; *m* — Iwarby

The **1st Lord** (Baron) **Bergavenny** *m* 2nd 15 Oct 1448 his 3rd cousin Catherine, dau of Sir Robert Howard and sis of 1st Duke of Norfolk (*qv*), and *d* 18 Oct 1476, having had further issue:

3 Margaret; *m* as his 2nd w 7th Lord (Baron) Cobham of the Jan 1312/3 *cr* (*see* 1949 edn) and *d* 30 Sept 1506, having had issue

4 Catherine; *m* Robert Tanfield

5 Anne; (?)*m* as his 2nd w 8th Lord (Baron) Strange (of Knokyn) and *d* on or after 26 Feb 1480/1 (*see* SAINT DAVIDS, V)

The 1st LORD (Baron) BERGAVENNY's est surv s,

GEORGE NEVILL(E), **2nd Lord** (Baron) **Bergavenny**; *b c* 1440; ktd 1471; *m* 1st before 1469 Margaret (*d* 28 Sept 1485), dau and heir of Sir Hugh Fenne, Under-Treasurer of England, of Soulton Burdeleys, Norfolk (a manor held by Grand Serjeanty, *i.e.*, in exchange for personal service, as Chief Larderer to the sovereign, a duty that was undertaken by the Lord (A)Bergavenny of the day or his deputy at every coronation from JAMES II's to GEORGE IV's inclusive as well as various coronations before that), and Braintree, Essex, Treasurer Household to HENRY VI; *m* 2nd, as her 4th husb, Elizabeth (*d* 1500), widow of (a) Sir Robert Bassett, Ld Mayor London, (b) Richard Naylor (*d c* 1483) and (c) John Stokker, both the latter being Londoners also, and *d* 20 Sept 1492, having had issue by his 1st w:

1 GEORGE NEVILL(E), **3rd Lord** (Baron) **Bergavenny**, KG (1513), KB (1483), PC (1516); *b c* 1469; Constable Dover Castle, Ld Warden Cinque Ports 1513, Keeper Ashdown Forest 1515, imprisoned 1521–22 on suspicion of conspiring with his f-in-law the Duke of Buckingham, Ch Larderer coronations of HENRY VIII and ANNE BOLEYN 1509 and 1533 respectively; *m* 1st Lady Joan FitzAlan (*dspm*), dau of 17th/10th Earl of Arundel (*see* NORFOLK, D), and had issue:

(1) Elizabeth; *m* as his 1st w 1st and last Earl of Bridgwater of the 1538 *cr*

1 (cont.) The **3rd Lord** (Baron) **Bergavenny** *m* 2nd Margaret (*dsps* in or after 1515), dau of William Brent, of Charing, Kent; *m* 3rd *c* June 1519 Lady Mary Stafford, dau of 3rd and last Duke of Buckingham of the 1444 *cr*; *m* 4th Mary Bro(o)ke alias Cobham, and *d* June 1535, having by his 3rd w had further issue:

(1) HENRY NEVILL(E), **4th Lord** (Baron) **Bergavenny**, KB (1553); *b* after 1527; one of the 26 peers who signed the letters patent 16 June 1553 settling the crown on LADY JANE GREY, Ch Larderer coronation of QUEEN MARY 1553; *m* 1st by 31 Jan 1555/6 Lady Frances Manners (*bur* Sept 1576), dau of 1st Earl of Rutland (*see* RUTLAND, D); *m* 2nd Elizabeth (*m* 2nd Sir William Sedley, 1st Bt, of Southfleet, Kent, and *d* 27 Feb 1618, by whom she was ggmother of Catherine Sedley, Countess of Dorchester, mistress of JAMES II), dau and coheir of Stephen Darrell, of Spelmonden, Horsmonden, Kent, and *dspm* 10 Feb 1586/7, leaving by his 1st w an only dau:

1a MARY Nevill(e), BARONESS LE DESPENSER; *b* 25 March 1554; *s* her f in the Mereworth estate in Kent and the Althorne estate, Essex, by agreement with her cousin Edward, the 6th Baron Abergavenny, though a previous entail had been drawn up by her gf the 3rd Baron Abergavenny by which his lands were to go to heirs male of his body; she claimed the barony of Bergavenny as heir general of her f against the claim of her cousin Edward (subsequently recognised as 6th Baron Abergavenny), who was only the heir male; the crown eventually (1604) awarded the barony of Bergavenny to Edward and in compensation terminated the abeyance in the barony of Le Despenser in her favour 25 May 1604 with precedence of 1264; *m* 12 Dec 1574, as his 2nd w, Sir Thomas FANE, of Badsell, Kent (*d* 13 March 1588/9), and *d* 28 June 1626, having had issue (*see* WESTMORLAND, E, and FALMOUTH, V)

(2) John; *d* young

(3) Thomas; *dsp*

(1) Catherine; *m* John St Leger, of Annersley, Devon; and had issue (*see* STUCLEY, Bt)

(2) Margaret; *m* John Cheney, s of Sir Thomas Cheney

(3) Dorothy; *m* as his 1st w her cousin 10th Lord (Baron) Cobham and *dspm* 22 Sept 1559

(4) Joan; *m* Sir Henry Pole

(5) Ursula; *m* Sir Wenham St Leger and *d* 1575, leaving issue (*see* DONERAILE, V)

(6) Mary; *m* 1st 1536 9th Lord (Baron) Dacre (*qv*) and had issue; *m* 2nd — Wootton, of N Tuddenham, Norfolk; *m* 3rd Francis Thursby and *d c* 1576

2 William NEVILL(E)

3 Edward (Sir), of Addington or Aldington Park, Kent; Sewer (official overseeing service at table) HENRY VIII's household, Esq of the Body, ktd 25 Sept 1513, Gentleman of the Chamber and Master Buckhounds 1516, HENRY VIII's Standard Bearer 1531, Constable Leeds Castle, Kent, 1534; *m* Eleanor, dau of 1st Lord (Baron) Windsor (*see* PLYMOUTH, E), and widow of 9th Lord (Baron) Scrope of Masham of the 1350 *cr*, and was beheaded 8 Dec 1538 on a charge of high treason (specifically for promoting the interests of his cousin Reginald Pole (Isee above)), having had issue:

(1) EDWARD NEVILL(E), **5th Lord**

(2) Henry (Sir), of Billingbear or Billingbere, nr Waltham St Lawrence, Berks; *m* Elizabeth, dau and heir of Sir John Gresham, and *d* 1593, having had issue:

1a Henry (Sir), of Billingbere; *b c* 1564; *educ* Merton Coll Oxford (MA 1605); MP New Windsor 1584–85 and 1593, Sussex 1588–89, Liskeard 1597–98, Kent 1601, Lewes 1603–04 and Berks 1604–11 and 1614, ironfounder in Sussex, Amb to France 1599, ktd 1599, implicated in Essex's Rising (*see* ESSEX, E, preliminary remarks) and consequently imprisoned in Tower of London 1600; *m* Anne, dau of Sir Henry Killigrew, and *d* 10 July 1615, leaving issue:

1b Henry (Sir), of Billingbere; *m* Elizabeth (she *m* 2nd Sir John Thoroughgood, of Clerkenwell, London), dau of Sir John Smith, of Ostenhanger, Kent, and *d* 29 June 1629, leaving issue:

1c Richard, JP and DL (Berks), of Billingbere; *b c* 1617; Gentleman of Privy Chamber to CHARLES I and Col royalist army in Civil War; *m* Anne, est dau of Sir John Heydon, of Baconthorpe, Norfolk, and *d* 1676, having had issue:

1d John, of Billingbere; *b* 23 July 1652; *dsp* Dec 1678

2d Richard, of Billingbere; *b* 12 Oct 1655; MP Berks; *m* Katherine, dau of 2nd Baron Grey of Warke of the Feb 1623/4 *cr*, and *d* 1717, leaving issue:

1e Grey; *b* 23 Sept 1681; MP Abingdon 1705, Wallingford 1708 and Berwick-on-Tweed 1715 and 1722; *m* Elizabeth (ld 16 Nov 1740), dau of Sir John Boteler, of Woodhall, and *d* 24 April 1723, having had a dau (*d* young)

2e Henry NEVILL(E) later GREY, of Billingbere; *b* 17 Aug 1683; took the name GREY instead of NEVILL(E), MP Wendover 1709; *m* Elizabeth (she *m* 2nd 1st Earl of Portsmouth (*qv*) and *dsp* July 1762), est dau of 2nd Baron Griffin of Braybrooke, and *dsp* 1740

1d Anne; *b* 14 Feb 1647; *m* Richard Raynsford of Dallington, Northants (*see* BRAYBROOKE, B)

2d Mirabell; *b* 16 Nov 1650

3d Elizabeth; *b* 6 May 1657

4d Catherine; *b* 23 June 1659; *m* Richard Aldworth, of Stanlake, Berks (*d* 1738), and *d* 1720, leaving issue:

1e Richard Neville ALDWORTH later NEVILLE; *b* 3 Sept 1717; *educ* Eton and Merton Coll Oxford; MP (Whig) Reading 1747, Wallingford 1754–61, Tavistock 1761–74, Under-Sec of State Southern Dept 1748–51, Jt Sec Cncl of Regency 1748 and 1750, Sec to Br Embassy Paris 1762, took name and arms of NEVILL(E) instead of ALDWORTH Aug 1762 on succeeding to the Billingbear estate following death of his aunt Countess of Portsmouth (*see* above); *m* Magdalen, dau of Francis Calendrini, First Syndic (magistrate or mayor) of Geneva, and *d* 17 July 1793, leaving issue:

1f RICHARD ALDWORTH later NEVILLE later still GRIFFIN, 2nd BARON BRAYBROOKE (*qv*)

1f Frances; *m* Francis Jalabert

5d Frances; *b* 19 May 1664; *m c* 1688, as his 1st w, Sir Richard Cocks, 2nd Bt (*see* SOMERS, B)

2c Henry; *b* 1620; *educ* Merton and Univ Colls Oxford; Parliamentarian in Civil War, memb CROMWELL's Cncl of State 1651 but banished from London by CROMWELL for extreme republicanism 1654, MP Reading 1658, imprisoned in Tower of London for allegedly conspiring to foment a rising in Yorks 1663, author of political squibs, travel fantasies, a Platonic dialogue which impressed Thomas Hobbes and translations of Macchiavelli's works; *m* Elizabeth, only child of Richard Staverton, of Heathly Hall, Warfield, Berks, and *d* 1694

1c Katherine; *m* Sir Thomas Lumsford, of Wilye, Sussex, Lt Tower of London

2c Mary; *m* — *Borell*

3c Philippa; *m* — *Jepson*

2b William; Fell Merton Coll Oxford

3b Charles; *d* 1626

4b Richard; LLD, Sub-Warden Merton Coll Oxford

5b Edward; Fell King's Coll Cambridge; *dsp* 1632

1b Elizabeth; *m* 1st William Glover; *m* 2nd Sir Henry Berkeley, of Yardington, Somerset; *m* 3rd Thomas Dyke

2b Frances; *m c* 1610 Sir Richard Worsley, 1st Bt, of Appuldercombe, IoW, of the 1611 *cr*, and left issue; *m* 2nd Jerome Brett and *d* between 18 Oct 1659 and 27 May 1661

3b Katherine; *m* Sir Richard Brooke(s), of Norton, Cheshire

4b Mary; *m* Sir Edward Lewknor, of Denham Hall, Suffolk

5b Dorothy; *m* Richard Cat(e)lyn, of Wingfield Castle, Suffolk

(1) Catherine; *m* Clement Throgmorton, of Hasley, Warwicks

(2) Frances; *m* 1st Sir Edward Waldegrave, of Borley, Essex (*see* WALDEGRAVE, E) and had issue; *m* 2nd Lord Chidiock Paulet, 2nd s of 1st Marquess of Winchester (*qv*)

(3) Elizabeth; *m* Thomas Eymes, of Yorks

(4) Mary; *m* Henry Dineley, of Charlton, Worcs

4 Thomas (Sir), PC, JP (Kent, Middx, Surrey, Sussex and Worcs), of Mereworth, Kent; *b c* 1480; Sheriff Staffs 1510 and 1515, MP Kent, Sec of State to HENRY VIII, Speaker H of C 1514, Memb Star Chamber 1519, Steward Westminster Abbey 1532; *m* 1st Catherine (*d* 20 Aug 1527), dau of 1st Lord Dacre of Gilsland (*see* DACRE, B) and widow of 8th Lord (Baron) FitHugh, and had issue:

(1) Margaret; *m* 1 May 1536 Sir Robert Southwell, Master of the Rolls

4 (cont.) Sir Thomas Nevill(e) *m* 2nd 28 Aug 1532 Elizabeth, widow of Robert Amadas, goldsmith, of London, and *d* 29 May 1542

5 Richard; Kt of Rhodes; living 1515

1 Jane; *m* by May 1520 her cousin 1st and last Lord (Baron) Montagu of the putative 1514 *cr* (*see* above) and *d* before 26 Oct 1538, leaving issue

2 Elizabeth; *m* Sir Edward Berkeley

The 4th LORD (Baron) BERGAVENNY's 1st cousin,

EDWARD NEVILL(E), **5th Lord** (Baron) **Bergavenny**, of Newton St Loe, Somerset; *m* 1st before 1550 Katharine (Maid of Honour to QUEEN MARY), dau of Sir John Brome, of Halton, Oxon; *m* 2nd Grisold (she *m* 2nd *c* 1589 4th Earl of Cumberland (*see* DE CLIFFORD, B) and *dsp* 15 June 1613), dau of Thomas Hughes, of Uxbridge, and *d* 10 Feb 1588/9, having had issue by his 1st w:

1 EDWARD NEVILL(E), **6th Lord** (Baron) **Bergavenny**, for whom *see* further below

2 Francis, of Chichester, Sussex; *m* Mary, dau and heir of Thomas Lewkenor, of Selsey, Sussex

3 George; *dsp*

4 Henry, of Bathwick, Somerset; *m* Eleanor, dau of Edward Poole, and had issue:

(1) Edward; *dsp* 1622

(2) Henry; *b c* 1604

(3) Thomas; *b c* 1606

(4) William; *b c* 1610

(5) George; *b c* 1612

(1) Catherine; *b c* 1603

(2) Frances; *b c* 1605

1 Margaret; *m* Sir Nicholas Lewkenor

2 Grisel; *m* Sir Henry Poole

3 Mary; *m* Edward Blount, of Kidderminster, Worcs

The 5th LORD (Baron) BERGAVENNY's est s,

EDWARD NEVILL(E), **6th Lord** (Baron) **Bergavenny**; *b c* 1550; MP Windsor 1588–89 and 1593; claimed 1598 the barony of Bergavenny, claim conceded 25 May 1604; *m* Rachel (*bur* 15 Oct 1616), 3rd dau of John Lennard, of Knole, nr Chevening, Kent, and *d* 1 Dec 1622, having had issue:

1 HENRY NEVILL(E), **7th Lord** (Baron) **Bergavenny**; *b* by 1580; *educ* Cambridge and Oxford (MA); *m* 1st by 1601 Lady Mary Sackville, dau of 1st Earl of Dorset (*see* SACKVILLE, B), and had issue:

(1) Thomas (Sir), KB; *m* Frances (*m* 2nd Sir Basil Brooke, of Madeley, Salop) dau of 4th Lord (Baron) Mordaunt (*see* MORDAUNT, Bt), and *dvp* and was *bur* 7 May 1628, having had issue:

1a Henry; *d* 1639

2a Charles; *d* 1637

1a Margaret; *m* Thomas Brooke, of Madeley, Salop, and left issue

(1) Cecily; *m* FitzWilliam Coningsby, of Hampton Court, Herefs

(2) Anne; Abbess Pontoise, France

(3) Elizabeth; *d* unm

(4) Mary; *d* unm

1 (cont.) The **7th Lord** (Baron) **Bergavenny** *m* 2nd by 1616 Catharine (*bur* 10 July 1649), yst dau of George Vaux and sis of 4th Lord (Baron) Vaux of Harrowden (*qv*), and was *bur* 24 Dec 1641, leaving further issue:

(2) JOHN NEVILL(E), **8th Lord** (Baron) **(A)Bergavenny**; *b c* 1614; *m* Elizabeth, dau and coheir of John Chamberlaine, of Sherborne Castle, Oxon, and *dsp* 23 Oct 1662

(3) GEORGE NEVILL(E), **9th Lord** (Baron) **(A)Bergavenny**; *m* Mary (*m* 2nd, as his 2nd w, Sir Charles Shelley, 2nd Bt, (*qv*), and was *bur* 14 Nov 1699), sis of Sir Henry Gifford, Bt, of Burstall, Leics, of the 1660 *cr*, and *d* 2 June 1666, having had issue:

1a GEORGE NEVILL(E), **10th Lord** (Baron) **(A)Bergavenny**; *b* 21 April 1665; *m* Honora (*d* 1 Jan 1706/7), dau of 1st Baron Belasyse of Worlaby of the 1644 *cr*, and *dsp* 26 March 1694/5

1a Mary, Bridget or Winifred; *m* Sir John Shelley, 3rd Bt, (*qv*), and had issue

(5) Frances; *d* unm

(6) Catherine; *m* 1st Sir Robert Howard, yr s of 2nd Earl of Suffolk (*see* SUFFOLK and BERKSHIRE, E); *m* 2nd Robert Berry, of Ludlow, Salop

(7) Elizabeth; *m* 1651Thomas Stonor (*d* 1683; *see* CAMOYS, B)

2 Edward; *d* unm

3 Christopher (Sir), of Newton St Loe, KB; *m* Mary, dau and coheir of Thomas Darcy, of Tolleshunt Darcy, Essex, and *d* 1649, having had issue:

(1) Richard, of Newton St Loe; *m* Sophia, dau of Sir George Carew, and *d* 1643, having had issue:

1a George, of Sheffield, Sussex; *m* Mary, dau of Sir Bulstrode Whitelocke, and had issue:

1b GEORGE NEVILL(E), **11th Lord** (Baron) **(A)Bergavenny**; *b c* 1659; Gent of the Bedchamber to GEORGE, PRINCE OF DENMARK (husb of QUEEN ANNE); *m* 22 Oct 1698 Anne (*m* 2nd 15 June 1744 1st Earl De La Warr (*qv*) and *d* 26 June 1748), dau of Nehemiah Walker, sea captain, and *d* 11 March 1720/1, having had issue:

1c Henry; *d* aged 7, killed accidentally by his mother, who had been beating him in a rage and who in throwing him to the ground fractured his skull

2c GEORGE NEVILL(E), **12th Lord** (Baron) **Abergavenny**; *b* 16 May 1702; *educ* Univ Coll Oxford; *m* 21 Feb 1722/3 Elizabeth, dau of Col Edward Thornicroft, of Westminster and est sis and coheir of Gideon Thornicroft, of Dodington and Linstead, Kent (she *m* 2nd Alured Pincke, of Lincoln's Inn and Tottenham High Cross, and *d* 4 March 1778), and *dspm* 15 Nov 1723, leaving two posthumous daus who *d* in infancy

3c EDWARD NEVILL(E), **13th Lord** (Baron) **Abergavenny**; *b c* 1705; *educ* Wadham Coll Oxford; *m* 6 May 1724 Katharine, dau of Lt-Gen William Tatton, of St Margaret's, Westminster (she *m* 2nd 14th Lord (Baron) Abergavenny; *see* below), and *dsp* 9 Oct 1724

1c Jane; *b* 8 March 1703; *m* John Abel Walter, of Busbridge, Surrey, and *d* 19 March 1786, having had issue

2c Ann; *b c* 1715; *d* unm March 1736/7

2b Edward; Cdr RN; *m* Hannah, dau of Jervoise Thorp, and *d* 12 Sept 1701 in Virginia, having had issue:

1c WILLIAM NEVILL(E), **14th Lord** (Baron) **Abergavenny**, for whom *see* further below

1c Mary; *m* Charles Chamberlain Rebow, of Smallfield Place, Surrey

(1) Anne; *b c* 1611; *m c* 17 Dec 1628 1st Baron Lucas of Shenfield and *d* 22 Aug 1660, having had issue (*see* LUCAS OF CRUDWELL, B)

4 John; *d* young

5 Thomas; *d* young

6 Charles; *d* young

1 Elizabeth; *m* 1st Sir John Grey; *m* 2nd Sir John Bingley

2 Mary; *m* just before 1608 1st Earl of Norwich and was *bur* 15 July 1648, having had issue (*see* GORING, Bt)

3 Catherine; *m* Sir Stephen Lessour, of Chiswick, Middx

4 Frances; *d* young

5 Margaret; *d* young

The 13th LORD (Baron) ABERGAVENNY's 1st cousin,

WILLIAM NEVILL(E), **14th Lord** (Baron) **Abergavenny**; Capt Yeomen of the Gd 1737, Master Jewel Office Feb 1738/9; *m* 1st 20 May 1725 Katharine (*d* 4 Dec 1729), widow of the 13th Lord Abergavenny, and had issue:

1 GEORGE NEVILL(E), **1st Earl of Abergavenny**

2 Edward; *b c* 19 Nov 1729

1 Catherine; *d* unm 1820

The **14th Lord** (Baron) **Abergavenny** *m* 2nd 20 May 1732 Lady Rebecca Herbert (*d* 20 Oct 1758), dau of 8th Earl of Pembroke and 5th Earl of Montgomery (*qv*), and *d* 21 Sept 1744, having had further issue:

2 William (Rev); *d* unm

The 14th LORD (Baron) ABERGAVENNY's er s,

GEORGE NEVILL(E), **1st Earl of Abergavenny** so *cr* 17 May 1784, Co Monmouth, and VISCOUNT NEVILL of Birling, Kent (both GB); *b* 24 June 1727 (GEORGE II stood sponsor); *educ* Ch Ch Oxford; Ld Lt Sussex 1757–61; *m* 5 Feb 1753 Henrietta (*d* 31 Aug 1768), dau of Thomas Pelham, of Stanmer, Sussex, sis of 1st Earl of Chichester (*qv*) and widow of Hon Richard Temple, of Romsey, Hants, and *d* 9 Sept 1785, having had issue:

1 HENRY NEVILL(E), **2nd Earl**

2 George Henry (Rev), of Flower Place, Surrey; *b* 6 Dec 1760; *m* 12 May 1787 Caroline (*d* 21 Dec 1841), dau of Hon Richard Walpole (*see* WALPOLE, B), and *d* 7 Aug 1844, having had issue:

(1) George (Rev); *b* 16 March 1792; rector Chiltington, Sussex; *d* unm 20 Sept 1825

(2) Henry Walpole (Rev); *b* 10 Nov 1803; rector Burgh Apton, Norfolk and Otley, Suffolk; *m* 28 May 1833 Frances (*m* 2nd 29 Oct 1840 Col Sir Hambleton Francis Custance, KCB (*d* 1893), of Weston House, Norfolk, and *d* 4 Oct 1892), yst dau of Sir Edmund Bacon, 9th and 10th Bt (*qv*), and ldsp 3 March 1837

(3) Reginald Henry, of Dangstein, Petersfield, Sussex, JP, DL (both Sussex); *b* 14 Sept 1807; *m* 2 Dec 1847 Lady Dorothy Fanny Walpole (*d* 24 March 1913), dau of 3rd Earl of Orford (*see* WALPOLE, B), and *d* 1 Sept 1878, having had issue:

1a Edward Augustus, JP (Sussex); *b* 28 Feb 1851; *m* 7 Aug 1877 Edith Fanny Owen (*d* 15 May 1937), est dau of Lt-Gen Edward Owen Leggatt, ISC, and *dsp* 10 Sept 1915

2a Horace John; *b* 22 Oct 1855; Lt KRRC Zulu War (medal); *m* 2 Jan 1880 Annie Harriett Martha (*d* 27 Dec 1931), dau of Henry Dickson Rowe, and *d* 10 Jan 1924, having had issue:

1b Frederick Reginald; *b* 17 Sept 1880; Lt RASC WW I; *m* 20 Aug 1927 Jeanne (*d* 17 June 1975), dau of Ignace Jean Fageol, of Paris, and *d* 20 Aug 1949, having had issue:

1c +John Robert Ralph [John Nevill Esq, 8 Radnor Cliff, Sandgate, Kent CT20 2JN; 5 Tite St, London SW3 4JU]; *b* 15 Feb 1928; *educ* Ampleforth; Lt DCLI, memb Hon Soc Gray's Inn, Kt Honour of Devotion SMO Malta, memb Court Gardeners' Co, Freeman City London, chm SE Regn ESU; *m* 30 July 1955 *Ann Margaret Mary (BA Oxon), dau of Archibald Corble, of Cookham, Berks, and has:

1d +Dominic John Frederick [Dominic Nevill Esq, 36 St George's Drive, London SW1]; *b* 27 June 1957; *educ* Worth and London U (BA 1979); *m* 1 May 1980 (*divorce* 19–) Amanda, dau of Howard King, of Leeds; *m* 2nd *Miriam, dau of Dr Sakoor, of Toronto, and by his 1st w has:

1e *Abigail Rosemary Jillian; *b* 15 July 1982

2e *Cordelia Magdalen; *b* 18 Oct 1984

2d +Ralph Stephen John; *b* 8 June 1959; *educ* Worth

3d +Christopher Henry Charles [Christopher Nevill Esq, Frogholt House, Frogholt, nr. Folkestone, Kent]; *b* 25 Oct 1962; *m* 28 March 1987 *Dominique, dau of Dr Paul Luder, of Staffisburg, Switzerland, and has:

1e +Gregory Paul John; *b* 11 Nov 1997

1e *Chantal Anne-Marie; *b* 11 Jan 1994

4d +Anthony Rupert Guy; *b* 8 Oct 1966; *educ* St Augustine's Ramsgate

1d *Cecilia Ann Frederica [Mrs Quinten Hollick, 12 Woottens Close, Comberton, Cambs CB3 7DA]; *b* 6 May 1956; *m* 23 Sept 1995 *Quinten Alexander Hollick, s of Dr Frank Hollick, Fell St John's Coll, Cambridge

2d *Caroline Mary; *b* 13 Aug 1960; *m* 11 Sept 1982 *William Sunnucks, s of James Sunnucks, DL, barrister, and has:

1e *Charles Rupert Nevill; *b* 14 Oct 1984

2e *Hugo James d'Urban; *b* 1 Nov 1990

1e *Georgina Anne Borradaile; *b* 25 April 1985

2e *Katie Ann Rochford; *b* 24 Sept 1993

1c *(Anne Mary) Frederica Dorothy [Mrs Ian Hastie, Cabos de Canezac, Montirat, Tarn, France]; *b* 17 Jan 1938; *m* 17 Dec 1960 *Ian George Hastie, only s of Andrew Hastie, of Salisbury, and has:

1d *Rupert Andrew Frederick Nevill; *b* 20 May 1962; *educ* Downside

2d *James Alexander Nevill; *b* 6 June 1967; *educ* Downside

1d *Caroline Ann Jeanne Frederica Nevill; *b* 13 July 1963

2b John Henry Adrian; *b* 22 Jan 1882; Lt (Gen Service), attached 2nd Bn Roy Irish Regt, served WW I 1914; *d* unm 29 April 1942

3b Robert Evelyn; *b* 9 July 1883; *d* 2 March 1884

4b Geoffrey Horace; *b* 13 Nov 1894; *d* 2 March 1895

3a Ralph Henry; *b* 4 Feb 1865; *educ* Eton and Magdalene Coll Cambridge; *d* 24 June 1930

1a Meresia Dorothy Augusta; *b* 14 Dec 1849; *d* unm 26 Oct 1918

(1) Catherine Caroline; *b* 5 Aug 1789; *d* 23 Jan 1794

1 Henrietta Nevill(e); *b* 24 May 1756; *m* 9 Sept 1799 Sir John Berney, 7th Bt (*qv*), and *d* 2 April 1833, having had issue

The 1st EARL OF ABERGAVENNY's er s,

HENRY NEVILL(E), **2nd Earl of Abergavenny**, KT (1814); *b* 22 Feb 1755; *educ* Ch Ch Oxford (MA 1776); MP Seaford 1784 and Mon 1784–85, Recorder Harwich; *m* 3 Oct 1781 Mary (*d* 26 Oct 1796), only child of John Robinson, MP, DCL, Sec to the Treasury, of Sion Hill and Wyke House, Isleworth, Middx, and *d* 27 March 1843, having had issue:

1 Henry George NEVILL(E), *Viscount Nevill*; *b* 22 May 1785; *d* unm & *vp* 8 April 1806

2 Ralph NEVILL(E), *Viscount Nevill*; *b* 21 Dec 1786; served RN: aboard HMS *Victory* at Trafalgar 1805, Capt 1811; *m* 2 Feb 1813 Mary Anne (*d* 6 June 1828), dau of Bruce Elcock, of Sloane St, Chelsea, and *dsp l**& *vp* 20 May 1826

3 JOHN NEVILL(E), **3rd Earl of Abergavenny**; *b* 25 Dec 1789; *educ* Christ's Coll Cambridge (MA 1818); rector Burgh Apton with Holveston, Norfolk, 1818–31, Otley, Suffolk, 1818–31, chaplain to the PRINCE REGENT 1818; *d* unm 12 April 1845

4 WILLIAM NEVILL(E), **4th Earl of Abergavenny**, for whom *see* further below

1 Mary Catherine; *b* 27 Feb 1783; *m* 2 Jan 1802 Thomas Myers and *d* 11 July 1807

2 Henrietta; *b* 14 July 1788; *d* unm 28 July 1827

The 3rd EARL OF ABERGAVENNY's yr bro,

WILLIAM NEVILL(E), **4th Earl of Abergavenny**; *b* 28 June 1792; *educ* Magdalene Coll Cambridge (MA 1816); rector Birling, Kent, vicar Frant, Sussex, chaplain to WILLIAM IV; *m* 7 Sept 1824 Caroline (*d* 19 May 1873), 2nd dau of Ralph Leeke, of Longford Hall, Salop, and *d* 17 Aug 1868, having had issue:

1 WILLIAM NEVILL, **5th Earl** and **1st Marquess of Abergavenny**, for whom *see* further below

2 Ralph Pelham, JP, DL (Kent); *b* 28 Nov 1832; High Sheriff Kent 1896; *m* 12 July 1860 Louisa Marianne (*d* 6 July 1919), 2nd dau of Sir Charles FitzRoy Maclean of Duart, 9th Bt (*qv*), and *d* 17 Aug 1914, having had issue:

(1) Ralph William Plantagenet NEVILL; *b* 12 April 1865; Lt 13th Hus; *d* unm 18 July 1902

(2) Percy Llewelyn; *b* 11 May 1877; *m* 8 June 1905 his cousin Marjorie (*d* 8 March 1945), only dau of Hon George Montacute Nevill (*see* below), and *d* 24 April 1927, leaving issue:

1a Michael George Ralph; *b* 19 June 1917; Lt Scots Gds WW II; *m* 27 July 1940, as her 1st husb, *Maureen Ethné David [Mrs John Balfour, Walnut Tree Farm, Birling, Maidstone, Kent] (she *m* 2nd 2 July 1947 Lt John Valentine Balfour, DSC, RNVR, s of Archibald Roxburgh Balfour and Pearl, 2nd dau of Arthur Price, only s of 6th s of Sir Rose Price, 1st Bt (*see* PRICE, Bt, of Trengwainton)), 2nd dau of Maj (Arthur) Tahu Gravenor Rhodes, MVO, Gren Gds, by his w Hon Helen Plunket, est dau of 5th Baron Plunket (*qv*), and was *ka* N Africa 28 April 1943, leaving:

1b +David Michael Ralph [David Nevill Esq, Birling Place, Birling, Maidstone, Kent]; *b* 20 June 1941; *educ* Bryanston; *m* 16 March 1972 *Katherine Mary, dau of Rossmore Derrick Westenra, of Christchurch, NZ, and has:

1c +Guy Michael Rossmore; *b* 12 Nov 1973; *educ* Bryanston and Southampton U (MA 1995)

1c *Anna Louise; *b* 16 Feb 1976

2c *Georgina Rose; *b* 16 May 1981

2b +Michael George Rathmore [Michael Nevill Esq, Walnut Tree Farm, Birling, Kent ME19 5JL]; *b* posthumously 14 July 1943; *educ* Eton

1a Joan Helen; *b* 26 April 1906; *m* 1st 14 Feb 1935 Lt Charles Austen Field-Marsham, (*das* Jan 1941); (*see* ROMNEY, E), and had issue; *m* 2nd 2 Oct 1950 *Maj Robert Edward Field-Marsham, (*d* 23 Nov 1996) er bro of her 1st husb, and *d* 18 Mar 1988

2a Sylvia Eleanor; *b* 6 Oct 1907; *d* unm 20 May 1981

3a Ruby Louisa; *b* 13 July 1909; *m* 3 Nov 1932 (*divorce* 1939) Kenneth Leslie Urquhart, est s of Leslie Urquhart, of Brasted Place, Kent, and *dsp* 1 Nov 1962

4a Rosemary; *b* 8 Feb 1912; *m* 17 Nov 1945 (*divorce* 1963) Maj Sir John Weston Brooke, 3rd Bt (*qv*), and *d* 11 March 1979, leaving issue

5a *Cicely Rose [Mrs Peter Nickols, Pinewood Lodge, Spofforth, N Yorks HG3 1AY]; *b* 23 June 1915; *m* 29 April 1947 Peter Richard Nickols (*d* 25 Oct 1990), only s of Richard Nickols, of Spofforth Hall, nr Harrogate, and has:

1b *Richard Henry; *b* 30 April 1948; *educ* Eton

2b *Charles Michael Ralph; *b* 29 Nov 1951; *educ* Trin Coll Glenalmond; *m* 14 March *Judith Frances Clarke and has:

1c *Honor Louisa; *b* 2 March 1985

2c *Sophie Alexandra; *b* 16 July 1987

1b *Rose Mary; *b* 29 Nov 1951; *m* 3 March 1979 *Stephen Lithgow Rickman and has:

1c *Struan Lithgow; *b* 31 Oct 1983

2c *Douglas Peter; *b* 19 Dec 1988

1c *Olivia Rose; *b* 27 Dec 1980

(1) Constance Emily; *b* 12 Dec 1863; *d* unm 4 Jan 1943

(2) Isabel Louisa; *b* 29 Dec 1864; *m* 15 Oct 1890 Maj Angus Howard Reginald Ogilvy, DSO, late 13th Hussars (*d* 4 July 1906), est s of Col Sir Reginald Howard Alexander Ogilvy, 10th Bt (*qv*), and *d* 21 Dec 1963, leaving issue

(3) Mary Frances; *b* 5 April 1869; *m* 1st 8 July 1891 3rd Viscount Hardinge (*qv*) and had issue; *m* 2nd 18 Oct 1928 her cousin 3rd Marquess of Abergavenny (*see* below) and *d* 31 Oct 1954

(4) Cicely Augusta; *b* 6 March 1872; *m* 14 Jan 1902 Philip Wyndham Cobbold, DL (*d* 28 Dec 1945), s of John Patteson Cobbold, MP Ipswich, and *d* 14 Oct 1958, leaving issue (*see* MANTON, B)

(5) Eleanor Georgiana; *m* 15 June 1901 Rowland Francis Meyrick (*d* 18 March 1953), 3rd s of Sir Thomas Charlton Meyrick, 1st Bt (*qv*), and *d* 12 Nov 1966 aged 93, leaving issue

1 Caroline Emily; *b* 31 May 1829; *d* unm 23 Feb 1887

2 Henrietta Augusta; *b* 18 June 1830; *m* 10 July 1855 Hon Thomas Edward Lloyd-Mostyn, MP (*dvp* 8 May 1861), est s of 2nd Baron Mostyn (*qv*), and *d* 25 Jan 1912, leaving issue

3 Isabel Mary Frances; *b* 6 Sept 1831; *m* 23 Feb 1854 Rev Hon Edward Vesey Bligh, JP, DL, of Fartherwell Hall, Kent (*d* 22 April 1908), 2nd s of 5th Earl of Darnley (*qv*), and *d* 18 Dec 1915, leaving issue

The 4th EARL OF ABERGAVENNY's est s,

WILLIAM NEVILL, **1st Marquess of Abergavenny**, Co Monmouth, and EARL OF LEWES, Sussex (both UK), so *cr* 14 Jan 1876, KG (1886), TD, JP (Kent and Mon); *b* 16 Sept 1826; *educ* Eton; Lt 2nd Life Gds 1849, Hon Col W Kent Yeo and Sussex Yeo, Ld Lt Sussex 1892–1905; *m* 2 May 1848 Caroline (*d* 13 Sept 1892), dau of Sir John van-den-Bempde-Johnstone, 2nd Bt, of Hackness Hall, Yorks, and sis of 1st Baron Derwent of Hackness (*qv*), and *d* 12 Dec 1915, having had:

1 REGINALD WILLIAM BRANSBY NEVILL, **2nd Marquess of Abergavenny**, JP (Kent 1880); *b* 4 March 1853; *educ* Eton; Lt West Kent Yeo; *d* unm 13 Oct 1927

2 HENRY GILBERT RALPH NEVILL, **3rd Marquess of Abergavenny**, DL (Sussex); *b* 2 Sept 1854; Lt-Col TA Res, formerly W Kent Yeo and Maj Sussex Imp Yeo; *m* 1st 12 Sept 1876 Violet (*d* 25 Dec 1880), est dau of Col Henry Dorrien Streatfeild, JP, DL, of Chiddingstone Castle, Kent, and had issue:

(1) Gilbert Reginald; *b* 6 April 1879; *d* 11 May 1891

(2) Geoffrey; *b* 6 April, *d* 14 April 1879

(1) Joan Marion, CBE (1920); *b* 16 July 1877; OStJ, Order of Mercy; *m* 2 June 1898 4th Marquess Camden (*qv*) and *d* 4 July 1952, leaving issue

2 (cont.) The **3rd Marquess** *m* 2nd 20 Oct 1886 Maud Augusta, LGStJ (*d* 15 July 1927), dau of William Beckett, MP (*see* GRIMTHORPE, B), and by her had issue:

(2) Marguerite Helen; *b* 30 Sept 1887; *m* 11 Feb 1907 21st Baron Hastings (*qv*) and *d* 7 June 1975, leaving issue

2 (cont.) The **3rd Marquess** *m* 3rd 18 Oct 1928 his cousin Mary Frances (*d* 31 Oct 1954), dau of Hon Ralph Nevill (*see* above) and widow of 3rd Viscount Hardinge, and *d* 10 Jan 1938 as the result of a hunting accident

3 George Montacute, JP, DL (both Sussex); *b* 23 Sept 1856; *m* 19 Oct 1882 Florence Mary, CBE, DGStJ (*d* 19 Dec 1929), only dau of Temple Soanes, of Brenchley House, Kent, by Alice, dau of Thomas Scurr Womersley, and *d* 10 Aug 1920, having had issue:

(1) GUY TEMPLE MONTACUTE, **4th Marquess**

(2) Rupert William; *b* 4 Sept 1884; Capt 15th Bn Rifle Bde; *das* 3 Dec 1918

(1) Marjorie; *b* 11 Oct 1886; *m* 10 June 1905 her cousin Percy Llewelyn Nevill (*d* 24 April 1927), only s of Hon Ralph Pelham Nevill, and *d* 8 March 1945, having had issue (*see* above)

4 William Beauchamp; *b* 23 May 1860; Lt 3rd Bn Roy West Kent Regt, ADC to Ld Lt Ireland; *m* 12 Feb 1889 Luisa Maria Carmen, Order of Mercy (*d* 3 Nov 1951), er dau of Don José Murrieta del Campo Mello y Urrutio, Marqués de Santurce, and *dsp* 12 May 1939

5 Richard Plantagenet, CMG (1909), CVO (1916), DL (Sussex); *b* 13 Jan 1862; *educ* Eton and Magdalene Coll Cambridge (BA); Priv Sec to Ld Pres Cncl 1885–92, Priv Sec and ADC to Govrs Victoria 1895–1901 and S Australia 1901–02 and Govrs-Gen Australia 1902–05, Chamberlain to Govr-Gen Australia 1908–14, Comptroller to Govrs-Gen Canada 1914–21, Order of Mercy (with bar); *d* unm 1 Dec 1939

1 Cicely Louisa; *b* 10 Sept 1851; *m* 16 April 1872 Col Hon Charles Gathorne Gathorne-Hardy (*d* 17 Feb 1919), 2nd s of 1st Earl of Cranbrook (*qv*), and *d* 1 May 1932, having had issue

2 Alice Maud; *b* Aug 1858; *m* 30 Sept 1884 Col Henry Courtenay Morland, JP, late 9th Lancers (*d* 30 June 1934), yr s of William Courtney Morland, JP, DL, of Court Lodge, Kent, and *d* 19 Feb 1898, having had issue

3 Idina Mary, JP (Sussex); *b* 5 May 1865; DJStJ, Order of Mercy and bar; *m* 28 Feb 1889 2nd and last Earl Brassey (*see* BRASSEY OF APETHORPE, B), and *d* 21 Feb 1951

4 Rose; *b* 7 Dec 1866; *m* 1st 14 June 1887 (*divorce* 1889) John Blundell Leigh, DL (*d* 27 July 1931), 2nd s of Henry Blundell Leigh, of Ammington Hall, Tamworth, Staffs, and had issue; *m* 2nd 29 Nov 1899 her 1st cousin once-removed 4th Earl of Cottenham (*qv*) and *d* 2 May 1913, leaving issue

5 Violet; *b* 7 Dec 1866; *m* 1st 17 Dec 1889 (*divorce* 1897) 3rd Earl Cowley (*qv*) and had issue; *m* 2nd 19 July 1898 Robert Edward Myddelton, DL, of Chirk Castle, Denbigh (*d* 12 Aug 1949), and *d* 28 March 1910, leaving further issue

The 3rd MARQUESS OF ABERGAVENNY's n,

GUY TEMPLE MONTACUTE NEVILL, later LARNACH-NEVILL (deed poll 17 June 1919), **4th Marquess of Abergavenny**, JP, DL (both Sussex); *b* 15 July 1883; Capt Scots Gds, Hon Maj 1920, formerly Sussex Yeo; *m* 30 Oct 1909 Isabel Nellie (*d* 5 Nov 1953), only child and heir of James Walker Larnach, of Brambletye, Sussex, Lanwades Hall, Newmarket, and Adderbury, Oxon, by his w Lady Isabel Boyle, dau of 9th Earl of Cork and Orrery (*qv*) and *d* 30 March 1954, leaving issue:

1 JOHN HENRY GUY LARNACH-NEVILL later NEVILL, **5th and present Marquess**

2 Rupert Charles Montacute LARNACH-NEVILL later NEVILL, CVO (1978), JP (E Sussex 1953), DL (E Sussex 1960); *b* 29 Jan 1923; *educ* Eton; Capt Life Gds, ADC to Lt-Gen Sir Brian Horrocks 1945–47, High Sheriff Sussex 1952, Treasurer to HRH THE DUKE OF EDINBURGH 1970–82, Priv Sec to HRH 1976–82, KStJ 1972, dir Sun Life Assurance Soc (v-chm 1971–82) and Australian Estates Ltd, v-pres Sussex Boy Scouts 1950–74, pres E Sussex Boy Scouts 1974–82, chm British Olympic Assoc 1966–77 (pres 1977), cdr Sussex St John's Cncl 1952–77, chm 1966–82, pres Br Show Jumping Assoc 1973–76; *m* 22 April 1944 *Lady (Anne) Camilla Evelyn Wallop, est dau of 9th Earl of Portsmouth (*qv*), and *d* 18 July 1982, having had:

(1) Guy Rupert Gerard; *b* 29 March 1945 (HM THE QUEEN stood sponsor); *educ* Eton; Page of Honour to HM THE QUEEN 1958–61; *m* 18 Feb 1982 *Lady Beatrix Mary Lambton [The Lady Beatrix Nevill, 39 Basuto Rd, London SW6; 251A Fulham Rd, London SW3], 2nd dau of Lord Lambton (formerly 6th Earl of Durham, *qv*), and formerly w of George William Bowdrey, and *d* 5 Feb 1993

(2) +CHRISTOPHER GEORGE CHARLES [Christopher Nevill Esq, Sham Farm, Eridge Green, Kent]; *b* 23 April 1955; heir presumptive; *educ* Harrow; *m* 1985 *Venetia V, er dau of Frederick Gerard Maynard, of Chelsea, and has:

1a George Rupert Gerard; *b* 27 June 1990 *d* 15 Sept 1990

2a *Sophie Alice Augusta; *b* 27 June 1990

(1) *Angela Isabel Mary [Mrs William Keating, 7 Durham Place, London SW3]; *b* 2 Jan 1948; *m* 12 March 1994 *William Keating

(2) *Henrietta Emily Charlotte [Mrs Timothy Purbrick, 35 Upper Addison Gdns, London W14]; *b* 21 June 1964 (HRH THE DUKE OF EDINBURGH stood sponsor); *m* 1991 *Maj Timothy Purbrick, 17th/21st Lancers, s of William Purbrick, and has:

1a *Rose; *b* 4 Nov 1997

2a *Lily; *b* 4 Nov 1997

1 Angela Isabel; *b* 3 Aug 1910; *m* 1st 20 Oct 1930 (*annulled* 1933), as his 1st w, Maj Sir Mark Vane Milbank, 4th Bt (*qv*); *m* 2nd 3 Oct 1933 7th Earl of Cottenham (*qv*) and *d* 26 May 1980, leaving issue

Seat: Eridge Park, Tunbridge Wells, Kent. Modern Eridge is predominantly a somewhat humdrum-proportioned, unadorned, vaguely neo-classical building. The architect, John Denman, drew up his plans in 1938–39 and claimed to have been influenced by Lutyens. Parts of the older castellated mansion were retained, notably the central towers and the stable block, Denman's original idea being to erect what is the present structure as the family wing of a much larger house. As it is, the old easterly wing was demolished in 1958, but Denman incorporated French-looking rounded tower protruberances with conical roofs at regular intervals along the facade. An orangery abuts one end of the house.

There seems to have been a manor house at Eridge in Tudor times. It was large enough to accommodate ELIZABETH I and her retinue for an entire week in 1576, when the **5th Lord Bergavenny** played host there. But no visual record of the house has survived and it was allowed to fall into disrepair, the Nevills apparently abandoning it in the early 17th century and not returning to take up residence for over 100 years. In the late 18th century Eridge underwent a dramatic revival of fortunes. The **2nd Earl of Abergavenny** decided to make it his principal seat and between 1790 and 1830 a fanciful creation in the prevailing Gothick taste arose where once the old Tudor building had stood. The architect, a Mr Taylor, is said to have been a brother of the family's governess and was an amateur — inasmuch as the distinction between professional and amateur was valid even as late as the last decade of the 18th century. After all, Richard Payne Knight, who with Uvedale Price has been suggested as an influence on the designer of Gothick Eridge, was a dilettante equally at home in Homeric scholarship. Another influence is thought to have been the **2nd Earl**'s father-in-law, John Robinson.

At all events the new Castle (for Eridge was so designated till well into the 20th century) erupted in a staggering, almost scrofulous wealth of heraldic beasts and other dynastic ornamentation, chiefly in the form of medallions on the elevations displaying an A (for Abergavenny), a bull's head, portcullis, rose or ship. The basic material seems to have been predominantly brick, rendered in something contemporaries referred to as 'Roman cement' (terracotta?). On the north front 16th-century masonry was recycled, presumably part of the old manor house. This north front was the most imposing, containing as it did the two round towers and central square one mentioned above as having survived till the 1950s, also a one-storey portal jutting forward from the left hand side to form the principal entrance. The south front was probably started at the beginning of the 40-year building programme. It was certainly more restrained in appearance, the windows, for instance, being classical rather than gothic. Even here, however, an iron walkway attached to the 1st-floor windows and running round to the eastern side of the house gave a foretaste of the Regency fashion for such devices. The interior apparently included a library with green scagliola columns and a fine Adam ceiling. When the house had become too big for modern living in the lean years after the War the **5th Marquess** allowed Mrs Langley Moore's Museum of Costume to instal its collection in the west wing.

The park proper, which covered over 1,000 acres until well into the second half of the 20th century, is claimed as the oldest known such enclosure for deer in England. It is mentioned in the Domesday Survey and was quite possibly part of the pre-Conquest lordship of Reredfelle (modern Rotherfield) held by Earl Godwin.

ABINGER

Arms: Chequy or and gules, a lion rampant ermine; on a canton azure a castle triple-towered argent. **Crest:** A Tuscan column chequy or and gules, supported on either side by a lion's jamb ermines erased gules. **Supporters:** On either side an angel, vested argent, tunic azure, wings or; in the exterior hand of each a sword in bend proper, pommel and hilt or. **Motto:** *Suis stat viribus* ('He stands by his own strength'). **Creation:** B. (UK) 12 Jan 1835.

THE 8TH BARON ABINGER, of Abinger, Surrey, and of the city of Norwich (James Richard Scarlett, DL (Essex 1968)) [The Rt Hon The Lord Abinger DL, 7 Cumberland St, London SW1V 4LS; Sheepcote House, Castle Hedingham, Essex CO9 3HA]; *b* 28 Sept 1914; *s f* 1943; *educ* Eton and Magdalene Coll Cambridge (BA 1936, MA 1946); Lt-Col RA WWII, RNXS 1968, company dir, farmer, v-pres

Byron Soc, former chm Keats-Shelley Meml Soc, memb: exec ctee CPRE, Halstead RDC and Braintree DC, pres Mid-Anglia Centre Nat Tst, former govr ESU, KStJ; *m* 4 April 1957 *Isla Carolyn, only dau of V-Adml James William Rivett-Carnac, CB, CBE, DSC, of Fornham House, Bury St Edmunds (*see* RIVETT-CARNAC, Bt), and has issue:

1 +JAMES HARRY [The Hon James Scarlett, 16 Thorncliffe Rd, London SW2]; *b* 28 May 1959; *educ* Eton; BSc, FRGS, FLS; *m* 19 Aug 1995 *Tracy, dau of Norman Cloutier, of Ottawa

2 +Peter Richard [The Hon Peter Scarlett, 33 Dagmar Rd, London SW12]; *b* 21 March 1961; *educ* Cheltenham; *m* 15 Aug 1992 *Sharon Elizabeth, dau of Derek Turl, of Exeter, Devon and has:

(1) +Harry Alexander; *b* 20 April 1997

(1) *Lucy Isla; *b* 8 Dec 1994

Lineage: BENJAMIN SCARLETT, of Eastbourne, Sussex; *m* 1625 Mary Kennard, also of Eastbourne, and had numerous issue, including an er s (Francis, merchant sea capt, served with Admls Penn and Venables capture of Jamaica 1655, granted lands in St Andrews Parish and elsewhere on Jamaica, Memb St Andrews in Legislative Assembly; *dsp*):

THOMAS, of Eastbourne; *m* and had, with other issue:

WILLIAM SCARLETT; *educ* Middle Temple; emigrated to Jamaica on inheriting estate of Waggwater, in St Andrews Parish, from his unc Francis Scarlett; was ancestor of:

ROBERT SCARLETT, of Duckett's Spring and other estates, St James Parish, Jamaica; *m* 2 Feb 1765 Elizabeth Wright, widow, dau of Philip Anglin, of Paradise Estate, Jamaica, by his w Mary, dau of John Lawrence, descended from Henry Lawrence, Pres of OLIVER CROMWELL's Cncl during the Protectorate, and had, with other issue, a 2nd s:

Sir JAMES SCARLETT, **1st Baron Abinger**, of Abinger, Surrey, and of the city of Norwich (UK), so *cr* 12 Jan 1835, PC, KC (1816); *b* 1769; *educ* Trin Coll Cambridge (BA 1790, MA 1794); barrister Inner Temple 1791; MP Peterborough 1819–30, Malton 1830–31, Cockermouth 1831–32 and Norwich 1832–34, ktd 1827, Attorney-Gen 1827 and 1829, Ld Ch Baron Exchequer 24 Dec 1834; *m* 1st 22 Aug 1792 Louise Henrietta (*d* 8 March 1829), 3rd dau of Peter Campbell, of Kilmorey, Argyllshire; *m* 2nd 28 Sept 1843 Elizabeth (*d* 13 Oct 1886), dau of Lee Steere Steere, formerly Witts, of Jayes, Surrey, and widow of Rev Henry John Ridley, rector Abinger, and *d* 7 April 1844, leaving by his 1st w:

1 ROBERT CAMPBELL SCARLETT, **2nd Baron Abinger**; *b* 5 Sept 1794; *educ* Trin Coll Cambridge (BA 1815, MA 1818); barrister Inner Temple 1818, MP Norwich 1835–38 and Horsham 1841–44, Br Min Florence; *m* 19 July 1824 Sarah (*d* 3 June 1878), 2nd dau of George Smith, Ch Justice Mauritius, and *d* 24 June 1861, leaving issue:

(1) WILLIAM FREDERICK SCARLETT, **3rd Baron Abinger**, CB (1877), DL (Inverness-shire); *b* 30 Aug 1826; *educ* Eton and Trin Coll Cambridge; Capt and Lt-Col Scots Fus Gds 1855, Maj 1868, Lt-Col 1874, Maj-Gen 1877, Lt-Gen 1882, served Crimean War, 5th Class Medjidie; *m* 23 Dec 1863 Helen/Ella/Eileen (*d* 13 Feb 1915), 2nd dau of Cdre George Allan Magruder, USN, and niece of Maj-Gen J B Magruder, and *d* 16 Jan 1892, leaving, with other issue:

1a JAMES YORKE MacGREGOR SCARLETT, **4th Baron Abinger**, JP (Invernessshire), DL; *b* 13 March 1871; Capt 2nd Bn Cameron Highrs 1900; *d* unm 11 Dec 1903

1a Helen Charlotte; *b* 18 Aug 1866; *m* 15 July 1885 Nicholas John Charlton, of Chilwell Hall, Notts (*d* 1892), and *d* 8 April 1948, leaving issue

2a Evelina; *b* 9 Aug 1867; *m* 1st 10 Feb 1887 Maj Henry Wykeham Brooke Tunstall Haverfield, RA (*d* 19 Jan 1895), and had issue; *m* 2nd 19 July 1899 Brig-Gen John Henry Balguy, RA, of Duffield, Derbyshire (*d* 27 Dec 1933); resumed by deed poll 1899 the name of Haverfield and *d* 21 March 1920

3a Gertrude Constance; *b* 28 Oct 1868; *d* 8 June 1869

(1) Henrietta Elizabeth; *b* 20 June 1825; *m* 28 July 1846 Hon Otway Fortescue Graham-Toler (*d* 23 April 1884), s of 2nd Earl of Norbury (*qv*), and *d* 4 March 1895, leaving issue

(2) Frances Mary; *b* 2 March 1828; *m* 17 Dec 1857 Rev Canon Sidney Lidderdale Smith, Preb Hereford and rector Brampton Ash, Northants (*d* 9 Oct 1903), and *d* 22 Aug 1920

2 Sir James Yorke, GCB; *b* 1 Feb 1799; Gen, cmded Heaby Bde Crimean War, Col 6th Dragoon Gds, C-in-C Aldershot Div, Cdr Legion of Honour, Kt of the Medjidie; *m* 19 Dec 1835 Charlotte Anne (*d* 9 Feb 1888 aged 82), 2nd dau and co-heir of John Hargreaves, of Ormerod House, and Bank Hall, Burnley, Lancs, and *dsp* 6 Dec 1871

3 Peter Campbell, CB, DL (Surrey); *b* 27 Nov 1804; Envoy Extrdy and Min Plen: Brazil 1855–58, Greece 1862–64 and Mexico 1865–67, Min Florence 1858–60; *m* 1st 22 May 1843 Frances Sophia Mostyn (*d* 27 Sept 1849), 2nd dau and co-heir of Edmund Lomax, of Parkhurst, Surrey; *m* 2nd 27 Dec 1873 Louisa Anne (*d* 19 March 1900), dau of James Wolfe Murray, of Cringletie, Lord Cringletie, a Ld of Session (*see* MURRAY, Bt, of Blackbarony), and widow of Edmond Jeannin, and *d* 15 July 1881, leaving issue by his 1st w:

(1) Leopold James Yorke Campbell, of Parkhurst, Surrey; *b* 9 Sept 1847; Lt-Col Scots Gds; *m* 16 Feb 1871 Bessie Florence (*d* 22 Sept 1934), dau and coheir of Edward Gibson and niece and adopted dau of Sir Percy Florence Shelley, 3rd Bt (*qv*), and *d* 21 Oct 1888, leaving issue:

1a SHELLEY LEOPOLD LAURENCE SCARLETT, **5th Baron Abinger**, JP (Hants); *b* 1 April 1872; Cdr RNVR, Capt and Hon Maj 3rd Bn Beds Regt WW I, Hon Attaché Stockholm 1897–99; *m* 8 Aug 1899 Lila Lucy Catherine Mary (*d* 7 June 1941), only dau of Sir William Arthur White, GCB, GCMG, PC, Amb Constantinople, and widow of Kammerherr Carl Emmanuel de Geijer, Swedish Diplomatic Serv, and *dsp* 23 May 1917

2a ROBERT BROOKE CAMPBELL SCARLETT, **6th Baron Abinger**; *b* 8 Jan 1876; barrister Inner Temple 1909, Assist Paymaster RNR, Lt RNVR; *m* 26 June 1917 Jean Marguerite (*d* 17 July 1954), dau of Edouard Japy, of Beaucourt, nr Belfort, France, and widow of Adolphe Steinhell, of Paris, and *dsp* 10 June 1927

3a Lawrence James Peter; *b* 27 April 1877; Midshipman RN; lost at sea in HMS *Victoria* 22 June 1893

4a HUGH RICHARD, **7th Baron**

5a Percy Gerald, CB (1941), MC, DL (Kent 1949); *b* 10 April 1885; *educ* Wellington; granted 18 July 1904 with his sisters and yr bros patent of precedence as the daus and yr sons of a baron, served WWs I (despatches, Brevet Maj) and II 1939–42, Brevet Lt-Col Shanghai Defence Force 1927–28, Maj-Gen cmdg Deccan District India 1938, Brig and Cdr 12th Inf Bde and Dep Constable Dover Castle 1936–38, Cdr 4th Indian Div 1939–40, Dir Mobilization 1940, DAG (A) 1940–42, Col The Buffs 1943–53, Kt Grand Cross Order of Dannebrog 1952; *m* 21 Nov 1928 Margaret Macdonald (*d* 2 Nov 1963), dau of Thomas Humphreys, JP, barrister, of 15 Waterloo Cresc, Dover, sis of Lt-Gen Sir (Edward) Thomas Humphreys, KCB, CMG, DSO, and widow of Col William Alleyne Macbean, RA, and *dsp* 5 Oct 1957

6a Leopold Florence; *b* posthumously 17 March 1889; Lt RN; *d* unm lost in Australian submarine AE 1 14 Sept 1914 after taking part in capture of German New Guinea

1a Ruth Hester Frances; *m* 11 Dec 1919 Lt-Col Francis Edmond Bray, MC, TD, DL, 4th Bn The Queen's Roy Regt (TA) (*d* 8 May 1950), s of Sir Reginald Bray, of The Manor House, Shere, Surrey, and *d* 28 April 1943, leaving issue

(1) Florence; *m* 5 March 1867 Sir John Walsham, 2nd Bt (*qv*), and *d* 21 Dec 1915, leaving issue

1 Mary Elizabeth Scarlett, *cr* 22 Jan 1836 BARONESS STRATHEDEN, of Cupar, Co Fife (UK); *m* 8 Sept 1821 1st BARON CAMPBELL (*see* STRATHEDEN and CAMPBELL, B) and *d* 25 March 1860, leaving issue

The 6th BARON's yr bro,

HUGH RICHARD SCARLETT, **7th Baron Abinger**, DSO (1916), JP, DL (both Inverness-shire); *b* 25 Nov 1878; Lt-Col RA, served S African War 1900–02 and WW I (despatches thrice), Brevet Lt-Col 1919; *m* 15 Oct 1913 Marjorie Ursula (*d* 17 Sept 1965), 2nd dau of John McPhillamy, of Blair Athol, Bathurst, NSW, and *d* 21 July 1943, leaving issue:

1 JAMES RICHARD SCARLETT, **8th and present Baron Abinger**

2 John Leopold Campbell, CBE (1973); *b* 18 Dec 1916; *educ* Eton and Magdalene Coll Cambridge (BA 1938, MA 1947); 2nd Lt 1940, Maj RA 1944 WW II (despatches twice), Ho Govr London Hosp 1962–72, Dep to Health Serv Commr 1973076, Esq OStJ; *m* 26 April 1947 *Bridget [The Hon Mrs John Scarlett, Bramblewood, Castle Walk, Wadhurst, E Sussex TN5 6DB], yr dau of Herbert Brown Crook, of 102 Stafford Court, London W8, and *d* 19 Aug 1994, leaving:

(1) +Hugh Lawrence; *b* 2 July 1953; *educ* Sherborne; *m* 12 Jan 1985 *Dinah, dau of Richard Pinsent, of Thora, NSW and has:

1a *Skye Michelle; *b* 21 Feb 1995

(2) +Felix James [Felix Scarlett Esq, Two Beeches, South Heath, Bucks HP16 9SH]; *b* 17 Feb 1958; *educ* Sherborne, Leeds U and RCA; *m* 1991 *Laura Stewart, only dau of Edward Petrie, of Dundee, Tayside, and has:

1a +Robert Campbell; *b* 27 Jan 1992

2a +Rory Maclaren; *b* 2 Oct 1993

3a +Fraser Stewart; *b* 1995

1a *Honor Katherine; *b* 1996

(1) *Sarah Elizabeth [Mrs Alistair Cairns, 2 Quarry Hill, Godalming, Surrey GU7 2NW]; *b* 30 July 1954; *educ* St Michael's Petworth and Cambridge; *m* 14 Sept 1996 *Dr Alistair Cairns, PhD, of Fife

3 Felix Lawrence, DFC; *b* 18 March 1920; *educ* Eton; S/Ldr RAF WWII; *kas* air operations July 1944

ACKNER

Arms: Sa. in fess issuant trom a barrulet wavy az., fimbriated arg., a representation of the bridge at Clare College Cambridge ppr., the whole between two whales spouting naiant counter naiant gold. **Crest:** Upon a helm with a wreath or and sa. a short-eared owl ppr., crowned or, supporting with the dexter claw a clarion az. **Supporters:** Two otters each holding in the mouth a trout gold, the compartment comprising a river bank with bulrushes growing therefrom ppr. **Motto:** *Non servimus justitiae silendo* ('We do no service by muzzling justice'). **Creation:** B. (LP, UK) 1986.

THE BARON ACKNER, of Sutton, Co of West Sussex (Desmond James Conrad Ackner, PC (1980) [The Rt Hon The Lord Ackner PC, Browns House, Sutton, W Sussex RH20 1PU]; *b* 18 Sept 1920; *educ* Highgate Sch and Clare Coll Cambridge (MA, Hon Fell 1983); RA WW II, barrister Middle Temple 1945, QC 1961, Bencher 1965, Chm Gen Cncl Bar, V-Pres Senate Four Inns of Court 1968–70 (Pres 1980–82), Recorder Swindon 1962–71, Judge Court Appeal Jersey and Guernsey 1967–71, High Court Judge Queen's Bench 1971–80, Ld Justice Appeal 1980–86, Treas Middle Temple 1984, Ld Appeal in Ordinary 1986–92, ktd 1970, memb: Law Advsy Ctee Br Cncl 1991– (chm 1980–90) and Lloyd's Arbitration Panel 1992–, Pres: Arbitration Appeal Tbnl Securties and Futures Authority 1994–, Appeal Commr Personal Investment Authority 1994–, Dir City Disputes Panel 1994–, Pres Soc of Sussex Downsmen 1993–96; *m* 1946 *Joan, dau of John Evans, JP, and widow of K B Spence, and has issue.

1 *Martin Stewart [The Hon Martin Ackner, Lands Farm, W Anstey, S Molton, Devon]; *b* 1951; *educ* Oundle and Birmingham U (BSc); *m* 1st 1976 Corina, dau of Vincent Scott; *m* 2nd 1983 *Janet, dau of C W Williamson

1 *Claudia Madeleine; *b* 1954; *educ* Roedean and Girton Coll Cambridge (BA); barrister; *m* 1978 *Iain Hamilton Douglas Hughes, s of Geoffrey Hughes, of Edinburgh

The BARON ACKNER adopted his stepdau (dau of K B Spence):

*Moelwyn Ulva [Mrs Michael Healy, Sylvan House, Goose Green, Gullane, E Lothian EH31 2AT]; *b* 1943, *educ* St Michael's Petworth and Switzeriand; *m* 1st 19– (*divorce* 19–) I K Bouckley; *m* 2nd 1980 *Michael Healy and has by her 1st husb:

(1) *Joanna Helen Sarah Brooke; *b* 1969; *m* 1993 *Simon William Young, twin s of Stephen Young, of Elgin

Lineage: Dr Conrad Ackner; *m* Rhoda — and had:

JAMES CONRAD, *cr* a **Baron**

ACKROYD

Arms: Azure on a pale between two oak leaves or a sword erect gules. **Crest:** A goat's head erased azure, armed or, charged on the neck with a rose argent, barbed and seeded proper. **Motto:** *Per fidem robur* ('Strength through faith'). **Badge:** Two hands couped proper grasping a torch or, enflamed also proper. **Creation:** Bt. (UK) 8 May 1956.

SIR TIMOTHY JOHN ROBERT WHYTE ACKROYD, 3RD BT, of Dewsbury, W R Yorks [Sir Timothy Ackroyd Bt]; *b* 7 Oct 1958; *s* f 1995; *educ* Bradfield and LAMDA; actor, appearances in plays include: *Agamemnon* (nominated most promising newcomer award West End Theatre Critics 1976), *A Sleep of Prisoners* (1983), *No Sex Please We're British* (1987), *Jeffrey Bernard Is Unwell* (1989, 1991); films include: *Luther* (1981), *Creator* (1984), *Pied Piper* (1989), *Lost in Africa* (1992). Dir Martingale Prods 1985, Tstee and Patron Tusk Tst 1990, Tstee Marjorie and Dorothy Whyte Meml Fund, and The Ackroyd Tst 1994, Freeman City London, Liveryman Carpenters' Co 1982

Lineage: JOHN ACKROYD, of Birkenshaw, Yorks; *b* 1790; *m* Johanna, dau of Joseph Parker, and *d* 1836, leaving:

JOHN ACKROYD, of Heckmondwyke, Yorks; *b* 1815; *m* Sarah, dau of Mark Barber, and *d* 1885, leaving, with a dau Susannah:

BENJAMIN BATLEY ACKROYD, of Dewsbury; *b* 1851; *m* Emily (*d* 21 Aug 1935), dau of John Armitage, of Dewsbury, and *d* 20 Aug 1934, leaving:

1 Victor Tattersfield; *b* 11 Dec 1886; *m* and *d* Sept 1939, leaving:

(1) *Brant; *b* 1922

(2) *Roy [Roy Ackroyd Esq, 1302 Carmel Drive, Mississauga, Ontario, Canada]; *b* 1925

2 **Sir Cuthbert Lowell Ackroyd, 1st Bt** (UK), so cr 8 May 1956, JP (City London 1945), DL (Kent 1962); *b* 4 Sept 1892; *educ* London U; Capt RA WW I, HG WW II, HAC; underwriting memb Lloyd's, City London: Common Cncllr 1940, Alderman 1945, Lt, Sheriff, Ld Mayor 1955–56; visiting magistrate Holloway Prison 1945–55, High Sheriff Kent 1964–65, Hon LLD Leeds 1956, Chm Victoria League 1959, Pres: Metropolitan Inst Blind, Nat Sunday Sch Union, Church Commr 1947–62, Charter Mayor Bromley 1964, Freeman Woolmen's Co, Master Carpenters' Co 1953, Freeman Belfast, Washington and Richmond (Virginia), V-Pres Br and For Bible Soc, Pres Govr RNLI, Nat Corpn Care Old People, Roy Assoc Deaf and Dumb, Govr Irish Soc 1964–67, RCA, FRSA, Cdr Orange-Nassau Netherlands, Offr Legn Honour, Grand Offr Order Merit Italy, Al Rafidain Iraq, KStJ; *m* 14 June 1927 Joyce Wallace, dau of Robert Whyte, JP, of Chislehurst, Kent, and *d* 11 April 1973, leaving:

(1) **Sir John Robert Whyte Ackroyd, 2nd Bt**; *b* 2 March 1932; *educ* Bradfield and Worcester Coll Oxford (BA 1955, MA 1958); 2nd Lt RA, Jordan 1951–52, Steward OUDS 1954, Patron London and Internat Sch of Acting 1983, Memb Cncl RCM 1981–91, Hon Sec RCM 1986–91, FRCM 1988, FRSA 1989, underwriting memb Lloyd's to 1969, sometime with Engrg and Planning Resources, latterly pensions consultant, V-Pres Dystonia Soc 1995, Hon Sec Pilgrims 1966, memb Cncl RZS 1987–95; *m* 23 March 1956 Jennifer Eileen McLeod (*d* 23 Sept 1997), dau of Henry George Stokes Bishop, and *d* 30 Aug 1995, leaving:

1a Sir TIMOTHY JOHN ROBERT WHYTE ACKROYD, **3rd and present Bt**

2a +ANDREW JOHN ARMITAGE; *b* 17 Sept 1961; heir presumptive; painter

1a *Jane Victoria McLeod [Mrs David Annesley, 77 Pk Ave N, London N8]; *b* 25 Feb 1957; sculptor; *m* 1992, as his 2nd w, *David Robert Ewart Annesley and has issue (*see* ANNESLEY, E)

2a *Kate Georgina McBride; *b* 9 March 1963; *m* 1986 *Fabrice Gilles Marion, est s of Roger Marion, of Paris, and has:

1b *Oscar; *b* 1991

1b *Oriane; *b* 1987

2b *Tiphaine Jennifer; *b* 1989

3b *Héloïse; *b* 1994

(2) +Christopher Lowell [Christopher Ackroyd Esq, Nutfield, Wickhurst Road, Weald, Sevenoaks, Kent TN14 6LX]; *b* 3 March 1934; *educ* Bradfield and Magdalene Coll Cambridge (BA 1957, MA 1961); *m* 17 June 1961 *Caroline Rachael Josephine, only dau of Eric Lewis, and has:

1a +Marcus Lowell; *b* 5 April 1964

1a *Vivyan Katy; *b* 20 Aug 1962; *m* 1987 *(David) Clive Whittaker, 2nd s of Kenneth Whittaker, and has:

1b *Giles; *b* 1988

2b *Harry; *b* 1992

3b *David; *b* 1995

ACLAND of Columb-John

Arms: Chequy argent and sable, a fess gules. **Crest:** A man's hand apaumée couped at the wrist in a glove lying fesswise to the sinister, thereon a falcon perched all proper, jessed and belled or. **Motto:** *Inébranlable* ('Unshakable'). **Creation:** Bt. (E) 21 Jan 1677/8 with precedence from 24 June 1644.

SIR JOHN DYKE ACLAND, 12TH BT, of Columb-John [Sir John Acland Bt, Sprydon, Broadclyst, Devon EX5 3JN]; *b* 13 May 1939; *s* f 1990; *educ* Clifton, Magdalene Coll Cambridge (MA) and U of WI (MSc); *m* 9 Sept 1961 *Virginia, yr dau of Roland Forge, of The Grange, Barnoldby-le-Beck, Lincs, and has issue:

1 +DOMINIC DYKE; *b* 19 Nov 1962; *educ* Edinburgh U (MA); *m* 1990 *Sarah Anne, 3rd dau of Ven Kenneth Unwin, and has issue:

(1) +Patrick; *b* 18 Nov 1993

(2) +Finlay; *b* 23 Sept 1995

(1) *Florence; *b* 18 Nov 1993

2 +Piers Dyke; *b* 2 Feb 1965; *educ* UCL (BSc, PhD); barrister Lincoln's Inn 1992; *m* 1993 *Lucinda M, dau of Dr John Draper Raiman, and has:

(1) *Harriet; b 1 April 1995

(2) *Alice Beatrice; *b* 23 Dec 1996

1 *Holly Dyke; *b* 21 July 1972

Lineage: BALDWIN ECCELIN; f of:

BALDWIN ACALEN, of Acalen, parish of Land Key, Devon, living *temp* HENRY III; ancestor (as was either directly or collaterally HUGH de ACALEN, *temp* HENRY II) of:

JOHN AKELAND, of Akeland; er brother of Sir John Acland, of Columb-John, High Sheriff Devon 1608; *m* Margaret, dau and coheir of Hugh Radcliffe, of Stepney, and had an est s:

HUGH ACLAND, of Acland; living 1620; *m* 1585 Margaret (aunt to George Monk, 1st Duke of Albemarle; see MONCK, V), dau of Thomas Monke, of Potheridge, and had, with other issue:

Sir ARTHUR ACLAND, of Acland and Columb John; ktd 1606; *m* Eleanor, dau and heiress of Robert Mallet, of Wooleigh or Woolley, Devon, and *d* 26 Dec 1610, having had, with other issue:

(Sir) JOHN ACLAND, 1st Bt(?) E), so *cr*(?) 24 June 1644, although no docket, patent or sign manual has been found enrolled owing to the confusion of the Civil War, in which he was a royalist, garrisoning Columb-John for CHARLES I and holding out after all other royalist forces in the county had captulated; *b c* 1591, Sheriff Devon 1641; *m* by 1635 Elizabeth (d by 25 Feb 1650/1), dau of Sir Francis Vincent, 1st Bt, by his 1st w Sarah, dau of Sir Amyas Paulet (*see* WINCHESTER, M), and *d* 24 Aug 1647, having had (with two daus, Eleanor, *m* Sir John Davie, Bt, and Susanna, *m* 1st Edward Halsall, *m* 2nd John Carleton):

1 (Sir) FRANCIS ACLAND, (?)2nd Bt(?); *d* unm 1649

2 (Sir) JOHN ACLAND, (?)3rd Bt(?); *b c* 1636; *m c* 1654 Margaret, dau of Dennis Rolle, of Stevenstone, Devon, by Margaret, dau of 1st Baron Poulett of Hinton St George (*see* 1970 edn POULETT, E), and *d* 1655, leaving:

(1) (Sir) ARTHUR ACLAND, (?)3rd Bt(?); *b c* 1655; *educ* Exeter Coll Oxford; *d* unm 1672

(1) Margaret; *m c* 10 May 1675, as his 1st w of two, 2nd Baron Arundell of Trerice, and *d* 26 March 1691, leaving issue

3 **Sir Hugh Acland, 1st** (or 5th) **Bt** (E), so *cr* 21 Jan 1677/8, which indicates that hard evidence of whatever *cr* had been made earlier was even then unobtainable, even though this new grant was with precedence of 24 June 1644; *b c* 1639; *educ* Exeter Coll Oxford; MP Barnstaple 1679 and Tiverton 1685–87; *m c* 19 March 1673/4 Anne (*bur* 15 March 1727/8), dau of Sir Thomas Daniel, of Beswick Hall, York, and was *bur* 9 March 1713/4, leaving, with five other s and a dau:

(1) John; *m* 24 March 1695/6 Elizabeth, dau of Richard Acland, of Fremington, and *dvp* (*bur* 20 May 1703), leaving, with other issue:

1a **Sir Hugh Acland, 2nd Bt**; *bapt* 26 Jan 1696/7; MP Barnstaple 1721–27; *m c* 9 May 1721 Cicely (*m* 2nd 13 Aug 1729 Rev Thos Troyte), est dau and eventually sole heir of Sir Thomas Wrothe, of Petherton Park, and *d* 29 July 1728, leaving an est s:

1b Sir THOMAS ACLAND later DYKE ACLAND, **3rd Bt** (added name following marriage); *b* 14 Aug 1722; MP Devon 1746–47 and Somerset 1767–68; *m* 7 Jan 1744/5 Elizabeth (*bur* 13 July 1753), only dau and heir of Thomas Dyke, of Tetton, Somerset, and *d* 24 Feb 1785, leaving:

1c John, of Pixton; *b* 18 Feb 1746; Maj 20th Foot, Col Devon Militia; *m* 3 June 1770 Lady Christian Harriot Caroline Fox Strangways (*d* 21 July 1815), 3rd dau of 1st Earl of Ilchester (*qv*), and *dvp* 31 Oct 1778, leaving:

1d **Sir John Dyke Acland, 4th Bt**; *b* 1778; *d* unm (*bur* 23 April 1785)

1d Elizabeth Kitty; *m* 26 April 1796 2nd Earl of Carnarvon (*qv*) and *d* 5 March 1813, leaving issue

2c **Sir Thomas Dyke Acland, 5th Bt**; *bapt* 18 April 1752; *m* 4 July 1785 his cousin Henrietta Anne (*m* 2nd 6 June 1795 Capt Hon Matthew Fortescue, RN, bro of 1st Earl Fortescue (*qv*); *d* 2 Sept 1841), only dau of Sir Richard Hoare, 1st Bt (*qv*), leaving, with anther s and two daus:

1d THOMAS DYKE ACLAND (Sir), **6th Bt**

2d Hugh Dyke; *b* 10 March 1791; *m* 12 June 1817 Ellen Jane (*m* 2nd 7 April 1835 Richard Hinckley, of Beacon Place, Lichfield; *d* 18 Oct 1870), dau of Dr Chappel Woodhouse, Dean Lichfield, and widow of Rev William Robinson, and *d* 24 March 1834, leaving issue:

1e Hugh Woodhouse; *b* 6 March 1818; *m* 5 Feb 1841 Mary, dau of Job Edwards, and *d* 7 March 1851, leaving issue:

1f John Woodhouse; *b* 9 June 1849; 57th Regt; *m* July 1875 Anne Waddell, dau of Col H P Hughes, RA

1f Ellen Mary Woodhouse; *m* 6 June 1867 Rev Frederick Wentworth Vernon (*d* 20 May 1906), s of Henry Charles Vernon, of Hilton Park, and *d* 20 July 1883, leaving issue

Sir THOMAS *d* 17 May 1794; his est s,

Sir Thomas Dyke Acland, 6th Bt ; *b* 29 March 1787; *educ* Ch Ch Oxford (MA, DCL); MP Devon 1812–18 and 1820–31, and N Devon 1837–57; *m* 7 April 1808 Lydia Elizabeth (*d* 23 June 1856), only dau of Henry Hoare, of Mitcham Grove, and had issue:

1 THOMAS DYKE ACLAND (Sir), **7th Bt**

2 Arthur Henry Dyke ACLAND later TROYTE (roy licence 1852 on inheriting estates of Rev Edward Berkeley Troyte, DCL), of Huntsham, Bampton, Devon; *b* 3 May 1811; *m* 15 Sept 1835 Frances (*d* 4 Aug 1856), dau of Robert Williams (*see* WILLIAMS, Bt,), and *d* 19 June 1857, leaving issue:

(1) Charles Arthur Williams, JP and DL (Devon), of Huntsham; *b* 11 May 1842; Col cmdg 1st Roy Devon Yeo Cav, Hon Col and Lt-Col cmdg 3rd Vol Bn Devon Regt; *m* 21 June 1864 Katherine Mary (*d* 5 June 1934), est dau of Sir John Walrond Walrond, 1st Bt, of Bradfield, Devon (*see* 1963 edn WALERAN, B), and *d* 11 April 1896, leaving issue:

1a Arthur Acland; *b* 30 March 1865; *d* 30 March 1883

2a Hugh Leonard ACLAND TROYTE, JP and DL (Devon), of Huntsham; *b* 18 Dec 1870; Lt-Col 4th Bn Devon Regt, 20th Hus, Indian Expdny Force Mesopotamia 1916; *m* 3 June 1899 Helen Jessie (*d* 1 Nov 1941), dau of Henry Chapman, of Wanstead, Essex, and was *ka* 17 April 1918

3a Gilbert John ACLAND TROYTE (Sir), ktd 1945, CMG (1917), DSO (1916), JP (Devon); *b* 4 Sept 1876; *educ* Eton and Trin Hall Cambridge; Lt-Col KRRC Boer War 1901 (dangerously wounded), Somaliland 1903–04, WW I (despatches seven times, Croix de Guerre, brevet), HG WW II, MP Tiverton 1924–45, CA Devon, Pres CLA 1937–39, Jt MFH Tiverton 1946–50; *m* 12 Oct 1909 Gwladys Eleanor (Id 21 Oct 1968), dau of Ernest Henry Godolphin Quicke, of Newton St Cyres, Devon, and *dsp* 27 April 1964

4a Herbert Walter ACLAND TROYTE, MC; *b* 13 Sept 1882; *educ* New Coll Oxford (BA); Maj Reserve Offrs TA WW I (despatches twice); *m* 3 Feb 1910, as her 1st husb (*divorce* 1921), Marjorie Florence, yr dau of Charles Guy Pym (*see* PYM, B), and *d* 24 Nov 1943, having had issue:

1b John; *b* 21 Jan 1914

1b Anne; *b* 12 June 1912; *m* 1st 1 July 1933 (*divorce* 1941) 5th Baron Ebury (*qv*) and had issue; *m* 2nd 23 Dec 1941 (divorce 1947) Henry Peregrine Rennie Hoare, er s of Harry Hoare, of Ellisfield Manor, Basingstoke; *m* 3rd 13 Nov 1947 Lt-Col Frederick Edwin Barton Wignall (*d* 9 Nov 1956) and had further issue; *m* 4th 25 Sept 1961 Anthony Freire Marreco, of Port Hall, Co Donegal, only s of Geoffrey Freire Marreco, and *d* 1982

1a Frances Lucy; *m* 8 May 1897 Brig-Gen Sir Francis Sudlow Garratt, KCMG, CB, DSO (*d* 23 June 1928), est s of Rev Sudlow Garratt, MA, and *d* 11 Nov 1921, leaving issue:

2a Cicely Mary; Sister Community St Mary the Virgin, Wantage; *d* 29 Dec 1960

(2) John Edward, JP (Dorset), of Wollaston House, Dorchester; *b* 20 Feb 1848; *educ* Ch Ch Oxon (MA); FSA; Capt, dropped name TROYTE; *m* 26 Oct 1882 Norah Letitia Nugent (*d* 1 March 1938), dau of Henry Hyde Nugent Bankes, of Studland Manor, Dorset, and *d* 15 Feb 1932, leaving issue:

1a Henry Vivian; *b* 27 Nov 1883; Capt 88th Fus BC Regt WW I (despatches), F/Lt RCAF WW II (despatches); *m* 1st 26 April 1910 Jeanne (*d* 8 Aug 1950), only dau of Henry van der Nest, Belgian Min Washington, and had issue:

1b John Ernest Vivian; *b* 1 April 1911; Capt Roy Westminster Regt, Canadian Army; *m* 1st 18 Dec 1935 Edith Eleanor Maud (*d* June 1953), dau of John Waterman, of Vancouver, BC; *m* 2nd 24 April 1954 Joan, dau of Dr L B Wilmot, MD, RAMC, of Fredericton, New Brunswick, and *d* 1982, leaving issue:

1c +Peter Vivian; *b* 2 Jan 1955

2c +Anthony Robert; *b* 20 March 1957

2b +Peter Theodore [Peter Acland Esq, 2700 Abbott Street, Kelowna, BC, Canada]; *b* 1 March 1914; Hon Maj Kumaon Rifles, Capt GS2 25th Canadian Inf Trg Bde, Maj Canadian Gren Gds

1b *Patricia Evelyn Leila [Mrs Robert Browne-Clayton, 4534 Gordon Drive, Kelowna, BC, Canada]; *b* 25 March 1920; *m* 16 June 1945 *Robert Denis Browne-Clayton, Lt PPCL Inf, only s of Capt Lionel Denis Clayton Browne-Clayton, RNR, of Browne's Hill, Co Carlow, and has issue:

1c *Patrick Robert [Patrick Browne-Clayton Esq, 385 5th St, Campbell River, BC, Canada V9 3X4]; *b* 13 March 1947; *educ* Notre Dame U Nelson BC (BSc)

2c +Peter Shane [Peter Browne-Clayton Esq, 1444 Lawrence Ave, Kelowna, BC, V1 6M8]; *b* 21 May 1949; *educ* BC U (BSc); *m* 1972 *Mary Elizabeth, dau of W C Law, of Vancouver, and has issue:

1d *Nicole Ann; *b* 1975

2d *Celia Jeanne; *b* 1977

1c *Jeanne Madeline [Miss Jeanne Browne-Clayton, 104 West 11th Ave, Vancouver, BC, Canada V6J 2B5]; *b* 19 Aug 1953; *educ* BC U (BSc)

1a (cont.) Capt H V Acland *m* 2nd 20 Oct 1951 *Inez Amelia, dau of Robert Everett Mutch, of Charlottetown, Prince Edward Island, and formerly w of William David Sweetwood, and *d* Jan 1968

2a Arthur Nugent ACLAND later FLOYER-ACLAND (added FLOYER 1928 under will of George William Floyer, of Stafford House), CB (1940), DSO (1918), MC (1915), DL (Dorset 1957); *b* 7 Sept 1885; *educ* Blundell's; Lt-Gen DCLI WW I (despatches seven times, Croix de Guerre), Waziristan NW Frontier 1937–38 (despatches) and WW II, Brig 3rd (Jhelum) Inf Bde 1936, Maj-Gen cmdg 43rd (Wessex) Div (TA) 1938; Mily Sec to Sec State War 1940–42; High Sheriff Dorset 1953; *m* 6 Dec 1913 Evelyn Stafford (*d* 4 March 1973), dau of Stafford Still, of Lincoln's Inn, and *d* 18 Feb 1980, leaving:

1b Stafford Nugent, CBE (1967); *b* 23 Dec 1916; *educ* Marlborough; Brig, Lt-Col cmdg 1st Bn KOYLI 1959–61, DCLI 1937–59, Brig cmdg 130 (West Country) Inf Bde (TA) 1963, Brig i/c Admin and Dep Cdr Land Forces Borneo 1965, Brig AQ HQ Northern Cmd 1967, Dep Col LI (Somerset and Cornwall) 1972; High Sheriff Dorset 1974; *m* 14 April 1950 *Patricia Egidia Hastings [Mrs Stafford Floyer-Acland, The Dairy House, W Stafford, Dorchester], est dau of Lt-Col Richard St Barbe Emmott, IA, by Hon Irene Mary Egidia Clifton-Hastings-Campbell, 3rd dau of 3rd Baron Donington (*see* LOUDOUN, E), and *d* 1994, leaving issue:

1c +Richard Stafford [Richard Floyer-Acland Esq, Mill House, Harley, Salop]; *b* 1 Jan 1952; *educ* Marlborough; Maj LI; *m* 1983 *Sarah Margaret, dau of Henry Millington Synge, and has issue:

1d +Charles Stafford; *b* 1987

1d *Olivia Joy; *b* 1985

2d *Beatrice Rose; *b* 1990

2c +Andrew Arthur [Andrew Floyer-Acland Esq, Old Grist, Coombe, Wotton under Edge, Glos]; *b* 8 Nov 1955; *educ* Marlborough and Durham U (BA); *m* 1987 *Penelope Lucy Priscilla, er dau of Julian Gerard Wathen (*see* STARKEY, Bt), and has issue:

1d +Toby Julian; *b* 1989

1c *Victoria Egidia [Mrs Nagi El-Bay, 1 Christchurch Rd, Malvern, Worcs]; *b* 8 May 1962; *educ* Bristol U (BA); *m* 1992 *Nagi El-Bay, est s of Saad El-Bay, of Heliopolis, Egypt, and has issue:

1d *Hani Stafford; *b* 1995

2d *Noorah Egidia; *b* 1993

3a John Bevil; *b* 14 March 1890; *educ* Blundell's; Capt Pacific Coast Rangers, Canadian Forces France WW I, staff Pacific Cmd WW II; *m* 7 March 1914 Marjorie, dau of Herbert Guernsey, and *d* 14 Nov 1966, having had issue:

1b Ian Hugh; *b* 17 Oct 1914; P/O RCAF, WW II; *kas* 18 March 1941

1b *Ione Vivienne [Mrs Charles Guthrie, 161 Acland Rd, Ganges, Salt Spring, Vancouver Island, BC, Canada]; *b* 23 Dec 1915; Headmistress Strathcona Lodge Sch 1959; *m* 19 Sept 1936 Charles Clement Guthrie (*d* 18 March 1966), 5th s of Alexander Guthrie, and has issue:

1c *Barnaby Fairbairn; *b* 1 July 1937; *educ* U of Victoria, BC (BA 1968)

2c *Nicholas Bruce; *b* 14 Nov 1938; *educ* U of BC (BSc 1960, BEd 1961); *m* 2 July 1966 *Anna, only dau of Rev E W Scott, MA, and has issue:

1d *Russell Sean; *b* 20 June 1967

2d *Ross Cameron; *b* 19 Sept 1968

3d *Ian Benjamin; *b* 1970

4d *Ryan David; *b* 1981

1d *Jennifer Sarah; *b* 1974

4a Charles Edward Bankes; *b* 24 Dec 1906; *educ* Blundell's; T/Lt-Col DCLI WW II

1a Lalage Mary Kathleen; *b* 18 Feb 1889; *m* 21 Aug 1915 her cousin Capt Hubert Guy Dyke Acland, DSO, RN (later 4th Bt; *see* ACLAND, Bt, of Oxford) and *d* 5 May 1961, leaving issue

2a Sibell Norah Carteret; *b* 21 Sept 1892; VAD WW I; *m* 23 April 1919 Lt-Col Osborne Victor Maude-Roxby, MBE, MC (*d* 25 Oct 1949), s of Capt Herbert Maude-Roxby, MVO, RN, and had issue:

1b John Leycester; *b* 25 March 1920; P/O RAF WW II; *das* 1 Nov 1940

2b *Guy Nigel [Guy Maude-Roxby Esq, 1581 Rena Crescent, West Vancouver, BC, Canada]; *b* 20 Feb 1921; *educ* U of BC (BA); Canadian Army WW II ; *m* 25 April 1958 *Claire Eileen, dau of Joseph Pollard, and has issue:

1c *Dean Victor; *b* 10 July 1961

2c *Craig Leycester; *b* 4 April 1965

1b *Sylvia Norah Grace; *b* 30 May 1926; *m* 27 March 1951 *Frederick Molyneaux Hackney, Supt Yukon Customs, s of Samuel John Hackney, of Nanaimo, BC, and has issue:

1c *David Samuel; *b* 9 April 1955

2c *Joel Bruce; *b* 17 Dec 1957

1c *Sibell Jeanne; *b* 3 Feb 1952

2c *Gail Patricia; *b* 10 Aug 1953

3a Fanny Veronica Margaret; *b* 22 March 1894; *d* unm 14 Oct 1966

4a Victoria Letitia; *b* 8 Feb 1897; *m* 14 March 1928 Maj-Gen Nigel William Duncan, CB, CBE, DSO, DL, Roy Tank Regt, s of George William Duncan, and had issue:

1b *Elizabeth Letitia [Mrs John Deverell, Pitlands House, Ramsdell, nr Basingstoke, Hants]; *b* 13 Dec 1929; *m* 26 June 1954 *Maj John Christopher Byron Deverell, RA, s of Maj John Latham Deverell, and has issue:

1c *John Duncan; *b* 1 May 1955; *educ* Eton; Maj Roy Scots Dragoon Gds; *m* 1993 *Susanne Christiana Kampert, of Dortmund, Germany, and has issue:

1d *John Conrad Christopher; *b* 1993

1c *Virginia Letitia; *b* 22 May 1957

2b *Janet Lyndsay Norah; *b* 24 Feb 1932; *m* 1 Feb 1956 *Maj Malcolm Vincent Chichester Firth, RA, only s of Col Cecil William Mallaby Firth, MC, and has issue:

1c *Richard Lyndsay Martin; *b* 23 Oct 1957; *educ* Downside and RMA Sandhurst; Capt 4th/7th Roy Drag Gds; *m* 1987 *Georgina Clare, dau of Capt Frederick Henry Beresford Mainwaring-Burton, DSC, RM

2c *Andrew William Mallaby; *b* 22 June 1960; *educ* Downside and Reading U (BSc); *m* 1989 *Amanda, dau of Christopher Marriot, of Whitchurch, Berks, and has issue:

1d *Edward Peter William; *b* 1993

3c *Patrick Nigel Vincent; *b* 23 June 1961; *educ* Downside; *m* 1986 *Susan, dau of Gerald Grehan, of Naas, Co Kildare, and has issue:

1d *Robert William Gerald; *b* 1988

2d *Ian James Duncan; *b* 1991

3d *James Andrew Donald; *b* 1994

4c *David Malcolm Angus; *b* 19 Nov 1964; *educ* Dauntsey's Sch and Exeter U (BA)

3b *Christina Lalage; *b* 6 April 1935; *m* 11 Aug 1959 *Maj Roger Halliburton Young, RA, only s of Maurice Lindsay Young, MD, MRCS, MRCP, and has issue:

1c *James Lindsay; *b* 20 July 1967; *m* 1993 *Helen, dau of Neville Wood, of Spofforth, Yorks

2c *Anthony Halliburton; *b* 16 June 1968; Capt Light Dragoons

(3) Reginald Henry Dyke (Rev); *b* 8 June 1851; *educ* Trin Coll Oxford (MA); Chaplain Pau, France, 1855–1922; *m* 8 Jan 1879 Charlotte Eliza (*d* 24 July 1917), yst dau of George Price (*see* PRICE, Bt), and *d* 17 April 1932

(1) Frances Lydia Dyke; *m* 21 July 1863 Rev Charles Sandford Bere (*d* 1889) and *d* 19 April 1922, leaving issue

(2) Harriet Dyke; *m* 8 Sept 1863 George Griffith, MA (*d* 7 May 1902), and *d* 6 Nov 1921, leaving issue

(3) Angelina Anne Dyke; *m* 22 July 1865 Rev James Dunn (*d* 1919), vicar St John the Baptist, Bath, and *d* 9 April 1935, leaving issue

(4) Mary Dyke; *m* 30 June 1864 Rev Walter Hook (*d* 27 March 1899), Preb Wells, and *d* 18 Aug 1924, leaving issue

(5) Joanna Dorothea Dyke; *m* 30 June 1864 Leonard Harper, barrister, of Bruton, Somerset, 2nd s of Rt Rev Henry John Chitty Harper, DD, Bp Christchurch, NZ, and *d* 8 May 1917, leaving issue

(6) Sarah Lucy Dyke; *d* 19 April 1863

3 Charles Baldwin Dyke; Lt RN; *d* at sea 1837

4 Sir HENRY WENTWORTH ACLAND 1st Bt (*see* ACLAND, Bt, of Oxford)

5 Peter Leopold Dyke (Rev); *b* 3 June 1819; MA; preb Exeter, RD, vicar Broadclyst 1845–96, sub-dean Exeter 1887; *m* 1st 24 April 1845 Julia (*d* 18 Sept 1851), dau of Rev Benjamin Barker, rector Shipdham, Norfolk, and had issue:

(1) Thomas Dyke, of Christchurch, NZ; *b* 3 July 1846; *m* 10 Oct 1874 Flora Margaret (*d* 1885), dau of Robert Watt, of Christchurch, and *d* 1892, leaving issue:

1a Leopold George Dyke, OBE (1919), MC; *b* 2 July 1876; Maj NZ Army Service Corps Boer War 1900–01 and WW I (despatches three times); author: *The Early Canterbury Runs*; *m* 7 Feb 1935 Emily (*d* 26 April 1960), dau of Very Rev Walter Harper, MA, Dean Christchurch, and widow of Hugh Maude Reeves, of Hororata, NZ, and *dsp* 7 April 1948

(2) Benjamin Dyke; *b* 18 Aug 1847; Cdr RN; *m* 8 Dec 1881 Clare Emily (*d* 27 Dec 1936), dau of Edward Cay, of Melbourne, and *d* 7 July 1909, leaving issue:

1a Baldwyn John Dyke; *b* 8 Feb 1883; Lt-Col Roy Canadian Art and RFA, Canadian staff WW I; *m* 1 July 1914 Helen Claire (*d* 4 Nov 1940), dau of John Breakey, of Quebec, and *d* 12 May 1941, leaving issue:

1b John Ben Dyke; *b* 10 Dec 1916; *educ* Rugby; *m* 1st 5 Feb 1941 (*divorce* 1950) Beatrice Margaret, 3rd dau of William Willes, and had:

1c +John William Brian Dyke [John Esq, 6 St John's Terrace, Devoran, Cornwall TR3 6NE]; *b* 14 Dec 1942; *educ* Bradfield; *m* 1968 *Georgina Scarborough and has issue:

1d +Peter; *b* 1978

1d *Samantha; *b* 14 Dec 1969; *m* 1994 *Wensley Grosvenor Haydon-Baillie, of Wentworth Woodhouse, Yorks, s of Malcolm Haydon-Baillie and Mrs Peter Murray-Lee

2d *Carina; *b* 1972

2c Peter Ben Dyke; *b* 14 Jan 1947; *educ* Bradfield; *k* car crash 22 June 1972

1b (cont.) John Acland *m* 2nd 18 Dec 1950 *Lorna May , dau of Capt Harry Woodthorpe Graham, MC, of Johannesburg, and *d* 1991, having by her had issue:

3c +Thomas Jeremy Dyke [Thomas Acland Esq, 86 Hurstbourne Rd, Forest Hill, London SE23]; *b* 21 Nov 1952; *educ* Plymouth Coll and by Pat England has:

1d *Joseph Peter Reynolds; *b* 1988

1d *Polly Jane Reynolds; *b* 1993

1c *Diana Jane Dyke; *b* 9 June 1954; *m* 1975 *Leonardo Martinez, of Menorca, and has issue:

1d *Maria-Carmen; *b* 1977

2a Hubert Edward Peter Dyke; *b* 12 Aug 1884; Capt 11th King Edward's Own Lancers (Probyn's Horse); *m* 5 Sept 1912 Dorothy Marion (*d* 7 April 1958), dau of Sir John Henry Thorold, 12th Bt (*qv*), and *d* 29 Oct 1953, having issue:

1b Benjamin Henry Dyke; *b* 22 Oct 1913; *d* 3 Feb 1914

2b Simon John Dyke; *b* 20 Sept 1916; F/Lt RAFVR WW II; *d* as POW Tokyo 30 Dec 1942

3b Roger Dyke; *b* 4 Feb 1920; *m* 1st 27 Oct 1945 (*divorce* 1951) Etta Sylvia, only child of Nicholas Galperin; *m* 2nd 25 Oct 1951 *Molly, dau of David MacLurg, of Washington, USA, and *d* 1984, having by her had issue:

1c +Simon Nicholas Dyke [Simon Acland Esq, Avalon, Camphill Devon Community, Hampstead Village, Devon]; *b* 6 July 1953; *m* 1981 *Kathleen Spellman and has issue:

1d *Rosemary Anjelica; *b* 1983

1b *Anne Dyke [Mrs Ian Gordon, The Old Laundry, Syston, nr Grantham, Lincs]; *b* 6 Aug 1915; Subaltern ATS; *m* 2 Oct 1948 Ian Graham Gordon (*d* 1993), only s of James Henry Gordon

3a Lauchlan Henry Dyke, MC; *b* 15 April 1889; *educ* Bath Coll and Magdalen Coll Oxford (BA); T/Capt RE WW I; *m* 3 Nov 1923 Doris Dar, yr dau of Hugh Davidson, and *d* 30 Jan 1969, leaving issue:

1b +Julian Dyke [Julian Acland Esq, 11 Dunton Cl, Four Oaks, Sutton Coldfield, Warwicks B75 5QD]; *b* 13 Sept 1924; *educ* St Paul's and Magdalen Coll Oxford (MA, MSc, BCh) and Sheffield U (PhD); Consultant Chemical Pathologist Manor Hosp Walsall 1971–90; *m* 18 March 1964 *Alison, MB, ChB, er dau of Arthur William Chapman, CBE, and has issue:

1c *Ann Sarah; *b* 26 Dec 1965

(3) Henry Dyke (Rev); *b* 4 March 1850; MA Oxon; rector Luccombe, Somerset; *m* 22 Jan 1878 Adelaide Clementina Hart (*d* 20 June 1941), 2nd dau of Richard Vaughan Davis, and *d* 8 Jan 1903, leaving issue:

1a Edward Leopold Dyke, CB (1937), MVO (1913), JP (1942), DL (1952) both Somerset; *b* 7 Dec 1878; *educ* Bedford Sch; Engr-R-Adml, cmdg RN Engr Coll Keyham 1930–33, Naval ADC to HM 1933, Maj HG WW II; *m* 12 Oct 1910 Phyllis Mary (*d* 25 Sept 1973), dau of Connell Whipple, MD, and *d* 11 March 1968, having had issue:

1b Peter Connell Duke; *b* 24 Sept, *d* 7 Oct 1920

1b *Adria Margaret [Mrs James Dennis, 37 Church St, Henley-on-Thames, Oxon RG9 1SE]; *b* 17 Jan 1914; *m* 1st 16 Jan 1935 Arthur Francis Procter (*d* 1970), of Eastwick Manor, nr Harlow, Essex, only s of Sir Henry Edward Edleston Procter, CBE; *m* 2nd 1971 Lt Col James Hawke Dennis, TD, Chev Legn Honour (*d* 1985), and by her 1st husb has issue:

1c *Susan Caroline; *b* 1939; *m* 1969 *Timothy Gordon Keown and has issue:

1d *David Nigel; *b* 1971

1d *Alice Belinda; *b* 1972

2a John Henry Dyke; *b* 24 June 1880; LRCP, MRCS, T/Capt RAMC, att Somerset LI; *m* 4 Nov 1914 Elizabeth Margaret, FCA (*m* 2nd 22 Dec 1926 Herbert Gwynne Evans, MC, FICA; *d* 25 June 1961), dau of Charles Corner, and was *ka* 12 July 1916

3a Rt Rev Richard Dyke; *b* 3 Oct 1881; *educ* Keble Coll Oxford (MA); Capt 1st Vol Bn Oxon LI; curate St Mary Slough 1905–10, SPG Missionary Ahmednagar India 1910, SPG Sec 1924–29, Bp Bombay 1920–47, Kaisar-i-Hind medal 1st Cl 1947, Assist Bp Bath and Wells 1948; *d* unm 4 Jan 1954

1a Katharine Anne; *b* 3 Oct 1881; *d* unm 1 Jan 1966

2a Adelaide Mary; *b* 3 July 1884; *d* unm 3 Dec 1972

3a Theodora Julia; *b* 19 June 1891; *d* unm 9 April 1977

(1) Katherine Dyke; *d* unm 29 May 1872

5 (cont.) The Rev Peter Acland *m* 2nd 12 Dec 1872 Julie (*dsp* 29 Oct 1906), dau of Philip Wappner, of Dusseldorf, and *d* 24 Oct 1899

6 John Barton Arundell; *b* 25 Nov 1823; MA Oxon; barrister; MLC NZ; *m* 17 Jan 1860 Emily Weddell (*d* 23 July 1905), est dau of Rt Rev Henry John Chitty Harper, DD, Bp Christchurch, and *d* 18 May 1904, having had issue:

(1) Barton Duke; *b* 1862; *d* 7 March 1863

(2) John Dyke, JP (Somerset); *b* 17 Feb 1863; *m* 14 May 1902 Mary Eveline (*d* 4 Aug 1961 aged 92), er dau of Rev Canon Harry Woodford St Hill, of Hawkes Bay, NZ, and *d* 24 April 1944, leaving issue:

1a +Thomas St Hill [Thomas Acland Esq, 12 Connelly St, Geraldine, S Canterbury, NZ]; *b* 8 April 1910; 2nd NZ Expdny Force WW II; *m* 14 Sept 1963 *Margaret Ellen, dau of John Musgrove and widow of Cdr John Swift Sharp, OBE, RD, RNR

1a *Emily Mary Dyke, JP (Somerset 1946) [Miss Emily Acland JP, Middle Croft, Bossington Lane, Porlock, Somerset]; *b* 5 Sept 1905; FANY and ATS WW II

(3) Henry Dyke; *b* 21 Sept 1867; *educ* Ch Ch Oxford (BA); barrister Inner Temple; memb Senate NZ U, Danish Consul Christchurch 1926, Order Dannebrog; *m* 25 April 1906 Elizabeth Grace (*d* 29 Oct 1942), 3rd dau of Hon James Watson, MLC, of Sydney, NSW, and *d* 12 Jan 1943, leaving issue:

1a Adrienne Maude; *b* 13 Dec 1907; *m* 1 Oct 1929 James Lyndon Macfarlane (*d* 30 Nov 1962), s of David Duncan Macfarlane, of NZ, and *d* 25 Feb 1950, leaving issue

2a *Philippa Mabel [Miss Philippa Acland, 8 Dublin St, Christchurch, NZ]; *b* 1 June 1914

(4) Hugh Thomas Dyke (Sir), CMG (1917), CBE (1919); *b* 10 Sept 1874; FRCS, LRCP; Col NZAMC Reserve Offrs Boer War 1900–01 and WW I (despatches), ktd 1933; *m* 15 April 1903 Evelyn Mary (*d* 6 April 1964), 2nd dau of John Lindsay Evans, and *d* 15 April 1956, having had issue:

1a Hugh John Dyke (Sir), KBE (1968), JP; *b* 17 Jan 1904; MP 1942–46, memb NZ Wool Bd, sheep farmer; *m* 12 June 1935 *Katherine Wilder, dau of John Davies Ormond, of Hawkes Bay, and *d* 1981, having had issue:

1b +John Barton Ormond [John Acland Esq, Mount Peel, South Canterbury, NZ]; *b* 13 March 1936; *m* 9 Dec 1961 *Dorothy Rosemary, dau of Allan Albert Hobson, of Hawkes Bay, and has issue:

1c +John Barton; *b* 3 Oct 1964

2c +Paul Hobson; *b* 30 Nov 1965

3c +Henry Dyke; *b* 1975

1c *Jessica Emily; *b* 6 May 1963

2c *Georgina Katharine; *b* 1969

3c *Alexandra Evelyn; *b* 1970

2b +Mark Arundell [Mark Acland Esq, Mount Somers Stn, Canterbury, NZ]; *b* 14 Feb 1939; *m* *Joanna, dau of John Quaife, and has issue:

1c +David Quaife; *b* 19–

2c +Benjamin Napier; *b* 19–

3c +Hamish Ormond; *b* 19–

3b +Simon Henry Harper (Rev) [The Rev Simon Acland, 27B Tite St, London SW3 4JR]; *b* 18 July 1941; *m* 1970 (*divorce* 1983) his cousin Nicola Hornby, dau of John Pavey, and has issue:

1c +Michael Bernard Pavey; *b* 1971

2c +Luke Simon Burgoyne; *b* 1980

1c *Kim Lin Ovans; *b* 1973

2c *Anna Katherine Hornby; *b* 1975

1b *Audrey Ann [Mrs Hamish McHardy, Tauroa, Haverlock N, NZ]; *b* 6 May 1937; *m* 1960 *Hamish McHardy and has issue:

1c *Jonathan Forbes; *b* 1962

1c *Kate Acland; *b* 1961

2c *Rebecca Thornley; *b* 23 Feb 1965

3c *Sarah Ormond; *b* 1966

4c *Emma Elizabeth; *b* 1968

2b *Evelyn Wilder; *b* 9 March 1947; *m* 1973 *James Leybourne Wallace (*see* JACKSON, Bt, of Arsley)

3b *Sarah Burgoyne; *b* 27 April 1951

2a Geoffrey Dyke; *b* 28 April, *d* 5 Aug 1905

3a Colin Dyke; *b* 16 June 1906; *educ* Christ's Coll Christchurch; S African forces WW II; *m* 1 Feb 1936 *Sybil Marjorie, dau of Thomas Arthur Warner, of Durban, and had issue:

1b +Hugh Thomas Dyke [Hugh Acland Esq, 17 Onehuka Rd, Melling, Lower Hutt, Wellington, NZ]; *b* 7 March 1940; *educ* Christ's Coll Christchurch (BAgSci 1964); *m* 3 Nov 1965 *Fredericka Scott, est dau of G A Hutton, of NZ, and has issue:

1c +Thomas Dyke; *b* 1972

1c *Susannah Scott; *b* 28 Oct 1967

2c *Annabel Emily; *b* 1970

1b *Mary Ann Warner; *b* 23 Oct 1936; *m* 1st 12 May 1964 (*divorce* 1968) Josef Maria Baukes; *m* 2nd 1970 *Christopher John Hindmarsh and has:

1c *John Marcos; *b* 1973

1c *Brigid Acland; *b* 1974

4a Michael Dyke; *b* 26 March 1911; Lt NZ Art WW II; *m* 15 June 1946 *Elizabeth Vibert, dau of Harry de Courcy McArthur, of Dunedin, NZ, and *d* 8 Jan 1994, leaving:

1b +Peter McArthur; *b* 4 April 1947

2b +Alastair Michael; *b* 19 March 1950; *m* 25 Feb 1989 *Margot, dau of Anthony Grace, and has:

1c *Monica; *b* 9 Sept 1991

2c *Elizabeth; *b* 1 July 1993

3b +Richard Hugh [Richard Acland Esq, 98 Fendalton Road, Christchurch 800, NZ]; *b* 19 June 1951; *m* 2 Dec 1978 *Nina Catherine, dau of Christopher Greeson, of NZ, and has:

1c +George Christopher; *b* 22 Sept 1983

1c *Emily Mary; *b* 24 Oct 1985

2c *Lucy Elizabeth; *b* 16 Nov 1988

1a Mary *b* 19, *d* 20 Jan 1910

2a *Elisabeth Evelyn Dyke; *b* 22 June 1913; *m* 15 Dec 1943 John Pavey (*d* 9 Sept 1953), s of Rev James Charles John Pavey, and has issue

(1) Agnes Dyke, OBE (1918); *m* 15 Sept 1885 Walter Empson, s of Rev Arthur John Empson (*d* 14 June 1934), of Eydon Rectory, Northants, and *d* 3 April 1945 aged 84, leaving issue

(2) Emily Dyke; *d* young 1864

(3) Mary Emily Dyke; *m* 1887 Frederick Villebois Lysaght, of NZ, and *d* 10 Jan 1916

(4) Harriet Dyke; *m* 30 Dec 1908 Maj Archibald Claude Douglas Spencer, Roy Irish Rifles (*d* 8 Nov 1929)

(5) Lucy Alice Dyke; *m* 19 Jan 1898 Oliver Scott Thomson (*d* 21 May 1928), s of William Thomson, of NZ, and *d* 6 Aug 1903, having had issue

(6) Elizabeth Dyke; *m* 12 May 1896 Charles Arthur Dunn (*d* 8 June 1949), est s of Rev James Dunn, of Bathwick, Bath, and *d* 13 Sept 1959, having had issue

(7) Emily Rosa Dyke; *m* 28 April 1915 John Herbert Berthon Williams (*d* 1916), of Havelock North, NZ, and *d* 12 June 1950, leaving issue

7 Dudley Reginald Dyke; *d* 1837

1 Lydia Dorothea; *d* 14 March 1858

2 Agnes Lucy; *m* 3 Aug 1848 Arthur Mills (*d* 12 Oct 1898), MP Exeter, and *d* 23 May 1895, leaving issue

Sir THOMAS *d* 22 July 1871; his s,

Sir Thomas Dyke Acland, 7th Bt, PC; *b* 25 May 1809; MA, Hon DCL Oxon, Fell All Souls; MP W Somerset 1837–47 and 1885–86 and N Devon 1865–85, Hon Col 3rd Vol Bn Devonshire Regt, Maj 1st Devonshire Yeo Cav; *m* 1st 14 March 1841 Mary (*d* 11 June 1851), est dau of Sir Charles Mordaunt, 8th Bt, of Massingham, and had, with other issue:

1 **Sir (Charles) Thomas Dyke, 8th Bt**, JP and DL (Somerset and Devon); *b* 16 July 1842; *educ* Ch Ch Oxford (MA); barrister Inner Temple 1867; CA and High Sheriff Devon 1903, Dep Warden Stannaries, MP E Cornwall 1882–35 and NE Cornwall 1885–92, Parly Sec BOT 1886, 2nd Ch Estate Commr, Maj and Hon Lt-Col 1st Devon Imp Yeo; *m* 1 Nov 1879 Gertrude (*d* 5 Aug 1920), 3rd dau of Sir John Walrond Walrond, 1st Bt, and sister of 1st Baron Waleran (see 1963 edn), and *dsp* 18 Feb 1919

2 ARTHUR HERBERT DYKE ACLAND (Sir), **9th Bt**

Sir **Thomas** *m* 2nd 18 June 1856 Mary (*d* 14 May 1892), dau of John Erskine, bro of 2nd Earl of Rosslyn (*qv*), and *d* 29 May 1898

The 8th Bt's bro,

Sir Arthur Herbert Dyke Acland, 9th Bt, PC; *b* 13 Oct 1847; *educ* Ch Ch Oxford (MA); Hon Fell Balliol, Steward Ch Ch 1879–85, Sr Bursar Balliol 1884–88, Hon LLD Leeds 1904 and Bristol 1912; MP Rotherham 1885–89, V-Pres Ctee Cncl Educn 1892–95; *m* 14 June 1873 Alice Sophia (*d* 5 July 1935), est dau of Rev Francis Macaulay Cunningham, MA, rector Brightwell, Oxon, and had issue:

1 FRANCIS DYKE ACLAND (Sir), **10th Bt**

2 Cuthbert Charles Dyke; *b* 30 May 1875; *d* 14 April 1882

1 Mabel Alice; *b* 17 April 1891; *m* 1 Feb 1919 Sir Frederick Carl Bovenschen, KCB, KBE, Jt Perm Under Sec War, s of Carl Bovenschen, and *d* 13 Feb 1975, leaving a dau

Sir ARTHUR *d* 9 Oct 1926; his s,

Sir Francis Dyke Acland, 10th Bt, PC (1915), JP (N R Yorks), JP and DL (Devon); *b* 7 March 1874; Jr Examiner Educn Dept 1900–03; MP Richmond Yorks 1906–10, Camborne 1910–22, Tiverton 1923–24 and N Cornwall 1932; PPS to Sec State War 1906–8, Fin Sec and memb Army Cncl 1908–10 and 1911, Under Sec For Affrs 1911–15, Fin Sec Treasury 1915, Parly Sec Bd Ag and Fisheries 1915–16; memb Senate London U, Chm: Cncl Bedford Coll and UK Dental Bd, Forestry Commr; *m* 1st 31 Aug 1905 Eleanor Margaret (*d* 12 Dec 1933), dau of Charles James Cropper, and had issue:

1 RICHARD THOMAS DYKE ACLAND (Sir), **11th Bt**

2 Arthur Geoffrey Dyke; *b* 17 May 1908; *educ* Rugby and Trin Coll Cambridge (BA 1930); Capt Border Regt; *m* 1 April 1932 (Winifred) Julian Dorothy, yr dau of Lt-Col Sydney Roden Fothergill, JP, DL, and *d* 14 Sept 1964, having had issue:

(1) +Oliver Geoffrey Dyke; *b* 20 Sept 1934; *educ* Heversham GS and Magdalene Coll Cambridge; late 2nd Lt Border Regt; *m* 25 July 1959 *Judith Veronica, 2nd dau of Peter Williams, and has issue:

1a +Peter Geoffrey Dyke; *b* 7 Aug 1961

2a +Francis Oliver Dyke; *b* 8 Nov 1963

3a +Christopher John Dyke; *b* 7 Sept 1966

(2) +Robin Julian Dyke; *b* 10 June 1937; *educ* Heversham GS and Magdalene Coll Cambridge

(3) +Edward Francis Dyke; *b* 23 April 1942; *educ* Heversham GS and RAC Cirencester; *m* Janet Anne, dau of — Ellenington, and has issue:

1a +Thomas Edward Dyke; *b* 11 Feb 1972

(4) Rowland Christopher Dyke; *b* 14 June 1951; *d* 18 July 1953

(1) Rose Ellen; *b* 21 Aug 1944; *d* 21 June 1959

2 (cont.) Mr and Mrs Arthur Acland also adopted:

*Martin Hilary Dyke; *b* 22 Oct 1953; *educ* The Lakes Sch Windermere

3 Cuthbert Henry Dyke; *b* 18 Nov 1910; *educ* Trin Coll Cambridge (BA 1932); Maj RE, High Sheriff Westmorland 1968

1 Eleanor Edith Dyke; *b* 12 Oct 1913; *d* 27 Feb 1924

Sir Francis *m* 2nd 10 Dec 1937 Constance (*d* 12 Oct 1940), dau of George Denis Darville Dudley, of Oxford, and *d* 9 June 1939

His son,

Sir Richard Thomas Dyke Acland, 11th Bt; *b* 26 Nov 1906; *educ* Rugby and Balliol Coll Oxford (BA 1927); barrister Inner Temple 1939; Lt 96th (Roy Devon Yeo) Field Bde RA; Pncpl Lecturer St Luke's Coll Exeter; MP Barnstaple 1935–45 and Gravesend 1947–55, Assist Lib Whip 1935–37, 2nd Ch Estates Commr 1950–51, Ldr Cwlth Parly Party 1944–45; *m* 15 April 1936 Anne Stella, ARIBA (*d* 1992), yr dau of Robert Greenwood Alford, of Chelsea, and *d* 24 Nov 1990, leaving issue:

1 Sir JOHN DYKE ACLAND, **12th and present Bt**

2 +Robert Dyke [Robert Acland Esq, 2020 Winston Ave, Louisville, KY, USA]; *b* 20 June 1941; *educ* Bryanston and London U (MB, BS London 1964), FRCS,

LRCP 1964; *m* 1st 24 Aug 1963 (*divorce* 1983) (Susan Maureen) Sarah, dau of Cdr James Wood, RN, of Liss Forest, Hants, and has issue:

(1) +Daniel James (Dyke); *b* 21 Feb 1969; *educ* Berkeley U Calif; has dropped forename Dyke

(1) *Beatrice Maud (Dyke); *b* 30 Dec 1966; *educ* Duke U Calif; has dropped forename Dyke

2 (cont.) Robert Acland *m* 2nd 1983 (*divorce* 1990) Susan Ann, dau of Thomas L Bishop, of Kentucky, and has further issue:

(2) +Benjamin Thomas; *b* 1984

(2) *Emily Grace; *b* 1986

3 +Henry Dyke [Dr Henry Acland, 1339 Talmadge St, Los Angeles, Calif, USA]; *b* 22 May 1943; *educ* Clifton and Magdalene Coll Cambridge (BA), DPhil (Oxon); *m* 8 June 1967 (*divorce* 1977) (Irene) Norma, dau of Percy Norman Gatley

4 William Dyke; *b* 17 Jan 1945; *d* 1945

ACLAND of Oxford

Arms: Chequy argent and sable, a fess gules, with in chief a mullet for difference. **Crest:** A man's hand apaumée lying fesswise to the sinister, couped at the wrist in a glove, thereon a falcon perched all proper. **Motto:** *Inébranlable* ('Unshakable'). **Creation:** Bt. (UK) 16 June 1890.

SIR (CHRISTOPHER) GUY DYKE ACLAND, 6TH BT, of St Mary Magdalen, Oxford, MVO (1990) [Lt-Col Sir Guy Acland Bt MVO, Buckingham Palace, London SW1A 1AA]; *b* 24 March 1946; *s* f 1983; *educ* All Hallows Sch and RMA Sandhurst; RA: commissioned 1966, BAOR 26 Field Regt 1967–70, UK and Hong Kong 3 RHA 1970–73, BAOR and UK 22 AD Regt 1974–77, psc 1978, staff HQ Eastern Dist 1979–80, cmded Q (Sanna's Post) Battery BAOR (5 Regt) 1981–83, GSO(2) Army Staff Duties Directorate MOD 1983–85, 2 i/c RHA BAOR 1986–88, Equerry to HRH THE DUKE OF EDINBURGH 1988–90 and HM THE QUEEN (also Dep Master Household) 1994–, GSO(1) Management Serv Orgn 3 MOD 1990–92; *m* 1971 *Christine Mary Carden, yr dau of Dr John Waring, of Totland Bay, IoW, and has:

1 +ALEXANDER JOHN DYKE; *b* 29 May 1973

2 +Hugh Anthony Waring Dyke; *b* 1976

Lineage: Sir THOMAS DYKE ACLAND, 10th Bt, of Columb-John, Devon (*qv*), had a 4th s:

Sir Henry Wentworth Acland, 1st Bt (UK), so *cr* 16 June 1890, KCB; *b* 23 Aug 1815; MD, DCL, LLD, FRS, Oxford: Regius Prof Medicine 1857–94, Radcliffe Librarian and Hon Student Ch Ch, memb GMC 1858–74 (Pres 1874–87),Hon Physician to HM EDWARD VII when PRINCE OF WALES; *m* 14 July 1846 Sarah (*d* 25 Oct 1878), est dau of William Cotton, DCL, FRS, of Walwood, Essex, and had:

1 WILLIAM ALISON DYKE (Sir), **2nd Bt**

2 Henry Dyke; *b* 14 Oct 1850; Lt Cornwall Vol Regt; FBI, FGS; *m* 16 Nov 1878 Margaret Hitchens (*d* 16 Jan 1939), est dau of John Jope Rogers, of Penrose-Helston, and *d* 4 April 1936, having had issue:

(1) Sarah Dyke; *b* and *d* 1879

3 Theodore Dyke; *b* 14 Nov 1851; *educ* Ch Ch Oxford (MA, MD, FRCP, MRCS); Brevet Lt-Col RAMC (T) and PMO Egyptian Army 1883; consulting physician and Govr St Thomas's and Brompton Hosps and King Edward's Sanatorium Midhurst, Hon consulting physician Min Pensions, Pres London Egyptian Medical Bd, Medical Advsr Sudan Govt, 2nd Cl Osmanieh, 4th Cl Medjidie, 2nd Cl Order Nile; *m* 12 April 1888 Caroline Cameron (*d* 20 March 1929), only surv dau of Sir William Gull, 1st Bt (*qv*), and *d* 16 April 1931, having had issue:

(1) Theodore William Gull; *b* 7 Nov 1890; *educ* Gresham's and King's Coll Cambridge (BA 1912, MA 1923); ARIC; Hon Curate St Luke's, Stanmore, Winchester, 1955–60, memb Cncl Missions Seamen, memb Bd CA, Christian Evidence Soc, Govrs St Olave's GS Fndn, Bishop's Coll Cheshunt and Standing Ctee Nat Soc, Headmaster King Edward VI Sch Norwich, deacon 1953, priest 1956; *m* 24 May 1944 *Mary Maxwell [Mrs Theodore Acland, Becton Lodge, Bereweeke Rd, Winchester], yst dau of Robert Maxwell Moffat, MD, and *d* 13 Oct 1960

(1) Aimee Sarah Agnes Dyke; *b* 14 May, *d* 17 Sept 1889

4 Herbert Dyke; *b* 9 April 1855; *d* 4 June 1877

5 Reginald Brodie Dyke (Sir), KC (1904), JP (Berks); *b* 18 May 1856; *educ* Univ Coll Oxford (MA); barrister Inner Temple 1881, Bencher 1913, Recorder Shrewsbury 1901–03 and Oxford 1903, Judge Advocate Fleet 1904, jr counsel Admlty 1897–1904, memb Roy Commn Legal Delay 1913, chm Berks QS, ktd 1914; *m* 12 Aug 1885 Helen Emma (*d* 31 Aug 1943), dau of Rev Thomas Fox, Rector Temple Combe, Somerset, and *d* 18 Feb 1924, leaving issue:

(1) Edward Fox Dyke; *b* 9 Nov 1891; *educ* Winchester; AEA, S/Ldr RAF WW I and WW II; *m* 29 March 1924 Beatrice (d 1972), dau of Dr John Wiseman Laver, of Grimston, Norfolk, and *d* 31 May 1978, leaving issue:

1a *(Barbara) Elizabeth [Mrs Richard Adams, Benwells, 26 Church St, Whitchurch, Hants RG28 7AR]; *b* 26 Feb 1929; FRSA, FSA; *m* 26 Sept 1949 *Richard George Adams, MA (Oxon), Hon FRSL, s of Dr Evelyn George Beadon Adams, and has issue:

1b *Juliet Vera Lucy; *b* 31 Jan 1958; MA (Oxon), AM (Stanford, USA); *m* 1981 *Peter Johnson, MA (Oxon), AM (Stanford, USA), MBA, DPhil, FRSA, and has issue:

1c *Robert Alasdair Edward; *b* 1994

1c *Lucy Charlotte Acland; *b* 1986

2c Sophia Helen Lara; *b* & *d* 1989

3c *Miranda Sylvia Louise; *b* 1991

2b *Rosamond Beatrice Elizabeth; *b* 17 April 1960; *m* 1983 *Michael Mahony and has issue:

1c *Sarah Elizabeth Louise; *b* 1989

2c *Grace Anna Kathryn; *b* 1991

2a *(Phyllis) Penelope Jane; *b* 22 Aug 1932; SRN; *m* 12 April 1958 *Glynn Meirion Owen, MBE, MSc, only s of William Owen, and has issue:

1b *William Edward; *b* 14 Jan 1959; *m* 1992 (*divorce* 1994) Rebecca Barnacle

1b *Eleri Jane; *b* 13 May 1961; SRN; Registered Sick Children's Nurse; *m* 1983 *Patrick Dodge and has issue:

1c *Thomas Patrick; *b* 1986

2c *Alan James; *b* 1989

1c *Emma Jane; *b* 1992

2c *Sîan Kathleen; *b* 1994

2b *Alys Mair; *b* 20 March 1964; *m* 1st 1990 (*divorce* 1992) David Marles; *m* 2nd 1995 *Peter Goodchild and has by him:

1c *Elke Marianne; *b* 1997

3a *Judith Sarah; *b* 7 July 1942

(2) Wilfred Reginald Dyke, AFC (1919), DFC (1919); *b* 26 June 1894; W/Cdr RAF WW I (despatches twice); *m* 4 Aug 1921 Mary Strange (d 1991), of Little Orchard, Hill Brow, Liss, Hants (*m* 2nd 23 May 1939 A/Cdre Thomas Edward Barham Howe, CBE), dau of Thomas Marshall, of Lee-on-Solent, and was *k* in a flying accident 1 Oct 1937, leaving issue:

1a *Joan Mary Louise [Mrs Peter Gould, Hambledon, 35 Stoke Rd, Cobham, Surrey KT11 3BG]; *b* 7 Feb 1923; 3rd Offr WRNS WW II; *m* 2 March 1946 *Lt-Cdr Peter Allen Ridd Gould, RN (ret), s of Maj Cyril Edward Gould, MC, RA, and has issue:

1b *Timothy Acland Ridd; *b* 17 July 1948; *educ* Bradfield; *m* 1976 (*divorce* 1994) Veronica Ruth Franklin and has issue:

1c *James Acland Ridd; *b* 1979

1c *Lucinda Jane Louise; *b* 1977

1b *Angela Mary; *b* 16 Oct 1950; *m* 1970 *Nicholas David Gooda and has issue:

1c *Edward Anthony; *b* 1970; *m* 1997 *Karen Anne Duff

1c *Anita Helen; *b* 1973

2a *Cynthia Helen [Mrs Robert Taylor, The Farm House, Enton Green, Godalming, Surrey]; *b* 9 Nov 1928; *m* 18 Dec 1953 *Robert Coston Taylor, yr s of Frederick Taylor, and has issue:

1b *Frederick Robert Acland; *b* 29 May 1961; BSc, LRPS

1b *Pamela Harriet; *b* 2 Aug 1957; *m* 1983 *George Goldsbrough, only sn of E Goldsbrough, of Johannesburg

(1) Hilda Mary; *b* 18 June 1890; *m* 1st 2 June 1914 Maj James Pearson Stockley, IA (*ka* 6 Jan 1916), s of Col Charles More Stockley, CB, and had:

1a John Acland Stockley; *b* 1916 *d* unm 8 Jan 1995

(1) (cont.) Mrs James Stockley *m* 2nd 15 Jan 1922 George Burt Geake, LDS, RCS (*d* 29 March 1968), s of Joseph Ford Geake, and *d* 3 Aug 1964

(2) Ruth Helen; *b* 10 March 1899; *d* unm 14 Nov 1977

6 Francis Edward Dyke; *b* 12 May 1857; MICE, MIME, Capt RA; *m* 8 Jan 1885 Marion Sarah (*d* 5 Feb 1937), dau of Rt Rev William Kenneth Macrorie, DD, Bp Maritzburg, and *d* 14 March 1943, leaving issue:

(1) Herbert Arthur Dyke; *b* 9 Oct 1886; *educ* Harrow and King's Coll Cambridge (BA); AMICE, MIMechE, Lt Cambridge U Rifle Vol Corps; *m* 22 Sept 1914 Maud Kathleen, er dau of Col George Ernest Branson, and *d* 25 May 1968, leaving issue:

1a Pauline Marjorie; *b* 14 Dec 1915; *d* unm 28 April 1936

2a Gwyneth Sybil, FCA; *b* 22 April 1918; *m* 1st 6 June 1942 F/Lt Roderick Stanley Emerson, RAFVR (*ka* 21 Feb 1944), s of George Emerson, of Argentina, and has issue:

1b *(George An)T(h)ony Dyke [Tony Emerson Esq, Oddington Lodge, Moreton-in-Marsh, Glos GL56 0VR]; *b* 5 Aug 1943; *educ* Eton and Magdalen Coll Oxford (BA); late Capt 17th/21st Lancers; *m* 1972 *Jillian Graham, dau of F Graham Roberts, OBE, and has issue:

1c *(George) Mark; *b* 1974

2c *Edward Anthony; *b* 1976

3c *William Robert; *b* 1982

2a (cont.) Mrs Roderick Emerson *m* 2nd 8 Nov 1962 Lt-Col Sir Henry Christopher Carden, 4th Bt (*qv*), and *d* 19 May 1996

3a *Stephanie Jane; *b* 9 May 1924; MChS; *m* 2 Aug 1947 Reginald Chase, LDS, RCS (*d* 1981), s of Reginald James Chase, and has issue:

1b *Philip Reginald [Philip Chase Esq, Warwick Court, Winchester, Hants]; *b* 27 March 1949; *educ* Seaford Coll; *m* 1st 1984 (*divorce* 1985)

Josephine Marian, dau of W T Whiting, of Cheadle Hume, Cheshire; *m* 2nd 1988 *Josephine Eleanor Weeks

2b *Douglas Martyn [Douglas Chase Esq, 17 Darlaston Rd, London SW19]; *b* 19 June 1955; *educ* Bradfield; *m* 1983 *Noëlle Mary Rose, dau of Mrs Barbara Thompson, of West Droyle, Chichester, and has issue:

1c *Guy William Thompson; *b* 1989

1c *Verity Jane; *b* 1986

(2) Kenneth Francis Dyke, Capt RN; *b* 16 Oct 1890; *m* 1st 15 July 1919 (*divorce* 1946) Katherine Farquharson, only dau of Robert Granbery Baillie, of Lanarks, and had issue:

1a Elizabeth Katherine Baillie; *b* 11 May 1920

(2) (cont.) Capt Kenneth Acland *m* 2nd 4 April 1946 Jean Elspeth Clare, dau of R-Adml Colin MacKenzie, CIE, DSO, and *d* 30 April 1975

(1) Charis Agnes; *b* 14 June 1888; *d* unm 24 Oct 1963

(2) Clemence Margaret; *b* 9 Oct 1889; Ambulance Driver WW I, CD WW II; MBOU; Research Assist Dept Tuberculosis Medical Sch Cardiff 1920–29; *d* unm 10 March 1973

7 Alfred Dyke, CBE (1920), JP (Devon); *b* 19 Aug 1858; Lt-Col Roy 1st Devon Yeo 1910–14 (TD), cmdg Base Depot Remounts BEF 1915, Assist Dir Labour 1917, Labour Cmdt Australia Corps 1918, KJStJ, Croix de Guerre; *m* 30 July 1885 Hon Beatrice Danvers Smith, DG StJ (*d* 4 Dec 1942), dau of Viscountess Hambleden (*qv*), and *d* 22 March 1937, leaving issue:

(1) Arthur William, OBE (1945), MC (1917), TD; *b* 20 Nov 1897; *educ* Eton; Lt-Col Gren Gds Reserve Offrs, Lt-Col 96th (Roy Devon Yeo) Field Bde RA WW I (wounded twice) and WW II (21st Army Gp HQ); OStJ; *m* 16 Dec 1926 Violet Gwendolen (d 1984), yr dau of Canon Hon Robert Grimston (*see* VERULAM, E), and *d* 1992, leaving issue:

1a +David Alfred, DL (Glos) [David Acland Esq DL, The Manor, Notgrove, nr Cheltenham, Glos]; *b* 21 Oct 1929; *educ* Eton and Ch Ch Oxford (MA); ch exec operating co W H Smith 1974; *m* 19 Oct 1960 *Serena Elizabeth, est dau of Cyril Hugh Kleinwort (*see* KLEINWORT, Bt), and has issue:

1b +Harry Alexander; *b* 22 March 1963; *m* 1st 1991 Catherine Juliet, MB, BS (*d* 1992 following a yachting accident), dau of Cdr Richard Masterman, RNR; *m* 2nd 1994 *Diana Chisell and by her has:

1c +Rory; *b* 1996

1c *Arabella Catherine; *b* 7 Feb 1998

1b *Lucy Henrietta; *b* 23 Jan 1962; *m* 1988 *Nicholas C Morris, yst s of C P Morris, of Radnor Walk, London SW3, and has issue:

1c *Leo; *b* 1991

1c *Pandora; *b* 1989

2a +Martin Edward, JP (Herts 1964) [Martin Acland Esq JP, Standon Green End, Ware, Herts SG11 1BN]; *b* 31 July 1932; *educ* Eton; Lt FF Yeo, late 11th Hus; High Sheriff Herts 1978; *m* 22 Sept 1956 *Anne Maureen, dau of Stanley Ryder Runton, and has issue:

1b +Michael Christopher Dyke; *b* 20 Aug 1958; *educ* Eton and RNC Dartmouth; Capt RM, ADC to Cmdt-Gen RM; *m* 1988 *Miranda Jane Elisabeth, est dau of John Bradshaw, of 11 Cheyne Place, London SW3, and has issue:

1c *Tara Katherine Elisabeth; *b* 1990

2c *Susanna Rose Juliet; *b* 1993

2b +Richard Arthur Dyke; *b* 7 July 1962; *educ* Eton, Wye Ag Coll and London U; *m* 1990 *Alison Jane, dau of Dr Bruce Osborne, and has issue:

1c +Thomas Alexander; *b* 1994

1c *Charlotte Emma Victoria; *b* 1992

2c *Emily Rosanna; *b* 9 Feb 1996

3b +Peter Edward Dyke; *b* 16 April 1964; *m* 1995 *Rachel, dau of John Hodge (ret)

3a +Charles Robert [Charles Acland Esq,Yeoman's, 4 Queens Rd, Cowes, IOW]; *b* 17 Sept 1937; *educ* Eton and RMA Sandhurst; Capt Gren Gds

(2) Peter Bevil Edward, OBE (1946), MC (1941), TD (1948), JP (Devon 1962); *b* 9 July 1902; *educ* Eton and Ch Ch Oxford; Devon: High Sheriff 1961, V-Lt 1962–93 (DL 1948–62), Sudan Political Service, T/Brig cmdg 1947–51 296 Field Regt Roy Devon Yeo RA (TA), Hon Col 1953, WW II (wounded, despatches), OSJ, 4th Cl Order Nile; *m* 7 July 1927 Bridget Susan (d 21 June 1996), JP (Devon 1950), yr dau of Rev Canon Herbert Barnett, and *d* 1993, leaving issue:

1a +John Hugh Bevil (Sir), KCB (1980), CBE (1978) [Maj-Gen Sir John Acland KCB CBE, Feniton Court, Honiton, Devon EX14 0BE]; *b* 26 Nov 1928; *educ* Eton; V-Lt Devon 1995– (DL 1984–95), Scots Gds: enlisted 1946, cmmnd 1948, served Malaya, Cyprus, Egypt, Germany, Kenya, Zanzibar, NI 1949–70, CO 2nd Bn 1968–71, Equerry to HRH THE LATE DUKE OF GLOUCESTER 1957–59, Head DRIT MOD 1975, cmded Land Forces Cyprus 1975-78, Hon Col: Exeter U OTC 1986–90, Roy Devon Yeo 1989–93, Roy Wessex Yeo 1989–93; memb Steering Gp Schools Health Educn Unit Exeter U 1986–92; GOC SW Dist 1978–81, Cdr Monitoring Force S Rhodesia 1979–80, Chm Exeter Cathedral Preservn Tst 1994–, Govr King's Sch Ottery St Mary 1994–; *m* 12 Nov 1953 *Myrtle Christian Euing, yr dau of Brig Alastair Wardrop Euing Crawford, DL, of Auchentroig, Buchlyvie, Stirlingshire, by his wife Helena Beatrice, 2nd dau of Adml Sir Charles Hope Dundas of Dundas, KCMG, and has issue:

1b +Peter John; *b* 24 Dec 1954; *educ* Radley and RMA Sandhurst; Lt Scots Gds 1975; *m* 1st 1979 (*divorce* 1990) Amanda, dau of Brian Ryrie, of Nairobi, and has issue:

1c *Katharine Elisabeth; *b* 1981

2c *Elizabeth Caroline; *b* 1983

1b (cont.) Peter Acland *m* 2nd *Cindy, dau of general Frederick Karsh, USME, and by her has:

3c *Bridget; *b* 1994

1b *Victoria Susan; *b* 20 Nov 1958; *m* 1986 *Thomas J Goddard, yst s of Maj David Goddard, and has issue:

1c *Luke; *b* 1992

1c *Rosanna; *b* 1990

2c *Helena; *b* 1995

2a +Antony Arthur (Sir), GCMG (1986, KCMG 1982, CMG 1976), GCVO (1991 , KCVO 1976) [Sir Anthony Acland GCVO GCMG, The Provost's Lodge, Eton College, Windsor, Berks SL4 6DH]; *b* 12 March 1930; *educ* Eton and Ch Ch Oxford; Dip Serv 1953091: Head Chancery Geneva 1966–68, Head Arabian Dept FCO 1970–72, Pncpl Priv Sec to For Sec 1972–75, Amb: Luxembourg 1975–77, Spain 1977–79, Washington 1986–91, PUS FCO 1982–86, dir Shell 1991–96, Booker plc 1992–, Provost Eton 1991–, chm cncl Ditchley Fndn 1991–, tstee Nat Portrait Gallery 19910, Hon LLD Exeter 1988, William and Mary Coll Virginia 1990 and Reading 1992; *m* 1st 6 Nov 1956 (Clare) Anne (*d* 1984), est dau of Francis Reynolds Verdon, and has:

1b +Simon Hugh Verdon; *b* 27 March 1958; *m* 1988 *Josephine, er dau of Michael Valentine, and has issue:

1c *Eloise; b 1992

2c *Olivia; b 1994

2b +Nicholas Antony Bevil; *b* 6 Feb 1960; *m* 1984 *Sophia Caroline Annabel, only dau of David John Yorke (*see* CLITHEROE, B), and has:

1c +Thomas; *b* 1989

2c +Hugh; *b* 1994

1c *Olivia; *b* 1990

1b *Katherine Mary; *b* 30 June 1965; *m* 20 Jan 1996 *George Weston, 2nd s of Garry Weston, of Pembridge Pla, London W11

2a (cont.) Sir Antony *m* 2nd 1987 *Mrs Jennifer McGougan, *née* Dyke (*see* RASHLEIGH, Bt)

(1) Angela Cicely Mary; *b* 26 Aug 1888; *m* 20 July 1927 Maj Aubrey George Wykeham Musgrave, MC (*d* 31 Dec 1958), yst s of Wenman Aubrey Wykeham Musgrave, of Barnsley Park, Cirencester, and Thame Park, Oxon, and *d* 2 Nov 1953, leaving:

1a *Jane; *b* 1930

(2) Katharine, OBE (1943, MBE 1919); *b* 28 Sept 1892; Mayor Chelsea 1959–61, Ch Cmdt ATS; *d* unm 6 Dec 1966

(3) Sarah Beatrice; *b* 11 Sept 1896; *m* 2 June 1917 Lt-Col Sir Cecil William Francis Stafford-King-Harman, 2nd Bt (*see* 1970 edn), and *d* 27 July 1979, leaving issue

1 Sarah Angelina; *b* 26 June 1849; FRPS, FRSA, FMS; *d* unm 2 Dec 1930

Sir HENRY *d* 16 Oct 1900; his est son,

Sir William Alison Dyke Acland, 2nd Bt CVO, JP (Oxon and Devon), DL (Devon); *b* 18 Dec 1847; FRGS, Adml Supt Gilbraltar Dockyard 1902–04; *m* 7 July 1887 his sis-in-law Hon Emily Anna Smith (*d* 28 Jan 1942), dau of Viscountess Hambleden (*qv*), and *d* 26 Nov 1924, leaving issue:

1 **Sir William Henry Dyke Acland, 3rd Bt**, MC, AFC, TD, JP and DL (Herts); *b* 16 May 1888; *educ* Eton and Ch Ch Oxford; Col TA, Lt-Col and brevet Col cmdg 96th (Roy Devon Yeo) Field Bde RA, Roy Scots Greys Reserve Offrs, RFC and RAF WW I (despatches, wounded), IDC 1938, CO Herts HG Bn WW II; Herts: High Sheriff 1951, CA 1952, 4th Cl St George Russia, Silver Jubilee Medal, 1937 and 1953 Coronation Medals; *m* 26 April 1916 Margaret Emily (*d* 21 May 1967), dau of Charles Theodore Barclay, of Fanshaws, Hertford, and *d* 4 Dec 1970, having had:

(1) *Elizabeth Margaret [Mrs Elizabeth O'Brien, Barnaderg, Letterfrack, Co Galway, Ireland]; *b* 24 July 1919; *m* 30 Aug 1943 (*divorce* 1968) Maj Edward Cecil O'Brien, OBE, and has issue (*see* INCHIQUIN, B)

(2) Juliet Mary, JP (Herts); *b* 20 Jan 1922; CC Herts; *m* 9 Dec 1939 Peter Robert Tabor, of Clibbons, Bulls Green, Datchworth, Herts, est s of Harry Ernest Tabor (*see* SOMERSET, D), and had issue:

1a *Robert Simon Dyke [Robert Tabor Esq, The Cotes, Llanrothal, Gwent]; *b* 27 Oct 1945; *educ* Eton; *m* 1970 *Brenda Frazer

2a *James Patrick [James Tabor Esq, Farthings Farm, Glastonbury, Somerset]; *b* 22 May 1950; *educ* Oundle; *m* 1977 *Jennifer Freeland and has:

1b *Harriet Sonia; *b* 1980

2b *Juliet Blanche; *b* 1982

3b *Veronica Joan; *b* 1985

1a *Rosemary Jill, JP (Bath and Wansdyke); *b* 28 March 1941; SRN, SCM; *m* 1st 8 Sept 1962 (*divorce* 1979) Richard Hawkesworth Horton-Fawkes, of Beacon House, Knebworth, Herts, s of Maj Le Gendre George William Horton-Fawkes, OBE, DL, of Farnley Hall, Yorks, and Brook Lodge, Wellow, Somerset, and has issue:

1b *David Hawksworth; *b* 6 March 1964

1b *Katharine Elizabeth; *b* 22 Aug 1965

2b *Jessica May; *b* 18 Sept 1967

1a (cont.) *Mrs Rosemary Horton-Fawkes *m* 2nd 1981 *Lt-Col Lionel Colin Tremellen, of Wellow, Somerset

2a *Theresa Mary [Mrs Lawrence Rawstorne, Tumblegum Farm, Alstonville, NSW, Australia]; *b* 20 June 1943; *m* 24 Oct 1964 *Laurence Atherton Rawstorne, only s of Richard Atherton Rawstorne, and has issue:

1b *Patrick Richard Guy; *b* 14 March 1968

1b *Joanna; *b* 18 March 1966; *m* 1987 *Gavan Murphy

2b *Amanda Juliet; *b* 1970

(3) Sarah Josephine; *b* 6 March 1930; *m* 15 April 1954 George Edward Brown, est s of Frederick William Brown, and *d* 18 Nov 1961, leaving two s

(4) *(Emily) Patricia [Mrs Kenneth Coles, The Old Rectory, Newtimbers, nr Hassocks, Sussex]; *b* 21 Nov 1931; *m* 8 July 1953 *Kenneth John Coles, yr s of Ernest James Coles, and has issue:

1a *Elizabeth Ann; *b* 16 Oct 1954

2 **Sir Hubert Guy Dyke Acland, 4th Bt**, DSO (1920); *b* 8 June 1890; Capt RN, WW I (despatches), staff FOIC NI WW II; Silver Jubilee and Coronation Medals; *m* 21 Aug 1915 his cousin Lalage Mary Kathleen (*d* 5 May 1961), dau of Capt John Edward Acland (*see* ACLAND, Bt, of Columb-John), and had issue:

(1) ANTHONY GUY, **5th Bt**

(2) James Alison, DSO (1944); *b* 6 June 1919; *educ* Nautical Coll Pangbourne and RMC Sandhurst; Lt Col 1st Recce Regt, RTR 1939–45, psc, Maj RTR, Mil Intell WW II, Malaya 1958–60; *m* 15 Jan 1942 *Diana Marcia, only dau of James Edward Briggs, and *d* 1993, leaving:

(1) +David James Dyke; *b* 25 Dec 1947; *educ* Nautical Coll Pangbourne; Cdr RN Fleet Air Arm 1969; *m* 1975 *Amanda Joy, SRN, er dau of John Alan Norman, and has issue:

1a +Thomas Alison Dyke; *b* 1977

2a +Timothy John Dyke; *b* 1978

(2) +Ion Andrew Dyke; *b* 24 Feb 1949; *educ* Nautical Coll Pangbourne; Lt-Cdr RNR, Master Mariner, with P&O 1967; *m* 1976 *Susan Jean, SRN, SCM, dau of John Jervis Chapman

(1) *Angela Marcia Dyke [Mrs Maurice FitzGibbon, 14 Burcote Rd, London SW18]; *b* 21 Oct 1946; *m* 1981 *Maurice FitzGibbon, er s of Maurice FitzGibbon, FRIC, FCS, MInstPl

Sir HUBERT *d* 6 May 1978; his est s,

Sir Antony Guy Acland, 5th Bt; *b* 17 Aug 1916; *educ* Winchester; Maj RA WW II; *m* 1st 13 Sept 1939 Avriel Ann (*d* 7 July 1943), only child of Capt Mervyn Edward John Wingfield-Stratford (*see* POWERSCOURT, V), and by her had issue:

1 *Gail Alison Jane; *b* 26 Feb 1942; *m* 17 Aug 1968 *Anthony James Rayment, s of Hubert Rayment

Sir Antony *m* 2nd 15 July 1944 *Margaret Joan, er dau of Maj Nelson Rooke, HLI, of Markham House, Badminton, Glos, by Marjorie, er dau of Sir Alexander Wood Renton, and *d* 14 Dec 1983, leaving further issue:

1 Sir (CHRISTOPHER) GUY DYKE ACLAND, **6th and present Bt**

2 *Caroline Barbara Margaret; *b* 13 May 1947; SRN, SCM; *m* 1972 *Peter Desmond George Sleigh, of Waimate, NZ, and has issue

ACTON

Arms: Quarterly, 1st and 4th gules semée of cross-crosslets fitchée or, two lions passant in pale argent (for ACTON); 2nd, quarterly, 1st and 4th azure, six fleurs-de-lys, three two and one argent, a chief dancettée of the last, 2nd and 3rd or, a cross patonce gules, over all an escutcheon also azure, thereon a tower argent, a chief dancettée of the last (for DALBERG); 3rd azure a lion passant or between three plates, each charged with a gryphon's head erased sable (for LYON). **Crest:** A human leg in armour flexed at the knee and couped at the thigh disgorging five drops of blood (for ACTON) [roy licence 23 Dec 1987, the new crest having long been associated with the ACTONs though never hitherto officially recorded at the College of Arms]. **Supporters:** On either side a lion guardant proper, gorged with a chain or and charged with a cross patonce gules. **Motto:** *Deo adjurante* ('With God assisting'). **Creations:** Bt. (E) 17 Jan 1643/4, B. (UK) 11 Dec 1869.

THE 4TH BARON ACTON OF ALDENHAM, Co Salop, and a **Baronet** (Sir Richard Gerald Lyon-Dalberg-Acton, Bt), also **Patrician of Naples** [The Rt Hon The Lord Acton, 152 Whitehall Court, London SW1A 2EL; 100 Red Oak Lane SE, Cedar Rapids, Iowa 52403, USA]; *b* 30 July 1941; *s* f 1989; *educ* St George's Coll Zimbabwe and Trin Coll Oxford (BA 1963, MA 1988); barrister Inner Temple 1976 (practised 1977–81), Manager Amalgamated Packaging Industs 1964–66, dir Coutts 1970–74, Sr Law Offr Min Justice, Legal and Parly Affrs Zimbabwe 1981–85; *m* 1st 28 Aug 1965 Hilary Juliet Sarah (*d* 25 Oct 1973), 2nd dau of Osmond Laurence Charles Cookson, MB, BS, MRCS, LRCP, of Perth, W Australia, and has issue:

1 +JOHN CHARLES FERDINAND HAROLD; *b* 19 Aug 1966; *educ* Winchester and Balliol Coll Oxford; *m* 7 Feb 1998 *Lucinda A F, dau of Brig James Percival of Marnhull, Dorset

The 4th BARON *m* 2nd 1 Jan 1974 (*divorce* 1987) Judith, writer, dau of Hon Sir Garfield Todd, former PM S Rhodesia; *m* 3rd 1988 *Patricia (law prof and writer), only dau of M Morey Nassif, of Cedar Rapids

Lineage: WILLIAM de Acton Burnel, Salop, lived *temp* EDWARD III; ancestor in the 9th generation of:

WALTER ACTON, of Aldenham, Salop; *m* his cousin Frances, dau of Edward Acton, of Acton Scott, Salop, and had:

Sir Edward Acton, 1st Bt (E), so *cr* 17 Jan 1643/4, of Aldenham Hall; *bapt* 20 July 1600; royalist in Civil War; *m* 1624 Sarah (*d* 30 Sept 1677), dau of Richard Mytton, of Halston, Salop, and *d* 1659, having had an est s:

Sir Walter Acton, 2nd Bt; MP; *m* Catherine, dau of Richard Cresset, of Cound, Salop, and *d* 1665, having had, with other issue:

1 **Sir Edward Acton, 3rd Bt**; MA Oxon; MP Bridgnorth 1698–1705; *m* Mary Walter and *d* 28 Sept 1716, leaving, with two yr s (Edward, *dsp*; John, DD, f of Edward, of Acton Scott; *m* Anne, est dau of William Gregory, of Woolhope, Herefs, and *d* July 1775, leaving an only dau Theresa Susannah, who *m* 21 April 1773 John Stackhouse, of Pendarves):

(1) **Sir Whitmore Acton, 4th Bt**; MP Bridgnorth 1710–13; *m* Elizabeth, dau of Matthew Gibbon (of the family of Edward Gibbon, the historian; *see* also below), and *d* 17 Jan 1731/2, leaving, with three daus (the est, Elizabeth, *m* Robert Barnston; the yst, Mary, *m* Rev Samuel Wanley, DD):

1a **Sir Richard Acton, 5th Bt**; *b* 1 Jan 1711/2; *m* 1744 Lady Anne Grey, dau of 3rd Earl of Stamford (*see* 1970 edn), and *d* 20 Nov 1791, having had two daus (*dsp*)

2 Walter; London merchant; *m* 1678 Catherine, dau of Oliver Pocklington, MD, and *d* 11 March 1718, leaving, with other issue (who, where in remainder, are so to btcy only):

(1) Edward; London banker; *m* Katherine, dau of John Steventon, and *d* 1728, having had (with John, Capt HEICNS, later Cdre-in-C Germanic Imp Navy Adriatic; and Katherine, w of John Darrell, of Richmond, Surrey):

1a Edward, of Besançon, Burgundy; *b* 11 June 1709; *m* Catherine (*d* 1767), dau of Francis Loijs de Gray, of Burgundy, and had, with other issue:

1b JOHN FRANCIS EDWARD (Sir), **6th Bt**

2b Joseph Edward; *b* 1737; Lt-Gen in serv of KING OF NAPLES, Govr Gaeta, Patrician Naples 1802; *m* Eleanora, Countess Berghe von Trips, of Düsseldorf, and *d* 12 Jan 1830, leaving:

1c Charles; *b* 1783; Cdre Roy Neapolitan Navy; *m* 12 April 1817 Zoe (*d* 1854), dau of Count d'Albon, and *d* 11 Oct 1863, having had:

1d Edward; *b* March 1818; *d* 1838

2d Richard; *b* 24 Feb 1822; *m* 1848 Giuseppina Troccoli and *d* 1880, leaving, with two daus:

1e Edward; *b* 1857; *m* 1888 Mary (*d* 1942), dau of Charles Acton, of Naples (*see* below), and *dsp* 1922

3d Ernest; *b* 24 March 1824; Capt Dragoons; *d* unm 1885

4d William; *b* 25 March 1825; V-Adml Italian Navy, Min Marine; *m* Mary (*d* 1905), dau of Marquis Ramirez, Min to the KING OF NAPLES, and *d* 1896, leaving issue:

1e Charles; *b* 1856; Col Bersaglieri Regt; *m* 1887 Annie Inglis (*d* 1923) and *d* 1905, leaving a s and dau

2e Henry; *b* 23 July 1858; Italian Min Plen; *m* 27 April 1892 Elly (*d* 12 Dec 1960), dau of Prince Cleon Rize Rangabe, of Greece, and *d* 22 Aug 1928, leaving issue:

1f Mary; *b* 1893; *m* 1st 2 March 1918 (*divorce* 1921) Count Carlo Andrea Pozzo di Borgo and had:

1g *Giovanna; *b* 1919; *m* 26 March 1947 Rene Saliege, of Paris, and has issue:

1h *Christian; *b* 5 April 1948

1h *Odile; *b* 12 July 1956

2g *Chantal; *b* 1922; *m* 30 April 1945 (*divorce* 1957) Jacques Daniel Brandela and has issue:

1h *Jean Marc; *b* 25 Dec 1946

2h *Serge; *b* 13 Sept 1948

1f (cont.) Mary *m* 2nd 17 March 1924 Dr Lucien Hirtzmann de Luttange(*d* 21 Dec 1965), s of Julien Hirtzmann de Luttange, and has further issue:

1g *Claude; *b* 21 June 1925; *m* 4 June 1946 *Monique, dau of Marcel Humbert, and has:

1h *Pascale; *b* 10 Oct 1948

2h *Dominique; *b* 12 Aug 1951

2g *Jean; *b* 3 May 1928; *m* 1957 *Claude de Michel and has issue:

1h *Laurent; *b* 27 Nov 1964

1h *Frédérique; *b* 7 Sept 1957

2h *Corinne; *b* 19 Dec 1962

2f Dorothy; *b* 20 April 1893; *m* 17 Nov 1921 Prince Raoul Bibica-Rosetti, Greek Amb to Canada (*d* 10 April 1967), s of Prince Salvator Bibica-Rosetti, Col Greek Army, and had:

1g *Roxane; *b* 3 Oct 1932; *m* 22 Jan 1956 (*divorce* 1980) Prince John Lobanow-Rostovsky, yr s of Prince Constantine Lobanow-Rostovsky, and has:

1h *Paul; *b* 23 Oct 1956

2h *Dimitry; *b* 14 Sept 1962

1h *Helena; *b* 7 Sept 1964

3f Marguerite; *b* 21 Nov 1896; *m* 25 March 1920 Lt-Col Gonsalvo Summonte, Italian Min Plen Lima, Peru (*d* 1 Nov 1959), s of Celestino Summonte, Mayor Naples, and had issue:

1g *Giancarlo; *b* 18 July 1924; *m* 11 Oct 1958 *Annamaria, dau of Dr Fabrizio Pietro Fabrizi, of Rome, and has issue:

1h *Fabrizio; *b* 5 Oct 1960

1h *Roberta; *b* 21 July 1963

2g *Enrico; *b* 17 Aug 1926; *m* 1956 *Mary, dau of Tommaso Mene, of Pescara, and has:

1h *Caterina; *b* 15 Feb 1957

2h *Lorenza; *b* 1 Sept 1958

1g *Elly; *b* 17 Aug 1921; *m* 21 April 1949 Dr Umberto Zanni, s of Michele Zanni, of Rome, and has:

1h *Raimondo; *b* 30 March 1952

2h *Jacopo; *b* 6 July 1953

1h *Cristina; *b* 6 Nov 1960

4f Roberta; *b* 11 Aug 1898; *m* 1920 Lt-Col Frank Phillips, DSO, MC (*d* 20 Aug 1938), and *d* 11 April 1953, leaving issue

1e Mary; *b* 1854; *d* 1919

5d Francis; *b* 29 Jan 1830; *m* 1863 Clotilde (*d* 1915), dau of Silvestro Burlamacchi, of Lucca, and *d* 1908, leaving issue:

1e Carolina Maria; nun; *b* 1864; *d* 1942

2e Maria Angelina; *b* 1866; *d* unm 11 Feb 1950

6d Ferdinand; *b* 16 June 1832; V-Adml Italy, Min Marine and War, ADC to the KING OF ITALY; *m* 16 Dec 1856 Ninfa (*d* 7 Aug 1885), dau of Marquis Ramirez, of Naples, and *d* 18 Feb 1891, having had:

1e Alfredo, KCB (Hon); *b* 12 Sept 1867; Adml Italian Navy, Ch Italian Naval Staff, *cr* 1925 an Italian baron, Bailiff SMO Malta, Senator and Min State; *m* 23 Oct 1907 Livia, Dame SMO Malta, Dame Grand Cross Constantinian Order St George 1959 (*d* 1963), dau of Prince of Cellamare Giudice Caracciolo, of Naples, and *d* 26 March 1934, leaving issue:

1f Ferdinando Amedeo Maria, 12th Prince of Leporano and a baron; *b* 27 Sept 1908; Kt SMO Malta, Bailiff and Kt Grand Cross Justice, Grand Inquisitor Constantinian Order St George, Patrician Naples, Grandee Spain 1st Cl, LLD, 1st Italian Grenadiers; *m* 15 June 1946 *Emilia (Dame Justice Constantinian Order St George), only dau of Count Gioacchino del Balzo di Presenzano and n of 8th Duke of Presenzano, and *d* 1979, leaving issue:

1g +Giovanni Alfredo Maria, 13th Prince of Leporano and a baron [Prince Ferdinand Leporano, Palazzo Cellamar a Chiaja, Naples; 58 Via Panama, Rome; La Chiusa, nr Cittanova di Calabria; Cannavá, nr Gioia Tauro, Italy]; *b* 26 Feb 1948; Patrician Naples, Kt Justice Constantinian Order St George 1969

1g *Maria Eleonora Carlotta [Princess Eleanora Taccone di Sitizano, Palazzo Cellences, Naples; Pizzo di Calabria, Italy]; *b* April 1949; Dame Justice Constantinian Order St George; *m* 1972 Pier Luigi Taccone di Sitizano, Patrician Tropea, Kt Justice Constantinian Order St George

2f +Francesco Eduardo Maria [Prince Francesco Cellamare Giudice Caracciolo, Palazzo Cellamare a Chiaja, Naples, Italy]; *b* 24 Aug 1910; Capt Italian Navy; Patrician Naples, *cr* 11 Jan 1940 a Baron of the Kingdom of Italy, Kt SMO Malta, Kt Justice Constantinian Order St George; *m* 11 June 1941 *Maria-Ida (Dame Justice Constantinian Order St George), only dau of Baron Giuseppe Ameglio, of Taranto, and has had issue:

1g Alfred; *b* 1 March 1942; *d* as the result of an accident 29 April 1946

2e Amedeo Ferdinand Maria; *b* 16 Jan 1871; V-Adml Italian Navy; Prince of Villa Santa Maria *jure uxoris*; *m* 3 June 1900 Anne, 10th Princess of Villa Santa Maria (Dame Grand Cross Constantinian Order St George; *d* 5 April 1969), dau of the Prince of Cellamare Giudice Caracciolo, of Naples, and *dsp* 25 Nov 1938

1e Anna Noemi; *m* 1889 Marquis Alfredo Lucifero, Capt Italian Navy (*d* 1909), and *d* 1927

2e Filomena Fernanda; *d* 1941

3e Mary Victoria; *m* 1902 Count Pietro Mencacci, of Rome, and *d* 1930

4e Mary Marguerite; *m* 1901 Thomas Messineo (*d* 1950) and *d* 12 Aug 1949

5e Gemma; *m* 1923 Count Zillo Zorzi (*d* 1958), of Venice and Rome, and *d* 23 June 1961

7d Emerich; *b* 16 Aug 1834; V-Adml Italian Navy; *d* unm 17 July 1901

8d Eugene Arthur Roger; *b* 12 Feb 1836; *m* 1879 Emilia Eden Spong (*d* 1895) and *d* 1895

9d Gustave; *b* 17 Feb 1838; Cdr Italian Navy; *m* Mathilde (*d* 1889), dau of Marshal Baron von Gablenz, and *dsp* 1880

10d Harold Edmund; *b* 15 April 1839; *m* 22 Dec 1870 Louisa Monica (*d* 1888), dau of John Nicholas Coulthurst, of Gargrave House, Yorks, and *d* 19 Feb 1902

1d Georgina Maria; *b* 12 May 1823; Lady Order Starry Cross; *m* 25 Aug 1847 Count Kurt zur Lippe-Weissenfeld (*d* 28 Dec 1895) and *d* 30 Dec 1891, leaving issue

2d Laura; *b* 4 March 1829; *m* 1st 6 April 1847 6th Prince of Camporeale (*d* 22 Jan 1863) and had issue; *m* 2nd 4 Sept 1864 Marco Minghetti (*d* 10 Dec 1886), PM Italy, and *d* 1915

2c Henry; *b* 10 July 1790; Capt 12th Lancers; *m* 2 Sept 1817 Charlotte, only dau of Dr Clugston, of Bombay, and had (with other issue):

1d Henry; Maj 4th Madras Cav; *m* Laura, dau of Col Hutchins, 4th Madras Cav, and *d* 16 April 1865, leaving issue:

1e Richard George; *b* May 1846; *m* 1885 Eugenie Mary (*m* 2nd 1893 Ven Archdeacon Lincoln R Vercoe, of Grand Rapids, Michigan, and *d* 1939), dau of James Adkins, of London, and *d* 22 Aug 1891, leaving issue:

1f Paul Reginald; *b* 31 July 1886; Lt US Army WW I; *m* 9 Feb 1907 Bertha Helen (*d* 1973), dau of Jules Le Duc, of Stone County, Mo., and *d* 6 Feb 1951, leaving issue:

1g Richard Le Duc; *b* 29 Dec 1913; *m* 19 Nov 1933 Alberta Althea, dau of Francis Joseph Budwiser, of Dubuque, Iowa, and *d* 1989, having had issue:

1h +Dennis Richard; *b* 21 Oct 1938; *m* 1st 2 June 1961 (*divorce* 1971) Susan Caroline, dau of Hartvige Ruddolph Miklethum, of Minneapolis, and has issue:

1i +Christopher Michael; *b* 21 Feb 1962

2i +Paul Reginald; *b* 5 May 1968

1i *Julia Ann; *b* 20 Sept 1964

1h(cont.) Dennis Acton *m* 2nd 1973 *Frances Lee, dau of Harold Stark, of Huntington Beach, California

2h +Paul Reginald; *b* 18 April 1943; *m* 1983 *Suzanne, dau of Eugene Erickson, of Minneapolis

1g *Pauline Laura; *b* 25 Dec 1907; *m* 1929 Charles Henry Heiney (*d* 1950) and has two s, two daus and an adopted dau

1f Gladys Mary; *b* 3 July 1888; *m* 28 Nov 1911 William Lindsay Thomson (*d* 27 Dec 1929), of Los Angeles, s of Peter N M I Thomson, and had a s

1e Charlotte Augusta Lousia; *m* 27 July 1865 Herbert Augustus Rous Jenner (*dsp* 1 April 1875)

2e Henrietta Georgina; *m* 8 Oct 1874 J A Briggs, BCS

1d Charlotte; *m* 28 July 1851 Douglas Baird (*see* KINTORE, E)), and *d* 30 Sept 1868, leaving issue

3c Francis; *b* 23 July 1796; Lt German Legion; *m* 2 Dec 1820 Esther, dau of Robert Fagan and widow of William Baker, and *d* 1865, leaving issue:

1d Richard; *b* 1827; *m* Irene, dau of Prince Pignatelli, and *d* 1858, leaving issue

2d Charles, of Naples; *b* 1829; *m* 1857 Michelina (*d* 1906), dau of Prince Pignatelli, and *d* 1908, having had issue

3d Edward; *b* 1833; *m* 1st 1859 Irene (*d* 1863), dau of Prince Pignatelli and widow of his bro Richard, and had issue; *m* 2nd Catherine Manganaro and *d* 1898, having by her had further issue

1c Mary Anne; *m* 1799 her uncle **Sir John Francis Edward Acton, 6th Bt** (*see* below)

2c Isabella; *m* 1812 Henry, Baron Dachenhausen

3 Richard; *m* and had:

(1) Catharine; *m* Edward Gibbon and with him was grandparent of Edward Gibbon the historian, to whom the 1st Baron Acton, another celebrated historian, was thus 2nd cousin twice-removed

The 5th Bt's 2nd cousin's s,

Sir John Francis Edward Acton , 6th Bt; *bapt* 3 June 1736; C-in-C Kingdom of Naples land and sea forces, PM Kingdom of Naples; *m* 1800 his niece Mary Anne (*d* 15 March 1873), er dau of Gen Joseph Edward Acton, and *d* Palermo 12 Aug 1811, having had, with other issue:

Sir FERDINAND RICHARD EDWARD ACTON later DALBERG-ACTON (roy licence 20 Dec 1833), **7th Bt**; *b* 24 July 1801; *m* Paris 9 July 1832 Marie Louise Pel(l)ina (*m* 2nd 25 July 1840 2nd Earl Granville (*qv*); *d* 14 March 1860), only child and heir of Em(m)erich Josef Wolfgang Heribert, 1st Duke of Dalberg *cr* 14 April 1810 and a Peer of France (so *cr* 17 Aug 1815), by Pellina, dau of the Marquis Brignole-Sale, of Genoa, and *d* 31 Jan 1837, leaving:

Sir John Em(m)erich Edward Dalberg-Acton, 8th Bt, and **1st Baron Acton of Aldenham**, Salop (UK), so *cr* (at the suggestion of Gladstone, who Acton revered but who he also greatly influenced, particularly over Irish Home Rule) 11 Dec 1869, KCVO (1897), JP and DL (Salop); *b* 10 Jan 1834; *educ* Oscott and privately in Munich under Prof von Döllinger; MP (Lib) Carlow 1859–65 and Bridgnorth 1865–66 (majority of one; unseated on petition; stood again unsuccessfully 1868), memb Roy Commn Historical MSS., memb Senate London U, Hon Dr Munich U 1872, FSA 1876, LLD Cantab 1888 and St Andrews, DCL Oxon 1887, Hon Fell All Souls 1890, Hon Fell Trin Coll Cambridge 1895, Tstee Br Museum, Ld in Waiting 1892–95, Regius Prof Modern History Cambridge 1895, ed *Rambler* (a lib catholic monthly) 1859–62 and (under its new name as a quarterly) *The Home and Foreign Review* 1862–64, co-fndr *English Historical Review* 1886, 1st ed *Cambridge Modern History*, author: *Lectures on Modern History* (1906), *The History of Freedom, and other Essays* (1907), *Historical Essays and Studies* (1907) and *Lectures on the French Revolution* (1910); *m* 1 Aug 1865 Maria Anna Ludomilla Euphrosina (*d* 3 April 1923), 2nd dau of Johann Maximilian, Count of Arco-Valley, by Anna Margareta Maria Juliana Pelina, Countess Marescalchi, and had:

1 RICHARD MAXIMILIAN, **2nd Baron**

2 John Dalberg; *b* 30 May 1872; *d* 16 April 1873

1 Mary Elizabeth Anne; *b* 15 Aug 1866; *m* 21 Oct 1901 Lt-Col Edward Bleiddian Herbert, DL, 17th Lancers (*d* 29 April 1931), 3rd s of John Arthur Edward Herbert, JP, DL, of Llanarth Court and Treowen, and *d* 9 Jan 1955, leaving issue

2 Annie Mary Catherine Georgiana; *b* 26 Sept 1868; *d* unm 30 Sept 1917

3 Elizabeth Mary Catherine; *b* 21 April 1874; *d* 1 Oct 1881

4 Jeanne Marie; *b* 12 March 1876; *d* 18 May 1919

The 1st BARON *d* 19 June 1902; his son,

Sir RICHARD MAXIMILIAN DALBERG-ACTON later LYON-DALBERG-ACTON (added name and arms of LYON by roy licence 1919), **9th Bt**, and **2nd Baron Acton of Aldenham**, KCVO, JP and DL (both Salop); *b* Bavaria 7 Aug 1870; *educ* Magdalen Coll Oxford; declared Br subject by Act of Parl 1911; Clerk FO 1894, 3rd Sec Dip Serv 1896, 2nd Sec 1900, 1st Sec 1908, Cnsllr Emb 1914, Chargé d'Affaires Berne 1904–06, Madrid 1906–07, The Hague 1908–1911, Darmstadt 1911–14, Berne 1915–16, Consul-Gen Zurich 1917–18, Envoy Extrdy and Min Plen Finland 1919–20, ret 1920; Ld in Waiting 1905–10 and 1910–15, Grand Offr Legn Honour, Grand Cross Dannebrog, Roy Red Cross Serbia; *m* 7 June 1904 Dorothy (*d* 17 March 1923), only child of Thomas Henry Lyon, DL, of Appleton Hall, Cheshire, and had issue:

1 JOHN EMERICH HENRY, **3rd Baron**

2 Richard William Heribert Peter, MBE; *b* 21 Feb 1909; T/Maj Intell Corps WW II; *m* 16 Dec 1937 Jill, only dau of Hugo C Ehlert, of Buenos Aires, and was *k* with her in an air crash nr Bathurst, Gambia, 7 Sept 1946

1 Marie Immaculée Antoinette; *b* 1 April 1905; Dame Honour and Devotion SMO; *m* 25 Feb 1933 (John) Douglas Woodruff, CBE (*d* 9 March 1978), s of Cumberland Woodruff, and *d* 5 April 1994

2 *(Dorothy Elizabeth Anne) Pelline; *b* 25 June 1906; *m* June 1928 Edward Joseph Eyre (*d* 6 Oct 1962), s of Edward Eyre, of New York, and Park Lane, and *d* by 11 April 1998, leaving:

(1) *Edward [Edward Eyre Esq,The Field House, Gt Durnford, Salisbury, Wilts SP4 6AT]; *b* 30 June 1929; barrister Inner Temple 1957; *m* 7 July 1969 *(Ethel) Mary, er dau of Cdr Charles Hardinge Drage, RN (ret), and widow of Roderick Andrew Joseph Fraser (*see* LOVAT, L), and has issue:

1a *Robert Edward John; *b* 24 June 1971

1a *Mathilda Elizabeth Mary Pelline; *b* 18 March 1970
2a *Virginia Margaret Dorothy; *b* 6 Feb 1974
3a *Constance Rose Octavia; *b* 10 Nov 1976
(2) *James Ainsworth Campden Gabriel (Sir), KCVO (1986, CVO 1978), CBE (1980, OBE 1975) [Maj-Gen Sir James Eyre KCVO CBE, Somerville House, E Garston, Berks RG16 7EY]; *b* 2 Nov 1930; *educ* Harvard (BA, LLB); Lt-Col cmdg Blues and Roys (RHG and 1st Dragoons) 1970–73, GOC London Dist and Maj-Gen cmdg Household Div 1983–86; dir Westminster Associates Ltd 1989–; *m* 20 Dec 1967 *Monica Ruth Esther, yr dau of Michael Joseph Smyth, MCh, FRCS, and has issue:
1a *James Patrick; *b* 29 Jan 1969; *m* 21 June 1997 *Sophie, yr dau of Christopher White
1a *Annabelle Catherine; *b* 7 Oct 1970
(3) *John Michael Simon William [John Eyre Esq, 20 East Bowery St, Newport, RI 02840, USA]; *b* 10 May 1935; *m* 9 July 1960 (*divorce* 1979) Susan, yr dau of Cdr Maxwell Cole, USN (ret), of Southampton, NH, and has issue:
1a *Michael John; *b* 12 Nov 1961
2a *Christopher Maxwell; *b* 9 Nov 1963
3a *Giles Stephen; *b* 5 July 1966
4a *Julian Patrick; *b* 1970
(4) *Peter Gervaise Joseph [Peter Eyre Esq, 62 Whitehall Ct, London SW1 2EL]; *b* 11 March 1940; actor
(5) *Patrick Giles Andrew [Patrick Eyre Esq, Manor Farm, Marcham, Abingdon, Berks]; *b* 11 March 1940; *educ* Downside and Trin Coll Oxford (MA); farmer 1965–72, barrister Inner Temple 1974, Master Supreme Court (Queen's Bench) 1992–; *m* 29 Sept 1977 *Victoria Mary, only dau of Charles Bathurst Norman, barrister, by Hon Doreen Gibbs (*see* WRAXALL, B), and formerly w of Capt Raymond Edward Barthorp, and has issue:
1a *Toby Charles Peter; *b* 1983
(1) *Dorothy Elizabeth Mary Pelline [Mrs Charles Remnick, Jonathans Landing, 15800 Windrift Drive, Jupiter, FL 33477, USA]; *b* 19 Nov 1938; *m* 1972 *Charles Gilbert Remnick
(2) *Caroline Elisa Margaret [Mrs Caroline Cooper, 18 Petersham House, Harrington Rd, London SW7]; *b* 7 Nov 1945; *m* 1978 (*divorce* 1979) Alan Cooper, s of Albert Cooper
3 *Helen Mary Grace [Princess Helen Rospigliosi, 602 Park West, London W2]; *b* 21 May 1910; *m* 6 July 1933 (*divorce* 1959) Prince Guglielmo Rospigliosi, s of Prince Lodovico Rospigliosi, and has issue (*see* NEWBURGH, E)
4 Gabrielle Marie Leopoldine; *b* 15 Dec 1912; *d* unm 2 Aug 1930
5 Joan Henrica Josepha Mary Clare; *b* 7 Aug 1915; *d* 14 Nov 1995
6 Margaret Mary Teresa; *b* 27 May 1919; *d* unm 9 Dec 1997
7 Ædgyth Bertha Milburg Mary Antonia Frances, OBE (1986); *b* 15 Dec 1920; *m* 7 July 1949 *John Alexander Callinicos, yst s of Alexander Theodore Callinicos, of Ithaca, Greece, and *d* June 1995, leaving:
(1) *Alexander Theodore [Dr Alexander Callinicos, 45 King Henry's Walk, London N1]; *b* 24 July 1950; *educ* Balliol Coll Oxford (PhD); lecturer York U; *m* 1977 *Joanna, dau of F Seddon, of Dore, Sheffield
(2) *Anastasius John [Anastasius Callinicos Esq, 21 Parham Rd, Harare, Zimbabwe]; *b* 12 Jan 1957; *educ* Exeter U; *m* 1985 *Alice, dau of Euan Robertson, of Harare, and has issue:
1a *Michael John; *b* 1986
1a *Helena Marie Immaculée; *b* 1986

The 2nd BARON *d* 16 June 1924; his er son,

JOHN EMERICH HENRY LYON-DALBERG-ACTON, **3rd Baron Acton of Aldenham**, CMG (1964), MBE (1945), TD, DL (Salop); *b* 15 Dec 1907; *educ* Downside, RMC Sandhurst and Trin Coll Cambridge; Maj RA (TA) WW II; *m* 25 Nov 1931 *Hon Daphne Strutt [The Rt Hon The Dowager Lady Acton, 46 Clarence Rd, Moseley, Birmingham B13 9UH], only dau of 4th Baron Rayleigh (*qv*), and *d* 23 Jan 1989, leaving:

1 RICHARD GERALD LYON-DALBERG-ACTON, **4th and present Baron Acton of Aldenham**
2 +(John) Charles [Prof The Hon Charles Acton, Westminster Diocesan Seminary, 28 Beaufort St, London SW3]; *b* 26 Jan 1943; *educ* St George's Coll Salisbury Zimbabwe and Gregorian U Rome; Prof Dogmatic Theology Westminster Diocesan Seminary
3 +Robert Peter [The Hon Robert Acton, Rutland House, Saxon St, Newmarket, Suffolk]; *b* 23 June 1946; *educ* St George's Zimbabwe; stud manager for Sheik Mohamed bin Rashid al Makhtoum; *m* 28 June 1974 *Michele, dau of Henri Laigle, and has issue:
(1) +Christopher Richard Henri; *b* 28 Sept 1977
(2) +Patrick John Pascal; *b* 9 June 1979
(3) +William Benjamin; *b* 1986
4 +Edward David Joseph [Prof The Hon Edward Acton, 365 Unthank Rd, Norwich NR4 7QG]; *b* 4 Feb 1949; *educ* St George's Zimbabwe, York U and St Edmund's Coll Cambridge (PhD 1976); Prof Modern European History UEA, author: *Alexander Herzen and the role of the Intellectual Revolutionary* (1979) etc; *m* 8 April 1972 *Stella Marie, only dau of Henry Conroy, and has issue:
(1) *Helen Marie; *b* 23 Jan 1974
(2) *Natalie Elizabeth; *b* 7 June 1977
5 +Peter Hedley [The Hon Peter Acton, Dancing Dicks, Blunts Hall Rd, Witham, Essex]; *b* 27 March 1950; *educ* Red Rice and RAC Cirencester; *m* 1981 *Anne, dau of James Sinclair, of Sandy, Orkney Isles, and has issue:
(1) +Simon Richard; *b* 1981
(1) *Emily; *b* 1989
1 *Pelline Margot [The Hon Mrs de Marffy von Versegh, Ealing Farm, PO Box 29, Mvurwi, Zimbabwe]; *b* 24 Dec 1932; *m* 30 June 1953 *Laszlo de Marffy von Versegh, s of Elemer Marffy, and has issue:
(1) *Denes [Denes de Marffy von Versegh Esq, Aston Upthorpe Stud, Aston Upthorpe, Oxon OX11 9EE]; *b* 1954; *m* June 1986 *Rachel, dau of Martin Lampard, of Tiverton, Devon, and has issue:
1a *Edmond; *b* Feb 1988
2a *Henry John; *b* Sept 1991
3a *George; *b* June 1994
1a *Hannah; *b* Sept 1989
(2) *Miklos [Miklos de Marffy von Versegh Esq, Ealing Farm, PO Box 29, Mvurwi, Zimbabwe]; *b* 1956; *m* April 1986 *Vibeke Jane, only dau of Christopher Culley, of Gweru, Zimbabwe, and has issue:
1a *Benjamin; *b* May 1992
2a *Hugh; *b* Feb 1997
1a *Lucinda; *b* Jan 1988
2a *Alice; *b* March 1990
(3) *Joseph [Joseph de Marffy von Versegh Esq, May Cottage, Hedsor Rd, Bourne End, Bucks SL8 5ES]; *b* 1957; *educ* St George's Coll Zimbabwe and Exeter U; *m* Sept 1987 *Anne Margaret Elizabeth, dau of Col Alexander W D Lewis, and has issue:
1a *Charles Alexander; *b* Dec 1989
2a *Alexander; *b* July 1991
(4) *Paul [Paul de Marffy von Versegh Esq, Roy Cottage, East St, Drayton, Somerset TA10 0JZ]; *b* 1958; *m* April 1987 *Lesley Anne, dau of Douglas Hall, of Bournemouth, and has issue:
1a *Tamas; *b* Oct 1987
2a *James; *b* Aug 1989
3a *William; *b* July 1992
(5) *Robert; *b* 1962; *m* 1989 *Katherine, dau of Martin Graham, of Harare, and has:
1a *Christopher; *b* July 1994
2a *Peter; *b* June 1996
1a *Philippa; *b* Oct 1992
(6) *Stephen [Stephen de Marffy von Versegh Esq, PO Box Wgt 211, Westgate, Harare, Zimbabwe]; *b* 1965; *educ* St George's Zimbabwe; *m* Sept 1995 *Dympha, dau of René Straatman, and has:
1a *Nicholas; *b* March 1996
(1) Gabriella; *b* 1960; *d* 1984
2 Charlotte; *b* 6 Dec 1934; *d* 1 March 1935
3 *Catherine [The Hon Mrs Joseph Corbett, The Old Rectory, Coates, nr Cirencester, Glos]; *b* 30 Sept 1939; *m* 20 Feb 1960 *Hon Joseph Mervyn Corbett, 4th s of 2nd Baron Rowallan (*qv*), and has issue
4 *Jill Mary Joan [The Hon Mrs Lampert, 46 Clarence Rd, Moseley, Birmingham B13 9UH]; *b* 15 June 1947; *m* 1 March 1969 *Nicholas Lampert, s of Eugene Lampert, PhD, of Keele U, by Katharine Sophy, only dau of Hon Sir Jasper Ridley, KCB, OBE, TD (*see* RIDLEY V), and has:
1a *Katharine; *b* 1969
2a *Frances; *b* 1971 and has issue:
1b *Jessica Katie Hakin; *b* 1996
5 *Mary Anne [The Hon Mrs Sheehy, 8 St Margaret's Rd, Oxford OX2 6RU]; *b* 30 March 1951; *m* 15 April 1972 *Timothy John Sheehy, only s of Matthew Joseph Sheehy, and has issue:
(1) *Jane Elizabeth; *b* 1973
(2) *Clare Ann; *b* 1975
6 *Jane [The Hon Mrs Smiley, 68 Lonsdale Rd, Oxford OX2 7EP]; *b* 25 Jan 1954; *m* 1st 13 Dec 1975 (*divorce* 1983) Charles Thomas Pugh (*d* 1989), s of Rev F W Pugh, and has issue:
(1) *Charlotte; *b* 1978
(2) *Rebecca; *b* 1979
6 (cont.) *The Hon Mrs Jane Pugh *m* 2nd 26 Aug 1983 *Xan de Crespigny Smiley, and has further issue (*see* SMILEY, Bt)

ADDINGTON

Arms: Vert a chevron engrailed plain cotised argent between three eagle's heads erased of the second, each gorged with a collar fleurettée gules. **Crest:** In front of a fasces fesswise proper an eagle's head as in the arms. **Supporters:** On either side an eagle argent, wings addorsed, gorged with a collar fleurettée gules, and pendant therefrom an escutcheon ermine charged with a rose gules.
Motto: *Alta petens* ('Seeking things on high').
Creation: B. (UK) 22 July 1887.

THE 6TH BARON ADDINGTON, of Addington, Co Buckingham (Dominic Bryce Hubbard) [The Rt Hon The Lord Addington, 9/11 Chalk Hill Rd, Thorpe Hamlet, Norwich NR1 1SC]; *b* 24 Aug 1963; *s* f 1982; *educ* Hewett Comprehensive Norwich and Aberdeen U (MA 1988)

Lineage: JOHN HUBBARD, of Stratford Grove, Essex; *b* Oct 1776; *m* 27 April 1801 Marianne (*d* 8 Jan 1851), dau of John Morgan, of Bramfield Place, Herts, and *d* 16 Aug 1847, having had an est s:

JOHN GELLIBRAND HUBBARD, **1st Baron Addington**, of Addington, Co Buckingham (UK), so *cr* 22 July 1887, PC; *b* 21 March 1805; Govr Bank England, MP (C) Buckingham 1859–68 and City London 1874–87, Chm Public Works Loan Ctee 1853–75; *m* 19 May 1837 Hon Maria Margaret Napier (*d* 17 April 1896), est dau of 9th Lord Napier and Ettrick (*qv*), and *d* 28 Aug 1889, leaving:

1 EGERTON HUBBARD, **2nd Baron Addington**, VD, JP (Bucks); *b* 29 Dec 1842; *educ* Ch Ch Oxford (MA); Hon Col Bucks Bn Oxon and Bucks LI, MP (C) Buckingham 1874–80 and N Bucks 1886–89, CA Bucks, High Steward Buckingham; *m* 3 June 1880 Mary Adelaide (*d* 3 Dec 1933), dau of Sir Wyndham Spencer Portal, 1st Bt (*qv*), and *d* 14 June 1915, leaving:

(1) JOHN GELLIBRAND HUBBARD, **3rd Baron Addington**, OBE (1919), TD, JP (Bucks 1930); *b* 7 June 1883; *educ* Eton and Ch Ch Oxford (BA 1906, MA 1954); Maj Bucks Bn Oxon and Bucks LI WW I 1914–19 (despatches), High Steward Buckingham, memb Bucks CC 1929 (Alderman 1952), Mayor Buckingam 1932–34, 1943–46 and 1951–52; *d* unm 20 July 1966

(2) RAYMOND EGERTON HUBBARD, **4th Baron Addington**; *b* 11 Nov 1884; *educ* Eton and Magdalen Coll Oxford (BA); *m* 11 Nov 1926 Margaret Favre (*d* 16 Jan 1963), dau of William MacCullum and widow of Edward Marriott Gibson, and *dsp* 17 Aug 1971

(3) Francis Spencer; *b* 1 July 1888; *educ* Eton and Magdalen Coll Oxford; Lt Oxon and Bucks LI, Roy Fus WW I, CD WW II, memb Buckingham Town Cncl 1936–45; *d* unm 11 July 1963

(1) Winifred Mary, MBE (1920); *b* 6 Sept 1881; *m* 10 Aug 1909 Capt Berkeley Cole Wilmot Williams, DL (*d* 10 Jan 1938), Yorks Regt, and *d* 1 Jan 1968, leaving issue

(2) Ruth Mary, JP (Bucks); *b* 30 Oct 1896; Mayoress Buckingham 1932–34, 1943–46 and 1951–52; *d* unm 23 Aug 1955

2 Francis Edward; *b* 11 Feb 1844; RN; *d* 25 Dec 1871

3 Cecil John, of Kingsbridge, Steeple Claydon, Bucks, JP; *b* 6 Sept 1846; Lt-Col Gren Gds Egypt 1882; *m* 15 April 1872 Helen Jane (*d* 27 April 1909), dau of Arthur Macdonald Ritchie, and *d* 10 March 1926, having had issue:

(1) John Francis, OBE (1919); *b* 5 June 1880; Gren Gds, Egyptian Civ Serv, Boer War 1902 and WW I T/Lt-Col spec list (despatches), Mil Govr Palestine; *m* 1st 16 Jan 1914 (*divorce* 1925) Gertrude Kathleen Frances (*d* following a car crash 8 June 1960), dau of Maj Cyril Wilson; *m* 2nd 28 May 1925 (*divorce* 1929) Barbara, dau of Capt James Spottiswoode Taylor, USN, and had issue:

1a Nicolette; *b* 5 May 1926; *m* 5 Sept 1953 Richard Joseph Pike (*d* 1992), yst s of Hubert Pike, and had issue:

1b *James Eben; *b* 1 July 1955

2b *William Joseph Fitzgerald; *b* 17 Feb 1960

(1) (cont.) John Addington *m* 3rd 2 Jan 1930 Betty Riversdale, dau of Horace West, Clerk H of C, and *d* 3 June 1953, having by her had issue:

1a JAMES HUBBARD, **5th Baron Addington**; *b* 3 Nov 1930; *educ* Eastbourne Coll and Chadacre Ag Inst; Br S Africa Police, S Rhodesia 1955–58; *m* 7 Oct 1971 (*divorce* 1974) Alexander Patricia [Patricia Lady Addington, Thorpe Hamlet, Norwich], yr dau of Norman Ford Millar, of The Angel Hotel, Halesworth, Suffolk, formerly of Glasgow and Burma, and *d* 1982, leaving:

1b DOMINIC BRYCE HUBBARD, **6th and present Baron Addington**

2b +MICHAEL WALTER LESLIE; *b* 6 July 1965; heir presumptive; *educ* Hewett Comprehensive Norwich, Manchester U (BA) and Leicester Poly (MA)

1b *Frances Linden; *b* 26 July 1962; *educ* Southampton U (BA); jnlst

2b *Sally-Anne; *b* 19 Oct 1966; *educ* SOAS London U (BA) and UCLA (MA)

2a +Peter; *b* 6 Oct 1932; *educ* Eastbourne Coll and Essex Ag Inst

(1) Muriel; *d* unm 19 June 1947

(2) Cicely Helen; *d* 1886

(3) Hilda Mary, JP (Bucks); *b* 27 May 1884

(4) Irene Margaret; *b* 21 Oct 1892; *educ* Reading U (BA 1940)

4 Arthur Gellibrand; *b* 6 Feb 1848; Sec Native Affrs Cape Colony, Accountant to Basutoland Govt; *m* 29 June 1881 Amy d'Esterée (*d* 20 Nov 1930), dau of Charles Hugh Huntly, CMG, Civil Commr and RM Albany, S Africa, and *d* 7 March 1896, having had issue:

(1) Gerald Napier; *b* 27 Aug 1882; *educ* Eton; Capt Irish Gds, Lt Rifle Bde, WW I (despatches, wounded); *m* 14 Jan 1908 Bertha Caroline (*d* 1969), 3rd dau of Rev Edward Southwell Garnier, MA, Rector Quidenham, and *d* 19 Oct 1939, leaving issue:

1a Ralph Arthur; *b* 22 Oct 1908; *educ* Eton; *m* 1st 8 June 1940 (*divorce* 1954) Hon Marian Woodruff, er dau of 1st and last Baron Ashfield (*see* 1940 edn) and formerly wife of (a) James Hart Rutland and (b) James Henry Royds, and had issue:

1b *Rosemary Jane; *b* 2 Sept 1942; *m* 3 July 1962 *Capt Andrew Peter Harold Parsons, Scots Gds, est s of Capt Thomas Edward Harold Thornbrough Parsons, of Carskley, Argyll, and Mrs William Eills Barrington Browne, of Ampney House, Cirencester, Glos, and has issue:

1c *James Alastair Thomas; *b* 5 March 1964

2c *Edward Charles William; *b* 7 Jan 1968

1c *Annabel Jane; *b* 29 Nov 1969

2b *Angela Mary; *b* 20 Sept 1945; *m* 1st 12 Jan 1965 (*divorce*) (Luke Edward) Timothy Hue Williams, s of Charles Anthony Hue Williams; *m* 2nd 1972 *Peter Anthony Charles Mordaunt (*see* MORDAUNT, Bt)

1a (cont.) Ralph Hubbard *m* 2nd 14 Sept 1954 Elizabeth Gertrude (*d* 1 Dec 1988 aged 88), yr dau of Stephen Cozens, of Mackney Manor, Wallingford, Berks, and formerly wife of (a) Henry Reginald Gambier Colclough, (b) Capt Michael Norton-Griffiths, RE (*see* NORTON-GRIFFITHS, Bt) and (c) George Paul Minchin Woodward, and *d* 1981

2a Thomas Edward; *b* 27 Dec 1911; *educ* Eton; S/Ldr RAuxAF WW II (despatches), factor to Sir John Buchanan-Jardine, Bt; *m* 23 Sept 1939 (*divorce* 1974) Bridget, dau of Charles Churchill Branch, OBE, and *d* 1985, leaving issue:

1b +Gerald Thomas Guy [Gerald Hubbard Esq, 19 Felden St, London SW6]; *b* 5 April 1947; *educ* Gordonstoun

2b +Charles Benjamin [Charles Hubbard Esq, 89 St Mark's Rd, London W6]; *b* 22 Sept 1950; *educ* Gordonstoun

1b *Harriet Anne [Mrs Michael Bailey, Great Dorweeke, Silverton, Exeter EX5 4BZ]; *b* 15 Oct 1943; *m* 31 Oct 1972 *Michael Frederick Bailey and has issue:

1c *Simon Douglas; *b* 1975

1c *Jessica Mary; *b* 14 July 1973

3a +Derek [Derek Hubbard Esq, Vine Cottage, The Street, Effingham, Surrey]; *b* 26 July 1920; *educ* Eton; Capt Sussex Yeo WW II (wounded); *m* 6 Oct 1951 *Joanne, dau of Donald D Maclean, of Croydon, and has issue:

1b *Rowan [Mrs Charles Collier-Wright, 2 Burcote Rd, London SW18 3LQ]; *b* 3 Oct 1954; *m* 1978 *Charles E H Collier-Wright and has issue:

1c *Robert Edward; *b* 1983

1c *Emma; *b* 1981

2c *Frances Alexandra; *b* 1986

2b *(Joanne) Candida; *b* 22 July 1957

1a *Susan d'Esterre [Mrs Herbert Carter, 12A The Hollies, Peter St, Shepton Mallet, Somerset]; *b* 24 Aug 1914; *m* 1st 10 Sept 1936 (*divorce* 1951) Edward Ernest Harrison, er s of Ernest Redford Harrison, and has issue:

1b *Martin Edward [Martin Harrison Esq, 8 Ravenscourt Rd, London W6]; *b* 4 April 1937; *educ* Harrow and Oriel Coll Oxford; manager Samuel Montagu 1968; *m* 11 June 1965 *Reziya, est dau of Dr Rasheed Ahmad, and has issue:

1c *Thomas Edward Henry; *b* 1969; *educ* Westminster and Wadham Coll Oxford

1c *Frances Catherine Saida; *b* 13 May 1966; *educ* Trin Hall Cambridge

1a (cont.) Mrs Susan Harrison *m* 2nd 21 Feb 1952 Capt Herbert John Tindall Carter, RHG (*d* 1980), er s of Arthur Herbert Carter, of Tydd Manor, Wisbech, Cambs, and has further issue:

1b *Carolyn Rachel [Mrs John House, 16 Town St, Shepton Mallet, Somerset BA4 5BJ]; *b* 14 April 1955; *m* 1st 1982 (*divorce* 1986) Alan Laurence Kelly and has issue:

1c *John Laurence; *b* 1 Sept 1983

1b (cont.) Mrs Carolyn Kelly *m* 2nd 11 Jan 1991 *John Richard House

(2) Basil Hope; *b* 1884; *d* 1885

(1) Kathleen d'Esterre; *b* 8 March 1886; *m* 11 Oct 1911 Rev Charles Hamilton Mylne (*d* 28 April 1941), Vicar E Meon, Hants, only s of Rev Townshend Webb Mylne, and had issue

(2) Dorothy Isabel, MBE (1951), DStJ (1955); *b* 7 April 1888; *d* unm 11 Jan 1964

(3) Noel Agnes; *b* 15 Dec 1892; *m* 30 Dec 1919 Walter Francis Glencairn Campbell (*d* 5 Sept 1935), Sr Commr Nairobi, 2nd s of Colin Glencairn Campbell, and had issue

5 Evelyn; *b* 18 March 1852; *educ* Ch Ch Oxford (MA); MP Lambeth 1896–1900, Dir Bank England 1890–1909, chm Guardian Assur 1900–30, Lt City London; *m* 25 Aug 1881 his sis-in-law Eveline Maude (*d* 29 Oct 1945), dau of Sir Wyndham Spencer Portal, 1st Bt (*qv*), and *d* 24 Aug 1934, having had issue:

(1) Harold Evelyn (Rt Rev), DSO (1918); *b* 12 Feb 1883; *educ* Eton and Ch Ch Oxford (MA); CF WW I (despatches, wounded), Rector Guisborough 1919–22, Chaplain Cheltenham Coll 1922–30, Vicar St John's Middlesbrough 1931–38, RD 1936, Hon Chaplain to HM GEORGE VI 1937–39, Bp Suffragan Whitby 1939–46; *d* unm 23 May 1953

(2) Eric Wyndham, JP (Kent); *b* 28 Oct 1885; *educ* Eton and Ch Ch Oxford; Lt Welsh Gds (SR) and Gds MGR; *m* 11 March 1918 Edith Sylvia (d 1977), dau of Herbert Picton Morris, and *d* 9 Feb 1946, leaving issue:

1a Evelyn Raymond HUBBARD later WHEATLEY-HUBBARD (deed poll 14 June 1949), OBE; *b* 22 Feb 1921; *educ* Eton; Coldstream Gds WW II; *m* 30 April 1949 *Ann Christobel, OBE, only child of Col Charles Joshua Hirst Wheatley, JP, DL, of Berkswell Hall, Leics, and *d* 1993, leaving issue:

1b +Thomas Henry; *b* 7 May 1952; *educ* Eton and Bristol U; *m* 28 April 1979 *Caroline M O, dau of Col Hilary Lewis, and has issue:

1c +Christopher Raymond; *b* 1982

2c +Andrew David; *b* 1984

1b *Caroline Sophia; *b* 1 May 1950

2a +Jasper Picton [Jasper Hubbard Esq, Hammonds, Horsmonden, Kent TN12 8EE]; *b* 28 Nov 1923; *educ* Eton and Ch Ch Oxford; *m* 6 Feb 1951 *Ethne Mary, only dau of Henry Charles Frederick Pelham-Clinton (*see* 1970 edn NEWCASTLE, D), and has issue:

1b John Louis Pelham; *b* 21 Oct 1954; *educ* Eton and Reading U; *d* 1996

1b *Charlotte Anne; *b* 24 Oct 1952

2b *Rose Mary; *b* 19 July 1957

1a *Virginia; *b* 4 May 1919

(3) Bertram John, MC; *b* 27 Aug 1895; *educ* Eton; Lt Gren Gds; *ka* 1 Dec 1917

1 Alice Eliza; *b* 2 Dec 1841; *d* unm 20 April 1931

2 Lucy Marian; *b* 19 May 1845; Sis Mercy; *d* 20 Nov 1893

3 Rose Ellen; *b* 13 Jan 1851; *d* unm 18 Aug 1933

4 Clemency; *b* 26 Oct 1856; *m* 4 Sept 1888 Maj-Gen Sir George Barker, KCB, RE (*d* 5 March 1930), s of Col George Barker, HEICS, and *d* 23 Feb 1940, having had issue

ADDISON

Arms: Per chevron vert and or in chief a snake embowed, head debruised between two garbs of the last and in base an anchor sable. **Crest:** In front of two keys in saltire, wards upwards, a sword point downwards or. **Supporters:** On either side a Lincolnshire red bull proper, the headstall also proper, charged with a sun in splendour or. **Motto:** *Servire est vivere* ('To serve is to live'). **Creations:** B. (UK) 22 May 1937, V. (UK) 6 July 1945.

THE 4TH VISCOUNT ADDISON (William Matthew Wand Addison) and **Baron Addison**, of Stallingborough, Co Lincoln [The Rt Hon The Viscount Addison, Church Barn, Oundle, Peterborough PE8 4AX], *b* 13 June 1945, *educ* King's Sch, Bruton, and Essex Inst of Ag, *m* 1st 10 Oct 1970 (*divorce* 1990) Joanna Mary, dau of John Ivor Charles Dickinson, of Blyborough Grange, Gainsborough, Lincs, and has issue:

1 +PAUL WAND, *b* 18 March 1973; *educ* Rannoch Sch Perthshire

1 *Sarah Louise, *b* 25 Nov 1971

2 *Caroline Amy, *b* 13 Oct 1979

The 4th VISCOUNT *m* 2nd 1991 *Lesley Ann, dau of George Colin Mawer, of Sudbeck Lane, Welton, Lincs

Lineage: ROBERT ADDISON, of Hogsthorpe, Lincs, *d* 15 Jan 1870, leaving:

ROBERT ADDISON, of Hogsthorpe and Stallingborough, Lincs, *b* 30 Nov 1838, *m* 30 May 1861 Susan (*d* 21 April 1913), dau of Charles Fanthorpe, and *d* 2 Sept 1899, leaving, with two other s and another dau:

1 CHRISTOPHER, **1st Viscount**

1 Carrie, *b* 14 Jan 1876 ; *d* unm 23 Jan 1947

2 Nellie, *b* 7 March, 1878, *m* 19 Feb 1949 Clarence Percival Ede, s of Richard Ede, of Saltash, Cornwall

3 Lizzie Fanthorpe, *b* 9 Oct 1870; *d* unm 27 March, 1958

ROBERT ADDISON's s,

CHRISTOPHER ADDISON, **1st Viscount Addison**, so *cr* 2 July 1945, as also previously 22 May 1937 BARON ADDISON, of Stallingborough, Co Lincoln (both UK), KG (1946), PC (1916), MD, BS (Lon), FRCS; MP (Lib) Hoxton 1910–18, Shoreditch 1918–22 and (Lab) Swindon 1929–31 and 1934–35; Parly Sec Board Educn 1914–15 and Min Munitions 1915–16, Min: Munitions 1916–17 and Reconstruction 1917–19, Pres Local Govt Bd 1919, Min Health 1919–21, Min without Portfolio 1921, Parly Sec Min Ag 1929–30 and Min Ag and Fisheries 1930–31; Sec State Dominion Affrs (name changed to Sec State Cwlth Rels 1947) and Leader Ho of Lds July 1945–Oct 1947; Ld Privy Seal and Ldr Ho of Lds 1947–51; Paymaster-Gen 1948–49; Ld Pres Cncl 1951; Chm MRC 1948–51; Hunterian Prof and examiner in Anatomy in Camb and Lond Us, Prof Anatomy U Coll Sheffield; Lecturer Anatomy St Bartholomew's Hosp, ed *Quarterly Medical Journal*, author *Politics from Within*; *b* 19 June 1869; *m* 1st 25 March 1902 Isobel Mackinnon (*d* 22 Aug 1934), dau of Archibald Gray, of 37 Holland Park, W, and had issue; *m* 2nd, 4 Nov 1937 (Beatrice) Dorothy (*d* 3 Sept 1982), dau of Frederick Percy Low, of Thames View House, Staines, Middx, and *d* 11 Dec 1951, leaving by his 1st w:

1 CHRISTOPHER ADDISON, **2nd Viscount Addison**, Maj S Staffs Regt WW II, mem London Stock Exchange (attached to Sutherland, Pershore, Millar & Co, stockbrockers); Pres Inst Motor Industry, Chm SW Met Regional Hosp Bd, Dir of various statutory and other companies *b* 8 Dec 1904; *educ* Univ Coll Sch, Hampstead, and Newton Coll Newton Abbot; *m* 10 Sep 1928 Brigit Helen Christine (*d* 1980), dau of Ernest Edwin George Williams, barrister, of Wimbledon, and *dspm* 18 Nov 1976, leaving issue:

(1) *Jacqueline Faith [The Hon Mrs Jacqueline Payne, 9A Kirk Park, Liberton Edinburgh, EH16 6HZ], *b* 2 March 1944, *m* 8 Oct 1966 (*divorce* 1985) Jeremy Warren Payne, yr s of Cecil Warren Payne, of Old Bursledon, Hants, and has:

1a *Katy Josephine; *b* 17 Dec 1972

2a *Christina Meriel; *b* 9 Oct 1975

3a *Anna Isabella; *b* 14 May 1978

(2) *Christine Gray [The Hon Mrs Tidborough, 2 Silver St, Willand, Cullompton, Devon], *b* 3 Sept 1946, *m* 28 Feb 1966 *Terry Frederick Tidborough, s of Victor Tidborough, of Cullompton, Devon

2 MICHAEL ADDISON, **3rd Viscount Addison**, F/Offr RAFVR 1941–45, civ serv 1936–65 (Treasury 1963–65) Chm Fulham (later Hammersmith) Borough Youth Cttee 1961–68, Sr Lecturer Polytechnic of Central London Sch Management Studies 1965–76, memb Roy Inst of Public Admin & Assoc Teachers of Management, *b* 12 April 1914, *educ* Hele's Sch, Exeter, and Balliol Coll Oxford (MA); *m* 22 Aug 1936 *Kathleen [The Rt Hon The Dowager Viscountess Addison, Old Stables, Maplehurst, W Sussex], only dau of Rt Rev and Rt Hon John William Charles Wand, KCVO, DD, Canon and Treasurer St Paul's Cathedral, formerly Bp London, and had issue:

(1) WILLIAM MATTHEW WAND, **4th and present Viscount**

(1) *Eleanor Brigit [The Hon Mrs Girling, 16 Heatherwood, Midhurst, W Sussex GU29 9LH], *b* 11 June 1938, *m* 27 Jan 1972 *Michael Girling, est s of Kenneth Girling, of Ipswich, Suffolk

(2) *Caroline Ruth [The Hon Mrs Wearing, 12 Hill St North, Richmond, Nelson, New Zealand], *b* 30 July 1942, *m* 29 May 1965 *John Hollis Wearing, er s of Hollis Wearing, of Rai Valley, Marlborough, NZ, and has:

1a *Patrick, *b* 28 Jan 1969

1a *Jacalyn Ruth, *b* 2 March 1966

1 Elizabeth Kate, *m* 3 Dec 1935 Edward Worsley Ashcroft, s of William Worsley Ashcroft, of Croydon, Surrey, and *d* July 1967, leaving issue

2 Isobel Gray, *m* 29 Aug 1932 Nicholas, s of Francis Augustus Cheshire, of St Petersburg, and had issue

AGNEW
of Great Stanhope Street

Arms: Per saltire argent and gules two cinquefoils in pale and as many saltires couped in fess, all counterchanged. **Crest:** An eagle rising regardant proper, each wing charged with a pale or, holding in the beak by the hilt a sword in bend sinister, also proper, and resting the dexter claw on a saltire gules. **Motto:** *Consilio et impetu* ('By wisdom and vigour'). **Creation:** Bt. (UK) 2 Sept 1895.

SIR JOHN KEITH AGNEW, 6TH BT, of Great Stanhope Street, London [Sir John Agnew Bt, Lawney's Farm, Rougham, Suffolk IP30 9LZ]; *b* 19 Dec 1950; *s f* 1994; *educ* Gresham's and RAC Cirencester

Lineage: The AGNEWs of Clendry, parish of Kirkcolm, on the Lochnaw estate, claimed descent from the Sheuchan branch of the AGNEWs of Lochnaw (*qv*).

THOMAS AGNEW, of Culhorn Inch, Wigtownshire; *b* Clendry; *m* 28 Feb 1751 Janet McMaster (*d* 19 Nov 1807) and *d* 30 Dec 1790, having had, with a yr s (Thomas, of Limekil, Inch; *bapt* 16 Nov 1760; executor and trustee to the last Thomas Agnew of Clendry (*d* 22 July 1822); *m* 19 Jan 1792 Mary McConnell (*d* 26 March 1804) and *d* 19 Dec 1835, leaving issue):

JOHN AGNEW, of Culhorn; *b* 10 Dec 1751; *m* 24 April 1794 Jane Glover, of Liverpool, and *d* by 16 Dec 1794, leaving:

THOMAS AGNEW, of Fairhope, Eccles, Lancs, JP (Salford); *b* 16 Dec 1794; Mayor Salford 1851, fndr Thos Agnew & Sons art dealers; *m* 19 Feb 1823 Jane Garnet (*d* 8 Oct 1864), dau and coheir of William Lockett, of Manchester, and *d* 24 March 1871, having had an est s:

Sir William Agnew, 1st Bt (UK), so *cr* 2 Sept 1895, JP (Lancs, Manchester and Salford); *b* 20 Oct 1825; MP (Lib) SE Lancs 1880–85 and Stretford 1885–86; *m* 25 March 1851 Mary (*d* 2 Sept 1892), est dau of George Pixton Kenworthy, of Peel Hall, Astley, Lancs, and had issue:

1 GEORGE WILLIAM (Sir), **2nd Bt**

2 Charles Morland, OBE (1918); *b* 14 Dec 1855; *educ* Rugby and Trin Coll Cambridge (MA); High Sheriff Herts 1930; *m* 22 Sept 1881 Evelyn Mary (*d* 14 April 1932), dau of William Naylor, and *d* 23 May 1931, leaving issue:

(1) (Charles) Gerald; *b* 30 July 1882; *educ* Rugby; T/Capt Manchester Regt WW I; *m* 11 July 1906 Olive Mary (*d* 30 March 1946), 2nd dau of Ven William Danks, Canon Canterbury, and *d* 29 June 1954, leaving issue:

1a Geoffrey William Gerald (Sir), CB (1975); *b* 11 July 1908; *educ* Eton and Trin Coll Cambridge (BA 1930); chm and md Thos Agnew & Sons, ktd 1973; *m* 25 April 1934 Hon Doreen Maud Jessel (*d* 1990), 3rd dau of 1st Baron Jessel (*see* JESSEL, Bt), and *d* 1986, leaving:

1b +Jonathan Geoffrey William [Jonathan Agnew Esq, Flat E, 51 Eaton Sq, London SW1W 9BE]; *b* 30 July 1941; *educ* Eton and Trin Coll Cambridge (BA 1963, MA 1972); *The Economist* 1964–65, World Bank 1965–67, Hill Samuel 1967–73 (dir 1971), Morgan Stanley 1973–82 (md 1977), fin consultant 1983–86, ch exec: ISRO 1986, Kleinwort Benson Gp 1987–93, chm Kleinwort Benson Ltd 1989–93, LIMIT plc and J G W Agnew and Co 1993–, memb cncl Lloyd's 1995–; *m* 1st 21 Oct 1966 (*divorce* 1985) Hon (Agneta) Joanna (Middleton) Campbell, yr dau of Baron Campbell of Eskan (LP; *see* 1970 edn), and has issue:

1c +Caspar Jonathan William; *b* 29 April 1967; *m* 6 April 1991 *Annabel J, er dau of Tim Summers, and has issue:

1d +Hector Jonathan Timothy; *b* 1993

2d *Daisy Matilda; *b* 1995

1c *Lara Joanna; *b* 1969

2c *Katherine Agneta; *b* 21 Oct 1971

1b (cont.) Jonathan Agnew *m* 2nd 1990 *Marie-Clare, er dau of Bernard Dreesmann, and has further issue:

3c *Clarissa Virginia; *b* 1992

2b +(Morland Herbert) Julian [Julian Agnew Esq, 22 Campden Hill Sq, London W8 7JY]; *b* 20 Sept 1943; *educ* Eton and Trin Coll Cambridge (BA 1965); *m* 1st 26 July 1973 Elizabeth Margaret, dau of William B Mitchell, and has issue:

1c +Thomas Julian Noel; *b* 21 Dec 1975

1c *Amelia Elizabeth; *b* 1979

2b (cont.) Julian Agnew *m* 2nd 1993 *Victoria, 2nd dau of Maj Henry Ronald Burn Callander, MC (*see* CROSSLEY, Bt), and has:

2c +Benjamin Geoffrey David Callander; b 6 Oct 1996

1b *Jennifer Maud; *b* 30 Jan 1937; *m* 24 May 1962 *$ILazell, PaulPaul Lazell, of 55 St James Gdns, London W11and Manor House, Kirkgate Lane, Wighton, Norfolk, only s of Henry George Leslie Lazell, and has issue:

1c *Sebastian Henry; *b* 6 Dec 1963; *m* 1989 *Belinda Mary, er dau of Peter Beck, and has:

1d *Frederick Henry; *b* 1990

2d *Hamish William; *b* 1992

2c *Dominic Geoffrey Paul; *b* 1972

1c *Natasha Jennifer; *b* 19 April 1967; *m* 1991 *Duncan James Bell, yst s of Harold Bell, and has issue:

1d *Joshua James; *b* 1994

2a +(Denys) Martin [Maj Martin Agnew, 107 Keverstone Ct, 95 Manor Rd, Bournemouth BH1 3BY]; *b* 9 July 1919; *educ* Eton and Trin Coll Cambridge (BA 1940); late Maj RA (Emergency Reserve), MTAI, gen manager Amex (S Africa), dir Wholesale Travel Ltd, v-chm Assoc S African Travel Agents, v-pres American Express Internat, dir World Wide Coaches and Horizon (Scotland); *m* 1st 9 Feb 1943 (*divorce* 1949) Monica, 2nd dau of Lt-Col Rev Samuel Foskett, MD, MA, and has issue:

1b +Jeremy Andrew Derrick [Jeremy Agnew, 3912 Linden Place, Colorado Springs, Colorado, USA]; *b* 10 Dec 1943; *educ* Eton, Colorado Coll (BA) and U of Colorado (BS); *m* 16 March 1968 *Mary Sylvia, dau of Van Kirk B Perkins, and has issue:

1c *Tracy Marie; *b* 1974

2c *Christine; *b* 1977

2a (cont.) Maj Martin Agnew *m* 2nd 23 Dec 1949 Josephine Anne, dau of Alan Ross, of Natal, S Africa, and by her has further issue:

2b +William George Morland; *b* 24 Aug 1955; *educ* Eton; *m* 1984 *Antonia Jane, yr dau of Capt Richard Lawrence Garnons-Williams

1b *(Emma Christianne) Annabel [The Most Hon The Marchioness Conyngham, Myrtle Hill, Andreas Rd, Ramsey, IoM]; *b* 3 Jan 1951; *m* 1987, as his 4th w, *7th Marquess Conyngham (*qv*)

2a (cont.) Maj Martin Agnew *m* 3rd 1974 Rosetta Mary, dau of Mrs Ethel Benjamin, of Johannesburg; *m* 4th 1988 *Mrs Rosemary Wylde

1a Sylvia Mary; *m* 21 Oct 1937 Christopher Richard Cecil Thursfield, yr s of Rev Richard Cecil Thursfield, Rector Cranford, Northants, and *d* 8 Aug 1961, leaving issue

(2) Kenneth Morland, DSO (1919), OBE, MC; *b* 25 May 1886; Lt-Col RA WW I (despatches, wounded, Croix de Guerre Italy); *m* 1st 20 Oct 1910 (*divorce* 1921) Edith (*d* 28 Oct 1950), only dau of Arthur Henry Laver, MD, MRCS, and had issue:

1a Joyce; *b* 23 June 1913; *m* 9 Nov 1940 *Maj Edwin Peter Holness, RA (ret), s of Edwin Cutler Holness, and *d* 2 Nov 1995

(2) (cont.) Lt-Col Kenneth Agnew *m* 2nd 29 Oct 1921 (*divorce* 1936) Louise (*d* 6 Oct 1965), dau of David Harris; *m* 3rd 5 March 1943 Lillian (*d* 10 Dec 1951), dau of George Matmerson, of Johannesburg, and formerly w of Roy Brown, and *d* 19 Aug 1951

(3) Alan Graeme; *b* 6 Dec 1887; Maj RA (TA) WW I (despatches); *m* 3 April 1913 Dorothy Cecil (*d* 27 Nov 1959), dau of William Winstanley Strode, and *d* 6 May 1962, leaving issue:

1a +Peter Graeme, MBE (1946) [W/Cdr Peter Agnew MBE, The Linhay, Trenarth Lane, Constantine, Cornwall TR11 5JN]; *b* 7 April 1914; *educ* Stowe and Trin Coll Cambridge (BA); W/Cdr RAFVR WW II; *m* 3 April 1937 *Mary Diana, only dau of James Philip Hervey, and has issue:

1b +Ian Hervey [Ian Agnew Esq, Oak Lodge, Ifield Wood, Crawley, Sussex]; *b* 19 Aug 1941; *educ* Stowe; late Lt Inns of Court and City Yeo (TA); *m* 4 April 1964 *Amanda Barbara, only dau of Maj Arnold Wyndham-Read, Inns of Court Regt, and Mrs Ursula Somerville Baker, of Water Hall, Ifield Wood, Sussex, and has issue:

1c +Mark Wyndham; *b* 2 Jan 1966

2c +Jonathan Graeme; *b* 27 Jan 1968

2b +James Philip [James Agnew Esq, Trenarth Cottage, Constantine, Cornwall TR11 5JN]; *b* 1 Oct 1947; *educ* Stowe; *m* Feb 1972 *Carol Ann, dau of Edward Garfield Williams, and has issue:

1c +William Edward Philip; *b* 1976

1c *Emma Victoria; *b* 1972

1b *Penelope Mary [Mrs Norman Davies, Lowfields Cottage, London Rd, Hartley Wintney, Hants RG27 8HY]; *b* 18 Oct 1939; *m* 14 Feb 1961 *Col Norman Thomas Davies, OBE, RHA, JP, late RA, s of Edward Ernest Davies, and has issue:

1c *Edward Peter; *b* 12 Feb 1962; Maj LI; *m* 19 Dec 1992 *Susan Mary, yr dau of Joseph Goble, of Harare, Zimbabwe, and has:

1d *Charles Jaspar Peter; *b* 25 March 1995

1d *Jemma Elizabeth Mary; *b* 1 May 1996

1c *Clare Mary [Mrs Nicholas Duffield, 43 Tonsley Hill, London SW18 1BE]; *b* 29 July 1962; *m* 7 June 1997 *Nicholas Thomas Duffield, er s of Capt R Duffield and Mrs Patricia Duffield

2b *Diana Nicola; *b* 22 Sept 1945; *m* 1st 6 June 1966 (*divorce* 1978) Anthony David Mayhew, yr s of Robert Evelyn Gurney Mayhew, and has issue:

1c *Anthony James; *b* 9 March 1969

2c *Gavin Mark; *b* 1971

1c *Louisa Clare; *b* 1973

2b (cont.) Mrs Diana Mayhew *m* 2nd 1983 (*divorce* 19–) Maj Antony Michael Tippet

1a *Jacquelin; *b* 6 Aug 1916; *m* 17 July 1937 Joseph Stanley Desmond Whitaker, only s of Stanley Milnes Whitaker, and has issue:

1b *Graeme Stanley [Graeme Whitaker Esq, Crowland, Ancaster, nr Grantham]; *b* 18 Sept 1938; *educ* Leys Sch Cambridge; *m* 29 Oct 1959 *Penelope Ann, dau of G/Capt Edwin Howard Walker, of Grendon Hall, Northampton, and has issue:

1c *Charles Alan; *b* 29 March 1962

2c *Anthony John; *b* 24 Aug 1964

1c *Bridget Ann; *b* 12 Oct 1960

2b *Nigel Glynne [Nigel Whitaker Esq, Broomfield House, Yatton, Keynell, nr Chippenham]; *b* 10 July 1940; *educ* Leys Sch and Trin Coll Cambridge (BA 1962); *m* 17 Jan 1964 *Patricia Caroline, only dau of Ian Falconer Stewart, and has issue:

1c *Jeremy Stewart; *b* 11 Aug 1964

1c *Patricia Frances; *b* 11 April 1967

3b *David Alan; *b* 28 Aug 1941; *educ* Leys Sch and Magdalene Coll Cambridge (BA 1962, VetMB, MRCVS 1965); *m* 17 Aug 1963 *Madeleine, yr dau of Ivan Louis Paux, of Berne, Switzerland, and has issue:

1c *Jean-François; *b* 9 Oct 1965

2c *Patrique; *b* 1969

1c *Marie Claude; *b* 2 Jan 1964

4b *Jonathan Milnes; *b* 10 March 1947; *educ* Leys Sch; *m* 1974 *Christine, dau of William Turner

(4) Hugh Ladas; *b* 6 June 1894; Cdr RN; md Thos Agnew & Sons 1931–39 (chm 1955–65), chm Govrs Bloxham Sch 1948–60, Pres BADA 1965–75; *m* 1st 6 July 1920 Mary Violet Maud (*d* 5 Dec 1932), dau of Hugh Davies, of Trinidad, and had issue:

1a Michael Hugh; *b* 11 July 1923; Sub-Lt RN WW II (despatches); *ka* 13 Nov 1943

1a Anne Mary; *b* 6 Aug 1926; *k* Arlberg disaster 22 Dec 1952

2a Susan Elizabeth; *b* 30 Sept 1930; *m* 24 April 1954 Robert Edward Michael Momber, BA, late Sub-Lt (S) RNVR, s of Robert Stephen Momber, and had issue:

1b *Robert Hugh; *b* 2 July 1956

2b *Adrian Michael; *b* 27 March 1958

(4) (cont.) Hugh Agnew *m* 2nd 28 April 1934 Gwendolen Ford Low (*d* 11 Sept 1975), yr dau of Ernest Albert Smith, and *d* 20 Dec 1975

(5) William Gladstone (Sir), KCVO (1947), CB (1941), DSO (1943) and bar (1944); *b* 2 Dec 1898; *educ* RNCs Osborne and Dartmouth; V-Adml, cmded HMS *Vanguard* roy tour S Africa 1947, served WWs I and II, Cdr Orange-Nassau 1948, Gen Sec Nat Playing Fields Assoc 1950–53; *m* 24 April 1930 Patricia Caroline (*d* 23 Aug 1977), yr dau of Col Alfred William Bewley, CMG, and *dsp* 12 July 1960

(1) Emily Margaret; *d* unm 26 June 1941

3 Walter; *b* 29 April 1861; *educ* Rugby and Trin Coll Cambridge (LLB); *m* 17 July 1886 Mabel (*d* 18 Aug 1956), dau of Charles Wilkin, and *d* 17 April 1915, having had issue:

(1) Victor Charles Walter; *b* 21 June 1887; *educ* Rugby and Trin Coll Cambridge (BA); Capt Suffolk Yeo; *m* 22 July 1913 Phyllis May Claude (*m* 2nd 18 Aug 1932 A/Cdre Andrew George Board, CMG, DSO, DL, RAF (ret)), dau of Claude Baggallay, KC, and *d* 4 Sept 1929, leaving issue:

1a (Charles) David; *b* 3 Sept 1916; *educ* Harrow; Lt-Col 15th/19th KRH WW II; *m* 3 Dec 1949 *Mary Lorna, 2nd dau of Rt Rev Henry St John Stirling Woollcombe, DD, Bp Selby, and *d* 1987, leaving issue:

1b +(David) Richard Charles; *b* 21 June 1953; *educ* Harrow; *m* 1978 *Charlotte Anne, yr dau of John Calkim Whately-Smith (*see* HOTHAM, B), and has issue:

1c +Dickon James; *b* 1983

1c *Joanna Woollcombe; *b* 1981

1b *Susan Lorna; *b* 31 Dec 1950; *m* 1976 Alastair Philip Hunter Smart (*d* 1992), and has issue:

1c *Angus David Alastair; *b* 1978

1c *Harriet Bridget; *b* 1981

2b *Vanda Jane; *b* 15 March 1959; *m* 1986 *Julian Edward Lambton and has issue (*see* DURHAM, E)

1a *Elizabeth Moran; *b* 7 May 1914; *m* 27 Oct 1938 Brig Brian Kingzett, CBE, MC, late RA, 2nd s of Norman Froggatt Kingzett, MBE, and has issue:

1b *Charles David; *b* 1 Jan 1942; *educ* Wellington

1b *Sarah Elizabeth; *b* 8 June 1945; *m* 10 Sept 1966 *James Anthony Lansley Sandow, s of G/Capt James Frederick Sandow, OBE, RAF (ret)

(2) Lewis Philip; *b* 16 March 1891; *d* 29 June 1898

(3) Richard Leslie; *b* 4 March 1900; *educ* Rugby and RMC Sandhurst; 2nd Lt 15th Hus 1918, ret as Capt 1936, Capt Northants Yeo 1937, Maj 1938, Maj

15th/19th Hus 1940, Lt-Col ER Yeo 1941, Lt-Col 146th Regt (RAC) Duke of Wellington's Regt 1943, Arakan Campaigns 1943–45 (despatches); High Sheriff Northants 1957; *m* 1st 20 July 1927 (*divorce* 1946) Leila May, only dau of Brig-Gen Anthony Courage, DSO, MC, Col 15th/19th Hus; *m* 2nd 1953 Hilda Dorothy (*d* 1993), dau of Thomas Henry Spinks, and *d* 1987, leaving issue:

1a +(Richard) Mark Walter [Lt Mark Agnew RN (ret), The Curate's House, Melbury Osmond, Dorchester, Dorset]; *b* 17 July 1930; *educ* RNC Dartmouth; ADC to Govr Malta 1954–55; *m* 1st 23 April 1955 (*divorce* 1963) Edwina Ottilie Jane, est dau of Maj-Gen Sir Robert Edward Laycock, KCMG, CB, DSO (*see* DUDLEY, E), and has issue:

1b *Leonie; *b* 28 March 1956; *m* 1979 *Daniel Davis, of New York, and has issue:

1c *Benjamin Daniel; *b* 1985

1c *Sarah Jane; *b* 1983

1a (cont.) Lt Mark Agnew *m* 2nd Jan 1972 Teresa Jane (*d* 1989), only dau of 7th Earl of Ilchester (*qv*) and widow of 9th Viscount Galway (*qv*); *m* 3rd 1992 *Elspeth, dau of Lt-Col A I Macpherson, of Lochgilphead, Argyll, and widow of Capt William Richard Dalrymple Gerard-Pearse, CBE, LVO, RN, of Dinder, Somerset

1a *(Leila) Rosemary [Mrs Robert Lyle, Pantyrhedyn, Gellywen, Dyfed SA33 6EA]; *b* 8 June 1928; *m* 1st 18 Dec 1948 (*divorce* 1959) Kenneth Malcolm Ritchie, only s of Kenneth Leslie Ritchie, and has issue:

1b *Linda Rosemary Anne; *b* 28 April 1951; *m* 1st 1973 F/Lt Nigel Corbishley (*d* 1984) and has issue:

1c *Benjamin James; *b* 1977

2c *Jonathan Piers; *b* 9 June 1979

3c *Rupert Charles; *b* 1982

1b (cont.) *Mrs Linda Corbishley *m* 2nd 1988 *F/Lt Michael Pichel-Juan

2b *Venetia Clare [Mrs Robert Sanders, 62 Lower Park Rd, Hastings, Sussex TN34 2LB]; *b* 7 Sept 1953; *m* 1972 *Robert Christopher Springett Sanders and has issue:

1c *Philip Malcolm; *b* 1982

1c *Katherine Joan; *b* 1974

2c *Josephine Rosemary; *b* 1980

3c *Sally Ann; *b* 1984

1a (cont.) Mrs Rosemary Ritchie *m* 2nd 6 Dec 1962 *Robert John Lyle, est s of Capt Robert Charles Lyle, and has further issue:

1b *Richard Charles Cecil [Richard Lyle Esq, 11 Galesbury Rd, London SW18]; *b* 13 April 1965; *m* 1993 *Joanna Mary Smith

1b *Lucinda [Mrs John Johnson, Rockstone, La Rue des Vaux de l'Eglise, St Martin, Jersey JE3 6BF]; *b* 19 Aug 1963; *m* 1989 *John Julian Peter Johnson and has issue:

1c *William Charles Eric; *b* 1994

2c *Charles Oliver Thomas; *b* 1997

1c *Elizabeth Daisy; *b* 1992

2a *Lavinia Mary; *b* 21 Dec 1933; *m* 1st 28 March 1952 (*divorce* 1956) Geoffrey Arnold Ellert, s of John Arnold Ellert by Barbara Jean, 2nd dau of Allan Havelock-Allan (*see* HAVELOCK-ALLAN, Bt), and has issue:

1b *Sally-Ann Barbara; *b* 13 Aug 1952; took name Rashleigh by deed poll 1970; *m* 1st 1973 Anthony Phillips and has issue:

1c *Melissa Mary; *b* 1976

2c *Victoria Clare; *b* 1978

3c *Antonia Melanie; *b* 1981

1b (cont.) *Mrs Phillips *m* 2nd 1992 *Philip M Boreham

2b *Serena Denise; *b* 31 Oct 1954; took name Rashleigh by deed poll 1970; *m* 1979 *Roderick Baird and has issue:

1c *Thomas Roderick; *b* 1982

1c *Rosemary Alice; *b* 1984

2c *Holly Madeleine; *b* 1987

2a (cont.) *Mrs Lavinia Ellert *m* 2nd 14 March 1956 *Jonathan Rashleigh, s of Vernon Leslie William Rashleigh, and has had further issue:

1b Julian Philip; *b* 5 May 1957; *d* 1993

3b *Elizabeth Jane; *b* 7 Dec 1961

(1) Phyllis Mary; *b* 30 Oct 1895; *m* 29 June 1918 Col Clifford Humphrey Lloyd, MC, RA, only s of Brig-Gen Frederick Charles Lloyd, CB, and had issue:

1a *Diana Mabel; *b* 12 May 1920, *m* 1st 22 March 1941 (*divorce* 1946) Capt Ian Hope-Johnstone, Roy Fus, only s of Col Hope-Johnstone, RA; *m* 2nd 28 Aug 1946 (*divorce* 1964) George Raymond Tibbitt, yr s of George Tracy Arthur Tibbitt, and has issue:

1b *Mark Julian Lloyd; *b* 27 Feb 1950; *educ* Eton

1b *Diana Olivia; *b* 16 Aug 1947

1a (cont.) *Mrs Diana Tibbitt *m* 3rd 1 June 1964 Hugo Romer Nicholson, s of Capt Eric Nicholson, 12th Roy Lancers, and Armorer, Countess of Breadalbane (*qv*)

4 Philip Leslie, JP (Northants); *b* 30 June 1863; *educ* New Coll Oxford (MA); FRAM; barrister, High Sheriff Northants 1924; *m* 12 Nov 1889 Alexandra Georgette (*d* 12 June 1957), er dau of Ewan Christian, of Alexandria, Egypt, and *d* 5 March 1938, having had issue:

(1) Ewan Siegfried; *b* 12 July 1893; Lt 5th Lancers (SR) WW I (despatches); *m* 1st 14 Feb 1917 (*divorce* 1929) Marion, dau of Frank Loughborough; *m* 2nd 23 Jan 1929 Constance Mary (*m* 2nd 24 Dec 1937 Theodore Rosser Kerby, MRCS, LRCP; *d* 10 May 1954), dau of Frederick John Newell, and *d* 8 March 1930

(1) Christine Elaine; *b* 15 Jan, *d* 13 Nov 1896

(2) Enid Jocelyn; *b* 13 July 1898; *m* 22 Nov 1919 Capt Roger Evans, MC, 7th Hus (*d* 22 Oct 1968), s of Roger Evans, and *d* 20 Feb 1921, leaving issue

1 Mary Caroline; *m* 5 June 1878 Arthur Graeme Ogilvie and *d* 2 Feb 1888, leaving issue

2 Florence; *m* 3 Dec 1880 Joseph John Bolton (*d* 2 Nov 1928) and *d* 2 Sept 1890, leaving issue

Sir WILLIAM *d* 31 Oct 1910; his est son,

Sir George William Agnew, 2nd Bt, JP (Lancs and W Suffolk); *b* 19 Jan 1852; *educ* St John's Coll Cambridge (MA); Lt-Col 2nd Bn Suffolk Vol Regt, MP W Salford 1906–18, High Sheriff Suffolk 1922; *m* 2 Oct 1878 Fanny (*d* 25 April 1937), yr dau of John Stuart Bolton, of Oulton Hall, Aylsham, Norfolk, and had issue:

1 JOHN STUART (Sir), **3rd Bt**

2 (George) Colin; *b* 28 Oct 1882; *educ* Rugby and King's Coll Cambridge; Lt WW I despatches, invalided)

1 Mary Emily; *m* 17 March 1904 William Burn Anderson (*d* 31 Jan 1948), est s of Jon Macvicar Anderson

2 Fanny Isabel, twin with her sister Mary Emily; *m* 4 March 1909 Brig-Gen Oswald Kesteven Chance, CMG, DSO, 5th Lancers (*d* 21 Sept 1935), s of William Edward Chance, and *d* 4 July 1967, leaving issue

3 Dorothy; *m* 4 July 1906 Hinton Arthur Stewart (*d* 18 Nov 1956), 2nd s of Hinton Daniell Stewart, and *dsp* 16 March 1940

4 Sybil Alice; *m* 22 May 1919 Maj-Gen John Talbot Wentworth Reeve, CB, CBE, DSO, Rifle Bde, s of Charles Sydney Wentworth Reeve, of Livermere Park, Bury St Edmunds, and *d* 17 Aug 1949, leaving issue

5 Cicely; *m* 10 June 1920 Norman Froggatt Kingzett, MBE (*d* 19 Jan 1947), er s of Charles Thomas Kingzett, and left issue (*see* TRITTON, Bt)

Sir GEORGE *d* 19 Dec 1941; his er son,

Sir John Stuart Agnew, 3rd Bt, TD, JP and DL (W Suffolk); *b* 16 Sept 1879; Maj Suffolk Yeo (TA) WW I, W Suffolk: CA, CC (ret 1952); *m* 14 April 1910 Kathleen (*d* 5 May 1971), 3rd dau of Isaac William Hewitt White, and *d* 27 Aug 1957, leaving:

1 **Sir (John) Anthony Stuart Agnew, 4th Bt**; *b* 25 July 1914; *d* unm

2 GEORGE KEITH (Sir) **5th Bt**

3 +Stephen William [Stephen Agnew Esq, 4a Prince Alfred Parade, Newport, NSW 2106, Australia]; *b* 31 July 1921; *educ* Rugby and Trin Coll Cambridge; Lt 7th Hus WW II (wounded); *m* 1st 28 June 1947 (*divorce* 1966) Elizabeth, dau of James Brooks Close, of Aldeburgh, Suffolk, and has issue:

(1) +John Stuart [John Agnew Esq, Fincham Farm, Rougham, Kings Lynn, Norfolk]; *b* 30 Aug 1949; *educ* Gordonstoun; *m* 1982 *Diana Margaret Zoë, er dau of Cdr Christopher Ellis Baker, RN, of Cley, Norfolk, and has issue:

1a +Jethro Luke; *b* 1988

2a +Edgar Christopher; *b* 1990

3a +Garth Stephen; *b* 1992

(2) +Bolton [Bolton Agnew Esq, Oulton Hall, Norwich, Norfolk]; *b* 1950; *educ* Gordonstoun; *m* 1989 *Clare Elizabeth, dau of Henry Everet Tinsley, of Langrick Grange, Boston, Lincs, and has issue:

1a +William Henry Bolton; *b* 1991

1a *Rosemary Brooks; *b* 1989

(3) +James Brooks Close [James Agnew Esq, Church Farm, Oulton, Norwich]; *b* 12 April 1953; *educ* Gordonstoun; *m* 1984 *Judith Dianne, dau of Edward Gilbert, and has issue:

1a *Catherine Penelope; *b* 1986

2a *Louise Frances Elizabeth; *b* 1988

(4) +Stephen Hardcastle [Stephen Agnew Esq, The Old Rectory, West Acre, Kings Lynn, Norfolk]; *b* 4 Dec 1954; *educ* Gordonstoun; *m* 1993 *Amanda, only dau of E W Trafford, of Wroxham, Norfolk

(5) +Theodore Thomas More [Theodore Agnew Esq, The Little Manor, Thorndon, Suffolk]; *b* 17 Jan 1961; *educ* Rugby; *m* 1993 *Clare Margaret, yr dau of John Joseph Buxton, of Horsey Hall, Gt Yarmouth (*see* BUXTON, Bt), and has:

1a *Madeleine Elizabeth Demetria; b 16 Aug 1995

(6) +St John Kenneth [St John Agnew Esq, 4 The Wheatcroft, Harborne, Birmingham]; *b* 25 Feb 1964; *educ* Rugby and Sheffield U; *m* 1992 *Jenny R, er dau of Gerald W Youngs

(1) *Margaret Elizabeth Diana; *b* 12 Jan 1952; *m* 10 Sept 1973 *Richard Eustace Thomas Gurney, only surv s of Samuel Edmond Gurney (*see* HERTFORD, M)

3 (cont.) Stephen Agnew *m* 2nd Mrs Adene Leona Cookson, dau of Vincent John Brady, and formerly w of John Cookson

The 4th Bt's bro,

Sir George Keith Agnew, 5th Bt, TD, JP (Suffolk 1949); *b* 25 Nov 1918; *educ* Rugby and Trin Coll Cambridge; Maj 258th (Suffolk Yeo) Medium Regt RA (TA), TAR Offrs WW II; *m* 10 July 1948 *Baroness Anne Merete Louise, yr dau of Baron Johann Schaffalitzky de Muckadell, of Rødkilde, Fyn, Denmark, and *d* 1994, leaving:

1 Sir JOHN KEITH AGNEW, **6th and present Bt**

2 +GEORGE ANTHONY [George Agnew Esq, Freewood Cottage, Bradfield St George, Bury St Edmunds, Suffolk]; *b* 18 Aug 1953; heir presumptive; *educ* Gresham's and UEA

AGNEW of Lochnaw

Arms: Argent a chevron between in chief two cinquefoils gules and in base a saltire couped azure. **Crest:** An eagle issuant and regardant proper. **Supporters:** Two heraldic tigers proper, collared and chained or. **Motto:** *Consilo non impetu* ('By counsel, not by rashness'). **Creation:** Bt. (NS) 28 July 1629.

SIR CRISPIN HAMLYN AGNEW OF LOCHNAW, 11TH BT, QC (1995) [Sir Crispin Agnew of Lochnaw Bt QC, 6 Palmerston Rd, Edinburgh, EH9 1TN]; *b* 13 May 1944; *s f* 1975; Chief of the Name and Arms of Agnew; *educ* Uppingham and RMA Sandhurst; Maj (ret) Roy Highland Fus, memb RN expdn E Greenland 1966, Ldr Army expdn Greenland 1968, Jt Services expdns: Antarctica 1970–71, Chilean Patagonia 1972–73 (leader), Army Nuptse expdn 1975, Jt Br and Roy Nepalese Army Everest expdn 1976, Army expdn Api NW Nepal 1980, advocate 1982, Slains Pursuivant of Arms to Earl of Erroll 1978–81, Unicorn Pursuivant 1981–86, Rothesay Herald 1986, memb Roy Co Archers; *m* 27 Sept 1980 *Susan, jnlst and broadcaster, dau of Jock Wykeham Strang Steel, (*see* STRANG STEEL, Bt), and has:

1 +MARK DOUGLAS NOEL; *b* 24 April 1991
1 *Isabel Sevilla Wilhelmina; *b* 1984
2 *Emma Rachel Elizabeth; *b* 1986
3 *Roseanna Celia Nancy; *b* 1989

Lineage: ANDREW AGNEW; Constable Lochnaw Castle, apptd hereditary Sheriff Wigton 1451, the post being held by successive AGNEWS till its abolition 1651; *d* 1455, leaving with two yr sons:

ANDREW AGNEW; Provost Wigton 1476; *m* a dau of Macdowall of Garthland and *d* 1483/4, having had an er s:

QUENTIN AGNEW of Lochnaw; Provost Wigton 1488; *m* 1469 Mariotta, 3rd dau of Robert Vaus of Barnbarroch, and *d* 1498, having had (with a yr s Michael and a dau, Mariotta):

PATRICK AGNEW of Lochnaw; *m c* 1499 Katherine, dau of Sir Robert Gordon of Lochinvar, and *d* 1513, having had, with three daus (including Margaret, *m* William Cairnis of Orchardton; *see* ROSSMORE, B):

ANDREW AGNEW of Lochnaw; *m* Agnes, dau of Sir Alexander Stewart of Garlies, and was *ka* Battle of Pinkie 1547, having had, with two yr sons (Gilbert, 1st of Galdenoch; Alexander, of Ardoch) and a dau:

PATRICK AGNEW of Lochnaw; *b* 1529; *m* 1550 Janet, dau of Sir James Gordon of Lochinvar, and *d* 1591, having had, with other issue:

1 ANDREW (Sir), for whom *see* below
2 Thomas; had:
(1) Patrick Agnew of Castlewigg; *s* an uncle in Barmeil; *m* Helen, dau of Anthony Dunbar of Machermore, and had:
1a Elizabeth; *m* William Agnew, 2nd s of Sir Andrew Agnew of Lochnaw (*see* below)

PATRICK's est s,

Sir ANDREW AGNEW of Lochnaw; Chamberlain Galloway by 1595; *m* 1576 Agnes, dau of Alexander Stewart, Yr of Garlies, and *d* 1616, leaving with other issue:

Sir Patrick Agnew, 1st Bt (NS), so *cr* 28 July 1629 with remainder to his heirs male whatsoever; *b c* 1578; MP Wigtownshire 1628–33 and 1643–47; *m* Margaret, dau of Sir Thomas Kennedy of Culzean (*see* AILSA, M), and *d* 1661, leaving an est s:

Sir Andrew Agnew, 2nd Bt; ktd *vp*, MP Wigtownshire 1644, 1647,1665, 1667 and 1669, memb Commn for governing Scotland 1649, Sheriff Kirkcudbrightshire and Wigtownshire during Interregnum 1656; *m c* 22 March 1625 Lady Anne Stewart, dau of 1st Earl of Galloway (*qv*), and *d* 1671, having had, with two daus (one of whom, Margaret, *m* 1656 John Maxwell of Monreith; *see* MAXWELL, Bt):

1 ANDREW (Sir), **3rd Bt**
2 William; *m* Elizabeth, dau and heir of Patrick Agnew of Castlewigg, and had issue:
(1) William; *d* unm 1738
(1) Agnes; *m* Charles Stewart of Tonderghie and had issue

Sir ANDREW's er son,

Sir Andrew Agnew, 3rd Bt; MP Wigtownshire 1685 and 1689–1702, memb Convention Estates 1689; *m c* 24 Oct 1656 Jean, dau of Sir Thomas Hay of Park, and was *bur* 9 June 1702, leaving an est s:

Sir James Agnew, 4th Bt; *m c* 22 June 1683 Lady Mary Montgomerie (*d* April 1742), dau of 8th Earl of Eglinto(u)n (*see* EGLINTON and WINTON, E), and *d* 9 March 1735, having had 21 children; the est s:

Sir Andrew Agnew, 5th Bt, JP; *b* 21 Dec 1687; Lt-Gen 1759, Govr Teignmouth Castle 1748; *m* 12 May 1714 Eleanor (*d* 29 May 1785), dau and eventually sole heir of Thomas Agnew of Croach, and *d* 21 Aug 1771, leaving a 5th s:

Sir Stair Agnew, 6th Bt; *b* 9 Oct 1734; *m* 1st 23 June 1763 Mary (*d* 9 April 1769), dau of Thomas Baillie of Polkemmet; *m* 2nd 11 April 1775 Margaret (*d* 30 May 1811), dau of Thomas Naesmyth of Dumblair, and *d* 28 June 1809, having by his 1st w had, with other issue:

ANDREW; Lt 12th Regt; *m* 21 May 1792 Hon Martha de Courcy, dau of 21st Baron Kingsale (*qv*), and *d* 11 Sept 1792, leaving:

Sir Andrew Agnew, 7th Bt; *b* 21 March 1793; *educ* Edinburgh and Oxford Us; V-Lt 1828 and MP Wigtownshire 1830–37; *m* 11 June 1816 Madeline (*d* 21 June 1858), dau of Sir David Carnegie, 4th Bt (*see* FIFE, D), and *d* 28 April 1849, having had issue:

1 ANDREW (Sir), **8th Bt**
2 John De Courcy Andrew; *b* 8 Oct 1819; Capt RN; *m* 1st 30 Oct 1849 Anne (*dsp* 13 July 1852), dau of Rev David Wauchope, Rector Warkton, Northants; *m* 2nd 17 Oct 1854 Patricia Elizabeth (*d* 2 Oct 1870), est dau of William Henry Dowbiggin and n of Lord Panmure, and had issue:
(1) Robert Wauchope; *b* 13 Nov 1861; *d* 22 Aug 1934
(2) Andrew William; *b* 1 Aug 1864; *d* unm
(3) Samuel Montagu, OBE (1918); *b* 22 Feb 1867; Capt RN Egypt 1882 and WW I; *d* unm 22 April 1929
(1) Georgina Anne; *m* 25 March 1885 Col James Ferguson of Kinmundy, DL, KC (*d* 25 April 1917), and *d* 2 March 1949, having had issue
(2) Madeline Mary; *d* unm 7 Dec 1942
2 (cont) Capt John Agnew *m* 3rd 14 May 1872 Patricia (*dsp* 16 July 1910), dau of Sir Alexander Ramsay of Balmain, 2nd Bt (*qv*), and *d* 20 Sept 1916
3 David Carnegie Andrew (Rev); *b* 3 May 1821; *m* 18 April 1855 Eleanora James Kerr Ross (*d* 22 March 1903), dau of George Bell, FRSE, and *d* 16 March 1887, leaving issue:
(1) Andrew David Carnegie; *b* 15 May 1856; *m* 28 Dec 1882 Minnie Dale (*d* 30 Oct 1928), dau of David Dale Buchanan, first Mayor Pietermaritzburg 1854, and *d* 4 Oct 1927, leaving issue:
1a Pearl Eleanor Isabella Jane
2a Ruby Geraldine
3a Amethyst Muriel Dale; *m* 12 Oct 1944 W Hulley (*d* 1947) and *dsp* 15 Nov 1966
4a Ivy Diamond Dale; *b* 1895
(1) Isabella Geraldine; *d* 1858
(2) Agnes Madeline Eleanora; *b* 9 Nov 1861; *m* 30 Nov 1897 James Macdonald, WS (*d* 17 July 1923), Dep Keeper Gt Seal Scotland, and *d* 4 July 1937
4 James Andrew; *b* 21 June 1823; CE; *d* 27 Jan 1918
5 Stair Andrew (Sir), KCB (1895), JP (Wigtownshire); *b* 6 Dec 1831; *educ* Trin Coll Cambridge (BA 1855, MA 1858); Lt 9th Regt; Legal Sec to Ld Advocate Scotland 1861–66 and 1868–70, Queen's Remembrancer Scotland 1870–81, Registrar-Gen Scotland 1881–1909; *m* 1 Dec 1870 Georgina (*d* 6 June 1916), dau of George More Nisbett, of Cairnhill, and *d* 12 July 1916, leaving issue:
(1) Stair Carnegie; *b* 16 Jan 1872; MA, LLB Cambridge; barrister; *m* 4 April 1918 Sylvia Bellville (*d* 12 Dec 1974), 2nd dau of Alexander Martin Bunster Bremner, barrister, and *d* 14 June 1940, leaving issue:
1a Douglas Martin Stair; *b* 23 Oct 1920; slr 1949; *m* 26 Feb 1951 *Christina Jeanette, dau of Harold Warburton, of Cromwell Crescent, and *dsp* 30 Dec 1954
1a *Lesley Stair [Sister Magdalen Mary, The English Convent, Bruges, Belgium]; *b* 1 June 1919; Augustinian Canoness 1945–
(2) Herbert Charles, OBE (1928); *b* 20 Nov 1880; Col RE WW I Mesopotamia (despatches twice); *m* 19 Aug 1919 Enys (*d* 1985), yst dau of James Watson, and *d* 15 June 1949, leaving issue:
1a David Michael; *b* 17 July 1920; *educ* Wellington; P/O RAF WW II; *ka* Nov 1940
2a +John Nevin; *b* 10 May 1922; *educ* Rugby and Ch Ch Oxford (BA 1943, MA 1947); Lt-Col Coldstream Gds, psc; *m* 1 June 1951 *, dau of Moffat Scott Thomson, and has issue:
1b +Andrew Robert [Andrew Agnew Esq, Spingfield, Lasswade, Midlothian]; *b* 12 Dec 1956; *m* 1981 *Patricia, dau of Sir Russell Fairgrieve, CBE, TD, of Galashiels, and has issue:
1c +Roy Duncan; *b* 1984
2c +Jonathan Michael; *b* 1986
1c *Christina Margaret; *b* 1982
2b +James Douglas [James Agnew Esq, Hendersyde, Kelso, Roxburghshire TD5 7ST]; *b* 16 Jan 1959; *m* 1984 *Elizabeth Mary, dau of Dr John Atherton Cameron, and has issue:
1c *Charlotte Elizabeth; *b* 1987
2c *Georgina Catherine; *b* 1990
3c *Alexandra Isobel; *b* 1992
1b *Jean Catherine; *b* 11 Aug 1953; *m* 1979 *Richard Swan, *s* of Lt-Col Sir William B Swan, KCVO, CBE, TD, JP, and has issue:
1c *Peter Alan; *b* 1982
1c *Nicola Anne; *b* 1981
2c *Alice Margaret; *b* 1984

3a +Patrick William; *b* 6 March 1927; *educ* Rugby and Trin Coll Cambridge (BA 1947, MA 1963); *m* 26 July 1958 *Anne Meryl Turner and has had issue:

1b David Martin; *b* 28 Oct 1959; Capt RHF; *k* 1984 in a helicopter crash while serving Frontier Force Oman

2b +Stephen William; *b* 4 April 1963

1b *Hazel Patricia; *b* 15 April 1961

(1) Mabel Mary; *d* unm 8 March 1940

(2) Georgina Constance; *m* 25 April 1913 (*divorce* 1933) Lt-Col Denis Wellesley Maxwell, 4th Gurkha Rifles, IA (*d* 16 May 1956), s of Sir William Maxwell, KCMG, and had issue

(3) Dora Charlotte; *d* unm 2 June 1940

6 Thomas Frederick Andrew; *b* 5 July 1834; *m* 9 Oct 1861 Julia (*d* 15 April 1934), dau of Charles Pelly (*see* PELLY, Bt), and *d* 20 Nov 1924, leaving issue:

(1) Douglas; *b* 5 Feb 1869; Capt RN China War 1900, WW I, Naval Tport Serv, Capt-Supt Lancs and Nat Sea Trg Homes, Wallasey; *m* 6 April 1904 Helen Louise Ann (*d* 11 June 1962), dau of Robert Thorpe, of Greenock, and *d* 4 Jan 1953, leaving issue:

1a (Frederick) Douglas, TD; *b* 18 Jan 1909; *educ* Repton; Maj 5th Bn King's Regt (TA), psc, WW II; *m* 1st 2 April 1938 (*divorce* 1950) Barbara, er dau of Reginald Thomas Booth Glasspool, MC, and *d* 198–, having had issue:

1b *Jocelyn [Mrs Raymond Jenner, 1c Park Hill Close, Carshalton Beeches, Surrey]; *b* 3 Oct 1940; *m* 5 June 1965 *Raymond Graham Jenner, s of Graham Bernard Newman Jenner, of Eastbourne, and has issue:

1c *Angus Donald Agnew; *b* 20 Oct 1966

2c *Bruce Roderick; *b* 1969

1a (cont.) Maj Douglas Agnew *m* 2nd 12 Oct 1951 *Vivien Elizabeth Willoughby, est dau of Harold Willoughby Bartlett, of Bourne End, Bucks, and *d* 198–

(2) Ernest Frederick; *b* 6 Jan 1871; *m* 21 Sept 1916 Evelyn Carr (*d* 8 Oct 1969), dau of Robert Carr Greenham, of Heswall, and *dsp* 3 Aug 1958

(3) Graham; *b* 8 Oct 1874; Capt 13th Bn Northumberland Fus; *m* 21 May 1908 Gwendolyn Rose (*d* 3 Nov 1935), dau of Frederick Lane Huddart, and was *ka* France *c* 25/27 Sept 1915

(4) Herman Maitland; *b* 29 March 1876; Lt 34th (Middx) Co Imp Yeo; *ka* Tweefontein 25 Dec 1901

(5) Percy Reginald; *b* 13 Jan 1878; Imp Yeo Boer War (wounded); *m* 15 June 1909 Ethel Adelaide Susan Wakefield (*d* 21 May 1962), and *d* 19 April 1952, leaving issue:

1a Kathleen Julia; *b* 8 May 1910; *m* 23 March 1940 William Robert Logie, s of William Robert Logie, of King's Lynn, and had issue:

1b *William Robert Agnew; *b* 16 Oct 1942; *educ* George Watson's Coll Edinburgh; *m* 1 May 1971 *Alison Grant Peterkin

1b *Johanna Susan [Mrs William Harvey, 31 Weald Rd, Brentwood, Essex]; *b* 2 April 1941; *m* 29 Jan 1966 *William Mortimer Harvey and has issue:

1c *Kate; *b* 1966

2c *Victoria; *b* 1967

2b *Margaret Kathleen [Mrs Andrew Boyd, The Bears Den, Upper St, Defford, nr Pershore, Worcs]; *b* 6 May 1944; *m* 6 Sept 1969 *Andrew Boyd

3b *Heather Alexander [Miss Heather Logie, Hillshead, Piper's Lane, Heswall, Cheshire]; *b* 8 Nov 1945

2a *Maud Susan Rosemary [Mrs Jarvis Campbell, The Moat Inn, Donegore, Dunadry, Co Antrim]; *b* 1 Dec 1911; *m* 1 Dec 1941 *Jarvis Hunniford Campbell, s of Jarvis Hunniford Campbell, of Belfast, and has issue:

1b *John Agnew; *b* 22 Oct 1949; *educ* Ballydare High Sch and Bath U; *m* 1974 *Kathleen Mary, yr dau of Alexander Shaw Ferguson Wilson

1b *Adelaide Elizabeth [Miss Adelaide Campbell, Rhinehurst Cottage, Colwood Lane, Warninglid, Sussex]; *b* 10 Sept 1943

2b *Eily Jane [Miss Eily Campbell, c/o The Moat Inn, Donegore, Dunandry, Co Antrim]; *b* 21 Jan 1945

3b *Dinah Mary; *b* 30 June 1953

3a *Poppy Eily, Uganda Independence Medal 1966 [Miss Poppy Agnew, Maresfield, Pipers Lane, Heswall, Merseyside L60 9HL]; *b* 25 Oct 1915

4a *Denise Frances; *b* 18 Jan 1917; *m* 8 Sept 1956 Ronald Maillard Stead, s of Augustus Maillard Stead, of S Norwood

5a *Nancy Marion [Mrs Philip Vellacott, Tan-y-Bryn, Franksbridge, Llandrindod Wells, Powys]; *b* 21 April 1919; *m* 29 July 1939 Philip Humphrey Vellacott, MA, s of Humphrey Doidge Vellacott, of Willesden, and has issue:

1b *Giles Wakefield [Giles Vellacott Esq, c/o Tan-y-Bryn, Franksbridge, Llandrindod Wells, Powys]; *b* 6 Jan 1949; *educ* Dulwich and Bangor U

1b *Julia Clare [Miss Julia Vellacott, 4 Compton Terrace, London N1]; *b* 23 May 1943

2b *Teresa [Mrs Leslie Holden, 44 Gt North Rd, London N6]; *b* 26 Sept 1944; *m* 23 Aug 1969 *Leslie Holden, er s of C L Holden

5a (cont.) Mr and Mrs Vellacott also adopted:

*Jason Henry; *b* 20 June 1961

(6) Harold Carnegie; *b* 6 March 1881; Lt King's Regt, Capt MGC WW I; *d* unm 22 Jan 1950

(1) Henrietta; *b* 21 May 1864; *d* unm 6 Feb 1962 aged 98

(2) Geraldine; *b* 19 Sept 1867; *d* unm 16 Feb 1919

(3) Ethel Patricia; *b* 9 Jan 1873; *d* unm 21 June 1965 aged 92

(4) Marion (Sister Agnes Marion); *b* 9 March 1885

7 Gerald Andrew; *b* 18 Dec 1835; Lt-Col 90th Light Infantry; served 1st Relief Lucknow, wounded 2nd Siege, DAAG Musketry Dublin; *m* 19 May 1870 Margaret Cunninghame (*d* 5 March 1924), only dau and heiress of William Bonar, of Warriston, Midlothian, and *d* 16 May 1927, leaving issue:

(1) Eva Mary; *m* 18 July 1906 Maj Archibald Campbell (*d* 5 Sept 1965), yr s of Archibald James Campbell of Auchendarroch, and *d* 20 April 1971 aged 94, leaving issue

1 Agnes; *m* 16 Oct 1845 Rev Thomas Blizzard Bell (*d* 10 Dec 1866) and *d* 1893, leaving issue

2 Martha; *m* 3 Oct 1848 Sheriff Frederick Lewis Maitland-Heriot of Ramornie, JP, DL (*d* 7 March 1881), of Ramornie Fife, and *d* 28 July 1904, leaving issue (*see* LAUDERDALE, E)

3 Mary Graham; *m* 23 June 1858 James Douglas (*dsp* 29 July 1878), of Cavers, and *d* 13 July 1885

The 7th Bt's est s,

Sir Andrew Agnew, 8th Bt, DL (Wigtownshire 1843); *b* 2 Jan 1818; Capt 4th Light Dragoons; MP Wigtownshire 1856–68; *m* 20 Aug 1846 Lady Louisa Noel (*d* 27 June 1883), est dau of 1st Earl of Gainsborough (*qv*), and *d* 25 March 1892, having had issue:

1 **Sir Andrew Noel Agnew, 9th Bt**, JP (Wigtownshire); *b* 14 Aug 1850; *educ* Harrow and Trin Coll Cambridge; barrister Inner Temple, Capt 1st Ayrshire and Galloway Artillery Vols, MP Lib U Edinburgh S 1900–06, V-Lt Wigtownshire 1893, memb Roy Co Archers; *m* 15 Oct 1889 Gertrude (*d* 3 April 1932), dau of Hon Gowran Charles Vernon (*see* LYVEDEN, B), and *d* 14 July 1928

2 Henry de Courcy, JP (Wigtownshire); *b* 1 Nov 1851; *m* 23 Dec 1885 Ethel Anne (*m* 2nd 27 July 1911 Edmund Charrington, AMInstCE; *d* 1 March 1928), dau of Capt Thomas William Goff, 7th Dragoon Gds, and *d* 6 March 1910, leaving issue:

(1) Dorothea Alma; *m* 14 May 1907 Harold Swann (*d* 7 Nov 1953), 2nd s of Sir Charles Ernest Swann, 1st Bt (*qv*), and *d* 27 Feb 1969, leaving issue

(2) Hazel Louisa; *m* 30 Oct 1913 (*divorce* 1926) 4th Viscount Combermere (*d* 8 Feb 1969; *qv*) and *d* 15 April 1943

3 Charles Hamlyn, JP (Wigtownshire); *b* 21 June 1859; Maj 4th Hus Burma 1885–87 and Rhodesia 1896; *m* 30 June 1897 (*divorce* 1908) Lillian Anne (*d* 15 Dec 1937), dau of Lt-Gen Sir John Wolfe Murray, KCB, RA, of Cringletie (*see* MURRAY, Bt, of Blackbarony), and *d* 31 March 1928, leaving issue:

(1) **Sir Fulque Melville Gerald Noel Agnew, 10th Bt** (later dropped title); *b* 6 Oct 1900; *educ* Harrow and Edinburgh U (BSc 1943); Lt 4th Bn Roy Sussex Regt (TA), MGC and RFC WW I (wounded, despatches), with US Army China 1926–29, Friends46 Ambulance Unit WW II; farmer S Africa 1944–53, Registrar U of Fort Hare, Sec Cambridge U Dept Educn 1960–65; *m* 9 Oct 1937 *Swanzie [Swanzie Lady Agnew of Lochnaw, 2/23 Croft an Righ, Abbey Hill, Edinburgh EH8 8EG], yr dau of Maj Esmé Nourse Erskine, CMG, MC (*see* BUCHAN, E), and *d* 28 Aug 1975, leaving:

1a Sir CRISPIN HAMLYN AGNEW OF LOCHNAW, **11th and present Bt**

4 Quentin Graham Kinnaird, DSO (1902), MVO (1903), JP and DL (Wigtownshire); *b* 8 Jan 1861; Col Roy Scots Fus Burma 1885–86, Tirah 1897–98, Boer War 1899–1902, Mil Sec Govr Gibraltar 1902–05, WW I Gallipoli and France; memb Gentlemen-at-Arms 1906; *m* 1st 9 Feb 1899 Evelyn Mary (*d* 28 Nov 1913), dau of Capt John Hobhouse Inglis Alexander, CB, RN, and had issue:

(1) David Quentin Hope; *b* 7 Feb 1900; *educ* Clifton; Col IA 3rd Afghan War 1919 and WW II Malaya and Burma (despatches); *m* 27 Aug 1927 Janet May Dilkes (*d* 4 Sept 1980), dau of Rev Charles Herbert Malden, MA, Rector Little Gransden, and *d* 27 April 1975, leaving issue:

1a +Andrew David Quentin [Dr Andrew Agnew, Garth House, Furnace, Machynlleth, Powys SY20 8PG]; *b* 31 Dec 1929; *educ* Trin Coll Glenalmond and Edinburgh U (BSc 1954), PhD U of Wales Bangor 1957; *m* 3 Aug 1957 *Shirley, dau of James Arnold Smithson, and has issue:

1b +David James; *b* 6 Sept 1960; PhD Glasgow 1985; *m* 24 Nov 1990 *Katherine Mary Batts and has issue:

1c +Ronan Samuel; *b* 14 Feb 1996

1c *Tansy May; *b* 25 Dec 1993

2b +Peter Jonathan; *b* 13 Sept 1963; BA York 1985; *m* 12 Aug 1995 *Kathleen Diana Newton

3b +Robin Andrew; *b* 30 April 1966; BSN Johns Hopkins 1994; *m* 11 July 1992 *Stacy Ann Evans

2a +Jonathan Herbert [Jonathan Agnew Esq, 11 Ulting La, Langford, Essex, CM9 6QB]; *b* 7 Nov 1933; *educ* Clifton and HMS *Conway*; Ch Offr Merchant Navy (NZ Shipping Co); *m* 17 May 1958 Mary Kathleen (*d* 13 Nov 1982), only dau of Brig Stannus Grant Gordon Fraser, MC, IA (ret), of Castle Douglas, and has issue:

1b +George Archibald Quentin; *b* 26 Feb 1962

2b +Michael Stannus; *b* 22 Oct 1965

1b *Susan Louise; *b* 11 Aug 1963; MA Aberdeen 1997

(2) John Andrew; *b* 26 Sept 1903; Cdr RN; *m* 7 April 1934 Ysabel August Aurelia (*d* 1979), dau of Ernesto Larios, of Algeciras, Spain, and *d* 3 May 1977, leaving issue:

1a +(Fulke) Quentin Ernesto [Maj Quentin Agnew, Monte de la Torre, Los Barrios, Prov de Cadiz, Spain]; *b* 27 Feb 1938; *educ* Stowe and RMA Sandhurst; Maj Roy Highland Fus (ret); *m* 1970 *Susan Georgina, est dau of G/Capt Frank Hastings Tyson, RAF (ret), of Diss, Norfolk, and has issue:

1b +Tomas Quentin; *b* 1972

2b +John Benedict; *b* 1976

1b *Luisa Beatriz; *b* 1973

(3) Patrick Alexander; *b* 19 Nov 1908; Capt 4th/5th Bn Seaforth Highrs WW II; *m* 1 Dec 1936 Baroness Johanna Elizabeth (*m* 2nd 4 Nov 1944 (*divorce* 1964) Brevet-Col William Stanley Baird, TD, and *d* 19–), dau of Baron Barthold Mackay (*see* REAY, L), and was *ka* 12 July 1943, leaving issue:

1a +Robin Andrew Patrick Mackay [Robin Agnew Esq, MS 897, Ravensbourne, Queensland 4352, Australia]; *b* 8 July 1940; *educ* Gordonstoun; *m* 2 Oct 1965 *Diane Clyde, dau of Humphrey Dinsdale Philips, of Brisbane, and formerly w of David Allan Bennett, and has issue:

1b +Gordon Alexander Mackay; *b* 15 May 1967

Robin Agnew adopted his wife's two children by her previous husb:

*Scott Andrew; *b* 14 Feb 1963

*Leigh Diane; *b* 25 Sept 1961

1a *Rosemary Joanna Evelyn [Mrs Rosemary Hannay Robertson, Suite 43, Private Bag X15, Hermanus 7200, CP, S Africa]; *b* 7 Oct 1938; *m* 1 Oct 1960 (*divorce* 1978) Arthur Struan Hannay Robertson, yr s of Geoffrey Douglas Hannay Robertson, of Claremont, CP, and has issue:

1b *Duncan Struan Alexander; *b* 1 Aug 1961
2b Jonathan Dougal; *b* 19 Aug 1962; *d* 1995
3b *Alastair James; *b* 1967
4b *Patrick Hamish; *b* 1970

(1) Suzanna Mary; *b* 11 Feb 1907; *m* 11 July 1942 Henry Nicolai Sclater Sclater, s of Rev Francis Saunderson Sclater, of Newick Park, Sussex, and *d* 1993, leaving:

1a *Patrick Henry [Patrick Sclater Esq, Old Farmhouse, Frith, Stalbridge, Dorset DT10 2SD]; *b* 9 Jan 1944; *educ* Charterhouse and RAC Cirencester; *m* 6 July 1968 *Rosalyn Heather, only dau of Urban George Eric Stephenson, and has issue:

1b *William Patrick; *b* 1969
2b *Alastair James; *b* 1971
3b *Peter Duncan; *b* 1976
1b *Heather Diana; *b* 1978

2a *Andrew Agnew [Dr Andrew Sclater, c/o The Cottage, Broughton, Stockbridge, Hants]; *b* 29 Aug 1949; *educ* Winchester, Cambridge (PhD) and Wye Coll (BSc); *m* 1st 6 Sept 1969 (*divorce* 1982) Joelle, yst dau of Lucien Patient, of Montrouge 92, France, and has issue:

1b *Julien Renaud; *b* 1970
1b *Chloe Elise; *b* 1974

2a (cont.) Dr Andrew Sclater *m* 2nd 1984 *Shelley, dau of George Day, of Wooler, Northumberland, and has further issue:

2b *James Nicolai; *b* 1983

4 (cont.) Col Quentin Agnew *m* 2nd 3 July 1916 Cicely Anne Churchhill (*d* 1 May 1964), yst dau of James Inskip, of Clifton Park House, Clifton (*see* CALDECOTE, V), and *d* 23 March 1937, having by her had further issue:

(4) Andrew Quentin; *b* 21 May 1917; Maj Roy Scots Fus WW II; *m* 4 July 1942 Diana (Im 2nd 2 April 1947 (*annulled* 1951) Harro Sandgren; *d* 20 March 1956), dau of Lt-Col Arthur William Hay Conyers-Baker, N Staffs Regt (PoW's), and was *ka* Normandy 26 June 1944

5 Gerard Dalrymple; *b* 24 April 1862; Lt The Buffs; *d* 24 Nov 1919

1 Madeline Diana Elizabeth; *m* 1st 7 Feb 1867 Thomas Henry Clifton, MP (*d* 31 March 1880), of Lytham Hall, Lancs, and had issue; *m* 2nd 30 Jan 1889 Sir James Hamlyn Williams-Drummond, 4th Bt (*d* 15 June 1913; *see* 1970 edn), and *d* 19 Oct 1907, having had further issue

2 Arabella Frances Georgiana; *d* unm 23 June 1910

3 Caroline Charlotte, twin with Arabella; *d* unm 15 Jan 1934

4 Louisa Lucia; *m* 10 July 1877 Duncan MacNeil (*d* 1892) and *d* 1913, leaving issue

5 Mary Alma Victoria; *m* 19 Aug 1875 11th Lord Kinnaird (*d* 30 Jan 1923; *see* 1970 edn) and *d* 19 Jan 1923, leaving issue

6 Catherine Carnegie; *d* young 31 March 1858

7 Rosina Constance; *m* 14 April 1898 Rev James and *d* 23 June 1920, leaving issue

8 Marguerite Violet Maud; *m* 23 July 1890 Lt-Col Sir Francis Dudley Williams Drummond, KBE, DL, and *d* 3 April 1939, leaving issue (*see* 1970 edn WILLIAMS-DRUMMOND, Bt)

AGNEW-SOMERVILLE

Arms: Quarterly, 1st and 4th, azure three mullets or, two and one, between seven cross-crosslets fitchée, three, two and one argent, a canton voided of the last charged with four mullets gules and as many cross-crosslets fitchée sable (for SOMERVILLE); 2nd and 3rd, parted per saltire argent and gules two cinquefoils in pale and as many saltires couped in fess, all counterchanged, a bordure azure (for AGNEW). **Crests:** 1 A demi-lion rampant sable, charged on the shoulder with a crosslet-crosslet fitchée between two mullets argent, 2 An eagle rising regardant proper, holding in its dexter claw a sword, hilted and pommelled or. **Mottoes:** *Consilio et impetu* ('By wisdom and vigour') and *Crains Dieu pourque tu viveras* ('Fear God and you will have eternal life'). **Creation:** Bt. (UK) 31 Jan 1957.

SIR QUENTIN CHARLES SOMERVILLE AGNEW-SOMERVILLE, 2ND BT, of Clendry, Kirkcolm, Co Wigtown [Sir Quentin Agnew-Somerville Bt, Mount Auldyn, Jurby Rd, Ramsey, IOM, IM8 3PF]; *b* 8 March 1929; inherited Somerville estate 1950 and added name and arms of SOMERVILLE under terms of will of his uncle by marriage 2nd and last Baron Athlumney (*see* 1929 edn), *s* f in btcy 1990; *educ* RNC Dartmouth and Greenwich; Sub-Lt RN 1950 (invalided); *m* 14 Dec 1963 *Hon (Margaret) April Irene Drummond, yst dau of 15th Baron Strange (*qv*), and hase:

1 +JAMES LOCKETT CHARLES; *b* 26 May 1970; *educ* Milton Abbey
1 *Amelia Rachel; *b* 21 Aug 1965
2 *Geraldine Margaret; *b* 19 May 1967

Lineage: JOHN AGNEW; f of:

THOMAS AGNEW, of Fairhope, Eccles, Lancs, JP (Salford); *b* 16 Dec 1794; fndr Thos Agnew & Sons, Mayor Salford 1851; *m* 19 Feb 1823 Jane Garnet (Id 8 Oct 1864), dau and coheir of William Lockett, of Manchester, and *d* 24 March 1871, having had, with four daus and as yst s Albert (*b* 13 Jan 1840, *d* 29 Nov 1877):

1 Sir WILLIAM AGNEW, 1st Bt (*see* AGNEW, Bt, of Great Stanhope Street)

2 Thomas; *b* 20 Nov 1827; *m* 7 April 1853 Anne (*d* 19 March 1906), dau of George Pixton Kenworthy; *d* 21 April 1883, leaving issue

3 John Henry, of Drywood Hall, Worsley; *b* 20 Nov 1830; *m* 7 April 1858 Elizabeth (*d* 13 May 1864), dau of John Standring, of Manchester, and *d* 27 Dec 1891, leaving issue

4 Charles Swain, of Davenham Lodge, Northwich, Cheshire; *b* 17 Nov 1836; *m* 28 July 1864 Edith (*d* 18 Feb 1910), only dau of William Bradbury, and *d* 8 Oct 1915, leaving issue:

(1) CHARLES LEONARD, for whom *see* below

(2) Frank, of Eccles Hall, Attleborough, Norfolk; *b* 1869; *educ* Rugby; co dir; *m* Edith Menzies and *d* 1920, leaving issue:

1a Edith Margaret; *b* 1899; *m* 1st 19 Feb 1919 Cdr Sir Thomas Lubbock Beevor, 6th Bt, RN (*kas* 29 April 1943; *qv*), and had issue; *m* 2nd 28 Aug 1944 R-Adml Robert Alexander Currie, DSC, of Thorpe Morieux Hall, Suffolk, s of John Currie

1 Edith Jessie; *m* H Heape

2 Mary; *m* F Brentford

CHARLES SWAIN AGNEW's est son,

CHARLES LEONARD AGNEW, of Peover Cottage, Knutsford, Cheshire; *b* 21 May 1867; *educ* Rugby; stockbroker, co dir; *m* 5 Aug 1897 Alice Rowley (*d* 21 March 1950), dau of John Nelson, and *d* 17 Feb 1928, leaving:

1 Walter Lockett; *b* 4 May 1898; *educ* RNCs Osborne and Dartmouth; Lt RN, ret 1923, rejoined 1939 as Lt-Cdr; *m* 10 May 1922 Rosamund Mildred (*d* 15 July 1961), er dau of FM Sir William Robert Robertson, 1st Bt (*see* ROBERTSON OF OAKRIDGE, B), and *d* 12 July 1942, leaving issue:

(1) *Rosamund Anne; *b* 15 Feb 1923; WRNS WW II; *m* 5 June 1945 *Hugo William Harvey Bowen, RNVR, s of Richard William Bowen, and has three adopted children

2 PETER GARNET (Sir), **1st Bt**

3 Arthur Brian; *b* 23 March 1903; *educ* Repton; farmed in NZ, managed rubber plantation Johore and Malaya, Cpl Johore Vol Engrs 1940, Japanese POW; *d* Dec 1942 working on Siam Rlwy

4 Charles Guy, JP; *b* 14 Feb 1908; *educ* Rugby and Jesus Coll Cambridge; *m* 10 March 1938 Enid Barbara (*d* 18 Feb 1971), dau of Samuel Richard Cobden Plimsoll, MC, and *dsp* 27 Jan 1973

CHARLES LEONARD AGNEW's 2nd son,

Sir Peter Garnett Agnew, 1st Bt (UK), so *cr* 31 Jan 1957, of Clendry, Kirkcolm, Co Wigtown; *b* 9 July 1900; *educ* Repton and RNC; ADC to Govr Jamaica 1927–28, Cdr RN WW II (despatches); memb House Laity Ch Assembly 1935–66, Church Commr England 1948–68, MP (C) Camborne 1931–50 and S Worcester 1955–66, PPS to: Pres BOT 1935–37, First Commr Works 1937–39, Assist Govt Whip May-July 1945, C Whip Aug 1945–Feb 1950, Chm Iran Soc 1966–73, Tstee Historic Churches Preservn Tst 1968–90, Pres European Centre Documenton and Info 1974–77, Order Homayoun Iran 1973, Grand Cross Civil Merit Spain 1977; *m* 1st 26 March 1928 Enid Frances (*d* 1 Dec 1982), er dau of Henry Boan, of Perth, W Australia, and widow of Lt Col Oscar Hyde East Marescaux, KSLI, and had issue:

1 Sir QUENTIN CHARLES SOMERVILLE AGNEW-SOMERVILLE, **2nd and present Bt**

Sir Peter *m* 2nd 1984 (*divorce* 1987) Mrs Julie Marie Watson and *d* 26 Aug 1990

AILESBURY

Arms: Quarterly, 1st and 4th or a saltire and chief gu., on a canton arg. a lion rampant az. (for BRUCE); 2nd and 3rd arg. a chevron gu., between three chapeaux, their fronts towards the sinister az. (for BRUDENELL). **Crests:** 1 A lion statant, tail extended az.; 2 A sea-horse naiant ppr. **Supporters:** Two savages ppr., wreathed round the loins and temples vert, each holding a banner of the arms of Bruce. **Motto:** Think and thank. **Creations:** Bt (E) 29 June 1611, B. (E) 26 Feb. 1627/8 (Brudenell of Stonton), E. (E) 20 April 1661 (Cardigan), B. (GB) 17 April 1746 (Bruce of Tottenham), E. (GB) 10 June 1776 (Ailesbury), M., E. (Bruce of Whorlton) and V. (Savernake) (UK) 17 July 1821.

THE 8TH MARQUESS OF AILESBURY, **Earl of Ailesbury**, **Earl of Cardigan**, **Earl Bruce of Whorlton**, **Viscount Savernake**, **Baron Brudenell of Stonton**, Co Leicester, **Baron Bruce of Tottenham**, and a **Baronet** (Sir Michael Sydney Cedric Brudenell Bruce, Bt) [The Most Hon The Marquess of Ailesbury, Luton Lye, Savernake Forest, nr Marlborough, Wilts SN8 3HP]; *b* 31 March 1926; *s* f 1974; *educ* Eton; Lt (Hon Capt) RHG, memb London Stock Exchange 1954 on; *m* 1st 17 March 1952 (*divorce* 1961) Edwina Sylvia de Winton, yr dau of Lt-Col Sir (Ernest) Edward de Winton Wills, 4th Bt (*see* WILLS, Bt, of Hazelwood), and has issue:

1 +DAVID MICHAEL JAMES, *Earl of Cardigan* [Earl of Cardigan, Savernake Lodge, Savernake Forest, nr Marlborough, Wilts]; *b* 12 Nov 1952; *educ* Eton, Rannoch and RAC Cirencester; 31st Hereditary Warden of Savernake Forest 1987–; *m* 1980 *Rosamond Jane, est dau of Capt W R M Winkley, of Wyke Champflower Manor, Bruton, Somerset, and has issue:

(1) +Thomas James, *Viscount Savernake*; *b* 11 Feb 1982

(1) *Catherine Anna, *b* 1984

1 *Sylvia Davina [The Lady Sylvia Gould, La Pulente, St Brelade, Jersey, CI]; *b* 19 June 1954; *m* 1987 *Peter M Gould, yst s of R C L Gould, of Jersey

2 *Carina Doune [The Lady Carina Brudenell-Bruce, Le Perchoir, rue du Carrefour, Trinity, Jersey, CI]; *b* 13 Jan 1956; *m* 26 June 1982 (*divorce* 1988) Anthony Le Brun, only s of Basil Le Brun, of Beauchamp, Sion, Jersey, and Mrs Elaine Le Brun, of Le Douet, Jersey, and has resumed her maiden name

The 8th MARQUESS *m* 2nd 10 July 1963 (*divorce* 1974) Juliet Adrienne Lethbridge, dau of Edward Hilary Lethbridge Kingsford, and by her has issue:

3 *Louise; *b* 13 July 1964

4 *Kathryn Juliot, *b* 24 Aug 1965

The 8th MARQUESS *m* 3rd 18 Sept 1974 (*divorce* 1992) Caroline Elizabeth, formerly w of Simon Romilly (er s of Eric Carnegie Romilly, JP, of Bradfield Court, Bodenham, Herefs) and only dau of Cdr Owen Frances MacTier Wethered, JP, RN, of Reward, Marlow, Bucks

Lineage: WILLIAM de BRUDENELL, of Dodington, Oxfordshire, extensive landowner *temp* HENRY III and EDWARD I, left a yr s:

RICHARD BRUDENELL, of Aynho, Northants; left, with other issue:

WILLIAM BRUDENELL, of Aynho; *m* Agnes, dau and heir of Thomas Grove (*see* GROVE, Bt), and had a 2nd s:

WILLIAM BRUDENELL, of Chalfont St Peter, Bucks; *m* Agnes, dau and heir of Richard Bulstrode, and had:

EDMUND BRUDENELL, of Ranes; *m* 1st Agnes, dau of Thomas Depden; *m* 2nd Philippa, dau of Peter Englefield, of Finchingfield, Essex, and by his 2nd w had:

Sir ROBERT BRUDENELL, King's Serjeant 1505, Judge King's Bench 1507 and Common Pleas 1509, Ld Ch Justice Common Pleas 1521, *b c* 1461; *m* 1st Margaret (*d* 1502), dau and coheir of Thomas Entwistle, of Stanton Wyvill, and widow of William Wyvill; *m* 2nd Philippa Power (*d* 28 March 1532) and *d* 30 Jan 1531, leaving by his 1st:

Sir THOMAS BRUDENELL, of Dean (Deene), Northants, Sheriff Rutland *c* 1538; *m* Elizabeth, est dau of Sir William Fitz William, and *d* 1 Dec 1586; his 4th s:

ROBERT BRUDENELL, of Dean, *m* 15 June 1570 Catherine, dau and heir of Sir Geoffrey Tayllard, of Doddington, Hunts, and *d* 4 July 1599, leaving an est s:

Sir Thomas Brudenell, **1st Bt** (E), so *cr* 29 June 1611, and **1st Earl of Cardigan** (E); so *cr* 20 April 1661 (as also 26 Feb 1627/8 BARON BRUDENELL OF STONTON, Co Leicester); ktd 1612; *m c* 1606 Mary (*d* 13 Oct 1664), dau of Sir Thomas Tresham, and *d* 16 Sept 1663, having had an er s:

ROBERT BRUDENELL, **2nd Earl of Cardigan**; *b* 5 March 1607; *m* 1st Mary, dau of 1st Viscount of Dunbar, and had a dau (*dsp*); *m* 2nd Anne (*d* 16 June 1696), dau of Thomas; Viscount Savage, and by her had, with other issue (including a dau Anna Maria, *m* 1st 11th Earl of Shrewsbury and Waterford (*qv*), *m* 2nd George Rodney Brydges; *see* RODNEY, B):

FRANCIS, Lord Brudenell, *m* Frances (*d* June 1696), dau of Thomas, Earl of Sussex, and *d* 1698, having had, with other issue:

1 GEORGE, **3rd Earl**

1 Dorothy; *m* 1st 3rd Earl of Westmorland (*qv*); *m* 2nd 1697 3rd Viscount of Dunbar and *dsp* 26 Jan 1739/40

2 Frances; *m* 1st 2nd Earl of Newburgh (*qv*); *m* 2nd 3rd Baron Bellew of Duleek (*see* BELLEW, B)

The 1st EARL *d* 16 July 1703; his gs,

GEORGE BRUDENELL, **3rd Earl of Cardigan**, Master Buckhounds 1712–15, *m* 15 May 1707 Elizabeth (*d* Dec 1745), est dau of 3rd Earl of Elgin (*see* ELGIN and KINCARDINE, E) and 2nd Earl of Ailesbury of the March 1663/4 *cr* and sis of Charles, 4th Earl of Elgin; the latter was *cr* 17 April 1746 BARON BRUCE OF TOTTENHAM, Wilts, with remainder to his n, Thomas Brudenell, afterwards 1st Earl of Ailesbury of the 1776 *cr* (*see* below), and *d* 5 July 1732, having had issue:

1 GEORGE BRUDENELL, 1st DUKE OF MONTAGU (so *cr* 1766; *see* MANCHESTER, D) and **4th Earl of Cardigan**, *b* 26 July 1712; *m* 7 July 1730 Mary (*d* 1 May 1775), only child of 2nd Duke of Montagu by Lady Mary Churchill, yst dau of 1st Duke of Marlborough (*qv*), and *d* 23 May 1790, having had, with three daus:

(1) JOHN BRUDENELL, *cr* BARON MONTAGU OF BOUGHTON, Co Northampton (GB), 8 May 1762, *b* 18 March 1734/5; *d* unm *vp* 11 April 1770

2 JAMES BRUDENELL, **5th Earl of Cardigan**, *cr* BARON BRUDENELL OF DEENE, Co Northampton (GB), 17 Oct 1780, *b* 20 April 1715; *m* 1st 24 Nov 1760 Anne (*d* 12 Nov 1786), sis of 2nd Earl of Dartmouth (*qv*); *m* 2nd 18 April 1791 Elizabeth (*d* 23 June 1822), dau of 3rd Earl Waldegrave (*qv*), and *dsp* 24 Feb 1811

3 Robert, MP Marlborough, Col of Foot, *b* 20 Sept 1726; *m* 27 Jan 1759 Anne (*d* 8 Oct 1803), dau of Sir Cecil Bisshopp, Bt, and *d* 20 Oct 1768, having had issue:

(1) ROBERT BRUDENELL, **6th Earl of Cardigan**, *b* 25 April 1760; *m* 8 March 1794 Penelope Anne (*d* 2 Feb 1816), dau of G J Cooke, and *d* 14 Aug 1837, having had, with other issue:

1a JAMES THOMAS BRUDENELL, **7th Earl of Cardigan**, KCB, Lt-Gen (commded Light Bde Crimean War in its famous charge), *b* 16 Oct 1797, *m* 1st 19 June 1826 Elizabeth Jane Henrietta (*d* 15 July 1858), sis of 1st Baron Tollemache (*qv*); *m* 2nd 20 Sept 1858 Adeline Louisa Maria (*m* 2nd 20 Aug 1873 Don Antonio Manuelo, Count de Lancastre in Portugal (*d* 1898); *d* 25 May 1915), only dau of Spencer Horsey de Horsey, of Great Glemham, Suffolk, by Lady Louisa Maria Judith Rous, dau of 1st Earl of Stradbroke (*qv*), and *dsp* 28 March 1868, when he was *s* by his kinsman, **2nd Marquess of Ailesbury** (*see* below)

4 THOMAS, **1st Earl of Ailesbury**

1 Frances, *m* 27 July 1749 Oliver Tilson

2 Mary, *m* 1st Richard Powys, MP (*d* before her), of Hintlesham Hall, Suffolk; *m* 2nd 20 June 1754 Thomas Bowlby, of North Bailey, Durham, and *d* 21 Feb 1813

The 4th and youngest son,

THOMAS BRUDENELL later BRUDENELL-BRUCE, **1st Earl of Ailesbury** (GB), so *cr* 10 June 1776, KT, *s* by special limitation to the barony of BRUCE OF TOTTENHAM on the death of his unc, 4th Earl of Elgin and 3rd Earl of Ailesbury of the earlier *cr*, and added the name and arms of BRUCE; *b* 30 April 1729; *m* 1st 17 Feb 1761 Susanna (*d* 4 Feb 1783), widow of Viscount Dungarvan and dau of Henry Hoare, of Stourhead, Wilts, and had issue:

1 George, *b* 1762 ; *d* unm 1783

2 CHARLES, **1st Marquess**

1 Caroline Anne, *d* unm 1824

2 Frances Elizabeth; *m* 1799 Sir Henry Wright Wilson, of Chelsea Pk, Middx, and *d* 1836. He *d* 1832

The **1st Earl** *m* 2nd 14 Feb 1788 Anne (*dsp* 8 Jan 1813), 3rd dau of 1st Earl of Moira, and *d* 19 April 1814

His only surv s,

CHARLES BRUDENELL-BRUCE, 2nd EARL and **1st Marquess of Ailesbury**, so *cr* 17 July 1821, as also VISCOUNT SAVERNAKE, of Savernake Forest, Wilts, and EARL BRUCE OF WHORLTON, Co York (all UK), KT; *b* 14 Feb 1773; *m* 1st 10 April 1793 Henrietta Maria (*d* 2 Jan 1831), dau of 1st Baron Berwick of Attingham, and had, with other issue:

1 GEORGE WILLIAM FREDERICK BRUDENELL-BRUCE, **2nd Marquess of Ailesbury**, KG (1864), *b* 20 Nov 1804, called up to Ho of Lds *vp* in his f's barony 1838; *s* kinsman as **8th Earl of Cardigan**, also his barony and baronetcy 27 March 1868; *m* 11 May 1837 Lady Mary Caroline Herbert (*d* 20 Jan 1892), dau of 11th Earl of Pembroke (*see* PEMBROKE and MONTGOMERY, E), and *d* 6 Jan 1878

2 ERNEST AUGUSTUS CHARLES, **3rd Marquess**

The **1st Marquess** *m* 2nd 20 Aug 1833 Maria Elizabeth (*d* 7 May 1893), yst dau of Hon Charles Tollemache (*see* TOLLEMACHE, B), and *d* 4 Jan 1856, having by her had issue:

3 Charles William, PC, Capt 1st Life Gds, hon Maj Roy Wilts Yeo, MP N Wilts 1865–74 and Marlborough 1878–85, V-Chamberlain to HM QUEEN VICTORIA 1880–85, *b* 18 June 1834, *m* 2 Feb 1860 Augusta Georgiana Sophia (*d* 10 Feb 1901), 3rd dau of Frederick Charles William Seymour and ggdau of 1st Marquess of Hertford (*qv*), and *dsp* 16 April 1897

The 2nd MARQUESS's bro,

ERNEST AUGUSTUS CHARLES BRUDENELL-BRUCE, **3rd Marquess of Ailesbury**, Ld-Lt Berks, *b* 8 Jan 1811; V-Chamberlain to HM QUEEN VICTORIA 1841–46 and 1852–58, *m* 25 Nov 1834 Hon Louisa Elizabeth (*d* 14 Oct 1891), 2nd dau of 2nd Baron Decies (*qv*), and *d* 18 Oct 1886, having had issue:

1 George John, Lt 14th Hussars, *b* 15 May 1839, *m* 7 Aug 1862 Lady Evelyn Mary (*m* 2nd 4 Dec 1869 Capt Henry Amelius Beauclerk Coventry (*d* 29 June 1885), est s of Henry Amelius Coventry (*see* COVENTRY, E); *m* 3rd 30 Aug 1877 Capt George William Hutton Riddell (*d* 9 Feb 1915) and *d* 7 Nov 1924), 2nd dau of 2nd Earl of Craven (*qv*), and *dvp* Ajaccio, Corsica, 28 May 1808, leaving issue:

(1) GEORGE WILLIAM THOMAS BRUDENELL-BRUCE, **4th Marquess of Ailesbury**, *b* 8 June 1863; *m* 6 May 1884 Dorothy Julia (*m* 2nd 28 March 1901 David Waddle Webster, JP, s of William Webster, of Arbroath; *d* 3 Sept 1917), est dau of Thomas Haseley, of Brighton, and *dsp* 10 April 1894

(1) Mabel Emily Louisa, *b* 10 Oct 1866, granted rank of marquess's dau 1887; *m* 1 Oct 1892 Robert Standish Sievier, only s of Robert Moore Sievier, and *d* 9 Jan 1930, leaving issue. He *d* 8 Oct 1939

2 James Ernest, barrister; *b* 30 June 1840, *d* 21 June 1876

3 HENRY AUGUSTUS, **5th Marquess**

4 Robert Thomas, Cdr RN, *b* 25 Jan 1845, *m* 4 March 1878 Emma (*d* 30 March 1921), dau of Capel Hanbury Leigh, of Pont-y-pool Park, Mon, and *d* 15 Feb 1912, having had issue:

(1) James Ernest John, of Deene Park, Northants, barrister Inner Temple 1901; T/Lt Northampton Yeo, *b* 27 Feb 1879, *educ* Harrow and Trin Coll Camb (BA and LLB 1900; MA 1906), *d* 11 April 1917 of wounds recd in action

(2) George Lionel Thomas BRUDENELL-BRUCE later BRUDENELL (roy licence 17 July 1917), of Deene Park and Stanton Wyville, Leics, *b* 26 Aug 1880, *educ* privately; *m* 6 Nov 1923 Mary Julia, JP Northants 1934–59 (*d* 20 Jan 1972), dau of Stephen Schilizzi (*see* RALLI, Bt), and *d* 8 Aug 1962, leaving issue:

1a +Edmund Crispin Stephen James George, DL Northants 1977 [Edmund Brudenell Esq DL, Deene Park, Corby, Northants; 18 Lochmore House, Ebury St, London SW1]; *b* 24 Oct 1928, *educ* Harrow and RAC Cirencester, *m* 8 Nov 1955 *Hon Marian Cynthia Manningham-Buller, JP, est dau of 1st Viscount Dilhorne, (*qv*), and has issue:

1b +Robert Edmund, *b* 12 Aug 1956; *educ* Stanbridge Earls Sch

2b +Thomas Mervyn, *b* 12 Aug 1956, *educ* Eton; *m* 1st 1984 Venetia Jane (*d* 1993), dau of Maj Robert Chaworth-Musters, of Felley Priory, Jacksdale, Notts, and has issue:

1c *Sophia, *b* 1985

2c *Victoria, *b* 1987

2b (cont.) Thomas Brudenell *m* 2nd 27 June 1996 *Mrs Amanda J Skiffington, dau of David Naylor-Leyland and the Countess of Wilton (*qv*)

1b *Anna Maria, *b* 6 Nov 1960; *educ* Benenden

1a Philippa Mary *b* 17 Nov 1924; *m* 18 Nov 1970 Michael Mendes Da Costa (*d* 22 March 1977) and *dsp* 25 Aug 1974

(3) Robert Hanbury, DSO (1919), Col Norfolk Regt GSO(2) 1916 WW I (despatches), Cdr 148th (3rd W R) Inf Bde 1933–36, *b* 24 Oct 1881, *educ* Harrow, *m* 1st 22 Oct 1913 Olive Ina Vera (*d* 21 April 1920), er dau of Charles Herbert Richardson, of Cedar Hurst, Co Down, and had issue:

1a Daphne Helen Anne, *m* 1st 20 Dec 1934 (*divorce* 1946) Cdr Reginald Hughes-Onslow, RN (ret), 2nd s of Maj Denzil Hughes-Onslow, of Balkissock, Ayrshire (*see* ONSLOW, E), and had issue; *m* 2nd 15 Aug 1946 *John Edward Mountague Bradish-Ellames, s of William Bradish-Ellames, of The Manor House, Little Marlow, Bucks, and had further issue; *m* 3rd as his 2nd w Hon Robert Francis Hubert Preston, 2nd s of 15th Viscount Gormanston (*qv*), and *d* 9 Dec 1992

(3) (cont.) Col Robert Brudenell-Bruce *m* 2nd 29 April 1922 Judith Iris (*d* 1981), yr dau of Maj Bertram Keppel (*see* ALBEMARLE, E), and *d* 12 Feb 1955, having by her had issue:

1a Chandos Robert Henry, Capt RHG, *b* 8 April 1923, *educ* Eton, *m* 12 Nov 1949 *Dana Moira Angela, 2nd dau of Stanhope Henry Joel, of Perot's Island, Southampton, Bermuda, and *d* 1993, leaving issue:

1b +Andrew Robert Joel, *b* 27 July 1951, *educ* Eton; *m* 1974 *Sophie, dau of Dr R S Inch, of 20 Harley Street, London W1, and has issue:

1c +Henry Robert Woolf, *b* 28 Aug 1976

1c *Alice Marie Antoinette, *b* 25 Oct 1974

2c *Christabel Marie-Jeanne, *b* 1981

3c *Florence Anne-Marie, *b* 1985

1b *Joanna Dana [Mrs Paul Farrant, The Chestnuts, Dunsfold, Surrey], *b* 2 Oct 1954; *m* 1st 7 Aug 1975 Charles FitzRoy (*d* car crash NZ 15 Oct 1975), er s of 6th Baron Southampton (*qv*); *m* 2nd 1977 *Paul Farrant and has:

1c *Thomas Robert Jack, *b* 1986

1c *Rebecca Dana, *b* 1979

2c *Francesca Joanna, *b* 1981

2b *Sara Vivien [Mrs Walter Hood, Flint Barn, Snailwell, Newmarket, Suffolk], *b* 14 Oct 1960; *m* 1985 *Walter (Wally) Hood and has issue:

1c *Talia Joelle, *b* 23 Feb 1996

(4) John Charles, MBE (1918), MLC Br Virgin Islands 1950–57, 2nd Sec Dip Serv 1916–18, on Peace Conference 1919, Assist-Commr and Sec-Gen Schleswig Commn 1919–20, Kt Cdr Dannebrog, OStJ, *b* 6 March 1885, *educ* Harrow, *m* 1st 29 Oct 1913 (*divorce* 1925) Else, dau of Capt C F Drechsel, of Copenhagen; *m* 2nd 1928 Sigrid Ellen (*d* 1980), dau of Anders Ammentorp, of Copenhagen, and *d* 13 Feb 1960, leaving issue:

1a +David John, *b* 1927

2a +Simon Robert [Simon Brudenell-Bruce Esq, 47 King's Rd, Paihia, BOI, New Zealand], *b* 8 Oct 1928, *m* 1st 11 Jan 1964 Christine Muriel, dau of William Hesketh Heald, of Pokeno, NZ, and has issue:

1b +Peter Gregory, *b* 9 Sept 1965

1b *Barbara Ann, *b* 28 March 1967

2b *Penelope Jane, *b* 1970

2a (cont) Simon Brudenell-Bruce *m* 2nd 1986 *Nina, dau of Andreas Skjoth, of Kolding, Denmark

3a Marc Hadrian, *b* 31 May 1930, *m* 1st 1953 (*divorce* 1957) —; *m* 2nd 14 Jan 1957 *Rayna Ellen, dau of Ernest Herbert Nicholas Howell, of Wanganui, NZ, and *d* following an accident 27 Feb 1965, leaving issue:

1b +Marc Raymond Christopher [Marc Brudenell-Bruce Esq, 38 Intrepid Dve, Mermaid Waters, Gold Coast, Qld, Australia], *b* 3 April 1962

1b *Karen Suzanne [Mrs Kempster, 1 Wainwright Ave, Mt Roskill, Auckland, New Zealand], *b* 23 Jan 1958; *m* 1983 — Kempster and has:

1c *Rochelle, *b* 1981

2c *Jade Michelle, *b* 1984

1a *Barbara Karen [Mrs Charles Zeese, 60–84 69th Ave, Ridgewood, NY, USA; 1211 N Miller Rd, Scottsdale, AZ, USA], *b* 8 Oct 1928, *m* 12 Sept 1953 *Charles, only s of Alfred Zeese, of New York, and has issue:

1b *Kevin Bruce [Kevin Zeese, 3619 Tallwood Terrace, Falls Church, VA, USA], *b* 28 Oct 1955; *m* 1976 (*divorce* 1994) Dina Smith; m 2nd 1995 *Kendra Wright and by his 1st w has:

1c *Alexander Bruce, *b* 1983

2c *Daniel Alfred, *b* 1988

3c *Stephen Taskova; *b* 1996

2b *Marc Charles [Marc Zeese, 1672 Woodbine Ave, Ridgewood, NY11385, USA], *b* 26 May 1957; *m* 1989 *Tatiana Taskova and has issue:

1c *Philip Taskova, *b* 1994

1c *Kristina Taskova, *b* 1990

1b *Eve Ellen [Mrs Todd Stevens, 1165 Old White Plains, RD Maroneck, NY, USA], *b* 1962, *m* 1988 *Todd Stevens and has issue:

1c *Jeremy Stevens; *b* 1994

1c *Sara Evelyn, *b* 1991

2a *Diana Mary [Diana Brudenell-Bruce, Little Denmark, Tortola, British Virgin Islands, WI]; *b* 13 July 1936; has issue:

1b *John Adam, *b* 1963

3a *Arabella Ann; *b* 13 March 1940, *m* 1962 (*divorce* 1969) Jack Ball, of Puerto Rico, and has issue:

1b *Robert J, *b* 1968

1b *Lesley Anne, *b* 1963

2b *Beth Sigrid, *b* 1965

3a (cont) Mrs Arabella Ball *m* 2nd 1972 *Morgan J Gatten and by him has:

1b *Michael J, *b* 1972

1 Frances Edith Agnes, *b* 6 June 1883, *m* 30 Jan 1907 Herbert Anderton Foster, TD, hon Col 2nd W R Bde RFA, 4th s of William Foster, DL, of Hornby Castle, Lincs, and had issue (*see* SHUTTLEWORTH, B). He *d* 17 Jan 1930

2 Helen Margaret, *b* 21 Feb 1887, *d* 2 May 1888

3 (Gwyneth) Marjorie, *b* 5 March 1890, *m* 16 Feb 1926 John Hayes Lord, US For Serv, s of Arthur Lord, of Plymouth, Mass, and *d* 7 March 1974, leaving issue:

(1) *Catherine [Mrs Jose Benardete, 845 Ackerman Ave, Syracuse 10, NY 13210, USA], *b* 22 Nov 1927, *m* 17 June 1961 *Jose Amado Benardete, est s of Prof Mair Jose Benardete, of New York

5 Charles Frederick, Maj Roy Wilts Yeo, MA Trin Coll Camb, JP and CC Wilts, JP Berks, *b* 4 March 1849, *m* 21 Aug 1873 Margaret (*d* 11 Sept 1913), dau of James Renshaw, of Broughton, Lancs, and *dsp* 31 May 1936

1 Louisa Caroline, *m* 19 Jan 1856 Sir Henry Meux, 2nd Bt, and *d* Dec 1894, leaving issue

2 Ernestine Mary, *m* 31 Aug 1865 3rd Earl of Listowel (*qv*) and *d* 27 Dec 1936, leaving issue

The 4th MARQUESS's unc,

HENRY AUGUSTUS BRUDENELL-BRUCE, **5th Marquess of Ailesbury**, Capt 9th Regt, Lt-Col 3rd Bn Duke of Edinburgh's Wiltshire Regt, MP Wilts 1886–92; *b* 11 April 1842; *m* 10 Nov 1870 Georgina Sophia Maria (*d* 23 June 1902), 2nd dau of George Henry Pickney, of Tawstock Court, Devon, and had issue:

1 GEORGE WILLIAM JAMES CHANDOS, **6th Marquess**

1 Ernestine Mary Alma Georgiana, *b* 6 Sept 1871; *m* 13 Jan 1898 Lt-Cdr Harry Brady Hunt, RNR, of Ballylean, Kildysart, Co Clare, s of William Lewis Hunt, and *d* 18 May 1953, having had issue. He *d* 1 Jan 1926

2 (Violet Louisa) Marjory, *b* 1 March 1880, *m* 9 July 1907 James Binney, MA, DL, JP, barrister, of Pampisford Hall, Cambs, and *d* 26 Aug 1923, leaving issue. He *d* 3 Sept 1935

The 5th MARQUESS *d* 10 March 1911; his only s,

GEORGE WILLIAM JAMES CHANDOS BRUDENELL-BRUCE, **6th Marquess of Ailesbury**, DSO (1900), TD, JP and DL Wilts, Argyll and Sutherland Highrs (M), Roy Wilts Yeo, Middx Yeo, Wilts Regt (SB), RASC and RFA (T), KGStJ, Boer War 1899–1900 (despatches, medal with four clasps), WW I 1915–19 (despatches) and WW II 1940–43 HG; *b* 21 May 1873; *m* 1st 21 March 1903 Caroline Sydney Anne (*d* 5 May 1941), only dau of John Madden, of Hilton Park, and had issue:

1 CHANDOS SYDNEY CEDRIC, **7th Marquess**

1 (Ursula) Daphne, *b* 21 Oct 1905, *m* 11 Dec 1944 Alfred Thomas Taylor and had issue:

(1) *Peter Alec, *b* 7 July 1945; *educ* Oratory

(2) *Martin Chandos, *b* 23 May 1952

2 Rosemary Enid, *b* 9 Feb 1907

The **6th Marquess** *m* 2nd 21 Feb 1945 Mabel Irene (*d* 26 June 1954), dau of John Samuel Lindsay, of Wrexham; *m* 3rd 9 July 1955 Alice Maude Emily (*d* 9 Feb 1960), widow of (a) Col John Henry Arthur Boyce, KORR, (b) Col Francis Byrne Johnson, KORR and (c) Col Rowland Money, OBE, KORR, and dau of Capt John Forbes Pinhey, 51st LI, and *d* 4 Aug 1961

His only s,

CHANDOS SYDNEY CEDRIC BRUDENELL-BRUCE, **7th Marquess of Ailesbury**, DL (1950), JP (1938), CC (1961) Wilts, *educ* Eton and Ch Ch Oxford, Maj RASC (TA) WW II (POW, escaped, despatches), author: *Youth Goes East*, *Amateur Pilot*, *The Wardens of Savernake*, *The Life and Loyalties of Thomas Bruce*; *b* 26

Jan 1904; *m* 1st 5 July 1924 Joan Houlton (*d* 24 July 1937), dau of Stephen Salter, of Pondwell House, Ryde, IOW, and had issue:

1 MICHAEL SYDNEY CEDRIC BRUDENELL-BRUCE, **8th and present Marquess of Ailesbury**

2 (Chandos Gerald) Piers, 2nd Lt RA 1948, *b* 9 Feb 1929, *educ* Harrow, *m* 1st 5 April 1951 (*divorce* 1957) Annie, only dau of Henry Angelé, of Yamaa-el-Mokra, Tangier; *m* 2nd 21 Jan 1958 *Nelida [The Lady Piers Brudenell-Bruce, Cortijo de la Plata, Zahara de los Atunes, Prov Cadiz, Spain], dau of Don Marino Garcia Villalba, of Madrid, and *d* 1974, leaving issue:

(1) *Tamara Angela, *b* 23 Feb 1966

(2) *Sandra Teresa, *b* 1969

The **7th Marquess** *m* 2nd 11 March 1944 (*divorce* 1948) Joyce Frances, formerly w of Peter Quennell and dau of Charles Warwick-Evans; *m* 3rd 20 Feb 1950 *Jean Frances Margaret [The Most Hon Jean Marchioness of Ailesbury, Bel au Vent, St Lawrence, Jersey, CI], widow of S/Ldr Richard Williamson, MBE, RAF, and dau of John Addison Wilson, of Bodicote, Banbury, Oxon, and *d* 15 July 1974, having by her had issue:

3 +Charles Adam, *b* 23 March 1951, *educ* Eton; late Lt Roy Hus; *m* 14 Sept 1996 *Teresa Chris, only dau of G T Simons, of Collingbourne Ducis, Wilts

AILSA

Arms: Argent, a chevron gules between three cross-crosslets fitchée sable, all within a double tressure flory counterflory of the 2nd. **Crest:** A dolphin naiant proper. **Supporters:** Two swans, wings inverted proper, beaked and membered gules. **Motto:** *Avise la fin* ('Take note of the outcome'). **Creations:** L. (S) 1457, E. (S) 24 Oct 1509, B. (UK) 12 Nov 1806, M. (UK) 10 Sept 1831.

THE 8TH MARQUESS OF AILSA, Earl of Cassillis, Lord Kennedy and **Baron Ailsa**, of Ailsa, Ayr (Archibald Angus Charles Kennedy) [The Most Hon The Marquess of Ailsa, Cassillis, Maybole, Ayrshire]; *b* 13 Sept 1956; *s f* 1994; *m* 1979 (*divorce* 1989) Dawn Leslie Anne, only dau of David A Keen, of 64 Rue Emeriau, Paris, and has issue:

1 *Rosemary Margaret; *b* 1980

2 *Alicia-Jane Lesley; *b* 1981

Lineage: DUNCAN de CARRICK, 1st EARL OF CARRICK; *fl c* 1150; gf of:

ROLAND of CARRICK; obtained from his unc Neil, 2nd Earl of Carrick (*dspm* 1256), a charter granting to him and his heirs the headship of the whole clan with the office of bailiary of Co Carrick; ancestor of:

JOHN KENNEDY, of Dunure; granted charters by DAVID II confirming that granted ROLAND of CARRICK and by Marjorie de Montgomerie the lands of Castlys and Stair, Kilmore, all Ayrshire; acquired from another Marjorie de Montgomerie (a cousin of the former) the barony of Dalrymple 1370 and 1376, and had a charter of his lands 1357/8 and again 1381; *d* soon after 1385, leaving an est s:

Sir GILBERT KENNEDY; a hostage to the English for liberation of DAVID II 1357; *m* Agnes, dau of Sir John Maxwell of Pollok (*see* HERON-MAXWELL, Bt), and had:

Sir GILBERT KENNEDY; *b* after 8 Nov 1408 had:

JAMES, Yr of Dunure; *m* 1404 Mary (*m* 3rd 13 Nov 1413 Sir William Graham (*see* MONTROSE, D); *m* 4th 1425 Sir William Edmonstone of Duntreath), dau of ROBERT III and widow of George, 1st Earl of Angus (*see* HAMILTON and BRANDON, D), and *dvp* by 8 Nov 1408, having had issue:

(1) John (Sir); a long-serving prisoner Stirling Castle, living 1434

(2) GILBERT, **1st Lord**

(3) James; Bp Dunkeld and St Andrews, Chllr Scotland, fndr St Andrews U; *d* July 1465

Sir GILBERT KENNEDY's gs,

GILBERT KENNEDY, of Dunure, **1st Lord Kennedy**, so *cr* between 27 May 1457 and 20 March 1457/8; one of the six regents of the kingdom during the minority of JAMES III 1466; *m* 1st Catherine, dau of 1st Lord Maxwell (*see* MAXWELL, Bt), and had issue; *m* 2nd Isabel (*d* 1484), dau of Sir Walter Ogilvie of Lintrathen (*see* AIRLIE, E) and widow of 1st Lord Glamis (*see* STRATHMORE and KINGHORNE, E), and *d* after 6 March 1478/9, leaving an est s:

JOHN KENNEDY, **2nd Lord Kennedy**; *m* 1st by 1459 Elizabeth, dau of 1st Lord Montgomery (*see* EGLINTON and WINTON, E), and had issue; *m* 2nd by 1471 Lady Elizabeth Gordon, dau of 1st Earl of Huntly (*see* HUNTLY, M) and widow of 2nd Earl of Erroll (*qv*), and by her (*d* 17 April 1500) had further issue; *d* by 23 May 1509, leaving an est s:

DAVID KENNEDY, **1st Earl of Cassillis**, so *cr* 24 Oct 1509, PC (S); *m* 1st Agnes, dau of William, Lord Borthwick (*qv*), and had issue; *m* 2nd Margaret (*dsp*), dau of Thomas Boyd, Earl of Arran (*see* KILMARNOCK, B), and widow of Alexander, 4th Lord Forbes (*qv*); *ka* battle of Flodden 9 Sept 1513, leaving:

GILBERT KENNEDY, **2nd Earl of Cassillis**; *m* Lady Isabel Campbell, dau of 2nd Earl of Argyll (*see* ARGYLL, D), and was *k* Aug 1527 leaving issue:

GILBERT KENNEDY, **3rd Earl of Cassillis**; *b* 1515; Ld Treas of Scotland 1554–58; assisted at the marriage of MARY STUART with FRANCIS, Dauphin of France, 1558 and may have been poisoned along with the other deputies attending the wedding after Scottish opposition to the French demand that Scotland form part of MARY's dowry angered the French; *m* Margaret, dau of Alexander Kennedy of Bargany and widow of William Wallace of Craigie, and *d* at Dieppe 28 Nov 1558 (the same night as his fellow deputies), having had:

1 GILBERT KENNEDY, **4th Earl of Cassillis**; *b c* 1541; *m* (contract 30 Sept 1566) Margaret (*m* 2nd 1st Marquess of Hamilton; *see* HAMILTON and BRANDON, D), dau of 7th Lord Glamis (*see* STRATHMORE and KINGHORN, E), and *d* 12 Dec 1576, leaving issue:

(1) JOHN KENNEDY, **5th Earl of Cassillis**; *b* 1575; Ld Treas Scotland 1599; *m* (contract 4 Nov 1597) Jean (*d* 23 June 1609), dau and heir of 4th Lord Fleming and widow of John, 1st Lord Maitland (*see* LAUDERDALE, E), Chcllr of Scotland; *dsp* by 14 Nov 1615

(2) Hew, *Master of Cassillis*; *m* (contract 2 Sept 1600) Katherine (*m* 2nd Sir James Stewart, Lord Ochiltree), dau of Uchtred Macdowall of Garthland; *d* by 25 March 1607, having had issue:

1a JOHN KENNEDY, **6th Earl of Cassillis**; Ld Justice Gen of Scotland 1649–51, memb of Cromwell's Ho of Lds; *m* 1st (contract Jan 1621/2) Lady Jean Hamilton (*d* 15 Dec 1642), dau of 1st Earl of Haddington (*qv*), and had issue; *m* 2nd 15 March 1644 Margaret (*bur* 22 April 1695), widow of Henry, Lord Ker, s of 1st Earl of Roxburghe (*see* ROXBURGHE, D); *d* April 1668, having had issue by his 2nd w (with two daus, Elizabeth and Mary):

1b JOHN KENNEDY, **7th Earl of Cassillis**; *m* 1st (contract 26 Dec 1668) Lady Susan Hamilton, dau of 1st Duke of Hamilton (*see* HAMILTON and BRANDON, D), and had, with other issue:

1c John, *Lord Kennedy*; *m* 18 June 1697 Elizabeth (*m* 2nd 22 March 1701 John Douglas, Earl of Selkirk and Ruglen, and *d* 10 March 1733/4), dau of Charles Hutchinson, of Owthorpe, MP Nottingham, and *dvp* 1700, leaving:

1d JOHN KENNEDY, **8th Earl of Cassillis**; *b* April 1700; Govr Dumbarton Castle; *m* (contract 6 Oct 1738) Lady Susan Hamilton (*d* 8 Feb 1763), dau of John Douglas, Earl of Selkirk and Ruglen (as above), and *dsp* 8 Aug 1759 when a dispute over the estates and title between William, Earl of March and Ruglen (heir of line) and Sir THOMAS KENNEDY, 4th Bt (kinsman and heir male; *see* below), was settled in the latter's favour by the Court of Session regarding the estates 29 Feb 1760 and by the Ho of Lds regarding the title 27 Jan 1762

1b (cont.) The **7th Earl** *m* 2nd 27 Feb 1697/8 Mary (*d* 12 Sept 1746), dau of John Fox, and *d* 23 July 1701, having by her had, with two daus (Elizabeth and Mary):

2c James; *dsp* by 1759

2a Gilbert; living 1617 and 1632

1a Jean; *m* William Stewart, of Carragar, Co Tyrone (*d* after 9 April 1665)

2 Thomas (Sir) of Culzean; ktd 1590; *m* by 28 April 1579, as her 2nd husb, Elizabeth (*m* 3rd (contract 4 April 1605) William Mewe of Rowallan and *d* Jan 1622), dau of David Makgill of Nesbit and Cranston-Riddell (*see* OXFUIRD, V) and was murdered 11 May 1602, having had, with other issue:

(1) Alexander (Sir) of Culzean; ktd 1632; *m* Agnes, dau of Thomas Kennedy of Ardmillian; *d* Sept 1652 leaving, with other issue:

1a John, of Culzean, JP Ayr; *m* 1st (contract 22 Feb 1645) Ann (*dsp*), dau of John Blair of Blair; *m* 2nd 1653 Margaret (*m* 2nd 1667 Sir David Ogilvy of Clova), est dau of John Hamilton, 1st Lord Bargany (*dormant* 1736), and *d* 1665, having had by her, with other issue:

1b Sir ARCHIBALD KENNEDY, 1st Bt, of Culzean (NS), so *cr* 8 Dec 1682; *m* Hon Elizabeth Leslie, dau of David, 1st Lord Newark, and *d* by 12 March 1711, having had with other issue:

1c Sir JOHN KENNEDY, 2nd Bt; *m* (contract 15 March 1705) Jean, dau of Capt Andrew Douglas of Mains; *d* by 28 Jan 1743, having had, with other issue (including Anne, *m* John Blair of Dunskey and had isssue; *see* HUNTER BLAIR, Bt):

1d Sir JOHN KENNEDY, 3rd Bt; *d* unm 10 April 1744

2d Sir THOMAS KENNEDY, 4th Bt, **9th Earl of Cassillis**; rep S peer 1774–75; *d* unm 30 Nov 1775

3d Sir DAVID KENNEDY, 5th and last Bt, **10th Earl of Cassillis**; advocate 1752, MP Ayrshire 1768–74, rep S peer 1776–90; *d* unm 18 Dec 1792 when the btcy expired

2a Alexander, of Craigoch and Kilhenzie; JP, Ayr; by his 1st w had a dau who *m* David Kennedy, of Drumellan, and had issue; *m* 2nd (contract 14 Dec 1683) Anna, dau of William Crawford, of Auchenames; *d c* 1698, having had by her, with other issue:

1b Archibald; Receiver-Gen and Collector of Customs of New York; *m* 1st —, dau of — Massam; *m* 2nd Dec 1736 Maria Walter, widow of Arent Schuyler; *d* 14 June 1763 aged 78, having had by his 1st w, with other issue:

1c ARCHIBALD KENNEDY, **11th Earl of Cassillis**; Capt RN; *m* 1st by June 1765 Katherine (*dsp* by 21 Jan 1768), only dau and heir of Peter Schuyler, of New Jersey; *m* 2nd 27April 1769 Anne (ld 29 Dec 1793)

dau of John Watts, of New York; *d* 30 Dec 1794, having had, with other issue:

1d ARCHIBALD, **1st Marquess**

2d John; *b* 1771; *m* 1800 Charlotte (*d* 27 May 1846), dau of Lawrence Gill; *d* 7 Aug 1859

3d Robert; *b* 1773; *m* Jane, sis of Alex Macomb, Gen US Army, and *d* 15 Nov 1843, leaving, with other issue:

1e John; Sec of Legation Naples and USA; *m* 5 Aug 1834 Amelia Maria (*d* 1896), only dau of Samuel Briggs; *d* 14 March 1845 leaving issue:

1f John Gordon (Sir), KCMG; *b* 18 July 1836; Dip Serv 1857–1905, Sec Legation Yedo 1878, Sec Embassy St Petersburg 1881, Rome 1885, Min and Consul-Gen Santiago 1888, Envoy Extrdy and Min Plen Romania 1897–1905, Grand Cross Order of Star of Romania; *m* 30 Oct 1877 Evelyn Adela (*d* 28 Nov 1939), dau of Col Hon Edward Bootle-Wilbraham (*see* SKELMERSDALE, B); *d* 2 Dec 1912 leaving with other issue:

1g Archibald Edward; *b* 7 Sept 1878; Capt Arygll and Sutherland Highrs; *ka* Le Cateau 26 Aug 1914

2g (Aubrey) Leo, MC; *b* 6 Feb 1885; MA Oxford; Capt Scots Gds, WW I 1914–19, KOYLI, Int Corps, and Scots Gds (Croce di Guerra); staff *The Times* 1910–14 and 1919–42, first dip correspondent BBC European Div 1942045; author: *Old Diplomacy and New, Britain Faces Germany, Salisbury (1830–1903), Portrait of a Statesman*; *m* 12 July 1921 Sylvia Dorothy (*d* 29 June 1968), est dau of Arthur Herbert Meysey-Thompson (*see* MEYSEY-THOMPSON, Bt); *d* 8 Dec1965 leaving issue:

1h *Elizabeth Dorothy [Mrs Jeremy Le Mesurier, 4 Gordon Place, London W8]; *b* 9 Aug 1922; *m* 1st 8 Sept 1945 (*divorce* 1958) Charles Russell-Scarr, s of Frederick Scarr, of Finchley, and has issue:

1i *(Aubrey) Mark Kennedy; *b* 27 Nov 1949; *educ* Eton; Capt RGJ; TV producer; assumed by deed poll 1978 name MEYSEY-THOMPSON; *m* 1975 *Catharine Diana Jane Herdman-Newton [Mrs Mark Meysey-Thompson Esq, Spellow Hill, Knaresborough, Yorks], and *d* 1987, leaving issue:

1j *James Leo Charles; *b* 1979

1j *Emma Catherine; *b* 1978

1i *Caroline Sarah [Ms Caroline Russell-Scarr, 64 Hatfield Rd, Chiswick, London W4 1AF]; *b* 14 May 1951

1h (cont) Mrs Elizabeth Russell-Scarr *m* 2nd 14 Oct 1960 her cousin *Jeremy John Le Mesurier, only s of Roderick Le Mesurier, of Alderney, CI, by Diana Elizabeth, dau of Arthur Herbert Meysey-Thompson (*see* MEYSEY-THOMPSON, Bt)

2h *(Horatia) Clare [Mrs Brian Heddy, Wynyards, Winsham, Chard, Somerset]; *b* 28 Aug 1926; *m* 1 Nov 1969 *Brian Huleatt Heddy, only s of Dr William Reginald Huleatt Heddy, of Blakesley Ave, London W5

3h *Diana Helen Marjorie; *b* 11 Feb 1929

3g Paul Adrian; *b* 11 Dec 1886; Capt Rifle Bde; *ka* 9 May 1915

4g John Patrick Francis; *b* 18 Sept 1891; T/Capt 5th Rifle Bde; *ka* 24 April 1918

1g Kathleen Yone; *b* 14 Aug 1880; *m* 25 Oct 1921 Hon Lionel Lindsay, MC (*d* 18 Aug 1965), s of 26th Earl of Crawford and Balcarres (*qv*); *d* 16 May 1970 leaving issue

2f William Robert (Sir), GCB; *b* 4 March 1838; Adml, C-in-C E Indies 1892–95 and the Nore 1900–01, served Crimea and China; *m* 11 June 1868 Edith Louisa (*d* 28 Nov 1936), dau of Capt Edward Stopford, RN (*see* COURTOWN, E); *d* 9 Oct 1916 leaving issue:

1g Alice Emily; *b* 7 June 1870; *m* 7 Dec 1911 her cousin George Waller Stopford (*d* 14 March 1959), s of James Sydney Stopford (*see* COURTOWN, E), and *d* 21 March 1939

3f Edward Briggs; *b* 28 Feb 1842; *m* 22 April 1875 Caroline Edith (*d* 29 Dec 1935), only child of Colville Coverley Jackson, BCS (*see* JACKSON, Bt), and *d* 6 Nov 1914 having had issue:

1g Edward Coverley; *b* 31 Aug 1879; Capt RN, served China 1900, WW I (despatches, Legion of Honour), WW II (despatches); *m* 21 Sept 1918 Rosalind Margaret Innes (*d* 1977), only child of Sir Ludovic James Grant, 11th Bt, of Dalvey (*qv*), and went down with his ship HMS *Rawalpindi* 23 Nov 1939 leaving issue:

1h +Ludovic Henry Coverley (Sir) [Sir Ludovic Kennedy, Ashdown, Avebury, Wilts SN8 1RF]; *b* 3 Nov 1919; *educ* Eton and Ch Ch Oxford (MA 1948); WW II 1939–45 as Lt RNVR; Cllr Navy Records Soc 1957–60; memb Lib Party Cncl 1964–67, fought (Lib) Rochdale by-election 1958 and gen election 1959; Rockefeller Fndn Atlantic Award Literature 1950; Librarian Ashridge Coll 1948–49, Lecturer for Br Cncl Finland, Sweden and Denmark 1955, Belgium and Luxembourg 1956, Newscaster ITN 1956–58, chm *This Week* (Assoc Rediffusion) 1959–60, Commentator *Panorama* 1960–63 (BBC), chm *Your Witness* (BBC), *Londoners**, *Face the Press* (ITA), presenter: *Time Out* 1964–65, *World at One* 1965–66 (both BBC), *The Middle Years* 1967 (ABC), *The Nature of Prejudice* 1968 (ATV), *Face the Press* 1968–69 and 1970–72 (Tyne-Tees), *Against the Tide* 1969 (Yorkshire TV), *Living and Growing* 1969–70 (Grampian V), *24 Hours* 1969–72, *Ad Lib* 1970–72, *Midweek* 1973–75, *Newsday* 1975–76, *Tonight* 1976–78, *A Life with Crime* 1979, *Change of Direction* 1979 (all BBC); author: *Sub-Lieutenant* (1942), *Nelson's Band of Brothers* (1951), *One Man's Meat* (1953), *Murder Story* (1954), *Ten Rillington Place* (1961), *The Trial of Stephen Ward* (1964), *Very Lovely People* (1969), *Pursuit: the chase and sinking of the* Bismarck (1974), *A Presumption of Innocence: the amazing case of Patrick Meehan* (1975), *Menace: the life and death of the* Tirpitz (1979), *The Portland Spy Case* (1979), *Wicked Beyond Belief* (1980), *The Airman and the Carpenter* (1985), *On My Way to the Club* (autobiog, 1989), *Euthanasia: the good death* (1990), *Truth to Tell* (1991), *In Bed with an Elephant: a journey through Scotland's past and present* (1995); *m* 25 Feb 1950 *Moira Shearer, actress and ballerina, only dau of Harold Charles King, of Queen's Gate, London SW7, and has issue:

1i +Alastair Charles Coverley; *b* 10 Feb 1963

1i *Ailsa Margaret; *b* 11 Aug 1952; *m* 29 July 1977 *Christopher Penny, yst s of Wilfred Penny, of 39 Salisbury Rd, Blandford Forum, Dorset

2i *Rachel Katherine; *b* 16 Nov 1956; *m* 1988 *Bill Hall, s of Prof Edward Thomas Hall, CBE, of Oxford

3i *Fiona Jane; *b* 20 Dec 1961

1h *Morar Margaret [Mrs Royce Ryton, Bonaly Tower, Colinton, Edinburgh 13]; *b* 6 Jan 1926; *m* 1st 24 Jan 1948 (*divorce* 1954) John Hamish Orr-Ewing (*see* ORR EWING, Bt) and has issue; *m* 2nd 6 Sept 1954 *Royce Thomas Carlisle Ryton, yr s of Reginald Thomas Ryton, of Ferring, Sussex, and has further issue:

2i *Charlotte Susan; *b* 15 Oct 1955

2h *Katherine; *b* 23 May 1927; *m* 29 April 1947 Ion Melville Calvocoressi, MBE, MC, Maj Scots Gds, only s of Matthew John Calvocoressi, and has issue:

1i *James Melville Ion; *b* 26 March 1948; *educ* Eton; *m* 1971 *Richenda Victoria Hanson, est dau of Peter Blandy, and has issue:

1j *Matthew James; *b* 1973

2j *Rupert Benedict; *b* 1976

3j *Cristopher John; *b* 1988

2i *Richard Edward Ion; *b* 5 May 1951; *educ* Eton; *m* 1976 *Francesca, only dau of David Temple Roberts, and has issue:

1j *Thomas David; *b* 1977

1j *Natalia Katherine; *b* 1980

2j *Hermione Beatrice; *b* 1984

3i *Andrew Matthew Ion; *b* 20 Sept 1953; *educ* Stanbridge Earls Sch

1i *Iona Rosalind; *b* 23 Sept 1957; *m* 1980 *Richard James Priestley, yr s of James Priestley, of Upton Manor, Upton, Hants, and has issue:

1j *Laura Katherine; *b* 1982

2j *Rosanna Victoria; *b* 1985

3j *Isabel Louise; *b* 1988

1g Mary Ethel; *b* 18 Aug 1876; *d* unm 1895

2g Margaret Amelia; *b* 19 March 1878; *m* 31 Oct 1908 Maj Heneage Frank Stopford, RHA (*ka* 15 Sept 1916), s of James Sydney Stopford, and *d* 22 Aug 1960, leaving issue (*see* COURTOWN, E)

4f Gilbert George; *b* 9 May 1844; MA Cambridge; barrister; Met Police Magistrate 1889–1907; *m* 6 Aug 1874 Alice (*d* 27 June 1944), dau of Edward Lyon, of Johnson Hall, Staffs; *d* 2 Jan 1909 leaving issue:

1g Gilbert Lyon; *b* 22 Oct 1875; Lt RNR, late 4th Bn Arg and Suth Highrs; *m* 1st 24 June 1903 (*divorce*) Mabelle Grace (*d* Jan 1938), yst dau of James Fairweather Low, of Baimakewan, Kincardineshire, and had issue:

1h Gilbert Ronald; *b* 27 March 1904; *educ* Harrow; WW II 1940–45 as Lt RANVR; *m* 20 June 1937 *Marion Beatrice, 2nd dau of Alfred Edward Cox, of Claremount, W Australia; *dsp* 18 June 1957

2h A son; *b* and *d* 30 Jan 1910

1g (cont.) Gilbert Kennedy *m* 2nd 1930 Noelle Evelyn Campbell (*d* 23 Feb 1955), dau of Gen Sir Richard Campbell Stewart, KCB, and widow of (a) Capt William K George and (b) his bro, Lt-Col Humphrey Hayes Kennedy (*see* below); *d* 11 Nov 1945

2g David Macomb; *b* 11 June 1878; 2/Lt 1st Bn Roy Scots Fus; *d* unm 19 Oct 1899

3g Humphfrey Hayes; *b* 19 Jan 1882; Lt-Col Seaforth Highrs, S African War 1901–02 (medal five clasps), NW Frontier India 1908 (medal with clasp), WW I; *m* 14 July 1917 Noelle Evelyn Campbell (*m* 2nd 1930 her bro-in-law Gilbert Lyon Kennedy (*see* above) and *d* 23 Feb 1955), dau of Gen Sir Richard Campbell Stewart, KCB, and widow of Capt William K George, Gloucester Regt; *ka* 29 July 1918

4g John de Navarre, OBE (1945); *b* 31 May 1888; QC (1947), Co Court Judge, Co of Peterborough, Ontario, Canada, 1952; author: *In the Shadow of the Cheka, Crime in Reverse, The Rain of Death, The History of the Department of Munitions and Supply*, and *Aids to Jury Charges, Criminal* (translated into French); *m* 1st 14 July 1914 Elsie Margaret (*d* 26 March 1969), dau of Edwin Charles Pinks, of Lindsell, EssexI, and had issue:

1h *Anne Macomb; *b* 24 July 1930; *m* 20 Aug 1953 *Frank Edward Dudas, only s of Frank Dudas, of Richmond Hill, Ontario, Canada, and has issue:

1i *Edward Tibor; *b* 26 June 1959

1i *Linda Julianna Kennedy; *b* 8 March 1956

2i *Yone Anne Pinks; *b* 18 Sept 1962

4g (cont.) Judge John Kennedy *m* 2nd 1970 *Marjorie Helen Troop, dau of Albert Morton, of Dudley, Worcs, and *d* 1979

The 11th EARL OF CASSILLIS's s,

ARCHIBALD KENNEDY, 1st Marquess of Ailsa, of the Isle of Ailsa, Co Ayr, so *cr* 10 Sept 1831, as also earlier 12 Nov 1806 BARON AILSA, of Alsa, Co Ayr (both UK), KT (1821), FRS; *b* Feb 1770; rep S peer 1796–1806; *m* 1 June 1793 Margaret (*d* 5 Jan 1848), 2nd dau and eventual heir of John Erskine of Dun, Forfarshire, and *d* 8 Sept 1846, having had, with three other daus:

1 Archibald, *Earl of Cassillis*; *b* 4 June 1794; *m* 1 May 1814 Eleanor (*d* 16 Nov 1832), only dau and heiress of Alexander Allardyce, of Dunnottar, and *dvp* 12 Aug 1832, having had, with two daus:

(1) ARCHIBALD, **2nd Marquess**

(2) Alexander; *b* April 1818; *d* unm Oct 1832

(3) John; *b* Sept 1819; *d* unm 3 Sept 1846

(4) David; *b* 17 Nov 1820; Capt EICS; JP, DL, Ayrshire; *m* 24 Feb 1873 Lady Mary Emily (*d* 25 Nov 1916), sis of 9th Earl of Cork and Orrery (*qv*) and widow of William Edward Hope Vere, of Craigie Hall, Scotland, and *d* 10 April 1905 leaving issue:

1a Evelyn Mary; *b* 11 May 1874; *m* 1st 17 Dec 1895 Charles Helbert Helbert (*d* 27 Jan 1903), s of Capt Federick Helbert Helbert, 5th Madras Light Cav, and had issue; *m* 2nd 30 Dec 1911 Lt-Col Arthur Molloy Kennard, DSO, RA (*d* 2 Jan 1917), s of Arthur Challis Kennard, of Eaton Place, London SW1, and *d* 2 July 1955, leaving issue

(5) Gilbert; *b* 14 July 1822; RN; *m* 26 Nov 1851 Margaret (*d* 24 March 1903), dau of Sir David Baird, 2nd Bt, of Newbyth (*qv*), and *d* 25 Nov 1901 leaving issue:

1a John Gilbert; *b* 1 May 1854; Capt 11th Roy Prussian Hussars, S Africa 1900–02 (two medals and five clasps); *m* 11 April 1882 Henrietta Maria Louise (*d* 3 Dec 1932), dau of Prof Oswald Achenbach, of Dusseldorf, and *d* 1 July 1923, leaving issue:

1b John Gilbert; *b* 1885; lost at sea 1904

2b Nigel Augustus; *b* 12 April 1886; Capt 3rd Bn Argyll and Sutherland Highrs; *m* 1st 30 April 1917 (*divorce* 1944) Gertrude Vera, 2nd dau of Brig-Gen Lionel Godolphin Brooke, CB, Connaught Rangers (*see* BROOKEBOROUGH, V), and had issue:

1c +Ian Michael Godfrey [Ian Kennedy Esq, The Camp Farm, Caynham, Ludlow, Salop]; *b* 7 May 1921; WW II 1941 as P/O RAF (invalided); *m* 1st 30 April 1960 Josephine Helen, est dau of John Leslie Price, of Warham Court, Breinton, Herefs, and *m* 2nd 29 July 1996 *Dr Fiona Alexander, dau of James R Alexander, of Leigh-on-Sea, Essex has by his 1st w issue:

1d +Angus Michael David; *b* 9 Aug 1962; MD, MRCP

1d *Virginia Anne Nicola; *b* 22 Dec 1964

1c *Lonia Hersey Joy; *b* 22 May 1924; *m* 24 July 1944 (*divorce* 1966) Lt Donald, MSA, RCNVR (ret), s of William James MacLean, of 2459 Marine Drive, W Vancouver, BC, and has issue:

1d *John Kennedy; *b* 30 June 1946; *m* 1983 *Rosemary, yr dau of FP Hillier, of Godalming, Surrey

2d *Alan Michael; *b* 27 April 1948; *m* 1971 *Sandra, dau of E McDonald, of Vancouver, BC, and has issue:

1e Sara Kennedy; *b* 1978

2e Gillian Anne; *b* 1983

3d *Brian William; *b* 9 Aug 1950

2b (cont.) Capt Nigel Kennedy *m* 2nd 22 Dec 1946 Dorothy Mary (*d* 12 June 1962), dau of William Henry Langley, of Victoria, BC, and widow of Lt-Col Richard Clive Cooper, Canadian Inf, and *d* 1 Sept 1957

1b Marguerite Cecilia; *b* 27 March 1894; *m* 1st 23 Jan 1918 (*divorce* 1924) Col Bodo von Borries, 12th Roy Prussian Dragoons, s of Col Hermann von Borries, and had a dau; *m* 2nd 20 Dec 1924 Lt-Gen Kurt Walter Wolff, s of Maximilian Wolff, of Potsdam

2b Clara; *b* 27 March 1894; *m* 1st 3 Nov 1920 Helmuth von Helster (*d* 7 May 1928), 5th Roy Prussian Lancers, s of Capt Alexander von Helster, and had a s and dau; *m* 2nd 1 Sept 1940 Leland Stanford Craft (*d* 9 March 1962), s of Richard Craft, of Vega, New York

2a Thomas Francis Archibald WATSON-KENNEDY, of Wiveton Hall, Cley, Norfolk; *b* 12 Nov 1856; Lt-Col 1st Bn QO Cameron Highrs; *m* 3 May 1907 Ethel Mary (*d* 27 Aug 1943), dau of Robert Fowler and widow of Sidney Watson, and *dsp* 30 May 1935

1a Mary Alice; *m* 6 May 1876 Alfred John Howard, of Warton Hall, Isleworth (*d* 22 Nov 1916), 4th s of Frederick John Howard, DL, and *d* 14 May 1942 leaving issue (*see* CARLISLE, E)

(6) William; *b* 30 Nov 1823; Capt RA; *m* 17 Sept 1846 Sarah Jane (*d* 5 Feb 1875), est dau of William M de Bois; *d* 5 March 1868 leaving issue:

1a William; *b* 13 Jan 1851; Offr 30th Regt; *m* 1874 Susan (*m* 2nd 17 Nov 1866 Capt George Arthur Trevor, Roy Sussex Regt), est dau of Edward Funnell; *dsp* 7 July 1883

1a Mary Oswald; *b* 28 June 1847

2a Mabel Esme; *b* 20 Oct 1862; *d* 5 Dec 1864

(7) Fergus; *b* 18 Feb 1826; HEICS; *d* 5 Oct 1852

(8) Nigel; *b* May 1828; *m* 1st 19 June 1858 Catherine Anne (*d* 1 Feb 1862), yst dau of Maj James Frere May, and had issue; *m* 2nd 5 Nov 1866 Elizabeth Charlotte (*d* 14 May 1884), sis of Sir John Neeld, 1st Bt, and widow of Rev Richard Prankerd Jones, of Charfield, Glos, and *d* 18 March 1878

(9) Adolphus Archibald; *b* 12 July 1832; *d* 20 June 1842

(1) Hannah Eleanor; *b* April 1815; *m* 5 July 1836 Sir John Andrew Cathcart, 5th Bt (*qv*); *d* 8 May 1877 leaving issue

2 John KENNEDY-ERSKINE of Dun, Forfarshire (added ERSKINE on inheriting Dun); *b* 4 June 1802; *m* 5 July 1827 Lady Augusta FitzClarence (*m* 2nd 24 Aug 1836 Lord John Frederick Gordon-Hallyburton (*d* 29 Sept 1878) (see HUNTLY, M), and *d* 8 Dec 1865), 4th illegitimate dau of WILLIAM IV and Mrs Jordan, and *d* 6 March 1831, having had issue:

(1) William Henry; *b* 1 July 1828; Capt 17th Lancers; *m* 18 Nov 1862 Catherine (*d* 18 Feb 1914), only surv child of William Jones, of Henllys, Carmarthenshire, and *d* 15 Sept 1870 leaving issue:

1a Augustus John William Henry; *b* 12 April 1866; Capt 5th Bde Scottish Div RA; *m* 3 Nov 1896 Alice Marjorie Cunningham (*d* 3 July 1940), dau of Revd A L R Foote, DD, of Rosehill, Forfarshire; *d* 2 Feb 1908 leaving issue:

1b Augustus John; *b* 14 Nov 1900

2b William Henry; *b* 14 Nov 1900; *m* Doreen —; *d* 21 May 1963

1b Violet Marjorie Augusta; *d* unm 25 Dec 1934

2b *Millicent Alison Augusta; *m* 17 July 1943 Lt-Col Thomas Maitland Lovett (*d* 1946), Gen List, late 4th Dragoon Gds, of Henlle Hall, Oswestry

1a Violet Augusta Mary Frederica; *b* 1 Sept 1863; *m* 27 Oct 1894 Maj Arthur Otway Jacob (*d* 1936), 20th Hus, 4th s of David Baldwin Jacob, JP, MD, FRCS, of Portlaoise, Queen's Co; *d* 9 Sept 1946 leaving issue

2a Millicent Augusta Vivian; *b* 12 Aug 1867; *d* 2 Nov 1883

(1) Wilhelmina; *b* 27 June 1830; *m* 17 April 1855 2nd Earl of Munster (*qv*) and *d* 9 Oct 1906, leaving issue

1 Margaret; *m* Thomas Radclyffe-Livingstone-Eyre, self-styled 7th Earl of Newburgh (*qv*)

The 1st MARQUESS's gs,

ARCHIBALD KENNEDY, **2nd Marquess of Ailsa**, KT (1859); *b* Aug 1816; Ld-Lt Ayrshire; *m* 10 Nov 1846 Julia (*d* 11 Jan 1899), 2nd dau of Sir Richard Mounteney Jephson, 1st Bt; *d* 20 March 1870 having had issue:

1 ARCHIBALD, **3rd Marquess**

2 Alexander; *b* 6 Oct 1853; Maj Black Watch and Hon Lt-Col 3rd Bn Black Watch; *m* 21 April 1881 Beatrice (*d* 8 Nov 1950), est dau of George Tomline Gordon, JP, DL, of Cuckney, Notts; *d* 4 April 1912 leaving issue:

(1) Irene Clare; *b* 1 March 1882; *m* 6 Dec 1906 John Bell (*d* 11 March 1948), JP, of The Hall, Thirsk, Yorks; *d* 9 Feb 1969 leaving issue (*see* KILMOREY, E)

(2) Hermione Julia; *b* 11 April 1883; *d* unm 18 Feb 1963

3 John; *b* 4 April 1859; Lt 4th Roy Scots Fus; *m* 12 Feb 1890 Adelaide Mary (*d* 30 Nov 1957), est dau of Col Alexander Learmouth, MP, formerly 17th Lancers, of Dean, Edinburgh; *dsp* 18 May 1895

1 Julia Alice; *b* 22 Nov 1849; *m* 15 Dec 1869 Col Robert William Web Follett (*d* 8 April 1921), Coldstream Gds, of Woodside, Old Windsor, yst s of Sir William Follett; *d* 22 Dec 1936

2 Evelyn Anne; *b* 24 Aug 1851; *m* 5 Nov 1885 Capt Sir Arthur Henderson Young (*d* 20 Oct 1938), GCMG, KBE, s of Col Keith Young, CB; *d* 24 Jan 1936 having had issue

3 Constance Eleanor; *b* 4 Oct 1855; *m* 28 April 1891 Col Lionel Grimston Fawkes (*d* 24 Aug 1931), JP, late RA, s of Major Richard Fawkes; *d* Oct 1946, having had issue

The 2nd MARQUESS's est s,

ARCHIBALD KENNEDY, **3rd Marquess of Ailsa**; *b* 1 Sept 1847; Lt and Capt Coldstream Gds, Lt-Cdr RNAV, hon Lt RNR, hon Capt RNVR; Ld-Lt Ayrshire 1919–37; Past Master Shipwrights' Co and a Yr Bro of Trinity Ho; hon LLD Glasgow 1904; *m* 1st 7 March 1871 Hon Evelyn Stuart (*d* 26 July 1888), 3rd dau of 12th Lord Blantyre, and had:

1 ARCHIBALD KENNEDY, **4th Marquess of Ailsa**, JP, DL (Ayrshire); *b* 22 May 1872; Maj 3rd Bn Roy Scots Fus, S Africa 1900–02 (two medals and five clasps), and WW I France, Jubilee and Coronation (1937) medals, Hon Col 4th/5th Bn Roy Scots Fus, 1930; memb Roy Co Archers, advocate Edinburgh, FRSGS; *m* 30 April 1903 Frances Emily, FSA Scot, DJStJ, Order of Mercy (*d* 29 Oct 1949), 3rd dau of Sir Mark John MacTaggart Stewart, 1st Bt, and *dsp* 27 Feb 1943

2 CHARLES KENNEDY, **5th Marquess of Ailsa**; *b* 10 April 1875; *educ* Eton and RAC Cirencester (silver medallist); formerly Capt Ayrshire Yeo and Lt 3rd Bn Roy Scots Fus, S Africa 1900–01 as Capt Prince of Wales's Light Horse (medal with two clasps); *m* 1st 15 Dec 1925 Constance Barbara (*d* 3 Nov 1931), dau of Edward Clarks, of Avishays, Chard, and widow of Adml Sir John Erskine Kennedy Baird, KCB; *m* 2nd 26 April 1933 Helen Ethel, MBE (1920) (*d* 17 Feb 1959), dau of James McDouall, JP, DL, of Logan, and widow of Richard John Cunninghame, MC, of Hensol, Stewartry of Kirkcudbright, and *dsp* 1 June 1956

3 ANGUS, **6th Marquess**

1 Evelyn; *b* 5 April 1876; *d* 9 Jan 1886

1 Aline; *b* 31 July 1877; *m* 17 Dec 1901 6th Baron Kilmaine (*qv*) and *d* 1 July 1957, leaving issue

The **3rd Marquess** *m* 2nd 3 Nov 1891 Isabella (*d* 9 Dec 1945), only dau of Hugh MacMaster, of Kausaui, NWP, India, and *d* 9 April 1938, having by her had further issue:

4 Hugh, MC (1918); *b* 19 Jan 1895; Lt-Col Coldstream Gds late Lt Ayrshire Yeo, WW I (despatches) and WW II; *m* 14 April 1925 *Katharine Louisa Clare, yst dau of Francis Henry Atherton, of Shalford, nr Guildford, and *d* 27 April 1970, leaving issue:

(1) Nigel; *b* 23 Jan 1926; *educ* Radley; *d* 1985

3 Marjory; *b* 4 Sept 1898; *m* 21 April 1921 Sir Laurence Pierce Brooke Merriam (*d* 27 July 1966), MC, JP, DL, Rifle Bde, yr s of Charles Pierce Merriam, JP, of Halstead, Essex, and had:

(1) Michael Kennedy; had a s (Andrew William Kennedy, *m* Elizabeth Finney (*see* PERTH, E); and dau (Teresa Anne, *m* Mark Woodhouse; *see* LICHFIELD, E)

The 5th MARQUESS's bro,

ANGUS KENNEDY, **6th Marquess of Ailsa**; *b* 28 Oct 1882; *educ* Eton; Capt RAF and Lt RNVR; *m* 28 Jan 1922 Gertrude Millicent (*d* 25 Aug 1957), yr dau of Gervas Weir Cooper, of Wordwell Hall, Bury St Edmunds, and *d* 31 May 1957, leaving issue:

ARCHIBALD DAVID KENNEDY, **7th Marquess of Ailsa**, OBE (1968), DL (Ayrshire 1960); *b* 3 Dec 1925; *educ* Nautical Coll Pangbourne; Lt Scots Gds, Lt Col Roy Scots Fus (TA), Chm Anglo-Somali Soc; *m* 7 April 1954 *Mary [The Most Hon Mary Marchioness of Ailsa, Cassilis, Maybole, Ayrshire], yst dau of John Burn, of Amble, Northumberland, and *d* 1994, having had issue:

1 ARCHIBALD ANGUS CHARLES KENNEDY, **8th and present Marquess of Ailsa**

2 +DAVID THOMAS [The Lord David Kennedy, Morriston, Culzean, Maybole, Ayrshire KA19 8LB]; *b* 3 July 1958; heir presumptive; *educ* Strathallan

Sch and Berks Ag; *m* 1991 *Anne, dau of Bernard Kelly, of Warwick, and has issue:

(1) +Archibald David; *b* 1995

(1) *Katherine Jean; *b* 1993

1 *Elizabeth Helen [The Lady Elizabeth Drummond, Pinkie Ho, Loretto Sch, Musselburgh, E Lothian EH21 7RE; Ach Nan Eun, Ellishader, Staffin, Isle of Skye]; *b* 23 Feb; *m* 1 July 1976 *Norman Walker Drummond, MA, BD, FRSA, Chaplain to HM THE QUEEN in Scotland, Headmaster Loretto Sch, yr s of Edwin P Drummond and Mrs Jill Drummond, of Glenely Ho, Odana Terrace, Greenock, and has issue:

(1) *Andrew; *b* 1977

(2) *Christian; *b* 1986

(3) *Ruaraidh; *b* 1993

(1) *Margaret; *b* 1980

(2) *Marie Clare; *b* 1981

AINSWORTH

Arms: Gules three battleaxes, two and one, and as many buckle's tongues to the dexter, one and two, argent. **Crest:** Between two battleaxes, blades outwards, argent a falcon, wings displayed and inverted or, beaked and legged gules, belled and jessed gold. **Motto:** *Spero meliora* ('I hope for better things'). **Creation:** Bt. (UK) 12 Jan 1917.

SIR (THOMAS) DAVID AINSWORTH, 4TH BT, of Ardanaiseig, Co Argyll [Sir David Ainsworth Bt, Flat 9, 80 Elm Park Gdns, London SW10 9PD; Ashley House, Wootton, Woodstock, Oxon OX20 1DX]; *b* 22 Aug 1926; *s* half-bro 1981; *educ* Eton; late Lt 11th Hus; merchant banker; *m* 6 May 1957 *Sarah Mary, dau of Lt Col Hugh Carr Walford, 17th/21st Lancers, and has issue:

1 +ANTHONY THOMAS HUGH; *b* 30 March 1962; *educ* Harrow

2 +Charles David; *b* 24 Aug 1966; *educ* Harrow; late Lt 11th Hus

1 *Serena Mary; *b* 13 March 1958; *m* 1987 *Stelios, of Corfu, and has issue:

(1) *Nicholas David; *b* 1987

(2) *George Stamatis; *b* 1988

2 *Tessa Jane; *b* 6 Aug 1959; *m* 1986 *Nicholas Cecil John Fortescue (*see* FORTESCUE, E)

Lineage: THOMAS AINSWORTH, of Blackburn-over-Darwen, later Backbarrow, N Lancs; *m* 1769 Sarah (*d* 1796), dau of David Barton, and *d* March 1785, having had, with an est s Joseph and a yst s Thomas:

DAVID AINSWORTH, of Preston; *m* Alice (*d* 1827), dau of Richard Hatton, of Park Lane, Lancs, and *d* 1819, having had (with three daus):

THOMAS AINSWORTH, JP, of The Flosh, Cumberland; *b* March 1804; High Sheriff 1861; *m* 1837 Mary Laurie (*d* Feb 1867), est dau of Rev John Stirling, DD, of Craigie, Ayrshire, and *d* 1881, having had, with other issue:

Sir John Stirling Ainsworth, 1st Bt (UK), so *cr* 12 Jan 1917, VD, JP (Argyllshire and Cumberland); *b* 30 Jan 1844; *educ* UCL (MA, LLB); Lt-Col 3rd Vol Bn Border Regt 1898-1902, High Sheriff Cumberland 1891, MP (Lib) Argyllshire 1903-18; *m* 5 Nov 1879 Margaret Catherine (*d* 8 Oct 1918), est dau of Robert Reid Macredie, and had issue:

1 THOMAS (Sir), **2nd Bt**

2 John Stirling; *b* 9 Nov 1889; Lt 11th Hus; *ka* Oct 1914

1 Janet Mary; *d* an infant 1880

2 Jean Barbara; *b* 3 Dec 1883; *m* 16 Feb 1905 12th Viscount Massereene and Ferrard (*qv*) and *d* 11 Dec 1937, leaving issue

3 Margaret Louise; *b* 18 June 1887; *m* 1st 5 Nov 1912 Arthur George Murray Smith, 2nd Life Gds (*d* 2 Nov 1914 of wounds recd in action), est s of George Murray Smith, of Gumley Hall, Harborough, and had issue; *m* 2nd 26 Nov 1924 John Pollock (*d* 30 Dec 1966), of Mountainstown, Navan, Co Meath, and *d* 5 July 1946, leaving further issue

Sir JOHN *d* 24 May 1923; his er s,

Sir Thomas Ainsworth, 2nd Bt, (JP Cumberland and Argyllshire); *b* 8 Feb 1886; *educ* Eton and Trin Coll Cambridge (BA); Lt 11th Hus (SR), Westmorland and Cumberland Yeo, Steward of INHS Ctee, Jt-MFH and Huntsman Meath 1922–25, MFH and Huntsman Co Galway 1925–26, Kildare 1926–27 and Tipperary 1928–32; *m* 1st 9 Feb 1911 (*divorce* 1925) Lady Edina Dorothy Hope Conyngham (*d* 13 April 1964), 4th dau of 4th Marquess Conyngham (*qv*), and had issue:

1 **Sir John Francis, 3rd Bt**; *b* 4 Jan 1912; *educ* Eton and Trin Coll Cambridge (BA 1933, MA 1937); FRHistS, Inspr Manuscripts Nat Library Ireland, External Lecturer Medieval Hist Univ Coll Cork 1966–81, Dist Commr Kildare Branch Irish Pony Club 1959-62, chm Dublin SPCA 1965-66 (V-Chm 1963-65 and 1966-67), Jt Huntsman Curragh Beagles 1964–81; *m* 1st 26 Aug 1938 (*divorce* 1946) Josephine, dau of Cdr Walter Randolph Bernard, RN (ret), by Millicent Olive, only dau of Augustus Edgar Graves (*see* GRAVES, B); *m* 2nd 19 Feb 1946 *Anita Margaret Ann [Anita Lady Ainsworth, 6 Aubury Park, Shankill, Co Dublin, Ireland], est dau of Harold Arthur Lett, of Kilgibbon and Ballynadara, Enniscorthy, Co Wexford, and *d* 1981

1 Iris Helen Hersey; *m* 22 April 1939 Nicholas St Vigor Fox, of Lough Park House, Castle Pollard, Co Westmeath, 3rd s of Maj Sir John St Vigor Fox, JP, DL, of Westholme House, Allton, Shepton Mallet, Somerset, and had issue:

(1) Nicholas Charles; *b* 1 May 1941; accidentally *k* while serving with Br S African Police S Rhodesia 15 April 1967

(2) *John St Vigor; *b* 15 Jan 1948

(1) *Charlotte Sylvia; *b* 25 Aug 1943

Sir Thomas *m* 2nd 10 Sept 1925 Marie Eleanor (May) (*d* 30 Dec 1969), dau of Compton Charles Domvile and formerly w of Evelyn Wenworth Hope-Johnstone (*see* ANNANDALE AND HARTFELL, E), and *d* 1 March 1971, having by her had:

2 Sir (THOMAS) DAVID AINSWORTH, **4th and present Bt**

AIRD

Arms: Gules, on a chevron between in chief two wolf heads erased and in base a mullet of six points within an increscent all argent, two falcon's heads erased sable. **Crest:** On a bull-headed rail fesswise, a lion rampant holding erect between the paws a spike point downwards, all proper. **Motto:** *Vigilantia* ('By vigilance'). **Creation:** Bt. (UK) 5 March 1901.

SIR (GEORGE) JOHN AIRD, 4TH BT, of Hyde Park Terrace, Paddington, London [Sir John Aird Bt, Grange Farm, Evenlode, Moreton-in-Marsh, Glos GL56 0NT]; *b* 30 Jan 1940; *s* f 1973; *educ* Eton, Ch Ch Oxford (MA) and Harvard (MBA); MICE 1966, Page of Honour to HM THE QUEEN 1955–57, chm: MATCON 1981–, Healthcare Devpt Servs 1995–, Advanced Fluid Systems Ltd 1996–; *m* 31 Aug 1968 *Margaret Elizabeth, yr dau of Sir John Harling Muir, 3rd Bt (*qv*), and has:

1 +JAMES JOHN; *b* 12 June 1978

1 *Rebecca; *b* 22 July 1970

2 *Belinda Elizabeth; *b* 14 May 1972

Lineage: JOHN AIRD, of Fortrose, Ross-shire; *d* 1823, leaving, with a yr s Alexander (*m* and had a dau):

JOHN AIRD, of Gt Cumberland Pla, London; *b* 1806; fndr 1845 John Aird & Sons (constructional engrs); *m* 2 Feb 1831 Agnes (*d* 29 July 1869), dau of Charles Bennett, of Lambeth, and *d* 9 April 1876, leaving a 2nd s:

Sir John Aird, 1st Bt (UK), so *cr* 5 March 1901, JP (Middx); *b* 3 Dec 1833; Hon Lt-Col Engr and Rlwy Staff Corps RE; Commr Ltcy City London, MP (C) Paddington N 1887–1906, Mayor Paddington 1900–01, Grand Cordon Medjidie; *m* 6 Sept 1855 Sarah (*d* 4 April 1909), dau of Benjamin Smith, of Lewisham, and had issue:

1 JOHN (Sir), **2nd Bt**

2 Malcolm Rucker, JP (Hants); *b* 4 Aug 1872; *m* 3 Nov 1898 Nellie Margaret (*d* 13 Sept 1954), dau of Jeremiah Dummett, and *d* 9 July 1934, leaving issue:

(1) Malcolm Henry, OBE (1945); *b* 5 Nov 1899; *educ* Harrow and RMC Sandhurst; Col 9th Lancers WW II (despatches), Offr US Legn Merit 1945; *m* 17 Aug 1922 Joan Meredith (*d* 1986), dau of Henry Sturgis, of 12 Chester St, London SW1, and *d* 9 July 1965, leaving issue:

1a +Malcolm Robin Meredith; *b* 16 Dec 1923; *educ* Canford; Capt Irish Gds WW II (wounded); *m* 1st 12 March 1946 (*divorce* 1955) Irma, dau of Erwin Spitzer; *m* 2nd 20 April 1955 *Barbara Kathleen Addison Shantz, dau of John Addison Wilson, and has issue:

1b +Julian Malcolm; *b* 1955

1b *Zandra Theresa Jane; *b* 1960; *m* 1989 *Michael Alistair Patrick Mercer, s of Maj P Mercer and Mrs J Davis

2a +Alastair Sturgis (Sir), GCVO 1997 (KCVO 1984 CVO 1977, LVO 1969) [Sir Alastair Aird GCVO, 31b St James's Palace, London SW1A 1BA]; *b* 14 Jan 1931; *educ* Eton and RMA Sandhurst; late Capt 9th/12th Roy Lancers (Prince of Wales's); HM QUEEN ELIZABETH THE QUEEN MOTHER: T/Equerry to 1960–64, Assist Priv Sec and Extra Equerry to 1964–73, Comptroller 1974– and Pv Sec and Equerry 1993–, Tstee RSAS Devpt Tst 1986–, Hon Bencher Middle Temple 1991; *m* 22 July 1963 *Fiona Violet, LVO (1980), Extra Ldy in Waiting to HRH PRINCESS MARGARET, COUNTESS OF SNOWDON, only dau of Lt-Col Ririd Myddelton, Coldstream Gds, LVO, hJP, DL, of Chirk Castle, Denbighshire (*see* LANSDOWNE, M), and has:

1b *Caroline Margaret Violet; *b* 18 June 1964 (HRH PRINCESS MARGARET, COUNTESS OF SNOWDON, stood sponsor); *m* 1989 *Capt Charles John Allfrey, Roy Hus (PWO) (*see* DAVENTRY, V)

2b *Henrietta Idina; *b* 9 June 1966; *m* 11 Dec 1996 *Francis Seidler, yr s of Francis Seidler, of San Francisco, and Mrs Daphne Seidler, of Horsted Keynes, Sussex

3a +Jeremy John [Jeremy Aird Esq, Quarry Wood Cottage, Burghclere, Newbury, Berks]; *b* 16 April 1936; *educ* Eton; late Capt 9th/12th Roy Lancers (Prince of Wales's); *m* 8 July 1967 *Mary Elizabeth, est dau of Lt-Col Sir (William) Richard des Voeux, 9th Bt (*see* 1940 edn), and has issue:

1b +David William; *b* 7 Dec 1968

2b *Catherine Rosemary Jean; *b* 1972

(2) Ronald, MC, TD; *b* 4 May 1902; *educ* Eton and Clare Coll Cambridge; T/Maj 4th Co London Yeo (TA) WW II (wounded); Assist Sec MCC 1926–53, Sec 1952–62, Pres 1968; *m* 16 April 1925 Viola Mary (*d* 18 April 1965), yr dau of Sir Godfrey Baring, 1st Bt (*qv*), and *d* 1986, leaving issue:

1a *Gillian Viola [Mrs Christopher Maude, Feildings, Hoe Lane, Flansham, Bogor Regis, W Sussex]; *b* 17 June 1930; *m* 1st 22 Nov 1951 (*divorce* 1961) Robert Ian MacDonald, s of Ian MacDonald, and has issue:

1b +Ian; *b* 1955

1b *Zara; *b* 1953; *m* 1980 *Daniel E Harris

1a (cont.) *Mrs Gillian MacDonald *m* 2nd 30 Nov 1962 *Christopher Michael Maude, s of Charles Wilfred Maude, and has further issue:

2b *Victoria Viola; *b* 15 Dec 1968

(3) Ian Basil, DSO; *b* 4 Jan 1905; T/Maj 4th Co London Yeo (TA) WW II; *kas* 17 Dec 1944

(1) *Ruth Sarah [Mrs Robert Brown, 14 Spring Walk, Wargrave, Berks]; *b* 29 July 1909; *m* 29 Feb 1940 *Robert Ross Buchanan Brown, CBE, yr s of Robert Cuthbert Brown, of Orange, NSW, Australia, and has issue:

1a *Ian Robert Aird; *b* 13 June 1946; *educ* Marlborough; *m* 1969 (*divorce* 1982) Tessa Elizabeth, dau of Desmond Pertwee, and has issue:

1b *Katherine; *b* 1972

2b *Emily; *b* 1974

3b *Rebecca Rose; *b* 1984

1a *Sarah Elizabeth; *b* 30 Jan 1944; *m* *— Penalver-Diaz

2a *Margaret Jane; *b* 9 Sept 1947; *m* *— Bryant

(2) Elizabeth Mary; *b* 29 Nov 1912

1 Sarah; *m* 10 July 1878 Basil Pym Ellis (*d* 5 Oct 1907) and *d* 31 May 1938, leaving issue

2 Jessie; *m* 19 June 1883 George Neill Abernethy (*d* 20 May 1923), of Broom Hall, Oxshott, Surrey, and *d* 17 Feb 1932, leaving issue

3 Kate; *m* 16 Oct 1884 Alfred William Thomas Bean and *dsp* 5 April 1905

4 Ada Eleanor; *m* 7 Feb 1889 Louis Miéville, barrister (*d* 11 June 1944), s of Jean Louis Miéville, and *d* 15 Nov 1947, leaving issue

5 Vida; *m* 5 July 1892 Rev Edward Paterson Anderson, MA, Vicar St John's, Paddington, and *d* 24 May 1947, leaving issue

6 Gertrude; *d* unm 8 Oct 1942

7 Dorothy; *m* 8 June 1899 Spyridion Mavrojani, JP, MA, BCL, barrister, Capt 5th Roy Fus (*d* 1 March 1930), s of Alexander Mavrojani, and *d* 2 Jan 1931, leaving issue

Sir JOHN *d* 6 Jan 1911; his son,

Sir John Aird, 2nd Bt, JP (Suffolk); *b* 6 Nov 1861; Maj RE Egypt 1884–85 (medal with clasp), 2nd Cl Osmanieh, Imperial Order and Grand Cordon Medjidie; *m* 20 April 1886 Alicia Ellen (*d* 8 March 1951), dau of James Hall Renton, of Park Lane, London W, and had issue:

1 JOHN RENTON (Sir), **3rd Bt**

2 Joseph Maurice; *b* 3 Nov 1904; *educ* Eton and Magdalen Coll Oxford (BA, 1926); T/Capt Roy Berks Regt WW II; *m* 1st 11 July 1934 (*divorce* 1958) Gwenyth Sheila, dau of Richard Dartrey and formerly w of Vincent Dominguez; *m* 2nd 16 Oct 1958 Betty Louise, twin dau of John Ralph Colson and formerly w of Maj Marcus Vincent, and *d* 26 June 1973

1 (Nellie) Phyllis; *m* 12 July 1910 Capt William Noel Cunliffe, 3rd Bn Shropshire LI (*d* 30 July 1933), 3rd s of Capt Ellis Brooke Cunliffe, and *d* 1976, having had issue (*see* CUNLIFFE, Bt)

2 Evelyn Dorothy; *m* 17 Nov 1921 Charles Ewald Scarisbrick (*d* 21 May 1962), only s of Charles Scarisbrick, and *d* 27 Feb 1957, leaving issue

The 2nd Bt *d* 20 Oct 1934; his er s,

Sir John Renton Aird, 3rd Bt, MVO (1936), MC, JP (1951), DL (1954); *b* 7 Aug 1898; Col Gren Gds WW I and WW II; Extra Equerry to HM GEORGE VI 1937–52 and HM THE QUEEN 1952–73, Equerry to HM EDWARD VIII as PRINCE OF WALES 1929036 (Extra Equerry 1936), ADC to Govr Bombay 1921–23 and HC Egypt 1926–27, Order St Olav; CC 1949 and CA 1958 Berks, Master Drapers' Co 1959; *m* 26 April 1939 *Lady Priscilla Heathcote-Drummond-Willoughby [The Lady Priscilla Aird, Wingrove House, Chipping Campden, Glos], yr dau of 2nd Earl of Ancaster (*see* WILLOUGHY DE ERESBY, B), and *d* 20 Nov 1973, leaving issue:

1 Sir (GEORGE) JOHN AIRD, **4th and present Bt**

1 *Susan Priscilla; *b* 26 Aug 1942

2 *Petra Daphne [The Rt Hon The Lady Willoughby de Broke, 19 Cranbury Rd, London SW6]; *b* 24 Sept 1944; *m* 1 May 1965 21st Baron Willoughby de Broke (*qv*) and has issue

3 *Amanda Alecia; *b* 27 Aug 1946

AIRLIE

Arms: Argent, a lion passant guardant gules, crowned with an imperial crown, and collared with an open one proper. **Crest:** A lady from the waist upwards affrontée azure, holding a portcullis gules. **Supporters:** Two bulls sable, armed, unguled and horned vert, with a garland of flowers about their necks proper. **Motto:** *A fin* ('To the end'). **Creations:** E. and L. (Ogilvy of Alith etc) (S) 2 April 1639, L. (S) 28 April 1491.

THE 8TH EARL OF AIRLIE, Lord Ogilvy of Airlie and **Lord Ogilvy of Alith** and **Lintrathen** (Sir David George Patrick Coke Ogilvy, KT (1985), GCVO (1984), PC (1984), JP) [The Rt Hon The Earl of Airlie KT GCVO PC JP, Cortachy Castle, Kirriemuir, Angus DD8 4LX; 5 Swan Walk, London SW3 4JJ]; *b* 17 May 1926; *s* f 1968; *educ* Eton; Capt Scots Gds, served with 2nd Bn Germany 1945, ADC to C-in-C and High Commr Austria 1947–48, Malaya 1948–49, RARO 1950; dir J Henry Schroder Wagg & Co 1961–84 (chm 1973–77) and Baring Stratton Investment Tst 1986–, chm: Schroders plc 1977–84, Gen Accident Fire and Life Assur 1987–97, Trans Europe Investment, Westpool Investment Tst, Ashdown Investment Tst 1968–82, Ld Lt Angus 1989– (DL 1964), Brig Roy Co Archers, Ld Chamberlain 1984–97, Perm Ld in Waiting 1998–, Chllr: Roy Victorian Order 1984–97 and Abertay U, Dundee, 1994–, memb exec ctee Pilgrims 1977–, Treas Scout Assoc, Roy Victorian Chain 1997; *m* 23 Oct 1952 *Virginia Fortune, Ldy of the Bed Chamber to HM THE QUEEN 1973–, memb: Industl Design Panel BR 1974– and Roy Fine Art Commn 1975–, tstee Tate Gallery 1983– and Nat Gallery 1989–, chm Tstees Nat Gallery Scotland 1997–, dau of John Barry Ryan, of Moorland Farm, Newport, Rhode Island, USA, by his w Margaret ('Nin'), dau of Otto Kahn, the German-born US financier, and has issue:

1 +DAVID JOHN, *Lord Ogilvy* [Lord Ogilvy, Airlie Castle, Kirriemuir, Angus DD8 5NG]; *b* 9 March 1958; *educ* Eton and Ch Ch Oxford (MA 1980); Page of Honour to HM THE QUEEN 1971–72, md Richard L Feigen UK Ltd (art dealers); *m* 1st 1981 (*divorce* 1990) Hon Geraldine Theodora Mary Gabriel Harmsworth, est dau of 3rd Viscount Rothermere (*qv*), and has issue:

(1) *Augusta Amadeus Caroline; *b* 3 Dec 1981

1 (cont.) *Lord Ogilvy m* 2nd 1991 *Tarka, dau of John Kings, of Austin, Texas, and has issue:

(1) +David Huxley, *Master of Ogilvy*; *b* 11 Dec 1991

(2) +Joseph Skene; *b* 21 March 1995

(3) +Michael Móir; *b* 20 Jan 1997

2 +Bruce Patrick Mark; *b* 7 April 1959

3 +Patrick Alexander; *b* 24 March 1971

1 *Doune Mabell [The Lady Doune Wake, The Stables, Courteenhall, Northants]; *b* 13 Aug 1953; *m* 16 April 1977 *(Hereward) Charles Wake, only s of Maj Sir Hereward Wake, 14th Bt (*qv*), and has had issue

2 *Jane Fortune Margaret [The Lady Jane Nairac, 23 Delaford Street, London SW6]; *b* 24 June 1955; *m* 30 Aug 1980 *François Nairac, s of Paul Nairac, of Vacoas, Mauritius, and has issue:

(1) *Jessica Doune; *b* 1985

(2) *Annabel Lydia; *b* 1988

3 *Elizabeth Clementina; *b* 4 June 1965

Lineage: GILIBRIDE, EARL OF ANGUS *temp* DAVID I; had, with other issue:

1 Angus; his successor in the Earldom

2 Magnus; *s* to the Earldom of Caithness through his mother

3 GILBERT

GILIBRIDE, EARL OF ANGUS's 3rd s,

GILBERT OGILVY; assumed the surname of Ogilvy from lands of that name in his possession, of which, with Powrie and Kyneithein in Angus, he had a charter 1172; from him descended:

Sir PATRICK OGILVY of Wester Powrie; had a charter of Kettins in Forfarshire from ROBERT I (THE BRUCE) and was *s* by his s:

PATRICK OGILVY of Wester Powrie; obtained from his n, Sir Patrick Ogilvy of Ogilvy, the lands of Wester Powrie; *m* Marjory, dau and eventual heiress of Robert Ramsay of Auchterhouse, and had a s:

WALTER OGILVY, of Wester Powrie and Auchterhouse; Hereditary Sheriff of Forfar; *s* to both Auchterhouse and the office of Sheriff on the death of his unc Sir Malcolm Ramsay *c* 1365; had, with an ers (Alexander, *d* unm):

Sir WALTER OGILVY, of Auchterhouse; Sheriff Forfar; *m* Isabel, dau and heir of Sir Malcolm Ramsay, and was *k* in a skirmish with robbers 1391, leaving issue:

1 Alexander (Sir), of Auchterhouse; Sheriff Angus 1403–23; had issue:

(1) Patrick (Sir), of Auchterhouse; Sheriff Angus and Justiciary; f of,

1a Alexander, of Auchterhouse; whose dau and heir Margaret, *m* James Stewart, Earl of Buchan, uterine bro of JAMES II

(2) Andrew (Sir), of Inchmartine; had issue (*see* SEAFIELD, E)

2 WALTER (Sir), of Lintrathen; for whom *see* further below

3 John, of Inverquharity (*see* OGILVY, Bt)

1 Marjory; *m* David, 3rd Earl of Crawford (*see* CRAWFORD and BALCARRES, E)

Sir WALTER OGILVY, of Auchterhouse's 2nd s,

Sir WALTER OGILVY of Lintrathen; High Treas Scotland under JAMES I; said to have *m* 1st an heiress of the Durward family, by whom he acquired Lintrathen, Forfarshire, and had:

1 JOHN (Sir), for whom *see* below

2 James

Sir WALTER (who had either by his 1st or 2nd w a dau Isabel, who *m* 1st shortly after 1427 Lord Glamis (*see* STRATMORE and KINGHORNE, E) and 2nd 1st Lord Kennedy (*see* AILSA, M) and *d* 1484); *m* 2nd Isabel, dau of Sir John Glen of Balmuto, and *d* 1440, having by her had:

3 Walter; ancestor of the OGILVYs of Deskford (*see* SEAFIELD, E)

4 David

5 Alexander

6 Patrick

7 George

Sir WALTER OGILVY, of Lintrathen's est s,

Sir JOHN OGILVY, of Lintrathen; had a charter of the lands and castle of Eroly (Airlie) 1459 and had his lands erected into the Barony of Lintrathen 1483; *m* 1st Marian, dau of Sir William Seton of Seton; *m* 2nd before 1447 Margaret, widow of James Dunbar, Earl of Moray, and had issue:

Sir JAMES OGILVY, of Airlie, **1st Lord Ogilvy of Airlie** (S), so *cr* 28 April 1491; Amb Denmark 1491; *m* 1st Elizabeth Kennedy and had an est s:

1 JOHN, **2nd Lord**

The **1st Lord** *m* 2nd by May 1478 Helen, dau of William, 2nd Earl of Angus (*see* HAMILTON and BRANDON, D), and widow of 2nd Lord Graham (*see* MONTROSE, D); *m* 3rd Jonet Lyle (*d c* 1525) and *d* by 25 Sept 1504, leaving two daus

The 1st LORD's est s,

JOHN OGILVY, **2nd Lord Ogilvy of Airlie**; ktd *c* 1495; *m* 1st by 14 Oct 1472 Mariot—; *m* 2nd Jean, est dau of 2nd Lord Graham (*see* MONTROSE, D), and had an er s:

JAMES OGILVY, **3rd Lord Ogilvy of Airlie**; *m* Margaret, dau of 7th Earl of Crawford (*see* CRAWFORD and BALCARRES, E), and had, with at least one dau (Margery, *m* John Lyon, 2nd of Cossins; *see* STRATHMORE and KINGHORNE, E):

JAMES OGILVY, **4th Lord Ogilvy of Airlie**; an Extrdy Ld of Session 1542; *m* Helen, dau of 3rd Lord Sinclair (*qv*), and *d* by 1549, having had, with other issue (including Helen, *m* 5th Lord Innermeath; *see* MORAY, E):

1 James, *Master of Ogilvy*; *m* Katherine (*m* 2nd Earl of Crawford), dau of Sir John Campbell of Calder, and was *ka vp* Battle of Pinkie 10 Sept 1547, leaving, with other issue:

(1) JOHN OGILVY, **5th Lord Ogilvy of Airlie**; *m* Jean, est dau of William, 7th Lord Forbes (*qv*), and *d* 1606, leaving issue:

1a JAMES OGILVY, **6th Lord Ogilvy of Airlie**; *m* 1st Jean, 4th dau of William Ruthven, 1st Earl of Gowrie (*see* CARLISLE, E), and had with other issue:

1b JAMES, **1st Earl**

1a (cont.) The **6th Lord Ogilvy of Airlie** *m* 2nd Elizabeth (*m* 2nd Alexander Auchmoutie), dau of Sir Archibald Napier of Merchistoun (*see* NAPIER, Bt, of Merchistoun), and *d* 1606

The **6th Lord Ogilvy of Airlie**'s s,

JAMES OGILVY, **1st Earl of Airlie**, so *cr* 2 April 1639, as also LORD OGILVY OF ALITH and LINTRATHEN (both S), with remainder '*haeredibus masculis sibi in patrimonio et statu succedentibus*', adherent of CHARLES I, fought at Battle of Kilsyth 1645; *m c* 1614 Lady Isabel Hamilton, 2nd dau of 1st Earl of Haddington (*qv*), and *d c* 1648, having had issue:

1 JAME, **2nd Earl**

2 Thomas (Sir); raised a regt for CHARLES I; *m* Lady Patricia Ruthven, dau of Patrick, Earl of Forth and Brentford (*extinct* 1651), and was *k* at Montrose's victory of Inverlochy 2 Feb 1645, leaving:

(1) Christian; *m* Sir James Ramsay, Bt, of Bamff (*see* 1970 edn)

(2) A dau; *m* — Fletcher, of Ballinshoe

3 David (Sir), of Clova; royalist Civil War

1 Helen; *m* Sir John Carnegy, of Balnamoon

2 Margaret Ogilvy; *m* Patrick Urquhart, of Meldrum

The 1st EARL's est s,

JAMES OGILVY, **2nd Earl of Airlie**; captured at royalist defeat at Philiphaugh 1645 and sentenced to death, escaped the night before his intended execution dressed in his sis's clothes; *m* 1st Helen, dau of George Ogilvy, 1st Lord Banff (*dormant* 1803); *m* 2nd Mary, dau of Sir John Grant, of Frenchie,and widow of Lewis Gordon, 3rd Marquess of Huntly (*qv*); *d c* 1704, leaving by his 1st w (with four daus) an only s:

DAVID OGILVY, **3rd Earl of Airlie**; *m* 8 May 1696 Lady Grizel Lyon, est dau of Patrick, 3rd Earl of Strathmore and Kinghorne (*qv*), and *d* 1717, having had, with a dau (Helen, *m* John Hamilton (*see* OGILVY-WEDDERBURN, Bt) and had issue):

1 James, *Lord Ogilvy*; Jacobite 1715, attainted *vp* by Act of Parl 1716, pardoned 1725 and returned home; *m* 6 Dec 1730 Anne (*m* 2nd Sir Alexander Macdonald, 14th of Sleat, Bt (*see* BOSVILLE MACDONALD, Bt), and *d* 27 Nov 1735), dau of David Erskine of Dun, a Ld of Session, and *dsp* 12 Jan 1731

2 John, self-styled 4th Earl of Airlie; *b* 1699; assumed the family honours on the *d* of his attainted er bro 1731; *m* 1722 Margaret (*d* 1767), est dau and coheir of David Ogilvy of Cluny, and *d* 24 July 1761, leaving, with other issue:

(1) David, self-styled 5th Earl of Airlie; joined Bonnie Prince Charlie at Edinburgh 1745, bringing with him a regt of 300 men chiefly of his own name and family, attainted by Act of Parl, escaped to France after the Battle of Culloden 1746 and getting command of a regt, called Ogilvy's, rose to the rank of Lt-Gen; obtained a Crown pardon 1778 and a Parly removal of disabilities (but not restoration of his honours) 1788; *m* 1st Margaret (imprisoned after Culloden but escaped to France where she *d* 1757), dau of Sir James Johnstone, of Westerhall, Bt, MP (*qv*); *m* 2nd 1770 Anne (*dsp* 27 Dec 1798), dau of James Stewart, of Blairhall, and *d* 3 March 1803, having had by his 1st w, with other issue (including Margaret, *m* John Wedderburn; *see* OGILVY-WEDDERBURN, Bt):

1a David, never assumed the title; *b* 4 Dec 1751; *dvp* unm and insane 6 April 1812

2a Walter Ogilvy; claimed Earldom but *d* before any decision was reached; *m* 1st Margaret (*dsp* 3 June 1780), dau of William Fullarton of Spynie; *m* 2nd 12 Nov 1780 Jane (*d* 11 June 1818), dau of John Ogilvy of Murkle (male heir of Walter Ogilvy of Balfour, s of James, 1st Lord Ogilvy of Airlie), and *d* 10 April 1819, having had, with other issue:

1b John; Capt Roy Scots; *d* Berbice 1809

2b DAVID, **4th Earl**

3b Donald, of Clova; *bapt* 10 May 1780; Col Forfar Militia, MP Forfarshire 1831–32; *m* Feb 1815 Maria (*d* 9 April 1843), 4th dau of James Morley, and *d* 9 April 1843, leaving with other issue:

1c Walter; *b* 30 Aug 1822; *m* 1879 Ellen (*d* 16 Jan 1896), dau of Alexander Smith, and *d* 30 April 1894, leaving issue:

1d Walter Donald Duncan; *b* 5 Nov 1883; *dsp*

1d Dorothea Sophia Elizabeth; *b* 15 Aug 1889

WALTER OGILVY's est surv s,

DAVID OGILVY, **4th Earl of Airlie**; *b* 16 Dec 1785; had his honours restored by Act of Parl 26 May 1826, rep S peer 1832–49, Ld Lt Forfarshire; *m* 1st 7 Oct 1812 Clementina (*d* 1 Sept 1835), only child and heiress of Gavin Drummond (3rd s of James Drummond of Keltie), by Clementina, sis and coheir of Alexander Graham of Duntrune (male heir of John, Viscount Dundee), and had, with other issue:

1 DAVID GRAHAM DRUMMOND, **5th Earl**

The **4th Earl** *m* 2nd 15 Nov 1838 Margaret (*d* 17 June 1845), only child of William Bruce, of Cowden, and gdau of William Bruce, of Newton, by his w Janet Bruce, of Clackmannan, and consequently heir of line and rep of the family of Clackmannan, and *d* 20 Aug 1849, having by her had further issue

The **4th Earl**'s s,

DAVID GRAHAM DRUMMOND OGILVY, **5th Earl of Airlie**, KT; *b* 4 May 1826; rep S peer 1850–81, Ld High Commr Church of Scotland 1872–73; *m* 23 Sept 1851 Hon Henrietta Blanche (*d* 5 Jan 1921), 2nd dau of 2nd Baron Stanley of Alderley (*see* STANLEY OF ALDERLEY, SHEFFIELD and, B), and *d* 25 Sept 1881, having had:

1 DAVID WILLIAM STANLEY, **6th Earl**

2 Lyulph Gilchrist, DSO; *b* 25 June 1861; Lt RASC (ATF), 2nd Lt Lanark Militia, Capt 2nd Brabant's Horse Boer War 1899–1901 (medal, despatches), Lt RASC WW I 1914–15; *m* 27 Aug 1902 Edith Gertrude (*d* April 1908), dau of Philip Henry Boothroyd, JP, of Waterdale Stock Ranch, Loveland, Colorado, USA, and *d* April 1947, leaving issue:

(1) +Jack David Angus; *b* 18 June 1903; *m* 1940 *Dorothy Stanley, of Boulder, Colorado

(1) Blanche Edith Maude; *b* 27 Sept 1905

1 Henrietta Blanche; *b* 8 Nov 1852; *m* 28 Sept 1873 Col Sir Henry Montague Hozier, KCB, 3rd Dragoon Gds (*d* 28 Feb 1907), bro of 1st Baron Newlands (*extinct* 1929), and *d* 23 March 1925, leaving issue (*see* MARLBOROUGH, D)

2 Clementina Gertrude Helen; *b* 19 June 1854; *m* 31 Dec 1874 1st Baron Redesdale (*qv*) and *d* 30 April 1932, leaving issue

3 Maude Josepha; *b* 16 Nov 1859; *m* 12 Oct 1886 Theodore George William Whyte (*d* 29 March 1903), of Estes Park, USA, 2nd s of John James Whyte, JP, DL, of Newton Manor, and *d* 3 April 1933, leaving issue

4 Griselda Johanna Helen; *b* 20 Dec 1865; *m* 22 Dec 1897 James Cheape (*d* 21 July 1943), of Strathtyrum, Fife, and *d* 12 Feb 1934, leaving issue

The 5th EARL's est s,

DAVID WILLIAM STANLEY OGILVY, **6th Earl of Airlie**, DL (Forfar); *b* 20 Jan 1856; Lt-Col 12th Lancers, 4th class Medjidie, Hon Col 3rd Vol Bn Black Watch, Scottish rep peer 1885–1900; *m* 19 Jan 1886 Lady Mabell Frances Elizabeth Gore, GCVO (1953), GBE (1920), DGStJ, Hon LLD St Andrews, Ldy of the Bedchamber to HM QUEEN MARY (*d* 7 April 1956), dau of 5th Earl of Arran, and was *ka* Diamond Hill, nr Pretoria, 11 June 1900, after leading his regt in a charge which saved the guns, and left issue:

1 DAVID LYULPH GORE WOLSELEY, **7th Earl**

2 Bruce Arthur Ashley, MVO 5th class (1922), MC (1919), DL (Angus 1936–51); *b* 15 March 1895; *educ* Wellington and RMC Sandhurst; Capt Reserve of Offrs 12th Roy Lancers, Life Gds and Irish Gds, Equerry to HRH THE PRINCE OF WALES 1921–30; *m* 28 April 1931 Primrose Eleanor (*d* 9 Dec 1961), er dau of Robert William O'Brien, of Bank of Ireland Ho, Drogheda, Co Louth, and *dsp* 29 Sept 1976

3 Patrick Julian Harry Stanley, MC; *b* 26 June 1896; Capt Irish Gds (Res); *ka* 9 Oct 1917

1 Kitty Edith Blanche; *b* 5 Feb 1887; author of children's books; *m* 1st 18 Sept 1906 (*divorce* 1925) Brig-Gen Sir Berkeley Vincent, KBE, CB, CMG (*d* 29 Jan 1963), s of Col Arthur Hare Vincent, 3rd Hus, of Summerhill, Co Clare, and had

issue; *m* 2nd 1 June 1926 Lt-Col Ralph Gerald Ritson, Inniskilling Dragoons (*d* 25 Oct 1966), 4th s of Ulrick Alexander Ritson, JP, DL, of Claf Hall, Muggleswick, Durham, and *d* 17 Oct 1969

2 Helen Alice Wylington; *b* 21 Nov 1890; Chm Cncl Married Women; *m* 1st 25 Nov 1909 Maj Hon Clement Betram Ogilvy Freeman-Mitford, DSO, 10th Hus (*ka dsp* May 1915), est s of 1st Baron Redesdale (*qv*), and had issue; *m* 2nd 11 July 1918 (*divorce* 1931) Lt-Col Henry Courtney Brocklehurst, 10th Hus and RAF (*ka* Burma 1942), 2nd s of Sir Philip Lancaster Brocklehurst, 1st Bt (*qv*), and had further issue; *m* 3rd 21 Feb 1933 Lt-Col Harold Bligh Nutting (*d* 7 July 1954), s of Philip Nutting, of Hazeley Hall, Warwick, and *d* Dec 1973

3 Mabell Griselda Esther Sudley; *b* 22 Jan 1892; one of HM QUEEN MARY's trainbearers Coronation 1911 (medal); *d* unm 4 Nov 1918

The 6th EARL's est s,

DAVID LYULPH GORE WOLSELEY OGILVY, **7th Earl of Airlie**, KT (1942), GCVO (1938, KCVO 1929), MC; *b* 18 July 1893; *educ* Eton; Lt-Col Scots Gds, 10th Roy Hus, Brevet-Col 4/5th Bn Black Watch (TA), WW I (despatches, wounded, MC) and WW II, Comdt Army Cadet Force (Scotland) 1943; rep S peer 1922–63, a Ld-in-Waiting to HM GEORGE V 1926–29, Ld-Lt Angus 1936–67, Ld Chamberlain to HM QUEEN ELIZABETH THE QUEEN MOTHER 1937–65; Chllr Order of Thistle 1956–66; Lt Roy Co of Archers, Hon LLD St Andrews 1958, Grand Offr Legion of Honour; *m* 17 July 1917 Lady Alexandra Marie Bridget Coke (*d* 1984), dau of 3rd Earl of Leicester (*qv*); *d* 28 Dec 1968, having had issue:

1 DAVID GEORGE PATRICK COKE OGILVY, **8th and present Earl of Airlie**

2 +Angus James Bruce (Sir) KCVO (1989) PC (1997) [The Rt Hon Sir Angus Ogilvy KCVO PC, Thatched House Lodge, Richmond, Surrey TW10 5HP]; *b* 14 Sept 1928; *educ* Eton and Trin Coll Oxford (MA); Capt Scots Gds (Res of Offrs, served 1946–48); dir Drayton Gp of Investment Tsts and other cos, chm Br Australian Investment Tst 1972–, memb Roy Co of Archers, V-Patron Toc H and Nat Children's Homes 1986–, Chm Nat Assoc of Youth Clubs; memb governing cncl Business in the Community 1984– and SPCK 1984–94, Tstee: Leeds Castle Fndn 1975–, GB-Saskawa Fndn 1985–, Prince's Youth Business Tst (chm Advisory Cncl 1986–) and Queen's Silver Jubilee Tst 1995–; Patron: Arthritis Care 1978–, Scottish Wildlife Tst 1974–90, Pres Imperial Cancer Research Fund 1964–94 (*s* by his w), V-Pres Friends of the Elderly and Gentlefolks' Help 1969–; *m* 24 April 1963 *HRH PRINCESS ALEXANDRA (Helen Elizabeth Olga Christabel), GCVO, only dau of HRH THE late DUKE OF KENT, KG, KT, GCMG, GCVO, PC, and HRH THE late PRINCESS MARINA, DUCHESS OF KENT (*see* Roy Family), and has issue:

(1) +James Robert Bruce; *b* 29 Feb 1964; *educ* St Andrews; publisher *Luxury Briefing* 1996–; *m* 1988 *Julia, md Hamilton & Inches, Edinburgh jewellers, est dau of Charles Frederick Melville Rawlinson, of Arkesden, Essex, and has:

1a +Alexander Charles; *b* 12 Nov 1996

1a *Flora; *b* Dec 1994

(1) *Marina Victoria Alexandra; *b* 31 July 1966; *m* 1990 (*divorce* 15 Oct 1997) Paul Julian Mowatt and has issue:

1a *Christian Alexander; *b* 1993

1a *Zenouska May; *b* 1990

3 +James Donald Diarmid [The Hon James Ogilvy, Sedgebrook Manor, Sedgebrook, Lincs NG32 2EU]; *b* 28 June 1934; *educ* Eton; Page of Honour to HM GEORGE VI 1947–51, Lt Scots Gds 1952–54, Egypt 1953–54; ptnr Rowe and Pitman (stockbrokers), dir Rowan Investment Managers, memb Roy Co of Archers, Govr Queen Charlotte's and Chelsea Hosps 1966–; *m* 1st 2 July 1959 (*divorce*) Magdalen June Ruth, only dau of Robert Ducas, of Pawling, New York, USA, by his 1st w Magdalen Mary Charlotte, est dau of Maj Herbert Marmaduke Joseph Stourton, OBE (*see* MOWBRAY, SEGRAVE and STOURTON, B); *m* 2nd 1980 *Lady Caroline Childe-Villiers, er dau of 9th Earl of Jersey (*qv*) and formerly w of (a) Viscount Melgund (later 6th EARL OF MINTO (*qv*)) and (b) Hon John Douglas Stuart (*see* STUART OF FINDHORN, V), and has issue by 1st w:

(1) +Shamus Diarmid Ducas; *b* 24 Jan 1966

(2) + [Diarmid Ogilvy Esq, 51d Eaton Sq, London SW1W 9BE]; *b* 12 April 1970; *educ* Eton

(1) *Laura Jane; *b* 27 April 1960; *m* 1990 *Philippe Goffin, yr s of Jean Goffin, of Brussels, and has issue:

1a *Sebastian; *b* 1992

(2) *Emma Louise; *b* 20 May 1962

1 *(Victoria) Jean Marjorie Mabell [The Rt Hon The Lady Lloyd, Clouds Hill, Offley, Hitchin, Herts]; *b* 21 Sept 1918; *m* 24 Jan 1942 2nd Baron Lloyd, MBE (*d* 1985; *see* 1970 edn), and has had issue

2 *Margaret Helen Isla Marion [The Lady Margaret Tennant, Lochnabo House, Elgin, Morayshire]; *b* 23 July 1920; WW II in WRNS; *m* 11 July 1946 *Capt Sir Iain Mark Tennant, KT, DL, Scots Gds, est s of Col Edward Tennant (*see* GLENCONNER, B), and has issue

3 Griselda Davina Roberta; *b* 12 June 1924; *m* 6 Nov 1948 (*divorce* 1968) Maj Peter Edward Gerald Balfour, Scots Gds, 2nd s of Brig Edward William Sturgis Balfour, CVO, DSO, OBE, MC, of Balbirine, Markinch, Fife, and *d* 8 June 1977, leaving issue

Seat: Cortachy Castle, Kirriemuir, Angus. Originally one of ROBERT I (THE BRUCE)'s hunting lodges in the early 14th century, Cortachy came into the hands of Sir William Ogilvy of Lintrathen about a hundred years later. The Sir William in question seems to have been a near kinsman of the Sir Walter Ogilvy of Lintrathen who was High Treasurer of Scotland under JAMES I and died in 1440 (*see* above). Subsequently the Ogilvys disposed of Cortachy but bought it back in the early 17th century, so that when their cheaf seat of Airlie Castle was sacked by Covenanters at the start of the Civil War the **1st Earl** was able to take up residence there instead.

CHARLES II stayed at Cortachy briefly in 1650, shortly after arriving in Scotland with a view to regaining his throne not just there but in England. The Castle was remodelled by W W Dickson in the early 19th century, about the time the **4th Earl** had his honours restored to him, when an entirely new wing was thrown out. Another wing was added for the **5th Earl** in the 1870s by David Bryce, the leading exponent of Scottish Baronial style softened by French flavouring. Bryce also enlarged Dickson's wing, crenellated the tops of the walls and capped the towers with 'witch's hats'. Internally he put in the plasterwork ceiling in the drawing room with downward-facing finials, making for a prettily stalactite effect. This was a copy of a similar ceiling at another Ogilvy property, Auchterhouse.

A few years later Bryce's wing largely burnt down, but after World War II Philip Tilden, who also worked on Chartwell for Sir Winston Churchill, was brought in to reconstruct it. The Castle today exhibits a lightness of touch very unlike most exercises in Scottish Baronial. The rendering on the elevations is nevertheless to be deprecated, though doubtless the climate requires it, and the rich brownish-red colouring of the crenellations constrast somewhat oddly with the grey slate of the conical roofs to the towers above and the cream rendering below.

AITCHISON

Creation: Bt. (UK) 31 Jan 1938.

SIR CHARLES WALTER DE LANCEY AITCHISON, 4TH BT, of Lemmington, Northumberland [Sir Charles Aitchison Bt, Park House, Barbon, Cumbria LA6 2LG]; *b* 27 May 1951; *s f* 1958; *educ* Gordonstoun; Lt 15th/19th King's Roy Hus 1974–78, RARO; ARICS; dir de Lancey Lands Ltd; *m* 1984 *Susan, yr dau of Edward Ellis, of Hest Bank, Lancs, and has issue:

1 +RORY EDWARD DE LANCEY; *b* 7 March 1986

1 *Tessa Charlotte; *b* 1982

Lineage: JOHN GORDON AITCHISON, of Devizes; f of:

Sir Stephen Harry Aitchison, 1st Bt (UK), so *cr* 31 Jan 1938, of Lemmington, Co Northumberland, JP (Northumberland and City and Co Newcastle-upon-Tyne); *b* 16 Jan 1863; ktd 1928; *m* 2 June 1891 Alice Mary (*d* 8 April 1932), dau of Walter de Lancey Willson, JP, of Kirklinton Park, Cumberland, and had issue:

1 WALTER DE LANCEY (Sir), **2nd Bt**

2 John Gordon, OBE (1944); *b* 5 Aug 1893; Cdr RN, official Commentator Hurlingham Polo Assoc; *m* 31 Oct 1919 Eveline Betty (*d* 16 July 1961), yr dau of William Tudor Sutherland, of Skibo Castle, Sutherland, and widow of Lt Arthur Walter Forbes, DSO, RN (*see* SEMPILL, L), and *d* 15 Aug 1964, leaving issue:

(1) Alastair Gordon; *b* 7 Aug 1920; *educ* Cranleigh and St John's Coll Cambridge (MA); LRCPI, LRCSI; *m* 16 Feb 1955 Marguerite Lucy, MB, BS Lond, MRCS Eng, LRCP Lond, yr dau of Col John Smith Sloper, OBE, and hads issue:

1a *Ann Marguerite; *b* 17 Aug 1955

2a *Eveline Lucy; *b* 23 May 1957

3a *Victoria; *b* 17 June 1958

4a *Alexandra Betty; *b* 18 March 1960

5a *Emily Sarah; *b* 3 Nov 1962

(2) Timothy John; *b* 19 July 1928; *educ* Charterhouse and St John's Coll Cambridge (MA); QALAS, ARICS; *m* 24 Oct 1955 June Rosemary, dau of John Herbert Whitfield, and had issue:

1a *Susan Jane; *b* 4 June 1960

3 Stuart Wilson; *b* 19 May 1896; *d* 3 Nov 1955

4 Stephen Villers; *b* 7 April 1902; *educ* Harrow and Christ's Coll Cambridge; *m* 1st 1925 Alice A Stamper and had issue:

(1) *Joan Alice [Mrs Cecil Bolt, c/o Box 714, Lahore, Pakistan]; *m* 17 March 1956 *Cecil Moncur Bolt, BSc, AMICE, and had issue

4 (cont.) Stephen Aitchison *m* 2nd 1955 *Jessie Ethel, dau of Vernon Lovell

1 Aline Mary; *m* 1918 Brig Harrison, IA

Sir STEPHEN *d* 26 Aug 1942; his est s,

Sir Walter De Lancey Aitchison, 2nd Bt; *b* 14 May 1892; *educ* Univ Coll Oxford (MA); FSA; *m* 18 April 1922 Sheena Lennox (*d* 21 Nov 1972), er dau of Charles Lennox Fraser, TD, MD, FRCS, FRCP, of Berwick-on-Tweed, and had issue:

1 STEPHEN CHARLES DE LANCEY (Sir), **3rd Bt**

2 Lennox Gordon Fraser; *b* 27 Sept 1925; *educ* Rugby and Trin Coll Oxford (BA 1949, MA 1954); *k* aeroplane accident 17 Sept 1966

3 +David Lachlan [David Aitchison Esq, The Red House, 2 Apperley Rd, Stocksfield, Northumberland NE43 7PE]; *b* 25 Nov 1928; *educ* Rugby; md Walter Willson Ltd and De Lancey Lands Ltd; *m* 12 Sept 1955 *Dorothy Hazel, 3rd dau of Swinburne Kindred Walton, and has issue:

(1) +Jeremy David; *b* 10 April 1959; *m* Oct 1991 *Ruth Mary, 3rd dau of Walter Timmis, and has:

1a +Harry Walter Jeremy; *b* 16 May 1994

1a *Rosanna Mary; *b* 2 April 1996

(1) *Dawn Elizabeth; *b* 10 Nov 1956; *m* Oct 1989 *John Michael Phillips, er s of Michael Phillips, and has:

1a *Nicholas George; *b* 17 June 1992

1a *Rachel Louise; *b* 24 Jan 1991

2a *Charlotte Elizabeth; *b* 17 Aug 1994

1 *Shena Diana [Miss Shena Aitchison, Weat Lea, Finwick, Berwick-on-Tweed TD15 2PJ]; *b* 3 May 1927

Sir WALTER *d* 14 Oct 1953; his est s,

Sir Stephen Charles De Lancey Aitchison, 3rd Bt; *b* 10 March 1923; *educ* Rugby and Univ Coll Oxford; Maj 13th/18th Hus (QMO), md Walter Wilson Ltd and De Lancey Lands Ltd; *m* 2 Sept 1950 *(Elizabeth) Anne Milburn, MB, BS (*m* 2nd 1974 Roland Antony Cookson, CBE, DCL (*d* 1991)), er dau of Lt-Col Edward Reed, and *d* 12 May 1958, leaving issue:

1 Sir CHARLES WALTER DE LANCEY AITCHISON, **4th and present Bt**

2 +(Stephen) Edward [Edward Aitchison Esq, Howden Dene Farm House, Corbridge, Northumberland]; *b* 27 March 1954; *educ* Fettes; chm and md Walter Willson Ltd and de Lancey Lands Ltd; *m* 1978 (*divorce* 19–) Mrs Harriet N Thomson, yr dau of Dr Henry Miller, and has issue:

(1) +Stephen Henry; *b* 1981

(1) *Amanda Jo; *b* 1983

ALANBROOKE

Arms: Or a cross engrailed per pale gules and sable, in the first quarter a crescent of the second. **Crest:** A brock proper. **Supporters:** On either side an officer of the Royal Horse Artillery in full dress proper, supporting with the exterior hand an escutcheon azure charged with seven barrulets wavy argent surmounted by a salmon rising gules. **Motto:** *Gloria finis* ('Let glory be the aim'). **Creation:** B. (UK) 18 Sept 1945, V. (UK) 29 Jan 1946.

THE 3RD VISCOUNT ALANBROOKE, of Brookebrough, Co Fermanagh, and **Baron Alanbrooke**, of Brookebrough, Co Fermanagh (Alan Victor Harold Brooke) [The Rt Hon The Viscount Alanbrooke, House of Lords, London, SW1A 0PW]; *b* 24 Nov 1932; *s* half-bro 1972; *educ* Harrow and Bristol U (BEd 1976); Capt RA

Lineage: Sir VICTOR ALEXANDER BROOKE, 3rd Bt, of Colebrooke, Co Fermanagh (*see* BROOKEBOROUGH, V) had a 5th s:

ALAN FRANCIS, **1st Viscount Alanbrooke**, of Brookeborough, Co Fermanagh, so *cr* 29 Jan 1946, as also previously 18 Sept 1945 BARON ALANBROOKE, of Brookeborough, Co Fermanagh (both UK), KG (1946), GCB (1945, KCB 1940, CB 1937), OM (1946), GCVO (1953), DSO (1917) and Bar (1918); *b* 23 July 1883; *educ* abroad and RMA Woolwich; WW I (despatches six times) and WW II (despatches), Cmdt Sch of Artillery 1929–32, Instr IDC 1932–34, Cdr 8th Inf Bde 1934–35; Inspr RA 1935–36, Dir Mily Trg War Off 1936–37, Cdr Mobile Div 1937–38, C-in-C AA Cmd (TA) 1938–39, GOC-in-C Southern Cmd 1939, cmdg 2nd Army Corps 1939–40, GOC-in-C BEF 1940, C-in-C Home Forces 1940041, Gen 1940 and FM 1944, CIGS 1941–46, ADC-Gen to HM GEORGE VI 1942–46; Col Cmdt RA 1939, RHA 1940, Glider Pilot Regt 1944 and HAC 1946–54, Master Gunner St James's Park 1946–56, Constable Tower London 1950–55; Ld Lt Co London 1950–56, Ld High Constable Coronation 1953, Pres London ZS 1950–54, Govt dir Anglo-Iranian Oil 1950–55, dir: Midland Bank 1947, Nat Discount Co 1948, Hudson's Bay Co 1948–58, Triplex Safety Glass 1954–56, chm Belfast Banking 1947, Freeman Belfast 1945 and City London 1946, Boyne Medal NI 1960, Grand Cross: Legn Honour, Netherlands Lion, Dannebrog, N Star Sweden, Grand Order Polonia Restituta 1st Cl, 1st Cl Suvarov USSR, Grand Cordon Leopold with palm Belgium, 1st Cl White Lion Czechoslovakia, 1st Cl Redeemer Greece, 1st Cl Trinity Ethiopia, Croix de Guerre, Belgian Croix de Guerre, Czechoslovak Croix de Guerre, American DSM, Hon DCL Oxon and Cantab, Hon LLD Queen's U Belfast 1945, Hon LLD: Bristol 1950, London 1951, Edinburgh 1953, Leicester 1957, Chllr Queen's U Belfast 1949; *m* 1st 28 July 1914 Jane Mary (*d* 24 April 1925), dau of Col John Mervyn Ashdall Carleton Richardson, of Rossfad, Co Fermanagh, and had issue:

1 THOMAS BROOKE, **2nd Viscount Alanbrooke**; *b* 9 Jan 1920; *educ* Wellington; RA WW II; writer, farm labourer, liner steward, water colour artist; *d* unm 19 Dec 1972

1 *Rosemary [The Hon Mrs Macdonald, Bottom Farm, Berkhamsted, Herts]; *b* 25 Oct 1918; *m* 13 July 1945 *Capt Macdonald, RA, s of Robert Macdonald, of Liverpool, and has issue:

(1) *Alastair Alan Graham; *b* 4 April 1947; *educ* T/S *Mercury*
(2) *Ian Ronald; *b* 11 Sept 1952; *educ* Ashlyn's Sch
(1) *Janey Rosemary; *b* 27 Nov 1949

The **1st Viscount** *m* 2nd 7 Dec 1929 Benita Blanche (*k* car crash 4 May 1968), est dau of Sir Harold Pelly, 4th Bt (*qv*), and widow of Sir Thomas Lees, 2nd Bt (*qv*), and *d* 17 June 1963, having by her had further issue:

2 ALAN VICTOR HAROLD BROOKE, **3rd and present Viscount Alanbrooke**

2 Kathleen Benita; *b* 23 Jan 1931; *m* 8 Aug 1953 *Lt-Cdr Robert Oliver Vesey Stoney, RN [Lt-Cdr Robert Stoney RN, Rosturk Castle, Westport, Co Mayo, Ireland], est s of Robert Vesey Stoney, RNVR, and *d* following a riding accident 20 Nov 1961, leaving issue

ALBEMARLE

Arms: Gu. three escallops arg. **Crest:** Out of a ducal coronet or a swan's head and neck arg. **Supporters:** Two lions ducally crowned or. **Motto:** *Ne cede malis* ('Do not give in to evil'). **Creations:** E. V. and B. (E) 10 Feb 1696/7.

THE 10TH EARL OF ALBEMARLE, Viscount Bury, Co. Lancaster, and **Baron Ashford**, of Ashford, Kent (Rufus Arnold Alexis Keppel) [The Rt Hon The Earl of Albemarle,Hurst Barns Farm, East Chiltington, E Sussex BN7 3QU]; *b* 16 July 1965, *s* gf 1965; *educ* St Christopher Sch Letchworth, Herts, and Centl Sch of Art (BA)

Previous creations under the name Albemarle: The names Aubemarle, Aumale and Aumarle, as well as the more familiar and modern Albemarle, are of the same origin. Aumale is a Norman town after which a county, or area under a count, was named. The first person known to have held a countly title associated with Aumale is in fact a woman, WILLIAM I THE CONQUEROR's sister Adelaide or Adelize.

Subsequent creations under the same designation were to Edward Earl of Rutland (see RUTLAND, D), who was promoted Duke of Aumale in 1397, and HENRY IV's second son Thomas, who was made Earl of Aumale in 1412. A few years later two of the Beauchamp Earls of Warwick (*qv*) enjoyed the title Count of Aumale.

The first peerage creation involving the modern version was to George Monck (*see* MONCK, V), who in 1660 was made Duke of Albemarle for his part in bringing about the Restoration. Monck descended from the Earl of Warwick granted the countship of Aumale in 1419. His dukedom became extinct with the death of his son in 1688.

JAMES II created one of his bastard sons Duke of Albemarle in 1696, after his deposition, but the title expired with its holder in 1702. The titular James III ('The Old Pretender') created George Granville Duke of Albemarle in 1721, but on the latter's nephew's death this title too, inasmuch as it had any validity, became extinct. Both the latter creations must be regarded as titular in that they were not by reigning sovereigns.

Lineage: The KEPPELS originate in the Dutch province of Guelderland.

WALTER van KEPPEL, Lord of Keppel, lived between 1179 and 1231; founded the monastery of Bethlehem, near Doetinchem; *m* Beatrix and had:

WALTER van KEPPEL, held the Lordship of Verwoelde; f of:

DEREK van KEPPEL, Lord of Verwoelde, living 1326; f of:

DEREK van KEPPEL, held Lordship of Verwoelde as fief under his cousin, Sweder Van Voorst, 1362; his eldest s,

WALTER van KEPPEL, Lord of Verwoelde, was ancestor of the Van Keppels, Lords of Verwoelde and the Voorst, whose representative was

ARNOLD JOOST van KEPPEL, **1st Earl of Albemarle**, so *cr* 10 Feb 1696/7, as also BARON ASHFORD, of Ashford, Co Kent, and VISCOUNT BURY, Co Lancaster (all E), KG (1700); *b* 1670 (s and heir of Osewalt van Keppel (*d* 1685) by Reinira Anna Gertruyde van Lintello tot de Mars), Ld of Voorst 1692, accompanied WILLIAM III to England 1688); *m* June 1701 Gertrude, dau and heir of Adam van der Duyn, Ld of St Gravenmoer, Holland, and *d* 30 May 1718, having had (with a dau, Sophia, *m* John Thomas, bro of Sir Edward Thomas, 3rd Bt, of Wenvoe, *qv*):

WILLIAM ANNE van KEPPEL, **2nd Earl of Albemarle**, KG (1749), KB (1725–49), PC (1751); *b* 5 June 1702 (QUEEN ANNE stood godmother in person, hence his second name); Gen Dutch armies, GB: Lt-Col 1st Foot, Col 3rd Horse Gds 1733, Brig-Gen 1739, Maj-Gen Feb 1741/2 (fought Battle of Dettingen 1743), Lt-Gen Feb 1744/5 and Col Coldstream Gds 1744–45 (fought Battles of Fontenoy 1745 and Culloden 1746), C-in-C Scotland 1746 Ld Bedchamper GEORGE II 1722–51, Govr Virginia 1737–54, Amb France 1749–54, Groom Stole 1751–54; *m* 21 Feb 1722/3 Lady Ann Lennox (*d* 20 Oct 1789), dau of 1st Duke of Richmond (*see* RICHMOND and GORDON, D), and had, with other issue:

1 GEORGE, **3rd Earl**

2 AUGUSTUS van KEPPEL, 1st and last VISCOUNT KEPPEL OF ELVEDEN, Co Suffolk (GB), so *cr* 22 April 1782 Adml, First Ld Admlty (with slight intermission) 1782–84, *b* 2 April 1725; *d* unm 3 Oct 1786, when the viscountcy expired

3 William, Lt-Gen, Gentleman of Horse to GEORGE III, C-in-C Ireland 1773, sometime MP, *b* 5 Nov 1727; *d* unm March 1782

4 Frederick (Rt Rev), DD, Bp Exeter 1762, Dean Windsor, Registrar Order Garter, *b* 19 Jan 1728, *m* 13 Sept 1758 Laura or Louisa, illegitimate dau of Sir Edward Walpole, KB (*see* WALPOLE, B), and *d* 27 Dec 1777, leaving, with other issue:

(1) Frederick, of Lexham Hall, Norfolk, *b* 12 Nov 1762; *m* 5 Aug 1796 Louisa (*d* 16 March 1832), dau of George Clive, MP, of Wormbridge, Herefs, and *d* 12 April 1830, leaving, with other issue:

1a Frederick Walpole, of Lexham Hall, *b* 23 May 1797; *m* 22 July 1848 Mary Anne (*d* 12 Jan 1880), widow of R R Wilson and dau of E Hodgkinson, and *d* 24 Dec 1858, leaving:

1b Louisa Maria Mary, *m* 6 Sept 1871 Thomas Edward Bagge (*see* BAGGE, Bt) and *dsp* 3 Feb 1882

2b Fanny Kunigunda Clive, *m* 4 Oct 1882 Charles Walpole Neville-Rolfe, of Heacham, Norfolk, and *d* 17 Jan 1891, leaving issue

2a William Arnold Walpole (Rev), of Lexham Hall, Rector Haynford, Norfolk, Registrar Diocese of Exeter, *b* 7 Oct 1804, *m* 7 Sept 1830 Frances Georgiana Sophia (*d* 7 June 1883), est dau of Robert Marsham, of Stratton Strawless, Norfolk, and *d* 26 Nov 1888, leaving:

1b Frederick Charles, Lt-Col Gren Guards, Equerry to HRH THE PRINCE OF WALES, *b* 25 Aug 1831; *d* unm 2 March 1876

2b William Henry Augustus, of Lexham Hall, Lt-Col 2nd Bde E Div RA, *b* 6 Aug 1845, *m* 10 July 1873 Hon Charlotte Elizabeth Eleanor Fraser (*m* 2nd 5 Dec 1903 Adml Sir Henry Frederick Stephenson, GCVO, KCB (*d* 16 Dec 1919); *d* 25 Feb 1923), dau of 17th Lord Saltoun (*qv*), and *d* 31 Oct 1889, having had:

1c Bertram William Arnold, Maj TFR, Staffs Yeo 1901–11, *b* 12 Jan 1876, *educ* Eton and Ch Ch Oxford; *m* 4 Oct 1898 Hon Alice Evelyn Agatha Hanbury Tracy (*d* 5 Nov 1955), dau of 4th Baron Sudeley (*qv*), and *d* 23 May 1949, leaving:

1d William Bertram Arnold Joost, MBE (1953), JP (1956) Port Loko Dist, Sierra Leone, W/Cdr RAAF 1934–56, Colonial Service, *b* 31 Aug 1909, *educ* Stowe, *m* 18 Aug 1962 *Nancy Ethel, formerly w of John Reeves and only dau of Percy Edgar Cross by Mrs Mary A Stannard

1d Marguerite Evelyn, *b* 8 Sept 1899; *d* unm 15 April 1968

2d Judith Iris, *b* 5 Nov 1900, *m* 29 April 1922 Col Robert Hanbury Brudenell-Bruce, DSO, 2nd surv s of Lord Robert Brudenell-Bruce, and had issue (*see* AILESBURY, M)

1c Frances Isabel Eleanor, *b* 20 July 1874, *m* 14 May 1902 Hon Harold Edward FitzClarence, MC, yst s of 2nd Earl of Munster (*qv*), and *d* 1 Feb 1951, leaving issue

2c Violet Eleanor, *b* 24 July 1881; *d* unm 15 Feb 1959

3b Edward George, MVO (1927), JP Norfolk, memb Gentlemen-at-Arms 1894–1928, Maj Highland LI and Manchester Regt, Lt-Col and hon Col 3rd Vol Bn Norfolk Regt, *b* 28 June 1847, *m* 1st 14 Dec 1875 Mary Cecilia Georgiana (*d* 29 July 1908), dau of Maj George King, and had:

1c Frederick George, Lt Norfolk Regt WW I, *b* 5 May 1878, *educ* Wellington, *d* unm 8 Jan 1949

2c Arnold Ramsay, Lt-Col KOYLI WW I, *b* 14 Sept 1879, *educ* Wellington, *m* 7 Nov 1922 Laura Margaret (*m* 2nd 19 April 1961 Sir Richard Arthur Pease, 2nd Bt (*qv*), of Hammersknott), dau of Hugh Martin, of Tullaghreine, Co Cork, and *d* 18 June 1930, leaving:

1d *June Cecilia; *b* 1924, *m* 1st 6 Feb 1946 Capt Edward Canning Loyd (*d* 7 Jan 1977), Coldstream Gds, est s of William Loyd (*see* BRABOURNE, B), and has:

1e *David William Arnold [David Loyd Esq, 17 Larkhall Rise, London SW4 6JB], *b* 4 Jan 1949, *educ* Eton; *m* 1985 *Mrs Anabel Laura Dorothy Stapleton, only dau of Hon Sir Charles Morrison, MP (*see* MARGADALE, B), and has:

1f *James Canning, *b* 1988

2f *Rupert Charles Percy, *b* 1990

1f *Tabitha Launa Mary, *b* 1992

1e *Caroline Evelyn [Mrs Anthony Hudson, Flat 3, Whittingstall Mansions, Whittingstall Rd, London SW6], *b* 16 Jan 1947, *m* 2 May 1968 *Anthony Havelock Hudson, er s of Sir Havelock Hudson, of The Rectory, Stanford Dingley, Berks, and Mrs Roger Houssemayne du Boulay, Anstey House, nr Buntingford, Herts

2d *Bridget Anne, *m* 5 Oct 1948 Lord Martin Fitzalan Howard, bro of 17th Duke of Norfolk (*qv*), and has issue

3d *Lavinia Mary, Governess to HRH PRINCE EDWARD 1969–71, *b* 23 June 1928; *m* 12 Oct 1971 Hon Richard Blackett Beaumont, 2nd s of 2nd Viscount Allendale (*qv*)

1c Evelyn Maud, *b* 15 April 1887; *m* 11 July 1911 4th Earl of Lichfield (*qv*) and *d* 16 April 1945, leaving issue

3b (cont.) Col Edward Keppel *m* 2nd 28 July 1933 Minna Helen Else, dau of Herman Rödel, of Vienna, and *d* 29 Nov 1934

1b Georgiana Gertrude Maria, *b* 6 Jan 1842; *d* unm 9 Dec 1900

The 2nd EARL *d* 22 Dec 1754; his est s,

GEORGE KEPPEL, **3rd Earl of Albemarle**, KG (1765), PC (1761); *b* 5 April 1724; MP Chichester 1745–64, ADC to HRH THE DUKE OF CUMBERLAND Battles of Fontenoy 1745 and Culloden 1746 (bore despatches announcing the victory to London), Maj-Gen 1756, Lt-Gen 1759, Gen 1772, Col King's Own Dragoons 1755–72, Govr Jersey 1761; *m* 20 April 1770 Anne (*d* 3 July 1824), yst dau of Sir John Miller, 4th Bt, of Chichester (*qv*), and *d* 13 Oct 1772, leaving:

WILLIAM CHARLES KEPPEL, **4th Earl of Albemarle**, GCH (1833), PC (1830); *b* 14 May 1772; Master Buckhounds 1806–07, Master Horse 1830–34 and 1835–41; *m* 1st 9 April 1792 Hon Elizabeth Southwell (*d* 14 Nov 1817), dau of 20th Lord (Baron) de Clifford (*qv*), and had issue (including a dau, Sophia, *m* 1819, as his 2nd w, Sir James Macdonald, 2nd Bt, of East Sheen; *see* BOSVILLE-MACDONALD, Bt); *m* 2nd 11 Feb 1822 Charlotte Susannah (*dsp* 13 Oct 1862), dau of Sir Henry Hunloke, 4th Bt,and *d* 30 Oct 1849; his est surv s by his 1st w:

1 AUGUSTUS FREDERICK KEPPEL, **5th Earl of Albemarle**, *b* 2 June 1794; offr 1st Foot Gds, MP Arundel 1820–26; *m* 4 May 1816 Frances (*m* 2nd 20 Aug 1860 Lt-Col Hon Peregrine Francis Cust, 4th s of 1st Baron Brownlow (*qv*); *d* 16 May 1869), dau of Charles Steer, and *dsp* 15 March 1851

2 GEORGE THOMAS, **6th Earl**

3 Henry (Sir), GCB, OM, Adml of the Fleet, DCL, Legn Honour, served Crimea, cdr destruction Chinese Fleet 1 June 1857, Groom-in-Waiting to HM QUEEN VICTORIA 1859–60, *b* 14 June 1809, *m* 1st 25 Feb 1839 Katherine Louisa (*dsp* 5 June 1859), dau of Gen Sir John Crosbie, GCH; *m* 2nd 31 Oct 1861 June Elizabeth (*d* 21 April 1895), dau of Martin John West, and *d* 17 Jan 1904, leaving:

(1) Colin Richard (Sir), GCVO, KCIE, CB, DSO, Adml, ADC to HM EDWARD VII 1907–08 and Extra Equerry 1909–10 and to HM GEORGE V 1910–12 and 1915–36, Equerry-in-Ordinary 1913–15, Extra Equerry to TM EDWARD VIII 1936 and GEORGE VI 1937 on, Serjeant-at-Arms H of C 1915–35, Extra Equerry to HRH THE late DUKE OF SAXE-COBURG-GOTHA, served Egypt and Sudan, *b* 3 Dec 1862, *m* 6 June 1889 Henrietta Mary (*d* 22 Feb 1957), Ldy-in-Waiting to HRH THE DUCHESS OF SAXE-COBURG-GOTHA, dau of Maj-Gen Richard Blundell-Hollinshead-Blundell, and *d* 6 July 1947, leaving:

1a Marie Henrietta Margaret, *b* 6 Jan 1891; *m* 24 July 1918 6th Earl of Romney (*qv*) and *dsp* 21 Jan 1976

2a Melita Agnes Mary, *b* 27 April 1892; *m* 11 Aug 1920 Maurice Robert Hely-Hutchinson, MC, Capt Irish Gds SR (*see* DONOUGHMORE, E), and had issue

(1) Maria Walpole, *b* 6 May 1865; *m* 3 Dec 1889 Adml Sir Frederick Tower Hamilton, GCVO, KCB, yr s of Capt Henry George Hamilton, RN, and *d* 20 Nov 1952, leaving issue (*see* BELHAVEN AND STENTON, L)

4 Thomas Robert (Rev), MA, Canon Norwich, Rector N Creake, *b* 17 Jan 1811; *m* 28 March 1833 Frances (*d* 31 Aug 1890), dau of Sir Thomas Barrett-Lennard, 1st Bt (*qv*), and *d* 20 April 1863, leaving:

(1) William George, of Old Buckenham Grange, Attleborough, Norfolk, JP and CC, Maj Bengal Army, *b* 5 June 1835, *m* 6 Dec 1864 Emily (*d* 12 April 1931), dau of J Houghton, of Myton, Warwicks, and *d* 17 Feb 1922

(2) Leicester Chantry, R-Adml; *b* 27 Aug 1837; *m* 27 Aug 1862 Emily (*d* 18 May 1913), dau of George Robinson, of Mauritius, and *d* 22 Sept 1917, having had a s and five daus (all *d* unm)

(3) Ellice (Rev), Rector Winfarthing, *b* 5 July 1841; *m* 27 April 1871 Alice Lydia (*m* 2nd 1887 Francis Hornor (*d* 27 March 1932); *d* 22 May 1932), 3rd dau of Rev John George Fardell, Rector Banham, Norfolk, and *d* 6 March 1883, leaving:

1a Derek Harold Ellice (Rev); Rector Tooting 1914–37, *b* 3 April 1875, *educ* Norwich GS, St John's Coll Oxford (MA, BD) and Ely Theological Coll, *m* 6 Oct 1908 Dora (*d* 16 Dec 1956), dau of Rev Arthur Herbert Knott, Vicar St Peter's, Dulwich, and *d* 20 March 1963, leaving:

1b Oswald Francis Arnold (Rev), Rector Woodsford, Dorset; *b* 4 Feb 1910, *educ* King's Coll Sch Wimbledon and King's Coll London (AKC 1934)

(4) Edward Frederick, RN, *b* 25 Nov 1843; *d* 18 March 1876

(5) George (Rev), Rector Intwood with Keswick 1904–27, *b* 19 April 1846; *m* 25 Nov 1874 Alice Le Neve (*d* 3 June 1933), 2nd dau of Rev Richard Hart, Vicar Catton, and *d* 21 Sept 1936, leaving a dau (*d* unm)

(6) Henry, Capt 3rd Bn Norfolk Regt, *b* 7 Aug 1848, *m* 9 June 1874 Alicia Menella (*d* 8 Jan 1892), yst dau of Sir Robert John Harvey, 1st Bt, of Langley Park (*see* 1931 edn), and *d* 1 June 1938, leaving, with an er dau (*d* unm):

1a Augusta Vera, *b* 13 Nov 1883, *m* 24 April 1912 Alfred Morland Jee, of Colkirk House, Norfolk, s of Alfred Stanistreet Jee, MICE, and had a s and two daus. He *d* 12 Jan 1982

(7) Thomas, *b* 1 July 1853; *m* 15 Feb 1876 his sis-inlaw Ida (*d* 2 May 1931), dau of Sir Robert Harvey, 1st Bt (*see* above), and *d* 11 July 1933, leaving, with three daus (*d* unm):

1a Thomas Robert Harvey, Maj IA, HG WW II, *b* 27 Sept 1881, *educ* Marlborough; *m* 1 Sept 1936 Judith Monica Constantia, dau of Frank Becher, of Dickleburgh Manor, Norfolk, and *dsp* 26 July 1943

(1) Augusta, *m* 16 March 1859 Charles North, of Rougham Hall, Norfolk, and *d* 17 Feb 1917, having had issue (*see* GUILFORD, E)

(2) Frances; *m* 5 March 1872 Rev Bryan O'Malley, MA, and *d* 10 Nov 1931, leaving issue. He *d* 12 Jan 1909

(3) Henrietta, *m* 3 Jan 1867 Alfred Edward Barrett, MRSCE, and *d* 14 Aug 1916, leaving issue. He *d* 1915

(4) Mary Jane, *d* unm 9 May 1905

(5) Maria, *m* 28 July 1874 Rev Henry Chichele Hart later Bampton (changed by deed poll 1916), Rector Cranwich, Norfolk, s of Rev Richard Hart, Vicar Catton, Norfolk, and *d* 17 May 1926, leaving issue. He *d* 31 Oct 1931

(6) May St Aubyn, *m* 19 Aug 1874 William Francis Chalmers Wigston, Lt 60th Rifles, only s of Adml Wigston, of Bittern Manor, Hants, and had issue

The 5th EARL's bro,

GEORGE THOMAS KEPPEL, **6th Earl of Albemarle**; *b* 13 June 1799; *educ* Westminster; 14th Foot: joined April 1815 (fought Waterloo), Maj-Gen 1858, Lt-Gen 1866, Gen 1874, MP E Norfolk 1832–35 and Lymington 1847–50, Sheriff Co Leitrim 1838, Groom-in-Waiting to HM QUEEN VICTORIA 1838–41, Equerry to HRH DUKE OF SUSSEX, author: *Memoirs of the Marquess of Rockingham* and *Fifty Years of My Life*; *m* 4 June 1831 Susan (*d* 3 Aug 1885), dau of Sir Coutts Trotter, 1st Bt, and *d* 21 Feb 1891, having had, with two er daus (*d* unm) and two yr daus (Louisa, *b* May 1836, *m* 30 Nov 1864 Capt Hon Frederick William Charteris, RN, 5th s of 8th Earl of Wemyss (*see* WEMYSS and MARCH, E), and *d* 12 March 1930, leaving issue; Augusta, *b* 26 April 1838, *m* 15 Oct 1873 Ernest Noel, 2nd s of Rev Hon Baptist Noel (*see* GAINSBOROUGH, E), and *dsp* 31 Jan 1902):

WILLIAM COUTTS KEPPEL, **7th Earl of Albemarle**, PC (1859), KCMG (1870); *b* 15 April 1832; *educ* Eton; ADC to HM QUEEN VICTORIA 1881, MP Norwich 1857–59, Wick 1860–65 and Berwick 1868–74, Lt-Col Civ Serv Rifles 1860, Lt Scots Gds 1848–53, Treasurer Household 1859–66, Under-Sec for War 1878–80 and 1885–86, called up to Ho of Lds *vp* in f's barony of Ashford 5 Sept 1876; *m* 15 Nov 1855 Sophia Mary (*d* 5 April 1917), 2nd dau of Hon Sir Allen Napier McNab, 1st Bt, PM Canada, and had:

1 ARNOLD ALLAN CECIL, **8th Earl**

2 Derek William George (Sir), GCVO, KCB, CMG, CIE, VD, Lt-Col PWO Civ Serv Rifles, Equerry: in Waiting to HRH THE DUKE OF YORK 1893–1901, in Ordinary to HRH THE PRINCE OF WALES 1901–10, in Ordinary and Dep Master Household to TM GEORGE V 1910–12 (Master Household and Extra Equerry 1912–36) and EDWARD VIII 1936, Extra Equerry to HM GEORGE VI 1937–44; Orders of: Dannebrog Denmark, Saviour Greece, Charles III Spain, White Eagle Serbia, Legn Honour, Rising Sun and Sacred Treasure Japan, Crown Belgium, Christ Portugal, Polar Star Sweden, White Lion Czechoslovakia, Crown Romania, Crown Italy, Star Ethiopia, Nile Egypt, Sardar-i-Ali Afghanistan, Al Rafidain Iraq, *b* 7 April 1863, *educ* Charterhouse, *m* 20 June 1898 Hon Bridget Louisa Harbord (*d* 24 Sept 1951), dau of 5th Baron Suffield (*qv*), and *d* 26 April 1944, having had:

(1) Victoria Mary Joan, *b* 2, *d* 14 Aug 1899 (TM KING GEORGE V and QUEEN MARY stood sponsors)

(2) Anne, *b* 2 Feb 1901 (TM KING GEORGE V and QUEEN MARY stood sponsors); *m* 1st 14 April 1931 (*annulled* 1933) Philip Mainwaring Broadmead, CMG, MC (later Sir Philip Mainwaring Broadmead, KCMG; *d* 23 May 1977), s of Col Henry Broadmead, Essex Regt; *m* 2nd 9 April 1936 Col Beresford Clayton Lockhart-Jervis, DSO, MC, s of James Thomas Jervis, and *d* 14 July 1951

(3) Victoria Winfred, *b* 29 April 1905; *d* unm 9 July 1976

3 George, MVO (1909), Lt-Col Res Offrs, Lt Gordon Highrs, Capt Norfolk RFA, WW I: Maj Roy Fus 1915–16, Col cmdg 2nd/4th Bn E Lancs Regt 1916–17 and 2nd/5th Bn Highland LI 1917–18, ADC Personal Staff 1919, *b* 14 Oct 1865, *m* 1 June 1891 Alice Frederica (*d* 11 Sept 1947), dau of Adml Sir William Edmonstone, 4th Bt (*qv*), and mistress of EDWARD VII 1898–1910, and *d* 22 Nov 1947, leaving:

(1) Violet, Cdr Italian Order Merit, Chev Legn Honour, Medaille d' argent arts, sciences, lettres, *b* 6 June 1894, *m* 16 June 1919 Maj Denys Robert Trefusis, MC, 2nd s of Hon John Schomberg Trefusis, CMG (*see* CLINTON, B) and *dsp* 1 March, 1970

(2) Sonia Rosemary, OBE (1959), DStJ, author *The Sovereign Lady*, *b* 24 May 1900, *m* 16 Nov 1920 (*divorce* 1947) Hon Roland Calvert Cubitt, Coldstream Gds, later 3rd Baron Ashcombe (*qv*), and *d* 1986, leaving issue

1 Gertrude Mary, *b* 9 Nov 1859, *d* 7 April 1860

2 Theodora, DGStJ, matron militia hospital France WW I, Medaille de la Reconnaisance Française (Ardent) (two medals); *m* 1 Feb 1887 Col Leslie Davidson, CB, RHA, JP, Gentleman Usher to HM GEORGE V, 2nd s of Patrick Davidson, and *d* 30 Oct 1945, leaving issue. He *das* 3 Aug 1915

3 Hilda Mary, VAD nurse WW I (1915 star, two medals), *b* 29 Aug 1864; *d* unm 7 Oct 1955

4 Leopoldina Olivia (Madam Keppel, a nun), *b* 14 Nov 1866; *d* 9 Aug 1948

5 Susan Mary, Grand Cordon Turkish Order Chefakat, *b* 5 May 1868, *m* 27 April 1896 Sir Walter Beaupré Townley, KCMG, Min Plen The Hague, 4th s of Charles Watson Townley, and *dsp* 26 June 1953. He *d* 5 April 1945

6 Mary Stuart, *b* 15 May 1869; *m* 16 Oct 1900 Maj-Gen Sir Harold Arthur Lewis Tagart, KCMG, CB, DSO, 15th Hus, s of Francis Tagart, JP, of Old Sneed Park, Glos, and *dsp* 21 Sept 1906. He *d* 18 March 1930

7 Florence Cecilia, *b* 24 Feb 1871, *m* 24 July 1902 12th Earl of Cork and Orrery (*qv*) and *dsp* 30 June 1963

The 7th EARL *d* 28 Aug 1894; his est s,

ARNOLD ALLAN CECIL KEPPEL, **8th Earl of Albemarle**, GCVO, CB, VD, TD, JP; *b* 1 June 1858; *educ* Eton; V-Lt Norfolk, Ld-in-Waiting to HM GEORGE V 1922–24, ADC to TM EDWARD VII and GEORGE V, Col Reserve of Offs, hon Lt-Col 1900, hon Col 5th Bn Norfolk Regt and formerly 4th Militia Bn and 2nd Vol Bn, Brig-Gen cmdg Norfolk Vol Inf Bde 1901–06, Col cmdg PWO Civ Serv Rifles 1892–1901, Lt-Col cmdg Inf Bn City Impl Vols S Africa 1900 (despatches, medal with four clasps), Lt Dorset Militia and Scots Gds, Grand Cross White Lion Czechoslovakia, Grand Cross Orange-Nassau; MP Birkenhead 1892–94, *m* 4 Jan 1881 Lady Gertrude Lucia Egerton (*d* 7 June 1943), only child of 1st and last Earl Egerton of Tatton (*see* 1956 edn), and had:

1 WALTER EGERTON GEORGE LUCIAN, **9th Earl**

2 Arnold Joost William, F/O RAF, Lt RFC, hon attaché Bucharest and Teheran, *The Times* correspondent Teheran 1912–14, special correspondent with expdn to Persian Mekran 1911, Photographic Offr 1st Wing RFC France WW I (1914–15 star, two medals), *b* 4 Aug 1884, *educ* Eton, *m* 1st 14 Feb 1921 (*divorce* 1938) Doris Lillian, dau of Oliver Carter; *m* 2nd 30 April 1938 Annie Margaret Blanche (*d* 14 Aug 1949), widow of Gerald Vyvyan Greenall, MC, and dau of Charles Oswald Purnell, of Wraysbury, Bucks; *m* 3rd 27 March 1952 Mildred, widow of F/O Allan Stanley Carter, RAF, and dau of William Stanley Rodber, and *dsp* 1 Oct 1964

3 Rupert Oswald Derek, Capt Coldstream Gds WW I (wounded, POW), *b* 27 July 1886, *educ* Eton and RMC Sandhurst, *m* 29 Jan 1919 (*annulled* 1921) Violet Mary (*d* 28 Feb 1968), only dau of Sir Humphrey de Trafford, 3rd Bt (*qv*), and *dsp* 7 May 1964

4 Albert Edward George Arnold, Lt 2nd Bn Rifle Bde WW I (despatches), *b* 12 Jan 1908 (HM EDWARD VII stood sponsor in person), *educ* Eton, *ka* 3rd Battle of Ypres 31 July 1917

1 Elizabeth Mary Gertrude, RRC 2nd Cl, VAD nurse WW I (star, two medals, despatches), *b* 4 Feb 1890, *m* 23 July 1923 Gen Sir Torquil George Matheson, 5th Bt (*qv*), and had issue

The 8th EARL *d* 12 April 1942; his est s,

WALTER EGERTON GEORGE LUCIAN KEPPEL, **9th Earl of Albemarle**, Maj Scots Gds, Lt-Col and Brev Col RA TA, WW I: Bde MG Offr 20th Inf Bde and 3rd Gds Bde (despatches) JP (1903) and V-Lt Norfolk 1940–44, KStJ, Pres Anglo-Netherlands Soc 1942065, member LCC (Centl Wandsworth) 1919, CC Norfolk 1943, CA 1957, ADC to Govrs-Gen Canada 1904–05 and India 1906 and Govr Orange River Colony; *b* 28 Feb 1882; *educ* Eton; *m* 1st 9 June 1909 Lady Judith Sydney Myee Wynn-Carrington (*d* 14 March 1928), 4th dau of 1st and last Marquess of Lincolnshire (*see* CARRINGTON, B), and had:

1 Derek William Charles, *Viscount Bury*, DL and JP Co Down, High Sheriff Co Down 1949, MFH E Down; Maj (hon Lt-Col) 13th/18th Roy Hus (QMO) WW II (seconded for flying duties RAF 1938–42, F/Lt 13 and 231 Sqdns, GSO(1) Ops (Air) HQ 21 Army Group 1944–45), *b* 18 Dec 1911, *educ* Eton, *m* 1st 10 Dec 1940 (*divorce* 1958) Lady Mairi Elizabeth Vane-Tempest-Stewart, JP, yst dau of 7th Marquess of Londonderry (*qv*), and had:

(1) *Elizabeth Mairi, *b* 3 Nov 1941, *m* 27 June 1962 (*divorce*) Alastair Michael Hyde Villiers, only s of Lt-Col Alastair Edward Hyde Villiers (*see* CLARENDON, E), and has issue; *m* 2nd 1980 (*divorce* 1988) 7th Baron Sudeley (*qv*)

(2) *Rose Deirdre Margaret [The Lady Rose Lauritzen, Palazzo da Silva, Canareggio 1468, Venice, Italy]; *b* 11 Dec 1943; *m* 3 April 1975 *Peter Lathrop Lauritzen, s of George F Lauritzen, of River Forest, Illinois, and has:

1a *Frederick Alexander Mark; *b* 14 Jan 1977

1 (cont) *Viscount Bury m* 2nd 20 March 1964 *Marina [Viscountess Bury, Hurst Barns Farm, East Chiltington, E Sussex BN7 3QU], ARIBA, AADipl, Chartered Architect, yr dau of Count Serge Orloff Davidoff and Hon Mrs Robinson (*see* HOWARD DE WALDEN, B), and *d* 8 Nov 1968, having by her had:

(1) RUFUS ARNOLD ALEXIS KEPPEL, **10th and present Earl of Albemarle**

2 Walter Arnold Crispian, DSC (1942), Lt-Cdr RN Fleet Air Arm WW II; *b* 6 Dec 1914, *educ* RNC Dartmouth, *m* 5 Nov 1941 *Aline Lucy, only dau of Brig-Gen John Harington, CB, CMG, DSO, of Chelmarsh Hall, Bridgnorth, Salop (*see* HARINGTON, Bt), and *d* 1986, leaving:

(1) +CRISPIAN WALTER JOHN [Crispian Keppel Esq, 15 Gresswell St, London SW6 6PR], *b* 29 Oct 1948; heir presumptive; *educ* Eton; *m* 1990 *Tina, er dau of Claus Ammann, of Stuttgart, and has:

1a *Christin Alexa, *b* 1991

(2) +Colin Rupert Harington [Colin Keppel Esq, Woodlands, Brockbridge Lane, Droxford, Hants SO 32 3Q2], *b* 14 Sept 1951; *educ* Eton; *m* 1981 *Frances May, dau of Cdr Francis Ommanney, DSC, RN, of Droxford, and has:

1a +Oliver George Rupert, *b* 1982

2a +William Richard Crispian, *b* 1986

1a *Isabel Frances Bridget, *b* 1984

(1) *Judith Cynthia Aline, *b* 18 Aug 1942, *m* 1st April 1964 (*divorce* 1980) Desmond Leon Corcoran, only s of Gerald Stuart Corcoran, of 31 Eaton Terrace, SW1, and has:

1a *Alexander Martin Desmond, *b* 28 Feb 1968

1a *Sibylla Monacella, *b* 27 May 1966; *m* 1992 *David J Whitmore, yr s of John Whitmore, of Hartfield, Sussex

2a *Aline Rose, *b* 1972

(1) (cont) Mrs Judith Corcoran *m* 2nd 1985 *Neil H Shand

3 Richard Edward Harry, *b* 3 Nov 1924, *educ* Stowe and Worcester Coll Oxford (BA); *d* unm 2 March 1953

1 *Cecilia Elizabeth [The Lady Cecilia McKenna, Rosteague, Portscatho, Cornwall]; *b* 12 April 1910; *m* 4 April 1934 Lt-Col David McKenna, CBE, RE, only s of Reginald McKenna, PC, and has:

(1) *Myee Miranda, MA Oxon; *b* 10 Aug 1935; *m* 19 July 1958 John Francis Hyde Villiers (*see* CLARENDON, E) and has issue

(2) *Pamela Primrose [Mrs Christopher Arnander, Old Wharf, Shillingford, Oxon], *b* 9 May 1937, *m* 7 April 1961 *Christopher James Folke Arnander, s of Per Erik Folke Arnander, 1st Sec Swedish Legn Rome, by Lady Anne Fummi, 2nd dau of 27th Earl of Crawford and Balcarres (*qv*), and has:

1a *Conrad David Folke, *b* 27 May 1963

2a *Michael Theodore Per, *b* 8 Dec 1964

3a *Magnus; *b* 10 March 1970

1a *Katharine Louise, *b* 16 May 1967

(3) *Sophia Mary [Mrs Sophia Wilson, Plas y Darren Ystradfellte, Powys]; *b* 11 June 1944, *m* 3 July 1965 (*divorce* 1971) John Boyd Wilson, yst s of Rev Percy Edward Wilson

2 *Cynthia Rosalie, *b* 25 June 1918, *m* 8 Dec 1944 Prof Sir Michael Moissey Postan (*d* 12 Dec 1981), Fell Peterhouse, Camb, s of Efim Postan, of Tighina, Bessarabia, and has:

(1) *Basil David, *b* 9 June 1946, *educ* Westminster, Strasbourg U and Corpus Christi Coll Oxford (BA 1967), *m* 29 June 1968 *Maria, est dau of Samuel Carr, of Paultons Square, SW3

(2) *Alexander Henry Keppel, *b* 25 Aug 1948; *educ* Westminster; *m* 1991 *Jane, er dau of Dr J Dillon, of Dublin

The **9th Earl** *m* 2nd 24 Feb 1931 *Diana Cicely, DBE (1956) [The Rt Hon The Countess of Albemarle DBE, Seymours, Melton, Woodbridge, Suffolk], hon DCL Oxon 1960, hon DLitt Reading 1959, hon LLD Lond 1960, Chm Albemarle Report on Youth and Devpt Commn 1948, V-Chm Br Cncl, memb Arts Cncl, life Tstee UK Carnegie Tst, only child of Maj John Archibald Grove, and *d* 14 July 1979, leaving further issue:

3 *Anne-Louise Mary, *b* 17 March 1932; *m* 25 Sept 1954 *Maj Sir Hew Fleetwood Hamilton-Dalrymple, 10th Bt (*qv*), and has issue

ALBU

Arms: Per chevron raguly or and vert, in dexter chief an acorn, in sinister chief a flower of a sugar bush, both slipped and leaved, and in base a bear sejant, all proper. **Crest:** The battlements of a tower or, issuant therefrom a demi-bear proper, holding in the dexter paw a flower of the sugar bush as in the arms. **Motto:** *Omnia bene evenient* ('May all turn out well'). **Creation:** Bt. (UK) 12 Feb 1912.

SIR GEORGE ALBU, 3RD BT, of Johannesburg, Transvaal, S Africa [Sir George Albu Bt, Glen Hamish Farm, PO Box 62, Richmond, Natal 3780, South Africa]; *b* 5 June 1944; *s f* 1963; *educ* Michaelhouse Natal, Cedara Ag Coll S Africa and London Tutorial Coll; late S African Light Horse Regt; *m* 23 April 1969 *(Joan) Valerie, dau of Malcom Millar, and has issue:

1 *Camilla Jane; *b* Durban 2 Aug 1972; *m* 4 May 1996 *Gary Neilsen, s of Denis Neilsen, of Ipswich, Qld

2 *Victoria Mary; *b* Durban 14 Jan 1976

Lineage: SIMON ALBU, of Berlin; *b* 26 Feb 1830; *m* 14 Dec 1856 Fanny Sternberg (*d* 24 Oct 1912) and *d* 26 Feb 1911, having had issue:

1 GEORGE (Sir), **1st Bt**

2 Felix; *b* 23 May 1859; *m* 18 July 1888 Evelina (*d* 13 March 1922), dau of Solomon Albu, and *d* 27 July 1895, leaving issue:

(1) Vivian Claud; *b* 24 July 1889; *educ* Charterhouse; RA WW I; *m* 25 Sept 1920 Dorothy Allison Alicia, er dau of Capt John Arden Bott, and *d* 23 Dec 1968, leaving issue:

1a *(Felix) Peter (Guy); *b* 14 July 1921; *educ* Cranleigh and Trin Coll Cambridge (MA); *m* 3 March 1951 *Valerie Patricia, er dau of Eric H Mayer, of St John's Wood, and has issue:

1b *Simon Timothy Arden; *b* 5 April 1952; *educ* King's Sch Ely

2b *Toby Guy; *b* 4 March 1955; *educ* Haileybury and ISC

1b *Sarah Josephine; *b* 9 Jan 1960

2a *Anthony Leopold; *b* 7 Aug 1927; *educ* Cambridge (BA Econ 1950); *m* 3 July 1954 *Barbara June (MA McGill), only dau of Harry E Wallace of London, Ontario, and has issue:

1b *Michael Andrew; *b* 15 Sept 1962

1b *Jennifer Lea; *b* 2 Sept 1960

1a *Evelyn Mary [Mrs Iain Robertson, Forfeits, Lymore Lane, Keyhaven, nr Lymington, Hants]; *b* 30 Dec 1923; *m* 1st 28 July 1944 Lt-Cdr Iain Ogilvie Robertson, RNVR, BSc (Edinburgh, Forestry) (*d* 6 April 1958), s of John James Robertson, and has issue:

1b *Iain Niall Ogilvie [Iain Robertson Esq, Field Grove, Durweston, nr Blandford, Dorset]; *b* 12 Aug 1947; *educ* Canford and RAC Cirencester (Dip Ag)

2b *James Patrick Oglivie; *b* 3 Nov 1954; *educ* Kingham Hill Sch Oxford

1b *Nicolette Ann Ogilvie; *b* 13 June 1945; *m* 14 Dec 1966 *Peter Knabe, s of Dr Kurt Knabe, of Hamburg, and has issue:

1c *Denise; *b* 14 Dec 1968

(2) Cecil Arthur; *b* 28 July 1890; *educ* Repton; RE WW I; *m* 9 Dec 1926 Blanche Hilda, only dau of Louis Lewis, of 61 Finchley Rd, London NW8

(1) Ethel; *b* 14 Feb 1892; *m* 11 March 1918 Campbell Walter Giffard, 4th Hus and MGC (*d* 30 Dec 1960), 2nd s of George Campbell Giffard, and *d* 23 Dec 1941, leaving issue

3 Leopold; *b* 10 March 1861; *m* 19 Aug 1901 Adelaide Veronica Elizabeth (*d* 14 Oct 1949), dau of Edgar Henry Burton, and *d* 19 March 1938, leaving issue:

(1) Veronica Evelyn; *b* 14 Oct 1902; *m* 1st 18 Jan 1927 (*divorce* 1935) Stanley Herbert Scott, yst s of Herbert Scott; *m* 2nd 25 Oct 1935 (*divorce* 1946) Antoni, s of Maziez Jurkiewicz, and had issue:

1a *Ann Veronica; *b* 27 June 1939

(1) (cont.) Mrs Veronica Evelyn Jurkiewicz *m* 3rd 23 May 1946 Count Ludomir Cienski, s of Count Tadeusz Cienski, and *d* 27 May 1970

4 Eugen; *b* 5 April 1871; *m* 11 May 1901 Jenny, dau of Isidore Fischer, of Eglan, W Prussia, and *d* 4 Feb 1935, leaving issue:

(1) Dorothea Lilli; *b* 15 June 1903; *m* 6 May 1933 Armando Vincenzo, Baron Lanni della Quara, San Marino Envoy Extrdy and Min Plen Republic, s of Baron Vincenzo Aniceto Lanni della Quara, and had issue(2) Susanne Ruth; *b* 4 April 1908; *m* 1st (*divorce*) — Schnitzler; *m* 2nd (*divorce*) — Arie; *m* 3rd 1945 — Morgenroth

1 Regina; *b* 27 Nov 1865; *m* 18 March 1894 Jacob Freudenthal (*d* April 1934), of 52 Eton Ave, Hampstead, and *d* 22 May 1950

2 Eveline; *b* 29 March 1869; *m* 23 Dec 1900 Professor Dr Theodore Flatau, of Berlin, and *d* 1935

SIMON ALBU's est son,

Sir George Albu, 1st Bt (UK), so *cr* 12 Feb 1912; *b* Berlin 36 Oct 1857; naturalised Transvaal 1887 and UK 1911; chm and md Gen Mining and Fin Corp Johannesburg, Danish Consul Denmark Johannesburg 1913, Order Dannebrog; *m* 9 Dec 1888 Gertrude Frederike Alice (*d* 18 April 1950), dau of Max Rosendorff, and had issue:

1 Walter George; *b* 23 July 1892; Lt Roy Irish Fus (SR) and Capt RAF WW I (Order Stanislaus Russia and Croix de Guerre with Palms); *d* 29 May 1920

2 GEORGE WERNER (Sir), **2nd Bt**

1 Charlotte Frederike; *m* 5 Sept 1933 Rt Rev Wilfrid Parker (*d* 22 June 1966), Bp Pretoria, s of Hon Cecil Thomas Parker (*see* MACCLESFIELD, E), and *dsp* 28 Nov 1965

2 Katherine Victoria; *m* 1913 Erroll Gordon Hay (*d* 2 Nov 1964) and had issue

3 Alice Ernestine; *m* 4 Sept 1924 Capt Nigel James Bengough, DL, and had:

(1) *Piers (Sir), KCVO (1986), OBE (1973), DL (Hereford and Worcester 1987) [Col Sir Piers Bengough KCVO OBE DL, Great House, Canon Pyon, Herefs HR4 8PD]; *b* 24 May 1929; *educ* Eton; 10th Roy Hus (PWO): cmmd 1948, cmded 1971–73, Hon Col 1983–90, memb: Jockey Club 1965– (Steward 1974–77, 1990–92), Horserace Betting Levy Bd 1978–81, Gentlemen-at-Arms 1981–, dir Cheltenham Steeplechase Co 1977–90, Hereford Racecourse 1974–, Ludlow Race Club 1979–, HM's Rep Ascot 1982–97; *m* 1952 *Bridget Shirley Adams and has:

1a *Andrew; *b* 1954

2a *Jonathan; *b* 1955

4 Irene Elsie; *b* 9 June 1900; *m* 7 Sept 1923 William Dalrymple, est s of Sir William Dalrymple, of Johannesburg, and *d* 24 June 1924

Sir GEORGE *d* 27 Dec 1935; his only surv son,

Sir George Werner Albu, 2nd Bt; *b* 3 Sept 1905; *educ* Rugby; Maj S African Forces WW II (despatches); chm Gen Mining and Fin Corp; *m* 1st 20 Oct 1928 Kathleen Betty (*d* 19 Feb 1956), dau of Edward Charles Dicey, of Parktown, Johannesburg, and had issue:

1 Sir GEORGE ALBU, **3rd and present Bt**

1 Georgina; *b* 9 Feb 1930; *m* 8 Feb 1951 Allan Goodman, twin s of J L Goodman, of Johannesburg, and had issue:

(1) *James Martin; *b* 18 March 1952

(2) *Charles Anthony; *b* 3 Dec 1953

(3) *John; *b* 1963

(1) *Philippa Mary; *b* 20 Aug 1955

(2) *Victoria

(3) *Mary Anne; *b* 21 July 1957

2 *Susan Nomakepu [The Hon Mrs David Stapleton-Cotton, The Old Buffers, Station Rd, Darling, Cape, S Africa]; *b* 8 June 1932; *m* 9 Feb 1955 *Hon David Peter Dudley Stapleton-Cotton, yr s of 4th Viscount Combermere (*qv*), and has issue

3 *Julia Mary [Mrs Julia Albu, PO Box 67250, Bryanston, S Africa]; *b* 13 June 1937; *m* 7 Feb 1957 (*divorce* 1978) Hon Michael John Harbottle Grimston, yst s of 1st Baron Grimston of Westbury (*qv*), and has issue

4 *Caroline [Mrs Philip Lorentz, 21 Ridge Rd, La Lucia, Durban 4051, S Africa]; *b* 10 June 1943; *m* 1969 *Philip G L Lorentz, and has issue:

(1) *William George; *b* 1971

(2) *Charles Gordon; *b* 1975

(1) *Marie Louise Caroline Rosie; *b* 1978

Sir George *m* 2nd 1956 Mrs Elsie Violet Taylor and *d* 18 Feb 1963

ALDENHAM and HUNSDON OF HUNSDON

Arms: Argent, three battleaxes erect within a bordure nebuly sable. **Crest:** In front of a rock a dexter arm embowed in armour, the hand gauntleted proper, bearing a battleaxe in bend sinister sable. **Supporters:** On either side a man habited in buff leather jerkin, gloves and boots, armed with a three-barred helmet, long gorget and sword, all proper, and holding in the exterior hand a battleaxe over the shoulder sable. **Motto:** *Tenax propositi* ('Tenacious of purpose'). **Creations:** B. (UK) 31 Jan 1896 (Aldenham) and 24 July 1923 (Hunsdon of Hunsdon).

THE 6TH BARON ALDENHAM, of Aldenham House, Herts, and **4TH BARON HUNSDON OF HUNSDON**, of Briggens, Co Hertford (Vicary Tyser Gibbs) [The Rt Hon The Lord Aldenham and Hunsdon, Aldenham Wood Lodge, Elstree, Herts]; *b* 9 June 1948; *educ* Eton, Oriel Coll Oxford and RAC Cirencester; Liveryman Merchant Taylors' Co; dir Montclare Shipping Co Ltd 1986–; *m* 1980 *Josephine Nicola, er dau of John Richmond Fell, of Lower Bourne, Farnham, Surrey, and has issue:

1 +HUMPHREY WILLIAM FELL; *b* 31 Jan 1989
2 +Thomas Antony John; *b* 1992
1 *Jessica Juliet Mary; *b* 1984

Barony of Hunsdon of Hunsdon: Henry Carey, first cousin through his mother (sister of ANNE BOLEYN) of ELIZABETH I, was created by her Baron Hunsdon of Hunsdon in Jan 1558/9 shortly after her accession. He had been MP for Buckingham in EDWARD VI's and MARY's reigns and was made a Privy Counsellor and Knight of the Garter a little later in ELIZABETH's. His mother had been HENRY VIII's mistress before the King fell in love with ANNE BOLEYN, indeed at the time Henry Carey was conceived. Accordingly it has been suggested that he was really HENRY VIII's son. If one assumes that Henry Carey's actual father was his official one, there is a connection with the Carys Viscounts Falkland (*qv*) through Henry's uncle Sir John Cary, grandfather of the 1st Viscount.

Lord Hunsdon of Hunsdon's son, the 2nd Baron, married a Spencer of Althorp, hence a connection of Diana Princess of Wales although unlike the Princess this Spencer lady was something of a blue-stocking, but he died without surviving male issue. His daughter, however, married into the Berkeley family (*see* BERKELEY, B).

In March 1627/8 the 4th Lord Hunsdon of Hunsdon was created Earl of Dover, having been promoted to a viscountcy (that of Rochford) nearly seven years earlier. Both the newer titles expired on the death of the 1st Earl's son in 1677, however. (His second wife was a Cokayne, hence the choice of title by the first Baron of the present creation, Herbert Gibbs, whose mother was a Cokayne, when ennobled in 1923.) The Barony of Hunsdon of Hunsdon seems to have continued till 1765, for its extinction at that date is presumptive rather than absolutely certain

Lineage: A family called Gibbs held a property called Venton or Fenton, Darlington, Devon, from RICHARD II's reign to 1570. They are thought to be the ancestors of the family of the same name of Clyst St George, Devon, early in the reign of HENRY VIII.

JOHN GIBBS, of Clyst St George; bought 1 May 1560 from Thomas, Lord Wentworth, a small estate called Pytt, which descended to ancestors of the Barons Aldenham and was bought back into the family 1859 (*see* WRAXALL, B).

GEORGE GYBBES, of Clyst St George; *m* Welthean (Gwenllian) — and had:

JOHN GIBBE, of Pytt; *d* July 1652, leaving an est s:

GEORGE GIBBS, of Clyst St George; *bapt* 3 Nov 1604; *m* Alice — and had, with four daus, three er s and a yst s:

ABRAHAM GIBBS, of Topsham, Devon; *bapt* 18 Aug 1649; *m* Tryphaena (*d* 1733), dau of William Rowe, of Shobroke, Devon, and *d* 1718, having had:

ABRAHAM GIBBS, of Topsham; *b* Feb 1687; *m* 1st Mary 2nd dau of Nehemiah Monke, of Topsham, and had issue; *m* 2nd Sarah Ewings, widow, 2nd dau and coheir of Robert Lyle, of Topsham, by Mary, dau of Nicholas Downe, and by her had an only s (whose issue is now extinct) and *d* Sept 1726, leaving by his 1st w:

GEORGE ABRAHAM GIBBS, of Exeter; surgn; *b* 1718; *s* his great-uncle George Gibbs (*d* 1723) at Pytt; *m* 1747 Anne, dau and coheir of Anthony Vicary, of Exeter, by Elizabeth, dau of Nicholas Munckley, of Exeter, and had, with four er s and six daus:

ANTONY GIBBS, London merchant; *b* 3 March 1756; *m* 3 Oct 1784 Dorothea Barnetta (*d* 24 Feb 1820), 2nd dau of William Hucks, of Knaresborough, and heir in her issue of her cousins Sarah and Anne Noyes, nieces and coheirs of Robert Hucks, of Aldenham, Herts, and Clifton Hampden, Oxon, and *d* 10 Dec 1815, having had, with other issue:

1 GEORGE HENRY, for whom see below

2 William, of Tyntesfield and Charlton, Wraxall, Somerset, and Pytt, London merchant; *b* 1790; *m* 1 Aug 1839 Matilda Blanche (*d* 22 Sept 1887), 3rd dau of Sir Thomas Crawley Boevey, 3rd Bt (*qv*), and *d* 3 April 1875, leaving issue:

(1) Antony, of Tyntesfield and Charlton, Somerset, and Pytt, JP and DL (Somerset); *b* 10 Dec 1841; *educ* Exeter Coll Oxford (MA); Maj N Somerset Yeo Cav, High Sheriff Somerset 1888; *m* 22 June 1872 Janet Louisa (*d* 10 Dec 1909), dau of John Louis Merivale, sr registrar Court of Chancery, and *d* 24 April 1907, having had issue:

1a GEORGE ABRAHAM GIBBS, 1st BARON WRAXALL (*qv*)

2a (Antony) Hubert, TD, JP (Devon); *b* 18 Sept 1874; *educ* Eton and Trin Hall Cambridge (MA); Maj N Somerset Yeo WW I; *m* 18 Oct 1899 (Mary) Mercy (*d* 16 Jan 1956), er dau of Col Evan Henry Llewellyn, MP N Somerset, of Langford Court, Somerset, and *d* 28 July 1957, having had issue:

1b Evan Llewellyn; *b* 17 May 1906; *educ* Eton and RMC Sandhurst; Capt Reserve of Offrs Coldstream Gds WW II, memb London Stock Exchange; *m* 28 April 1930 Monica Elizabeth (*m* 2nd 24 Oct 1957 Lt-Col Walter Pearce-Serocold, DSO, TD (*see* PRICHARD-JONES, Bt), yr s of Col Oswald Pearce-Serocold, CMG, DL, JP, of Taplow Hill Bucks, and *d* 8 July 1973), yr dau of Sir Edmund Charles Wyldbore Smith, of 68 Cadogan Place, London SW (*see* SMITH-MARRIOTT, Bt), and was *ka* nr Dunkirk 1 June 1940, leaving issue:

1c *Michael Edmund Hubert [Michael Gibbs Esq, 19 Caroline Place, London W2 4AN]; *b* 31 March 1932; *educ* Eton and Ch Ch Oxford (MA); *m* 31 March 1960 *Helen Antonia, only dau of Cdr Edward St John Edmonstone, RN (ret), of Barcombe Old Rectory, nr Lewes, Sussex (*see* EDMONSTONE, Bt), and has issue

2c *Peter Evan Wyldbore (Sir) KCVO (1997); [Lt-Col Sir Peter Gibbs KVCO, Leigh House, Chagford, Devon TQ13 8HH]; *b* 1 Feb 1934; *educ* Eton; Lt-Col Coldstream Gds; *m* 1st 30 Jan 1957 (*divorce*) Jane Duncombe, only dau of Col Arthur Howard Eckford Howell, DSO, TD, of 5 Headford Place, London SW1, by Beryl Stuart, yr dau of Sir Frank Henry Bowater, 1st Bt (*see* BOWATER, Bt, of Friston), and has issue:

1d *Nicholas Roland Antony; *b* 18 Nov 1957
2d *Simon Evan Alexander; *b* 8 June 1962
1d *Camilla Jane Evadne; *b* 16 July 1959

2c (cont.) Sir Peter *m* 2nd 11 June 1976 *Mrs E Sally Tyser and has by her:

3d *Evan Rupert Michael; *b* 27 April 1977

1c *Evadne Jane; *b* 17 May 1938; *m* 17 Nov 1958 *Sir Howard Christian Sheldon Guinness (*see* GUINNESS, Bt) and has issue

2b *Antony [Maj Antony Gibbs, Brook Farm, Sidford, Devon EX10 9PT]; *b* 26 Oct 1909; *educ* Stowe; Maj Coldstream Gds WW II; *m* 5 Sept 1939 *June Audrey, er dau of John Reginald Chichester, of Lurley Manor, Tiverton, Devon, and has issue:

1c *(Antony) Julian [Julian Gibbs Esq, 11 Fernshaw Rd, London SW10 0BT]; *b* 4 Nov 1942; *educ* Eton; late Coldstream Gds; *m* 1st 22 May 1968 (*divorce* 1992) Mary-Anne Amy, dau of Capt Reginald Percy Phillips, of Hale, Rudgwick, Sussex; *m* 2nd 17 Dec 1997 *Hon Alexandra, former w of Nicholas Edward Hugo Meynell (*see* HALIFAX, E), and er dau of 2nd Baron Killearn (*qv*)

1c *Victoria Anne [Mrs Antony Pemberton, Trumpington Hall, Haslingfield, Cambridge]; *b* 24 Nov 1944; *m* 7 Jan 1967 *Antony Francis Pemberton, er son of Sir Francis William Wingate Pemberton, CBE, DL, of Trumpington Hall, and has:

1d *Richard Francis Antony; *b* 9 July 1970; *educ* Eton, RAC Cirencester and Wye Ag Coll; *m* 4 Oct 1997 *Helen Rachel, dau of Raymond Boileau, of Rampisham Manor, Dorset

2d *Charles Jeremy; *b* 23 June 1972; *educ* Eton, Newcastle U and RAC Cirencester

1b Elaine Blanche; *m* 16 Sept 1925 His Honour Judge (Samuel) Richard Edgedale, QC (*d* 5 April 1966), son of Samuel Edgedale, of Littleton Hall, Chester, and *d* 19–, leaving issue:

1c William Richard; *b* 28 Feb 1931; *educ* Eton; Lt-Col The Life Gds; *m* 1st 19 July 1954 (*divorce*) Mary, est dau of Guy Arthur Newman, JP (*see* NEWMAN, Bt, of Cecil Lodge), and had issue; *m* 2nd *Anne Virginia, dau of Maj G W Murray Smith, of Iverk, Piltown, Co Kilkenny, and *d* 22 July 1996

1c Elizabeth Eve; *b* 28 Aug 1926; *m* 16 Jan 1952 11th Baron Suffield (*qv*) and *d* 1995, leaving issue

2c Mercy Maud; *b* 4 Nov 1928; *d* 2 Feb 1995

2b Elizabeth Mercy; *d* 17 Feb 1997

3b *Pamela Mary; *m* 10 March 1944 *Maj Charles Henry Liddell, MC, JP, Rifle Bde, (*see* RAVENSWORTH, B) and has issue

3a William, CVO; *b* 20 Nov 1877; *educ* Eton and Magdalen Coll Oxford (MA); Lt-Col 7th Hussars, S Africa 1901–02 (medal with five clasps) and WW I, Croix de Guerre, Exon Yeomen of the Guard 1926; *m* 22 July 1911 Ruby Mabel, yst dau of Henry Arthur Brassey, MP, of Preston Hall, Kent (*see* BRASSEY OF APETHORPE, B), and *d* 25 Jan 1963, having had issue:

1b Diana Anstice Williamina; *m* 15 June 1940 Maj Sir Charles Edward Mott-Radclyffe, MP, Rifle Bde, only s of Lt-Col Charles Edward Radclyffe, DSO, Rifle Bde, of Little Park, Wickham, Hants, and *d* 27 June 1955, leaving three daus

2b *Marigold Ruby

4a John Evelyn, MC; *b* 22 Dec 1879; *educ* Eton and RMC Sandhurst; Col Coldstream Gds, S Africa 1901–2 (medal with three clasps) and WW I; *m* 2 Sept 1919 Lady Helena Frances Augusta Cambridge (*d* 22 Dec 1969), yr dau of 1st Marquess of Cambridge (*see* 1970 edn), and *d* 11 Oct 1932

5a Louis Merivale; *b* 24 April 1883; *d* 1 May 1884

6a Eustace Lyle; *b* 10 March 1885; *educ* Eton; Capt North Somerset Yeo; merchant; *d* 13 Feb 1915 of wounds received in action

7a Lancelot Merivale, CVO, DSO, MC and bar; *b* 23 Dec 1889; *educ* Eton; Brig Coldstream Gds WW I and WW II; memb Gentlemen-at-Arms 1939–59; *m* 1st 10 July 1929 Hon Marjory Florence Maxwell (*d* 5 May 1939), er dau of 11th Baron Farnham (*qv*), and had issue:

1b *David Evelyn [David Gibbs Esq, Martin House, Swallowcliffe, Wilts SP3 5PF]; *b* 22 March 1931; *educ* Eton; late Coldstream Gds; memb London Stock Exchange; *m* 6 June 1959 *Phyllida Lovaine, yr dau of Lt-Col Piers Standish Plowden (*see* PLOWDEN, B) and has issue:

1c *Giles Evelyn Somerset; *b* 6 Nov 1962

2c *Crispin Lancelot; *b* 14 Dec 1966

1c *Quenelda Marjory; *b* 1 July 1960

7a (cont.) Brig Lancelot Gibbs *m* 2nd 25 Feb 1942 (*annulled* 1945) Diana Primrose, yst dau of Percy Quilter (*see* QUILTER, Bt), and *d* 8 Dec 1966

1a Albinia Rose, of Thornbury Park, Glos; *b* 31 March 1876; *m* 2 Dec 1899 Richard Alexander Bennett (*d* 16 July 1951), er son of Rev Alexander Sykes Bennett, MA, Vicar of St Stephen's, Bournemouth, and *d* 3 Oct 1941, leaving issue

2a Anstice Katharine; *b* 12 Sept 1881; *m* 16 June 1903 Rev Arthur Stafford Crawley, MC and Bar, MA (*d* 8 Oct 1948), Canon of Windsor, Chaplain to HM GEORGE VI, 6th son of George Baden Crawley, and *d* 8 Jan 1963, leaving issue

3a Janet Blanche; *b* 15 April 1887; *m* 23 Feb 1915 her cousin Col William Otter Gibbs (*see* below) and *d* 4 June 1974, leaving issue

(2) William; *b* 14 Jan 1846; *d* unm 11 June 1869

(3) George Abraham; *b* 25 March 1848; *d* unm 23 Feb 1870

(4) Henry Martin, of Barrow Court, Barrow Gurney, Somerset, JP (Somerset); *b* 30 May 1850; Lord of the Manor of Barrow Gurney; High Sheriff Somerset 1897; *m* 22 June 1882 Emily Anna (*d* 5 July 1928), 5th dau of Ven William Bruere Otter, Archdeacon of Lewes, and *d* 22 April 1928, having had issue:

1a William Otter, JP (Somerset 1924–46), DL (Somerset); *b* 13 Sept 1883; *educ* Eton and RMC Sandhurst; Hon Col 5th Bn Somerset LI (TA), Maj 10th Hus WW I (despatches), ADC to HM GEORGE VI 1938, High Sheriff Somerset 1936; *m* 23 Feb 1915 his cousin Janet Blanche (*d* 4 June 1974), dau of Antony Gibbs, DL, of Tyntesfield (*see* above), and *d* 22 March 1960, leaving issue:

1b Martin Antony, JP (Wilts 1966); *b* 12 March 1916; *educ* Eton and RMC Sandhurst; Maj Coldstream Gds (ret 1952), WW II; High Sheriff Wilts 1974; *m* 17 Jan 1947 *Elsie Margaret Mary [Mrs Martin Gibbs, Sheldon Manor, Chippenham, Wilts], er dau of Sir Hew Hamilton-Dalrymple, 19th Bt (*qv*), and *d* 1995, leaving issue:

1c *Antony William Hew [Antony Gibbs Esq, The Home Farm, Barrow Gurney, Bristol]; *b* 6 Nov 1947; *educ* Eton and Worcs Coll Oxford; *m* 1974 *Lady Virginia Rous, dau of 5th Earl of Stradbroke (*qv*), and has issue:

1d *Abram; *b* 17 Sept 1976

2d *William Martin; *b* 1986

1d *Mary; *b* 24 Sept 1975

2d *Emily-Anna; *b* 30 May 1978

3d *Elizabeth Rose; *b* 6 Oct 1979

4d *Margaret Blanche; *b* 1988

1c *Mary Blanche; *b* 16 Jan 1949; *educ* London U (BA); *m* 4 July 1971 *Rupert Leander Ridge, The Light Infantry, yr son of Maj Robert Vaughan Ridge, The Manor Farm, Brockley, Somerset, and has issue:

1d *Thomas Leander; *b* 1972

2d *Edward Francis; *b* 1976

1d *Marian Sophia; *b* 1973

2d *Adeline Dyce Albinia Rose; *b* 1979

2c *(Anstice) Bridget; *b* 25 Sept 1951; *m* 19 Aug 1978 *Anthony Richard (Tonino) Howard, yr son of Hon Edmund Howard, and has issue (*see* HOWARD OF PENRITH, B)

3c *Cecily Ann Albinia (Lal); *b* 11 Oct 1952; *m* 24 Aug 1975 Robert Ian Mayson Mathers (*k* in a traffic accident 1992), yr son of Mayson Alexander Mathers, of Coopers Cross, Curry Rivel, Somerset, and has issue:

1d *John Alexander Joseph; *b* 1978

2d *Simon Martin; *b* 1984

3d *Ralph Michael; *b* 1987

1d *Alice Mary Albinia; *b* 22 May 1976

2d *Imogen Blanche; *b* 1982

4c *Katharine Rose; *b* 9 March 1955

5c *Julia Margaret; *b* 9 March 1957; *m* 1986 *Julian Alexander Stanley, of 5 The Park, London NW11, and has issue:

1d *Isaac Martin; *b* 1990

1d *Madeline Leah; *b* 1988

2d *Elinor Katherine Eve; *b* 1992

2a Noel Martin; *b* 25 Dec 1884; *educ* Eton; *ka* at Kahe, German E Africa, 20 March 1916

3a Francis Antony Woodard, MC (Rev); *b* 17 Dec 1885; *educ* Eton; T/CF during WW I; Rector of Walkern, Herts, 1922–36, Vicar of Fairford, Glos, 1936–; *m* 5 June 1923 Agnes Mary Denise, dau of Rev Mark Ernest Ruddock, and *d* 3 Aug 1946, leaving issue:

1b *Henry Francis [Maj Henry Gibbs, Fieldways, Bagshot Rd, West End, Cobham, Surrey]; *b* 23 June 1928; *educ* Eton and RMA Sandhurst; Maj Coldstream Gds; *m* 29 March 1957 *Patience Janet, yr dau of Alexander John Buckley Rutherford, CBE, of Assendon Lodge, Henley-on-Thames, and has issue:

1c *Nicholas Francis; *b* 14 Sept 1962

1c *Claire Matilda; *b* 15 April 1958

2c *Belinda Mary; *b* 6 Nov 1959

1b *Emily Matilda Jeanne [Mrs Van Duren Burton, Long Bars, St George's Hill, Weybridge, Surrey]; *b* 13 Dec 1924; *m* 7 Feb 1953 *Capt Van Duren Burton, 12th Roy Lancers, est son of Van Duren Burton, and Mrs F T Segerman, and has issue:

1c *Robert Antony; *b* 4 Sept 1958

1c *Philippa Denise; *b* 18 Sept 1953

2c *Henrietta Susan; *b* 5 Oct 1955

2b *Anne Denise Perpetua; *b* 7 March 1926; *m* 7 Oct 1950 *Ian Norman Mitchell, of Trull, Tetbury, Glos, son of Maj Alexander Black Mitchell, of Poulton Priory, Glos, and has issue:

1c *Simon Alexander Francis; *b* 31 July 1951; *educ* Harrow

2c *Michael Ian; *b* 10 Aug 1955; *educ* Harrow

3c *John Crispin; *b* 12 July 1958

1c *Janet Denise; *b* 18 Sept 1953

3b Caroline Mary Blanche; *b* 8 Aug 1932; *d* unm 27 Feb 1965

4a Roland Vicary; *b* 16 March 1887; *d* 19 July 1909

5a Guy Melvil, TD; *b* 15 Dec 1889; *educ* Eton; Maj N Somerset Yeo WW I and WW II; *m* 6 Aug 1914 Margaret Olivia (*d* 29 Sept 1964), est dau of Henry Percy St John (*see* BOLINGBROKE and ST JOHN, V), and *d* 14 March 1959, leaving issue:

1b *Martin St John Valentine, CB (1958), DSO, TD, JP, DL (Wilts 1972) [Col Martin Gibbs CB DSO TD JP DL, Ewen Manor, Cirencester, Glos]; *b* 14 Feb 1917; *educ* Eton; Hon Col Roy Wilts Yeo (TA), WW II (despatches); High Sheriff Glos 1958; *m* 5 July 1947 *Mary Margaret, er dau of Lt-Col Philip Mitford, of Berryfield, Lentran, Inverness-shire, and widow of Capt Michael Desmond Hamilton Wills, MC, Coldstream Gds (*see* DULVERTON, B), and has issue:

1c *Caroline Margaret; *b* 30 May 1949

2c *Mary Elizabeth; *b* 28 March 1951; *m* 1980 *Sir Geoffrey Newman 6th Bt, of Marnhead (*qv*) and has issue

2b *Roland Christopher (Sir), GCB (1976, KCB 1972), CBE (1968), DSO (1945), MC (1943) [Field-Marshal Sir Roland Gibbs GCB CBE DSO MC, Patney Rectory, Devizes, Wilts SN10 3QZ]; *b* 22 June 1921; *educ* Eton and RMC Sandhurst; FM 1979, Brig late 60th Rifles and The Parachute Regt, WW II in N Africa, Italy and NW Europe, cmded 16 Parachute Bde 1963–66, Chief of Staff, Middle East Cmd from 1966, CGS 1976–79, ADC-Gen to HM THE QUEEN 1976–79; Ld-Lt Wilts 1989–96, Constable HM Tower of London 1985–90, Col-Cmdt 2nd Bn RGJ 1971–78, Parachute Regt 1972–77, KStJ 1990; *m* 27 Oct 1955 *Davinia Jean, er dau of Lt-Col Eion James Henry Merry, MC, of Lucknam Park, Chippenham, Wilts, by Jean Trefusis, only dau of Hon Arthur Owen Crichton (*see* ERNE, E), and has issue:

1c *Aidan (Joe) Merry; *b* 9 Feb 1957

2c *James Roland Melvil; *b* 20 Dec 1958

1c *Melissa Margaret Jean; *b* 9 June 1966

1b *Anna Patricia; *b* 24 Oct 1915; *m* 22 June 1940 *Rupert Edward de Zoete, late 12th Royal Lancers, of 31 Gilston Rd, London SW10, yr son of Herman Walter de Zoete, of The Rookery, Sproughton, Ipswich, and has issue:

1c *Timothy Rupert; *b* 8 May 1942; *educ* Harrow; *m* 2 July 1969 *Moyra Dawnay

2b *Ursula Mary [Mrs Edward Gibb, Forge House, Taynton, nr Binford, Oxon]; *b* 20 May 1919; *m* 14 Dec 1939 Michael Edward Gibb, MA, MIStructE, MASCE (*d* as the result of a motor accident 10 Aug 1970), 3rd son of Sir Alexander Gibb, GBE, CB, of House of Gruinard, Ross-shire, and has issue:

1c *Rosemary Ursula; *b* 27 Oct 1940

2c *Diana Elizabeth; *b* 22 Feb 1945; *m* 16 Feb 1967 *Hon Trevor Garro Trefgarne, 2nd son of 1st Baron Trefgarne (*qv*)

3c *Janet Emily; *b* 11 Dec 1946

6a Ralph Crawley-Boevey; *b* 24 July 1891; *educ* Eton and Magdalen Coll Oxford; Capt N Somerset Yeo, WW I and WW II (Hon Lt-Col CMP); *m* 5 Aug 1915 Dorothy Elizabeth (*d* 9 March 1951), 3rd dau of Rev William Thomas Houldsworth, and *d* 10 Aug 1957, leaving issue:

1b *Peter Houldsworth [Peter Gibbs Esq, Combend Manor, Elkstone, Glos]; *b* 14 Nov 1921; *educ* Bryanston; Capt Scots Gds WW II; *m* 4 Dec 1946 *Audrey Hamilton, yst dau of Frederick Noel Hamilton Wills, of Miserden Pk, Stroud, and has issue (*see* DULVERTON, B)

2b *William Gilbert (Rev) [The Rev Canon William Gibbs, Guilsborough Vicarage, Northampton NN6 8PU]; *b* 7 April 1931; *educ* Haileybury and Bishop's Coll Cheshunt; served in Coldstream Gds 1950–54, ordained 1958, Curate of St Mary's, Kensington 1961–63, Priest-in-Charge, St George's, Campden Hill, London W8 1963–68, Vicar of Guilsborough with Hollowell 1968; *m* 17 June 1958 *Lady Sarah Bingham, yr dau of Col 6th Earl of Lucan (*qv*), and has issue

1b *Mary Elizabeth; *b* 5 June 1919; *m* 6 June 1946 Capt Sir Alexander Somerled Angus Bosville-Macdonald of Sleat, 16th Bt (*qv*), and has issue

2b *Jane [Miss Jane Gibbs, 21 Parliament Hill, London NW3]; *b* 11 Sept 1924

3b *Susan [Mrs Richard Carr-Gomm, Batheaston, Avon]; *b* 4 April 1927; *m* 21 Oct 1957 *Maj Richard Culling Carr-Gomm, Coldstream Gds, 3rd son of Mark Culling Carr-Gomm, late of Ockley Lodge, Keymer, Hassocks, Sussex, and has issue:

1c *David Culling; *b* 9 May 1967; *m* 4 Sept 1997 *Rosalind, dau of Robert Holness, of Middx

1c *Anna Mary; *b* 12 Aug 1958

2c *Elizabeth Dorothy; *b* 18 Nov 1959

3c *Harriet Jane; *b* 9 April 1964

3b (cont.) Maj and Mrs Richard Carr-Gomm adopted:
*Adam Richard; *b* 1 July 1966

7a Lionel Cyril; *b* 15 Feb 1893; *educ* Eton; Capt N Somerset Yeo WW I; *m* 1st 1 July 1925 (*divorce* 1932) Mary, 2nd dau of Albany Hawke Charlesworth, of Grinton, and had issue:

1b (Rothesay) Timothy; *b* 26 Jan 1927; *educ* Eton; late Coldstream Gds; *m* 10 Oct 1953 *(Ann) Caroline [Mrs Timothy Gibbs, Creaton Lodge, Creaton, Northampton], dau of Lt-Col Cecil Bury, of Creaton Lodge, Northampton, and *d* 1990, leaving:

1c *Joanna Mary; *b* 7 Aug 1954

2c *Henrietta Elizabeth; *b* 15 Dec 1956

2b Nicholas Albany; *b* 11 Jan 1929; *educ* Eton and RMA Sandhurst; with 9th Queen's Roy Lancers 1948–56 (Br Jt Servs Mission Washington, DC 1953–54), with Internat Bank for Reconstruction and Development Washington 1960; *m* 15 Jan 1962 *Hon Elizabeth Beatrice Baring, yr dau of 1st Baron Howick of Glendale (*qv*), and *d* 1984, leaving issue:

1c *Andrew Lionel John; *b* 28 March 1966

1c *Mary Camilla; *b* 2 Feb 1964

2c *Eliza Jane; *b* 6 March 1968

7a (cont.) Capt Lionel Gibbs *m* 2nd 1 Nov 1933 Elizabeth Sonia (*m* 2nd 23 Jan 1946 2nd Viscount Harcourt (*see* 1970 edn) and *d* 30 Oct 1959), 2nd dau of Sir Harold Snagge, KBE, of 13 St Leonard's Terrace, London SW3, and *d* 25 Dec 1940

1a Matilda Blanche; *b* 20 Nov 1888; *d* 14 Jan 1889

2a *Mary Albinia; *b* 5 Nov 1894; *m* 9 Aug 1923 Lt-Col Edward William Tremayne Miles, MC, Roy Dragoons (*d* 22 Sept 1943), est son of Capt Frederick Tremayne Miles, and has issue:

1b *Peter Tremayne (Sir), KCVO (1986) [Sir Peter Miles KCVO, Mill House, Southrop, Lechlade, Glos GL7 3NU]; *b* 26 June 1924; *educ* Eton and RMC Sandhurst; Capt late Roy Dragoons; dir Gerrard and Reid Ltd 1959–80; Keeper Privy Purse and Treasurer to HM THE QUEEN 1981–87, Receiver-Gen Duchy of Lancaster 1981–87, memb Prince of Wales's Cncl 1981–87; *m* 25 July 1956 *Philippa Helen, dau of Edmund Bernard Marcellin Tremlett, and has:

1c *(Edward) Napier Tremayne; *b* 1 Aug 1958

2c *Patrick William; *b* 1 June 1960

1c *Davinia Mary Evelyn; *b* 8 Jan 1964

2b *Robert William (Rev) [The Rev Robert Miles, Dalmahoy Rectory, Kirknewton, Midlothian]; *b* 18 Feb 1927; *educ* Eton and Magdalene Coll Cambridge; ordained 1952, Rector of St Mary, Dalmahoy, Warden of Provincial Youth House 1965; *m* 26 April 1966 *Heather Katharine, dau of Maj-Gen Angus Lyell Collier of Glassburn, CBE, MC, JP, DL

(1) Dorothea Harriett; *b* 12 June 1840; *d* 20 Sept 1914

(2) Alice Blanche; *b* 27 Oct 1843; *m* 16 Aug 1866 Rev Alfred Gurney, MA, son of Rev Hampden Gurney, and *d* 12 March 1871, leaving issue

(3) Albinia Anne; *b* 7 June 1853; *d* 17 April 1874

3 Joseph (Rev); *b* 23 July 1801; *educ* Mr Phillip's Sch, Turnham Green, and Worcester Coll Oxford (BA 1828); Vicar of Clifton Hampden, Berks, 1830; *m* 14 Sept 1831 Emily (*d* 7 Sept 1869), dau of Rev Charles Vaughan, of Crickhowell, Brecon, by his wife Emilia Monck, and *d* 22 March 1864, having had issue:

(1) Joseph Henry; *b* 3 June 1832; *d* 1833

(2) George Louis Monck; *b* 28 April 1838; *m* 5 Jan 1864 Laura Beatrice (*d* 3 Aug 1911), est dau of Sir Arthur Hallam Elton, 7th Bt (*qv*), and *d* 26 Nov 1881, leaving issue:

1a Joseph Arthur; *b* 25 Nov 1867; *educ* Eton and Ch Ch Oxford; author and humanitarian; *d* unm 13 May 1899

2a George Harold; *b* 28 Feb 1869; *m* 2 Sept 1897 Anne Everilda Caroline, er dau of Thomas Wingfield Webber, JP, DL, of Kellavil, Queen's Co, and *d* 28 Dec 1926, leaving issue:

1b George Arthur Elton; *b* 27 Oct 1898; *educ* Wellington, RMA Woolwich and Pembroke Coll Cambridge; Lt-Col RE; *m* 22 Sept 1989 *Suzanne East, of Michael March, Romney, Sussex

1b Beatrice Mary; *b* 26 May 1900; *m* 28 Jan 1930 Dan Charles Frederick Tighe, est son of Wilfred Tighe, of Rosanna, Co Wicklow, and had two s

3a Stanley Vaughan; *b* 1 Jan 1872; *educ* Charterhouse, privately and New Coll Oxford; *d* unm 7 Oct 1907

4a Antony Edmund; *b* 27 Dec 1873; Maj Roy Glos Hus; *m* 24 Oct 1906 Euphemia Constance (*m* 2nd 25 July 1934 Cyril Chester Chester-Master (*d* 18 April 1961), 2nd son of Thomas William Chester Chester-Master, JP, of the Abbey, and Knole Park, Glos, and *d* 21 April 1966), dau of Thomas Alford Houston-Boswell-Preston, JP, DL, of Tweedhill, Berwick-on-Tweed (*see* HOUSTON-BOSWALL, Bt), and *d* 12 May 1922, leaving issue:

1b Sylvia Mary; *b* 10 Dec 1907; *m* 16 Nov 1935 George Arthur Loveday, er son of Arthur Frederick Loveday, OBE, and *d* 5 Jan 1967, leaving two s

1a Mabel Beatrice; *m* 5 Sept 1888 Sir Charles Fortescue Brickdale, JP (*d* 20 Sept 1944), est son of Matthew Inglett Fortscue-Brickdale, barrister Lincoln's Inn, and *d* 11 March 1944, leaving issue

2a Lillian Mary; *m* 15 Nov 1888 Maj-Gen Sir Henry Hallam Parr, KCB, CMG (*d* 4 April 1914), 2nd son of Thomas Clements Parr by Julia Elizabeth, est dau of Sir Charles Abraham Elton, 6th Bt (*qv*), and *d* 15 July 1925, having had three s (all dsp)

3a Agnes Hilda; *m* 20 Sept 1892 Maj-Gen Charles Frederick Gordon Young, 6th Bengal LI (*d* 17 March 1956), s of Col G Gordon Young, IA, and *d* March 1934, leaving issue

4a Beatrice Rhoda; *m* 1st 23 July 1896 Cyril Grant Cunard, JP, yst son of William Cunard (*d* 17 April 1914), and had issue (*see* 1970 edn CUNARD, Bt); *m* 2nd 4 April 1918 Capt Walter Hilton Curran (*d* 14 July 1931), son of John Curran, of Rockvale, Co Tipperary, and *d* 10 Aug 1945, leaving a further dau

5a Helen Laura; *m* 1900 Lauriston Leonard Batten, KC, JP (*d* 31 July 1934), son of Rayner Winterbotham Batten, FRCP, of Gloucester, and *dsp* April 1947

(3) Joseph Hucks; *b* 14 Oct 1840; *m* 13 June 1867 Mary Rider (*d* 11 Jan 1924), yst dau of Richard Budd, MD, of Barnstaple, and *d* 23 March 1886, having had issue:

1a Richard William Sidney; *b* 28 March, *d* 26 Aug 1868

2a Edward; *b* 6 Sept 1869; *d* 1 Nov 1876

3a Leonard Albert, MC; *b* 27 Sept 1875; *m* Mary Scott (*d* Dec 1961) and *dsp* *c* 1950

4a Stanley Rider, MC, TD, Croix de Guerre; *b* 17 Dec 1880; *educ* Radley and St Thomas's Hosp; Maj RAMC; *m* 27 Sept 1909 Margaret Ellen (*d* 24 Sept 1955), dau of Dr Joseph Harper, of Barnstaple, N Devon, and *d* 17 July 1935, leaving issue:

1b *Peter Joseph; *b* 9 July 1910; *educ* Radley, BNC Oxford (MA) and the Sorbonne; WW II 1940–41 (invalided); Headmaster King's Coll Jr Sch Wimbledon 1965; *m* 16 April 1936 *Mary Frances Hillary, dau of Ernest Augustus Rootham, of Barnstaple, N Devon, and has issue:

1c Margaret Frances; *b* 20 Sept 1937; *m* 14 Aug 1965 John Roger Beavis, s of Alfred Edward Beavis, of Burnham-on-Sea, Somerset, and had issue:

1d *Judy Frances; *b* 4 June 1968

2c *Ann Elizabeth; *b* 24 Jan 1948

1a Evelina Antonia Hermenegilda; *b* 28 Feb 1871; *m* 10 June 1897 John Robinson Harper, CBE, TD, JP (*d* 30 April 1947), son of Dr Joseph Harper, of Barnstaple, and *d* 28 April 1960, leaving a s and dau

(4) George Henry (Rev); *b* 15 Sept 1842; *educ* Marlborough and Exeter Coll Oxford (BA); Rector of Hutton Somerset 1869; *m* 3 Sept 1868 Mildred (*d* 22 Sept 1926), est dau of Capt John Mordaunt, JP, 17th Lancers, of Gatcombe Court, Flax Bourton, Somerset (*see* MORDAUNT, Bt), and *d* 29 Oct 1896, having had issue:

1a Henry Mordaunt; *b* 9 April 1880; *d* unm 19 Aug 1944

2a Joseph Francis Vaughan; *b* 8 Dec 1887; *educ* Haileybury; farmer in S Africa 1920–29, FO 1943–45; *m* 27 July 1921 Hon Dorothy Annesley, yst dau of 1st Baron Annesley (11th Viscount Valentia; *qv*), and *d* 4 March 1961, leaving issue:

1b *Caryl Antony Vaughan [Caryl Gibbs Esq, 57 Warwick Gdns, London W14 8PL]; *b* 12 Dec 1926; *educ* Loretto; late Lt Gren Gds; *m* 17 April 1959 *Christiana Maria-Theresa, only dau of Erich Oswald von Machanek zu Marienthal, of Gasse-Tschermak Gasse 23, Vienna XIX, and formerly w of Hamish Reid-Bennie, and has issue:

1c *Nicola Jane; *b* 27 Sept 1960

2c *Alexandra Henrietta; *b* 30 Nov 1966

1b *Brenda Mary [Mrs Cecil Edwards, Glendon Court, Upton Bishop, Herefs]; *b* 20 April 1929; *m* 12 Jan 1957 Cecil Ralph Timothy Edwards, Lt Welsh Gds (Res), s of Herbert Cecil Ralph Edwards, CBE, of Suffolk House, Chiswick Mall, London W4, and has issue:

1c *333 James Timothy; *b* 27 Oct 1957

2c *Simon Martin Ralph; *b* 16 Nov 1959

3c *Stephen Jonathan Hugh; *b* 10 April 1967

1c *Jane Alexandra; *b* 18 June 1961

2c *Katharine Mary; *b* 15 July 1963

1a Emily; *b* 9 June 1869; *d* unm 5 Feb 1962

2a Mildred Blanche; *b* 9 Aug 1870; *d* unm 30 June 1953

3a Mary Balmain; *b* 17 Dec 1871; *d* 25 June 1875

4a Ethel Mary; *b* 31 May 1873; *d* unm 16 Jan 1961

5a Olive; *b* 26 March 1876; *m* 1908 Maj-Gen Stukeley Torkington, of Hartley, Cranbrook, Kent, and *dsp* 8 May 1963

6a Annie Rose; *b* 22 April, *d* 28 June 1877

(5) William Cobham (Rev); *b* 28 July 1845; *educ* Jesus Coll Cambridge; Vicar St Andrew's, Exwick, nr Exeter 1873, and Abingdon 1878, Rector of Hagley, Worcs, 1884; *m* 6 Feb 1879 Annie Katharina (*d* 11 Dec 1924), dau of Ven. Archdeacon John Downhall, and *d* 14 March 1918, having had issue:

1a John Stanley, MC (Rev Canon); *b* 21 Nov 1879; *educ* Haileybury, Keble Coll Oxford and Cuddesdon Theological Coll; Rector Shipton Moyne Glos 1937–50; *m* 24 April 1924 Mary Rosamond (*d* 17 Feb 1966), er dau of Norman McCorquodale, JP, of Winslow Hall, Bucks (*see* 1970 edn McCORQUODALE OF NEWTON, B), and *d* 30 Jan 1952, leaving issue:

1b *Beresford Norman; *b* 27 Feb 1925; *educ* Eton and RAC Cirencester; Capt RHG (Blues) WW II, FRICS, FLAS, land agent and chartered surveyor; *m* 22 Aug 1956 *Mary Jane, only dau of William Arthur Norman Thatcher, of Over Worton, Middle Barton, Oxford, and has issue:

1c *John William; *b* 5 Nov 1957

2c *David Norman; *b* 22 Sept 1965

1c *Cecily Sheila; *b* 9 Feb 1960

2c *Alice Rosamond; *b* 8 March 1963

1b *Mary Sheila; *b* 8 March 1927; *m* Sept 1949 *21st Earl of Morton (*qv*) and has issue

2a William Beresford; *b* 1 Feb 1881; *educ* Wellington and RMC Sandhurst; Lt-Col Worcs Regt; *ka* 3 Sept 1916

3a George Louis Downall, DSO; *b* 30 July 1882; Capt RN (ret), WW I (despatches) and WW II; *m* 21 Sept 1926 Susan Fayth (*d* 5 Feb 1942), er dau of Francis Robert Harding-Newman, JP, FLAS, of Nelmes, Essex, and *d* 31 Oct 1956, leaving issue:

1b *Anne Susan Downall; *b* 20 Jan 1928; *m* 15 Sept 1951 *Edward Maynard Liddon, of Elmfield, Higher Durston, Taunton, Somerset, son of John Henry Churchill Liddon, of Blundells, West Monkton, Taunton, Somerset, and has issue:

1c *Timothy John; *b* 19 April 1957

1c *Susan Patricia; *b* 3 Nov 1954

1b *Mary Bridget; *b* 8 March 1937; *m* 5 Aug 1961 *Maj John Samuel Byard White, late The Somerset and Cornwall LI, of Bridge House, Bickenhall, Taunton, Somerset, son of Col Harold Samuel White, MC, TD, DL, of Fosgrove, Taunton, Somerset, and has issue:

1c *Jenifer Sarah; *b* 3 June 1963

2c *Catherine Angela; *b* 6 Nov 1965

4a Edward Reginald; *b* 9 Oct 1885; *educ* Halleybury and Keble Coll Oxford; Chaplain Gds Div; *ka* April 1918

5a Alfred Joseph, DSO, MC; *b* 26 May 1887; *educ* Marlborough and RMA Woolwich; WW I as Bde Maj 32nd Divl Artillery 1915–18 (wounded), AMS Eastern Command 1921–23; *dsp* 31 Dec 1969

1a Mary Katherine Pyndar; *b* 5 Aug 1884; *d* unm Dec 1949

(6) Stanley Vaughan; *b* 30 Nov 1846; *d* unm at Kingston, Jamaica, 25 Feb 1870

(1) Emily Harriett; *m* Ven. Alfred Pott, MA, Archdeacon of Berks, and had five s and five daus

(2) Dorothea Barnetta; *m* Rev George Heberden, Rector of Ranmore, Surrey, and had six s and four daus

(3) Harriet Theresa; *m* 7 Nov 1872 Lt-Col James Sparrow Mordaunt, late Leinster Regt (*d* 19 Dec 1927), est son of Capt John Mordaunt, 17th Lancers, and *d* 21 July 1925, leaving issue (*see* MORDAUNT, Bt)

The est son,

GEORGE HENRY GIBBS, of Aldenham, Herts, and Clifton Hampden, Oxon; *b* 24 Aug 1785; London merchant; *m* 7 July 1817 his cousin Caroline, 6th dau of Rev Charles Crawley, LLB, Rector of Stowe Nine Churches, Northants (*see* CRAWLEY-BOEVEY, Bt), and *d* 21 Aug 1842, having had, with other issue:

1 HENRY HUCKS, **1st Baron**

2 John Lomax (Rev), of Speen House, Newbury, Berks; *b* 28 March 1832; MA; Vicar of Clifton Hampden Oxon 1864–74 and Exwick, Devon, 1878–85, Rector Clyst St George 1885–97; *m* 3 Jan 1860 Isabel Marianne (*d* 22 March 1920), 2nd dau of Robert Bright, of Abbot's Leigh, near Bristol, by Caroline, dau of Thomas Tyndall, of The Fort, Bristol, and *d* 12 Jan 1914, having had issue:

(1) John Arthur; *b* 27 Oct 1860; *educ* Winchester and Keble Coll Oxford (MA); *m* 14 Jan 1902 Emily Gertrude Franck (*d* 27 Nov 1960), 3rd dau of Rev James Franck Bright, DD, Master Univ Coll Oxford, and *d* 9 July 1949, having had issue:

1a *Christopher John, OBE (1967); *b* 6 Dec 1902; *educ* Winchester and Univ Coll Oxford (MA); Lt Col RA (TA); FLAS, ARICS, land agent and surveyor, Ch Land Agent Nat Tst 1961; *m* 8 Sept 1942 *Margaret Evelyn, 3rd dau of Capt Robert Henry Ramsay Mackay, OBE, RN, of Petham, nr Canterbury, Kent, and has issue:

1b *Julian Robert [Julian Gibbs Esq, The Old Vicarage, Staunton-upon-Hine-Heath, Salop]; *b* 20 May 1949; *educ* Winchester; *m* 8 Jan 1977 *Juliet Marguerite Celia Gore, er dau of Col Philip Maitland Gore Anley, R Northumberland Hus, of Rycroft House, Bolney, Sussex, and has issue:

1c *Joseph; *b* 10 July 1977

1c *Florence Margaret; *b* 16 July 1979

2c *Dorothea; *b* 26 Sept 1981

1b *Isabel Margaret Ramsay [Mrs John Howell, 1 Church St, Mere, Wilts BA12 6DS]; *b* 8 Dec 1944; *m* 1st 17 Sept 1966 (*divorce* 1977) John Anthony Austin Harrison, yst son of Rev Roger Montagu Harrison, of St Ambrose Vicarage, Bournemouth, Hants; *m* 2nd 21 July 1978 *John Brooke Howell, and by her 1st husb has:

1c *Eleanor Margaret; *b* 9 Jan 1971

2a Antony James; *b* 29 April 1904; *educ* Eton and Univ Coll Oxford (MA, DM, MRCS, LRCP); *m* 21 Oct 1937 *Helen Margaret, only dau of William Wood Leuchars, of Waystrode, The Ridgeway, Pyrford, Surrey, and *d* 14 June 1993, leaving:

1b *Antony Richard [Antony Gibbs Esq, 6 Tarleton Gdns, London SE23 3XN]; *b* 25 May 1939; *educ* Bradfield, Byam Shaw Sch of Drawing and Painting, and Kingston Sch of Art (NDD, FCSD, FRSA); founding dir Hop Design; *m* 4 Sept 1964 *Mary Janet, 2nd dau of Frank Day, of Kingston-on-Thames, and has issue:

1c *Rupert Nicolas Antony [Rupert Gibbs Esq, 47 St Mary's Rd, Reigate, RH2 7JH]; *b* 28 April 1968; *educ* Ravensbourne Sch of Art (BA)

1c *Emily Jo [Miss Emily Gibbs, 128 Fortress Rd, London NW5]; *educ* Wolverhampton U (BA); proprietor Emily Jo Gibbs Design

2b *John William [John Gibbs Esq, 50a Redcliffe Sq, London SW10]; *b* 25 Aug.1941; *educ* Bradfield and London Sch of Printing and Graphic Arts; *m* 4 Nov 1967 *Anya, dau of Hans Coper, of Cherry Tree Farm, Spring Gdns, nr Frome, Somerset, and has issue:

1c *Ella; *b* 8 Aug 1968

3b *David Michael [David Gibbs Esq, 14 Westgate Terrace, London SW10]; *b* 15 May 1944; *educ* Bradfield and Loyola Coll, U of Montreal

4b *Raymond Martin; *b* 14 Oct 1947; *educ* Bradfield

3a Evelyn Arthur; *b* 2 July 1906; *d* 7 July 1917

4a *Martin Franck (Rev); *b* 28 May 1912; *educ* Eton and Univ Coll Oxford; Vicar of Wootton Berks 1943–57, Rector Brightwell-cum-Sotwell Berks 1957–61, RD Wallingford 1961–67, Vicar St German's Roath 1967

(2) Robert Tyndall; *b* 20 May 1865; *m* 3 April 1893 Emily Fraser (*d* 24 May 1947), 2nd dau of Rev George Handcock, of Bath, and *d* 4 Oct 1942, leaving issue:

1a Robert Claud; *b* 17 April 1895; Lt-Cdr RN; *m* 15 March 1930 Walda, dau of Edwin Gruhn, of 19 Stettinerstrasse, Berlin N20, and *d* 10 June 1949, having had issue:

1b *Terence Claud [Terence Gibbs Esq, 40 Thorpe Lea Rd, Peterborough, Cambs]; *b* 9 March 1934; *educ* Ewell Castle Sch, Ewell, Surrey

2b *John Francis [John Gibbs Esq, Stone House, Hill Top View, Dacre Banks, Harrogate, N Yorks HG3 4BH]; *b* 15 April 1936; *educ* Ardingly; 2nd Lt RA; *m* 12 Oct 1961 *Margaret Patricia, est dau of John Cecil Jackson, of Narborough, Leicester, and has issue:

1c *Patricia Helen [Mrs John Bissell, 12 Snape Court, Currumbin Waters, Qld 4223, Australia]; *b* 8 Nov 1963; *m* 4 Jan 1989 *John Philip Bissell, s of Eric Bissell, of Teignmouth, S Devon

2c *Erika [Mrs Ronald Magill, 19 Rosemary Close, High Wycombe, Bucks]; *b* 15 March 1966; *m* 17 Oct 1990 *Ronald David Magill, er s of James Magill, of Denver, Colo, and has:

1d *Alice Sara; *b* 13 Aug 1992

2d *Abby Christina; *b* 1 Oct 1994

1b Iris Walda; *b* 12 May, *d* 9 June 1932

2b Jacqueline Sylvia; *b* 19 April 1938; SRN 1960, SCM 1963; *m* 25 Sept 1972 *Alan Martin and *d* 14 April 1997, leaving:

1d *Conor James; *b* 12 June 1996

1d *Lydia Denise [Mrs Gary Hancock, 31 Clifton Rd, Wallington, Surrey]; *b* 26 May 1976; *m* 19 April 1997 *Gary Michael Hancock

3b Iris Emily; *b* 30 Oct 1939; *d* 15 May 1957

(3) Reginald (Rev); *b* 29 June 1867; *educ* Lancing and Keble Coll Oxford (MA); Vicar of Clifton Hampden Oxon 1893–1923 and Aldenham Herts 1923–40; *m* 4 Jan 1899 Lucia (*d* 10 Jan 1940), 2nd dau of Conolly Thomas McCausland, JP, DL, of Drenagh, Co Derry, and *d* 27 Oct 1940, having had issue:

1a Michael McCausland (Very Rev); *b* 1 Sept 1900; *educ* Lancing and Keble Coll Oxford (MA); Rector of Bulawayo S Rhodesia 1936–42, Archdeacon of Matabeleland 1937–42, Rector of St Saviour's, Claremont, Cape Town, S Africa 1942–48, Dean and Rector of St George's Cathedral, Cape Town, 1948–54, Dean of Chester 1954; *m* 4 Aug 1926 Edith Marjorie (ld 18 Oct 1968), est dau of John Spenser Ward, of Long Whittenham, Berks, by his wife Beatrix, dau of Sir Charles Gordon Cumming Dunbar of Northfield, 8th Bt (*qv*), and *d* 27 July 1962, leaving issue:

1b *Denis Dunbar [Denis Gibbs Esq, 16 London Rd, Lichfield, Staffs]; *b* 19 July 1927; *educ* Ruzawi Sch, S Rhodesia, Diocesan Coll, Cape Town, and Keble Coll Oxford (DM 1962, MRCP); *m* 11 April 1953 *Rachel Elizabeth, est dau of Geoffrey Bernard Youard, of Hartley Court, Longfield, nr Dartford, Kent, by Hon Rosaline Joan, 6th dau of Baron Atkin, PC (see 1940 edn), and has issue:

1c *Nicholas Mark; *b* 17 Dec 1954

1c *Sarah Mary; *b* 20 July 1956

2b *John Michael Francis; *b* 8 March 1929; *educ* Ruzawi Sch, S Rhodesia, Diocesan Coll, Cape Town, and Keble Coll Oxford (MA); Pncpl Coll of Citizenship, Salisbury, Rhodesia 1960; *m* 14 Aug 1954 *Carol Margaret, est dau of Mr Justice Faure Williamson, of Johannesburg, and has issue:

1c *Michael Alban; *b* 21 June 1955

2c *Dominic Faure; *b* 12 Feb 1959

3c *Peter Denys; *b* 20 Jan 1961

1c *Caroline Mary; *b* 31 Oct 1956

3b *Peter McCausland; *b* 30 Sept 1934; *educ* Diocesan Coll Cape Town, and Keble Coll Oxford (BA); *m* 21 July 1961 *Judith Ann, dau of John Richard Orgill, of Lancaster, and has issue:

1c *Simon Michael; *b* 20 Feb 1962

1c *Joanna Bridget; *b* 24 Nov 1965

1b *Mary Elizabeth; *b* 7 Jan 1932; *educ* Cape Town U (BSocSc 1955); *m* 29 Oct 1965 *Maurice Fraser Carver, Headmaster of Ruzawi Sch Rhodesia 1951056, 2nd son of Frank Carver, of 109 Wentworth Rd, Harborne, Birmingham, by Annie Jane Harriet Creswell

2b *Bridget Anne Susan [Mrs John Perry, c/o University of Botswana, Lesotho and Swaziland, Roma, nr Maseru, Lesotho]; *b* 14 April 1942; *educ* London U (BA); *m* 1 April 1967 *John Walton Beauchamp Perry, 2nd son of Roland Perry, MC, of Underhill Cottage, Oswestry, Salop

2a *Thomas Reginald (Rev); *b* 3 Nov 1902; *educ* Lancing; Curate at South Bank, Yorks, 1927–31 and 1934–38, Priest-in-Charge St Ninian's Whitby 1938–44, Vicar South Bank Yorks 1944–49, Chaplain St Hilda's Sch Whitby 1949, attached to Universities' Mission to Central Africa 1931–34

3a Denis Lucius Alban, DSO (1942) and bar (1944); *b* 15 Oct 1905; *educ* Lancing and RMC Sandhurst; Lt-Col Queen's (Roy W Surrey) Regt, gazetted 1926, India and Sudan 1926–28, Capt and Adj 2nd Bn 1937, Staff Coll 1939, Staff Capt GHQ and Bde Maj 144 Bde BEF France 1939–40, cmded 1st/6th Queen's 1942 in Egypt (Alamein), POW Italy 1942–43 (escaped), cmded 2nd Warwicks 1944–45, Normandy, Holland, Germany, cmded 1st Queen's Malaya 1947–48, Cmdt Eaton Hall Offr Cadet Sch 1948–50; memb House of Laity Church Assembly 1965; *m* 17 Oct 1933 *Lady Hilaria Agnes Edgcumbe, est dau of 6th Earl of Mount Edgcumbe (*qv*), and *d* 1984, leaving issue

1a Bridget Julia; *b* 29 Aug 1907; *d* unm 22 June 1935

2a *Joanna Isabel; *b* 29 Aug 1907; *m* 1 Oct 1945 Dr Victor Bremner Purvis, son of Rev John Bremner Purvis, Rural Dean of Bedlington, Northumberland, and has issue:

1b *Christopher Thomas Bremner; *b* 15 April 1950; *educ* Bradfield

1b *Lucia Elizabeth; *b* 3 Oct 1946

(4) Francis Lomax; *b* 23 Jan 1869; *m* 26 April 1909 Sylvia Beatrice (*d* 21 Aug 1940), dau of George Edward Cokayne (*see* CULLEN OF ASHBOURNE, B), and *dsp* 28 Dec 1943

(1) Caroline Blanche; *b* 27 Nov 1861; *d* unm 23 Nov 1945

(2) Isabel Alice; *b* 27 Dec 1862; *m* 3 July 1890 Dudley Julius Medley (*d* 14 Oct 1953), Hon LLD, Prof History Glasgow U, son of Julius George Medley, Bengal Engineers, and *d* 17 April 1942, leaving issue

(3) Mary Beatrice; *b* 16 Feb 1871; *d* 20 May 1886

(4) Ethel Constance; *b* 27 Nov 1872; *m* 3 Jan 1922 Reginald Herbert Bruce Dickson, er son of Rev Robert Bruce Dickson, late Vicar of Speen, Berks, and *d* 11 March 1961

1 Mary Dorothea; *b* 4 May 1833; *m* 2 Dec 1856 George Edward ADAMS later COKAYNE (roy licence 15 Aug 1873), Clarenceux King of Arms, MA, FSA, barrister (*d* 6 Aug 1911), yst s of William Adams, LLD, by Hon Mary Anne Cokayne, gdau of 5th Viscount Cullen, and *d* 11 March 1906, leaving issue (*see* CULLEN OF ASHBOURNE, B)

The er son,

HENRY HUCKS GIBBS, **1st Baron Aldenham**, of Aldenham, Herts (UK), so *cr* 31 Jan 1896, JP (Herts and Middx); *b* 31 Aug 1819; *educ* Rugby and Exeter Coll Oxford (MA); sr ptnr Antony Gibbs & Sons 1875, High Sheriff Herts 1884, Commr Ltcy City London, MP (C) City of London 1891–92, Dir Bank of England 1853–1901 (Govr 1875–77), FSA, FGS; *m* 6 May 1845 Louisa Anne (*d* 17 April 1897), 3rd dau of William Adams, LLD, of Thorpe, Surrey, Advocate Doctors'

Commons, by Hon Mary Anne Cokayne (*see* CULLEN OF ASHBOURNE, B), and *d* 13 Sept 1907, having had issue:

1 ALBAN GEORGE HENRY GIBBS, **2nd Baron Aldenham**; *b* 23 April 1846; *educ* Eton and Ch Ch Oxford (MA); FSA, Lt City London, MP City of London 1892–1906; *m* 18 Feb 1873 Bridget (*d* 27 Feb 1896), 6th surv dau of Alexander James Beresford Beresford-Hope, PC, MP, by Lady Mildred Arabella, est dau of 2nd Marquess of Salisbury (*qv*), and *d* 9 May 1936, leaving:

(1) GERALD HENRY BERESFORD GIBBS, **3rd Baron Aldenham**; *b* 9 Jan 1879; *educ* Eton and Ch Ch Oxford (BA); *m* 9 May 1905 Lillie Caroline (*d* 1 Sept 1950), est dau of Rev William Thomas Houldsworth, Vicar St Andrew's, Wells Street, London W, and *dsp* 21 March 1939

(1) Catherine Louisa; *b* 3 Jan 1875; *d* unm 5 May 1967

(2) Mildred Dorothea, OBE (1920); *b* 2 May 1876; WW II (CD); *d* unm 14 May 1961

2 Walter Antony; *b* 19 Jan 1850; *d* 16 July 1858

3 Vicary, JP (Herts); *b* 12 May 1853; *educ* Ch Ch Oxford (BA); London merchant, ed *Complete Peerage*, barrister, MP St Albans 1892–1904; *d* unm 13 Jan 1932

4 HERBERT COKAYNE GIBBS, **1st Baron Hunsdon of Hunsdon**, of Briggens, Co Hertford (UK), so *cr* 24 July 1923, JP (Herts); *b* 14 May 1854; *educ* Trin Coll Cambridge (MA); bought the Manor of Hunsdon and the Briggens estate 1908, High Sheriff Herts 1913, Chevalier Legion of Honour; *m* 12 Feb 1885 Anna Maria (*d* 30 Dec 1938), 4th dau and coheir of Richard Durant, of High Canons, Herts, and Sharpham, Devon, by Charlotte, dau of Col Alexander Wilton Dashwood (*see* DASHWOOD, Bt, of Kirtlington Park), and *d* 23 May 1935, leaving issue:

(1) WALTER DURANT, **4th Baron Aldenham** and **2nd Baron Hunsdon**

(2) Geoffrey Cokayne (Hon Sir), KCMG (1955, CMG 1945); *b* 20 July 1901; *educ* Eton and Ch Ch Oxford; Assist Sec Min Ec Warfare WW II, Master Grocers' Co 1938, chm: Antony Gibbs & Sons, Advsy Cncl Export Credits Guarantee Dept, Managing Tstees Nuffield Fndn (ret 1973) and Nuffield Provincial Hosps Tst, Nat Corp Care of the Aged, Imp Rels Tst, Australia and New Zealand Bank, Barclays Overseas Devpt Corp, Australian Mutual Provident Soc (UK); *m* 6 Oct 1926 Helen Margaret CBE (1961), JP (Herts 1942, Oxon 1950) (*d* 1979), yst dau of Charles Frederick Henry Leslie, of Epcombs, Hertingfordbury, and *d* 6 July 1975, leaving issue:

1a +David Charles Leslie [David Gibbs Esq, AM, 21 William St, S Yarra, VICT 3141, Australia]; *b* 15 Aug 1927; *educ* Eton and Ch Ch Oxford (MA); dir: Antony Gibbs & Sons, Marsh and McLennan Gp (Aust), pres World Wide Fund for Nature (Aust), dir: John Swire and Sons, Pty Ltd, Victoria State Opera etc, Tstee Museum of Victoria, Australia and New Zealand Banking Gp; *m* 20 March 1965 *Charmian Fleur, only dau of Dalzell Pulteney Mein, of Toolang, Coleraine, Victoria, Australia, and has issue:

1b +Hugo Dalzell; *b* 7 Dec 1967

2b +Justin Geoffrey; *b* 18 Feb 1969

1b *Emma Victoria; *b* 27 Sept 1966

2b *Arabella Sarah; *b* 20 June 1970

2a +Stephen Cokayne [Stephen Gibbs Esq, Dougarie, Isle of Arran, KA27 8EB]; *b* 18 July 1929; *educ* Eton; 2nd Lt KRRC 1948–49, Maj QVR (TA) 1960–63; dir: Charles Barker plc and Vaux Gp plc; *m* 21 Nov 1972 *Lavinia Winifred, est dau of Sir Edmund Castell Bacon, 13th Bt (*qv*), and has:

1b +James Edmund Geoffrey; *b* 13 Jan 1975; *educ* Glenalmond and RAC Cirencester

2b +William Stephen; *b* 8 Nov 1978; *educ* Eton

1b *Emily Anna Maria; *b* 19 Oct 1973; *educ* W Heath and European Business Sch London

3a +Julian Herbert; *b* 26 Nov 1932; *educ* Eton; 2nd Lt KRRC 1951–53, Lt Queen's Westminster TA 1953–55; dir Antony Gibbs (Life and Pensions) Ltd

4a +Roger Geoffrey (Sir) [Sir Roger Gibbs, 23 Tregunter Rd, London SW10]; *b* 13 Oct 1934; *educ* Eton and Millfield; dir Arsenal Football Club 1980 and Roy Nat Pension Fund for Nurses, chm Gerrard and Nat Discount Co plc 1975, Wellcome Tstee 1983, ktd 1994

5a +Christopher Henry [Christopher Gibbs Esq, Manor House, Clifton Hampden, Abingdon, Oxon; L6 Albany, London W1]; *b* 29 July 1938; *educ* Eton. Stanbridge Earls and U of Poiters; owns art shop; Tstee J Paul Getty Jr Charitable Trust 1985–

1a *Elizabeth Helen [Mrs Valentine Fleming, Stonewall Park, Chiddingstone Hoath, Edenbridge, Kent]; *b* 29 July 1938; *m* 14 June 1963 *Valentine Patrick Fleming, est son of Capt Michael Valentine Paul Fleming and Mrs James Currie Thomson, of Aston Dene, Stevenage, Herts (*see* BORTHWICK, Bt), and has issue

(3) Humphrey Vicary (Sir), PC (1969), GCVO (1969, KCVO 1965), KCMG (1960), OBE (1958); *b* 22 Nov 1902; *educ* Eton and Trin Coll Cambridge; Govr S Rhodesia 1959–69, MP Wankie (S Rhodesia) 1948–54, chm: Rhodesia NFU and Natural Resources Bd, Hon DCL UEA 1969, Hon LLD Birmingham, KStJ 1960; *m* 17 Jan 1934 Molly Peel, DBE (1969), CSTJ (*d* 20 March 1997), 2nd dau of John Peel Nelson, of Bulawayo, and *d* 1990, leaving issue:

1a +Jeremy Herbert [Jeremy Gibbs Esq, Upper Kennards, Leigh, Kent, TN11 8RE]; *b* 26 May 1935; *educ* Diocesan Coll, S Africa, and Ch Ch Oxford (MA); *m* 8 April 1958 *Alison Douglas, dau of Lt Col Douglas McCrone Martin, (*see* STRATHCLYDE, B) and has:

1b *Elizabeth Belinda; *b* 9 Jan 1959; *m* 1988 *Ferrill D Roll, of 92 Norwood Ave, Upper Montclair, NJ 07043, USA, yst son of M W Roll, of New Mexico, USA, and has issue:

1c *James Herbert; *b* 1992

1c *Helen Mary; *b* 1990

2c *Alice Elizabeth; *b* 1993

2b *Barbara Anne Camilla; *b* 8 Dec 1961

3b *Lucinda Jane; *b* 20 April 1965

4b *Arabella Sophie; *b* 4 Jan 1967

2a +Nigel Henry Vicary [Nigel Gibbs Esq, Cyrene, Horcott, Fairford, Glos]; *b* 24 April 1937; *educ* Ruzawi Sch, Marandellas, Diocesan Coll, Rondebosch, Prince Edward Sch, Salisbury, and RAC Cirencester; *m* 9 Sept 1967 *Barbara Boitumelo, 2nd dau of Rev Canon Edward George Paterson, of Salisbury, Rhodesia, and has issue:

1b +Paul Humphrey Paterson; *b* 5 July 1968; *m* 1992 *Claire Diane, only dau of Peter Freeman, of Johannesburg, S Africa

2b +Douglas Robert Nigel; *b* 1972

1b *Mairi Rosalind Diana; *b* 1970

3a +Timothy Durant [Timothy Gibbs Esq, Silver St House, South Cerney, Cirencester, Glos GL7 5TP]; *b* 27 Dec 1938; *educ* Ruzawi Sch, Marandellas, Rhodesia, and Diocesan Coll, Rondebosch; *m* 1978 *Susan Heather, dau of Graham Melville Rankine, and widow of Robert Duncan Bothwell Fleming, and has issue:

1b +James Rankine Fleming; *b* 13 Oct 1979

1b *Caroline Rose; *b* 7 June 1981

3a Mr and Mrs Timothy Gibbs adopted:

*Alexander FLEMING-GIBBS; *b* 14 June 1974

*Sarah Victoria FLEMING-GIBBS; *b* 10 June 1977

4a +Kenneth Richard; *b* 6 May 1941; *educ* Ruzawi Sch, Marandellas, Diocesan Coll, Rondebosch, and U of Cape Town (BSc Civ Engrg); civ engr; *m* 28 Dec 1966 *Mary Elizabeth Frances, only dau of Francis Beamish, of East London, S Africa, and has issue:

1b +Vicary James; *b* 3 May 1973

1b *Sara Jane; *b* 27 June 1970

5a +Simon Humphrey [Simon Gibbs Esq, Brunswick Cottage, Church St, Kelvedon, Essex]; *b* 8 Oct 1947; *educ* Peterhouse, Rhodesia, and Reading U; *m* 1974 *Philippa Mary, dau of Terence Astley Brand, and has issue:

1b +Nicholas Geoffrey; *b* 1979

2b +Thomas Humphrey; *b* 1982

1b *Susannah Kate; *b* 1985

(1) Winifred Marian, JP; *m* 28 July 1912 Col Sir Charles Edward Ponsonby, 1st Bt (*qv*), and had issue

(2) Barbara Louisa, OBE (1961); *b* 4 March 1896; *d* unm 24 Feb 1964

(3) Rosalind Mary; *b* 5 Feb 1898

5 Kenneth Francis (Ven); *b* 2 April 1856; *educ* Winchester, Ch Ch Oxford (MA), and Leeds Clergy Sch, DD (Lambeth) 1929; Archdeacon St Albans 1909–33, Chaplain to HM GEORGE V 1921, Vicar of Aldenham 1884–913; *m* 5 June 1894 Mabel Alice, JP (*d* 20 March 1953), dau of Charles Edward Barnett, of Edge Grove, Aldenham, and *d* 1 Feb 1935, having had issue:

(1) Alan Christopher Henry; *b* 25 June 1895; *d* 20 Aug 1908

(2) Leonard Charles Michael; *b* 29 Sept 1896; *educ* Winchester; Capt Coldstream Gds (SR), dir Antony Gibbs & Sons and Bank of London and S America; *d* unm 26 Aug 1955

(3) Raymond Kenneth; *b* 17 Sept 1901; *educ* Winchester; Lt-Col Herts Regt; *m* 7 June 1941 *Kathleen, dau of Rev William Hartley Carnegie, Canon and Sub-Dean of Westminster Abbey and Rector of St Margaret's, Westminster, by his 1st w Albinia Frances, dau of Sir Thomas Hyde Crawley-Boevey, 5th Bt (*qv*)

(4) Bernard Vicary; *b* 2 Jan 1905; *educ* Winchester; Maj RA (TA); *d* 17 March 1995

(5) +Andrew Antony, MBE (1945), TD (1945) [Maj Andrew Gibbs MBE TD, Kilvington Hall, Thirsk, Yorks]; *b* 31 March 1914; *educ* Winchester and Ch Ch Oxford (BA 1937, MA 1946); Maj Herts Regt TARO WW II (despatches), dir (local) Barclays Bank Oxford Dist 1947–53, Shrewsbury Dist 1953, York Dist 1961, full dir 1962, Fell Corpn of SS. Mary and Nicolas (Woodard Schs Midland Div), Govr St Edward's Sch Oxford, Hon life memb BRCS; *m* 9 May 1947 *Elizabeth Joan, yr dau of Maj Eric Charles Montagu Flint, DSO, of Hembury Castle, nr Torrington, Devon, and widow of Capt Peter George William Savile Foljambe (*see* LIVERPOOL, E), and has issue:

1a +John Kenneth Andrew [John Gibbs Esq, The White Cottage, Old Heathfield, E Sussex]; *b* 9 Oct 1948; *educ* Winchester; FCA; dir Balfour Williamson & Co 1988–97, and Intramar 1997–; *m* 7 Jan 1978 *Julia Margaret, only dau of Maurice Edwards, of Mullets, Piddletrenthide, Dorset, and has issue:

1b +Simon Andrew Maurice; *b* 27 Nov 1985

1b *Emma Elizabeth; *b* 5 Nov 1979

2b *Louisa Mary; *b* 11 Dec 1981

2a +Alan Francis [Alan Gibbs Esq, 16 Edwardes Sq, London W8]; *b* 25 Feb 1953; *educ* Winchester and Ch Ch Oxford; *m* 1982 *Francine Nicola, est dau of Nicholas Preston, of Park Farm, Beverston, Tetbury, Glos, and has:

1b +Alfred Andrew Vicary; *b* 27 Dec 1997

2a (cont.) Mr and Mrs Alan Gibbs also adopted:

*Leo Antony Francis; *b* 1988

*Fleur Elizabeth; *b* 1990

(1) Dorothea Louisa; *b* 29 Sept 1897; *m* 15 May 1924 Sir William Macnamara Goodenough, 1st Bt (*qv*), of Filkins Hall, Lechlade, Glos, and has issue

(2) Anstice Ros (Dame), DCVO (1967), CBE (1960); *b* 2 Jan 1905; Ch Commr and Chm Br Cwlth Girl Guides' Assoc 1956–66, V-Chm Ctee World Assoc Girl Guides and Girl Scouts 1957–60

6 Henry Lloyd; *b* 21 July 1861; Lt City of London; *m* 17 Aug 1887 Alice Mary (*d* 5 Oct 1942), 4th dau of Gen Charles Crutchley, of Sunninghall Park, Berks, and *d* 14 Sept 1907, having had issue:

(1) Maurice Antony Crutchley; *b* 9 June 1888; *educ* Eton and Ch Ch Oxford (BA 1910); joined Australian Ordnance Corps 1940, ret as Capt 1947; *m* 1st 10 Jan 1912 (*divorce* 1924) Elma (*d* 1973), er dau of Sir William Gordon Gordon-Cumming, of Altyre, 4th Bt (*qv*), and had issue:

1a Ronald Gordon Vicary; *b* 4 Sept 1918; *educ* Eton; F/O RAF WW II; *ka* 31 Oct 1942

1a *Daphne Marion [Mrs Percy Agar, La Haut, Dominica, WI]; *b* 8 Nov 1912; *m* 5 Jan 1934 Percy Kirwan Agar (*d* 12 July 1954), son of Edward Ashton Agar, of La Haut, Dominica, and has issue:

1b *Antony Edward [Antony Agar Esq, La Haut, Dominica, WI]; *b* 30 April 1936; *m* 12 July 1967 *Madeleine Carmel, dau of Stephen Morrison, of Nova Scotia, and has issue:

1c *Stephen Kirwan; *b* 6 June 1968
2c *Maurice Ashton; *b* 1970
1c *Madeleine Daphne; *b* 1972
2c *Francillia; *b* 1975
1b *Elizabeth Anne; *b* 1938; *m* 26 April 1958 *Mark Varvill, of Lane End House, Ellamore Lane, W Wittering, W Sussex, son of Michael Noel Varvill, of Harbour Cottage, W Wittering, and has issue:
1c *Richard Antony; *b* 23 Sept 1961
1c *Katherine Mary; *b* 27 Oct 1963
(1) Maurice Antony Crutchley Gibbs *m* 2nd 3 May 1933 Margaret Falkiner (*d* Aug 1964), only dau of Daniel Grant McBean, of Fairley Grange, NSW, and formerly wife of Reginald Francis Egerton, RN, and *d* 1974
(2) Ronald Charles Melbourne; *b* 24 Aug 1894; *educ* Eton; 2nd Lt Scots Gds; *ka* 28 Oct 1914
(1) Helen Bridget, MBE (1948); *b* 18 Feb 1896; *m* 24 Jan 1917 Sir Ian Leslie Orr Ewing, MP, est son of Charles Lindsay Orr Ewing, MP, and had issue (*see* ORR EWING, Bt)
(2) Christian Louisa; *b* 14 May 1898 (HRH PRINCESS CHRISTIAN stood sponsor); *d* 27 Aug 1899
(3) Sibella Mary; *b* 20 Nov 1899; *d* 16 Feb 1900
1 Edith Caroline; *b* 2 Nov 1848; *d* unm 25 July 1942

The 3rd BARON ALDENHAM's cousin and 1st BARON HUNSDON OF HUNSDON's s,

WALTER DURANT GIBBS, **4th Baron Aldenham** and **2nd Baron Hunsdon of Hunsdon**; *b* 11 Aug 1888; *educ* Eton and Trin Coll Cambridge (BA); Capt Herts Yeo, chm: Antony Gibbs & Sons, Westminster Bank and Australian Pastoral Co; *m* 6 Nov 1919 Beatrix Elinor (*d* 17 July 1978 aged 87), dau of Herbert Woodfield Paul and widow of Algernon Hyde Villiers (*see* CLARENDON E), and *d* 30 May 1969, having had issue:

1 Vicary Paul; *b* 11 Feb 1921; *educ* Eton; Capt Gren Gds WW II; *m* 19 Sept 1942 *Jean Frances, CVO (1953), Ldy-in-Waiting to HM THE QUEEN when Princess Elizabeth 1945, Extra Woman Bedchamber to HM THE QUEEN 1953, dau of Capt Angus Valdimar Hambro, MP (*see* HAMBRO, B), of Milton Abbas, Dorset, and was *ka* Nijmegen 20 Sept 1944, leaving issue:
(1) Susan Frances; *b* 14 May *d* 1 July 1943
(2) Jennifer Susan; *b* 12 May 1944; Ldy-in-Waiting to HM QUEEN ELIZABETH THE QUEEN MOTHER 1993–; *m* 1974 *Cdr Michael Charles Gordon-Lennox, RN, of Fishers Hill, Iping, Midhurst, W Sussex (*see* RICHMOND and GORDON, D)

2 ANTONY DURANT GIBBS, **5th Baron Aldenham** and **3rd Baron Hunsdon of Hunsdon**; *b* 18 May 1922; *educ* Eton and Ch Ch Oxford; Lt RNVR WW II, Master Merchant Taylor's Co 1977; *m* 16 July 1947 *Mary Elizabeth [The Rt Hon Mary Lady Aldenham and Hunsdon, Rathgar, The Avenue, Sherborne, Dorset DT9 3AH], only dau of Walter Parkyns Tyser, of Gordonbush, Brora, Sutherland, and *d* 1986, leaving issue:
(1) VICARY TYSER GIBBS, **6th and present Baron Aldenham** and **4th and present Baron Hunsdon of Hunsdon**
(2) +George Henry Paul [The Hon George Gibbs, The Old Manor Farmhouse, Hempton Rd, Deddington, Oxon OX15 0TL]; *b* 17 June 1950; *educ* Rannoch; *m* 1st 1973 (*divorce* 1989) Janet Elizabeth, er dau of Harold Leonard Scott, of Middle Farm House, Bassingbourne, and has issue:
1a +Piers Antony Scott; *b* 11 Aug 1973
2a +Corin William Tyser; *b* 7 April 1976
(2) (cont.) The Hon George Gibbs *m* 2nd 1992 *Elizabeth, dau of Prof Geoffrey Wingfield Harris, CBE, FRS
(3) William Humphrey Durant; *b* 14 Oct 1954; *educ* Eton; *d* as a result of a road accident 14 Sept 1973
(1) *Antonia Mary [The Hon Mrs Johnson, Manor Farm, Middle Chinnock, Somerset TA18 7PN]; *b* 10 July 1958; dir Anthony Reynolds Gallery, London 1985–; *m* 1989 *Simon H Johnson, s of E A Johnson of Walmer, Kent, and has issue:
1a *Edmund Antony Gibbs; *b* 1992
1a *Maud Eleanor Gibbs; *b* 1990
2a *Isabel Beatrice Gibbs; *b* 1995

ALDERDICE

Creation: B. (LP, UK) Aug 1996.

THE BARON ALDERDICE, of Knock, in the City of Belfast (John Thomas Alderdice) [The Rt Hon The Lord Alderdice, House of Lords, London SW1A 0PW]; *b* 28 March 1955; *educ* Ballymena Acad and Queen's U Belfast; Sr Ho Offr Belfast City Hosp 1979–80, Registrar: Holywell and Whiteabbey Hosps 1980–81, Shaftesbury Square Hosp 1981–82, and Belfast City Hosps 1982–83, Sr Tutor and Sr Registrar Belfast City Hosp and Queen's U Belfast 1983–87, Exec Med Dir S and E Belfast Health and Soc Servs Tst 1993–, Dir NI Inst Human Relns 1991–94, Alliance parly candidate Belfast E 1987 and 1992 gen elections and NI in Euro election 1989, European Lib, Dem and Reform Party: memb Exec Ctee 1987–, Treas 1995–, V-Pres Lib Internat 1992–, Tstee Ulster Museum 1993, leader Alliance Party NI 1987– (memb Exec Ctee 1984, chm Policy Ctee 1985–87, V-Chm March-Oct 1987), consultant psychotherapist E Health and Soc Servs Bd Belfast 1988–; *m* 1977 *Dr Joan Margaret Hill and has two sons and a dau

Lineage: Rev DAVID ALDERDICE; *m* *Helena Shields and has:

JOHN THOMAS, *cr* a **Baron**

ALDINGTON

Arms: Gules a pale ermine, on a chief argent, masoned sable, three saffrons, stalked and leaved proper. **Crest:** Out of the battlements of a tower or a cubit arm proper, the hand grasping a hurt. **Supporters:** Dexter, a stag proper; sinister, a black labrador dog proper, pendent from the neck of each by its own chains a portcullis or. **Motto:** *Spes* ('Hope'). **Creation:** B. (UK) 29 Jan 1962.

THE 1ST BARON ALDINGTON, of Bispham, Co Borough of Blackpool (Sir Toby Austin Richard William Low, KCMG (1957), CBE (1945, MBE 1944), DSO (1941), TD and clasp (1950), PC (1954), DL (Kent 1973)) [The Rt Hon The Lord Aldington KCMG CBE DSO TD PC DL, Knoll Farm, Aldington, Kent TN25 7BY]; *b* 25 May 1914; *educ* Winchester and New Coll Oxford (BA 1936, MA 1960, Hon Fell (1976)); barrister Middle Temple 1939; KRRC (TA), WW II Greece, Crete, Western Desert and Tunisia 1940–42, Staff 8th Army Sicilian Campaign 1943, Lt-Col Staff 13 Corps Italy, Brig BGS 5 Corps 1944–45 (Croix de Guerre avec palmes, 1945 Cdr USA Legn Merit); MP (C) Blackpool N 1945–62, Parly Sec Min Supply 1951–54, Min State BOT 1954–57, chm: Select Ctee Nationalised Industs 1957–61, dep chmn C Pty 1959–63, chmn Ho Lds Select Ctee Overseas Trade 1984–85, Sub-Ctee A Ho Lds Euro Communities Ctee 1989–93, Westland Aircraft 1977, Jt Chm Jt Special Ctee Industry 1972, dir: Grindlays Bank 1946–51, Nat & Grindlays Bank, GEC, AEI, Exporters Refinance Corp, v-chm: Sun Alliance, dir John Brown & Co, London Assur, English China Clays, Nat Discount Co, Wm Brandt's Sons & Co, Lloyds; *m* 10 April 1947 *(Felicite Ann) Araminta, er dau of Sir Harold Alfred MacMichael, GCMG, DSO, of Folkestone, and formerly w of Capt Paul Humphrey Armytage Bowman, Coldstream Gds (*see* BOWMAN, Bt), and has issue:

1 +CHARLES HAROLD STUART [The Hon Charles Low, 59 Warwick Sq, London SW1]; *b* 22 June 1948; *educ* Winchester, New Coll Oxford and INSEAD (Fontainebleau); md Deutsche Bank AG (London Branch) 1988; *m* 1989 *Regine, dau of Erwin von Csongrady-Schopof, of Bielefeld, Germany, and has issue:
(1) +Philip Toby Augustus; *b* 1 Sept 1990
(1) *Louisa Charlotte Patience; *b* 1992
(2) *Marie-Therese Sophie Araminta; *b* 1992

1 *(Priscilla) Jane (Stephanie), LVO (1995, MVO 1985); *b* 4 Sept 1949; *educ* Cranborne Chase, Westfield Coll London and Courtauld Inst Art; Curator Print Room Roy Library Windsor Castle 1975–, author *Royal Landscape* (1997); *m* 13 Dec 1975 *Hugh Ashley Roberts, CVO, Dir Roy Collection and Surveyor Queen's Works Art 1996–, yst s of Rt Rev Edward Roberts, former Bp of Ely, and has issue:
(1) *Sophie Jane Cecilia; *b* 28 March 1978; *educ* Downe House and York U

(2) *Amelia Frances Albinia; *b* 1982; *educ* Downe House

2 *(Lucy) Ann Anthea [The Hon Mrs Laing, Logie House, Forres, Morayshire IV36 0QN]; *b* 29 April 1956; *educ* Cranborne Chase and Camberwell Sch Art; *m* 2 Feb 1979 *Alasdair North Grant Laing, est s of Alexander Grant Laing, MC, by Graeme Elizabeth, yr dau of Adml Sir Frederick Hew George Dalrymple-Hamilton of Bargany, KCB, gs of 10th Earl of Stair (*qv*), and has issue:

(1) *Alexander William Grant; *b* 7 March 1982; *educ* Stowe

(2) *Frederick Charles Grant; *b* 1985

(1) *Emma Mary Grant; *b* 19 April 1980; *educ* St Mary's Calne

Lineage: STEPHEN PHILPOT LOW, JP and DL (Kent), of Sydenham, Kent, and Parliament St, Westminster; *b* 5 Jan 1827; *m* 1st 15 Aug 1846 Emily (*d* 15 May 1852), dau of William Austin, of Saffron Waldron, Essex, and had a dau; *m* 2nd 8 March 1853 Hannah (*d* 10 Oct 1864), dau of William Austin, and *d* 1 Feb 1895, having by her had:

1 Frederick (Hon Sir) (Mr Justice Low), KC (1902), of 51 Sloane Sq, London SW1; *b* 21 Nov 1856; barrister Middle Temple 1890, Recorder Ipswich 1906,ktd 1909, MP Norwich 1910–15, High Court Judge (King's Bench) 1915; *m* 28 June 1882 Katherine Eliza (*d* 4 Nov 1953), 4th dau of Charles Thompson, of Pk Sq, St Marylebone, and *d* 4 Sept 1917, leaving issue:

(1) Stephen Philpot (Sir), of 26 Pembridge Gdns, London W2; *b* 17 Sept 1883; barrister Middle Temple 1906, Min Labour: Slr's Dept 1920, Assist Slr 1925–33, Slr BOT 1934–48 and Min Fuel and Power 1942–48, ktd 1938; *m* 8 Dec 1906 Bertie Faith (*d* 6 May 1962), dau of R Crosse, and *d* 25 Oct 1955, leaving issue:

1a Stephen Philpot; *b* 21 Sept 1907; *d* 21 Aug 1962

2a John Philpot; *b* 16 July 1910; *d* 5 March 1967

3a *Harold Philpot, TD; *b* 1 Feb 1913; *educ* Westminster; TA 1936, Lt-Col Middx Regt WW II; *m* 10 Oct 1936 (Audrey) Cynthia (*d* 1994), dau of William Ernest Falconer, MD, and has issue:

1b *Nicholas Philpot; *b* 28 July 1941; *m* 27 July 1965 *Virginia Sandford, yr dau of Joseph P Smyth Jr, of New York

2b *Stephen Peregrine; *b* 20 April 1949

(1) Hannah Austin; *b* 23 Aug 1885; *m* 8 Aug 1911 Francis Trevelyan Villiers Bayly, barrister Middle Temple, and had issue

(2) Esther Jessie; *b* 6 Dec 1886; *m* 5 Dec 1908 Jasper Webb Knight, of Bolney Court, Shiplake, Oxon, and had issue

2 Sidney, of Melbourne, Australia; *b* 13 March 1861; barrister Middle Temple

3 AUSTIN (Sir)

4 Harold, of 10 Evelyn Gdns, Kensington; *b* 12 Oct 1863; *educ* Gonville and Caius Coll Cambridge (MA); MRCS Eng; *d* 1932

1 Edith; *b* 20 Nov 1857; *d* unm 14 Jan 1885

The 3rd s,

Sir AUSTIN LOW, CIE (1919), JP (London and Bucks), of The Old House, Wexham, Bucks; *b* 25 April 1862; *educ* Dr Jones's Sch, Sydenham; chm Grindlay, dir Nat Provincial Bank and London Assur, ktd 1928; *m* 10 Feb 1885 Mary Stephanie (*d* 27 May 1937), dau of Stephen Octavius Jay, of Burton Constable, Yorks, and *d* 12 Jan 1956, having had issue:

1 Frederick Stephen, MC (1918), JP (Bucks 1946); *b* 5 April 1887; *educ* Charterhouse; Maj RFA WW I, HG WW II; *m* 1st 20 March 1915 Gladys (*d* 3 March 1942), dau of Sidney Leetham, of Elm Bank, York, and had issue:

(1) Antony Frederick Leetham; *b* 4 March 1916; Maj RA; *ka* Singapore 17 Feb 1942

1(cont.) Maj Frederick Low *m* 2nd 1 Feb 1947 *Dorothy, dau of Arthur Hunter Denham Gillies, of Whitehall Court, London SW1, and by her had issue:

(2) *George Stuart Hunter of Spain; *b* 6 March 1949; *educ* Harrow; *m* 1997 (*divorce* 1985)

(3) *Alan Frederick of Cape Town; *b* 28 Feb 1954; *educ* Harrow; *m* 1978 *Manya Romano and has:

1a *Joshua James Austin; *b* 1980

2a *Daniel Stuart; *b* 1982

3a *Benjamin John Frederick; *b* 1984

2 Stuart, DSO; *b* 1 Dec 1888; Lt-Col RGA (TA) WW I; chm Grindlays Bank; *m* 1st 19 July 1913 (*divorce* 1929) Hon Lucy Gwen Atkin (*d* 22 Aug 1957), est dau of Baron Atkin (*see* 1940 edn), and had issue:

(1) TOBY AUSTIN RICHARD WILLIAM, **1st Baron**

(2) Charles Stuart; *b* 2 Feb 1916; *educ* Sherborne and Ch Ch Oxford (BA 1937); barrister Grays Inn 1961; *m* 6 Oct 1953 (*divorce* 1963) Rosemarie (*d* 1985), dau of Hugo Heidecker, of Nuremberg and London, and *d* July 1986, leaving:

1a *Peter Michael Stuart of Atlanta, Ga; *b* 12 March 1958; *educ* Harrow; *m* March 1986 *Lele Shannon and has issue

(1) *Gwen Mary Patience [Mrs Denis Martin, 2 Mulberry Fields, Loop St, Sandwich, Kent CT13]; *b* 28 May 1917; *m* 1st 7 July 1938 (*divorce* 1951) Henry Lewis Whitworth Jones (*d* Nov 1990), s of Lt-Col Seymour Whitworth Jones, of Hill House, Fleet, Hants, and has a s and dau; *m* 2nd 31 March 1953 Denis Hemmant Rolleston Martin (*d* 1987), s of Arthur Wilfred Martin, of Sevenoaks, and has another s

2 (cont.) Stuart Low *m* 2nd19– *Mrs Phyllis Lacey Pellatt (*m* 3rd June 1948 Ralph Nye) and *d* as a result of enemy action at sea 10 Dec 1942

1 Katherine; *b* 13 Dec 1885; *m* 1st 25 June 1915 Capt Reginald Raynor Nye, Roy Scots (*ka* 17 Dec 1915), s of Edwin Nye; *m* 2nd 3 June 1919 (*divorce* 1930) Edwin Angas Roberts (*d* Oct 1955), s of Edward Roberts; *m* 3rd 23 Dec 1932 Edgar Kershaw Middleton (*d* Feb 1949), s of John Middleton, and *dsp* 7 May 1970

2 Mary Dorothy; *b* 20 Sept 1893; *m* 28 April 1917 Capt Gordon Cooper Wilkinson, RN (*d* 7 June 1966), s of Dr John Cooper Wilkinson, and had a s and dau

ALEXANDER of Edgehill

Arms: Azure, on a chevron between three lymphads, sails furled, oars in action or, as many grenades fired proper. **Crest:** In front of a talbot's head erased sable, gorged with a collar gemel gules, two crescents or. **Motto:** *Vita perit labor non moritur* ('Life perishes; toil does not'). **Creation:** Bt. (UK) 2 July 1921.

SIR DOUGLAS ALEXANDER, 3RD BT, of Edgehill, Stamford, Connecticut, USA [Sir Douglas Alexander Bt, 2499 Windsor Way Ct, Wellington, FL 33414, USA]; *b* 9 Sept 1936; *s* unc 1983; *educ* Rice U (MA 1961) and U of NCa (PhD 1987); sometime Assoc Prof French NY State U and Pres Edgehill Investment Co, currently with Cowen & Co; *m* 9 Aug 1958 *Marylon, dau of Leonidas Collins Scatterday, of Worthington, Ohio, and has had:

1 +DOUGLAS GILLESPIE; *b* 24 July 1962; *educ* Reed Coll Portland Oregon (BA 1984); *m* 1993 *Marsha Sue, dau of Robert Fink, of Cleveland, Ohio

2 +Andrew Llewellyn; *b* 14 Jan 1967; *educ* Bowdoin Coll Brunswick Maine (BA 1989); *m* 1996 *Rachel Elle, dau of Gerald Gehrke, of Litchfield, Conn.

1 Helen Douglas; *b* and *d* 1959

2 Elizabeth Collins; *b* and *d* 1961

Lineage: ANDREW ALEXANDER, of Errol, Perthshire; *b* Jan 1795; *d* Jan 1859, leaving:

ANDREW ALEXANDER, of Errol; *b* 29 July 1832; *m* 28 June 1857 Harriet Newell (*d* 29 Dec 1906), dau of Samuel Hayward, and *d* 8 Nov 1914, leaving:

Sir Douglas Alexander, 1st Bt (UK), so cr 2 July 1921, of Edgehill, Stamford, Conn., USA; *b* 4 July 1864; barrister Canada 1886, pres Singer Mfg Co NY 1905–49; *m* 28 Sept 1892 Helen Hamilton (*d* 19 March 1923), dau of George Hamilton Gillespie, of Hamilton, Canada, and *d* 22 May 1949, leaving:

1 **Sir Douglas Hamilton Alexander, 2nd Bt**; *b* 6 June 1900; *educ* Princeton (BA 1921); *d* 1983

2 Archibald Gillespie; *b* 29 March 1907; Lt-Cdr US Coast Gd (R) 1942–51; *m* 17 June 1932 Margery Isabel, dau of Arthur Brown Griffith, of Media, Penn., and *d* 1978, leaving:

(1) Sir DOUGLAS ALEXANDER, **3rd and present Bt**

(2) +Archibald Bonsall [Archibald Alexander, 6540 Cholla Dve, Scottsdale, Arizona 85253, USA]; *b* 30 Jan 1940; *m* 1967 *Catherine Clair, dau of John Cyril Biggins, of Montclair, NJ, and has issue:

1a +Sean Hamilton; *b* 1970

1a *Cristina Cripps; *b* 1969; *m* 27 April 1996 *Brodie Ransom, s of Cynthia Celick Heimel, of Los Angeles

(1) *Margery Griffith [Mrs Frederick J Ramsey III, 68 Florence Rd, Riverside, Connecticut 06878, USA; *b* 30 May 1945; *m* 1st 1969 (*divorce* 1971) Richard Danch Cleland; *m* 2nd 1972 *Frederic James Ramsey III

1 Elizabeth Agnes; *b* 22 June 1895; *d* unm 14 Sept 1944

2 Helen Douglas; *b* 20 April 1897

ALEXANDER of Sundridge Park

Arms: Barry wavy of ten azure and argent a lion rampant gules holding a trident erect or, on a chief of the second three lymphads sable with pennons flying gules. **Crest:** On a bundle of sticks fesswise banded or a cock proper, collared gold. **Motto:** *Semper vigilans* ('Always watchful'). **Creation:** Bt. (UK) 19 Nov 1945.

SIR CHARLES GUNDRY ALEXANDER, 2ND BT, of Sundridge Park, Kent [Sir Charles Alexander Bt, Hollytree Farmhouse, N Cadbury, Yeovil, Somerset BA22 7DD]; *b* 5 May 1923; *s* f 1959; *educ* Bishops Stortford Coll and St John's Coll Cambridge (BA 1943, MA 1947); Lt (E) RN WW II; AIMarE, chm Alexander Shipping, dir Houlder Bros, Houlder Line, Ore Carriers, Newcastle Protection and Indemnity Assoc, Leadenhall Tport, Hull, Blyth & Co, Master Merchant Taylors' Co 1981, Prime Warden Shipwrights' Co 1983; *m* 1st 16 Dec 1944 Mary Neale, only child of Stanley Robert Richardson, and has issue:

1 +RICHARD [Richard Alexander Esq, Wealden Hall, Pilgrim's Way, Detling, Kent ME14 3JY]; *b* 1 Sept 1947; *educ* Bishop's Stortford Coll; MIPR, Liveryman Merchant Taylors' Co, Freeman City London; *m* 1971 *Lesley Jane, dau of Frederick William Jordan, and has issue:

(1) +Edward Samuel; *b* 1974

(2) +James Gundry; *b* 1977

1 *Jennifer; *b* 14 June 1949

Sir CHARLES *m* 2nd 1979 *Eileen Ann, dau of Gordon Stewart, of Inveresk, Finchampstead

Lineage: W ALEXANDER, of Rochester, Kent; *b* 1729; *m* Elizabeth Day and *d* 1785, having had, with five other children:

WILLIAM ALEXANDER; *b* 1769; fndr Alexander Discount Co; *m* Ann Barber and *d* 1819, having had, with five er and three yr children:

SAMUEL ALEXANDER; *b* 26 Aug 1809; *m* Sarah Gundry and *d* 1884, having had, with six other children, an est s:

EDWARD ALEXANDER, of Highgate; *b* 26 Jan 1839; *m* 25 Jan 1877 Cora (*d* 4 Feb 1939), dau of William Zwicker, and *d* 30 March 1925, leaving issue:

1 Charles Edward; *b* 1877; *d* 1945

2 Waldemar Joseph; *b* 5 Jan 1879; *m* 12 Jan 1927 Kathleen Lydia, dau of James Cass, and *d* 2 Nov 1954, leaving issue:

(1) *Stephen Patrick Cass [Stephen Alexander Esq, 71 Hillway, London N6]; *b* 27 June 1928

(1) *Anne Elizabeth Gundry [Mrs Peter Reeves, 10 Acacia Rd, Hawthorndene, S Australia]; *m* 10 Jan 1961 *Peter Reeves, PhD, and has issue:

1a *Michael David; *b* 12 Aug 1962

2a *James; *b* 7 Dec 1963

3 FRANK SAMUEL (Sir), **1st Bt**

4 Victor William; *b* 6 April 1887; *educ* Bootham Sch York and New Coll Oxford (MA), L és L Paris; *m* 9 Sept 1927 Elizabeth Tiefaine, 3rd dau of Rev James Harris Cullen, of The Mission House, Alofi, Niu233, S Pacific, and *d* 14 Jan 1963, having had issue:

(1) Christopher Edward; *b* 25 Jan 1929; *educ* Bootham Sch York and New Coll Oxford; *d* unm 24 April 1953

(1) *Margaret Casilda Tiefaine [Mrs Robert Watkins, Delaval Vicarage, Seaton Sluice, nr Whitley Bay, Northumberland]; *b* 19 Jan 1932; *m* 18 May 1957 *Rev Robert Henry Watkins, Vicar Delaval, s of Henry David Watkins, of Bristol, and has issue:

1a *Jeremy Christopher; *b* 12 Sept 1959

2a *Nicholas Henry; *b* 31 March 1962

1a *Rowena Margaret; *b* 22 May 1958

2a *Eleanor Tiefaine; *b* 27 May 1964

1 Irma Casilda Anna; *b* 27 April 1880; *d* unm 14 Nov 1964

2 Melita Cora; *b* 12 Sept 1891; *d* unm 10 March 1969

3 Eva Mary; *b* 27 May 1895; *d* unm 22 Dec 1987

The 3rd s,

Sir Frank Samuel Alexander, 1st Bt (UK), so *cr* 19 Nov 1945, JP (City London); *b* 17 June 1881; *educ* Highgate Sch; Capt and Adj 72nd Heavy Artillery Bde WW I (despatches); shipowner and shipbroker; City London: Common Cnclman 1934, Alderman 1938, Sheriff 194041, Ld Mayor 1944–45, chm Baltic Exchange 1939–46, dir Alexander Shipping, Houlder Line, Waxed Papers Ltd, Yorkshire Insur, London & Provincial Marine & Gen Insur, ktd 1942; *m* 16 Feb 1922 Elsa Mary (*d* 20 Jan 1959), er dau of Sir Charles Henry Collett, 1st Bt (*qv*), and *d* 18 July 1959, leaving:

1 Sir CHARLES GUNDRY ALEXANDER, **2nd and present Bt**

2 +John Edward [John Alexander Esq, Dene Court, Oldfield Dve, Heswall, Wirral, Cheshire]; *b* 1 Aug 1924; *educ* Bishops Stortford Coll; Lt RNVR WW II; AICS; chm Crichton Brown and Mersey Insulation, dir Alexander Shipping; *m* 11 April 1953 *Maureen Kettlewell, 2nd dau of William Walter Dickson, MB, ChB, of George Farm, Speen, Bucks, and has issue:

(1) +Jonathan Charles; *b* 3 Jan 1957

(1) *Catherine; *b* 9 Nov 1954

1 *Elizabeth Jane [Mrs Peter Boult, Little Holt, Bull Lane, Chislehurst, Kent BR7 6NX]; *b* 14 March 1927; *m* 11 June 1949 *Lt-Col Peter Walter Swinton Boult, TD, est s of Peter Swinton Boult, MC, and has issue:

(1) Nigel Peter Alexander; *b* 12 May 1952; *educ* St Edward's Sch Oxford; *d* 1984

(2) *Geoffrey Pattisson; *b* 6 June 1957

(1) *Rosanne Margaret; *b* 27 April 1950

(2) *Alison Judith; *b* 16 Jan 1955

2 *Margaret Mary [Mrs Neville Wells, Durant Hollies, Hookwood Park, Limpsfield, Surrey RH8 0DU]; *b* 24 Nov 1929; *m* 19 May 1951 *Neville Manwaring Wells, only s of Maj Stanley Walter Wells, MBE, and has issue:

(1) *Michael Edward Alexander; *b* 29 July 1956

(2) *Martin Charles Stanley; *b* 20 Jan 1959

(1) *Frances Mary; *b* 2 Oct 1954

ALEXANDER OF TUNIS

Arms: Per pale argent and sable a chevron, in base a crescent, all counterchanged; on a canton azure a harp or, stringed argent. **Crest:** An arm in armour embowed, the hand holding a sword proper, hilt and pommel or. **Supporters:** Dexter, a piper of the Irish Guards, holding under the interior arm a bagpipe; sinister, a Sepoy of the 3rd/2nd Punjabi Regiment, holding in the exterior hand a rifle proper, each charged on the shoulder with an escutcheon barry nebuly of six argent and azure. **Motto:** *Per mare, per terras, per astra* ('By land, by sea, by the stars'). **Creations:** V. (UK) 1 March 1946, E. and B. (UK) 14 March 1952.

THE 2ND EARL ALEXANDER OF TUNIS, Viscount Alexander of Tunis, of Errigal, Co Donegal, and **Baron Rideau**, of Ottawa and of Castle Derg, Co Tyrone (Shane William Desmond Alexander) [The Rt Hon The Earl Alexander of Tunis, 59 Wandsworth Common West Side, London SW18 2ED]; *b* 30 June 1935; *s* f 1969; *educ* Harrow and Ashbury Coll Ottawa; Lt Irish Gds (ret 1958), Govt Whip 1974, patron Br-Tunisian Soc 1979–, dir Pathfinder Fin Corp (Toronto) 1980–, Internat Hosps Gp 1981–, chm Canada Meml Fndn 1989–, Pres Br-American-Canadian Assoc 1989–94, Freeman and Liveryman Mercers' Co; *m* 14 July 1971 (*divorce* 1976) Hilary, dau of John van Geest; *m* 2nd 22 July 1981 *Hon Davina Mary Woodhouse, LVO (1991), yst dau of 4th Baron Terrington (*qv*), and has issue:

1 *Rose Margaret; *b* 23 April 1982

2 *Lucy Caroline; *b* 1984

Lineage: The 4th EARL OF CALEDON (*qv*) had a 3rd s:

HAROLD RUPERT LEOFRIC GEORGE ALEXANDER, **1st Earl Alexander of Tunis**, so *cr* 14 March 1952, as also BARON RIDEAU, of Ottawa and of Castle Derg, Co Tyrone, and previously 1 March 1946 VISCOUNT ALEXANDER OF TUNIS, of Errigal, Co Donegal, KG (1946), PC (UK and Canada 1952), OM (1959), GCB (1942, CB 1938), GCMG (1946), CSI (1936), DSO, MC; *b* 10 Dec 1891; *educ* Harrow and RMC Sandhurst; served WW I (wounded three times, despatches five times and Legn of Honour), T/Brig and Bde-Cdr India 1934, Maj-Gen 1937, Gen 1942, ADC to HM EDWARD VIII 1936, Col 3rd Bn 2nd Punjab Regt 1937, Cdr Nowshera Bde India 1934–38 (despatches twice) and 1st Div Aldershot 1938–40, GOC-in-C Southern Cmd 1940–42, Burma 1942, C-in-C Middle East 1942, Deputy C-in-C Allied Forces N Africa 1943, C-in-C Allied Armies Italy 1943–44, SAC Mediterranean 1944–45, Govr-Gen and C-in-C Canada 1946–52, Mof Defence 1952–54, ADC-Gen to HM GEORGE VI 1944–46, Col Irish Gds 1947, Chllr Order St Michael and St George 1956–60 (Grand Master 1960–67), Constable Tower London 1960–65, Ld-Lt Co London 1957–65 and Gtr London 1965–66, Govr Harrow 1952–63, Hon Freeman and Liveryman Mercers' Co, KStJ, Grand Cross Legn Honour, Orders: St Anne Russia, Suvorov 1st Cl USSR, Grand Cross George I and Redeemer Greece, Legn Merit and DSM USA, Virtuti Militari 5th Cl Poland; *m* 14 Oct 1931 Lady Margaret Diana Bingham, GBE (1954), DStJ, JP (1956) (*d* 17 Aug 1977), yr dau of 5th Earl of Lucan (*qv*), and *d* 16 June 1969, leaving:

1 SHANE WILLIAM DESMOND ALEXANDER, **2nd and present Earl Alexander of Tunis**

2 +Brian James [The Hon Brian Alexander, 11 The Little Boltons, London SW10 9LJ]; *b* 31 July 1939; heir presumptive; *educ* Harrow and Grenoble U; Lt Irish Gds

1 *Rose Maureen [The Lady Rose Crossman, Cheswick House, Berwick-on-Tweed, Northumberland]; *b* 28 Oct 1932; v-chm Berwick-upon-Tweed Presern Tst 1989; *m* 20 Jan 1956 *Lt Col Humphrey Crossman, RA, JP, DL, High Sheriff Berwick-upon-Tweed 1990, s of Maj-Gen Francis Linidisfarne Morley Crossman, CB, DSO, MC, and has issue:

(1) *David Lindisfarne Alexander; *b* 14 Nov 1956; *m* 1985 *Mrs Jane Lusk, dau of S J Hamp-Adams, of Harare, and has issue:

1a *Alice Patricia; b 1986

2a *Sophie Rose; b 1988

(1) *Emma Margaret [Mrs Christopher Baldwin, Twyssenden Manor, Goudhurst, Kent]; *b* 13 Oct 1959; *m* 1984 *Christopher William Kennard Baldwin, s of Peter Godfrey Kennard Baldwin, and has issue:

1a *John Lindsay Alexander; *b* 1989

1a *Isabelle Rose; *b* 1992

Lord and Lady Alexander also adopted:

*Susan Mary [Mrs Andrew Hamilton, 8 Herondale Ave, London SW18]; *b* 26 Feb 1948; *m* 18 Sept 1970 *Andrew Paulet Hamilton, s of Capt (Hubert Charles) Paul(et) Hamilton, Roy Irish Fus (*see* WILLIAMS-WYNNE, Bt), and has issue:

(1) *Alexander Caspar Paulet; *b* 1974

(1) *Romany Celia Margaret; *b* 1971

(2) *Imogen Laetitia Alice; *b* 1981

ALEXANDER OF WEEDON

Arms: Per fess azure and gules, between two swords in pale, points upward argent, hilts, pommels and quillons or, a tower argent pierced of a cross gules masoned proper and with a portcullis or infess with two towers each issuant in the flanks masoned and with a portal gold. **Crest:** Upon a chapeau gules encircled by a coronet rayonny or and doubled ermine, a lion sejant or, head and mane gules, collared ermine, supporting by its staff or, spearheaded also or, a banner of the arms fringed argent and gules. **Supporters:** Dexter, a lamb statant erect in trian aspect, collared ermine, unguled or; sinister, a lion statant erect or, head and mane in trian aspect gules, collared ermine. **Motto:** I plead to serve. **Creation:** B. (LP, UK) 1988.

THE BARON ALEXANDER OF WEEDON, of Newcastle-under-Lyme, Co Stafford (Robert Scott Alexander, QC (1973, NSW 1983)) [The Rt Hon The Lord Alexander of Weedon QC, House of Lords, London SW1A 0PW]; *b* 5 Sept 1936; *educ* Brighton Coll (Pres Cncl 1993–) and King's Coll Cambridge (BA 1959, MA 1963); barrister Middle Temple 1961, Bencher 1979, V-Chm Bar Cncl 1984–85, Chm 1985–86, Judge Courts Appeal Jersey and Guernsey 1985–88, Chm: Panel on Takeovers and Mergers 1987–89, Nat West Bank 1989–, Tstees Crisis 1990–96 and Cncl Justice 1990–, Tstee: Nat Gallery 1987–93 and The Economist 1990–, non-exec dir RTZ 1991–96, London Stock Exchange 1991–93, Dep-Chm SIB 1994–96, Chm Ho Lds Delegated Powers and Deregulation Ctee, Memb UK Panel on Sustainable Devpt, Presentn Fell King's Coll London 1995, FRSA 1991, Hon LLD Sheffield 1991, Buckingham 1992, Keele 1993, Exeter 1994; *m* 1st 1963 (*divorce* 1973) Frances Rosemary, *née* Pughe; *m* 2nd 1978 Elizabeth *née* Norman; *m* 3rd 1985 *Marie, *née* Sugrue and formerly w of — Anderson, and by his 1st w has had, with another s (*d* young):

1 *David Robert James; *b* 1964

2 *William Richard Scott; *b* 1969

1 *Mary Frances Anne; *b* 1966

Lineage: SAMUEL JAMES ALEXANDER, of Newcastle, Staffs; *m* Hannah May Trevitt and had:

ROBERT SCOTT ALEXANDER, QC, *cr* a **Baron**

ALLEN OF ABBEYDALE

Arms: Barry of twelve azure and argent, two swords in saltire, points in base proper, hilts, pommels and quillons or, surmounted by a representation of the tower of Beauchief Abbey proper. **Crest:** Within a wreath of holly proper a boar's head erased behind the ears argent, holding in the jaws a dice gold. **Supporters:** On either side a tricolour cavalier King Charles spaniel, the compartment comprising a grassy mount, growing therefrom sprigs of holly, all proper. **Motto:** *Ad recta tende* ('Hold to the right'). **Creation:** B. (LP, UK) 1976

THE BARON ALLEN OF ABBEYDALE, of the City of Sheffield (Sir Philip Allen, GCB (1970, KCB 1964, CB 1954)) [The Rt Hon The Lord Allen of Abbeydale GCB, Holly Lodge, Englefield Green, Surrey, TW20 0JP]; *b* 8 July 1912; *educ* King Edward VII Sch Sheffield and Queens' Coll Cambridge (MA, Hon Fellow); Dep Chm Prison Commn 1950–52, Assist U-Sec Home Office 1952–55 (joined 1934), Dep Sec Min Housing and Local Govt 1955–60, Dep U-Sec Home Office 1960–62, Second Sec Treasury 1963–66, PUS Home Office 1966–72, Memb Security Commn 1973–91, Chm Gaming Bd 1977–85; *m* 1938 *Marjorie Brenda, dau of Thomas John Colton Coe, of Sheffield

Lineage: ARTHUR ALLEN, of Sheffield; *m* Louie Tipper and had a yr s:

PHILIP, *cr* a **Baron**

ALLENBY

Arms: Per bend argent and gules, in the sinister three crescents two and one of the second, and in the dexter three horse's heads erased, one and two, of the first, all within a bordure azure. **Crest:** Issuant out of a crescent gules a demi-lion proper. **Supporters:** Dexter, a horse regardant or; sinister, a camel regardant argent. **Motto:** *Fide et labore* ('With faith and work'). **Creation:** V. (UK) 7 Oct 1919.

THE 3RD VISCOUNT ALLENBY OF MEGIDDO and **OF FELIXSTOWE**, Co Suffolk (Michael Jaffray Hynman Allenby) [The Rt Hon The Viscount Allenby of Megiddo, Newnham Lodge, Newnham, Hants RG27 9AJ]; *b* 20 April 1931; *s* f 1984; *educ* Eton and RMA Sandhurst; Lt-Col Roy Hus (PAO), formerly 11th Hus, Malaya 1953–56, ADC to Govr Cyprus 1957–58, Bde-Maj 51st Bde Hongkong 1967–69, cmdg Roy Yeo (TA) 1974–77, GSO(1) Instr Nigerian Staff Coll Kaduna 1977–79, chm Quickrest 1987–90, Chm ILPH 1997–, Dep Speaker Ho Lds 1993–; *m* 29 July 1965 *Sara Margaret, only dau of Lt-Col Peter Milner Wiggin, JP (*see* WIGGIN, Bt), and has issue:

1 +HENRY JAFFRAY HYNMAN; *b* 29 July 1968; *m* 29 Sept 1996 *Louise Victoria Green

Lineage: HYNMAN ALLENBY, of Felixstowe House, Suffolk, s of Hynman Raddish Allenby, of Kenwick Hall and Garnsgate Hall; *b* 1823; *m* Catherine Anne (*d* 31 Oct 1922 aged 92), dau of Rev T C Cane, of Brackenhurst, Southwell, Notts, and *d* 1879, leaving, with other issue:

1 EDMUND HENRY HYNMAN, **1st Viscount Allenby of Megiddo** and **of Felixstowe**, Co Suffolk (UK), so *cr* 7 Oct 1919 (with remainder, in default of his own male issue, to his bro Frederick and the latter's heirs male), GCB (1918, KCB 1915, CB 1902), GCMG (1917), GCVO (1934); *b* 23 April 1861; *educ* Haileybury and RMC Sandhurst; Col Life Gds and 16th/5th Lancers, joined 6th Inniskilling Dragoons 1882, Bechuanaland 1884–85, Zululand 1888, Capt 1889, Adj 1889–93, psc 1896, Maj 1897, Boer War 1899–1902 (despatches three times, two brevets two medals, eight clasps), Lt-Col cmdg 5th Roy Irish Lancers 1902, Col 1905, cmded 4th Cav Bde 1905–09, Maj-Gen 1909, Inspr Cav 1910–14, WW I: GOC 1st Cav Div BEF 1914, Cav Corps 1914–15, 5th Army Corps 1915, 3rd Army 1915–17, Lt-Gen 1916, Gen 1917, C-in-C Egy[ptian Expdny Force Palestine Campaign, took Jerusalem 9 Dec 1917 and wn Batle of Megiddo against Turks 19 Sept 1918, FM 1919 (despatches seven times, thanks of Parliament and £50,000 for his services , 1914 star, two medals), Hon Col: 5th Bn Welsh Regt, Warwicks Yeo, Cinque Ports (Fortess) Engrs RE, TA, Hon LLD Cantab, Aberdeen, Edinburgh, Toronto, New York, Hon DCL Oxon, Chm King's Roll Nat Cncl, Freeman Jerusalem, Rector Edinburgh U, CB 1902, KCB 1915, US DSM, Livingstone Gold Medallist Roy Geographical Soc Scotland, KJSt J; *m* 30 Dec 1896 Adelaide Mabel, DGStJ and Grand Cordon El Kemal Egypt (*d* 20 March 1942), dau of Horace Edward Chapman, of Donhead House, Salisbury, Wilts, and *dsps* 14 May 1936, having had:

(1) Horace Michael Hynman, MC; *b* 11 Jan 1898; *educ* Wellington; Lt RHA; *d* 29 July 1917 from wounds recd in action

2 Frederick Claude Hynman, CBE (1919), JP (Northumberland); *b* 21 Sept 1864; *educ* HMS *Britannia*; Capt RN; *m* 28 Aug 1901 Edith Mabel (*d* 28 Jan 1956), dau of John Munton Jaffray (*see* JAFFRAY, Bt), and *d* 1 Aug 1934, leaving:

(1) DUDLEY JAFFRAY HYNMAN ALLENBY, **2nd Viscount Allenby of Megiddo** and **of Felixstowe**; b 8 Jan 1903; *educ* Eton and RMC Sandhurst; Lt Col 11th Hus WW II; *m* 1st 10 July 1930 (*divorce* 1949) Gertrude Mary Lethbridge, dau of Edward Geoffrey Stanley Champneys, of Otterpool Manor, Sellindge, Kent, and had issue; *m* 2nd 13 April 1949 Daisy, CStJ, dau of Charles Francis Hancox and formerly wife of (a) Carl Arthur Bendix and (b) Col Lionel George Cotterill Neame, Coldstream Gds, and *d* 1984, leaving by his 1st w:

1 MICHAEL JAFFRAY HYNMAN ALLENBY, **3rd and present Viscount Allenby of Megiddo** and **of Felixstowe**

(2) (Claude) William Hynman; *b* 13 Aug 1912; *educ* Stowe; Lt-Col 11th Hus Reserve Offrs, WW II; granted by roy warrant 28 Jan 1939 rank of viscount's yr s; *m* 1st 1 July 1939 (*divorce* 1948) Sheila Patsey, yst dau of G P Price, of Beechfield, Petworth, Sussex; *m* 2nd 11 Sept 1951 *Barbara Marion [The Hon Mrs William Allenby, 29 Hovedene, Cromwell Rd, Hove, Sussex BN3 3EH], yr dau of John Hall, of Felpham, Sussex, and *d* 2 Dec 1975

(1) Ivy Catherine; *b* 5 March 1904; *d* 9 Feb 1915

ALLENDALE

Arms: Gules a lion rampant or, armed and langued azure, between eight crescents in orle of the second. **Crest:** A bull's head erased quarterly argent and gules, charged with a mullet sable. Supporters: Dexter, a lion argent semée of crescents gules; sinister, a bull, quarterly argent and gules, horns of the first, tipped or. **Motto:** *Fide sed cui vide* ('Trust, but see whom you trust'). **Creations:** B. (UK) 20 July 1906, V. (UK) 5 July 1911.

THE 3RD VISCOUNT ALLENDALE, of Allendale and Hexham, Co Northumberland, and **Baron Allendale**, of Allendale and Hexham, Co Northumberland (Wentworth Hubert Charles Beaumont, DL (Northumberland 1961)) [The Rt Hon The Viscount Allendale DL, Bywell Hall, Stocksfield-on-Tyne, Northumberland NE43 7AE; Allenheads Hall, Hexham, Northumberland]; *b* 12 Sept 1922; *s* f 1956; *educ* Eton; F/Lt RAFVR WW II (wounded, POW), ADC to Viceroy India 1946–47, Hon A/Cdre No 3508 (Co Northumberland) Fighter Control Unit RAuxAF, Steward Jockey Club 1963–65, Pres Northumberland and Durham Assoc Bldg Socs, OStJ; *m* 10 Feb 1948 (*divorce* 1984) Hon Sarah Field Ismay, 2nd dau of Gen 1st and last Baron Ismay, KG, GCB, CH, DSO, PC (*see* 1963 edn), and has:

1 +WENTWORTH PETER ISMAY [The Hon Wentworth Beaumont, Bywell Castle, Stocksfield-on-Tyne, Northumberland]; *b* 13 Nov 1948; *educ* Harrow; *m* 14 Feb 1975 *Theresa Mary Magdalene, 2nd dau of Francis Ambrose More O'Ferrall (*see* JACKSON, Bt, of The Manor House, Birkenhead), and has issue:

(1) +Wentworth Ambrose Ismay; *b* 11 June 1979

(1) *Lucy Harriet; *b* 30 April 1981

(2) *Alice Theresa; *b* 1983

(3) *Martha Rose; *b* 1986

2 +Mark Henry [The Hon Mark Beaumont, Newbrough Hall, Hexham, Northumberland NE47 5AJ]; *b* 21 July 1950; *educ* Eton; *m* 17 April 1982 *Diana Elizabeth, yst dau of Lt-Col John Elliott Benson, and has issue:

(1) +George Richard Benson; *b* 1987

(2) +John Wentworth; *b* 1989

3 +Charles Richard [The Hon Charles Beaumont, Swallowship House, Hexham, Northumberland NE41 1RJ]; *b* 8 March 1954; *educ* Eton and RAC Cirencester; *m* 27 Oct 1979 *Charlotte Sybil, yst dau of Lt-Col Richard Ian Griffith Taylor, DSO, MC, JP, DL, of Chipchase Castle, Northumberland, by his 2nd w Hon Cecily Eveline, yst dau of 1st and last Baron Buckland (*see* 1928 edn), and has issue:

(1) +Edward; *b* 1983

(2) +Harry; *b* 1987

(1) *Laura; *b* 1985

Lineage: THOMAS BEAUMONT, of Flockton, Yorks, had a yr s:

GEORGE BEAUMONT,of The Oaks, Darton, Yorks; *m* Sarah — (*bur* Oct 1646) and was *bur* Oct 1666, having had:

1 John, of Wooley Moorhouse; *b* 27 May 1622; *m* Helen (*m* 2nd Matthew Wilkinson, of Greenhead), dau of Thomas Townsend, of Hoyland, and *dvp* 1652, having had a dau (Helen,; *d* young)

2 George, of York; *b* 1633; Danzig merchant, fndr sch at Darton; *d* unm after 24 Jan/July 1668

3 WILLIAM, for whom *see* below

1 Sarah; *b* 1625; *m* 18 Oct 1656 Josiah Wordsworth (*d* 18 Feb 1709 aged 82), of Waterhall, Peniston, and *d* 16 Feb 1691, leaving issue; the poet William Wordsworth was of this family

2 Mary; *m* Jonathan Shaw, of Hall Broom, Bradfield

GEORGE BEAUMONT's 3rd son,

WILLIAM BEAUMONT; *bapt* 5 Sept 1638; *m* 26 June 1662 Jane (*d* 29 May 1719 aged 68), dau of William Milner, of Burton Grange, Yorks, and was *bur* 18 Dec 1713, leaving issue:

1 GEORGE, for whom *see* below

2 Thomas, of Chapelthorpe; *d* 30 April 1731 aged 52 (*bur* at Darton)

3 Jonathan

1 Mary; *m* James Smith, of Manningham, and *dsp*
2 Jane; *m* Abraham Hall, of Booth Town, Halifax
3 Anne; *m* Thomas Dobson, of Bingley
4 Sarah; *m* Roger Coates

WILLIAM BEAUMONT's est son,

GEORGE BEAUMONT, of Chapelthorpe; *m* 20 Dec 1688 Gertrude (*bur* 11 Sept 1713), dau of John Bagshawe, of Hucklow, Derbys, and was *bur* 12 June 1712, having had issue:

1 GEORGE, for whom *see* below
2 Thomas (Rev); Rector Bulwell, Notts; *d* unm 1771
1 Jane; *m* 1713 Abel Smith, banker (*d* Dec 1756), of E Stoke and Nottingham, and *d* 1743, leaving issue (*see* CARRINGTON, B)
2 Mary; *m* John Grammar, of Pledwick, Yorks
3 Gertrude; *m* Thomas Hall, of Carcolston, Notts
4 Sarah; *d* 14 July 1695
5 Elizabeth; *bur* at Sandal
6 Hannah; *m* Rev Andrew Burnaby (*d* 27 Dec 1776), Vicar St Mary's Leicester, Preb Lincoln, and *d* 22 July 1757, leaving issue; from this marriage descends HM QUEEN ELIZABETH THE QUEEN MOTHER

GEORGE BEAUMONT's er son,

GEORGE BEAUMONT, of The Oaks; *bapt* 24 Aug 1696; *educ* Trin Hall Cambridge; *m* 23 April 1723 Frances (*d* 14 April 1735), dau of Richard Beaumont, of Whitley Beaumont, Yorks, and *d* 27 Jan 1735, leaving issue:

1 THOMAS, for whom *see* below
2 George Beaumont (Rev); *b* 1726; LLB; Rector St Nicholas and Gedling, Notts; *m* Elizabeth (*d* 25 Nov 1792 aged 60), dau of John Green, and *d* 17 May 1773, having had issue:
(1) Thomas (Rev), of Bridgford Hill, Notts; *b* 1754; *educ* Jesus Coll Cambridge (MA); *m* 24 Feb 1777 Charlotte (*d* 9 Nov 1830), dau of William Huthwaite, of Nottingham, and *d* 25 Aug 1835, having had a dau (Mary Elizabeth, *d* 19 Jan 1786)
(2) George, of Crossland Hall, Leeds; *m* Ann, dau of Francis Ridsdale, Leeds merchant, and had seven daus (all *d* unm bar the 7th: Elizabeth, *m* 10 April 1828 Lt-Gen H Huthwaite and had issue)
(3) Richard Henry, of Aston, Warwicks; *b* 1761; Capt 84th Regt; *m* 1795 Ann, dau of William Walford, of Penn Bank, Staffs, and *d* 1828, leaving issue:
1a George, of Bridford Hill, Notts; *b* 1796; *m* 1821 Anne (*d* 26 July 1870 aged 73), dau of John Shilcock, of Redmile, Leics, by Theodosia, dau of Rev Henry Hough, Rector Redmile, and *d* 26 March 1882, having had issue:
1b Richard Henry, of Old Trafford, Lancs; *b* 1824; *m* 1854 Mary Purcell, dau of Robert Crofts Bullen, JP, of Ballythomas, Co Cork, and *d* 1884, leaving, with other issue:
1c Hubert Blackett; *b* 9 Dec 1859; *m* 18 Jan 1889 Mary Ellen, dau of Thomas Steele, of Carrington, and had issue
2c Robert Bullen; *b* 27 Jan 1865; *m* 23 Sept 1887 Maude Mary Copley (*d* 24 Aug 1910), dau of William Waterfall, of Sheffield, and had issue:
1d Glynne Wentworth; *b* 6 April 1890; *educ* Southport Sch; FRIC (1927); with Huson & Hardwick, analytical and consulting chemists, Liverpool from 1905; *d* unm 21 Dec 1975
1d Mary Katherine; *b* 29 Dec 1888; *m* Ellis Daniel Mather (*d* 11 July 1961), of Liverpool, and *dsp* 11 March 1961
2b George, of Old Hall, E Bridgford, and later of Bridgford Hill; *b* 1 Dec 1825; land agent; *m* 1861 Emma (*b* 1839; *d* 15 July 1907), 5th dau of Rev Charles Heycock, of Pytchley House, Northants, and *d* 17 March 1899, having had, with other issue:
1c Charles; *b* 22 April 1862; *educ* Repton; *m* Naomi Carpendale and *d* 5 Jan 1904, leaving issue
2c Richard Henry, of the Burgage, Southwell, Notts; *b* 7 Oct 1865; *educ* Repton; slr; registrar Notts; *m* 1907 Edith (*d* 20 May 1963), dau of Ven Egbert Hacking, Rector Holme Pierrepoint, Archdeacon Newark, and *d* 20 June 1952, leaving, with other issue:
1d *Richard Melville, of The Burgage; *b* 7 Dec 1909; *educ* Repton; slr; *m* 30 May 1960 Mary (*d* 15 July 1997), dau of Maj John Pickard Becher, of Southwell
2d *Thomas; *b* 18 Feb 1916; *educ* Repton and Clare Coll Cambridge (MA); RE WW II Africa, India and Burma, slr, assist clerk W Sussex CC; *m* 3 Dec 1949 *Jillian Mary, dau of Geoerge William Weeks, of Colner House, Bosham, and has issue:
1e *Edward Melville; *b* 27 May 1952; *educ* Lancing
2e *William Henry; *b* 28 Jan 1958
1e *Susannah Louise; *b* 29 March 1961
3c Walter Noel; *b* 7 Jan 1867; *educ* Repton and Caius Coll Cambridge (MA); assist master Cheam Sch; *m* Edith Roberts and *d* 10 Dec 1943, having had issue
4c Rupert Kendall, of E Bridgford; *b* 1870; *m* 3 Sept 1903 Gladys Mary (*d* 1953), yr dau of William Deeping Warwick, of Balderton Hall, Newark, and *d* 22 Dec 1933, leaving issue:
1d George William; *b* 4 July 1904; *educ* Shrewsbury and Trin Coll Cambridge; *m* 24 June 1942 Margaret Evelyn Mowatt and has issue:
1e *Myrtle Everilde; *b* 12 Feb 1943; *m* *P Deer
2e *Frances Charlotte; *b* 23 May 1946
2d Gladys Emma; *b* 19 May 1907; *m* 1931 Richard Francis Turney Granger, FRAS (*d* 19 Jan 1948) and had:
1e *Christopher Francis Kendall; *b* 15 Sept 1935
1e *Daphne Caroline; *b* 15 May 1933; *m* Henry Halkyard and has two s
3d *Everilde Mary; *b* 15 April 1912; *m* 1940 Charles Harold Moor, tobacco farmer (*d* 1952), and has issue:
1e *Charles; *b* 14 Dec 1948
1e *Sylvia Catherine; *b* 11 June 1942; *m* 23 June 1962 *Brian Nugent and has a dau
2e *Everilde Elaine; *b* 11 Feb 1945; *m* 20 April 1963 *Angus Ogilvy and has a s
3e *June Lynnette; *b* 22 June 1946
6c Claude Frederick; *b* 1871; *m* Nellie (*d* 1915 aged 29) and *d* 1911
1c Georgina Annie; *b* 15 April 1864; *m* 23 Aug 1892 Dr Archibald Campbell of Mull of Kintyre, and *d* 16 May 1950, having had a s and two daus
2c Catherine Everilde; *b* 1869; *m* Kenneth St Clare Carruthers and *dsp* 1926
3c Christine Louise; *b* 1874; *d* unm 1921
3b John Walter; *b* 1828; *educ* Derby Sch; *d* 1848
4b Henry, Town Clerk Grantham; *b* 28 June 1830; *educ* Derby Sch; *m* 1st 25 Sept 1855 Elizabeth (*d* 1869), yst dau of John Stuart Edwards, of Stanton Lacey, Salop, and had, with other issue:
1c Henry Stuart; *b* 25 Sept 1858; *d* 1890
2c George Walter Glynne; *b* 4 Jan 1860; *m* Rose Osgodby and *d* 1904, leaving a dau
4b (cont.) Henry Beaumont *m* 2nd 6 June 1872 Elizabeth Anne (*d* 1934), dau of James Lewis, of Aigburth, Liverpool, and *d* 7 Oct 1882, having by her had issue:
3c Lewis Grote, Liverpool merchant; *b* 2 July 1873; *educ* Marlborough and Trin Coll Cambridge; *m* 1904 Constance Shenton, dau of Walter Glynn, and *d* 16 Oct 1940, leaving issue
4c Henry, OBE, Lt-Col Lancs Fus; *b* 7 Oct 1881; *educ* Wellington and RMA Sandhurst; *m* 1917 Dorice, yst dau of Alfred Hoole, and *d* 17 Aug 1964, leaving issue:
1d *Arthur Timothy, Capt 16th/5th Lancers; *b* 1 May 1918; *educ* Wellington and RMA Sandhurst; *m* 1st 1947 (*divorce* 1954) Donna Ray Swanburg, of USA, and has, with two daus:
1e *Richard
1e *Christine
2e *Kendra
1d (cont.) Arthur Beaumont *m* 2nd 31 Aug 1956 *Jean Mary, dau of Percy Robert Bladon, and by her has issue:
2e *Adam Robert; *b* 2 Sept 1957
3e *Sarah Anne; *b* 31 May 1960
1d *Stella; *b* 22 July 1922; *m* 24 April 1948 *Louis Henry James Lillywhite, s of Louis Patterson Lillywhite, and has issue:
1e *Louis Beaumont; *b* 21 Aug 1949
2e *Sally Elizabeth; *b* 4 Oct 1951
2d *Everilde; *m* 1st 9 June 1945 (*divorce* 1952) Geoffrey Edward Meek, s of Edward J. Meek, and has issue:
1e *Carola; *b* 5 Oct 1946
2e *Vanessa; *b* 12 Jan 1949
2d (cont.) Mrs Everilde Meek *m* 2nd 28 Nov 1952 Dr William Roy Barrett, MRCS, LRCP, s of Dr William Claude Percy Barrett, and has further issue:
1e *Simon; *b* 13 Dec 1952; *educ* Dover Coll
2e *Jonathan; *b* 14 Oct 1954; *educ* Dover Coll
3d *Anne; *m* 19 July 1953 *Richard Sydney Easton, of Braydon Oak, Marlborough, Wilts, s of Frederick Easton, of London, and has issue:
1e *Kerry; *b* 23 Aug 1954
2e *Alanna; *b* 4 Dec 1955
2c Everilde Anne; *b* 1877; *m* 25 May 1899 Maj Edward Francis Oakeley, 2nd s of Sir Charles Oakeley, 4th Bt (*qv*), and *d* 20 April 1968, leaving issue
3c Mary; *b* 1879; *m* 1905 Nevile Reid, of Hanworth, and *d* 15 Nov 1968, leaving issue. He *d* 9 Dec 1950
5b Thomas Elliott, slr; *b* 20 Oct 1838; *educ* Trin Coll Cambridge (MA); *m* 1882 Elizabeth Maria, widow of George Wolstenholme, JP, of Kenwood Park, Sharrow, Sheffield, and dau of William John Rundle, MD, of Gosport, and *d* 19 March 1899
1b Theodosia; *b* 1822; *d* unm 1850
2b Frances; *d* unm
3b Anne Charlotte; *m* 15 Sept 1859 Frederick Ward, s of T Asline Ward, of Park House, Sheffield, and had issue
2a Henry, of Edgbaston, Warwicks; *b* 8 March 1801; *m* 1 Sept 1823 Elizabeth, dau of James Taylor, of Birmingham, and had issue:
1b James Taylor; *b* 4 July 1831
(4) Walter; *b* 1767; *m* Caroline Clarkson, of Loudwater (*d* 4 March 1861 aged 89), and *d* 12 April 1841, having had a dau (*d* young)
(5) Henry, *dsp*, young
(6) Abel; *bapt* 23 Sept 1772; *m* Jane Waite (*d* 26 Oct 1834) and *dsp* 24 Jan 1838
(1) Frances; *b* 28 April 1756; *m* William Elliott, of Gedling House, Notts
(2) Charlotte; *b* 9 Dec 1765; *m* Rev John Swete, of Oxton House, Devon
1 Susannah; *m* Rev John Walter, Rector Bingham, Notts, and *dsp* June 1804

The er son,

THOMAS BEAUMONT, of The Oaks; *b* 18 Feb 1723; *m* Anne (*b* 1 Jan 1725; *d* 14 Dec 1778), dau of Edward Ayscough, and *d* 6 Feb 1783, leaving:

THOMAS RICHARD BEAUMONT, of Bretton Hall, Yorks, and Hexham Abbey, Northumberland, Col 21st Light Dragoons, MP Northumberland 1795–1818; *b* 29 April 1758; *m* Diana Wentworth (*d* 10 Aug 1831), illegitimate dau but heir of Sir Thomas Wentworth, 5th and last Bt, who took the name BLACKETT, and *d* 31 July 1829, leaving issue:

1 THOMAS WENTWORTH, for whom *see* below
2 William; *b* 9 Sept 1794; *d* 1872
3 Richard; *b* 25 Jan 1799; Capt RN; *m* 9 Feb 1832 Hon Susan Hussey Macdonald (*d* 5 Nov 1879), dau of 3rd Baron Macdonald (*qv*), and *d* 2 Nov 1877, leaving issue:

(1) Godfrey Wentworth; *b* 1835; *educ* Eton; Lt-Col; *m* 10 March 1863 Anna Maria (*d* 11 Aug 1918), dau of Sir Edward Blackett, 6th Bt (*qv*), and *d* 23 Aug 1876, having had, with other issue:

1a Ronald Wentworth; *b* 23 Aug 1864; *m* 1889 Margaret Anne (*d* 1943), dau of Thomas Harrison, and *d* 1930, leaving issue:

1b Bosville Wentworth (additional name of Ronald dropped legally); *b* 10 April 1901; S/Ldr RCAF; *m* 10 Oct 1930 Veronica Cook-Nelson, of Glasgow, and *d* 17 Jan 1961, leaving issue:

1c *Audrey Veronica; *b* 12 Sept 1931; *m* 24 Oct 1953 Maj Thomas Finlayson Davie, Canadian Intell Corps, s of Thomas Wilson Davie, of Portsoy, Banffshire, and has issue:

1d *Michael Wentworth; *b* July 1954

1d *Gayle Kimberly; *b* 20 June 1957

2d *Karen Lynn; *b* 12 April 1960

1b Ronalda Bruce Margaret Wentworth; *b* 1890; *m* 1 Dec 1917 Charles John Rowley, s of John Richard Frederick Rowley, and had issue (*see* ROWLEY, Bt, of Hill House)

2b Ailsa Francis Wentworth; *b* 1894; *m* Reginald Oliver Gray and had issue:

1c *Audrey; *b* 1919; *m* 30 June 1945 *Maj David Charles Blair, Roy Sigs, Assist Engr-in-Ch GPO, s of John Blair, and has issue:

1d *Robert; *b* 7 July 1946; *educ* Haberdashers' Sch, Aske

2d *Patrick; *b* 14 Nov 1949; *educ* Penarth County Sch

3d *Andrew; *b* 12 April 1954; *educ* St Dunstan's Coll

1d *Anne; *b* 8 April 1945; *m* 24 Sept 1966 *Colin Richard Davis, s of Alwyn Thomas Davis

2c *Diana; *b* 1925

3b Diana Wentworth Blackett; *b* 1899

4b Olva Velorna Wentworth; *b* 16 July 1903; *m* 1st 24 Jan 1925 (*divorce* 1946) Kenneth Godfrey Macmillan, MBE, AEA, ACP, s of Capt John Bathgate Macmillan, of Kobe, Japan, and had issue:

1c *Ian Alexander [Ian Macmillan Esq, Westminster Hotel, Rhyl, Flintshire]; *b* 21 Jan 1929; *educ* Gordonstoun; *m* 7 July 1958 *Pauline Mary Margaret, dau of Herbert Riley, of Blackpool, and has issue:

1d *Peter Timothy Alexander; *b* 13 May 1959

4b (cont.) Mrs Olva Macmillan *m* 2nd 24 Nov 1951 Ivan Godfrey Stanley, MC (*d* 13 Jan 1973), s of Harry Frank Stanely; *m* 3rd 25 May 1974 her former husb *Kenneth Godfrey Macmillan

2a Ernest Godfrey; *b* 22 Dec 1874; *educ* Emmanuel Coll Cambridge; *m c* 1921 Constance Ida Hay Currie (*d* 1952) and *d* Jan 1967

1a Marion Edith; *m* 2 Sept 1897 Maj Robert Bell Turton (*d* 18 March 1938), of Kildale Hall, Yorks, and *d* 13 Sept 1959, leaving issue

(2) Dudley; *d* unm

(3) Richard; *b* 1838; *educ* Eton and Trin Coll Cambridge; sheep farmer NZ; *m* 1885 Annette Rutter and *d* 1893, having had, with other issue:

1a Diana; *b* 1887; *m* 1915 Capt George Kenneth Benton, 3rd Dragoon Gds (*d* 2 March 1936), and *d* 1948, leaving issue

(4) Cecil William; *b* 1843; *educ* Eton; Cdr RN; *d* unm 1888

(1) Diana; *b* 11 June 1834; *m* 5 April 1864 Melchior Bolivar, 5th Count Gurowski (*d* 14 Jan 1908), Consul-Gen Austria-Hungary at Nice, s of Adam, 4th Count Gurowski, and had issue

(2) Averil; *b* 1841; *m* 10 Nov 1870 1st Baron Swansea (*qv*) and *d* 14 Jan 1934 aged 92, leaving issue

(3) Gwendoline; *b* 9 July 1849; *m* 1st 9 July 1973 Hugh Pigot, barrister (*d* 21 Oct 1907), s of Charles Henry Pigot (*see* PIGOT, Bt); *m* 2nd 29 April 1911 Col Thomas Mayhew; *m* 3rd Rev William Joseph de Kilpeck (*d* Jan 1939 aged 92), Rector Corfe Castle 1899–1937, s of Joseph Killpack, of Leicester

4 Edward Blackett, of Darfield, Yorks; *b* 2 May 1802; *m* 25 April 1825 Jane, dau of William Lee, of Grove, by Sophia, 2nd dau of Sir Thomas Wentworth Blackett, and *d* 7 June 1878, leaving issue:

(1) Frederick Edward Blackett; *b* 22 Oct 1833; *educ* Harrow; Capt RE, Turkish medal and medal for Lucknow; MP S Durham 1868–80; *d* 20 Aug 1899

(2) Charles Edward; *b* 27 Feb 1841; *educ* Cheltenham

(1) Sophia; *b* 20 April 1829; *m* 20 April 1852 Rev Hon Percival George Willoughby, Rector Durweston-cum-Bryanston, bro of 8th Baron Middleton (*qv*), and *d* 15 Jan 1898, leaving issue

(2) Louise; *m* 23 Aug 1871 Samuel Warren, QC, and *d* 1913 aged 82

(3) Lucy Matilda; *m* 14 Oct 1863 George Margesson (*d* 4 March 1911), of Van and Oakhurst, Surrey, and Woodringfold and Findon Place, Sussex, and *d* 6 June 1909, leaving issue

5 Henry Ralph; *b* 3 Feb 1807; *m* 19 May 1831 Katherine (*m* 2nd 6 May 1845 Capt James Anlaby Legard (*see* LEGARD, Bt); *d* 12 March 1887), dau of Sir George Cayley, 6th Bt (*qv*), and *d* 21 June 1838, leaving issue:

(1) Henry Frederick, of Whitley Beaumont, JP, DL; *b* 10 March 1857; MP S Yorks; *m* 1 Sept 1857 Maria Johanna (*d* 10 July 1925 aged 90), only surv dau of William Garthorpe, of Wiganthorpe, and *d* 6 Oct 1913, leaving two s and eight daus

(2) Richard Thomas; went to Western Australia; *m* and *dsp*

(3) George; *d* young

(1) Emily; *m* 19 June 1855 Rev Richard Hugh Cholmondeley (*d* 10 Aug 1911), of Condover Hall, Salop, Vicar Leaton, and *d* 11 April 1895, leaving issue

(2) Mary Catherine; *d* unm

1 Diana; *b* 15 Jan 1796

2 Marianne; *b* 25 Sept 1797; *m* 21 Sept 1837 Edward Booth, of Catsfield, Battle, Sussex, s of Edward Taylor Booth, of Norwich, and *d* 9 Feb 1858, leaving issue:

(1) Edward Thomas; *b* 2 June 1842; *educ* Harrow; ornithologist; *d* 8 Feb 1890

3 Sophia; *b* 25 Sept 1803; *m* Alexander Trensch, Baron de Buttlar Brandenfels, and *dsp* 26 Jan 1849

The est son,

THOMAS WENTWORTH BEAUMONT, of Bretton Hall, Wakefield, and Bywell Hall, Northumberland; *b* 5 Nov 1792; MP Northumberland 1818–26 and 1830–37 and Stafford 1827; *m* 22 Nov 1827 Henrietta Jane Emma Hawks (*d* 22 Nov 1861), dau of John Atkinson, of Maple Hayes, Staffs, and *d* 20 Dec 1848, leaving issue:

1 WENTWORTH BLACKETT, **1st Baron**

2 Walter; *b* 12 Feb 1832; *educ* Harrow; founded Beaumont Scripture prizes there; *d* unm 1895

3 Somerset Archibald, of Shere, Guildford, DL (Northumberland); *b* 6 Feb 1835; FRGS, MP Newcastle-on-Tyne 1860–65 and Wakefield 1868–74; *d* unm 8 Dec 1921

4 Dudley Zamoiski; *b* 18 Sept 1836; *educ* Harrow and Ch Ch Oxford; barrister Lincoln's Inn; *m* 1st and had issue:

(1) Harold Ernest

(1) May Eliza; *m* 27 April 1905 Robert Henry Verschoyle (*d* 1911), s of Richard John Verschoyle, of Tanrago, Co Sligo, and *dsp* 30 April 1948

4 (cont.) Dudley Beaumont *m* 2nd and *d* 15 Dec 1907, having had further issue two daus

1 Emma Diana; *m* 23 March 1858 Rev Stopford Augustus Brooke, MA LLD (*d* 18 March 1916), and *d* 20 June 1874, leaving issue

2 Florence; *m* 1st 12 Nov 1858 (*divorce*) George Edward March, CMG (*d* 29 May 1922), s of Thomas March, and had issue; *m* 2nd 15 July 1866 Baron Vincenzo Palumbo

The est son,

WENTWORTH BLACKETT BEAUMONT, **1st Baron Allendale**, of Allendale and Hexham, Co Northumberland (UK), so *cr* 20 July 1906, JP and DL (Northumberland and W R Yorks) and JP (Co Durham); *b* 11 April 1829; MP S Northumberland 1852–85 and Tyneside 1886–92; *m* 1st 6 March 1856 Lady Margaret Anne de Burgh (*d* 31 March 1888), 4th dau of 1st Marquess of Clanricarde (*see* SLIGO, M), and had issue:

1 WENTWORTH CANNING BLACKETT, **2nd Baron** and **1st Viscount**

2 Edward de Grey; *b* 2 March 1862; Maj Lancashire Hus and 16th Lancers; *d* unm 23 Nov 1940

3 Hubert George; *b* 6 April 1864; *educ* Oxford (BA); MP Eastbourne 1906–10, High Sheriff Bucks 1919, KGStJ; *m* 26 May 1900 Elisa Mercedes, LGStJ (*drowned* off Leghorn 10 Aug 1917), er dau of Michael Paul Grace, of Battle Abbey, Sussex, and Belgravia, and *d* 14 Aug 1922, leaving issue:

(1) Michael Wentworth, TD, JP (1927–47) and DL (1938) (both Bucks); *b* 8 Feb 1903; *educ* Eton, Oundle and RMC Sandhurst; Maj 90th (Bucks and Berks Yeo) Field Bde RA (TA), formerly Lt Coldstream Gds; MP Aylesbury 1929–38, PPS to Parly Sec Bd Educn 1931–32; CC (Bucks 1925–34); MFH: Bicester and Warden Hill 1945–47, Kildare 1953–59; *m* 1st 29 Feb 1924 Hon Faith Pease (*d* 16 Feb 1935), yr dau of 1st Baron Gainford (*qv*), and had issue:

1a +TIMOTHY WENTWORTH BEAUMONT (Rev), *cr* BARON BEAUMONT OF WHITLEY (LP; *qv*)

(1) (cont.) Maj Michael Beaumont *m* 2nd 30 Dec 1935 *Doreen Christian [Mrs Michael Beaumont, Harristown House, Brannockstown, Co Kildare, Ireland], only dau of Sir Herbert William Davis-Goff, 2nd Bt (*see* 1939 edn), and *d* 19 Dec 1958

1 Margaret Harriet; *b* 1856; *m* 19 May 1881 3rd Baron Poltimore (*qv*) and *d* 4 Aug 1931, leaving issue

2 Violet Augusta; *b* 1858; *d* 1862

3 Amy Virginia; *b* 1859; *m* 2 Nov 1880 2nd Baron Brabourne (*qv*) and *d* 19 May 1949, having had issue

The **1st Baron** *m* 2nd 17 Feb 1891 Edith Althea (*d* 19 May 1927), dau of Lt-Gen Henry Meade-Hamilton, CB, and widow of Maj-Gen Sir George Pomeroy-Colley, KCSI, CB, CMG, and *d* 13 Feb 1907

His s,

WENTWORTH CANNING BLACKETT BEAUMONT, **2nd Baron Allendale** and **1st Viscount Allendale**, of Allendale and Hexham, Co Northumberland (UK), so *cr* 5 July 1911, JP and DL; *b* 2 Dec 1860; *educ* Trin Coll Cambridge (MA); Capt and Hon Maj Yorkshire Hus; MP Hexham 1895–1907; V-Chamberlain Household (Govt Whip) 1905–07, Capt Yeoman Gd (Dep Ch Whip Ho of Lds) 1907–11, Ld in Waiting (Govt Whip) 1911–16; *m* 12 Nov 1889 Lady Alexandrina Louisa Maud Vane-Tempest (*d* 31 July 1945), dau of 5th Marquess of Londonderry (*qv*), and had issue:

1 WENTWORTH HENRY CANNING, **2nd Viscount**

2 Ralph Edward Blackett, CBE (1967), TD, JP (1932) and DL (1961) (both Montgomeryshire); *b* 12 Feb 1901; *educ* Eton and Ch Ch Oxford (BA 1923, MA 1953); Lt-Col 636 LAA Regt RA (RWF), TA; MP Portsmouth Centl 1931–1945, PPS to PMG 1935–40 and Sec State War 1942–45, High Sheriff Montgomeryshire 1957, V-Lt 1962–77, Devpt Commr 1952–69, Chm Montgomeryshire CAEC 1948–69, memb Cncl Tbnls 1958–77, chm Machynlleth UDC 1964–66, memb Welsh Ec Cncl 1965, memb Cncl Small Industries Rural Areas 1969; *m* 22 March 1926 Helena Mary Christine (*d* 26 Aug 1962), yr dau of Brig-Gen Cecil Wray, CB, CMG, CVO, TD, and *d* 18 Sept 1977, leaving issue:

(1) John Ralph, JP and DL (Powys); *b* 22 April 1927; *educ* Eton and Ch Ch Oxford (MA 1952); MP Mrewa, Fedn Rhodesia and Nyasaland 1962–63; *m* 26 June 1951 *Audrey Lilian Christie, yr dau of Edward Thomas Hickling, of York, and *d* 1992, leaving:

1a +Ralph Wentworth Christopher [Ralph Beaumont Esq, Llwyngwern Farm, Machynlleth, Powys]; *b* 4 April 1952; *educ* Peterhouse Rhodesia; *m* 1979 *Nicole Marie Blanche, dau of R J Dubreuil, of Niort, France, and has issue:

1b +Christopher Henry Louis; *b* 1982

1b *Aline Mary Helena; *b* 1985

2a +Nigel Canning Vane; *b* 8 Jan 1954; *educ* Shrewsbury; *m* 1991 *Nicola Carron Toy, dau of R T West, of Brighton, and has issue:

1b *Francesca Daisy; *b* 1992

3a +Andrew John Blackett; *b* 27 March 1956; *educ* Shrewsbury; Maj RWF; *m* 1988 *Jane Margaret, only dau of Colin Weedon, of Bournemouth, and has issue:

1b +Henry George Canning; *b* 1993

1b *Lucinda Eleanor Christine; *b* 1991

4a +Hugh Edward Stewart; *b* 25 March 1959; *educ* Shrewsbury; *m* 1988 *Susan Elizabeth, dau of Elfed Jones, of Wellington, Salop, and has issue:

1b *Charlotte Louise Margaret; *b* 1991

5a +Peter John Tempest; *b* 29 Dec 1964; *educ* Wrekin; *m* 1993 *Jill Nicola, only dau of B R Rodgers, of Keighley, Yorks, and has issue:

1b +Harry-John Tempest; *b* 1993

1a *Louise Christine Winsmore; *b* 27 March 1956; *m* 1987 *Allan N Markham, of Zambia, and has issue:

1b *Lyon Frederick; *b* 1991

1b *Lilly-Anne Winsmore; *b* 1988

(2) +David Christopher [David Beaumont Esq, Poolspringe, Much Birch, Hereford and Worcester]; *b* 15 Feb 1929; *educ* Eton and King's Coll Durham U (BSc 1952); *m* 1st 17 March 1954 (*divorce* 1974) Marion Edith, yst dau of Henry John Mallard and formerly w of Thomas Harkness Davison, of Salisbury, S Rhodesia, and has issue:

1a +Timothy David; *b* 27 July 1955; *educ* King's Sch Bruton

1a *Sally Aline Christine; *b* 12 Dec 1956

(2) (cont.) David Beaumont *m* 2nd 1977 *Valerie Margaret, dau of Talbot Wrigley Roberts

(1) *Diana [Mrs Brian Outhwaite, Roseberry House, Westbourne, Emsworth, Hants]; *b* 22 July 1934; *m* 18 Dec 1954 *Capt Brian Robert Outhwaite, RN, only s of Cdr Cedric Robert Leonard Outhwaite, DSC, RNVR, by Helen, yr dau of Capt Arthur Herbert Kennedy, and has issue:

1a *Mark Robert Canning; *b* 27 April 1957; *educ* Sherborne; Maj RTR (ret); *m* 1988 *Sarah Elizabeth, only dau of Michael Hipwell, of Affpuddle, Dorset, and has issue:

1b *Catherine Rossana; *b* 1992

2a *James Edward; *b* 4 Feb 1961; *educ* Stowe

3a *Charles Cedric; *b* 12 June 1965; *educ* Sherborne

1 Margaret Helen, CBE (1958); *b* 13 Nov 1892; *m* 8 Feb 1917 5th Earl Fortescue (*qv*) and *d* 10 June 1958, leaving issue

2 Aline Mary de Burgh; *b* 23 April 1895; *m* 12 Nov 1925 (*divorce* 1939) Geoffrey Richard Purcell Gilpin, DSC, 2nd s of Peter Purcell Gilpin, and *d* 15 April 1967, having had:

(1) *Patricia Margaret Aline; *b* 22 Aug 1926; *m* Oct 1962 *David Roy MacGregor

(2) *Beatrice May Edith, MBE; *b* 4 Sept 1928

3 Diana; *d* an infant 31 Jan 1897

4 Agatha Violet; *b* 26 Dec 1903; OStJ; *m* 1 June 1933 Sir John Victor Thomas Woolrych Talt Perowne, KCMG (*d* 8 Jan 1951), est s of Col John Thomas Woolrych Perowne, VD, TD, of St James's Court, London SW, and *d* 15 Jan 1994, having had:

(1) *John Florian Canning [John Perowne Esq, The White House, Bramerton, Norwich, NR14 7DW]; *b* 20 Aug 1942; *educ* Eton and Corpus Christi Coll Cambridge (BA 1964, MA 1968); slr; *m* 12 Oct 1968 *Elizabeth Mary, only dau of Rev Shirley Beckett Freeman, of The Rectory, Long Bredy, Dorset, and has issue:

1a *John Matthew Gregory; *b* 10 April 1983

(1) Mr and Mrs John Perowne also adopted:

*Anastasia Emily; *b* 10 July 1975; *educ* Norwich High Sch, Mouleton Combe and Durham U (BSc)

*Clementine Sophia; *b* 11 Jan 1979; *educ* Norwich High School

(1) Rachel Penelope; *b* 10 May 1938; *d* 4 Feb 1940

The 1st VISCOUNT *d* 12 Dec 1923; his est son,

WENTWORTH HENRY CANNING BEAUMONT, **2nd Viscount Allendale**, KG (1951), CB (1948), CBE (1943), MC, JP, DL; *b* 6 Aug 1890; *educ* Eton and Trin Coll Cambridge (BA 1912); Hon Col 4th Bn KOYLI 1928–39, Lt-Col and Brevet Col Northumberland Hus Yeo, Capt 2nd Life Gds, WW I ; Ld-Lt Northumberland 1949–56, Perm Ld in Waiting 1954, Ld in Waiting to HM GEORGE VI, MFH Badsworth 1936–45, Steward Jockey Club 1947–50, Chm W R Unemployment Centres 1937–41, Hon DCL Durham U 1951; *m* 20 July 1921 Violet Lucy Emily (*d* 1979), er dau of Sir Charles Hilton Seely, 2nd Bt (*qv*), and *d* 16 Dec 1956, leaving:

1 WENTWORTH HUBERT CHARLES BEAUMONT, **3rd and present Viscount Allendale**

2 +Richard Blackett CVO (1996) [The Hon Richard Beaumont CVO, Flat 1, 13–16 Embankment Gdns, London SW3 4LW]; *b* 13 Aug 1926; *educ* Eton; RNVR 1944, Sub-Lt 1946–48; PA to 1st Viscount Monckton of Brenchley Hyderabad 1947–48, ADC to Sir Donald MacGillivray Malaya 1954–55, with James Purdey & Sons 1949 (dir 1952, chm 1971), Master Gunmakers' Co 1969 and 1985, author: *Purdey's, The Guns and the Family* (1984); *m* 12 Oct 1971 *Lavinia Mary, yr dau of Lt-Col Arnold Ramsey Keppel (*see* ALBEMARLE, E)

3 +(Edward) Nicholas Canning (Sir), KCVO (1994, LVO 1976, CVO 1986), DL (Berks 1982); *b* 14 Dec 1929; *educ* Eton; Capt (ret) Life Gds; Sec Ascot Authority and Clerk Course 1969, V-Lt Berks 1989–94, Pres Baillie St John Ambulance Bde 1988; *m* 8 Oct 1953 *Jane Caroline Falconer, er dau of Alexander Lewis Paget Falconer Wallace, TD, JP, of Candacraig, Strathdon, Aberdeenshire, and has issue:

(1) +Thomas Wentworth; *b* 27 Jan 1962

(2) +Henry Alexander Nicholas; *b* 25 July 1966; Page Honour to HM QUEEN ELIZABETH THE QUEEN MOTHER, 1979–82

4 +Matthew Henry [The Hon Matthew Beaumont, Bearl House, Stocksfield, Northumberland NE43 7AJ]; *b* 10 April 1933; *educ* Bradfield; underwriting memb Lloyd's 1961; *m* 1st 14 April 1959 (*divorce* 1972) Anne Christine Margaret, er dau of Gerald John Hamilton, and has issue:

(1) +Justin George Gerald; *b* 12 Jan 1960

(1) *Charlotte Catherine Lucinda; *b* 29 May 1962; *m* 1987 *Lord Cardross, est s of 17th Earl of Buchan (*qv*)

4 (cont.) The Hon Matthew Beaumont *m* 2nd 13 Oct 1973 *Belinda Jane Elizabeth, er dau of Maj Harold David Cuthbert (*see* MILNES-COATES, Bt)

5 George Andrew; *b* 21 June 1938 (HM QUEEN ELIZABETH THE QUEEN MOTHER stood sponsor); *educ* Eton; *k* flying accident NZ 3 Jan 1960

1 *Ela Hilda Aline, OStJ [The Rt Hon The Countess of Carlisle, Naworth Castle, Brampton, Cumbria]; *b* 27 May 1925; *m* 3 Oct 1945 12th Earl of Carlisle (*qv*) and has issue

Seat: Bywell Hall, Northumberland. An enterprising design by James Paine, one of what has been identified as his 'Villa' series, Bywell has a particularly noteworthy garden front, in which a triple pediment with dentillated cornices surmounts a three-storey, five-bay facade. The ground floor contains a central, round-topped door and curved pediments to two outer windows, each of which is flanked by twin alcoves, the whole of that floor being adorned with stylised unpointed stonework. On the second storey vestigial balustrades adorn the windows, with again curved pediments to the outer windows. The central bays are interspersed with four pilasters that join the ground floor to the base of the triple pediment.

ALLEYNE

Arms: Per chevron gules and ermine in chief two lion's heads erased or. **Crest:** Out of a ducal coronet, a horse's head argent.

Motto: *Non tua te moveant sed publica vota* ('Let not your own interests move you but rather the wishes of the public').

Creation: Bt. (GB) 6 April 1769.

SIR JOHN OLPHERTS CAMPBELL ALLEYNE, 5TH BT, of Four Hills, Barbados [The Rev Sir John Alleyne Bt, 2 Ash Grove, Guildford, Surrey GU2 5UT]; *b* 18 Jan 1928; *s* f 1983; *educ* Eton and Jesus Coll Cambridge (BA 1950, MA 1955); ordained deacon 1955, priest 1956, curate Southampton 1955–58, Chaplain: Coventry Cathedral 1958–62, Clare Coll Cambridge 1962–66 and Bp Bristol 1966–68, Vicar Speke 1971–73, Rector 1973–75, Rector Weeke, Hants, 1975–93; *m* 28 Sept 1968 *Honor Emily Margaret, er dau of Albert William Irwin, of Linkview Park, Upper Malone, Belfast, and has issue:

1 +RICHARD MEYNELL; *b* 23 June 1972

1 *Clare Emma Gila; *b* 26 Oct 1969

Lineage: GEORGE ALLEYNE, of Chartley, Staffs, and Grantham, Lincs, had:

RICHARD ALLEYNE, of Grantham; *m* 1st —; *m* 2nd Isabella, dau of John Sheldon, of Beoley, Worcs, and *d* 6 Sept 1559, having by her had further issue; his only s by his 1st w:

JOHN, of Grantham; *dvp*, leaving, with an er s (John, *b c* 1535, *m* Dorothy, dau of Alderman Clerk, of London, and had four s):

RICHARD ALLEYNE; *m* Margaret, dau of John Wisdom, London merchant, and had:

Rev RICHARD ALLEYNE, DD, rector Stowting, Kent, inherited land in E Greenwich which had belonged to his ggf; *m* Christian and *d* Oct 1651, leaving a 3rd s:

REYNOLD ALLEYNE; one of the first Englishmen to settle Barbados, where he built up an estate and a mansion he called Mount Alleyne; *m* Mary Skeet (*m* 2nd John Turner,of Boston, Mass., and later Barbados) and had:

ABEL ALLEYNE; memb Barbadian Cncl, Lt-Gen Barbados; *m* Elizabeth Denzy and had, with an est s, a yst s and four daus:

REYNOLD ALLEYNE; built the mansion of Four Hills, Barbados, memb Legislative Assembly, Ch Judge Bridge Court Barbados; *m* Elizabeth, dau and coheir of John Gay, and had an est s:

JOHN ALLEYNE, of Four Hills; *educ* Magdalen Coll Oxford; *m* 24 Nov 1718 Mary (*d* 1742), dau of William Terril, of Cabbage-tree Hall (sole heiress of her mother Rebecca, dau and coheiress of Thomas Spair, of Mount Steadfast), and *d* 1730, having had, with a dau (Rebecca, *m* as his 2nd w 1st Earl of Radnor; *qv*) an only surv s:

Sir John Guy Alleyne, 1st Bt (GB), so *cr* 6 April 1769; *b* 28 April 1724; memb LegislativeAssembly for St Andrew's 1757, Speaker 1767–97; *m* 1st 19 Oct 1746 Christina (*d* 1782), 4th dau and coheir of Joseph Dottin, of Black Rocks, by Anne, only dau and heir of Edward Jordan, and had a s (*d* in infancy); *m* 2nd 29 June 1786 Jane Abel, dau of Abel Alleyne, and *d* 1801, having had, with five daus, an only surv s:

Sir Reynold Abel Alleyne, 2nd Bt; *b* 10 June 1789; *m* 20 Sept 1810 Rebecca (*d* 5 June 1860), 3rd and yst dau of John Olton, of Harrow, Barbados, and had, with four daus:

1 JOHN GAY NEWTON (Sir), **3rd Bt**
2 Reynold Fitzherbert Beresford; *b* 7 Aug 1825; Judge Assist Court Appeal Barbados; *m* 23 April 1854 Anna Maria Best (*d* 3 June 1913), 3rd dau of Sir Robert Boucher Clarke, CB, Ch Justice Barbados, and *d* 24 Sept 1889, leaving issue:
(1) Reynold Beresford Senhouse; *b* 1 March 1858; *d* unm 1898
(2) William Newton; *b* 25 Dec 1859; *m* Ethel Florence (*d* 23 Nov 1967), dau of John Mason, of Bulkeley, Barbados, and *d* 1910, leaving:
1a William Norman; *b* 1903; *d* 18 Oct 1971
(1) Emily Rebecca; *m* 5 July 1876 Henry Alleyne Pile (*d* May 1933), of Warleigh, Barbados, and *d* 28 July 1941, leaving issue
(2) Agnes Martin; *m* 1882 James Francis Browne (*d* 8 Oct 1901), of Merton Lodge, Barbados, and *d* 13 Nov 1944, leaving issue
3 Bouverie; *b* 19 July 1828; Colonial Sec Grenada and St Vincent; *m* 17 Aug 1856 Charlotte Agnes Emma (*d* 24 April 1895), yst dau of Lt-Gen Sir William Macbean George Colebrooke, CB, RA, Govr Barbados, and *d* 25 Oct 1861, leaving issue:
(1) Bouverie Colebrook; *b* 14 Jan 1861; Lt RNR; *m* Ada Clements and *d* Feb 1901, leaving:
1a Mabel Charlotte; *d* unm 15 Aug 1961
(1) Charlotte; *d* 1873
(2) Gertrude; *d* unm 20 March 1943

Sir REYNOLD *d* 14 Feb 1870; his est son,

Sir John Gay Newton Alleyne, 3rd Bt, JP (Derbys); *b* 8 Sept 1820; MICE, CA Derbys, V-Pres Iron and Steel Inst, Warden Dulwich Coll 1843–51; *m* 11 March 1851 Augusta Isabella (*d* 9 Sept 1910), dau of Sir Henry FitzHerbert, 3rd Bt (*qv*), and *d* 20 Feb 1912, leaving, with four other daus (*d* unm):
1 Reynold Henry Newton; *b* 16 May 1852; *m* 4 Jan 1879 Susanna (*d* 9 Feb 1947), 3rd dau of John Meynell, of Meynell Langley, Derbys, and *dvp* 6 April 1908, leaving, with four other daus (*d* unm):
(1) JOHN MEYNELL (Sir), **4th Bt**
(2) Reynold Meynell; *b* 6 March 1892; Cdr RN, WW I and WW II; *d* 4 May 1978
(1) Alice; *m* 10 June 1911 Charles Tertius MacLean Plowright, MB, BCh, MRCS, LRCP, Capt RAMC (*d* 16 Oct 1935), s of Charles Bagge Plowright, MD (Durham), FRCS, and *d* 28 Oct 1956, leaving issue
2 Anthony FitzHerbert; *b* 1858; *d* 30 Dec 1859
1 Agnes Rebecca Augusta; *m* 7 Sept 1880 Frederick Channer Corfield, JP (*d* 4 Dec 1904), of Ormonde Fields, Codnor, Derbys, and Chatwall Hall, Leebotwood, Salop, est s of Rev Frederick Corfield, Vicar Shirley, Derbys, and *d* 6 April 1941, leaving issue
2 Judith; *m* 7 Sept 1880 William de Burgh Jessop, JP (*d* 10 April 1894), of Overton Hall, Derbys, and *d* 1 Feb 1492, leaving issue
3 Rebecca Olton; *m* 7 Nov 1883 Frederic Charles Arkwright, JP, DL (*d* 18 July 1923), of Willersley, Derbys, and *d* 9 March 1944, leaving issue

Sir JOHN *d* 20 Feb 1912; his grandson,

Sir John Meynell Alleyne, 4th Bt, DSO (1918), DSC; *b* 11 Aug 1889; Capt RN, WW I (wounded, despatches) and WW II; *m* 20 Dec 1920 Alice Violet (*d* 1985), dau of James Campbell, and *d* 17 Dec 1983, leaving:
1 Sir JOHN OLPHERTS CAMPBELL ALLEYNE, **5th and present Bt**
1 *Eileen Violet; *b* 11 May 1923
2 *Rosemary [Mrs John Perry, Greenacres, Minstead, Lyndhurst, Hants]; *b* 26 April 1925; *m* 6 Dec 1954 John Perry (*d* 10 Dec 1954), yst s of Capt John Perry, MC, of Birdhill, Co Tipperary

ALPORT

Arms: Barry wavy arg. and az., on a bend or a Tudor Rose arg. on gu. between two oyster shells gu. **Crest:** A demi-lion or gorged with a mural crown gu. within a Norman arch ppr. **Supporters:** Dexter, a representation of a Roman centurion supporting a vexillum of the XX Legion ppr.; sinister, a representation of an Ancient Briton ppr.
Motto: *Ferio tego* ('I strike (and) I defend').
Creation: B. (LP) (UK) 16 Feb 1961.

THE BARON ALPORT, of Colchester, Essex (Cuthbert James McCall Alport, TD (1949), PC (1960), DL (Essex 1974)) [The Rt Hon The Lord Alport TD PC DL, The Cross House, Layer de la Haye, Essex CO2 0JG]; *educ* Haileybury and Pembroke Coll Camb (BA 1934, MA 1941, Pres Cambridge Union 1935); MP (C) Colchester 1950–61, High Steward Colchester 1967–, barrister Middle Temple 1944, joined Artists' Rifles (TA) 1934, served WW II with Roy Welch Fus and KAR (E Africa), GSO1 E Africa Cmmd 1944–45, hon Lt-Col, tutor Ashridge Coll 1935–37, assist sec Cons Pty Educn Dept 1937–39, Dir Conservative Political Centre 1945–50, Assist PMG 1955–57, Parly U-Sec CRO 1957–59, Min State CRO 1959–61, Br HC Fedn Rhodesia and Nysaland 1961–63, Special Rep Salisbury, Rhodesia, 1967, Master Skinners' Co 1969–70, UK Rep Cncl Europe 1964–65, dir: Industl Finance and Investment Ltd and Leslie Langton Hldgs, author: *Kingdoms in Partnership* (1937), *Hope in Africa* (1952) and *The Sudden Assignment* (1965); *b* 22 March 1912, *cr* a life peer as BARON ALPORT, of Colchester, Essex, 16 Feb 1961; *m* 26 Oct 1945 Rachel Cecilia (*d* 13 July 1980), only dau of Lt-Col Ralph Charles Bingham, CVO, DSO, of 10 Evelyn Gdns, London SW1 (*see* LUCAN, E), and has issue:
1 *Arthur Edward Bingham; *b* 22 May 1954; *educ* Haileybury and Exeter U (BSc 1976); *m* 14 July 1979 *Anne Vivian, est dau of P A Grove-White, of Crown Piece, Wormingford, Colchester, and has issue:
(1) *Robert Michael Bingham; *b* 23 Aug 1983
1 *Cecilia Alexander Rose [The Hon Mrs Lang, St Margaret's Vicarage, King's Lynn, Norfolk]; *b* 3 Sept 1946; *m* 23 Aug 1969 *Rev Geofrey W F Lang, MA, s of Frederick Lang, of Saint Cross, Croxley Green, Herts, and has issue:
(1) *Oliver James Alport; *b* 23 April 1971
(1) *Imogen Eileen Cecilia; *b* June 1973
2 *(Lavender) Lilias Carole; *b* 13 Dec 1950; *m* 17 June 1974 *Ian C Taylor, s of H S Taylor, and has issue:
(1) *Arthur Lawrence Alport; *b* 27 Dec 1972
(2) *Ralph George Alport; *b* 13 May 1980

Lineage: EDWARD ALPORT, of Stourbridge, Worcs, merchant; b 25 Nov 1750; *m*; and *d* 4 July 1792, leaving issue:

JAMES SWAINE ALPORT, of London and Nova Scotia; *b* 1780; *m*; and *d* 1852, leaving issue:

HENRY ROSE ALPORT; *m* Eleanor Parker, of Warley Hall, Essex, and had issue:

ARTHUR CUTHBERT ALPORT, of Great Warley, Essex, and Cape Colony, S Africa; *b* 1844; *m* Eleanor, est dau of James Thwaites, and *d* 1888, leaving issue:
1 ARTHUR CECIL, of whom presently
2 Sidney
1 Grace
2 Dorothy

The eldest son,

Prof ARTHUR CECIL ALPORT, MD, FRCP, of Cairo; *b* 1880; *m* 1907 Janet (*d* 3 March 1976), dau of James McCall, of Caitloch, Dunfriesshire, and *d* 17 April 1959, leaving issue:
1 Arthur Cuthbert; *d* young
2 CUTHBERT JAMES McCALL, *cr* a **Baron**

ALTON OF LIVERPOOL

Creation: B. (LP, UK) 1997.

THE BARON ALTON OF LIVERPOOL, of Mossley Hill, Co Liverpool (David Patrick Alton) [The Rt Hon The Lord Alton of Liverpool, 25 N Mossley Hill Rd, Liverpool L18 8BL]; *b* 15 March 1951; *educ* Edmund Campion Sch Hornchurch and Christ's Coll of Educn Liverpool; memb Liverpool City Cncl 1972–80 (Dep Leader, Chm Housing 1978); MP (Lib) Liverpool Edge Hill 1979–97; Lib Party Spokesman: Environment and Race Rels 1979–81, Home Affrs 1981–82, NI 1987–88; Lib Ch Whip 1985–87; memb: Select Ctee Environment 1981–85, H of C Privileges Ctee 1994–; All Party Gps: Drugs Misuse, Mental Health (V-Chm), Pro-Life (Treas), Street Children (Chm) 1992–, Ukraine (Sec); Chm: Cncl Educn Cwlth, Lib Candidates Ctee 1985; Nat Pres Nat League Young Libs 1979, Co-Fndr Movement for Christian Democracy Britain 1990; Pres Liverpool Old People's Hostels Assoc, V-Pres: AMA 1979–, Liverpool YMCA; Nat V-Pres Life; Chm Forget-me-Not Appeal; Tstee: Crisis at Christmas, Liverpool Hostels for Victims of Violent Crime, Western Care Assoc; Patron: Jubilee Campaign for Release Prisoners of Conscience 1986–, Belfast Tst Integrated Educn; author: *What Kind of Country?* (1987), *Whose Choice Anyway?* (1988), *Faith in Britain* (1991); *m* 1988 *Dilys Elizabeth, yr dau of Rev Philip Bell, and has two sons and a dau

Lineage: FREDERICK ALTON; *m* Bridget — and had:

DAVID PATRICK, *cr* a **Baron**

ALTRINCHAM

Arms: Sable three owls argent, a chief azure, issuant from the base thereof a sun in splendour or. **Crest:** A grenade sable fired proper between two roses argent barbed and seeded, also proper. **Supporters:** (not currently borne since barony disclaimed) On either side a lion gules gorged with a chain collar, pendent therefrom a portcullis or, and supporting a date palm fructed proper. **Motto:** *Servire et servare* ('To serve and to preserve'). **Creation:** B. (UK) 1 Aug 1945.

John Edward Poynder Grigg [John Grigg, 32 Dartmouth Row, London SE10 8AW]; *b* 15 April 1924; *s f* as 2nd Baron Altrincham 1 Dec 1955, disclaimed Barony for life 31 July 1963; *educ* Eton and New Coll Oxford; Lt Gren Gds WW II, ed *The National and English Review* 1954–60, jnlst *Guardian* 1960–70, *The Times* 1986–93, chm London Library 1985–91 (pres 1996–), pres Blackheath Soc, Govr Nehru Meml Tst, FRSL, author: *Two Anglican Essays* (1958), *The Young Lloyd George* (1973), *Lloyd George: The People's Champion* (1978), *The Victory That Never Was* (1980), *Nancy Astor: Portrait of a Pioneer* (1980), *Lloyd George: From Peace to War 1912–1916* (1985), *The History of* The Times, *Vol 6: the Thomson Years* (1993), part-author: *Is the Monarchy Perfect?*; *m* 3 Dec 1958 *(Marian) Patricia, only dau of Harold Ernest Campbell, and has adopted:

*Alexander Henry Campell; *b* 4 April 1966; *educ* Westminster
*Edward William Jonathan; *b* 3 April 1969; *educ* Westminster

Lineage: HENRY BIDEWELL GRIGG, CIE, ICS; Political Resident Travancore; *m* Elizabeth (*d* Jan 1920), er dau of Sir Edward Deas-Thomson, Colonial Sec NSW, and *d* 1894, leaving:

EDWARD WILLIAM MACLEAY GRIGG, **1st Baron Altrincham**, of Tormarton, Co Gloucester (UK), so *cr* 1 Aug 1945, PC (1944), KCMG (1928, CMG 1919), KCVO (1920, CVO 1919), DSO (1918), MC; *b* 8 Sept 1879; *educ* Winchester and New Coll Oxford (BA 1902); Lt-Col Army Special Res WW I (despatches), Hon-Col RA (TA) 1944, Mil Sec to HRH THE PRINCE OF WALES tours Canada, Australia and NZ 1919–21, Priv Sec to PM 1921–22, Sec Rhodes Tst, dir Reuters 1923–25, Govr and C-in-C Kenya 1925–30, chm Milk Reorgn Commn 1932, MP (Nat Lib) Oldham 1922–25 and (C) Altrincham 1933–45, Parly Sec Min Inf Sept 1939, Fin Sec War Off April 1940, Jt U-Sec War 1940–42, Min Res Middle E 1944–45, author: *The Greatest Experiment in History, Britain Looks At Germany, British Foreign Policy*, Chevalier Order Leopold II Belgium, Offr Legn Honour; *m* 31 Jan 1923 Hon Joan Alice Katherine Dickson-Poynder (*d* 1987), only child of 1st and last Baron Islington, PC, GCMG, GBE, DSO (*see* 1936 edn), and *d* 1 Dec 1955, leaving:

1 JOHN EDWARD POYNDER GRIGG, **briefly 2nd Baron Altrincham**
2 +ANTHONY ULICK DAVID DUNDAS [The Hon Anthony Grigg, 11 Horbury Mews, London W11 3NL]; *b* 12 Jan 1934; heir presumptive; *educ* Eton and New Coll Oxford; 2nd Lt Gren Gds 1952–53; *m* 2 March 1965 *Eliane de Cassagne de Beaufort, 2nd dau of the Marquis de Miramont, and has:
(1) +(Edward) Sebastian; *b* 18 Dec 1965; *educ* Eton; Parly candidate Heywood and Middleton 1997 gen election; *m* 1993 *Rachel Sophia, jnlst *Daily Telegraph*, dau of Lawrence Kelly (*see* CAMROSE, V), and has:
1a +Edward Laurence Dundas De Miramont; *b* 11 Feb 1995
2a +Anthony George Seymour Sebastian; *b* 10 March 1997
(2) +Steven Thomas; *b* 13 March 1969; *educ* Eton
(1) *Anne Casilda; *b* 1 March 1967
1 Annabel Desirée; *b* 19 Nov 1931

ALVINGHAM

Arms: Per pale argent and azure, a chevron between three chaplets of roses counter-changed. **Crest:** A falcon close, belled or, preying on a mallard proper. **Supporters:** On either side a falcon, wings expanded, belled or, gorged with a chaplet of roses azure. **Badge:** A rose gules, barbed, seeded, leaved and slipped, between two branches of laurel in saltire proper, enfiled with a baron's coronet or. **Motto:** Who dares wins. **Creation:** B. (UK) 10 July 1929.

THE 2ND BARON ALVINGHAM, of Woodfold, DL (Oxon 1996) Co Palatine of Lancaster (Robert Guy Eardley Yerburgh, CBE (1978, OBE 1972) DL (Oxon)1996) [Maj-Gen The Rt Hon The Lord Alvingham CBE, DL Bix Hall, Henley-on-Thames, Oxon]; *b* 16 Dec 1926; *s f* 1955; *educ* Eton; Maj-Gen late Coldstream Gds, UK, Palestine (1948), Tripolitania, BAOR, FARELF, Br Guiana, Head of Staff CDS 1972–75, Dep Dir Army Staff Duties 1975–78, Dir Army Quartering 1978–81 (ret 1981); *m* 31 March 1952 *Beryl Elliott, only dau of William David Williams, of Knowle Holt, Hindhead, Surrey, and has issue:

1 +ROBERT RICHARD GUY [The Hon Robert Yerburgh, Valley Farm House, Bix Bottom, Henley-on-Thames, Oxon]; *b* 10 Dec 1956; *educ* Eton; late Capt 17th/21st Lancers; *m* 31 Oct 1981 (*divorce* 1993) Vanessa, yr dau of Capt Duncan Kirk, of Sheaves Farm, Loxwood, Sussex, and has issue:
(1) +Robert William Guy; *b* 16 Sept 1983
(2) +Edward Alexander Henry; *b* 1986
1 (cont.) Capt The Hon Robert Yerburgh *m* 2nd 1994 *Karen, er dau of Antony Baldwin
1 *Susannah Elizabeth [The Hon Mrs Moss, 24 Rusham Rd, London SW12 8TH]; *b* 13 June 1953; *educ* Priorsfield; *m* 9 June 1979 *Edward Ian James Gray Moss, 2nd son of Ernest Frederick Moss, of The Gardens, Sprotborough, S Yorks, and has issue:
(1) *Alice Elinor; *b* 1983
(2) *Victoria Elizabeth; *b* 1986
(3) *Theodora Katherine Rose; *b* 1992

Lineage: GERMUND; enfeoffed of lands at Grainthorpe, Lincs, and of the advowson of the church there by Alain, Count of Brittany, 1040–89; had:

ALVERIC Fitz GERMUND, of Grainthorpe; had:

KETEL CROC, of Grainthorpe; had:

OSBERT; presented by his f to the living of Grainthorpe, which he resigned on his marriage; had, with an est s (Hamelin Croc, who held land in Alvingham of the Count of Brittany and left issue) and a yst s (Richard):

HAMELIN de YERBURGH; *m* Hawis — and *d* by 15 Oct 1195, leaving:

ACE Fitz HAMELIN de YERBURGH; granted lands in Yerburgh and Grainthorpe to Alvingham Priory for the souls of his parents; *m* Nicola — and had:

ROBERT Fitz ACE de YERBURGH; had:

JOHN Fitz ROBERT de YERBURGH; living 1285; had:

RICHARD Fitz JOHN de YERBURGH; *d* by 1316; had:

JOHN de YERBURGH; MP Lincs 1325; *m* Elizabeth — and had:

ROBERT de YERBURGH, of Cockerington and Grimoldby; *m* Isobel, dau of Sir John Ewerby, and had, with an er s (William, had issue, *see* DERAMORE, B):

JOHN de YERBURGH, of Cockerington; living 1401; had:

RICHARD YERBURGH, of Cockerington; living 1437; had:

ROGER YERBURGH/YARBURGH; held lands of Cockerington St Mary, Lincs, *c* 1455; had:

WILLIAM YERBURGH, of Cockerington St Mary; *b* by 1460; sold lands in Cockerington to his s Richard 20 April 1537; *m* Agnes — (predeceased him) and had:

1 Robert, *dvp*
2 RICHARD, for whom *see* below
3 Thomas, of Alvingham, Lincs
4 John, of Cockerington

The 2nd son,

RICHARD YARBURGH/YERBURGH; bought 1541 a messuage and 54 acres at Over Toynton, Lincs, from Thomas, s of Simon Eve; also held lands at Cockerington St Mary; *d* between 26 May and 19 June 1545, leaving an est s:

ROBERT YERBURGH, of Cockerington St Mary; *m* Janet — and was *bur* 13 Dec 1593, leaving an est s:

GEORGE YERBURGH, of Covenham St Bartholomew; also held lands in Cockerington and Skedbrooke; *m* 8 Aug 1596 Anne Gentle and *d* 13 June 1610, leaving:

ROBERT YERBURGH, of Boston; also held lands at Cockerington; *m* Jane — and was *bur* 24 Oct 1678, leaving:

ROBERT YERBURGH, of Boston; Parly Commr Lincs 1650, Parly army offr; *m* Mary — and was *bur* 2 Oct 1717, leaving:

GEORGE YERBURGH; *bapt* Boston 24 Sept 1674; *m* 8 June 1699 Alice, dau of John Gainsborough, of Frampton, and was *bur* at Frampton 24 March 1734, leaving an est surv s:

JOHN YERBURGH, of Frampton, JP; *bapt* 6 Jan 1707; *m* 1st 1730 Mary, dau of Rev Samuel Coddington, vicar of Boston; *m* 2nd Elizabeth, dau of — Pulvertoft and widow of Dymoke Cawdron, and was *bur* 18 May 1780, leaving by his 1st w:

RICHARD YERBURGH, of Frampton, JP, DL; *bapt* 16 April 1742; *m* 1767 Bridget (*d* 1823), dau of Thomas Arnall, of Heckington, and *d* 1806, leaving:

RICHARD YERBURGH (Rev); *bapt* 7 Dec 1774; *educ* Pembroke Coll Cambridge (DD); Vicar Sleaford 40 years; *m* 9 Oct 1811 Elizabeth, dau of John Eardley Norton, of Little Stanmore, Middx, and *d* 1851, leaving an only s:

RICHARD YERBURGH (Rev); *bapt* 5 May 1817; *educ* Harrow and Christ's Coll Cambridge; Vicar Sleaford, Rector High Bickington; *m* 1st 1846 Susan (*d* 1860), dau of John Higgin, of Wenning Cottage and Greenfield, Lancs, and had issue:

1 Richard Eustre, CB; *b* 25 Feb 1847; Exchequer and Andit Department 1869–1908; *m* 20 April 1876 Emma (*d* 7 Nov 1931), dau of Naunton Henry Vertue, of Richmond, Surrey, and *d* 15 Jan 1939, leaving issue:

(1) Richard Eustre Vertue; *b* 8 Dec 1879; *m* 1st 1 Dec 1906 Gladys Eileen (*d* 6 Nov 1911), 4th dau of Col Ernest Lindsay Marryat, RE, and had issue:

1a *Richard Eustre Marryat (Rev), ED; *b* 12 Jan 1908; *educ* U of BC (MA); WW II 1940–1946 in RCASC (ret as Maj), Chaplain with Canadian Army Special Force Korea 1952–52; Vicar of Vanderhoof, BC, formerly Vicar of Ocean Falls, BC, and Rector of Kimberley, BC, a Canon of Diocese of Kootenay 1954; *m* 2 Jan 1934 *, yr dau of Arthur Brooke Osborne-Smith, of Vernon, BC, and has issue:

1b *Richard Eustre Brooke [Richard Yerburgh Esq, Box 790, Fernie, BC, Canada]; *b* 23 Oct 1934; *m* 22 Dec 1956 *Patricia Ethel, 2nd dau of George Quail, of Fernie, BC, and has issue:

1c *Laurie Anne; *b* 17 Sept 1957

2c *Sheila Colleen; *b* 26 May 1960

3c *Judith Marion; *b* 8 Aug 1963

2b *Christopher Richmond Brooke, CD; *b* 6 June 1936; *m* 16 July 1959 *Christina Alma, only dau of Ralph Yarwood, of Kimberley, BC, and has issue:

1c *Shelly Louise; *b* 24 March 1962

2c *Deborah Ann; *b* 5 Dec 1965

2a Robert; *b* 1 April 1910; *d* an infant

3a *Ernest Robert Marryat; *b* 4 Nov 1911; MA U of BC (1940), BEd U of BC (1946); *m* 15 April 1941 *Elizabeth Nora, yr dau of Most Rev Walter Robert Adams, MA, DD, formerly Archbp of the Yukon, and has issue:

1b *Mark Robert [Mark Yerburgh Esq, 397 Lexington Ave, Waltham, Mass, USA]; *b* 4 Aug 1942; *educ* Drew U, Madison, New Jersey (BA); *m* 17 Jan 1965 *Linda Marjorie, only dau of Vernon Larrabee, of Dover, Mass., USA, and has issue:

1c *Hugh Christopher; *b* 14 Dec 1965

1b *Susan Mary; *b* 6 Sept 1944; *educ* Boston Coll Sch of Nursing (BS)

2b *Clare Elizabeth; *b* 3 Oct 1950

(1) (cont.) Richard Yerburgh *m* 2nd 8 April 1915 Mary Eleanor, dau of Rev Albert Frederick Thornhill, and *d* 18 Dec 1941, having by her had issue:

1a *Winifred Prudence Mary; *b* 21 Jan 1916; *m* 10 Nov 1948 Maj Claude Dampier Buckle, MBE, IA (ret), 2nd son of Lewis Mansfield Buckle, of Victoria, BC, and has issue:

1b *Jonathan Lewis Stewart; *b* 19 Jan 1950

2b *Mark Richmond; *b* 7 Jan 1955

1b *Jane Mary; *b* 22 June 1951

(1) Ethel Lennox Vertue; *b* 22 March 1877; *m* Nov 1898 Lt-Col Frederick Thwaites Lund, 9th Lancers (*d* Nov 1914), and *d* 18 Feb 1951, leaving issue

2 John Eardley; *b* 8 Jan 1850; *m* 8 Aug 1878 Annie (*d* 25 Feb 1917), only dau of Joseph Royden, of High Carrs, Roby, Lancs (*see* ROYDEN, Bt), and *d* 9 Dec 1924, leaving issue:

(1) Annie Royden; *b* 2 July 1897; *m* 27 April 1905 Granville Bevan (*d* 26 Nov 1950), 2nd son of Frederick Lincoln Bevan, of Chipstead Place, Sevenoaks, and *d* 19 Oct 1967, leaving issue

(2) Ethel Mary; *b* 10 Nov 1880; *m* 1st 11 June 1907 (*divorce* 1931) Maj Alexander John Lainson, DSO, late KRRC (*d* 6 June 1931), er son of John Arthur Lainson, of Horringer House, Suffolk; *m* 2nd 17 Feb 1931 Leslie Freke Thwaites (*d* 1961), son of John Thwaites, DL, of Troy, Blackburn, Lancs, and *d* 16 Aug 1965

(3) Dorothea Gertrude; *b* 23 Aug 1882; *m* 16 Dec 1911 her cousin Robert Daniel Thwaites Yerburgh, later 1st Baron Alvingham (*see* below), and *d* 10 Feb 1927, leaving issue

(4) Olive Shirley; *b* 29 Oct 1884; *m* 14 July 1908 Edward Manuel Magor, MBE (*d* 13 June 1954), 2nd son of Richard Blormey Magor, of Tylhus, Ingatestone, Essex, and had issue

3 Robert Armstrong; late of Woodfold

4 Edmond Rochfort (Rev); *b* 30 June 1855; *educ* Magdalene Coll Cambridge (BA); Rector of Wrentham, Suffolk; *m* 17 Jan 1890 Constance (*d* 31 Oct 1960), dau of John Thwaites, DL, of Troy, Witton, Lancashire, and *d* 29 Aug 1924, leaving issue:

(1) Richard Edmond Rochfort; *b* 4 Sept 1891; *d* unm 1969

(2) Oswald Rochfort (Rev); *b* 10 Nov 1900; *educ* Magdalene Coll Cambridge (MA) and Wells Theological Coll; Vicar of Steeple Ashton, Wilts from 1932, Rural Dean Bradford-on-Avon 1942–52, Canon of Salisbury and Preb of Wilsford and Woodford 1950, Rector of Studland, Dorset, 1959, RD Purbeck 1961; *m* 3 Dec 1930 *Cicely Joan, yst dau of Charles Cornelius Savile, 19 Roy Crescent, Bath, and *d* 25 June 1966, leaving issue:

1a *John Rochfort [Lt-Col John Yerburgh, The Cottage, Hartlip, Kent]; *b* 14 Sept 1931; *educ* Marlborough and RMA Sandhurst; Lt-Col RE; *m* 17 Aug 1963 *Gillian Elizabeth, only dau of Derek Plint Clifford, of Hartlip Place, Sittingbourne, Kent, and has issue:

1b *Toby William Rochfort; *b* 9 Oct 1965

1b *Sophia Jane Clifford; *b* 8 Jan 1967

2a *Peter Charles (Rev) [The Rev Peter Yerburgh, Cathedral Sch, Wells, Somerset]; *b* 14 Sept 1931 (twin); *educ* Marlborough, Magdalene Coll Cambridge (MA 1957) and Wells Theological Coll; ordained 1955, Curate St James 1956–58, Chaplain Wells Cathedral Sch 1958

3a *David Savile (Rev) [The Rev David Yerburgh, St John's Vicarage, Churchdown, Gloucester]; *b* 10 June 1934; *educ* Marlborough and Magdalene Coll Cambridge (BA 1957, MA 1961); ordained 1959, Curate Cirencester 1959–63 and Bitterne Park, Southampton 1963–67, Vicar St John the Evangelist, Churchdown, 1967

(1) Mary; *b* 24 Nov 1893

5 Harry Beauchamp; *b* 25 Oct 1856; *m* 1st 21 Sept 1880 Sophia (*d* 13 Nov 1897), dau of William Sewell, of The Warren, Loughton, Essex, and had issue:

(1) William Higgin Beauchamp (Rev); *b* 19 Aug 1881; MA Oxford; Rector of Bredon, Worcs 1920, Vicar Kineton, T/Chaplain RN 1916–18; *m* 27 June 1925 Frances Sylvia (*d* 29 Oct 1939), dau of Henry Bazely Wolryche-Whitmore, of Royal Hill, Tewkesbury, and *d* 3 June 1937, leaving issue:

1a *Sylvia Mary Douglas; *b* 18 Dec 1927

2a *Margaret Rosamund; *b* 29 April 1930; *m* 28 April 1962 Maj Anthony Leslie Thres, The Sherwood Foresters (ret), son of Leslie Walter Thres, DFC, of Lane End, Barrow Point Lane, Pinner, Middx, and has issue:

1b *Douglas William Yerburgh; *b* 2 April 1963

2b *Jeremy Anthony Yerburgh; *b* 7 April 1965

(2) Ralph Richmond, MBE; *b* 5 March 1886; MICE; *m* 1 Sept 1917 Selina Marie, dau of Frederick Fuchs, and *d* 14 March 1959, leaving issue:

1a *Charles Beauchamp Ralph [Charles Yerburgh Esq, 10 Walsingham Rd, Enfield, Middx]; *b* 1 June 1929

(1) Madeline Edith; *m* 30 March 1932 George Smith Tovey (*d* 21 April 1948), of Parkstone, Dorset, and *d* 18 July 1943

(2) Osyth Mary; *m* 14 Dec 1937 Alfred John Healey, son of Alfred Healey, of Sandhurst Lodge, Regent's Park, London NW, and *d* 20 Feb 1959

5 (cont.) Harry Yerburgh *m* 2nd 18 April 1899 Amy Beatrix (*d* 25 Oct 1948), dau of Maj-Gen Archibald Harenc, and *d* 27 July 1929, having by her had issue:

(3) Vere Archibald Harenc; *b* 24 Feb 1899; *d* 11 Aug 1901

6 Oswald Pryor Wardell-Yerburgh (Rev); *b* 23 Feb 1858; *educ* Trin Coll Dublin (MA); Vicar of Tewkesbury Abbey and Walton, Cardiff, Hon Canon of Gloucester and Rural Dean of Winchcombe, Proctor in Convocation 1908; *m* 21 Jan 1889 Edith Wardell (*d* 22 July 1941), only child of Arthur Potts, JP, of Hoole Hall, Cheshire, when he added by roy licence the name Wardell, and *d* 14 Nov 1913, leaving issue:

(1) Arthur, DSC; *b* 13 July 1891; *educ* RNCs Osborne and Dartmouth; Cdr RN; *m* 1st 7 Sept 1921 (*divorce* 1931) Enid Florence, yr dau of John Till, of Kemerton Court, Glos, and had issue:

1a *John Gerald Oswald [Dr John Yerburgh, 6 Old Northwick Lane, Worcester]; *b* 6 Nov 1925; *educ* Stowe, Trin Coll Cambridge (MA) and St Bartholomew's Hosp (MB, BChir, BPM); *m* 30 Aug 1950 *Brenda Eileen, dau of George Charles Warner Bennett, and has issue:

1b *John Philip; *b* 1 Aug 1951; *educ* Stowe

2b *Tom Charles; *b* 7 Dec 1962

(1) (cont.) Cdr Arthur Yerburgh *m* 2nd 1 Aug 1931 Marion Georgina, dau of Charles Cooper, and *d* 20 March 1953, having by her had issue:

2a *Richard Geoffrey Robert [Richard Yerburgh Esq, 9 The Downlands, Warminster, Wilts BA12 0BD]; *b* 6 Jan 1935; *educ* Sherborne; *m* 11 Feb 1957 (*divorce* 1981) Karin Astra, dau of Rene Paul Ferdinand Kangro; *m* 2nd 3 Sept 1983 *Patricia Ann Davor Aubrey Lopes and by his 1st w has issue:

1b *Astra Karina; *b* 21 July 1958

2b *Vicki Eva; *b* 18 Feb 1960

1a Sarah; *b* and *d* 14 Jan 1933

(2) Geoffrey Bassett; *b* 28 Sept 1893; *educ* Eton and Trin Coll, Cambridge (BA); F/Sub-Lt RNAS; *m* 24 April 1935 Elizabeth Alis Georgina, only dau of Gordon Lloyd Trevor Kenyon, of Tree Tops, Amersham, Bucks (*see* KENYON, B), and *d* 15 Feb 1944, leaving issue:

1a *Oswald Kenyon; *b* 21 May 1936; *educ* Eton; *m* 19 March 1960 *Daphne Anne, only dau of Arthur Dennis Whitley, of Hampton Hill, Middx, and has issue:

1b *Peter Geoffrey; *b* 12 March 1964

1b *Susan Elizabeth; *b* 14 Nov 1961

2a Hugh Arthur; *b* 11 Jan 1938; *educ* Eton and Bristol U (BSc); Sr Analyst Plesseys Radar Corp, Assist Master Eton, Oarsman (Olympic Silver Medallist, Diamond Sculls Winner); *m* 2 April 1966 *Janet Clouston Bewley (Poppy) (*m* 2nd 19 May 1973 David J Cooksey, son of Dr Frank Cooksey, of Aldeburgh, Suffolk, Olympic fencer), est dau of Dr Ian Aysgarth Bewley Cathie, of Barton House, Barton-on-the-Heath, Warwicks, and was *k* in a motor accident 28 Jan 1970, leaving issue:

1b *Atlanta Jane; *b* 6 Dec 1969

(1) Hilda; *b* 5 Dec 1889; *d* unm 22 April 1941

1 Susan Edith; *b* 1848; *m* 1872 Ven William Bonsey, MA (*d* Jan 1909), Archdeacon of Lancaster, and *d* 18 June 1924, leaving issue

2 Mary Florence; *b* 1854; *d* unm 1878
3 Rachel; *b* 1856; *d* an infant
4 Lucy Isabel (twin with Oswald Pryor); *m* 1885 Rev Walter Loveband, MA (*d* 11 April 1945), Vicar of Ifield and Rural Dean of Cuckfield, Sussex, and *d* 17 June 1922, leaving issue
5 Charlotte Elizabeth; *d* an infant 22 Dec 1860

The Rev Richard Yerburgh *m* 2nd 1863 Anne (*d* 1880), dau of Charles Kirk, of Sleaford, and *d* 30 Aug 1886, having by her had further issue:
6 Anne Constance; *d* Jan 1909
7 Mabel Stanley; *m* 16 Jan 1902 Edward James Morton, DL (*d* May 1914), of Heathfield, Woverley, Worcs, son of Edward Morton, JP, of Heathfield, and *d* Feb 1943

The 3rd son,
ROBERT ARMSTRONG YERBURGH, of Woodfold Park, Blackburn, Caythorpe Court, Lincs, Freeby, Melton Mowbray, and Barwhillanty, Parton, Scotland, JP (Kirkcudbright), DL (Lancs); *b* 17 Jan 1853; *educ* Univ Coll Oxford; barrister Middle Temple 1880, Maj 2nd Vol Bn Cheshire Regt, MP Chester 1886–1906 and 1910–16, Pres Navy League, CC Lancs; *m* 8 Aug 1888 Elma Amy (*d* 6 Dec 1946), only child of Daniel Thwaites, JP, DL, of Woodfold Park, Blackburn, and *d* 18 Dec 1916 before letters patent were issued ennobling him, despite roy approval having been obtained, leaving issue:
1 ROBERT DANIEL THWAITES, **1st Baron**
2 Richard Guy Cecil, OBE; *b* 5 Nov 1882; Maj Irish Gds, Croix de Guerre, Croce di Guerra Italy; *m* 27 Oct 1921 Hilda Violet Helena (*m* 2nd 10 Nov 1931 Maj-Gen Sir (Arthur) Guy Salisbury-Jones, GCVO, CMG, CBE, MC, formerly Coldstream Gds, son of Arthur Thomas Salisbury-Jones, of 82 Cornwall Gdns, London SW7), est dau of Sir Maurice William Ernest de Bunsen, 1st and last Bt, GCMG, GCVO, CB (*see* 1932 edn), and *d* 13 March 1926, leaving issue:
(1) *John Maurice Armstrong [John Yerburgh Esq, Barwhillanty, Parton, Kirkcudbrightshire]; *b* 23 May 1923; *educ* Eton; WW II in Irish Gds, V-Ld Lt of Dumfries and Galloway (Stewartry Div) 1990–; *m* 2 March 1973 *Anne Jean Mary, dau of (N) Peter Maclaren, of Brooklands, Crocketford, Kirkcudbrightshire, and has issue:
1a *Oscar Guy Hamelin; *b* 16 Oct 1983
1a *Henrietta; *b* 31 Dec 1973
2a *Arabella; *b* 16 March 1975
3a *Roseanna; *b* 27 Dec 1977
4a *Matilda; *b* 3 May 1979
(2) *Oscar Guy de Bunsen [Oscar Yerburgh Esq, 51 Elsworthy Rd, London NW3]; *b* 17 June 1925; *educ* Eton; WW II in RAF; *m* 23 Jan 1953 *Alicia, only dau of Horace Marshall, of Grimston Lodge, Tadcaster, Yorks

The er son,
ROBERT DANIEL THWAITES, **1st Baron Alvingham**, of Woodfold, Co Palatine of Lancaster (UK), so *cr* 10 July 1929; *b* 10 Dec 1889; *educ* Harrow and Univ Coll Oxford; Brevet-Maj RASC, MP (U) S Dorset 1922–29; *m* 1st 16 Dec 1911 his cousin Dorothea Gertrude (*d* 10 Feb 1927), 3rd dau of John Eardley Yerburgh, of Wavendon Lodge, Bucks (*see* above), and had issue:
1 ROBERT GUY EARDLEY YERBURGH, **2nd and present Baron Alvingham**
1 *Dorothy Joan [The Hon Mrs Turner, Old Rectory Farm, Cheselbourne, Dorchester, Dorset]; *b* 12 April 1913; *m* 1934 Lt-Col William Aspinall Turner, late the Queen's Bays, est son of Col James Aspinall Turner, JP, DL, of Broughton Grange, Grange-over-Sands, Lancs, by his wife Dorothy Vernon, 3rd dau of Harry Clegg, JP, of Plas Llanfair, Anglesey, and has issue:
(1) *Adrian Vernon Aspinall [Adrian Turner Esq, The Old Rectory, Cheselbourne, Dorchester, Dorset]; *b* 4 Oct 1946; *educ* Stowe; *m* 1975 *Jacquelyn Ann, est dau of Wallace A Seymour, of Summerfold, Child Okeford, Dorset, and has issue:
1a *William Aspinall; *b* 1980
2a *Charles James Aspinall; *b* 1982
3a *Nicholas John Aspinall; *b* 1988
(1) *Caroline Sarah]; *b* 22 Dec 1943; *educ* Cranborne Chase; *m* 15 May 1965 *Robin Gilman Arculus, MA, ACA, only son of Frederick Minshull Arculus, of Folly Bridge, Long Hanborough, Oxon, and has issue:
1a *James Edward Gilman; *b* 1 Sept 1970
2a *Henry William; *b* 1974
2 *Marjorie Elizabeth [The Hon Mrs Setchim, 134 Lynton Rd, London W3]; *b* 7 Oct 1916; *m* 1st 1938 Abdul Hamid Mustafa Risk, son of M M Risk, of Amrous, and has issue:
(1) *Diana; *b* 1940
2 (cont.) The Hon Mrs Marjorie Risk *m* 2nd 8 Jan 1952 *Leon Setchim, son of Michon Setchim, and has further issue:
(1) *David Maurice; *b* 1952; *m* 1977 *Marion Helena Grundy, of Dublin, and has issue:
1a *James Ashley Yerburgh; *b* 1983
(2) *Richard Victor; *b* 1954; *m* 1989 *Elizabeth Mary, only dau of H F Andrews, of Tilehurst, Reading

The **1st Baron** *m* 2nd 30 July 1936 Maud Lytton Grey, dau of Charles Lytton Grey Morgan, of Fairlight, nr Hastings, and formerly w of R E Bright, and *d* 27 Nov 1955

AMHERST OF HACKNEY

Arms: Quarterly, 1st and 4th, barry of ten argent and azure, six escutcheons, three, two and one sable, each charged with a lion rampant of the first, a mullet for difference (for CECIL); 2nd and 3rd, gules, three tilting spears, two and one or, headed argent (for AMHERST). **Crest:** On a chapeau gules doubled ermine a garb or, supported by two lions rampant, the dexter argent, the sinister azure. **Supporters:** Two herons proper, collared or.
Motto: *Cor unum via una* ('One heart, one way').
Creation: B. (UK) 26 Aug 1892.

THE 4TH BARON AMHERST OF HACKNEY, Co London ((William) Hugh Amherst Cecil) [The Rt Hon The Lord Amherst of Hackney, Hillside House, Hyde, nr Fordingbridge, Hants SP6 2HD]; *b* 28 Dec 1940; *s f* 1980; *educ* Eton; dir E A Gibson, Shipbrokers Ltd; *m* 30 March 1965 *Elisabeth, dau of Hugh Humphrey Merriman, DSO, MC, TD, of Hazel Hall, Peaslake, Surrey, and has issue:
1 +(HUGH) WILLIAM AMHERST CECIL; *b* 17 July 1968; *educ* Eton
1 *Aurelia Margaret Amherst; *b* 19 July 1966; *m* 1990 (*divorce* 1993, resumed maiden name) Giles Wilson Mervyn Crewdson (*see* GRIMTHORPE, B)

Previous peerages under title Amherst: Jeffrey Amherst, who won his reputation during the war against the French in North America, where he was Commander in Chief between 1758 and 1764, was created Baron Amherst of Holmesdale in 1776 and 12 years later, since he was childless, Baron Amherst of Montreal with remainder to his nephew. This first Lord Amherst refused an earldom when offered it in 1795. The nephew in question, William Pitt Amherst, was less self-effacing. In 1826 he was promoted to a viscountcy and further created Earl Amherst of Arracan, commemorating an area of Burma he had caused to be conquered by the British Crown two years earlier shortly after being appointed Governor General of Bengal. To this distinction he added that of marrying two Dowager Countesses of Plymouth in succession. All these titles expired with the death of the 5th Earl in 1993.

The somewhat remote link between the 1st Baron of the present (Amherst of Hackney) creation, who lived at Amherst in Kent, and the original Amhersts is set out below. In addition, he quartered the undifferenced arms of those Amhersts with the arms of his father's family.

Lineage (of Amherst): THOMAS AMHERST, of Amherst, Kent, ancestor of the Earls Amherst (*see* 1970 edn); had an est s:

NICHOLAS AMHERST, of Juddy's Lands in Tudeley; *d* 1660, leaving:

GEORGE AMHURST [*sic*]; *educ* Oxford (BA 1580); Vicar Yalding, Kent; *m* Margaret Eagles and *dvp*, leaving:

NICHOLAS AMHERST, of E Farleigh; *m* Elizabeth, dau of Stephen Norton, and *d* 1662, leaving:

NICHOLAS AMHERST; *b c* 1617; *m* Jane Fletcher and *d* 1679, leaving a yr s:

NICHOLAS AMHERST; had:

Capt JOHN AMHURST [*sic*], RN; *b c* 1724; *m* 1st —; *m* 2nd Mary, dau and heir of Francis John Tyssen, of Hackney, and *d* 1788, leaving:

Amelia; *m* 1794 WILLIAM GEORGE DANIEL later TYSSEN (*see* below)

Lineage (of Daniel): GERALD/GARRETT DANIEL, otherwise MacDANIEL or MacDONNELL, of Dublin and Clognagh, Co Mayo, held in 1657 the lands of Castellafy in Borrishoole, Co Mayo; *m* Mary — and *d* 1710, having had, with an est s, three yr s and a dau:

NICHOLAS DANIEL; *bapt* 12 May 1695; *m* 9 July 1730 Elizabeth Lovett (*bur* 1 Aug 1754) and was *bur* 11 June 1752, leaving an est s:

JOHN DANIEL; *bapt* 12 June 1734; *m* 23 Oct 1762 Dorcas, dau and eventual heir of Thomas Auchmuty, of the Auchmutys of Bryanstown, Co Longford, originally of Scottish descent, and *d* 20 Nov 1790, having had a 3rd s:

WILLIAM GEORGE DANIEL later DANIEL-TYSSEN (added by sign manual 14 March 1814 with arms), of Westbrooke House, Dorset; High Sheriff Kent 1825; *m* 21 June 1794 Amelia (*bur* 13 Aug 1851), only surv dau and heiress of Capt John Amhurst, RN (*see* above), through whom his descendants acquired the manors of Hackney, Middx, and Foulden Hall, Norfolk, and was *bur* 13 Jan 1838, leaving an est s:

WILLIAM GEORGE TYSSEN DANIEL later DANIEL-TYSSEN later still TYSSEN-AMHURST (sign manual 6 Aug 1852), of Didlington, Hackney, and Foulden Hall; *b* 18 Dec 1801; High Sheriff Norfolk 1843; *m* 13 April 1834 Mary (*d* 9 Feb 1854), est dau of Andrew Fountaine, of Narford Hall, Norfolk, and *d* 30 Dec 1885, leaving, with a yr s and two daus:

WILLIAM AMHURST DANIEL-TYSSEN later TYSSEN AMHURST (roy licence 6 Aug 1852) later still TYSSEN-AMHERST (roy licence 16 Aug 1877), **1st Baron Amherst of Hackney**, Co London (UK), so *cr* 26 Aug 1892 with special remainder to his est dau and her heirs male, JP (Norfolk, Middx and Westminster), DL (Middx); *b* 25 April 1835; *educ* Eton and Ch Ch Oxford; High Sheriff Norfolk 1866, MP (C) W Norfolk 1880–85 and SW Norfolk 1885–92, KJStJ; *m* 4 June 1856 Margaret Susan, DJStJ (*d* 2 Nov 1919), only child of Adml Robert Mitford, of Hunmanby Hall, Yorks, and Mitford Castle, Northumberland, and had issue:

1 MARY ROTHES MARGARET, **Baroness Amherst of Hackney**

2 Sybil Margaret, DJStJ; *d* unm 21 June 1926

3 Florence Margaret, DJStJ; *d* unm 9 Aug 1946

4 Margaret Mitford, DJStJ; *d* unm 19 Dec 1923

5 Alicia Margaret, CBE (1920, MBE 1918), DGStJ; *m* 16 Feb 1898 1st Baron Rockley (*qv*), and *d* 14 Sept 1941, leaving issue

6 Geraldine Margaret; *m* 30 April 1890 Capt Malcolm Drummond, of Megginch Castle, Perthshire, and *d* 24 Aug 1956, leaving issue (*see* STRANGE, B)

7 Beatrice Margaret; *d* 20 Nov 1881

The 1st BARON *dspm* 16 Jan 1909; his est dau,

MARY ROTHES MARGARET Tyssen-Amhurst later Tyssen-Amherst, **Baroness Amherst of Hackney** in her own right, OBE, DJStJ; *b* 25 April 1857; *m* 2 Sept 1885 Col Lord William Cecil, CVO (*see* EXETER, M), and had issue:

1 William Amherst, MC; *b* 30 June 1886; Capt Gren Gds WW I; *m* 14 April 1910 Gladys (granted by roy warrant 25 Aug 1920 rank of baron's widow; *d* 30 May 1947), only child of Henry Charles Baggallay, of Heatherhurst Grange, Frimley, Surrey, and was *ka* Battle of the Aisne 16 Sept 1914, leaving issue:

(1) WILLIAM ALEXANDER EVERING, **3rd Baron**

(2) Henry Kerr Auchmuty; *b* 1 April 1914; *educ* Eton; Lt Parachute Regt WW II; granted by roy warrant 8 Jan 1921 rank of baron's yr s; *m* 15 Dec 1938 Elizabeth Rohays Mary (*m* 2nd 24 July 1944 Capt Sir Cecil Charles Boyd-Rochfort, KCVO (*d* 1983), yst son of Maj Rochfort Hamilton Boyd-Rochfort, JP, of Middleton Park, Co Westmeath, and *d* 1993), only dau of Maj-Gen Sir James Lauderdale Gilbert Burnett of Leys, 13th Bt, CB, CMG, DSO (*see* 1956 edn), and was *ka* N Africa between 30 Nov and 2 Dec 1942, leaving issue:

1a +John Strongbow Amherst [John Cecil Esq, The Old Rectory, Monks Sherborne, nr Basingstoke, Hants]; *b* 20 Oct 1939; *educ* Eton; Lt Scots Gds (Res); *m* 18 Jan 1966 *(Elizabeth) Clare, 2nd dau of Charles Michael Hughes, of Penton Manor, nr Andover, Hants, and has issue:

1b +Richard Strongbow Amherst; *b* 1 Aug 1973

2b +Michael John Amherst; *b* 14 Feb 1977

1b *Miranda Elizabeth Rohays; *b* 21 Aug 1974

2a +James Comyn Amherst [James Burnett of Leys, House of Crathes, Banchory, Kincardineshire]; *b* 24 July 1941; *educ* Eton; recognized in the surname of Burnett of Leys by decree of Lyon Court 15 July 1966; *m* 7 July 1971 *Fiona Mercedes, 2nd dau of Lt-Col Harold Pedro Joseph Phillips, of Checkendon Court, Checkendon, Mending, and has issue:

1b +Alexander James Amherst; *b* 1973

2b +Victor Cecil Tobias; *b* 1982

1b *Eliza Amelia; *b* 1977

3a +Henry Richard Amherst [Henry Cecil Esq, Warren Place, Newmarket, Suffolk, CB8 8QQ]; *b* posthumously 11 Jan 1943; *educ* Canford; racehorse trainer; *m* 1st 18 Oct 1966 (*divorce* 1990) Julia, dau of Sir (Charles Francis) Noel Murless, of Warren Place, Newmarket, and has:

1b +(Arthur) Noel Amherst; *b* 3 Feb 1973

1b *Katrina Henrietta Amherst; *b* 17 June 1971

3a (cont.) Henry Cecil *m* 2nd 1992 Natalie Payne and by her has:

2b +Jake Henry Richard Amherst; *b* 22 Feb 1994

4a +David Henry Amherst [David Cecil Esq, The Horse and Hound, Lambourne, Berks]; *b* 11 Jan 1943; *educ* Canford; former racehorse trainer, publican; *m* 1st 6 Aug 1966 (*divorce* 1972) Hon Fiona Elizabeth Cameron Corbett, only dau of 2nd Baron Rowallan (*qv*), and has issue:

1b +Rupert Laurence Amherst; *b* 27 May 1967

2b +Benjamin David Amherst; *b* 6 Aug 1968; *m* 14 March 1998 *Jennie, dau of Fred Sahadi, of California

4a (cont.) David Cecil *m* 2nd 19 March 1973 (*divorce* 1995) Vanessa Josephine Bronislawna, yst dau of Captain Wladyslaw Gallica, of Vale House, Little Somerford, Wilts, and has further issue:

1b *Anoushka Henrietta Amherst; *b* 7 April 1975

2b *Sapphire Rose; *b* 1981

2 Thomas James Amherst; *b* 9 Nov 1887; *educ* Eton; Capt 10th Bn KRRC WW I (wounded); *m* 29 July 1912 Vera Agnes, yr dau of Hedworth Trelawny Barclay, and *d* 4 Oct 1955, leaving:

(1) +Barclay James Amherst [Barclay Cecil Esq, Belmont Lodge, Belmont Road, Maidenhead, Berks]; *b* 13 April 1913; *educ* Stowe; WW II as Lt Australian Forces; *m* 1st 24 May 1941 (*divorce* 1949) Suzanne Jocelyn, dau of Frederick William Dennett, of Melbourne, Australia, and had issue:

1a +Timothy Dennett Amherst; *b* 26 Sept 1942; *educ* Stowe

2a +Jonathan Peter Hedworth; *b* 1 Oct 1944; *educ* Stowe

(1) (cont.) Barclay Cecil *m* 2nd 1972 *Jessica Iliffe Lane [Mrs Barclay Cecil, Upcross Hotel, Berkeley Ave, Reading, Berks RG1 6HY], dau of Rev Thomas Ernest Matthews of Grantham, Lincs, and *d* 1987

3 John Francis Amherst; *b* 30 June 1890; *educ* Eton and New Coll Oxford; 1st Sec Dip Serv; *m* 29 April 1924 (*divorce* 1934) Cornelia Stuyvesant (*d* 1976), only dau of George Washington Vanderbilt, and *d* 22 Oct 1954, leaving issue:

(1) +George Henry Vanderbilt [George Cecil Esq, 2 Arboretum Rd, Biltmore, NC 28813, USA]; *b* 27 Feb 1925; WW II in RNVR; *m* 30 April 1955 *Nancy, dau of Charles Dexter Owen, of Biltmore, and has issue:

1a +John Francis Amherst Vanderbilt; *b* 28 March 1956; *m* 1993 *Sarah, dau of Thomas M Mettler, of Palm Beach, Florida, and has issue:

1b +Thomas Amherst Vanderbilt; *b* 1994

2b +Hugh Brownlow Amherst; *b* 1995

2a +Christopher Henry Amherst; *b* 31 Aug 1965; *m* 1992 *Ruth, dau of William H Taft, Jr, of Greenville, NC, and has issue:

1b +George Henry Vanderbilt II; *b* 1994

1b *Rachel Taft Amherst; *b* 1996

1a *Edith Anne Cecil; *b* 11 Sept 1957; *m* 1983 (*divorce* 1991, when returned to maiden name) Nicholas M C Stancioff, son of John Stancioff, and has issue:

1b *Charlotte Eloïse; *b* 1988

2a *Catherine Amherst; *b* 13 May 1959; *m* 1982 (*divorce* 1997) William M Whitehouse and has issue:

1b *Timothy Amherst; *b* 1984

2b *Henry Meredith; *b* 1986

3b *Brooks Cecil; *b* 1989

3a *Margaret Elizabeth; *b* 2 March 1961; *m* 1987 *John B Sinnott, of Pittsburgh, and has:

1b *Peter Cecil; *b* 1991

2b *David Stuyvesant; *b* 1993

1b *Mollie Amherst; *b* 1989

4a *Louisa Owen; *b* 31 Aug 1965; *m* 1994 *W W Rodes Harrison, of New York

(2) +William Amherst Vanderbilt [William Cecil, 7 Frith Drive, Biltmore Forest, Asheville, NC 28803, USA]; *b* 17 Aug 1928; *m* 5 Oct 1957 *Mary Lee, dau of John J Ryan, of New York, and has issue:

1a +William Amherst Vanderbilt; *b* 3 July 1958; *m* 1983 *Virginia Lee, dau of Robert A Rott, of Asheville, NC, and has issue:

1b +Ryan Jordan Vanderbilt; *b* 1987

2b +William Robert Vanderbilt; *b* 1994

2b +Aubrey Lea Amherst; *b* 1990

(2) (cont.) Mr and Mrs William Cecil adopted 1972:

*Diana Marshall Ryan; *b* 1957; *m* 1985 *George Wiley Pickering, son of George Wiley Pickering, of Black Mountain, NC, and has issue:

1b *Chase Kennedy Cecil; *b* 1987

2b *Devon Lee Cecil; *b* 1991

4 Henry Mitford Amherst, OBE (1935); *b* 9 March 1893; Cdr RN, T/S/Ldr RAF 1934–36, WW I and II; memb House of Laity Church Assembly 1953–55 and 1960–62, Chevalier Order Redeemer Greece, OStJ; *m* 27 Jan 1923 Hon Yvonne Cornwallis (*d* 1983), 3rd dau of 1st Baron Cornwallis (*qv*), and *d* 6 Jan 1962, leaving issue:

(1) +(Oswald) Nigel Amherst (Sir), KBE (1979), CB (1977) [Rear-Adml Sir Nigel Cecil KBE CB, c/o C Hoare & Co, 37 Fleet St, London EC4P 4DQ]; *b* 11 Nov 1925; *educ* RNC Dartmouth; Capt RN 1966, cmded Dartmouth Tr Sqdn 1969–71, Sr Br Naval Offr S Africa and Naval Attaché Cape Town 1971–73 (as Cdre), Naval ADC to HM THE QUEEN 1975, R Adml 1975, NATO Cdr SE Mediterranean 1975–77, Cdr Br Forces and Flag Offr Malta 1975–79, Lt Govr IoM and Pres Tynwald 1980–85, OStJ 1971, KStJ 1980, FIMgt 1980; *m* 6 April 1961 *Annette (CStJ 1980), er dau of Maj Robert Edward Barclay, of Bury Hill, nr Dorking, Surrey, and has:

1a +Robert Barclay Amherst; *b* 22 Dec 1965

(1) *Rachel Mary; *b* 24 Jan 1924; *m* 6 March 1954 *Brig Mortimer Cecil Lanyon, MBE, MC, RA, of Woodman's Farm House, W Meon, Hants, er son of Maj Louis Frank Lanyon, of Hambledon House, Hambledon, Hants, and has issue:

1a *Robert Henry Mortimer; *b* 4 Sept 1962

1a *Charlotte Yvonne; *b* 20 Feb 1955; *m* 1977 Maj Paul Alistair Strutt (*see* RAYLEIGH B)

2a *Victoria Clare [Mrs Angus Ramsay, Woodmans Farm House, West Meon, Hants GU22 1JJ]; *b* 14 Oct 1956; *m* 1987 *Maj-Gen Angus Ramsay, RHF, s of Col A I Ramsay, of Dalry, Kirkcudbright, and has:

1b *James Ivor Iain; *b* 1990

1b *Alexandra Rachel Iona; *b* 1988

(2) Alison Yvonne; *b* 22 Aug 1931; *m* 22 June 1961 *John Alfred Leavett-Shenley, High Sheriff Hants 1985–86, DL Hants [John Leavett-Shenley Esq DL, The Holt, Upham, Hants SO32 1HR], s of Ernest Alfred Leavett-Shenley, and *d* Oct 1990, leaving:

1a *Christopher John; *b* 15 Aug 1963

2a *Mark Henry; *b* 19 Feb 1967

1a *Katherine Yvonne; *b* 13 Sept 1965

BARONESS AMHERST *d* 21 Dec 1919; her gs,

WILLIAM ALEXANDER EVERING CECIL, **3rd Baron Amherst of Hackney**, CBE (1963); *b* 31 May 1912; *educ* Eton and Trin Coll Cambridge (BA 1933); Maj RHG (Blues) WW II MEF 1940–45, OStJ; *m* 14 Sept 1939 *Margaret Eirene Clifton [The Rt Hon Margaret Lady Amherst of Hackney, 138 Cranmer Ct, Sloane Ave, London SW3], yst dau of Brig-Gen Howard Clifton Brown, MP, of Holmbush, Faygate, Sussex (*see* BROWN, Bt), and *d* 22 July 1980, leaving issue:

1 (WILLIAM) HUGH AMHERST CECIL, **4th and present Baron Amherst of Hackney**

2 +Anthony Henry Amherst; *b* 1 April 1947; *educ* Eton; *m* 1st 23 Oct 1969 (*divorce* 1974) Fenella Jane, only dau of David George Crichton, MVO, of 77 Cadogan Gdns, London SW3 (*see* ERNE, E); *m* 2nd 20 Nov 1974 *Jane Elizabeth, 2nd dau of Maj Philip Norman Elston Holbrook, of 4 Sloane Court East, London SW3, and by her has issue:

(1) +Henry Edward Amherst; *b* 2 Nov 1976

(2) +Thomas Anthony Amherst; *b* 1981

(1) *Georgiana Helen Amherst; *b* 4 June 1979

1 *Angela Margaret Amherst [The Hon Mrs Reid, Queenford Farm, Dorchester-on-Thames, Oxon, OX10 7PH]; *b* 16 May 1955; *m* 7 June 1980 (Gavin) Ian Reid, yr son of Col (Percy Fergus) Ivo Reid, OBE, DL, of The Glebe House, Marston St Lawrence, Banbury, Oxon, and has had:

(1) *Nicholas Andrew; *b* 1981

(1) Susanna Claire; *b* and *d* 1987

(2) *Jessica Mary; *b* 1988

AMOS

Creation: B. (LP, UK) 1997.

THE BARONESS AMOS, of Brondesbury, London Borough of Brent (Valerie Amos) [The Rt Hon The Baroness Amos, House of Lords, London SW1A 0PW]; *b* 13 March 1954; *educ* Warwick and Birmingham Us and UEA; with Lambeth 1981–82, Camden 1983–85 and Hackney 1985–89 (Hd Training, Hd Management Services) Borough Cncls; management consultant 1984–89; Ch Exec Equal Opportunities Commn 1989–94; md Quality and Equality 1994–; dir Hampstead Theatre 1992–; dir Amos Fraser Bernard 1995–; memb: Advsy Ctee Centre Educnl Devpt, Appraisal and Research Warwick U 1991–, Gen Advsy Cncl BBC, Ctee King's Fund Coll 1992–, Cncl Inst Employment Studies 1993–; External Examiner: Northumbria U 1989–93, Liverpool U 1992–; dep Chm Runnymede Tst 1990–; Tstee Women's Therapy Centre 1989–

Lineage: E MICHAEL AMOS; *m* Eunice — and has:

VALERIE, *cr* a **Baroness**

AMPTHILL

Arms: Argent, a lion rampant gules, on a chief sable three escallops argent, a mullet or for difference. **Crest:** A goat statant argent, charged with a mullet sable for difference. **Supporters:** Dexter, a lion; sinister, a heraldic antelope, both gules, ducally gorged, lined, armed and unguled or, each charged with a mullet or for difference.
Motto: *Che sara sara* ('What will be, will be').
Creation: B. (UK) 11 March 1881.

THE 4TH BARON AMPTHILL, of Ampthill, Co Bedford (Geoffrey Denis Erskine Russell, CBE (1986), PC (1995)) [The Rt Hon The Lord Ampthill CBE PC, 6 Nth Court, Gt Peter St, London SW1P 3LL]; *b* 15 Oct 1921; *s f* 1973; *educ* Stowe; WW II as Capt Irish Gds, Dep Speaker Ho Lds 1983–, Chm Ctees Ho Lds 1992–94 (Dep Chm 1981–92), dep chm Express Newspapers 1989 and United Newspapers 1991; *m* 1st 20 July 1946 (*divorce* 1971) Susan Mary, yr dau of Hon Charles John Frederic Winn, of Nostell Priory, Wakefield, Yorks (*see* St OSWALD, B), and has issue:

1 +DAVID WHITNEY ERSKINE [The Hon David Russell, 46 Ebury Mews, London SW1W 9NY]; *b* 27 May 1947; *educ* Stowe; *m* 15 Nov 1980 *April McKenzie, yst dau of Paul Arbon, of New York, and has issue:

(1) *Christabel Joan Susan; *b* 18 Dec 1981

(2) *(Pauline Alexandra) Daisy; *b* 15 Nov 1983

2 James Nicholas Geoffrey; *b* 22 July 1948; *educ* Stowe; *d* following a car crash 17 Oct 1969

3 +Anthony John Mark; *b* 10 May 1952; *educ* Stowe; *m* 1985 (*divorce*) Christine L, er dau of John O'Dell, and has issue:

(1) +William Odo Alexander; *b* 1986

1 *Vanessa Mary Linda; *b* 18 Sept 1960; *m* 24 June 1983 (*divorce*) Charles Ivor Angus Burt, er s of Ivor B Burt, of Moreton House, Highgate, and has:

(1) *James Ivor Geoffrey; *b* 1984

(1) *Emma Louise Victoria; *b* 1986

The 4th BARON *m* 2nd 28 March 1972 (*divorce* 1987) Elisabeth Anne Marie, dau of Claude Henri Mallon, of Paris

Lineage: The 9th DUKE OF BEDFORD (*qv*) had a yr bro:

Lord ODO WILLIAM RUSSELL, **1st Baron Ampthill**, of Ampthill, Co Bedford (UK), so *cr* 11 March 1881, GCB (1874), GCMG (1879), PC (1872); *b* 20 Feb 1829; entered Dip Serv 1849: attaché Vienna, FO 1850–52, Paris 1852, Constantinople 1854, Sec Washington 1857, Sec of Legation Florence 1858, Naples 1860, sole UK rep Rome 1858–70, Assist Under-Sec For Affrs 1870–71, special mission to German Army HQ Versailles Nov 1870–March 1871, Amb Berlin 1871–84; *m* 5 May 1868 Lady Emily Theresa Villiers, VA, Ldy Bedchamber to HM QUEEN VICTORIA 1885–1901 (*d* 22 Feb 1927), 3rd dau of 4th Earl of Clarendon (*qv*), and *d* 25 Aug 1884, having had issue:

1 ARTHUR OLIVER VILLIERS, **2nd Baron**

2 Odo William Theophilus Villiers (Sir), KCMG, KCVO, CB; *b* 3 May 1870 (THE QUEEN OF THE NETHERLANDS stood sponsor); *educ* Eton and abroad; Attaché Dip Serv 1892, Rome 1893, Athens 1894, 3rd Sec 1894, St Petersburg 1896, 2nd Sec Rome 1898, Buenos Aires 1899, Vienna 1900, Berlin 1903, 1st Sec 1905, Assist Priv Sec For Sec 1905–08, Counsellor Vienna 1908–14, Dip Sec to For Sec 1915, Envoy Extrdy and Min Plen Berne 1919–22, Vatican 1923–28, The Hague 1928–33; *m* 25 June 1910 Countess Marie Louise Rex (Cross Pro Ecclesia et Pontifice Vatican; *d* 16 Nov 1966), dau of Count Rudolf Karl Casper Rex, Saxon Min Austro-Hungarian Court, and *d* 23 Dec 1951, leaving issue:

(1) +Cosmo Rex Ivor [Cosmo Russell Esq, Parapet Ho, Lenham, Maidstone, Kent ME17 2QJ]; *b* 12 March 1911; *educ* Eton and Trin Coll, Oxford; Maj Queen's Westminsters, KRRC, WW II (despatches), CC Berks 1949, Counsellor Secretariat Gen Cncl Europe 1949–63, Cncllr Roy Borough New Windsor 1947–49, US Bronze Star Medal, Offr Order Orange Nassau with Swords; *m* 6 Sept 1941 *Agnes Mary, est dau of Rev Canon Richard Edward Parsons, of Moor Park Coll, Farnham, Surrey (*see* ROSSE, E), and has issue:

1a +Nicholas Odo Richard Desmond [Nicholas Russell Esq, 3 Court Farm Cottages, Udimore, Sussex]; *b* 9 Dec 1946; *educ* Strasbourg, Brickwall Sch, Northiam, and Munich U; overseas relief and development consultant; *m* 1982 *Rashida Anwar

2a +John Drummond Athelstan; *b* 22 March 1948; *educ* Strasbourg and Brickwall Sch, Northiam; Lt Irish Gds 1967–70 (Res); *m* 28 Nov 1968 *(Mai) Toril, est dau of Fynn Kristian Tennfjord, former Head Social Affs Dept Cncl of Europe, of Norway, and has issue:

1b +Rory Finn Cosmo; *b* 1984

1b *Maikki Natacha; *b* 19 May 1969

2b *Natacha Anne; *b* 6 June 1971

3b *Tatiana Agnes; *b* 1973

1a *Cecilia Hester Marie-Louise Constance; *b* 22 Oct 1942; *m* 31 March 1965 *Peter Robert Nutting, er son of Capt Arthur Ronald Stansmore Nutting, OBE, MC, of North Breache Manor, Ewhurst, Surrey, and has issue (*see* NUTTING, Bt)

2a *Jennifer Rose Ann [Mrs Julian Goldsmid, 24 Scarsdale Villas, London W8 6PR]; *b* 12 April 1945; *m* 26 April 1966 *Julian Nicholas Goldsmid, only son of Vivian Goldsmid, of Monk's Alley, Binfield, Berks, and has issue:

1b *Tara Alexandra; *b* 24 Nov 1970

3a *Theodosia Mary; *b* 15 June 1952; *m* 3 July 1976 *Christopher Gouldstone, late Lt Queen's Lancs Regt, of Thorndene, Pluckley, Ashford, Kent, son of Peter Gouldstone, and has issue:

1b *Edward Oliver; *b* 1981

1b *Emma Charlotte Elizabeth; *b* 1979

4a *Katharine Agnes; *b* 7 Jan 1955

(2) Alaric Charles William; *b* 16 March 1912; *educ* Eton; Maj Queen's Westminsters, KRRC, WW II,; memb London Stock Exchange; *m* 6 April 1940 *Iris Charmian [Mrs Alaric Russell, 44 Linver Rd, London SW6 3RD], yr dau of Noel Van Raalte, of Bursledon, Hampshire, by his wife Iris Enid Florence, only dau of James Reginald Graham, of Scaurbank, Longtown, Cumberland (*see* GRAHAM, Bt, of Netherby), and *d* 1986, leaving issue:

1a +Michael Noel [Michael Russell Esq, 10A Highbury New Pk, Islington, London N5 2BD]; *b* 26 July 1941; *educ* Eton

1a *Amanda Charmian; *b* 21 Aug 1946; *m* 29 Sept 1966 *Martyn Anthony Hedley, of 2 Milbourne Grove, London SW10 9SN, er son of Anthony Miles Hedley, of Bailiff's Cottage, Crawley Down, Sussex, by Elizabeth Alice, yr dau of Maj Cuthbert Blundell, of Slangham Place, Haywards Heath, Sussex

(3) +David Hastings Gerald; *b* 27 Aug 1915; Lt RNVR WW II, actor RSC, consultant to Krug 1972–95, viticulturist 1995–; *m* 8 June 1940 *Hester Clere, 2nd dau of Rev Canon Richard Edward Parsons, of Moor Park Coll, Farnham, Surrey (*see* ROSSE, E), and has issue:

1a +Wriothesley David Xavier [Wriothesley Russell Esq, 19 Adams Row, S Audley St, London W1]; *b* 16 April 1941; *educ* Eton and Trin Coll Dublin; *m* 1992 *Melissa Tan Hui Chui

2a +Rupert Edward Odo [Rupert Russell Esq, Highleaze House, Oare, Marlborough, Wilts]; *b* 5 Nov 1944; *educ* Selwyn Ho Sch Montreal and Rannoch Sch Perths; slr 1973, memb Law Soc, chm Cities of London and Westminster Conservative Assoc 1979–83 (V-Pres 1984); *m* 9 Dec 1981 *Catherine Jill, dau of William Gulliver, and formerly w of 5th Baron Brougham and Vaux (*qv*)

3 Victor Alexander Frederick Villiers, CBE (1959, OBE 1919), JP (Beds); *b* 27 June 1874 (HM QUEEN VICTORIA and HIM THE EMPRESS FREDERICK OF GERMANY stood sponsors); *educ* Wellington and New Coll Oxford (BA 1909); barrister, Bencher Inner Temple 1934, Recorder Bedford 1929–48, Lt-Col 5th Bn Beds Regt, WW I (despatches twice); *m* 23 Aug 1905 Annora Margaret Bromley (*d* 21 June 1949), yst dau of George Edward Martin, DL, of Ham Court, Worcs, and *d* 11 March 1965, leaving issue:

(1) Averil, OBE (1956, MBE 1946); *b* 24 July 1906; *d* unm 15 Aug 1963

(2) Rosemary; *b* 3 Oct 1907; *m* 12 Dec 1935 Lt-Col William Douglas Gosling, MBE, TD, DL, est son of Maj William Sullivan Gosling, of Hassobury, and had issue:

1a *Petronella Margaret [Mrs Charles Humphreys, The Folly, Farnham Green, Bishops Stortford Herts]; *b* 27 Dec 1936; *m* 20 Feb 1965 *Charles

William Humphreys, est son of Sydney George Gordon Humphreys, of Corfu, Chaddesley Glen, Canford Cliffs, Dorset, and has issue:
1b *Christopher Charles; *b* 27 Jan 1968
1b *Lucinda Ferelith; *b* 28 Oct 1966
2a *Lucy Annora [Mrs Murphy, 11 Thurloe Court, Chelsea, London SW3]; *b* 4 March 1938; *m* *— Murphy
3a *Gwendolin Frances; *b* 30 June 1946
(3) *Angela Irene; *b* 29 Sept 1912; *m* 19 July 1938 *Robert Alexander Bennett Gosling, of Mutton Hall, Wetherden, Stowmarket, Suffolk, yst son of Maj Willian Sullivan Gosling, of Hassobury, and *d* 1996, leaving:
1a *Alexander Bennet [Alexander Gosling Esq, 32 Auburn Grove, East Hawthorn, Victoria 3123, Australia]; *b* 10 June 1940; *educ* Eton and King's Coll Cambridge; dir AIM Electronics Ltd; *m* 1st 11 June 1963 (*divorce* 1987) Mary Fiona, yr dau of Duncan James Macrae, of 22 The Little Boltons, London SW10; *m* 2nd 1989 *Wirat Sukprem and by his 1st w has:
1b *Henrietta Mary; *b* 8 June 1966; *m* 1990 *Nicholas R Worthington, of 90c Beaufort St, London SW3, s of Philip Michael Worthington, of The Knoll House, Knossington, Leics, and has:
1c *Victoria Mary; *b* 1994
2b *Louisa Katherine; *b* 22 April 1968
2a *Andrew Edward [Andrew Gosling Esq, 36 Yorrick Rd, W Mersea, Essex CO5 4HU]; *b* 26 Oct 1944; *educ* Eton; *m* 1st 11 June 1966 Rosemary Ailsa, er dau of Col John Lyon Corbett-Winder, OBE, MC, of Vaynor Park, Berriew, Montgomery, and has issue:
1b *Amanda Sophia Jane; *b* 30 May 1968
2b *Catherine Angela Rose; *b* 1970
2a (cont.) Andrew Gosling *m* 2nd 1977 *Imogen Margaret, est dau of Humphrey Fisher Crosby Halahan, of Foxearth, Winterbourne Houghton, Blandford, and has further issue:
3b *Matilda Anne; *b* 1979
3a *Robert Anthony [Robert Gosling Esq, Pulham Cottage, Wetherden, Stowmarket, Suffolk IP14 3LQ]; *b* 1 April 1948; *educ* Eton; *m* 1969 *Clarissa Beatrice, yr dau of Maj John Whitcombe, of the Malt Ho, Roundway Village, Devizes, Wilts, and has issue:
1b *Richard Bennet; *b* 1972; *educ* Eton and Cambridge
1b *Charlotte Arabella Ida; *b* 1974; *educ* Downe House and Cambridge
1a *Annabel Victoria [Mrs Nathaniel Sebag-Montefiore, 180 Kensington Pk Rd, London W11 2ER]; *b* 1942; *m* 1965 *Nathaniel Charles Sebag-Montefiore, only son of Oliver Sebag-Montefiore, of Brook Hall, Finchingfield, Essex, and has issue:
1b *Matthew Oliver; *b* 1971
1b *Victoria Alice; *b* 1969
4 Alexander Victor Frederick Villiers, CMG (1918), MVO (1908); *b* 27 June 1874 (HM QUEEN VICTORIA and TIM THE EMPEROR AND EMPRESS FREDERICK OF GERMANY stood sponsors); *educ* Wellington and RMC Sandhurst; Gren Gds S Africa 1899–1902 (despatches twice and brevet Maj), WW I (despatches three times), Legion of Honour, Cdr Order Crown of Belgium, Brig-Gen 1926, GSO War Off 1908–10, Mil Attaché Berne with rank of Brig-Gen 1919–20, special mission Chile 1920, Romanian Boundary Cmmr 1921–26, dir Sun Insur Office, Sun Life Assur Soc, Steward NGRC; *m* 11 Feb 1909 Marjorie Gladys (*d* 28 April 1949), dau of Claude Hume Campbell Guinness (*see* GUINNESS, Bt) by his 1st w Gladys Helen Louisa, 2nd dau of Col Hon Hercules Langford Boyle Rowley (*see* LANGFORD, B), and *d* 3 Jan 1965, leaving issue:
(1) (William) Rodney Villiers, MC; *b* 15 March 1914; *educ* Wellington; Lt-Col Rifle Bde WW II (T/Lt-Col whilst cmdg Chin Hills Bn in Burma); *m* 3 April 1950 *Diana Marigold [Mrs Rodney Russell, 43 Upper Headland Park Rd, Preston, S Devon TQ3 1JG], er dau of Lt-Cdr Arthur Trafford, of Paignton, Devon, and *d* 7 Dec 1994, leaving:
1a +Rupert Alick Villiers; *b* 16 May 1951; *educ* Wellington; *m* 1974 *Laura Suzanne Golds and has issue:
1b +Christopher John; *b* 1983
1b *Elinor Kate; *b* 1991
1a *Sarah Caroline Villiers; *b* 20 April 1956; *m* 13 Jan 1979 (*divorce* 1984) Brian Roy Wort
(2) +Stephen Alexander Villiers [Stephen Russell Esq, Godford Land, Honiton, Devon]; *b* 30 Nov 1916; *educ* Wellington; Capt Black Watch WW II (POW); *m* 24 July 1945 *Ailsa Mary, 2nd dau of William Hope Pilcher, of The Gows, Invergowrie, Dundee, and has issue:
1a +John Alick Stephen Villiers; *b* 22 May 1946; *educ* Wellington; *m* 1975 (*divorce* 1986) Verity Elizabeth Anne Murray and has issue:
1b +Alick Robin; *b* 1976
2b +Guy James Villiers; *b* 1983
1b *Rosie Alice Swallow; *b* 1978
1a *Camilla Mary Louise; *b* 3 March 1949; *m* 1978 *Robin Geoffrey Murray, and has issue:
1b *Charles Tobias Heatley; *b* 1978
2b *William Barnaby Robin; *b* 1980
2a *Lucy Marjorie Eileen; *b* 6 July 1954; *m* 1974 *Christopher Nigel Gordon Smith and has:
1b *Ben Christopher Gordon; *b* 1979
1b *Flora Eileen Ailsa; *b* 1981
1 Constance Evelyn Villiers; *b* 1 Jan 1872; *d* unm 27 Sept 1942
2 Augusta Louise Margaret Romola Villiers; *b* 14 March 1879 (HIM THE EMPRESS AUGUSTA OF GERMANY and TRH THE DUKE AND DUCHESS OF CONNAUGHT stood sponsors); *d* unm 15 Nov 1966

The 1st BARON AMPTHILL's est son,

ARTHUR OLIVER VILLIERS RUSSELL, **2nd Baron Ampthill**, GCSI, GCIE, JP and DL; *b* 19 Feb 1869; *educ* Eton and New Coll Oxford; Chm Beds CC, Private Sec to: Colonial Sec 1895–1900, Govr Madras 1900–06, ad interim Viceroy India 1904, Hon Col 3rd Bn Beds and Herts Regt, Lt Roy 1st Devon Yeo Cav, cmded 3rd and 8th Bns Beds Regt and 13th Bn Leics Regt WW I (despatches twice, Brevet Col); Pro Grand Master Utd Grand Lodge Freemasons of England; *m* 6 Oct 1894 Lady Margaret Lygon (*d* 12 Dec 1957), CI (1900), GCVO (1946), GBE (1918), DGStJ and Kaisar-i-Hind gold medal (1906), Ldy Bedchamber to HM QUEEN MARY, 3rd dau of 6th Earl Beauchamp (*see* 1970 edn), and *d* 7 July 1935, having had issue:
1 JOHN HUGO, **3rd Baron**
2 Guy Herbrand Edward (Sir), GBE (1953, CBE 1943), KCB 1951 (CB 1948), DSO (1944); *b* 14 April 1898; *educ* RNCs Osborne and Dartmouth; Adml, WW I (despatches) and WW II (despatches), Adml cmdg Reserves 1949–51, C-in-C Far East Station 1951–53, 2nd Sea Ld 1953–55, Cmdt IDC 1955–57, 1st and Pncpl Naval ADC to HM THE QUEEN 1954–58, Chm Nat Assoc Boys' Clubs 1958–63, Chm Missions to Seamen 1960–65, Govr Radley 1958 (Chm 1964), Cranleigh Sch 1960 and Wellington 1961, Chm Exec Ctee Gordon Boys' Sch 1965; *m* 16 Feb 1939 Hon Helen Elizabeth Blades (d 16 Nov 1995), dau of 1st Baron Ebbisham (*see* 1970 edn), and *d* 25 Sept 1977, leaving issue:
(1) +James Rowland [Dr James Russell, Sheepcote, Harrow Court, Stockbury, nr Sittingbourne, Kent ME9 7UQ]; *b* 28 March 1940; *educ* Radley, Clare Coll Cambridge (MA 1965) and Middx Hosp (MA, MB, BChir 1964, DObst, RCOG 1968); Surgn-Lt RN 1964–68; *m* 2 Sept 1965 *Glenys Pearl, only dau of Herbert George Lofting, of Nairobi, Kenya, and has:
1a +Robert James Russell; *b* 23 Aug 1966; *educ* Radley and Middx Hosp; Maj RAMC, MRCP 1997; *m* 1994 *Melanie Alexandra, dau of Bruce Cumming, of Chilham, Kent, and has:
1b +Angus George Skeoch; *b* 16 March 1995
1a *Katharine May; *b* 11 Dec 1968; *educ* Roy Ballet Sch; choreologist Ballet Rambert; MCSP Edinburgh U 1996
2a *Elizabeth Sarah; *b* 1970; *educ* Gordonstoun and Exeter U
3a *Mary Glenys; *b* 1973; *educ* Eggleston Hall and St Andrews
(2) +Oliver Henry [Oliver Russell Esq, Ballindalloch Castle, Banffshire]; *b* 7 May 1942; *educ* Radley and Magdalene Coll Cambridge (BA 1965); Page Honour to HM THE QUEEN 1957–59, memb Roy Co Archers; *m* 16 Sept 1967 *Clare Nancy, DL, only child of Sir Ewan George Macpherson-Grant, 6th Bt (*see* 1970 edn), and has issue:
1a +Guy Ewan; *b* 27 Aug 1968; *educ* Eton; Page Honour to HM THE QUEEN 1981–83
2a +Edward Oliver; *b* 1970; *educ* Eton
1a *Lucy Clare Nancy; *b* 1972
(1) *Margaret Elizabeth; *b* 11 Oct 1945; *educ* St Margaret's Sch Bushey; *m* 4 Nov 1975 *James Anthony Fowell Buxton, er son of Maj Robert James Buxton, MRCS, LRCP, DOMS, RAMC, of Galhampton Manor, North Cadbury, Yeovil, Somerset, and has issue (*see* BUXTON, Bt)
3 Edward Wriothesley Curzon, OBE (1946); *b* 2 June 1901; *educ* Eton and Trin Coll Cambridge (MA); W/Cdr RAFVR WW II, assist ed *Morning Post* 1932–35, managing ed 1935–37; *m* 11 Oct 1941 *Barbara [Mrs Arthur Farwell, Tall Pines, 308 Hearthstone Ridge, Landrum, S Carolina 29356, USA; Pony's Point, Iona, CBI, Nova Scotia, Canada] (*m* 2nd 1988 Arthur Farwell), dau of Baron Serge Alexandrovich Korff, of Russia, and *d* 1982, leaving issue:
(1) *Diana; *b* 20 Dec 1943
(2) *Margaret Angela; *b* 10 March 1946; *m* 1992 *Stephen Howell
4 Leopold Oliver, OBE (1944), TD (1945); *b* 26 Jan 1907; *educ* Eton; Brig Beds and Herts Regt TA WW II, Assist Sec BOT 1946–47, Dir BIM 1947–56, Dir-Gen Cement and Concrete Assoc 1958, memb Bd Govrs Nat Hosp Nervous Diseases 1963; *m* 9 May 1935 (*divorce* 1954) Rosemary, only dau of Capt Charles John Wintour, RN (*see* KEYES, B), and *d* 1988
1 *Phyllis Margaret, OBE (1946) [The Hon Mrs Thorold OBE, 55 Ebury Mews, London SW1]; *b* 3 June 1900; Ldy-in-waiting to HRH THE late PRINCESS ROYAL 1963–65, Extra Ldy-in-Waiting 1965, WW II with BRCS (despatches), OStJ 1909; *m* 4 April 1940 (*annulled* 1942) William George Preston Thorold (*see* THOROLD, Bt)

The 2nd BARON AMPTHILL's est son,

JOHN HUGO RUSSELL, **3rd Baron Ampthill**, CBE (1945); *b* 4 Oct 1896; Capt RN, WWs I and II, Croix de Guerre with Palms 1945, US Legion of Merit; *m* 1st 18 Oct 1918 (*divorce* 1931) Christabel Hulme (*d* 16 Feb 1976), dau of Lt-Col John Hart, Leinster Regt, of Broadhurst, Heathfield, Sussex, by Blanche Anstruther, 4th dau of Capt David Holland Erskine, 92nd Regt (*see* ERSKINE, B), and had issue:
1 GEOFFREY DENIS ERSKINE RUSSELL, **4th and present Baron Ampthill**
The **3rd Baron** *m* 2nd 22 Feb 1937 Sibell Faithfull (*d* 13 Sept 1947), dau of Thomas Wilkinson Lumley; *m* 3rd 24 July 1948 *Adeline Mary Constance [The Rt Hon Adeline Lady Ampthill, Flat 3, 75 Holland Pk, London W11], est dau of Canon Henry Evelyn Hone, Vicar and RD Godalming, by Adeline Mabel Ellen, only dau of Frederick George Alexander Lane, JP, and *d* 3 June 1973, leaving by her:
2 +John Hugo Trenchard [The Hon John Russell, Ringstead Farm, Dorchester, Dorset DT2 8NF]; *b* 13 Oct 1950; *educ* Eton; *m* 9 Oct 1976 *Susanna Helen, yr dau of Peter Merriam, of Holton Lodge, Holton St Mary, Suffolk, s of Sir Lawrence Pierce Brooke Merriam, MC, JP, DL, by Lady Marjory Kennedy, yst dau of 3rd Marquess of Ailsa (*qv*), and has:
(1) +Henry John Trenchard; *b* 1977; *educ* Eton
(2) +James Peter Faber; *b* 1980; *educ* Eton
(1) *Rose Susanna; *b* 1992
1 *Georgina Adeline Villiers; *b* 3 Jan 1952; *m* 1981 Charles Francis Hoare (*d* 1991), s of Col Charles Edward Hoare

AMWELL

Creation: B. (UK) 16 July 1947.

THE 3RD BARON AMWELL, of Islington, Co London (Keith Norman Montague) [The Rt Hon The Lord Amwell, House of Lords, London SW1 0PW]; *b* 1 April 1943; *educ* Ealing GS and Nottingham U (BSc CE 1964); CEng, FICE, CGeol, FGS, MIHT, consulting civil engr 1965–, dir: Thorburn Hldgs 1994–, Thorburn Colquhoun (consulting engrs) 1994–; *m* 5 May 1970 *Mary, only dau of Frank Palfreyman, and has issue:

1 +IAN KEITH; *b* 20 Sept 1973

2 +Christopher James; *b* 24 Feb 1977

Lineage: JOHN MONTAGUE, of Amwell, London; *m* Mary Ann Manderson (*d* March 1931) and had:

FREDERICK MONTAGUE, **1st Baron Amwell**, of Islington, Co London (UK), so *cr* 16 July 1947, CBE (1946); *b* 8 Oct 1876; newsboy, shop assist, ad copy writer, political agent, lecturer, Pte 18th (S) Bn KRRC 1915–16 and Lt 1st (G) Bn Northants Regt 1917–19 WW I, Alderman Islington Cncl 1919–25, MP (Lab) W Islington 1923031 and 1935–47, Under-Sec Air 1929–31, Parly Sec Mins Tport 1940–41, Aircraft Prodn 1941–42, chm Grand Opera Prodns (Carl Rosa Management) 1950–55; *m* 25 Nov 1911 Constance Mary (*d* 28 Jan 1964), dau of James Craig, and *d* 15 Oct 1966, leaving:

1 FREDERICK NORMAN MONTAGUE, **2nd Baron Amwell**; *b* 6 Nov 1912; *educ* Highbury Co Sch; ARAeS, aircraft design engr; *m* 29 July 1939 *Kathleen Elizabeth, dau of Arthur Percival Fountain, and *d* 1990, leaving issue:

(1) KEITH NORMAN MONTAGUE, **3rd and present Baron Amwell**

(1) *Sheila Elizabeth; *b* 12 Feb 1949

1 *Constance [The Hon Mrs Slade, 24 Kershaw Rd, Swindon, Wilts]; *b* 2 March 1915; *educ* N London Collegiate Sch; *m* 1 June 1938 *Albert Henry Cecil Slade, s of Cecil Slade, of Chalfont St Giles, and has issue:

(1) *David [David Slade Esq, 27 Howitt Rd, London NW3]; *b* 10 April 1943; *educ* William Ellis Sch Highgate

(1) *Lesley; *b* 13 Dec 1946; *m* *— Crenell

(2) *Stephanie; *b* 25 Feb 1956

2 *Betty [The Hon Mrs Dudley, 76 Eastcourt Rd, Burbage, Wilts SN8 3AJ]; *b* 15 Oct 1920; *educ* St Aidan's High Sch Hornsey; *m* 13 Jan 1941 John Forbes Dudley (*d* 10 July 1995), s of Arthur Dudley, of Hampstead, and has issue:

(1) *Lysbeth [Mrs Kenneth Hall, The Anchorage, The Chalks, Chew Magna, Bristol BS40 8SN]; *b* 23 March 1947; *m* 1972 *Kenneth John Hall

ANELAY OF ST JOHNS

Creation: B. (LP, UK) Aug 1996.

THE BARONESS ANELAY OF ST JOHNS, of St Johns, Co Surrey (Dame Joyce Anne Clarke, DBE (1995, OBE 1990), JP (NW Surrey 1985)) [The Rt Hon The Baroness Anelay of St Johns DBE JP, House of Lords, London SW1A 0PW]; *b* 17 July 1947; *educ* Enfield Co Sch, Bristol U, London U Inst of Educn and Brunel U; schoolmistress 1969–74, chm: Woking Citizens' Advice Bureau 1988–93 (vol advsr 1976–85), SE Area C Womens' Ctee 1987–90 (v-chm exec ctee 1990–93) and Govrs Hermitage First and Middle Schs 1981–88, memb: Social Security Appeal Tbnl 1983–, Social Security Advsy Ctee 1989–, Nat Union C Party 1987– (V-Pres 1996–97), Women's Nat Commn 1990–93, Oppn Spokesman Soc Security and Home Affairs 1997–, Oppn Whip Ho Lds 1997–, FRSA 1991; *m* 1970 *Richard Alfred Anelay, QC, s of Maurice Alfred Anelay

Lineage: STANLEY CHARLES CLARKE; *m* Annette Marjorie — and had:

JOYCE ANNE, *cr* a **Baroness**

ANGLESEY

Arms: Sable, on a cross engrailed, between four eagles displayed argent, five lions passant-guardant of the field. **Crest:** A demi heraldic tiger sable, maned, tufted and ducally gorged argent. **Supporters:** Two heraldic tigers sable, maned, tufted and ducally gorged argent. **Motto:** *Per il suo contrario* ('By means of its own opposite'). **Creations:** B. (E) 3 Dec 1549, Bt. (I) 4 July 1730, E. (GB) 19 May 1784, M. (UK) 4 July 1815.

THE 7TH MARQUESS OF ANGLESEY, Earl of Uxbridge, Co Middx, **Baron Paget**, of Beaudesert, Co Stafford, and a **Baronet** (Sir George Charles Henry Victor Paget, Bt) [The Most Hon The Marquess of Anglesey, Plâs-Newydd, Llanfairpwll, Anglesey LL61 6DZ]; *b* 8 Oct 1922 (TM GEORGE V and QUEEN MARY stood sponsors); *s* f 1947; *educ* Eton; Maj RHG (Blues) WW II, V-Lt Anglesey 1960–83 (DL 1960), Ld-Lt Gwynedd 1983–89, Tstee: Nat Portrait Gallery 1979–90 and Nat Heritage Memorial Fund 1980–90, CC 1951–67, Pres Anglesey C Assoc 1947–90, FSA 1951, FRHist Soc, Hon FRIBA, FRSL, Cdre Roy Welsh Yacht Club 1947, Freeman City of London 1948, memb Roy Fine Art Cmmn 1965–71, memb Historic Buildings Cncl Wales 1954–90 (Chm 1977–90), V-Pres Army Historical Research Soc, memb Cncl Nat Army Museum 1970–79, Hon Treasurer Br Danilo Dolci Tst, Hon Fell Roy Cambrian Acad, dir Nationwide Bldg Soc, V-Chm Nat Tst Ctee Wales, memb Bd Welsh Nat Opera Co 1954–61; V-Pres Nat Museum Wales 1957–62 (Pres 1962–67), Pres Friends of Friendless Churches 1959–90, memb Redundant Churches Fund 1970–78, author: *The Capel Letters 1814–1817* (ed, 1955), *One Leg: the Life and Letters of 1st Marquess of Anglesey* (1961), *Sergeant Pearman's Memoirs* (1968), *A History of the British Cavalry* vols I-VIII; *m* 16 Oct 1948 *(Elizabeth) Shirley Vaughan, DBE (1983, CBE 1977), Chm Nat Fedn Women's Insts 1966–1969 and Welsh Arts Cncl, memb Roy Comm Environmental Pollution, Wales and the March Telecommunications Branch, memb IBA, Chm Br Cncl Drama and Dance Advsy Ctee, a Tstee Pilgrim Tst 1982–, V-Chm Civic Tst for Wales, only dau of Charles Langbridge Morgan, MA, LLD, author, of 16 Campden Hill Sq, London W8, by Hilda Vaughan, author, and g-dau of Sir Charles Langbridge Morgan, CBE, and has issue:

1 +CHARLES ALEXANDER VAUGHAN, *Earl of Uxbridge* [Earl of Uxbridge, Plâs-Newydd, Llanfairpwll, Gwynedd LL61 6DZ]; *b* 13 Nov 1950 (HM QUEEN MARY stood sponsor); *educ* Eton, Exeter Coll Oxford and Sussex U (MA, DPhil); *m* 1986 *Georganne Elizabeth Elliott, dau of Col John Alfred Downes, MBE, MC, of Tudor Cottage, Whittlesford, Cambridge, by his 1st w Anne Elliot-Deacon, and has:

(1) +Benedict Dashiel Thomas, *Lord Paget*; *b* 11 April 1986

(1) *Clara Elizabeth Isis; *b* 1988

2 +Rupert Edward Llewellyn [The Lord Rupert Paget, 58 Castle St, Beaumaris, Anglesey]; *b* 21 July 1957; *educ* Westminster and Oxford Air Training Sch; *m* 1982 *Louise Victoria, yst dau of Peter Hugh Youngman, of Charsfield Hall, Woodbridge, Suffolk, and has issue:

(1) +Jack William Kyffin; *b* 1989

(1) *Lily Florence Angharad; *b* 1992

1 *Henrietta Charlotte Eiluned; *b* 31 July 1949; *m* 16 Feb 1980 *Timothy Megarry, son of William Megarry, of Putney, London SW15

2 *(Elizabeth) Sophia Rhiannon [The Lady Sophia Keir, Lakelands Farm, Plaistow Rd, Kirdford, W Sussex RH14 0JR]; *b* 14 May 1954; *m* 1983 *Robert D Keir, son of James Dewar Keir, QC, of Crossways, High St, Dormansland, Surrey, and has issue:

(1) *(Owen) Samuel; *b* 1986

(2) *(James) Oliver Dewar; *b* 1987

3 *Amelia Myfanwy Polly; *b* 12 Sept 1963; *m* 1984 *Andrew M Singleton, 2nd son of Sir Edward Singleton (*see* 1970 edn SCOTT, Bt, of Great Barr), and has:

(1) *Henry Edward; *b* 1993

(1) *Isabella Polly; *b* 1990

Anglesey, other creations under name of: *see* JERSEY, E, and VALENTIA, V.

Lineage (of Paget): WILLIAM PAGET, of Wednesbury, Staffs, alleged by the genealogist Sir William Dugdale to have been born of a father of humble socioeconomic status; Serjeant-at-Mace City of London; had, with two other sons and a dau (Mrs Smith):

Sir WILLIAM PAGET, **1st Baron Paget**, of Beaudesert, Co Stafford (E), so *cr* 3 Dec 1549, KG (Feb 1546/7), PC (1543); *b c* 1506; *educ* St Paul's, Trin Hall Cambridge and U of Paris; employed in houehold of Stephen Gardiner Bp Winchester, Clerk to Signet by Oct 1531, Clerk PC 1540, Clerk of Parls 1541–50, Amb France 1541–43, a Pncpl Sec of State 1543–48, ktd Jan 1543/4, Duchy Lancaster: Jt Chllr 1546–47 and Chllr 1547–52, Comptroller Household 1547–50, MP Staffs 1547–49, Jt Ld Lt Staffs and Middx 1551, Ld Privy Seal Jan 155/6–58, among the land holdings granted him by HENRY VIII were Beaudesert, Staffs, and W Drayton, Middx; he acquired Burton-on-Trent Abbey following the Dissolution of the Monesteries 1536 and 1539; *m c* 1530 Anne, allegedly dau of Henry Preston, gs of Thomas Preston, of Preston, Lancs, and Nether Levens, Westmorland, and *d* 9 June 1563, leaving:

1 Sir HENRY PAGET, **2nd Baron Paget**, KB (1553); MP Arundel 1555 and Lichfield 1559 and 1562–63; *m* 20 May 1567 Catherine (*m* 2nd Sir Edward Car(e)y, of Aldenham, Herts (*see* FALKLAND, V), and *d* 30 Dec 1662), dau of Sir Henry Knyvett, of Buckenham, Norfolk, and *d* 28 Dec 1568, having had:

(1) Elizabeth; *d* an infant; it is a moot point whether she inherited the Barony, the question of its status (*i.e.*, as a creation by writ of summons, which would have been heritable by heirs general, or some other mechanism such as letters patent, being unresolved, though the weight of belief tends to the theory that it is heritable only by heirs male)

2 THOMAS PAGET, **3rd Baron Paget**; *b c* 1544; *educ* Gonville and Caius Coll Cambridge; attainted (Act of Parl March 1586/7) with his bro Charles for working on behalf of MARY QUEEN OF SCOTS; *m* 1565 (separated March 1581/2) Nazareth (*d* 16 April 1583), dau of Sir Henry Newton, of Barr's Court, Somerset, and widow of Thomas Southwell, of Wood Rising, Norfolk, and *d* 1590, leaving an only s:

(1) WILLIAM PAGET, **4th Baron Paget**; *b* 1572; *educ* Ch Ch Oxford; attainder reversed 19 March 1603/4, barrister Middle Temple Feb 1610/1, memb Cncl Virginia Co March 1611/2; *m* by 19 June 1602 Lettice, dau and coheir of Henry Knollys, of Kingsbury, Warwicks, and *d* 29 Aug 1628, leaving, with at least one dau (Margaret, *m* Sir William Hicks, 1st Bt; *see* SAINT ALDWYN, E) an est s:

1a WILLIAM, **5th Baron Paget**, KB (Feb 1625/6); *b* 13 Sept 1609; *educ* Ch Ch and Wadham Coll Oxford; Parly Ld Lt Bucks 1642, later royalist, fighting for CHARLES I Battle of Edgehill Oct 1642; *m* 28 June 1632 Lady Frances Rich (*bur* 12 Sept 1672), dau of 1st Earl Holland, and *d* 19 Oct 1678, having had, with other issue:

1b WILLIAM PAGET, **6th Baron Paget**; *b* 10 Feb 1637; Ld Lt Staffs 1689–1713, Amb Vienna 1689–93 and Sublime Porte 1693–1702; *m* 1st (licence 20 July 1616) Frances (*bur* 7 Nov 1681), dau of Francis Pierrepont, yr s of 1st Earl of Kingston (*extinct* 1773), and had issue:

1c HENRY PAGET, **7th Baron Paget** and 1st EARL OF UXBRIDGE of the 19 Oct 1714 *cr* (also *cr vp* 1 Jan 1711/2 BARON BURTON, of Burton, Co Stafford (both GB)), PC (1714); *b c* 1663; MP (Tory) Staffs 1695–1711, a Ld of Treasury 1710–11, Capt Yeomen Gd 1711–15, Ld Lt Staffs 1713–15; *m* 1st (licence 2 Jan 1685/6) Mary (*bur* 9 Nov 1734), er dau and coheir of Thomas Catesby, of Whiston, Northants, and had issue:

1d Thomas Catesby, *Lord Paget*; *b* 1689; MP (Tory) Staffs 1715–27, Gentleman Bedchamber to GEORGE II, author: *Miscellanies in Prose and Verse*; *m* 6 May 1718 Lady Elizabeth Egerton (*d* 18 Feb 1735/6), dau of 3rd Earl of Bridgwater (*see* GREY EGERTON, Bt), and *dvp* 4 Feb 1741/2, leaving:

1e HENRY PAGET, **8th Baron Paget** and 2nd and last EARL OF UXBRIDGE; *bapt* 22 Jan 1719; *educ* St John's Coll Oxford; *d* unm 16 Nov 1769, when the Earldom of Uxbridge and Barony of Burton expired, but the Barony of Paget passed to his cousin (*see* below)

1d Mary; *m* Stephen Metcalf and *dsp* by 1769

1c (cont.) The **7th Baron** *m* 2nd 7 June 1739 Elizabeth (*dsp* 2 Sept 1749), dau of Sir Walter Bagot, 3rd Bt, and *d* 30 Aug 1743

1b (cont.) The **6th Baron** *m* 2nd Isabel (*bur* 18 Dec 1685), dau of Sir Anthony Irby, of Boston (*see* BOSTON, B), and *d* 26 Feb 1712/13, having by her had further issue:

2c William; *d* young

2b Henry; settled in Ireland; *m* 1st Anne (*d* 15 Dec 1683), dau of Robert Sandford, of Sandford, Salop, and by her had seven s (*dsp*); *m* 2nd (licence 29 March 1684) Mary, dau of Col Hugh O'Rorke, Sheriff Co Leitrim, by Joan, dau of Humphrey Reynolds, of Loughseur, Co Leitrim, and by her had:

1c Thomas; Brig-Gen, Groom Bedchamber 1727, Govr Minorca; *m* Mary (*d* 15 Feb 1740/1), dau and coheir of Peter Whitcombe, of Great Braxted, Essex, and *d* 1741, leaving:

1d CAROLINE Paget; *m* 19 April 1737, as his 1st w, **Sir Nicholas BAYLY, 2nd Bt**, of Plasnewydd (*see* below; he *m* 2nd Anne Hunter (*d* 18 May 1818) and *d* 9 Dec 1782), and had:

1e HENRY (Sir), **3rd Bt** and **9th Baron Paget**

2e Nicholas; *b* 1749; Lt-Col 1st Foot Gds, Col Roy W Middx Militia; allegedly *m* Fanny, dau of Rev — Nettlefold, of Kent, and *d* 7 June 1814, leaving issue

3e Paget; Capt RN; *m* 25 Aug 1791 — (*m* 2nd William Henry Ireland), dau of Col Pepper, and *d* 15 Nov 1804, leaving issue

1c Dorothy; *m* 1706 Sir Edward Irby, 1st Bt, and *d* 1734, leaving issue (*see* BOSTON, B)

1 Griselda, *m* as his 2nd w Sir Thomas Rirett and had issue (*see* PLYMOUTH, E)

Lineage (of Bayly): The Rt Rev LEWIS BAYLY, Bp Bangor; *d* 26 Oct 1631, leaving:

NICHOLAS BAYLY; Govr Isles of Arran; had:

Sir Edward Bayley, 1st Bt (I), so *cr* 4 July 1730, of Plâsnewydd, Anglesey; *m* 28 Aug 1708 Dorothy (*d* 16 Aug 1745), 5th dau of Hon Oliver Lambart, 2nd son of 1st Earl of Cavan (*qv*), and *d* Sept 1741, leaving issue:

1 NICHOLAS (Sir), **2nd Bt**

2 Edward (Very Rev); Dean of Ardfert, DD; *m* 13 Jan 1738 Catherine, dau of Capt James Price, of Hollymount, Co Down, and widow of John Savage, of Portaferry, and had issue:

(1) Dorothea; *m* 19 June 1759 Sir Thomas Butler, 6th Bt (*d* 7 Oct 1772), and *d* 1824, leaving issue

3 Lambart; barrister; *m* Jan 1743 Elizabeth, dau of John Rotton, and *d c* 1747, leaving issue:

(1) Edward (Rev); *b* 10 Oct 1743; Rector of Killuring, Wexford; *m* 1st 6 March 1773 Elizabeth (*d* 5 Jan 1781), dau of Richard Symes, of Ballyarthur, and had issue:

1a Henry Lambart (Rev), of Ballyarthur, Co Wicklow; *b* 26 Nov 1774; *m* 29 Aug 1802 Selina (*d* 18 July 1852), dau of Sir Charles Levinge, 5th Bt (*qv*), and *d* 25 July 1827, leaving with other issue:

1b Edward Symes, of Ballyarthur, Co Wicklow, JP and DL; *b* 9 April 1807; Sheriff 1837, Lt-Col Wicklow Artillery, and sometime Capt 34th Regt; *m* 20 June 1835 Catherine (*d* 1808), dau of Maurice FitzGerald, Knight of Kerry (Isee FitzGERALD, Bt, of Valentia), and *d* 26 Nov 1884, leaving with other issue:

1c Edward Richard, of Ballyarthur, JP and DL; *b* 20 June 1845; Lt Col and Hon Col Wicklow Artillery, late The Buffs (E Kent Regt); *m* 10 Aug 1875 Adelaide Alicia (*d* 24 Nov 1930), dau of Col Charles Tottenham, of Woodstock (*see* ELY, M), and *d* 11 Oct 1907, leaving issue:

1d Edward Archibald Theodore, DSO (1917), of Ballyarthur, Woodenbridge, Co Wicklow; *b* 19 June 1877; Maj late Roy Welch Fus, attd Egyptian Army 1908, Govr W Desert Province Frontier Admin Egypt 1924–30, S African War 1899–1902 (severely wounded, two medals, seven clasps), Sudan 1908 (medal and clasp) and in 1910 (medal and three clasps), WW I (despatches), 3rd Cl Order Nile, Cdr Crown of Italy; *m* 11 April 1921 Ileene Caroline Ethel Otway (*d* 17 Oct 1960), only dau of Maj Arthur Augustus Hamlet Inglefield, of Old Church House, Beckington, Bath, and *d* 10 Dec 1959, leaving issue:

1e + (in remainder with his s to btcy only) Edward Archibald Richard [Edward Bayley Esq, Ballyarthur, Arklow, Co Wicklow, Ireland]; *b* 20 Sept 1922; *educ* St Columba's Coll, Trin Coll Dublin and Trin Coll Oxford; *m* 30 May 1964 *Rosemarie Evelyn Gisela Steins, only dau of Paul Heinrich Johann Minkley, of Frankfurt-on-Main, Germany, and has issue:

1f +Edward Alexander Christian Lambart; *b* 19 Oct 1967

1f *Selina Ileene Suzanne Rosemarie; *b* 24 May 1965; *m* 1986 *Robert J Kavanagh, of Raheen, Beech Rd, Arklow, Co Wicklow, and has issue:

1g *Emma-Sarah Rosemarie Isabelle; *b* 6 Aug 1988

2f *Catriona Louise Alicia Lucinda; *b* 15 March 1977

1e *Adelaide Elizabeth Mary; *b* Sept 1923; *m* 2 Aug 1955 *Patrick Mullen, of Kilqueeney, Avoca, Co Wicklow, son of John Mullen, of Abbeyshrule, Co Longford, and has issue:

1f *Anthony Patrick Theodore; *b* 11 Aug 1956; *educ* De La Salle Coll and U Coll Dublin; *m* 1980 *Aileen Mary, yst dau of Frederick Shackleton, of 3 Kenure Lawns, Rush, Co Dublin, and has issue:

1g *Benjamin Anthony; *b* 1983

2g *Patrick William; *b* 1984

1g *Constance Elizabeth Joy; *b* 1989

2g *India Margaret Eileen; *b* 1993

1f *Annabelle Sandra; *b* 11 Dec 1957

2e *Rosabelle Ileene Zahra; *b* 14 April 1931; *m* 9 Oct 1957 W/Cdr Donald Brian Robinson, RAF, of Green Acres, nr Chepstow, Gwent, er son of Maj Dudley Clare Robinson, MC, of Balvonie, 1 Shimna Pk, Newcastle, Co Down, and has issue:

1f *Colan Denis; *b* 8 July 1958; *m* 1988 *Jane Hilary Shrimpton, and has issue:

1g *Matthew Conor; *b* 1988

1g *Anna Kirsten; *b* 1990

2f *Timothy Rupert; *b* 31 Aug 1965

1f *Judith Sarah; *b* 3 March 1962

2d Charles John; *b* 8 Sept 1878; *educ* Radley; Maj late Roy Inniskilling Fus, WW I; *m* 21 Feb 1915 Deborah, dau of James Callinan Holland, of Bridge House, Dungarvan, Co Waterford, and *dsp* 10 Dec 1955

1d Adela Maude; *b* 27 Jan 1880; *m* 10 April 1916 Lt-Col Arthur Lovell Hadow, CMG, late Norfolk Regt (*d* 19 April 1968, aged 90), yr son of Rev John Lovell Gwatkin Hadow, and *d* 20 June 1963, having had issue

2d Kathleen Isabel; *b* 6 March 1882; *m* 18 July 1949 Gerald Noel FitzRichard Barry, MInstCEI, AMIHVE (*d* 20 Aug 1961), son of Richard FitzRichard Barry, Crown Slr, of Birr, Co Offaly, and *d* 2 Nov 1951

2c Maurice Spring Rice; *b* 17 Jan 1850; *m* 19 March 1880 Jeanie Theodora, dau of Capt Hayes, 44th Regt, and *d* 9 Dec 1900, leaving issue:

1d Crofton Talbot BAYLY-VANDELEUR, of Wardenstown, Co Westmeath; *b* 27 Oct 1881; assumed by Roy Licence 26 April 1911 the name and arms of VANDELEUR on succeeding to the Wardenstown estate; *m* 24 Nov 1915 Ruth Sidney, er dau of Abel John Layard, of Turley House, Winsley, Bath, and *d* 26 Oct 1927, leaving issue:

1e *Nesta; *b* 28 July 1917; *m* 16 April 1958 *Neville Moore, of Ulverscroft Grange, Markfield, Leics, yst son of Harry Herbert Moore, of Ulverscroft Grange

2e *Joan; *b* 27 Sept 1918

1d *Dorothy Mary; *b* 19 May 1884; *m* 8 Nov 1915 Lt-Col John Espenett Knott, CMG, DSO, late 8th Bn Roy Inniskilling Fus (*d* 1 Nov 1959), son of Herbert Knott, JP, of Sunny Bark, Wilmslow, Cheshire, and had issue:

1e John Maurice Wakefield; *b* 1 Jan 1920; WW II (despatches); *ka* Libya 11 June 1942

2e *William Espenett Bayly [William Knott Esq, Coombe Farm, Presteigne, Radnorshire]; *b* 23 Jan 1922; WW II with RM; *m* 28 May 1968 *Charlotte Teresa, dau of John Stobart Keith, slr, of The Cottage, Manuden, nr Bishops Stortford, Herts

2d Henry Edward; *b* 1889; *d* Jan 1923

3d Maurice Fitzgerald; *b* 1891; WW I in RCE; *d* of wounds 6 Aug 1918

(1) (cont.) The Rev Edward Bayly *m* 2nd 6 Aug 1793 Mildred (*d* 22 May 1831), dau of Joshua Davis, and *d* 21 Dec 1825, having by her had, with other issue:

2a Edward (Rev); *b* 13 March 1789; Rector of Horetown, Co Wexford; *m* 3 Jan 1827 Ellen Josephine (*d* 14 May 1871), dau of Rev Joseph Miller, and *d* 2 May 1858, leaving with other issue:

1b Edward (Rev); *b* 26 Dec 1827; Chaplain at Genoa; *m* 27 Sept 1854 Mary Elizabeth (*d* 1883), dau of Capt T Mosse, and *d* 1883, leaving issue:

1c Edward; *b* 26 July 1855; *d* unm

1c Helen Thomasine Margaret; *m* 18 April 1912 Brig-Gen Skerett Edward George Lawless, late RA (*d* 7 March 1936), and *d* 24 May 1947

(2) John (Very Rev); *b* 28 July 1747; DD; Dean of Killaloe; *m* 22 Sept 1772 Mary, dau of William Wall, and *d* 24 June 1831, leaving issue (with a dau Letitia), an only son:

1a Paget Lambart; *b* 1776; Capt 7th Hus; *m* Elizabeth (*d* 8 Feb 1872), dau of Samuel Shaw, and *d* 1845, leaving, with other issue:

1b Paget; Maj-Gen in the Army; *dsp*

2b John, CB, JP and DL (Dunbartonshire); *b* 9 Feb 1821; Gen in the Army (ret), Col Cmdt RE, FSA; *m* 5 July 1854 Jane (*d* 14 Aug 1908), only dau of Humphry Ewing Crum-Ewing of Strathleven, Ld-Lt Dunbartonshire, and *d* 12 March 1905, leaving issue:

1c Paget Lambart (Rev); *b* 18 July 1863; MA Pembroke Coll Cambridge; Rector of Newton St Loe, nr Bristol 1908–25; *m* 23 July 1896 Hon Blanche Louisa O'Brien (*d* 19 Jan 1945), dau of 13th Baron Inchiquin (*qv*), and *d* 1 Aug 1928

1c Helen Tolmie Dick; *m* 17 Nov 1880 Charles John Cathcart Douglas, DL (*d* 25 April 1926), 2nd son of Sir John Douglas, GCB, of Glenfinart, Argyllshire, and *d* 8 Oct 1935, leaving issue

2c Florence Elizabeth; *m* 1 Dec 1887 Thomas Denroche Smith, late BCS (*d* 21 Aug 1925), and *d* 6 Dec 1930, having had issue

3c Jane Coventry Ewing; *m* 15 June 1898 Rev Arthur William Dorman, MA, Vicar of Hinton Charterhouse, Somerset, and *d* 28 Feb 1910, leaving issue

1b Ellen; *d* 10 March 1912, aged 79

4 Charles, Capt RN; *m* Anne, dau of — Graves, of Moseley Hall, Worcs

Sir EDWARD *d* 28 Sept 1741; his est son,

Sir Nicholas Bayly, 2nd Bt; *b* 1709; *educ* Trin Coll Dublin; MP Anglesey 1734–41, 1747–61 and 1770–74; Ld-Lt Anglesey 1763; *m* 1st 19 April 1737 Caroline (*d* 7 Feb 1766), dau and heiress of Brig-Gen Thomas Paget (*see* above, **Lineage (of Paget)**), and had, with other issue:

Sir HENRY BAYLY later PAGET, **3rd Bt, 9th Baron Paget** (in which title he *s* his cousin 1769, taking name and arms of PAGET only by roy licence 29 Jan 1770; *see* above) and **1st Earl of Uxbridge**, Co Midx (GB), so *cr* 19 May 1784; *b* 18 June 1744; *m* 11 April 1767 Jane (*d* 9 March 1817), est dau of Very Rev Arthur Champagne, Dean Clonmacnoise, and ggdau of 2nd Earl of Granard (*qv*), and had issue:

1 HENRY WILLIAM, **1st Marquess**

2 William, Capt RN; *d* unm 1795

3 Arthur (Sir), GCB, PC; *b* 15 Jan 1771; *m* 16 Feb 1809 Lady Augusta Fane, 2nd dau of 10th Earl of Westmorland (*qv*), and *d* 26 July 1840, leaving issue:

(1) Stewart Henry; *b* 30 May 1811; Police Magistrate at Gibraltar; *m* 27 Feb 1834 Charlotte Jemima (*d* 3 March 1895), 4th dau of Sir Robert Williams, 9th Bt (*see* WILLIAMS-BULKELEY, Bt), and *d* 4 Aug 1869, having had issue:

1a Arthur Cecil Henry; *b* 16 March 1839; V-Adml; *m* 16 June 1870 Sophia Caroline (*d* 23 Dec 1939), dau of Rev Charles Bushe, and *d* 10 July 1924, leaving issue:

1b Stewart Charles Augustus; *b* 5 Jan 1872; *d* unm 28 Sept 1956

1b Kathleen Annie; *m* 25 April 1900 Falconer Lewis Wallace, OBE, JP, DL (*d* as the result of an accident 21 Oct 1944), of Candacraig, Aberdeen, only son of Alexander Falconer Wallace, and *d* 22 Nov 1942, leaving issue

2b Gladys Alwyn; *m* 15 July 1911 Henry LONSDALE later DANBY (deed poll 1941) and was *k* by enemy action 10 May 1941

1a Augusta Henrietta; *m* 4 Dec 1873 Capt Edward Brodrick Hughes Hartwell, RN, 2nd son of Sir Brodrick Hartwell, 2nd Bt (*qv*), and *d* 22 July 1883, leaving issue

2a Caroline Annie; *d* 28 Oct 1922

3a Charlotte Julia; *m* 25 Oct 1865 George Banks Bennie (*d* 15 Nov 1908), of Denford, Hungerford, Berks, and 20 Lowndes St, London SW, and *d* 19 Nov 1935, leaving issue

(2) Cecil Augustus; *b* 1821; *d* 1843

(3) Amelius; *b* 1821; *d* 1843

(4) Augustus Berkeley (Rt Hon Sir), GCB, PC; *b* 16 April 1823; Amb Extrdy and Min Plen to Italy 1876–83, to Austria 1883–93; *m* 20 Oct 1860 Countess Walburga Ehrengarde de Hohenthal (*d* 11 Oct 1929), late Dame d'Honneur to PRINCESS FREDERICK WILLIAM of Prussia (PRINCESS ROYAL), est dau of Charles Frederic Anthony de Hohenthal, Count of the Austrian Empire, and *d* 11 July 1896, having had issue:

1a Victor Frederick William Augustus; *b* 14 Aug 1861; Lt-Col late RA, WW I in France; *m* Sept 1901 Juliana Fortescue (*d* 22 May 1906), dau of Capt Henry Turner Uniacke, of Laywell Park, S Devon, and *d* 28 June 1927

2a Ralph Spencer (Rt Hon Sir), KCMG (1909), CVO (1907), PC (1919); *b* 20 Nov 1864; entered Diplomatic Serv 1888, Chargé d'Affaires Bangkok 1902–04, Envoy Extrdy and Min Plen there 1904–09, Min Resident Munich 1909–10, Envoy Extrdy and Min Plen Belgrade 1910–13, Assist Under-Sec of State Foreign Affairs 1913–15, Ch Commr Red Cross and St John of Jerusalem 1915–16, Envoy Extrdy and Min Plen to King of Denmark 1916–18, Amb Extrdy and Min Plen Rio de Janeiro 1918–20, had 1st class Order of White Eagle of Serbia; *m* 28 Oct 1907 Louise Margaret Leila Wemyss, GBE (1917), Grand Cordon Order of St Sava of Serbia (*d* 24 Sept 1958), dau of Gen Rt Hon Sir Arthur Henry FitzRoy Paget, PC, GCB, KCVO (*see* below), and *dsp* 11 May 1940

1a Alberta Victoria Sarah Caroline; *b* 7 Aug 1863 (HM QUEEN VICTORIA stood sponsor); DStJ; *m* 11 Aug 1883 1st Earl of Plymouth (*qv*), and *d* 22 Aug 1944, having had issue

(1) Laura Caroline Jane; *m* 3 Aug 1842 2nd Baron Templemore (*see* DONEGALL, M), and *d* 9 Dec 1871, leaving issue

(2) Rosa Maria; *m* 1st 10 March 1842 Maj-Gen John Douglas, CB, 11th Hus (*dsp* 10 May 1871), of Glenfinart, Argyllshire; *m* 2nd 16 March 1872 William John Waters, and *dsp*

(3) Agnes Charlotte; *m* 27 Feb 1854 Lord George Augustus Frederick Paget, KCB, and *d* 10 March 1858, leaving issue (*see* below)

4 Edward (Sir), GCB; *b* 3 Nov 1775; Gen, Col 28th Foot, Govr Chelsea Hosp; *m* 1st 22 May 1805 Frances (*d* 30 May 1806), dau of 1st Baron Bagot (*qv*), and had:

(1) Francis Edward (Rev); *b* 24 May 1806; Rector of Elford, Staffordshire, Rural Dean; *m* 2 June 1840 Fanny (*d* 30 July 1890), dau of Rev William Chester (*see* BAGOT, B), and *d* 4 Aug 1882, leaving issue:

1a Howard Francis; *b* 22 April 1858; *m* 15 May 1884 Alice Catharine (*d* 8 March 1934), dau of Rev Preb John Thomas Jeffcock, Rector of Wolverhampton, and *d* 18 March 1935, having had issue:

1b Francis Edward Howard; *b* 4 June 1886; *educ* Brasenose Coll Oxford; Lt Gren Gds SR; *m* 1st 8 June 1909 (*divorce* 1918) Anna Maria (Nancy) (*d* 25 March 1965), yst dau of George Richard Dyott, of Whittington Court, Lichfield, and had issue:

1c Edward Francis Howard; *b* 6 Sept 1910; *educ* Cheltenham; Capt Gren Gds, WW II; *m* 28 Oct 1948 (*divorce* 1972) Bridget (*d* 1981), est dau of Charles Harold Ellis, of Willington House, Maidstone, and *d* 1985, leaving issue:

1d *Caroline Charlotte; *b* 22 June 1950; BSc; *m* 1974 *Hensel John Peters, of Jamestown, St Helena, S Atlantic Ocean, and has issue:

1e *Howard Hensel; *b* 1974

1e *Nicole Maria; *b* 1982

1c *Elizabeth Beatrice Howard; *b* 10 Jan 1913; *m* 1 Dec 1938 (*divorce* 1968) Maj Charles Rochfort-Boyd, RA (ret) (*d* 1979), only son of Col Henry Charles Rochfort-Boyd, DSO, RHA

1b (cont.) Francis Paget *m* 2nd 25 March 1922 Jane Florence (*d* 17 Aug 1970), er dau of Capt Charles Francis Lang, and *d* 9 April 1945

2b Salisbury Howard; *b* 7 March 1889; 15th Bn 4th Inf Bde, Australian IF, Dardanelles 1915 (wounded); *m* 5 Nov 1915 Florence May dau of Arthur James McMahon, of Waterford, and *d* 9 Feb 1940, leaving issue:

1c William Howard; *b* 20 Sept 1919; lost at sea in HMS *Repulse* 12 Dec 1940

2c John Henry Howard; *b* 17 May 1925; *m* Grace, only dau of E Tunnicliffe of Austrey, Warwickshire, and *d* 1983, leaving issue:

1d *Deborah Anne [Mrs Norman Sanford, 69 Child Drive, Aurora, Ontario L4G 1Y8, Canada]; *b* 24 Jan 1952; *m* 1972 *Norman Edward Sanford, and has issue:

1e *Stephen Andrew; *b* 1980

2e *Michael Benjamin; *b* 1982

2d *Kathryn Mary; *b* 1956; *m* 1979 *William John Scrafton

3b John Howard; *b* 20 Sept 1890; *d* 1894

4b Louis Michael Howard; *b* 19 Oct 1895; late Lt Roy Fus, WW I; *m* 1st 15 Jan 1923 Eveline Tisle (*d* 7 Aug 1965), dau of Edmund Frank Angell, of Sidcup, Kent; *m* 2nd 27 July 1968 Marie Jeanette, er dau of Frederick James Foot, of Wairoa, NZ

5b George Howard; *b* 4 Feb 1897; Capt 2/3 Gurka Rifles, WW I (wounded twice); *m* 12 March 1920 Kathleen (who *m* 2nd 28 July 1923 Maj Thomas Arthur Hughes, IMS, son of Patrick Hughes, of Armagh, and *d* 1967), only dau of Samuel Dinham Byles, of Crow's Nest, Poltuan, Cornwall, and was *ka* Waziristan 11 Dec 1921

6b Patrick Everard Howard; *b* 21 Nov 1903; *d* 18 Nov 1911

1b Mary Frances Howard; *b* 9 May 1885; *m* 26 June 1906 Maj Richard Archibald Dyott, BCI, barrister (*d* 28 May 1965), est son of George Richard Dyott, JP, of Whittington Court, Lichfield, and *d* 18 Dec 1960, leaving issue

2b Fanny Desirée Howard; *b* 26 Aug 1892; *m* 1st 19 Jan 1917 Kenelm Mitchill Dyott, Surg RN (*ka* 13 Dec 1917), son of George Richard Dyott, JP, of Whittington Court, Lichfield; *m* 2nd 28 May 1925 Lt-Col Sir Charles George Wickham, KCMG, KBE, DSO (*d* 20 July 1971), of Ashdene Comber, Co Down, Inspr-Gen Roy Irish Constabulary, yst son of William Wickham, of Chestnut Grove, Boston Spa, Yorks, and *d* 19 Oct 1946

3b Hilda Beatrice Howard; *b* 23 May 1894; *m* 6 Oct 1919 Henry Edward Raymond Barker (*d c* 1930), and *d* 17 Feb 1937, leaving issue

4b Alice Katharine Howard; *b* 10 Oct 1898; *m* 22 May 1924 Capt Roderic Cecil Williams, dir of Prisons (*d* 28 May 1966), son of Col Henry David Williams, CMG, JP, DL, of Lambert House, Dorchester, and had:

1c *Roderic Greville David [Cdr Roderick Williams RN (ret), 16 Trowbridge Pk, Ilchester, Somerset]; *b* 26 Sept 1927; *educ* RNC Dartmouth; Cdr RN; *m* 15 Dec 1950 *Susan Margaret, dau of W/Cdr Robert Leslie Edward, and has issue:

1d *Nigel David Blackstone; *b* 8 Dec 1952; *educ* Cheltenham

2d *Timothy Nicholas Edward; *b* 15 June 1954; *educ* Cheltenham

2c *Michael Montague; *b* 15 Aug 1930; *educ* Marlborough

1c *Patricia Jane [Mrs Michael Aston, 14 College Rd, Cheltenham, Glos]; *b* 15 Aug 1930 (twin); *m* 7 May 1955 *Maj Michael Aston, Intell Corps, son of Arthur Vincent Aston, CMG, MC, of The Mill House, Swallowcliffe, Salisbury, Wilts, and has issue:
1d *Roderic Charles Mark; *b* 17 Aug 1956
2d *Salisbury Edward Henry; *b* 4 Feb 1959
5b Charlotte Gabrielle Howard; *b* 7 Oct 1900; *m* 2 Nov 1929 Joseph Harold Hodgetts (*d* 29 July 1965), son of William Hadley Hodgetts, of Model Farm, Elford, and has issue:
1c *Harold Patrick [Harold Hodgetts Esq, Model Farm, Elford, Tamworth, Staffs]; *b* 2 Aug 1933; *m* 22 Sept 1956 *Mary, dau of Eric William Watts, of Hollies Farn, Lee Maston, Sutton Coldfield, Warwicks, and has issue:
1d *George Harold; *b* 14 Feb 1958
2d *Charles Patrick; *b* 4 Nov 1960
3d *Edward William; *b* 23 Jan 1932
1c *Mary Undine; *b* 25 May 1932; *m* 26 July 1958 John Keith Sykes, barrister, of 50 Knowles Hill Rd, Newton Abbot, S Devon, son of Edgar Sykes, and has issue:
1d *Adam Keith; *b* 18 April 1964
1d *Abigail Charlotte; *b* 3 Jan 1960
2d *Gabrielle Ann; *b* 3 July 1961
3d *Emma Frances; *b* 23 March 1963
4d *Rebecca Marguerite (twin); *b* 18 April 1964
1a Agatha Mary Frances; *d* unm 14 June 1932
2a Rosalind Frances Emily; *d* unm 29 Jan 1925
3a Minna Frances Jane; *d* unm 1940
4a Ada Gertrude Frances; *d* unm 17 March 1931
5a Geraldine Louisa Frances; *d* 9 Jan 1863, aged 10
6a Gwendolen Margaret Frances; *m* 11 Aug 1982 Rev Lewis Jones (*d* 10 May 1931), late Vicar of Wold Newton, Yorks, and *d* 7 Jan 1938, leaving issue
4 (cont.) Sir Edward *m* 2nd 22 Feb 1815 Lady Harriet Legge (*d* 11 March 1855), dau of 3rd Earl of Dartmouth (*qv*), and *d* 13 May 1849, having by her had issue:
(2) Henry William; *b* 14 Feb 1818; Maj; *m* 23 Sept 1851 Anne Matilda Catherine (who *m* 2nd 8 June 1880 Maj-Gen Sir William Drummond Scrase Dickins, KCB (*dsp* 29 June 1914), 3rd son of Charles Scrase Dickins, of Coolhurst, Sussex, and *d* 23 June 1901), dau of Gen Sir George T Walker, 1st Bt, GCB, and *d* 17 Jan 1853, leaving issue:
1a Edward; *b* 1852; *d* 31 May 1863
(3) Patrick Lewis Cole; *b* 10 Feb 1820; Lt-Col late Scots Fusilier Gds; *m* 23 Oct 1855 Frances (*d* 14 Jan 1912), yst dau of Rev Richard Garth, of Morden, Surrey, and *d* 17 July 1879, leaving issue:
1a Henry Patrick Edward; *b* 8 July 1870; Lt 3rd Bn Rifle Bde; *d* unm 17 June 1893
1a Gertrude Frances; *m* 9 Sept 1884 Col Phelips Brooke Hanham, and *d* 16 Sept 1922, leaving issue (*see* HANHAM, Bt)
2a Florence Mary Emily; *d* unm 11 March 1947
3a Violet Evelyn; *m* 27 Nov 1906 Rev George Ranking, CF (*ka* 20 Nov 1917), Vicar of Fenhurst, Sussex, son of Harvey Ranking, and *d* 1946
4a Mildred Eileen May; *b* 17 Nov 1865; *m* 12 Oct 1880 Col Henry Lloyd Powell, DSO, JP, DL, late RA (*d* 29 Aug 1941), son of Thomas Powell, of Coldra, Newport, Mon, and *d* Jan 1955, leaving issue
(4) Edward Heneage (Rev); *b* 23 July 1828; Vicar of Hoxne; *m* 20 Nov 1856 Hon Emma Mary (*d* 30 March 1895), 3rd dau of 3rd Baron Auckland (*qv*), Bp of Bath and Wells, and *d* 29 Sept 1884, leaving issue:
1a Henry Edward Clarence, CBE (1919), JP; *b* 20 March 1860; Lt-Cdr RNVR, formerly Police Cmmr at Calcutta, Afghanistan 1880 (medal); *m* 1st 5 July 1899 Maria Caroline (*d* 26 Dec 1933), dau of Thomas Simon Bolitho, of Trengwainton; *m* 2nd 10 April 1934 Lucy Grace (*d* 17 July 1965), dau of Bernard Hamilton, of Springfield, Taplow, Bucks, and *d* 10 Aug 1940
2a Hugh Arthur; *b* 29 May 1862; *m* 31 July 1902 Catherine Honoria (*d* 5 Aug 1943), dau of Capt Arthur Watson de Capell Brooke, 4th Hus, and *d* 7 April 1924, having had issue:
1b Clarence Arthur Edward; *b* 15 July 1909; *educ* Eton and Hertford Coll Oxford; editoral dir Pan Books; WW II, Capt RA attached Intell Corps; *m* 24 Jan 1942 Cynthia Mary (*d* 1977), dau of Herbert Hutchings, of Langton Cottage, Stoodleigh, Devon, and *d* 1991, having had issue:
1c +Hugh Charles Edward [Hugh Paget Esq, 27 Highbury Hill, London N5 1SU]; *b* 11 Nov 1946; *educ* Eton and Merton Coll Oxford; *m* 1977 *Eleanor Mary, only dau of Rev Canon Williiam Wallis, and has issue:
1d +Francis Andrew Edward; *b* 1984
1d *Lucy Caroline Eleanor; *b* 1981
1c *Caroline Hermione; *b* 4 Sept 1942; *m* 30 Sept 1966 *Dr Theodore Bennett Robbins, of Box 57, North Pomfret, Vermont 05053, USA, yr son of Chandler Robbins II, of Eastern Point, Gloucester, Mass, USA
2c *Frances Catherine; *b* 14 Dec 1947
3c *Selina Mary; *b* 15 May 1950
1b Honoria Barbara; *b* and *d* 23 April 1908
3a Eden Wilberforce, CBE (1918); *b* 9 Sept 1865; *m* 14 Dec 1898 Gertrude Amy (*d* 30 Jan 1961), dau of William Mawdsley Charnley, of Preston, and *d* 20 Nov 1955, leaving issue:
1b Charles Edward Eden; *b* 18 May 1903; *d* unm 14 Oct 1968
4a Eric Morton; *b* 21 Nov 1867; *m* 24 May 1904 Georgina Byng (*d* 14 Sept 1916), dau of Herbert Byng Paget, of Darley House, Darley Dale, Derbys, and *d* 24 Feb 1929, having had issue:
1b Sylvia; *b* 24 Nov; *d* 31 Dec 1911
2b Mamaine; *b* 7 Sept 1916; *m* 25 April (*divorce* 1954) Arthur Koestler, writer, only son of Henrik Koestler, of Budapest, Hungary, and *dsp* 2 June 1954
3b *Celia Mary; *b* 7 Sept 1916 (twin); *m* 1st 23 June 1942 (*divorce* 1946) Charles Cecil Patrick Kirwan; *m* 2nd 10 May 1954 Arthur John Goodman (*d* (BA); Chaplain to the Community of the Holy Cross, Haywards Heath; *d* 9 21 June 1964), son of Joseph Goodman, and by him has issue:
1c *Mark Eden; *b* 9 May 1957
1c *Ariane; *b* 14 Aug 1955; *m* 1984 Andrew Dykes Scott Bankes (*d* 1987) (*see* SPICER, Bt)
5a Claude Edmund; *b* 21 July 1869; *m* 27 Aug 1895 Maude Ross (*d* 31 Dec 1926), dau of Frederick Purser, of New Zealand, and *d* 18 Feb 1922, leaving issue:
1b Jillian; *m* 27 June 1931 Lt-Cdr John Frederick Barker, RN (*ka* 8 June 1940), son of Engr Capt Henry Charles Day Barker, RN, of Cliff House, Kingsand, Cornwall, and *d* 31 May 1943, leaving issue
(1) Frances Jane; *m* 19 Sept 1843 2nd Marquess of Ormonde (*see* MOUNT GARRETT, V) and *d* 26 Aug 1903, leaving issue
(2) Caroline; *m* 15 Dec 1853 Rev Hon John Venables Vernon, yst son of 3rd Baron Vernon (*qv*), and *dsp* 17 July 1894
5 Charles (Sir), GCH; *b* 7 Oct 1778; V-Adml; *m* 7 March 1805 Elizabeth Araminta (*d* 17 Aug 1843), dau and coheir of Henry Monck, and *d* 27 Jan 1839, leaving issue:
(1) Charles Henry; *b* 15 July 1806; Capt RN; *m* 1st Jan 1836 Elizabeth Annals (*dsp* 27 Jan 1839); *m* 2nd 24 Jan 1840 Emily Caroline (who *m* 2nd 19 July 1848 Capt John Ballard Gardiner), dau of Henry M'Clintock, and niece of John M'Clintock, of Drumcar, Co Louth, and *d* 26 May 1845, leaving issue:
1a Charles Henry Monck; *b* 19 May 1842; late Capt 29th Foot; *m* 30 Sept 1873 Anna Matilda Margaret (*d* 28 Feb 1828), yst dau of Rev Jonathan Chase Matchett, Vicar of St Mary, Norwich, and *d* 17 March 1903, leaving issue:
1b Charles Henry FitzClarence; *b* 16 July 1874; *d* 20 Jan 1920
1b Louise Caroline; *m* 28 Jan 1915 Rev Gilbert Adolphus Rideout, MA (*d* 21 March 1927), late Rector of Rusper, Horsham, Sussex, and *d* 1 May 1947
2b Dorothy; *d* unm 14 July 1957
2a Alfred FitzClarence; *b* 2 Sept 1844; *d* 20 Sept 1916
(2) Edward James (Rev); *b* 16 July 1811; *m* Oct 1841 Emma (*d* 24 May 1806), dau of Gen Thewles, and *d* 30 Aug 1859, having had issue:
1a Horatio Edward; *b* 22 Dec 1842; Lt 27th Regt; *d* 9 May 1869
2a Charles Berkeley; *b* 4 June 1849; *m* 1st 17 Sept 1874 Frances (*dsp* 9 Dec 1877), 4th dau of Capt T Sibbald, RN; *m* 2nd 27 May 1880 Annie (*d* 10 Feb 1931), dau of William Sibbald, and *d* 8 Jan 1920, having by her had issue:
1b Edward William Berkeley; *b* 1881; *d* unm 18 Dec 1960
2b Charles Francis; *b* 2 Aug 1882; *d* unm 5 July 1904
1b Frances Anne; *m* 1 Sept 1927 Rev Neville Blunt (*d* 10 March 1965)
2b Eleanor Georgina; *m* 25 Oct 1911 William Roaf Grubbe (*d* 14 Oct 1955), son of William Charles Grubbe, of Weston, Ontario
3b Mary Letitia; *b* 1 Sept 1895; *m* 7 Aug 1954 George John Spreull, QC, MA, LLB (*d* 26 Feb 1956), son of John Spreull, of Spreull's Court, Glasgow
3a Edward Clarence (Very Rev); *b* 14 Aug 1851; DD; Dean of Calgary, Canada; *d* unm March 1927
1a Fanny Elizabeth; *d* unm 11 April 1904
2a Eleanor Caroline; Sister of Community of Sisters of the Church; *d* 11 Sept 1940
3a Frederica Maria; *d* unm 14 June 1898
(3) Brownlow Henry; *b* 8 May 1819; Lt RN; *d* unm at sea 1843
(1) Elizabeth Jane; *m* 25 March 1845 Maj William Berners, RHA, and *d* 13 June 1866, leaving issue
(2) Caroline; *m* 10 Dec 1832 Hon Algernon Henry Champagne Capell, brother of 6th Earl of Essex (*qv*), and *d* 11 June 1880, leaving issue
(3) Louisa Augusta; *m* 2 Aug 1828 Capt William Augustus Broadhead, 7th Hus (*d* 12 July 1860)
(4) Georgina; *m* 8 April 1841 Capt William Henry Kennedy, RN (*d* 13 Oct 1864), and *d* 8 Nov 1901, leaving issue
(5) Frederica Georgiana Augusta; *d* unm 12 Sept 1835
(6) Jane Frances Elizabeth; *m* 1st 19 Aug 1845 John Horne (*dsp* 9 Jan 1850), nephew of Sir William Horne; *m* 2nd 1851 Lt-Col Philip Sambrooke Crawley, Coldstream Gds, who *d* her widower, 6 Jan 1905
6 Berkeley Thomas; *b* 2 Jan 1780; *m* 22 Nov 1804 Sophia Askell (*d* 18 Feb 1859), dau of Hon William Bucknall, and *d* 26 Oct 1842, having had issue:
(1) Frederick; *b* 9 March 1807; Col Coldstream Gds; MP Beaumaris; *m* 26 Nov 1856 Maria Georgiana (*d* 27 Sept 1900), est dau of Charles William Pascoe Grenfell, MP (*see* GRENFELL, B), and *d* 4 Jan 1866
(2) Catesby, of Aspley Guise, Woburn; *b* 29 Nov 1809; Capt 7th Foot; *m* 1st 28 Aug Florinda Frances (*d* 28 Feb 1842), est dau of Capt Thomas Monck Mason, RN, and had issue:
1a Berkeley, DL (Middx); *b* 9 Feb 1841; *m* 22 Aug 1865 Gertrude Fanny (*d* 31 Dec 1906), 2nd dau of Rt Rev Hon Henry Montagu Villiers, DD, Bp of Durham (*see* CLARENDON, E), and *d* 21 Jan 1910, having had issue:
1b Frederick Catesby Villiers; *b* 30 Oct 1867; *educ* Trin Coll Cambridge (BA); V Consul Taranto; *dsp* 19 Feb 1896
2b Leopold Cecil, JP (ER Yorks); *b* 26 Jan 1871; *m* 1 July 1897 Christina Jessie (*d* 22 March 1929), dau of Samuel MacKenzie, and *d* 3 April 1934, having had issue:
1c Berkeley; *b* 1 Aug 1898; Lt Argyll and Sutherland Highrs; *d* 2 Dec 1921
2c Edward Catesby; *b* 7 April 1903; *educ* Harrow and Trin Coll Cambridge (BA); late Maj 5th Royal Inniskilling Dragoon Gds and Lt Yorks Hus (TAR), WW II 1940–45; *m* 1 Nov 1940 *Sibyl Gladys Rodney (who *m* 3rd 2 Nov 1963 Col Thomas Cromwell Williamson, DSO and bar, of Casa Tabraza Apartado 46, San Pedro de Alcantara, Malaga, Spain (*d* 1987), son of Sydney Williamson of Heligan, Pentewan, St Austell, Cornwall), yr dau of Col Charles Edward Duff, CB, and formerly wife of Lt-Col Robert Albert Glanville Bingley, CVO, DSO, OBE, 11th Hus, of Pegglesworth, Andoversford, Glos, and *d* 1 April 1963, leaving issue:

1d +(Anthony) Berkeley [Berkeley Paget Esq, c/o 8 Symons St, Sloane Sq, London SW3 2TJ]; *b* 29 April 1946; *educ* Harrow; *m* 1st 1976 (*divorce* 1979) Judith Mary Parry, and has:

1e +William Berkeley; *b* 5 July 1976

1d (cont.) Berkeley Paget *m* 2nd 1981 *Gabriele Mathilde Langer, of Munich, and by her has:

2e +Catesby Langer; *b* 1982

3e +Rodney Langer; *b* 1984

1d *Diana Jenefer; *b* 14 Aug 1943

1c Evelyn Mary; *b* 13 Feb 1901; *m* 4 April 1923 Lt-Col Louis Rowlatt Kettle, MFH, late 5th Inniskilling Dragoon Gds (*d* 27 Oct 1954), only surv son of Louis Coke Kettle, Capt S Staffs Regt, and *d* 4 Nov 1953, leaving issue

2c Rachel; *b* 14 March 1906; *m* 13 Oct 1927 George Nevill Deas, late 8th King's Irish Hus (*d* 11 Nov 1968), only son of George Deas, of Edinburgh, and has issue:

1d *Elizabeth Anne; *b* 24 April 1931; *m* 21 Jan 1961 *Douglas James Collins, of Hardwick House, Pembridge, Herefordshire, yr son of James Gordon Fenn Collins, of Wyecliff House, Brienton, Herefs, and has issue:

1e *Edward Simon James; *b* 31 Aug 1963

1e *Lucinda Jane; *b* 28 Nov 1965

2d *Rosemary Rachel [Mrs Simon Firbank, Bourton, Dorset]; *b* 12 June 1936; *m* 1st 29 July 1956 Sir Peter George Culcheth Holcroft, 3rd Bt (*qv*), and has issue: *m* 2nd *Simon Firbank

3b Ernest Villiers (Rev); *b* 10 April 1872; *educ* Selwyn Coll Cambridge Oct 1928

4b Algernon Berkeley; *b* 1 Nov 1877; *m* 5 Jan 1909 Elizabeth Anne Henniker (*d* 11 May 1925), er dau of Sir John Henniker-Heaton, 1st Bt (*qv*), and *d* 24 March 1928, having had issue:

1c Victor Berkeley; *b* 27 Sept 1911; Capt RA, formerly a Midshipman in Merchant Service, served WWII; *d* 1990

1c Elizabeth; *b* 21; *d* 25 Oct 1909

1c Rose, twin with her sister Elizabeth; *m* 5 July 1933 Eric Stafford Nuttall, s of John Stafford Nuttall, of Bonis Hall, Prestbury, Cheshire, and *d* 11 Oct 1981, leaving:

1d *Michael John Berkeley (Rev) [The Ven Michael Nuttall, The Rectory, Adare, Co Limerick, Ireland]; *b* 29 Aug 1936; *educ* Hurstpierpoint and King's Coll London (AKC); ordained 1961, Curate Chapel Allerton 1961–64, Stanningley, Ripon, 1964–68, Vicar Gipton 1968–76, Rector Witham Gp of Parishes (Lincoln) 1976–83, Team Vicar Bottesford with Ashby 1983–88, Rector Adare Union 1988–, Archdeacon Limerick 1992–; *m* 10 Oct 1964 *Valerie Doreen, er dau of George Edwin Rignall, of Leeds, and has:

1e *Richard Francis; *b* 10 Aug 1965; *m* 8 June 1991 *Heather, er dau of John Ramsden, of Scunthorpe, and has:

1e *Erin Rose; *b* 21 March 1994

2e *Andrew John; *b* 20 June 1967

2d *Edward James Stafford [Edward Nuttall Esq, Flat 25, Westley Close, Winchester, Hants SO22 9LA]; *b* 24 April 1938; *educ* Peter Symonds Sch, Winchester, and Newland Park Coll, Chalfont St Giles

1d *Elizabeth Mary; *b* 26 July 1946; *m* 20 July 1974 *William Nigel Radcliffe, yr s of Percy Radcliffe of Sulby, IoM, and has:

1e *Nicholas John; *b* 8 July 1977

1e *Claire Frances; *b* 1 Oct 1975

1b Eleanor Frances; *b* 12 Aug 1866; *d* unm 16 Nov 1946

2b Sybil Mary; *b* 9 May 1869; *m* 14 Sept 1912 Cdr Edward Louis Dalrymple Boyle, CMG, RN, son of Capt Robert Boyle, RA (*see* GLASGOW, E), and *d* 22 April 1947

3b Mildred Florence, MBE (1927); *b* 3 Sept 1873; clerk in the Foreign Office (ret 1952); *d* unm 9 Aug 1956

4b Florinda Frances; *b* 23 July 1875; *m* 16 Nov 1899 John Kenneth Crawley (*d* 29 Nov 1943), s of George Baden Crawley, and *d* 16 March 1901, leaving issue

5b Inez Gertrude; *b* 26 July 1881; *m* 12 Jan 1905 Adml Cole Cortlandt Fowler, CB (*d* 24 May 1936), 2nd son of Maj-Gen Charles John Fowler, RE, and *d* 5 April 1971, leaving issue

(2) (cont.) Capt Catesby Paget *m* 2nd 23 Oct 1851 Adelaide (*d* 26 Aug 1860), est dau of Rev Hon Miles John Stapleton (*see* STAPLETON, Bt), and by her had further issue:

2a Miles; *b* 5 Nov 1854; *d* unm 1886

1a Ruth Anne; *d* unm 21 Nov 1903

2a Rachel Maria; *b* 20 Jan 1858; *m* 17 May 1888 Frederick Pratt-Barlow, and *d* 31 Aug 1940, leaving issue. He *d* Aug 1893

3a Adelaide Stapleton; *d* unm 31 Jan 1914

(2) (cont.) Capt Catesby Paget *m* 3rd Sept 1862 Emily (*d* 7 July 1924), dau of Richard Armit, and *d* 16 July 1878, having by her had issue:

3a Catesby; *b* 4 Aug 1868; *d* 22 Dec 1930

4a Geoffrey; *b* 9 Nov 1869; *d* unm 28 Nov 1932

4a Mary; *b* 8 Dec 1863; *d* unm 24 Jan 1939

5a Cherry; *d* unm 9 May 1941

6a Sophia; *b* 15 Jan 1871; *m* 9 April 1896 Sir Ernest Musgrave Harvey, 1st Bt, KBE (*qv*), and *d* 30 Dec 1952, leaving issue

(3) Leopold Grimston, of Park Homer, Wimborne, Dorset; *b* 9 July 1824; Col late RA; *m* 3 Nov 1846 Georgiana Theodosia (*d* 28 Feb 1919), only child of Rev John Fitz Moore Halsey, of Gaddesten Park, Herts (*see* HALSEY, Bt), and *d* 5 June 1892, having had issue:

1a Harold, CB (1897), DSO (1900); *b* 9 Sept 1849; Col late 7th Hus, Sudan and S Africa; *d* unm 2 Feb 1933

2a Claude; *b* 3 Oct 1851; Cdr RN (ret); *m* 21 July 1880 Theodosia (*d* 17 March 1920), dau of John Henry Parnell, of Avondale, Co Wicklow (*see* CONGLETON, B), and was accidentally *drowned* 30 Jan 1917, leaving issue:

1b Cyril Nevil, VD; *b* 7 Feb 1891; Lt-Col IA (Gen List), WWs I and II; barrister Gray's Inn 1912; MIA Burma 1938–40, chm Public Serv Commn Burma 1946–47 and Ceylon 1947–50; *m* 25 Feb 1928 Eveleen Mary (*d* 1983), dau of Barnaby Lanktree, of Cork, and *d* 1980, leaving issue:

1c Richard Berkeley; *b* 22 Dec 1928; *educ* Downside, New Coll, Oxford (MA) and Cornell U (MBA); *m* 21 Aug 1965 (*divorce* 1986) Nicola Mary, est dau of Archibald Baird Murray, of Old Pk, Warninglid, Sussex, and *d* 6 Aug 1991, leaving:

1d +Edward Berkeley; *b* 13 Oct 1977

1d *Henrietta Elizabeth; *b* 20 Aug 1966

2d *Annabelle Mary; *b* 28 Sept 1968

3d *Charlotte Patricia; *b* 11 March 1971

1c *Mary Patricia [Mrs Lawrence Butterfield, Shepherd's Wood, Sheffield Park, E Sussex TN22 3QX]; *b* 17 March 1931; *m* 20 Sept 1969 *Maj Lawrence Butterfield, TD, FRIBA, FCIArb

2c *Caroline Eve Mary [Mrs Francis Smith, 20 Hampstead Gdns, London NW11]; *b* 29 Sept 1935; *m* 1st 2 Aug 1956 (*divorce* 1984) Anthony Coade Aljoe, son of Robert Aljoe, of 10 Frognal Gdns, London NW3, and has issue:

1d *Mark Coade; *b* 9 Sept 1959; *m* 1988 Sally Hancock

2c (cont.) Mrs Anthony Aljoe *m* 2nd 1984 *Francis J B Smith

3a Cecil George (Rev); *b* 19 June 1853; MA, Ch Ch Oxford; *m* 4 Jan 1887 Innes Elizabeth (*d* 29 Dec 1944), dau of Charles Berkeley Skinner, of The Chantry, Ipswich, and *d* 24 April 1929, leaving issue:

1b Francis Austin Elliott; *b* 7 Aug 1890; Roy Fus; *ka* 31 July 1916

2b Bernard Leopold; *b* 29 June 1892; *educ* Malvern and U Coll Reading; WW I with Artists Rifles and 2nd/13th London Regt in France, Macedonia, Palestine and Egypt, WW II with Oxon and Bucks LI and Roy Berks Regt, Western Airways 1941–43, sometime worker for War Graves Commn; *m* 12 Oct 1935 *Violet Gwendoline, dau of Lennox Robertson, FRIBA, of 14 Chargot Rd, Llandaff, and *d* 1974, leaving issue:

1c +Michael Robertson [Michael Paget Esq, 207 Aldwick Rd, Bognor Regis, W Sussex]; *b* 22 Dec 1936; *educ* King's Sch, Bruton, and St Luke's Coll Exeter; a composer and teacher, late Cpl Greenjackets Bde, Cyprus 1956–59; *m* 29 July 1960 *Betty May dau of Edwin Hobbs Browning, of Weston-super-Mare, Somerset, and formerly wife of Ernest Ralph Hobden, and has issue:

1d *Gerardine Carol-Louise; *b* 2 Aug 1961

2d *Sarah Catherine; *b* 2 March 1962

3b John Christopher; *b* 14 March 1895; Capt RGA; *ka* 26 April 1917

4b Dudley Noel; *b* 11 Dec 1896; *d* 6 Feb 1897

5b Michael Theodore; *b* 23 Dec 1897; 2nd Lt Lancs Fus; *ka* 17 Aug 1917

6b Martin Charles; *b* 20 July 1900; *d* 3 March 1931

7b Felix Barnaby; *b* 11 June 1904; *educ* St Edward's Sch, Oxford; *m* 1st 23 July 1932 Marjorie Therese (*d* 16 Feb 1962), er dau of Lt-Col Charles Seaver-Smith, RAMC (ret), of Fallowfield, Manchester, and had issue:

1c *Susan Jane Seaver; *b* 3 Oct 1933; dentist; *m* 14 Sept 1957 *John Keith Wood, MSc, PhD, AMIEE, of 147 Prescot Rd, Aughton, Ormskirk, Lancs, only son of John Wood, of 61 Millfield Rd, Chorley, Lancs, and has issue:

1d *Jonathan Piers Martin; *b* 3 April 1962

1d *Carolyn Jane; *b* 7 April 1965

2d *Elizabeth Anne; *b* 2 May 1967

2c *Carolyn Elizabeth; *b* 26 Feb 1935; *m* 18 Aug 1962 Arthur James Sanderson, ACH (*d* 1986), of 3 Pedmore Court Rd, Pedmore, nr Stourbridge, Worcs, son of Fred Sanderson, of 19 Green St, Fallowfield, Manchester 14, and has issue:

1d *Wendy Elizabeth; *b* 30 April 1967

2d *Helen Louise; *b* 13 June 1965

3d *Clare Marjorie *b* 1970

7b (cont.) Felix Paget *m* 2nd 9 May 1964 Dora Josephine Adams, MRCS, LRCP (*d* 1990), dau of William Adams Clark, MD, of 44 High St, Penge, London SE20, and *d* 1985

1b Averil Mary; *b* 15 Nov 1887; *m* 14 June 1921 Ronald John Barcham Leney (*d* 9 March 1965), son of Augustus Leney, of Orpines, Wateringbury, Kent, and had issue:

1c *Robin Christopher Paget; *b* 25 April 1928

1c *Anne Frances; *b* 12 Oct 1922; late WAAF

2b *Cecily Innes; *b* 21 June 1902

4a Alwyn de Blaquiere Valentine; *b* 14 Feb 1855; Lt-Col and Brevet Col, late Durham Light Infantry, memb Gentlemen-at-Arms; *m* 2 Feb 1882 Florence Talbot (*d* 9 Nov 1943), 2nd dau of Sir James Laing, DL, of Etal Manor, Northumberland, and *d* 14 May 1931, leaving issue:

1b Rupert Alwyn; *b* 14 Dec 1882; late Lt RW Kent Regt and Capt 24th Bn Roy Fus; *m* 6 Feb 1923 Amy Bessie (*d* 14 Sept 1970, aged 91), 2nd dau of Adam Dugdale, of Griffin Lodge, Blackburn, and Gilmonby Hall, Bowes, Darlington, and *dsp* 1 Feb 1946

1b Gladys Theresa; *b* 17 Sept 1885; WW I as nursing memb Br Red Cross; *d* unm 3 Feb 1965

2b Florence Eleanor (Elsie); *b* 25 Sept 1887; *m* 16 July 1919 Adam Norman Dugdale, JP (*d* 8 Jan 1948), er son of Adam Dugdale, of Griffin Lodge, Blackburn, and *d* 27 Jan 1965, leaving issue

3b Kathleen Louisa; *b* 6 June 1896; *m* 1st 26 April 1919 (Idivorce 1927) Capt John Holt-Schooling, Middx Regt, son of John Holt-Schooling, of 19 Linton Rd, Hastings, Sussex, and had issue; *m* 2nd 17 April 1928 Allan Gibson Hughes, late Capt KSLI (*d* 9 April 1938), of Chalfont, Shrewsbury, er son of Harry William Hughes, of Kingsland, Shrewsbury, and had further issue; *m* 3rd 6 Dec 1944 Leslie Doriam Cadman, late The Black Watch, son of George Cadman, of The Cottage, Purston, Yorks, and *d* 5 July 1973

5a Arthur Leopold; *b* 19 Aug 1856; late Maj and Hon Lt-Col 4th Bn Gloucester Regt; *m* 29 Jan 1885 Ina Blanche Georgie (*d* 6 July 1910), dau of Lord Otho Augustus FitzGerald, PC, MP (*see* LEINSTER, D), and *d* 1 March 1906, leaving issue:

1b Desmond Otho; *b* 8 May 1898 (twin); Lt KRRC; *ka* 21 March 1918

2b Oswald Leopold; *b* 8 May 1898 (twin); Capt late Durham LI, WW I (POW 1918), North-West Frontier 1930, WW II, Brevet Maj MEF; *m* 14 Oct 1931 Barbara Mackintosh (*d* 5 Sept 1968), 2nd dau of Arthur Forman Balfour Paul, MC, FRIBA, of Peffermill, Craigmillar, and *d* 22 Feb 1955, leaving issue:

1c *Susan Blanche; *b* 3 Nov 1933; *m* 29 Nov 1956 Capt William Mitchell Miller, MVO, late Gren Gds, of Craighill, Kinellan Rd, Edinburgh 12, yr son of Geoffrey William Mitchell Miller, of 4 West Bay Rd, North Berwick, and has issue:

1d *Richard Neville Mitchell; *b* 28 Oct 1964

1d *Anna Caroline; *b* 5 Feb 1959

2d *Victoria Jane; *b* 18 Aug 1961

1b *Cynthia Geraldine Ursula; *b* 29 Oct 1888; *m* 21 Aug 1921 Nicholas Henry Lambert (*d* 1 Aug 1943), 2nd son of Ambrose Lambert, JP, of New Grove, Co Kilkenny, and had issue:

1c *Desmond Ambrose [Maj Desmond Lambert, Dysertmore, New Ross, Co Wexford, Ireland]; *b* 15 June 1923; *educ* Downside; late Maj Irish Gds; *m* 7 May 1957 *Olive, yr dau of Oliver Hardy Eustace-Duckett, of Castlemore, Tullow, Co Carlow, and has issue:

1d *Nicholas Patrick; *b* 23 Feb 1958

2d *Patrick Nicholas; *b* 5 Oct 1959

1d *Eliza Patricia; *b* 7 Dec 1962

1c Patricia Mary; *b* 13 Nov 1924; *m* 2 March 1962 Count Gunnar Bernstorff, of Berkeley Forest, New Ross, Co Wexford, yr son of Count Bechtold Bernstorff, and *dsp* 3 Sept 1962

6a Wellesley Lynedoch Henry, CB, CMG, MVO; *b* 2 March 1858; Brig-Gen (ret), late cmdg RA 6th Corps, S African War 1899–1900 (despatches three times, medal, six clasps, brevet), WW I (despatches); *m* 29 Feb 1888 Isabelle Louise (*d* 5 Aug 1942), dau of William Hudson Swire, and *d* 11 June 1918, leaving issue:

1b Leo Berkeley, MC (1918); *b* 15 Nov 1889; Maj late Royal Tank Corps, formerly Rifle Bde; *m* 20 Oct 1917 Elizabeth Frances (*d* 25 April 1965), dau of Sir Henry James Vansittart-Neale, KCB, of Bisham Abbey, Berks, and *d* 26 July 1951, having had issue:

1c Berkeley Henry Vansittart; *b* 11 Feb 1919; Lt KRRC, WW II; *ka* Middle East 28 Oct 1942

2c Guy Leo; *b* 27 July 1921; Lt KRRC, WW II; *ka* Italy 26 Oct 1944

1b Mary Rance; *b* 11 March 1894; *m* 2 March 1916 Maj Kenelm Essex Wingfield Digby, RHA, 2nd son of John Kenelm Digby Wingfield Digby, MP, of Sherborne Castle, Dorset, and Coleshill Park, Warwicks, and *d* 20 Dec 1933, leaving issue

7a Lennox Dudley; *b* 4 Feb 1861; *d* 18 Feb 1881

8a Ralph; *b* 28 Jan 1863; *m* 30 Nov 1898 Geraldine Mary (*d* 24 Dec 1960), only dau of Sir Richard George Glyn, 3rd Bt (*qv*), of Gaunt's House, Wimborne, and *d* 5 Feb 1940

9a Mark John, JP (Parts of Lindsey, Lincs); *b* 13 Jan 1864; *m* 19 April 1898 Frances Carr (*d* 5 June 1941), yst dau of Capt Carr Stuart Glyn, of Woodleaze, Wimborne (*see* GLYN, Bt), and *d* 22 May 1938, leaving issue:

1b +John Francis; *b* 6 Aug 1903; *educ* Rugby; *m* 29 March 1932 Ann Millicent (*d* 1981), dau of Peter Arthur Blundell, of Ridgelands, Cooparoo, Brisbane, Australia, and had issue:

1c +Peter Jeremy Valentine, RD [Lt-Cdr Peter Paget RD RNR, 75 Little Walden Rd, Saffron Walden, Essex]; *b* 14 Feb 1933; *educ* Malvern; Master Mariner, Lt-Cdr RNR; *m* 1st 12 Oct 1963 Helene Boye (*d* 1978), er dau of Capt Thorolf Boye Hansen, of Ormey, Stavanger, Norway; and has issue:

1d +Mark Sebastian Boye; *b* 4 July 1967

2d +Charles John Leopold; *b* 1974

1d *Caroline Elizabeth Astrid; *b* 4 July 1964

1c (cont.) Lt-Cdr Peter Paget *m* 2nd 19– *Mrs Sara Veronica Mills, only dau of Mrs Joycella Colbourne, of 44 Gold St, Saffron Walden, Essex

1c *Sarah Ann Victoria; *b* 12 Aug 1945; *m* 4 April 1968 *James Lewis, RIBA, of 101 High St, Marshfield, nr Chippenham, Wilts, son of Stanley James Lewis, of 3 Mostyn Ave, Littleover, Derby, and has issue:

1d *Brett; *b* 1970; *m* 1992 *John Benjamin Gardener, of Nailey Farm, St Catherine's, Bath, and has issue:

1e *Benjamin James; *b* 1993

1d *Kim; *b* 1973

2c *Jane Melanie; *b* 12 July 1947; *m* 14 Oct 1967 *Lt-Col Richard Seymour Corkran, Gren Gds, of Crockfords, Waltham St Lawrence, Berks, only son of Maj Giles Seymour Corkran, of The Old Thatch, Hellingly, Hailsham, Sussex, and has issue:

1d *Claire Melanie; *b* 1973

2d *Alexandra Frances Louise; *b* 1976

1b Evelyn Mary Selina; *b* 6 Aug 1900; *m* 17 April 1926 (*divorce* 1930) Lt Col Osmund John Francis Fooks, late 14/20th Hus (*d* 28 Nov 1970), 2nd son of Edward John Fooks, of Langton Green, Kent, and *d* 22 Aug 1976, leaving issue

(4) Lennox; *d* 26 June 1827

(1) Gertrude Jane; *m* 16 Dec 1828 2nd Viscount Guillamore (*see* 1953 edn) and *d* 22 Oct 1871

(2) Eleanor; *m* 8 Oct 1825 1st Baron Hylton (*qv*), and *d* 23 July 1862, leaving issue

(3) Matilda Susannah (Hon); Maid-of-Honour to QUEEN VICTORIA; *d* 17 May 1871

7 Brownlow; *d* young 1797

1 Caroline; *m* April 1792 Hon John Thomas Capell, 2nd son of 4th Earl of Essex (*qv*), and *d* 9 July 1847, leaving issue

2 Jane; *m* April 1797 8th Earl of Galloway (*qv*), and *d* 30 June 1842

3 Louisa; *m* 1801 Lt-Gen Sir James Erskine, 3rd Bt, of Torrie, Fife (*d* 1825); *m* 2nd Lt-Gen Sir George Murray, GCB, PC (*d* 28 July 1846), and *d* 23 Jan 1842

4 Charlotte; *m* 15 Oct 1805 2nd Earl of Enniskillen (*qv*), and *d* 26 Jan 1817, leaving issue

5 Mary; *m* 27 June 1803 2nd Baron Graves (*qv*), and *d* 29 April 1835, leaving issue

The 1st EARL *d* 13 March 1812, when he was *s* by his est son,

HENRY WILLIAM PAGET, **2nd Earl of Uxbridge** and **1st Marquess of Anglesey** (UK), so *cr* 4 July 1815, KG (1818), GCB (1815), GCH (1816), PC (1827), KMT (1815), KSG (1815); *b* 17 May 1768; *educ* Westminster and Ch Ch Oxford (MA 1786); Lt-Col of a Regt of Inf; exhanged into Hussars, with whom served Peninsular Campaign, cmded united British, Hanoverian and Belgian Cavalry Waterloo, where towards the close of the battle he was wounded in his right knee, necessitating amputation, Ld Lt Ireland 1828–29 and 1830–33, Master-General Ordnance 1827–28 and 1846–52, FM 1846, Col RHG (Blues) 1842–54, Ld Lt and Custos Rotulorum Anglesey 1812–54 and Staffs 1849–54, Constable Caernarvon Castle, Ranger Snowden Forest, V-Adml N Wales and Carmarthen, Capt Cowes Castle; *m* 1st 5 July 1795 (*divorce* 29 Nov 1810) Lady Caroline Elizabeth (*d* 16 June 1835), dau of 4th Earl of Jersey (*qv*), and had, with other issue:

1 HENRY, **2nd Marquess**

2 William; *b* 1 March 1803; Capt RN; *m* 22 Jan 1827 Frances (*d* 6 May 1875), dau of Lt-Gen Francis, Baron de Rottenburg, and *d* 17 May 1873, having had issue:

(1) William Henry; *b* 13 March 1829; Maj-Gen IA, Hon Col 25th Cav IA; *m* 25 June 1878 Rosalind Margaret, OBE (*d* 16 June 1932), 2nd dau of Peter Northall Laurie, of Pax Hill Pk, Sussex, and *d* 16 May 1904, leaving issue:

1a Bertha Frances; *m* 16 Oct 1913 Maj-Gen George Jasper Farmer, CB, CMG, late Lancashire Fus (*d* 3 Nov 1958), Lt-Govr and Sec Roy Hosp, Chelsea 1928–33, son of Maj-Gen William Roberts Farmer, of Bedford House, Hants, and *d* 15 Nov 1951, leaving issue

(2) Frederick George Charles; Cdr RN; *d* 3 March 1866

(3) Charles Augustus; *b* 17 March 1832; Lt RN; *m* 8 Sept 1857 Emily Anna (who *m* 2nd 1 Jan 1866 Rt Hon Sir John Charles Ready Colomb, PC, KCMG (*d* 27 May 1909), and *d* 16 June 1907), dau of Robert S Palmer, and was accidentally *k* 19 Aug 1864, on board HMS *Phæton* at sea in the West Indies, leaving issue:

1a Anna Blanche Constance; *m* 22 Nov 1883 Col Ulick George Campbell de Burgh, CB (*d* 17 Nov 1922), 2nd son of Thomas de Burgh, of Old-town, Co Kildare, and *d* 2 Aug 1915, leaving issue

3 Arthur; *d* 1825

1 Caroline; *m* 10 April 1817 5th Duke of Richmond (*qv*), and *d* 12 March 1874, leaving issue

2 Jane; *m* 24 April 1824 2nd Marquess Conyngham (*qv*), and *d* 28 Jan 1876, leaving issue

3 Georgina; *m* 19 Oct 1833 2nd Baron Crofton (*qv*), and *d* 9 Nov 1875, leaving issue

4 Augusta; *m* 27 July 1820 1st Baron Templemore (*see* DONEGALL, M), and *d* 9 June 1872. leaving issue

The **1st Marquess** *m* 2nd 1810 Charlotte (*d* 8 July 1853), dau of 1st Earl Cadogan (*qv*), and formerly wife of Hon Sir Henry Wellesley, GCB, afterwards 1st Earl Cowley (*qv*), and by her had issue:

4 Clarence Edward (Sir), PC, GCB; *b* 17 June 1811; Adml, Sec Admlty 1859–66, C-in-C Mediterranean 1866–70, MP Sandwich 1847–52 and 1857–76; *m* 7 April 1852 Martha Stuart (*d* 23 March 1895), dau of Adml Sir Robert Walter Otway, 1st Bt, GCB, and *d* 22 March 1895, leaving issue:

(1) FitzRoy Richard Clarence; *b* 13 Aug 1853; Capt 3rd Bn Leicestershire Regt and Lt Gren Gds; *d* 30 April 1934

(1) Alma Martha; *m* 9 July 1890 Henry Aldenburg Bentinck, yr son of Charles Aldenbury Bentinck, of Terrington St Clements, Norfolk (*see* PORTLAND, E), and *d* 7 March 1947

(2) Emily Olivia Georgina; *d* unm 24 Dec 1953, aged 97

5 Alfred Henry, CB; *b* 29 June 1816; Gen, Equerry and Clerk-Marshal of the Roy Household, MP Lichfield 1837–65; *m* 8 April 1847 Cecilia (*d* 3 May 1914), 2nd dau and coheir of George Thomas Wyndham, of Cromer Hall, Norfolk, by his wife Maria Augusta, afterwards Countess of Listowel, dau of V-Adml William Lukyn later Wyndham, of Felbrigg Hall, Norfolk, and *d* 24 Aug 1888, leaving issue:

(1) Arthur Henry FitzRoy (Sir), PC (I 1912), GCB (1913), KCVO (1906); *b* 1 March 1851; Gen, Col East Kent Regt, late cmdg 1st Bn Scots Gds, King of Arms of the Order of the British Empire, ADC-Gen to HM GEORGE V 1910–14, GOC-in-C Irish Cmd 1912–14, Ashanti, Sudan, Burma and S Africa, Grand Offr Legion of Honour; *m* 27 July 1878 Mary, LGStJ (*d* May 1919), dau of Paran Stevens, of New York, USA, and *d* 9 Dec 1928, having had issue:

1a Albert Edward Sydney Louis, MVO; *b* 23 May 1879 (HRH THE PRINCE OF WALES stood sponsor); Capt and Brevet Lt-Col 11th Hussars, GSO(1) 1916, S African War 1899–1901 (medal with four clasps), WW I from 1914 (wounded, despatches twice, brevet); *das* unm 2 Aug 1917

2a Arthur Wyndham Louis, MC; *b* 6 March 1888; *educ* Wellington; Capt Irish Gds (SR); Hon Attaché Diplomatic Serv, Rio de Janeiro 1919–21 and Paris 1921–28, Equerry to HM QUEEN MARY 1936–40, an Extra Equerry from 1940; *m* 24 July 1928 Rosemary Victoria (*d* 1970), er dau of Brig-Gen Noel Armar Lowry-Corry, DSO (*see* BELMORE, E), and *d* 28 Feb 1966 leaving issue:

1b +David Arthur FitzRoy [David Paget Esq, East Kennett Manor, Marlborough, Wilts]; *b* 20 May 1929; *educ* Eton and Ch Ch Oxford; late Scots Gds

1b *Rosaline Louise [Mrs Clive Cameron, East Kennett Manor, Marlborough, Wilts]; *b* 15 Feb 1931; *m* 16 April 1958 *Clive Bremner Cameron, MD, er son of Maj Clive Rutherford Cameron, MBE, late New Zealand Imp War Graves Commn, Cairo, and has issue:

1c *James Paget; *b* 20 June 1961

2c *Andrew Wyndham Armar; *b* 4 March 1965

1c *Sarah Louise; *b* 12 Feb 1959

3a Reginald Scudamore George; *b* 6 March 1888 (twin with his brother); Capt late Irish Gds; *m* 22 Dec 1920 Minna Louise (*d* 1 Nov 1936), dau of G A Classenius, of Chicago, and widow of Laurens Rider, of New York, and *d* 11 June 1931

1a Louise Margaret Lelia Wemyss, GBE (1917), Grand Cordon of St Sava of Serbia; *m* 28 Oct 1907 Rt Hon Sir Ralph Spencer Paget, PC, KCMG, CVO, 2nd son of Rt Hon Sir Augustus Berkeley Paget, PC, GCB (*see* above), and *dsp* 24 Sept 1958

(2) Alfred Wyndham (Sir), KCB, KCMG, DSO; *b* 26 March 1852; Adml 1914, Capt and Cdre RNR 1914–18, R-Adml cmdg Coast of Ireland 1908–11, Egypt and Suakin, WW I; *m* 7 May 1906 Viti (*d* 13 Sept 1918), er dau of Sir William Macgregor, PC, GCMG, CB, and *d* 17 June 1918, leaving issue:

1a *Honor Cecilia; *b* 18 June 1907; *m* 1st 25 April 1928 (*divorce* 1930) Cdr Vivian Russell Salvin Bowlby, RN, son of Col Robert Russell Bowlby, Loyal N Lancs Regt (*d* 23 July 1972); *m* 2nd 15 April 1936 (*divorce* 1946) Ralph Glenhill, son of — Glenhill, of Portland, Oregan, USA; *m* 3rd 11 Nov 1952 (*divorce* 1957) Count de Vibraye

(3) George Thomas Cavendish; *b* 24 May 1853; Maj Imp Yeo, T/Maj 1916, Russo-Turkish campaign 1877–78, Zulu War 1879, S Africa 1900–01 in Paget's Horse, which he raised; *m* 29 Aug 1916 (*divorce* 1922) Dorothy St Vincent, er dau of Edward St Vincent Parker-Jervis (*see* St VINCENT, V), and *d* 28 Jan 1939

(4) Gerald Cecil Stewart; *b* 15 Oct 1854; Lt Herts Yeo Cav and Capt Northumberland Artillery Militia, Matabele War and S Africa 1900; *m* 2 Jan 1877 Lucy Annie Emily (*d* 15 April 1927), yr dau of Richard Gardiner, MP, and *d* 25 Oct 1913, leaving issue:

1a Dorothy Cecilia; *b* 30 Nov 1878; *m* 1st 28 Oct 1902 Capt Christopher Egerton Balfour, DSO (*d* 29 Aug 1907), son of Archibald Balfour, and had issue; *m* 2nd 9 Aug 1912 Reginald Charles Lowry-Cory, son of Armar Henry Lowry-Corry, and *d* 10 Feb 1936, leaving issue (*see* BELMORE, E)

2a *Lettice Mina; *b* 25 July 1880; *m* 1st 5 Jan 1904 Lt-Col Ronald Percy Hamilton Bernard, late Rifle Bde (*d* 2 Feb 1921), est son of Percy Brodrick Bernard, late Rifle Bde; *m* 2nd 27 May 1922 Lt-Col Hon Charles Christopher Joseline Littleton, DSO, 3rd son of 3rd Baron Hatherton, CMG (*qv*), and *d* 6 Dec 1969

(5) Sydney Augustus; *b* 19 April 1857; late Lt Machine Gun Section, XIIth Imp Yeo, S Africa 1900; *m* 13 March 1906 Marie Elizabeth (*d* 26 Sept 1942), dau of William P Dolan, of Philadelphia, USA, and *dsp* 16 Sept 1916

(6) ALMERIC HUGH PAGET, BARON QUEENBOROUGH, of Queenborough, Co Kent (UK), so *cr* 18 Jan 1918, GBE (1926), JP (London and Suffolk); *b* 14 March 1861; *educ* Harrow; Hon Fell Corpus Christi Coll Cambridge; High Sheriff 1909; MP Cambridge 1910–17, V-Cdre Roy Thames Yacht Club, Govr Guy's Hosp, Pres Miller Gen Hosp (Greenwich), Nat Union C and U Assocs 1928–29 and 1940–41 and E Provincial Div of the Assoc 1909–46 (also Centl Cncl Assoc 1940), memb Cncl RZS, Pres Roy Soc St George, KJStJ; *m* 1st 12 Nov 1895 Pauline (*d* 22 Nov 1916), dau of Hon William C Whitney, sometime Sec US Navy, and had issue:

1a Olive Cecilia, of Leeds Castle, Maidstone, Kent; *m* 1st 16 July 1919 (*divorce* 1925) Hon Charles John Frederick Winn (*see* SAINT OSWALD, B), and had issue; *m* 2nd 11 May 1925 (*divorce* 1931) Arthur Thomas Filmer Wilson-Filmer (*d* 17 April 1968), son of Arthur Stanley Wilson, of Tranby Croft, Hull; *m* 3rd 4 Nov 1931 (*divorce* 1944) Sir Adrian William Maxwell Baillie, 6th Bt, JP, MP (*d* 8 Jan 1947), and *d* 9 Sept 1974, leaving further issue

2a Dorothy Wyndham; *b* 1905; *d* unm 9 Feb 1960

(6) (cont.) The 1st BARON QUEENBOROUGH *m* 2nd 19 July 1921 Edith (*d* 1 Jan 1933), dau of William Starr Miller, of New York, and *dspm* 22 Sept 1949, when the Barony expired, having by her had further issue:

3a *Audrey Elizabeth; *b* 4 May 1922; *m* 1st 25 Jan 1945 Cmdt Christian Martell, DFC, French Air Force, Officier de la Legion d'Honneur, Croix de Guerre avec Douze Palmes, Silver Star, Liberation Cross (*k* in an aircraft accident 31 Aug 1945); *m* 2nd 3 Dec 1946 (*divorce* 1956) Alexander Ronan Nelson, son of Capt Thomas Arthur Nelson, and has issue:

1b *(Thomas) Lorne; *b* 29 June 1947; *educ* Eton and Brasenose Coll Oxford; *m* 1979 *Georgina Mary, dau of Hon Michael Astor (*see* ASTOR, V), and has issue

1b *(Audrey) Caroline; *b* 16 Jan 1949; *m* 1978 2nd Baron Egremont and 7th Baron Leconfield (*qv*) and has issue

2b *Elizabeth Christian; *b* 1 June 1950

3a (cont.) Mrs Audrey Nelson *m* 3rd 3 July 1956 Lt-Cdr Claud Peter Harcourt Lucy, RN, son of Claud Arthur Lucy, of London; *m* 4th 12 March 1982 Sir Thomas Musker, and *d* 1991

4a *Enid Louise; *b* 14 July 1923; *m* 11 Dec 1947 (*divorce*) Capt Count Rolland de la Poype, Armée de l'Air, Legion d'Honneur, est son of Count de la Poype, of Paris, and has had issue:

1b Charles Henri; *b* 3 Nov 1949; *d* an infant

1b *Isabelle Victoria; *b* 28 March 1951

5a *Cicilie Carol [Mrs Robert Evans, Gainsford House, Cowden, Kent TN8 7JD]; *b* 18 April 1928; *m* 10 Dec 1949 *Capt Robert Victor John Evans, Welsh Gds, son of Brig John Meredith Jones Evans, CBE, MC, of Wishanger, Churt, Farnham, Surrey, and has had issue:

1b *John Almeric; *b* 13 Sept 1950; *educ* Eton

2b *Michael Hugh; *b* 11 Nov 1956

1b Camilla Carol; *b* 22 Jan 1952; *d* 13 Feb 1963

2b *Patricia Antoinetta; *b* 18 July 1959

(1) Victoria Alexandrina; *d* 2 Feb 1859

(2) Evelyn Cecilia (Hon); Maid-of-Honour to HM QUEEN VICTORIA; *d* unm 17 May 1904

(3) Violet Mary; *m* 22 Oct 1889 2nd Baron Blythswood (*dsp* 30 Sept 1916; *see* 1940 edn), and *d* 13 June 1908

(4) Amy Olivia; *b* 3 June 1858: *d* unm 14 Feb 1948

(5) Alberta Victoria; *d* unm 28 July 1945

(6) Alice Maud; *m* 2 Oct 1897 Capt Claud Edward Stracey-Clitherow, late Scots Gds (*see* STRACEY, Bt), and *d* 24 Dec 1925

(7) Alexandra Harriet; *m* 17 June 1889 1st and last Baron Colebrooke, PC, GCVO (*d* 28 Feb 1939), and *d* Nov 1944, leaving issue

(8) Guinevere Eva; *m* 22 Oct 1891 Reginald Charles Hart-Dyke, and *d* 26 Feb 1894, leaving issue (*see* DYKE, Bt)

6 George Augustus Frederick, KCB; *b* 16 March 1818; Gen in the Army, Col 4th Hus, Inspr-Gen Cav, Offr Legion of Honour, Kt Order of the Medjidie (3rd class), Lt-Col 4th Light Dragoons at the Alma and Balaclava, Brig-Gen cmdg Light Cav Bde in the Crimea, MP Beaumaris 1847–57; *m* 1st 27 Feb 1854 Agnes Charlotte (*d* 10 March 1858), dau of Rt Hon Sir Arthur Paget, PC, GCB (*see* above), and had issue:

(1) Cecil Stratford; *b* 25 Sept 1856; late Capt 5th Bn KRRC; *m* 28 Feb 1882 Mary, dau of James Hay Erskine Wemyss of Wemyss (*see* WEMYSS, E), and *d* 26 Feb 1936, having had issue:

1a A son; *b* 17 Aug *d* 28 Nov 1886

2a Louis George, AFC; *b* 26 Feb 1891; F/Lt late RAF; *m* 29 March 1934 Harriet, only dau of George Bullock, of New York

1a Agnes Millicent Augusta Dorothy Canning; *b* 28 March 1883; *d* unm 2 Jan 1935

(2) Charles; *b* 4 March 1858; *d* 31 Aug 1867

6 (cont.) Lord George Paget *m* 2nd 6 Feb 1861 Louisa Elizabeth (*m* 2nd 25 April 1881 6th Earl of Essex (*qv*) and *d* 25 Jan 1914), yr dau of Charles Heneage, and *d* 30 June 1880

6 Emily; *m* 4 Aug 1832 John, 1st and last Earl Sydney (*extinct* 1890), and *d* 6 March 1893, aged 83

7 Mary; *m* 6 Sept 1838 7th Earl of Sandwich (*qv*), and *d* 20 Feb 1859, leaving issue

8 Adelaide; *m* 29 Nov 1851 Hon Frederick William Cadogan, yst son of 3rd Earl Cadogan (*qv*), and *d* 21 Aug 1890, leaving issue

The 1st MARQUESS *d* 29 April 1854; his est son,

HENRY PAGET, **2nd Marquess of Anglesey**, PC; *b* 6 July 1797; Col, MP Anglesey; called up to Ho Lds *vp* as Baron Paget of Beaudesert 15 Jan 1833; Ld-Lt Anglesey; *m* 1st 5 Aug 1819 Eleanora (*d* 3 July 1828), 2nd dau of Col John Campbell of Shawfield and niece of 6th and 7th Dukes of Argyll (*qv*), and had issue:

1 HENRY WILLIAM GEORGE PAGET, **3rd Marquess of Anglesey**; *b* 9 Dec 1821; MP S Stafford 1854–57; *m* 7 June 1845 Sophia (*d* 7 Dec 1901), dau of James Eversfield, of Denne Park Sussex, and *dsp* 30 Jan 1880

1 Eleanora Caroline; *m* 4 Feb 1847 Sir Sandford Graham of Kirkstall, 3rd Bt (*dsp* 2 May 1875), and *d* 17 Nov 1848

2 Constance Henrietta; *m* 6 Aug 1846 11th Earl of Winchilsea (*qv*), and *d* 5 March 1878, leaving issue

The **2nd Marquess** *m* 2nd 27 Aug 1833 Henrietta Maria (*d* 22 March 1844), 3rd dau of Rt Hon Sir Charles Bagot, GCB, and by her had issue:

2 HENRY PAGET, **4th Marquess of Anglesey**, DL; *b* 25 Dec 1835; V-Adml N Wales and W Carmarthen, Hon Col Queen's Own Staffordshire Yeo Cav and 2nd Vol Bn Roy Welch Fus; granted with his sisters rank of marquess's dau/yr s 9 July 1906; *m* 1st 24 Aug 1858 Elizabeth (*dsp* 5 Nov 1873), dau of Joseph Norman; *m* 2nd 2 Feb 1874 Blanche Mary (*d* 14 Aug 1877), dau of J C Curwen Boyd, of Merton Hall, Wigtownshire, and had issue:

(1) HENRY CYRIL PAGET, **5th Marquess of Anglesey**; *b* 16 June 1875; Lt 2nd Vol Bn Roy Welch Fus; *m* 20 Jan 1898 his cousin Lilian Florence Maud (*m* 2nd 11 Dec 1909 John Francis Grey Gilliat (*d* 22 Sept 1948), son of Howard Gilliat, of Abbots Ripton Hall, Hunts, and *d* 20 Feb 1962), er dau of Sir George Chetwynd, 4th Bt (*qv*), and *dsp* 14 March 1905

2 (cont.) The **4th Marquess** *m* 3rd 26 June 1880 Mary Livingstone, LGStJ (*d* May 1931), dau of J P King, of Sandhills, Georgia, USA, and widow of Hon Henry Wodehouse, brother of 1st Earl of Kimberley (*qv*), and *d* 13 Oct 1898

3 Alexander Victor, DL (Staffs); *b* 25 April 1839; Hon Lt RN Artillery Vols (Liverpool Bde); *m* 26 Aug 1880 Hon Hester Alice (*d* 17 March 1930), 2nd dau of 2nd Viscount Combermere (*qv*), and *d* 26 Oct 1896, leaving issue:

(1) CHARLES HENRY ALEXANDER, **6th Marquess**

(2) Victor William, MC (1918); *b* 17 May 1889; Capt RHG (Blues) WW I; *m* 1st 16 Jan 1913 (*divorce* 1921) Olive Mary (the actress Olive May) (*d* 24 Nov 1947), dau of George Meatyard, of Kensington, London W, and had issue:

1a +Henry Alexander Reginald; *b* 20 Nov 1914; late Lt Welsh Gds; *m* 4 June 1938 *Sonia, dau of Count Paul Chatoulenco, and has issue:

1b *Tessa Ann; *b* 3 May 1947

1a *Peggy Hester Pauline; *b* 18 Nov 1913; *m* 1st 28 Feb 1935 Lt Nigel Arthur St George Gibbes, 8th Hus (*d* of wounds received in action in the Middle East, May 1942), er son of Arthur Gibbes, of Wickenden, Sharpthorne, Sussex, and has issue; *m* 2nd 1 Jan 1944 (*divorce* 1950) Maj Samuel Peter Barrow, MC, RA, est son of Hugh Barrow, of Pike House, Kingswood, Surrey, and has further issue; *m* 3rd Ian Coward, of Saintpaulia, Carlo Flamingo, St Tal-Virtu, Malta GC

(2) (cont.) Lord Victor Paget *m* 2nd 29 March 1922 (*divorce* 1932) Hon Bridget Colebrooke (*d* as the result of an accident 27 Jan 1975), yr dau of 1st and last Baron Colebrooke, and by her had issue:

2a +Nicholas David; *b* 16 Oct 1924; *educ* Eton; Hon Capt RHG (Blues) 1942–47 (wounded); *m* 1st 23 May 1952 (*divorce* 1956) Mrs Heather Betty Bevis, dau of Charles Smetham, of Surrey; *m* 2nd 7 Sept 1956 Mrs Moya Lillian Hayim (*d* 5 May 1962), dau of Capt William John Enwright, OBE, DSO, RNR, of Auckland, NZ; *m* 3rd 1962 Ellen Bridget O'Neill (*d* 1963), and by her has issue:

1b +John David; *b* 1962

1b *Jane Bridget; *b* 1963

2a *Ann; *b* 19 May 1923

(2) (cont.) Lord Victor Paget *m* 3rd 7 Oct 1935 Mavis (*d* 1977), dau of William Crockford, of Chislehurst, Kent, and widow of (a) Lt Henry Mark Hector Robinson, RN and (b) Maj Herbert Macmillan Dawson, MC, and *d* 11 Feb 1952

(1) Winifred Constance Hester; *m* 1st 23 April 1904 Viscount Ingestre, MVO (*dvp* 8 Jan 1915), only son of 20th Earl of Shrewsbury and Waterford (*qv*), and had issue; *m* 2nd 2 Aug 1917 Richard Edmunds Pennoyer (*d* 17 Nov 1968,

aged 83), er son of Albert Adams Pennoyer, of Berkeley, California, USA, and *d* 18 April 1965, leaving further issue

(2) Beatrice Eleanor, CBE (1919), Mayor of Wilton 1942–46 and 1954; *m* 21 Jan 1904 15th Earl of Pembroke and Montgomery, MVO (*qv*), and *d* 8 Feb 1973, leaving issue

4 Berkeley Charles Sydney; *b* 5 March 1844; Hon Maj Staffordshire Yeo Cav; *m* 5 June 1877 Florence (*d* 26 May 1936), only dau of William Henry Chetwynd, of Longdon Hall, Staffs (*see* CHETWYND, Bt), and *d* 25 Nov 1913, leaving issue:

(1) Rowland Edward; *b* 8 Dec 1878; Maj 21st Bn KRRC, late Lt 1st Bn Roy Sussex Regt, S Africa 1900–02, WW I 1915–16 (wounded); *m* 28 June 1913 Maude Erskine (*d* 28 June 1975), dau of James Cran, of Vancouver, BC, and *d* 29 Jan 1954, having had issue:

1a (William Edward) Sydney; *b* 20 Aug 1916; 2nd Lt Roy Sussex Regt, WW II; *m* 25 May 1940 *Justine (*m* 2nd 22 Oct 1945 (*divorce* 1956) Capt James Allan Leslie Pritchard, Roy Sussex Regt, son of Maj Frank Vernon Pritchard), est dau of Maj Harcourt Sawyer, of Lyminster, Sussex, and was *ka* Eritrea 8 April 1941

(1) Muriel Helen Florence, CBE (1918); *b* 3 Jan 1878; *m* 21 Dec 1896 Hon Rupert Evelyn Beckett, brother of 2nd Baron Grimthorpe (*qv*), and *d* 20 April 1941, leaving issue

3 Florence Cecilia; *b* Aug 1842; *m* 1st 16 July 1864 4th and last Marquess of Hastings (*dsp* 10 Nov 1868); *m* 2nd 9 June 1870 Sir George Chetwynd, 4th Bt (*qv*), and *d* 3 Feb 1907, having had issue

The **2nd Marquess** *m* 3rd 8 March 1860 Ellen Jane (*d* 2 June 1874), dau of George Burnand, and *d* 7 Feb 1869

The 5th MARQUESS's cousin,

CHARLES HENRY ALEXANDER PAGET, **6th Marquess of Anglesey**, GCVO (1928), DL (Anglesey); *b* 14 April 1885; Capt late Reserve of Off RHG (Blues), ADC to GOC Egypt 1915, Assist Mily Sec to GOC Ireland 1916, WW I, WW II as Lt-Col Home Gd; Ld-Lt Anglesey 1942–47; Mayor Burton-on-Trent 1911, Ld Chamberlain to HM QUEEN MARY 1922–47; Order of the Nile 4th Cl, Grand Cross Star of Italy and Romania, Grand Cross Order of Ismail, Grand Cordon Star of Ethiopia, Grand Cross of Star Afghanistan, Cdr Legn of Honour; *m* 3 Aug 1912 Lady Victoria Marjorie Harriet Manners (*d* 3 Nov 1946), dau of 8th Duke of Rutland (*qv*), and *d* 21 Feb 1947, leaving:

1 GEORGE CHARLES HENRY VICTOR PAGET, **7th and present Marquess of Anglesey**

1 (Alexandra Mary) Caroline Cecilia; *b* 15 June 1913; *m* 14 July 1949 Sir (Charles) Michael Robert Vivian Duff, 3rd Bt, and *d* 22 May 1973, having adopted:

*Charles David

2 *Elizabeth Hester Mary; *b* 28 Oct 1916; *m* 7 June 1939 Raimund von Hofmannsthal (*d* 20 March 1974), son of Hugo von Hofmannsthal, and had:

(1) *Octavian Charles Hugo; *b* 13 Feb 1946; *educ* Millfield

(1) *(Sarah) Arabella Marjorie; *b* 14 Jan 1942; *m* 17 July 1964 (*divorce* 1969) Baron (Frederick Patrick) Piers von Westenholz, er son of Baron Henry Frederick Everard von Westenholz, of Little Blakesware, Widford, Herts

3 Mary Patricia Beatrice Rose; *b* 19 Jan 1918; *d* 28 March 1996

4 *Rose Mary Primrose [The Lady Rose McLaren, Old Bodnod, Eglwysbach, Colwyn Bay, N Wales, LL28 5RF] *b* 21 July 1919; *m* 3 April 1940 Hon John Francis McLaren (*d* 23 March 1953), 2nd s of 2nd Baron Aberconway (*qv*), and has issue

5 *Katharine Mary Veronica (twin) [The Lady Katharine Farrell, Cuttmill House, Watlington, Oxon OX9 5BA]; *b* 8 Oct 1922; *m* 1st 16 April 1941 (*divorce* 1948) Lt-Col Jocelyn Eustace Gurney, DSO, MC, DL, late Welsh Gds (*d* 22 May 1973), 2nd son of Sir Eustace Gurney, of Walsingham Abbey, and Spowston Hall, Norfolk, and has:

(1) *Judith Marjorie Katherine [Mrs James Bowen, Rishworth Hall Cottage, Sowerby Bridge, W Yorks HX6 4QN]; *b* 1942; *m* 1964 *James Bowen

5 (cont.) Lady Katharine Gurney *m* 2nd 21 Jan 1949 *Maj Charles Farrell, MC, late Scots Gds, For Serv, yst s of Gerald William Farrell, and by him has:

(1) *Gerald Charles William; *b* 1956; *m* 1981 *Joanna Rosemary, yr dau of Col Philip Turner van Straubenzee, DSO, of Spennithorne House, Leyburn, N Yorks, and has:

1a *Frederick Desmond Casimir; *b* 1987

2a *William Arthur; *b* 1992

(1) *Louisa Caroline Mary; *b* 1949; *m* 1970 (*divorce* 1993) Robin James Lane Fox, writer, yst s of James Henry Lane Fox, FRICS, of Middleton House, Middleton Cheney, Oxon, and has issue

(2) *Diana Mary; *b* 1958

(3) *Marjorie Elizabeth Mary; *b* 1962

Seat: Plâs Newydd, Anglesey, Gwynedd. Built to James Wyatt's neo-Gothick designs in the 18th century, this building is chiefly famous for its Rex Whistler mural in the dining room. The artist is the subject of a one-room museum elsewhere in the house, as is the Waterloo hero the **1st Marquess**. There is a fine view over the Menai Straits to the Snowdon range beyond.

ANNALY

Arms: Arg., on a chevron engrailed between three roses gu., a cross crosslet or. **Crest:** A cubit arm ppr., charged with a chevron engrailed gu., thereon a cross crosslet or, in the hand three roses gu. slipped ppr. **Supporters:** Dexter, a horse arg., caparisoned with the trappings of the 14th Regt. of Light Dragoons ppr.; sinister, an Irish wolfhound ppr., gorged with an antique crown and chained or. **Motto:** *Vi et virtute* ('By strength and virtue'). **Creation:** B. (UK) 19 Aug 1863.

THE 6TH BARON ANNALY OF ANNALY AND RATHCLINE, Co Longford (Luke Richard White) [The Rt Hon The Lord Annaly, Heath Farm, North Street, Fritwell, Oxon OX6 9QS]; *b* 29 June 1954; *s f* 1990; *educ* Eton, RMA Sandhurst and RAC Cirencester; Lt Roy Hus 1974–78, RARO, Ld-in-Waiting 1994–; *m* 11 June 1983 *Caroline Nina, yr dau of Col Robert Hugh Garnett, MBE, KSLI, (*see* GLENARTHUR, B) and has:

1 +LUKE HENRY; *b* 20 Sept 1990

1 *Lavinia Marye; *b* 1987

2 *Iona Elizabeth, b 1989

Barony of Annaly: Two earlier creations under this name (more precisely ANNALY OF TENELICK) were conferred on members of the Gore family (*see* ARRAN, E) in the second half of the 18th century.

Lineage: LUKE WHITE, of Woodlands, Co Dublin, High Sheriff 1804, MP Leitrim 1812–24, High Sheriff Co Longford 1806, was said to have made the greatest amount of money from commerce ever in Ireland up to that time, doing so by bookselling and running a lottery office. He bought the Earl of Carhampton's estate of Luttrelstown (so named from the Carhampton family name of Luttrell), just outside Dublin. He was *b* 1740 and *m* 1st (licence 7 Feb 1781) Elizabeth, dau of Andrew de la Mazière, of Dublin, of a Huguenot family, and had issue; *m* 2nd 1800 Arabella (*d* Feb 1853), dau of William Fortescue, and *d* 1824 having had a further s; his 4th s by his 1st w:

HENRY WHITE, **1st Baron Annaly of Annaly and Rathcline**, Co Longford (UK), so *cr* 19 Aug 1863; *b* 1789; Ld Lt Co Longford, MP Co Longford 1837–47 and 1857–63 and Co Dublin 1823–32, joined 14th Light Dragoons 1811, served Peninsular War (present Badajoz and Salamanca (medal with clasps)); *m* 3 Oct 1828 Ellen (*d* 12 May 1868), dau of William Soper Dempster, of Skibo Castle, Sutherland, and *d* Sept 1873, having had an est s:

LUKE WHITE, **2nd Baron Annaly of Annaly and Rathcline**, KP, DL Co Dublin; Lt-Col Longford Militia, Lt-Col Dublin Militia; MP (Lib) Co Clare 1859–60, Co Longford 1861–62 and Kidderminster 1862–65; Capt 13th Light Dragoons; a Ld of Treasury 1862–65, State Steward to Ld-Lt of Ireland 1868–74, Ld-Lt Co Longford 1873–74; *b* 26 Sept 1829; *m* 24 Aug 1858 Emily (*d* 22 Jan 1915), dau of James Stuart, and had:

1 LUKE, **3rd Baron**

2 Henry Frederick, DSO, Lt-Col late Gren Guards, ADC and Mil Sec to Ld Lt Ireland; served Sudan campaign 1884–85 (medal with clasp and bronze star) and S Africa 1899–1902, present Relief of Mafeking (DSO, Queen's medal with three clasps, King's medal with two clasps, wounded), *b* 1 April 1859; *d* unm 17 Aug 1903

3 Charles James, Ch Commr Police Rhodesia 1892–95, brevet Major, late Capt Roy Fus, served Matabeleland campaign 1893 and 1896 (medal and clasp), on staff World War I 1914–19 (despatches twice, brevet Major); Order of St Sava of Serbia, *b* 24 June 1860, *m* 11 Dec 1901 Evelyn (*d* 31 Aug 1946), dau of Francis B Bulkeley-Johnson, and *d* 8 Sept, 1930, leaving issue:

(1) Margaret Lucia, *b* 12 Nov 1902, *m* 24 April 1948 Capt Sir Gervase Ralph Edmund Blois, 10th Bt (*qv*)

4 Robert, CB (1919), CMG (1916), DSO (1918), Lt-Col late 10th (Service) Bn Roy Fus, Brig-Gen cmdg 184th Inf Brigade, BEF; raised and cmded 10th Bn Roy Fus 1914; hon Brig-Gen 1918, formerly Maj and brevet Lt-Col Reserve of Officers, Roy Welch Fus, served Nile Expedition 1884–85 (medal and clasp and bronze star), S Africa 1896 and 1900 (medal with five clasps) and WW I (despatches six times, twice wounded, brevet), *b* 26 Oct 1861; *d* unm 19 Nov 1936

5 Francis William, OBE (1919), Maj late General List, temp Maj and superintendent Remount Servs 1915, served World War I (despatches twice), *b* 23 May 1873; *m* 14 July 1910 Anna Elizabeth (*d* 20 June 1956), formerly w of H Sladden and 2nd dau of C Jaeger, and *d* 15 July 1931

1 Ellen Harriet, *m* 29 Jan 1874 14th Baron Inchiquin (*qv*) and *d* 2 March 1913, leaving issue

2 Alice Emily, DBE (1920), *m* 26 Aug 1879 3rd Earl of Leicester (*qv*) and *d* 24 April 1936, leaving issue

3 Violet, *m* 18 March 1899 Lord Percy St Maur, 2nd s of 14th Duke of Somerset (*qv*), and *d* 2 July 1927, leaving issue

The 2nd BARON *d* 17 March 1888; his est s,

LUKE WHITE, **3rd Baron Annaly of Annaly and Rathcline**, GCVO, DL (Co Longford), JP and DL (Northants); Ld of Bedchamber to HRH THE PRINCE OF WALES 1908–10, Perm Ld-in-Waiting to HM GEORGE V 1910–21, hon Col (late cmdg) Northants Yeo, formerly Capt Scots Guards, served Eqyptian Campaign 1882 (medal with clasp and bronze star); Grand Offr Legion of Honour France; *b* 25 Feb 1857; *m* 24 July 1884 Hon Lilah Georgiana Augusta Constance Agar-Ellis (*d* 27 Jan 1944), only dau of 3rd Viscount Clifden (*see* 1970 edn), and had issue:

1 LUKE HENRY, **4th Baron**

1 Lilah Charlotte Sarah, *b* 22 Dec 1889, *m* 1 June 1911 Col John George Lowther, CBE, DSO, MC, TD, DL, late 11th Hus, s of George William Lowther (*see* LOWTHER, Bt), and *d* 20 Dec 1976, leaving issue. He *d* 19 March 1977

2 Lucia Emily Margaret, Maid of Honour to HM QUEEN ALEXANDRA 1919–22, JP (1944) Notts, served World War I overseas with YMCA and BRCS Nursing Service, *b* 3 Dec 1890, *m* 24 June 1922 8th Viscount Galway (*qv*) and had issue

The 3rd BARON *d* 15 Dec 1922; his only son,

LUKE HENRY WHITE, **4th Baron Annaly of Annaly and Rathcline**, MC, JP (Northants); *educ* Charterhouse; Maj 11th Hus WW I, P/O RAFVR 1940, Legion of Honour, *b* 7 Aug 1885, *m* 9 April 1919 Lady Lavinia Emily Spencer (*d* 9 May 1955), 2nd dau of 6th Earl Spencer (*qv*), and had issue:

1 LUKE ROBERT, **5th Baron**

1 *Elizabeth Patricia [The Hon Mrs King, 20 The Craig Rd, Downpatrick, Co Down]; WAAF WW II; *b* 5 Nov 1923, *m* 10 Feb 1945 Lt-Cdr James Osborne King, DSC, DL, RNVR (*d* 2 May 1995), s of James King, of Carnasure, Comber, Co Down, and has issue:

(1) *James [James King Esq, Rademon, Crossgar, Co Down BT30 9HD]; *b* 14 Jan 1952; *educ* Eton; *m* 1981 *Sally Louisa, dau of Alan Walker-Gray, of Northwood, Middx, and has issue:

1a *James Charles Osborne, *b* 1984

2a *Dillon Alexander Jolyon, *b* 1987

3a *Justin Sheridan Vere, *b* 1990

(1) *(Elizabeth) Lavinia Sara [Mrs Lavinia Montgomery, Riverview, Pallamallawa, NSW 2399, Australia], *b* 8 Jan 1946 (HM THE QUEEN stood sponsor); *m* 14 June 1969 (*divorce* 1990) David Hugh Montgomery and has:

1a *Matthew Hugh, *b* 24 Sept 1970

2a *Alexander James, *b* 1974

(2) *Patricia Rose [Mrs Antony North, PO Box 781336, Sandton 2146, South Africa], *b* 23 Dec 1947; *m* 1 Aug 1970 *Antony D G North, s of Douglas North, of Northdene, Constantia, Cape Town, and has issue:

1a *Christopher Douglas Antony, *b* 1976

2a *Richard James Patrick, *b* 1978

1a *Georgina Chloë Shallcross, *b* 1972

The 4th BARON *d* 1970; his only s,

LUKE ROBERT WHITE, **5th Baron Annaly of Annaly and Rathcline**, ptnr W Greenwell & Co, Liveryman Haberdashers' Co 1953, Freeman City of London, F/Offr RAF 1944–48, RAuxAF 1948–51; *b* 15 March 1927; *educ* Eton and Trin Coll Cambridge; *m* 1st 23 July 1953 (*divorce* 1956) Lady Marye Isabel Pepys (*d* 4 June 1958), est dau of 7th Earl of Cottenham (*qv*), and had:

1 LUKE RICHARD WHITE, **6th and present Baron Annaly of Annaly and Rathcline**

The **5th Baron** *m* 2nd 26 Jan 1960 (*divorce* 1967) Jennifer Margaret, only dau of Rupert Sausmarez Carey, OBE, of East Hoe Manor, Hambledon, Hants, and had further issue:

1 *Doone Patricia, *b* 16 June 1961; *m* 4 Nov 1995 *Julian G Smith, only s of Antony Smith, of Orcheston, Wilts

2 *Caroline Davina, *b* 8 Feb 1963

The **5th Baron** *m* 3rd 1984 *Beverley Elizabeth [The Rt Hon Beverley Lady Annaly, 33 Chipstead St, London SW6 3SR], fndr Anastasia Tst 'Sign' Campaign for Deaf People, dau of William Maxwell and formerly w of Michael Healy, and *d* 1990, leaving by her:

3 *Georgina Elisabeth Healy; *b* 1973

ANNAN

Creation: B. (LP) (UK) 16 July 1965.

THE BARON ANNAN, of the Royal Burgh of Annan, Co Dumfries (UK), so *cr* 16 July 1965 (Nöel Gilroy Annan, OBE (1946)) [The Rt Hon the Lord Annan OBE, 45 Ranelagh Grove, London SW1W 8PB]; *b* 25 Dec 1916; *educ* Stowe and King's Coll Cambridge; WW II: Mil Intell Directorate 1940–42, Staff Coll Camberley 1942, Jt Intell Staff War Cabinet Off 1943–44, Intell Staff SHAEF 1944–45, Lt-Col 1945, GSO(1) Political Div Br Control Commn Germany 1945–46; Cambridge: assist tutor King's Coll 1947–56, lecturer politics 1948–66, Provost King's Coll 1956–66 and UCL 1966–1978, V-Chllr London U 1978–81, Pres London Library 1980–96, Tstee: Churchill Coll Cambridge 1958–76 and Br Museum 1963–80, Chm: Tstees Nat Gallery 1980–85 (Tstee 1978–85), Deptl Ctee teaching Russian in schs 1960, Educn Ctee Gulbenkian Fndn 1957–64 and Acad Planning Bd Essex U 1965–70, memb: V-Chllrs and Pncpls Ctee 1966–81, Acad Advsy Ctee Brunel Coll 1964–, Public Schs Advsy Ctee 1966–70, Acad Planning Bd UEA 1964–71, Dir Roy Opera House Covent Gdn 1967–78, Fell Eton 1956–66, Govr Stowe 1945–66, author: *Leslie Stephen* (1951), *The Intellectual Aristocracy* (1956), *Roxburgh of Stowe* (1965), *Our Age* (1990), *Changing Enemies* (1995), Cdr Order King George the Hellenes 1963; *m* 30 June 1950 *Gabriele, dau of Louis Ferdinand Ullstein, of Berlin, and has issue:

1 *(Amanda) Lucy [The Hon Mrs de Grey, 38 Stockwell Park Close, London SW19 0DG]; *b* 13 June 1952; *m* 3 Sept 1977 *Spencer Thomas de Grey, (*see* WALSINGHAM, B), and has:

(1) *Felix Nicholas; *b* 1992

(1) *Georgia Catharine; *b* 1988

2 *Juliet Louise [The Hon Mrs Le Fanu, 24 Grafton Sq, London SW4 0DB]; *b* 7 Jan 1955; *m* 1987 *Dr Richard James Le Fanu, 2nd s of Richard Le Fanu, and has:

(1) *Frederick James; *b* 1898

(1) *Allegra Frances; *b* 1992

Lineage: — ANNAN; *b c* 1741; farmer at Cults and Kinneswood and Canon Mills, nr Edinburgh; *m* and had with a yst s:

DAVID ANNAN, of Cults and Kinneswood; *b* 1787; *m* and *d* 1842, leaving, with three other s and two daus:

JOHN ANNAN; *b* 29 April 1792; *m* Agnes (*b* 18 Feb 1791; *d* 18 Aug 1857), 2nd dau of John Bell, and *d* 1 Aug 1869, leaving issue:

1 Thomas, of Lenzie, nr Glasgow; fndr with his bro Robert of T & R Annan, of Glasgow, art dealers; *m* Mary Craig and had issue:

(1) John; *b* 1862; *m*, *d* 1947, leaving issue:

1a Thomas Craig; *b* 1894; *m* and *d* 1964, leaving issue:

1b *John; *b* 1920; *m* *Marion McColl and *d* 1995, leaving:

1c *Hamish Craig; *b* 1952

2c *Douglas McColl; *b* 1956

2a Ellison; *d* 1967

(2) James Craig; *d* unm

(3) Thomas Craig; CA; emigrated to USA

(4) William Craig; *b* 1870; with Bengal & NW Rlwy India; *d* 1964

(5) David; banker and merchant

(1) Sophie Forrester; *d* unm

(2) Agnes Bell; *b* 2 Jan 1875; *d* unm 4 March 1976

2 ROBERT, for whom *see* below

3 John

4 Stephen; *b* 13 Sept 1835; *d* 31 Dec 1894

5 David

1 Margaret; *b* 23 June 1828; *m* William Stuart Robertson and *d* 18 Aug 1857, leaving a dau

JOHN ANNAN's 2nd son,

ROBERT ANNAN, of Glasgow; *b* 18 May 1826; *m* 1854 Frances Purcell Fox (*d* 1900), and *d* 1893, leaving issue (with two daus, Margaret, *m* Alexander MacKendrick, of Glasgow, and had two s and two daus; and Frances):

JOHN ANNAN, of Glasgow and London; *b* 9 Nov 1856; *educ* Glasgow U; FCA, sr ptnr Annan Dexter & Co, London, 1895; *m* 8 Aug 1884 Marion (*d* 21 May 1931), est dau of James Gilroy, of High St, Lanark, by Agnes Frame, and *d* 28 Oct 1908 leaving issue:

1 Robert; *b* 16 May 1885; *educ* Uppingham and Columbia U New York; Capt RE WW I, chm Consolidated Goldfields S Africa 1944–60 (pres 1960); *m* 27 Sept 1911 Dely (*d* 25 Dec 1967), yr dau of Everett Loraine Weston, of New York, and had issue:

(1) *John, MBE (1945), TD [John Annan Esq MBE TD, 35 Burke's Rd, Beaconsfield, Bucks]; *b* 6 Dec 1912; *educ* Marlborough and Trin Coll Cambridge; Maj WW II, slr 1939, ptnr Elvy Robb & Co; *m* 17 Sept 1938 Pamela Harwood (*d* 9 July 1972), dau of Henry Vincent James, of Radlett, Herts, and has issue:

1a *Robert; *b* 7 March 1950; *educ* Shiplake Coll

1a *Allela Harwood; *b* 7 Jan 1940; *m* 28 Aug 1969 *Maj Roderick Stuart Cochase-Dyet, 9/12th Roy Lancers (POW), yst s of Col John Cochase-Dyet, MC, TD

2a *Virginia; *b* 18 Oct 1946

(2) *Everett Weston [Everett Annan Esq, 4 Church Rd, Spratton, Northants]; *b* 15 Nov 1915; *educ* Uppingham

2 JAMES GILROY; *b* 27 Nov 1886; *educ* Uppingham and King's Coll Cambridge; Capt RA; md Moull & Sons 1925, E Telegraph 1926, Middle West Utilities London 1927, dir Dyer & Dyer 1933 and Pontifex & Emmanuel 1934, chm Gen Ceylon Tea Co 1950, Chev Legn d'Honneur; *m* 12 March 1913 Fannie Mildred (*d* 4 Oct 1969), yst dau of Thomas Sylvester Quinn, of Brooklyn, and *d* 31 May 1965, leaving issue:

1 *Thomas Quinn; *b* 13 Jan 1914; *educ* Stowe and Manchester U; Fleet Air Arm and Intell Corps WW II; mining engr with Mill Close Miles 1936–39, Taquah and Abosso Mines 1939–43 and 1944–46, RO Stokes & Co 1945–55, Denver Equipment Co 1955–61, lecturer Ealing Tech Coll 1965; *m* 8 Jan 1936 *Dora, dau of Harry Priestley, of Oldham, Lancs, and has had issue:

(1) *Roger James Gilroy; *b* 6 March 1937; *educ* Harrow County Sch and Exeter U

(2) Malcolm Laurence; *b* 8 Nov 1943; *educ* Harrow County Sch; *d* 2 Feb 1961

(1) *Judith Valerie; *b* 29 Nov 1941; *m* 2 April 1963 *Robin Wright, only s of Robert Wright, of Cardiff, and has issue:

1a *A dau; *b* 26 Oct 1970

2 NOEL GILROY, *cr* a **Baron**

ANNANDALE AND HARTFELL

Arms: Argent, a saltire sable, on a chief gules three cushions or. **Crest:** A winged spur or. **Supporters:** Dexter, a lion rampant argent, armed and langued azure, crowned with an imperial crown or; sinister, a horse argent furnished gules. **Motto:** *Nunquam non paratus* ('Aye ready'). **Creations:** E, and L. (S) 23 April 1662 with precedence of 18 March 1642/3.

THE 11TH EARL OF ANNANDALE AND HARTFELL and **Lord Johnstone** (Patrick Andrew Wentworth Hope Johnstone of Annandale and of that Ilk, [The Rt Hon The Earl of Annandale and Hartfell DL, c/o House of Lords, London SW1A 0PW]; *b* 19 April 1941; *s f* as *de jure* 11th Earl 1983 (claim to earldom allowed by H of Lds Ctee for Privileges 1985), 26th Chief of Clan Johnstone, 11th Hereditary Steward of Annandale and 11th Hereditary Keeper of Lochmaben Palace; *educ* Stowe and RAC Cirencester; chm Roy Jubilee and Prince's Trusts for Dumfries and Galloway 1984–88, underwriting memb Lloyd's 1976–, dir Murray Lawrence Lloyd's Membs' Agency 1988–, (V-Lt Nithsdale and Annandale and Eskdale Districts 1992– (DL 1987)); *m* 1969 *Susan Josephine, only dau of Col Walter John Macdonald Ross, CB, OBE, MC, TD, JP, DL, of Netherhall, Castle Douglas, Dumfriesshire, and has:

1+ DAVID PATRICK WENTWORTH, *Lord Johnstone, Master of Annandale and Hartfell*; *b* 13 Oct 1971; *educ* Stowe and St Andrews U (BSc)

1 +Julia Claire; *b* 1974; *educ* Stannes Sch Windermere and W of England U Bristol

Annandale, Earldom of, previous creation:

Between 1622 and 1658 this title was held by a father and son, John and James Murray, cadets of the MURRAYs of Cockpool (*see* MANSFIELD and MANSFIELD, E).

Lineage: Sir JOHN JOHNSTONE (apparently s of Gilbert of Johnston(e), Dumfriesshire, who was living July 1249 and was probably s of Sir Gilbert Johnstone, who *fl* 1194–*c* 1249 and is thought to have been s of John, who seems to have settled in Johnston, to which he gave the name, *c* 1170–94); living 1296; had:

GILBERT of Johnstone; living 1309; had, with an er s (John):

GILBERT of Johnstone; *d c* 1370, leaving:

Sir JOHN JOHNSTONE; living 1377; Warden West March; *d* by 1413, leaving:

Sir ADAM JOHNSTONE of that Ilk; present Scots victory over English at Sark 23 Oct 1448, helped suppress the rebellion of the Douglases against the king 1455, for which he was granted the lands of Pettinain, Lanarks; *m* 1st — and had issue; *m* 2nd after 1433 Janet, probably dau of George Dunbar, 11th Earl of March, and widow of William Seton (by whom she was mother of George, 1st Lord Seton), and *d* by May 1455, having by her had four other sons (Gilbert; Patrick; Archibald; William); his s by his 1st w:

Sir JOHN JOHNSTONE of that Ilk; *b* by 8 Nov 1438; Warden West March 1459; *d* in or after Feb 1492/3, having had:

JAMES JOHNSTONE Yr , of Johnstone; *dvp* after 8 June 1478, leaving, with an er s (*dsp*):

Sir ADAM JOHNSTONE of Johnstone; *m* 1st —; *m* 2nd Marion Scott (living March 1511), widow of Archibald Carruthers, Yr of Mouswald, and, *d* by 2 Nov 1509, having had, almost certainly by his 1st w, with a yr s (William, living 1519):

JAMES JOHNSTONE of Johnstone; of age by 1504; had a charter of the lands of Whiteriggs and Meiklehouse 1516; *m* Mary, est dau of 3rd Lord Maxwell (*see* MAXWELL, Bt), and *d* Aug 1524, leaving, with other issue:

JOHN JOHNSTONE of Johnstone; *b* 1507; had various charters of lands 1542, 1545 and 1550; fought Battle of Pinkie 1547, Commr to settle Border disputes 1552; *m* 1st Elizabeth Jardine and had, with other issue:

1 James; *b* by 31 Oct 1539; *m* Margaret Hamilton and *dvp* by May 1552, leaving:

(1) JOHN (Sir)

(1) Jean; *m* 1st William, Master of Carlyle; *m* 2nd *c* 1572 6th Lord Saltoun (*qv*) of Abernethy; *m* 3rd William Kerr of Ewinstoun (*see* LOTHIAN, M)

2 Robert

1 Dorothea; *m* John Maitland of Auchencastle/Auchingassel

2 Margaret; *m* C Irving of Bonshaw

JOHN JOHNSTONE *m* 2nd Nicola, dau of Sir James Douglas, 7th of Drumlanrig (*see* QUEENSBERRY, M), and *d* 8 Nov 1567, having by her had:

3 John

4 James; *b* after 1559

The gs,

Sir JOHN JOHNSTONE of Johnstone; of age 1568, Justice-Gen 1570, Warden West March 1580–1581 and 1582–1585, ktd 1584; *m* Margaret, dau of Sir William Scott, Yr of Buccleuch (*see* BUCCLEUCH and QUEENSBERRY, D), and *d* 5 June 1587, leaving:

1 JAMES (Sir), his heir

1 Elizabeth; *m* Alexander Jardine, Yr of Applegirth

2 Margaret; *m* by Nov 1594 James Johnstone of Westerhall

3 Grizel; *m* 1st Sir Robert Maxwell of Orchardton; *m* 2nd Patrick Vans, Yr of Barnarroch and had issue

The son,

Sir JAMES JOHNSTONE of Johnstone; *b c* 1567; ktd 1590, Warden West March 1596; *m* 1588 Sarah, sis of 5th Lord Herries (*qv*), and was murdered 6 April 1608 by 8th Lord Maxwell (*see* MAXWELL, Bt), leaving an only s:

JAMES JOHNSTONE, 1st EARL OF HARTFELL, so *cr* 18 March 1642/3, as also LORD JOHNSTON OF LOCHWOOD, MOFFATDALE, AND EVANDALE, as also earlier 20 June 1633 LORD JOHNSTON OF LOCHWOOD (all S); *b* 1602; acquired by charter territorial barony of Newbie 1609; royalist Civil War, fighting Battles of Kilsyth and Philiphaugh 1645, captured after Philiphaugh and narrowly escaped execution; *m* 1st 1622 Lady Margaret Douglas (*d* 1640), dau of 1st Earl of Queensberry (*see* QUEENSBERRY, M), and had:

1 JAMES, **1st Earl**

2 William, Col Swedish and French Armies; *dsp* 1656

1 Mary; *m* 1st Sir George Graham of Esk, Bt (*qv*); *m* 2nd Sir George Fletcher of Huttonhall

2 Janet; *m* Sir William Murray of Stanhope, Bt

3 Margaret; *m* Robert Dalzell, Yr of Glenae

4 Bethia

The 1st EARL *m* 2nd Elizabeth, dau of Sir Samuel Johnston, 1st Bt, of Elphinstone and widow of John Seton of Pitmedden (*see* SETON, Bt, of Pitmedden); *m* 3rd 1647 Lady Margaret Hamilton, 3rd dau of 1st Earl of Haddington (*qv*), and widow of David, Lord Carnegie (*see* FIFE, D), and *d* March 1653

His er s,

JAMES JOHNSTONE, 2nd EARL OF HARTFELL (which he resigned 1657 with a view to a regrant, since under the terms of sucession of the earldom as they then stood a 4th cousin would have inherited to the detriment of his daus; the legality of the surrender was challenged as it occurred under the Protectorate) and 1st EARL OF ANNANDALE AND HARTFELL, so *cr* 13 Feb 1661, as also VISCOUNT OF ANNAND [*sic*], LORD JOHNSTON OF LOCHWOOD, LOCHMABEN, MOFFATDALE AND EVANDALE (all S), with the precedence of the resigned Earldom (*i.e.*, of 18 March 1642/3) and with remainder to heirs male, est heirs female of his body and the est heirs male of the body of such heirs female bearing the name and arms of Johnston(e), failing whom to his nearest heirs whatsoever; in 1662, when the EARL's yr son was dead and his er one seemed near death, so that he would soon be left with daus only, he obtained from CHARLES II (23 April) a charter of novodamus erecting his estates into a territorial earldom and lordship, a docquet attached to the charter creating him **Earl of Annandale and Hartfell**, also LORD JOHNSTONE (both S, again with precedence of 18 March 1642/3), with remainder to 'heirs male, whom failing, his eldest heir female without division, and the lawful heirs male of the body of the said eldest female bearing the name and arms of Johnston, which arms they shall be bound always to assume and bear always, whom all failing, the nearest heirs whomsoever of James, Earl of Hartfell', so that he now held two identically worded hereditary honours, each with a different destination, the 1661 *cr* being implicitly in the first instance to heirs male whomsoever — otherwise why seek a charter of novodamus a year later? — and the 1662 *cr* being explicitly to heirs male of the body etc — which would secure the title to his daughters and their issue at the expense of more distant cousins, even if male, although such persons were not precluded from inheriting the 1661 creation; PC (S, 1661); *b* 1625; MP Dumfriesshire Protectorate E Parl 1654–56; at the Restoration the EARL petitioned CHARLES II for recompense on account of the family's suffering during the Civil War and was accordingly made, in addition to his titles of honour, Hereditary Steward of Annandale and Hereditary Keeper of Lochmaben Palace 1661; *m* 29 May 1645 Lady Henrietta Douglas (*d* 1673), dau of 1st Marquess of Douglas (*see* HAMILTON and BRANDON, D), and *d* 16 July 1672, having had, with four other daus (*dsp*):

1 James, *Lord Johnstone*; *b* 17 Dec 1660; *bapt* 23 Dec 1661; *d* in infancy 1661/2

2 WILLIAM, **2nd Earl**

3 John; *b* 3 Sept 1665; *educ* Glasgow and St Andrews Us; Ensign Earl of Dumbarton's Regt (later The Roy Scots) 1685, Capt 1686, on mil courses France and

Italy 1687–88, led Jacobite mutiny of Roy Scots at Sleaford (Lincs) 1689, committed to the Tower and Newgate, released on bail and joined JAMES II in exile 1690, Col Jacobite and French Armies, pardoned by QUEEN ANNE and granted roy charter of Stapleton Tower, Dornock, Dumfriesshire, 1702 (this property was formerly part of the Annandale estates but had been surrendered to the Crown by the 1st Marquess for the specific purpose of an immediate regrant to his bro), entered service of FREDERICK-AUGUSTUS I, ELECTOR OF SAXONY; commnd Roy Saxon Army and Col von Johnston (later von Zuhlen) regt of cuirassiers 1710; Maj-Gen and GOC Polish cav div 1711; *m* 19 June 1713 Catherine Christine (*m* 2nd 1722 Duke of Glucksburg and *dsps* 1726), est dau of Count Detler Sievert von Ahlefeldt, and *d* Poland 29 Dec 1714, leaving:

(1) An only dau; *b* 1714; *d* in infancy 1715

4 George; *b* 21 June 1667; *d* 10 May 1674

1 Mary; *m* 18th Earl of Crawford and (2nd Earl of) Lindsay (*qv*)

2 Margaret; *m* Sir James Montgomerie of Skelmorlie (*see* EGLINTON and WINTON, E)

3 Henrietta; *b* 21 Jan 1668/9; *m* 15 May 1684 Sir John Carmichael of Bonningtoun, Lanarks

The 1st EARL's 2nd but est surv son,

WILLIAM JOHNSTONE, **2nd Earl of Annandale and Hartfell** and 1st MARQUESS OF ANNANDALE, so *cr* 24 June 1701, as also EARL OF HARTFELL, VISCOUNT OF ANNAND, LORD JOHNSTON OF LOCHWOOD, LOCHMABEN, MOFFATDALE AND EVANDALE (all S), with remainder to heirs male whomsoever, KT (1704), PC (1714); *b* 17 Feb 1664; Hereditary Steward Annandale and Hereditary Keeper Lochmaben Palace; *educ* Glasgow U; raised and cmded two anti-Jacobite Troops of Horse against Viscount Dundee 1689, implicated in the Montgomery Plot and committed to the Tower but pardoned 1690, Extrdy Ld of Session and a Ld of the Treasury 1693, Pres Parl (S) 1695, Ld High Commr Gen Assembly Church of Scotland 1701 and 1711, Ld Privy Seal (S) 1702, Pres Privy Cncl (S) 1702–1706, Sec of State (S) 1705–1706, opposed Union with England 1707, rep S peer 1707, 1710 and 1715, Keeper Gt Seal 1714, Ld-Lt Dumfriesshire, Kirkcudbrightshire and Peeblesshire 1715; *m* 1st 1682 Sophia (*d* 13 Dec 1716), dau and sole heir of John Fairholm of Craigiehall, and had:

1 JAMES JOHNSTONE, **3rd Earl of Annandale and Hartfell** and 2nd MARQUESS OF ANNANDALE; *b c* 1688; Hereditary Steward of Annandale and Hereditary Keeper of Lochmaben Palace, MP Dumfriesshire 1708 (disallowed as he was a peer's est s); spent much of his adult life in Italy, amassing a huge art collection, much of which was later kept at Hopetoun House; in 1726 executed a deed of entail settling the Annandale lands and titles on his sister HENRIETTA's family the Hopetouns, thus disinheriting his half-bros; *d* unm Napes 10 Feb 1730

2 John; *b* 3 Aug 1688; *d c* 1694

3 William; *b* Aug 1696; fought a duel against Capt Roe of the Foot Gds March 1720 in which both were wounded; *d* unm 24 Sept 1721

1 HENRIETTA; *b* 11 Nov 1682; heir female under the 1662 charter; *m* 31 Aug 1699 1st Earl of Hopetoun (*see* LINLITHGOW, M) with whom she tried, on her er bro the **3rd Earl**'s death 1730, to enforce her bro's entail but was opposed by her step-mother Marchioness Charlotte (*see* below), acting on behalf of her infant son, the latter party winning judgment 1733; *d* 25 Nov 1750, leaving an er s:

(1) JOHN HOPE, 2nd EARL OF HOPETOUN; *b* 7 Sept 1704; *s f* as Earl of Hopetoun 1742 and mother as heir general to the Annandale inheritance 1750; apptd Curator Bonis (Trustee in Lunacy) for his half-uncle **4th Earl** (*see* below), 1747; *m* 1st 14 Sept 1753 Lady Anne Ogilvy (*d* 1759), 2nd dau of 2nd Earl of Seafield (*qv*), and had, with other issue:

1a JAMES HOPE later HOPE JOHNSTONE (added so as to inherit the Annandale estates), 3rd EARL OF HOPETOUN and *de jure* 5th EARL OF ANNANDALE AND HARTFELL, his f's heir not only in the Hopetoun lands and titles but as Curator Bonis for **4th Earl** (on whose death 1792 he became heir gen instead of Curator Bonis and took possession of the Annandale estates as beneficial owner; claimed 1795 the Annandale Earldom, basing his claim on the terms of the remainder attached to the 1661 creation, but no progress made before his death); *b* 23 Aug 1741; Hereditary Steward Annandale and Hereditary Keeper Lochmaben Palace, rep S peer 1784–90 and 1794–96, Ld Lt and Hereditary Sheriff Co Linlithgow, *cr* 3 Feb 1809 BARON HOPETOUN OF HOPETOUN, Co Linlithgow (UK), with remainder in default of male issue to the heirs male of his f; *m* 16 Aug 1766 Lady Elizabeth Carnegie (*d* 1793), est dau of 6th Earl of Northesk (*qv*), and *d* 29 May 1816, when he was *s* in the Hopetoun lands and titles by his half-bro and in the Annandale inheritance by his est dau, having had:

1b ANNE, *de jure* COUNTESS OF ANNANDALE AND HARTFELL in her own right

2b Jane Elizabeth; *d* unm 1786

3b Georgina; *m* 20 Nov 1793 Colonel Hon Andrew Johnstone-Cochrane (*see* DUNDONALD, E) and *d* 17 Sept 1797, leaving issue

4b Jemima; *m* 1803 her cousin Adml Sir George Hope-Vere, GCB, RN (*see* LINLITHGOW, M), of Carriden, W Lothian, and *d* 29 Aug 1808

5b Lucinda; *d* unm 1800

(1) (cont.) The 2nd EARL OF HOPETOUN *m* 2nd 30 Oct 1762 Jane (*d* 1767), dau of Robert Oliphant of Rossie, Perthshire, and *d* 12 Feb 1781, having had a 2nd s:

2a JOHN HOPE, 4th EARL OF HOPETOUN

The **2nd Earl of Annandale and Hartfell** and 1st MARQUESS OF ANNANDALE *m* 2nd 20 Nov 1718 Charlotte Van Lore (*m* 2nd Col John Johnstone of Westerhall (*ka* Cartagena 1741) and was ancestor with him of the BARONs DERWENT; *qv*), dau and sole heiress of John Vanden-Bempdé, of Hackness Hall, N Yorks, and Pall Mall, Middx, and *d* Bath 14 Jan 1721, having by her had:

4 GEORGE JOHNSTONE, **4th Earl of Annandale and Hartfell** and 3rd MARQUESS OF ANNANDALE; *b* 29 May 1720; Hereditary Steward of Annandale and Hereditary Keeper of Lochmaben Palace; insane by 1744 and declared as such by an Inquest in Chancery 1747; his half-nephew the 2nd Earl of Hopetoun, then his half-great-nephew the 3rd Earl of Hopetoun became Curatores Bonis (Trustees in Lunacy); *d* unm 29 April 1792, when all his titles became dormant, though the 3rd Earl of Hopetoun inherited the Annandale estates

5 John; *b* posthumously 8 June 1721; *d* unm Oct 1741

The *de jure* 5th EARL's est dau,

ANNE Hope later Hope Johnstone, *de jure* COUNTESS OF ANNANDALE AND HARTFELL in her own right; *b* 13 Jan 1768; Hereditary Steward Annandale and Hereditary Keeper Lochmaben Palace; claimed the Annandale peerages 1816 on the same basis as her f's argument, but no progress made before her death; *m* 8 July 1792 her cousin Adml Sir William HOPE later JOHNSTONE, GCB (*see* LINLITHGOW, M), and *d* 28 Aug 1818, having had issue:

1 JOHN JAMES, *de jure* 7th EARL

2 William James (Sir), KCB; *b* 28 July 1798; Adml RN; *m* 26 April 1826 Eleanora (*d* 12 July 1891), est dau of Sir Thomas Kirkpatrick, 5th Bt (*qv*), and *d* 11 July 1878, having had issue:

(1) Jane Anne; a nun; *d* 29 Jan 1871

(2) Ellen Lucy; *m* 3 Oct 1865 Capt John D'Arcy, RN (*d* 1894), and had issue

(3) Alicia Isabella; *d* unm 3 Dec 1893

3 Charles James; *b* 29 Jan 1801; Cdr RN; *m* 23 April 1826 Eliza (*d* 31 Oct 1885), dau of Joseph Wood and *d* 14 April 1835 leaving issue:

(1) Charles James; *b* posthumously 11 June 1835; Maj-Gen RA; *m* 17 May 1859 Mary Fanny Ellen (*d* 10 Sept 1914), est dau of William Hankey, of Middlesex Hall, W Lothian, and *dsp* 6 Oct 1888

(1) Anne Williamina; *m* 10 Feb 1886 Gen Charles Fanshawe, RE (*d* 9 Dec 1901), son of Gen Edward Fanshawe, CBE, RE, and *d* 14 Jan 1899 having had issue

(2) Mary Josephine; *d* 22 Dec 1903

4 George James; *b* 30 July 1802; Capt RN; *m* 29 July 1826 Maria (*d* 10 Sept 1844), dau of Joseph Ranking, and *d* 21 May 1842 leaving issue:

(1) William George; *b* 1830; Capt RN; *m* 21 April 1858, Emily (who *m* 2nd 1882 John Mason Stead and *d* 7 Sept 1907), yst dau of William Stead, and *d* 1870 having had issue:

1a William John; *b* 1863; *d* 26 Sept 1921

2a Charles Henry Edmund, of 77 Pah Road, Epsom, Auckland, NZ; *b* 1867; *m* 1st 30 April 1901 Elizabeth *d* 1922), 2nd dau of George Samuel Wright, of Brunswick, NZ, and had issue:

1b George William; *b* 5 Feb 1902; *m* 1st 8 Jan 1925 (*divorce* 1932) Dorothy Charity, dau of Frederick Beasley Hartley, of Birkenhead, NZ; *m* 2nd 1933 (*divorce* 1946) Amelia Daphne, dau of Thomas du Auverue de Thierry, of Puniho, Laranaki, NZ, and by her had issue:

1c Graeme William; *b* 20 June 1934; *m* 1961 *Robin, dau of Edward Herbert, of Sydney, NSW, Australia, and *d* 1979, leaving issue:

1d +Gregory William; *b* 1963

2d +Bruce Edward; *b* 1968

1d +Trudy Anne; *b* 1963; *m* 1989 *Paul John Neave, RNZAF, and has issue:

1e +Ryan Matthew; *b* 1993

1d +Nerida Mae; *b* 1972

1c +Carolyn Anne; *b* 1938; *m* 1960 *Gordon John Bracher, of 14 Reiman St, New Lynn, Auckland, NZ, and has issue:

1d +Jonathan Charles; *b* 1963; *m* 1989 *Sonia Claudette Mary, dau of Edward John Galea Phipps

1d +Louise Jane; *b* 1961; *m* 1983 *Geoffrey Stuart David Cooke, of Christchurch, NZ, and has issue:

1e +Nathaniel David John; *b b* 1986

1e +Sophia Jane; *b* 1988

2e +Elizabeth Ann; *b* 1990

3e +Juliette Rose *b* 1992

1b (cont.) George Hope Johnstone *m* 3rd 1946 Helen Louisa (*d* 1964), dau of William Taylor, of Howick, Scotland, and *d* 1985

2b Charles James, of Rotuna, Waikato, NZ; *b* 20 Feb 1907; *m* 27 July 1933 Ellen Sarah, dau of Henry John Bennett Gason, of Temuka, NZ, and *d* 1964 having had issue:

1c Violet June; *b* 6 July 1934; *d* 1936

2c +Robyn [Mrs Robyn Hope Johnstone, PO Box 101330, N Shore Mail Centre, NZ]; *b* 28 Aug 1945; *m* 1954 (*divorce* 1992; resumed maiden name) Glen Douglas Ireland, of Kaiwaka, NZ, and has:

1d +Kim Joanne; *b* 1967

2d +Gina Diana; *b* 1969; *m* 1990 *Matthew Harrison

3d +Jodi Hope; *b* 1971

1b Emily Elizabeth; *b* 7 June 1903

2b Florence Muriel Hope Johnstone; *b* 1 July 1904; *m* 1932 Reginald Percy Castaing, 3rd son of Henry Theodore Castaing, of Christchurch, NZ, and had a dau

3b Evelyn Violet; *b* 26 March 1906

2a (cont.) Charles Hope Johnstone *m* 2nd 1929 Helen Muriel, dau of Thomas Revell, of Christchurch, NZ

1a Emily Alicia; *d* unm 16 Sept 1938

2a Florence Blanche; *m* 1890 Rev C Girdwood Thompson (*d* 1916), rector Wheathampstead, Herts, and *d* 1942

(1) Edith Firenze Georgina; *m* 20 Sept 1855 Carl Wilhelm Peter Eisen, Lt in serv of Grand Duke of Baden

1 Elizabeth; *d* unm Zofingen, Switzerland, 1 Nov 1864

2 Mary; *m* 3 Feb 1840 Rt Rev Hon Hugh Percy, DD, Bp Carlisle (*see* NORTHUMBERLAND, D), and *dsp* 22 Nov 1851

The *de jure* COUNTESS's est son,

JOHN JAMES HOPE later HOPE JOHNSTONE, *de jure* 7th EARL OF ANNANDALE AND HARTFELL; *b* 29 Nov 1796; Hereditary Steward Annandale, Hereditary Keeper Lochmaben Palace; MP Dumfries; claimed the 1661 Annandale peerages 1820, advised to advertise for rival claimants 1826 but got no credible response, claim disallowed 11 June 1844, presented further petition 1876 but *d* before making further progress; *m* 8 July 1816 Alicia Anne, only dau of Col George Gordon of Hallhead, Aberdeenshire, and *d* 11 July 1876, having had issue:

1 William James; *b* 1819; *m* 7 Dec 1841 Hon Octavia Sophia Bosville Macdonald (*d* 22 Jan 1897), yst dau of 3rd Baron Macdonald (*qv*), and *dvp* 17 March 1850, leaving issue:

(1) JOHN JAMES HOPE JOHNSTONE, *de jure* 8th EARL OF ANNANDALE AND HARTFELL, JP, DL; *b* 5 Oct 1842; *educ* Eton; Hereditary Steward of Annandale and Hereditary Keeper of Lochnaben Palace; Capt Gren Gds, formerly Rifle Bde; MP Dumfriesshire 1874–80; continued 1876 petition claiming the 1661 Annandale peerages December 1876, became mentally unsound 1877 and claim continued by Curator Bonis, claim disallowed 30 May 1879; *d* unm 26 Dec 1912

(2) Percy Alexander, of Ardsallagh, Co Meath; *b* 13 Aug 1845; Capt 60th Rifles; *m* 28 March 1878 his cousin Evelyn Anne (*d* 8 Jan 1940), dau of Capt George Gordon Hope-Johnstone (*see* below) and *d* 7 Aug 1899 leaving issue:

1a EVELYN WENTWORTH, *de jure* 9th EARL

1a Constance Violet; *b* 19 Nov 1880; *m* 5 Aug 1908 Capt Lewellyn Heywood Jones, 5th Lancers (*d* 19–), and *d* 1965, having had issue:

1b Hugh; *b* 1909; 10th Roy Hus and RAF; *m* 1937 Perena Grace (*d* 1985), est dau of Sir Edward Ernest Pearson, JP, and formerly wife of Capt Marcus George Roddick, 10th Roy Hus, and *d* 1969, having had issue:

1c +Llewellyn [Llewellyn Heywood Jones Esq, 29 Flag Walk, Eastcote High Rd, Pinner, Middx]; *b* 1937; *educ* Gordonstoun; Master Mariner, Merchant Navy 1955–70, civ servant with US Navy Mily Sealift Cmd Off UK 1970–; *m* 1976 *Irene Dorothy, SRN, dau of John Maurice Andrews, of 18 Winchester Rd, Bexleyheath, Kent, and has issue:

1d +Benjamin John; *b* 1980

1d +Perena; *b* 1978

1c +Imogen Iris; *b* 1944; *m* 1965 *Christopher Bowly, of Tulla Lodge, Emly, Co Tipperary, and has issue:

1d +Hamish; *b* 1966

1d +Samantha; *b* 1970

1b Olwen; *b* 1911; *m* 1940 Anthony Abel Smith, 10th Roy Hus (*d* 1979), and *d* 1980, having had issue:

1c +Timothy Bertram [Timothy Abel Smith Esq, 30 Dawson Pl, London W2]; *b* 1941; *educ* Eton; *m* 1965 *Susanna Mary, est dau of Douglas Collins, and has issue:

1d +Lucy; *b* 1969

2d +Julia; *b* 1971

2a Alice; *b* 1883

(3) Wentworth William, of Skeynes, Edenbridge, Kent; *b* 22 Jan 1848; Capt 7th Hus; *m* 22 Jan 1879 Mary Beatrice (who *m* 2nd 27 Oct 1914 Peter Bevan Warrall, of New York), dau of James Christie, of Melbourne Hall, Yorks, and *dsp* 25 Oct 1910

(1) Alice; *d* unm 15 Sept 1881

2 George Gordon; *b* 18 Oct 1820; *m* 18 Aug 1845 Adelaide Mary Wentworth (*d* 7 Sept 1873), 2nd dau of Sir George Sinclair, 2nd Bt, of Ulbster (*qv*), and *d* 14 July 1866 having had issue:

(1) Charles Cecil Gordon; *b* 26 July 1846; *m* 1 June 1871 Elizabeth Agnes, dau of Edmund Grundy, and *d* 13 May 1931, leaving issue:

1a George Wentworth; *b* 21 April 1872; *m* 19 April 1900 Annie Eleanor (*d* 1957), only dau of Thomas Hack, and *d* 26 Aug 1920, leaving issue:

1b +George Ernest Gordon [George Hope Johnstone Esq, 28 Roding Cl, Elmbridge Village, Cranleigh, Surrey]; *b* 1901; *m* 1st 27 July 1926 Anna Dorothea Florence (*d* 2 Jan 1959), only dau of Hon (Edward) Grenville Gore-Langton (*see* TEMPLE OF STOWE, E); *m* 2nd 1940 Aileen Stephen (*d* 1987), dau of Alfred Ewing, and by her has:

1c +John Wentworth Gordon [John Hope Johnstone Esq, Town House 32, 4165 Fieldgate Dve, Mississauga, Ontario L4W 2M9, Canada]; *b* 1944; *m* 1st 19– (*divorce* 1975) Trudy, dau of Dennis Delmar Dalquist, and has issue:

1d +Jared; *b* 1972

2d +Jodi; *b* 1974

1c (cont.) John Hope Johnstone *m* 2nd 1979 *Patricia, dau of Philip Fisher

2a Edmund William Gordon; *b* 21 Jan 1873; *m* 4 Aug 1909 Mary Ceely (*m* 2nd 2 Oct 1934 Maj Gerard Irvine, and *d* 7 Aug 1935), 4th dau of Maurice Ceely Maude, (*see* HAWARDEN, V), and *d* 4 Feb 1925

3a David Percy, MC; *b* 1 Nov 1876; T/Capt Gen List, WW I; *m* 26 Jan 1926 Sylvia Wyke, widow of Capt Arthur John Dillon Preston, of Swainston, Co Meath

1a Frances Ellinor

(2) William James; *b* 25 July 1855; *m* 17 Feb 1877 Emily Mary (*d* 19 Feb 1933), dau of Capt Edward Bailie, and *d* 9 Aug 1919 leaving issue:

1a George Granville, of Johannesburg, S Africa; *b* 29 Nov 1880; *m* 1913 (*divorce* 1915) Princess Marie Louise Augustine, dau of Prince Felix Wilhelm Ludwig of Hohenlohe-Oeringen, of Wurttemburg, and widow of Prince Albrecht of Waldeck and Pyrmont, and had:

1b William August Ludwig Vernon Alexander; *b* 5 July 1914; Maj Gren Gds, WW II, ret 1946, rejoined Army Res of Offrs 1949; *m* 27 March 1943 (*divorce* 1951) Pamela Maud (*m* 2nd Ambrose Cadogan; *see* CADOGAN, E), er dau of Lt-Col John Murray Cobbold, of Glemham Hall, Suffolk, and *d* 1993, leaving issue:

1c +Philip William HOPE-JOHNSTONE later HOPE-COBBOLD (deed poll 1995) [Maj Philip Hope-Cobbold, Glemham Hall, Little Glemham, Woodbridge, Suffolk IP13 0BT]; *b* 27 Dec 1943; *educ* Radley and RMA Sandhurst; late Maj 13/18th Roy Hus; *m* 1968 (*divorce* 1984) Antonia Jay, dau of Jack Yuan Hutton-Potts, and has:

1d +Thomas William; *b* 1974; *educ* Stowe

2d +Timothy Mark; *b* 1976; *educ* Stowe

2c Charles John Victor; *b* 26 Jan 1948; *educ* Radley and Grenoble and Madrid Us; farmer; *d* 10 Sept 1994

2a Charles John; *b* 8 Jan 1883; *educ* King's Coll Cambridge; WW I as Lt Norfolk Regt (TF); ed *The Burlington Magazine*, lecturer Peking 1939 and Istanbul Us 1943–48

3a Henry Murray, MC; *b* 13 March 1886; Capt and A/Lt-Col Roy Fus, Egyptian Army WW I 1914–17; *ka* 31 July 1917

4a William Gordon Tollemache; *b* 5 July 1887; Lt 4th Bn Roy Fus, formerly Roy Berks Regt and IA; *ka* 25 Oct 1914

1a Adelaide Olivia; *b* 18 Aug 1879; *m* 1906 Maj Oswald Walter Brinton, 21st Lancers (*d* 17 May 1941)

2a Wentworth Frances; *b* 18 Feb 1882; *m* 9 May 1912 Maj Ferdinand William Cavendish-Bentinck, CMG, KRRC (ret), son of William George Frederick Cavendish-Bentinck, BA, FSA, JP (*see* PORTLAND, E)

(1) Evelyn Anne; *m* 28 March 1878 her cousin Capt Percy Alexander Hope Johnstone, and *d* 8 Jan 1940 leaving issue (*see* above)

3 John Charles; *dsp*

4 Robert Gordon; *b* 1829; *m* 26 Sept 1855 Agnes (*d* 14 Feb 1909), dau of Col John Swanson, and *d* 15 Jan 1890 leaving issue:

(1) Gordon Frank; *b* 25 March 1861; *m* 1890 Isabel (*d* 1892), dau of Breden Camp, and *d* 20 Sept 1913 leaving:

1a Isabel

(1) Anne Eleanor; *m* 15 April 1890 Edwin Baily, MBE, MB, CM (*d* 4 Dec 1930), and *d* 18 March 1922 leaving issue

5 Charles; *b* 23 Nov 1830; Lt RN; *d* 17 July 1855

6 David Baird; Capt 92nd Highrs; *m* 1st 25 Jan 1860 (*divorce*) Margaret Elizabeth, dau of Lt-Col William Grierson (*see* GRIERSON, Bt); *m* 2nd 1874 Eliza (who *m* 3rd 17 Jan 1888 Charles Edward Webb), 2nd dau of T Archer and widow of R W Harris, and *dsp* 28 Dec 1886

1 Anne Jemima

2 Lucy Wilhelmina

3 Alice; *m* 10 April 1845 Sir Graham Montgomery, 3rd Bt, of Stanhope (*qv*), and *d* 16 Dec 1890 leaving issue

The *de jure* 8th EARL's nephew,

EVELYN WENTWORTH HOPE JOHNSTONE, *de jure* 9th EARL OF ANNANDALE AND HARTFELL; *b* 9 May 1879; Hereditary Steward of Annandale, Hereditary Keeper of Lochmaben Palace; *m* 1st 25 July 1905 Eileen (*d* 18 April 1909), est dau of Gustavus Villiers Briscoe, of Bellinter, Co Meath, and had issue:

1 PERCY WENTWORTH, *de jure* 10th EARL

The *de jure* 9th EARL *m* 2nd 1 May 1916 (*divorce* 1925) Marie Eleanor, dau of Compton Charles Domvile, and by her had further issue:

1 +Jean Evelyn [The Lady Jean Elwes, Flat 4, 24 Collingham Gdns, London SW5 0HL]; *b* 9 July 1917; *m* 4 April 1950 Capt Robert Philip Henry Elwes, MBE, MC (*d* 1976), 16th/5th Lancers, son of Capt Robert Hamond Arthur Elwes, JP, RASC (ret), of Congham House, Norfolk, and has:

(1) +Sarah Jane; *b* 1951; *m* 1975 *(Arthur) Guy Galbraith (*see* HAMPDEN, V), of Newbold Revel, Haddington, E Lothian, and has issue

The *de jure* 9th EARL *m* 3rd 30 Oct 1926 Mary Evelyn (*d* 1962), dau of John Locke, of Kilbeggan, Co Westmeath, and formerly w of John Bearmore Batten, and *d* 26 Oct 1964

The *de jure* 9th EARL's only son,

PERCY WENTWORTH HOPE JOHNSTONE, *de jure* 10th EARL OF ANNANDALE AND HARTFELL; *b* 2 Jan 1909; *educ* Sherborne and RMC; Hereditary Steward of Annandale and Hereditary Keeper of Lochmaben Palace; Maj 155th Field Regt RA, Lt 16th/5th Lancers WW II Far East (POW); recognised by Lord Lyon King of Arms as Ch of the Name and Arms of Johnstone and matriculated Arms as such in the Public Register of All Arms and Bearings Scotland 4 Feb 1983; claimed in 1982 the 1662 peerages (which being created with remainder to a different set of heirs from the 1661 ones — hitherto the sole subject of petitioning — were considered in quite another, and as it proved more favourable, light) but *d* before making further progress; *m* 1st 7 July 1932 (*divorce* 1939) Phyllis Athena, only child of Edgar Errol Napier MacDonnell, CMG; *m* 2nd 26 July 1940 Margaret Jane (*d* 5 May 1998), dau of Herbert William Hunter-Arundell, of Barjarg, Auldgirth, Dumfriesshire, and *d* 5 April 1983, having had issue:

1 PATRICK ANDREW WENTWORTH HOPE JOHNSTONE, **11th and present Earl of Annandale and Hartfell**

1 +Eileen Elizabeth [The Lady Eileen Duncan, Newlands, Kirkmahoe, Dumfriesshire]; *b* 3 Oct 1948; *m* 1969 *Andrew Walter Bryce Duncan, son of Sir Arthur Bryce Duncan, and has:

(1) +John Walter Bryce; *b* 1971

(2) +Edward James Bryce; *b* 1974

(3) +Henry Andrew Bryce; *b* 1975

ANNESLEY

Arms: Paly of six argent and azure, a bend gules. **Crest:** A moor's head, couped at the shoulders in profile proper, wreathed round the temples argent and azure. **Supporters:** Dexter, a Roman soldier in armour or, short sleeves and apron azure, face, arms and legs bare, the latter sandalled or, on his head a helmet (or cap) gold, on the top thereof three feathers argent and azure, in his exterior hand an antique shield proper; sinister, a Moorish prince in armour or, short sleeves and apron azure, face, neck, arms and legs proper, on the latter boots gold, behind him a sheaf of arrows proper, fastened by a pink ribbon, wreathed round the temples argent and azure, in his exterior hand a bow proper. **Motto:** *Virtutis amore* ('By love of virtue'). **Creations:** B. (I) 20 Sept 1758, V. (I) 14 Nov 1766, E. (I) 17 Aug 1789.

THE 10TH EARL ANNESLEY, of Castlewellan, Co Down, **Viscount Glerawly**, of Co Fermanagh, and **Baron Annesley**, of Castlewellan Co Down (Patrick Annesley) [The Rt Hon The Earl Annesley, 35 Spring Rise, Egham, Surrey]; *b* 12 Aug 1924; *educ* Strode's GS Egham; late RN; *m* 21 June 1947 *Catherine, only dau of John Burgess, of Edinburgh, and has issue:

1 *Jane Margaret [The Lady Jane Gamester, The Retreat, 23 Wendover Rd, Staines, Middx TW18 3DE]; *b* 15 June 1948; *m* 8 Dec 1966 *Vernon Hugh Gamester, only s of Edward Arthur Gamester, and has issue:

(1) *Carl Vernon; *b* 1970

(1) *Colette Louise; *b* 17 June 1967

(2) *Juliet Dawn; *b* 17 Jan 1969

2 *Nora Kathleen [The Lady Nora Binning, 6 Barons Way, Egham, Surrey]; *b* 27 March 1950; *m* *John Bathurst Shaw Binning, s of John Bathurst Shaw Binning, and has issue:

(1) *Gareth John; *b* 19 July 1971

(2) *Gavin Douglas; *b* 10 March 1977

(1) *Madeleine Rachel; *b* 2 July 1969

(2) *Carina Lorraine; *b* 9 July 1975

3 *Patricia Catherine [The Lady Patricia Morehead, 133 Oriental Rd, Woking, Surrey]; *b* 30 Dec 1952; *m* 29 June 1974 *David Sidney Morehead, s of Sidney Morehead, and has issue:

(1) *Duncan Patrick David; *b* 11 July 1977

(2) *George Sydney; *b* 1984

(1) *Danielle Simone; *b* 12 June 1975

4 *Frances Elizabeth; *b* 27 July 1957

Lineage: FRANCIS ANNESLEY (1663–1750), of Thorganby, Yorks (*see* VALENTIA, V, under which particulars of an earlier Barony of Annesley of Newport Pagnel are given) had by his 1st w a 6th and yst s:

WILLIAM ANNESLEY, **1st Viscount Glerawly** (so written in the patent in error for Glenawley, also known as Clanawley, a barony in west Co Fermanagh), of Co Fermanagh, so *cr* 14 Nov 1766, as also previously 20 Sept 1758 BARON ANNESLEY, of Castlewellan, Co Down (both I); *b c* 1710; barrister Dublin 1738, MP (I Parl) Midleton, Co Cork, 1741–58, inherited his f's Castlewellan estate 1750, Sheriff Co Down 1750; *m* 16 Aug 1738 Lady Anne Beresford (*d* 12 May 1770), est dau of 1st Earl of Tyrone (*see* WATERFORD, M), and *d* 12 Sept 1770, having had, with other issue:

1 FRANCIS CHARLES ANNESLEY, **1st Earl Annesley**, of Castlewellan, Co Down (I), so *cr* 17 Aug 1789 with special remainder to his bro; *b* 27 Nov 1740; MP (I Parl) Downpatrick 1761–70; *m* 8 Feb 1766 Mary (*d* 25 Aug 1791), dau and heiress of Richard Grove, of Ballyhimmock, Co Cork; went through a form of marriage after 25 Aug 1791 with Sophia Connor, who was already married to one of his gmekeepers, and *dspl* 10 Dec 1802, having by her had, together with an est illegitimate s born before even the bogus marriage and who *d* at sea aged 14:

(1) George de la Poer Beresford; *b c* 1799; *educ* RMC Sandhurst; *d* unm, *bur* 18 Feb 1814

(2) Francis Charles; *d* in infancy 9 March 1803

1 (cont.) The **1st Earl** also had by Dorothy McIlroy four other sons, all *b* before his real w's death

2 RICHARD ANNESLEY, **2nd Earl Annesley**, PC (I 1798); *b* 14 April 1745; barrister Dublin 1770, MP (I Parl) Coleraine 1776–83, St Canice 1783–90, Newtownards 1790–96, Blessington 1797–1800, Clogher Feb-March 1800 and Midleton April-Dec 1800, Commr Customs 1786–95 and Excise 1795–1810 (both I); *m* 25 Sept 1771 Anne (*d* 30 June 1832), only dau and heiress of Robert Lambert, of Dunlady, Co Down, and *d* 9 Nov 1824, having had, with other issue:

1 WILLIAM RICHARD ANNESLEY, **3rd Earl Annesley**; *b* 16 July 1772; MP (Whig) Downpatrick 1815–20; *m* 1st 19 May 1803 (*divorce* 8 June 1821) Lady Isabella St Lawrence (*d* April 1827), dau of 2nd Earl of Howth (*see* 1909 edn), and had issue:

(1) Mary; *m* 16 Feb 1828 William John MacGwire, of Rostrevor, Co Down, and *d* 1837, leaving issue

1 (cont.) The **3rd Earl** *m* 2nd 15 July 1828 Priscilla Cecilia (*d* 29 March 1891), 2nd dau of Hugh Moore, of Eglantine, Co Down, and *d* 25 Aug 1838, having by her had issue:

(1) WILLIAM RICHARD ANNESLEY, **4th Earl Annesley**; *b* 21 Feb 1830; MP (C) Gt Grimsby 1852–57, rep I peer 1867–74; *d* unm 10 Aug 1874

(2) HUGH ANNESLEY, **5th Earl Annesley**, JP and DL (Co Down); *b* 26 Jan 1831; *educ* Eton and Trin Coll Dublin (BA); Lt-Col Scots Fus Gds, Kaffir War 1851–53 and Crimea 1854, MP (C) Co Cavan 1857–74, rep I peer 1877–1908; *m* 1st 4 July 1877 Mabel Wilhelmina Frances (*d* 17 April 1891), est dau of Col William Thomas Markham, of Cufforth Hall, Yorks, and had issue:

1a FRANCIS ANNESLEY, **6th Earl Annesley**; *b* 25 Feb 1884; Sub-Lt RNVR WW I; *m* 14 Sept 1909 Evelyn Hester (*m* 3rd 15 May 1919 Guy Aylwin; *d* 16 June 1947), est dau of Alfred Edward Miller Mundy, DL, of Shipley Hall, Derbys, and formerly w of Capt Hugh Robert Edward Harrison, of Caerhowel, Montgomeryshire, and was *ka* in an aeroplane over Ostend 5 Nov 1914

1a Mabel Marguerite; *b* 25 Feb 1881; *m* 14 Jan 1904 Gerald Sowerby, Lt RN (*d* 6 Nov 1913), yst s of Thomas Charles Johnson Sowerby, of Gainford, Co Durham, and *d* 19 June 1959, leaving issue (*see* RODEN, E)

(2) (cont.) The **5th Earl** *m* 2nd 2 July 1892 Priscilla Cecilia (*d* 9 Oct 1941), dau of William Armitage Moore, of Arnmore, Co Cavan, and *d* 15 Dec 1908, having by her had:

2a Clare; *b* 30 June 1893

3a Constance Mary; *b* 24 Oct 1895; *educ* RADA; actress and writer (including autobiography *After Ten Years* 1931); *m* 6 May 1915 (*divorce* 1924) (William) Miles Malleson, the celebrated character actor (*d* 15 March 1969), s of Edmund Taylor Malleson, and *d* 5 Oct 1975

(3) Robert John; *b* 15 Feb 1834; 11th Hussars; *d* 28 Sept 1854

(4) Arthur; *b* 20 Sept 1835; Capt Gren Gds; *m* Nov 1867 Clara (*d* 24 Sept 1923), only dau of George Weston, of Norwich, and *dsp* 25 April 1881

(5) George, of Castlewellan, Co Down; *b* 22 Feb 1837; *m* 1st 23 Feb 1859 his cousin Anna Clementina, dau of James Annesley (*see* below); *m* 2nd June 1861 Georgina Henrietta (*d* 6 Nov 1892), dau of William Henry Daniel, of Auburn, Co Westmeath, and *d* 4 Sept 1903, leaving issue:

1a Josephine; *m* 6 Aug 1884 Col Sir (Herbert) Stuart Sankey, KBE, CVO, JP, DL, MA (*d* 5 April 1940), Remembrancer City London, est s of Lt-Col H T Sankey, and *d* 12 Sept 1945, leaving issue

(6) William Octavius Beresford, of Painswick, Glos; *b* 29 Nov 1838; *m* 16 May 1860 Caroline (*d* 6 Jan 1869), dau of John Mears, of Bagshot, and *d* 20 July 1875, leaving issue:

1a WALTER BERESFORD ANNESLEY, **7th Earl Annesley**; *b* 10 Feb 1861; *m* 1st 21 June 1893 Maud Fleming (*d* 2 July 1923), dau of Haynes Bingham Higginson, of Rock Ferry, Cheshire, and had issue; *m* 2nd 23 Jan 1924 Mabel Frances (*d* 10 July 1931), dau of John Burnet and formerly w of Petrus Aganoor, and *d* 7 July 1934; his s by his 1st w:

1b BERESFORD CECIL BINGHAM ANNESLEY, **8th Earl Annesley**; *b* 4 April 1894; P/O RAFVR 1941, Lt 6th Bn Roy Fus; *m* 1st 30 July 1921 (*divorce* 1941) Edith Constance (*d* 7 July 1950), only dau of Maj Albemarle Alexander Rawlinson, 8th Hus, and formerly w of Lord Kilconnell (*see* CLANCARTY, E); *m* 2nd 7 Dec 1945 Josephine Mary (d 1977), fndr and nat chm American Friends of Britain WW II, dau of Philip Brandell, of New York, and widow of Capt George John Seymour Repton, Irish Gds, and *dsp* 29 June 1957

1a Sarah; *m* 3 Sept 1884 Seymour Peel Nash, s of Rev Robert Seymour Nash, Canon Salisbury, and *d* 17 Oct 1938, leaving issue

2a Florence Cecilia; *m* 12 June 1888 Frank Proctor (*d* 9 July 1898), s of Rev George Proctor, MA, and *d* 22 June 1959, having had issue

3a Katherine Maud; *m* 8 July 1890 George Henry Thompson, s of George Thompson, of Southampton, and *d* 29 Dec 1952, leaving issue

2 Robert; *b* 1 June 1773; *m* Mary Anne (*d* 31 March 1845), dau of James Gandon, of Canon Brook, the celebrated architect, and *d* 21 April 1825, having had, with other issue:

(1) James; *b* 1799; Br Consul Barcelona and Amsterdam; *m* 21 June 1826 Clementine (*d* 12 Oct 1868), dau of Baron de Brockhausen, of Prussia, and *d* 29 Sept 1859, leaving issue:

1a William Richard; *b* 23 May 1827; Maj-Gen; *m* 3 March 1862 Isabel (*d* 28 April 1927), 2nd dau of Rev Hon James Norton and n of 3rd Baron Grantley (*qv*), and *d* 29 March 1896, leaving:

1b William Richard Norton, DSO; *b* 12 June 1863; Maj QOR W Kent Regt, Sudan 1885–86, GSO(3) 1914; *m* 20 Aug 1890 Edith Mackenzie (*d* 21 Dec 1938), dau of Robert Davidson, CSI, of Clayton, Fife, and *d* 29 Nov 1914, leaving issue:

1c William Robert Bathurst; *b* 30 May 1892; F/Lt RAF, Lt RE (TF); *d* 16 Aug 1927

2b Arthur James Patrick; *b* 1 Aug 1869; Capt 3rd Bn Roy W Kent Regt, T/Maj 11th Serv Bn, Ashanti Expdn 1896 (Star), Boer War 1900–02 (Medal), WW I; *m* 1st 18 Dec 1899 (*divorce* 1914) Florence Lilian Jane, dau of Frederick Burcher; *m* 2nd 23 April 1915 Winifred Mabel (*m* 3rd 8 June 1949 Henry George Carpenter), yr dau of Vincent Cornelius Garman, MD, LSA, of Heigham Hall, Norwich, and widow of Robert William Martin, of Victoria, BC, and *d* 1 Jan 1934, leaving issue:

1c Sheila Isabel Ina; *b* Nov 1921; Div Pres BRCS, Dir 1960; *m* 1st 6 Aug 1942 W/Cdr George Harcus Sheehan, RAF (*ka* Aug 1942), s of James Arthur Sheehan, of Sydney, NSW; *m* 2nd 26 Sept 1944 Maj Eric Weston Tory, TD, Dorsetshire Regt, est s of Clement Edward Tory, of Higher Burton House, Dorchester, and had:

1d *Patrick James Weston [Patrick Tory Esq, Perrysfield Farm, Broadham Green, Oxted, Surrey]; *b* 1 July 1945; *educ* Cranleigh

2d *Robert Michael Annesley [Robert Tory Esq, 11 Highview Court, Wray Common Rd, Reigate, Surrey]; *b* 12 Dec 1946; *educ* Cranleigh; *m* 11 July 1970 *Faith Charlotte Grant, yr dau of — Grant, of Woodhurst Park, Oxted, Surrey

3d *Charles Peter Hamilton; *b* 20 Dec 1952; *educ* Cranleigh

1d *Frances Shelagh; *b* 27 April 1950

3b James Harry Sydney; *b* 29 Nov 1875; Maj RAF; *m* 14 Dec 1920 Violet Adelaide, yr dau of Harry Withers, of Sydney Place, Bath, and *dsp* 3 Jan 1949

1b Clementine Mary Sophie; *d* 21 June 1878

2a Arthur Adolphus; *b* 23 Feb 1833; Br Consul Portland, Maine; *m* 1863 Martha (*d* 7 Sept 1883), dau of Edmund Austin, and *d* 4 May 1887, having had issue:

1b Arthur Albert O'Donel Valentia; *b* 27 Feb 1867; *m* 21 April 1888 Elizabeth Mary (*d* 24 April 1909), dau of Embertus van Ooms, Netherlands Consul, and *d* 6 Jan 1947, leaving issue:

1c ROBERT, **9th Earl**

1c Elizabeth; granted rank of earl's dau 10 July 1964; *m* 7 Dec 1926 Eric Carwardine Francis, FSA, RWA, FRIBA, yr s of George Carwardine Francis, of Chepstow, and had issue:

1d *Katharine Annesley; *b* 13 April 1930; *m* 29 Oct 1955 *John Alexander Henderson, 14th/20th King's Hus, of Wicks Manor, Tolleshunt Major, Essex, s of Col Thomas Lisle Henderson, of Milverton, Somerset, and had issue:

1e *Fergus Alexander; *b* 25 July 1956

1e *Emma Annesley; *b* 1 Oct 1958

2d *Julie Carwardine; *b* 30 May 1938; *m* 3 April 1958 *Robert Tracy Whitford, s of Robert Henry Whitford, of Swansea, and has had two s and two daus

2b Clementine Martha; *b* 8 Aug *d* 11 Sept 1872

3a James O'Donel; *b* 23 Dec 1834; 68th Foot; *m* 10 Dec 1860 Sybil (*d* 16 Jan 1924), only dau of William Henry Gommonde and n of Sir Edmund Filmer, 8th Bt, MP (see 1916 edn), and *d* 24 July 1884, leaving issue:

1b Euphemia Constance; *m* 13 July 1892 George Frederick Nicholas Beresford Annesley (*see* below) and *dsp* 1893

2b Anna Clementine; *d* 7 Nov 1937

3b Alice Mary; *m* 27 April 1892 Lt-Col Charles Frederick Herbert Davidson, Argyll and Sutherland Highrs, and *d* 30 June 1952

4a Robert Eugene Hyde; *b* 22 Sept 1837; Maj 10th Regt; *m* 1st 2 June 1873 Eveline Edith (*d* 1893), 3rd dau of Henry Steel; *m* 2nd 2 July 1894 Constance Mary (*m* 2nd — Tebbs; *d c* 1936), dau of Thomas Gray Hill, of Manchester, and *dsp* 8 April 1904

5a Francis Charles; *b* 13 Feb 1845; Capt 28th Regt; *m* 1st 10 Sept 1865 Matilda (*d* 4 Sept 1872), dau of Col Cowper Rochfort, and had:

1b Francis Charles Cowper; *b* 25 Nov 1866; Burma Police; *m* 19 Nov 1896 Hon Mabel Wynn (*d* 14 Feb 1970 aged 97), sis of 4th Baron Newborough (*qv*), and *d* 12 Feb 1924

2b James Howard Adolphus, CMG (1917), DSO (1900); *b* 3 March 1868; Lt-Col 6th Dragoon Gds (Carabiniers), Tirah 1897–98 (despatches, medal two clasps), S Africa 1899–1902 (despatches, two medals, eight clasps), WW I (wounded, despatches); *m* 29 Nov 1900 Helene Marie (*d* 13 April 1949), yst dau of Charles Edward Johnston, and *d* 22 April 1919, leaving issue:

1c Patricia Moyra; *b* 26 April 1904; *m* 1st 4 Feb 1926 A/Cdre Sir Henry Nigel St Valery Norman, 2nd Bt, CBE, AAF (*kas* 19 May 1943; qv), and had issue; *m* 2nd 6 Oct 1944 Sir Walter Robert Dempster Perkins, er s of Walter Frank Perkins, of Boldre, Hants

2c Sheila Cecilia Louise; *b* 4 Aug 1905; *m* 25 July 1934 Lt-Col Christopher John Burlison, OBE, TD, BA (*d* 23 Dec 1958), only s of John Clement Burlison, and had:

1d *John James; *b* 26 March 1940; Capt 2nd Gurkha Rifles; *educ* Ampleforth

1d *Cecilia Margaret; *b* 19 Aug 1936; *m* 5 April 1961 Maj Edward Martin Shewell Turner, RA, only s of Brig Charles Edward Francis Turner, CBE, DSO, and has issue

3c Dorothy Maud; *b* 30 Oct 1906; Polish Gold Cross of Merit

1b Clementina Maude; *m* 1st 1892 (*divorce* 1906) Maj Francis Denis Jack Annesley, 1st Bn the Buffs (*see* below); *m* 2nd 12 Oct 1907 Spencer Oswald Heinemann, s of Emil Heinemann, and *dsp* 3 April 1949

2b Constance Maude; *d* unm

3b Blanche Wilhelmina Dorothea; *m* 1 June 1892 Brig-Gen George Harvey Nicholson, CB, CMG, JP (*d* 13 June 1942), s of William Smith Nicholson, JP, of Eastmore, IoW, and *d* 15 Jan 1955, leaving issue

5a (cont.) Capt Francis Annesley *m* 2nd 11 May 1876 Marion Emily (*d* 4 April 1877), est dau of John Campbell Dicker, and *d* 6 March 1878

1a Anna Clementina; *m* 23 Feb 1859 her cousin Hon George Annesley (*see* above) and *dsp* 6 Sept 1860

3 Arthur ANNESLEY later GROVE-ANNESLEY (added on inheriting the estate of Ballyhimmock, Castletownroche, Co Cork (subsequently called Annes Grove), from his aunt Countess Annesley, dau and heiress of Richard Grove); *b* 9 Nov 1774; Lt-Gen; *m* 28 Dec 1814 Elizabeth, only child of John Mahon, of Bessborough, Co Tipperary (*see* MAHON, Bt), and *d* 7 Nov 1849, having had with other issue:

(1) Richard, of Annes Grove; *b* 2 Dec 1815; *m* 7 Aug 1878 Sara Augusta Ruth (*m* 2nd 1 Oct 1907 Harold Locke; *d* 23 Nov 1929), dau of Rev Canon John Abraham Bolster, MA, and *d* 1892, having had issue:

1a Richard Arthur, of Annes Grove; *b* 20 June 1879; *educ* Harrow; Lt NI Horse; *m* 7 March 1907 Hilda Margaret (*d* 4 March 1961 aged 92), yr dau of Sir Francis Edmund Workman-Macnaghten, 3rd Bt, PC, and *d* 4 Feb 1966, leaving:

1b (Richard Francis) Michael Grove; *b* 2 Sept 1908; *educ* Eton and privately; E African Forces in Africa and Asia, Lt KAR 1941–45, manager (mining section) Booth & Co (Africa) 1951; *m* 1st 1931 (*divorce* 1939) Elizabeth, dau of J Anderson, of Edinburgh, and had issue:

1c *Diana Elizabeth Doreen [Mrs Robin Duff, Box 67419, Bryanston, nr Johannesburg, S Africa]; *b* 15 June 1932; *m* 1 May 1954 *Robin Keitley Duff, Kenya Govt Admin, s of Keith Mitchell Keitley Duff, of Molo, Kenya, and has:

1d *Hugh Robert Keitley; *b* 1958

1d *Margaret Jean Keitley; *b* 1955; *m* 1982 *Nikola Vujovic, of Yugoslavia

1b (cont.) Michael Annesley *m* 2nd 1 July 1939 *Elsie Susannah, dau of Jacob Daniel Krige, of Stellenbosch, and formerly w of Reginald de Beer, of Johannesburg, and *d* 1979, having had further issue:

1c +Richard David Fergus Robert [Richard Annesley Esq, Kensington Park, Adelaide, Australia]; *b* 11 March 1940; Rhodesian Police Corps; *m* 1st 1966 (*divorce*) Marina Soares, of Salisbury, Rhodesia, and has issue:

1d +Michael Richard Edward; *b* 1970

2d +Robert Patrick Sean; *b* 1971

1c (cont.) Richard Annesley *m* 2nd *Mary Hurley, of Durban, Natal, and has further issue:

3d +James Richard; *b* 1980

4d +Paul Daniel; *b* 1982

2c *Rozanne Mary; *b* 12 Nov 1942; *m* 1967 David Worsley, of Rivermead, Henley-on-Klip, Transvaal, S Africa, and has issue:

1d *Nicolette Grace; *b* 1971

2d *Justine Elizabeth Mary; *b* 1975

2b Edmund Patrick Grove, OBE (1957); *b* 11 Sept 1911; *educ* Harrow; md W M Valentine Ltd, London, 1958–66, formerly md Omo Sawmills of Nigeria Ltd (ret 1957); *m* 7 Dec 1939 *Ruth [Mrs Edmund Annesley, Annes Grove, Castletownroche, Co Cork, Ireland], er dau of Arthur Norman Rushforth, of Jersey, and *d* 27 Feb 1975, leaving issue:

1c +(Arthur) Noël Grove [Noël Annesley Esq, 103 Dulwich Village, London SE21 7BJ]; *b* 28 Dec 1941; *educ* Harrow and Worcester Coll Oxford; Dep chmn Christie's and Christie's Internat plc 1992–; *m* 7 Sept 1968 *Caroline Susan Aurea, er dau of Thomas Henry Waldore Lumley, of London W9, and has issue:

1d +Marcus Robert Grove ; *b* 27 March 1972; *educ* Harrow and Birmingham U

2d +James Alexander Grove; *b* 22 May 1974; *educ* Alleyn's Sch

2c +(Francis) Patrick Grove [Patrick Annesley Esq, Annes Grove, Castletownroche, Co Cork, Ireland]; *b* 1 Dec 1943; *educ* Harrow and Univ Coll Oxford (MA); *m* 30 Nov 1968 *Jane Frances, er dau of Egbert James Neville Holder, of Squire's Hill, Tilford, Surrey, and has issue:

1d *Melanie Jane Ruth; *b* 1969; *m* *Paul Muende

2d *Cressida Mary Siobhan; *b* 18 Feb 1971

1b *Diana Patricia (twin) [Mrs Martin Hill, 260 Snowden Lane, Princeton, NJ 08540, USA]; *b* 11 Sept 1911; *m* 3 Dec 1932 (William) Martin Hill, MA, CMG (*d* 1976), sometime Assist Sec Gen UN, s of William Henry Hill, of Currabinny, Co Cork,and has issue:

1c *Colin Patrick Annesley Martin [Colin Hill Esq, 104 Bayard Lane, Princeton, NJ 08540, USA]; *b* 28 June 1941; *educ* Groton, Princeton (BA) and Trin Coll Dublin (MLitt); *m* 9 July 1966 *Margaret Lydia Faith, 2nd dau of Maj Charles Robert Purdon Coote, of Bearforest, Mallow, Co Cork (*see* COOTE, Bt), and has issue:

1d *Sebastian Martin Coote; *b* 7 April 1967

2d *Brendan Colin Charles; *b* 27 March 1970; *m* 21 June 1997 *Sophie, dau of Jodie Procter of Eugene, Oregon

3d *Orlando William Eyre; *b* 1980

1d *Cordelia Diana Margaret; *b* 1978

2a William John; *b* and *d* 7 May 1881

3a Warden Beresford; *b* 15 June 1882; *educ* Harrow; Lt 3rd Bn E Kent Regt

(2) John Charles; *b* 28 Oct 1819; *m* 1870 Belinda Murphy and *d* 4 Jan 1904, leaving issue:

1a John; *b* 1871; *m* June- and *d* 10 Feb 1951, leaving issue:

1b John

2b Albert

1b Charlotte; *m* — Colestock

1a Charlotte; *m* 22 June 1901 Michael Joseph Barry, 2nd s of Thomas Barry, of Ballyanihan House, Rockmills, and *d* 1954, leaving issue

2a Elizabeth; *m* 25 March 1903 F J Smith

(3) William; *b* 12 Feb 1826; Capt 6th Foot; *m* 8 March 1866 Eliza, 2nd dau of J Taylor, of Good Hope, Jamaica, and *dsp* 6 April 1873

(4) Henry Robert; *b* 22 April 1831; County Inspr RIC; *m* 20 Nov 1862 Kathleen Letitia (*d* 25 Dec 1919), only dau of Benjamin Tilly, and *d* 3 Nov 1908, having had issue:

1a Arthur Geoffrey; *b* 24 June 1867; Dist Inspr RIC; *m* 22 June 1898 Mary Edith (*d* 17 June 1972 aged 93), dau of William J Roe, of Kingstown, Co Dublin, and *d* 12 Jan 1954, leaving issue:

1b Stella Edith; *b* 23 Oct 1899

2b *Phyllis Kathleen Rhona [Mrs Averell Daniell, Oak Lodge, 21 Hillside St, Hythe, Kent CT21 5EJ]; *b* 31 Jan 1907; *m* 29 May 1934 Brig Averell John Daniell, CBE, DSO, RA, only s of Col Oswald James Daniell, and had issue:

1c *Patrick John, CBE (1987) [Col Patrick Daniell CBE, Abbey Cottage, Itchen Abbas, Winchester, Hants]; *b* 1939; Col RA (ret)
2c *Michael Hugh [Michael Daniell Esq, 1 Wolvercote Court, Wolvercote Green, Oxford]; *b* 1946; *m* 1983 *Susan Jane Winsor and has issue:
1d *Timothy Edward Winsor; *b* 1988
1d *Helena Rose Winsor; *b* 1986
2d *Esther Marianna Winsor; *b* 1992
1c *Susan Mary; *b* 1937; *m* 1973 *Guy Vivian Fennell Robinson, of 46 Carson Rd, Dulwich, London SE21, and has issue:
1d *Thomas James Daniell; *b* 1977
2d *Philip Henry Guy; *b* 1979
2a Vivian Warden; *b* 10 Oct 1871; *d* 27 Dec 1895
1a Ethel Dawson; *m* 6 April 1899 F W Westray and *d* 23 Sept 1935, leaving issue
2a Violet Mable; *m* 1915 John Riversdale Bolster and *d* 26 March 1938
4 Francis Charles; *b* 21 Nov 1775; Capt RN; *m* 31 July 1813 Mary (*m* 2nd April 1834 Rev J Dickson; *d* Dec 1854), dau of William Radcliffe, and *d* 5 Aug 1832, having had issue:
(1) Richard Arthur; *b* 21 Nov 1814; *m* 17 Dec 1836 Frances (*d* 1867), yst dau of Capt Barnewall, and *dsp* 1856
(2) Stephen Francis Charles; *b* 21 Nov 1817; Lt-Gen, Lt-Col 10th Foot; *m* 30 July 1851 Henrietta Selina (*d* 30 April 1893), dau of Rev William Annesley (*see* above), and *d* 24 Nov 1887, leaving issue:
1a Francis Charles; *b* 27 Sept 1855; Lt-Col Roy Fus; *m* 1881 Lillie, dau of Jacob Conrad, of Br Guiana, and *dsp* 19 April 1903
1a Frances Priscilla Mary; *m* 27 Dec 1871 Col Gerrard Paul Townshend, Lincs Regt (*d* 7 Oct 1908), of Caldecote Hall, Warwickshire, and *d* 21 Dec 1937, leaving issue
2a Catharine Roberta Henrietta; *d* 15 July 1938
3a Mary Maria; *m* 22 Sept 1898 Capt Arthur William Curtis, RFA (*d* 9 March 1900), and had issue
(3) Francis Charles; *b* 30 June 1819; Capt 63rd Foot; *m* and *dsp* 30 May 1854
(4) Robert Michael Smith; *b* 21 Nov 1825; Lt-Col Bengal Army; *m* 24 July 1866 Jane Hume (*m* 2nd 9 April 1889 Maj-Gen C E Layard; *d* 6 May 1901), dau of Sir George Anderson, KCB, and *d* 13 Dec 1887, having had issue:
1a Arthur Stephen Robert, CMG (1919); *b* 12 Jan 1869; Lt-Col and Brevet Col IA; *m* 5 Dec 1895 Kate Talbot (*d* 11 June 1939), dau of Maj-Gen William Howey, and *d* 28 June 1939, leaving issue:
1b *Vera Kathleen; *m* 10 March 1921 Cdr Wilfrid Edmund Warner, DSC, RN (*d* 19 June 1951), yst s of Rev Henry James Warner, and has issue:
1c *Elizabeth Vivienne Annesley; *b* 20 Dec 1921; *m* 1st 20 Dec 1941 Loyezeleur Campbell Smith (*d* 6 Jan 1949), s of George Alexander Smith, of Glasgow, and has issue:
1d *Heather Jane [Mrs Roger Alwen, 11 Bywater St, London SW3 4DX]; *b* 30 Oct 1944; *m* 5 Dec 1964 *Roger Norman Alwen, yr s of Walter Jame Alwen, of Seal, Kent, and has issue:
1e *Mark James; *b* 22 Feb 1967
2e *Jonathan David; *b* 1977
1e *Kate Annesley; *b* 17 Feb 1969
1c (cont.) Mrs Loyezeleur Campbell Smith *m* 2nd 10 Oct 1952 Harold Basil Toller Foy (*d* 1979), s of Harold Toller Foy, of Sevenoaks
2a William Henry, CMG (1919), DSO (1917); *b* 5 May 1876; Lt-Col Roy W Kent Regt, AA and QMG 1916; *m* 29 April 1905 Gertrude Agnes, dau of Samuel Burton Relf, and *d* 28 June 1934
1a Mabel Jeannie; *m* 3 Oct 1889 Maj William Thomas Wilson Scott, Bedfordshire Regt (*d* 10 Aug 1942), s of Richard Scott, of Scottsborough, Co Monaghan, and has issue
2a Ethel Emily Anna; *m* 17 July 1894 William Norris (*d* 12 June 1919), 3rd s of Capt William Norris, Rifle Bde, and *d* 29 Sept 1939, leaving issue
3a Alice Mary; *d* unm 6 Oct 1918
4a Eva Edwardes; *m* 5 Feb 1902 Freeman Archibald Grant Haynes (*d* 15 March 1915), s of Oliver Grant Haynes, and *d* 29 April 1956, leaving issue
(5) William Henry; *b* 4 Oct 1830; Capt RN; *m* 5 May 1863 Lucy Ann (*d* 14 Jan 1874), dau of Denis Kelly, and *d* 27 March 1875, leaving issue:
1a Francis Denis Jack; *b* 3 June 1864; T/Maj 8th Bn E Surrey Regt,Capt 1st Bn the Buffs, S Africa War 1900–02; *m* 1882 (*divorce* 1906) Clementina Maude (*d* 6 April 1949), est dau of Francis Charles Annesley (*see* above), and *d* 23 March 1929
2a William Robert Ewart; *b* 7 July 1872; Capt Roy Berks Regt Boer War 1899–1900; *m* 15 April 1906 Eleanor Mary (*d* 1969), dau of Surg-Maj William Ferguson, and *d* 22 Feb 1917, having had issue:
1b William Alan Cecil; *b* 25 Sept 1907; *educ* Malvern and RMC Sandhurst; Maj RASC, late Roy Berks Regt; *m* 14 Aug 1935 Dorothy Vaughan (*d* 1971), er dau of Frank Yewdall, ICS, and *d* 1976, leaving issue:
1c +David Robert Ewart [David Annesley Esq, 77 Park Ave N, London N8]; *b* 9 April 1936; *educ* Scotch Coll Adelaide; F/O RAF; sculptor; *m* 1st Oct 1960 (*divorce* 1968) Patricia, dau of V I Jones, of London, and has issue:
1d +Benjamin; *b* 13 July 1963
1c (cont.) David Annesley *m* 2nd 1992 *Jane Victoria McLeod, er dau of Sir John Robert Whyte Ackroyd, 2nd Bt (*qv*), and has further issue:
2d +William Henry McLeod; *b* 1992
2c +William Gerald; *b* 27 Nov 1937; *educ* Scotch Coll Adelaide
3c +Simon Richard; *b* 23 Oct 1939; *educ* Scotch Coll Adelaide; *m* 1961 *Janine, dau of Ramand Varin, of France, and has issue:
1d +Emmanuel; *b* 16 Oct 1961
1c Jane; *b* 5 March, *d* 3 April 1942
2c *Sarah Elizabeth; *b* 25 May 1943; *m* 1962 *Henry William Peter Thompson, of 34 Southam Rd, Greystone Park, Harare, Zimbabwe, and has issue:
1d *Howard Luke; *b* 4 July 1964
2d *Paul David; *b* 1966

3a Albemarle Cator, DSO; *b* 12 Jan 1874; Maj Roy Fus, T/Lt-Col cmdg 8th Serv Bn, Boer War 1899–1901 (despatches), WW I 1914–16 (despatches); *m* 23 Nov 1901 Florence Lalande (*d* 23 May 1920), dau of John Hurdis Ravenshaw, of Richmond, Surrey, and *dsp* 8 July 1916 of wounds recd in action
1a Elizabeth Mary; *m* 23 April 1892 Maj Harry Crewe Godley, DSO, Northamptonshire Regt (*d* 19 Feb 1907), s of Lt-Col H R C Godley, 28th Regt, of Fonthill, Co Dublin, and *d* 26 Feb 1958, leaving issue
(1) Catherine Mary; *m* 12 June 1856 William Nevin Wallace, JP, DL (*d* 14 Jan 1895), of Downpatrick and Waterfront House, Newcastle, Co Down, and *d* 30 Dec 1877, leaving issue
(2) Anna Maria Wilhelmina; *m* 17 July 1849 Capt Owen Phibbs Knott, RN (*dsp* 1884), and *d* 7 Dec 1907
(3) Elizabeth Catherine; *m* 4 Oct 1854 Randall Howe, JP (*d* 1885), and *d* 20 Feb 1907, leaving issue

The 8th EARL's 3rd cousin once-removed,

ROBERT ANNESLEY, **9th Earl Annesley**; *b* 20 Feb 1900; RN WW I, Roy Signals WW II, civil servant; *m* 19 April 1922 Nora (*d* 1992), yst dau of Walter Harrison, of Sapperton, Cirencester, Glos, and *d* 21 Feb 1979, leaving:
1 PATRICK ANNESLEY, **10th and present Earl Annesley**
2 +PHILIP HARRISON [The Hon Philip Annesley, 17 Folly Mill Gdns, Bridport, Dorset DT6 3RN]; *b* 29 March 1927; heir presumptive; *educ* Strode's GS Egham; late REME; *m* 24 March 1951 Florence Eileen (*d* Jan 1995), only dau of John Arthur Johnston, of Gillingham, Kent
3 +Michael Robert [The Hon Michael Annesley, 16 Coltash Rd, Furnace Green, Crawley, W Sussex]; *b* 4 Dec 1933; *educ* Strode's GS Egham; RAF 1949, Warrant Offr 1968 (ret 1973), memb Assoc Licensed Aircraft Engrs and Technologists, Fell Internat Assoc of Book-Keepers 1997; *m* 23 June 1956 *Audrey Mary, only dau of Ernest Stanley Goodwright, of Dartford, Kent, and has issue:
(1) +Michael Stephen; *b* 26 July 1957; *m* 1983 *Angela, 2nd dau of David Matthews, of Chipping Norton, Oxon, and has issue:
1a +Michael David; *b* 28 Jan 1984
1a *Zara Jane; *b* 28 Jan 1984
(2) +Robert Francis; *b* 8 Sept 1962; *m* 1992 *Sharon Anne, 5th dau of John Fraser, of Stevenage, Herts
(1) *Sheila Marie; *b* 18 Aug 1961

ANSON

Arms: Argent three bendlets engrailed gules, in the sinister canton a crescent of the second. **Crest:** Out of a ducal coronet or a spear erect proper. **Motto:** *Nil desperandum* ('Never despair'). **Creation:** Bt. (UK) 30 Sept 1831.

SIR PETER ANSON, 7TH BT, CB (1974) [Rear-Adml Sir Peter Anson Bt CB, Rosefield, 81 Boundstone Rd, Rowledge, Farnham, Surrey, GU10 4AT]; *b* 31 July 1924; *s* f 1951; *educ* RNC Dartmouth; RN (ret 1974): WW II SW Pacific 1941–45 (POW), Flag Lt to C-in-C Mediterranean 1950–52, Flag Lt and Sqdn Communicns Offr to V-Adml Sir Manley Power, KCB, CBE, DSO, Flag Offr Aircraft Carriers 1956–57, cmdg HMS *Alert* Far E Station 1957–58, Staff RN Tactical Sch 1959–60, cmdg HMS *Broadsword* 1961–62, Dep-Dir Weapons Radio (Naval) 1963–64 (Dir 1965–66), CO HMS *Naiad* and Capt (D) Londonderry Sqdn 1966–68, cmdg HMS *Mercury* and Capt HM Signal Sch 1968–70, Cdr Naval Forces Gulf 1970–72 and Assist Ch Def Staff (Signals) 1972–74, assist mktg dir Marconi 1975, CEng, FIEE, chm Marconi Space Systems 1985 (md 1984, divnl manager Satellites 1977) and UK Industl Space Ctee 1980–82; *m* 16 April 1955 *Elizabeth Audrey, barrister, only dau of R-Adml Sir (Charles) Philip Clarke, KBE, CB, DSO, of Pine Needles, Avon Run Rd, Christchurch, Hants, and has issue:

1 +PHILIP ROLAND [Philip Anson Esq, 34 Martello Rd, Eastbourne, E Sussex BN22 7SS]; *b* 4 Oct 1957; *educ* Charterhouse and Chelsea Coll London (Bpharm); with Boots Ltd 1979–84, Waremoss Ltd 1984–96, E Moss Ltd 1996–; chm SE England Regn Pharmaceutical Soc 1995–

2 +Hugo William; *b* 30 April 1962; *m* 1986 *Sharon E, dau of L J Gardner, of Palmers Green, London

1 *Louisa Frances [Mrs Michael Barnsley, 335 Pennbrooke Trace, Duluth, SA 30155–1879, USA; *b* 28 Jan 1956; *m* 1978 (*divorce* 1985) Robert W A Cuthill and has issue; *m* 2nd 1994 Dr Michael F Barnsley and by him has:
(1) *Rose Alice; *b* 24 July 1995
2 *Sarah Elizabeth; *b* 4 Sept 1966; *m* 1992 *Robert Van Lieshout and has:
(1) *Edward Henry; *b* 16 May 1995
(2) *David Thomas; *b* 8 Aug 1997

Lineage: Sir William Anson, 1st Bt (UK), so *cr* 30 Sept 1831, KCB; *b* 13 Aug 1772, unc of 1st Earl of Lichfield (*qv*); served Army Peninsular War; *m* 26 Jan 1815 Louisa Frances Mary (*d* 25 July 1837), only child of John Dickenson by Mary, only child of Charles Hamilton, s and heir of Lord Archibald Hamilton (*see* HAMILTON and BRANDON, D), and *d* 14 Jan 1847, leaving an est s:

Sir John William Hamilton Anson, 2nd Bt; *b* 26 Dec 1816; *m* 27 July 1842 Elizabeth Catherine (*d* 3 July 1903), dau of Maj-Gen Sir Denis Pack, KCB, by Lady Elizabeth Beresford, yst dau of 1st Marquess of Waterford (Iqv), and was *k* in a rlwy accident 2 Aug 1873, having had issue:
1 **Sir William Reynell Anson, 3rd Bt**, PC (1911), JP (Oxford); *b* 14 Nov 1843; *educ* Eton (Fell 1883) and Balliol Coll Oxford; barrister Inner Temple 1869, Bencher 1900, Oxford: Fell All Souls 1867 (Warden 1881),Vinerian Reader English Law 1874–81, V-Chllr 1898–99, Chllr Diocese of Oxford 1899–1912, MP (Lib U) Oxford U 1899–1914, Parly Sec Bd Educn 1902–05, Tstee Nat Portrait Gallery 1904 and Br Museum 1911, CA Oxford, Chm QS Oxford, author: *Principles of the English Law of Contract* and *The Law and Custom of the Constitution*; *d* unm 4 June 1914
2 John George Beresford; *b* 28 March 1845; *d* 18 Feb 1852
3 Frederick Arthur, of Piraki, Akaroa, NZ; *b* 6 Nov 1850; *educ* Eton and Trin Coll Oxford; *m* 23 Feb 1878 Agnes (*d* 7 April 1923), 2nd dau of James F Roberts, of Akaroa, and *d* 11 Dec 1913, leaving issue:
(1) **Sir Denis George William Anson, 4th Bt**; *b* 14 Aug 1888; *educ* Eton and Trin Coll Oxford; barriste Inner Temple 1913; *d* unm drowned Thames 3 July 1914
(1) Ella Francis Olive; *b* 12 Nov 1880; *m* 26 July 1906 Charles John Crawford (*d* 19 March 1940), yst s of James Coutts Crawford, of Overton, Lanarks, and *d* 30 Oct 1954, leaving issue
(2) Agnes Margaret; *m* 1st 27 June 1912 Horace Edward Wilkie Young (*d* 20 Feb 1914), V-Consul Levant Consular Serv, 2nd s of Sydney Young, of Hyndford House, Chelsea, and had issue; *m* 2nd 31 July 1923 Charles Evelyn David Gladstone (*d* 23 July 1942), 2nd s of Rev David Thomas Gladstone, Vicar Rye, Sussex; *m* 3rd 3 Dec 1954 Capt Henry Whyham, RA (*d* 17 April 1961), s of Rev George Whyham, of Hereford
(3) Janet Katharine Mary; *m* 23 Aug 1914 George Kenneth Thompson Fisher, of Sussex, T/Capt Norfolk Regt (*d* 3 Sept 1917 of wounds received in action), er son of Rt Rev George Carnac Fisher, Bp Islington, and *d* 30 Nov 1938, leaving issue
(4) Anne Evelyn; *m* 10 Oct 1912 Capt Thomas Edmund Sotheron-Estcourt, JP, RSG (*d* 25 Jan 1958), of Estcourt Park, Tetbury, Glos, and had issue
4 Algernon Horatio, JP (Cheshire); *b* 3 Aug 1854; R-Adml; *m* 9 April 1896 Hon Adela Vernon (*d* 1 Jan 1931), dau of 6th Baron Vernon (*qv*), and *d* 12 Nov 1913, leaving issue:
(1) **Sir John Henry Algernon Anson, 5th Bt**; *b* 13 Jan 1897; Lt RN; *das* lost at sea 10 March 1918
(2) EDWARD REYNELL (Sir), **6th Bt**
1 Louisa Elizabeth Annie; *m* 7 Oct 1880 Rev Donald Campbell (*d* 4 Dec 1909), Rector Oakford, Devon, Hon Canon Norwich, and *d* 28 Nov 1920, leaving issue
2 Mary Louisa; *d* unm 11 Feb 1899
3 Elizabeth Georgiana; *d* unm 2 Sept 1930
4 Florence Helen; *d* unm 29 Sept 1944
5 Margaret Mildred; *m* 8 Sept 1886 Rev Frederick George Buller (*d* 1 June 1932), Rector Oakford 1909–24, and *d* 4 Nov 1947, leaving issue
6 Gertrude Christina; *d* unm 22 Feb 1937
7 Janet Katharine Olive; *m* 5 Dec 1899 Herbert Elphinstone Montgomery, son of Capt Thomas Henry Montgomery (*d* 24 Feb 1943), of Hattonburn, Kinross-shire, and *d* 22 June 1937, leaving issue (*see* MONTGOMERY, Bt)

The 5th Bt's brother,

Sir Edward Reynell Anson, 6th Bt; *b* 31 Jan 1902; *educ* Trin Coll Cambridge; WW I as Midshipman RN, WW II as Lt-Col RA; *m* 17 Oct 1923 (Frances) Alison (*d* 29 April 1997) only dau of Hugh Pollock (*see* MONTAGU-POLLOCK, Bt), and *d* 26 June 1951, leaving:
1 Sir PETER ANSON, **7th and present Bt**
2 +John (Sir), KCB [Sir John Anson KCB, 18 Church Rd, Barnes, London SW13 9HN]; *b* 3 Aug 1930; *educ* Winchester and Magdalene Coll Cambridge (BA 1953, MA 1959); Treasury 1954–90, Priv Sec to Chllr Exchequer 1957–58, UK Exec Dir IMF and World Bank 1980–83, Cnsllr (Fin) Br Emb Paris 1968–70, 2nd Perm Sec Treasury 1987–90; *m* 20 July 1957 *Myrica, dau of Harold Fergie-Woods, of Beech Court, Liphook, Hants, and has issue:
(1) +Christopher Edward, MA, PhD; *b* 22 May 1958; *m* 1986 *Susan Melanie, PhD, dau of P Robinson, of Cleveleys, Lancs, and has issue:
1a +Thomas Anthony; *b* 1987
2a +Matthew David; *b* 1990
3a +Joshua Daniel; *b* 1993
(2) +Timothy John; *b* 27 Jan 1967
(1) *Rachel Mary, BA; *b* 6 Dec 1961; *m* 1984 *Michael John Snelson, son of D L Snelson of Handforth, Cheshire, and has issue:
1a *William Lawrence; *b* 1991
1a *Katherine Louise; *b* 1989
(2) *Elizabeth Margaret; *b* 2 Nov 1968

ANSTRUTHER

Arms: Argent, three piles issuing from the chief sable. **Crest:** Two arms embowed in armour, the hands gauntletted and grasping a pole-axe, all proper. **Supporters:** Two falcons, wings expanded proper, armed gules, jessed and belled or. **Motto:** *Periissem ni periissem* ('I should have perished had I not gone through it'). **Creations:** Bt. (NS) 28 Nov 1694 (of Balcaskie) and (NS) 6 Jan 1700 (of Anstruther).

SIR RALPH HUGO ANSTRUTHER OF THAT ILK, 7TH BT of Balcaskie and **12TH BT** of Anstruther, GCVO (1993, KCVO 1976, CVO 1967), MC (1943), DL (Fife 1960, Caithness 1965) [Maj Sir Ralph Anstruther Bt GCVO MC DL, Balcaskie, Pittenweem, Fife KY10 2RD; Watten Mains, Caithness KW1 5UH]; *b* 13 June 1921; Hereditary Carver to the Sovereign, Hereditary Master Roy Household Scotland; *s* gf as 7th Bt of Balcaskie 1934 and cousin as 12th Bt of Anstruther 1980; *educ* Eton and Magdalene Coll Cambridge (BA 1940); Maj (RARO) Coldstream Gds WW II (wounded) and Malaya 1948–50 (despatches); memb Roy Co Archers; Assist Priv Sec to HM QUEEN ELIZABETH THE QUEEN MOTHER 1959–64, Equerry to HM 1959–, Treasurer 1961–

Lineage (of Anstruther of that Ilk): WILLIAM de CANDELA, feudal Ld (territorial baron) of Anstruther 1100 (at that time nobles customarily took surnames from their lands; one of the few to do otherwise was the above, who already had a noble name and was one of the leading territorial barons in Fife); *d c* 1153; f of:

WILLIAM de CANDELA, Ld of Anstruther; benefactor BalmerinoAbbey; *d c* 1165; f of:

HENRY; dropped de CANDELA in favour of ANSTRUTHER; *fl c* 1221, benefactor Dryburgh Monastery; f of:

HENRY de ANSTRUTHER, Ld of Anstruther, benefactor Balmerino and Dryburgh Abbey/Monastery, crusader under LOUIS IX; swore fealty for barony of Anstruther to EDWARD I of England 1292 and 1296; f of:

WILLIAM de ANSTRUTHER, Ld of Anstruther; f of:

HENRY de ANSTRUTHER of Anstruther; f of:

RICHARD de ANSTRUTHER of Anstruther; *d* between 1406 and 1437; f of:

ROBERT de ANSTRUTHER of Anstruther; *m* Elizabeth Balfour (*see* BALFOUR OF BURLEIGH, L) and *d* between 1460 and 1488, leaving an est s:

ANDREW ANSTRUTHER of Anstruther; granted charter of his barony of Anstruther 1483, fought at Scottish defeat of Flodden 1513; *m* 1st Christina, dau of Sir James Sandilands of Calder (*see* TORPHICHEN, L) and widow of David Hepburn of Waughton (*see* BUCHAN-HEPBURN, Bt); *m*(?) 2nd(?) Janet Borthwick; f (by 1st(?) w?) of:

JOHN ANSTRUTHER of Anstruther; *m* 1st Margaret Douglas, dau of Thomas Douglas of Lochleven (*see* MORTON, E); *m* 2nd Elizabeth, dau of Spens of Wormiston; *d* 1548, leaving:

ANDREW ANSTRUTHER; *m* Margaret, dau of Thomas Abercrombie of Abercrombie, and was *ka vp* Battle of Pinkie 1547, leaving:

JOHN ANSTRUTHER of Anstruthor; *m* Margaret, dau of George Clephane of Carslogie (*see* NORTHAMPTON, M), and had issue:

Sir JAMES ANSTRUTHER of Anstruther; apptd by JAMES IV Hereditary Grand Carver 1585, Master Household 1595; *m* 1571 Jean, dau of Sir Thomas Scott of Abbotshall, and *d* 1606, having had:
1 William (Sir), of Anstruther KB 1603; Gentleman Bedchamber to JAMES VI/I; *m* 1601 Euphemia, dau of Sir Andrew Wemyss of Myrecairnie, Fife, a Ld of Session, and *dsp* 1649
2 Robert (Sir), PC, of Wheatley, Yorks, which came to him through his w; Gentleman Bedchamber to JAMES VI/I, Amb Denmark 1620 and in Germany 1627, 1629 and 1630; *m* Mary, dau of Sir Edward Swift and sis of Viscount Carlingford, and was *bur* 9 Jan 1644/5, leaving, with other issue:
(1) Philip (Sir), of Anstruther; royalist Civil War, captured Battle of Worcester 1651, fined and his estates sequestrated until the Restoration; *m* Christian, dau of Gen Sir James Lumsden of Innergely (mil cdr under GUSTAVUS ADOLPHUS OF SWEDEN) and had, with two other sons:

1a WILLIAM (Sir), for whom *see* below

2a James (Sir), of Airdrie; *m* Katherine (*m* 2nd Maj Andrew Quhyt; *m* 3rd Lord Edward Murray; *see* ATHOLL, D), dau of John Skene of Hallyards, and had:

1b Gen Philip Anstruther of Airdrie, MP; *d* unm

3a ROBERT (Sir), **1st Bt**, of Balcaskie (*see* below, under **Anstruther of Balcaskie**)

4a Philip (Sir), of Anstrutherfield; *m* Elizabeth, dau and heir of James Hamilton, and *d* 1722, leaving, with other issue:

1b Philip

1b Christian; *m* 1st Sir William Weir, 2nd Bt; *m* 2nd 1740 6th Earl of Traquair (*see* MORAY, E)

5a Alexander (Sir); *m* 8 March 1694 Jean Leslie, self-styled Lady Newark (*d* 21 Feb 1740), and *d* 1743, having had by her, with other issue:

1b William, self-styled 3rd Lord Newark

2b Alexander, self-styled 4th Lord Newark; had issue (*see* REDESDALE, B)

1 Jean; *m* 1609, as his 3rd w, James douglas, 2nd s of 6th Earl of Morton (*qv*)

2 Jean; *m* Sir William Riddell (*see* RIDDELL, Bt)

Sir PHILIP *d* 1702; his est s,

Sir WILLIAM ANSTRUTHER of Anstruther; MP 1681–1707, Ld of Session as Lord Anstruther 1699; *m* 1677 Lady Helen Hamilton, dau of 4th Earl of Haddington (*qv*), and *d* 24 Jan 1711, leaving issue:

Sir John Anstruther, 1st Bt, of Anstruther (NS), so *cr* 6 Jan 1700; *b* 1673; MP Fifeshire 1721; *m* 24 Jan 1717 Lady Margaret Carmichael, est dau of 2nd Earl of Hyndford (through whom the Anstruthers inherited the Hyndford estates), and *d* by 25 April 1754, leaving issue:

Sir John Anstruther of that Ilk, 2nd Bt; *b* 27 Dec 1718; *m* 4 Oct 1750 Janet (*d* 17 Feb 1802), dau of James Fall, of Dunbar, and *d* 4 July 1799, having had, with other issue:

1 Sir PHILIP ANSTRUTHER later ANSTRUTHER-PATERSON (added on marriage), **3rd Bt**; *b* 13 Jan 1752; *m* 17 Feb 1778 Anne (*d* 11 March 1822), only child of Sir John Paterson, Bt (*see* POLWARTH, L), and *dsp* 5 Jan 1808

2 JOHN (Sir), **4th Bt**

3 Robert; *b* 31 Dec 1757; Col 68t Regt; MP Anstruther Easter; *m* 9 May 1801 Anne (*d* 27 Sept 1804), dau of Col Nairne, and had, with a dau and another s:

(1) Philip; *b* 26 May 1802; Colonial Sec Ceylon; *m* 27 July 1838 Mary Frances (*d* 31 Dec 1913), dau of James Alexander Stewart Mackenzie of Seaforth (*see* GALLOWAY, E), and *d* 22 May 1862, leaving issue:

1a Robert Durham; *b* 11 May 1841; Capt 106th Regt; Govr Pentonville Prison; *m* 7 May 1864 Florence Sophia (*d* 1 April 1932), dau of F Wise, of Leamington, and *d* 9 March 1890, leaving issue:

1b Philip Francis; *b* 29 April 1869; *m* 2 April 1907 Edith, yst dau of John Bradford, of St Margaret's, Paignton, and *dsp* 10 Sept 1941

1b Florence Mary; *d* unm Nov 1937

2b Edith Sophia; *d* 18 Nov 1919

3b Elizabeth Ethel; *d* unm 22 Oct 1948

4b Constance Lucy; *d* unm 10 Oct 1958

5b Armine Clementine; *d* unm 5 Feb 1919

2a Philip Morrison; *b* 23 Sept 1846; *m* Mary Adams and *dsp* 12 April 1899

3a Stewart Mackenzie; *b* 5 July 1848; *m* 29 June 1893 Mary Elizabeth (*d* 26 Aug 1937), est dau of Henry Roberts, and *dsp* 4 Feb 1898

4a John Newdegate; *b* 5 April 1850; *m* 15 June 1874 Georgina Julia, dau of Daniel Farley, of Henwick, Worcs

5a Keith Francis George; *b* 3 Feb 1854; FRGS; *m* 28 Nov 1878 Maria Catherine Geraldine (*d* 23 Aug 1921), dau of William Dallas Bernard, and *d* 24 July 1915, leaving issue:

1b Pearl Annie Geraldine Keith; *b* 19 May 1882; *m* 3 Nov 1914 Charles Edward Matthew Windspear Broadley (*d* 8 Feb 1943), barrister and Ecclesiastical Commr, er s of Charles Robert Broadley, and *dsp* 3 Feb 1945

6a Henry Lewis; *b* 25 April 1856; RMLI; went to Australia *c* 1800

7a Charles William; *b* 8 Sept 1858; *d* unm 22 Dec 1887

1a Mary Helen; *m* 9 Dec 1858 William Reirson Arbuthnot (*d* 31 May 1913), of E Grinstead, yst s of George Arbuthnot, JP, of Elderslie, Surrey, and *d* 21 May 1912, leaving issue (*see* ARBUTHNOT, Bt, of Kittybrewster)

2a Annie Nairn; *m* 23 Jan 1869 Col Charles Edward Stewart, CB, CMG, CIE (*d* 26 Dec 1904), and *d* 6 April 1931, leaving issue (*see* GALLOWAY, E)

3a Jemima Stewart; *b* 6 Jan 1845; *d* Jan 1874

4a Caroline Petre; *m* 19 Jan 1892 Duncan Mackay (*d* 1917), of Durinish and Carver's Croft, Plockton, and *d* 1 Jan 1928

Sir PHILIP's yr bro,

Sir John Anstruther, 4th Bt, and 1st Bt (GB) of the 18 May 1798 *cr*, PC; *b* 27 March 1753; Ch Justice Supreme Court of Judicature Bengal 1798–1806; *m* Maria (*d* 14 June 1833), dau of Edward Brice, of Berners St, London, and *d* 26 Jan 1811, having had issue:

1 Sir JOHN ANSTRUTHER later CARMICHAEL-ANSTRUTHER (added surname with arms on inheriting the Lanarks estate of the Carmichaels on the death of the 6th and last Earl of Hyndford 1817), **5th Bt**, and 2nd Bt, MP; *m* 11 Jan 1817 Jessie (*m* 2nd 27 March 1928 Robert Bullock Marsham, DCL, Warden Merton Coll Oxford; *d* 27 Dec 1880), dau of Maj-Gen David Dewar, of Gilston House, Fife, and *d* 28 Jan 1818, leaving:

(1) **Sir John Carmichael-Anstruther, 6th Bt**, and 3rd Bt; *b* 6 Feb 1818; accidentally shot by a school-fellow nr Eton 31 Oct 1831

2 WINDHAM (Sir), **7th Bt**, and 4th Bt

1 Marianne; *m* 27 March 1828 her cousin James Anstruther, WS, and *d* 19 June 1859, leaving issue

Sir JOHN's unc,

Sir Windham Carmichael-Anstruther, 7th Bt, and 4th Bt, DL (Lanarks); *b* 6 March 1793; Maj County Militia; *m* 1st 24 July 1824 Meredith Maria (*d* 10 April 1841), 2nd dau of Charles Wetherell, and had issue:

1 **Sir Windham Charles James Carmichael-Anstruther, 8th Bt**, and 5th Bt; *b* 1825; MP S Lanarks 1874–80, Convenor Lanark 1894, V-Lt Lanarks (DL previously); *m* 4 Sept 1872 Janetta (*d* 11 Sept 1891), only dau of Robert Barbour, of Bolesworth Castle, Cheshire, and *d* 26 Jan 1898, leaving issue:

(1) **Sir Windham Robert Carmichael-Anstruther, 9th Bt**, and 6th Bt, DL (Lanarks; *b* 26 March 1877; 2nd Lt Lanarks Imp Yeo; *m* 16 April 1901 Frederica Sylvia (*m* 2nd 2 Dec 1905 Maj Hon Algernon Henry Charles Hanbury-Tracy, CMG (*d* 3 Dec 1915), 2nd s of 4th Baron Sudeley (*qv*); *d* 5 Sept 1958), yst dau of Sir Frederick Darley, PC, GCMG, Lt-Govr and Ch Justice NSW, and *d* 26 Oct 1903, leaving issue:

1a **Sir (Windham) Frederick Carmichael-Anstruther, 10th Bt**, and 7th Bt; *b* 30 April 1902; *m* 23 July 1925 Katharine Mary (*m* 2nd 25th Sept 1930 (*divorce* 1940) John Robert Follett (*d* 4 June 1953), only son of Brig-Gen Gilbert Burrell Spencer Follett, DSO, MVO, Coldstream Gds, and had issue), dau of Daniel Arthur Neilson, of Wentbridge House, Pontefract, Yorks, and *dsp* 29 Nov 1928

Sir Windham *m* 2nd 10 May 1841 Anne Constance (*d* 21 June 1856), dau of Allen Williamson Grey, and by her had issue:

2 Windham George Conway; *b* 31 July 1846; 85th Regt; *m* 14 Feb 1867 Ellen Anne Katharine (*d* 29 March 1983), er dau of John Adam, HEICS, and *d* 13 Sept 1898, leaving issue:

(1) Gerald Yorke; *b* 24 Jan 1871; *m* 1900 Ellen Caroline (*d* 1902), dau of J Milne, of Cape Colony, and *d* 28 June 1910, leaving issue:

1a **Sir Windham Eric Francis Carmichael-Anstruther, 11th Bt**, and 8th and last Bt, DL (Lanarks 1940); *b* 29 May 1900; *educ* Marlborough; Gp Cmdt 34 and 38 Gp ROC WW II; *m* 1st 4 April 1932 (*divorce* 1948) Fay Sibyl Marie, only child of Ernest Rechnitzer, of 45 Charles St, London W1, and Warninglid Grange, Haywards Heath, Sussex; *m* 2nd 26 July 1948 Joanne, dau of William Coates, of Brighton, Sussex, and *d* 1980, when the GB btcy expired but the NS one passed to his kinsman (*see* below)

(2) Eric George Basil; *b* 10 Feb 1874; *m* and *d* 7 Jan 1934

(3) Hugh John Elphinstone; *b* 27 Nov 1875; Capt Roy Welch Fus and Assist Provost Marshal, Matabeleland Relief Rhodesia 1896, S African War, WW I, WW II in HG; *m* 11 Sept 1906 Ada Marie (*d* 17 Dec 1958), 2nd dau of Thomas Clark, of Putney, and *d* 6 Jan 1960, leaving issue:

1a Averil Nina; *b* 10 June 1907; *m* 10 Oct 1947 Hugh Thompson Dickinson, 3rd s of Robert Dickinson, of Styford Hall, Northumberland

(1) Maud Ellen Constance; *m* 6 Feb 1888 (*divorce* 1898) Maj-Gen John Christopher Swann, CB (*d* 10 May 1939), IA, s of Very Rev Robert Swann, Dean Nassau, and *d* 25 Jan 1925, leaving issue

(2) Mildred Helen Mary; *m* 19 Dec 1895 John Christopher Nevile, 3rd s of Rev Christopher Nevile, of Thorney Hall, Notts, and *d* 24 May 1939, leaving issue

(3) Muriel Vere; *b* 10 April 1881; *m* 17 Jan 1912 Harold Adam Whyte (*d* 15 July 1932), 3rd s of Robert Whyte, of Forfar, and *d* 4 Oct 1942

1 Mariana Constance; *d* unm 2 Nov 1883

2 Marian Alice; *m* 18 Feb 1875 Capt Charles Roger (*d* 25 March 1907), 70th Regt, of Chiefswood, Melrose, and *d* 2 April 1929

Sir Windham *m* 3rd 30 Sept 1859 Mary Ann (*dsp* 31 Dec 1905), 2nd dau of John Parsons, and *d* 15 Sept 1869

Lineage (of Anstruther of Balcaskie): Sir Robert Anstruther, 1st Bt, (NS), so *cr* 28 Nov 1694 (3rd s of the Sir Philip Anstruther of Anstruther who *d* 1702; *see* above); *bapt* 24 Sept 1658; bought Balcaskie, Fife, 1698; *m* 1st Sophia (*dsp*), dau and heir of David or James Kinneir of Kinneir; *m* 2nd 12 March 1687 Jean, dau and heir of William Monteith of Wrea, by whom he had six s and two daus (Christian *m* Sir J Henderson of Fordel, Bt, and Jean, *m* James Makgill, *de jure* 4th Viscount of Oxfuird; (*qv*)); *m* 3rd 13 Sept 1703 Marion, dau of Sir W Preston of Valleyfield, Bt, by whom he had a s Charles, Maj Army (*dsp*), and four daus (Anne *m* Jas Durham of Largo, Agnes, Isabel and Prestina) and *d* March 1737, leaving by his 1st w an est s:

Sir Philip Anstruther, 2nd Bt; *b* 1688; *m c* 21 Aug 1738 Catharine (*d* 11 Feb 1759), only dau of Lord Alex Hay, s of 1st Marquess of Tweeddale (*qv*), and had, with other issue:

1 ROBERT ANSTRUTHER (Sir); **3rd Bt**

2 John; *b* 13 May 1736; Col; *m* Dec 1774 Grizel Maria, dau and heiress of John Thomson of Charleton (*see* SINCLAIR, L), and *d* 10 Feb 1815, having had (with two daus and two yr s; *dsp*):

(1) John ANSTRUTHER later ANSTRUTHER-THOMSON (added on inheriting the Charleton estate); *b* 15 April 1776; *m* 27 April 1807 Clementina (*d* 29 Oct 1877), only dau of William Adam, of Blair Adam, MP, Baron Exchequer, Ld Ch Commr Jury Court and Ld-Lt Kinross, by Hon Eleanor Elphinstone, dau of 10th Lord Elphinstone (*qv*), and *d* 10 April 1833, leaving, with other issue:

1a John, of Charleton, Fife, and Carntyne, Lanarks; *b* 8 Aug 1818; offr 9th Lancers and 13th Light Dragoons, Hon Col Fife and Forfar Imp Yeo, VD, JP and DL (Fife); *m* 1st 25 Sept 1852 Caroline Maria Agnes Robina (*d* 12 Feb 1882) only child of Rev John Hamilton Gray, of Carntyne, and had issue:

1b John St Clair ; *b* 4 June 1853; *d* unm 4 July 1873

2b Charles Frederick St Clair ANSTRUTHER-THOMSON later ANSTRUTHER, DSO (1900), MVO (1905), DL, of Charleton, Fife; *b* 6 May 1855; Brevet-Col cmdg 2nd Life Gds Boer War 1899–1900 (despatches); memb Roy Co Archers, OStJ, Offr Legn of Honour, Kt Cdr Sword Sweden and Isabel la Catolica Spain; *m* 14 Jan 1882 Agnes Dorothea (*d* 7 Feb 1941), 3rd dau of James Alexander Guthrie, of Craigie, Forfarshire, and *d* 21 Oct 1925, having had:

1c John Arnold St Clair; *b* 23 Feb 1888; Lt 3rd Dragoon Gds (Carabiniers), ADC to Govr-Gen Australia 1914; *ka c* 30 Oct 1914

1c Grizel Margaret St Clair, of Charleton, Colinsburgh, Elie, Fife; *m* 18 April 1911 Baron Knut Bonde, Counsellor Legn, Swedish Dip Serv, of Gimmersta, Julita, Sweden (*d* 7 March 1952), s of Baron Carl Carlsson Bonde, of Ericsberg, Sweden, and *d* 10 May 1970 leaving issue

3b William ANSTRUTHER later ANSTRUTHER-GRAY (added on inheriting maternal gf's estates 1904), of Kilmany, Cupar, Fife, and Carntyne, Lanarks, JP (Fife), JP and DL (Lanarks and Glasgow); *b* 6 Sept 1859; Lt-Col

TAR, Maj Scottish Horse and RHG (Blues), ADC to Govr S Australia 1880–91; MP St Andrews 1906–10 and 1910–18, CC (Fife), FSA, FRGS; *m* 26 Jan 1891 Clayre Jessie, CBE (1934), JP (*d* 22 Oct 1958), dau of Andrew Tennant, of Essenside, Gleneig, S Australia, and *d* 17 April 1938, leaving issue:

1c Sir WILLIAM JOHN ST CLAIR ANSTRUTHER-GRAY, 1st and last Bt (UK), so *cr* 4 July 1956, and BARON KILMANY (LP, UK), of Kilmany, Fife, so *cr* 2 June 1966, MC (1943), PC (1962); *b* 5 March 1905; *educ* Eton and Ch Ch Oxford (MA); Ld Lt Fife (1974, DL 1953), MP (C) Lanarks N 1931045 and Berwick and E Lothian 1951–66, PPS to Sec Overseas Tde 1935, Parly Under Sec Scotland 1935, Fin Sec Treasury 1936 and Sec State Scotland 1938, Assist PMG May-July 1945, Dep Chm Ways and Means 1959–62, Chm: Ways and Means and Dep Speaker 1962–64, 1922 Ctee 1964–66, Maj Res Offrs Coldstream Guards WW II, Crown Nominee Scotland GMC 1952–65, memb Nat Hunt Ctee, PC 1962, owner and trainer of race horses; *m* 4 Oct 1934 Monica Helen, OBE (1946) (*d* 1985), only child of Geoffrey Lambton (Isee DURHAM, E), and *d* 1985, leaving issue:

1d *Diana Mary, *b* 16 June 1936, *m* 11 April 1959 *James Charles Macnab of Macnab, JP, est s of Lt-Col James Alexander Macnab, TD, MA, FCA, and has issue:

1e *James William Archibald MacNab of MacNab, yr; *b* 22 March 1963; *m* 1994 *Dr Jane Louise, dau of Dr David Mackintosh, of Exmouth

2e *Geoffrey Charles, *b* 20 Aug 1965

1e *Virginia Mary, *b* 29 July 1960; *m* 1986*Richard Laurence Oliphant Fyffe, er s of Laurence Fyffe, MC, JP, DL, and has issue:

1f *Alice Catherine; *b* 1989

2f *Emma Cicely; *b* 1992

2e *Katharine Monica, *b* 29 Feb 1968

2d *Jane Caroline, *b* 1 Oct 1943; *m* 28 July 1962 *Hon George Anthony Weir, PhD, 3rd s of 2nd Viscount Weir (*qv*), and has issue; *m* 2nd F Graham Gillies (*d* 1992)

1c Ruth Mary St Clair; *d* 25 Oct 1916

2c Jean Helen St Clair, CBE (1954); Ch Commr Girl Guides 1949–56; *m* 6 Feb 1923 4th Baron Stratheden and Campbell (*qv*) and *d* 9 Aug 1956, leaving issue

4b Arthur St Clair ANSTRUTHER-THOMSON; *b* 19 Nov 1872; Lt 1st Fife Light Horse Vols; *d* unm 16 Oct 1904

1b Clementina Caroline; *d* 7 July 1921

2b Rosia Mary; *m* 1st 20 Dec 1892 Col David Bryce Burn, 18th Hus (*d* 3 July 1915); *m* 2nd 11 May 1920 Edward Chapman Clayton, of Cottesmore, Oakham (*d* 22 Dec 1935), and *d* 13 Feb 1956

3b Olivia Beatrice Louisa; *m* 9 Dec 1895 Francis William Blackburne (*d* 11 July 1921), of Tankardstown, Slane, Co Meath, and *d* 17 Nov 1941, leaving issue

1a (cont.) Col John Anstruther-Thomson *m* 2nd 17 June 1891 Isabel (*d* 27 Feb 1918), 2nd dau of Gen Robert Bruce (bro of 1st Baron Aberdare (*qv*)), and *d* 8 Oct 1904, having by her had issue:

4b Rachel Jean; *m* 25 June 1923 (*divorce* 1943) Michael Willoughby Gordon-Cumming, yst s of Sir William Gordon-Cumming, 4th Bt (*qv*), and *dsp* 17 Sept 1968

2a William Adam; *b* 4 Dec 1823; Lt-Col, Cdr Bodyguard Govr-Gen India, ADC to Sir Charles Napier, Scinde Campaign, present actions of Meeance and Hyderabad (medal); *m* 15 Nov 1849 Isabella Eliza (*d* 11 Oct 1924 aged 93), dau of Gen James Steel, and *d* Calcutta 3 Aug 1865, leaving issue:

1b Charles James Anstruther; *b* 15 Dec 1859; Maj 17th Lancers; *m* 28 July 1894 Olive (*d* 16 Oct 1935), yst dau of Wyndham Slade, of Montys Court, Taunton (*see* SLADE, Bt), and *d* 7 June 1948, having had issue:

1c William; *b* 11 Dec 1897; *d* unm 12 April 1940

1c Clementina Susan Adelaide; *d* unm 23 April 1929

Sir PHILIP *d* 1763, and was *s* by his est son,

Sir Robert Anstruther, 3rd Bt; *b* 19 April 1733; *m* 17 Aug 1763 Lady Janet Erskine (*d* 14 Oct 1770), yst dau of 5th Earl of Kellie (*see* MAR and KELLIE, E), and had issue:

1 Robert; *b* 3 March 1768; served Flanders 1793–94, QMG Egypt 1800, Adj-Gen Ireland 1802, Brig-Gen Portugal 1808, present Battle of Vimiera, cmded rearguard Sir John Moore's retreat to Corunna 12 Jan 1809; *m* 16 March 1799 Charlotte Lucy, only dau of Lt-Col James Hamilton, Coldstream Gds (gs of 4th Duke of Hamilton; *see* HAMILTON and BRANDON, D), and *dvp* 14 Jan 1809, leaving issue:

(1) RALPH ABERCROMBY (Sir), **4th Bt**

(2) James Hamilton ANSTRUTHER later LLOYD-ANSTRUTHER, of Hintlesham Hall, Suffolk, JP and DL; *b* 20 Dec 1806; Capt 46th Regt; *m* 1st 6 Dec 1838 Georgiana Charlotte (*d* 21 Sept 1843), est dau of Hon Lindsey Merrik Peter Burrell (*see* 1915 edn GWYDYR, B), and had issue:

1a Robert Hamilton, JP and DL (Suffolk); *b* 21 April 1841; Lt-Col Rifle Bde; MP SE Suffolk 1886–92; CA E Suffolk; *m* 5 July 1871 Gertrude Louisa Georgiana (*d* 17 July 1927), est dau of Francis Horatio FitzRoy (*see* GRAFTON, D), and *d* 24 Aug 1914, having had issue:

1b FitzROY HAMILTON LLOYD-ANSTRUTHER later ANSTRUTHER-GOUGH-CALTHORPE (Sir), 1st Bt (*qv*)

2b Reginald; *d* an infant 1875

1b Rosalind Gertrude; *m* 14 Feb 1895 Brig-Gen Noel Armar Lowry-Corry, DSO, Gren Gds, est s of Armar Henry Lowry-Corry, and *d* 2 June 1903, leaving issue (*see* BELMORE, E)

1a Pricilla Barbara Elizabeth; nun; *d* 3 Aug 1899

(2) Capt James Hamilton LLOYD-ANSTRUTHER *m* 2nd 1 Nov 1847 Hon Georgiana Christiana Barrington (*d* 11 July 1881), dau of 5th Viscount Barrington (*qv*), and *d* 23 Dec 1882, having by her had issue:

2a Francis William; *b* 20 Feb 1849; Lt-Col 3rd Bn Suffolk Regt, *d* unm 4 Jan 1918

3a James, JP (Dorset); *b* 9 Jan 1852; *m* 29 June 1907 Hon Eleonora Chetwynd, MBE (*d* 20 Feb 1949), est dau of 7th Viscount Chetwynd (*qv*), and *d* 22 March 1947

4a Basil; *b* 1 Dec 1852; Col 1st Bn Manchester Regt; *m* 25 April 1899 Adela Maria (*d* 22 March 1915), dau of Sir Robert Loder, 1st Bt, and widow of Maj-Gen Hon Alexander Stewart (*see* GALLOWAY, E), and *d* 27 Dec 1932

5a Cecil; *b* 1 Dec 1852; Ch Clerk Parly Off Ho of Lds; *m* 4 Aug 1904 Bertha Mary (*d* 26 July 1958), yst dau of John Capel Philips, of The Heath House, Tean, Stoke-on-Trent, and *d* 24 Feb 1939

(1) Jane; *m* 21 Jan 1822 John Dalyell (*d* 7 Oct 1843), of Lingo, Fife, and *d* 13 March 1865, leaving issue

(2) Charlotte Lucy; *d* unm 5 Jan 1890 aged 84

(3) Elizabeth Christian; *m* 2 Nov 1837 Rev WH Deane (*d* 30 Nov 1854), Rector Hintlesham, and *d* 7 Dec 1893, leaving issue

2 Alexander (Sir), of Thirdpart, Fife; *b* 10 Sept 1769; Advocate-Gen Madras, Recorder Bombay; *m* 14 March 1803 Sarah (*d* 15 Dec 1865), dau of Thomas Prendergast, of Croane, and widow of Capt W Selby, HEICS, and *d* 16 July 1819, leaving issue:

(1) Robert, of Thirdpart, Fife; *b* 18 May 1805; Lt-Col; *m* 1 Oct 1832 Louisa (*m* 2nd 15 Aug 1861 Andrew Bonar (*d* 15 Feb 1874), yst s of Andrew Bonar, of Kimmerghame, Berwickshire; *d* 3 Oct 1903), yst dau of Lt-Gen Sir Howard Elphinstone, 1st Bt, and *dsp* 26 Feb 1856

(2) Philip, CB, of Thirdpart, Fife; *b* 12 Sept 1807; Maj-Gen: China War 1840–42, Punjab Campaign 1846, Kaffir War 1851, Burma Expdn 1853–54; *d* unm 18 Feb 1884

(3) Thomas Andrew; *b* 3 Feb 1810; HEICS; *m* 7 Jan 1841 Sophia, yst dau of Arthur Vansitart, of Shottesbrook, Berks, and *d* 14 April 1876, leaving issue:

1a Philip Robert; *b* 30 June 1841; Lt-Col 94th Regt; *m* 12 Jan 1875 Zaida Mary (*d* 18 April 1922), est dau of Sir Thomas Erskine, 2nd Bt, of Cambridge, and *d* of wounds recd in action 26 Dec 1880, leaving issue:

1b Philip George, DL, of Colinsburgh, Fife; *b* 25 Oct 1875; Maj and Brevet-Lt-Col Seaforth Highrs Boer War 1899–1902 (severely wounded, two medals, six clasps) and WW I (wounded twice, despatches, Order St Stanislas Russia 3rd Cl with swords); *d* unm 19 Aug 1940

2b Robert Abercrombie, DSO (1917); *b* 3 Aug 1879; Maj RFA Boer War 1900 and WW I (despatches); *d* unm 27 Aug 1945

1b Mary Rosamond; *m* 21 Nov 1900 Edward Windsor Hussey (*d* 17 Oct 1952 aged 97), of Scotney Castle, Kent, and *d* 19 July 1958

2a George John; *b* 4 Dec 1842; Capt RN; *d* unm 19 Jan 1888

3a Alexander William ANSTRUTHER later ANSTRUTHER-DUNCAN; *b* 3 Oct 1847; Col RA; *m* 26 April 1897 Catherine Henrietta Adamina (*d* 22 Oct 1932), dau of Adam Aldexander Morrison-Duncan, of Naughton, Fife, and *dsp* 18 Oct 1902

4a Ralph Nicholas; *b* 4 Nov 1851; *d* 10 Sept 1882

5a William Thomas; *b* 12 Dec 1857; *d* June 1898

(4) George Buchan; *b* 1811; RN; *d* unm Jan 1836

(1) Janet Catherine; *d* an infant 1804

(2) Janet Catherine; *d* unm 1884

(3) Catherine Louisa *d* an infant 5 Dec 1810

(4) Louisa Anne Erskine; *m* 25 June 1860 Gen Sir Frederick William Hamilton, KCB (*see* BELHAVEN AND STENTON, L), and *d* 29 Aug 1888

(5) Elizabeth Colville; *m* 17 Jan 1839 William Graham of Airth (*d* 21 Jan 1883) and *d* 26 Dec 1895, leaving issue

3 Philip; *b* 4 Oct 1770; RN; *d* 23 July 1796

1 Janet; *m* 39 Sept 1797 Sir Thomas Andrew Lumsden Strange (*d* 16 July 1841), Ch Justice Madras, and *dsp* 1798

2 Catherine; *d* unm 22 Sept 1820

3 Elizabeth; *m* 23 Feb 1787 Col Colin Campbell of Stonefield (*d* 1839), and *d* 1839, leaving issue

Sir ROBERT *d* 2 Aug 1818; his grandson,

Sir Ralph Abercromby Anstruther, 4th Bt; *b* 1 March 1804; Capt Gren Gds; *m* 2 Sept 1831 Mary Jane (*m* 2nd 14 Nov 1868 William Talbot Talbot-Crosbie (*d* 4 Sept 1899), of Ardfest Abbey, Co Kerry; *d* 26 Aug 1886), est dau of Maj-Gen Sir Harry Torrens, KCB, and *d* 18 Oct 1863, having had, with other issue:

Sir Robert Anstruther, 5th Bt; *b* 28 Aug 1834; Lt-Col Gren Gds; MP Fifeshire 1864–80 and St Andrews 1885–86, Ld-Lt Fife; *m* 20 July 1857 Louisa Maria Chowne (*d* 25 Jan 1913), dau of Rev William Knox Marshall, Preb Hereford, and had issue:

1 RALPH WILLIAM (Sir), **6th Bt**

2 Henry Torrens, JP (Bucks and Fife); *b* 27 Nov 1860; advocate Scotland; MP St Andrews 1886–1903, Jr Ld Treasury (Govt Whip) 1895–1903, memb Conseil d'Administration Suez Canal Co 1903; *m* 24 Aug 1889 Hon Eva Hanbury-Tracy, DBE (*d* 19 June 1935), est dau of 4th Baron Sudeley (*qv*), and *d* 5 April 1926, leaving issue:

(1) Douglas Tollemache; *b* 15 July 1893; *educ* Eton; chm Comtucs Ltd and Garden Shops Ltd; *m* 1st 9 Dec 1914 (*divorce* 1925) Enid (*d* 18 Dec 1964), 2nd dau of Lord George Granville Campbell, s of 8th Duke of Argyll (*qv*), and had issue:

1a Adrian Fagus Campbell; *b* 28 April 1917; *d* as the result of a fall 2 Jan 1932

2a +IAN FIFE CAMPBELL [Ian Anstruther Esq, Springs, Barlavington, Petworth, Sussex]; *b* 11 May 1922; heir presumptive; *educ* Eton and New Coll Oxford; Capt late Roy Corps of Signals and Attaché Br Emb Washington, DC; author; memb Roy Co of Archers; *m* 1st 7 March 1951 (*divorce* 1963) Geraldine Honor, er dau of Capt Gerald Stuart Blake, MC, of Clock House, Lindfield, Sussex, and has issue:

1b *Emily Kate Campbell; *b* 25 Jan 1953

2a (cont.) IAN ANSTRUTHER *m* 2nd 15 Nov 1963 *Susan Margaret Walker, dau of Henry St John Brading Paten, and by her has further issue:

1b +Sebastian Paten Campbell; *b* 13 Sept 1962

2b +Tobias Alexander Campbell; *b* 16 Dec 1968

2b *Rachel Whittome Campbell; *b* 28 Aug 1965

3b *Harriet Joan Campbell; *b* 24 March 1967

4b *Eleanor Thurloe Campbell; *b* 30 March 1971

1a *Janet Finetta Campbell [Mrs Janet Baker, Westwood, Bucklebury, Cold Alley, Newbury, Berks RG16 9NN]; *b* 11 July 1920; *m* 1st 4 Oct 1945 (*divorce* 1959) Rev William Pritchard Cole, MBE, CF, s of B T Cole, of Carmarthen, and has issue:

1b *Michael Henry Campbell; *b* 1945

1b *Janet Barbara Campbell; *b* 1947

1a (cont.) Mrs Janet Cole *m* 2nd 5 July 1968 (*divorce* 1983) Clive Ernest Baker, s of Lionel Baker, of Thatcham, Berks

(1) (cont.) Douglas Anstruther *m* 2nd 15 Oct 1925 Evelyn Mabel (*d* 1981), yst dau of Sir John Wormald, KBE, of N Stoke, Oxon, and *d* 23 July 1956, having by her had further issue:

2a Jean Dionis; *b* 3 Sept 1927; *m* 2 Sept 1949 Capt Richard David Somerset Drew-Smythe, MFH, er s of Col Henry James Drew-Smythe, MC, TD, MS, FRCS, FRCOG, of the Little Farm, Tockington, Glos, and *d* 5 April 1961, leaving a s and a dau

(1) Joyce; *b* 6 June 1901; author: *Mrs Miniver*; *m* 1st 4 July 1923 (*divorce* 1947) Anthony James Oliphant Maxtone Graham (*d* 8 June 1971), er s of James Maxtone Graham, of Colotquhay and Redgorton, Perthshire, and had issue; *m* 2nd 1 March 1948 Adolf Kurt Placzek, of Columbia U, s of Oswald Placzek, of Vienna, and *d* 20 July 1953

3 Robert Hamilton, CMG (1907); *b* 10 June 1862; Adml, Sr Naval Offr Danube 1900–02, N Sea Fisheries 1902–04, Newfoundland Fisheries 1906–08, Cdr Hong Kong 1912, Sr Offr coast of China 1914–16, 2nd class Order Rising Sun Japan; *m* 6 Jan 1890 Edith Flora (*d* 22 Feb 1944), dau of William Felton Peel, and *d* 26 Sept 1938, leaving issue:

(1) Philip Noel, DSO (1916), MC; *b* 2 Sept 1891; *educ* Sherborne; Col cmdg 1st Bn Roy W Kent Regt, Staff-Capt Malta 1928, Bde-Maj Canal Bde (wounded), Skipper Admlty Ferry Serv 1943–44; *m* 1st 6 Jan 1920 (*divorce* 1931) Mary Hope (*d* 23 March 1963), er dau of Harold Chaloner Lewin, of Bromley, Kent, and had issue:

1a +Robert Lewin [Robert Anstruther Esq, Windy Ridge, Pear Tree Lane, Dymchurch, Kent]; *b* 21 Aug 1924; *educ* Eastbourne Coll; FRICS; F/Lt RAFVR WW II; *m* 15 April 1950 *Nathalie Rosemary Nathalie, only dau of Cdr (E) Guy Ernest Williamson, MBE, MIMechE, RN, of Bickley, Kent, and has issue:

1b +Peter Robert; *b* 2 Oct 1955; *educ* Sevenoaks Sch; *m* 1981(*divorce* 1984) Joanna Mary, dau of Ken Herring, OBE, and has issue:

1c *Charlotte Daisy; *b* 1982

1b *Catherine Jane; *b* 28 Sept 1951; *m* 1981 (*divorce* 196) Robert Adrian Emerson and has issue:

1c *Nicolas; *b* 1980

2c *Joseph; *b* 1983

2b *Sally Elizabeth [Mrs Philip Johnson, 36 Palm Beach Ave, Hythe, Kent]; *b* 5 April 1958; *m* 1st 1978 (*divorce* 19–) James Trevor Reader and has issue:

1c *Mark Richard James; *b* 1981

1c *Rebecca Claire; *b* 1979

2b (cont.) Mrs Sally Reader *m* 2nd 1984 (*divorce* 1991) John Michael Smith and by him has:

2c *Victoria Wendy; *b* 1984

2b (cont.) Mrs Sally Smith *m* 3rd 1995 *Philip Johnson

1a *Jean Mary [Mrs Robert Blackall, The Little House, 2E Southlands Grove, Bromley, Kent BR1 2DQ]; *b* 17 July 1921; *m* 28 July 1951 F/Lt Robert (Robin) Owen Blackall, RAF (*k* on air/sea exercises over N Sea 25 June 1952), s of Norman Blackall, of Berkhamsted, Herts

(1) (cont.) Col Philip Anstruther *m* 2nd 2 Sept 1937 (*divorce* 1951) Mrs Mary Were, dau of Edwin Edwards, of Matamata, NZ; *m* 3rd 30 July 1952 *Marion Frances (Bunty), dau of Capt Ivor Macgregor, DSC, RNR, and formerly w of Philip Charles Secretan, and *d* 26 Feb 1960

4 Arthur Wellesley, CB (1908); *b* 5 March 1864; Capt Fife Art Militia; Priv Sec to Pres Bd Ag and Fisheries 1892–98, Ch Clerk to Bd 1898–1902, Asst Sec 1902–20; *m* 1st 26 April 1893 Hon Mary Elma Cumming-Bruce (*dsp* 11 Feb 1894), dau of 5th Baron Thurlow; *m* 2nd 21 Oct 1901 (Louisa Adele) Rose (*d* 21 Oct 1962 aged 94), dau of William Hume Trapman, of Charleston, S Carolina, and Roland Gdns, London SW, and *d* 20 Oct 1938, leaving issue:

(1) Alexander Meister, CB (1953), OBE (1946); *b* 26 July 1902; *educ* Malvern; Col RE (T/Brig 1946, Brig 1951) WW II, Ch Engr Br Troops Egypt 1950–53, Ch Engr W Cmd UK 1953, ret 1956; Fell Ancient Monuments Soc, dir Nubold Devpt Ltd 1956 (Chm 1959–65) and Boathire Internat (1967); *m* 16 May 1939 Barbara Ivy, dau of Abraham Ashman, of Hitchin, Herts, and formerly w of Frederick A Macquisten

(2) Peter Ralph; *b* 10 Oct 1907; *educ* Malvern; *m* 1st 29 Oct 1949 (*divorce* 1954) Joan Elizabeth Theresa Powell, dau of James Gilbert Saunders, of London; *m* 2nd 9 June 1962 *Mary Virginia, dau of Morgan Berkeley More, of New York

(1) Margaret Elizabeth; *b* 21 June 1906; F/Offr WRAF WW II

1 Mary Evelyn; *b* July 1859; *d* 2 Jan 1921

Sir ROBERT *d* 21 July 1886, and was *s* by his est son,

Sir Ralph William Anstruther, 6th Bt, JP (Fife) and JP and DL (Caithness); *b* 5 July 1858; Lt-Col (late cmdg) and Hon Col 6th/7th Bn Black Watch, Capt RE, Egyptian Expdn 1882 (medal with clasp, bronze star), Bechuanaland Expdn 1884–85, WW I (Legn of Honour); Ld-Lt Fife, Hon LLD St Andrews; *m* 5 Aug 1886 Mildred Harriet, CBE (1918) (*d* 25 April 1952), dau of Edward Hussey, of Scotney Castle, Kent, and *d* 30 Sept 1934, having had issue:

1 Robert Edward, MC; *b* 4 April 1890; Capt Black Watch (Roy Highrs) WW I (T/Col, twice wounded, despatches, Croix de Guerre with palms); *m* 16 June 1919 Marguerite, only dau of Hugo de Burgh, of Ballinapierce, Co Wexford, and *d* from the effects of wounds 22 July 1921, leaving issue:

(1) Sir RALPH HUGO ANSTRUTHER, **7th and present Bt**

1 Margaret Christian; *b* 16 Aug 1887; *d* unm 8 Sept 1925

2 Magdalen Janet; *b* 19 April 1889; *m* 14 Aug 1911 Lt-Col Sir Thomas Wilfred Hargreaves John Erskine of Cambo, 4th Bt, DSO, and *d* 15 Feb 1953, leaving issue (*see* ERSKINE, Bt, of Cambo)

3 Sarah Katherine, JP (Fife 1943); *b* 28 Sept 1894; *d* unm 22 Dec 1952

4 Elizabeth Mildred Louisa; *b* 29 April 1896; *m* 20 Oct 1920 Maj Julian Neil Oscar Rycroft, DSO, MC, only s of Maj-Gen Sir William Henry Rycroft, KCB, KCMG, and *d* 11 Sept 1932, leaving issue (*see* RYCROFT, Bt)

5 Gertrude Mary; *b* 9 March 1900; Headmistress St James's Sch W Malvern 1948–60, Assist Prof English Hood Coll Maryland 1961–62, Coffey Coll Nevada 1962–64; *d* unm 10 April 1975

ANSTRUTHER-GOUGH-CALTHORPE

Arms: Quarterly, 1st and 4th, chequy or and az., a fess erm., for distinction a canton erm. (for CALTHORPE); 2nd, gu. on a fess arg., between three boar's heads couped or, a lion passant az., for distinction a canton erm (for GOUGH); 3rd, arg. three piles sa.
Crests: 1 A boar's head couped erect az., charged for distinction with an erm spot. arg. (for CALTHORPE), 2 (dexter) A boar's head couped arg., pierced through the cheek with a broken spear gu., charged for distinction with an erm. spot az. (for GOUGH), 3 (sinister) Two arms in armour embowed, holding in the gauntlets a battle-axe in fess, all ppr. (for ANSTRUTHER).
Motto: *Gradu diverso via una* ('In one direction but by different steps').
Creation: Bt. (UK) 1 July 1929.

SIR EUAN HAMILTON ANSTRUTHER-GOUGH-CALTHORPE, 3RD BT, of Elvetham Hall, in the parish of Elvetham, Hants [Sir Euan Anstruther-Gough-Calthorpe Bt, c/o Brooks's Club, St James's St, London SW1A 1LN]; *b* 22 June 1966; *s* gf 1985; *educ* Harrow and RAC Cirencester; property manager

Lineage: Lt-Col ROBERT HAMILTON LLOYD-ANSTRUTHER, of Hintlesham (*see* ANSTRUTHER, Bt), had:

Sir FitzROY HAMILTON LLOYD-ANSTRUTHER later ANSTRUTHER-GOUGH-CALTHORPE (roy licence 7 Nov 1910), **1st Bt** (UK), so *cr* 1 July 1929, JP, Perm Staff Offr i/c Motor Res Staff WW I, Portuguese Mil Order of Avis 3rd Cl; *b* 5 July 1872; *m* 11 Oct 1898 Hon Rachel Gough Calthorpe (*d* 25 May 1951), est dau and coheir of 6th Baron Calthorpe (*see* 1970 edn), and had:

1 RICHARD HAMILTON (Sir), **2nd Bt**

1 Frances Jean; *b* 29 June 1910; *m* 14 Sept 1942 His Hon Judge (Frank Alleyne) Stockdale, JP, 5th Roy Inniskilling Dragoon Gds, er s of Sir Frank Stockdale, GCMG, CBE, and *d* 19–, leaving:

(1) *James Arthur FitzRoy [James Stockdale Esq, Moons Mill, Tinkers Lane, Hadlow Down, E Sussex]; *b* 16 Oct 1948; *educ* Eton and Southampton U (LLB); barrister Gray's Inn 1972; *m* 1974 *Jane Mary Gabriel, er dau of William Hazzard, and has issue:

1a *John Francis; *b* 1978

1a *Kathryn Jane; *b* 1980

2a *Philippa Rachel; *b* 1982

3a *Elinor Victoria; *b* 1985

(1) Sarah Victoria; *b* 2 Aug 1943; *m* 30 Oct 1965 *Christopher Norman Anthony Castleman, MA, only son of Mrs James Spring-Rice-Pyper, and *d* 1979 leaving issue:

1a *Jonathan William; *b* 1971

1a *Amanda Lucy; *b* 12 Oct 1967

(2) *Frances Jane [Mrs Charles Deacon, 9 Dinorbin, 79/81 Woodcote Rd, Wallington, Surrey]; *b* 23 Jan 1946; *m* 10 June 1967 *Charles Julian Deacon, MA, er son of Lt-Col Robert Stanley Deacon, of Park Ho, Madeley, Cheshire, and has issue:

1a *Julian Mark; *b* 1972

1a *Rebecca; *b* 1970

2 *Barbara; *b* 24 Oct 1911; *m* 4 Feb 1932 2nd Baron Luke (*qv*) and has issue

Sir FitzROY *d* 29 Sept 1957; his only son,

Sir Richard Hamilton Anstruther-Gough-Calthorpe, 2nd Bt, CBE (1946), DL (1955), JP (1950), Hon LLD Birmingham 1950, CC Hants 1949, CA Hants 1956, chm Hants CC 1967, Brig RSG WW II (Croix de Guerre), dir: Artizans and Gen Properties, Rowton House Ltd and Lloyds Bank S Regn, Conservator River Thames; *b* 28 March 1908; *educ* Harrow and Magdalene Coll Cambridge (BA 1930, MA 1936); *m* 20 July 1939 Nancy Moireach (*d* 15 Dec 1976), only dau of Vernon Austen Malcolmson, MA, JP, of Aston Bury, Stevenage, Herts, and had issue:

1 Niall Hamilton, ARICS (1966), ptnr Strutt & Parker; *b* 20 July 1940; *educ* Harrow, RAC Cirencester and Coll of Estate Management; *m* 2 April 1964 *Martha (Martia) Rodman (*m* 2nd 1975 *Sir Charles Christian Nicholson, 3rd Bt (*qv*)), 2nd dau of Stuart Warren Don, of 1 Hyde Park St, W2, and *d* as the result of a motor accident 26 Jan 1970, leaving issue:

(1) Sir EUAN HAMILTON ANSTRUTHER-GOUGH-CALTHORPE, **3rd and present Bt**

(1) *Lara Nancy Don; *b* 17 Sept 1968

2 Michael Richard, AAI; *b* 30 Oct 1943; *educ* Harrow and Coll of Estate Management

3 +John Austen [John Anstruther-Gough-Calthorpe Esq, Shroner Wood, Martyr Worthy, Winchester, Hants]; *b* 14 July 1947; *educ* Harrow; *m* 1st 27 May 1977 (*divorce* 1986) Lady Mary Gaye Georgiana Lorna Curzon, 3rd dau of 5th Earl Howe (*qv*), and has issue:

(1) +Jacobi Richard Penn; *b* 10 May 1983

(1) *Georgiana Moireach Gay; *b* 14 Oct 1978

(2) *Isabella Amaryllis Charlotte; *b* 1980

3 (cont.) John Anstruther-Gough-Calthorpe *m* 2nd 1987 *Vanessa Mary Theresa, yst dau of Lt-Cdr Theodore Bernard Peregrine Hubbard, RN (see NORFOLK, D), and formerly w of David St Vincent Llewellyn (*see* LLEWELLYN, Bt), and has further issue:

(3) *Gabriella Zanna Vanessa; *b* 1989

(4) *Octavia Elsa; *b* 1991

ANTRIM

Arms: Quarterly, 1st and 4th grand quarters, quarterly 1st, or a lion rampant gules; 2nd, or, a dexter arm issuant from the sinister fess point out of a cloud proper, in the hand a cross-crosslet fitchée erect azure; 3rd, argent, a ship with sails furled sable; 4th, per fess azure and vert a dolphin naiant in fess proper (for McDONNELL); 2nd and 3rd grand quarters, quarterly, 1st and 4th, azure, a sun in splendour or; 2nd, gules, on a chevron argent three mullets of the field; 3rd, sable on a chevron between three unicorn's heads argent, as many mullets of the field (for KERR). **Crests:** 1 A dexter arm embowed fessways, couped at the shoulder, vested or, cuffed argent, holding in the hand a cross-crosslet fitchée erect azure (for McDONNELL), 2 A sun in splendour or (for KERR). **Supporters:** Dexter, a savage wreathed about the temples and loins with ivy, all proper; sinister, a falcon, wings inverted proper, beaked, membered and belled or.
Motto: *Toujours prest* ('Always ready').
Creation: V. and E. (I) 19 June 1785.

THE 9TH EARL OF ANTRIM and **Viscount Dunluce** (Alexander Randal Mark McDonnell) [The Rt Hon the Earl of Antrim, Deer Park Cottage, Glenarm, Co Antrim BT44 0BQ]; *b* 3 Feb 1935; *s f* 1977; *educ* Downside, Ch Ch Oxford and Ruskin Sch of Art (Dip Fine Art); FRSA, restorer Tate Gallery 1965, restorer Grade I 1968, keeper conservation 1975, Memb Exec Ctee City and Guilds London Art Sch and Court RCA, dir Ulster TV, Fishmongers' Co: Prime Warden 1995–96, 4th Warden 1996–97; *m* 1st 9 Feb 1963 (*divorce* 1974) Sarah Elizabeth Anne, 2nd dau of St John Bernard Vyvyan Harmsworth, of Valley Holme, Horsted Keynes, Sussex (*see* ROTHERMERE, V), and has issue:

1 +RANDAL ALEXANDER ST JOHN *Viscount Dunluce*; *b* 2 July 1967; *educ* Gresham's

1 *Flora Mary; *b* 7 Nov 1963

2 *Alice Angela Jane; *b* 5 Dec 1964

The 9th EARL *m* 2nd 21 Oct 1977 *Elizabeth, er dau of Michael Moses Sacher (*see* MARKS OF BROUGHTON, B), and by her has:

3 *Rachel Frances; *b* 24 Feb 1978

Lineage: IAIN, LORD OF THE ISLES (*see* BOSVILLE MACDONALD, Bt); had by his 2nd w MARGARET, dau of ROBERT II KING OF SCOTS, a 2nd s:

IAIN *Mor* ('The Great'), LORD OF THE ISLES, of Duniveg and Glyns; *m* Margery, dau and heir of John Byset, Lord of the Glyns, Co Antrim, and was murdered by one James Campbell before 1427, having had, with a yr s: (Ranald *Bane*, ancestor of Clanranald Bane, of Largie, Kintyre):

Sir DONALD *Balloch* ('The Freckled'); *b c* 1407; cdr the rebellion in the Isles 1431, invaded Lochaber, defeated the King's Army under the Earls of Caithness and March and ravaged the adjacent districts, then withdrew to his mother's lands in Ulster; *m* —, dau of Con O'Neill, of Edenduffcarrick, and *d* 1476, leaving, with a dau (*m* Con O'Neill, Chief or Prince of Clannaboy; *see* O'NEILL, B):

IAIN *Mor*; *m* Sabina, dau of Phelim O'Neill, called 'Baccach' ('the Lame') and had:

Sir IAIN *Cathanach* MacIAN (from being fostered by the O'Cathans in Ulster); headed the Clan Ian Vor when the Lordship of the Isles was finally forfeited 1493, stormed the Castle of Dunaverty in South Kintyre, then held for the King, and hanged the Governor in the sight of the King and his Fleet 1494; *m* Sheela Savage and soon after 1494 was seized by his kinsman John Mac Ian MacDonell of Ardnamurchan and brought to Edinburgh, when he and four of his six sons were executed for high treason, leaving an est s:

ALEXANDER *Cathanach* MacIAN; with his surv brother Angus Ilach fled to Ireland after the execution of their father and brothers, supported Sir Donald MacDonald of Lochalash against the Govt 1517, again rebelled 1529 and ravaged the lands of the Campbells; in 1531 he and his followers were pardoned and granted lands in the South Isles and Kintyre; sent to Ireland 1532 with 8,000 men to assist the Scots in Ulster against the English; *m* Katherine, dau of John MacIan MacDonnell, and *d* by 1540, having had, with three daus (one of whom, Alice, *m* Sir Moyses Hill; *see* DOWNSHIRE, M), three er sons and two yst ones:

SORLEY *Buie* MACDONNELL; appointed by his est bro Lord of the Route, Co Antrim 1558; on his bro's death he seized the family's Irish estates and after fighting the native Irish and the English submitted to ELIZABETH I; since by birth a Scot, was made a free denizen of Ireland 14 April 1573; *m* Mary (*d* 1590), dau of 1st Earl of Tyrone (*see* O'NEILL, B), and had:

1 Alexander; *dsp*

2 RANDAL MacSORLEY, 1st EARL

3 James MacSorley (Sir); *dsp*

4 Encas or Angus

1 A dau; *m* Peter Hill (*see* DOWNSHIRE, M)

SORLEY *Buie d* 1589, his est surv son,

Sir RANDAL Mac SORLEY Mac DONNELL, 1st EARL OF ANTRIM, so *cr* 12 Dec 1620, as also earlier 28 May 1618 VISCOUNT DUNLUCE (both I), PC (1620); Ld Lt Co Antrim 1620, joined Sir Arthur Chichester with 500 Foot and 40 Horse against O'Neill, had a grant of the region of the Route and the Glyns, Co Antrim, 28 May 1603; *m* 1604 Alice, dau of 3rd and last Earl of Tyrone, and *d* 10 Dec 1636, having had, with six daus (including Anne, the est, *m* 1st Christopher, Lord Delvin, est s of 1st Earl of Westmeath (*qv*), *m* 2nd by 18 Jan 1626/7 14th Lord (Baron) Slane; another dau *m* George Gordon, 3rd s of 13th Earl of Sutherland (*qv*); another, Mary, *m* 1st 2nd Viscount Dillon (*qv*) and 2nd 6th Baron Louth (*qv*)):

1 RANDAL Mac SORLEY Mac DONNELL, 2nd EARL and 1st MARQUESS OF ANTRIM (I), so *cr* 26 Jan 1644/5; *b* 1609; ktd March 1638/9, royalist (albeit ineffective) Civil War; *m* 1st April 1635 Lady Catherine Manners, dau and heir of 6th Earl of Rutland (*see* RUTLAND, D) and widow of George Villiers, 1st Duke of Buckingham (*see* JERSEY, E); *m* 2nd by 20 March 1655/6 Rose, dau of Sir Henry O'Neill (*see* O'NEILL, B), but *dsp* 3 Feb 1682, when the Marquessate expired

2 ALEXANDER Mac DONNELL, 3rd EARL OF ANTRIM, PC (1685); *b* 1615; Ld Lt Co Antrim; attainted under CROMWELL, restored 1660, Jacobite in Ireland 1689–90, when again attainted but being subsequently included in the Treaty of Limerick 1691 his lands and honours were restored; *m* 1st Lady Elizabeth Annesley (*dsp* 4 Sept 1672), 2nd dau of 1st Earl of Anglesey of the 1661 *cr* (see VALENTIA, V); *m* 2nd Helena (*d* 7 Oct 1710), 3rd dau of Sir John Burke, of Derrymaclaghtry, Co Galway, and *d* 10 Dec 1699, having by her had, with a dau (Mary, *m* Henry Wells, of Brambridge, Otterbourne, Hants):

(1) RANDAL Mac DONNELL, 4th EARL OF ANTRIM; *b* 1680; *m* Rachel Skeffington (*m* 2nd Robert Hawkins Magill, of Gill Hall, Co Down (*d* 10 April 1745), and *d* 13 April 1739), dau of 3rd Viscount Massereene (*see* MASSEREENE and FERRARD, V), and had:

1a ALEXANDER, 5th EARL

1a Helena; *d* unm June 1783

The 4th EARL *d* 19 Oct 1721; his only son,

ALEXANDER Mac DONNELL, 5th EARL OF ANTRIM, PC; *b* 22 July 1713; Govr Co Antrim; *m* 1st 10 April 1735 Elizabeth (*d* 18 March 1736), dau of Matthew Pennefather, Comptroller and Accountant-Gen Ireland, and had an only dau (*b* 7 Feb 1736, *d* an infant); *m* 2nd 2 Jan 1739 Anne (*d* 15 Jan 1755), est dau and heir of Charles Patrick Plunkett, MP, of Dillons Town, Co Louth, and by her had issue:

1 RANDAL WILLIAM, 6th EARL

1 Rachel; *m* 13 Aug 1777 Joseph Sanford

2 Elizabeth Helena; *m* 22 Aug 1777 Lt-Col James Callander, 13th Dragoons, and *d* 1796, leaving issue

The 5th EARL *m* 3rd 5 July 1755 Catherine, yst dau of Thomas Meredyth, of Newtown, Co Meath, and widow of James Taylour (*see* HEADFORT, M), and *d* 13 Oct 1775

His son,

RANDAL WILLIAM Mac DONNELL, 6th EARL OF ANTRIM (1618 *cr*) and **1st Earl of Antrim**, also VISCOUNT DUNLUCE (both I), so *cr* 19 June 1785 with special remainder to his daughters by primogeniture and their male issue, since he had no male issue, also 1st and last MARQUESS OF ANTRIM (I), so *cr* 18 Aug 1789 but without such special remainder, KB (1779, also nominated KP but never installed owing to his reluctance to give up the KB), PC (I 1786); *b* 4 Nov 1749; *m* 3 July 1774 Hon Letitia Morres (*d* 7 Dec 1801), est dau of 1st Viscount Mountmorres (*see* DE MONTMORENCY, Bt) and widow of Hon Arthur Trevor (*see* TREVOR, B) and *d* 29 July 1791, when all his honours expired except those *cr* 1785, leaving:

1 ANNE KATHARINE Mac Donnell, **Countess of Antrim** in her own right; *b* 11 Feb 1778; *m* 1st 25 April 1799 Sir Henry VANE-TEMPEST, 2nd Bt (*dspm* 1 Aug 1813; *see* LONDONDERRY, M), and had:

(1) FRANCES ANNE EMILY Vane-Tempest; *m* 3 April 1849 3rd Marquess of Londonderry (*qv*) and *d* 20 Jan 1865, leaving issue

1 (cont.) The **Countess** *m* 2nd 24 May 1817 Edmund PHELPS later McDONNELL (roy licence 27 June 1817) (he *d* 30 May 1852 aged 72) and *dspm* 30 June 1834

2 Letitia Mary; *b* 11 Feb 1778, twin with her est sister but *d* unm in her lifetime

3 CHARLOTTE McDonnell, **Countess of Antrim**; *b* 12 Aug 1779; *m* 18 July 1799 V-Adml Lord Mark Robert Kerr (*d* 9 Sept 1840), 3rd s of 5th Marquess of Lothian (*qv*), and *d* 26 Oct 1835, having had, with other issue:

(1) Charles Fortescue, *Viscount Dunluce*; *b* 4 April 1810; *dvm* unm 26 July 1834

(2) HUGH SEYMOUR KERR later McDONNELL (roy licence 27 June 1836), **4th Earl of Antrim**; *b* 7 Aug 1812; *m* 3 May 1836 Lady Laura Cecilia Parker (*d* 26 Jan 1883), 5th dau of 5th Earl of Macclesfield (*qv*), and *d* 19 July 1855, leaving:

1a Helen Laura; *m* 15 Oct 1864 Sir Malcolm MacGregor of MacGregor, 4th Bt (*qv*), and *d* 17 March 1922, leaving issue

(3) MARK KERR later McDONNELL (roy licence 8 Nov 1855), **5th Earl of Antrim**, DL (Co Antrim); *b* 3 April 1814; Capt; *m* 27 April 1840 Jane Emma Hannah (*d* 21 April 1892), dau of Maj Turner Macan, of Cardiff, Co Armagh, and had issue:

1a WILLIAM RANDAL, **6th Earl**

2a Mark Henry Horace; *b* 18 Aug 1852; Lt 18th Regt; *m* 19 Aug 1892 Emily Fanny Dorothy (*d* 12 July 1925), dau of Sir George Osborn, 6th Bt (*qv*), and *dsp* 23 April 1909

3a Hugh Seymour; *b* 18 July 1855; *d* 24 Oct 1879

4a Alexander; *b* 23 June 1857; Ch Clerk Ho Lds; *d* unm 9 Dec 1945

5a Schomberg Kerr (Sir), GCVO, KCB; *b* 22 March 1861; Maj 5th Bn Cameron Highrs, Capt 1st London RV, Hon Lt, Boer War 1900, WW I 1915, Ch Intell Offr London Dist 1914–15, FSA, Pncpl Priv Sec to PM 1888–1902, Sec to Commrs Works 1902–12; *m* 26 Feb 1913 Ethel Henry (*d* 14 April 1916), dau of Maj Alexander Henry Davis, of La Floridiana, Naples, and formerly w of Capt Harrison, and *d* 23 Nov 1915 from wounds recd in action

1a Caroline Elizabeth; *m* 27 April 1881 Rev Hon Alberic Edward Bertie, Rector Gedding, Notts, s of 6th Earl of Abingdon, and *d* 23 Feb 1930, leaving issue (*see* LINDSEY and ABINGDON, E)

2a Mabel Harriet, CBE (1920); *m* 6 June 1878 Henry Charles Howard, of Greystoke Castle, Cumberland, and *d* 31 Dec 1942, leaving issue (*see* NORFOLK, D)

3a Evelyn; *d* unm 1 June 1947

4a Jane Grey, CStJ; *m* 1 June 1886 21st Baron Clinton (*qv*) and *d* 27 Aug 1953, leaving issue

5a Helena (Nina); *m* 12 April 1888 Capt Charles Barrington Balfour, CB (*d* 31 Aug 1921), of Newton Don, Kelso, and Balfour House, Balgonie, Fife, and *d* 11 Jan 1948, leaving issue

The 5th EARL *d* 19 Dec 1869; his est son,

WILLIAM RANDAL McDONNELL, **6th Earl of Antrim**, DL (Co Antrim); *b* 8 Jan 1851; *m* 1 June 1875 Louisa Jane, VA (*d* 2 April 1949), Ldy Bedchamber in Ordinary to TM QUEEN VICTORIA and QUEEN ALEXANDRIA, 3rd dau of Gen Hon Charles Grey, and gdau of 2nd Earl Grey (*qv*), and had issue:

1 RANDAL MARK KERR, **7th Earl**

2 Angus, CB (1919), CMG (1918); *b* 7 June 1881; *educ* Eton; MP Dartford 1924–29, Col Canadian Rlwy Tps Res, WW I 1916–19, Hon Attaché Washington 1941–45; *m* 13 Dec 1913 Ethelwyn Sylvia Arthur (*d* 3 April 1948), 2nd dau of Henry Arthur Jones and formerly w of M V Leveaux, and *dsp* 22 April 1966

1 Sybil Mary, CStJ; *b* 26 March 1876; *m* 6 March 1897 1st Baron Bicester (*qv*), and *d* 16 April 1959, leaving issue

The 6th EARL *d* 19 July 1918; his er son,

RANDAL MARK KERR McDONNELL, **7th Earl of Antrim**, DL (Co Antrim); *b* 10 Dec 1878; *m* 2 July 1904 Margaret Isabel (*d* 19 April 1974 aged 95), yst dau of John Gilbert Talbot, PC (*see* SHREWSBURY and WATERFORD, E), and had:

1 RANDAL JOHN SOMERLED, **8th Earl**

2 +James Angus Grey, MBE (1946) [The Hon James McDonnell MBE, 36 Farley Ct, Melbury Rd, London W14]; *b* 3 Aug 1917; *educ* Eton; 2nd Lt 7th Bn Roy Norfolk Regt WW II 1939–40 (POW); *m* 19 Oct 1939 *Jeanne Irene, dau of Col Stanley Leonard Barry, CMG, CBE, DSO, MVO, of Hampton Gay Manor, Oxon (*see* BARRY, Bt), and has issue:

(1) +Sorley James; *b* 10 Aug 1940; *educ* Eton; *m* *Ngawaiata Mei, dau of Te Nagaelie Wauikau, of Wellington, NZ, and has issue:

1a *A dau; *b* 23 March 1970

(1) *Louisa; *b* 16 July 1946

1 *Rose Gwendolen Louisa, DCVO (1973, CVO 1964); *b* 23 May 1909; Woman of the Bedchamber to HM THE QUEEN 1953; *m* 22 April 1933 Francis Anthony Baring, only son of Maj Hon Hugo Baring, OBE (*ka* June 1940), and *d* 1993, leaving issue (*see* REVELSTOKE, B)

2 *Jean Meriel [The Lady Jean Philipps, Slebech Park, Haverfordwest, Dyfed]; *b* 1 Sept 1914; *m* 31 Aug 1939 Hon William Speke Philipps (*d* as the result of an accident 5 Sept 1975), yst son of 1st Baron Milford (*qv*),and has issue

The 7th EARL *d* 15 June 1932; his er son,

RANDAL JOHN SOMERLED McDONNELL, **8th Earl of Antrim**, JP (1934) and DL (both Co Antrim); *b* 22 May 1911; *educ* Eton and Ch Ch Oxford; Capt RNVR WW II, cmdg Ulster Div RNVR 1954–57, V-Lt Co Antrim 1955, Hon Attaché Teheran 1932, Clerk Ho Lds 1932–34, Chm: Nat Tst NI 1947–64, T&AFA Co Antrim 1950–62, Nat Tst 1965–77, Ulster TV, Bd Govrs St Peter's Hosp London, Hon Col 429 Coast Regt RA (TA) 1954–59, Hon FRIBA 1972; *m* 11 May 1934 Angela Christina (*d* 1984), yst dau of Sir (Tatton Benvenuto) Mark Sykes, 6th Bt (*see* SYKES, Bt, of Sledmere) and *d* 26 Sept 1977, having had:

1 ALEXANDER RANDAL MARK McDONNELL, **9th and present Earl of Antrim**

2 A son; *b* 4, *d* 5 Feb 1936

3 +Hector John [The Hon Hector McDonnell, The Old Rectory, Glenarm, Co Antrim]; *b* 1 March 1947; *educ* Eton and Ch Ch Oxford; *m* 15 Feb 1969 (*divorce* 1974) Catherine Elizabeth, yr dau of Ronald Chapman, of Buttermilk Hall, Brill, Bucks, and has issue:

(1) +Colquitto Angus; *b* 1972

(1) *Hannah Margaretta; *b* 1 Feb 1971

1 Christina Alice; *b* 18 Sept 1938; *educ* Slade Sch of Art (Dip Fine Art); *m* 23 Jan 1963 *Joseph Andrew Christopher Hoare, of Hartridge Manor Farm, Cranbrook, Kent TN17 2NA, only son of Sir Reginald Hervey Hoare, KCMG, of Pine Crest, Hawley, Camberley, Surrey, and 80 Harley House, Marylebone Rd, London NW1, and *d* 19–, leaving issue:

(1) *Charles William Reginald; *b* 23 June 1966

(1) *Jane Alice Patience; *b* 23 Dec 1963

(2) *Lucy Mary Christina; *b* 24 Oct 1968

ANTROBUS

Arms: Lozengy or and azure, on a pale gules three estoiles of the first. **Crest:** Issuing out of rays proper a unicorn's head couped argent, horned and maned or, gorged with a wreath of laurel proper. **Supporters:** Two horses proper. **Motto:** *Dei memor, gratus amicis* ('Mindful of God, grateful to friends'). **Creation:** Bt. (UK) 22 May 1815.

SIR EDWARD PHILIP ANTROBUS, 8TH BT, of Antrobus, Co Palatine of Chester [Sir Edward Antrobus Bt, Box 1953, Parklands 2121, S Africa, or 54a, 3rd Ave, Parktown, North Johannesburg, S Africa]; *b* 28 Sept 1938; *s f* 1995; *educ* Witwatersrand U (BSc (Eng) 1961) and Magdalene Coll Cambridge (BA 1965, MA 1969); *m* 7 Oct 1966 Janet (*d* 1990), er dau of Philip Walter Sceales, of Hyde Park, Johannesburg, S Africa; *m* 2nd 29 Nov 1996 *Rozanne Penelope, dau of Neville Simpson, of Durban and by his 1st w has:

1 +FRANCIS EDWARD SCEALES; *b* 1972; *educ* Cape Town U (BSc)

1 *Barbara Joanna; *b* 27 Jan 1968

2 *Sarah Diana; *b* 1970

Lineage: The chief seat of this Cheshire family, Antrobus Hall, was sold by Henry Antrobus in 1460 to Thomas Venables, nephew of Sir William Venables, of Bolyn, whose branch of the VENABLESES lived there for several generations; the lands were, however, redeemed by:

EDMUND ANTROBUS, of Odrode, Astbury, nr Chester, s of another Edmund Antrobus, of Odrode (ggs of the above-mentioned Henry Antrobus of Antrobus Hall); left, with an er s:

PHILIP ANTROBUS, of Congleton; *m* Anne, dau of John Vardon, of Congleton, and had an est s:

PHILIP ANTROBUS, of Congleton; *m* 1745 Mary, dau of Thomas Rowley, of Overton, Staffs, and had, with other issue (*d* unm):

1 **Sir Edmund Antrobus, 1st Bt** (UK), so *cr* 22 May 1815, with remainder to his ns, of Antrobus Hall, which he bought; FRS and FSA; *d* unm 6 Feb 1826

2 John; *m* 1791 Anne (*d* 1793), only dau of Gibbs Crawfurd, MP Queenborough, and *d* 27 April 1794, having had:

(1) **Sir Edmund Antrobus, 2nd Bt**; *b* 17 May 1792; *m* 16 Oct 1817 Anne (*d* 1 Dec 1885, aged 85), only dau of Hon Hugh Lindsay, yst s of 5th Earl of Balcarres (*see* CRAWFORD and BALCARRES, E), and *d* 4 May 1870, having had issue:

1a **Sir Edmund Antrobus, 3rd Bt**, JP and DL (Wilts); *b* 3 Sept 1818; High Sheriff 1880; MP E Surrey 1841–47 and Wilton 1855–77; *m* 11 Feb 1847 Marianne Georgiana (*d* 3 Feb 1903), dau of Sir George Dashwood, 4th Bt (*see* DASHWOOD, Bt, of Kirtlington Park), and *d* 1 April 1899, having had, with three daus:

1b **Sir Edmund Antrobus, 4th Bt**; *b* 25 Dec 1848; Col Gren Gds; *m* 2 March 1886 Florence Caroline Mathilde (*d* 19 Feb 1923), dau of Jules Alexander Sartoris, of Hoppesford Hall, Warwicks, and *dsps* 11 Feb 1915, having had:

1c Edmund; *b* 23 Dec 1886; Lt Gren Gds; *ka vp* 24 Oct 1914

2b Robert Lindsay; *b* 9 Aug 1857; *d* 6 March 1891

3b **Sir Cosmo Gordon Antrobus, 5th Bt**, JP (Wilts); *b* 22 Oct 1859; barrister Inner Temple; *d* unm 29 June 1939

2a Hugh Lindsay; *b* 1 Jan 1823; *m* 8 Sept 1859 Mary (*d* 31 Dec 1900), dau of Adml Sir Charles Adam, of Blair-Adam, KCB (*see* ADAM, Bt), and *d* 18 March 1899, leaving issue:

1b Charles; *b* 18 June 1860; *d* 22 Aug 1861

1b Marion Lindsay; *m* 1st 25 Oct 1886 Capt Henry Gerard Leigh, 1st Life Gds (*d* 7 Jan 1900), est son of Henry Blundell Leigh, of Ammington Hall, Tamworth, Staffs; *m* 2nd 16 April 1910 Lt-Col Reginald Halsey (*d* 30 May 1927), 5th son of Rt Hon Sir (Thomas) Frederick Halsey, 1st Bt (*qv*), and *d* 27 Dec 1927

2b Katherine Mary; Order Precious Crown Japan; *m* 5 May 1886 Maj-Gen Laurence George Drummond, CB, CBE, MVO, JP, DL, Scots Gds, and *d* 9 Sept 1947, leaving issue (*see* PERTH, E)

3b Helen; *m* 11 Feb 1888 Maj Evelyn George Hammond Atherley, RHG (Blues) (*d* 15 Feb 1935), and *dsp* 1922

4b Elizabeth; *d* unm 16 Nov 1944

3a Robert Crawfurd, JP (Middx and London); *b* 21 March 1830; *m* 2 Aug 1873 Emily (*d* 21 Dec 1936), dau of Col John Ireland Blackburne, JP, DL, MP, of Hale Hall, Lancs, and widow of William John Hope Edwardes, of Netley, Salop, and *d* 12 Feb 1911, leaving issue:

1b **Sir Philip Humphrey Antrobus, 6th Bt**, MC (1918); *b* 22 July 1876; *educ* Eton; Lord of the Manor of Amesbury, Capt Irish Gds (SR) WW I (wounded twice, despatches); *m* 29 Nov 1919 Olive Geraldine Emma, Polish Gold Cross of Merit, dau of Louis Theobald Dillon FitzGibbon (*see* DILLON, V), and widow of Jordan Dumaresq, of Boston, and *dsp* 11 July 1968

1b Sybil Mary; *b* 19 Jan 1875; *m* 20 Sept 1904 Sir Henry Tindal Methold, JP (*d* 29 Jan 1952), Master in Lunacy, son of Thomas Tindal Methold, of Hepworth House, Suffolk, and *d* 24 March 1932, leaving issue

2b Margaret Freda Evelyn; *b* 4 Aug 1879; *m* 24 Aug 1904 Hon Gilbert de St Croix Rollo, yst son of 10th Lord Rollo (*qv*) of Duncrub, and *d* 26 Oct 1959, leaving issue

4a John Edward; *b* 24 Sept 1831; *d* 21 April 1845

5a Frederick (Rev), of the Oratory, South Kensington; *b* 4 Aug 1837; 2nd Sec Dip Serv; *d* 12 July 1903

1a Jane; *m* 3 Aug 1843 Rev Sir Gilbert Frankland Lewis, 2nd Bt (*d* 18 Dec 1883), Preb of Worcester, and *d* 20 Oct 1899, leaving issue

2a Anne; *m* 9 Dec 1847 Rt Hon Sir Henry George Elliot, GCB, 2nd son of 2nd Earl of Minto (*qv*), and *d* 17 Dec 1899, leaving issue

3a Harriet Coutts; *d* young 1826

4a Caroline; *m* 2 Oct 1860 Hon Humphrey de Bohun Devereux, 4th son of 14th Viscount Hereford (*qv*), and *d* 22 Dec 1903

5a Anna Maria; *m* 8 Nov 1859 Cosmo Duff Gordon, and *d* 26 Jan 1898, leaving issue (*see* DUFF-GORDON, Bt)

(2) Gibbs Crawfurd, of Eaton Hall, Cheshire, JP, DL; *b* 27 May 1793; High Sheriff 1834, MP Aldborough, Yorks; *m* 1st 25 June 1827 Jane (*d* 24 Nov 1829), dau of Sir Coutts Trotter, 1st Bt (*see* CRAWFORD and BALCARRES, E), and had issue:

1a John Coutts, of Eaton Hall, Cheshire, JP; *b* 23 Nov 1829; MA Cambridge; barrister, Hon Lt-Col Earl of Chester's Yeo Cav, CC Cheshire, High Sheriff 1868; *m* 1st 29 Sept 1855 Fanny (*d* 20 Sept 1863), dau of Clement Swetenham, JP, DL, of Somerford Booths, Cheshire, and had:

1b Crawfurd John; *b* 16 June 1862; *m* 6 June 1900 Marie (*d* 16 March 1930), widow of Dennis Pierce, and *d* 10 Sept 1943

1b Eleanor Margaret; *d* unm 1873

2b Blanche Helen; *d* unm 26 Nov 1954 aged 96

3b Jane Mary Evelyn; *m* 23 Nov 1899 as his 2nd wife Arthur Francis Thomas Cooper (*d* 8 Dec 1918) and *d* 26 July 1937, having had issue

1a (cont.) John Antrobus *m* 2nd 10 Jan 1865 Mary Caroline (*d* 11 Sept 1872), 4th dau of Geoffrey Joseph Shakerley (*see* SHAKERLEY, Bt), and by her had issue:

2b Geoffrey Edward; *b* 15 Sept 1867; *m* 3 Dec 1898 Mary Atherstone (*d* 28 April 1954), dau of Hilton Barber, JP, of Halesowen, Cradock, Cape Province, S Africa, and *d* 16 July 1958, leaving:

1c **Sir Philip Coutts Antrobus, 7th Bt**; *b* 10 April 1908; WW II 1939–42 (POW), Lord of the Manor of Amesbury; *m* 1st 28 Aug 1937 Dorothy Mary (*d* Sept 1973), dau of Rev William George Davis, of The Rectory, Tarkastad, Grahamstown, S Africa, and sometime of Australia, and had:

1d Sir EDWARD PHILIP ANTROBUS, **8th and present Bt**

2d +Michael Ronald [Michael Antrobus Esq, PO Box 433, Cradock 5880, Cape Province, S Africa]; *b* 21 Oct 1939; Dip of Ag (SA); *m* 27 Jan 1968 *Sandra, dau of J H Moolman, Middleton, Cape Province, S Africa, and has:

1e +Philip Michael; *b* 1973

1e *Cherie Joann; *b* 1969

2e *Elizabeth Ruth; *b* 1971

1d *Patricia Jennifer [Mrs Michael Montgomery, c/o Lloyds Bank, Gentlemans Walk, Norwich]; *b* 25 Aug 1948; *m* 1971 *Maj Michael George Rodgers Montgomery, RE, and has issue:

1e *Charles George Philip; *b* 1979

1e *Geraldine Claire Margaret; *b* 1977

1c (cont.) **Sir Philip** *m* 2nd 1975 Doris Primrose (*d* 1986), dau of Harry George Watts and widow of Thomas Ralph Dawkins; *m* 3rd 1991 *Esmé Florence Bayes [Lady Antrobus, West Amesbury House, Amesbury, Wilts], dau of Dudley Charles Windsor and widow of Frank Herbert Mawer and *d* 1 Aug 1995

2c +Crawfurd Ralph [Crawfurd Antrobus Esq, PO Box 390, Grahamstown, 6140, S Africa]; *b* 29 Sept 1915; WW II (wounded); *m* 12 July 1943 *Sheila Marcia, dau of Ven Archdeacon Alfred Edward McKenzie, of Cradock, CP, S Africa, and has issue:

1d +Geoffrey Gordon [Prof Geoffrey Antrobus, 5 South St, Grahamstown, CP 6140, S Africa]; *b* 28 Oct 1944; *educ* St Andrew's Coll Grahamstown, U of Natal (MSc Ag 1967) and Rhodes U (PhD); ecomonist with S African Dept of Ag, Registrar (Acad) to U of Fort Hare 1988–90, Prof Economics Rhodes U Grahamstown 1991–; *m* 1973 *Margaret Elizabeth, dau of Roy Nettleton Gordon, and has issue:

1e +Charles Crawfurd; *b* 1982

2e +Richard Roy; *b* 1982

1e *Helen Catherine; *b* 1976

2e *Shirley Jean; *b* 1977

1d *Margaret Jean [Mrs Margaret Baker, Jacques House, Kingswood Coll, Grahamstown, S Africa]; *b* 9 Nov 1947; *m* 8 March 1969 (*divorce* 1988) John Rodney Baker, son of John Howard Baker, of Durban, Natal, and has issue:

1e *John Andrew; *b* 1971

2e *Bruce Stephen; *b* 1975

1e *Carol Lynn; *b* 1973

1c *Ida Dorothy; *b* 3 Aug 1909; *m* 1st 7 July 1937 (*divorce* 1940) Frank Thomas Hayes Jr, son of Frank Thomas Hayes Sr, of Grafton, PO Cathcart, CP, S Africa, and has issue:

1d *Heather Ann; *b* 1938; *m* 4 May 1963 *Leonard Erie Twentyman-Jones, of Erldun, PO Trapp's Valley, Bathurst, CP, S Africa, son of Graham Villiers Twentyman-Jones, and has issue:

1e *Leonard Hilton; *b* 2 June 1965

1e *Lee-Ann; *b* 7 April 1964

2e *Julie; *b* 19 Sept 1968

1c (cont.) *Mrs Ida Hayes *m* 2nd 23 March 1944 *Cyril Embleton Hilton Barber Standen, of PO Conway, CP, S Africa, son of Charles Evelyn Barber, of Haledowen, Cradock, CP, S Africa, and has further issue:

1d *Charles Geoffrey Hilton; *b* 11 April 1947

2d *Valerie May Hilton; *b* 24 June 1948; *m* 1974 *William Gerald Sieberhagen, of 16 Bay View Rd, Wynberg, Cape Prov, S Africa, and has issue:

1e *Hilton John; *b* 1978

2c *Mary Shakerley; *b* 4 March 1913; *m* 19 June 1937 *Edward Mounsey Gilfillan, JP, of Conway Farm, PO Conway Station, CP, S Africa, son of Edward Thornhill Gilfillan, JP, of Brincliffe PO, Tafelberg Station, Middleburg, CP, S Africa, and has issue:

1d *Edward Crawfurd; *b* 27 May 1940; *m* 1968 *Ruth-Mary MacJannet, and has issue:

1e *Edward Hugh; *b* 1970

2e *Ross Mounsey; *b* 1974

1e *Claire Mary; *b* 1972

2d *Philip Mounsey; *b* 25 Oct 1950; Dr Vet Sc

1d *Camilla Mary; *b* 29 May 1938; *m* 1968 *Henry Guerney Gush, and has issue:

1e *Giles Joseph Guerney; *b* 1968

2e *Andrew; *b* 1970

2d *Jocelyn Mary; *b* 26 Dec 1948; *m* 1978 *Christiaan Visser, and has issue:

1e *Richard; *b* 1982

1e *Christine; *b* 1982

3b Philip; *d* young 1874

4b Ralph Edmund; *b* 4 Sept 1871; *m* 16 Nov 1901 Millicent (*d* 15 April 1937), yst dau of Edward Lindsey de Morgan, and *d* 2 April 1927, leaving issue:

1c Geoffrey John; *b* 26 May 1904; *educ* Emmanuel Coll Cambridge (BA 1926); *m* 1st 22 Jan 1938 Mary Dorothea (*d* 22 Aug 1950), dau of Adrian Van der Byl, of Cape Town, and had issue:

1d *Prunella Mary [Mrs David Burt, Silton Hoe, Peaslake, Surrey GU5 9SR]; *b* 26 Oct 1938; *m* 10 March 1961 *David Lyndon Burt, only son of Maj Robert Frederick Burt, of Upwey, Newdigate, Surrey, and has issue:

1e *Lyndon Oliver Antrobus; *b* 23 Nov 1965

1e *Nicola Katherine; *b* 10 June 1962

2d *Chloe Louise; *b* 8 Oct 1943; *m* 1969 *Alan Douglas Saunders, of Gordon Heights, Constantia, Cape Town, and has issue:

1e *Thandi Antonia; *b* 1973

2e *Lucy; *b* 1975

1c (cont.) Geoffrey Antrobus *m* 2nd 29 June 1954 Antonia Marie (*d* 1994), dau of William Henry Carlin, of Durban, S Africa, and formerly w of Harry Berrington Blew, and *d* 1990

2c +Edmund Shakerley Alexander [Edmund Antrobus Esq, 20A Sherwood Rd, Forest Town, Johannesburg 2193, S Africa]; *b* 1 Nov 1919; *educ* Magdalene Coll Cambridge (BA 1946), and McGill U Montreal (MSc 1949, PhD 1955); WW II 1940–45 as Capt RA; *m* 7 June 1947 *Shelagh Elizabeth, twin dau of Clive Noble Rich, of The Old Farm House, Fyfield, Abingdon, Berks, and has issue:

1d +(Edmund) Bayard [Bayard Antrobus Esq, 6 Dunkeld Rd, Bournemouth, Dorset BH3 7EN]; *b* 27 June 1949; *m* 1978 *Gillian Van Hasselt, and has issue:

1e *Sara Kate; *b* 1988

2e *Lucy Jane; *b* 1989

3e *Olivia Sage; *b* 1991

2d +Bryan Ralph [Bryan Antrobus Esq, 95 Kerry Rd, Johannesburg, S Africa]; *b* 22 March 1951; *m* 1982 *Rosemary Logie and has had:
1e +Nicholas Hugh; *b* 1986
1e Caroline Elizabeth; *b* 1984; *d* 1994
2e *Megan Elizabeth; *b* 1996
3d +Christopher Adrian [Christopher Antrobus Esq, 51 Rothesay Ave, Craighall Park, Johannesburg, S Africa]; *b* 16 Dec 1952; *m* 1979 *Ann Tuffin and has:
1e *Kyra Liza; *b* 1984
2e *Jacinta Leigh-Ann; *b* 1986
4d +Robin Clive [Robin Antrobus Esq, 28 Broadbent Loop, Leeming, Perth, W Australia 6155]; *b* 6 June 1954; *m* 1982 *Theresa Susan, dau of Arthur Allenby Noble, and has issue:
1e *Courtney Lynne; *b* 1990
1c Joan Margaret; *b* 15 Oct 1902; *d* unm 1975
2c Frances Millicent Eleanor; *b* 30 Sept 1910; *d* 4 Feb 1921
4b Dora Katharine; *d* unm 30 Jan 1919
1a (cont.) John Antrobus *m* 3rd 6 Feb 1875 Mary Egidia (*d* 1 July 1911), yst dau of Gen Hon Sir James Lindsay, KCMG (*see* CRAWFORD and BALCARRES, E), and *d* 19 Dec 1916, having by her had issue:
5b Jocelyn James (Rev), JP (Somerset); *b* 9 May 1876; *educ* New Coll Oxford (MA); Rector of Bishops Hatfield, Herts, 1917–36; *m* 10 June 1915 Justine Mary Louisa (*d* 17 June 1964), dau of Maj William Affleck King, 17th Regt, and *d* 10 Sept 1953, leaving issue:
4c +Charles Hugh [Lt-Col Charles Antrobus, Wootton House, Wootton Rivers, nr Marlborough, Wilts]; *b* 18 April 1916; *educ* Eton and Magdalene Coll Cambridge (MA); Lt-Col RA, WW II 1939–45 (despatches); *m* 7 July 1945 *Pamela, 2nd dau of Lt-Col Huntley Gordon Spencer, TD, JP, DL, of South Hill House, Cranmore, Shepton Mallet, Somerset
1c *Mary Elizabeth [Miss Mary Antrobus, 16 Prospect Place, Camden Rd, Bath]; *b* 6 June 1918
6b Cecil Hugh; *b* 25 Sept 1877; Capt 6th Bn Cameron Highrs, S Africa 1900 (Queen's medal with five clasps), WW I 1914–15; *ka* France 25/26 Sept 1915
7b Walter Guy; *b* 27 March 1879; *educ* Charterhouse; with Marshall's Horse S Africa 1901–02; *m* 19 Dec 1907 Kathleen Frances, 2nd dau of Gen Arthur Broadwood, CVO, and *d* 19 April 1963, leaving issue:
1c Robert Michael; *b* 7 April 1910; Govt Land Surveyor with S African Rlwys, memb Inst Land Surveyors of Transvaal, Natal and Cape Province; WW II 1940–45 in SA Engr Corps (invalided); *m* 1st 26 Nov 1938 (*divorce* 1948) Janet Lyle Holmes, only dau of Neil Mackay, of 140 Main Rd, Sea Point, Cape Town, and had issue:
1d +Norman Hugh [Norman Antrobus Esq, 17 Plover St, Horizon Extension 1 Roodepoort, Transvaal]; *b* 12 March 1940; *m* 5 Oct 1963 *Barbara Gwen, dau of E J M Gravett, of Pietermartizburg, Natal, and has issue:
1e +Stephen Craig; *b* 3 Oct 1965
1e *Liane Mary; *b* 18 Nov 1966
1c (cont.) Robert Antrobus *m* 2nd 3 Oct 1959 *Peggy, dau of Douglas Graham and widow of Donald Halley, and *d* 2 Oct 1961
2c +Henry Lindsay [Henry Antrobus Esq, PO Box 428 Umtentweni, Natal 4235]; *b* 17 June 1916; *educ* Witwatersrand U (Bsc Eng); WW II 1941– 45 as Lt SA Engr Corps; *m* 17 June 1943 *Mary Lammie, only child of Thomas Howie, of Wankie, Zimbabwe, and has issue:
1d +Ronald James; *b* 25 April 1950
1d *Rosemary Lindsay; *b* 10 July 1947
2d *Helen Kathleen; *b* 23 Oct 1951
3c +Dennis Ronald; *b* 11 Dec 1920; *educ* Witwaterstrand U (BSc Eng 1949); WW II 1940–45 in SA Engr Corp (POW); *m* 25 March 1950 *Audrey Eleanor, yr dau of William James McGill, of Rustenburg, SA, and has issue:
1d +Dennis Mark; *b* 18 Nov 1956
1d *Sally Elizabeth; *b* 22 Dec 1952
1c *Frances Joan; *b* 26 Dec 1912; *educ* Rhodes U Coll, S Africa (BSc 1933); WW II 1942–46 in S African Mily Nursing Serv
2c *Penelope Maude; *b* 31 May 1914; *m* Capt Charles Alexander, KOSB (*ka* Dardanelles 25 April 1915)
8b Charles Alexander; *b* 16 Dec 1880; Capt KOSB; *ka* Dardanelles 25 April 1915
9b Ronald Henry, MC, JP (Cheshire 1948), DL (1952); *b* 8 Nov 1891; *educ* Charterhouse; Lt-Col RA WW I (despatches three times) and WW II; High Sheriff Cheshire 1960, memb Cheshire Rivers Bd; *m* 24 Nov 1921 Muriel Kathleen (*d* 1980), est dau of Richard Henry Gosling, of Hawthorn Hill, Bracknell, Berks, by his wife Kathleen Maria Swinnerton, yr dau of Sir Henry Swinnerton Dyer, 10th Bt (*qv*), and widow of Capt Henry Miles Chetwynd-Stapleton (*see* CHETWYND, V) and *d* 1980, having had issue:
1c +John Ronald Lindsay [John Antrobus Esq, The School House, 18 School Lane, Eaton, nr Congleton, Cheshire, CW12 2NG]; *b* 12 June 1926; *educ* Eton, Magdalene Coll Cambridge (BA 1950, MA 1955) and Trin Coll Oxford; late Lt Duke of Wellington's Regt, Palestine 1947–48 as Lt 17th/21st Lancers, late Lt R Irish Hus; *m* 1st 16 Feb 1952 (*divorce* 1960) Ann, est dau of Cdr Denys Royds Brocklebank, RN, of Longbridge House, nr Warminster, Wilts] (*see* CRAWFORD and BALCARRES E), and has issue:
1d +Nigel John Lindsay [Nigel Antrobus Esq, Grey Wall, Ship St, E Grinstead, W Sussex]; *b* 19 March 1953; *educ* Michael Hall Sch, Forest Row, Sussex
2d +James Hugh Lindsay [Dr James Antrobus, 5 Beech Cliffe, Warwick CV34 5HY]; *b* 10 Nov 1954; *educ* Michael Hall Sch, Forest Row, Sussex, and London U (Charing Cross Hosp Med Sch) (BSc, MB, BS, FRCA); *m* 1983 *Elizabeth Anne, yr dau of Bryan Jarman Wright, of Norwich, Norfolk, and has issue:
1e +Philip Edward; *b* 1987
1e *Lucy Elizabeth; *b* 1989
1c (cont.) John Antrobus *m* 2nd 22 Nov 1961 (*divorce* 1966) Margaret Jane, only child of Dr J H Penman, of Eskbank, Mid-Lothian; *m* 3rd 26 Aug 1966 *Rochelle Christine, yr dau of Theodore William Candee, of Pasadena, California, USA, and by her has issue:
3d +Richard Henry Lindsay; *b* 5 June 1967; *educ* Keele U (BA 1991)
4d +Charles Edward Lindsay; *b* 11 July 1968; *educ* Brighton U (BEng 1997)
1d *Rosemary Caroline Lindsay; *b* 4 Sept 1969; *educ* Salford U (BA 1997)
2d *Jane Elizabeth Lindsay; *b* 18 Dec 1972
3d *Catherine Mary Lindsay; *b* 24 Jan 1975
5b Mabel Dorothy; *b* 21 Aug 1882; *m* 12 April 1918 Henry Lister Reade, son of Henry Lister Reade, of West Street, Congleton, Cheshire, and *d* 8 Oct 1942, leaving issue
(2) (cont.) Gibbs Antrobus *m* 2nd 12 Jan 1832 Hon Charlotte Crofton (*d* 29 Sept 1839), 2nd dau of Sir Edward Crofton, 2nd Bt, by Anne, Baroness Crofton in her own right (*see* CROFTON, B), and *d* 21 May 1861, having by her had issue:
1a Anna Maria; *m* 1864 Rev Francis Richard Bryans MA (*d* 1909), of Clevelands House, Babbacombe, Devon, er son of Rev Francis Bryans, MA, Vicar of Backford, Cheshire, and *d* 1915, leaving issue

ARBUTHNOT of Edinburgh

Arms: Azure, a crescent between three mullets, two and one, argent; the whole within a bordure or, charged with three boar's heads couped gules. **Crest:** A peacock's head proper. **Supporters:** Dexter, a wyvern vert vomiting flames; sinister, a greyhound argent, collared and line reflexed over the back gules. **Motto:** Innocent and true. **Creation:** Bt. (UK) 3 April 1823.

SIR KEITH ROBERT CHARLES ARBUTHNOT, 8TH BT, of Edinburgh [Sir Keith Arbuthnot Bt, Whitebridge, Peebles, Peeblesshire EH45 9HS]; *b* 23 Sept 1951; *s* f 1983; *educ* Wellington and Edinburgh U; *m* 22 May 1982 *Anne Rosemary, yr dau of Brig Peter Moore, of Hastings Hill House, Churchill, Oxon, and has issue:
1 +ROBERT HUGH PETER; *b* 2 March 1986
2 +Patrick William Martin; *b* 13 July 1987
1 *Alice Elizabeth Mary; *b* 22 March 1990

Lineage: ROBERT ARBUTHNOT, of Haddo, Aberdeenshire; *m* Mary, dau of John Urquhart, of Cromarty, and had:

Sir William Arbuthnot, 1st Bt (UK), so *cr* 24 Aug 1822 (patent 3 April 1823) on occasion of banquet given by the Magistrates and Town Cncl of Edinburgh in honour of GEORGE IV on his visit to Edinburgh; *b* 24 Dec 1766; Sec to the Bd of Tstees for Manufactures, Ld Provost Edinburgh 1822–23; *m* 13 Sept 1800 Anne (*d* 19 July 1846), dau of John Alves, of Shipland, and had, with other issue:
1 ROBERT KEITH (Sir), **2nd Bt**
2 John Alves, of Coworth Park, Old Windsor, Berks, JP; *b* 3 Oct 1802; *m* 2 June 1832 his cousin Mary (*b* 29 April 1812, *d* 30 March 1859), dau of George Arbuthnot, of Elderslie, Surrey, and *d* 29 Aug 1875, leaving issue:
(1) William, of The Ham Manor, Newbury, Berks, and formerly of Coworth Park, JP and DL (Berks); *b* 14 April 1833; *m* 1st 5 Jan 1858 Adolphine Eliza Macleod (*d* 12 Dec 1858), dau of Edward Lecot, French Consul Madras; *m* 2nd 12 July 1865 Margaret Rosa (*d* 11 May 1918), dau of John Campbell, of Kilberry, Argyllshire, and *d* 9 Feb 1896, having by her had issue:
1a Adolphine Mary; *m* 22 Dec 1897 Charles Edward Brownrigg (*d* 7 June 1942), 2nd s of Thomas Marcus Brownrigg, Assist Inspr-Gen RIC, and *d* 18 Dec 1904, having had a s (*d* an infant) and two daus,
2a Alice Marion; *m* 18 April 1900 Edward Herbert Fox (*d* 17 Oct 1928), of Adbury Park, Newbury, Hants, son of William Fox, of Adbury, Hants, and had issue
(2) George, of Norton Court, Glos, JP and DL (Herefordshire), JP (Glos); *b* 9 Jan 1836; Col late RA, MP Hereford 1871–74 and 1878–80; *m* 12 Oct 1870 Caroline Emma Nepean (*d* 16 March 1927), yst dau of Capt Andrew Nepean Aitchison, HEICS, and *d* 26 Dec 1912, leaving issue:

1a John Bernard, MVO (1902); *b* 17 May 1875; Maj late Scots Gds, S Africa 1900–01, WW I (despatches), KStJ; *m* 8 June 1903 Olive (*d* 12 Sept 1953), only dau of Sir Henry Arthur Blake, GCMG, and *d* 16 Sept 1950, leaving:

1b David George; *b* 7 April 1905; *educ* Eton and Corpus Christi Coll Cambridge (MA); CStJ, FZS, ADC to Govr-Gen S Africa 1941–42, Mil Censorship Cape Town 1942–45, Hon memb Discharged Soldiers & Demobilisation Ctee Cape Town 1945–48; *m* 1st 17 May 1933 (*divorce* 1946) Hon Elizabeth Dorothy Kemeys-Tynte, later 10th Baroness Wharton (*qv*), and *d* 14 Nov 1985, leaving issue

2b Terence John; *b* 8 Oct 1906; *educ* Eton; G/Capt RAF (ret), Mohmand ops 1933, NW Frontier 1935 (despatches), Waziristan 1936–37, WW II (despatches), Croix de Guerre, Offr Order of Leopold of Belgium, OStJ; *m* 20 April 1937 Karin Gunborg (*d* 19 June 1983), dau of Carl Adolph Sundgren, of Hudiksvall, Sweden, and *d* 31 Dec 1995, leaving:

1c +(John Sten) Robert (Robin) [Robin Arbuthnot Esq, Flat 6, 86 Redcliffe Gdns, London SW10]; *b* 3 Jan 1941; *educ* Sherborne and Architectural Assoc; *m* 1st 8 Oct 1971 (*divorce* 1982) Elizabeth Marjorie, dau of Baron Plumb (LP, *qv*); *m* 2nd 1984 *Swee Lien Ong, dau of Boon Bah Ong, of Petaling Jaya, W Malaysia, and by her has issue:

1d +James Robert Yu-Ming; *b* 24 Sept1984

1d *Jennifer Mei-Chen; *b* 21 Nov 1987

1c *Susan Christine [Mrs John Minchin, 354 Moyne Dve, West Vancouver, BC, Canada]; *b* 17 April 1939; *m* 23 Dec 1970 B John Minchin (*d* July 1987), 3rd son of Dr R L H Minchin, of Nelson, NZ, and has issue:

1d *Karen Christine; *b* 9 April1972

2d *Joanna Lesley; *b* 5 Jan 1975

2c *Diana Karin; *b* 8 June 1942; *m* 4 Feb 1963 *Geert Holger Sonderhoff, of 316 Stevens Dve, W Vancouver, Canada, son of Karl Sonderhoff, of Hamburg, Germany, and has issue:

1d *Terence Sven; *b* 17 Sept 1965

2d *Stefan Andrew; *b* 10 Sept 1967

3b Bernard Kieran Charles, DSC; *b* 8 Nov 1909; Cdr RN; *m* 15 April 1939 Rosemary Harold (*d* 1978), dau of Lt-Col Harold Thompson, DSO, Roy Scots Fus, and *d* 14 Sept 1975, leaving issue:

1c *Shirley; *b* 9 March 1949; *m* 2 May 1970 *Ormiston Gauvain Nigel Murray, of Myrtle Grove, Youghal, Co Cork, only son of Dr Ronald Ormiston Murray, of S Kensington, and has:

1d *Simon Peregrine Gauvain; *b* 2 Aug 1974

1d *Iona Louise Arbuthnot; *b* 1972

2c *Penelope Anne; *b* 23 Dec 1953; *m* 1983 *Michael Drake Stewart, of Stokestown, New Ross, Co Wexford, and has issue:

1d *Kerry Blake (a dau); *b* 1987

4b Richard Henry Myles, MBE; *b* 17 Aug 1911; *educ* Trin Coll Cambridge (BA); Maj Roy Signals, WW II (despatches); *m* 28 April 1939 *Marjorie Helen [Mrs Joseph van der Schrieck, 17 Hays Mews, London W1] (who *m* 2nd 15 Sept 1948 Joseph Richard van der Schrieck, son of Henry Egide van der Schrieck, of 42 Parklaan, Rotterdam), yr dau of Dr Ralph Miller, and *das* Italy 16 Oct 1943

1b (Irene) Joan Grace; *b* 1904; *d* 17 March 1997

2b *Patricia Evangeline Anne; *b* 1914; author: *The Years of the Week*; *m* 1st 10 Oct 1933 (*divorce* 1940) Arthur Cecil Byron, only s of Cecil Byron, and has had a deceased s; *m* 2nd 1940 Claud Cockburn, the jnlst (*d* 15 Dec 1981), of Brook Lodge, Youghal, Co Cork, s of Henry Cockburn, CB, and has:

1c *Alexander Claud; *b* 6 Jan 1941; *educ* Glenalmond and Keble Coll Oxford; writer; *m* 13 Dec 1968 (*divorce* 1973) Hon Emma Christina Tennant, er dau of 2nd Baron Glenconner (*qv*), and formerly wife of (a) Sebastian Yorke (*see* HARDWICKE, E) and (b) Christopher John Penrice Booker, and has:

1d *Daisy Alice; *b* 1969

2c *Andrew Myles; *b* 7 Jan 1947; *educ* Glenalmond and Worcester Coll Oxford; TV producer; *m* 1977 *Leslie Corkhill, dau of Christopher Redlich, of Hillsborough, California, and has:

1d *Chloe; *b* 1979

2d *Olivia; *b* 1984

3c *Patrick Oliver; *b* 5 March 1951; *educ* Glenalmond and Trin Coll Oxford; *m* 1981 *Janet, dau of Rt Rev Hugh William Montefiore, BD, Bp Birmingham, and has:

1d *Henry Claud; *b* 1982

2d *Alexander; *b* 1987

2a Hugh Archibald; *b* 4 Dec 1885; *m* 1917 (*divorce* 1928) Mabel Eleanor, dau of Henry Jackson, and *dsp* 28 Dec 1950

3a Ronald George Urquhart; *b* 8 Oct 1891; Lt 16th Lancers, attd RAF; *kas* flying 3 Dec 1918

1a Frances Muriel; *b* 22 Nov 1871; *m* 1st 6 July 1910 Stephen K I Brichta (*d* 19 Oct 1924; *m* 2nd 1929 Gilbert Amos Reeve, Indian Police, and *d* 7 Sept 1933

2a Dorothy Gertrude; *b* 20 Jan 1878; *m* 3 Feb 1904 Brig-Gen Hugh Frederick Bateman-Champain, CMG, late IA (*d* 7 Oct 1933), 2nd son of Col Sir John Bateman-Champain, KCMG, RE, and *d* 25 April 1958, leaving issue

3a Mary Christobel; *b* 12 Sept 1879; *m* 1st 23 Oct 1907 George Archibald Wallace Young, er son of Archibald Young, of Wellington House, Lancs, and had issue; *m* 2nd 3 June 1914 Capt Alexander Gifford Ludford-Astley, 14th Hus (*ka* 5 March 1917), yst son of Rev Benjamin Buckler Gifford Ludford-Astley JP, Rector of Cadeby, Leics, and had further issue; *m* 3rd 27 April 1922 Col Edgar James Bridges, MC, late 14th Hus (*d* 8 Jan 1960), son of John Henry Bridges, of Fedderate, Aberdeenshire, and The Court, Eastbourne

(3) Charles George; *b* 20 Oct 1846; a dir Bank of England, one of HM Lts City of London; *d* unm 27 Sept 1928

(4) Hugh Lyttelton; *b* 27 Sept 1851; *m* 1st 25 Sept 1879 Elizabeth Fountaine, MBE (1920) (*d* 21 April 1920), dau of Fountaine Walker, of Ness Castle, Inverness-shire, and had issue:

1a Henry Charles; *b* 1 May *d* 31 Aug 1894

1a (Alice) Maud; *b* 14 July 1880; *m* 15 Jan 1918 her cousin **Sir Dalrymple Arbuthnot, 5th Bt** (*qv*), and *d* 16 Oct 1969

(4) (cont.) Hugh Arbuthnot *m* 2nd 16 Sept 1922 Justine Henriette (*d* 14 March 1947), dau of Colin George Ross, of Gruinard, Ross-shire, and widow of Henry Robert Mansel Porter, of Birmingham, and *d* 28 Jan 1929

(1) Eliza; *d* young

(2) Gertrude; *d* young

(3) Anne; *d* unm 16 Aug 1909

(4) Mary; *d* unm 4 Oct 1930

(5) Florence; *d* unm 17 Jan 1932

(6) Jane; *d* 1891

(7) Alice Magdalen; *d* young 1869

3 George Clerk, of Mavisbank, Midlothian; *b* 7 Oct 1803; *m* 1st 7 Nov 1837 Agnes (*d* 12 March 1842), dau of John Rait, of Anniston, and has issue:

(1) Emily; *m* 27 Nov 1860 1st Baron Inverclyde (*d* 12 Feb 1901; *see* 1956 edn) and *d* 14 Feb 1901, leaving issue

3 (cont.) George Arbuthnot *m* 2nd 10 Jan 1845 Caroline (*d* 9 Aug 1911), yst dau of James Hay, of Collepriest, by Lady Mary Ramsay, 4th dau of 8th Earl of Dalhousie (*qv*), and *d* 21 Feb 1876, having by her had issue:

(1) George (Ven); *b* 24 May 1846; Archdeacon Coventry, Vicar Arundel and Stratford; *m* 19 Nov 1885 Margaret Evelyn (*d* 1 Dec 1951), dau of Very Rev Herbert Mortimer Luckock, Dean Lichfield, and *d* 9 Nov 1922

(2) Charles Ramsey; *b* 5 Feb 1850; Adml, ADC to HM; *m* 8 Jan 1880 Emily Caroline (*d* 5 Dec 1910), dau of R-Adml Charles Frederick Schomberg, and *d* 30 Sept 1913, leaving issue:

1a Geoffrey Schomberg (Sir), KCB (1942), DSO (1919); *b* 18 Jan 1885; Adml, Naval ADC to HM 1936, 4th Sea Ld Admlty and Ch of Supplies and Transport 1937, C-in-C E Indies Station 1941, WW I (despatches), Legion of Honour; *m* 22 Oct 1913 Jessie Marguerite (*d* 3 Aug 1947), 2nd dau of William Henderson, of Berkeley House, Frome, and *d* 4 Oct 1957, having had issue:

1b Peter Charles Reginald; *b* 10 Sept 1915; *educ* RNC Dartmouth; Lt RN WW II; *kas* 23 Dec 1941

2b Michael Geoffrey Henderson; *b* 28 Sept 1919; *educ* Stowe; Lt RNVR; *m* 24 April 1948 *(Nicole) Patricia [Mrs Michael Arbuthnot, 5 Egerton Place, London SW3 2EF], er dau of Lt-Col Richard Leslie Halliburton Collins, of Thurston House, Bury St Edmunds, and *d* 11 June 1967, leaving:

1c +Peter Geoffrey [Peter Arbuthnot Esq, 4 Gt Western Terrace, Glasgow GL2 0UP]; *b* 18 Sept 1950; *educ* Stowe and Trin Coll Cambridge; *m* 1 Dec 1979 *Belinda, er dau of Herbert Terry-Engell, of Guernsey, CI, and has issue:

1d +James Nicholas; *b* 5 Nov 1982

1d *Harriet Emily; *b* 2 May 1984

1b *Mary Marguerite [Mrs Walter Clough-Taylor, Marvins, Kingston Deverill, Warminster, Wilts]; *b* 12 Aug 1914; *m* 24 Sept 1934 Lt-Col Walter Stuart Clough-Taylor RWF (*d* 1988), yr s of Lt-Col Edward Harrison Clough-Taylor, by Lady Mary, dau of 5th Earl Castle Stewart (*qv*), and has:

1c *Juliet Mary [Mrs Colin Paul, Yew Tree Cottage, Halland, Lewes, Sussex, BN8 6PW]; *b* 3 Feb 1935; *m* 1st 27 May 1961 (*divorce*) Timothy Charles Austin Horn, of Bickton Mill, Fordingbridge, Hants, son of Gp/Capt Charles Horn, RAF, and has issue:

1d *Francis William Austin; *b* 24 Oct 1962

1d *Charlotte Mary; *b* 29 Nov 1965

1c (cont.) *Mrs Juliet Horn *m* 2nd 1978 *Colin Malcolm Paul

1a Evelyn Mary, OBE (1920); *m* 24 April 1924 Septimus Tristram Preun (*d* 19 Feb 1936), and *d* 25 March 1939

2a Beatrice Caroline; *m* 21 April 1906 Capt Robert Henry Ramsay Mackay, OBE, JP, RN (*d* 18 Aug 1954), son of Henry Ramsay Mackay, of Petham House, Canterbury, and *d* 8 July 1953, leaving issue

(3) James; *b* 21 July 1855; *m* 1st 22 April 1879 (*divorce* 1896) Mary Steward, dau of Capt RN Taylor, and had issue:

1a (George) Ramsay; *b* 28 June 1880; *educ* Glenalmond; *m* in Hull 22 April 1910 Rose Anna Branson (*d* 1973), and *d* 27 Nov 1932, leaving issue:

1b +George Ramsay [George Arbuthnot Esq, 56 Wimborne Cl, Midmere Ave, Bransholme by Hull, Yorks]; *b* 20 Nov 1930; *m* 11 Feb 1950 *Sheelah Margaret Inchbold, and has issue:

1c +Graham Stewart; *b* 9 Oct 1952; *educ* Salthouse High Sch

1c *Glynis Kathleen; *b* 18 March 1954; *m* 7 Jan 1977 (*divorce* 1988) John Campbell, son of Gilbert Campbell, and has issue:

1d *Jamie John; *b* 1980

1d *Zöe; *b* 1978

2c *Colleen; *b* 7 Oct 1964; *m* 1984 *Philip Dolan, and has issue:

1d *Kelly Arbuthnot; *b* 1986

2d *Lynsey Caroline Arbuthnot; *b* 1988

3c *Alison Georgina; *b* 18 Feb 1967

1b *May; *b* 1911; *m* 29 Jan 1930 John (Jack) Pilling, and had issue:

1c *John

2c *George

3c *Reginald

1c *Shirley

2b *Ruby Molly [Mrs Reginald Mullet, 17 Pitman Ave, Barton-on-Humber, Lincs]; *b* 5 May 1912; *m* 1941 Reginald Mullet

3b *Ivy [Mrs Norman Chilvers, 52 Graham Ave, Hull, Yorks]; *b* 17 Nov 1913; *m* 17 July 1931 (William Charles) Norman Chilvers, and has issue:

1c *Raymond Dennis; *b* 7 Dec 1932; *d* 1994

2c *David; *b* 16 Dec 1937

3c *Michael Charles; *b* 8 Jan 1949

4c *Charles Aorderey; *b* 27 Dec 1952

5c *Malcolm Roy; *b* 11 Sept 1954

1c *Betty Doreen; *b* 29 May 1934
2c *Joyce; *b* 14 Aug 1936
3c *Joan Mary; *b* 7 Dec 1944
4c *Audrey Lynn; *b* 1952
4b Frances Noel; *b* 25 Dec 1914; *m* 3 March 1935 Sidney Jenner, and had issue:
1c *Sidney; *b* 20 Feb 1936
1c *Sandra; *b* 26 Aug 1946
2c *Susan; *b* 13 Nov 1951
5b *Queenie Steward [Mrs Lesley Fox, 7 Snowhill Close, Bransholme by Hull, Yorks]; *b* 21 July 1923; *m* 7 Sept 1941 *Lesley Fox, having issue:
1c *Norman; *b* 28 March 1942
2c *Raymond *b* 18 June 1948
1c *Sylvia; *b* 1 May 1953
2a Charles Gwynne (Guy); *b* 21 May 1881; *d* 7 July 1881
3a Francis Clemente; *b* Feb 1883; *d* unm 1905
(3) (cont.) James Arbuthnot *m* 2nd 22 Oct 1897 Mary Margaret (*dsp* 26 Aug 1905), only dau of Lowry Mann, of Earleston, Cheshire, and *d* 16 April 1913
4 Archibald Francis; *b* 8 Jan 1805; *m* 12 Dec 1837 Hon Gertrude Sophia (*d* 21 Nov 1882), dau of Field Marshal 1st Viscount Gough (*qv*), and *d* 31 March 1879, having had issue:
(1) William, CB; *b* 27 Sept 1838; Maj-Gen late 14th Hus, AAG Horse Gds 1885–92; *m* 1st 26 April 1865 Hon Alice Charlotte (*k* by lightning 21 June 1865), 4th dau of 4th Baron Rivers (*see* 1880 edn); *m* 2nd 20 July 1869 Selina (*d* 26 Nov 1877), 7th dau of Sir Thomas Moncreiffe of that Ilk, 7th Bt (*see* ERROLL, E), and by her had issue:
1a Gerald Archibald; *b* 19 Dec 1872; 2nd Lt Gren Gds, late Lt RNVR, in RN 1886–92; MP Burnley Jan-Dec 1910, Assist Priv Sec to Pres Bd of Ag 1895–99, Assist Priv Sec to Pres Local Govt Bd 1901–02, Assist Priv Sec to Ch Sec Ireland 1905–06; Vice-Chllr Primrose League 1912; *m* 6 Feb 1894 (Mary Johanna Antoinette) Dulcie (*d* 24 Nov 1945), yr dau of Charles Oppenheim, and was *ka* 25 Sept 1916, leaving issue:
1b Frances Gertrude; *m* 23 March 1918 (*annulled* 1921) Kenneth Lindsay Stewart, son of William Lindsay Stewart, of Stanmore, Lanarks, and *d* 28 April 1938
2b *Cynthia Isabelle Theresa; *m* 27 July 1925 (*divorce* 1941) Stephen Ian Fairbairn (*d* 5 Dec 1968), yr son of Stephen Fairbairn, of 38 Gt Cumberland Place, London W, and has had issue:
1c Jerome Stephen Gerald; *b* 27 Feb 1933; *d* 4 June 1945
1c Jennifer Selina; *b* 8 Dec 1927; *m* 6 Oct 1949 *5th Baron Manners (*qv*), and *d* May 1996, leaving issue
3b Dorothea Helen Mary; *m* 10 Aug 1927 Hubert Hawkes Woodward, of 89 Peel St, London W8, son of John Hawkes Woodward, of Quorn, Leics, and *d* 12 Jan 1942
(1) (cont.) Maj-Gen William Arbuthnot *m* 3rd 2 Dec 1879 Edith Anne (*m* 2nd 1 Aug 1894 Guy, Count de Miremont (*d* 21 Jan 1928), and had issue (*see* ERROLL, E), and *d* 21 Aug 1931), dau of Maj-Gen J L Pearse, and *d* 12 Sept 1893
(2) Hugh Gough; *b* 29 Jan 1840; one of HM Lts City of London; *m* 9 June 1864 Caroline (*d* 15 March 1927), yst dau of Rev Capel Molyneux (*see* 1939 edn MOLYNEUX, Bt), and *d* 1 June 1905, leaving issue:
1a Lionel Gough, MBE (1919); *b* 24 Sept 1867; Capt Lancashire Fus, Order White Eagle Serbia 5th Cl; *m* 1st 18 April 1894 (*divorce* 1913) Violet Rebecca (*d* 11 Nov 1951), yst dau of Sir John Henry Morris, KCSI, of S Kensington; *m* 2nd 9 June 1927 Ada Ellen (*d* 15 March 1963), dau of Lt-Col H M G Brunker, The Cameronians, and widow of James Thomas Sydenham, and *d* 16 May 1942
2a Capel Robert; *b* 27 Nov 1868; *d* Jan 1870
1a Constance Gertrude; *m* 25 Jan 1900 Ernest Luxmoore Marshall, of 1 Prince's Court, First Ave, Hove, Sussex, son of F Marshall, late of the Court of Stannaries of Cornwall, and *d* 21 Nov 1929
(2) Archibald Ernest, of Westfield Meadow, Hayling Island; *b* 5 Jan 1841; Maj late 8th Madras Light Cav; *m* 14 Nov 1872 Anne Elizabeth (*d* 13 May 1922), dau of W W Ball, of Cape Town, and widow of Surgn-Maj Alexander Russell Atkinson, Bengal Army, and *d* 11 May 1923, leaving issue:
1a Archibald Hugh; *b* 7 Dec 1875; Lt-Col late 7th Gurkha Rifles, IA, WW I, cmded Field Force Persian Frontier 1913–14, Naga Hills 1916, received thanks of Govts of India, E Bengal and Asam, 3rd Afgan War 1919, invalided from Zhob Valley Field Force 1922; *m* 1st 25 Feb 1900 Gertrude Alice (*d* 11 Nov 1918), est dau of Rev Frederick Charles Green, Vicar of Denmead, Hants, and had issue:
1b Archibald Hugh Gough; *b* 12 Nov 1900; Lt-Cdr RN, WWs I and II; *m* 1st 2 July 1935 (*divorce* 1954) Molly Irene Frances, dau of Arthur William Weeks; *m* 2nd 18 Feb 1955 (Emma) Mary (*d* 26 Sept 1994), dau of Rev Gilbert Ambrose Bell, of Stowupland, nr Stowmarket, Suffolk, and *d* 2 Jan 1959, leaving by her:
1c *Viola Jane; *b* 30 Oct 1957
2b Patrick Charles; *b* 26 Nov 1902; *educ* Haileybury; Maj IARO, WW II Middle East (despatches), late tea-planter in N Bengal; *m* 15 Oct 1952 *Evelyn Margaret [Mrs Patrick Arbuthnot, Quay Head, Sampford Peverell, Tiverton, Devon, EX16 7BS], dau of George Robert Crawford, of Leamington, Warwicks, formerly of Cartington, Northumberland, and *d* 27 March 1988, leaving:
1c +Patrick Hugh Alexander [Patrick Arbuthnot Esq, 41 Merivale Sq, Oxford OX2 6QX]; *b* 28 Dec 1954; *educ* Blundell's and Sidney Sussex Coll Cambridge; *m* 5 Sept 1986 *Susan Elizabeth, dau of John Frederick Shaw, of Auckland, NZ, and has issue:
1d +Charles Alexander; *b* 4 Feb1990
2d +Robert Hugh; *b* 14 Oct 1991
1d *Roseanna Louise; *b* 30 Aug 1997
2c +Colin Hugh David; *b* 7 Sept 1957; *educ* Blundell's and Sidney Sussex Coll, Cambridge (MA, MS, PhD Cantab)
3b Ernest Douglas; *b* 15 Sept 1905; *educ* Blundell's and Balliol Coll Oxford; Political Offr Abyssinian Frontier WW II; *m* 15 April 1939 *(Eveline) Mary, dau of Harold Morgan, of Worksop, Notts, and *d* 1984, leaving issue:
1c +Antony Hugh Gough [Antony Arbuthnot Esq, Runham, Norfolk]; *b* 5 Oct 1948; *educ* Blundell's; *m* 1974 Frances, dau of S/Ldr F W Williamson, of Garveston, Norfolk, and has issue:
1d +Rupert; *b* 14 Nov 1981
1d *Emily Kate; *b* 29 Sept 1977
2c +Robin Douglas; *b* 17 Oct 1951; *educ* Blundell's; *m* 1979 *Elizabeth Anne, dau of F C Palmer, of Yarmouth, Norfolk, and has issue:
1d *Kitty Anne; *b* 16 May 1980
2d *Amy Elizabeth; *b* 23 May 1984
1c *Ann Faith; *b* 8 Dec 1941; JP, BA, MB, BS, MRC (Psych); *m* 1966 *Raymond Barker, and has issue:
1d *Kate Abigail; *b* 1973
2d *Lucy Grace; *b* 1975
1b *Sheila Gertrude Tollemache [Mrs Roy Dunlop, Meadow Cottage, Aldingbourne, nr Chichester, W Sussex]; *b* 1917; WW II as Subaltern ATS; *m* 9 April 1942 *Maj Roy Dunlop, MBE, Derbyshire Yeo, son of Robert Dunlop, slr, of Falkland Mansions, Glasgow, and has issue:
1c *Robert Andrew [Robert Dunlop Esq, Alding Farm, Aldingbourne, W Sussex]; *b* 19 March 1948; *educ* Tonbridge; *m* 1985 *Catherine Jennifer Ewart and has:
1d *Robert James; *b* 1987
2d *Archibald Montgomery; *b* 1994
1d *Letitia Annabel; *b* 1989
1c *Caroline Jane; *b* 11 Oct 1944; *m* 1973 *James Lawrence Monro, MB, BS, FRCS, of Rolle House, East Tytherley, nr Salisbury, Wilts, and has issue:
1d *Charles Reed; *b* 1975
2d *Andrew James; *b* 1981
1d *Rosanne Elspeth; *b* 1978
2c *Elspeth Marilyn [Miss Elspeth Dunlop, Meadow Cottage, Aldingbourne, Chichester]; *b* 19 Oct 1951; MB, BS, DA, DRCOG
1a (cont.) Lt-Col Archibald Arbuthnot *m* 2nd 2 Feb 1920 Marjory (*d* 1975), dau of Rev Howard Beech, Rector Barlavington and Burton with Coates, Sussex, and *d* 3 Jan 1957, having by her had:
2b *Faith Deborah Etrenne [Mrs Edmund Grattan, Quoins, Pound Place, Petworth, W Sussex]; *b* 1 Jan 1921; WW II as Subaltern ATS; *m* 14 June 1948 Edmund (O'Donnel) Colley Grattan, FRCS, Colonial Med Serv, Kenya (*d* 1985), son of Colley Edmund George Hume Grattan, of Tyrconnel Lodge, Canford Cliffs, Dorset, and has issue:
1c *Howard Colley Arnout Hugh; *b* 13 May 1949; *educ* Wellington
2c *Clive Edmund Hume [Clive Hume Esq, Downham Lodge Farmhouse, Barnham Broom Rd, Wymondham, Norfolk]; *b* 22 July 1953; *educ* Wellington and King's Coll Cambridge; MRCP; *m* 1980 *Diana Mary, dau of Lt-Cdr William John Prowse, RN, and has issue:
1d *Amanda Mary Winifred; *b* 1983
2d *Harriet Lucy; *b* 1988
3d *Abigail Frances; *b* 1991
4d *Claudia Etrenne; *b* 1994
1c *Sarah Faith Madalyn [Mrs Ian Mackie, Beggearn Huish Manor, Beggearn Huish, Somerset]; *b* 18 Aug 1950; *m* 1981 *Ian Charles Mackie, ARICS, and has issue:
1d *Alistair Graham; *b* 1983
2d *Neil Edmund; *b* 1986
3d *Ewan James Stuart; *b* and *d* 1988
4d *Edward James Stephen; *b* 1991
2c *Clare Winifred Melissa; *b* 7 Aug 1956
2a Ernest Kennaway, DSO (1917); *b* 3 Sept 1876; Capt RN WW I (despatches four times, promotion); Ch Constable Oxfordshire from 1921, had Roy Humane Soc's bronze medal and Order St Maurice and St Lazarus of Italy; *m* 1st 1 June 1910 Edith Elizabeth (Evie Greene, the actress) (*d* 11 Sept 1917), dau of Richard Bentley Greene, of Southsea; *m* 2nd 15 Jan 1920 Gladys (*d* 10 May 1946), dau of William Butland Mann, of Broadhampstead, S Devon, and *d* 12 June 1945, having had by her:
1b +John Keith, OBE (1967) [Lt-Cdr John Arbuthnot OBE RN, 11 Ivory St, Ipswich, Suffolk IP1 3QP]; *b* 15 Aug 1927; Lt-Cdr RN (ret 1967), WW II, Korea 1951 and 1954, cmded: HMS *Santon* 1957–58, HMS *Dartington* 1958–59, Naval Staff Coll 1959, Naval Staff 1960–61, Ch Exec Malta-Gozo Air Services (ret 1992); *m* 2 July 1949 *Susan Philippa, only dau of Kenneth Petrie Letts, of Tickerage Mill, Blackboys, Sussex, by Mrs John Stephen Giles Eyre, of Garde, Wych Cross, Sussex, and has:
1c +Richard Keith [Richard Arbuthnot Esq, 87 Haverhill Rd, London SW12]; *b* 1 Oct 1950; *educ* Earnley Sch, Chichester; *m* 1st 14 Jan 1978 (*divorce* 1980) Jacqueline Hazel, dau of George William White; *m* 2nd 4 Aug 1984 (*divorce* 1991) Anne L Pitman *m* 3rd 27 June 1997 *Samaita Sharma
2c +Charles Petrie [Charles Arbuthnot Esq, 76 Constable Rd, Ipswich, Suffolk IP4 2UL]; *b* 25 Nov 1959; *m* Penelope Jane, only dau of J F J Dickinson, of Kirby-le-Stoken, Essex, and has
1d *Emily Jane; *b* 6 March 1997
1c *Sally Anne; *b* 19 March 1954; *m* 1st 18 July 1972 (*divorce* 1978) Richard Drumbell-Howie; *m* 2nd 17 Sept 1983 Brian Bovey (*d* April 1994)
2c (Philippa) Jane; *b* 8 Oct 1961; WPC, Chelsea Police Station; *k* in IRA bomb attack on Harrods 17 Dec 1983
2b +Peter Kennaway [Peter Arbuthnot Esq, Winstons, Fieldgate Close, Monks Gate, Horsham, Sussex]; *b* 21 Sept 1930; Lt RN (ret), Korea 1952; *m* 11 May 1957 *Mia, est dau of Maj Percy Montague Nevile, of Skelbrooke, nr Doncaster, and has issue:

1c +Matthew Kennaway; *b* 18 Aug 1959
2b (cont.) Pete Arbuthnot adopted:
*Katherine Jane; *b* 14 Oct 1964; *m* 1987 *Keith Robert Howe, of 12 Rushwood Cl, Haywards Heath, W Sussex, yst son of F J Howe, of Newcastle-upon-Tyne
*Emma Mary; *b* 1 July 1966; *m* 26 Sept 1992 *Nigel S Dent, of Beeding, son of C R Dent, of Steyning
3a William Patrick; *b* 28 April 1878; Col RM, WW I with 4th Cruiser Sqdn and 1st Battle Sqdn, Instr in Naval Gunnery; *m* 30 June 1904 Olive (*d* 5 April 1957), only dau of Hon William Gregory Walker, late Justice Supreme Court, New South Wales, and *d* 12 Aug 1949, leaving issue:
1b Olive Joan; *b* 2 April 1905; *m* 28 July 1926 Lt-Col Charles Walter Adair, RM, of Maen House, Burton Bradstock, Dorset, er son of V-Adml Charles Henry Adair, of Hendon, Southampton, and *d* 27 May 1979, leaving issue:
1c *Arbuthnot James; *b* 11 June 1931; *educ* Trin Coll Glenalmond; Maj RA (Army Air Corps); *m* 10 Jan 1959 *Gillian Marjorie, only dau of Herbert Mettam, of The White House, Pirbright Rd, Farnborough, Hants, and has issue:
1d *William Henry; *b* 28 Dec 1961
1d *Catherine Elizabeth; *b* 6 April 1960
2c *Patrick Charles Hugh; *b* 6 June 1942; *educ* Nautical Coll Pangbourne; *m* 1968 *Gloria Rosalind Ogston and has:
1d *Andrew Patrick; *b* 1970
2d *James William; *b* 1975
1c *Anthea Arbuthnot [Mrs John D'Aeth, 41 Roy Hosp Sch, Ipswich, Suffolk]; *b* 28 Aug 1928; *m* 11 Oct 1959 *Rev John Echlin D'Aeth, yr son of Walter Lionel D'Aeth, of BC, Canada, and has issue:
1d *Jack Theodore; *b* 4 Sept 1959
1d *Sybil Mary; *b* 8 Dec 1961
2b *Patricia Gwyn; *b* 27 March 1906; *m* 17 Sept 1931 Henry Bartle Frere (*d* 1977), only son of Sir Bartle Henry Temple Frere, of Mangreen Hall, Norwich, Norfolk, and has had issue:
1c Bartle Henry Arbuthnot; *b* 27 Nov 1937; *d* 1 July 1941
1c *(Henrietta) Julia Arbuthnot [Miss Julia Adair, Halfway House, Scoulton, nr Norwich, Norfolk; Broad Farm, South Walsham]; *b* 22 May 1942
1a Editha Gertrude; *b* 1874; *m* 30 July 1903 Basil Stephenson (*d* 1950), yst son of Thomas Stanley Stephenson, formerly of Kobe, Japan, and *d* 18 Nov 1964, aged 91, leaving issue
(4) Robert George; *b* 20 May 1843; barrister; *m* 22 Dec 1885 Helen Mary (*d* 20 June 1926), dau of Sir William Muir, KCSI, DCL, Pncpl Edinburgh U, and *d* 19 March 1890, leaving issue:
1a Robert Wemyss Muir, MC (1918); *b* 25 July 1889; *educ* Eton and Trin Coll Cambridge (BA 1910); Capt RFA (SR) WW I (wounded twice, Croix de Guerre); *m* 3 July 1915 Mary (*d* 1986), est dau of Norman Coghill, of Almington Hall, Market Drayton, and *d* 10 Jan 1962, leaving issue:
1b +Andrew Robert Coghill (Rev) [The Rev Andrew Arbuthnot, Monksfield House, Tilford, Farnham, Surrey]; *b* 14 Jan 1926; *educ* Eton; Capt late Scots Gds, WW II 1944–45 (wounded), chm Arbuthnot Latham Holdings Ltd 1974–81, dir Sun Alliance and London Ins 1970–91, ordained a priest 1975; *m* 9 Aug 1952 *Mrs Audrey Eileen Dutton-Barker, only dau of Denys Billinghurst Johnson, MC, of Midhurst, Sussex, and has issue:
1c +Charles Robert Denys [Charles Arbuthnot Esq, 17 Frewin Rd, London SW18 3LR]; *b* 12 June 1956; *educ* Eton and Cambridge (MA); *m* 1985 *Jennifer Rosemary, dau of C T Arden-White, of Wormley, Surrey, and has issue:
1d +Alexander Barnabas David; *b* 1993
1d *Kezia Louise; *b* 1987
2d *Johanna Rachel; *b* June 1989
1c *Caroline Rose; *b* 16 April 1954; *m* 1st 1977 (*divorce* 1988) Paul J Francis Clusker and has:
1d *Rowan; *b* 7 June 1978
1d *Jade; *b* 29 Aug 1980
2d *Sacha; *b* 1984
1c (cont.) Mrs Caroline Clusker *m* 2nd 1988 *Andrew Gueter, and by him has:
2d *Christian; *b* 1986
3d *Samuel; *b* 1990
1b *Juliet Mary Gough [Mrs Guy Halsey, Whitehouse Farm, Gaddesden Row, nr Hemel Hempstead, Herts HP2 6HG]; *b* 2 April 1917; *m* 23 Sept 1939 Lt-Col Guy Marsden Halsey, (*see* HALSEY, Bt), and has issue:
1c *Nicholas Guy, TD DL (Herts 1998) [Maj Nicholas Halsey TD DL, The Golden Parsonage, Gaddesden Row, Hemel Hempstead, Herts HP2 6HG]; *b* 14 June 1948; *educ* Eton and RAC Cirencester; Maj RGJ (V); FRICS; High Sheriff Herts 1995; *m* 7 Aug 1976 *Viola Georgina Juliet, dau of Maj George Thorne, MC, DL, ERD (*see* PEEL, E), and has:
1d *Guy Francis Johnston; *b* 1981
2c *Robert Frederick; *b* 1950; *educ* Eton and RAC Cirencester; FCA; *m* 1976 *Elizabeth Virginia, dau of John Holman, and has issue:
1d *Daniel John; *b* 1978
2d *Samuel Treve; *b* 1983
2b *Elizabeth Christian; *b* 4 Dec 1918; *m* 7 Oct 1943 *S/Ldr Frank Ernest Cameron Cox, RAFVR, of The Jolly Sailors Inn, Brancaster Staithe, Norfolk, son of Ernest Henry Cameron Cox, of 20 Belvedere Court, London SW15, and has issue:
1c *Oliver Robert Frank; *b* 16 Sept 1945; *educ* Eton; *m* 19– *Victoria — and has:
1d *Alexander Francis; *b* 24 June 1980
1d *Antonia; *b* 1981
2c *Christopher Peter; *b* 27 Nov 1946; *educ* Eton; *m* 19– *Sylvie, dau of Jean Escaude, and has:
1d *Gregory Pierre; *b* 1970
2d *Ludovic; *b* 1972
1c *Virginia Frances Elizabeth; *b* 20 May 1949
1a Jean Marjorie; *m* 3 June 1913 Maj Arthur Frederick Dudgeon, OBE (*d* 12 Aug 1959), yr son of Ellis Frederick Dudgeon, of Gogar Bank, Midlothian, by his wife Emily Augusta, 2nd dau of Joseph John Henley, CB, JP, DL, of Waterperry, Oxon, and had issue:
1b John Arbuthnot; *b* 6 Nov 1919; *educ* Winchester; *d* 19–
1b Emily Mary; *b* 25 March 1914; *d* 24 Nov 1978
2b *Elizabeth Arbuthnot [Mrs Gregor Grant, The Manor Hse, Ronmorkie, Ross-shire]; *b* 4 April 1915; *m* 19 Nov 1936 Gregor James Grant, MC, KAR, yst s of John Peter Grant of Rothiemurchus, and has:
1c *James MacAlpine Gregor, TD [Maj James Grant TD, Roskill House, Munlochy, Ross-shire IV8 8PA]; *b* 18 Feb 1938; *educ* Eton and RAC Cirencester (MRAC); NDA, memb Roy Co Archers; *m* 29 July 1967 *Sara Marjory, yr dau of Brig William Alexander MacKenzie of Gairloch, DSO, OBE, and has issue:
1d *Annabel Elizabeth; *b* 24 July 1968
2d *Clare Marjory; *b* 16 Sept 1970; *m* 23 Sept 1995 *Rupert Lumsden, Yr of Banchory and has issue
3d *Lucy Sara; *b* 21 Dec 1975
2c *Andrew Arthur Gregor [Andrew Grant Esq, 30 Halford Rd, London SW6]; *b* 9 Jan 1948; *educ* Eton and Trin Coll Oxford; *m* 19– *Clare, dau of Cdr Robert Phillimore, (*see* PHILLIMORE, B) and has:
1d *Angus; *b* 1978
2d *Alexander; *b* 19–
1d *Hannah; *b* 1981
3c *Hamish Duncan Gregor; *b* 13 June 1958; *m* 19– Vanessa — (*d* 1997)
1c *Elspeth Jean; *b* 25 Jan 1940; *educ* Edinburgh U (MA); *m* 24 July 1964 *William Galloway Miller Ritchie, of 50 Ormidale Terrace, Edinburgh 12, only son of Dr William Miller Ritchie, of Bonhill, Bishopton Rd, Stockton-on-Tees, and has issue:
1d *Nicholas William; *b* April 1966
1d *Hermione Elizabeth; *b* 5 May 1968
2c *Victoria Mary [Miss Victoria Grant, 108 Cranmer Ct, Sloane Ave, London SW3]; *b* 1 Aug 1941; *educ* Edinburgh (MSAOT)
3c *Fiona Marjorie; *b* 24 April 1943; *m* 26 Feb 1968 *Frederick George Blackwood, of Gogar, Rongai, Kenya, and has issue:
1d *Arthur Frederick; *b* 9 Oct 1968
4c *Julia Emily; *b* 10 July 1950
3b *Jean Arbuthnot; *b* 4 April 1915; *m* 20 Nov 1937 Power Maurice Anderson, of Grassymead, Botley, Southampton SO3 2BR, and has issue:
1c *Jeremy Dudgeon; *b* 29 April 1941; *educ* Charterhouse and Edinburgh U (BSc Eng); *m* 15 June 1968 *Jill Ellis
2c *Keith Maurice; *b* 25 March 1943; *educ* Charterhouse
3c *Alastair Maurice; *b* 7 Aug 1950; *educ* Charterhouse
4c *Colin Dudgeon; *b* 7 Aug 1950; *educ* Charterhouse
1c *Priscilla Jean; *b* 4 March 1947
2a Elizabeth Gertrude Gough; *b* 25 July 1889 (twin with Robert); *d* unm 11 Nov 1976
(5) George Gough (Sir); *b* 28 Aug 1847; MLC Madras and Chm Madras Chamber of Commerce; *m* 9 Sept 1873 Isabella (*d* 25 Aug 1929), dau of Rev Hon Richard Cavendish Boyle (*see* CORK and ORRERY, E), and *d* 3 May 1929, leaving issue:
1a Cecilia Albinia; *m* 10 Oct 1903 Lt-Col Hon Robert Lygon, MVO, late Gren Gds (*d* 13 Jan 1952), 3rd son of 6th Earl Beauchamp (*see* 1970 edn), and *d* 19 March 1956, leaving issue
(1) Frances; *m* 27 Nov 1866 Rt Hon Sir John Henry Kennaway, 3rd Bt, PC, CB (*qv*), and *d* 23 Oct 1922, leaving issue
(2) Anne Gertrude Grace; *d* unm 9 Feb 1912
5 James Edward (Hon), of Bon Air, Mauritius; *b* 12 Jan 1809; *m* June 1837 Harriet Frances (*d* 11 March 1910), dau of Gen William Staveley, CB, and *d* 29 Sept 1868, leaving issue:
(1) George Ireland; *b* 1847; *m* 1876 May Cumming (*d* 18 Sept 1915), dau of D Munro, and *d* 24 March 1900, leaving issue:
1a Alister Dare Staveley; *b* 11 July 1881; Capt RE (3rd Sappers and Miners), WW I (wounded); *ka* 8 March 1916
1a Frances Ella; *d* unm 18 Sept 1957
2a Madeline Winifred Louise Ogilvy; *m* 17 April 1912 Col Norman Doncaster Noble, DSO, RE (*d* 21 Sept 1955), yst son of Col C S Noble, late IA, and *d* 3 March 1963, leaving issue
(1) Mary Rose; *m* 1st 1856 Clinton Francis Berens Dawkins (*d* 24 Aug 1859), 3rd son of Col Henry Dawkins, of Overn Norton, Oxon; *m* 2nd 23 Dec 1861 Charles Edmund Banks, Sec to the Cncl of Mauritius
(2) Anne; *m* 21 May 1862 Edward Douglas, and *d* 26 Jan 1937, leaving issue (*see* QUEENSBERRY, M)
(3) Harriet Gertrude; *d* unm 12 March 1939
(4) Louisa FitzGerald L'Estrange; *d* unm 15 March 1947
(5) Emily Frederica; *m* Feb 1879 Walter Fox Williamson Wells, late ICS (*d* 24 Nov 1928), and *d* 3 Feb 1929, leaving issue
(6) Charlotte Elizabeth; *m* 1896 Cdr Frederick George Loring, RN, and *d* 7 Oct 1933, leaving issue
(7) Frances Henrietta; *d* unm 23 June 1926

Sir WILLIAM *d* 18 Sept 18–; his est son,

Sir Robert Keith Arbuthnot, 2nd Bt; *b* 9 Sept 1801; *m* 20 March 1828 Anne (*d* 6 March 1882), yr dau of Field-Marshal Sir John Forster FitzGerald, GCB, and had, with other issue:
1 WILLIAM WEDDERBURN (Sir), **3rd Bt**

2 Robert Keith (Rev); *b* 10 Aug 1838; Vicar of St James's, Ratcliffe, London, E; *m* 17 June 1868 Mary Agnes (*d* 14 March 1908), dau of Rev Canon Edward T Vaughan, Canon of St Albans, late Rector of Harpenden, and *d* 5 Dec 1894, leaving issue:

(1) Robert Edward Vaughan, CSI (1922); *b* 15 Jan 1871; ICS, Commr of Settlements and Land Records Burma 1915–19, Fin Commr Burma 1919, additional memb Govr-Gen's Leg Cncl; *m* 19 April 1899 Ethel Mary (*d* 30 Sept 1965, aged 101), dau of Maj Charles Wyndham, late 9th Bengal Cav, and *d* 22 Oct 1922, leaving issue:

1a Elynth Mary Arbuthnot; *b* 1 Feb 1900; *m* 9 June 1924 Ferrante 9th Count Capponi, V-Adml Italian Navy (*d* 29 April 1965), er s of Piero, 8th Count Capponi, of Palazzo Capponi, Florence, and *d* 27 Jan 1977, leaving:

1b *Neri Piero Roberto 10th Count Capponi [Count Capponi, 36 Via dei Bardi, Florence 50125, Italy]; *b* 5 Sept 1925; Judge (Ecclesiastical) Tuscan Tribunal; *m* 16 April 1958 *Flavia, yr dau of Romano Lodi-Fé, Min Plen, of Rome, and has:

1c *Nicolo Piero; *b* 20 March 1961

2c *Piero Zanobi; *b* 13 July 1965

3c *Sebastiano Marca; *b* 29 March 1971; *m* 24 June 1995 *Ginerva, only dau of Count Giulinelli, of Ferrara, and has:

1d *Buonamico Maria; *b* 7 May 1995

2d *Ferrante Maria; *b* 6 March 1997

1c *Tessa Elena; *b* 3 March 1959; *m* 26 June 1985 *Jakub Borawski, only s of Ludwik Borawski, of Warsaw, and has:

1d *Zygmunt Maria; *b* 26 Aug 1987

1d* Cosima Maria; *b* 11 April 1986

2d *Flavia Maria; *b* 3 May 1989

1b *Diamante Tessa Luisa; *b* 7 Aug 1927; *m* 1st 20 June 1949 (*divorce* 1971) Marchese Agostino Cornaggia-Medici, of Florence, and has:

1c *Beatrice; *b* 26 Feb 1950; *m* 9 Sept 1972 *Marchese Rolando Roveereto di Rivanazzano and has:

1d *Marco; *b* 17 Oct 1977

1d *Flavia; *b* 26 Feb 1975

2c *Ilaria; *b* 12 July 1954; *m* 4 Oct 1973 *Angiolo Logi and has:

1d *Lorenzo; *b* 8 Jan 1986

1b (cont.) Marchesa Diamante Cornaggia-Medici *m* 2nd 18 Jan 1986 *Richard Lawrence Westinghouse

(2) Henry FitzGerald; *b* 16 July 1873; Dep Conservator Indian Forestry Serv, Madras; *m* 31 Dec 1900 Ivy (*d* 10 March 1959), dau of John W Minchin, of Clovelly, Ootacamund, Madras, and *d* 26 May 1917, having had issue:

1a +Hugh FitzGerald; *b* 13 Oct 1903; *educ* St Edward's Sch Oxford; *m* 6 Sept 1928 *Kathleen Phyllis (Peggy) (*d* 1982), only dau of Reginald Walter Sheppard, of Looe, and *d* 1990, having had issue:

1b Robert Ian FitzGerald (Robin); *b* 8 Oct 1933; *educ* Haileybury; 2nd Lt Roy Warwicks Regt; *d* of gunshot wounds while serving in Korea, 25 Dec 1953

2b +Patrick Stephen FitzGerald; *b* 24 May 1936; *educ* Haileybury; *m* 14 Oct 1967 *Jennifer Anne, dau of Sidney George Roe, of 43 Claygate Rd, London W13, and has issue:

1c +Simon Charles FitzGerald; *b* 10 Feb 1969

1b *Rosemary Elizabeth FitzGerald; *b* 27 Oct 1930; *educ* Headington Sch Oxford and Bristol U (BA 1952); *m* 19 Jan 1957 *William Allen Humpherson, FRCO, BDS, LRAM, of The White Cottage, Somerset Rd, Reigate, Surrey, son of Victor William Humpherson, of Tanglewood, Rowant, Sussex, and has issue:

1c *Robert William; *b* 3 March 1958

2c *Michael Hugh; *b* 27 July 1962

3c *Edward Allen; *b* 1970

1c *Susan Linley; *b* 21 May 1960

1a Julia Mary Agnes; *b* 16 Dec 1901; *d* 16 May 1909

2a *Madeline Ivy [Mrs Geoffrey Teed, The Halt, 2 Lowercroft, Fairford, Glos]; *b* 26 April 1908; *m* 2 June 1928 Geoffrey Wilmot Teed (*d* 1989), son of Harry Williamson Teed, of Cranbourne, Bromley Common, Kent, and has:

1b *Christopher Litherland [Christopher Teed Esq, 18 Delves Wood Rd, Beaumont Park, Huddersfield, Yorks]; *b* 21 Feb 1933; *educ* Tonbridge; *m* 7 Jan 1978 *Mary Rose, dau of Alan Edward Hearn, of Harold Wood, Essex, and widow of Arthur Tilbrook

2b *Hugh Arbuthnot [Hugh Teed Esq, 65 Fisherton St, Salisbury, Wilts SP22 7SU]; *b* 17 April 1936; *educ* St George's, Harpenden; *m* 30 April 1966 *Marjorie Gillian, BA, only dau of Charles Theodore Law-Green, of Bradford, Yorks, slr and notary public, and has issue:

1c *Jane Arbuthnot; *b* 25 April 1970

2c *Caroline Green; [Mrs Jeremy Strutt, 8 Kings Rd, Cowplain, Waterlooville, Hants]; *b* 9 June 1972; *m* 28 June 1997 *Jeremy David Strutt, est s of Roger Anthony Strutt, of Ferring, W Sussex

1b *Ruth Sinclair [Mrs Derek Hale, Glade House, 54 Weir Rd, Kibworth, Beauchamp, Leics LE8 0LP; *b* 1 Oct 1930; *educ* St Thomas's Hosp (MDSP 1952); *m* 6 March 1954 Derek Hale, AMPOH, s of Harry Hale, of Blackpool, and has:

1c *Jonathan Wilmot [Jonathan Hale Esq, Brandywell, Queens Sq, Chalford Hill, Glos]; *b* 17 July 1964; *m* 1993 *Gaynor, dau of E R Astin, LLB of Budleigh Salterton, and has:

1d *Victoria Madeline; *b* 1997

1c *Christine Morley; *b* 13 May 1956; *m* 1984 *Michael Andrew Hollis, of 36 Fleckney Rd, Kibworth Beauchamp, Leics, and has issue:

1d *Nicholas Elkin; *b* 1987

2d *Matthew Jonathon; *b* 1990

1d *Sarah Morley; *b* 1986

2c *Deborah Sinclair; *b* 2 March 1959; has issue by John Martin Stew:

1d *Edward Christopher; *b* 1992

2b *Aurea Wilmot [Mrs Christoper Hart, 38 High St, Marshfield, Chippenham, Wilts]; *b* 8 Feb 1943; *educ* St Paul's Sch; *m* 28 Dec 1968 *Christopher James Collier Hart, only son of James Joseph Collier Hart, of Frampton Cotterell, Bristol, and has issue:

1c *Barnaby Teed; *b* 27 June 1975

1c *Alexandra Prinz; *b* 21 Oct 1972

3a Katherine Rose; *b* 18 Sept 1913; *m* 30 Dec 1943 Robert Theodore Gladstone (*d* 25 April 1962), son of Samuel Henry Gladstone, of Darley Ash, Bovingdon, Herts, and *d* 8 Feb 1980

(3) Hugh Keith; *b* 20 July 1874; Lt RN; *d* unm 16 Feb 1903

(1) Geraldine Mary; *b* 1 May 1869; *m* 3 Sept 1896 Henry Edward Hamill Stewart, son of John Hamill Stewart, of Fulwood Park, Cheltenham, and *d* 11 July 1956, leaving issue

(2) Constance Margaret; *b* 3 March 1879; *m* 23 April 1913 Lt-Col Robert Denbigh Keyworth, late 52nd Oxf and Bucks LI (*d* 15 May 1956), son of Maj Charles Keyworth, 52nd LI, and *d* 18 Oct 1949, leaving issue

Sir ROBERT *d* 4 March 1873; his est son,

Sir William Wedderburn Arbuthnot, 3rd Bt; *b* 22 Aug 1831; Maj 18th Hus; *m* 11 June 1863 Alice Margaret (*d* 5 May 1889), 4th dau of Rev Matthew Carrier Tompson, Rural Dean and Vicar of Alderminster, Worcs, and *d* 5 June 1889, leaving:

1 **Sir Robert Keith Arbuthnot, 4th Bt**, KCB (posthumous 1916, CB 1916), MVO (1904); *b* 23 March 1864; entered RN 1877, Sub-Lt 1883, Lt 1885, Cdr 1897, Capt 1902, Cdre 1910–12, R-Adml 1912, ADC to HM GEORGE V 1911–12, R-Adml cmdg 9th Cruiser Sqdn 1913, 2nd Battle Sqdn 1913–14, cmdg 1st Cruiser Sqdn 1915–16; *m* 11 Dec 1897 Lina (*d* 29 May 1935), dau of Col Alexander Caldcleugh Macleay, CB, and was *ka* Battle of Jutland 31 May 1916, leaving:

(1) Rosalind Desirée; *b* 28 Feb 1906; *m* 29 May 1926 Anthony John Anson, er son of Hon Claud Anson, and had issue (*see* LICHFIELD, E)

2 DALRYMPLE (Sir), **5th Bt**

3 Reginald Ramsay; *b* 25 April 1869; Capt Roy Irish Regt; *dsp* of wounds red in action S Africa 3 Sept 1900

4 William FitzGerald; *b* 29 Oct 1875; *educ* Eton; Maj 3rd Bn Seaforth Highrs WW I; OStJ; *d* unm 12 Dec 1955

1 Aline Henriette; *d* unm 13 Feb 1913

The 4th Bt's brother,

Sir Dalrymple Arbuthnot, 5th Bt, CMG (1915), DSO (1915), JP (Salop); *b* 1 April 1867; Col late RFA, Hon Brig-Gen 1920, Chitral 1895 (medal with clasp), S African War 189901902 (despatches, two medals, five clasps), WW I (despatches eight times, Brevet), cmded 12th Corps 1916, WW II (CD), had Order St Maurice and St Lazarus of Italy; *m* 15 Jan 1918 his cousin (Alice) Maud (*d* 16 Oct 1969), only dau of Hugh Lyttelton Arbuthnot, of 26 Cadogan Sq, London SW (*see* above), and *d* 31 March 1941, leaving:

1 **Sir Robert Dalrymple Arbuthnot, 6th Bt**; *b* 4 July 1919; *educ* Eton and Magdalene Coll Cambridge; Maj 24th Lancers WW II; *ka* Normandy 30 June 1944

2 **Sir Hugh FitzGerald Arbuthnot, 7th Bt**; *b* 2 Jan 1922; *educ* Eton; Capt Welsh Gds WW II; MFH Ludlow 1948–52, Cotswold 1952–64, Duke of Buccleuch's 1964–83; *m* 1st 17 Aug 1949 Elizabeth Kathleen (*d* 20 May 1972), er dau of S/Ldr George Gilbert Algernon Williams, of Currall Hall, Tenbury Wells, Worcs, and had:

(1) Sir KEITH ROBERT CHARLES ARBUTHNOT, **8th and present Bt**

(2) +David William Patrick; *b* 7 March 1953; *educ* Wellington; *m* 1988 *Diane, only dau of John Yeomans, of Hill House, Baughurst, Hants, and has:

1a *Phoebe Elizabeth; *b* 1988

2a *Rosanna Mary; *b* 1989

(1) *Christian Aline [Mrs John Morley, Mount Ulston, Jedburgh, Roxburghshire]; *b* 6 July 1950; *m* 1973 *(Geoffrey) John Morley (*see* HOOD, V) and has:

1a *William Everard Hugh; *b* 1980

1a *Aline Elizabeth Georgina; *b* 1974

2a *Emily Alice; *b* 1977

2 (cont.) **Sir Hugh** *m* 2nd 1977 *Julia Grace, only dau of Lt-Col Frederick Gerard Peake, CMG, CBE, of Hawkslee, St Boswells, Roxburghshire, and formerly wife of — Grant, and *d* 3 July 1983

ARBUTHNOT of Kittybrewster

Arms: Azure a crescent between three mullets argent, a bordure gules charged with two escallops in chief and a buck's head cabossed or in base, and in centre chief (overlapping bordure) an inescutcheon argent. **Crest:** A peacock's head and neck proper, accompanied on either side by a spray of strawberry leaves vert, each flowered of a cinquefoil argent. **Motto:** *Deum laudans* ('Praising God'). **Creation:** Bt. (UK) 26 Feb 1964.

SIR WILLIAM REIERSON ARBUTHNOT, 2ND BT, of Kittybrewster, Aberdeen [Sir William Arbuthnot Bt, 37 Cathcart Rd, London SW10 9JG]; *b* 2 Sept 1950; *educ* Eton and Coll of Law London; *s f* 1992; with Arbuthnot Latham Hldgs 1970–76, Joynson-Hicks & Co 1978–81, underwriting memb Lloyd's 1972–, Cncl of Lloyd's 1998–, dep-chm High Premium Gp 1994–; div ALM Ltd 1997–, Liveryman Grocers' Co

Lineage: GEORGE ARBUTHNOT, of Elderslie, Surrey, and Madras, JP; *b* 4 Dec 1772 (yr bro of Sir William Arbuthnot, 1st Bt, of Edinburgh; *qv*); *m* 26 April 1810 Elizabeth (*d* 29 Sept 1834), dau of Donald Fraser, and *d* 3 Nov 1843, leaving a 5th s:

WILLIAM REIERSON ARBUTHNOT, of Plawhatch, Sussex; *b* 28 Jan 1826; MLC Madras, chm Bank of Madras and Madras Chamber Commerce; *m* 9 Dec 1858 Mary Helen (*d* 21 May 1912), er dau of Philip Anstruther, Colonial Sec Ceylon (*see* ANSTRUTHER, Bt), and *d* 31 May 1913, having had issue:

1 George Anstruther; *b* 27 March 1860; *d* 15 Jan 1861

2 Philip Stewart Mackenzie; *b* 27 March 1863; settled S Africa 1920, Hon Sec Highland Soc London; *m* 11 Dec 1906 Ada Jane (*d* 14 Oct 1946), est dau of William John Evelyn, JP, DL, of Wotton, Surrey, and *d* 16 June 1936, leaving issue:

(1) Mary Evelyn; *b* 14 Aug 1907; *d* 1 Jan 1995

3 Keith Fraser; *b* 27 May 1864; *m* 1899 Mabel Constance Elizabeth, dau of Gen David Robertson, and *d* 31 Oct 1914, leaving issue:

(1) Joyce Frances, OBE; *b* 1 Aug 1902; *m* 15 Dec 1931 Capt Ivan Beale Colvin, RN (*d* 12 Oct 1962), only s of Lt-Col Cecil Hodgson Colvin, CB, DSO, and *d* Sept 1983, leaving issue

4 William Reierson; *b* 15 Dec 1866; *educ* Eton; Chm Standard Bank S Africa, ptnr Arbuthnot, Latham & Co London; *m* 5 Dec 1907 Mabel (*d* 6 March 1947), only dau of Francis Henry Slade, of New York, and *d* 23 June 1938, leaving issue:

(1) Helen Marion; *b* 27 Sept 1910; *d* 2 Jan 1981

(2) Caroline Elizabeth Mabel; *b* 10 Aug 1912; *m* 23 March 1944 Ralph Ernest Watkins Grubb, of Mayes House, nr E Grinstead, Sussex, (*d* 14 March 1996), s of Rev Ernest Watkins Grubb, of Shepherdswell Vicarage, nr Dover, and *d* 6 Dec 1989 leaving issue

5 Harold Denison, of Merristwood, Worplesdon, and Field Place, Compton, Surrey; *b* 15 Sept 1868; *educ* Eton; *m* 28 April 1898 Annie Grace (*d* 10 May 1956), dau of Charles Edward Lambert, of The Manor House, Effingham, Surrey, and *d* 5 Jan 1944, having had issue:

(1) Clive Denison, Capt RN WWs I and II; *b* 1 Aug 1900; *m* 15 April 1935 Pansy (*d* 16 Feb 1983), dau of Charles Grey Howick Davis, Auditor-Gen Jamaica, and *d* 15 Feb 1965, leaving:

1a *David Charles Denison; *b* 20 June 1938; *educ* Shrewsbury; Welsh Gds; *m* 1st Dec 1959 (*divorce* 1963) Rosemary, dau of George Richmond, and has issue:

1b *Katherine; *b* 8 Nov 1960

1a (cont.) David Arbuthnot *m* 2nd 16 March 1967 *Felicity Anne Clarendon-Hyde

1a *Vania Joy [Mrs Peter Oxley, Queen Camel Hse, nr Yeovil, Somerset BA22 7NF]; *b* 6 Dec 1936; *m* 3 Feb 1959 *Peter John Reginald Oxley, only s of Lt-Col Richard George Reginald Oxley, of Queen Camel, Somerset, and has issue:

1b *Stephen David Richard; *b* 23 Nov 1959

2b *Timothy Peter Charles; *b* 13 May 1962

1b *Rachel Mary; *b* 23 Dec 1966

(2) David Denison; *b* 14 Oct 1906; *d* 4 March 1915

(1) Thelma Grace; *b* 3 Oct 1911; *m* 1st 8 Oct 1932 (*divorce* 1950) Somerset Struben de Chair, yr s of Adml Sir Dudley Rawson Stratford de Chair, KCB, KCMG, MVO, of Wentworth, Surrey, and had issue; *m* 2nd 20 Oct 1960 Sir Jocelyn Morton Lucas, 4th Bt (*qv*), and *d* 23 Jan 1974

6 KENNETH WYNDHAM, for whom *see* below

7 Andrew Carmichael, of Sinah Warren, Hayling Island, Hants, and Woodlands, Chiddingfold, Surrey; *b* 6 Aug 1877; *educ* Charterhouse; *m* 19 June 1911 Jessie Evelyn (*d* 2 Jan 1951), dau of Charles Edward Lambert, of The Manor House, Effingham, Surrey, and *d* 1 July 1953, leaving issue:

(1) (Evelyn Helen) Anne; *b* 23 June 1912; *m* 19 Dec 1942 *Brig Henry Beveridge Latham, of Wimbledon, yr s of Thomas Ringrose Latham, of Toorak, Melbourne, Australia, and *d* 25 Aug 1986, leaving issue

(2) (Ursula) Bridget; *b* 10 May 1914; *m* (*divorce*) Norman Jenkins and *d* 19–

8 Malcolm Alexander, OBE (1919); *b* 23 Sept 1878; *educ* Trin Coll Cambridge; WW I as Maj Seaforth Highrs (wounded); *m* 8 Jan 1906 Florence Jessie (*d* 30 Dec 1973), dau of Gen George Saunders Theophilus Boileau, of Goulburn, NSW, and *dsp* Jan 1956

WILLIAM ARBUTHNOT's 6th son,

KENNETH WYNDHAM ARBUTHNOT; *b* 23 July 1873; Maj Seaforth Highrs, Relief Force Chitral Campaign 1895, Nile Expedition 1898, Battle of Khartoum, Boer War 1900–02 (despatches), Brevet Maj 1902, Adj 4th Vol Bn 1907–08, Bde-Maj Gordon Inf Bde (Scottish Cmd) 1911–14, WW I; *m* 26 April 1911 Janet Elspeth, est dau of Maj Robert Dunbar Sinclair-Wemyss, Gordon Highrs, of Wedderburn Castle, Duns, Berwickshire, and was *ka* 2nd Battle Ypres 25 April 1915, leaving issue (with a yr s Robert Michael Wemyss; *b* 9 March 1914; *educ* Eton and Trin Coll Cambridge; *d* unm 29 Aug 1946):

Sir John Sinclair-Wemyss Arbuthnot, 1st Bt (UK), so *cr* 26 Feb 1964, of Poulton Manor, Ash, Kent, MBE (1944), TD (1951); *b* 11 Feb 1912; *educ* Eton and Trin Coll Cambridge (BA 1933, MA 1938); Maj RA WW II, TARO 1948–62; MP (C) Dover 1950–64; PPS Min Pensions 1952–55 and Health 1956–57, memb Public Accounts Ctee 1955–64, Chm Ctees and T/Chm H of C 1958–64, Parly Chm Dock and Harbour Authorities Assoc 1961–64, memb House of Laity Ch Assembly 1955–75, a Church Commr England 1962–77, Tstee Lambeth Palace Library 1964–77, 2nd Ch Estates Commr 1962–64; Chm Estates and Agency Hldgs, Dir Ecclesiastical Insur Office, Underwriting Memb Lloyd's, Jt Hon Sec Assoc Br Chambers Commerce 1953–59, V-Pres TSB Assoc 1962–76, Dir Folkestone and Dist Water Co; *m* 3 July 1943 *(Margaret) Jean [Lady Arbuthnot, 7 Fairholt St, London SW7 1EG], yr dau of (Alexander) Gordon Duff, of Folkestone, Kent, and *d* 13 June 1992, leaving:

1 Sir WILLIAM REIERSON ARBUTHNOT **2nd and present Bt**

2 +JAMES NORWICH, PC (1998) [Rt Hon James Arbuthnot Esq PC MP, House of Commons, London SW1 0AA]; *b* 4 Aug 1952; heir presumptive; *educ* Eton and Trin Coll Cambridge (MA); barrister Inner Temple 1975 and Lincoln's Inn 1977; MP (C) Wanstead and Woodford 1987–97, and NE Hants 1997–, PPS to: Min State Armed Forces 1988–90, Sec of State DTI 1990–92, Assist Govt Whip 1992–94, Parly Under-Sec State DSS 1994–95, Min State Def Procurement 1995–97, Oppn Chief Whip 1997–; *m* 1984 *Emma Louise, dau of (John) Michael Broadbent, and has issue:

(1) +Alexander Broadbent; *b* 1 May 1986

(1) *Katherine Rose Joste; *b* 14 July 1989

(2) *Eleanor Sophie Duff; *b* 11 Aug 1992

1 *Elizabeth Mary [Miss Elizabeth Arbuthnott, 3 Edith Grove, London SW10 0JZ]; *b* 27 May 1947; *educ* St Mary's Sch Calne and Kent U (BA)

2 *Louise Victoria [Mrs David Lancaster, Beech House, Ramsdell, Hants RG26 5PR]; *b* 26 Oct 1954; *educ* St Mary's Sch Calne and Exeter U (LLB); slr; *m* 1984 *David Bernard Lancaster, slr, only s of Maj Bernard Thomas Lancaster, of Salisbury, Wilts, and has issue:

(1) *Rachel Alice; *b* 18 March 1985

(2) *Rebecca Saskia; *b* 12 June 1987

(3) *Tamara Louise; *b* 16 Nov 1988

3 *Alison Jane [Miss Alison Arbuthnot, 18 Clonmel Rd, London SW6 5BJ]; *b* 9 April 1957; *educ* Benenden and New Hall Cambridge (BA); slr

ARBUTHNOTT

Arms: Azure, a crescent between three mullets argent. **Crest:** A peacock's head couped proper, beaked or. **Supporters:** Two wyverns, wings expanded, tails nowed vert, spouting fire proper. **Motto:** *Laus Deo* ('Praise be to God'). **Creations:** L. and V. (S) 16 Nov 1641.

THE 16TH VISCOUNT OF ARBUTHNOTT and **Lord Inverbervie** (Sir John Campbell Arbuthnott, KT (1996), CBE (1986), DSC (1945)) [The Rt Hon The Viscount of Arbuthnott KT CBE DSC, Arbuthnott House, by Laurencekirk, Kincardineshire AB30 1PA]; *b* 26 Oct 1924; *s* f 1966; *educ* Fettes and Gonville and Caius Coll Cambridge (BA 1949, MA 1967); WW II in RNVR (FAA), FRICS, FLAS, FRSE, LLD, Ag Land Serv Min of Ag 1949–55, Sr Land Agent Nature Conservancy in Scotland 1955–67, memb Countryside Commn Scotland 1968–71, Chm Red Deer Conservancy 1969–75, Pres Scottish Landowners Fedn 1974–79, Ld-Lt Grampian Region (Kincardineshire) 1977–, Prior OStJ Scotland 1983–95 (OStJ 1972); *m* 3 Sept 1949 *Mary Elizabeth Darley, er dau of Cdr Christopher Bernard Oxley, DSC, RN, of Morley, Herts, and has:

1+(JOHN) KEITH OXLEY, *Master of Arbuthnott* [The Master of Arbuthnott, Kilternan, Arbuthnott, Kincardineshire AB3 1NA]; *b* 18 July 1950; *educ* Fettes and N Scotland Coll of Ag Aberdeen (Higher Nat Dip, Dip Farm Business, Organisation and Management); *m* 19 Jan 1974 *Jill Mary, er dau of Capt Colin Farquharson, of Whitehouse, Alford, Aberdeenshire, and has:

(1) +Christopher Keith; *b* 29 July 1977

(1) *Clare Anne; *b* 24 June 1974

(2) *Rachel Sarah; *b* 24 Aug 1979

1 *Susanna Mary [The Hon Mrs Smith, Warren Farm House, Finmere, Bucks]; *b* 1 May 1954; *educ* Overstone Sch Northants and Dorset House Sch of Occupational Therapy Oxford (MBAOT); *m* 27 May 1978 *Hugh Turnbull Bradbridge Smith, yr son of Lewis Smith, of Darnlee, Melrose, Roxburghshire, and has:

(1) *Andrew Keith Turnbull; *b* 21 Feb 1981

(1) *Emma Charlotte; *b* 7 Sept 1983

Lineage: HUGH de SWINTON, feudal Ld of Aberbothenoth/Arbuthnott, in the Mearns, which he acquired from Walter Olifard/Oliphant, whose predecessor, Osbert/Olifard, described as a Crusader, had been granted them by the Crown; allegedly *m* —, dau of the said Osbert, and had:

DUNCAN de ABERBOTHENOTH; *b* by 1206; *d* in or after 20 March 1238; had an er s:

HUGH de ABERBOTHENOTH; *d* in or after 20 March 1238, leaving:

HUGH de ABERBOTHENOTH; *d* in or after 2 Aug 1282, leaving:

DUNCAN de ABERBOTHENOTH; *d* 13 Dec 1314, having had, with a dau (*m* Straiton of Lauriston):

DUNCAN de ARBUTHNOTT; *b* by *c* 1330; *d* in or after 15 Dec 1368, leaving:

HUGH de ARBUTHNOTT; *d c* 1355, leaving:

PHILIP de ARBUTHNOTT; of age by 25 April 1355; had a new charter of his lands from Douglas, Lord of Galloway and Bothwell, 25 Oct 1372; *m* 1st Janet, dau of Sir William Keith, Marschal Scotland (*see* KINTORE, E), and had two daus; *m* 2nd Margaret, dau of Sir James Douglas of Dalkeith (*see* MORTON, E,) and by her had, with a dau (Margaret, *m* 24 Feb 1410 Sir William Monypenny, yr s of Thomas Monypenny of Pitmilly):

HUGH ARBUTHNOTT OF THAT ILK; of age by 26 May 1404; *m* Margaret (*d* 1419), dau of Sir Robert Keith, Great Marischal of Scotland, and *d* on or after 13 March 1446), leaving, with a dau (Margaret, *m* Andrew Menzies, Provost Aberdeen):

ROBERT ARBUTHNOTT OF THAT ILK; *m* Giles Ogilvy and *d* 1450, having had, with five yr sons and and a dau:

DAVID ARBUTHNOTT OF THAT ILK; *m* Elizabeth Durham (*d* 1488), of Grange, and *d* 1470, having had, with a yr s and four daus:

ROBERT ARBUTHNOTT OF THAT ILK; had a charter of the lands of Portatown, Kincardine, Feb 1487/8 and Arduthie 20 Oct 1488, MP (S Parl) 1487 and 1491; *m* 1st Margaret, dau of James Wishart of Pitarrow, and had a s (*d* young); *m* 2nd (contract 10 Sept 1475) Mariot (*d* 1518), dau of Sir James Scrymgeour of Dudhope (*see* DUNDEE, E), and *d c* 1506, having by her had, with three yr sons and seven daus:

JAMES ARBUTHNOTT OF THAT ILK; *m* (contract 31 Aug 1507) Janet, dau of John Stewart, Earl of Atholl (*see* MORAY, E), and *d* on or after 7 March 1521, having had, with two yr sons and a dau:

ROBERT ARBUTHNOTT OF THAT ILK; *m* 1st (contract 2 March 1526) Katherine (*dsps* 15 June 1529), dau of John Erskine of Dun; *m* 2nd Christian (will dated 12 July 1553), dau of Robert, Lord Keith, s of 2nd Earl Marischal (*see* KINTORE, E), and by her had four sons and four daus; *m* 3rd by 13 April 1558 Helen, dau of George Clephane of Carslogie, and *d* by 18 Oct 1579, having by her had, with three yr sons and four daus:

ANDREW ARBUTHNOTT OF THAT ILK; *m* 1st (contract 7 Aug 1553) Elizabeth (*d* 28 Oct 1563), dau of Robert Carnegie of Kinnaird (*see* FIFE, D); *m* 2nd by 24 Nov 1575 Margaret Hoppringil and *d* 16 March 1606, leaving by his 1st w, with other issue, including an er s (Sir Robert of that Ilk, MP Kincardineshire 1621, *m* (contract 21 June 1582) Lady Mary Keith (*dsp* 11 March 1619/20), dau of 4th Earl Marischal (*see* KINTORE, E), but having no issue, got a Crown regrant 9 Jan 1616 erecting all the estates into the free Barony of Arbuthnott in favour of his nephew Robert, and *dsp* Sept 1631):

JAMES ARBUTHNOTT of Arrat; *m* (contract 24 Nov 1590) Margaret (*m* 2nd David Carnegie of Balmachie), dau of John Livingstone of Dunipace, and *d* 1606, having had:

Sir ROBERT ARBUTHNOTT OF THAT ILK; *m* 1st (contract 23 Dec 1615) Lady Margaret Keith (*dsp*), dau of 5th Earl Marischal (*see* KINTORE, E); *m* 2nd (contract 29 April 1617) Margaret (*m* 2nd 1653 Sir James Haldane of Gleneagles), dau of 6th Lord (Fraser of) Lovat (*qv*), and *d* 15 March 1633, having by her had, with three yr sons and three daus:

ROBERT ARBUTHNOTT, **1st Viscount of Arbuthnott**, so *cr* 16 Nov 1641, as also LORD INVERBERVIE (both S); *m* 1st *c* 1639 Marjory (*d* 22 Dec 1651), 4th dau of 1st Earl of Southesk (*see* FIFE, D) and widow of William Hallburton of Pictur, and had a s and dau (Margaret, *m c* 22 April 1659 Sir John Forbes, 3rd Bt, of Monymusk; *see* STUART-FORBES, Bt); *m* 2nd 30 June 1653 Catherine (*m* 3rd 1660 3rd Lord Fraser (*see* SALTOUN, L) and *d* 18 Oct 1663), 3rd dau of 7th Lord (Fraser of) Lovat (*qv*) and widow of Sir John Sinclair of Dunbeath, and *d* 10 Oct 1655, having by her had a further s and dau; his s by his 1st w:

ROBERT ARBUTHNOTT, **2nd Viscount of Arbuthnott**; *m* 1st (contract 25 March 1658) Lady Elizabeth Keith (*d* Feb 1664), dau of 8th Earl Marischal (*see* KINTORE, E), and by her had:

1 ROBERT ARBUTHNOTT, **3rd Viscount of Arbuthnott**; *bapt* 8 Oct 1661; *m* 3 May 1683 Anne (*d* June 1695), dau of 14th Earl of Sutherland (*qv*), and *d* Aug 1694, leaving, with other issue:

(1) ROBERT ARBUTHNOTT, **4th Viscount of Arbuthnott**; *bapt* 24 Nov 1686; *d* unm 8 May 1710

(2) JOHN ARBUTHNOTT, **5th Viscount of Arbuthnott**; *m* 1710 Jean, dau of William Morrison, of Preston Grange, Haddington, but *dsp* 8 May 1756

1 Margaret; *m* 1677 Sir Thomas Burnett, 3rd Bt, of Leys (*see* SETON, Bt, of Pitmedden), and had issue

The **2nd Viscount** *m* 2nd (contract 30 July 1667) Catherine (*m* 2nd (contract 29 Oct 1684) Sir David Carnegie of Pitarrow, 1st Bt, ancestor of Earl of Southesk (*see* FIFE, D), and *d* 4 Nov 1692), dau of Robert Gordon of Pitlurg, and *d* 16 June 1682, having by her had, with other issue:

2 John, of Fordoun; *m* (contract 30 May 1695) Margaret, dau of Sir James Falconer of Phesdo, a Ld of Session, and was *bur* 10 Jan 1737, having had, with other issue:

(1) James; banker in Edinburgh; *d* unm Aug 1727

(2) JOHN ARBUTHNOTT, **6th Viscount of Arbuthnott**; *m* 1st (contract 16 April 1740) Mary (*dspms*), dau and coheir of Robert Douglas, of Bridgeford; *m* 2nd (contract 4 July 1749) Jean (*d* 18 March 1786), dau of Alexander Arbuthnot of Findowrie, and *d* 20 April 1791, leaving an est surv s:

1a JOHN ARBUTHNOTT, **7th Viscount of Arbuthnott**; *bapt* 25 Feb 1754; *m* 27 Dec 1775 Isabella (*d* 4 March 1818), 2nd dau of William Graham of Morphie, Kincardineshire, and *d* 27 Feb 1800, leaving issue

The 7th VISCOUNT's est s,

JOHN ARBUTHNOTT, **8th Viscount of Arbuthnott**; *b* 16 Jan 1778; Ld Lt Kincardineshire, rep S peer 1818–20 and 1821–47; *m* 25 June 1805 Margaret (*d* 12 Dec 1870), sis of 6th Earl of Airlie (*qv*), and *d* 10 Jan 1860, leaving, with other issue:

1 JOHN ARBUTHNOTT, **9th Viscount of Arbuthnott**; *b* 4 June 1806; *m* 5 June 1837 Lady Jean Graham Drummond Ogilvy (*d* 4 March 1902), est dau of 6th Earl of Airlie (*qv*), and *d* 26 May 1891, having had, with other issue:

(1) JOHN ARBUTHNOTT, **10th Viscount of Arbuthnott**; DL (Kincardineshire); *b* 20 July 1843; Lt 49th Foot; *m* 20 April 1871 Anna Harriet (*d* 23 April 1892), only dau of Edmund Allen, of Inchmartin, Perthshire, and *dsp* 30 Nov 1895

(2) DAVID ARBUTHNOTT, **11th Viscount of Arbuthnott**; *b* 29 Jan 1845; *d* unm 24 May 1914

(3) WILLIAM ARBUTHNOTT, **12th Viscount of Arbuthnott**; *b* 24 Oct 1849; *d* unm 8 Nov 1917

2 Walter, of Hatton, near Montrose; *b* 21 Nov 1808; Capt 52nd LI; *m* 16 May 1835 Anna Maria (*d* 17 March 1891), yst dau of Brook Taylor Ottley, of Delaford, Co Dublin, and *d* 5 Jan 1891, leaving, with other issue:

(1) WALTER CHARLES WARNER ARBUTHNOTT, **13th Viscount of Arbuthnott**; *b* 22 Oct 1847; Lt-Col (ret) RA, Afghan War 1880; *m* 15 Jan 1878 Emma Marion Hall (*d* 27 Jan 1930), dau of Rev John Hall Parlby, JP, of Manaton, Devon, and *d* 9 Aug 1920, having had issue:

1a Walter St John Mayne; *b* 30 Sept, *d* Nov 1880

2a JOHN OGILVY ARBUTHNOTT, **14th Viscount of Arbuthnott**; *b* 15 Sept 1882; rep S peer 1944–55, enlisted Calgary Light Horse Canadian Army Feb 1917, Lt late Welsh Gds; Ld Lt Kincardineshire, Convenor Kincardineshire CC, Pres Kincardine TA Assoc; Silver Jubilee Medal (1935), Coronation Medals 1937 and 1953; memb Scottish Advsy Air Cncl Bd; *m* 6 June

1914 *Dorothy, OBE (1951 (Silver Jubilee and Coronation Medals), yst dau of Adml Charles Lister Oxley, of The Hall, Ripon, York, and *dsp* 17 Oct 1960

3a Hugh Robin Claud; *b* 12 Sept 1884; Capt late 5th Bn Black Watch, WW I (1914 medal); *m* 4 Sept 1915 Katherine Alice (*d* 20 Sept 1962), dau of William Tindall Lucas, JP, of The Hall, Welwyn, Herts, and *d* 15 Jan 1930

1a Georgina Muriel; Médaille de la Reconnaissance Française (1945); *m* 17 Oct 1923 David Crawford Fullerton Lindsay Carnegie (*d* 19 Feb 1935), of Kinblethmont, Arbroath, Angus, and *d* 22 Dec 1973

2a Violet Anna; *d* 1 Jan 1884

3a Norah Gertrude; of Cairnhill, Forfar, Angus

3 Hugh; *b* 13 Aug 1812; Lt-Col 3rd Madras Light Cav; *m* 2 Jan 1854 Susannah Morrison (*d* 12 June 1920), dau of John Campbell, and *d* 5 Feb 1866, leaving issue:

(1) John Campbell, CIE (1808); *b* 6 April 1858; Pres Assam LC, Indian CS 1879–1914, formerly Commr Surma Valley; *m* 21 July 1887 Jeannie Sinclair (*d* 3 April 1947), dau of Robert Hamilton, and *d* 20 May 1923, leaving issue:

1a Hugh Hamilton; *b* 24 Feb 1894; Lt 67th Punjabis, IA, WW I (despatches twice); *das* Kut-al-Amara 28 Dec 1915

2a ROBERT KEITH, **15th Viscount**

1a Jeannie; *b* 15 Dec 1888; *m* 21 Nov 1911 Rev Sir Nicholas Dodd Beatson-Bell, KCSI, KCIE (*d* 12 Feb 1936), vicar Cornish Hall End, Essex, son of Andrew Beatson-Bell, of Kilduncan, Fife, and *d* 28 Feb 1970, leaving issue

2a Margaret Ogilvy; *b* 9 Aug 1892; *m* 7 Jan 1915 Lt-Col Hastings Roy Harington, 8th Gurkha Rifles (*d* 26 Dec 1942), son of Col Hastings Norman Victor Harington, late IMS, having had issue:

1b Hugh; *b* 6 April 1916; *educ* Fettes; Capt 4/8th Gurkha Rifles, WW II; *ka* Arakan, Burma, 8 Feb 1943

2b *Timothy [Timothy Harington Esq, Kelston Ranch, PB 235A, Salisbury, Zimbabwe]; *b* 1 Nov 1926; *educ* Eastbourne Coll; *m* 30 March 1959 *Jean, er dau of Maj-Gen Sir Lancelot Cutforth, KBE, of Glade Earlydene, Ascot, Berks, and has issue:

1c *Hugh Cutforth; *b* 4 Sept 1963

1c *Joanna Lucy; *b* 20 May 1961

2c *Louise Mary; *b* 31 Jan 1967

1b *Pamela [Mrs Ronald Montague-Jones, 10 Battlemead, Swanage, Dorset]; *b* 14 June 1919; *m* 7 May 1955 Brig Ronald Montague-Jones, CBE, son of Edgar Montague Jones, late Headmaster St Albans Sch, Herts, and has issue:

1c *Roy Ronald; *b* 21 July 1958; *m* 19– *Henry Price and has:

1d *Christopher Henry; *b* 13 Oct 1991

2d *Patrick Roy; *b* 4 Feb 1994

3a Susannah Mary; *b* 14 May 1901; *m* 6 Aug 1925 Lt-Col Adrian Kelso Hamilton, DSO, MC, Black Watch (*d* 15 April 1960), only son of Maj Keith Randolph Hamilton, DSO, and had issue:

1b *Bruce Meade, MBE (1965); *b* 27 Dec 1926; *educ* Sherborne; Col Black Watch; *m* 5 Dec 1953 *Mary Elizabeth, dau of R A Walter, of Westwood, Balthayock, Perthshire, and has issue:

1c *Roderick Adrian; *b* 25 Aug 1959

1c *Catherine Elizabeth; *b* 22 March 1963

1b *Isabel Mary; *b* 5 Dec 1929; *m* 6 Jan 1951 *Lt-Col Ian Ranald Critchley, Black Watch, only son of Lt-Col Ranald Drury Critchley, Rajputana Rifles, of Park Close, Tetbury, Glos, and has issue:

1c *Rowland Bruce Ranald; *b* 21 Oct 1953

2c *Adrian Hugh; *b* 27 March 1961

1c *Anna Mary; *b* 30 Nov 1951

2c *Julia Clare; *b* 21 Nov 1956

(2) Hugh Corsar; *b* 5 Oct 1860; CE; *m* 27 Dec 1886 Marianne, JP (*d* 27 July 1943), 6th dau of Archibald Gibson, and *d* 6 Feb 1915, leaving issue:

1a John; *b* 26 June 1894; Lt 2nd Bn Gren Gds; *das* 16 Sept 1916

2a Hugh; *b* 20 June 1896; *educ* Cheltenham; Lt-Col 5th Bn Border Regt (TA), late Capt 9th Bn Highland LI, WWs I and II (despatches, Legion of Merit (USA), and US Bronze Star); *m* 18 April 1923 *Jess Agnes [Mrs Hugh Arbuthnott, 35 Loch Dve, Helensburgh, Dunbartonshire], dau of Robert Henderson, of Mount Hooly, and *d* 26 Nov 1961, leaving issue:

1b +Hugh John [Hugh Arbuthnott Esq, Ardmoy, Rhu, Argyll G84 8NH]; *b* 19 June 1924; *educ* Sedbergh and Emmanuel Coll Cambridge (BA 1950, MA 1955); late Capt RE, WW II 1945 (wounded, despatches); *m* 2 Oct 1954 Dorothy Ferguson (*d* April 1991), only dau of Sir William Lang Denholm, of Glenmill Kilmacolm, Renfrewshire, and has:

1c *Carolyn Ann; *b* 9 Dec 1955; *m* 1981 *Hugh Alexander Normand, of Garden Cottage, Ardoch, Cardross, Dunbartonshire, and has issue:

1d *William Alexander; *b* 11 Sept 1984

2d *Andrew John Charles; *b* 6 Aug 1989

1d *Margaret Catherine; *b* 15 Dec 1986

2c *Sarah Jean [Mrs Jeremy MacLehose, Clantive House, Littleheath Rd, Fontwell, W Sussex; *b* 24 Jan 1957; *m* 31 March 1978 *Jeremy Spencer James MacLehose, s of (Norman) Donald MacLehose, DSO (and nephew of Baron MacLehose of Beoch *qv*), and has issue:

1d *Benjamin Donald Robert; *b* 9 Feb 1981

2d *Fergus Donald Hugh; *b* 15 Sept 1988

1d *Anna Margaret; *b* 6 April 1983

3c *Susan Mary [Mrs Roger Clegg, Braeside, 257 Bangor Rd, Newtonards, Co Down]; *b* 22 March 1962; *m* 1983 *Roger James Clegg, of Braeside, 257 Bangor Rd, Newtonards, Co Down, and has issue:

1d *James Hugh; *b* 8 Dec 1988

1d *Victoria Rebecca; *b* 24 March 1986

4c *Christine Elizabeth; *b* 20 Nov 1966

1b *Mary [Mrs Laurence Young, Plovers, East Boldre, Hants]; *b* 8 Feb 1926; (BSc (Hons) 1946); *m* 3 Oct 1949 *Col Laurence MacLellan Young, MBE, MC, RE, of Plovers, East Boldre, Brockenhurst, Hants, son of William MacLellan Young, of Bridge of Allan, and has issue:

1c *Alice Mary; *b* 10 Oct 1951; *m* 1972 *Peter James Summerhayes, of The Paddock, Borthwood Lane, Sandown, IoW, and has issue:

1d *Catherine Elizabeth; *b* 4 Feb 1976

2d *Christina Mary; *b* 4 Feb 1976

3d *Kirsty Alice; *b* 1 Nov 1979

2c *Christina Jess; *b* 16 June 1954; *educ* Imp Coll London (PhD); *m* 1978 *David Peter Turner, of White Hart Cottage, Brinkley Newmarket, Suffolk, and has issue:

1d *James Peter; *b* 1984

1d *Catriona Jane; *b* 11 Aug 1982

2b *Marianne Jean Elspeth [Mrs William Woods Ballard, Oliver's Cottage, Capel St Mary, Ipswich, Suffolk]; *b* 11 Nov 1937; *m* 1 April 1967 *William Richard Woods Ballard, yr son of Lt-Col Basil Woods Ballard, CIE, MBE, of Shepherds Oak, Crawley, Down, Sussex, by his w Eileen Rose, only dau of Hugh Wilson Molesworth, CBE (*see* MOLESWORTH, V), and has:

1c *Hugh William; *b* 22 Nov 1968

2c *Andrew James; *b* 19 March 1976

3a Archibald, MBE (1946), ED; *b* 8 July 1898; *educ* Cheltenham; WW I 1917–18 as Lt RE (severely wounded), and WW II as Maj Malay States Vol Forces; chartered accountant; *m* 18 Sept 1931 *Barbara Joan [Mrs Archibald Arbuthnott, The Mill House, Tidmarsh, nr Pangbourne, Berks], yr dau of John Hughman Worters, of The White Ho, Chipstead, Surrey, and *d* 12 March 1977, leaving issue:

1b +John [John Arbuthnott Esq, The Old Rectory, Llangynhafal, Clwyd]; *b* 21 May 1933; *educ* Sedbergh and Emmanuel Coll Cambridge (BA 1955, MA 1960); *m* 7 April 1956 *Ann, yr dau of Arthur Frederick Garton, of 5 Gwynn Ho, Lower Sloane St, London SW1, and has issue:

1c +Ian [Ian Arbuthnott Esq, 4 Broadleaze, Hook, Hants]; *b* 25 July 1958; *m* 1986 *Jane, dau of Gary Redshaw, of Penllan Stoney La, Llanbedr, Ruthin, Clwyd, and has issue:

1d *Hannah; *b* 20 April 1994

2c +David [David Arbuthnott Esq, Crenny, 15 Acorn Way, Shawbirch, Telford, Salop]; *b* 28 March 1961; *educ* Aberdeen U (MA); *m* 1987 *Dawn Grace, dau of John Frederick Kirby, of Birmingham, and has issue:

1d +Christopher John; *b* 4 June 1991

1d *Jennifer Ann; *b* 12 Sept 1989

1c *Fiona, MCSP; *b* 25 Feb 1957; *m* 1984 *Andrew Graham Sneddon, of Ty-Draw, Efenechtyd, Ruthin, Clwyd, and has issue:

1d *John Andrew; *b* 14 Oct1986

1d *Emily Fiona; *b* 9 Aug 1988

2d *Laura Alice; *b* 16 Aug 1990

2c *Jane; *b* 9 Dec 1966; *m* *Robert Nicholas Shannon, of Crowborough, E Sussex, son of Robert Henry Shannon, of Belfast, and has:

1d *Jack Robert; *b* 26 June 1997

1d *Kate Ruth; *b* 6 Nov 1994

2b +Robert, CBE (1991) [Robert Arbuthnott Esq CBE, Glazeley Old Rectory, nr Bridgnorth, Shropshire, WV16 6AB]; *b* 28 Sept 1936; *educ* Sedbergh, Emmanuel Coll Cambridge (BA 1960, MA 1964); 2nd Lt Black Watch 1955–57, Br Cncl 1960–93; *m* 19 May 1962 *(Sophie) Robina, er dau of Robin Arthur Axford, of Burlington Gdns, and has issue:

1c +Robert Keith; *b* 27 June 1968

1c *Alison Mary; *b* 10 Dec 1963

2c *Catherine Anne [Mrs Owen Wheatley, 182D Elm Rd, Kingston-on-Thames, Surrey]; *b* 5 Feb 1965; *m* 1992 *Owen Wheatley

4a Robert, MBE (1945), TD (1941), DL (Dunbartonshire 1961) Ld Lt 1968; *b* 22 Sept 1900; *educ* Cheltenham; FICE, FIMechE; WW II with Manchester Regt and REME (TA) Europe; memb Roy Co of Archers; *d* 198–

1a Jean; *b* 6 Nov 1887; *m* 5 Sept 1911 Alexander Cavendish, Malayan CS (ret) (*d* 25 July 1960), er son of Alexander Carnegie Cavendish, of Madras, and had issue:

1b *Alexander Arbuthnott, DSC; *b* 24 April 1914; Lt-Cdr RN, WW II; *m* 11 Nov 1943 *Katherine Virginia Mary, dau of Gilbert Hooper, of The Chine, Muswell Hill, London N, and *d* 1996, leaving:

1c *Alexander Gilbert James; *b* 7 Jan 1957

1c *Diana Valerie Frances [Mrs Diana Cavendish, 3270 Kempton Ave, Oakland, CA 94611, USA]; *b* 13 May 1945; *m* 19– John Cross, and has issue

1b Jean May; *b* 19 Jan 1918; FANY; ATS WW II; *d* 1996

4 David, CSI; *b* 13 April 1820; late Madras CS; *m* 8 Sept 1847 Eliza (*d* 16 June 1913), dau of Thomas Forbes Reynolds, of Wallington, Surrey, and *d* 27 July 1901, having had issue:

(1) John Pelly; *b* 1 April 1851; *d* unm 19 May 1878

(2) Lindsay George; *b* 14 Jan 1853; Dep Inspr-Gen Police Madras 1902–08; *m* 1st 3 Oct 1907 Gertrude Forbes (*d* 9 Jan 1924), dau of Clifford E F Nash, barrister, of Cheltenham, and had issue:

1a +Bernard David Ogilvy; *b* 7 Aug 1908

1a *Margaret Wedderburn; *b* 7 May 1913; *m* 30 June 1939 Lt-Col Hew Angus Christopher Blair-Imrie, DSO, MC, Black Watch, attd Gordon Highrs (*ka* 18 Aug 1944), yr s of Lt-Col Hew Francis Blair-Imrie, CMG, OBE, JP, of Lunan, Angus, and has issue

(2) (cont.) Lindsay Arbuthnott *m* 2nd 9 July 1924 Gertrude Amy (*d* 21 Aug 1940), dau of John Gaskolin, and *d* 31 May 1927

(3) David; *b* 20 March 1856; Lt 67th Foot; *d* unm 6 Sept 1878

(4) Donald Stuart, CE; *b* 23 Dec 1860; *m* 2 Feb 1892 Anne Elizabeth (*d* 23 Oct 1944), dau of James Brand, of Glasgow, and *d* 29 Sept 1918, leaving issue:

1a David; *b* 19 Nov 1892; *educ* Stonyhurst; RC priest; *d* unm 18 June 1969

2a James Gordon; *b* 10 March 1894; *educ* Stonyhurst; Cdr RN (ret), WWs I and II, ret May 1920; *m* 21 April 1931 *Margaret Georgina, dau of John Wolley Hyde, of Seaview, Instow, N Devon, and had issue:

1b John Hyde; *b* 7 March 1932; *educ* RNC Dartmouth; Lt RN (ret); *m* 29 Dec 1955 *Patience Sarah (*m* 2nd 11 May 1990 *David Hillier) [Mrs David Hillier, Hausse Cambe, 46700 Mauroux, France], er dau of Charles Wainman, of Hinton St George, Somerset, and *d* 1981, leaving:

1c +Anthony St John Gordon; *b* 25 Nov 1956; *m* 1980 *Susan, yr dau of George Humphreys, of Herts

2c +Nicholas Charles [Nicholas Arbuthnott Esq, The Ridings, Wilcote Finstock OX7 3DX]; *b* 4 Oct 1958; *educ* Ampleforth and Corpus Christi Coll Oxford; *m* 1st 1989 (*divorce* 1991) Tracey, yr dau of Lesley Brett, of Eltham Park, Kent; *m* 2nd 199– *—

2b +Hugh James, CMG (1984) [Hugh Arbuthnott Esq CMG, 65 Winchendon Rd, London SW6 5DH]; *b* 27 Dec 1936; *educ* Ampleforth and New Coll Oxford; late 2nd Lt Black Watch; For Serv 1960–96, Amb: Romania 1986–89, Portugal 1989–93 and Denmark 1993–96, author: *Common Man's Guide to the Common Market* (ed, with G Edwards, 1979); *m* 29 May 1964 *Vanessa Rose, only dau of Edward Dyer, of Tunbridge Wells, and has had:

1c +Dominic Hugh; *b* 11 June 1965

2c Justin Edward James; *b* 8 Sept 1967; *educ* Edinburgh U; *d* in a boating accident 1989

3c +Giles Sebastian; *b* 30 March 1970

1b *Georgina Mary [Mme Christian Toulet, Le Boute, 46800 Montcuq, France]; *b* 22 June 1940; *m* 25 Oct 1968 (*divorce* 1982) William Robert Sparling, s of Wilfred Eustace Sparling, of Beauvallon, Ste Maxime, France; *m* 2nd 1988 *Christian Toulet and has by him:

1c *Christophe Jean James Alexandre; *b* 1979

1c *Claire Margaret Suzanne; *b* 1984

2b *Elisabeth Grace [Mrs Rupert Evans, St Jacques, St Peter Port, Guernsey, CI GY1 1SW]; *b* 29 Aug 1945; *m* 21 Dec 1967 *Rupert Arthur Rees Evans, barrister, only s of Philip Evans, of Bournemouth, Hants, and has:

1c *Marcus James Julius; *b* 1972

1c *Frances Imogen; *b* 13 June 1975

2c *Adelaide Grace; *b* 1978

3a John St Clair; *b* 27 Aug 1898; *educ* Downside and RMC Sandhurst; late Capt IA and S/Ldr RAF, WWs I and II; *m* 1st 30 May 1932 Constance Clare (*d* 16 Nov 1964), dau of Frank Fairlie, of Beldorny, Nairn; *m* 2nd 14 March 1967 *Catherine Wellborn [Mrs John Arbuthnott, Buttermilk Cottage, Barford St Michael, Deddington, Oxon], dau of Thomas Redman Morgan, of Aiken, S Carolina, USA

4a Donald Charles; *b* 10 Dec 1901; *educ* Beaumont; *d* 6 Nov 1930

5a Hugh Forbes; *b* 17 Jan 1906; *educ* Wimbledon Coll and Wadham Coll Oxford (BA 1928, MA 1930); Headmaster Penryn Sch 1934, formerly Master of Arisford and Oratory Schs, Kt of Honour and Devotion SMO Malta; *m* 7 Aug 1937 Janet Elizabeth (*d* 1990), only dau of V-Adml Herbert John Temple Marshall, Gayton Hall, Ross, Herefordshire, and *d* 1982, leaving issue:

1b +Robert Marshall; *b* 26 Sept 1938; *educ* privately

2b +James Francis [Maj James Arbuthnott, Stone House Cottage, Kidderminster, Worcs]; *b* 27 April 1940; *educ* Downside and RMA Sandhurst; Maj Black Watch, Kt of Honour and Devotion SMO Malta; *m* 20 July 1974 *Hon Louisa Nina Hughes-Young, yst dau of 1st Baron St Helens (*qv*), and has issue:

1c +John Patrick; *b* 1977

2c +Albert Michael; *b* 1988

3c +Walter Francis; *b* 1991

1c *Elizabeth Nina; *b* 1980

2c *Florence Mary; *b* 1981

3b +Simon David [Simon Arbuthnott Esq, Winterfold Ho, Chaddesley Corbett, Worcs]; *b* 16 March 1942; *educ* Downside and Ch Ch Oxford (BA 1963); teacher Penryn Sch; *m* 5 Sept 1970 *Suzanne Ruth, er dau of Allen Mainwaring Parker, of The Wadhouse, Heightington, Bewdley, Worcs, and has issue:

1c +Thomas; *b* 10 June 1969

2c +Edward Alexander Hugh; *b* 1980

1c *Lucy Margaret; *b* 9 April 1972

2c *Katherine Anne; *b* 1976

4b +Charles Philip [Charles Arbuthnott Esq, The Old Manse, Caputh, by Murthly, Perthshire]; *b* 13 Feb 1946; *educ* Downside and RMA Sandhurst; *m* *Lindsay C, dau of Angus Sillars, of Stuckenduff, Shandon, Dunbartonshire, and has issue:

1c +Magnus Malcolm James; *b* 1989

2c +A son; *b* 1994

1c *Molly Victoria; *b* 1987

5b +Hugh Andrew [Hugh Arbuthnott Esq, 13 Rosenau Rd, London SW11]; *b* 15 June 1948; *educ* Downside; *m* 1974 *Elizabeth Jane, dau of Col Lionel James Showers, DSO, of Kingston St Michael, Wilts, and has issue:

1c +Hugh Frederick Archibald; *b* 1982

1c *Arabella Elizabeth; *b* 1979

6b +Nicholas Octavius [Nicholas Arbuthnott Esq, 10 Atwood Rd, London W6]; *b* 28 Feb 1952; *educ* Downside; *m* 1984 *Vanessa Julie, dau of Richard Mather, of Kendal, Cumbria, and has issue:

1c +George Arthur Harben; *b* 1986

2c +Edmund; *b* 1992

1c *Rose Elizabeth Marshall; *b*1987

2c *Florence (Flora) Lily Nott; *b* 1990

1b *Margaret Mary; *b* 23 Dec 1943; *m* 26 July 1968 *Hon Hugh Desmond Donovan, er son of Baron Donovan, PC (LP; *see* 1970 edn), and had issue

2b *Janet Felicity; *b* 28 March 1950; *m* 1980 *William George McMorran, and has issue:

1c *Donald Hugh; *b* 1983

1c *Roland Francis; *b* 1985

1c *Hugo Edmund; *b* 1988

6a Charles Reynolds (Rev); *b* 4 March 1908; *educ* Wimbledon Coll; SJ; *d* 29 April 1966

7a +Edmund Stephen (Very Rev) [The Very Rev Canon Edmund Arbuthnott, 14 Westbrook, Worthing, W Sussex BN11 1RF]; *b* 9 Nov 1909; *educ* Wimbledon Coll and Christ's Coll Cambridge (BA 1938, MA 1942); Canon St George's Cathedral Southwark 1956

1a Edith Gertrude; *b* 11 April 1895; *d* 1967

2a Margaret; *b* 30 April 1896; *d* 1899

3a Anne; *b* 9 July 1897; *m* 23 April 1930 John Cyril Taylor Rains, barrister; *d* Dec 1981

4a Eliza Mary

5a Mary Frances Clementina; *m* 24 June 1930 Philip Adrian Flood (*d* 1 March 1971), 2nd son of Dr Flood, of Meadowside, Warwick Park, Tunbridge Wells, and had issue:

1b *Timothy Adrian; *b* 21 March 1931; *educ* Beaumont, Rome and — Coll Oxford (BA 1963); monk

2b *David Gybrian; *b* 8 May 1933; *educ* Beaumont; Maj 2nd Roy Tank Regt

3b *John Charles Arbuthnott; *b* 18 Feb 1947; *educ* Beaumont

1b *Mary Ann Theresa; *b* 16 May 1935; nun

2b *Philippa Mary [Mrs Clive Beck, 1 Parkside Gdns, London SW19]; *b* 24 June 1937; *m* 28 April 1960 *Clive Beck, 2nd son of Sir Edgar Charles Beck, CBE, of 3 Ilchester Place, London W14, and has issue:

1c *David Clive; *b* 28 July 1962

2c *Andrew Philip; *b* 22 Sept 1964

3c *Simon Charles; *b* 30 Dec 1965

1c *Nicola Anne; *b* 17 Feb 1961

2c *Emma Louise; *b* 19 Dec 1967

3c *Sarah Antonia; *b* 16 July 1971

(1) Margaret Frances; *d* unm 11 Jan 1917

(2) Louisa Curzon; *d* unm 11 Jan 1919

(3) Eliza Clementina Mary; *d* unm 8 Feb 1940

The 14th VISCOUNT's cousin,

ROBERT KEITH ARBUTHNOTT, **15th Viscount of Arbuthnott**, CB (1945), CBE (1944), DSO (1938), MC, DL (Kincardineshire 1959); *b* 21 Aug 1897; *educ* Fettes and RMC Sandhurst; Maj-Gen late Black Watch, Col Black Watch (RHR) 1960–64, WWs I and II (despatches), Palestine 1938–39 (despatches), GSO(2) Staff Coll 1938, Lt-Col 1944, cmdg 11th Inf Bde Italy 1942–44 and 78th Inf Div 1944–46, Maj-Gen 1945, Ch Br Mil Mission Egyptian Army 1946, Ch of Staff Scottish Cmd 1948–49, Cdr Highland Dist and 51st (Highland) Inf Div (TA) 1949–52, ret 1952; Ld Lt Kincardineshire 1960–66, Cdr US Legn of Merit; *m* 10 Jan 1924 Ursula (*d* 1989), dau of Sir William Collingwood, KBE, of Dedham Grove, Colchester, Essex, and *d* 15 Dec 1966, leaving:

1 JOHN CAMPBELL ARBUTHNOTT, **16th and present Viscount of Arbuthnott**

2 +(William) David, MBE (1964) [Col The Hon David Arbuthnott MBE, The Old Manse, Trochry, Dunkeld, Perthshire PH8 0DY]; *b* 5 Nov 1927; *educ* Fettes and RMA Sandhurst; Col Black Watch (ret), Korea 1952–53, Kenya 1953–55, NI 1974 (despatches); *m* 30 April 1955 *Sonja Mary, est dau of Charles Newbigging Thomson, CBE, DSO, TD, DL, of The Gdn Ho, Panmure, Carnoustie, and has issue:

(1) +Charles Robert [Charles Arbuthnott Esq, Harveiston Farmhouse, Dollar, Clackmananshire, FK14 7PX]; *b* 4 Oct 1956; *educ* Fettes and Silsoe Coll Carnfield Inst of Technology (BSc Engrg); *m* 23 May 1987 *Patricia Diane, dau of Barrington Brooke, of Mukoko, Glendale, Zimbabwe, and has issue:

1a +David Barrington; *b* 6 May 1989

2a +James Brooke; *b* 30 Aug 1990

(1) *Georgina Margaret; *b* 22 Oct 1964; *educ* Fettes and St Andrews (MA)

(2) *Elizabeth Christian; *b* 31 Oct 1967

3 +Hugh Sinclair [The Hon Hugh Arbuthnott, Cairnhill, Forfar, Angus DD8 3TQ]; *b* 14 Nov 1929; *educ* Fettes, Gonville and Caius Coll Cambridge (MA 1952) and Edinburgh U (LLB 1953); Lt Black Watch (TARO); Shell Internat Petroleum Co 1950–83; *m* 21 Sept 1963 *Anne Rosamund, only dau of Charles Bentley Terdre, of Appledore, Cherry Walk, High Salvington, Worthing, Sussex, and has issue:

(1) +(Hugh) James Hamilton; *b* 5 Aug 1967; *m* 11 May 1996 *Sally, yr dau of Geoffrey Davies, of Hatch End, Middx

(1) *Katherine Anne; *b* 14 Jan 1970

1 *Christian Keith Arbuthnott [The Hon Mrs Bing, The Lodge, Church St, Edzell, Brechin, Angus DD9 7TQ]; *b* 1 Oct 1933; *educ* Edinburgh U (MA 1954); *m* 13 Nov 1954 *Cdr Peter John Bing, OBE, RN (ret), son of William Leslie Bing, of High Hedges, Crowborough, Sussex, and has:

(1) *Alan Charles (Rev) [The Rev Alan Bing, Mulberry Way, Roundswell, Barnstaple, Devon]; *b* 29 March 1956; *educ* Christ's Hosp and St Edmund Hall Oxford (MA); ordained 1992; *m* 1985 *Wendy Margaret, er dau of Dennis Capstick, of Simonstone, Lancs, and has:

1a *Alison Ursula; *b* 1988

2a *Emma Florence; *b* 1990

3a *Julia Margaret; *b* 1993

(2) *Robert Adrian [Robert Bing Esq, 17 Grasmere Ave, London W3 6JT]; *b* 11 March 1958; *educ* Christ's Hosp and Magdalene Coll Cambridge (MA 1980); ARICS 1982; *m* 1991 *Sarah Frances, yr dau of Laurence Greenwood, of Silvertrees, Coldwaltham, W Sussex, and has:

1a *Henry Jarvis; *b* 1992

2a *Adam Laurence; *b* 1997

1a *Eleanor Mary; *b* 1994

(3) *Andrew John Collingwood [Andrew Bing Esq, Auldbar, Station House, Balgavies, Forfar, Angus DD8 2TH]; *b* 21 Oct 1960; *educ* Christ's Hosp and Edinburgh U (MA 1984); Dip in Marketing 1985; *m* 1993 *Isobel Donald (Zoë), yr dau of John Wilson Muir, of Woodburn Gdns, Aberdeen, and has:

1a *Katherine Isobel Collingwood; *b* 1996

(1) *Sarah Lucy; *b* 22 July 1969; *educ* Marlborough, Edinburgh U (MA 1992) and Coll of Law, London; slr

ARCHDALE

Arms: Quarterly, 1st and 4th, azure a chevron ermine between three talbots passant or (for ARCHDALE); 2nd, or a chevron sable (for MERVYN); 3rd, quarterly, 1st and 4th, azure three fleurs de lys or, 2nd and 3rd, gules three gem-rings gold, all within a bordure or charged with a tressure flory gules, in the centre point an inescutcheon argent charged with a tilting spear and sword saltire-ways points upwards proper (for MONTGOMERY). **Crest:** Out of a ducal crest-coronet or a heraldic tiger's head argent, maned, tufted and armed sable. **Motto:** *Data fata secuta* ('The allotted destiny is followed'). **Creation:** Bt. (UK) 25 June 1928.

SIR EDWARD FOLMER ARCHDALE, 3RD BT, of Riversdale, Co Fermanagh, DSC (1943) [Capt Sir Edward Archdale Bt DSC RN, 19 Dermott Rd, Comber, Co Down BT23 5LG]; *b* 8 Sept 1921; *s f* 1955; *educ* Copthorne Sch and RNC Dartmouth; Capt RN, served WW II (despatches); *m* 24 July 1954 (*divorce* 1978) Elizabeth Ann Stewart, only dau of Maj-Gen Wilfred Boyd Fellowes Lukis, CBE, RM (ret), of Scotts Paddock, Meonstoke, Hants, and has had:

1 +NICHOLAS EDWARD; *b* 2 Dec 1965

1 Annabel Frances; *b* 14 Feb 1956; *d* April 1996

2 *Lucinda Grace; *b* 27 April 1958; *m* 1991 *Targino Luedy Kalid Filho and has:

(1) *Sibylla Archdale; *b* 1993

Lineage: EDWARD ARCHDALE, of Riversdale, Co Fermanagh, 3rd s of Col Mervyn Archdall, of Castle Archdale, Co Fermanagh, JP and DL; *b* 4 March 1775; *educ* St Mary's Hall Oxford (BA 1803); High Sheriff Co Fermanagh 1813, raised and cmded Lurg and Magheraboy True Blue Inf 1798; *m* 2 Oct 1809 Matilda (*d* 10 July 1859), dau of William Humphrys, of Ballyhaise, Co Cavan, and *d* 12 May 1864, having had a 5th s:

NICHOLAS MONTGOMERY ARCHDALE, of Crock na Crieve and Riversdale, JP and DL (Co Longford), JP (Co Fermanagh); *b* 18 Feb 1820; High Sheriff Co Fermanagh 1861; *m* 27 Jan 1852 Adelaide Mary (*d* 6 Jan 1926), 4th dau of Rev John Grey Porter, of Belle Isle, Co Fermanagh, Rector Kilskeery, Co Tyrone, and *d* in the hunting field 2 Feb 1877, leaving an est s:

Sir Edward Mervyn Archdale, 1st Bt (UK), so *cr* 25 June 1928, of Riversdale, PC (I 1921, NI 1922), JP and DL (Co Fermanagh); *b* 26 Jan 1853; Lt-Cdr RN, High Sheriff Co Fermanagh 1884, MP N Fermanagh 1898–1903 and 1916–22, Tyrone and Fermanagh 1921–29 and Enniskillen 1929–43 NI Parl, Min Ag NI 1921–33, Pres Belfast Chamber Commerce 1929; *m* 10 June 1880 Alicia Bland (*d* 10 May 1924), yst dau of Quintin Fleming, of Chapelville, Liverpool, and had issue:

1 NICHOLAS EDWARD (Sir), **2nd Bt**

2 William Porter Palgrave, CBE (1943); *b* 1 Dec 1883; *educ* Portora Roy Sch; *m* 27 April 1918 Alice Edith Palgrave (*d* 17 June 1963), 3rd dau of Charles Alexander Price Chetwynd-Talbot, Consul-Gen Boston (*see* SHREWSBURY and WATERFORD, E), and *d* 2 Nov 1956, leaving issue:

(1) +Mervyn Talbot, DL (Co Tyrone 1974) [Mervyn Archdale Esq DL, The Cottage Farm, Knockmoyle, Omagh, Co Tyrone]; *b* 30 Oct 1924; *educ* Westminster and Campbell Coll Belfast; High Sheriff Co Tyrone 1985; *m* 19 April 1951 *Aureole Helen, yst dau of Rev Canon Robert Hamilton Whelan, of Lislimnaghan Rectory, Omagh, Co Tyrone, and has issue:

1a +Peter Mervyn [Peter Archdale Esq, 8 Linkside, Clevedon BS21 7DD]; *b* 17 July 1953; *educ* Portora Roy Sch; Lt-Cdr RN; *m* 1976 *Caroline Anne, dau of N R C Griffin, and has issue:

1b +Jonathan Talbot; *b* 1982

1b *Kathryn Emma; *b* 1984

1a *Geraldine Angel; *b* 25 June 1952

(1) Angel; *b* 17 Nov 1919; *m* 1st — Jansma and had issue:

1a *Simon Anthony (adopted by his stepfather 1947) [Simon von Benckendorff Esq, 16 Westmead, Woking, Surrey GU21 3BS]; *b* 7 Aug 1943; *educ* Dauntsey's; *m* 1st 16 April 1966 (*divorce* 1972) Susan Alexandra, dau of Alexander Fyvie-Gauld, of Northwells, Bembridge, IoW, and had issue:

1b *Alexander Talbot; *b* 6 May 1969

1b *Samantha Palgrave; *b* 8 April 1967

1a (cont.) Simon von Benckendorff *m* 2nd 1980 *Belinda Fay, dau of J Hetherington, and has further issue:

2b *Louisa Alice; *b* 1982

(1) (cont.) Mrs Jansma *m* 2nd 19 Oct 1946 Paul von Benckendorff (*d* 24 Dec 1996), only s of Johann von Benckendorff, of Jendel, Estonia, by Baroness Budberg, and *d* 28 Jan 1990, having by him had:

1a *Carolyn [Mrs Peter Medak, 32 Phillimore Court, Argyll Rd, London W8]; *b* 6 Nov 1947; *m* 9 Dec 1972 *Peter Gyula Medak, film dir, s of Gyula Medak, of Budapest, and has issue:

1b *Joshua Paul; *b* 11 Nov 1974

1b *Cornelia Daisy Angel; *b* 1975

2a *Philippa (twin) [Mrs Roger Law, 38 Cromwell Ave, Bromley, Kent]; *b* 6 Nov 1947; *m* 1977 *Roger Fraser Law and has issue:

1b *Helen; *b* 1979

2b *Kate; *b* 1981

(2) Kathleen; *b* 15 Sept 1922; *m* 15 Nov 1958 *Anthony Robert Whelan, s of Rev Canon Robert Hamilton Whelan, of Lislimnaghan Rectory, Omagh, Tyrone, and bro of Aureole Helen (*see* above), and *d* 2 May 1988, leaving:

1a *Nicholas Robert; *b* 13 Feb 1960; *m* 10 Oct 1987 *Elizabeth Anne Harrison

1a *Sarah Deborah; *b* 10 Feb 1963; *m* 19– *Anthony Eaton and has:

1b *Georgina; *b* 17 July 1996

3 Audley Quintin; *b* 3 April 1886; *educ* Winchester; Lt-Col RHA WW I (wounded, despatches) and WW II; *m* 22 March 1922 Mary Edith Haigh (*d* 1987), dau of Oliver Bury, JP, of Chelsea, and *d* 1978, leaving:

(1) *Rosemary [Mrs William Twiston-Davies, The Faulds, Rockliffe, Carlisle, Cumbria]; *b* 22 Jan 1923; *m* 16 July 1949 William Anthony Twiston-Davies (*d* 1989), er s of Sir Leonard Twiston Davies, KBE, FSA, of Rockfield Park, Mon, and has:

1a *Audley William [Audley Twiston-Davies Esq, Mynde Park, Much Dewchurch, Herefs HR2 8DN]; *b* 13 Nov 1950; *educ* Radley; *m* 1985 *Hon Caroline Mary Elaine Harbord-Hamond, dau of 11th Baron Suffield (*qv*), and has:

1b *Thomas Audley; *b* 1994

1b *Antonia Rose; *b* 1987

2b *Sophie Louise; *b* 1990

3b *Zoë Caroline; *b* 1992

2a *Nigel Anthony [Nigel Twiston-Davies Esq, Grange Hill Farm, Naunton, Cheltenham, Glos]; *b* 16 May 1957; *educ* Radley; *m* 1st 1981 (*divorce* 1987) Hon Sara Emma Hamilton-Russell, dau of 10th Viscount Boyne (*qv*); *m* 2nd 1988 *Catherine B, yst dau of John Farey, of Bredon's Norton, nr Tewkesbury, and has:

1b *Sam; *b* 1992

2b *William; *b* 1994

1a *Alexandra Rosemary; *b* 4 April 1954; *m* 1986 *Robin L F Burgess, of Scaleby, Cumbria, er s of Sir John Lawrie Burgess, OBE, TD, JP, DL, of Carlisle, and has:

1b *James; *b* 1994

1b *Rose Charlotte; *b* 1987

2b *Catherine; *b* 1989

3b *Rachel; *b* 1992

2a *Penelope Auriol; *b* 12 Feb 1959; *m* 1982 *Giles H Mounsey-Heysham, of Castletown House, Rockcliffe, Carlisle, s of Maj R H G Mounsey-Heysham, and has issue:

1b *Toby; *b* 1984

2b *Benjamin; *b* 1986

3b *Rory; *b* 1989

1b *Anna; *b* 1991

(2) *Judith Penelope [Miss Judith Archdale, Tre-Evan, Llangarron, Ross-on-Wye, Hereford and Worcester]; *b* 7 Nov 1924

(3) *Anne Alicia, MBE (1973); *b* 24 June 1928

4 Dominick Mervyn; *b* 4 April 1892; *educ* Felsted and Wye Ag Coll; Lt KAR; *ka* 13 Nov 1916

5 Humphrys, DSC; *b* 29 July 1896; Capt RN WW I and WW II; *m* 26 May 1944 Mary Katherine, 2nd Offr WRNS (*d* 15 May 1975), only dau of Robert Leslie Gilbert, formerly of W Australia, and *d* 24 Aug 1972, leaving issue:

(1) +Gilbert Humphrys [Gilbert Archdale Esq, 35 Milson Rd, London W14]; *b* 22 July 1947; *educ* Tonbridge; *m* 1984 *Susan Anne, er dau of Dennis John Boyles, of Enton, Surrey, and has issue:

1a +Thomas Robert Humphrys; *b* 1988

2a +Peter Charles Alexander; *b* 1991

1 Angel; *b* 10 Aug 1882; *m* 31 Aug 1909 Percy Marmaduke Tottenham, CBE, of Crowborough, Sussex (*d* 27 Jan 1975), er s of Capt Francis Loftus Tottenham. of Coolmore, Crowborough, and *d* 14 April 1973, leaving issue

Sir EDWARD *d* 1 Nov 1943; his est s,

Sir (Nicholas) Edward Archdale, 2nd Bt, CBE (1920); *b* 11 June 1881; V-Adml, ADC to HM GEORGE V 1929, WW I with submarine flotillas (despatches); Gen Inspector Min Home Affrs NI 1931–46; *m* 22 July 1920 Gerda (*d* 17 Dec 1969), 2nd dau of Frederik Christian Sievers, of Copenhagen, and *d* 28 July 1955, leaving issue:

1 Sir EDWARD FOLMER ARCHDALE, **3rd and present Bt**

1 Alice Gerda (Patty); *b* 9 June 1923; *m* 31 March 1949 (*divorce* 1965) Maj Peter Courage, 1st King's Dragoon Gds (ret), est s of Lt-Col John Hubert Courage, of Kirkby Fleetham Hall, Northallerton, Yorks, and *d* 1988, leaving:

(1) *John Mervyn; *b* 30 June 1950; *educ* Tabley House
(1) *Gerda Veronica; *b* 16 Aug 1952
(2) *Susan Rose; *b* 1 Aug 1956
(3) *Belinda Jane; *b* 9 Aug 1958

ARCHER OF SANDWELL

Creation: B. (LP, UK) 1992.

THE BARON ARCHER OF SANDWELL, of Sandwell, Co of West Midlands (Peter Kingsley Archer, PC (1977), QC (1971)) [The Rt Hon The Lord Archer of Sandwell PC, 7 Old School Court, Wraysbury, Berks]; *b* 20 Nov 1926; *educ* Wednesbury Boys' High Sch, UCL (BA, LLB, Fell 1978) and LSE (LLM); barrister Gray's Inn 1952, Bencher 1974, MP (Lab) Rowley Regis and Tipton 1966–74 and Warley W 1974–92, PPS to Attorney Gen 1967–70, memb UK Delegn UN Gen Assembly 1969, Chm: Amnesty Internat (Br Section) 1971–74 and Soc Lab Lawyers 1971–74 and 1980–93, Slr-Gen 1974–79, Crown Court Recorder 1982–, Oppn Frontbench Spokesman: Legal Affrs 1981–82, Trade 1982–83, Shadow Sec NI 1983–87, Chm Cncl on Tbnls 1992–, Pres: Fabian Soc 1993–, World Disarmament Assoc 1993– and Methodist Homes for the Aged 1992–, author: *The Queen's Courts* (1956), *Social Welfare and the Citizen* (ed, 1957), *Communism and the Law* (with Lord Reay, 1963), *Freedom at Stake* (1966), *Human Rights* (1969), *Purpose in Socialism* (jt author, 1973), *The Role of the Law Officers* (1978), *More Law Reform Now* (ed, 1984); *m* 1954 *Margaret Irene, da of Sydney John Smith, of London, Ontario, and has:

1 *John Kingsley; *b* 1962; *educ* Watford GS and Corpus Christi Coll Cambridge

Lineage: CYRIL KINGSLEY ARCHER, MM; *m* May Baker and had:

PETER KINGSLEY, *cr* a **Baron**

ARCHER OF WESTON-SUPER-MARE

Creation: B. (LP, UK) 1992.

THE BARON ARCHER OF WESTON-SUPER-MARE, of Mark, Co Somerset (Jeffrey Archer) [The Rt Hon The Lord Archer of Weston-super-Mare, The Old Vicarage, Grantchester, Cambs CB3 9ND]; *b* 15 April 1940; *educ* Wellington Sch Somerset and BNC Oxford; sometime PT instr Dover Coll, Member GLC for Havering 1966–70, MP (C) Louth 1969–74, Pres Somerset AAA 1973, FRSA 1973, Dep Chm C Party 1985–86, Tstee RWS 1989–, author: *Not a Penny More, Not a Penny Less* (1975), *Shall We Tell The President?* (1977), *Kane and Abel* (1979), *A Quiver Full of Arrows* (1980), *The Prodigal Daughter* (1982), *First Among Equals* (1984), *A Matter of Honour* (1986), *A Twist in the Tale* (1988), *As the Crow Flies* (1991), *Honour Among Thieves* (1993), *Twelve Red Herrings* (1994), *The Proprietors* (1996); *m* 1966 *Mary Doreen, PhD, dau of Harold Norman Weeden, and has issue:

1 *Will(iam) Harold; *b* 1972; *educ* Eton and Georgetown U, Washington DC; with European Comm'n's Human Rights Office 1996–97; gen manager Playhouse Theatre Charing Cross 1997

2 *James Howard; *b* 1974; *educ* Stanford U California

Lineage: WILLIAM ARCHER; *m* Lola Cook and had:

JEFFREY HOWARD, *cr* a **Baron**

ARGYLL

Arms: Quarterly, 1st and 4th, gyronny of eight or and sable (for CAMPBELL); 2nd and 3rd, argent, a galley or lymphad sable, sails furled, flag and pennants flying and oars in action proper (for the lordship of LORNE); behind the arms two badges of honour in saltire: 1 A baton gules, powdered with thistles or, ensigned with an imperial crown proper, thereon the crest of Scotland (for the office of Hereditary Great Master of the Household in Scotland), 2 A sword proper, hilt and pommel or (for the office of Lord Justice Gen of Scotland, now no longer hereditary in the family). **Crest:** A boar's head fesswise, erased or, armed argent, langued gules. **Supporters:** Two lions guardant gules. **Motto:** *Ne obliviscaris* ('Forget not'). **Creations:** L. (S) 1445 (Campbell), 17 April 1470 (Lorne), 22 Feb 1626 (Kintyre); E. (S) 1457 (Argyll); Bt. (NS) 13 Dec 1627; D., M., E., V., L. (S) 23 June 1701; B. (GB) 22 Dec 1766 (Sundridge) and 20 May 1776 (Hamilton of Hameldon), D. (UK) 7 April 1892.

THE 12TH DUKE OF ARGYLL (S), **5th Duke of Argyll** (UK), **Marquess of Kintyre** and **Lorne**, **Earl of Argyll**, **Earl of Campbell and Cowall**, **Viscount of Lochow** and **Glenyla**, **Lord Campbell**, **Lord Lorne**, **Lord of Kintyre**, **Lord Inverary**, **Mull**, **Morvern** and **Tirie**, **Baron Sundridge**, of Coomb Bank, Co Kent, **Baron Hamilton of Hameldon**, Co Leicester, and a **Baronet** (Sir Ian Campbell, Bt, of Lundie) [His Grace The Duke of Argyll DL, Inveraray Castle, Argyllshire PA32 8XF]; *b* 28 Aug 1937; *s* f 1973, also as Chief of Clan Campbell (Mac Cailein Mor), Hereditary Grand Master Roy Household Scotland, Adml Western Coasts and Isles, Keeper Great Seal Scotland, Keeper Dunstaffnage, Carrick, Tarbert and Dunoon Castles; *educ* Le Rosey, Trin Coll Glenalmond and McGill U; Capt Argyll and Sutherland Highrs (ret), memb Roy Co Archers, chm Beinn Bhuidhe Holdings 1977–, dir S Campbell & Son 1982–, Aberlour Glenlivet Distillery Co, White Heather Distillers, Muir Mackenzie & Co 1973–, Visual Sound Programmes 1970–, Pres: Roy Caledonian Schs, Argyll Scouts Assoc, Highland Soc of London 1985–90, Hon Col Argyll and Sutherland Highrs Bn ACF 1981–91, Ld Lt Argyll and Bute 1994– (DL 1987–94), FRSA 1953, KStJ 1975; *m* 4 July 1964 *Iona Mary, only dau of Sir Ivar Iain Colquhoun of Luss, 8th Bt (*qv*), and has issue:

1 +TORQUHIL IAN, *Marquess of Lorne*; *b* 29 May 1968; Page of Honour to HM THE QUEEN 1981–83; *educ* Trin Coll Glenalmond and RAC Cirencester

1 *Louise Iona; *b* 26 Oct 1972; *educ* Gordonstoun

Lineage: Sir GILLESPIC CAMBELL of Menstrie, Clackmannanshire; *d c* 1280, leaving:

Sir COLIN CAMPBELL of Lochow; *m* possibly a dau of Sinclair/St Clai of Roslin and was *k c* 1294 at the Ath-dearg (red ford) of Lorn fighting Alexander, Lord of Lorne (thus starting a feud between the Houses of Lochow and Lorne which only ended when the 1st Earl of Argyll (*see below*) *m* the Lorne heiress *c* 1465), leaving issue:

1 NEIL/NIGEL, for whom *see* below

2 Donald; ancestor of the Earls of Loudoun (*qv*)

3 Dugald (Sir) of Torsa, Laird of Menstrie; swore fealty to EDWARD I 1296 but later joined ROBERT BRUCE

(?)4 Arthur, (Sir); Constable Dunstaffnage; also swore fealty to EDWARD I but later joined ROBERT BRUCE(?). (Some writers doubt his paternity.)

4/5 Duncan; living 1296

5/6 Gillespic

Sir COLIN's est son,

Sir NEIL/NIGEL CAMPBELL of Lochow; ktd *c* mid-1280s, joined ROBERT THE BRUCE 1296 in struggle against the English, one of the great Barons of Parl which met at Ayr 26 April 1315 and fixed the succession to the Crown; *m* 1st by 1303 —, yr dau of Andrew Crawford, and had, with other issue:

1 COLIN (Sir), for whom *see* below

Sir NEIL allegedly *m* 2nd Margaret Cameron, possibly widow of Hubert de Multon, and by her had issue:

2 Duncan Campbell Macdhonnachie of Inverawe; ancestor of the CAMPBELLs of Inverawe

Sir NEIL *m* 3rd *c* 1312 Lady Mary Bruce (*m* 2nd 1316 Sir Alexander Fraser of Touchfraser, Gt Chamberlain of Scotland), sis of ROBERT THE BRUCE (who granted the couple and their son John all the Scottish lands of David de Strathbogie, 11th Earl of Atholl), and *d* by 1316, having by her had issue:

3 JOHN CAMPBELL of Moulin, 1st and last EARL OF ATHOLL (S), so *cr c* 1320; *b c* 1313; *m c* 1320 Joanna, dau of Sir John Menteith of Rusky and widow of Malise, 7th Earl of Strathe(a)rn (originated by 1124), but *dspl* Battle of Halidon Hill 19 July 1333, when the title expired

4 Dougal; living 1323; had:

(1) John; had:

1a Margaret/Mariota; *m* as his 2nd w her 2nd cousin Sir Colin Campbell of Lochow (*see* below)

Sir NEIL's est son,

Sir COLIN CAMPBELL of Lochow (which lands, united with those of Ardsheodnish, he was granted in free barony 10 Feb 1315); hereditary Keeper Dunoon Castle from *c* 1334; allegedly *m* Helena, dau of Sir John Mor, son of the Earl of Lennox, and *d* by 2 May 1343, having had, with two yr s (Dugal, John) and a dau, plus allegedly an illegitimate s (Niall, ancestor of the CAMPBELLs of Melfort):

Sir ARCHIBALD/ GILLESPIC CAMPBELL, Ld of Lochow; granted by DAVID II 2 May 1343 many forfeited lands, did homage to ROBERT II 26 March 1371; (?)*m* 1st a dau of Sir John Menteith(?); *m*(?2nd?) Mary (or Isabella), dau of Sir John Lamont of that Ilk, and *d* by 1394, leaving, with a yr s (Duncan, claimed by the CAMPBELLs of Glenfeochan as their ancestor):

Sir COLIN CAMPBELL, Ld of Lochow; *m* 1st Margaret, 2nd dau of Sir John Drummond of Stobhall and sis of ANNABELLA, Queen Consort of ROBERT III, by whom he had no issue; *m* 2nd by 1 April 1387 his 2nd cousin Margaret/Mariota (*see* above) and *d* by 1414, having had, with six other s (John of Barbreck, ancestor of the CAMPBELLs of Inverliver and claimed by the CAMPBELLs of Succoth (*see* that Bt) as their ancestor via a cadet branch; Colin of Ardkinglass, *m* 1396 Christina, dau of Robert Maclayman/Lamont of Inveryne and was ancestor of the CAMPBELLs of Ardentinny, Auchnawillan, Carrick, Dergachy and Clachan; Dugall Mor of Dunstaffnage, *m* a dau of Macdonald of the Isles and was ancestor of the CAMPBELLs of Glenamackrie, Scammadale, Torry and Crackaig; Donald, living 1442; Patrick; Celestin), plus allegedly two illegitimate s (Dugall Dean of Argyll, living 1442; Duncan, ancestor of the CAMPBELLs of Duntroon):

DUNCAN CAMPBELL (Sir) of Lochow, **1st Lord Campbell** (S), so *cr* 1445, PC (S); Justiciar and Ld of Argyll, a hostage for ransoming by the English of JAMES I 1424, for whom he collected the ransom and took it to Windsor, his annual income then being 1,500 marks, larger than any other hostage's; *m* 1st Lady Marjory/Marcelline Stewart (*d* by Aug 1432), dau of Robert, Duke of Albany, Regent of Scotland, and had:

1 Archibald/Celestin/Gillespic, *Master of Campbell*; *m* 1st Elizabeth, dau of John, 3rd Lord Somerville, and had:

(1) COLIN, **1st Earl**

1 (cont.) Archibald etc, *Master of Campbell*, allegedly *m* 2nd —, dau of Murdoch, Duke of Albany, and *dvp* by March 1440

The **1st Lord Campbell** *m* 2nd by 12 March 1439/40 Margaret, dau of Sir John Stewart of Blackhall and Ardgowan, illegitimate s of ROBERT III, and *d* late 1453, having by her had:

2 Colin (Sir); ancestor of the CAMPBELLs of Glenorchy, Lawers (*see* LOUDOUN, E), Glenlyon, Monzie, Barcaldine (*see* that Bt) and Breadalbane (*see* BREADALBANE AND HOLLAND, E)

3 Neil of Ormidale; ancestor of the CAMPBELLs of Ormidale

4 Duncan of Kilmichael; ancestor of the CAMPBELL Bts of Auchinbreck (*qv*)

5 Archibald; ancestor of the CAMPBELLs of Otter

His gs,

COLIN CAMPBELL, **1st Earl of Argyll** (S), so *cr* 1457; Master King's Household 1464, Ld High Chllr Scotland 1483; *m c* 9 April 1465 Elizabeth/Isabel Stewart (*d* 26 Oct 1510), est dau of 2nd Lord Lorne, was *cr* 17 April 1470 LORD LORNE together with a conveyance to him of the lands and lordship of Lorne on the resignation of his wife's unc Walter Stewart, Lord Innermeath (*see* MORAY, E), and *d* 10 May 1493, leaving, with at least three daus (Catherine, *m Bronnach* ('The Gluttonous') of Dowart (*see* MACLEAN, Bt, of Dowart); Isabel, *m* William, Master of Drummond; (*see* PERTH, E); Mary, *m* Angus, illegitimate s of 11th and last Earl of Ross; *see* BOSVILLE-MACDONALD, Bt) an er s:

ARCHIBALD CAMPBELL, **2nd Earl of Argyll**; Master Household to JAMES IV, Lt-Gen of the Isles 1500; *m* Elizabeth Stewart, dau of 1st Earl of Lennox (*see* MORAY, E), and was *ka* cmdg the Scottish vanguard at the defeat by the English of Flodden 9 Sept 1513, leaving, with other issue (including daus Catherine/ Elizabeth, *m* 1st Lachlan Maclean of Dowart (*see* MACLEAN, Bt, Of Dowart), *m* 2nd Archibald Campbell of Anchinbrech and had issue (*see* CAMPBELL, Bt of Anchinbrech); Janet *m* 2nd Earl of Atholl of the 1457 *cr* (*see* MORAY, E); Margaret *m de jure* 6th Earl of Mar, *qv*)

1 COLIN, **3rd Earl**

2 Archibald, of Skipinche/Skipnish; *m* 1st —; *m* 2nd by 1535, as her 2nd husb, Janet, sis of 6th Earl of Angus (*see* QUEENSBERRY, M) and widow of 6th Lord Glamis (*see* STRATHMORE and KINGHORNE, E), and had, with a s (John, *m* as her 3rd husb, Marion, dau of Hugh Montgomerie of Hazlehead; *see* EGLINTON and WINTON, E), an only dau (*m* her cousin Campbell of Ardentinny)

3 John (Sir), of Calder; ancestor of the Earls Cawdor (*qv*)

The 2nd EARL's est son,

COLIN CAMPBELL, **3rd Earl of Argyll**; Lt of the Borders, Warden of the Marches, Heritable Sheriff Argyllshire, Justice-Gen Scotland, Master of the King's Household 1528; *m c* 28 Feb 1506/7 Jean Gordon, dau of 3rd Earl of Huntly (*see* HUNTLY, M), and *d* by 26 March 1529, leaving an est s:

ARCHIBALD CAMPBELL, **4th Earl of Argyll**; Justiciary of Scotland and Master of the Household 1529, one of the first Scots nobles to turn Protestant, accordingly becoming a Ld of Congregation; *m* 1st by 26 March 1529 Lady Helen Hamilton, dau of 1st Earl of Arran (*see* ARRAN, E, preliminary remarks), and *d* 1558, leaving:

1 ARCHIBALD CAMPBELL, B5th Earl of Argyll, PC (S, 1571); *b c* 1532; made Justiciar Scotland 1558 by MARY QUEEN OF SCOTS, opposed her 1565 and helped plot Darnley's murder, nevertheless cmded (albeit indecisively) MARY's forces at the Battle of Langside 1568, only to come to an agreement with the Regent Morton 1572 and by the latter be made Ld Chllr; *m* 1st *c* 1 July 1553 (*divorce* 23 June 1573) Jean Stuart (*d* 7 Jan 1587/8), illegitimate dau of JAMES V by Elizabeth, dau of John Bethune of Creich; *m* 2nd *c* 5 Aug 1573 Lady Janet Cunningham (*m* 2nd 1583 Humphrey Colquhoun of Luss (*see* that Bt) and *dsp* 1584), 2nd dau of 6th Earl of Glencairn (*see* CUNING-HAME, Bt), and *dsp* 12 Sept 1575

The **4th Earl** *m* 2nd 21 April 1541 Lady Margaret Graham, dau of 3rd Earl of Menteith, by whom he had, with other further issue:

2 COLIN, **6th Earl**

1 Margaret; *m* 11 Jan 1563/4 1st Lord Doune (*see* MORAY, E), and *d* Feb 1571/2, leaving issue

2 Janet; *m* Hector Maclean of Dowart and had issue (*see* MACLEAN, Bt, of Dowart)

The **4th Earl** *m* 3rd Katherine, dau of Lachlan Maclean (*see* MACLEAN, Bt of Dowart), and *d* by 2 Dec 1558

The 5th EARL's half-bro,

Sir COLIN CAMPBELL of Boquhan, **6th Earl of Argyll**; Ld Chllr Scotland 1579; *m* 1st *c* 14 Oct 1551 Joan Stewart (*dsp*), dau of 1st Lord Methven (*see* MORAY, E); *m* 2nd between May 1571 and 26 Feb 1571/12 Lady Agnes/Annabel (*d* 16 July 1588), dau of 4th Earl Marischal (*see* KINTORE, E) and widow of 1st Earl of Moray (the Regent), and *d* 10 Sept 1584, having by her had:

1 ARCHIBALD, **7th Earl**

2 Colin, of Lundie, Angus, Forfar; *m* 26 June 1599 his cousin Maria, sis of Duncan Campbell of Glenorchy and widow of 6th Earl of Menteith, and had issue:

(1) **Sir Colin Campbell of Lundie, 1st Bt** (NS), so *cr* 13 Dec 1627 with remainder to his heirs male whatsover; his son or gs:

1a **Sir Colin Campbell of Lundie, 2nd Bt**; *dspm* by 1696, leaving a dau and coheir Katherine (*m* 1696 Alexander Russell of Noncoffer), but the btcy passed to his cousin the **1st Duke of Argyll** (*see* below)

The 6th EARL's er son,

ARCHIBALD CAMPBELL, **7th Earl of Argyll**; *b* 1575; Justice-Gen of Scotland; turned RC by 1618 and fought for PHILIP III OF SPAIN against the Dutch, being accordingly outlawed as a traitorous rebel 16 Feb 1618/9 (pardoned 22 Nov 1621); *m* 1st 24 July 1592 Lady Agnes Douglas (*d* 3 May 1608), dau of 7th Earl of Morton (*qv*) and an RC who influenced her husb's conversion, and had, with three other daus:

1 ARCHIBALD CAMPBELL, **8th Earl** and **1st Marquess of Argyll**

1 Mary; *b c* 1622; *m* 20 March 1641/2, as his 2nd w, 2nd Lord Rollo (*qv*) of Duncrub and was *bur* 12 Jun 1669

The **7th Earl** *m* 2nd 30 Nov 1610 Anne (author; *d* 12 Jan 1634/5), dau and coheir of Sir William Cornwallis, of Brome, and *d* by 29 Nov 1638, having by her had, with other issue:

2 JAMES CAMPBELL, **Lord of Kintyre** (S), so *cr* 22 Feb 1626 with remainder to heirs male, further *cr* 28 March 1642 EARL OF IRVINE and LORD OF LUNDIE with remainder to the heirs male of his body, and *dsp* by 16 March 1646, when the latter titles expired but the former passed to his half-bro, the **1st Marquess of Argyll**

The 7th EARL's er s,

ARCHIBALD CAMPBELL, **1st Marquess of Argyll** (S), so *cr* by letters patent 15 Nov 1641, PC (S 1628); *b* probably 1607; *educ* St Andrews; resigned 1628 to CHARLES I the hereditary Justiciarship of Scotland, reserving to himself and his heirs the jurisdiction of the Western Isles, Argyll, and wherever else he had lands in Scotland (ratified by Parl 1633); Extrdy Ld of Session 1634; Covenanter, and though successful in spreading Presbyterianism forcibly throughout Angus, Atholl and Badnoch was defeated by Montrose (*see* MONTROSE, D) at Battles of Inverlochy 2 Feb 1644/5 and Kilsyth 15 Aug 1645; renewed the Covenant 1648 in concert with CROMWELL but in 1650 supported CHARLES II in Scotland in exchange for a pledge to *cr* him a duke and KG, only to reach an accommodation with Ld Protector CROMWELL once more in 1653; MP Aberdeenshire 1658–59; on going to London to welcome CHARLES II at the Restoration in 1660 he was imprisoned, found guilty of high treason and attainted 1661; *m* by 6 Aug 1626 his cousin Lady Margaret Douglas (*d* 13 March 1677/8), 2nd dau of 8th Earl of Morton (*qv*), and was beheaded 27 May 1661, when all his titles were forfeited, leaving, with three daus and a yr s (Neil, *m* Lady Vere Kerr, sis of 1st Marquess of Lothian,(*qv*):

ARCHIBALD CAMPBELL, **9th Earl of Argyll** (restored to all his predecessor's titles bar the marquessate 16 Oct 1663, together 15 Oct 1667 with the estates), PC (S 1664); *b* 26 Feb 1628/9; Col Foot Gds, fought as royalist Battles of Dunbar 3 Sept 1650 and Worcester 3 Sept 1651 (as Lt-Gen); imprisoned and sentenced to death at Restoration 26 Aug 1662 but set free 4 June 1663, Extrdy Ld of Session 1674–81, refused to subscribe to the Test Act, sentenced to death for high treason 19 Dec 1681, escaped from Edinburgh Castle disguised as a page holding up the train of his step-dau Lady Sophia Lindsay and fled to Holland, following which he was attainted and stripped of his titles, Gen pro-Monmouth forces Scotland 1685 but the campaign proved a fiasco and he was captured and beheaded 30 June 1685; *m* 1st 13 May 1650 Lady Mary Stuart (*d* May 1668), dau of 4th Earl of Moray (*qv*), and had, with three daus:

1 ARCHIBALD CAMPBELL, **1st Duke of Argyll** (S), so *cr* 23 June 1701, as also MARQUESS OF KINTYRE and LORN, EARL OF CAMPBELL AND COWALL, VISCOUNT OF LOCHOW AND GLENYLA, and LORD OF INVERARY, MULL, MORVERN, and TIRIE, with remainder to heirs male whatsoever, having been acknowledged EARL OF ARGYLL by the Convention of Estates in Scotland shortly before his f's attainder was formally reversed 5 June 1689, also s cousin as 3rd Bt by 1696, PC (S 1689); proposed to JAMES II that he fight against his own f's pro-Monmouth invasion 1685 but in 1688 switched to WILLIAM III; Extrdy Ld of Session 1694–1703, Col 4th Horse Gds 1696–1703, a Ld of Treasury 1696–1703; *m* 12 March 1677/8 Elizabeth (*d* 9 May 1735), dau of Sir Lionel Tollemache, 3rd Bt (*qv*), of Helmingham, Suffolk, by Elizabeth, Countess of Dysart (*see* DYSART, E) in her own right and widow of 1st Duke of Lauderdale (*see* LAUDERDALE, E), and *d* 25 Sept 1703, having had:

(1) JOHN CAMPBELL, **2nd Duke of Argyll**, 1st and last BARON OF CHATHAM and EARL OF GREENWICH, Kent (both E), so *cr* 26 Nov 1705, as also 27 April 1719 DUKE OF GREENWICH (GB), KG (March 1709/10), KT (Feb 1703/4–March 1709/10), PC (GB Feb 1708/9); *b* 10 Oct 1680; Extrdy Ld of Session 1704–08, High Commr S Parl 1705, strongly pro-Protestant succession (which with the Duke of Somerset (*qv*) he helped secure by an unsolicited appearance before the PC at its crucial session of 30 July 1714) and Union of English and Scottish Parls, Col: 4th Horse Gds 1703–15, 3rd Foot 1707–11, RHG 1715–16, 1733–40 and Feb-March 1742 and 3rd Horse (later 2nd Dragoon Gds) 1726–33, Brig-Gen 1704, Maj Gen 1706, Lt Gen 1709, Gen 1711, FM Jan 1735/6, served War Spanish Succession 1708–10, Amb Spain Jan 1710/1, Govr Minorca 1712–April 1714 and Oct 1714–16, cmded Hanoverian troops in defeating Jacobites Battle of Sheriffmuir 13 Nov 1715, Ld Lt Surrey 1715–16 and Argyllshire and Dunbartonshire 1715–43, Ld Steward Household 1718/9–25; *m* 1st *c* 30 Dec 1701 Mary (*dsp* 16 Jan 1716), dau of Thomas Browne later Duncombe (*see* FEVERSHAM, B); *m* 2nd 6 June 1717 Jane (Maid-of-Honour to QUEEN ANNE; *d* 16 April 1767), dau of Thomas Warburton, of Winnington, Cheshire (s of Sir George Warburton, 1st Bt, of Arley), and *dspms* 4 Oct 1743, when his E and GB titles expired, having by her had, with four yr daus:

1a CAROLINE Campbell, 1st and last BARONESS OF GREENWICH, Co Kent (GB), so *cr* 19 Aug 1767; *b* 17 Nov 1717; *m* 1st 2 Oct 1742 Francis SCOTT, Earl of Dalkeith, est s of 2nd Duke of Buccleuch (*d* 1 April 1750; *see* BUCCLEUCH and QUEENSBERRY, D); *m* 2nd 18 Sept 1755 Hon Charles TOWNSHEND, PC, s of 3rd Viscount Townshend (*see* TOWNSHEND, M), and *dspms* 11 Jan 1794, when the Barony expired

(2) ARCHIBALD CAMPBELL, **3rd Duke of Argyll**, 1st and last EARL AND VISCOUNT OF ILAY, LORD ORANSAY, DUNOON, AND ARASE (S), so *cr* 19 Oct 1706, PC (1711); *b* June 1682; *educ* Eton, Glasgow U and Utrecht; a Ld S Treasury 1705–06, a Commr Treaty Union E and S Parls, rep S peer 1707–13 and 1715–61, Ld Justice-Gen S 1710–61, Ld Clerk Registrar 1714–16, Keeper Gt Seal 1733–61, fought under bro at Sheriffmuir 1715 (wounded), granted £21,000 (over £1,250,000 in late 1990s terms) for abolition of hereditary justiciarship of Argyllshire and the Isles, shrievalty of Argyll and regality of Campbell 1747, built Inveraray Castle; *m c* 19 Jan 1712/3 Anne (*dsp* 1 Sept 1723), dau of Maj Walter Whitfield, MP Romney, and *dspl* 15 April 1761, when the 1706 titles expired

(1) Anne; *m* 1st 2nd Earl of Bute (*see* BUTE, M); *m* 2nd 19 Sept 1731 Alexander Fraser, 7th of Strichen (*see* LOVAT, L), and *d* 20 Oct 1736, leaving issue

2 John, of Mamore; sentenced to death 1685 for his part in his f's rebellion, pardoned and forfeiture annulled 1689, MP (S) Argyllshire 1700, (GB) Dumbarton 1708–22 and 1722–27; *m* 1692 Elizabeth (*d* 13 April 1758), dau of 8th Lord Elphinstone (*qv*), and *d* 7 April 1729, leaving, with other issue (including William, *m* as her 3rd husb Bridget, widow of (a) Edward Evers and (b) Sir Cordell Firebrace, 3rd and last Bt (*see* PARKER, Bt, of Melford Hall), and Primrose, *m* 11th Lord (Fraser of) Lovat, *qv*):

(1) JOHN, **4th Duke**

3 Charles; forfeited for participation in his f's rebellion, forfeiture rescinded 1689, MP (S) Campbelltown 1700; *m* 1st 1678 Sophia (*d* 1698), 2nd dau of 1st Earl of Balcarres (*see* CRAWFORD and BALCARRES, E) and his f's step-dau, through whom the Earl of Argyll's escape from Edinburgh Castle was effected; *m* 2nd Bettie Bowles and by her had issue

4 James, of Burnbank and Boquhan; on 14 Nov 1690, with the aid of Archibald Montgomery and Sir John Johnston of Caskieben, Bt (*see* ANNANDALE AND HARTFELL, E), forcibly carried off and married Mary, an heiress of 13 and dau of Sir George Wharton; marriage annulled by Act of Parl and, while Johnston was executed at Tyburn, Campbell escaped to Scotland and was afterwards Col of Dragoons, MP Renfrew 1699–1707 and Ayr 1708–10; *m* Hon Margaret Leslie (*d* 17 April 1755), 4th dau of 1st Lord Newark (dormant or extinct 1694), and had issue

The **9th Earl** *m* 2nd 28 Jan 1670 Anne (*bur* 29 May 1707), 2nd dau of 1st Earl of Seaforth (*see* CROMARTIE, E) and widow of 1st Earl of Balcarres (*see* CRAWFORD and BALCARRES, E), who was imprisoned in Edinburgh Castle on the rumour of her husb's invasion

The 3rd DUKE's cousin,

JOHN CAMPBELL, **4th Duke of Argyll**, KT (1765), PC (1762); *b c* 1693; Lt-Col 1712, Col: 39th Foot 1737–38, 21st Foot 1738–52, N Br Dragoons (later Scots Greys) 1752–70, Brig-Gen 1743, Maj Gen 1744, Lt Gen 1747, Gen 1765, fought Battle of Dettingen 1741, Groom Bedchamber 1727–60, MP (Whig) Bute 1713–15, Elgin burghs 1715–22 and 1725–27 and Dunbartonshire 1727–61, rep S peer 1761–70, Govr Limerick 1761–70; *m* 1720 Mary (*d* 18 Dec 1760), dau of 2nd Lord Bellenden of Broughton (*see* ROXBURGH, D), and *d* 9 Nov 1770, having had five children; his est s:

JOHN CAMPBELL, **5th Duke of Argyll**, also 1st BARON SUNDRIDGE, of Coomb Bank, Kent (GB), so *cr vp* 22 Dec 1766 with remainder to his bros; *bapt* June 1723; MP (Whig) Glasgow 1744–61 and Dover 1765–66, C-in-C Scotland 1767–78, Ld Lt Argyllshire 1794–1800, FM 1796; *m* 3 March 1759 Elizabeth (*bapt* 7 Dec 1733, Ldy of Bdchamber to QUEEN CHARLOTTE 1761–84; a beauty of the Court of GEORGE III, who greatly admired her; lcr 20 May 1776 **Baroness Hamilton of Hameldon**, Leicester (GB); *d* 20 Dec 1790), 2nd dau of John Gunning (*see* GUNNING, Bt), and widow of 6th Duke of Hamilton (*see* HAMILTON and BRANDON, D), and *d* 24 May 1806, having had:

1 George John, *Earl of Campbell*; *b* 17 Feb 1763; *d* 12 July 1764

2 GEORGE WILLIAM CAMPBELL, **6th Duke of Argyll** and **3rd Baron Hamilton** (inherited his mother's Barony of Hamilton on death 1799 of his half-bro 8th Duke of Hamilton); *b* 22 Sept 1766; MP (Whig) St Germans 1790–96, Ld Lt Argyll 1800–39, Keeper Gt Seal of Scotland 1827–39, Ld Steward Household 1833–34 and 1835–39; *m* 29 Nov 1810 Lady Caroline Elizabeth (*d* 16 June 1835), dau of 5th Earl of Jersey (*qv*) and formerly w of 1st Marquess of Anglesey (*qv*), and *dspl* 22 Oct 1839 (an illegitimate dau *m* George Innes; *see* INNES, Bt of Balvenie

3 JOHN DOUGLAS EDWARD HENRY, **7th Duke**

1 Augusta; *m* Col Henry Clavering and *d* 22 June 1831, leaving issue

2 Charlotte Susan Maria; authoress; *m* 1st 21 June 1796 Col John Campbell (*d* 15 March 1809), son of Walter Campbell of Shawfield, and had issue; *m* 2nd 17 March 1818 Rev Edward John Bury (*d* 1832) and *d* 1 April 1861

The 6th DUKE's bro,

JOHN DOUGLAS EDWARD HENRY CAMPBELL, **7th Duke of Argyll**; *b* 21 Dec 1777; MP (Whig) Argyllshire 1799–1822; *m* 1st 3 Aug 1802 Elizabeth (*dsp* 9 Dec 1818), est dau of William Campbell of Fairfield; *m* 2nd 17 April 1820 Joan (*d* 22 Jan 1828), dau and heir of John Glassel of Long Niddry, by Helen, dau of John Buchan of Leatham (*see* BUCHAN-HEPBURN, Bt), and by her had issue:

1 John Henry; *b* 11 Jan 1821; *d* 27 May 1837

2 GEORGE DOUGLAS, **8th Duke**

1 Emma Augusta; *m* 26 Aug 1870 Sir John Mcneill, GCB, PC (*d* 17 May 1883), and *d* 30 May 1893

The **7th Duke** *m* 3rd 8 Jan 1831 Anne Colquhoun (*d* 25 Feb 1874), est dau of John Cunninghame of Craigends and widow of Dr George Cunningham Monteath, and *d* 25 April 1847

The 7th DUKE's only surv son,

GEORGE DOUGLAS CAMPBELL, **8th Duke of Argyll** and 1st DUKE OF ARGYLL (UK), so *cr* 7 Aug 1892 , KG (1883), KT (1856), PC (1853); *b* 30 April 1823; Ld Privy Seal 1852–55, 1859–66 and 1880–81, PMG 1855–58, Sec of State India, DCL, LLD, FRS, Chllr St Andrews, Tstee Br Museum, author: *The Reign of Law*; *m* 1st 31 July 1844 Lady Elizabeth Georgiana Sutherland-Leveson-Gower, VA, CI (*d* 25 May 1878), est dau of 2nd Duke of Sutherland (*qv*), and had issue:

1 JOHN DONALD SUTHERLAND CAMPBELL, **9th Duke of Argyll**, KT (1871), PC (1875), GCMG (1878), GCVO (1901), DL (Dunbartonshire); *b* 6 Aug 1845; *educ* Eton and Trin Coll Cambridge (Hon LLD 1902); MP (Lib) Argyllshire 1868–78 and S Manchester (Lib U) 1895–1900, Ld Lt Argyllshire 1900, Pres Argyllshire TFA, Govr-Gen 1878–83, Govr and Constable Windsor Castle 1892–1914, Hon LLD Glasgow 1907, Chllr Order St Michael and St George, Roy Victorian Chain, Prussian Order Black Eagle; *m* 21 March 1871 HRH PRINCESS LOUISE CAROLINE ALBERTA, VA, CI, GCVO, GBE, DGStJ, Col-in-Chief Princess Louise's Argyll and Sutherland Highrs, Pres Nat Tst, Hon Freeman Roy Borough Kensington (*d* 3 Dec 1939), 4th dau of HM QUEEN VICTORIA, and *dsp* 2 May 1914

2 Archibald, JP and DL (Argyllshire); *b* 18 Dec 1846; Capt 5th Vol Bn Princess Louise (Argyll and Sutherland) Highrs; *m* 12 Jan 1869 Janey Sevilla (*d* 15 July 1923), 3rd dau of James Henry Callander, of Craigforth, Stirling, and Ardkinglas, Argyll, and ward of his f, **8th Duke**, and *d* 29 March 1913, leaving:

(1) NIALL DIARMID CAMPBELL, **10th Duke of Argyll**; *b* 16 Feb 1872; *educ* Ch Ch Oxford (BA 1896); Hon Col 8th Bn Argyll and Sutherland Highrs 1914–29, Ld Lt Argyllshire; *d* unm 20 Aug 1949

(1) Elspeth Angela; *b* 2 Nov 1873; granted by roy warrant 22 Aug 1914 rank of duke's dau; *d* unm 28 Oct 1942

3 Walter; *b* 30 July 1848; *m* 14 April 1874 Olivia Rowlandson (*m* 2nd 14 June 1890 Allan Gordon; *d* 17 Aug 1892), only dau of John Clarkson Milns, of Asory House, Bute, and *d* 2 May 1889, leaving:

(1) Douglas Walter; *b* 6 March 1877; *educ* Charterhouse and Trin Coll Cambridge; 30th Lancers WW I, IEF; *m* 1st 28 Nov 1899 Aimee Marie Suzanne (*d* 9 Feb 1920), dau of John Lawrence, of New York, and had:

1a IAN DOUGLAS, **11th Duke**

(1) (cont.) Douglas Campbell *m* 2nd 17 June 1920 Lilian Elizabeth Lutley (*d* 8 April 1957), only dau of Philip Lutley Sclater, of Odiham Priory, Hants (*see* BASING, B), and widow of Harington Morgan, Judge Civil Courts of Justice, Khartoum, and *d* 5 Jan 1926 of illness contracted in WW I

(1) Lilah Olive; *b* 10 Oct 1875; *d* unm 6 July 1960

4 George Granville; *b* 25 Dec 1850; Lt RN; *m* 8 May 1879 Sybil Lascelles (*d* 1 May 1947), only child of James Brace Alexander, and *d* 21 April 1915 leaving:

(1) Ivar; *b* 14 May 1890; 2nd Lt 3rd Bn Argyll and Sutherland Highrs; *das* 8 Jan 1916

(1) Joan; *b* 5 Aug 1887; JP; *d* unm 18 July 1960

(2) Enid; *b* 8 July 1892; *m* 1st 9 Dec 1914 (*divorce* 1925) Douglas Tollemache Anstruther, only son of Henry Torrens Anstruther, and had issue (*see* ANSTRUTHER, Bt); *m* 2nd 18 Aug 1925 (*divorce* 1931) Col Lancelot Holland, DSO, Seaforth Highrs (*d* 29 July 1943), son of Henry Holland and Mrs James Wason, and *d* 18 Dec 1964

5 Colin; *b* 9 March 1853; MP Argyll 1878–85, LLB, barrister 1886; *m* 21 July 1881 (*judicial separation* 1884) Gertrude Elizabeth (*b* 1857; author: *Topo, A Tale About English Children in Italy* (as G B Brunefille, 1878), *A Book of the Running Brook and of Still Waters* (1885), *Etiquette of Society* (1886), *Darrell Blake, a Study* (1889), playwright: *Bud and Blossom* and (with Clothilde Graves) *St Martin's Summer*, art ed *World* (newspaper) 1889–1903, fndr/co-ed *Realm* 1894095, ed *Ladies' Field* 1901–03; *d* 2 Nov 1911), yr dau of Edmund Maghlin Blood, of Brickhill, Co Clare, and Thurloe Sq, S Kensington, London, and *dsp* 19 June 1895

1 Edith; *b* 7 Nov 1849; *m* 23 Dec 1868 7th Duke of Northumberland (*qv*) and *d* 6 July 1913, leaving issue

2 Elisabeth; *m* 17 July 1880 Lt-Col Edward Harrison Clough Taylor, 23rd Roy Welch Fus (*d* 1 April 1921), son of Edward Clough-Taylor, JP, DL, of Kirkham Abbey and Firby Hall, Yorks, and *d* 24 Sept 1896, leaving issue

3 Victoria; *b* 22 May 1854; *d* unm 6 July 1910

4 Evelyn; *b* 17 Aug 1855; *m* 10 Aug 1886 James Baillie-Hamilton, son of Adml William Alexander Baillie-Hamilton (see HADDINGTON, E), and *d* 22 March 1940

5 Frances; *b* 22 Feb 1858; Hon DLitt Durham (1919), Hon LLD Edinburgh (1921); *m* 12 May 1879 Eustace James Anthony Balfour, 5th son of James Maitland Balfour, of Whittingehame, E Lothian (*see* BALFOUR, E), and *d* 25 Feb 1931, leaving issue

6 Mary Emma; *b* 22 Sept 1859; *m* 4 July 1882 Rt Rev Hon Edward Carr Glyn, Bp of Peterborough (*d* 14 Nov 1928), son of 1st Baron Wolverton (*qv*), and *d* 22 March 1947, leaving issue

7 Constance Harriet; *b* 11 Nov 1864; *m* 27 June 1891 Charles Emmott (*d* 18 Feb 1910), of North Bailey, Durham, son of Thomas Emmott, of Brookfield, Oldham, and bro of 1st and last Baron Emmott, and *d* 9 Feb 1922, leaving issue

The **8th Duke** *m* 2nd 13 Aug 1881 Amelia Maria (*d* 4 Jan 1894), dau of Rt Rev Thomas Legh Claughton, DD, Bp of St Albans, and sis of Sir Gilbert Henry Claughton, Bt (*see* 1921 edn), and widow of Col Hon Augustus Henry Archibald Anson, VC (*see* LICHFIELD, E); *m* 3rd 30 July 1895 Ina Erskin, VA (*d* 24 Dec 1925), formerly Extra Woman of the Bedchamber and Private Sec to HM QUEEN VICTORIA, yst dau of Archibald McNeill, of Colonsay, Argyll, and *d* 24 April 1900

The 10th DUKE's 1st cousin once-removed,

IAN DOUGLAS CAMPBELL, **11th Duke of Argyll**, TD (1953); *b* 18 June 1903; *educ* Milton, Mass., USA, and Ch Ch Oxford; Capt 8th Bn Argyll and Sutherland Highrs (TA), WW II (POW 1940–45), KStJ; *m* 1st 12 Dec 1927 (*divorce* 1934) Hon Janet Gladys Aitken, only dau of 1st Baron Beaverbrook (*qv*), and had issue:

1 *Jeanne Louise; *b* 10 Dec 1928; jnlst; *m* 1st 1962 (*divorce* 1963), as his 2nd w, the writer Norman Mailer, son of Isaac Barnett Mailer, and has issue:

(1) *Kate; *b* 1962

1 (cont.) Lady Jeanne Mailer *m* 2nd March 1964 *John Sergeant Cram, son of Henry Sergeant Cram, of Foot Point Plantation, Bluffton, USA, and has further issue:

(2) *Cusi Charlotte Campbell Sergeant; *b* 1967

The **11th Duke** *m* 2nd Nov 1935 (*divorce* 1951) Louise Hollingsworth Morris (*d* 10 Feb 1970), only dau of Henry Clews, of Château La Napoule, Alpes Maritimes, France, and formerly wife of Hon Andrew Nicolas Armstrong Vanneck, MC (*see* HUNTINGFIELD, B), and by her had issue:

1 IAN CAMPBELL, **12th and present Duke of Argyll**

2 +Colin Ivar; *b* 14 May 1946; *educ* USA and Trin Coll Glenalmond; deep sea diver; *m* 23 March 1974 (*divorce* 1975) Georgia/Georgie Ariana (author: *The Substance and Shadows* and *A Life Worth Living* (1997)), dau of Michael Ziadie, of Jamaica

The **11th Duke** *m* 3rd 22 March 1951 (*divorce* 1963) Margaret (*d* 1993), only dau of George Hay Whigham, of 48 Upper Grosvenor St, London W1, and formerly wife of Charles Sweeny (*see* also RUTLAND, D); *m* 4th 15 June 1963 Mathilda Coster (*d* 6 June 1997), dau of Stanley Mortimer, of Lichfield, Conn., and formerly w of Prof Clemens Heller, of Paris U, and *d* 7 April 1973, having by her had:

2 Elspeth; *b* 29 April, *d* 4 May 1967

Seat: Inveraray Castle, Argyll. The Gothick exterior is by Roger Morris, who began work in 1744, although its actual execution was superintended by William Adam and his sons John and Robert. A little over a century later the top storeys burnt down and Anthony Salvin designed a less than wholly harmonious replacement. The designer chiefly responsible for Inveraray's appearance inside was Robert Mylne, who was not commissioned till nearly 30 years after the castle had been begun by Morris. His work is in complete contrast to the fantasy appearance of the exterior, being high classical, with copious plasterwork and painted panelling. Especially noteworthy is the dining room, with its grisaille effect and ornamentation by Biagio Rebecca (who also, with Angelica Kauffmann, painted the Royal Academy's lecture room in Somerset House).

ARMSTRONG

Arms: Quarterly, 1st and 4th, argent, issuing from the sinister a dexter arm embowed habited gules, the hand grasping the trunk of an oak tree eradicated and broken at the top proper (for ARMSTRONG); 2nd and 3rd, argent, two ravens hanging palewise sable suspended from an arrow gules headed and feathered proper piercing both their heads fessways (for MURDOCH). **Crests:** 1 An arm in armour embowed, the hand grasping the broken trunk of an oak tree, all proper (for ARMSTRONG), 2 A raven rising sable pierced through the breast by an arrow as in the arms (for MURDOCH). **Motto:** *Invictus maneo* ('I remain unconquered'). **Creation:** Bt. (UK) 18 Sept 1841.

CLARENCE FRANCIS ARMSTRONG, 6TH BT, of Gallen Priory, King's Co, CMG (1959) [Sir Andrew Armstrong Bt CMG, 5 Thamesfield Court, Wargrave Rd, Henley-on-Thames, Oxon RG9 2LX]; *b* 1 May 1907; *s* cousin 1987; *educ* St Edmund's Ware and Christ's Coll Cambridge (BA 1928); Cadet Colonial Admin Serv Western Pacific 1929, Admin Offr Nigeria 1940, Sr Dist Offr 1949, Admin Offr Staff Grade 1954, Perm Sec Min Mines and Power Fedn Nigeria 1957, ret 1961; *m* 1st 8 Jan 1930 Phyllis Marguerite (*d* 18 Jan 1930), dau of Lt Col Roland Henry Waithman, DSO; *m* 2nd 17 June 1932 Laurel May (*d* 1988), er dau of Alfred Wellington Stuart, of Lakeba, Fiji, and *d* 21 Dec 1997, having had:

1 Andrew Michael Kingsley; *b* 30 June 1935; *educ* Ampleforth and Christ's Coll Cambridge (BA); *d* 23 Aug 1969

2 +CHRISTOPHER JOHN EDMUND STUART, MBE (1979) [Lt-Col Christopher Armstrong MBE, Sheepridge House, Lordswood Lane, Chilworth, Hants SO16 7JG]; *b* 15 Jan 1940; *educ* Ampleforth and RMA Sandhurst; Lt-Col RCT; *m* 1972 *Georgina Elizabeth Carey, 2nd dau of Lt-Col WG Lewis, of Hayling Island, Hants, and has issue:

(1) +Charles Andrew; *b* 1973

(2) +James Hugo; *b* 1974

(3) +Sam Edward; *b* 1986

(1) *Victoria Jane; *b* 1980

Lineage: ANDREW ARMSTRONG; migrated from Scotland to NI *c* 1600 and settled in Co Fermanagh; royalist at outbreak of 1641 Uprising, offr of horse under CHARLES I; *m* 1st — Alexander and had, with a dau:

1 Andrew; left issue

ANDREW ARMSTRONG *m* 2nd Elizabeth Johnson and by her had, with other issue:

2 EDMUND, for whom *see* below

ANDREW ARMSTRONG *m* 3rd in his 74th year Mrs Jane Stephenson and *d* 1671 aged 95, having had by her, with other issue:

3 Archibald; ancestor of the ARMSTRONGs of Ballylin and the ARMSTRONG Bts of Ashburn Place (*see* 1940 edn)

ANDREW ARMSTRONG's 2nd son,

EDMUND ARMSTRONG, of Stonetown, Co Kildare; royalist, fought Battle of Worcester 1651 and taken prisoner; *m* Mary, dau of William Hamilton, of Liscloony, King's Co, and had, with seven other s and two daus:

WILLIAM ARMSTRONG, of Stonestown; *m* Alice, dau of Francis Coghlan, of Kilcolgan Castle, King's Co, and *d* 1717 or 1718 in his 80th year, having had, with a yr s and two daus:

EDMUND ARMSTRONG, of Gallen, King's Co, JP; High Sheriff King's Co 1730 and Co Kildare 1731; heir not just to his f but also his uncs, Andrew and Charles, who had bought estates in Co Kildare; *m* 1722 Elizabeth, 2nd dau of George Holmes, of Liscloony, MP Banagher, and *d* 15 April 1745, having had, with other issue:

ANDREW ARMSTRONG, of Gallen, JP (King's Co); *b* 2 May 1729; High Sheriff 1751, Col Vols; *m* 1752 Constantia Maria, 2nd dau of John Pigot, of Brockley Park, Queen's Co, by Constantia Maria, dau of Sir Roger Burgoyne, and had an est s:

EDMUND ARMSTRONG, of Gallen; *b* 14 Dec 1754; barrister 1779, High Sheriff 1818; *m* 4 Feb 1783 Elizabeth (*d* 1825), sis of 1st Baron Ashtown (*qv*), and *d* 12 Dec 1827, having had an est s:

Sir Andrew Armstrong, 1st Bt (UK), so *cr* 18 Sept 1841; *b* 19 Oct 1785; MP 1841–52, High Sheriff King's Co 1811 and 1836, Capt King's Co Militia, Receiver-Gen Stamp Duties; *m* 1 Jan 1835 Frances Fullerton (*d* 19 March 1890), dau of George Alexander Downing Fullerton, of Westwood, Hants, and Ballintoy Castle, Co Antrim, and *d* 27 Jan 1863, having had, with other issue:

1 **Sir Edmund Frederick Armstrong, 2nd Bt** (Rev), JP (King's Co); *b* 27 May 1836; Vicar Borris-in-Ossory, Queen's Co, RD; *m* 14 June 1865 Alice (*d* 8 Dec 1875), est dau of William W Fisher, and *d* 24 April 1899, leaving issue:

(1) **Sir Andrew Harvey Armstrong, 3rd Bt**, JP (King's Co); *b* 23 May 1866; Capt 3rd Bn Leinster Regt (Roy Canadians), T/Capt 5th (Serv) Bn Connaught Rangers Imp Yeo Boer War 1900–01, High Sheriff 1914; *d* unm 3 June 1922

(2) **Sir Nesbitt William Armstrong, 4th Bt**; *b* 3 July 1875; *m* 1910 Clarice Amy, dau of John Carter Hodkinson, of Maryborough, Victoria, Australia, and *d* 21 Sept 1953, having had issue:

1a **Sir Andrew St Clare Armstrong, 5th Bt**; *b* 20 Dec 1912; RAE (2nd AIF) WW II; *d* unm 1987

2a Gaven Patrick O Hara; *b* 12 June 1918; *d* 1920

1a *Edith Fisher [Mrs Clarence Cliff, 33 Freyburg St, Lyall Bay, Wellington, NZ]; *b* 1910; *m* 8 Feb 1933 Clarence Albert Cliff (*d* 1981), s of James Pendarves Cliff, of Geraldine, NZ, and has issue:

1b *Frances; *b* 23 Jan 1938; *m* 21 April 1962 *Julius Joseph Eugene Dienes de Mezökövesd, s of Julius Louis Dienes de Mezökövesd, and has issue:

1c *Katherine; *b* 1970

(1) Beatrice Frances; *b* 6 July 1868; *d* unm 7 Dec 1958

(2) Gertrude Adelaide; *b* 30 Dec 1871; *m* 8 Feb 1906 Sir Francis Hare Clayton, OBE (*d* 18 Oct 1956), est s of Charles Hare Clayton, of Ditton Hill, Surrey, and *d* 11 Feb 1962

(3) Constantia Jessie; *b* 3 Feb 1873; *d* unm 24 Nov 1965

(4) Katherine Edith; *b* 18 April 1874; *d* unm 12 Sept 1948

2 George Alexander; *b* 5 Dec 1843; *m* 1877 Elizabeth Patricena (*d* 1887), dau of Very Rev John Armstrong, Dean Kilfenora, and *dsp* 21 July 1891

3 Andrew Charles; *b* 5 Feb 1845; Lt 2nd Foot, Capt 3rd Bn Prince of Wales's Leinster Regt; factories inspr; *m* 1st 5 Feb 1874 Alice Maria (*d* 13 Jan 1881), yst dau of Sir Thomas William Clinton Murdoch, KCMG, and had issue:

(1) Edmund Clarence Richard; *b* 23 Feb 1879; FSA, MRIA; Keeper Irish Antiquities Nat Museum Dublin 1914–23, Bluemantle Pursivant of Arms 1923; *m* 10 Feb 1906 Mary Frances (*d* 14 May 1953), 2nd dau of Sir Francis Richard Cruise, MD, DL, of 93 Merrion Sq W, Dublin, and *d* 29 March 1923, leaving issue:

1a Sir ANDREW CLARENCE FRANCIS MARK ARMSTRONG, **6th Bt**

2a +(Edmund Charles) Mark [Mark Armstrong Esq, Free Hill House, Westbury-sub-Mendip, Somerset, BA5 1HJ]; *b* 17 Feb 1914; *educ* St Edmund's Ware and St John's Coll Cambridge (BA 1935); Lt (S) RNR WW II; civ serv MOD (ret 1977), replaced by deed poll 1945 forenames Clarence Charles with Charles Mark; *m* 1st 14 Oct 1939 (*divorce* 1949) Patricia Phyllis Vassall, dau of Edward Robert Vassall Adams, of Horns Cross, Devon, and Mrs James Hay; *m* 2nd 16 Aug 1951 Dorice (*d* 1983), dau of William Harold Austin, of Marlow, Bucks, and has issue:

1b +Mark Simon Warneford [Mark Armstrong Esq, 20 Boulevard Princesse Charlotte, MC 98000, Monte Carlo]; *b* 27 Oct 1954; *educ* Roy Naval Sch Malta, Kent U and Sorbonne (BA 1977); with Sotheby's Monaco; *m* 1992 *Roselyne Jeanne Thérèse, dau of Roberto Moro, of Cavalaire-sur-Mer, Var, France, and has issue:

1c +Alexander Edmund Roberto; *b* 29 Dec 1994

1c *Anne-Victoire Emily; *b* 1993

2b +Sean Andrew [Sean Armstrong Esq, Free Hill House, Westbury-sub-Mendip, Wells, Somerset]; *b* 27 Oct 1954; *educ* Roy Naval Sch Malta and Bristol U (BSc 1976, MBA 1992)

3b +Patrick Austin; *b* 27 Oct 1954; *educ* Roy Naval Sch Malta and Merrist Wood Ag Coll Surrey; horticulturist

1a Katherine Mary; *b* 1909; *m* 4 Sept 1937 Jerrold E Vassall Adams (*d* 1989), of Medmenham, Bucks, est s of Edward Robert Vassall Adams, of Horns Cross, Devon, and *d* 1996, having had:

1b (Paul) Rory; *b* 4 Oct 1941; *educ* Stonyhurst; MD, PhD, BS; Surgn-Lt RN; *m* 7 Dec 1967 *Nicola [Dr Nicola Adams, High Hedges, Brookthorpe, Glos, GL4 OUS], er dau of Dr R Lissau, and *d* 1983, leaving issue:

1c +Guy Luke; *b* 11 Oct 1969

2c +Daniel Francis; *b* 19 Aug 1971

1b *Augusta Frances [Mrs Michael Regester, 4 Abbey Cottages, Medmenham, Bucks SL7 2HB]; *b* 25 Sept 1938; *m* 1st 1958 (*divorce* 1972) Alastair Ian Hamish Valentine, of Marlow, 2nd s of Guy Valentine, of S Rhodesia, and has had:

1c *Hamish Guy; *b* 28 Nov 1958; *m* 1981 (*divorce* 1990) Sarah Alexandra MacDermott, of Perth, W Australia

2c Alastair Rory; *b* 11 Jan 1961; *d* 1988

3c *Ranald Andrew; *b* 28 June 1962; *m* 1996 *Debra Ellen Kennedy, of Melbourne, Australia

1c *Katherine Ann; *b* 10 Dec 1959; *m* 1984 *Michael Das Gupta, of Perth, W Australia, and has issue:

1d *Nathan Lee; *b* 1987

1d *Jessica Dawn; *b* 1983

2d *Hannah Catherine; *b* 1993

1b (cont.) Mrs Augusta Valentine *m* 2nd 1972 (*divorce* 1984) Christopher K Keele and has further issue:

2c *Stephanie Jane; *b* 1974

1b (cont.) Mrs Augusta Keele *m* 3rd 1984 *Michael John Carr Regester

2b *Sarah Catherine [Mrs Richard Holland, 29 Victoria Park Ave, Toronto, M4E 351, Canada]; *b* 7 Aug 1945; *m* 1971 *Richard Thomas Holland and has issue:

1c *Derek Simon; *b* 1977

2c *Toby Michael; *b* 1984

1c *Camilla Juliet; *b* 1973

(1) Mary Ann Katharine; *m* 1st 1 Jan 1902 (*divorce* 1920) her cousin Nevill Alexander Drummond Armstrong (*d* 21 Nov 1954) and had issue (*see* below); *m* 2nd 20 Oct 1920 John Butler Aitken, 2nd s of Rev George Aitken, BA, of BC, and *d* 27 April 1954

(2) Mildred Amy; *d* 1884

(3) Muriel Agnes Kavanagh; *m* 15 Jan 1908 James Douglas Graham and *d* 9 May 1923, leaving issue

3 (cont.) Capt Andrew Armstrong *m* 2nd 25 July 1888 Annie Beatrice (*d* 30 March 1949), dau of John Lorimer, of Ayleston, Leics, and *d* 5 Oct 1895, having by her had issue:

(2) John Andrew; *b* 17 Feb 1892; Assist DC Lawra Gold Coast, Capt 3rd Bn Lancs Fus; *m* 1 Jan 1935 Pauline (*d* 1983), yr dau of Maj Charles Oswald Nicholson Williams, of Pulborough, and *d* 1974, leaving issue:

1a *Jill Sara; *b* 29 June 1937; *m* 21 March 1958 *Capt Alexander Maxwell-Hyslop, late 17th/21st Lancers, er s of Capt Alexander Henry Maxwell Hyslop, AM, RN (ret), of Cornwall, and has issue:

1b *Lucinda Frances [Mrs Charles Moubray, 22 Narbonne Ave, London SW4]; *b* 2 March 1959; *m* 1985 *Charles John Moubray, s of Michael Moubray, of Ridlington House, Rutland, and has issue:

1c *James; *b* 1987

2b *Zara Belinda; *b* 3 Sept 1962; *m* 1988 *Maj James Pollock, Irish Gds, s of Brig J P O'H Pollock, of Upper Froyle, Hants

(4) Nadine Alice; *m* 4 Feb 1919 Maj Vernon Robert Guise, OBE, MC, RA, only s of Rev Vernon Lane Guise, Rector Stopham, Pulburough, and had issue (*see* GUISE, Bt)

4 Frederick William; *b* 19 Feb 1846; *d* same year

5 Montagu Fullerton; *b* 8 March 1852; *m* 3 April 1873 Florence Angelica Sophia (*d* 10 July 1936), dau of Charles John Proby, Consul Florence, and *d* 9 Feb 1926, leaving issue:

(1) Nevill Alexander Drummond, OBE (1919); *b* 18 April 1874; Lt-Col RM, Capt 16th Bn Manitoba Regt WW I (despatches) and WW II, Cmdt Canadian Corps Sniping Sch France 1916–18, Cmdt RM Corps Sniping Sch 1942–45, Ch Scout Canadian Army 1918, FRGS, author: *Yukon Yesterdays*; *m* 1 Jan 1902 (*divorce* 1920) his cousin Mary Anne Katharine (*d* 27 April 1954), dau of Capt Andrew Charles Armstrong (*see* above), and *d* 21 Nov 1954, leaving issue:

1a Eileen Molly Nevill; *b* 1 April 1903

(2) Jack Proby; *b* 27 May 1878; Consul Tegucigalpa 1911, Actg 1st Sec Legn Guatemala 1919–20, ret 1920; *m* 25 Oct 1912 Maria Dominga Alvarenga, dau of John Molina, and *d* 21 Feb 1953, leaving issue:

1a Montagu John Proby, DSC (1942); *b* Nov 1913; *educ* Harrow and Merton Coll Oxford; Lt-Cdr RNVR WW II (despatches)

2a *Martha Florence; *b* 16 Nov 1921; *m* 1st 1944 (*divorce* 1956) Elmer Page Madsen; *m* 2nd 1958 *James Worth Thornton, of Virginia, USA, only s of Sir Henry Worth Thornton, KBE, MInstCE, of Montreal

(3) Charles Francis; *b* 1881; Capt Egypt Coast Gd; *d* unm 11 Dec 1904

(4) Frederick Edmund John; *b* 1889; Lt 181st Pioneer Regt IA; *m* 6 Feb 1915 Stella (*d* 31 July 1966), er dau of J R Morgan, of Weymouth, and *d* 27 Oct 1919, leaving issue:

1a *Beatrice; *b* 24 Feb 1916; *m* 11 Dec 1937 *Cdr Edric Guy Phillip Bromfield Knapton, DSC, RN, of Inkpen, Berks, yst s of Capt A L K Knapton, RN, and has issue:

1b *Guy Augustus Bromfield [Guy Knapton Esq, c/o Barclays Bank Ltd, Godalming, Surrey]; *b* 9 Sept 1940; *educ* Downside and Pembroke Coll Cambridge (MA 1967); *m* 23 July 1966 *Catherine Margaret Ffoulkes, dau of Francis Herbert Walker, of Middlesbrough, Teesside, and has issue:

1c *A son; *b* 2 March 1971

2b *Julian Richard Anthony; *b* 29 Dec 1954

1b *Vanessa Josephine Stella; *b* 15 April 1944

2b *Maria Victoria Gwendolyn; *b* 24 Sept 1947

3b *Louise Elizabeth Teresa; *b* 4 Sept 1956

2a *Madeline; *b* 29 March 1917; *m* 1942 (*divorce* 1967) Bernard Michael Edmund O'Mahoney and has issue:

1b *Kevin Edmund; *b* 9 June 1943; *d* 1983

2b *Hugh Frederick Michael; *b* 17 Aug 1948

3b *Stephen Lawrence Thomas; *b* 24 Dec 1956

1b *Philippa Katherine; *b* 20 Dec 1944

2b *Deirdre Lillian Mary; *b* 5 Jan 1958

(1) Madeline Ruth; *m* 4 March 1913 John Collis Snaith (*d* 8 Dec 1936), s of J Snaith, of W Bridgford, Nottingham, and *d* 12 March 1931

(2) Stella Elizabeth Constance; *d* unm 5 June 1935

(3) Frances Evelyn; *m* 19 Dec 1906 Sir Ernest Frederic Goodhart, 2nd Bt (*qv*), and *d* 3 Jan 1953, leaving issue

(4) Beatrice Helen; *m* 26 Sept 1911 Robert Cox (*d* 1952), s of Robert Cox, MP, and *d* leaving issue

6 Charles Nesbitt Frederick; *b* 25 Jan 1858; *m* 22 Dec 1882 (*divorce* 1900) Melba Helen Porter (Dame Nellie Melba, the singer), GBE (1927, DBE 1918) (*d* 23 Feb 1931), dau of David Mitchell, of Melbourne and Doonside, Richmond, Australia, and *d* Sept 1948, leaving issue:

(1) George Nesbitt; *b* 16 Oct 1883; Lt 3rd Bn Roy Berks Regt; *m* 1st 18 Dec 1906 (*divorce* 1908) Phoebe Georgina Frances (Ruby) (*d* 1939), only dau of Lt-Col Jocelyn Otway, of 7 Park Lane, London W; *m* 2nd 20 Feb 1913 Evelyn Mary (*d* 1973), dau of Michael Doyle, of Brisbane, Queensland, and *d* 1971, having by her had issue:

1a Frederick; *b* 20, *d* 21 Nov 1920

1a *(Helen) Pamela Fullerton Melba, raised to the rank of a baron's widow 1955 [The Rt Hon Pamela Lady Vestey, Coome Cottage, Coldstream, Victoria, Australia]; *b* 14 Sept 1918; *m* 27 Sept 1939 Capt Hon William Howarth Vestey, Scots Gds (*ka* Italy 25 June 1944), only s of 2nd Baron Vestey (*qv*), and has issue

ARMSTRONG OF ILMINSTER

Creation: B. (LP, UK) 1988.

THE BARON ARMSTRONG OF ILMINSTER, of Ashill, Co Somerset (Sir Robert Temple Armstrong, GCB (1983, KCB 1978, CB 1974), CVO (1975)) [The Rt Hon The Lord Armstrong of Ilminster GCB CVO, House of Lords, London SW1A 0PW]; *b* 30 March 1927; *educ* Eton (Fell 1979–94) and Ch Ch Oxford (Hon Student 1985); Treasury: joined 1950, Assist Pncpl 1950–55, Pncpl 1955–64, Assist Sec: Cabinet Office 1964–66 and Treasury 1967–68, Jt Pncpl Priv Sec to Chllr Exchequer 1968, Under Sec Treasury 1968–70, Pncpl Priv Sec to PM 1970–75, Home Office: Dep Under Sec 1975–77 and PUS 1977–79, Sec to Cabinet 1979–87, Head Home Civ Serv 1981–87, Dir: RAM 1975– (Hon Fellow 1985), ROH 1988–93 (Sec to Dirs 1968–87), Cncl Management Roy Philharmonic Soc, Rhodes Tst 1975–, Pilgrim Tst 1987–, D'Oyly Carte Opera Tst 1988–93, Leeds Castle Fndn 1988–97, Shell Transport and Trading (non-exec) 1988–, NM Rothschild & Sons 1988–, BAT Industs 1988–97, Carlton TV 1991–95, Bank of Ireland 1991–, Chm: Tstees V&A 1988–97, Biotechnology Investments 1989–, Bristol and West Bldg Soc 1993–96, Hon Bencher Inner Temple 1986, Chllr Hull U 1994–; *m* 1st 1953 (*divorce* 1985) Serena Mary Benedicta (*d* 1994), er dau of Sir Roger James Ferguson Chance, 3rd Bt (*qv*); *m* 2nd 1985 *(Mary) Patricia, only dau of Charles Cyril Carlow, and by his 1st w has:

1 *Jane Orlanda; *b* 1954

2 *Teresa Brigid; *b* 1957

Lineage: A E ARMSTRONG, of Peterborough; had an only s:

Sir THOMAS HENRY WAIT ARMSTRONG, FRCM, DMus, of 1 E St, Olney, Bucks; *b* 15 June 1898; *educ* Chapel Roy Choir Sch St James's, King's Sch Peterborough, Keble Coll Oxford and RCM; organist Ch Ch Oxford 1935–55, Pncpl RAM 1955–68, ktd 1958; *m* 1926 Hester, 2nd dau of Rev W H Draper, and *d* 26 June 1994, leaving:

ROBERT TEMPLE, *cr* a **Baron**

ARMYTAGE

Arms: Gules, a lion's head erased between three cross crosslets argent. **Crest:** A dexter arm embowed, couped at the shoulder, habited or, the cuff argent, holding in the hand proper a staff gules, headed and pointed or. **Motto:** *Semper paratus* ('Always ready'). **Creation:** Bt. (GB) 4 July 1738.

SIR (JOHN) MARTIN ARMYTAGE, 9TH BT, of Kirklees, Co York [Sir Martin Armytage Bt, 5 St James's Place, Cheltenham, Glos GL50 2EG]; *b* 26 Feb 1933; *s* f 1983; *educ* Eton and Worcester Coll Oxford

Lineage: WILLIAM ARMYTAGE (descended from John Armytage, Hull of Wrigbowls, living mid-12th century); *m* 2nd 1583 Margery, dau of Richard Beaumont, of Emily Park, Yorks, and widow of Henry Knight, of Knight Hill, Surrey, and *d* between 16 June and 30 Oct 1606, having by his 1st w had, with another s and a dau:

1 John, of Kirklees; High Sheriff Yorks 1615; *m* Winifred, only dau and heir of Henry Knight, of Knight Hill, Surrey, and had with other children (*d* young):

(1) John; *m* 1622 Dorothy, dau of Cyrill Arthington, of Arthington, Yorks, and *dsp* 1624

(2) Sir FRANCIS ARMYTAGE, 1st Bt (E), so *cr* 15 Dec 1641; *b c* 1600; *m* 1629 Catherine (*bur* 13 Jan 1666), dau of Christopher Danby, of Farnley, nr Leeds, and was *bur* 12 June 1644, having had, with other issue:

1a Sir JOHN ARMYTAGE, 2nd Bt, JP, DL; *bapt* 15 Dec 1629; High Sheriff Yorks 1668; *m* 1651 Margaret (*bur* 10 Feb 1695), 2nd dau of Thomas Thornhill, of Fixby, Yorks, and was *bur* 9 March 1676/7, having had, with other issue:

1b Sir THOMAS ARMYTAGE, 3rd Bt; *bapt* 10 May 1652; *educ* Univ Coll Oxford; *d* unm between 28 Feb 1693/4 and 26 May 1694

2b Sir JOHN ARMYTAGE, 4th Bt; *bapt* 14 April 1653; *d* unm 2 Dec 1732

3b Sir GEORGE ARMYTAGE, 5th Bt; *bapt* 23 Aug 1660; *d* unm (*bur* 24 April 1736)

2a Francis, of South Kirby, Yorks; *bapt* 3 Jan 1631/2; *m* Mary, dau of Robert Trappes, of Nidd, Yorks, and had an only surviving son:

1b Sir THOMAS ARMYTAGE, 6th and last Bt; *bapt* 31 July 1673; *d* unm 12 Oct 1737, when the baronetcy expired

(1) Elizabeth; *m* 1626 Sir John Savile (*d* July 1650), of Lupset, Yorks, and *d* 1638

2 Edward, of Keresforth Hill, Yorks; *m* 1st 26 Oct Elizabeth, only dau and heir of Edward Hanson, of Little Royd, Yorks, and had issue; *m* 2nd Jane, dau of John Popley, of Moorehouse, and widow of Thomas Cutler, of Field Head, Yorks, by whom he also had issue; his s by his 1st w:

(1) John, of Keresforth Hill; *b* 1610; *m* 1st Mary, dau and heir of Matthew Whitley, of Shelf, Yorks, and had issue; *m* 2nd Elizabeth, dau of John Dransfield, of Elland, Yorks, and by her had, with other issue:

1a George, of Keresforth Hill; *b* 1661; *m* 1690 Magdalen, dau of Francis Usher, of Barnsley, and had, with five other s and three daus:

1b **Sir Samuel Armytage, 1st Bt** (GB), so *cr* 4 July 1738; *bapt* 5 May 1695; inherited the estates of his cousin the 6th and last Bt of the 1641 *cr*; High Sheriff Yorks 1739; *m* Anne (*d* Nov 1738), dau of Thomas Griffith, of Llanvylian, Montgomeryshire, and *d* 19 Aug 1747, having had, with other issue:

1c **Sir John Armytage, 2nd Bt**; *b* 13 July 1732, MP York 1754–58; *d* unm, *k* near St Cass, on the coast of France, 10 Sept 1758

2c GEORGE (Sir), **3rd Bt**

1c Anne Marian; *m* 1st Thomas Carter, MP, er s of Thomas Carter, PC, of Robertstown and Rathually, Co Meath; *m* 2nd 18 Sept 1766 Capt John Nicholson (*d* 29 March 1782), of Balrath Bury, Co Meath

Sir JOHN's yr bro,

Sir George Armytage, 3rd Bt; *b* 25 Dec 1734; MP Yorks 1761–68, High Sheriff Yorks 1755; *m* 10 April 1760 Anna Maria (*d* 21 March 1788), est dau and coheir of Godfrey Wentworth, of Woolley Park, and *d* 21 Jan 1783, having had, with other issue:

Sir George Armytage, 4th Bt; *bapt* 11 June 1761; High Sheriff Yorks 1791; *m* 1st 12 Aug 1783 Mary (Id 13 Aug 1790), est dau of Sir Harbord Harbord, 2nd Bt (*see* SUFFIELD, B), and had issue; *m* 2nd 6 Dec 1791 Mary (*d* 25 July 1834), dau of Oldfield Bowles, of North Aston, Oxon, and by her had, with other issue:

1 John, of Heath, Wakefield; *b* 7 Oct 1792; *m* 2 Oct 1818 Mary (*d* 21 April 1871), only dau of William Assheton, of Downham Hall, Lancs (*see* CLITHEROE, B), and *dvp* 24 May 1836, leaving, with other issue:

(1) George (Sir), **5th Bt**

2 Henry; *b* 29 Oct 1796; Col Coldstream Gds; *m* 1st 12 June 1819 Charlotte, only dau of Legendre Starkie, of Huntroyd. Lancs, and had, with other issue:

(1) Henry; *b* 1 Feb 1828; Col Coldstream Gds; *m* 12 April 1851 Hon Fenella Fitzhardinge Berkeley (*d* 20 Nov 1903), dau of 1st Baron Fitzhardinge of Bristol (*see* BERKELEY, B), and *d* 18 April 1901, leaving issue:

1a Percy, CVO (1920, MVO 5th Cl 1902 and 4th Cl 1911); *b* 8 March 1853; Gentleman Usher to TM EDWARD VII 1903–10 and GEORGE V 1910–27, Extra Gentleman Usher to HM GEORGE V 1927, Chevalier Legn of Honour and Order Lion and Sun, OStJ; *m* 25 April 1888 Rosetta Philippa (*d* 31 Dec 1902), dau of Col Cameron, of Danygraig, Glam, and widow of Capt Charles Stannard Eustace, of Robertstown, Co Kildare, and *d* 4 June 1934

2a Horace, Lt King's Own Liverpool Regt and West India Regt; *b* 28 July 1856; *d* unm 28 May 1898

3a William; *d* young

1a Maude Charlotte; *d* unm 15th April 1917

2a Constance; *m* 17 Oct 1876 J Critchley Martin, of Narborough Hall, Swaffham, and *d* 31 May 1923, leaving issue

3a Alice; *m* 17 July 1907 Capt Frederic Whitworth Jones, KOYLI (*d* 27 June 1935), est s of Henry Whitworth Jones

2 (cont.) Col Henry Armytage *m* 2nd 26 Aug 1858 Frances Sarah (*m* 2nd 28 July 1863 Arthur Pott, DL, of Bentham, and *d* 1887), dau of Robert William Branding, of Low Gosforth, Northumberland, and *d* 30 Oct 1861

Sir GEORGE *d* 14 July 1836; his grandson,

Sir George Armytage, 5th Bt, DL (Yorks); *b* 3 Aug 1819; *educ* Rugby, Harrow and Oriel Coll Oxford; *m* 1 June 1841 Eliza Matilda Mary (*d* 2 March 1898), 2nd dau of Sir Joseph Radcliffe, 1st Bt (*qv*), of Rudding, Yorks, and had:

1 GEORGE JOHN (Sir), **6th Bt**

2 Arthur Henry, JP (E R Yorks); *b* 27 Aug 1845; Lt-Col RHA; *m* 24 June 1870 Katherine Harriet (*d* 7 Jan 1938), 2nd dau of Ralph Creyke, of Rawcliffe and Marton, Yorks, and *d* 5 May 1927, leaving issue:

(1) Arthur Ralph; *b* 2 May 1884; *d* 5 Aug 1885

(1) Dorothy Harriet; *m* 13 Feb 1908 Lt-Col Henry Halford Dawes, OBE, TD, E Kent Yeo (*d* 17 Feb 1940), yr s of Sir Edwin Sandys Dawes, KCMG, of Mount Ephraim, Kent, and *d* 20 Jan 1934, leaving issue

(2) Lilac Gwendolen; *m* 9 Feb 1916 Evelyn St Vincent Parker-Jervis (*d* 26 Dec 1957), 3rd s of William Robert Parker-Jervis, DL, of Meaford and Park Hall, Staffs (*see* St VINCENT, V), and *dsp* 22 Feb 1956

(3) Frances Guinevere; *m* 2 Dec 1916 Maj Humphrey Ernest Bowman, CMG, CBE, Egyptian CS (*d* 23 March 1965), s of John Frederick Bowman, of Garramor, Arisaig, and *d* 13 Feb 1923, leaving issue (*see* BOWMAN, Bt)

3 William Edward; *b* 7 Sept 1847; *d* 1 Dec 1861

4 Francis Reginald; *b* 9 July 1849; MA Oxon; barrister; *d* unm 9 Dec 1907

1 Harriet Matilda; *d* unm 10 Oct 1865

Sir GEORGE *d* 9 March 1899; his est son,

Sir George John Armytage, 6th Bt, DL (W R Yorks and City of York); *b* 26 April 1842; Chm Lancs and Yorks Rlwy, High Sheriff Yorks 1907, FSA; *m* 1st 11 May 1871 Ellen (*d* 4 July 1890), dau of Rev Ayscough Fawkes, of Farnley Hall, York, and had issue:

1 GEORGE AYSCOUGH (Sir), **7th Bt**

2 John Hawksworth; *b* 19 May 1873; Assist Inspr BOT; *m* 8 Feb 1912 Everilda Frances (took by deed poll 19 May 1938 the name Armytage-Creyke; *d* 9 Jan 1977 aged 87), only dau of Ralph Creyke, DL, of Rawcliffe Hall and Marton, Yorks, and *d* 30 June 1944, leaving issue:

(1) Walter John; *b* 27 March 1913; *educ* Eton; Lt KRRC WW II (despatches, POW); *m* 1st 10 July 1947 (*divorce* 1958) Daphne Frances Mary, only dau of Thomas Grant Fletcher, of Ardmulchan, Navan, Co Meath, and formerly w of Philip Alwyn Lucas, and had issue:

1a +Julian Ralph Fitzroy [Julian Armytage Esq, 18 Lowndes Sq, London SW1]; *b* 23 Feb 1948; *educ* Milton Abbey; *m* 1st 1973 (*divorce* 1982) Laura Diana, only child of Capt Ian Charles Palliser Galloway, of Tynte Park, Dundairn, Co Wicklow; *m* 2nd 1983 *Julia, dau of Lawrence George Buchanan, and by her has issue:

1b *Georgina Caroline; *b* 1986

2b *Edwina Frederica; *b* 1992

1a *Clare Frances Elizabeth; *b* 13 May 1950; *m* 1973 (*divorce* 1983) Jonathan E Clarke

(1) (cont.) Walter Armytage *m* 2nd 22 Jan 1959 Marion Elizabeth (*d* 1986), only child of Maj David Mitchell Anderson, DL, LLD, of Creevy Rocks, Saintfield, Co Down, and widow of Edward John Wakefield D'Arcy, and *d* 1980, having by her had further issue:

2a *Diana Marion; *b* 21 Jan 1960

(1) *Ellen Elizabeth [Mrs Duncan Crow, Little Bendrose, Finch Lane, Amersham Common, Bucks]; *b* 23 May 1915; *m* 1st 25 July 1940 (*divorce* 1945) John Antony de Berniere Hallows, only s of Dr Norman Frederic Hallows, of The Hermitage, Marlborough, Wilts; *m* 2nd 30 Aug 1945 *(Henry) Duncan Crow, only s of Henry Crow, OBE, MA, barrister, of Edinburgh

1 Winifred Harriett; *b* and *d* 1875

2 Edith Beatrice, JP (Bucks); *m* 19 July 1905 Marjoribanks Keppel North, MICE, 2nd surv s of Charles North, of Rougham, Norfolk, and *d* 21 Oct 1973, leaving issue (*see* GUILFORD, E)

Sir George *m* 2nd 6 April 1893 Mary Georgiana (*d* 14 Aug 1920), dau of Henry Anthony Littledale, of Bolton Hall, Yorks, and *d* 8 Nov 1918

His er son,

Sir George Ayscough Armytage, 7th Bt, CMG (1918), DSO (1917), JP (W R Yorks); *b* 2 March 1872; Brig-Gen cmdg an Inf Bde WW I (despatches four times, Brevet Lt-Col 1916), Col 1920, Lt-Col KRRC and Col cmdg 2nd W R Inf Bde (TA) 1921–22, Croix de Guerre; *m* 12 July 1899 Aimée (*d* 24 Sept 1955), 3rd dau of Sir Lionel Milborne-Swinnerton-Pilkington, 11th Bt (*qv*), and had issue:

1 JOHN LIONEL (Sir), **8th Bt**

2 Reginald William, GC (formerly Albert Medal, 1928), CBE (1959); *b* 18 May 1903; R-Adml, Ch Inspr Naval Ordnance 1956–59, V-Pres Ordnance Bd 1959–60 (Pres 1961); *m* 27 Oct 1928 Sylvia Beatrice (*d* 27 July 1996), 2nd dau of Lt-Col Charles Russell Staveley-Staveley, of Pamflete, Holbeton, S Devon, and *d* 1984, leaving issue:

(1) +DAVID GEORGE, CBE (1981) [Capt David Armytage CBE RN, Sharcott Manor, Pewsey, Wilts SN9 5PA]; *b* 4 Sept 1929; heir presumptive; *educ* RNC Dartmouth; Capt RN; cmded: HMS *Minerva* 1968–70, HMS *Scylla* 1976, HMS *Jupiter* 1977, 7th Frigate Sqdn 1976–77, Standing Naval Force Atlantic 1980–81, Defence Policy Staff 1970–72 and Naval Assist to 1st Sea Ld 1972–74, ADC 1981; Sec Gen Br Diabetic Assoc 1981–92; *m* 3 April 1954 *Antonia Cosima, er dau of Count Cosmo Diodono de Bosdari, of Cape Province, S Africa, by Enid, only dau of Lt-Col Sir Peter Carlaw Walker, 2nd Bt (*see* WALKER-OKEOVER, Bt), and has:

1a +Hugh Anthony [Hugh Armytage Esq, 6 Ponsonby Place, London SW1P 4PT]; *b* 6 Aug 1955

2a +Charles David [Charles Armytage Esq, The Flint House, Ashmansworth, Berks RG15 9SG]; *b* 26 Dec 1962; *m* 1987 *Katharine (Katie) Alexandra, yr dau of Dr Anthony Cooper Sudell Bloomer, of 11 Devonshire Pl, London, W2, and has issue:

1b +Harry Charles George; *b* 1992

2b +Alexander Hugh Edward; *b* 17 Sept 1995

1a *Davina Jane [Mrs David Chappel, The Cottage, Sharcott Manor, Pewsey, Wilts SN9 5PA]; *b* 6 Aug 1956; *m* 15 Jan 1977 *Lt-Col David Martin Chappel, 4th/7th R Dragoon Gds, s of Dr H M Chappel, and has issue:

1b *William David George; *b* 1987

2b *Rupert Henry Edward; *b* 1989

3b *Jeremy David Hugh; *b* 1990

(2) +Maurice John Reginald [Maurice Armytage Esq, Maplehurst, Staplehurst, Tonbridge, Kent]; *b* 4 July 1932; *educ* Wellington and Magdalene Coll Cambridge (BA); *m* 7 July 1956 *Brioni Katherine, er dau of Gerald Wellington Williams, of Shernfold Park, Frant, Sussex, and has issue:

1a *Lucinda Jane Brioni; *b* 1 April 1959; *m* 1983 *Maj Mark Andrew Tilden Hibbert-Hingston, Coldstream Gds, er s of Andrew Donovan Huntly Hibbert-Hingston (*see* DENBIGH and DESMOND, E), and has issue:

1b *Jonathan; *b* 1985

2b *Nicholas; *b* 1988

3b *James; *b* 1989

1b *Edwina; *b* 1986

2b *Joy; *b* 1991

2a *Nicola Susan Katharine [Mrs Richard Woosnam, Langton House, Langton Malton, N Yorks YO17 9QW]; *b* 10 April 1959; *m* 1981 *Maj Richard Bowen Woosnam, 15th/19th King's Roy Hussars, er s of Charles Woosnam, and has issue:

1b *David Ralph William; *b* 1983

1b *Katharine Patricia Mary; *b* 1985

3a *Jane Annette; *b* 23 March 1961

(3) +Roderick (Roddy) Charles [Roderick Armytage Esq, Broughs Farm, Middleham, nr Leyburn, N Yorks]; *b* 5 Aug 1934; *educ* Wellington; *m* 5 April 1961 Susan (*d* 23 July 1996), only dau of Maj Reginald Talbot Whitehead, of Bryn Rhydderch, Abergavenny, and has issue:

1a +Marcus David; *b* 17 July 1964

1a *Gaye (Gee); *b* 10 Sept 1965

1 Barbara Ellen; *b* 24 March 1906; *m* 3 June 1930 (*divorce* 1949) Col Henry David Makgill-Crichton-Maitland, OBE, REME (*d* 1970), only s of Cdr Coventry Makgill-Crichton-Maitland, RN, and *d* 12 Dec 1994, leaving issue (*see* LAUDERDALE, E)

Sir GEORGE *d* 15 Aug 1953, and was *s* by his er son,

Sir John Lionel Armytage; 8th Bt; *b* 23 Nov 1901; *educ* Eton and RMC Sandhurst; Capt KRRC; *m* 1st 7 June 1927 (*divorce* 1946) Evelyn Mary Jessamine (*m* 2nd 1946 (*divorce* 1950) Capt John Samuel Pontifex-Cooper; *m* 3rd 1950 Lt-Col John Warwick Tainton Wooldridge (*d* 1973); *m* 4th 1960 her 2nd husb Capt John Samuel Pontifex-Cooper), dau of Edward Herbert Fox, of Adbury Park, Newbury, Hants, by Alice Marion, 2nd dau of William Arbuthnot, of Coworth Park, Berks (*see* ARBUTHNOT, Bt, of Edinburgh), and had issue:

1 Sir (JOHN) MARTIN ARMYTAGE, **9th and present Bt**

1 *Ann [Mrs David Featherstonhaugh, Plas Kinmel, Abergele, Denbighs]; *b* 14 Aug 1928; *m* 1st 16 Dec 1948 (*divorce* 1960) Francis Richard Anson (*d* 1989), er s of Maj William Alfred Anson, of The Manor, Leamington, Warwicks, and has issue (*see* LICHFIELD, E); *m* 2nd 20 Nov 1962 (*divorce* 1971) Philip John Warburton-Lee, only s of Capt Bernard Armitage Warburton-Lee, VC, RN, of Broad Oak, Salop, and has further issue:

(1) *John Henry Bernard; *b* 19 Oct 1963

1 (cont.) Mrs Ann Warburton-Lee *m* 3rd 3 July 1972, as his 2nd w, *Maj David Henry Featherstonhaugh, JP, DL, late Coldstream Gds

Sir John Lionel *m* 2nd 8 Nov 1949 *(Maria) Margarete [Lady Armytage, Kirklees Park, Brighouse, York], only dau of Paul Hugo Tenhaeff, of Bruenen, Niederhein, and *d* 21 June 1983, having by her had:

2 *Christina Mary [Mrs Richard Cornish, 12 Market Place, Bradford on Avon, Wilts]; *b* 15 Sept 1952; *m* 1980 *Richard Cornish

ARNOTT

Arms: Per chevron argent and azure, in chief two mullets and in base a crescent counterchanged, on a chief of the second three mullets of the first. **Crest:** A tower on a rock proper, with a pennon of one point, flotant, azure. **Motto:** *Speratum et completum* ('Hoped for and realized'). **Creation:** Bt. (UK) 12 Feb 1896.

SIR ALEXANDER JOHN MAXWELL ARNOTT, 6TH BT, of Woodlands, Shandon, Co Cork [Sir Alexander Arnott Bt, 11 Palmerston Rd, Dublin 6]; *b* 18 Sept 1975; *s f* 1981

Lineage: ROBERT ARNOTT of Auchtermuchty, Fifeshire, sometime of Strathmiglo, Fifeshire; living 1800; *m* 16 Sept 1785 Janet (otherwise Jessie), dau of James Page, of Auchtermuchty, and had, with a yr s and four daus:

JOHN ARNOTT, of Auchtermuchty, Co Fife; *b c* 1787; *m* 1st Elizabeth, dau of Alexander Paton, of Greedybank, Fifeshire; *m* 2nd Ellen Leyburn; *m* 3rd before 1851 Elizabeth Nichol and *d* 16 Sept 1878, having had, with an er and yr s and two daus:

Sir John Arnott, 1st Bt (UK), so *cr* 12 Feb 1896, JP (City and Co Cork); *b* 26 July 1814; MP Kinsale 1859–63, Mayor Cork 1859–61; philanthropist and promoter of Irish industries; *m* 1st 20 Jan 1852 Mary (*d* 29 July 1866), dau of John James McKinlay, of Stirling, and had issue:

1 JOHN ALEXANDER (Sir), **2nd Bt**

2 David Taylor; *b* 28 April 1855; *m* 1st 1890 Ethel Marion Napier (*d* 21 Nov 1893), only dau of Capt Frederic John Bell, 47th Regt, and had issue:

(1) John Frederic, MC; *b* 2 June 1892; *educ* Bradfield; Capt late Wilts Regt, WW I (despatches) and WW II in S Saskatchewan Regt; *m* 23 April 1919 Phyllis (*d* 25 May 1967), dau of James Cundell, of Kingston-upon-Thames, and *d* 10 Jan 1967, leaving issue:

1a (John) Anthony; *b* 23 March 1921; *educ* Cheltenham; Lt-Cdr RNVR WW II (despatches); FRICS, FAI; Superintendent Lands and Surveys Sarawak; *m* 18 Nov 1944 *Jean Barbara [Mrs Anthony Arnott, Devon Cottage, Bourton, Dorset], yst dau of Charles Lovett Gill, FRIBA, of The White House, Odiham, Hants, and *d* 1980, leaving:

1b +John David [John Arnott Esq, 100 Richmond Rd, Bristol BS6 5ER]; *b* 29 Dec 1947; *educ* Cheltenham, Birmingham U and Liverpool U (BA); *m* 12 March 1971 *Jennifer Mary Dooley and has issue:

1c +John Andrew; *b* 1974

2c +Myles Anthony; *b* 1980

1b *(Ann Margaret) Amabel [Mrs Peter Bolton, 7 Silver St, Wells, Somerset, BA5 1UN]; *b* 29 Aug 1945; *educ* Keele U (BA); *m* 1st 7 June 1969 Robert Edward Hughes, of Liverpool, er s of E R Hughes, of Liverpool; *m* 2nd 1981 *Peter Bolton and has issue:

1c *Gabriel Peter; *b* 1982

1c *Mary Christabel; *b* 1985

1a *Patricia Ruth [Mrs Evrard Burke, 3 Uigshadder, by Portree, Isle of Skye]; *b* 7 Feb 1920; WAAF WW II; *m* 7 Dec 1961 Evrard Burke (formerly Bourque) (*d* 17 July 1963), s of Philip Bourque, of Delcambre, Louisiana

(1) Marie Ethel; *m* 26 Aug 1919 George Graeff Barber, s of George Barber, of Walsingham House, Chislehurst, Kent, and *d* 11 March 1961 leaving a dau

2 (cont.) David Arnott *m* 2nd 11 Dec 1895 Blanche Emma (*d* Jan 1962), only dau of John Girdwood, JP, of Prospect House, Carrickfergus, and *d* 22 July 1915, having by her had issue:

(2) David Terence Edmond; *b* 27 Sept 1899; Lt 17th/21st Lancers; *d* unm 27 May 1933

3 Mangerton William, of Drumdiah, Killeagh, Co Cork, JP (Cork); *b* 14 Aug 1856; High Sheriff 1896; *m* 10 Nov 1886 Eliza Mary (*d* 17 July 1898), est dau of Thomas Arnott, of Blairmore, Argyllshire, and *d* 16 Dec 1901, leaving:

(1) Eliza Mary; *m* 1st 30 April 1913 William Maule Reginald Wingate (*d* 12 April 1927), s of Rev George Wingate, of Stratton, Cornwall; *m* 2nd 12 Nov 1928 Arthur Ralph Stephens, barrister, Zanzibar (*d* 10 Aug 1947), s of Rev James Stephens, of Lowestoft, Suffolk, and *d* 1 Feb 1956

1 Rosina; *b* 16 Aug 1852; *m* 30 Oct 1872 William Johnson, Capt 6th Inniskilling Dragoons (*d* 1899), of Fern Bank, Oddington, Glos, and *d* 25 Dec 1926, leaving issue

2 Margaret Jane; *b* 10 April 1859; *m* 1st 28 Sept 1880 Francis Augustus St Maur Shiel, Lt North Cork Rifles (*d* 21 Sept 1887), and had issue; *m* 2nd 6 Aug 1892 Maj Harry Wetherell Rowden, late Wiltshire Regt, and *d* 5 Aug 1936, leaving further issue

Sir John *m* 2nd 7 Nov 1872 Emily Jane (*d* 2 Oct 1938), 3rd dau of Rev Edward Loftus Fitzgerald, Rector Ardagh, Co Cork, and by her (who added by roy licence 20 Sept 1902 the surname FITZGERALD) had further issue:

4 Loftus Percival; *b* 7 Nov 1873; Capt and Hon Maj Special Res of Offrs, late 3rd Bn Leinster Regt; *d* unm 2 Dec 1956

5 Cecil John Maxwell; *b* 4 Aug 1882; late Lt 3rd Bn Leinster Regt; *d* unm 31 Aug 1954

3 Emmeline Louisa; *m* 16 Sept 1896 Capt Godfrey Herbert Bloomfield (*d* 21 Nov 1946), of Lisnafillon House, Gracehill, Co Antrim, only surv s of Fitz-Maurice Gustavus Bloomfield, JP, of New Park, Co Waterford, and *d* 10 Aug 1966, leaving issue

4 Jessie Alexandra; *m* 17 Oct 1917 Lt-Gen Sir William Pulteney Pulteney, GCVO, KCB, KCMG, DSO (*d* 14 May 1941), s of Rev Richard Thomas Pulteney Pulteney, Rector Ashley, Northants, and *d* 16 Jan 1971 aged 94

5 Lily Eleanor; *m* 12 Aug 1902 Arthur Edward Rogers (*d* 1 Jan 1950), s of Lt-Col John Thornton Rogers, DSO, of Sevenoaks, Kent, and *d* 12 Dec 1967, having had issue

6 Florence Geraldine; *m* 24 June 1906 Maj Henry Herbert Ronald White, DSO, OBE, Capt KRRC (*d* 12 March 1939), only s of Maj-Gen Henry George White, DL, of Lough Eske Castle, and *d* 26 July 1958, leaving issue

7 Mary Louisa Mabel; *m* 5 May 1915 Capt Sir Francis Hugh Brooke, 2nd Bt (*d* 4 Nov 1954), of Summertown, and had issue

Sir JOHN *d* 28 March 1898, and was *s* by his son,

Sir John Alexander Arnott, 2nd Bt, JP and DL (Co Cork); *b* 16 Nov 1853; Maj and Hon Lt-Col 4th Bn Cheshire Regt; *m* 27 Sept 1881 Caroline Sydney, DBE (1918), LGStJ, JP (*d* 28 Dec 1933), est dau of Sir Frederick Martin Williams, 2nd Bt, of Tregullow, Cornwall, and *d* 26 July 1940, having had issue:

1 John, MC; *b* 25 July 1885; Capt 15th Hus WW I (despatches twice); *ka* 30 March 1918

2 **Sir Lauriston John Arnott, 3rd Bt**; *b* 27 Nov 1890; *educ* Wellington; Capt 3rd Bn Roy Irish Rifles WW I (twice wounded); *d* unm 2 July 1958

3 ROBERT JOHN (Sir), **4th Bt**

4 Thomas John; *b* 12 April 1899; *educ* Eton; Maj 15th Hus WW II (despatches, US Silver Star); *m* 29 Sept 1927 Lettice Mary (*d* 1986), yst dau of Lt-Col Charles Montagu Crompton-Roberts, of Drybridge, Monmouth, and *d* 16 July 1979, leaving issue:

(1) +Peter John [Peter Arnott Esq, Flat 38, Braemar, Kersfield Rd, London SW15]; *b* 25 Jan 1929; *educ* Eton; Lt (ret) 15th/19th Hus

(2) +Guy [Guy Arnott Esq, 12/500 Marine Parade, Biggera Waters, Queensland 4216, Australia]; *b* 9 Nov 1932; *educ* Eton; late Lt 15th/19th Hus; *m* 29 Nov 1963 Diana (*d* 1982), est dau of D Staines and Mrs Williams, of Wahroonga, Queensland

(1) Marigold Winifred; *b* 15 Nov 1931; *m* 2 April 1955 *Capt David Miller, BA, Roy Dragoons, s of Lynden Roberts Miller, of Georgestown, by Lady Patricia Beresford, yst dau of 6th Marquess of Waterford (*qv*), and has issue

(2) *Caroline [Miss Caroline Arnott, Poole Keynes House, Cirencester, Glos]; *b* 28 April 1934

1 Margaret Christian Salome; *m* 14 Sept 1904 Maj Hugh Blenkinsop Spence, W Yorkshire Regt (*d* 31 Dec 1923), s of Joseph Spence, of E Acton House, East Acton, and *d* 14 March 1952, leaving issue

2 Mary Christian; *m* 10 March 1915 Capt Count Richard van Cutsem, late 4th Bn Leinster Regt (*d* 4 Oct 1960), Privy Chamberlain of Sword and Cape to HH POPE PIUS XI, and *d* 26 May 1936, leaving issue

3 (Lina) Victoria (twin with her sister); *m* 28 Feb 1916 6th Baron de Freyne (*qv*) and *d* 25 Oct 1974, leaving issue

Sir LAURISTON's bro,

Sir Robert John Arnott, 4th Bt; *b* 19 Aug 1896; *educ* Eton; Lt and Adj KRRC WW I France and Salonica; *m* 17 June 1926 Emita Emelia (*d* 19 Jan 1948), dau of Francis James, of Royston, Herts, and had issue:

1 JOHN ROBERT ALEXANDER (Sir), **5th Bt**

2 +Eric John [Eric Arnott Esq, Trottsford Farm, Headley, Hants; 11 Milford House, 7 Queen Anne St, London W1]; *b* 12 June 1929; *educ* Harrow and Trin Coll Dublin (MB, Bch 1954); FRCS (1962); *m* 19 Nov 1960 *Veronica Mary, only dau of Capt Arvid Lanqué Querfeld von der Seedeck, of Hartley Wintney, Hants, and has issue:

(1) +Stephen John; *b* 19 Feb 1962; *m* 1989 *Katherine Jane Keep, dau of Colin Thompson, of The Old House, Sutton Veny, Wilts, and has issue:

1a +Oliver Timothy John; *b* 1990

1a *Lara Georgina Emma; *b* 1992

2a *Isabella Anastasia; b 25 May 1996

(2) +Robert Lauriston John; *b* 12 Aug 1971

(1) *Tatiana Amelia; *b* 20 March 1963; *m* 1986 *Nicholas Paul Whishaw, est s of Michael Whishaw, of Anaheim Hills, California, and has issue:

1a *Timothy Alexander; *b* 1988

Sir ROBERT *d* 25 July 1966; his er son,

Sir John Robert Alexander Arnott, 5th Bt; *b* 9 April 1927; *educ* Harrow; Lt Roy Irish Fus; London ed *Irish Times*; *m* 1974 *Ann (Annie) [Lady Arnott, 11 Palmerston Rd, Dublin, Ireland], dau of Terence Alphonsus Farrelly, of Kilcar, Co Cavan, and *d* 1981, leaving issue:

1 Sir ALEXANDER JOHN MAXWELL ARNOTT, **6th and present Bt**

2 +ANDREW JOHN ERIC; *b* 20 June1978; heir presumptive

ARRAN

Arms: Gules a fess between three cross crosslets fitchée or.
Crest: A wolf rampant argent, collared gules.
Supporters: Two horses argent. **Motto:** *In hoc signo vinces* ('In this sign thou shalt conquer'). **Creations:** Bt. (I) 10 April 1662, B. and V. (I) 15 Aug 1758, E. (I) 12 April 1762, B. (UK) 7 Nov 1884 (Sudley of Castle Gore).

THE 9TH EARL OF ARRAN OF THE ARRAN ISLANDS, Co Galway, **Viscount Sudley of Castle Gore**, Co Mayo, **Baron Saunders of Deeps**, Co Wexford, **Baron Sudley of Castle Gore**, Co Mayo (Sir Arthur Desmond Colquhoun Gore, Bt) [The Rt Hon The Earl of Arran, Crocker End House, Nettlebed, Oxon]; *b* 14 July 1938; *s* f 1983; *educ* Eton and Balliol Coll Oxford; late 2nd Lt Gren Gds; co-owner Border Incident (racehorse), Assist Manager *Daily Mail* 1972–73, md Clark Nelson 1973–74, Assist Gen Manager *Daily* and *Sunday Express* June-Nov 1974, dir Waterstone & Co 1984–87; Govt Whip 1987–89, Parly Under-Sec Armed Forces MOD 1989–92, NI Off 1992–94, DoE 1994, Dep Govt Ch Whip 1994–95; Chm Children's Country Holiday Fund; *m* 28 Sept 1974 *Eleanor (Nell), Pres Calvert Tst 1997–, er dau of Bernard Henry Richard van Cutsem, of Exning, Suffolk, and has issue:

1 *Laura Melissa FORTESCUE-GORE; *b* 14 June 1975

2 *Lucy Katherine FORTESCUE-GORE; *b* 26 Oct 1976

Earldom of Arran: Two creations under this name in the peerage of Scotland are separately noticed in the articles KILMARNOCK, B, and ABERCORN, D. For previous creations in the Irish peerage *see* MOUNTGARRET, V

Lineage: GERARD GORE; *b c* 1516; Alderman City London (s of John Gore), granted land in Surrey; *m* Helen (*d* 13 Feb 1607/8), dau of Ralph Davenant, of Davenant Land, Essex, and *d* 11 Dec 1607, having had, with other issue:

1 John (Sir); Ld Mayor London 1624; ancestor of the Earls Temple of Stowe (*qv*)

2 Sir PAUL GORE, 1st Bt, of Manor Gore (*qv*); had issue, with an er s (2nd Bt of Manor Gore):

(1) **Sir Arthur Gore, 1st Bt** (I), so *cr* 10 April 1662, of Newtown Gore, Co Mayo; High Sheriff Cos Mayo and Galway 1656, Constable Fort Falkland 1660, Maj Coy of Foot 1660, MP Co Mayo 1661–66; *m* Eleanor, dau of Sir George St George, Bt, of Carrickdrumrusk, Co Leitrim (*see* SAINT GEORGE, Bt), and had issue (with seven daus, of whom Catherine *m* Brig-Gen Gore; Eleanor *m* Edward Wingfield (*see* POWERSCOURT, V); Anne *m* John French, of French Park; Lettice *m* Hon William Caulfeild (*see* CHARLEMONT, V)):

1a Paul; *m* 23 Dec 1682 Anne (*d* 3 March 1725), est dau of Sir John Gore, of Sacombe, Herts, and *dvp* 20 Oct 1689, leaving with other issue:

1b ARTHUR (Sir), **2nd Bt**

2b John, Captain RN; *d* unm 1741

1b Catherine; *m* Rev Peter Mahon, Dean Elphin (*d* Feb 1739), and left issue

2a Arthur; *m* —, widow of — Baynes, and *d* 13 June 1693, leaving:

3a William, of Woodford, Co Leitrim; ancestor of the Barons Harlech (*qv*)

4a George; 2nd Justice I Court Common Pleas; *m* 4 Feb 1702 Bridget, dau and eventually sole heir of John Sankey, of Tenelick, Co Longford, and had issue:

1b Arthur; MP Co Longford; *d* March 1758

2b JOHN GORE, 1st and last BARON ANNALY OF TENELICK, Co Longford (I), of the 17 Jan 1766 *cr*, PC (I 1764), KC (1749); *b* 2 March 1718; barrister King's Inns 1742, MP (I Parl) Jamestown 1747–60 and Co Longford 1761–64, Slr-Gen I 1760–64, Ch Justice I Court King's Bench 1764, Speaker I Ho of Lds 1767 and 1769; *m* 26 Nov 1747 Frances, 2nd dau of 1st Viscount Wingfield (*qv*), and dsp 3 April 1784, when the barony expired

3b HENRY GORE, 1st and last BARON ANNALY OF TENELICK, Co Longford (I), of the 23 Sept 1789 *cr*; *b* 8 March 1728; MP Co Longford 1758–60 and 1768–69 and Lanesborough 1761–68, Sheriff Co Longford 1765; *m* 4 July 1764 Mary, only dau of Skeffington Randal Smyth, of Leigh, Queen's Co, s of Edward Smyth, Bp Down and Connor, by Hon

Mary Skeffington (*see* MASSEREENE and FERRARD, V), and *dsp* 5 June 1793, when the Barony expired

Sir ARTHUR *d* 20 Dec 1697; his grandson,

Sir Arthur Gore, 2nd Bt; *b c* 1685; High Sheriff Co Mayo 1711, MP Donegal Borough 1713–14 and Co Mayo 1715–41; *m* Elizabeth, est dau of Maurice Annesley, of Little Rath, Co Kildare (gs of 1st Viscount Valentia; *qv*), and *d* 10 Feb 1741, having had, with three yr s and three daus:

Sir ARTHUR GORE, **3rd Bt**, and **1st Earl of Arran of The Arran Islands**, Co Galway, so *cr* 12 April 1762 (also 15 Aug 1758 BARON SAUNDERS OF DEEPS, Co Wexford, and VISCOUNT SUDLEY OF CASTLE GORE, Co Mayo; all I), PC (I 1748); *b* 1703; *educ* Trin Coll Dublin (BA 1722); barrister King's Inns 1730, MP Donegal Borough 1727–58, High Sheriff Co Wexford 1738, Custos Rotulorum Co Mayo 1762–73; *m* 16 March 1730/1 Jane (*d* 20 March 1747), dau and heiress of Richard Saunders, of Saunders Court, Co Wexford, and widow of William Worth, and *d* 17 April 1773, leaving issue:

1 ARTHUR SAUNDERS, **2nd Earl**

2 Richard; *bapt* 31 July 1734; MP Castlebar; *m* and had issue:

(1) John; Capt; *m* and had issue:

1a Richard Frederick John; *b* 1836; *m* 1874 Susan Jane (*d* 1937), dau of William Stephenson, of Meaford, Canada, and widow of Frederick Featherstonhaugh, of Co Wicklow, and *d* 1914, leaving issue:

1b Frederick John; *b* 1879; Lt Australian Res Offrs WW I; *m* 1918 Constance Victoria, dau of William Somerville Paul

2b Edward; *b* 1880; *m* 1913 Constance May Campbell (*d* 1958), dau of George William Campbell Wilson, and *d* 1935, leaving issue:

1c Isabelle Ada Louie Langton; *b* 1915; *m* 1944 Lloyd Baine Beck, US Med Corps, and had issue:

1d *Juanita Ann; *b* 1949

3b Arthur Charles; *b* 1884

1b Mary Eileen; *b* 1887; *m* 1911 Ernest Noel Mills

3 Paul; *m* Anne, dau of William Leonard, and had, with other issue:

(1) Arthur, of Ballina, Co Mayo; *b* 1763; *m* 1st Anne, dau of J Mayne; *m* 2nd Martha Sophia, dau of Edward Butler, and *d* 16 Sept 1825, leaving issue:

1a Annesley Paul; Maj 33rd Regt; *m* 1st 13 Aug 1874 Caroline Elizabeth (*dsp* 21 April 1875), dau of T W Flavell, of Mundesley, Norfolk; *m* 2nd 30 Dec 1876 Margaret Elizabeth, dau of Henry Solomon, and *dsp* 1903

2a Frederick William; Lt-Col 3rd Regt; *m* 7 Jan 1868 Millicent (*d* 9 Jan 1908), dau of Sir Robert Miller Mundy, KCMG, and *d* 2 Jan 1909, leaving issue:

1b Leicester; *b* 19 Nov 1868; *m* 17 Sept 1898 Sophia Harris (*d* 19 June 1926), dau of Francis Mitchell, of Chard, Somerset, and *d* 8 June 1931, leaving issue:

1c Ruth Sophia Joan, CStJ; *b* 9 April 1902; *m* 23 Aug 1924 Baron Coutanche (LP; *see* 1970 edn) and *d* 7 Aug 1973, leaving issue

1b Millicent Sophia; *m* 6 July 1904 Percival Hedley Anderson (*d* 20 Nov 1964), only s of Matthew Wheatley Anderson, of Quebec, and *d* 31 March 1966, leaving issue

(2) Ralph; *b* 1786; Cdr RN; *m* 1807 Frances, dau of Alexander Hay, and *d* 1859, leaving issue:

1a William John; *b* 1810; *m* Harriet Salmon and *d* 1889, leaving issue:

1b Charles Arthur; *b* 1845; *m* 1st 1883 Mary Goacher (*d* 1894) and had issue:

1c William Charles Paul Hay; *b* 1894; *m* 1st 1924 Ethel Mildred (*d* 1939), dau of John Winchcombe Howard Packer, of Newbury; *m* 2nd 1943 Iris Amy, dau of James Alexander Cutmore Clarke, of Bannockburn, Tasmania

1c Cecilia Mary; *b* 1884; *m* 1908 Albert Reynolds

1b (cont.) Charles Gore *m* 2nd 1907 Constance Gertrude (*m* 3rd 1928 John James Sayers (*d* 1955); *d* 1971), dau of John Burch and widow of Henry William Willis, and *d* 1926, having by her had issue:

2c Evelyn May; *b* May 1908; *m* 1934 Edward Clement Fernandes, MRCS, LRCP, of Bangalore, India, and *d* Sept 1956, leaving issue

3c *Constance Joyce Gwendoline [Mrs Ernest Killingback, 5 Orchard Crescent, Enfield, Middx]; *b* Sept 1911; SRN; *m* 12 Aug 1937 Ernest Killingback, BSc, ARCS (*d* 30 Aug 1939), and has issue:

1d *Peter Gore [Peter Killingback Esq, 58 Highfields Dve, Loughborough, Leics LE11 3JT]; *b* 7 March 1939; *educ* King Edward VI GS Aston, London Sch of Pharmacy (B Pharm) and Manchester U (MSc); *m* 12 Oct 1968 *Janet Mary (BSc Aberdeen), dau of Eric Frank Reason, of London N14, and has issue:

1e *David Gore; *b* 1971

2e *Christopher Michael; *b* 1975

1b Harriet Cecilia

2b Frances

3b Alice Sophia; *m* and had issue

4b Angelina; *m* Siddon Crook, of W Tarring, Sussex

5b Fanny Elvira; *m* Howard Ninnis (*d* 1886) and had issue

2a Ralph; *d* 1892, leaving:

1b Herbert, with Inland Revenue

(1) Anne; *m* Rev Richard Eyre (*d* 25 Nov 1831), Rector Eyrecourt, Co Galway, and *d* 21 Aug 1847, leaving issue

(2) Maria; *m* Capt Robert Eyre and had issue

1 Joanna; *m* 1st 29 Aug 1750 Philip Doyne (*dsp* 11 March 1765), of Wells, Co Wexford; *m* 2nd Michael Daly (*d* 23 Oct 1808), of Mount Pleasant, Co Galway

2 Elizabeth; *m* 15 July 1764 Sir John Evans Freke, Bt, and had issue (*see* CARBERY, B)

The 1st EARL's est son,

ARTHUR SAUNDERS GORE, **2nd Earl of Arran of the Arran Islands**, KP (1783), PC (I 1771); *b* 25 July 1734; MP Donegal borough 1759–60 and 1768–73 and Co Wexford 1761–68; *m* 1st 24 July 1760 Hon Catherine Annesley (*d* 23 Nov 1770), only dau of William, Viscount Glerawly (*see* ANNESLEY, E), and had issue:

1 ARTHUR SAUNDERS GORE, **3rd Earl of Arran of the Arran Islands**; *b* 20 July 1761; MP (Tory) Baltimore 1783–90 and Co Donegal 1800–06; *m* 29 Dec 1787 Mary (*d* 31 Aug 1832), only dau and heir of Sir John Tyrell, Bt, of Heron Hall, and *dsp* 20 Jan 1837

2 William John; *b* 16 Nov 1767; Col; *m* 30 May 1798 Caroline (*d* 7 June 1836), yst dau and coheir of Sir Thomas Pym Hales, 4th Bt, and *d* 15 Jan 1836, having had issue:

(1) PHILIP YORKE, **4th Earl**

(2) William John Pym; *b* 28 Oct 1804; Army Capt; *d* 23 April 1859

(3) Annesley Henry (Rev); *b* 1 Dec 1808; Rector Withcall, Lincs; *m* 20 May 1865 Emma (*d* 21 May 1854), yr dau of Gen John Reeve, of Leadenham, Lincs, by Lady Susan Sherard, 6th dau and coheir of 5th Earl of Harborough (*see* 1859 edn), and *d* 11 May 1877

(4) Robert; *b* 1810; Capt RN, Chargé d'Affaires Uruguay; *d* 4 Aug 1854

(5) Charles Alexander; *b* 10 Oct 1811; Commr Woods and Forests 1839–85; *m* 2 April 1845 Lady Augusta Lavinia Priscilla Ponsonby (*d* 19 Nov 1904), 2nd dau of 4th Earl of Bessborough (*qv*), and *d* 6 July 1897, leaving issue:

1a Francis Charles (Sir), KCB (1911); *b* 19 May 1846; barrister Inner Temple 1870, Recorder Canterbury 1893–94, slr Inland Revenue 1984–1911; *m* 14 Aug 1879 Constance Mary (Id 8 July 1925), dau of Lt-Gen Robert Bruce, bro of 1st Baron Aberdare (*qv*), and *d* 12 Feb 1940, leaving issue:

1b Arthur Charles; *b* 18 July 1880; *educ* Radley; Lt Connaught Rangers Boer War 1900–02; *m* 1st 12 Feb 1913 (*divorce* 1924) Rosamond Edna (*d* 24 June 1941), dau of William Hiden; *m* 2nd 7 June 1926 (*divorce* 1928) Florence, dau of Edward Sutherland, of Portland, Oregon; *m* 3rd 10 Feb 1934 Audrey Elizabeth Guelph, dau of Maynard L Young, of Philadelphia, and widow of Harold Mead, of San Francisco, and *dsp* 17 April 1963

2b Charles Henry, OBE (1918), JP (Berks); *b* 28 Nov 1881; *educ* Radley and Trin Coll Oxford (MA 1928); Fell and Bursar Queen's Coll Oxford, Govr Radley and Giggleswick Sch, dir Supplies and Tport Egyptian Army (Order Nile 3rd Cl); *m* 1st 18 Jan 1911 Marguerite (*d* 30 Dec 1918), dau of Walter Langley; *m* 2nd 15 April 1920 Hon Violet Kathleen Annesley (*d* 4 Sept 1963), 2nd dau of 11th Viscount Valentia (*qv*), and *d* 20 June 1941, leaving issue:

1c +PAUL ANNESLEY, CMG (1964), CVO (1961) [Paul Gore Esq CMG CVO, 1 Burkitt Rd, Woodbridge, Suffolk IP12 4JJ]; *b* 28 Feb 1921; heir presumptive; *educ* Winchester and Ch Ch Oxford (MA); Capt 16th/5th Lancers WW II, Colonial Admin Serv Uganda 1948–65, Dep Fin Sec Mauritius 1955–59, Fin Sec Gambia 1959–62 (Dep Govr 1962–65); *m* 9 March 1946 *$IGore, Gillian MaryGillian Mary, est dau of Capt Tom Edmund Allen-Stevens, of Wicklesham Lodge, Faringdon, and has issue:

1d +Charles Alexander; *b* 11 July 1947; *educ* Radley and Southampton U; *m* 1st 1970 (*divorce* 1971) Penelope, yr dau of R C Caunce, of Maidenhead; *m* 2nd 1984 *Susan Diana, dau of M J Hardy, and *d* 1985

2d +William Henry [William Gore Esq, 106 Simpsons Rd, Bardon, Qld, Australia 4064]; *b* 12 Aug 1950; *educ* Radley; *m* 1st 1980 Mrs Cecilia Nell McBean (*d* 1990), dau of R Cox, of Brisbane, and has issue:

1e +Charles David; *b* 1985

1e *Letitia Sarah; *b* 1982

2d (cont.) William Gore *m* 2nd 1993 *Mrs Rosemary Lindholm, dau of R Payne, of Brisbane

3d +Nicholas David; *b* 7 Sept 1952; *educ* Radley; *m* 1983 *Christine Mary, dau of H W Clothier, of Evercreech, Somerset, and formerly w of C B Tilley, and has issue:

1e +Alastair Mark; *b* 1984

2e +Robert William; *b* 1986

1c *Ursula Mary; *b* 31 July 1922; *m* 20 Sept 1947 Cdr Edward Graham Ducat-Hamersley, RN, of Batchfoot House, Upwey, Weymouth, Dorset (*d* 1987), yr s of Hugh Charles Claude Ducat-Hamersley, of Pyrton Manor, Oxon, and has issue:

1d *Penelope Tara; *b* 10 Aug 1948; *m* 1973 *Stephen Hayes and has issue:

1e *Timothy; *b* 1975

1e *Kirsty; *b* 1977

2e *Rosemary; *b* 1980

2d *Priscilla Rosemary; *b* 23 May 1951; *m* 1st 1982 David Henderson (*d* 1989), of Qld, Australia, and has issue:

1e *Nathan Edward Vivien; *b* 1982

1e *Kelly Letitia; *b* 1984

2e *Tara Gae; *b* 1988

2d (cont.) Mrs David Henderson *m* 2nd 1994 *Keith Nobes, of Qld

3d *Felicity; *b* 24 Sept 1954; *m* 1978 Gerald Brian O'Brien, of Winchester, and has issue:

1e *Katherine; *b* 1983

2e *Eleanor; *b* 1987

4d *Joanna; *b* 26 May 1957; *m* 1st 1980 (*divorce* 1983) Charles Robert Sindell; *m* 2nd 1983 (*divorce* 1988) George Bentham Walker and by him has issue:

1e *Hugh Simon; *b* 1985

4d (cont.) Mrs Joanna Walker *m* 3rd 1990 *Stephen Lockwood, of NSW, and has further issue:

2e *Thomas Edward; *b* 1990

1e *Alice Sophie; *b* 1992

2c *Rosemary Kathleen; *b* 20 Aug 1924; WRNS; *m* 3 May 1945 Lt (A) Arthur Emerson Mabin, RNZNVR (*d* 1986), s of Edward Ernest Bayley Mabin, of Nelson, NZ, and has issue:

1d *Richard Peter; *b* 15 June 1965; *m* 1990 *Elizabeth Katurah, yr dau of James Doble, of Stoney Stratton, Somerset and has issue
1d *Susan Kathleen; *b* 9 May 1946; *m* 1968 *Leslie Howard Cook and has issue:
1e *Timothy Peter; *b* 1972
1e *Sarah Kathleen; *b* 1974
2e *Helen Ruth; *b* 1976
2d *Caroline Ruth; *b* 10 Dec 1947
3d *Helen Rosemary; *b* 10 Nov 1950; *m* 1973 *Alan Archibald Winwood and has issue:
1e *Derek Emerson; *b* 1978
2e *Christopher Alan; *b* 1982
3e *Thomas Willem; *b* 1984
1e *Joanna Rosemary; *b* 1980
4d *Victoria Jane, PhD; *b* 28 Dec 1953; *m* 1st 1983 Willem Louis Fritz van der Broek (*d* 1984); *m* 2nd 1987 *Christopher Mannings Sutton, PhD, of Wellington, NZ, and has issue
3b John Francis, CVO (1941), TD; *b* 15 May 1885; *educ* Radley and Trin Coll Oxford (BA 1907, MA 1943); Capt Beds Yeo WW I (despatches), barrister Inner Temple, chm Midhurst Bench 1944–58, author and jnlst, James Tait Black Meml Prize for official memoir of KING GEORGE V 1942; *m* 14 April 1926 Lady Janet Helena Campbell (*d* 2 Nov 1982 aged 83), er dau of 4th Earl Cawdor (*qv*), and *d* 24 July 1983, leaving issue:
1c +Charles John [Charles Gore Esq, Port na Mine, Taynuilt, Argyll, PA35 1HU]; *b* 11 June 1932; *educ* Eton; *m* 10 June 1961 *Jean, yr dau of Maj Charles Ian Fraser of Reelig, CBE, TD, JP, DL, Albany Herald of Arms, of Reelig, Kirkhill, Inverness-shire, and has issue:
1d +(Ian) Simon Francis; *b* 3 March 1965; *m* 1993 *Sarah E, yr dau of Colin Frizzell, of Chuffs House, Holyport, Berks, and has:
1e +Samuel Charles Fraser; *b* 20 Aug 1994
2e +Milo Thomas Spencer; *b* 30 Nov 1995
1e *Marnie Rose; *b* 18 Nov 1997
2d +John Alexander Charles; *b* 21 Nov 1971
1d *Helena Mary; *b* 30 Dec 1962; *m* 1992 *Michael J Baylerand has:
1e *Amelia Jane; *b* 26 March 1993
1c *Moyra [Miss Moyra Gore, Littlehay, Burley, Hants]; *b* 21 Jan 1927
2c *Mary Elizabeth; *b* 19 Jan 1929; *m* 15 June 1957 *Sir Charles Edward Coleridge Cave, 4th Bt (*qv*), and has issue
1b Evelyn Mary; *b* 22 June 1883; *d* unm 5 June 1951
2a Spencer William; *b* 10 March 1850; Surveyor Ecclesiastical Commrs; *m* 9 Jan 1875 Amy Margaret (*d* 5 Dec 1944), est dau of Edmund James Smith, of Whitehall Place, London SW1, and *d* 1906, having had issue:
1b George Pym; *b* 30 Nov 1875; T/Lt Welsh Gds; *m* 15 Sept 1914 Alexandra Leila (*d* 9 Dec 1970), only child of Rev Canon Frederick Alfred John Hervey, CVO (*see* BRISTOL, M), and widow of Sir Walter Clervaux Chaytor, 5th Bt (*qv*), and *d* 25 June 1959, having had issue:
1c Victoria Maud Lavinia Mary; *b* 19 Sept 1915; *m* 16 Sept 1944 (*divorce* 1955) Lt Ian Alexander Kennedy, 16th/5th Lancers, s of Maj J Y M Kennedy, MC, and had:
1d *Lavinia Susan; *b* 1 July 1948; *m* 1st 1970 (*divorce* 1983) Timothy Scott Bigland, s of T S Bigland, and has issue:
1e *Alexandra Rosalind; *b* 1977
1d (cont.) Mrs Lavinia Bigland *m* 2nd, as his 2nd w, *Richard Hugh Chaytor Vaux, late Maj RAPC, of Upper Rakehanger, Liss, Hants, only s of Gp Capt Hugh Manford Vaux, of Low Startforth Hall, Barnard Castle, Co Durham (*see* CHAYTOR, Bt), and has further issue:
2e *Philippa Clare Marisa; *b* 1986
3e *Lucinda Mary Diana; *b* 1987
2c Anne Georgiana Mary; *b* 12 Aug 1917; *d* 17 April 1918
2b Spencer Frederick; *b* 26 May 1878; *m* 18 Jan 1912 Mary Joanna (*d* 8 Dec 1968), dau of Capt John Kerr, and *d* 27 March 1914, leaving issue:
1c +Frederick John Pym, CBE (1987) [Frederick Gore Esq CBE, Flat 3, 35 Elm Park Gdns, London SW10 9QF]; *b* 8 Nov 1913; *educ* Lancing and Trin Coll Oxford; Maj RA WW II; head painting St Martin's Sch Art 1951–79 (V-Pncpl 1961–79), RA 1964, Tstee Imp War Museum 1967–84; *m* 1st 1945 (*divorce*) Lili Renée, dau of L Gaber, and has issue:
1d *Georgiana Sarah; *b* July 1950; PhD; *m* 19– *Laurent Christophe Michel Wierre and has issue:
1e *Natasha Anouk Eva; *b* 1991
1c (cont.) Frederick Gore *m* 2nd *Constance Irene, only dau of William Henry Smith, of Brentford, Middx, and by her has issue:
1d +Charles David [Charles Gore Esq, Flat 1, 2A Coleherne Mews, London SW10]; *b* 1954; *educ* Westminster PhD; has:
1e *James Spencer; *b* 1988
2d *Geraldine Lucy; *b* 1957; BA
1c Margaret Elizabeth; *b* 13 Oct 1912; *m* 1940 Samuel Richard Cowie (*d* 1979), of Meopham, Kent, and *d* 1994, leaving issue:
1d *Christopher Frederick [Christopher Cowie Esq, 45 Wynn Rd, Tankerton, Kent]; *b* 1941; *m* 1965 *Corinna, dau of Col H V Ewbank, Roy Signals, and has issue:
1e *Malcolm Ambrose; *b* 1981
1e *Charmian Philippa; *b* 1969
2d *John Richard, BA; *b* 1944
3d *Martin George Charles, BA (Japan) [Martin Gore Esq, 5-25-10 Kotokuji, Kagoshima, Japan]; *b* 1956; *m* 1985 *YokoTatsuo Matsumoto, of Kagoshima, and has issue:
1e *Spencer Richard; *b* 1989
1e *Katherine Melissa; *b* 1987
1d *Frances Mary [Miss Frances Cowie, 30 High St, Watlington, Oxon]; *b* 1947

1b Kathleen Amy; *m* 22 Feb 1919 William Allan Smith-Masters (*d* 27 Aug 1937) and *d* 24 Feb 1965
2b Florence Emily Frances; *m* 29 Dec 1910 Lt-Cdr Nigel de Grey, CMG, OBE, RNVR (*d* 25 May 1951), yr s of Rev Hon Arnold de Grey, and *d* 28 May 1963, leaving issue (*see* WALSINGHAM, B)
3a Charles (Rt Rev); *b* 22 Jan 1853; MA, Oxon: DD, Hon DCL, Hon LLD Cantab and Birmingham, Hon DD Edin and Durham, PhD Athens, Hon Fell Balliol and Trin Colls Oxford, Fell King's Coll London, V-Pncpl Cuddesdon 1880–83, Librarian Pusey House 1884–93, Vicar Radley 1893–94, Canon Westminster 1894–1902, Bp: Worcester 1902–05, Birmingham 1905–11 and Oxford 1911–19; *d* unm 17 Jan 1932
1a Emily Caroline Augusta; *b* 27 May 1848; *d* unm 1912
2a Caroline Maria; *m* 14 Aug 1883 Lt-Col Henry Arthur Lascelles, MVO, Rifle Bde, of Woolbeding, Midhurst, Sussex, and *d* 6 Nov 1945, leaving issue (*see* HAREWOOD, E)
(1) Mary Catherine; *m* 3 Sept 1828 George Hayward Lindsay, of Glasnevin, Co Dublin, s of Bp Kildare, and *d* 28 April 1885, leaving issue (*see* CRAWFORD and BALCARRES, E)
(2) Elizabeth Anne; *d* 21 Sept 1868
(3) Emily Jane; *d* unm 14 Dec 1899
1 Anne Jane; *m* 1st 1783 Henry Hatton, of Clonard, Co Wexford; *m* 2nd 3 April 1800 1st Marquess of Abercorn (*see* ABERCORN, D) and *dsp* May 1827
2 Elizabeth Araminta; *m* Henry Monck
3 Catherine Charlotte; *m* 25 Jan 1783 6th Baron Carbery (*qv*) and *dsp* 23 Feb 1852
4 Jane; *m* Dudley Loftus, of Killyon, and *d* 1831

The **2nd Earl** *m* 2nd 1771 Anne (*d* 1779), dau of Rev Boleyn Knight, of Otley, Yorks, and by her had issue:
3 George (Very Rev); *b* Feb 1774; LLD, Dean Killala; *m* 1st Anne (*d* 16 Sept 1819), dau of Robert Burrowes, of Stradone, Co Cavan, and had issue:
(1) Arthur Saunders; Lt HEICS; *d* 1837
(2) Thomas; *b* 17 March 1818; Maj 88th Regt; *d* 5 July 1872
(3) Robert, of Raveagh, Clogher, Co Tyrone, JP; *b* 1 Sept 1819; *m* 16 Aug 1852 Elizabeth (*d* 4 May 1908), dau of Lt-Col Hugh Gore Edwards, of Raveagh, and *d* 13 June 1899, leaving issue:
1a Hugh; *b* 11 June 1853; Lt Tyrone Militia; *d* 7 June 1933
2a Robert George; *b* 22 Sept 1859; *m* 19 Sept 1901 Ida Mary (*d* 26 Jan 1949), est dau of Maj William Bridger, and *dsp* 2 Feb 1941
3a Arthur Saunders; *b* 23 June 1861; *d* 29 June 1924
4a John Ribton; *b* 15 Nov 1868; *d* unm 10 March 1907
1a Frances Sophia; *b* 3 Nov 1863; *m* 1886 Maj James Browne, Devonshire Regt, and *d* 8 Oct 1949, leaving issue:
2a Mary Elizabeth (twin with sis Frances); *m* 25 April 1889 Alfred Ormond Jordan and *d* 1891
3a Emily; *b* 7 July 1868; *m* Aug 1901 Byron Brenan, CMG, FRIC (*d* 26 Feb 1927), s of Col Edward Fitzgerald Brenan, and *d* 3 March 1956
(1) Sophia; *m* 13 Dec 1823 James Exham Purefoy Turbett (*d* 1868), of Owenstown, Co Dublin, only child of Robert Turbett, of Greenmount, Co Dublin, and *d* 13 Dec 1882
(2) Frances; *m* 12 Dec 1834 John Sankey (*d* 2 Jan 1873) and *d* 14 Feb 1898, leaving issue
(3) Louisa; *m* 1st May 1839 William John Waldron (*d* 8 Nov 1856), of Balla Lodge, Mayo; *m* 2nd 12 Sept 1859 Owen H F O'Malley
(4) Anne; *m* 16 Sept 1857 Arthur Frederick Lloyd, Registrar High Court Justice I
3 (cont.) The Very Rev George Gore *m* 2nd 3 Feb 1820 Sophia (*d* Dec 1821), dau of Sir George Ribton, 2nd Bt (*see* 1901 edn), and by her had issue:
(4) John Ribton (Ven); *b* 3 Nov 1820; Archdeacon Achonry, Rector and Vicar Dromard, Co Sligo, Canon Killala, RD; *m* 2 Aug 1844 Frances Brabazon (*d* 1896), dau of John Dunsford Ellard, of Renmore, Co Galway, and *d* 1894, leaving issue:
1a John Ellard; *b* 1 June 1845; CE; *d* unm 6 July 1910
2a George Anthony Ellard, JP (Devon); *b* 15 Dec 1846; Brevet Lt-Col RM, memb Gentlemen-at-Arms; *m* 27 May 1905 Bessie Frances (*d* 25 Sept 1924), dau of Rev T Coulthard, Vicar Plymstock, and widow of Richard Cory, JP, of Langdon Court, Devon, and *dsp* 6 March 1915
3a Arthur Saunders; *b* 6 Dec 1848; *m* 1st 26 Sept 1878 Frances Elizabeth (*dsp* 1879), only dau of William Fraser, of Madras; *m* 2nd 23 Nov 1881 Elizabeth (*d* 17 Aug 1950), dau of James Baldwin, of Bath, formerly of Mount Pleasant, Co Cork, and *d* 24 Jan 1901, having had issue:
1b Arthur Henry Baldwin; *b* 26 Dec 1883; *m* 14 Oct 1913 Margaret Jane, dau of John Douglas Browne, of Los Angeles, and *d* 24 Sept 1953, leaving issue:
1c +Arthur Francis Baldwin; *b* 29 Sept 1914; *m* 6 Dec 1939 *Helen Claire, dau of James J Mullen, of Whitehall, Montana, and has issue:
1d +James Arthur; *b* 12 Aug 1950
1d *Judith Ann; *b* 21 Dec 1940; *m* 1964 *Fernando Joseph Ramirez, of Fountain Valley, California, and has issue:
1e *Jane Ellen; *b* Nov 1965
2e *Anne Marie; *b* 1969
2d *Nancy Jane; *b* 4 May 1942
3d *Margaret Frances; *b* 31 Oct 1946
4d *Pamela Elizabeth; *b* 3 June 1948; *m* 1969 *Paul Everett Adkins and has issue:
1e *Jennifer Claire; *b* 1975
5d *Jill Marie; *b* 4 March 1957
6d *Martha Jane; *b* 27 June 1959
2c John Douglas; *b* 7 Oct 1916; BS; *m* 4 July 1946 *Evelyn Mae (Lynn) Wagner (*m* 2nd 1978 Gerald Louis Artaud (*d* 1979) of Los Angeles) and *d* 1976, leaving issue:
1d +John Douglas; *b* 31 Aug 1947

1d *Theresa Ann; *b* 22 March 1951; *m* 1973 *Jon Patrick Ferguson and has issue:
1e *Stacy Ann; *b* 1975
2e *Dana Marie; *b* 1978
2d *Margaret Jane; *b* 8 Sept 1957; *m* 1978 *John Fisher
2b John Ribton; *b* 1886; *m* 10 May 1913 Valentine Ansiebel, dau of James Curran, and *d* May 1939, leaving issue:
1c Patricia Ellard; *b* 2 Aug 1914; *m* 1st 17 April 1934 Clayton Dougherty (*d* 25 July 1935), s of Charles Richard Dougherty, of Bakersfield, California; *m* 2nd 5 Sept 1937 Edward Newell Wead Steele, of Sausalito, Calif, s of Stanley Steele, and had issue:
1d *John Stanley; *b* 1939; *m* 1st 1960 Donna McColly and has issue:
1e *Timothy Edward; *b* 1961
1d (cont.) John Steele *m* 2nd 1970 *Terry Dee Sanborn and has further issue:
2e *Todd William; *b* 1970
1d *Valerie Ann; *b* 1941; *m* 1961 *Thomas Arthur Benge
1b Margaret Frances; *b* 13 Nov 1882; *m* 10 Nov 1909 Walter Samuel Sisson (*d* 24 Dec 1947), s of Charles James Sisson, of Bramcote, Notts, and *dsp* 23 May 1953
2b Mabel (Jill); *b* 9 Feb 1891; *m* 27 Jan 1959 Chambré Baldwin (*d* 1969), s of James Baldwin, of Bath, formerly of Mount Pleasant, Co Cork
4a Ribton; *b* 12 March 1852; Lt-Col Res Ofrs, Maj 1st Bn Roy Sussex Regt; *m* 24 Nov 1881 Ada Sophia (*m* 2nd 5 May 1930 Lt-Col A Mackenzie-Penderel (*d* 1940); *d* 14 Nov 1944), dau of Robert Dendy, of Chichester, and *d* 28 Sept 1924, having had issue:
1b Arthur Ribton; *b* Sept, *d* 16 Dec 1888
2b Gerard Ribton; *b* 2 May 1893; Lt 1st Bn Roy Welch Fus; *d* 20 Dec 1914 of wounds recd in action
1b Ada Mary Frances; *b* 15 Sept 1882; *m* 9 Jan 1919 Capt Robert John Mackessack, MD, MA, RAMC (*d* 1970), of Tiraluin, Nairn, and had issue:
1c *John Ribton Gore; *b* 12 July 1921; *educ* Edinburgh U (MB, ChB); *m* Jan 1955 *Nicolette, dau of Henry Freston, of Alderley Edge, Cheshire, and has had issue:
1d Simon Fraser; *b* Jan 1957; *d* 3 April 1958
1c *(Evelyn) Mary; *b* 1 May 1924; *m* 19 June 1954 Maj Robert Henry Brydges Oatts, KOSB, of Fonthill Gifford, Wilts, er s of Col H A Oatts, of Argyll, and has had issue:
1d *Andrew Robert Brydges; *b* 7 Sept 1955
2d Nicholas; *b* and *d* 10 Jan 1957
3d *Jeremy Roderick Henry; *b* 6 Jan 1958
1d *Victoria Mary; *b* 21 July 1960
2b Esmée Kathleen; *b* 23 March 1885; *d* unm 6 June 1947
3b Mabel Pauline; *b* 17 April 1887; *m* 2 July 1918 Richard Vandeleur Bourke (*d* 10 April 1952), of Co Limerick, and *d* 23 Sept 1961, leaving issue
4b Evelyn Esther; *b* 11 July 1894; *d* 3 Nov 1915
1a Elizabeth Sophia Rebecca; *b* 22 Dec 1850; *m* 1 Sept 1885 Rev Robert Blair, MA (*d* 1933), Rector Magheracross, Fermanagh, and *d* 1921, leaving issue
3 (cont.) The Very Rev George Gore *m* 3rd June 1823 Maria (*dsp* 22 Feb 1856), widow of Thomas Bunbury Isaac, of Hollywood House, Co Down, and *d* 27 Aug 1844
5 Maria Louisa; *m* 19 Jan 1800 James Knox-Gore (*d* 21 Oct 1818), of Broadlands Park, Co Mayo, MP, and *d* 6 March 1827, leaving issue
6 Eleanor; *m* 25 May 1801 Hon Frederick Cavendish and *d* 25 March 1812, leaving issue (*see* WATERPARK, B)
The **2nd Earl** *m* 3rd Jan 1781 Elizabeth (*d* 5 June 1829), dau of Richard Underwood, and *d* 8 Oct 1809, having by her had further issue:
4 Saunders; *b* 1783; *d* 1813
5 John; *d* 1814
6 Charles Stephen (Sir), GCB, KH; *b* 26 Dec 1793; Gen, Col 6th Foot, Lt-Govr Chelsea Hosp; *m* 13 May 1824 Sarah Rachel (*d* 17 Oct 1880), dau of James Fraser, of Nova Scotia, and *d* 4 Sept 1869, leaving issue:
(1) James Arthur Charles; *b* 10 April 1826; Maj 71st Regt; *m* 19 July 1854 Catherine Louise (*d* 16 March 1921), 3rd dau of Col John Bazalgette, and *d* 3 Jan 1901, leaving issue:
1a Arthur Charles Fraser; *b* 10 July 1857; *m* 22 April 1897 Mary (*m* 2nd 14 June 1917 Hugh Austin Neame, of Johannesburg), dau of Anders Ohlsson, Swedish Consul S Africa, and *d* 22 Sept 1914
2a James Walmer; *b* 7 Nov 1859; *d* unm
3a Edward John Mounsey; *b* 26 July 1863; Brevet Lt-Col London Regt; *m* 25 May 1899 Hon Emilia Herbert Fullarton Napier (*d* 6 April 1932), dau of FM 1st Baron Napier of Magdala (*qv*), and *d* 2 Dec 1949, having had issue:
1b Arthur Sydney Napier; *b* 18 Sept 1901; *d* 27 Oct 1910
2b +Humphry Gerard Napier [Maj Humphry Gore, The Red Cottage, South Park, Sevenoaks, Kent]; *b* 2 Aug 1916; *educ* Sherborne; 2nd Lt Gordons SRO, WW II Maj Roy Ulster Rifles, served Singapore 1949 (despatches); *m* 6 May 1948 *Leslie Marshall, dau of Benjamin Bostwick Peabody, of New York, and has issue:
1c +Mark Staveley, BA; *b* 26 Aug 1952; *educ* Bembridge Sch
2c +Brendon Bostwick, BSc; *b* 8 Sept 1955; *educ* Tonbridge; *m* 1990 *Helen Elizabeth, yst dau of P A Merker, of Fleet, Hants, and has:
1d +Charles James Napier; b 21 Feb 1995
3c +Timothy Francis [Timothy Gore Esq, Longfield House, Seal Hollow Rd, Sevenoaks, Kent TN13 3SL]; *b* 22 July 1957; BA, BSc, ARICS; *m* 1989 *Amanda S, twin dau of P F Kingsley, of Sussex, and has:
1d +Edward Charles Theodore; *b* 1994
1d *Emma Philippa; *b* 1991
2d *Celia Frances; *b* 1992

1b Irene Frances Cecilla; *b* 18 Jan 1908; *m* 1947 (*divorce*) William James Curtis, of Evercreech, Somerset
4a Charles Arran; *b* 30 Dec 1864
5a William Stuart; *b* 11 May 1868; *m* 1894 Emily Winn (*d* 1956) and *d* 1946, leaving issue:
1b William James Stuart; *b* 1894; *m* Lillian May, dau of James Knight
2b Erroll Napier; *b* 1897; *m* 1926 Alma Maude (*d* 1978), dau of William Edward Kessell, and *d* 1968, having had issue:
1c William Erroll; *b* 1926; *m* 1951 *Joan Hetherington and *d* 1969, leaving issue:
1d +William Arran; *b* 1965
1d *Jennifer Louise; *b* 1957; *m* 1977 *Jonathan Smith and has issue:
1e *Justin William; *b* 1987
1e *Jacqueline Louise; *b* 1984
2e *Jessica Ashleigh; *b* 1991
2d *Susan Michelle; *b* 1959; *m* 1979 *Steven Cole and has had issue:
1e Christopher Steven; *b* 1980; *d* 1983
2e *Mathew Dean; *b* 1984
3d *Alyson Maree; *b* 1961; *m* 1991 *Christopher John Gearing and has issue:
1e *Jack Ernest; *b* 1993
4d *Catherine Anne; *b* 1968
2c +Stuart Maxwell; *b* 1929; *m* 1988 *Leovegilda Marcos and has issue:
1d +Benjamin Laurence Stuart; *b* 1990
1d *Kylie-Anne Shirley; *b* 1989
3c +Ian Winn Bazelgette; *b* 1932; Maj Australian Staff Corps; *m* 1961 *Evelyne Phyllis, dau of Maj Charles William Sayers, of Melbourne, and has issue:
1d +Robert Ian Charles; *b* 1966; *m* 1991 *Tina Marie Kelly and has issue:
1e +Thomas Ian; *b* 1992
1d *Belinda Jane; *b* 1967; *m* 1992 *William Anthony Tyrewartha and has issue:
1e +William Ian Alexander; *b* 1993
4c +Laurence James; *b* 1935
1c *Pamela Mary; *b* 1939; *m* 1961 (*divorce* 1967) Graham Richard Westwood and has issue:
1d *Nicholas Ian Richard; *b* 1964
1d *Jo-Anne Louise; *b* 1963
3b Vere Hunt; *b* 1899
1b Gwendoline Arran; *b* 1908; *m* 1931 Michael Ernest Seymour and *d* 1993, leaving issue (*see* CULME-SEYMOUR, Bt)
6a Frederick George; *b* 26 July 1870; Lt W Kent (Queen's Own) Yeo, late Lt Thorneycroft's Mounted Inf Boer War 1900 (medals with clasps) and SW Africa 1915; believed *dec* S Africa
7a Sydney Hamilton; *b* 18 June 1872; *d* unm 3 Aug 1906
8a Staveley Napier, MC; *b* 15 Nov 1875; Lt 24th Bn Roy Fus, Lt 3rd Bn Oxford LI Matabele, Boer and Zulu Rebellions, SW Africa and France WW I (wounded, despatches); *m* 30 Nov 1916 Isabelle Margaret, dau of Philip Frith and gdau of the painter William Powell Frith, RA, and *d* 19–, having had issue:
1b John Staveley; *b* 10 Sept 1917; *d* 10 Sept 1921
1a Catherine Margaret Bazalgette; *m* 1st 18 July 1889 Montague C T Stevenson; *m* 2nd 23 Feb 1897 William Brooke Prance and *d* 22 May 1936
2a Mary Maude Nina; *d* unm 19 Dec 1928
(2) Charles Clitheroe, MVO (1914); *b* 7 Sept 1839; Col Lt-Col Roy Irish Rifles, Indian Mutiny 1857–59, Transvaal 1881; *m* 1st 27 Jan 1875 Maria Harriet Elizabeth (*d* 15 Feb 1881), 2nd dau of Rev Thomas Cator, MA, and had issue:
1a Charles Savile Lumley; *b* 9 Dec 1876; Assist Priv Sec to 1st Govr-Gen Australia; *d* unm 4 Feb 1902
(2) (cont.) Col Charles Gore *m* 2nd 24 Oct 1882 Lavinia (*d* 16 May 1912), dau of Francis Charles FitzRoy (*see* GRAFTON, D), and *d* 13 Aug 1926
(3) Frederick Augustus; *b* 8 May 1844; Lt-Col late 2nd Bn York and Lancaster Regt; *m* 8 March 1886 Alice (*d* 1 April 1930), dau of Edward W H Schenley, and *d* 2 Jan 1931
(1) Eliza Amelia, VA; Ldy Bedchamber to HM QUEEN VICTORIA; *m* 20 Sept 1848 19th Earl of Erroll (*qv*) and *d* 11 March 1916, leaving issue
(2) Adelaide Rachel; *m* 10 March 1864 Lt-Gen George Whitworth Talbot Rich, CB (*see* 1970 edn RICH, Bt), and *dsp* 2 Sept 1893
7 Edward; *b* 1797; Capt RN; *m* 28 Oct 1822 Mary Anne Douglas (*d* 4 Aug 1880) and *d* 10 Jan 1879, leaving issue:
(1) Augustus Frederick, CMG; *b* 1 Feb 1826; Lt-Govr St Vincent, FRGS; *m* 26 Jan 1861 Eliza Arabella (*d* 24 Jan 1884), est dau of Rt Rev William P Austin, DD, Bp Guiana, and *d* 21 Sept 1887, leaving issue:
1a Cecilia Emily; *b* 22 June 1862
2a Mary Mehitabel; *d* young
3a Charlotte Elizabeth; *d* unm 8 Nov 1948
4a Adelaide Isabella; *d* unm 17 May 1947
5a Dora Letitia; *d* unm 27 Feb 1914
(1) Cecilia Elizabeth; *m* 23 Nov 1848 Adolphus Meetkerke (*d* 1879) and *d* 26 Oct 1903
(2) Mary Anne; *d* unm 13 April 1910
7 CECILIA LETITIA Gore; *m* 1st 14 May 1815 Sir George Buggin (*d* 12 April 1825); took by roy licence 2 May 1831 her mother's name UNDERWOOD; *m* 2nd 1831 HRH AUGUSTUS FREDERICK, DUKE OF SUSSEX (*d* 21 April 1843), 6th s of GEORGE III, was *cr* 10 April 1840 DUCHESS OF INVERNESS (UK), and *dsp* 1 Aug 1873
8 Isabella; *m* 2 March 1816 Rev Hon Charles Douglas, bro of 17th Earl of Morton (*qv*), and *d* 30 Nov 1838, leaving issue

9 Julia; *m* 23 Dec 1821 Robert Manners Lockwood and *d* 21 Aug 1891 aged 91, leaving issue

The 3rd EARL's n,

PHILIP YORKE GORE, **4th Earl of Arran of the Arran Islands**, KP (1841); *b* 23 Nov 1801; *m* 1 March 1838 Elizabeth Marianne (*d* 27 April 1899), 2nd dau of Gen Sir William Francis Patrick Napier, KCB (n of 7th Lord Napier and Ettrick; *qv*), by Caroline Fox, gdau of 1st Baron Holland (*see* ILCHESTER, E), and had:

1 ARTHUR SAUNDERS WILLIAM CHARLES FOX, **5th Earl**

2 Augustus Frederick Napier; *b* 7 Dec 1840; *d* 19 Jan 1849

1 Caroline Annesley; *m* 21 Aug 1869 8th Lord Ruthven of Freeland (*see* GOWRIE, E), and *d* 16 Dec 1914, leaving issue

2 Elizabeth Augusta; *d* unm 26 May 1933

3 Mary Napier; *m* 30 July 1889 Herbert Brisbane Ewart, 2nd s of Lt-Gen Charles Brisbane Ewart, CB, Lt-Govr Jersey, and *d* 2 Feb 1927, leaving issue

The 4th EARL *d* 25 June 1884, his only surv s,

ARTHUR SAUNDERS WILLIAM CHARLES FOX GORE, **5th Earl of Arran of the Arran Islands**, KP (1898); *b* 6 Jan 1839; *educ* Eton; Ld lL Co Mayo 1889–1901; *cr* 7 Nov 1884 BARON SUDLEY OF CASTLE GORE, Co Mayo (UK); *m* 1st 21 Feb 1865 Edith (*d* 3 Oct 1871), yr dau of Robert, Viscount Jocelyn, and gdau of 3rd Earl of Roden (*qv*), and had issue:

1 ARTHUR JOCELYN CHARLES, **6th Earl**

1 Mabell Frances Elizabeth, GCVO (1953), GBE (1920), DGStJ, Hon LLD St Andrews, Ldy Bedchamber to HM QUEEN MARY; authoress; *m* 19 Jan 1886 8th Earl of Airlie (*qv*) and *d* 7 April 1956, leaving issue

2 Cicely Alice, OStJ, Extra Ldy Bedchamber to HM QUEEN ALEXANDRA; *m* 17 May 1887 4th Marquess of Salisbury (*qv*) and *d* 5 Feb 1955, leaving issue

3 Esther Georgiana Caroline, DGStJ; *m* 26 July 1894 2nd Viscount Hambleden (*qv*) and *d* 11 Oct 1955, leaving issue

The **5th Earl** *m* 2nd 29 July 1889 Winifred Ellen (*d* 12 Nov 1921), Ldy-in-waiting to HRH PRINCESS CHRISTIAN 1886–89, dau of John Reilly, of St Bridgids, Co Dublin, by Hon Augusta Sugden, dau of 1st Baron St Leonards, and widow of Hon John Montagu Stopford, Gren Gds (*see* COURTOWN, E), and by her had issue:

4 Winifred Helena Lettice; *b* 11 Aug 1891; *d* unm 6 Dec 1958

The 5th EARL *d* 14 March 1901; his only s,

ARTHUR JOCELYN CHARLES GORE, **6th Earl of Arran of the Arran Islands**, KP (1909), PC (I 1917), JP and DL (Co Mayo), JP (Co Louth and Herts), DL (Essex); *b* 14 Sept 1868; Capt, Brevet-Maj and Adj RHG (Blues) Boer War 1900 (brevet, medal with four clasps), Lt-Col cmdg 15th Bn Co London Regt 1904–08 and OTC Ireland 1910–11, re-joined RHG 1914 (invalided), memb London TA&AFA; Ld lL Co Donegal 1917–20, KGStJ; *m* 1st 16 Aug 1902 Maud Jacqueline Marie Beauclerk, DGStJ (ld 6 March 1927), only dau of 3rd Baron Huyssen van Kattendyke, of Kattendyke, Zeeland, Holland, and had issue:

1 ARTHUR PAUL JOHN JAMES CHARLES GORE, **7th Earl of Arran of the Arran Islands**; *b* 31 July 1903; *educ* Winchester and New Coll Oxford (BA); Lt 5th Bn Essex Regt (TA), ADC to Govr-Gen and C-in-C Union S African 1931–32; author and translator; *d* unm 28 Dec 1958

2 ARTHUR KATTENDYKE STRANGE ARCHIBALD GORE, **8th Earl of Arran of the Arran Islands**; *b* 5 July 1910; *educ* Eton and Balliol Coll Oxford; Assist Press Attaché Br Legn Berne 1939–40, Attaché Lisbon 1941–42, Dep Dir Overseas Gen Div Min of Inf 1943–45, Dir Secretariat COI 1945–49, Dir Daily Mail Gen Tst, Chm Children's Country Holidays Fund, Hon Treas Moorfields Eye Hosp, columnist *Evening News*; *m* 11 June 1937 *Fiona Bryde [The Rt Hon Fiona Countess of Arran, Pimlico House, Hemel Hempstead, Herts], est dau of Sir Iain Colquhoun of Luss, 7th Bt (*qv*), and *d* 1983, leaving issue:

1 ARTHUR DESMOND COLQUHOUN GORE, **9th and present Earl of Arran of the Arran Islands**

2 Philip; *b* 22 March 1943

The **6th Earl** *m* 2nd 17 Dec 1929 Lilian Constance (*d* 25 Jan 1962 aged 87), dau of Joseph Quick, of Cross Deep Place, Twickenham, and widow of Francis Browne, of Pycroft Place, Chertsey, and *d* 19 Dec 1958

ARTHUR

Arms: Or on a chevron azure, between two clarions in chief gules and a kangaroo sejant in base proper, two swords, the points upwards also proper, points and hilts of the first, on a chief of the third a horse courant argent. **Crest:** In front of two swords in saltire proper, pommels and hilts or, a pelican in her piety sable, the nest or. **Motto:** *Stet fortuna domus* ('May the fortune of the house be maintained'). **Creation:** Bt. (UK) 5 June 1841.

SIR STEPHEN JOHN ARTHUR, 6TH BT, of Upper Canada [Sir Stephen Arthur Bt, c/o Trio, 43 Woollcombe St, Timaru, New Zealand]; *b* 1 July 1953; *s* f 1985; *m* 1978 (*divorce*) Carolyn Margaret, dau of Burnie Lawrence Diamond, of Cairns, Qld, Australia, and has issue:

1 +BENJAMIN NATHAN; *b* 27 March 1979

1 *Amanda; *b* 1975

2 *Melanie; *b* 1976

Lineage: JOHN ARTHUR, originally of Cornwall, later of Plymouth, Devon; *b* 1683; *m* 29 April 1730 Sarah, dau of Philip Westlake, of Plympton St Mary, Devon, and *d* 25 June 1760, leaving:

JOHN ARTHUR, of Plymouth; *bapt* 6 Sept 1732; *m* 3 March 1767 Catherine (*d* 31 May 1818), dau of Thomas Cornish, of E Portlemouth, Devon, and *d* 24 Jan 1788, having had a 4th s:

Sir George Arthur, 1st Bt (UK), so *cr* 5 June 1841, KCH; *b* 21 June 1784; Lt-Gen , Col 50th Regt, DCL, ktd 1837, Lt-Govr Honduras, Van Diemen's Land and Upper Canada, Govr Bombay, Actg Govr-Gen India 1846; *m* May 1814 Eliza Ord Ussher (*d* 14 Jan 1855), 2nd dau of Lt-Gen Sir John Frederick Sigismund Smith, KCB, RA, and *d* 19 Sept 1854, having had, with other issue:

1 **Sir Frederick Leopold Arthur, 2nd Bt**; *b* 20 Dec 1816; Col; *m* 24 April 1856 Lady Elizabeth Hay (*m* 2nd 22 Nov 1883 Rev Canon Ernest Edward Dugmore, Vicar Parkstone, Dorset (*d* 10 March 1925); *d* 24 Feb 1902), 4th dau of 11th Earl of Kinnoull (*qv*), and *d* 1 June 1878, leaving issue:

(1) **Sir George Compton Archibald Arthur, 3rd Bt**, MVO (1909); *b* 30 April 1860; Lt 2nd Life Gds and Herts Imp Yeo, Hon Capt, Egypt 1882, Nile 1884–85, Imp Yeo and Staff Boer War 1900–01 and WW I, Personal Priv Sec to Sec State War 1914–16, FRSL, Chesney Gold Medal, Chevalier Legn Honour, Offr Crown Belgium; *m* 11 Aug 1898 Kate Harriet (*d* 28 Jan 1950), dau of Horatio Brandon and widow of Arthur Raymond Yates, and *dsp* 14 Jan 1946

(2) Leonard Robert Sunkersett, CMG; *b* 23 Dec 1864; Capt Prince Consort's Own Rifle Bde; Colonial Sec Gold Coast, Priv Sec to Govr-Gen Australia; *d* unm 13 Dec 1903

(1) Frederica Louisa Juliana; *m* 28 April 1881 Alfred Edmund William Darby, JP, DL (*d* 23 July 1925), est s of Alfred Darby, of Coalbrookdale, Salop, and *d* 23 March 1946, leaving issue

2 Charles Viney; *b* 20 June 1823; Bombay Light Cav; *d* 1 Nov 1847

3 Edward Penfold; *b* 24 Feb 1825; Col Bombay Staff Corps; *m* 1847 Emma Isabella Wilson (*d* 13 Feb 1912), dau of Capt Thomas Alexander Souter, 44th Regt, and *d* 9 June 1870, having had, with other issue:

(1) George Arthur; *b* 19 Jan 1851; *m* 19 Aug 1873 Helen (*d* 16 April 1878), dau of Neale Thomson, of Camphill, Glasgow, and *d* 20 Sept 1878, leaving issue:

1a Edward Malcolm; *b* 1874; Lt 4th Bn S Wales Borderers; *m* 1906 Evelyn (*d* 31 Dec 1947), dau of Edward George Kerr, of Timaru, NZ, and *d* 4 June 1928, leaving issue:

1b GEORGE MALCOLM (Sir), **4th Bt**

1b Edith Doreen; *b* 14 Sept 1912; *m* 8 April 1939 Paul Dare Rodgers, of Palmerston N, NZ (*d* 16 Dec 1961), and had:

1c *Anthony Paul [Anthony Rodgers Esq, 32 Sheen St, Dunedin, NZ]; *b* 20 Jan 1945; *m* 4 May 1968 *Carol Anne, dau of — Guthrie, of Timaru, NZ

2c *Peter Stanlan; *b* 29 Nov 1949

1c *Janet Mary [Mrs Gerald Marlow, 11 Athol Place, Timaru, NZ]; *b* 19 Sept 1940; *m* 25 May 1963 *Gerald James Joseph Marlow and has issue:

1d *Nicholas Paul James; *b* 28 March 1964

1d *Jacinta Anne Louise; *b* 22 Jan 1966

2d *Susan Bridget Marie; *b* 11 July 1967
2c *Margaret Jill; *b* 17 Dec 1942; *m* 28 Oct 1967 *Daniel Joseph Sherry, of Christchurch, NZ
3c *Juliet Anne; *b* 16 Feb 1946
4c *Joan Dorothy; *b* 6 July 1948
2a George Frederick Neale; *b* 10 April 1878; KAR; *m* 20 Sept 1905 Edith Lavender (*d* 20 Aug 1966), dau of Joseph Horace Taylor, of Kensington, and *d* 16 Jan 1939, leaving issue:
1b +George Leonard, JP; *b* 27 March 1908; MPC, MEC, Maj SA Army Staff Corps WW II, DAAG Br Forces Palestine 1943–44, attd 2nd Bn Roy Inniskilling Fus Italy 1945, memb Br Mil Mission Greece 1945, DAAG Natal 1949–57, Cabinet Min Health and Tport Natal; *m* 22 April 1936 *Gladys Raina, dau of George Percy Farr, of Bedford, CP, S Africa, and has had issue:
1c Leonard Compton; *b* 1 Feb 1942; *d* 11 Feb 1956
2c +Gavyn Farr; *b* 13 Sept 1951; *educ* Harrow and Ch Ch Oxford (MA); barrister Middle Temple 1975
2b +Archibald John; *b* 3 Sept 1909
4 Sigismund Montagu; *b* 26 Aug 1828; *d* 28 Aug 1855
5 John Raynor, of Normandy Park, Guildford; *b* 20 Nov 1830; Bombay CS; *m* 6 Oct 1864 Aileen (*d* 15 June 1916), 3rd dau of Hon Stephen Edmond Spring Rice (*see* MONTEAGLE OF BRANDON, B), and *d* 19 Nov 1903, having had issue:
(1) Sigismund Raynor; *b* 9 Feb 1867; Indian CS; *m* 2 Sept 1891 Constance Eleanor (*d* 27 Oct 1947), dau of Sir Charles Parry Hobhouse, 3rd Bt (*qv*), and *d* 8 Feb 1920, having had issue:
1a George Raynor; *b* 1 Aug 1892; *d* 16 May 1894
2a John Sigismund (Rev), MC; *b* 24 Aug 1894; *educ* Charterhouse and Oriel Coll Oxford (BA 1921, MA 1944); CF 1941–44, Maj RARO and F/O RAF; Vicar and RD Beaminster 1953–62, Vicar Market Lavington, Wilts, Chaplain Dauntseys Sch 1944–53; *m* 6 July 1925 Constance Amy Farquhar (*d* 1980), 2nd dau of Joseph Sladen, ICS, and *d* 16 Dec 1974, leaving issue:
1b Leonard John Henry; *b* 20 April 1926; *educ* Aldenham and Magdalene Coll Cambridge (MB, BCh 1951); MRCP (London) 1957; Capt RAMC, RMO 1st DLI 1952–54; *m* 27 Feb 1954 *Hon Janet Stella Brain [The Hon Mrs Arthur, Royal Oak Cottage, Church Broughton, Derbys], only dau of 1st Baron Brain (*qv*), and *d* 1983, leaving issue:
1c +Robert Leonard Sigismund; *b* 16 April 1955
1c *Linet Stella; *b* 7 Sept 1956
2c *Tansy Amy Anne; *b* 4 April 1959
3c *Elaine Fay; *b* 25 Feb 1961
4c *Hazel Jane; *b* 2 Aug 1964
5c *Ruth Gilly; *b* 29 Oct 1966
1b *Flora Jessamine Mary [Mrs Charles Elliott, 35 Cook St, Northgate, Brisbane, Queensland, Australia]; *b* 23 June 1928; *educ* St Hugh's Coll Oxford (MA); *m* 8 May 1954 *Charles Edward Elliott, BM, BCh, er s of Charles James Elliott, of Toowong, Brisbane, and has issue:
1c *Charles John Peter [Charles Elliott Esq, PO Box 161, Pomona 4568, 164 Arthy's Rd, Cooran 4569, Qld, Australia]; *b* 19 Jan 1955; *m* 1982 *Elizabeth Mary, dau of Denley Keeling, and has issue:
1d *Charles Leonard George; *b* 1983
2d *James Leonard; *b* 1984
3d *Henry Robert; *b* 1988
4d *Georgina Mary-Jane; *b* 1990
2c *John Michael [John Elliott Esq, 104 Cavendish St, Nundah, Brisbane, Qld 4012, Australia]; *b* 14 Oct 1956; *m* 1986 *Barbara Jane, dau of Bernard Russell Arthur Stuart, and has issue:
1d *Conor Stuart; *b* 1992
1d *Caitlin Elaine; *b* 1988
2d *Sally Brenda; *b* 1990
3c *Thomas George [Thomas Elliott Esq, 3791 West 3rd Ave, Vancouver, BC, Canada]; *b* 29 March 1958; *m* 1982 *Gwenneth Mary, dau of John Stanley Shaw, and has issue:
1d *Tristan; *b* 1989
2d *Reece; *b* 1991
1d *Tyne Rebecca; *b* 1993
1c *Mary Jessamine; *b* 17 Dec 1960; *m* 1990 *Lee Cameron Thompson and has issue:
1d *Eliot George; *b* 1991
1d *Rachel Rebecca; *b* 1993
2d *Lucy Jane; *b* 1972
2b *Rose Eleanor [Mrs Edward Longman, The Vicarage, Back Lane, Cerne Abbas, Dorset DT2 7JW]; *b* 22 March 1931; *educ* St Hugh's Coll Oxford (MA); *m* 27 May 1961 *Rev Edward George Longman, Priest-in-Charge, St Mary's, Cerne Abbas, er s of George Frederick Norton Longman, JP, of Somerset, and has:
1c *Harold John; *b* 4 March 1962, MA Cantab; *m* 1989 *Alison Louise, dau of Col William Armstrong, and has:
1d *Edward Ian Armstrong; *b* 1997
1d *Margaret Amy Armstrong; *b* 1994
2c *Peter George; *b* 2 Aug 1965; *m* 1994 *Melanie Joy, dau of Terry James Pitcher
3c *George Roland; *b* 7 March 1969; BSc; *m* 1996 *Dáša, dau of Vladimir Hloušek
1c *Anna Frances; *b* 2 Aug 1963; MA Oxon; *m* 1996 *Philip Rutnam
3b *Cecil Lucy Sylvia [Mrs Richard Vooght, Rose Cottage, Over, Almondsbury, Bristol]; *b* 8 Oct 1939; *m* 1980 *Richard Denis Vooght, of Bristol, and has:
1c *Jenny Madeleine Rose; *b* 1981
2c *Abigail Katharine Amy; *b* 1983
3a Leonard Charles; *b* 23 Feb 1898; *d* 8 March 1911
4a (Oswald) Raynor (Sir), KCMG (1957, CMG 1953), CVO (1953), JP (E Sussex 1962); *b* 16 Dec 1905; *educ* Charterhouse and Corpus Christi Coll Cambridge; Commr Cyprus 1937, Ch Commr Cyprus 1948, Colonial Sec Bermuda 1951–54, Govr and C-in-C Falkland Islands 1954–57, Govr and C-in-C Bahamas 1957–60, KStJ; *m* 8 May 1935 Mary Elizabeth, MBE, SSStJ (*d* 1994), only dau of Rt Hon Sir Cecil Arthur Spring Rice, GCMG, GCVO (*see* MONTEAGLE OF BRANDON, B), and *d* 4 Dec 1973 following an accident, leaving issue:
1b +Thomas Sigismund Raynor [Thomas Arthur Esq, Burwash Glebe, Etchingham, Sussex]; *b* 19 Jan 1940; *educ* Eton and Oriel Coll Oxford (MA); *m* 26 March 1966 *Angela Susan Clare, er dau of Lt-Col Roland Theodore Wroughton MacLeod, of Lanark, and has issue:
1c +George Raynor Macleod; *b* 1969
1c *Juliet Caroline; *b* 19 Sept 1966
2c *Valentine Bridget; *b* 11 Sept 1968; *m* 1991 *Hugo S Akerman, of Ragnall Farm, Carswell Marsh, Faringdon, Oxon, est s of John Akerman, of London, and has issue:
1d *Valentine Cosima; *b* 1994
3c *Alexandra Maxine; *b* 1973
1b *Caroline Ann Florence; *b* 19 Aug 1937; *educ* Somerville Coll Oxford (MA) and Goldsmith's Coll London U; *m* 15 Jan 1972 *Courtney Kenny, of Ballinrobe, Co Mayo, and 14 Grange Grove, London N1, only s of Stanhope Kenny, of Ballinrobe, and has issue:
1c *Courtney Arthur Francis; *b* 1983
1a Lucy Eleanor; *b* 20 Jan 1904; MB, BS (London) 1929, LRCP, MRCS (Eng), FRSM; *m* 1st 25 July 1929 (*divorce* 1953) Charles Edward Murray Elliott, s of Frank Louis Dumbell Elliott, CB, of Wimbledon, and had issue:
1b *Anthony Charles Raynor [Anthony Elliott Esq, c/o Coutts & Co, 440 Strand, London WC2]; *b* 28 Jan 1937; *educ* Radley and Trin Coll Cambridge (BA 1960); slr; *m* 16 July 1960 *Christina, dau of Capt William Theobald Hindson, MEMech, RN (ret), of Newtown, Hants, and has issue:
1c *Nicholas Charles Raynor; *b* 23 Dec 1964
2c *Paul William Anthony; *b* 15 March 1967
2b *Timothy John [Timothy Elliott Esq TD, Larkhill, Haynes, West End, Beds MK45 3RB]; *b* 5 Oct 1940; *educ* Radley and Neuchâtel U and Trin Coll Cambridge (MA); *m* 1964 *Julia Margaret Clare, dau of Donal O'Donovan, and has issue:
1c *Hugh Stephen Murray; *b* 1965; *educ* Bedford Sch and Trinity Coll Cambridge (MA); *m* 1989 *Maria Antonia Martin Elena, of Salamanca, Spain, and has:
1d *Edward Arthur; *b* 1993
1d *Alba Sofia; *b* 1995
1c *Lucy Eleanor Catherine; *b* 1964 *educ* Bedford High Sch and Trin Coll Cambridge (MA) ACA;
2c *Alice Margaret Sophie; *b* 14 March 1970; *educ* Bedford High Sch and Trin Coll Cambridge (PhD)
1b *Rosalind Ann [Mrs John Hinton, Tower House, Clifton Down Rd, Bristol BS8 4AG]; *b* 30 Oct 1930; *educ* Roy Free Hosp (MB, BS 1954, D(Obst) RCOG 1955); *m* 14 July 1956 *Lt-Cdr Rev John Dorsett Owen Hinton, RN (ret), of The Vicarage, Pucklechurch, Bristol, s of Capt John Charles Dorsett Hinton, of Exmouth, and has issue:
1c *Jeremy Charles Dorsett; *b* 16 April 1961
2c *John Murray Raynor; *b* 30 July 1964
1c *Sarah Margaret; *b* 12 July 1958
1a (cont.) Mrs Lucy Elliott *m* 2nd 15 June 1953 Denys Otho Hamson, OBE, MC (*d* 14 June 1963), s of Charles Edward Hamson, of Istanbul
(2) Oswald George, Indian CS; *b* 16 July 1869; *d* 20 March 1896
(3) Edmund John; *b* 29 March 1873; Maj 7th Bombay Lancers WW I (despatches); *m* 1 Aug 1921 Kathleen Emily Isabel Ada (*m* 2nd 20 Feb 1958 Arnold Richmond), dau of George Penn Simkins, CB, and *d* 26 Jan 1953, leaving:
1a +George Henry Edmond; *b* 25 March 1927; GIMechE; *m* 8 July 1950 *Kathleen, dau of Frederick Joseph Bow, of Bristol, and has issue:
1b +Robert George; *b* 15 Dec 1950; *m* 1969 *Janice Margaret, dau of Gerald Poolman, of 266 Tavy House, Plymouth, and has issue:
1c +Neil Robert; *b* 1970
2c +Kieron Gerald; *b* 1970
1a *Leonora Kathleen; *b* 22 Feb 1923; *m* 1st 10 Sept 1945 F/Sgt John Francis Bingham, RAF, s of William Henry Bingham; *m* 2nd *— Wallis, of Margate
(4) Henry Bartle Compton; *b* 14 Oct 1879; Maj RFA; *ka* 10 Aug 1916
(1) Aileen Mary; *b* 3 Sept 1865; *m* 28 Sept 1892 Sir Henry Charles Miller Lambert, KCMG, CB (*d* 9 Feb 1935), er s of Henry Thomas Lambert, JP, of Bletchingley, Surrey, and *d* 10 April 1944, leaving issue
(2) Leonora Frances; *b* 22 Jan 1871; *d* unm 21 Nov 1956
(3) Christina Lucy; *b* 31 Dec 1875; *m* 30 Dec 1905 Robert Vaughan Johnson, s of Henry R Vaughan Johnson (*d* 1 Jan 1954) by Hon Cecilia, dau of 1st Baron Campbell (*see* STRATHEDEN AND CAMPBELL, B), and *d* 9 March 1962, leaving issue
1 Isabella Maria; *m* 1st 19 April 1842 Compton Charles Domvile (*dsp* 19 March 1852), er s of Sir Compton Pocklington Domville, 1st Bt (*see*1970 edn); *m* 2nd 18 Feb 1868 Charles J Malton and *d* 22 July 1891

Sir GEORGE's 1st cousin twice-removed,

Sir George Malcolm Arthur, 4th Bt; *b* 26 March 1908; *m* 24 March 1928 *Doris Fay [Dowager Lady Arthur, 421 Waimea Rd, Wakatu, Nelson, New Zealand], yst dau of Joseph Wooding, JP, of Woodland Grange, S Canterbury, NZ, and had issue:

1 BASIL MALCOLM (Sir), **5th Bt**
1 *Helen Fay; *b* 28 Jan 1931; *m* 1st 1949 (*divorce* 1981) Morton King and has:
(1) *Donald Malcolm; *b* 1950
(2) *Peter Morton; *b* 1955
(1) *Yvonne Jane; *b* 1951
(2) *Maree Fay; *b* 1960

1 (cont.) Mrs Helen King *m* 2nd 1982 *Peter William Caird, of 8RD Waimate, S Canterbury, NZ

2 *Maureen Beatrice; *b* 22 Sept 1933; *m* 1st 1953 (*divorce* 1972) James Warren Patterson; *m* 2nd 1976 *James Wright McLauchlan, of Nydia Bay, Private Bag, Haverlock, Marlborough, NZ, and has by her 1st husb:

(1) *Warren John; *b* 1954

(2) *James Bartley; *b* 1956

(3) *Desmond Bruce; *b* 1965

(1) *Moira Fay; *b* 1957

(2) *Rosana Mae; *b* 1961

3 Evelyn Jennifer; *b* 2 May 1939

4 *Elizabeth Adele; *b* 4 Jan 1948; *m* 1972 *Lindsay Gerald Dawkins, of 129 Wellington St, Picton, Marlborough, NZ, and has issue:

(1) *Hayden Gerald; *b* 1977

(1) *Leah Janette; *b* 1973

Sir GEORGE *d* 27 July 1949; his only son,

Sir Basil Malcolm Arthur, 5th Bt; *b* 18 Sept 1928; MP Timaru 1962; *m* 1st 2 Jan 1950 (*divorce* 1983) Elizabeth Rita, 2nd dau of Alan Mervyn Wells, JP, of Temuka, NZ, and had issue:

1 Sir STEPHEN JOHN ARTHUR, **6th and present Bt**

1 *Marilyn Jane [Mrs W Keeman, 37 Pohutukawa Ave, Howick, Auckland, New Zealand]; *b* 1 Oct 1950; *m* 1972 *W B M Keeman, of Howick, and has:

(1) *Zane Basil Cornelius; *b* 1974

(2) *Kris William Reginald; *b* 1981

(1) *Lauriely Elizabeth Wanda; *b* 1976

2 *Cheryl Dawn; *b* 7 Sept 1951; *m* 1971 *G L Blanchard, of 1RD Springbrook, Timaru, NZ

Sir Basil *m* 2nd 1983 *Sandra Colleen, dau of William Boaz, of Whangarei, NZ, and *d* 1985

ASHBOURNE

Arms: Ermine, three keys fesswise in pale azure and in chief as many trefoils slipped vert. **Supporters:** Dexter, a female figure representing Mercy, her exterior hand resting on a sword, point downwards, all proper; sinister, a female figure representing Justice, holding in her left hand a sword, point upwards, and in her right a balance, all proper, each figure charged on the breast with a trefoil slipped vert, and each standing on a fasces, also proper.
Crest: On a bank of reeds a pelican in her piety, all proper.
Motto: *Cœlestes pandite portæ* ('Open, oh ye heavenly gates').
Creation: B. (UK) 4 July 1885.

THE 4TH BARON ASHBOURNE, of Ashbourne, Co Meath ((Edward) Barry Greynville Gibson) [The Rt Hon The Lord Ashbourne, 107 Sussex Rd, Petersfield, Hants GU31 4LB]; *b* 28 Jan 1933; *s* f 1983; *educ* Rugby; RN 1951–72: Midshipman 1952, Sub-Lt 1953, Lt 1955, specialised in Torpedo and Anti-Submarine Warfare, Lt-Cdr 1963, cmded HMS *Crofton* 1963–64, RN Staff Course 1965, HMS *Phoebe* 1966, Staff Cdr Naval Forces Gulf 1967; with Kitcat and Aitken, stockbrokers, 1972–73 and 1976–79, Vickers, da Costa, stockbrokers, 1973–76, Save and Prosper Gp 1979–81, GT Management 1981–88; Directorate Naval Operations and Trade (MOD) 1989–93; pres Petersfield branch E Hants C Assoc; v-pres Hampshire Autistic Soc; chm: Joshua Christian Tst, All Party Roy Yacht Parly Gp, Lords and Commons Family and Child Protection Gp; memb Select Ctee on EC; *m* 25 March 1967 *Yvonne Georgina, dau of Mrs Flora Ham, of Malin, Co Donegal, and has issue:

1 +(EDWARD) CHARLES D'OLIER; *b* 31 Dec 1967; *educ* Christ's Hosp and Oxford; stockbroker Cazenove and Co 1994–

2 +(William) Rodney Colles; *b* 20 Oct 1970

3 +Patrick Mayne; *b* 1977; *educ* Canford

Lineage: WILLIAM GIBSON, of Lodge Park, Co Meath; had issue:

WILLIAM GIBSON, JP (Co Tipperary), of Rockforest, Co Tipperary, and 22 Merrion Sq, Dublin; *b* 15 Feb 1808; *m* 1st 27 Oct 1831 Louisa (*d* 4 Dec 1853), dau of Joseph Grant, of Dublin, barrister, and had, with other issue, a 2nd s:

1 EDWARD, **lst Baron**

WILLIAM GIBSON *m* 2nd 24 April 1856 Charlotte (*d* 3 June 1909), dau of John Hare, of Deer Park, Co Tipperary, and *d* 20 Feb 1872, having had further issue:

1 Fanny Elizabeth

WILLIAM GIBSON's 2nd s,

EDWARD GIBSON, **1st Baron Ashbourne**, of Ashbourne, Co Meath (UK), so *cr* 4 July 1885, PC (I 1877, GB 1885), QC (1872), JP (Co Meath); *b* 4 Sept 1837; *educ* Trin Coll Dublin (BA 1858, MA 1861); called Irish Bar 1860, Bencher King's Inns 1877, Hon LLD Trin Coll Dublin 1881 and Hon Bencher Gray's Inn 1886; MP (C) Dublin U 1875–85, Attorney-Gen Ireland 1877–80, Ld Chllr Ireland with Cabinet seat 1885–86, 1886–92 and 1895–1905, author *Pitt: some chapters of his life and times*; *m* 4 April 1868 Frances Maria Adelaide (*b* 24 Dec 1849; *d* 21 March 1926), 2nd dau of Henry Cope Colles, barrister, and *d* 22 May 1913, having had:

1 WILLIAM GIBSON, **2nd Baron Ashbourne**, JP (Cos Meath and Dublin); *b* 16 Dec 1868; *educ* Merton Coll Oxford (MA) and Trin Coll Dublin (BA); *m* 7 Jan 1896 Marianne (*d* 17 Aug 1953), dau of Henri Roger Conquerre de Monbrison, of Paris, and *dsp* 21 Jan 1942

2 Henry d'Olier Grant; *b* 13 June 1870; Lt RA; *d* unm 11 Dec 1905

3 Edward Graves Mayne, JP (Co Dublin); *b* 28 July 1873; *educ* Wellington, Trin Coll Cambridge (MA) and Trin Coll Dublin; barrister King's Inns Dublin, Lt 5th Bn Leinster Regt; *m* 1st 15 Aug 1900 Mary Phillips (*d* 19 Dec 1919), dau of Henry Russell Greg, of Lode Hill, Cheshire, and had issue:

(1) EDWARD RUSSELL, **3rd Baron**

(2) John Mayne; *b* 6 June 1906; *educ* Sherborne; *m* 9 Jan 1935 Penelope, JP (1951) (she *m* 2nd 27 Dec 1947 Cecil Batstone Cook (*d* 23 July 1965), only s of Horace Batstone Cook, of London, and had further issue), er dau of Alexander Mayall, of Bealings End, Woodbridge, Suffolk, and *d* 26 Feb 1939, leaving issue:

1a Nicholas Mayne; *b* 27 Nov 1938; *educ* Haileybury; *k* in a motor accident at Cape Town 13 April 1957

(3) (William) David, OBE (1944), TD; *b* 22 March 1914; *educ* Sherborne and Trin Coll Cambridge (BA 1936, MA 1948); 2nd Master and modern languages teacher Clifton (housemaster 1936–65), Col Gen Staff WW II (despatches twice); *m* 6 Jan 1947 *Sabina (formerly Sabine) [The Hon Mrs David Gibson, Buckley Cottage, Batson, Salcombe, Devon], dau of Dr Ernst Landsberg, of 31 Rosemead Av, Cape Town, S Africa, and *d* 1993, leaving issue:

1a *Celia Mary; *b* 6 Sept 1948; *m* 1977 (*divorce* 1993) Robert Sommers and has issue:

1b *Dominic Alexander; *b* 1977

1b *Abigail Jane; *b* 1980

2b *Jessica Sarah; *b* 1982

2a *Monica Anne [Mrs Monica Harding, 13 Kingston Av, Stony Stratford, Milton Keynes, Bucks MK11 1DS]; *b* 25 Sept 1951; *m* 1973 (*divorce*1985) Andrew Vaughan Harding and has issue:

1b *James Lee; *b* 19 July 1977

1b *Louise; *b* 21 Jan 1975

3a *Philippa Constance [Miss Gibson, Maes-y-Morfa, Llangrannog, Llandysul, Dyfed SA44 6RU]; *b* 5 Jan 1953

(1) Erica Alba; *m* 23 Oct 1920 Patrick Hope Rutland, yr s of Charles Rutland, MD, and had issue:

1a *Jeremy Charles; *b* 1930

2a *Jonathan Patrick; *b* 1935

(2) *Kathleen Mary [The Hon Mrs Russell, Fairmead Court, 6 College Rd, Rondebosch, Cape Town, S Africa]; *b* 1908; *m* 16 Dec 1930 James Hamilton Russell, MA, LLB (*d* 1981), 2nd s of Verner Wallace Russell, of Cape Town, and has issue:

1a *Michael Anthony Hamilton [Prof Michael Russell, 14 Court Lane Gdns, London SE21 7DZ]; *b* 1932; *educ* Oxford (MA); BM, BCh, FRCP, FRCPsych (London); Prof of Addiction, Maudsley Hosp, London; *m* 1962 *Audrey Anne Timms and has issue:

1b *James Hamilton; *b* 1974

2b *Nicholas Hamilton; *b* 1977

2a *Timothy Patrick Hamilton [Timothy Hamilton-Russell Esq, De Mond House, 317 Tenth St, PO Box 2043, Hermanus 7200, Western Cape, S Africa]; *b* 1934; *m* 1958 *Athene Wendy Isobel, dau of William Aubrey Bindon, and has issue:

1b *Anthony James; *b* 1962; *m* *Arabella Sabina Lilian, only dau of Hon David Anthony Lawrence Caccia (*see* 1970 edn CACCIA , B), and has issue:

1c *Olivia Sabina; *b* 1992

2c *Ella Maria; *b* 1992

2b *Patrick David; *b* 1969; *m* 1995 *Caroline Dicey

1b *Bridgid Mary; *b* 1960; *m* 1980 *Scipion Vernede and has:

1c *Monica Athene; *b* 1991

2c *Amelia Victoria; *b* 1992

2b *Julia Kathleen; *b* 1965; *m* 1992 *Robert David Marshall (*see* MONTAGU-POLLOCK, Bt)

3a *David Patrick Hamilton [The Rt Rev The Lord Bishop of Grahamstown, Bishopsbourne, 17 Durban St, Grahamstown 6140, S Africa]; *b* 1938; Bp Grahamstown; *m* 1980 *Dorothea Mary Madden and has issue:

1b *Sipho Matthew; *b* 1981

2b *Thabo Andrew; *b* 1983

4a *Robin James [Robin Russell Esq, 161 Court Lane, London SE21 7EE]; *b* 1947; *m* 1977 (*divorce* 1989) Imogene Veronica King and has issue:

1b *George; *b* 1982

2b *Thomas Richard Henry; *b* 1984

1b *Frances; *b* 1977

2b *Virginia; *b* 1979

1a *Jill Mary [Mrs Anthony Hall, 20 Unthank Rd, Norwich, Norfolk NR2 2RA]; *b* 1935; *m* 1965 Anthony Ronald Hall (*d* 1991) and has issue:

1b *Catherine Sian; *b* 1967; *m* 1995 *Benjamin Conway Greenwood and has:

1c *Alexandra Rosalind; *b* 1996

2b *Marion Ruth; *b* 1970

2a *Diana Elizabeth Hamilton [Prof Diana Russell, 2432 Grant St, Berkeley, CA 94703, USA]; *b* 1938; *educ* Cape Town U (BA), LSE and Harvard (MA, PhD); Prof Emerita of Sociology, Mills Coll, author

(3) Elizabeth Marion; *m* 6 March 1936 Neil Richardson, 2nd s of William Richardson, of York, and *d* 15 Aug 1960, leaving three sons and a dau

3 (cont.) Edward Gibson *m* 2nd 1 June 1922 Deloraine Amy Norah (*d* 16 Aug 1962), 2nd dau of C W E Henslowe, PWD, India, and *d* 26 April 1928

4 (Ernest) Victor; *b* 3 Jan 1875; barrister King's Inns Dublin, T/Cdr RNVR and Hon Lt Army, Boer War 1900 and 1902; *m* 1st 28 April 1905 Mary Wood Salisbury (*dsp* 21 Sept 1905), dau of Joseph L R Wood, of New York; *m* 2nd 8 Dec 1909 Caroline (*d* 15 Oct 1951), dau of Frederic de Billier, of New York, and *d* 14 Jan 1922, leaving by her:

(1) +John Frederic, DSC [John Gibson Esq DSC, 687 Erickson Rd, Campbell River, BC, Canada]; *b* 6 May 1919; Lt RNVR WW II (despatches), author; *m* 1st 18 Oct 1941 (*divorce* 1946) Margaret Andrina, only dau of Andrew Booth, of Beverley, E Yorks, and has issue:

1a +Victor Russell [Victor Gibson Esq, Barn Hill House, 15 Parsonage Lane, Market Lavington, nr Devizes, Wilts]; *b* 4 Nov 1942; *educ* Nautical Coll Pangbourne; *m* 1968 *Pamela Cherry, dau of Edward Cupitt-Eggleshaw, and has issue:

1b +Geoffrey Andrew; *b* 1971

2b +Neil Henry; *b* 1975

(1) (cont.) John Gibson *m* 2nd 17 March 1947 *Lorna Mary, dau of John Pickering, of Kinta, Oakleigh Park S, London N20, and by her has issue:

2a +Simon John [Simon Gibson Esq, 31844 Conrad Av, Clearbrook, BC, Canada V2T 2K3]; *b* 26 March 1952; *m* 1976 *Joy Beatrice, dau of Walter Sidney Ridgway, of Vancouver, BC, and has issue:

1b *Shari-Anne Joy; *b* 1980

2b *Alisa Julie; *b* 1982

1a *Julia de Billier; *b* 1959; *m* 1985 *Evert van der Zee and has issue:

1b *Matthew James; *b* 1988

(1) *Amelie Sheila; *b* 25 Aug 1916; *m* 10 Feb 1940 *Capt (Ralph) Neville

1a *Neil Theodore Ralph; *b* 16 June 1944; *educ* Bradfield and King's Coll Cambridge

2a *Keith Neville; *b* 12 May 1951; *educ* Marlborough

1a *Amelie Camilla; *b* 18 April 1941; *m* 12 Oct 1963 *Pyers Pennant, est s of Judge David Edward Thornton Pennant, of Parkbury, Balcombe Rd, Poole, Dorset, and has issue:

1b *Jeremy Bankes; *b* 16 Jan 1965

2b *Donald Neville Hugo; *b* 27 Feb 1966

1 Elizabeth Mary; *m* 6 June 1893 5th Baron Bolton (*qv*) and *d* 9 Dec 1943, leaving issue

2 Violet Albina; went to Rome 1926 and tried to assassinate Mussolini by shooting; *d* unm 2 May 1956

3 Frances Maud; *m* 2 July 1904 Alexander Horsbrugh Porter (*d* 4 Feb 1946), 2nd s of Sir Andrew Porter, 1st Bt (*see* HORSBRUGH-PORTER, Bt), and *d* 5 March 1957, leaving issue

4 Constance Anna; went to Rome 1926 to secure her sis Violet's release from prison; *d* unm 7 Aug 1960

The 2nd BARON ASHBOURNE'S n,

EDWARD RUSSELL GIBSON, **3rd Baron Ashbourne**, CB (1950), DSO (1943), JP (Devon 1955–65), DL (Devon 1962–65); *b* 1 June 1901; *educ* RNCs Osborne and Dartmouth and Gonville and Caius Coll Cambridge; served WW I 1917–1918 in HMS *Superb*, HMS *Dreadnought* and HMS *Monarch*, specialised in submarines 1925, served in L3, L4 and L12, cmded H48 and Pandora, Cdr 1934, on staff of Adml Sir Dudley Pound 1939, Capt 1939, WW II: on staff of Adml Sir Max Horton 1940–42, took part in assault on Sicily, cmded HMS *Ariadne* 1943–45, 3rd Submarine Flotilla 1945, Naval Staff at Admlty 1945–47, cmded HMS *Mauritius* 1947–48, R-Adml 1948, UK Naval Rep Mily Staff Ctee UN 1948–50, Flag Offr Gibraltar and Adml Supt HM Dockyard Gibraltar 1950–52, V-Adml 1952; Legion of Merit (US) 1944, OStJ, Co Pres Devon St John's Ambulance Bde 1962–65; *m* 20 July 1929 Reta Frances (*d* 20 Jan 1996), er dau of Ernest Manning Hazeland, of Hong Kong, and *d* 3 Sept 1983, leaving issue:

1 (EDWARD) BARRY GREYNVILLE GIBSON, **4th and present Baron Ashbourne**

1 Oonagh Elizabeth; *b* 20 April 1935; *m* 2 Feb 1963 *John William Jeffrey, s of William Jeffrey, of The Old House, Medbourne, Market Harborough, Leics, and *d* June 1991, leaving issue:

(1) *(Edward) Paul John; *b* 7 Dec 1966

(1) *Katharine Helen; *b* 9 Aug 1964; *m* 19 May 1995 *Roy Margolis but retained her maiden name

ASHBROOK

Arms: Quarterly, 1st and 4th, argent two chevronels between three ravens, each having an ermine spot in its beak sable, and between the chevronels three pellets; 2nd and 3rd, gules three towers argent. **Crest:** A raven, having an ermine spot in its beak. **Supporters:** Two tigers regardant proper, ducally collared and chained or. **Motto:** *Mens conscia recti* ('A mind conscious of rectitude'). **Creations:** B. (I) 27 Oct 1733, V. (I) 30 Sept 1751.

THE 11TH VISCOUNT ASHBROOK and **Baron Castle Durrow**, Co Kilkenny (Michael Llowarch Warburton Flower, JP (Cheshire 1983)) [The Rt Hon The Viscount Ashbrook JP DL, The Old Parsonage, Arley Green, Northwich, Cheshire CW9 6LZ]; *b* 9 Dec 1935; *s* f 1995; *educ* Eton and Worcester Coll Oxford (MA); 2nd Lt Gren Gds 1955, slr 1963, ptnr: Farrer & Co 1966–76, March Pearson & Skelton (Manchester) 1986–, V-Lt Cheshire 1990– (DL 1982–90), chm HHA Gardens; *m* 8 May 1971 *Zoë Mary, yst dau of Francis Henry Arnold Engleheart, JP, of The Priory, Stoke-by-Nayland, Suffolk, and has issue:

1 +ROWLAND FRANCIS WARBURTON; *b* 16 Jan 1975

2 +Harry William Warburton; *b* 11 Jan 1977

1 *Eleanor Filumena; *b* 1973

Lineage: Sir WILLIAM FLOWER had, with another s (Sir William, PC (*c* 166?); soldier in Ireland at time of 1641 Uprising, *m* Frances, dau of Walter Weldon, of St John's Bower, Co Kildare, and widow of William Savage):

JOHN FLOWER; had:

THOMAS FLOWER, of Finglas, Co Dublin, and Durrow, Queen's Co; *m* 1st Jan 1683 Mary, sis of 1st Viscount Palmerston(*see* TEMPLE OF STOWE, E,) and had issue; *m* 2nd — Jeffreys and by her had two other children, Jeffreys and Catherine; his s by his 1st w:

WILLIAM FLOWER, **1st Baron Castle Durrow**, Co Kilkenny (I), so *cr* 27 Oct 1733, PC (I 1735); *bapt* 11 March 1685; *educ* Ch Ch Oxford; MP Co Kilkenny 1715–27 and Portarlington 1727–33, High Sheriff Co Kilkenny 1731; *m* by 1717 Edith, dau of Hon Toby Caulfeild, of Clone, Co Kilkenny (*see* CHARLEMONT, V), and *d* 29 April 1746, having had, with another s and two daus (*see* NORMANTON, E):

HENRY FLOWER, **1st Viscount Ashbrook** (I), so *cr* 30 Sept 1751; Cornet of Horse 1710, Capt 1711; *m* 9 March 1740 Elizabeth (*d* 10 Feb 1759), dau of Lt-Gen William Tatton, and *d* 27 June 1752, having had, with two daus (Elizabeth, *d* unm 1831; Mary, *m* 8 Jan 1788 Rev John Nicholl, Rector Remenham (*dsp* 16 July 1830)):

WILLIAM FLOWER, **2nd Viscount Ashbrook**; *b* 25 June 1744; *educ* Ch Ch Oxford; *m* 1766 Elizabeth (*m* 2nd 20 Jan 1790 Rev John Jones, DD, and *d* 22 Feb 1808), dau of Thomas Ridge, of Oxford, and *d* 30 Aug 1780, having had, with three daus:

1 WILLIAM FLOWER, **3rd Viscount Ashbrook**; *b* 19 Oct 1767; *educ* Eton and Trin Coll Oxford; *d* unm 6 Jan 1802

2 HENRY JEFFREY FLOWER, **4th Viscount Ashbrook**; *b* 6 Nov 1776; sometime Capt 58th Foot; Ld Bedchamber 1832–37; *m* 1st 26 May 1802 Deborah Susannah (*d* 24 March 1810), only dau and heiress of Rev William Maximilian Freind, Rector Chinnor, Oxon, and gdau and heiress of Thomas Walker, of Woodstock, and had issue; *m* 2nd 22 June 1812 Emily Theophila (*d* 9 April 1885 aged 94), est dau of Sir Thomas Metcalfe, 1st Bt (*see* 1970 edn), and *d* 4 May 1847, having by her had a surv dau; his only surv s by his 1st w:

(1) HENRY JEFFREY FLOWER, **5th Viscount Ashbrook**; *b* 17 June 1806; High Sheriff Co Kilkenny 1834; *m* 7 June 1828 Frances (*d* 15 June 1886 aged 83), dau of Sir John Robinson, 1st Bt, of Rokeby Hall, Co Louth (*see* 1883 edn), and *d* 3 Aug 1871, having had, with three daus (*see* RAVENSDALE, B):

1a HENRY JEFFREY FLOWER, **6th Viscount Ashbrook**, DL (Queen's Co); *b* 26 March 1829; Ensign 52nd Foot 1848, ret 1853, High Sheriff Queen's Co 1856; *m* 4 Sept 1860 (*divorce* 1877) Emily, est dau of John Frederick Abington, of Esher, Surrey, and *dsps* 14 Dec 1882

2a WILLIAM SPENCER FLOWER, **7th Viscount Ashbrook**, DL; *b* 23 March 1830; *educ* Eton and Trin Coll Dublin (BA 1851); sometime Offr 52nd Foot;

m 25 June 1861 Augusta Madeline Henrietta (*d* 5 Jan 1906), est dau of George Marton, of Capernway Hall, Lancs, and *d* 25 Nov 1906, having had:

1b Lucy Adelaide Frances; *d* an infant 20 Aug 1862

2b Adelaide Caroline; *d* an infant 6 Oct 1874

3a ROBERT THOMAS FLOWER, **8th Viscount Ashbrook**; *b* 1 April 1836; Lt-Col 4th Bn Leinster Regt Roy Canadians; *m* 18 July 1866 Gertrude Sophia (*d* 8 Nov 1911), er dau of Rev Sewell Hamilton, of Bath, and had issue:

1b LLOWARCH ROBERT, **9th Viscount**

2b Reginald Henry; *b* 15 June 1871; *m* 10 May 1901 Katherine (Kate) Ella (*d* 14 Nov 1957), dau of Col Edward William Cumming, Cameron Highrs, of Crover, Co Cavan, and *d* 6 Feb 1938, leaving issue:

1c *Mollie Frances, RN; *b* 26 March 1902; *m* 1st 20 April 1929 (*divorce* 1945) John Albert Peacey, s of Albert Henry Peacey, of Victoria, BC; *m* 2nd 14 June 1947 Maj Wilfrid Vincent Townshend Allen, s of Alfred William Bevan-Allen

2c Honor Florence; *b* 6 Jan 1904; *m* 23 May 1923 Terence Dampier Dyson, s of Arthur Dyson, and had issue:

1d *Peter Spencer Dampier; *b* 6 Feb 1926; RCNVR WW II (Service Medal, Vol Service Medal, Atlantic Star with Pacific Bar); *m* 5 Nov 1952 *Margaret Helen Stevens, of Rutland, BC, and has issue:

1e *Steven Dampier; *b* 5 July 1962

1e *Helen Honor; *b* 1953

2e *Katherine Mary; *b* 1955

3e *Virginia Ann; *b* 1957

2d *Terence Alexander; *b* 24 Aug 1942

1d *Pamela Florence; *b* 15 Feb 1924

2d *Virginia Nina; *b* 30 Jan 1925; *m* 1946 *Arthur Orsi, of Lakerview Heights, RR1, Westbank, BC, Canada, and has issue:

1e *Kim Arthur; *b* 1959

1e *Judith Ann; *b* 1947; *m* Aug 1966 *Henry Grant Maddock, of 364 Christlebon Ave, Kelowna, BC, Canada, and has issue:

1f *Jacqueline Lee; *b* May 1968

1b Frances Mary; *m* 2 Sept 1893 Harry Ernest White (*d* 1923), 2nd son of Gen Sir Robert White, KCB, of Aghaboe, Queen's Co

2b Eva Constance Gertrude; *d* unm 6 Nov 1928

3b Gertrude; *d* unm 1956

The 9th VISCOUNT *d* 9 March 1919; his est son,

LLOWARCH ROBERT FLOWER, **9th Viscount Ashbrook**, DL (Queen's Co); *b* 9 July 1870; *m* 14 Feb 1899 Gladys Lucille Beatrice (*d* 18 June 1968 aged 91), dau of Gen Sir George Wentworth Alexander Higginson, GCB, GCVO, and *d* 30 Aug 1936, leaving:

1 DESMOND LLOWARCH EDWARD FLOWER, **10th Viscount Ashbrook**, KCVO (1977), MBE (1945), JP (Cheshire 1946–68), DL (Cheshire 1949); *b* 9 July 1905; *educ* Eton and Balliol Coll Oxford (BA 1927); chartered accountant 1933, Maj RA (TA) and on Staff WW II, memb Cncl Duchy Lancaster 1957–95, V-Lt Cheshire 1961–68, BTA award for Arley Hall Gardens 1976; *m* 8 Nov 1934 *Elizabeth [The Rt Hon Elizabeth Viscountess Ashbrook, Woodlands, Arley, Northwich, Cheshire], er dau and coheir of Capt John Egerton-Warburton, of Arley Hall, Cheshire (*see* GREY EGERTON, Bt), and *d* 5 Dec 1995, leaving:

(1) MICHAEL LLOWARCH WARBURTON FLOWER, **11th and present Viscount Ashbrook**

(2) Anthony John Warburton; *b* 6 June 1938; *educ* Eton; *m* 23 July 1970 *Bridget Karen [The Hon Mrs Anthony Flower, Prouts Farm, Hawkley, Liss, Hants], yr dau of J Duncan, and *d* 1991, leaving issue:

1a *Alexandra Jane; *b* 24 Feb 1972

(1) *Jane Mary Elizabeth [The Hon Mrs Foster, 18 Stanley Gdns, London W11]; *b* 8 Dec 1943; *educ* LMH Oxford (BA) and LSE (MSc); *m* 6 May 1967 *Charles Francis Foster, yr s of Brig Thomas Francis Vere Foster, CBE, MC, and has issue:

1a *Rupert Rowland; *b* 25 Nov 1970

1a *Antonia Elizabeth; *b* 22 Feb 1969

2a *Cordelia Rose; *b* 1974

1 Eileen Augusta Sybil; *d* unm 1 Nov 1959

ASHBURNHAM

Arms: Gules, a fess between six mullets argent. **Crest:** Out of a ducal coronet or an ash tree proper. **Motto:** Will God, and I shall. **Creation:** Bt. (E) 15 May 1661.

SIR DENNY REGINALD ASHBURNHAM, 12TH BT, of Broomham, Sussex [Sir Denny Ashburnham Bt, Little Broomham, Church Lane, Guestling, Hastings, E Sussex TN35 4HS]; *b* 24 March 1916; *s* f 1953; *educ* Nautical Coll Pangbourne; Capt S Staffordshire Regt; *m* 22 June 1946 *Mary Frances, dau of Maj Robert Pascoe Mair, of Nicholls, Udimore, Sussex, by May Frances Urquhart, yr dau of John Turner, JP, DL, of Turner Hall and Tipperty, Aberdeenshire, and has had issue:

1 John Anchitel Fleetwood; *b* 25 June 1951; *educ* Shiplake Coll Henley; *m* 1975 *Corinne A [Mrs John Merricks, The Manor, Icklesham, Winchelsea, E Sussex] (*m* 2nd 1982 John Philip Merricks, of The Manor, Icklesham, Winchelsea, E Sussex), dau of D W J O'Brien, of The Grey House, Hooe Common, Battle, E Sussex, and *d* 1981, leaving issue:

(1) +JAMES FLEETWOOD; *b* 17 Dec 1979; *educ* Sherborne

(1) *Henrietta Mary; *b* 1 Oct 1981

1 *Frances; *b* 11 Sept 1947; *m* 1973 *Robert Charles Taylor, of Summerhayes, Pett, Hastings, E Sussex, and has issue:

(1) *Robert Denny; *b* 1982

(1) *Ellen Frances; *b* 1979

2 *Honor Rosemary; *b* 19 July 1949; *m* 1981 *Frank Cooke, of Broomhill Farm, Camber, Rye, E Sussex, and has issue:

(1) *Matthew John; *b* 1983

(1) *Lucy Frances; *b* 1981

(2) *Alice Mary; *b* 1985

Lineage: This family derives its name from Ashburnham, anciently Esburnham or Oseburnham, a hamlet situated on the Ashburn (a small stream in Sussex).

REGINALD de OSEBURNHAM; living 1166; held at one time land in Hoo, Cheliland and Denne, Sussex; had:

STEPHEN de ESBURNHAM; at one time held land at Dudewell, Sussex; had:

Sir RICHARD de ESBURNHAM; *m* Margaret, dau of Sir John Maltravers, and had:

Sir RICHARD de ESBURNHAM; held *temp* HENRY III two knights' fees of Alice, Countess of Eu; *m* Katherine, dau of Sir Richard Peverell, and had, with a yr s (Sir Bartholomew; held of HENRY III *c* 1254 land worth £20 p.a. (over £480,000 in late 1990s terms) summoned *c* 1254 to attend the King at London in Easter with horse and arms and to march to Portsmouth so as to proceed to Gascony to oppose the King of Castile):

Sir HAMOND de ESBURNHAM; *m* Maud, dau of Thomas Elton, of Elton, Sussex, and had:

Sir RICHARD ESBURNHAM; *m* Isabel, dau of Sir Thomas Morville, and had:

Sir JOHN ESBURNHAM; summoned *c* 1299 to attend EDWARD I in London with horse and arms; *m* Joan, dau of Richard Covert, of Sullington, Sussex, and had, with a dau (Mabel, *m* Simon Lunsford):

JOHN ESBURNHAM; Sheriff Surrey and Sussex *c* 1396, MP Sussex *c* 1397–98; *m* Mary, dau of — Isley, of Sundbridge, Kent, and had:

JOHN ASHBURNHAM, Sheriff Surrey and Sussex *c* 1402, a Commr of Array for Sussex *c* 1416; *m* Elizabeth Finch and had an only s:

THOMAS ASHBURNHAM; living *c* 1434; *m* Sarah, dau and heir of Henry Waunsey, descended from Sir Nicholas de Waunsey, Sheriff Surrey and Sussex *c* 1250, and had, with two other s (in cluding an er one, John, ancestor of the Earls of Ashburnham; *see* 1924 edn):

RICHARD ASHBURNHAM; *m* —, dau and heiress of Sir John Stoneling, of Broomham, Sussex, through whom he acquired that estate, and had:

THOMAS ASHBURNHAM, of Broomham; *m* Elizabeth, dau of John Dudley and aunt of John Dudley, Duke of Northumberland, and had an only s:

THOMAS ASHBURNHAM, of Broomham; *m* Bennet, dau and heiress of John Cromer, brother of Sir William Cromer, of Tunstall, Kent, and had, with four yr s and six daus:

LAURENCE ASHBURNHAM, of Broomham; *m* Eva, dau of Richard Adams, of Sussex, sister and heiress of Stephen Adams, of Harrietsham, Kent, and widow of John Levet, and had an er s:

ADAM ASHBURNHAM, of Broomham; MP Winchelsea 1592; *m* Elizabeth, er dau of Rodger Twisden, of Royden Hall, Kent, and *d* 5 June 1597, leaving, with a yr s (Edward, Rector Tonbridge, Kent; *m* 1639 Anne, widow of 1 Hutchinson):

LAWRENCE ASHBURNHAM, of Broomham; *b c* 1583; *m* Bridget, est dau of Sir George Fleetwood, of The Vatch, Bucks, and had an est s:

Sir Denny Ashburnham, 1st Bt (E), so *cr* 15 May 1661, of Broomham; Commr of Excise, Victualler Navy, MP Hastings 1660 and 1685; *m* 1st Frances, dau of John Ashburnham and aunt of 1st Baron Ashburnham (*see* 1924 edn ASHBURNHAM, E,), by whom he had an only surviving dau; *m* 2nd 1675 Ann, dau of Sir David Watkins, and *d* 1697, leaving, with other issue:

1 **Sir William Ashburnham, 2nd Bt**, of Broomham; Commr Alienation Off, Chamberlain Exchequer, MP Hastings; *m* 7 June 1701 Margaret (*d* 1742), dau of Sir Nicholas Pelham, of Catsfield Place, Sussex (*see* CHICHESTER, E,), and *dsp* 7 Nov 1756

2 **Sir Charles Ashburnham, 3rd Bt**; *d* 3 Oct 1762, leaving an est s:

(1) **Rev Sir William Ashburnham, 4th Bt**; *b* 1710; Dean of Chichester 1741, Canon Residentiary St Paul's Cathedral 1753, Bp of Chichester 1754; *m* 1736 Margaret, dau of Thomas Pelham, of Lewes, and *d* 4 Sept 1797, having had an only surv s:

1a **Sir William Ashburnham, 5th Bt**, of Broomham; *b* 5 March 1738/9; MP Hastings 1761 and 1768; *m* April 1766 Alice (*d* 10 Jan 1777), dau of Rev Francis Woodgate, Vicar of Mountfield, Sussex, and *d* 21 Aug 1823, having had, with other issue:

1b **Sir William Ashburnham, 6th Bt**, of Broomham; *b* 21 June 1769; *m* 7 July 1825 Juliana (*d* 22 Feb 1865), dau of Rev William Humphrey, Rector of Sele, and Vicar of Kemsing, Kent, and *dsp* 23 March 1843

2b John (Sir), **7th Bt**

3b George; *b* 12 Aug 1774; *m* Hannah — (*d* 30 June 1884) and had, with four other s and two daus:

1c John Woodgate; *b* 5 Jan 1840; *m* 13 Jan 1864 Julia Letitia (*d* 29 April 1912), dau of Rt Rev Nathaniel James Merriman, DD, 3rd Bp of Grahamstown, and *d* 1888, having had issue:

1d John Anchitel; *b* 6 Feb 1865; Ch Magistrate Johannesburg; *m* 20 June 1894 Jean (*d* 6 July 1937), dau of Rev R Price, and *d* 20 June 1939, leaving issue:

1e Phyllis Elizabeth; *b* 1895; *m* 1st 6 April 1918 Lt-Col John William James Clark-Kennedy, S African Police (*d* 19 June 1939), est son of Capt Alexander William Clark-Kennedy, Coldstream Gds, of Knockgray, and had a dau; *m* 2nd 7 March 1961 Colin Charlwood Frye, OBE, FRIC (*d* 13 April 1968), son of John Nicholas Frye, of Saffron Walden, Essex

2e Jean Margaret Julia; *b* 1899; *m* 15 July 1922 John Pratt-Johnson, MC, MB, BS, MRCS (*d* 1960), and had a s and twin daus

2d Bertram; *d* 1873

3d Laurence Piers; *b* 15 July 1875; *m* 25 Oct 1926 Sarah Agnes (*d* 13 Oct 1953), dau of Maj Thomas Warcup Kirkbride, of Nantwich, Cheshire, and *dsp* 21 May 1951

1d Mabel Julia; *m* 1888 Gerald Callander, MD (*d* 1892)

2d Cecil Mary; *m* 8 May 1894 Cdr Basil William Reid Hall, RN (*see* HALL, Bt, of Dunglass), and *d* 8 Feb 1919

3d Katharine Piers; *d* unm 16 April 1905

4d Gladys Maud; *m* 30 Sept 1905 William John Grant, of Bulawayo, and had issue

The 6th Bt's bro,

Rev Sir John Ashburnham, 7th Bt; *b* 26 Dec 1770; Chllr Cathedral and Preb Chichester, Rector of Guestling and Vicar of Pevensey; *m* 1st 4 July 1804 Fanny (*d* 11 April 1838), 4th dau of William Foster, of Hollington, Sussex, and had, with other issue:

1 ANCHITEL (Sir), **8th Bt**

2 Cromer (Sir), KCB; *b* 13 Sept 1831; Maj-Gen, Col-Cmdt KRRC, Lt-Col cmdg 3rd Bn Indian Mutiny 1857, Afghanistan 1878–80, Boer War 1881, Egyptian Campaign 1882, Sudan campaign 1884; *m* 26 July 1864 Urith Amelia (*d* 22 Dec 1928), 3rd dau of Capt George Bohun Martin, CB, RN, of East Bridgford, Notts, and *d* 25 Feb 1917, having had issue:

(1) Cromer; *b* 25 April 1866; Maj KRRC; *m* 11 June 1903 Ethel Mary (*d* 4 Feb 1947), 2nd dau of William James Menzies, of Crowhurst Park, Battle, and *d* 11 Sept 1919

(2) John; *b* 19 Aug, *d* 7 Sept 1873

(1) Urith Amelia; *m* 18 Oct 1904 Rev John Brand (*d* 11 Dec 1922), Vicar of St Mary's Platt, Borough Green, Kent, son of Thomas Brand, and *d* 4 Feb 1958

(2) Editha; *b* 7 Sept 1878; *m* 28 Oct 1913 Claud Willie Wemyss Carbery (*d* 5 May 1947), er s of William Edward Carbery, of the Bank of Australia, and *dsp* 20 May 1963

Sir John *m* 2nd Anne (*dsp* 1873), dau of Thomas Harman, and *d* 1 Sept 1854

His er son,

Sir Anchitel Ashburnham, 8th Bt, of Broomham, Sussex, JP; *b* 8 Feb 1828; declared by Ho Lds Privileges Ctee 1858 a coheir of the Barony of Grandison; *m* 7 June 1859 Isabella (*d* 4 Jan 1907), est dau of Capt George Bohun Martin, CB, RN, of East Bridgeford, Notts, and *d* 2 Dec 1899, leaving:

1 Sir ANCHITEL PIERS ASHBURNHAM later ASHBURNHAM-CLEMENT (roy licence 1899), **9th Bt**, JP; *b* 22 Aug 1861; *m* 4 Dec 1895 Elizabeth Ellen (*d* 28 April 1935), dau of George Burry Clement, of Silverhill, St Leonards-on-Sea, and *d* 5 Aug 1935

2 **Sir Reginald Ashburnham, 10th Bt**; *b* 26 Aug 1865; *m* 10 Sept 1921 Mildred (*d* 11 April 1942), dau of Rev Burrell Hayley, formerly Rector of Catsfield, Sussex, and widow of Walter Cheeseman, of Hill House, Crowhurst, Sussex, and *dsp* 29 Jan 1944

3 FLEETWOOD (Sir), **11th Bt**

4 Lawrence; *b* 21 May 1870; *m* 26 April 1904 Rosalie Winifred, only dau of Talbot Barnard, of The Hoo, Kempston, Beds, and *d* 7 Oct 1944, leaving issue:

(1) Doreen Winifred; *b* 15 May 1905; *m* Feb 1945 Sydney Jackson Ruffner, son of S Ruffner, of Los Angeles, and *d* 1991, leaving:

1a *Virginia Rosalie; *b* 194–

5 Piers; *b* 1 June 1871; *d* unm 6 Aug 1946

1 Isabella; *b* 5 April 1860; *m* 12 Jan 1881 Herbert Curteis (*d* 28 Oct 1919) ,of Windmill Hill Place, and *d* 1 Sept 1938, leaving issue

2 Maud; *b* 22 Nov 1863; *d* unm 16 April 1952

3 Bridget; *b* 14 March 1876; *m* 1921 Ronald Cloke (*d* 1954)

The 10th Bt's bro,

Sir Fleetwood Ashburnham, 11th Bt; *b* 2 March 1869; *m* 30 July 1908 Elfrida (*d* 19 Oct 1953), dau of James Kirkley, JP, of Cleadon Park, Co Durham, and *d* 5 March 1953, having had:

1 Anchitel Fleetwood; *b* 26 May 1911; *educ* Stowe; T/Maj RASC, late Lt Roy Sussex Regt, WW II 1939–40; *m* 28 Dec 1938 *Kathleen Marjory, dau of Lt-Col Frederic Wilfred Bagnall Willett, DSO, of Cudwell, Scaynes Hill, Sussex, and *das* Palestine 20 Dec 1940

2 Sir DENNY REGINALD ASHBURNHAM, **12th and present Bt**

3 Piers Wilfrid; *b* 27, *d* 28 May 1918

1 *Honor Elfrida [Mrs Ernest Boorman, 22 Heathlands, Westfields, Hastings, E Sussex]; *b* 23 April 1920; *m* 31 March 1951 *Ernest James Boorman, son of Frederick Boorman, of Court Lodge, Udimore, nr Rye, Sussex

ASHBURTON

Arms: Azure a fess or, in chief a bear's head proper, muzzled and ringed or, differenced by a cross formy fitchy azure.
Crest: A mullet erminois between two wings, argent.
Supporters: On either side a bear proper, muzzled, collared and chained or, each charged on the shoulder with a cross patée fitchée of the last. **Motto:** *Virtus in arduis* ('Fortitude under difficulties').
Creation: B. (UK) 10 April 1835.

THE 7TH BARON ASHBURTON, of Ashburton, Devon (Sir John Francis Harcourt Baring, KG (1994), KCVO (1990, CVO 1980), DL (Hants 1994)) [The Rt Hon The Lord Ashburton KG KCVO DL, Lake House, Northington, Alresford, nr Winchester, Hants SO24 9TG]; *b* 2 Nov 1928; *educ* Eton (Fell 1982) and Trin Coll Oxford (MA, Hon Fell 1989, Hon Fell Hertford Coll Oxford 1976–97); chm Baring Bros 1974–89, Barings plc 1985–89 (non-exec dir 1989–94) and Accepting Houses Ctee 1977–81, dir: Pye Hldgs 1967–79, Roy Insur 1964–82, Trafford Park Estates 1964–77, Harris and Ptnrs, Toronto, Outwich (SA), Johannesburg 1967–77, chm Outwich Investment Tst 1968–86 and Baring Stratton Investment Tst 1986–, memb Cncl CBI 1976–79, V-Pres Gen Cncl Br Bankers Assoc 1977–81, Pres Overseas Bankers Club 1977–78, Receiver-Gen Duchy of Cornwall 1974–90, Ld Warden Stannaries and Keeper Privy Seal Duchy of Cornwall 1990–94, dir: Dunlop Hldgs 1981–84, BP 1982–95 (chmn 1992–95), Rhodes Tstee 1970 (Chm 1987), Tstee Nat Gallery 1981–87, dir Bank of England 1983–91, ktd 1983, memb Br Tport Docks Bd 1966–71; *m* 1st 25 Nov 1955 (*divorce* 1984) Hon Susan Mary Renwick, est dau of 1st Baron Renwick (*qv*), and has issue:

1 +MARK FRANCIS ROBERT [The Hon Mark Baring, Abbotstone Farm House, nr Arlesford, Hants]; *b* 17 Aug 1958; *educ* Eton and Ch Ch Oxford; *m* 29 Oct 1983 *Miranda, 2nd dau of Capt Charles St John Graham Moncrieff, (*see* PETO, Bt of Barnstaple), and has:

(1) +Frederick Charles Francis; *b* 1990

(2) +Patrick Robin John; *b* 1995

(1) *Aurea Rose; *b* 1988

(2) *Flora; *b* 2 May 1997

2 +Alexander Nicholas John; *b* 15 Feb 1964; *educ* Eton and Oriel Coll Oxford; *m* 1992 *Lucy Caroline, yr dau of Gen Sir David William Fraser, GCB, OBE, and has issue (*see* SALTOUN, L)

1 *Lucinda Mary Louise; *b* 20 Oct 1956; *educ* N Foreland Lodge, Aigton and London U; *m* 1978 *Hon Michael John Wilmot Malet Vaughan, 2nd son of 8th Earl of Lisburne (*qv*) and has issue

2 *Rose Theresa; *b* 7 Dec 1961; *educ* St Mary's Calne, Marlborough and St Andrews U; *m* 1994 *Barnaby Hugh Rogerson, 2nd s of Cdr Keith Rogerson, RN, and has:

1a *Molly Frances Tripoli; *b* 1995

The 7th BARON *m* 2nd 1987 *Sarah Cornelia, dau of John George Spencer-Churchill (*see* MARLBOROUGH, D), and formerly wife of James Colin Crewe

Lineage: Sir FRANCIS BARING, 1st Bt (*see* NORTHBROOK, B), had a 2nd s:

ALEXANDER BARING, **1st Baron Ashburton**, of Ashburton, Devon, so *cr* 10 April 1835, PC (1834); *b* 27 Oct 1774; DCL Oxford, MP Taunton 1806–26, Callington 1826–31, Thetford 1831–32 and N Essex 1832–35, Pres BOT and Master of the Mint 1834–35, Tstee Br Museum 1829–49 and Nat Gallery 1835–48; *m* 23 Aug 1798 Anne Louisa (*d* 5 Dec 1848), est dau of William Bingham, of Philadelphia, US Senator, and *d* 12 May 1848, leaving:

1 WILLIAM BINGHAM BARING, **2nd Baron Ashburton**, PC (1845); *b* June 1799; MP Thetford 1826–30 and 1841–48, Callington 1830–31, Winchester 1832–37, Staffordshire N 1837–41, Sec Bd Control 1841–45, Paymaster Forces and Treasurer Navy 1845–46, Cdr Legn of Honour; *m* 1st 12 April 1823 Harriet Mary (*d* 4 May 1857), est dau of 6th Earl of Sandwich (*qv*), and had:

(1) Alexander Montagu; *b* 10 Nov 1828; *d* 5 Feb 1830

1 The **2nd Baron** *m* 2nd 17 Nov 1858 Louisa Caroline (*d* 2 Feb 1903), yst dau of James Stewart Mackenzie, PC, and *dspms* 23 March 1864, having by her had:

(1) Mary Florence; *m* 30 April 1884 5th Marquess of Northampton (*qv*) and *d* 1 June 1902, leaving issue

2 FRANCIS BARING, **3rd Baron Ashburton**; *b* 24 May 1800; MP Thetford; *m* Dec 1832 Hortense Eugenie Claire (*d* 15 Dec 1882), dau of Hugues Bernard Maret, Duke of Bassano, Min of NAPOLEON I, and had issue:

(1) ALEXANDER HUGH, **4th Baron**

(2) Denzil Hugh; *b* 1837; *d* at Nice, 26 May 1866

(1) Marie Anne Louisa; *m* 10 Feb 1858 6th Duke of Grafton (*qv*) and *dsp* 8 April 1928

The 3rd BARON *d* 6 Sept 1868; his er s,

ALEXANDER HUGH BARING, **4th Baron Ashburton**, DL; *b* 1835; MA; MP Thetford 1857–67; *m* 5 Jan 1864 Hon Leonora Caroline Digby (*d* 19 Aug 1930), 2nd dau of 9th Baron Digby (*qv*), and had issue:

1 FRANCIS DENZIL EDWARD, **5th Baron**

2 Frederick Arthur; *b* 18 Sept 1867; Capt Hampshire Yeo (Carabiniers); *m* 30 April 1890 Laura Louisa (*d* 13 Nov 1951), dau of Frederick Hobson, of Hockley House, Alresford, Hants, and *d* 26 Feb 1961, leaving issue:

(1) Evelyn Claire; *b* 22 March 1891

3 Alexander Henry, JP; *b* 4 Sept 1869; CC and CA Hants 1915–48; *d* unm 21 Jan 1948

4 Guy Victor; *b* 26 Feb 1873; Lt-Col Coldstream Gds Res, MP Winchester 1906–16; *m* 16 July 1903 Olive Alethea (*d* 5 March 1964), yst dau of Hugh Colin Smith (*see* BICESTER, B), and was *ka* 15 Sept 1916, having had:

(1) Oliver Hugh; *b* 19 May 1904; *d* 19 Jan 1908

(2) Simon Alexander Vivian; *b* 22 Nov 1905; *educ* Eton; Lt Welsh Gds; *m* 1st 1 May 1935 (*divorce* 1946) Jeanne, dau of Felix Salmond, of New York, and had issue:

1a +Julian Guy Alexander [Julian Baring Esq, Manor Farm, Bradley, Alresford, Hants]; *b* 9 Dec 1935; *educ* Eton; *m* 1971 *Isla, dau of Sir Frank Samuel Tait, of Toorak, Melbourne, Victoria, Australia, and has issue:

1b +Justin Frank Alexander; *b* 1971

1b *Rebecca Alexandra Viola; *b* 1973

(2) (cont.) Simon Baring *m* 2nd 24 Oct 1946 Pamela Rachel (*d* 1985), only dau of Sir Mark Beresford Russell Grant-Sturgis, KCB, of Hillersdon House, Cullompton, Devon, and formerly wife of Allan Alexander Cameron, and *d* 2 Nov 1962, having had further issue:

2a +Francis Esmond [Francis Baring Esq, Hill House, Monkwood, Alresford, Hants]; *b* 10 Oct 1948; *educ* Eton; *m* 1978 *Nicolette Mary Irving, dau of (Frederic) Alan (Irving) Muntz, of Les Hauts de Claires, Montauroux 83770, France, and has issue:

1b +Simon Esmond Charles; *b* 1983

1b *Sophie Edwina; *b* 1980

1a *Camilla Jane; *b* 26 Oct 1952; *educ* City and Guilds Coll of Art; *m* 1986 *John Nicholas Robbins, and has issue:

1b *Daniel John; *b* 1986

2b *Willie Francis; *b* 1987

(3) Amyas Evelyn Giles; *b* 21 Jan 1910; *educ* Gresham's and Magdalene Coll Cambridge; *m* 1st 25 May 1935 (*divorce* 1949) Mona Montgomerie (*d* 1988), only dau of Col Willoughby Brooking Mullins, of Ambersham House, Midhurst, Sussex, and formerly w of Maj William Frederick Husband, and had:

1a *Claire Leonora [Mrs Claire Ward, 7 Callow St, London SW3; Villa Cetinale, Sovicille, Siena, Italy]; *b* 29 Feb 1936; *m* 21 Nov 1956 (*divorce* 1974) Hon Peter Alistair Ward, yr surv son of 3rd Earl of Dudley (*qv*), and has issue

(3) (cont.) Amyas Baring *m* 2nd 23 May 1949 *Peggy Michell], only dau of Surgn V-Adml Sir Arthur Gaskell, KCB, OBE, FRCS, of Greenwood, Fareham, Hants, and formerly wife of George Clive Reeves, and *d* 1986

(4) Aubrey George Adeane, DFC; *b* 3 May 1912; *educ* Eton and Caius Coll Cambridge; S/Ldr RAFVR WW II, chm Twickenham Film Studios; *m* 30 May 1952 *Marina [Mrs Aubrey Baring, 22 Farley Court, Melbury Rd, London, W14 8LJ], er dau of Basil Bessel and formerly w of Sir Charles Richard Andrew Oakeley, 6th Bt (*qv*), and *d* 1987, leaving:

1a +Alexander Esmond; *b* 26 June 1953; *educ* Milton Abbey and Trin Coll Oxford; *m* 1986 *Zein El Guindi and has:

1b +Adam Alexander Aubrey; *b* 1988

1b *Lara Louise; *b* 1987

2a +Adrian Hugh Vasili; *b* 4 Jan 1962; *educ* Westminster and King's Coll London

1a *Louise Olivia [Mrs Eric Franck, 7 Victoria Sq, London SW1]; *b* 28 July 1955; *m* 5 Feb 1997 *Eric Franck, only s of Col Louis Franck, CBE, of Gstaad, Switzerland

(5) Esmond Charles, OBE (1946); *b* 11 March 1914; *educ* Eton and Trin Coll Cambridge; Lt-Col RAC (TA) WW II (Legion of Honour, Croix de Guerre); *m* 1st 16 April 1936 (*divorce* 1951) Zalia (*d* 1986), yst (twin) dau of Sir Harold Edward Snagge, KBE (*see* AVEBURY B), and had issue:

1a +Oliver Alexander Guy [Oliver Baring Esq, Deane House, Overton, Hants]; *b* 8 Sept 1944; *educ* Eton; head of S African and African corporate finance SBC Warburg; *m* 23 Sept 1967 *Veronica, only dau of Capt Ian Alexander Henderson (*see* FARINGDON, B), and has:

1b +Rupert Esmond Ian; *b* 24 Dec 1968

2b +Esmond Oliver Mark; *b* 18 March 1978

3b +Thomas Edward Joseph; *b* 1979

1b *Emma Rose; *b* 20 March 1970

2a +Guy Esmond [Guy Baring Esq, c/o Con Zinc Rio Tinto, Collins St, Melbourne, Victoria, Australia]; *b* 18 Nov 1945; *educ* Milton Abbey; *m* 17 June 1967 *Raina Elizabeth (*d* 1979), dau of David Campbell, of Palerang, Bungendore, NSW, Australia, and has issue:

1b +Ben; *b* 2 Dec 1970

2b +Ned; *b* 8 March 1975

1b *Samantha Jane; *b* 5 Feb 1969

1a *Caroline Venetia; *b* 29 Jan 1937; *m* 1 June 1957 *(Henry) Giles Francis Lascelles (*d* 20 April 1998), and has issue (*see* HAREWOOD, E)

2a *Patricia; *b* 14 Oct 1938; *m* 1st 19 Jan 1965 (*divorce* 19–), as his 3rd w, Maj Henry Claude Lyon Garnett, CBE, late RHG (Blues) (*d* 1990), of 22 Chelsea Sq, London SW3, only son of Capt Claude Lionel Garnett, RA, and has issue:

1b *Charles Henry Esmond; *b* 1 May 1966

1b *Henrietta Patricia; *b* 11 Feb 1968; *m* 8 Dec 1995 *Patrick Mansergh-Wallace, est s of Dr John Mansergh-Wallace and Dr Vivienne Paula Wallace

2a (cont.) Mrs Patricia Garnett *m* 2nd 1986, as his 2nd w, *Hon Mark Hugh Wyndham, of Newmans Cottage, Froxfield Green, Petersfield, Hants (*see* EGREMONT, LECONFIELD and, B)

(5) (cont.) Lt-Col Esmond Baring *m* 2nd 21 Jan 1960 Judith (*m* 3rd 15 Feb 1965 3rd Marquess of Linlithgow (*qv*) and *d* 1991), dau of Stanley Matthew Lawson, of Cincinatti, Ohio, and formerly w of John Symonds Radway, and *d* 24 Nov 1963

(1) Olivia Constance Leonora, JP (Hants 1950); *b* 3 July 1908; *m* 11 Oct 1941 Maj Cecil Henry Feilden (*d* 1983), Coldstream Gds (SR), of Bramdean House, Alresford, Hants, yr son of Maj Percy Henry Guy Feilden, JP, DL, of Cokethorpe, Witney, Oxon, and *d* 9 March 1975, leaving issue:

1a *Victoria Rose; *b* 6 Aug 1942

2a *Mary Henrietta; *b* 17 March 1944

5 Caryl Digby; *b* 13 Jan 1880; *educ* Eton and RMC Sandhurst; Lt Coldstream Gds Boer War 1899–1902, WW I; *m* 28 Nov 1907 Ivy (*d* 24 June 1971), dau of Humphrey Brooke Firman, JP, of Stone Court, St Leonards-on-Sea, and *d* 12 July 1956, leaving issue:

(1) +Denzil [Denzil Baring Esq, 81 Cadogan Sq, London SW1]; *b* 24 March 1909; *educ* Eton; Capt Roy Signals WW II

(1) *Leonora Jacqueline [Miss Leonora Baring, 81 Cadogan Lane, London SW1]; *b* 2 Aug 1912

1 Lilian Theresa Clare; *b* 28 May 1874; *m* 5 March 1906 Lt-Col Frederick Loch Adam, MVO, Scots Gds (*d* 31 March 1907), Mil Sec to Viceroy India, yst son of William Patrick Adam, CIE, DL, of Blair-Adam, Kinross-shire, and *dsp* 15 Nov 1962 aged 88

2 Dorothy Mary; *b* 28 Sept 1885; *d* 11 April 1893

The 4th BARON *d* 18 July 1889; his est son,

FRANCES DENZIL EDWARD BARING, **5th Baron Ashburton**, DL (Hants); *b* 20 July 1866; Maj Hampshire Yeo (Carabiniers); *m* 1st 25 July 1889 Hon Mabel Edith Hood (*d* 18 Jan 1904), est dau of 4th Viscount Hood (*qv*), and had issue:

1 ALEXANDER FRANCIS ST VINCENT, **6th Baron**

1 Venetia Marjorie Mabel; *b* 30 April 1890; Maid of Honour to HM QUEEN MARY; *d* 15 July 1937

2 Aurea Versa; *b* 11 Aug 1891; *m* 10 Jan 1917 Maj Charles James Balfour, DL, Scots Gds (*d* 18 Aug 1939), son of Charles Barrington Balfour, of Balgonie and Newton Don, and *d* 26 Nov 1975

3 Angela Mildred; *b* 9 Dec 1893; *d* unm 13 March 1995

4 Violet Alma Madeline; *b* 12 Sept 1895; *d* unm 18 July 1924

The **5th Baron** *m* 2nd 19 Feb 1906 Frances (*d* 31 March 1959), dau of James Caryll Donnelly, of New York, and *d* 27 March 1938

His est son,

ALEXANDER FRANCIS ST VINCENT BARING, **6th Baron Ashburton**, KG (1969), KCVO (1961), JP (Hants 1951), DL (1951); *b* 7 April 1898; *educ* Eton and RMC Sandhurst; Lt Roy Scots Greys 1917–23, F/Lt AAF 1939, G/Capt AAF 1939–44, Hants: CC 1945 and 1955, Ld Lt and custos rotulorum (and IOW) 1960–73, V-Lt 1951–60, DL 1973 High Steward Winchester 1967, memb Hants TAA 1951–60, Pres 1960–67, Pres E Wessex TAA 1968, Receiver-Gen Duchy Cornwall 1961–1973, Chm: Hants and IOW Police Authority 1961–67, Hants Police Authority 1967, dir: Baring Bros 1962–68 (md 1928–62), Alliance Assur 1932–68 and Pressed Steel 1944–66, memb London Ctee Hong Kong and Shanghai Banking Corp 1935–39, Treasurer King Edward VII Hosp Fund for London 1955–64, Tstee King George's Jubilee Tst 1949–68, St Cross Hosp Winchester 1961 and Chantrey Bequest 1963, KStJ 1960; *m* 17 Nov 1924 Hon Doris Mary Thérèse Harcourt (*d* 1981), est dau of 1st Viscount Harcourt (*see* VERNON, B), and *d* 1991, leaving:

1 JOHN FRANCIS HARCOURT BARING, **7th and present Baron Ashburton**

2 +(Robin) Alexander [The Hon Alexander Baring, 183 Abbotstone, Itchen Stoke, Hants]; *b* 15 Jan 1931; *educ* Eton; late Sub-Lt RNVR; *m* 25 Feb 1960

*Anne Caroline Thalia, er dau of Maj Edward Fitzhardinge Peyton Gage, (*see* GAGE, V), and has:

(1) *Francesca Rhiannon; *b* 6 Dec 1963; *m* 1990 *Stuart Douglas

ASHCOMBE

Arms: Chequy or and gules, on a pile argent a lion's head erased sable. **Crest:** A Doric column proper, in front two falchions in saltire argent, pommels and hilts or. **Supporters:** Dexter, a stonemason proper, holding in the exterior hand a mallet sable; sinister, a carpenter proper, holding in the exterior hand a pair of compasses or. **Motto:** *Felix qui prudens* ('Happy is he who takes care for the morrow'). **Creation:** B. (UK) 22 Aug 1892.

THE 4TH BARON ASHCOMBE OF DORKING, Surrey, **AND OF BODIAM CASTLE**, Sussex (Henry (Harry) Edward Cubitt) [The Rt Hon The Lord Ashcombe, Sudeley Castle, Winchcombe, Cheltenham, Glos GL54 5JD; Flat 6, 53 Drayton Gdns, London SW10 9RX]; *b* 31 March 1924; *s f* 1962; *educ* Eton; WW II with RAF; Consul-Gen in London for Monaco 1961–68; *m* 1st 12 Sept 1955 (*divorce* 1968) Ghislaine, only dau of Cornelius William Dresselhuys, of Long Island, USA, and Edith, Viscountess Kemsley (*qv*), and formerly w of 6th Earl of Caledon (*qv*); *m* 2nd 1 Jan 1973 (*divorce* 1979) Hon Virginia Carington, yr dau of 6th Baron Carrington (*qv*); *m* 3rd 1979 *(Mary) Elizabeth, dau of Dr Davis Henry Chips, of Lexington, Kentucky, and widow of (Geoffrey) Mark Dent-Brocklehurst, of Sudeley Castle (*see* TREVOR, B)

Lineage: THOMAS CUBITT, yeoman, of Mayton Hall, Frettenham, Norfolk, living before 1677; had an est s:

THOMAS CUBITT, of Mayton Hall; *b* 1681; *m* Mary Dewing and *d* 1729, leaving a yr s:

WILLIAM CUBITT; *m* 1746 Mary Hall and left, with an er s:

JONATHAN CUBITT, of London; *m* Agnes Scarlett and *d* 1806, leaving, with a yr s (William, Ld Mayor London 1860–62, *d* 1863):

THOMAS CUBITT, of Denbies, Surrey; *b* 1788; builder who erected the Belgravia, Bloomsbury, Lowndes and Westminster urban estates on land belonging to the Dukes of Bedford and Westminster and Lord Southampton (*qqv*); *m* 1819 Mary Anne, dau of Samuel Warner, and *d* 20 Dec 1855, leaving an est s:

GEORGE CUBITT, **1st Baron Ashcombe of Dorking**, Surrey, **and of Bodiam Castle**, Sussex (UK), so *cr* 22 Aug 1892, PC (1880), DL (Surrey and Middx); *b* 4 June 1828; MA Trin Coll Cambridge; Hon Col 5th Bn Roy W Surrey Regt; MP (C) W Surrey 1860–85 and Mid-Surrey 1885–92, Second Church Estates Commr 1874–79; *m* 14 June 1853 Laura (*d* 7 July 1904), dau of Rev James Joyce, Vicar of Dorking, and had issue:

1 Geoffry George; *b* 31 May 1854; *dvp* 6 June 1855
2 Thomas Edmund Wilfred; *b* 5 Aug 1859; *dvp* 17 May 1865
3 Henry, **2nd Baron**
1 Helen Laura, CBE (1920); *d* unm 16 Aug 1939
2 Mary Agnes; *m* 23 April 1884 Rev Edward Arthur Chichester, MA (*d* 30 Sept 1925), Hon Canon Winchester, late Vicar of Dorking, and *d* 6 Feb 1944, leaving issue (*see* O'NEILL, B)
3 Adelaide Laura; *m* 20 Oct 1891 Richard Anthony Fuller-Maitland (*d* 24 Jan 1919), and *d* 3 Nov 1922
4 Mildred Sophia; *m* 4 Oct 1883 George William Tallents, BA Oxford, JP (*d* 17 Dec 1924), barrister, and *d* 9 March 1930, leaving issue
5 Mabel Georgina; *d* 5 Nov 1865
6 Beatrice Hayward; *m* 8 April 1891 William Archibald Calvert (*d* 26 July 1943), of Ockley Court, Surrey, and *d* 12 Feb 1963, leaving issue

The 1st BARON *d* 26 Feb 1917; his only surv son,

HENRY CUBITT, **2nd Baron Ashcombe of Dorking and of Bodiam Castle**, CB, TD; *b* 14 March 1867; MA Trin Coll Cambridge; Col Surrey Vol Regt, Hon Col 4th Bn The Queen's Roy Regt, Lt-Col and Hon Col cmdg Surrey Yeo (TD) 1901–12, Chevalier Legn Honour, MP (C) SE Surrey 1892–1906, Ld Lt and Custos Rotulorum Surrey 1905–39, Pres Surrey TAA 1908; *m* 21 Aug 1890 Maud Marianne (*d* 7 March 1945), dau of Col Archibald Motteux Calvert, RA, of Ockley Court, Surrey, and had issue:

1 Henry Archibald; *b* 3 Jan 1892; Capt and Adj Coldstream Gds, Chevalier Legn Honour; *ka* 15 Sept 1916
2 Alick George; *b* 16 Jan 1894; Lt 15th Hus; *ka* 24 Nov 1917
3 William Hugh; *b* 30 May 1896; Lt 1st Roy Dragoons; *d* 24 March 1918 of wounds recd in action
4 ROLAND CALVERT, **3rd Baron**
5 Archibald Edward, JP (Bucks); *b* 16 Jan 1901; *educ* Jesus Coll Cambridge; Maj 98th (Surrey and Sussex Yeo) Field Bde RA (TAR); *m* 1st 9 Nov 1926 (*divorce* 1933) Lady Irene Helen Pratt (*d* 1976), er dau of 4th Marquess Camden (*qv*), and had issue:

(1) Alick John Archibald; *b* 10 Aug 1927; *educ* Eton; Capt Roy Dragoons; *m* 1st 1 Dec 1956 Rosemary Priscilla (*d* 6 Aug 1957), er dau of Thomas Cecil Gouldsmith, of Coneysthorpe, Yorks; *m* 2nd 30 June 1961 *Jennifer Faith [Mrs Tim Collins, Chetwode Manor, Buckingham, Bucks] (*m* 2nd 1986 J E H (Tim) Collins), yr dau of Lt-Gen William Henry Ewart Gott, CB, CBE, DSO, MC, of Wyther Grange, Leeds, and *d* 1983, leaving issue:

1a *Amanda Jane; *b* 27 April 1966; *m* 1995 *Rupert Sweeting, s of Christopher Sweeting, of Churchill, Oxon
2a *Belinda Carey; *b* 19868

5 (cont.) Maj The Hon Archibald Cubitt *m* 2nd 25 Sept 1934 (*divorce* 1949) Sibell Margaret, er dau of Ronald Collet Norman, JP, of Moor Place, Much Hadham, Herts, and *d* 13 Feb 1972, having by her had further issue:

(2) (Mark) Robin; *b* 13 June 1936; *educ* Gordonstoun; *m* 21 July 1962 (*divorce* 1984) Juliet Perpetua, yr dau of Edward Woodall, OBE, of The Red House, Clifton Hampden, Abingdon, Berks, and *d* 1991, having had issue:

1a +MARK EDWARD [Mark Cubitt Esq, 9 Hartismere Rd, London SW6 7TT]; *b* 29 Feb 1964; heir presumptive; *m* 1992 *Melissa Mary, dau of Maj Charles Hay, of Boldre, Hants, and has:
1b +Richard Robin Alexander; *b* 14 June 1995
2b +Ronald Charles Edward; *b* 13 Feb 1997
2a +David Antony; *b* 9 July 1966
3a +Hugo John; *b* 19 July 1967

(1) Mary Sibell; *b* 21 April 1938; *d* 5 April 1940
(2) *Priscilla Margaret; *b* 30 May 1941; *m* 14 Oct 1964, as his 3rd w, 11th Earl of Harrington (*qv*), and has issue

6 (Charles) Guy, CBE (1973), DSO (1943), TD (1944), DL (1955); *b* 13 Feb 1903; *educ* Eton and RMC Sandhurst; Col 98th (Surrey and Sussex Yeo) Field Regt RA (TA), formerly Lt Res of Offrs Roy Dragoons WW II (despatches), Hon Col Surrey Yeo 1951; Jt MFH Crawley and Horsham 1928–33, Actg Master 1933–39, Pres British Horse Soc 1952, CC (1954), CA (1965) Surrey, High Sheriff Surrey 1955; *m* 13 July 1937 Rosamund Mary Edith (*d* 1984), only dau of Sir Montague Aubrey Rowley Cholmeley, 4th Bt (*qv*), and *d* 1979, having had issue:

(1) +Hugh (Guy) (Sir), CBE (1977), JP (Surrey 1964), DL (Gtr London 1978) [Sir Hugh Cubitt CBE JP DL, Chapel House, West Humble, Dorking, Surrey]; *b* 2 July 1928; *educ* RNCs Dartmouth and Greenwich; Lt RN Korea 1950–51, Flag-Lt to Adml B J S M Washington 1952 and C-in-C Nore 1953, ret 1953; FAI (1964); memb Westminster City Cncl 1963 (Ld Mayor 1977–78), High Sheriff Surrey 1983, memb Bd Green Cloth Verge of Palaces 1980–, chm Rea Bros Gp 1995–, dir PSIT plc, ktd 1982; *m* 26 June 1958 *Linda Ishbel, yr dau of Hon Angus Dudley Campbell, CBE, of Doddington Cottage, Nantwich, Cheshire (*see* COLGRAIN, B), and has issue:

1a +Jonathan Guy; *b* 4 Nov 1962; *educ* Eton and Exeter U
1a *Joanna Mary; *b* 27 May 1960; *m* 1986 *Charles William Smyth-Osbourne (*see* RAMSDEN, Bt)
2a *Victoria Jane [Mrs Crispin Harding Rolls, Rock Cottage, Buckingham Rd, S Holmwood, Dorking, Surrey]; *b* 23 Dec 1964; *m* 1987 *Crispin Martin Hardinge-Rolls, son of Maj Christopher Hardinge-Rolls, of Pwll-y-Cwm, The Hendre, Monmouth, Gwent, and has issue:
1b *George Christopher; *b* 1992
1b *Sophie Elizabeth; *b* 1990

(1) *Sylvia Rosemary [Mrs Ronald Dallas, Primrose Hill, Westonbirt, Glos]; *b* 19 Jan 1930; *m* 25 July 1951 *Maj Ronald James Grant Dallas, 3rd The King's Own Hus (ret), s of Lt-Col Douglas Dallas, and has had issue:

1a *Nigel Alexander; *b* 20 Sept 1962
1a Caroline Rosemond; *b* 9 April 1952; *m* 1981 *Philip T Shearing, and *d* 1992
2a *Jennifer Mary [Mrs Simon King, Southview, Sandford, nr Crediton, Devon]; *b* 20 April 1954; *m* 1st 1975 (*divorce* 1986) Philip S W Hawkins, son of Capt O S W Hawkins, RN (ret); *m* 2nd 1987 Roger Babington Hill; *m* 3rd 1993 *Simon King

(2) *Celia Mary; *b* 7 Dec 1939; *m* 30 April 1962 *7th Baron Carew (*qv*) and has issue

The 1st BARON *d* 27 Oct 1947; his est surv son,

ROLAND CALVERT CUBITT, **3rd Baron Ashcombe of Dorking and of Bodiam Castle**, DL (Surrey); *b* 26 Jan 1899; *educ* Eton and RMC Sandhurst; Lt Coldstream Gds, V-Lt Surrey 1940; *m* 1st 16 Nov 1920 (*divorce* 1947) Sonia Rosemary, OStJ, dau of Lt-Col Hon George Keppel, MVO (*see* ALBEMARLE, E), and had issue:

1 HENRY EDWARD CUBITT, **4th and present Baron Ashcombe of Dorking and of Bodiam Castle**
2 Jeremy John; *b* 7 May 1927; *educ* Eton; Lt Coldstream Gds; *m* 17 Jan 1952 (*divorce* 1957) Diana Edith, er dau of Cdr (E) Peter Du Cane, OBE, RN (ret), of Haselbech Grange, Maidwell, Northants, and *d* 12 Jan 1958, leaving issue:

(1) *Sarah Victoria [Mrs Sarah Hutton, Flat 3, 13 Cranley Gdns, London SW7 3BB]; *b* 13 Sept 1953; *m* 31 July 1975 (*divorce* 1981) David Hutton, est son of Thomas Hutton, of Birdswood, Ashley Park, Walton-on-Thames, Surrey

1 Rosalind Maud; *b* 11 Aug 1921; *m* 2 Jan 1946 *Maj Bruce Middleton Hope Shand, MC and bar, late 12th Roy Lancers, V-Ld-Lt E Sussex 1974–92, only s of Philip Morton Shand, of 9 Norland Sq, London W11, and bro of Lady Howe of Aberavon (*qv*), and *d* 1994, leaving issue:

(1) *Mark Roland; *b* 28 June 1951; *educ* Milton Abbey; author: *Travels on My Elephant* 1991; *m* 1990 *Clio, dau of Edward René David Goldsmith

(1) *Camilla Rosemary; *b* 17 July 1947; Patron National Osteoporosis Society 1997–; *m* 1973 (*divorce* 1996) Brig Andrew Henry Parker-Bowles, OBE, Blues and Royals, and has issue (*see* MACCLESFIELD, E)

(2) *(Sonia) Annabel; *b* 2 Feb 1949; *m* 27 April 1972 *Simon John Elliot, only son of ACM Sir William Elliot, GCVO, KCB, KBE, DFC and bar, of Stourpaine House, nr Blandford, Dorset, and 30A Hill St, London W1, by Rosemary, dau of Lt-Col Sir John Robert Chancellor, GCMG, GCVO, CBE, DSO, and has issue:

1a *Benjamin William; *b* 1975

1a *Alice Rosalind; *b* 1977

2a *Catherine Camilla; *b* 1981

The **3rd Baron** *m* 2nd 6 Aug 1948 Idina Joan (*d* 9 Oct 1954), only dau of Col Robert Edward Myddelton, of Chirk Castle, Denbighshire, and formerly w of John Charles Trueman Mills; *m* 3rd 2 July 1959 Jean (*k* air crash Nantes 5 March 1973), dau of Charles Tuller Garland, of Moreton Hall, Moreton Morrell, Warwicks, and formerly wife of (a) Arthur Turberville Smith-Bingham, (b) Sir Robert George Maxwell Throckmorton, 11th Bt (*see* 1970 edn), and (c) Greville Pollard Baylis, and *d* 28 Oct 1962

Ashley of Stoke

Creation: B. (LP, UK) 1992.

THE BARON ASHLEY OF STOKE, of Widnes, Co Palatine of Cheshire (Jack Ashley, CH (1975), PC (1979)) [The Rt Hon The Lord Ashley of Stoke CH PC, House of Lords, London SW1A 0PW]; *b* 6 Dec 1922; *educ* Ruskin Coll Oxford and Gonville and Caius Coll Cambridge (Pres Union 1951); shop steward convenor and Nat Exec Ctee memb Chemical Workers' Union 1946, Councillor Borough of Widnes 1946, BBC Radio Producer 1951–57, Sr TV Producer 1957–66, Memb Gen Advsy Cncl BBC 1967–69 and 1970–74, MP (Lab) Stoke on Trent 1966–92, PPS to Sec State Ec Affrs 1967–68 and Sec State DHSS 1974–76, memb Lab NEC 1976–78, author: *Journey into Silence* (1973); *m* 1951 *Pauline Kay, dau of Clarence Adley Crispin, of Liverpool, and has issue:

1 *Jacqueline; *b* 1954; *m* 1987 *Andrew Marr and has:

(1) *Harry Cameron; *b* 1989

(1) *Isabel Claire; *b* 1991

2 *Jane Elizabeth; *b* 1958; *m* 1992 *Martin Rosenbaum and has:

(1) *Ben; *b* 1992

3 *Caroline; *b* 1966; *m* 1993 *Richard Dewdney

Lineage: JOHN ASHLEY; had:

JACK, *cr* a **Baron**

Ashton of Hyde

Arms: Sable on a pile between two crescents in base argent, a mullet pierced of the first. **Crest:** On a mount vert a mower proper, vested paly argent and sable, in the act of whetting his scythe, also proper. **Supporters:** Dexter, a mower proper, vested paly argent and sable, holding in the exterior hand a scythe also proper; sinister, a boar argent semée of mullets sable pierced. **Motto:** *Fide et virtute* ('With faith and valour'). **Creation:** B. (UK) 28 June 1911.

THE 3RD BARON ASHTON OF HYDE, of Hyde, Cheshire (Thomas John Ashton TD, JP (Oxon 1965)) [The Rt Hon The Lord Ashton of Hyde TD JP, Fir Farm, Upper Slaughter, Bourton-on-the-Water, Glos GL54 2JR]; *b* 19 Nov 1926; *s f* 1983; *educ* Eton and New Coll Oxford (BA 1950, MA 1955); Maj Roy Glos Hus (TA), formerly Lt 11th Hus; dir Barclays Bank; *m* 18 May 1957 *Pauline Trewlove, er dau of Lt-Col Robert Henry Langton Brackenbury, OBE, of Yerdley House, Long Compton, Shipston-on-Stour, and has issue:

1 +(THOMAS) HENRY [The Hon Henry Ashton, Broadwell Hill, Moreton-in-Marsh, Glos]; *b* 18 July 1958; *educ* Eton and Trin Coll Oxford; late Roy Hus (PWO), Lt Roy Wessex Yeo; *m* 1987 *Emma Louise, dau of Colin Allinson, of Bath, and has issue:

(1) *Harriet Emily; *b* 1990

(2) *Isobel Louise; *b* 1992

(3) *Flora Juliet; *b* 1995

2 +John Edward; *b* 8 Jan 1966; *educ* Eton

1 *Charlotte Trewlove; *b* 22 Feb 1960; *m* 1987 *Andrew D Bartlett, only son of D W Bartlett and Mrs J D Potts, of Macclesfield, Cheshire, and has issue:

(1) *Oliver William; *b* 1991

(2) *Hugh Alistair; *b* 1994

2 *Katharine Judith; *b* 30 Jan 1962; *m* 1987 *Douglas J Lawson, son of Harry D Lawson, of 58 Seafield Rd, Broughty Ferry, Dundee, and has issue:

(1) *James Alexander; *b* 1988

(2) *Robert Douglas; *b* 1991

(1) *Anna Katharine; *b* 1994

Lineage: The ASHTONs, settled in Cheshire since the 16th century, are allegedly a branch of the ASHTONs of Stoney Middleton, who descended from the ASHTONs of Ashton-under-Lyne.

JOSEPH ASHTON, of Werneth, Hyde, Cheshire, living 1698; had:

SAMUEL ASHTON, of Gerrards, Hyde, Cheshire; *b* 1674; *m* Jane, dau of John Kinder, of Bredbury, Cheshire, and *d* 1754, leaving a 5th s:

BENJAMIN ASHTON, of Gerrards; *b* 1718; *m* 1742 Elizabeth, dau of Edward Lees, of Hazlehurst, Ashton-under-Lyne, and *d* 1791, leaving:

SAMUEL ASHTON, of Gerrards; *b* 1742; *m* Mary (*d* 1825), dau of J3ohn Oldham, of Hyde, and had, with other issue:

1 Samuel, of Gerrards and Pole Bank, Cheshire, JP (Cheshire, Lancs and Derbys); *b* 1773; *m* Mary, dau of Thomas Turner, of Godley, and *d* 1836, leaving issue

2 THOMAS, for whom *see* below

3 James, of Newton Lodge, Cheshire; *b* 1777; *m* Elizabeth, dau of George Astley, and *d* 1841, leaving issue

4 Robert, of Croughton and Hyde, Cheshire, JP (Derbys and Lancs); *b* 1797; *m* Lucy, est dau of Joseph Horsfield, and *dsp* 1856

SAMUEL ASHTON *d* 1812; his 2nd son,

THOMAS ASHTON, of Hyde, JP (Lancs and Chester); *b* 1775; *m* 1804 Harriot, dau of Thomas Booth, of Godley, and *d* 1845, leaving a 2nd s:

THOMAS ASHTON, of Hyde, Cheshire, and Ford Bank, Didsbury, JP (Cheshire), JP and DL (Lancs); *b* 8 Feb 1818; High Sheriff 1883; Hon LLD Victoria U; *m* 14 April 1852 Elizabeth (*d* 1 Jan 1914), dau of Samuel Stillman Gair, of Penketh Hall, Liverpool, and *d* 21 Jan 1898, having had an est s:

THOMAS GAIR ASHTON, **1st Baron Aston of Hyde**, Co Chester (UK), so *cr* 28 June 1911, JP (Lancs, Cheshire and Sussex); *b* 5 Feb 1855; MA Univ Coll Oxford, Hon Fell 1923; MP (Lib) Hyde 1885–86 and Luton 1895–1911; *m* 2 Dec 1886 Eva Margaret (*d* 4 Jan 1938), dau of John Henry James, JP, slr, of Kingswood, Watford, Herts, and had issue:

1 Thomas Henry; *b* 8 Oct 1887; *d* 20 Sept 1897

2 THOMAS HENRY RAYMOND, **2nd Baron**

1 Marion Evelyn; *m* 4 April 1913 Maj Robert Wood, Roy Warwicks Regt (*d* 5 March 1940), s of Thomas Robert Wood, of Toronto, Canada

2 Margaret Joan; *m* 2 Oct 1925 Hugh Whistler, JP, FZA (*d* 7 July 1943), son of Maj Fuller Whistler, MA, JP, of Battle, Sussex, and had:

(1) *Ralf Ashton [Ralf Whistler Esq, The Old Rectory, Sandhurst, Hawkhurst, Kent]; *b* 9 Aug 1930; *educ* Eton and Selwyn Coll Cambridge (MA); *m* 25 July 1953 *Jane (BA McGill), dau of Ivan Agar McCarthy, of 900 Sherbrooke St W, Montreal, and has issue:

1a *Brian Hugh; *b* 9 Oct 1954; *educ* Eton

2a *Nicholas McCarthy; *b* 25 Dec 1955; *educ* Eton

3a *John Daniel Ralf; *b* 7 May 1964

1a *Clare Evelyn Joan; *b* 23 July 1958

2a *Lucy Julia; *b* 18 May 1960

(1) *Benedicta [Miss Benedicta Ashton, Hammonds, Caldbec Hill, Battle, E Sussex]; *b* 30 July 1927; *educ* Newnham Coll Cambridge (MA 1953)

The 1st BARON *d* 1 May 1933; his son,

THOMAS HENRY RAYMOND ASHTON, **2nd Baron Ashton of Hyde**, JP (1944), DL (1957) (both Glos); *b* 2 Oct 1901; *educ* Eton and New Coll Oxford (BA 1924, MA 1934); Maj Roy Glos Hus (TA); MFH Heythrop 1934–52, CC Glos 1962; *m* 10 June 1925 *Marjorie Nell, JP (Glos 1949) (*d* 1993), dau of Hon Marshall Jones Brooks, of Portal, Tarporley, Cheshire (*see* CRAWSHAW, B), and *d* 21 March 1983, having had issue:

1 THOMAS JOHN ASHTON, **3rd and present Baron Ashton of Hyde**

1 Susan; *b* 11, *d* 15 Aug 1931

2 Judith Marjorie; *b* 10 Jan 1934; *d* 10 Sept 1943

ASHTOWN

Arms: Argent, a lion passant gules between three fleurs-de-lys azure, on a chief of the last a sun in splendour or. **Crest:** A dexter arm embowed in armour, the hand grasping a scimitar, all proper. **Supporters:** Dexter, a lion gules, semée-de-lys and ducally crowned or; sinister, a stag proper, armed and hoofed, ducally gorged and lined or. **Motto:** *Virtutis fortuna comes* ('Fortune is the companion of virtue'). **Creation:** B. (I) 27 Dec 1800.

THE 7TH BARON ASHTOWN (Sir Nigel Clive Cosby Trench, KCMG (1976, CMG 1966)) [The Rt Hon The Lord Ashtown KCMG, 4 Kensington Ct Gdns, Kensington Ct Place, London W8 5QE]; *b* 27 Oct 1916; *s* kinsman 1990; *educ* Eton and Corpus Christi Coll Cambridge; Maj KRRC WW II (despatches); Dip Serv 1946–76, Counsellor Tokyo 1961–63 and Washington 1963–67, Cabinet Office 1967–69, Amb: Korea 1969–71 and Portugal 1974–76, Assist U-Sec Civ Serv Selection Bd 1971–73, Memb Police Prison and Fire Service Selection Bds 1977–86; *m* 1st 1 Dec 1939 Marcelle Catherine (*d* July 1994), yst dau of Johan Jacob Clotterbooke Patyn van Kloetinge, of Zeist, The Netherlands, and has:

1 +RODERICK NIGEL GODOLPHIN [The Hon Roderick Trench, Bassetts, Coggins Mill Lane, Mayfield, Sussex]; *b* 17 Nov 1944; *educ* Eton and Stanford U, USA (BA); *m* 1st 27 June 1967 Janet Merle (*d* 1971), yr dau of Harold Hamilton-Faulkner, of Redwood City, Calif, USA, and Mrs O A Cecil, of Kingsbridge, Devon, and has issue:

(1) +Timothy Roderick Hamilton; *b* 29 Feb 1968; *educ* Sherborne and London U

1 (cont.) The Hon RODERICK TRENCH *m* 2nd 10 Jan 1973 *Susan Barbara, only dau of L F Day, FRCS, DLO, of Cooden, Sussex, and formerly w of Michael R J Wright, and by her has:

(1) *Victoria Susan; *b* 24 Aug 1977

The 7th BARON *m* 2nd 17 Dec 1997 *(Dorothea) Mary Elizabeth, dau of Lt-Col Richard George Edward Minchin and formerly w of HSH Hans Heinrich XVII Wilhelm Albert Eduard, 4th Prince of Pless (*see* DE LA WARR, E)

Lineage: FREDERIC TRENCH (*see* CLANCARTY, E); *d* 1669, leaving, with an er s:

Very Rev JOHN TRENCH, Dean of Raphoe; *m* Anne, est dau of Richard Warburton, of Garryhinch, Queen's Co, and *d* 1725, having had, with three yr sons and two daus (Anne, *m* 11 July 1719 Sir John Caldwell, Bt; Judith, *m c* 10 June 1726 Sir Samuel Cooke, Bt):

FREDERICK TRENCH, of Moate, Co Galway; *m* 1718 Mary, dau and coheir of Richard Geering, Clerk Court of Chancery, and *d* 1758, having had an only surv s:

FREDERICK TRENCH, of Moate and Woodlawn, Co Galway; *bapt* 3 Nov 1724; *m* 20 Aug 1754 Mary (*d* 1819), er dau and coheir of Francis Sadleir, of Sopwell Hall, Co Tipperary (and sis of Catherine, *m* 1st John Bury and had issue; *see* 1875 edn CHARLEVILL, E; *m* 2nd 1st Baron Dunally *qv*), and *d* 27 Nov 1797, having had, with other issue:

1 FREDERICK TRENCH, **1st Baron Ashtown**, of Moate, Co Galway (I), so *cr* 27 Dec 1800, with remainder to the heirs male of the body of his deceased father, for supporting the Union; *b* 17 Sept 1755; MP (I Parl) Maryborough 1785–90 and Portarlington 1798–1800, (UK) Portarlington 1800; *m* 25 May 1785 Elizabeth (*d* 1844), only dau and heiress of Robert Robinson, MD, and *dsp* May 1840

2 Francis, of Sopwell Hall; *b* 29 July 1757; *m* 11 June 1802 Mary, 2nd dau of Henry Mason, of Shrewsbury, and *d* Nov 1829, leaving with other issue:

(1) FREDERICK MASON, **2nd Baron**

3 Thomas (Very Rev), Dean of Kildare; *b* 1761; *m* 1786 Mary, est dau of Walter Weldon, of Rahinderry, MP (*see* WELDON, Bt), and *d* April 1834, leaving, with six daus (of whom Jane *m* Charles Grimston and had issue; *see* LEGARD, Bt):

(1) Henry, of Glenmalyre, Ballybrittas, Queen's Co, DL; *b* 29 May 1806; *m* 27 Nov 1833 Elizabeth Anne Caroline (*d* 1898), est dau of Charles Launcelot Sandes, of Indiaville, Queen's Co, and *d* 28 Feb 1888, having had issue:

1a Thomas Sandes, of Glenmalyre, JP (Co Cork), JP and DL (Queen's Co); *b* 29 March 1840; Capt 4th Bn Leinster Regt; *d* 25 Nov 1921

2a Charles Stewart, of Clay Hill, Virginia, N America; *b* 20 Aug 1843; *m* 16 Sept 1873 Ellen Adelaide (*d* 5 May 1935), dau of Charles Marryat, and *d* 11 May 1886, leaving issue:

1b Henry Marryat; *b* 16 Jan 1876; *m* 14 June 1904 Juliet Benham (*d* 23 March 1946), est dau of William Seaman, of Staten Island, USA, and *d* 14 April 1948, leaving issue:

1c *Edith Katharine [Mrs Albert Dorr, 11 Jackson Ave, Mystic, Conn, USA]; *b* 21 June 1905; *m* 21 June 1930 Albert Irwin Dorr (*d* 26 April 1947), son of Frederic Edward Dorr, of Boston, Mass

2b Frederick Steuart; *b* 6 Oct 1877; *d* 20 March 1886

3b Thomas Perceval, of Ashfield, Ballybrittas; *b* 28 March 1880; *m* 27 July 1921 Phyllis Clare Hume (*d* 1968), yst dau of Arthur Hume-Spry, ICS, and *d* 3 July 1924, leaving issue:

1c Thomas Perceval Hume; *b* posthumously 14 Aug 1924; *educ* Rossall; *d* 19–

4b Albert Charles (Rev), MC; *b* 25 Jan 1884; Rector of St Andrew's Church, Scarborough, Tobago 1940–58, Vicar of Hartlip, nr Sittingbourne, Kent 1938–40, formerly Chaplain at Holy Trinity, Bangalore, Madras, Hon CF (and formerly at RAF Stn, Heliopolis); *m* 11 Oct 1913 Marion Isabella (*d* 27 May 1954), only dau of Foster Hewison-Thompson, of Westoe, Durham, and *d* 11 June 1964, leaving issue:

1c *Ethel Alberta; *m* 15 May 1963 Rev John Douglas How, of All Saints Rectory, Queens Park, Port of Spain, Trinidad, WI, 2nd son of Sydney How

1b Mary Caroline; *b* 1 July 1874; *m* 17 Nov 1904 Capt Thomas Henry Kemmis (*d* 17 Dec 1915), of Shaen, Queen's Co, and *d* 18 May 1952, leaving issue

2b Edith Frances; *b* 22 Jan 1879

3b Nora Creina; *b* 17 Nov 1881; *m* 3 March 1915 Hans Emil Fletz (*d* 16 Aug 1950), son of Fredinand Emil Fletz, of Zurich, and *d* 27 May 1964, leaving issue

4b Gertrude Iola; *b* 4 Dec 1882; *d* unm 1913

3a Henry Walter; *b* 3 July 1845; Col cmdg 100th Regtl Dist and 1st Bn Leinster Regt; *m* 21 June 1887 Ada Blanche (*d* 25 Aug 1943), dau of Richard Warburton, of Garryhinch, DL Queen's Co, and *d* 25 Aug 1911, leaving issue:

1b Aleyne Elizabeth; *b* 14 Aug 1888; *d* unm 6 July 1958

2b Nora Mary; *b* 1890

4a Frederick Perceval; *b* 27 March 1849; Capt RN; *d* unm 10 May 1895

1a Maria Georgina; *d* unm 21 Aug 1909

2a Elizabeth Jane; *d* unm 16 April 1919

3a Frances Lydia; *d* 8 Nov 1936

(2) Richard, commonly called William Steuart; *b* 16 Nov 1808; *m* 9 April 1832 Elizabeth Susanna (*d* 1887), dau of J Sealy Townsend, Master in Chancery, and *d* 1872, having had issue:

1a Thomas Weldon; *b* 11 Feb 1833; *d* unm 15 Aug 1872

2a John Townsend; *b* 17 Feb 1834; *m* 1st 20 Aug 1870 Agnes (*dsp* 8 Jan 1872), dau of Herman Merivale, CB, Under-Sec for India; *m* 2nd 25 April 1874 Leonora (*d* 19 Dec 1902), dau of George Cecil Gore Wray, of Ardnamona, Co Donegal, and *d* 9 Aug 1909, having by her had issue:

1b John Steuart; *b* 9 April 1879; Maj IA Res Offrs, Assist Traffic Manager Indian State Rlwys; *d* 16 Dec 1922

2b George Frederick (Rev); *b* 7 Jan 1881; *educ* Radley and Selwyn Coll Cambridge (BA 1902, MA 1908); Vicar of Milland 1945–51, Gen Supt Missions to Seamen 1931–45, formerly Supt and Rural Dean, Lloydminster, Saskatchewan, Canada, and Pncpl Emmanuel Coll Sask, T/CF 1914–19 (despatches twice), Assist Home Sec CMS, Hon CF 1921; *m* 28 June 1919 Muriel Leonore (*d* 8 March 1974), est dau of Leslie Stephen Robertson, MICE, and *d* 23 April 1966, leaving issue:

1c *Leonore Elisita [Mrs Denis Powell, Old Fox Cottage, Heath End Rd, Gt Kingshill, Bucks HP15 6HS]; *b* 4 Nov 1920; *educ* Girton Coll Cambridge (BA); *m* 3 Feb 1945 *(Henry) Denis (Whitwell) Powell, MA, MB, ChB, FRCS, late F/Lt RAFVR, only son of Henry Jenkyn Powell, MA, and has issue:

1d *John Denis Trench; *b* 22 July 1951; *educ* Monkton Combe Sch

1d *Margaret Leonore [Mrs Frank Taylor, PO Box 2020, Gaborone, Botswana]; *b* 7 Dec 1945; *m* 21 Sept 1968 *Frank William Taylor, 2nd son of Claude Napier Taylor, of Toka, S Africa, and has:

1e *Michael John; *b* 1970; *m* 1996 *Katrin Willcocks

2e *Peter Hugh; *b* 1972; *m* 1994 *Naomi Starbuck and has:

1f *Rebekah Joy; *b* 1997

3e *Christopher David; *b* 1979

2d *Janet Elisita; *b* 3 Jan 1949; *m* 1st 1972 *Derek Peacock; *m* 2nd 1991 *Murray Frankland and by her 1st husb has:

1e *Timothy Simon; *b* 1978

2e *Anthony Robert *b* 1980

3d *Clare Louise; *b* 21 Dec 1954; *m* 1st 1979 *Philip Marshall Garside; *m* 2nd 1991 *Murray Frankland and by her 1st husb has:

1e *Douglas Paul; *b* 1982

2e *Alan Nigel; *b* 1984

3e *Ian Richard; *b* 1987

2c *Bridget Wray; *b* 15 Oct 1928; MAOT, OT Reg; *m* 19 Sept 1959 *Robin Blakeway Dickens, BSF, BCRF, of 18, 3144 Sherman Rd, Duncan, BC, Canada, yst son of Charles Davis Dickens, of 3175 W 39th Ave, Vancouver, BC, Canada, and has issue:

1d *Mark Lester; *b* 21 June 1961

1d *Lynn Catherine; *b* 24 May 1963; *m* 1985 *Mark Hayden Lane

1b Mary Laura Beatrice; *b* 25 March 1875; *d* 1 June 1883

2b Charlotte Violet; *b* 14 July 1877; *d* unm 6 Oct 1948

3b Leonore Wray; *b* 3 Sept 1885; *m* 24 Sept 1912 John Methuen Coote, OBE, 2nd son of Sir Algernon Charles Plumptre Coote, 12th Bt (*qv*), and *d* 7 June 1969, leaving issue

1a Anna Maria; *m* 15 Dec 1862 Lt-Gen George Neeld Boldero, Roy Scots Fus (*d* 5 May 1898), son of Lt-Col Henry George Boldero, MP Chippenham, Wilts, and *d* 1 Dec 1903, leaving issue

4 William, of Cangort Park, King's Co; *b* 1769; *m* 18 June 1798 Sarah Elizabeth Frances Henrietta Ricarda, only child of Hon Robert Moore, and gdau of 5th Earl of Drogheda (*qv*), and *d* April 1849, having had issue:

(1) Frederic FitzWilliam (Rev); *b* 11 March 1799; *m* 16 Feb 1835 Louisa Alice (*d* 16 Dec 1878), yst dau of Rt Hon Robert Ward, of Bangor Castle, Co Down (*see* BANGOR, V), and *d* 3 Dec 1869, having had issue:

1a William Robert (Rev); *b* 9 Oct 1838; LLM Cambridge; Hon Canon Carlisle, Vicar Kendal, Westmorland; *m* 18 Jan 1877 Edith Anne Hamilton (*d* 4 Dec 1892), est dau of Charles Langton, DL, of Liverpool, and *d* 4 July 1913, having had issue:

1b Frederick Charles; *b* 25 Nov 1877; *educ* Trin Coll Cambridge (MA); *d* 25 Jan 1940

2b William Langton, MC; *b* 10 Nov 1880; *educ* Trin Coll Cambridge (MA); late Lt-Col W Yorks Regt; *m* 15 Nov 1927 Dorothy Alice (*m* 2nd 24 July 1934 Herbert Philip Wynne Humphreys (*d* 17 Nov 1965), son of Rev S Humphreys, of Hendre, Pwylheli, N Wales, and *d* 14 April 1968), yst dau of James Charles Fidler, and *dsp* 27 June 1932

3b Robert Hamilton; *b* 10 Nov 1880; *educ* Trin Coll Cambridge (MA); *m* 9 Dec 1914 Alice Matilda (*d* 10 March 1959), er dau of Reginald Carter Nelson

4b John Roy; *b* 2 Sept 1884; *educ* Ch Ch Oxford (BA); late Capt 6th Bn Liverpool Regt; *m* 12 Feb 1930 Mary Ailsie, dau of Thomas Lome, and *dsp* 10 Feb 1948

1b Louisa Jessie; *b* 16 May 1879; *educ* Lady Margaret Hall Oxford, and Dublin U (BA); *d* unm 11 March 1966

2b Mary Ellinor; *b* 14 June 1883; *m* 4 July 1907 Capt Francis Stanfield Symons (*d* 15 Feb 1941), son of Francis Standfield Symons, of Streatham, and had issue

2a Frederick Ward; *b* 1 May 1840; *d* 4 Jan 1854

3a John Henry; *b* 21 March 1842; *d* unm 25 Dec 1870

4a Robert Fitz Frederick (Rev); *b* 14 Nov 1848; *m* 28 Aug 1808 Margaret Geraldine (*d* 3 Aug 1871), 2nd dau of Rev Francis Hewson, Rector of Dungastown, Co Wicklow, and *dsp* 4 June 1869

5a Louis; *b* 21 March 1846; BA Trin Coll Cambridge; *m* 21 June 1877 Mary Anne (*d* 5 March 1897), dau of William Robert Ward (*see* BANGOR, V), and *d* 25 Jan 1940, leaving issue:

1b John Henry; *b* 4 Aug 1878; *educ* Trin Coll Cambridge (MA, MB, BCh); Capt late RAMC; *d* unm 13 Jan 1955

2b Bernard Frederic; *b* 17 July 1880; Lt-Col (ret) RM, WW II; *m* 8 Sept 1943 Mary Audrey, yr dau of Rev Robert Fetzer Taylor, of Grundisburgh House, Suffolk, and *dsp* 10 Oct 1967

3b Claud William (Rev); *b* 23 Oct 1881; *educ* Trin Coll Cambridge (MA, LLB); T/Lt RNVR 1918; *d* unm 8 Oct 1956

4b Geoffrey FitzLouis; *b* 16 Oct 1885; *educ* Bradfield and UCL; AMICE; Capt RE WW I (despatches); *m* 5 March 1927 Olive Muriel (*d* 1984), dau of George Constance, and *d* 29 April 1971, leaving issue:

1c *Joanna Mary; *b* 5 April 1937; *m* 11 April 1959 *Timothy Francis Cox, of Priors Mesne, Aylburton, Lydney, Glos, est son of Maj Henry Francis Cox, of The Manor House, Blockley, Glos, and has issue:

1d *Dermot Francis [Dermot Cox Esq, Lee Farm Cottage, Free Street, Bishops Waltham, Hants]; *b* 24 Jan 1963; *m* 1989 *Heather Ann Jackson and has:

1e *Naomi Josephine; *b* 1995

1d Miranda Josephine; *b* 30 Dec 1961; *m* 1985 *Andrew Thomas Doran, of The Manor House, Blockley, Glos, and *d* 1994, leaving:

1e *Dominic Henry; *b* 1988

1e *Fionnuala Mary; *b* 1987

1b *Harriette Louisa; *b* 3 Oct 1891; *m* 30 Nov 1917 T/Capt Guy Middleton Davison, RE (*d* 30 Nov 1918)

1a Sarah Louisa; *d* unm 8 Oct 1880

(2) Henry, of Cangort Park; *b* 8 Oct 1807; *m* 22 Oct 1836 Hon Georgina Mary Amelia Bloomfield (*d* 13 Jan 1893), dau of 1st Baron Bloomfield of Oakhampton and Redwood (*see* 1849 edn), and *d* 7 March 1881, leaving:

1a Henry Bloomfield, of Huntington, Queen's Co, JP (Co Tipperary); *b* 24 Nov 1840; *m* 11 Aug 1870 Jessie Maria (*d* 23 Jan 1919), only child of W C F Rawlins, HEICS, and *d* 12 Dec 1900, leaving issue:

1b Henry William Bloomfield; *b* 17 May 1873; Lt Oxf LI; *dvp* 29 Jan 1898, unm

2b Frederick Charles Bloomfield; *b* 23 April 1878; *m* 20 July 1905 Catherine Anne Swetenham, MBE (*m* 2nd 27 Jan 1926 Rev James Godfrey MacManaway, MP NI Parl (*d* 22 Oct 1951), yst son of Rt Rev James MacManaway, Bp of Clogher, and *d* 27 Jan 1951), only child of Sir Thomas Lecky, of Greystone Hall, Limavady, and was *ka* 1 July 1919

1b Constance Georgiana Bloomfield; *m* 1 Feb 1899 Brig-Gen Edward Dalrymple White, CMG, Oxford and Bucks LI (*d* 18 Aug 1929), and *d* 19 April 1944

2b Mildred Blanche Bloomfield; *m* 1st 2 June 1897 George Arthur Pomeroy Vernon, LLD (*d* 9 Jan 1918), son of John Edward Vernon, of Erne Hill, Belturbet, Co Cavan, and had issue; *m* 2nd 20 Feb 1930 Sir John Hubert Plunkett Murray, KCMG (*d* 27 Feb 1940), Lt -Govr Papua, and *d* 26 Jan 1960

3b Jessie Angel Bloomfield; *b* 21 July 1885; *d* 11 May 1889

2a William Thomas, of Redwood, Co Tipperary, JP (Co Tipperary and King's Co); *b* 5 Sept 1843; barrister; High Sheriff King's Co 1885; *m* 10 Jan 1877 Elizabeth Ida (*d* 27 Nov 1920), dau of Colin George Campbell, of Stonefield, and *dsp* 8 Dec 1911

3a Benjamin Bloomfield, of Cloughjordan, Co Tipperary, JP (Co Monaghan), DL (Co Tipperary); *b* 28 Nov 1846; *m* 25 July 1889 Dora Agnes Caroline (*d* 7 April 1899), yst dau of Christopher Turnor, of Stoke Rochford, Lincs, and *d* 24 Jan 1926, leaving issue:

1b Sheelah Georgiana Bertha; *b* 28 May 1890; *m* 15 Oct 1924 Langlois Massy Lefroy, OBE, yr son of Lt-Col Augustine Hugh Lefroy, JP, DL (*d* 5 April 1957), of Carrigglas Manor, Co Longford, and *d* 13 May 1972

2b Theodora Caroline; *b* 17 July 1891; *d* unm 14 Feb 1971

1a Harriott; *d* unm 25 Jan 1940

2a Georgiana Sarah; *m* 24 June 1869 Francis William Lloyd-Edwards (*d* 20 Jan 1890), of Nanhoron, N Wales, and *d* 13 Nov 1912, leaving issue

3a Louisa Charlotte; *m* 20 July 1870 Col James Gore-Booth, late RE, and *d* 26 Oct 1926, leaving issue (*see* GORE-BOOTH, Bt)

4a Isabella Catherine; *m* 3 Jan 1883 Rev Herbert Francis Chenevix Trench (*d* 5 May 1900), Vicar of Orpington, Kent, son of Archbp of Dublin, and *d* 25 Jan 1927, leaving issue (*see* below)

5a Blanche Helen; *m* 19 Dec 1896 Archfield John Mackey (*d* 27 Feb 1936), of Hurst House, Twyford, formerly Recorder of Andover, 2nd son of Lt -Col John Alexander Mackey, of Fairhill, Exeter, and *d* 20 March 1937

(1) Harriet; *m* April 1832 Ven Evans Johnson, Archdeacon of Ferns, and *d* Oct 1840

(2) Anne Margaret; *m* 24 Oct 1839 Guy Atkinson, of Cangort, who *d* 28 Nov 1859, leaving issue

5 Charles; *b* 1772; *m* 27 Nov 1807 Anna Maria (*d* 19 Dec 1847), est dau of Luke White, of Woodlands, Co Dublin (*see* ANNALY, B), and *d* 6 April 1840, leaving with other issue:

(1) Frederick Charles TRENCH later TRENCH-GASCOIGNE (added with arms by roy licence), of Parlington, Yorks, VD, JP and DL; *b* May 1814; Hon Col 2nd Yorks Vol Eng; *m* 16 Jan 1850 Mary Isabella (*d* 22 Oct 1891), est dau and coheir of Richard Oliver Gascoigne, of Parlington, Yorks, and Castle Oliver, Co Limerick, and *d* 12 June 1905, leaving issue:

1a Frederick Richard Thomas, DSO (1900), of Parlington, Lotherton Hall, Aberford, Leeds, and Craignish Castle, Ardfern, Argyllshire, JP (W R Yorks); *b* 4 July 1851; Hon Col, Capt RHG (Blues) and Lt-Col and Hon Col Yorks Hus, Nile Expdn 1884–85, S Africa 1899–1900, OStJ; High Sheriff Yorks 1923; *m* 16 Feb 1892 Laura Gwendolen Douglas, CBE (1918), DJStJ (*d* 10 July 1949), yst dau of Sir Douglas Galton, KCB, and *d* 2 June 1937, having had issue:

1b Alvary Douglas Frederick (TRENCH-)GASCOIGNE (Sir), GBE (1953), KCMG (1948, CMG 1942); *b* 6 Aug 1893; *educ* Eton; WW I as Lt Coldstream Gds (despatches); Dip Serv 1921–53, Political Rep Japan with rank of Amb 1946–51, Amb USSR 1951–53; *m* 1st 15 May 1916 (*divorce* 1935) Sylvia, er dau of Brig-Gen Wilbur Elliott Wilder, 5th Cavalry US Army, and had issue:

1c Douglas Wilder; *b* 11 Nov 1917; Capt Coldstream Gds WW II; *ka* Aug 1944

1c Yvonne TRENCH GASCOIGNE later STUDD-TRENCH-GASCOIGNE (deed poll 1959); *b* 5 May 1919; *m* 15 Oct 1952 Charles Kynaston Studd, late F/Lt RAF (*d* 25 Aug 1959), son of Edward Fairfax Studd, of Oxton House, Exeter, and *dsp* 17 Jan 1973

1b (cont.) Sir Alvary Gascoigne *m* 2nd 23 Feb 1935 Lorna Priscilla, OBE, RRC (*d* 19 June 1979), dau of Edmund Ernest Leatham, of Wentbridge House, Pontefract, and *d* 18 April 1970

2b Edward Oliver; *b* 9 July, *d* 16 Aug 1896

1b Cynthia Mary; *b* 6 Feb 1898; *m* 10 April 1924 6th Baron Sandys (*qv*), and *d* 1990, leaving issue

6 Richard; *b* 1774; barrister; *m* 3 March 1803 Melesina Chenevix (*d* 27 May 1827), dau and sole heiress of Rev Richard Chenevix, and gdau and heiress of Rt Rev Richard Chenevix, Bp of Waterford (in 1873 all his living descendants added CHENEVIX before TRENCH), and widow of Col Richard St George, of Hatley Manor, Co Leitrim, and *d* 16 April 1860, having had:

(1) Francis(Rev); *b* 1805; Rector of Islip, Oxfordshire; *m* 6 Dec 1837 Mary Caroline (*d* 4 March 1886), dau of Rev William Marsh, DD, and *d* 3 April 1886, having had issue:

1a Richard William Francis; *b* 2 June 1849; *d* 12 Aug 1860

1a Mary Melesina; *m* 11 Oct 1894 Rev Thomasin Albert Stoodley, BCL Oxford, sometime Rector of Dowsby, Lincoln

2a Maria Marcia Fanny; *m* 12 Jan 1875 Capt Frederick Farrer, late Madras Army, and *d* his widow, 7 April 1926, leaving issue

(2) Richard (Most Rev), PC; *b* 9 Sept 1807; DD, DCL; Archbp Dublin 1864–84; *m* 1 June 1832 his cousin Hon Frances Mary Trench (*d* 5 Nov 1890), sis of **2nd Baron Ashtown** (*see* below), and *d* 27 March 1886, having had:

1a Richard; *b* 18 Feb 1836; *d* 27 May 1861

2a Frederic, CMG; *b* 10 Oct 1837; Maj-Gen late 20th Hus, Mil Attaché St Petersburg 1883–86; *m* 17 July 1873 Mary Frederica Blanche (*d* 4 Nov 1924), dau of Charles Blood Mulville, Capt 3rd Dragoon Gds, and *d* 17 Aug 1894, leaving:

1b Richard Samuel Dermot; *b* 6 Oct 1881; *d* unm 1 June 1909

2b Julius Francis, OBE (1944), DSO (1918), DL (Berwicks); *b* 2 Nov 1885; served WW I (despatches, Brevet-Maj), Mesopotamia 1920 (medal and clasp); *m* 21 Oct 1929 Winifred Mary Frances (*d* 14 July 1982), yr dau of Sewallis Evelyn Shirley, of Ettington and Lough Fea, Carrickmacross (*see* FERRERS, E), and *dsp* 15 Jan 1948

1b Mary Anne Rose; *m* 29 Nov 1900 George Baily Michell (*d* 24 May 1929), of Frampton-on-Severn, Glos, only son of Maj-Gen George Bruce Michell, IA, and *d* 11 June 1944

2b Frederica Gwen; *m* 28 Nov 1905 Frederick Lechmere Paton (*d* 4 Jan 1937), MA Oriel Coll Oxford, barrister, and *d* 9 Dec 1941, having had issue

3b Frances Melesina; *d* unm 28 Sept 1977

3a Charles; *b* 26 Jan 1839; Col (ret) RA; *m* 14 Feb 1874 Emily Mary (*d* 3 Oct 1919), est dau of Gen Sir John Henry Lefroy, KCMG, CB, FRS, LLD, FSA, Govr Bermuda and Tasmania, and *d* 15 Oct 1933, having had:

1b Richard Henry (Sir), CIE, OBE; *b* 4 April 1876; Lt-Col late IA, Indian Police Dept, sometime Under-Sec Foreign Office, India, China 1900 (medal with clasp); *m* Sept 1913 Evelyn May (*d* 14 Nov 1977, aged 91), only child of Capt Harry Evelyn Stracey Pocklington, 15th Hus, only son of Lt-Col George Henry Pocklington, DL, of Chelsworth, Suffolk, and *d* 3 Sept 1954, leaving issue:

1c +Charles Pocklington, MC [Maj Charles Trench, MC, Lisnamoe House, Ballymachey, Nenagh, Co Tipperary, Ireland]; *b* 29 June 1914; *educ* Winchester and Oxford U; Maj formerly Hodson's Horse, Indian Pol Serv and Colonial Admin Serv Kenya; author: *The Royal Malady, George II*, etc; *m* 1st 14 Jan 1946 (*divorce* 1954) Patricia Jane (*d* 19 Jan 1963), only dau of Maj George Foster Gretton, 7th Hariana Lancers, of 62 Melton Ct, London SW7, and has:

1d Richard Hugh Roger; *b* 11 March 1949; *m* Jo — and *d* 18 May 1997, leaving:

1e +Jack

2e +Alex

1e *Anna

1d *Charlotte Ann; *b* 7 Oct 1946

2d *Priscilla Jane; *b* 6 Oct 1947

1c (cont.) Maj Charles Trench *m* 2nd 2 Oct 1954 *Mary Elizabeth, dau of Lt-Col George Kirkbride, of Mullion, Cornwall, and by her has further issue:

3d *Lucy; *b* 8 June 1956; *m* 1995 *Robert Collingwood

4d *Georgia; *b* 8 Feb 1959; *m* 1983 *Dr Nicholas Gordon Martin, of 37 Burns Rd, Toowong, Qld 4066, Australia

1c *(Evelyn) Jane; *b* 28 Sept 1917; *m* 28 June 1950 *Richard Christian Allhusen, of Bradenham Hall, Thetford, Norfolk, est s of Frederick Henry Allhusen CMG, DSO, of Fulmer House, Bucks, and has issue:

1d *Christian Henry [Christian Allhusen Esq, Manor House, Bradenham, Thetford, Norfolk IP25 7QU]; *b* 1956; *m* 1986 *Penelope Amanda, yr dau of Colin G C Rae, of Little Weston House, Yeovil, Somerset, and has issue:

1e *Benjamin Christian Thomas; *b* 17 May 1989

2e *Matthew John Oliver; *b* 28 Nov 1991

1e *Natasha Sophie Tasmin; *b* 4 Nov 1993

2e *Sabrina Isabella India; *b* 9 Sept 1996

2d *Richard Frederick [Richard Allhusen Esq, The Old Parsonage, Hinxton, Cambs CB10 1RS]; *b* 1960; *m* 1989 *Katrina Jane, yr dau of I R P Haig, of Brockstone House, Dunley, Worcs

1d *Elizabeth Mary [Mrs William Durlacher, Whalebone House, Langham, Colchester, Essex, CO4 5PX]; *b* 1952; *m* 1977 *William P Durlacher, s of Jack Durlacher, and has:

1e *Emma Jane; *b* 1980

2e *Susanna Mary; *b* 1982

2d *Rosalind Jane; *b* 1954; *m* 1985 *Nicholas Charles Thoresby Pawson, only son of K V F Pawson, of Haggas Hall, Weeton, Yorks, and has:

1e *Iona Elizabeth; *b* 1988

2e *Georgia Catherine; *b* 1991

2b Charles Godfrey, CIE (1931); *b* 30 Dec 1877; *educ* Loretto and Lincoln Coll Oxford (BA 1900); ICS; *m* 8 Sept 1910 Margaret May (*d* 1981), est dau of John Holmes Blakesley, CE, of 67 The Ave, Kew Gdns, London, and *d* 1 Sept 1964, leaving issue:

1c Christopher John, MBE (1946); *b* 27 July 1911; *educ* Shrewsbury and Balliol Coll, Oxford (BA 1936, MA 1946); Dep County Educn Offr Kent CC, County Educn Offr Warwicks, Liveryman Mercers' Co; *m* 11 Aug 1936 *Mary Elizabeth Catherine, er dau of George Henry Allen, of Branksome, Poole, and *d* 10 July 1971, leaving issue:

1d +Timothy Christopher John [Timothy Chenevix-Trench Esq, 196 Broom Rd, Teddington, Middx]; Tech Offr ICI; *b* 5 Oct 1938; *educ* King's Canterbury and Corpus Christi Coll Oxford (BA 1961); *m* 1st 2 Sept 1961 (*divorce* 1973) Penelope Mary Travers, er dau of George Cummings Walton, of Island Cottage, Maidensgrove, Henley-on-Thames, and has:

1e *Katharine Rae [Mrs Timothy Reilly, 25 Aldebrooke Rd, London SW12]; *b* 8 June 1964; *m* 1984 (*divorce* Feb 1989) Dr Robert Neil Summers Slater, only s of Robert Slater of Childswickham, Worcs, and has:

1f *Thomas Alexander; *b* 1986

1e (cont.) Mrs Katharine Slater *m* 2nd 6 July 1991 *Dr Timothy Reilly and by him has:

2f *Sam; *b* 2 Jan 1993

1f *Sophie; *b* 31 Jan 1995

2e *Alison Mary; *b* 20 Aug 1965; *m* 1983 *Jonathan Robert Hill, s of Fl-Lt F G Hill, and has:

1f *Maximililan Alexander; *b* 29 Jan 1993

1f *Charlotte Rachel; *b* 31 March 1990

3e *Phillida Clare; *b* 25 May 1969

1d (cont.) Timothy Chenevix-Trench *m* 2nd 1977 Stella-Maris Melhuish (*d* 9 March 1997), dau of Edwin Samuel Henderson, Supt CID, Burma

2d +John Richard [John Chenevix-Trench Esq, Skrinis House, Glenalmond Coll, Perthshire]; *b* 20 Feb 1948; *educ* King's Canterbury, and U of Newcastle-upon-Tyne; *m* 1970 *Pauline, dau of James Stephen Alexander, of 2 Seawood Place, Grange Over Sands, Cumbria, and has:

1e +Christopher Hamish; *b* 1977

1e *Alix; *b* 1983

1d *Elizabeth Mary; *b* 16 May 1941; *educ* Somerville Coll Oxford (BA 1963); *m* 25 July 1964 *Anthony Saville Stephen Rowe, MA, BM, BCh, MRCP, of Woodtown, Sampford Spinney, Yelverton, Devon, only son of Stephen V Rowe, of 30 Montpelier Crescent, Brighton, Sussex, and has issue:

1e *Jonathan Stephen; *b* 1969

2e *James Benedict; *b* 7 Aug 1970; *m* 9 Aug 1997 *Sophie, dau of James Rowlatt, of Hinton St Mary, Dorset and has:

1e *Antonia Jane; *b* 2 March 1967; *m* 1993 *Jonathan Katz and has:

1f *Oliver; *b* 199–

2f *James; *b* 199–

2c Richard Blakesley; *b* 28 Oct 1912; *educ* Shrewsbury; Lt-Cdr RN WW II (despatches); *m* 10 April 1939 *Nancy Carey [Mrs Richard Chenevix-Trench, 21 Church Rd, Davenport Green, Wilmslow, Cheshire], only dau of James Munro, of Shanghai, and *d* 16 May 1979, leaving:

1d *Fenella Anne [Mrs Richard Townsend, 129 Broadleaf Crescent, Ancaster, Ontario, Canada]; *b* 25 Nov 1943; *m* 22 Nov 1969 *Richard Law Townsend, 2nd s of Dr R L H Townsend, of Cape Town, and has:

1e *Simon Andrew; *b* 26 Jan 1974

3c +Godfrey Maxwell, DSC and bar [Cdr Godfrey Chenevix-Trench DSC and bar RN (ret), Kelling, Holt, Norfolk]; *b* 14 Oct 1917; *educ* Shrewsbury; Cdr RN WW II; history teacher; *m* 17 March 1945 *Nancy Louise (2nd Offr WRNS), dau of Rev Arthur Clarkson Birch, of Cloughton Vicarage, Scarborough, Yorks, and has:

1d *Juliet; *b* 29 Sept 1947; *m* 1973 *Graham Duncan Campbell, of Perth, W Australia, and has:

1e *Ian Neil; *b* 1977

2e *Duncan Alastair; *b* 1981

2d *Frances Claire; *b* 12 Nov 1949; *m* 1972 (*divorce* 1985) Christopher Maurice White, of Montreal, Prov Quebec, Canada, and has issue:

1e *Colin Stephen Maxwell; *b* 1974

4c Anthony, JP (Berks 1960); *b* 10 May 1919; *educ* Shrewsbury and Ch Ch Oxford (MA 1948); Capt RA WW II 1939–42 (POW); Assist Master Shrewsbury Sch 1948, Housemaster 1952–55, Headmaster: Bradfield 1955–63, Eton 1963–70, Fettes 1970, memb Lord Robbins Comm on higher education, FRSE, FRSA; *m* 15 Aug 1953 Elizabeth Chalmers (*d* 1991), dau of Capt Sir Stewart Dykes Spicer, 3rd Bt, RN (*qv*), and *d* 21 June 1979, leaving issue:

1d +Richard Thomas Chalmers [Richard Chenevix-Trench Esq, 20 Hill Crest, 22 Plunketts Rd, The Peak, Hong Kong]; *b* 9 Dec 1958; *m* 1985 *Sarah Jane, est dau of Raglan Charles Wykeham, of Northroyd, Crimphill, Englefield Green, Surrey, and has:

1e +Harry Chalmers; *b* 1988

2e +James William Reynolds; *b* 1990

3e +Marcus; *b* 1993

2d +Jonathan Charles Stewart; *b* 24 March 1961

1d *Josephine Dykes; *b* 6 Oct 1954; *m* 22 July 1978 *John George Richards Homfray, s of Maj Herbert Franklin Richards Homfray, of Penllyn Court, Cowbridge, Glam, and has:

1e *Matthew Anthony; *b* 1980

2e *Thomas Richards; *b* 1983

1e *Virginia; *b* 1987

2d Laura Lefroy; *b* 6 Oct 1954; *m* 1981 *Nicholas John Ford, Lt RN, yr son of Air Marshal Sir Geoffrey Ford, and *d* 1988, leaving:

1e *Peter Anthony Alexander; *b* 1982

2e *Alexander Charles Richard *b* 1984

3e *Edward Christopher Gillespie; *b* 1987

3b Francis Maxwell; *b* 23 Sept 1879; Maj RFA WW I (despatches); *m* 28 March 1914 Sibyl (*m* 2nd 7 Dec 1921 William Fox Bruce, DSO, MC (*see* ABERDARE, B), and *d* 2 March 1954), dau of Alfred Owen Lyon, of Elm Park Gdns, London SW, and was *ka* 31 Oct 1914

4b Christopher; *b* 14 April 1881; Lt RE; *das* unm S Africa 13 April 1902

5b Lawrence, CMG (1919), DSO (1918); *b* 24 March 1883; Col RE, AQMG N Cmd India 1933–37, Legion of Honour; *m* 15 June 1908 Winifred Ross (*d* 2 Nov 1969), 3rd dau of Edward Henry Tootal, of Kensington, and *d* 11 Nov 1958, leaving:

1c Elizabeth; *b* 13 June 1909; *m* 9 April 1932 Brig Charles Deane Steel, CMG, OBE, late RE, of Little Hill, Nettlebed, Henley-on-Thames, Oxon, yr s of Dr Gerard Steel, of Leominster, Herefs, and *d* 10 June 1973, leaving:

1d *Christopher Charles [Christopher Steel Esq, Bullens, Bradfield College, Berks]; *b* 15 Jan 1939; *educ* Shrewsbury; *m* 31 July 1963 *Anthea Victoria, only dau of Col Edward Thirlwell Wilson

2d *Francis Gerard; *b* 10 May 1941; *educ* Shrewsbury

2c *Katharine Anne [Mrs George Leicester, The Gables, Hopton Cangeford, Ludlow, Salop]; *b* 13 May 1912; *m* 1st 19 Jan 1932 Lt-Col George William Frederic Leicester, Cheshire Regt (*d* 25 Feb 1944), er s of Maj William Frederic Leicester, and has issue (*see* 1967 edn LEICESTER, Bt); *m* 2nd 1945 Lt-Col Alec Frankland, OBE (*d* 9 March 1969), and by him had:

1d *Philip; *b* 1946; *educ* Tonbridge

2d *John; *b* 1949; *educ* King's Canterbury; *m* 1975 *Mary Faith Elizabeth Townsend, dau of Lionel Becher Somerville-Large, MRIA, of Blackrock, Co Dublin, and has:

1e *William Becher Chenevix; *b* 1983

1e *Anna; *b* 1978

1d *Sarah; *b* 1947; *m* 1969 *Dr Peter Morris of Ware, Herts, and has:

1e *Patrick; *b* 1982

1e *Leila; *b* 1980

6b Ralph, CB (1940), OBE (1919), MC (1916); *b* 15 Dec 1885; Col (T/Brig) Roy Signals, Dep Dir Staff Duties War Office 1937, Cmdt Signal Trg Centre 1938, Signal Offr-in-Ch BEF (A/Maj-Gen) 1939–40; *m* 2 Dec 1916 Meriel Edith (*d* 1985), dau of Rev Dr George Edward Jelf, DD, Master of the Charterhouse, and *d* 1 May 1974, leaving:

1c +John Gordon [John Chenevix-Trench Esq, Windmill Farm, Coleshill, Amersham, Bucks HP7 9LZ]; *b* 17 Oct 1920; *educ* Wellington and RMA Woolwich; Capt Roy Signals WW II; author; *m* 22 Sept 1944 Ann

Patricia (*d* 3 July 1997), est dau of Norman Moore, of 34 Jubilee Pl, London SW3, and has:

1d +Maxwell John [Maxwell Chenevix-Trench Esq, Windmill Farm, Coleshill, Bucks HP7 0LZ]; *b* 17 June 1952; *educ* Wellington; *m* 1991 (*divorce* 19–) Chou Ern, dau of Lam-Tai Lim, of Selangor, Malaysia

1d *Jessica; *b* 15 July 1949; *m* 1st 12 Sept 1970 (*divorce* 1976) Jonathan Yardley, of 36 Beaumont Ct, Sutton Lane, Chiswick, London W4, yr son of F T Yardley, of Beaconsfield, and has:

1e *Thomas James; *b* 1974

1d (cont.) Mrs Jessica Yardley *m* 2nd 1976 *George Laurence and by him has:

2e *Benjamin George; *b* 1981

1e *Catherine Ann; *b* 1978

2c Maxwell; *b* 25 Oct 1921; Lt RE, WW II; *ka* 10 April 1943

3c Philip Roger; *b* 22; *d* 24 May 1924

1c *Susan Meriel; *b* 8 Sept 1925; *m* 8 July 1950 Oscar Patrick Wood (*d* 1994), of Christ Church, Oxford, er s of Sydney Herbert Wood, CB, MC, of Ealing, and has:

1d *Charles William; *b* 12 March 1955; *m* 1985 *Mary Rose, dau of Rex Cooper, of East Bergholt, Suffolk, and has issue:

1e *Oscar Giles Chenevix; *b* 1986

1e *Amelia Claire Lucy; *b* 1988

2e *Georgia Charlotte; *b* 1991

2d *Silas James London; *b* 19 April 1965

1d *Lucy Melesina; *b* 27 Dec 1956

7b Alfred Saward, MC; *b* 10 Dec 1887; *educ* Wellington, Trin Coll Cambridge (BA) and McGill U (BSc); Maj RE, WW I (despatches) and WW II; *m* 1st 3 Feb 1920 Helen Winifred (*d* 29 Oct 1945), only dau of George Fowler; *m* 2nd 26 April 1949 *Sylvia Mary Crawford, twin dau of Francis Crawford Caffin and *d* 3 Nov 1963, leaving by his 1st w:

1c +Dudley Alfred; *b* 7 Oct 1928; *educ* Bradfield; late Lt RA; *m* 15 Jan 1955 *Isobel Margaret Logie, dau of William Low McDonald, of Port Elizabeth, S Africa, and has:

1d *Jennifer Elizabeth; *b* 23 April 1957

2d *Helen Winifred; *b* 5 May 1959

1c *Gillian [Mrs James Notley, Redcote, 48 Port Hill Gdns, Shrewsbury]; *b* 22 Dec 1920; *m* 16 Dec 1947 Maj James Thomas Benedictus Notley, DSO, late Duke of Cornwall's LI, only s of Capt James Thomas Benedictus Notley, RN, of S Devon, and has:

1d *Christopher John Marwood; *b* 25 Jan 1949; *educ* Cokethorpe Sch; Maj 1st Bn LI; *m* 1st 1977 (*divorce* 1982) Christine Louise, dau of Patrick Hugh Ash, of Haughley, Suffolk; *m* 2nd 1987 *Alison Jane Leila, dau of Colin Biggs, of IoW

1d *Helen Ann Hamilton; *b* 10 Nov 1950; *m* 11 Sept 1971 (*divorce* 1987) Timothy Rowland Hunt, yst s of John Rowland Hunt, of Borratton Hall, Salop, and has issue:

1e *Benjamin Rowland; *b* 1973

1e *Nina Katheryn; *b* 1974

1b Emily Maude; *d* unm 27 April 1937

4a Arthur Julius; *b* 5 July 1840; *d* at Calcutta, 23 Oct 1860

5a Alfred; *b* 4 Nov 1849; *m* 27 Nov 1873 Ella (*d* 18 Feb 1934), yst dau of James Moore, of Dalchoolin, Co Down, and *d* 13 March 1938

6a Herbert Francis (Rev); *b* 21 Dec 1850; MA Cambridge; Vicar St Peter's in Thanet, Kent; *m* 3 Jan 1883 Isabella Catharine (*d* 25 Jan 1927), dau of Henry Trench, of Cangort Park, King's Co (*see* above), and *d* 5 May 1900, leaving:

1b Arthur Henry, CIE (1919); *b* 28 April 1884; Col RE, Inspecting Offr Rlwys MOT 1927–47; *m* 18 Dec 1913 Dorothy Pauline (*d* 19 Sept 1950), est dau of Allan Gibson Steel, KC, Recorder Oldham, and *d* 12 Jan 1968, leaving:

1c +Reginald Allan; *b* 1 Sept 1920; Maj RE; *m* 23 Nov 1957 *Sophie Sybella Strathern, dau of Air Ch Marshal Sir Douglas Claude Strathern Evill, GBE, KCB, DSC, AFC, RAF, DL, and has:

1d +Ivo Richard; *b* 31 March 1959; *m* 1982 *Joelle, dau of Rene Bezert, of Marseilles, France, and has:

1e *Sophie Armella Francoise; *b* 1982

2d *Angus; *b* 7 Nov 1960

1d *Katharine; *b* 12 Dec 1964

2d *Jessica Sophia; *b* 11 Aug 1966

1c *Margaret Georgiana [Mrs Patrick Synge, Farthings, School Lane, Fittleworth, Pulborough, W Sussex RH20 1JB]; *b* 30 March 1915; WW II in FANY; *m* 14 April 1944 Maj Patrick Millington Synge, Intell Corps (*d* 1982), son of Edward Millington Synge, ARE, of Clare Cottage, W Byfleet, Surrey, and has:

1d *Arthur Hugh Millington; *b* 4 Aug 1951; *educ* Rugby and Wye Coll London U (BSc), MBA Kingston; botanist Roy Botanic Gdns Kew 1973–87, dir 'Plant Talk' 1995

2d *Robert Patrick; *b* 21 Jan 1957; *educ* Stowe; *m* 1992 *Susan Jean Frances Wixley

2c *Dorothy Anne [Mrs Roderick Wilson, Three Chimneys, Fittleworth, W Sussex]; *b* 25 Nov 1916; 2nd Offr WRNS WW II; *m* 10 April 1942 Roderick Peter Garratt Wilson (*d* 1994), s of Sir Roderick (Roy) Wilson, of Wood End, Pyrford, Woking, and has:

1d *Nicholas Allan Roy (Sir) [The Hon Mr Justice Wilson, 31 Sutherland Pl, London W2]; *b* 9 May 1945; *educ* Bryanston and Worcester Coll Oxford (BA); barrister Inner Temple 1967; QC and Recorder Crown Court 1987, High Court Judge Family Division 1993–, ktd 1993; *m* 1974 *Margaret, barrister Middle Temple 1966, dau of Reginald Francis Higgins, and has:

1e *Matthew Roderick Benjamin; *b* 1977

1e *Camilla Jessica; *b* 1981

1d *Francesca Dorothy (Rev); *b* 8 Aug 1952; MA Cantab, Dip Theol; *m* 1985 John Dudley Dixon, MBE, DSC (2 stars) (*d* 1996)

2b Charles Reginald; *b* 5 March 1888; *educ* Merton Coll Oxford (BA); A/Maj Notts and Derbys Regt WW I (despatches); *m* 28 Jan 1915 Clare Cecily, yst dau of Henry Blunt Howard, of Bark Hart, Orpington, and was *ka* 21 March 1918, leaving:

1c *Isabel Clare [Mrs John Fletcher, 20 Tullis Close, Sutton Courtenay, Oxon]; *b* 4 Nov 1915; *educ* Bedford Coll, London (Dip Soc Studies 1936); *m* 10 Aug 1939 *(Clarence) John Molyneux Fletcher, MA Oxford, PhD California, FSA, yr s of Clarence George Eugene Fletcher, CBE, and has:

1d *Anthony John [Prof Anthony Fletcher, 2 Bluecoat Court, Durham]; *b* 24 April 1941; *educ* Wellington and Merton Coll Oxford (MA); *m* 29 July 1967 *Tresna Dawn, (BA), dau of Charles Henry Railton Russell, of Southgate, London, and has:

1e *Crispin Hilary Trench; *b* 1970

2e *Dickon Anthony Railton; *b* 1972

2d *Martin Chenevix; *b* 22 Dec 1942; *m* 1972 *Diana Cantillon, and has issue:

1e *Nicholas Cantillon; *b* 1975

1e *Alison Chenevix; *b* 1973

1d *Joanna Delle; *b* 9 July 1946; *m* 1992 *Cdr Robert Walker, RN (ret)

2d *Hilary Clare; *b* 27 Sept 1951; *m* 1976 *John Bennett, and has issue:

1e *Charlotte Louise; *b* 1981

2e *Rowena Clare; *b* 1982

3b Herbert; *b* 26 May 1892; *m* 1 Sept 1922 Marjorie (*d* 11 April 1962), dau of Robert Carstairs Bell, of Melbourne, and *d* 23 June 1971, having had issue:

1c Robert Hugh; *b* 22 July 1923; *d* 5 Jan 1924

1c *Frances Robina; *b* 26 Nov 1925; *m* 27 Jan 1953 *Raymond Robert Lockyer, ARIBA, of The Old Manor Cottage, Broadwell, nr Lechlade, Glos, est son of Cuthbert James Lockyer, of The Mill House, Clapton, nr Crewkerne, Somerset, and has issue:

1d *Sarah Frances Chenevix; *b* 13 Oct 1954; *educ* Benenden; *m* 1982 *Peter Hickman, son of W J Hickman, and has issue:

1e *Emma Charlotte; *b* 1985

2e *Lucy Elizabeth; *b* 1987

2d *Victoria Robina Chenevix; *b* 14 July 1957

2c *Valerie Hester; *b* 18 May 1929; *educ* Reading U (BA 1952); *m* 5 Dec 1959 *David McKie Kerslake, OBE, DSc, MB, BS, of Lime Tree Cottage, Yateley, Camberley, Surrey, son of John Kerslake, of Henfield, Sussex, and has issue:

1d *Michael John Chenevix; *b* 21 May 1962

3d *Caroline Julia Chenevix; *b* 30 May 1961

1b Monica Mary; *b* 27 Aug 1886; *d* young

2b Margaret Isabel; *b* 29 July 1889; *d* unm 8 May 1936

3b Frances Georgiana; *b* 3 Feb 1891; *m* 17 April 1918 Diarmid Coffey (*m* 2nd his wife's cousin Sheela Wilbraham FitzJohn, er dau of Prof Wilbraham FitzJohn Trench (*see* below), and *d* 7 July 1964, s of George Coffey, of 5 Harcourt Terrace, Dublin, and *d* 30 Oct 1918

1a Melesina Mary; *m* 7 Jan 1864 Cholmeley Austen Leigh (*d* 30 Sept 1899), est son of Rev J E Austen Leigh, and *d* 2 March 1918, leaving issue

2a Edith; *m* 17 Aug 1882 Most Rev Reginald Stephen Copleston, DD (*d* 19 April 1925), late Bp of Calcutta, and *d* 2 Nov 1942, leaving issue

3a Helen Emily; *m* 16 Feb 1871 Capt Arthur Blundell George Sandys Hill, est son of Lord George Hill, and *d* 25 June 1935, leaving issue (*see* DOWNSHIRE, M)

4a Frances Harriet; *d* unm 14 Dec 1941

5a Rose Julia; *m* 8 June 1876 Samuel Henry Butcher, Hon LLD and LittD (*dsp* 29 Dec 1910), son of Rt Rev Samuel Butcher, Bp of Meath (*see* 1935 edn DANESFORT, B), and *d* 7 April 1902

(3) Philip Charles, of Botley, Hants, JP; *b* 20 July 1809; *m* 21 Nov 1846 Ellen Maria (*d* 2 Aug 1872), dau of Thomas Turner, HEICS, and *d* 9 Feb 1888, leaving issue:

1a Philip Francis; *b* 7 June 1849; *m* 13 April 1882 Frances Angel (*d* 21 Feb 1947), dau of Robert Reeves, of Fitzwilliam Place, Dublin, and *d* 6 April 1911, leaving issue:

1b Philip Gervais, late Lt KRRC; *b* 11 Oct 1886; *d* 15 Dec 1916

2b Robert Denis; *b* 11 Feb 1899; *educ* Winchester; late Capt KRRC, WW I 1918, and WW II (Japanese POW 1942–45)

1b Muriel Emily; *b* 17 Dec 1882; *d* 24 April 1982

2b Melesina Gladys, JP; *b* 11 Sept 1884; *m* 3 July 1912 Herbert William Deedes, JP, late KRRC (*d* 2 Aug 1966; *see* DEEDES, B), er s of Col Herbert George Deedes, and *d* 16 Jan 1966, leaving issue

3b Oonagh Frances; *b* 1 Feb 1895

2a Charles; Capt Bengal Staff Corps; *b* 31 Oct 1856; *d* 2 Aug 1891

3a George Frederick, CIE (1911); *b* 23 June 1859; Lt-Col late IA(ret), formerly Indian Pol Dept Base Cmdt 1916, had Order of the Crown of Italy, and of the White Eagle of Serbia, 4th class; *d* 20 Dec 1937

4a Richard Bayley; *b* 23 Oct 1861; *m* 16 July 1889 Gwendoline, MBE (*d* 9 Jan 1948), dau of Sir John Heron-Maxwell, 7th Bt (*qv*), and *d* 5 April 1933, leaving:

1b Hugo; *b* 24 July 1890; Capt 5th Bn Rifle Bde SR WW I; *m* 12 June 1920 (*divorce* 1933) Emma Margaret Florence (*d* 12 July 1948), dau of Sir Robert McAlpine, 1st Bt (*qv*), and *d* 13 Aug 1965, having had:

1c Richard; *b* 1 Jan 1922; P/O RAFVR WW II; *kas* while flying, 10 March 1942

2c +Brian Robert David [Brian Chenevix-Trench Esq, 13 Holland Park, London W11]; *b* 10 July 1927; *m* 1st 11 Feb 1956 (*divorce*) Elizabeth Bridget Penelope, 2nd dau of K R J Saxon, of 17 Keswick Rd, Boscombe, Hants; *m* 2nd 2 Nov 1963 *Elspeth Charlesworth, yr dau of T D Ross, OBE, of Windmill Way, Stamford, Lincs

2b Eric; *b* 17 Dec 1892; *educ* Malvern; late Lt Roy Fus and RASC, Mech Tport, WW I 1914–18; *m* 1st 6 July 1929 Helen Frances (*d* 1 Dec 1965), dau of Rev Ernest George Beckwith, of Mortimer Vicarage, Berks, by his wife Charlotte Evelyn, dau of Charles Patrick Stewart (*see* GALLOWAY, E); *m* 2nd 7 Sept 1967 *Theano, dau of Emmanuel Schilizzi, and *dsp* 31 Aug 1971

3b Ivor; *b* 7 Dec 1892; Lt 8th Bn Wiltshire Regt WW I (wounded); *m* 20 June 1918 Doris Mary (*d* 22 April 1951), est dau of John Francis Gaskell, of Cambus O'May, Aberdeenshire, and *d* 27 May 1960, leaving issue:

1c *Diana Doris; *b* 6 March 1920; *m* 1st 8 May 1943 (*divorce* 1947) Capt Charles Brodie Knight, Welsh Gds, only son of Capt Charles M Knight, MC, and Mrs Broomfield Knight, of 54 Crompton Court, London SW3; *m* 2nd 2 July 1947 Capt Gilbert Wadham Younghusband, late RHG (Blues), of Pickering, Ontario, Canada, son of Leigh Younghusband, of Brookfield, Horton, Bucks, and adopted:

*Antony Mark; *b* 26 July 1950

*Wendy Martell; *b* 6 Sept 1952

4b Lionel Geoffrey; *b* 14 Oct 1901; *m* 23 June 1925 Doris Maud (*m* 2nd 25 April 1933 George Sweeting (*d* 16 Feb 1957), yr son of A C Sweeting, of Paxton Hall, St Neots, Hunts, and *d* 1980), er dau of Charles D Turrall, of Downes, Torrington, N Devon, and *d* 22 Sept 1930, leaving issue:

1c +(Keith Everard) George [George Chenevix-Trench Esq, The Old Mill, Worton, Devizes, Wilts]; *b* 20 March 1926; *educ* Stowe; late Sub-Lt RNVR; *m* 5 April 1952 (*divorce* 1972) Bridget, only dau of Lt-Col K R O'Brien, MC, Roy Ulster Rifles, of The Old Oak House, Westham, Sussex, and has:

1d +Guy Charles; *b* 15 July 1955; *m* 1982 *Sarah A, yr dau of John Speakman, of Bickacre, Essex, and has:

1e *Olivia Kate; *b* 1985

2e *Poppy; *b* 1987

2d +Rupert George; *b* 14 Sept 1957; *m* 1988 *Susannah Rainey, dau of Robert Craik, of the Old Rectory, Mawdesley, Lancs, and has:

1e +Frederic George; *b* 1989

1e *Fleur Melesina; *b* 1992

1a Mary Eliza; *d* unm 20 March 1926

2a Ellen Melesina; *m* 21 April 1882 Sir Algernon Charles Plumptre Coote, 12th Bt (*qv*), and *d* 21 April 1923, leaving issue

3a Catherine Louisa Anne; *m* 1st 12 Nov 1872 Lt-Col Robert Bartholomew, late Bengal Cav (*d* 1918), of The Cleave, Northam, Bideford, son of Rev Christopher Bartholomew, and had issue; *m* 2nd 30 Aug 1921 Capt Frederick Henry Peere Williams-Freeman, RN (ret) (*d* 3 Oct 1939), yr son of Frederick Peere Williams-Freeman, of Greatham, Sussex, and *d* 25 July 1926

4a Melesina Ethel Maude, LGStJ; *m* 7 July 1892 Capt Alfred Charles Seton Christopher, of 40 Carlyle Sq, London SW, JP, late Seaforth Highrs, KJStJ (*d* 12 Oct 1934), son of Rev Alfred Millard William Christopher, Hon Canon Ch Ch Oxford, and *d* 22 May 1924

(4) William; *dsp*

7 John, of St Catherine's Park, Leixlip, Co Kildare; *b* 1776; *m* 30 July 1807 Jean, est dau of James Currie, MD, FRS, of Ellerslie, Liverpool, and *d* 1858, having had issue:

(1) Frederic FitzJohn (Rev); *b* 10 Oct 1808; MA; Rector of Staplestown, Leighlin; *m* 6 April 1838 Elizabeth (*d* 24 Feb 1902), dau of John Maconchy, of Edenmore, Co Dublin, and *d* 25 June 1859, leaving issue:

1a John Alfred; *b* 5 Feb 1839; *m* 25 May 1866 Jenetta Wilbraham (*d* 14 June 1925), est dau of Wilbraham Taylor, Gentleman Usher to HM QUEEN VICTORIA, and *d* 28 March 1922, leaving, with other issue:

1b Wilbraham FitzJohn; *b* 22 Feb 1873; *educ* Christ's Coll Cambridge (MA); LittD Dublin, Prof English Literature Trin Coll Dublin; *m* 29 Dec 1903 Mary Alicia (*d* 3 Feb 1930), est dau of Edward Cross, of Hollywood, Co Down, and *d* 14 July 1939, leaving issue:

1c Patrick Mackenzie FitzJohn; *b* 16 Jan 1905; *m* 1st 29 July 1926 (*divorce* 1930) Frances Cautley, dau of Cecil Cautley Baker; *m* 2nd 24 Nov 1930 Eveleen (*d* 1945), dau of John Hayden, and by her had issue:

1d *Patricia Anne [Mme Pierre Verstraete, Chemin des Oisillons, 1009 Pully, Switzerland]; *b* 1930; *m* 8 Sept 1954 Pierre Edouard Marie Ghislain Verstraete, of Lausanne, s of Jacques Verstraete, and has:

1e *Philippe Jacques Marie Ghislain; *b* 16 Sept 1957

2e *Jacques Michel Marie Ghislain; *b* 7 May 1962; *m* 1982 *Lorraine Court, and has issue:

1f *Maud; *b* 1981

2f *Zoë; *b* 1983

1e *Catherine Jacqueline Marie Ghislaine; *b* 2 March 1955; *m* 1977 *Peter Carp, and has:

1f *Benoît; *b* 1983

2f *Henri; *b* 1986

3f *Alain; *b* 1988

1f *Sarah; *b* 1981

2e *Brigid Louise Marie Ghislaine; *b* 25 Sept 1956; *m* 1980 *Edouard Chanson and has:

1f *Sophie; *b* 1984

2f *Léa; *b* 1986

3f *Céline; *b* 1988

3e *Anne Bernadette Marie Ghislaine; *b* 6 Jan 1960; *m* 1982 *Patrice Droz and has:

1f *Olivier; *b* 1985

1f *Meryem; *b* 1983

2f *Nadège; *b* 1990

3f *Béatrice; *b* 1991

2d *(Eveline) Mary [Mrs Mary Lane, 2571 Heron St, Victoria BC Canada]; *b* 16 Feb 1932; *m* 22 Dec 1952 (*divorce* 1987) Thomas William Lane, BA, LLB, barrister, Sub-Lt RNVR, of Fulford Harbour, BC, 3rd s of Thomas William Lane, of St Cloud, Beauparc, Co Meath, and has:

1e *William Alan; *b* 6 Oct 1955; *m* 1980 *Janet Elinor, dau of Thomas Merville de Blois, of Toronto, and has:

1f *Helen Eilis de Blois; *b* 1984

2f *Heather Fiona de Blois; *b* 1988

1e *Patricia Sheela; *b* 9 June 1954; *m* 1993 *Kenneth Malcolm Maclure, of Victoria, BC, and has:

1f *Troy Liam Chalmers Alexander; *b* 1994

1c (cont.) Patrick Trench *m* 3rd 1947 Winifred Frances, (*d* 1992) dau of Arthur Edward Stidolph and *d* 27 Feb 1948, having by her had:

3d *Brid; *b* 16 Oct 1942; *m* 1962 *Michael Frederick Strutt, s of Frederick Strutt, of Pontypool, Gwent, and has:

1e *Patrick; *b* 1962

1e *Catherine; *b* 1964

2e *Anna; *b* 1965

3e *Siân; *b* 1978

2c +Chalmers Edward FitzJohn [Chalmers Trench Esq, Killrian, Slane, Co Meath, Ireland]; *b* 27 Nov 1909; *educ* Sidney Sussex Coll, Cambridge (BA), and Trin Coll, Dublin (BA); *m* 5 July 1940 Beatrice Esther (*d* 1980), dau of Charles St George Orpen, of Lisheens, Carrickmines, Co Dublin, and has:

1d +Fiachra Terence Wilbraham [Fiachra McMahon Trench Esq, Easton House, Delgany, Co Wicklow]; *b* 7 Sept 1941; *educ* Trin Coll Dublin (BA) and U of Cincinnati (M Mus); Assoc of Roy Irish Acad of Music; added name McMAHON 1983; *m* 1st 25 Sept 1965 (*divorce* 1980) Michaela Fredericka, dau of Edgar H Maus, of Hamilton, Ohio, and has:

1e +Michael Chalmers Wilbraham; *b* 4 Feb 1966

1d (cont.) Fiachra McMahon Trench *m* 2nd *Hanora Carmel, yst dau of Joseph McMahon, of Nenagh, Co Tipperary, and by her has:

2e +Oisin Patrick; *b* 1984

3e +Rian Charles; *b* 1986

2d +Brian Arthur Wilbraham; *b* 13 July 1945; *educ* Trin Coll, Dublin (BA); has issue by Judith Bowles, MA, dau of E A Bowles, of Melton, Humberside:

3e *Danny Eric Trench Bowles; *b* 25 Nov 1993

3e *Nora Trench Bowles; *b* 29 Nov 1987

3d +Patrick Chalmers Wilbraham [Patrick Trench Esq, 259 Lea Bridge Rd, London E10]; *b* 24 July 1955; *m* 1988 *Julia Catherine, dau of Dorian Cresswell Cooke, and has:

1e +Liam Patrick Alexander; *b* 1988

2e +James Chalmers Dorian; *b* 1991

1d *Beatrice Mary Wilbraham [Mrs Beatrice Bol, 54 Southern Drive, Ottawa, Ontario, Canada]; *b* 28 Jan 1948; *m* 1st 14 Dec 1968 (*divorce* 1976) Sydney Douglas Saunders, BA, BAI Trin Coll, Dublin, er s of Sidney Edwin Saunders of Dublin; *m* 2nd 1983 *Gerald Adrian Bol, er s of Gerrit Bol, of Utrecht, Netherlands, and Essex, Ontario, and by him has:

1e *Kieran Gerrit; *b* 1986

1c *Sheela Wilbraham FitzJohn [Mrs Sheela Strunz, Glendarragh, Newtownmountkennedy, Co Wicklow, Ireland]; *b* 9 March 1907; *m* 1st 15 Aug 1929 (Hugh) Diarmid James Coffey (*d* 7 July 1964), s of George Coffey, of Dublin, and widower of her cousin Frances Georgina (*see* above); *m* 2nd 1971 Erwin Strunz (*d* 1995), of Clonmannon Vige, Ashford, Co Wicklow and by her 1st husb has:

1d *(Donal) Manus George [Manus Coffey Esq, Glendarragh Hill, Newtownmountkennedy, Co Wicklow, Ireland]; *b* 4 June 1935; *m* 26 Sept 1959 *Patricia Ann, dau of Daniel Taylor, of Glasgow, and has:

1e *Aedan Diarmid Cailean; *b* 27 Jan 1961; *m* 1 Sept 1994 *Margaret Philomena, dau of John Sullivan, of Cork, and has:

1f *Sean Cailean; *b* 22 June 1996

1e *Fiona Ann Champagné; *b* 13 June 1962

1d *Saive Frances Mary; *b* 16 June 1930

2d *Helen Dairine; *b* 28 Dec 1933

2c Jean Martha Netta FitzJohn; *b* 20 Dec 1908; *m* 1st 15 May 1937 (*divorce* 1951) F/Lt Charles Green, RAF, and had:

1d Timothy John Chalmers; *b* 7 June 1941; *d* unm 1961

2c (cont.) Mrs Jean Green *m* 2nd 17 Nov 1951 Andrea Dudley Richard, 9th Count Metaxa, Cdr RN; *m* 3rd *Hugh Crichton Roberts, of Kensington, and *d* 15 April 1974

1b Evelyn Wilbraham; *d* unm 2 June 1942

2b Ada Wilbraham; ed of magazine in raised type for the blind; *d* unm 22 April 1959

3b Gertrude Wilbraham; *d* unm 29 Feb 1956

2a William Wallace; *b* 9 Aug 1840; *m* 1st 14 July 1864 Elizabeth French (*d* 16 March 1867), dau of Thomas Allin, of Avoncore, Co Cork, and had issue:

1b Frederick Herbert; *b* 12 Nov 1865; MA Oxford; Fell All Souls; formerly Sr Examiner Bd of Educn; *m* 15 July 1891 Lilian Isabel (*d* 20 April 1961, aged 92), dau of Robert Fox, of Grove Hill, Falmouth, and *d* 11 June 1923, leaving issue:

1c WALLACE TALBOT TRENCH later WALDO TRENCH-FOX (deed poll 19 July 1934), MC; *b* 11 May 1892; WW I as Maj Canadian Militia, Croix de Guerre; Nigerian CS; CC Cornwall; *m* 1 June 1933 Janet Mary Kennedy (*d* 1987), dau of MacIvor Bassett, and *d* 11 March 1954, leaving:

1d +Robert Trench, CBE (1993) [Robert Fox Esq CBE, Cheriton House, Alresford, Hants]; *b* 1 Jan 1937; *educ* Winchester and Univ Coll Oxford (MA); *m* 6 Sept 1962 *Lindsay Garrett, 3rd dau of Sir Donald Forsyth Anderson (*see* LEWELLYN, Bt), and has:

1e +Barclay Trench; *b* 27 April 1971

2e +Caspar Lloyd; *b* 6 Oct 1972

1e *Fenella Garrett; *b* 23 Oct 1964; *m* 8 Sept 1990 *John Francis Dernie and has:

1f *Oliver Garrett; *b* 13 March 1995

2f *Joshua George; *b* 8 May 1997

2e *Tamara Forsyth; *b* 24 June 1967; *m* 8April 1995 *Robert Denzil Onslow and has issue (*see* ONSLOW,E)

1d *Jill Trench [Mrs Donald Morison, Boskenna, St Martin in Meneage, Helston, Cornwall]; *b* 3 April 1935; High Sheriff Cornwall 1996–97; *m* 1st 27 Dec 1955 Lt Rodney Francis Power Carne, RN (presumed drowned off Australia while on active service with Fleet Air Arm 26 Feb 1959), yst s of Capt William Power Carne, CBE, RN, of Tresahor Vean, Constantine, Cornwall, and has:

1e *Rupert Barclay Power; *b* 6 Nov 1958; *m* 1994 *Julie Evans, of Chichester, and has:

1f *Jerrick Achilles; *b* 1996

1e *Nicola Trench; *b* 9 April 1957; *m* 1985 *Eric McClean, of Co Tyrone, and has:

1f *Angus Carne; *b* 1990

1f *Kirsten Valentine; *b* 1988

1d (cont.) Mrs Rodney Carne *m* 2nd 25 Feb 1961 *Capt Donald Barns Morison, RN, s of Engr R-Adml Richard Barns Morison, CMG, RN, of Woodchurch, Crapstone, Devon, and by him has:

2e *Barnaby Daniel Barns; *b* 23 Dec 1964

1e *Candida Trench; *b* 23 June 1963; *m* 1990 *Robin Spencer, of The Wirral, and has:

1f *Samuel Peter Nelson; *b* 1992

1f *Freya Jill; *b* 1995

2d *Rachel Trench; *b* 9 March 1943; *m* 26 April 1965 *Raymond Joseph Morin, of 52 Bellevue Ave, Haverhill, Mass, USA, BSc (Architecture), Dip (Town & Country Planning), yr s of A Morin, of Haverhill, Mass

2c Desmond Patrick; *b* 14 July 1893; WW I (wounded); *m* 1st 1916 Elfrida Mary Eliott (*d* 27 Feb 1942), dau of Rev Canon Daniel Eliot Young, formerly Vicar of Penzance, and had issue:

1d John Patrick, DSO; *b* 2 Dec 1918; F/Lt RAF WW II; *ka* 8 March 1943

2d +Antony Barclay; *b* 11 Nov 1919; F/Lt RAFVR, WW II 1939–43 (POW); AMIEE (England); consulting engr Ontario; *m* 1st 26 Dec 1940 Sheila Mary, dau of Lawrence Lois Keith, of 59 The Ridge, Hastings, Sussex, and has issue:

1e +Simon Patrick; *b* 23 July 1946

2d (cont.) Antony Trench also adopted:

*Pamela Mary; *b* 16 April 1956

2d (cont.) Antony Trench *m* 2nd 1981 *Doris Lynne, dau of Alvin Radcliffe James, of St Elizabeth, Jamaica

1d Pamela Joan; *d* unm 15 Dec 1939

2d *Heather Mavis; *b* 1925; *m* 25 June 1948 *Robin Krohn Pooley, Headmaster, Dane Court School, Pyrford, Surrey, yst son of Hugh Francis Pooley, of Dane Court School, Pyrford, and nephew of Sir Ernest Pooley, 1st Bt, KCVO (*see* 1963 edn), and has:

1e *Peter John [Peter Pooley Esq, 18 Rivermead Rd, St Leonards, Exeter, Devon EX2 4RL]; *b* 1 Dec 1950; *educ* Bryanston; *m* 1986 *Lynn Kimber, and has issue:

1f *Alice Jane; *b* 1990

1e (cont.) Mr and Mrs Pooley also adopted:

*Catherine Susan; *b* 9 March 1958; *m* 1984 *Robert Drake, of Cour de la Bruyère, 27210 Manneville la Raoult Beuzeville, France, and has issue:

1g *Jason Paul; *b* 1980

1g *Georgia; *b* 1985

2g *Jessica; *b* 1989

3g *Madeleine Barbara; *b* 1991

2c (cont.) Desmond Trench *m* 2nd 15 April 1947 Hilda Olive (*d* 1993), dau of Alfred Arthur John Akhurst, of 38 Seafield Rd, Southborne, Hants, and formerly wife of Antony Weare, and *d* 5 Dec 1967

1c Romola; *d* unm 17 June 1930

2c Avice Blanaid; *m* 1934 (*divorce* 1938) John Hanbury Martin, yst son of Waldyve Alexander Hamilton Martin, JP, DL, of Byams, Marchwood, Hants

3c Maeve; *m* 1st 28 Nov 1928 Cyril Hay Shaw (*d* 2 Dec 1937); *m* 2nd 23 April 1945 Percy Richards (*d* 19 May 1957), and *d* 20 Dec 1963

1b Ethel Agnes; *d* unm 18 Nov 1926

2a (cont.) William Trench *m* 2nd 21 April 1870 Catherine Sabine (*d* 31 Dec 1913), dau of Adml Sir Bartholomew James Sullivan, KCB, and *d* 12 Feb 1883, having by her had issue:

2b Claud Llewellyn (Pomeroy); *b* 5 Feb 1881; served as a trooper in S African Constabulary in S African War (medal with three clasps) and as Driver RASC (MT) WW I (two medals); *m* 27 Dec 1911 Annie Elizabeth, er dau of William Charles Davis, of Glen Valley, Saskatchewan, Canada, formerly of Cheltenham, and *d* 5 April 1945, having had issue:

1c Wallace Frederick; *b* 31 Dec 1912; *d* 5 Jan 1913

1c *Muriel Ellen, SRN, RSCN; *m* 1st 27 April 1939 George Edward Bonner, RASC (*ka* France 21 May 1940), son of Bertie Bonner, of 17 Prospect Rd, Child's Hill, London NW2; *m* 2nd 7 June 1948 William Leslie Walter Davison, of Wilmurand, Church Lane, Lelant, nr St Ives, Cornwall, son of Walter Davison, of 24 Lion Rd, Lower Edmonton, London N9, and has issue:

1d *Andrea Elaine; *b* 9 April 1951

2c *Eileen Elizabeth [Mrs Cecil Knight, Cheriton House, Alresford, Hants]; *m* 1937 *Cecil H F Knight, of Wigston Magna, Leics, and has:

1d *Bernard Cecil Frank; *b* 1939; Coldstream Gds; *m* 1965 *Jacqueline Ann, dau of William John Rudkin, of 94 Heacham Dve, Leicester, and has:

1e *Paul; *b* 1968

1d *Elizabeth Ann [Mrs Elizabeth Heighton, The Birches, 11A Willow Pk Dve, Wigston, Leicester]; *b* 1937; *m* 1956 (*divorce* 1973) John David Heighton, and has:

1e *David Peter; *b* 1957

2e *Brian John; *b* 1958; *m* 1977 *Ellen Lucell Glover, and has issue:

1f *Richard James Brian; *b* 1981

2f *Alexander Charles Luke; *b* 1983

1f *Claire Samantha Lucell; *b* 1978

1e *Suzanne Elizabeth; *b* 1961

2d *Catherine Beryl [Mrs Patrick Roddy, 5 Highcroft, Husbands Bosworth, Leics]; *b* 1945; *m* 1968 *Patrick James Roddy, and has:

1e *Christopher James; *b* 1970

1e *Paula Louise; *b* 1972

3d *Hazel Mary [Mrs Martin Oliver, 9 Dalby Rd, Anstey, Leics]; *b* 1949; *m* 1975 *Martin Oliver, and has:

1e *Nigel Edward Llewellyn; *b* 1985

1e *Heidi Joanne; *b* 1974

2e *Gwen Georgina; *b* 1976

3e *Jaqui Eve Marie; *b* 1979

4e *Ruth Christina; *b* 1982

3c *Jean Olive, RSCN; *m* 1 June 1944 *Denis Stannard Waring Foreman, RASC, of 61 Roehampton Dve, Wigston Fields, Leics LES 1HU, son of William Stannard Foreman, of 11 Hungerford St, Cheltenham, and adopted:

*Martin John [Martin Foreman Esq, 15 Midland Cottages, S Wigston, Leics LE8 2BU]; *b* 1957; *m* 1989 *Sarah J M Colbert, and has issue:

1e *Ian James; *b* 1990

*Jill Rosemary [Mrs Jill Egginton, 47 Winford Cres, Leicester LE3 1TA]; *b* 1948; *m* 1973 (*divorce* 1980) Alan Egginton and has issue:

1e *Robert John; *b* 1975

2e *David Paul; *b* 1979

2b Frances Sarah; *m* 16 April 1904 Isaac John Trew Colquhoun, BA (*d* Nov 1944), son of Thomas Colquhoun, of Rockfort, Buncrana, Co Donegal, and *d* 6 Aug 1958

3b Kathleen Elizabeth; *d* unm 30 June 1952

3a George Frederic, JP Kerry; *b* 6 Aug 1841; *educ* Trin Coll, Dublin (BA); FSI; *m* 1st 25 May 1868 Frances Charlotte (*d* 13 Jan 1907), yst dau of William Talbot Crosbie, of Ardfert Abbey, Co Kerry, and had issue:

1b Ernest Frederic Crosbie, CBE (1920); *b* 6 Aug 1869; *educ* Trin Coll Dublin (MA); MICE; Col late Engrg and Rlwy Staff Corps RE, TD, formerly Ch Engr LMS Rlwy, Past Pres Inst of Civ Engrs; *m* 3 April 1895 Netta Wilbraham (ld 9 May 1950), est dau of Herbert Wilbraham Taylor, JP, of Hadley Bourne, Barnet, Herts, and *d* 15 Sept 1960, having had issue:

1c Maurice Crosbie; *b* 29 April 1896; F/O RAF 45 Sqdn; *k* whilst flying 24 April 1923

2c Dermot George Crosbie; *b* 3 Jan 1904; *educ* Charterhouse and Trin Coll Cambridge (MA); chartered accountant; *m* 17 June 1938 *Nancy Muriel [Mrs Dermot Trench, El Mirador, MG-CA19, Javea, Alicante, Spain], dau of Dr Stewart Arthur Smith, of Sydney, Australia, and *d* 1984, leaving issue:

1d +Anthony Crosbie; *b* 1 April 1941

1d *Patricia Ann; *b* 16 July 1944; *m* 1976 *Roger A Nuttall, of 46 Grayton Rd, London NW3, and has issue:

1e *Tom Oliver; *b* 1977

1e *Peggy Ellen Nan; *b* 1980

3c Brian Morley Crosbie; *b* 16 April 1908; *educ* Charterhouse and New Coll Oxford (BA 1929, MA 1936); slr; *m* 11 June 1938 Harriett Milward (*d* 1981), er dau of John Lyons Agnew, of Ontario, and *d* 1979, leaving:

1d *Jonathan Agnew [Jonathan Trench Esq, 29 West Parade, Norwich]; *b* 2 March 1939; *educ* Gordonstoun and Ch Ch Oxford (BA 1963); *m* 25 Jan 1969 *Sarah, dau of Don Cameron Williams, of Kansas City, Missouri, USA, and has issue:

1e *Mary Olivia; *b* in Bangkok, 20 May 1972

1d *Amanda Milward [Mrs Amanda Radice, 12A Caithness Rd, London W14 0JB]; *b* 21 Sept 1941; *m* 15 April 1961 (*divorce* 1979) Jonathan Radice, and has:

1e *James Heneage; *b* 4 Nov 1961

2e *Daniel Brett; *b* 2 April 1967

4c Desmond Ernest Crosbie; *b* 23 Sept 1911; F/Lt RAF; *m* 5 May 1937 *Dorothy Waugh [Mrs William Spencer, Erme Wood, Ivybridge, Devon] (who *m* 2nd 9 May 1953 Maj William Spencer, 3rd son of Ralph Spencer, of Nether Wilton, Northumberland), dau of Maj H C Shewell, RGA, and was *ka* 26 Feb 1941, leaving issue:

1d *Josephine Crosbie; *b* 7 Aug 1938; *m* 24 April 1965 *David N McCowan, of Pursehouse St, W Goroka, Territory of New Guinea, and has issue:

1e *Jonathan David; *b* 19 Dec 1965

1e *Deborah Kate; *b* 14 Sept 1967

2d *Kerry Deborah; *b* posthumously 22 Aug 1941; *m* 2 July 1965 *Michael Honnor, of Wilkeysmoor, Cornwood, Ivybridge, Devon, son of Col N P Honnor, and has issue:

1e *Julius Desmond; *b* 1973

2e *Seth Michael; *b* 1976

5c Peter Crosbie; *b* 21 Sept 1912; formerly P/O RAFVR, WW II; *m* 1st 6 June 1941 (*divorce* 1946) Nan Dorice Hunter; *m* 2nd 1947 *Joy Seymour [Mrs Peter Trench, 26A Wells Drive, London NW9 8DG], dau of H Shave, of Calcutta, and *d* 30 Nov 1969, having by her had issue:

1d +Colin Crosbie; *b* 1949; *m* 1st 1972 (*divorce* 1975) Susan Ann Saunders; *m* 2nd 1976 *Susan Wooldridge, and by her has issue:

1e *Jacqueline; *b* 1979

2e *Joanna; *b* 1984

3e *Michelle; *b* 1985

1c Noreen Charlotte; *b* 2 Nov 1899; *m* 21 Jan 1922 Sir Stephen Lewis Holmes, KCMG, MC, MA, Ch Ch Oxford, UK High Commr Australia 1952–56, (*d* 1980), er surv s of Basil Holmes, JP, and *d* 1990, leaving:

1d Michael Trench; *b* 1923; *educ* Eton and Ch Ch Oxford (MA); slr; had by Janet Mary Wakefield Logie (*d* 1992):

1e *Theodora; *b* 1957; MA Oxon; *m* 1990 *Stephen Andrew McCubbin and has:

1f *Michael; *b* 1993

1d (cont.) Michael Holmes *m* 1968 *Thelma Heather Storch and *d* 1975, leaving by her:

2e *Charlotte Clemency Magor; *b* 1971

2d *Richard Tilt [Richard Holmes Esq, 1 Baronsmead Rd, London SW13 9RR]; *b* 1924; *educ* Charterhouse and Ch Ch Oxford, Fl/Lt RAFVR; *m* 1954 *Susan Byrne, dau of C H B Chatteris, and has:

1e *Jasper Stephen; *b* 1962

1e *Prudence Mary [Mrs Norman Beckett, 32 Barleyfields, Didcot, Oxon]; *b* 1956; *m* 1983 *Norman Graham Beckett and has:

1f *Matthew Graham; *b* 1983

2f *Adam Richard; *b* 1986

2e *Miranda Jane [Miss Miranda Holmes, 14 Burcot Farm Cottages, Burcot, nr Abingdon, Oxon]; *b* 1959; by *David John Scott has:

1f *Amy Clare; *b* 1986

2f *Olivia Jane; *b* 1988

1d *Jennifer Prudence Trench [Mrs Cholmondeley Darvall, 41 William St, Rose Bay, Sydney, NSW 2029, Australia]; *b* 1929; *m* 1953 *Cholmondeley Darvall, QC, of Sydney, Australia, and has:

1e *Cholmondeley [Cholmondeley Darvall Esq, 9 Prospect St, Waverley, NSW 2024, Australia]; *b* 1957; *educ* Macquarie U (BA)

1e *Cassandra Holmes [Mrs Michael Bartolomei, 45 Imperial Ave, Bondi, NSW 2026, Australia]; *b* 1964; *educ* Sydney U (BA); *m* 1996 *Michael James Bartolomei

2b George David; *b* 6 March 1872; *d* 26 Nov 1877

3b Lionel Aime; *d* an infant March 1876

4b William Launcelot Crosbie, CIE (1936); *b* 22 July 1881; *educ* The Leys Sch Cambridge and Trin Coll Dublin (BA 1904); MICE; Ch Engr Sind; *m* 1st 19 March 1910 Margaret Zephanie (*d* 30 Oct 1934), yst dau of Rev W P Huddleston, and had:

1c George Shan Crosbie; *b* 6 Aug 1913; *educ* Stowe; Lt-Col RA WW II (despatches, POW); *m* 1 Dec 1945 *Myrtle Sheila [Mrs George Trench, 105 Walsall Rd, Four Oaks, Sutton Coldfield, Warwicks B74 4NP], est dau of H Jerrett, of Crofton, Meols, Cheshire, and *d* 8 April 1995, leaving:

1d +Barney George Crosbie [Barney Trench Esq, 83 Rue Marie Therese, Brussels 1210, Belgium]; *b* 17 Sept 1947; *educ* St Edward's Sch Oxford and St Catherine's Coll Oxford; *m* 3 Sept 1982 *Marjorie (Midge) Shirley and has:

1e +Felix William Crosbie; *b* 14 Dec 1986

1d *Margaret Felicity; *b* 29 Dec 1953

2c David Clive Crosbie (Sir), GCMG (1969, KCMG 1962, CMG 1960), MC (1944), DL (Dorset 1979); *b* 2 June 1915; *educ* Tonbridge and Jesus Coll Cambridge (MA); entered Colonial Serv 1938, WW II with Solomon Islands Def Force, Lt-Col 1945, jssc 1949, Assist Sec Hong Kong 1950, idc 1958, Dep Colonial Sec Hong Kong 1959–60, HC Western Pacific Territories 1961–64, Govr Hong Kong 1964–71, KStJ; Hon LLD U Hong Kong 1968; *m* 18 Aug 1944 *Margaret [Lady Trench, Church House, Church Rd, Shillingstone, Dorset], dau of Jay D Gould, of New York, and *d* 1988, leaving:

1d *Katherine Elizabeth [Mrs Christopher Down, 5A Bronsart Rd, London SW6 6AJ]; *b* 28 Dec 1956; *m* 1984 *Christopher John Down, s of Frederick William Down

1c Ruth Zephanie Charlotte; *b* 5 Jan, *d* 3 Aug 1918

4b (cont.) William Trench *m* 2nd 12 Nov 1935 Eileen Beatrice Cecil (*d* 1980), dau of Henry Carmichael Marsh, of Hove, and *d* 2 June 1949

1b Elizabeth Mary; *b* 16 Jan 1871; *m* 24 March 1896 Lt-Col Rev William Edward Wingfield, DSO, and *d* 25 Nov 1939 leaving issue (*see* POWERSCOURT, V)

2b Ruth Emma; *b* 28 Sept 1879; *m* 30 March 1904 Lt-Col Michael Biddulph, OBE, (*see* BIDDULPH, B), and *d* 10 Dec 1930.

3b Emily Olive Victoria, MBE (1948); *b* 2 April 1887; *m* 22 May 1923 Mark Edwin Botham, son of Thomas Earlam Botham, of Congleton, Cheshire

3a George Trench *m* 2nd 7 Sept 1910 Edith (*d* 6 March 1954), yr dau of Sir Samuel Lee Anderson, of Dublin, and *d* 11 Nov 1915

4a James Currie; *b* 24 June 1848; *m* 6 March 1883 Annie Gertrude (*d* 18 Sept 1944), er dau of John Haughton, of Adreigh, Athy, Co Kildare, and *d* 25 Jan 1936, leaving issue:

1b Frederic FitzCurrie; Capt RTC WW I; *b* 1 June 1889; *m* 1 Aug 1911 Harriette Elizabeth (*d* 1964), yst dau of Thomas Fagan, JP, Racefield of Kingstown, Co Dublin, and *d* 5 Sept 1961, leaving:

1c Doreen Virginia; *m* 1st 31 March 1934 John Richard Needham and had two sons and a dau; *m* 2nd 5 Sept 1952 (*divorce* 1963) Stuart William Glover, MA, PhD; *m* 3rd 1963 Charles Richard Holdom, of Esher, Surrey, and *d* 14 Feb 1969

2b Alfred Lionel; *b* 7 Sept 1894; *d* 7 April 1912

1b Aileen Agnes; *b* 14 Jan 1891; *m* 28 July 1936 Louis W E Evans (*d* 29 June 1952)

2b Muriel Constance; *b* 22 Jan 1892; *m* 30 March 1920 Raymond Croisdale Stevenson, ARIBA (*d* 23 Dec 1962), only s of Thomas Alfred Stevenson, of Stamford Hill, London, and *d* 2 Nov 1964

3b Amy Feodora; *b* 27 Jan 1896; *m* 5 Sept 1922 James Alfred Stuart-Watt, of Dublin (*d* 1975), s of Stuart Watt, of Kenya, and had:

1c *Lionel Robert [Lionel Stuart-Watt Esq, 3 Ystrad Bldgs, Trethomas, Newport, Gwent]; *b* 17 March 1924; *m* 24 Oct 1959 *Elizabeth Maureen, only dau of Edward Colston Buckley, of Trethomas, Mon, and adopted:

*Janet Elizabeth; *b* 7 March 1964

2c Peter Alfred Brian; *b* 29 April 1925; *d* 13 July 1952

3c David Maiben; *b* 26 Aug 1929; *d* 27 Oct 1931

4b Maria Helene Elizabeth; *b* 19 Dec 1897; *d* unm 4 Feb 1964

5a Arthur Francis; *b* 25 March 1849; *d* June 1896

1a Agnes Deborah; *m* 30 April 1872 as his 1st wife John Chaigneau Colvill, 2nd s of John Chaigneau Colvill, of Coolock House, Co Dublin, and *d* 23 Nov 1895. He *d* 21 April 1927

2a Jean Helen Georgina; *m* 28 May 1874 Emil Moritz von Bernus, of Frankfurt and Schardau Falkenstein im Taunus. and *d* 17 Dec 1934. He *d* 1913

(2) James Currie; *b* 1809; *d* 1832

(3) Francis Arthur; *b* 11 Jan 1816; *m* 27 Jan 1848 Emily (*d* 7 April 1848), yst dau of George Littledale, and *d* 14 Aug 1868, having had issue:

1a Arthur, JP (Cos Cavan and Fermanagh); *b* 6 March 1851; *m* 11 Dec 1883 Lilian Jean Maria (*d* 19 March 1951), dau of Rev John Edmund Trench (*see* below), and *d* 15 April 1934, having had issue:

1b Vera Esteile Stephanie Marie-de-las-Mercedes; *m* 28 July 1906 Richard Arthur Austen Leigh, son of Cholmeley Austen Leigh, and *dsp* 11 Dec 1927

2b Yvonne Olga Gabrielle Marie-Angèle; *m* 5 May 1937 René de Lessert (*d* 1956), of the Château de Vincy, Gilly, Switzerland, and *dsp* 1956

2a George Harry; *b* 14 Oct 1852; *m* 29 Nov 1906 Caroline Beatrice (*d* 12 June 1928), est dau of Col Eugene Hay Cameron RA, and *d* Sept 1929

3a Francis Ponsonby, MB and CM Edin; *b* 25 Oct 1854; *d* 2 Jan 1925

4a Frederic John; *b* 27 Dec 1855; *d* 13 March 1900

1a Harriet Helena; *m* 1st 24 March 1870 Maj-Gen Alfred George Huyshe, CB (*d* 6 Aug 1886); *m* 2nd1889 Capt Charles Sedgfield Donner, RN (*d* 1892), and *d* 12 Oct 1937

2a Lucy Alice; *d* unm 28 Aug 1906

3a Florence Jane Constance; Sister of All Saints Community, Bombay; *d* 1 Jan 1915

4a Blanche Emily; *m* 1st 18 Dec 1889 Charles George Buchanan Dunlop (*d* 2 Sept 1897), and had issue; *m* 2nd 1905 Richard Durant Robinson (*d* 9 Nov 1909), of Les Myrtes, Cap d'Antibes, France, and *d* 26 Sept 1937

5a Harriet Evelyn; *d* unm 9 July 1882

(4) John Edmund (Rev); *b* 6 Oct 1818; MA; *m* 2 April 1856 Anne (*d* 1909), dau of J Cuff Gildea, of Cloona Castle, Co Mayo, and *d* 15 Oct 1860, leaving issue:

1a Frederic John Arthur, CVO (1906), DSO (1902); *b* 2 Feb 1857; Col RA, Zululand 1879, S Africa 1901–02, Mil Attaché Berlin 1906–10; *m* 14 Feb 1900 Anne Somerville (*d* 1 July 1941), dau of John Craddock, of Tuscaloosa, Alabama, and *dsp* 23 March 1942

1a Lilian Jean Maria; *m* 11 Dec 1883 Arthur Trench (*see* above), and *d* 19 March 1951

(1) Lucy Henrietta; *m* 13 Nov 1844 William W Pole Piggott (*d* 1886), of Kilcavan, and *d* 1895

(2) Sophia Mary; *d* unm 23 July 1809

The 1st BARON's n,

FREDERICK MASON TRENCH, **2nd Baron Ashtown**; *b* 25 Dec 1804; *m* 1st 29 Aug 1831 Harriette Georgiana (*d* 25 Feb 1845), yst dau of Thomas Cosby, of Stradbally Hall, Queen's Co; *m* 2nd 10 Feb 1852 Elizabeth (*d* 23 Feb 1893), 2nd dau and co-heir of Richard Oliver Gascoigne, of Parlington, Yorks, and *d* 12 Sept 1880, having by his 1st w had:

1 Frederick Sydney Charles; *b* 18 April 1839; *m* 30 April 1867 Lady Anne Le Poer Trench (*d* 12 March 1924), est dau of 3rd Earl of Clancarty (*qv*), and *dvp* 2 March 1879, leaving:

(1) FREDERICK OLIVER TRENCH, **3rd Baron Ashtown**, DL Co Galway; *b* 2 Feb 1868; rep I peer 1908–15; *m* 11 Jan 1894 Violet Grace (*d* 2 Sept 1945), yst dau of Col Robert Ashworth Godolphin Cosby, of Stradbally Hall, Queen's Co, and *d* 20 March 1946, having had:

1a Frederic Sydney; *b* 9 Dec 1894; Lt KRRC WW I 1914–16 (wounded three times); *d* 16 Nov 1916 of wounds received in action the previous day

2a ROBERT POWER TRENCH, **4th Baron Ashtown**; *b* 27 April 1897; Lt 3rd Bn Roy W Surrey Regt; *m* 1st 20 Oct 1926 (*divorce* 1938) Geraldine Ida (*d* as the result of an accident 11 Oct 1940), 4th dau of Sir Henry Foley Grey, 7th Bt (*see* LAMBERT, Bt); *m* 2nd 27 June 1950 his cousin Oonah Anne (*d* 1984), er dau of Brig-Gen Lewis Frederic Green-Wilkinson, CMG, DSO, by his wife Hon Sarah May Trench, sister of 3rd Baron Ashtown (*see* above), and *dsp* 3 Nov 1966

3a Arthur Cosby; *b* 3 July 1899; *d* 29 Nov 1918

4a DUDLEY OLIVER TRENCH, **5th Baron Ashtown**, OBE (1961); *b* 11 July 1901; *educ* Wellington and RMC Sandhurst; Lt-Col KRRC, Assist Instr Netheravon Wing Small Arms Sch 1929–31, Adj: KRRC 1932, 11th London Regt (TA) 1935–36 and 16th London Regt 1936–38, WW II with KRRC (despatches); Assist Ch Constable War Dept Constabulary 1947–64; *m* 1st 1 Dec 1932 Ellen Nancy (*d* 10 March 1939), yr dau of William Garton, of Brixedone, Bursledon, Hants, and had issue:

1b *Anne Rosemary; *b* 19 Dec 1936; *m* 1st 1 Oct 1958 Capt Timothy Patrick Arnold Gosselin, Scots Gds (*d* 17 March 1961), only son of Brig Arthur Nicholas Gosselin, CBE, DSO, of Warickdale, Symington, Ayrshire, and has issue:

1c *Nicola Jane; *b* 13 Aug 1960

1b (cont.) The Hon Mrs Gosselin *m* 2nd 2 March 1962 *Maj Greville Wyndham Tufnell, Gren Gds, Clerk of the Cheque and Adj Yeomen Gd, of The Old Rectory, North Cerney, Cirencester, Glos, son of Maj Kenneth

Edward Mortimer Tufnell, MC, of West Soke Farm, Silchester, nr Reading, Berks, and has further issue:

2c *Caroline Elizabeth; *b* 1 April 1963

3c *Belinda Sheelagh Anne; *b* 18 June 1964

4c *Georgina Frances; *b* 27 Oct 1966

2b *Jacqueline Noel; *b* 22 Dec 1940; *m* 14 April 1966 *Alastair Gordon Eadie, dir IDV (UK) Ltd, W A Gilbey and Morgan Furze Ltd, of Bourne Orchard, Brickendon, Herts, yr son of Col James Alister Eadie, DSO, TD, DL, of Bramfield House, Herts, and has issue:

1c *James Alastair; *b* 4 June 1967

2c *Christopher John; *b* 16 March 1969

3c *Edward Charles; *b* 1972

4a (cont.) The **5th Baron** *m* 2nd 28 Nov 1955 Sheelah Adrienne Sarah (*d* 9 July 1963), yr dau of Brig-Gen Lewis Frederic Green-Wilkinson, CMG, DSO, by his wife Hon Sarah May Trench, sister of 3rd Baron Ashtown (*see* above); *m* 3rd 27 Jan 1966 Frances Natalie (*d* 19 Sept 1979), dau of Maj Hermon Barker-Hahlo, of La Petite Vallée, Rue de Putron, St Martin, Guernsey, CI, and widow of James Fenwick de Sales La Terriere, of Dunalastair, Perthshire, and *dspm* 19 Aug 1979

1a Grace Mary; *b* 7 May 1896; SRN, WWs I and II; *d* unm 18 Jan 1975

(2) William Cosby, of Clonodfoy Castle, Co Limerick, JP; *b* 23 Jan 1869; High Sheriff 1805; *m* 7 Sept 1893 Frances Elizabeth (*d* 30 Oct 1950), only dau of Walter Taylor Newton Shawe Taylor, DL, of Castle Taylor, Co Galway, and *d* 12 March 1944, having had:

1a Percy Richard Oliver; *b* 31 July 1894; Capt Roy West Surrey Regt; *ka* 25 Jan 1917

2a Walter Frederick Oliver; *b* 10 March 1899; late F/O RFC and RAF, WW I 1917–19; Dir Kenya Farmers' Assoc 1930; *m* 1st 8 Feb 1921 Norah Maude (*d* 28 April 1958), yr dau of Ven John Richard Hedges Becher, Archdeacon of Ross, and had:

1b John Cecil Oliver; *b* 23 Sept 1923; P/O RAF, WW II; *ka* Middle East 22 Oct 1942

2b Kieran Hedges Oliver; *b* 24 May 1929; *d* unm 20 May 1960

1b *Olga Ann Oliver [Mrs Olga Hindley, PO Box 377, Richmond, Natal, S Africa]; *b* 3 March 1922; *m* 5 June 1947 (*divorce*) William Hugh Hindley, son of Charles Edward Hugh Hindley, of Dar-es-Salaam, and has issue:

1c *Michael Edward Oliver; *b* 28 June 1950; *m* 1977 *Jane Mary Brimacombe, of Devizes, Wilts, and has issue:

1d *Alexander William Oliver (John); *b* 1980

2d *Lawrence Hugh John; *b* 1982

3d *Thomas Henry Walter; *b* 1984

1d *Caroline Jane; *b* 1988

2c *Douglas William John; *b* 16 July 1963

1c *Sheila Rachel; *b* 16 Nov 1949; *m* 1981 *Christopher Davis

2b Rachel; *b* and *d* 2 Nov 1926

3b *Norah Susan Oliver; *b* 23 Dec 1936; *m* 2 Nov 1957 *Walter Stuart Gash, MBE, of Rocklea, Mitchell Rd, Walliston, W Australia 6076, son of Alexander Gash, of Nairobi, Kenya, and has issue:

1c *Maureen Susan; *b* 20 March 1959; *m* 1980 *Gregory John Gittos, of 5 Cooper Ridge, Winthrop, W Australia 6150, and has issue:

1d *Michael John; *b* 1987

1d *Lisa Marie; *b* 1988

2c *Shelia Ann; *b* 26 Nov 1960; *m* 1981 (*divorce* 1985) Kevin John McDowall

2a (cont.) Walter Trench *m* 2nd 3 Feb 1960 *Marian Gwendolyn, dau of Robert Young, of Beech House, Woolley, Yorks, and *d* 22 March 1960

3a Algernon Oliver; *b* 22 June 1900; *m* 24 Nov 1928 Muriel Dorothy (*d* 1954), est dau of Frank Thorne, of Weston-super-Mare, and *d* Dec 1955, leaving issue:

1b CHRISTOPHER OLIVER TENCH, **6th Baron Ashtown**; *b* 23 March 1931; *educ* Owen Sound High Sch, Ontario; with Canadian Imperial Bank of Commerce 1950–57; *d* unm 1990

4a A son; *b* 28 Feb 1908; *d* an infant

(3) Sydney; *b* 9 Jan 1877; *m* 6 Nov 1905 Elinor Mary (who *m* 3rd 7 Jan 1908 Brig-Gen Ronald Campbell Machachlan, DSO, Rifle Bde (*ka* 11 Aug 1917)), dau of J C Cox of Sydney, NSW, and widow of William Martins Le Poer Trench of Coorheen, Vancouver (*see* CLANCARTY, E), and *dsp* 16 Dec 1905

(1) Charlotte Anne; *b* 13 Jan 1871; *m* 11 March 1903 Alan Theodore Smythe (*d* 7 Jan 1941), est son of Richard Altamont Smythe, of Courtnafaraga, Killiney, and *d* 28 Aug 1947, leaving issue

(2) Sarah May; *b* 17 Aug 1873; *m* 18 May 1904 Brig-Gen Lewis Frederic Green-Wilkinson, CMG, DSO, Legion of Honour, late Rifle Bde (*d* 11 April 1950), son of Lt-Gen Frederic Green-Wilkinson, CB, and *d* 30 March 1934, leaving issue

2 Cosby Godolphin, of Sopwell Hall, Cloughjordan, Co Tipperary, JP and DL (Co Tipperary), JP (Co Waterford); *b* 6 Jan 1844; late Capt 1st Dragoons; High Sheriff Tipperary 1886; *m* 19 June 1873 Maria (*d* 4 Nov 1938), est dau of Sir Richard Musgrave, 4th Bt (*qv*), and *d* 9 Dec 1925, having had issue:

(1) Charles Sadleir Musgrave, JP and DL (Co Tipperary); *b* 15 April 1874; *educ* Eton; formerly Capt and Adj Northumberland Fus; *m* 11 Feb 1914 Helen Cowley (*d* 14 Oct 1937), 5th dau of Robert Lidwill Brown, of Clonboy, Co Clare, and *d* 16 May 1958, leaving issue:

1a Cosby Patrick Musgrave; *b* 14 Jan 1915; *educ* Eton and Trin Coll, Dublin (BA 1939); *m* 17 May 1956 *Julia Violetta May dau of Frank Porch, and widow of Frank Louis Whiting, and *dsp* 29 April 1983

(2) Edward Cosby; *b* 1 May 1881; formerly Hon Attaché Diplomatic Serv; *m* 5 Feb 1910 Evelyn de Courcy (*d* 22 Nov 1965), est dau of Col de Courcy Daniell, late RA, and *dsp* 21 Oct 1961

(3) Clive Newcome; *b* 7 July 1884; *m* 27 Jan 1910 Kathleen Maud Marion (*d* 1979), 2nd dau of Maj Ivar MacIvor, CSI, and *d* 24 Feb 1964, leaving issue:

1a NIGEL CLIVE COSBY TRENCH, **7th and present Baron Ashtown**

1a *Lois Eileen, JP (Nairn) [The Hon Mrs Mackintosh-Walker JP, Geddes House, Nairn]; *b* 14 Dec 1910; *m* 20 March 1937 Capt Charles Algernon Mackintosh-Walker, MBE, late QO Cameron Highrs (*d* 1 Sept 1964), est son of Thomas Charles Bruce Mackintosh-Walker, MBE, DL, of Geddes, Nairn, and has:

1b *(Charles) James [James Mackintosh-Walker Esq, Geddes House, Nairn]; *b* 17 May 1939; *educ* Rugby; *m* 14 Oct 1967 *Elizabeth Margaret, dau of Charles Stewart, CMG, OBE, of the Cottage, Dunvegan, Skye, and has had:

1c Ewen Charles; *b* 22 March 1970; *d* 1980

2c *Andrew Eneas; *b* 1976

1c *Maria Jane; *b* 24 Dec 1968

2c *Sarah Emily; *b* 1972

1b *Serena Mary; *b* 30 March 1946; *m* 1st 12 Oct 1968 (*divorce* 1976) Hugh Robert Norton, of Flat 2, 9–11 Richmond Bldgs, Dean St, London W1, 2nd son of Leslie C Norton; *m* 2nd 1976 *Dr Kenneth Mitchell Nuttall

(4) Hubert Roland; *b* 3 Feb 1887; *d* unm 29 Dec 1911

1 Charlotte Elizabeth; *d* 19 Dec 1854

2 Harriette Mary; *m* 6 Feb 1883 Hon Frederick Le Poer Trench, 2nd son of 3rd Earl of Clancarty (*qv*), and *d* 16 July 1884

ASKE

Arms: Argent a martlet sable between two bars azure, each charged with as many cross-crosslets of the first. **Crest:** In front of a Saracen's head proper wreathed around the temples argent and azure, two roses argent. **Creation:** Bt. (UK) 21 Jan 1922.

SIR CONAN ASKE, 2ND BT, of Aughton, East Riding of Yorks [The Rev Sir Conan Aske Bt, 167 Malvern Rd, Worcester WR2 4NN]; *b* 22 April 1912; *s* f 1954; *educ* Rugby and Balliol Coll Oxford (MA); Hon Maj E Yorks Regt, Civil Affrs Offr Res Area Ethiopia and Ogaden 1949–51; *m* 1st 13 Dec 1948 Vera (*d* 17 July 1960), yr dau of George Rowbotham, of Iffley, Oxford, and formerly w of Roland Faulkner; *m* 2nd 23 Aug 1965 Rebecca (*d* 21 Jan 1996), yr dau of Hugh Fraser Grant, of Wick, Caithness

Lineage: ROBERT ASKE, of Bubwith, Yorks; had:

EDWARD ASKE, of Hull; had:

Sir Robert William Aske, 1st Bt (UK), so *cr* 21 Jan 1922, TD, KC (1934), JP (Surrey); *b* 29 Dec 1872; *educ* London (LLD, Gold medallist); Lt-Col TA Res, slr 1894, Dep Sheriff Hull 1906–08, barrister Middle Temple 1914, Bencher 1942, MP (Lib) Newcastle-upon-Tyne E 1923–24 and 1929–45, ktd 1911; *m* 1st 17 Feb 1899 Edith (*d* 20 Jan 1900), dau of Charles McGregor; *m* 2nd 2 June 1909 Edith (*d* 22 June 1918), dau of Sir Walter Herbert Cockerline, JP, and *d* 10 March 1954, leaving:

1 Sir CONAN ASKE, **2nd and present Bt**

2 +ROBERT EDWARD [Robert Aske Esq, 45 Holland Rd, London W14]; *b* 21 March 1915; heir presumptive; *educ* Harrow and Balliol Coll Oxford (MA); *m* 20 Jan 1940 *Joan Bingham, only dau of Capt Eric Bingham Ackerley, of White Lodge, Cobham, Surrey, and has issue:

(1) +Robert John Bingham [Robert Aske Esq, 20 Christopher Rd, E Grinstead, Sussex]; *b* 12 March 1941; *educ* King's Sch Canterbury

1 *Margaret; *b* 6 April 1910; *m* 22 Dec 1936 Richard Du Vivier, CBE, MA, of 45 Chatsworth Rd, Ealing, London W5, son of James Eastwood Du Vivier, of La Ferme, Lacthem-St Martin, nr Ghent, Belgium, and has issue:

(1) Charles Richard; *b* 8 April 1938; *educ* Malvern and King's Coll Cambridge; *d* 1992

(2) *Hugh Michael [Hugh Du Vivier Esq, 43 Britannia Rd, London SW6 2HJ]; *b* 13 Feb 1945; *educ* Malvern and Trin Coll Dublin; *m* 1969 *Jacqueline Sarah, dau of Harry Reginald Albert de Belleroche, of 38 De Vere Gdns, London W8, and has issue:

1a *Juliet Amy; *b* 1979

1a *Katherine Lucy Sarah; *b* 1984

(1) *Carol Anne [Mrs Allan Shaw, 28 La Roche Dve, Humewood 6001, Port Elizabeth, S Africa]; *b* 8 July 1941; *m* 1st 1963 (*divorce* 1969) Bearnard O'Riain, of Dun Laoghaire, Co Dublin, and has issue:

1a *Manus Justin; *b* 1966

1a *Natasha Selina; *b* 1963

(1) (cont.) Mrs Carol O'Riain *m* 2nd 1978 *Cmdt Allan Joseph Shaw and has issue:

2a *Nicholas Simon Dominic; *b* 1978

3a *Simon Philip Benedict; *b* 1984

(2) *Nicola Jill [Mrs Gordon Prosser, 7 Hooley Range, Heaton Moor Rd, Stockport, Cheshire SK4 4HU]; *b* 20 March 1953; *m* 1975 *Gordon Walter Prosser and has issue:

1a *Alexander Marcos; *b* 1978

2a *Hugh Angus; *b* 1980

3a *Giles Henry James; *b* 1983

4a *Edward Hamish Neal; *b* 1987

2 *Audrey Vivienne; *b* 20 Oct 1917

ASTOR

Arms: Or, a falcon resting on a dexter hand couped at the wrist proper and gauntletted gules, in chief two fleurs-de-lys of the last. **Crest:** From a mount vert a falcon rising proper, ensigned by three mullets gold. **Supporters:** Dexter, a North American Indian; sinister, a North American fur trapper, each habited, accoutred and holding in the exterior hand a rifle, all proper. **Motto:** *Ad astra* ('To the stars'). **Creations:** B. (UK) 26 Jan 1916, V. (UK) 23 June 1917.

THE 4TH VISCOUNT ASTOR, and **Baron Astor,** of Hever Castle, Kent (William Waldorf Astor) [The Rt Hon The Viscount Astor, Ginge Manor, Wantage, Oxon OX12 8QT; 27 Egerton Gdns, London SW3 2DE]; *b* 27 Dec 1951, *s f* 1966; *educ* Eton; Tstee Stanley Spencer Gallery, Cookham, 1974–, Ld-in-Waiting 1990–93, Dept Nat Heritage 1992–93, Parly U-Sec DSS and Dept Nat Heritage 1993–95, Oppn Spokesman Ho Lds 1997–; *m* 14 Jan 1976 *Annabel Lucy Veronica, dau of Timothy Angus Jones, of 40 Albert St, London NW1, by Hon Mrs Pandora Astor (*see* below and CLIFFORD OF CHUDLEIGH, B), and formerly wife of Sir Reginald Adrian Berkeley Sheffield, 8th Bt (*qv*), and has issue:

1 +WILLIAM WALDORF; *b* 18 Jan 1979

2 +James Jacob; *b* 1981

1 *Flora Katherine; *b* 7 June 1976

Lineage: JOHN JACOB ASTOR, of New York; *m* Charlotte Augusta (*d* 1887), dau of Thomas Stanyarne Gibbes, and *d* 1890, leaving an only child:

WILLIAM WALDORF, **1st Viscount Astor,** of Hever Castle, Kent, so *cr* 3 June 1917, as also previously 26 Jan 1916 BARON ASTOR, of Hever Castle, Kent (both UK); *b* 31 March 1848; BA Columbia U; lawyer (USA 1875); memb New York State Legislature 1878 and 1881, US Min Italy 1882–88, naturalized in UK 1899; *m* 6 June 1878 Mary Dahlgren (*d* 22 Dec 1894), dau of James William Paul, of Philadelphia, and had issue:

1 WALDORF, **2nd Viscount**

2 JOHN JACOB ASTOR, *cr* BARON ASTOR OF HEVER (*qv*)

1 Pauline, JP (Surrey 1920); *m* 29 Oct 1904 Lt-Col Herbert Henry Spender Clay, CMG, MC, PC, MP (*see* STRATHMORE AND KINGHORNE, E), and *d* 5 May 1972, leaving issue

The 1st VISCOUNT *d* 18 Oct 1919; his er son,

WALDORF ASTOR, **2nd Viscount Astor,** DL (Devon); *b* 19 May 1879; MA New Coll Oxford; T/Maj and Inspr QMG Servs London Dist 1914–17, Hon Col Devon Heavy Bde RA (TA) 1929; MP (Lib) Plymouth 1910–18 and Plymouth Sutton 1918–19, PPS to PM 1917–18, Parly Sec Min Food 1918–19 and Min of Health 1919–21, Lt City London, chm Departmental Commn on Tuberculosis, State Med Research Ctee, League of Nations Ctee on Nutrition 1936–37, Roy Inst Internat Affrs 1935–49, Hon Freeman City London 1934 and City of Plymouth 1936, Master Musicians' Co 1935–36, Ld Mayor Plymouth 1939–44, High Steward Maidenhead; *m* 3 May 1906 Nancy Witcher, CH (1937), MP Plymouth (Sutton) 1919–45 (first woman MP to take seat), Hon Freeman Plymouth 1959, Hon LLD Exeter (1959), Hon LLD Birmingham and Hon D Litt Reading, Hon LLD Coll of William and Mary, Williamsburg, Va. (*d* 2 May 1964), dau of Chiswell Dabney Langhorne, of Mirador, Greenwood, Virginia, USA, and formerly w of Robert Gould Shaw, and had issue:

1 WILLIAM WALDORF, **3rd Viscount**

2 +(Francis) David Langhorne, CH 1994 [The Hon David Astor CH, The Manor House, Sutton Courtenay, Abingdon, Berks; 24 St Anne's Terrace, London NW8; 9 Cavendish Ave, NW8 9JD]; *b* 5 March 1912; *educ* Eton and Balliol Coll Oxford; WW II as Capt RM (Croix de Guerre); foreign ed *The Observer* 1945–48, proprietor/ed 1948–1975; *m* 1st 1 Aug 1945 (*divorce* 1951) Melanie Mathilda Elena, dau of Philip Hauser, of Berne, Switzerland, and has issue:

(1) *Frances Christine Langhorne; *b* 1 March 1947; *m* 13 April 1970 *Dr Miles Frankel, of Kilbrack House, Doneraile, Co Cork, son of Dr Eric Frankel, of 20 Herncon Hill, London E11

2 (cont.) The Hon David Astor *m* 2nd 28 Feb 1952 *Bridget Aphra, est dau of Maj Cyril Wreford, of Yew Tree House, Goosey, Faringdon, Berks, and by her has further issue:

(1) +Richard David Langhorne; *b* 28 April 1955; *m* 1990 *Sarah G H, dau of James Skinner, and has issue:

1a *Bonny Jane; *b* 1992

(2) +Thomas Robert Langhorne; *b* 25 April 1962

(2) *Alice Margaret Frances [Mrs Mark Grindon-Welch, Stockadon Farm, Loddiswell, Kingsbridge, Devon TQ7 4EQ]; *b* 7 Sept 1953; *m* 1st 1972 (*divorce* 1985) Lawrence Woodward, and has issue:

1a *William Lawrence; *b* 1978

1a *Jessica Alice; *b* 1980

(2) (cont.) Mrs Alice Woodward *m* 2nd 1987 *Mark Thomas Luke Grindon-Welch and has further issue:

2a *Adam Thomas Richard; *b* 1988

2a *Rose Aphra Elizabeth; *b* 1991

(3) *Lucy Aphra Nancy; *b* 6 Jan 1958

(4) *Nancy Bridget Elizabeth [Mrs Sean Naidoo, 89 Carlton Mansions, Randolph Ave, London NW1 8UG]; *b* 7 Oct 1960; *m* 1990 *Séan V Naidoo, son of Stanley Naidoo, of Johannesburg, and has issue:

1a *Cara Mary; *b* 1992

3 Michael Langhorne; *b* 10 April 1916; *educ* Eton; Capt late RA (TA); MP (C) Surrey E 1945–51, memb Cncl of Arts Cncl 1968, author: *Tribal Feeling* (1963) and *Brand* (novel, 1968); *m* 1st 28 Nov 1942 (*divorce* 1961) Barbara Mary Colonsay (*d* 1980), only dau of Capt Ronald Frank Rous McNeill, and Mrs John Dewar, of 8 Hyde Park Gdns, London W2, and had:

(1) +David Waldorf, CBE (1994) [David Astor Esq CBE, Bruern Grange, Milton-under-Wychwood, Oxon]; *b* 9 Aug 1943; *educ* Eton and Harvard U; Lt Roy Scots Greys 1962–65, Chm CPRE; *m* 19 Sept 1968 *Clare Pamela, er dau of Cdr Michael Beauchamp St John, DSC, RN (ret), of Bepton Lodge, Midhurst, Sussex (*see* SAINT JOHN OF BLETSO, B), and has issue:

1a +Henry Waldorf; *b* 17 April 1969

2a +Thomas Ludovic David; *b* 1972

1a *Joanna Colonsay Clare; *b* 23 June 1970

2a *Rose Nancy Langhorne; *b* 9 June 1979

(2) +James Colonsay Langhorne; *b* 2 Dec 1945; *educ* Eton; *m* 29 Oct 1972 *Jane M S, dau of Charles de Chazal, of 11 Ossington St, London W2, and has issue:

1a +Tobias; *b* 1980

1a *Katharine Tamsin; *b* 1976

(1) *(Kathleen Nancy) Jane; *b* 9 Aug 1949

(2) *Georgina Mary; *b* 10 March 1952; *m* 1st 3 Nov 1973 (*divorce* 1979) Hon Anthony Ramsay (*see* DALHOUSIE, E) and has issue:

1a *Alexander Simon; *b* 1977

(2) (cont.) Mrs Georgina Ramsay *m* 2nd 1979 *Lorne Nelson, of Kilmaronaig, Connel, Argyll (*see* ANGLESEY, M), and has further issue:

2a *Thomas Michael; *b* 1979

1a *Alice Catherine; *b* 1981

2a *Clare Emma; *b* 1983

3 (cont.) The Hon Michael Astor *m* 2nd 12 July 1961 (*divorce* 1968) (Patricia David) Pandora (*d* 1988), 2nd dau of Hon Sir Bede Edmund Clifford, GCMG, CB, FRGS, of Queen Anne Farm, Jacob's Well, Guildford (*see* CLIFFORD OF CHUDLEIGH, B), and formerly w of Timothy Angus Jones; *m* 3rd 1970 *Judith Caroline Traill [The Hon Mrs Michael Astor, Red Brick House, Bruern, Churchill, Oxon], dau of Paul Innes and formerly w of John Moynihan, and *d* 1980, having adopted his stepson (*Joshua Paul Michael ASTOR, *b* 16 Nov 1966, *educ* Eton) and leaving by her:

(3) *Polly Michael; *b* 1971

4 +John Jacob (Sir), MBE (1945), ERD (1989), JP (1960–74) and DL (1962) (both Cambs) [Maj The Hon Sir John Astor, MBE ERD JP DL, The Dower House, Hatley Pk, Hatley St George, Beds SG19 3HI]; *b* 29 Aug 1918; *educ* Eton and New Coll Oxford; Maj Life Gds WW II Italy, France, Germany and Norway (Legion of Honour, Croix de Guerre), MP (C) Plymouth (Sutton) 1951–59, PPS to Fin Sec Treasury 1951–53; Chm: Govg Body Nat Inst Ag Engrg 1963–68, Ag Research Cncl 1968–78; NEDC Ag Industry 1978–73, memb Horserace Betting Levy Bd 1976–80, Horserace Totalisator Bd 1983–85, Steward Jockey Club 1968–71 and 1983–85, High Sheriff Cambs and Isle of Ely 1967, ktd 1978; *m* 1st 1944 (*divorce* 1972) Ana Inez (*d* 1992), yr dau of Dr Don Miguel Angel Carcano, Hon KCMG, Hon KBE, Argentine Amb UK, and has had issue:

(1) +Michael Ramon Langhorne; *b* 29 Sept 1946; *educ* Eton; *m* 1979 *Daphne, dau of Edward Mortimer Morris Warburg, of Westpoint, Conn.

(2) John William; *b* 29 Nov 1962; *d* 9 March 1963

(1) *Stella Inez; *b* 18 May 1949; *m* 1974 (*divorce* 19–) Martin Wilkinson, of Cwm Hall, Clunton, Craven Arms, Salop, s of Martin Wilkinson, of Thornton Hall, Banbury, Oxon, and has:

1a *Matthew Miguel Angel; *b* 1977

1a *Alice Ana Maria; *b* 1975

4 (cont.) Sir John *m* 2nd 1976 (*divorce* 1985) Mrs Susan Sheppard (*d* 1997), dau of Maj Michael Eveleigh, of Lyddington, Leics; *m* 3rd 1988 *Mrs Marcia de Savary

1 Nancy Phyllis Louise; *b* 22 March 1909; *m* 27 July 1933 3rd Earl of Ancaster (*see* HEATHCOTE, Bt, of London), and *d* 2 March 1975, leaving issue

The 2nd VISCOUNT *d* 30 Sept 1952; his est son,

WILLIAM WALDORF ASTOR, **3rd Viscount Astor**; *b* 13 Aug 1907; *educ* Eton and New Coll Oxford; Lt-Cdr (SR) RNVR, memb Pilgrim Trust 1930–31, Sec to Earl of Lytton League of Nations Ctee of Enquiry in Manchuria 1932, in Unemployment Dept Nat Cncl Soc Serv 1933–34, MP (C) Fulham (E) 1935–45 and Wycombe 1951–52, PPS to 1st Ld Admlty 1936–37 and Home Sec 1937–39, High Steward Maidenhead, Grand Cross of Merit with star and sash SMO Malta; *m* 1st 14 June 1945 (*divorce* 1953) Hon Sarah Katharine Elinor Norton (*m* 2nd 1953 (*divorce* 1965) Lt-Col Thomas Michael Baring, Derbyshire Yeo; *see* NORTHBROOK, B), only dau of 6th Baron Grantley (*qv*), and had issue:

1 WILLIAM WALDORF ASTOR, **4th and present Viscount Astor**

The **3rd Viscount** *m* 2nd 26 April 1955 (*divorce* 1960) Philippa Victoria, est dau of Lt-Col Henry Philip Hunloke, TD, of Pendower House, Ruan High Lanes, S Cornwall, and Lady Anne Montague (*see* DEVONSHIRE, D), and had further issue:

1 *Emily Mary [The Hon Mrs James Anderson, 14 Shalcomb St, London SW10 0HX]; *b* 9 June 1956; photographer; *m* 1st 1984 Alan M C L Gregory, er son of Donald Gregory, of San Francisco; *m* 2nd 1988 (*divorce* 1996), as his 2nd w, James Ian Anderson (*see* PERTH, E), insur broker

The **3rd Viscount** *m* 3rd 14 Oct 1960 *(Janet) Bronwen Alun [The Rt Hon Bronwen Viscountess Astor, Tuesley Manor, Godalming, Surrey], model, yst dau of Judge (Sir John) Alun Pugh, of The Old Rectory, Dunsfold, Surrey, and *d* 7 March 1966, having by her had:

2 *Janet Elizabeth [Countess of March and Kinrara, Goodwood, Chichester, W Sussex PO18 0PX; 7 Charles St, London W1X 7HB]; *b* 1 Dec 1961; *educ* New Coll Oxford (BA) and King's Coll, London (MA); *m* 1991 as his 2nd w Charles Henry, Earl of March and Kinrara, only s of 10th Duke of Richmond and (5th Duke of) Gordon (*qv*)

3 *Pauline Marian [The Hon Mrs Case, Turville Lodge, Turville Heath, Oxon]; *b* 26 March 1964; *m* 1990 *George C V Case, s of Denis Case, of Marlow, Bucks, and has:

(1) *Magdalena Beatrice; *b* 1994

(2) *Nancy Mary; *b* 30 Dec 1996

ASTOR OF HEVER

Arms: Argent, eight barrulets sable overall resting on a dexter hand couped at the wrist proper, gauntleted gules, a falcon also gules, in chief two fleurs-de-lys of the last. **Crest:** Rising from a mount vert a falcon proper ensigned by three mullets or. **Supporters:** Dexter, the figure of Aesculapius; sinister, that of Mercury, both proper.
Motto: *Ad astra* ('To the stars'). **Creation:** B. (UK) 21 Jan 1956.

THE 3RD BARON ASTOR OF HEVER (John Jacob Astor, DL (Kent 1996)) [The Rt Hon The Lord Astor of Hever DL, Frenchstreet House, Westerham, Kent TN16 1PW]; *b* 16 June 1946; *educ* Eton; *s f* 1984; Lt The Life Gds 1966–70, Malaysia, Hong Kong, Ulster; md Honon et Cie 1982, Astor France 1989, Pres Astor Enterprises Inc 1983, Sec Anglo-Swiss Parly Assoc 1992, Jt Treasurer Br-S African Parly Assoc, V-Pres Hearing Research Tst; *m* 1st 18 July 1970 (*divorce* 1990) Fiona Diana Lennox, dau of Capt Roger Edward Lennox Harvey, of Parliament Piece, Ramsbury, Wilts, and has issue:

1 *Camilla Fiona; *b* 8 May 1974

2 *Tania Jentie; *b* 18 April 1978

3 *Violet Magdalene; *b* 1980

The 3rd BARON *m* 2nd 1990 *Hon Elizabeth Constance, yr dau of 2nd Viscount Mackintosh of Halifax (*qv*), and formerly wife of (a) Timothy Cutting and (b) Nicholas Chagrin, and by her has:

1 +CHARLES GAVIN JOHN; *b* 10 Nov 1990

4 *Olivia Alexandra; *b* 21 Aug 1992

Lineage: JOHN JACOB ASTOR, **1st Baron Astor of Hever**, of Hever Castle, Co Kent (UK), so *cr* 21 Jan 1956, JP (1929–62) and DL (1936–62) (both Kent); *b* 20 May 1886 (yr son of 1st Viscount Astor; *qv*); *educ* Eton; joined 1st Life Gds 1906, ADC to Viceroy India 1911–14, WW I (twice wounded, Chev Legion of Honour), cmded Household Siege Battery, Lt-Col 5th Bn City of London HG 1940–44, Hon Col 23rd London Regt (TA) 1928–49 and Kent and Sussex RGA (TA) 1927–46; ch proprietor *The Times* 1922–66, MP (C) Dover 1922–45, Alderman LCC 1922–25, Lt City London, memb Govt Broadcasting Ctee 1923 and 1935, memb Gen Advsy Cncl BBC 1937, Pres Press Club, Pres Newspaper Press Fund, Pres Cwlth Press Union, Chm 4th, 5th, 6th, and 7th Imp Press Conferences, Hon Freeman Dover, memb POUNC 1933, dir: GWR 1929–48, Barclays Bank 1942–52, Hambro's Bank 1934–60, The Times Publishing Co (to 1962), Phoenix Assur (v-chm 1941–52, chm 1952–58), London Guarantee and Accident, Monotype Corp, memb Cncl St Dunstan's 1922–62, Pres Nat Assoc for Employment of Regular Sailors, Soldiers and Airmen 1936–62, Pres Kent Cncl Br Legn 1934–62, V-Pres RCM 1934–62, Chm Middx Hosp 1938–62 and Middx Hosp Med Sch 1945–62, Pres MCC 1937, Kent County Cricket Club 1929, OEA 1942 (Chm 1939–49) and Hurlingham Club (Chm 1929–49), Master of Guild St Bride's Church Fleet Street 1955–62; Hon degrees Us Perth (W Australia) 1925, London 1939 and McGill (Canada) 1950; won Public Sch Racquets 1905 and Army Racquets (singles and doubles) 1908); *m* 28 Aug 1916 Lady Violet Mary Elliot-Murray-Kynynmound, DStJ (*d* 3 Jan 1965), yst dau of 4th Earl of Minto (*qv*) and widow of Lord Charles George Francis Mercer Nairne, MVO (*see* LANSDOWNE, M), and had issue:

1 GAVIN, **2nd Baron**

2 +Hugh Waldorf, JP (Berks 1953) [Lt-Col The Hon Hugh Astor JP, Folly Farm, Sulhamstead, Reading, Berks RG7 4DF; 79 Ashley Gdns, Thirleby Rd, London SW1P 1HG]; *b* 20 Nov 1920; *educ* Eton and New Coll Oxford; WW II as Lt-Col Intell Corps; joined staff The Times Publishing Co 1947 (dir 1956, dep chm 1959–66), Chm The Times Bookshop 1960 (resigned 1967), dir Hutchinson Ltd, Winterbottom Trust Ltd, Hambros Bank Ltd, Phoenix Assur and Olympia Ltd (Dep Chm 1971–73); High Sheriff Berks 1963–64 Tstee THF (Chm Cncl Tstees 1971), Dep Chm Middx Hosp 1962–64, Govr Bradfield and Gresham's, 6th Renter Warden Fishmonger's Co 1975 (Prime Warden 1976–77), KtCdr Star Ethiopia; *m* 8 Nov 1950 *Emily Lucy, est dau of Sir Alexander Davenport Kinloch, 12th Bt, of Gilmerton (*qv*), and has issue:

(1) +Robert Hugh; *b* 27 Jan 1958; *m* 1991 *Diana M, dau of Dr Louis Murray, of Johannesburg, and has:

1a +Nicholas Louis Robert; *b* 8 Feb 1996

2a +Jonathan Hugh; *b* 11 April 1997

(2) +James Alexander Waldorf; *b* 16 Sept 1965; *m* 21 Sept 1996 *Janine, est dau of James Valentine, of Reading, Mass., and has:

1a *Lucy Valentine; *b* 21 Feb 1998

(1) *Virginia Lucy; *b* 5 Aug 1951; *m* 1984 *Richard Denis Wyer McGillycuddy, The McGillycuddy of the Reeks, and has issue:

1a *Tara Virginia; *b* 1985

2a *Sorcha Alexandra; *b* 1990

(2) *Rachel Mary; *b* 29 Sept 1955; *m* 1985 *Hon Edward Nicholas Ward, yr son of 7th Viscount Bangor (*qv*), and has issue

(3) *Jean Violet; *b* 25 Jan 1962; *m* 1982 *John Maximilian Halford-Thompson, yr son of Lt-Col Peter Halford-Thompson, of Manor Lodge, Longworth, Abingdon, Oxon, and has issue:

1a *Guy; *b* 1986

2a *Hugh Maximilian; *b* 1988

3a *Ralph Mark; *b* 1993

3 John; *b* 26 Sept 1923; *educ* Eton; WW II 1942–46 as F/Lt RAFVR; MP (C) Newbury 1964–74, PPS to Min Overseas Development 1970, CC Berks 1953, CA 1960; *m* 1st 19 July 1950 Diana Kathleen (*d* 1982), 4th dau of George Henry Drummond, of Mount Rule, IoM (*see* PERTH, E), and had issue:

(1) +(John) Richard [Richard Astor Esq, Kirby House, Inkpen, nr Newbury, Berks]; *b* 20 Nov 1953; *educ* Eton and RMA Sandhurst; *m* 7 July 1977 *Katherine Mary, er dau of Brig Sir Jeffrey Lionel Darell, 8th Bt, MC (*qv*), and has issue:

1a +Charles John; *b* 1982

1a *Emily Mary; *b* 1980

2a *Tamara Sarah Diana; *b* 1989

(2) +(George) David; *b* 8 July 1958; *m* 1983 *Marianne Piroska Julia, only dau of John Hurleston Leche, of Carden, Cheshire, and has issue:

1a +Thomas David; *b* 1987

1a *Amy Violet; *b* 1989

(1) *Elizabeth Kathleen; *b* 22 July 1951

3 (cont.) The Hon John Astor *m* 2nd 1982 *Penelope Eve (*m* 3rd 1995 8th Marquess of Lansdowne, *qv*), dau of Cdr George Francis Norton Bradford, RN, and formerly wife of David Rolt, and *d* 1987

The 1st BARON *d* 19 July 1971; his est son,

GAVIN ASTOR, **2nd Baron Astor of Hever**, DL Sussex (1956) and Kent (1966); *b* 1 June 1918; *educ* Eton and New Coll Oxford; Capt The Life Gds, WW II; High Sheriff Sussex 1955, Ld-Lt and Custos Rotulorum Kent 1972, Seneschal Canterbury Cathedral 1973, Chm The Times Publishing Co 1959–66, Co-Ch Proprietor *The Times* 1962–66, Life Pres Times Newspapers Ltd 1967, dir Electrolux Ltd, Monotype Corp and Alliance Assur, Chm Cncl (Pres 1972) Cwlth Press Union, Chm 9th Cwlth Press Union Conf India and Pakistan 1961 and 10th Conf West Indies 1965, Chm Centl Cncl Roy Cwlth Soc 1972–75, Pres The Pilgrims 1977; *m* 4 Oct 1945 *Lady Irene Violet Freesia Janet Augusta Haig [The Rt Hon Irene Lady Astor of Hever, 11 Lyall St, London SW1X 8DH; Hollytree House, Frenchstreet, Westerham, Kent, TN16 1PW], yst dau of 1st Earl Haig of Bemersyde (*qv*), and *d* 1984, leaving:

1 JOHN JACOB ASTOR, **3rd and present Baron Astor of Hever**

2 +Philip Douglas Paul [The Hon Philip Astor, Flat 3, 6 Embankment Gdns, London SW3 4LJ]; *b* 4 April 1959 (HRH THE DUKE OF EDINBURGH stood sponsor); *educ* Eton and Ch Ch Oxford; barrister

1 *Bridget Mary [The Hon Mrs Smith, Sellack House, Sellack, Ross-on-Wye, Herefs HR9 6QP]; *b* 16 Feb 1948; *m* 1st 1980 (*divorce* 1986) Count Arthur Tarnowski, yr s of Count Hieronim Tarnowski, of Poland, and has:

(1) *(John) Sebastian Gavin; *b* 1981

(2) *Lucian Francis Philip; *b* 1984

1 (cont.) Countess Tarnowska *m* 2nd 1989 *Geofrey Richard Smith, 4th son of James William Smith, of Eywood House, Titley, Herefs, and by him has:

(1) *Moya Morvenna Irene; *b* 1987

2 *(Elizabeth) Louise [The Hon Mrs Ward, Sauvey Castle Farm, Withcote, Oakham, Leics LE15 8DT]; *b* 1 March 1951; *m* 1st 1979 (*divorce* 1981) David John Shelton Herring; *m* 2nd 1985 *David Joseph Ward, FRCS, MB, BS, son of Joseph Ward, FRCOG, MRCP, LRCP, of Tancrey, Fordwich, Canterbury, Kent, and has:

(1) *Oliver Gavin Joseph; *b* 1985

(1) *Victoria Mary; *b* 1987

3 *Sarah Violet [The Hon Mrs Lopes, Gnaton Hall, Yealmpton, Plymouth, Devon PL8 2HU]; *b* 30 Sept 1953; *m* 22 Feb 1975 *Hon George Edward Lopes, yr s of 2nd Baron Roborough (*qv*), and has issue

ATHOLL

Arms: Quarterly, 1st, paly of six or and sable (for ATHOLL); 2nd, or a fess chequy azure and argent (for STEWART); 3rd, argent on a bend azure three stag's heads cabossed or (for STANLEY); 4th, gules, three legs in armour proper, garnished and spurred or, flexed and conjoined in triangle at the upper part of the thigh (ensigns of ISLE OF MAN); over all an escutcheon en surtout azure three mullets argent within a double tressure flory or, ensigned of a Marquess's coronet (chiefship of MURRAY). **Crests:** 1 A mermaid holding in her dexter hand a mirror and in her sinister a comb, all proper (for MURRAY), 2 A demi-savage proper, wreathed about the temples and waist with laurel, his arms extended and holding in the right hand a dagger, in the left a key, all proper (for ATHOLL), 3 A peacock's head and neck proper, accompanied on either side by two arms from the elbows proper and vested in maunches azure doubled argent. **Supporters:** Dexter, a savage proper, wreathed about the temples and loins with juniper, his feet in fetters, the chain held in his right hand, proper; sinister, a lion rampant gules, armed and langued azure, gorged with a plain collar of the last charged with three mullets argent. **Mottoes:** 1. (dexter) *Tout prest* ('Quite ready'); 2. (centre) Furth fortune and fill the fetters; 3. (sinister) *Praite* ('Ready'). **Creations:** L. (S) 25 April 1604 (Murray of Tullibardine); E. (Tullibardine) and L. (Murray, Gask and Balquhidder) (S) 30 Jan 1627/8 (with precedence of 10 July 1606); M. (Athole), E. (Tullibardine), V. (Balquhidder) and L. (Murray, Balvany and Gask) (S) 17 Feb 1676; D., M. (Tillibardin), E. (Strathtay and Strathardle), V. (Balwhidder, Glenalmond and Glenlyon), L. (Murray, Balvenie and Gask) (S) 30 June 1703. (D., M., E., V. and L. (S, Jacobite) 1 Feb 1716/7).

THE 11TH DUKE OF ATHOLL, Marquess of Athole, Marquess of Tillibardin, Earl of Atholl, Earl of Tullibardine, Earl of Tullibardin, Earl of Strathtay and Strathardle, Viscount of Balquhidder, Viscount of Balwhidder, Viscount of Glenalmond and Glenlyon, Lord Murray, Gask and Balquhidder, Lord Murray, Balvany and Gask, Lord Murray, Balvenie and Gask, also Duke of Rannoch, Marquess of Blair, Earl of Glen Tilt, Viscount Glenshie and Lord of Strathbran in Jacobite peerage (John Murray) [John Murray Esq, PO Box 137, Haenertsburg 0730, S Africa]; *b* 19 Jan 1929; s cousin 1996 as 11th Duke etc and Chief of the name of Murray but reportedly has decided not to use the title; BSc (Eng); *m* 15 Dec 1956 *Margaret (Peggy) Yvonne, only dau of Ronald Leonard Leach, of Louis Trichardt, S Africa, and has:

1 +BRUCE GEORGE RONALD, *Marquess of Tullibardine*; *b* 6 April 1960; Lt Transvaal Scottish; *m* 1984 *Lynne Elizabeth, est dau of Nicholas Andrew, of Bedfordview, S Africa, and has:

(1) +Michael Bruce John; *b* 1985

(2) +David Nicholas George; *b* 1986

(1) *Nicole; *b* 1987

2 +Craig John; *b* 1963; Cpl Transvaal Scottish; *m* 1988 *Inge, 2nd dau of Auke Bakker, of Bedfordview, S Africa, and has issue:

(1) +Carl; *b* 1993

(1) *Shona; *b* 1995

1 *Jennifer; *b* 8 Feb 1958; *m* 1979 (*divorce* 1985) — Purdon, and has issue:

(1) *Grant Clive; *b* 1981

(1) *Charlene; *b* 1983

Atholl, other titles under name of: A dignitary known as a Mormaer held what was later called an Earldom of Atholl in Scotland towards the close of the 1st millennium AD. (The designation Atholl could also be spelt Athole and was sometimes referred to as Asce(l)les.) The first person designated Earl of Atholl/Athole was Madach, most probably a nephew of MALCOLM III KING OF SCOTS, though he may have been a son of Donald Bane rather than MALCOLM's brother Melmare. This was around 1115. The Earldom passed to Madach's male descendants until nearly a century later, when his elder great-great granddaughter Isabel became Countess of Atholl in her own right. She married Thomas, known as 'of Galloway' and younger brother of the then Lord of Galloway, but within some thirty years the Earldom became vested in her younger sister Fernelith, whose daughter subsequently inherited the title, so that towards the end of the 13th century it was held by men of the Strathbogie family, one of them having married Fernelith's heiress daughter.

With the English King EDWARD I's temporary ascendancy in Scotland, the Earldom came under forfeiture and was very briefly assigned by EDWARD to his father-in-law Ralph de Monthermer Earl of Gloucester. Between late summer of 1307 and spring 1308 the new King of England EDWARD II restored it to the Strathbogies (*see* STRABOLGI, B), though the continued existence of the Earldom thereafter is bedevilled by the question of who was rightful sovereign of Scotland at the time. Since ROBERT I BRUCE (THE) effectively ruled by 1314, when the then Earl of Atholl rebelled against him and was deprived of his title, its existence must be deemed to have ceased at that date, even though documents prepared under the aegis of English sovereigns continued to refer to an Earl of Ascelles (Atholl) for several decades afterwards.

Meanwhile in Scotland the title Earl of Atholl was conferred several times in succession over the next century and a half, usually on various connections of the sovereign. In the 1320s there was Sir John Campbell of Moulin, a cousin of DAVID II; in Feb 1341/2 Robert Stewart, grandson of ROBERT I through his mother Marjory (he later ascended the throne as ROBERT II whereupon his Earldom merged with the Crown, though he revived it for two of his sons successively, Robert in 1403 and Walter in 1404); in 1398 ROBERT III's son David; and in about 1457 Sir John Stewart of Balveny, whose mother Joan was a former Queen of Scots. In each of these cases the title was only held for a single generation, indeed in one case for as little as three years.

Only Sir William Douglas of Liddesdale (*see* MORTON, E), created Earl of Atholl in 1341, had no close tie of marriage or blood with the sovereign, and he resigned the title for the benefit of the future ROBERT II (*see above*) almost as soon as it was conferred on him. The last pre-Murray creation was in May 1595/6 in favour of the second husband of the widow of the last Earl of Atholl of the creation of *c* 1457 (*see* MORAY, E).

Lineage: FRESKIN; possibly a Fleming by descent; held extensive lands in Moray and Strathbrock in Linlithgow and *d* by 1171; alleged ancestor of the Earls of Sutherland (*qv*) and undoubted gf of:

WILLIAM MORAY of Petty; probable ancestor of:

Sir MALCOLM MORAY/MURRAY; Sheriff Perthshire; *m* —, dau and heir of Sir Geoffrey de Gask, through whom he acquired the lands of Gask, and *d c* 1280, leaving:

Sir WILLIAM MURRAY; *m c* 1284 Ada, dau of Malise, Seneschal of Strathearn, thus acquiring the lands of Tullibardine, Perthshire; *d* in or after 1296; his s:

ANDREW MURRAY of Tullibardine; supported Edward Balliol's candidature for throne of Scotland 1332 and contributed to Balliol's victory at Battle of Dupplin by fixing a stake to show a ford in the River Earn; imprisoned and executed at Perth as a traitor 7 Oct 1332, leaving:

Sir WILLIAM MURRAY of Tullibardine; granted charter of those lands by Malise, Earl of Strathearn, *c* 1333; *d c* 1352, leaving:

Sir JOHN MURRAY of Tullibardine; had charter of Pitcairly, Fifeshire, and *d c* 1358; leaving:

WALTER MURRAY of Tullibardine, his grants of which, plus other lands in the Earldom of Strathearn and Pitcairly, Fife, were confirmed by DAVID II 1362; *m* Margaret le Baird and *d* 1390, leaving:

Sir DAVID MURRAY of Tullibardine; acquired Camsyny and Barneglis in Strathearn from Sir Malcolm Drummond, a grant confirmed by Eufemia, Countess Palatine of Strathearn, 1389; *m* as her 2nd husb Isabel, dau of Sir John Stewart of Innermeath (*see* MORAY, E), and had, with other issue:

Sir DAVID MURRAY of Tullibardine; acquired Polgour in 1430, Fendoch, half of Ardoch and half of Kintoches in 1443; founded Collegiate Ch of Tullibardine 1445; obtained Lethendy and Cultrannoch 1446; Auditor Exchequer 1448 and 1450, Bailie Earldom of Strathearn and Keeper Methven Castle; *m* 1430 Margaret, 2nd dau of Sir John Colquhon of Luss (*see* COLQUHOUN, Bt), and *d* 1451/2, leaving, with other issue (including Patrick (*see* MURRAY, Bt of Ochtertyre) and Mariot, *m* Sir Malcolm Drummond; *see* PERTH, E) an est s:

WILLIAM MURRAY of Tullibardine; Sheriff Perth, Keeper Doune Castle; *m* Margaret (*m* 2nd George Clephane of Carslogie), dau of 1st Lord Gray (*qv*), and *d c* 1459, having had, with other issue:

Sir WILLIAM MURRAY of Tullibardine; *b c* 1444; confirmed as Steward, Forester and Coroner of Strathearn by charter 1483 and Parl 1492; *m* Lady Mary Keith, dau of 1st Earl Marischal (*see* KINTORE, E), and *d* 10 Feb 1524/5, having had, with other issue:

Sir WILLIAM MURRAY of Castleton, which he acquired with the lands of Drumdewan 1490; *m* Lady Margaret Stewart, dau of 1st Earl of Atholl of the 1457 *cr* (*see* MORAY, E), and was *ka vp* Battle of Flodden 9 Sept 1513, having had, with other issue:

Sir WILLIAM MURRAY of Tullibardine; served heir to his uncle, Sir John, in the lands of Polgour and Clow 1527, acquired Wester Locheane in Strathearn 1558; *m c* April 1538 Katherine, dau of Sir Duncan Campell of Glenorchy (for whose early ancestry *see* ARGYLL, D), and *d* 30 Jan 1562, leaving, with a dau (Annabel, *m* 17th Earl of Mar, *qv*):

Sir WILLIAM MURRAY of Tullibardine; Jt Govr JAMES VI and Keeper Stirling Castle 1572, Comptroller Scotland; *m* 15 April 1547 Lady Agnes Graham, 3rd dau of 2nd Earl of Montrose (*see* MONTROSE, D), and *d* 16 March 1583, having had, with other issue (including William and Mungo (Sir)):

JOHN MURRAY (Sir), 1st EARL OF TULLIBARDINE, so *cr* 10 July 1606, as also LORD MURRAY, GASK AND BALQUHIDDER and earlier 25 April 1604 LORD MURRAY OF TULLIBARDINE (all S), PC (S 1592); *b c* 1550; Master Household *c* 1578–92, ktd *c* 1584; *m* by 15 Nov 1576 Catherine, dau of 2nd Lord Drummond (*see* PERTH, E), and *d* between 29 July and 3 Aug 1613, having had, with other issue (*see* MANSFIELD and MANSFIELD, E):

1 WILLIAM MURRAY, 2nd and last EARL OF TULLIBARDINE, which on the understanding that the King would revive the Earldom of Atholl for his (WILLIAM's) issue by his 2nd w he resigned 1 April 1626 so that it could be regranted to his bro Patrick (*see* below), since he wished the Earldoms of Tullibardine and Atholl to descend in two different branches of the Murrays (Patrick, however, died before the regrant could take place), PC (S Jan 1616/7 and March 1625/6); *b c* 1574; helped rescue JAMES VI from the attempted abduction by the Earl of Gowrie (*qv*) and his bro at Perth 1600, accordingly made hereditary Sheriff Perthshire; *m* 1st (contract 3 Oct 1599) Cecilia (*dsp*), sis of 1st Earl of Wemyss (*qv*); *m* 2nd Sept 1604 Dorothea, est dau and heir of 5th Earl of Atholl of the 1457 *cr* (*see* MORAY, E), and was *bur* 30 July 1627, when by the terms of the surrender the Earldom of Tullibardine and the Lorships of Murray and Murray of Tullibardine seem to have been vested in the Crown, having had:

(1) JOHN MURRAY, **1st Earl of Atholl** (S), so *cr* 17 Feb 1628/9; royalist Civil War; *m* 6 June 1630 Jean, dau of Sir Duncan Campbell of Glenorchy (for whose early ancestry *see* ARGYLL,D,) and *d* June 1642, having had, with two daus (*d* young):

1a JOHN, **2nd Earl**

2a Mungo (Sir) of Garth; *d* unm

1a Jean; *d* 1688

2a Anne; *m* her cousin **2nd Earl of Tullibardine** (*see* below) and *dsp*

(1) Mary; *m* Sir John Moncreiffe of that Ilk, 1st Bt (*see* ERROLL, E)

(2) Anne; *m* June 1595 1st Earl of Kinghorne (*see* STRATHMORE AND KINGHORNE, E)

2 Sir PATRICK MURRAY of Redcastle, **1st Earl of Tullibardine**, *cr* 30 Jan 1627/8 but with precedence of the earlier *cr* of 1606, with remainder to his heirs male whatsoever, KB (1603), PC (1630); *b* by 16 April 1579; *m* 1st by 18 Jan 1604 Prudence — but by her had no issue; *m* 2nd between 1609 and 26 July 1613 Elizabeth (*d* by 1656), dau and coheir of John Dent and widow of Sir Francis Vere (*see* SAINT ALBANS, D), and *d* 5 Sept 1644, having had, with other issue (including four yr sons, all *dsp*) :

(1) JAMES MURRAY, **2nd Earl of Tullibardine**, PC (S 1661); *bapt* 22 Sept 1617; Covenanter; *m* 1st 3 June 1643 Lady Lilias Drummond, 2nd dau of 2nd Earl of Perth (*qv*), and had:

1a Patrick, *Lord Murray*; *b* 1644; *d c* 1664

2a James, *Lord Murray*; *b* 1645; *d c* 1670

1a Elizabeth; *b* 1654

(1) (cont.)The **2nd Earl** *m* 2nd 1664 his cousin Lady Anne Murray, dau of **1st Earl of Atholl** (*see* above) and had issue (including Mary, *m c* 1635 Sir John Moncrieff, 1st Bt *see* MONCRIEFF, B); *m* 3rd 1667 Lilias (*m* 2nd 4th Earl of Perth (*qv*) and *d c* 1685), est dau of Sir James Drummond of Machany (*see* PERTH, E), and *dspms* Jan 1670

3 Robert

1 Lilias; *m c* 15 April 1591 John Grant, 5th of Freuchie (*see* STRATHSPEY, B)

The 1st EARL OF ATHOLL's er son,

JOHN MURRAY, **2nd Earl of Atholl**, **3rd Earl of Tullibardine** and **1st Marquess of Athole** (S), so *cr* 17 Feb 1676, as also EARL OF TULLIBARDIN [*sic*] VISCOUNT OF BALQUHIDDER, LORD MURRAY, BALVANY and GASK, KT (1687), PC (S 1660); *b* 2 May 1631; royalist Civil War, Hereditary Sheriff Fife, Justice Gen Scotland 1663–76, Capt Gen Roy Co Archers 1670–1703, Col 4th Horse Gds 1671–78, Keeper Scotttish Privy Seal 1672–89, Extrdy Ld of Session 1673–89, leading opponent of uprising by Duke of Argyll (*qv*) on behalf of Duke of Monmouth 1685; *m* 5 May 1659 Lady Amelia Sophia Stanley (*d* 22 Feb 1703), 4th but 3rd surv dau (and in her issue heir) of 7th Earl of Derby (*qv*), and *d* 6 May 1703, having had, with other issue, including two yr sons (CHARLES MURRAY, *cr* EARL OF DUNMORE; *qv*; James, f of Catherine, 1st w of 5th Lord Rollo (*qv*) of Duncrib) and a dau (Amelia, *m* 9th Lord (Fraser) of Lovat; *qv*)):

JOHN MURRAY, **1st Duke of Atholl**, so *cr* 30 June 1703, as also MARQUESS OF TILLIBARDIN [*sic*], EARL OF STRATHTAY AND STRATHARDLE, VISCOUNT OF BALWHIDDER [*sic*], GLENALMOND AND GLENLYON, AND LORD MURRAY, BALVENIE AND GASK, Co Perth (S), with remainder, in default of his own male issue, to the sons of his deceased f, and earlier 27 July 1696 EARL OF TULLIBARDIN, VISCOUNT GLENALMOND, AND LORD MURRAY (S) for life only, KT (Feb 1703/4), PC (S *temp* WILLIAM III, GB 1712–14); *b* 24 Feb 1659/60; a Pncpl Sec State Scotland, High Commr S Parl 1696–98, Chllr St Andrews U 1697–1724, Ld Privy Seal Scotland 1703 and 1713–14, against Act of Union of 1707, Ld High Commr Gen Assembly Ch Scotland 1712–14, Extrdy Ld of Session 1712–24, rep S peer 1710–15, Ld Lt Perthshire 1715–24; *m* 1st 24 May 1683 Lady Katharine Douglas later Hamilton (*d* 11 Jan 1707), dau of William Duke of Hamilton and Anne, Duchess of Hamilton (*qv*) in her own right, and had, with two other sons and five other daus:

1 John, *Marquess of Tullibardine*; *b* 6 May 1684, *ka* Battle of Malplaquet 11 Sept 1709

2 William, *Marquess of Tullibardine*, Duke of Rannoch, Marquess of Blair, Earl of Glen Tilt, Viscount Glenshie and Lord of Strathbran (all S), so *cr* by titular James III 1 Feb 1716/7 with remainder to heirs male; *b* 14 April 1689; RN; Jacobite 1715, accordingly attainted 17 Feb 1715/6 and his titles settled on his yr bro by Parl; escaped abroad and returned to Scotland with a Spanish force 1719, but after a fresh Jacobite defeat returned to the Continent and lived in exile under the name Kateson; took part in '45 Uprising, when arrested and imprisoned Tower of London, where *d* unm 9 July 1746

3 JAMES MURRAY, **2nd Duke of Atholl**, KT (Feb 1733/4), PC (Jan 1733/4); *b* 28 Sept 1690; Capt and Lt-Col 1st Foot Gds, later Lt-Col Roy Scots, MP (Whig) Perthshire 1715–24, Ld Privy Seal 1733–63, rep S peer 1733–36, *s* cousin 10th Earl of Derby (*qv*) as 7th BARON STRANGE 1736, Keeper Gt Seal of Scotland 1763–64; *m* 1st 28 April 1726 Jane (*d* 13 June 1748), sis of Sir John Frederick, 1st Bt (*qv*), and widow of James Lannoy, of Hammersmith, and had, with two sons (*d* in infancy):

(1) Jane; *m* 3 March 1747 17th Earl of Crawford and Balcarres (*qv*) and *dsp* & *vp* 10 Oct 1747

(2) CHARLOTTE; *b* 13 Oct 1731; BARONESS STRANGE in her own right; *m* 1753 her cousin **3rd Duke of Atholl** and *d* 13 Oct 1805, leaving issue (*see* below)

3 The **2nd Duke** *m* 2nd 7 May 1749 Jean (*m* 2nd 2 Sept 1767 Gen Lord Adam Gordon (*d* 1801), 2nd s of 2nd Duke of Gordon (*see* HUNTLY, M), and *d* 22 Feb 1795), dau of John Drummond, 10th of Lennoch and 3rd of Megginch (for whose early ancetry *see* PERTH, E), and *dspms* and without further issue by her 8 Jan 1764

4 Charles; *b* 24 Sept 1691; Cornet 5th Dragoons, Jacobite 1715, cmded a regt Battle of Preston, when captured and tried as a deserter and sentenced to be shot, but reprieved and *dsp* (*bur* 28 Aug 1720)

5 George; *b* 4 Oct 1694; Ensign Roy Scots 1712; Jacobite 1715, escaped abroad; returned with his bro Marquess of Tullibardine 1719, when allegedly wounded at Battle of Glenshiel; again escaped, again returned 1724, pardoned, Jacobite again '45 Uprising, when Lt-Gen throughout the campaign; attainted after Culloden 1746 but again escaped abroad, the attainder being held by a decision 7 Feb 1764 of the House of Lords not to have affected his son's right of succession since he predeceased his son; *m* 3 June 1728 Amelia, only surv child and heiress of James Murray of Glencarse and Strowan, and *d* Medemblick, Holland, 11 Oct 1760, having had, with other issue:

(1) JOHN, **3rd Duke**

(1) Amelia; *b* 17 May 1732; *m* 1st 1750 as his 2nd w, John Master of Sinclair (*see* SINCLAIR, L); *m* 2nd 18 April 1754, as his 1st w, James Farquharson of Invercauld and *d* 24 April 1777

1 Susan; *m* 25 April 1716 2nd Earl of Aberdeen (*see* ABERDEEN AND TEMAIR, M) and *d* 22 June 1725, leaving issue

The **1st Duke** *m* 2nd (contract 26 June 1710) Mary (*d* 17 Jan 1767), dau of 11th Lord Ross, and *d* 14 Nov 1724, having by her had four sons and with two other daus:

2 Mary; *m* 1749 3rd Earl of Seafield (*qv*) and had issue

The 2nd DUKE's n,

JOHN MURRAY, **3rd Duke of Atholl**, KT (1767); *b* 6 May 1729; Capt 54th Foot, MP (Tory) Perthshire 1761–64, rep S peer 1766–74; *m* 23 Oct 1753 his cousin Charlotte, BARONESS STRANGE in her own right (*d* 13 Oct 1805; *see* above), only surv child and heiress of **2nd Duke of Atholl** (with whom he sold their sovereignty of the Isle of Man 1765 to the Br Govt for £70,000 cash down (over £3,600,00) in late-1990s terms) and £2,000 (over £103,000 in late-1990s terms) p.a. for their joint lives, reserving their real estate ownership rights), and *d* 5 Nov 1774, leaving:

1 JOHN MURRAY, **4th Duke of Atholl** and 1st EARL STRANGE and BARON MURRAY, of Stanley, Co Gloucester (both GB), so *cr* 18 Aug 1786, also *s* mother as BARON STRANGE 1805, KT (1800), PC (1797); *b* 30 June 1755; fndr Atholl Highrs (raised 1777), rep S peer 1780–84, FRS; sold remaining property and privileges in IOM to the Crown for £409,000 (over £18m in late-1990s terms); *m* 1st 26 Dec 1774 Jane (*d* 4 Dec 1790), est dau of 9th Lord Cathcart (*qv*), and had, with other issue:

(1) JOHN MURRAY, **5th Duke of Atholl**; *b* 26 June 1778; *educ* Eton; Ensign 61st Regt 1797; *d* unm and insane 14 Sept 1846

(2) JAMES MURRAY, 1st BARON GLENLYON, of Glenlyon, Co Perth (UK), so *cr* 9 July 1821, KH; *b* 29 May 1782; Maj-Gen; *m* 19 May 1810 Lady Emily Frances Percy (*d* 21 June 1844), 2nd dau of 2nd Duke of Northumberland (*qv*), and *d* 12 Oct 1837, leaving issue:

1a GEORGE AUGUSTUS FREDERICK JOHN, **6th Duke of Atholl**, KT (1853); *b* 20 Sept 1814; offr 2nd Dragoon Gds; *m* 29 Oct 1839 Anne, VA (*b* 17 June 1814; Mistress Robes Feb-Dec 1852; *d* 18 May 1897), dau of Henry Home-Drummond, of Blair Drummond, Perthshire, and *d* 16 Jan 1864, leaving an only child:

1b JOHN JAMES HUGH HENRY MURRAY later STEWART-MURRAY (registered Lyon Office 1 Dec 1865), **7th Duke of Atholl**, KT (1868); *b* 6 Aug 1840 ; *s* 12 Feb 1865 his unc 4th Duke of Northumberland (*qv*) as LORD (Baron) PERCY, Perthshire: Ld Lt 1878, Hereditary Sheriff and Pres TFA, Hon Col 3rd Bn Black Watch, Col-in-Ch S African Scottish Regt, Lt and Capt Scots Fusilier Gds, Chllr Order of the Thistle 1913; *m* 29 Oct 1863 Louisa (*d* 8 July 1902), est dau of Sir Thomas Moncreiffe of that Ilk, 7th Bt (*see* ERROLL, E), and *d* 20 Jan 1917, having had:

1c John, *Marquess of Tulibardine*; *b* 30, *d* 31 Aug 1869

2c JOHN GEORGE STEWART-MURRAY, **8th Duke of Atholl**, KT (1918), PC (1921), GCVO (MVO 1902), CB, DSO (1898); *b* 15 Dec 1871; T/Brig-Gen and Bde Cdr HQ Unit 1918, Col-Cmdt Scottish Horse, Hon Col 10th Bn Liverpool Regt; Hon Col 3rd Bn Black Watch SR, Hon Brig-Gen (ret) TA 1927, ADC to HM GEORGE V 1920–31, Capt and Brevet Maj RHG (Blues), Nile Expdn 1898 (despatches twice, two medals, two clasps), Boer War (despatches twice, Queen's medal with six clasps, King's medal with two clasps, brevet), WW I (despatches), Order White Eagle Serbia 3rd Cl with swords, Ld Lt Perthshire, Pres Perthshire TAA, MP (C) W Perthshire 1910–17, Ld High Commr Gen Assembly Ch of Scotland 1918, 1919 and 1920, Ld Chamberlain 1921–22, Grand Master Mason Scotland 1908–13, Freedom Edinburgh 1928; *m* 20 July 1899 Katharine Marjory, DBE (1918), (LLD Glasgow, Manchester and Leeds, FRCM, Hon DCL Oxford, Durham, McGill and Columbia (New York), MP (Lab) Kinross and W Perthshire and Kinross 1923–38, Parly Sec Bd Edcn 1924–29, and *d* 21 Oct 1960), 4th dau of Sir

James Henry Ramsay, 10th Bt, of Banff (*see* 1970 edn), and *dsp* 16 March 1942

3c George; *b* 17 Feb 1873; Maj 1st Bn Black Watch, S African War (despatches, Queen's medal, five clasps, King's medal, two clasps), WW I; *ka* 14 Sept 1914

4c JAMES THOMAS STEWART-MURRAY, **9th Duke of Atholl**; *b* 18 Aug 1879; Maj 1st Bn Cameron Highrs Boer War (Queen's medal, four clasps, King's medal, two clasps), WW I (wounded, POW); *d* unm 8 May 1957, when the Earldom of Strange and Barony of Murray *cr* 1786 expired and the Barony of Strange (*qv*) fell temporarily into abeyance

1c Dorothea Louisa; *b* 25 March 1866; *m* 5 Feb 1895 Maj-Gen Sir Harold Goodeve Ruggles-Brise, KCMG, CB, MVO (*d* 24 June 1927), Gren Gds, yst son of Sir Samuel Ruggles-Brise, KCB, of Spains Hall, Essex (*qv*), and *d* 28 Dec 1937

2c Helen; *b* 20 April 1867; *m* 28 Dec 1916 David Alexander Tod (*d* 6 Sept 1933), of Tirinie, Blair Atholl, and *d* 1 Dec 1934

3c Evelyn; *b* 17 March 1868; *d* unm 30 July 1940

2a James Charles Plantagenet; *b* 8 Dec 1819; Col Scots Fusilier Gds, Groom-in-Waiting to HM QUEEN VICTORIA; Crimea; *m* 6 Nov 1851 Elizabeth Margery (*d* 11 Oct 1888), only dau of G Fairholme, (*see* FORBES), and *d* 3 June 1874, having had issue

1a Charlotte Augusta Leopoldina; *m* 10 June 1847 Rev Court Granville (*d* 1871), Hon Canon of Durham, Incumbent of Alnwick, and *d* 2 May 1889

2a Frances Juliet; *m* 16 Jan 1840 Hon Charles Henry Maynard (*see* 1865 edn MAYNARD, V), and *d* 4 Nov 1868

1(cont.) The **4th Duke** *m* 2nd 11 March 1794 Margery (*d* 3 Oct 1842), est dau of 16th Lord Forbes (*qv*) and widow of John Mackenzie, Lord Macleod (*see* CROMARTIE, E), and *d* 29 Sept 1830, having by her had:

(3) Charles; *b* 1799; *d* Aug 1824

(1) Catherine; *d* young 1796

2 George (Rt Rev); *b* 30 Jan 1761; Bp St David's; *m* 18 Dec 1780 Anne Charlotte, Ldy-in-Waiting to QUEEN CHARLOTTE (*d* 27 April 1844), dau of Lt-Gen Francis Grant, MP (*see* STRATHSPEY, B), and *d* 1803, having had, with other issue:

(1) John; RN; *d* 1803

(2) George (Rt Rev), DD; *b* 12 Jan 1784; Bp of Sodor and Man 1814, and Rochester 1827; *m* 9 May 1811 Lady Sarah Maria Hay (*d* 11 July 1874), 2nd dau of 10th Earl of Kinnoull (*qv*), and *d* 16 Feb 1860, having had, with other issue:

1a George Edward (Rev); *b* 1 Sept 1818; Rector of Southfleet; *m* 18 July 1848 Penelope Frances Elizabeth Pemberton (*d* 5 Oct 1910), yst dau of Brig-Gen Austin, and *d* 14 Sept 1854, leaving issue:

1b George Herbert (Sir), PC, GCB, GCVO, ISO; *b* 27 Sept 1849; MA and Hon Student Ch Ch Oxford; FO 1873–80, Treasury 1880–97, Chm Bd Inland Revenue 1897–99, Sec to GPO 1899–1903, Perm Sec Treas 1903–11; *m* 23 Sept 1879 Hon Helen Mary Mulholland, CBE, DGStJ (*d* 19 Feb 1932), est dau of 1st Baron Dunleath (*qv*), and *d* 4 April 1936, leaving:

1c George Evelyn Pemberton (Sir), KCB (1919); *b* 25 July 1880; Priv Sec to Ld Pres Cncl 1905–07 and Pres Bd Educn 1907–09, on Bd of Edcn 1903–11, Commr Customs and Excise 1911–14, Sec to GPO 1914–34, Chm Bd Customs and Excise 1934; *m* 10 Jan 1906 Muriel Mildred Elizabeth (*d* 30 Aug 1961), est dau of Philip Beresford Hope, JP, of Bedgebury Park, and *d* 30 March 1947, having had:

1d George Anthony, OBE; *b* 7 Jan 1907; *educ* Eton and Ch Ch Oxford (BA); Lt-Col Scottish Horse (TA), WW II; *m* 25 Aug 1930 Hon Angela Pearson, Chm Westminster Press Prov Newspapers Ltd (*m* 2nd 5 June 1950 Lt-Col Robert Mordan Thorne Campbell Preston, MC, TD, of Ardchattan Priory, Connel, Argyll), 3rd dau of 2nd Viscount Cowdray (*qv*), and was *ka* Italy April 1945, having had:

1e GEORGE IAIN MURRAY, **10th Duke of Atholl**, DL (Perth and Kinross 1980); *b* 19 June 1931; *educ* Eton and Ch Ch Oxford (BA 1952, MA 1964); rep S peer 1958–63, dep chm Westminster Press Gp to 1974 (chm 1974–96), chm Trident Gp Printers to 1975, BPM Hldgs 1972–83, dir Pearson Longman 1975–83, memb Red Deer Comm, Ctee on preparation of legislation 1973–75, Pres Scottish Landowners Fedn 1986–91 (V-Convener 1971–76, Convener 1976–79), Chm RNLI 1979, V-Pres Nat Tst Scotland 1977–96, Pres Internal Sheepdog Soc 1982–83 and 1988–89; *d* unm 27 Feb 1996

2e John Colin; *b* 30 June 1933; *d* 17 June 1934

3e A son; *b* and *d* 17 Dec 1936

1c Irene Helen, MBE (1919); *b* 9 Nov 1882; *m* 23 June 1903 (*divorce* 1921) Capt Marshall Owen Roberts, Scots Gds (*d* 3 July 1931), s of Marshall Owen Roberts, of New York, and had issue

2b Arthur Mordaunt, CB (1909), MVO (1908); *b* 20 Jan 1852; Lt-Col and Brevet-Col RA, Assist-Cmdt RMA Woolwich 1900–04, Cmdt Duke of York's RM School 1907–09, served Afghanistan; *m* 1st 15 Jan 1895 Isabel (*d* 30 June 1896), dau of Richard Laurence Pemberton, of Hawthorn Tower, Co Durham, and had issue:

1c Helen Isabel; *b* 7 June 1896; *d* unm 23 June 1957

2b (cont.) Col Arthur Murray *m* 2nd 18 Oct 1898 Mabel Meliora (*d* 24 Dec 1964), est dau of Frederick Francis Nicholson, of Wynnstay, Lancashire, and *d* 23 May 1920, having by her had issue:

1c (Arthur) Stewart Pakington; *b* 9 Sept 1899; *educ* Eton and RMC Sandhurst; Brig Gren Gds WW II (ret 1948, Hon Brig); *m* 30 Sept 1961 Winifreda Irene, dau of Edmund Henry Bevan, of Hilston Park, Mon

2c Godfrey Pemberton, DSO (1945); *b* 13 June 1901; *educ* Radley and RMC Sandhurst; Lt-Col Seaforth Highrs WW II; Queen's Messenger 1951, Superintendant Queen's Messengers 1957–85; *m* 3 Dec 1934 *Mary Isabel, dau of Dr D Brownlee, and *d* 1985, having had issue:

1d *Susan Elizabeth; *b* 18 Sept 1935; *m* 6 June 1959 *David Hill, son of Cdr George Walter Hill, RN (ret), of Kent and has issue:

1e *Simon Sebastian; *b* 7 Sept 1961

2e *David Alexander; *b* 31 Aug 1964

3e *Tobias Hunter; *b* 14 Feb 1967

2d *Mary Jennifer [Mrs James Vickers, 45 Beever Rd, Ashford, Kent]; *b* 15 Oct 1939; *m* 1964 *James Vickers, and has issue:

1e *Sandra; *b* 6 June 1965

3c Harry George Felix; *b* 20 Sept 1905; *d* 13 Jan 1906

1c Olive Penelope, MBE; *b* 28 Jan 1908; *m* 1st 1928 (*divorce* 1942) Charles Russell Wood; *m* 2nd 1948 Sir (Walter) Charles Norton MBE, MC (*d* 22 Oct 1974), slr, s of Walter Percy Norton, and had by her 1st husb:

1d *Peter; *b* 1930

3b Douglas Stuart (Rev); *b* 28 May 1853; *educ* Exeter Coll Oxford (MA); Rector of Blithfield Staffs 1879–1919; *m* 22 April 1879 Harriet Georgina Isabel (*d* 11 Nov 1921), only dau of Rev Canon Hon George Thomas Orlando Bridgeman (*see* BRADFORD, E), and *d* 19 March 1920, leaving:

1c Walter, OBE (1918), MC (1916); *b* 13 Aug 1882; Lt-Col RE; *m* 15 Aug 1911 Evelyn, est dau of William Edward Adie, of Buxton, and *d* 8 Nov 1945, leaving issue:

1d Donald Stuart; *b* 13 Nov 1917; Maj RA, WW II; *m* 12 June 1948 *Margaret Ann (Peggy), dau of Ernest Simmons, of The Glebe House, Boughton Aluph, Ashford, Kent, and *d* 1985, leaving issue:

1e *Elizabeth Anne; *b* 25 April 1949; *m* 1978 *John Kneafsey Kelsey, and has issue

2e *Jean Margaret; *b* 27 April 1951; *m* 1975 *Nils Bertil Eidestedt, and has issue

1d *Jean Pamela [Mrs James Fraser, Tomoaine, Tomich, by Beauly, Inverness-shire]; *b* 3 July 1920; *m* 4 Oct 1947 *Col James Andrew Fraser, MC, RA, er son of Cdr John Fraser, OBE, RN, of Godalming, Surrey, and has issue:

1e *Simon John; *b* 11 Jan 1950; *educ* Milton Abbey

2e *Donald James; *b* 15 March 1951; *educ* Milton Abbey

1e *Jean Catherine; *b* 16 April 1954; *m* 1973 *Daniel Letts

2c George; *b* 20 Nov 1884; Maj RFA, WWs I and II; *m* 17 Jan 1928 *Joan [Mrs G Murray, Box 111, Louis Trichardt 0920, N Transvaal, S Africa], 3rd dau of William Edward Eastwood, of Buffelspoort, Mara, N Transvaal, and *das* S Africa, 21 June 1940, leaving issue:

1d JOHN MURRAY, **11th and present Duke of Atholl**

3c Leonard; *b* 31 Dec 1896; Lt Lancs Hus, att RFC; *ka* 13 March 1917

4c Edward; *b* 8 Jan 1899; Lt Rifle Bde; *m* 23 April 1936 *Irma, only dau of Anton Kubálek, of Roundhay, and *dsp* 30 July 1964

1c Emily; *b* 2 Oct 1886

2c Mabel; *b* 4 Nov 1888; *d* unm 13 Oct 1949

3c Margaret; *b* 29 Jan 1894

1b Alice Lillian; *m* 25 Jan 1871 Rev John Duncan (*d* 28 Jan 1907), Vicar Calne, Wilts, and Canon Salisbury, and *d* 22 Feb 1922, leaving issue

2b Marian Georgina; *d* unm 14 Feb 1932

2a Francis Henry (Rev); *m* and had issue

3a Robert Hay, JP (Bucks), DL (Surrey); *b* 26 Sept 1826; High Sheriff 1869, barrister; *m* 8 May 1849 Elizabeth (*d* 20 April 1914), dau of Samuel Gregson, MP, and *d* 1 June 1908, leaving:

1b Robert Evelyn Hay; *b* 1 Oct 1851; *m* 5 June 1879 Frances Charlotte (*d* 15 March 1917), only dau of Rev Edward Jackson, of Thruxton, Herefs, and *d* 23 Feb 1910, leaving issue:

1c Eleanor Marjorie Hay; *b* 24 Nov 1880; *m* 29 July 1911 Sir John Fischer Williams, KC, CBE (*d* 17 May 1947), son of John Williams, and *d* 14 Oct 1961, leaving issue

2c Augusta Muriel Hay; *m* 1st 10 June 1914 Philip Algernon Tillard (*ka* 19 Nov 1916), son of Algernon Tillard, of Stukeley Hall, Hants; *m* 2nd 2 Oct 1919 Capt Geoffrey Charlton Wolryche-Whitmore (*d* 5 March 1969), son of Col Francis Alexander Wolryche-Whitmore, of Dudmaston Hall, and *dsp* 19 Dec 1951

3c Audrey Frances Hay; *b* 22 July 1884; *d* unm 20 Nov 1968

4c Rhona Evelyn Hay; *m* 17 Dec 1915 Capt Claude Spence McNab, Cameron Highrs, and had issue

5c Mary Sancta Hay; *m* 16 March 1918 Richard Charles Farrow (*d* 20 Feb 1950), of Victoria, BC, Canada, son of Charles Henry Farrow, and *d* 29 July 1937, leaving issue

1b Eleanor Augusta; *m* 17 Oct 1878 Lionel Knight Rice (*d* 27 June 1929), son of Edward Royds Rice, of Dane Court, and *d* 10 Dec 1938

2b Edith Selina; *m* 5 June 1883 Robert Leigh Pemberton (*see* KINGSDOWN, B), and *d* 22 Sept 1925, leaving issue

3b Alice Lima; *m* 17 Oct 1878 Walter Edward Archer, CB (*d* 19 Aug 1917), 4th son of Capt Clement R Archer, of Hampton, Middx, and *d* 18 Feb 1936, leaving issue

4b Augusta Eleanor; *m* 20 April 1881 Lt-Gen Ormelie Campbell Hannay, Argyll & Sutherland Highrs (*ka* Paardeburg, South Africa, 18 Feb 1900), son of Col Simon Fraser Hannay, of Sorbie, and *d* Nov 1943, leaving issue

5b Mary Louisa; *m* 7 Sept 1882 Arthur Egerton Leigh (*d* 4 Nov 1914), of Sherborne, Dorset, yst son of Col Egerton Leigh, of Cheshire, and *d* 7 Oct 1922, leaving issue

4a Herbert Harley (Sir), KCB; *b* 4 Nov 1829; Govr Newfoundland 1894–98, Chm HM Customs; *m* 12 July 1859 Charlotte Letitia Caroline (*d* 1884), est dau of Lt-Gen Charles G J Arbuthnot, and *d* 11 March 1904, leaving surv issue:

1b Stewart Lygon; *b* 5 July 1863; Col Gordon Highrs; *m* 16 Nov 1895 Harriet Sophia (*d* 22 Feb 1948), dau of Col John Clark Kennedy, CB, of Knockgray; *d* 27 April 1930, leaving issue:

1c Elsie Dorothea Isabel; *m* 21 Dec 1931 John Stewart Heber, son of Gottlob Heber, and had issue:

1d *James William, MB, BS Lond 1962, MRCS Eng, LRCP Lond 1962; *b* 25 June 1938; *m* 26 Nov 1960 *Margaret Lesley, dau of A N Cooper, of Tilehurst, Reading, and has issue:

1e *Andrew John; *b* 27 Nov 1963

2e *Jeremy Mark; *b* 23 March 1966

1d *Janet Elizabeth; *b* 25 Sept 1934; *m* 22 Dec 1956 *Robert Bruce Holgate Butler, son of Albert Butler, of Tenterden, Kent, and has issue:
1e *Susan Elizabeth; *b* 12 Feb 1958
2e *Anne Judith; *b* 17 July 1960
3e *Jennifer Allison; *b* 31 March 1963
2c *Christian Charlotte [Mrs R Williams, 1 Verandah Cotts, Cricket Green, Hartley Wintney, Hants]; *m* 27 Nov 1937 Ronald Peers Williams (*d* 13 Nov 1968), yr son of Harry Williams, of Torquay, and has issue:
1d *Richard Murray; *b* 27 April 1947; *m* 1980 *Linda, dau of Dennis Akehurst, of Denbury, and has issue
1d *Jennifer Mary [Mrs Colin Willmott, The Middle Barn, Alexanders Lane, Privett, Alton. Hants GU34 3PW]; *b* 30 March 1940; *m* 20 March 1965 *Colin Willmott, yr son of Theodore Harold Wilmott, and has issue:
1e *Giles Benedict Paddington; *b* 29 April 1967
1e *Victoria; *b*. 4 Nov 1965
2d *Susan; *b* 19 Dec 1942
3d *Penelope Ann [Mrs Abraham Wax, 219 E 69th St, New York 10021, NY, USA]; *b* 23 Nov 1944; *m* 1971 *Abraham Wax, and has issue:
1e *David Israel; *b* 1980
1e *Rebecca; *b* 1981
3c Joan Margaret Vere; *b* 1 Oct 1909; *m* 9 Sept 1933 Henry Robert Stewart, only son of Rev Edward Hamilton Stewart, and had issue:
1d *Richard John; *b* 25 March 1936; *m* 1 Sept 1958 *Morag McLellen, dau of James Duncan Stewart, of Whitekirk, E Lothian, and has issue:
1e *Robert Murray; *b* 31 May 1959
2e *Roderick Iain; *b* 8 Aug 1960
3e *Alisdair James; *b* 15 July 1961
1e *Careen Ann; *b* 26 Oct 1962
2d *Geoffrey Edward; *b* 2 Nov 1938; *m* 6 Nov 1965 *Valerie Louise, est dau of Maj A E Twells, of Salisbury, Rhodesia
2b Gerald Ottway Hay; *b* 24 July 1868; *m* 3 June 1905 Charlotte (*d* 18 Nov 1944), yr dau of Dudley George Cary Elwes, of Conway, Florida, USA, and *d* 11 May 1951, leaving issue:
1c Herbert Frederick; *b* 8 March 1906; Sgt Som LI; *m* 28 May 1942 *Doris Mary, dau of Henry Walter Rowsell, of Taunton, and *d* 1971, leaving issue:
1d *Kathleen Elizabeth [Mrs Richard May, The Shop, Rorrington, Chisbury, Salop SY15 6BX]; *b* 31 Aug 1943; *m* 1969 *Richard John May Capt 2nd Bn LI, and has issue
2c Douglas Gerald; *b* 3 Sept 1907; *m* 2 March 1940 Elsie Brenda (*d* 1986), yr dau of Earle R Waight, and had issue:
1d +Julian Charles [Julian Murray Esq, c/o R Australian Yacht Sqdn, Outer Harbour, S Australia 5018]; *b* 9 July 1946
3c Stewart Hay; *b* 9 Feb 1909; *m* 7 Sept 1939 *Freda [Mrs Stewart Murray, Folly House, Folly Lane, Lacock, Wilts], dau of Charles Woodland, of Ashill, Somerset, and *d* 1988, leaving issue:
1d +John Stewart [John Murray Esq, Houndall Wood, Sparkwell, Plymouth]; *b* 23 Sept 1940; *m* 1970 *Alison, dau of Humphrey Tremblath, of Reigate, and has issue:
1e +Charles Humphrey Stewart; *b* 1971
1e *Jennifer Mary Ellen; *b* 1974
2d +Peter Gerald Stewart [Peter Murray Esq, 31 Priory Ave, London W4]; *b* 6 April 1944; *m* 1967 *Jane, dau of Alexander Wood, of Ashtead, and has issue:
1e +Rupert Hay; *b* 1969
2e +William Alexander; *b* 1972
1e *Sophie Elizabeth; *b* 19–
2e *Alice Adelaide; *b* 1981
3d +Geoffrey Charles Stewart [Geoffrey Murray Esq, 46 Rylett Rd, London W12 9ST]; *b* 20 June 1948; *m* 1983 *C Lynne, dau of Stewart Murray, of Ealing, and has issue:
1e +James Stewart; *b* 1983
2e +George Andrew Stewart; *b* 1986
4c Arthur Frank; *b* 25 April 1911; *m* 2 Oct 1937 Ruby Joyce (*d* 14 Aug 1995), dau of Arthur Hooper, of Ashill, Som, and *d* 26 May 1996, leaving:
1d *Anne Jennifer [Mrs Neil Jarman, The Shrubber, 21 Middleton Rd, Ringwood, Hants BH24 1RN]; *b* 19 July 1939; *m* *Neil Jarman and has issue:
1e *Ian; *b* 1960; *m* 1989 *Elizabeth Caroline Foster and has:
1f *Stephen Andrew; *b* 1994
1e *Frances Ann; *b* 1962; *m* 1989 *Richard Allen and has:
1f *Jennifer Helen; *b* 1992
2e *Rebecca; *b* 1965; *m* Sept 1994 *John Percival and has:
1f *Alexander James; *b* 1997
5c +Keith Robert [Keith Murray Esq, 2 Windrush Place, Northmoor, Exford]; *b* 27 July 1912; RE; *m* 4 Feb 1941 *Ellen Georgina, dau of Charles Woodland, of Ashill, Som, and has issue:
1d +Andrew Keith; *b* 15 Dec 1946
1d *Joan Ursula; *b* 21 Jan 1945
1c Kathleen Margaret Augusta; *b* 3 April 1916; *d* 1996
3b Keith Norman Ward; *b* 31 Aug 1873; *d* 15 Sept 1936
1b Mona Elizabeth Louise; *d* unm 13 June 1929
2b Maud Louisa Rosalind; *d* unm 29 April 1925
3b Isobel Salisbury Mabel; *d* unm 8 Sept 1960
5a Frederick William (Rev); *b* 8 May 1831; *educ* Ch Ch Oxford (MA); Rector of Stone, Kent 1859–1906, Hon Canon of Rochester; *m* 18 Aug 1864 Kathleen Cortlandt (*d* 26 Oct 1914), 3rd dau of Rev William Gorst Harrison, and *d* 2 Nov 1913, leaving issue:
1b Frederick Auriol (Rev); *b* 27 Nov 1865; *educ* Keble Coll, Oxford (MA); Vicar of Stourport, Worcs; *m* 4 Jan 1893 Jessie (*d* 2 April 1955), dau of George Gaviller Styles, of Knockhall, Greenhithe, Kent, and *d* 12 Feb 1939, having had issue:
1c Maurice Austin; *b* 4 Jan 1895; Lt Essex Regt; *ka* 1915
2c (George) Ronald Auriol; *b* 2 April 1900; *educ* King's Coll Lond (BSc Eng); *m* 1 Sept 1926 Phyllis (*d* 1978), est dau of Walter Langford Rowley, of Birlingham Grange, Worcs, and *d* 8 Nov 1961, leaving issue:
1d +Brian Austin Walter [Brian Murray-Gourlay Esq, The Old Smithy, School Lane, S Chard, Somerset]; *b* 17 July 1927; RN; *m* 4 April 1953 (*divorce* 1962) Margaret, yr dau of William Bryant, of Cribbs Causeway, Glos; *m* 2nd 1973 *Patricia Mary, dau of Daniel Fewtrell, of Dudley, Staffs, and formerly wife of Charles Desmond Small, and has issue by 1st wife:
1e +Hugh William Auriol [Hugh Murray Esq, 2 Vale View Cotts, Milton Lilbourne, Pewsey, Wilts]; *b* 27 May 1960; *m* 1987 *Fiona Joan, yst dau of Capt John Rumble, of Lymington, Hants, and has issue:
1f *Alice Auriol; *b* 1992
1d *Auriol Mary; *b* 13 April 1933; *m* 5 Oct 1957 *Capt Frederick Ernest Herring, Roy Norfolk Regt, yst son of John Herring, of Jesmond, Northumberland, and has issue:
1e *Jonathan James Auriol; *b* 27 July 1959
2e *Christopher John Murray; *b* 18 Sept 1962
2b Charles Hay (Rev); *b* 17 April 1869; Rector of Kirkby Knowle, Yorks; *m* 26 April 1906 Mabel (*d* 10 July 1953), est dau of Samuel Charles Umfreville, of Ingress Abbey, Greenhithe, and *d* 11 Oct 1923, having had issue:
1c (Francis) Ralph Hay (Sir), KCMG (1962, CMG 1950), CB (1957); *b* 3 March 1908; *educ* Brentwood and St Edmund Hall Oxford (BA); joined BBC 1934, seconded FO 1939, Allied Control Commn Austria 1945, Special Commr's Staff SE Asia 1946, Counsellor: FO 1948 and Madrid 1951–54, Min Cairo 1954–56, Assist U-Sec FO 1957–61, Dep U-Sec 1961, Amb Greece 1962–67, Govr BBC 1967–83, Chm CSM Parly Consultants 1975; *m* 10 April 1935 Countess Mauricette Vladimira Marie Kuenburg (*d* 21 June 1996), only child of Count Bernhard Kuenburg, of Payerbach, Lower Austria, and *d* 1983, leaving:
1d +Ingram Bernard Hay, TD [Lt-Col Ingram Murray TD, 23 Dunton Rd, Stewkley, Leighton Buzzard, Beds]; *b* 21 May 1937; *educ* Bedford Sch and St Edmund Hall, Oxford (BA); Lt-Col RE 1956–57, TARO; *m* 14 Sept 1963 *Juliet Anne Thackeray, dau of Capt J M T Ritchie and Mrs A R Dickinson, and has:
2e +Alastair James Hay; *b* 10 May 1968; *m* June 1995 *Katherine Perry
1e *Xenia Margaret Thackeray; *b* 10 May 1966
2e *Francesca Helen Anne; *b* 16 Feb 1970
2d +Nicholas Julyan Edward [Nicholas Murray Esq, The Old Vicarage, Aston Abbots, Aylesbury, Bucks]; *b* 7 March 1939 *m* 14 July 1973 *Caroline Ann, est dau of Capt Alan McClintock, of Nenagh, Co Tipperary, and has:
1e *Anstice Aileen Thérèse; *b* 1981
3d +Simon Anthony [Simon Murray Esq, Easton Hill House, Dunsford, Exeter, Devon]; *b* 9 July 1948; *m* 26 July 1975 *Lesley-Ann, JP, dau of Robert Freeman Wright, of Leighton Buzzard, and has issue:
1e +Joshua Robert Darroch; *b* 1980
1e *Hannah Lisl; *b* 1982
1d *Georgina Theresa [Mrs Roy Ashworth, The Old Forge Cottage, Petworth Rd, Chiddingfold, Surrey GU8 4TY]; *b* 26 Dec 1942; *m* 1965 *Roy Ashworth, yr s of F A Ashworth, of Nairobi, Kenya, and has issue
2c Stephen Umfreville Hay; *b* 6 Sept 1912; *educ* Brentwood and RADA; WW II in RASC, Capt Gen List; actor; *m* 26 April 1937 *Joan Alestha, dau of John Joseph Moy Butterfield, of London, and *d* 31 March 1983, leaving:
1d *Amanda [Mrs George Tarry, The Old Stables, Roeheath, Cinder Hill, Chailey, E Sussex BN8 4HR]; *b* 15 Sept 1942; actress; *m* 1975 *George Tarry
1c Anna Kathleen; *b* 31 March 1907; *d* 1983
2c Sybilla Angela; *b* 29 Sept *d* 14 Oct 1909
3b Maurice William (Rev); *b* 14 July 1870; Rector of Chulmleigh, N Devon 1920–39; *m* 29 June 1909 Eva Margaret (*d* 7 May 1958), er dau of Charles Hubback Watson, of Stone Castle, Kent, and *d* 3 Oct 1942, leaving issue:
1c Kathleen Joan; *b* 7 Sept 1911; *m* 1958 Alfred Roberts (*d* 1976), of Pulborough, Sussex and *d* 8 Oct 1996
2c Margaret Elizabeth; *b* 20 Jan 1915; *m* 27 Nov 1943 Cecil George McCullagh, yr s of Isaac John McCullagh, of Portadown, NI, and Kimberley, S Africa, and adopted four children
3c *Ursula Mary [Mrs Alan White, 89 High St, Tenterden, Kent]; *b* 1919; *m* 27 Sept 1941 Maj Alan A White, Border Regt (*d* 1993), of Cookham Dean, Berks, and has issue:
1d *Christopher Douglas [Christopher White Esq, 11 Cornwall Mews South, Grenville Place, London SW7 4RZ]; *b* 1943; *m* 1987 *Maria Eulallia Pessoa, and has issue:
1e *Douglas Alan Pessoa; *b* 1987
2d *David Ian (twin) [David White Esq, 2 Balliol Cotts, Wadhurst, E Sussex]; *b* 1943; *m* 1972 *Margaret Ann Griffith, and has issue:
1e *Jonathan Alan; *b* 1974
2e *Daniel Edmund; *b* 1977
4b Cecil Austin; *b* 13 Mar 1872; *m* 6 May 1908 Elizabeth, 2nd dau of Frederick Chambers, of Bridgewater, and widow of J Bevan of Cape Town, and *d* 15 July 1927

1b Mildred Sarah Maria; *b* 24 Oct 1874; *m* 21 Nov 1907 Arthur James Warburton Kitchin CIE, ICS (*d* 22 April 1957), son of Rev Joseph Laxton Kitchin, of Teignmouth, and *d* 21 Jan 1957

2b Geraldine Mary; *b* 18 April 1876; *m* 5 Jan 1905 Gilbert Edward Chetwynd Talbot (*d* 26 March 1950), yr son of Col Hon Sir Wellington Patrick Manvers Chetwynd Talbot, KCB, and *d* 12 Feb 1953, leaving issue (*see* SHREWSBURY and WATERFORD, E)

3b Lilian Augusta; *m* 14 March 1900 Walter de Merindol Malan, ICS, est son of Rev Arthur N Malan, DD, of Sandhurst, and *d* 12 Dec 1913, leaving issue

(3) Charles; HEIC CS, Bengal; *m* 1806 Anne Amelia (*m* 2nd George Warde, HEIC CS), 2nd dau of Thomas Dashwood (*see* DASHWOOD, Bt, of Kirtlington Park), and *d* 1808

(4) Edward (Rev); *b* 5 Nov 1798; Vicar of Northolt, Middx, and Prebendary of St Paul's; *m* 14 Feb 1822 Ruperta Catherine (*d* 5 Sept 1871), only child of Sir George Wright, Bt, and *d* 1 July 1852, leaving issue:

1a Augustus George Ernest; *b* 1823; Cdr RN; *d* 1872

2a Charles Edward Gostling, JP, DL; *b* 12 May 1825; Hon Col 2nd Vol Bn Middx Regt; High Sheriff 1890, barrister; *m* 1st 21 March 1850 Emily (*d* 18 Jan 1859), only child of Rev John Whalley Gostling, of Whitton Park, Middx, and had issue:

1b Augustus; *b* 5 Feb 1854; *d* 14 May 1886

1b Rosalind Emma; *m* 13 Feb 1879 1st Baron Roundway (*d* 17 June 1925), and *d* 8 Nov 1938, having had issue

2b Julia Ruperta; *m* 1st 7 July 1875 William Hale Willats (*d* 16 July 1893), of Denton Court, Canterbury, est son of William Willats, and had issue; *m* 2nd 20 June 1894 Col Morgan Samuel Crofton, CB, DSO (*dsp* 9 Jan 1916; *see* CROFTON, Bt, of Mohill), and *d* 30 March 1949

3b Emily; *m* 28 Nov 1878 Henry John Conant (*d* 17 May 1914), and *d* 18 June 1881, leaving issue

2a (cont.) Col Charles Murray *m* 2nd 10 Dec 1878 Margaret Frances Elizabeth (*d* 30 June 1910), only dau of Rev John W Conant, and *d* June 1892, having by her had issue:

2b Fane Wright Stapleton; *b* 16 Oct 1879; Capt 12th Lancers; *ka* 30 Oct 1914

3b Cecil de Grey; *b* 4 Dec 1880; Lt 1st Bn York and Lancaster Regt, Maj RASC and Lt-Col cmdg 12th Cadet Bn Essex Regt, Boer War, WW I (despatches), WW II; *m* 1st 8 Dec 1910 (*divorce* 1945) Theodora Lockhart, dau of James T Jervis, MICE; *m* 2nd 24 May 1945 Ivy Noel Campbell, dau of William Augustus Kennedy Gostling, and *dsp* 18 June 1956

4b Rupert Auriol Conant; *b* 29 Sept 1882; Capt Seaforth Highrs; *m* 12 Aug 1913 Ivy Maud (*m* 2nd 12 Nov 1918 Brig Hector Robert Hume Greenfield, CBE, Argyll & Sutherland Highrs, son of Lt-Col Hume Greenfield, JP, of Argyll, and *d* 22 July 1947), dau of Sir Henry Edward Dering, 10th Bt, and *das* 11 March 1915, leaving issue:

1c Anthony Ian Rupert, OBE (1957, MBE 1944); *b* 13 June 1914; *educ* Eton and RMC Sandhurst; Col Seaforth Highrs WW II (despatches); *m* 26 May 1944 Alexandra Elizabeth (*d* 1991), only dau of Lt-Col Alexander Dalziel Mackenzie, CVO, DSO, of Farr, Inverness-shire, and *d* 1993, leaving issue:

1d +John Rupert [John Murray Esq, Old Cardinham, Bodmin, Cornwall PL30 4ED]; *b* 7 Sept 1945; *educ* Eton and Sorbonne; *m* 1977 *Valerie Margaret, dau of Eric V Sanders, and has issue:

1e +Edward Ian; *b* 1977

2e +George John; *b* 1979

2d +(Ian) James; *b* 22 July 1947; *educ* Eton and RMA Sandhurst; Lt QO Highrs; *m* 1976 *Christina Anne, yr dau of Arthur Carr, MC, and has issue:

1e *Emma Juliette; *b* 1977

2e *Clare Patience Frances; *b* 1979

3e *Alice Christina; *b* 1983

3d +Andrew Edward; *b* 2 Nov 1950; *educ* Gordonstoun and Dijon U

5b Stracey Montagu Atholl; *b* 7 March 1888; *m* 10 June 1926 Irene Margaretta (*d* 1972), yr dau of Capt William Wheat Waring, and *d* 1970, leaving issue:

1c +Edward William Atholl [Edward Murray Esq, Highfield, Derby Rd, Haslemere, Surrey]; *b* 30 June 1927; *educ* Northampton GS; *m* 1st 22 Aug 1959 Anne Oakeley (*d* 1972), only dau of Maj Loraine Macgregor Kerr, MC, W Yorks Regt, of New Romney, Kent, by Ellen Beatrice, er dau of Sir Charles John Oakeley, 5th Bt (*qv*); *m* 2nd 1974 *Elizabeth Dawn, dau of H D Harman, MC, and has issue by 1st wife:

1d +James Henry Atholl; *b* 7 July 1960

1d *Charlotte Melloney Loraine; *b* 19 Feb 1964

2c +Fane Robert Conant [Fane Murray Esq, Park House Farm, Baldersdale, Barnard Castle, Co Durham]; *b* 19 March 1929; *educ* Northampton GS; *m* 27 April 1962 *Margaret Carisina, only dau of Lt-Col Leslie George Gray-Cheape, MBE, JP, DL, of Carse Gray, Forfar, and has:

1d +Rupert Charles; *b* 15 March 1963

1d *Emma Jane; *b* 3 June 1965

4b Nina, MBE (1946); *b* 19 Sept 1889; *m* 18 Aug 1916 Maj Harry Colmore, 7th Hussars and RFC (*d* 28 Sept 1937), son of George Harry Colmore, of Hathern, Leics, by Emily Laura, yst dau of Rev Samuel Vere Dashwood (*see* DASHWOOD, Bt, of Kirtlington Park), and had issue:

1c *Peter Dashwood Murray; *b* 22 Nov 1919; *educ* Sherborne; WW II in E Africa and Ethiopia

5b Gwladys, MBE (1946); *b* 8 Jan 1891; *m* 9 July 1913 (*divorce* 1947) Sir Philip Lee Brocklehurst, 2nd Bt (*d* 28 Jan 1974), and had issue

1a Louisa Ruperta; *m* 20 June 1848 Edward Colston (*d* 20 Dec 1864), of Roundway Park, Wilts, and *d* 20 Nov 1900, leaving issue (*see* 1940 edn ROUNDWAY, B)

2a Emma Selina; *m* 25 April 1854 Maj Robert Bartholomew Lawes, DL (*d* 11 Nov 1907), of Old Park, Dover, and *d* 1896, leaving issue

3 William; *b* 20 March 1762; *m* 14 June 1789 Mary Anne (*d* 29 May 1827), dau of James Hodges, and *d* 29 Dec 1796, leaving, with a dau (Mary Anne, *d* 22 Dec 1868):

(1) James Arthur; *b* 25 May 1790; V-Adml; *m* 1st 13 Dec 1821 Harriet (*d* 27 July 1829), dau of William Coupland, and had issue:

1a James; *b* 3 July 1829; Lt RE; *k* 18 June 1855 Sebastopol

1a Harriet Coupland; *m* 7 Oct 1852 Harvey Winson Fellows (*d* 13 Jan 1907), and *d* 8 Feb 1893, leaving issue

(1) (cont) V-Adml James Murray *m* 2nd 3 May 1838 Julia (*d* 31 Dec 1878), dau of John Delmé, of Cams Hall, and *d* 6 March 1860, having by her had issue:

2a William Frederick; *b* 5 Jan 1845; Cdr RN

3a George Delmé; *b* 6 Oct 1854; *m* 3 July 1877 Sarah (*d* 31 Dec 1939), dau of Alphonse Loney, and *d* 1 April 1915 leaving issue:

1b George Arthur Delmé, DSO; *b* 23 Jan 1879; Maj Shropshire LI, S African War (Queen's and King's medals with clasps), WW I (despatches, DSO); *m* 29 Nov 1906 Dorothea Emily Anne (*d* 31 March 1938), dau of T Alexander Webb, of Waynwern, Mon, and *d* 30 Sept 1944, leaving:

1c +George Philip Alexander, DSO (1945), MBE [Lt-Col George Delmé Murray DSO MBE, Yew Tree Cott, Knowbury, Ludlow, Salop]; *b* 13 July 1921; Lt-Col KSLI, formerly T/Maj IA; WW II Burma (wounded); *m* 29 Dec 1951 *Alison Elizabeth, yr dau of Col William John Beddows, MC, TD, JP, DL, of Ackleton House, nr Wolverhampton, Staffs, and has:

1d *Caroline Alison [Mrs John Howson, The Dingle, Ditton Priors, Bridgnorth, Salop WV16 6SX]; *b* 6 May 1953; *m* 1979 *John William Howson and has:

1e *William George Frederick; *b* 15 Dec 1982

2e *Edward James Philip; *b* 25 Sept 1985

2d *Rosemary Janet [Mrs James Budgett, Park Farm, Kirtlington, Oxon OX5 3JQ]; *b* 3 Sept 1956; *m* 1979 *James Frederick Budgett, and has issue:

1e *Charles George Arthur; *b* 6 Nov 1981

1e *Georgina Patrica Alison; *b* 23 June 1985

1c Dorothea Agnes Cecilia; *b* 11 July 1908

2c Eleanor Joan Medora; *b* 8 Jan 1911; *m* 7 June 1933 Thomas Angus Lyall Paton, CMG, BSc, MICE, FASCE, only son of Thomas Lyall Paton, of St John, Jersey, CI, and *d* 7 Jan 1964, leaving two sons and two daus

3c Corin Georgina Florence; *b* 27 March 1919; *m* 6 March 1947 William R Wilson, of Dawlish, Devon, son of Harold Byrne Wilson

2b Reginald William Hugh; *b* 15 Aug 1881; *m* 15 Oct 1917 Emily Maud Satchell

3b William Henry; *b* 7 Oct 1883; *m* 22 Nov 1908 Winifred Mary Wilson, and *dsp* 18 Sept 1943

4b Algernon Charles; *b* 24 Feb 1887; Capt Seaforth Highrs WW I; *d* 18 Dec 1964

1b Julia Cecilia; *b* 6 Oct 1882; *d* 1911

2a Julia Frances Delmé; *m* 18 Dec 1862 Adml Sir Richard Vesey Hamilton, GCB (*d* 17 Sept 1912), and *d* 4 June 1897, leaving issue

3a Mary Ann; *m* A E Harston, and *d* 1891

4a Margaret Amelia; *m* Martin Seal, and *d* 1910

5a Louisa Mary; *m* 13 Nov 1872 Cdr Hugh H Hannay, RN, and *d* 18 Feb 1874

4 Henry; *b* 13 June 1767; *m* 8 Dec 1786 Eliza (*d* 20 Dec 1847), dau of Richard Kent, of Liverpool, and *d* 3 Dec 1805, leaving issue, with five daus:

(1) Richard; *b* 19 Oct 1787; Lt-Col; *m* 1st 1 June 1811 Catherine (*d* 30 April 1817), dau of J J Bacon, and had issue:

1a Henry; *b* 4 April 1815; Col RA; *m* 22 Dec 1840 Isabella (*d* 20 Nov 1870), dau of Rev John Oliver, and *d* 8 March 1864, leaving issue:

1b Richard Paget (Rev), MA; *b* 26 Dec 1842; Vicar of Shapwick, Dorset; *m* 1st 4 July 1868 Emily Blanche (*d* 1877), dau of Gen James Webber Smith, CB, and had issue:

1c Henry James Stewart; *b* 30 Nov 1874; Capt RE WW I; *m* 28 June 1919 Maude Amelia (*m* 2nd 1947 Thomas Rosser Dummer (*d* 17 April 1959), of Cape Town, S Africa, and *d* 1974), yst dau of George Jonathan Mills, of Norwich, and *d* 17 March 1942, leaving issue:

1d *Margaret Dorothea [Mrs Stanley Miller, PO Box 14204, Bredell, Transvaal, S Africa]; *b* 2 March 1926; *m* 14 Dec 1946 *Stanley Alastair Miller, of Le Tremouille, 104 Third Ave, Bredell, Transvaal, son of Robert Ashley Miller, and has issue:

1e *Pamela Ann [Miss Pamela Miller, No 1 Shiraz, 26 Arum Rd, Bloubergrant, 7441 CP, S Africa]; *b* 30 April 1949

2e *Sheila Frances; *b* 15 Oct 1950; *m* 1981 *Anthony John Foxcroft, of Roodepoort, Transvaal, and has:

1f *Samantha; *b* 17 Feb 1986

3e *Wendy Margaret [Mrs Mark Everingham, 44 Slim St, Melville, Hamilton, New Zealand]; *b* 29 April 1954; *m* 1st 1977 (*divorce* 1982) David Foxcroft; *m* 2nd 1989 *Mark Everingham and has issue by both husbs

1c Mona Blanche; *b* 6 April 1872; *d* unm Aug 1961

1b (cont.) The Rev Richard Paget *m* 2nd 20 April 1880 Ada Constance (*d* 6 Feb 1943), dau of Henry Richard Woodhouse, and *d* 29 Oct 1908, having by her had issue:

2c Athole Evelyn (Rev); *b* 26 Nov 1881; *educ* Keble Coll Oxford (MA); *m* 16 Jan 1917 Ellen Emily (*d* 13 Feb 1960), 4th dau of Henry Frederic Tiarks, JP, of Foxbury, Chislehurst, Kent, and *d* 27 April 1962, leaving issue:

1d *Anne [Mrs John Page, 67B, High St, Codford, nr Warminster, Wilts]; *b* 14 Jan 1920; MusB Durham U; *m* 11 May 1954 John Edward Page (*d* 30 June 1964), er son of Edward Page, of Orpington, Kent, and has issue:

1e *Edward John Atholl; *b* 3 Aug 1956

2e *Henry Stewart Murray; *b* 3 Aug 1956

3e *Thomas Patrick Murray; *b* 18 June 1960

1e *Susan Margaret; *b* 10 April 1955; *m* 1974 (*divorce* 1986) Julian Marc Piers Bryant, and has issue:
1f *Polly Louise; *b* 1976
2f *Sophie Catherine; *b* 1978
3f *Emma Charlotte; *b* 1980
3c Arthur Hugh; *b* 9 Feb 1883; ICS; *d* unm 22 May 1909
4c Edward Douglas; *b* 29 Feb 1884; slr; 2nd Lt 11th Bn (attached 8th Bn) Black Watch; *ka* 20 July 1916, unm
2c Violet Constance (Sister Constance, OMSE); nun
3c Ethel Mary
4c Muriel Gladys Angela; *d* unm 6 Oct 1970
2b Henry; *b* 20 March 1850; Lt-Col Roy Munster Fus; *m* 1880 Marianne (*d* 4 Oct 1903), dau of C M Farquharson, Judge Supreme Court Jamaica, and *d* 8 Jan 1909, leaving issue:
1c Henry Francis Farquharson; *b* 6 July 1881; Maj Black Watch, Boer War, WW I (despatches); *m* 1 Jan 1915 Madeline Elizabeth (*d* 18 March 1966), dau of Arthur Henry Giles, of Bristol and Weston-Super-Mare, Dep Inspr-Gen Bengal Police; *ka* 1917, leaving issue:
1d Ian Henry, MC (1945); *b* 29 Jan 1916; *educ* Wellington and RMC Sandhurst; Lt-Col (Hon Col) RHF WW II (wounded), Naval and Mil Attaché Br Emb Warsaw 1960–61; *m* 20 April 1940 Eleanor Fownes (*d* 14 Nov 1983), dau of Rev Geoffrey Lionel Porcher, BD, Rector Weston-Super-Mare, by Marjorie Fownes, and *d* 1990, leaving issue:
1e *Alison Fownes [Mrs Oliver Wilkins, Victoria House, St Keyne, Liskeard, Cornwall PL14 4SG]; *b* 11 June 1941; *m* 1970 *Oliver William Wilkins, and has issue:
1f *Geoffrey James Murray; *b* 1976
1f *Andrea Caroline Fownes; *b* 1975
2e *Jacqueline Dorothea Fownes [Miss Jacqueline Murray, 13 Wheatley Way, Chalfont St Peter, Bucks SL9 0JE]; *b* 2 Oct 1942
1c Mona Anna; *m* 11 July 1907 Adml Sir Thomas Jackson, KBE, CB, MVO (*d* 7 July 1945), son of Adml Sir Thomas Sturges Jackson, KCVO, and *d* 20 May 1945, leaving issue
3b John Oliver; *b* 9 July 1851; *d* unm 1887
4b Edward Dudley; *b* 13 March 1854; *m* 1st 1889 Margaret (*d* 1912), dau of Thomas Cawkwell, of Auckland, NZ; *m* 2nd 1916 Emily May Mona Murray Gawne, and *d* 10 Nov 1930
5b Charles Nathaniel; *b* 27 March 1855; *m* 1885 Annie Isabel, dau of W C Wright, of Cambridge, NZ, and *d* 6 Sept 1922, leaving issue:
1c Atholl Alma Emily Clare; *m* 1910 John Nicholas Quick, and had issue
2c Kathleen Stewart; *m* 1913 Joseph Wilford Sanderson, and has issue
6b Arthur Silver (Rev), MA; *b* 13 Aug 1858; Vicar of Horningsham, Warminster; *m* 15 Dec 1887 Rose Evelyn (*d* 10 May 1941), dau of Henry Richard Woodhouse, and *d* 8 Oct 1932, leaving issue:
1c Arthur Evelyn Francis; *b* 28 Sept 1888; *educ* Marlborough and Exeter Coll Oxford (BA); barrister Middle Temple 1929, Sr Resident Admin Serv Nigeria, Silver Jubilee 1935 and Coronation 1937 medals; *m* 21 May 1927 Louise Isabelle (*d* March 1996), dau of Lt-Col Addis Delacombe, DSO, of Shrewton Manor, Wilts, and had:
1d +James Stewart [James Murray Esq, Lewtrenchard Manor, Lewdown, nr Oakhampton, Devon]; *b* 26 Nov 1941; *educ* Diocesan Coll, Rondebosch, Cape Town, and Stellenbosch U (BSc (Agric) 1965); *m* 1979 *Susan Janet Elizabeth, dau of Wyndham John Williams, and widow of AVM Thomas James Hanlon, CB, CBE, and has issue:
1e +Duncan William; *b* 1980
2e +Henry Stewart; *b* 1983
3e +Angus Ian (twin); *b* 1983
1d*Jean Evelyn Louise [Mrs Jonathan Oliphant, White Lodge, Startley, Chippenham, Wilts SN15 5HE]; *b* 6 Jan 1932; *educ* Stellenbosch U (BA 1953); *m* 7 Feb 1959 *Capt Jonathan Beresford Oliphant, 7th Duke of Edinburgh's Own Gurkha Rifles, son of Rev Donald Aden Oliphant, MA, of Alton, Hants, and has issue:
1e *Angus Laurence; *b* 31 Jan 1966; *m* 1995 *Siobhan Alexandra Forbes Painter
1e *Catriona Jane; *b* 30 Sept 1960
2e *Janet Elizabeth; *b* 1 July 1963; *m* 1994 *William Kerrison Gotch Hutchings and has:
1f *Eleanor Charlotte Margaret; *b* 1995
2c Kenneth Andrew Silver; *b* 9 June 1904; *d* unm 9 Nov 1991
3c Douglas Vivian; *b* 2 Dec 1905; *educ* Westminster and Gonville and Caius Coll Cambridge (MA); *m* 1st 17 Aug 1932 (*divorce* 1958) Isabel Mary Farquhar, dau of Dr Andrew Grierson Fausset-Farquhar, of Kincardineshire; *m* 2nd, 16 July 1958 *Beryl Violet [Mrs Douglas Murray, 6 Courtmead, South Stoke, Bath BA2 7EB], yr dau of Lt-Col John Henry Wybergh, and by her had:
1d +Hamish Douglas [Hamish Murray Esq, Horseshoe Cottage, Faulkland, Somerset BA3 5XA]; *b* 3 Sept 1959; Merchant Navy; *m* 1993 *Kate Watson, only dau of Albert Edwar Watson, and has:
1e *Imogen Ann; *b* 23 Aug 1995
2d +Andrew Vivian [Andrew Murray Esq, No 2 Cottages, Newbarns, Inverkeilor, Arbroath, Angus]; *b* 11 Oct 1961; RM; *m* 1988 *Anne Towns, and has issue:
1e +James Andrew; *b* 1988
1e *Claire Beryl; *b* 1991
1d *Anne Beryl Charlotte de la Trémoïlle; *b* 2 May 1963; *m* 1988 *George Coronis and has:
1e *Douglas Michael; *b* 1990
2e *Seymour Luke; *b* 29 Aug 1996
1e *Clementine Aspasia; *b* 1989
2e *Portia Marie Violet; *b* 1993

1c Anne Evelyn Charlotte de la Trémoïlle; *m* 26 July 1916 John Christopher Scrimgeour Law, son of Rev W J Law, and *d* 3 March 1941, leaving issue
1b Isabella Sophia (Sister Petronella); *d* 12 April 1907
2b Elizabeth Emily; *d* 4 March 1927
3b Mona; *d* unm 7 Dec 1934
1a Elizabeth Anne; *d* unm 1863
2a Emily Maria; *b* 19 April 1814; *m* 28 April 1835 Edward Moore Gawne (*d* 8 Feb 1872), Speaker H of Keys, IOM, and *d* 11 May 1889, leaving issue
(1) (cont) Lt-Col Richard Murray *m* 2nd 1819 Margaret (*d* 8 Nov 1864), dau of William Tennison, and *d* 16 Oct 1843, having by her had:
3a Margaret Tennison; *d* unm 13 June 1859
5 Charles MURRAY later MURRAY-AYNSLEY (roy licence) (Very Rev); *b* 21 Oct 1771; Dean Bocking; *m* 18 June 1793 Alicia (*d* 18 June 1813), dau of George Mitford and heiress of her great-uncle Gawen Aynsley, and *d* 5 May 1808, leaving issue:
(1) John, of Undertown, Herefs, JP, DL; *b* 2 June 1795; *m* 24 June 1820 Emma Sarah (*d* 27 Feb 1877), dau of Samuel Peach, of Tockington House, and *d* 25 March 1870, having had issue:
1a Charles, CB, JP; *b* 21 Sept 1821; V-Adml; *m* 9 Dec 1861 Augusta Judith (*d* 16 June 1893), dau of William Gilbert Campion, and *d* 1 April 1901, leaving issue:
1b John Francis; *b* 27 Oct 1866; Capt RN; *d* unm 10 May 1904
1b Alicia Harriet; *m* 15 Jan 1891 Rev Alfred Evans VINTER later MURRAY-AYNSLEY (taken with arms by roy licence 15 Aug 1904; *d* 27 Nov 1920), Pncpl Bishop's Stortford Trg Coll, and *d* 1923, leaving issue
2a James Athole; *b* 18 June 1823; Capt in the Army; *m* 23 Oct 1855 Hannah Maria, dau of John Justin, of Ledbury, Herefs, and *d* 28 March 1869, leaving issue:
1b Clara Adelaide; *b* 15 Oct 1867; *m* 1888 Rev Samuel Martin Young, MA, Vicar Holy Trinity, Southall, Middx, and Rural Dean, and had issue
3a John Cruger (Rev), JP (Herefs); *b* 21 Feb 1825; Rector Walton and Weston; *m* 6 July 1852 Harriet Georgina Maria (*d* 6 Aug 1898), dau of Rev Frederick Manners-Sutton (*see* RUTLAND, D), and *dsp* 19 Jan 1913
4a George Herbert; *b* 4 Sept 1826; Maj-Gen Madras Army; *m* 12 Feb 1848 Emily (*d* 18 Aug 1894), yst dau of Robert Hand, and *d* 10 Dec 1887, having had issue:
1b Charles Edward; *b* 31 Jan 1851; *m* 20 Oct 1880 Fanny, dau of Rev A Fennell, and *d* 20 April 1918
2b John Percy; *b* 6 June 1853
1b Emma; *m* 8 Oct 1867 Maj Charles Bateman Prust, 60th Rifles, and *d* his widow, 28 Sept 1923, leaving issue
2b Clara Emily Stewart; *m* 5 Oct 1889 Owen Armstrong, and *dsp* 3 Sept 1894
3b Maud; *m* 24 Dec 1881 Maj C M T Western, RA, and *d* 3 March 1898, leaving issue
4b Alice Elizabeth; *m* 15 April 1882 Maj G F A Norton, RA, and *d* 31 Jan 1896, leaving issue
5a Hugh Percy; *b* 8 Oct 1828; *m* 7 June 1859 Elizabeth (*d* July 1893), dau of Thomas Campbell, and *d* 1917, having had issue:
1b John Henry, MRCS (Eng), LRCP (Lond); *b* 24 July 1860; *m* 27 April 1891 Elizabeth Anderson, only dau of Andrew Key, MD
2b Charles Percy; *b* 9 Jan 1862; *m* 1st 5 Oct 1911 Ina Winifred (*d* 1918), dau of D Prins, MD, and *d* 1936, leaving issue:
1c *Elizabeth [Mrs John Simpson, Dalvey, Turakina, New Zealand]; *b* 1912; *m* 1935 *John Duncan Simpson, of Dalvey, and had issue:
1d *Charles William; *b* 1936
2d *Duncan Murray; *b* 1938; *m* 1961 *Judith Margaret Mary, dau of H Simmons, of Hawkes Bay, NZ, and has issue:
1e *Michael Paul; *b* 1961
2e *Toby Duncan; *b* 1963
1d *Patricia Mary; *b* 1940
2b (cont) Charles Murray-Aynsley *m* 2nd 1921 Gladys (*d* 1959), dau of Francis Turnor, and *d* 6 Sept 1936, having by her had issue:
1c +Francis Percy [Francis Murray-Aynsley Esq, Wi Waka, Eketahuna, New Zealand]; *b* 1924; *m* 1950 *Diana Gray, dau of W Gray Young, of Lowry Bay, Wellington, NZ, and has:
1d +Charles William; *b* 1955
2d *Susan Jane; *b* 1951
2d *Bridget Anne; *b* 1952
2c *Beatrice Mary; *b* 1923; *m* 24 Jan 1948 *John Tansley, est son of Alfred Tansley, of Invercargill, NZ, and has issue:
1d *Sara Lorraine; *b* 20 Aug 1949; *m* 1968 *Grant Alistair Marshall
2d *Philippa Ann; *b* 18 Aug 1952
3d *Pamela Winifrid; *b* 10 July 1961
3b Archibald Cruger; *b* 23 July 1864; *m* 24 April 1901 Blanche, yst dau of William Gerard, and *dsp* Oct 1903
4b George; *b* 19 Nov 1865; *m* 1st 1916 Blanche (*d* 1927), dau of W Gerard; *m* 2nd 1933 Ann, dau of D McVeigh
1b Agnes Athole; *d* unm Dec 1901
2b Emma Mary
3d Helen Elizabeth; medal of Queen Elisabeth of Belgium; *m* 26 March 1913 Beauchamp Lasseter Lane, who *d* 1924
1a Emma Athole Murray; *d* 19 Dec 1843
(1) Charlotte; *m* 28 Jan 1812 Gen Sir John Oswald, GCB (*d* 6 June 1840), and *d* 27 Feb 1827, leaving issue
(2) Atholl Keturah; *m* 5 June 1826 Rev Sir Herbert Oakeley, 3rd Bt (*d* 27 March 1845; *qv*), and *d* 26 Jan 1844, leaving issue
(3) Elizabeth Anne; *d* unm 7 June 1880
1 Charlotte; *d* unm 1808

2 Amelia; *m* 1st Thomas Ivie Cooke, Capt in the Army; *m* 2nd Sir Richard Gamon, Bt, and *d* 1818
3 Jane; *m* John Grosset Muirhead (*d* 1836), and *d* 14 June 1846
4 Mary; *m* Rev George Martin (*d* 1822), and *d* 1814, leaving issue

Seat: Blair Castle, Pitlochry, Perthshire, Tayside Region. Only one tower dates from the 13th century, the era of the building's first construction. Such castellated features as survive are predominantly 19th-century, although the actual remodelling of the original castle to give a house took place a hundred or so years earlier. Inside is a celebrated staircase, which was brought 400 miles north from London. At the time of going to press it was reported that the late **(10th) Duke** had set up a trust to care for the estate and castle. The latter is said to be Scotland's premier tourist attraction among comparable sights.

ATTENBOROUGH

Creation: B. (LP, UK) 1993.

THE BARON ATTENBOROUGH, of Richmond upon Thames in the London Borough of Richmond upon Thames (Sir Richard Samuel Attenborough, CBE (1967)) [The Rt Hon The Lord Attenborough CBE, Old Friars, Richmond Green, Surrey TW9 1NQ]; *b* 29 Aug 1923; *educ* Wyggeston GS for Boys Leicester and RADA; F/Sgt Airgunner and Cameraman RAF WW II, film producer and dir; actor, films include: *In Which We Serve* (1942), *Brighton Rock* (1948), *The Angry Silence* (1959), *The Great Escape* (1962), *Seance on a Wet Afternoon* (1963), *Guns at Batasi* (1964), *The Flight of the Phoenix* (1965), *The Sand Pebbles* (1966), *10 Rillington Place* (1970), *Jurassic Park* (1992) and *Miracle on 34th Street* (1994); producer: *Whistle Down The Wind* (1961), *The L-Shaped Room* (1962), (and dir) *Oh! What A Lovely War* (1969); dir: *Young Winston* (1972), *A Bridge Too Far* (1977), *Magic* (1978), (also producer) *Gandhi* (1980–81), *A Chorus Line* (1985), *Cry Freedom* (1987), *Chaplin* (1992), *Shadowlands* (1993), Chm BAFTA 1969–70 (V-Pres 1971–), RADA 1970–, Capital Radio 1972–92, Help A London Child 1975–, UK Tstees Waterford-Kamhlaba Sch Swaziland 1976–, Duke of York's Theatre 1979–82, BFI 1982–92, Goldcrest Films and TV 1982–87, Channel 4 TV 1987–92, Dir Young Vic 1974–84, Govr Nat Film Sch 1970–81, Tstee Tate Gallery 1976–82, Tate Fndn 1986– and Fndn for Sport and the Arts 1991–, Pro-Chllr Sussex U 1970–, Freeman Leicester 1990, Hon DLitt Leicester 1970, Kent 1981 and Sussex 1987, Hon DCL Newcastle 1974, Hon LLD Dickinson Penn 1983, Fellow BAFTA 1983, BFI 1992 and King's Coll London 1993, Cdr Ordre des Arts et des Lettres, Chevalier Legion Honour, ktd 1976; *m* 1945 *Sheila Beryl Grant, JP (the actress Sheila Sim), dau of Stuart Grant Sim, of Hove, Sussex, and has:

1 *Michael John; *b* 1950; *educ* Westminster and Sussex U (BA); exec producer and dir RSC; *m* 1st 1971 (*divorce* 1976) Jane (the actress Jane Seymour), dau of Benjamin John Frankenberg, MRCS, LRCP, FRCOG, of Hillingdon, Middx; *m* 2nd 1984 *Karen Esther, yr dau of Sydney Victor Lewis, of London SW1, and by his 2nd w has:
(1) *Thomas Frederick Richard; *b* 1986
(1) *William Grant Oliver; *b* 1991
1 *Jane Mary; *b* 1955; *educ* Lady Eleanor Holles Sch and Sussex U; arts admin; *m* 1982 *Michael Holland, 2nd s of George Holland, of Heathfield, Sussex, and has:
(1) *Samuel George William; *b* 1984
(2) *Alice Jane; *b* 1987
(3) *Lucy Elizabeth; *b* 1989
2 *Charlotte Isabel; *b* 1959; *educ* Lady Eleanor Holles Sch and Bristol U; actress; *m* 1993 *Graham Sinclair

Lineage: FREDERICK LEVI ATTENBOROUGH; had:
RICHARD SAMUEL, *cr* a **Baron**

ATTLEE

Arms: Azure, on a chevron or between three hearts or winged argent as many lions rampant sable.
Crest: On a mount vert two lions rampant addorsed or.
Supporters: On either side a Welsh terrier sejant proper.
Motto: *Labor omnia vincit* ('Labour conquers all').
Creation: E. and V. (UK) 16 Nov 1955.

THE 3RD EARL ATTLEE and **Viscount Prestwood**, of Walthamstow, Co Essex (John Richard Attlee) [The Rt Hon The Earl Attlee, House of Lords, London SW1A 0PW]; *b* 3 Oct 1956; *s f* 1991; *educ* Stowe; *m* 1993 *Celia Jane, yst dau of Dexter Plummer, of Bishops Stortford, Herts

Lineage: JOHN ATTLEE; had:
RALPH ATTLEE; *bur* at Cobham, Surrey, 12 March 1619, leaving:
ABRAHAM ATTLEE; *bapt* Cobham 12 Feb 1618; had:
JOHN ATTLEE; had:
JOHN ATTLEE; churchwarden Dorking, Surrey, 1725; had:
1 JOHN, for whom *see* below
2 Richard; *bapt* 7 July 1725; said to have gone to America
1 Ann; *bapt* 26 Sept 1727
2 Elizabeth; *bapt* 24 Nov 1728; *m* 4 May 1759 John Stillwell

JOHN ATTLEE's er son,
JOHN ATTLEE, of Dorking; *bapt* 1 Jan 1722; *m* 1 June 1762 Elizabeth Searde (*bur* 11 Jan 1767), and *d* 4 Nov 1788, leaving issue:
JOHN ATTLEE; *bapt* 6 Sept 1763; *m* 1788 Ann Piper (*d* 22 Aug 1846), and was *bur* 8 Nov 1821, leaving:
1 RICHARD, for whom *see* below
2 John; *d* 28 Feb 1827
1 Ann; *m* John Wells, and had issue
2 Elizabeth; *m* John Phelps, and had issue

JOHN ATTLEE's er son,
RICHARD ATTLEE, of Holly House, Dorking; *b* 1 July 1795; *m* 18 Sept 1827 Harriott (*b* 16 July 1801; *d* 1876), and *d* 28 July 1873, having had:
1 John, of Rose Hill, Dorking, Surrey; *b* 14 July 1828; *m* 1st Sarah Ann Bartlett, and had issue; *m* 2nd Elizabeth Waller, and *d* 27 Dec 1913, having had, with other issue:
(1) Wilfred Henry Waller; BA Cambridge (1897); MD (1904), MRCP London (1925), MRCS Eng (1900); *m* 8 April 1920 Emily Bridget, yr dau of Charles Cornelius Maconochie, CBE, KC, of Avontown, Linlithgow, W Lothian, and *d* 27 Feb 1962, leaving, with two daus and a s:
1a *David Charles [David Attlee Esq, Brockley House, Leintwardine, Salop]; *b* 1922; *educ* Eton and Trin Coll Oxford; served Irish Gds WW II; *m* 10 Dec 1955 *Rosemary, gdau of 1st Baron Elton (*qv*), and has issue
2 Richard; *b* 1 March 1833; *d* 1846
3 William; *b* 17 Nov 1834; *m* Sophy Pulford and *d* 16 Sept 1897, having had issue
4 Simmonds (Rev); *b* 6 Oct 1836; *m* Elizabeth Wood and *d* 1 June 1918, having had issue
5 Charles; *b* 7 May 1838; *m* Elizabeth Wilson and *d* 25 July 1900, having had, with other issue:
(1) Edward Guy; had issue:
1a Charles Guy; manager Lloyds Bank Worcester, Pres Worcester Chamber of Commerce; *d* unm July 1956 aged 42, *k* while climbing in the Alps
(2) Hugh Guthrie; BA
(1) Florence Ethel
6 HENRY, for whom *see* below
7 James; *b* 6 June 1844; *m* Elizabeth Butler and *d* 28 Aug 1925, having had, with other issue:
(1) Elizabeth Madeline; *d* unm July 1963
(2) Elsie

1 Elizabeth; *b* 6 Nov 1829; *m* William Wood, and *d* 31 Jan 1909, leaving issue
2 Harriott Ann; *b* 13 Oct 1831; *m* Richard Flint, and *d* 1 April 1905, having had issue
3 Emily; *b* 3 Feb 1840; *m* Rev Canon William B Calvert, and *dsp* 17 March 1929

RICHARD ATTLEE's 6th son,

HENRY ATTLEE, of Westcott, Portinscale Road, Putney, DL (City of London); *b* 23 Dec 1841; slr, Pres Incorporated Law Soc; *m* 11 Aug 1870 Ellen Bravery (*b* 4 July 1847; *d* 19 May 1920), dau of Thomas Simons Watson, of The Gables, Wandsworth Common, and *d* 19 Nov 1908, leaving issue:

1 Robert Bravery; *b* 7 July 1871; *educ* Haileybury and Oxford; *d* 14 May 1953
2 Bernard Henry Bravery (Rev); *b* 6 May 1873; *m* A Ethel Garnock-Jones, and *dsp* 1943
3 Thomas Simons; *b* 18 Oct 1880; *educ* Haileybury and Corpus Christi Coll Oxford (MA); FRIBA; *m* 1913 Kathleen Ida Mary Medley (*d* 13 Oct 1965), and *d* 11 Oct 1960, leaving issue:
(1) *Christopher Sebastian Bravery [Christopher Attlee Esq, Perran, Dalewood Road, Orpington, Kent]; *educ* Shrewsbury and Corpus Christi Coll Oxford (MA); *m* *Clarinda Campbell Allen, and has issue:
1a *Richard Christopher Bravery [Richard Attlee Esq, 82 Osborne Rd, Jesmond, Newcastle upon Tyne]; *b* 1945; *m* 15 June 1968 *Stella Marie, dau of Robert Wills, of 15 Penfold Close, Capenhurst, nr Chester
2a *Andrew David Simons; *b* 1949
(2) *Hereward Patrick Lovelace [Hereward Attlee Esq, Leory Croft, Perranar-Worthal, Truro; 6 Keats Grove, Hampstead, London NW3]; *educ* Shrewsbury and Ch Ch Oxford (MA); For Serv, Chev Order Leopold II of Belgium, Croix de Guerre; *m* *Margaret Mary Brennan, MA, and has:
1a *Jeremy Patrick Simons (Rev), SJ [The Rev Jeremy Attlee SJ, Stonyhurst College, via Blackburn, Lancs]; *b* 20 June 1942; *educ* Beaumont and Campion Hall Oxford (MA)
2a *Thomas Joseph Simons; *b* 12 April 1950
1a *Patricia Marianne Bravery; *b* 28 Sept 1943; *educ* Sorbonne (L ès L); *m* 24 Aug 1968 *Harvey Peters, of 35 Hornsey Lane Gdns, London N6, son of William Albert Peters, of 101 Hoppers Rd, Winchmore Hill, London N21
2a *Margaret Clare; *b* 1 Oct 1946; *m* 24 May 1969 *Peter William Hill, of Ipswich
3a *Catherine Mary Sinclair; *b* 29 Sept 1956
4 CLEMENT RICHARD, **1st Earl**
5 Laurence Gillespie; *b* 6 Nov 1884; *educ* Haileybury and Lincoln Coll Oxford (BA); Maj RASC; *m* 1921 Letitia Rotton, MBE (1919) (*d* 17 Feb 1973), and *d* 3 May 1969, leaving issue:
(1) *Donald Laurence, CB (1978), LVO (1964), DL (Devon 1991) [AVM Donald Attlee CB LVO DL, Jerwoods, Culmstock, Cullompton, Devon EX15 3JU]; *b* 2 Sept 1922; *educ* Haileybury; AVM RAF (1975); Pilot trg in Canada 1942–44, Flying Instr 1944–48, Trg Cmd 1949–52, 12 Sqdn 1952–54, Air Min Air Staff 1954–55, RAF Staff coll 1956, 59 Sqdn 1957–59, CO (W/Cdr) Queen's Flight 1960–63, HQ RAF Germany 1964–67, CO RAF Brize Norton, Oxford 1968–69, IDC 1970, MOD Policy Staff 1971–72, Dir RAF Recruiting 1973–74, Air Cdre Intell 1974–75, AOA (AVM) Trg Cmd 1975–77, ret 1977; fruit farmer 1977–, Memb Mid Devon DC 1982– (V-Chm 1987–89), chm Mid Devon Business Club 1985–87, Div Mid Devon Enterprise Agency 1983–93; *m* 1952 *Jane Hamilton, dau of R M H Young, of Tichborne Grange, Alresford, Hants, and has:
1a *Charles Hamilton; *b* 24 May 1955; *m* 1 Sept 1984 *Anne, dau of Geoffrey Hinton, of Bexley, and has:
1b *John Patrick Hamilton; *b* 18 Dec 1988
2b *Fergus; *b* 26 April 1984
1b *Edwina Katherine Jane; *b* 24 Jan 1986
2b *Annecy Agatha Harriet; *b* 26 Dec 1991
3b *Constance; *b* 26 April 1994
1a *Carolyn Jane; *b* 12 June 1957; *m* 1 July 1989 *Kevin Moloney, s of Danny Moloney of Weston-super-Mare, and has:
1b *Callum Johnathan; *b* 24 March 1993
1b *Freya Elizabeth; *b* 16 Aug 1990
2a *Jenny Louise; *b* 2 March 1963; *m* 27 Oct 1989 *Luke Ellis, s of Dr Ellis of Oxford, and has:
1b *Max Barnaby; *b* 9 Dec 1990
2b *Rory Daniel; *b* 9 April 1995
1b *Holly Jane; *b* 18 April 1993
(2) *Paul Henry [Paul Attlee Esq, Yew Tree Cottage, Church Lane, Frisby on the Wreake, Melton Mowbray LE14 2NQ]; *b* 1924; *m* 1947 *Sheila Rosemary Garnham, and has issue:
1a *William Paul; *b* 10 June 1954
2a *Timothy Laurence; *b* 10 May 1961
1a *Elizabeth Jane; *b* 2 Oct 1949
2a *Lucy; *b* 18 Feb 1952
(3) *Theodore Mark [Theodore Attlee Esq, North Gables, 201 Wigston Rd, Oadby, Leics]; *b* 1931; *educ* Tonbridge and Queens' Coll Cambridge (BA); *m* 1958 *Margaret Joan Eteson, MCSP, and has issue:
1a *Hilary Anne; *b* 20 July 1959
2a *Judith Claire; *b* 13 June 1961
1 Mary; *b* 1875; a missionary in S Africa 1915–50; *d* unm 1956
2 Dorothy Janet; *b* 1877; *m* 1900 Wilfrid Fletcher (*d* Feb 1959), of Atherton House, 4 St Marks Ave, Salisbury, Wilts, and *d* 1920, having had issue
3 Margaret Ellen; *b* 1878; *d* unm 8 March 1964

HENRY ATTLEE's 4th son,

CLEMENT RICHARD ATTLEE, **1st Earl Attlee**, so *cr* 16 Nov 1955, as also VISCOUNT PRESTWOOD, of Walthamstow, Co Essex (both UK), KG (1956), OM (1951), CH (1945), PC (1935); *b* 3 Jan 1883; *educ* Haileybury and Univ Coll Oxford (MA, Hon Fell 1943); WW I as Maj S Lancs Regt (wounded), barrister Inner Temple 1905 (Hon Master), practised till 1909, joined Fabian Soc, ILP and Nat Union of Clerks 1908, Sec Toynbee Hall 1910, Lecturer Ruskin Coll 1911, tutor and lecturer social science LSE 1913–23, First Lab Mayor Stepney 1919, Alderman 1920–27, First Chm London Lab Mayors and ex-Mayors' Assoc 1919; MP (Lab) Limehouse 1922–50 and W Walthamstow 1950–55, PPS to Ldr Oppn 1922, Under Sec of State for War 1924, memb Indian Statutory Commn 1927, Chllr Duchy Lancaster 1930, PMG 1931, Dep Ldr PLP 1931, Ldr PLP and Oppn 1935 and 1951–56, Ld Privy Seal 1940–42, Dep PM 1942–45, Dominions Sec 1942–43, Ld Pres Cncl 1943–45, PM 1945–51, Min Def July 1945–Jan 1946, author: *The Social Worker, The Town Councillor, The Will and the Way to Socialism, The Labour Party in Perspective, Purpose and Policy, As it Happened* (autobiography); Hon DCL Oxford, Hon LLD Cambridge 1946, London 1947, Wales 1949, Glasgow 1951, Nottingham 1953, Aberdeen 1956, Madras 1957, Ceylon 1961, Hon DLitt Reading 1948, FRS, Hon FRIBA, Er Bro Trin House, Freeman and Liveryman Innholders' Co 1946, Freeman Merthyr Tydfil 1946, Birmingham 1947, Greenwich 1948, Dartford 1948, Stepney 1948, Leeds 1951, Manchester 1954, Oxford 1956, Aberdeen 1956, Bristol 1959, City of London 1954, Hon Fell Queen Mary Coll London U 1948, LSE 1960; *m* 10 Jan 1922 Violet Helen (*d* 7 June 1964), 10th child and yst dau of Henry Edward Millar, of Heathdown, Hampstead Heath (*see* INCHYRA, B), and had issue:

1 MARTIN RICHARD, **2nd Earl**
1 *Janet Helen [Mrs Harold Shipton, 4 North Kingshighway, St Louis, MO 63108, USA]; *b* 25 Feb 1923; does not use courtesy title having taken American citizenship 1973; *m* 15 Nov 1947 *Prof Harold William Shipton, only son of Albert William Shipton, of Shrewsbury, and has:
(1) *Ann Helen; *b* 15 Aug 1948; *m* 1st 1969 (*divorce* 1994) Charles William Nandell and has a s and four daus; *m* 2nd 1993 *Michael Zateslo
2 *Felicity Ann [The Lady Felicity Harwood, Appledore, 6 Hubert Day Close, Beaconsfield, Bucks HP9 1TL]; *b* 22 Aug 1925; *m* 2 April 1955 John Keith Harwood, OBE (*d* 1989), son of Col George Edward Harwood, of Putney, and has issue:
(1) *Richard James Attlee; *b* 8 June 1963; *m* 21 Nov 1997 *Miranda, dau of Alan Kemp, of Wickham Bishops, Essex
(1) *Penelope Ann; *b* 17 Jan 1956; *m* 1990 *Richard Charles Anthony Robertson, only son of A H Robertson, of Strasbourg, France, and has issue:
1a *Joseph Keith; *b* 1993
(2) *Joanna Patricia; *b* 16 May 1958, *m* 1st 30 June 1979 (*divorce* 1984) Philip Michael Darcey Pinniger, yst son of T Keith Pinniger and Mrs Margaret Orchard, of Baymoot, Thaxted, Essex, and has issue:
1a *Thomas George; *b* 1981
(2) (cont.) Mrs Joanna Pinniger *m* 2nd 1988 *Martin Roundell Greene, only son of George Roundell Greene, of Beaconsfield, Bucks, and has further issue:
2a *Charles George; *b* 1988
(3) *Sally Alexandra; *b* 11 May 1960; *m* 1985 *Michael P Camps, er son of David Camps, of Bosham, W Sussex, and has issue:
1a *Alice Beatrice; *b* 1990
2a *Elizabeth Ann; *b* 1994
3 *Alison Elizabeth [The Lady Alison Davis, Westcott, Beacon Rise, Sevenoaks, Kent TN13 2NJ; *b* 14 April 1930; *m* 8 March 1952 *Richard Lionel Lance Davis, son of Maj Arthur Owen Lance Davis, of Hinckley, Leics, and has issue:
(1) *Jennifer Alison; *b* 17 Feb 1953; *m* 1978 *Christopher James Lochen, er son of Harald Olaf Lochen, of Sevenoaks, Kent
(2) *Tessa Meriel; *b* 11 Nov 1955; *m* 1976 *Michael Robert Dormon, son of Jack Barrett Dormon, of Hadley Wood, Herts
(3) *Belinda Jane; *b* 24 Nov 1957; *m* 1979 *Atholl Christopher Johnston, yr son of Christopher Kitchin Johnston, of Belfast

The 1st EARL *d* 8 Oct 1967; his only son,

MARTIN RICHARD ATTLEE, **2nd Earl Attlee**; *b* 10 Aug 1927; *educ* Millfield and Southampton Nautical Coll; Merchant Navy 1945–50, memb HAC 1951–55, MIPR 1964, Assist PRO SR BR 1970–77, Mktg Dir SOS Talkswan Co 1977, owner Prestwood Publicity 1967; *m* 1st 16 Feb 1955 (*divorce* 1988) Anne Barbara, est dau of James Henderson, CBE, author, of Sydney Place, Bath, Somerset, and had issue:

1 JOHN RICHARD ATTLEE, **3rd and present Earl Attlee**
1 *Jane Elizabeth; *b* 29 March 1959

The **2nd Earl** *m* 2nd 1988 *Margaret (Gretta) Deane only dau of Geoffrey Gouriet, CBE, of Paper House, Hampton Court, Middx, and *d* 1991

AUBREY-FLETCHER

Arms: Quarterly , 1st and 4th, sa. a cross engrailed arg. between four plates, each charged with an arrow of the first (for FLETCHER); 2nd and 3rd, az. a chevron between three eagle's heads erased or (for AUBREY). **Crests:** 1 A horse's head arg., charged with a trefoil gu. (for FLETCHER), 2 An eagle's head erased or (for AUBREY).
Motto: *Martis, non Cupidinis* ('Make war not love').
Creation: Bt. (GB) 20 May 1782.

SIR HENRY EGERTON AUBREY-FLETCHER, 8TH BT [Sir Henry Aubrey-Fletcher Bt, Estate Office, Chilton, Aylesbury, Bucks HP18 9LR]; *b* 27 Nov 1945; *s* f 1992; *educ* Eton; chm Chilton House Nursing Home 1987–, dir Fox FM ILR 1987– and Mix 96 ILR 1994–, memb: Cncl CLA 1987–, Landscape Advsy Ctee Dept Tport 1990–94, Cncl Berks Bucks Oxon Wildlife Tst 1992–, Cncl NT 1995–, High Sheriff Bucks 1995–96; *m* 14 July 1976 *(Sara) Roberta, yr dau of Maj Robert Gilliam Buchanan, TD, KOSB, of Blackpark Cottage, Evanton, Ross-shire, and has issue:

1 +JOHN ROBERT; *b* 20 June 1977
2 +Thomas Egerton; *b* 1980
3 +Harry Buchanan; *b* 1982

Lineage (of Aubrey): WILLIAM AUBREY, DCL; *b c* 1529; *educ* Oxford (BCL 1549, DCL 1554, Fell All Souls), Pncpl New Inn Hall 1550, Regius Prof Civil Law Law 1553–59, memb Cncl of Wales, Chllr to Archbp Canterbury, a Master Court of Requests, MP Carmarthen 1554, Brecon 1558, Hindon 1559, Arundel 1562 and Taunton 1592; *d* 25 June 1595, leaving, with six daus:

1 Edward
2 THOMAS (Sir), for whom *see* further below
3 Richard; f of:
(1) John; the antiquary and author of the *Brief Lives*

The 2nd s,

Sir THOMAS AUBREY, of Llantrithyd, Glam; *m* Mary, dau of Anthony Mansel(l), and had issue:

Sir JOHN AUBREY, 1st Bt (E), so *cr* 23 July 1660, having been granted a warrant of baronetcy by CHARLES I April 1644; *b c* 1606; *educ* Wadham Coll Oxford and Gray's Inn; *m c* 1650 Mary, dau of Sir Richard South, goldsmith of Cheapside, by Elizabeth, dau of Richard Gosson, a London grocer, and was *bur* 25 March 1679, leaving an only surv son:

Sir JOHN AUBREY, 2nd Bt; *b c* 1650, Sheriff Glam 1685–86, MP Brackley 1698–1700; *m* 1st 1 March 1678/9 Margaret, 15th child of Sir John Lowther, 1st Bt, of Lowther (*see* LONSDALE, E); *m* 2nd after June 1680 Mary (*dsp* 1717), widow of William Jephson and dau and coheir of William Lewis, of the Van, Glam, and Boarstall and Brill, Bucks, by Margaret, dau and heiress of Laurence Banaster, of Boarstall and Brill, whereby the Aubreys came into possession of the Boarstall estate, which had allegedly never been sold since the reign of EDWARD THE CONFESSOR but had passed by inheritance from the original grantee via the Handlos, de la Poles, Jameses, Redes and Dynhams to the Banasters and from them to the Aubreys, and *d* Sept 1700 from injuries incurred by falling from his horse, having by his 1st w had an only son:

Sir JOHN AUBREY, 3rd Bt; *b* 20 July 1680; *educ* Jesus Coll Oxford; MP Cardiff 1706–10, Sheriff Glam 1710–11; *m* 1st 20 June 1701 his stepmother's maid Mary (*d* July 1714), dau of John Stealy, and had issue; *m* 2nd Frances (*dspm*), dau of William Jephson by his stepmother Mary; *m* 3rd 1 Feb 1724/5 Jane Thomas and *d* 16 April 1743, having had no issue by his 3rd w, female issue only by his 2nd and an only surv son by his 3rd:

1 Sir JOHN AUBREY, 4th Bt; *b c* 1707; *d* unm 14 Oct 1767
2 Sir THOMAS AUBREY, 5th Bt; *m* 18 July 1738 Martha, dau of Richard Carter, of Chilton, Bucks, and *d* 4 Sept 1786, leaving issue:
(1) Sir JOHN AUBREY, 6th Bt; *b* 4 June 1739; *educ* Westminster and Ch Ch Oxford (DCL 1763); MP Wallingford 1768–74 and 1780–84, Aylesbury 1774–80, Bucks 1784–90, Clitheroe 1790–96, Aldborough 1796–1812, Steyning 1812–20 and Horsham 1820–26, Ld Commr Admlty 1782, a Ld of Treasury 1783–89, bought 1783 the Dorton estate, Bucks; *m* 1st 9 March 1771 Mary, er dau and coheir of Sir James Colebrooke, 1st Bt, and sis of Emma, Countess of Tankerville, and had a s (*d* young from accidental poisoning); *m* 2nd 26 May 1783 his 1st cousin Martha Catherine, dau and heir of George Richard Carter, of Chilton, Bucks, and *dspl* (his illegitimate dau Mary *m* 7 May 1792 Samuel Whitcombe, of Hempstead Court, Glos) 14 March 1826
(2) Richard; *b c* 1745; Lt-Col Glam Militia; *m* Frances, dau of Hon Wriothesley Digby (2nd s of 5th Baron Digby, *qv*), and *d* April 1808, leaving issue:
1a Sir THOMAS DIGBY AUBREY, 7th and last Bt; *b* 2 Dec 1782; *educ* St John's Coll Cambridge; Sheriff Bucks 1815–16; *m* 9 Dec 1813 Mary, dau of Thomas Wright, of London, and n of Rev Robert Verney, formerly Wright, of Middle Claydon, Bucks (whose w Catherine inherited the Middle Claydon estate from her half-sis Mary, Baroness Fermanagh in her own right; *see* VERNEY, Bt, of Claydon), and *dsp* 5 Sept 1856, when the baronetcy became extinct
(3) Thomas; *m* and *dspm* 15 Jan 1814, leaving issue:
1a Elizabeth Sophia; *b* 31 Jan 1792; *m* 3 Feb 1814 Charles Spencer Ricketts (*d* 17 Feb 1867), of Connaught Place, London, and had, with other issue:
1b Charles Aubrey RICKETTS later AUBREY (roy licence 7 March 1874, but retained arms of RICKETTS, quartering them with those of AUBREY); *b* 1 Nov 1814; *dsp* 28 Dec 1901
1 ELIZABETH, *m* Henry Lintot, of Southwater, Sussex, and *d* 20 Jan 1735, leaving an only child:
(1) CATHERINE Lintot; *m* **Sir Henry Fletcher, 1st Bt** (*see* below)

Lineage (of Fletcher): WILLIAM FLETCHER, of Cockermouth, Cumberland; *m* —, a dau of Swinburn of Huthwait, and had:

HENRY FLETCHER, of Cockermouth Castle; received MARY QUEEN OF SCOTS on her flight into England after the defeat of her supporters at the Battle of Langside 1568 and gave her a robe of red velvet; *d* 1574, leaving, with other issue:

1 William, ancestor of the FLETCHERs of Moresby
2 Lancelot, ancestor of the FLETCHERs of Tallantire
3 Thomas, of Cockermouth; *m* Jane Boleen and had, with other issue:
(1) Richard (Sir), of Cockermouth, and Hutton-in-le-Forest, Cumberland; *m* 1st — Richmond and had three children (*d* unm); *m* 2nd Barbara, dau of Henry Crackenthorpe, of Newbiggen, and by her had, with five daus (including Mary, *m* Sir John Lowther, 1st Bt, of Lowther; *see* LONSDALE, E):
1a Sir HENRY FLETCHER, 1st Bt (E) of the 19 Feb 1640/1 *cr*; *m c* 1638 Catherine (*m* 2nd Thomas Smith, Bp Carlisle), sis of Sir William Dalston, 1st Bt, and was *k* leading a royalist regt in the Civil War at the skirmish of Rowton Heath, Cheshire, 24 Sept 1645, having had, with three daus and another s (*dvp*):
1b Sir GEORGE FLETCHER, 2nd Bt, of Hutton-in-le-Forest, MP Cumberland 1661–1700, *m* 1st 27 Feb 1654/5 Alice, dau of 1st Baron Coleraine of Coleraine of the 1625 *cr*, and had, with other issue:
1c Sir HENRY FLETCHER, 3rd Bt; MP Cockermouth 1689–90, monk; *d* unm 19 May 1712, when the btcy expired
1c Catherine, *m* Lionel Vane, of Longnewton, Co Durham, and was ancestor of the VANE-TEMPEST Bts (*see* LONDONDERRY, M) and FLETCHER-VANE Bts (*see* BARNARD, B)
1b (cont.) Sir GEORGE *m* 2nd Lady Mary *née* Johnstone, widow of Sir George Graham, 2nd Bt (*see* GRAHAM, Bt, of Esk), and dau of 1st Earl of Hartfell (*see* ANNANDALE AND HARTFELL, E), and *d* 23 July 1700, leaving issue by her, all of whom *dsp*
(2) Philip; gf of:
1a Richard; f of:
1b PHILIP Maj; *d* 1744 at an advanced age, leaving, with a dau:
1c JOHN
2c Philip, ancestor of the FLETCHERs of Kenward

The elder son,

JOHN FLETCHER, of Clea Hall, Cumberland; *m* 1st Mary, dau of Ewan Christian, and had no surv issue; *m* 2nd Isabella, dau and coheir of John Senhouse, of Netherhall, Cumberland, by whom he had, with four er sons:

1 HENRY (Sir), **1st Bt**
1 Grace, *m* William Taylor
2 Jane, *m* Thomas Benson

The 5th son,

Sir Henry Fletcher, 1st Bt (GB), so *cr* 20 May 1782, of Clea Hall, Dir HEICS, MP Cumberland 1768–1802; *m* Oct 1768 Catherine (*d* 17 Oct 1816), dau and sole heir of Henry Lintot, of Southwater, Sussex, by Elizabeth, est dau of Sir John Aubrey, 3rd Bt (*see* above), and had:

1 HENRY (Sir), **2nd Bt**
1 Catherine

He *d* 29 March 1807; his s,

Sir Henry Fletcher, 2nd Bt; *b* 4 Feb 1772; *m* 19 March 1801 Frances Sophia (*d* 9 Feb 1828), 4th dau of Thomas Wright Vaughan, of Woodstone, and *d* 10 Aug 1821, having had, with another s (*d* unm):

1 **Sir Henry Fletcher, 3rd Bt**, *b* 18 Sept 1807; *m* 26 June 1834 Emily Maria (*d* 30 Jan 1888), 2nd dau of George Browne, Memb Cncl Bombay, and *d* 6 Sept 1851, having had, with other issue:
(1) Sir HENRY FLETCHER later AUBREY-FLETCHER after he inherited his cousin Charles Aubrey Aubrey's estates 1901 (roy licence 1 Jan 1903), **4th Bt**, PC (1901), CB (1900), JP (Surrey, Sussex and Bucks), DL (Sussex); *b* 24 Sept 1835; *educ* Eton; Col cmdg Sussex and Kent Vol Inf Bde 1897–1904, Lt Gren Gds, MP (C) Horsham 1880–85 and Lewes 1885–1910, Groom-in-Waiting to HM QUEEN VICTORIA 1885–86; *m* 10 May 1859 Agnes (*d* 5 Feb 1916), yst dau of Col Sir John Morrillyon Wilson, CB, KH, of the Roy Hosp, Chelsea; the name and arms of AUBREY; *dsp* 19 May 1910
(2) Edward, Lt RN; *b* 17 Nov 1841; *m* 26 April 1871 Louisa (*d* 1890), est dau of Henry Coore, of Scruton Hall, Yorks, and *dsp* 16 Nov 1881
(3) LANCELOT (Sir), **5th Bt**
(4) Philip (Rev); Kt Cdr Order Holy Sepulchre; *b* 30 Oct 1848; *educ* Exeter Coll Oxford (MA); *d* 13 Jan 1928

(5) John Lowther; *b* 9 Sept 1851; *m* 22 March 1893 Emily (*d* 1937), widow of Cecil Henry Weston and dau of William Burkwood, and *d* 24 June 1928, leaving:

1a Grace Vaughan; *b* 1891

2a Jacquetta Mary; *b* 1894; *m* 1919 Capt Ronald G Seaburne May, Sherwood Foresters (*d* 1940), and had:

1b *Daphne; *b* 1923

2b *Jacquetta Jane; *b* 1929

(1) Adelaide Maria; *m* 30 June 1863 Horace Edward Chapman, JP, and *d* 21 Aug 1926, leaving issue. He *d* 6 March 1907

(2) Eliza Emily; *m* 30 Oct 1890 William Victor Foster, s of William Foster, of Wilbury Road, Hove, and *d* 3 Aug 1935. He *d* 24 April 1923

Sir HENRY AUBREY-FLETCHER's brother,

Sir LANCELOT FLETCHER later AUBREY-FLETCHER (roy licence 23 June 1910), **5th Bt**; *b* 13 March 1846; *m* 1st 9 Oct 1875 Gertrude Isabella (*d* 1878), dau of John Howell, and had a s (*d* an infant); *m* 2nd 18 April 1882 Emily Harriet (*d* 19 April 1911), dau of Rev Nugent Wade, MA, Canon Bristol, and by her had:

1 HENRY LANCELOT (Sir), **6th Bt**

1 Kathleen Margaret; *b* 15 Jan 1884; *m* 20 Nov 1916 Capt Hugh Carleton Charsley Tufnell, RE, er son of Carleton Fowell Tufnell, of Watendone Manor, Kenley, Surrey, and *d* 27 Feb 1959, having had issue. He *d* 6 July 1945

Sir LANCELOT *m* 3rd 3 June 1913 Aileen Mary (*d* 28 June 1968), yr dau of John Macpherson, barrister, and *d* 5 Jan 1937

Sir LANCELOT's son,

Sir Henry Lancelot Aubrey-Fletcher, 6th Bt, CVO (1957), DSO (1918), DL (1934), JP and CA, Ld Lt Bucks 1954–61, High Sheriff 1925, memb Gentlemen at Arms 1936 (Standard Bearer 1955, Lt 1956–57); *educ* Eton and New Coll Oxford, Maj (ret) Gren Gds, T/Lt-Col and AA&QMC 1919, served WWs I (wounded, brevet, Croix de Guerre) and II 1940–45 (2nd in cmd Gds Depot Caterham), KStJ, author: *A History of the Foot Guards* and (as Henry Wade) of several novels; *b* 10 Sept 1887; *m* 1st 11 Oct 1911 Mary Augusta, OStJ (*d* 29 June 1963), dau of Rev Robert William Chilton, Rector Gt Horkesley, Essex; *m* 2nd 4 Dec 1965 *Nancy Cecil [Nancy Lady Aubrey-Fletcher, Barnfield, Delly End, Hailey, Oxon], widow of Maj Charles Reynolds and dau of Joseph Cecil Bull, and *d* 30 May 1969, leaving by his 1st w:

1 JOHN HENRY LANCELOT (Sir), **7th Bt**

2 Nigel Chilton; F/Lt RAFVR WW II 1941–45; *b* 10 April 1914; *educ* Eton; *m* 7 Nov 1942 *Areta Mae [Mrs Nigel Aubrey-Fletcher, 4 Monmouth Court, Church Lane, Lymington, Hants SO41 3RB], dau of Frederick Lees, of Hamilton, Ontario, Canada, and *d* 1980, leaving:

(1) +Philip Nigel [Philip Aubrey-Fletcher Esq, 9 Kings Satern Rd, Lymington, Hants SO41 9QS]; *b* 9 Dec 1944; *educ* Millfield; *m* 1969 *Susan Anne, only dau of W/Cdr M L Bathe, RAF (ret), and has:

1a *Caroline Susan; *b* 1973

2a *Elizabeth Claire; *b* 1976

(2) +David Lancelot [David Aubrey-Fletcher Esq, Chapel Cottage, 15 Chapel St, Tring, Herts H23 6BL]; *b* 9 Dec 1944; *educ* Millfield; *m* 1974 *Carolyn Cochrane, only dau of Kenneth F Neale, of Beoley, Worcs, and has:

1a *Sophie Rebecca; *b* 1976

3 +Lancelot Philip [Lancelot Aubrey-Fletcher Esq, Wychden, Chobham, Surrey]; Capt (ret) Gren Gds, served WW II 1939–40 (wounded, POW); *b* 30 Oct 1919; *educ* Eton; *m* 2 Dec 1952 Audrey Muriel (*d* 1993), only dau of (Frederick) Ronald Oliver, of Kensington, by Sybil Maud Elizabeth, only dau of Lt-Col Hon Ranulph Allsopp (*see* HINDLIP, B), and has:

(1) +Mark Lancelot; *b* 1964; *educ* Harrow

(1) *Jane Elizabeth; *b* 1961; *m* 1st 1988 Jonathan Mark Davies, only s of Frank Antony Davies, of Valewood Farm House, Haslemere, Surrey, and has:

1a +James Robert, *b* 1988

1a *Katrina Elizabeth, *b* 1991

2a *Alexandra Sophie, *b* 1993

(1) (cont.) Mrs Davies *m* 2nd 199– *Desmond Barron and by him has:

2a *Angus; *b* 19–

3a *Harry; *b* 2 Sept 1997

3a *Charlotte; *b* 2 Sept 1997

4 +Edward Henry Lancelot, DL (Northants) [Lt-Col Edward Aubrey-Fletcher DL, Stanford Hall, Lutterworth, Leics LE17 6DH], Lt-Col Gren Gds (ret); *b* 6 May 1930; *educ* Eton and New Coll Oxford (BA 1952); *m* 1st 11 March 1953 Bridget Mary (*d* 6 Jan 1977), er dau of Brig Sir Henry Robert Kincaid Floyd, 5th Bt (*qv*); *m* 2nd 1981 *Baroness Braye in her own right (*qv*) and by his 1st w has:

(1) +Richard Edward Henry, Capt Gren Guards; *b* 5 May 1954; *educ* Bradfield and RMA Sandhurst (Sword of Honour 1973), Lt-Col Gren Gds (despatches 1988); *m* 1980 *Caroline Margaret Jolley, stepdau of Maj Henry Charles Blosse-Lynch, Irish Gds, of Headly, Newbury, Berks, and has:

1a +George Richard Edward, *b* 1985

(2) +Patrick John Kincaid [Patrick Aubrey-Fletcher Esq, Home Farm House, Ascott Pk, Wing, Bucks LU7 0PP]; *b* 12 Oct 1955; *educ* Bradfield and RAC Cirencester; *m* 1977 *Elizabeth Ann, er dau of Victor Sheerman, and has:

1a *Rebecca Louise, *b* 1981

2a *Victoria Mary; *b* 1982

(1) *Gillian Mary; *b* 25 Sept 1958; *m* 1991 *Miles Courtenay Ambler, yr s of Capt Quintin Ambler, of Little Orchard, Chapmanslade, Wilts, and has:

1a *Henry Richard Edward; *b* 1994

1a *Camilla Mary; *b* 1992

1 Mary Elizabeth; *b* 14 April 1923; *m* 10 Sept 1951 Algernon Putland Devaynes Smyth (*d* 1980), only s of Capt Charles Devaynes Smyth, of Stoney Lodge, Brockenhurst, Hants, and *d* 1994, leaving:

(1) *Charles Henry Devaynes; *b* 29 Jan 1955; *educ* Eton; *m* 1980 *Virginia Anne, only dau of Maj James Lionel d'Esterre Darby, of Kensington

(1) *Caroline Dorothy [Mrs Peter Gee, 20 St Mary's Terrace, Hastings, E Sussex TN 34 3LS]; *b* 5 Nov 1952; *m* 1st 1981 (*divorce* 1992) Adrian Brandham Bishop Stroude; *m* 2nd 1995 *Peter Anthony Gee

Sir HENRY's eldest son,

Sir John Henry Lancelot Aubrey-Fletcher, 7th Bt, JP Bucks; *b* 22 Aug 1912; *educ* Eton and New Coll Oxford (BA 1936), High Sheriff Bucks 1961, Lt-Col Gren Gds (SR) WW II, barrister Inner Temple 1937, Metropolitan Magistrate 1959, Dep Chm Bucks QS 1959–71, Recorder Crown Court 1972; *m* 25 April 1939 Diana Mary Fynvola (*d* 1997), only child of Lt-Col Arthur George Edward Egerton, Coldstream Gds (*see* 1956 edn EGERTON OF TATTON, B), and *d* 1992, having had:

1 Sir HENRY EGERTON AUBREY-FLETCHER, **8th and present Bt**

1 Susan Mary Fynvola; *b* 21 Feb 1940; *m* 5 Jan 1965 Hon Richard Oliver Stanley, MP, bro of 18th Earl of Derby (*qv*), and *d* 29 Feb 1976

AUCKLAND

Arms: Gules on a chevron argent, between three garbs or, banded vert, as many escallops sable. **Crest:** A dexter arm in armour embowed proper, holding a garb or, the forearm encircled by an annulet gules. **Supporters:** Dexter, a horse guardant argent, charged on the shoulder with a fleur-de-lys or; sinister, a horse argent, charged on the shoulder with a castle or. **Motto:** *Si sit prudentia* ('If there be but prudence'). **Creations:** B. (I) 18 Nov 1789 and (GB) 22 May 1793.

THE 10TH BARON AUCKLAND, of West Auckland, Co Durham (GB), and **Baron Auckland** (I) (Robert Ian Burnard Eden) [The Rt Hon The Lord Auckland, House of Lords, London SW1A 0PW]; *b* 25 July 1962; *s* f 1997; *educ* Blundell's; *m* 1986 *Geraldine Caroll

Lineage: Sir ROBERT EDEN, 3rd Bt, of West Auckland (*see* EDEN OF WINTON, B) had a 3rd s:

WILLIAM EDEN, **1st Baron Auckland** (I), so *cr* 18 Nov 1789, as also 22 May 1793 BARON AUCKLAND, of West Auckland, Co Durham (GB); *b* 1744; *educ* Ch Ch Oxford (MA); barrister, Auditor Greenwich Hosp 1771–1814, Under-Sec of State for the Northern Dept 1772–78, MP Woodstock 1774–84, Heytesbury 1784–93 and (I Parl) Dungannon 1781–83, Ld of Trade 1776–82, Ch Sec Ireland 1780–82, Envoy France 1785–87, Amb Spain 1787–89 and Netherlands 1789–93, Jt PMG 1798–1804, Pres BOT 1806–07; *m* 26 Sept 1776 Eleanor (*d* 18 May 1818), 2nd dau of Sir Gilbert Elliot, 3rd Bt, of Headshaw (*see* MINTO, E), and *d* 28 May 1814, having had, with other issue, (including a dau, Mary Louisa, *m* Andrew WEDDERBURN COLVILE; later COLVILE; *see* OGILVY-WEDDERBURN, Bt):

1 William Frederick Elliot; *b* 19 Jan 1782; a Teller Exchequer; drowned Thames 19 Jan 1810

2 GEORGE EDEN, **2nd Baron Auckland** and 1st and last EARL OF AUCKLAND, so *cr* 21 Dec 1839, as also BARON EDEN OF NORWOOD, Co Surrey, GCB; *b* 25 Aug 1784; MA Ch Ch Oxford; barrister, Dep Teller Exchequer 1809–12, MP Woodstock 1810–14, Auditor Greenwich Hosp 1814–29, Commr 1829034, Pres BOT 1830–34, 1st Ld Admlty 1834–35 and 1846–49, Govr-Gen India 1835–41; *d* unm 1 Jan 1849, when the Earldom and Barony of Eden expired

3 ROBERT JOHN, **3rd Baron**

The 2nd BARON's brother,

ROBERT JOHN EDEN, **3rd Baron Auckland**; *b* 10 July 1799; DD Cambridge; Bp Sodor and Man 1847–54 and Bath and Wells 1854–69; *m* 15 Sept 1825 Mary (*d* 25 Nov 1872), est dau of Francis Edward Hurt, of Alderwasley, Derbys, and had, with other issue:

1 WILLIAM GEORGE, **4th Baron**

2 Henry Johnes; *b* 18 Sept 1830; RN; *d* 10 Feb 1853

3 Ashley (Sir), KCSI, CIE; *b* 13 Nov 1831; Lt-Govr Bengal 1876–82, Memb Cncl India 1882–87; *m* Eva Maria (*d* 10 Jan 1877), yst dau of V-Adml Rowland Money, CB, and formerly wife of (a) H E H Palmer, IA, and (b) J M Bellew, and *d* 9 July 1887

4 Robert Henley Shaw, of Tyddynllan, Llandrillo, Merioneths, JP (Worcs and Merioneths); *b* 25 Sept 1840; *m* 27 Nov 1862 Jessie Ellen (*d* 23 Jan 1927), est dau of Rev Frederick Hildyard, Rector Swanington, Norfolk, and *d* 28 Dec 1916, leaving issue:

(1) Robert Hildyard Henley; *b* 16 Dec 1863; *m* 14 April 1887 Maud Effie Mary (*d* 15 Aug 1957), yr dau of Baron Otto von Guttenberg, of Bavaria, and *d* 21 Aug 1932, leaving issue:

1a Dulcibella; *b* 23 May 1891; *m* 1st 29 July 1914 (*divorce* 1924) Llewellyn Arthur Hugh-Jones (*d* 8 Jan 1970), er son of Llewellyn Hugh-Jones, of Chevet Hey, Wrexham, and had issue:

1b *Brenda Mary [Mrs Brenda Keighley, 2 Motcomb St, London SW1]; *b* 1916; *m* 1st 1941 F/Lt Derek Rawnsley, RAF (*ka* 1943); *m* 2nd 1949 (*divorce* 1952) Geoffrey Keighley, OBE (*d* 1966), and has issue:

1c *Jonathan Eden; *b* 1950

2b *Margaret Claire; *b* 1920; *m* 1st 1939 Philip Dalton Worthington, MBE (*d* 1964), and has issue:

1c *Richard Philip [Richard Worthington Esq, King's Farm House, Stratfield Saye, Hants]; *b* 1941; *m* 1967 *Sara, dau of Capt Michael Collender (*see* COVENTRY, E), and has issue:

1d *Camilla; *b* 1968

1c *Margaret Joan [Mrs Johnny Mangers, 6 Pembroke Gdns Clo, London W8]; *b* 1943; *m* 1968 *Johnny Pierre Mangers

2c *Rosemary Claire; *b* 1950

2b (cont.) Mrs Margaret Claire Worthington *m* 2nd 1969 as his 2nd wife Lt-Cdr Thomas Dorrien Smith, JP, RN (ret) (*d* 5 Dec 1973), of Tresco Abbey, Isle of Scilly

1a (cont.) Mrs Dulcibella Hugh-Jones *m* 2nd 1 Dec 1924 Eustace Gurney Pelly (*d* 13 Feb 1954), 2nd son of John Gurney Richard Pelly, of Theydon Place, Epping, Essex (*see* PELLY, Bt)

2a Phyllis Eleanor; *b* 31 May 1893; *m* 28 June 1916 Capt Robert Henry Evans, MBE, JP (*d* 11 Dec 1960), and had issue

3a Betty; *b* 24 May 1896; *m* 1st 6 Jan 1920 Maj Hugh B Hartley (*d* 15 Sept 1928), only son of T W Hartley, JP, of Gainford, Darlington, and had a dau; *m* 2nd 11 May 1933 Lt-Col Roger Palmer Landon, MC, RA (*d* 3 Oct 1936), 2nd son of Col Asalbie Landon, and *d* 2 June 1965, leaving a further dau

(2) William Annesley; *b* 21 April 1868; MRCS, LRCP; *m* 23 Jan 1895 Mabel Louisa Homfray (*d* 13 Feb 1951), dau of Sir Robert Pinsent, KCB, DCL, and *d* 5 Aug 1939, leaving issue:

1a Edward Hildyard; *b* 1 Aug 1898; *m* 14 Jan 1942 Annie (*d* 1981), dau of Ernest Sylvester, of Midnapore, RR I, Alberta, Canada, and *d* 25 Dec 1968, leaving issue:

1b +Ernest John [Ernest Eden Esq, RRH 2, Barrhead, Alberta, Canada]; *b* 28 May 1943; *m* 1967 *Alison Carolyne, dau of — Wilde, of Edmonton, Alberta, and has issue:

1c +Buckley John; *b* 1974

1c *Heidi Anne; *b* 1969; *m* 1991 *Dereck Spence

2b +William Edward [William Eden Esq, Box 13, Newbrook, Alberta, Canada]; *b* 7 Aug 1945; *m* 1967 *Maureen T O'Hagan, and has issue:

1c +Joseph Edward; *b* 1970

2a Robert Annesley; *b* 8 May 1900; *d* unm 24 April 1963

3a George Henley, TD; *b* 3 May 1904; Maj RA, WW II; *m* 1st 1928 (*divorce* 1949) Avril Edith (*d* 18 Jan 1966), dau of R O Simmons, and had issue:

1b *Annesley Kathleen [Mrs David Brown, 151 Oakwood Ct, London W14]; *b* 1928; *m* 9 Aug 1949 *David George Warre Yeats Brown, 2nd son of Col Frederick Victor Yeats Brown, of The Little House, Quenington, nr Fairford, Glos, and has issue:

1c *Richard Andrew; *b* 12 June 1955

1c *Caroline Jane; *b* 28 May 1950

2c *Sarah Kate; *b* 9 July 1961

2b *Avril Jane [Mrs Peter Horley, PO Box 2892, Rivonia 2128, S Africa]; *b* 1930; *m* 10 May 1957 *Peter Milne Horley, s of W/Cdr Walter G Horley, of Claremont, Cape Town, and Mrs Richard Parton, of Rye, Sussex, and has:

1c *Rupert; *b* 24 Dec 1958

3b *Sally Mabel Henley; *b* 4 Oct 1932; *m* 30 April 1964 *Johann Leusink, son of Johan Gerard Leusink, of Hengelo, Netherlands, and has:

1c *Andrew Hamilton Henley; *b* 1968

3a (cont.) Maj George Eden *m* 2nd 1951 (*divorce* 1974) Doreen Rosamund Averil Tobeason; *m* 3rd 1974 *Stella Frances, dau of W H Duplock, and *d* 1982

4a Frederick Reeve; *b* 30 June 1908; *m* 1953 *Beatrice Helena, dau of Montague Smith, and *d* 1989, leaving issue:

1b *Sarah Ursula [Mrs Michael Adams, 91 The Common, Earlswood, Birmingham, B94 5SJ]; *b* 1954; *m* 1977 *Michael Adam James Adams, and has issue:

1c *Ross Henley; *b* 1983

2c *Euan George; *b* 1986

1a Ursula; *b* 17 Aug 1896; WW I (despatches), WW II 1939–43 as Subaltern ATS

(1) Mabel Kate; *m* 25 Jan 1893 Lewis Alexander Wallace (*d* 6 May 1929), of Hawford House, Worcs, son of George Wallace, of Eardiston, Worcs, and *d* 17 Nov 1939, leaving issue

(2) Alice Mary; *m* 5 Nov 1889 Rev Harold Smith, MA (*d* Sept 1938), Rector of Himley, Dudley, son of Alfred Smith, and *d* 27 Jan 1931, leaving issue

The 3rd BARON *d* 25 April 1870; his est son,

WILLIAM GEORGE EDEN, **4th Baron Auckland**, DL; *b* 19 Jan 1829; Chargé d'Affaires Karlsruhe 1859–61; *m* 1st 8 Oct 1857 Lucy Walbanke (*d* 12 May 1870), yst dau of John Walbanke Childers, of Cantley, Yorks, and had issue:

1 WILLIAM MORTON EDEN, **5th Baron Auckland**, JP (Yorks); *b* 27 March 1859; T/Maj 6th Serv Bn Dorsetshire Regt 1914–15, formerly Capt 2nd Bn Dorsetshire Regt and 3rd Bn Yorks Regt; *m* 2 April 1891 Sybil Constance (*d* 22 April 1955), est dau of Col George Morland Hutton, CB, of Gate Burton, Lincs, and *d* 31 July 1917, having had:

(1) William Alfred Morton; *b* 15 June 1892; Lt KRRC; *ka* 2 March 1915

(2) FREDERICK COLVIN GEORGE EDEN, **6th Baron Auckland**; *b* 21 Feb 1895; Assoc Inst of Naval Architects, WW II as F/O RAFVR, Assist to Air Attaché Paris 1940; *m* 1st 2 June 1917 (*divorce* 1925) Susan Livingstone (*d* 15 Jan 1966), dau of Augustus Griffin Hartridge, of Jacksonville, Florida, USA, and had:

1a *Susan Constance [The Hon Mrs Bridges, Estancia Viamonte, Rio Grande, Tierra del Fuego, Argentina]; *b* 5 Sept 1918; *m* 1st Mexico City 19 Nov 1942 (*divorce* 1956) Jose Diaz de Rivera, son of Jose Diaz de Rivera, of Asturias, Spain, and has issue:

1b *Dennis Pakenham DIAZ De RIVERA later BRIDGES; *b* 18 April 1944; *m* *Allyn Conant Pryor

1a (cont.) The Hon Mrs Susan Diaz de Rivera *m* 2nd 5 Jan 1957 Guillermo Pakenham Bridges, OBE, MBE (*d* 1980), Hon V-Consul Rio Grande, Argentina, son of William Samuel Bridges, of Tierra del Fuego, Argentina

(2) (cont.) The **6th Baron** *m* 2nd 25 April 1939 Mrs Constance Caroline Hart-Faure (*d* 23 Dec 1946), dau of Benno Hart, of San Francisco, and was *k* in a London air raid 16 April 1941

2 George; *b* 29 May 1861; *m* 19 April 1888 Amy Violet (*d* 10 Dec 1926), 3rd dau of Col Hon Charles Rowley Hay-Drummond (*see* KINNOULL, E), and *d* 14 June 1924, leaving issue:

(1) GEOFFREY MORTON EDEN, **7th Baron Auckland**, MBE (1919); *b* 17 Feb 1891; *educ* Eton; Capt RASC (TF), formerly Lt 6th Serv Bn E Surrey Regt, WW I (despatches twice), and WW II 1939–40; Govr Star and Garter Home for disabled ex-service men; *m* 30 April 1919 Dorothy Ida (*d* 24 July 1964), yst dau of Rev Francis Clyde Harvey, Vicar of Hailsham, Sussex, and Preb of Chichester, and *d* 21 June 1955, leaving:

1a *Joan Edith, JP (Essex 1966) [The Hon Mrs Franklin JP, Hea Corner, Felsted, Dunmow, Essex]; *b* 31 Jan 1920; *m* 1st 6 Sept 1941 Rev Alfred Lisinea Pond (*d* 21 July 1947), Vicar Nettleden with Potten End, son of Chaloner Pond, and has issue:

1b *Rosemary Jane; *b* 8 Nov 1942; *m* 23 April 1966 *John Edward Rendall, of Sherborne Lodge, Adelaide Rd, Teddington, Middx, only son of Anthony Rendall, of Hawkshill Way, Esher, Surrey, and has issue:

1c *Angus Mark; *b* 1975

1c *Amelia Jane; *b* 1969

2c *Sophie Charlotte; *b* 1971

2b *Sarah Joan [Mrs David Platts, 6 Eddiscombe Rd, London SW6 4UA]; *b* 16 Dec 1945; *m* 1972 *David Alexander Platts, and has issue:

1c *Charles Alexander; *b* 1976

1a (cont.) The Hon Mrs Pond *m* 2nd 31 Aug 1948 Rev Arthur Harrington Franklin, MBE, TD, MA, SCF, TA (*d* 14 March 1996), er s of Maj Percival Charles Franklin, of Rawdon Cottage, Cross Deep, Twickenham, and by him has:

3b *Elizabeth [Mrs Michael Lance, 85 Ayer Rd, Williamsville, New York, 14221, USA]; *b* 30 July 1949; *m* 11 July 1970 *Dr Michael Peter Withycombe Lance, son of M R Lance, of Farnham, Surrey, and has:

1c *Tom; *b* 1979

1c *Emma; *b* 1977

4b *Caroline [Mrs Kenneth Leafe, Ivy House, Broughton, nr Huntingdon, Cambs]; *b* 12 Oct 1952; *m* 1979 *Lt-Cdr Kenneth J Leafe, RN, and has:

1c *Alistair James Farquhar; *b* 1984

1c *Emily Jane; *b* 1982

2c *Charlotte Alice; *b* 1993

2a *Elizabeth [The Hon Mrs Mason, Gable Cottage, Alton Hall Lane, Stutton, nr Ipswich, Suffolk]; *b* 23 May 1928; *m* 27 Nov 1954 Maj Frederic Edward Isdale (Robin) Mason, Roy Anglian Regt (*d* 1995), only s of Fred Mason, of St Margarets-on-Thames, and has:

1b *Timothy Robin [Timothy Mason Esq, The Anchorage, Bristol Hill, Shotley, Suffolk]; *b* 16 July 1957

2b *Edward Geoffrey; *b* 3 Dec 1961; *m* 1987 *Joanna E, yr dau of J H Beckly, of Manor Farm, Bower Chalke, Wilts, and has:

1c *Hector; *b* 1994

1c *Georgina Sophie; *b* 1991

1b *Catherine Elizabeth [Mrs Charles Shelbourne, Caswell, Walnut Hill, Surlingham, Norwich NR14 7DQ]; *b* 22 Sept 1955; *m* 1989 *Charles Robin Shelbourne, er s of G R Shelbourne, of Langore, Cornwall, and has:

1c *Freya Anna; *b* 1992

(2) TERENCE, **8th Baron**

(3) Vivian Francis; *b* 19 March *d* 22 May 1898

(1) Ivy Maude; *b* 18 Aug 1899; WW II in Women's Land Army; granted rank of baron's dau 1942; *m* 24 June 1927 John Dawson, of White Gates, Potters Heath, Welwyn, Herts

3 Francis; *b* 26 Dec 1863; *d* 23 Feb 1864

4 Francis Fleetwood; *b* 16 Feb 1865; *d* 22 March 1898

1 Dulcibella; *b* 23 April 1860; *m* 1 Jan 1885 Robert Nassau Sutton-Nelthorpe, OBE, of Scawby, Lincs, and *d* 6 April 1925, leaving issue (*see* SUTTON, Bt)

2 Agnes; *b* 5 July 1862; *d* unm 1 Nov 1935

3 Mary; *b* 15 May 1867; *m* 10 Feb 1904 8th Viscount Chetwynd (*qv*), and *d* 22 Jan 1925, leaving issue

The **4th Baron** *m* 2nd 6 July 1872 Lady Mabel Emily Finch-Hatton (*dsp* 7 Nov 1872), 2nd dau of 11th Earl of Winchilsea and Nottingham (*qv*); *m* 3rd 20 July 1875 Edith (*m* 2nd 10 June 1877 Philip Symons (*d* 4 Jan 1926), son of Edward Symons, and *d* 28 March 1931), yst dau of Sir William Eden, 6th Bt, of West Auckland (*see* EDEN OF WINTON, B), and *d* 7 Feb 1890, having by her had issue:

5 Robert Evelyn, MC; *b* 1 May 1876; Maj TA Res, formerly RHA (TF); *d* 4 Nov 1943

6 Ashley Morland, JP (Co Durham); *b* 5 Aug 1878; Lt Special List and Staff Lt during WW I; *d* unm 16 Jan 1943

The 7th BARON's brother,

TERENCE EDEN, **8th Baron Auckland**, MC and bar; *b* 3 Nov 1892; *educ* Eton;, WW I as Capt MGC (despatches), Maj RAC (TA) WW II; *m* 12 Sept 1925 Evelyn Vane Drummond of Cromlix (*s* to her f's estate, recognised in this style by Lord Lyon 1954 and *d* 23 Nov 1971), 3rd dau of Col Arthur William Henry Drummond of Cromlix (*see* KINNOULL E), and *d* 14 Sept 1957, leaving:

1 IAN GEORGE EDEN, **9th Baron Auckland**; *b* 23 June 1926; *educ* Blundell's; Roy Signals 1945–48 and Sharpshooters (TA) 1948–53; underwriting memb Lloyd's 1956–68, Master Broderers' Co 1967–68, Pres ROSPA, insur consultant Olford Blackmore & Co, dir CJ Sims & Co, memb New Zealand Soc; *m* 28 Aug 1954 *Dorothy Margaret, JP (Surrey 1965), yr dau of Henry Joseph Manser, of Beechwood, Friday St, Eastbourne, Sussex, and *d* 28 July 1997, leaving:

(1) ROBERT IAN BURNARD EDEN, **10th and present Baron Auckland**

(1) *(Margaret) Fiona [The Hon Mrs Shouler, 137 Appledore Ave, Wollaton, Nottingham]; *b* 12 Dec 1955; *m* 14 April 1979 *Michael Howard Shouler, yr son of John Richard Shouler of Bramcote, Notts, and has:

1a *Benjamin; *b* 1987

1a *Elizabeth; *b* 1982

2a *Katherine; *b* 1983

3a *Abigail; *b* 1989

(2) *Rachel Audrey; *b* 9 June 1959; *m* 20 June 1981 *Bramwell M Paton, s of John B Paton, and has:

1a *Alexander Robert; *b* 1983

2a *Joe Bramwell; *b* 1986

1a *Charlotte Jane; *b* 1985

2 +Ronald John [The Hon Ronald Eden, Mill Dam, Cromlix, Dumblane, Perthshire FK15 9JT]; *b* 5 March 1931; *educ* Trin Coll Glenalmond and Ch Ch Oxford (MA); *m* 1 June 1957 *Rosemary Dorothy Marion, yr dau of Sir John (Frederick) Ellenborough Crowder, JP, MP, Charlestown, St Austell, Cornwall, and 72 Chester Sq, London SW1, by Florence Gertrude, est dau of Alfred Ralph William George Petre (*see* PETRE, B), and has issue:

(1) +Henry Vane; *b* 11 March 1958; *m* 1988 *Alicia Claire, yr dau of Christopher James Blois Needham (*see* KILMOREY, E), and has had:

1a Harry; *b* and *d* 1989

2a +Oliver; *b* 1990

1a *Roseanna; *b* 1992

2a *Annabel; *b* 20 Oct 1995

(2) +Edward John; *b* 22 June 1959; *m* 1990 *Victoria M C, est Dau of Maj D P T Deshon, of Hartley Mauduit House, Alton, Hants, and has:

1a +William; *b* 1991

1a *Charlotte; *b* 1996

AUSTIN

Arms: Gules eight mullets, three, three and two argent, a bordure dovetailed or, charged with four thistles, leaved and slipped proper.
Crest: A dexter arm embowed in fess, couped at the shoulder, vested or, cuff indented ermine, the hand proper holding a cross bottony fitchée gules, resting on the arm a mullet of the last.
Motto: Trust in God and he will give strength.
Creation: Bt. (UK) 16 July 1894.

SIR ANTHONY LEONARD AUSTIN, 6TH BT, of Red Hill, Castleford, West Riding of Yorks [SirAnthony Austin Bt, Stanbury Manor, Morwenstow, Bude, Cornwall EX23 9JQ]; *b* 30 Sept 1930; *s* bro 1995; *educ* Downside; *m* 1st 26 June 1956 (*divorce* 1966) Mary Annette, dau of Richard Kelly, of Greenogue, Kisallaghan, Co Dublin, and has issue:

1 +PETER JOHN; *b* 29 July 1958

2 +Nicholas Michael James; *b* 1 June 1960

1 *Caroline Dorothy; *b* 31 March 1957

Sir ANTHONY *m* 2nd 1967 *Aileen Morrison Hall, dau of William Hall Stewart, and has further issue:

2 *Rebecca Dorothy Mary; *b* 1968

Lineage: JOHN AUSTIN, of Manor House, Kippax, Yorks; *m* Hannah (*d* 31 May 1866), dau of James Fawcett, of Kippax, and had, with other issue:

Sir John Austin, 1st Bt (UK), so *cr* 16 July 1894, of Red Hill, Castleford, Yorks, JP (W R Yorks); *b* 9 March 1824; MP (Lib) Osgoldcross 1886–1906; Chm Visiting Ctee County Justices York Castle; *m* 1866 Agnes (*d* 31 May 1910), dau of Samuel Standish Byron, JP, of West Ayton, nr Scarborough, and had issue:

1 WILLIAM MICHAEL BYRON (Sir), **2nd Bt**

2 John Standish Thomas Joseph, JP (W R Yorks); *b* 30 March 1875; *educ* Trin Hall Cambridge (MA); 2nd Lt RASC WW I; *m* 11 Aug 1908 Gwendolyne Audrey Beverley (*d* 9 Dec 1959), dau of Capt Beverley Robinson, of Hyde Lodge, Winchester, and *d* 2 Sept 1941, leaving issue:

(1) John Standish Beverley; *b* 6 Aug 1909; *educ* Ampleforth and Downside

(1) Audrey Mary; *b* 13 Nov 1910; *m* 2 Sept 1950 Ralph Dixon Brown, 2nd son of Lionel Dixon Dixon Brown, of 12 Carlton Rd, London W5

(2) Janetta Agnes Gwendolyne; *b* 21 July 1912; F/O WRAF

3 Wilfred Charles; *b* 1877; *d* 1883

4 Joseph Edward; *b* 3 April 1881; Lt 9th Coy London Bn London Regt (TF) WW I; *m* 8 July 1914 Katherine Matilda (*d* 1968), dau of John Ryan, MD, FRCSI, of Castleconnell, Co Limerick, and *d* 10 Sept 1938, leaving issue:

(1) Edward John Byron; *b* 11 April 1918; *d* 5 Aug 1928

(2) Charles Anthony Byron; *b* 19 Nov 1920; *d* 22 Nov 1921

(3) John Patrick Standish; *b* 27 Sept 1922; *kas* 4 April 1945

(4) +Richard Joseph Byron [Richard Austin Esq, 65 Chatsworth Ct, Pembroke Rd, London W8]; *b* 16 March 1926; *educ* Ampleforth

(1) *Joan Agnes Mary; *b* 18 Feb 1917; *m* 23 April 1949 *Michael Laurence Bexon, MC, son of MacAlister Bexon, CBE, of Stoneways, Amersham Rd, High Wycombe, Bucks, and has issue:

1a *Julian Michael Adrian; *b* 17 Feb 1950; *educ* Beaumont, Stonyhurst and St John's Coll Oxford

2a *Dominic Edmund Christian; *b* 7 Jan 1954; *educ* Worth

1 Agnes Mary Philomena; *d* unm 1940

2 Elizabeth Hannah Mary; *m* 3 Feb 1892 Louis Eugene Will (*d* 1939), and *d* 1938, leaving issue

3 Frances Mary; *m* 1898 John Henry Charles Baker (*d* 1951), and *d* 9 Sept 1950, having had two s (*dec*)

4 Emmeline Jane Mary; *m* 26 June 1903 William Bernard Slesser (*d* 1940), er son of Ernest Theodore Slesser, and *d* 22 Oct 1968 aged 95, leaving issue

5 Alice Eleanor Mary; *d* unm 20 May 1954

Sir JOHN *d* 30 March 1906; his est son,

Sir William Michael Byron Austin, 2nd Bt, JP (W R Yorks); *b* 27 Nov 1871; Capt RASC, Capt Yorks Mounted Brig T&S Column ASC (TF), WW I with Yorkshire Dragoons; *m* 3 Sept 1896 Violet Irene (*d* 18 July 1962), dau of Alexander Fraser, JP, of Westerfield House, nr Ipswich (*see* 1970 edn FRASER OF LONSDALE, B), and *d* 13 Nov 1940, having had issue:

1 **Sir John Byron Fraser Austin, 3rd Bt**; *b* 14 July 1897; *educ* Downside and RMC Sandhurst; Flt Cdr RFC and with 7th Hus RFC WW I and later with Somaliland Camel Corps and KAR Tanganyika WW II, cmded IA Bn Burma (despatches); *m* 1st 10 June 1953 (*divorce* 1958) Sheila Jean, only dau of Duncan McNaught, of Ayr, and formerly wife of Col Harry Carlisle Boyce, CBE, RA; *m* 2nd 25 March 1960 *Rhoda Noreen, dau of Herbert Lloyd Pinches, of Eastbourne, and widow of Col Charles Vincent Donglas Rose, and *d* 1981

2 **Sir William Ronald Fraser Austin, 4th Bt**; *b* 20 July 1900; *m* 1st 20 Feb 1926 Dorothy Mary (*d* 10 July 1957), yr dau of L A Bidwell, FRCS, and had issue:

(1) **Sir Michael Trescawen Austin, 5th Bt**; *b* 27 Aug 1927; *educ* Downside; WW II in RNVR; sometime MFH Braes of Derwent; *m* 30 Jan 1951 *Bridget Dorothea Patricia, dau of Francis Farrell, of Miltown, Clonmellon, Co Meath, and *d* 3 Aug 1995, leaving:

1a *Mary; *b* 3 Nov 1951; *m* 1981 *John Orchard, of Mill-Roy, Budleigh Salterton, Devon

2a *Jane [Miss Jane Austin, Goldburn, Okehampton, Devon EX20 3BD]; *b* 9 Sept 1954

3a *Susan; *b* 12 Feb 1956; *m* 1978 *Anthony Farrell, of Station House, Ballivor, Co Meath, and has issue:

1b *Sean Patrick; *b* 1982

1b *Bridget; *b* 1980

(2) Sir ANTHONY LEONARD AUSTIN, **6th and present Bt**

2 **Sir William** *m* 2nd 1958 *Mary Helen Farrell and *d* 1989

1 Marjorie Irene Gwendoline; *m* 17 June 1924 Maj Leslie Lawson de Ste Croix, OBE, late RASC, son of Philip Charles de Ste Croix, of Jersey, and had a s

2 Violet Cecily; *m* 12 May 1932 Brig Douglas Hugh Moffatt Carbery, MC, DFC, RA (*d* 27 April 1959), son of Hugh John Carbery, of Cork, and had issue:

(1) Anne Irene [Mrs Alexander Brown, 1 Midmar Ave, Morningside, Edinburgh 10]; *b* 6 July 1935; WRNS; *m* 10 Nov 1956 *Lt-Cdr Alexander Leonard Dominic Brown, RN, son of Alexander Brown, of Prestwick, Scotland, and has issue:

1a *Hamish Alexander Douglas; *b* 29 Dec 1961

1a *Sally-Anne; *b* 12 Sept 1958

3 Muriel Agnes Jane; *m* 30 April 1930 (*divorce* 1940) Lt-Col Maurice Charles Frye, OBE, 1st Bn 1st Punjab Regt, IA, and had issue:

(1) *John Maurice; *b* 14 Oct 1935; *educ* Lancing; formerly Assist Inspr N Rhodesian Police

AVEBURY

Arms: Argent on a mount vert a stork close ermine, on a chief gules three estoiles of the field. **Crest:** A stork, wings elevated ermine, resting the dexter claw on an antique shield azure, bordured or, charged with a lion rampant guardant argent. **Supporters:** On either side a stork, wings elevated ermine, gorged with a chain or, suspended therefrom an escutcheon gules charged with an estoile argent. **Motto:** *Auctor pretiosa facit* ('The perpetrator of a deed confers the value it holds'). **Creations:** Bt. (UK) 9 April 1806, B. (UK) 22 Jan 1900.

THE 4TH BARON AVEBURY, of Avebury, Wilts, and a **Baronet** (Sir Eric Reginald Lubbock, Bt) [The Rt Hon The Lord Avebury, House of Lords, London SW1A 0PW]; *b* 29 Sept 1928; *s* cousin 1971; *educ* Upper Canada Coll, Harrow and Balliol Coll Oxford (BA); Lt Welsh Gds (Reserve) 1949–51; with Rolls-Royce 1951–56, production engr 1956–60, Charterhouse Gp 1960–62, MP (Lib) Orpington 1962–1970 (Lib Whip 1963–70), consultant Morgan Grampian Ltd 1970, chm Digico Ltd 1971, dir CL Projects Ltd, Pres Data Processing Management Assoc 1972–75, Fluoridation Soc 1972, Conservation Soc 1973, memb Cncl Inst Race Relations 1972–74, memb Roy Commn on Standards of Conduct in Public Life 1974–76; *m* 1st 2 Sept 1953 (*divorce* 1983) Kina-Maria, BSc London 1970, only dau of Count Joseph Henry O'Kelly de Gallagh, of 41 Roland Gdns, London SW7, and has issue:

1 +LYULPH AMBROSE JONATHAN [The Hon Lyulph Lubbock, 53 Worlds End Lane, Green St Green, Orpington, Kent BR6 6AF]; *b* 15 June 1954; *educ* St Olave's GS Orpington and Birmingham U; *m* 14 May 1977 *Susan Carol, yr dau of Kenneth Henry MacDonald, and has issue:

(1) +Alexander Lyulph Robert; *b* 17 Jan 1985

(1) *Vanessa Adelaide Felicity; *b* 15 April 1983

2 +Maurice Patrick Guy; *b* 5 Nov 1955; *m* 1982 *Diana Rivia Tobin, and has issue:

(1) *Olivia Adelaide; *b* 30 Nov 1990

1 *Victoria Sarah Maria [The Hon Ms Lubbock, 225 Evering Rd, London E5 8AL]; *b* 27 April 1959; has retained maiden name *m* 1983 *Alan Binnie, and has issue:

(1) *Archie; *b* 1983

(2) *Alastair; *b* 1985

The 4th BARON *m* 2nd 1985 *Lindsay Jean, dau of Gordon Neil Stewart and Pamela Hansford Johnson (Lady Snow; *see* 1970 edn), writer, and by her has further issue:

3 +John William Stewart; *b* 8 Aug 1985

Lineage: JOHN LUBBOCK, of N Walsham, Norfolk; *m* Elizabeth, dau of William Webster, of Calthorp, and had an only s:

Rev WILLIAM LUBBOCK; Rector of Lamas, Norfolk; *m* Elizabeth (*d* 10 March 1764), dau of Thomas Cooper, and *d* 20 April 1754, leaving:

1 **Sir John Lubbock, 1st Bt** (UK), so *cr* 9 April 1806, with remainder, in default of male issue, to his n; *bapt* 20 Aug 1744; merchant and banker London; *m* 12 Oct 1771 Elizabeth Christiana (*d* 1846), dau of Frederick Commerell, of Hanwell, and *dsp* 24 Feb 1816

2 William, of Lamas; *bapt* 6 July 1746; *m* 7 Oct 1773 Anne (*d* 30 Nov 1773), only dau and heir of Thomas Woodrow, of Hobbis, Norfolk, and had:

(1) JOHN WILLIAM (Sir), **2nd Bt**

(1) Anne Elizabeth; *m* Hugh William Brown and *d* 4 March 1855

(2) Maria; *m* Rev WJ Blake

The 1st Bt's n,

Sir John William Lubbock, 2nd Bt; *bapt* 26 Aug 1774; merchant and banker; *m* 1 Aug 1799 Mary, dau of James Entwisle, of Rusholme, Manchester, and *d* 22 Oct 1840, leaving an only child:

Sir John William Lubbock, 3rd Bt; *b* 26 March 1803; V-Pres Roy Soc, scientific author; *m* 29 June 1833 Harriet (*d* 12 Feb 1873), dau of Lt-Col George Hotham, of York, and had, with other issue (of whom those with + are in remainder to the btcy only):

1 JOHN, **1st Baron**

2 Henry James, JP and DL; *b* 7 Feb 1838; High Sheriff Co London 1894 and 1897; *m* 8 May 1866 Frances Mary (*d* 5 Aug 1922), yst dau of Rev Henry Turton, incumbent Betley, Staffs, and *d* 25 Jan 1910, leaving issue:

(1) Henry; *b* 27 June 1868; *educ* Eton and RMC Sandhurst; Lt 4th Bn Bedfordshire Regt; *d* unm 24 Dec 1957

(2) Geoffrey; *b* 18 May 1873; *educ* Eton and Trin Coll Oxford; Maj N Somerset Yeo, S Africa 1900–02, WW I (wounded, despatches twice); High Sheriff Co London 1912; *m* 13 Nov 1907 Marguerite Agaranthe (*d* 26 May 1943), dau of Col Charles William Miles, of Burtonhill, Malmesbury, Wilts, and widow of Sir Charles Tennant, 1st Bt (*see* GLENCONNER, B), and *d* 31 Dec 1932, leaving issue:

1a Peter Geoffrey; *b* 10 Jan 1909; *educ* Eton; md Peter Lubbock Travel Ltd

2a David Miles; *b* 5 March 1911; *educ* Eton and Trin Coll Cambridge; WW II as Lt (A) RNVR (despatches, POW), md James Simpson and Son (Peterhead) Ltd; *m* 7 July 1939 Hon Helen Anne Boyd Orr (*d* Dec 1994), yr dau of 1st and last Baron Boyd-Orr, DSO, MC, MD, FRS, LLD, and *d* Sept 1992, having had:

1b +Geoffrey Orr; *b* 30 June 1946; *educ* Eton and Magdalene Coll Cambridge; *m* 1981 *Fiona Constance, yst dau of Col Homer E Harris, of Mass, USA, and has issue:

1c *Francesca Eriminta Alessandra; *b* 1985

2c *Caroline Angelica; *b* 1989

2b +(John Nicholas) Andrew [Andrew Lubbock Esq, Harwood Mill, Bonchester Bridge, Hawick, Roxburgh]; *b* 1 Aug 1948; *educ* Eton; *m* 12 March 1977 *Jane Louisa, dau of Col Charles King, OBE, of Hale House, Cucklington, Somerset, and has issue:

1c +Hamish Percy Elliot; *b* 4 Sept 1977

2c +James Alexander George; *b* 1982

1c *Sammie Elizabeth Ursula; *b* 1980

3b +Kenneth Miles Boyd; *b* 14 July 1950; *educ* Eton; *m* 1975 *Moira Baillie, of Helensburgh, Dunbartonshire, and has:

1c +John Angus Elliot; *b* 1981

1c *Julia Janet Roxanne; *b* 1989

1b *Ann Patricia [Mrs John Gooch, The Schoolhouse, Oathlaw, Forfar, Angus]; *b* 25 Aug 1941; *m* 1972 *John Daniel Gooch, VRD, and has issue (*see* GOOCH, Bt, of Clewer Pk)

(3) Rupert Egerton; *b* 7 May 1886; Capt RN; *m* 18 Dec 1912 Vera Isabel (*d* 11 Oct 1962), only dau of George Reginald Wingrove, of Shanghai, and *das* 8 May 1943, leaving issue:

1a Rupert James; *b* 21 April 1916; *educ* Nautical Coll, Pangbourne; Capt 5th Bn Leics Regt (TA) WW II 1939–40 (POW); *m* 21 July 1954 Jeanette Patricia (*d* 1 Oct 1976), only dau of Anton van Beugen Bik, of Broughton, Esher, Surrey, and *d* 1981, leaving issue:

1b + Guy Rupert Anthony; *b* 4 April 1956

2b +David Alexander; *b* 22 Feb 1958

1b *Fiona Jeanette Ariane; *b* 9 July 1960

2a +Christopher William Stuart [Christopher Lubbock Esq, New Barn House, Great Horkesley, Essex]; *b* 4 Jan 1920; *educ* Charterhouse and Brasenose Coll, Oxford; WW II as Lt RNVR, barrister Inner Temple 1947; *m* 11 June 1947 *Hazel Gordon, yst dau of Gordon Chapman, of Woodpeckers, Delamere, Cheshire, and has issue:

1b +(Rupert) James Gordon [James Lubbock Esq, 139 Ramsden Rd, London SW12]; *b* 7 April 1948; *educ* Charterhouse; *m* 1982 *Miranda Jane, est dau of Stephen St Clair McNeile, of 18 Redesdale St, London SW3, and has issue:

1c +Richard Christopher Sinclair; *b* 1983

1c *Sophie Caroline; *b* 1986

1b *Victoria Margaret; *b* 4 Oct 1950; *m* 1977 *Geoffrey Richard Humphrey Edwards, of 44 St Barnabas Rd, Cambridge, and has issue:

1c *Charles David Christopher; *b* 1979

2c *Guy William Humphrey; *b* 1983

1c *Chloë Elizabeth Rose; *b* 1981

1a *Nancy Diana Mary; *b* 4 Oct 1914; *m* 22 May 1937 Sir Charles Gerald Stewkley Shuckburgh, 12th Bt (*qv*), and has issue

(1) Evelyn Mary; *b* 26 May 1897; *m* John Verity, JP, MIEE (*d* 6 April 1905), of Sandrigebury, and *d* 22 Aug 1949, leaving issue

(2) Cecil Blanche; *m* 9 June 1888 Riversdale Francis John Grenfell, of The Hall, Welwyn, Herts, and *d* 8 Oct 1931, leaving issue (*see* GRENFELL, B)

(3) Margaret Muriel; *m* 17 July 1906 Ernest Tatham Richmond, FRIBA, Egyptian CS (*d* 5 March 1955), son of Sir William Richmond, KCB, and *d* 25 March 1959, leaving issue

3 Nevile (Sir) KCMG; *b* 31 March 1839; Pres W India Ctee 1909–14; *m* 1st 18 June 1861 Harriet Charlotte (*d* 20 Nov 1878), dau of Western Wood, MP, of North Cray Place (*see* WOOD, Bt, of Hatherley House), and had issue

(1) Charles Western; *b* 5 June 1862; *m* 1 Oct 1884 Margaret Ellen (*m* 2nd 13 May 1895 Herbert Sadler (formerly Bergmann; *d* 29 Sept 1940), son of Herbert Joseph Bergmann, and *d* 16 March 1958), only dau of Richard N Thornton, of Knowle, Sidmouth, and *d* 16 April 1890, leaving issue:

1a Humphrey Thornton; *b* 30 Aug 1886; Hon Capt 28th London Regt (Artists Rifles); memb London Stock Exchange; *m* 9 Sept 1916 Elma Vera (*d* 30 June 1958), dau of Everard Britten-Holmes, and *dsp* 12 Aug 1962

1a Madeleine Alice; *b* 27 July 1885; *m* 31 Jan 1912 George Norman Ferrers-Guy, T/Capt Worcestershire Regt (*d* 4 Dec 1944), son of Tom Ferrers-Guy, and *d* 8 Nov 1965, leaving issue (*see* GREY, B)

(2) Hugh Nevile; *b* 6 Dec 1865; 2nd Lt Roy Defence Corps; *m* 1st 17 June 1890 (*divorce* 1934) Margaret Agnes (*d* 18 April 1959), est dau of Henry Frederic Tiarks, of Foxbury, Chislehurst, and had issue:

1a Ralph Hugh, MC (1918); *b* 16 March 1891; F/O No 906 (Co of Middx) Balloon Sqdn AAF and Maj RFA; *m* 1st 8 June 1914 (*divorce* 1922) Adelaide Margaret Constance, yst dau of Samuel Hynman Montgomerie, DL (formerly Allenby), by his wife Lady Sophia Montgomerie, er dau and co-heir of 14th Earl of Eglinto(u)n and (2nd Earl of) Winton(*qv*), and had:

1b *Ursula Egidia [Mrs Peter Bellamy, West End Cottage, Eythorne, nr Dover, Kent]; b 13 June 1919; m 4 Jan 1941 *Peter Bellamy, and has issue:

1c *Geraldine Anne; b 1943; m 1964 *Michael Wyant Littlebourne

1a (cont.) Maj Ralph Lubbock m 2nd 5 Dec 1923 Louise (d 1987), dau of James Charles Vogel, of Durban, Natal, S Africa, and d 31 Aug 1961, having by her had issue:

1b +John Ralph [John Lubbock Esq, 31 Crompton Court, London SW3]; b 23 Dec 1925; educ Malvern; WW II 1943–45 as Capt Coldstream Gds; m 1st 7 Dec 1950 (divorce 1957) Patricia Helen Winifred, only child of Brig-Gen Hon Roger Brand, CMG, DSO, 5th son of 2nd Viscount Hampden (qv), and by her had:

1c Hugh Roger; b 3 Oct 1951; educ Eton; PhD Cantab, Fell Churchill Coll Cambridge; k in a motor accident in Rio de Janeiro 1981

1b (cont.) John Lubbock m 2nd 15 April 1957 (divorce 1961) Jane Marjorie, 2nd dau of Maj Evelyn Ronald Moncrieff Fryer, MC, Gren Gds, of Nine Acres, Selborne, Hants, and by her has further issue:

2c +Thomas Nevile; b 28 Dec 1957

1b (cont.) John Lubbock m 3rd 1963 (divorce 1966) Helene Gladys Frances, only dau of Maj William Fergusson Thomson; m 4th 1967 Anne Elizabeth, dau of Frank Colville Pearce, and by her has:

3c +Stephen Henry Ralph; b 1970; m 11 Oct 1997 *Melissa Caroline, est dau of Ian Yates

1c *Elizabeth Serena; b 1967

1b (cont.) John Lubbock m 5th *Margaret Dorothy Pearce and by her has:

1c +Roderick John; b 6 March 1981

2c *Rosemary Margaret; b 14 Feb 1984

2a Mark Hugh; b 17 Nov 1898; educ Eton; m 15 Jan 1930 Beatrice Isabel, only dau of Edgar Howe, of 44 Hans Mansions, London SW3

1a Agnes Margaret; b 24 Sept 1893; m 1st 23 Feb 1924 (divorce 1927) Alfred Wallace Turner, only son of Dr Alfred Turner, of Plympton House, Plympton, S Devon; m 2nd 9 Nov 1927 Samuel Guy Loveridge (d 16 Sept 1961), son of Walter Loveridge, of The Mount, Codsal, Wolverhampton

2a Mary Harriet Margaret; b 22 Sept 1903; m 6 July 1928 Paul Schoeffler, yr son of Paul Schoeffler, of Dresden, and had issue:

1b *Peter Walter Paul [Peter Schoeffler-Lubbock Esq, Woodmuir, 10 Clifton Rd, Chesham Bois, Amersham, Bucks]; b 2 Nov 1931; educ Radley; m 29 Oct 1955 *Patricia Gladys, yst dau of Louis Hofmens, of 4161 Oxford Ave, Montreal, Canada, and has issue:

1c *Paul Geoffrey; b 21 Nov 1958

1c *Andrea Mary; b 24 Sept 1964

(2) (cont.) Hugh Lubbock m 2nd 22 Nov 1934 Lilian (d 16 Feb 1937), dau of William John Spanner, and widow of Alexander M Sommerville, of China, and d 7 Nov 1938

(3) Arthur Nevile; b 1 March 1869; m 5 Nov 1895 Alice Ellen (d 14 Jan 1944), dau of Henry Frederic Tiarks, of Foxbury, Chislehurst, and d 8 Sept 1939, leaving issue:

1a +Ivo Arthur [Ivo Lubbock Esq, Hazelbridge Court, Chiddingfold, Surrey]; b 12 June 1908; educ Eton

1a Gillian; b 6 Aug 1906; m 14 July 1927 2nd Viscount Chelmsford (qv), and d 22 April 1978, leaving issue

(4) Bertie Nevile; b 2 May 1872; educ Marlborough; d unm 9 Jan 1965

(5) Ernest Nevile; b 25 March 1875; drowned at sea 1918

(6) Reginald Nevile; b 19 May 1876; educ Repton; Lt RNVR; m 21 March 1907 Lilian Stephenson (d Aug 1942), 2nd dau of William Stephenson Swift, of Walkeringham, Lincs, and d 14 March 1942, leaving issue:

1a Ruth Elizabeth Stephenson; m 20 Aug 1931 Thomas Marshall Bell, MB, BChir, MRCS, LRCP, son of Maj Herbert Alfred Bell, of Lindum Clo, Wragby Rd, Lincoln, and had issue:

1b *Michael Nevile Marshall; b 11 Oct 1933; educ Charterhouse and Christ's Coll, Cambridge (MA); slr; m 5 June 1964 *Joyce Violet, dau of Eustace Graham Long, of London, and has issue:

1c *Francis Graham Thomas; b 6 Oct 1965

2b *Robin John Marshall [Robin Bell Esq, 3 The Ave, Burton on Stather, Scunthorpe, Lincs]; b 21 Feb 1935; educ Charterhouse and Christ's Coll, Cambridge (MA, MB 1960, BCh 1959)

(1) Edith Harriet; b 22 May 1867; m 2 April 1919 Hon Norman Lubbock (d 11 Nov 1926), 2nd son of 1st Baron Avebury (see below), and d 24 Dec 1950

(2) Maud; b 18 June d 24 Aug 1870

(3) Madeleine; b 25 April d 9 July 1874

3 (cont.) Sir Nevile Lubbock m 2nd 15 Sept 1881 Constance Ann (d 20 June 1939), 9th dau of Sir John Frederick William Herschel, 1st Bt (qv), and d 12 Sept 1914, having by her had issue:

(7) Alexander Nevile; b 2 Nov 1883; Lt-Cdr RN; drowned on active service 28 April 1918

(4) Margaret Constance Nevile; b 6 July 1882; m 1st 24 April 1912 Bertram Emil Hambro (see HAMBRO, B), and had issue; m 2nd 15 May 1919 Lt-Col Charles Norman Cavendish Boyle, MC, late Rifle Bde (see CORK and ORRERY, E), and d 28 Jan 1969

(5) Sybil; b 26 Jan 1885; m 2 Nov 1912 Lt-Col Edward Boyd Maxwell, OBE, MC, late RFA, 2nd son of James Maxwell, and d 25 July 1966, leaving issue

(6) Hilda Francesca; b 12 March 1886; m 20 June 1929 Paul Cairn Vellacott, CBE, DSO (d 15 Nov 1954), Master of Peterhouse, Cambridge 1939–54, Headmaster of Harrow 1934–39, son of William Edward Vellacott, FCA, of Winterbourne, Budleigh Salterton, and dsp 9 April 1970

(7) Rosemary; b 24 March 1887; m 12 Jan 1921 Christopher Carlile (d 27 March 1964), 3rd son of Prebendary Wilson Carlile, CH, and d 9 Dec 1942, leaving issue (see CARLILE, Bt)

(8) Alice Mildred; b 28 Aug 1888; d unm 4 Nov 1958

(9) Dorothy; b 8 July 1890; m 30 June 1933 Frederick George Bonham-Carter (d 13 Dec 1968), son of Henry Bonham-Carter

4 Beaumont William; b 12 Oct 1840; d unm 19 March 1909

5 Montagu; b 24 May 1842; MD, FRCP, MRCS; m 1st 14 Nov 1872 Lora (d 1 Aug 1882), yst dau of Capt George Hotham, RE (see HOTHAM, B), and had issue:

(1) Montagu Hotham; b 11 May 1876; Lt-Cdr RN (ret); d 22 July 1926

(2) Ronald Hotham; b 22 March 1878; d 1886

(3) George Hotham; b 5 March 1882; d 1886

(1) Alice Harriet; d an infant 1873

5 (cont.) Dr Montagu Lubbock m 2nd 1 Feb 1888 Nora (d 25 July 1918), est dau of Nottidge Charles Macnamara, FRCS, of The Lodge, Chorleywood, Herts, and d 8 April 1925

6 Frederic; b 1 May 1844; m 11 Nov 1869 Catherine (d 18 May 1934), only dau of John Gurney, of Earlham Hall, Norfolk, and d 22 June 1927, having had issue:

(1) Guy, CMG (1917), DSO (1916); b 9 Oct 1870; educ Eton; Col RE, Brig-Gen 1921, WW I (despatches, Legion Honour), Order White Eagle Serbia 3rd Cl with swords; m 16 April 1912 Lettice Isabella (d 1980), 3rd dau of Robert Harvey Mason, DL, of Necton Hall, Swaffham, Norfolk, and d 3 March 1956, leaving issue:

1a +Joseph Guy [Joseph Lubbock Esq, High Elms, Waldringfield, Woodbridge, Suffolk]; b 20 May 1915; educ Eton and Trin Coll Cambridge (BA 1937); late Capt RE, WW II; m 28 April 1941 *Ruth Cecilia, 2nd dau of Maj Quintin Edward Gurney, DL, of Bawdeswell Hall, Norfolk, and has issue:

1b *Jennifer [Mrs Jennifer Lubbock, 2 Rectory Lane, Mulbarton, Norwich NR14 8AG]; b 20 May 1942; m 1st 22 Oct 1966 (divorce 1974) Marchese Giorgio Ciaralli-Parenzi, s of Gilberto Ciaralli, and has:

1c *Andrew; b 5 Nov 1969

1c *Elena; b 12 Dec 1967; m 1994 *Giuseppe Pizzini and has:

1d *Vivien; b 20 Oct 1994

2d *Eve; b 30 Sept 1996

1b (cont.) Marchese Jennifer Ciaralli-Parenzi m 2nd 1975 (divorce 1989) Michael Wynne Parker, and by him has:

2c *Sarah Ruth Isabella; b 1978

3c *Fiona Alice Elizabeth; b 1981

2b *Catherine; b 14 Jan 1944; m 13 Jan 1968 *Stuart Jennings, MB, BS London LRCP, MRCS, s of Oliver Jennings, of Devizes, Wilts, and has:

1c *Mark; b 1970; m 1993 *Sarah Louise Hesketh

2c *Samuel; b 1971

3b *Lucinda [Mrs John Harkness, Hill House, Geldeston, Beccles, Suffolk NR34 0LX]; b 11 Dec 1948; m 1st 1974 Thomas Henry Carew (d 1978), yr s of Cdr Hon Peter Cuthbert Carew, RN (see CAREW, B), and has issue:

1c *Rachel Catherine; b 9 June 1978

3b (cont.) Mrs Thomas Carew m 2nd 1983 *John Martin Harkness, and by him has:

1c *Edward John; b 1984

1c *Alice Elizabeth; b 1986

(2) Cecil; b 15 Feb 1872; educ Eton; a Lt of the City of London, Dir Bank of England; m 14 April 1898 Edith (d 14 Dec 1960), dau of Ven Charles Wellington Furse, Archdeacon of Westminster, and d 18 Jan 1956, leaving:

1a Michael Ronald, MBE (1942); b 31 May 1906; educ Eton and Trin Coll, Oxford (MA); Col Royal Signals (TA) WW II (despatches three times), Order King George I of Greece; m 1st 1 May 1929 (divorce 1956) Diana Beatrice (d 1976), dau of Henry Ernest Crawley (see CRAWLEY-BOEVEY, Bt), and had:

1b +Jeremy Michael [Jeremy Lubbock Esq, 1390 Kelton Ave, Apt 301, Los Angeles, CA 90024, USA]; b 4 June 1931; late Lt Durham LI; m 1st 1956 (divorce 1959) Jill Caroline, dau of Eric Nicholls, and has issue:

1c +Justin Roger; b 18 Dec 1956

1b (cont.) Jeremy Lubbock m 2nd 6 Sept 1963 *Shelagh Mary, dau of Richard Lang, MB, of Kenilworth, Cape, S Africa, and by her has issue:

1c *Lindsay Brigid; b 17 March 1965

1b (cont.) Jeremy Lubbock m 3rd 1974 (divorce 1987) his cousin Philippa Harriet, er dau of Lt-Col Charles Arthur Chadwyck-Healey (see CHADWICK-HEALEY, Bt), and by her has:

2c +Rowan Mark; b 23 Jan 1981

2c *Holly Andrée; b 29 Aug 1976

2b +John David Peter; b 18 March 1945; educ Radley; m 1977 *Eleanor Sloane, and has issue:

1c +Daniel John; b 1978

2c +Patrick; b 1980

1b *Judith Caroline Gurney [Mrs Martin Marriott, Morris Farmhouse, Baverstock, Dinton, Wilts SP3 5EL]; b 4 May 1934; m 10 Nov 1956 *Martin Marriott, yst son of Rt Rev Philip Selwyn Abraham, MA, DD, 6th Bp of Newfoundland, by Elizabeth Dorothy Cicely, dau of Sir John Arthur Ransome Marriott, and has:

1c *Charles John Philip; b 13 Feb 1964

1c *Virginia Elizabeth [Mrs Patrick O'Conor, 51 Downs Park West, Westbury Park, Bristol BS6 7QL]; b 12 May 1958; m 1987 *Patrick Francis O'Conor

2c *Rebecca Jane; b 4 Oct 1960

2b *Jessica Rose [Mrs David Brook, c/o Lloyds Bank, 19 High St, Evesham, Worcs WR11 4DQ]; b 23 Dec 1937; m 14 Jan 1961 Air V-Marshal David Conway Grant Brook, CBE, RAF, and has:

1c *William Alexander Darville; b 31 Aug 1965

1c *Julie Nicola; b 30 Dec 1961

3b *Joanna [Mrs Michael Seligman, Crown Lodge, Newnham, Basingstoke, Hants, RG27 9AN]; b 29 Jan 1941; m 16 Oct 1965 *Michael Coleridge Seligman, s of R J Seligman, of Deane House, Basingstoke, Hants, and has:

1c *Simon Michael Hugo; b 29 May 1966

2c *Thomas Reginald James; b 1975

1c *Kate Sophia; b 1 Oct 1968

1a (cont.) Col Michael Lubbock *m* 2nd 1 Jan 1957 (*divorce* 1975) Inga Olga, dau of Eugene Ivan de Rudez, of Zagreb, Yugoslavia, and widow of Col Geoffrey Gore Moule, and by her issue:

4b *Inga Cecilia; *b* 6 Oct 1957

1a (cont.) Col Michael Lubbock *m* 3rd 1976 *Elizabeth Christina [Mrs Michael Lubbock, 30/655 Richmond Rd, Ottawa, Ontario, Canada], dau of John Sutherland, of Ontario, Canada, and *d* 1989

1a Cynthia Margaret; *b* 1 Nov 1899; *m* 20 April 1921 Alexander Henry Melvill Wedderburn, CBE (*d* 23 Dec 1968), son of Alexander Dundas Ogilvy Wedderburn, CBE, KC, and had issue (*see* OGILVY-WEDDERBURN, Bt)

2a Joan Catherine [Mrs Joan Cunliffe, 12a St Olave's Court, St Petersburgh Place, London W2]; *b* 10 Feb 1903; *m* 5 Nov 1925 (*divorce* 1952) 2nd Baron Cunliffe (*d* 24 Nov 1963; *qv*), and had issue

3a *Margaret Hester [Mrs William Rathbone, Greenbank Mill Lane, Dyer's Hill, Charlbury, Oxon, OX7 3QG]; *b* 24 March 1910; *m* 16 Nov 1932 William Rathbone, est son of William Rathbone, of 2 Lord North St, Westminster, London SW1, and has issue

4a *Viola, JP (Sussex 1951) [Viola Lady Chadwyck-Healey JP, 38 Castle Court, River Pk, Marlborough, Wilts SN8 1NH]; *b* 19 Dec 1912; *m* 2 May 1939 Lt-Col Charles Arthur Chadwyck-Healey, OBE, RA, of 4 Nethergate St, Sudbury, Suffolk, 2nd son of Sir Gerald Edward Chadwyck-Healey, 2nd Bt (*qv*), and has issue

(3) Samuel Gurney; *b* 6 Aug 1873; *educ* Eton and King's Coll, Cambridge (MA); assist master Eton 1897–1934 and Farnborough Sch 1934–37, Chev Order Leopold Belgium; *m* 21 Dec 1915 Irene (*d* 11 Jan 1971), dau of Tobias Scharrer, and *d* 29 Jan 1958, leaving:

1a Ian Gurney; *b* 16 Oct 1917; *educ* Eton; actor; *m* 1st 8 Oct 1938 (*divorce* 1943) Lys De la Tour, dau of Ernest Alexander Dunlap, of Jacksonville, Illinois; *m* 2nd *Gunvor Callisen and *d* 9 June 1977

1a *Rachel Gurney [Mrs Rachel Rhodes, 17 Paultons House, Paultons Sq, London SW3]; *b* 5 March 1920; *m* 4 Aug 1945 (*annulled* 1950) Capt Denys Rhodes, er s of Capt Arthur Tahu Rhodes, MVO, of Mount Offham, West Malling, Kent, and has:

1b *Sharon Gurney [Mrs Simon Gough, Old Hall Farmhouse, Barney, Norfolk NR21 0AD]; *b* 16 June 1950; *m* 1970 *Simon Peter Gough, son of Michael Gough, actor, and has issue:

1c *Samuel Gurney; *b* 1975

2c *Dickon Graves; *b* 1979

1c *Tamasin Rachel; *b* 1973

2c *Daisy Diana; *b* 1976

(4) Percy, CBE (1952); *b* 4 June 1879; *educ* Eton and King's Coll Cambridge (MA); author; *m* 8 Dec 1926 Lady Sybil Marjorie Cuffe (*d* 31 Dec 1943), 2nd dau of 5th Earl of Desart (*see* 1934 edn), and widow of William Bayard Cutting, and *dsp* 2 Aug 1965

(5) Roy, of Riding Oaks, Hildenborough, Tonbridge, Kent; *b* 1 Oct 1892; *educ* Eton and King's Coll Cambridge (BA 1914, MA 1919); Fell Peterhouse 1919–60; *m* 26 April 1919 Yvonne (*d* 1987), dau of Sydney George Vernham, and *d* 1985, leaving:

1a +Jocelyn Roy; *b* 12 April 1920; *educ* Eton and Peterhouse Cambridge (BA 1941, MA 1945, MusB 1946); *m* 1st 15 Aug 1948 (*divorce* 1976) Frances Georgette Coningsby, est dau of Capt George Ashmead-Bartlett and formerly wife of George Derek Pepys Whiteley, and has had:

1b A son; *b* 25, *d* 28 Sept 1953

1b *Annina Nicolette Mary; *b* 18 May 1949

1a (cont.) Jocelyn Lubbock *m* 2nd 1976 *Adriana Camarca, of Rome, and *d* 1992

2a Hubert Timothy; *b* 2 July 1923; *educ* Eton and Peterhouse, Cambridge (BA 1944, MA 1948); *m* 1 Jan 1958 *Barbara Anne [Mrs Hubert Lubbock, Beech Mount, Bircham Rd, Reepham, Norwich], dau of Henry Montgomery Caruth, of 6 Grove Pk, Bury St Edmunds, Suffolk, and *d* 1991, leaving:

1b Catherine Fiona; *b* 1 May 1960; *m* 1986 *Neil Atkinson, and *d* 19–, leaving:

1c *Samuel Lawrence; *b* 1990

1c *Rebecca Louise; *b* 1987

2c *Elizabeth Anne; *b* 1994

2b *Lucinda Anne [Mrs Christopher Copage, Bawburgh, Norfolk]; *b* 3 June 1964; *m* 1987 *Christopher Copage

(6) Alan (Sir), JP (1934), DL (1951), both Hants; *b* 13 Jan 1897; *educ* Eton and King's Coll, Cambridge (MA 1922, Fell 1923–28); Maj RA, WW I 1915–18 as Lt RGA, and WW II 1939–45, Assist Mil Attaché Br Emb Madrid 1940–45; FSA, High Sheriff Hants 1949, CA Hants, Vice-Chm CC 1948, Chm 1955–67, memb Nat Parks Commn 1954–61, Chm Cncl U of Southampton 1957–69, Pro-Chllr 1967, memb Roy Commn to inquire into law relating to common land in England and Wales 1955–58, memb War Works Commn 1959–64, V-Chm Exec Cncl County Cncls Assoc 1963 (Chm 1965), ktd 1963; *m* 20 April 1918 Helen Mary (*d* 1987), only child of John Bonham-Carter, JP, DL, of Adhurst St Mary, Hants, and *d* 1990, having had issue:

1a +Roger John, DSC [Lt-Cdr Roger Lubbock DSC RNR (ret), Weatherall Lodge, Well Rd, London NW3]; *b* 27 Feb 1922; *educ* Eton and King's Coll, Cambridge (BA 1948, MA 1952); Lt-Cdr RNR, WW II; *m* 25 Jan 1955 *Moyra, dau of John Newton Mappin Fraser, and formerly wife of Maj Douglas Sutherland, and has:

1b +Guy John; *b* 6 May 1957

2b +Paul Nigel; *b* 27 April 1960; *m* 1984 *Lucinda, only dau of Ronald Simms, of St Johns Wood, London NW8, and has issue:

1c +Oliver Guy; *b* 1990

1c *Alice Helen; *b* 1988

2a +Martin [Lt-Cdr Martin Lubbock RNVR (ret), Brown's Copse, Heyshott, Midhurst, Sussex]; *b* 22 Feb 1925; *educ* Eton and King's Coll Cambridge; Lt-Cdr RNVR WW II; *m* 9 Aug 1957 *Elizabeth, dau of Roland Marshall, of W Kirby, Yorkshire, and formerly w of Baron Selwyn-Lloyd, and has:

1b +Toby Mark; *b* 13 Oct 1959; *m* 1990 *Bridget A, dau of Geoffrey Sleddon, of Deopham, Norfolk

2b +Robin Alan; *b* 25 June 1961

(1) Violet Catherine; *m* 7 June 1905 Sir Charles Evelyn Pym, CBE, JP, DL (*see* PYM, B), and *d* 21 Jan 1927, leaving issue

7 Alfred; *b* 31 Oct 1845; *m* 1 Oct 1874 Louisa (*d* 13 April 1943), est dau of Charles William Herman Wallroth, of Leigh, Kent, and *d* 17 July 1916, having had issue:

(1) Alfred Basil, MC; *b* 9 Sept 1876; Capt RFA, S Africa 1901–02 and WW I 1914; *m* 15 Jan 1912 Dorothy Mary (*d* 15 Nov 1944), 7th dau of Charles William Warner, CB, barrister, and widow of Cdr Thomas Ulric Thynne, RN (Isee BATH, M), and *dsp* 3 Sept 1944

(2) Robin; *b* 24 Jan 1879; *dsp* 28 Dec 1898

(3) Merlin Gordon, DSO (1921), MC; *b* 12 April 1884; Maj RFA, WW I (Croix de Guerre) and Mesopotamia 1919–20; *m* 29 July 1912 Mary Clermont (Clare) (*d* 2 June 1933), dau of Clermont Livingston, and widow of W M Wightman, and was *k* in the hunting field 23 Dec 1951

(1) Nora; *b* 19 Aug *d* 24 Sept 1875

(2) Inez Alfreda; *m* 1st 16 Jan 1901 (*divorce* 1943) Sir Harold Edward Snagge, KBE (*d* 19 March 1949), 2nd son of Sir Thomas William Snagge, JP, DL, Judge of County Courts, and had issue; *m* 2nd 24 April 1948 1st and last Baron Rushcliffe, PC, GBE (*d* 18 Nov 1949), and *d* 4 May 1955

8 Edgar; *b* 22 Feb 1847; LLB; a Lt for City of London, High Sheriff Lincolnshire 1907; *m* 26 June 1886 Amy Myddleton (*m* 2nd 25 March 1914 2nd Baron Kesteven (*dsp* 23 July 1915), and *d* 13 April 1941), only dau of Christopher Gilbert Peacock, of Greatford Hall, Stamford, and *d* 9 Sept 1907, having had issue:

(1) Nancy Induna Frances Caroline; *b* 17 Sept 1897; *m* 9 July 1925 Hon James Knyvett Estcourt Howard (*d* 5 Dec 1964), son of 18th Earl of Suffolk (*qv*), and *d* 13 Dec 1972, leaving issue

(2) Bridget Myfanwy Gian; *b* 11 Nov 1900; *m* 1st 29 June 1921 (*divorce* 1935) Capt George Cartmel Barker, 16th Lancers (*k* in a hunting accident 23 Oct 1945), est son of Lt-Col Frederick George Barker, CBE, of Stanlake Park, Twyford, and had issue; *m* 2nd 10 Dec 1935 (*divorce* 1947) Baron Louis Philippe Mortimer de Cabrol de Moute, 2nd son of Baron Roger de Cabrol de Moute, of 9 Rue de Siam, Paris, and Villa Lassence, Pau, and *d* 7 Feb 1966

(3) Marigold Rosemary Joyce; *b* 15 May 1903; *m* 1st 4 Sept 1935 4th Earl of Londesborough (*qv*), and had issue; *m* 2nd 19 July 1948 (*divorce* 1954) Zygmunt Stanislaw de Lubicz-Bakanowski, formerly Capt 18th Lancers, Polish Army, son of Waclaw de Lubicz-Bakanowski, of Medyngianz, Poland, and *d* 15 May 1976

1 Diana Hotham; *m* 1856 William Powell Rodney and had issue (*see* RODNEY, B)

Sir JOHN *d* 21 June 1865; his est son,

Sir John Lubbock, 4th Bt; and **1st Baron Avebury**, of Avebury, Wilts (UK), so *cr* 22 Jan 1890, PC, JP, DL (Kent); *b* 30 April 1834; MP (Lib) Maidstone 1870–80 and London U 1880–1900; V-Chllr U of London 1873–80, Commr of Ltcy for London, Chm LCC 1890–92, Ld Rector St Andrews U 1907–13, Pres Soc of Antiquaries, Tstee Br Museum, foreign sec Roy Academy, V-Pres Roy Soc, Cdr Legion of Honour, memb Prussian Order Pour le Mérite, Hon DCL Oxford, Hon LLD Cambridge, Dublin, St Andrews and Edinburgh, FRS; *m* 1st 10 April 1856 Ellen Frances (*d* 20 Oct 1879), only child of Rev Peter Hordern, of Chorlton-cum-Hardy, and had:

1 JOHN BIRKBECK LUBBOCK, **2nd Baron Avebury**, DL (Kent); *b* 4 Oct 1858; ptnr Coutts and Co; *d* unm 26 March 1929

2 Norman; *b* 16 Dec 1861; Lt 3rd Middx VA, trooper 13th Bn Duke of Cambridge's Own Imp Yeo Boer War 1900; *m* 2 April 1919 Edith Harriet (*d* 24 Dec 1950), est dau of Sir Nevile Lubbock, KCMG (*see* above), and *dsp* 11 Nov 1926

3 Rolfe Arthur; *b* 19 Sept 1865; *m* 10 March 1894 Ethel Turner (*d* 13 Jan 1959), yst dau of Thomas Acland Lawford, and *dsp* 11 May 1909

1 Amy Harriet; *b* 15 March 1857; *m* 1st 15 March 1877 Andrew Walter Mulholland (*dvp* 2 June 1877), est s of 1st Baron Dunleath; *m* 2nd 18 March 1884 Ferdinand Suydam Van Zandt, of New York, USA (*d* 2 March 1892); *d* 19 May 1929, leaving issue

2 Constance Mary; *m* 3 Feb 1882 1st Earl Buxton (*d* 15 Oct 1934; *see* BUXTON, Bt), and *d* 3 Nov 1892, leaving issue

3 Gertrude; *d* unm 23 Feb 1934

The **1st Baron** *m* 2nd 17 May 1884 Alice Augusta Laurentia Lane (*d* 11 March 1947), dau of Gen Augustus Henry Lane Fox-Pitt-Rivers, DCL, FRS, of Rushmore, Wilts, and *d* 28 May 1913, having by her had issue:

4 Harold Fox Pitt; *b* 10 June 1888; *educ* Eton and Trin Coll Cambridge (MA); Lt Gren Gds (R), Capt West Kent Yeo, WW I; ptnr Coutts & Co; *m* 10 June 1914 Hon Dorothy Charlotte (*m* 2nd 4 April 1923 1st Baron Wardington; *qv*), er dau of 1st and last Baron Forster, by his wife Rachel Cecily, dau of 1st Baron Montagu of Beaulieu (*qv*), and was *ka* 4 April 1918, leaving issue:

(1) JOHN LUBBOCK, **3rd Baron Avebury**; *b* 13 May 1915; *educ* Eton and Balliol Coll Oxford; *m* 1st 24 Feb 1938 (*divorce* 1945) Cecily Kathleen, dau of Dr Nathaniel Alexander Knox Sparrow; *m* 2nd 31 July 1946 (*divorce* 1955) Diana Mary Margaret Westcott, yr dau of Capt Edward Westcott King, RA, formerly of Malaya, and had issue:

1a *Emma Rachel [The Hon Mrs Page, Lepe House, Exbury, Hants]; *b* 16 April 1952; *m* 23 July 1977 *Michael Charles Page, est son of Maj-Gen C E Page, of Church Farm House, Old Bosham, Sussex, and has issue:

1b *Sophie Elizabeth; *b* 1982

2b *Natasha Diana; *b* 1984

(1) The **3rd Baron** *m* 3rd 22 Dec 1955 *Betty Gay, dau of William Oscar Ingham, of Poulton-le-Fylde, Lancs, and formerly wife of — Goode, and *dspm* 21 June 1971

(1) (Ursula) Moyra; *b* 5 Dec 1917; granted rank of baron's dau 26 Aug 1931; *m* 7 April 1938 (*divorce* 1949) Dorian Joseph George Williams, OBE, TV equestrian sports commentator 1951–80, er son of Col Vivian Dunbar Stanley Williams, OBE, of East Burnham Park, Farnham Royal, Bucks

5 Eric Fox Pitt, MC; *b* 16 May 1893; Capt and F/Cdr RFC WW I (despatches); *ka* 11 March 1917

6 Maurice Fox Pitt; *b* 17 Oct 1900; *educ* Eton and Balliol Coll Oxford; *m* 9 Jan 1926 Hon Mary Katherine Adelaide Stanley (*d* 1981), est dau of 5th Baron Stan-

ley of Alderley (*see* STANLEY OF ALDERLEY, SHEFFIELD and, B), and *d* 26 April 1957, leaving issue:

(1) ERIC REGINALD LUBBOCK, **4th and present Baron Avebury**

(1) *Alice Olivia Maureen [The Hon Mrs Alice Keighley, 19 Beach Rd, Collaroy, NSW 2097, Australia]; *b* 19 Nov 1926; *m* 10 May 1951 (*divorce* 1974) William Geoffrey Keighley, barrister, MLC, son of AW Keighley, of Sydney, Australia, and has issue:

1a *Francis Stephen; *b* 21 March 1953

2a *John William; *b* 6 June 1959

1a *Pamela Jane; *b* 23 Sept 1956

2a *Josephine Clare; *b* 6 Feb 1961

4 Ursula; *b* 6 Feb 1885; *m* 22 Oct 1906 Lt-Col Adrian Grant Duff, CB, Black Watch (Roy Highrs) (*ka* Sept 1914 Battle of the Aisne), 3rd son of Rt Hon Sir Mountstuart Grant Duff, PC, GCIE, and *d* 15 Jan 1959, leaving issue

5 Irene; *b* 30 March 1886; *m* 5 Dec 1905 Sir Edward Henry Pelham, KCB (*d* as the result of an accident 18 Dec 1949), of Currant Hill, Westerham, Kent, er son of Henry Francis Pelham, Pres Trin Coll, Oxford, and *d* 14 Feb 1961, leaving issue (*see* CHICHESTER, E)

AYKROYD of Birstwith Hall

Arms: Azure on a chevron ermine between three stag's heads erased or as many crosses patonce sable. **Crest:** In front of a stag's head erased and gorged with a wreath of oak proper two crosses as in the arms. **Motto:** *In veritate victoria* ('Victory in truth').
Creation: Bt. (UK) 23 March 1929.

SIR JAMES ALEXANDER FREDERIC AYKROYD, 3RD BT, of Birstwith Hall, Co York [Sir James Aykroyd Bt, Birstwith Hall, nr Harrogate, Yorks HG3 2JW; 5 Highbury Terrace, London N5 1UP]; *b* 6 Sept 1943; *s* unc 1993; *educ* Eton, U of Aix en Provence and U of Madrid; sr export dir James Buchanan & Co Ltd 1965–83, md Martini & Rossi SA 1983–87, sr ptnr Aykroyd Mktg Consultants 1987–, chm Alexander Muir & Son 1993–; *m* 1973 *Jenifer Marshall and has issue:

1 *Gemma Jane Aykroyd; *b* 1976

2 *Victoria Louise Aykroyd; *b* 1977

Lineage: WILLIAM AYKROYD, of Bradford, had, with an er s (f of Sir William Aykroyd, 1st Bt, of Lightcliffe; *qv*).

WILLIAM EDWARD AYKROYD, of Ashdown, Apperley Bridge, Yorks, JP; *b* 11 March 1847; Mayor Bradford 1898; *m* 7 April 1869 Alice (*d* 24 May 1911), dau of Henry Milnes, of Manningham, Yorks, and *d* 1 March 1927, leaving issue:

1 Henry Edward; *b* 31 Aug 1871; Lt-Col 49th Div RFA (TD); *d* 31 March 1929

2 FREDERICK ALFRED (Sir), **1st Bt**

3 Percy Clifford; *b* 27 April 1877; *m* 6 April 1921 Constance Muriel (*d* 12 Jan 1968), dau of Lewis Gordon Hill, of Lake View, Bradford, and *d* 27 Nov 1946

1 Ada; *m* 28 June 1899 Cromwell Walter Jones, MA (*d* 12 July 1968), s of John Lambert Jones, of Dublin and *d* 19 April 1941, leaving issue

2 Beatrice Emily; *m* 2 June 1897 Joseph Harold Smith (*d* 26 March 1947), of Ranby Hall, nr Retford Notts, s of Isaac Smith, and *d* 23 April 1956, leaving issue

WILLIAM EDWARD AYKROYD's 2nd son,

Sir Frederick Alfred Aykroyd, 1st Bt (UK), so *cr* 23 March 1929, JP (W R Yorks and Liberty of Ripon); *b* 25 June 1873; High Sheriff Yorks 1941; *m* 8 April 1902 Lily May (*d* 22 March 1964), er dau of Sir James Roberts 1st Bt, JP, LLD, of Milner Field (*qv*), and *d* 31 Dec 1949, leaving:

1 **Sir Cecil William Aykroyd, 2nd Bt**; *b* 23 April 1905; *educ* Charterhouse and Jesus Coll Cambridge (BA1925); dir Nat Prov Bank Ltd (Bradford and dist local br); *d* unm 1993

2 (Frederic) Howard Aykroyd; *b* 10 Oct 1907; *educ* Rugby and Jesus Coll Cambridge (BA 1928); *m* 12 July 1932 (Ruth) Joan (d 1992), er dau of Carlton Oldfield, and *d* 1978, leaving:

(1) *Mary Elizabeth Wendy Carlton; *b* 26 May 1934; *m* 21 June 1955 *Nigel David Sykes Porter, Scots Gds, of Saltwick House, Stannington, nr Morpeth, Northumberland, only s of Lt-Col Bruce Dennistoun Sykes Porter, KDG

(2) *Joanna Jane; *b* 5 June 1937; *m* 17 Dec 1960 Maj Christopher Jonathan Pumphrey, TD, Northumberland Hus, of Bolam West Houses, Middleton, Morpeth, Northumberland, er s of Lt-Col Jonathan Moberly Pumphrey, OBE, TD, JP, DL, MIME, Northumberland Hus, and has:

1a *Edward Jonathan Lawrence Pumphrey; *b* 15 Dec 1963

2a *Andrew Charles Pumphrey; *b* 18 Sept 1965

1a *Sara Rose Pumphrey; *b* 4 March 1962

(3) *Victoria Margaret Aykroyd; *b* 1 April 1939; *m* 28 April 1962 *Robert Fleming, only s of Maj Philip Fleming JP, DL, of Barton Abbey, Steeple Aston, Oxon, and has issue

3 Bertram Aykroyd; *b* 17 Sept 1915; *educ* Charterhouse and Trin Coll Cambridge; Capt KOYLI WW II (despatches); *m* 1st 5 Oct 1938 (*divorce* 1947) Margot, DBE (*m* 2nd Roy Smith, MC, TD), er dau of Leonard Graham-Brown, FRCS, and had issue:

(1) Sir JAMES ALEXANDER FREDERIC AYKROYD, **3rd and present Bt**

(1) *Jean Margaret Elizabeth [Mrs Timothy Eastwood, The Old Vicarage, Moreton Pinkney, Northants NN11 6SD]; *b* 2 March 1940; *m* 1st 8 Sept 1962 (*divorce* 1972) Michael Frederick David Morley, er s of Brig Michael Frederick Morley, MBE, and has issue:

1a *Harry Michael Charles; *b* 16 June 1965

2a *Edward James Cecil; *b* 17 Sept 1967

(1) (cont.) Mrs Jean Morley *m* 2nd 1984 *Col Timothy John Seymour Eastwood, RA

3 (cont.) Bertram Aykroyd *m* 2nd 28 Sept 1949 *Catalina [Mrs Bertram Aykroyd, Houghtons, East Harting, Hants GU31 5LU], only dau of Henry Marchington, and *d* 1983, having by her had further issue:

(2) Jeremy Charles; *b* 28 July 1950; *educ* Eton and Trin Coll Cambridge; *d* 1982

(3) +TOBY NIGEL BERTRAM [Toby Aykroyd Esq, 37 Pembridge Villas, London W11 3EP]; *b* 13 Nov 1955; heir presumptive; *educ* Eton and St Catharine's Coll Cambridge (MA)

(1) *Rachel [Mrs Charles Helmore, Wyndham Cottage, Rogate, Hants GU31 5BL]; *b* 14 March 1952; *m* 1981 *Charles Patrick Helmore and has issue:

1a *Max David Charles Helmore; *b* 1984

2a *Caspar William Helmore; *b* 1987

1 Margaret Roberts; CStJ; *m* 2 Sept 1924 Col George Hammond Aykroyd, TD, BA, RA (*d* 30 Sept 1972), yst s of Sir William Henry Aykroyd, 1st Bt (*see* AYKROYD, Bt, of Lightcliffe), and had issue

AYKROYD of Lightcliffe

Arms: Azure on a chevron ermine between three stag's heads erased or as many crosses couped sable. **Crest:** In front of a stag's head erased, gorged with a wreath of oak proper, two crosses as in the arms. **Motto:** *In veritate victoria* ('Victory in truth').
Creation: Bt. (UK) 16 June 1920.

SIR WILLIAM MILES AYKROYD, 3RD BT, of Lightcliffe, Yorks, MC (1944) [Sir William Aykroyd Bt MC, Buckland Newton Place, Dorchester, Dorset DT2 7BX]; *b* 24 Aug 1923; *s* f 1965; *educ* Charterhouse; Lt 5th Roy Inniskilling Dragoon Gds WW II; dir Hardy Amies Ltd

Lineage: WILLIAM AYKEROID, of Heptonstall, Yorks living 1424; f of:

RICHARD AYKEROIDE; *m* Emmote de Greenwood and had, with an er s (Richard, of Wadsworth; ancestor of the Folkerthorpe AYKROYDs):

JOHN AYKEROIDE, of Heptonstall; *d* by 1479; had:

THOMAS AYKEROIDE; *d* 1521; had:

ROBERT AYKEROIDE, of Warley Yorks; *d* by 1570; had:

ROBERT AYKEROIDE, of Greenhurst, Heptonstall; *m* Agnes — and *d* 1582, leaving:

EDWARD AYKEROID, of Heptonstall; had:

RICHARD AYKEROID, of Ovenden, Halifax; *d* by 27 Aug 1616, leaving:

SAMUEL AYKROYD, of Warley, Halifax; *m* 12 April 1591 Susan Hemingway and had, with other issue:

SAMUEL AYKROYD, of Hipperholme, Halifax; *b* Jan 1592; had:

MICHAEL ACKROYD, of Thornton, Bradford; *b* May 1620; *m* 26 Jan 1646 Sarah Deane and had:

JOHN AYKROYD, of Allerton, Yorks; *b* Dec 1647; *d* Oct 1728, leaving a 3rd s:

RICHARD AYKROYD, of Allerton; *b* Jan 1679; *m* Mary Marshall (*d* May 1749) and *d* Aug 1755, leaving:

JEREMY AYKROYD, of Allerton; *b* June 1719; *m* May 1747 Sarah Usher, of Thornton, and had:

JOSEPH AYKROYD, of Horton Bradford; *b* March 1758; had:

CHARLES AYKROYD, of Thornton; *b* Feb 1778; *m* Susanna — and had, with other issue:

WILLIAM AYKROYD, of Bradford; *b* 4 May 1808; *m* 22 Feb 1836 Mary Constantine (*d* 27 June 1881), of Bradford, and *d* 7 July 1879, leaving with other issue (*see* AYKROYD, Bt, of Birstwith):

ALFRED AYKROYD, of Oakwood, Manningham, Yorks, JP; *b* 29 Jan 1841; *m* 4 June 1862 Ellen (*d* 4 July 1925), dau of Henry Milnes, of Nearcliffe, Manningham, and *d* 18 April 1890, leaving:

1 WILLIAM HENRY (Sir), **1st Bt**

2 Alfred Constantine; *b* 23 April 1869; *m* 3 June 1896 Wilhelmina Mary (*d* 27 Nov 1957), dau of William Ruddell, of Dublin, and *d* 23 Feb 1945, leaving issue:

(1) Wallace Ruddell, CBE (1943); *b* 30 July 1899; *educ* Leys Sch Cambridge and Trin Coll Dublin (MB, BCh 1924, MD 1928, ScD 1938); RAF WW I, dir Nutrition Div FAO Washington 1946; *m* 18 Oct 1930 Freda Kathleen, dau of Harry Brazier Buttery, of Bridgnorth, Salop, and *d* Feb 1979, leaving:

1a *(Ian) Peter Lister [Peter Aykroyd Esq, Stranges, Upton, Hants SP11 0JS]; *b* 1 June 1932; *educ* Charterhouse and Ch Ch Oxford; *m* 1st 13 April 1957 (*divorce* 1978) Susan Audrey, dau of Frank William Ives, of Chieveley, Berks, and has adopted:

*James Stephen; *b* 17 April 1960

*William Daniel; *b* 14 March 1962; *m* 1 May 1994 *Angela, yr dau of Donald Maclellan, of Symington, Ayrshire

*Sophia Mary; *b* 10 Nov 1966

1a (cont.) Peter Aykroyd *m* 2nd 21 Oct 1980 *Veronica Jane Drake-Brockman, er dau of John Brown, of Clifton, Bristol

1a *Gillian Lucy [Mrs Brisbane Somerville-Large, Arlands Inch, Thomastown, Co Kilkenny, Ireland]; *b* 24 Sept 1934; *educ* Millfield and Trin Coll Dublin; *m* July 1958 *Brisbane Peter, yr s of William Collis Somerville-Large, FRCSI and has adopted :

*Vanessa Townshend [Mrs Patrick Breese, PO Box 759, Airlie Beach, Qld, Australia]; *b* 13 July 1969; *m* Oct 1992 *Patrick Breese

2a *Juliet Wilhelmina [Mrs Nicholas Lacey, Reeds Wharf, 33 Mill St, London SE1 2BA]; *b* 16 May 1944; *educ* St Paul's and St Anne's Coll Oxford; *m* 1981 *Nicholas Stephen Lacey and has:

1b *Laetitia Eleanor; *b* 1978

2b *Theodora Cecilia Candida; *b* 1980

(2) Franklin Milnes; *b* 9th Sept 1901; *educ* Leys Sch Cambridge and Gonville and Caius Coll Cambridge

(1) Phyllis; *b* 10 June 1898; *educ* Trin Coll Dublin (PhD 1926); *d* unm 12 Feb 1975

(2) Winifred Mary; *b* 12 March 1901; LRAM; *m* 7 Sept 1932 John Wilfrid Parkes, MSc, FRIC, FCI (*d* 18 Sept 1967), and *d* 5 Oct 1993, leaving:

1a *Andrew John Aykroyd [Andrew Parkes Esq, The Boulders, Sydenham Rd, Dublin 14, Ireland]; *b* 17 July 1939; MA Cantab; chartered patent agent; *m* 11 Sept 1965 *Delyth Jones and has issue

2a *Wilfrid Duncan; *b* 29 June 1948

1a *Janet Elizabeth [Mrs Brian Pasley, 7 Woodlawn Crescent, Churchtown, Dublin 14, Ireland]; *b* 24 Sept 1933; *educ* Trin Coll Dublin (BA, Dip Soc Sci); *m* 2 April 1959 *Brian J O Pasley and has issue

2a *Susan Mary [Miss Susan Parkes, 24 Beaumont House, 60 Terenure Rd East, Dublin 6, Ireland]; *b* 16 Oct 1936; *educ* Trin Coll Dublin (MA, MLitt, FTCD)

(3) Olive Elizabeth; *b* 20 June 1913; *educ* Trin Coll Dublin (PhD 1938); *m* 9 Dec 1941 Thomas Walter Freeman

3 Herbert Edward; *b* 21 Aug 1872; *d* 6 July 1923

1 Mary Ellen; *d* unm 17 April 1950

2 Edith Emily; *m* 23 April 1896 Rev Samuel William Scadding (*d* 19 Nov 1945), Vicar Southminster, Essex, and *d* 21 May 1946, leaving issue

3 Henrietta Maude; *m* 7 Sept 1904 Harold Nichols Pochin, MBE (*d* 23 Feb 1932), 2nd s of John Pochin, and had issue

4 Charlotte Ruth; *d* unm 25 July 1953

ALFRED AYKROYD's est son,

Sir William Henry Aykroyd, 1st Bt (UK), so *cr* 16 June 1920, JP (W R Yorks); *b* 8 May 1865; High Sheriff Yorks 1926, OStJ; *m* 29 Jan 1890 Emma Louisa (*d* 5 Sept 1946), dau of Alderman Ezra Waugh Hammond, JP, of Horton Hall, Bradford, and had issue:

1 ALFRED HAMMOND (Sir), **2nd Bt**

2 Harold Hammond, OBE (1935), MC, TD, JP; *b* 7 April 1896; *educ* Rugby; Col TA, Lt-Col and Brevet-Col 4th Bn Duke of Wellington's Regt (W Riding) WW I, High Sheriff Yorks 1957; *m* 1st 14 Dec 1926 (*divorce* 1938) Nina Marguerite, yr dau of Edward John Hulse, OBE, JP, of Oakdene, Duffield Rd, Derby, and had issue:

(1) *Susan; *b* 1 Feb 1931; *m* 1st 8 Dec 1951 (*divorce* 1958) John Kenneth Benney, RE, s of Ernest George Benney, and has issue:

1a *Cecilia Anne; *b* 14 Oct 1952

(1) (cont.) Mrs Susan Benney *m* 2nd 1968 *Christopher John Day, of Sandhill House, Gunnislake, Cornwall

(2) *Sally Mary [Mrs Christopher Stoddart, The Old Cottage, High St, Whixley, York]; *b* 3 Aug 1934; *m* 9 July 1960 Christopher Boyd Stoddart (*d* 1984), 2nd s of Frank Boyd Stoddart, and has:

1a *Mark Harold Boyd; *b* 27 Sept 1966; *m* 1990 *Suzanna Baynard and has:

1b *Tom Lawrence Boyd; *b* 1993

1b *Araminta Sophie; *b* 1994

1a *Margaret Jane; *b* 5 June 1962; *m* 1987 *Steven Bentley and has:

1b *Christopher Alan; *b* 1990

2b *Tobias Frank; *b* 1993

2 (cont.) Col Harold Aykroyd *m* 2nd 29 Dec 1941 *Kathleen [Mrs Harold Aykroyd, The Glebe House, Aldborough, Boroughbridge, N Yorks], est dau of Harry Tyrrell-Gray, FRCS, MD, MCh (Cambridge), and *d* 6 Jan 1974, having by her had:

(3) *Harriet Louisa; *b* 15 Oct 1951; *m* 17 Sept 1977 *John Flinders Highley, est s of S M Highley, and has:

1a *Samuel Thomas George; *b* 1981

2a *Henry William Charles; *b* 1985

3 George Hammond, TD; *b* 1 July 1900; *educ* Rugby and Trin Coll Cambridge (BA 1923); Col Res Offrs RA, MFH; *m* 2 Sept 1924 Margaret Roberts, CStJ (*d* 1981), only dau of Sir Frederic Alfred Aykroyd, 1st Bt, of Birstwith Hall (*qv*), and *d* 30 Sept 1972, leaving:

(1) +MICHAEL DAVID [Michael Aykroyd Esq, The Homestead, Killinghall, Harrogate, Yorks]; *b* 14 June 1928; heir presumptive; *educ* in USA; Capt Yorks Yeo; *m* 19 April 1952 *Oenone Gillian Diana, only dau of Donald George Cowling, MBE, and has:

1a +Henry Robert George [Henry Aykroyd Esq, Cushnie, Auchterless, Turriff, Aberdeen]; *b* 4 April 1954; *educ* Charterhouse; *m* 1975 *Lucy Merlin, yst dau of Col Jack Houghton Brown, and has:

1b +George Jack; *b* 8 Jan 1977

2b +Bertie Thomas; *b* 1983

1b *Emma Rachel; *b* 1978

2b *Kate; *b* 1989

3b *Rose (twin); *b* 1989

1a *Annabel Mary Diana; *b* 3 Jan 1956; *m* 1979 *Robin Guy Graham and has issue (*see* GRAHAM, Bt, of Norton Conyers)

2a *Sarah Jane Elizabeth [Mrs Guy Davis, The Caretaker's Flat, Shardeloes Park, Bucks]; *b* 25 June 1960; *m* 1985 *Guy Matthew Davis, s of James Davis

3a *Susannah Margaret Victoria; *b* 11 June 1964

(2) (John) Richard; *b* 16 Nov 1934; *educ* Eton; *m* 1st 16 Feb 1963 (*divorce* 1974) Catherine Marthe, est dau of Dr George Vettier, and has:

1a *Bettina Dominique; *b* 21 Nov 1963

(2) (cont.) Richard Aykroyd *m* 2nd 29 Nov 1974 *Lavinia Mary, dau of Patrick Thomas Beasley (*see* WILTON, E), and formerly w of Confrey A Phillips, and *d* 1 Feb 1997, having by her had:

2a *Serena Mary; *b* 21 Aug 1976

3a *Clare Lavinia; *b* 4 Oct 1978

(3) +David Peter [David Aykroyd Esq, Sweethills, Nun Monkton, Yorks YO5 8ET]; *b* 6 June 1937; *educ* Eton; 2nd Lt Coldstream Gds; *m* 30 Oct 1958 *(Lydia) Huldine, yr dau of Richard Pigott Beamish, of Castlelyons, Co Cork, and has:

1a Nicholas William; *b* 20 May 1962; *d* 1989

1a *Amanda Huldine; *b* 2 June 1960

2a *Emily Sorrell; *b* 9 Nov 1970; *m* 8 June 1996 *Luke Thomas Penwicke-Clennell, yr s of Warren Penwicke-Clennell, of Kirk Hammerton, Yorks

3a *Matilda Rose; *b* 15 March 1978

(1) *Patricia Jean [Miss Patricia Aykroyd, 1 Clara Place, Topsham, Exeter, Devon]; *b* 28 Oct 1925; SRN, SCM

1 *Mary Hammond, OBE (1945); *b* 15 Aug 1902; formerly regnl adminr Leeds WVS

Sir WILLIAM *d* 3 April 1947; his est son,

Sir Alfred Hammond Aykroyd, 2nd Bt; *b* 3 June 1894; *educ* Charterhouse; Maj RFA, High Sheriff Yorks 1952, Pres Yorks Ag Soc 1954, MFH; *m* 12 Nov 1919 Sylvia, dau of Frank Walker, of Huddersfield, and widow of Lt-Col Foster Newton Thorne, and *d* 29 April 1965, leaving:

1 Sir WILLIAM MILES AYKROYD, **3rd and present Bt**

1 Ann Prudence; *b* 28 Nov 1920; SRN, CStJ (1967); *m* 11 April 1944 *Douglas Ferris Hewat Jaboor, MB, ChB (*see* SCARSDALE, V), s of Dr Ferris Jaboor, and had issue:

(1) *Philip; *b* 10 June 1953; *educ* Charterhouse

(1) *Sarah [Mrs Simon Wilson, 18 Bowater St, London SW3]; *b* 29 Jan 1947; *m* 11 April 1968 *Simon James Curzon Wilson, s of Maj Walter James Lytimar Wilson, DSO, of Herbertstown Stud, Dunboyne, Co Meath, and has two s

(2) *Victoria Anne [Mrs Barry Paterson, Madam's Hill, Easthope, Much Wenlock, Salop]; *b* 24 May 1948; *m* 13 Jan 1968 *Barry Paul Paterson, s of Edward Victor Paterson, and has:

1a *A son; *b* 14 April 1969

AYLESFORD

Arms: Argent, a chevron between three griffins passant sable. **Crest:** A griffin passant sable. **Supporters:** Dexter, a griffin sable, ducally gorged or; sinister, a lion or, ducally gorged azure. **Motto:** *Aperto vivere voto* ('To live with will unfettered'). **Creations:** B. (E) 15 March 1703, E. (GB) 19 Oct 1714.

THE 11TH EARL OF AYLESFORD, Kent, and **Baron of Guernsey** (Charles Ian Finch-Knightley, JP (1948), DL (1954) (both Warwicks)) [The Rt Hon The Earl of Aylesford JP DL, Packington Old Hall, Coventry, West Midlands CV7 7HG]; *b* 2 Nov 1918; *s f* 1958; *educ* Oundle; Capt Black Watch WW II (wounded), Ld-Lt W Midlands 1974–93 (V-Lt 1964–74), County Cmmr Boy Scouts Warwicks 1949–74, memb Advsy Ctee World Wild Life Fund 1970–, KStJ; *m* 21 March 1946 Margaret Rosemary (*d* 1989), only dau of Maj Austin Arnold Tyer, MVO, TD, MICE, of Tunstall, Wadhurst, and has:

1 +CHARLES HENEAGE, *Lord Guernsey* [Lord Guernsey, Packington Hall, Meriden, Coventry, CV7 7HF]; *b* 27 March 1947; *educ* Oundle and Trin Coll Cambridge; V Ld-Lt W Midlands 1990– (DL 1986–90) *m* 18 Feb 1971 *Penelope Anstice, only dau of Keneth Arnold Gibbs Crawley, TD (*see* CRAWLEY-BOEVEY, Bt), of 20 Alexander Sq, London SW3, and has:

(1) +(Heneage) James Daniel; *b* 29 April 1985
(1) *Rachel Louise; *b* 20 Nov 1974
(2) *Kate Pamela; *b* 20 Nov 1974 (twin)
(3) *Alexandra Rosemary; *b* 5 Oct 1977
(4) *Laura Charlotte; *b* 10 Aug 1982

1 *Sarah Elizabeth Jane; *b* 14 July 1950; *m* 5 Sept 1974 *(Angus) Nigel Garnet Maclean, 8th of Kilmoluaig, yr s of Maj Gordon Maclean, of Poachers Lodge, Odiham, Hants, and has:

(1) *Angus Charles; *b* 29 Oct 1976
(2) *Ian Andrew; *b* 31 July 1980

2 *Clare Charlotte Rosemary [The Lady Clare Remington-Hobbs, 11a Porchester Terrace, London W2 3TH]; *b* 13 Sept 1959; *m* 1985 *James Remington-Hobbs, son of C Remington-Hobbs, of Normandy, France, and has issue:

(1) *Jonathan Ian; *b* 1986
(2) *Alexander Charles; *b* 1988

Lineage: The 1st EARL OF NOTTINGHAM (*see* WINCHILSEA and NOTTINGHAM, E); had a 2nd s:

HENEAGE FINCH, **1st Earl of Aylesford** (GB), so *cr* 19 Oct 1714, as also earlier 15 March 1702/3 BARON OF GUERNSEY (E), PC (1714), KC (1677); *b* 1649; *educ* Ch Ch Oxford; barrister Inner Temple, MP (Tory) Oxford U 1679, 1689–98 and 1701–03 and Guildford 1685–87, Slr-Gen 1678, dismissed by JAMES II 1686, subsequently the pncpl advocate defending the seven Bishops, Chllr Duchy of Lancaster 1714–16; *m* 16 May 1678 Elizabeth (*d* 1 Sept 1743), dau and coheir of Sir John Banks, Bt, of Aylesford, and *d* 22 July 1719, leaving, with other issue (including John, *m* 1726 Elizabeth, dau of John Savile (*see* MEXBOROUGH, E) and Frances *m* Sir John Bland, 5th Bt; *see* RAVENSDALE, N) an est s:

HENEAGE FINCH, **2nd Earl of Aylesford**; *b* 1683; MP (Tory) Maidstone 1704–05, Surrey 1710–19, Master Jewel Office 1711–16; *m* 9 Dec 1712 Mary (*d* May 1740), dau and heir of Sir Clement Fisher, Bt, of Packington, Warwicks, and *d* 29 June 1757, leaving:

HENEAGE FINCH, **3rd Earl of Aylesford**; *bapt* 6 Nov 1715; *educ* Ch Ch Oxford (MA 1735, DCL 1761); MP (Tory) Leics 1739–41 and Maidstone 1741–47 and 1754–57; *m* 6 Oct 1750 his cousin Lady Charlotte Seymour (*d* 15 Feb 1805), dau of 6th Duke of Somerset by his 2nd w Charlotte, dau of Daniel, Earl of Winchilsea and Nottingham, and had with other issue:

1 HENEAGE, **4th Earl**

2 Charles; *b* 4 June 1752; *m* 28 Dec 1778 Jane (*d* Nov 1811), dau of Watkin Wynne, heiress of the Wynnes of Voelas, Denbighshire, and the Griffiths of Cefnamwich, and *d* 17 Dec 1819, having had, with other issue:

(1) Charles Wynn Griffith-Wynne, of Voelas; *b* 4 March 1780; MP; *m* May 1812 Sarah (*d* 19 May 1860), 5th dau and coheir of Rev Henry Hildyard, of Stokesley, Yorks, and *d* 22 March 1865, leaving, with other issue:

1a Charles Wynne Finch, of Voelas, JP and DL; *b* 14 June 1815; MP Caernarvon; *m* 1st 15 June 1840 Laura Susan (*d* 7 March 1851), dau of Richard Pollen, of Rodbourne, Wilts, and had:

1b Charles Arthur, of Voelas and Cefnamwich, JP and DL (Caernarvonshire) and JP (Denbighs); *b* 6 April 1841; Lt-Col Scots Gds; *m* 29 Oct 1889 Maud Emily (*d* 2 Aug 1945), dau of Col Hon Richard Charteris (*see* WEMYSS and MARCH, E), and *d* 4 Dec 1903, leaving:

1c Charles Richard; *b* 29 Sept *d* 28 Nov 1890

2c John Charles, CBE (1956), MC (1916), JP (Denbighshire 1915 and Caernarvonshire 1924), DL (Caernarvonshire 1947), of Voelas, Betws-y-Coed, N Wales; *b* 31 Aug 1891; *educ* Eton and RMC Sandhurst; Col Coldstream Gds WW I (despatches twice, wounded), and WW II, Denbighs: High Sheriff 1949, Ld-Lt 1951–66 (V-Lt 1949, DL 1947), Chm Welsh Ag Land Sub Commission 1948, Dep Chm Ag Land Commission 1954–63, memb Nature Conservancy 1956–63, KStJ; *m* 17 Feb 1914 Alice Mary Sybil, MBE (1949) (*d* 31 March 1970), 2nd dau of Rt Rev Hon Edward Carr Glyn, DD, Bp Peterborough (*see* WOLVERTON, B), and *d* 15 March 1982, leaving issue:

1d +Charles Edward Ifan [Charles Wynne Finch Esq, Cefnamwich, Tudweiliog, Pwlhelli, Caernarvonshire]; *b* 11 Jan 1929; *educ* Eton and RMA Sandhurst; late Capt Coldstream Gds, High Sheriff Denbighshire 1963; *m* 28 Jan 1967 *Rosemary Dorothea, yst dau of Lt-Col Clive Grantham Austin, JP, DL, RHA, of Roundwood, Micheldever, Hants, and has issue:

1e +David Heneage; *b* 19 April 1970
1e *Mary Davina; *b* 1 March 1968
2e *Harriet Jane; *b* 24 May 1971

1d *Elizabeth Jane Myfanwy [Mrs Alexander Malcolm, Phillips House, Much Marcle, Ledbury, Hereford and Worcester]; *b* 5 Feb 1918; *m* 8 June 1948 *Alexander Dougal Malcolm, yst s of Ronald Malcolm, of 3 Mulberry Walk, London SW3, and has issue:

1e *James Ronald; *b* 1951; *m* 1978 *Sandra Lee, dau of Charles Wilson Thomas, of Salt Lake City, Utah, USA, and has issue:

1f *Peter Thomas; *b* 1979
1f *Lucy Caitlin; *b* 1983

1e *Janet Mary; *b* 1949; *m* 1984 *James Hume Greenfield, and has issue:

1f *Harry Alexander Hume; *b* 1985
1f *Katherine Mary; *b* 1987

2e *Elizabeth Anne; *b* 1960

2d *Olwen Mary [Mrs Olwen Wake, The Bantam House, White Roding, Dunmow, Essex]; *b* 22 Oct 1924; *m* 22 July 1944 (*divorce* 1969) Lt Roger Wake, RN (ret) (*d* 1988), 2nd son of Maj-Gen Sir Hereward Wake, 13th Bt (*qv*), and has issue

3c William Heneage (Sir), ktd 1960, MC, JP (Caernarvonshire); *b* 18 Jan 1893; *educ* Eton; Col Scots Gds WW I (wounded twice, despatches twice), attd Egyptian Army 1919–26 (4th Cl Order Nile), and WW II, Ld-Lt Caernarvonshire 1941–60, CStJ; *m* 17 Oct 1929 Gladys, OStJ (*d* 24 Feb 1969), dau of John Isaac Waterbury, of Fairfield House, Convent Station, New Jersey, USA, and *dsp* 16 Dec 1961

2b Edward Heneage, of Stokesley, Yorks, JP (Denbighs and NR Yorks); *b* 9 Dec 1842; *educ* Eton and Trin Coll Cambridge (BA 1864); barrister; *m* 1st 9 June 1870 Ada (*d* 28 Sept 1873), dau of Henry L'Estrange Styleman Le Strange, of Hunstanton, Norfolk, and had issue:

1c Heneage; *b* 30 April 1871; *educ* Eton and New Coll Oxford (MA); *d* unm 26 Nov 1939

2b (cont.) Edward Wynne Finch *m* 2nd 24 Feb 1876 Emily Caroline (*d* 6 Dec 1947), dau of George Marwood, of Busby Hall, Yorks, and *d* 7 Jan 1914, having by her had:

2c Arthur, JP (NR Yorks); *b* 15 Oct 1878; *educ* Marlborough; Capt late 4th Bn Green Howards; *m* 3 June 1926 Florence Irene Harriet (*d* 1978), dau of Very Rev Charles Thomas Ovenden, Dean of St Patrick's Dublin, and *d* 25 Nov 1936, leaving:

1d *Anne; *b* 4 Sept 1927; *m* 16 Jan 1954 (*divorce* 1968) John Vavasour Earle, MA, MB, ChB, Cambridge, only s of Edward Vavasour Earle, of Venture, Cross-in-Hand, Sussex, and has:

1e *Belinda Diana; *b* 25 Oct 1957
2e *Jenny Ruth; *b* 1 Sept 1959
3e *Polly Joan; *b* 11 Aug 1961

3c Griffith; *b* 16 Oct 1880; *educ* Marlborough; Maj late KRRC; *m* 27 Jan 1926 Helena (*d* 19 Nov 1964), dau of Edward Samuel Smith, of Rutland Sq, Dublin, and *d* 18 June 1935

1c Helen; *b* 14 Jan 1877; *d* unm 21 Dec 1928

3b John Seymour; *b* 16 Feb 1845; Maj late RHG; *d* unm 22 Jan 1906

1b Edith Sarah; *b* 5 Oct 1849; *d* 18 July 1858

1a (cont.) Charles Wynne Finch *m* 2nd 7 Sept 1863 Jamesina Joyce Ellen (*d* 6 July 1892), dau and coheir of John Stewart, MP, and widow of Henry L'Estrange Styleman Le Strange, of Hunstanton, Norfolk, and *d* 3 March 1874

The 3rd EARL *d* 9 May 1777; his est son,

HENEAGE FINCH, **4th Earl of Aylesford**; *b* 4 July 1751; Ld Steward Household; *m* 18 Nov 1781 Lady Louisa Thynne (*d* 28 Dec 1832), dau of 1st Marquess of Bath (*qv*), and *d* 21 Oct 1812, leaving an est surv s:

HENEAGE FINCH, **5th Earl of Aylesford**; *b* 24 April 1786; FSA; *m* 23 April 1821 Lady Augusta Sophia Greville (*d* 2 March 1845), 4th dau of 2nd Earl of Warwick (*see* WARWICK, BROOKE and, E), and *d* 3 Jan 1859, leaving an er s:

HENEAGE FINCH, **6th Earl of Aylesford**; *b* 24 Dec 1824; *m* 7 May 1846 Jane Wightwick (*d* 21 Oct 1911), only child of John W Knightley, of Offchurch Bury, Warwicks, and *d* 10 Jan 1871, having had, with other issue:

1 HENEAGE FINCH, **7th Earl of Aylesford**, DL (Warwicks); *b* 21 Feb 1849; *m* 8 Jan 1871 (separated 22 May 1877) Edith (*d* 23 June 1897), having given birth 4 Nov 1881 to a s, Guy Bertrand, whose reputed f was 8th Duke of Marlborough,

qv), 3rd dau of Col Peers Williams, MP, of Temple House, Berks, and *dspm* Texas 13 Jan 1885, leaving:

(1) Hilda Joanna Gwendoline; *b* 25 July 1872; *m* 12 April 1898 Lt-Col Sir Malcolm Donald Murray, GCVO, CB, CIE (*d* 2 Aug 1938), late Seaforth Highrs, and *d* 13 Aug 1931, leaving issue (*see* DUNMORE, E)

2 CHARLES WIGHTWICK, **8th Earl**

2 Alexandra Louise Minna; *b* 9 July 1875 (HM QUEEN ALEXANDRA stood sponsor); *m* 1st 10 Sept 1901 Philip Samuel Danby (*d* 22 Dec 1909), son of Rev Samuel Danby, and had issue; *m* 2nd 19 April 1911 Robert William Emmet (*d* 13 May 1933), slr, 2nd s of George N Emmet, of Kensington, London W, and *d* 18 July 1959, leaving further issue

The 7th EARL's brother,

CHARLES WIGHTWICK FINCH, **8th Earl of Aylesford**, JP, DL; *b* 7 June 1851; Hon Col S Staffs Regt, late Maj 3rd Bn S Staffs Regt, and Capt and Hon Maj Warwicks Yeo Cav; *m* 1st 4 Feb 1873 Hon Georgiana Agnes Bagot (*dsp* 14 April 1874), dau of 3rd Baron Bagot (*qv*); *m* 2nd 16 April 1879 Marcella Araminta (Ella) Victoria (*d* 6 May 1930), yst dau of John Ross, of Benena Abbots, Hunts, and widow of Capt John Wingfield Linton, of Hemingford, Hunts, and *d* 16 Sept 1924, having by her had issue:

1 Heneage Greville, *Lord Guernsey*; *b* 2 June 1883; *educ* Eton and RMC Sandhurst; Capt Warwicks Yeo and Irish Gds; *m* 11 June 1907 Hon Gladys Cecil Georgina Fellowes (*d* 4 Aug 1952), dau of 2nd Baron de Ramsay (Iqv), and was *ka* 14 Sept 1914, leaving issue:

(1) HENEAGE MICHAEL CHARLES FINCH, **9th Earl of Aylesford**; *b* 31 Oct 1908; *educ* Eton; Capt RA WW II (despatches); *m* 18 April 1940 Pamela Elizabeth (*d* 1990), er dau of Col Hon Charles John Coventry, CB, of Earls Croome Court, Worcester (*see* COVENTRY, E), and formerly w of Lt-Cdr James George Greville Dugdale, RN (ret), and was *ka* Wormhondt 28 May 1940

2 CHARLES DANIEL, **10th Earl**

3 Ronald William Edward; *b* 28 Sept 1889; Lt Canadian Forces, late Midshipman RN; *m* 19 July 1920 Grace Edith (*d* 30 Dec 1968), dau of Walter Langley, of 55 Egerton Gdns, London SW, formerly of Victoria BC, and *dsp* 27 July 1948

1 Violet Ella; *m* 14 Dec 1904 Maj Eustace Crawley, 12th Lancers (*ka* 2 Nov 1914), 2nd son of George Baden Crawley, and *dsp* 26 Feb 1960

2 Muriel Gladwys; *m* 27 July 1901 William Worthington Worthington, JP (*d* 25 Nov 1949), of Maple Hayes, and *d* 26 April 1940, leaving issue (*see* NORMAN, Bt, also FEVERSHAM, B)

The 9th EARL's uncle,

CHARLES DANIEL FINCH later FINCH-KNIGHTLEY (added 1912), **10th Earl of Aylesford**, JP (Warwicks); *b* 23 Aug 1886; Capt late 7th Bn Rifle Bde and Canadian Forces, formerly in Merchant Service, WW I (wounded), Mil Sec to Govr-Gen Australia 1918–20; *m* 7 Feb 1918 Aileen Jane Chartres (*d* 30 Aug 1977), only dau of William McCormac Boyle, of Armagh, N Ireland, and *d* 20 March 1958, leaving:

1 CHARLES IAN FINCH-KNIGHTLEY, **11th and present Earl of Aylesford**

2 Anthony Heneage, JP (Hunts and Peterborough 1965); *b* 27 April 1920; *educ* Oundle; Lt and T/Capt The Black Watch WW II (despatches), Dep Chm Huntingdon Bench, Pres Hunts Conservative Club; *m* 12 June 1948 *Susan Mary [The Hon Mrs Anthony Finch-Knightley JP, Broomleigh, Huntingdon Rd, Brampton, Cambs PE18 8PB], only dau of Maj-Gen Geoffrey Woodroffe Palmer, CB, CBE, of Chilwell, Notts, and *d* 15 Oct 1995, leaving:

(1) *Minette Jane, MBE (1990); *b* 29 May 1950; *m* 1983 (*divorce*, when resumed maiden name) Nicholas Redfern, and has:

1a *James Heneage Stuart; *b* 17 Sept 1983

(2) *Joanna Elizabeth [Mrs Christopher Anthony, The Old Coach House, 45A Huntingdon Rd, Brampton, Cambs PE18 8PB]; *b* 10 June 1954; *m* 1987 *Christopher Paul Anthony, 2nd son of Kenneth Anthony, of Hillandale, Oxted, Surrey, and has issue:

1a *Charles Henry; *b* 2 June 1996

1a *Harrington Arthur Heneage; *b* 19 June 1992

1a *Charlotte Susan; *b* 13 May 1990

AYLMER

Arms: Argent, a cross sable, between four Cornish choughs proper. **Crest:** Out of a ducal coronet or a Cornish chough rising proper. **Supporters:** Two marines vested with fur caps, brown jackets and blue breeches, their waists girt with bunting and dressed at all points like complete sailors, the dexter holding in his exterior hand a forestaff, and the sinister, a deep-sea line, the plummet pendant, all proper. **Motto:** Steady. **Creations:** Bt. (I) by 6 Nov 1662, B. (I) 1 May 1718.

THE 13TH LORD AYLMER, BARON OF BALRATH, Co Meath, and a **Baronet** (Sir Michael Anthony Aylmer, Bt) [The Rt Hon The Lord Aylmer, Dovecot House, Jesse's Lane, Long Crendon, Bucks HP18 9AG]; *b* 27 March 1923; *s* cousin 1982; *educ* privately and Trin Hall Cambridge (BA 1944, LLB 1945, MA 1948); slr 1948; *m* 5 May 1950 *Countess Maddalena Sofia Maria Gabriella Cecilia Stefania Francesca, only dau of Count Arbeno Attems di Santa Croce, of Aiello dei Friuli, Italy, by Sofie, est dau of Prince Maximilian Karl Fredrich zu Löwenstein-Wertheim-Freudenberg, and has:

1 +(ANTHONY) JULIAN [The Hon Julian Aylmer, 16 Edgarley Terrace, London SW6 6QF]; *b* 10 Dec 1951; *educ* Westminster and Trin Hall Cambridge (MA); slr 1976; *m* 1990 *Belinda Rosemary, only dau of Maj Peter Henry Parker (*see* MACCLESFIELD, E), and has:

(1) +Michael Henry; *b* 21 March 1991

(1) *Rosemary Sofia; *b* 11 Dec 1993

1 *Gioia Francesca [The Hon Mrs Shaw, 25 Willow Dve, Southwold, Bicester, Oxon OX6 9XA]; *b* 14 Sept 1953; *m* 1991 *Andrew Robert Shaw, and has issue:

(1) *Elizabeth Margaret Louise; *b* 10 Feb 1993

(2) *Imogen Madeleine Rose; *b* 13 Sept 1995

Lineage: Sir GERALD AYLMER, of Dollardstown, Co Meath (2nd son of Bartholomew Aylmer, of Lyons); Chief Justice of Ireland 1535–59; *d* 1560, leaving:

BARTHOLOMEW AYLMER; *m* Ellen, dau of Thomas Warren, of Navan, Co Meath, and *dvp* 1553, having had, with other issue:

NICHOLAS AYLMER; *b c* 1544; Auditor-Gen Ireland; *m c* 1561 Margaret, dau and coheir of 7th Lord (Baron) Killeen (*see* 1970 edn FINGALL, E) by Alice, dau of Sir Christopher Barnewall, and *d* 1608, leaving:

CHRISTOPHER AYLMER, of Balrath; had:

GERALD AYLMER, of Balrath; lawyer; Catholic and royalist 1649; *m* 1st — and had issue; *m* 2nd after 1629 Mary, dau of Sir Richard Fitzwilliam, of Mount Merryon, and widow of Matthew Plunkett, 5th Lord Louth (*qv*), and *d* 1662, leaving an est s:

Sir Christopher Aylmer, 1st Bt (I), so *cr* by 6 Nov 1662, of Balrath, Co Meath; *m* by 11 Aug 1639 his stepsister Margaret Plunkett (*d* 4 Dec 1683), 3rd dau of 5th Lord Louth (*qv*), and *d* Sept 1671, having by her had:

1 **Sir Gerald Aylmer, 2nd Bt**; *m* Jan 1664/5 Mary, sister of Sir Patrick Bellew, 1st Bt, and *d* June 1702, leaving, with a 3rd s:

(1) **Sir John Aylmer, 3rd Bt**; *m* Alice (*m* 2nd Dominick Meade, of Tullyheady; *m* 3rd 7 March 1718/9 Thomas Lyster, of Athleague, Co Roscommon; *m* 4th Rev Oliver Carter), sister of George Browne, and *dsp* 2 April 1714

(2) **Sir Andrew Aylmer, 4th Bt**; *m* Catherine (*d* March 1746/7), dau of Edward Hussey, of Westown, Co Dublin, and *d* 5 Nov 1740, leaving an only s:

1a **Sir Gerald Aylmer, 5th Bt**; *d* unm 12 July 1745

(4) Patrick Aylmer, of Mayfield, Co Kildare; *d* 1739, leaving an only s:

1a **Sir Matthew Aylmer, 6th Bt**; *b* 10 April 1724; *m* Dorothea Lord (*d* 1791) and *dsp* 11 May 1776

2 MATTHEW AYLMER, **1st Lord Aylmer, Baron of Balrath**, Co Meath (I), so *cr* 1 May 1718; offr RN *temp* JAMES II, R-Adml of the Red *temp* WILLIAM and MARY, Govr Greenwich Hosp, Ranger Greenwich Park, R-Adml GB 1720; *m* Sarah (*d* 1710), dau of Edward Ellis, of London, and *d* 18 Aug 1720, leaving:

(1) HENRY, **2nd Baron**

(1) Elizabeth; *m* 1st Chester Moore (*dsp*); *m* 2nd V-Adml Sir John Norris, PC (*d* 1749), of Hempsted Park, Capt of Deal Castle, and had issue

(2) Lucy; *m* Hugh Fortescue, of Filleigh and Wear Gifford, and had issue (*see* FORTESCUE, E)

3 George; Capt RN

1 Catherine; *m* 1st Sir Nicholas Plunket, of Dublin; *m* 2nd Michael Warren, of Warrenstown, Co Meath

The 1st BARON's only son,

HENRY AYLMER, **2nd Lord Aylmer, Baron of Balrath**; *m* June 1716 Elizabeth (*d* 12 Jan 1749/50), dau of Henry Priestman, Commr RN *temp* WILLIAM and MARY, and *d* 26 June 1754, having had:

1 Matthew; *b* 1717; Capt Foot Gds; *dsp* & *vp* 1748

2 HENRY AYLMER, **3rd Lord Aylmer, Baron of Balrath**; *b* 21 May 1718; Capt RN; *m* Anne (*d* 28 Sept 1756), dau of William Pierce, of Virginia, N America, and *d* 7 Oct 1766, leaving, with an only dau (Anne, *m* — Tencke), an only s:

(1) **Sir Henry Aylmer, 7th Bt** (*s* kinsman 11 May 1776), and **4th Lord Aylmer, Baron of Balrath**; *b c* 1750; *m* 23 Feb 1774 Catherine (*m* 2nd Howel Price, *d* Jan 1805), dau of Sir Charles Whitworth, of Leyborne, and sister of 1st and last Earl Whitworth (*see* RAVENSDALE, B), and *d* 22 Oct 1785, leaving:

1a MATTHEW AYLMER later WHITWORTH-AYLMER (roy licence 1825 on death of his uncle, Earl Whitworth), **5th Lord Aylmer, Baron of Balrath**, GCB; *b* 24 May 1775; Gen, Col 18th Foot, Govr-Gen Canada 1831–35; *m* 4 Aug 1801 Louisa Anne (*d* 13 Aug 1862), 2nd dau of Sir John Call, 1st Bt, of Whiteford, Cornwall, and *dsp* 23 Feb 1850

2a Henry; *b* 1776; drowned at St Petersburg 1798, unm

3a FREDERICK WILLIAM AYLMER, **6th Lord Aylmer, Baron of Balrath**, KCB; *b* 12 Oct 1777; Adml; *d* unm 5 March 1858

4a James Thomas; *b* in 1785; *d* unm Calcutta 5 Aug 1813

1a Rose Whitworth; *d* in India 1800

3 Philip; *b* 1721; *d* young, unm

4 John (Rev); MA; *bapt* 25 May 1723; Prebendary of Bristol, and Rector of St Alban's, Wood Street, London; *m* 4 June 1755 Elizabeth (*d* 5 Sept 1779), dau of John Henry Vassmer, and *d* 16 Feb 1793, leaving, with three other s (Henry, *d* unm Oct 1787; George; Charles), a 2nd s:

(1) John; *b* 16 June 1759; Adml of the Red; *m* 1st 2 Sept 1784 Martha (*d* 7 July 1809), dau of Stephen Cazalet, and had issue:

1a John, of Melbourne, Quebec, Canada; *b* 19 Aug 1795; Capt RN; *m* 12 July 1812 Elizabeth, dau of Henry Coates, and *d* 21 Jan 1849, having had issue:

1b Athalmer; *b* 16 June 1813; *d* 25 March 1829

2b UDOLPHUS AYLMER, **7th Lord Aylmer, Baron of Balrath**; *b* 10 June 1814; Col Canadian Militia; *m* 28 June 1871 Mary Eliza (*d* 14 Sept 1881), dau of Edward Journeaux, JP (formerly of Dublin), of Melbourne, Canada, and *d* 29 Nov 1901, having had issue:

1c MATTHEW AYLMER, **8th Lord Aylmer, Baron of Balrath**; *b* 28 March 1842; Maj-Gen, Adj-Gen and Inspr-Gen Canadian Forces, Lt 7th Roy Fus; *m* 20 Oct 1875 Amy Gertrude (*d* 14 Sept 1935), 2nd dau of Hon John Young, of Montreal, and *d* 11 June 1923, leaving:

1d JOHN FREDERICK WHITWORTH AYLMER, **9th Lord Aylmer, Baron of Balrath**; *b* 23 April 1880; *m* 3 July 1928 *Emma Gertrude, 4th dau of Colin Black, CE, ME, of Victoria, BC, and *dsp* 4 Nov 1970

2d KENNETH ATHALMAR AYLMER, **10th Lord Aylmer, Baron of Balrath**; *b* 23 June 1883; *m* 25 Sept 1924 Eleanor Katherine (*d* 1970), 3rd dau of John Francis Rogers, of Swanington, Norfolk, and *dsp* 1 May 1974

3d BASIL UDOLPHUS AYLMER, **11th Lord Aylmer, Baron of Balrath**; *b* 20 May 1886; *m* 1st 28 Feb 1916 Bessie Irving, ARRC (*d* 12 Nov 1956), dau of Joseph Watson, of Westward Park, Wigton, and had issue:

1e Matthew; *b* 29 May 1917; *ka* Normandy 1 July 1944

3d (cont.) The **11th Baron** *m* 2nd 3 Oct 1960 *Helen Cooper, dau of Thomas Hogg, of Toronto, Canada, and widow of Frederick Gordon Riseborough, and *d* 13 March 1977

1d Amelia Winifred; *m* 31 Dec 1919 Henry Perry-Leake, CE, JP (*d* 8 May 1937), of Balfour, BC, son of Henry Leake, of Herts, by Anne Perry, and *dsp* 7 Aug 1960

2d Florence Gwendolyn; *b* 28 March 1891; *m* 11 June 1914 Robert Arthur Scott-Lauder (*d* 24 Jan 1964), yr son of Dep Surgn-Gen Henry Scott-Lauder, of Edinburgh, and *d* 4 Dec 1967, leaving three daus

2c Henry; *b* 25 April 1843; Lt RM Artillery, Lt-Col Canadian Militia, barrister, MP Canadian Parl, Sheriff Dist of St Francis; *m* 5 Oct 1870 Louisa Blanche Fanny, est dau of Henry Aspinall

3c Edward Francis; *b* 6 March 1848; *d* 16 Nov 1868

4c Frederick Whitworth; *b* 4 Feb 1850; Capt Canadian Militia; CE; *m* 1899 Emma Meredith (*d* 14 Dec 1949 aged 91), dau of R Lang, and *d* 21 Sept 1920

1c Isabella; *m* 17 July 1872 Henry Lovell Aylmer (*d* 3 June 1882), of Richmond, Quebec, est son of Maj-Gen Henry Aylmer, RA, and *d* 12 July 1939, leaving issue (*see* below)

2c Eliza Jane; *d* unm 1893

3b Henry; *b* 10 Aug 1816; granted with sis rank of baron's dau/yr s 15 May 1867; *m* 2 Nov 1846 Eliza (*d* 1880), dau of Henry Atkins, and *d* 1900, leaving issue:

1c John Athalmer; *b* 28 Aug 1847; MEIC; *m* 1883 Mary Christine (*d* 1957), dau of Judge Pringle, of Ontario, and *d* 11 April 1934, leaving issue:

1d Edith Christine; *m* 1910 L F Cross, and *d* May 1954, leaving issue

2d Mary Dorothy; *m* 1919 Eric G McDougall (*d* 1943), and *d* Jan 1971

3d Muriel Esmée; *m* 15 June 1921 George Meredith Morrison (*d* Nov 1967), and *d* Jan 1982, leaving:

1e *John Alexander Aylmer [John Morrison, 1273 Anoka St, Ottawa K1V 6O3, Ontario, Canada]; *b* 15 Jan 1924

1e *Beverley Ann [Miss Beverley Morrison, 80 Certwright St, Kingston, Ontario K7M 1P7, Canada]; *b* 26 July 1925

2c Henry Brooke; *b* 12 Nov 1852; CE; late Capt Canadian Militia; *m* 1901 Bertha Amelia Coates (*d* 9 Feb 1932), and *d* 30 June 1932

1c Elizabeth Anne; *d* unm

2c Christiana Louisa; *d* unm 1901

1b Caroline Amelia Sophia; *b* 4 Oct 1820; *m* 10 Feb 1850 Rev William Valentine Lloyd (*d* 1896), Rector of Haselbech, Northamptonshire, and *d* 1898, leaving issue

(1) (cont.) Adml John Aylmer *m* 2nd 2 Nov 1809 Frances (*d* 17 June 1862), 2nd dau of Rev Thomas Horner Pearson, and sister of Gen Sir Thomas Pearson, KCB, and *d* 19 April 1841, having by her had issue:

2a Henry; *b* 6 Jan 1813; Maj-Gen RA; *m* 28 Oct 1847 Charlotte Louisa (*d* 20 April 1895), dau of John Gwatkin, of Parc Behan, Cornwall, and *d* 31 March 1904, having had issue:

1b Henry Lovell; *b* 26 Aug 1848; *m* 17 July 1872 his cousin Hon Isabella Aylmer (*d* 12 July 1939), est dau of 7th Baron Aylmer (*see* above), and *d* 3 June 1882, leaving issue:

1c Arthur Lovell; *b* 22 July 1873; *m* 1st Sept 1900 Georgina Henrietta Emmeline (Ghetta) (*d* 7 April 1936), dau of Lt-Col James Fielding Sweeney, and had issue:

1d HUGH YATES AYLMER, **12th Lord Aylmer, Baron of Balrath**; *b* 5 Feb 1907; *m* 12 Aug 1939 *Althea [The Rt Hon Althea Lady Aylmer, 601–1159 Beach Dve, Victoria, BC V8S 2N2, Canada], est dau of Lt-Col John Talbot, IA, and *d* 6 Dec 1982, leaving:

1e *Ann Kathleen [The Hon Mrs Miller, 6–1701 Chesterfield Ave, N Vancouver, BC, Canada, V7M 2N9]; *b* 4 Dec 1941; *m* 13 Oct 1972 *Gregor Byron Miller and has issue:

1f *Jonathan Brown Aylmer; *b* 23 Jan 1975

1c (cont.) Arthur Aylmer *m* 2nd 16 Oct 1937 Charlotte Giselle (*d* 4 Jan 1968), dau of George Cornell Yates, of Oil Springs, Ontario, Canada, and *d* 1961

2c Henry Adolphus Paget; *b* 30 Dec 1876; QC (Canada); *m* 1st 5 June 1912 Annie Hall (*d* 25 June 1916), 3rd dau of J J Shillington, of Strandtown, Belfast; *m* 2nd 18 Oct 1922 Anne Munro, 2nd dau of Judge David Sage Williams, of Ocala, Florida, USA, and *dsp* 4 June 1959

1c Mary Louisa Ethel; *b* 20 Feb 1875; *m* 13 Jan 1906 Maj-Gen William Richard Blackwell, CB, CMG, late RAMC (*d* 9 July 1946), er son of Capt T S Blackwell, of Dublin, and *d* 1942, leaving issue

2b Frederick Arthur; *b* 21 Oct 1849; Lt-Col and Brevet Col late RA; *m* 21 Jan 1890 Constance Isabella (*d* 14 Oct 1923), dau of Charles William Grenfell, MP, of Taplow Court, Bucks (*see* GRENFELL, B), and *d* 29 March 1918, having had issue:

1c Christopher; *b* 24 Oct 1890; *educ* Malvern and abroad; Lt late Wilts Regt; *m* 1st 1 June 1922 (*divorce* 1927) Marjorie Marianne Ellison, dau of Percival Ellison Barber, of Sheffield, by his wife Jessie, 2nd dau of Alfred Harrison Smith, of Carlton Hall, Worksop, and widow of Reginald Barber, and had issue:

1d MICHAEL ANTHONY AYLMER, **13th and present Lord Aylmer, Baron of Balrath**

1c (cont.) Christopher Aylmer *m* 2nd 18 April 1931 Margaret, dau of Robert Brotherton, of Antwerp, and *d* 6 Feb 1955

2c Edward Arthur, DSC; *b* 20 March 1892; Capt RN, WW I (despatches) and WW II (despatches, 3rd Cl Order George I of Greece with swords); *m* 8 Jan 1925 Gwladys Phoebe (*d* 21 Sept 1968), yst dau of David Evans, JP, of Ffrwdgrech, Brecon, and *d* 1974, leaving issue:

1d +Gerald Edward [Dr Gerald Aylmer, The Old Captains, Hereford Rd, Ledbury, Herefs HR8 2PX; 18 Albert St, Jericho, Oxford OX2 6AZ]; *b* 30 April 1926; *educ* Winchester and Balliol Coll Oxford (BA 1950, MA, DPhil); WW II in RN; Master St Peter's Coll Oxford 1978–91, memb Roy Commn Historical MSS 1978– (Chm 1989–94), Pres Roy Historical Soc 1984–88; *m* 6 Aug 1955 *Ursula Adelaide, only dau of Maj Brian George Michael Frederick Nixon, of Llangrove, Ross-on-Wye, Herefs, and adopted:

*(Thomas) Bartholomew; *b* 10 Feb 1962

*Emma Clare; *b* 5 March 1964

3c Henry Gerald; *b* 18 May 1896; *educ* Cheltenham; Maj Res of Offrs, late Essex Regt, formerly Lt Roy Dublin Fus, WW I (France 1915–18) and WW II (Home Defence Forces); *m* 19 Jan 1927 Nancy (*d* 1991), dau of Drake Hollick, of The Old House, Sheering, Harlow, Essex, and *d* 1978, leaving issue:

1d +John Henry [John Aylmer Esq, Hilltop House, The Hill, Burford, Oxon OX18 4HX]; *b* 1 July 1936; *educ* Radley; Gren Gds 1954–56; memb London Stock Exchange 1968–; *m* 1st 10 July 1959 (*divorce* 1970) Venetia Mary, er dau of Ian Thomas Henderson, of Pond House, Crawley, Winchester, Hants, by his wife Monica Wingfield, yst dau of Sir Edward Wingfield Verner, 5th Bt (*see* 1970 edn), and has issue:

1e *Miranda Jane; *b* 18 May 1962; *m* 1987 *Simon M A Webster, of 15 Harrison's Lane, Ringmer, nr Lewes, E Sussex, est son of P M Webster, of Blackstone Grange, Henfield, W Sussex, and has issue:

1f *Sophie Charlotte Monica; *b* 1990

2e *Juliet Rose; *b* 23 Oct 1965

1d (cont.) John Aylmer *m* 2nd 1971 *Margaret Gillian Elliot, dau of John Musker

1d Constance Bridget; *b* 17 April 1928; *m* 12 Jan 1951 Geoffrey Ralph Merton, MC, 4th son of Sir Thomas Ralph Merton, KBE, DSc, FRS, of Stubbings House, Maidenhead Thicket, Berks, and had issue:

1e *Flavia Jane; *b* 1 Dec 1951

2e *Laura Rachel; *b* 1 Dec 1952

3e *Claudia Bridget; *b* 9 July 1962

2d *Rachel Moyra *b* 29 Jan 1930; *m* 4 April 1951 *Maj Sir Philip Digby Pauncefort-Duncombe, 4th Bt (*qv*), and has issue

4c Claud; *b* 23 Sept 1900; Lt-Col RA; *m* 19 July 1928 *Margaret Victoria [Mrs Claud Aylmer, c/o 17 Mill Lane, Old Marston,Oxford OX3 0PX] (who *m* 2nd 1 Dec 1954 Cdr John Rodolf Perronet Thompson, RN (*d* 16

March 1965), son of Maj-Gen Charles William Thompson, CB, DSO, of Trent Meadows, Puddletown, Dorchester, Dorset, and resumed the name AYLMER by deed poll 1982), er dau of Frank Hemming, of Franklyns, Great Waltham, Essex, and *d* 12 Oct 1952, leaving issue:

1d +Richard Grenfell [Richard Aylmer Esq, Cromwell's House, 17 Mill Lane, Old Marston, Oxon, OX3 OPY]; *b* 11 Jan 1932; *educ* Wellington and London U (BA 1952); Capt (ret) RA; *m* 11 April 1964 *Marelyn Joyce, only dau of Sir James Miller, GBE, JP, DL, of Belmont, Ellersly Rd, Edinburgh 12, and has issue:

1e +Christopher James; *b* 22 May 1966; *m* 1992 *Cheryl Janice, yr dau of Clive Perrett, of Stratford-upon-Avon

2e +Kenneth Malcolm; *b* 20 Oct 1970; *m* 1996 *Illona Rebecca Melanie Dixon, yr dau of Stephen Dixon, of Oxford

1c Rose Caroline Georgiana; *b* 28 Oct 1893; *m* 14 May 1918 Henry Francis Lascelles, late Welsh Gds (*d* 31 Aug 1937), 2nd son of Lt-Col Henry Arthur Lascelles, Rifle Bde, of Woolbeding, Midhurst, Sussex, and had issue (*see* HAREWOOD, E)

2c Constance Evelyn; *b* 12, *d* 15 May 1899

3b Charles Paget; *b* 28 April 1853; *d* 28 Oct 1870

1b Charlotte Louisa Mary; *b* 18 March 1851; *d* unm 1 Feb 1941

2b Frances Veryan; *b* 7 Jan 1856; *d* 28 Oct 1919

3a Frederick Charles; *b* 24 July 1814; Lt-Col 89th Regt, Kt Legion of Honour and Medjidie; *m* 22 Sept 1853 Maria Anne, yst dau of John Gwatkin, of Parc Behan, Cornwall, and *dsp* 20 March 1882

AYLMER, Bt

Arms: Argent, a cross sable between four Cornish choughs proper. **Crest:** A Cornish chough proper rising out of a ducal coronet or. **Motto:** Hallelujah. **Creation:** Bt. (I) 25 Jan 1621/2.

SIR RICHARD JOHN AYLMER, 16TH BT, of Donadea, Co Kildare [Sir Richard Aylmer Bt, 3573 Lorne Ave, Montreal, Quebec H2X 2A4, Canada]; *b* 23 April 1937; *s f* 1987; *m* 16 June 1962 *Lise, dau of Paul Emile Demers, of Montreal, Canada, and has issue:

1 +FENTON PAUL; *b* 1965; *educ* Selwin House Sch and Concordia U; *m* 19– *Pina, dau of Mrs Velia Mastromonaco

1 *Genevieve; *b* 1963

Lineage: JOHN AYLMER *m* late 14th century Helen, dau and heir of John Tyrrell of Lyons, Co Kildare, thus acquiring that manor and other lands; ggggf of:

RICHARD AYLMER; *b* 1509; bought 1558 from 10th Earl of Ormonde and (3rd Earl of) Ossory (*see* MOUNTGARRET, V) the territorial barony of Oughterany, Co Kildare, including the manor of Donadea, and *d* 1559, leaving a 3rd s:

Sir Gerald Aylmer, 1st Bt (I), so *cr* 25 Jan 1621/2, of Donadea, Co Kildare; *b c* 1548; lawyer, ktd 1598; *m* 1st 1587 Mary (*dsp* 28 Nov 1611), dau and coheir of Henry Travers (son and heir of Sir John Travers, 1st Master of the Ordnance in Ireland), and widow of 3rd Viscount Baltinglass; *m* 2nd 1611 Julia (*d* 2 Nov 1617), dau of 3rd Lord (Baron) Delvin (*see* WESTMEATH, E), and *d* 19 Aug 1634, leaving, with a dau (Julia Lettice, *m* Sir Richard Barnewall, 2nd Bt; *qv*), an est s:

Sir Andrew Aylmer, 2nd Bt; *b* 1613; *m* 1634 Ellen, sister of 1st Duke of Ormonde (*see* MOUNTGARRET, V), and *d* after 11 July 1671, having had, with other issue:

GARRET/GERALD AYLMER; *b* 1635; Army Capt; *m* 1661/2 Jane, dau and heir of Philip FitzGerald of Alloone, Co Kildare, through whom he acquired large estates near the Hill of Allen, Co Kildare, and *dvp* 20 Dec 1663, leaving, with a dau (Elizabeth):

Sir FitzGerald Aylmer, 3rd Bt; *b* 1663; *m* June 1681 Lady Ellen Plunkett (*m* 2nd Michael Fleming), 2nd dau of 3rd Earl of Fingall (*see* 1970 edn), and *d* 9 June 1685, having had, with a yr s (Luke; *b* 1684; *dsp* 1706):

Sir Justin Aylmer, 4th Bt; *b* 24 Feb 1682; *m* 1702 Ellice (*m* 2nd Philip Roche; *m* 3rd 1714 Luke Dillon, of Clonbrock; *m* 4th 1718 John Dillon, of Mile Abbey, and *d* 27 Aug 1741), dau of Sir Gerald Aylmer, 2nd Bt, of Balrath (*see* AYLMER, B), and *d* 1711, having had, with a yr s (Peter Justin, *dsp* young):

Sir Gerald Aylmer, 5th Bt; *b* 1703; *m* Oct 1726 Lucy (*m* 2nd Nov 1737 Robert Fisher), dau of Adml Sir John Norris, of Hempstead, Kent, and *d* 6 Jan 1737, leaving, with two daus (Lucy, Elizabeth):

Sir FitzGerald Aylmer, 6th Bt; *b* 14 Sept 1736; MP Co Roscommon 1761–68, Old Leighton 1769–76, Kildare 1776–83 and Harristown 1783–94, High Sheriff Co Kildare 1761; *m* 15 Aug 1764 Elizabeth, dau and heir of Fenton Cole, of Silver Hill, Co Fermanagh, and *d* 11 Feb 1794, having had an est s:

Sir Fenton Aylmer, 7th Bt; *b* 12 May 1768; High Sheriff Co Kildare 1795; *m* 4 June 1795 Jane Grace (*d* 31 Dec 1827), sis of 6th Baron Carbery (*qv*), and *d* 23 May 1816, leaving issue:

1 **Sir Gerald George Aylmer, 8th Bt**, DL (Co Kildare); *b* 26 May 1798; High Sheriff 1827, Lt 1st Dragoon Gds; *m* 24 April 1826 Maria (*d* 9 May 1879), est dau and coheir of Col James Hodgson, HEICS, of Carlisle, and *d* 8 Feb 1878, leaving:

(1) **Sir Gerald George Aylmer, 9th Bt**, JP (Cos Dublin, Meath and Kildare); *b* 26 May 1830; High Sheriff Co Kildare 1854; *m* 6 April 1853 Alicia Hester Caroline (*d* 6 March 1907), dau of Conway Richard Dobbs, of Castle Dobbs, Co Antrim, and *d* 25 June 1883, leaving issue:

1a **Sir Justin Gerald Aylmer, 10th Bt**; *b* 17 Nov 1863; *d* unm 15 March 1885

1a Caroline Maria, of Donadea Castle, Co Kildare, which she inherited from her bro; *d* 13 May 1935

2a Helen Charlotte Nichola; *d* young

2 ARTHUR PERCY (Sir), **11th Bt**

3 William Josiah (Rev); *b* 6 Dec 1802; settled in Akaroa, New Zealand; *m* 24 Nov 1830 Elizabeth Frances (*d* 1880), est dau of Rev Henry Lambart Bayly, of Ballyarthur (*see* ANGLESEY, M), and *d* 9 Aug 1883, having had issue:

(1) Justin John; *b* 11 Aug 1831; RM, New Zealand; *m* 1st 1855 Caroline (*d* 28 June 1861), dau of Rev W Slatter, and had issue:

1a Selina Frances; *m* 16 March 1876 Warner William Warren Westenra (*d* 1906), of Canterbury, New Zealand and *d* 14 Aug 1929, leaving issue

2a Lucy Catherine; *m* 1879 John George Thomson (*d* 1904), of New Zealand, and *d* 1935, leaving issue

3a Geraldine; *d* unm 1929

4a Helen; *m* 1881 Thomas Noel Brodrick, OBE, ISO (*d* 1931), of Hamner Springs, Canterbury, New Zealand, son of Thomas Brodrick, of Invercargill, NZ, and *d* 6 Jan 1930, leaving issue

(1) (cont.) Justin Aylmer *m* 2nd 1869 Sarah Anne Cockerill (*d* 1897), dau of Dr Samuel Beswick, of Canterbury, NZ and *d* 12 Jan 1885, having by her had further issue:

1a Justin Arthur; *b* 12 Aug 1870; *m* 1895 Annie Laura (*d* 6 Aug 1937), dau of T H Harper, of Wanganui, NZ

2a FitzGerald Beswick; *b* 8 Jan 1872; *d* 1 June 1873

(2) William Henry; *b* 22 Aug 1833; settled in NSW, Australia; *m* 1st 1861 Henrietta, dau of Dr Martin, and had issue:

1a Percy Gordon; *b* 6 Aug 1865; *m* 13 Feb 1888 Eliza Anne (*d* 31 Aug 1951), dau of William Haddon, and *d* 3 Dec 1923, leaving issue:

1b Arthur William; *b* 23 July 1889; *m* 23 Sept 1924 Daisy, dau of William Goodall, of Firth Cliffe, New York and *d* 7 June 1964, leaving issue:

1c *Constance Elizabeth; *b* 1931; *m* 31 Aug 1953 Charles T Brown, and has issue:

1d *Kenneth Aylmer; *b* 8 March 1959

1d *Janette Lockwood; *b* 15 Feb 1957

2b Justin Kenneth; *b* 28 May 1898; *m* 23 Oct 1918 Winifred Clare Mullins, and *d* June 1951, leaving issue:

1c +Francis Gordon [Francis Aylmer, 61 Gipps St, Smithfield, NSW, Australia]; *b* 7 Aug 1919; *m* *Dura Marion Onus, of Inverell, NSW, and has issue:

1d +Michael

2d +Peter

3d +Anthony

1d *Marion Dura

2c +Ernest Austin; *b* 15 March 1921; *m* 26 June 1943 *Jean Elsie, dau of James Alfred Walker, of 13 Potter Ave, Earlwood, Sydney, NSW, Australia, and has issue:

1d +David Ernest; *b* 12 Dec 1945

2d +Philip Kenneth Raymond; *b* 3 Jan 1952

3d +James Raymond; *b* 16 Feb 1953

1d *Margaret Jean; *b* 29 May 1944

2d *Irene Clare; *b* 21 Sept 1950

3c +Kenneth Richard; *b* 17 May 1922; *m* 1952 *Trudy, dau of W Everingham

4c +Bruce William; *b* 17 Nov 1927; *m* *Elizabeth Law, and has issue:

1d +Robert

1d *Barbara

1c *Marjorie Irene, JP; *b* 11 Sept 1924; *m* 10 May 1946 *John Michael McGann, son of John William Charles McGann, of 60 King George Rd, Lakemba, NSW, Australia, and has issue:

1d *Beverley Gay; *b* 1 Jan 1948

2d *Lynette Joy; *b* 14 Aug 1950

3d *Jeannette Ellen; *b* 10 Nov 1953

3b Frederick Gordon; *b* 26 July 1900; *m* 1940 *Alma [Mrs Frederick Aylmer, 48 Maxim St, West Ryde, Sydney, NSW 2114, Australia], dau of — Elton, of Marombra, NSW, and *d* 10 July 1954, leaving issue:

1c *Carolyn Ann; BSc, BA; *b* 1946; *m* 1970 *Ronald Bucholtz

2c *Margaret Susan; *b* 1948; *m* 1969 *Alan Robert Underwood, and has issue:

1d *Julie; *b* 1975

2d *Fiona; *b* 1978

1b Constance Lenore; *b* 21 May 1891; *m* 24 April 1920 John Joseph Mullins

2b Inez Amy; *b* 8 Dec 1896; *m* 26 March 1921 Cyril Frederick Mullins (*d* 1955)
3b Edith Mildred; *b* 6 Oct 1899; *d* 11 May 1918
4b *Phyllis Lilian; *b* 16 July 1904; *m* 16 June 1925 Raymond Robert Brown, and has issue:
1c *Robert Aylmer; *b* 31 Dec 1932
1c *Aline Mildred; *b* 21 March 1927
5b Muriel Eileen; *b* 23 April 1907
2a William; *b* 1867; *d* in infancy
1a Edith Maude; *m* Frederick Blakiston Holland
2a Inez; *d* unm 5 June 1943
(2) (cont.) William Aylmer *m* 2nd 1874 Elizabeth (*d* 30 Jan 1936), dau of Dr Gordon, of Sydney, and *d* 1882, having by her had issue:
3a Blanche Emily
4a Ida Mildred
5a Madge Irene
6a Muriel Lilian
7a Lenore
(3) FitzGerald George; Midshipman, RN; *d* unm on board HMS *Tweed* off Rio
(4) Arthur Freke; *d* 1866 at Valparaiso
(5) Henry Lambert; *b* 1844; *m* 7 Aug 1883 Matilda (*d* 21 June 1950), dau of Alexander Mee, and *d* 24 Nov 1890, having had issue:
1a Mercy Frances; *m* 15 Dec 1915 James Lawrence Menzies, and had issue
2a Dorothy; *m* 19 Nov 1925 John MacPherson (*d* 19 March 1951), son of Allan MacPherson, of Dunsandel, Canterbury, NZ, and had issue
(1) Selina Percy; *m* March 1856 Richard Westenra, est son of Capt Westenra, of Christchurch, Canterbury, NZ, and had issue
(2) Catherine Charlotte; *m* 1861 James Rattray, of Dunedin, Otago, NZ and had issue
4 John Freke, of Green Bank, Bray, Co Wicklow; *b* 6 May 1807; *m* 22 May 1832 Anna, 3rd dau of Robet Austin Parrish, of Philadelphia, Pennsylvania, and *d* 22 Dec 1874, leaving issue:
(1) Margaret Susan; *m* 29 Dec 1828 John Aylmer (*d* 5 March 1857), of Courtown, Co Kildare, and *d* Dec 1892, leaving issue

The 10th Bt's great-uncle,

Sir Arthur Percy Aylmer, 11th Bt, JP; *b* 31 Aug 1801; MA Trin Coll Dublin; *m* 12 Dec 1833 Martha (*d* 3 Feb 1887 aged 77), dau of Richard Reynell, of Killynon, Co Westmeath, and *d* 7 May 1885, having had:
1 Fenton John; *b* 24 Dec 1835; Capt 97th Regt, Crimea (medal and clasp with the order of Medjidie); *m* 9 June 1857 Isabella Elinor (*d* 27 Dec 1908), er dau of George Darling, of Fowberry Tower, Northumberland, and *d* 9 April 1862, having had issue:
(1) **Sir Arthur Percy FitzGerald Aylmer, 12th Bt**; *b* 2 March 1858; *m* 1st 27 Nov 1878 Annie (*d* 1884), dau of John Sanger; *m* 2nd 1885 (*divorce* 1886) Anne, dau of J Douglas Reid, of New York, and formerly wife of George Stelle, of Chicago, and *dsp* 5 Dec 1928
(2) George Darling; *d* young
(3) **Sir Fenton John Aylmer, 13th Bt**, VC, KCB; *b* 5 April 1862; Lt-Gen RE, Col-Comdt RE (1922), AG India 1912–15; served in Burma 1886-87 (despatches, medal and clasp), Hazara Field Force 1891 (despatches and clasps), Hunza-Nagar Expedition 1891–92 (despatches, wounded, clasp, brevet majority), Isazal Field Force 1892, Chitral Expedition 1895 (despatches, medal and clasp, brevet Lt-Col) and WW I as AG India and Corps Cdr in Mesopotamia 1915–16 (despatches); *m* 1913 Elsie Julie (*d* 18 July 1934), dau of Frederick Oppermann, of Hanover, and widow of Sir Herbert Hope Risley, KCIE, CSI, and *dsp* 3 Sept 1935
(1) Helen Cecilia Adelaide; *d* unm 14 July 1914
2 John Evans Freke; *b* 23 Feb 1838; Capt 54th Regt; MP Maidstone 1880–85; *m* 3 July 1861 Frances Margarita (*d* 4 July 1920), dau of James Thomson, Hanseatic Consul at Gibraltar, and *d* 14 Oct 1907, leaving issue:
(1) GERALD ARTHUR EVANS FREKE (Sir), **14th Bt**
(2) Henry Evans-Freke, CBE (1922), R-Adml, Order of St Stanislas of Russia and American DSM; *b* 6 Sept 1878; *m* 4 Jan 1910 Edith Winifred (*d* 5 Nov 1952), dau of Vet-Col Sir Francis Duck, KCB, FRCVS, and *d* 16 Aug 1933, leaving issue:
1a +John Francis; *b* 27 Dec 1910; late RAF
2a Michael Arthur; *b* 24 Sept 1913; S/Ldr RAF; *das* 1939
(1) Amy Geraldine Frances; *d* unm March 1943
(2) Nina Florence Mary; *m* 4 Oct 1886 Arthur Thomas Marson MA, JP (*d* 5 Jan 1927), of Wix, Merrow, nr Guildford, Surrey, and *d* 21 Dec 1936, leaving issue
(3) Dora Gertrude Aylmer; *d* unm 15 Feb 1955
(4) Grace Marion; *m* 10 Feb 1913 Arthur Grayhurst Hewat (*d* 15 Dec 1951), est son of John Grayhurst Hewat, of Surbiton, Surrey, and *d* Feb 1955, leaving issue
(5) Elfrida Fenton; *m* 7 June 1917 James Henry Nicholson (*d* 8 March 1943), son of Henry Nicholson, of Stanhope, Co Durham, and had issue
3 Richard Reynell; *b* 24 Dec 1840; *dsp* in NZ, 1896
4 Arthur Percy Barnard; *b* 24 March 1845; *d* unm 22 May 1875
1 Harriet Elizabeth; *m* 17 Feb 1857 Eaton Joseph Travers (*ka* at Delhi, Aug 1857), son of Gen Sir Robert Travers, and *d* 11 March 1918, leaving issue
2 Jane Grace; *d* unm 13 Feb 1923
3 Catherine Charlotte; *d* unm 3 April 1910
4 Geraldine Maria; *m* 9 July 1861 Robert Constable Hall (*d* 19 Oct 1888), of Cork, and *d* 11 Oct 1904, leaving issue
5 Elizabeth Nannette; *d* unm 18 Sept 1893
6 Martha Josepha Helena; *m* 24 April 1884 Capt Richard Arthur Herbert Townshend, late 13th Light Inf (*d* 1930), of Beach House, Bantry, and *d* 29 Oct 1919
7 Anna Angelina

The 13th Bt's cousin,

Sir Gerald Arthur Evans Freke Aylmer, 14th Bt; *b* 15 Oct 1869; *m* 13 Sept 1898 Mabel Howard, dau of Hon James K Ward, MLC Quebec, and *d* 3 April 1939, leaving issue:
1 FENTON GERALD (Sir), **15th Bt**
1 Margaret Lydia; *m* 10 May 1924 Donald Henry MacFarlane, MBE, MC, son of Henry MacFarlane, and had issue:
1 *Margaret Ann Aylmer; *b* 1926; Anglican nun
2 *Monica Aylmer; *b* 1929
3 *Rose Aylmer [Mrs Edmund McIntyre, 131 Price Edward Avenue, Valois, PQ, Canada]; *b* 1935; *m* 1959 *Edmund Hugh McIntyre, and has issue

Sir GERALD's only son,

Sir Fenton Gerald Aylmer, 15th Bt; *b* 12 March 1901; *m* 18 Feb 1928 Rosalind Boultbee, dau of John Percival Bell, of Hamilton, Ontario, Canada, and *d* 1987, leaving:
1 Sir RICHARD JOHN AYLMER, **16th and present Bt**
1 *Rosalind Alice [Mrs Milton Cameron, 2197 Queen's Avenue, W Vancouver, BC V7V 2Y1]; *b* 1 Jan 1941; *m* 1st 10 April 1965 (*divorce* 1973) Michael Neal Denis, s of Denis White, of Victoria, BC, Canada; *m* 2nd 1977 *Milton Cameron and adopted:
*Michael Aylmer; *b* 1968
*Anna Rosalind; *b* 1970

BACKHOUSE

Arms: Per saltire or and azure a saltire engrailed ermine between two roses in pale gules, barbed and seeded proper, and as many passion crosses in fess of the first. **Crest:** In front of a rock proper thereon an eagle displayed vert, holding in each claw a passion cross or, a serpent on its back, the tail nowed also proper.
Motto: *Confido in deo* ('I trust in God').
Creation: Bt. (UK) 6 March 1901.

SIR JONATHAN ROGER BACKHOUSE, 4TH BT, of Uplands; *b* 30 Dec 1939; *s* f 1944; *educ* Ampleforth and BNC Oxford; dir WH Freeman and Co; *m* 11 July 1997 *Sarah, dau of James Stott of Cromer, Norfolk

Lineage: JONATHAN BACKHOUSE; *b* 1747; *m* 12 May 1774 Anne Pease and *d* 1826, leaving:

JONATHAN BACKHOUSE, of Polam, Darlington; *b* 19 Jan 1779; banker; *m* 23 April 1811 Hannah Chapman (*d* 6 May 1850), er dau of Joseph Gurney, of Lakenham Grove, Norfolk, and *d* 7 Oct 1842, leaving issue:
1 EDMUND
1 Jane Gurney; *m* 10 Oct 1844 Robert Barclay Fox (*d* 10 March 1855), of Falmouth, Cornwall, and *d* 10 April 1860, leaving issue
2 Anne; *m* John Hodgkin, of London, and *d* Dec 1845, leaving issue

JONATHAN BACKHOUSE's s,

EDMUND BACKHOUSE, JP (Co Durham and Yorks), of Trebah, Falmouth; *b* 28 Nov 1824; MP Darlington 1868–80; *m* 22 Sept 1848 Juliet Mary (*d* 3 Dec 1898), only dau of Charles Fox, of Trebah, and *d* 7 June 1906, having had, with other issue (including a dau Sarah Juliet, *m* 1876 Horatio Pym and had issue; *see* PYM, B):

Sir Jonathan Edmund Backhouse, 1st Bt (UK), so *cr* 6 March 1901, JP (N R Yorks and Co Durham), of The Rookery, Middleton Tyas, N R Yorks; *b* 15 Nov 1849; *m* 29 Nov 1871 Florence (*d* 11 Oct 1902), yst dau of Sir John Salusbury Trelawny, 9th Bt (*qv*), and *d* 27 July 1918, having had:
1 **Sir Edmund Trelawny Backhouse, 2nd Bt**; *b* 20 Oct 1873; *educ* Winchester and Merton Coll Oxford; FRGS, FRSA, memb Nat Geog Soc Washington, DC, memb Internat Dip Acad Paris, Prof Peking U 1902–13, Prof of Chinese King's Coll London 1913; *d* unm 8 Jan 1944
2 Roland Charles; *b* 15 Dec 1874; *d* 18 Dec 1877

3 Oliver CB (1915); *b* 4 June 1876; Adml, served Somaliland 1904 (despatches) and WW I, Cdr 2nd Naval Bde Antwerp 1914 and Dardanelles 1915 (despatches twice, Legion of Honour and Croix de Guerre), cmded HMS *Orion* Battle of Jutland 1916 (despatches), Silver Medal of Italy, cmded HMS *Royal Sovereign* Allied occupation Constantinople 1920, Supt Sheerness Dockyard 1923–25, Adml Supt Devonport Dockyard 1927–31; *m* 15 Dec 1920 Margaret Susan (*d* 26 Nov 1973), er dau of Charles William Dyson Perrins, JP, DL, of Ardross, Ross-shire, and Davenham, Malvern, and *dsp* 25 March 1943

4 Roger Roland Charles (Sir), GCB (1938, KCB 1933), GCVO (1937), CMG (1917); *b* 24 Nov 1878; Adml of the Fleet 1934, First and Pncpl Naval ADC to HM GEORGE VI 1938, 3rd Sea Ld Admlty and Controller Navy 1928–32, V-Adml cmdg First Battle Sqdn Med Fleet 1932–34, C-in-C Home Fleet 1935–38 and First Sea Ld and Ch Naval Staff 1938–39; *m* 4 June 1907 Dora Louisa MBE (1946) (*d* 3 Jan 1958), 6th dau of John Ritchie Findlay, of Aberlour, DL (*see* FINDLAY, Bt), and *d* 15 July 1939, leaving:

(1) JOHN EDMUND (Sir), **3rd Bt**

(2) Richard Miles; *b* 9 April 1911; *m* 1st 9 June 1948 (*divorce* 1951) Angela Mary, er dau of Peter Haig-Thomas (*see* NORMANTON, E) and widow of Capt Count Richard Dudley Melchior Gurowski, Scots Gds; *m* 2nd 21 Dec 1951 *Edeltraud Margaretha [Mrs Richard Backhouse, 73 Divinity Rd, Oxford OX4 1LH], dau of Hofrat Dr Hans Perz and Mrs Perz-Schonegger, of Vienna, and *d* 23 Sept 1969, leaving:

1a *Louise Maria Theodora; *b* 16 Aug 1955; *m* 1984 *Maj Jonathan Arthur Francis Howard, Roy Hus (PWO), and has issue (*see* CARLISLE, E)

2a *Julia Maria Florence [Mrs Paul Taylor, 41 Hambalt Rd, London SW4 9EQ]; *b* 12 July 1956; *m* 1990 *Paul Cameron Taylor, s of J A Taylor, of Westbourne, Bournemouth, and has issue:

1b +John Maximilian; *b* 1993

1b *Marie-Louise Florence; *b* 1992

(1) Florence; *b* 17 Feb 1908; *m* 22 Dec 1934 V-Adml Sir Hilary Worthington Biggs, KBE, CB, DSO, er s of Lt-Col Charles William Biggs, RE, of 4 Montpelier Grove, Cheltenham, and had issue:

1a *Geoffrey William Roger (Sir), KCB (1993) [V-Adml Sir Geoffrey Biggs KCB, c/o Naval Secretary, Victory Building, HM Naval Base, Portsmouth PO1 3LS]; *b* 23 Nov 1938; *educ* Charterhouse and RNC Dartmouth; Lt-Cdr RN, Cdr 1975, Capt 1980, R-Adml 1990, V-Adml 1992, mil advsr ICL and DESC 1995–; *m* 1st 19 Aug 1967 (*divorce* 1978) Marcia Zoe de Cambourne, er dau of Maj-Gen Henry Lowther Ewart Leask, CB, DSO, OBE, Col Roy Highland Fus, of Frogmorton, Greywell, Basingstoke, Hants, and has:

1b *William; *b* 29 Nov 1968

2b *Anthony; *b* 24 May 1970

1a (cont.) Sir Geoffrey *m* 2nd 1981 Caroline Ann Daly and by her has:

1b A dau; *b* 19–

2a *Michael Richard [Michael Biggs Esq, Hill House, Meonstoke, Hants]; *b* 31 Oct 1942; *educ* Charterhouse

1a *Elizabeth [Mrs James Walmsley, 4 Beech Ride, Sandhurst, Berks]; *b* 9 Oct 1936; *m* 20 Sept 1958 *Capt James Walmsley, RM, s of Col Arthur Wyndham Walmsley, of 4 Mermaid St, Rye, Sussex, and has issue:

1b *James Patrick; *b* 29 Feb 1960

2b *David Christopher; *b* 8 March 1962

2a *Rachel Mary; *b* 10 Nov 1944; *m* 17 May 1969 *Capt John Michael Curtis, Roy Hants Regt, est s of John Curtis, of Gastons, Kilmeston, Alresford, Hants and has:

1b *A dau; *b* 28 Aug 1970

(2) Ruth Dora; ARRC, AIMSW

(3) Barbara Constance; *m* 28 April 1938 (*divorce* 1960) Cdr David Charles Kinloch, DSO, OBE, RN (*d* 17 Nov 1969), 2nd s of Rev Canon Michael Ward Kinloch, OBE, MA, rector Moreton, Dorset, and *d* 1 Oct 1968, leaving issue

(4) Joan Margaret Backhouse; *m* 8 Jan 1944 Lt Archibald Norman Macpherson, RN, s of Lt-Col Archibald Duncan Macpherson, CIE , and had:

1a *Allan Alisdair; *b* 7 Feb 1951; *educ* Stowe

2a *Angus John; *b* 17 March 1953; *educ* Stowe

1a *Susan Margaret; *b* 1 April 1947

5 Miles Roland Charles, DSO (1902) and bar; *b* 24 Nov 1878; *educ* Eton and Trin Hall Cambridge; Lt-Col TA, Northumberland Hus Yeo (TD), T/Lt-Col cmdg 8th Bn York Regt 1917, Hon Capt 1914, served S Africa 1899–1902 and WW I (despatches), V-Pres Internat Sleeping Car Co, dir La Protetrice Insur Co Paris and Brixton Estate Ltd; *m* 14 Sept 1904 Olive (*d* 16 Sept 1954), 2nd dau of Geoffrey Fowell Buxton, CB, (*see* BUXTON, Bt), and *d* 15 May 1962, leaving:

(1) Roger Trelawny; *b* 5 Sept 1905; *educ* Harrow; High Sheriff Co Durham 1962, Maj Roy Rifles of Canada, WW II, dir Barclays Bank Darlington, Darlington Building Soc; *m* 22 April 1938 *Beatrice (Betty) Ada Janet, only dau of Capt Hedleigh St George Bond, Roy Canadian Engrs, of Toronto, and *d* 6 Nov 1977, leaving issue:

1a *Jane Trelawny [Mrs Duncan Eyre, Silvester Cottage, Hudswell, Richmond, N Yorkshire]; *b* 6 Oct 1939; *m* 1st 27 July 1962 (*divorce* 1982) Michael Lake Coghlan, est s of Kenneth Lake Coghlan, of Vine Cottage, Liphook, Hants; *m* 2nd 1982 *Duncan Irwin Eyre and has by her 1st husb:

1b *Henry Trelawny Lake; *b* 21 Feb 1964

2b *Benjamin Patrick Lake; *b* 11 Dec 1970

1b *Jane Louise Lake; *b* 12 Nov 1962; *m* 1994 *Stevan Caldwell, of NSW, and has:

1c *Amy; *b* 1994

2c *Mary Beatrice; *b* 1997

2b *Serena Mary Lake; *b* 16 March 1969; *m* 1996 *Thomas Montgomery and has:

1c *Jack Thomas; *b* 1996

2a *Avery St George [Mrs Jeremy Fraser, Stutton Vale Farm, Tattingstone, Ipswich, Suffolk IP9 2PA]; *b* 25 Nov 1941; *m* 1st 15 June 1963 (*divorce* 1973) Colin Frohawk Burrell, est s of Roy Herbert Adams Burrell, OBE, Indian Police, of The Grange, Tadcaster, Yorks, and has:

1b *Oliver Roy St George BACKHOUSE (deed poll 1990); *b* 9 Sept 1966

1b *Katharine Victoria; *b* 20 June 1964; *m* 1st 1989 (*divorce* 1995) Peter John Bowrings; *m* 2nd 19– *Roderic Mark Robert Lloyd and by her first husb has:

1c *Oscar Peter James; *b* 1989

2a (cont.) Mrs Avery Burrell *m* 2nd 1978 *Jeremy James Fraser, s of Maj Hugh Munro Fraser, and by him has:

2b *Juliet Avery Virginia; *b* 1980

3a *Elizabeth Este [Mrs Angus Fraser, Hornton Hall, Banbury, Oxon OX17 6DF]; *b* 19 April 1943; *m* 7 June 1969 Angus Hugh Fraser (*d* 1994), s of Maj Hugh Munro Fraser, of Charlton Musgrove, nr Wincanton, Somerset, and Mrs D-H de Pass, formerly of Arlingon, nr Polegate, Sussex, and has:

1b *Sophie Lavinia; *b* 1971

2b *Camilla Elizabeth; *b* 1973

3b *Emma Caroline; *b* 1977

(2) Jonathan of Breewood Hall, Gt Horkesley, Essex ; *b* 16 March 1907; *educ* RNC Dartmouth; Maj RA WW II, dir J Henry Schroder and Co; *m* 23 March 1934 Alice Joan (*d* 1984), dau of Brig-Gen Charles Richard Woodfroffe, CMG, CVO, CBE, RA, of N Wells, Bembridge, IoW, and *d* 1993, leaving:

1a +David Miles [David Backhouse Esq, South Farm, Fairford, Glos]; *b* 30 Jan 1939; *educ* Eton; *m* 18 Jan 1969 *Sophia Ann, only dau of Col Clarence Henry Southgate Townsend, of South Farm, and has:

1b +Benjamin Jonathan; *b* 1974

1b *Cilla Gael; *b* 1972

2a +William [William Backhouse Esq, Layer Marney Wick, Colchester, Essex CO5 9UT]; *b* 29 May 1942; *educ* Eton; *m* 4 Nov 1971 *Deborah Jane, yst dau of Hon David Edward Hely-Hutchinson (*see* DONOUGHMORE, E), and has:

1b +Timothy James; *b* 20 March 1981

1b *Harriet Diana; *b* 26 June 1975

2b *Tessa Louise; *b* 6 May 1977

1a *Joanna [Mrs Jeremy Wyatt, Hawkins Farm, Monk Eleigh, Tye, Ipswich, Suffolk IP7 7JW]; *b* 18 July 1936; *m* 10 May 1956 Jeremy James Norris Wyatt (*d* 1988), s of Sir Miles Dermot Norris Wyatt, CBE, of Alresford Hall, Colchester, Essex, and has:

1b *Thomas; *b* 27 May 1967

1b *Sarah; *b* 13 Oct 1957

2b *Nell Victoria; *b* 20 May 1959

3b *Carina May; *b* 9 Oct 1963

(3) Wilfrid Jasper, MBE (1941); *b* 28 July 1913; *educ* Rugby; Maj Roy Signals WW II (despatches); *m* 29 July 1946 *Nancy Catherine [Mrs Wilfred Backhouse, Horsey Island, Kirby-le-Soken, Essex], dau of Maj Lindsay Edward Bury, CB, of Millichope Cottage, Munslow, Craven Arms, and widow of David Haig-Thomas, and *d* 1980, leaving:

1a +Joseph Lindsay; *b* 2 April 1953

1a *Mary [Mrs Angus Bancroft, Water Farm, Raydon, Hadleigh, Suffolk]; *b* 5 Aug 1947; *m* 1973 *Angus Bancroft and has:

1b *William Harry; *b* 1978

1b *Anna Charlotte; *b* 1975

2a *Hannah Margaret [Mrs Robert Skepper, Ferry Farm, Sudbourne, Woodbridge, Suffolk]; *b* 30 Nov 1948; *m* 1968 *Robert Braeme Skepper and has had:

1b *Jonathan Henry Alexander; *b* 1971

1b *Jane Rachel Nancy; *b* 1969

2b Georgina Alexandra; *b* 1976; *d* 1996

3b *Poppy Joanna Alice; *b* 1998

(1) Una Patricia; *b* 23 April 1911; *m* 7 Oct 1938 (*divorce* 1961) Douglas Raymond Collins, Lt-Cdr RNVR, yr s of Richard Johnson Douglas Collins, of Annascaul, Co Kerry, and had:

1a *Christopher Douglas [Christopher Collins Esq, Hawthorn Farm, Gt Missenden, Bucks]; *b* 19 Jan 1940; *educ* Eton; FCA; owner and rider of racehorses; *m* 1976 *Susan Anne Lumb and has:

1b *Edward Douglas; *b* 10 Oct 1979

1b *Lorna Patricia; *b* 24 Dec 1981

2a *Benjamin Jasper; *b* 8 Dec 1951; *educ* Eton

1a *Susanna Mary [Mrs Timothy Abel Smith, 36 Campden St, London W8]; *b* 21 Aug 1942; *m* 7 July 1965 *Timothy Bertram Abel Smith, only s of Col Anthony Abel Smith, OBE, of Stoneham Lodge, Stowmarket, Suffolk, and has issue:

2a *Belinda Patricia; *b* 24 June 1946

3a *Annabella; *b* 2 Nov 1947; *m* 1975 *James Desmond Buxton (*see* BUXTON, Bt)

1 Harriet Jane, DBE (1929); *b* 12 March 1880; *m* 9 July 1901 Sir John Ritchie Findlay, 1st Bt, KBE (*qv*), and *d* 24 July 1954, leaving issue

Sir EDMUND's nephew,

Sir John Edmund Backhouse, 3rd Bt; *b* 30 April 1909; Maj RA WW II; *m* 3 June 1937 Jean Marie Frances (*m* 2nd 28 Feb 1953 (*divorce* 1966) William Nicol Gray, CMG, DSO, er s of Dr William Gray, of W Hartlepool, and had further issue; *m* 3rd Norman Sharpe), only dau of Lt-Col Gavin Robert Vernon Hume Gore, MC, and *d* of wounds Normandy 29 Aug 1944, leaving issue:

1 Sir JONATHAN ROGER BACKHOUSE, **4th and present Bt**

2 +OLIVER RICHARD [Oliver Backhouse Esq, 141 Quickley Lane, Chorleywood, Herts WD3 5PD]; *b* 18 July 1941; heir presumptive; *educ* Ampleforth and RMA Sandhurst; *m* 14 Dec 1970 *Gillian Irene, only dau of L W Lincoln, of 8 Sandy Lodge Court, Northwood, Middx, and adopted a s and dau

1 *Jenifer Ann [Mrs Arthur Reed, Flat 4, 69 Charlwood St, London SW1V 4PG]; *b* 24 March 1938; *m* 25 April 1959 Arthur Wreford Reed (*d* 1989), 2nd s of A A G Reed, of Christchurch NZ, and has issue:

(1) *Dominic Wreford; *b* 1 April 1962

(2) *Rupert Wreford; *b* 8 Dec 1964

(1) *Catherine Anna; *b* 17 Jan 1960

(2) *Suzanne Belinda; *b* 6 March 1961; *m* 1 May 1992 *Guido Lombardo, er s of Remo Lombardo, of Paris, and has:
1a *Giacomo Willoughby; *b* 23 Sept 1996
1a *Isabella Mariantonietta; *b* 23 Sept 1996
2 Jane Elizabeth; *b* 13 May 1943; *d* 17 March 1946
3 *Judith Mary [Mrs Filippo Lo Giudice, via di Sta. Eufemia II, 00187 Rome, Italy]; *b* posthumously 20 Feb 1945; *m* 1st 9 Aug 1967 (*divorce* 1971) Garth Bently Gibson, only s of Burchell Gibson and Mrs Ena Fraser; *m* 2nd 26 May 1973 *Filippo Lo Giudice, er s of Avvocato — Lo Giudice, of Rome, and has:
(1) *Barbaro; *b* 1982
(1) *Barbara; *b* 1975
(2) *Francesca; *b* 1987

BACON

Arms: Gules on a chief argent, two mullets pierced sable. **Crest**: A boar passant ermine. **Motto**: *Mediocria firma* ('Moderation is stable'). **Creations:** Bt. (E) 2 May 1611 and 29 July 1627.

SIR NICHOLAS HICKMAN PONSONBY BACON, 14TH BT, of Redgrave, Co Suffolk, and **15TH BT**, of Mildenhall, Co Suffolk [Sir Nicholas Bacon Bt, Raveningham Hall, Norwich, Norfolk NR14 6NS]; *b* 17 May 1953; *s* f 1982, also as Premier Baronet of England; *educ* Eton and Dundee U (MA); Page of Honour to HM THE QUEEN 1966–69, barrister Gray's Inn; *m* 1981 *Susan, dau of Raymond Dinnis, of Edenbridge, Kent, and has issue:
1 +HENRY HICKMAN; *b* 23 April 1984
2 +Edmund; *b* 1986
3 +Nathaniel; *b* 1989
4 +Thomas Castell; *b* 1992

Lineage: Sir NICHOLAS BACON, PC, of Redgrave Hall, Suffolk, and Gorhambury, Herts; *b* 1510; Ld Keeper Gt Seal 1558–Feb 1578/9; *m* 1st Jane, dau of William Fernley, of W Creting, Suffolk, and had:
1 NICHOLAS (Sir), **1st Bt**
2 Nathaniel (Sir), KB, of Stiffkey, Norfolk; *m* 1st Anne, illegitimate dau of Sir Meautys Thomas Gresham, the financier; *m* 2nd Dorothy, dau of Sir George Hopton, and by his 1st w had three daus
3 Edward, of Shrubland Hall, Suffolk; *m* Helen, dau and heiress of Thomas Littel, of Shrubland Hall, Ipswich; ancestor of the BACONs of Shrubland Hall and Earlham
Sir NICHOLAS *m* 2nd Anne, dau of Sir Anthony Cooke, of Gidea Hall, Essex, and *d* 20 Feb 1578/9 leaving:
4 Anthony; *d* unm
5 FRANCIS BACON, 1st and last VISCOUNT ST ALBAN [*sic*], so *cr* 27 Jan 1620/1, as also earlier 12 July 1618 BARON OF VERULAM, Co Hertford (both E), PC (1616–25), QC (1595), KC (1603); *b* 22 Jan 1560/1; *educ* Trin Coll Cambridge and Gray's Inn; MP Melcombe Regis 1584–86, Taunton 1586–March 1586/7, Liverpool 1588–March 1588/9, Middx 1592–93, Ipswich Oct 1597–Feb 1597/8, Oct-Dec 1601 and March 1603/4–Feb 1610/1 and Cambridge U April-June 1614, ktd 1603, Slr-Gen 1607–13, Clerk Cncl Star Chamber 1608, Cncllr Colony of Virginia 1609, Attorney-Gen 1613–17, Ld Keeper Gt Seal March 1616/7–Jan 1617/8, Ld Chllr Jan 1617/8–21 (by the close of his term of office he had been fined £40,000 (almost £2m in late-1990s terms) and imprisoned Tower of London for bribery, pardoned Jan 1620/1); *m* 10 May 1606 Alice (*m* 2nd 20 April 1626 Sir John Underhill and *d* 29 June 1655), dau and coheir of Benedict Barnham, Alderman London, and *dsp* 9 April 1626, when his titles expired
Sir NICHOLAS BACON's est s,
Sir Nicholas Bacon, 1st Bt (E), so *cr* 22 May 1611 (the first ever of the new order); *b* 1540; Ld of several manors and advowsons in Norfolk and Suffolk, ktd 1578; *m* 1564 Anne (*d* 19 Sept 1616), dau and heiress of Edmund Butts, of Thornage, Norfolk, and *d* 12 Nov 1624, leaving issue:
1 **Sir Edmund Bacon, 2nd Bt**, MP Norfolk; *m* Phillippa Wotton (*d* 1 Oct 1626), dau and coheir of 1st and last Baron Wotton of Marley, and *dsp* 10 April 1649
2 **Sir Robert Bacon, 3rd Bt**; *m* 1st Anne (*bur* 27 Sept 1640), dau of Sir John Peyton, 1st Bt, of Isleham, and had, with other issue:
(1) Robert; *m* Catherine, dau of Grave Violet, of Pinkney House, Norfolk, and *dvp* 25 Aug 1652, leaving, with three daus:
1a **Sir Edmund Bacon, 4th Bt**; *m* 1650 Elizabeth (*m* 2nd 1686 John Tate, Serjeant-at-law), dau and coheir of Sir Robert Crane, Bt, of Chilton, Suffolk, and *dspms* 12 Sept 1685, having had, with six s and six other daus:
1b Frances; *m* Walter Norborne, of Calne, Wilts
2b Elizabeth; *m* William Ettrick, of the Middle Temple
3b Susannah; *m* Charles Morris, of Loddington, Leicestershire
4b Philippa; *m* her cousin **Sir Edmund Bacon, 4th Bt**, of Gillingham (*see* below)
(2) Butts; *m* Catherine, dau and coheir of Sir John Tracey, of Stanhoe, Norfolk, and *d* Jan 1662, having had:
1a **Sir Robert Bacon, 5th Bt**; sold Redgrave to Ld Chf Justice Holt and moved to Garboldisham; *m* Elizabeth (*d* 21 Dec 1686), dau of Daniel Chandler, and *d* 31 Jan 1704, leaving issue:
1b **Sir Edmund Bacon, 6th Bt**; MP Norfolk; *m* 27 Nov 1712 Mary (*d* 14 Sept 1727), dau of Sir Robert Kemp, Bt, and sole heir of her mother, Letitia, dau of Sir Robert King, of Great Thurlow, and *dspm* 30 April 1755
3 **Sir Butts Bacon, 1st Bt**, of Mildenhall, Suffolk (E), so *cr* 29 July 1627; *m* Dorothea (*d* 4 Sept 1657), dau of Sir Henry Warner, of Mildenhall, and widow of Robert Jermyn, and *d* 29 May, 1661 leaving issue:
(1) **Sir Henry Butts Bacon, 2nd Bt**, of Herringfleet, Suffolk; *m* Barbara, dau of William Gooch, of Mettringham, Suffolk, and *d c* 1671, leaving a dau (Anne, *m* her cousin Sir RICHARD BACON, 3rd and last Bt, of Gillingham; *see* below)
1a **Sir Henry Bacon, 3rd Bt**, of Gillingham, Norfolk, and Herringfleet; *m* 29 June 1671 Sarah (*d* 3 Feb 1727), dau of Sir John Castleton, 2nd Bt, of Shipdom, Norfolk, and Sturston, Suffolk, and was *bur* 13 Jan 1685/6, leaving issue:
1b **Sir Edmund Bacon, 4th Bt**, of Gillingham; *bapt* 6 April 1672; MP Orford 1700–08; *m* 1st Dec 1688 his cousin Philippa (*bur* 12 July 1710), 4th dau and coheir of **Sir Edmund Bacon, 4th Bt**, of Redgrave, and had issue:
1c **Sir Edmund Bacon, 5th Bt**; *b* 7 Aug 1692; MP Thetford 1727–38; *m* 7 Nov 1724 Susan, dau of Sir Isaac Rebow, and *d* 4 Oct 1738, leaving a dau (Susan *m* Francis Schutz)
1d **Sir Edmund Bacon, 6th Bt**; *b* 7 Aug 1725; *d* unm 6 April 1750
2c **Sir Henry Bacon, 7th Bt**; *b* 5 Oct 1693; *d* unm April 1753
3c **Sir Richard Bacon, 7th Bt**, of Redgrave (as which *s* cousin 1755), and **8th Bt**, of Mildenhall (as which had *s* er bro 1753); united the btcies of both branches of the family; *b* 22 Feb 1695; *m* 1st 29 Dec 1720 Bridget Mayhew (*d* 6 Jan 1725/6); *m* 2nd 18 July 1729 Lucy (*d* 17 Aug 1765), a coheir of the Barony of FitzWalter (*qv*), dau of Thomas Gardiner, of Tolleshunt, Essex, and *dsps* 26 March 1773
1b (cont.) **Sir Edmund** *m* 2nd 16 April 1713 Mary, dau of John Castell, of Raveningham, Norfolk, and *d* 10 July 1721, leaving further issue:
4c Castell, of Raveningham; *b* 1713; *m* Elizabeth, dau of Richard Dashwood, of Cley, Norfolk, and *d* 13 April 1770, leaving:
1d EDMUND (Sir), **8th** and **9th Bt**
2d Dashwood; *b* 1752; *m* Anne Barbara Ogilvie, of St Christopher's, and *d* 1812, leaving:
1e Edmund C; Capt RN; had:
1f Katherine Elizabeth; *m* 22 April 1847 John Thomas (*see* THOMAS, Bt, of Wenvoe) and *d* 25 May 1886
1c Mary; *m* Philip Bedingfeld
4 Nicholas, of Gillingham, Norfolk; *m* 1st Anne, dau of Sir James Weston, Baron of the Exchequer, and had issue; *m* 2nd 26 Oct 1622 Margaret, dau of Eustace Darcy, of Bury St Edmunds, and had:
(1) Anne; *m* 23 June 1636, as his 1st w, Sir John Rous, 1st Bt (*see* STRADBROKE, E)
(1) Sir NICHOLAS BACON, 1st Bt (E), so *cr* 7 Feb 1661/2, of Gillingham; *bapt* 31 Oct 1623; *m* 31 May 1647 Elizabeth (*m* 2nd 14 April 1670 Sir William Godbold), dau of Richard Freston, of Mendham, Norfolk, and *d* 3 Aug 1666, leaving issue:
1a Sir EDMUND BACON, 2nd Bt; *d* unm (*bur* 5 Nov 1683)
2a Sir RICHARD BACON, 3rd and last Bt; *m* his cousin Anne, dau of **Sir Henry Bacon, 2nd Bt**, of Mildenhall (*see above*), and was *dsp* 8 Oct 1685, when the btcy expired and the Gillingham estate passed to his w's family
5 Nathaniel (Sir), KB of Culford Hall, Suffolk; painter, Rector Great Ryburgh; *m* Jane (*d* 1 July 1627), dau of Hercules Meautys and widow of Sir William Cornwallis, and had two daus (Anne, *m* 1st Sir Thomas Meautys; *m* 2nd Sir Harbottle Grimston (*see* VERULAM E); Jane, *d* unm), *dspm*
1 Elizabeth *m* by 1600 Sir Robert Mansel (*see* MANSEL, Bt)
The 7th/8th Bt's nephew,
Sir Edmund Bacon, 8th and **9th Bt**; *b* 14 Oct 1749; *m* 29 Jan 1778 Anne (*d* 26 Aug 1813), est dau of Sir William Beauchamp-Proctor, 1st Bt (*qv*), and *d* 5 Sept 1820, leaving, with other issue:
1 **Sir Edmund Bacon, 9th** and **10th Bt**; *b* 6 July 1779; *m* 27 Aug 1801 his cousin Mary Anne Elizabeth (*d* 24 Oct 1820), dau of Dashwood Bacon, of Ottery St Mary, Devon, and *d* 30 May 1864, leaving two s (*dsp*) and three daus
2 Nicholas; *b* 6 June 1786; *m* 14 Oct 1813 Jane (*d* 1888), 2nd dau of Alexander Bowker, of Lynn, and *d* 9 Feb 1863, leaving issue:
(1) HENRY HICKMAN (Sir), **10th** and **11th Bt**
(2) Francis (Rev), of The Hall, Much Hadham; *b* 17 Feb 1824; *m* 19 June 1855 Caroline Cecilia (*d* 6 Oct 1897), 4th dau of Peter Clement Cazalet, of Kemp Town, Brighton, and *d* 28 June 1882, leaving, with other issue:
1a Reginald Cazalet (Rev); *b* 3 Jan 1861; *educ* Trin Coll Cambridge (MA); *m* 16 July 1890 May Blanche (*d* 5 April 1942), 2nd dau of Rev William Rimington, Vicar Norton, Norfolk, Rector Gilston Harlow 1890–99, and *d* 27 March 1927, leaving issue:
1b Francis Rimington, Capt, Scottish Rifles; *b* 29 June 1891; *educ* Trin Coll Cambridge (BA); *m* 11 June 1919 Winifred Marie (*d* 26 Dec 1973),

dau of Col George Henry Brook Coats, CB, of 5 Powis Square, Brighton, and *d* 13 Aug 1947, leaving issue:

1c +Roger David Coats [Roger Bacon Esq, 2 Caledon Rd, Poole, Dorset BH14 9NN]; *b* 18 July 1922; *educ* Downside and Trin Coll Cambridge; -Capt Irish Gds; *m* 8 Feb 1947 *Phyllis Eleanore Claire, dau of Roland Oliver, of Hong Kong, and has:

1d *Sarah Antina Oliver; *b* 24 Jan 1948

2d *Fiona Jane Oliver; *b* 4 June 1950

3d *Veronica Claire; *b* 26 July 1953

4d *Diana Mary; *b* 21 Sept 1958

5d *Jennifer Lindsay; *b* 26 Oct 1963

2c +Anthony Peter Coats [Dr Anthony Bacon, 10 Buccleuch Rd, Branksome Park, Poole, Dorset BH13 6LE]; *b* 23 Aug 1924; *educ* Downside and Trin Coll Cambridge; physician Scarborough Hospitals Gp, MD, FRCP; *m* 6 Dec 1947 *Helen, MB, BChir, dau of Harold Jaques, of Westfield, Bradford, and has:

1d +Hugh Francis [Hugh Bacon Esq, Les Ruettes Farm, LeGron, St Saviours, Guernsey, CI]; *b* 16 March 1952; *educ* Downside and Trin Coll Cambridge; *m* 1 July 1977 *Tania Mary Smart and has:

1e +Thomas Hugh; *b* 3 April 1981

1e *Joanna Mary; *b* 30 July 1979

2e *Marina Tania; *b* 3 Oct 1983

3e *Susannah Helen; *b* 3 Feb 1991

2d +Peter Jaques FRCS [Peter Bacon Esq, Poplar House Farm, Snainton, nr Scarborough, N Yorks]; *b* 21 Sept 1953; *educ* Downside and St Thomas's Hosp Medical Sch; *m* 10 Dec 1977 *Susan, dau of David Montague Rowse, and has:

1e +Nicholas David; *b* 30 May 1980

2e +George Anthony Hugh; *b* 8 Jan 1986

1e *Diana Mary Louise; *b* 5 Jan 1982

2e *Annabel Jane Elizabeth; *b* 18 April 1984

1d *Annette Susan; [Mrs Paul Rosen, Rupert's Bell, Bell Lane, Henley-on Thames, Oxon]; *b* 13 Oct 1959; FRCS; *m* 19 Aug 1985 *Paul Henry Rosen and has:

1e *Harry Samuel; *b* 30 May 1996

2d *Patricia Margaret; [Mrs Paul Kelly, The Coach House, Little Gaddesden, Herts HP4 1PH] *b* 21 Aug 1962; *m* 7 May 1988 *Paul Kelly and has:

1e *Frederick George Bacon; *b* 22 April 1997

1 Jane; *m* 9 May 1832 William Hutton, of Gate Burton (*d* 5 Dec 1877), leaving issue

2 Anne Elizabeth; *m* 7 May 1837 John Henry Barker (*d* 28 Jan 1876), of Bakewell, Derbys, and *d* 1899, leaving issue

The 9th/10th Bt's nephew,

Sir Henry Hickman Bacon, 10th and 11th Bt; *b* 5 April 1820; Capt 3rd Dragoon Gds, High Sheriff Lincs 1867; *m* 17 March 1853 Elizabeth (*d* 29 Nov 1885), dau and coheir of Sir Thomas Beckett, 3rd Bt (*see* GRIMTHORPE, B), and *d* 14 Nov 1872, leaving issue:

1 **Sir Hickman Beckett Bacon, 11th** and **12th Bt**, JP, DL; *b* 14 April 1855; Lt Gren Gds, CA parts of Lindsey, Lincs, High Sheriff 1887, Chm CC 1914–24; *d* unm 13 April 1945

2 NICHOLAS HENRY (Sir), **12th** and **13th Bt**

3 Edmund; *b* 15 Jan 1860; Lt KRRC; *d* 13 Aug 1886

4 Thomas Walter, JP (Essex); *b* 16 Sept 1863; *m* 30 May 1901 Edith Mary (*d* 18 April 1950), dau of Alexander Samuel Leslie-Melville, of Branston Hall, Lincs (*see* LEVEN and MELVILLE, E), and *d* 2 Dec 1950, leaving issue:

(1) +Anthony Walter, F/Lt AAF [Anthony Bacon Esq, Leiston Old Abbey, Leiston, Suffolk IP16 4RF]; *b* 10 March 1902; *educ* Eton and Trin Coll Cambridge (BA 1923); *m* 9 Jan 1941 Lola Mary Stanley (*d* 15 Feb 1998), yr dau of Charles Stanley Martin, of Dowlais, Glamorgan, and has:

1a +Christopher Nicholas [Christopher Bacon Esq, Boundary Farm, Framsden, Stowmarket, Suffolk]; *b* 5 Sept 1945; *educ* Eton; *m* 1977 *Margaret Ann, yst dau of J L W Craig, of the Wheelwrights, Brandeston, Woodbridge, Suffolk, and has issue:

1b +Nathaniel John; *b* 29 Aug 1978

1b *Catharine Anne; *b* 1979

(2) Francis Thomas, OBE (1967); *b* 21 Dec 1904; *educ* Eton and Trin Coll Cambridge (BA 1925, MA 1946); Churchill Gold Medal of Soc Engrs 1973, consultant on fuel cells to Energy Conversion Ltd, Basingstoke, FRS 1973; *m* 4 Aug 1934 *Barbara Winifred [Mrs Francis Bacon, 34 High St, Little Shelford, Cambs CB2 5ES], yst dau of Godfrey Keppel Papillon, of Barrasford, Northumberland, and *d* 1992, having had:

1a Francis Richard; *b* 1 July 1937; *educ* Eton; *d unm* 16 April 1960, accidentally drowned

2a +Edward Thomas Godfrey, OBE [Edward Bacon Esq OBE, 17 Abingdon Court, Abingdon Villas, London W8 6BS]; *b* 11 Dec 1939; *educ* Eton and Fitzwilliam Ho Cambridge (BA 1963, MA 1966); FRS; *m* 1980 *Angelina Mary, dau of Alphonse Morhange, and has:

1b +Francis Edward Alphonse; *b* 1982

1b *Veronica Elizabeth; *b* 1984

1a *(Elizabeth) Daphne [Mrs Giles Vivian-Neal, Welbeck Ho, Brooke, Norfolk]; *b* 13 Oct 1935; *m* 30 Aug 1958 *Giles Arthur Vivian-Neal, yr s of Arthur Westall Vivian-Neal, MC, JP, DL, of Poundisford Park, Taunton, Somerset, and has issue:

1b *Henry Arthur; *b* 25 Jan 1963

2b *James Francis; *b* 12 Sept 1968

1b *Gina Rosemary; *b* 2 July 1960

2b *Marianne Clare; *b* 17 Sept 1961

(3) Christopher Henry; *b* 12 Feb 1906; *educ* Eton and Trin Coll Cambridge (BA 1927); *m* 15 June 1940 Diana Sybil Richmond (*d* 27 Aug 1995), dau of Frederick Richmond Brown (*see* BROWN Bt), and *d* 26 Aug 1956, leaving:

1a +Richard Anthony [Richard Bacon Esq, Devondale, Beh's Lane, Uralba Rd, Alstonville, NSW 2477, Australia]; *b* 23 May 1943; *educ* Stowe; *m* 1973 *Doreen Nan, dau of John Keillar, and has issue:

1b *Georgina Louise; *b* 1974

2b *Philippa Jane; *b* 1977

2a +Tim(othy) Roger [Tim Bacon Esq, Ramsden Farm, Stone, Kent TN30 7JB]; *b* 4 Dec 1947; *educ* Eton; *m* 1985 *Marylyn Rowan Ogilvie, twin dau of Arthur Grant, and has:

1b *Rosalind Sarah; *b* 1987

2b *Laura Charlotte; *b* 1988

1a *Elizabeth Anne [Mrs Pierre Bartlett, Leeswood Hall, Mold, Clwyd]; *b* 15 Feb 1942; *m* 1971 *Pierre Bartlett, twin s of John A Bartlett, of Hatton Lodge, Hatton Heath, Chester, and has issue:

1b *Nicholas Michael; *b* 16 May 1972

2b *Andrew Christopher; *b* 1977

1b *Suzannah Louise; *b* 11 July 1973

1b *Georgina Louise; *b* 1974

5 Richard Castell; *b* 20 Feb 1866; *educ* Eton and Trin Coll Cambridge (BA 1888, MA 1893); High Sheriff Lincs 1914, Capt Roy Defence Corps, Lt Sherwood Rangers Yeo Cav; *d unm* 12 Jan 1961

1 Frances Elizabeth; *m* 28 Dec 1882 Ralph Creyke, of Rawcliffe Hall, Yorks (*d* 16 April 1908), and *d* 2 Feb 1944, leaving issue

2 Mary Rose; *m* 14 Feb 1895 Sir Charles Burton Barrington, 5th Bt (*qv*), and *d* 1 March 1943, leaving issue

The 11th/12th Bt's bro,

Sir Nicholas Henry Bacon, 12th and **13th Bt**, JP (Norfolk); *b* 22 Oct 1857; High Sheriff 1895, Capt 4th Dragoon Gds Egyptian Campaign 1882; *m* 22 June 1893 Constance Alice, CBE (*d* 11 Feb 1962 aged 91), yst dau of Alexander Samuel Leslie Melville, of Branston Hall, Lincs, (*see* LEVEN and MELVILLE, E), and *d* 1 Jan 1947, leaving issue:

1 EDMUND CASTELL (Sir), **13th** and **14th Bt**

1 Margery Frances; *b* 24 Nov 1894; *m* 7 Jan 1920 Lt-Col Sir Charles Samuel Rowley, 6th Bt (*qv*), and *d* 15 March 1977, leaving issue:

2 Albinia Joane; *b* 3 Jan 1897; *m* 9 Jan 1924 Brig Wilson Theodore Oliver Crewdson, CB, RA, (*d* 5 July 1997) s of Wilson Crewdson, of Southside, St Leonards-on-Sea, and *d* 8 Dec 1961, leaving issue

3 Bridget Louisa; *b* 25 Dec 1897; *m* 24 July 1934 Lt-Col William Noel Arnold, MC, TD, s of Charles Arnold

4 Constance Rhoda Elizabeth; *b* 21 Aug 1899; *m* 1 Oct 1919 Gerard William Reginald Fane, DSC, late Capt RAF, of Feering Place, Kelvedon, Colchester, Essex, 2nd s of Sydney Algernon Fane (*see* WESTMORLAND E), and *d* 26 March 1969, leaving issue

5 Katherine Mary; *b* 15 July 1906; *m* 22 July 1930 John Fowell Buxton, est s of Henry Fowell Buxton, of Easneye, Ware, Herts (*see* BUXTON, Bt), and *d* 27 March 1970, leaving issue

The 12th/13th Bt's est s:

Sir Edmund Castell Bacon, 13th and **14th Bt**; JP (Norfolk 1944), DL (1939); *b* 18 March 1903; *educ* Eton and Trin Coll Cambridge; Ld Lt Norfolk 1949–82, High Steward Norwich Cathedral and Gt Yarmouth, Pro-Chllr UEA, Hon Col 308 (Suffolk and Norfolk Yeo) Field Regt RA (TA) 1961–67, Lt-Col 55th (Suffolk Yeo) AT Regt, RA (TA), WW II (despatches), KStJ, chm Br Sugar Corp 1957–68 and Ag EDC 1966–82, dir Lloyds Bank; *m* 15 Jan 1936 *Priscilla Dora [Priscilla Lady Bacon DL, Orchards, Raveningham, Norfolk], est dau of Col Sir Charles Edward Ponsonby, 1st Bt (*see* DE MAULEY, B), and *d* 1982, leaving:

1 Sir NICHOLAS HICKMAN PONSONBY BACON, **14th and present and 15th and present Bt**

1 Joanna Constance; *b* 12 March 1937; *m* 18 May 1957 Hon Edward Roundell Palmer (*d* 1 Aug 1974), yst s of 3rd Earl of Selborne (*qv*), and had issue

2 *Lavinia Winifred; *b* 7 June 1939; *m* 21 Nov 1972 Stephen Cokayne Gibbs, (*see* ALDENHAM and HUNSDON OF HUNSDON, B)

3 *Elizabeth Albinia [Mrs Ronald Hoare, Roydon Hall, Diss, Norfolk]; *b* 15 Jan 1944; *m* 11 Sept 1971 *Ronald James Hoare, s of Wilfred Hoare, of Orwell House, Milnathorp, Kinross, and has issue:

(1) *Jocelyn Charles Stewart; *b* 1974

(1) *Selina Albinia; *b* 1976

(2) *Nicola Clare; *b* 1977

4 *Sarah; *b* 1 June 1947; *m* 18 July 1970 *Sir Paul Douglas Nicholson and has issue (*see* LAWSON-TANCRED, Bt)

Seat: Raveningham Hall, Raveningham, Norfolk. The Raveningham estate came to the Bacons through Mary, the Castell heiress who was second wife of Sir Edmund, 4th Baronet of the 1627 creation. Her family had held it since a little over half a millennium earlier. The house was completely rebuilt in the early 19th century and added to around the end of the same century with porticos, porches, an oculus in the pediment, a dormer storey and wings outside together with imposing ceilings inside, including a perfectly adequate Adam-style one in the drawing room.

BADDELEY

Arms: Argent a sword erect between two crosses couped gules, on a chief of the last a hind trippant between two garbs or. **Crest:** An arm couped and erect vested azure cuff argent the hand holding an open book buckled and clasped proper between two crosses as in the arms. **Motto:** *In te Domine confido* ('In thee, O Lord, I trust'). **Creation:** Bt. (UK) 24 Nov 1922.

SIR JOHN WOLSEY BERESFORD BADDELEY, 4TH BT, of Lakefield, Parish of St Mary Stoke Newington, Co London [Sir John Baddeley Bt, Springwood, Sandgate Lane, Storrington, Sussex RH20 3HJ]; *b* 27 Jan 1938; *s f* 1979; *educ* Bradfield; *m* 1st12 May 1962 (*divorce* 1992) Sarah Rosalind, only dau of Colin Crofts, of Scarborough, and Mrs John Holman, of 12 Langbury Lane, Ferring, Sussex, and has issue:

1 *Sara Alexander; *b* 4 June 1964; *m* 1989 *Andrew C E Turner, er s of D E Turner, of W Chiltington, Sussex, and has issue:

(1) *Peter Andrew John; *b* 1982

2 *Anna Victoria; *b* 5 Nov 1965; *m* 1992 *Brian A Chambers, est s of D B Chambers, of Rutherglen, Victoria, Australia, and has:

(1) *William; *b* 199–

(2) *Thomas Donald; *b* 18 Feb 1995

3 *Emma; *b* 1972

Sir JOHN 2nd 16 April 1998 *Mrs Carol Quinlan, *née* Greenham

Lineage: JOHN BADDELEY, of Ash Grove Ho, Hackney, Middx; *m* Frances (*d* 4 Jan 1870), dau of James Beresford, of Hackney, and *d* 6 July 1869, leaving issue:

Sir John James Baddeley, 1st Bt (UK), so *cr* 24 Nov 1922, JP (Co London); *b* 22 Dec 1842; Lt and Sheriff City of London 1908–09, Alderman 1912, Ld Mayor 1921–22, ktd 1909; *m* 1st 13 Aug 1868 Mary Elizabeth (*d* 6 Nov 1906), dau of William Locks, of Hackney; *m* 2nd 25 July 1912 Florence Bertha, JP (Middx), DG StJ (*d* 7 April 1962), dau of Joseph Douglas Mathews, DL, FRIBA, FSICC, of Highbury New Park, and *d* 28 June 1926, having had by his 1st w:

1 JOHN WILLIAM (Sir), **2nd Bt**

2 Mark; *b* 1 Dec 1871; *m* 10 Sept 1918 Mabel Annie, dau of John Frederick Trigg, and *d* 15 Oct 1930, leaving issue:

(1) +MARK DAVID; *b* 10 May 1921; heir presumptive; *educ* Cambridge House Sch and Cliftonville Coll Margate

(1) *Mabel Joyce

3 Bernard Beresford; *b* 20 March 1876; *m* 31 July 1900 Ethel Emily (*d* 9 June 1955), dau of Sir David Burnett, 1st Bt (*qv*), and *d* 23 Feb 1956, leaving issue:

(1) Paul Bernard; *b* 31 May 1903; *educ* Charterhouse FCA; *m* 1 June 1954 Barbara Joan (*d* 3 Sept 1968), dau of Harry Tilling Burnett and widow of H J Hobson

(2) +Allan Beresford; *b* 7 May 1909; *educ* The Leys Sch and Christ's Coll Cambridge (BA 1931, MA 1926); late Capt RE; *m* 4 April 1945 *(Dorothy) Ronwen, dau of H J Head, of Four Marks, Alton, Hants, and has issue:

1a +Paul Allan; *b* 15 Aug 1948; *educ* Kingswood Sch Bath; *m* 1977 *Lesley, dau of R G Springett and has:

1b +Thomas Sands; *b* 1978

2b +Samuel Joseph; *b* 1980

2a +John Burnett; *b* 25 June 1951

1a *Rozanne Mary; *b* 11 April 1946; *m* 1973 *Ashley Beeby and has:

1b *Morgan Douglas; *b* 1978

2b *Joshua John; *b* 1981

(1) Marjorie Gertrude Baddeley; *m* 11 Sept 1935 William John Hunt Montgomery Beattie, MD, FRCS, FRCOG, er s of John Montgomery Beattie, of Wash Common, Newbury, Berks

4 Sydney; *b* 6 Oct 1878; slr; *d* unm 2 Jan 1968

5 Allan; *b* 23 May 1884; Lt-Cdr RN, served WW I and II, author and journalist; *m* 22 Dec 1914 Constance, dau of Walter Baddeley, of Woodford Green, and *dsp* 4 Feb 1943

1 Mary Frances; *m* 28 Sept 1898 Walter Ellis (*d* 1917), s of Thomas Henry Ellis, and had issue

2 Edith Florence; *m* 9 April 1896 Maj Walter Henry Wellesman, TD, JP (Herts), of Dudley House, Manor Rd, Barnet, barrister, and *d* 10 Nov 1919, leaving issue

3 Doris; *m* Herbert Vivian Beedell and *d* his widow 10 Jan 1938

4 Ruth; *m* 1902 Herbert Hitchcock and *dsp* 1964

The 1st Bt's est s,

Sir (John) William Baddeley, 2nd Bt, of Lakefield; *b* 24 Aug 1869; *educ* privately; Alderman Cripplegate Ward 1924–30, Lt City London, Master Stationers' and Newspaper Makers' Co 1937; *m* 3 April 1894 Catherine Mary Ann (*d* 7 Sept 1956), dau of Matthew Shaw, of Stamford Hill, London, and *d* 28 Dec 1951, having had issue:

1 Sir JOHN BERESFORD BADDELEY, 3rd Bt, for whom *see* further below

2 William Shaw, MBE (1942), of The Mill House, Mugswell, Chipstead, Surrey; *b* 15 Sept 1903; *educ* Lancing; S/Ldr RAFVR WW II; *m* 26 March 1935 *Mary Joyce Somers, dau of Sidney Somers Brister, of Kings Walk Ho, Tadworth, and *dsp* 22 April 1971

1 Kathleen Mary; *b* 15 Jan 1895; *m* 21 Feb 1918 David John Adams-Lewis, MB, BS, of Hafren Hall, Carmarthen, s of Benjamin Adams-Lewis, and *d* 16 Oct 1951

2 Betty Mary, JP (Wilts); *b* 10 June 1909; *m* 5 Nov 1938 Donald George Matthews Blanchard, s of Thomas George Blanchard, of The Manor, Burbage, Wilts, and *d* 20 Oct 1996, leaving:

(1) *Peter Donald [Peter Blanchard Esq, Manor Farm, Burbage, Wilts]; *b* 12 March 1945; *educ* Marlborough and Wye Coll Kent (BSc 1967); NDA; *m* 10 July 1982 *Pamela Anne, dau of Basil Constanduros, of Burbage, and has:

1a *Thomas Peter; *b* 1984

(1) *Diana Mary, JP (Wilts) [Mrs Simon Faux JP, Culley's Farm, Clench Common, Marlborough, Wilts]; *b* 28 July 1939; *m* 11 Jan 1964 *Simon John Valsey Faux, s of Sydney Ewart Faux, of Mersey Hampton, Cirencester, Glos

(2) *Anne Catherine [Mrs Timothy Holgate, 4 Manor Farm Cottages, Etchilhampton, Wilts SN10 3JR]; *b* 21 July 1942; *m* 7 April 1973 *Timothy David Holgate and has:

1a *Mark Edward; *b* 30 June 1975

1a *Clare Susannah; *b* 25 May 1977

2a *Amy Louisa; *b* 22 Sept 1979

(3) *Mary Patricia [Mrs Peter Stibbard, The Old House, Preston, Ramsbury, Wilts]; *b* 19 May 1950; *m* 1978 *Peter Stibbard and has issue:

1a *Andrew George; *b* 1983

The 2nd Bt's est s,

Sir John Beresford Baddeley, 3rd Bt; *b* 23 Nov 1899; *educ* Lancing and RMC Sandhurst; md Baddeley Bros (London); *m* 4 June 1929 Nancy Winifred (*d* 25 Oct 1994), dau of Thomas Wolsey, of Smallburgh Hall, Norwich, and *d* 27 Jan 1979, leaving issue:

1 Sir JOHN WOLSEY BERESFORD BADDELEY, **4th and present Bt**

1 *Susan (Sue) Catherine [Mrs Anthony Harris, Corner Cottage, Middle St, Petworth, W Sussex]; *b* 26 Jan 1932; *m* 27 Oct 1956 *Anthony Philip Harris, er s of R M Harris, of Red Garth, Reigate, Surrey, and has issue:

(1) *Ian Robert Beresford; *b* 7 Feb 1958; *m* 1988 *Rosie, dau of Rotin Tebaki, of the Solomon Islands, and has:

1a *William Atoia Beresford; *b* 1992

1a *Emily Kirika; *b* 1989

2a *Lucy Teromita; *b* 1993

(2) *Michael Anthony; *b* 14 Sept 1959; *m* 1988 *Joanna Mary, dau of R-Adml Peter Marsden, of Niton, IoW, and has:

1a *Thomas Wolsey; *b* 1991

2a *Henry Beresford; *b* 1993

3a *Edward Holman; *b* 1996

(3) *David John Tindall; *b* 7 May 1961; *m* 1989 *Deborah L M, dau of R H Green, of Ludlow, Salop, and has:

1a *Robert Anthony; *b* 1991

1a *Isabelle Margaret; *b* 1990

(4) *Peter Wolsey; *b* 11 March 1964; *m* 1989 *Amelia Angela, dau of Nigel Azis of W Burton, W Sussex, and has:

1a *Jack Wolsey; *b* 1991

2a *Nicholas Peter; *b* 1993

(5) *Andrew Charles; *b* 4 July 1966

(1) *Lucinda Jane; *b* 15 Feb 1963; *m* 1991 *Andre John Neumann, s of R Neumann, of Wellington, NZ, and has:

1a *Benjamin Charles; *b* 1993

2a *Fergus Guy; *b* 1997

(2) *(Shirley) Ann [Mrs Alan Grout-Smith, Saddlers, Church Lane, Bury, W Sussex]; *b* 29 Oct 1934; *m* 7 April 1956 *Alan Richard Anthony Grout-Smith, yr s of P Grout-Smith, of Aldwick, Sussex, and has issue:

1a *John Alan Beresford; *b* 4 March 1962

1a *Nicola Susan; *b* 8 Feb 1958

2a *Sally Caroline; *b* 16 Jan 1960

BADEN-POWELL

Arms: Quarterly, 1st and 4th, per fess or and argent a lion rampant guardant gules between two tilting spears erect proper (for POWELL); 2nd and 3rd, argent a lion rampant proper, on the head a crown vallary or, between four crosses patées gules and as many fleurs-de-lys azure alternately (for BADEN). **Crests:** 1 A lion passant or, in the paw a broken tilting spear in bend proper, pendent therefrom by a riband gules, an escutcheon resting on a wreath sable, charged with a pheon or (for POWELL), 2 Out of a crown vallary or a demi-lion rampant gules, on the head a like crown, charged on the shoulder with a cross patée argent and supporting with the paws a sword erect proper, pommel and hilt gold (for BADEN). **Supporters:** Dexter, an officer of the 13th/18th Hussars in full dress, his sword drawn over his shoulder proper; sinister, a Boy Scout supporting a staff, also proper. **Motto:** *Ar nyd yw pwyll pyd yw* ('Where there is danger will be a Powell'). **Creations:** B. (UK) 17 Sept 1929), Bt. (UK) 4 Dec 1922.

THE 3RD BARON BADEN-POWELL, of Gilwell, Co Essex, and a **Baronet** (Sir Robert Crause Baden-Powell, Bt) [The Rt Hon The Lord Baden-Powell, Clandon Manor Farm, Back Lane, East Clandon, Guildford, Surrey GU4 7SA]; *b* 15 Oct 1936; *s f* 1962; *educ* Bryanston; served RN 1955–57, V-Pres Scout Assoc 1982– (Ch Scouts Commissioner 1965–82, pres W Yorks Scout Cncl 1972–88, memb Ctee Cncl Scout Assoc 1972–78 (memb 1965–)), chm: Quarter Horse Racing UK 1985–88 and Br Quarter Horse Assoc 1990 (memb Cncl 1984–90), pres Camping and Caravanning Club 1992–, former dir Boulton Bldg; *m* 1 Aug 1963 *Patience Hélène Mary, CBE (1986) (*b* 27 Oct 1936; *educ* St Peter's Diocesan Sch Bulawayo; V-Pres Girl Guides Assoc 1990– (Ch Commissioner 1980–85, Internat Commissioner 1975–79), pres: Cwlth Youth Exchange Cncl 1982–86, Surrey Cncl for Voly Youth Servs 1986– and Nat Playbus Assoc 1979–, dir: Laurentian Financial Gp 1981– and Fieldguard Ltd 1986–, tstee Painshill Pk Tst 1992–, sometime dir Nynex Cable Communications Surrey Ltd, patron: Surrey Antiques Fair 1969– and Woodlarks Camp Site for Disabled 1978–), dau of Maj Douglas Myers Batty (*d* 1982), of Melsetter, Rhodesia (now Zimbabwe)

Lineage: ROBERT POWLE/POWELL, of Mildenhall, Suffolk; *b c* 1508; attorney; *m* Johane (*bur* 6 March 1590), dau of John Dobson, of Mildenhall, and *d* before 1589, leaving a 3rd s:

BARNABIE POWELL; *b* by 1543; *m c* 1573 Agnes (*bur* 8 Sept 1594), dau of John Webb, of Mussels, in Barton Mills, Suffolk, where he had already settled, and *d* 1602, leaving an est s:

DAVID POWELL; *b c* 1580; *m* 22 May 1615 Agnes Ellis (*d c* 1657) and *d* 1656, leaving a s:

DAVID POWELL; sold the Barton Mills property 1679 and moved to Burwell, Cambs; *m* Bridget (*bur* 18 July 1708) and was *bur* 6 April 1694, leaving a s:

JOHN POWELL; *b* Barton Mills 1662; yeoman, moved to Hawsted, Suffolk; *m* Katharine (*d* 1752), dau of Henry Murton, of Boxted, Suffolk, and *d* Hawsted 1725, having had issue, with four yr sons and a dau:

DAVID POWELL, of Clapton, Middx; *b* 27 Jan 1695; went to London 1712, merchant in Old Broad St, Ld of the Manor of Wattisfield, Suffolk; *m* 27 April 1723 Susanna (*b* 2 April 1696; *d* 20 Aug 1762), dau and coheir of Edward Thistlethwayte, of Winterslow, Wilts, and The Close, Sarum, Registrar to Bp Salisbury, by his w Susanna, dau of Andrew Baden, of New Sarum, and *d* Clapton 10 Feb 1784, leaving issue:

1 DAVID POWELL, for whom *see* further below

2 Baden POWELL, of Bench House, Loughton, Essex; *bapt* 29 March 1731; *d* unm Clapton 31 Aug 1802

3 Thomas POWELL, of The Chestnuts, Tottenham, Middx; *bapt* 24 Aug 1735; *m* 1st 5 May 1770 Catherine (*d* 27 June 1780), dau of Dr Smith, physician to CATHERINE II ('The Great') of Russia, and had issue; *m* 2nd 11 Aug 1786 Clarissa (*d* 30 Jan 1847), dau of James Madden, of Fulham, and *d* 5 Nov 1820, having by her had issue

4 James POWELL, of Wattisfield, Suffolk; *bapt* 29 July 1737; *m* 8 Nov 1775 Anne (*d* 27 Aug 1831), dau of Rev Thomas Cornthwaite, 46 yrs Vicar Hackney, and *d* 25 Feb 1824, having had, with other issue:

(1) Rev Thomas Baden POWELL; *b* 14 Oct 1786; *educ* Oriel Coll Oxford (BA 1808, Fell 1808–12); rector Newick, Prebendary Chichester; *m* 22 May 1811 Sarah Louisa (*d* 13 April 1835), dau of Rev Nathaniel Cotton, rector Thornby, Northants, and *d* 25 April 1868, having had, with other issue:

1a Rev William POWELL; *b* 25 Jan 1817; *educ* Exeter Coll Oxford (BA 1839); barrister Inner Temple 1846, rector Newick 1868; *m* 2 Nov 1862 Isabella Vandamme Mackenzie (*d* May 1886) and *d* 28 Jan 1885, leaving issue:

1b Thomas Baden POWELL, of Newick, Bradfield 1877–79 and of New Coll Oxford; *b* 2 Jan 1864

2b William George POWELL, of Newick, Bradfield 1877–82; *b* 25 Jan 1865; *m* 24 Aug 1899 Maida Randall (*d* 1911) and had issue:

1c Thomas Baden POWELL; *b* Aug 1900

DAVID POWELL (of Clapton)'s est s,

DAVID POWELL, of Little St Helens, London, Homerton, London, and Horton Kirby, Kent; *b* 13 Dec 1725; Treasurer St Luke's Hosp, London, 1794; *m* 15 Aug 1761 Laetitia (*d* 27 April 1801), dau and heiress of John Clark, of St Botolph's, Bishopsgate, and *d* Homerton 31 Jan 1810, having had, with other issue:

1 David, JP, of Bench House, Loughton, Essex; *b* 22 Nov 1764; *m* 1st 20 Dec 1798 Mary (*d* 12 March 1809), only child of Harry Townsend by Mary, dau of Robert Williamson, of Cockermouth, Cumberland, and had issue, with four daus:

(1) Harry Townsend (Rev); *b* 11 Jan 1800; *educ* Harrow and Oriel Coll Oxford (BA 1821); vicar Stretton-on-Dunsmore; *m* 30 Sept 1834 Harriet Elizabeth (*d* 28 June 1881), dau of H Grimes, of Coton House, Warwick, and *d* 13 June 1854, leaving, with other issue:

1a Henry Clark (Rev); *b* 25 Feb 1838; MA, rector Wylye, Wilts; *m* June 1863 Georgina Albinia (*d* 1911), dau of Henry Norris, and *d* 5 May 1901, having had issue

(2) David, of Heath Lodge, Hampstead; *b* 15 Jan 1806; *m* 1st 28 June 1831 Elizabeth Martha (*d* 1 Oct 1833), dau of Joseph Morris, of Ampthill, Beds, and had a dau; *m* 2nd 17 Nov 1837 Caroline (*d* 14 Oct 1865), dau of Thomas Pryor, of Hampstead, and *d* 6 April 1882, having had, with other issue:

1a David; *b* 16 April 1840; Govr Bank of England; *m* July 1867 Lucy Elizabeth (*d* Nov 1902), dau of Arthur Pryor, of Hylands, and *d* Sept 1897, having had issue

2a Henry Pryor; *b* 14 Feb 1847; *m* July 1875 Helena, dau of E U Eddis, and *d* 12 Dec 1905, having had issue

1 (cont.) David Powell, *m* 2nd 9 Aug 1810 Grezell (*d* 21 Feb 1852), dau of Samuel Hoare, of Hampstead, and was *k* by lightning 15 May 1832, having had, with two other sons:

(3) Thomas Edward (Rev); *b* 22 Aug 1823; *educ* Oriel Coll Oxford (BA 1845); Vicar Bisham, Berks; *m* 5 Jan 1847 Emma (*d* 24 Feb 1919), 5th dau of Edgar Corrie (gs of William Corrie, of Dumfries), of Purley Lodge, Croydon, and afterwards of Arlington Manor, Newbury, and *d* 8 Feb 1901, leaving issue

2 Baden, of Langton, and Speldhurst, Tunbridge Wells, Kent; *b* 21 Nov 1767; High Sheriff Kent 1831; *m* 21 Nov 1795 Hester (*d* 7 June 1848), dau of James Powell, of Clapton, and *d* 24 July 1844, leaving issue, with two daus:

(1) Baden (Rev); *b* 22 Aug 1796; *educ* Oxford (MA); vicar Plumstead, Kent, Savilian Prof Geometry Oxford 1827, VPRS, FRAstS, FRGS; *m* 1st 17 July 1821 Eliza (*dsp* 13 March 1836), dau of Vincent Francis Rivaz, of Hackney; *m* 2nd 27 Sept 1837 Charlotte (*d* 14 Oct 1844), dau of William Pope, of Hillindene, Middx, and had issue, with three daus:

1a Baden Henry, CIE; *b* 23 Aug 1841; Judge of Ch Court, Lahore, Conservator of Forests, Punjab, author; *d* unm 2 Jan 1901

(1) (cont.) The Rev Baden Powell *m* 3rd 10 March 1846 Henrietta Grace (*d* 13 Oct 1914), dau of V-Adml W H Smyth, DCL, FRS, and sis of Professor Piazzi Smyth, Astronomer Royal for Scotland, also gniece of 1st Earl Nelson (*qv*), and *d* 11 June 1860, having had issue (with two sons *d* young), all of whom by roy licence 30 April 1902 added the surname BADEN:

2a (Henry) Warrington Smyth, KC; *b* 3 Feb 1847; barrister Inner Temple, Admlty Barrister, Lt RNR; *m* 13 Sept 1913 Cicely Hilda (*d* 7 May 1955), dau of James Farmer, of Brownhills, St Andrews, Fife, and *d* 24 April 1921

3a George Smyth (Sir), KCMG (1888, CMG 1884); *b* 24 Dec 1847; *educ* St Paul's, Marlborough and Balliol Coll Oxford (MA, LLD); MP (C) Liverpool (Kirkdale Div) 1885–98, FRS, author on political, financial and colonial subjects; *m* 8 April 1893 Frances (*d* 29 Oct 1913), dau of Charles Wilson, of Glendouran, Cheltenham, and *d* 20 Nov 1898, leaving issue:

1b Donald Ferlys Wilson; *b* 5 Oct 1897; *educ* Oriel Coll Oxford (MA 1925, BSc 1926); geologist, Sub-Lt RNAS 1916, 2nd Lt Rifle Bde 1917–18, Roy Observer Corps 1939–44; *m* 25 Oct 1924 Muriel Jane Thomson (*d* 16 Dec 1967), dau of James Duncan, of London, and had issue:

1c David Duncan; *b* 20 Jan 1926; *d* 7 Sept 1939

2c *Francis Robert; *b* 16 Sept 1929; *educ* King's Coll Cambridge (MA); Lt RE 1953, ARIBA, AADipl, Pres Architectural Assoc 1968–69; *m* 26 July 1958 *Charlotte Elizabeth, ARIBA, AADipl, yr dau of Digby Percy Cornwall Neave, of Loddon Court, Spencer's Wood, Reading, Berks, and has issue:

1d *Edward James; *b* 5 Feb 1968

2d *Matthew Toby; *b* 7 Jan 1969

1b Maud Kirkdale; *b* 27 July 1895; *m* 23 March 1920 William Harvey Moore, QC (*d* 4 July 1961), est s of W R Moore, of High Bullen, Chulmleigh, N Devon, and had issue

4a Francis Smyth; *b* 29 July 1850; MA Oxford, barrister Inner Temple, painter and sculptor; *m* 28 May 1902 Florence Sydney (*d* 17 Oct 1914), dau of James Watt, and had issue:

1b Robert Harold; *b* 1903; *m* 24 Nov 1932 Annie Elizabeth Spinks and *d* 29 Jan 1998, leaving:

1c *Margaret Mary; *m* 11 July 1962 *Hans Franzke, 2nd s of J Franzke

5a ROBERT STEPHENSON SMYTH, **1st Baron**

6a Baden Fletcher Smyth; *b* 22 May 1860; Maj Scots Gds, served Nile Expdn 1884–85, Gds Camel Corps (medal, clasp, and Khedive's Star), ADC to Sir Anthony Musgrave 1888, ADC and Priv Sec to Sir Henry Norman in Queensland 1889–90, served S African War and WW I, Pres Aeronautical Soc 1902–09; *d* unm 3 Oct 1937

(2) Charles, JP (Kent), of Speldhurst, Tunbridge Wells; *b* 30 July 1807; *m* 28 Oct 1851 Emily Ann (*d* 21 May 1890), dau of James Eyre Watson, of Fillongley Grange, Warwicks, and *d* 17 March 1885, leaving issue

(3) Henry; *b* 6 March 1809; MD Oxford; *m* Jan 1842 Mary Sophia, dau of James Eyre Watson, and *d* May 1867, leaving issue

The Rev Baden POWELL's 5th surv s,

Sir ROBERT STEPHENSON SMYTH POWELL later BADEN-POWELL, **1st Bt**, and **1st Baron Baden-Powell**, OM (1937), GCMG (1927), GCVO (1923, KCVO 1909), KCB (1909, CB 1900), DL (Hants); *b* 22 Feb 1857; *educ* Charterhouse; served India, also Afghanistan 1880–81, Zululand 1888 (despatches, star, Brevet Lt-Col), Ashanti Expdn 1895–96, S African War 1896 (despatches, Brevet Col) and 1899–1901 (commanded defence at Siege of Mafeking 1899–1900: despatches, Maj-Gen), raised 1901 S African Constabulary which he commanded till 1903, Inspector-Gen Cavalry GB and I 1903–07, Divisional-Gen TF 1908–10, founded Boy Scouts 1908 and Girl Guides 1910 (Acclaimed Ch Scout of the World 1920), *cr* 4 Dec 1922 a Baronet (UK) and 17 Sept 1929 a Baron (UK), Grand Offr Order of Christ (Portugal), Chevalier Order Redeemer (Greece), Grand Cross: Dannebrog (Denmark) and St Alfonso XII (Spain), Order Merit (Chile), Grand Cross Legion of Honour, Order Crown of Belgium and Polonia Restituta, Hungarian Order of Merit (1st Class), Lithuanian Order of Geminidas, Czechoslovak Order White Lion (1st Class for Military Merit) and Grand Order Merit Austria, Waterier Peace Prize 1937; *m* 30 Oct 1912 Olave St Clair, GBE (1932), (*b* 22 Feb 1889; Co Commr Girl Guides Sussex 1916, Ch Commr Girl Guides GB and Empire, World Ch Guide 1930, 1914–18 War Medal, Order Merit Poland 1933, White Rose Finland 1934, Grand Cross Roy Order Phoenix Greece 1949, Order Honour and Merit Haiti 1951, Order Sun Peru 1959, Order of Bernardo O'Higgins Chile 1959, Order of Vasco Nuñez de Balboa Panama 1959, L'Ordre Nationale du Cèdre de Lebanon 1960, L'Ordre Grand de la Couronne de chêne Luxembourg 1960, Order Sacred Treasure Japan 1963, Hon Freeman Poole; *d* 25 June 1977), yr dau of Harold Soames, of Lilliput, Dorset, and *d* Kenya 8 Jan 1941, leaving issue:

1 ARTHUR ROBERT PETER, **2nd Baron**

1 Heather Grace; *b* 1 June 1915; *m* 24 June 1940 W/Cdr John Hall King, BA, RAF, er s of Leslie King, MB, BCh, and *d* 23 May 1986, having had:

(1) Michael Robert Hall; *b* 26 Sept 1942; *educ* Charterhouse and Oxford Sch of Architecture; missing believed drowned while sailing on SS *Heraklion* off Crete 7/8 Dec 1966

(2) Timothy John; *b* 22 Feb 1946; *educ* Charterhouse; *m* 28 Aug 1971 *Marion [Mrs Timothy King, Easter Langlee, By Galashiels, Selkirkshire TD1 2NU], dau of Herbert Ingram, of Beds, and widow of Christopher Parrott, of Hook House, Hook Norton, and *d* July 1975, leaving:

1a *Natasha; *b* 17 May 1973

2 *Betty St Clair, CBE (1997) [The Hon Mrs Clay CBE, Ford Lodge, Wiveliscombe, Somerset]; *b* 16 April 1917; Assist Commr Guides (England); *m* 24 Sept 1936 *Gervas Charles Robert Clay, Resident Commr Overseas Civ Serv N Rhodesia (ret), Dir Rhodes-Livingstone Museum 1961–64, er s of Gerard Arden Clay, of Kitwe, N Rhodesia (now Zambia), and has issue:

(1) *Robin Baden; *b* 16 April 1939; *educ* Michaelhouse, Natal, Pierrepont Ho Sch Frensham, Surrey, UK, and Loughborough Coll UK; civ engr; *m* 1971 *Susan, er dau of Rev Charles Patrick de Candole, of Witchampton Rectory, Dorset, and has issue:

1a *Toby; *b* 1973

1a *Annabella; *b* 1975

(2) *Nigel Gerard Arden [Nigel Clay Esq, c/o Tsetse Control Dept, PO BOX 65, Choma, Zambia]; *b* 10 Feb 1943; *educ* Peterhouse Rhodesia and Rhodesia U; *m* 23 Aug 1969 *Elaine Isobel Nora, only dau of Albert Hughes, of Mavis Bank, Bodorgan Rd, Bournemouth, Hants, and has issue:

1a *Gerard; *b* 1970

2a *Adam; *b* 1975

1a *Olivia; *b* 1973

(3) *Crispin David Powell [Crispin Clay, Centourus High School, Windhoek, Namibia]; *b* 15 Nov 1944 *educ* Peterhouse Rhodesia and St David's Coll Lampeter, Wales, UK (BA 1967); *m* 1973 *Ortrud Wiese, of Windhoek, Namibia, and has issue:

1a *Eric; *b* 1974

(1) *Gillian Ella St Clair [Mrs William Clay, Coed Hills, St Hilary, Cowbridge, Glamorgan]; *b* 14 June 1937; *educ* St Anne's Diocesan Coll, Natal, S Africa; *m* 16 Nov 1968 her 3rd cousin *William Leigh Strudwick Clay, yst s of John Charles Clay, JP, DL, of The Cottage, St Hilary, Cowbridge, and has issue:

1a *Rawley; *b* 1971

1a *Daphne; *b* 1970

The 1st BARON's only s,

ARTHUR ROBERT PETER BADEN-POWELL, **2nd Baron Baden-Powell**; *b* 30 Oct 1913; *educ* Charterhouse and RMC Sandhurst; FRSA, Dr Humane Letters, Lincoln, Ill, USA, Fell Roy Cwlth Soc, Freeman City of London, memb Mercers' Co, served Br S Africa Police 1934–37 and Native Affairs Dept S Rhodesia (now Zimbabwe) 1937–45; *m* 3 Jan 1936 Carine (*d* 1993), dau of Clement Hamilton Crause Boardman, of Johannesburg, S Africa, and *d* 9 Dec 1962, having had issue:

1 ROBERT CRAUSE BADEN-POWELL, **3rd and present Baron Baden-Powell**

2 +(DAVID) MICHAEL [The Hon Michael Baden-Powell, 18 Kalang Road, Camberwell, Melbourne, Victoria 3124, Australia]; *b* 11 Dec 1940; heir presumptive; *educ* Pierrepont Ho Sch, Surrey; memb Mercers' Co, Freeman City of London, insur consultant and agent Australian Mutual Provident Soc 1972–; *m* 20 Aug 1966 *Joan Phillips, only dau of Horace William Berryman, of Camberwell, and has issue:

(1) +David Robert; *b* 6 Jan 1971

(2) +Alexander Peter; *b* 1973

(3) +Myles Warrington; *b* 1975

1 *Wendy Dorothy Lilian [The Hon Wendy Baden-Powell, 4/16 Allambee Ave, Camberwell, Victoria 3124, Australia]; *b* 16 Sept 1944; *educ* Sorbonne

BAGGE

Arms: Lozengy paly bendy argent and gules, two flanches or, on a chief of the last an annulet between two cinquefoils of the second.
Crest: A pair of wings addorsed or, semé of annulets gules.
Motto: *Spes est in Deo* ('My hope is in God').
Creation: Bt. (UK) 13 April 1867.

SIR (JOHN) JEREMY PICTON BAGGE, 7TH BT, of Stradsett Hall, Norfolk, DL (Norfolk 1996) [Sir Jeremy Bagge Bt DL, Stradsett Hall, King's Lynn, Norfolk PE33 9HA]; *b* 21 June 1945; *s f* 1990; *educ* Eton; FCA, memb King's Lynn and W Norfolk Cncl 1981–95, Hon Alderman 1995, Freeman City London; *m* 25 Jan 1979 *Sarah Margaret Phipps, dau of Maj James Shelley Phipps Armstrong (*see* SMITH, Bt), and has:

1 +ALFRED JAMES JOHN; *b* 1 July 1980

2 +Albert Daniel Bracewell; *b* 1 April 1985

1 *Alexandra Mary Pleasance; *b* 26 Dec 1982

Lineage: EDMUND BAGGE, tenant of the Manor of Shipdham, Norfolk, 1473; had:

EDWARD BAGGE, of Shipdham; *m* Alice — (living 1499) and had, with a yr s (John, *d c* 1530):

STEPHEN BAGGE, of Shipdham; *m* Alice — and *d c* 26 Oct 1530, having had a 2nd s:

EDMUND BAGGE, of Shipdham; *m* Jean — and *d c* 24 Jan 1560, leaving, with an er s (William, *d c* 1580):

RALPH BAGGE, of Shipdham and Cockley Cley, Norfolk; *m* Cecilia— and *d c* 28 Oct 1641, having had a yst s:

SIMON BAGGE, of Cockley Cley; *d* 1671, leaving, with an est s (Francis, of Flitcham, Norfolk, *d* by 1699, leaving issue) and yst s (Simon, *b* 1640, Fell Caius Coll Cambridge, *d unm* 1681):

JOHN BAGGE, of Cockley Cley; *m* 1656 Mary, dau of John Carter, of Northwold, and *d c* 2 Oct 1702, having had, with four yr s (Charles, of Boughton, *d* by 1745; Simon; Stephen; Richard, *d* 1736):

JOHN BAGGE, of Lynn, Norfolk; *m* 1st 1692 Sarah, dau of Samuel Thacker, of Lynn, and widow of Geoffrey Gynn, and had two s (Samuel and John) and two daus; *m* 2nd Susan Cranwell and *d* 1741, leaving by her, with four other s:

WILLIAM BAGGE, of Islington Hall, Norfolk; *b* 1700; *m* Jane (*d* 7 Jan 1790), dau of Peter Dixon and heiress of her bro Thomas Dixon, of Islington Hall, and had a 2nd s:

THOMAS BAGGE, of Stradsett Hall, Norfolk, and Islington Hall; *bapt* 1 Jan 1740; *m* 1st 20 July 1768 Pleasance (*bur* 1 Nov 1790), dau and coheir of Philip Case, of Stradsett and Gaywood, and had, with other issue (including two daus who *m* Sir Thomas Preston, 1st Bt (*qv*), and his yr bro Edward):

1 THOMAS PHILIP

THOMAS BAGGE *m* 2nd 17 Nov 1800 Anne (*d* 15 Aug 1807), dau of Thomas Lee-Warner, of Walsingham, and widow of his cousin Charles Elsden Bagge, MD, and *d* 19 Aug 1807, having by her had issue:

1 Anne Philip; *b* 3 March 1802; *m* 21 July 1829 Capt William Simon Houghton FitzRoy, of Kempston, Norfolk, gs of 1st Baron Southampton (*qv*), and *d* May 1860

THOMAS BAGGE's s,

THOMAS PHILIP BAGGE, of Stradsett and Islington, JP, DL; *b* 29 July 1771; *m* 28 April 1808 Grace (*d* 27 Jan 1834 aged 56), yst dau of Richard Salisbury, of Castle Park, Lancs, and *d* 3 June 1827, having had an est s:

Sir William Bagge, 1st Bt (UK), so *cr* 13 April 1867, of Stradsett Hall; *b* 7 June 1810, MP (C) W Norfolk; *m* 11 July 1833 his cousin Frances (*d* 27 May 1887), 4th dau of Sir Thomas Preston, 1st Bt, of Beeston St Lawrence (*qv*), and *d* 12 Feb 1880, leaving issue:

1 **Sir William Henry Ernest Bagge, 2nd Bt**, of Stradsett; *b* 9 Aug 1840; *m* 26 Oct 1865 Alice (*m* 2nd 11 July 1889 William Wainwright (*d* 23 Jan 1929) and *d* 21 May 1935), 2nd dau of Alfred Giles, MP, and *dsp* 23 Oct 1881

2 ALFRED THOMAS (Sir), **3rd Bt**

1 Frances Henrietta; *d unm* 16 Jan 1892
2 Emilia Jane; *m* 16 June 1864 Maj Charles Wells Archdale, 85th Regt, of Cottishall, Norfolk, and *d* 23 Dec 1916, leaving issue
3 Caroline Thomazina; *d unm* 4 May 1911
4 Edith Mary; *d unm* 31 Jan 1927

Sir WILLIAM's yr bro,

Sir Alfred Thomas Bagge, 3rd Bt, JP, DL, of Stradsett Hall; *b* 5 July 1843; Capt RN; *m* 11 July 1872 Millicent Case (*d* 22 May 1918), 5th dau of John Grant Morris, JP, of Allerton Priory, Liverpool, and *d* 16 Feb 1916, having had issue:

1 William John Preston; *b* 6 May; *d* 10 Sept 1874
2 **Sir Alfred William Francis Bagge, 4th Bt**, JP (1930 Norfolk), of Stradsett Hall; *b* 14 Sept 1875; *educ* Eton and King's Coll Cambridge (BA, LLB), barrister Inner Temple 1899, Capt 4th Bn Norfolk Regt (T) WW I, Judge Norwich Guildhall Court 1922, Dep Chm QS 1932; *d unm* 3 March 1939
3 JOHN PICTON (Sir), **5th Bt**
4 Henry Percy, MC; *b* 20 April 1879; *educ* Eton and Clare Coll Cambridge (BA); Maj TFR WW I (wounded); *m* 30 Aug 1928 Marjorie Aubrey (*d* 5 July 1951), dau of Cdr Alexander Young Crawshay Mainwaring Spearman, RN (*see* SPEARMAN, Bt), and *d* 25 Nov 1942, leaving issue:
(1) *Mary Pleasance [Mrs Amir Garakani, 7 Stack Ho, Cundy St, London SW1]; *b* 28 July 1929; *educ* Newnham Coll Cambridge (BA); *m* 15 July 1953 *Amir Feridun Garakani, s of Sayyid Mohammad Garakani, of Teheran
1 Lilian Mary; *b* 13 March 1883, MA, Fell and Bursar Newnham Coll Cambridge 1920–34; *m* 15 Dec 1920 Rev Frederick Hugh Lacy, MA, Rector Northwold, Norfolk (*d* 16 March 1943), s of Charles James Lacy, of Fleet, Hants, and *dsp* 2 Oct 1968
2 Gwendolen Millicent; *b* 21 Feb 1887; *d unm* 18 Aug 1908

Sir ALFRED's yr bro,

Sir (John) Picton Bagge, 5th Bt, CMG (1929), ED, DL; *b* 19 Oct 1877; *educ* Eton and King's Coll Cambridge (BA); Consular Serv 1903, Commercial Sec 1st Grade Russia 1918, Berne 1921 and Brussels 1922, Dir For Div Dept Overseas Trade 1928, ret 1937; *m* 24 May 1910 Olive Murial Mary (*d* 21 Aug 1965), yr dau of Samuel Taylor Mendel, of Manley Hall, Manchester, and Easthorpe Hall, Malton, Yorks, and *d* 23 Dec 1967, having had issue:

1 **Sir John Alfred Picton Bagge, 6th Bt**, ED,DL; *b* 27 Oct 1914; *educ* Eton and abroad; Maj Inns of Court Regt, WW II with Cheshire Yeo in Palestine, Sudan and Br Mil Missions Ethiopia and Bulgaria, KStJ (1975, CStJ 1959); *m* 1 June 1939 (Elizabeth) Helena (Lena) (*d* 17 Feb 1996), 2nd dau of Daniel James Davies, CBE, Commr Newfoundland in London, and *d* 17 June 1990, leaving:
(1) Sir (JOHN) JEREMY PICTON BAGGE, **7th and present Bt**
(2) +(Alfred) James Stephen; *b* 7 Dec 1952; *educ* Eton; Lt RARO, 2nd Lt Blues and Royals 1972–76, barrister 1979, ptnr Norton Rose 1993; *m* 10 Oct 1981 *Victoria Imogen Lyndon Skeggs, dau of Michael Andrew Lyndon Skeggs, of Dalgheal, Evanton, Ross-shire, and has:
1a *Edwina Rose; *b* 7 March 1985
(3) +Thomas (Tom) Philip; *b* 4 May 1955; *educ* Eton, RMA Sandhurst and RAC Cirencester, FRICS 1987; Lt Blues and Royals 1974–78; ptnr Strutt and Parker 1987
(1) *Christabel Rosemund [Mrs Peter Dimmock, Windlesham Park, Windlesham, Surrey GU20 6AT]; *b* 3 March 1940; *educ* Benenden; High Sheriff Gter London 1990; *m* 1st 19 Dec 1963 James Hinton Scott (*d* 1988), est s of Maj Archibald Craufurd Scott, by Hon Ruth Mary Dawnay, only dau of 9th Viscount Downe (*qv*), and has:
1a *Anthony Craufurd; *b* 11 Oct 1964; *educ* Charterhouse and RMA Sandhurst; Capt Blues and Royals 1986–91
1a *Lucinda Ruth; *b* 17 Aug 1966; *educ* W Heath
2a *Sarah Rosamund;*b* 14 Feb 1968; *educ* W Heath; *m* 9 Dec 1995 *Ivor Engel
(1) (cont.) Mrs James Scott *m* 2nd 8 June 1990, as his 2nd w, *Peter Dimmock, CVO, OBE
(2) *Rosaleen Pleasance [Mrs Jonathan Buxton, 62 Endlesham Rd, London SW12 8JL]; *b* 3 July 1947; *m* 4 April 1972 *Capt Jonathan James Buxton, 17th/21st Lancers (*see* BUXTON, Bt), and has issue
(3) *Elizabeth Mary Frances [Mrs Dean Rasheed, Arkaba Station, Hawker, S Australia 5434, Australia]; *b* 27 Sept 1949; *educ* E Hadden Hall Sch; *m* 13 June 1981 *Dean Rasheed and has:
1a *Edward James; *b* 14 April 1985
1a *Lucy Elizabeth; *b* 27 April 1983
2 (Thomas) Peter, of Reed Bank, Ashford Road, Bearstead, Kent; *b* 29 Jan 1917; Maj RA WW II, dir Houchin Ltd Ashford 1968; *educ* Eton; *m* 1st 5 June 1947 (*divorce* 1951) Mary Armine, only dau of Brig Leonard William Henry Mathias, DSO, of Hambutts Orchard, Painswick, Glos, and widow of Maj Denis Brestram Radley, Duke of Cornwall's LI; *m* 2nd 2 Oct 1954 *Sorel Venetia, yr dau of Col Clarence Preston Gunter, CIE, OBE, and *d* 4 Oct 1977
1 Audrey Rosamund; *b* 19 Jan; *d* 15 May 1913

Seat: Stradsett Hall, Stradsett, Norfolk. It was Philip Case, whose daughter Pleasance was paternal grandmother of the **1st Baronet**, who is responsible for Stradsett's coming to the Bagges. He had bought it as an Elizabethan house in 1747 from a family called Goldsmith, who in turn had bought it soon after it was built from the original owners the Picots. The standard Elizabethan E-shape remains but in the early 18th century the house was remodelled and sash windows inserted to give a Georgian aspect. At the same time the south garden was given its beautiful iron gates. In 1810–13 the Park was landscaped by John Loudon with plans to build a new house on the north side of the lake but these were abandoned and the present house was again remodelled in 1819.

BAGOT

Arms: Erm. two chevronels az. **Crest:** Out of a ducal coronet a goat's head arg., attired or. **Supporters:** Two goats arg., attired or.
Motto: *Antiquum obtinens* ('Possessing antiquity').
Creations: Bt. (E) 31 May 1627, B. (GB) 17 Oct 1780.

THE 9TH BARON BAGOT OF BAGOT'S BROMLEY, Co Stafford, and a **Baronet** (Sir Heneage Charles Bagot, Bt) [The Rt Hon The Lord Bagot, Tyn-y-Mynydd, nr Llithfaen, Gwynedd LL53 6PD; 16 Barclay Rd, London SW6 1EH]; *b* 11 June 1914; *s* half-bro 1979; *educ* Harrow; Maj 6th Gurkha Rifles; *m* 29 Nov 1939 *Muriel Patricia Moore, yst dau of Maxwell James Moore Boyle, of Tullyvin Ho, Co Cavan, and has issue:

1 +CHARLES HUGH SHAUN; *b* 23 Feb 1944; *educ* Abbotsholme; *m* 1986 *Sally A, dau of D G Blunden, of Farnham, Surrey, and formerly w of — Stone, and has:
(1) *Grace Lorina Kitty; *b* 1993
1 *Caroline Patricia [The Hon Mrs Garner-Clarke, Tradsfield Ho, St Martins, nr Oswestry, Salop]; *b* 6 May 1942; *m* 1st 1962 (*divorce* 1985) Hugh Alexander James Cameron-Rose (*d* 1993) and has issue:
(1) *Hugh Charles; *b* 1962
(1) *Georgina Louise Stella; *b* 1968
1 (cont.) The Hon Mrs Caroline Cameron-Rose *m* 2nd 1991 *Peter Garner-Clarke

Lineage: — BAGOT held Bramshall, Staffs, at the time of the Domesday Survey 1086; a man who was possibly his s was living *c* 1129; the latter's s or gs:

HERVEY Fitz BAGOT, of Bramshall; was living 1166 and held three knight's fees; had:

HERVEY BAGOT later D E STAFFORD; *m* Millicent, sis of Robert de Stafford, and had issue: (*see* STAFFORD, B)

A cadet,

WILLIAM BAGOT, of Bagot's Bromley; held two-thirds of a knight's fee from Robert de Stafford 1166; had:

SIMON BAGOT; held Bagot's Bromley 1198; *d* by 1203; had:

Sir HUGH BAGOT, of Bagot's Bromley; *m* Alice — and *d* 1256, having had:

Sir RICHARD BAGOT, of Bagot's Bromley; living 1256; *m* Christian, dau of Sir William Mauveslin, of Rydeware, and *d* by June 1271, having had:

Sir WILLIAM BAGOT, of Bagot's Bromley; living 1276; *m* Hawyse/Avice — and *d* 1290, having had:

JOHN BAGOT, of Bagot's Bromley; *m* Lucy — and *d c* 1333, having had:

Sir JOHN BAGOT, of Bagot's Bromley; a minor 1334; served under Ralph, Lord (Baron) Stafford, in campaign Scotland 1336; present Battle of Crécy 1346 and Siege Calais 1346–47; *m* Eglina (*m* 2nd Sir William de Pounfreth), dau and coheir of Sir Anketill Mallory, of Kirkby Mallory, and *d* 1349, having had:

RALPH BAGOT, of Bagot's Bromley; minor in 1349; *m* Elizabeth, dau and eventual heir of John/Richard de Blithfield, Staffs, who brought him the manors of Blithfield and Littlehay, Staffs, and *d c* 1376, leaving, with a yr s (Sir William, one of RICHARD II's intimates):

Sir JOHN BAGOT, of Blithfield and Littlehay; served with John of Gaunt 1386 in Spain, Lt Calais 1408, fought Agincourt 1415; *m* Beatrice, dau of Sir John Villlers, and *d* 1437, leaving, with at least one dau (Joan, *m* John Curzon; *see* SCARSDALE, V):

RICHARD BAGOT, of Blithfield; *b* by 1388; High Sheriff Staffs 1451–52; *d* after 1475, leaving:

RICHARD BAGOT, of Blithfield; High Sheriff Staffs 1478; *m* Isabella (*d* 1477), dau of Sir Robert Aston, of Tixall, and was *k* Bosworth 1485, leaving:

JOHN BAGOT, of Blithfield; MP Staffs 1477; *m* 1st Isabella, dau of John Curzon, of Essex, and widow of John Eyton; *m* 2nd Agnes Kniveton and *d* on or after 25 Oct 1489, leaving by his 1st w:

Sir LEWIS BAGOT, of Blithfield; served France 1513, present Field of Cloth of Gold 1520; *m* 1st of his five wives Emma/Lucy Kniveton and had a s (John, *m* —, dau of Sir Thomas Botler, and *dsp* & *vp*) and four daus; *m* 3rd Anna, dau of Sir Nicholas Montgomery, and *d* 1534, having by her had, with two yr sons:

THOMAS BAGOT, of Blithfield; *m* Jane (*d* 13 March 1557), dau of Richard Astley, of Patshull, and *d* 13 May 1541, leaving:

RICHARD BAGOT, of Blithfield, DL Staffs; minor 1541; *m* Mary (*bur* 22 March 1608), dau of William Saunders, of Welford, Northants, and *d* 2 Feb 1596/7, leaving an est s:

WALTER BAGOT, of Blithfield; *b* 24 Oct 1557; *m* by June 1584 Elizabeth (*bur* 3 Dec 1638), dau of Roger Cave, of Stanford, Northants, by Margaret, sis of 1st Baron Burghley (*see* EXETER, M), and *d* 17 May 1623, leaving an est s:

Sir Hervey Bagot, 1st Bt (E), so *cr* 31 May 1627, of Blithfield; Staffs: High Sheriff 1626, MP 1628–42; *b* 8 Feb 1590; *m* 1st Katherine (*d* 16 Feb 1622), dau of Humphrey Aldersley, of Weddington, Warwicks, and had issue; *m* 2nd Anne, dau of Sir Clement Fisher and widow of Sir Thomas Dilke, of Maxstoke, and *d* 27 Dec 1660, having by his 1st w had an est s:

Sir Edward Bagot, 2nd Bt; MP Staffs 1660; *b* 23 May 1616; *m* 9 May 1641 Mary (*d* 22 Oct 1686), dau and heir of William Lampard and widow of John Crawley, and *d* 30 May 1673, having had, with 11 other s and five daus, a 3rd and est surv s:

Sir Walter Bagot, 3rd Bt; MP Staffs 1678–95; *b* 21 March 1644; *m* 25 June 1670 Jane (*d* 20 July 1695), dau and sole heir of Charles Salusbury, of Bachumbydd, Denbighs, who brought him the Pool Park estate, and *d* 15 Feb 1704, leaving an est surv s:

Sir Edward Bagot, 4th Bt; MP Staffs 1698–1708; *b* 21 Jan 1673/4; *m* 15 April 1697 Frances (*m* 2nd Sir Adolphus Oughton, Bt, and *d* 1714), dau and heiress of Sir Thomas Wagstaffe, of Tachbrooke, Warwicks, and *d* May 1712, having had an only surv s:

Sir Walter Wagstaffe Bagot, 5th Bt; LLD, MP Newcastle-under-Lyme, Staffs, and Oxford; *b* 3 Aug 1702; *m* 27 July 1724 Lady Barbara Legge (*d* 29 Oct 1765), est dau of 1st Earl of Dartmouth (*qv*), and *d* 28 Jan 1768, having had issue:

1 WILLIAM, **1st Baron**

2 Charles BAGOT later CHESTER (Act of Parl 1755; his descendants are in remainder to the btcy only); *b* 1 Sept 1730; *m* 5 Oct 1765 Catherine (*d* 31 May 1819), dau of Hon Heneage Legge (*see* DARTMOUTH, E), and *d* 2 April 1793, having had, with other issue:

(1) William (Rev); MA, Rector Denton, Norfolk; *b* 27 May 1775; *m* 8 Jan 1810 Hon Elizabeth Wilson (*d* 10 Feb 1865), dau of 10th Baron Berners (*qv*), and *d* 22 Nov 1838, having had, with other issue:

1a William Heneage; *b* 1810; *d* 1811

2a Charles Montagu, of Chicheley Hall, Bucks, DL, JP; Lt-Col; *b* 18 Jan 1813; *m* 7 Sept 1843 Maria (*d* 1893), dau of Maj Sandham, RA, and *d* 17 Nov 1879, having had issue:

1b Charles Anthony, JP (Bucks); *b* 15 April 1846; *d unm* 10 Jan 1910

2b George Paget; *d* young 1866

3b Henry; *b* 7 SepT 1850; *d* 1902

4b John Greville (Rev); MA, vicar Gilling, Yorks; *b* 15 May 1852; *m* 1883 Amy (*d* 25 Feb 1915), dau of Arthur Hughes, and *d* 13 Jan 1923, having had issue:

1c Greville Arthur Bagot; *b* 3 April 1891; Lt 3rd Bn N Staffs Regt; *ka* 13 Oct 1914

2c Anthony James Bagot, MC, of Chicheley Hall; Maj RA (TAR) IA RO WW I (despatches) and WW II; *b* 29 Dec 1892; *m* 29 July 1924 Gladys Mabel (*d* 1974), er dau of Rev Frederick Charles Stamer, MA (*see* STAMER, Bt), and *d* 5 Nov 1952, leaving issue:

1d +(John) Greville Bagot, MC [Maj Greville Chester MC, The Old Rectory, North Crawley, Newport Pagnell, Bucks]; *b* 20 May 1925; Maj Coldstream Gds WW II

3c George Bagot, MC; *b* 6 Sept 1894, Lt Durham LI and MG Corps WW I (twice wounded); *d* unm 13 June 1970

4c Henry Montagu Bagot; *b* 1896, Lt 12th Lancers; *m* 17 May 1924 Alyce Amy Maude Tranchell (*d* 1934) and *d* 1969, leaving issue:

1d Greville Derrick Bagot; *b* 1925

2d +Hugh Malcolm [Hugh Chester Esq, 76 Aylesbury Crescent, Bedminster Down, Bristol BS3 5NN]; *b* 1929; *m* 1972 *Pauline Lillian, dau of Thomas Nicholls and formerly w of Lionel Butt

5c Lewis Charles Bagot; *b* 29 Aug 1898, 2nd Lt Lancs Fus; *ka* 5 April 1918

6c Hugh Bagot; *d* an infant 19 Feb 1902

1c Dorothy Mary; *m* 1st 8 Feb 1916 Maj Robert Frances Ruck Keene, RA (*d* 2 Feb 1918), s of Maj Gen John Edward Ruck Keene, RA, JP, and had issue; *m* 2nd 20 July 1922 Herbert St John Durnford, MICE (*d* 1951), s of Rev Frances Edward Durnford, and *d* 25 Aug 1976, leaving further issue

2c Kathleen Agnes Chester; *m* 1931 Masuto Veno (*d* 1965) and had issue

5b Algernon Stewart McKenzie Bagot (Rev); *b* 30 Dec 1853; *educ* Keble Coll Oxford (MA); *m* 11 June 1884 Emily Mary Dillman (*d* 5 Aug 1928), only dau of Rev Edward Manners Dillman Pyne, MA, and *d* 12 March 1930, having had issue:

1c Charles Edward Sandham Bagot; Midshipman RN; *b* 26 Jan 1886; *d* unm 6 Jan 1903

2c Walter Greville Bagot, MC (1918); *b* 15 March 1887; Capt 3rd Gurkha Riffles WW I (despatches, wounded); *d* 28 March 1918 of wounds received in action in Palestine

1c Sylvia Viole Bagot; *b* 18 Oct 1889; *d* 21 March 1890

2c Muriel Bagot; *b* 28 Sept 1891; *d* unm 24 May 1960

1b Fanny Maria; *m* 19 Sep 1876 Lt-Col Charles William Selby-Lowndes, Argyll Sutherland Highrs (*d* 2 Nov 1921), only s of Rev Charles William Selby-Lowndes, JP, Rector N Crawley, Bucks, and *d* 12 Feb 1928, leaving issue

2b Louisa Grace; *d* unm 6 July 1936

3b Mary Isabella; *d* unm 1944

4b Katherine; *d* unm 1952

5b Margaret Isabel; *d* unm 1946

(2) John, of Ashstead, Surrey, Lt-Gen RA; *b* 3 Aug 1770; *m* 17 May 1821 Sophia Elizabeth (*d* 19 May 1879), dau of Charles Stuart, of Airdroch, and *d* 19 May 1857, having had issue:

1a John CHESTER later ST LEGER (1863), of Park Hill, Yorks; JP and DL; *b* 6 May 1823, Col 53rd and 85th Regts; *m* 8 April 1858 Philippa (*d* 1909), dau of John Bonfoy Roper, of Abbot's Ripton Hall, MP Hunts, and *d* 9 Aug 1905, having had issue:

1b Arthur John Bonfoy, JP (Herts), Maj KRRC; *b* 25 Nov 1859; *m* 8 April 1896 Hilda Geraldine (*d* Jan 1961), 2nd dau of Col Sir Gerard Smith, KCMG, Govr W Australia, and *d* 22 March 1939, leaving issue:

1c Brenda Mary; *b* 11 July 1897; *m* 24 July 1918 Achille SABBE later ST LEGER (roy licence 1940), 1st Belgian Guides (*d* 2 Oct 1962), and had issue:

1d Anthony Rene; *b* 26 July 192–; Lt RN 1920; *ka* 1943

2d Julian, ARIBA; *b* 29 Oct 1927; *m* 1 April 1950 (*divorce* 1954) Patricia, yst dau of Sir Eric Alexander Ogilvy Hutchison, 2nd Bt (*qv*), and had issue:

1e Harriet Claire; *b* 12 Oct 1951

2c Vera; *b* 29 July 1900; *m* 2 Sept 1964 Ian Alexander Beith, s of Alexander Beith, of The Cliff, Knutsford, Cheshire

2b Henry Berners; Indian Police; *b* 26 Oct 1861; *m* 31 Aug 1921 Sylvia, dau of Douglas Kingsford, barrister, and *d* 1945

3b Reginald Warham Anthony; *b* 15 Feb 1866; *m* 1888 Amy Eva (*d* 1942), dau of George Sloan, of Dumfries, and had:

1c Gaspard Douglas Anthony; *b* 1890; *m* 1914 Ivy (*d* 1974), dau of William S West, and *d* 1974, leaving:

1d John Douglas; *b* 1920; *d* 1941

1d *Ivy; *b* 1915; *m* 1939 *Charles P Leonard and has:

1e *Anne Carol; *b* 1940; *m* 1962 *William Denno and has:

1f *Nicole; *b* 1963

2f *Lori; *b* 1967

2d *Virginia May [Mrs David Hunter, 3616 Lone Wolf Trail, St Augustine, FL 32086, USA]; *b* 1922; *m* 1964 *David Hunter

2c Geoffrey Bayard; *b* 1892; *m* 1919 Grace Elizabeth (*d* 1934), dau of Robert Baylor, and had:

1d Jean Mary; *b* 1923; *d* 1989

2d *Claire Amy [Mrs H Charles McNally, 335 Old Army Rd, Basking Ridge, NJ 07920, USA]; *b* 1928; *m* 1952 *H Charles McNally and has:

1e *Robert Charles; *b* 1953; *m* 1977 *Jacqueline Port and has:

1f *Austin Charles; *b* 1986

1f *Ashley Jacqueline; *b* 1983

2f *Caroline Taylor; *b* 1987

1e *Jan Barbara; *b* 1955

2e *Jane Hoefer; *b* 1959; *m* 1982 *Douglas E Brandt

3c Roderic Craufurd; *b* 1894; *m* 1916 Cora Irene (*d* 1932), dau of Giles Curtis Gass, and *d* 1949, leaving:

1d *(Roderic) Harry [Harry St Leger 25 Dirks Terrace, Highland, NY 12528, USA]; *b* 1919; *m* 1950 *Doris J, dau of Eugene Geary, and has had:

1e Thomas; *b* and *d* 1951

1e Nancy J; *b* 1953; *m* 1978 (*divorce* 1990, resumed maiden name) Roy L Post

1d *Beverly Cora; *b* 1917; *m* 1955 George Howard Hurd (*d* 1987)

4c Victor Robert; *b* 1896

1c Evangeline; *b* 1900

1b Gwendoline Mary Hope; *m* 9 April 1885 Frederic William Brooke (*d* 26 Dec 1952), of Totscott, Witham, Essex, s of John William Brooke, JP, of Sibton Park, Suffolk, DL, and *d* 27 June 1954, leaving issue

2b Georgiana Harriet; *m* 12 April 1888 John Walter Parry-Cooke, JP, of Darsham House, Suffolk (*d* 26 Sept 1939), and *d* 8 Nov 1947, leaving issue

3b Ursula Beatrice Philippa; *m* 20 Dec 1888 Francis Egbert Hollomd, JP, of Leiston Old Abbey, Suffolk (*d* 19 April 1953), s of Rev Edmund Hollond, of Benhall Lodge, Suffolk, and *d* 4 Feb 1933, leaving issue

2a Heneage Charles BAGOT-CHESTER; *b* 12 Feb 1836, JP Suffolk, Col Res Forces, late 27th and 29th Regts, served Indian Mutiny and NW Frontier; *m* 11 March 1865 Madeline Elizabeth (*d* 3 Feb 1919), only dau of Richard Mansel Oliver Massey, of Tickford Abbey, Bucks, and Kinrara and widow of Thomas Bowen Sheriffe, of Henstead Hall, Suffolk, and *d* 9 Aug 1912, leaving issue:

1b Greville John Massey; *b* 22 Oct 1868; Capt and Brev Major Res Of Offrs, Scots Gds, Boer War 1899–1901 (two medals, six clasps) and WW I (despatches twice, Brevet); *ka* 28 Nov 1917

2b Hugh Augustus; *b* 21 April 1871; Capt Staff Yeo, Capt 3rd Loyal Lancs Regt, served S Africa 1900 (medal and three clasps) and WW I as ADC to 9th Div (three medals); *m* 1st 13 Jan 1895 (*divorce* 1908) Margaret Kathleen Julia (*d* 10 Feb 1951), dau of Col Richard E Oakes, DSC; *m* 2nd 15 April 1913 Clotilde Mary Hamilton (*d* 1 Feb 1964), est dau of Hon Arthur Henry Browne (*see* KILMAINE, B), and *d* 6 Jan 1938, having by her had issue:

1c *Peggy Mary Clotilde [Mrs Peggy Harley, 16 Swan Court, Flood St, London SW3]; *b* 6 Jan 1914; *m* 1st 1 Dec 1937 (*divorce* 1946) Wallace Stuart Finlayson (the actor and stage dir Wallace Douglas), yr s of Capt Robert Finlayson, of 162 Sloane Street, London SW; *m* 2nd 16 Aug 1947 (*divorce* 1954) Ralph Harley

1a Sophia Elizabeth; *m* 5 Aug 1845 Lord Alfred Hervey (*d* 15 April 1875) and *d* 20 Sept 1892, leaving issue (*see* BRISTOL, M)

2a Mary; *m* 18 Feb 1846 her cousin Rev Charles Walter Bagot (*d* 10 Sept 1884) and *d* 15 April 1899, leaving issue (*see* below)

3a Barbara Wilhelmina; *m* 12 Feb 1862 Rev Hon William Howard (*dsp* 12 May 1881) and *d* 26 April 1909 (*see* EFFINGHAM, E)

(3) William; *m* Isabel, dau of Rev William Legard (*see* LEGARD, Bt)

3 Walter (Rev), of Pipe Hall, Staffs; *b* 2 Nov 1731; Rector Blithfield and Leigh; *m* 1st 7 Sept 1773 Anne, dau of William Swinnerton, of Butterton, Staffs, and had issue; *m* 2nd Mary Ward and *d* 1806, having had further issue

4 Richard BAGOT later HOWARD; *b* 13 Nov 1733; *m* 25 Feb 1783 Frances, yst child of William Howard, Viscount Andover, and eventually heir of her nephew, Henry, Earl of Suffolk and Berkshire (*qv*), and *d* 18 Feb 1819, leaving an only dau and heiress:

(1) Mary; *m* 9 July 1807 Hon Fulke Greville UPTON later HOWARD (*dsp* 4 March 1846), bro of 1st Viscount Templetown (*see* 1970 edn), and *d* 10 Oct 1877

5 Lewis (Rt Rev), DD; Bp Bristol, Norwich and St Asaph; *b* 1 Jan 1740; *m* Mary (*d* 17 Aug 1799), dau of Hon Edward Hay, and *dsp* June 1802

6 Thomas; *b* 14 Feb 1746; barrister Lincoln's Inn 5 May 1766; *d* at Naples

The 5th Bt's est s,

WILLIAM BAGOT, **1st Baron Bagot of Bagot's Bromley**, Co Stafford (GB), so *cr* 17 Oct 1780; *b* 28 Feb 1728; MP (Tory) Staffs 1754–80; *m* 20 Aug 1760 Elizabeth Louisa (*d* 4 Feb 1820), dau of 2nd Viscount Bolingbroke and St John (*qv*), and *d* 22 Oct 1798, having had, with other issue:

1 WILLIAM BAGOT, **2nd Baron Bagot of Bagot's Bromley**; *b* 11 Sept 1778; LLD, FSA, FLS, FZS, FHS; *m* 1st 30 May 1799 Hon Emily FitzRoy (*d* 8 June 1800), 4th dau of 1st Baron Southampton (*qv*), and had a dau (Louisa Barbara, *d* in infancy); *m* 2nd 17 Feb 1807 Lady Louisa Legge (*d* 13 Aug 1816), est dau of 3rd Earl of Dartmouth (*qv*), and *d* 12 Feb 1856, having her had, with three daus:

(2) WILLIAM BAGOT, **3rd Baron Bagot of Bagot's Bromley**; *b* 27 March 1811; Hon Col Staffs Yeo, a Ld-in-Waiting; *m* 13 Aug 1851 Hon Lucia Caroline Elizabeth Agar-Robartes (*d* 22 Jan 1895), sis of 2nd Viscount Clifden (*see* 1970 edn), and *d* 19 Jan 1887, having had:

1a WILLIAM BAGOT, **4th Baron Bagot of Bagot's Bromley**, JP Staffs and Derbys; *b* 19 Jan 1857; ADC to Govr-Gen Canada 1879–84, Gentleman Usher Privy Chamber 1885–87 and a Ld-in-Waiting 1896–1901, Capt 3rd S Staffs Regt, Lt-Col 2ic Staffs Imp Yeo; *m* 25 July 1903 Lilian Marie (*d* 21 Feb 1958), dau of Henry May, of Maryland, USA, and *dspm* 23 Dec 1932, leaving issue:

1b Barbara; *b* 1 Jan 1905; *m* 1 June 1934 (*divorce* 1945) Oscar Crosby Sewall, s of Oscar Trufant Sewall, of Bath, Maine, USA, and had issue

2a Walter Lewis, DSO, Maj Gren Gds, Staff IVth Army Corps BEF and Dir Min Munitions WW I, served Nile Expdn 1898 (wounded, two medals and clasp), S Africa 1900–02 (despatches, two medals, six clasps); *b* 22 April 1864; *m* 6 Feb 1892 Margaret Jane Caroline (*d* 14 June 1941), dau of Hon Frederick Cadogan (*see* CADOGAN, E), and *d* 26 May 1927, having had issue:

1b Edward Luke Henry, 2nd Lt Welsh Gds; *b* 18 Oct 1896; *ka* Somme 10 Sept 1916

1b Marjorie Olive; *b* 21 Nov 1893; *d* unm 14 Nov 1954

1a Georgina Agnes; *m* 4 Feb 1873 8th Earl of Aylesford (*qv*) and *dsp* 14 April 1874

2a Louisa; *m* 1st 22 Feb 1879 Hamar Alfred Bass, MP, of Byrkley Lodge, Staffs, bro of 1st Baron Burton (*qv*), and had issue; *m* 2nd 28 Nov 1901 Rev Bernard Day Douglas Shaw, Vicar of The Annunciation, Bryanston Street, London W1, and *d* as the result of an accident 18 May 1942. He *d* 7 Aug 1922

3a Constance; *d* unm 1 Feb 1898

4a Katherine Jane; *m* 17 Sep 1898 Col David Murray Smythe, of Methven Castle, Perthshire, and *d* 13 Jan 1952, leaving issue. He *d* 10 Feb 1928

5a Elizabeth Sophia Lucia, DGStJ; *m* 13 Oct 1888 Sir Francis Alexander Newdigate Newdegate, GCMG, of Arbury, Nuneaton, Warwicks, and Harefield, Middlesex, and *d* 29 Dec 1940, leaving issue. He *d* 2 Jan 1936

(2) Hervey Charles (Rev), MA, Rector Blithfield; *b* 17 Dec 1812; *m* 16 July 1873 Frances Mary (*d* 13 July 1902), dau of Thomas Dickin, and *dsp* 3 Jan 1879

(3) Alfred Walter; *b* 4 April 1816; *d* 19 June 1891

2 Charles (Sir), GCB, PC, MP; Under-Sec State For Affrs, Min Plen USA, Amb St Petersburg, The Hague and Vienna, Govr-Gen Canada 1841; *b* 23 Sept 1781; *m* 22 July 1806 Mary Charlotte Anne (*d* 2 Feb 1845), est dau of 3rd Earl of Mornington (*see* WELLINGTON, D), and *d* 19 May 1843, leaving, with other issue (including Georgiana Augusta *m* 1843 Alexander Mackenzie Fraser; *see* LOVAT, L):

(1) Charles, JP (Staffs); *b* 20 May 1808; Col Gren Gds, Col 3rd Bn KOSB, Assist Master of Ceremonies to HM QUEEN VICTORIA; *m* 7 July 1846 Sophia Louisa (*d* 7 Nov 1908), dau of V-Adml Hon Josceline Percy (*see* NORTHUMBERLAND, D), and *d* 25 Feb 1881, leaving issue:

1a Josceline FitzRoy, of Levens Hall, Westmorland, JP, DL; *b* 22 Oct 1854; CC Westmorland, Capt Gren Gds Boer War 1899–1901 (despatches), ADC to Govr-Gen Canada 1882–83 and 1888–89, Maj and Hon Lt-Col Westmorland and Cumberland Imp Yeo, MP S Westmorland 1892–1906 and 1910–13, Parly Sec to Sec Treasury 1897–98 and Home Sec 1898–1900; *m* 11 June 1885 Theodosia, RRC, DGStJ, memb Roy Red Cross Serbia, Medaille Queen Elisabeth Belgium, granted rank of bt's widow by roy warrant 12 April 1913 (*m* 2nd 3 June 1920 Rev Sidney Bellingham Swann, Vicar Lindfield, Sussex, and *d* 21 Feb 1940), 3rd dau of Sir John Leslie, 1st Bt, of Glaslough (*qv*), and *d* 1 March 1913, having been nominated 1 Jan 1913 a Bt (the title being conferred on his son due to his own death before the actual creation could take place), leaving:

1b Sir ALAN DESMOND BAGOT, 1st and last Bt (UK), so *cr* 19 April 1913; *b* 20 Feb 1896; Lt RHG, Lt 12th Lancers WW I; *d* unm 11 Jan 1920, when the btcy expired

1b Dorothy; *b* 10 July 1886; *m* 9 May 1905 Henry Melville Gaskell, JP (*d* 21 Oct 1954), only s of Capt Henry Brooks Gaskell, JP, 9th Lancers, of Kiddington Hall, Oxon, and *d* 1974, having had, with an er s :

1c *Oliver Robin GASKELL later BAGOT (roy licence 1936 on *s* to Levens Hall under terms of will of his maternal uncle), TD, JP (Westmorland 1948), DL (Cumberland 1967) [Oliver Bagot Esq TD JP DL, Levens Brow, Kendal, Cumbria]; *b* 1914; *educ* Eton and Trin Coll Cambridge; Lt 4th Bn Border Regt (TA) WW II (POW), FRICS; *m* 1938 *Annette Dorothy, dau of Paymaster-Cdr F R Stephens, RN, and has:

1d *Charles Henry, JP (Cumbria 1991) [Charles Bagot Esq JP, Levens Hall, Kendal, Cumbria]; *b* 1946; FRICS; *m* 1975 *Susan Elizabeth, dau of Ian Alexander Ross, and has:

1e *Richard Alexander; *b* 1981

2e *Harry Josceline; *b* 1983

1e *Jessica Mary; *b* 1977

2e *Laura Elizabeth; *b* 1979

1d *Priscilla [Mrs Erik Smith, Tithe Barn, Forde Abbey, Chard, Somerset TA20 4HN]; *b* 1939; *m* 1st 1960 (*divorce* 1964), as his 1st w, Sir Humphry Wakefield, 2nd Bt (*qv*); *m* 2nd 1967 *Erik George Sebastian Smith and by him has:

1e *Miranda; *b* 1968

2e *Susanna; *b* 1970

2d *Elizabeth Dorothy [Mrs Mark Roper, Forde Abbey, Chard, Somerset]; *b* 1947; *m* 1967 *Mark Roper (*see* LOVELACE, E) and has issue:

1e *Katherine Alice; *b* 1968

2e *Victoria Jane; *b* 1970

3e *Lucinda; *b* 1972

3d *Lucinda Rose Mary [Mrs Lucinda Sclater, Cook House, Levens, Cumbria LA8 8PU]; *b* 1950; *m* 1969 (*divorce* 1993) Michael Victor Sclater and has:

1e *Josceline Mark; *b* 1972

2e *Henry Rupert; *b* 1975

2b Marjorie Constance Bagot, MBE; *m* 7 Sept 1910 Maj James Winstanley Cropper, JP, DL (*d* 8 Nov 1956), of Ellergreen, Kendal, Westmorland, and *d* 15 Nov 1951, leaving issue

3b Mary; *m* 14 June 1910 Sir Vincent Strickland Jones, KBE (*d* 1 May 1967), 2nd s of Rev Canon William Jones, MA, Vicar Burneside, Westmorland, and had issue

2a Alan Charles, JP, DL Staffs; *b* 1 June 1856; *d* unm 10 April 1885

3a Richard, of Levens, Grand Officer Order Crown Italy, Kt SMO Malta; *b* 8 Nov 1860; *d* 11 Dec 1921

1a Alice Mary; *d* 22 Nov 1922

(2) George Talbot; *b* 14 June 1820; *m* 20 Aug 1885 Charlotte Margaret (*d* 1 Oct 1897), dau of W T Blair, and *dsp* 22 Nov 1907

(3) Alexander, Col BCS; *b* 10 June 1822; *m* 28 Oct 1852 Gertrude Letitia (*d* 8 Sept 1898), dau of Brig-Gen Robert Dampier Halifax, and *d* 20 Oct 1874, leaving issue:

1a Charles FitzRoy Alexander Halifax; *b* 20 Oct 1853; *m* 1st 17 Aug 1881 (*divorce* 1890) Emily Maynard Palmer (*d* 1901), dau of Col Charles Oldfield; *m* 2nd 9 Feb 1891 Beatrice Laura (*d* 27 Sept 1922), widow of Gen John Studholme Brownrigg, CB, and dau of Chevalier L Desanges, and *d* 1901, having by her had issue

2a Francis Robert William; *b* 15 Nov 1858; *d* 11 March 1861

(1) Wilhelmina Frederica; *m* 17 Nov 1846 Adm Henry Bagot

3 Richard (Rt Rev), DD, Dean Canterbury 1827–45, Bp Oxford 1829–45 and Bath and Wells 1845–54; *b* 22 Nov 1782; *m* 22 Dec 1806 Lady Harriet Villiers (*d* 18 Oct 1870), dau of 4th Earl of Jersey (*qv*), and *d* 15 May 1854, having had, with four daus:

(1) Edward Richard, of Ashtead Park, Surrey; Maj-Gen, Kt Redeemer Greece; *b* 4 Jan 1808; *m* 15 Jan 1842 Matilda (*d* 4 July 1889), widow of Maj Frederick Oswald Perkins and 2nd dau of Henry Perkins, of Hanworth Park, Middx, and *d* 20 July 1874, leaving issue:

1a Ponsonby, Lt-Col Scots Gds; *b* 11 June 1845; *d* unm 6 Dec 1921

2a Villiers Spencer, Lt-Col Rifle Brigade; *b* 7 April 1847; *d* unm 24 March 1929

1a Evelyn; *m* 25 Sep 1869 Augustus Woodley Bernal and *d* 21 April 1877, leaving issue

2a Ethel; *m* 21 Jan 1873 Maj-Gen George Paton, CMG, and *d* 11 Oct 1885, leaving issue. He *d* 30 July 1931

(2) William; *b* 22 June 1809; *d* Nov 1810

(3) Henry; V-Adml; *b* 12 July 1810; *m* 1st 17 Nov 1846 his cousin Wilhelmina Frederica (*d* 15 April 1852), dau of Rt Hon Sir Charles Bagot, GCB, and had issue:

1a Arthur Greville, 60th Foot; *b* 29 Sept 1849; *m* 1st 5 Feb 1878 Mary Isabella (*d* 7 Dec 1905), dau of Henry Scott, and had issue:

1b Hervey Ronald Henry; *b* 1 Oct 1885; *d* 2 Feb 1888

2b Frederic Spencer Wellesley, Lt Sussex Regt; *b* 1888; *ka* 1916

1a Arthur Bagot *m* 2nd 10 Dec 1913 Mary Lilian (*d* 15 Oct 1936), widow of L Kinglake and dau of Rev H Wall, Rector of Huntspill, Somerset, and *d* 7 June 1915

(3) (cont.) V-Adml Henry Bagot *m* 2nd 9 Feb 1858 Eleanor (*d* 25 Nov 1886), dau of Edward Sacheverell Chandos-Pole, of Radbourne Hall, Derbys, and *d* 30 Nov 1877, having by her had:

2a Henry Richard Reginald; *b* 15 Aug 1860; *m* 25 March 1890 Frances Anna Mary (*m* 2nd 3 Feb 1909 Henry Bennett Ewins-Barwell-Ewins (*d* 4 April 1920), of Marston Trussell, Northants, and *d* 11 Feb 1915), only child of William Walter Bagot, of Pipe Hayes Hall, Warwicks, gs of Rev Walter Bagot (*see* above), and *d* 17 July 1908, leaving:

1b Mabel Arden; *b* 18 April 1896; *m* 1st 15 Dec 1921 Richard Alexander Douglas Liebert, s of Capt Edward Bernhard Liebert, 18th Hus, of Swinton Hall, Lancs (*d* 17 Aug 1931), *m* 2nd 1 March 1932 (*divorce* 1943) Michael Haworth-Booth, est s of Digby Clifton Haworth-Booth, and *d* 28 April 1965, leaving issue

3a Claud Leveson; *b* 9 April 1865; *d* 6 March 1930

4a GERALD WILLIAM BAGOT, **5th Baron Bagot of Bagot's Bromley**; *b* 13 May 1866; *d* unm 5 April 1946

1a Florence Eleanor; *b* 15 Feb 1859; *m* 2 March 1886 (*divorce* 1908) Charles Frederick Heneage Bagot, s of Rev Charles Walter Bagot, and *d* 26 Sept 1940, leaving issue (*see* below)

2a Mabel Harriet; *b* 27 Nov 1863; *d* 7 May 1872

3a Agnes Mary; *b* 9 Sept 1867; *d* unm 1944

(4) Charles Walter (Rev), MA Oxon 1842, Chllr Bath and Wells and Registrar Oxford, Rector Castle Rising, Norfolk; *b* 11 Feb 1812; *m* 18 Feb 1846 Mary (*d* 15 April 1899), 2nd dau of Lt-Gen John Chester, and *d* 10 Sept 1884, leaving issue:

1a Lewis Richard Charles (Rev), MA Oxon 1873, Vicar of Stanton Lacy, Salop; *b* 2 Dec 1846; *m* July 1872 Celia Cator (*d* 10 Jan 1927), 4th dau of Rev Henry Jodrell, Rector of Gisleham, Suffolk (*see* JODRELL Bt), and *d* 13 Feb 1922, leaving issue:

1b CARYL ERNEST BAGOT, **6th Baron Bagot of Bagot's Bromley**, Lt Irish Gds (SR) WW I; *b* 9 March 1877; *m* 1st 6 Feb 1911 Margaret (*d* 10 Aug 1937), dau of James MacMenemy; *m* 2nd 1 March 1940 (*divorce* 1972) Nancy Constance (*m* 2nd 14 Sept 1965 George Kenneth Whitehead, s of Percy Kay Whitehead, of Greenbank, Bury, Lancs), dau of Francis Aldborough Spicer, of Sydney, Australia, and *d* 5 Aug 1961, having adopted:

*Caryl Rosemary; *b* 7 Dec 1960

1b Ysolde Cicely; *m* 12 Oct 1899 Bertram Gordon Snell, s of Col Francis William Snell, and *d* 12 Oct 1964 aged 90. He *d* 20 July 1952

2b Gladys Mary Beatrice; *m* 18 Jan 1905 Frank Herbert Leake, s of Edward Leake, of Castle Square, Ludlow, and *d* 2 Aug 1944, leaving issue. He *d* 27 March 1949

3b Enid Avice; *m* 18 Sept 1905 Capt Reuben James Charles Jewitt (*d* 5 Nov 1958), s of James Joseph Jewitt, of Bedford Lodge, Newmarket, and had:

1c *Dermod James Boris, DSC, Cdr RN; *m* 1st 1 March 1941 (*divorce* 1951) Pamela Mary, dau of Furse Fairfax Vidal Scrutton, and has issue:

1d *Sarah Mary; *b* 20 Oct 1943; *m* 16 July 1966 Lt James Nigel Best, RM, s of Capt J E Best, of Periton House, Minehead, Somerset, and has issue:

1e *James Philip; *b* 28 Aug 1967

2d *Penelope Anne; *b* 20 July 1946; *m* 1 April 1967 Peter Allanson-Bailey, s of Maj T N Allanson-Bailey, of Oare Manor, Brendon, N Devon, and has issue:

1e *Samantha Anne; *b* 2 Sept 1968

1c (cont.) Cdr Dermod Jewitt *m* 2nd 19 Sept 1960 *Emma Jane, dau of Reginald Martin Vick, OBE, TD, MCh, FRCS, and by her has issue:

1d *Charles James Bagot; *b* 7 Dec 1965

2a Ernest Alfred John; *b* 30 March 1848; *m* 15 Feb 1879 Ethel Julia (*d* 10 Nov 1941), 2nd dau of Rev Charles Thoroton Hildyard, and *dsp* 14 Aug 1901

3a Walter Wagstaffe; *b* 25 March 1852; *d* unm 18 March 1882

4a Charles Frederick Heneage; *b* 25 Jan 1858; *educ* Marlborough and Haileybury; *m* 1st 2 March 1886 (*divorce*1906) Florence Eleanor (*d* 26 Sept 1940), est dau of Adml Henry Bagot (*see* above), and had issue:

1b HARRY ERIC BAGOT, **7th Baron Bagot of Bagot's Bromley**; *b* 4 Feb 1894; *educ* Marlborough; Capt RFA and RFC; *m* 1st 11 July 1951 (*divorce*) Kathleen Elizabeth Saddler (*d* 1972), widow of Noel Murray Puckle, of Melbourne, Australia; *m* 2nd 13 Nov 1972 Mrs Mary Hewitt (*d* 8 July 1997)and *dsp* 20 June 1973

2b REGINALD WALTER BAGOT, **8th Baron Bagot of Bagot's Bromley**; *b* 24 Aug 1897; *educ* Wellington; Maj RM; *m* 1st 1922 (*divorce* 1934) Winfred Gweyneth Bowen; *m* 2nd 1934 Millicent Brenda (*d* 1980), only dau of Henry White Bowden, of Great Missenden, Bucks, and *d* 1979

1b Margaret Anne; *b* 1887; *m* 17 April 1917 Edward Richard Marker, yr s of Richard Marker, DL, of Coombe, Devon, and *d* 22 Feb 1954, leaving issue. He *d* 30 Oct 1949

4a (cont.) Charles Bagot *m* 2nd 17 July 1909 Alice Lorina (*d* 30 March 1975), dau of Thomas Farr, and *d* 2 June 1939, having by her had:

3b HENEAGE CHARLES BAGOT, **9th and present Baron Bagot of Bagot's Bromley**

5a Hugh Villiers; Lt 3rd Bn Norfolk Regt; *b* 14 July 1860; *d* 8 Feb 1919

1a Mary; *m* 22 Dec 1885 Sir (William) Algernon Law, KCMG, CB, and *d* 11 Feb 1909, leaving issue (*see* ELLENBOROUGH B)

2a Adela Sophia Harriet; *m* 1 June 1876 Rt Hon Edmond Robert Wodehouse, PC, MP (*see* KIMBERLEY, E), and *d* 25 April 1921

3a Mildred Emily Barbara; *m* 13 June 1882 Cdr Charles Elphinstone Fleming Cunninghame Graham, MVO, RN, and *d* 15 Nov 1935, leaving issue. He *d* 8 June 1917

(5) Lewis Francis (Rev); *b* 18 Feb 1813; *m* 13 June 1848 Catherine (*d* 11 Aug 1891), dau of Rev Hon John Evelyn Boscawen (*see* FALMOUTH, V) and *dsp* 13 Aug 1870

(6) George, Maj, memb Household of Ld Lt Ireland; *b* 5 May 1818; *m* 17 June 1861 Mary Eleanor Frances (*m* 2nd 30 April 1868 Thomas Astell St Quintin, 10th Hus, and *d* 28 Oct 1869), dau of 3rd Baron Kilmaine (*qv*), and *dsp* 9 May 1867

(7) Richard; *b* 21 Feb 1821; *d* 6 Jan 1840

(8) Frederic (Rev), DCL, Rector Harpsden, Oxon, Prebendary Wells, Register Oxford; *b* 23 Jan 1822; *m* 29 Oct 1862 Charlotte Anne Philippine (*d* 8 Dec 1925), only dau of Brice Pearse, of Ashlyns, Gt Berkhamsted, and *d* 1 Jan 1892, leaving issue:

1a Cecil Villiers; *b* 5 Sep 1865; *educ* Pembroke Coll Oxford (MA); *m* 18 June 1903 Ethel (*d* 4 Jan 1944), yr dau of Jesse Garratt, of Wateringbury, Kent, and *d* 21 July 1940, leaving issue:

1b Charles Frederic Villiers, OBE (1955); Lt-Col RA, Essex Regt, WW II (despatches), Assist Mil Sec HQ Western Cmd 1952–55, AAG War Office 1956–59, Queen's Messenger 1961; *b* 18 May 1912; *educ* Radley; *m* 1st 26 June 1939 Lucy Violet Kathleen de la Cloche (*d* 5 July 1972), er dau of Harold Henry Marriott, of 60 Gt Cumberland Place, W1, and had:

1c +Richard Charles Villiers; *b* 26 April 1941

2c +Julian William D'Arcy; *b* 24 Dec 1943

1c *Harriet Anne Elizabeth [Mrs Julian Greene, 27 Brockwell Park Gdns, London SE24]; *b* 20 July 1951; *m* 1978 *Julian Patrick Greene and has:

1d *John Charles Henry; *b* 1985

1d *Lucy Diana Sylvia; *b* 1989

2c *Patricia Mary [Mrs Terence Maguire, 87 Lea St, Kidderminster, W Midlands DY10 1SN]; *b* 5 May 1953; *m* 1984 *Terence B A Maguire

1b (cont.) Col Charles Bagot *m* 2nd 1975 *Anne Drabble [Mrs Charles Bagot, The Red House, Brockdish, Diss, Norfolk], er dau of Arthur Calver, of Docking, Norfolk, and *d* 1986

1b Helen Cecilia Mary; *b* 19 June 1905; *m* 17 April 1940 (William) Thomas Keble, MA (*d* 19 Oct 1965), s of Preb Thomas Charles Keble, of Lichfield, and *d* 9 Nov 1974, leaving issue

2b *Millicent Jessie Eleanor, CBE (1967, MBE 1949); *b* 28 March 1907; *educ* LMH Oxford (MA 1932)

2a Harold Frederic; *b* 9 Feb 1867; *d* unm 16 Oct 1894

3a Sidney Charles (Rev), Rector of Rous Lench, Evesham, Worcs; *b* 10 April 1873; *educ* Keble Coll Oxford (MA); *d* unm 11 March 1933

1a Mary Harriet Agnes; *d* unm 19 Aug 1914

BAGRI

Arms: Per pale sable and gules six swordblades three bend sinisterwise issuant from the dexter three bendwise issuant from the sinister their points crossing in saltire or. **Crest:** Issuing from a demi-kalasa sable garnished or a lotus flower also or. **Badge:** Three lotus flowers in pairle slips outwards and conjoined to the fimbriation or of a roundel gules. **Supporters:** Two elephants the dexter gules with housings on the back and forehead sable garnished tasselled and fringed or the sinister sable with like housings gules garnished tasselled and fringed or each semy of cinquefoils tusked and unguled argent the tusks banded or and holding aloft with the trunk a lotus flower slipped also or. **Motto:** Truth always triumphs. **Creation:** B. (LP, UK) 1996.

THE BARON BAGRI, of Regent's Park, City of Westminster (Raj Kumar Bagri, CBE (1995)) [The Rt Hon The Lord Bagri, Metdist Ltd, 80 Cannon St, London EC4N 6EJ]; *b c* 1930; chm: London Metal Exchange 1992– (memb management ctee 1973–, dir 1983–), Metdist Ltd 1959– and Rajiv Gandhi Fndn, dir Minmetco, bd memb Bagri Fndn; *m* *Usha Maheshwary (co sec Minmetco) and has, with a dau:

1 *Apurv; *b* 1959; dir Minmetco, bd memb Bagri Fndn

BAILEY

Arms: Arg. on a fess between three martlets gu. a bezant between two sprigs of mimosa ppr. **Crest:** A demi-female figure with arms extended ppr., habited az., trimmed at the collar, cuffs and shoulders arg., holding in each hand a sprig of mimosa as in the arms. **Motto:** *Virtus castellum meum* ('Virtue is my fortress'). **Creation:** Bt. (UK) 12 Feb 1919.

SIR DERRICK THOMAS LOUIS BAILEY, 3RD BT, of Cardock, in the Province of the Cape of the Good Hope and Union of South Africa, DFC [Sir Derrick Bailey Bt DFC, Bluestones, Alderney, Channel Islands]; *b* 15 Aug 1918; *s* half-bro 1946; *educ* Winchester and Ch Ch Oxford; Capt SAAF, 2nd Lt S African Irish, WW II; *m* 1st 18 July 1946 (*divorce* 19–) (Katharine) Nancy, only dau of Robert Stormonth Darling, WS, of Rosebank, Kelso; *m* 2nd 1980 (*divorce* 1990) Jean Roscoe (*d* 1996) and by his 1st w has issue:

1 +JOHN RICHARD [John Bailey Esq, 67 Darley Rd, Randwick, NSW 2031, Australia]; *b* 11 June 1947; *educ* Winchester and Christ's Coll; *m* 11 June 1977 *Philippa Jane, only dau of John Sherwin Mervyn Pearson Gregory, of Monnington House, Monnington-on-Wye, Herefs, and has issue:

(1) +James Edward; *b* 7 Sept 1983

(2) +Michael Abe; *b* 1987

(1) *Anna; *b* 1980

2 +Thomas Noel [Thomas Bailey Esq, Lower Brinsop Court Farm, Hereford and Worcester HR4 7AZ]; *b* 23 Dec 1948; *educ* Bradfield; *m* 1987 *Penelope Jane, dau of F B Aggas, of Kibworth, Leics, and has issue:

(1) +Peter Robert; *b* 1988

(2) +Charles Richard; *b* 1990

(3) +Jack Frederick; *b* 1994

3 +William Abe [William Bailey Esq, Poortje Stud, PO Box 83, Colesberg 5980, Cape Prov, S Africa]; *b* 21 May 1950; *educ* Winchester; *m* 1982 *Nikki, dau of Vernon Langerman, of Cape Town, and formerly w of — Riley, and has issue:

(1) +David Moir; *b* 1983

(1) *Camilla; *b* 1985

4 +Patrick James [Patrick Bailey Esq, Upton Court, Upton Bishop, Ross-on-Wye, Hereford and Worcester HR9 7UN]; *b* 17 March 1959; *educ* Bradfield; *m* 1st 6 Aug 1983 (*divorce* 1986) Hon Lucy Jane, yst dau of 10th Viscount Boyne (*qv*); *m* 2nd 17 March 1990 *Sarah, yr dau of Brian J Hammond, of White Leas, Sopworth, Chippenham, Wilts, and by her has:

(1)+Edward William; *b* 22 May 1997

(1) *Jemima Jane; *b* 28 July 1994

(2) *Lucinda Mary; *b* 28 July 1994

(3) *Annabel Lettice; *b* 22 May 1997

1 *Patricia Rosemary; *b* 21 Oct 1951; *m* 1986 *Anthony Howard Collins, of Llantellen, Skenfrith, Gwent, and has:

(1) *Edward; *b* 1989

(2) *Sam; *b* 1991

(1) *Tara; *b* 1987

Lineage: JOHN BAILEY, of Manor House, Laycock, Keighley, W R Yorks; *d* 28 Nov 1873, leaving:

THOMAS BAILEY, of Queenstown, S Africa; *b* 30 Jan 1836; *m* 29 July 1860 Ann Drummond (*d* 27 May 1872), dau of Peter McEwan, of Nuthill, Crieff, Perthshire, and had:

1 ABE (Sir), **1st Bt**

1 Mary; *m* 20 Oct 1886 William Henry Clapham, of Tower House, Skipton, Yorks, and *d* 13 June 1946, leaving issue

2 Alice Maude; *m* 16 Oct 1894 Thomas Henry Haggas, of Myrtle Grove, Keighley, and Walmsgate Hall, Lincs, and *d* 9 July 1950, leaving issue

3 Susanah Janet; *d* unm 20 Feb 1929

THOMAS BAILEY *d* 29 May 1905; his only son,

Sir Abe Bailey, 1st Bt (UK), so *cr* 12 Feb 1919, KCMG (1911), JP Sussex, Lt City London, Liveryman Framework Knitters' Co, Capt Sussex Imp Yeo, Maj S African Forces and DAQMG 6th Mounted Bde S Africa 1914–15, memb Johannesburg Ctee during Jameson's Raid 1895, raised and financed troops to suppress Zulu Rebellion 1907 and Sharpshooters for W Front WW I 1915, Boer War 1900–02 with rank of Col, SW Africa WW I 1914–15; MLA Cape of Good Hope 1902–05, Transvaal 1907–10 and Union of S Africa for Krugersdorp 1915–24; *b* 6 Nov 1864; Croix de Guerre and Cornwell Scouts' Decoration; *m* 1st 17 July 1894 Caroline Mary (*d* 23 March 1902), er dau of John Paddon, of Sydenham, and Kimberley, S Africa, and *d* 10 Aug 1940, had issue:

1 **Sir John Milner Bailey, 2nd Bt**; *b* 15 June 1900; *m* 1st 12 Dec 1932 (*divorce* 1935) Diana (*d* 19 Oct 1963), est dau of Sir Winston Spencer Churchill (*see* MARLBOROUGH, D); *m* 2nd 18 Oct 1939 (*divorce* 1945) Muriel, formerly w of Count Alexandre Orlowski and dau of J Henry Mullins, of New York; *m* 3rd 4 May 1945 *Stella Mary, dau of Charles Du Plessis Chiappini, of 2 Stephen Street, Cape Town, and *dsp* 13 Feb 1946

1 Cecil Marguerite; *b* 8 June 1895; *m* 16 March 1919 Maj William Francis Christie (*d* May 1948), MD, RAMC, son of Dugald Christie, CMGP, FRCP, and *d* 29 June 1962

Sir Abe *m* 2nd 5 Sept 1911 Hon Mary Westenra, DBE (1930) (*d* 29 Aug 1960), only dau of 5th Baron Rossmore (*qv*), and by her had:

2 Sir DERRICK THOMAS LOUIS BAILEY, **3rd and present Bt**

3 +James Richard Abe , DFC (1944), S/Ldr RAFVR WW II; *b* 23 Oct 1919; *educ* Winchester and Ch Ch Oxford (BA 1947); *m* 1st 1958 (*divorce* 1963) Gillian Mary (*d* 19–), dau of John Kilgour Parker, of Cape Town, S Africa, and has:

(1) +Jonathan Alcuin Abe; *b* 4 Aug 1959

3 (cont.) James Bailey *m* 2nd 16 April 1964 *Barbara Louise, dau of Harry Epstein, of 22 Central Avenue, Illovo, Johannesburg, and by her has had:

(2) Alaric James Abe; *b* 9 Nov 1965; *d* 1986

(3) +Prospero James Thomas; *b* 1969

2 Mittie Mary Starr; *b* 1 Aug 1913; *m* 1st 23 May 1934 (*divorce* 1935) Robin Grant Lawson (*das* 10 April 1944), 2nd s of Sir John Grant Lawson, 1st Bt (*see* 1970 edn); *m* 2nd 4 Dec 1935 (*divorce* 1947) William Frederick Lloyd (*d* 1960), 2nd s of Samuel Janson Lloyd, JP, of Pipewell, Northants, and had issue; *m* 3rd 1947 (*divorce* 1958) George Edward Frederick Rogers, and *d* 10 April 1961

3 Ann Hester Zia; *b* 15 Aug 1918; *m* 6 Sept 1939 (*divorce* 1948) Pierce Nicholas Netterville Synnott, CB, er s of Nicholas Joseph Synnott, JP, of Furness, Naas, Co Kildare, and had issue

4 *Noreen Helen Rosemary; *b* 27 July 1921; *m* 1st 27 Jan 1941 W/Cdr Peter Anker Simmons, DFC, RAF (*d* 13 May 1947 as the result of an aeroplane accident), s of R C Simmons, of Salisbury, Zimbabwe, and has:

(1) *Richard James [Richard Simmons Esq, Manutsa Farm, PO Box 84, Hoedspruit, Eastern Transvaal, S Africa]; *b* 1944; *m* 1981 (*divorce* 1982) — and has:

1a *Justin Rorke James; *b* 1982

(1) *(Noreen) Starr [Mrs Philip Harper, Tebula, PO Box 2442, Tzaneen, S Africa]; *b* 1941; *m* 1st 1967 (*divorce* 1975), as his 2nd w, Sir Vivyan Edward Naylor-Leyland, 3rd Bt (*qv*); *m* 2nd 1986 *Philip Thomas Harper

1 (cont.) Noreen Simmons [Mrs Noreen Raben-Levetzau, L'Ermitage, rue de Souers, Vineuil, St Firmin, 60500, Chantilly, France; 94 Pretoria Ave, Atholl, Johannesburg, S Africa]; *m* 2nd 8 Aug 1947 (*divorce* 1951) Count Peter Christian Raben (*d* 26 April 1969), s of Count Siegfried Raben-Levetzau, of 8 Wilton Street, London SW1, and has:

(2) *Paul Michael; *b* 1949

(1) Alexandra Louise; *b* 1948; *d* 1984

BAILLIE

Arms: Az. nine mullets, three, three, two and one or within a bordure counter-nebuly arg. and sa. (for BAILLIE). **Crest:** Out of clouds ppr. a star of eight points or. **Supporters:** Two lions guardant arg. **Motto:** *In caligine lucet* ('It shines in the dark'). **Creation:** Bt. (UK) 14 Nov 1823.

SIR GAWAINE GEORGE HOPE BAILLIE, 7TH BT, of Polkemmet, Linlithgowshire [Sir Gawaine Baillie Bt, Freechase, Warninglid, Sussex RH17 5SZ]; *b* 8 March 1934; *s f* 1947; *educ* Eton and Cambridge U; *m* 28 Dec 1966 *Lucille Margot, only dau of Senator Louis Philippe Beaubien, of Montreal, Canada, and formerly w of Peter Melvill-Gardner, and has issue:

1 +ADRIAN LOUIS; *b* 26 March 1973

1 *Liza Katharine; *b* 8 April 1969

Lineage: THOMAS BAILLIE of Polkemmet (descended from the BAILLIEs of Jervistowne, who were descended from the BAILLIEs of Carphin, who were cadets of the BAILLIEs of Lamington); *m* 1600 Elizabeth Polwarth, of Cathlaw, and had, with other issue:

THOMAS BAILLIE; *m* 1625 Alison, dau of Sir Hames Muirhead of Lauchop, and was *k* 1645 at the Battle of Kilsyth under the royalist Marquess of Montrose (*see* MONTROSE, D), leaving, with a dau:

THOMAS BAILLIE; *m* 1644 Margaret, dau of William Baillie of Carphin, and *d* 1660, leaving, with other issue:

THOMAS BAILLIE; *m* 1667 Ann, *d* au of Thomas Inglis of Murdiston, Stirlingshire, and *d* 1704, having had issue:

THOMAS BAILLIE; became heir of line of his mother's family; *b* 1678; *m* Ann, dau and ultimate successor of Patrick Cockburn of E Borthwick, and *d* 1758, leaving, with other issue:

THOMAS BAILLIE; *b* 22 April 1708; *m* 1731 Isabel Walker, dau of the minister of Kirkuds, and *d* 22 April 1784, leaving, with other issue:

WILLIAM BAILLIE of Polkemmet; advocate 1758, Ld of Session as Lord Polkemmet 14 Nov 1793 (resigned 1811); *m* 1st 3 Dec 1768 Margaret, dau of Sir James Colquhoun, 4th Bt, of Luss (*qv*); *m* 2nd 15 April 1803 Janet, sis of Sir John Sinclair, 1st Bt, of Ulbster (*see* THURSO, V), and *d* 14 March 1816, having by his 1st w had, with other issue:

Sir William Baillie, 1st Bt (UK), so *cr* 14 Nov 1823, of Polkemmet; *b* 25 July 1782; *m* 1815 Mary Lyon (*d* 17 Dec 1872), dau of James Dennistoun of Colgrain (and coheir of her mother Margaret, dau of Robert Dreghorn of Blochairn), and *d* 28 Jan 1854, having had, with other issue:

1 **Sir William Baillie, 2nd Bt**, DL and JP, MP Linlithgowshire 1844–47, Convener Linlithgowshire; *b* 2 Feb 1816; *m* 14 April 1846 Mary (*d* 7 June 1910), est dau of Stair Hathorn Stewart, of Physgill, Wigtownshire, and *dsp* 21 July 1890

2 James Dennistoun; *b* 1817; *d* 1 May 1876

3 Robert; *b* 1818; *d* 12 May 1883

4 Thomas; *b* 21 June 1823; *m* 1849 Elizabeth, dau of James Ballinghall, of Australia, and *d* 7 Jan 1889, leaving issue:

(1) **Sir George Baillie, 3rd Bt**, of Polkemmet, BA Cambridge, JP Victoria and NSW; *b* 20 Oct 1856; *d* unm 2 April 1896

(2) ROBERT ALEXANDER (Sir), **4th Bt**

(3) William; *b* 25 April 1861; *m* 1892 Mary (*d* 1946), er dau of Rev Walter Fellows, MA, Vicar St John's, Toorak, Melbourne, and *d* 24 April 1928, leaving:

1a Helen Elizabeth Jacqueline, CMB, City of London Maternity Hosp; *b* 17 Feb 1893; *d* 1970

2a Alison Hope; *m* 1st 1936 F/Lt P R M Barker, RAA F (*d* 1946); *m* 2nd 1949 *Kenneth Charles Watson and *d* 1975

3a Julia Mary Alexandra; *b* 1905; *m* 1943 Leonhard Adam, LLD, DPhil (*d* 9 Sept 1960), s of Michael Meinhard Adam, of Berlin, and *d* 1993, leaving:

1b *Mary Clare [Mrs Moshe Murvitz, 22 Micha St, Apt 1, Tev Aviv 63111, Israel]; *b* 22 Jan 1945; *m* 1st 1964 (*divorce* 1969) Gabriel A Michaelides; *m* 2nd 1981 *Moshe Murvitz and by him has:

1c *Batia Leonora; *b* 1982

(1) Mary Dennistoun; *m* 5 Aug 1874 Col Thomas Caradoc Rose Price, CB (*d* 3 July 1911), and *d* 22 March 1899, leaving issue (*see* PRICE, Bt)

(2) Elizabeth Janet, OBE (1918); *m* 25 March 1885 Brig-Gen Hon William Edwin Cavendish, MVO, late Gren Gds (*d* 28 Aug 1931), and *d* 2 May 1935, leaving issue (*see* CHESHAM, B)

5 John Hope; *b* 1825; *d* 1837

6 Alexander Hope; *b* 15 Oct 1827; *m* 30 April 1878 Edith Caroline (*d* 7 Aug 1928), 2nd dau of Fairfax Fearnley, of Sutton, Notts, and *dsp* 19 Sept 1883

7 George Augustus Frederick, Capt Haddington Artillery Militia; *b* 31 July 1833; *m* 16 Feb 1871 Mary Gertrude (*d* 6 Nov 1922), 4th dau of Benjamin Peyton Sadler, RN, and *d* 7 April 1882, leaving issue:

(1) William Lyon Dennistoun, Capt Roy Scots Fus; *b* 11 Aug 1872; *ka* at Frederickstad S Africa 25 Oct 1900

(1) Catherine Gertrude Penual; *d* unm 17 Feb 1936

(2) Janet Hope Peyton; *d* unm 8 Jan 1964

(3) Mary Gertrude Colquhoun; *m* 25 Nov 1915 Lt-Col Mordaunt John Fortescue FitzGerald, DSO, late RA (*d* 17 Nov 1947), and *dsp* 18 Aug 1958

The 3rd Bt's bro,

Sir Robert Alexander Baillie, 4th Bt, BA Oxford, Maj cmdg Australian Sqdn King's Colonials Imp Yeo; *b* 24 Aug 1859; *m* 13 July 1887 Isabel (*d* 1 Feb 1945), dau of David Elliot Wilkie, of Ratho Byres, Midlothian, and *d* 16 Oct 1907, leaving:

1 **Sir Gawaine George Stuart Baillie, 5th Bt**; Lt 2nd Dragoons, Scots Greys; *b* 29 May 1893; *ka* France 7 Sept 1914

2 **Sir Adrian William Maxwell Baillie, 6th Bt**, DL and JP, MP Linlithgow 1931–35 and Tonbridge 1937–45, Dip Serv 1921–28 (ret as 2nd Sec), Lt 2nd Dragoons, Scots Greys, Res of Offrs; *b* 5 May 1898; *m* 4 Nov 1931 (*divorce* 1944) Hon Olive Cecilia (*d* 9 Sept 1974), est dau of 1st and last Baron Queenborough (*see* ANGLESEY, M), and *d* 8 Jan 1947, leaving issue:

(1) Sir GAWAINE GEORGE HOPE BAILLIE, **7th and present Bt**

BAILLIEU

Arms: Sa. on a pile between two eagle's heads erased or three escutcheons gu., each charged with a fleur-de-lys of the second. **Crest:** Upon a billet fesswise az., charged with three plates, a martlet sa., holding in the beak a fleur-de-lys as in the arms. **Supporters:** Dexter, a yellow Labrador dog ppr.; sinister, a kangaroo, also ppr. **Motto:** *Sans changer* ('Without changing'). **Creation:** B. (UK) 13 Feb 1953.

THE 3RD BARON BAILLIEU of Sefton, Cwlth of Australia, and Parkwood, Co Surrey (James William Latham Baillieu) [The Rt Hon The Lord Baillieu, 56 Rose St, Armadale, Melbourne 3143, Australia]; *b* 16 Nov 1950; *s f* 1973; *educ* Radley, Monash U Melbourne (BEc 1977); late 2nd Lt Coldstream Gds; *m* 1st 1974 (*divorce* 1985) Cornelia Masters, yst dau of William Conkling Ladd, of 61 Cadogan Sq, London SW1; *m* 2nd 1987 *Clare, dau of Peter Stephenson, of Benalla, Victoria, Australia, and by his 1st w has issue:

1 +ROBERT LATHAM; *b* 2 Feb 1979

Lineage: JEAN BAPTISTE BAILLIEUX, of Liège; *b* 1698; *m* 1st 27 Nov 1723 Isabelle Bodson; *m* 2nd Barbe Noel Molinet (*d* 7 March 1767) and *d* Liège 14 June 1744 having by her had further issue; by his 1st w he had, with two yr sons (Charles, *bapt* 30 Oct 1725; Jean Baptiste, *bapt* Liège 22 Feb 1727):

ETIENNE BAILLIEUX, of Liège; *bapt* 2 April 1718; *m* 17 Oct 1740 Dieudonné (*d* 1789), dau of Jacques Werpin, and *d* Liège 12 April 1791, having had, with four er s:

ETIENNE LAMBERT BAILLIEUX; *bapt* 24 March 1752; *m* 23 Nov 1772 Agathe Elizabeth (*m* 2nd Charles Le Clercq), dau of Pascal Pieltain by Agathe Duchesnem, and *d* St Severin, Liège, 2 Feb 1781, having had, with other issue:

ETIENNE LAMBERT BAILLIEUX, of 5 Unity Street and 3 Berkeley Crescent, Bristol; *bapt* Liège 14 Sept 1773; *m* 1st 13 Sept 1801 Anne Taylor, widow (*d* 27 Nov 1811), and had issue:

1 LAMBERT FRANCIS

2 Pascal; *bapt* 19 July 1804

1 Anne; *bapt* 18 Jan 1807; *m* James George, of Bristol, and *d c* 1849

2 Elizabeth twin; *bapt* 18 Jan 1807, living 1848–49

ETIENNE BAILLIEUX *m* 2nd 26 Nov 1812 Sarah Hawksley and *d* 8 Nov 1816 having by her had:

3 Frederick Joseph Hawksley; *b* 25 May 1815; *m* Mary Ann Farrow (*d* 6 Dec 1881), and *d* 9 April 1890, leaving issue:

(1) Sarah Maria

The est son,

LAMBERT FRANCIS BAILLIEU; *bapt* 24 Aug 1802; *m* 25 Oct 1829 Elizabeth (*bapt* 19 June 1804; *d* 13 Jan 1876), dau of Joseph Lloyd Morgan, of Haverfordwest, Pembs, and *d* 6 Sept 1861, having had issue:

1 William Henry; *b* 1 March 1830; *d* 11 March 1869

2 James (twin); *b* 13 Feb; *d* 15 Feb 1831

3 JAMES GEORGE, of whom presently

4 John Lloyd; *b* 15 July 1833; *d* 15 March 1834

5 John Pietain; *b* 1 Nov 1834

6 Frederick Joseph; *b* 28 July 1836; *m* 7 March 1858 Anne Maria (*d* 26 April 1893), dau of John Davies, sea captain, of Haverfordwest, and *d* 17 Aug 1875, having had issue

7 Charles; *b* 23 Sept 1841; *m* 8 Oct 1864 Elizabeth (*d* 10 July 1870), dau of William James, of Haverfordwest, and *d* 17 Aug 1875, having had issue

8 Lambert Francis; *b* 23 Oct 1944; *m* 1 June 1876 Eliza Caroline (*d* 11 April 1930), dau of Edwin Jarvis, of Cardiff, and *d* 28 April 1911, having had issue

9 Alfred; *b* 20 Feb 1846; *m* 6 Oct 1872 Jane Hughes-Jones, of Haverfordwest (*d* 24 April 1920), and *d* 25 Feb 1873

10 Richard Phillips Lloyd; *b* 26 May 1847; *m* 1st 5 Dec 1870 Sarah (*d* 21 Aug 1871), dau of John Davies, of Neath, Glam; *m* 2nd 11 Oct 1873 Keziah, widow of — Morgan, and dau of William Glover, of Cardiff, and *d* 27 Jan 1906

11 Thomas Patrick Crawford; *b* 17 March 1852; *m* 9 July 1900 Martha (*d* 1 Oct 1926), dau of John Whitney, of Carmarthen, and *d* 8 Feb 1909

1 Anne (twin); *b* 13 Feb; *d* 17 Feb 1831

2 Anne Elizabeth; *b* 31 March 1838; *m* 31 Oct 1869 James Davies, of Haverfordwest, and *d* 4 March 1877, leaving issue

3 Margaret Jane; *b* 8 Nov 1839; *m* Nov 1868 Hugh Bryans, merchant, of Queenscliff, Victoria, Australia, and *d* 1 Sept 1925, having had issue

4 Catherine Maria; *b* 19 Sept 1843; *d* 26 Jan 1845

LAMBERT BAILLIEU's 3rd son,

JAMES GEORGE BAILLIEU, of Queenscliff, Victoria, and Merrylands, Canterbury, Victoria, Australia; *b* 13 March 1832; *m* 3 Nov 1853 Emma Lawrence (*bapt* 25 Nov 1838; *d* 3 Jan 1908), dau of James Pow, of Barrow Hill Farm, Farmborough, Somerset, and *d* 10 Dec 1897, having had issue:

1 James Lambert; *b* 17 June 1855; *m* 5 Sept 1881 Elizabeth Mary Dod, and *dsp* 11 Dec 1900

2 WILLIAM LAWRENCE, of whom presently

3 George Francis; *b* 17 Aug 1860; *m* 30 Oct 1894 Agnes, dau of William Sheehan, of Queenscliff, Victoria, and *d* 1906, leaving issue:

(1) Reginald Francis, MC; *b* 17 March 1896; *m* 9 Oct 1923 Florence Chapman, of Melbourne, Australia, and *d* 18 Jan 1965, having had issue:

1a *Ronald George; *b* 10 Oct 1924; *m* 10 Dec 1949 *Gabrielle, dau of John Griffin Money, of W Australia, and has issue:

1b *Andrew Edward; *b* 13 Jan 1952

2b *Richard Francis; *b* 9 Aug 1954

3b *Timothy James; *b* 5 Nov 1961

1b *Bronwyn; *b* 10 Nov 1950

2a Richard Forster; *b* 28 June 1927; *d* 1 May 1943

(1) Agnes Beryl; *b* 22 Jan 1898; *m* Walter Frederick Stewart (*d* 16 May 1937), and *d* 29 Jan 1967, leaving issue

(2) (Margery) Merlyn, DBE (1960), OBE (1948); *b* 8 Jan 1900; *m* 1920 Sidney Myer (*d* 1934), and had with other issue:

1a *Sidney Baillieu Myer, AC 1990, MA (Cantab) [Sidney Myer Esq, Level 45, 55 Collins St, Melbourne, Victoria 3000, Australia]; dir N M Rothschild & Son Australia; *b* 11 Jan 1926; *educ* Geelong GS, Pembroke Coll Cambridge (MA); *m* 15 Dec 1955 Sarah J, dau of Samuel Hordern, CMG, OBE (*see* below), and has issue

(3) *Vida Finetta; *b* 5 March 1903; *m* Ian McEacharn, and has issue

4 Robert Frederick; *b* 6 June 1862; missing, presumed *ka* S African War 1900

5 Charles Formby Pieltain; *b* 2 Nov 1864; *educ* Melbourne U (MB 1887); *dsp* Dec 1903

6 Edward Lloyd Morgan; *b* 2 Nov 1867; *d* unm 14 July 1939

7 Arthur Sidney, OBE; *b* 27 April 1872; *m* 15 Nov 1899 Ethel Mary (*d* Nov 1932), dau of Hon David Ham, MLC, of Ballarat, Victoria, Australia, and *d* 10 Oct 1943, having had issue:

(1) Jack Kingsbury; *b* 29 Sept 1900; *m* 1925 Grace Lavers, and *dsp* 21 April 1926

(2) *Darren, MA Cambridge; *b* 30 April 1903; *m* 18 March 1936 *Diana Margaret, dau of Maj W J Knox, MC, Australian Forces, and has issue:

1a *Ian Arthur Knox; *b* 18 July 1938; *educ* Oxford (BA); *m* 1967 *Marianne, 2nd dau of J N Dalhoff, of Nelson, NZ, and has issue:

1b *James Clive Knox; *b* 26 June 1968

2a *David McArthur, (BA) U of W Australia; *b* 13 July 1942; *m* 19— Claire —, of Melbourne, and has:

1b *Charles Edward; *b* 26 Dec 1971

3a James George; *b* 18 Oct 1948; *d* unm as a result of an accident in USA 29 Sept 1972

4a *William John; *b* 15 Aug 1951

5a *Edward Norman; *b* 31 July 1953

1a *Fiona Mary; *b* 14 Sept 1940

2a *Katharine Jean; *b* 7 Jan 1946

(3) *Everard; *b* 9 Dec 1912; *m* 19– *Betty Mary, dau of James William Balfe, of Sydney, NSW, and has issue:

1a *Sarah Mary Christine; *b* 9 Aug 1950

(1) *Lelda Sunday; *b* 15 Oct 1905; *m* 19– *John Reed

8 Richard Percy Clive; *b* 15 Oct 1874; *m* 28 March 1900 Mary Affleck Ramsay (*d* 18 Dec 1968), and *d* 1941, leaving issue:

(1) *Marshall Lawrence, (BA) Cambridge; *b* 19 Sept 1902; *m* 15 Oct 1930 *Nancy Elizabeth Willsallen, and has issue:

1a *(Richard) Lawrence, (BA) Cambridge; *b* 5 Nov 1934; *m* 15 May 1965 (*divorce*) Charlotte Susannah, dau of Sir Cyril Hugh Kleinwort (*see* KLEINWORT, Bt) and has issue:

1b *Richard; *b* 19–

1b *Joanne Alice Serena; *b* 20 May 1968

2a *Ian Marshall; *b* 6 June 1936; *m* 27 April 1961 *Judith Anne, dau of Alan Evans, of 6 Landen Place, Toorak, Victoria

1a *Jacqueline Elizabeth; *b* 17 Aug 1932; *m* 15 Dec 1954 *David Hunter White, of Havilah, Mudgee, NSW Australia, and has issue:

1b *Hunter Baillieu; *b* 13 Oct 1955

2b *Peter Baillieu; *b* 3 Jan 1959

1b *Sarah Jacqueline; *b* 1 Jan 1957

(2) Ian Clive, BA Oxford; *b* 11 Aug 1904; *m* 1st 15 May 1929 (*divorce* 1951) Joanna Edith, yr dau of Roland Danvers Brinton, MD, MRCP (*see* 1970 edn STOCKS, B); *m* 2nd *Mary Minns, and *d* 31 Dec 1978, leaving issue

1a *Colin Clive, late Lt Coldstream Gds; *b* 2 July 1930; *m* 1st 5 Oct 1955 Diana, dau of Aubrey Clare Robinson, of Roppeleghs, nr Haslemere, Surrey, and has issue:

1b *Amanda Jane; *b* 15 Dec 1956

2b *Victoria Constance; *b* 4 July 1964

1a (cont.) Colin Baillieu *m* 2nd 28 Sept 1968 *Renata, er dau of Franz Richter, of W Berlin and has issue:

1b *Alexander; *b* 7 May 1972

2b *Danveb; *b* 21 March 1976

(1) *Mary Ramsay; *b* 17 Jan 1901; *m* Harry Davies

(2) *June; *b* 11 July 1909; *m* 1934 Samuel Hordern, CMG, OBE (*d* 25 July 1960), son of Sir Samuel Hordern, KBE, of Sydney, and has issue:

1a *Samuel; *b* 4 Jan 1937

1a *Sarah J; *b* 1 Feb 1935; *m* 15 Dec 1955 *Baillieu Myer, son of Sidney Myer, and Dame Merlyn Myer, DBE, and has issue (*see* above)

9 Norman Horace; *b* 17 June 1878; *d* unm 22 Aug 1955

10 Maurice Howard Lawrence; *b* 21 Sept 1883; *m* 12 March 1912 Beatrice Marie St John Madden (*d* 10 Oct 1957), and *d* 26 July 1961, leaving issue:

(1) *John Madden; *b* 31 Dec 1912; *m* 9 March 1938 *Elizabeth Darling, and has issue:

1a *Anthony John; *b* 6 Jan 1949

2a *Michael Harold Charles; *b* 30 Jan 1953

1a *Joanna Darling; *b* 24 Dec 1946

(1) *(Beatrice) Sandra; *b* 19 Feb 1921; *m* 26 Sept 1950 *William Alexander Stewart, and has issue:

1a *Judith Margaret; *b* 20 Oct 1953

2a *Alexandra Beatrice; *b* 9 April 1957

1 Emma Elizabeth; *b* 22 Nov 1856; *m* 4 Sept 1895 Edward Latham, and had issue

2 Anne Finetta; *b* 2 Nov; *d* 21 Dec 1866

3 Amy Adelaide; *b* 1 Feb 1870; *m* 28 Sept 1904 Edward Herbert Shackell (*d* 6 May 1932), son of James Shackell, of Hungtingtower Road, Armadale, Melbourne, Victoria, Australia, and *d* 19 Feb 1966 aged 96, leaving issue

4 Florence Frances *b* 22 Feb 1876; *m* 14 Dec 1921 John Seymour Teulon, and *d* 8 Aug 1961

JAMES BAILLIEU's 2nd son,

WILLIAM LAWRENCE BAILLIEU, of Sefton Mount, Macedon, Victoria, Australia; *b* 29 April 1859; *m* 1887 Bertha Martha (*b* 6 Nov 1865; *d* 28 July 1925), dau of Edward Latham, of Melbourne, Australia, formerly of Liverpool (and gdau of Capt Thomas Atkins by his former w Bertha, dau of Dr Edward Luttrell, ninth in descent from Sir Andrew Luttrell, of Dunster Castel, Somerset), and *d* 6 Feb 1936, leaving issue:

1 CLIVE LATHAM, **1st Baron**

2 Harry Latham, MC, of Torrumbarry, Echuca, Victoria, Australia; *b* 28 April 1891; *educ* Jesus Coll Cambridge; *m* Oct 1922 Margaret Christie (*m* 2nd 1945 Harold Timon Coldham, of Poresea, Victoria, Australia, who *d* March 1964), only dau of William Sydney Robinson, of Arundel Farm, Keilas, Victoria, Australia, and *d* 9 Feb 1944, leaving issue:

(1) *Peter Lawrence; *b* 22 July 1927

(2) *Gavin; *b* 1 Nov 1933

(1) *Barbara Margaret; *b* 8 July 1924; *m* 1st — Deasey; *m* 2nd *— Bostock

(2) *Elizabeth Anne; *b* 24 April 1926

3 Tom Latham, DFC, memb Australian Jockey Club Ctee 1947; *b* 7 April 1898; *m* 7 Sept 1926 Ruth Marian Coleman, and had issue:

(1) *Tom Lawrence; *b* 17 Sept 1929; *m* 10 Oct 1957 *Jan Harvey Wilson, and has issue:

1a *Etienne; *b* 21 Dec 1959

1a *Katrina Elizabeth; *b* 4 Dec 1961

2a *Nicola Anne; *b* 4 March 1965

3a *Yvette Marian; *b* 4 June 1967

(1) *Lois Latham; *b* 22 Dec 1927; *m* 19— *Dr Victor Geoffrey Abram, and has issue:

1a *Peter Geoffrey; *b* 25 March 1953

2a *William Geoffrey; *b* 28 Oct 1957

1a *Kerry Ann Lois; *b* 18 Aug 1954

2a *Jillian Ruth; *b* 13 June 1962

(2) *June Leslie; *b* 2 June 1933; *m* 26 April 1957 *Douglas Allan Pickering, and has issue:

1a *Robin Baillieu; *b* 20 Feb 1960

1a *Jane Baillieu; *b* 4 Dec 1961

4 James Latham; *b* 3 Aug 1899; *educ* Melbourne U (LLB); *d* unm 18 July 1934
1 Vere Latham; *b* 10 Nov 1892; *d* 10 Dec 1949
2 Bertha Latham; *b* 12 March 1896; *m* 23 Oct 1918 Robert Ramsay, of Santosa, Albany Road, Toorak, Melbourne, Australia, and *d* 22 Aug 1957, having had issue
3 *Claire Latham; *b* 20 Feb 1902; *m* 30 April 1931 *Robert James Vicars, CBE, son of Robert Vicars of Cheltenham, Sydney, Australia, and has issue
4 Amy Latham; *b* 30 July 1904; *m* 24 July 1929 Julian Ormond Smith, MBE, FRCS (Eng), MRCS (Eng), LRCP (Lond), MD (Melb), FRACS, and *d* 24 May 1948, leaving issue

WILLIAM BAILLIEU's est son,

CLIVE LATHAM BAILLIEU, **1st Baron Baillieu**, of Sefton, in the Cwlth of Australia, and of Parkwood, Co Surrey (UK), so *cr* 13 Feb 1953, KBE (1938, OBE 1918), CMG (1929); Maj AIF, T/Lt-Col RAF, WW I 1915–18 (despatches), Australian rep Imp Wireless and Cable Conf 1928 and on Imp communications Advsy Cttee 1929–39, FBI 1945–47 (dep pres 1944–45), 1st Pres BIM 1959 (hon fell 1960), Australian rep Imp Ec Ctee 1930–47, exec memb Export Cncl 1940, dir-gen Br Purchasing Commn Washington 1941–42 and Br Supply Cncl N America 1941–43, Head Br Raw Materials Mission Washington 1942–43, Br Rep Combined Raw Materials Bd Washington 1942–43, Head Br Trade Mission to Argentine 1948, memb Nat Investment Cncl 1946–48, chm Dunlop Rubber Co Ltd 1949–57 (dep chm 1945–49, pres from Oct 1957), jt pres Dalgety and NZ Loan Ltd 1962, chm Centl Mining and Investment Corp 1945–59 (dep chm 1959–64), dir Midland Bank Ltd, English Scottish and Australian Bank Ltd, barrister Inner Temple 1914, chm ESU 1951 (dep chm 1947–51, dep pres 1965); *b* 24 Sept 1889; *educ* Trin Coll Melbourne U and Magdalen Coll Oxford (MA 1913); *m* 24 Feb 1915 Ruby Florence Evelyn (*d* 21 Oct 1962), dau of William Clark, of Windlesham Moor, Windlesham, Surrey, formerly of Beenham Court, Newbury, Berks, and had issue:

1 WILLIAM LATHAM, **2nd Baron**
2 +Robert Latham, MBE (1945), TD [The Hon Robert Baillieu MBE TD, 9 Abingdon Court, Abingdon Villas, London W8; Little Barhams, Priors Way, Aldeburgh, Suffolk]; slr 1954, md DFC (UK) 1973–, Dawnay Day & Co 1973–, Henry Ansbacher Co Ltd, C H Goldrei, Fourcard and Son Ltd, and View Forth Investment Tst Ltd, dir Banque Belge Ltd; Maj Middx Yeo WW II (despatches); *b* 18 July 1917; *educ* Winchester and Magdalen Coll Oxford (BA 1946, MA 1953); *m* 14 May 1949 *Delphine Mary, yr dau of Edgar Hastings Dowler (*see* REYNOLDS, Bt), and has issue:
(1) +Simon; *b* 17 July 1951; *educ* Ampleforth; *m* 1977 *Jane Brebner, of Dunkeld, Johannesburg, and has issue:
1a +James; *b* 1982
1a *Nicole; *b* 1979
2a *Karen; *b* 1986
(2) +Anthony Robert; *b* 15 March 1956; *m* 1980 (*divorce* 1988) Clare Veronica, dau of Richard Gubbins, of The Old Post House, Phoenix Green, Hartley Witney, Hants, and has issue:
1a *Emma Louise; *b* 1986
(1) *Mary Clare; *b* 3 July 1950; *m* 12 July 1974 (*divorce* 1985) James Neil Percival Cranston, and has issue:
1a *Sophie Louise; *b* 22 July 1976
2a *Georgina Clare; *b* 5 May 1978
(2) *Celia Maria; *b* 1 Sept 1953; *m* 1977 *William Bryant Style, and has issue (*see* STYLE, Bt)
3 +Edward Latham, Capt RA and RHA WW II (invalided), memb London Stock Exchange, chm Nat Mutal Life Assur Assoc Australasia (London br), dir ANZ Bank, RTZ Corp, Embankment Tst Ltd, Australasian Tst Ltd and Hoare & Co Govett, memb Court of Assistants Merchant Taylors' Co, ptnr Govett, Sons & Co, Dep Grand Master United Grand Lodge of England; *b* 17 Oct 1919; *educ* Winchester and BNC Oxford (BA 1942, MA 1947); *m* 6 June 1942 *Betty Anne Jardine, dau of Henry Leslie Jardine Taylor, of Crofton Lodge, Sunningdale, Berks, and has issue:
(1) +Christopher Latham; *b* 12 Dec 1949; *educ* Radley; *m* 1984 *Jane, only dau of Robert Bowie, of Bayford, Somerset, and has issue:
1a +Charles Latham; *b* 1985
2a +Edward Latham; *b* 1990
1a *Olivia Clare; *b* 1987
(2) +Philip Latham; *b* 27 June 1958; *m* 1985 *Lucinda Rosalie, er dau of Francis Rokeby Black, FCA (*see* CADMAN, B), and has issue:
1a *Sacha Frances; *b* 27 Dec 1989
2a *Francesca Caroline; *b* 27 March 1994
(1) Sarah Bridget Latham; *b* 27 Oct 1946; *d* 1 April 1947
(2) *Annette Leslie; *b* 4 July 1955; *m* 1986 *Christopher Aylwin, er son of John Aylwin, FRCS, and has issue:
1a *Patrick John; *b* 1990
1a *Camilla Louise; *b* 1993
1 *Yvette Latham [The Hon Mrs Wilson, Durford Knoll, Upper Durford Wood, Petersfield, Hants]; *b* 30 Sept 1922; *m* 20 July 1946 *Robert Ruttan Wilson, s of Arthur Alling Wilson, of San Francisco, California, and has:
(1) *Nenon Baillieu; *b* 25 Oct 1948
(2) *Elizabeth Ruttan; *b* 15 Oct 1950
(3) *Merilyn Yvette; *b* 6 Feb 1953
(4) *Deborah Baillieu; *b* 14 Oct 1955

The 1st BARON *d* 18 June 1967; his est son,

WILLIAM LATHAM BAILLIEU, **2nd Baron Baillieu**; *b* 10 Dec 1915; *educ* Winchester and Magdalen Coll Oxford (BA 1937, MA 1951); WW II 1939–40 as 2nd Lt RA (invalided), assist master St Peter's Sch, Seaford, Sussex; *m* 1st 11 Aug 1945 (*divorce* 1961) Anne Bayliss [Mrs Anthony Dodd, Ridgewood, Parry Inlet, via Denmark, W Australia 6333; Ridgewood Manor, Uckfield, Sussex] (*m* 2nd 1964 *(Harry) Anthony Rupert Dodd), er dau of Leslie William Page, of Southport, Qld, Australia, and had:

1 JAMES WILLIAM LATHAM BAILLIEU, **3rd and present Baron Baillieu**
2 +David Clive Latham; *b* 2 Nov 1952; *educ* Seaford and Radley; slr

The **2nd Baron** *m* 2nd 10 Feb 1962 *Mrs Delia Muriel Champion and was *k* in a motor accident 18 April 1973

BAIRD of Newbyth

Arms: Gu. in chief within an increscent and estoile of eight points arg., in base a boar passant or, on a canton erm. a sword erect ppr., pommel and hilt gold. **Crests:** 1 A Mameluke mounted on a horse and holding in his dexter hand a scimitar, all ppr., 2 A boar's head erased or. **Motto:** *Vi et virtute* ('By strength and valour'). **Creation:** Bt. (UK) 13 April 1809.

SIR DAVID CHARLES BAIRD, 5TH BT, of Newbyth, Co Haddington [Sir David Baird Bt, Novar, Barrhill Rd, Dalbeattie DG5 4JX]; *b* 6 July 1912; *s* unc 1941; *educ* Eton and Cambridge

Lineage: Sir ROBERT BAIRD, 1st Bt, of Saughton (*qv*); had a 2nd surv s:

WILLIAM BAIRD, of Edinburgh, merchant and baillie (local magistrate); *m* 13 Feb 1697 Catherine, dau of Sir W Binning, Ld Provost Edinburgh, and *d* Sept 1737, leaving, with other issue:

WILLIAM BAIRD, heir to his cousin, Sir John Baird, 2nd Bt, of Newbyth of the Feb 1679/80 *cr*; *m* Alicia, 4th dau of Robert Johnston, of Hilltown, Berwicks, and *d* 5 Jan 1765, having had, with other issue:

1 Robert, of Newbyth; *m* 1st Jan 1779 his cousin Hester (*dsp* 6 July 1789), dau of Wynne Johnston, of Hilltown; *m* 2nd 16 Aug 1791 Hersey Christina Maria (*d* July 1829), 2nd dau of David Gavin, of Langton, Berwicks, by Lady Elizabeth Maitland, dau of 7th Earl of Lauderdale (*qv*), and *d* 10 June 1828, having by her had, with other issue:
(1) DAVID (Sir), **2nd Bt**
(2) John, Midshipman RN; *kas* Algiers of a head wound Sept 1806
(3) Wynne, Capt RN; *b* 1799; *m* 12 Nov 1824 Madelina Susan (*d* 15 July 1827), dau of Lt-Col Henry Andrew Cerjat, 6th Inniskilling Dragoons, and *d* 1835, leaving, with a dau (Anne Charlotte, *d* an infant):
1a Robert Henry, Lt Rifle Bde; *b* 19 Sept 1825; *m* 22 Jan 1853 Elizabeth Maria (*d* 6 Dec 1912), dau of George Goff, yr bro of Joseph Goff, of Hale Park, Hants, and *d* 14 May 1905, having had issue:
1b Robert George; *b* 23 May 1864; *m* 3 Jan 1893 Mabel Charlotte (*d* 16 June 1957 aged 87), dau of Rev William Moundeford Bramston, and *d* 31 Dec 1938, leaving issue:
1c Robert Douglas, MC (1918), Maj Rifle Bde WW I and Waziristan 1920–21 (wounded, star, two medals); *b* 19 Dec 1893; *educ* Winchester; *m* 8 June 1926 Alice Patience (*d* 29 Sept 1995), dau of Cecil Gordon Crawley, CBE, of 19 Cranley Place, London SW7, and *d* 9 Dec 1969, leaving:
1d *Dawn [Mrs Geoffrey Loyd, Remenham House, Ocle Pychard, Herefs]; *b* 3 June 1927; *m* 1 March 1968, as his 2nd w, *Geoffrey Haig Loyd (*see* OAKELEY, Bt), 2nd s of Wilfred Haig Loyd
2c George Henry William, Maj Seaforth Highrs WW II; *b* 10 Jan 1903; *educ* Eton; *m* 22 Jan 1931 Catherine Augusta (*d* 1986), yst dau of Capt Francis William Forester, of Hurdcott House, Salisbury (*see* FORESTER, B), and *d* 1992, leaving:
1d Angus George David; *b* 2 Dec 1934; *educ* Eton; *m* 30 Sept 1961 *Fiona Elizabeth Hildred [Mrs Angus Baird, Hartsfield House, Westland Green, Little Hadham, Ware, Herts SG11 2AJ], est dau of John Sholto Fitzpatrick Cooke, CBE, of Ferry Quarter, Strangford, Co Down, and *d* 15 Dec 1996, leaving:
1e +Andrew James; *b* 23 Oct 1970
1e *Nicola Laura; *b* 23 March 1964
2e *Eliza Caroline; *b* 23 July 1967
1d *Diana Catherine [Mrs Julian Jenkinson, Folly Faunts House, Goldhanger, Maldon, Essex CM9 8AP]; *b* 21 Dec 1931; *m* 24 July 1953 *Julian Charles Lewis Jenkinson (*see* JENKINSON, Bt) and has:
1e *Dermot Julian; *b* 2 Dec 1954
1e *Karen Barbara; *b* 19 Sept 1957
2e *Laura Louise Diana; *b* 7 Oct 1966
1c Elizabeth Mabel, JP; *b* 17 Aug 1895; *d* unm 24 March 1957

1b Elizabeth Alice; *d* unm 8 Oct 1925
2b Anne Henrietta; *m* 1879 Hermann van Muyden (*d* 1893) and *d* 13 Nov 1945, leaving issue
3b Ella Sophia Mary; *m* 23 April 1887 Ferdinand de Charrière de Severy, of Lausanne, and *d* 24 April 1938, leaving issue
(1) Elizabeth; *m* 1817 Lt-Col William Wauchope, of Niddrie, Midlothian, and has issue
(2) Christina Maria Hersey; *m* 25 July 1833 7th Viscount Strathallan (*see* PERTH, E) and *d* 14 Feb 1867, leaving issue
2 **Sir David Baird, 1st Bt** (UK), so *cr* 13 April 1809, with remainder, in default of male issue, to his est bro and the latter's heirs male, GCB, PC; *b* 6 Dec 1757; headed storming-party taking of Seringapatam 4 May 1799 (*see* also CORNWALLIS, B); C-in-C capture of Cape of Good Hope, also served Egypt (insignia of the Crescent from Sultan of Turkey), bombardment of Copenhagen and Retreat to Corunna (lost an arm); Gen, Col 24th Foot; *m* 4 Aug 1810 Anne Preston Menzies Campbell, of Fernton and Cochlane (*d* 28 May 1847), er dau and heiress of Maj Patrick Preston, Yr. of Valleyfield, and *dsp* 18 Aug 1829
3 Joseph, Maj-Gen; *m* 27 Feb 1802 Hon Heather Charlotte Tonson (*d* 27 June 1850), dau of 1st Baron Riversdale, and *d* Cape of Good Hope 4 April 1816, leaving issue

The 1st Bt's nephew,

Sir David Baird, 2nd Bt, Capt Army; *b* 1795; *m* 10 Aug 1821 Lady Anne Kennedy (*d* 2 Nov 1877), est dau of 1st Marquess of Ailsa (*qv*), and had issue:
1 Robert Wynne; drowned 15 Oct 1845
2 Archibald; drowned 15 Oct 1845
3 DAVID (Sir), **3rd Bt**
4 John Erskine Kennedy (Sir), KCB, Adml, Naval ADC; *b* 16 Sept 1833; *m* 6 March 1905 Constance Barbara (*m* 2nd 15 Dec 1925 Lord Charles Kennedy, 2nd son of 3rd Marquess of Ailsa (*qv*), and *d* 3 Nov 1931), est dau of Edward Clarke, of Avishays, Chard, and *dsp* 8 Dec 1908
5 William Arthur, Capt 42nd Highlanders; *b* 1839; *d* of wounds recd Ashanti Campaign
6 Frederick, Lt 6th Foot, Capt Haddington Militia; *b* 1841; *d* 1884
7 Jonathan Peel, JP Lanarks; *b* 9 Jan 1844; *m* 7 Nov 1867 Emily Diana Frances (*d* 23 Sept 1926), only dau of Col Sir George Ashley Maude, KCB (*see* HAWARDEN, V), and *d* 22 April 1915, having had issue:
(1) Edward Ashley, Lt-Cdr RN; *b* 4 Jan 1870; *d* 28 Feb 1902
(2) Randolph Eustace Wemyss, OBE (1919), Lt-Col 3rd Bn Highland LI, Lt-Col Royal Scots Fus, Govr Peterhead (1923–27) and Barlinnie (1927–29) Prisons, Perm Sec Prisons Dept Scotland 1929, served S Africa 1901–02 (medal with three clasps) and France WW I; *b* 27 June 1879; *d* unm 23 Nov 1935
(1) Helena Emily; *d* unm 3 April 1908
(2) Alice Anne, jt-fndr St James's Sch Malvern and Headmistress 1896–1948; *d* unm 10 Aug 1959
(3) Katrine Maclean, jt-fndr St James's Sch Malvern, Head Mistress and co-fndr Abbots Hill Sch Hemel Hempstead 1912–30; *d* unm 2 Sept 1932
(4) Mary Isabel, co-fndr Abbots Hill Sch Hemel Hempstead; *d* unm 1 March 1927
(5) Diana Margaret; *d* unm 28 Sept 1961
(6) Georgina Marian; *d* unm 4 May 1922
(7) Constance Kennedy, MBE (1918) (despatches); *d* unm 9 March 1923
1 Margaret; *m* 26 Nov 1851 Lord Gilbert Kennedy (*d* 25 Nov 1901), bro of 2nd Marquess of Ailsa (*qv*), and *d* 24 March 1908, leaving issue
2 Hersey Maria Christina Elizabeth; *d* unm 4 June 1908
3 Alice Anne; *m* 1866 Rev Hon Arthur Charles Baillie-Hamilton (*d* May 1910), and *d* 16 Jan 1908, leaving issue (*see* HADDINGTON, E)

Sir DAVID *d* 8 Jan 1852; his est surv son,

Sir David Baird, 3rd Bt, DL and JP Haddington, JP and Commr of Supply, Edinburgh, Maj 98th Foot and 74th Highlanders, served Kaffir War 1851–52, staff of Sir Colin Campbell (afterwards Lord Clyde) Crimea and Indian Mutiny (medals and brevet); *b* 26 Jan 1832; *m* 15 June 1864 Hon Ellen Stuart (*d* 19 April 1927), 2nd dau and coheir of 12th Lord Blantyre (*see* 1900 edn), and *d* 13 Oct 1913, leaving:
1 **Sir David Baird, 4th Bt**, MVO (1909), DL and JP; Capt Black Watch, Roy Highrs, ADC to Govr Malta 1890 and GOC Scottish Cmd; *b* 6 May 1865; *m* 1901 Lilian Gertrude (*d* 30 April 1941), widow of Maj Ernest Maxwell Willshire, Black Watch (*see* 1940 edn WILLSHIRE, Bt), and dau of Maj-Gen James Davidson, and *d* 6 Jan 1941, leaving issue:
(1) Jean Marjorie; *d* unm 16 Dec 1961
2 William Arthur, of Lennoxlove, Haddington, and Wedderlie, Gordon; *s* to Lord Blantyre's estates 1900, DL and JP E Lothian, JP Renfrewshire, Maj Lothians and Border Horse Yeo; *b* 20 March 1879; *m* 28 Jan 1908 Lady Hersey Constance Evelyn Conyngham (*d* 6 Aug 1962), 3rd dau of 4th Marquess Conyngham (*qv*), and *d* 6 June 1933, leaving issue:
(1) Sir DAVID CHARLES BAIRD, **5th and present Bt**
(2) Robert Walter Stuart, served WW II 1939–41, with Lothian and Border Yeo (prisoner); *b* 5 March 1914; *m* 1st 21 April 1938 (*divorce* 1960) Maxine Christine, only child of Rupert Darrell, of New York, and had issue:
1a +CHARLES WILLIAM STUART [Charles Baird Esq, 12 Falstaff St, Sunnybank Hills, Brisbane, Qld 4109, Australia]; *b* 8 June 1939; heir presumptive; *educ* Switzerland; *m* March 1965 *Jane Joanna, est dau of Brig A Darley Bridge, of 12 Mulberry Walk, London SW3, and has issue:
1b *Tara Francesca Stuart; *b* 1970
2b *Senta Louise Stuart; *b* 1973
3b *Petra Helen Stuart; *b* 1975
(2) (cont.) Robert Baird *m* 2nd 1960 *Maria Florine [Mrs Robert Baird, 16 rue des Granges, Geneva 1204, Switzerland], and *d* 1989, leaving further issue:
1a *Frances; *b* 1960
(1) Evelyn Frances; *b* 26 Oct 1908; *d* unm 21 Feb 1957
(2) Margaret Stuart; *b* 17 Sept 1910; *m* 2 Aug 1938 Marcus Humphrey Ure Spurway (*d* 1989), and *d* 21 Aug 1997, leaving:
1a *Humphrey John [Humphrey Spurway Esq, Linnhouse, Livingstone, W Lothian, Scotland]; *b* 14 March 1942; *educ* Fettes and RAC Cirencester; *m* 28 Dec 1968 *Rosaline Avril Orr, yr dau of George Edward Orr Walker, MBE, TD, QC, of Newark Castle, Ayr, and has issue:
1b *Charles; *b* 1972
2b *Mark; *b* 1973
3b *Guy; *b* 1974
1b *Kalitza; *b* 1977
2a *George Henry; *b* 23 May 1945; *educ* Fettes
3a David Marcus; *b* 26 Sept 1946; *d* 26 July 1949
1a *Kalitza Mary Stuart [Mrs Patrick Campbell Fraser, Borthwickshiels, Hawick, Roxburghshire]; *b* 7 June 1939; *m* 14 Oct 1961 *Patrick Alexander Campbell Fraser and has issue:
1b *Fiona Margaret; *b* 17 Feb 1963
2b *Lucinda Caroline; *b* 15 Nov 1964
3b *Theresa Elizabeth; *b* 27 Sept 1967
2a *Theresa Frances; *b* 13 Feb 1941; *m* 16 July 1966 *Richard Dawnay Innes (*see* DOWNE, V), of Playford Hall, Ipswich, yst s of Lt-Col James Archibald Innes, DSO, JP, of Horringer Manor, Bury St Edmunds, Suffolk, and has:
1b *Antonia Frances; *b* 5 March 1967
2b *Sara Evelyn; *b* 15 March 1969
3b *Johanna; *b* 1970
4b *Katherine; *b* 1973
(3) *Hersey Ellen [Mrs Hersey Gordon-Duff, Spring Cottage, Hardgate, Castle Douglas, Kirkcudbrightshire, Scotland]; *b* 5 Oct 1916; *m* 29 Sept 1939 (*divorce* 1959) Maj Lachlan Cecil Gordon-Duff, The Gordon Highlanders, yr s of Capt Lachlan Gordon-Duff, of Drummuir and Park, Banffshire, and has:
1a *Simon Lachlan [Simon Gordon-Duff Esq, Lodge Farm, Stowood, nr Beckley, Oxon OX3 9SR], Capt Scots Gds, mentioned in despatches 1968; *b* 25 July 1942; *educ* Eton; *m* 1990 *Caroline Edith Mary Craig, er dau of Col Charles Neil Howard, MC, late Black Watch (*see* DENBIGH and DESMOND, E)
2a *Robert Andrew [Robert Gordon-Duff Esq, Corrie, Port Appin, Argyllshire]; *b* 18 March 1945; *educ* Eton and RAC Cirencester; *m* 1973 (*divorce* March 1997) Caroline Orby, formerly w of Michael Robarts and dau of Maj Robert Clifton Gascoigne (*see* MUNRO, Bt, of Foulis-Obsdale), and has:
1b *Hersey Diana; *b* 1973
1b *Philippa Sophie; *b* 1976
1 Evelyn, OBE (1918); *b* 1871; *m* 19 Feb 1903 Hon Ronald Thomas Graham Murray, Maj 3rd Bn Black Watch, SR (*d* 24 Sept 1934), only s of 1st Viscount Dunedin (*see* 1940 edn), and *dsp* 3 Jan 1947
2 Hilda; *b* 22 April 1875; *m* 7 July 1908 Curtis Walter Lampson, CBE (*d* 9 Aug 1952), er s of Norman George Lampson, DL, and *d* 4 Aug 1946, leaving issue (*see* KILLEARN, B)
3 Mabel; *b* 15 May 1880; *d* unm 14 Sept 1945
4 Cecilia; *b* 18 May 1881; *d* 24 April 1891

BAIRD of Saughton Hall

Arms: Gules a sanglier passant or, on a canton ermine a sword paleways proper. **Crest:** A boar's head erased or. **Motto:** *Vi et virtute* ('By strength and valour'). **Creation:** Bt. (NS) 28 Feb 1695/6.

SIR (JAMES) ANDREW GARDINER BAIRD, 11TH BT, of Saughton Hall, Edinburgh; *b* 2 May 1946; *s* f 1997; *educ* Eton; *m* 1984 (*divorce* 1988) Jean Margaret, dau of Brig Sir Ian Liddell Jardine, 4th Bt (*see* JARDINE, Bt, of Godalming), and has:
1 +ALEXANDER; *b* 28 May 1986

Lineage: GILBERT BAIRD of Posso had a 2nd s:

ANDREW BAIRD, of Lavoroklaw, Fifeshire, held the lands of Auchmedden 13 Feb 1534; *m* Bessy Learmonth, of Balcomy, and *d* 10 Feb 1543, leaving:

GEORGE BAIRD, of Auchmedden; *m c* 10 Aug 1550 Elizabeth, dau of Alexander Keith, of Troup, and *d* 29 May 1593, leaving an est s:

GILBERT BAIRD, of Auchmedden; *m* 1578 Lilias, dau and heir of Walter Baird, of Ordinhivas, and *d* 23 Feb 1620, leaving, with an est s (George, ancestor of the BAIRDs of Auchmedden), and two intermediary ones:

JAMES BAIRD, of Newbyth, Haddington; Commr Ecclesiastical Court *temp* CHARLES I; a warrant was issued by CHARLES I for creating him Lord Doveran but he *d* before the patent passed the Seals; *m* Bethia, dau of Sir John Dempster, of Pitliver, and *d* 1655, having had, with two daus:

1 Sir JOHN BAIRD; *bapt* 10 Sept 1620; Ld of Session as Lord Newbyth; *m* Margaret, dau of Sir William Hay of Linplum, bro of 1st Earl of Tweeddale (*see* TWEEDDALE, M), and *d* 27 April 1698, leaving:

(1) Sir WILLIAM BAIRD, 1st Bt (NS), so *cr* 4 Feb 1679/80, of Newbyth; *b* 12 Nov 1654; *m* 1st Helen (*d* 22 April 1701), dau of Sir John Gilmore, of Craigmillar (*see* GILMOUR OF CRAIGMILLAR, B); *m* 2nd Mary (*dsp* 23 Oct 1756), dau of 7th Lord Sinclair (*qv*), and *d* 17 Feb 1737, leaving by his 1st w:

1a Sir JOHN BAIRD, 2nd and last Bt; *b* 13 Oct 1686; MP Edinburgh; *m* Janet (*m* 2nd Gen Hon James St Clair of Dysart (*see* SINCLAIR, L); *dsp* 8 Jan 1766), only dau of Hon Sir David Dalrymple of Hailes, 1st Bt (*extinct* 1829; *see* STAIR, E), and *dsp* Sept 1745, when the btcy expired and the estates passed to his cousin William Baird (*see* BAIRD, Bt, of Newbyth)

2a Alexander; *m* 1st Ann, dau of Wauchope of Niddry; *m* 2nd Margaret, dau of Lord Belhaven (*see* BELHAVEN AND STENTON, L), but *dsp* 1743

2 **Sir Robert Baird, 1st Bt** (NS), so *cr* 28 Feb 1695/6, of Saughton Hall, Midlothian; *m* Elizabeth (*bur* 18 Oct 1676), dau of Michael Fleming, of Ratho Byres, and was *bur* 2 March 1697, having had, with a yr surv s (William, ancestor of the BAIRD Bts of Newbyth, *qv*):

(1) **Sir James Baird, 2nd Bt**; *m* 1st 1689 Margaret (*bur* 8 March 1694), dau of Hamilton of Mountain Hall, and had two s and two daus; *m* 2nd Elizabeth, dau of Sir John Gibson of Addiston, and *d* May 1715, having by her had issue (now extinct); his s by his 1st w:

1a **Sir Robert Baird, 3rd Bt**; *b c* 1690; *m* 1st 1729 Janet (*d* 11 June 1733), dau of Robert Baikie, of Tankerness, Orkney; *m* 2nd Helen Hope (*d* March 1741) and *d* 8 Sept 1742, leaving, with another s and a dau, an est s:

1b **Sir David Baird, 4th Bt**; *b c* 1729; Lt 1st Royals; *d* unm 1 July 1745 from wounds recd Battle of Fontenoy

2b **Sir William Baird, 5th Bt**; Capt RN; *m* 1750 Frances (*d* 7 Dec 1811), dau of Col James Gardiner, of Bankton, and *d* 17 Aug 1771, leaving:

1c **Sir James Gardiner Baird, 6th Bt**; Lt-Col 28th Light Dragoons War American Independence and Flanders; *m* 1st 1781 Henrietta, 3rd dau of Wynne Johnston, of Hilltown, and had issue; *m* 2nd 15 July 1818 Mary (*d* 14 Jan 1826), dau of Robert Watt and widow of James Symington; *m* 3rd 1827 Wortley Cornelia Anne, dau of William Moir, of New Grove, and *d* 23 June 1830; his est surv s by his 1st w:

1d William; Army Capt; *m* 28 March 1809 Lucy, est dau of Thomas Dickson, of Prospect House, Southampton, and *dvp* 1823, having had, with other issue:

1e **Sir James Gardiner Baird, 7th Bt**, DL; *b* 20 Aug 1813; Capt 10th Hus, Hon Col 1st Midlothian Artillery Vol Corps, ADC, Ensign-Gen Roy Co Archers; *m* 13 March 1845 Henrietta Mary (*d* 3 Nov 1896), est dau of John Wauchope, of Edmondstone, Edinburgh, and sis of Sir John Don-Wauchope, 8th Bt, DL (*qv*), and *d* 6 Jan 1896, leaving an only surv s:

1f **Sir William James Gardiner Baird, 8th Bt**, JP (Midlothian and E Lothian); *b* 23 Feb 1854; Lt 7th Hus, Lt-Col and Hon Col Lothians and Berwickshire Imp Yeo; Commr of Supply Midlothian; *m* 3 April 1879 Hon Arabella Rose Evelyn Hozier (*d* 18 June 1916), est dau of 1st Baron Newlands (*see* 1970 edn, SPENCER-CHURCHILL, B), and *d* 19 April 1921, leaving:

1g **Sir James Hozier Gardiner Baird, 9th Bt**, MC (1915); *b* 25 Nov 1883; *educ* Eton; Maj 4th Bn Bedfordshire Regt, Capt 4th Bn Argyll and Sutherland Highrs, WW I (despatches, wounded), and WW II (Nat Def Force and Green Howards); *m* 1st 8 June 1921 Blanche Celia (*d* 8 Jan 1922), dau of John Louis Denton, of Massachusetts; *m* 2nd 24 March 1923 Joan Violet, of Waterfall, Bantry, Co Cork, yst dau of Thomas Barker, of Matlock, Derbys, and *dsp* 3 Aug 1966

2g William Frank Gardiner; *b* 18 April 1885; Capt 4th Bn Beds Regt, Lt 7th Dragoon Gds and Scots Gds; *m* 24 Nov 1910 Violet Mary (*d* 17 Oct 1947), 5th dau of Richard Benyon Croft, JP, DL, of Fanhams Hall, Ware, Herts (*see* CROFT, Bt, of Croft Castle), and *d* 5 Nov 1914 of wounds recd in action, leaving:

1h **Sir James Richard Gardiner Baird, 10th Bt**, MC (1945); *b* 12 July 1913; *educ* Eton and Univ Coll Oxford; Capt RA and Kent Yeo WW II; *m* 22 Feb 1941 *Mabel Ann (Gay) Tempest [Lady Baird, Church Farm House, Guist, Norfolk NR20 5AJ], dau of Algernon Gill, of Toronto, and *d* 13 March 1997, having had:

1i William Robert Gardiner; *b* 2 Jan, *d* 5 Jan 1943

2i Sir (JAMES) ANDREW GARDINER BAIRD, **11th and present Bt**

3i +(William) Julian Gardiner [Julian Baird Esq, 7 Bettridge Rd, London SW6]; *b* 12 May 1947; *educ* Milton Abbey; *m* 1984 *Nichola Bridget Halsall, dau of Lt-Col Cecil West, OBE, of Hythe, Kent

1i *Lavinia Mary Arabella [Miss Lavinia Baird, 25 Broadhinton Rd, London SW4 0LT]; *b* 5 April 1951

2h William Henry Gardiner; *b* 11 Oct 1914; *educ* Eton; Maj Bombay Grenadiers WW II; *m* 1st 10 Oct 1946 (*divorce* 1966) Helen Mary, est dau of Edward Charles Rich, MA, and had:

1i +Mervyn Edward Hozier [Mervyn Baird Esq, 22 The Terrace, Sunninghill, nr Ascot, Berks SL5 9NH]; *b* 28 Dec 1947; *educ* Milton Abbey; *m* 10 Feb 1970 *Isobel F, dau of Stewart Winzor, of S Australia, and has issue:

1j +James Edward Hozier; *b* 6 Oct 1976

1j *Mirella Frances Hozier; *b* 14 Aug 1973

2i +Roderick Frank Gardiner [Roderick Baird Esq, 161 Craigleith Rd, Edinburgh EH4 2EB]; *b* 4 July 1955; *educ* The Elliott Sch Putney; *m* 1985 *Julia Mary, er dau of Gerald Barry, WS, of Humbie, E Lothian, and has issue:

1j *Arabella Elizabeth Gardiner; *b* 1987

1i *Judith Mary Gardiner [Mrs David Cosby, Ballycreen House, Aughrim, Co Wicklow, Ireland]; *b* 4 Jan 1951; *m* 4 July 1974 *David Ashworth Sydney Phillips Cosby, 3rd s of Maj Errold Ashworth Sydney Cosby, of Stradbally Hall, Co Laois, and has two sons

2h (cont.) William Baird *m* 2nd 1966 *Catherine Gwendolyn [Mrs William Baird, 71 The Cloisters, Pegasus Grange, Oxford OX1 4QQ], dau of James Smart, OBE, of Ottawa, and *d* 1989

1h Lilias Mary; *b* 26 Sept 1911; *m* 31 Jan 1934 Thomas Lloyd, er s of Lt-Col Thomas Owen Lloyd, CMG, of Minard, Argyll, and *d* Oct 1938, leaving issue

1g Frances Harriet; *b* 5 June 1880; *m* 22 Nov 1910 John Eduff Blagrave Swinton, 32nd of that Ilk (*d* 23 March 1931), of Swinton Bank, Peeblesshire, and *dsp* 4 June 1955

2g Mary Rose; *d* 29 May 1882 aged three months

BAKER OF DORKING

Creation: B. (LP, UK) 19 April 1997

THE BARON OF DORKING, of Iford, Co Sussex (Kenneth Wilfred Baker, CH (1992), PC (1984)) [The Rt Hon The Lord Baker of Dorking CH PC, House of Lords, London SW1A 0PW]; *b* 3 Nov 1934; *educ* St Paul's and Magdalen Coll Oxford; Lt RA, Artillery Instr Libyan Army 1953–55; memb Twickenham Borough Cncl 1960–62; MP (C) Acton 1968–70, St Marylebone 1970–83, Mole Valley 1983–97, memb: H of C Public Accts Ctee 1969–70, Exec 1922 Ctee, Parly Sec CSD 1972–74, PPS to Leader Oppn 1974–75, Min State DTI 1981–84, DOE 1984–85; Sec State: DOE 1985–86, DES 1986–89; Chllr Duchy Lancaster 1989–90, Home Sec 1990–92; Chm: Hansard Soc 1978–81, C Party 1989–90; Sec-Gen UN Conf Parliamentarians World Population and Devpt 1978; author: *I Have No Gun But I Can Spit* (ed, 1980), *London Lines* (ed, 1982), *The Faber Book of English History in Verse* (ed, 1988), *Unauthorized Versions: poems and their parodies* (ed, 1990), *The Faber Book of Conservatism* (1993), *The Turbulent Years: my life in politics* (1993); *m* 1963 *Mary Elizabeth Gray-Muir and has a s and two daus

Lineage: W M BAKER, OBE; *m* — Harries and had:

KENNETH WILFRED, *cr* a **Baron**

BAKER WILBRAHAM

Arms: Quarterly, 1st and 4th, argent, three bends wavy azure, a canton ermine (for WILBRAHAM); 2nd and 3rd, per pale argent and or, on a saltire nebuly sable, five escallops of the first, on a chief of the third a lion passant of the second (for BAKER). **Crests:** 1 A wolf's head erased argent, charged on the neck with a cross crosslet azure (for WILBRAHAM), 2 A dexter arm embowed vested azure, charged with three annulets interlaced or, cuffed argent, holding in the hand proper an arrow of the last. **Motto:** *In porto quies* ('There is rest in port'). **Creation:** Bt. (GB) 19 Sept 1776.

SIR RICHARD BAKER WILBRAHAM, 8TH BT, of Loventor, Co Devon, DL (Cheshire 1992) [Sir Richard Baker Wilbraham Bt DL, Rode Hall, Scholar Green, Cheshire ST7 3QP]; *b* 5 Feb 1934; *s* f 1980; *educ* Harrow (Govr 1982–92); late Lt Welsh Gds, High Sheriff Cheshire 1991, dir J Henry Schroder Wagg and Co Ltd 1969–89, Tstee Grosvenor Estate 1981–, Dir Christie Hosp NHS Trust 1990–96, chm Bibby Line Gp 1992–97 (dir 1989), dep chm Brixton Estate plc 1994 (dir 1985), dir Majedie Investments plc 1989–, Govr Nuffield Hosps 1990–, a Church Commr 1994–, Renter Bailiff Weavers' Co 1993–94 and Upper Bailiff 1994–95, Tstee Dyson Perrins Museum of Worcester Porcelain 1993–, Govr The King's Sch Macclesfield 1986–, memb Gen Cncl King Edward's Hosp Fund for London 1986–; *m* 2 March 1962 *Anne Christine Peto, est dau of Charles Peto Bennett, OBE, of La Haute, Fliquet, Jersey, CI, and Fru Farnes, of Oslo, and has issue:

1 +RANDLE; *b* 28 May 1963; *educ* Harrow; *m* 17 May 1997 *Amanda Jane, est dau of Robert Glossop, of Dogmersfield, Hants

1 *Sibella Caroline; *b* 20 Feb 1965; *m* 3 Sept 1994 *Timothy, s of Peter Makower, of Barnes, SW London, and has:

(1) *Noah; *b* 30 March 1997

2 *Charlotte Cecilia Anne; *b* 24 Jan 1968

3 *Alice Maria Elisabeth; *b* 7 May 1971

Lineage (of Baker): The Rev AARON BAKER; *b* 1652, son of John Baker, of Alvington, Devon; *educ* Oxford; Rector of West Alvington, Devon; *m* Martha Thompson and had:

Rev GEORGE BAKER; *b* 1687; *educ* Eton (Scholar) and King's Coll Cambridge (Scholar, DD and Fell); Vicar of Modbury, Archdeacon of Totnes and Preb Exeter Cathedral; *m* 1st 1713 Bridget Harris and had a s; *m* 2nd Mary, dau of Rt Rev Stephen Weston, Bp of Exeter; his s by his 1st w:

Sir George Baker, 1st Bt (GB), so *cr* 19 Sept 1776, of Loventor in Totnes; *b* 1723; *educ* Eton and King's Coll Cambridge (BA 1745, MA 1749, MD 1756, Fell); FRS, FSA; physician first at Stamford, Lincs, then London 1761, Physician Queen Consort's household, Physician in Ordinary to the Queen Consort by 1776, Physician in Ordinary to GEORGE III, Pres Coll of Phyicians 1785–90, 1792–93 and 1795, ret 1798; *m* 28 June 1768 Jane (*d* 13 July 1813), dau of Roger Morris, of York, and had issue:

1 FREDERICK FRANCIS (Sir), **2nd Bt**

1 Maria Charlotte; *m* 1 May 1821 Lt-Col Sir John Hutton Cooper, 1st and last Bt, MB, FRS (*dsp* 24 Dec 1828)

Sir GEORGE *d* 15 June 1809; his only son,

Sir Frederick Francis Baker, 2nd Bt; *b* 13 May 1772; *educ* Balliol Coll Oxford (MA); FRS, FSA; *m* July 1814 Harriet (*d* 15 Nov 1845), 3rd dau of Sir John Simeon, 1st Bt (*qv*), and had issue:

1 GEORGE (Sir), **3rd Bt**

2 Frederick Francis; *b* 29 Jan 1822; *d* 2 June 1892

3 Henry Cooper; *b* 8 Jan 1826; *d* 12 Jan 1892

1 Jane Maria; *m* 26 Nov 1840 Sir John Simeon, 3rd Bt (*d* 21 May 1870), and *d* 24 Aug 1860, leaving issue

Sir FREDERICK *d* 1 Oct 1830; his est son,

Sir George Baker, 3rd Bt; *b* 16 June 1816; *educ* Ch Ch Oxford (BA); *m* 1st 2 June 1840 Mary Isabella (*d* 6 May 1855), 2nd dau of Robert Nassau Sutton, yr s of Sir Richard Sutton, 1st Bt (*qv*), and had issue:

1 Sir FREDERICK EDWARD BAKER later RHODES (changed name by roy licence 29 Oct 1878 under terms of will of Ambrose Rhodes, of Bellair in Heavitree, Devon), **4th Bt**; *b* 12 July 1843; *d* unm 4 Oct 1911

2 GEORGE BARRINGTON (Sir), **5th Bt**

3 Francis Manners; *b* 10 Feb 1852; Lt 73rd Regt; *d* 1878

1 Isabella Maria; *m* 14 Dec 1865 Charles Oliver Frederick Cator (*d* 10 Dec 1876), and *d* 1 Dec 1927, leaving issue

2 Alice Emily Jane; *m* 11 Nov 1885 Rt Rev Charles Sandford, DD (*dsp* 8 Dec 1903), Bp of Gibraltar, and *d* 1 June 1901

3 Evelyn Nina Frances; *m* 23 Aug 1877 3rd Baron Hampton (*qv*), and *d* 19 Aug 1904, leaving issue

Sir George *m* 2nd 16 Nov 1858 Augusta Catherine (*d* 19 Nov 1893), yst dau of Sir Robert Fitzwygram, 2nd Bt (*see* WIGRAM, Bt), and *d* 27 Aug 1882

The 4th Bt's brother,

Sir GEORGE BARRINGTON BAKER later BAKER WILBRAHAM (added with arms by roy licence 14 July 1900), **5th Bt**; *b* 26 Jan 1845; *educ* Corpus Christi Coll Oxford (MA); barrister Lincoln's Inn; *m* 4 April 1872 Katharine Frances (*d* 8 Feb 1945), only child of Gen Sir Richard Wilbraham, KCB, of Rode Hall, Cheshire, nephew of 1st Baron Skelmersdale (*qv*; *see* also below), and had issue:

1 Wilbraham George; *b* 15 Nov 1873; *d* 16 March 1875

2 PHILIP WILBRAHAM (Sir), **6th Bt**

1 Katharine Mary, MBE (1920), STh (Lambeth) 1931; *m* 25 July 1899 Rev Piers John Benedict Foulkes, MA Oxford (*d* 7 June 1927), Hon Canon Chester, and *d* 25 March 1937

2 Margaret Isabel; *m* 28 April 1914 Rev Martin Stewart Ware, MA Cambridge (*d* 8 June 1934), Hon Canon Winchester, of Tilford House, Tilford, Farnham, Surrey, and *d* 26 Feb 1968, leaving issue

3 Sibylla Frances; *m* 30 Dec 1920 Ven Percy Barnabas Emmet, MA Oxford (*d* 10 Sept 1963), formerly Archdeacon of Nandyal, S India, son of Rev William Edward Emmet, and *dsp* 10 March 1969

Sir GEORGE *d* 28 Aug 1912; his only surv son,

Sir Philip Wilbraham Baker Wilbraham, 6th Bt, KBE (1954), JP (Cheshire); *b* 17 Sept 1875; *educ* Harrow and Balliol Coll Oxford (BA 1898, MA 1901); barrister Lincoln's Inn 1901, and a Bencher 1942; formerly Fell All Souls, DCL Lambeth 1936; High Steward Congleton, Dean of the Arches, Master of the Faculties, Judge Provincial Courts Canterbury and York, Vicar-Gen Province of Canterbury 1934–, Commissary to Dean and Chapter St Paul's Cathedral 1942–, First Church Estates Commr 1939–54, Sec Nat Assembly Church of England 1920–39, formerly Vicar-Gen Province of York, Chllr Dioceses of York, Durham, Chester, Chelmsford and Truro; *m* 8 Aug 1901 Joyce Christabel (*d* 25 Aug 1958), yr dau of Rt Hon Sir John Henry Kennaway, 3rd Bt, PC, CB (*qv*), and had issue:

1 RANDLE JOHN (Sir), **7th Bt**

1 *Joyce Katharine, MBE (1959) [Miss Joyce Baker Wilbraham MBE, Flat 2, 23 Onslow Sq, London SW7]; *b* 29 June 1902; *educ* Somerville Coll Oxford (MA); Adminr Married Quarters Min of Supply 1949–60, Fell Inst of Housing Managers, Civilian Housing Adminr Min of Defence 1961

2 Mary Frances; *b* 19 Aug 1904; *m* 1 April 1937 Elliott Perkins, Prof of History and former Master of Lowell House, Harvard U, of 18 Hawthorn St, Cambridge, Mass. (*d* 4 March 1985) est s of Thomas Nelson Perkins, of Westwood, Mass. and *d* 6 March 1994

3 Elisabeth Sibylla; *b* 1 May 1908; *m* 24 Sept 1938 Lt-Col Hugh Maurice Carstairs Jones-Mortimer, JP, DL, Welsh Gds, of Hartsheath, Mold, Flintshire, only s of Wilson Cuthbert Bevan Jones-Mortimer, of Plas Newydd, Llanfair-Dyffryn-Clwyd, Denbighshire, and *d* 16 June 1989, leaving:

(1) *Maurice Carstairs [Dr Maurice Jones-Mortimer, Hartsheath, Mold, Clwyd CH7 4HP]; *b* 17 Jan 1940; *educ* Eton and Ch Ch Oxford (MA 1966, DPhil 1968); Research Fell Birmingham U 1969–72, Sr Research Assoc Biochemistry Dept Cambridge 1975–85

(1) *Loraine Elisabeth; *b* 27 Jan 1947; *m* 1970 (*divorce* 1986) Alvin Randolph Martin (*d* 1992), BA Dartmouth, MA PhD Harvard

(2) *Johanna Favell [Mrs Peter Kaufmann, 17 Burgess Hill, London NW2 2DD]; *b* 9 May 1949; *m* 1981 *Peter Gerald Dorian Kaufmann and has:

1a *Miranda Clare; *b* 15 April 1982; *educ* St Paul's Girls Sch

2a *Augusta Jane; *b* 2 Aug 1984; *educ* Francis Holland Sch

3a *Olivia Katharine; *b* 20 April 1986; *educ* Clifton

Sir PHILIP *d* 11 Oct 1957; his only son,

Sir Randle John Baker Wilbraham, 7th Bt, JP (1954), DL (1959) Cheshire; *b* 31 March 1906; *educ* Harrow and Balliol Coll Oxford (BA 1928); WW II as S/Ldr RAuxAF; High Sheriff 1953, High Steward Congleton, Pres Chartered Land Agents Soc 1958, Fell Chartered Land Agents Soc; *m* 26 Feb 1930 Betty Ann, CBE (1973) (*d* 2 Oct 1975), er dau of Matt Torrens, of The Grove, Hayes, Kent, by his w Lilian Edith, yr dau of Sir Thomas George Fardell, JP, MP, and *d* 24 Feb 1980, leaving:

1 Sir RICHARD BAKER WILBRAHAM, **8th and present Bt**

1 *Letitia Ann [Mrs Timothy Kirkbride, Little Hill Farm, Buckland St Mary, nr Chard, Somerset TA20 3SS]; *b* 6 Feb 1931; *m* 30 April 1960 *Timothy George Kirkbride, MA, yr s of Lt-Col George Kirkbride, IPS (ret), of Meres Vean, Mullion, Cornwall, and has issue:

(1) *George Edward; *b* 31 March 1967

(1) *Harriet Ann; *b* 15 Sept 1964; *m* 11 Sept 1993 *Anthony Leonard Clinton Bloomer, son of Arnold Euston Moore Bloomer (*see* VIVIAN, B), and has issue:

1a *Alice Letitia Clinton; *b* 17 Sept 1996

Lineage (of Wilbraham):

RANDLE WILBRAHAM, of Rode (see SKELMERSDALE, B) had by his 2nd w Sibylla Egerton:

Sir RICHARD WILBRAHAM, KCB, of Rode; High Steward Congleton; *m* Elizabeth, dau of William Egerton, of Gresford, and had:

KATHARINE FRANCES; *m* 4 April 1872 **Sir George Barrington Baker, 5th Bt** (*see* above)

BALDWIN OF BEWDLEY

Arms: Arg. on a saltire sa. a quatrefoil or. **Crest:** A cockatrice sejant, wings addorsed arg., combed, wattled and beaked or, gorged with a crown vallary, lined and reflexed over the back gold, and charged on the shoulder with a rose gu., barbed and seeded ppr. **Supporters:** On either side a white owl ppr., the sinister holding in the beak a sprig of broom, also ppr. **Motto:** *Per Deum meum transilio murum* ('With the help of my God I leap over the wall'). **Creation:** V. and E. (UK) 8 June 1937.

THE 4TH EARL BALDWIN OF BEWDLEY and **Viscount Corvedale**, of Corvedale, Co Salop (Edward Alfred Alexander Baldwin) [The Rt Hon The Earl Baldwin of Bewdley, Manor Farm House, Godstow Rd, Upper Wolvercote, Oxford OX2 8AJ]; *b* 3 Jan 1938; *s* f 1976; *educ* Eton and Trin Coll Cambridge (BA 1961, MA 1966); late 2nd Lt Intelligence Corps; *m* 1970 *Sarah MacMurray, est dau of Evan Maitland James, of Upwood Park, Abingdon, Berks, and has issue:

1 +BENEDICT ALEXANDER STANLEY, *Viscount Corvedale*; *b* 28 Dec 1973; *educ* Bryanston and Newcastle U (BMus 1996)

2 +James Conrad; *b* 13 March 1976; *educ* Bryanston

3 +Mark Thomas Maitland; *b* 24 July 1980; *educ* Bryanston

Lineage: RICHARD BALDWIN, of Munslow Salop (allegedly descended from the BALDWINs of Diddlebury); Collector Subsidies there 1523; *m* — Portman and had:

WILLIAM BALDWIN, of Munslow; *m* Elizabeth, dau of Richard Jenkes, and had, with other issue:

THOMAS BALDWIN, of Munslow; *m* Elizabeth (*d* Nov 1574), dau of Edward Norton, of Collington, and *d* Feb 1585, having had, with other issue:

JOHN BALDWIN, of Munslow; *b* 1544; *m* 1st 29 Oct 1571 Anne (*d* Nov 1581), dau of Edward Crowther, of Munslow, and had issue, including three daus; *m* 2nd Margery — (*d* 1620) and *d* June 1605, leaving by his 1st w:

WILLIAM BALDWIN, of Munslow; *b* 1573; *m* 27 April 1595 Joyce (*d* 1619), dau of Roger Forester (son of John Forester, of Watling Street, by Joyce, dau of Philip Upton; *see* FORESTER, B), of Watling Street, Salop, and had, with other issue:

EDWARD BALDWIN, of Much Wenlock and Astley Abbots, Salop; *b* 1605; *m* Catherine, dau of Francis Lokier, of The March, Much Wenlock, and *d* 1667, having had, with other issue:

THOMAS BALDWIN, of Shrewsbury; *d* by 1713, having had, with an er son (Samuel, living 1713) and a dau (Ann, *m* 1 June 1699 Thomas Harris, of Shrewsbury):

JOHN BALDWIN, of Broseley, Salop; *m* Mary — (*d* Dec 1765) and *d* Sept 1761, having had, with other issue:

JOHN BALDWIN, of Broseley; *b* 1725; *m* 8 Jan 1748/9 Mary (*d* 8 Oct 1811), dau of George Pearce, of Broseley, and *d* June 1757, having had, with an er and yr son (John, *b* 1749; William Pearce, of Madeley, Salop, *b* 1754, *m* 1782 Ann Pugh and *d* 1822):

THOMAS BALDWIN, of Shrewsbury and Stourport, Worcs; *b* 1751; *m* 1 Jan 1784 Mary Gough (*d* 7 Feb 1820), of St Mary's, Shrewsbury, and *d* 26 April 1823, having had, with other issue:

GEORGE PEARCE BALDWIN, of Stourport; *b* 17 May 1789; *m* 1st 16 April 1812 Anne Hill (*d* Feb 1819) and had issue:

1 Pearce, of Stourport; *b* 20 July 1813; *m* 17 Sept 1856 Hannah Myra (*d* Oct 1882), dau of Edward Evans, of Thornloe House, Worcs, and *dsp* 6 April 1861

2 William Hill; *b* 8 March 1817; *d* 11 May 1863

GEORGE BALDWIN *m* 2nd 4 Oct 1822 Sarah Chalkey (*d* 25 Feb 1874), dau of Rev Jacob Stanley, of Alnwick, Northumberland, and *d* 1 Oct 1840, having by her had:

3 George; *b* 8 April, *d* 17 Oct 1824

4 George, of Stourport; *b* 16 March 1826; *m* 7 March 1854 Amy Ellen Poole (*d* 16 Jan 1873) and *d* 5 March 1881, leaving issue

5 Stanley, of Stourport and W Didsbury, Lancs; *b* 4 Feb 1828; *d* 21 Sept 1907

6 Edward; *b* 26 May 1832; *d* 26 April 1848

7 ALFRED

1 Sarah Anne; *b* 19 April 1830; *m* 1861 George Robinson (*d* 1871), of Leicester, and *d* 15 Dec 1919

2 Mary Jane; *b* 16 Jan 1834; *m* 17 Nov 1864 George Gwynn Brown, of Mitton Grange, Stourport, and *d* 18 Jan 1908, leaving issue

3 Lucilla; *b* 16 March 1836; *m* 20 April 1859 William Harrison Livesey, and *d* Nov 1916, leaving issue

4 Eliza; *b* 2 Sept 1837; *m* 8 June 1864 Thomas Bond Worth, and *d* July 1914, leaving issue

GEORGE BALDWIN'S 7th son,

ALFRED BALDWIN, of Wilden House, Stourport, DL and JP Worcs and Staffs; MP Bewdley 1892–1908, chm and dir GWR; *b* 4 June 1841; *m* 9 Aug 1866 Louisa (*d* 16 May 1925), dau of Rev G B Macdonald, of Wolverhampton, and *d* 13 Feb 1908, leaving issue:

STANLEY BALDWIN, **1st Earl Baldwin of Bewdley**, so *cr* 8 June 1937, as also VISCOUNT CORVEDALE, of Corvedale, Co Salop (both UK), KG (1937), PC (GB 1920, Canada 1927), JP (Worcs 1897); *b* 3 Aug 1867; *educ* Harrow and Trin Coll Cambridge (MA); MP (C) Bewdley 1908–37, Fin Sec Treasury 1917–21, Pres BOT 1921–22, Chllr Exchequer 1922–23, Ld Privy Seal 1932–33, Ld Pres Cncl 1931–35, PM and 1st Ld Treasury 1923–24, 1924–29 and 1935–37; Rector Edin U 1923–26, Glasgow U 1928–31, Chllr St Andrews U 1929–47, Cambridge U 1930–47, Pres Classical Assoc 1926, Er Bro Trin House 1927, memb Academie des Sciences Morales et Politiques (Institut de France) 1930, Hon Master Bench Inner Temple 1936, Pres MCC 1938–39, High Steward Tewkesbury 1939 , FRS, Hon LLD Cambridge, St Andrews, Birmingham, Edin, Lond, Liverpool, Wales and Queen's U Belfast, Hon DCL Oxford and Durham; *m* 12 Sept 1892 Lucy, GBE, DGStJ (*d* 17 June 1945), est dau of Edward Lucas J Ridsdale, of The Dean, Rottingdean, Sussex, and *d* 14 Dec 1947, having had issue:

1 OLIVER RIDSDALE BALDWIN, **2nd Earl Baldwin of Bewdley**; *b* 1 March 1899; *educ* Eton; MP Dudley 1929–31 and Paisley 1945–47, served WW I 1916–18, Armeno-Turkish War 1920–21 and WW II 1940–45 as Maj Intelligence Corps, Govr and C-in-C Leeward Islands 1948–50, author; *d* unm 10 Aug 1958

2 (ARTHUR) WINDHAM, **3rd Earl**

1 Diana Lucy; *b* 8 April 1895; *m* 1st 24 Nov 1919 (*divorce* 1934) Capt Richard Gordon Munro, 4th Dragoon Gds (later Sir Gordon Munro, KCMG, MC) (*d* 4 Oct 1967), and had issue; *m* 2nd 24 Feb 1934 Capt George Durant Kemp-Welch, Gren Gds (*k* by enemy action in the Gds Chapel 18 June 1944)

2 Leonora Stanley; *b* 10 July 1896; *m* 20 June 1922 Capt Hon Sir Arthur Jared Palmer Howard, KBE, CVO (*d* 26 April 1971), son of Baroness Strathcona and Mount Royal (*qv*), and *d* 1989, leaving issue

3 (Pamela) Margaret; *b* 16 Sept 1897; *m* 2 April 1919 Sir (Herbert) Maurice Huntington-Whiteley, 2nd Bt (*qv*), and *d* 14 Aug 1976, leaving issue

4 Esther Louisa (Betty); *b* 16 March 1902

The 2nd EARL's bro,

(ARTHUR) WINDHAM BALDWIN, **3rd Earl Baldwin of Bewdley**; *b* 22 March 1904; *educ* Eton and Trin Coll Cambridge; WW II in RAF, dir GWR and Equitable Life Assur Soc 1938–74; *m* 25 Aug 1936 Joan Elspeth (*d* 1980), yst dau of Charles Alexander Tomes, of New York, and *d* 1976, leaving issue:

1 EDWARD ALFRED ALEXANDER BALDWIN, **4th and present Earl Baldwin of Bewdley**

BALFOUR

Arms: Arg. on a chevron engrailed, between three mullets sa. as many otter's heads erased of the first. **Crest:** A palm tree ppr. **Supporters:** Two otters ppr., collared or. **Motto:** *Virtus ad æthera tendit* ('Virtue strives towards heaven'). **Creation:** E. and V. (UK) 5 May 1922.

THE 4TH EARL OF BALFOUR and **Viscount Traprain**, of Whittingehame, East Lothian (Gerald Arthur James Balfour, JP (E Lothian 1970)) [The Rt Hon The Earl of Balfour JP, Whittingehame Tower, Haddington, East Lothian EH41 4QA]; *b* 23 Dec 1925; *s* f 1968; *educ* Eton and HMS *Conway*; Master Mariner; farmer; CC East Lothian 1960–74, WW II in Merchant Navy; *m* 14 Dec 1956 Natasha Georgina (*d* 22 Sept 1994), dau of Capt George Anton, of Archangel, N Russia, and formerly w of J C Lousada

Lineage: JAMES BALFOUR, yr son of John Balfour, of Balbirnie; *m* Lady Eleanor Maitland (*d* 23 May 1869), dau of 8th Earl of Lauderdale (*qv*), and *d* April 1845, leaving, with other issue:

JAMES MAITLAND BALFOUR, of Whittinghame, E Lothian, and Strathconan, Ross-shire; *b* 5 Jan 1820; *m* 15 Aug 1843 Lady Blanche Mary Harriet Gascoigne-Cecil (*d* 16 May 1872), 2nd dau of 2nd Marquess of Salisbury, KG (*qv*), and *d* 23 Feb 1856, having had issue:

1 ARTHUR JAMES BALFOUR, **1st Earl of Balfour**, so *cr* 5 May 1922, as also VISCOUNT TRAPRAIN of Whittingehame, East Lothian (both UK), with special remainder, in default of his own issue male, to his bro Gerald and heirs male of the latter's body, failing whom to the grantee's nephew Francis and the heirs male of his body, failing whom to the grantee's yr nephew Oswald and the heirs male of his body, KG (1922), PC (GB 1885, I 1887), OM, DL, JP; *b* 25 July 1848; *educ* Trin Coll Cambridge (MA 1873); MP (C) Hertford 1874–85, E Manchester 1885–1906 and City of London 1906–22, FRS, FBA, Ld Rector St Andrews 1886 and Glasgow 1890, Chllr Edinburgh U 1891 and Cambridge U 1919, Er Bro Trin House, Pres Local Govt Bd 1885–86, Sec for Scotland with seat in Cabinet 1886–87; Ch Sec Ireland 1887–91, 1st Ld Treasury and Leader H of C 1891–92 and 1895–1905, Leader Oppn 1892–95 and 1906–11, PM and 1st Ld Treasury 1902–05, Ld Privy Seal 1902–03, 1st Ld Admlty 1915–16, For Sec 1916–19, Ld Pres Cncl 1919–22 and 1925–29, Hon LLD Edin, St Andrews, Cambridge, Dublin, Glasgow, Manchester, Liverpool, Birmingham, Leeds, Sheffield and Bristol, Hon DCL Oxford, Durham, Columbia; LittD Cardiff, DPh Cracow, LLD Athens and Leeds; *d* unm 19 March 1930

2 Cecil Charles; *b* 22 Oct 1849; *d* unm 5 April 1881

3 Francis Maitland, LLD, FRS, Prof Animal Morphology Cambridge; *b* 10 Nov 1851; *d* 19 July 1882

4 GERALD WILLIAM, **2nd Earl**

5 Eustace James Anthony, MA, FSA, FRIBA, FZS, Col Lond Scottish RV, ADC to HM EDWARD VII; *b* 8 June 1854; *m* 12 May 1879 Lady Frances Campbell (*d* 25 Feb 1931), dau of 8th Duke of Argyll (*qv*), and *d* 14 Feb 1911, having had issue:

(1) Francis Cecil Campbell, CIE (1919), CVO (1953), CBE (1931), MC, Sudan Political Serv 1906–31, Lt-Col 6th Bn Northumberland Fus, Mil Sec to Govr Madras 1924–26, Govr Red Sea Province Sudan 1927–28 and Mongalla Province 1929–31, WW I 1917–19 in Mesopotamia (despatches), Order of the Nile 3rd Cl, Order Lion and Sun Persia 2nd Cl; *b* 8 Dec 1884; *educ* Eton; *m* 31 Aug 1920 Hon Phyllis Evelyn Goschen (*d* 1976), er dau of 2nd Viscount Goschen (*qv*), and *d* 16 April 1965, leaving issue:

1a +EUSTACE ARTHUR GOSCHEN [Eustace Balfour Esq, Le Pavillon, Ancenis-les-Bois, 44440 Riaillé, France, Savignac, Nanteuil de Bourzac, 24320 Verteillac, France]; *b* 26 May 1921; heir presumptive; *educ* Eton; Capt Scots Gds WW II N Africa and Italy (wounded); *m* 1st 28 Sept 1946 (*divorce* 1971) Anne, dau of Maj Victor Yule, IA; *m* 2nd 1971 *Paula Susan Cuene-Grandidier, dau of John Maurice Davis, MBE, and by his 1st w has:

1b +Roderick Francis Arthur [Roderick Balfour Esq, Burpham Lodge, Burpham, Arundel, Sussex]; *b* 9 Dec 1948; *educ* Eton; memb London Stock Exchange 1975–81, dir Union Discount Co of London 1983–90 and Rothschild Tst Corp, Liveryman Clothworker's Co 1986; *m* 1971 *Lady Tessa Mary Isabel Fitzalan-Howard, er dau of 17th Duke of Norfolk (*qv*), and has:

1c *Willa Anne; *b* 1973; *m* 17 May 1997 *George William Franks, yst s of Anthony Franks, of Beckett's Grove, Matfield, Kent

2c *Kinvara Clare Rachel; *b* 1975

3c *Maria Alice Jubilee; *b* 1977

4c *Candida Rose; *b* 1984

2b +Charles George Yule [Charles Balfour Esq, 15 Oakley St, London SW3]; *b* 23 April 1951; *educ* Eton; md NASDAQ, memb Roy Co Archers; *m* 1st 1978 Audrey Maragaret, dau of Henry Peregrine Rennie Hoare, of Stourton, Wilts (*see* BRISTOL, M); *m* 2nd 1987 *Reichsgräfin (Countess) Svea Maria Cecily Lucrezia, er dau of Reichsgräf Ernst Friedrich von Goëss, of Staupitzhof, Austria, and by her has:

1c +George Eustace Charles; *b* 1990

1c *Eleanor Cecily Isabelle; *b* 1989

1a Janet Christine Goschen *b* 8 Nov 1923; *m* 22 July 1944 (*divorce* 1962) 3rd Baron Hardinge of Penhurst (*qv*), and *d* 18 March 1970, leaving issue

(2) Oswald Herbert Campbell, CMG (1923), OBE (1944), Lt-Col KRRC, Mil Sec to Govr-Gen Canada 1921–23, chm High Grade Steels; *b* 1894; *d* unm 16 Oct 1953

(1) Blanche Elizabeth, JP Leics; *m* 18 Nov 1902 Edgar Trevelyan Stratford Dugdale, JP, Capt Leics Yeo (*d* 14 Oct 1964), yr bro of Sir William Francis Straford Dugdale, 1st Bt, of Merevale and Blyth (*qv*), and *d* 16 May 1948, leaving issue

(2) Joan Eleanor Campbell; *m* 11 March 1915 Maj Hon Edward Cecil Lascelles, DSO, MC (*d* 18 Aug 1935), 2nd son of 5th Earl of Harewood (*qv*), and *d* 10 May 1939

(3) Alison Catherine Campbell; *m* 20 April 1913 Arthur Dawson Milne, CMG, Lt-Col E Africa Medical Serv (*d* 12 Feb 1932), son of Very Rev A J Milne, LLD, Minister of Fyvie, and *d* 3 Sept 1955, leaving issue

1 Eleanor Mildred, Pncpl Newnham Coll Cambridge, LittD Victoria U, LLD Birmingham, St Andrews and Edin Us; *m* 1876 Henry Sidgwick, Prof Moral Philosphy, Cambridge, MA, LittD (*d* 28 Aug 1900), and *d* 10 Feb 1936

2 Evelyn Georgiana Mary; *m* 19 July 1871 3rd Baron Rayleigh (*qv*), and *d* 7 April 1934, leaving issue

3 Alice Blanche; *d* unm 12 June 1936

The 1st EARL's bro,

GERALD WILLIAM BALFOUR, **2nd Earl of Balfour**, PC (GB 1900, I 1895); *b* 9 April 1853; *educ* Trin Coll Cambridge (MA); Hon LLD Cambridge, MP (C) Leeds Centl 1885–1906, Ch Sec Ireland 1895–1900, Pres BOT 1900–05; *m* 21 Dec 1887 Lady Elizabeth Edith Lytton (*d* 28 March 1942), est dau of 1st Earl of Lytton (*qv*), and had issue:

1 ROBERT ARTHUR LYTTON, **3rd Earl**

1 Ruth, CBE (1941), MB, BS, MRCS, LRCP; *m* 26 Dec 1914 Brig Edward William Sturgis Balfour, CVO, DSO, OBE, MC, DL, Scots Gds, of Balbirnie (*d* 23 Dec 1955), and *d* 30 Aug 1967, leaving issue

2 Eleanor; *m* 7 Dec 1917 Hon Galbraith Lowry Egerton Cole (*d* 6 Oct 1929), 3rd son of 4th Earl of Enniskillen, KP (*qv*), and had issue

3 Mary Edith *b* 21 Jan 1894

4 Evelyn Barbara, Hon Life V-Pres Soil Assoc, author: *The Living Soil*; *b* 16 July 1898; *educ* Reading U

5 Kathleen Constance Blanche; *b* 1912; *educ* Newnham Coll Cambridge (BA 1934, MA 1949); *m* 23 Aug 1933 Richard Charles Oldfield, MA, Hon Prof Edinburgh U (*d* 27 April 1972), son of Sir Francis du Pre Oldfield, and *d* 20 Aug 1996, leaving:

(1) *Frances Elizabeth; *b* 10 May 1935; *educ* Edin U (BSc 1958) and London U (PhD 1961); *m* 11 July 1963 (*divorce* 1983) Roderick Whitfield, MA, PhD, Assist Keeper Dept Oriental Antiquities BM, and has:

1a *Aldous Francis; *b* 1970

1a *Martha Ming; *b* 15 July 1965

2a *Tanya Thisbe; *b* 14 April 1967

(2) *Margaret Cayley, PhD, Lecturer English Lit U of Ife Nigeria; *b* 12 July 1939; *educ* Bristol U (BA 1962, MA 1965); *m* 1960 *Agbo Folarin, of Ife U, Nigeria, and has issue:

1a *Oliver Abiola Raschid; *b* 1973

2a *Akinola Amos; *b* 1978

1a *Evelyn Adeola; *b* 1970

The 2nd EARL *d* 14 Jan 1945; his only son,

ROBERT ARTHUR LYTTON BALFOUR, **3rd Earl of Balfour**; *b* 31 Dec 1902; *educ* Eton and Trin Coll Cambridge; Lt RNVR WW II; chm and md Bruntons (Musselburgh) Ltd, part-time dir Scottish Gas Bd 1958–65 and Nat Coal Bd Scottish Div 1951–63; V-Convenor E Lothian CC 1937–38, chm Scottish Special Housing Assoc 1938–44; Regnl Controller (Scotland) Min Fuel and Power 1942–46, chm Scottish Div NCB 1946–51, Nat Govr Scotland BBC 1956–60, chm Roy Commn on Scottish Affrs; *m* 12 Feb 1925 Jean Lily West Roundel (*d* 1981), 4th dau of Rev Canon Cooke-Yarborough, Rector Puttenham (*see* COOKE, Bt), and *d* 27 Nov 1968, leaving issue:

1 GERALD ARTHUR JAMES BALFOUR, **4th and present Earl of Balfour**

2 Andrew Maitland; *b* 16 Sept 1936; *d* as the result of an accident 27 April 1948

1 *Evelyn Jean Blanche; *b* 22 March 1929; *m* 11 Dec 1948 *Michael William Brander, late 10th Hus, and has issue:

(1) *Andrew Michael; *b* 27 June 1949; *educ* St John's Coll Cambridge; *m* 1988 *Donna Spielman

(1) *Kathleen Jean; *b* 12 Sept 1950; *m* 1976 *Ian McCall and has issue:

1a *Angus; *b* 1979

2a *Andrew; *b* 1980

(2) *Evelyn Anne; *b* 9 June 1952

2 *Alison Emily [The Lady Alison Kremer, Widworthy Barton, Honiton, Devon EX14 9JS]; *b* 16 Nov 1934; *m* 8 May 1963 *Thomas Kremer, son of Bernard Kremer, of Budapest, and has issue:

(1) *David Lytton; *b* 10 Feb 1964; *m* 1995 *Karen Holloway and has:

1a *Jack Lytton; *b* 1997

(1) *Amanda Lili; *b* 10 Feb 1966

(2) *Kim Madeleine; *b* 10 June 1969

BALFOUR OF BURLEIGH

Arms: Quarterly, 1st and 4th, argent, on a chevron sable, an otter's head erased of the first; 2nd and 3rd, or a saltire and a chief gules, the latter charged with a mullet argent. **Crests:** 1 On a rock a mermaid, holding in her dexter hand an otter's head, and in her sinister a swan's head erased proper, 2 A dexter arm in fess embowed in armour, holding in the hand a sceptre in bend sinister or. **Supporters:** Dexter, an otter proper; sinister, a swan, wings inverted proper. **Mottoes:** *Omne solum forti patria* ('The entire earth is the brave man's homeland'); *Fuimus* ('We have been').
Creation: L. (S) 16 July 1607.

THE 8TH LORD BALFOUR OF BURLEIGH (Robert Bruce) [The Rt Hon The Lord Balfour of Burleigh, Brucefield, Clackmannan]; *b* 6 Jan 1927; *s* f 1967; *educ* Westminster; late RN; CEng, FIEE, FRSE, manager then Dir and Gen Manager English Electric Co of India Ltd, Madras, Gen Manager English Co Ltd, Netherton, Liverpool, and D Napier and Son, dir Bank of Scotland and Unbrako Ltd, Coventry; Chllr Stirling U to 1998; *m* 1st 30 Oct 1971 (*divorce* 1993) Jennifer, dau of E S Manasseh and formerly w of John Edward Jocelyn Brittain Catlin, and has:

1 *VICTORIA; *b* 7 May 1973; heiress presumptive

2 *Ishbel; *b* 28 Sept 1976

The 8th LORD *m* 2nd 1993 *Dr Janet Morgan, MA, PhD, dau of Dr Frank Morgan

Lineage (of Balfour): Sir JOHN BALFOUR, of Balgarvie, which JAMES II granted him and erected into a free barony 1446; *d* by 1486, leaving:

MICHAEL BALFOUR, of Burleigh; had a feu-charter of the lands of Burleigh and Tulery 1456; *m* Margaret — and had:

MICHAEL BALFOUR, of Burleigh and Balgarvie; *m* *c* July 1502 Margaret Muschat and *d* after 28 Jan 1524/5, leaving:

DAVID BALFOUR of Burleigh; *m* Agnes Forester and *d* by 1531, leaving, with two yr sons and two daus (including Margaret, *m* as his 1st w Sir Robert Douglas of Lochleven; *see* MORTON, E):

MICHAEL BALFOUR, of Burleigh; *m* Christina, dau of John Bethune of Creich, and *d* 29 Nov 1577, leaving an only child:

MARGARET; *m* 1st Sir James Balfour, of Pittendreich and Monquhany, Fife (*d* 1590), Pres Court of Session; *m* 2nd Sir Robert Melville and *d* 1584, leaving, with five yr sons and three daus:

Sir MICHAEL BALFOUR, **1st Lord Balfour of Burleigh** (S), so *cr* 16 July 1607, PC; Amb to Duke of Tuscany and Lorraine 1606; granted 7 Sept 1614 a charter of the Barony of Kilwinning with the title LORD OF KILWINNING to him and his heirs and assigns whatever; *m* 1st Oct 1577 Marion Adamson; *m* 2nd Margaret (*d* 1625), dau of Lundin of that Ilk, and *d* 15 March 1619, leaving issue:

MARGARET BALFOUR, *de jure* LADY BALFOUR OF BURLEIGH; *m* 1606 Robert ARNOT (son of Robert Arnot, of Newton, Chamberlain of Fife), who assumed the surname of BALFOUR on his marriage and sat in Scottish Parl as **2nd Lord Balfour of Burleigh** in right of his w 1621, PC (S), Pres Scottish Parl 1640–1641, a Commr Treaty of Peace with England 1640 and 1641; he *m* 2nd Margaret — (*d* June 1639) and *d* 10 Aug 1663, having had by her (with at least one dau, Anna, who *m* as his 1st w 2nd Earl of Wemyss; *see* WEMYSS and MARCH, E) an only s:

JOHN BALFOUR, **3rd Lord Balfour of Burleigh**; *m* 1649 Isabella, dau of Sir William Balfour, of Pitcullo, Lt Tower of London, and *d* by 27 Feb 1697, leaving, with six daus:

1 ROBERT, **4th Lord**

2 John, of Fernie; Lt-Col, Jacobite 1715, attainted 1716; *m* (contract 7 Oct 1684) Barbara, dau of Rt Rev Arthur Ross, Archbp of Glasgow, and *d* 8 Sept 1725, leaving an est s:

(1) Arthur, of Fernie; restored to that estate 1720 and 1738; *m* 1st (contract 21 Feb 1736) Dorothy Sandford, widow of Christopher Crackenthorp, of Crackenthorp, Westmorland; *m* 2nd (contract 31 July 1740) Janet, dau of George Paterson, of Dunmuir, and *d* 1 Feb 1746, leaving issue:

1a Sandford, of Fernie; *dsp* 1769

2a John, of Fernie; *dsp* 1765

3a Francis, of Fernie, MD; *m* the dau of Balfour, of Dunbog, Fifeshire, and *d* 7 May 1818, leaving issue:

1b Francis, of Fernie; *m* 1829 Margaret (*d* March 1853), dau of Graham Bower, of Kincaldrum, Forfarshire, and *d* 3 Dec 1854, leaving issue:

1c Francis Walter, of Fernie, DL (Fife); *b* 8 Jan 1830; Maj Rifle Bde; claimed the Lordship of Balfour as heir male 1862; *m* 25 Oct 1866 Jane Amelia (*d* 9 Feb 1898), dau of Patrick Small Keir, DL, of Kindrogan, Perthshire, and *d* 24 Feb 1909, leaving issue:

1d Francis, of Kindrogan, JP (Cos Perth and Fife); *b* 25 Aug 1867; *m* 22 April 1903 Katherine Morgan, dau of Harry W Chubb, of Burlington, Chislehurst, and *d* 2 Aug 1926, leaving issue:

1e Francis Keir; *b* 29 April 1905; *educ* Eton and Clare Coll Cambridge; *m* 15 Dec 1932 *Katharine Augusta, dau of Maj Sir George Alexander Dolby, of Silwood Pk, Sunninghill, and *dsp* 3 Nov 1974

2e Patrick Small Keir; *b* 10 Sept 1910; *educ* Repton; *m* 1 Feb 1936 *Lila Camila [Mrs Patrick Balfour, 103 Greenleaf Gdns, Polgate, East Sussex BH6 6PH], dau of Basil Edward Spicer, and *d* 1967, leaving issue:

1f +Robert William Keir [Robert Balfour Esq, 6 Millicent St, Leongatha, Victoria 3953, Australia]; *b* 28 April 1942; *educ* St Michael's, Heacham; *m* 8 Aug 1964 *Evelyn Mary Douglas and has issue:

1g +Michael Patrick Keir; *b* 8 Aug 1965

1f Mary Camilla; *b* 21 Nov 1937; *d* unm 29 June 1963

2f *Frances Norah [Mrs Hugh Tregarthen, 99 Hopetoun Ave, Vaucluse, Sydney 2050, Australia]; *b* 6 Feb 1941; *m* 15 Nov 1965 Hugh Manning Tregarthen of 10 Lawson St, Paddington, NSW, Australia and has issue:

1g *Carolyn Mary; *b* 1967; *m* 1991 Stephen Noel Manns, and has issue:

1h *Emelia Jane; *b* 1994

2g *Sarah Jane; *b* 1970

3g *Susan Manning; *b* 1971

3f *Sheila Katherine; *b* 13 March 1946; *m* 1st 1966 (*divorce* 1975) Jan Owen Sikorski; *m* 2nd 1989 *Ronald Leslie Patterson, RAAOC, of Henty, NSW, Australia and has issue by 1st husb:

1g *Ian Patrick; *b* 1971

1g *Tanya Mary; *b* 1966; *m* 1988 *Philip Pitt and has issue:

1h *Christopher Leigh; *b* 1983

2h *Flynn Edward James; *b* 1990

1h *Kirsten Mary Marie; *b* 1988

2g *Katharine Louise; *b* 1968

1e Katherine Amelia; *b* 13 May 1907; *m* 1940 Valentine Palmer (*d* at sea as a result of enemy action 1941), and *dsp* 16 Aug 1952

2d William Keir, JP (Co Fife); *b* 9 Dec 1869; *m* 12 April 1910 Mary (*d* 29 Sept 1952), dau of Sir Michael Barker Nairn, 1st Bt (*qv*), and *d* 10 Sept 1941

2c James Bower; *b* 1832; Lt RN; *m* 1859 Martha Maria (*d* 1863), dau of G H Emerson, and *d* 1864, leaving issue

3c Graham Montague; Lt Madras Army; *d* unm

1a Elizabeth

2a Barbara

3 Henry, of Dunbog; Maj of Dragoons, MP Fife, f of Henry Balfour of Dunbog, who *m* Katherine Porterfield

1 Margaret; *m* Nov 1670 3rd Lord Rollo (*qv*) of Duncrub

The 3rd LORD's est son,

ROBERT BALFOUR, **4th Lord Balfour of Burleigh**; *m* Margaret, only dau of 1st Earl of Melville (*qv*), and *d* July 1713, leaving issue:

1 ROBERT BALFOUR; **5th Lord Balfour of Burleigh**; tried 4 Aug 1709 for the murder of Henry Stenhouse, a schoolmaster at Inverkeithing, and sentenced 29 Nov 1709 to beheading 6 Jan 1710; escaped from prison a few days before sentence due by exchanging clothes with his sis; Jacobite 1715, attainted 13 Nov 1715 (attainder reversed 1869 in favour of the heir of his sis Mary, w of Maj Alexander Bruce, of Kennet (*see* below)); *d* unm and was *bur* 20 March 1757

1 Margaret; *d* unm Edinburgh 12 March 1769

2 MARY Balfour; *m* 6 Aug 1714 Maj Alexander BRUCE, of Kennet (*d* 8 Aug 1747) (*see* below), and *d* 7 Nov 1758, leaving issue:

(1) ROBERT, for whom *see* below

(1) Margaret Bruce; *m* 9 April 1738 Sir Laurence DUNDAS, of Kerse, 1st Bt (*d* 21 Sept 1781), and *d* 11 Oct 1802, leaving issue (*see* ZETLAND, M)

Lineage (of Bruce): DAVID BRUCE, of Green, nr Clackmannan, yr son of Sir David Bruce, of Clackmannan (*see* ELGIN, E), was f of:

ARCHIBALD BRUCE; *m* 1st 16 June 1568 Margaret (*d* Sept 1579), only dau and heir of Robert Bruce, of Wester Kennet; *m* 2nd 1596 Grizel Forrester and *d* 1609, leaving by his 1st w:

ROBERT BRUCE, of Kennet; served heir to his mother 6 Feb 1580; *m* 3 July 1599 Elizabeth, dau of Alexander Gall, of Maw, Fifeshire, and *dvp* 1606, leaving:

ROBERT BRUCE, of Kennet; *m* 1627 Agnes (*d* 1664), dau of Patrick Murray, of Perdowie, by Margaret, dau of Lord Colville of Culross (*qv*), and *d* after 4 Oct 1671, leaving an est s:

DAVID BRUCE, of Kennet; *m* 1656 Margery (*d* by 20 Nov 1714), dau of David Young, of Kirkton, Fife, and *d* 1673, leaving, with an est s (David, *d* unm by 20 Jan 1704), four yr sons and two daus:

JAMES BRUCE, of Kennet; Capt Earl of Leven's Regt of Foot 1689, Brig-Gen; *m* 1690 Mary, dau of Sir Alexander Swinton of Mersington, Senator Coll of Justice, and widow of John Fletcher, of Aberlady, and *d* Aug 1728, leaving, with three yr sons and three daus:

ALEXANDER BRUCE, of Kennet; served War of Spanish Succession in Flanders, Maj of a regt raised by Glasgow to support the Hanoverians in 1715; *m* 6 Aug 1714 Mary (*d* 7 Nov 1758), 2nd dau of Robert Balfour, 4th Lord Balfour of Burleigh (*see* above), and *d* 8 Aug 1747, leaving:

ROBERT BRUCE, of Kennet; *b* 24 Dec 1718; Ld of Session as Lord Kennet 1764, a Ld of Justiciary 1769; *m* 6 June 1754 Helen (*d* 1786), dau of George Abercromby, of Tullibody, and sis of Gen Sir Ralph Abercromby, and *d* 8 April 1785, leaving an est s:

ALEXANDER BRUCE, of Kennet; *b* 17 July 1755; *m* 13 Feb 1793 Hugh (*d* Dec 1851), dau of Hugh Blackburn, of Glasgow, and *d* 12 July 1808, leaving an est s:

ROBERT BRUCE, of Kennet; *b* 8 Dec 1795; Gren Gds Peninsula War and Waterloo, MP Clackmannan 1820–41, claimed the Lordship of Balfour of Burleigh but *d* before the case was decided; *m* 1st 12 April 1825 Anne (*dsp* 9 May 1846), dau of William Murray, of Touchadam and Polmaise; *m* 2nd 22 April 1848 Jane Dalrymple Hamilton, dau of Sir James Fergusson, of Kilkerran, 4th Bt, and *d* 13 Aug 1864, leaving issue:

1 ALEXANDER HUGH, **6th Lord**

1 Henrietta Anne; granted 6 May 1870 rank of Ld of Parl's dau; *m* 26 Nov 1874, as his 2nd w, Claud Hamilton Hamilton, JP, DL (*d* 30 Aug 1900), 12th of Barns and Cochno, Dumbartonshire, and of Dunmore Pk, Stirling, and *d* 27 Jan 1911, leaving issue

ROBERT BRUCE, of Kennet's only son,

ALEXANDER HUGH BRUCE, **6th Lord Balfour of Burleigh**, KT, PC, GCMG, GCVO, JP and DL (Clackmannanshire), JP (Perth, Stirling and Fife); *b* 13 Jan 1849; *educ* Eton and Oriel Coll Oxford (BA 1871, MA 1874); Capt Stirlingshire Militia; the Ho of Lds Privileges Ctee resolved 23 July 1868 that the 6th Lord's f Robert would have been entitled to the peerage but for the attainder of 1715, and an Act of Parl was passed 19 March 1869 removing the attainder; rep S peer 1876–1921, Ld-in-Waiting 1887–88, Parly Sec BOT 1888–92, Sec for Scotland 1895–1903, Chllr St Andrews 1907, Ld Warden of Stannaries Cornwall and Devon 1908–21, Capt Roy Co of Archers, Hon DCL Oxford, Hon LLD: Edinburgh, Glasgow, St Andrews, N Wales and Aberdeen Us; *m* 21 Nov 1876 Lady Katherine Eliza Gordon (*d* 28 Feb 1931), yst dau of 5th Earl of Aberdeen (*see* ABERDEEN AND TEMAIR, M), and *d* 6 July 1921, having had:

1 Robert, *Master of Burleigh*; *b* 25 Sept 1880; Capt Argyll and Sutherland Highrs, attd Egyptian Army 1910–14, 4th Cl Medjidie, S Africa 1900–2 (Queen's medal with three clasps, King's medal with two clasps), Sudan 1912 (medal with clasp) and WW I; *ka* 26 Aug 1914

2 GEORGE JOHN GORDON, **7th Lord**

1 Mary, OBE (1920), JP (Midlothian); *b* 24 Aug 1877; *m* 26 April 1910 Sir John Augustus Hope, 16th Bt, MP (*qv*), and *d* 18 Feb 1957, leaving issue

2 Jean Hamilton; *b* 18 March 1879; Woman Bedchamber to HM QUEEN MARY 1935–38, Extra Woman Bedchamber 1938–39; *d* unm 15 Jan 1939

3 Victoria Alexandrina Katherine; *b* 13 Sept 1898; probation offr London Juvenile Courts 1931–37, Dep Govr Borstal Inst 1937–40, Dep Govr Manchester Prison 1940–43, Govr Borstal Inst 1943–46, Govr Duke Street Prison Glasgow 1946–51; *d* unm 25 Nov 1951

The 6th LORD's only surv s:

GEORGE JOHN GORDON BRUCE, **7th Lord Balfour of Burleigh**, JP and DL (Clackmannanshire); *b* 18 Oct 1883; Capt and Brevet Maj Intell Corps and 7th Bn Argyll and Sutherland Highrs TAR, WW I (wounded, despatches four times, 1914 star, Brevet of Maj, Legn of Honour), rep S peer Scotland 1922–63, chm Lloyds Bank 1946–54, Freeman Roy Borough of Kensington 1965, Chm: MRC 1936–48, Kensington Housing Tst 1926–49, Bd of Land Tax Commrs City of London; *m* 2 June 1919 (Violet) Dorothy Evelyn, MBE (1920), pioneer of anaesthetised childbirth, Hon Sec Mrs Dighton Pallock Fund (*d* 28 Oct 1976), yr dau of Richard Henry Done, JP, DL, of Salterswell, Tarporley, Cheshire, and *d* 4 June 1967, leaving issue:

1 ROBERT BRUCE, **8th and present Lord Balfour of Burleigh**

2 +George John Done, does not use courtesy title [George Bruce Esq, 6 Pembroke Walk, London W8 6PQ]; *b* 28 March 1930; *educ* Westminster and Byam Shaw Sch of Drawing and Painting; Pres Roy Soc Portrait Painters 1991–94 (Hon Sec 1970–84, V-Pres 1984–89)

1 *Lætitia Mary, JP (Northumberland 1959) [The Hon Mrs Telfer, 5 Ruthven Court, Adderstone Crescent, Newcastle-upon-Tyne NE2 2HH]; *b* 29 Dec 1920; MB and ChB (St Andrews 1946); V-Pres NE Cncl on Addictions 1983–, Pres W Northumberland Branch NSPCC 1980–; *m* 8 July 1955 Ian Metcalfe Telfer, MRCGP (*d* 1988), er s of John Telfer, MCom, FSAA, of Kingarth, Moorside, Fenham, Newcastle-upon-Tyne, and has:

(1) *John Bruce; *b* 15 June 1956; BA

(2) *George Metcalfe; *b* 9 Oct 1961; Dip RSA, MD; *m* 1992 *Susan Elizabeth, dau of Michael Bernard Allen, of Rose Cottage, 11 Stoneheads, Whaley Bridge, Stockport

(1) *Mary Daubeny; *b* 30 March 1958; BSc, MSc; *m* 1990 *Kenneth Francis Douthwaite, and has issue:

1a *Matthew Geoffrey Ian; *b* 1991

2a *Christopher Robert; *b* 1993

1a *Rebecca Rosemary; *b* 1995

2 *Katherine, does not use courtesy title [Miss Katherine Bruce, 25 Kew Green, Richmond, Surrey]; *b* 27 Nov 1922; *educ* Somerville Coll Oxford; reassumed maiden name by deed poll 1 July 1975; *m* 23 Nov 1946 (*divorce* 1961) Thomas Riviere Bland, MC, er s of Charles Riviere Bland, and has issue:

(1) *Charles Riviere; *b* 17 July 1949; *educ* Westminster; *m* 1980 *Julie Louise, dau of Sir Edgar Charles Beck, CBE, and has issue:

1a *William Reviere; *b* 1990

1a *Jemima Katherine Agnes; *b* 1983

2a *Daisy Prudence Harriet; *b* 1986

(1) *Susanna Katherine; *b* 11 Sept 1947; *m* 1986 *Général Philippe Saint-Loubert Bié, and has issue:

1a *Thomas Georges Bland; *b* 1988

2a *Louise Margaret; *b* 1 July 1953

3 *Jean; *b* 13 July 1924; WRNS WW II; *m* 1st 12 Nov 1949 (*divorce* 1971) John Shirley Ward, est s of John Shirley Ward Jr, of Pasadena, Calif, USA; and has issue:

(1) *John Shirley ; *b* 28 March 1960; *m* 1987 (*divorce* 1994) Monica Lanz

(1) *Lætitia; *b* 4 Aug 1951; *m* 1980 *Dr Paul Buehrens, and has issue:

1a *Thomas; *b* 1984

2a *Daniel; *b* 1986

(2) *Reavis Mary; *b* 14 June 1955; *m* 1987 *Gotfried Hilz Ward, and has issue:

1a *Sonia; *b* 1988

2a *Christine; *b* 1993

3 (cont.) *The Hon Mrs Jean Ward *m* 2nd 1974 *John Herbert Poole, of Pasadena

4 *Margaret Bruce [The Hon Mrs Worthy, 33 Sloane Gdns, London SW1; Keepers Cottage, Hare Warren Hollow, Merrow Downs, Guildford, Surrey GU1 2HJ]; *b* 1 Sept 1934; *m* 24 Nov 1967 *David Graham Worthy, MA Oxford, yr son of Marcus Gerald Worthy, of Sunnyside, Minster Rd, Godalming, Surrey, and has issue:

(1) *Henry Jonathan David Bruce; *b* 23 June 1971

BALFOUR OF INCHRYE

Arms: Arg. on a chevron indented sa. between in chief a rose gu. and in base a saltire couped az. an otter's head erased of the first, a bordure engrailed of the third. **Crest:** A dexter hand grasping an olive branch, all ppr. **Supporters:** Dexter, an otter per fess or and az.; sinister, a peregrine falcon ppr., bells arg., jesses sa. **Motto:** *Adsit Deus* ('God be with me'). **Creation:** B. (UK) 5 July 1945.

THE 2ND BARON BALFOUR OF INCHRYE (Ian Balfour) [The Rt Hon The Lord Balfour of Inchrye, House of Lords, London SW1A 0PW]; *b* 21 Dec 1924; *s* f 1988; *educ* Eton and Magdalen Coll Oxford; WW II 1942–45 in RN; *m* 28 Nov 1953 *Josephine Maria Jane, only child of Morogh Wyndham Percy Bernard, of 8 Bloomfield Terrace, London SW1 (*see* 1970 edn BANDON, E), and has:

1 *Roxane [The Hon Mrs Laird Craig, 30 Coltbridge Terrace, Edinburgh EH12 6AE]; *b* 8 Sept 1955; *m* 8 April 1978 *Adrian Laird Craig, yr s of W/Cdr A J Laird Craig, DSO, DFC, AFC, MBE, and has:

(1) *Robert Joseph; *b* 1982

(1) *Mary Ann Josephine; *b* 1984

(2) *Alethea Katharine; *b* 1986

Lineage: ALEXANDER BALFOUR, Cellarman 1499 to JAMES IV, from whom he leased Inchrye, Fifeshire, 1501; *b* 1470; *m* Jane Wemyss and had, with other issue:

DAVID BALFOUR of Powis and Inchrye; *b c* 1500; *m* Katharine Abercrombie and *d* 1580, leaving, with other issue:

JAMES BALFOUR, Minister Guthrie and 1589 St Giles, Edinburgh; *b* 1540; *m* as his 1st w his cousin Barbara, dau of Richard Melvill of Baldowy, Minister of Maryton, and *d* 1613, leaving by her:

ANDREW BALFOUR, Minister Kirknewton, W Midlothian; *b* 1587; *d* 7 July 1624, leaving issue:

JAMES BALFOUR, Advocate, Clerk of Session; *b* 1619; *m* Beatrice Chalmers (*bur* 23 June 1666), of Balbitham, Aberdeenshire, and had:

JAMES BALFOUR, merchant, Govr Darien Co; *b* 1652; *m* 1679 Helen, gdau of Sir John Smith, of Grotchall, nr Edinburgh, and *d* 1703, leaving issue:

JAMES BALFOUR 1st of Pilrig; *b* 1681; *m* 10 Sept 1704 Louisa, dau of Robert Hamilton (*see* STIRLINGHAM-ILTON, Bt) and left, with an est son (James, 2nd of Pilrig, advocate, Prof Moral Philosophy and Public Law Edin U, *b* 1705), a seventh s:

JOHN BALFOUR, of Edinburgh, publisher; *b* 1715; *m* 4 Jan 1747 Catherine, dau of Ludovic Cant, of Thurston, E Lothian, and *d* 1796, leaving issue:

JAMES BALFOUR, of Riga, merchant; *m* 1780 Anna Gertrude (*b* 1760; *d* 1811), dau of Carl George Haatz, of Riga, and *d* 1795, leaving, with other issue, including another son (John Lewis, *b* 1784, *d* on or after 7 July 1842):

CHARLES BALFOUR, of London, merchant; *b* 1786; *m* 1 July 1826 Maria Caroline (*d* 4 July 1876), only dau of Sir John Edward Harington, 8th Bt (*qv*), and *d* by 1876, leaving, with other issue:

HARINGTON BALFOUR, ICS; *b* 1827; *m* 2 July 1863 Isabella Anne (*d* 14 April 1923), est dau of Sir David Kinloch, 9th Bt, of Gilmerton (*qv*), and *d* 1910, leaving issue:

NIGEL HARINGTON BALFOUR, OBE, of Belton, Camberley, Surrey; *b* 1873; Col; *m* 1894 Grace Annette Marie (*d* 24 Jan 1965), dau of Henry Robarts Madocks, BCS, of Glanywern and Llay Hall, Denbighshire, by Hon Amelia Anne Napier, 2nd dau of 1st Baron Napier of Magdala (*qv*), and had issue:

1 Sydney Harington, Lt-Cdr RN; *m* 7 June 1932 Doreen Isabella Mary (*d* 1957), only dau of Alexander FitzPatrick Grant, and was *kas* 11 Jan 1941

2 HAROLD HARINGTON, **1st Baron**

1 Islay Monica Mary; *m* 1933 Cdr Herbert Wyndham Williams, RN (ret), and *d* 16 March 1952, leaving issue

NIGEL BALFOUR's 2nd son,

HAROLD HARINGTON BALFOUR, **1st Baron Balfour of Inchrye**, of Shefford, Co Berks (UK), so *cr* 5 July 1954, PC (1941), MC and bar; *b* 1 Nov 1897; *educ* Chilverton Elms, Dover, and RNC Osborne; WW I with 60th Rifles, RFC and RAF, MP (C) Isle of Thanet 1929–45, Parly U-Sec Air 1938–44, Min Resident W Africa 1944–45, Pres Fedn Chambers Commerce Br Empire League 1951–56 and Empire Industries Assoc 1956–61, dir BEA 1955–66; *m* 1st 15 Dec 1921 (*divorce* 1946) Diana Blanche (*d* 4 June 1982), 2nd dau of Sir Robert Grenville Harvey, 2nd Bt (*see* 1931 edn), and had:

1 IAN BALFOUR, **2nd and present Baron Balfour of Inchrye**

The **1st Baron** *m* 2nd 2 Jan 1947 *Mary Ainslie [The Rt Hon Mary Lady Balfour of Inchrye, End House, St Mary Abbots Place, London W8 6LS], yr dau of Baron Albert Peter Anthony Profumo, KC, of Avon Carron, Avon Dassett, Warwicks, and *d* 1988, leaving further issue:

1 *Mary Ann [The Hon Mrs Martin Janson, Uppat House, Brora, Sutherland]; *b* 22 July 1949; *m* 14 Feb 1974 *Hon Martin Dearman Sutherland Janson and has issue (*see* SUTHERLAND, E)

BALL

Arms: Arg. on a chevron gu. between three fireballs ppr. a galley with one mast, sails furled, pennon flottant, in stern of the first. **Crest:** An arm in armour embowed arg. charged with two ogresses, the hand grasping a fireball as in the arms. **Motto:** On. **Creation:** Bt. (UK) 23 June 1911.

SIR CHARLES IRWIN BALL, 4TH BT [Sir Charles Ball Bt, Killybegs, Eddystone Rd, Thurlestone, Kingsbridge, Devon TQ7 3NU]; *b* 12 Jan 1924; *s f* 1978; *educ* Sherborne; served RA 1942–47, Capt 1946, FCA 1960; dir Kleinwort, Benson Ltd 1964–76 (v-chm 1974–76); dep chm Assoc Br Ports Holdings 1982–; Clockmakers' Co: Liveryman 1960, memb Ct of Assists 1979–87, Master 1985; *m* 1st 2 Sept 1950 (*divorce* 1983) Alison Mary, only dau of Lt-Col Percy Holman Bentley, MBE, MC, of 4 Castle Court, Farnham, Surrey, and has issue:

1 +RICHARD BENTLEY [Richard Ball Esq, Evenshade, Sandown Rd, Esher, Surrey KT10 9TT]; *b* 29 Jan 1953; *educ* Sherborne and Leicester U; ACA; *m* 1991 *Beverley Ann, dau of Bertram Joffre Wright, and has

(1) *Anna Frances; *b* 24 Feb 1996

1 *Diana Margaret [Miss Diana Ball, 56 Barrons Way, Comberton, Cambridge]; *b* 20 April 1955

Sir CHARLES *m* 2nd 14 May 1994 *Christine Trilby Knowles, dau of William Bedo Hobbs

Lineage: NICHOLAS BALL, of Chudleigh, Devon; ggf of:

THOMAS BALL, of Southwood; aged 100 in 1620; alleged ancestor of:

ROBERT BALL, Mayor Youghal, Co Cork, 1690; *b* Bampton, Devon, 20 Nov 1651; *m* 28 Sept 1675 Elizabeth, dau of Thomas Vaughan, of Youghal, and *d* 17 Jan 1724, having had, with other issue:

HENRY BALL, of Sandy Hill, Co Cork, and Keane, Devon, Mayor of Youghal 1722 and 1729; *b* 25 Jan 1685; *m* 23 Aug 1728 Ruth (*d* 16 June 1749), dau of Jonas Stawell, of Kilkearns and Kilbrittain, Co Cork, and *d* 21 June 1741, having had, with other issue:

ROBERT BALL, of Youghal, Co Cork, sold the rest of the Ball property in Devon; *b* 10 July 1729; *m* 23 July 1749 Mary (*d* Oct 1805), dau of Bent Croker by Mary, dau of Gregory Salter, and *d* 31 Jan 1802, leaving, with other issue:

1 Henry, of Rocksboro', Co Cork, Lt 15th Foot War American Independence; *b* 18 Dec 1750; *d* unm 1807/8

2 Bent, of Rocksboro', Capt 63rd Foot; *b* 25 Sept 1753; *m* 25 Sept 1785 Catherine, dau of Joshua Hamilton, son of Hon Henry Hamilton, MP (*see* BOYNE V), and *d* 12 Oct 1832, leaving issue

3 Bob Stawell, of Youghal; five times Mayor Youghal; *b* 18 Sept 1768; *m* 20 Jan 1799 Mary (*d* 11 May 1862), dau of Roger Green, of Youghal, by his 2nd w Mary Ellis, and *d* 5 Jan 1841, having had with other issue:

(1) Robert, of Dublin, Hon LLD Trin Coll Dublin 1850; naturalist, Pres Geological Soc of Ireland, Treasurer Roy Irish Acad, Dir Trin Coll Museum; *b* 1 April 1802; *m* 21 Sept 1837 Amelia Gresley (*d* 1 March 1895), dau of Thomas Hellicar, of Bristol, by Catherine, dau of John Gresley, ggs of John Gresley, bro of Sir George Gresley, 1st Bt (*see* 1970 edn), and *d* 30 March 1857, having had, with four daus:

1a Robert Stawell (Sir), MA and LLD, Dublin, Hon MA Cambridge, FRS, FRAS, DSc, astronomer, Lowndean Prof of Astronomy and Geometry Cambridge, Fell King's Coll, Astronomer Royal Ireland 1874–92, ktd 1886, Dir Cambridge Observatory 1892–1913; *b* 1 July 1840; *m* 5 Aug 1868 Frances Elizabeth (*d* 6 Aug 1919), dau of William Edward Steele, MD, Dir Science and Art Museum, Dublin, and *d* 25 Nov 1913, leaving issue:

1b Robert Steele, AMICE; *b* 17 Dec 1869; *educ* Boston (BSc) and Cambridge Us (Hon MA); *m* 2 Sept 1903 Olga, 2nd dau of John Edmund Sturge, of Montserrat and Birmingham, and *d* 23 July 1957, leaving:

1c Robert Sturge, served WW II; *b* 3 Feb 1909; *educ* Marlborough and King's Coll Cambridge (MA, DipAg); *m* 13 May 1939 *Kathleen (*m* 2nd 17 Sept 1942 David Edward Fielden, of Spring Hill, PO, Nakuru, Subukia, Kenya, est s of Lt-Col Edward Anthony (Mark) Fielden, MC, of Court-of-Hill Salop), dau of Thomas Grant, of Silver Bridge, Co Down, and was *ka* Abyssinian Border 30 July 1940, leaving issue:

1d *Robert Grant, AIAgrE, area sales manager Massey Ferguson (Export) Ltd; *b* 3 July 1940; *educ* Marlborough and King's Coll Cambridge (BA, DipAg, MA 1967)

1c *Stella Elizabeth; *b* 4 June 1907; *m* 7 Oct 1943 Robert Ogle Barnes, OBE, son of Robert Samuel Wemyss Barnes, AMICE, of Durban and New Milton, and has issue:

1d *Robert Ogle Ball; *b* 26 Aug 1944; *educ* Repton and Pembroke Coll Cambridge (BA)

2b William Valentine (Sir), ktd 1946, OBE (1918), barrister Lincoln's Inn 1897, joined Middle Temple 1919, Bencher Lincoln's Inn 1945, Examiner of the Court 1919, Master Supreme Court 1921–44, Sr Master and King's Remembrancer 1944–47, Master Clockmakers' Co 1953, WW I with Anti-Aircraft Corps and as Civil Liabilities Commr; *b* 10 Feb 1874; *educ* Royal Sch Armagh, Tonbridge, Trin Coll Dublin and King's Coll Cambridge (BA 1895, MA 1898); *m* 9 Oct 1903 Kathleen Mary (*d* 30 April 1957), dau of George Butt, ICS, and *dsp* 25 Nov 1960

3b Charles Rowan Hamilton, MRCS Lond 1901; *b* 24 June 1876; *m* 30 Sept 1907 Anne Josephine (*d* 25 Oct 1965), dau of George Cowie, of Courtfield Road, London SW5, and *d* 9 March 1964, leaving:

1c *Peter Halley, MRCS, LRCP, DOMS, Col RAMC WW II, Adviser in Ophthalmology to MOD (Army); *b* 25 Jan 1910; *educ* Haileybury and Pembroke Coll Cambridge; *m* 9 March 1937 *Mary Le Geyt, dau of James Rae Pearson, CIE, ICS, and has had issue:

1d Anthony Rae; *b* 5 July 1947; *d* 19 March 1963

1d *Rosemary Drummond; *b* 8 Jan 1945; *m* 28 March 1968 *William Anthony Snow, yst s of Brig James Elliot Snow, OBE, RAMC, of Echo Barn, Farnham, Surrey

2d *Josephine Grace; *b* 5 July 1947

4b Randal Gresley, Col Royal Inniskilling Fus WW I (wounded); *b* 23 July 1881; *m* 8 July 1914 Evelyn Iris (*d* 3 July 1953), dau of Sir Robert Holmes, of Dublin, and *d* 2 Aug 1934, leaving issue:

1c *Pamela Gresley; *b* 2 April 1917; *m* 18 April 1939 Maj-Gen John Edward Longworth Morris, CB, CBE, DSO, son of Col Arthur Edward Morris, of Edenderry, Co Offaly, and has:

1d *Virginia Gresley; *b* 3 July 1944

2d *Angela Longworth; *b* 7 Sept 1948

1b Frances Amelia; *m* H B Meakin, and *d* Jan 1959

2b Mary Agnetta; *m* 5 Aug 1903 Sir Joseph Barcroft, CBE, FRS, FRCOG (*d* 21 March 1947), er son of Henry BarcroftDL, JP of The Glen, Newry, Co Armagh, and *d* 8 July 1962, leaving issue

2a Valentine, CB, Hon LLD Trin Coll Dublin, FRS, MRIA, geologist, Dir Science and Art Museum Dublin; *b* 14 July 1843; *m* 18 Sept 1879 Mary (*d* 19 Feb 1936), dau of John Stewart-Moore, of Moyarget, Co Antrim, and *d* 15 June 1895, having had:

1b John Stewart Valentine; *b* 1884; *d* 1941

2b Robert Gordon, Capt RAMC WW I; *b* 1888; *d* 3 Feb 1920

1b Katherine Stewart; *b* 1880; *d* 1881

2b Maude Mary, painter, memb Roy Dublin Soc and Roy Zoological Soc of Ireland; *b* 5 April 1883; *d* unm 7 April 1969

3b Ethel Gresley, sculptress, memb Roy Dublin Soc and Roy Zoological Soc of Ireland; *b* 1886; *d* unm 3 July 1959

3a **Sir Charles Bent Ball, 1st Bt** (UK), so *cr* 23 June 1911, of Merrion Square, Dublin, and Killybegs, Co Donegal; Hon Surgn to HM, Pres Roy Acad of Medicine Ireland, Regius Prof Surgery Trin Coll Dublin; *educ* Trin Coll Dublin (BA, MCh, MD, Medical Scholar, Sr Moderator, Gold Medal Natl Science), FRCS Ireland, Hon FRCS England, Lt-Col RAMC 1914; *b* 21 Feb 1851, ktd 3 Feb 1903; *m* 23 July 1874 Annie Julia (*d* 24 Sept 1940), est dau of Daniel Kinahan, JP, of Roebuck Park, Dublin, and *d* 17 March 1916, having had issue:

1b **Sir (Charles) Arthur Kinahan Ball, 2nd Bt**; *b* 29 March 1877; *educ* Trin Coll Dublin (BA, MD, MCh); Moderator Natl Science, FRCSI, Regius Prof of Surgery Dublin U, Surgn Sir Patrick Dun's Hosp, Dublin, Consultant Surgn Monkstown Hosp, Stewart Instn and Drogheda Cottage Hosp, Maj RAMC; *m* 25 April 1907 Elizabeth Smyth (*d* 7 March 1904), dau of Joseph Smyth Wilson, of Berkeley, California, and *dspm* 21 Dec 1945, having had:

1c Barbara Ann; *d* an infant 30 Oct 1911

2b George Stawell; *b* 19 July 1884; *d* 10 March 1888

3b NIGEL GRESLEY (Sir), **3rd Bt**

4b Ivan Hellicar; *b* 23 July 1894; *m* 27 April 1929 Dorothy (*d* 1992), dau of Charles E Gill, and *d* 26 March 1963, leaving issue:

1c *Ursula Pamela Joyce [Mrs Herbert Lewis, Strath Isla, Wothorpe Drift, Wothorpe, Stamford, Lincs]; *b* 1930; *m* 31 March 1959 *Herbert John Lewis, and has issue:

1d *Peter John; *b* 11 Aug 1961

1d *Joanna Mary; *b* 11 Feb 1964

2d *Sarah Catherine; *b* 30 July 1966

2c *Dorothy Lucia Annie [Miss Dorothy Ball, 2 Abbots Way, Neston, S Wirral, Cheshire L64 3SU]; *b* 1933

1b Minnie Gwendoline; *d* unm 22 Dec 1963 aged 88

2b Nina Evelyn; *m* 9 Oct 1912 Oliver Murphy (*d* 3 Jan 1944), barrister, yst son of Isaac James Murphy, of Armagh, and *d* 14 Jan 1968 aged 88, leaving issue

3b Mabel Vaughan; *m* 1 July 1911 William Geoffrey Harvey, MD, FRCPI (*d* 2 Nov 1958), er s of Reuben James Harvey, MD, of Dublin, and *d* 23 July 1968 aged 87, leaving issue

4b Annie Muriel Kift; *d* unm 14 April 1976 aged 87

The 2nd Bt's bro,

Sir Nigel Gresley Ball, 3rd Bt; *b* 27 Aug 1892; *educ* St Columba's and Trin Coll Dublin (MA, DSc); FLS, Prof Botany U Coll Colombo 1924–43, Lecturer Botany King's Coll London 1944–55, Reader Botany 1955–57, Special Lecturer Botany 1957–59, Capt 8th Service Bn Roy Dublin Fus; *m* 28 Dec 1922 Florine Isabel (*d* 4 Oct 1995), est dau of Col Herbert Edwardes Irwin, Roy Warwicks Regt, and *d* 1978, leaving issue:

1 Sir CHARLES IRWIN BALL, **4th and present Bt**

2 +Ronald Herbert [Ronald Ball Esq, 31 Waterlip Cottage, Cranmore, Shepton Mallet, Somerset BA4 4RN]; ARIBA, Capt Gren Gds 1943–47; *b* 19 Nov 1925; *educ* Sherborne; *m* 1st 15 April 1950 Pamela Mary (*d* 23 June 1969), er dau of John Morton, of Hunningham Grange, Warwicks; *m* 2nd 1970 (*divorce* 1980) Diana Joy Maitland, dau of Lt-Col James Pridham, of 54 Elm Park House, Fulham Rd, London SW10, and by his 1st w has:

(1) +Christopher Nigel Morton [Christopher Ball Esq, 31 Waterlip Cottage, Cranmore, Shepton Mallet, Somerset BA4 4RN]; *b* 3 Nov 1951; *educ* Sherborne; *m* 1974 *Melanie, dau of Col David James Fenner, of 1 Riverside Cottage, Lyme Regis, Dorset, and has:

1a +Peter Jonathan; *b* 14 Feb 1981

1a *Amelia Kate; *b* 14 Jan 1983

(2) +Jonathan Gresley [Jonathan Ball Esq, The Headlands, Luntley, nr Pembridge, Hereford and Worcester HR6 9EJ]; *b* 1956; *m* 1981 *Molly, dau of Christopher Major, and has issue:

1a +Christopher James; *b* 1984

1a *Katherine Elizabeth; *b* 1987

2a *Joanna Rachel; *b* 1987

(3) +Rupert Valentine [Rupert Ball, Treasure Chest, Parque Don José, Costa del Silencio, Arona, Tenerife, Spain]; *b* 1958; *m* 1981 *Christine, dau of Cliff Hampson, of 46 Hereford Rd, Blackburn, Lancs, and has issue:

1a +James Irwin Hampson; *b* 1992

1a *Emma Frances; *b* 1983

(1) *Susan Mary [Mrs Susan Allen, PO Box 438, Woollahra, NSW 2025, Australia]; *b* 16 Aug 1953; *m* 1979 (*divorce* 1981) Steven Rhead Allen

1 *Valerie Margaret; *b* 1929 [Mrs Christopher Winn, 8 Broadlands Court, Kew Gardens Rd, Richmond, Surrey]; *m* 28 March 1953 *Christopher Elliott Winn, and has issue:

(1) *David Elliott [David Winn Esq, 219 Hempstead Rd, Hempstead, nr Gillingham, Kent]; *b* 24 July 1958; *m* 20 Feb 1988 *Esther Maria Lewis, dau of Salvatore Antonio Consilio and has:

1a *Catherine Elizabeth; *b* 16 June 1988

2a *Stephanie Fay; *b* 12 July 1991

(1) *Joanna Margaret [Mrs Anthony Green, Oak Cottage, Hill House Hill, Liphook, Hants]; *b* 21 July 1955; *m* 1979 *Anthony Oliver Bay Green and has:

1a *Barnaby Oliver Bay; *b* 1983

1a *Samantha Margaret Bay; *b* 1981

2a *Susannah Katharine Bay; *b* 1986

(2) *Fiona Anne [Mrs Charles Brett, St Swithun's Gate, Kingsgate Rd, Winchester, Hants SO23 9QQ]; *b* 7 March 1957; *m* 1985 *Charles Christopher Carter Brett and has:

1a *Luisa Annabel Carter; *b* 1987

2a *Claudia Alessandra Isabel; *b* 1990

Banbury of Southam

Arms: Erm. a cross patée gu. between five stars of six points, each within an annulet, three in chief and two in base, all of the last. **Crest:** A demi-antelope ppr., holding between the forepaws a cross patée and charged on the shoulder with a garb gu. **Supporters:** On either side a collie dog ppr., charged on the shoulder with a cross patée gu. **Motto:** *Moneo et munio* ('I warn and I protect'). **Creations:** Bt. (UK) 6 Jan 1903, B. (UK) 21 Jan 1924.

THE 3RD BARON BANBURY OF SOUTHAM, of Southam, Co Warwick and a **Baronet** (Sir Charles William Banbury Bt) [The Rt Hon The Lord Banbury of Southam, The Mill, Fossebridge, Glos GL54 3JN]; *b* 29 July 1953; *s* f 1981; *educ* Eton; *m* 1st 1984 (*divorce* 1986) Lucinda Elizabeth Scarlett, er dau of John Frederick Edward Trehearne; *m* 2nd 1989 *Inger Marianne Norton, dau of — Wiegert, and by her has:

1 *Charlotte Rosa; *b* 1990

2 *Poppy Isobel; *b* 1991

Lineage: THOMAS BANBURY, Prior of Burcester (Bicester); *d* 1486; possibly kin to:

HENRY BANBURY; *m* Elizabeth — (*d* 1557) and had, with a dau (Alys, *b* 1541):

WILLIAM BANBURY; *b* 21 June 1544; *m* 6 Nov 1582 Joan Fenton and had:

WILLIAM BANBURY; *b* 12 Nov 1584; *m* Jane — and had:

THOMAS BANBURY; *b* 1 Jan 1617; *m* Margaret — (*d* 1691) and *d* 1698, leaving issue:

EDMUND BANBURY; *b* 1654; *m* 1697 Elizabeth Garrett (*d* 8 Oct 1705) and *d* 30 Jan 1721, having had, with an er son (Thomas, *b* 18 Feb 1698, *d* unm Sept 1731) and dau (Elizabeth, *b* 30 Aug 1702, *m* Richard Overton):

WILLIAM BANBURY; *b* 30 Oct 1700; *m* Hannah, dau of E Horley, and *d* 21 Aug 1733, having had, with other issue:

WILLIAM BANBURY; *b* 6 Dec 1730; *m* 13 May 1756 Ann (*d* 1768), widow of S Snell, dau of George Worth, of Church Lawford, and gdau of Michael and Judith Worth, of The Manor House, Newnham Regis, and *d* 1770, having had, with other issue:

WILLIAM BANBURY, of Warlies Park, Waltham Abbey, Essex, and 77 Lombard St, London; banker, joined the business of his maternal unc Michael Worth; *b* 12 Sept 1766; *m* 1st 5 Nov 1795 Mary (*d* March 1811), dau of John Massu, of a French family, by his w Mary Beverley, and had a son (*d* an infant) and three daus; *m* 2nd Dec 1811 Margaret, dau of Joshua Knowles by Mary Mitchell, and *d* 1852, having by her had, with other issue:

1 William, of 77 Lombard St; *b* 12 Dec 1813; *m* 16 April 1845 Harriet (*d* 31 Dec 1899), dau of James Grout, and *d* 13 Feb 1893, having had issue:

(1) William, Capt 90th LI; *b* 15 May 1848; *dsp* 26 June 1876

(2) Edward; *b* 15 Aug 1859; *m* 15 Dec 1883 Frances Mary (*d* 28 Dec 1925), 2nd dau of Adml Sir William King Hall, KCB and *d* 16 Feb 1933, leaving issue:

1a William Michael Victor, Capt 11th Bn Rifle Brigade WW I; *b* 13 Oct 1884; *ka* 17 Aug 1917

2a Francis Edward, 2nd Lt Coldstream Gds SR 1915–17; *b* 12 Feb 1894; *d* unm 6 Jan 1956

1a Margaret Louise; *b* and *d* May 1889

2a Elizabeth; *d* in childhood

(2) Margaret; *d* unm 29 July 1929

2 Frederick, of Shirley House, Surrey; *b* 1827; *m* Feb 1850 Cecilia Laura (*d* 4 Jan 1904), dau of William Cox, of Woodford Hall, Essex, and *d* 13 Aug 1890, leaving, with other issue:

(1) FREDERICK GEORGE, **1st Baron**

(2) George; *b* 18 Feb 1852; *m* 9 May 1876 Nina (*d* 8 Jan 1909), only child of Thomas Chay Beale, of Shanghai, and *d* 13 Feb 1932, leaving issue:

1a George Chay; *b* 27 Feb 1877

2a Cecil Edmund, JP (E Sussex 1909–23); Maj 11th Res Regt Cavalry, served Boer War, WW I (despatches) and WW II as Ch Staff Offr Herts HG; *b*

19 March 1878; *m* 14 Nov 1905 Baroness Lily de Brienen (*d* 18 June 1948), 2nd dau of Baron de Brienen, of Clingendaal, The Hague, Holland, and *d* 18 Jan 1963

3a Ralph Edgar, Capt Roy Fus WW I (wounded); *b* 2 Jan 1881; *m* 1st 26 April 1910 Cecil Phoebe (*d* 16 Feb 1918), yr dau of Lt-Col Arthur Balfour Haig, CVO, RE, and *d* 31 Dec 1957

(1) Nina; *m* 1st 6 July 1903 Lt Philip Arthur Flower, The Buffs (*d* 21 April 1910), and had issue; *m* 2nd 17 Oct 1912 Francis William Murray Sturges (*d* 31 Oct 1945), 3rd son of Canon Edward Sturges, Rector Wokingham, and *d* 13 Nov 1952, leaving further issue

(3) Edmund; *b* 2 Oct 1853; *m* 16 Oct 1913 Lady Beatrice Mary Capell (*d* 22 Jan 1954), dau of 6th Earl of Essex (*qv*), and *d* 3 Jan 1938, leaving issue:

1a *John Edmund; *b* 15 Nov 1914; *m* 4 April 1941 *Lelia Elizabeth, only dau of Gilbert Russell, of Sydney, Australia

FREDERICK BANBURY's est son,

Sir Frederick George Banbury, 1st Bt, and **1st Baron Banbury of Southam**, of Southam, Co Warwick (both UK), so *cr* 6 Jan 1903 and 21 Jan 1924 respectively, PC (1922), JP Hunts, Wilts and London; MP (C) Peckham 1892–1906 and City of London 1906–24; *b* Dec 1850; *educ* Winchester; *m* 3 July 1873 Elizabeth Rosa (*d* 7 Jan 1930), dau of Thomas Barbot Beale, of Brettenham Park, Suffolk, and had issue:

1 Charles William, Capt Coldstream Gds, served Boer War 1900–02 and WW I; *b* 11 Feb 1877; *educ* Eton and Univ Coll Oxford; *m* 26 April 1913 Josephine Marguerite (*m* 2nd 18 June 1925 Maj Hon Rupert Cecil Craven, OBE (*d* 9 July 1959), 2nd son of 3rd Earl of Craven (*qv*), and *d* 13 April 1971), dau of José Reixach, and was *ka* 16 Sept 1914, leaving issue:

(1) CHARLES WILLIAM, **2nd Baron**

(1) *Mary Heritage; *b* 28 March 1914; granted rank of baron's dau 7 Oct 1938; *m* 1st 28 March 1941 Siegfried Guido Buchmayr (*d* 1963), son of Maximilian Buchmayr, of Hof Gastein, Austria; *m* 2nd 5 Dec 1964 *Richard D Greenough, s of Col Charles E Greenough, of New York, and Mrs Norman Thwaites, of Aldbury Common, Herts, and by her 1st husb has had:

1a *Siegfried Beale [Siegfried Buchmayr, 137 Rowayton Ave, Rowayton, CT 06853, USA]; *b* 1942; *m* 1987 *Renée Bernier, and has issue:

1b *Siegfried Brandon; *b* 1987

2b *Trevor Banbury; *b* 1989

2a Norbert Gant; *b* 26 Jan 1942; *k* in a motor accident 1981

3a *Charles Rupert; *b* 1942; *m* 19– *Katharine —

(2) Florence Evelyn; *d* unm 29 Sept 1958

The 1st BARON *d* 13 Aug 1936; his gs,

CHARLES WILLIAM BANBURY, **2nd Baron Banbury of Southam**; Glos: DL 1965, CC 1958, CA 1967, 2nd Lt Coldstream Gds Res of Offrs, Capt 12th Lancers, WW II (despatches); *b* posthumously 18 May 1915; *educ* Stowe; *m* 1 Nov 1945 (*divorce* 1958) Hilda Ruth (*m* 2nd 1959 Maj Robert O G Gardner, MC (*d* 1987); *m* 3rd 1988, as his 3rd w, Richard Frederick Norman), 2nd dau of Archibald Hamilton Rowan Carr, of Cultra, Co Down, and *d* 1981, leaving issue:

1 CHARLES WILLIAM BANBURY, **3rd and present Baron Banbury of Southam**

1 *Carolyn; *b* 27 March 1947; *m* 16 April 1977 Christopher (Kim) J A North (*k* in a motor accident 1988)

2 *Anna Josephine; *b* 5 Jan 1950; *m* 1970 (*divorce* 1981) Michael Gordon Croose Parry, and has issue:

(1) *Sophie Ruth Flora; *b* 1976

BANGOR

Arms: Quarterly, 1st and 4th, az. a cross patonce or (for WARD); 2nd and 3rd, gu. three cinquefoils erm., on a chief or a human heart of the first (for HAMILTON). **Crest:** A Saracen's head affrontée, couped below the shoulders ppr., wreathed about the temples or and az. and adorned with three ostrich feathers. **Supporters:** Dexter, a knight in complete armour, all ppr., on his breast a cross moline gu., behind him a flowing crimson robe, a cross moline arg. on the sinister side of it, on the helmet a plume of feathers of the last, his dexter hand resting upon a drawn sword also ppr., pommel and hilt or, the point to the ground; sinister, a Turkish prince, vested in robes of blue and gold, the habit reaching to the ankles, white stockings, yellow sandals, gold sash and fringe round his waist, behind him a loose brown robe of fur, on his head a white turban with black feathers, his hands chained together by a long chain ppr. **Motto:** *Sub cruce salus* ('Salvation beneath the Cross'). **Creations:** B. (I) 30 May 1770, V. (I) 11 Jan 1781.

THE 8TH VISCOUNT BANGOR, of Castle Ward, Co Down, and **Baron Bangor**, of Castle Ward, Co Down (William Maxwell David Ward) [The Rt Hon The Viscount Bangor, 31 Britannia Rd, London SW6 2HJ]; *b* 9 Aug 1948; *s f* 1993; *educ* St Edward's Sch Oxford and UCL; *m* 1 Oct 1976 *Sarah Mary Malet, biographer as Sarah Bradford, dau of Brig Hilary Anthony Hayes, DSO, OBE, and formerly w of Anthony John Bradford, of Lisbon

Previous creation: An Earldom of Bangor was one of the subsidiary dignities conferred on the Duke of Schomberg when he was made Duke of Leinster some nine months after the Battle of the Boyne, at which he had played a leading part on WILLIAM III's side. It and all his other titles expired with him in 1719.

Lineage: BERNARD WARD, of Carrickshannagh, Co Down (which he acquired from the Earl of Kildare (*see* LEINSTER, D) *c* 1570 and renamed Castle Ward); *m* — Leigh, of High Leigh, Cheshire, and *d* by 12 Sept 1584, leaving issue:

NICHOLAS WARD, of Castle Ward; Clerk, Comptroller and Surveyor-Gen Ordnance 1599–1602; *m* by 1584 Joan, dau of Ralph Leycester, of Toft, Cheshire, and had, with several daus:

1 BERNARD

2 Sir ROBERT WARD, 1st and last Bt (I), so *cr* 9 Dec 1682, of Killough, Co Down; High Sheriff 1661 and 1667, ktd 1670; *b* 1610; *m* by April 1661 Mary, dau of Henry Leslie, Bp Meath, and widow of Robert Echlin, of Ardquin, and *dspms* 1691, when the btcy expired, having had:

(1) Charles; *m* 15 Dec 1681 Catherine (*m* 2nd Charles King, of Dublin, and *d* 1694), est dau of Sir John Temple (*see* TEMPLE OF STOWE, E), and *dsp* & *vp*

3 Charles; Col; *k* Battle of Worcester 1651

4 Nicholas; had:

(1) Arthur; *m* Anne Flowerdue and *d* 24 Aug 1674, leaving two sons (Nicholas; Arthur; both *d* young) and two daus (of whom one *m* Rev William Dunkin)

NICHOLAS WARD's est son,

BERNARD WARD, of Castle Ward; *b* 1606; *m* Anne, dau of Richard West, of Ballydugan, Co Down, and had, with other issue:

NICHOLAS WARD, of Castle Ward; MP Downpatrick 1661–66; *b* 1630; *m* Sarah, dau and coheir of Theophilius Buckworth, Bp Dromore, by Sarah Ussher, and had, with other issue:

BERNARD WARD, of Castle Ward; *b* 1654; *m* 1681 Anne, dau of Richard Ward, of Newcastle-under-Lyme, and sis of Michael Ward, Bp Derry, and was *k* in a duel 1690, having had, with an est and yst s and two daus:

MICHAEL WARD, of Castle Ward; MP Co Down 1715, Judge King's Bench Ireland 1725; *b* 1683; *m* 1709 Anne Catherine, dau and coheir of James Hamilton, of Bangor, Co Down, and *d* 19 Feb 1759, leaving, with two daus (Anne, *m* Sir John Parnell, 1st Bt (*see* CONGLETON, B); Sophia, *m* Arthur Upton, of Castle Upton, Co Antrim), an only surv son,

BERNARD WARD, **1st Viscount Bangor** of Castle Ward, Co Down, so *cr* 11 Jan 1781, as also earlier 30 May 1770 BARON BANGOR, of Castle Ward, Co Down (both I); *bapt* 6 Sept 1719; MP Co Down 1745–70; *m* Dec 1747 Anne (*d* Feb 1789), widow of Robert Hawkins Magill, of Gill Hall, Co Down, and 2nd dau of 1st Earl of Darnley (*qv*), and *d* 20 May 1781, leaving, with four daus:

1 NICHOLAS WARD, **2nd Viscount Bangor**; *bapt* 5 Dec 1750; MP Bangor 1771–76; *d* unm 11 Sept 1827

2 Edward, MP Co Down; *b* 30 April 1753; *m* 15 Feb 1783 his cousin Lady Arabella Crosbie (*d* 10 Nov 1813), dau of 1st Earl of Glandore by Theodosia, dau of 1st Earl of Darnley (*qv*), and *d* Nov 1812, leaving, with four daus:

(1) EDWARD SOUTHWELL, **3rd Viscount**

(2) John Petty; *b* 17 July 1791; BCS, granted with siblings 2 Feb 1836 rank of viscount's daus/yr s; *m* 18 Aug 1817 Eleanor (*d* 13 Sept 1862), dau of John Erskine, of York, and *d* 23 March 1869, having had, with other issue:

1a Edward Wolstenholme (Sir), KCMG; Maj-Gen RE, Dep Master Royal Mint Sydney 1854–67 and Melbourne 1867–76, MLC NSW 1860–65; *b* 17 Aug 1823; *m* 21 Nov 1857 Anne Sophia (*d* 13 March 1923), est dau of Hon Robert Campbell, MP, of Sydney, and *d* 5 Feb 1890, leaving issue:

1b John Petty; *b* 1864; *d* unm 19 Dec 1893

2b Edward Crosbie; *b* 1 May 1872; *m* 2 Nov 1901 Alice Sara Boyd (*d* 1940), only dau of Col Spencer Edward Orr, of Dullatur, Camberley, Surrey, and *d* 24 Oct 1926, leaving issue:

1c John Crosbie, Maj S Wales Borderers; *b* 15 March 1911; *m* 1936 Margaret Llewellyn (*d* 1983), dau of Rev Llewellyn Christopher Watson Bullock, of Gt Wigborough, Colchester, and *d* 1952, leaving:

1d +Christopher John Robert Crosbie [Maj Christopher Ward, The Old House, Longbridge Deverill, Warminster, Wilts BA12 7DJ]; Maj 2nd KEO Gurkas, formerly S Wales Borderes; *b* 8 July 1937; *educ* Wellington and RMA Sandhurst; *m* 1979 *Caroline Fiona, dau of James Alan Gerald Harley, MC, of Lower Lodge, Wyck Rissington, Glos, and has:

1e +Robert James Crosbie; *b* 1986

1e *Arabella Louise Crosbie; *b* 1980

2e *Sophie Ann Crosbie; *b* 1982

2d +David Edward Crosbie [David Ward Esq, St Olaf, Sellafirth, Yell, Shetland ZE2 9DG]; *b* 26 Feb 1941; *educ* Wellington; *m* 1976 *Christine Julia, dau of Travers Burnell Christopher Christie, of Nelson, NZ

1c Anne Elizabeth; *b* 24 July, *d* 23 Sept 1917

3b Guy Bernard Campbell, DSO (1918); Lt-Col S Wales Borderers Boer War 1900 and WW I (Croix de Guerre with palm); *b* 4 Nov 1875; *m* 5 Nov 1904 Beatrice Constance Charlotte (*d* 18 Jan 1959), yst dau of Hon Charles Lennox Butler (*see* DUNBOYNE, B), and *d* 24 March 1933, having had:

1c Cyril Edward; *b* 15 Oct 1913; *d* 1915

1c *Constance Isabel [Mrs Charles Mackness, 7 Minford Gardens, London W14 0AN]; *b* 11 Aug 1905; *m* 23 Dec 1932 Lt Charles Lawrence Mackness, The Buffs (*ka* 6 Oct 1943), only child of William Reginald Mackness, Consular Service, and has issue:

1d *Caroline Anne [Mrs John Sullivan, Campagne Florent, 04280 Cereste, Alpes de Haute, Provence, France]; *b* 28 April 1940; *m* 1 June 1968 *John Sullivan, and has:

1e *Mercedes Emma; *b* 23 Oct 1969

1b Elinor Erskine (Anne); *m* 14 June 1883 Henry Sheehy Keating, QC, LLD (*d* 12 Dec 1897), only son of Rt Hon Sir Henry Keating, of Headley Park, Hants, and gs of Henry Sheehy Keating, KCB, of Headley Park, by Mary Anne, est dau of Capt James Singer, of Annadale, Co Dublin, and *d* Jan 1887, leaving issue

2b Frances Sophia; *d* unm 15 Aug 1932

3b Henrietta Lucy Hamilton; *d* unm 2 Dec 1925

4b Evelyn Mary Montgomery; *m* 11 May 1901 Sir Arthur George Ramsay Mackenzie, 11th Bt, of Coul (*qv*), and *d* 10 May 1908, leaving issue

2a George Innes Crosbie; *b* 1834; *d* 1848

3a John Petty Hamilton; *b* 15 Aug 1835; *d* unm 1878

4a William Erskine (Sir), KCSI, Bengal Civ Serv 1861–96, MA Trin Coll Cambridge, Ch Commr Assam 1891–96; *b* 4 Feb 1838; *m* 17 March 1866 Alicia Caroline (*d* 23 Aug 1928), dau of Edward Palmer, of Calcutta, and *d* 24 Dec 1916, leaving issue:

1b George Louis Steuart, Maj IA; *b* 2 April 1869; *m* 24 April 1905 Alice Muriel (*d* Nov 1958), yst dau of G Denis B Harrison, of Clifton, and *d* 1920, leaving issue:

1c Denis Erskine, Maj RTR; *b* 8 Oct 1912; *m* 20 April 1942 *Kathleen Beryl Kyle (Susan) (*m* 4th 1978 Stanley Chapman) [Mrs Stanley Chapman, 87 Dartford Rd, Sevenoaks, Kent], dau of Maj Raymond Kyle Cotter, MC (*see* COTTER, B), and previously w of Reginald Barnes Elwin, ICS, and was *ka* El Alamein 27 Oct 1942

2b John Petty; *b* 25 Dec 1871; *m* 20 Nov 1906 Rose Gladys May (*d* 17 Nov 1937), est dau of Rev Richard Marsh Marsh-Dunn, vicar of St Nicholas, Shaldon, Devon, and *d* 22 Jan 1956, leaving issue:

1c Richard Erskine (Sir), GBE, KCB (1971), DSO and bar (1943), MC; Lt-Gen RTR WW II, GOC 1st Div 1965, Cdr Br Forces Hong Kong 1970; *b* 15 Oct 1917; *educ* Marlborough; *m* 12 Aug 1947 *Stella Elizabeth [Lady Ward, Bellsburn, 18 Lower St, Rode, Somerset BA3 6PU], dau of Brig Philip Neville Ellis, of Rhyllech, Pwllheli, Caernarvs, and *d* 1989, leaving issue:

1d +Anthony Richard Bangor [Anthony Ward Esq, Lower Bowden House, Pangbourne, Berks RG8 8JL]; *b* 5 May 1960; *m* 1989 *Caroline Wallace, est dau of Giles Walker, of IoM, and has issue:

1e +Archie Erskine Bangor; *b* 1990

2e +Maximilian Richard Petty; *b* 1992

2d +Jeremy Neville [Jeremy Ward Esq, 266 Camberwell New Rd, London SE5 0RP]; *b* 10 March 1961; *m* 1984 *Elizabeth, only dau of Vernon Butterworth, of Thornton, Cleverlys, Lancs, and has issue:

1e +Oliver Richard Xavier; *b* 1985

2e +Frederick; *b* 1988

1d *Léonie [Mrs David Chalmers Brown, Berrycroft Farmhouse, Ashbury, Wilts SN6 8LX]; *b* 15 Feb 1949; *m* 1983 *David James Chalmers Brown, son of W Chalmers Brown, of Balerno, Midlothian, and has issue:

1e *Alexandra; *b* 1985

2e *Isobel; *b* 1988

2d *Stephanie Rachel [Mrs John Lace, 58 Dukes Ave, London W4 2AF]; *b* 7 Oct 1952; *m* 1981 *John David Lace, and has issue:

1e *William John Edward; *b* 1985

2e *Thomas Charles; *b* 1988

3e *Toby Richard; *b* 1988

1e *Jessica Elizabeth Rachel; *b* 1983

1c *Myrtle Josephine; *b* 1907; *m* 1st 20 Nov 1929 (*divorce* 1972) Donald Stuart Denholm Fraser (*d* 1986), 2nd son of Col Howard Alan Denholm Fraser, CB, RE; *m* 2nd 10 May 1972 Theodore Alfred Raymond (*d* 1988), of Horizons Ord, Banff, Grampian, and by her 1st husb has issue:

1d *June, ARCA [Mrs Allen Cull, 5 Combemartin Rd, London SW18 5PP]; *b* 30 Aug 1930; PPCSD, MInst Pkg; *m* 7 Oct 1963 *Allen Hans Cull, and has issue:

1e *Zoë Gail; *b* 1970; BA

2d *Sally [Mrs Clive Freshwater, The Hall, Kincraig, Inverness-shire]; *b* 3 Feb 1936; *m* 1971 *Clive Freshwater, and has issue:

1e *Duncan; *b* 1971

2e *Andrew; *b* 1973

3e *Jonathan; *b* 1977

3d *Joanna [Dr Joanna Fraser, 1021 Elliot Rd South, Lethbridge, Alberta, T1K 3V2, Canada]; *b* 20 July 1950; MSc, PhD

3b Noel Edward; *b* 22 Dec 1872; *m* 1st 10 Oct 1898 (*divorce* 1922) Jessie Mabel (*d* 22 March 1968), dau of James B Wood, of Assam, and had issue:

1c James Palmer; WW II N Africa and Italy as Maj RASC; *b* 6 Jan 1902; *educ* Aldenham; *m* 5 Oct 1931 *Yvonne Lockington (*m* 2nd 1977 Arthur George Kelly, who *d* 1983), dau of Cedric Lockington Flood, Supt Zoological Gardens, Phoenix Park, Dublin, and *d* 1976, leaving issue:

1d +Michael James [Michael Ward Esq, 20 Cluny Grove, Killiney, Co Dublin, Ireland]; *b* 11 Dec 1934; *m* 10 Sept 1959 *Jocelyn Mary, dau of Arthur George Kelly, of Athlone, and has had issue:

1e Jeremy Charles Arthur James; *b* 4 Dec 1960; *educ* St Andrews; *d* 1983

1e *Alexandra Rowena; *b* 27 June 1963; *educ* Glengara Park and Trin Coll Dublin

2d +Patrick Erskine, RD [Capt Patrick Ward RD RNR, 57 Intwood Rd, Cringleford, nr Norwich, NR4 6AA]; *b* 18 May 1937; *educ* Nautical Coll Pangbourne; *m* 1st 3 March 1962 (*divorce* 1972) Eldrith Janet, dau of John Barwis Delbridge, of 6 Library Buildings, 8th Avenue, Fort Street, Bulawayo, and has issue:

1e +Richard John Bangor; *b* 4 April 1967

1e *Julia Helen Yvonne; *b* 25 April 1963

2e *Janette Elizabeth Barwis; *b* 15 Oct 1964

2d (cont.) Capt Patrick Ward *m* 2nd 1972 *Sarah Elizabeth, dau of John Williams, of Ash, Bocking, Surrey, and has issue:

2e +James Julian Erskine; *b* 1977

3e +Timothy John; *b* 1979

2c Jack Lionel, OBE; *b* 10 June 1910; *educ* Bradfield, Trin Coll Cambridge (BA), Konservatorium Frankfurt and RCM; *m* 1 Feb 1939 *Beatrice Mary Caroline [Mrs Jack Ward, Hope Cottage, Church Rd, Rotherfield, E Sussex TN6 3LE], dau of George Austin Wareham, of King's Langley, Herts, and *d* 1986, leaving issue:

1d +Edward Nicholas [Edward Ward Esq, Hookwood House, Shipbourne, Tonbridge, Kent]; *b* 13 Dec 1945; *educ* Winchester and Trin Coll Cambridge (BA 1967); *m* 1973 *Felicity Lilian Beatrice, dau of John Richard Gibbs, of Bromley, Kent, and has had issue:

1e *Lucy Beatrice Alice; *b* 1974; *educ* Sevenoaks and St Andrews

2e *Emily Charlotte Holly; *b* 1982

3e Holly; *b* and *d* 1982

1d *Gillian Elizabeth; *b* 27 Nov 1939

1c Phyllis Reaskine; *b* 1 Feb 1900; *m* 5 Jan 1925 David Manson, MB, ChB, LDS (*d* 1950), son of James Manson, of Alness, Scotland, and *d* 1 April 1965

3b (cont.) Noel Ward *m* 2nd 22 May 1922 Muriel, dau of Edward Dalton, of Leeds, Yorks, and *d* 22 June 1944, having by her had issue:

3c +Noel Erskine [Noel Ward Esq, Penrowan, New Rd, Boscastle, N Cornwall]; Lt 8th Gurkha Riffles, IA; *b* 9 Feb 1925; *educ* Marlborough; *m* 1st 1948 June Margaret, dau of Albert Ellerton-Long, of Gravesend; *m* 2nd 1977 Jacqueline Ann Aylwin (*d* 1990), dau of James Cyril Lodge, and by his 1st w has issue:

1d +Jonathan Philip [Jonathan Ward Esq, 109A Tankerton Rd, Tankerton, Whitstable, Kent]; *b* 1951; *educ* St Edmund's Sch; *m* 1980 *Pauline, dau of Howard Moore Gentry, and has issue:

1e +Michael John; *b* 1983

1e *Sarah-Jane; *b* 1981

2d +Graeme David; *b* 1955; RN; *m* 1977 *Janet Gates, dau of Sidney Brewer, and has issue:

1e +Colin; *b* 1977

1e *Michelle; *b* 1980

4b Lancelot Bangor, Fin Dept Govt India 1905–35; *b* 14 Sept 1883; *educ* Trin Coll Cambridge (BA); *m* 21 Nov 1910 Agnes Frances Jean (*d* 23 Aug 1959), 2nd dau of Rev Richard Marsh Marsh-Dunn, vicar of St Nicholas, Shaldon, Devon, and *d* 13 July 1959, having had issue:

1c Anthony Bangor, Maj 1st/10th Gurkha Rifles WW II; *b* 19 Sept 1918; *ka* Burma 11/12 May 1944

1c *Pamela Erskine; *b* 8 Nov 1920; *m* 20 Sept 1946 *James Routledge, and has issue:

1d *David Patrick; *b* 14 Feb 1952

2d *Martin John; *b* 22 Nov 1954

2c *Margaret Jean; *b* 8 Nov 1920; *m* 30 July 1945 Walter Ralph Melford, US Army, son of George Mecklenburg, of Chemnitz, Germany, and has issue:

1d *Anthony George Bangor; *b* 10 Oct 1947

2d *Michael Ralph; *b* 18 Feb 1950

1d *Greta Jean; *b* 10 Oct 1947

1b Mabel Reskine; *m* 14 May 1896 Basil Copleston Allen, CSI, ICS (*d* 22 Sept 1935), and *d* 21 May 1956, leaving issue

(3) Henry; *b* Dec 1795; Rector Killinchy, Co Down; *m* 15 Sept 1823 Anne (*d* 19 Jan 1875), dau of Rev Henry Mahon, of Killigally, and *d* 31 May 1874, having had, with other issue:

1a Crosbie; *b* 10 Feb 1833; *m* 13 Jan 1857 Margaret (*m* 2nd 2 July 1868 John George Cooke, 53rd Regt, and *d* 14 Dec 1912), yst dau of James Townsend, of Canterbury, NZ, and *d* 10 Nov 1867, leaving issue:

1b Edward William Townsend; *b* 26 May 1861; *m* 1895 Florence (*d* 28 June 1946), widow of Ogle Peck, of Toronto, and dau of Alexander Morten, and *d* 1921, leaving issue:

1c Margaret Flora; *b* 16 Jan 1899

1b Harriette Louisa Frances; *m* 1885 Burnett Silver, and *d* 10 Aug 1948, having had issue

2a John Hamilton; *b* 16 Oct 1834; *m* 15 April 1857 Marcia (*d* 25 July 1915), dau of James Townsend, and *d* 24 Oct 1914, having had issue:

1b Edward Robert; *b* 1859; *m* 1901 Edith Georgina (*d* 1948), dau of Albert George Sheriff, and *d* 1941, leaving issue:

1c Albert Edward Hamilton; *b* 1902; *m* 1932 *Violet Kate, dau of John Henderson Jones, and *d* 1976, leaving issue:

1d +John Albert; *b* April 1933; *m* 1956 *Judith Mary, dau of Richard R Lamdin, and has issue:

1e +Stuart John; *b* Dec 1964

1e *Fiona Marion; *b* 1956

2c +Robert Hamilton; *b* 1906

3c +John Hamilton [John Ward Esq, 14 Green Park Way, Chillngton, Kingsbridge, S Devon]; *b* 1907; *m* 23 June 1939 *Peggy Elizabeth Louise, dau of William Allen Hazeldine, of Hill Dean, 1 Roundwood Way, Banstead, Surrey, and has issue:

1d +Edward Hamilton [Edward Ward Esq, 38 Cambridge Park, Twickenham, Middx]; *b* 13 Sept 1944; *m* 1971 *Jean Audrey, dau of Alfred Hudson

2d +Roger Hamilton [Roger Ward Esq, 42 Redruth House, Grange Rd, Sutton, Surrey]; *b* 31 March 1947

1c *Marcia Hamilton; *b* 1904; *educ* Lond U (BA)

2c Edith May Hamilton; *b* 1909; *d* 10 Nov 1921

3c Emily Hamilton; *b* Nov 1913; *d* 1915

2b Henry Rawson; *b* 1861; *d* 1896

1b Louisa Margaret; *b* 1858; *d* unm 1945

2b Alicia Theodora; *b* 1864; *m* 11 April 1901 John O Blackrall, (BA), of Penshurst, Kent, son of Rev T O Blackrall, and *d* 5 Dec 1943, leaving issue

3b Marcia Burges; *m* 30 July 1913 George Curtis Candler, MBE (*d* 1947), and *d* 1950

4b Katherine Mary; *b* 1869; *m* 1911 James Edward Monaghan, of New York, and *d* 20 April 1936

5b Mary; *b* 1872; *d* unm 1951

6b Frances; *b* 1874; *m* 4 Sept 1929 Edward Erita, RBA, FRSA (*d* March 1954), and *dsp* 4 Jan 1960

7b Arabella Crosbie; *m* 9 July 1902 Rev Canon Horace Rollo Meyer, Hon Canon St Albans (*d* 6 March 1953), and *d* 1 Dec 1960, leaving issue

8b Anne Charlotte Elizabeth; *b* 1878; *d* unm 1957

3a Thomas Lawrence; *b* 2 Sept 1837; *educ* Trin Coll Dublin (BA); *m* 21 Feb 1871 Elizabeth Mary (*d* 1927), dau of David Green, of NZ, and *d* 1926, leaving issue:

1b Henry Crosbie; *b* 9 Jan 1873; *d* 1965

2b Edward Michael; *b* 1874; *d* 1891

3b Frederic Valentine; *b* 10 Dec 1878; *m* 30 June 1908 Florence Grace (*d* 1961), dau of Dr James Dalziel, of Auckland, NZ, and *d* 1960, leaving issue:

1c Kathleen Florence Mary; *b* 1909; *m* 19– *William Samuel Hazelwood, of 3 Te Reinga View, Tawa, Wellington, NZ, and *d* 1989, leaving issue:

1d *Robert William; *b* 1940; *m* 1963 *Mary Eagles, and has issue:

1e *Mark; *b* 1967

1e *Anne; *b* 1969

2e *Lisa; *b* 1971

1d *Barbara Grace [Mrs Gregory Burgoyne, 83 Castor Crescent, Porirua, Wellington, New Zealand]; *b* 1944; *m* 1965 Gregory Burgoyne (*d* 1993), of Melbourne, Australia, and has issue:

1e *Debbie; *b* 1966

2e *Sharon; *b* 1968

3e *Wendy; *b* 1972

2c *Doreen Mabel Valerie [Mrs Blondie Henderson, 15 Mason St, Lower Hutt, Wellington, New Zealand]; *b* 1915; *m* 1939 *Blondie Henderson

4b Thomas Lawrence; *b* 29 Jan 1886; *d* 192–

1b Annie Louisa; *d* unm 1895

2b Elizabeth Alice; *m* 1909 Arnott John Fernie (*d* 6 April 1959), yr son of Dr Andrew Fernie, of Barnstaple, Devon, and *d* 17 Sept 1966, leaving issue

3b Mary Clifford; *m* 9 April 1907 William Richard Stanley Hickson (*d* 30 Nov 1930), er s of Stanley Hickson, of Wellington, NZ, and had issue:

1c *Lawrence Stanley; *b* 22 July 1910

1c *Mary Clifford; *b* 3 Dec 1912; *m* 10 April 1945 *Gerald Frodsham Watkinson, s of Frodsham Watkinson, of Wellington, NZ, and has issue:

1d *Gerald Clifford; *b* 21 Nov 1951

2d *Edward Paul; *b* 13 April 1955

1d *Joan Elizabeth; *b* 10 Feb 1949

2c *Alison May; *b* 1 May 1918; *m* 17 Sept 1945 *Samuel Whaler Burkitt, of Christchurch, NZ, and has issue:

1d *Janice Anne; *b* 16 Jan 1947

4a William Somerset; Marine Surveyor; *b* 20 March 1839; *m* 7 Jan 1879 Mary Augusta (*d* 2 Oct 1942), 4th dau of Rev John Gordon, and *d* 28 June 1919, leaving issue:

1b Mildred Frances; *b* 1879; *d* 1898

2b Winifred Harriet; *b* 1881; *m* 10 May 1904 Henry Louis King (formerly Mahon), DL, of Ballykin, King's Co (*d* 22 Jan 1922), and *d* 13 Nov 1964, leaving issue

5a Francis Michael; *b* 21 Sept 1847; *m* 19 Oct 1875 Anne Jane (*d* 1934), dau of James Clarke, of Felmingham, and *d* 21 Jan 1908, leaving issue:

1b Alva Crosbie; *b* 1881; *d* 1908

2b Basil Edward; *b* 1886; *m* 1912 Hazel Smith (*d* 1948), and *d* 1953, leaving issue:

1c *Caroline Anne [Mrs Darrell Walker, 624 San Miguel Ave, Berkeley, California 94707, USA]; *b* 1914; *m* 1st 1939 Robert Frederick McKean (*d* 1966); *m* 2nd 1967 *Darrell Wiltse Walker, and by her 1st husb has issue:

1d *Robert Basil; *b* 1943; *m* 1967 *— and has issue:

1e *Jacob Frederick; *b* 1969

2e *Aaron Robert; *b* 1970

3e *Nathaniel Basil; *b* 1973

1d *Barbara Anne; *b* 1940; *m* 1960 *Ray Donald Konig, and has issue:

1e *Kathleen Ann; *b* 1966

2e *Colleen Ann; *b* 1970

2d *Patricia Ann [Mrs Ramish Ramchandani, 2503 Lincoln Ave, Alameda, Calif 94501, USA]; *b* 1951; *m* 1979 *Ramish Ramchandani

3b Geoffrey Glandore; *b* 1891; *d* 1900

1b Muriel Mary *b* 1876; *m* 24 May 1906 William Somerville Clarke, son of Rev Charles Granville Clarke, of Tunbridge Wells, and has issue

2b Edith Marion; *b* 1877; *d* unm 9 Nov 1964

3b Alice Geraldine *b* 1878; *m* 29 June 1909 Charles Dudley Gresham, and *d* 19 April 1962

1a Arabella; *m* March 1845 her cousin William Robert Ward (*d* 1 April 1879) and *d* 6 Jan 1908, leaving issue (*see* below)

2a Harriette; *m* 30 April 1857 her cousin Robert Edward Ward (*d* 29 Nov 1904), of Bangor Castle, Co Down, and *d* 4 March 1881, leaving issue (*see* below)

3 Robert; Col S Down Militia; *b* 14 July 1754; *m* 1st 1782 Sophia Frances (*d* 1793), 3rd dau of Richard Chapel Whaley, of Whaley Abbey, Co Wicklow, and had, with other issue:

(1) Michael Edward; Min Plen Dresden; *b* 5 Feb 1789; *m* 14 Sept 1815 Lady Matilda Stewart (*d* 3 Oct 1842), dau of 1st Marquess of Londonderry (*qv*), and *d* 12 Sept 1832, leaving issue:

1a Robert Edward, of Bangor Castle, DL and JP; Lt 10th Hus; *b* 10 Nov 1818; *m* 30 April 1857 his cousin Harriette (*d* 4 March 1881), dau of Rev Hon Henry Ward (*see* above), and *d* 29 Nov 1904, leaving issue:

1b Matilda Catherine; *m* 27 June 1878 5th Baron Clanmorris (*qv*), and *d* 14 Feb 1941, leaving issue

1a Anne Catherine; *m* 5 Sept 1849 Robert Stewart Kennedy (*d* 6 July 1854), of Cultra, Co Down, and *d* 20 June 1904, leaving issue

3 (cont.) The Hon Robert Ward *m* 2nd 1797 Louisa Jane (*d* 18 Feb 1911), 2nd dau and coheir of Rev Abraham Symes, DD, and by her had issue:

(2) Bernard John (Rev); Vicar Peterchurch; *b* 26 May 1798; *m* 31 Aug 1824 Isabella Frances (*d* 1884), dau of Robert Phillipps, of Longworth, Herefs, and *d* 24 Jan 1832, leaving issue:

1a Robert, of Sodstone House, Narberth, Pembs, MA Oxford, JP and CC Pembs; *b* 20 June 1825; *m* 7 April 1858 Elizabeth, dau of William Cockerill, of Northampton, and *dsp* 16 July 1904

2a Bernard Edward; Lt-Col 60th Rifles; *b* 9 Jan 1827; *m* 1st 29 Nov 1860 Gertrude Maria (*d* 5 March 1864), est dau of Rowland W Chesterfield, Madras CS, and had issue:

1b Bernard Rowland, CMG (1917); Col RE; *b* 16 Jan 1863; *m* 1st 5 Dec 1891 Jeanie (*d* 11 April 1925), dau of John Milner Duffield, Gibraltar CS; *m* 2nd 6 Nov 1926 Amy Margaret (*d* June 1946), widow of Reginald Arbouin Nelson, MA, LLM, barrister, and yr dau of Arthur Nelson, of Salmonby, Lincs, and *d* 30 April 1933, having by his 1st w had:

1c Bernard Mordaunt; Capt Res of Offrs 1st Dragoon Gds WW I; *b* 20 Jan 1893; *d* unm 12 Oct 1945

2b Lionel (Rev); Vicar Frampton-on-Severn, Glos, 1902–36; *b* 29 Feb 1864; *educ* Lincoln Coll Oxford (MA); *m* 22 Jan 1913 Jessie (*d* 5 May 1930), dau of John Barrett, of Massingham, Norfolk, and *dsp* March 1944

2a (cont.) Lt-Col Bernard Ward *m* 2nd 31 Aug 1869 Charlotte Eugenia (*d* 22 Feb 1904), er dau of Samuel George Smith, of Sacombe Park, Herts, and *d* 18 Nov 1894, having by her had issue:

3b Edward Francis, DSO (1917); Lt-Col KRRC; *b* 21 June 1870; *d* 11 Nov 1935

4b Bernard John Hamilton, OBE (1919); Capt RN; *b* 13 March 1875; *m* 4 Nov 1908 Annie Lilias (*d* 1978), dau of Ralph Dalyell, CB, of Lingo (*see* WARWICK, BROOKE and E), and *d* 20 Sept 1938, leaving issue:

1c +Bernard Ralph Henry, OBE (1946) [Lt-Cdr Bernard Ward OBE RN (ret), Trott's Close, Trott's Lane, Westerham, Kent TN16 1SD]; *b* 4 April 1911; Civ Serv 1957; *m* 1st 1943 (*divorce* 1951) Tamara Estrya Jasvoin; *m* 2nd 22 June 1955 Marion Violet (*d* 1958), dau of Capt Percy William Rimington, OBE, RN; *m* 3rd 8 June 1961 *Daphne Thalia, dau of John Lumsden, MBE, and by her has issue:

1d +Nicholas Ralph Dalyell [Nicholas Ward Esq, 5 Seaton Close, Highcliffe on Sea, Christchurch, BH23 5HP]; *b* 29 Jan 1964; *m* 1991 *Victoria Anne, dau of Leslie Francis Carr, of Highcliffe on Sea, and has issue:

1e *Emily Stephanie; *b* 1992

1d *Annie Christabel [Mrs Andrew Forbes, 70 Hillingdon Ave, Sevenoaks, Kent TN13 3RA]; *b* 3 Sept 1965; *m* 1992 *Andrew Peter Forbes, and has issue:

1e *Frances Rose; *b* 1988

2e *Ruby Ann; *b* 1993

1c (cont.) Lt-Cdr and Mrs Bernard Ward also adopted:

*John Louis Frederic; *b* 1959; *educ* UEA (BA 1981); Roy Hong Kong Police 1982; *m* 1985 *Melanie Bayoneta, dau of Salcedo Isidro, of The Philippines, and has issue:

1e *Louisa Marie Christabel; *b* 1986

(cont.) Mr and Mrs John Ward also adopted:

*Dean Salcedo; *b* 1984

2c Nicholas Edward; Lt RN Air Arm; *b* 15 Sept 1913; lost at sea in HMS *Glorious* 2 June 1940

1c *Barbara Mary; *b* 17 Jan 1910; *m* 1st 31 Aug 1940 Cdr Richard Scobell Palairet, RN (*d* 18 Dec 1953); *m* 2nd 31 July 1957 Sir John Francis Hedges, CBE, only son of Maj Francis Reade Hedges, of Wallingford Castle, Berks

5b Wilfrid Henry; *b* 24 Aug 1876; *m* 10 Jan 1907 Kate, er dau of John Nash Gray, and *dsp* 28 Oct 1952

1b Eugenia Gertrude; *d* unm Dec 1957

2b Violet Ella Mary; *m* 22 July 1905 her cousin Capt John Richard Le Hunte Ward, CBE, RN (*d* 13 Feb 1953), and *d* 22 Oct 1962 aged 89, leaving issue (*see* below)

3b Rose Isabella; *d* unm 8 Nov 1907

3a Thomas Le Hunte, CB; Adml, Naval ADC; *b* 4 Aug 1830; *m* 29 April 1869 Helen Mary (*d* 28 Feb 1930), dau of George Maconchy, of Rathmore, Co Longford, and *d* 24 Sept 1907, having had issue:

1b John Richard Le Hunte, CBE; Capt RN; *b* 18 March 1870; *m* 22 July 1905 his cousin Violet Ella Mary (*d* 22 Oct 1962 aged 89), 2nd dau of Col Bernard Edward Ward (*see* above), and *d* 13 Feb 1953, having had issue:

1c Edward Le Hunte; Lt-Col Roy Norfolk Regt WW II; *b* 16 Oct 1906; *educ* Bromsgrove and RMC Sandhurst; *m* 1 Aug 1946 *Flora [Mrs Edward Ward, Linney Water, Eastern Rd, Ashburton, S Devon TQ13 7AP], dau of Capt William Balfour Macdonald, DSO, RN, by Jane Isabelle Capel, yr dau of Lt-Col Capel Henry Miers, JP, of Eastbach Court, Glos, and *d* 1987, having adopted:

*Antonia Janet Elizabeth [Mrs Daryl Youé, Linney Water, Eastern Rd, Ashburton, S Devon TQ13 7AP]; *b* 1947; *m* 1975 *Daryl George Youé, and has issue:

1e *André; *b* 1978

2e *Dominic; *b* 1980

*Fynvola Mary Isabel [Mrs Carlo Bernabucci, 28 via Anton Cechov Apt 10, Rome 00142, Italy]; *b* 1949; BA; *m* 1975 *Carlo Angelo Bernabucci, and has issue:

1e *Ivan; *b* 1976

2e *Matteo; *b* 1978

2c Michael Bernard John; Maj RTR; *b* 17 Feb 1910; *educ* Bromsgrove,and RMC Sandhurst; *m* 25 Jan 1944 Marjory (*d* 7 July 1966), widow of Capt Arthur Thomas Reginald Symonds, Queen's Roy Regt, and dau of Bernard Noel Langdon-Davies, of 61 Valley Road, Welwyn Garden City, and *d* 1963, leaving issue:

1d John Michael Barrie; *b* 16 Dec 1945; *educ* Wellington; *m* 1974 *Anne Christine Hotchkiss [Mrs John Ward, The Victoria Tavern, Station Rd, Shrivenham, Wilts], and *d* 1992, leaving issue:

1e +Thomas Edward Le Hunte; *b* 1980

1e *Charlotte Jane; *b* 1977

2e *Catherine Sophie; *b* 1979

1c Sophia Eugenia; *b* 21 Sept 1908; *d* 3 July 1909

1b Sophia Louisa; *m* 4 June 1896 Frederick Anderson, JP (*d* 5 Jan 1940), son of James Anderson, of Hillhead, Glasgow, and Auchendarrock, Dunoon, Argyllshire, and *d* 27 April 1967 aged 96, leaving issue

2b Alice Mary Le Hunte; *m* 17 June 1905 Robert Walter, CMG, Colonial CS (*d* 21 March 1959), 2nd son of Maj Frederic Edward Walter, MVO, BA, and *d* 18 Jan 1955, leaving issue

1a Sophia Mordaunt; *b* 11 Sept 1828; *m* 10 June 1856 her cousin Solomon Augustus Richards, of Ardamine, Co Wexford (*d* 13 Jan 1874), and *d* 10 Aug 1899, leaving issue

(3) James Hamilton, V-Adml; *b* 23 Dec 1802; *m* 26 July 1839 Hon Elizabeth Dorcas (*d* 24 June 1898), dau of 3rd Baron Dufferin and Claneboye (*qv*), and *d* 16 June 1873, leaving issue:

1a Robert Frederick; Lt RN; *b* 10 Oct 1846; *m* 22 July 1879 Rose Edith (*d* 2 Feb 1933), dau of Simon Watson Taylor, of Eriestoke Park, Wilts, and *d* 5 March 1891, leaving issue:

1b Hamilton Frederick; Maj Irish Gds, MLC Kenya Colony 1922–31, served Boer War 1900–01, WW I and WW II; *b* 3 Sept 1880; *educ* Eton; *m* 27 May 1913 Violet Enid Jane (*d* 1972), dau of Sir Henry Conway Belfield, KCMG, and *d* 1971, leaving issue:

1c +John Frederick; *b* 3 June 1923; Capt Irish Gds; *m* 17 May 1950 *Pamela [Mrs John Ward, Kabazi, PO Box 153, Nakuru, Kenya], yr dau of Lt-Col George Archibald Swinton Home, DSO, OBE, of Soy, Kenya Colony, and has issue:

1d +Edward; *b* 1958

1d *Sarah; *b* 1953

1c *Sheila Maria Jane [Mrs Alexander Reynard, 675 Pretorius St, Arcardia, Pretoria 0083, S Africa]; *b* 26 Oct 1914; *m* 7 Oct 1939 *Alexander Frederick Reynard, only son of Maj Claude Edward Reynard, of Malindi, Kenya, and has issue:

1d *Edward Anthony; *b* 1945; *m* 1969 *Margaret Marian, dau of Thomas Allan Fairbairn, of Millbrae Head, Kirkton Manor, Peebles, and has issue:

1e *Iain Michael; *b* 1971

2e *Robert Neil; *b* 1974

2d *John William; *b* 1947; *m* 1974 (*divorce* 1989) Sandra Dianne, dau of Willacy Guy Goulding, of 273 Pasteur Rd, Rembrandt Park, S Africa, and has issue:

1e *Angela Lynne; *b* 1979

2e *Jennifer Susan; *b* 1983

1d *Monica Mary; *b* 1942; *m* 1983 *Michael William Atkinson, civ engr, son of William Charles Atkinson, of Johannesburg

1b Mabel Hariot Julia, twin; *m* 27 Feb 1906 Edwyn Guy Markham (*d* 13 April 1931), er son of Lt-Gen Sir Edwin Markham, KCB, and *d* 24 June 1964, leaving issue

(4) William Robert, Sec Legation The Hague; *b* 14 Oct 1806; *m* March 1845 Arabella (*d* 6 Jan 1908), 2nd dau of Rev Hon Henry Ward (*see* above), and *d* 1 April 1879, leaving issue:

1a Edward, MBE (1918), Lt-Col RGA, Assist Inspr Shells Min Munitions; *b* 10 Oct 1852; *m* 20 Feb 1900 Harriette Caroline Adeline (Etta) (*d* 14 March 1937), yst dau of John Steuart Maconchy, of Kilvare, Templeogue, Co Dublin, and *d* 20 Feb 1929, leaving issue:

1b Charlotte Hazel; *b* 1900

1a Alice Louisa; *m* 5 Jan 1869 Maj James Nugent Blackwood Price, KRRC (*d* 27 Jan 1927), of Saintfield, Co Down, and *d* 8 Sept 1928, leaving issue

2a Mary Ann; *m* 21 June 1877 Louis Trench, and *d* 5 March 1897, leaving issue (*see* ASHTOWN, B)

3a Charlotte; *m* 1884 Adolf Heinrich Preschlin (*d* 1 Dec 1934), of Oberutzwil, Switzerland, and *dsp* 23 Jan 1913

The 2nd VISCOUNT's nephew,

EDWARD SOUTHWELL WARD, **3rd Viscount Bangor**; *b* March 1790; *m* 14 Feb 1826 Harriet Margaret (*m* 2nd 4 Oct 1841 Maj Andrew Nugent (*d* 6 April 1899), son of Andrew Nugent, of Portaferry, and *d* 4 July 1880), dau of 6th Baron Farnham (*qv*), and *d* 1 Aug 1837, leaving issue:

1 EDWARD WARD, **4th Viscount Bangor**; *b* 23 Feb 1827; rep I peer 1855; *d* unm 14 Sept 1881

2 HENRY WILLIAM CROSBIE, **5th Viscount**

3 William John; Adml (ret), Naval ADC to HM QUEEN VICTORIA; *b* 9 Dec 1829; *m* 29 April 1875 Evelyn Sophia (*d* 24 Sept 1925), yst dau of Col Hon Richard Hare, bro of 2nd Earl of Listowel (*qv*), and *dsp* 20 Nov 1900

4 Bernard Matthew, CB; Lt-Gen, Col Suffolk Regt, 47th and 32nd Foot, served Crimea; *b* 26 Aug 1831; *m* 1st 27 June 1865 Emily Maria (*d* 1 June 1868), er dau of John La Touche, DL, JP, of Harristown, Co Kildare, and had issue:

(1) Ernest Otway WARD later WARD LA TOUCHE (roy licence 8 July 1921); Lt 5th Bn Roy Irish Rifles, Inspr Congested Dists Bd Ireland 1893–1900, Inspr Crown Lands Transvaal 1903–21, served Boer War 1900–01 (medal and four Clasps); *b* 3 Sept 1867; *m* 2 April 1909 Feodora, dau of Charles Daniel, of Bloemfontein, and *d* 23 Nov 1965, having had issue:

1a Pamela Annette; *b* 16 Jan 1918; *m* 8 June 1938 Mervyn Charles Balston, son of Lt-Col George Richard Balston, DSO (*see* below), and *d* 13 Nov 1958

(1) Rose Florence; *b* 29 Aug 1866; *m* 10 Dec 1889 Brig-Gen John Hotham, CB, RA (*d* 16 Nov 1932), and *d* 5 Jan 1944, leaving issue (*see* HOTHAM, B)

4 (cont.) Lt-Gen The Hon Bernard Ward *m* 2nd 11 Feb 1873 Laura (*d* 12 Feb 1928), est dau of Maj-Gen Evan Maberly, CB, RA, and *d* 27 June 1918, having by her had issue:

(2) Herbert Bernard, Capt Roy Irish Fus Boer War 1899–1902; *b* 5 March 1876; *m* 16 April 1918 Evelyn Annie (*d* 26 Nov 1925), 4th dau of Sir Daniel Dixon, 1st Bt, PC, MP (*see* GLENTORAN, B), and *d* 3 June 1957, leaving issue:

1a Diana, WW II 1941–46 with St John Amb Bde and WRNS; *b* 29 Dec 1918; *m* 19 Jan 1967 *W Richard M Gemmill, yst son of W Gemmill, of Johannesburg

(3) Evan Bernard, DSO (1919); Lt-Col Duke of Cornwall's LI, served Boer War 1899–1902 and WW I (despatches); *b* 30 Oct 1878; *m* 30 Nov 1914 Margaret Dorothy Norah, yr dau of T W Waller, of 31 Sussex Square, Brighton, and *dsp* 20 Nov 1966

(4) Bernard Lawrence; *b* 23 June; *d* 4 Oct 1880

(5) Maxwell William Bernard; *b* 24 Aug 1889; *m* 1st 28 Aug 1919 (*divorce* 1931) Ruth Elizabeth, only dau of John Flasby Laurence Whittingdale, OBE, MD, of Sherborne, Dorset and Thornton-in-Lonsdale, Yorkshire; *m* 2nd 9 May 1934 *Josephine, widow of Guy Nelson Brown and yst dau of Rev Canon Hugh Robert Coulthard, MA, Vicar Breage, Cornwall, and *d* 12 Jan 1960, leaving by his 1st w issue:

1a Bernard Maxwell, LVO; Maj 4th Regt RHA, memb London Stock Exchange, assoc memb Vickers da Costa & Co; *b* 28 April 1921; *educ* Sherborne; *m* 1 June 1948 Sunniva (*d* 29 Jan 1962), er dau of Sir Basil Hamilton Hebden Neven-Spence, MP, of Hall of Uyea, Shetland, and 15 Ashley Place, SW1, and *d* 1991, leaving issue:

1b +Maxwell Colin Bernard [Maxwell Ward Esq, Stobshiel House, Humbie, E Lothian EH36 5PD]; *b* 22 Aug 1949; *educ* Harrow and St Catharine's Coll Cambridge; *m* 1982 *Sarah, yr dau of Lt-Col Peter William Marsham, MBE (*see* ROMNEY, E), and has issue:

1c +Charles Bernard Maxwell; *b* 1986

2c +Frederick Peter Neven; *b* 1989

1c *Laura Sunniva; *b* 1984
2c *Antonia Hersey; *b* 1993
2a +John Maxwell [John Ward, PO Box 72, Kwe Kwe, Zimbabwe, S Africa]; *b* 19 Sept 1922; *educ* Sherborne; MRCS Eng and LRCP Lond 1945, MFGP (SA) 1975; *m* 1 May 1948 *Evelyn Millicent, only dau of John Philip Usher, of Singapore, and has issue:
1b +Peter Evan; *b* 4 June 1949
2b +Michael John; *b* 22 Feb 1951
3b +Nicholas Crosbie; *b* 7 Sept 1956
1b *Philippa Jane; *b* 3 Sept 1957
(2) Evelyn Margaret; *b* 23 Nov 1873; *d* unm 30 Dec 1962
(3) Hildred Laura *b* 25 July 1877; *m* 2 Jan 1909 Capt Mervyn James Hamilton, Gordon Highlanders (*d* 28 Nov 1914 of wounds recd in action), of Cornacassa, Co Monaghan, only son of Dacre Mervyn Archdale Hamilton, DL, of Cornacassa, and *d* 28 Feb 1971, leaving issue
(4) Edith Marion; *b* 10 Dec 1882; *m* 27 Feb 1906 Lt-Col George Richard Balston, DSO, RFA (*d* 21 April 1967 aged 88), and *d* 27 Dec 1957, leaving issue
(5) Doreen Harriette; *b* 8 Oct 1884
(6) Constance Katherine; *b* 18 Aug 1891; *m* 15 Dec 1926 Paul André Pilette (*d* 1972), only surv son of Theodore Pilette, of Brussels

The 4th VISCOUNT's bro,

HENRY WILLIAM CROSBIE WARD, **5th Viscount Bangor**, DL and JP Co Down; *b* 26 July 1828; *educ* Rugby and Sandhurst; rep I peer 1885–1911, Capt 43rd LI Kaffir War 1851–53; *m* 1st 6 Dec 1854 Mary (accidentally *k* 31 Aug 1869), yst dau of Rev Henry King, of Ballylin, King's Co; *m* 2nd 8 April 1874 Elizabeth (*d* 11 Jan 1919), only surv dau and heiress of Maj Hugh Eccles, of Cronroe, Co Wicklow, and by his 1st w had issue:

1 Henry Somerset Andrew; *b* 30 Aug 1857; *d* 10 July 1860
2 Edward William Henry, Lt Rifle Brigade; *b* 2 Jan 1863; *d* 10 July 1887
3 MAXWELL RICHARD CROSBIE, **6th Viscount**
1 Harriette Mary; *m* 22 Nov 1881 Maj-Gen John Edmund Waller, 19th Punjab Inf (*d* 4 Dec 1934), of Aughnacloy, Killiney, Co Dublin, and *d* 6 Nov 1941
2 Kathleen Annette Norah; *d* unm 28 Sept 1945
3 Bertha Jane, DGStJ; *m* 9 Aug 1883 Sir Robert John Kennedy, KCMG, DL (*d* 11 Nov 1936), of Cultra, Co Down, and *d* 21 Aug 1936, leaving issue
4 Mary Henrietta; *d* 9 Dec 1861
5 Emily Georgiana; *d* unm 26 Feb 1935

The 5th VISCOUNT *d* 23 Feb 1911; his only surv son,

MAXWELL RICHARD CROSBIE WARD, **6th Viscount Bangor**, OBE (1919), PC (NI 1931); *b* 4 May 1868; rep I peer, Memb NI Senate (Speaker 1930), Parly Sec to PM NI 1929, Lt-Col RGA; *m* 5 Jan 1905 Agnes Elizabeth (*d* 12 May 1972 aged 94), 3rd dau of Dacre Archdale Hamilton, of Cornacassa, Co Monaghan, and had issue:

1 EDWARD HENRY HAROLD, **7th Viscount**
1 Mary Helen Kathleen; *b* 2 April 1909; *m* 4 April 1934 *Peter Mansfield Weatherby, 2nd son of Edward Mansfield Weatherby, of Brill House, Brill, Aylesbury, Bucks, and *d* 19–, leaving issue:
(1) *Simon Maxwell; *b* 31 Dec 1938; *educ* Winchester and Columbia U New York; *m* 25 July 1964 *Caroline Ann, yr dau of Lt-Col Conolly Robert McCausland, MC, DL, JP, of Drenagh, Limavady, Co Londonderry, and has issue:
1a *Maxwell Peter; *b* 26 Feb 1965
1a *Rebecca Margaret; *b* 13 Nov 1966
(1) *Juliet Mary; *b* 1 April 1935; *m* 1 June 1963 *Florin Virgil Cucos, yr son of DI Constantin Cucos, of Roman, Romania, and has issue:
1a *Peter Constantine; *b* 26 Dec 1964
1a *Maria Emma; *b* 10 Jan 1964
2 *Helen Elizabeth [The Hon Helen Ward, 7 Chelsea Lodge, 58 Tite St, London SW3]; *b* 9 May 1912
3 *Margaret Bertha [The Hon Mrs Smith, 21 Chesil Court, Chesil Manor St, London SW3]; *b* 29 Sept 1914; *m* 1st 20 Jan 1938 (*divorce* 1947) Lt-Col Desmond Charles Forde, Coldstream Gds (*d* 31 Jan 1961), 2nd s of Maj William George Forde, of Seaforde, Co Down; *m* 2nd 5 July 1947 (*divorce* 1962) Gavin Robert Sligh, yr s of Robert Scott Sligh, of Pednor House, Chesham, Bucks; *m* 3rd 1969 *Maj Dennis Eric Smith, and by her 1st husb has:
(1) *Patrick Matthew Desmond, JP and DL Co Down; *b* 1940; *educ* Eton; *m* 1965 *Lady Anthea Geraldine Lowy-Corry, dau of 7th Earl Belmore (*qv*), and has:
1a *Matthew Galbraith; *b* 1967
2a *Charles Patrick; *b* 1972
3a *Finnian Nicholas; *b* 1982
1a *Emily Louise; *b* 1966; *m* 1 July 1995 *Peter T W Mackie, yr s of Denis Mackie, of Lissanoure, Co Antrim
(1) *Sylvia Helena [Miss Sylvia Forde, Flat 9, 110 Elm Park Gardens, London SW10 9PF]; *b* 1938

The 6th VISCOUNT *d* 17 Nov 1950; his only son,

EDWARD HENRY HAROLD WARD, **7th Viscount Bangor**; *b* 5 Nov 1905; *educ* Harrow and RMA Woolwich; Reuters correspondent China and Far East, BBC news observer Libya 1941, antique dealer (ran shop 'Trad' in London's Portobello Rd); *m* 1st 29 April 1933 (*divorce* 1937) Elizabeth, est dau of Thomas Balfour, JP, of Wrockwardine Hall, Wellington, Salop; *m* 2nd 14 Aug 1937 (*divorce* 1947) May Kathleen (*d* 9 May 1969), dau of William B O Middleton, of Shanghai; *m* 3rd 12 Nov 1947 (*divorce* 1951) Leila Mary (*d* 23 Feb 1959), 2nd dau of David Rimington Heaton, DSO, of The Cottage, Downderry, Torpoint, Cornwal, and by her had issue:

1 WILLIAM MAXWELL DAVID WARD, **8th and present Viscount Bangor**

The **7th Viscount** *m* 4th 1951 *Marjorie Alice, formerly w of — Simpson and dau of Peter Banks, of St Leonards-on-Sea, Sussex, and *d* 1993, having by her had issue:

2 +(EDWARD) NICHOLAS [The Hon Nicholas Ward, 9 Kildare Terrace, London W2]; *b* Feb 1953; heir presumptive; *educ* Westminster and Edinburgh U (MA); TV producer, formerly investment analyst Smith New Court Securities; *m* 1985 *Rachel Mary, dau of Hon Hugh Waldorf Astor (*see* ASTOR OF HEVER, B), and has issue:
(1) *Anna Roxelana; *b* 1987
(2) *Zoë Rachel; *b* 1990
1 *Sarah [The Hon Mrs Dawkins, Savile House, Mansfield Rd, Oxford; 13 Durham Terrace, London W2]; *b* 1951; formerly actress as Lalla Ward, now illustrator; *m* 1st 1980 (*divorce* 1982), as his 3rd w, Tom Baker, actor; *m* 2nd 1992 *Dr (Clinton) Richard Dawkins, DSc, of New College, Oxford, Prof for the Understanding of Science

BANNERMAN

Arms: Gules, a banner displayed argent, thereon a canton azure charged with St Andrew's Cross of the second (badge of Scotland). **Crest:** A demi-man in armour holding in his right hand a sword proper. **Supporters:** two armed men proper. **Motto:** *Pro patria* ('For one's country'). **Creation:** Bt. (NS) 28 Dec 1682.

SIR DAVID GORDON BANNERMAN, 15TH BT, of Elsick, Kincardineshire, OBE (1976) [Sir David Bannerman Bt OBE, 3 St George's Rd, St Margarets, Twickenham, TW1 1QS]; *b* 18 Aug 1935; *s* bro 1989; *educ* Gordonstoun and New Coll Oxford (MA 1959); 2nd Lt QO Cameron Highrs 1954–56, Overseas Civ Serv Tanzania 1960–63, with MOD 1963–97; *m* 25 June 1960 *Prudence Mary, er dau of Rev Philip Frank Ardagh-Walter, Vicar Woolton Hill, Hants, and has:

1 *Clare Naomi; *b* 24 April 1961; *m* 1991 *Michael Angus O'Neill, only son of Shane O'Neill, of Bletchton, Cheshire, and has:
(1) *Alexander Constantine Bannerman; *b* 16 May 1996
(1) *Constance Isobel Bannerman; *b* 17 Aug 1994
2 *Margot Charlotte; *b* 6 Aug 1962
3 *Arabella Rose; *b* 31 Jan 1965
4 *Clodagh Isobel Rose; *b* 1975

Lineage: The BANNERMANs claim to have been hereditary banner-bearers to the kings of Scotland, presumably before 1298 since the Earls of Dundee (*qv*) have held that position since then.

DONALD BANNERMAN; physician to DAVID II; had a charter of Waterton and other lands near Aberdeen 1366; had a (?)yr(?) s:

ALEXANDER BANNERMAN; Provost Aberdeen 1382, had a charter of Elsick (in the barony of Cowie in the Mearns) from Sir Alexander Fraser 1387.

ALEXANDER BANNERMAN of Elsick; *s* to Waterton and Elsick 1609, sold former to John Johnston of that Ilk and of Caskieben 1611 (*see* JOHNSTON, Bt, of Caskieben) and *m* 1586 his dau Elizabeth, leaving, with a dau (Margaret, *m* 1608 John Gordon, Yr of Haddo, ancestor of the Earls of Aberdeen; *see* ABERDEEN AND TEMAIR, M):

ALEXANDER BANNERMAN of Elsick; *m* 1st Margaret, dau of William Forbes of Tolquhon; *m* 2nd Marjory (*m* 2nd Sir John Fletcher, King's Advocate), dau of Sir John Leslie, 1st Bt of Wardes (*see* LESLIE, Bt), and by his 1st w had:

ALEXANDER BANNERMAN of Elsick; had a Crown charter of the barony of Pitmedden 1641, wounded his cousin Sir John Gordon of Haddo in a duel 1644; *m* 1st Marion, est dau of Alexander Hamilton, of East Binning, Linlithgowshire, and had issue:

1 ALEXANDER (Sir), **1st Bt**
2 George, of Dunboig; King's Advocate; *m* Elizabeth, dau of Oliphant of Bachilton, Perthshire, and *dsp* 1690

ALEXANDER BANNERMAN *m* 2nd — and *d c* 1666, having had further issue:

3 Robert; Min of Newton 1681, deprived as a non-juror 1689; *m* 1719 Margaret, dau of Sir Mark Carse of Cockpen, and had issue
4 John; Gds Offr *temp* JAMES II, whom he followed into exile

The est son,

Sir Alexander Bannerman of Elsick, 1st Bt (NS), so *cr* 28 Dec 1682; *m* 15 Feb 1670 Margaret, 2nd dau of Patrick Scott of Thirlstane, and *d* 11 April 1711, having had issue:

1 **Sir Alexander Bannerman, 2nd Bt**; *m* Isabella (*d* 13 June 1743), dau of Sir Donald Macdonald of Sleat, 3rd Bt (*see* BOSVILLE MACDONALD, Bt), and *d* Feb 1742, having had, with three daus:

(1) **Sir Alexander Bannerman, 3rd Bt**; cmded a Jacobite regt at Culloden 1746, then fled to France; *m* Isabella, heiress of the Trotters of Horsley, Yorks, and *d* at Paris 1747, leaving issue:

1a **Sir Alexander Bannerman, 4th Bt**; sold Elsick after involvement in lawsuits and threatened forfeiture following his f's and his own alleged participation in the rebellion of 1745; *m* 1764 Elizabeth, dau of Marmaduke Sedgwick, and *d* 13 June 1770, leaving:

1b Elizabeth, of Strachan; *m* Sir Alexander Ramsay, of Balmain, Bt (*qv*)

2b Mary, of Blackhall; *m* Francis Russell

2a **Sir Edward Bannerman, 5th Bt**; Maj 36th Regt; *d* unm 1 Oct 1796

1a Isabella

2 Francis; *d* unm

3 Patrick (Sir); Jacobite Provost Aberdeen 1715, ktd by Old Pretender, imprisoned by Hanoverian authorities in Carlisle but escaped to France; *m* 1714 Margaret, dau of Sir Charles Maitland of Pitrichie, and *d* 1733, leaving, with a yr s and three daus:

(1) Alexander, of Aberdeen; *b* 1715; *m* 1737 Margaret, dau and heir of Thomas Burnett of Kirkhill, and *d* 1782, leaving issue:

1a Sir ALEXANDER BANNERMAN later BURNETT (1777) later still (1796) BANNERMAN again, **6th Bt**; MD Aberdeen; *b* 20 Dec 1741; *m* 1768 Mary, dau of James Gordon, of Banchory, and *d* 29 Dec 1813, having had, with other issue:

1b Thomas; *d* in India unm

2b **Sir Alexander Bannerman, 7th Bt**; *b* 19 Dec 1769; *m* 15 Nov 1800 Rachel (*d* 13 Nov 1847), yr dau of John Irvine, Gothenburg merchant, and *dsp* 31 May 1840

3b **Sir Charles Bannerman, 8th Bt**; *b* 18 Aug 1782; *m* 14 Aug 1821 Anne (*d* 1838), dau of Charles Bannerman (yst bro of 6th Bt), and *d* 18 June 1851, having had issue:

1c **Sir Alexander Bannerman, 9th Bt**; *b* 6 April 1823; V-Lt Aberdeenshire, bought back part of the Elsick estate; *m* 1st 25 Sept 1860 Lady Arabella Diana Sackville (*d* 9 Feb 1869), dau of 5th Earl De La Warr (*qv*), and had:

1d Ethel Mary Elizabeth; *m* 1 Aug 1891 10th Earl of Southesk (*see* FIFE, D), and *d* 10 Dec 1947, leaving issue

1c (cont.) The **9th Bt** *m* 2nd 20 Jan 1874 Lady Katherine Ashburnham (*d* 30 Sept 1885), dau of 4th Earl of Ashburnham (*see* 1924 edn), and *dsp* 21 April 1877

1c Margaret; *d* young

2c Mary; *d* young

3c Anne Catherine; *d* 1847

2a Thomas, of Aberdeen; *b* 1743; *m* Jane, dau of George Simpson, of Hazelhead, and *d* Jan 1820, leaving issue:

1b Alexander (Sir); *b* 8 Oct 1788; MP Aberdeen 1833–47, Govr Prince Edward Island 1851–54, Bahamas 1854–57, Newfoundland 1857–64; *m* 14 Jan 1824 Margaret (*d* 24 Dec 1878), dau of Alexander Gordon, and *dsp* 30 Dec 1864

2b Thomas; *b* 3 Oct 1795; *m* 22 June 1824 Jane, dau of George Hogarth, and *d* 14 April 1863, leaving issue:

1c **Sir George Bannerman, 10th Bt**; *b* 4 June 1827; *m* 5 Oct 1869 Anne Mary (*d* 11 Aug 1909), est dau of Richard Brooke, FSA, of Handford, Cheshire, and *d* 3 Dec 1901, having had:

1d **Sir Alexander Bannerman, 11th Bt**; *b* 16 Dec 1871; Maj RE, Lt-Col cmdg 2nd/5th N Staffs Regt, Boer War (despatches, two medals, five clasps), Russo-Japanese War 1904–05 with Japanese Army at Siege Port Arthur (Brevet Maj, Japanese War Medal, Japanese Orders Rising Sun 4th Cl and Sacred Treasure 4th Cl), WW I; *m* 12 May 1920 Joan Mary, only child of Frederic Dundas Harford, CVO (*see* HARFORD, Bt), and *dspm* 10 March 1934, leaving:

1e *Eve Mary [Mrs Cecil Symmes, 39 Karu Crescent, Waikanae, New Zealand 6454]; *b* 12 March 1921; *m* 27 Jan 1951 (Thomas) Cecil (Leyburn) Symmes (*d* 1991), only son of Maj H C Symmes, of Cambridge, and has issue:

1f *Howard Alexander [Howard Symmes Esq, 5 Connaught Terrace, Wellington, New Zealand]; *b* 11 Feb 1954; *m* 1989 *Jane Williams, and has:

1g *Kirk Thomas; *b* 1992

1g *Hilary Mary; *b* 1994

2f *George Weymouth [George Symmes Esq, 5 Fletcher Crescent, Crofton Downs, Wellington 6004, NZ]; *b* 20 May 1956; *m* 1989 *Veronica Anne Challies and has:

1g *Rose Laura; *b* 1994

1d Eleanor; *m* 12 July 1905 Harry Colvin Colvin-Smith, MICE, AKC (*d* 18 Sept 1948), 2nd son of Surg-Gen Sir Colvin Colvin-Smith, KCB, KHS, and *d* 30 March 1955, leaving issue

1c Jane; *m* 22 Aug 1855 Maj-Gen Millington Henry Synge (*dsps* 10 Sept 1907), 5th s of Sir Edward Synge, 2nd Bt (*qv*), and *d* 13 Jan 1915

2c Euphemia; *d* unm 1918

3c Margaret; *d* unm 30 March 1906

4c Elizabeth; *m* 19 Jan 1869 A P Hogarth, and *d* 6 Feb 1877, leaving issue

5c Thomasina; *m* 28 April 1866 Francis Logie Pirie, MA, and *d* 1889, leaving issue

3a Charles; *m* Margaret, dau of Patrick Wilson of Finzeauch, and *d* Sept 1813, leaving, with two other s and four daus:

1b Alexander; *d* in India

2b Patrick Wilson, of Elmsfield, Aberdeen; *b* 18 Dec 1794; *m* 5 Sept 1826 Anna (*d* 8 March 1884), dau of Sir William Johnston of that Ilk and of Caskieben, 7th Bt (*qv*), and *d* 16 Sept 1854, leaving, with other issue:

1c William, CB; *b* 23 Sept 1828; Gen IA, Col 104th Wellesley Rifles 1900–14, Punjab 1848–49, NW Frontier 1849, Persia 1857, Indian Mutiny 1858–59, China 1860, Afghanistan 1879–80; *m* 10 Sept 1868 Louisa Constance (*d* 26 Aug 1915), dau of Robert Goddard, of Monkstown, Co Dublin, and *d* 10 Feb 1914, leaving issue:

1d Wyndham Philip; *b* 16 Feb 1870; Lt-Col 31st Lancers, IA, Dongola Expdn 1896 (two medals with clasp), NW Frontier 1898–1900, WW I; *m* 1st 17 June 1901 Mary Augusta Mosley (*d* 2 June 1910), est dau of George Ashwin Cheeke, and had issue:

1e Diana Mary Wyndham; *b* 12 Jan 1908; *m* 2 Aug 1933 (*divorce* 1959) Capt (E) Sydney Alick Harrison Smith, CBE, RN, son of Paymaster R-Adml Sir Francis Harrison Smith, KCB, of Pewsey, Wilts, and has issue:

1f *Christopher Francis; *b* 24 Jan 1939; *m* 7 Dec 1968 *Angela Jill, dau of Maj Eric Forbes Mervyn-Smith, of Godalming, Surrey

1f *Sheila Mary; *b* 7 March 1936; *m* 21 Sept 1957 *David Ewing Cox, yr s of Joseph Pariss Cox, of Rugby, Warwicks, and has issue:

1g *Patricia Mary; *b* 27 Feb 1959

2g *Susan Elizabeth; *b* 30 July 1961

2f *Penelope Ann; *b* 30 April 1943

1d (cont.) Wyndham Bannerman *m* 2nd 4 Oct 1928 Dorothy Beatrice, widow of Dr John Ferguson, and *d* 15 Jan 1930

2d Oriel William Erskine; *b* 13 Dec 1877; Capt 15th Lancers, IA; *m* Sept 1907 Emile Henriette (*m* 2nd — Ramsay-Gordon), dau of Capt Charles Lousada, 9th Regt, and *das* 3 Feb 1915

2c Patrick Wilson; *b* 23 Dec 1833; Col IA; *m* 20 May 1859 Flora Lindsay (*d* 1 July 1917), dau of Maj-Gen T A Vanrenen, and *d* 1 Dec 1912, leaving issue:

1d ARTHUR D'ARCY GORDON (Sir), **12th Bt**

1d Emily Catherine Florence; *m* 15 Dec 1897 Col Augustus Charles Twentyman, CB (*d* 24 March 1913), late 4th Regt, son of William Holme Twentyman, DL, and *d* 31 March 1933

2d Ada Mary Campbell; *m* 1st 6 July 1898 Lt-Col Cyril Henry Moore (*d* 16 March 1912); *m* 2nd 15 April 1919 Maj-Gen Sir Alfred Percy Blenkinsop, KCB, CMG (*d* 3 Nov 1936), 4th son of Lt-Col William Blenkinsop, and *d* 29 July 1964

3c Charles Bromhead; *k* at Delhi 8 Sept 1857

4c Arthur Johnston; *b* 26 April 1839; Lt-Col Bombay Staff Corps Afghan War 1879–80 (medal), DL Aberdeenshire; *d* 20 Sept 1936

5c Alexander D'Arcy; *b* 27 Feb 1848; *d* 3 Oct 1927

6c Edward Mordaunt; *b* 14 Jan 1850; *m* 1st 8 July 1873 Anne Christina (*d* 30 May 1902), dau of James Hay Mackenzie, and had issue:

1d Kenneth Mordaunt; *b* 15 May 1874; *ka* 1916

2d D'Arcy; *b* 30 Oct 1875; *m* 1896 Mary (*d* 1962), dau of Rev Richard Dennett, DCL, and *d* 1952, leaving issue:

1e Halcro D'Arcy; *b* 11 Feb 1898; hon Lt Roy Pioneer Corps

1e Thora; assumed forename of D'Arsy as surname; *m* 18 Nov 1931 Raymond Frederick Budden (*d* 1972), Met Office Air Ministry

3d Eric Edward; *b* 17 May 1878; *d* young

4d Vere; *b* 7 Aug 1879

5d Bertrand, DSO (1917); *b* 1883; Cdr RN WW I (despatches); *m* April 1909 Vera (*d* 1976), dau of Edward Stuart, and *d* 21 Oct 1954, leaving issue:

1e *Sheila Christina [Lady Walsham, 19 Beckford Close, Tisbury, Wilts]; *m* 21 Nov 1936 R-Adml Sir John Scarlett Warren Walsham, 4th Bt (*d* 1992; *qv*), and has issue

6d Roger; *b* 1885; *d* 1966

7d Nigel Johnston; *b* 1892; Lt RFA WW I

1d Marjorie Hay; *b* 1890; *d* young

6c (cont.) Edward Bannerman *m* 2nd 29 Jan 1907 Jean (*d* 10 Aug 1951), er dau of William Clarke Dale, and *d* 29 March 1923, having by her had issue:

8d Mordaunt Francis; *b* 22 Dec 1907; S/Ldr RAFVR; *m* 1st 16 Oct 1937 (*divorce* 1946) Aileen Salisbury, yst dau of Elford Virtue, of Godalming, and had issue:

1e Nigel Mordaunt, LRCP, MRCS; *b* 27 Feb 1943; *educ* Marlborough and Guy's Hosp; *m* 1971 *Jane Alison [Mrs Nigel Bannerman, 18 Pilgrims Close, Farnham, Surrey], er dau of Paul Taylor, of Milford, Godalming, Surrey, and *d* 1975, leaving issue:

1f *Henrietta Jane; *b* 1973

8d (cont.) Mordaunt Bannerman *m* 2nd 1 Dec 1950 *Edna Gladys, yst dau of David Hamilton Thompson, of Cardiff

9d Douglas Edward; *b* 26 Jan 1917; Lt Roy Fus WW II; *ka* Italy 22 Jan 1944

The 11th Bt's cousin,

Sir Arthur D'Arcy Gordon Bannerman, 12th Bt, KCVO (1928), CIE (1903); *b* 20 Feb 1866; *educ* Harrow and RMC Sandhurst; Lt-Col IA, Resident Kashmir 1917–21, Political ADC to Sec State India 1921–28, Gentleman Usher to HM GEORGE V 1928, Extra Gentleman Usher to TM EDWARD VIII 1936, GEORGE VI 1937–52 and THE QUEEN 1952–55; *m* 1st 7 June 1889 Virginia Emilie (*d* 19 June 1915), dau of William J Guthrie Bedford, and had issue:

1 **Sir Donald Arthur Gordon Bannerman, 13th Bt**; *b* 2 July 1899; *educ* Harrow and RMC Sandhurst; Lt-Col QO Cameron Highrs, WWs I and II, Sr Control Offr CCG 1945–48, housemaster Gordonstoun 1948–52, assist master Fettes 1952–69, author: *A Short Family History* and *Random Recollections*; *m* 27 July 1932 *Barbara Charlotte [Dowager Lady Bannerman, Cecil Court, 2 Priory Rd, Kew TW9 3DG], yr dau of Lt-Col Alexander Cameron, OBE, IMS, of Southwold, and *d* 16 Sept 1989, leaving issue:

(1) **Sir Alexander Patrick Bannerman, 14th Bt**; *b* 5 May 1933; *educ* Gordonstoun and RAC Cirencester; QO Cameron Highrs 1952–54; *m* 1977 *Joan Mary [Joan Lady Bannerman, 73 New Causeway, Reigate, Surrey RH2 7PP], dau of John Henry Wilcox, of Tadcaster and *d* 21 Nov 1989

(2) Sir DAVID GORDON BANNERMAN, **15th and present Bt**
(1) *Ruth Mary Charlotte; *b* 30 July 1937; *m* 11 Oct 1958 Michael Joseph Orgill Massey, MA, MB, Bchir MFOM (*d* 1989), s of Stanley Orgill Massey, MRCS, LRCP, of Birmingham, and has issue:
1a *Jonathan David Orgill; *b* 22 April 1962; BEng (Hons)
2a *William Michael Orgill; *b* 3 May 1964
3a *James Richard Orgill; *b* 18 Feb 1966
1a *Alexandra Mary Orgill; *b* 21 Aug 1959; MB, BS
2a *Charlotte Elizabeth; *b* 3 Nov 1960; MB, BS
(2) *Janet Elizabeth Naomi [Mrs Warren Jackson, 7 Gildridge Rd, Whalley Range, Manchester]; *b* 30 July 1937; ARCM (1959); *m* 15 July 1966 Warren Jackson, MA, s of George Warren Jackson, of Northampton, and has issue:
1a *Catherine Elizabeth; *b* 13 July 1967; BA 1989
2a *Ruth Helen Isobel; *b* 6 April 1969
1 Charlotte Elizabeth; *b* 19 April 1902; *m* 20 Nov 1937 Gerald Derek Lockett, MBE, yr s of Richard Cyril Lockett, and *d* 1992 leaving:
(1) *Jeffrey Bannerman; *b* 1939
(2) *Richard Bannerman; *b* 1942

Sir Arthur *m* 2nd Nov 1918 Philippa (*d* 3 Jan 1949), dau of Edward Jocelyn Baumgartner, of Supreme Court, Gibraltar, and widow of Lt-Col C S Vores, RA, and *d* 27 April 1955

BARBER, Baron

Creation: B. (LP, UK) 1974.

THE BARON BARBER, of Wentbridge, W Yorks (Anthony Perrinott Lysberg Barber, TD, PC (1963), DL (W Yorks 1987)) [The Rt Hon The Lord Barber TD PC DL, House of Lords, London SW1A 0PW]; *b* 4 July 1920; *educ* Retford GS and Oriel Coll Oxford (MA); LLB London; WWII: Lt RA and pilot RAF (POW, despatches); barrister Inner Temple 1948; MP (C) Doncaster 1951–64, Altrincham and Sale 1965–74, PPS to Parly U-Sec Air 1952–55, Assist Whip 1955–57, Ld Commr Treasury 1957–58, PPS to PM 1958–59, Ec Sec Treasury 1959–62, Fin Sec Treasury 1962–63, Min Health 1963–64, Chm C Party Orgn 1967–70, Chllr Duchy Lancaster 1970, Chllr Exchequer 1970–74, Pres Nat Union of C and U Assocs 1973; Chm: Standard Chartered Bank 1974–87, Cncl Westminster Medical Sch 1975–84; V-Chm Cncl Westminster and Charing Cross Medical Sch 1984–; Memb: Franks Ctee on Falklands 1982–83, Br Memb Eminent Persons Gp on S Africa 1986; Chm RAF Benevolent Fund 1991–; Hon Fell Oriel Coll Oxford 1971, author *Taking the Tide* (memoirs, 1996); *m* 1st 1950 Jean Patricia (*d* 1983), dau of Milton Asquith, of Wentbridge, W Yorks, and has:
1 *Louise Patricia Lysberg; *b* 1951
1 *Josephine Julia Asquith [The Hon Mrs Bradby, Hollesley Lodge, nr Woodbridge, Suffolk IP12 3RT]; *b* 1953; *m* 1989 *William J L Bradby, s of James Bradby, of Spetisbury, Dorset
The BARON BARBER *m* 2nd 1989 *Rosemary, formerly w of John Surgenor and dau of Rev Canon Fearnly Youens

Lineage: JOHN BARBER, CBE; had:
ANTHONY PERRINOTT LYSBERG, *cr* a **Baron**

BARBER, Bt

Arms erm. two chevronels between three fleurs-de-lys gu., a bordure embattled also gu. **Crest:** In front of two swords in saltire, points upward ppr., hilts and pomels or, a bull's head erased, also ppr. **Motto:** *In Deo spes* ('My hope lieth in the Lord'). **Creation:** Bt. (UK) 25 July 1960.

SIR (THOMAS) DAVID BARBER, 3RD BT [Sir David Barber Bt, Windrush House, Inkpen, Hungerford, Berks RG17 9QY]; *b* 18 Nov 1937; *s f* 1995; *educ* Eton and Trin Coll Cambridge (BA 1961, MA 1966); late Lt S Notts Hus Yeo, 2nd Lt RA 1957–58; *m* 1st 15 May 1972 (*divorce* 1975) Amanda Mary, dau of Frank Rabone, of Beacon Barn Farm, Coton, Milwich, Staffs, and widow of Maj Michael Healing, Gren Gds, and has issue:
(1) +THOMAS EDWARD; *b* 14 March 1973; *educ* Eton and St Aidan's Coll Durham (BA 1994)

Sir DAVID *m* 2nd 1978 *Jeannine Mary, dau of Capt Timothy John Gurney, Coldstream Gds, of The White House, Hare St, Buntingford, Herts (*see* 1940 edn DE BATHE, Bt), and formerly w of John Richard Boyle (*see* CORK and ORRERY, E), and by her has:
(2) +William Samuel Timothy; *b* 1982
(1) *Sarah Emily; *b* 1981

Lineage: JOHN BARBER; *m* Sarah —, and had, with a yr son (Edward, *b* 1709) and dau (Mary, *b* 1707):

FRANCIS BARBER; *b* 1687; *m* 1731 Elizabeth (*d* 1787), dau of John Fletcher, and *d* 1762, having had, with three er sons (John, *b* 1734; Francis, *b* 1735; Robert, *b* 1737) and four daus (Elizabeth, *b* 1733; Mary, *b* 1739, *d* 1740; Mary, *b* 1741; Anne, *b* 1743):

THOMAS BARBER; *b* 1738; *m* Sophia Hutchinson and had, with three daus (Ruth Eliza, *m* 1803 John Borne; Sophia, *m* 1797 Hugh Campbell; Anne, *m* 1794 Richard Cheslym (*d* 1843) and *d* 1823):

THOMAS FRANCIS PHILIP HUTCHINSON BARBER; *b* 1778; *m* Hannah Jackson (*d* 1844) and had, with two daus (Anne, *m* 1822 George Robinson; Eliza, *m* 1839 Francis Read Grammar):

THOMAS BARBER; *b* 1805; *m* 1st 1843 Hannah Coates; *m* 2nd Elizabeth, dau of John Lewis Pasteur, and by his 1st w had, with an est son (George) and a dau (Hannah, *m* Duncan Macdonald Forbes, MD):
1 THOMAS
2 Robert; *b* 1848; *m* 1874 Elizabeth Catherine Baker and *d* 1929, leaving, with two er sons (Thomas Gerrard; Robert), a yr son (Harold Wordsworth) and two daus (Evelyn Mary; Gerrardine Ethel):
(1) Walter Browne, of Beacon Hill House, Hucknall, Notts, and Salruck House, Renvyle, Galway; had:
1a Robert Heberden, Northamptonshire Regt; *m* 14 June 1941 *Eileen Mary Louisa, only dau of Capt Harvey Alexander Brabazon Combe, MBE, of Oaklands Park, Sussex, and was *ka* Normandy 6 June 1944, leaving issue

THOMAS BARBER's 2nd son,
THOMAS BARBER, of Lamb Close, Eastwood, Notts, JP; *m* 1st Lavinia Bertha (*d* 1870); *m* 2nd Frances Anne (*d* 1930), dau of —Spragge, of Ottawa, Canada, and had issue:
1 (THOMAS) PHILIP (Sir), **1st Bt**
2 Kenneth; *d* 1890 aged 12
3 William Douglas, MC (1915), JP (1939) Notts, Col (ret) KRRC (joined 1901) WW I, cmded 2nd Bn Northamptonshire 1929–33, Col 1923 (ret 1937); *b* 1881; *educ* Eton; *m* 1st Dorothy Bourke; *m* 2nd 1937 *Mary Catherine, widow of Charles Francis Darley, of Thorne, Yorks, and Ranby Hall, Retford, Notts, and dau of William Bain, of Moray Place, Edinburgh, and *dsp* 26 April 197–
4 Norman Elsdale; *b* 1888; *d* 1951
1 Gwendolen; *m* Rev Ernest Clapin Wilson, MA
2 Grace JP (1934), Notts, WW I with 1st Br Field Hosp for Serbia; *b* 1879; *educ* Cheltenham Ladies Coll; *d* unm 1955
3 Rosamond; *m* Guy Mellor, and *d* 26 Jan 1968
4 Cecily; *d* 1892 aged 6

THOMAS BARBER's est son,
Sir (Thomas) Philip Barber, 1st Bt (UK), so *cr* 25 July 1960, DSO (1918), TD (1917), DL (Notts 1918), JP (Notts 1902), of Greasley, Notts; *b* 6 Jan 1876; *educ* Eton and Trin Coll Cambridge (BA 1897); Hon LLD Nottingham 1955, Notts: CC 1898–1925, CA 1925–61 (chm 1931–45), High Sheriff 1907, Boer War 1900–01 with Imp Yeo (despatches), and WW I (despatches twice), Hon Col 307 S Notts Hus Yeo RHA (TA) 1944–56, Pro-Chllr Nottingham U 1949–61; *m* 17 April 1902 Beatrice Mary (*d* 12 Nov 1962 aged 85), dau of Lt-Col William Ingersoll Merritt, of St Catherines, Ontario, Canada, and left issue:
1 Thomas Cecil; *b* 9 Feb 1903; *educ* Eton; *m* 1928 *Joyce Mary (*m* 2nd 18 Sept 1933 (*divorce* 1948) Col John Sidney North FitzGerald, CVO, MBE, MC (*d* 1976), son of Francis FitzGerald, CBE, of Wroxton, Banbury (*see* 1970 edn NORTH, B); *m* 3rd 20 May 1948 Lt-Col Arthur Frederick Reginald Wiggins, who *d* 1961), dau of Dr Edward Hedley, MBE, of The Cottage, Thursley, Surrey, and *d* 10 Jan 1930, leaving issue:
(1) *Susan Jane; *b* 1930; *m* 1st 17 April 1951 (*divorce* 1965) Ian Hope Johnstone, only son of Col Hope Johnstone, RA, of Pyt House, Tisbury, Wilts; *m* 2nd David Day (*d* 1970), and by her 1st husb has issue:
1a *Robin Philip Wentworth; *b* 22 Jan 1956
1a *Rosanna Jane; *b* 8 March 1958; *m* 1982 *Andrew Hugh Hope, and has issue:
1b *Clara Harriet; *b* 1984
2 WILLIAM FRANCIS BARBER (Sir), **2nd Bt**
1 Joan; *b* 7 May 1907; *m* 1934 Rev Canon Sydney John Galloway (*d* 1969) and *d* 1995
2 *Beatrice Naomi [Mrs Charles Stewart, The Manse, Moorgreen, Newthorpe, Notts]; *b* 27 April 1911; *m* 5 Dec 1939 F/Lt Charles David Stewart, RAF (*ka* 1940)
3 *Honor [Mrs Noel Hunt, Limehurst, Hallam Rd, Southwell, Notts]; *b* 21 May 1914; *m* 8 Feb 1947 Cdr Noel Hunt, RNVR (*d* 1974)

Sir PHILIP *d* 11 July 1961; his 2nd son,
Sir William Francis Barber, 2nd Bt, TD (1942), JP (1952) Notts, High Sheriff 1964–65; *b* 20 Nov 1905; *educ* Eton; Lt-Col 307 S Notts Hus Yeo 1947–50, Hon Col 1961–66, WW II as Maj S Notts Hus Yeo RHA in Palestine, Egypt, N Africa and NW Europe; *m* 1st 28 Oct 1936 (*divorce* 1978) Diana Constance (*d* 1984), dau of Lt-Col Thomas Lloyd, CMG, of Minard, Argyll; *m* 2nd 1978 *Jean Marie [Jean Lady Barber, Lamb Close House, Eastwood, Notts NG16 3QX], widow of Dr Harry Carew Nott, of Adelaide, Australia, and *d* 1 April 1995, having by his 1st w had issue:

1 Sir (THOMAS) DAVID BARBER, **3rd and present Bt**

1 *Diana Mary [Mrs Nicholas Davie-Thornhill, Hinderclay Hall, Diss, Norfolk]; *b* 20 Sept 1939; *m* 6 March 1965 (*divorce* 1991) Nicholas Bache Barlow Davie-Thornhill, er son of Humphrey Bache Christopher Davie-Thornhill, of Stanton Hall, Matlock, Derbyshire (see BARLOW, Bt, of Bradwell Hall and has issue

BARBER OF TEWKESBURY

Creation: B. (LP, UK) 1992.

THE BARON BARBER OF TEWKESBURY, of Gotherington, Co Glos (Sir Derek Coates Barber) [The Rt Hon The Lord Barber of Tewkesbury, Chough House, Gotherington, Glos GL52 4QU]; *b* 17 June 1918; *educ* RAC Circencester (MRAC); served WWII (invalided); memb Cheltenham RDC 1948–52; Dist Advsy Offr Nat Ag Advsy Serv MAFF 1946–57, Ag Advsr Glos 1957–72, MAFF Assessor: Pilkington Ctee Ag Educn 1966, Ag and Horticultural Trng Bd 1968, Fndr Memb Farming & Wildlife Advsy Gp 1969, environment consultant Humberts 1972–93; Chm BBC Centl Ag Advsy Ctee 1974–80, memb: Ordnance Survey Advsy Bd 1982–85, Bd RURAL Cncl 1983–94, Bd CEED 1984–, Centre for Ag Strategy 1985–91, Cncl Br Tst Ornithology 1987–90, Cncl Rare Breeds Survival Tst 1987– (Pres 1991–95), Ag Research Insts Assoc 1991–96; ktd 1984; Chm: RSPB 1976–81 (Pres 1990–91), Countryside Commn 1981–91, New Nat Forest Advsy Bd 1991–, Booker Countryside Advsy Bd 1990–95; V-Pres Ornithological Soc Mid-East 1987–97; Pres: Glos Naturalists' Soc 1981–, RASE 1991–92, Owl and Hawk Tst 1992, Br Pig Assoc 1995–97; Patron Lancs Heritage Tst 1990–; memb Ho Lds: Sub Ctee D on Food and Ag 1992–96, Select Ctee on Sustainable Devpt 1994–95; Hon FRASE 1986; Hon DSc Bradford 1986, FRAgS 1992, FIAgrM 1992, author: *Humbert's Commentary* (ed, 1973–88), *Farming for Profits* (with Keith Dexter 1961, 2nd ed 1967), *Farming in Britain Today* (with J G S and Frances Donaldson 1969, 2nd ed 1972), *Farming with Wildlife* (ed, 1971), *A History of Humberts* (1980); *m* 1st 19– (*divorce* 1981) —; *m* 2nd 1983 *Rosemary Jennifer Brougham, dau of Lt-Cdr Randolph Brougham Pearson, RN

Lineage: THOMAS SMITH-BARBER; *m* Elsie Coates and had:

DEREK COATES SMITH-BARBER later BARBER, *cr* a **Baron**

BARCLAY

Arms: Azure, a chevron between three crosses patée or. **Crest:** A sword erect proper, hilted and pommelled or. **Motto:** *Crux Christi nostra corona* ('The cross of Christ is our crown').

Creation: Bt. (NS) 22 Oct 1668.

SIR COLVILLE HERBERT SANFORD BARCLAY, 14TH BT, of Pierston, Ayrshire [Sir Colville Barclay Bt, 23 High St, Broughton, Stockbridge, Hants SO20 8AE]; *b* 7 May 1913; *s* unc 1930; *educ* Eton and Trin Coll Oxford (MA); 2nd Sec Dip Serv 1938–41, Lt-Cdr RNVR WW II; painter: exhibitor RA, RBA London Gp, Bradford City and Brighton Art Galleries; Chm Roy Lond Homoeopathic Hosp 1970–74 and League of Friends 1974–84, botanical expdns Crete, Turkey, Cyprus, Réunion, Mauritius and Nepal 1966–81, author: *Crete, checklist of vascular plants* (1986); *m* 19 March 1949 *Rosamond Grant Renton, yr dau of Dr Walter Armstrong Elliott, of Chandler's Ford, Hants, and has issue:

1 +ROBERT COLRAINE [Robert Barclay Esq, Av Linen de P Machado 1005, Jardim Botanica, 22470–040 Rio de Janeiro, Brazil]; *b* 12 Feb 1950; *educ* Eton and UEA; *m* 1980 *Lucilia Saboia, yr dau of Carlos Saboia de Albuquerque, of Ipanema, Rio de Janeiro, and has issue:

(1) +Henry William Saboia; *b* 16 Jan 1982

(1) *Caroline Saboia; *b* 21 Dec 1983

2 +(Alistair) James Elliot [James Barclay Esq, 8 Redcliffe Gdns, London SW10 9EU]; *b* 23 July 1952; *educ* Eton

3 +(Colville) Edwin Ward [Edwin Barclay Esq, Watts Farm, River Lane, Pulborough, W Sussex RH20 1NG]; *b* 6 July 1956; *educ* Charterhouse and Aberdeen U; Hon Treas Psionic Soc 1997–, dir Barclay Forestry 198–; *m* 1992 *Fiona M, dau of Robin Bell, of Uckfield, Sussex, and has issue:

(1) +Frederick Colville Beresford; *b* 1993

Lineage: DAVID BARCLAY, of Pierston, Ayr; held part of the territorial Barony of Kellie, Forfar, 1442 and Nether (for Barclay) Pierston in 1443, both through his w Helen, dau of Sir William Douglas of Pierston by the dau and heir of Sir John Stewart of Pierston, whose charter of that estate had been granted by ROBERT BRUCE (*see* GALLOWAY, E); he *d c* 18 Feb 1461/2, leaving;

DAVID BARCLAY of Pierston; *d c* 24 April 1489; his est s:

NINIAN BARCLAY of Pierston; *m* Agnes Bruce (living 1509/10); *d* by 11 April 1502, leaving:

WILLIAM BARCLAY of Pierston; *m* Marion Cunningham (living 1534) and *d* by 20 April 1529, leaving:

ROBERT BARCLAY of Pierston; *m c* 15 Sept 1518 Katherine (*m* 2nd John Boyle, of Ballykewin, and had further issue; *see* GLASGOW, E), dau of Wallace of Cairnhill, and *d c* 21 Feb 1531/2, having had, with an er s (John, served heir to his f 7 Nov 1539, *d* unm 1550):

WILLIAM BARCLAY of Pierston; served heir to his bro 23 Jan 1551/2; *m* Janet, dau of Hugh Montgomerie of Stane, gs of 1st Earl of Eglinton (*see* EGLINTON and WINTON, E), and *d* 17 July 1584, leaving an est s:

WILLIAM BARCLAY of Pierston; *m c* 10 May 1565 Isobel, dau of Robert Hamilton, yr of Dalmuir, and *d* 26 June 1586, leaving an est s:

WILLIAM BARCLAY of Pierston; *b* 1570; *m* 24 May 1592 Jean (*d* July 1631), est dau of John Boyle of Kelburne (*see* GLASGOW, E), and *d* Aug 1628, leaving an est s:

ROBERT BARCLAY of Pierston; had a Crown charter of Drummuir 25 June 1627; *m* 1st *c* 29 Dec 1619 Agnes Wallace; *m* 2nd *c* Aug 1631 Janet, est dau of John Campbell of Sankstown, and *d* 1644, leaving, with an est s (William, had a Crown charter of Pierston 9 Jan 1643/4, retoured heir to his f 5 Sept 1644, *m* —, dau of Sir Ludovic Houstoun of that Ilk, and *dsp c* 4 July 1661):

Sir Robert Barclay, 1st Bt (NS), so *cr* 22 Oct 1668, of Pierston; retoured heir to his bro 4 July 1661; had a State charter of Whytfoord, Renfrew, 3 July 1657; merchant and Baillie of Edinburgh, fitted out privateers 2nd Dutch War 1665–67; Commr Supply, Excise and Militia Ayrshire 1678; *m* 1st 4 Aug 1653 Catharine (*bur* 7 March 1658/9), dau of Alexander Lockhart, of Edinburgh, and had:

1 Alexander; *bapt* 17 Dec 1654; *dvp* unm *c* 28 Dec 1681

2 ROBERT (Sir), **2nd Bt**

The **1st Bt** *m* 2nd 28 Sept 1659 Barbara (*bur* 7 April 1697), dau of James Deans, of Edinburgh, had 13 Sept 1667 a charter to himself and his heirs male by her of the lands of Busbie, Knockintubber and Hallbarns, in Kilmaurs, Ayrshire, and *d* Sept 1694, having by her had four other s and two daus

The 1st Bt's est surv s by his 1st w,

Sir Robert Barclay, 2nd Bt; *b* 21 Feb 1658/9; Commr of Supply Ayrshire 1704; *m* Bethia (*d* 21 Jan 1730/1), dau of Sir Robert Baird, 1st Bt, of Saughton (*qv*), and *d* 15 Aug 1717, having had issue:

1 **Sir Robert Barclay, 3rd Bt**; *bapt* 11 Jan 1676/7; Jacobite 1715; sold Pierston 22 Aug 1720; *d* unm in exile at Aix-la-Chapelle 1728

2 John; *bapt* 6 March 1677/8; *d* young

3 JAMES (Sir), **4th Bt**

4 David; *d* unm

1 Elizabeth; *m* her cousin William Barclay of Warrix, Provost of Irvine, and had issue

2 Bethia; *m* Barclay of Bennets, Ayrshire

3 Margaret; *m* Archibald Houston, yst son of Sir Patrick Houston, 1st Bt, of Houston

The 3rd Bt's bro,

Sir James Barclay, 4th Bt; MD Glasgow, Surgn RN; *m* —, er dau and coheir of Capt William Blois, RN, of Taunton Dean, Somerset, and *d* 12 Jan 1755, leaving an only surv child:

Sir William Blois Barclay, 5th Bt; *b c* 1710; RN; *m* 18 March 1746/7 Susannah (*d* 28 March 1791), dau of William Church, Surgn, of Gloucester, and *d* 7 June 1756, having had issue:

1 **Sir William Barclay, 6th Bt**; *b* 22 May 1748; Lt Bengal Army; *d* unm at Calcutta 1769

2 **Sir James Mantle Barclay, 7th Bt**; *b* 2 Oct 1750; Capt RN; *d* unm 12 June 1793

3 ROBERT (Sir), **8th Bt**

1 Susannah; *m* 22 June 1782 Thomas de Mounteney, of Newbold Verdon, Leics, and *d* 5 Jan 1825, leaving issue

2 Elizabeth; *d* in infancy

The 7th Bt's bro,

Sir Robert Barclay, 8th Bt; *b* 13 Sept 1755; MP Newport 1802–07, Collector Internal Revenue Mauritius 1813–35; *m* 1st 20 Nov 1780 Elizabeth (*d* 13 March 1788), est dau of John Tickell, of Glasnevin, Dublin, and *d* 14 Aug 1839, having had, with other issue:

1 Robert Brydges; *b* 22 May 1782; Maj 71st Regt Peninsular War (wounded); *m* 5 May 1809 Jane (*d* 16 March 1868), dau of Arthur Williams, of Dungannon, Co Tyrone, and *dvp* 8 Aug 1825, leaving issue:

(1) **Sir Robert Barclay, 9th Bt**; *b* 24 July 1819; Lt 25th Foot; *d* unm 19 May 1859

(2) Thomas Tickell; *b* 1822; Clerk RN; *d* unm 11 Dec 1847

(3) John Graves; *b* 1823; *d* 1834

The **8th Bt** *m* 2nd 20 June 1802 Harriet Alicia (*d* 16 Feb 1859), dau and coheir of Dep Commr-Gen Thomas Durell, RHG (Blues), and widow of Baron de Cronstadt, and by her had issue:

2 Henry; *b* 23 Aug 1803; *d* in infancy

3 DAVID WILLIAM (Sir), **10th Bt**

4 George Augustus Frederick; *b* 30 May 1807; *d* Jan 1819

The 9th Bt's half-unc,

Sir David William Barclay, 10th Bt; *b* 5 Sept 1804; Capt 56th and 99th Regts, ADC to Govr Mauritius, MLC Mauritius 1846–64; *m* 1st 16 Feb 1829 Lise Josephe de Rune (*d* 22 March 1867), yst dau of Charles Malo de Rune, of Mauritius, and *d* 23 Nov 1888, having had issue, with four daus:

1 COLVILLE ARTHUR DURELL (Sir), **11th Bt**

2 Frederick Charles d'Epinay; *b* 26 March 1831; Maj-Gen, ADC to Govr Mauritius, Kaffir War (medal); *m* 18 July 1854 Isabella Caroline (*d* 6 Nov 1915), dau of Martin West, Lt-Govr Natal, and *dsp* 28 Dec 1890

3 William Malo de Rune; *b* 29 Aug 1842; Lt 24th Foot; *m* 3 Sept 1863 Harriet Jane (*d* 4 Dec 1919), only dau of Francis Charles Leslie, of Castlewellan, Co Down, and Kincraigie Castle, Co Donegal, and *d* 4 June 1938, having had issue:

(1) David Francis Glenville; *b* 10 Sept 1864; *d* 1915

(2) Francis Charles Leslie; *b* 8 March 1866; Lt-Col Boer War (medals); *dsp* 1907

(3) William Malo de Rune; *b* 19 June 1871; *m* 15 April 1898 Nellie Grace Inall Hamilton, and *d* 1917, leaving issue

1a Leslie William Hamilton, MBE (1963); *b* 1899; WW I with Australian Forces; *m* 1927 Mabel Dobson Freene, and *d* 1983, leaving issue:

1b *Beverley Lesley Lorraine [Miss Beverley Barclay, 2 Denmark Court, Buderim, Queensland 4556, Australia]; *b* 1936; *educ* Sydney C of E GS

(4) Frederick Arthur D'Epinay; *b* 24 Sept 1875; FIANZ; *m* 14 April 1904 Laura Gwendolen (*d* 14 Sept 1939), dau of Craddock Beauchamp, of Picton, NZ, and *d* 9 May 1955, leaving issue:

1a William Cradock de Rune; *b* 28 June 1906; WW II with NZ Forces (invalided); *m* 10 Aug 1943 *Frances Berenice, dau of W F Aplin, of Wellington, NZ, and *d* 1992, leaving issue:

1b *Elizabeth Beauchamp [Mrs Anthony Leatherbarrow, 14B Stephen St, Upper Hutt, New Zealand]; *b* 8 Aug 1945; *m* 1967 *Anthony Leatherbarrow, and has issue:

1c *Clifford Beau; *b* 1975

1c *Catherine Anne; *b* 1972

2a Beauchamp d'Epinay; *b* 19 Aug 1911; *m* Feb 1935 *Margaret Katherine (who *m* 2nd 1945 Ian M Rutherford, MB, ChB, DOMS, DLO), dau of James Begg, of Dunedin, NZ, and was *ka* Hong Kong Dec 1941, leaving issue:

1b +James Fergus [James Barclay Esq, Cruachan, RD1 Miller's Flat, Central Otago, New Zealand]; *b* 29 Feb 1940; BAgr; *m* 5 Dec 1964 *Sally Elizabeth, only dau of Hugh Stuart Fleming, MB, ChB, of Hove, Sussex, and has issue:

1c +Andrew James; *b* 23 Aug 1967

2c +Hamish Beauchamp; *b* 2 Feb 1969

1c *Fiona Jane; *b* 1972

1b *Margaret Elizabeth [Mrs John Gibbs, Millers Flat, Central Otago, New Zealand]; *b* 21 April 1936; *m* 13 Dec 1958 *John Michael Gibbs, MB, ChB, FFARCS, FFARACS, est son of Douglas Gibbs, MB, ChB, of Auckland NZ, and has issue:

1c *David Douglas; *b* 6 Nov 1966

1c *Margaret Jennifer; *b* 19 Sept 1959

2c *Hilary Eva; *b* 12 Feb 1961

2c *Helen Dorothy; *b* 1970

2b *Frances Beauchamp [Mrs Robert Campbell, 3 Over Place, Knutsford, Cheshire WA16 8NN]; *b* 15 Aug 1938; *m* 12 June 1966 *Robert Campbell, C Eng, BSc Engr, MICE, MIStructE, s of Walter Edward Campbell, of Kenton, Middx, and has:

1c *James Robert [James Campbell Esq, Warren Heath, Ipswich, Suffolk]; *b* 10 Aug 1968; Bsc, MCIOB; *m* 14 Sept 1996 *Penelope Jane Hewitt

2c *Alastair John; *b* 21 Nov 1969; B Eng, ACA;

1c *Margaret Elizabeth; *b* 29 Dec 1966

(5) Geoffrey Dashwood Zobel; *b* 1877; *d* unm 19 April 1901

(6) Aubrey Henri de Rune; *b* 20 Jan 1880; *m* 17 Sept 1903 Alice Anne (*d* 1969), er dau of Sir Edward Osborne Gibbes, 3rd Bt (*see* 1940 edn), and *d* March 1950, having had issue:

1a Aubrey Geoffrey de Rune; *b* 29 April 1914; Capt AIF WW II; *ka* New Guinea 1942

1a *Betty Theodosia [Mrs Russell Gellatley, 3 Harbour St, Wollongong 2500 NSW, Australia]; *m* 26 Dec 1936 *Russell Gellatly, est son of Francis Mephan Gellatly, LLD, of Sydney, NSW, and has issue:

1b *Peter Russell; *b* 22 March 1947; *m* 5 May 1967 *Marilyn Fay, est dau of Peter Fletcher, of Dural, NSW

2a *Susan Alice [Mrs Roy Lucena, 50 Grace Ave, French's Forest, NSW, Australia]; *b* 19 June 1939; *m* 16 Sept 1961 Roy Lancaster Lucena (*d* 1975), est son of Henry Lancaster Lucena, of Wollongong, NSW, and has issue:

1b *Peter Blair Lancaster; *b* 21 Feb 1964

1b *Karen Jane; *b* 29 Oct 1962

2b *Belinda Marie; *b* 1969

(1) Theodosia Leslie; *m* 1st 1891 William Thomas Locke Travers, barrister (*dsp* 26 April 1903); *m* 2nd 1905 Lt-Col Edward James Faudon Wood, late IA (*d* 11 Feb 1931), and *d* 22 April 1958, leaving issue

(2) Constance Durell; *m* 1892 Charles Armstrong, and had issue

(3) Enid Harriet Durell; *d* unm

4 Henry Thomas de Rune; *b* 5 Oct 1849; CS British Guiana; *m* 28 Oct 1878 Ellen Eliza (*d* 20 Sept 1935), yr dau of Thomas Frederick Henley, CE, of London, and *d* 16 Sept 1921, leaving:

(1) Leslie George de Rune; *b* 3 Oct 1879; Capt late Roy Ulster Rifles, S African War (two medals, four clasps), WW I (two medals, 1914 star and clasp); *m* 15 June 1926 Dorothea (*d* 1971), est dau of Rev Charles Herbert Griffith, MA, late Vicar of St Michael's, Folkestone, and *d* 1 Feb 1965, leaving issue:

1a +Ninian de Rune [Ninian Barclay Esq, 111 St Helens Rd, Hastings, E Sussex]; *b* 28 Nov 1927; *m* 1971 *Aileen Margaret, er dau of Maj Hayes, and has issue:

1b +Robert David; *b* 1972

1b *Anna Marie; *b* 1974

2a +Michael George [Michael Barclay, 27611 Santa Clarita Rd, Saugus, California 91350, USA]; *b* 1 April 1932; LAC RAF 1950–52; *m* 18 July 1953 *Agnes Joy, yr dau of A Batehup, of Northiam, Sussex, and has issue:

1b *Wendy Margaret; *b* 16 June 1954

2b *Beverley Ann; *b* 17 Aug 1959

(2) Frederick David Henry de Rune; *b* 11 Oct 1881; *das* 10/11 May 1941, unm

Sir David *m* 2nd 19 Sept 1872 Emily (*d* 18 June 1910), 2nd dau of James Edward Stacey, of Kingston, Surrey, and by her had issue:

5 David Hamilton Dashwood; *b* 12 April 1877; presumed *d c* 18 June 1910

The 10th Bt's est son,

Sir Colville Arthur Durell Barclay, 11th Bt, CMG; *b* 20 Dec 1829; Receiver-Gen Mauritius and Auditor-Gen Ceylon, Cdr Legion of Honour; *m* 8 May 1855 Louise Melanie (*d* March 1930), yst dau and coheir of Edouard Jullien de Belzim, of Mauritius, and *d* 18 Feb 1896, having had issue:

1 **Sir David Edward Durell Barclay, 12th Bt**; *b* 30 March 1858; Capt 19th Hus Egypt 1882 (wounded), Sudan (medal with three clasps, bronze star), T/Capt and Rlwy Staff Offr 1914–18; *m* 9 Oct 1889 Letitia (*d* 5 April 1923), dau of Hon Amias Charles Orde-Powlett (*see* BOLTON, B), and *dsp* 2 Oct 1918

2 **Sir Robert Cecil de Belzim Barclay, 13th Bt**; *b* 18 June 1862; *m* 11 Oct 1926 Therese Marie Camille (*m* 2nd 193– Baron de Pierre Bourg), dau of E Pouget, and *dsp* 18 March 1930

3 Colville Adrian de Rune (Sir), PC, KCMG, CB, CBE, MVO; *b* 17 Sept 1869; Envoy Extrdy and Min Plen Sweden 1919–24, Hungary 1924–28, Amb Extrdy and Plen Portugal 1928–29; *m* 10 April 1912 Sarita Enriqueta (*m* 2nd 29 July 1931 1st and last Baron Vansittart, GCB, GCMG, MVO (*d* 14 Feb 1957; *see* 1956 edn)), dau of Herbert Ward, and *d* 2 June 1929, leaving issue:

(1) Sir COLVILLE HERBERT SANFORD BARCLAY, **14th and present Bt**

(2) +Cecil Edward Sanford [Cecil Barclay Esq, 44 Church St, Eye, Suffolk IP23 7BD]; *b* 13 Nov 1914; *educ* Eton and Magdalen Coll Oxford (BA); *m* 1st 16 Feb 1939 (*divorce* 1957) Yvonne Eleanor Mutch, dau of Sir William Edward Leonard Shenton; *m* 2nd 17 Jan 1958 *Marcia Isobel Mary, dau of John Horatio Macoun, and by her has issue:

1a *Melanie Sarita; *b* 12 Nov 1958; *m* 1985 *Roger William Stephen Hale, and has issue:

1b *John William Sanford; *b* 1988

1b *Harriet Sarita; *b* 1989

(3) +Robert Charles Sanford, JP Kent (1960) [Maj Robert Barclay JP, Green Bank South, Grundisburgh, nr Woodbridge, Suffolk IP13 6TD]; *b* 14 Feb 1918; *educ* Eton and Magdalen Coll Oxford; Maj Intell Corps WW II, Chevalier Legn Hon, Croix de Guerre; *m* 1st 29 Jan 1941 (*divorce* 1964) Camilla (*d* 4 May 1997), yr dau of Sir George Menteth Boughey, 9th Bt (*qv*); *m* 2nd 6 March 1964 Alice Molly (*d* 1985), dau of Sidney Blackman, and has issue by 1st wife:

1a +Peter John [Peter Barclay Esq, 8 Broomhill Rd, London SW18]; *b* 27 Dec 1941; *educ* Eton; *m* 25 June 1964 (*divorce* 1973) Angela Mary, er dau of Harold Francis Blackborow, of Rodmarton, Cirencester, Glos, and has issue:

1b +Alasdair James; *b* 16 Jan 1968

2b +Piers David; *b* 2 June 1972

2a +Michael George [Michael Barclay Esq, Frostland Farm, Newchurch, Romney Marsh, Kent]; *b* 22 Aug 1945; *educ* Eton; *m* 1973 *Susan, dau of James Thompson, and has issue:

1b *Philippa; *b* 1973

2b *Sasha; *b* 1976

3a +Jonathan Robert [Jonathan Barclay Esq, The Old Vicarage, Stoke Holy Cross, Norwich NR14 8AB]; *b* 9 March 1947; *educ* Eton; *m* 28 June 1969 *Clare Amabel, only dau of Capt Philip Cecil Langdon Yorke, OBE, RN (ret) (*see* HARDWICKE, E), and has issue:

1b +Timothy Robert; *b* 23 Dec 1984

1b *Emily Rose; *b* 2 July 1976

4a +Christopher Richard [Christopher Barclay Esq, 29 Bicester Rd, Richmond, Surrey]; *b* 24 Oct 1949; *educ* Eton; *m* 1986 *Linda Anne, dau of Joseph Redshaw, and has issue:

1b *Leonora Sophie; *b* 1989

2b *Chloe Imogen; *b* 1989

1 Emma Louisa; *m* 21 Dec 1875 Vicomte Henri Perot de Chazelle, and *dsp* 21 Nov 1898

BARING

Arms: Az. a fess or, in chief a bear's head couped ppr., muzzled and ringed gold. **Crest:** A mullet erminois between two wings arg. **Motto:** *Probitate et labore* ('By uprightness and labour'). **Creation:** Bt. (UK) 4 Feb 1911.

SIR JOHN FRANCIS BARING, 3RD BT, of Nubia House, IoW [Sir John Baring Bt, 89 June Road, North Salem, NY 10560, USA]; *b* 21 May 1947; *s* unc 1990; *educ* Eton, RAC Cirencester and LSE; chm Hackman, Baring & Co 1994–; *m* 15 July 1971 *Elizabeth Anne, yst dau of Robert David Henle Pillitz, of Juramento 3437, Belgrano, Buenos Aires 30, Argentina, and has issue:

1 +JULIAN ALEXANDER DAVID; *b* 10 Feb 1975

2 +James Francis; *b* 1984

1 *Andrea Hermione; *b* 5 April 1977

Lineage: Sir FRANCIS BARING, 1st Bt (*see* NORTHBROOK, B); had a 3rd s:

HENRY BARING, of Cromer Hall, Norfolk; *b* 18 Jan 1776; *m* 1st 19 April 1802 Maria Matilda, 2nd dau of William Bingham, of Philadelphia, USA, and had, with other issue:

1 HENRY BINGHAM

HENRY BARING *m* 2nd 9 July 1825 Cecilia Anne (*d* 21 Oct 1874), dau of V-Adml William Windham, of Cromer Hall, Norfolk, and by her had issue:

2 EDWARD CHARLES, *cr* BARON REVELSTOKE (*qv*)

3 EVELYN BARING, *cr* EARL OF CROMER (*qv*)

HENRY BARING *d* 13 April 1848; his est son,

Maj HENRY BINGHAM BARING; *b* 4 March 1804; MP Callington 1831–32 and Marlborough 1832–68, a Ld Treasury; *m* 1st 30 June 1827 Augusta (*d* 8 Jan 1853), dau of 6th Earl of Cardigan (*see* AILESBURY, M); *m* 2nd 1854 Marie de Martinoff (*dsp* 9 Aug 1903) and by his 1st w had:

1 CHARLES

2 Henry, Capt 17th Lancers; *b* 6 Sept 1831; *m* 22 March 1888 Harriette Emily (*d* 12 Aug 1950), dau of Edward George Cubitt, of Honing Hall, Norfolk, and *d* 13 April 1929, leaving issue (*see* NORTHBROOK, B)

3 Francis, Lt-Col Scots Gds, Adj Yeomen Gd; *b* 16 March 1833; *d* unm 21 Feb 1895

1 Mary Emily; *m* 1st 18 May 1857 (*divorce* 1864) Richard Lewis Mostyn Williams-Bulkeley, afterwards 11th Bt (*qv*), and had issue; *m* 2nd 27 July 1867 Lt John Oakley Maund, RMA

2 Augusta; *d* unm 2 April 1867

HENRY BARING *d* 25 April 1869; his est son,

Lt-Gen CHARLES BARING, Coldstream Gds; *b* 26 June 1829; *m* 25 Aug 1860 Helen (*d* 17 Jan 1914), dau of Rt Hon Sir James Graham, 2nd Bt, PC, GCB, of Netherby (*qv*), and had issue:

1 GODFREY (Sir), **1st Bt**

1 Mabel; *b* 21 June 1861; *m* 3 Sept 1884 Richard Tassell Anthony Grant (*d* 1 July 1902), of Staffa, IoW, and *d* 7 May 1917

2 Olivia; *b* 14 May 1863; *m* 8 July 1886 Sir Richard James Graham, 4th Bt, of Netherby (*qv*), and *dsp* 21 March 1887

CHARLES BARING *d* 7 Feb 1890; his only son,

Sir Godfrey Baring, 1st Bt (UK), so *cr* 4 Feb 1911, KBE (1952), DL, JP Hants, High Sheriff 1897; CA IoW, chm IoW CC 1898–1957 and IoW Co Bench 1934, Alderman London CC 1920–22, chm RNLI, MP (Lib) IoW 1906–10 and Barnstaple 1911–18, PPS to Parly U-Sec Colonies 1908–10 and Pres Bd Educn 1911–13, Lt 3rd Bn Hampshire Regt; *b* 18 April 1871; *m* 1st 26 Jan 1898 Eva Hermione, MBE, JP Hants (*d* 9 June 1934), only child of Alexander Aeneas Mackintosh of Mackintosh, DL, JP; *m* 2nd 22 Jan 1937 Brenda Margery (*d* 18 July 1953), yr dau of Canon Joseph Sewell Blake, MA, and *d* 24 Nov 1957, having by his 1st w had issue:

1 **Sir Charles Christian Baring, 2nd Bt**, DL (Hants 1962), JP (IoW 1956); chm IoW Bench 1962, WW I with Coldstream Gds (wounded), WW II as Maj Coldstream Gds, Prison Serv 1936–38, Home Office Inspr 1946–49, Warden Prisons Bermuda 1952–53, memb Bd of Visitors Parkhurst Prison IoW 1956; *b* 16 Dec 1898; *educ* Eton; *m* 19 Feb 1948 *Jeannette, dau of Henry Charles Daykin, and *d* 1990

2 Raymond Alexander, Capt KRRC (TAR); *b* 7 July 1912; *educ* Eton; *m* 9 June 1938 Margaret Fleetwood, OBE, JP, DL (*m* 2nd 1991, as his 2nd w, 6th Earl of Malmesbury (*qv*) and *d* 25 Dec 1994), yst dau of Col Robert William Pigott Clarke Campbell-Preston, of Ardchattan Priory, Argyllshire, and *d* 23 Aug 1967, leaving:

(1) (Charles) Peter, 2nd Lt RHG; dir WH Smith and Son (Hldgs); *b* 24 May 1939; *educ* Eton; *m* 1st 1964 (*divorce* 1974) Sarah, yr dau of Lt-Col William Gill Withycombe, of Providence House, Sutton, Thirsk, Yorks, and had:

1a *Arabella; *b* 2 July 1965

2a *Henrietta; *b* 4 Sept 1966

(1) (cont.) Peter Baring *m* 2nd 1976 *Susannah Jane [Mrs Peter Baring, 31 Grantley St, Shelton, Shrewsbury SY3 5LA], dau of Dr William Ezra Smith, of Bashaw, Alberta, Canada, and *d* 1987, leaving:

3a *Gabriella Louise; *b* 1977

4a *Olivia; *b* 1980

(2) Sir JOHN FRANCIS BARING, **3rd and present Bt**

(3) +(Andrew) Michael (Godfrey) [Michael Baring Esq, Ravenscourt House, Ravenscourt Park, London W6]; *b* 16 Feb 1949; *educ* Eton and — Coll Oxford; *m* 1976 *Anstice Mary Blanche, dau of Alfred George Cardale, of Newbury, Berks, and has:

1a +Alexander Francis; *b* 1978

2a +Edward George; *b* 1980

3a +Andrew Thomas; *b* 1983

1a *Rosalind Mary Blanche; *b* 1986

(1) *Ann Hermione [Mrs Alistair Buchanan, Hill Barn, Great Bedwyn, Marlborough, Wilts]; *b* 21 May 1941; *educ* Southampton U (PhD 1990), Fellow St Hilda's Coll Oxford 1994; *m* 20 July 1963 *Alistair John Buchanan, and has:

1a *Catherine Ann Louise; *b* 9 Nov 1965

2a *Teresa Margaret; *b* 10 Sept 1967

3a *Helen Hermione; *b* 1973

1 *Helen Azalea; *b* 8 Nov 1901; *m* 17 Dec 1928 William Piers Thursby (*d* 3 June 1977), yr son of Rev Harvey William Gustavus of Culverlands, Burghfield, Berks

2 Viola Mary; *b* 8 Feb 1905; *m* 16 April 1925 Maj Ronald Aird, MC, RAC (TA), 2nd son of Malcolm Aird, of Woolton House, Newbury, Berks, and gs of Sir John Aird, 1st Bt (*qv*), and *d* 18 April 1965, leaving issue

BARLOW of Bradwall Hall

Arms: Per pale erm. and gu. three chevrons counterchanged, over all two lions combatant or. **Crest:** A lion sejant affrontée or, holding erect in the forepaws a cross crosslet fitchée gu. **Motto:** *Qui non proficit deficit* ('Who fails to make his way slips back'). **Creation:** Bt. (UK) 20 July 1907.

SIR JOHN KEMP BARLOW, 3RD BT, of Bradwall Hall, Sandbach, Cheshire [Sir John Barlow Bt, Bulkeley Grange, Malpas, Cheshire SY14 8BT]; *b* 22 April 1934; *s* f 1986; *educ* Winchester and Trin Coll Cambridge (BA 1956, MA 1958); High Sheriff Cheshire 1979, chm Thomas Barlow & Bro Ltd and Majedie Investment plc, Jt MFH Cheshire 1987–; *m* 30 June 1962 Susan, er dau of Col Sir Andrew Marshall Horsbrugh-Porter, 3rd Bt, DSO (*qv*), and has issue:

1 +(JOHN) WILLIAM MARSHALL [William Barlow Esq, 4 Wharfedale St, London SW10]; *b* 12 March 1964; *educ* Eton and Liverpool U; *m* 1991 *Sarah Hilary, dau of John Nobes, of Windsor, Berks, and has issue:

(1) +John William Oakley; *b* 4April 1993

2 +Thomas David Bradwall; *b* 17 Jan 1966; *educ* Eton; *m* 1993 *Emily Melissa, only dau of Anthony Andrew Ward Kimpton, of Tarrington, Herefs (*see* HAZLERIGG, B)

3 +(Andrew) Michael Kemp; *b* 14 Dec 1966; *educ* Harrow; *m* 23 Aug 1997 *Veronica yr dau of Andrew Buxton (*see* BUXTON, Bt)

4 +Charles James Bulkeley; *b* 22 Sept 1970

Sir JOHN *m* 2nd 21 May 1998 *Mrs Pauline Windsor, of Cheshire

Lineage: JOHN BARLOW, of Oak Estate, Chorley, Cheshire; *m* Mary — and had, with other issue:

HENRY BARLOW, of Oak Estate; *b* there 3 March 1720; *m* 6 April 1744 Mary Bolton (*b* 15 March 1723), and had, with other issue:

JOHN BARLOW, of Oak Estate; *b* 21 May 1748; *m* 22 Feb 1786 Elizabeth Beely (*d* 9 Oct 1821), and *d* 27 Sept 1818, having had, with an er son (Henry, *b* 8, *d* 17 Jan 1787):

JOHN BARLOW, of The Oak, Chorley; *b* 28 April 1789; *m* 5 May 1812 Deborah (*d* 19 Nov 1850), dau of Ralph Neild, of The Rileys, Chorley, and *d* 14 Sept 1846, leaving, with other issue:

1 John, of Edinburgh; *b* 20 Sept 1815; *m* 1 Jan 1851 Eliza (*d* 18 March 1894), dau of Thomas Nicholson, and *d* 29 Jan 1856, leaving issue:

(1) Alfred; *b* 14 Oct 1851; *d* young

(2) John Henry; *b* 13 Sept 1855; *m* 17 July 1895 Mabel (*d* 24 April 1956), dau of Frederick Goodall Cash, and *d* 8 Aug 1924, leaving issue:

1a *John Cash; *b* 10 Dec 1901; *m* 26 June 1926 Enid, dau of Walter Priestman, of Edgbaston, Birmingham, and has issue:

1b *John Roger; *b* 19 Aug 1930; *m* 3 Aug 1963 *Mary, dau of Clarence Biddle, of 25 Elmfield Road, Castle Bromwich, and has issue:

1c *Annabel; *b* 7 July 1963

2a *Frederick Ralph; *b* 9 July 1910; *m* 17 Sept 1936 *Joan Mary, dau of William Barber, and has issue:

1b *David John, Dip Ed, Dip ESL, BBC Hindi, Tamil and Bengali Programme Organiser; *b* 20 Oct 1937; *educ* Oxford (MA); *m* 20 Aug 1958 *Jill, dau of Charles Frank Roberts, of London, and adopted:

*John Henry Patrick; *b* 5 Nov 1965

*Andrew (*b* Bryan Timothy); *b* 22 April 1966

2b *Anthony Ralph, Gen Manager Roy Acad of Dancing, Head Press and Publicity London Festival Ballet; *b* 19 Jan 1941; *educ* Manchester U (BA)

3b *Stephen Hugh; *b* 22 Nov 1945

4b *Nicholas Philip; *b* 24 Aug 1958

1b *Rosemary Joan; *b* 17 March 1947

1a *Mary Millior; *b* 13 July 1904; *m* 25 March 1939 *Alfred William Braithwaite, and has issue:

1b *Anna Millior; *b* 18 Oct 1942

2b *Caroline May; *b* 3 June 1948

2a Phyllis Deborah; *b* 15 May 1907; *d* 9 June 1909

(1) Mary Eliza; *b* 22 Sept 1853; *d* unm 14 Feb 1899

2 THOMAS of whom presently

JOHN BARLOW's yr son,

THOMAS BARLOW, of Bradwall Hall, Sandbach and of Torkington Lodge, Hazel Grove, Cheshire, and Bryn Eiras, Colwyn Bay, N Wales, Lord of The Manor of Bradwall, JP Cheshire; *b* 1 June 1825; *m* 9 Aug 1855 Mary Ann (*d* 25 Oct 1905), dau of George Emmott, CE, of Wood Bank, Disley, Cheshire, and *d* 23 Dec 1897, having had issue:

1 JOHN EMMOTT (Sir), **1st Bt**

2 Frank, of Woodville, Marple, nr Stockport, Cheshire JP and CA Cheshire, chm Mersey and Irwell Joint Ctee 1913–28; *b* 26 March 1859; *m* 8 March 1883 Mary (*d* 4 Aug 1941), est dau of Thomas Carver, JP, of The Hollins, Marple, and *d* 30 Sept 1929, leaving issue:

(1) Frank Russell; *b* 18 Dec 1883; *d* 10 Dec 1886

(2) Harold Carver, Lt 20th Lancs Fus, attached RAF; *b* 29 Aug 1891; *ka* 18 July 1917

(1) Eveleen Mary; *b* 18 Jan 1885; JP (1922) Cheshire; *m* 17 July 1934 Roger Pilkington Young, only surv son of Col Thomas Pilkington Young

(2) Alice; *b* 9 May; *d* 22 Aug 1886

(3) Jessie Marjory; *b* 4 Aug 1887; *m* 14 May 1914 Reginald Hollington (*d* 2 July 1947), 2nd son of Alfred Jordan Hollington, DL, JP, of Enfield, Middlesex and had issue

(4) Hilda Ethel; *b* 22 June 1889; *m* 16 Feb 1926 Christian Frederick Budenberg, MC, est son of C F Budenberg, of Somerville, Marple

(5) May; *b* 8 May 1896; *m* William Morris

(6) Frances Winifred; *b* 11 Aug 1897

3 Lionel, of Prior's Court, Newbury, Berks, barrister Inner Temple; *b* 18 July 1864; *educ* Cambridge (MA); *m* 8 May 1889 Margaret Alice (*d* 1919), yst dau of William Shuter, and *dsp* 31 Oct 1901

4 Percy, of Torkington House, Acton, London W3 and of Morden House, Littlestone, Kent, MP Bedford 1906–10, MA Cambridge, JP Middx, dep chm Willesden Div Petty Sessions 1921, Sheriff of Middx 1927, barrister Inner Temple 1892; *b* 11 July 1867; *m* 12 April 1892 Clara Frances (*d* 12 March 1940), est dau of William Staple Lee Midelton, of Somerset, and *d* 18 June 1931, leaving issue:

(1) Christopher Neild, Capt KRRC WW I; *b* 25 Nov 1893; *educ* Charterhouse, and Pembroke Coll Cambridge (BA); *m* 29 Jan 1920 Hon Dorothy Emmott, of Milcombe House, nr Banbury, Oxon, yr dau of 1st and last Baron Emmott (*see* 1926 edn), and *d* 10 March 1964, leaving issue:

1a *Christopher Edward Emmott, served Roy Signals WW II; *b* 26 Aug 1922; *educ* Eton; *m* 27 March 1957 *Marea, er dau of Eric Hughes, of Balwyn, Melbourne, Australia, and adopted:

*David Michael; *b* 20 Dec 1960

*Anne Louise; *b* 15 March 1964

1a Diana Veronica Ann, SRN (1949), SCM (1951), HV (1953), RSCN (1946); *b* 9 Sept 1925; *educ* Roedean; *d* unm 1 Aug 1977

(2) Sydney Ralph Midelton, Lt KRRC and Capt RGA WW I, WW II CD; *b* 4 July 1895; *educ* Charterhouse and Pembroke Coll Cambridge; *m* 5 Feb 1925 Nina Muriel, 4th dau of Rev Ewart Barter, and had issue:

1a Ralph; *b* 29, *d* 30 Nov 1926

1a *Annie Nina; *b* 20 March 1928; *m* 4 July 1949 Denis Fforde Creswell, and has issue:

1b *Ralph Denis Fforde; *b* 11 Nov 1954; *educ* Bradfield

2b *Robin Bruce Barlow; *b* 10 Feb 1960

3b *Paul Denby Thomas; *b* 23 July 1961

1b *Kathleen Nina; *b* 5 Sept 1950

2a *Betty Midelton; *b* 8 Aug 1930; *m* 3 April 1954 *Nicholas Lister Villiers, er son of Cdr Thomas Hyde Villiers, RN (ret), and has issue (*see* CLARENDON, E)

3a *Iris Patricia; *b* 27 July 1933

(1) Frances Ida Marguerite; *b* 23 Jan 1897; *m* 19 March 1923 Charles Burton Philips (*d* 4 April 1968)

(2) Helen Beatrice Beryl; *b* 18 July 1899; *m* 19 Sept 1922 Maj-Gen Edmund Charles Beard, CB, CBE, MC, yr son of Charles Thomas Beard, CB, and *d* 18 Feb 1968, leaving issue

THOMAS BARLOW's est son,

Sir Emmott Barlow, 1st Bt (UK), so *cr* 20 July 1907, JP (Cheshire and Somerset); CA Cheshire, MP (Lib) Frome 1892–95 and 1896–1918, barrister Inner Temple, sr ptnr Thomas Barlow and Bro of Manchester and London and Barlow and Co of Calcutta, Shanghai, Singapore and Kuala Lumpur (FMS); *b* 16 April 1857; *m* 13 July 1895 Hon Anna Maria Heywood (*d* 28 May 1965 aged 91), sis of 3rd Baron Denman (*qv*), and had issue:

1 JOHN DENMAN (Sir), **2nd Bt**

2 Thomas Bradwall; *b* 7 March 1900; *m* 8 July 1943 Elizabeth Margaret (*d* 1988), dau of Hon Bertrand George Sackville-West (*see* SACKVILLE, B), and *d* 1988, leaving issue:

(1) +Henry Sackville, OBE (1989) [Henry Barlow OBE, PO Box 10139, 50704 Kuala Lumpur, Malaysia]; *b* 4 July 1944; *educ* Eton and Trin Coll Cambridge (MA); FCA

(1) *Anna Elizabeth [Miss Anna Barlow, Thornby House, Northampton]; *b* 5 Jan 1949

1 Nancy Mary Emmott; *b* 14 May 1896; *m* 4 July 1917 Capt Francis Leopold Faure Deneys, OBE, JP, late Leinster Regt (*d* 31 May 1959), and *d* 29 March 1957 leaving issue

2 (Anna) Elizabeth *b* 20 Sept 1905; *m* 12 Nov 1930 Humphrey Bache Christopher DAVIE later DAVIE-THORNHILL (roy licence April 1959), er son of Col Bertie George Davie and Mrs Flora Helen Frances Davie-Thornhill, of Stanton, Matlock, Derbyshire, and *d* 21 April 1976, leaving issue:

(1) *Nicholas Bache Barlow [Nicholas Davie-Thornhill, Stanton Hall, Matlock, Derbys]; *b* 3 Sept 1936 (*divorce* 1991); *educ* Eton and Merton Coll Oxford; *m* 6 March 1965 (*divorce* 1991) Diana Mary, only dau of Sir William Francis Barber, 2nd Bt, TD, JP (*qv*), and has:

1a *John Philip Bache; *b* 27 Jan 1966

2a *Adrian George Barber; *b* 12 June 1968

(2) *Michael William John DAVIE, MB, BCh; *b* 13 Oct 1943; *educ* Eton and Trin Hall Cambridge

(1) *Bettine Eva Frances; *b* 20 April 1933; *m* 30 April 1955 *David Francis Ferrand, TD, 2nd son of Lt-Col Stafford Hubert Ferrand, DSO, MC, of Howden Lodge, Spennithorne, Leyburn, Yorks, and has:

1a *Richard Davie; *b* 5 June 1956

2a *Thomas David; *b* 15 Oct 1966

1a *Flora Elizabeth Francis; *b* 10 Nov 1959

Sir EMMOTT *d* 17 Sept 1932; his er son,

Sir John Denman Barlow, 2nd Bt, JP (Cheshire 1935); MP (C) Eddisbury 1945–50 and Middleton and Prestwich 1951–66, chm C Trade and Industry Ctee H of C, ptnr Thomas Barlow and Bro of Manchester and London, dir Manchester Chamber of Commerce, Barclays Bank Ltd and Calico Printers Assoc, chm Blantyre Tea Holdings 1974; *b* 27 June 1898; *m* 27 June 1928 Hon Diana Helen Kemp (*d* 1986), yr dau of 1st Baron Rochdale (*see* ROCHDALE, V), and *d* 1986, leaving:

1 Sir JOHN KEMP BARLOW, **3rd and present Bt**

2 +George Bradwall [George Barlow Esq, Robin's Cob, Henbury, Macclesfield, Cheshire]; *b* 11 Jan 1938; *educ* Radley; *m* 21 Oct 1967 *Daphne Anne, er dau of Henry Read Birtwistle, of Great Dudland, Sawley, Clitheroe, Lancs, and has:

(1) +Jeremy George Reed; *b* 18 Dec 1968

(2) +Edward Bradwall; *b* 1972

(1) *Deborah Jane Kemp; *b* 1970

3 +Mark Henry Denman [Mark Barlow Esq, Waldridge Manor, Stockwell Lane, Meadle, Aylesbury, Bucks]; *b* 11 Jan 1938 (twin); *educ* Radley; *m* 17 May 1968 *Rosemary Alexandra, yst dau of John Alan Bell, of Anglesey, and has:

(1) +Andrew Mark Egerton; *b* 1972

(1) *Camilla Frances; *b* 29 Sept 1970

1 *Jennifer Beatrice; *b* 12 Feb 1932; has:

(1) *Sacha Jane Anna [Ms Jennifer Barlow, Flat 3, 9 Kensington Park Gardens, London W11]; *b* 1971; *educ* Yehudi Menuhin Sch and USC Los Angeles

BARLOW of Fort William

Arms: Arg. on a chevron engrailed gu., between three cross-crosslets fitchée az., two lions passant-counter-passant, supporting an eastern crown or; in the centre chief point a branch of olive and another of palm in saltire ppr. **Crest:** Issuing out of an eastern crown or a demi-lion arg., the paws supporting a cross-crosslet fitchée az. between (dexter) a branch of olive and (sinister) another of palm, ppr. **Supporters:** On either side an angel ppr., vested arg., zoned and on the head an eastern crown or, the dexter holding in the exterior hand a balance gold and in the other a book ppr., the sinister bearing in the exterior hand an olive branch and in the other an escroll ppr. **Motto:** *Sis plus in primis* ('May you be more than those who came before you'), (over the crest) *Dilige pacem* ('Choose peace'). **Creation:** Bt. (UK) 29 June 1803.

SIR CHRISTOPHER HILARO BARLOW, 7TH BT, of Fort William, Bengal [Sir Christopher Barlow Bt, 18 Winter Avenue, St John's, NF A1A 1T3, Canada]; *b* 1 Dec 1929; *s* f 1946; *educ* Eton and McGill U (BArch); MRAIC; past pres Newfoundland Architects Assn; *m* 17 May 1952 *Jacqueline Claire de Marigny, er dau of John Edmund Audley, of Chester, and has had issue:

1 Crispin Richard Audley; *b* 15 Sept, *d* 29 Oct 1956

2 +CRISPIAN JOHN EDMUND AUDLEY [Crispian Barlow Esq, 22 Milford Rd, Plumstead, Cape Town, S Africa]; *b* 20 April 1958; Inspr Hong Kong Police; *m* 1981 *Anne Wai Ching Siu and has issue:

(1) *Jennifer Claire Audley; *b* 1990

1 *Persephone Claire [Mrs Robert Booth, The Timbers, Church Rd, Kettleburgh, Woodbridge, Suffolk IP13 7LE]; *b* 11 Dec 1953; *m* 1975 *Robert Eric Booth, and has issue:

(1) *Katherine Claire; *b* 1982

(2) *Sophie Elizabeth Barlow; *b* 1986

2 *Caroline Claire [Mrs James Jordan, 11813 Silent Valley Lane, Gaithersburgh, MD, USA]; *b* 26 Jan 1960; *m* 1986 *James Cass Jordan

Lineage: WILLIAM BARLOW, of S Audley Street, London (s of Hugh Barlow, of Forbridge, Staffs); *bapt* 8 Jan 1682; *m* Elizabeth (*d* May 1741), dau of William Ford, and *d* 30 Sept 1743, leaving, with other issue:

WILLIAM BARLOW, of Bath; *m* 17 Feb 1757 Hilare (*d* 18 Feb 1774), dau of Robert Butcher, of Walthamstow, Essex, and *d* 29 May 1798, having had, with other issue:

1 Robert (Sir), Adml, GCB; *b* 25 Dec 1757; *m* 8 Sept 1785 Elizabeth, dau of William Garrett, of Worthing House, Hants, and *d* 11 May 1843, leaving, with other issue:

(1) Robert, Bengal CS; *b* 26 Dec 1788; *m* 17 April 1813 Catherine (*d* 25 Aug 1861), dau of William Wilberforce Bird, MP, and *d* 18 March 1845, leaving issue

(2) William (Rev), Canon Chester, Col Madras Cav; *b* 4 Dec 1789; *m* 1st Louisa (*d* 7 May 1837), dau of Robert Jones Adeane, of Babraham, Cambridge, and had issue; *m* 2nd 27 July 1846 Anne (*dsp* 23 July 1878), dau of Rev Frederick Hotham (*see* HOTHAM, B), and *d* 8 Dec 1848

(2) Hilare; *m* 1st 27 Feb 1817 her cousin Capt George Ulric Barlow, 69th Foot (*dsp* 29 June 1824; *see* below); *m* 2nd 26 March 1829 1st Earl Nelson (*qv*); *m* 3rd 7 Feb 1837 George Thomas Knight (*d* 1867), and *dsp* 22 Dec 1857

2 Thomas William (Rev), Preb Bristol, Vicar Halberton; *b* 12 Oct 1760; *m* 12 Jan 1798 Frances (*d* May 1838), dau of John Bockett, of S Mimms, Middx, and *d* 18 Jan 1821, leaving issue

3 **Sir George Hilaro Barlow 1st Bt** (UK), so *cr* 29 June 1803, GCB (KCB 1806); *b* 20 Jan 1763; joined HEIC CS 1778, Sub-Sec to Supreme Govt Revenue Depart 1788, Sec 1796, memb Cncl Bengal 1801 and April 1802, Provisional Govr-Gen India 1805–07, Govr Madras 1807–13; *m* 16 April 1789 (*divorce* 30 April 1816) Elizabeth, dau of Burton Smith, of Co Westmeath, and *d* 18 Dec 1846, having had, with other issue:

(1) **Sir Robert Barlow, 2nd Bt**; joined HEIC CS 1817, Judge Native Supreme Court Calcutta; *b* 24 Sept 1797; *m* 27 Sept 1832 Augusta Louisa (*d* 19 Nov 1836), 3rd dau of Maj-Gen — Seymour, RA, Govr St Lucia, and *d* Jan 1857, leaving issue:

1a **Sir Morison Barlow, 3rd Bt**; Capt 7th Hus and 9th Lancers Indian Mutiny (medal with clasp for Lucknow); *b* 3 Nov 1835; *d* unm 10 April 1889

(2) Richard Wellesley, Bengal CS; *b* 10 Sept 1804; *m* 2 March 1835 Maria (*m* 2nd 27 Feb 1843 Lt-Col Charles Henry Nicholetts, Bengal Cavalry), 2nd dau of Maj-Gen Sir William Nott, GCB, and *d* 14 April 1839, leaving issue:

1a RICHARD WELLESLEY (Sir), **4th Bt**

1a Maria Charlotte Exmouth; *m* 7 Jan 1857 William Southey Whiteside (*d* 12 Oct 1900), Madras CS, est s of Rev John W Whiteside, DD, Vicar Scarborough, and *d* 20 Oct 1927, leaving issue

The 3rd Bt's cousin,

Sir Richard Wellesley Barlow, 4th Bt, MLC and Madras CS; *b* 30 Jan 1836; *m* 14 June 1860 his sister's sis-in-law Annie Catherine (*d* 8 July 1886), dau of Rev John W Whiteside, DD, and niece of Lord Ch Justice Whiteside, and *d* 10 Aug 1904, having had, with a yr s (Ulric Richard Wellesley, *b* Aug 1862, *d* an infant):

Sir Hilaro William Wellesley Barlow, 5th Bt, CB (1913), CMG (1918); Col RA, Supt Roy Laboratory Woolwich 1902–16, served Min Munitions; *b* 19 June 1861; *m* 29 July 1891 Victoria Katherine (*d* 3 May 1963 aged 95), est dau of Col Hugh Robert Hibbert, 7th Roy Fus, of Birtles Hall, Cheshire, and Broadgate, Barnstaple, and had issue:

1 RICHARD HUGH (Sir), **6th Bt**

2 Christopher Mark; WW II as S/Ldr RAFVR; *b* 14 Jan 1908; *educ* Stowe and King's Coll Cambridge (MusB 1935, MA 1938); *d* 29 June 1990

1 Annie Katherine, MA Cambridge; *d* unm 11 Aug 1964

2 *Mildred Hilare; *m* 31 July 1923 Richard John Routh, MA, and has issue:

(1) *Francis John, FRCO; *b* 15 Jan 1927; *educ* Malvern, King's Coll Cambridge (MA) and RAM; *m* 1 Sept 1956 *Virginia Chloe, yr dau of Geoffrey George Raphael, of Chilston House, Burwash, Sussex, and has issue:

1a *Simon Christopher; *b* 4 March 1958

1a *Christina Phoebe; *b* 11 July 1961

2a *Belinda Rosalind; *b* 4 April 1970

(2) *Richard Michael, BA; *b* 9 Oct 1934; *m* 18 Aug 1964 *Brenda, dau of William Parkinson, of Bolton, Lancs, and has issue:

1a *Daniel William; *b* 11 Aug 1965

2a *Christopher Benjamin; *b* March 1968

(1) *Hilary Katherine; *b* 25 Sept 1924; *m* 5 Aug 1949 *Stephen Malet Tunnicliffe, 3rd son of Rev William John Wheldale Tunnicliffe, MA, Vicar Middleton, Staffs, and has issue:

1a *Timothy Hugh; *b* 4 June 1950; *educ* Heath GS Halifax

2a *Stephen Jacob Routh; *b* 13 May 1952; *educ* Heath GS Halifax

3a *Richard John; *b* 5 June 1958

3 Ruth Beatrice; *d* unm 30 Oct 1958

Sir HILARO *d* 16 Oct 1941; his er son,

Sir Richard Hugh Barlow, 6th Bt, AFC, W/Cdr RAF WW II; *b* 30 June 1904; *m* 8 Dec 1928 *Rosamund Sylvia [Mrs Leonard Morrison, Laurel Cottage, Parracombe, Barnstaple, N Devon EX31 4QQ] (*m* 2nd 31 Jan 1950 Rev Leonard Haslett Morrison, MA (*d* 1985), barrister, only son of Lt-Col Robert Victor Morrison, IMS), yr dau of Francis Swithin Anderton, and was *k* in a plane crash near Quito, Ecuador, 3 Dec 1946, leaving issue:

1 Sir CHRISTOPHER HILARO BARLOW, **7th and present Bt**

2 +David Peter [David Barlow Esq, 1335 Franklin Terrace, Victoria, BC V8S 1C8 Canada], late Lt Gloucester Regt; *b* 8 Jan 1931; *educ* Eton and Peterhouse Cambridge; *m* 24 June 1958 *Mary June, dau of W S Emmerton, of Victoria, BC, Canada, and has issue:

(1) +Peter Stephen; *b* 28 Sept 1961

(2) +Richard Owen; *b* 7 Oct 1963; *m* 19– *Karen Varrelman and has:

1a +Alexander Hudson; *b* 5 Sept 1996

(1) *Rosemary Sylvia Mary; *b* 26 Jan 1968; *m* 19— *Christopher Thakray

3 +Anthony Donald [Anthony Barlow Esq, 4 The Grange, Evesham Rd, Cheltenham, Glos GL52 3AE]; late Lt RSAC; *b* 12 May 1935; *educ* Stowe; *m* 30 Mar 1961 (*divorce* 19–) Ginette Alice, dau of Joseph Burki, of Courrendlin, Switzerland; *m* 2nd 19– *Patricia Jennifer Bond and by her has issue:

(1) +Nicholas Hugh; *b* 1973

1 *Lucinda Mary [Mrs Edward Chubb, Blackbird Cottage, Woodside Lane, King's Stanley, Stonehouse, Glos]; *b* 22 March 1941; *m* 9 Feb 1962 *Edward James Chubb and has:

(1) *Richard John; *b* 6 Aug 1963

(2) *William Maurice; *b* 1969

BARLOW of Wimpole Street

Arms: Arg. on a pile sa. between two torches erect in base, fired ppr., an eagle displayed with two heads of the field. **Crest:** In front of a staff erect entwined by a serpent ppr. an eagle's neck erased with two heads arg., thereon a rose gu. **Motto:** *Sicut aquila juvenescam* ('I will become young as an eagle').
Creation: Bt. (UK) 7 March 1902.

SIR THOMAS ERASMUS BARLOW, 3RD BT, of Wimpole Street, London, DSC, DL (Bucks 1976) [Sir Thomas Barlow Bt DSC DL, 45 Shepherds Hill, London N6 5QJ]; *b* 23 Jan 1914; s f 1968; *educ* Winchester; served RN 1932–64, Capt 1954, CSO to Flag Offr Submarines 1960–62, Cdre HMS *Drake* Devonport 1962–64; *m* 9 July 1955 *Isabel, yst dau of Thomas Munn Body, MRCS, LRCP, DL, JP, of Middlesbrough, Yorks, and has issue:

1 +JAMES ALAN [James Barlow Esq, 45 Shepherds Hill, London N6 5QJ]; *b* 10 July 1956; *educ* Highgate and Manchester U (BSc); metallurgist; ptnr Glassdrumman House Annalong 1984–93; maître d'hotel Galgorm Manor 1993–95, consultant North Star Ventures, Fort St John, BC, Canada 1995–

2 +Philip Thomas; *b* 31 Dec 1960; *educ* Highgate and Sheffield U (MB); *m* 25 July 1992 *Susan Jane Wilkins, dau of James Wilkins, of Letchworth, Herts, and has:

(1) +Joshua Samuel; *b* 10 May 1996

(1) *Natasha Anne; *b* 14 Oct 1993

(2) *Katie Emma; *b* 9 June 1995

1 *Monica Anne; *b* 7 March 1958; *educ* St Mary's Bushey and Bristol U (MA, PhD)

2 *Teresa Mary; *b* 6 Oct 1963; *educ* St Mary's Bushey and York U (BSc); *m* March 1997 *Julian Scott

Lineage: THOMAS BARLOW, of Edgworth, Lancs; *bapt* 5 Jan 1788; *m* 9 July 1820 Maria Smith (*d* 7 May 1825), of Tottington, Lancs, and *d* 23 Nov 1849, leaving, with other issue:

JAMES BARLOW, of Greenthorne, Edgworth, JP; *b* 23 April 1821; *m* 29 July 1843 Alice (*d* 22 Sept 1888), dau of James Barnes, of Edgworth, and *d* 16 Aug 1887, leaving issue:

1 THOMAS (Sir), **1st Bt**

2 John Robert, of Greenthorne, JP, MA; *b* 7 March 1852; *d* 16 July 1923

1 Maria; *m* 14 April 1891 Frank Ainsworth (*d* 22 July 1898), of Lostock, Lancs, and *d* 1937, leaving issue

2 Alice; MA Cantab; *d* 31 Oct 1919

3 Annie Elizabeth Finney; *d* unm 1942

JAMES BARLOW's est son,

Sir Thomas Barlow, 1st Bt (UK), so *cr* 7 March 1902, KCVO (1901), FRCP, FRS, MD Lond, BSc Lond, Consulting Physician to U Coll Hosp and Hosp for Sick Children Gt Ormond St, Emeritus Prof Clinical Medicine U Coll Lond, Hon LLD Aberdeen, St Andrews, Harvard, McGill, Toronto and Edin, Hon DCL Durham, Hon DSc Victoria U Manchester and Lond, Hon MD Christiania and Dublin, Fell U Coll Lond, Physician Roy Household 1896–1901, Physician Extrdy to TM QUEEN VICTORIA 1899–1901, EDWARD VII 1901–07 and GEORGE V 1910–36, PRCP 1910–15, Pres Internat Congress Medicine 1913; *b* 4 Sept 1845; *m* 28 Dec 1880 Ada Helen (*d* 1 Dec 1928), dau of Patrick Dalmahoy, WS, of Edinburgh, and had issue:

1 JAMES ALAN NOEL (Sir), **2nd Bt**

2 Thomas Dalmahoy (Sir), GBE (1946, KBE 1934), Dir-Gen Civilian Clothing, memb Industl and Export Cncl 1941–45, Pres Jt Ctee Cotton Trade Orgnsns and Manchester Chamber Commerce, chm Barlow and Jones Ltd Manchester and District Bank; *b* 23 Feb 1883; *educ* Marlborough and Trin Coll Cambridge (BA 1904, MA 1909); *m* 15 Feb 1911 Esther Sophia, JP Manchester (*d* 24 March 1956), yr dau of Henry Gaselee, of Linden Gdns, Bayswater, and *d* 22 Nov 1964, leaving issue:

(1) Basil Stephen, chm Man-Abell Hldgs; *b* 15 Feb 1918; *educ* Marlborough and Trin Coll Cambridge (MA); *m* 1st 17 Aug 1940 (*divorce* 1950) Harriette, yst dau of His Honour Judge (Robert) Peel, OBE, KC, of Knowlmere Manor, Clitheroe (*see* 1956 edn WORSLEY-TAYLOR, Bt); *m* 2nd 15 April 1950 *Gerda Theresia [Mrs Basil Barlow, Stancombe Park, Dursley, Glos GL11 6AU], dau of Prof Dr Zaar Ferrari de Grado, of Graz, Austria, and *d* 1991, having by her had:

1a +Nicholas Dalmahoy; *b* 18 May 1951; *educ* Eton

1a *Maria Theresa; *b* 25 July 1953; *m* 1977 (*divorce* 1996) Martin William Llewellyn

2a *(Esther) Alexandra; *b* 31 Aug 1956

(1) *Theodora Gertrude [Mrs Theodora Winter, Flat 76, Hurlingham Court, Ranelagh Gdns, London SW6]; *b* 21 Feb 1912; *m* 10 Dec 1936 (*divorce* 1953) Carl Winter (*d* 21 May 1966), son of Carl Friedrich Adolf Winter, of Melbourne, Australia, and has issue:

1a *Robert Stephen; *b* 22 May 1939; *m* 17 Dec 1966 *Nicola Anne, 3rd dau of A/Cdre R C Mead, CBE, DFC, AFC, of Rottingdean, Sussex

2a *John Barlow; *b* 13 March 1944; *m* *Alison Mary, 3rd dau of Alexander Robson Bruce, CMG, OBE, of Highgate

1a *Caroline Helen; *b* 28 May 1942

(2) Penelope Sophia, MA, JP; *b* 10 April 1914; *m* 14 Aug 1943 *Raymond William Baldwin, and *d* 1995, having had:

1a *Thomas Raymond; *b* 10 April 1947; *educ* Winchester and Trin Coll Cambridge

1a Alice Margaret; *b* 9 July 1944; *m* 27 July 1968 *Rev Andrew Talbot-Ponsonby and *d* 1989, leaving issue (*see* SHREWSBURY and WATERFORD, E)

2a *Rosalind Penelope; *b* 26 Sept 1949

3 Patrick Basil, MA Oxford, Private Gren Gds WW I; *b* 23 Oct 1884; *d* 18 Jan 1917 from injuries incurred on active service

1 Helen Alice Dorothy; *b* 4 May 1887; *d* unm 16 Sept 1975

2 Gertrude Mary; *b* Aug 1888; *d* 22 July 1889

Sir THOMAS *d* 12 Jan 1945; his est son,

Sir (James) Alan (Noel) Barlow, 2nd Bt, GCB (1947), KBE (1938), JP Bucks; *b* 25 Dec 1881; MA Oxon, Hon Fell Corpus Christi Coll Oxford, Hon LLD Glasgow, FSA; Pncpl Priv Sec to PM 1933–34, Under-Sec Treasury 1934–39, 3rd Sec 1939, Jt 2nd Sec 1942, chm Nat Gallery 1948–55, pres Oriental Ceramic Soc and Bucks Archaeological Soc, gave his collections of Persian Pottery to the Ashmolean 1953 and Chinese Porcelain to U of Sussex 1967; *m* 6 April 1911 Emma Nora (*d* 1989), yr dau of Sir Horace Darwin, KBE, FRS, of Cambridge, and *d* 28 Feb 1968, leaving issue:

1 Sir THOMAS ERASMUS BARLOW, **3rd and present Bt**

2 +Erasmus Darwin [Erasmus Barlow Esq, Elbrook House, Ashwell, Baldock, Herts], MRCS Eng and LRCP Lond 1940, DPM 1951, FRCPsych, Sr Lecturer Psychological Medicine and Hon Consultant Physician St Thomas's Hosp, chm Cambridge Instrument Co Ltd, dep chm George Kent Ltd, dir Gp Investors Ltd and Gillett & Sibert Ltd, dir CIC Investment Hldgs, chm Bath Inst of Med Engrg 1975, v-chm Mental Health Research Fund; *b* 15 April 1915; *educ* Marlborough and Trin Coll Cambridge (MA, MB, BCh 1941); *m* 9 July 1938 *Brigit Ursula Hope, dau of Ladbroke Black, of Whitefields, Gt Missenden, Bucks, and has issue:

(1) +(Thomas) Jeremy Erasmus [Jeremy Barlow Esq, 20 Leverton St, London NW5 2PJ]; *b* 25 July 1939; *educ* Westminster, RCM, Trin Coll Cambridge (BA) and RAM, MA, ARCM, ARAM; *m* 11 Aug 1962 (*divorce* 1994) Jane Marian, dau of Bernard Hollowood, of Blackmoor Paddock, Shamley Green, Surrey, and has:

1a +Josiah Bernard; *b* 1973

(1) (cont.) Mr and Mrs Thomas Barlow also adopted:

*Mark Thomas Duncan; *b* 4 June 1967

*Thomas Daniel; *b* 1972

* Susan Marian Deborah; *b* 1970

(1) *Camilla Ruth; *b* 2 June 1942; *m* 1st 22 May 1965 (*divorce* 1973) Martin Christopher Mitcheson, MB, BChir, DPM, only son of Dr Victor Steele Mitcheson, of Hythe, Kent, and has issue:

1a *Luke Thomas Patrick; *b* 17 March 1966

1a *Amy Brigit; *b* 18 May 1967

(1) (cont.) Mrs Camilla Mitcheson *m* 2nd 1974 *Anthony Whitworth-Jones, and has issue:

2a *Eleanor Gwen; *b* 1975

(2) *Gillian Phyllida [Mrs Fabian Peake, 1 Woodstock Rd, London NW]; *b* 4 April 1944; *m* 23 July 1966 *Fabian Benedict Peake, yr son of Mervyn Peake, writer and artist, and has issue:

1a *Edward; *b* 1981

2a *Lewis; *b* 1981

1a *Florence; *b* 1973

2a *Clover; *b* 1975

3a *Tabitha; *b* 1978

3 +Andrew Dalmahoy, MRCP Lond 1944 [Andrew Barlow Esq, 10 Wimpole St, London W1M 7AB]; paediatrician W Middx Hosp 1953; *b* 16 Sept 1916; *educ* Eastbourne Coll and Trin Coll Cambridge (BA 1938, MA, MB, BChir), *m* 13 Nov 1951 *Yvonne Rosalind, dau of Walter Tanner, and has issue:

1a +Martin Thomas; *b* 16 June 1953; *educ* St Paul's

1a *Clare Yvonne; *b* 24 Sept 1954

4 +Horace Basil, FRS (1969), Prof Physiology Berkeley California 1964–73, Fell Trin Coll Cambridge 1950–54 and King's Coll Cambridge 1954–64, Prof Physiology Cambridge; *b* 8 Dec 1921; *educ* Winchester, Trin Coll Cambridge (MB, BCh 1947) and Harvard (MD); *m* 22 Dec 1954 (*divorce* 1970) Ruth Chattie, yst dau of Myer Head Salaman, MD, of 21 Argyll Road, London W8, and has issue:

(1) *Rebecca Nora; *b* 12 May 1956

(2) *Natasha Helen; *b* 29 Jan 1958

(3) *Naomi Jane; *b* 25 March 1963

(4) *Emily Anne; *b* 25 March 1967

4 (cont.) Horace Barlow *m* 2nd 1980 *Elisabeth Miranda, dau of J Weston Smith, of Hampstead, and has further issue:

(1) +Oscar Hugh; *b* 1986

(5) *Ida Lucy; *b* 1988

(6) *Pepita Elisabeth; *b* 1990

1 Joan Helen; *b* 26 May 1912; *d* unm 21 Feb 1954

2 *Hilda Horatia [Mrs John Padel, 16 Staverton Road, Oxford OX2 6XJ]; *b* 14 Sept 1919; *m* 27 Dec 1944 *John Hunter Padel, BA, MB, BS, DPM, and has issue:

(1) *Oliver James; *b* 31 Oct 1948; *educ* U Coll Sch

(2) *Felix John; *b* 9 Nov 1955; *educ* U Coll Sch

(3) *Adam Frederick; *b* 9 Nov 1958

(1) *Ruth Sophia; *b* 8 May 1946

(2) *Nicola Mary; *b* 3 Oct 1951

BARNARD

Arms: Azure, three sinister gauntlets or. **Crest:** A dexter hand in armour couped at the wrist proper holding a sword argent, pommel and hilt or. **Supporters:** Dexter, a griffin argent plain collared azure thereon three sinister gauntlets or; sinister, an antelope or, plain collared azure, thereon three martlets gold. **Motto:** *Nec temere nec timide* ('Neither rashly nor timidly'). **Creation:** B. (E) 25 July 1698.

THE 11TH BARON BARNARD OF BARNARD'S CASTLE in the Bishopric of Durham ((Harry) John Neville Vane, TD (1960), JP (Co Durham 1961)) [The Rt Hon The Lord Barnard TD JP, Raby Castle, PO Box 50, Staindrop, Co Durham DL2 3AY]; *b* 21 Sept 1923; *s* f 1964; *educ* Eton and Durham U (MSc); served RAFVR 1942–47 (F/O 1945), Lt Northumberland Hus (TA) 1948, Lt-Col cmdg Northumberland Hus 1964–66, Hon Col 7th (Durham) Bn LI 1979–89, Co Durham: Ld-Lt and Custos Rotulorum 1970–88 (DL 1956–70), CC 1952–61, Jt MFH Zetland 1963–65, Pres Durham Co Branch BRCS 1969–87 (Patron 1993), V-Chm Cncl BRCS 1987–93 (memb cncl 1982–85), Pres N of England TAVR Assoc 1974–77, KStJ; *m* 8 Oct 1952 (*divorce* 1992) Lady Davina Mary Cecil, est dau of 6th Marquess of Exeter (*qv*), and has issue:

1 +HENRY FRANCIS CECIL [The Hon Henry Vane, The Old Lodge, Staindrop, Darlington DL2 3LN]; *b* 11 March 1959 (HRH THE DUCHESS OF GLOUCESTER stood sponsor); *educ* Eton, Edinburgh U (Bsc) and Durham U (MBA)

1 *Carolyn Mary; *b* 5 May 1954; has issue:

(1) *Nicola Lauren; *b* 1988

2 *Elizabeth Anne; *b* 17 May 1956; *m* 1982 *Glyn M Deacon, er s of A Deacon, and has issue:

(1) *Jessica Anne; *b* 1982

(2) *Laura Sophie; *b* 1984

3 *Sophia Rosalind; *b* 24 Jan 1962; *educ* Cobham Hall and Westfield Coll London U (BSc); *m* 1986 *Simon B Phillips, yst s of Peter J Phillips, of Gustard Wood, Wheathampstead, Herts, and has issue:

(1) *Oliver John; *b* 1989

(2) *Benjamin James; *b* 1994

(1) *Emily Josephine; *b* 1992

4 *Louise Cicely; *b* 30 May 1968; *educ* Cobham Hall and St Martins' Sch of Art and Design (BA)

Lineage: JOHN VANE or FANE, of Tonbridge, Kent (*see* WESTMORLAND, E), had a 4th and yst s:

JOHN FANE, of Hadlow, Kent; *m* Joan, dau and coheir of Sir Edward Haute, and *d* before 1553/4, leaving issue:

HENRY FANE, of Hadlow Place, Kent; Ld of Manors of Hadlow and Shipbourne (*s* his cousin Sir Ralph Fane 1553); took part in Sir Thomas Wyatt's insurrection 1553, committed to the Tower and attainted but pardoned, MP Winchelsea; *m* Elizabeth, dau of Henry White, of Christchurch, Hants, and widow of Sir John Godsalve, and *d* 11 June 1580, leaving issue:

HENRY FANE, of Hadlow; *b c* 1560; *m* 1st 1578 his cousin Mary (*dsp*), sole dau and heir of Thomas Fane, of Burston; *m* 2nd 1584 Margaret, dau of Roger Twysden, of E Peckham, Kent, and *d* 1596 at Rouen in command of English forces sent to assist HENRY IV of France, and by his 2nd w had issue, with three daus and two yr s (Sir Ralph and Charles):

Sir HENRY FANE later VANE, the Elder, PC (1630); *b* 18 Feb 1589; *educ* Brasenose Coll Oxford and Gray's Inn; adopted the alternative version of the family name, sold Hadlow and bought Fairlawn, Kent, where he and his descendants principally lived for the next century, also Raby Castle, Co Durham (*see* ABERGAVENNY, M), ktd 1611, MP Lostwithiel 1614, Carlisle 1621–26, Retford 1628, Wilton 1640 (Short and Long Parls) and Kent 1653; Amb to GUSTAVUS ADOLPHUS KING OF SWEDEN 1631, Commr Admlty 1632 and Colonies 1636, Comptroller 1629 and Treasurer 1639 Household, Sec of State 1640–41 (dismissed all his roy posts 1641, whereupon he threw in his lot with Parl), took an active part in the prosecution of the Earl of Strafford, against whom he was allegedly biased because the latter was *cr* Baron Raby of Raby Castle, a title Sir Henry coveted himself as Raby's owner; *m* 1612 Frances (*d* 2 Aug 1663), dau and coheir of Thomas D'Arcy, of Tolleshunt Darcy, Essex (descended from Guicciardini, the noble Florentine historian), and *d* 1654, leaving with other issue:

1 HENRY (Sir)

2 George (Sir), of Long Newton, Durham; ktd 22 Nov 1640; *m* Elizabeth, dau of Sir Lionel Maddison, of Rogerley and Newcastle-upon-Tyne, and had issue; ancestor of the Vane Bts of Hutton Hall, Cumberland (*see* LONDONDERRY, M)

3 John VANE; *bur* 19 Oct 1618

4 Sir Walter VANE; *bapt* 6 Oct 1619; DCL Oxford, Col Holland Regt afterwards 3rd Foot (Buffs); *bur* 1676 at The Hague, having been mortally wounded at Battle of Senaffe

1 Anne; *m* Sir Thomas Liddell, 2nd Bt (see RAVENSWORTH, B), and had issue

Sir HENRY VANE'S est s,

Sir HENRY VANE the Younger, of Raby Castle and Fairlawn, Kent; *bapt* 26 May 1613; *educ* Westminster and Magdalen Hall Oxford; attached to embassies at Vienna, Leiden and Geneva, ktd 23 June 1640, as an enthuisiastic Puritan emigrated to Massachusetts so he could practise his faith freely (Govr 1636–37), Jt-Treas Navy 1639, MP Hull Short and Long Parls also Whitchurch 1658, lighted on the crucial papers among his f's documents which brought about Strafford's downfall, led the impeachment of Archbp Laud, Parly Commr (twice), leading Parliamentarian in Civil War but never endorsed CHARLES I's execution, Memb Cncl of State 1649, Ch Commr Navy during Commonwealth and Protectorate and was chiefly responsible for streamlined administrative measures that led to the defeat of Van Tromp in the Dutch Wars, fell out with CROMWELL over proposals to widen the franchise (he being pro, but Cromwell favouring a more militaristic arrangement for ordering Parl), imprisoned in Carisbrooke Castle Sept–31 Dec 1656 on suspicion of encouraging Anabaptists and other subversive movementsthroughout the Protectorate. At the Restoration Vane was arrested, but though CHARLES II pardoned him the ultra Parl of 1661 voted for his execution and he was beheaded on Tower Hill 14 June 1662; *m* 1 July 1640 Frances, dau of Sir Christopher Wray, Bt, of Glentworth and Ashby, Lincs, and had, with other issue:

CHRISTOPHER VANE, **1st Baron Barnard of Barnard's Castle** in the Bishopric of Durham (E), so *cr* 25 July 1698, PC (1688); *bapt* 21 May 1653; MP (Whig) Co Durham 1675–79; *m* (licence 9 May 1676) Elizabeth Holles (*d* 9 Nov 1725), est dau of 3rd Earl of Clare of the 1624 *cr*, and sis of 1st Duke of Newcastle of the 1694 *cr*, and *d* 28 Oct 1723, having had, with other issue:

1 Henry; *b* and *d* 1676

2 GILBERT, **2nd Baron**

3 WILLIAM VANE, 1st VISCOUNT VANE, so *cr* 13 Sept 1720, as also BARON VANE OF DUNGANNON, Co Tyrone (both I); *b c* 1680; MP: (Whig) Co Durham 1708–10, Kent 1715–22 and 1734, Steyning 1727–34; *m* (settlement 15 Nov 1703) Lucy (*d* 27 March 1742), 2nd dau of William Jolliffe, of Caverswell Castle, Staffs, by Lady Mary Hastings, dau of 6th Earl of Huntingdon (*qv*), and *d* 20 May 1734, having had issue:

(1) Christopher; *b* 1704; *educ* King's Coll Cambridge; *dvp* unm 19 July 1721

(2) John; *b* 1707; *dvp* unm 5 Feb 1723/4

(3) WILLIAM HOLLES VANE, 2nd VISCOUNT VANE; *b* 4 Feb 1713/4; *educ* Ch Ch Oxford; *m* 19 May 1735 Frances (*d* 31 March 1788), dau of Francis Hawes, of Purley Hall, Berks, Dir South Sea Co, and widow of Lord William Hamilton (*dsp* 11 July 1734), 2nd s of 4th Duke of Hamilton and (1st Duke of) Brandon (*qv*), and *dsp* 5 April 1789, when his titles expired

The 1st BARON BARNARD's 2nd s,

GILBERT VANE, **2nd Baron Barnard of Barnard's Castle**; *bapt* 17 April 1678; *m* Jan 1704 Mary (*d* 8 Aug 1728), dau and heiress of Morgan Randyll, MP, of Chilworth, and *d* 27 April 1753, having had, with other issue:

1 HENRY VANE, **3rd Baron Barnard of Barnard's Castle** and 1st EARL OF DARLINGTON, Co Durham, so *cr* 3 April 1754, as also VISCOUNT BARNARD OF BARNARD'S CASTLE (both GB) PC (1742); *b c* 1705; MP (Whig) Launceston 1726–27, St Mawes 1727–41, Ripon 1741–47 and Co Durham 1747–53, V-Treasurer and Paymaster Gen (I) 1742–44, a Ld of Treasury 1749–55, Ld-Lt Durham 1753–58, Jt Paymaster Forces 1755–56; *m* 2 Sept 1725 Lady Grace FitzRoy (*d* 29 Sept 1763), 2nd dau of 1st Duke of Cleveland and Southampton (*see* GRAFTON, D), and *d* 6 March 1758, leaving issue:

(1) HENRY VANE, **4th Baron Barnard of Barnard's Castle** and 2nd EARL OF DARLINGTON; *b* 1726; *educ* Ch Ch Oxford and Cambridge (MA 1749); Capt 1st Foot Gds 1747, Lt-Col Coldstream Gds 1750, Col 1779, MP (Whig) Downton 1749–53 and Co Durham 1753–58, Ld-Lt Co Durham 1758–92, Govr Carlisle 1763–92, Master Jewel Office 1763–82; *m* 19 March 1757 Margaret (*d* 4 Sept 1800), dau of Robert Lowther, Govr Barbados, and sis of 1st Earl of Lonsdale (*qv*), and *d* 8 Sept 1792, having had issue:

1a WILLIAM HARRY VANE, **5th Baron Barnard of Barnard's Castle**, 3rd EARL OF DARLINGTON and 1st DUKE OF CLEVELAND, so *cr* 29 Jan 1833, as also BARON RABY OF RABY CASTLE, Co DURHAM, and earlier 5 Oct 1827 MARQUESS OF CLEVELAND (all UK), KG (1839); *b* 27 July 1766; *educ* Ch Ch Oxford; MP (Whig) Totnes 1788–90, Winchelsea 1790–92, Ld-Lt and V-Adml Durham, Col Durham; *m* 1st 19 Sept 1787 Lady Katherine Margaret Powlett (*d* 17 June1807), 2nd dau and coheir of 6th and last Duke of Bolton of the 1689 *cr* (*see* WINCHESTER, M); *m* 2nd 27 July 1813 Elizabeth (*d* 31 Jan 1861 aged 84), dau of Robert Russell, market gardener, and *d* 29 Jan 1842, having had issue by his 1st w:

1b HENRY VANE, **6th Baron Barnard of Barnard's Castle** and 2nd DUKE OF CLEVELAND, KG (1842); *b* 6 Aug 1788; *educ* Ch Ch Oxford; MP Co Durham 1812–15,Winchelsea 1816–18, Tregony 1818–26 and Totnes 1826–30, Lt-Col 75th Foot 1824, Maj-Gen 1851, Lt-Gen 1857, Gen 1863 and Col Durham Militia; *m* 18 Nov 1809 Sophia (*dsp* 9 Jan 1859), est dau of 4th Earl Poulett, KT (*see* 1970 edn), and *dsp* 18 Jan 1864

2b WILLIAM JOHN FREDERICK VANE later POWLETT (roy licence 14 April 1813) later still VANE again (roy licence 4 March 1864), **7th Baron Barnard of Barnard's Castle** and 3rd DUKE OF CLEVELAND; *b* 3 April 1792; *educ* Brasenose Coll Oxford U (MA 1812); MP Winchelsea 1812–15, Co Durham 1815–31, St Ives 1846–52 and Ludlow 1852–57; *m* 3 July 1815 Caroline (*d* 31 Oct 1883 aged 91), 4th dau of 1st Earl of Lonsdale, KG (*qv*), and *dsp* 6 Sept 1864

3b HARRY GEORGE VANE later POWLETT (roy licence 18 Nov 1864), **8th Baron Barnard of Barnard's Castle** and 4th and last DUKE OF CLEVELAND, KG (1865); *b* 19 April 1803; *educ* Oriel Coll Oxford (BA 1829); attaché Paris Embassy 1829, Sec Stockholm Legation 1839–41, MP (Lib) S Durham 1841–59 and Hastings 1859–64, Hon DCL Oxford 1876 and Durham 1882; *m* 2 Aug 1854 Catherine Lucy Wilhelmina (*d* 18 May 1901), only dau of 4th Earl Stanhope (*see* 1967 edn STANHOPE, E) and widow of Archibald, Lord Dalmeny (*see* ROSEBERY, E), and *dsp* 21 Aug 1891, when all his titles expired bar the barony of Barnard

1b Louisa Catherine; *b* 4 Jan 1791; *m* 29 July 1813 Maj Francis Forester (*d* 21 Oct 1861), Roy Horse Gds (*see* FORESTER B), and *d* 8 Jan 1821, leaving issue

2b Caroline Mary; *b* 8 Feb, *d* 11 May 1795

3b Augusta Henrietta; *b* 26 Dec 1796; *m* 2 June 1817 Mark Milbank (*d* 21 Oct 1881), of Thorp Perrow and Barningham Park, Yorks (*see* MILBANK, Bt), and *d* 13 Sept 1874, leaving issue

4b Laura; *m* 24 Feb 1823 Lt-Col William Henry Meyrick

5b Arabella; *b* 2 June 1801

1a Grace; *b* 3 Dec 1757; *d* an infant

2a Elizabeth; *b* 28 April 1759; *d* 1765

(2) Frederick; *b* 26 June 1732; *m* 1st Henrietta, dau of Sir William Meredyth, 2nd Bt, of Henbury, of the 1639 *cr*; *m* 2nd Jane (*d* 7 April 1813), dau of Arthur Lysaght, and had issue by his 1st w:

1a A dau; *m* 22 Feb 1795 Capt — Metcalfe

(3) Raby; *b* 2 Jan 1736; *dsp* 23 Oct 1769

(1) Harriet; *d* 1758

(2) Mary; *m* 1752 Ralph Carr, of Cocken, Co Durham

(3) Anne; *bapt* 25 June 1726; *m* 1st 20 March 1745/6 (*divorce* 1757) Charles Hope-Vere (*see* LINLITHGOW, M); *m* 2nd Brig-Gen George Monson (*see* MONSON, B)

2 Morgan, of Bilby Hall, Notts; *b* 1706; barrister Middle Temple, Comptroller Stamp Office 1729; *m* 1st 28 Feb 1731 Margaretta (*d* 1 May 1739), dau of Robert Knight, of Barrells, Warwicks, and sis and eventually heir of 1st and last Earl of Catherlough (I) of the 1763 *cr*; *m* 2nd 19 Feb 1742 Anna Maria (*dsp* 19 July 1756), dau of Edward Fowler, of Feltham, s of Rt Rev Edward Fowler, Bp Gloucester; *m* 3rd 18 Dec 1759 Mary (*dsp* 11 July 1771), dau of William Woodyear, of Crookhill, Yorks, and *d* 14 Nov 1779, leaving issue by his 1st w:

(1) Morgan, of Bilby Hall; *b* 5 Dec 1737; *m* 1st 4 July 1760 Anna Maria Margaret Upton (*dsp* 15 July 1771); *m* 2nd Sarah Brookes (*dsp* 1779); *m* 3rd 9 May 1780 Catharine (*m* 2nd 21 May 1791 John Dore, and *d* 5 Sept 1839), dau of John Brookes, and *d* 11 Nov 1789, having had issue by his 3rd w:

1a John Henry; *b* 12 April 1788; *m* 15 April 1808 Elizabeth (*d* 19 Nov 1865), 3rd dau of Richard Nicholson, of Glandford Bridge, Lincs, and *d* 10 June 1849, leaving issue:

1b (Sir) Henry Morgan, DL (Durham); *b* 29 Nov 1808; barrister Inner Temple 1853, Sec to Charity Commn, ktd 1883; *m* 6 July 1853 Louisa (*d* 16 Dec 1878), dau and coheir of Rev Richard Farrer, of Ashley, Northants, and *d* 22 April 1886, having had issue:

1c HENRY DE VERE VANE, **9th Baron**

2c (Rev) Gilbert Holles Farrer; *b* 26 Sept 1855; *educ* Trin Coll Cambridge (MA); FSA, rector Wem, Salop 1895–1905, granted with siblings rank of baron's dau/yr s 12 Aug 1892; *m* 24 June 1891 Mary (*d* 29 July 1921), dau of E B Steadman, of High Ercall Hall, Salop, and *d* 27 June 1905, leaving issue:

1d Mary Louisa; *b* 25 March 1892; *d* unm 29 June 1909

3c Ralph John; *b* 14, *d* 28 July 1858

4c William Lyonel, JP, DL (both Durham); *b* 30 Aug 1859; chm Durham TFA, Maj 1st Bn Durham LI, Lt-Col and Hon Col cmdg 6th Bn Durham LI 1903–11; *m* 27 Jan 1904 Lady Katharine Louisa Pakenham (*d* 9 March 1954), dau of 4th Earl of Longford (*qv*), and *d* 23 Jan 1920, leaving issue:

1d William Morgan VANE later FLETCHER-VANE, 1st BARON INGLEWOOD (*qv*)

1d Katharine Selina; *b* 13 July 1906; *m* 1 Oct 1932 Hugh Bullock Hall (*d* 17 June 1949), s of Maj Alexander Cross Hall, of Gt Rollright Manor, Oxon, and *d* 14 April 1992, leaving:

1e *Alexander Bullock [Alexander Hall Esq, Craiglearan, Moniaive, Thornhill, Dumfriesshire DG3 4JD]; *b* 11 Nov 1934; *educ* Eton and RAC Cirencester; NDA, served Welsh Gds and Durham LI 1953–55; *m* 25 July 1964 *Rosalind Mary, only child of Cdr Robert Brian Halliwell, DSO, RN, of Twomerkland, Moniaive, Dumfriesshire, and has:

1f *Robert Hugh Bullock; *b* 28 Dec 1965; BSc, MSc; *m* 17 Dec 1994 *Diane, er dau of Gerald Cheek, of Port Stanley, Falkland Islands

2f *Richard Alexander Bullock; *b* 13 June 1971; BA, MTh; *m* 29 July 1995 *Annabel Barbara, only dau of David Moon

1f *Rosemary Joan Katharine; *b* 25 April 1967; BA; *m* 24 July 1993 *Jonathan Mark Hutchinson, only s of Denis Hutchinson, of Forest Grove, Stockton Lane, York

2e *David Bullock; *b* 22 May 1936; *educ* Eton; *m* 1st 22 April 1961 Susan Stephanie, yr dau of Samuel William Prittie Perry-Aldworth, of Littlestone-on-Sea, Kent, and has:

1f *Katrina Favell; *b* 16 June 1968

2e (cont.) David Hall *m* 2nd 30 Dec 1971 *Ellen Turner and has further issue:

1f *Mark Bullock; *b* 8 Nov 1973

2f *Andrew Bullock; *b* 11 Feb 1976

1e *Elizabeth Katharine Favell [Miss Elizabeth Hall, Broomfield Bank, Moniaive, Thornhill, Dumfries]; *b* 15 Sept 1938

2e Margaret Cicely; FIHM; *b* 24 Dec 1910; *d* 19–

1c Louisa Henrietta; *b* 18 Oct 1856; *m* 10 Nov 1891 William Blackstone Rennell (*d* 11 Dec 1912), of 62 Eaton Place, London SW, and *d* 6 Dec 1923

2b Frederick Nicholson; *b* 19 Dec 1809; *educ* Cambridge U (BA); Maj Hants Militia, a clerk H of Lds; *d* unm 10 Feb 1878

(1) Margaret; *d* unm

3 Thomas, of Staindrop Hall; *d* unm 1758

1 Anne, 'the beautiful Vanella,' Maid of Honour to QUEEN CAROLINE, *d* unm 11 March 1736, mistress of FREDERICK PRINCE OF WALES and by him had, with a dau who *d* an infant:

Fitz-Frederick; *b* 4 June 1732; *d* an infant

The 4th and last DUKE OF CLEVELAND's 3rd cousin once removed,

HENRY DE VERE VANE, **9th Baron Barnard of Barnard's Castle**, JP and DL (Durham); *b* 10 May 1854; *educ* Eton and Brasenose Coll Oxford (BA1876); barrister Inner Temple 1879, Hon DCL Durham, memb Senate Durham U 1912–19, FSA, Hon Col 4th Bn Durham LI; claim to the peerage allowed by Ho of Lds 30 May 1892; *m* 28 June 1881 Lady Catherine Sarah Cecil (*d* 14 March 1918), 3rd dau of 3rd Marquess of Exeter (*qv*), and *d* 28 Dec 1918, having had issue:

1 Henry Cecil; *b* 19 Sept 1882; Maj Yorks Hus, temp Maj RFA, ADC to Govr Madras 1903–07; *m* 25 Aug 1914 Lady Enid Victoria Rachel Fane (*m* 2nd 1 Sept 1922 Maj Herbert Broke Turnor, MC, JP, DL, of Little Ponton Hall, Grantham, and Stoke Rochford, Grantham, Lincs, est s of Algernon Turnor, CB, and *d* 9 Sept 1969, leaving issue), dau of 13th Earl of Westmorland (*qv*), and *dsp* & *vp* 9 Oct 1917 of an illness contracted on serv in France

2 CHRISTOPHER WILLIAM, **10th Baron**

3 Ralph Frederick; *b* 8 June 1891; *educ* Trin Coll Cambridge (BA); Capt Durham LI; *m* 5 June 1917 Kathleen Airni (*d* 7 Feb 1965), only surv child of Capt Gilbert Mair, NZC, sometime Judge Native Land Court, of Ohinimutu, Rotorua, NZ, and *dsp* 6 June 1928

The 9th BARON's 2nd s,

CHRISTOPHER WILLIAM VANE, **10th Baron Barnard of Barnard's Castle**, CMG (1930), OBE (1955), MC (1918), JP (1920), DL (1927); *b* 28 Oct 1888; *educ* Eton and Trin Coll Cambridge (BA); served WWI (wounded twice), Maj Westmorland and Cumberland Yeo, attd to Serv Bn Border Regt 1917, Maj 6th Bn Durham LI 1922, Lt-Col cmdg 1925–31, Hon Col 6th Durham LI 1943, Zone Cdr Durham Home Gd 1940, Ld-Lt Durham 1958–64, Jt MFH 1920–30, MFH 1930–37, Jt MFH 1937–64 the Zetland, Co Commr Durham Co Boy Scouts Assoc; *m* 14 Oct 1920 Sylvia Mary, JP Durham, Ch Cmdt ATS (*d* 1993), only dau of Herbert Straker, of Hartforth Grange, Richmond, Yorks, and *d* 19 Oct 1964, leaving issue:

1 (HARRY) JOHN NEVILLE VANE, **11th and present Baron Barnard of Barnard's Castle**

2 Gerald Raby; *b* 2 Dec 1926; *educ* Eton and Trin Coll Cambridge (BA)

1 *Rosemary Myra [The Hon Mrs Rosemary Gore-Booth, The White House, Gainford, Darlington DL2 3DN]; *b* 4 Nov 1921; served WWII in VAD, memb: RDC Barnard Castle 1961, Co Exec Ctee Durham Co Fedn Women's Inst 1962–; *m* 14 Aug 1948 (*divorce* 1954) Angus Josslyn Gore-Booth (later Sir Angus, 8th Bt (*qv*)) and has issue

Seat: Raby Castle, Staindrop, Co Durham. The origins of Raby date back to its occupancy by the NEVILLs (*see* ABERGENNY, M). Construction of the Great Hall, for instance, is thought to have been started in the 1320s, in the time of the 1st Lord (Baron) Neville (of Raby), who died in the spring of 1331. It continued under his successors, the 2nd and 3rd Lords, who reigned (the term is no exaggeration, given the family's ascendancy in the North) 1331–67 and 1367–88. It was during this long-drawn-out period that the Great Hall was extended north and south and towards its end that such luxuries as kitchens were added, these apparently dating from the late 1370s. John Lewyn, a master mason who worked on Durham Cathedral and one of a handful of craftsmen in the medieval building industry whose names have come down to us, has been suggested as the man immediately responsible for them. But despite the NEVILLs employing the 14th-century equivalent of Smallbone of Devizes, Raby was not the family's chief stronghold. Its low-lying position made it too hard to defend compared with Barnard Castle, say, although the nearby lake to the immediate south, which remains to this day, must have been a useful source of moat-filler.

Nevertheless Raby commemorates its earliest occupants in several respects, chiefly the Neville Gateway, Joan's Tower (possibly named after Joan de Monmouth, wife of Geoffrey fitz Robert fitz Maldred, who later took his mother's family's name of de Nevill(e)) and lastly the Bulmer Tower on the east flank. (The de Bulmer heiress Emma, probably of Saxon rather than Norman origin, had married Geoffrey de Nevill(e) some two centuries earlier, but her dowry was the basis of much of the family's wealth.) Other notable features dating from the Middle Ages include Clifford's Tower, at 80 feet the tallest of them all, and the Kitchen Tower, with its deeply cut frontal trench running vertically up and down.

With the eclipse of the NEVILLs following the disastrous rising of the Northern Earls in 1569 Raby was taken into the possession of the Crown. In 1613 JAMES I granted it to his favourite Robert Carr, Earl of Somerset (*see* LOTHIAN, M), but with Carr's disgrace it reverted again to the Crown. Sir Henry Vane the Elder, whose cousins preferred the spelling Fane and had conferred on them the formerly NEVILL-held Earldom of Westmorland, took a lease on Raby in 1616 and bought it outright ten years later. Whatever work was done in the following century has left little trace and it is thought Vane's chief purpose in acquiring the estate was the land. But he did keep the castle in reasonable repair, cannibalising

Barnard Castle, which he pulled down, and using its stones on Raby. He also added an external arcade on the east side of the courtyard, its balustraded roof serving as a balcony for diners sallying forth from the Great Hall above. He also regularised the appearance of the central block by inserting a two-storey, five-bay facade with triangular pediments and adorned by another balustrade.

Raby was much knocked about during the Civil War and again at the beginning of GEORGE I's reign by the **1st Baron Barnard**, apparently out of sheer malice towards his son Gilbert, later **2nd Baron**. Two hundred workmen were brought on site to strip the lead off the roof, the glass from the window frames and the doors from their hinges. They even ripped up the floors. Trees were felled in their hundreds and the parkland was let to a farmer, who ploughed it over. But it was only in the mid-19th century that Vane's alterations, which sound on the whole rather agreeable, were swept away, this time by the well-intentioned but in fact far more destructive 'improving' hand of William Burn, the meddlesome architect who also worked on Bowhill (*see* BUCCLEUCH and QUEENSBERRY, D). With Gilbert's accession a golden age at last dawned. He had already won an injunction against his father to prevent any further damage. He now brought in James Paine, whose splendid, gently curvaceous Hunter's Gallery at Raby has been called the Morning Star of the Gothick Revival, anticipating as it does Horace Walpole's Strawberry Hill. Sadly for Gilbert his troubles with Raby were not entirely over. At some point before 1750 a fire destroyed the central southern-flank tower, leaving an unsightly gap-toothed countenance that was not made good till the end of the century. Nor did all Paine's projects see completion, his plan to gothicise the windows, for instance, coming to nothing, though his transformation of part of Joan's Tower as apartments for the 3rd Duke of Cleveland of the 1670 creation (brother-in-law of the **3rd Baron**) did get put in hand.

Such work by Paine as survives includes the Stucco Room, probably the Alcove Room (off the Hunter's Gallery), whose fluted Tuscan-order columns provide a screen between the bed area and the 'dead space' of the rest, and much of the interior of the west wing between Joan's and Clifford's Towers. Gilbert's son the **3rd Baron**, promoted Earl of Darlington the year after his father's death, employed a less distinguished north-country architect, John Carr of York, at first using him for minor alterations but gradually working up to large-scale projects, notably the extraordinary transmuting of the hall into a massive vaulted chamber which would allow a coach and horses to enter. This was all the more necessary because the courtyard was proving too small for 18th-century vehicles. It was nevertheless a bold stroke, the taming of an essentially outdoors activity, to wit carriage-driving, being completed by Carr's addition of twin fireplaces which in the 1780s were together with the piers given a warm blood-red hue by the London scagliola specialist Joseph Brown(e). The effect on a cold winter's night of stepping from one's wheeled conveyance immediately into a welcoming, if melodramatic, interior was well described by the dramatist George Colman the Younger. Carr also worked on the Round Tower, creating an additional drawing room. His plans for an entirely new facade, however, were never executed.

The early 19th century saw the doing over of Carr's drawing room in the Chinese taste for a projected visit by the PRINCE OF WALES (later GEORGE IV). But the principal alterations were much later, around the mid-century, when Burn began his association with Raby. He removed medieval vaulting from the Bulmer and Clifford Towers, inserted over-large window glazing, made copious use of new stone which contrasted starkly with the mellowed fabric of the older work, and in particular demolished a wooden roof over the Baron's Hall. In the field of detailed ornament he swept away 14th-century tracery in the Chapel and plastered over individual medieval furnishings of the first importance and great rarity. Despite the return of High Victorian style to favour in recent years, Burn's contribution to Raby at the expense of older work is largely regrettable.

BARNETT

Creation: B. (LP, UK) 1983.

THE BARON BARNETT, of Heywood and Royton, in Greater Manchester (Joel Barnett, PC (1975), JP (Lancs (1960)) [The Rt Hon The Lord Barnett PC JP, Flat 92, 24 John Islip St, London SW1P 4LG; 7 Hillingdon Rd, Whitefield, Manchester M25 7QQ]; *b* 14 Oct 1923; *educ* Centl High Sch Manchester; WWII: RASC, Br Mil Govt Germany; Hon Treas Manchester Fabian Soc 1953–65; consultant Hacker Young, Manchester (sr ptnr 1954–74); Cncllr Prestwich Cncl 1956–65; MP (Lab) Heywood and Royton 1964–83, memb: Public Accounts Ctee 1965–71 (Chm 1979–83), Public Expenditure Ctee 1971–74, Select Ctee Tax Credits 1973–74, Chm PLP Ec and Fin Gp 1967–70 and 1972–74 (V-Chm 1966–67), oppn spokesman Treasury 1970–74, Ch Sec Treasury 1974–79, Cabinet Memb 1977–79, oppn spokesman Treasury Ho Lds 1983–86; memb: Hallé Ctee 1982–93, Unisys Internat Advsy Bd 1989–; Tstee: V&A 1983–, O U Fndn 1994–; V-Chm Govrs BBC 1986–93; Chm: Hansard Soc 1984–90, Br Screen Finance Ltd 1985–, Building Socs Ombudsman Cncl 1987–96, Birkbeck Coll Appeal Ctee 1992–; Pres RIPA 1988–92; Hon Visiting Fell Strathclyde U 1980–, Hon LLD Strathclyde 1983, Hon Fell Birkbeck Coll 1994, FCCA, author: *Inside the Treasury* (1982); *m* 1949 *Lilian Stella, dau of Abraham Goldstone, and has issue:

1 *Erica Hazel; *b* 1951

Lineage: LOUIS BARNETT; *m* Ettie — and had:

JOEL, *cr* a **Baron**

BARNEWALL

Arms: Erm. a bordure engrailed gu. **Crest:** From a plume of five ostrich feathers or, gu., az., vert and arg., a falcon rising of the last. **Motto:** *Malo mori quam foedari* ('I prefer to die than be dishonoured'). **Creation:** Bt. (I) 21 Feb 1622/3.

SIR REGINALD ROBERT BARNEWALL, 13TH BT, of Crickstown Castle, Co Meath [Sir Reginald Barnewall Bt, Innisfree, 39 Normandie Court, Mount Tamborine, Qld 4272, Australia]; *b* 1 Oct 1924; *s f* 1961; *educ* Xavier Coll Melbourne; wool grower and grazier, cattle breeder, airline operator, orchardist and land developer, WW II: Offr Roy Australian Engrs, AIF S Pacific Islands, Allied Intelligence Bureau, GHQ, SWPA 1939–45, cmded B Sqn Victorian Mounted Rifles, Royal Australian Armoured Corps, 1952–56, md Southern Airlines Ltd of Melbourne 1953–58, fndr and operations manager Polynesian Airlines W Samoa 1958–62, dir: Eildon Aviation, J Roy Stevens Pty Ltd, Island Airways Pty Ltd 1964–68, chm and md Orchid Beach (Fraser Island) Pty Ltd— tourist resort operators 1965–72, Coastal-Air Co (Qld) 1971–76; *m* 1st 8 June 1946 Elsie Muriel (*d* Jan 1962), dau of Thomas Matthews Frederick, of Brisbane, Australia, and has had issue:

1 John Reginald; *b* 5 Sept; *d* 29 Oct 1953

1 *Mary Catherine; *b* 18 May 1947; *m* 1979 *Peter Lynch, of Toowoomba, Qld

2 *Frances Patricia; *b* 4 July 1948; *m* 1969 *Michael Curley, of Brisbane

3 *Margaret Ann; *b* 6 July 1952

Sir REGINALD *m* 28 June 1962 *Maureen Ellen, dau of William Daly, of S Caulfield, Vict, Australia, and by her has:

2 +PETER JOSEPH [Peter Barnewall Esq, 26 Tirrabella St, Carina Heights, Qld 4152, Australia]; *b* 26 Oct 1963; *educ* St Joseph's Coll Nudgee and Qld U (B Ag Sc Econ); offr 2nd/14th Light Horse QMI RAAC 1982–; *m* 29 Oct 1988 *Kathryn Jane, dau of Hugh Carroll, of Brisbane, and has:

(1) +Christopher Patrick; *b* 3 June 1995

(2) +Richard Joseph; *b* 23 April 1997

(1) *Jessica Rose; *b* 10 Nov 1992

Lineage: Sir MICHAEL de BERNEVAL/BARNEVAL; settled in Ireland late 12th century; had:

ALANUS de BERNEVAL; had, with an er s (Hugo; memb KING JOHN's expdn to Ireland 1212; granted land at Drumenagh and Terenure, Co Dublin, 1216; *dsp* by 24 Jan 1220/1):

REGINALD de BERNEVAL; had the lands at Drumenagh and Terenure restored him 24 Jan 1228/9; *d* in or after 28 Sept 1234, leaving:

ULPHRAM/WOLFRAM de BERNEVAL, of Drumenagh; Constable Dublin Castle 1279, 1280 and 1281, Sheriff Dublin 1284 and 1289; *m* Mary, only dau and heiress of Sir William Molyneux, of Moylagh, Co Meath, and had:

REGINALD de BERNEVAL; *m* —, dau of Sir Conway Clifford, and *d* in or after 1299, leaving:

REGINALD de BERNEVAL, of Drumenagh; *d* 1331, leaving:

ULPHRAM de BERNEVAL, of Drumenagh; *m* Sarah, dau of — Berford, of Moymet, and had:

REGINALD de BERNEVAL; *m* Jannetta, dau of Cusac of Killeen, and *d* in or after 1374, leaving, with an er s (Wolfram/Ulphram, held the manor of Ballythermot 1400; his descendants continued at Drumenagh till JAMES I's reign, when his line terminated in an heiress, Elizabeth, dau of Marcus Barnewall, of Drumenagh, who *m* James Barnewall, of Bremore, and sold the property 1 Feb 1607 to Sir Adam Loftus, of Rathfarnham; *see* ELY, M):

NICHOLAS de BERNEVAL, of Crickstown, Co Meath; *m* — Clifford and *d* by 1386, leaving:

Sir CHRISTOPHER de BERNEVAL, of Crickstown; *m* Eleanor, dau of Sir Nicholas Rochford, of Rathcoffie, Co Kildare, and Kilbride, Co Meath, and had issue:

1 CHRISTOPHER (Sir), his successor

2 John, of Frankstown; Sheriff Co Meath 1435–36, ancestor of the Viscounts Barnewall of Kingsland (extinct 1834)

3 Barnaby; a Baron of the Exchequer

The est son,

Sir CHRISTOPHER BARNEWALL, of Crickstown; Serjeant-at-Law 1408, Ld Treasurer Ireland 1436, Ch Justice King's Bench 1446; *m* Matilda Drake, dau and heiress of the last feudal Ld of Drakestown and Drakerath, and had, with a yr s (1st BARON TRIMLESTOWN, *qv*):

Sir NICHOLAS BARNEWALL, of Crickstown; Ch-Justice Court Common Pleas Ireland 1461; *m* Ismay, dau and heiress of Sir Robert Serjeant, of Castleknock, Co Dublin, and had, with a yr s (Edmund, ancestor of the BARNEWALLs of Dunbrow):

CHRISTOPHER BARNEWALL, of Crickstown; *m* Alice Butler, dau of 8th Baron of Dunboyne (*qv*), and had issue:

1 EDMUND

2 George; ancestor of the BARNEWALLs of Arrodstown, whose representative George Barnewall, of Cookstown, was living 1615

3 Robert; ancestor of the BARNEWALLs of Moylagh, whose rep Patrick Barnewall *s* to the estate 1632

4 Barnabas, whose line ended with his gs, Edmund Barnewall

Sir CHRISTOPHER's est son,

EDMUND BARNEWALL, of Crickstown; *m* Elizabeth, dau of Sir Thomas Plunkett, of Dunsoghly, and *d* 7 Aug 1511, having had, with two daus (Anne, *m* Oliver Nugent, of Drumcairne; Genet; *m* Sir Robert Dillon):

Sir CHRISTOPHER BARNEWALL, of Crickstown; *m c* 1517 Catherine Fleming, dau of 8th Lord (Baron) Slane, and had, with other issue (including Maud, *m* 1580 Richard Nugent; *see* NUGENT Bt, of Donore) an est s:

Sir PATRICK BARNEWALL, of Crickstown; ktd 1566; known from his large land holdings as 'the Knight of the Broad Acre'; *m* his cousin Margaret, dau of Sir Patrick Barnewall, of Turvey, and had, with other issue:

1 RICHARD (Sir)

2 Robert, of Stackallan, Co Meath; living 1615; *m* Alison, dau of James Brandon, of Dundalk, and was ancestor of the BARNEWALLs of Stackallan

3 John, of Cookstown; *m* Mary, dau of James Brandon, of Dundalk, and had a son George

Sir PATRICK *d* by 1603; his est son,

Sir RICHARD BARNEWALL, of Crickstown; *m* Elizabeth, dau of Sir Oliver Plunkett, of Rathmore, Co Meath, and had, with other issue:

1 PATRICK (Sir), **1st Bt**

2 James, a soldier in Spain; *dsp*

3 John, a Franciscan monk

4 Barnaby, a Capuchin friar, several times reader, guardian, and reader of divinity in France; Superior of the Irish Capuchins in Ireland

Sir RICHARD's est son,

Sir Patrick Barnewall, 1st Bt (I), so *cr* 21 Feb 1622/3, of Crickstown; *m* Cicely Fleming (*d* 1628), dau of 11th Lord (Baron) Slane, and *d* 21 June 1624, having had, with three daus:

1 **Sir Richard Barnewall, 2nd Bt**; *b* 21 Dec 1602; much of his land was sequestrated after CROMWELL's arrival in Ireland; after the Restoration he recovered only his castle and 2,000 acres immediately surrounding it; *m* 1st 1621 Thomasina (*d* 1628), dau of Edward Dowdall, of Athlumney, Co Meath, and had issue:

(1) Mary; *m* Capt Andrew Kindelan

1 (cont.) **Sir Richard** *m* 2nd Julia, dau of Sir Gerald Aylmer, 1st Bt, of Donadea (*qv*), and *d* soon after 1660, having had, with five other s and five more daus:

(1) **Sir Patrick Barnewall, 3rd Bt**; MP Co Meath 1680 and 1690; granted 1,261 acres in the barony of Clare, Co Galway, *c* 1689; *m* Frances (*d* 1709), dau of Richard Butler, of Kilcash and Garryricken, bro of James, 1st Duke of Ormonde (*see* MOUNTGARRET, V), and *d* after 26 March 1695, having had:

1a **Sir George Barnewall, 4th Bt**; *d* unm 22 Oct 1735, when his estates passed to his sisters

1a Ellen; *m* 1703 4th Earl of Mount Alexander

2a Frances; *d* unm 23 May 1758

3a Elizabeth; *d* unm by 17 Sept 1728

4a Mary; *d* unm 1750

2 John, of Athronan; *m* his cousin Anne, dau of James Barnewall, of Bremore, and had, with a yr s and three daus:

(1) James, of Roskeen, Queen's Co; *m* Margaret, dau of Col John Legge, unc of 1st Baron Dartmouth (*see* DARTMOUTH, E), and *d* 1692, leaving, with a dau (Anne, *m* William Dillon, of Flemingstown):

1a Barnaby, of Ballyard; *m* Jane, dau of Kedagh Geoghegan, of Carne and Jamestown, and had, with two other s and a dau:

1b **Sir George Barnewall, 5th Bt**; *dsp* 1750

2a George; *dsp*

3a James; *m* Margery, dau of Kedagh Geoghegan (*see* above), and *d* 20 Nov 1709, having had, with three other sons:

1b **Sir Thomas Barnewall, 6th Bt**; *m* —, dau of Mulhall, of Kilcauligar Castle, Queen's Co, and had:

1c Marcella; *m* 1st Arthur Geoghegan, of Jamestown, Co Westmeath; *m* 2nd Theobald Dillon, of Mount Dillon, Co Roscommon; *m* 3rd Thomas Dillon, est son of Thomas Dillon, of Sung, Co Mayo. He *d* 1790

3 George; *d* unm Dec 1686

4 James; *b* after March 1615; Lt-Col of Horse; *m* 1653 his cousin Mabel, widow of 2nd Earl of Fingall (*see* 1970 edn) and dau of 1st Viscount Barnewall of Kingsland, and *d* by 23 July 1661, leaving, with two daus (Eleanor, *d* unm; Mabel, *m* Edward Hussey, of Westown):

(1) George; *b* by 21 Nov 1664; *m* —, dau of James Dillon, of Huntstown, and had, with an er s (*m* Margaret Barnewall, of Arrodstown, and *dsp*):

1a Bartholomew, of Ballyhost, Co Westmeath; *m* Jane, dau of Edward Geoghegan, of Castletown Geoghegan, and *d* 1736, having had, with two daus:

1b Robert, of Moyrath, Co Meath; *b* 1702; *m* 1723 Bridget, dau of Henry Piers, of Lisloughan, and widow of Richard Barnewall, of Clonylogan, Co Meath, and had, with other issue:

1c BARTHOLOMEW (Sir), *de jure* 7th Bt

2b James (Rev), parish priest of Mullingar, Co Westmeath

3b Thomas; *d* on board ship on his way to Groningen

The 6th Bt's cousin,

BARTHOLEMEW BARNEWALL, de jure 7th Bt, but did not assume the title, of Ballyhost, Co Westmeath, and Boyne Lodge and Greenanstown, Co Meath; *m* 1748 Mary (*d* 24 March 1802), 2nd dau of John Colt and sis and heiress of Isaac Brand Colt, of Brightlingsey Hall, Essex, and *d* 1802, having had issue:

1 **Sir Robert Barnewall, 8th Bt**, of Greenanstown, Co Meath; *b* 6 Oct 1757; established right to btcy 1821; *m* lst 1786 Catherine Rose (*d* 10 Feb 1790), est dau and eventual coheir of Charles Aylmer, of Painstown, Co Kildare, and had:

(1) Bartholomew; *d* young

(2) **Sir Aylmer John Barnewall, 9th Bt**; Lt 35th Regt, served in Holland and at Waterloo; *b* 30 Dec 1789; *m* 29 Sept 1836 his cousin Esmay Mary (*d* 5 March 1879), est dau of Christopher Barnewall, of Meadstown, Co Meath, and *d* 22 Jan 1838, leaving:

1a **Sir Reginald Aylmer John de Barneval Barnewall, 10th Bt**; *b* 16 Feb 1838; *d* unm 18 April 1909

1 (cont.) **Sir Robert** *m* 2nd 1795 Margaret Jane (*d* 1844), est dau of George Palmer, of Dublin, Govr Bank of Ireland, and *d* 27 Aug 1836, having by her had:

(1) Mary Anne; *m* Cargles Ruxton, of Rahanna, Co Louth, and *dsp*

2 John, of Kilmurry, Co Meath; *m* Anne, dau of Joseph Brown, of Kilpatrick, Co Westmeath, and had:

(1) Bartholomew, offr Co Meath Militia; *m* Barbara, dau of Dr Chambers, surgeon of the Kilkenny Militia, and had:

1a John Aylmer; *b c* 1812; settled in Australia 1840; *m* 1st 19 May 1840 Ellen Saunders (*d* 10 Jan 1877) and had:

1b JOHN ROBERT (Sir), **11th Bt**

1b Catherine Lucy; *m* Robert Rennie, and *d* 3 June 1920

2b Barbara; *m* Thomas Tossol

3b Eleanor; *m* William McMartin

4b Sarah; *d* an infant

5b Maritza; *b* 30 June 1852; *m* Robert Nicholas, and *d* 31 Oct 1931

6b Adeline; *b* 15 Oct 1854; *m* Francis Downey, of Main St, Eltham, Victoria, Australia, and *d* 11 Jan 1947, leaving issue

7b Eliza; *b* 12 June 1857; *m* 17 Dec 1884 John O'Rourke, of Thornton, Victoria, Australia, and *d* 6 Nov 1945, leaving issue

8b Francesina; *b* 26 May 1861; *d* unm 1 May 1892

1a (cont.) John A Barnewall *m* 2nd 25 April 1879 Annie Reid (*d* 4 Nov 1886), and *d* at Upper Thornton, 23 Jan 1890, having by her had issue:

2b Alfred George; *b* 9 May 1880; *m* 1915 Sarah, dau of J Footter, of Violet Town, Victoria, and *d* 27 Jan 1952, having had:

1c +Patrick Joseph, JP; *b* 1915; served WW II with 2nd/9th Australian Field Regt; *m* 1949 *Daphne Mavis, dau of Charles Turner Lockhart, and has:

1d Robert Charles; *b* 1957

2d *Naomi Patricia; *b* 1955

2c +John Robert; *b* 1917; md 2/9th Aust Field Regt Roy Australian Artillery AIF WW II Syria and New Guinea; *m* 1946 *Marietza Elizabeth, dau of Henry James O'Rourke, of Tullamore, NSW, and has:

ld +John Jeffrey; *b* 1951; *m* 1976 *Frances Erica, dau of Eric Ernest Virieux, of Glen Garry, Tasmania, and has:

1e *Tammie Elizabeth; *b* 1980

2e *Alison Louise; *b* 1983

1d *Marietza Anne; *b* 1947

2d *Linda Mary; *b* 1955

3d *Dorothea Larree; *b* 10 May 1959; *m* 10 June 1989 *Kevin David Chapman and has:

1e *Alexander Kevin; *b* 6 Jan 1994

1e *Emma Clair; *b* 28 Oct 1990

3c +Francis Richard [Francis Barnewall Esq, Whitemark, Flinders Island, Tasmania, Australia]; *b* 1922; served WW II 1939–45 with AIF in SW Pacific; *m* 1951 *Margaret Mary, dau of L Lyons, of Euchuca, Victoria, Australia, and has issue:

1d +Brian Francis; *b* 1956; *m* 1981 *Judith Diane, dau of Thomas Bowland, of Whitemark, Flinders Is, Tasmania, and has issue:

1e *Holly Renae; *b* 1985

2e *Rhianna Kate; *b* 1987

1d *Kerry Teresa

2d *Dianne Margaret

4c George Raymond; *b* 1923; *d* 6 June 1988

5c Terence James [Terence Barnewall Esq, 53 Seignior St, Junee, NSW 2663, Australia]; *b* 1935; *m* 1st 1957 Jannete, dau of Robert Smith, of Junee; *m* 2nd 1978 *Marie Patricia, dau of Fredric Davies, of Sydney, and formerly w of John Layton, and has issue by 1st w:

1d *Judith Margaret; *b* 1959; *m* 1979 *Warren Wright, and has issue:

1e *Daniel Leigh; *b* 1981

2e *Nathan Warren; *b* 1983

2d *Teena Merrie; *b* 1965; nurse, Canberra ACT

1c Kathleen Joyce; *b* 1919; *d* 20 April 1991

2c Sidna Mary (twin); *b* 1919; *d* 1921

3b Bartholomew John; *b* 29 Jan 1882; *d* unm 18 July 1948

4b Robert Benjamin; *b* 18 Jan 1885; *d* 1959

2a Robert, settled in America in 1840

3a Benjamin, settled in Australia

(2) Robert; *d* unm at Rio de la Flache, S America

(3) John; *b* Sept 1793; *m* lst 1819 Sophia Barrington (*d* 1823, aged 23), and had issue:

1a Henry Charles; *b* 16 July 1820; *m* 15 Jan 1844 Henrietta Mary, dau of John Woollett, of London, and *dsp* 6 June 1900

(3) (cont.) John Barnewall *m* 2nd July 1829 Margaret (*dsp* 7 Feb 1877), dau of W Madden, of Limerick, and *d* 10 Dec 1869
(4) Samuel, emigrated to America
(5) William, emigrated to America
(1) Mary; *m*.— Chambers
(2) Ellen; *m* — Lewis
(3) Katherine, a nun at Tullamore
(4) Anne
(5) Elizabeth
(6) Theresa
3 Bartholomew Patrick; *b* 1764; *m* 1806 Margaret (*d* 1815), dau of Theobald Bourke, Dublin, and *dsp* 1849
1 Mary; *m* Tyrrell O'Reilly, of Adamstown, Meath
2 Elizabeth; *m* Thomas Fitzgerald, of Geraldine, Co Kildare, and had issue

The 10th Bt's cousin,

Sir John Robert Barnewall, 11th Bt; *b* 14 April 1850; *m* 14 Oct 1884 Grace (*d* 17 May 1921), dau of Arthur Richard Blennerhassett, and had:
1 REGINALD JOHN (Sir), **12th Bt**
2 Arthur Walter Aylmer; *b* 15 Aug 1890; *m* 17 March 1921 Hilda, dau of Thomas Triffit, and *d* Aug 1961, leaving issue:
(1) Alfred Reginald; *b* 10 July 1921; *m* 25 Nov 1950 *Daisy Mabel, dau of Charles Newman, and *d* 26 Oct 1980, leaving issue:
1a +Graeme David [Graeme Barnewall Esq, 20 Lachlan Court, Sunbury, VIC 3429, Australia]; *b* 2 Aug 1957; *m* 28 Nov 1987 *Lindy Jean, dau of James Donaldson, and has:
1b *Samantha Kate; *b* 2 Feb 1994
2b *Amy Louise; *b* 28 May 1996
2a +Ronald William [Ronald Barnewall Esq, PO Box 1632 Swan Hill, VIC 3585, Ausralia]; *b* 8 June 1960; *m* 23 Aug 1986 *Susan Jennifer, dau of Raymond Welsford and has:
1b *Alexandra Rose; *b* 11 July 1993
2b *Rebecca Jayne; *b* 30 Jan 1995
3a +Michael James [Michael Barnewall Esq, 2 Bishop Place, W Melton, VIC 3337, Australia]; *b* 12 Nov 1962; *m* 17 April 1988 *Glenda Michelle, dau of Michael Condon, and has issue:
1b *Jessica Kate; *b* 21 Nov 1990
2b *Sarah Jane; *b* 15 Oct 1992
3b *Allison Mae; *b* 9 Aug 1996
1a *Kate Lorraine; *b* 31 Dec 1951; *m* 5 March 1988 *William Robert Capper, s of Robert Hordern Capper
2a *Margaret Anne; *b* 26 Nov 1953; *m* 12 Jan 1974 *Ian Lawrence Hemming, s of Sidney James Hemming and has:
1b *Travers Jorge; *b* 28 June 1976
1b *Bonny Louise; *b* 4 June 1979; has:
1c *Tia Victoria LEE; *b* 30 Aug 1997
3a *Sandra Maree; *b* 15 May 1970; *m* 8 Jan 1994 *Vaughan Edward Manders, s of Edward Walter Manders and has:
1b *Isabel Paige; *b* 16 Aug 1997
(2) John Robert; *b* 23 Dec 1922; *m* 29 April 1950 *Joan Catherine, dau of Shadrack Allen, and *d* 18 Nov 1995, leaving:
1a +John Robert; *b* 17 May 1952; *m* 10 Oct 1981 *Jennifer Hooper, and has:
1b *Ann Louise; *b* 19 Jan 1986
2b *Laura Mary; *b* 5 June 1989
2a +Kieran Gerard; *b* 30 July 1958
3a +Anthony Brian; *b* 31 March 1960; has:
1b *Jack; *b* 8 Nov 1990
4a +Mark Raymond; *b* 14 June 1961; *m* 1994 *— and has:
1b *Madeleine Grace; *b* 15 March 1997
1a *Eileen Mary; *b* 16 March 1951; *m* 25 June 1971 *Ken Hoffman, s of George Hoffman and has:
1b *Katrina Mary; *b* 18 Oct 1973
2b *Mandy Lee; *b* 8 Aug 1977
2a *Catherine Frances; *b* 28 Feb 1955; *m* 30 Oct 1982 *David Kehoe, s of John Kehoe and has:
1b *Joseph John; *b* 16 Sept 1993
1b *Monica Anne; *b* 16 April 1984
3a *Clare Therese; *b* 10 July 1970
(3) Henry Marcus Joseph [Henry Barnewall Esq, 56 Elizabeth Dve, Rosebud, VIC 3939, Australia]; *b* 10 May 1924; *m* 3 July 1976 *Barbara Ruth Mary, dau of Reginald Lindsley, and widow of John Douglas Bays
(4) Kevin Arthur; *b* 4 Aug 1925; *m* 30 July 1949 *Marjorie Joyce, dau of Charles Body, and had:
1a Ross David; *b* 4 Aug 1950; *m* 3 March 1973 *Dianne Robyn [Mrs Ross Barnewall, 17 Landale Ave, Croydon, VIC 3136, Australia], dau of Victor Jordan (formerly Vitto Giordano), and *d* 16 April 1989, leaving:
1b +David Matthew; *b* 27 Sept 1973
2b +Daniel Leigh; *b* 7 July 1976
3b +Benjamin Scott; *b* 9 Oct 1978
2a +Murray Charles [Murray Barnewall Esq, Hennessy St, Port Campbell, VIC 3269]; *b* 16 Jan 1954; *m* 11 Dec 1976 *Lesley Christine, dau of Ronald O'Brien, and has issue:
1b *Brooke; *b* 23 Feb 1978
2b *Lisa; *b* 30 Aug 1979
3a +Kevin Bruce; *b* 9 Dec 1956
1a *Dianne Maree [Mrs Michael Primmer, 4 Morrison St, Colac, VIC 3250]; *b* 17 Nov 1952; *m* 14 Nov 1970 *Michael John Primmer, son of Roy Charles Primmer, and has:
1b *Michael John; *b* 22 Feb 1976
2b *Matthew Scott; *b* 22 Feb 1976 (twin)
1b *Leanne Maree; *b* 2 June 1971; *m* 20 Sept 1992 *Malcolm Lindsay Williamson and has:
1c *Jayden Leigh; *b* 21 April 1993
1c *Ashlee Maree; *b* 6 March 1995
2b *Jacqueline Louise; *b* 21 Oct 1972; *m* 5 April 1997 *Jason Demajo and has:
1c *Randall Terrence USHER; *b* 28 Dec 1992
2a *Debra Michelle [Mrs Robert Phibbs, 15 Olympus Dve, Croydon, VIC 3136, Australia]; *b* 21 June 1962; *m* 21 April 1984 *Robert James Phibbs, s of Mervyn John Phibbs, and has issue:
1b *Cody James; *b* 4 April 1990
1b *Loran Michelle; *b* 27 April 1988
(5) Patrick Thomas; *b* 17 Sept 1928; *m* 11 Oct 1947 *Mavis Leone, dau of Charles Cooper, and *d* 26 Feb 1996, leaving:
1a Dennis John; *b* 1948; RAN, served Vietnam War in HMAS *Brisbane*; *d* 1971
1a Suzanne Elizabeth; *b* and *d* 1952
2a *Annette Lynne; *b* 6 May 1954; *m* 7 July 1973 *Wayne George Peterson and has:
1b *Dennis Norman; *b* 28 April 1980
1b *Amanda Patricia; *b* 22 July 1976
1 Eleanor Grace; *b* 25 May 1886; *d* 19 Aug 1886

Sir JOHN *d* 23 Sept 1936; his est son,

Sir Reginald John Barnewall, 12th Bt; *b* 8 June 1888; *m* 29 April 1922 Jessie Ellen, dau of John Fry, and *d* 1 Nov 1961, having had issue:
1 Sir REGINALD ROBERT BARNEWALL, **13th and present Bt**

BARRAN

Arms: Per saltire gules and sable a bear passant or, muzzled of the second, between two mascles palewise of the third. **Crest:** In front of a tower gules, charged with three mascles interlaced in pale, a lion's jamb erased and fesswise or. **Motto:** *Amor patriæ* ('Love of one's country'). **Creation:** Bt. (UK) 11 Feb 1895.

SIR JOHN NAPOLEON RUTHVEN BARRAN 4TH BT, of Chapel Allerton Hall, Chapel Allerton, West Riding, Co York, and Queen's Gate, St Mary Abbots, Kensington, Co London [Sir John Barran Bt, 17 St Leonard's Terrace, London SW3 4QG; The Hermitage, E Bergholt, Suffolk C07 6RB; Middle Rigg Farm, Sawley, N Yorks HG4 3HA]; *b* 14 Feb 1934; *s* f 1974; *educ* Winchester and UCL (BA 1994); late Lt 5th Inniskilling Dragoon Gds, served Br High Commn Ottawa 1964–67, Head Info Tech COI 1985–87; *m* 7 Sept 1965 *Jane Margaret, only child of Sir Stanley George Hooker, CBE, FRS, PhD, of Orchard Hill, Milbury Heath, Wootton-under-Edge, by Hon Margaret, only dau of 1st Baron Bradbury (*qv*), and has:
1 +JOHN RUTHVEN; *b* 10 Nov 1971
1 *Susannah Margaret; *b* 1981

Lineage: JOHN BARRAN, of London; *b* Oct 1790; *m* 1812 Elizabeth (*d* 12 Jan 1841), dau of Henry Fletcher, and *d* 3 Feb 1880, having had issue:

Sir John Barran, 1st Bt (UK), so *cr* 11 Feb 1895, JP (Leeds and W R Yorks); *b* 3 Aug 1821; MP (Lib) Leeds 1876–85 and Otley 1886–95, Mayor Leeds 1870 and 1871, Life Govr and Treas Leeds U, LLD, Pres Leeds Chamber Commerce; *m* 1st 22 Dec 1842 Ann (*d* 15 Jan 1874), dau of M Hirst, of Leeds; *m* 2nd 10 Jan 1878 Eliza (*d* 4 May 1917), dau of William Brown, of Helensburgh, Dunbartonshire, and widow of John Bilton, of Scarborough, and by his 1st w had issue:
1 John, of Chapel Allerton, Leeds; *b* 25 Dec 1844; *m* 22 June 1870 Eliza Henrietta (*d* 2 March 1929), dau of Edward Nicholson, of Matthews Green, Wokingham, and *dvp* 19 Feb 1886, leaving issue:
(1) JOHN NICHOLSON (Sir), **2nd Bt**
(2) Philip Austyn, JP (Leeds); *b* 20 March 1876; *educ* Christ's Coll Cambridge (BA); Maj 1st W R Bde RFA (TF), chm Leeds Maternity Hosp; *m* 2 Jan 1908 Dorothy Currer (*d* 30 Jan 1956), only dau of Arthur Currer Briggs, of Leeds, and *d* 8 Feb 1953, having had issue:

1a Philip Henry, F/Lt AAF WW II; *b* 20 April 1909; *ka* Battle of Britain 11 July 1940

2a (Arthur) Haworth; *b* 14 April 1911; *educ* Repton and St John's Coll Cambridge (BA 1933); *m* 27 March 1945 *Rosa, dau of John Russell Greenwood, of The Oval, Tranmere Park, Guiseley, Yorks, and *d* 1991, having had issue:

1b +Jonathan Haworth [Jonathan Barran Esq, 13 Tumene Drive, Owhata, Rotorua, NZ]; *b* 17 Nov 1946; *educ* Badingham Coll; *m* NZ *Lindsay, dau of C P Ward, of Wellington, NZ, and has issue:

1c +Alastair Haworth; *b* 1973

1c *Rachel Louise; *b* 15 April 1976

1b Helen Margaret; *b* 23 Nov 1949; *d* 6 Jan 1953

2b *Elizabeth Claire; *b* 3 April 1954; *m* 1977 *David George Glendinning, and has issue:

1c *Richard David Peter; *b* 1981

2c *Hamish Donald; *b* 1986

3c *Thomas John; *b* 1990

1c *Sophie Rosa; *b* 1984

3a +Donald Austyn Nicholson [Dr Donald Barran, 3 Gt Western Terr, Glasgow W2]; *b* 17 Aug 1922; *educ* Repton and Trin Coll Cambridge (BA 1942, MB, BCh 1945), FFARCS 1954

1a *Dorothy Stella Margaret [Mrs Sloan Allison, The Cottage, Longbarn, Cardross, Dunbartonshire]; *b* 4 June 1919; *m* 6 March 1943 *(Joseph William) Sloan Allison, DSC, CA, only s of Joseph Allison, of Ashfield House, Balloch, Dunbartonshire, and has issue:

1b *(Joseph) Philip Sloan [Philip Allison Esq, 4 Raeburn St, Edinburgh EH4 1HY]; *b* 6 Feb 1944; *educ* Rugby and Churchill Coll Cambridge; *m* 1976 *Caroline Margaret, dau of James Roxburgh Paton, of Gullane, and has issue:

1c *James Austyn Sloan; *b* 1978

2c *Gerard Joseph Roxburgh; *b* 1982

3c *Peter William Donald; *b* 1987

1c *Catherine Margaret Elaine; *b* 1980

1b *Judith Stella Elaine [Mrs Simon Stone, 120 Divinity Rd, Oxford]; *b* 6 Dec 1948; *m* 1968 *Cdr Simon Hugh Stone, RN, and has issue:

1c *Charlotte Anne; *b* 1972

2c *Harriet Jane; *b* 1974

2b *Dorothy Lucy Louise; *b* 20 Jan 1950

(1) Ruth; *m* 1st 7 Nov 1900 Francis Edward Montague Donner (*d* 22 Sept 1927), of Mere Court, Chelford, Cheshire, and had issue; *m* 2nd 30 Sept 1942 Rev Canon Albert Darell Tupper-Carey (*d* 21 Sept 1943), Hon Chaplain to HM, son of Rev — Tupper-Carey, RD, of Chalke, and *d* 11 Sept 1948

(2) Lorna; *d* unm 2 April 1965 aged 91

(3) Edith; *d* unm 10 Sept 1953

(4) Margaret Elma; *d* unm 11 Sept 1916

(5) Dorothy Hilda; *m* 21 April 1909 Lt-Col Alfred James Napier Bartlett, DSO, OBE, DL, Oxon and Bucks LI (*d* 2 Feb 1956), of The Red House, Iffey, Oxford, yst son of John Edward Bartlett, DL, JP, of Peverel Court, Aylesbury, Bucks, and *d* 4 July 1949, leaving issue

(6) Nathalie Beatrice; *m* 16 April 1914 Maj Anthony Drummond Boden, Rifle Brigade (*ka* 25 Sept 1914), son of Henry Boden, of The Friary, Derby, and had issue:

1a *Patrick Anthony Drummond, OBE (1957), MC (1942); *b* 12 March 1915; *educ* Eton and Trin Coll Cambridge (BA 1936); Lt-Col Rifle Bde WW II 1943–45; *m* 29 Dec 1959 *Rosemary Jane, formerly w of Lt-Col Owain Hubert John Foster and only dau of Lt-Col Norman Hugh Huttenbach, DSO, OBE, MC, and has issue:

1b *John Peter; *b* 1 June 1961

2 Major; *b* 1 Dec 1846; *d* unm 21 Sept 1866

3 Charles, of Berry Pomeroy, Totnes, JP Devon 1894; *b* 22 Nov 1849; chm Dart Dist Bd Conservators and Totnes Dist Cottage Hosp Ctee; *m* 8 June 1876 Louisa Annie (*d* 2 April 1939), dau of John McNab, of Midtonfield, Renfrewshire, and *d* 7 Nov 1929, having had:

(1) Charles Marcel; *b* 2 April 1877; *m* 4 April 1907 Jessie Henderson, est dau of Thomas Pollok, of Liverpool, and was drowned in a storm at sea 9 Sept 1924

(2) Kenneth Gerald McNab; *b* 17 March 1886; *m* 2 June 1937 Frances Annie, 3rd dau of John Strang, of Garthowen, Castle Hill, Sydney, NSW, and *d* 13 Feb 1938

(3) Colin Adair, Capt 52nd LI; *b* 6 June 1893; *m* 17 July 1913 Christine Ida Leslie, dau of Francis Gassiot Houghton, and *dsp* 13 Oct 1964

(1) Muriel Louise; *m* 6 March 1913 John Hamilton Cumming, MRCS, LRCP (*d* 18 Nov 1936, and *d* 16 April 1952

4 Alfred, of Giggleswick, Settle, JP (W R Yorks and Leeds); *b* 29 June 1851; *m* 1st 8 Aug 1883 Lily Maria (*d* May 1885), dau of Thomas Scattergood, MRCS, and had issue:

(1) Claude Roulston, JP WR Yorks, Lt RGA (SR); *b* 1 May 1885; *educ* Marlborough and Trin Coll Cambridge (BA); *m* 10 Oct 1911 Edith (*d* 19 May 1973 aged 83), 2nd dau of Arthur Gaunt, of Stanningley Hall, Leeds, and *d* 17 Jan 1942, leaving issue:

1a (Lilian) Joan; 2nd Offr WRNS WW II 1940–46; *b* 23 July 1912; *d* 24 April 1996

2a Katharine Muriel; MB, ChB (Leeds) 1940; *b* 21 Aug 1913; *d* 28 Aug 1995

4 (cont.) Alfred Barran *m* 2nd 6 April 1904 Anne Mabel (*d* 6 Aug 1950), only dau of Capt Thomas Candler Wharton, 97th Regt, and *d* 12 Oct 1927, having by her had issue:

(2) Richard Wharton; *b* 21 March 1905; *educ* Wellington; *m* 15 June 1936 (Marie) Eileen (*d* 3 March 1995), dau of George Crabbe, of Sri Lanka, and *d* 19 July 1961, leaving issue:

1a *Valerie Anne Heather [Mrs Malcolm Chase, Byways, 12 Kent Rd, Fleet, Hants GU13 9AH]; *b* 11 July 1941 *m* 25 June 1977 *Malcolm G Chase and has:

1b *Jennifer Marianne Alison; *b* 1978

2b *Sarah Elizabeth Lucy; *b* 1979

(3) George Fletcher, MRCS, LRCP 1933, MB and BCh 1934, MD 1947; *b* 18 Aug 1908; *educ* Wellington and Trin Coll Cambridge (BA 1929); *m* 3 Oct 1936 Clare Mary Elizabeth (*d* 20 March 1998), dau of Albert Dudley, of London, and had:

1a +George Wharton [George Barran Esq, Rose Farm, East Runton, Norfolk]; *b* 26 Aug 1939; *educ* Douai Sch; *m* 1st 1967 Sue Russell, and has:

1b +Nicholas George; *b* 1968

1a (cont.) George Barran *m* 2nd 1984 *Sally Elizabeth, dau of David Charles Jeffcott Mansfield, of Suffolk, and by her has:

2b +George Arthur Mansfield; *b* 1985

1b *Elizabeth Margery; *b* 1986

2a +Richard Martin [Richard Barran Esq, 9 Evesham Walk, London, SE5 8SJ]; *b* 10 Dec 1941; *educ* Douai Sch

3a +Hugh Paull [Hugh Barran Esq, 1 Church Walk, N Petherton, Somerset TA6 6SE]; *b* 29 June 1943; *educ* Douai Sch; *m* 1973 *Anthea Janet, yst dau of R W Baker-Beall, of Beer, Devon, and has issue:

1b +Rowland Paull; *b* 1974

1b *Alice Matilda; *b* 18 Feb 1978

1a *Rosemary Clare [Mrs Rae Tugwell, The Village Shop, Minstead, Hants SO43 7FY]; *b* 7 March 1947; *m* 1974 *Capt Rae Tugwell, RA, and has:

1b *David Alexander Barran; *b* 1978

1b *Laura Clare; *b* 1976

5 Henry, JP (W R Yorks), of Moor Allerton, nr Leeds, and Madehurst Lodge, barrister; *b* 5 Oct 1856; *educ* Trin Hall Cambridge (MA, LLM); *m* 10 Feb 1891 Rosalie Mary (*d* 2 Jan 1914), est dau of Edgar Flower, JP, of Middlehill, Broadway, Worcs, and *d* 7 May 1942, leaving issue:

(1) Henry Vernon Flower, BA Cambridge, barrister Inner Temple 1921, Lt RFA SR; *b* 30 July 1894; *m* 21 July 1921 Cicely (*d* 1985), er dau of V-Adml Francis Wade Caulfeild, CBE (*see* CHARLEMONT, V), and *d* 21 June 1943, leaving issue:

1a *Mary Rosalie [Mrs Giles Heron, The Cottage, Glaisdale, Whitby, Yorks YO21 2PZ]; *b* 14 Oct 1922; *educ* St Anne's Coll Oxford (BA 1955); *m* 5 Jan 1963 *(Antony) Giles Heron

2a Alethea Katharine; *b* 13 July 1925; *m* 18 Oct 1950 *Rev John Manifold Courtenay (*d* 25 Aug 1988), s of Rev John Manifold Courtenay, and *d* 21 April 1977

3a Bridget Flower; *b* 19 May 1927; *m* 2 Dec 1949 *Denis Martin Browne, ARIBA, AADip ARIAS, Dip Dist TP, AMPTI, er son of Elliott Martin Browne, CBE, of London, and *d* 20 Feb 1989, leaving:

1b *Thomas Martin; *b* 18 Jan 1951; *educ* Edinburgh Acad

2b *Henry Francis; *b* 17 Sept 1962

3b *Roland Anthony; *b* 12 Dec 1964

1b *Helen Mary; *b* 14 Nov 1952

4a *Elfrida Cicely [Mrs Martin Cordeaux, 15 Lee Rd, Lincoln LN2 4BJ]; *b* 5 April 1929; *m* 2 March 1957 *Martin Bennett Cordeaux, son of Capt Edward Cawdron Cordeaux, DSO, OBE, DL, RN, of Louth, Lincs, and has issue:

1b *Charles Nicholas [Charles Cordeaux Esq, 136 Victoria Ave, Kingston-upon-Hull, E Yorks]; *b* 5 July 1958; *m* 1987 *Margaret Elizabeth, dau of William M A Davidson, of Hopeman, Elgin, Moray, and has issue:

1c *Michael Robert; *b* 1992

2c *Mark Edward; *b* 1995

1c *Heather Claire; *b* 1988

1b *Elizabeth Katharine; *b* 8 July 1961; *m* 1985 *Ritchie Hardin and has:

1c *Liam Alexander; *b* 1985

1c *Lauren Siobhan; *b* 1987

2b *Cicely Jane; *b* 14 April 1964; *m* 1992 *Kevin Skelton and has:

1c *Katherine Cicely; *b* 1995

5a *Selina Elizabeth [Mrs Michael Makower, Gogar House, Blairlogie, by Stirling]; *b* 24 May 1934; *m* 1 Oct 1960 *Michael Stanley Makower, 2nd son of Anthony Makower, MA, AIMM, of 15 Addison Crescent, London W14, by Sylvia Evelyn, MA, 2nd dau of Henry Goulburn Willouhly Chetwynd, AMICE, and has issue (*see* CHETWYND, V)

6a *Christabel Lucy; *b* 24 Feb 1939

(1) Elaine Isabel Flower; *d* 6 Sept 1981

6 Rowland Hirst (Sir); MP N Leeds 1902–18, memb Ct Leeds U, ktd 1917; *b* 7 Aug 1858; *m* 1st 10 Feb 1887 (*divorce* 1899) Rose Cardew (*d* 19 Jan 1952), dau of Rev Gilbert Bradley; *m* 2nd 7 April 1909 Louise Buchanan (*d* 24 Aug 1947), dau of J Stevenson Brown, of Montreal, and *d* 6 Aug 1949, having by his 1st w had issue:

(1) Rowland Noel, Capt 2nd Life Gds; *b* 25 Dec 1887; *m* 12 March 1917 Auriol Camilla Sharlia Blanche (*m* 2nd 25 Feb 1924 Sir James Allan Horne (*d* 3 Feb 1944) and *d* 7 Sept 1930), only dau of Hon Alistair George Hay, son of 12th Earl of Kinnoull (*qv*), and *das* 19 March 1919

(2) Hugh Bradley, MC; *b* 13 May 1889; Capt 1st W R Bde RFA (TF) WW I; *m* 21 Nov 1917 Estelle, dau of Frank Lockhart Cox, of 85 Cadogan Gdns, London, and *d* 19 May 1975, leaving issue:

1a +Hugh Rowland Murray [Hugh Barran Esq, Hildenley, Malton, Yorks]; *b* 14 April 1929; *m* 19 Feb 1957 *Diana Buttercup, only child of Capt Eric Geoffrey Dawnay, of Hildenley (*see* DOWNE, V), and has issue:

1b +Patrick Robin; *b* 28 Feb 1959; *m* 23 Sept 1989 *Miranda Jane, dau of Christopher John Spence, of Chieveley Manor, Newbury, Berks (*see* ROPNER, Bt), and has issue:

1c +Hugo Jeremy; *b* 1993

1c *Daisy Charlotte; *b* 1991

2c *Camilla Violet; *b* 27 April 1997

2b +Nicholas Eric Hugh; *b* 16 Jan 1964; *m* 1990 *Emma Louise Moya, only dau of Robert George Gee (*see* SHREWSBURY and WATERFORD, E), and has issue:

1c +Toby Nicholas Hugh; *b* 2 Feb 1995
1c *Hebe Elisabeth Blair; *b* 1993
1b *Annabelle Clare [Mrs Edward McMullan, 16 Acfold Rd, London SW6 2AL]; *b* 11 Dec 1960; *m* 4 Nov 1989 *Edward B McMullan, and has issue:
1c *Alexander; *b* 15 April 1991
2c *James; *b* 4 Oct 1996
1c *Poppy Victoria Ines; *b* 31 July 1992
2b *Verena April; *b* 6 June 1968; *m* 1993 *William A Ritson, s of Capt Tim W Ritson, of Ebnal Grange, Malpas, Cheshire, and has:
1c *Harry William; *b* 8 Oct 1997
1c *Alice; *b* 199–
1a *Jean Lockhart; *b* 8 Oct 1919
2a *Estelle Elspeth; *b* 6 Feb 1921
3a *Ann Lockhart [Mrs John Robinson, The Normans, Bilbrough, York]; *b* 7 Oct 1930; *m* 6 Sept 1950 *Maj John Francis Leetham Robinson, MC, 12th Roy Lancers, est s of Maj John Robinson, of Aldersyde, Dringhouses, York, and has issue:
1b *Hugh Andrew Leetham [Hugh Robinson Esq, Sandwith Lodge, Bilbrough, Yorks]; *b* 12 Dec 1955; *m* 1980 *Amanda Jane Menage, and has issue:
1c *Oliver Leetham; *b* 1981
1c *Georgina; *b* 198–
1b *Marian Lockhart [The Hon Mrs Michael Bourne, 50 Bradbourne St, London SW6]; *b* 28 Sept 1951; *m* 1985 *Hon Michael Kemp Bourne, son of Baron Bourne, GCB, KBE, CMG, LP, (*see* 1970 edn)
2b *Caroline Mary [Mrs John Edwards, 26 Summerfield Ave, London NW6]; *b* 18 June 1957; *m* 1987 *John Edwards, and has issue:
1c *Thomas; *b* 1991
1c *Kate; *b* 1990
3b *Joanna Susan [Mrs Martin Drake, 98 The Mount, York]; *b* 11 March 1961; *m* 1982 *Capt Martin James Butterfield Drake, Duke of Wellington's Regt, and has issue:
1c *James; *b* 1988
1c *Lucie; *b* 1985
(1) Rose Sylvia; *m* 20 June 1918 Capt Brevet Maj Harold Abbot Ryott, 6th Bn Northumberland Fus (*d* 18 June 1954), and had issue
(2) Gwendoline Cardew; *m* 23 Oct 1919 John Ughtred Thornton Shuttleworth (*d* 1966), and had issue
1 Elizabeth; *m* 3 March 1875 William Town, of The Hills, Bingley, and *d* 1892, having had issue
2 Anne; *m* 25 Dec 1867 Rev Lundy Edward William Foote (*d* 25 Dec 1925), Vicar St Peter's Harrogate, and *d* 1930, leaving issue
3 Eliza; *m* 8 Aug 1907 Sir Nathan Bodington, LittD, LLD (*dsp* 12 May 1911), V-Chllr Leeds U, and *d* 21 Jan 1941
4 Louisa; *m* 8 Sept 1909 Harry Manfield (*d* 9 Feb 1923), of Moulton Grange, Pitsford, Northampton, er son of Sir Moses Philip Manfield, MP, and *d* 20 Feb 1944

Sir JOHN *d* 3 May 1905; his gs,

Sir John Nicholson Barran, 2nd Bt, JP (W RYorks); *b* 16 Aug 1872; *educ* Winchester and Trin Coll Cambridge (BA 1894); MP (Lib) Hawick Burghs 1909–18, PPS to: PMG, Pres Local Govt Bd, Home Sec, For Sec and PM 1910–16, chm Port and Transit Exec Ctee 1920–21; *m* 1st 18 Nov 1902 Alice Margarita (*d* 1 July 1939), est dau of Rev Leighton Parks, DD, Rector St Bartholomew's, New York; *m* 2nd 14 Nov 1946 Esther Frances, er dau of Hon Francis Marion Bates Fisher, of Ngongotaha, Rotorua, NZ, and by his 1st w had:
1 JOHN LEIGHTON (Sir), **3rd Bt**
2 Edward Nicholson; *b* 30 March 1910; *educ* Winchester and Trin Coll Cambridge (BA 1931, MA 1935); Capt 5th Inniskilling Dragoon Gds SR WW II; *m* 1st 4 Dec 1940 (*divorce* 1953) Daphne Margaret, only dau of Herbert William Bird, of Norther, Cranleigh, Surrey, and has:
(1) +Nicholas Dudley Edward; *b* 17 Jan 1942; *educ* Harrow and U of California (BSc Business Admin 1967); *m* 11 April 1964 *Feliksa, dau of Feliks Pabilionis, of Omaha, Nebraska, and has issue:
1a +Antony Nicholas; *b* 13 May 1967
2a +Daniel Nicholas; *b* 20 Aug 1968
(2) +Stephen William Edward; *b* 11 April 1944; *educ* Winchester and Trin Coll Cambridge
(1) *Alice Daphne Margarita; *b* 22 Nov 1946; *m* 20 Sept 1975 *Giovanni Battista Liugi Dalle Nogare, est s of Gino Nogare, of Vicenza, Italy, and has issue
2 (cont.) Edward Barran *m* 2nd 28 Jan 1955 *Patricia Helen [Mrs Edward Barran, Ackworth Grange, East Hardwick, Pontefract, Yorks WS8 3EG], est dau of Alexander Granville Blake, ICS, of Ascot, and *d* 20 Aug 1994 leaving by her:
(3) +Charles Patrick Edward; *b* 5 Dec 1955
(2) *Frances Margarita [Mrs John de Moraville, Frethorne House, Wantage, Oxon]; *b* 10 May 1958; *m* 15 July 1979 *John de Moraville, s of Capt de Moraville
3 +David Haven [Sir David Barran, Brent Eleigh Hall, Sudbury, Suffolk CO10 9NP]; *b* 23 May 1912; *educ* Winchester and Trin Coll Cambridge (BA 1934); pres Asiatic Petroleum Corp (NY) 1958–61, chm Shell Transport Trading Gp Ltd 1966–72, dir Rheem Mfg Co New York, Drayton Corp and Drayton Gp Marine Midland Bank, Internat Marine Banking Co 1973–, Glaxo Hldgs 1973– and BICC 1973–, chm Hampton Gold Mining Areas 1973–, Tstee Anglo-German Fndn Study Industl Soc 1973–, dir Samuel Montagu 1974–, BL 1975– and Standard Chartered Bank 1977–; ktd 1971; *m* 29 March 1944 *Jane Lechmere, 2nd dau of Nicholas Lechmere Cunningham Macaskie, QC, of 27 Kensington Sq, London W8, and has had issue:
(1) Tristram Cosmo; *b* 17 July 1945; *educ* Downside; *m* 5 Nov 1973 *Miranda Clare Frances [Mrs Tristram Barran, The 'Oldall, Brent Eleigh, Sudbury, Suffolk CO10 9NP], yst dau of Maj Sir (Robert) Crichton Mitchell Cotts, 3rd Bt (*qv*), and *d* 1992 in a motor accident, leaving issue:
1a +Ferdinand Roc; *b* 1974
2a +Giuseppe Maria; *b* 1978
1a *Petra Sely; *b* 1975
(2) +Julian Mark Lechmere [Julian Barran Esq, Welham Farm, Shepton Montague, Castle Cary, Som]; *b* 27 May 1947; *educ* Downside; *m* 1st 19 July 1970 Mary, dau of Sir Edward Playfair, KCB, and has issue:
1a +Leo David; *b* 17 Dec 1973
2a +Laurence Edward; *b* 8 Aug 1977
1a *Tabitha Jane; *b* 24 March 1972
(2) (cont.) Julian Barran *m* 2nd 1986 *Diana, dau of Cosmo de Bosdari, and has further issue:
3a +Cosmo Ralph; *b* 1990
3a +Milo; *b* 17 Jan 1996
4a +Hugh; *b* 17 Jan 1996
2a *Emily Dolores; *b* 1988
(3) +Marius Peregrine Lechmere [Marius Barran Esq, 64 St Marks Rd, London W10 6NN]; *b* 18 Feb 1949; *educ* Downside and Trin Coll Cambridge; *m* 22 Jan 1972 *Veronica Tessa, yst dau of Prof Alphonsus Ligouri d'Abreu, OBE, ChM, MB, FRCS Eng, of Coughton, Warwicks, and has issue:
1a *Perdita Elizabeth; *b* 1972
2a *Lorna Marina; *b* 1974
3a *Phoebe Alice; *b* 1981
4a *Amy Louise; *b* 1984
(4) +Adrian Stuart Lechmere; *b* 20 May 1959
(1) *(Jane) Francesca [Mrs Philip Scoones, 199 Goldhawk Rd, London W12]; *b* 26 Dec 1950; *m* 1980 *Philip Anthony Francis Scoones, and has issue:
1a +Benedict Boniface Nicholas; *b* 1983
1a *Eleanor Jane; *b* 1981
(2) *Lalage Margarita; *b* 6 Sept 1957; *m* 27 Jan 1996 *Stephen Reeve-Tucker, 4th s of Lt-Col T S W Reeve-Tucker, of Ross-on-Wye, Herefs
(3) *Calista Maria [Mrs William Lucy, 10 Grace's Rd, London SE5 8PA]; *b* 28 Aug 1960; *m* 1986 *William Walrond Lucy, only son Maj D P V Lucy, of The Chantry, Ilminster, Som, and has issue:
1a *Tancred Edmund Walrond; *b* 1992
1a *Laetitia Alice Haven; *b* 1989
1 Elise Margarita; *b* 3 June 1906; *m* 14 Nov 1941 16th Viscount Mountgarret (*qv*), and *d* 8 Aug 1968

Sir JOHN *d* 8 July 1952; his est son,

Sir John Leighton Barran, 3rd Bt; *b* 24 March 1904; *educ* Winchester and Trin Coll Cambridge (BA 1925); JP and CC W R Yorks 1952, Cdr RNV (S)R WW II, dir City Investing Co (New York and Zurich) 1972–; *m* 5 March 1929 Hon Alison Mary Hore-Ruthven (*d* 2 Oct 1973), 3rd dau of 9th Lord Ruthven (*see* CARLISLE, E), and *d* 28 Dec 1974, leaving issue:
1 Sir JOHN NAPOLEON RUTHVEN BARRAN, **4th and present Bt**

BARRETT-LENNARD

Arms: Quarterly, 1st and 4th, or on a fess gu. three fleurs-de-lys of the field (for LENNARD); 2nd and 3rd, party per pale arg. and gu. barry of four counterchanged (for BARRETT), all within a bordure wavy sa. **Crest:** Out of a ducal coronet or an Irish wolf-dog's head per fess arg. and erm., charged on the neck with an escallop per fess nebulée gu. and sa. **Mottoes:** 1 *Pour bien désirer* ('To wish well'), 2 *La bondad para la medra* ('Goodness through improvement'). **Creation:** Bt. (UK) 30 June 1801.

SIR HUGH DACRE BARRETT-LENNARD, 6TH BT, of Belhus, Essex [The Rev Sir Hugh Barrett-Lennard Bt, The Oratory, London SW7 2RW]; *b* 27 June 1917; *s* cousin 1977; *educ* Radley and Pontifical Beda Coll Rome; 2nd Lt London Scottish 1940, Capt Essex Regt WW II (despatches); RC priest, ordained 1950

Lineage: Sir Thomas Barrett-Lennard, 1st Bt (UK), so *cr* 30 June 1801, of Belhus; *b* 6 Jan 1762 (illegitimate s and testamentary heir of 17th Lord (Baron) Dacre (*qv*); FSA; *m* 1st 15 Feb 1787 Dorothy (*d* 26 Oct 1830), dau of Sir John St Aubyn, 3rd Bt, of Clowance, Cornwall (*see* SAINT LEVLAN, B), and had:

1 Thomas; MP Maldon; *b* 4 Oct 1788; *m* 1st 3 Aug 1815 Margaret, 2nd dau of John Wharton, of Skelton Castle, Yorks; *m* 2nd 30 June 1825 Mary (*d* 1844), only dau and heiress of Bartlett Bridger Shedden, of Adlham Hall, Suffolk, and *d* 9 June 1856, having by her had:

(1) **Sir Thomas Barrett-Lennard, 2nd Bt**, JP, DL and CA Essex, High Sheriff 1865, DL Co Monaghan, High Sheriff 1868; *educ* St Peter's Coll Cambridge (MA); *b* 29 Dec 1826; *m* 18 Jan 1853 Emma (*d* 8 June 1916), dau of Rev Sir John Page Wood, 2nd Bt (*qv*), and *d* 16 Jan 1919, leaving issue:

1a **Sir Thomas Barrett-Lennard, 3rd Bt**, JP, DL Essex, JP Norfolk, barrister Middle Temple; *b* 25 Oct 1853; *m* 21 June 1884 Mary (*d* 2 April 1932), dau of Rev Canon William Price, Vicar Llanarth, Mon, and *dsp* 18 Sept 1923

2a Charles Dacre; *d* an infant 31 Jan 1860

3a **Sir Richard Fiennes Barrett-Lennard, 4th Bt**, JP Essex; *b* 17 May 1861; *educ* Clare Coll Cambridge (MA); *m* 27 April 1892 Lepel Julia (*d* 16 Dec 1959), dau of Rev Henry Thornton Pearse, MA, and *d* 6 Sept 1934, leaving:

1b **Sir (Thomas) Richard Fiennes Barrett-Lennard, 5th Bt**, OBE (1977), JP (Essex 1926–37 and Norfolk 1941–66); *b* 12 Dec 1898; *educ* Brighton Coll and Clare Coll Cambridge (BA 1920, MA 1924); v-pres Norwich Union Life Assur Soc and v-chm Norwich Union Fire Insur Soc, dir Scottish Union & Nat Ins Co and Maritime Insur Co, chm E Anglian TSB; KStJ; *m* 26 July 1922 Una Kathleen Finora (*d* 20 Nov 1985), dau of Hon John Donohoe FitzGerald, KC, s of Baron FitzGerald (*see* 1898 edn), and *d* 28 Dec 1977, leaving:

1c *Anne [Mrs John Pollock, Rose Ash House, S Molton, Devon EX36 4RB]; *b* 2 Dec 1923; *m* 4 May 1949 *Rev John Charles Pollock (*see* POLLOCK, Bt)

1b Marjorie Lepel; *b* 6 Aug 1894; Kaisar-i-Hind silver medal; *m* 27 Feb 1926 Sir Charles Dalrymple Belgrave, KBE (*d* 28 Feb 1969), Fin Advsr to Ruling Sheikhs of Bahrain 1926–57, and *d* 19 Nov 1970, leaving issue

1a Evelyn Laura Mary; *m* 5 June 1877 Lt-Col Frederick Ekins Blakeney Loraine, RA (*d* 4 April 1914), 2nd surv s of Sir John Lambton Loraine, 10th Bt (*see* 1956 edn), and *d* 17 Nov 1939, leaving issue

2a Emma Isolda; *m* 7 Jan 1881 Hon John Donohoe FitzGerald, KC (*d* 11 May 1918), 2nd s of Baron FitzGerald (*see* 1889 edn), and *d* 11 Aug 1938, leaving issue

3a Dorothy Ada; *d* 28 July 1864

4a Anna Cristabel; *m* 1895 Lt Gerard Henry William O'Shea, Essex Regt, and *d* 23 Sept 1945, leaving issue

5a Barbara Joyce Frances; *m* 12 June 1893 Alfred Hastings Warren and had issue

(2) Dacre (Rev); Rector Aldham; *b* 19 Jan 1829; *educ* St Peter's Coll Cambridge (MA); *m* 1st 1855 Elizabeth, dau of Henry Lelliott; *m* 2nd 1881 Sarah (*d* 22 March 1903), dau of John Liversage, and *d* April 1910, having by her had issue:

1a Dacre; *b* 9 Aug 1884; *m* 1915 Mabel Ella, dau of James Sage, of Aldham, and *d* 1948, leaving:

1b *Viva Dacre [Miss Viva Barrett-Lennard, Gable Cottage, Aldham, Hadleigh, Suffolk]; *b* 1923

(3) St Aubyn; MA, barrister Inner Temple, Ensign 17th Regt; *b* 8 Jan 1831; *m* 8 May 1862 Jane, widow of Lt-Col — Aubrey and dau of F Sparks, and *dsp* 1 April 1866

(4) Charles Edward; Lt 5th Dragoon Gds; *b* 13 Jan 1835; *m* 1st 18 Feb 1856 Fanny (*d* 5 April 1857), dau of Rev D Darnell, Rector Welton, Northants; *m* 2nd 4 Dec 1873 Anna Meredith, dau of Chaplin Aaron Harris, of Baltimore, Md., and *d* 17 July 1874, leaving by his 1st w:

1a Emma Frances Mary; *d* young 29 Feb 1860

(5) John (Rev); MA Cantab, Lt RE, Rector Crawley, Sussex; *b* 20 Feb 1839; *m* 9 April 1861 Isabella Jane (*d* 29 March 1933), 2nd dau of Sir John Lambton Loraine, 10th Bt (*see* 1956 edn), and *d* 13 Dec 1898, having had issue:

1a Herbert Loraine (Rev); Rector Crawley; *b* 9 Oct 1863; *educ* Selwyn Coll Cambridge; *m* 27 Nov 1928 Beatrice Ella (*d* 3 May 1960), 3rd dau of Walter Fox, of The White Ho, Rockford, Essex, and *d* 13 June 1934

1a Emily Isabella; *d* young 1867

2a Constance Keppel; *d* unm 9 Jan 1927

2 John; *b* 30 Dec 1789; *m* 23 July 1814 Dorothy Anne (*d* 19 Nov 1888 aged 93), 2nd dau of Sir Walter Stirling, 1st Bt (*see* 1850 edn), and *d* 16 Dec 1856, having had issue:

(1) Thomas Stirling George; *m* 7 Sept 1841 Frederica (*m* 2nd 13 July 1846 William Whitaker), dau of Col Joseph Brooks, and *dsp* 7 April 1845

(2) George; Dip Serv; *b* 1817; *m* 1st 1840 Jessie, dau and coheir of J M Drummond Nairne, of Dunsinane Castle, Perth, and had issue:

1a Thomas George; Capt 5th Dragoon Gds; *b* 1842; *m* 1873 Edith, dau of John Mackenzie, and *d* Feb 1908, leaving issue:

1b Fiennes Cecil Arthur (Sir); barrister Lincoln's Inn 1905, Judge Supreme Court Straits Settlements and FMS, Judge Appeal Court Johore and Kedah 1920–25, Ch Justice Jamaica 1925–32, ktd 1926, Lecturer Birkbeck Coll London 1932–38, Legal Assist Min Ag and Fisheries 1942–56, served Boer War (wounded) and E Africa WW I; *b* 2 April 1880; *educ* Bonn U; *m* 18 Sept 1916 Winifrede Mignon (*d* 27 Dec 1969), dau of Alfred Berlyn, and *d* 26 Jan 1963, leaving issue:

1c Rev Sir HUGH DACRE BARRETT-LENNARD, **6th and present Bt**

2b Aylmer Guy Howard, Army Lt WW I (wounded); *b* 6 Aug 1881; *m* 1925 *Cicely Anne, dau of William George Hunter, of Hawkes Bay, NZ, and *d* March 1936, leaving issue:

1c Cynthia Jane Fiennes; *b* 12 Sept 1926; *educ* Victoria U Coll Wellington (BA)

3b Eric Gordon, Lt RFC; *b* 1886; *d* following a car crash 8 June 1950

1b Dorothy Margaret Ivy; *b* 1884; *d* unm 3 July 1955

(2) (cont.) George Barrett-Lennard *m* 2nd 5 Aug 1858 Sarah (*d* 19 Jan 1925), dau of William Bradbury, of Everton, and *d* 11 March 1896, having by her had issue:

2a George; *dsp* 23 May 1886

3a Henry; *dsp* 1897

4a Trenchard Goodenough; *b* 10 Sept 1872; *m* 3 June 1903 Rosa (*d* 13 Jan 1962), dau of W J Hall, of Cheadle Hulme, Cheshire, and *d* 28 Feb 1945, leaving issue:

1b Dacre; *b* 21 June 1906; *m* 19 Nov 1938 *Una [Mrs Dacre Barrett-Lennard, 37 The Cliff, Wellington Rd, Wallasey, Merseyside L45 2NL], dau of Leo Burn, of Wallasey, Cheshire, and was *ka* 27 Nov 1944, leaving issue:

1c *Paula [Mrs David Staines, 1 Old Orchard, Hawthorne Lane, Wilmslow, Cheshire SK9 5DH]; *b* 12 Sept 1943; *m* 1969 *David Ambrose Staines, and has issue:

1d *Dacre Ambrose; *b* 1977

1d *Rachel; *b* 1975

2b Roy; *b* 23 July 1909; *m* 20 July 1939 Joyce Christine Elizabeth (*d* 1985), dau of Stuart Robert Drinkwater, of Coventry, and *d* 4 Jan 1969, leaving issue:

1c +RICHARD FYNES [Richard Barrett-Lennard Esq, Top Flat, 8 Flexbury Park, Flexbury, Bude, Cornwall EX23]; *b* 6 April 1941; heir presumptive

2c +Peter John [Peter Barrett-Lennard Esq, Forest House, Forest Rd, E Horsley, Surrey KT24 3BX]; *b* 26 Sept 1942; *m* 20 June 1979 *Sonja, dau of Vladimir Belacic, of Zagreb, and has issue:

1d +Simon James; *b* 12 Aug 1980

1c *Penelope Anne; *b* 27 Dec 1948

1a Gertrude; *m* 18 June 1894 Charles Rutz, s of Jakob Rutz, of Zurich, and *d* 6 Dec 1939

(3) Henry; *b* 28 May 1818; *m* 31 Aug 1845 his cousin Elizabeth (*d* 28 May 1855), dau of George Barrett-Lennard (*see* below), and *d* 31 Aug 1899, leaving issue:

1a Francis; *b* 17 Dec 1848; *d* 12 Oct 1924

3 George; *b* 26 June 1796; *m* 1st 7 Nov 1820 Elizabeth (*d* 28 July 1867), est dau and coheir of Edmund Prideaux, of Hexworthy, Cornwall; *m* 2nd 18 March 1868 Elizabeth (*d* 1886), widow of Col — Beaumont and dau of Robert Abraham Silvera, and *d* 4 March 1870, leaving by his 1st w:

(1) Edmund Thomas Henry, of Annandale, W Australia; *b* 20 Nov 1823; *m* 1853 Elizabeth Ann, dau of Charles Smith, of W Australia, and *d* 22 July 1895, leaving issue:

1a Edmund George; *b* 1855; *m* 1881 Fanny Emily (*d* 2 Dec 1934), dau of James William Broun, of Beverley, W Australia, and *d* 27 Jan 1931, leaving issue:

1b Edmund Thomas Dacre; *b* 1882; *m* 1907 Kathleen Rosina (*d* 12 Aug 1939), dau of Thomas D Pettigrew, and *d* 8 Aug 1945, leaving issue:

1c Geoffrey; *b* 1908; *m* 30 Jan 1933 *Lorna Margaret, dau of A B Lodge, of York, W Australia, and *d* 1988, leaving issue:

1d +John [John Barrett-Lennard Esq, Annandale, Box 24, Beverley, W Australia 6304]; *b* 2 Feb 1949; *m* 1976 *Leita Catherine, dau of R A McLean, of Beverley, W Australia, and has issue:

1e +James Dacre; *b* 1981

1e *Claire; *b* 1979

2e *Marie; *b* 1984

1d *Sarah Margaret [Mrs Archibald Fraser, Lot 6, Brookman Rd, Meadows, S Australia 5201]; *b* 1936; *m* 20 May 1963 *Archibald Stewart Fraser, and has issue:

1e *John Buchanan; *b* 1966

2e *Geoffrey Lodge; *b* 1968

1e *Catherine Margaret; *b* 1971; *m* 1996 *David Alexander Edgar

2d *Judith [Mrs Robert Magill, 77 Forrest St, Beverley 6304, W Australia]; *b* 24 Dec 1938; *m* 7 June 1969 Robert Henry Magill (*d* 1974), and has issue:

1e *Peter John; *b* 1972

2e *David James Henry; *b* 1974

1e *Catherine Elizabeth; *b* 1970

2c Edmund Thomas Keith; *b* 1911; *m* 1938 *Margaret [Mrs Edmund Barrett-Lennard, Woonderlin, Beverley, W Australia], dau of A V Clarke, of Beverley, W Australia, and *d* 19–, leaving issue:

1d +Edmund Timothy Dacre; *b* 1941

2d +Douglas John [Douglas Barrett-Lennard Esq, Woonderlin, Beverley, W Australia]; *b* 1944; *m* 1974 *Dorothy Marianne, er dau of Gordon Derwent Crosthwaite, of Glenroa, Margaret River, W Australia, and has issue:

1e +Derwent Thomas Keith; *b* 1976

3d +Richard [Richard Barrett-Lennard Esq, Milepool, Beverley, W Australia]; *b* 1950; AMF Vietnam; *m* 1975 *Lorna Jean, dau of Donald A Sprigg, of Strathallen, Wagin, W Australia, and has issue:

1e +Michael James; *b* 1978

2e +Jeremy; *b* 1980

1d *Helen Mary [Helen Barrett-Lennard, Forrest St, Beverley, W Australia]; *b* 1939; *m* 1959 —, and has issue:

1e *Christopher James Blake; *b* 1960

2e *Thomas William Timothy; *b* 1966

1e *Catherine Jane Blake; *b* 1962

3c +Antony Leslie [Antony Barrett-Lennard Esq, 84/31 Williams Rd, Nedlands, W Australia 6009, Australia]; *b* 1913; *m* 1943 *Ethel Barbara Adams, and has issue:

1d +Antony John William; *b* 1953; *m* 1981 *Alison, dau of P R Bremner, of Beverley, W Australia, and has issue:

1e +Benjamin James; *b* 1987

1e *Jodie Louise; *b* 1985

1d *Carmen Lesley; *b* 1944

2d *Jill Kathleen; *b* 1946; *m* 1974 *Allan Wall, and has issue:

1e *Timother Lawler; *b* 1976

1e *Carmen Belinda; *b* 1978

3d *Sally Anne; *b* 1950; *m* 1979 *George Jenkin Ellis Smith, and has issue:
1e *Thomas William; *b* 1983
1e *Hilary Rebecca; *b* 1981
2b Francis; *b* 29 Dec 1882; *m* 1910 Elsie Selena (*d* 1950), dau of Thomas George Walker, and *d* 7 June 1959, having had issue:
1c +Thomas Edmund [Thomas Barrett-Lennard Esq, Drumclyer, Beverley, W Australia]; *b* 1916; farmer; *m* Jan 1948 *Lesley Vernon, dau of Vernon Bland Gibson, of Perth, W Australia, and has issue:
1d +Graham Francis; *b* 1953; *m* 1984 *Dina Campbell, dau of John Pike Campbell Curlewis, of Toronto, NSW, and has issue:
1e +Edmund George; *b* 1986
1e *Marika Joan; *b* 1984
1d *Felicity Anne; *b* 1949; BEd Dip PE; *m* 1977 *Russell John Perry, PhD, BSc, s of Alfred Trevor Perry, of Perth, W Australia, and has issue:
1e *Philippa Louise; *b* 1982
2e *Elizabeth Emma; *b* 1985
2d *Jennifer Jane; *b* 1950; WATC; *m* 1975 *Vernon Ashley, s of Julius Vernon Brockman, of Busselton, W Australia, and has issue:
1e *James Julius; *b* 1977
2e *Ashley Edmund Vernon; *b* 1980
3d *Dinah Louise [Mrs Ronald Fleming, Glenesk, Muchea, W Australia]; *b* 1955; WATC, BHSAI; *m* 1987 *Ronald John Fleming
2c Francis Graham; RAAF attd RAF; *b* 1923; *ka* over Germany 1944
1c *Launa; *b* 1911; *m* 1940 *Horace Arnold Butler, of Beverley, W Australia, and has:
1d *Lennard Wilfred; *b* 1944
1d *Frances Merrilyn; *b* 1943
3b Henry; *b* 15 June 1884; *m* 8 May 1912 Muriel Ellen, dau of John Trevelyan, and *d* 1960, leaving issue:
1c +Trevor Henry [Trevor Barrett-Lennard Esq, Camblebren, Gairdner River, W Australia]; *b* 18 Jan 1922; AIF WW II, farmer; *m* 1951 *Audrey, yr dau of Albert E Wilhelm, of Beverley, W Australia, and has issue:
1d +Cameron [Cameron Barrett-Lennard Esq, Beaming Hill, Gairdner River, W Australia]; *b* 1952; *m* 1979 *Kathryn Faye, dau of Colin V Ellis, of Victoria, and has issue:
1e +Dale Cameron; *b* 1982
1e *Deanna Jane; *b* 1981
2e *Krystelle Amy; *b* 1985
2d +Brent; *b* 1957; *m* 1984 *Jillian Elizabeth, dau of William E Meier, of Toocelup, Bremer Bay, W Australia, and has issue:
1e +Clay; *b* 1988
1e *Holly Elizabeth; *b* 1985
1d *Leonie Gaye; *b* 1954; *m* 1977 *Raymond John Ward, of Bridgetown, W Australia, and has issue:
1e *Benjamin Trevor; *b* 1978
2d *Belinda Anne [Mrs Graham Yuill, PO Box 8, Esperence, W Australia]; *b* 1963; *m* 1987 *Graham John Yuill, and has issue:
1e *Rhys Raymond; *b* 1989
1e *Kyra Corrine; *b* 1990
4b Alexander Forrest; *b* 28 May 1895; *m* 31 Oct 1917 Evan Mary (*d* 1973), dau of Edward Berry, and *d* 1941, leaving issue:
1c +Alexander Dacre [Alexander Barrett-Lennard Esq, Belhus, Box 58, Beverley, W Australia]; Sgt RAAF; *b* 1921; *m* 1949 *Dorothea Ann, dau of James Davidson Weaver, of Beverley, W Australia, and has issue:
1d +Gregory Dacre; *b* 1958; *m* 1985 *Margaret Louise, dau of Alan J Croft, of City Beach, W Australia, and has issue:
1e +Jackson Dacre; *b* 1988
1e *Alix Louise; *b* 1990
2e *Rebecca Ann; *b* 1992
1d *Susan [Mrs Phillip Hill, PO Box 225, Beverley, W Australia 6304, Australia]; *b* 1950; *m* 1st 1971 Kenneth Charles Baston, and has issue:
1e *George Derek; *b* 1974
2e *Richard Charles; *b* 1976
1d (cont.) Mrs Susan Baston *m* 2nd 1981 *Phillip James Hill, and has further issue:
3e *Guy Philip; *b* 1982
2d *Meredith; *b* 1953; *m* 1973 *Philip Anthony Cockerill, of W Australia, and has issue:
1e *Benjamin Dacre; *b* 1976
2e *Joseph Anthony; *b* 1978
3e *Samuel Charles; *b* 1980
4e *Zachary Philip; *b* 1984
3d *Vicki; *b* 1955
1c *Peggy Amy [Mrs Durward Toleman, 208 Mahoney's Rd, Burwood East, 3151, Victoria, Australia]; *b* 1918; *m* 1946 Durward Toleman (*d* 1981), and has issue:
1d *David Forrest; *b* 1952; *educ* U of Melbourne (BSc, BCom)
2d *Michael Fiennes; *b* 1955; *m* 1985 *Suzanne Joy, dau of Bruce Herbert Whitaker, of Donvale, Victoria, and has issue:
1e *Kate Suzanne; *b* 1986
2e *Penny Nicole; *b* 1988
1b Emily Eliza; *m* 1911 John Richard Norris, of Queensland, and *d* 10 Sept 1935, leaving issue
1a Amy Eliza; *m* 1880 Alexander Forrest, CMG, MLA (*d* 20 June 1901), of W Australia, and *d* 1898, leaving issue

(2) Henry (Rev); *b* 12 Sept 1828; *d* 20 Sept 1866
(1) Hebe Dorothy; *m* 1 May 1849 Francis Cortlandt Arnold Wallinger, and *d* 19 May 1880, leaving issue
(2) Elizabeth; *m* 31 Aug 1845 her cousin Henry Barrett-Lennard, and *d* 8 May 1855, leaving issue (*see* above)
(3) Julia Georgina; *m* 26 July 1883 Rev Albert Philip Cornwall, Vicar Barnham, Sussex, and *d* 6 May 1900
4 Henry (Rev); *b* 18 Jan 1798; *m* 26 April 1821 Hebe Dorothy, yst dau and coheir of Edmund Prideaux, of Hexworthy, Cornwall, and *d* 17 Aug 1870
5 Edward Pomeroy, of St Leonards, Middle Swan, W Australia; *b* 19 June 1799; *m* 28 Sept 1837 Elizabeth Frances (*d* 1878), dau of Robert Graham, and *d* 29 June 1878, leaving:
(1) Edward Graham; *b* 30 Nov 1839; *m* 9 Jan 1862 Mary Ann (*d* 1884), est dau of Hon John W Hardey, MLC, of Grove Ho, Perth, W Australia, and *d* 1888, leaving issue:
1a George Hardey, of St Leonards, Guildford, Swan River, W Australia; *b* 4 Dec 1862; *m* 13 Jan 1886 Amy (*d* 23 March 1937), dau of Hon Edmund Ralph Brockman, of Henley Pk, W Australia, and *d* 8 Oct 1917, leaving issue:
1b George Graham; *b* 30 Dec 1887; *m* 1911 Maud Gladys Hastings, dau of G W Hester, of Dalgarup Pk, Bridgetown, W Australia, and *d* 1968, having had issue:
1c +Fynes [Fynes Barrett-Lennard Esq, Marri Hieghts, Gingin, W Australia 6503]; *b* 14 May 1915; *m* 1949 *Florence Ray, dau of W C Williams, of W Australia, and has issue:
1d +Kingsley Ian Michael [Mr Kingsley Barrett-Leonard, 12 Collier St, Applecross, W Australia 6153]; *b* 9 Nov 1954; *m* 1979 *Kerry Dawn Howard and has:
1e +Andrew Graham; *b* 25 May 1989
1e *Alison Louise; *b* 31 Oct 1985
2d +William Ashley Dacre; *b* 25 Nov 1957; *m* 1979 *Shirley May Brimblecombe and has:
1e +Denholm; *b* 13 Sept 1986
1e *Joanne Elaine; *b* 24 Sept 1983
1d *Wendy Roslyn [Mrs David Webb, 48a Tain St, Applecross, W Australia 6153]; *b* 19 Feb 1950; *m* 1st 1972 Ralph Dunstan Pomery; *m* 2nd 3 Nov 1990 *David Webb and by her 1st husb has:
1e *Sharon Anne; *b* 10 April 1974
2e *Michelle Louise; *b* 27 Jan 1977
2d *Helen Elizabeth [Mrs Kimberley Clifton, 9 Riley Road, Claremont, W Australia 6010]; *b* 13 Sept 1951; *m* 1974 *Kimberley John Clifton and has:
1e *Matthew Adam, *b* 29 Sept 1981
1e *Kendall Jane; *b* 1 Nov 1977
2e *Rachel Susan; *b* 28 April 1979
2c +Douglas Graham [Douglas Barrett-Lennard Esq, The Crescent, Gingin, W Australia]; *b* 1916; *m* 1943 *Olive, dau of Alec Davidson, of Bonnie Rock, W Australia, and has had:
1d +David Thomas [David Barrett-Lennard Esq, Belhus, Upper Swan, W Australia]; *b* 1945
2d +Peter Dacre; *b* 1947
1d *Joan [Mrs Keith McMullan, Caprice Rd, Geraldton, W Australia]; *b* 1945; *m* 1970 *Keith McMullan
2d Rosalind; *b* 1951; *d* 1958
3d *Kaye Julie; *b* 1959
3c +Lancelot [Lancelot Barrett-Lennard Esq, Averley Downs, Kondut, W Australia], MB, BS Adelaide; *b* 1918; *m* 1943 *Patricia Ida, dau of W Porter, of Toodefay, W Australia, and has:
1d +Michael Scott; *b* 1949
2d +Richard John Stirling (Rev) [The Rev Dr Richard Barrett-Lennard, 16 Bellairs Rd, Kardinya, W Australia 6163]; *b* 1951; MA Oxon, PhD; *m* 1st 1973 (*divorce* 1990) Rosalind, dau of Robert Willis; *m* 2nd 1990 *Julie Louise, dau of Leslie Gibson, and by his 1st w has:
1e +David John; *b* 1978
2e +Jeremy Robert; *b* 1981
3d +Simon Hugh; *b* 1957
1d *Patricia Ruth; *b* 1947; *m* 1972 *Richard Stevenson
2d *Kathleen Ann; *b* 1954
4c Michael Godfrey; Fl/Sgt RAAF WW II; *b* 1920; *ka* 1943
5c +Godfrey Trevor, PhD Chicago U 1959, Prof Psychology Waterloo U; *b* 1926; *educ* U of W Australia (BSc 1947, BA 1950); *m* 1948 *Helen MPS, dau of William J Love, of Mosman Pk, W Australia, and has issue:
1d +John Graham; *b* 8 March 1953
2d +Lance Godfrey; *b* 23 Sept 1955
1d *Siri Anne; *b* 10 June 1960
2d *Katherine Gail (twin); *b* 10 June 1960
3d *Judith Helen; *b* 15 Aug 1966
6c +Irwin Prescott [Irwin Barrett-Lennard Esq, St Leonard's, Kondut, W Australia]; *b* 1929; *educ* Perth U (BSc Agric 1952, MSc 1953); *m* 1953 *Berwine Ruth, dau of Dr Leigh Cook, of Stirling Highway, Claremont, W Australia, and has issue:
1d +Edward Graham; *b* 1953
2d +Hugh Anthony; *b* 1955
3d +James Irwin; *b* 1961
1d *Ann Mary; *b* 1958
1c *Hester [Mrs Hubert Shields, Glenvar, Wongan Hills, W Australia 6603, Australia]; *b* 1913; *m* 6 Feb 1937 *Hubert Leake Shields and has issue:
1d *Graham Michael; *b* 1946; *m* 1969 *Lynette, dau of John Gale, of Yelbeni, W Australia, and has issue:
1e *Michael Graham; *b* 1973

1e *Marnie Jane; *b* 1974
2e *Kellie Anne; *b* 1977
2d *Peter William Hubert; *b* 1950; *m* 1980 *Mary Charm, dau of Frederick Hamilton, of Moora, W Australia, and has issue:
1e *William Hubert; *b* 1984
2e *Stuart Frederick; *b* 1986
1e *Philippa Robin; *b* 1981
3d *Anthony Hubert; *b* 1955
1d *Robin Wendy; *b* Dec 1937; *m* 1961 *Dr Roy Montague Green, MSc, and has issue:
1e *Julie Anne; *b* 1964
2e *Cathy Susan; *b* 1965
2d *Waverley Hester; *b* 1939; *m* 1970 *Robin Ladyman, of Katanning, W Australia, and has:
1e *Lara; *b* 1972
2e *Tanya; *b* 1974
3d *Christine Mary [Mrs Robert Weise, Highbury 6313, W Australia]; *b* 1944; *m* 1967 *Robert Weise, and has issue:
1e *Michael William; *b* 1969
2e *Timothy; *b* 1971
3e *Anthony; *b* 1973
4d *Elizabeth Ann; *b* 1953; *m* 1980 *John Casey, of Auckland, NZ, and has issue:
1e *Nicola Simone; *b* 1985
2e *Asha; *b* 1987
2b Trevor St Aubyn; *b* 29 March 1889; *m* 1st 1912 Susan Mary (*d* 1939), dau of C W Ferguson, of W Australia, and had issue:
1c +Ferguson [Ferguson Barrett-Lennard Esq, W Swan Rd, W Swan 6056, W Australia]; *b* 1913
2c +Donald; *b* 1916; *m* 1940 his cousin *Dorothy, dau of C O Ferguson (*see* below), and has had issue:
1d Bruce; *b* 1 Sept 1944; *d* 29 March 1951
2d +Brian; *b* 5 July 1952
1d *Flora; *b* 25 Sept 1947; *m* 1972 *Lawrence Alec Smith, and has issue:
1e *Kathryn Rachel; *b* 1980
1c *Rosemary; *b* 1918; *m* 1946 *Rodney Charles Nordfelt and has issue
2b (cont.) Trevor Barrett-Lennard *m* 2nd 1942 Emily Edith (*d* 1968), dau of John Edward Wedge, and by her has issue:
2c *Barbara [Mrs Stuart Green, 25 Gloucester St, Victoria Park 6100, W Australia]; *b* 1948; *m* 1968 *Stuart William Green, and has issue:
1d *Philip Edward Spencer; *b* 1968
2d *Julian St Aubyn; *b* 1973
1d *Rosemarie Catherine; *b* 1970
3c *Elizabeth [Mrs Gregory Harris, 7 Rubida Court, Boronia 3155, Victoria, Australia]; *b* 1949; *m* 1968 *Gregory Allan Harris, and has issue:
1d *Trevor Allan; *b* 1968
2d *Daniel Raymond; *b* 1974
3b Kingsley Dacre; *b* 4 May 1890; *d* 1919
4b Douglas; *b* 27 May 1894; *ka* Gallipolli 1915
5b Forrest; *b* 10 Aug 1897; *d* 1915
6b St Aubyn Edward; *b* 31 Oct 1899; *m* 1933 Betty Corona (*d* 1981), dau of Edward Sydney Simpson, DSc, BE, of Mill Point, S Perth, W Australia, and *d* 1956, leaving issue:
1c George Simpson; *b* 6 Nov 1934; *m* 1961 *Angela Clare [Mrs Frank Bazely, The Rectory, Yule Ave, Middle Swan, W Australia 6056, Australia] (*m* 2nd 1978 Rev Frank Bazely), dau of Alfred Raymond Stevens, of W Swan, W Australia, and *d* 1972, leaving issue:
1d +David Anthony; *b* 1966; *m* 1993 *Julieanne, dau of Theodore Charles Fisher, of Lockridge, W Australia
2d +Michael John; *b* 1972
1d *Susan Fairlie; *b* 1963; *m* 1990 *Philip Stephen Hall, s of Ronald Alan Hall, of Red Hill, W Australia, and has issue:
1e *Teresa Elisabeth; *b* 1992
2e *Kate Louise; *b* 1993
2c +Richard St Aubyn [Richard Barrett-Lennard Esq, Beermullah, PO Box 29, Gingin, W Australia 6503]; *b* 5 April 1938; *m* 7 Aug 1965 *Sandra, est dau of Keith Irwin Bedford Smith, of Alfred Cove, W Australia, and has issue:
1d +Nigel Dacre; *b* 1968
2d +Philip St Aubyn; *b* 1972
1d *Amy Wilson; *b* 1 June 1966
3c +John Dacre; *b* 6 June 1940; *m* 1970 *Lynette Marie, er dau of Robert Atkinson, of W Perth, W Australia, and has issue:
1d +Mark Robert; *b* 1970
2d +Timothy Stewart; *b* 1972
3d +Daniel Thomas John; *b* 1977
1d *Bethwyn Ruth; *b* 1975
7b Septimus; *b* 1901; *d* 1962
1b Hebe Dorothy; *m* 1910 C O Ferguson, and *d* 11 Nov 1965, leaving issue (*see* above)
2b Vera; *m* 1918 C T P Ewing
2a Edward Ernest; *b* 31 Dec 1870; *m* Grace Sewell, and *d* 1897, leaving issue
3a Victor Dacre; *b* 22 June 1874; *m* Feb 1906 Blanche Isabell (*d* 1958), yst dau of Robert Allen, of S View, Adelaide, S Australia, and *d* 17 Jan 1930, having had issue:
1b Dacre; *b* 30 Nov 1906; *m* 1943 *Maisie, dau of J Vile, of Aubrey, NSW, and *d* 1962, leaving:
1c +John Dacre [John Barrett-Lennard Esq, Mobedine, York, W Australia]; *b* 4 May 1944; *educ* U of W Australia (B Comm 1966); *m* 1972 *Margaret, dau of Peter Lee, of Cottesloe, W Australia, and has issue:
1d +Dacre; *b* 1974
2d +Peter John; *b* 1977
1d *Elizabeth May; *b* 1982
2b Victor Dudley; *b* 1 Aug 1908; *m* *Jane Harpers, dau of G H Lukin, of Guildford, W Australia
3b Ernest Stuart; *b* 25 April 1910; *m* 1939 *Lorraine, dau of Allen Mair, of Swanbourne, W Australia, and *d* 1980, leaving issue:
1c +Robert Allan; *b* 4 June 1941; *educ* U of W Australia (BSc Ag 1964); *m* 1965 *Judith Anne, dau of Horace Joseph Stone, of Merredin, W Australia, and has issue:
1d *Clare Lois; *b* 4 Aug 1967
2d *Melissa; *b* 1969
1c *Sandra Lorraine; *b* 23 Nov 1942; *m* 1966 *Geoffrey Wackett, of Quairadina, W Australia, and has issue:
1d *Andrew; *b* 1968
2c *Jennifer Jill; *b* 14 June 1947
4b John Allen; Sgt RAAF WW II; *b* 6 Nov 1921; *kas* 1943
1b Mary Isabell; *b* 17 July 1912; *d* 13 July 1929
2b *Lucille [Mrs John Chellew, 57 Watkins Rd, Claremount, W Australia]; *b* 27 Oct 1914; *m* 1940 John Hill Chellew (*d* 1981), and has issue:
1c *John Alexander; *b* 26 July 1949; *m* 1974 *Penny, dau of Malcolm Devine, of Melrose Station, Leonora, W Australia, and has issue:
1d *Cameron John; *b* 1977
1d *Amanda Jane; *b* 1981
2c *William Lennard; *b* 22 April 1951; *m* 1976 *Billie Keiller, and has issue:
1d *Duncan; *b* 1985
1d *Jacqui (twin); *b* 1985
1c *Mary Diane; *b* 24 Nov 1941; *m* 1965 *John Kingsley Baldock, of Wattle Grove, W Australia, and has issue:
1d *Jeremy John; *b* 1971
1d *Catherine Jane; *b* 27 Oct 1968
2d *Judith Mary (twin); *b* 1971
2c *Margaret Anne; *b* 22 Oct 1947; *m* Dec 1969 *Andrew Henry Skreiner, and has issue:
1d *Hugh Michael; *b* 1976
1d *Anna Nadine; *b* 1973
3c *Elizabeth Jill; *b* 20 Jan 1953; *m* 1st 1977 David Arthur Cannon; *m* 2nd 1982 *Dr Henly Harrison, and has issue:
1d *Amy Elizabeth; *b* 1982
3b *Flora Grace; *b* 21 March 1919; *m* 3 Aug 1944 *John Richard Fountayne-England, MB, BS, 2nd s of R F England, of Echuca, Victoria, and has issue:
1c *John Dacre Fountayne; *b* 1 Aug 1945
1c *Jane Anne Fountayne; *b* 30 Oct 1950
2c *Caroline Margaret Fountayne; *b* 29 Sept 1961
4a Arthur St Aubyn; *b* 19 Feb 1876; *m* 1907 Fanny Susan (*d* 24 Nov 1949), only dau of Samuel Henry Viveash, of Swan, W Australia and *d* Oct 1954, leaving issue:
1b Arthur Viveash; *b* 1910; *m* 23 Feb 1952 Joan (*d* 1994), only dau of Frederick Short, of W Australia, and *d* 1983, leaving:
1c *Jane Margaret; *b* 3 Feb 1953; *m* 1973 *Bernard Drag, of Cirencester, Glos, and has:
1d *Timothy Viveash; *b* 1979
1d *Heather Rosalie; *b* 1976; *m* 1995 *Stewart Neil Garlick, of Katanning, W Australia
2b +Frank St Aubyn [Frank Barrett-Lennard Esq, 17 Martock Way, Karrinyup, W Australia 6018, Australia]; *b* 1912; *m* 29 July 1942 *Constance Rosalie, only dau of Ven Archdeacon Lionel Walpole Parry, of Perth, W Australia, and has issue:
1c *Rosalie Susan [Mrs Kim Sears, 8 Bent St, City Beach, 6015, W Australia]; *b* 15 April 1945; *m* 1st 29 July 1966 Ian Maxwell Greenham (*d* 1988), s of David Ian Greenham, Australian Dip Serv; *m* 2nd 1991 *Kim Sears and by her 1st husb has issue:
1d *Anthony Ian St Aubyn; *b* 1970
1d *Deborah Susan; *b* 20 Oct 1968; *m* 10 Dec 1994 *Geoffrey Michael Riley, of Perth
2c *Marian Ruth; *b* 9 March 1947; *m* 1977 *S/Ldr Roger Ashton Clark, RAAF, and has:
1d *Paul Robert; *b* 1980
2d *Nicholas James; *b* 1982
3c *Constance Anne; *b* 2 Jan 1951; *m* 1st 1972 (*divorce* 19–) Neil Bates; *m* 2nd 29 July 1995 *Michael John O'Donoghue, of Exmouth, W Australia
4c *Jennifer Robyn; *b* 5 May 1954; *m* 1978 *Bryce Edward Hayes-Thompson, of Doodlakine, W Australia, and has issue:
1d *Owen Bryce; *b* 1980
2d *David Frank; *b* 1983
1d *Ruth Verna; *b* 1985
3b +Edward Guy [Edward Barrett-Lennard Esq, Nundah, Northam, W Australia; 7 Albert St, S Perth, W Australia]; *b* 1919; *m* 19 March 1960 *Dymity Ann, dau of V W Shotter, of Perth, and has:
1c +Edward William; *b* 26 Jan 1967
2c +Guy St Aubyn; *b* 19 July 1969
1c *Lindal Dymity; *b* 7 Jan 1963; *m* 1988 *Herbert Dennis Wessels, of Bannister Springs, Boddington, W Australia
1b Ruth Ellen; *b* 1908; *m* 18 March 1960 *Don Turner, and *d* May 1960

5a John Evelyn; *b* 24 June 1881; *m* 1911 Frances Amy (*d* 16 Sept 1954), dau of Edward Kay Courthope, of Perth, W Australia, and *d* 17 Sept 1967, leaving issue:

1b *Frances Josephine [Mrs Geoffrey Gwynne, 9 Alexander Rd, Dalkeith, W Australia 6009, Australia]; *m* 19 Oct 1940 Geoffrey Howard Gwynne (*d* 27 Feb 1984), yr s of Lewis Howard Gwynne, of W Perth, and has issue:

1c *John Howard [John Gwynne Esq, 66 Riley Road, Dalkeith, W Australia 6009]; *b* 14 Feb 1946; *educ* W Australia U (BSc); *m* 18 April 1969 *Deborah Judith, dau of A B Walton, of Perth, and has issue:

1d *Christopher Howard; *b* 13 Sept 1976

1d *Belinda Judith; *b* 16 Nov 1972

2d *Katherine Anne; *b* 16 Nov 1972

1c *Geraldine Frances [Mrs Jens Jorgensen, 9 Alexander Road, Dalkeith, W Australia 6009]; *b* 22 Aug 1941; *m* 23 Aug 1967 *Jens Dalhoff Jorgensen, of Aalborg, Denmark, and has issue:

1d *Michael Dalhoff; *b* 3 Aug 1971

1d *Frances Dalhoff [Mrs Scott Leary, Seppentine Rd, Albany, W Australia 6330]; *b* 27 Nov 1968; *m* 24 March 1990 *Scott Leary and has:

1e *Daniel Scott; *b* 13 Aug 1996

2d *Pia Dalhoff; *b* 21 Jan 1982

2c *Angela Madeline; *b* 1953

2b *Judith [Mrs Ashburton Clark, Unit 23, 31 Williams Rd, Nedlands, W Australia]; *b* 1914; *m* 25 Jan 1941 Ashburton Hall Clark (*d* 1975), s of Samuel Henry Clark, of Onslow, W Australia, and has issue:

1c *John Jeremy; *b* 1941; *m* 1969 *Geraldine Lesley, dau of L J Locke, of Perth, and has:

1d *Anthony Phillip; *b* 1974

1d *Catherine Roseanne; *b* 1971

1c *Frances Louise [Mrs Trevor Tyson, 68 Lawley Cres, Mt Lawley, W Australia 6050]; *b* 1946; *m* 1974 *Trevor William Tyson and has:

1d *Dale Lee; *b* 1982

2c *Angela Madeline Gwynne [Miss Angela Clark, 9 Alexander Rd, Dalkeith, W Australia]; *b* 22 Jan 1953

3b *Anne [Mrs Edward Watkins, 37 Fifth Ave, Mt Lawley, W Australia 6050]; *b* 27 Sept 1916; *m* Edward A Glyn Watkins (*d* 1985) and has issue:

1c *Jonathan George Glyn; *b* 8 June 1948; *m* 6 July 1986 *Rhonda Evelyn, dau of Thomas Burton, and has issue:

1d *Isaac Thomas Edward; *b* 4 March 1987

2c *Daniel Glyn [Daniel Watkins Esq, Kerralong, Arthur River, W Australia 6315]; *b* 25 Feb 1955; *m* 26 Oct 1986 *Frances Anne, dau of Eugene Patrick O'Callaghan, of Perth, and has issue:

1d *Chauncy Patrick; *b* 14 Feb 1990

2d *Hamish Eugene; *b* 13 Feb 1993

3d *Edward Connor; *b* 31 Oct 1996

1d *Bridget Glyn; *b* 6 Oct 1987

1c *Miranda Glyn [Mrs Andrew Forte, 27 Swan St, Henley Brook, W Australia 6055]; *b* 16 July 1952; *m* 20 Aug 1977 *Andrew Forte and has issue:

1d *Woodrow Andrew; *b* 6 Nov 1983

1d *Georgina Amy; *b* 12 April 1979

4b Prudence; *b* 3 April 1918; *m* 29 March 1946 Frank Ernest Heymanson (*d* 17 Feb 1989), only s of Ernest L Heymanson, of Toorak, Melbourne, and d 9 May 1995, leaving:

1c *Simon John [Simon Heymanson Esq, 4 Plover Way, Stirling, W Australia 6021]; *b* 5 Nov 1953; *m* 1st 1975 Jane Carruthers and has issue:

1d *Jonathan Simon; *b* 11 Feb 1976

1d *Kate Louise; *b* 15 Dec 1977

1c (cont.) Simon Heymanson *m* 2nd 28 Oct 1990 *Concetta Carratazzolo and by her has:

2d *Antonina; *b* 30 Jan 1994

3d *Rebecca; *b* 21 Feb 1996

1c *Janet Louise [Mrs Patrick Nodwell, 33 Summerhays Dve, Karrinyup, W Australia 6018]; *b* 19 March 1947; *m* 21 Jan 1976 *Patrick John Nodwell and has issue:

1d *Joanne Helen; *b* 21 Feb 1977

2d *Emma Louise; *b* 18 Oct 1979

3d *Shelly Prudence; *b* 31 March 1983

2c *Jennifer Anne [Mrs Jack McAdam, 24 Thomas St, Freemantle, W Australia 6121]; *b* 23 July 1950; *m* 19– *Jack McAdam and has issue:

1d *Samson Roscoe; *b* 15 Sept 1976; *m* 29 Nov 1997 *Alina Price

2d *Luke; *b* 21 Dec 1986

5b Charlotte Virginia; *b* 16 Oct 1920; *m* 7 May 1945 *Alleyne Bruce Giles and *d* 1 Jan 1971, leaving:

1c *John Nicholas; *b* 22 Dec 1946; *m* 30 March 1974 *Christine Linfoot and has:

1d *Natalie Simone; *b* 17 March 1976

2d *Kelly Vanessa; *b* 7 July 1978

2c *Richard Courthope [Richard Giles Esq, 612 River Road, Dwellingup, W Australia 6213]; *b* 25 Jan 1953; m 26 Oct 1974 *Barbara Flower and has:

1d *Daniel Peter; *b* 14 Feb 1978

1d *Kirsten Jasmine; *b* 21 March 1980

1c *Susanne Virginia [Mrs John Dowling, 26 Garland Rd, Rollystone, W Australia 6111]; *b* 10 July 1949; *m* 9 Jan 1971 *John Herbert Dowling and has:

1d *Paul Brian; *b* 15 Oct 1978

1d *Karen Mena; *b* 16 Jan 1976

6b Evelyn; *b* 5 Oct 1925; *d* 5 May 1966

1a Elizabeth; *m* E Light, and had issue

2a Flora May; *m* William G Lefroy, and had issue

3a Mary Maud; *d* unm 10 Sept 1877

4a Amelia Grace; *m* Richard Hildreth Francis Rockett, MB, BS, Hon Capt AAMC (res), and had issue

(1) Fanny Helen; *m* 4 Oct 1870 Frederick Morton Eden (*d* 11 March 1917), est son of Bp of Moray, and *d* 14 April 1918, leaving issue (*see* EDEN OF WINTON, B)

(2) Rosa Georgina; *m* 23 June 1868 Rev Benjamin Newman Cherry (*d* 7 Feb 1905), of Brickendon Grange, Herts, Rector Clipsham, Oakham, and *d* 1 Oct 1921, leaving issue

6 Dacre (Rev); *b* 3 Jan 1801; *m* 4 Oct 1825 Rachel Anna (*d* 1 July 1847), est dau of Jeremiah Ives, of St Katherine's Norfolk, and *d* 21 Jan 1839, having had issue:

(1) Dacre Ives, Capt Duke of Cornwall's LI, previously 6th Inniskillin Dragoons; *b* 21 March 1829; *m* 1st 3 Nov 1877 Anna Statira (*d* Jan 1892), dau of Rev Nicholas Devereux, DD, of Ballyrankin Ho, Co Wexford; *m* 2nd 17 Dec 1892 Jane, widow of Augustus Binstead, of Bray, Co Wicklow, and dau of Samuel Mellor, and *dsp* 17 Dec 1897

(2) Percy Charles; *d* 13 July 1877

(1) Georgina Matilda Keppel; *m* 8 Feb 1866 Walter Buchan Young

7 Charles; *b* 24 May 1802; *m* 12 June 1838 Elizabeth Amelia (*d* 1899), est dau of Robert Nicholson, of Bradley, Co Durham, and *d* 22 March 1891, leaving issue:

(1) Robert Charles; *d* 21 Jan 1911

(1) Blanche; *d* unm 30 April 1924

1 Dorothy Anne; *m* 1 Oct 1822 William John St Aubyn, 3rd s of Sir John St Aubyn, Bt (*see* 1839 edn)

2 Julia Elizabeth; *m* 1st 23 Oct 1823 Charles Dalston Nevinson, MD, and had issue; *m* 2nd 21 July 1865 Capt J D Macdonald, and *d* 15 Feb 1874

3 Charlotte Maria; *m* 1 Dec 1830 Maj Charles Baillie Brisbane, 34th Regt, s of R-Adml Sir Charles Brisbane, KCB, and *d* 1884, leaving issue

4 Frances; *m* 28 March 1833 Rev Hon Thomas Robert Keppel and *d* 31 Aug 1890, leaving issue (*see* ALBEMARLE, E)

Sir Thomas *m* 2nd 20 June 1833 Georgina Matilda (*d* 7 May 1873), widow of H D Milligan and dau of Sir Walter Stirling, 1st Bt, of Faskine (*see* 1850 edn), and *d* 25 June 1857, having by her had further issue:

8 Walter James, Lt 16th Lancers; *b* 1 April 1835; *m* 18 Feb 1854 Caroline (*d* 6 June 1922), dau of Samuel Dormer, and *d* 6 June 1899, leaving issue:

(1) William; *b* 27 May 1857; *m* 1st 6 Oct 1880 Margaret (*d* 1890), dau of Capt — Boswell, of Peterborough, Ontario, and had issue:

1a Walter James, Chartered Accountant; *b* 17 Sept 1883; *m* 27 July 1904 Mary Graham (*d* 1967), 2nd dau of James Lawther, of Russell, Canada, and *d* 1954, having had issue:

1b +Walter James, late Lt RCNVR; *b* 9 April 1914; *m* 23 Dec 1947 *Beatrice Elizabeth, est dau of Dr C T Crowdy, of Montreal, and has issue:

1c +James Thomas; *b* 1956

1c *Elizabeth Jane; *b* 16 Aug 1948

2c *Deborah Dacre; *b* 26 Sept 1949

3c *Naomi Barbara; *b* 15 Jan 1952

2b Dacre Lowther; Lt Seaforth Highrs WW II; *b* 6 May 1918; *ka* Italy 18 Oct 1943

1b Caroline Mary; *b* 3 Feb 1908; *m* 2 June 1931 *Capt Richard Walter Underhill, OBE, RCNVR, and has issue

2b *Margaret; *b* 3 Oct 1911; *m* 26 July 1936 *Col Donald Spankie, OBE, Canadian Inf, and has issue

2a Hardinge, served WW I; *b* 1890; *m* 1st 1922 Annie dau of Harry Wyles, of Victoria, BC, Canada; *m* 2nd 1930 Leontine Leffler (*d* 1975), of New York, and *d* 1959, leaving issue:

1b *Joan; *b* 1 Jan 1933; *m* 12 March 1955 *Roy Hubbard and has:

1c *Catherine Julia; *b* 28 Sept 1957; *m* 19– (*divorce* 1991) and has:

1d *Edward Joseph; *b* 19 Aug 1978

2d *Eric Michael; *b* 27 May 1988

2c *Annabel Joan; *b* 31 July 1962; *m* 8 Aug 1991 *Alberto Bayante and has:

1d *Maxwell Arthur; *b* 6 June 1992

3c *Dorothy Jean; *b* 26 Dec 1963

2b Mildred; *b* 17 Oct 1935; *m* 16 June 1957 *Eli Friedman [Dr Eli Friedman, SUNY Health Science Center, 450 Clarkson Ave, Brooklyn, NY 11203, USA], and *d* 21 Sept 1997, leaving:

1c *Amy Louise; *b* 29 June 1959; *m* 25 Aug 1985 *Simon Meguira and has:

1d *Benjamin Joseph; *b* 15 Nov 1988

2d *Jeremy Eli; *b* 19 June 1992

1d *Sharon Rachel; *b* 28 June 1994

2c *Rebecca Alicia; *b* 17 Oct 1960; *m* 14 Oct 1984 *Dr Yair Caspi and has:

1d *Matan; *b* 3 Oct 1997

1d *Ruth; *b* 6 April 1988

2d *Lee; *b* 6 Dec 1990

3c *Sarah Jo; *b* 5 March 1963; *m* 12 June 1988 *Christian Eric Grethlein and has:

1d *David Jacob; *b* 8 Dec 1993

1d *Karen Elizabeth; *b* 8 Aug 1990

1a Georgina Boswell; *m* 2 Dec 1903 D'Arcy E Boulton, est s of Maj — Boulton, and had issue

2a Mary Caroline Pearl; *m* 31 Oct 1911 V-Adml Harry Rowlandson Godfrey, CB, DSO (*d* 17 Feb 1947), s of Lt-Col Charles J Godfrey, MSC, and had issue

3a Gladys Dacre; *m* 1909 Frederick Jancowski, of Alberta, and had issue

(1) (cont.) William Barrett-Lennard *m* 2nd 1892 Laura Sophia (*d* 22 Nov 1900), dau of Thomas Garnier Johnson, of Manitoba, and by her had:
3a William Louis, MC (1919), Lt Canadian Inf WW I (wounded); *b* 1893; *m* 1920 Agnes Mildred, dau of Nathaniel Dowsett, of Lethbridge, Alberta
4a Charles, WW I with Canadian Inf; *b* 1895; *m* Florence Sylvia Shafer, of Vancouver
4a *Mabel Sophia; *m* 15 June 1918 Brig Arthur Harry Langham Godfrey, DSO, MC, AIF (*ka* 1942), only s of C E R Godfrey, of Romsey, Victoria, Australia, and has issue:
1b *John Elliott; *b* 1919; Australian mil forces; *m* 19– *Patricia, only dau of A/Cdre Owen (Washington) de Putron, CBE
2b *Edward Arthur; *b* 1921
3b *Charles Lovett; *b* 1924
1b *Mildred Isabel; *b* 1922
5a Mildred Keppel; *d* 18 March 1909
(2) Hardinge, AMICE, Croix de Chevalier du Mérite Agricole France; *b* 21 April 1859; *m* Clara (*d* 10 Oct 1910), dau of Francis West
(3) John, CBE (1919), Lt-Col Gen List, served Boer War 1900 and WW I (Legion of Honour); *b* 14 Dec 1863; *m* 20 Oct 1887 Mary Emma (*d* 29 Jan 1948), est dau of J Gardiner, of Richmond, and *d* 29 March 1935, leaving issue:
1a Dacre Fiennes (Rev), Vicar Arkesden Essex; *b* 16 Aug 1888; *educ* Keble Coll Oxford (BA 1911); *m* 1st 1919 Charlotte Dorothy Evelyn (*d* Feb 1937), 2nd dau of Rev Henry Chichele Bampton, and had issue:
1b +Richard Dacre; *b* 1921
2b +Michael Henry [Michael Barrett-Lennard Esq, 12 Chisholm Court, St Peters Rd, London W6]; *b* 1923
3b +John Fiennes; *b* 1926; *m* 1984 *Monica Anne, dau of Henry John Wood
1b *Evelyn Mary; *b* 26 June 1927; *m* 18 May 1964 *Lt-Cdr Derek Charles Godfrey, RN (ret), son of V-Adml Harry Rowlandson Godfrey, CB, DSO, and adopted 12 Sept 1968:
*Ian Charles; *b* 22 Jan 1966
2b *Rachel Margaret [Mrs Maurice Dickenson, 26 Grange Ave, New Duston, Northants NN5 6SR]; *b* 1928; *m* 1950 Maurice Harry Dickenson (*d* 1993), and has issue:
1c *Trevor David; *b* 1955
1a (cont.) The Rev Dacre Barrett-Lennard *m* 2nd 20 July 1940 Irene Phyllis (*d* 1986), dau of Mark Moss, of Rock Hall, Cressing, and *d* 1975, having by her had issue:
4b +Philip Francis Dacre [Philip Barrett-Lennard Esq, Six Mile House, Acle Rd, Great Yarmouth, Norfolk NR30 1TH]; *b* 24 Oct 1947; *m* 1986 *Josephine Albertina Elizabeth, dau of Joseph Albert Colchester
(4) Villiers; *b* 29 July 1865; *m* 1885 Laura (*d* 27 Sept 1954), dau of George Clement, of Nottingham, and *d* 7 March 1903, leaving issue:
1a John Villiers; *b* 1889; *d c* 1930
2a Richard; *b* 1892; *m* 24 Dec 1917 Kathleen (*d* 1988), dau of Alfred Blake, of Ross, Herefs, and *d* 1967, leaving issue:
1b +Robert Villiers; *b* 1924
1b *June Rosemary [Miss June Barrett-Lennard, 85 Compton Place, Carpenders Park, Herts]; *b* 1922
1a Caroline; *m* 5 Sept 1908 William Barrett, FSA (*d* 1958), resumed her maiden name and *d* 5 Dec 1963, leaving issue
2a Dorothy Mabel; *b* 1890; *m* 1914 John Henry Cecil Murray, est s of J O D Murray, ICS; *m* 2nd 1931 Percival Robert Hopkins (*d* 1956), and by her 1st husb had issue:
1b *John Keith Lennard; *b* 1916; *m* 1939 *Evelyn Dawn, dau of Col E V Anderson, and has:
1c *Evelyn Anne; *b* 1944
(1) Mary Jane Matilda; *m* 31 Jan 1880 John Hugh Mouat (*d* 3 Feb 1926), of Barrett's Park, Heathfield, Sussex

BARRINGTON

Arms: Arg. three chevronels gu., a label of three points vert, a canton of the second, charged with a trefoil, slipped or. **Crest:** Out of a crown vallery or a hermit's bust with a cowl, vested paly arg. and gu. **Motto:** *Ung durant ma vie* ('I will be true to one ideal while I live'). **Creation:** Bt. (UK) 30 Sept 1831.

SIR ALEXANDER FITZWILLIAM CROKER BARRINGTON, 7TH BT, of the City of Limerick [Sir Alexander Barrington Bt, Swains, North End, Henley-on-Thames, Oxon RG9 6LF]; *b* 19 Nov 1909; *s* bro 1980; *educ* Shrewsbury and Ch Ch Oxford; WW II as Capt Intelligence Corps 1939–42 (POW 1942–45)

Lineage: SAMUEL BARRINGTON, of Limerick; living 1691; had issue:

BENJAMIN BARRINGTON, Sheriff Co Limerick 1714; had issue:

BENJAMIN BARRINGTON, Sheriff Co Limerick 1729; *m* 1724 Anne, dau of John Waltho, of Anna, by Catharine, dau of Joseph Croker, of Ballynagard, and had, with other issue:

MATTHEW BARRINGTON, of Limerick; *m* Jane, dau of John Canter, of Ballyvard, and was *bur* 13 June 1765, leaving issue:

Sir Joseph Barrington, 1st Bt (UK), so *cr* 30 Sept 1831; *b* 21 Feb 1764; fndr with his sons of the hospital in Limerick bearing their name; *m* 1787 Mary (*bur* 1 Nov 1829), dau of Daniel Baggott, of Limerick, and had, with other issue:
1 MATTHEW (Sir), **2nd Bt**
2 Daniel, Clerk of the Crown Limerick; *b* 14 Oct 1792; *m* 22 Oct 1829 Anne (*d* 5 Feb 1892), dau of Richard Williams, of Drumcondra Castle, Co Dublin, and *d* 5 Feb 1842, leaving issue:
(1) Joseph Thomas, Col Army Ordnance Dept, formerly RA; *b* 4 Sept 1834; *m* 14 Dec 1861 Emma (*d* 1921), dau of Thomas Evans, of Glamorgan, and *d* 24 Feb 1913, having had issue:
1a Richard Mordaunt, Capt Hampshire Regt; *b* 23 Feb 1806; *d* 19 July 1909
2a Thomas Percy, Lt-Col Roy Irish Rifles Res of Offrs, late W Yorks Regt, served in Ashanti 1895–96, NW Frontier of India, 1908, and WW I 1915–18 (despatches); *b* 11 Sept 1867; *m* 7 June 1906 Constance Mabel (*dec*), yst dau of Andrew R Houghton, of Leamington, and *d* 19 May 1951, having had issue:
1b Thomas Guy, 2nd Lt W Yorks Regt; *b* 7 Feb 1912; *d* 9 April 1934
3a William D'Olier, Capt RE; *b* 19 Aug 1870; *d* unm 13 May 1903
4a Joseph Croker; *b* 9 Jan 1880; *d* 1962
5a John Frederick, DSO (1919), Lt-Col (hon Col) late RA, served in Somaliland 1902–04, and WW I 1915–19 (despatches), and WW II (O/C Troops Trinidad, BWI), Coronation Medal 1937; *b* 30 Aug 1881; *m* 15 April 1916 Christine Mary Stella (*d* 15 May 1962), dau of C Kuhling, of N Ferriby, E Yorks, and *d* 10 April 1961, leaving issue:
1b +JOHN WILLIAM [Maj John Barrington, PO Box 894, Invermere, BC VOA 1K0, Canada], heir presumptive; Maj Roy Irish Fus (ret 1948); Palestine 1939 (medal with two clasps), served WW II in Italy (1939–45 star, Italy star, two medals) (POW 1943–45), GHQ Middle E 1947–48; *b* 28 Oct 1917; *educ* Stowe, and RMC Sandhurst; *m* 1st 19 Sept 1948 Annie (*d* 1985), dau of Florian Wotton, of Loostrasse 01, Coiro, Grisons, Switzerland; *m* 2nd 1986 *Evelyn Carol Paterson, dau of Oscar Broten, of Oslo, and by his 1st w has issue:
1c +Benjamin [Benjamin Barrington Esq, 44 Cherovan Dve SW, Calgary, Alberta T2V 2P2, Canada]; *b* 23 Jan 1950; *m* 1980 *Carola Christel Mogck, and has issue:
1d +Patrick Benjamin; *b* 1988
1d *Marisa Christel; *b* 1982
2c +Reto; *b* 25 Dec 1953; *m* 1976 *Shelly Ann Lapham, and has issue:
1d *Lauren Anne; *b* 1984
2d *Amy; *b* 1986
1c *Annette; *b* 2 Aug 1952; *m* 1984 *David Clinckett, and has issue:
1d *Nicole; *b* 1985
2d *Claire; *b* 1987

2b +Peter Malet, MC and bar, TD [Maj Peter Barrington MC TD, Thorn Cottage, The Green, Chiddingfold, Surrey GU8 4TU], Maj RA (TA) WW II (despatches three times, 1939–45 Star, Africa Star, NW Europe Star, two medals); *b* 28 Feb 1920; *educ* Wellington; *m* 8 Dec 1945 *Joan Warren, yr dau of Col Guy Warren Meade, DSO, MC, of Pitch Place Farm, Thursley, Surrey, and has had issue:

1c +Charles Peter [Charles Barrington Esq, The Lodge, Gt Bealings, nr Woodbridge, Suffolk IP13 6NW]; *b* 5 Oct 1946; *educ* Wellington; ACA 1970; *m* 1969 *Ann Elizabeth, dau of H B Foster, and has issue:

1d *Elizabeth Ann; *b* 1973

2c Peter David *b* 1 April 1949; *d* 19-

3c +Michael; *b* 7 April 1951

1a Annie Evelyn; *m* 25 Sept 1895 5th Baron Castlemaine (*qv*), and *d* 14 Nov 1955, leaving issue

(2) Richard Williams, Capt HEICS; *b* 4 Jan 1838; *m* 30 Oct 1873 Henrietta Maria Jane (*d* 21 March 1933), dau of John Johnstone, of Halleaths, Dumfriesshire, and Castlenau House, Surrey, and *d* 15 Oct 1900, leaving issue:

1a John Lawrence; *b* 16 Oct 1875; *d* 31 Oct 1918

2a Richard Irving Williams; *b* 21 May 1892; *m* 6 April 1922 Constance Elizabeth Mary (*m* 2nd 4 March 1930 Maj Alan Murdoch, TD (*ka* Singapore 7 Jan 1942); *m* 3rd 6 Nov 1946 Maj (Cecil) James Traill, Seaforth Highrs (*d* 31 March 1968), and *d* as a result of a road accident 28 Sept 1972), only dau of Henry Manders, and *d* 20 Nov 1928, leaving issue:

1b +Lawrence Hew Williams [Maj Lawrence Barrington, Oddington Lodge, Moreton-in-Marsh, Glos]; Maj Roy Wilts Yeo (PWO), Capt Coldstream Gds, served in Malaya 1948–50 (despatches); *b* 18 June 1928; *educ* Eton and RMA; *m* 1st 14 Oct 1950 (*divorce* 1968) (Patricia) Anne Isabella, only dau of Ralph William Whitson, of Carlton House, Symington, Lanarkshire, and has issue:

1c +Rupert Hew Williams; *b* 5 Jan 1963; *m* 1991 *(Ann) Olivia, er dau of Nicholas Ronald Nutting (*see* NUTTING, Bt), and has issue:

1d +Dominic Hew Williams; *b* 1994

2d +Edward Alexander; *b* 1 Aug 1997

1c *Serena Henrietta Williams [Mrs Adrian Underwood, 757 Wandsworth Rd, London SW8 3JF]; *b* 3 Oct 1956; *m* 12 Nov 1977 *Adrian Michael Campbell Underwood and has:

1d *Charles Edward Thomas; *b* 27 Nov 1982

1d *Katherine Anne; *b* 8 Oct 1984

1b (cont.) Lawrence Barrington *m* 2nd Sept 1968 *Merle Aurelia, formerly w of Christopher John Spence and er dau of Sir Leonard Ropner, 1st Bt, of Thorp Perrow (*qv*), and by her has further issue:

2c *Shaun Richard Williams; *b* 9 July 1969

1a Alice Henrietta; *m* 1st 6 July 1898 William Keswick, DL, JP, MP (*d* 9 March 1912), of Eastwick Park, Gt Bookham, Surrey, son of Thomas Keswick, of Beech Grove, Annan, Dumfries, and had issue; *m* 2nd 4 Sept 1915 Cyril Cameron Pyke, OBE (*d* 7 Nov 1951)

2a Helen Lucy Johnstone; *m* 26 April 1905 John Molesworth Staples (*d* 22 May 1948), est son of Maj-Gen Thomas Staples, and had issue (*see* STAPLES, Bt)

1 Anne; *m* 29 Nov 1866 Col Walter Carr Mackinnon, 3rd Buffs, and *d* 1886, leaving issue

2 Maryanne Charlotte; *m* 3 Sept 1857 John Bayly, DL, JP (*d* 15 Nov 1890), of Desborough, Co Tipperary, and *d* 31 Aug 1870, leaving issue

Sir JOSEPH *d* 10 Jan 1846; his est son,

Sir Matthew Barrington, 2nd Bt, Crown Slr Munster 1932–61; *b* 21 May 1788; *m* 1 Jan 1814 Charlotte (*d* 18 Nov 1858), dau of William Hartigan, of Dublin, and *d* 1 April 1861, having had, with six daus:

1 **Sir William Hartigan Barrington, 3rd Bt**; *b* 4 Oct 1815; *m* 14 March 1859 Elizabeth Olivia (*d* May 1907), 2nd dau of Henry Darley, of Wingfield, Co Wicklow, and *d* 14 July 1872, leaving:

(1) Charlotte Jessy; *m* 4 June 1901 Rev George Digby Scott, Rector Bray, Co Wicklow, and Chllr Ch Ch Cathedral, son of the Archdeacon of Dublin, and *d* 12 Aug 1951, leaving issue

(2) Maria Louisa Olivia; *d* unm 19 Aug 1947

2 **Sir Croker Barrington, 4th Bt**, DL; *b* 12 July 1817; *m* 12 April 1845 Anna Felicia (*d* 7 June 1873), est dau of John Beatty West, MP Dublin, and had, with five other daus:

(1) CHARLES BURTON (Sir), **5th Bt**

(2) Croker, of Barrington Bridge, Co Limerick, barrister King's Inns Dublin 1876; *b* 1851; *educ* Trin Coll Dublin (MA); *m* 7 Oct 1890 Florence Jane (*d* 16 July 1935), yst dau of John Bayly, DL, JP, of Desborough, Co Tipperary, and *d* 24 June 1926, having had issue:

1a William Matthew; *b* 11 May 1895; *d* 12 March 1897

2a Croker Edmund, MC, Brig RA WW I 1916–19 (despatches, two medals) and WW II (despatches); *b* 2 Sept 1897; *m* 26 July 1933 Gwendolen Mary, only child of Maj Frederick Arthur Bligh, RA, of Brittas, Nobber, Co Meath, and was *kas* Burma 17 July 1944

1a Florence Mary, Hon Life memb BRCS, 3rd Cl Order St George Russia; *d* unm 9 Nov 1968

2a Evelyn Victoria Muriel; *m* 29 July 1922 Maj Reginald Fosbery Nation (*d* Feb 1969), Roy Fus, Chevalier Legion Honour, and *d* 3 Feb 1929

(3) William Matthew; *b* 1855; *d* 10 June 1883

(4) John Beatty, JP Cos Limerick and Tipperary and Limerick City, High Sheriff Co Limerick 1912, served WW I 1915–19 (Legion Honour, Croix de Guerre); *b* 18 July 1859; *educ* Trin Coll Dublin (BA); *m* 2 Aug 1887 Catherine Charlotte (*d* 3 April 1937), est dau of John Bayly, DL, JP, of Desborough, Co Tipperary, and *d* 16 Sept 1926, leaving issue:

1a John, Maj RA WW I 1917–19 and WW II, Perm Pres Courts Martial Mil Govt Germany; *b* 2 June 1899; *educ* Wellington and RMA Woolwich; *m* 1st 23 Jan 1928 (*divorce* 1947) Joan Mary, er dau of William Bellingham Jameson, of The Roundel, Wittersham, Kent; *m* 2nd 30 April 1949 Margaret Eileen, widow of Maj B E Hickson, 16th Light Cav IA, and dau of Rev Henry Brownrigg Hewson, Rector Clonaslee and Acranches, France, and *dsp* 4 Jan 1961

1a Mary Charlotte Gladys; *m* 20 April 1911 Colin Algernon Campbell (*d* 3 Jan 1957), of Colgrain, Dumbartonshire, and had issue (*see* 1970 edn CAMPBELL OF ESKAN, B)

2a Marjory *m* 27 July 1915 Michael King-French, Capt RFA (*d* 21 June 1950), son of William Michael French, of 15 Lower Pembroke Street, Dublin, and had issue:

1b *Lancelot Michael; *b* 20 Sept 1916; *educ* Winchester; *m* 3 June 1939 *Mary, dau of William McMullan, of The Moorings, Limavady, Co Londonderry, and has had issue:

1c *Iona Sarah; *b* 17 March 1940; *m* Oct 1967 *Albert Pratt, DSc

2c *Primrose Madawe; *b* 4 May 1947

3c Wanda; *b* 25 April 1929; *d* 29 April 1948

(1) Anna Josephine; *m* 3 June 1891 John Naper George Pollock, DL, JP (*d* 13 Feb 1905), of Mountainstown, Co Meath, and *d* 2 July 1947, leaving issue

Sir CROKER *d* 4 July 1890; his est son,

Sir Charles Burton Barrington, 5th Bt, MBE (1919), DL and JP Co Limerick, High Sheriff (1879), MA Trin Coll Dublin, Hon Col (SR) Limerick City Roy Field Res Artillery, S Div; *b* 1848; *m* 14 Feb 1895 Mary Rose (*d* 1 March 1943), yst dau of Sir Henry Hickman Bacon, 11th Bt (*qv*), and *d* 12 Aug 1943, having had issue:

1 **Sir Charles Bacon Barrington, 6th Bt**; *b* 6 June 1902; *educ* Eton; *m* 7 Aug 1930 Constance Doris, dau of Ernest James Elkington, of London, and *d* 1980, leaving issue:

(1) *Victoria Elizabeth Josephine [Miss Victoria Barrington, Barrihurst Bungalow, Cranleigh, Surrey]; *b* 30 Nov 1940

(2) *Diana Mary Rose (retained maiden name) [Mrs Diana Barrington, Serridge Lodge, Trafalgar, Cinderford, Glos]; *b* 11 May 1946; *educ* Leicester U (BA 1968); *m* 17 July 1968 *Thomas Manuel, yr s of Anthony Manuel and Mrs James Cuoco, of Angola, New York, and has:

1a *Jessica Barrington; *b* 9 March 1977

2 Sir ALEXANDER FITZWILLIAM CROKER BARRINGTON, **7th and present Bt**

1 Winifred Frances; *b* 5 July 1897; *d* 14 May 1921

BARROW

Arms: Sa. two swords in saltire, points upwards arg., pommels and hilts or, between three fleurs-de-lys, one in chief and two in flaunch, and an anchor erect in base of the last. **Crest:** On a mount vert a squirrel sejant cracking a nut, all ppr., charged on the shoulder with an anchor. **Motto:** *Parvum sufficit* ('Little suffices'). **Creation:** Bt. (UK) 30 March 1835.

SIR RICHARD JOHN UNIACKE BARROW, 6TH BT, of Ulverstone, Co Lancaster; *b* 2 Aug 1933; *s* f 1960; *educ* Beaumont; Capt Irish Gds 1956 (ret 1960), with Internat Computers and Tabulators Ltd 1960–73; *m* 8 July 1961 (*divorce* 1974) Alison Kate, yr dau of Capt Russell Grenfell, RN, of Downton, Salisbury, Wilts, and Mrs Lindsay-Young, of The Loom House, Dedham, Essex, and has:

1 +ANTHONY JOHN GRENFELL; *b* 24 May 1962; *educ* Dulwich and Edinburgh U (MA); *m* 1990 (*divorce* 1996) Rebecca Mary Long and has:

(1) *Bryony Helen Ann Lambert; *b* 22 Jan 1996

1 *Nony Mary Louise; *b* 5 Aug 1963; *m* 19 Dec 1992 *Simon Alastair Hugh Kerr-Smiley, s of Lt Hector Robert Kerr-Smiley, QO Highrs TAR (*see* SMILEY, Bt), and has issue

2 *Frances Teresa Catherine; *b* 16 April 1971; BSc, ARICS

Lineage: Sir John Barrow, 1st Bt (UK), so *cr* 30 March 1835 (only son of Roger Barrow, of Ulverstone (*d* 1794), by Mary Dawson, and gs of Roger Barrow, of Patterdale, Westmorland); *b* 19 June 1764; 2nd Sec Admlty, fndr RGS; *m* Aug 1798 Anna Maria (*d* 15 Dec 1857), only dau of Peter John Trüter, of Cape of Good Hope, Memb Court of Justice, and *d* 1848, leaving, with other issue:

Sir George Barrow, 2nd Bt, CMG; Ch Clerk Colonial Office, Sec and Registrar Order of St Michael and St George; *b* 22 Oct 1806; *m* 23 July 1832 Rosamond Hester Elizabeth (*d* 9 Jan 1906), dau of William Pennell, Consul-Gen Brazil, and sister-in-law and adopted dau of Rt Hon John Wilson Croker, and had, with five daus:

1 JOHN CROKER (Sir), **3rd Bt**

2 George Staunton (Rev), MA, Vicar Stowmarket, Suffolk; *b* 20 Oct 1834; *m* 7 April 1864 Florence Mary (*m* 2nd 1896 Charles Lomer, of Stow Thorma, Westgate-on-Sea, and *d* 20 April 1930), est dau of John Nicholles, and *d* 10 Aug 1884, having had issue:

(1) John Wilson Croker; *b* 31 Jan; *d* 23 Feb 1868

(1) Annie Reta; *b* 20 Sept 1865; *m* 26 July 1892 Frederick Banister (*d* 25 Dec 1927), of Fairfield, Epsom, and *d* 12 Nov 1953, leaving issue

(2) Ida Florence; *b* 18 Aug 1869; *m* 27 Sept 1910 William Henry Oakes, and *d* 22 July 1949

(3) Gillian Mary; *b* 18 Sept 1872; *d* 10 May 1938

(4) Rosamond Nony; *b* 16 Nov 1875

(5) Evelyn Marguerite; *b* 14 Oct 1880; *m* 11 May 1909 her cousin Capt Francis Alexander Clutterbuck, DSO, RN, and had issue

3 William Pennell, Lt RN; *b* Jan 1841; *d* 6 July 1873

Sir GEORGE *d* 27 Feb 1876; his est son,

Sir John Croker Barrow, 3rd Bt, JP Kent; MA Oxford, barrister Lincoln's Inn; *b* 8 July 1833; *m* 2 Dec 1857 Emily Jane (*d* 23 Jan 1911), est dau of James Nathaniel Merriman, MD, of Kensington, and *d* 23 Sept 1900, having had, with two daus (Emily Agnes, *d* 1951; Mary Mercy, nun):

Sir Francis Laurence John Barrow, 4th Bt; *b* 11 Aug 1862; architect and ornithologist; *m* 1st 7 Jan 1890 Winifred Sarah (*d* 21 Feb 1932), 2nd dau of William Crozier Steward, of Castgate, Whitehaven; *m* 2nd 21 April 1932 Edith, dau of William Townsend, and by his 1st w had issue:

1 WILFRED JOHN WILSON CROKER (Sir), **5th Bt**

2 Cuthbert Joseph; *b* 24 May *d* 4 Oct 1900

3 Alfred Francis Lendon; *b* 12 May 1904; *m* 1933 *Ruth [Mrs Alfred Barrow, 13 The Lindens, Great Austins, Farnham, Surrey GU9 8LA], only dau of William Sydney Milsum, of Frensham, Surrey, and *d* 29 April 1989, leaving:

(1) +John Lendon [John Barrow Esq, 31 Lingfield Ave, Torkington Park, Hazel Grove, Cheshire]; *b* 1934; *m* 1961 *Maureen Ann, dau of Alfred Stanley Gover, and has issue:

1a +Paul Lendon; *b* 1966

1a *Nicola Mary; *b* 1963

(2) +Antony Francis [Anthony Barrow Esq, Street Farm, Tilford, Farnham, Surrey]; *b* 1937; *m* 1962 *Alexa, dau of Raleigh Ashlin Skelton, and has issue:

1a +Kevin Mark; *b* 1963

1a *Katherine Laura; *b* 1965

(3) +Simon William [Simon Barrow Esq, Oratory School, Woodcote, Reading, Berks]; *b* 1942; *m* 1977 *Brenda Cora, dau of Dermot Ernest Kelly, and has issue:

1a +Julian Alexander Dermot; *b* 1981

1a *Jennifer Ann; *b* 1979

(1) *Susanne Mary [Mrs Charles D'Arcy, Norreys, Heath Lane, Crondall, Farnham, Surrey] ; *b* 1946; *m* 1st 1972 (*divorce* 1983) Patrick Hugh Walker-Taylor; *m* 2nd 1987 *Charles D'Arcy, and by her 1st husb has issue:

1a *Timothy Patrick; *b* 1974

1a *Alice Mary; *b* 1976

2a *Sally Anne; *b* 1981

(2) *Catherine Ruth [Mrs Christopher Price, 9 Tilney Close, Alton, Hants GU34 2BG]; *b* 1950; *m* 1976 *Christopher John Price and has:

1a *Robert Christopher; *b* 1981

1a *Sarah Kate; *b* 1978

4 Edward Joseph Merriman, Lt-Cdr (S) RNR; *b* 19 June 1912; *m* 1938 Mary Ellen, dau of John William Allen, of Shrewsbury, and *d* 1988, leaving issue:

(1) +Timothy John; *b* 17 Oct 1946; BVSC; MRCVS; *m* 1969 *Fiona, dau of Eric Lord, of Croydon, Surrey

(1) *Susan Diana Margaret [Mrs Geoffrey Clarke, 5 Thruston Close, Grestun Manor, Abingdon, Oxon OX14 5RD]; *b* 29 Sept 1938; *m* 1963 (*divorce* 1979) Peter McConnell; *m* 2nd 1980 *Geoffrey Lindsay Clarke, ACIOB, and by her 1st husb has:

1a *Simon John; *b* 1969

1a *Julie Mary [Mrs William Humphries, 51 St Amand Drive, Abingdon, Oxon OX14 5RG]; *b* 1967; *m* 1987 *William Alexander Humphries and has:

1b *Edward Simon Alexander; *b* 1992

1b *Emma Diana Lindsay; *b* 1988

2a *Sarah Frances; *b* 1971

(2) *Marylin Elizabeth Emily [Mrs John Butler, Rope Walk Cottage, Lyth Hill, Shrewsbury, Salop SY3 0BS]; *b* 5 Aug 1944; *m* 1970 *John Richard Butler, FSVA, and has:

1a *Jane Mary; *b* 1972

1 *Mildred Mary Wilfred; *b* 28 Nov 1901; *m* 1st 26 Oct 1922 Edward Stanhope Benhow Rowe, of Shanghai (*d* 1941); *m* 2nd 1949 Gerald Dun, of St Vincent, WI, and by her 1st husb has had:

(1) Edward Francis; *b* 29 Apr 1926; *d* 19–

(2) *John Oswald Barrow; *b* 15 June 1930

(3) *Anthony Courteney; *b* 2 Jan 1934

(1) *Ursula Mary; *b* 18 Aug 1923

(2) *Jocelyn Francis; *b* 9 Jan 1925

Sir FRANCIS *d* 9 June 1950; his est son,

Sir Wilfred John Wilson Croker Barrow, 5th Bt, FR HistS, FRGS, FZS, Maj Roy Fus WW I, Regnl Offr Min House Security 1941, Dep Sr Regnl Offr 1943–44; *b* 28 Dec 1897; *educ* Stonyhurst, Oxford and RMC Sandhurst; *m* 27 April 1926 (Gwladys) Patricia, only surv dau of Richard Gordon FitzGerald Uniacke, MA, FSA, and *d* 11 Jan 1960, leaving issue:

1 Sir RICHARD JOHN UNIACKE BARROW, **6th and present Bt**

1 *Rosamond Mary Geraldine [Mrs George Sterling, Castletown, Coolbawn, Co Tipperary, Ireland]; *b* 29 Jan 1927; *m* 27 April 1956 *George Myles Sterling, and has issue:

(1) *Myles Patrick; *b* 21 Jan 1958

(2) *Andrew David; *b* 9 Aug 1963

(2) *Natalie Rosamond; *b* 14 Dec 1960

2 *Ann Patricia [Mrs Ann Carr, Fellover, St Breward, nr Bodmin, Cornwall]; *b* 31 Jan 1928; *m* 17 Oct 1951 (*divorce* 1960) Maj Anthony Richard Carr, RA (ret), only son of E J A Carr and Lady (John) Darwood, and has issue:

(1) *Julian Antony Robie; *b* 23 Dec 1955

3 *Angela Mary Philippa [Mrs Geoffrey Swaine, 9 Oaktree Close, Ealing, London W5]; *b* 26 May 1940; *m* 13 July 1968 Geoffrey Swaine (*d* 31 July 1992), only s of Sydney Swaine, of Wingfield House, Lawshall, Bury St Edmunds, Suffolk, and has:

(1) *Jonathan David; *b* 6 Jan 1971

(1) *Mary Angela; *b* 18 Sept 1972

BARRY

Arms: Azure, two lions passant guardant, or.
Creation: Bt. (UK) 22 Feb 1899.

SIR (LAURENCE) EDWARD ANTHONY TRESS BARRY, 5TH BT, of St Leonard's Hill, Clewer, Berks, and Keiss Castle, Caithness and **5th Baron De Barry** in Portugal [Sir Edward Barry Bt, 4 The Gables, Argos Hill, Rotherfield, E Sussex TN6 3QJ]; *b* 1 Nov 1939; *s f* 1977; *educ* Haileybury; Capt Gren Gds 1958–64; *m* 1st 14 Sept 1968 (*divorce* 1991) Fenella, dau of Mrs Hilda Hoult, of Knutsford, Cheshire; *m* 2nd 1992 *Elizabeth Jill, dau of Geoffrey Bradley, of Fishtoft, Boston, and has issue by his 1st w:

1 +WILLIAM RUPERT PHILIP TRESS; *b* 13 Dec 1973

1 *Alexandra Diana Frances Louise; *b* 1977

Lineage: Sir ROBERT BARRY, of Stanton Barry Manor; summoned to serve overseas 7 July 1297, performed mil service in person against the Scots 1301, MP Bucks 1297, 1307 and 1312, Northants 1313 and 1318; blazoned the Barry arms 'de azure, a ij lupards passaunz de or' in the Roll of Arms of the reign of EDWARD II and in other ancient Rolls of that period.

Sir WILLIAM BARRY, of Stanton Barry Manor; living 1390; also blazoned his arms, this time in the Roll of Arms of the reign of RICHARD II.

According to the entry for Barry of Eynsham in the Heralds' Visitation of Oxfordshire in 1566 the right to these arms was proved by LAWRENCE BARRY, of Hampton Gray Manor, Oxon.

The first names recorded by him were (slightly paraphrased for intelligibility): 'RICHARD BARRY, of Eynsham, Oxon, gent, a yr bro (presumably of LAWRENCE BARRY); *m* Agnes, dau of Richard Merrye, of Eynsham, gent, and had issue an est s:

JOHN BARRY'

RICHARD BARRY, of Eynsham, was living 1476; f(?) of:

JOHN BARRY, of Eynsham and Oxford (Mayor 1539–40), and of Hampton Gray Manor, Oxon; *m* 1st Margaret —; *m* 2nd Elyn — and *d* 1546, leaving issue by his 2nd w:

1 LAWRENCE

2 George

3 Richard

1 Agnes; *m* Anthony Daubeney, of Cirencester, Glos

JOHN BARRY's est s,

LAWRENCE BARRY, of Eynsham and Hampton Gray Manor; *m* Jane, dau of Richard Buckner, of Whitley, Berks, and *d* 1576, leaving, with other issue, a 3rd s:

FRANCIS BARRY, of Thame, Oxon; *m* Frances (who *m* 2nd 21 Dec 1612 Michael Saunders, of Thame), dau of Edward Croft, MP Leominster 1571 (*see* CROFT, Bt, of Croft Castle), and had, with other issue, a 2nd s:

VINCENT BARRY, JP, of Thame and Hampton Gay Manor; *b* 1598; *educ* Oriel Coll Oxford (BA 1617) and Gray's Inn (admitted 26 May 1620); *m* Elizabeth, dau of Robert Scrope, of Wormsley, Oxon, and *d* 19 July 1666, leaving issue:

1 VINCENT
2 Adrian; *m* and had issue
3 Robert; *b* 1629
4 Rev Francis; *b* 1632; *educ* Oriel Coll Oxford (BA 1656); vicar Kingsey, Bucks, 1666; *d* 1694
1 Elizabeth; *b* 1637; *d* 1639
2 Sarah; *b* 1640
3 Katherine; *b* 1642; *d* 1659

VINCENT BARRY's est s,

VINCENT BARRY, JP (Oxon), of Hampton Gray Manor; *b* 1628; barrister Gray's Inn 1646; *m* Jane, dau of Thomas Southby, of Stanford-in-the-Vale, Berks, and *d* 1679, leaving, with other issue:

VINCENT BARRY; *bapt* 25 May 1660; *educ* Oriel Coll Oxford (MA 1683); vicar Fulham 1691; *m* Rebecca (*d* 1713) and *d* 3 Dec 1708, leaving, with other issue, a 5th s:

JOHN BARRY, of King Street, St Botolph, Aldgate; *bapt* 3 Sept 1702; *m* 23 Feb 1760, as his 2nd w, Mary Culwick (*b* 1734), of All Hallows, City of London, and *d* 1763, leaving issue:

JOHN BARRY, of Montagu St, London; *b* 1762; *m* Elizabeth Lewis (*b* 1765; *d* 1828), of St George's, London, and *d* 1830, leaving, with other issue, a 3rd s:

CHARLES BARRY, of The Priory, Orpington, Kent; *b* 28 June 1790; *m* 22 Aug 1820 Harriet (*d* 11 Nov 1862), dau of Robert Ades, of Brede Place, Sussex, and *d* 13 Aug 1866, leaving issue, with four yr s and nine daus:

Sir Francis Tress Barry, 1st Bt (UK), so *cr* 22 Feb 1899, DL (Caithness), of St Leonard's Hill, Clewer, Berks, and Keiss Castle, Wick, Caithness; *b* 8 June 1825; 1st BARON DE BARRY in Portugal; MP Windsor 1890–1906, Br V-Consul for Spanish Province of Biscay, Actg Consul for Provinces of Biscay, Santander and Guipuycoa 1847, Cdr Order of Christ of Portugal and Cross of Naval Merit of Spain; *m* 4 June 1851 Sarah Douglas (*d* 1 Aug 1926), only child of Arthur Herron, of Beckley, Sussex, and *d* 28 Feb 1907, leaving issue:

1 Francis Tress; *b* 8 Aug 1856; *d* unm 10 Sept 1888
2 EDWARD ARTHUR (Sir), **2nd Bt**
3 Douglas Herron; *b* 5 Dec 1861; *m* 22 Jan 1884 Rose Grace (*d* Oct 1939), dau of Peter Gowlland, of Gloucester Terrace, Hyde Park, and *d* March 1945, leaving issue:
(1) Ronald Tress; *b* 23 Jan 1888; Capt Scots Gds, served WW I (wounded); *m* 1st 1909 (*divorce* 1913) Elspeth Sophia Louisa Sinclair and had issue:
1a Marjory Hermione; *b* 1910; *m* 3 Sept 1934 Dr William Wilson (*d* 1 Dec 1969), er s of Dr Wilson, of Irvine, Ayrshire, and *dsp* 29 April 1940
(1) (cont.) Ronald Tress Barry *m* 2nd 1919 Madge Dorrington, dau of Richard Bangay, MD, of Saxlingham, Norfolk, and widow of N A Loggin
(1) Dorothy Grace; *b* 26 Feb 1885; *m* 15 April 1913 Kenneth Delmar Barrett (*d* 15 Nov 1925), 2nd s of Charles Rolls Barrett, of Pelton Fell, Co Durham, and *d* 14 Nov 1949, leaving issue
(2) Audrey Rose; *b* 15 Oct 1895; *m* 19 July 1922 (*divorce* 1945) Maj Leslie Fitzroy Richard, RA (*d* 5 March 1947), s of Walter M Richard
4 William James, JP (Norfolk); *b* 18 March 1864; High Sheriff Norfolk 1912; *m* 25 Jan 1896 Lady Grace Murray, MBE (*d* 23 Sept 1960), dau of 7th Earl of Dunmore (*qv*), and *d* 1 July 1952, leaving issue:
(1) Gerald, MC; *b* 18 Dec 1896; *educ* Eton; Lt-Col The Black Watch (RHR); served WW I Coldstream Gds, WW II with The Black Watch, Dep Mil Sec Eastern Army of India 1942–43; *m* 28 Feb 1923 *Lady Margaret Pleydell-Bouverie, 4th dau of 6th Earl of Radnor (*qv*), and *d* 21 Feb 1977, leaving issue:
1a +Richard John [Richard Barry Esq, Hampton Fields, nr Circencester, Glos]; *b* 14 Nov 1938; *educ* Ruzawi Sch, S Rhodesia, Michaelhouse, S Africa, and Gresham's Sch Holt; *m* 4 Dec 1965 *Jillian Frances, yr dau of Lt-Col Anthony Leslie Novis, MC, of Fryern House, Storrington, Sussex, and has issue:
1b +James Tress; *b* 8 June 1967
2b +Anthony Gerald; *b* 11 June 1969
1b *Bridget Margaret; *b* 1973
1a *Anne; *b* 28 April 1924; *m* 24 Feb 1950 *6th Marquess of Aberdeen and Temair (*qv*) and has issue
2a *Diana; *b* 30 Oct 1927; *educ* U of Cape Town (BA); *m* 1st 17 Oct 1951 (*divorce* 1959) Kenneth Robert Motion, yr s of Andrew Kenneth Motion, MFH, of Brick House Farm, Naughton, Ipswich, and has issue:
1b *Richard Peter; *b* 1954
1b *Sarah; *b* 1955
2a (cont.) Mrs Diana Motion *m* 2nd 11 June 1959 (*divorce* 1984) Nathaniel Edward Sherwood, s of John Edward Newman Sherwood, of Prested Hall, Kelvedon, Essex, and has further issue:
2b *David Gerald; *b* 1960
3a *Patricia Helen; *b* 22 July 32; *m* 26 June 1958 *Peregrine Michael Hungerford Pollen, only s of Sir Walter Michael Hungerford Pollen, MC, JP, of Norton Hall, Mickleton, Glos (*see* POLLEN, Bt), and has issue
4a Gillian Margaret; *b* 15 Jan 1934; *m* 10 Dec 1953 (*divorce* 1964) Edward Alexander Martin, er s of Brig Edwyn Sandys Dawes Martin, DSO, OBE, MC, of Sparkford Hall, Yeovil, by his w Margaret Ayliffe Ellinor, er dau of David Charles Guthrie, JP, of Craigie, Forfarshire, and has issue:
1b *Alexander; *b* 14 Feb 1956
1b *Margaret; *b* 18 Dec 1957
2b *Helena; *b* 4 Jan 1960
3b *Georgina; *b* 22 Feb 1961
5a *Pamela Rosemary [Mrs Colin Peterson, Balldown Farmhouse, Sparsholt, Hants]; *b* 14 Nov 1938 (twin with Richard); *m* 1 Jan 1966 *Colin Vyvyan Peterson, yst s of Sir Maurice Drummond Peterson, GCMG, of The Little House, Wargrave, Berks, and has issue:
1b *Andrew Drummond; *b* 26 April 1967
2b *Thomas Richard; *b* 1970
1b *Helen Margaret; *b* 1969
2b *Alice Diana; *b* 1974
(2) Hubert Wyndham; *b* 6 Oct 1898; Cdr RN, served WW I and WW II; *m* 19 Aug 1936 *Violet Agatha, er dau of Col Sir Edward Archibald Ruggles-Brise, 1st Bt, and *d* 1992, leaving issue:
1a +William Edward [William Barry Esq, 12 Kensington Pk Mews, London W11 2EY; Malt House Farmhouse, Manningford Abbots, Wilts SN9 6HY]; *b* 6 Jan 1938; *educ* Eton and Trin Coll Cambridge; Lt KRRC; *m* 21 May 1965 *Juliet Alexandra Sarah, only child of James Herbert Lonsdale Musker (*see* LAUDERDALE, E), and has issue:
1b *Catherine Jane; *b* 13 Nov 1968; *educ* St Paul's Girls Sch, Durham U (Msc) and Imperial Coll (MSc)
2a +James Hubert; *b* 27 April 1947; *educ* Eton and RAC Cirencester
1a *Rosemary; *b* 17 Feb 1939; *m* 18 Dec 1963 *Alastair Pinckard Leslie, only s of Hon John Wayland Leslie, of E Kintrockat, Brechin, Angus (*see* ROTHES, E), and has issue
2a *Susan; *b* 5 May 1945; *m* 12 Nov 1969 *4th BARON GLENARTHUR (*qv*)
(1) Esther Joyce; *b* 3 July 1906
(2) *Nancy Elizabeth; *b* 31 July 1910; *m* 22 Oct 1935 *George Nigel Capel Cure, TD, JP, V-Lt Essex, only s of Maj George Edward Capel Cure, and has issue:
1a *(George) Ronald [Ronald Capel Cure Esq, Blake Hall, Ongar, Essex]; *b* 21 Oct 1936; *educ* Eton; *m* 1st 21 Feb 1968 Caroline Ann (*d* 1986), only dau of Giles Yarnton Mills, of La Maison Blanche, Puys sur Dieppe, Seine Maritime, France, and has issue three s; *m* 2nd 25 Aug 1995 *Mrs Isabella Doble, dau of Col W H Whitbread
2a *Michael; *b* 9 Oct 1947; *educ* Eton
1a *Sarah Virginia [The Hon Mrs Thomas Lindsay, The Old Rectory, Ashmore, Salisbury, Wilts SP5 5AG]; *b* 27 Oct 1938; *m* 20 April 1961 *Hon Thomas Richard Lindsay, yst s of 28th Earl of Crawford and Balcarres (*qv*), and has issue
5 Stanley Leonard, CMG (1915), CBE (1919), DSO (1900), MVO (1915), JP (Bucks 1935), DL (Oxon); *b* 31 Dec 1873; Ld of the Manor of Long Crendon, Bucks, and High Sheriff Bucks 1935, Maj 10th Roy Hus and Brevet-Col (Col T A) Res of Offrs, memb Hon Corps Gentlemen-at-Arms 1923, served S African War 1899–1902 (despatches, Brevet Maj), cmdg 3rd Bn Northants Regt 1914, ADC to C-in-C BEF France 1914–15, in attendance on HRH THE PRINCE OF WALES in France 1914–15 (despatches, Brevet Col, Chevalier Legion of Honour), chm CPRE Oxon and chm Area Ctee Oxon, Bucks and Berks under Physical Training and Recreation Act 1937; *m* 1st 5 June 1906 Hannah Mary (*d* 28 March 1923), est dau of James Hainsworth, of 34 Phillimore Gdns, London W8, formerly w of Col William MacGeorge, 6th Dragoon Gds, and *d* 22 Dec 1943, leaving issue:
(1) *Jeanne Irene [The Hon Mrs James McDonnell, Hoebridge Cottage, Balls Cross, Petworth, Sussex; 36 Farley Ct, Melbury Rd, London W14]; *b* 12 July 1915; *m* 19 Oct 1939 *Hon James Angus Grey McDonnell, yst son of 7th Earl of Antrim (*qv*), and has issue
5 (cont.) Stanley Leonard Barry *m* 2nd 3 Feb 1927 Laline Annette (*d* 22 April 1969), er dau of William Harvey Astell, JP, DL, of Woodbury Hall, Sandy, Beds, and widow of Lt-Col Arthur Preston Hohler, DSO, 10th Bn Middx Regt (*see* ERROLL, E and GORT, V), of Long Crendon Manor, Oxon
1 Alice Maria; *b* 12 May 1852; *m* 20 June 1876 Henry Neve Goodhart (*d* 11 Oct 1880), s of Charles Emmanuel Goodhart, of Langley Pk, Beckenham, Kent, and *d* 31 Dec 1939, leaving issue
2 Grace Isabel; *b* 20 April 1866; *m* 5 June 1889 Harry Holmes (*d* 21 Dec 1931), of Balgreggan, Stranraer, Wigtownshire, est s of Harry Holmes, JP, DL, of Grey Towers, Hornchurch, Essex, and *d* 31 July 1947, leaving issue

Sir FRANCIS's est surv s,

Sir Edward Arthur Barry, 2nd Bt, JP; *b* 25 April 1858; 2nd BARON DE BARRY of Portugal, V-Lt Berks, High Sheriff 1907, Lt-Col Berks Yeo, served WW I; *m* 1st 31 Jan 1883 Kathleen Ellen (*d* 4 Dec 1885), dau of Percy Bicknell, of Shinrone, Co Tipperary, and had issue:

1 CLAUDE FRANCIS (Sir), **3rd Bt**
2 Gerald Tress; *b* 24 Nov, *d* 11 Dec 1885

Sir Edward *m* 2nd 10 Feb 1891 Eleanor Margaret (*d* 11 Feb 1916), dau of Col Courtenay Harvey Saltren Scott, of Pennant Hall, Abermule, Montgomeryshire, and *d* 23 July 1949, leaving further issue:

3 Edward Courtenay Tress; *b* 23 Jan 1896; Lt, served WW I 1914 in Berks Yeo and RE, WW II in RA; *d* unm 23 Feb 1959
1 Cicely Eleanor; *b* 24 Dec 1892; *m* 16 Oct 1918 Philip Poore (*d* 28 April 1937), 4th s of Maj Robert Poore, 8th Hus (*see* POORE, Bt), and had issue
2 Margaret Colquhoun; *b* 5 Nov 1894; VAD WW I 1917–19; *m* 12 July 1919 Capt James Cifton Colquhoun, MBE, Highland LI, s of James Colquhoun, of Humboldt House, Tunbridge Wells, and had issue:
(1) *James Barry; *b* 1931
(2) *William Balliol; *b* 1934
(1) *Elizabeth; *b* 1924
(2) *Margaret; *b* 1927
3 Rosamonde; *b* 25 Dec 1901; *m* 22 Jan 1925 Gen Sir Sydney Frederick Muspratt, KCB, CSI, CIE, DSO, IA, s of Henry Muspratt, ICS, and had issue:
(1) *John Scott [John Muspratt Esq, 47 Dominion Circuit, Forrest, Canberra, ACT, Australia]; *b* 16 Oct 1925; *m* 6 May 1957 *Elizabeth Barrett, yr dau of John Davis Canning, of Waipukurau, NZ, and has issue
(2) David Barry; *b* 2 Jan 1928; *educ* Peterhouse and Cambridge (MA); *m* 5 Oct 1963 *Rosemary Anne, er dau of Col E D Rash, of Larkshayes, Grundisburgh, nr Woodbridge, Suffolk, and *d* 19–, leaving:
1a *Jonathan David; *b* 8 Feb 1965
1a *Rosalind Mary; *b* 25 Sept 1966

Sir EDWARD's est s,

Sir Claude Francis Barry, 3rd Bt; *b* 16 Dec 1883; *educ* Harrow; *m* 1st 16 Dec 1908 (*divorce* 1927) Angela Doris Manners (*d* 13 June 1960), er dau of Herbert Charles Hume-Spry, of the The Priory, Thornbury, Glos, and had issue:

1 RUPERT RODNEY FRANCIS TRESS (Sir), **4th Bt**

1 Kathleen Manners Tress; *b* 2 Oct 1909; *m* 5 June 1934 Edgar Freshman, FRCS, and had issue:

(1) *Roger David Barry [Roger Freshman Esq, c/o Mobil (S Africa) Ltd, Box 1043, Johannesburg, S Africa]; *b* 22 Oct 1938; *educ* Radley and Bristol U (BSc); 2nd Lt, 3rd Roy Tank Regt

(1) *Judy Rosemary [Mrs R W M Hunt, Brooklands, Nowick, Natal, S Africa]; *b* 30 June 1935; *m* 19– *R W M Hunt and has issue:

1a *James William Miles; *b* 1 May 1964

2a *Rex Anthony; *b* 5 Aug 1968

1a *Philippa Tress; *b* 10 May 1962

2a *Tessa Molly; *b* 10 Aug 1966

(2) *Angela Carolyn Tress [Mrs Robert Bartlett, The Clock House, Challock, Ashford, Kent]; *b* 15 Sept 1941; *m* 1967 *Capt Robert Anthony Bartlett, 1st Bn Middx Regt (DCO), er s of P N Bartlett, of The Old Manor, Bloxham, nr Banbury, Oxon, and has issue:

1a *Christopher Noel; *b* 28 Jan 1968

1a *Reynell Angela; *b* 3 Jan 1970

2 *Sheila Yvonne Elizabeth Doris; *b* 20 July 1915; *m* 21 June 1941 *Col John Loftus Carter, late RM (*see* ELY, M), s of Alexander John Carter, of The White House, Pitdown, Sussex, and has issue:

(1) *Brian Loftus, OBE (1989); *b* 16 June 1945; *educ* Clifton; Col RM; *m* 1st 1969 (*divorce* 1971) Caroline Jane Halsey and has issue:

1a *Andrew Charles Loftus; *b* 1971

(1) (cont.) Col Brian Carter *m* 2nd 1973 *Eva Jorum Berglund, of Horten, Norway, and has issue:

1a *Anneli Victoria Solveig; *b* 1980

(1) *Sally Elizabeth [Mrs David Gow, The Oak House, Church Lane, Aldington, Kent]; *b* 29 Nov 1943; *m* 1970 *David William Mearns Gow and has issue:

1a *William Hugh Mearns; *b* 1971

1a *Amanda Elizabeth Mearns; *b* 1973

Sir Claude *m* 2nd 20 Dec 1927 Violet Gwendoline Pretyman, (*d* 18 Jan 1957), yr dau of Alfred Darby, of Brentwood, Essex, and *d* 25 Oct 1970

Sir CLAUDE's only s,

Sir Rupert Rodney Francis Tress Barry, 4th Bt, MBE (1945); *b* 6 Dec 1910; *educ* King's Sch Canterbury and RMC Sandhurst; Maj 1st Green Jackets (43rd and 52nd) WW II 1939–40 (POW), dir St John Ambulance Assoc Cheshire 1960; *m* 1st 7 March 1936 Diana Madeline (*d* 22 Sept 1948), only dau of Rowland O'Brien Thompson, of 8 Harley Gdns, London SW10, and had issue:

1 Sir LAURENCE EDWARD ANTHONY TRESS BARRY, **5th and present Bt**

1 *Armorel Madeleine Frances Tress [Mrs Peter Lambert, Half Moon House, Rectory Lane, Halesworth, Suffolk IP19 8AF]; *b* 11 Dec 1936; *m* 5 Sept 1959 *Maj Peter Miles Lambert, Gren Gds, only s of Peter Jocelyn Lambert, MC, by Lettice, dau of Maj Cecil Wellesley (*see* WELLINGTON, D), and has issue

Sir Rupert *m* 2nd 12 May 1951 *Sheila Georgina Veronica [Sheila Lady Barry, Brisley Rise, Willesborough Lees, Ashford, Kent], only dau of Maj George Joseph Francis White, MBE, 43rd LI, of Longacre, Andover Rd, Winchester, and *d* 1977, leaving further issue:

2 +Timothy Rupert Francis Tress; *b* 1 Nov 1952; *educ* Sutton Valence Sch; late Capt RMP; *m* 1977 *Valerie, yst dau of Mrs M D M Reid, of Otterburn, Northumberland, and has issue:

(1) *Victoria Louise Frances Tress; *b* 1982

(2) *Georgina Alicia Frances Tress; *b* 1985

(3) *Henrietta Elizabeth Frances Tress; *b* 1990

3 +Nicholas Mark Francis Tress [Nicholas Barry Esq, The Kennels, Lenacre St, Eastwell, Ashford, Kent]; *b* 22 Oct 1957; *m* 1985 *Fiona Mary, yr dau of John Rankin, QC, of Prospect House, Boughton, Faversham, Kent, and has issue:

(1) *Lucy Arabella Frances Tress; *b* 1987

(2) *Katharine Rose Frances Tress; *b* 1989

4 +Jonathan Rodney Francis Tress [Jonathan Barry Esq, Eyhorne Manor, Hollingsbourne, Kent]; *b* 12 Feb 1960

2 *Tara Caroline Frances Tress [Mrs Peter Kortlang, The Duck Farm, Sandy Hurst Lane, Ashford, Kent TN25 4PD]; *b* 22 Feb 1954; *m* 1977 *(Fokko) Peter Anthony Kortlang, only s of C F H F Kortlang, of Willesborough Lees, Kent, and has issue:

(1) *Piers Anthony Fokko Tress; *b* 1978

(2) *Christian Rupert Fokko Tress; *b* 1988

(1) *Lavinia Cordelia Frances Tress; *b* 1982

(2) *Venetia Sophia Frances Tress; *b* 1984

3 *Xandra Georgina Frances Tress [Mrs Simon Cox, c/o Brisley Rise, Willesborough Lees, Ashford, Kent]; *b* 21 Nov 1962; *m* 25 May 1996 *Maj Simon John Cox, RA, er s of J C Cox of Umberleigh, Devon

BARTLETT

Arms: Argent, two barrulets dancettée between in chief two cinquefoils and in base a crescent, issuant therefrom a cross formée fitchée all azure. **Crest:** A demi-eagle displayed azure winged or and supporting with the beak a pennon of the first, charged with the arms. **Motto:** *Fortitudine et fidelitate* ('With fortitude and fidelity'). **Creation:** Bt. (UK) 7 Feb 1913.

SIR ANDREW ALAN BARTLETT, 5TH BT, of Hardington-Mandeville, Somerset [Sir Andrew Bartlett Bt, Hardington House, Ermyn Way, Leatherhead, Surrey KT22 8TW]; *b* 26 May 1973; *s* f 1998

Lineage: ROBERT BARTLETT, of Hardington, Somerset; *b* 2 May 1803; *m* 6 Nov 1827 Anne Guppy (*d* 12 Nov 1871) and *d* 15 April 1885, leaving issue:

Sir Herbert Henry Bartlett, 1st Bt (UK), so *cr* 7 Feb 1913, of Hardington Mandeville, Somerset; *b* 30 April 1842; chm Perry & Co, of Bow, civil engrg contractors, Freeman City of London, thrice Master Pattenmakers' Co, fndr Bartlett Sch of Architecture, UCL; *m* 18 April 1874 Ada Charlotte (*d* 24 Dec 1933), dau of Joseph Barr, of Ampthill Sq, London, and *d* 28 June 1921, having had issue:

1 Herbert Evelyn; *b* 27 Feb 1875; *d* unm 8 Aug 1917

2 Hardington Arthur; *b* 21 Nov 1878; *m* 2 July 1902 Irene, dau of Prof Henry Robinson, and *d* 11 Jan 1920, leaving issue:

(1) **Sir Basil Hardington Bartlett, 2nd Bt**; *b* 15 Sept 1905; *educ* Repton and Corpus Christi Coll Cambridge (BA); Lt-Col Intell Corps, served WW II (despatches, wounded); *m* 5 Jan 1937 (*divorce* 1960) Mary, only dau of Sir Ian Zachary Malcolm of Poltalloch, KCMG, JP, DL, and *d* 1985, leaving issue:

1a *Julia Jane [Mrs John Atkinson, 12 Brookside, Cambridge CB2 1JE]; *b* 31 Dec 1937; *m* 1966 *John Atkinson and has had:

1b *Thomasina Kate; *b* 27 Feb 1967

2b *Teresa Mary; *b* 2 Oct 1968

3b Cressida Jane Elizabeth; *b* 9 Feb 1971; *d* 2 May 1994

2a *Lucy Mary Le Breton [Mrs Adrian Bridgewater, Manor Farm, Gt Eversden, Cambs CB37 7HW]; *b* 16 April 1941; *m* 7 Nov 1969 *Adrian Alexander Bridgewater, only s of Maj P A C Bridgewater (*see* VIVIAN, B), and has issue:

1b *Benjamin Hardington; *b* 1979

1b *Nancy Le Breton; *b* 1971

2b *Daisy Maud; *b* 1973

3a *Annabel Kate [Mrs Anthony McCall, 214 W 17th St, Apt PHC, New York, NY 10011–5347, USA]; *b* 4 Aug 1945; *m* *Anthony David McCall and has issue:

1b *Hardington Alexander William; *b* 1988

(2) **Sir Henry David Hardington Bartlett, 3rd Bt**, MBE (1944); *b* 18 March 1912; *educ* Stowe and Corpus Christi Coll Cambridge; Hon Maj RA, Lt-Col RA (TA), served WW II; *m* 1st 8 Dec 1936 (*divorce* 1974) Kathleen Rosamund, 2nd dau of Lt-Col W H Stanbury, of Park Lodge, Park Rd, Ashtead, Surrey; *m* 2nd 1974 Joyce Lillian (*d* 1982), dau of Malcolm Odell, of Surbiton; *m* 3rd 1982 *Jeanne Margaret Esther [Jeanne Lady Bartlett, Brockley Place, Brockley, Bury St Edmunds, Suffolk IP29 4AG], dau of Charles William Brewer, of St John's Wood, and *d* 13 Sept 1989, leaving by his 1st w:

1a **Sir John Hardington Bartlett, 4th Bt**; *b* 11 March 1938; *educ* St Peter's Guildford; author and engr; FRSA, MInst PI; Freeman: Pattenmakers' Co and City London; *m* 1st 1966 Susan Elizabeth (*d* 1970), dau of Norman Waldock, of Gt Bookham, Surrey, and had:

1b *Nicola Jane; *b* 1969

1a (cont.) **Sir John** *m* 2nd 1971 *Elizabeth Joyce [Lady Bartlett, Hardington House, Ermyn Way, Leatherhead, Surrey KT22 8TW], dau of George Thomas Raine, of Kingston-upon-Thames, Surrey, and *d* 8 April 1998, leaving by her:

1b Sir ANDREW ALAN BARTLETT, **5th and present Bt**

2b +STEPHEN; *b* 1975; heir presumptive

2a +Simon Hardington [Simon Bartlett Esq, Cobweb Cottage, 23 Lower Town, Sampford Peverell, Devon EX16 7BJ]; *b* 21 July 1940; *educ* St

Peter's, Guildford; *m* 1967 (*divorce* 1972) Antoinette Lois, dau of Gaston Charpentier, and has issue:

1b *Rebecca Rosamund; *b* 1969

3a +Christopher Mandeville [Christopher Bartlett Esq, 1 Redlands Bank Cottages, Mid Holmwood, Dorking, Surrey RH5 4ES]; *b* 3 April 1942; *educ* St Peter's, Guildford; *m* 1966 *Brenda June, dau of Eric Thorne, of Beech Cottage, Coneyhurst Lane, Ewhurst, Surrey, and has issue:

1b +Paul David; *b* 1968

1b *Sarah Jane; *b* 1972

(1) (Irene) Theodora; *b* 25 May 1908; *d* unm 7 Feb 1998

3 Robert Dudley; *b* 8 Oct 1880; Lt RNVR; *m* 1st 14 Jan 1906 Maud Violet (*d* 30 July 1930), dau of George Joseph Martin, of Boston, Lincs; *m* 2nd 17 Dec 1931 Mrs Yvonne Mignon (Barry) Miller, dau of Charles Edward Simons, and *d* 18 Nov 1963

4 Eric Oscar; *b* 26 Aug 1882; *m* 16 Jan 1907 Irene, dau of Lawrence Alport, of 100 Lexham Gdns, London W, and *d* 1968, leaving issue:

(1) *Betty Frances; *b* 11 March 1908; *m* 20 May 1933 Gordon Bushell Hedley (*d* 22 May 1969), late Bengal Pilot Serv, and has issue:

1a *Richard; *b* 1940

1a *Anne Wilhelmina Betty; *b* 1934

(2) *Mary Augusta; *b* 28 Feb 1911; *m* 1st 20 Jan 1934 F/Lt Roy James Oliphant Bartlett, RAF (*d* 7 Oct 1936), s of Capt Howard Bartlett, of Rustington, and has issue:

1a *Peter Howard Oliphant; *b* 1937

1a *Jill Rose Alyne Charlotte; *b* Dec 1934; *m* 1955 *Stuart Bollam and has issue:

1b *Miles Stuart; *b* 1957

1b *Kim Pauline; *b* 1956

(2) (cont.) Mrs Roy Bartlett *m* 2nd 1941 *G/Capt James Douglas Ferrier Bruce, RAF, and by him has:

2a *Mhairi Christina Deborah; *b* 1945

5 Philip Mandeville (Rev); *b* 19 Oct 1884; *educ* Ch Ch Oxford (MA 1911); Preb St Paul's 1950, Rural Dean Poplar 1951, vicar St Saviour with St Gabriel and St Stephen, Poplar, 1952–58; *d* unm 16 Aug 1958

6 Norman Edwin; *b* 20 Sept 1888; late Maj RFA (TF); *m* 1st 20 Dec 1917 (*divorce* 1928) Mary Adelaide Leslie (*d* 1981), yr dau of Norman R Foster, of 47 Murray Rd, Wimbledon, London SW, and had issue:

(1) +Norman Alaric [Lt-Cdr Norman Bartlett RN (ret), Lonesome Pine, Bickenhall, Taunton, Som]; *b* 7 April 1920; Lt-Cdr and pilot Flying Branch RN (ret), WW II despatches; *m* 1945 *Mary Paterson Waugh and has issue:

1a +Michael Alaric; *b* 1946; *m* 1st 1967 Sheila Taylor and has issue:

1b +Colin; *b* 1967

2b +Glen; *b* 1971

1a (cont.) Michael Bartlett *m* 2nd 1983 *Linda Ireson and has issue:

3b +Andrew; *b* 1984

4b +Gary; *b* 1986

1a *Carol Ann; *b* 1948; *m* 1985 *Harry Page

(1) *Hazel Leslie [Mrs Philip Elwood, 21 Garstons, Bathford, Avon BA1 7TE]; *b* 24 Sept 1922; *m* 1st 1947 George Edward Short (*d* 8 Aug 1962), of Wimbledon; *m* 2nd 1966 Philip John Elwood (*d* 1979), s of Timothy Walter Elwood, of Norfolk, and has had by her 1st husb:

1a Edward Louis; *b* 15 July 1949; *d* 31 Oct 1967

1a *Jennifer Anne; *b* 21 March 1942; *m* 1st 1964 (*divorce* 19–) James William Price; *m* 2nd 1978 *Vivian Leslie Stuart Stokes and has issue by her 1st husb:

1b *Hamish Dudley; *b* 1965

2a *Angela Jill; *b* 2 April 1948; *m* 1970 (*divorce* 19–) Brian K Rogers and has issue:

1b *Thomas Edward George; *b* 1977

2b *Jamie Alexander Francis Forgan; *b* 1988

1b *Tiffany Roberta Kate; *b* 1974

3a *Catherine Leslie; *b* 15 Dec 1952; *m* 1st 1977 (*divorce* 19–) Mark Hoy; *m* 2nd 1987 *Alan Jones and by him has issue:

1b *Nicola Suzanne; *b* 1988

2b *Elizabeth Lesley; *b* 1991

6 (cont.) Norman Bartlett *m* 2nd 25 June 1928 Sheila (*d* 1993), dau of Frederick Page Barton, of Villa Louis, Monte Carlo, and Mrs Hill, of 11 Bentinck Terr, London SW8, and *d* 1972, leaving further issue:

(2) +Derek [Maj Derek Bartlett, Fiveways, Warfield, Bracknell, Berks]; *b* 13 May 1930; Maj Life Gds (ret), with Vickers da Costa; *m* 25 Jan 1956 *Joan Patricia, dau of Robert Joshua Breyfogle, of Field Cottage, Sunningdale, Berks, and has issue:

1a +Peter Mandeville; *b* 21 July 1960

2a +Robert Hardington; *b* 3 April 1965

1a *Jonica Mary; *b* 10 Feb 1958

(2) *Edwina [Mrs Esmond Boldero, Gyles Croft, Bellingdon, Chesham, Bucks]; *b* 15 May 1933; *m* 3 Nov 1956 *Capt Esmond Dunn Boldero, Life Gds (ret), only surv s of Sir Harold Esmond Arnis Boldero, MA, DM, FRCP, of 63 Hill St, London W1, and has issue:

1a *Jonathan Dunn; *b* 21 Aug 1958; Capt Life Gds

1a *Alexandra [Mrs Nicholas Tapner, 13 Woodstock Rd, London W4 1D5]; *b* 13 May 1964; *m* 1988 *Nicholas Rory Tapner

2a *Louisa; *b* 21 June 1966

1 Ada Nora; *b* 4 Dec 1876; *m* 2 Dec 1916 Evelyn Ronald Brodrick Cloete Graham, FRGS (*d* 13 Oct 1961), slr and commr for oaths, s of Lawrence Graham, of Hardelot, Pas de Calais, France, and *dsp* 12 March 1962

2 Ruby Hilda; *b* 24 Aug 1886; *d* unm 24 May 1964

3 Olive Florence Ivy; *b* 28 Jan 1892; *m* 17 Nov 1917 Maj Edward Cartwright Young, RA (TA Res), s of Lt-Col E W Young, IMS, and *d* 18 Sept 1926

BARTTELOT

Arms: Quarterly, 1st and 4th, sable, three sinister gloves pendent argent, tasselled or (for BARTTELOT); 2nd and 3rd, per fess indented argent and gules, four crescents countercharged (for STOPHAM). **Crests:** 1 A swan couchant, wings endorsed argent, 2 A castle with three turrets sable. **Motto:** *Mature* ('In good time'). **Creation:** Bt. (UK) 14 June 1875.

SIR BRIAN WALTER DE STOPHAM BARTTELOT, 5TH BT, of Stopham, Sussex, OBE (1989), DL (W Sussex 1988) [Col Sir Brian Barttelot Bt OBE DL, Stopham Park, Pulborough, Sussex RH20 1DY]; *b* 17 July 1941; *s* f 1944; *educ* Eton and RMA Sandhurst; Col Coldstream Gds (ret 1992), Equerry to HM THE QUEEN 1970-72, Mil Sec to Maj-Gen cmdg London Dist and Household Div 1978–80, Lt-Col cmdg Coldstream Gds 1987-92, Col Foot Gds 1989-92, memb Hon Corps Gentlemen at Arms 1993-, Liveryman Gunmakers' Co 1980, High Sheriff W Sussex 1997–98 (V-Ld Lt 1994–), chm Exec Ctee Standing Cncl Baronetage 1996–; *m* 20 Nov 1969 *Hon (Mary Angela) Fiona Weld-Forester, Ch Pres St John Ambulance 1996–, yst dau of 7th Baron Forester (*qv*), and has:

1 *Isabel Emily; *b* 5 March 1971; *m* 19 July 1997 *Luke Sanders, s of Andrew Sanders, of Hempstead, Essex

2 *Sophie Rosalind; *b* 17 April 1973

3 *Ursulina May; *b* 1 May 1978

4 *Emma Amelia; *b* 1981

Lineage: WILLIAM BARTTELOT, of Stopham, Sussex; f of:

JOHN; f of:

RICHARD, of Stopham; *b* 1216; f of:

ADAM BARTTELOT; mentioned in Sussex Subsidy Roll 1295; f of:

THOMAS BARTTELOT de STOPHAM; on Subsidy Roll 1326–27; f of:

JOHN; f of:

ADAM, of E Preston and Stopham; *m* Assoline, dau of John de Stopham, and *d c* 1371, leaving issue:

JOHN BARTTELOT, during the Hundred Years War took the castle of Fontenay in France, for which EDWARD THE BLACK PRINCE granted him a castle as his crest; *m* Joan er dau and coheir of William de Stopham (*d* 1399), thus acquiring that Manor, and *d* 1428, leaving:

JOHN BARTTELOT, of Stopham; fought at Agincourt 1415, MP Sussex 1434; *m* Joan, dau and heir of John Lewknor, s of Sir Thomas Lewknor, and *d* 1453, leaving, with other issue:

1 RICHARD, for whom *see* further below

2 Thomas, of Oakhurst; MP Midhurst 1448; *m* Elizabeth, dau and heiress of William de Oakhurst, and *d* 1489

JOHN BARTTELOT's est s,

RICHARD BARTTELOT, of Stopham; *m* Petronella Walton, and *d* 1482, leaving issue:

JOHN BARTTELOT, of Stopham; *m* Olyff, dau of John Artour, of London, and *d* 1493, leaving issue:

1 John, of Stopham; *m* Katherine, sis of Sir John Dawtrey, of Moor House, Petworth, Sussex, and *dsp* 1528

2 Richard; *m* Elizabeth, dau of John Gates; predeceased his bro (at Tournay, France) 1514, leaving issue:

(1) WILLIAM, for whom *see* further below

(2) Thomas; ancestor of the BARTTELOTs of Glos

(3) Edmund, of Ernley; *d* 1591, leaving issue

JOHN BARTTELOT's gs,

WILLIAM BARTTELOT, of Stopham; *m* Anne, dau of William Covert, of Hascombe, Surrey, and *d* 1601 aged 97, having had issue:

ROBERT BARTTELOT; *m* 1st Barbara, dau of Thomas Onley, of Pulborough, and had an only dau, Elizabeth; *m* 2nd Mary, dau of John Apsley, of Thakeham, and *d* 1573, leaving issue by his 2nd w:

1 Richard, of Stopham; *m* 1st Mary, dau of Richard Covert, of Slaugham; *m* 2nd Rose, dau of Richard Hatton, of Thames Ditton, Surrey, and *d* 1614 aged 50, leaving issue by his 1st w:

(1) Walter, of Stopham; MP Bramber 1625-26; *m* Mary (*d* 1626), dau of John Middleton, of Hills Place, Horsham, and *d* Jan 1640, leaving, with an er dau and four yr daus:

1a Mary; *m* her cousin Henry Barttelot (*see* below)

2 John; *dsp*

3 HENRY, for whom *see* further below

ROBERT BARTTELOT's 3rd s,

HENRY BARTTELOT, of Stopham Feodar, Sussex; *m* Ann, dau of John Marlott, of Muntham and Itchinfield, and had:

HENRY; *b* 1618; *m* his cousin Mary (*see* above) and had, with other issue:

1 WALTER, for whom *see* further below

2 Henry, of Fittleworth; High Sheriff Surrey; *d* 1710

HENRY BARTTELOT's er s,

WALTER BARTTELOT, of Stopham; *m* Anne (*d* 1690), dau of Thomas Bettesworth, of Halnaker, Sussex, and *d* 1702, leaving, with other issue:

WALTER, of Stopham; *b* April 1665; *m* 1st Isabel (*d* 1707), dau of Rev Edmund Barker, rector Buriton, Hants; *m* 2nd 1710 Mary (*d* June 1721), widow of John White, of Steyning, Sussex, and *d* Jan 1744, having had, with other issue:

Rev WALTER; rector Rottingdean and Preb Chichester; *m* Barbara (*d* 1742), dau of George Smyth, of Binderton, Sussex, and *dvp* Oct 1743, leaving an only s:

WALTER, of Stopham; High Sheriff Sussex 1754; *m* 1750 Elizabeth (*d* 1767), dau of Thomas Hooker, of Gt Chart, Kent, and *d* June 1764, having had an est s:

WALTER BARTTELOT later SMYTH (replaced to comply with the will of his great-aunt Mary Hamilton, dau of George Smyth and sis of Barbara Smyth (*see* above)), of Stopham; *b* 19 March 1751; *m* 9 June 1772 Philadelphia (*d* May 1809), dau of Rev John Wickens, DD, rector Petworth and Tillington, Sussex, by his w Philadelphia, dau of Robert Mitford, of Mitford Castle, Northumberland, and coheir of the Osbaldeston estates, and *d* 2 Feb 1837, leaving a 3rd s:

GEORGE SMYTH later BARTTELOT (replaced 1837), JP, DL (Sussex), of Stopham; *b* Aug 1788; offr RHA Peninsular War (war medal with five clasps); *m* 22 Nov 1819 Emma (*d* 1877), yst dau of James Woodbridge, of Richmond, Surrey, and *d* 28 Nov 1872

GEORGE BARTTELOT's est s,

Sir Walter Barttelot, 1st Bt (UK), so *cr* 14 June 1875, CB, PC (1892), JP, DL (both Sussex); *b* 10 Oct 1820; *educ* Rugby; MP (C) W Sussex 1860-85 and Sussex NW or Horsham 1885-93, Col 2nd Regt Sussex Roy Vols, sometime Capt 1st Roy Dragoons; *m* 1st 28 April 1852 Harriet (*d* 29 July 1863), 4th dau and coheir of Rev Sir Christopher Musgrave, 9th Bt (*see* MUSGRAVE, Bt, of Hartley Castle), of Edenhall, Cumberland, and *d* 2 Feb 1893, leaving issue by his 1st w:

1 WALTER GEORGE (Sir), **2nd Bt**

2 Edmund Musgrave; *b* 28 March 1859; Maj 1st Bn RF, served Afghan Campaign (medal and clasp) and Egypt (medal and clasp), afterwards in Africa with Emin Pasha Expdn; assassinated Central Africa 19 July 1888

1 Amy; *d* an infant

2 Edith Harriet; DBE (1918); *m* 12 June 1884 Gen Sir Henry Crichton Sclater, GCB, GBE, RA (*d* 26 Sept 1923), 3rd s of James Henry Sclater, of Newick Pk, Sussex, and *d* 29 March 1927

3 Evelyn Fanny; *m* 29 March 1883 Charles Munro Sandham (*d* 1892), of Rodmell, Sussex, and *d* 27 April 1947, leaving issue

4 Blanche; *d* unm 28 March 1876

5 Ada Mary; *m* 17 Oct 1882 Maj-Gen William Frederick Cavaye (*d* 30 Jan 1926), of Birchenbridge, Horsham, late Roy Sussex Regt, and *d* 23 June 1954 aged 91

Sir Walter *m* 2nd 30 April 1868 Margaret (*d* 28 Jan 1893), only child and heir of Henry Boldero, of S Lodge, St Leonard's Forest, Sussex

Sir WALTER's er s,

Sir Walter George Barttelot, 2nd Bt, JP (Sussex and Devon), DL (Sussex), of Stopham; *b* 11 April 1855; Maj 2nd Vol Bn Roy Sussex Regt, late Maj 1st Devon Yeo, previously Capt 5th Dragoon Gds; *m* 3 June 1879 Georgiana Mary (*m* 2nd 22 Oct 1902 Beville Molesworth St Aubyn, yr s of Rev Sir Hender Molesworth-St Aubyn, 12th Bt (*qv*), and *d* 6 Feb 1946), only dau of George Edmond Balfour, of The Manor, Sidmouth, and was *ka* S Africa 23 July 1900, leaving issue:

1 WALTER BALFOUR (Sir), **3rd Bt**

2 Nigel Kenneth Walter; *b* 9 April 1883; Lt-Cdr RN WW I (despatches); *m* 10 Jan 1906 Dorothy Maud (*m* 2nd 14 July 1923 V-Adml Sir Frank Forrester Rose, KCB, DSO (*d* 3 March 1955), and *d* 2 March 1961), est dau of Frederick Aldcroft Kay, and was *ka* off Heligoland 28 Aug 1914, leaving issue:

(1) +James Nigel Walter [Cdr James Barttelot RN (ret), Crowpits, Stopham, Pulborough, W Sussex]; *b* 27 June 1911; Cdr RN (ret), WW II; *m* 1st 3 Dec 1936 Rachel Mildred (*d* 20 Nov 1964), 3rd dau of Raymond Courage, of Edgcote, Banbury, and has issue:

1a +Nigel Michael Anthony [Nigel Barttelot Esq, Wingcroft, Marten, Wilts]; *b* 15 March 1941; *educ* Eton; *m* 1 Feb 1971 *Serena L H, dau of F W Brett, of The Little Cottage, Hurst, Twyford, Berks, and has issue:

1b +Piers Nigel Edward; *b* 21 May 1976

1b *Sasha Rachel; *b* 1972

2b *Olivia Henrietta; *b* 29 May 1974

3b *Hannah; *b* 1981

2a +David James Raymond [David Barttelot Esq, 49 Grandison Rd, London SW11 6LS]; *b* 28 Feb 1946; *educ* Eton; Liveryman Armourers' and Brasiers' Co 1980; *m* 1st 1973 (*divorce* 1980) Lucinda Jane, dau of Cdr G R Callingham, RN (ret); *m* 2nd 1983 *Charmian, er dau of Cdr John S Kerans, DSO, RN (ret), of 44 Gordons Way, Oxted, Surrey

1a *Carol Rachel Mildred [Mrs Carol Macmillan, Altyre House, Great Horkesley, nr Colchester, Essex CO6 4AB]; *b* 4 Feb 1938; *m* 7 Oct 1961 (*divorce* 1988) Torquil Robin Armour Macmillan, yr s of John Armour Macmillan and Mrs Margery Babington O'Cock, of 26 Chestnuts Cl, Haywards Heath, Sussex, and has issue:

1b *James Armour; *b* 12 June 1965; *m* 1986 *Susan Margaret Falle and has issue:

1c *Joshua; *b* 1990

2c *Benedict; *b* 1993

1c *Sophie Charlotte; *b* 1987

2b *Andrew Giles; *b* 6 April 1968

3b *Timothy Iain; *b* 19 June 1969; *m* 25 Oct 1996 *Kirsty Rawlings and has:

1c *Ella Georgia; *b* 10 July 1997

1b *Lucinda Jane Carol [Mrs John Brezak, Crowpits, Pulborough, Sussex RH20 1ED]; *b* 23 Feb 1963; *m* 1989 *John Brezak and has issue:

1c *Tiffany; *b* 1992

2c *Audrey; *b* 1994

(1) (cont.) Cdr James Barttelot *m* 2nd 28 May 1965 (Sara) Patricia (*d* 14 Jan 1998), dau of Lt-Col Herbert Valentine Ravenscroft and widow of Brig Sir Walter de Stopham Barttelot, 4th Bt, DSO (*see* below)

1 Irene Margaret Mary; *m* 5 Jan 1910 Maj Francis Alexander Atchis, Hants Regt, s of Col Atchis, RA, and *d* 5 Jan 1932, leaving issue

Sir WALTER's est s,

Sir Walter Balfour Barttelot, 3rd Bt, DSO (1916); *b* 22 March 1880; Maj and Brevet Lt-Col Coldstream Gds, Mily Attaché Teheran 1918, Bde Maj and GSO S African War 1899-1902 (despatches, two medals, eight clasps) and WW I (despatches, four times, wounded 1914, Star, Croix de Guerre, Brevet); *m* 17 Nov 1903 Gladys St Aubyn (*m* 2nd 30 April 1920 Capt Neston William Diggle, CMG, RN (ret) (*d* 17 Dec 1963), s of Wadham Neston Diggle, of Bratton House, Westbury, Wilts, and *d* 12 Jan 1976 aged 94), dau of William Collier Angove, of Onslow Gdns, London SW, and was *ka* Teheran 23 Oct 1918, leaving issue:

1 WALTER De STOPHAM BARTTELOT (Sir), **4th Bt**

2 William Frederick Geoffrey Nelson; *b* 21 Oct 1905; *educ* Wellington; Lt-Col RE WW II, AIEE, later with Taylor Woodrow; *m* 20 Dec 1930 Jane Elizabeth (*d* 1990), only dau of Duncan Stirling, of Santiago, Chile, and has:

(1) +Richard James Walter Stuart; *b* 3 Feb 1932; *educ* Wellington

(1) *Elizabeth (Lisa) Georgiana Margaret; *b* 16 March 1933; *m* 1st 2 July 1955 (*divorce* 1973) James Drury Edward Kelly, Essex Regt, only s of Lt-Col Arthur Hamilton Kelly, of Forge Cottage, Lyminster, Sussex, and has:

1a *Thomas James Barttelot; *b* 2 May 1956; *m* 1981 (*divorce* 1986) Sarah Jane St Clair Weir and has issue:

1b *Louis Frederick Charles; *b* 1986

1a *Rose Jane Elizabeth; *b* 15 Sept 1958; *m* 1984 *John Charles Harding and has issue:

1b *Minnie Apphia Rose; *b* 1990

2b *Patience Elizabeth Ann; *b* 1992

(1) (cont) Mrs Elizabeth Kelly *m* 2nd 1973 *Nigel John Petrie Mermagen, of Richmond House, Chard, Somerset

Sir WALTER's er s,

Sir Walter de Stopham Barttelot, 4th Bt, DSO (1944); *b* 27 Oct 1904; Maj Coldstream Gds, WW II 1939–44 as T/Lt-Col and A/Brig (despatches); *m* 7 May 1938 (Sara) Patricia, OStJ (1965) (*m* 2nd 28 May 1965 *Cdr James Nigel Walter Barttelot, RN (ret) (*see* above)), dau of Lt-Col Herbert Valentine Ravenscroft, JP, of The Abbey, Storrington, Sussex, and was *ka* Normandy 16 Aug 1944 whilst cmdg 6th Gds Tank Brigade, leaving issue:

1 Sir BRIAN WALTER De STOPHAM BARTTELOT, **5th and present Bt**

2 +ROBIN RAVENSCROFT [Robin Barttelot Esq, Targrove, Fittleworth, Sussex]; *b* 15 Dec 1943; heir presumptive; *educ* Seaford Coll and U of W Australia (BA); *m* 1987 *Teresa, er dau of Kenneth Greenlees, and has:

(1) +Hugo Ravenscroft; *b* 7 April 1990

(1) *Emily Rose; *b* 1988

BASING

Arms: Quarterly, 1st and 4th, gules a chevron, between in chief two bezants, and in base a portcullis chained or (for BOOTH); 2nd and 3rd, argent a cross gules between two penguins proper in the 1st and 4th quarters, and two martlets azure in the 2nd and 3rd quarters (for SCLATER). **Crests:** Dexter, a horse's head erased proper, bridled and reined or, charged with a roundel argent, thereon a boar's head erect and erased sable (for BOOTH); sinister, between two sprigs of oak proper, fructed or, a woodcock's head erased proper, gorged with a collar argent, charged with a saltire azure (for SCLATER). **Supporters:** Dexter, a winged lion, queue fourchée; sinister, an eagle sable; each gorged with a saltire azure affixed to the collar, a chain reflexed over the back argent, the wings charged on the covert and secondary feathers with three cogwheels in chevron or. **Motto:** God is my source.
Creation: B. (UK) 7 July 1887.

THE 5TH BARON BASING OF BASING BYFLETE AND OF HODDINGTON, both in Co Southampton (Neil Lutley Sclater Booth) [The Rt Hon The Lord Basing, 112 E 74th St, New York, NY 10021, USA]; *b* 16 Jan 1939; *s* f 1983; *educ* Eton and Harvard U (BA); dir Akroyd & Smithers Inc (NYC); *m* 19 Sept 1967 *Patricia Ann, dau of George Bryan Whitfield, of 598 Prospect St, New Haven, Connecticut, and has:

1 +STUART ANTHONY WHITFIELD; *b* 18 Dec 1969; *educ* The Collegiate Sch; *m* 28 June 1997 *Kirsten Erica, dau of Eric Henry Oxboel
2 +Andrew Linbrey; *b* 1973; *educ* The Collegiate Sch

Lineage: The Rev ANTHONY SCLATER, DD, from a Northumbrian branch of the Sclater family which allegedly originated in Slaughter, Glos, was vicar Leighton Buzzard 1553–1625; *d* in his 96th year, leaving issue:

1 William, DD; *b* 1575; vicar Pitminster, Somerset; theological author; f of:
(1) William, DD; vicar Colhampton
2 John
3 CHRISTOPHER

The Rev ANTHONY SCLATER's yst s,

Rev CHRISTOPHER SCLATER, DD; vicar Leighton Buzzard; *d* in his 63rd year, leaving issue:

Rev WILLIAM SCLATER; *educ* Corpus Christi Coll Oxford; royalist Cornet and Lt of Horse Civil War; imprisoned for royalism; later ordained, incumbent: Hadley, Middx, 1662, and St James's, Clerkenwell, 1666 and rector Clifton, Beds; *d* 1690, leaving issue:

Rev FRANK SCLATER, DD; Fell Corpus Christi Coll Oxford; *dvp* 12 May 1685 aged 35, leaving issue:

Rev CHRISTOPHER SCLATER, MA; *b* 1679; rector Loughton then Chingford, both Essex; *m* 1707 Elizabeth, est dau of John May, of Worting, Hants, and had, with other issue, a 2nd s:

RICHARD SCLATER; *b* 1712; Alderman City of London; *m* 1st Magdalen, yst dau of John Limbrey, of Tangier Pk and Hoddington House, Hants, and had issue:

1 THOMAS LIMBREY SCLATER later SCLATER MATHEW (added by roy sign manual as rep through his maternal gf of the MATHEWs of Hoddington House, of Tangier Pk and Hoddington House); *dsp* 1809
1 ELIZABETH SCLATER; who *s* her bro in the estates; *d* unm 1814

RICHARD SCLATER *m* 2nd Penelope, dau of Philip Lutley, of Bromcroft Castle and Loughton Hall, Salop, by his w Penelope, dau of Richard Barneby, of Brockhampton, Herefs, and by her had issue:

2 Rev BARTHOLOMEW LUTLEY SCLATER, for whom *see* further below
2 Penelope Lutley, of The Tything, Worcs, and Hoddington House; *d* unm 1844

RICHARD SCLATER's 2nd s,

Rev BARTHOLOMEW LUTLEY SCLATER, MA; Fell Oriel Coll Oxford; rector Whittingham, Northumberland; *m* Elizabeth Rebecca (*d* 1825), only surv dau and heiress of George Bristow, of Ashford, Middx, and *d* 1804, having had an est s:

WILLIAM LUTLEY SCLATER, JP, of Hoddington House; *b* 22 Jan 1789; Chm Magistrates Basingstoke Div, MA; *m* 26 July 1821 Anne Maria (*d* 1 April 1879), dau of William Bowyer, of The King's Remembrancer's Office, by his w Dorothy, dau of Thomas Tomkyns, of Bucknall, Herefs, and *d* 15 Dec 1885, leaving, with other issue:

1 GEORGE, **1st Baron**
2 Philip Lutley; *b* 4 Nov 1829; Fell Corpus Christi Coll Oxford; MA, DSc, PhD, FRS; barrister Lincoln's Inn; *m* 16 Oct 1862 Jane Anne Eliza (*d* 25 May 1915), yst dau of Sir David Hunter Blair, 3rd Bt (*qv*), and *d* 27 June 1913, leaving issue:
(1) William Lutley; *b* 23 Sept 1863; *m* 1 Feb 1896 Charlotte Seymour, CBE (*d* 1942), dau of William Proctor Mellen, of Colorado Springs, USA, and was *ka* July 1944
(2) Bertram Lutley; *b* 22 Feb 1866; Capt RE; *d* unm 24 July 1897
(3) Guy Lutley; *b* 15 Aug 1868; Capt RN; *m* 2 Sept 1907 Evelyn Muriel, only dau of Edward Chappell, of The Close, Odiham, Hants, and was lost in HMS *Bulwark* off Chatham 26 Nov 1914, leaving issue:
1a Claude Edward Lutley, DSO and bar; *b* 24 Jan 1910; MA, Cdr RN (ret), Fell and Bursar King's Coll Cambridge 1955-63, Sec Bath Club 1964; *m* 2 March 1935 Helen Mansel, only dau of Cdr Mansel Brabazon Fiennes Colvile, DSO, RN, of King's Barn, Odiham, Hants, and had issue:
1b *Edward Guy Lutley [Lt-Cdr Edward Sclater RN, Abington Pigotts Hall, Royston, Herts]; *b* 21 June 1936; *educ* Gordonstoun; Lt-Cdr RN; *m* 14 Dec 1963 *Elizabeth Eleanor, er dau of Montague George de Courcy Ireland, of Abington Pigotts Hall, and has issue:
1c *Rupert Edward Lutley Pigott; *b* 9 Dec 1967
2c *A son; *b* 8 Nov 1970
1c *Alice Eleanor Pigott; *b* 22 Oct 1965
2b *Christopher John Lutley [Christopher Sclater Esq, 22 Nirvana Rd, Brighton Beach, Durban, S Africa]; *b* 5 Nov 1939; *educ* Gordonstoun; *m* 2 Nov 1968 *Angela, 2nd dau of Henry Cole, of Durban
3b *Nigel William Lutley; *b* 13 Sept 1943; *educ* Gordonstoun and RMA Sandhurst; RA; *m* 23 July 1965 *Jennifer, only dau of W G Crabbie, of 9 Essex Rd, Barton, Edinburgh 4, and has issue:
1c *Niall Lutley; *b* 9 Aug 1966
1c *Mary Charlotte; *b* 19 March 1969
1b *Penelope Caroline; *b* 12 Nov 1949
2b *Anne Mary; *b* 24 June 1952
1a Elizabeth Flora Lutley; *b* 10 Dec 1912; *m* 28 Sept 1933 Maj-Gen Edward Barrington de Fonblanque, CB, CBE, DSO, Inspector-Gen Fedl Home Gd Malaya 1951, yr s of Lester Ramsay de Fonblanque, of Guildford House, Farnham, Surrey, and had issue:
1b *Hugh Barrington; *b* 27 Oct 1937
2b *John Robert; *b* 20 Dec 1943
1b *Patricia Constance; *b* 23 Dec 1934
2a *Susan Muriel; *b* 27 Jan 1914; *m* 6 Jan 1954 *Lt-Col Hugh Vincent Rose, late Gurkhas, only surv s of Col Hugh Rose, of Scobitor, Widecombe-in-the-Moor, S Devon, and has issue:
1b *Philip Timothy; *b* 31 Oct 1960
(4) Arthur Lutley; *b* 24 Sept 1873; *m* 5 Aug 1911 Mabel Frances Clifton (*d* 9 Sept 1919), 2nd dau of Rev John Clough, of Wilford Rectory, Nottingham, and *d* Rhodesia 2 May 1922
1 Lillian Elizabeth Lutley; *m* 2 Nov 1909 Harington Morgan (*d* 11 May 1914), 5th s of Walter Morgan, formerly Ch Justice Madras Presidency, Judge Civ Courts of Justice the Sudan; *m* 2nd 17 June 1920 Douglas Walter Campbell (*d* 5 Jan 1926), only s of Lord Walter Campbell (*see* ARGYLL, D), and *d* 8 April 1957
3 Frederick Booth; *b* 22 Aug 1838; *d* 9 Dec 1856

WILLIAM LUTLEY SCLATER's est s,

GEORGE SCLATER later SCLATER BOOTH (added by roy licence 1857 to comply with terms of will of Mrs Anna Maria Booth), **1st Baron Basing of Basing Byflete and of Hoddington**, both in Co Southampton (UK), so *cr* 7 July 1887, PC (1874), DL (Hants); *b* 19 May 1826; *educ* Winchester and Balliol Coll Oxford (BA 1847, MA 1850); barrister Inner Temple 1851, MP (C) Hants 1857–87, Parly Sec Poor Law Bd 1867–68, Fin Sec Treasury March-Dec 1868, Pres Local Govt Bd 1874–80, Govr Winchester Coll, Public Works Loan Commr, Official Verderer New Forest, FRS 1876; *m* 8 Dec 1857 Lydia Caroline (*d* 5 July 1881), only dau of Col George Birch, of Clare Pk, Hants, and *d* 22 Oct 1894, leaving issue:

1 GEORGE LIMBREY SCLATER BOOTH, **2nd Baron Basing of Basing Byflete and of Hoddington**, CB (1902), JP, DL (both Hants); *b* 1 Jan 1860; *educ* Eton and Balliol Coll Oxford (BA); Lt-Col and Brevet-Col 1st Roy Dragoons and Hon Brig-Gen 1918; *m* 12 Dec 1889 Mary (*d* 1 June 1904), dau of John Hargreaves, of Maiden Erleigh, Berks, and Whalley Abbey, Lancs, and *d* 8 April 1919, leaving issue:
(1) JOHN LIMBREY ROBERT SCLATER BOOTH, **3rd Baron Basing of Basing Byflete and of Hoddington**, TD, DL (Hants 1939–50, Dorset 1959); *b* 3 Dec 1890; Lt-Col and Brevet-Col late cmdg 43rd Wessex Div Roy Corps of Signals, TA, Hon Col 1934, formerly Capt and Brevet Maj 1st Roy Dragoons, memb Dorset TA Assoc 1948-69, served WW I (1914 star, two medals), WW II with RE Movement Control, Dorset: CC 1947, CA 1963; *m* 27 Feb 1924 Mary Alice Erle (*d* 21 Oct 1970), yr dau of Lt-Col Richard Erle Bens, E Yorks Regt, and *d* 2 Oct 1969, leaving issue:
1a *Diana Penelope Florence [The Hon Mrs Bailward, Causeway House, Radipole, nr Weymouth, Dorset DT4 9RX]; *b* 29 Jan 1925; served FANY WW II; *m* 1 Aug 1946 *James Tennant Bailward, Colonial Serv 1940–58, er twin s of Cdr Maurice William Bailward, RN (ret), of Penny's Hill Lodge, Ferndown, Dorset, and has issue:
1b *Christopher John [Christopher Bailward Esq, Horsington Manor, Horsington, Templecombe, Somerset]; *b* 1949; *m* *Anne, dau of Lt-Col G E Gray, of Colehill, Wimborne, Dorset, and has issue:
1c *James Richard; *b* 1978
2c *Thomas William; *b* 1981
3c *Robert John (twin); *b* 1981

1c *Kate Louise; *b* 1976

1b *Clare Penelope [Mrs Brian Jayes, Wayside, Old Horsely Rd, Nailsworth, Glos]; *b* 1947; *m* *Brian Jayes, s of P H Hayes, of Lindfield, Sussex, and has issue:

1c *Andrew Patrick Harris; *b* 1977

1c *Rosamund Sarah; *b* 1974

2a *Barbara Amy; *b* 5 April 1926; served WRNS WW II; *m* 27 April 1961 *Peter Michell Luttman-Johnson, only s of Frederic Michell Luttman-Johnson, of Crouchland, Plaistow, Billingshurst, Sussex, and has issue:

1b *William Michell [William Luttman-Johnson Esq, Waldegrave Farm, Hartest, Suffolk IP29 4EA]; *b* 9 Dec 1963; *m* 1992 *Lucilla Jane, est dau of David Adams, of Earls Colne, Essex

1b *Anne Elizabeth; *b* 2 July 1962

2b *Catherine Mary; *b* 20 Oct 1966; *m* 24 Aug 1996 *Ian Guiver, er s of P Guiver, of Leigh-on-Sea

3a *Gabrielle Mary [The Hon Mrs Seth-Smith, The Triangle, Wildhern, Andover, Hants SP11 0JE]; *b* 18 Jan 1929; *m* 18 April 1953 *Cdr Martin Parnell Seth-Smith, RN, only surv s of Brig Hugh Garden Seth-Smith, DSO, of Little Chaffey, Bourton, Dorset, and has:

1a *Nicholas John; *b* 20 Aug 1961; *m* 30 July 1994 *Sally Anne, dau of David Wright

1a *Imogen Gabrielle [Mrs Jeremy Charles-Jones, Charlam Farm House, Ampney St Peter, Glos]; *b* 18 Jan 1963; *m* 7 Sept 1996 *Jeremy Charles-Jones, es s of Hugh Charles-Jones

(1) Joan Penelope; *b* 19 Oct 1892; *m* 16 Jan 1919 Capt Roger Grenville Peek, 9th Lancers (*kas* 23 March 1921 in Ireland), 2nd s of Sir Cuthbert Peek, 2nd Bt (*qv*), and *d* 23 Feb 1976, leaving issue

(2) Lydia Joyce; *b* 20 Feb 1898; *m* 11 Jan 1921 Maj Anthony Harley Mark Bell, MC (*d* 5 June 1964), est s of Col Mark Bell, VC, CB, ADC, RE, and had issue

2 Charles Lutley, JP (Hants); *b* 6 May 1862; *educ* Balliol Coll Oxford (BA); barrister Inner Temple; *m* 18 April 1900 Ellen Geraldine (*d* 12 Jan 1957), yst dau of George Jones, of Mitton Manor, Staffs, and widow of William Tudor Frere, barrister, and *d* 23 Jan 1931, leaving issue:

(1) GEORGE LUTLEY SCLATER BOOTH, **4th Baron Basing of Basing Byflete and of Hoddington**; *b* 7 Dec 1903; *educ* Winchester; *m* 1st 16 March 1938 (*divorce* 1944) Jeanette (*d* 17 Nov 1957), dau of Neil Bruce MacKelvie, of NY; *m* 2nd 18 July 1951 Cynthia (*d* 1982), dau of Charles W Hardy, of Salt Lake City, Utah, and widow of Carl H Beal, of Los Angeles, and *d* 18 Sept 1983, leaving issue:

1a NEIL LUTLEY SCLATER BOOTH, **5th and present Baron Basing of Basing Byflete and of Hoddington**

3 Anthony Bohun; *b* 1865; Naval Cadet; *d* 1880

4 Walter Dashwood, CB (1917), CMG (1919), DSO (1915), JP (Hants); *b* 15 Feb 1869; Col late RHA and Hon Brig-Gen, WW I (wounded despatches); *m* 24 June 1913 Frances Mary (*d* 8 July 1949), est dau of Rowland Burdon, CBE, of Castle Eden, Co Durham, and *d* 10 Jan 1953, leaving issue:

(1) John Walter Limbrey; *b* 26 Jan 1922; *m* April 1947 *Kathleen Mary (who *m* 2nd 21 Sept 1971 Robert Courtney Brooks, of Odiham, Hants), yr dau of Richard Fouracre, of Hale Farm, Old Basing, Basingstoke, and *d* 27 Feb 1965

(1) Eleanor Mary; *b* 3 April 1914; *d* unm 3 June 1997

(2) Nora Frances; *b* 8 April 1916; *d* 10 May 1989

1 Diana Maria Penelope; *d* unm 20 Nov 1900

2 Theodora Mary; *m* 1st 11 April 1889 Remington Walter White-Thomas (*d* 1916), Bd of Educn, est s of Sir Robert White-Thoms, KCB, of Broomford Manor, Exbourne, N Devon; *m* 2nd 3 Jan 1922 her late husband's yst bro, Col Sir Hugh Davie White-Thomas, KBE, CB, CMG, DSO (*d* 24 Feb 1922), and *d* 7 March 1936

3 Penelope Magdalen; *m* 3 Aug 1886 Charles A Bovill (*d* 5 May 1932), of 60 Pont St, London SW, s of B S Bovill, and *d* 2 Jan 1934, leaving issue

4 Lydia Katharine; *m* 30 Dec 1893 Frank Walkinshaw (*d* 14 July 1934), only s of W Walkinshaw, of Hartley Grange, Hartley Wintney, Hants, and *d* 25 April 1946, leaving issue

5 Eleanor Birch, CBE (1918); *m* 19 July 1898 Henry Wilson Fox, MP (*d* 22 Nov 1921), and *d* 7 Oct 1963 aged 92, leaving issue

6 Amy Cicely; Order of Mercy 1920; *m* 6 April 1893 Francis Marshall (*d* 3 Oct 1922), of Shapely, Winchfield, Hants, and *d* 19 March 1937

BASSAM OF BRIGHTON

Creation: B. (LP, UK) 2 Aug 1997.

THE BARON BASSAM OF BRIGHTON, of Brighton, Co E Sussex ((John) Steven Bassam) [The Rt Hon The Lord Bassam of Brighton, House of Lords, London SW1A 0PW]; *b* 11 June 1953; *educ* Sussex and Kent Us; social worker E Sussex CC 1976–77, legal advsr N Lewisham Law centre 1979–83, policy advsr Camden Cncl 1983–84; GLC (Police Ctee) 1984–86; London Strategic Policy Unit 1986–; Assist Sec Police, Fire, Environmental Health and Consumer Affrs AMA 1988–97, Leader (Lab) Brighton and Hove Cncl 1987–97 (Brighton Cncl to 1996, memb 1983–97), Head Environmental Health and Consumer Issues Local Govt Assoc 1997–; has had by *Jill Whittaker two sons (one decd) and two daus

Lineage: SYDNEY STEVENS BASSAM; *m* Enid — and had:

(JOHN) STEVEN, *cr* a **Baron**

BATES of Bellefield

Arms: Argent, on a fess azure a quatrefoil between two fleurs-de-lys of the field, in chief two quatrefoils, and in base a fleur-de-lys, both azure. **Crest:** A stag's head erased azure, attired or, charged on the neck with two quatrefoils in pale, and pierced by as many arrows in saltire, all or. **Motto:** *Labore et virtute* ('By labour and virtue').
Creation: Bt. (UK) 13 May 1880.

SIR GEOFFREY VOLTELIN BATES, 5TH BT, of Bellefield, Co Lancaster, MC (1942) [Sir Geoffrey Bates Bt MC, Gyrn Castle, Llanasa, Holywell, Clwyd CH8 9BG]; *b* 2 Oct 1921; *s* unc 1946; *educ* Radley; High Sheriff Flintshire 1969, Maj Cheshire Yeo, formerly Capt 8th Hus, served WW II; *m* 1st 12 July 1945 Kitty (*d* 2 June 1956), dau of Ernest Kendall Lane, of Saskatchewan, Canada, and has issue:

1 +EDWARD ROBERT; *b* 4 July 1946; *educ* Gordonstoun

2 +Richard Geoffrey [Richard Bates Esq, Pirates House, Bowen Bay, Bowen Island, BC, Canada VON 1GO]; *b* 13 March 1948; *m* 1971 Diana Margaret Rankin (*d* 1990) and has:

(1) +James Geoffrey; *b* 14 March 1985

(1) *Margot Zoë; *b* 1976

(2) *Nichola Sarah; *b* 1979

Sir GEOFFREY *m* 2nd 31 July 1957 Hon Olivia Gwyneth Zoë FitzRoy (*d* 24 Dec 1969), 2nd dau of 2nd Viscount Daventry (*qv*); *m* 3rd 1971 *Juliet Eleanor Hugolyn Whitelocke-Winter, dau of Cdr G Whitelocke, RN, and Mrs Whitelocke, of Cerrigllingdion Hall, Denbigh, and widow of Edward Colin Winter, and has by his 2nd w:

1 *Celina Zoë; *b* 7 Oct 1958; *m* 19– *Timothy M Radcliffe, only s of R J Radcliffe, of Bodedern, Anglesey, and has issue:

*Olivia Philippa Zoë; *b* 1993

2 Sarah Rose; *b* 4 Jan 1960; *d* as a result of an accident 5 March 1977

Lineage: Sir Edward Bates, 1st Bt (UK), so *cr* 13 May 1880, JP and DL (Lancs and Hants), MP (C) Plymouth 1871–80 and 1885–92, of Manydown Pk, Hants, and Gyrn Castle; *b* 17 March 1816; only surv s of Joseph Bates, of Spring Hall, W Riding Yorks (*d* 11 Nov 1846), by his w Rebekah, dau of Joseph Walker, of Ardsley, W Riding; *m* 1st 1837 Charlotte Elizabeth (*d* Feb 1843), est dau of Cornelius Umfreville-Smith, HEICS, and had issue three daus; *m* 2nd 25 June 1844 Ellen (*d* 20 April 1905), dau of Thomas Thompson, of Hessle, E Riding Yorks, and *d* 17 Oct 1896, leaving with other issue:

1 EDWARD PERCY (Sir), **2nd Bt**

2 Gilbert Thompson, JP (Renfrewshire); *b* 22 April 1847; *m* 13 July 1876 Charlotte Thaxter (*d* 27 Nov 1936), dau of George Warren, of Woolton, and *d* 30 March 1917, leaving issue:

(1) Stanes Geoffrey; *b* 2 June 1884; Capt 7th Hus and Adj N Somerset Yeo; *ka* 13 May 1915

(1) Mary; *m* 21 Feb 1903 Sir Edward Lionel Fletcher, CBE (*d* 20 June 1968), s of Alfred Fletcher, DL, of Allerton, and *d* 27 Feb 1935, leaving issue

3 Sydney Eggers, JP (London and Hants), of Manydown Pk, Hants; *b* 28 April 1851; *m* 9 July 1878 Elizabeth Jessie (*d* 13 Oct 1940), 3rd dau of Col George Grenville Malet, 3rd Bombay Light Cavalry (*see* MALET, Bt), and *d* 3 March 1924, leaving issue:

(1) Arthur Sydney, DSO (1915), TD, JP (Hants); *b* 18 June 1879; Brevet-Col, late cmdg London Rifle Bde, served WW I (despatches four times), Croix de Guerre; *m* 26 April 1905 Mary da Costa, OStJ (*d* 18 Jan 1962), est dau of Lt-Col Charles Robert Crosse, CMG, MVO, Roy W Kent Regt, and *d* 7 May 1958, leaving issue:

1a *Anne Mary [Mrs John Oliver-Bellasis, Beech House, Wootton St Lawrence, Basingstoke, Hants RG23 8PE]; *b* 1915; *m* 29 July 1939 Lt-Col John Oliver-Bellasis, DSO, JP, DL (*d* 1979), Roy Fus, yr s of Capt Richard John Erskine Oliver-Bellasis, JP, DL, of Shilton House, Coventry, and has issue:

1b *Charles Arthur John [Charles Oliver-Bellasis Esq, The Old Rectory, Boxford, nr Newbury, Berks]; *b* 1 Oct 1940; *educ* Winchester and RAC Cirencester; FRICS, MRAC; *m* 1972 *Julia Elizabeth, dau of Lt Cdr John Errol Manners, DSC, RN, of Laurel House, Gt Cheverell, Devizes, Wilts, and has issue:

1c *John Edward; *b* 1976

2c *Richard Charles; *b* 1977
1c *Clare Elizabeth; *b* 1974
2b *Hugh Richard [Maj Hugh Oliver-Bellasis, Wootton House, Wootton St Lawrence, Basingstoke, Hants RG23 8PE]; *b* 11 April 1945; *educ* Winchester and RMA Sandhurst; Maj Welsh Gds (ret 1977), FRAgS; *m* 1971 *Daphne Phoebe, yr dau of Arthur Christopher Parsons (*see* ROSSE, E), and has:
1c *Joanna Gwenda; *b* 8 April 1975
2c *Nicola Mary; *b* 12 June 1978
(1) Norah Ellen; *d* 28 Nov 1922
(2) Edith Mary; *m* 27 Sept 1923 William Lamb (*d* 15 Sept 1936), s of Rev William Lamb, of Ednam, Scotland
(3b) Dorothy Eileen Bates; *m* 18 May 1948 Thomas More, MBE (*d* 21 Sept 1948), s of Francis More, CA, of Edinburgh
1 Anne Millicent; *m* 25 Nov 1874 Donald Ninian Nicol, DL (*d* 27 July 1903), of Ardmarnock, Argyll, and *d* 7 March 1946, leaving issue
2 Mabel Stenhouse; *m* 20 Feb 1873 Frederick Bellairs Thompson (*d* 1882), of Bellefield, West Derby, and *d* April 1931, having had issue
3 Norah Greame; *m* 9 Dec 1880 Stanes Brocket Henry Chamberlayne (*d* 5 March 1931), of Witherley Hall, Atherstone, yst s of Henry Thomas Chamberlayne, of Stoney Thorpe, Warwicks, and *d* 20 Dec 1939, leaving issue

Sir EDWARD's s,

Sir Edward Percy Bates, 2nd Bt, JP, DL, of Gyrn Castle; *b* 17 Aug 1845; High Sheriff Flintshire 1899; *m* 20 April 1876 Constance Elisabeth (*d* 18 April 1930), 2nd dau of Samuel Robert Graves, MP Liverpool, and *d* 31 Dec 1899, leaving issue:

1 **Sir Edward Bertram Bates, 3rd Bt**; *b* 7 March 1877, of Manydown Pk, Hants, and Gyrn Castle, Flintshire; *d* unm 6 March 1903
2 **Sir Percy Elly Bates, 4th Bt**, GBE (1920), JP (Cheshire); *b* 12 May 1879; High Sheriff Cheshire 1920, Hon Capt RNR 1935; Freedom City of London 1935; Offr Legion of Honour, Crown of Italy, chm Cunard Steam Ship Co and Cunard White Star, dir Midland Bank and GWR; *m* 20 June 1907 Mary Ann Lefroy (*d* 30 July 1973 aged 93), yr dau of Very Rev William Lefroy, DD, Dean Norwich, by Mary Ann, dau of Charles MacIver, fndr Cunard Steamship Co, and *d* 16 Oct 1946, leaving issue:
(1) Edward Percy; *b* 15 Oct 1913; *educ* Winchester and Trin Coll Cambridge; P/O RAF WW II; *ka* 1 Jan 1945
3 Cecil Robert, DSO (1918); *b* 3 Feb 1882; Maj late RFA, served WW I 1914 (despatches); *m* 27 June 1918 Hylda Madeleine (*d* 29 Dec 1960), dau of Sir James Heath, 1st Bt, and widow of Capt George Millais James, and *d* 5 March 1935, leaving issue:
(1) Sir GEOFFREY VOLTELIN BATES, **5th and present Bt**
(1) Audrey Cecil; *b* 15 July 1919; *m* 28 March 1942 (*divorce* 1957) Maj Hon Thomas Heron Hazlerigg, Leics Yeo, 2nd s of 1st Baron Hazlerigg (*qv*), and has issue
4 Frederic Alan, MC (1918), AFC (1919), DL (Flintshire); *b* 16 Aug 1884; late Capt Denbigh Yeo, Maj RAF, served WW I (despatches four times); High Sheriff Denbighshire 1935; *m* 5 July 1932 Elizabeth Barberie, dau of Thomas Fair, of Clifton Hall, Preston, and *dsp* 24 June 1957
5 Denis Haughton, MC, TD; *b* 25 Aug 1886; Col TA, Hon Col Duke of Lancaster's Own Yeo, served WW I 1914–19 (despatches), chm Cunard Steam Ship Co and Cunard White Star; *m* 12 Dec 1922 Aline Mary (*d* 1974), MA Oxon 2nd dau of Edward Tipping Crook, JP, of Woodlands Hall, Bridgnorth, and *d* 13 Sept 1959, leaving:
(1) +Philip Edward, VRD [Maj Philip Bates VRD, 2 Squirrels Cottages, Poles Lane, Woodside, Lymington, Hants SO41 8AD]; *b* 19 July 1925; *educ* Shrewsbury; Maj RM (Commando) WW II; *m* 22 April 1952 *Mary Patricia Carol, yr dau of Lt-Col Clive Vincent Moberly Bell, OBE, of 4 Down St, London W1, and has issue:
1a +Hugh Percy [Hugh Bates Esq, Hathaway House, Lower Pennington Lane, Lymington, Hants]; *b* 9 Jan 1953; *educ* Milton Abbey; *m* 1977 *Angela Roberta Wall and has issue:
1b +James Edward; *b* 1984
1b *Kathryn Ann; *b* 1981
2a +Denis Moberly [Denis Bates Esq, Wisteria Cottage, Minstead, Lyndhurst, Hants SO4 7FX]; *b* 8 Aug 1954; *educ* Milton Abbey; *m* 1979 *Hilary Mackay and has issue:
1b +Alastair Martin; *b* 1987
1b *Jennifer Jane; *b* 1985
1a *Patricia Mary; *b* 11 Jan 1956; *m* 1978 *Dr Anthony Yates and has issue:
1b *Colin Robert; *b* 1979
2b *Robert Mark; *b* 1981
3b *Christopher John; *b* 1983
4b *William Anthony; *b* 1987
2a *Carol Elisabeth [Mrs Brian Thomas, 17 Clifton Rd, Parkstone, Poole, Dorset]; *b* 28 June 1957; *m* 1981 *Brian Hedley Thomas and has issue:
1b *Sophie Patricia; *b* 1983
2b *Nicola Hedley; *b* 1985
(1) *Denise Elisabeth; *b* 25 Jan 1928; *m* 10 Sept 1958 *Rev Thomas Michael Rylands, rector Malpas, Cheshire, s of Thomas Edleston Rylands, and has issue:
1a *Thomas Gordon; *b* 27 Sept 1959; *educ* Shrewsbury and Birmingham U (BSc); *m* 1985 *Jane Lesley, dau of Alan Goode, and has issue:
1b *Thomas Christopher; *b* 1987
2b *Peter Michael; *b* 1993
1b *Louise Victoria; *b* 1989
2a *Mark James (Rev); *b* 11 July 1961; *educ* St Hild and St Bede Coll, Durham (BA); *m* 1986 *Rev Amanda, dau of Peter Craig Byrom, OBE, and has issue:
1b *Samuel George Ambrose; *b*1990
1b *Frances Elisabeth; *b* 1988
1a *Alison Joane; *b* 27 Feb 1963; *educ* Moreton Hall and City and Guilds Coll of Art
6 Austin Graves, DSO (1918), MC (1917); *b* 19 Aug 1891; *educ* Clifton; barrister 1918, Lt-Col late RA, served WW I (wounded despatches three times), WW II 1939–43; *m* 15 Dec 1920 Jean Christian Marguerite (*d* 1982), dau of Col James Hunter, of Anton's Hill, Berwickshire, and *d* 11 Sept 1961, leaving issue:
(1) +Jeremy Dickson, ACGI; *b* 1 April 1932; *educ* London U (BSc 1955); *m* 1978 *Elizabeth Marjorie, dau of H W Rudd, of High Pines, Woodend Dve, Sunninghill, Ascot, Berks, and has issue:
1a +Thomas James Dickson; *b* 1980
1a *Sarah Marjorie; *b* 1981
(2) +Martin Graves [Martin Bates Esq, 17 Queen's Gate Place, London SW7 5NY]; *b* 26 June 1935; *educ* Clifton and St Edmund Hall Oxford (BA); *m* 2 Oct 1965 *Susan Myfanwy Prudence, only dau of Capt Robert Edward Dudley Ryder, VC, RN (ret), of The Old Rectory, Wolferton, King's Lynn, Norfolk (*see* HARROWBY, E), and has issue:
1a +Oliver Robert Hunter; *b* 29 March 1969
1a *Susannah Hilaré Myfanwy; *b* 15 May 1970
7 Maurice Halifax; *b* 9 Aug 1898; Lt-Col RA, served WW I 1917–18; *m* 21 March 1922 May Francis (*d* 25 Feb 1969) (who *m* 2nd 24 Oct 1927 Brig Ralph Emers Pickering, CBE, The Queen's Roy Regt (*d* 27 March 1962), s of Thomas Pickering, of The Hillhouse, Gilsland), est dau of Sir Edward Arthur Henry Blunt, KCIE, OBE, ICS (*see* BLUNT, Bt), and *d* 23 Sept 1925, leaving issue:
(1) *Ann Maurice [Miss Ann Bates, Little Hatchett, Hatchett Lane, Beaulieu, Brockenhurst, Hants SO42 7WA]; *b* (posthumous) 26 Dec 1925

BATES of Magherabuoy

Creation: Bt. (UK) 7 June 1937.

SIR RICHARD DAWSON HOULT BATES, 3RD BT, of Magherabuoy, Co Londonderry; *b* 12 May 1956; *s* f 1998

Lineage: RICHARD DAWSON BATES, of Belfast; slr; *m* 11 April 1872 Mary (*b* 17 March 1845; *d* 1 May 1931), dau of Prof Robert Foster Dill, MD, MRCS, of Belfast, and *d* 1881, leaving issue, with three daus:

1 John ; *dsp* 1874
2 **Sir (Richard) Dawson Bates, 1st Bt** (UK), so *cr* 7 June 1937, OBE (1919), PC (I 1921, NI 1922), JP (Co Down), DL (Belfast); *b* 23 Nov 1876; slr 1900, ktd 11 Feb 1921, MP (U) Belfast, E Belfast 1921–29 and Belfast Victoria 1929–43, Min Home Affrs NI 1921–43, v-pres UU Cncl; *m* 8 April 1920 Jessie Muriel (*d* 31 Oct 1972), yst dau of Sir Charles John Cleland, KBE, MVO, of Bonville, Maryhill, Glasgow, and *d* 9 June 1949, leaving issue:
(1) Sir (JOHN) DAWSON BATES, **2nd Bt**, MC (1943); *b* 21 Sept 1921; *educ* Winchester and Balliol Coll Oxford (BA 1949); FRICS, FLAS 1960, Maj Rifle Brigade WW II, S Midlands Area Agent Nat Tst; *m* 30 April 1953 *Mary Murray [Lady Bates, Butleigh House, Glastonbury, Somerset BA6 8SU], only dau of Lt-Col Joseph Murray Hoult, RA, of Norton Place, Lincoln, and Voorspoed, Tokai, CP, S Africa, and *d* 12 July 1998, leaving:
1a Sir RICHARD DAWSON HOULT, **3rd and present Bt**
2a +Charles Joseph Dill; *b* 25 April 1959; *m* 1984 *Suzanne C, yr dau of David Beaumont, of Much Hadham, Herts, and has issue:
1b +Patrick Charles Beaumont; *b* 1990
2b +Oliver James Beaumont; *b* 1993
1b *Claudia; *b* 1988
1a *Drusilla Mary Cynthia; *b* 25 Feb 1954; *m* 1983 *Gervase R Belfield, est s of Eversley Belfield, of Beauchamp, Sark, CI, and has issue:
1b *Laura Daisy; *b* 1987
(2) *Matilda May; *b* 1992

BATH

Arms: Quarterly, 1st and 4th, barry of ten or and sa. (for BOTEVIL(L)E); 2nd and 3rd, arg., a lion rampant, tail nowed and erected gu. (for THYNNE). **Crest:** A reindeer statant or. **Supporters:** Dexter, a reindeer or gorged with a plain collar sa.; sinister, a lion tail nowed and erected gu. **Motto:** *J'ay bonne cause* ('I have good reason'). The lion device in the arms, which is reminiscent of the arms of the Scottish kings, is said to have been granted to Sir Thomas Thynne by Protector Somerset in the mid-16th century to commemorate his victory over the Scots, at which Sir Thomas assisted. **Creations:** Bt (E) 15 June 1641, B. and V. (E) 11 Dec 1682, M. (GB) 18 Aug 1789.

THE 7TH MARQUESS OF BATH, **Viscount Weymouth**, Co Dorset, **Baron Thynne of Wermister** [*sic*], Co Wilts, and a **Baronet** (Sir Alexander George Thynn, Bt) [The Most Hon The Marquess of Bath, Longleat Warminster, Wilts BA12 7NN]; *b* 6 May 1932; *s* f 1992; *educ* Eton and Ch Ch Oxford; Lt Life Gds 1951–52 and Roy Wilts Yeo (TA) 1953–57, self-styled 'painter and decorator', also artist, novelist and songwriter, dir: Cheddar caves 1956– and Longleat Entrprises 1964–, pres Verulam Inst 1976–86, fought: Westbury and Wells 1974 and 1979 gen elections respectively as Wessex Regionalist and Wessex European election 1979 as Wessex Regionalist and European Fedl Pty candidate, author (as Alexander Thynn(e)): *The Carry Cot* (1972), *Lord Weymouth's Murals* (1974), *A Regionalist Manifesto* (1975), *The King is Dead* (1976) and *Pillars of the Establishment* (1980), *m* 9 May 1969 *Anne Abigail Gyarmathy (Anna Gael, former actress, currently author and jnlst), of Budapest and Los Angeles, and has issue:

1 +CEAWLIN HENRY LASZLO, *Viscount Weymouth*; *b* 6 June 1974; *educ* Bedales, Richmond U, Va, USA, and UCL

1 *Lenka Abigail, *b* 20 Oct 1969; *educ* Univ Coll Oxford

Earldom of Bath: John Bourchier, 11th Lord (Baron) Fitzwarin of the notional 1295 creation, was created Earl of Bath in 1536. Through his paternal grandmother he descended from Thomas of Woodstock, s of EDWARD III. His son the 2nd Earl married as one of his wives a sister of the Earl of Rutland (*see* RUTLAND, D) and his grandson the 3rd Earl married a sister of the Earl of Bedford (*see* BEDFORD, D). This creation became extinct in 1654.

A second creation under this title was made in 1661 in favour of John Granville, son of the Royalist commander Sir Bevil Granville (*see* TEMPLE OF STOWE, E for remoter ancestry). His grandson died in 1711 aged 17, when this earldom too became extinct. In 1742 William Pulteney, a leading opponent of Sir Robert Walpole (*see* WALPOLE, B), was created Earl of Bath. As his son predeceased him the earldom became extinct on his own death in 1764, though his first cousin's granddaughter, whose father had assumed the name Pulteney, was created Baroness of Bath [*sic*] in 1792 and Countess of Bath in 1803. Meanwhile a sister of the 2nd Earl of Bath of the 1661 creation had married the 1st Baron Carteret of Hawnes of the 1681 *cr* and after his death been created Countess Granville in her own right. Lady Granville's granddaughter married the 2nd Viscount Weymouth, and their grandson was created Marquess of Bath (*see* below).

Lineage: The Thynnes' original name is said to have been Botfield or Botevil(l)e, derived from a Shropshire place name.

The heralds' Visitations of Shropshire of 1584 and 1623 begin the pedigree with RALPH BOTEVILE, of Stretton, Shropshire, who *m* Ann, dau of John Higgons, of Stretton, and had, with other issue:

1 THOMAS BOTFIELD, BOTVILE, de la INNE or THYNNE

2 William, Master Household to HENRY VIII, collected and published the works of Chaucer with notes 1542; f of:

(1) Francis THYNNE, Lancaster Herald

RALPH's er s,

THOMAS THYNNE, of Stretton; *m* Margaret, dau and heir of Thomas Eynes, of Stretton and maternal gdau of Humphrey Gatacre, Esq of the Body to HENRY VI, and had an est s:

Sir JOHN THYNNE, Secretary to Protector Somerset (*see* SOMERSET, D) in the campaign against the Scots of 1547, ktd 1547 after the Battle of Pinkie; started construction Jan 1567 of Longleat, the building continuing till 1579; *m* 1st Christian, dau of Sir Richard Gresham, Ld Mayor London and sis and heir of Sir Thomas Gresham, and had issue; *m* 2nd Dorothy, dau of Sir William Wroughton, of Broad Hinton, Wilts, and *d* 21 May 1580, having had five other s (one of whom was Sir Egremont Thynne, Serjeant-at-Law) and two daus (one of whom, Dorothy, *m* Edward Grenville; *see* KINLOSS, L, Lineage (of Grenville)); his est s by his 1st w:

Sir JOHN THYNNE, of Longleat; *m* Joan, yst dau of Sir Rowland Hayward, Ld Mayor London, and had an est s:

Sir THOMAS THYNNE; *m* 1st Maria, dau of George, Lord Audley, and had surviving issue:

1 James (Sir), of Longleat, *m* Lady Isabella Rich, dau of Henry, Earl of Holland, but *dsp* 12 Oct 1670

2 Thomas (Sir), of Richmond, Surrey, *m* 6 Sep 1642, Stuarta, dau and coheir of Dr Walter Balquanquill, Dean Durham, and had:

(1) Thomas; *b* 1648, known as 'Tom of Ten Thousand', who *s* to Longleat and lived there in great magnificence; *m* 15 Nov 1681 Lady Elizabeth Percy, dau and heir of 5th and last Earl of Northumberland of the 1557 *cr* (Isee NORTHUMBERLAND, D), and was murdered in his coach in Pall Mall 12 Feb 1682

Sir THOMAS THYNNE *m* 2nd Catherine, dau of Hon Charles Lyle-Howard and n of Viscount Bindon

The est surv s of the 2nd marriage,

Sir Henry Frederick Thynne, 1st Bt (E), so *cr* 15 July 1641, of Kempsford; *b* 1 March 1615; *m* Mary, dau of Thomas, 1st Lord Coventry, and *d* 6 March 1680, having had, with other issue:

1 **Sir Thomas Thynne, 2nd Bt**, and **1st Viscount Weymouth**, Co Dorset, so *cr* 11 Dec 1682, as also BARON THYNNE OF WERMISTER, Co Wilts (both E), with remainder in the event of failure of his male issue to his bros and their male issue; MP Oxford U 1674–79 and Tamworth 1679–81; *m* Frances (*d* 17 April 1712), dau of 3rd Earl of Winchilsea (*see* WINCHILSEA and NOTTINGHAM, E), and *d* 28 July 1714, having had an only s:

(1) Henry; *b* 8 Feb 1675; *m* by licence 29 April 1695 Grace (*d* 3 April 1725), dau and heiress of Sir George Strode, Serjeant-at-Law, of Leweston, Dorset (2nd s of Sir John Strode, of Parnham, by Anne, dau of Sir John Wyndham), and *dvp* 20 Dec 1708, having had two daus

2 James; LLD, MP; *d* unm 15 March 1709

3 Henry Frederick; Clerk PC; *m* Dorothy, dau and coheir of Francis Philips, of the Inner Temple and Kempton Pk, Middx, barrister, and *d* 1705, leaving (with a dau Dorothy, *m* 1st Lord Chedworth, Baron of Chedworth; *see* HOWE, E):

(1) Thomas; *m* Lady Mary Villers, dau of Edward, 1st Earl of Jersey, and *d* 24 Apr 1710, leaving a posthumous s:

1a THOMAS THYNNE, **2nd Viscount Weymouth**, *b* 21 May 1710, *m* 1st 6 Dec 1726 Lady Elizabeth Sackville (*dsp* 19 June 1729), dau of Lionel, Duke of Dorset (*see* SACKVILLE, B); *m* 2nd 1733 Lady Louisa Carteret (*d* 25 Dec 1736), dau of 1st Earl Granville, and *d* 13 Jan 1751, having by her had issue:

1 THOMAS, **1st Marquess**

2 Henry Frederick THYNNE later CARTERET (assumed on inheriting the Carteret estates of his maternal uncle Robert, last Earl of Granville), 1st BARON CARTERET OF HAWNES, Co Bedford (GB), so *cr* 29 Jan 1784, with special remainder to the yr sons of his bro; *b* 17 Nov 1735; PMG; *d* unm 17 June 1826

The 2nd VISCOUNT's er s,

THOMAS THYNNE, **1st Marquess of Bath** (GB), so *cr* 18 Aug 1789, KG (1778), PC (1765); *b* 13 Sept 1734; *educ* St John's Coll Cambridge; Ld Lt Ireland April-July 1765, Sec State for North Jan-Oct 1768 and South 1768–70 and 1775–79; *m* 22 May 1759 Lady Elizabeth Cavendish Bentick (*d* 12 Dec 1825 aged 91), est dau of 2nd Duke of Portland (*see* PORTLAND, E), and *d* 19 Nov 1796, leaving:

1 THOMAS THYNNE, **2nd Marquess of Bath**, KG (1823); *b* 25 Jan 1765; *educ* Winchester and St John's Coll Cambridge; MP (Tory) Weobley 1786–90 and Bath 1790–96, Ld Lt Somerset 1819–37, FSA, FLS; *m* 14 April 1794 Hon Isabella Elizabeth Byng (*d* 1 May 1830), 3rd dau of 4th Viscount Torrington (*qv*), and had, with three other s and three daus:

(1) Thomas, *Viscount Weymouth*, *b* 9 April 1796, *m* 11 May 1820 Harriet Matilda (*m* 2nd Count Inghirami and *d* 18 June 1873), dau of Thomas Robbins, and *dsp* 16 Jan 1837

(2) HENRY FREDERICK, **3rd Marquess**

(3) John (Rev), of Haynes Park, Bedfordshire, DD, canon and Sub-Dean Westminster, *b* 7 Nov 1798, *m* 2 March 1824 Anne Constantia (*d* 22 Apr 1866), dau of Rev Charles Cobbe Beresford (*see* WATERFORD, M), and *d* 9 Feb 1881, having had issue:

1a George Emillus, *b* 6 Dec 1824; *d* 9 Aug 1838

2a Francis John, of Haynes Park, JP, DL Beds, *b* 17 June 1830, *m* 30 June 1864 Edith Marcia Caroline (*d* 9 Apr 1876), dau of Richard Brinsley Sheridan, MP, and *d* 30 Jan 1910, leaving issue:

1b Bevil Granville Carteret, Lt 3rd Bn Bedfordshire Regt, *b* 17 Apr 1867; *d* 14 March 1922

2b Algernon Carteret, DSO, Lt-Col Roy N Devon Hus, late Capt N Somerset Yeo Cav and 3rd Bn Bedfordshire Regt, served S Africa 1900–02 and WW I, *b* 9 April 1868, *m* 13 Feb 1904 Anita Constance Edith (*d* 27 Jan 1961 aged 90), widow of Francis Phillips and dau of Edward Bonham, and was *ka* 6 Nov 1917

4b George Augustus Carteret, Capt Roy N Devon Hus and Lt N Somerset Imp Yeo, served S Africa 1900–01 and WW I, *b* 28 Oct 1869, *educ* Pembroke Coll Camb (BA), *m* 13 March 1915 Hon Gladys Isabel Annette Adderley (*d* 16 Oct 1960), yst dau of 2nd Baron Norton (*qv*), and *d* 13 April 1945, leaving issue:

1c +John Granville [Maj John Thynne, Hays House, Shaftesbury, Dorset], Maj RHG WW II; *b* 28 April 1917, *educ* Stowe, *m* 19 Jan 1946 Marianne Madeleine (*d* 1990), est dau of Baron John de Jenner, of Berne and Alexandria, and has issue:

1d +Bevil Granville de Jenner, *b* 5 April 1947, *educ* Stowe; *m* 1970 *Gertrude Dagnie, dau of Arvid K Ekman, of Sweden, and has issue:

1e +Christopher John Granville; *b* 1972

2e +Richard Charles Granville; *b* 1977

2d +Richard George Granville [Richard Thynne Esq, Tads Cottage, Froxfield, Hants]; *b* 26 Sep 1950, *educ* Stowe; *m* 1st 1973 Elizabeth, dau of Geoffrey Barton, and has issue:

1e +Piers James Carteret; *b* 1976

1e *Serena Katherine Nora; *b* 1980

2d (cont.) Richard Thynne *m* 2nd 1991 *Mrs Yvonne Watkins, dau of Maj Cuthbert Chudleigh

1d *Joanna Sybil Marcia, *b* 22 Aug 1949; *m* 1985 *Graham Gordon and has issue:

1e *Edward Alexander; *b* 1986

1e *Jenna Elizabeth; *b* 1988

4b Francis Carteret, *b* 9 Oct 1870; *d* 24 Feb 1876

1b Marcia Selina Helena, *d* unm 7 May 1950

2b Margaret Carteret, *d* unm 7 Nov 1938

3b Isabel Carteret, *m* 26 Oct 1911 Sir Alfred George Lascelles, Ch Justice Ceylon 1911–14, and *d* 12 Aug 1965 aged 89, leaving issue (*see* HAREWOOD, E)

3a Arthur Christopher (Rev), hon canon Truro, rector Kilkhampton, Cornwall, *b* 9 Nov 1832, *m* 28 June 1859 Gwenllian Elizabeth Fanny Isabel (*d* 14 March 1905), est dau of Russell Kendall, of Walthamstow, and *d* 2 Jan 1908, leaving issue:

1b William Francis Granville, *b* 15 Jan 1862, *m* 11 June 1914 Evelyn Agneta (*d* 22 June 1930), dau of Rev Horace Meyer, vicar Christ Church, Clifton, and *d* 15 Apr il1934

2b John Granville, served on special duty as Scout during Reils Rebellion 1885, *b* 15 March 1865, *m* 1887 Mary Elizabeth (*d* 21 Jan 1857), dau of William Linklater, of Hudson Bay Service, and *d* 6 Nov 1943, leaving issue:

1c Mary Ethel, *b* 27 Feb 1888, *m* 7 June 1911 George Gilbert Batstone, s of William Batstone, of West Newton, Mass, and *d* 17 Nov 1950, leaving issue

3b Arthur Granville, *b* 15 Feb 1867; *m* 2 April 1891 Amy (*d* 28 Nov 1949), dau of Capt Charles A Hamilton, of Montreal, and *dsp* 30 May 1948

4b Denis Granville, CMG (1919), Capt RN (ret), served WWs I and WW II as Lt RNVR, Russian Order of St Stanislas 2nd Cl with swords, *b* 17 Oct 1875, *m* 5 April 1921 Anne May, widow of Adm Noel Grant, CB, and dau of E Allen, and *dsp* 18 Dec 1955

5b Richard Granville, Lt Scots Gds WW I (wounded), *b* 3 Dec 1878, *m* 1st 7 June 1911 Gladys (*d* 28 Dec 1919), yst dau of William Neave Hill, of Hans Crescent, London SW; *m* 2nd 19 March 1921 (*divorce*) Honor Margaret (*d* 30 Nov 1967), only dau of Lt.-Col Thomas Duncan William Dunn, Hampshire Regt; *m* 3rd — and *d* 29 Feb 1952

6b Hugh Edward Granville, T/Capt RE WW I (despatches twice), *b* 26 March 1881, *m* Nov 1907 Marguerite (*d* 19 May 1964), dau of W Hearne, of Buenos Aires, and *d* 14 Jan 1952, leaving issue:

1c Christopher William Granville, served WW II with Australian Forces (wounded); *b* 24 Feb 1910, *m* 2 March 1954 *Emilienne Legrain, widow of Leon Lefèvre, of Paris

1c Marguerite Isabel Gwenllian Granville, *b* 28 Oct 1908, *m* 7 June 1930 Clifford Charles Gulliver, s of Charles Gulliver, of Bexhill and had issue:

1d John Clifford Granville, *b* 16 April 1931; *d* 20 Aug 1941

2d *Michael Charles Granville; *b* 20 March 1933, *m* 8 Aug 1958 *Deirdre, dau of William Alan Gordon Ellis, and has issue:

1e *David Charles Granville, *b* 15 April 1960

2e *Ross John Granville, *b* 3 March 1962

3e *Alan James Granville, *b* 8 June 1963

3d *Anthony Francis Granville; *b* 6 Oct 1943, *m* 4 Dec 1965 *Rosalind Jane, dau of Archibald Lorimer Brown Corson, and has issue:

1e *Karen Anita Granville, *b* 17 March 1968

4d *Timothy Edward Granville, *b* 25 May 1945

1d *Ann Marguite Granville, *b* 23 April 1936

2c *Grace Marian Granville [Mrs Kenneth Thomson, Hanger Mill, Salcombe, Devon TQ8 8LU], *m* 9 June 1934 *Kenneth Taylor Thomson, yr s of R Greig Thomson, of Roundhay, Leeds, and has issue:

1d +Peter Granville [Peter Thynne Esq, Thrybergh Hall, Thrybergh, nr Rotherham, Yorks], golf professional, *b* 11 Jul 1936, *m* 6 Oct 1962 *Marion, dau of Francis Harry Smith, and has issue:

1e +Christopher Granville, *b* 21 Jan 1966

1e *Sally Frances, *b* 2 April 1964

2d +Jeremy Clayton [Jeremy Thynne Esq, Hurworth Cottage, Hurworth-on-Tees, Co Durham]; *b* 5 July 1938, *m* and has two s and a dau

3d +Robert Hugh, *b* 6 April 1942, *m* 1968 and has a s

1b Sophie Gwenllian Granville, *b* 1 Jan 1861; *d* 2 Jan 1923

2b Mary Granville, *b* 8 May 1863; *d* unm 7 Jan 1960

3b Anne Constantia Granville, *b* 11 March 1870; *d* unm 20 March 1943

4b Grace Granville, *b* 25 Jan 1873, *m* 23 July 1914 Evelyn Howard-Jones, of 49 Lupus Street, SW1, and *d* 26 May 1952. He *d* Jan 1951

5b Margaret Ethel Granville, *b* 9 Oct 1883, *m* 15 Nov 1916 Maj-Gen Sir George de la Poer Beresford, CB, MC, IA, and *d* 30 Dec 1963, leaving issue (*see* DECIES, B)

4a William Frederick, Capt 2nd Bn Rifle Bde, *b* 8 Aug 1834; *d* Lucknow 11 March 1858

5a Alfred Walter, Lt.-Col Gren Guards, JP Beds, *b* 15 June 1836; *d* unm 1 Nov 1917

6a John Charles, DL Beds, barrister, Receiver-Gen to Chapter of Westminster, *b* 14 Apr 1838, *educ* Exeter Coll Oxford (MA), *m* 25 April 1871 Mary Elizabeth (*d* 30 Jul 1934), yr dau of Sir John Atholl Murray MacGregor, 3rd Bt, and *d* 11 March 1918, having had issue:

1b Lionel Charles, *b* 3 Jan 1875; *d* 21 May 1883

1b Joan Emily Mary, *m* 11 June 1898 4th Earl Cawdor (*qv*) and *d* 26 July 1945, leaving issue

2b Agatha Lilian, *m* 19 April 1904 3rd Baron Hindlip (*qv*) and *d* 11 Dec 1962, leaving issue

3b Mary Beryl, *d* unm 8 Dec 1937

7a Reginald Thomas (Sir), KCB (1902), Maj-Gen in command of troops NE District 1894–1902, formerly cmdg 3rd Bn Gren Gds, served Zululand, Egypt and Sudan, *b* 23 Dec 1843, *m* 6 May 1890 Louise (*d* 18 Jan 1933), widow of Maj William Ewing and dau of Douglas Du Bois, and *d* 30 Dec 1926, leaving issue:

1b Katharine Angela, MBE (1920); *b* 20 April 1893, *m* 4 Oct 1933 Sir Vincent Wilberforce Baddeley, KCB, s of Rev Joseph Jeremiah Baddeley, rector Chelsfield, Kent. He *d* 25 Jul 1961

2b Beatrix Elaine, JP, *b* 20 Feb 1895, *m* 27 Oct 1923 Lt.-Col (Edward) Roger Pratt, MC, DL, RA, of Ryston Hall, Downham, Norfolk, and *d* 25 Dec 1969, leaving issue. He *d* 18 Jan 1966

1a Emily Constantia, *m* 1st 12 Aug 1863 Capt Eustance John Wilson-Patten, 1st Life Gds, and had issue; he *d* 17 Dec 1873; she *m* 2nd 29 Nov 1875 3rd Marquess of Headfort (*qv*) and *d* 16 July 1926, having had further issue

2a Selina Charlotte, *d* unm 26 Jul 1913

(4) Charles (Rev), rector Longbridge and Kingston Deverell, Wilts, canon Canterbury, later RC priest; *b* 9 Feb 1813, *m* 18 Jul 1837 Harriet Francis Bagot (*see* BAGOT, B) and *d* 11 Aug 1894, leaving, with other issue:

1a Charles Ernest, barrister, Assist Slr to HM's Customs 1880–1906, *b* 26 Feb 1849, *m* 8 June 1880 Annie Harriet (*d* 6 Jan 1937), only dau of Sir Francis Seymour Haden, of Woodcote Park, Hants, and *d* 28 May 1906, leaving issue:

1b Roger Charles Seymour, MBE (1936), T/Sec Br Legation Holy See 1919–38, *b* 19 Jan 1885; *d* 17 Jan 1938

1b Mary Harriet, *b* 25 July 1881; *d* unm 9 May 1950

2a Gertrude Harriet, *m* 28 April 1858 4th Earl of Kenmare (*see* 1949 edn) and *d* 28 Feb 1913, having had issue. He *d* 9 Feb 1905

2 GEORGE THYNNE, 2nd BARON CARTERET OF HAWNES, PC (1804); *b* 23 Jan 1770; *educ* St John's Coll Cambridge; MP (Tory) Weobley 1790–1812, a Ld Treasury 1801–04, Comptroller Household 1804–12; *m* 9 May 1797 Hon Harriet Courtenay, 5th dau of 2nd Viscount Courtenay (*see* DEVON, E), and *dsp* 19 Feb 1838

3 JOHN THYNNE, 3rd and last BARON CARTERET OF HAWNES, PC (1804); *b* 28 Dec 1772; *educ* St John's Coll Cambridge; MP (Tory) Weobley May-Dec 1796 and Bath 1796–1832, V-Chamerlain Household 1804–12; *m* 18 June 1801 Mary Anne, dau of Thomas Master, of Cirencester Abbey, Glos, by Mary, sis of 1st Baron Sherborne (*see* 1970 edn), and *dsp* 10 March 1849, when the barony expired

The 2nd MARQUESS *d* 27 March 1837; his s,

HENRY FREDERICK THYNNE, **3rd Marquess of Bath**, Capt RN, *b* 24 May 1797, *m* 10 April 1830 Harriet (*d* 2 Jan 1892), dau of 1st Baron Ashburton (*qv*), and had:

1 JOHN ALEXANDER, **4th Marquess**

2 Henry Frederick, PC, MP S Wilts 1859–85, DL Wilts, Treasurer Household 1875–80, Maj Wilts Yeo Cav, *b* 2 Aug 1832, *m* 1 June 1858 Lady Ulrica Frederica Jane St Maur (*d* 26 Jan 1916), 2nd dau of 12th Duke of Somerset (*qv*), and *d* 28 Jan 1904, having had issue:

(1) Henry Frederick Boteville, *b* 14 Apr 1860; *d* unm 8 May 1887

(2) Thomas Ulric, Cdr RNR and Capt and hon Maj 3rd and 4th Bns Highland LI, *b* 14 June 1861, *m* 10 March 1898 Dorothy Mary (*m* 2nd 15 Jan 1912 Capt Alfred Basil Lubbock, MC (*d* 3 Sep 1944), est s of Alfred Lubbock (*see* AVEBURY, B), and *d* 15 Nov 1944), dau of Charles William Warner, CB, and *dsp* 20 April 1911

(3) John Alexander Roger, *b* 1 Sep 1863; *d* unm 10 Apr 1914

(4) Ulric Oliver, CMG (1918), CVO (1946), DSO (1900), TD, Col late cmdg R Wilts Yeo, TA (hon Col 1938–46), memb Corps of Gentlemen-at-Arms 1922–46 (Standard Bearer 1945–46), late Lt KRRC, served Chitral Expdn 1895, S Africa 1900 (despatches) and WW I (despatches), *b* 6 July 1871, *educ* Charterhouse and RMC Sandhurst; *m* 1st 16 May 1899 Marjory (*d* 17 Nov 1950), er dau of Edward Wormald, of Sheepwell House, Herts, and 15 Berkeley Sq, W1, and had issue:

1a Oliver St Maur, TD (1940), Lt-Col Roy Wilts Yeo WW II (despatches), pres London Master Printers' Assoc 1948–49, pres Br Fedn Master Printers 1963–64; *b* 24 Oct 1901, *educ* Eton and New Coll Oxford (BA 1923), *m* 8 June 1936 Mary Wroughton (*d* 1992), dau of Herbert Francis Morris and formerly w of Maj Richard Wale Gordon Dill, MC, and *d* 1 May 1978, leaving:

1b +Sheridan Ulric [Sheridan Thynne Esq, Patterdale, Ferry Road, S Stoke, Berks], Lt Royal Wilts Yeo; *b* 14 June 1939, *educ* Eton, *m* 12 Sep 1964 *Eve Clare, dau of Lt-Cdr George James Cardew, RN, of Manor Cottage, Goring on Thames, Oxon, and has:

1c +Piers Mark; *b* 20 June 1977

1c *Louisa Sarah; *b* 10 Nov 1965

2c *Marika Helen; *b* 2 April 1973

3c *Tamara Jane; *b* 19 Dec 1974

2a Edward Wormald; *b* 17 March 1905; *d* unm 8 Oct 1925

3a Brian Sheridan, CBE (1946), AFC, G/Capt RAuxAF WW II (despatches); *b* 29 Nov 1907, *educ* Eton, *m* 1st 9 Oct 1940 (*divorce* 1949) Mrs Naomi Bourn, only dau of C E Waters, of Sydney, NSW, and had:

1b *Harriet Anne; *b* 10 Sept 1941

3a (cont.) G/Capt Brian Thynne *m* 2nd 10 Nov 1952 Fernanda Herrero (*d* 1987), dau of the Marquis de Aledo, of Madrid, and *d* 1985, having by her had:

2b *Ulrica Maria Teresa; *b* 27 Jan 1954

3b *Jane Georgiana; *b* 3 Feb 1955; *m* 1979 *Javier Arzola and has:

1c *David; *b* 1981

1c *Raquel; *b* 1982

1c *Esther; *b* 1990

1a *Ulrica Marjory; *b* 5 May 1911; *m* 19 Feb 1936 (*divorce* 1961) Maj George Anthony Murray Smith, DL, MFH, RHG, of Gumley Hall, Market Harborough, s of Arthur Murray Smith, 2nd Life Gds

(4) (cont.) Col Ulric Thynne *m* 2nd 19 Dec 1951 Elspeth Stiven (*d* 25 March 1955), widow of 1st and last Baron Invernairn (*see* 1936 edn) and est dau of David Tullis, of Glencairn, Rutherglen, and *d* 30 Sept 1957

(1) Alicia Rachel, *d* 16 Aug 1938

(2) Alice Ruth Hermione, *m* 25 Apr 1889 Alexander Edward Lane Fox-Pitt-Rivers, of Rushmore, Wilts, and *d* 2 Aug 1948, leaving issue. He *d* 19 Aug 1927

1 Louisa Isabella Harriet, *m* 29 Apr 1862 Gen Hon Sir Percy Robert Basil Feilding, KCB, and *d* 26 June 1919, having had issue (*see* DENBIGH and DESMOND, E)

2 Alice, *d* 1847

The 3rd MARQUESS *d* 24 June 1837; his er s,

JOHN ALEXANDER THYNNE, **4th Marquess of Bath**, Ld Lt Wilts, hon Col Wilts Yeo Cav, Chm Wilts CC; *b* 1 March 1831, *m* 20 Aug 1861 Frances Isabella Catherine (*d* 31 Oct 1915), est dau of 3rd Viscount de Vesci (*qv*), and had:

1 THOMAS HENRY, **5th Marquess**

2 John Boteville, Lt 9th Lancers, *b* 27 May 1867; *d* unm 19 May 1887

3 Alexander George, DSO (1917), of Norton Hall, Daventry, MP Bath 1910–18, Maj Roy Wilts Yeo and T/Lt-Col cmdg service Bn Wilts Regt, served S Africa 1900–02, Somaliland 1903–04 and WW I (wounded, despatches, Croix de Guerre), *b* 17 Feb 1873; *ka* 16 Sep 1918

1 Alice Emma, CBE (1920), *m* 14 Nov 1883 Sir Michael Hugh Shaw-Stewart, 8th Bt (*qv*), and *dsp* 26 Jan 1942

2 Katherine Georgina Louisa, *m* 22 Oct 1901 1st Earl of Cromer (*qv*) and *d* 4 March 1933, leaving issue

3 Beatrice (twin with her bro John), *d* unm 5 Dec 1941

The 4th MARQUESS *d* 20 Apr 1896; his est s,

THOMAS HENRY THYNNE, **5th Marquess of Bath**, KG, CB, PC (1922), JP; *b* 15 July 1862; *educ* Balliol Coll Oxford (MA); Ld Lt Somerset, Pres TAA, Chm: Wilts CC, QS 1906–23, Freedom of Bath 1929, Pro-Chllr Bristol U 1937, KJStJ, Master Horse 1922–23, Hon Col Roy Wilts Yeo, Hon Col 4th Bn Somerset LI (TA), Lt-Col and Hon Col cmdg Roy Wilts Yeo, MP (C) Frome 1886–92 and 1895–96, U-Sec India 1905; *m* 19 April 1890 Violet Caroline (*d* 29 May 1928), dau of Sir Charles Mordaunt, 10th Bt (*qv*), and *d* 9 June 1946, having had:

1 John Alexander, *Viscount Weymouth*; *b* 29 Nov 1895; 2nd Lt RSG; *ka* 13 Feb 1916

2 HENRY FREDERICK THYNNE, **6th Marquess of Bath**, ED, JP (Wilts 1938); *b* 26 Jan 1905; *educ* Harrow and Ch Ch Oxford; CC Wilts; Maj Roy Wilts Yeo (TA), WW II (wounded), MP (C) Frome 1931–35, memb Cncl Duchy Cornwall 1933–36; Bronze and Silver Stars USA; *m* 1st 27 Oct 1927 (*divorce* 1953) Hon Daphne Winifred Louise Vivian (*d* 5 Dec 1997), er dau of 4th Baron Vivian (*qv*), and had:

(1) Thomas Timothy; *b* 13 Oct 1929, *d* 14 Sept 1930

(2) ALEXANDER GEORGE THYNNE later (from 1976) THYNN, **7th and present Marquess of Bath**

(3) +Christopher John [The Lord Christopher Thynne, Britmore House, Donhead St Andrew, Dorset SP7 9EB]; late 2nd Lt Life Gds; *b* 9 April 1934; *educ* Eton, *m* 6 June 1968 *Antonia Mary, only dau of Maj Sir Anthony Frederick Mark Palmer, 4th Bt (*qv*), and has:

1a *Sophie Emma, *b* 6 Dec 1968

(4) Valentine Charles, late 2nd Lt The Life Guards; *b* 3 Nov 1937; *educ* Eton; *m* 22 March 1961 (*divorce* 1971) Veronica Ann, only dau of Col G E Jacks, IA, of Stratford, NZ, and had:

1a +Lucien, *b* 2 June 1965; *educ* Milton Abbey

2a *Xenia Laura [Mrs David Mason, 20 Ingate Terrace, London SW8 3RR], *b* 11 March 1962; *m* 1989 Joshua David Mason (*d* 1991), s of Richard Mason

(4) (cont.) Lord Valentine Thynne *m* 2nd 1971 (*divorce* 1976) Susanne Caroline, dau of Edgar Alder and formerly w of Christopher Hodgson Moore; *m* 3rd 1977 *Liese Maria [The Lady Valentine Thynne, 16 Bedford St, Bath BA1 6AF], dau of Kenneth Dennis, of Bristol, and formerly w of Karl Martin Weschke, and *d* 1979

(1) Caroline Jane, *b* 28 Aug 1928; *educ* RADA; Hon LLD Bristol, involved with over 60 charities in the Avon, Glos and Wilts area; *m* 5 July 1950 11th Duke of Beaufort (*qv*) and *d* 22 April 1995, leaving issue

2 (cont.) The **6th Marquess** *m* 2nd 15 July 1953 *Virginia Penelope [The Most Hon The Dowager Marchioness of Bath, Job's Mill, Crockerton, Warminster, Wilts], dau of Alan Leonard Romaine Parsons, of The Baas, Broxbourne, Herts, by Viola (dau of Sir Herbert Beerbohm Tree), and formerly w of Hon David Tennant (*see* GLENCONNER, B), and *d* 1992, having by her had:

(2) *Silvy Cerne; *b* 22 Dec 1958; *m* 1989 *Iain McQuiston and has:

1a *Milo Henry Cerne; *b* 1992

1a *Eve Iris; *b* 1990

1 (Alice) Kathleen Violet; *b* 27 March 1891; *m* 8 July 1919 Lt-Col Hon Oliver Hugh Stanley, DSO (*see* STANLEY OF ALDERLEY, SHEFFIELD and, B), and *d* 4 Oct 1977, leaving issue

2 Emma Margery, OBE (1943); *b* 5 July 1893; regnl administrator WVS 1939–45, CC Wilts 1946–51; *m* 15 Oct 1921 (*divorce* 1942) 6th Marquess of Northampton (*qv*)

3 Mary Beatrice, Ldy of Bedchamber to HM THE QUEEN (now QUEEN ELIZABETH THE QUEEN MOTHER) 1937–47; *b* 6 May 1903; *m* 1st 24 Nov 1927 (*divorce* 1947) 3rd Baron Nunburnholme (*qv*) and had issue; *m* 2nd 27 Nov 1947 Sir (James) Ulick Francis Canning Alexander, GCB, GCVO, OBE, PC, er s of James Dalison Alexander, DL, of Oakbank, Sevenoaks, and *d* 11 Dec 1974. He *d* 4 April 1973

Seat: The same Sir Thomas Thynne who is said to have received the grant of a lion device on his coat of arms by Protector Somerset (*see* section **Arms**) had a little earlier taken advantage of the dissolution of the monasteries to buy in 1540 an Augustinian priory past which flowed a river called the Long Leat. He built a mansion on the site, probably to his own designs, but it burnt down almost immediately after completion. He tried again, enlisting the help this time of Robert Smythson, his master mason and the sole distinguished architect of his time in England whose name has come down to us. The result is substantially the present building. Longleat is claimed as the first Elizabethan mansion built in the style of the Italian Renaissance. Alterations since the 16th century include the great staircase and the ground-floor east passage by Sir Jeffry Wyattville *c* 1810 and rather heavier, Italianate changes made by the **4th Marquess** in the 1870s. The grounds were landscaped by Lancelot 'Capability' Brown.

BATHO

Arms: Gu. on a fess arg. two castles of the first, over all a sword in pale, point upwards, ppr. **Crest:** A dragon sejant or, gorged with a mural crown gu. and holding in the dexter claw a sword as in the arms. **Motto:** *Nec parvis sisto* ('Neither do I hesitate at trifles').
Creation: Bt. (UK) 19 Oct 1928.

SIR PETER GHISLAIN BATHO, 3RD BT, of Frinton, Co Essex [Sir Peter Batho Bt, Park Farm, Saxmundham, Suffolk IP17 1DQ]; *b* 9 Dec 1939; *s* f 1990; *educ* Ampleforth and Writtle Farm Inst; CC Suffolk 1989–93; *m* 29 Oct 1966 *Lucille Mary, dau of Wilfred Francis Williamson, of The White House, Saxmundham, Suffolk, and has issue:

1 +RUPERT SEBASTIAN GHISLAIN [Rupert Batho Esq, 4 Hedgerow Cottages, Gasbeck, Suffolk IP6 9SD]; *b* 26 Oct 1967; *educ* Harper Adams Ag Coll; *m* 29 April 1995 *Jo-Anne Louise, dau of Rodney F Hellawell, of Kesgrave, Ipswich

2 +Alexander Francis Ghislain [Alexander Batho Esq, 10 Archway Cottages, Leiston, Suffolk IP16 4AR]; *b* 26 May 1970; *m* 18 June 1994 *Zoe Elizabeth, dau of Nigel J Miller, of Aldburgh, and has:

(1) *Bethany Frances Ghislaine; *b* 16 Feb 1996

3 +Hugh Charles Ghislain; *b* 22 May 1973; *educ* UCL

Lineage: Sir Charles Albert Batho, 1st Bt (UK), so *cr* 19 Oct 1928 (yst son of William Smith Batho, of Highgate); *b* 7 Oct 1872; Lt City London, Alderman Aldgate Ward City London, Sheriff 1925–26, Ld Mayor London 1927–28, Govr The Irish Soc; a ships' store and export merchant, memb Baltic Exchange, Govr Guy's, St Bartholomew's, St Thomas's and Bridewell and Bethlem Hospitals, dir LNER; Belgian Medaille du Roi Albert, Afghan Order Sirdar el Ali 1928, chm Cattle Markets Ctee 1916, Music Ctee 1918 and 1919, Gen Purposes Ctee 1921, Freeman City Londonderry 1937; CStJ, ktd 1926; *m* 10 Feb 1897 Bessie (*d* 19 Dec 1961), 4th dau of Benjamin Parker, of Broadlands, Oulton Broad, Suffolk, and had issue:

1 MAURICE BENJAMIN (Sir), **2nd Bt**

1 Madeline, JP City of Birmingham 1947; *b* 3 Oct 1901; *m* 9 July 1925 Leslie Somerville Gathergood, MA , MD (*d* 5 Aug 1968), barrister, son of Benjamin William Gathergood, MD (Aberdeen), of Aylmer Hall, Tilney St Lawrence, Kings Lynn, Norfolk, and *d* 22 Dec 1968

Sir CHARLES *d* 29 Jan 1938; his only son,

Sir Maurice Benjamin Batho, 2nd Bt; *educ* Uppingham; WW II in KRRC (T/Lt-Col), sub-dir Syrian Wheat Collection Scheme of the Spears Mission 1943, Teheran Regnl Advsr Iranian Min Finance on Cereals Collection 1944, dep dir Rice Procurement Govt Bengal 1945, dir and gen manager Reed Paper and Bd Sales Ltd, dir London Paper Mills Co Ltd, Empire Paper Mills Ltd, Reed Bd Mills (Colthrope) Ltd and Castrol (Overseas) Ltd; *b* 14 Jan 1910; *m* 28 May 1934 Antoinette Marie (*d* 1994), dau of Baron d'Udekem d'Acoz, of Ghent, and *d* 1990, leaving issue:

1 Charles Graham Paul Maurice John Ghislain; *b* 21 March 1935; *d* following an accident 30 Jan 1942

2 Sir PETER GHISLAIN BATHO, **3rd and present Bt**

3 +Richard Ghislain [Richard Batho Esq, Carlton, Marden, Hereford and Worcester HR1 3ES]; *b* 30 Nov 1941; *educ* Ampleforth and Wye Coll London U (BSc); *m* 20 June 1970 *Georgina Catherine Ann Gwynne, dau of William Reginald Gwynne Chadwick, of the Croft, Monmouth Rd, Abergavenny, Gwent, and has issue:

(1) +Charles William Ghislain; *b* 1971; *educ* Belmont Abbey

(1) *Sarah Catherine Ghislain; *b* 27 April 1974

1 *Anne Madeline Bessie Ghislaine [Mrs Stephen Oliver, St Briavels, Wetherden, Stowmarket, Suffolk]; *b* 5 April 1938; *m* 31 Oct 1964 *Stephen Robert Morgan Oliver, and has issue:

(1) *Felix Benjamin Morgan; *b* 3 March 1966; *m* 4 June 1993 *Jean Katharine Mary Dinsdale-Young and has issue:

1a *Ruaraid Jack; *b* 3 Oct 1996

1a *Miranda Jean; *b* 28 Sept 1994

(2) *Alban Geoffrey Morgan; *b* 29 Feb 1968

(3) *Damian Paul Morgan; *b* 30 Oct 1970; *m* 10 April 1994 *Nanette Whittingham

(4) *Justin Edmund Morgan; *b* 22 May 1978

2 *Jacqueline Ghislaine [Mrs Ian Bruce-Jones, Little Garth, The Street, Walberswick, Southwold, Suffolk IP18 6UH]; *b* 22 Oct 1947; *m* 1987 *Ian David Bruce-Jones

BATHURST

Arms: Sa. two bars erm., in chief three crosses pattée or. **Crest:** A dexter arm embowed, habited in mail, holding in the hand all ppr. a spiked club or. **Supporters:** Two stags arg., each gorged with a collar gemel ermines. **Motto:** *Tien ta foy* ('Keep thy faith'). **Creations**: B. (GB) 1 Jan 1711/2 and (Apsley) 24 Jan 1771, E. (GB) 27 Aug 1772.

THE 8TH EARL BATHURST OF BATHURST, Sussex, **Baron Bathurst of Battlesden**, Co Bedford, and **Lord Apsley, Baron of Apsley**, Sussex (Henry Allen John Bathurst) [The Rt Hon The Earl Bathurst DL, Manor Farm, Sapperton, nr Cirencester, Glos GL7 6LE]; *b* 1 May 1927; *s* gf 1943; *educ* Eton, Ridley Coll Canada and Ch Ch Oxford; late Capt Roy Glos Hus (TA) 1949–57, Lt 10th Roy Hus 1948, Ld-in-Waiting1957–61, Jt Parly U-Sec Home Office 1961–62, Govr Hosp of St Lawrence Cirencester 1944– and RAC Cirencester 1948, Chllr Primrose League Glos Branch 1959, CPRE, memb Cncls CLA (chm Glos Branch 1968) and Timber Grower's Orgn, pres: Roy Forestry Soc 1976–78, Inst of Sales and Mktg Management 1981– and Assoc Professional Foresters 1983, DL Glos 1960–86, Jt MFH VWH 1949–65; *m* 1st 20 March 1959 (*divorce* 1976) Judith Mary, only dau of Amos Christopher Nelson, of Springfield House, Foulridge, Colne, Lancs, and has:

1 +ALLEN CHRISTOPHER BERTRAM, *Lord Apsley* [Lord Apsley, Cirencester Park, Cirencester, Glos GL7 2BT]; *b* 11 March 1961; *m* 1st 1986 (*divorce* 1994) Hilary Jane, yr dau of John F George, of Weston Lodge, Albury, Surrey, and has:

(1) +Benjamin George Henry; *b* 6 March 1990

(2) *Rosie Meriel Lilias; *b* 1992

1 (cont.) *Lord Apsley m* 2nd *8 June 1995 *Sara, dau of Christopher Chapman, of Ilminster, Somerset, and Mrs Marguerite Chapman, of Kenya

2 +Alexander Edward Seymour [The Hon Alexander Bathurst, Tarlton Farmhouse, Tarlton, Cirencester, Glos GL7 6PA]; *b* 8 Aug 1965; *educ* Harrow, RMA Sandhurst and RAC Cirencester, Capt Roy Hus (Prince of Wales's Own) (commissioned 1985) Capt Roy Glos Hus; *m* 1992 *Emma Gae, dau of J L Sharpe, FRCS, and has:

(1) +Harry John Seymour; *b* 3 July 1996

1 *Henrietta Mary Lilias; *b* 17 Oct 1962

The 8th EARL *m* 2nd 17 Jan 1978 *Gloria Wesley, only dau of Harold Edward Clarry, of Vancouver, BC, and widow of David Rutherston, of Jaymes Court, Bisley, Glos

Lineage: LAWRENCE BATHURST, of Cranbrook, Kent; had:

LAWRENCE BATHURST, of Canterbury and Cranbrook; had:

LAWRENCE BATHURST, of Canterbury, Cranbrook and Staplehurst Kent; *m*—, dau of Robert Chapman, and was *bur* 1549 aged 92, leaving, with two other sons (Robert, of Horsmonden, Kent, ancestor of the extinct or dormant Bathurst Bts, of Lechlade, Glos; John, of Staplehurst):

EDWARD BATHURST, of Staplehurst; living 1558; had:

LAUNCELOT BATHURST; Alderman London, Ld Manor of Franks, Kent; *b* 1529; *m* Judith, dau of Barnard Randolph, of London and Wardis, Sussex, and had, with other issue:

GEORGE BATHURST, of Hothorpe, Northants; *b* 1587; *m* 1610 Elizabeth (*d* 1650), dau and coheir of Edward Villiers, of Hothorpe, and had, with 12 other sons (including Dr Ralph Bathurst, DD, MD, Dean Wells, Chaplain to CHARLES II, Pres Trin Coll Oxford, *b* 1620, fndr memb Roy Soc) and four daus:

Sir BENJAMIN BATHURST, of Paulersbury, Northants; MP, Govr: Roy African Co *temp* CHARLES II and HEIC 1688–89, Treasurer Household to Princess Anne of Denmark, Cofferer to QUEEN ANNE; *m* Frances (*d* 7 June 1727), dau of Sir Allen Apsley, of Apsley, Sussex, and *d* 27 April 1704, leaving, with other issue:

ALLEN BATHURST, **1st Earl Bathurst of Bathurst**, Sussex, so *cr* 27 Aug 1772, as also 1 Jan 1711/2 BARON BATHURST OF BATTLESDEN, Beds (both GB), PC (1742); *b* 16 Nov 1684; *educ* Trin Coll Oxford; MP (Tory) Cirencester 1705–11/2, Capt Gentlemen Pensioners 1742–44; *m* 6 July 1704 his 1st cousin Catherine (*d* 8 June 1768), dau and eventual heiress of Sir Peter Apsley, of Apsley, Sussex, and *d* 16 Sept 1775, leaving with other issue, including an er s (Benjamin, MP Gloucester, *m* 26 Nov 1732 Elizabeth, dau of 4th Earl of Elgin (*see* ELGIN and KINCARDINE, E), and *dsp* & *vp* 23 June 1767):

HENRY BATHURST, **2nd Earl Bathurst of Bathurst**, PC (1771); *b* 20 May 1714; barrister 1736, MP (Tory) Cirencester 1735–54, KC 1746, Judge Court Common Pleas 1754–71, Ld Chllr 1771–78; *cr* 24 Jan 1771 LORD APSLEY, BARON OF APSLEY, Sussex (GB); Ld Pres Cncl 1779–82; *m* 1st 19 Sept 1754 Anne (*dsp* 4 Feb 1758), widow of Charles Phillipps and dau of—James; *m* 2nd 14 June 1759 Tryphena (*d* 2 Dec 1807), dau of Thomas Scawen Maidwell, of Northants, by Tryphena, only dau and heiress of Lord James Russell, 5th son of 1st Duke of Bedford (*qv*), and *d* 6 Aug 1794, leaving by her:

HENRY BATHURST, **3rd Earl Bathurst of Bathurst**, KG (1817), PC (1793); *b* 22 May 1762; *educ* Ch Ch Oxford; MP (Tory) Cirencester 1783–94, a Ld Admlty 1783–89 and Treasury 1789–91, last Teller Exchequer before post's abolition 1790–1834, Commr India Bd 1793–1802, Jt Clerk of the Crown 1801–16 and (solely) 1816–34, Master Mint 1804–06 and 1807–12, Pres BOT 1807–12, For Sec Oct-Dec 1809, Sec War and Colonies 1812–27, Ld Pres 1828–30; *m* 1 April 1789 Georgina (*d* 20 Jan 1841),sis of 4th Duke of Richmond (*see* RICHMOND and GORDON, D), and *d* 27 July 1834, leaving, with other issue:

1 HENRY GEORGE BATHURST, **4th Earl Bathurst of Bathurst**; *b* 24 Feb 1790; *educ* Eton and Ch Ch Oxford; MP (Tory) Weobley Jan-Sept 1812 and Cirencester 1812–34, a Commr India Bd 1812–18; *d* unm 25 May 1866

2 WILLIAM LENNOX BATHURST, **5th Earl Bathurst of Bathurst**; *b* 14 Feb 1791; *educ* Ch Ch Oxford; Fell All Souls; MP (Tory) Weobley 1812–16, Dep Teller Exchequer 1816–30, barrister 1821, Commr Victualling RN 1825–29, Jt Sec BOT 1830–47, Jt Clerk PC 1830–60, DCL; *d* unm 24 Feb 1878

3 Thomas Seymour, Lt-Col; *b* 22 Oct 1793; *m* 6 Oct 1829 Julia (*d* 21 Feb 1877), only dau of John Peter Hankey, London banker and merchant, and *d* 10 April 1834, leaving issue:

(1) ALLEN ALEXANDER, **6th Earl**

(1) Mary Selina; *d* unm 16 March 1883

The 5th EARL's nephew,

ALLEN ALEXANDER BATHURST, **6th Earl Bathurst of Bathurst**; *b* 19 Oct 1832; *educ* Eton and Trin Coll Cambridge; MP (C) Cirencester 1857–78; *m* 1st 31 Jan 1862 Meriel Leicester (*d* 6 July 1872), 2nd dau of 2nd Baron de Tabley (*see* 1895 edn), and had issue:

1 SEYMOUR HENRY, **7th Earl**

2 Lancelot Julian; *b* 24 Jan 1868; *d* 14 June 1928

3 (Allen), Benjamin, DL Glos; Lt-Col TFR cmdg 5th Bn Gloucs Regt, Hon Capt, MP E Glos 1895–1906 and 1910–18; *b* 25 June 1872; *m* 22 April 1902 Augusta Ruby, dau of Lord Edward Spencer-Churchill (*see* MARLBOROUGH, D), and *d* 8 Oct 1947, leaving issue:

(1) Peter, G/Capt RAF WW II; *b* 1 March 1903; *educ* Clare Coll Cambridge (BA 1925); *m* 7 July 1927 *Lady (Elizabeth) Ann [The Lady Ann Bathurst, 12A Northanger Ct, Grove St, Bath], only dau of Capt Hon Chandos Graham Temple-Gore-Langton (*see* TEMPLE OF STOWE, E), and *d* 1970, leaving:

1a +(David) Benjamin, GCB (1991, KCB 1987), DL (Som 1996) [Admiral of the Fleet Sir Benjamin Bathurst GCB, DL, c/o Coutts & Co, 440 Strand, London WC2]; *b* 27 May 1936; *educ* Eton and RNC Dartmouth; Adml and C-in-C Fleet, Allied C-in-C Channel and C-in-C E Atlantic 1989, Adml of the Fleet 1995–; V-Ch Def Staff 1991–93, Ch Naval Staff and 1st Sea Lord, 1st and Pncpl Naval ADC to HM THE QUEEN 1993–95; *m* 29 Aug 1959 *Sarah Christian Pandora, yst dau of Maj (Basil Arthur) John Peto (*see* PETO, Bt, of Barnstaple), and has issue:

1b +Benjamin John; *b* 15 April 1964; *m* 10 Feb 1996 *Katherine, dau of S/Ldr Peter Ellison and Mrs John Lendrum

1b *Alice Patrica; *b* 24 May 1962

2b *Anna Christian; *b* 15 Oct 1968

3b *Lucilla Ruby; *b* 28 Dec 1970

2a +Timothy Seymour [Timothy Bathurst Esq, College Farm House, Tetbury Rd, Cirencester, Glos]; *b* 26 March 1939; *educ* Eton; late 2nd Lt The Rifle Bde, dir Arthur Tooth & Sons Ltd, Bruton Street W1 (ret) and David Carritt and Artemis Fine Arts (UK); *m* 1st 1 Oct 1960 (*divorce* 1973) (Elizabeth) Mary, twin dau of Philip Michael Armitage, of Southend Cottage, Henley-on-Thames, and has:

1b +Jonathan Chandos Seymour [Jonathan Bathurst Esq, 4 Kit Lane, Checkenden, Reading RG8 0TY]; *b* 5 March 1965; *m* *Sharon Elizabeth, est dau of Anthony Chinnery, and has:

1c *Lara Elizabeth; *b* 24 June 1997

1b *Joanna Mary [Mrs Hugh Nevile, 21 Cromwell Grove, London W11 2DE]; *b* 9 April 1963; *m* 1989 *Hugh Simon Nevile (*see* MOWBRAY, SEGRAVE and STOURTON, B) and has:

1c *Max Henry; *b* 24 June 1994

2c *Thomas Michael; *b* 27 Nov 1996

2b *Elizabeth Sarah [Mrs Simon Reid, 15 Brackenbury Gdns, London W6 0BP]; *b* 12 March 1968; *m* 1993 *Simon Dale Reid, son of Hubert Reid, of The Old Rectory, Marton, Cheshire, and has:

1c *Imogen Elizabeth; *b* 2 Feb 1997

2a (cont.) Timothy Bathurst *m* 2nd 1973 *Charlotte Anne, formerly w of Richard Belloc-Lowndes and dau of Capt Richard Formby, and by her has:

3b *James Seymour; *b* 20 Dec 1976

1 Georgina Meriel; *b* 25 July 1863; *m* 25 Feb 1885 Sir George William Buchanan, GCB, GCMG, GCVO, PC (*d* 20 Dec 1924), and *d* 25 April 1922, leaving issue (*see* BUCHANAN, Bt)

The **6th Earl** *m* 2nd 6 June 1874 Evelyn Elizabeth (*d* 1 March 1927), only dau of George James Barnard Hankey, of Fetcham Park, Surrey, and by her had:

2 Evelyn Selina; *m* 18 June 1898 Maj George Coryton Lister (*d* 30 May 1903), son of Sir Thomas Villiers Lister, KCMG, and *d* 16 April 1946, leaving issue

The 6th EARL *d* 2 Aug 1892; his est son,

SEYMOUR HENRY BATHURST, **7th Earl Bathurst of Bathurst**, CMG, TD, JP, DL (Glos), *b* 21 July 1864; CC Glos, Tstee Nat Portrait Gallery, Pres Glos TAA, Hon Col 1903, cmdg 4th Bn Gloucester Regt 1893–1908, Hon Col 6th Bn Gloucester Regt 1908–33; *m* 15 Nov 1893 Hon Lillas Margaret Frances Borthwick (medal of Queen Elizabeth of Belgium and Offr Legn Hon; *d* 30 Dec 1965), only surv child of 1st and last Baron Glenesk (*see* 1908 edn), and *d* 21 Sept 1943, having had:

1 Allen Algernon *Lord Apsley*, DSO (1918), MC (1917); *b* 3 Aug 1895; *educ* Eton and Ch Ch Oxford (BA); Lt-Col Roy Glos Hus, TD, DL and JP Gloucs, MP Southampton 1922–29 and Bristol Centl 1931–42, PPS to: Parly Sec Overseas Trade Dept 1922–24, Min Tport 1925–29 and Min Co-ordination Defence 1936, pres UK Pilot's Assoc 1925, chm Western Airways and Western Air Transport Co Ltd, dir Morning Post; author: *The Amateur Settlers*, served overseas WW I 1915–19, WW II 1939–42 with Arab Legion 1941–42; *m* 27 Feb 1924 Viola Emily Mildred, CBE (1952), Ch Cdr ATS 1938–40, MP Bristol Centl 1943–45, Govr RAC 1945 and Burdon Neurological Inst 1945, Pres Cirencester and Tewkesbury C Assoc 1947, memb Glos TA&RAFA, dir Western Airways Ltd, Nat Chm Women's Section Br Legion 1942–48, MFH VWH (Bathurst) 1946–55, authoress (*d* 20 Jan 1966), er dau of Capt Bertram Charles Christopher Spencer Meeking, of Richings Park, Bucks, and was *kas* Malta 17 Dec 1942, leaving:

(1) HENRY ALLEN JOHN BATHURST, **8th and present Earl Bathurst of Bathurst**

(2) +George Bertram [The Hon George Bathurst, Hullasey House, Tarlton, Glos]; Capt (ret 1967) Roy Wilts Yeo (TA), formerly Lt 10th Roy Hus; *b* 12 March 1929; *educ* Eton, Trin Coll Oxford (MA) and RAC Cirencester; Capt Roy Wilts, Lt 10th Hus; *m* 1973 *Susan, dau of Malcolm Messer, of Tarlton, and has:

1a +William Malcolm; *b* 1978

2 William Ralph Seymour, TD, FSA, of Cold Ashton Manor, Chippenham, Wilts, JP (Bristol 1957), High Sheriff Glos 1952, Capt Roy Glos Hus, served WW II, Master Soc Merchant Venturers Bristol 1958–59, Prov Grand Master Masonic Province of Glos 1950; *b* 21 Sept 1903; *educ* Eton and Trin Coll Oxford (BA 1925, MA 1929); *m* 12 July 1932 Helen Winifred (*d* 30 Oct 1972), er dau of Lt-Col Harry Heathcoat-Amory, of Hele Manor, Dulverton (*see* HEATHCOAT-AMORY, Bt), and was *k* in a car crash 10 Sept 1970

3 Ralph Henry; *b* 3 Sept 1904; *educ* Eton and Trin Coll Oxford (MA); *d* unm 5 Dec 1965

1 Meriel Olivia; *b* 3 Sept 1894; *m* 4 May 1916 Capt Lord Alastair Mungo Graham, RN, 3rd son of 5th Duke of Montrose (*qv*), and *d* 18 Jan 1936, leaving issue

Seat: Cirencester Park, Cirencester, Glos. Sir Benjamin Bathurst, father of the **1st Earl**, bought the estate in 1695 from a family called Danvers, who had built the main house some 100 years earlier. Sir Benjamin's new acquisition was not modernised till 1710, and even then the alterations were a shade perfunctory, with wings being removed and no more than a new face being superimposed on the bones of the old house's front elevation. For its size, the remodelled building proved somewhat cramped inside. The Oxford master mason used for the job, William Townesend, is known to have been competent, so he was presumably working to a tight budget.

Yet the **1st Earl**, who had inherited back in 1704, could be lavish enough if his heart was in it. After his political eclipse following the death of QUEEN ANNE he showed what he could do, in 1716 adding the Oakley estate west of Cirencester to his existing property and in concert with his friend the poet Alexander Pope laying out on the plateau towards Sapperton a park that the late James Lees-Milne called one of the grandest in all 18th-century England. Lord Bathurst was especially sensitive to the colour of landscaped grounds, selecting species of trees which would show off each other's foliage to the best advantage according to the season. He was also a gifted amateur architect, as his Hexagon or Pope's Seat, together with Alfred's Hall, show. But these were ornamental buildings, little more than follies. Straightforward domestic architecture seems to have bored him. On his death in 1775 the main house was found to be dangerously rickety and the **2nd Earl**, his son, feared demolition was the only answer.

The new owner only survived his father 19 years, however, and towards the end of the Napoleonic Wars Robert Smirke was brought in by the **3rd Earl** to see what could be done in retaining the house. It seems to have been Smirke who built the north wing, though he did carry out some demolition, notably the sweeping away of the west porch. In 1830 or thereabouts he returned, remodelling what is now the entrance front on the eastern side of the house to accommodate more spacious and harmoniously proportioned rooms inside.

BAUER

Creation: B. (LP, UK) 1983.

THE BARON BAUER, of Market Ward, City of Cambridge (Peter Thomas Bauer) [The Rt Hon The Lord Bauer, House of Lords, London SW1A 0PW]; *b* 6 Nov 1915; *educ* Scholae Piae Budapest and Gonville and Caius Coll Cambridge (MA, Fell 1946–60 and 1968–); FBA, Reader Ag Economics London U 1947–48, lecturer economics Cambridge 1948–56, Smuts Reader Cwlth Studies Cambridge 1956–60, Prof Economics LSE 1960–83, Prof Emeritus 1983–, Hon Fell 1997–; author: *Markets, Market Control and Marketing Reform* (co-author, 1968), *Indian Economic Policy and Development* (1972), *Dissent on Development* (1972), *Aspects of Nigerian Development* (1974), *Equality: The Third World of Economic Delusion* (1981), *Reality and Rhetoric: Studies in the Economics of Development* (1984), *The Development Frontier* (1991)

Lineage: ALADAR BAUER had issue:

PETER THOMAS, *cr* a **Baron**

BAYNES

Arms: Sa. a shin-bone in fess, surmounted of another in pale arg., on a canton of the last a vulture, ppr. **Crest:** A cubit arm, vested az., cuffed erminois, the hand holding a jaw-bone arg. **Supporters:** On either side a savage wreathed with holly about the head and waist, holding a club over his exterior shoulder, all ppr. **Motto:** *Furor arma ministrat* ('Rage supplies weapons'). **Creation:** Bt. (UK) 29 June 1801.

SIR JOHN CHRISTOPHER MALCOLM BAYNES, 7TH BT, of Harefield Place, Middlesex [Lt-Col Sir John Baynes Bt, Talwrn Bach, Llanfyllin, Powys SY22 5LQ]; *b* 24 April 1928; *s f* 1979; *educ* Sedbergh, RMA Sandhurst and Edinburgh U (MSc); Lt-Col QO Highrs, served Cameronians (Scottish Rifles) 1948–68, Malaya 1950–53 (despatches), Order of the Sword 1st Cl Sweden 1965, author: *Morale* (1967), *The Soldier in Modern Society* (1970), *The Jacobite Rising of 1715* (1971), *Urquhart of Arnhem* (1993); *m* 2 June 1955 *Shirley Maxwell, only dau of Robert Allan Dodds, of Foxbury, Lesbury, Alnwick, Northumberland, and has issue:

1 +CHRISTOPHER RORY [Christopher Baynes Esq, Greywalls, Findon, Sussex]; *b* 11 May 1956; *m* 1992 *Sandra Finwala, dau of Thomas Desmond Merriman and has:

(1) +Alasdair William Merriman; *b* 1993

(2) +Fergus Joseph Malcolm; *b* 31 Jan 1996

2 +Timothy Peter [Timothy Baynes Esq, Muirton of Drumlochy, Blairgowrie, Perthshire PH10 6TD]; *b* 6 Aug 1957; *m* 1986 *Estelle Anne Gabrielle, er dau of Nicholas John Dennys Parry de Winton, of Valley Farm, Brancaster, Norfolk, and has issue:

(1) +Rory Nicholas Aimery; *b* 1992

(2) +Adam John Stuart; *b* 7 Dec 1994

3 +Simon Robert Maurice; *b* 21 April 1960; *m* 1992 *Margaret Anne Mary, yr dau of Sydney Boag, of Boar's Hill, Oxford

4 +William John Walter; *b* 2 Jan 1966

Lineage: WALTER BAYNE, of Limley, Yorks (descended from a family of Yorkshire origin settled at Middlesmoor in Nidderdale in 1484); *d* 1616, having had, with other issue:

CHRISTOPHER BAYNES, of Kilburn Hall, Yorks; *b* 1603; *m* 1st 1625 Margaret, widow of James Bayne, of Ravensthorp, and had an er s (Christopher; barrister; *b* 1634, *m* Katherine, dau of Stephen Wilks, of Sawley, and *dsp* 15 April 1695, leaving Kilburn to his half-bro); *m* 2nd Elizabeth Dawson, and *d* 10 Aug 1678, leaving by her:

WILLIAM BAYNES; *b* 13 July 1661; *m* 1719 Tabitha, dau of George Prickett, of York, Serjeant-at-Law, Recorder York, and *d* 24 Jan 1731, leaving issue:

WILLIAM BAYNES, of Kilburn Hall and Harefield Place, Middx; Gentleman of the Privy Chamber to GEORGE II and GEORGE III; *b* 19 Jan 1719; *m* Mary, 2nd dau of Christopher Roberts, of London, and *d* 23 Nov 1798, leaving, with other issue:

Sir Christopher Baynes, 1st Bt (UK), so *cr* 29 June 1801, of Harefield Place, DL, JP; *b* 6 Aug 1755; Offr RHG, Maj-Cmdt 1796 Uxbridge Gentlemen and Yeomanry Cavalry (later Middx Yeo); *m* 1 March 1788 Nanny (*d* 15 Dec 1842), dau of William Gregory, of Cowes, IoW, and *d* 16 March 1837, having had, with two other sons and a dau:

Sir William Baynes, 2nd Bt; *b* 28 Nov 1789; *m* 14 Dec 1815 Julia (*d* 21 Jan 1881), 4th dau of Gen Sir John Smith, GCH, Col Cmdt RHA, and had, with a 3rd s and four daus:

1 WILLIAM JOHN WALTER (Sir), **3rd Bt**

2 Walter Francis; *b* 16 Dec 1823; *m* 23 Sept 1853 Amelia Sarah (*d* 7 Aug 1910), yr dau of William Malton, and *d* 10 Sept 1914, leaving issue:

(1) Walter Malton; *b* 31 Aug 1854; *d* unm 24 June 1946

(2) Nigel William Francis, Maj Glos Regt WW I (wounded); *b* 21 March 1878; *m* 1st 26 Oct 1904 Phoebe (*d* 22 March 1906), 4th dau of John Grant Morris, of Allerton Priory, Lancs, and Kincora, Torquay; *m* 2nd 25 Jan 1912 Gladys Marie, widow of Maj Edward Reginald Talbot (*see* TALBOT DE MALAHIDE, B), and dau of T W Shortridge, and *d* 19 March 1915, having by his 1st w had issue:

1a Katherine Phoebe; *b* 1905; *d* 1908

(1) Amy Helen; *d* unm

(2) Ethel Frances; *d* unm 12 April 1933

1 Mary Anne Louisa; *m* 8 Sept 1857 Maj-Gen Thomas de Coney Hamilton, VC, JP (*d* 3 March 1908), 4th son of James John Hamilton, of Ballymacoll, and *d* 21 May 1913, having had issue

Sir WILLIAM *d* 1 Jan 1866; his est son,

Sir William John Walter Baynes, 3rd Bt, JP; *b* 5 June 1820; *m* 17 June 1845 Margaret (*d* 17 July 1911), 3rd dau of Daniel Stuart, of Wykham Park, Oxon, and *d* 26 Oct 1897, having had issue:

1 **Sir Christopher William Baynes, 4th Bt**; *b* 14 Sept 1847; *m* 20 June 1872 Amy Ruperta (*d* 28 Jan 1919), est dau of Edward Colston, of Roundway Park, Wilts, and *d* 29 July 1936, leaving:

(1) **Sir William Edward Colston Baynes, 5th Bt**, MC; *b* 23 Feb 1876; *educ* Trin Coll Cambridge (MA, LLM); barrister Inner Temple 1900, licencié en droit Paris 1905, Judge Native Court of First Instance Egypt, Egyptian CS 1906–22, Capt Coldstream Gds (SR) and Staff Capt London Dist WW I; *d* unm 17 Sept 1971

(2) Ronald Christopher, civ engr GWR, PASI, Lt 8th City of London Regt WW I, attd Min Munitions 1917–19; *b* 12 Nov 1878; *educ* Harrow and UCL; *m* 12 Feb 1930 Cecilia (*d* 4 July 1968), only dau of Maj Charles Russell Day, Oxon LI, and *dsp* 22 June 1953

(1) Christobel Ruperta; *d* unm 5 Dec 1940

(2) Dorothy Julia BAYNES later COLSTON-BAYNES (deed poll 1946); author (as Dormer Creston): *In Search of Two Characters* (Roy Lit Soc award 1946), *Fountains of Youth, The Youthful Queen Victoria* and *The Regent and his Daughter*

2 Donald Stuart, CE; *b* 17 Sept 1848; *m* 8 June 1881 Annie (*d* 7 Oct 1933), yst dau of Rev Edward Ravenshaw, Rector W Kington, Wilts, and *d* 5 Jan 1932

3 Roderick Walter, CE; *b* 8 May 1852; *d* unm 31 Oct 1944

4 Malcolm Charles (Rev), Rector Ringwould Kent 1907–15; *b* 15 Aug 1853; *educ* Trin Coll Cambridge (MA); *m* 14 April 1885 Margaretha (*d* 17 Aug 1936), er dau of Rev Arthur Cazenove, Hon Canon Rochester, and *d* 23 May 1941, leaving issue:

(1) RORY MALCOLM STUART (Sir), **6th Bt**

(2) Keith Stuart, artist *b* 11 Nov 1887; *educ* Harrow and Trin Coll Cambridge; *d* unm 17 April 1977

(3) Ivan Cazenove Stuart; *b* 11 July 1891; *d* 28 Dec 1902

(1) Isla Margaretha Stuart *m* 29 Jan 1918 Rev Maurice Henry FitzGerald, MA, Canon Emeritus Bristol (*d* 17 Feb 1963), er son of Gerald Augustus Robert FitzGerald, KC, and *d* 13 Oct 1972

(2) Morah Susan Stuart; *m* 17 Dec 1914 Maj Ralph Beecroft Horsfield, BA, Essex Regt (*d* 31 Oct 1966) and *d* 13 Dec 1980, leaving:

1a Nigel James; *b* 19 Sept 1915; *d* 23 April 1987

2a *David Ralph, OBE (1962) [Maj-Gen David Horsfield OBE, Preybrook Farm, 3 Preywater Rd, Wookey, Wells, Somerset BA5 1LE]; ADC to HM THE QUEEN 1968–69, CEng FIEE, Brig Roy Signals (Col Comdt 1972–78), served WW II, Maj-Gen 1969; *b* 17 Dec 1916; *educ* Oundle, RMA Woolwich and Clare Coll Cambridge (MA); *m* 12 June 1948 *Sheelah Patricia Royal, dau of Thomas George Royal Eagan, of Rose Cottage, Tisbury, Wilts, and has issue:

1b *Crispin David Stuart; *b* 18 Sept 1952; *educ* Oundle

2b *Hugo Malcolm Beecroft; *b* 29 Aug 1955; *educ* Oundle

1b *Antonia Clare Margaretha; *b* 22 March 1954

2b *Claudia Ann Gisele; *b* 18 Nov 1957

3a Malcolm John Maurice; *b* 1 May 1920; *d* unm 15 Oct 1947

5 Gilbert Samuel, Maj 60th Roy Rifles, served Afghan War 1878–79, 1st Boer War 1881 and E Sudan 1884; *b* 10 April 1855; *d* unm 20 March 1935

6 Kenneth Schalch, JP Inverness-shire; Lt-Col 79th QO Cameron Highrs, served Egyptian and Sudan Wars 1882–85 (despatches twice, brevet, medal with five clasps, bronze star) and WW I (despatches); *b* 20 Feb 1857; *m* 6 Feb 1893 Florence Stewart Meetkerke (*d* 28 May 1953), yr dau of Rev Alexander Ewing, Vicar Walmer, Kent, and *dsp* 16 March 1940

7 Edward Neil, FSA; *b* 1 April 1861; *m* 31 July 1888 Charlotte Augusta, OBE (*d* 8 July 1949), er dau of Hon Augustus Anthony Frederick Irby (*see* BOSTON, B), and *d* 20 Jan 1951, having had issue:

(1) Edward Stuart Augustus, OBE (1950), FRES, Dept of Overseas Trade 1918–40, Dominions Office 1941–46, UK Trade Commr Ireland 1946–54, T/Capt 11th Bn KRRC, served WW I (wounded), Hon Citizen New York 1940; *b* 25 June 1889; *educ* Radley; *m* 9 Nov 1918 Helen Mary (*d* 23 July 1979), widow of John Stanley White and dau of George Alfred Meredith, of Britwell, Epsom, Surrey, and *d* 1972, leaving issue:

1a +Anthony Edward George [Anthony Baynes Esq, School Hill, Little Minster, Minster Lovell, Oxon], artist, Sub-Lt RNVR WW II; *b* 28 March 1921; *educ* Radley

(2) George Kenneth, King's Messenger, T/Lt 11th Bn KRRC; *b* 1 Feb 1891; *m* 6 June 1921 Lilias Mary Wilson (*d* 23 Dec 1938), only dau of Hon Lord Ashmore (a Ld of Session), of Ashmore, Perthshire, and *d* 10 Sept 1936

(1) Margaret Agnes; *m* 28 Jan 1908 Jere Osborne (*d* 1919), of Hawthornden, Clifton, Bristol, and *d* 25 April 1937

(2) Eleanor Mary; *d* 14 April 1851

The 5th Bt's cousin,

Sir Rory Malcolm Stuart Baynes, 6th Bt; Lt-Col Cameronians (Scottish Rifles) WW I 1914–15 (wounded), Palestine 1936 and WW II, CC 1946, CA 1958 Somerset; *b* 16 May 1886; *educ* Harrow; *m* 8 June 1925 Audrey (*d* 6 Jan 1947), only dau of Edward Giles, CIE, and *d* 29 April 1979, leaving issue:

1 Sir JOHN CHRISTOPHER MALCOLM BAYNES, **7th and present Bt**

BAZLEY

Arms: Per pale az. and sa. a bee volant or between three fleurs-de-lys arg. **Crest:** A cubit arm erect ppr. between two branches of oak in orle vert, charged with a bee as in the arms and holding a chapeau gu., doubled or. **Motto:** *Finem respice* ('Consider the end'). **Creation:** Bt. (UK) 30 Nov 1869.

SIR THOMAS JOHN SEBASTIAN BAZLEY, 4TH BT, of Hatherop, Co Gloucester [Sir Thomas Bazley Bt, Eastleach Downs Farm, Eastleach Martin, Cirencester, Glos GL7 3PX]; *b* 31 Aug 1948; *s* f 1997; *educ* St Christopher Sch and Magdalen Coll Oxford

Lineage: JOHN BAZLEY, of Warrington, Lancs; living 1750; had:

THOMAS BAZLEY; *b* 15 Jan 1773; merchant with mathematical and literary interests; *m* Anne, dau of C Hinton, of Horwich, nr Bolton-le-Moors, and had, with other issue:

Sir Thomas Bazley, 1st Bt (UK), so *cr* 30 Nov 1869, of Tolmers, Herts, JP and DL Glos and Lancs; *b* 27 May 1797; Pres Manchester Chamber Commerce 1845–1859, MP (Lib) Manchester 1857–80, Offr Legion Honour; *m* 2 June 1828 Mary Maria Sarah (*d* 22 Aug 1897), 2nd dau of Sebastian Nash, of Clayton, Lancs, and *d* 18 March 1885, leaving issue:

Sir Thomas Sebastian Bazley, 2nd Bt, of Hatherop, Glos; JP (Glos and Cheshire), DL (Glos), High Sheriff Glos 1874; *b* 30 April 1829; *educ* Trin Coll Cambridge (MA); *m* 1 Nov 1855 Elizabeth (*d* 1 May 1890), dau of Robert Gardner, of Chaseley, Manchester, and *d* 5 Jan 1919, having had issue:

1 Gardner Sebastian, of Hatherop Castle, Fairford, Glos; *b* 14 Oct 1863; MA Oxon, barrister Inner Temple, DL, JP and CC Glos, High Sheriff 1901, Lt 3rd Bn Yorks Regt and Capt 4th Bt Glos Regt; *m* 5 Jan 1903 Ruth Evelyn (*m* 2nd 2 Sept 1913 Cdr Francis Charles Cadogan, RN (*see* CADOGAN, E), and *d* 14 March 1962), er dau of Sir Edward Stafford Howard, KCB, of Thornby Castle (*see* NORFOLK, D), and *dvp* 22 June 1911, leaving issue:

(1) **Sir Thomas Stafford Bazley, 3rd Bt**; *b* 5 Oct 1907; *educ* Harrow and Magdalen Coll Oxford; fndr Marigold Health Foods, WW II with intell servs and Min Info; *m* 15 Oct 1945 *Carmen, only dau of Jacinto Tulla, of 11 Stanley Gdns, London W11, and *d* 14 April 1997, leaving:

1a Sir THOMAS JOHN SEBASTIAN BAZLEY, **4th and present Bt**

2a +ANTHONY MARTIN CHRISTOPHER; *b* 23 Feb 1958; heir presumptive; m 27 April 1996 *Claudia Patricia Montoya Cano, dau of Sr Ovidio Montoya, of Colombia, and has:

1b *Zoë Tulia; *b* 18 Nov 1997

3a +John Francis Alexander; *b* 23 Feb 1961

1a *Catherine Elisabet Annemarie; *b* 16 Aug 1950

2a *Virginia Isabella Marged; *b* 19 April 1953

(2) Anthony Gardner, CC Glos, 2nd Lt 5th Bn Glos Regt; *b* 4 June 1911; *m* 9 Feb 1934 *Anne (*m* 2nd 1 July 1944 2nd Baron Howard of Penrith (*qv*)), dau of John Beaumont Hotham (*see* HOTHAM, B), and *d* 23 May 1937, leaving:

1a Juliet Anne; *b* 7 July 1935; *d* 2 Jan 1943

2a *Susan Antonia [Mrs Susan Vicary, Dean Farm, Coln St Aldwyn, Cirencester, Glos GL7 5AX]; *b* 5 May 1937; *m* 1st 14 June 1958 (*divorce* 1970) Peter Humphrey Alexander Van Oss, and has issue:

1b *Mark Peter Anthony; *b* 10 April 1959; *m* 1985 *Caroline Elizabeth, dau of Ian Maxwell Scoggins, of High Thicket, Dockenfield, nr Farnham, Surrey, and has issue:

1c *Emily Atalanta; *b* 1988

2c *Francesca Camilla; *b* 1989

3c *Octavia Rose; *b* 1994

2b *Anthony Tom Francis; *b* 8 March 1961

1b *Juliet Anne Favell; *b* 8 March 1961; *m* 1991 *Robert Gwyn Palmer and has:

1c *Xanthe Hope; *b* 11 Feb 1995

2c *Syrie Favell; *b* 20 May 1997

2b *Katharine Susanna; *b* 8 June 1964

2a (cont.) Mrs Susan Van Oss *m* 2nd 11 Dec 1970 (*divorce* 1984) William J Vicary, and has further issue:

3b *William Sebastian; *b* 1973

(1) Elisabeth Rachel; *b* 6 Jan 1904; *m* 16 Oct 1930 Christopher Evelyn Blunt, OBE, 2nd son of Rev Arthur Stanley Vaughan Blunt, OBE, MA, and had issue:

1a *Simon Wilfrid; *b* 20 Sept 1933; *educ* Michael Hall and Trin Coll Cambridge; *m* 2 Sept 1964 *Julia Miranda, dau of Colin Alfred Lampson, and has issue:

1b *Christopher Mark; *b* 13 Oct 1967

1b *Amanda Claire; *b* 17 June 1966

2a *Anne Caroline; *b* 2 Dec 1931; *m* 29 Aug 1964 *Prof Karl Frederick Morrison, son of Prof Karl Morrison, of U of Mississippi, and has issue:

1b *Andrew David; *b* 9 July 1965

1b *Sarah Christina; *b* 3 Nov 1966

3a *Judith Elisabeth; *b* 18 Nov 1937; *m* 12 May 1962 *Julian Edwin Hamby Mustoe, and has issue:

1b *James William *b* 13 Aug 1963

1b *Sophia Louise; *b* 3 Oct 1967

(2) Francis Catharine Ruth; *b* 16 Dec 1905; *m* 8 Jan 1932 Richard Arthur Warren Hughes, OBE, of Mor Edrin, Talsarnau, Merionethshire, and had issue (*see* HUGHES, Bt)

(3) *Rachel Constance; *b* 2 May 1909; *m* 25 Jan 1939 *(Edward John) Ronald Bennett, son of Rev Edward Herbert Bennett, of Rendcomb, Glos, and has issue:

1a *John Sebastian [John Bennett Esq, Colbourne House, Ufton, Warwicks CV33 9PE]; *b* 4 Jan 1942; *educ* Marlborough and Trin Coll Oxford; *m* 1971 *Sara Hermione, only dau of Maj Inglis Jones, of Saddlewood, Camberley, Surrey, and has issue:

1b *William James Alexander; *b* 1978

2b *Alexander Thomas Edward; *b* 1985

1b *Jemima Charlotte; *b* 1974

2b *Camilla Sophie; *b* 1976

2a *Henry Christopher [Henry Bennett Esq, The Shrubbery, Linton, Cambs CB1 6SY]; *b* 26 June 1946; *educ* Marlborough and Warwick U; *m* 1991 *Sarah Margaret Diana, dau of John Louis Arnott Bowles (*see* 1970 edn BARWICK, Bt), and has issue:

1b *Jonathan Ronald Sebastian; *b* 1991

3a *Charles Michael; *b* 18 Aug 1948; *educ* Marborough; *m* 1975 *Barbara Joyce, dau of George Hammond, of NY, USA, and has issue:

1b *George Christopher; *b* 1976

2b *Henry Arthur; *b* 1985

1b *Emma Reese; *b* 1983

4a *Edward Alexander (twin); *b* 18 Aug 1948; *educ* Marlborough; *m* 1993 *Tarja Hannele, dau of Kapteeni Evp Tenho Taavetti Reponen, of Kaijala, Finland

1a *Victoria; *b* 2 March 1940; *m* 10 Oct 1964 *Henry Alexander Fowell Buxton, only son of Maj John Fowell Buxton, TD (*see* BUXTON, Bt), and has issue

1 Elizabeth Mary; *m* 1883 Gen Sir Edward Pemberton Leach, VC, KCB, KCVO, RE (*d* 26 April 1913), 2nd son of Lt-Col Sir George Archibald Leach, KCB, and *d* 9 Jan 1940, leaving issue

2 Annie Caroline; *m* 16 Feb 1887 Frederic Pocock Bulley, JP (*d* 3 Aug 1940), of Lullingworth, Painswick, Glos, and *d* 25 June 1944, leaving issue

3 Francis Annette Ellen; *m* 5 Jan 1892 Richard Assheton, DSc, FRS (*d* 23 Oct 1915), 2nd son of Ralph Assheton, of Downham Hall, Lancs and *d* 19 June 1945, leaving issue (*see* CLITHEROE, B)

4 Jessie Marion Atkinson; *m* 20 April 1911 Rev Frederick Douglas Bateman, MA (*d* 20 May 1933), and *d* 8 June 1947

5 Lucy Maud Mary; *m* 27 July 1898 Robert Dimsdale, of Ravenshill, Eastleach, Lechlade (*d* 23 Sept 1950), 3rd son of Baron Dimsdale (*see* 1956 edn Foreign Titles), and *d* 24 Feb 1960, leaving issue

BEARSTED

Arms: Gu., on a chevron between two lion's heads erased in chief and in base a naval crown or, a human heart gu. **Crest:** A dexter arm embowed ppr., grasping a battleaxe arg., the head charged with two triangles interlaced sa. **Supporters:** Dexter, a horse arg.; sinister, a dragon gu., each charged on the shoulder with a human heart or. **Motto:** *Facta non verba* ('Deeds, not words'). **Creation:** Bt (UK) 26 Aug 1903, B. (UK) 15 June 1921, V. (UK) 16 June 1925.

THE 5TH VISCOUNT BEARSTED, of Maidstone, Co Kent, **Baron Bearsted,** of Maidstone, Co Kent, and a **Baronet** (Sir Nicholas Alan Samuel, Bt) [The Rt Hon The Viscount Bearsted, 9 Acacia Rd, London NW8 6AB]; *b* 22 Jan 1950; *s* f 1996; *educ* Eton and New Coll Oxford; *m* 30 Jan 1975 *Caroline Jane, yr dau of Dr David Sacks, MRCS, LRCP, of 38 Elgin Ave, London W9, and has issue:

1 +HARRY RICHARD; *b* 23 May 1988

1 *Eugenie Sharon; *b* 17 Jan 1977

2 *Natalie Naomi; *b* 18 May 1979

3 *Zoe Elizabeth; *b* 27 July 1982

4 *Juliet Samantha; *b* 1986

Lineage: SAMUEL BEN AMSCHEL, of Amersfoort, Holland, settled London *c* 1750; f of:

MARCUS SAMUEL; f of:

SAMUEL SAMUEL, of London; *b* 1762; merchant; *m* Leah Keyser (*d* 24 Nov 1860) and *d* 30 Dec 1855, leaving:

MARCUS SAMUEL, of London; *b* 4 April 1799; merchant, opened 1833 a curio shop near the Tower of London dealing in sea shells among other objects, later expanding under his son Marcus Jr to encompass kerosene oil imports and eventually a fleet of tankers to transport the oil, hence the name Shell Transport and Trading; *m* Abigail (*d* 11 Dec 1874), dau of Abraham Moss, of London, and *d* 24 Nov 1872.

His 2nd s,

Sir Marcus Samuel, 1st Bt, so *cr* 20 Aug 1903, as also 16 June 1925 **1st Viscount Bearsted,** of Maidstone, Kent, and earlier 15 June 1921 BARON BEARSTED, of Maidstone, Kent (all UK), JP (Kent), of Mote Pk, Maidstone, Kent; *b* 5 Nov 1853; Ld of the Manor of Mote, Hon LLD Sheffield and Cambridge, Sr Alderman and Lt City of London (Sheriff 1894–95), Ld Mayor London 1902–03, Grand Offr Legion of Honour, Cdr Orders of Leopold of Belgium and Rising Sun of Japan; ktd 1898 for public servs rendered in connection with the salvage of HMS *Victorious*; *m* 19 Jan 1881 Fanny Elizabeth (*d* 16 Jan 1927), only dau of Benjamin Benjamin, and *d* 17 Jan 1927, leaving:

1 WALTER HORACE, **2nd Viscount**

2 Gerald George; *b* 6 May 1886; *educ* Eton; Lt Roy W Kent Regt, *ka* 7 June 1917

1 Nellie; *b* 2 July 1883; *m* 1st 7 April 1903 Maj Walter Henry Levy, DSO (*d* 9 June 1923), late RASC, est s of Henry Levy, of 11 Hyde Pk Place, London W; *m* 2nd 23 May 1930 Basil Ionides (*d* 23 Sept 1950), yst s of Luke Ionides, and *d* 14 Nov 1962, leaving issue

2 Ida Marie; *b* 22 April 1890; *m* 27 April 1911 Robert Montefiore Sebag-Montefiore, LCC, Capt E Kent Yeo, BA Balliol Coll Oxford, barrister (*d* 19 Nov 1915 of wounds recd in action), est s of Arthur Sebag-Montlefiore, of E Cliff Lodge, Ramsgate, and *d* 21 April 1940, having had issue

The 1st VISCOUNT's s,

WALTER HORACE SAMUEL, **2nd Viscount Bearsted,** MC; *b* 13 March 1882; *educ* Eton and New Coll Oxford; Capt late Queen's Own W Kent Yeo, Hon A/Cdre Auxiliary Air Force 1930–37, Lt City of London, Tstee Nat Gallery 1936–43 and Tate Gallery 1938–42, served WW I (despatches) and WW II 1939–43 as Col Intell Corps; *m* 23 July 1908 Dorothea Montefiore (*d* 19 Dec 1949), er dau of E Montefiore Nicholls, of 11 Queen's Gate, London SW, and *d* 1948, having had:

1 MARCUS RICHARD SAMUEL, **3rd Viscount Bearsted,** TD (1945), DL (Warwicks 1950); *b* 1 June 1909; *educ* Eton and New Coll Oxford; Maj Warwicks Yeo WW II 1939–44 (wounded), dir: Hill Samuel Gp, The Investment Tst Ltd (1928), Alliance Assur, Lloyds Bank, Sun Alliance and London Insur, Samuel Properties, Tanker Finance, tstee and chm Whitechapel Art Gallery, Jt MFH Warwicks 1935–56 (chm 1960–86); *m* 1st 15 Jan 1947 (*divorce* 1966) Elizabeth

Heather, er dau of Geoffrey Frimston-Williams, of 72 Cadogan Sq, London SW1, and left issue:

(1) *Felicity Ann [The Hon Mrs Waley-Cohen, 18 Gilston Rd, London SW10]; *b* 3 April 1948; *m* 9 Dec 1975 *Robert Bernard Waley-Cohen, yr s of Sir Bernard Nathaniel Waley-Cohen, 1st Bt (*qv*), and has issue

(2) Camilla Elizabeth; *b* 27 Oct 1949; *d* 29 Dec 1962

1 (cont.) The **3rd Viscount** *m* 2nd 24 Jan 1968 Jean Agnew (*d* 31 Oct 1978), dau of R A Wallace, of 13 Clarendon Crescent, Edinburgh, and formerly w of Maj John Somerville, and *d* 1986

2 PETER MONTEFIORE SAMUEL, **4th Viscount Bearsted**, MC (1943), TD (1951); *b* 9 Dec 1911; *educ* Eton and New Coll Oxford; Maj Warwicks Yeo TA WW II (despatches), dep chm Hill Samuel Gp 1965–82 (dir 1965–87), dir: M Samuel & Co 1935 (dep chm 1948), Shell Tport & Trading 1938–82, Samuel Properties 1961–68, Mayborn Gp plc 1946–96, pres Norwood Home for Jewish Children 1962–79; *m* 1st 11 Oct 1939 (*divorce* 1942) Dierdre du Barry, dau of Thomas Franklin Marshall du Lavey, of Tiffenden Manor, High Halden, Kent; *m* 2nd 20 March 1946 Hon Elizabeth Adelaide (*d* 14 July 1983), dau of Baron Cohen (LP, *see* 1970 edn) and widow of Capt Arthur John Pearce-Serocold, Welsh Gds; *m* 3rd 1984 *Nina Alice Hilary [The Rt Hon Nina Viscountess Bearsted, 9 Campden Hill Court, London W8 7HX], widow of (Car)Michael Charles Peter Pocock, CBE, sometime chm Shell, and *d* 9 June 1996, leaving issue by his 2nd w:

(1) NICHOLAS ALAN SAMUEL, **5th and present Viscount Bearsted**

(2) +Michael John [The Hon Michael Samuel, 24 Hyde Pk Gate, London SW7]; *b* 2 Nov 1952; *educ* Eton; *m* 6 March 1980 *Julia Aline, yr dau of James Edward Alexander Rundell Guinness (*see* GUINNESS, Bt), and has:

1a +Benjamin Peter Marcus; *b* 1989

1a *Natasha Vivienne; *b* 25 June 1981

2a *Emily Elizabeth; *b* 11 July 1983

3a *Sophie Alexandra; *b* 1986

(1) *Sarah Virginia [The Hon Mrs Mullins, Moorhill House, Brannockstown, Naas, Co Kildare, Ireland]; *b* 26 June 1947; *m* 1st 22 May 1969 (*divorce* 1978) Duncan John Lloyd Fitzwilliams, yr s of Charles Collinsplatt Lloyd Fitzwilliams, TD, DL, JP, of Cilgwyn, Cardiganshire; *m* 2nd 14 July 1980 *Brian Mullins, 2nd s of Col William Mullins

3 +Anthony Gerald [The Hon Anthony Samuel, 29 St Leonard's Terr, London SW3 4QG; Woodbury House, Longparish, Hants SP11 6PB], *b* 18 Feb 1917; *educ* Eton and New Coll Oxford, served WW II as Capt Intelligence Corps, *m* 1st 20 Nov 1946 (*divorce* 1961) Mary Eve, only dau of John Comyn Higgins, CIE, ICS, of Alford, Lincs, and has issue:

(1) *Jacqueline Eve [Mrs Jack O'Halloran, Rue a l'Eau 46, 1380 Marasnsart, Belgium]; *b* 7 Aug 1948; *m* 1st 1978 (*divorce* 19–) Robert Rusk; *m* 2nd 1988 *Jack O'Halloran, of California, and has by him:

1a *Slaine Aoife, *b* 1988

(2) *Daphne Lavina [Mrs Daphne Petro, 154 Ave de la Concorde, 06190 Roquebrune, Cap Martin, France]; *b* 13 March 1951, *m* 1980 (*divorce* 1985) Leo Petro and has issue:

1a *Marco Antonio Cerreto; *b* 1985

3 (cont.) The Hon Anthony Samuel *m* 2nd 6 July 1962 (*divorce* 1966) Jennifer, dau of Maj Kenneth Alfred Bridge Puckle, RM, of Farnham; *m* 3rd 1 Aug 1966 *Jean Mercy, dau of M C Haystead

1 Daphne Isobel, *b* 21 April 1913; *d* 14 Feb 1914

BEATTY

Arms: Az., a beehive beset with nine bees volant or, a chief arg., charged with the cross of St George gu. **Crest:** A demi-lion gu., holding in the dexter paw a crescent or. **Supporters:** Dexter, a sailor of the Navy; sinister, a soldier of the Royal Marines, both ppr. **Motto:** *Non vi sed arte* ('Not by force but by art'). **Creation:** E., V. and B. (UK) 27 Sept 1919.

THE 3RD EARL BEATTY, Viscount Borodale, of Wexford, Co Wexford, and **Baron Beatty,** of the North Sea and of Brooksby, Co Leicester (David Beatty) [The Rt Hon The Earl Beatty, House of Lords, London SW1A 0PW]; *b* 21 Nov 1946; *s f* 1972; *educ* Eton; *m* 1st 26 June 1971 (*divorce* 1982) Ann, yr dau of A Please, of Wokingham, Berks; *m* 2nd 1984 *Anoma Corinne, dau of Ray Wijewardene, of Colombo, Sri Lanka, and has by his 1st w:

1 +SEAN DAVID, *Viscount Borodale*; *b* 12 June 1973

2 +Peter Wystan; *b* 1975

Lineage: DAVID BEATTY, of Dublin, was f of:

EDWARD BEATTY, of Dublin, *m* 7 July 1740 Mary Brock, of Glasnevin, and *d* 1794, leaving:

DAVID BEATTY, of Dublin, *m* 1782 Olivia Maria Bell and *d* 1794, leaving:

Capt DAVID BEATTY, of Borodale, Co Wexford, *b* 1787, *m* 1813 Elizabeth, er dau of John Martin, of Cork, Sheriff Cork 1780, and *d* 1855, leaving issue:

DAVID BEATTY, of Borodale, JP; *b* 1815; *m* 1st 1838 Mary Elizabeth, dau of Robert Longfield, of Cork; *m* 2nd 1851 Margaret Charlotte, 4th dau of Harry Alcock, of Wilton castle, Co Wexford, and *d* 5 April 1881, leaving by his 1st w:

DAVID LONGFIELD BEATTY, of Borodale, Capt 4th Hus, *b* 28 Apr 1841, *m* 1st Katherine Edith (*d* 1896), dau of Nicholas Sadleir, of Dunboyne Castle, Co Meath, by Mary Anne Frances, dau of Richard Moore, of Summerhill, Clonmel, Co Tipperary, and had issue:

1 Charles Harold Longfield, DSO (1900), Capt and hon Maj 6th Bn Roy Warwicks Regt, *b* 16 Jan 1870, *m* 31 Jan 1905 Lucy Alice (*d* 1 May 1968), widow of Major John S Langlands, and *d* 17 May 1917, leaving issue:

(1) Charles

2 DAVID, **1st Earl**

3 William Vandeleur, Maj 19th QO Hus, *m* 21 Jan 1925 (*divorce* 1941) Hon Victoria Alexandrina Sibell, 3rd dau of 4th Baron Southampton (*qv*), and *d* 23 Jan 1953

4 Richard George, Capt 36th (Jacob's) Horse, attached 1st DYO Lancers IA, served S Africa 1900–02 with 4th Bn and 1st Mtd Inf Bn, Roy Warwickshire Regt Orange River Colony, Transvaal and Cape Colony (two medals, four clasps), Extra ADC to Gen Aldersen 1901, WW I NW Frontier, Shabkardar 1915 (1914 star, two medals), Supt Remount Dept Lahore and Baluchistan 1911–14, *b* 2 Nov 1881, *m* 21 Oct 1907 Florence Mary (*d* 21 April 1938), yr dau of John Bywater, of London, and *d* 9 June 1915, leaving:

(1) John Lionel, served WW II with 14th/20th King's Hus, *b* 8 Jun 1910, *educ* Harrow, *m* 22 July 1954 Stella, yst dau of George Owen, of Pembury, Kent, and had issue:

1a *Joanna Elisabeth, *b* 1 Jan 1956

2a *Kathleen Eva Margaret Le Hunte, *b* 3 Sept 1957

3a *Jill Lucinda, *b* 20 Dec 1958

(2) William Richard Le Hunte, Cdr RN, Naval Ordnance Inspection Dept, served WW II, *b* 5 Dec 1913, *m* 22 July 1939 Eva (Eve) Miriam Lancaster, yst dau of Henry William Putley, of London and Hove, and *d* 20 Jan 1975, leaving issue:

1a *Angela Miriam; *b* 3 Jan 1942

(3) David Lion; *b* 22 Feb, *d* 18 Dec 1915

(1) Helen Ethel Kathleen; *b* 7 Dec 1908; *d* 27 Feb 1951

1 Kathleen Roma, *m* 5 Oct 1899 Lt-Col Miles Rafe Ferguson Courage, DSO, late RA, s of Edward Courage, of Shenfield, Essex, and *d* 18 Dec 1949, leaving issue. He *d* 4 April 1961

Capt DAVID LONGFIELD BEATTY *m* 2nd 9 Jan 1899 Anita Georgina Edith (*m* 2nd — Letts, of Enniscorthy, Co Wexford), yr dau of Capt Henry Studdy, RN, and *d* 4 April 1904, having by her had further issue:

5 Henry Longfield, F/Lt RAF, *d* 15 Feb 1935 as the result of a flying boat disaster

Capt D L BEATTY's 2nd s,

DAVID BEATTY, **1st Earl Beatty**, so *cr* 27 Sept 1919, as also BARON BEATTY, of the North Sea and of Brooksby, Co Leicester, and VISCOUNT BORODALE, of Wexford, Co Wexford (all UK), when he recd thanks of Parl and a grant of £100,000 for his servs in WW I, GCB (1916, KCB 1914, CB 1911), OM (1917), GCVO (1917, KCVO 1916, MVO 1905), DSO (1896), PC (1927), Adml of the Fleet, Rector Edinburgh U, Hon LLD Aberdeen, Hon DCL Oxford, V-Pres Roy Empire Soc, *educ* RN Acad Gosport, entered RN 1884, Lt 1892, Cdr 1898, Capt 1900, R-Adml 1910, V-Adml 1915, Adml and Adml of the Fleet 1919, served Dongola Expdn 1896 (despatches), Nile Expdn 1897–98, present Battles of Atbara and Khartoum (despatches, 4th Cl Medjidie), China 1900 (wounded, despatches, medal and clasp), and WW I, ADC to HM EDWARD VII 1908–10, Naval Sec 1st Ld Admlty 1912, cmded 1st Battle Cruiser Sqdn 1913–16, C-in-C Grand Fleet 1916–18, 1st Sea Lord 1919–27, Br Delegate Washington Conference 1921, Grand Offr Legion of Honour, Order St George of Russia 4th Cl; *b* 17 Jan 1871, *m* 22 May 1901 Ethel (*d* 17 July 1932), only dau of Marshall Field, of Chicago, USA, and *d* 11 March 1936, having had:

1 DAVID FIELD, **2nd Earl**

2 Peter Randolph Louis, served WW II in RNVR, *b* 2 Apr 1910, *educ* Eton, *d* unm 26 Oct 1949

The 1st EARL's er s,

DAVID FIELD BEATTY, **2nd Earl Beatty**, DSC (1942), Cdr RN (ret), *educ* RNCs Osborne and Dartmouth, served WW II 1939–45; Dep Dir Combined Ops Dept Admiralty 1944–45; PPS to Parly Sec Admlty, MP Peckham 1931–36, Jt Under Sec Air May-July 1945, Lt Leics Yeo (TA) 1933, mem LCC 1937, chm: Navy League 1937 (pres 1939–44), Br Empire and Cwlth Games Cncl England 1954, Home Oil Co of Canada 1966–72, *b* 22 Feb 1905; *m* 1st 21 April 1937 (*divorce* 1945) Dorothy (*d* 11 May 1966), formerly w of Harry Ester Reynolds Hall and yr dau of Thomas Sarsfield Kent Power, of Virginia, USA; *m* 2nd 7 Feb 1946 (*divorce* 1950) Dorothy Rita, sometime ferry pilot ATA, widow of Sgt Richard Edward Bragg, RAF, and dau of Michael James Furey, of New Orleans, and had issue:

1 DAVID BEATTY, **3rd and present Earl Beatty**

The **2nd Earl** *m* 3rd 5 July 1951 (*divorce* 1958) Adele (*m* 3rd 1960 Stanley Donen, the film dir, and *d* 1990), formerly w of William O'Connor, of Los Angeles, and dau of M Dillingham, of Oklahoma City, and by her had:

1 *Diana Adrienne [The Rt Hon The Viscountess Gage, The Cottage, Charwelton, Daventry, Northants], *b* 13 Sep 1952; *m* 1974 *8th Viscount Gage (*qv*) and has issue

The **2nd Earl** *m* 4th 3 Dec 1959 *Diana, dau of John Blundell, of Hayling Island, Hants, and adopted dau of Capt Duncan Kirk (*m* 2nd 1973 John Grenfell Nutting, of Chicheley Hall, Newport Pagnell, Bucks, er s of Rt Hon Sir (Harold) Anthony Nutting, 3rd Bt, *qv*), and *d* 10 June 1972, having by her had:

2 +Nicholas Duncan, *b* 1 April 1961; *educ* Eton and Exeter U (BA); *m* 1990 *Laura Mary Catherine, dau of Charles William Lyle Keen (*see* HOWE, E), and has issue:

(1) *David Brin Charles; *b* 1992

2 *Miranda Katherine; *b* 18 Feb 1963; *m* 1989 *(Iain) Alan Stewart, yst s of Sir Dugald Leslie Lorn Stewart, of Appin, KCVO, CMG, 16th Chief of Clan Stewart of Appin, and has issue:

(1) *Alexandra Katherine; *b* 1991

(1) *Augusta Lileas; *b* 1994

BEAUFORT

Arms: Quarterly, 1st and 4th, azure, three fleurs-de-lys or (for France); 2nd and 3rd, gules three lions passant-guardant in pale or (for England), all within a bordure company argent and azure. **Crest:** A portcullis or, nailed azure, with chains pendant thereto gold. **Supporters:** Dexter, a panther argent, flames issuant from the mouth and ears proper, gorged with a plain collar and chained or, and semée of torteaux, hurts and pommes alternately; sinister, a wyvern, wings addorsed vert, holding in the mouth a sinister hand couped at the wrist gules. **Motto:** *Mutare vel timere sperno* ('I scorn to change or fear'). **Creations:** D. (E) 2 Dec 1682, M. (E) 2 March 1642/3, E. (E) 1 Feb 1514.

THE 11TH DUKE OF BEAUFORT, Marquess of Worcester and **Earl of Worcester** (David Robert Somerset) [His Grace The Duke of Beaufort, Badminton House, Glos GL9 1DB; 90 Eaton Terrace, London SW1]; *b* 23 Feb 1928; *s* kinsman 1984; *educ* Eton; Hereditary Keeper Raglan Castle, late Lt Coldstream Gds, Pres Br Horse Soc 1988–90, chm Marlborough Fine Art Ltd; *m* 5 July 1950 Lady Caroline Jane Thynne (*d* 22 April 1995), only dau of 6th Marquess of Bath (*qv*), and has issue:

1 +HENRY ('Bunter') JOHN FITZROY, *Marquess of Worcester* [Marquess of Worcester, The Cottage, Badminton, S Glos]; *b* 22 May 1952; *educ* Eton; *m* 1987 *Tracy Louise, TV actress, yr dau of Hon Peter Alistair Ward (*see* DUDLEY, E), and has:

(1) +Robert (Bobby), *Earl of Glamorgan*; *b* 20 Jan 1989

(2) +Alexander; *b* 3 Sept 1995

(1) *Isabella Elsa; *b* 1991

2 +Edward Alexander; *b* 1 May 1958; *educ* Millfield; *m* 1982 *Hon (Georgina) Caroline Davidson, 2nd dau of 2nd Viscount Davidson (*qv*) and has issue:

(1) *Francesca; *b* 1984

(2) *A dau; *b* 1992

3 +John Robert; *b* 5 Nov 1964; *educ* King's Sch Bruton; *m* 1990 (*divorce* 1996) as her 2nd husb, Lady Cosima ('Cozzy') Maria Gabriella, nominally yr dau of 9th Marquess of Londonderry (*qv*) and formerly w of Cosmo Fry, and has:

(1) +Lyle David; *b* 1991

(1) *Romy Caroline; *b* 1993

1 *Anne Mary, *b* 21 Jan 1955; *educ* King's Coll London (BA 1976); writer; *m* 1988 *Matthew Xavier Maillard Carr, s of Sir Raymond Carr (*see* STRICKLAND-CONSTABLE, Bt)

Earldom of Worcester: In 1138 STEPHEN conferred the Earldom of Worcester on Waleran, son of Robert de Beaumont Earl of Leicester by a granddaughter of HENRY I of France. This was among other things an attempt to secure Waleran's support in his struggle against MATILDA or MAUD following the death of HENRY I of England, one of whose leading military men Waleran had been. Under STEPHEN's successor HENRY II the Earldom seems not to have been recognised.

In 1397 a younger brother of the Earl of Northumberland was created Earl of Worcester but rebelled against HENRY IV in 1403, so that his honours were forfeited (*see* NORTHUMBERLAND, D). Nearly 20 years later Richard de Beauchamp, Lord Bergavenny or Beauchamp de Bergavenny (*see* ABERGAVENNY, M), was created Earl of Worcester but on his death without surviving male issue the Earldom seems to have reverted to the Crown. Later in the 15th century an Earldom of this name was conferred on John Tiptoft, 2nd Lord (Baron) Tiptoft. Tiptoft was Treasurer and Constable of England and had a nasty reputation for enforcing EDWARD IV's will during the Wars of the Roses, when he used to impale his victims on stakes. During HENRY VI's temporary restoration he was himself executed. His son and heir died fifteen years later, when the Earldom became extinct.

Lineage: EDWARD III'S 4th s:

JOHN OF GAUNT; had issue (originally illegitimate but legitimised by papal decree 1396 and confirmed by letters patent 20 RICHARD II) by Catherine Swynford:

Sir JOHN BEAUFORT (Beaufort being the name of a castle in Champagne belonging to his f), KG (*c* 1397); *b c* 1371; *cr*: 10 Feb 1396/7 EARL OF SOMERSET and 29 Sept 1397 MARQUESS OF DORSET and MARQUESS OF SOMERSET (all E; he was degraded from both marquessates 1399 following accession of HENRY IV), Constable of England 1404; *m* by 28 Sept 1397 Lady Margaret de Holand, dau of Thomas, Earl of Kent, by Alice, dau of Richard FitzAlan, Earl of Arundel (*see* NORFOLK, D), and *d* 16 March 1409/10, leaving, with other issue:

1 HENRY BEAUFORT, 2nd EARL OF SOMERSET; *bapt* 26 Nov 1401; *d* unm 1418

2 JOHN BEAUFORT, 3rd EARL OF SOMERSET, KG (c 1440); *b c* April 1404; *cr* 28 Aug 1443 EARL OF KENDAL and DUKE OF SOMERSET (both E); *m c* 1442 Margaret, dau of John Beauchamp, of Bletso, by Edith, dau of Sir John Stourton (*see* MOWBRAY, SEGRAVE and STOURTON, B), and widow of Sir Oliver St John (*see* SAINT JOHN OF BLETSO, B), and *dspm* 27 May 1444, when the Earldom of Kendal and Dukedom of Somerset expired, leaving:

(1) Margaret; *b* 31 May 1443; *m* 1st between 28 Jan and 7 Feb 1449/50 (*divorce* by 24 March 1452/3), as his 1st w, John de la Pole, 2nd Duke of Suffolk of the 1448 *cr*; *m* 2nd 1455 Edmund Tudor, 1st Earl of Richmond of the 1452 *cr* (*d* 3 Nov 1456), by whom she was mother of HENRY VII; *m* 3rd by 1464 Sir Henry Stafford, 2nd s of 1st Duke of Buckingham of the 1444 *cr* (*see* STAFFORD, B); *m* 4th by Oct 1473 1st Earl of Derby (*qv*) and *d* 29 July 1504

3 EDMUND, 4th EARL

1 Joan; *m* as her 1st husb Feb 1423/4 JAMES I of Scotland and with him was ancestor of the STUART dynasty who reigned over both England and Scotland

The 3rd EARL OF SOMERSET's yr bro,

Sir EDMUND BEAUFORT, 4th EARL OF SOMERSET and 1st DUKE OF SOMERSET, as which *cr*:31 March 1448, as also earlier 28 Aug 1442 EARL OF DORSET and 24 June 1443 MARQUESS OF DORSET (all E), KG (1436); *b c* 1406; Constable of England 1450; *m* by 1436 Lady Eleanor Beauchamp, dau of Richard Earl of Warwick (*see* WARWICK, BROOKE and, E) and widow of 8th Lord (Baron) De Ros (*qv*)of Helmsley, and was *k* fighting on the Lancastrian side at the Yorkist victory of St Albans 22 May 1455, leaving, with at least two daus (Eleanor, *m* 1st 5th Earl of Ormonde (*see* 1970 edn) and 2nd SirRobert Spencer and had issue (*see* NORTHUMBERLAND, D); Margaret, *m* 1st Humphrey, Earl of Stafford, s of 1st Duke of Buckingham of the 1444 *cr* (*see* STAFFORD, B) and had issue; *m* 2nd Sir Richard Darell)

HENRY BEAUFORT, 2nd DUKE OF SOMERSET; *b c* April 1436; as a Lancastrian was attainted 1461 during EDWARD IV's ascendancy and all his titles forfeited (later pardoned and had them restored March 1462/3, the pardon and restoration being in their turn revoked Jan 1464/5; this revocation too was declared null after his death by HENRY VII 1485); beheaded following his defeat by the Yorkists at Hexham 1464, leaving illegitimate issue by Joan Hill:

CHARLES SOMERSET, **1st Earl of Worcester** (E), so *cr* 1 Feb 1513/4, KG (1498), PC (1498); *b c* 1460; ktd 1485, Capt Yeomen of the Gd by 1 March 1485/6, Constable Hemsley Castle, Yorks, 14 May 1487, Capt and Adml of the Fleet 1488, took part in Siege of Boulogne Oct 1490, *cr* 17 July 1497 Kt Banneret at Battle of Blackheath when HENRY VII defeated an attack on London by Cornish rebels, V-Chamberlain 1498, Jt Amb to HOLY ROMAN EMPEROR MAXIMILIAN I 28 Sept 1501–July 1502, Steward Ewyas Lacy and Monmouth 1503, Constable Pains Castle, Radnorshire, and Montgomery Castle 1504, Amb to France June-Aug 1505, Ld Chamberlain 1508 and 1509 (1 Feb 1513/4 for life) and in this capacity as Ld Chamberlain was largely in charge of the organisation of the Field of Cloth of Gold 1520, Constable: Ruthin Castle, Monmouth Castle and the Three Castles 21 May 1509, Cardiff Castle 22 Aug 1509, Abergavenny Castle 25 Sept 1510 (all for life), Sheriff Glam 22 Aug 1509 (for life), called to Parl 1509 by writs apparently addressed to him as LORD HERBERT in right of his w (though he may also thereby have been designated LORD (Baron) SOMERSET), Jt Steward and Constable Usk Castle and Dynas Castle 20 Sept 1514; *m* 1st 2 June 1492 Elizabeth Herbert, according to later doctrine rightful Baroness Herbert of the 1461 *cr* (*d* between 29 Jan 1508/9 and 21 March 1512/3), only dau and heiress of 2nd Earl of Huntingdon of the 1472 *cr* by his w Mary, sis of ELIZABETH, EDWARD IV's QUEEN; *m* 2nd Elizabeth West, dau of 8th Lord (Baron) de la Warr (*see* DE LA WARR, E), by whom he had several children (*see* GREY, B); *m* 3rd Eleanor Sutton or Dudley (*m* 2nd as his 2nd w Leonard Grey, afterwards Viscount Grane (beheaded 28 July 1541), dau of 2nd Lord (Baron) Dudley (*see* DUDLEY, B), and *d* 15 April 1526, leaving issue by his 1st w:

HENRY SOMERSET, probably *s* his mother on her death as 4th LORD (Baron) HERBERT and his f on the latter's death as **2nd Earl of Worcester**, Jt Constable Ruthin Castle, Cardiff Castle, Pains Castle and Montgomery Castle, Jt Sheriff Glam, Jt Ch Steward Abergavenny and Jt Steward Ewyas Lacy 21 June 1510, Jt Steward Monmouth and Jt Constable Monmouth Castle and the Three Castles 5 July 1510, Jt Steward and Constable Usk Castle 6 May 1514 and Dynas Castle 20 Sept 1514, Steward and Constable Brecknock Castle 26 May 1523, ktd 1523, Jt Coroner Usk and Constable Caerleon Castle 30 March 1525; *m* 1st (papal dispensation 15 June 1514) his cousin Margaret Courtenay (*dsp* before 15 April 1526), dau of 9th Earl of Devon (*qv*) by his w Katherine, yst dau of EDWARD IV; *m* 2nd *c* 1527 Elizabeth (*d* between 20 April and 23 Oct 1565), dau of Sir Anthony Browne, Standard-Bearer to HENRY VII, by his w Lucy Nevill(e), dau of 1st Marquess of Montagu of the 1461 *cr* (*see* ABERGAVENNY, M), and *d* 26 Nov 1549, leaving by his 2nd w, with a yst dau (Jane, *m* Sir Edward Ma(u)nsel(l); *see* MANSEL, Bt):

WILLIAM SOMERSET, **3rd Earl of Worcester**, KG (1570), KB (1546/7); *b c* 1527; Gent Privy Chamber 1546, memb Cncl in Marches of Wales Nov 1553, took part in the defence of London against Sir Thomas Wyatt Feb 1553/4, Dep Earl Marshal of England 2 April 1571, Lt Order of the Garter 22 April 1579; *m* 1st by 29 Jan 1549/50 Christian North, dau of 1st Lord North (*see* GUILFORD, E); *m* 2nd Theophila (*m* 2nd William Paratt, of Pantglas), dau of Sir John Newton (otherwise Cradock), of E Harptree, Somerset, and Barr's Court, Glos, and *d* 21 Feb 1588/9, leaving issue by his 1st w:

EDWARD SOMERSET, **4th Earl of Worcester**, KG (1593), PC (1601); *b c* 1550; Amb to Scotland June 1590, memb cncl Marches of Wales Dec 1590, Dep Master of the Horse Jan 1597/8, Master of the Horse April 1601–2 Jan 1615/6, Ld-Lt Glam and Mon 1602–28, a Commr Treasury 16 June-July 1614, Ld Privy Seal 1616–28; *m* Dec 1571 Lady Elizabeth Hastings (*d* 24 Aug 1621), dau of 2nd Earl of Huntingdon (*qv*), and *d* 3 March 1627/8, having had issue, with five other sons:

1 William, *Lord Herbert; b* 1575/76; *educ* Magdalen Coll Oxford (MA); ktd 1596; *dvp* and unm *c* 21 Jan 1597/8

2 HENRY, **1st Marquess**

3 THOMAS SOMERSET, VISCOUNT SOMERSET, of Cashel, co Tipperary (I), so *cr* 8 Dec 1626, KB (1604/5); *m* 1631 Helena Barry, dau of 5th Viscount Buttevant and widow of 10th Earl of Ormonde (*see* ORMONDE, M), and *dsps* 1650, having had:

(1) Helena; *d* unm

The 4th EARL OF WORCESTER's est s,

HENRY SOMERSET, **1st Marquess of Worcester** (E), so *cr* 2 March 1642/3 (also promised the Dukedom of Somerset, for which he received a warrant dated 6 Jan 1644/5, but letters patent were never issued); *b* 1576/7; *educ* Magdalen Coll Oxford; memb cncl Marches of Wales June 1601, called up to Ho of Lds *vp* in his f's supposed Barony as LORD HERBERT 31 Jan 1603/4, Jt Ld-Lt Glam and Mon 1626–31, conducted the defence of Raglan Castle 3 June–19 Aug 1646 when besieged by Parly forces; *m* 16 June 1600 Lady Anne Russell (*d* 8 April 1639), gdau of 2nd Earl of Bedford (*see* BEDFORD, D), and *d* 18 Dec 1646, having had, with eight other sons and four daus:

EDWARD SOMERSET, **2nd Marquess of Worcester**; *b c* 9 March 1602/3; memb cncl Marches of Wales 12 May 1633, Lt-Gen S Wales and Monmouth April 1643, cdr roy forces defeated by Parl AT Highnam, Glos, 24/25 March 1642/3, allegedly *cr* 1 April 1644 BARON BEAUFORT OF CALDECOT CASTLE, Co Monmouth, and EARL OF GLAMORGAN, with special remainder to his male issue, by Margaret O'Brien, his 2nd w, failing which to the heirs male of his body and those of his f. The usual entries to this effect were made in the docquet books for April 1645 in the Signet Office and the Privy Seal Office but the Letters Patent for this creation never passed the Great Seal, although he was almost invariably styled Earl of Glamorgan by CHARLES I and others until he s his f as **2nd Marquess of Worcester** in 1646; during a mission to Ireland to raise troops for CHARLES he signed on the former's behalf the so-called Glamorgan Treaty 25 Aug 1645 with the Confederate Catholics and an engagement 20 Dec following with the Papal Nuncio Rinuccini; arrested 26 Dec 1645 and imprisoned; Freeman Waterford 26 Feb 1645/6, Burgess Galway 1 Aug 1647, Memb New Supreme Cncl of Confederate Irish 26 Sept 1646, Gen of forces in Munster Sept 1646–12 June 1647, sentenced to banishment and death by H of C March 1648/9, imprisoned Tower of London 27 July 1652–5 Oct 1654, but after the Restoration his estates were restored. He was interested in mechanics and is said to have anticipated the steam engine in some of his experiments; author *Century of Inventions* (1663); *m* 1st *c* 1628 Elizabeth (*d* 31 May 1635), dau of Sir William Dormer (*see* DORMER, B); *m* 2nd Aug 1639 Lady Margaret O'Brien (*m* 2nd *c* June 1679 Donogh Kearney (*bur* 4 May 1718), of Gray's Inn, Mddx, Gent Usher to titular James III, and *dsps* 26 July 1681), 2nd dau and coheir of 4th Earl of Thomond (*see* INCHIQUIN, B), and *d* 3 April 1667, having had by his 1st w:

1 HENRY, **1st Duke**

1 Anne; *m c* 1652 6th Duke of Norfolk (*qv*) and *d* 1662, leaving issue

2 Elizabeth; *m* 2 Aug 1654 1st Marquess of Powis (*see* POWIS, E) and *d* 16 March 1690/1, leaving issue

The 2nd MARQUESS OF WORCESTER's s,

HENRY SOMERSET, **1st Duke of Beaufort** (E), so *cr* 2 Dec 1682 because among other reasons of his descent from EDWARD III, KG (1672), PC (1672); *b* 1629; MP Mon 1660–67, Ld-Lt: Glos, Herefs and Mon 1660–89, Col Regt of Foot 1660, Col Regt of Horse 1661, Ld Pres Wales, Ld-Lt N and S Wales 1672–89, Col 11th Regt of Foot 1685, Ld-Lt Isle of Purbeck 1687, refused to subscribe the oaths of allegiance to WILLIAM III and lived in retirement; *m* 17 Aug 1657 Mary Capel (*d* 7 Jan 1715/16), dau of 1st Baron Capell of Hadham (*see* ESSEX, E) and widow of Henry Seymour, Lord Beauchamp (*see* SOMERSET, D), and *d* 21 Jan 1699/1700, having had, with four daus:

1 Henry, *Lord Herbert; d* an infant

2 Charles, *Marquess of Worcester; b* Dec 1660 (CHARLES II stood sponsor); *educ* Ch Ch Oxford (MA 1681/2); Col 11th Regt of Foot 1685–87, MP (Tory) Mon 1685–87 and 1689–95, Glos 1685 and Monmouth and Brecknock 1685; *m* 5 June 1682 Rebecca (*m* 2nd 15 April 1703 1st and last Baron Granville, of Potheridge, Devon, and *d* 17 July 1712), dau of Sir Josiah Child, of Wanstead, Essex, Govr HEIC, and sis of 1st Earl Tylney of the 1731 *cr*, and *dvp* 13 July 1698, having had:

(1) HENRY, **2nd Duke**

(1) Henrietta; *m* 30 April 1713 2nd Duke of Grafton (*qv*)

3 Arthur; *m* Mary, dau and heir of Sir William Russell, 1st and last Bt, of Langherne, Carmarths, of the 1660 *cr*, and widow of Hugh Calverley Cotton, er s of Sir Robert Cotton, 1st Bt, of Combermere (*see* COMBERMERE, V), and had:

(1) Mary; *m* Algernon Greville, MP Warwick 1699–1705, and had issue (*see* WARWICK, BROOKE and, E)

(2) Elizabeth

(3) Anne; *m* Uvedale Price, the landscape gardener

The 1st DUKE OF BEAUFORT's gs,

HENRY SOMERSET, **2nd Duke of Beaufort, KG (1712), PC (1710)**; *b* 2 April 1684; Ld-Lt Hants 1710–14 and Glos 1712–14, Capt Gentlemen Pensioners 1712–14, Tory; *m* 1st 7 July 1702 Lady Mary Sackville (*dsps* 18 June 1705), only dau of 6th Earl of Dorset; *m* 2nd 26 Feb 1705/6 Rachel Noel (*d* 13 Sept 1709), 2nd dau and coheir of 2nd Earl of Gainsborough (*qv*); *m* 3rd 14 Sept 1711 Mary Osborne (*m* 2nd 4th Earl of Dundonald and *dsp* 4 Feb 1722), yst dau of 2nd Duke of Leeds (*see* 1963 edn), and *d* 24 May 1714, leaving issue by his 2nd w:

1 HENRY SOMERSET later SCUDAMORE (Act of Parl 1730), **3rd Duke of Beaufort** ; *b* 26 March 1707; *educ* Westminster and Univ Coll Oxford (DCL 1725); High Steward Hereford 1729, Tory; *m* 28 June 1729 Frances Scudamore (*m* 2nd Charles FitzRoy later FitzRoy Scudamore, of Holme Lacy, Herefs, illegitimate s of 2nd Duke of Grafton (*qv*), by whom she left one dau Frances, heiress of the Scudamore estates, who *m* 11th Duke of Norfolk (*qv*), and *d* 27 Feb 1749/50), only child and heir of 2nd Viscount Scudamore (I) from whom he was divorced 2 March 1743/4 on account of her adultery with William Talbot (subsequently Earl Talbot; *see* SHREWSBURY and WATERFORD, E) by whom she had a child named Frances Matthews, and *dsp* 24 Feb 1744/5

2 CHARLES NOEL SOMERSET, **4th Duke**

The 3rd DUKE OF BEAUFORT's yr bro,

CHARLES NOEL SOMERSET, **4th Duke of Beaufort**; *b* 12 Sept 1709; *educ* Westminster and Univ Coll Oxford (MA 1727, DCL 1736); MP (Tory) Mon 1731–34 and Monmouth Borough 1734–45; *m* 1 May 1740 Elizabeth (*d* 8 April 1799), dau of John Symes Berkeley, of Stoke Gifford, Glos, and sis and heir of 4th Lord (Baron) Botetourt of the 1305 *cr* and coheir to the said Barony, and *d* 28 Oct 1756, having had issue, with five daus:

HENRY SOMERSET, **5th Duke of Beaufort**, KG (1786); *b* 16 Oct 1744; *educ* Oriel Coll Oxford; Grand Master Freemasons (E) 1767–72, Master of the Horse to QUEEN CHARLOTTE 1768–70, Ld-Lt Mon 1771–1803, Brecknockshire 1787–1803 and Leics 1787–99, DCL 1763, obtained 4 June 1803 a patent terminating the abeyance of the BARONY OF BOTETOURT in his favour; *m* 2 Jan 1766 Elizabeth (*d* 15 June 1828), dau of Adml Hon Edward Boscawen (*see* FALMOUTH V), and *d* 11 Oct 1803, having had, with other issue (*see* SUTHERLAND, D):

1 HENRY CHARLES, **6th Duke**

2 Charles Henry; *b* 12 Dec 1767; Col 1st W India Regt, Govr Cape of Good Hope; *m* 1st June 1788 Elizabeth Courtenay (*d* 1815), 4th dau of 2nd Viscount Courtenay (*see* DEVON E), and had, with other issue:

(1) Henry (Sir), KCB, KH, of Roehampton Lodge, Surrey; *b* 30 Dec 1794; Lt-Gen, Col 25th Foot, C-in-C Bombay; *m* 1 April 1817 Frances Sarah (*d* 16 March 1886), dau of Adml Sir Henry Heathcote (*see* HEATHCOTE, Bt, of Hursley) and *d* 15 Feb 1862, leaving, with other issue (including a dau Leonora Louisa, *m* 1804 Montague Johnstone; *see* JOHNSTONE, Bt):

1a Charles Henry, CB; *b* 1819; Col 72nd Foot; *m* 1848 Christina Emma (*d* 13 Oct 1863), est dau of R W Thompson, and *d* 4 Nov 1863, leaving issue:

1b William Henry; *b* 10 Oct 1849; Capt RN; *m* 11 Aug 1892 Kate Eliza Bramley (*d* 10 Oct 1909), est dau of Capt Edwin George Mainwaring, 91st Highrs, and *d* 18 Aug 1922, leaving issue:

1c Nina Evelyn Mary; *b* 3 Nov 1893; *d* —

2b Henry Plantagenet; *b* 19 May 1852; MLA Stanley, Qld Parl, Australia; *m* 5 July 1879 Katherine Rose (*d* Feb 1935), est dau of David Cannon McConnel, of Cressbrook, Qld, and *d* 11 April 1936, having had issue:

1c Edward Kingsley Plantagenet; *b* 18 May 1890; *d* 26 Jan 1891

2c Charles William Henry Rollo, MC; *b* 24 Jan 1895; Capt Australian Cwlth Mil Force WW I Gallipoli and France (despatches); *m* 10 Aug 1925 Glory Kathleen, (*d* 1973), 3rd dau of Frederick Albert Turner, of Glenbardi, Toogoolawah, Qld, and *d* 20 Feb 1936, leaving issue:

1d +Arthur Henry [Arthur Somerset Esq, 31 Rangeview St, Aspley 4034, Brisbane, Qld 4034, Australia]; *b* 30 May 1926; served RAN Pacific WW II; *m* 7 Oct 1950 *Dorothy Joan, only dau of William Harrison, of Cresley Rd, Albion, Brisbane, Qld, and has had issue:

1e Rollo William Charles; *b* 8 March, *d* 10 March 1952

2e +Arthur Rollo Henry Plantagenet; *b* 18 Nov 1953; *educ* Qld U (BCom); *m* 2 June 1979 *Marion Lyle, dau of D V Graham, of Brisbane, Qld, and has issue:

1f *Katherine Lee; *b* 1981

2f *Victoria Anne; *b* 1984

3e +John William Plantagenet; *b* 30 Jan 1965; *educ* Qld U (BCom); *m* 1989 *Margaret Judith, dau of Ivan Bowen, of Brisbane, and has issue:

1f +Justin Mitchell Plantagenet; *b* 1993

1f *Kristina Margaret; *b* 25 March 1996

1e *Andrea Helen; *b* 8 Sept 1957; *educ* Qld U (MEd); *m* 1988 *Andrew L M Todd and has:

1f *Phillip William Andrew (triplet); *b* 1994

2f *Oliver James; *b* 3 April 1996

1f *Maima Louise Somerset (triplet); *b* 1994

2f *Rachelle Alexandra Somerset (triplet); *b* 1994

1d *Patricia Honor [Mrs Norman Butler, 110 Esplanade, Golden Beach, Coloundra, Qld 4551, Australia]; *b* 15 Oct 1928; *m* 5 Dec 1953 *Norman David Thomas Butler and has issue:

1e *Luke Norman; *b* 1954; *m* 1988 *Margaret, est dau of J R R D Field, of Brisbane, and has:

1f *Micah; *b* 1989

2e *Robert David; *b* 1957; LLB; *m* 1995 *Gayle Karen, 2nd dau of M W H Bice, of Maleny, and has:

1f *Elizabeth Kathleen; *b* 1997

1e *Gloria Patricia; *b* 1962; B Nurs Dist; *m* 1982 (*divorce* 1995) Trevor John Kennedy and has:

1f *Brendan James; *b* 1986

2f *Lachlan Gene; *b* 1987

2d *Barbara Joan [Miss Barbara Somerset, 110 Esplanade, Golden Beach, Caloundra, Qld 4551, Australia]; *b* 2 Oct 1933

3c Hereward Henry Plantagenet, JP, of Broadacres, Dourong, via Tingoora, Qld, Australia; *b* 2 Dec 1900; *m* 27 June 1923 Jean Castle (*d* 1987), 2nd dau of Frederick Albert Turner, of Glenbardi, Toogoolawah, Qld, and *d* 1989, leaving issue:

1d +Edward Plantagenet [Edward Somerset Esq, 79 Guy St, Warwick, Qld 4370, Australia]; *b* 15 Dec 1924; served RAAF 1943–45; *m* 7 June 1952 *Elsie Joy, only dau of Stanley Morrow, of Booyong, Lismore, NSW, Australia and has issue:

1e Richard John Plantagenet; *b* 30 Aug 1960; *m* 1982 *Elizabeth Mary, dau of Frank Neal, of Tara, Qld, and *d* 1991, leaving issue:

1f *Gilliam Maree; *b* 1985

2f *Sarah Jane; *b* 1987

3f *Heidi Louise; *b* 1990

1e *Pru-Ellen [Mrs Stuart Barkla, Rosscoe Downs, Cunnamulla, Qld 4490, Australia]; *b* 27 March 1956; *m* 1976 *Stuart Charles Barkla and has issue:

1f *Alina Jane; *b* 1983

2f *Zoë Ann; *b* 1986

2d +David Plantagenet [David Somerset Esq, Peek-a-Do, Taroom, Qld 4420, Australia]; *b* 25 June 1926; *m* 7 Aug 1953 *Margaret Pamela, 2nd dau of David Victor Staines, of Jandowae, Qld, and has had issue:

1e *Jennifer Margaret [Mrs Stuart Stirling, Willwood, Pittsworth, Qld 4356, Australia]; *b* 30 Sept 1954; *m* 1976 *Stuart James Stirling and has issue:

1f *Jillian Elizabeth; *b* 1978

2f *Rebecca Lynn; *b* 1981

3f *Roslyn Ann; *b* 1984

2e *Kerri-Jane; *b* 20 Feb 1957

3e *Erica Jan [Mrs Harry Perrett, Cattle Downs, Wandoan, Qld 4419, Australia]; *b* 12 Jan 1959; *m* 1983 *Harry Sibun Perrett and has:

1f *Edward Sibun; *b* 1984

1f *Hilary Elizabeth; *b* 1986

2f *Jessica Victoria; *b* 1989

3f *Sophie Jayne; *b* 1993

3d +Robert Plantagenet, AM (1992), JP [Robert Somerset Esq AM JP, Caboonbah, Proston, Qld 4613, Australia]; *b* 11 Feb 1930; *m* 19 Oct 1952 *Leslie Rawdon, only dau of Rawdon Briggs, JP, of Swindon, Mt Perry, Qld, and has:

1e +Robert Plantagenet; *b* 21 Jan 1959; *m* 1990 *Georgina Jane Persse, yst dau of David Rokeby Robinson, of Lorraine, Longreach, Qld, and has:

1f +Benjamin Plantagenet; *b* Jan 1995

2f +Macartney Plantagenet; *b* Jan 1996

1e *Leslie Ann, JP [Mrs Ian Haselwood JP, S Westgrove, Injune, Qld 4454, Australia]; *b* 27 June 1953; *m* 1974 Ian Robert Haselwood (*d* 1997) and has:

1f *Georgina Leslie; *b* 1984

2e *Katherine Nina [Mrs Lindsay Marshall, Yurunga Farm, Beechmont, via Nerang, Qld 4211, Australia]; *b* 18 June 1957; *m* 1978 *Lindsay George Joseph Marshall and has:

1f *Lachlan Colvin; *b* 1981

2f *Adam Lindsay; *b* 1983

3e *Victoria Joyce [Mrs Paul Bartlett, 'Anandale', Trangie, NSW 2823, Australia]; *b* 12 Jan 1967; *m* 1993 *Paul Arthur Bartlett

4e *Jane Elizabeth; *b* 16 Nov 1968; *d* 1973

4d +William Plantagenet [William Somerset Esq, Warra Willa, Brolga Rd, Beandesert, Qld 4285, Australia]; *b* 6 July 1934; served in RAN 1951–58; *m* 18 Nov 1961 *Marion Helene, er dau of Maiben Hay Blackman, of Brisbane, Qld, Australia, and has:

1e +Mark William Plantagenet; *b* 27 Jan 1965; *m* 1990 *Anne Marie, 2nd dau of Terence Michael Murphy, of Dalby, Qld and has issue:

1f +Brent Michael John Plantagenet; *b* 1990

1f *Krystie Lee; *b* 1992

2e +Steven Plantagenet; *b* 20 Aug 1968; *m* 1992 *Sharlene Michelle Payne and has:

1f *Alexandra Elizabeth; *b* 1997

1e *Christine Helene; *b* 6 Jan 1963; *m* 1988 *Nicholas John Case and has:

1f *Fenton Vaughan; *b* 1992

1f *Stephanie Helene; *b* 1988

5d +Charles Plantagenet [Charles Somerset Esq, Caraweena, MS612, Kingaroy, Qld 4610, Australia]; *b* 11 May 1944; *m* 1978 *Pamela Dorothy, dau of Guy Oakes McIver, of Braeside Bell, Qld, and has issue:

1e +Miles Plantagenet; *b* 1979

2e +Scott Plantagenet; *b* 1981

1d *Susan JP (Qld) [Mrs Susan Hassall, JP, 18 Diana St, Mundubbera, Qld 4626, Australia]; *b* 5 Nov 1945; *m* 16 Aug 1969 (*divorce* 1991) Heath Hill Hassall and has:

1e *Rem Hill; *b* 29 Dec 1970

1e *Martine Dione; *b* 1974

1c Mary Georgiana; *b* 18 June 1880; *m* 1917 John Arthur Turnor, JP, and *d* 21 April 1970, leaving issue

2c Joan; *b* 23 Sept 1881; *m* Aug 1918 George Sharpe and *d* 20 Feb 1921, leaving issue

3c Christiana; *b* 1 June 1884; *d* unm 30 Nov 1960

4c Gwendolin Frances; *b* 13 May 1888; *d* unm 4 March 1970

5c Vida; *b* 1891; *d* young

6c Doris Henrietta; *b* 1 Feb 1893; *m* 2 Jan 1917 Aldred Richard Waite, of 3rd Avenue, Mayes Estate, Caloundra, Qld, Australia, s of A R Waite, of Battle Abbey, Sussex, and NZ, and *d* 19–, leaving issue

7e Ealhswith Anne Matilda; *b* 11 Aug 1897; *m* 1921 Percival Dent Ridgway Drane (*d* 1962), of 34 Hale St, Margate, Qld, Australia, and *d* 19–, leaving issue

3b Charles FitzRoy Maclean; *b* 19 Nov 1855; Lt RN (ret); *d* unm 1895

1b Georgina Frances Emma, sister All Saints Convent Cape Town; *b* Nov 1853; *d* unm 17 June 1889

2a Henry George Edward; *b* 28 Dec 1829; Col 3rd Buffs, Mily Kt of Windsor; *m* 15 Oct 1853 Harriette Lade (*d* 28 Sept 1916), dau of Maj — Coast, 52nd Regt, and *d* 5 April 1920, having had issue:

1b Henry Calthorpe; *b* 2 Feb 1856; Capt 2nd Bn Buffs, Staff Offr of Cadets, Melbourne; *m* 1880 Bertha Clothilde (*d* 1931), dau of Dr P Reilly, of Mauritius, and *d* 3 March 1904, leaving issue:

1c Henry George FitzRoy; *b* 1885; served AIF WWI; *m* 1913 Honore (*d* 30 Sept 1956), dau of J Olive, of Ravenswood, Qld, and *d* 13 May 1958, leaving issue:

1d Vivienne Constance; *b* 1914; *m* 1941 (*divorce* 1951) James Rodsted and *d* 10 Sept 1970, leaving issue

2d *Margot [Mrs Donald Campbell, 9/11 Lovett St, Manly Vale, NSW, Australia]; *b* 1916; *m* 1943 *Donald Campbell and has issue:

1e *Bruce Ronald; *b* 1946

1e *Anne-Marie; *b* 1944

2c Charles William Clifford; *b* 3 July 1887; *d* 19 March 1890

3c Alan Wyndham; *b* 1890; Lt Australian Inf WWI; *ka* Nov 1916

4c Edward Harold; *b* 1893; *d* 1913

1c Marguerite Constance; *b* 1881; *m* Charles Edwin Hibberd and *d* 9 May 1961

2c Violet Bertha; *b* 1882; *m* 1929 Louis O'Keefe (*d* 18 March 1930), of Melbourne, and *d* 21 Feb 1964

2b Charles Wyndham, CB (1918), CMG (1917), MVO (1911); *b* 24 June 1862; Col IA, Hon Brig-Gen 1919, late 48th Pioneers IA, served Burma 1886–89, Chitral 1895, NW Frontier India 1897–98, Tirah 1897–98 and WW I; *m* 14 Nov 1901 Elinor Barbara Alice (*d* 3 Aug 1935), yst dau of Arthur Pearce Howell, ICS, and *d* 12 Nov 1938, leaving issue:

1c Alan FitzRoy; *b* 21 Sept 1902; Maj RASC; *m* 18 April 1927 Nell Lauder (*d* 15 Jan 1951), dau of Harold English Pyman, of Edinburgh, and *d* 18 June 1940, leaving issue:

1d +Robin FitzRoy MBE (1997) [Robin Somerset Esq MBE, 91 Edgar Rd, Winchester, Hants]; *b* 21 May 1930; *educ* Eton, Balliol Coll Oxford and RMA Sandhurst; Capt Rifle Bde; *m* 1977 *Sarah Marguerite, er dau of V-Adml Sir Charles Piercy Mills, KCB, CB, DSC, of Aldeburgh, Suffolk, and has issue:

1e +Charles FitzRoy; *b* 1981

1e *Anne Marguerite; *b* 21 Nov 1978

1d *Barbara Carol [Miss Barbara Somerset, Aldehaven, Leiston Rd, Aldeburgh, Suffolk IP15 5QA]; *b* 21 June 1933; *educ* Girton Coll Cambridge

1b Frances Constance; *d* unm 13 Aug 1959

3a FitzRoy Maclean Henry; *b* 1 Nov 1839; Ch of Police, Hanover, Cape of Good Hope; *m* 18 July 1867 Ellen Amelia (*d* 12 Dec 1911), est dau of David Arnot, and *d* 29 June 1907, having had issue:

1b Henry Edward; *b* 16 April 1868; served Cape Mtd Rifles 1884, Langeberg Campaign and Boer War (wounded four times), with Cullinan's Horse German SW Africa and S African Inf France, Egypt and Br E Africa WW I

2b William Grimmer; *b* 16 Feb 1870; served Cape Mounted Police Langeberg Campaign; *m* 1904 Annie, dau of J Pienaar, of Colesberg, and *dsp* 22 May 1929

3b Henry Plantagenet; *b* 25 Jan, *d* 28 Jan 1880

4b FitzRoy Henry; *b* 1 Feb 1881; served Langeberg Campaign Boer War 1899–1902 and WWI; *m* 28 Aug 1902 Martha Johanna, dau of Philip Watermeyer, MP, of Hanover, S Africa, and *d* 13 April 1946, having had issue:

1c +Raglan Henry; *b* 27 May 1903; boilermaker Daggafontein Mines; *m* 23 May 1928 *Hendrica Alida, dau of John Gabriel van der Berg, of Bloemfontein, and has had issue:

1d +Eugene; *b* 31 March 1929; *m* 11 Aug 1951 *Valerie Rene, dau of D T Stewart, of Benoni, S Africa, and has issue:

1e *Sharon; *b* 9 May 1952

2e *Geraldine; *b* 2 June 1954

2d +John FitzRoy; *b* 4 Feb 1933

1d *Eunice; *b* 30 Aug 1931

2d Desirée; *b* 1937; *d* 1940

2c +Philip Arthur; *b* 21 Jan 1905

3c FitzRoy Henry; *b* 13 Dec 1909; served WW II S African Forces; *m* Rachel McCullough and *d* 1945 of wounds recd in action

4c William Grimmer; *b* 16 Sept 1912; *d* 6 Sept 1932

5c +Harry Edward [Harry Somerset Esq, 1 Raydora Mansions, Roxburgh Rd, Selection Park, Springs 1568, S Africa]; *b* 10 June 1914; *m* 1939 *Muriel Elizabeth Watkins and has:

1d +Ronald Arthur [Ronald Somerset Esq, 1 Raydora Mansions, Roxburgh Rd, Selection Park, Springs 1568, S Africa]; *b* 4 Feb 1940; *m* 1966 (*divorce* 1973) Lesley Drummond and has issue:

1e +Grant Bradford; *b* 1967

1d *Beryl Louisa [Mrs Arie de Lange, 19 Rogers Rd, Selection Park, Springs 1567, S Africa]; *b* 15 Nov 1946; *m* 1966 *Arie David de Lange and has issue:

1e *David John; *b* 1969

1e *Shaye Beryl; *b* 1967

1c *Lilian Blanche [Mrs Thomas Grieve, Floreat, 8 Paschendaele Rd, Delville, Germiston, S Africa]; *b* 24 Jan 1907; *m* 1st 1 Aug 1933 Richard William Flagg (*d* 22 May 1940); *m* 2nd 1 Feb 1949 Thomas Grieve and has issue by 1st husb:

1d *John Richard; *b* 15 Feb 1937
1d *Marjorie; *b* 30 Nov 1935
2c Violet; *b* 14 Nov 1911; *d* 21 March 1913
3c *Winifred Mary; *b* 25 Dec 1925; *m* 1948 Derek Edgerton Moult and has:
1d *Adrian Thomas; *b* 1951
1d *Kathleen Dawn; *b* 1949
5b Charles James Edward; *b* 9 July, *d* 3 Dec 1883
1b Anne Isabel; *b* 20 Aug 1871; *m* 14 March 1892 William Heathcote Somerset Murray (*d* 25 Aug 1925), s of James Murray, and *dsp* 1942
2b Frances Sarah; *b* 6 June 1873; *m* 1907 Walter James Hinks, of 15 Sixth Avenue, Fish Hoek, CP, S Africa, s of Joseph Hinks, of Orkney House, Taplow, and *d* 1960, leaving issue
3b Louisa Blanche; *b* 5 Jan 1875; *m* 7 April 1902 John Henry Gauntlett Loubser (*d* 30 Sept 1964), s of Michael Matthew Loubser, of Fernkloof, Port Elizabeth, S Africa, and *d* 29 June 1961, leaving issue
4b Frances Grace Mary; *b* 22 Dec 1876; *m* 1901 Hector Vaughan Heberden, of Wadza, S Rhodesia, and *d* Jan 1936, leaving issue
5b Muriel Maude; *b* 21 Sept 1878; *m* 4 May 1909 James Wingate White, of 1a Bellevue St, Bloemfontein, OFS, S Africa, est s of James White, ICS and *d* 24 April 1958, leaving issue
(2) Villiers Henry Plantagenet (Rev); *b* 12 Feb 1803; Rector Honiton, Devon; *m* 8 Aug 1844 Frances Dorothy (*d* 7 Feb 1885), est dau of John Henry Ley, of Trehill, Devon, by Lady Frances Hay, dau of 7th Marquess of Tweeddale (*qv*), and *d* 3 Feb 1855, leaving:
1a Henry Plantagenet (Rev); *b* 14 Sept 1845; *educ* Queen's Coll Oxford (MA); Rector and RD Crickhowell, Brecon; *m* 1st 4 Jan 1881 Charlotte Elizabeth (*d* 16 June 1886), dau of Lt-Col Rose Wynter; *m* 2nd 7 July 1898 Elizabeth (*d* 26 Dec 1927), dau of J A Walton, of Richmond, Yorks, and *d* 14 July 1926, having had issue by his 1st w:
1b Richard Henry Plantagenet; *b* 11 Oct 1882; *d* unm 26 March 1907
2b Charles Henry Plantagenet; *b* 2 Nov 1884; Lt Tank Corps; *d* unm 5 May 1953
3b Noel Henry Plantagenet; *b* 24 Dec 1885; Capt RASC; *m* 26 Oct 1915 Helen Barbara (*d* 1 April 1952), dau of Joseph Arderne Ormerod, MD, FRCP, of Greenhill, Upham, Hants, and 25 Upper Wimpole St, London W, and *d* 7 Sept 1921, leaving issue:
1c *Mary Arderne Frances [Miss Mary Somerset, Lavenders, 151 Elsley Rd, London SW11]; *b* 13 May 1920
1b Frances Georgiana; *b* 12 Oct 1881; *d* 1 Dec 1883
2b Charlotte Rose Mary; *b* 4 Sept 1883; *d* unm 25 May 1968
2a John Henry William; *b* 29 Jan 1848; *m* 1st 3 Sept 1889 Mary de Chair (*d* 19 March 1892), 5th dau of Rev W C Denshire, of Thetford Ho, Lincs, and had issue:
1b Villiers Henry Plantagenet; *b* 16 Aug 1890; Private 10th Bn 2nd Inf Bde, 1st Canadian Contingent; *ka* 23 April 1915
2a (cont.) John Somerset *m* 2nd 14 Nov 1893 Isabel Maud (*m* 2nd — Larking), yst dau of Frederick Courtney, and *d* 2 March 1928, having had further issue:
1b Isabel Maud Mary de Chair; *b* 29 Oct 1894
1a Frances Dorothea Charlotte; *d* unm 24 Oct 1925
2a Mary Isabella Frances; *d* unm 28 April 1929
2 (cont.) Lord Charles Somerset *m* 2nd 9 Aug 1821 Mary (*d* 11 June 1860), 2nd dau of 4th Earl Poulett (*see* 1970 edn), and *d* 20 Feb 1831, having had further issue:
(3) Poulett George Henry, CB; *b* 19 June 1822; MP Mon, Col Coldstream Gds; *m* 1st 15 April 1847 Barbara Augusta Norah (*d* 4 June 1870), dau of John Mytton, of Halston, Salop, and had issue:
1a Vere Francis John; *b* 20 Dec 1854; *m* 28 Dec 1875 Annette Katherine (*d* 5 Oct 1889), dau of Col Richard Frederick Hill, DL (*see* HILL, V), and *d* 10 Oct 1909, leaving issue:
1b William Francis; *b* 1876; *m* 1st 1899 Laura Helen (*d* 1926), dau of W H Thomas, of Port Sydney, Ontario, Canada; *m* 2nd 1927 Ann Margaret Vibert (*d* 1955), dau of C V Laurence, of Allensville, Ontario, Canada, and *d* 7 March 1942, having had issue by his 1st w:
1c William Vere; *b* 1901; *d* 1920
2c Lionel Francis, of Port Sydney, Muskoko, Ontario, Canada; *b* 1903; *m* 1937 *Wanda Gertrude, dau of Arthur W Clarke, of Port Sydney, and *d* 1981, leaving:
1d +Lionel Vere; *b* 1938; *m* 1970 *Janet Mary, dau of Maj David Colin Heggie, MD, GM, of Brampton, Ontario, and has:
1e +Scott Edward; *b* 1973
2e +Steven Arthur; *b* 1975
1e *Tammy Lee; *b* 1978
2d +Cyril Henry; *b* 1940; *m* 1st 1963 (*divorce* 1972) Bonnie Erin, dau of Lloyd W Wood, of Port Sydney, Ontario, and has issue:
1e *Robin Marie; *b* 1964; *m* 1982 *John Joseph Fiorini, of Shannon Hall, and has issue:
1f *John Cyril; *b* 1984
2f *Joey Michael; *b* 1985
3f *Matthew Dominic; *b* 1988
1f *Mikhele Erin; *b* 1987
2d (cont.) Cyril Somerset *m* 2nd 1981 *Gale Eileen, dau of John William Russell, of Moncton, New Brunswick, and has further issue:
1e *Ashley Gale; *b* 1982
3d +William John; *b* 1944; *m* 1978 *Beverly Ann, dau of George Robert Stewart, of 37 Wright Ave, Toronto, Ontario, and has:
1e +Trevor John Stewart; *b* 1985
1e *Amanda Carol; *b* 1981
3c; Henry FitzRoy *b* 1905; *d* 1925
1c Hele na Louisa, of Port Sydney, Muskoko, Ontario, Canada; *b* 1902
2c *Jessie Catherine; *b* 1907; *m* 1944 *Brodie Kay, s of Alfred Kay, of Port Sydney, Ontario, and has:
1d *William Douglas; *b* 6 July 1949; *m* 1979 *Cynda Campbell and has:
1e *Courtney Eileen; *b* 19–
3c *Leonora Mary; *b* 1909; *m* 1936 George Simmens, (*d* 1973) of Ferris, Ontario, and has:
1d *Donald Wayne; *b* 1 Jan 1938; *m* 1970 *Elaine Mary, dau of Robert Bailey, of Cartier, Ontario, and has:
1e *David Robert; *b* 1974
2e *Kirk William; *b* 1976
3e *Donald Glenn; *b* 1980
1d *Norma Helen [Miss Norma Simmens, 129 Whitney Ave, North Bay, Ontario, Canada]; *b* 6 April 1944
2b Charles; *b* 2 June 1878; *m* 8 Feb 1913 *Doris Amy [Mrs Charles Somerset, 16 Allenby Rd, Dalkeith 6009, W Australia], 3rd dau of Edward George Cronin, and *d* 1941, leaving issue:
1c +Henry Charles FitzRoy [Henry Somerset Esq, 16 Allenby Rd, Dalkeith 6009, W Australia]; *b* 15 Feb 1919; *educ* Guildford GS; *m* 1946 *Patricia Barr, 3rd dau of Rudolph George Barr Goyder, and has issue:
1d +Charles Nigel FitzRoy; *b* 18 Feb 1953
1d *Virginia FitzRoy; *b* 31 Dec 1947
2d *Suzette FitzRoy; *b* 1 May 1950
3d *Mary Ursula FitzRoy; *b* 11 Nov 1958
4d *Georgina Patricia FitzRoy; *b* 13 June 1963
2c +Claud Edward Ralph; *b* 1925
1c *Mary Poulett; *b* 1916
2c *Diana; *b* 1918
3c *Suzette; *b* 1920
3b Hugh; *b* 1879; *m* 1911 Elizabeth Jane (*d* 1963), dau of William Verron, of Herodsfoot, Cornwall, and *d* 23 Feb 1953, leaving issue:
1c Annette Joan, of Argyle Ho, Camelford, Cornwall; *b* 1915
4b Claude; *b* 1881; *d* 13 March 1942
5b Vere Edward; *b* 1884; MRCS, LRCP, Temp Capt Army Med Serv; *m* 28 April 1910 Gladys Mildred (*d* 1980), dau of Richard Baker, of Exeter, Devon, and *d* 23 Dec 1961, leaving issue:
1c *Vere Murielle Cecily Idina Somerset, has resumed her maiden name; *b* 14 Jan 1912; *m* 1st 11 April 1934 F/Lt Dudley Scorgie, AFC, RAFVR, est s of Robert Lind Scorgie, of Montrose, Bassett Ave, Southampton; *m* 2nd 1959 (*divorce* 1978) Capt Alan Abraham, late RASC, and has issue by her 1st husb:
1d *Vere Roderick [Vere Scorgie Esq, 27 Bicton St, Exmouth, Devon]; *b* 17 April 1938
2d *Annette Idina; *b* 30 Dec 1939; *m* 15 Dec 1966 *(Peter) Alan Crow, s of John Crow, of Cherrington Manor, Newport, Salop, and has issue:
1e *Christopher John; *b* 1973
2e *Timothy; *b* 1975
1e *Camille Bettina; *b* 1970
2a Henry Charles FitzRoy; *b* 23 Aug 1860; Capt 3rd Bn Shropshire LI; *m* 1st 1889 Amy (*d* 1889), dau of Henry Cox; *m* 2nd 17 April 1894 Barbara Salter (*d* 17 Oct 1894), widow of James Alfred Cochrane, of Riverina, Australia; *m* 3rd 22 July 1897 Isabella Goodsir (*d* 13 Feb 1941), dau of John Mowat, of Glasgow, and widow of John Anthony Inglis, and *d* 28 July 1925, having had issue by his 3rd w:
1b Henry Vere FitzRoy; *b* 10 June 1898; *educ* Radley and Corpus Christi Coll Oxford (MA); Fell Worcester Coll Oxford; *d* unm 2 Sept 1960
2b Charles Alexander, of Malt Ho Barn, Kingsley, Hants; *b* 21 Aug 1901; *educ* Radley; late Capt RA; *m* 1st 15 June 1926 Audrey Vernon (*d* 21 July 1935), 2nd dau of George W L Thompson, of Olton, Warwicks; *m* 2nd 22 Jan 1955 Winifred May (*d* 1996), 2nd dau of J A Helyar, of Windyridge, East Coker, Somerset, and *d* 1981, leaving by his 1st w:
1c *(Audrey) Barbara, AMIA [Mrs Barbara Ellingham, The Old Granary, Stoneputts Manor, Seal, Kent TN15 0ER]; *b* 18 March 1929; *m* 2 Oct 1954 (*divorce* 1960) Jeremy Paul Ellingham, of Brockenhurst, Hants, and has:
1d *Hugh Vere Alexander [Hugh Ellingham Esq, Seal, Kent]; *b* 17 Oct 1957; *educ* Marlborough and Reading U (BSc), ARICS; *m* 1979 *Angela, est dau of T A Jackson, of Lincoln, and has:
1e *Marcus Charles Anthony; *b* 1988
2e *Luke William Alexander; *b* 1990
2e *Hugo Robert Vere; *b* 1992
2d *(Charles Henry) Mark [Mark Ellingham Esq, 7 Parliament Hill, Hampstead, NW3]; *b* 8 April 1959; *educ* Marlborough and Bristol U (BA); *m* 1991* Natania Maria, yst dau of Dr Clifford Jansz, of London, and has:
1e *Miles Arthur Almo; *b* 1996
(3) (cont.) Col P G H Somerset *m* 2nd 10 Sept 1870 Emily (*m* 2nd 25 Aug 1882 Richard John Kinkead, MD (*d* 18 March 1928), of Forster House, Galway, and *d* 7 Sept 1919), dau of John Hubert Moore, of Cherry Hill, Cheshire, and *d* 7 Sept 1875, having had further issue:
1a Cecily Mary Poulett; *m* 7 April 1896 Capt William Francis Annesley Wallace (*d* 30 March 1934), of Pew Hill House, Chippenham, Wilts, est s of William Nevin Wallace, DL, JP, of Downpatrick and Waterfoot House, Co Down and *d* 19 June 1951, leaving issue
1 Mary Sophia; *d* 11 Nov 1869
2 Augusta Anne; *m* 1 Aug 1863 Sir Henry Winston Barron, 2nd Bt (*d* 1872; *see* 1900 edn) and *d* 27 Dec 1881
3 Robert Edward Henry, GCB, KTS; *b* 19 Dec 1776; Gen, Col 4th Dragoons; *m* 17 Oct 1805 Louisa Augusta Courtenay (*d* 9 Feb 1823), dau of William, Viscount Courtenay (*see* DEVON E), and *d* 1 Sept 1842, leaving, with other issue:

(1) Edward Arthur, CB; *b* 21 Feb 1817; Gen Army; Kt Medjidie, Chevalier Legn Honour; *m* 13 Sept 1849 Agatha (*d* 13 Aug 1912), dau of Sir William Miles, 1st Bt (*qv*), and *d* 12 March 1886, having had issue:

1a Edward William Henry; *b* 25 Jan 1866; Lt Rifle Bde; *d* unm 20 March 1890

1a Agatha Georgiana; *m* 17 April 1879 Maj Charles Arthur Baldwyn Knyvett Leighton (*d* 18 May 1889), Roy Welch Fus (*see* LEIGHTON, Bt), and *dsp* 10 May 1940

2a Evelyn Somerset; *b* 20 Nov 1857; *m* 7 Sept 1882 George Caulfeild Prideaux Brune (*d* 21 July 1906), gs of 2nd Baron Kilmaine (*qv*), and *d* 1 July 1883, leaving issue

3a Ada Frances, CBE (1939), JP Mon, DJStJ; *m* 3 Aug 1886 Sir Henry Mather-Jackson, 3rd Bt (*qv*) and *d* 17 March 1949, leaving issue

4a Maude Catherine; *d* unm 6 June 1946

5a Lilian; *m* 29 Dec 1892 Sir Frederick Archdale Palmer, 6th Bt (*qv*), of Wanlip Hall, Leics, and *d* 22 Jan 1947, leaving issue

6a Blanche Louisa; *m* 4 Feb 1892 John George Burdon (*d* 15 Jan 1930), of East Park, Hexham, Northumberland, and *d* 20 Aug 1946, leaving issue

7a Muriel; *m* 7 Nov 1894 Rev William Neville (*d* 27 June 1939), rector East Knoyle, Salisbury (*see* BRAYBROOKE, B), and *d* 25 Nov 1951

8a Hilda; Sister of Mercy, Community of the Sisters of the Church; *d* 16 May 1965

4 Arthur John Henry; *b* 12 Feb 1780; *m* 23 June 1808 Elizabeth Boscawen (*d* 2 March 1872), est dau of 3rd Viscount Falmouth (*qv*), and *d* 18 April 1816, leaving issue:

(1) George Henry (Rev), MA; *b* 30 March 1809; rector St Mabyn, Cornwall; *m* Sept 1835 Philida Elizabeth (*d* 16 Aug 1889), dau of Sir William Pratt Call, 2nd Bt (*see* 1903 edn), and *d* 12 Oct 1882, having had issue:

1a Arthur William Henry; *b* 1843; *d* April 1869

2a George Edward; *b* 1844; Lt RN; *d* 19 Jan 1870

3a FitzRoy John Henry; *b* 1851; *educ* Hertford Coll Oxford (BA)

1a Anne; *d* unm 20 Feb 1929

2a Frances Elizabeth; *d* unm 29 March 1920

3a Mary Georgiana; *d* 1865

4a Louisa Bessy; *d* 1867

5a Elizabeth Anne; *m* 1 Jan 1873 George Airey Talbot Stapleton (*d* 16 Feb 1908) and *d* Feb 1940, leaving issue (*see* STAPLETON, Bt)

6a Blanche Emma; *d* 1867

7a Alice Catherine; *d* unm 29 Sept 1916

8a Rose Octavia; *m* 28 Jan 1886 Edgar Hanbury (*d* 12 Oct 1917), of Eastrop Grange, Wilts, and *d* 26 Feb 1887, leaving issue

(2) Arthur Edward; *b* 28 Aug 1813; *m* 12 Feb 1850 Frances (*d* 23 Oct 1882), dau of Rev Hon John Evelyn Boscawen (*see* FALMOUTH, V), and *d* 9 Sept 1853, leaving issue:

1a Edith; *m* 3 June 1885 Bertram Savile Ogle, JP (*d* 5 Jan 1930), s of Maj Arthur Ogle, 9th Regt, and *d* 24 Nov 1928

2a Florence; *m* 20 May 1879 John Henry Oglander (formerly Glynn), JP, DL, FSA (*d* 16 April 1924), of Nunwell, IoW, and *d* 3 Aug 1921, leaving issue

(1) Elizabeth Anne; *d* unm 1835

5 William George Henry (Rev); *b* 2 Sept 1784; Preb Bristol; *m* 1st 29 June 1813 Elizabeth (*d* 1843), dau of Lt-Gen Sir Thomas Molyneux, 5th Bt (*see* 1940 edn); *m* 2nd 1844 Frances Westby (*d* 31 Aug 1854), dau of Henry Brady and widow of C O'Callaghan, and *d* 14 Jan 1851, leaving issue by his 1st w:

(1) Henry Charles Capel; *b* 20 June 1816; Col Army; *m* 10 Sept 1840 Alice Elizabeth (*d* 29 Aug 1892), only dau of Lt-Gen Sir Maurice Charles O'Connell, KCH, and *d* 17 Jan 1905, having had, with other issue:

1a Charles Bruce Henry; *b* 18 July 1841; 3rd Buffs; *m* 31 July 1862 Victoria Alice Anne (*d* 20 Dec 1919), dau of William FitzGibbon, of Sidney Ho, Cork, and *d* April 1889, leaving:

1b May; *d* 1 March 1938

2b Geraldine Amy Caroline Alice; *m* 27 Jan 1905 Vladimir de Kossikowsky (*d* 1917), Chamberlain to Tsar of Russia, and *d* 28 Dec 1943

3b Rose Marguerite; *m* 15 Nov 1893 Basil Guy Oswald Smith (*d* 13 July 1928), of Shottesbrooke Park, Berks, and *d* 3 Aug 1942, leaving issue

4b Sybil Mary Blanche; *m* 4 June 1901 Maj George Frederick Molineux Montgomerie (*ka* 22 Oct 1915), Gren Guards, of Garboldisham Hall, Norfolk, and *d* 21 March 1932, leaving issue

2a FitzRoy William Henry; *b* 19 Dec 1845; *m* 14 Dec 1869 Anna Martha, dau of Capt William Geary, RN, and *d* 18 Oct 1878, leaving issue:

1b Henry Charles FitzRoy; *b* 27 Oct 1870; *m* 1920 Winifred Marion, dau of George Bartram, of London, and *d* 19 Nov 1940, leaving issue:

1c +Francis Charles; *b* Nov 1921; *m* Sept 1945 *Sheila Marion, dau of Aldred Davis, of Yass, NSW, Australia, and has:

1d *Susan; *b* 1952

2b Raglan; *b* 15 April 1872; *m* 1892 Madeleine Blanche, dau of George Newland, and *d* 18 July 1940, leaving issue:

1c FitzRoy Raglan, of 5th Floor, Colonial Muthal Buildings, Queen St, Brisbane, Qld, Australia; *b* 1901; *m* 1924 Alma Lauderdale, dau of Henry Lauderdale Maitland, of Melbourne, Australia, and *d* 1985, leaving:

1d +Raglan FitzRoy, BM, BS [Raglan Somerset Esq, 67 Westering Rd, Christmas Hills, Victoria 3775, Australia]; *b* 1925; served 2/10 Australian Commando Sqdn (despatches) WW II in SW Pacific; *m* 1954 *Lenore Beatrice, dau of Oswald William Miller, of Brisbane, and has:

1e +Stephen Raglan [Stephen Somerset Esq, 112 Arundel St, Park Orchards, Victoria 3114, Australia]; *b* 1956; *m* 1980 *Antoinette Rose Briggs and has:

1f *Elise Ann; *b* 1987

2f *Olivia Rose; *b* 1991

1b Lola Alice; *m* 1929 Noel Lauderdale Maitland, of Lochiel Flats, Toorak Rd, Hamilton, Brisbane, Qld, Australia, and has issue

2b Blanche; *b* 2 June 1909; *m* 1st 1934 Kenneth Peter Robertson, s of Dr W H Robertson, CMG, CBE, of Craigston, Brisbane, Queesland, Australia; *m* 2nd 1958 *James Richard Lambert Hyne, s of Harry Hyne, of Maryborough, Qld, Australia and *d* 1990, leaving by her 1st husb:

1c *Peter Kenneth [Peter Robertson Esq, 125 Long St, Cleveland, Qld 4163, Australia]; *b* 1936; Capt RAAMC (ret); *m* 1977 *Carole Mary Underwood

1c *Susan Blanche [Mrs Warren Murray, 4 Court St, Ormiston, Qld 4160, Australia]; *b* 1938; *m* 1957 *Lt-Col Warren John Murray and has:

1d *Kenneth Peter; *b* 1958

2d *Neill Julian; *b* 1960

1b Elizabeth Alice; *d* unm 24 Jan 1949

2b Helen Susan; *d* unm 11 June 1934

(2) William (Rev); *b* 3 Oct 1822; LLB (Cambridge), Rector Wollastone, Glos; *m* 1st 2 Aug 1842 Helen (*d* 6 May 1849), only dau of Capt James Donald, 94th Foot, and had issue: one s and two daus; *m* 2nd 24 Sept 1850 Georgiana Amelia (*d* 1896), dau of Maj-Gen W L Darling, and *d* 29 May 1902, having had, with other issue:

1a FitzRoy George Henry (Rev); *b* 9 Aug 1852; *m* Feb 1881 Julia Hannah (*d* 11 Dec 1947), dau of Hugh Munro, and *dsp* 7 April 1889

2a John Plantagenet Edward Arthur Henry; *b* 22 Aug 1853; *d* unm 30 March 1878

3a Raglan Turberville Henry, JP; *b* 20 April 1859; *m* Oct 1884 Elizabeth Horatia Anne (*d* 3 May 1929), dau of Rev Horatio Nelson Nelson-Ward, rector Radstock, and *d* 2 June 1938, leaving issue:

1b Raglan Horatio Edwyn Henry, QC (1947); *b* 1885; *educ* Queens' Coll Cambridge (BA Scholar); barrister Gray's Inn and Middle Temple, Recorder Oswestry 1933–37 and Gloucester 1937, Dep Chm Mon QS, T/Capt Army; *m* 6 Nov 1915 his cousin Adelaide Millicent Blanche Gwendolen, JP (*d* 20 Jan 1958), only dau of Arthur William FitzRoy Somerset, DL, of Castle Goring, Sussex (*see* below), and *d* 29 April 1956, leaving issue:

1c *Anna Millicent Horatia FitzRoy, OBE [Mrs William Tribe OBE, Hill House, Raglan, Gwent]; *b* 12 Sept 1929; *m* 6 Nov 1950 *William John Francis Tribe, only s of William Harold Tribe, barrister, and has issue:

1d *William John Raglan Horatio; *b* 22 Jan 1955; *m* 1st 1975 (*divorce* 1983) Maria Magdalena Hernas, of Wroclaw, Poland; *m* 2nd 1983 (*divorce* 1987) Ana, dau of Dr Janet Rutherford Esquivel; *m* 3rd 1987 *Ruth, dau of Lawrence Corner, and has issue by his 2nd w:

1e *Charles William Edward; *b* 1986

2d *Raglan Horatio Andrew Harold; *b* 13 Aug 1961; *m* 1987 *Susan Elizabeth, dau of John Bennett, of Cheshire

1d *Mary Anna Kathleen Horatio; *b* 26 Sept 1958; *m* 1982 *Ian Geoffrey Arthur, s of Colin Arthur, of Llangibby, Gwent, and has issue:

1e *Rebecca Horatia Jean; *b* 1988

1b Lily Horatia Ethel Georgiana; author: *The Somerset Sequence*; *m* 3 Feb 1913 Lt-Col Hugh Norcott Durant, JP (*d* 24 March 1948), of Twyn-y-corras, Kentchurch, Hereford, Roy Irish Rifles, s of Charles Durant, of Lydney, Gloucester

4a Charles Edward Henry; *b* 15 May 1862; *m* 25 Feb 1908 Edith (*d* 26 Oct 1932), dau of Lionel Weatherly, MD, of Bournemouth, and *d* 1 Dec 1939, having had issue:

1b William; *b* and *d* 29 July 1910

2b William Raglan Henry Guy, of Ashbrook Hall, Hollington, St Leonards-on-Sea, Sussex; *b* 5 Nov 1912; *m* 1st 2 Feb 1932 (*divorce* 1950) Edna Margaret, dau of Ernald Drybrough-Smith, MD, FRCS, of Hastings, and had issue:

1c +William Michael John Charles [William Somerset Esq, Somerville, 9 Overslade Close, E Hunsbury, Northampton NN4 0RZ]; *b* 8 June 1934; *m* 1967 *Constance Langley and has issue:

1d +John Reginald; *b* 1970

2c +Malcolm John; *b* 1947

1c *Rosemary Margaret Drybrough [Mrs Herbert Liquorish, Northfield, 44 North St West, Uppingham, Leics LE15 9S6]; *b* 3 Jan 1933; *m* 1951 *Herbert Paul Liquorish, RHG, and has issue:

1d *Michael Paul; *b* 1952; served RN; murdered 1973 Antigua

1d *Susan Carlotta Anne; *b* 1953

2d *Deri Jane; *b* 1957; *m* 1987 *Tyrone Maloney, of St Peter's, Barbados, and has issue:

1e *Antoine Michael Bevan; *b* 1992

1e *Tamara Chantel; *b* 1985

2e *Tiahra Charmain; *b* 1986

3d *Cherilyn Mary; *b* 1959; *m* 1978 (*divorce* 1981) Terrance Carr and has issue:

1e *Cheryl Marie; *b* 1978

4d *Karin Melinda; *b* 1963

2b (cont.) William Somerset *m* 2nd 1955 *Evelyn, dau of William Lee, of Bradford, and *d* 1981 having had further issue:

3c +Nicholas Anthony; *b* 1956; *d* 1981

2c *Stephanie Lynn; *b* 1960

3c *Amanda Jayne; *b* 1961; *d* 1971

3b +Herbert Michael John Charles [Herbert Somerset Esq, Ashbrook Hall, Hollington, St Leonards-on-Sea, Sussex]; *b* 14 Aug 1920

1b *Charlotte Georgiana Rose Mary, BA (Oxford); *b* 12 April 1909; *m* 25 Sept 1933 *Jules Omer John Malfroy, LLM, s of Camille M Malfroy, of Wellington, NZ, and has issue

2b Anne Blanche Edwina Alma; *b* 5 Feb 1918; *d* unm 23 May 1977

(3) FitzRoy Molyneux Henry, of The Priory, Frimley, Surrey; *b* 29 Dec 1823; Col (ret) RE; *m* 1st 1 March 1849 Jemima Drummond (*d* 19 June 1874), 4th dau of J M Drummond Nairne, of Dunsinane, Perthshire; *m* 2nd 5 Sept 1882 Emily (*d* 28 March 1897), dau of Rev George A Biedermann and widow of W

H H Hartley, of Lyegrove, Glos, and *d* 22 Feb 1901 having had, with other issue, by his 1st w:

1a FitzRoy James William Henry; *b* 1850; *d* 19 Jan 1859

2a Arthur William FitzRoy, DL, JP Sussex; *b* 20 Sept 1855; *m* 25 July 1887 his cousin Gwendolin Adelaide Katherine Georgiana Matilda (*d* 24 Sept 1942), dau of Col Sir Alfred Plantagenet Frederick Charles Somerset, KCB, DL, of Enfield Court, Middx (*see* below), and *d* 8 Jan 1937, leaving:

1b Arthur Plantagenet Francis Cecil; *b* 28 Sept 1889; Lt late Serv Bn Roy Fus, served in WWI 1915 (wounded); *m* 8 Nov 1916 Mary Frances Elizabeth, est dau of Fenton George Randolph, of Chichester, Sussex (*see* NEPEAN, Bt),and *d* 13 Oct 1957, leaving issue:

1c +(John) FitzRoy Pechell [FitzRoy Somerset Esq, Holt Farm House, Clapham, nr Worthing, Sussex]; *b* 14 Oct 1923; *educ* Wellington and London U (BSc Estate Management); ARICS, QALAS, late KRRC WW II 1942–45 (wounded); *m* 13 Sept 1952 *Daphne Marigold, yr dau of Col Clement Topham, OBE, MC, of Nairobi, Kenya, and has:

1d +Clement Charles FitzRoy [Clement Somerset Esq, Longdean House, Clapham, nr Worthing, W Sussex]; *b* 10 March 1956; *m* 1986 *Sara Ann, dau of Roy James Lally, of Worthing, and has:

1e +William Henry Pechell Somerset; *b* 22 July 1994

1e *Georgina Katherine Ella; *b* 1987

1d *Annabel Mary [Mrs Robert Smyth, Altmover House, Dungiven, Co Derry]; *b* 14 June 1953; *m* 1979 *Robert Matthew Smyth and has:

1e *Emily Margaret; *b* 1980

2d *Philippa Margaret; *b* 2 July 1965; *m* July 1995 *Stephen Wright and has:

1e *Henry Somerset; *b* April 1997

1c *Cecily Mary Adelaidet [Mrs Lawrence Howe-Ely, 1 Piras Gdns, Oxford Rd, Avondale, Harare, Zimbabwe]; *b* 18 Nov 1919; Jr Cdr ATS WW II; *m* 9 Jan 1946 Maj Lawrence James Howe-Ely, 60th Rifles, (*d* April 1996) yr s of F Howe-Ely, of Salisbury, Rhodesia, and has:

1d *Christopher Lawrence Somerset [Christopher Howe-Ely Esq, c/o SA Eagle Insurance Company, PO Box 226, Cape Town, S Africa]; *b* 25 Dec 1946; *m* 1984 *Linda Gilbee, of Port Elizabeth, S Africa, and has:

1e *Michael; *b* 1987

2e *Andrew; *b* Dec 1994

2d *Michael James FitzRoy [Michael Howe-Ely Esq, c/o Ministry of Commerce and Industry, Harare, Zimbabwe]; *b* 27 Oct 1950; *m* 1980 *Mary Anne, dau of George Piers, of Pregrave Farm, Harare, and has:

1e *Piers Lawrence; *b* 1985

1e *Caroline Louise; *b* 1982

1d *Anne Diana Mary [Mrs George Papasavvas, 25 Kew Dr, Highlands, Harare, Zimbabwe]; *b* 19 Oct 1948; *m* 1972 George Constantine Papasavvas (*d* 1983) and has:

1e *Alexander Lawrence; *b* 1979

1e *Christina Helena; *b* 1978

2e *Georgina Zoe (twin); *b* 1983

3e *Suzanna Cecily (twin); *b* 1983

2c Diana Millicent; *b* 1 Aug 1921; served WW II (VAD); *m* 3 April 1943 Cdr Geoffrey Inderwick Palmer, RN, yr s of J H Palmer, of Hillsborough, Rustington, Sussex, and *d* 25 Feb 1985, leaving:

1d *Juliet Elizabeth [Lady Cooper, West End House, Donhead St Andrew, Shaftesbury, Dorset SP7 9DY]; *b* 9 Feb 1945; *m* 9 Sept 1967 *Maj-Gen Sir Simon Christie Cooper KCVO, Life Gds, Master HM's Household, only s of Maj-Gen Kenneth Christie Cooper, CB, DSO, OBE, of West End House, and has:

1e *Jonathan Francis Christie; *b* 21 March 1969; *m* 29 June 1996 *Pollyanna Fenella, yr dau of Christopher Hughes, of Furneaux Pelham, Herts

1e *Venetia Elizabeth Somerset; *b* 8 Jan 1971

2d *Anthea Somerset; *b* 1 April 1947

3d *Catherine Annabella Inderwick; *b* 20 Nov 1952

2b FitzRoy Aubrey, MC; *b* 21 Dec 1892; Lt 13th Serv Bn Cheshire Regt; *ka* 7 July 1916

1b Adelaide Millicent Blanche Gwendolin, JP (Mon); *b* 13 Oct 1888; *m* 6 Nov 1915 her cousin Raglan Horatio Edwin Henry Somerset (*d* 29 April 1956), and *d* 20 Jan 1958, leaving issue (*see* above)

(4) John Plantagenet Edward Henry; *b* 1826; *d* 1838

(5) Boscawen Thomas George Henry (Rev), MA; *b* 2 June 1833; rector Crickhowell; *m* 1st 24 Sept 1863 Florence Smallwood (*dsp* 8 May 1874), yst dau of John Were Clarke, of Bridwell Ho, Devon; *m* 2nd 14 Nov 1878 Sophia Vernon Powys (*d* 5 April 1935), 3rd dau of Rt Rev Hon Horatio Powys, Bp Sodor and Man (*see* LILFORD, B), and *d* 13 June 1893, having had issue by his 2nd w:

1a William Horace Boscawen; *b* 7 Nov 1880; *educ* Exeter Coll Oxford (MA); Capt Mon Regt; *m* 23 July 1921 Rubie Drummond-Nairne (*d* 27 Dec 1977 aged 91), only dau of William Redston Warner, and *d* 7 Sept 1946, leaving issue:

1b +FitzRoy Douglas Boscawen [FitzRoy Somerset Esq, Thackit Eaves, Highclere, Newbury, Berks]; *b* 19 Nov 1923; *educ* Marlborough and Exeter Coll Oxford (BA 1949, MA 1957); Colonial Administrative Serv Nigeria 1950–57, Assist Advr Aden 1957–68, Lt KSLI WW II (wounded), assist master Duncan Ho Sch Moffat and Cheam Sch 1970–86; *m* 15 Sept 1962 *Sheila Jean, est dau of Dr Douglas James Bowie Wilson, of Faringdon, High Wycombe, Bucks, and has issue:

1c +Douglas William Boscawen; *b* 22 May 1965; *educ* Marlborough, Bristol U (BSc) and Queen's Coll Oxford (PhD); lecturer Aberdeen U; *m* 29 June 1995 *Dr Mary Joan, dau of Rev John Macleod, of Stornaway, Lewis

1c *Eirene Helen Giffard [Miss Eirene Somerset, 30A Belmont Rd, St Andrews, Bristol]; *b* 23 June 1963; *educ* Downe Ho; RGN and RM

1b *Helen Jane Boscawen [Mrs Henry Lock, Winterborne, W Stafford, Dorchester]; *b* 12 Aug 1925; *educ* Oxford U (MA 1950); *m* 8 July 1950 *Henry Ensor Fossett Lock, MA, only s of Maj Henry Osmond Lock, of York Ho, Dorchester, and has:

1c *Edward Henry Somerset [Edward Lock Esq, 39 Park Rd, Chiswick, London W4 3EX]; *b* 27 April 1953; *educ* Marlborough and London U (BA); *m* 1987 *Caroline Metcalfe and has:

1d *Anthony Henry; *b* 1989

1d *Emma Ruth; *b* 1991

2c *Charles John Somerset; *b* 15 April 1955; *educ* Marlborough and Keble Coll Oxford (BA, PhD); *m* 1st 1979 (*divorce* 1991) Helen Mogilandsky; *m* 2nd 1993 *Nicoletta Isar and has issue by his 1st w:

1d *Nicholas Walter; *b* 1981

1d *Nadezhda Caroline; *b* 1980

2d *Persephone; *b* 1987

3c *Richard Michael Somerset; *b* 14 Oct 1959; *educ* Marlborou gh and Balliol Coll Oxford (BA); *m* 1991 *Julia Bernhardt

1c *Amanda Mary Somerset; *b* 3 Feb 1966; *educ* Sherborne; *m* 1996 *Alan Victor Hill

2a Edward Boscawen Aylmer (Rev); *b* 16 Aug 1885; *educ* Exeter Coll Oxford (MA); Vicar: Mexborough, Yorks, 1930–37, Grinton with Marrick, nr Richmond, Yorks, 1938–43 and Middleton Tyas 1943–45; *m* 1 June 1920 Hilda Anna (*d* 15 June 1970), yst dau of Sir Montagu Cotterill, CMG, MB, FRCS, and *dsp* 25 March 1957

6 John Thomas Henry; *b* 30 Aug 1787; Col Army; *m* 4 Dec 1814 Lady Catherine Annesley (*d* 25 June 1865), dau of 1st Earl of Mountnorris (*see* VALENTIA, V), and *d* 3 Oct 1846, leaving, with other issue:

(1) Alfred Plantagenet Frederick Charles (Sir), KCB, JP, DL (Middx, Westminster and Essex), of Enfield Court, Middx, and Castle Goring, Sussex; *b* 5 Sept 1829; Hon Col 7th Bn Rifle Bde; *m* 24 Sept 1857 Adelaide Harriet (*d* 30 June 1920), yst dau of V-Adml Sir George Richard Brooke-Pechell, 4th Bt, MP (*see* 1956 edn), and *d* 26 March 1915, leaving:

1a Gwendoline Adelaide Katherine Georgiana Matilda; *m* 25 July 1887 her cousin Arthur William FitzRoy Somerset (*d* 8 Jan 1937), and *d* 24 Sept 1942, leaving issue (*see* above)

7 FitzROY JAMES HENRY, *cr* BARON RAGLAN (*qv*)

The 5th DUKE's est s,

HENRY CHARLES SOMERSET, **6th Duke of Beaufort**, KG (1805); *b* 22 Dec 1766; *educ* Westminster and Trin Coll Oxford (MA 1786); MP (Tory) Monmouth 1788–90, Bristol 1790–96 and Glos 1810–35, Ld Lt and Custos Rotulorum: Mon and Brecon 1803–35 and Glos 1810–35, V-Adml Gloucester, Constable St Briavel's Castle, Warden Forest of Dean 1812–35, High Steward Bristol 1834–35; *m* 16 May 1791 Charlotte Sophia Leveson-Gower (*d* 12 Aug 1854), dau of 1st Marquess of Stafford (*see* SUTHERLAND, D), and *d* 23 Nov 1835, having had, with seven other daus (see INCHIQUIN, B, and HUNTLY, M):

1 HENRY, **7th Duke**

2 Granville Charles Henry, PC, MP; *b* 27 Dec 1792; *m* 27 July 1822 Emily (*d* 4 Jan 1869), dau of 1st Baron Carrington (*qv*), and *d* 23 Feb 1848, having had three sons and two daus

1 Charlotte Sophia; *m* 12 Aug 1823 4th Baron Calthorpe (*qv* 1970 edn) and *d* 12 Nov 1865, leaving issue

The 6th DUKE's er s,

HENRY SOMERSET, **7th Duke of Beaufort**, KG (1842); *b* 5 Feb 1792; ADC to Duke of Wellington in Portugal and Spain 1812–14, Ld of Admlty 1815–19, Maj 1819, MP (Tory) Monmouth 1813–32, W Glos Jan-Nov 1835, High Steward Bristol 1836–53; *m* 1st 25 July 1814 Georgiana Frederica (*d* 11 May 1821), dau of Hon Henry FitzRoy (*see* SOUTHAMPTON, B), and had two daus; *m* 2nd 29 June 1822 Emily Frances (*d* 2 Oct 1889), dau of Charles Culling Smith by Lady Anne Wellesley (*see* WELLINGTON, D), and *d* 17 Nov 1853, having had, with a further six daus:

HENRY CHARLES FitzROY SOMERSET, **8th Duke of Beaufort**, KG (1867), PC (1858); *b* 1 Feb 1824; *educ* Eton; Lt Life Gds 1843, Capt 7th Dragoons 1847, Lt Col 1858, ADC to Duke of Wellington 1842 and Viscount FitzHardinge 1842–46, MP (C) E Gloucester 1846–53, High Steward Bristol 1854–99, Master of the Horse 1858–59 and 1866–68, Ld-Lt Mon 1867–99; *m* 8 July 1845 Lady Georgiana Charlotte Curzon (*d* 14 May 1906), est dau of 1st Earl Howe (*qv*), and *d* 30 April 1899, having had, with other issue:

1 HENRY ADELBERT WELLINGTON FitzROY SOMERSET, **9th Duke of Beaufort**, JP, DL (Mon and Glos); *b* 19 May 1847; Cornet RHG 1865, Capt 1869, Hereditary Keeper Raglan Castle, High Steward Bristol 1899 and Gloucester, Hon Col Glos Yeo, ADC to HM QUEEN VICTORIA 1899; *m* 9 Oct 1895 Louise Emily, DGStJ, JP Glos (*d* 11 Oct 1945), dau of William Henry Harford, DL, of Oldown, Almondsbury, Glos, and widow of Baron Carlo de Tuyll, and *d* 27 Nov 1924, leaving issue:

(1) HENRY HUGH ARTHUR FitzROY SOMERSET, **10th Duke of Beaufort**, KG (1937), PC (1936), GCVO (1930); JP (1927), DL (1923); *b* 4 April 1900; *educ* Eton and RMC Sandhurst; Ld Lt and custos rotulorum Bristol and Glos, Ld-Lt Glos 1974–84, Ld High Steward Bristol, Gloucester and Tewkesbury, Hereditary Keeper Raglan Castle, Master of the Horse 1936–84, Steward Tewkesbury 1948–84, Chllr Bristol U 1965, served RHG, Hon Col 21st (Roy Glos Hus) Armoured Car Co T&AVR 1969–71, Hon Col Roy Glos Hus, Dep Col Warwick Yeo 1971–72 and Hon Col 1972, MFH Beaufort, Pres: MCC 1952–53, Br Olympic Assoc, Br Horse Soc, Hunters Improvement and Nat Light Horse Breeding Soc 1957–68, Grand Cross Legion of Honour France, Order of: Leopold Belgium, Faithful Service Romania, House of Orange, Grand Offr Orange Nassau Netherlands, St Olav Norway, Dannebrog Denmark, North Star Sweden, Order of Menelik II Ethiopia and Christ Portugal; Roy Victorian Chain 1953, KStJ; *m* 14 June 1923 Lady (Victoria Constance) Mary Cambridge, CStJ (*d* 1987), er dau of 1st Marquess of Cambridge, GCB, GCVO, CMG (*see* 1970 edn), and *dsp* 5 Feb 1984, when the Baronies of Botetourt and Herbert (*qv*) fell into abeyance between the descendants of his sis Lady Blanche Douglas (*see* below)

(1) Blanche Linnie; *b* 15 April 1897; *m* 1st 11 June 1918 6th Earl of Saint Germans (*qv*) and had issue; *m* 2nd 15 July 1924 Capt George Francis Valentine Scott Douglas (*d* 12 June 1930), 15th Hus, and *d* 30 Aug 1968, leaving further issue (*see* 1970 edn DOUGLAS, Bt, of Springwood)

(2) Diana Maud Nina; *b* 12 Sept 1898; *m* 19 Sept 1925, as his 2nd w, Capt Lindsey Harry Compton Shedden (*d* 1971), er surv s of Lewis William Shedden, of Pont-y-Pardy, Caerphilly, Cardiff, and *d* 6 May 1935

2 Henry Richard Charles, PC, JP (Herefs and Mon), DL (Mon); *b* 7 Dec 1849; MP Mon 1871–80, Comptroller Roy Household 1874–79; *m* 6 Feb 1872 Lady Isabella Caroline (*d* 12 March 1921), er dau and coheir of 3rd Earl Somers (*see* SOMERS, B), and *d* 10 Oct 1932, leaving issue:

(1) Henry Charles Somers Augustus, OBE, JP (Surrey), DL (Worcs and Herefs); *b* 18 May 1874; Lt 1st Herefs Vol Rifles, served S African War and on Staff WW I (despatches twice, 1914 Star, Legion of Honour); *m* 1st 23 Jan 1896 (*divorce* 1920) Lady Katherine Beauclerk (*d* 1 Feb 1958), dau of 10th Duke of St Albans (*qv*); *m* 2nd 28 Jan 1932 Brenda (*d* 17 July 1946), only dau of Robert Woodhouse and widow of 3rd Marquess of Dufferin and Ava (*see* DUFFERIN AND CLANEBOYE, B), and *d* 25 Nov 1945, having had issue by his 1st w:

1a Henry Robert Somers FitzRoy de Vere, DSO (1918); *b* 3 March 1898; *educ* Eton; Capt Reserve of Offrs Coldstream Gds; *m* 2 Dec 1922 *Bettine Violet [Mrs Henry Somerset, The Round House, Netton, Salisbury, Wilts], yr dau of Maj Charles Edward Malcolm (*see* MALCOLM, Bt), and *d* 27 Feb 1965, having had issue:

1b John Alexander; *b* 1 Jan 1925; *educ* Eton; Lt Coldstream Gds WW II; *ka* 15 April 1945 Germany

2b DAVID ROBERT SOMERSET, **11th and present Duke of Beaufort**

1b Anne Elizabeth; *b* 1 Nov 1929; granted rank of duke's dau 1985, author: *Unnatural Murder* (1996) and other historical works; *m* 10 Nov 1953 *Maj David Alwyne Carne Rasch, CVO, DSO, DL, of Avon Cottage, Lower Woodford, Salisbury (*see* RASCH, Bt), and *d* 1995, leaving issue

2a John Beauclerk; *b* 5 Oct 1901; Sub-Lt RN; *d* 26 Sept 1921

3a Edward Victor; *b* 2 July 1903; 2nd Lt Coldstream Gds; *d* 23 Sept 1929 as a result of an aeroplane accident

3 (Henry) Arthur George; DL Wilts; *b* 17 Nov 1851; Maj RHG; *d* 26 May 1926

4 Henry Edward Brudenell; *b* 6 July 1853; Maj GlosYeo Cav, memb Gentlemen-at-Arms; *m* 17 Aug 1880 Fanny Julia (*d* 17 Aug 1939) (*m* 2nd 2 July 1898 Maj John Gratwicke Blagrave (*d* 12 Feb 1926), yst dau of Sir Alexander Beaumont Churchill Dixie, 10th Bt (*see* 1970 edn), and had issue:

(1) Henry FitzRoy Edward; *b* 7 Sept 1886; Lt Roy Mon RE (mil); *m* 12 March 1908 Evelyn Juliet (*m* 2nd 1915 Capt Frederick Agnew Gill, late 3rd Dragoons, and *d* Oct 1942), est dau of W L Adamthwaite, of Cirencester, Glos, and *d* 23 May 1913, leaving issue:

1a Georgina Brenda (Betty); *b* 17 Oct 1908; *m* 27 Oct 1939 (*divorce* 1957) Maj Sir John Stanley Vincent Marling, 4th Bt (*qv*), and *d* 29 June 1961, leaving issue

Seat: Badminton House, Glos. The **1st Duke** set about transforming what had been a manor house into the Palladian mansion one sees today. But it was the **3rd Duke** who is responsible for most of the present appearance. He carried out an almost total remodelling, with the result that the south drawing room is today the only example of the 17th-century building still in existence. The **3rd Duke** employed William Kent, who added the top floor to counter a sense of the house's being overshadowed by the avenues of trees planted by his employer's predecessor. The pediment and cupolas over the main entrance are also Kent's work, as is the extension either side. In addition he decorated the splendid entrance hall.

BEAUMONT

Arms: Az. semée of fleurs-de-lys, a lion rampant or. **Crest:** On a chapeau az., semée of fleurs-de-lys, doubled erm., a lion passant with tail extended or. **Motto:** *Erectus non elatus* ('Exalted, not elated'). **Creation:** Bt. (E) 21 Feb 1660/1.

SIR GEORGE HOWLAND FRANCIS BEAUMONT, 12TH BT, of Stoughton Grange, Co Leicester [Sir George Beaumont Bt, Stretton House, Manor Court, Stretton-on-Fosse, nr Moreton-in-Marsh, Glos GL56 9SB]; *b* 24 Sept 1924; *s* f 1933; *educ* Stowe; late Lt KRRC, served WW II in Coldstream Gds, Warrant Offr Roy Australian Inf 1952–58; *m* 1st 11 June 1949 (*divorce* 1951) Barbara, 2nd dau of William Singleton, of Windhill, Whiteleaf, Prince's Risborough, Bucks; *m* 2nd 27 Dec 1963 (*divorce* 1986) Henrietta Anne, dau of Dr Arthur Waymouth and Mrs R M H Rodwell, of Berks, and by her has issue:

1 *Georgina Brienne Arabella; *b* 12 June 1967

2 *Francesca Renée Henrietta; *b* 12 June 1967

Lineage: ENGILBERT COUNT OF BRIENNE 954; a Frank who with his bro wrested Brienne-le-Château, on the River Aube in Champagne, from LOUIS IV OF FRANCE and established himself there in control of the county, which was one of the seven peerages of Champagne; *d* after 968, leaving, with a dau (Ingeltrude, *m* Milon III, Count of Tonnerre, and *d* by 980):

ENGILBERT II COUNT OF BRIENNE; living 950–987; *m* Adele — and had issue:

ENGILBERT III COUNT OF BRIENNE; *b c* 970; *m* 1st Windismodis, dau of Humbert II, Seigneur of Salins (son of Humbert I, son of Aubrey, Count of Macon), and had two sons (of whom the yr Guy had an er s, Lietard, Count of Cerciaci 1050); *m* 2nd Aeiis, dau of Renard, Count of Sens, and *d* after 1008, having by her had a dau (*m* 1020 Stephen, Sire of Joinville 1005–27); his er son:

ENGILBERT IV COUNT OF BRIENNE; *b* 995; *m* Peronelle — and *d* after 1031, leaving:

WALTER I COUNT OF BRIENNE; *m* his cousin Eustachie, eventual heiress of the county of Bar-sur-Seine, dau of Milon, Count of Tonnerre, by Azeka of Bar, and *d* 1089/90, having had, with a dau (*m* Fulk IV Le Rechin, Count of Anjou (*d* 1109)):

1 Engilbert; *b* 1060; became a monk 1072; *dvp* 1085

2 ERARD I

3 Walter; living 1141

4 Milon II, Count of Bar-sur-Seine 1085, Seigneur of Juilly; *b* 1075; *m* Maud de Noyers and *d* after 1125, leaving issue:

(1) Guy, Count of Bar; *m* Peronelle, dau of Anseri de Chacenay, Baron of Chacenay in Champagne, and *d* after 1159, having had issue:

1a Milon III, Count of Bar; *m* Agnes, Dame de Braine (*m* 2nd 1152 Robert of France Count of Dreux, yr son of LOUIS VI OF FRANCE), dau of Guy de Baudemont, Seigneur of Braine, and *d* Oct 1151, having had, with two sons (Walter, William, *d* young):

1b Peronelle, Countess of Bar in her own right 1168–74; *m* Hugh de/du Puiset, Vicomte of Chartres (son of the Hugh de/du Puiset *cr* Count of Jaffa in the Holy Land by BALDWIN I OF JERUSALEM and cousin or perhaps f by another w of the Hugh de/du Puiset who bought the Earldom of Northumberland in 1189; *see* NORTHUMBERLAND, D, preliminary remarks), and *d* at Durham Nov 1189, leaving issue

2a Manasses, Count of Bar 1151–68; became a priest 1169, Duke-Bp of Langres and Peer of France 1179; took part in the Third Crusade against Saladin 1190; *d* unm 1193

3a William, living 1139

4a Guy, living 1139

5a Thibaut, Seigneur of Bragelogne 1151–1204; *m* Margaret de Chacenay, dau of James I, Baron of Chacenay, and left issue:

1b Peronelle, held half the county of Bar 1218–23, when she sold it to the Count of Champagne; *m* Guy de Chappes (*d* 1220), and *d* Dec 1236

2b Agnes; *m* Philip de Plancy (*d* 1240)

1a Ermesent; *b* 1159; *m* 1st Anseau II, Seigneur of Trainel (*d* 1184); *m* 2nd Thibaut I, Count of Bar-le Duc (*d* 1214), and *d* 1214

(2) Renard, Abbot of Citeaux 1133; *d* Jan 1151

(3) Herbert the Fat, Sire of Ville-sur-Arce; *m* Aimée, heiress of Ville-sur-Arce, and *d* 1167, leaving issue

ENGILBERT IV's son,

ERARD I, COUNT OF BRIENNE; took part in the First Crusade 1097; *m* Alice, Dame de Ramerupt, dau of Andrew, Sire of Ramerupt, yr son of Hilduin de Montdidier, Count of Roucy, and *d* after 1125, having had, with a dau (Felicity, *b* 1110, *m* 1st Simon, Sire de Broyes (*d* 1152), *m* 2nd 1154 Geoffrey III the Old, Sire de Joinville, Seneschal of Champagne (*d* 1188), and *d* 1154):

WALTER II, COUNT OF BRIENNE, Sire of Ramerupt; took part in Second Crusade 1147–52; *m* 1st Humbeline — (*d* after 1138); *m* 2nd Adeliz, dau of Andrew de Baudemont, Seigneur of Braine-sur-Vesle and Seneschal of Champagne, and *d c* 1158, having by his 1st w had issue:

1 Guy, living 1133; *dvp*

2 ERARD II, his successor

3 John, Abbot of Beaulieu 1156–92

4 Andrew, Sire of Ramerupt; cmded the advance party of French troops in the Third Crusade; *m* Nov 1167 Adele, Dame de Venisy (*m* 2nd Gaucher de Joigny, Seigneur of Château-Renard, yr son of Renaud III, Count of Joigny), dau and heiress of Anseau, Seigneur of Venisy, and was *k* at the Siege of Acre 14 Oct 1189, leaving issue:

(1) Erard, Sire of Ramerupt and Venisy; claimed the County of Champagne in right of his 2nd w but the Peers of France decided against him at Melun 1216, though he was compensated with other lands 1221; *m* 1st Helisende, widow of Thomas, Count du Perche, and dau of Hugh II, Count of Rethel; *m* 2nd 1214 Philippine (*b* 1195), dau and coheir of HENRY KING OF JERUSALEM and Count of Champagne, and *d* after 1244, leaving by her:

1a Henry, Sire of Ramerupt; *m* Margaret, dau of John I 'the Wise', Count of Châlon and the Auxonnois, and was *k* at the Battle of Mansourah Egypt during the Seventh Crusade 8 Feb 1250

1b Erard, Sire of Ramerupt; *m* Maud —, and *d* after 1278

2a Erard, Sire of Ramerupt, *k* Seventh Crusade

1a Mary; *m* 1st Gaucher III, Seigneur de Nanteuil-la-Fosse (*d* 1241); *m* 2nd Hugh II, Seigneur de Conflans

2a Sybil, Abbess of Ramerupt

3a Isabel, Dame de Ramerupt; *m* 1258 Henry V, Count of Grandpré (*d* 1287)

4a Margaret; *m* 1st 1234 Anseau, Sire de Dampierre; *m* 2nd Dietrich van Beveren, Castellan of Dixmude, and *d* a nun at Flines 1275

5a Jeanne, Dame de Sens; *m* 1250 Matthew III, Sire de Montmorency, known as the 'Premier Christian Baron' (*d* 1270)

(1) Isabel; *m* 1st Miles, Seigneur de Pougy (*d* 1219); *m* 2nd Philip de Courtenay, Marquis of Namur (*d* Siege of Avignon 1226; *see* DEVON, E), and *d* after 1225

(2) Agnes; *m* Milon VII de Noyers

1 Eustache, living 1133–65

2 Mary; *m* William III, Castellan of St Omer (*d* 1175)

WALTER II's son,

ERARD II COUNT OF BRIENNE; took part in Third Crusade; *m* 1166 Agnes de Montfaucon, dau of Richard II, Count of Montbeliard, and *d* Siege of Acre 8 Feb 1191, leaving issue:

1 WALTER III COUNT OF BRIENNE, also DUKE OF APULIA; took part in Third Crusade; *m* 1200 Mary-Elvira de Hauteville (*m* 2nd 1206 Giacomo Sanseverino, Lord of Tricarico; *m* 3rd Tegrimo Guidi), sis and heiress of WILLIAM III OF SICILY and dau of TANCRED, KING OF SICILY and COUNT OF LECCE; claimed to be King of Sicily in right of his wife, was recognised by POPE INNOCENT III as Prince of Taranto and invested by him with the County of Lecce May 1200, but *d* June 1205 of wounds received in fighting against forces of the Holy Roman Emperor in an attempt to establish his claim, leaving, with other issue:

(1) WALTER IV COUNT OF BRIENNE, called 'the Great', also COUNT OF JAFFA (from 1239) and ASCALON in the Holy Land and COUNT OF LECCE; *b* 1205; *m* 1233 Mary of Luisignan, dau and eventual coheir of HUGH I KING OF CYPRUS, and *d* in Cairo a captive of the Mamelukes, by whom he had been captured during the Battle of Gaza 1244, leaving:

1a JOHN II COUNT OF BRIENNE; *m* Mary, widow of Hugh de Rethel, Seigneur of Beaufort, and dau of Siger d'Enghien, and *dsp* Sept 1260

2a HUGH COUNT OF BRIENNE and LECCE, which he recovered after taking part with Charles of Anjou in the conquest of Naples *c* 1268; unsuccessful claimant (through his mother) to the Regency of Jerusalem 1264; had best claim to Crown of Cyprus 1267 but did not press it; Baron of Karytena in Greece in right of his 1st w; Regent of Athens from 1288 during his w's nephew's minority; *m* 1st after 1275 Isabel de La Roche (*d* 1279), widow of Geoffrey, Baron of Karytena and Lord of Thebes, dau of Guy I Duke of Athens, and had a s and dau (Agnes-Isabel, *m* 1297 John II, Count of Joigny, and *d* 1324); *m* 2nd 1291 his 1st w's sis-in-law Helena Angelina Comnena, widow of William I Duke of Athens and dau of John Angelus Sebastocrator of Thessaly and Duke of Neopatras (illegitimate son of Michael II Despot of Epirus) and *d* of wounds 9 Aug 1296 received in the defence of Brindisi on behalf of the Angevins, having by her had a yr dau (Jeannette, *m* 1310 Nicholas Sanudo Duke of Naxos and *d* 1341); his s by his 1st w:

1b WALTER V COUNT OF BRIENNE and LECCE, also DUKE OF ATHENS (as which he *s* through his mother 1308); hired Catalan mercenaries to help him recover territory in Greece from the Byzantines but later fell out with them and was *k* in battle 15 March 1311 trying to expel them, after which they seized his Duchy of Athens; *m* 1305 Jeanne (*d* 16 Jan 1354), dau of Gaucher V de Chastillon, Count of Porcean and Constable of France, and had:

1c WALTER VI COUNT OF BRIENNE and LECCE, titular Duke of Athens (which he failed to reconquer 1331–32), but actual ruler only of Argolis; King of France's Lt in Thiérache 1339; Lord of Florence by election 1342 but deposed 1343; *m* 1st Dec 1325 Margaret, dau of Philip I Prince of Taranto by Thamar, dau of Nicephorus Angelus, Despot of Epirus, and had a s (Walter of Brienne, *k vp* 1332 by the Catalans during his f's attempt to recover Athens); *m* 2nd 1344, as her 1st husb, his cousin Jeanne, dau of Raoul, Count of Eu and Guines (Isee below), and was *k* fighting as Constable of France in the defeat of the French by the English at Poitiers 19 Sept 1356, having by her had two daus (Jeanne and Margaret, both *d* young)

1c Isabel, heiress of Argolis, of Brienne and Lecce; *m* 1321 Walter IV, Seigneur d'Enghien (*k* Battle of Poitiers 1356), and *d* July 1362; ancestress of the Luxembourg and Lomenie Counts of Brienne

3a Amaury; *dsp* 1270

2 William; *m* Eustachie (*m* 2nd 1201 William I de Champlitte, Prince of Achaea (*d* 1209/10); *m* 3rd *c* 1215 William I of Champagne, Count of Sancerre (*d* 1219), and *d* after 1235), sis of PETER de COURTENAY, EMPEROR-elect OF BYZANTIUM (*see* DEVON, E), and *d* March 1201, leaving issue:

(1) Andrew; *d* 1215

(1) Elvis; *m* John, Vicomte of St Florentin (*d* July 1235)

3 Andrew, living 1177–81

4 JOHN I, of whom below

1 Ida; *m* Arnoul, Seigneur de Risnel, and had a dau (Margaret, *m* Balian I, Lord of Sidon)

ERARD II's yr son,

JOHN I de BRIENNE, KING OF JERUSALEM in right of his w (as which crowned 1210, reigning at Acre since Jerusalem itself was in Saracen hands) and EMPEROR OF BYZANTIUM, so elected 1229 (aged 80) by the Frankish Latins as colleague for BALDWIN II, a minor, despite his having been among the Crusaders who turned aside from their mission to the Holy Land to sack Byzantium 1204; *b c* 1148; took part in Third Crusade; Regent County of Brienne for his nephew 1205–21; led Fifth Crusade 1218–19; *m* 1st 15 Sept 1210 MARY, QUEEN OF JERUSALEM in her own right (*d* 1212), dau and heiress of Conrad, Marquis of Montferrat, by ISABEL OF ANJOU, QUEEN OF JERUSALEM, dau of AMAURY I, KING OF JERUSALEM, and *d* 21 March 1237, having become a Franciscan friar, having had issue:

1 ISABEL/YOLANDE, QUEEN OF JERUSALEM; *m* 9 Nov 1225 the HOLY ROMAN EMPEROR FREDERICK II and *d* 31 April 1228, aged 16, leaving issue

JOHN I *m* 2nd 1214 Stephania (*dsp* 1219), dau and heiress of LEO II, KING OF ARMENIA; *m* 3rd 1223 Berengaria (*d* 12 April 1237), dau of ALFONSO IX, KING OF CASTILE AND LEON, and by her had further issue:

1 Alfonso, Count of Eu, Gt Chamberlain of France 1258; *m* Mary of Lusignan (*d* 1252), dau and heiress of Raoul d'Issoudun, Count of Eu, and *d* at Tunis 25 Aug 1270, having had (with an er son Raoul, *dvp*, and a dau Blanche, Abbess of Maubuisson lez Pontoise in 1309) issue:

(1) John, Count of Eu; *m* Beatrice (*d* 1304), dau of Guy de Chastillon, Count of St Paul, and *d* 1294, leaving issue:

1a John, Count of Eu and Guines; *m* Jeanne (*d* 1331), dau and heiress of Baldwin, Count of Guines, and was *k* fighting the Flemings Battle of Courtrai 1302, leaving (with a dau Margaret, *m* Guy II, Vicomte of Thouars):

1b Raoul, Count of Eu and Guines, Constable of France 1330, Amb to England 1331; *m* Jeanne, dau and heiress of Dreux IV de Mello, Seigneur of l'Orme and Château-Chinon, and was *k* in a tournament at Paris 18 Jan 1344, leaving issue:

1c Raoul, Count of Eu and Guines, Constable of France; *m* 1340 Catherine (*m* 3rd 1352 William I of Flanders, Count of Namur, and *d* 18 June 1388), widow of Azzo Visconti, Lord of Milan, and dau of Louis II of Savoy, Lord of Vaud in Switzerland, Senator of Rome, and *dspl* 19 Nov 1351, being beheaded while held in secrecy by the French King for allegedly having pledged the County of Guisnes to the English King as ransom after beng captured by the English 1346, leaving an illegitimate son (John du Bois, Seigneur de la Maison Fort, legitimated and ennobled 1395)

1c Jeanne, heiress of Eu and Guines; *m* 1st 1344 her kinsman WALTER VI COUNT OF BRIENNE (*see* above); *m* 2nd 1357 Louis d'Evreux, Count of Etampes, Peer of France (*d* 1400), and *d* 6 July 1389

1a Margaret; *m* John of Flanders, Seigneur de Dampierre

2a Jeanne; *m* 1st Raymond V, Vicount of Turenne; *m* 2nd Renaud, Vicounte of Amiens

3a Maud, Abbess of Maubuisson lez Pontoise

2b John, Grand Butler of France 1258, Amb to Castile 1275; *m* 1st MARY (*dsp*), widow of ALEXANDER II KING OF SCOTS and dau of Enguerrand III 'the Great', Sire of Coucy; *m* 2nd Jeanne, Dame du Château du Loir, dau of Geoffrey IV, Vicomte of Châteaudun, and and *d* 1296, having by her had issue:

1c Blanche, Dame de La Loupelande; *m* 1269 William de Fiennes, Baron of Tingry

3 LOUIS, of whom below

1a Mary; *m* 19 April 1229 BALDWIN II De COURTENAY EMPEROR OF BYZANTIUM (*d* 1273) and *d* after 5 April 1275

JOHN I's yr son,

LOUIS of Acre, VICOMTE OF BEAUMONT in right of his w; *m* by 1253 Agnes, sis and heiress of Richard II, Vicomte of Beaumont (*d* 17 Sept 1242), and dau of Raoul VI, Vicomte of Beaumont in Maine (the family having been hereditary Viscounts of the Maine since at least 936, with Roscelin II, Viscomte 1145–76, marrying Constance, illegitimate dau of HENRY I OF ENGLAND, and Ermengarde de Beaumont (whose sis Constance *m* Roger de Toenior de Conches; *see* STAFFORD, B) marrying 1186 WILLIAM THE LION KING OF SCOTS), and had issue:

1 JOHN VICOMTE OF BEAUMONT; *m* 1263 Jeanne de La Guerche, Dame de Pounance, dau of Geoffrey, Seigneur of La Guerche; and *d* after 1305, leaving, with a yr son (Richard) and two daus (Anne, *m* Payen de Chourses, Seigneur of Malicorne; Isabel, *m* Geoffrey, Seigneur d'Ancenis):

(1) ROBERT VICOMTE OF BEAUMONT; *m* (contract 25 Aug 1303) Mary, Dame de Chastelais, dau of Maurice VI, Sire of Craon, and *d* 20 Sept 1327, leaving, with three daus (Mary, Abbess of Ronceray; Jeanne, *m* John of Amboise, Seigneur of Chaumont; Margaret, *m* Bernard, Vicomte of Ventadour):

1a JOHN II VICOMTE OF BEAUMONT; *m* 1st Isabel, dau of John III, Sire of Harcourt, Viscomte of Châtelherault, and had issue:

1b Jeanne, Dame du Hommet

2b Mary; *m* William Chamaillart, Seigneur d'Antenaise, and left issue, being the eventual heiress of Beaumont-le-Vicomte in Maine, and from her that fief descended in the female line to the Houses of Alençon and Bourbon

1a (cont.) JOHN II *m* 2nd Margaret de Poitiers, dau of Aymer IV, Count of Valentinois, and by her had further issue:

1b LOUIS II VICOMTE OF BEAUMONT; *m* 1357 Jeanne de Bourbon (*m* 2nd Bouchard VII, Count of Vendôme and Castres), dau of James I, Count of La Marche and Ponthieu, but *dsp*, *k* Battle of Cocherel 6 May 1364

2b Geoffrey, Seigneur du Lude; *m* Jeanne, Dame de Beaucay (*m* 2nd 1360 Charles d'Artois, Count of Longueville and Pezenas, and *d* March 1402), dau and heiress of Hugh, Seigneur of Beaucay, and *dsp* by 1360

3b Jeanne, a nun

4b Margaret; *m* Bouchard de Vendôme, Seigneur de Feuillet, living 1373

2 Louis, Bp Durham; *d* 24 Sept 1333

3 HENRY, 1st LORD (Baron) BEAUMONT

1 Margaret; *m* Bohemund VII, Prince of Antioch and Count of Tripoli (*dsp* 19 Oct 1287), and *d* 9 April 1328

2 Jeanne, Dame de Loue; *m* 11 Nov 1286 Guy VIII de Montmorency, Sire of Laval, Count of Caserta (*k* 22 Aug 1295), and *d* 1310

3 Mary *m* Henry III d'Avaugour, Baron of Mayenne and Goello

4 Isabel; *m* John de Vesci, fedual Ld of Alnwick, and *dsp* 1334

LOUIS VICOMTE OF BEAUMONT *d* after 1263; his yr son,

HENRY BEAUMONT, EARL OF BUCHAN (E), so *cr* 23 Jan 1333/4 (*see* also BUCHAN, E, preliminary remarks), as also 1st LORD (Baron) BEAUMONT (E), so *cr* 4 March 1308/9 by writ of summons according to later doctrine, Lord of the Isle of Man 1310, PC and Constable of England 1322, ktd by 1308, Envoy to France 1312–31, Constable of the (English?) Army, 1333, English Justiciar of Scotland 1338; *m c* 1310 Alice (*d* 1349), dau of Alexander Comyn, Sheriff of Aberdeen, and niece and heir of line of John Comyn, Earl of Buchan, and *d* 10 March 1339/40, leaving issue:

1 JOHN, 2nd LORD

2 Richard

3 John

4 Thomas, of Bolton Percy

1 Alice

2 Elizabeth *m* (contract 1330) 3rd Lord (Baron) Audley (*qv*) and *d* 27 Oct 1400

3 Joan; *m* Fulk 3rd Lord (Baron) FitzWarin, KG (*d* of plague 1349)

4 Isabel; *m c* 1337 Henry 1st Duke of Lancaster (*d* of plague 24 March 1360/1), gggs in the male line of HENRY III (of England), and *d* on or after 23 March 1336, having had two daus (Matilda/Maud, *m* 1st Ralp, s of Ralph 1st Earl of Stafford, *m* 2nd Wilhelm I, Duke of Bavaria, *dsp* 1362; Blanche, *m* as his 1st w John of Gaunt, Duke of Lancaster, 4th s of EDWARD III, and was mother of HENRY IV)

5 Beatrice; *m* Charles I, Count of Dammartin

6 Catherine; *m* David of Strathbogie, Earl of Atholl (*k* Battle of Kilblane 30 Nov 1335), and *d* 11 Nov 1368

The 1st LORD's est son,

JOHN de BEAUMONT, 2nd LORD (Baron) BEAUMONT, so *cr* by writ of summons to Parl but never summoned as Earl of Buchan; *b c* 1318; ktd 1338; *m* by June 1337 Eleanor (*m* 2nd 1345 Richard FitzAlan, 10th/3rd Earl of Arundel, *see* NORFOLK, D), dau of Henry, 3rd Earl of Lancaster (ggs of HENRY III), and *d* May 1342, leaving issue:

1 HENRY de BEAUMONT, 3rd LORD (Baron) BEAUMONT; *b* Brabant 1340; *m* Margaret de Vere (*m* 2nd Sir Nicholas Lovain and 3rd Sir John Devereux), dau of 7th Earl of Oxford (*see* SAINT ALBANS, D), and *d* 17 June 1369, leaving, with other issue:

(1) JOHN de BEAUMONT, 4th LORD (Baron) BEAUMONT, KG (1393), PC (1389); *b* 1361; Adml of the N and Warden of W Marches towards Scotland 1389, Castellan Cherbourg 1390, Constable Dover Castle and Warden Cinque Ports 1392, Envoy France 1395; *m* Catherine (*d* 1426), dau and heiress of Thomas de Everingham, of Laxton, Notts, and *d* 9 Sept 1396, leaving with a dau (Margaret, *m* 3rd Lord (Baron) Botreaux; *see* LOUDOUN, E):

1a HENRY de BEAUMONT, 5th LORD (Baron) BEAUMONT, KB (1399); *b* 1380; ktd 1399, a Commr to negotiate peace with France 1410–11; *m* by July 1405 Elizabeth (*d* 1428), dau of 5th Lord (Baron) Willoughby de Eresby (*qv*), and *d* late summer 1413, leaving, with three daus (Eleanor; Katherine; Anne, a nun at Barking):

1b JOHN de BEAUMONT, 1st VISCOUNT BEAUMONT, the first ever of this rank of peerage in England, so *cr* 12 Feb 1439/40, as also previously 27 July 1436 COUNT OF BOULOGNE (a policy pursued by HENRY V and HENRY VI of granting fiefs and titles to leading English nobles in English-occupied France to consolidate their hold on the area), KG (1441), KB (1426), PC (1434), Gt Chamberlain 1450 and Constable 1445–50 of England, feudal Vicomte of Beaumont in Maine (conferred on him by HENRY VI 18 Jan 1440/1); *b* 1409; *m* 1st between summer 1425 and summer 1436 Elizabeth Phelip (*d* 1440), dau and heiress of William, held to have been 1st Lord (Baron) Bardolf of the notional 1437 *cr*; *m* 2nd after 1442, as her 3rd husb, Lady Katherine Nevill(e), dau by his 2nd w of 1st Earl of Westmorland (*see* ABERGAVENNY, M), and was *k* fighting on the Lancastrian side at the Yorkist victory of Northampton 10 July 1460, leaving, with an er s (Henry, *dvp*):

1c WILLIAM de BEAUMONT, 2nd VISCOUNT BEAUMONT; *b* 1438; ktd by late summer 1460; captured by the Yorkists at the Battle of Towton and attainted by their Parl 1461, restored 1470 but again forfeited for opposing EDWARD IV 1471, restored once more after HENRY VII's victory at Bosworth 1485; *m* 1st by 4 March 1461 Lady Joan Stafford, dau of 1st Duke of Buckingham (*see* STAFFORD, B); *m* 2nd 24 April 1486 Elizabeth (*m* 2nd 13th Earl of Oxford (*see* ST ALBANS, D) and *d* 26 June 1537), dau and heiress of Sir Richard Scrope, yr son of Henry, 4th Lord (Baron) Scrope (of Bolton), and *dsp* 19 Dec 1507, when the Viscountcy and French honours expired but the Barony of Beaumont fell into abeyance (*see* NORFOLK, D)

1c Joan; *m* 1st 8th Lord (Baron) Lovel (*d* 9 Jan 1464/5) and had issue (*see* NORFOLK, D); *m* 2nd 1465 Sir William Stanley (*see* DERBY, E) and *d* 5 Aug 1466

1b Henry; had:

1c Henry, of Wednesbury, Staffs; *m* Joan, dau and heiress of William Leventhorpe, of Wednesbury, and had issue:

1d Henry, of Wednesbury; *m* Eleanor Sutton, dau of 3rd Lord (Baron) Dudley (*qv*), and left issue:

1e Henry (Sir), of Wednesbury; had issue:

1f John (Sir), of Wednesbury; *dspm*, leaving issue:

1g Joan, heiress of Tinmore, Staffs; *m* William Babington, yr son of Thomas Babington, of Dethick, Derbys

2g Dorothy, heiress of Wednesbury; *m* Humphrey Comberford, of Comberford

3g Eleanor; *m* Humphrey Babington (bro of the above William Babington)

2 THOMAS (Sir), of whom below

3 Richard

1 Eleanor, a nun at Amesbury

2 Margaret, a nun at Dartford

3 Elizabeth; *m* by 1411 William, 3rd Lord (Baron) Botreaux (*d* 16 May 1462; *see* ST DAVIDS, V)

The 4th LORD's yr son,

Sir THOMAS BEAUMONT, Seigneur of Basqueville Normandy 1426, Captain of Château-Gaillard, Warden Cinque Ports and Constable Dover Castle; *m* 1426 Philippine, dau and heiress of Thomas Maureward, of Cole Orton alias Overton Quatermarsh, Leics, and had issue:

1 JOHN, his heir

2 Thomas, of Thringston, nr Cole Orton, living 1495; *m* Anne, dau of Sir Robert Moton, of Peckleton, Leics, and had issue:

(1) Thomas, of Thringston, leased lands in Cotes Hodington, Broughton, Prestwould, Wimeswould and Loughborough to his cousin John Beaumont, of Cole Orton and another *c* 1530; *m* Anne Harcourt and *d* 1531/2, leaving, with two daus (Mary, *m* Richard Storey, of Braunston; Dorothy, *m* John Rigmalden):

1a John; Master of the Rolls; surrendered all his manors and goods to the Crown, but the estate of Gracedieu Priory, Leics (bought by him and his w 1539) was restored to his w 1557; *m* 1st Isabel, dau of Lawrence Dutton, of Dutton, Cheshire, and by her had a dau (Anne, *m* 1st—Dutton, *m* 2nd Thomas Ashby, of Loseby); *m* 2nd Elizabeth, dau and coheir of Sir William Hastings, bro of 1st Earl of Huntingdon (*qv*), and by her had:

1b Francis, Justice Court of Common Pleas 1592/3–98, MP Aldborough 1572; *m* Anne, dau of Sir George Pierrepont, of Holme Pierrepont, Notts, and widow of Thomas Thorold, of Marston, Lincs, and *d* 22 April 1598, leaving issue:

1c Henry (Sir), of Gracedieu; ktd 1603; *m* Barbara (*m* 2nd Sir Henry Harpur, Bt), dau of Anthony Faunt, of Foston, Leics, and *dspm* 13 July 1605 (aged 24), leaving issue:

1d Barbara; *m* 1st John Harpur, of Swarkeston, Derbys (*dsp*); *m* 2nd 1629 Sir Wolstan Dixie, 1st Bt (*see* 1970 edn), and *d* Dec 1666, leaving issue

2c Sir JOHN BEAUMONT, 1st Bt (E), so *cr* 31 Jan 1626/7, of Gracedieu; *b c* 1582; poet; *m* Elizabeth, dau of John Fortescue, gs of Sir Geoffrey Pole (*see* ABERGAVENNY, M), and *d* 19 April 1627, leaving issue:

1d Sir JOHN BEAUMONT, 2nd Bt, of Gracedieu; *b* 24 June 1607; royalist Col Civil War; *k* Siege Gloucester Sept 1643

2d Francis; *b* 13 Jan 1608; Jesuit; *d* unm

3d Henry; *b* 13 April 1610; *d* unm

4d Gervase; *b* 23 May 1614; *d* 4 June 1621

5d George; *b* 23 Nov 1616; *d* unm

6d Sir THOMAS BEAUMONT, 3rd and last Bt, of Gracedieu; *b* 29 April 1620, *dspm* 7 July 1686, when Gracedieu passed to his est dau and her husb, but was sold by them; *m* Vere (*m* 2nd George Lane), only child of Sir William Tufton, 1st Bt, and *dspm* 7 July 1666, when the btcy expired, having had, with four other daus (*d* young):

1e Cicely; *m* her cousin Robert Beaumont, of Barrow-Upon-Trent (*see* below), and *d* 1697, leaving issue

2e Vere; *m* Sir John Rayney, 3rd Bt (*d* Feb 1704)

3e Mary; *m* George Morton, of Sileby

4e Jane; *m* Charles Byerly, of Belgrave

5e Anne; *m* Robert Pawley

7d Charles; *b* 6 Feb 1622; *d* unm

1d Helen; *b* 5 June 1611; *d* unm

2d Anne; *b* 26 Sept 1612; *d* in infancy

3d Catherine; *b* 31 July 1615

4d Mary; *b* 7 July 1617; *m* 1st Sir Edmond Williams; *m* 2nd John Tasborough

3c Francis; the dramatist; *b* 1584; barrister Inner Temple 1600; *m* Ursula, dau and coheir of Henry Isley, of Sundridge, Kent, and *d* 6 March 1615/6, leaving issue:

1d Elizabeth; allegedly *m* a Scottish Col and was living 1682

2d Frances; living unm 1700, memb household of Duke of Ormonde (*see* ORMONDE, M)

2b Henry; barrister Inner Temple; *d* aged 42

1b Elizabeth; *m* by 1 June 1557, as his 1st w, 3rd Baron Vaux of Harrowden (*qv*)

2a Edward, of Barrow-upon-Trent, Derbys; living 1550; *m* Anne Milgate, heiress of Lockington, Leics, and was ancestor of the BEAUMONTs of Barrow-upon-Trent, who held the estate there till the second half of the 19th century

Sir THOMAS *d* 1457; his er son,

JOHN BEAUMONT, of Cole Orton and Godeby; *m* Joan, dau of Sir John D'Arcy, of Torksey, yr son of 5th Lord (Baron) D'Arcy de Knayth (*qv*), and was *k* Battle of Towton 29 March 1461, his estates being forfeited posthumously, leaving, with an est s (John (Sir), of Cole Orton and Godeby, KB (1490), *b* 1446, restored to his f's estates 1485, *dsp* 11 Aug 1531) and four yr ones (Henry; William; Richard; Robert, all *dsp*):

GEORGE BEAUMONT, of Overton Quatermarsh; *m* Joan, dau and heiress of Sir Thomas Pauncefote, of Northall, Gloucs and *d* 1531, having had issue:

1 WILLIAM; *m* Mary (*d* 2 July 1539), dau of Sir William Basset, of Fledburgh, Notts, and *dvp* 1529, leaving issue:

(1) RICHARD, of whom below

(2) George; settled in Sussex; *m* Elizabeth, dau of Nicholas Leigh, of Addington, Surrey, and had issue:

1a George; settled in Kent; *m* Elizabeth Leigh, widow of Robert Lusher, and had, with a dau (Margaret):

1b Henry; Fell All Souls 1571, Dean Windsor 1622; *d* 30 June 1637

2b Thomas, of Giltisham, Devon; living 1606; *m* 1st Elizabeth, dau of Thomas Glidd; *m* 2nd Dorothy, dau of Nicholas Bluet, and had, with three other sons (Henry; John; Thomas) and two daus (Grace; Dorothy):

1c Glidd; Fell All Souls 1602

1c Elizabeth; *m* Matthew Wren, Dean Windsor

(3) Edward; *d* unm

(4) Simon

(5) John (Rev); Rector of Cole Orton

(6) Anthony, of Glenfield, Leics; *m* Anne, dau of Thomas Armstrong, of Corby, Lincs, and had, with three sons (Maurice; Thomas, both *d* unm; Francis, *m* twice and had issue):

1a MARY Beaumont, COUNTESS OF BUCKINGHAM in her own right, so *cr* 1618 for life; *m* 1st Sir George VILLIERS, of Brokesby, High Sheriff Leics (*d* 4 Jan 1605/6) (*see* JERSEY, E); *m* 2nd 19 June 1606 Sir William RAYNER; *m* 3rd Sir Thomas COMPTON, bro of 1st Earl of Northampton (*see* NORTHAMPTON, M), and *d* 19 April 1632, leaving issue

(7) William

(1) Cicely; *m* Henry Fenton

(2) Katherine; *m* Leonard Bardsey

2 Edmund; *m* Katherine Laxham and had a dau (Mary, *m* Sir Matthew Charnock)

1 Anne; *m* 1st — Francis, of Tickenhall, Derbys; *m* 2nd William Turner

GEORGE BEAUMONT's gs and heir,

RICHARD BEAUMONT, of Cole Orton and Godeby; *m* Colette (*m* 2nd William Villiers, of Brokesby), dau and heiress of Richard Clerke, of Willoughby (*see* CLERKE, Bt), er bro of Sir John Clerke, and *d* 18 Oct 1538, leaving issue:

1 NICHOLAS, his heir

2 Thomas

1 Mary; *m* 1st — Sharpe; *m* 2nd — Hatcliffe

2 Avery; *m* Thomas Findern, of Findern, Derbys, and *d* 1601

3 Anne; *m* William Kilden

4 Dorothy; *dsp*

RICHARD BEAUMONT's er son,

NICHOLAS BEAUMONT, of Cole Orton; MP Leics *temp* ELIZABETH I; *b* 1529; *m* Anne (*d* 7 Sept 1581), dau of William Saunders, of Welford, Northants, and *d* 9 July 1585, leaving issue:

1 Henry (Sir), of Cole Orton, MP Leics 1589, High Sheriff 1594, ktd 1603; petitioned unsuccessfully for the Viscountcy of Beaumont to be revived in his favour; *m* Elizabeth (*d* 26 March 1608), sis and heiress of Humphrey Lovis and dau of John Lovis, citizen of London, and *d* 31 March 1607, leaving issue:

(1) Sir THOMAS BEAUMONT, 1st Bt (E), so *cr* 1619, and 1st VISCOUNT BEAUMONT OF SWORDS, Co Dublin (I), so *cr* 20 May 1622; MP Leics, ktd 1603, High Sheriff Leics 1610–11; *m* by 1614 Elizabeth (*b* 1570), dau and heiress of Henry Sapcote, of Bracebridge, Lincs, by Eleanor, dau and coheir of Robert Sapcote, of Elton, Hunts, and *d* 1624/5, leaving, with five yr daus (Katherine; Frances; Eleanor; Anne; Jane):

1a SAPCOTE BEAUMONT, 2nd VISCOUNT BEAUMONT OF SWORDS; *b* 10 May 1614; *m* 1st 28 May 1632 Bridget (*d* May 1640), yr dau of Sir Thomas Monson, 1st Bt, and had:

1b THOMAS BEAUMONT, 3rd VISCOUNT BEAUMONT OF SWORDS; *bapt* 10 April 1634; *m* Mary, dau of Sir Erasmus de la Fontain, of Kirby Bellars, Leics, but *dsp* 11 June 1702, when the btcy and Viscountcy expired, leaving Cole Orton to **Sir George Beaumont, 4th Bt** (*see* below)

2b John, MP Nottingham 1685, Lt-Col Duke of Berwick's Regt; on 10 Sept 1688, in the affair of the 'Portsmouth Captains', resisted JAMES II's attempt to leaven the English Army with a number of Irish Roman Catholics, for which he was court-martialled and cashiered; took part in the Whig Revolution Dec 1688, when made Colonel of his Old Regt, fighting for WILLIAM III Battle of the Boyne 1690; MP Hastings 1688 and 1690; served Flanders and Scotland until 1695; Govr Dover Castle; fought a duel with Sir William Forrester, whom he disarmed, after a quarrel in Parl May 1695; *m* 1st Felicia Mary, dau of Sir Hatton Fermor (*see* HESKETH, B), and widow of Sir Charles Compton (*see* NORTHAMPTON, M); *m* 2nd Philippa, dau of Sir Nicholas Carew, of Beddington Surey, *dsp* 3 July 1701

1b Elizabeth, eventual heir general; *bapt* 20 March 1632/3; *m* 8 Aug 1650 Sir John Hotham, 2nd Bt (*see* HOTHAM B)

1a (cont.) The 2nd VISCOUNT *m* 2nd by 1643 Anne (*d* Sept 1678), dau of Sir William Villiers, Bt, and *d* 1658, having by her had issue:

3b William; *b* 1643; *dsp*

2a Henry; *b* 1616

3a Thomas, *k* at Worcester 1642

4a Robert; *d* Cambridge U

1a Elizabeth; *m* 1st 1623 Sir Thomas Waldron, of Charley Leics (*d* 1628); *m* 2nd Henry Hastings, s of Sir Henry Hastings, of Kirby and Braunston, Leics (gs of 1st Earl of Huntingdon, *qv*), and had issue by him

2a Mary; *m* Francis Manby

2 Francis, Master of the Charterhouse; *dsp* 18 June 1624

3 Thomas (Sir); *m* Catherine (*d* 1621), dau and heiress of Thomas Farnham, of Bedworth, Leics, and *d* 27 Nov 1614, leaving issue:

(1) Henry (Sir), of Stoughton Grange; *m* Elizabeth, dau of Sir William Turpin, of Knaptoft, and *d* April 1648, leaving issue:

1a THOMAS (Sir), **1st Bt**

(1) ELIZABETH Beaumont, BARONESS [*sic*] OF CRAMOND (S) in her own right, so *cr* 29 Feb 1627/8, with remainder to her 2nd husb's s by his 1st w, to the exclusion of her own flesh and blood by her 1st husb; *m* 1st Sir John Ashburnham, of Ashburnham, Sussex (*d* 1620; *see* 1924 edn ASHBURNHAM, E), and had issue; *m* 2nd 14 Dec 1626, as his 2nd w, Sir Thomas RICHARDSON (Ch Justice King's Bench; *m* 1st 20 July 1595 Ursula, 3rd dau of John Southwell, and by her had an only surv s, Thomas, *Master of Cramond*, whose son s his gf's 2nd w as 2nd Baron of Cramond) and was *bur* 3 April 1651

4 Huntingdon, of Bedworth, Warwicks; *m* after 1616 — Holland

1 Dorothy; *m* William Read, of Barton, Berks

2 Catherine; *m* 1st Anthony Byron (*dvp*), est s of Sir John Byron (*see* BYRON, B); *m* 2nd Henry Berkeley, of Wymondham, Leics

NICHOLAS BEAUMONT's ggs,

Sir Thomas Beaumont, 1st Bt (E), so *cr* 5 March 1657/8 and again (since Interregnum creations were ruled invalid at the Restoration) 21 Feb 1660/1, of Stoughton Grange; MP Leics, memb Ctee New Model Army 1644–45, High Sheriff Leics 1668–89; *m* Elizabeth, dau and coheir of Sir Nicholas Trott, of Quickswood, Herefs, by Mary, dau and coheir of Sir George Perient, and *d* 11 Aug 1676, having had, with two daus (Jane; Mary):

1 **Sir Henry Beaumont, 2nd Bt**, MP Leics 1679–87; *bapt* 2 April 1638; *m* 2 April 1662 Elizabeth (*d* 30 Sept 1727), dau of George Farmer, Prothonotary Common Pleas, and *d* 27 Jan 1688/9, leaving, with two daus:

(1) **Sir Thomas Beaumont, 3rd Bt**; Offr JAMES II's Horse Gds, joined WILLIAM III, who made him Lt-Col of Dragoons and Standard Bearer 1st Troop of Gds; fought against Jacobites in Ireland; *d* unm 5 Dec 1690

(2) **Sir George Beaumont, 4th Bt**, MP Leicester 1702–37, DCL Oxford, Commr Privy Seal 1712, a Ld Admlty 1714; *d* unm 9 April 1737, leaving the Stoughton estate to his surv sisters and his n, William Busby

(3) Henry; *d* unm

(4) Basil; R-Adml; *d* Goodwin Sands in a storm 27 Nov 1703

(5) **Rev Sir Lewis Beaumont, 5th Bt**, MA Oxford, Rector Pyecombe, Sussex, Preb Chichester; *m* Elizabeth, widow of Rev — Temple and dau of — Courtenay, and *dsp* 23 Dec 1738

(6) Charles, blown up in the Downs Sept 1700 in the man-of-war *Carlisle*

2 Thomas (Rev); *m* Susannah, dau of Rev William Oldys, DD, and *d* 15 Jan 1710, having had four sons (only one of whom left issue, a dau) and two daus (Elizabeth, *m* William Hayley, MD; Arabella)

3 William, of Gt Dunmow, Essex; *m* Jane, dau of John Watts, of Leics, by Jane, dau of Sir Thomas Burton, 2nd Bt, of Stockerston, and was *bur* 1719, leaving issue:

(1) William, of Gt Dunmow; *m* Elizabeth, dau of William Jordan, of Charlwood, Surrey, and had, with other issue:

1a **Sir George Beaumont, 6th Bt**; *bapt* 16 March 1726; *m* 26 March 1751 Rachel (*d* 5 May 1814), dau of Michael Howland, of Stonehall, Essex, and *d* 4 Feb 1762, leaving issue:

1b **Sir George Howland Beaumont, 7th Bt**, FRS, DCL, and FSA, MP Beeralston 1790–96, Tstee Br Museum, painter, collector and patron of art; friend of Wordsworth; a fndr Nat Gallery; *b* 6 Nov 1753; *m* 6 May 1778 Margaret (*d* 14 July 1829), dau of John Willes, of Astrop, Northants, and gdau of Lord Ch Justice Willes, and *dsp* 7 Feb 1827

2a Thomas, of Buckland, Surrey, had issue:

1b Thomas, of Buckland; *m* 29 Jan 1799 Bridget (*d* 16 April 1842), yst dau of Rev William Davie and niece of Sir John Davie, of Creedy, and was *bur* 3 Feb 1818, leaving, with other issue:

1c GEORGE HOWLAND (Sir), **8th Bt**

2c Thomas Davie; *b* 1801; *d* 1824

3c William Francis Bertie, of Buckland; *bapt* 23 Oct 1808; *m* 30 May 1833 Frances Mary Caroline (*d* 30 July 1834), dau of John Smith, of Bury St Edmunds, and *d* 10 March 1837, leaving issue:

1d Francis Henry, of Buckland Court, Surrey, DL, JP and CA Surrey; *b* 1 April 1834; *educ* Oriel Coll Oxford (MA); *m* 1 July 1856 Mary Emily (*d* 11 Jan 1923), 3rd dau of Evan Baillie, of Dochfour, Inverness, by Lady Georgiana Montagu, dau of 5th Duke of Manchester (*qv*), and *d* 21 Jan 1929, leaving issue:

1e Francis Montagu, of Buckland Court; Maj KRRC; *b* 27 Sept 1857; *m* 21 July 1904 Sybil Anne (*d* 25 May 1949), yst dau of Higford Higford, of Hartsfield, Betchworth, and *d* 14 April 1936, leaving issue:

1f *Crystal Katherine [Mrs Leslie Earl, Henspark Cottage, Dulverton, Somerset]; *b* 10 Dec 1908; *m* 30 Aug 1930 Leslie James Earl (*d* 1988), and has:

1g *Diana Crystal; *b* 1931; *m* 1st 1952 (*divorce* 1959) R E Williams, and has:

1h *Janice Diana; *b* June 1953

1g (cont.) Mrs Diana Williams *m* 2nd 1959 *David Francis Bassett, and has further issue:

1h *Earl Jonathan; *b* 6 July 1960

2h *Gwenda Margaret; *b* 8 Sept 1962

2g *Rosemary Margaret [Mrs Vernon Hammett, West Anstey, South Molton, Devon]; *b* 1934; *m* 1954 *Vernon Hammett, and has issue:

1h *Peter; *b* 25 Sept 1962

1h *Joanna; *b* 8 Jan 1960; *m* 1982 (*divorce* 1989) Graham Howard, of S Molton, and has issue:

1i *Samuel John; *b* 1985

1i *Jemma Grace Louise; *b* 1984

3g *Lesley Anne [Mrs Philip Veysey, Venford Farm, Dulverton, Somerset]; *b* 20 May 1950; *m* 1975 *Philip Veysey, and has issue:

1h *James William Philip; *b* 1979

2h *Benjamin Stewart; *b* 1980

1h *Rachel Ruth; *b* 1982

2e Spencer William Montagu, Cdr RN; *b* 3 July 1864; *d* unm 25 April 1914

1e Evelyn Jane Mary; *d* 22 Oct 1862

2e Beatrice Caroline, OStJ; *m* 18 May 1899 Col Sir Percival Scope Marling, 3rd Bt, VC, CB (*qv*), and *d* 28 July 1941

3e Mary Georgiana; *m* 19 June 1884 Henry Claude Fuller (*d* 22 April 1926), and *d* 7 June 1951, leaving issue

4e Hilda Augusta Katherine MBE; *m* 1 Feb 1899 Robert Massy Dawson Saunders, DL, JP (*d* 30 Dec 1941), of Charleville Park, Co Cork, est son of Thomas Saunders, JP, LLD, of Saunders Park, Co Cork, and *d* 17 April 1930, leaving issue

The 7th Bt's cousin,

Sir George Howland Willoughby Beaumont, 8th Bt; *b* 16 Dec 1799; *m* 16 June 1825 Mary Anne (*d* 15 Feb 1834), est dau of Dr William Howley, Archbp Canterbury, and *d* 7 June 1845, having had, with other issue (including a dau; *see* HEYGATE, Bt):

Sir George Howland Beaumont, 9th Bt, High Sheriff Leics 1852; *b* 12 Sept 1828; *m* 1st 4 June 1850 his cousin Pauline Menzies (*d* 9 Dec 1870), 3rd dau of William Hallows Belli, HEICS, and niece of Dr Howley, Archbp of Canterbury, and had issue:

1 GEORGE HOWLAND WILLIAM (Sir), **10th Bt**

2 Francis Howley; *b* Naples 11 Feb 1854; *d* 3 Jan 1875

3 Frederick Louis Maureward; *b* 17 June 1862; *m* 1st 21 Nov 1900 Helen Mary (*d* 22 Aug 1924), dau of Decimus Sturges, barrister; *m* 2nd 27 Aug 1927 Isabella Mary Rachel (*d* 1942), dau of Richard Pierce, of Liverpool, and *dsp* 26 Nov 1948

4 Henry Cecil Charles, Capt 1st Bn Scots Gds WW I (severley wounded); *b* 24 April 1864; *m* 1st 19 Dec 1894 Jessie Leigh (*d* 1916), dau of George A Fellows, of New York; *m* 2nd 21 June 1919 Marie Adele (*d* 18 June 1948), widow of Carl von Brunelius and dau of Albert Tachard, Ministre Plenipotentiaire for France 1870, and *dsp* 13 Feb 1944

1 Lina Mary Howley; *m* 19 Oct 1876 Col Gawn William Rowan Hamilton (*d* 22 April 1930), of Killyleagh Castle, Co Down, and *d* 6 June 1934, leaving issue

2 Eleanor Grace Caroline; *d* unm 16 Dec 1870

Sir George *m* 2nd 4 April 1872 Octavia Willoughby (*d* 19 June 1901), widow of Maj J R S Wallis, of Drishane Castle, Co Cork, and illegitimate dau of 7th Baron Middleton (*qv*), and *d* 8 June 1882

His est son,

Sir George William Beaumont, 10th Bt, JP Leics, Capt RHA; *b* 10 March 1851; *m* 24 Feb 1880 Lillie Ellen (*d* 17 Aug 1946), 2nd dau of Maj-Gen George Aytun Craster, RE, and *d* 21 June 1914, leaving:

Sir George Arthur Hamilton Beaumont, 11th Bt, JP, Maj KRRC WW I (wounded); *b* 18 Jan 1881; *m* 17 Nov 1923 Renee Muriel (*m* 2nd 20 Oct 1934 Capt Oswald Marmaduke Dalby Bell (*d* 25 June 1949), yst son of Hon Sir Joshua Peter Bell, KCMG, of Queensland, Australia; *m* 3rd (*divorce*) Lisle Hawkins and *d* 1987), 2nd dau of Maj-Gen Sir Edward Northey, GCMG, CB, of The Glebe Farm, Hinton Waldrist, Faringdon, Berks, and Woodcote House, Epsom, and *d* 2 Oct 1933, leaving issue:

1 Sir GEORGE HOWLAND FRANCIS BEAUMONT, **12th and present Bt**

1 (Eleanor) Brienne; *b* 10 June 1927; *m* 18 Nov 1954 *Maj Hugh Abdy Collins, 1st Bn the Buffs, only son of Michael Abdy Collins, OBE, MD, BS, of The Elms, Old Dover Road, Canterbury

BEAUMONT OF WHITLEY

Arms: Gules, a lion rampant or, armed and langued azure, between eight crescents in orle of the second. **Crest:** A bull's head erased quarterly argent and gules, charged with a mullet sable. **Supporters:** Dexter, a phoenix; sinister, a pelican vulning herself proper. **Motto:** *Ich kann nicht anders* ('I cannot do otherwise') **Creation:** B. (LP, UK) 1967.

THE BARON BEAUMONT OF WHITLEY, of Child's Hill, Greater London (Rev Timothy Wentworth Beaumont) [The Rev and Rt Hon The Lord Beaumont of Whitley, 40 Elms Rd, London SW4 9EX]; *b* 22 Nov 1928; *educ* Eton, Gordonstoun and Ch Ch Oxford (MA); Vicar: Ch Ch Kowloon,Hong Kong 1957–59 (resigned holy orders 1973, resumed them 1984), St Philip and All Souls, Kew, and St Luke's, Kew, 1986–91; periodical owner: *Prism* 1960–65, *New Christian* 1965–70, *New Outlook* 1972—74 (also ed), chm Studio-Vista Ltd 1963–68, Lib Party: Hon Treas 1962–63, Head Orgn 1965–66, Chm 1967–68, Pres 1969–70, Leader Br Delegn Parly Assemblies Cncl Europe and WEU 1977–79, V-Chm Lib Gp Cncl Europe 1978, Ho Lds Spokesman educn, arts and environment 1971–85 and (Lib Dem) conservation and countryside 1993–, memb Lib Dem Fedl Policy Ctee 1992–95, Chm Inst Research Mental Retardation 1972–74; Pres Br Fedn Film Socs 1974–80, co-ordinator The Green Alliance 1977–80, author: *The Selective Ego: the diaries of James Agate* (ed, 1976), *Where Shall I Place My Cross?* (1987) and *The End of the Yellow Brick Road* (1997); *m* 1955 *Mary Rose, dau of Lt-Col Charles Edward Wauchope, MC, of Sandhill House, Rogate, Sussex, and has:

1 *Hubert Wentworth [The Hon Hubert Beaumont, Harristown House, Brannockstown, Co Kildare, Ireland]; *b* 1956; *educ* Gordonstoun and South Bank Poly; *m* 1980 *Katharine Emma, only dau of Col Richard Francis Abel Smith, of Blidworth Dale, Notts (*see* 1956 edn ATHLONE, E), and has:

(1) *George Wentworth; *b* 24 Aug 1985

(2) *Richard Christian; *b* 1989

(3) *Michael; *b* 1991

(1) *Amelia May; *b* 1983

2 Alaric Charles Blackett; *b* 22 April 1958; *k* in a road accident 2 Dec 1980 unm

1 *Atalanta Armstrong; *b* 1961; *m* 1987 *Dr Stephen Francis Bungay, er s of E W G Bungay, of Chester, and has:

(1) *Felix Nicholas; *b* 1990

(2) *Caspar Stephen; *b* 1994

2 *Ariadne Grace; *b* 1963; *m* 1990 *Mario Calvo-Platero, yr s of Guido Calvo-Platero, of Milan, and has:

(1) *Oliver Guido; *b* 1991

(2) *Milo Alaric; *b* 1992

(1) *Clio; *b* 1995

Lineage: Maj MICHAEL WENTWORTH BEAUMONT, TD (*see* ALLENDALE, V); had:

Rev TIMOTHY WENTWORTH, *cr* a **Baron**

BEAVERBROOK

Arms: Argent two barrulets wavy azure between in chief two maple leaves slipped and in base a thistle eradicated gules, a bordure sable charged with eight bezants. **Crest:** Upon a drum proper a cock gules wattled, armed and legged or. **Supporters:** On either side a beaver regardant holding in the mouth a fish proper. **Motto:** *Res mihi non me rebus* ('Things for me, not me for things'). **Creations:** B. (UK) 2 Jan 1917, Bt (UK) 3 July 1916.

THE 3RD BARON BEAVERBROOK, of Beaverbrook, New Brunswick, and of Cherkley, Surrey, and a **Baronet** (Sir Maxwell William Humphrey Aitken, Bt) [The Rt Hon The Lord Beaverbrook, House of Lords, London SW1A 0PW]; *b* 29 Dec 1951; *s f* (who, however, had disclaimed the barony for life) 1985; *educ* Charterhouse and Pembroke Coll Cambridge; with Beaverbrook Newspapers 1973–77, dir Ventech 1983–86 and chm Ventech Healthcare Corp 1986 and 1988–92, chm Beaverbrook Fndn 1985–92 (tstee 1974–92), Govt: Spokesman DTI and Home Office 1986 and Whip 1986–88, memb cncl Homeopathic Tst 1986–92, chm Nat Assoc Boys Clubs 1989–92, Treasurer: European Democratic Union 1990–92 and Conservative Pty 1990–92 (Dep Treasurer 1988–90); *m* 19 July 1974 *Susan Angela, est dau of Francis More O'Ferrall, of Hermongers, Rudgwick, W Sussex, by Angela, dau of Sir Anthony Mather-Jackson, 6th Bt, JP, DL (*see* JACKSON, Bt, of the Manor House, Birkenhead), and has:

1 +MAXWELL FRANCIS; *b* 17 March 1977; *educ* Ampleforth

2 +Alexander Rory; *b* 1978

1 *Charlotte Susanna; *b* 1982

2 *Sophia Violet Angela; *b* 1985

Lineage: The Aitken ancestors of the Barons Beaverbrook have been traced back to 1613. A local minister in Torphichen, West Lothian (a place about halfway between Edinburgh and Glasgow), where the 1st Lord Beaverbrook's father was born, once established from baptismal records the existence of a continuous line of Aitkens in that parish. From 1720, and possibly even earlier, they were tenant farmers of the Hopes, Earls of Hopetoun and subsequently Marquesses of Linlithgow (*qv*).

The **1st Baron**, founder of the family's fortunes in modern times, is one of the towering figures of 20th-century Britain (figuratively speaking only: he stood 5 7" fully grown). He was dominant not just in politics and journalism but in social life and relatively arcane areas such as experimental literature (he supported William Gerhardie). He also extended his patronage to such diverse literary figures as Barbara Cartland, Michael Arlen and Arnold Bennett and to the pianist Harriet Cohen.

His passion for protectionism, expressed right down to the end of his life in terms of Empire Free Trade, cannot be understood without grasping the importance of tariff barriers against the considerable threat of US competition, as it seemed to many contemporaries, in the Canada of his youth. His North American background is important in another way. It made him much more influential than any native Briton in persuading US industrialists to speed up production of munitions during his mission to the USA in World War II.

Beaver Brook (*sic*) is a logging site occupied mostly by French inhabitants a few miles from Lord Beaverbrook's childhood home of Newcastle, New Brunswick. The stream there is insignificant, so it is probably just a legend that Lord Beaverbrook chose his title because he remembered beavers when fishing in it during his childhood. Rudyard Kipling, a close personal friend till the two men fell out over Irish independence, is said to have tried to persuade Lord Beaverbrook to get the beaver supporters made fiercer-looking when the latter was contemplating the design of his armorial bearings. The University of New Brunswick, which Beaverbrook supported with great generosity, later incorporated beavers into its coat of arms as a gesture of respect.

Of Beaverbrook's two wives, his first, Gladys, is less well-known. But her husband reckoned her a better public speaker than himself, and his striking success in entering Parliament only ten days after being adopted as the Conservative candidate, to say nothing of the fact that he had only been living in the UK for four months, owed much to her fine clothes and attractive appearance.

There is still controversy among professional historians over exactly how important Beaverbrook's role was in the selection of Bonar Law as leader of the Conservative Party in 1911 following Balfour's resignation, the overthrow of Asquith as Prime Minister in 1916, changes in government policy following the *Daily Express*-inspired Empire Free Trade campaign of 1929–31 (which was partly conducted by Beaverbrook out of detestation of Baldwin), the events surrounding the Abdication of 1936 (again related to his detestation of Baldwin) and the boosting of aircraft production for the war effort in 1940–42. It is enough here to say that his contribution to every one of these events cannot be ignored. He was the first ever Minister of State, a rank specifically created for him by Churchill. As an old friend he shored up Churchill's morale at a critical point in World War II. He is indisputably one of the founders of 20th-century popular journalism.

JOHN AITKEN; *m c* 1790 Elizabeth Donaldson (*d* 1857 aged 80) and *d* 1840 aged 88, having issue: together with at least two other s (John, who *d* 1836 aged 35, and William, who *d* 24 Jan 1833 aged 14) and at least one dau (Margaret, who *d* 1803 aged 13), a s:

ROBERT AITKEN, who was as early as the 1840s renting from Lord Hopetoun the smallholding of Wester Tartraven and Lime Craig of Silvermine (usually abbreviated to Silvermine, from there once having been extraction of that metal nearby in the early 17th century). The extent of Robert s holding was around 99 Scottish acres. His f and gf had also been tenants on the Tartraven estate. Robert invested in real estate in the neigbouring market town of Bathgate; *m* —, of Bathgate, and *d* 1875, having had, with an er s and dau and two or three yr children (one of whom, Ann, emigrated to Canada to keep house for her minister bro and *m* Arthur Noble, her bro s bro-in-law):

Rev WILLIAM CUTHBERT AITKEN; *b* 28 Feb 1834; *educ* Bathgate Acad and Edinburgh U; licensed to preach the gospel Sept 1858, ordained 1864, Ch of Scotland minister at: Cobourg, Ontario, Canada 1864–65, Vaughan, Maple, Ontario, 1865–80 and Newcastle, New Brunswick, 1880–1902; *m* 8 May 1867 Jane (*d* 6 Aug 1927), dau of Joseph Noble (emigrated from Co Tyrone, Ireland, to Ontario in the 1840s) by his w Sarah Macquarrie (descended from the chiefs of Ulva, off Mull, in western Scotland, via one Hector Macquarrie, who emigrated from Mull to the USA 1802 and thence to Ontario since he was pro-British at the time of the War of 1812) and *d* 13 Dec 1913, having had issue (together with a dau Katie, older than the 1st Lord Beaverbrook, who *d* of diphtheria aged six):

1 (Robert) Traven Donaldson; *b* 23 April 1873; *educ* Dalhousie U, Halifax, Nova Scotia (BA, LLB); Maj ASC Canadian Expditionary Force WW I; *m* 1st 3 June 1901 Agnes Jean (*d* by the winter of 1906/7), dau of Samuel Thomson, KC, and had issue:

(1) (Agnes) Jean Thomson; *b* 4 Jan 1904; *m* 26 July 1929 Sir Thomson McLintock, 2nd Bt (*qv*; *d* as a result of a motor accident 23 Dec 1953), and *d* 199–, having had issue

(2) *Lillian Katherine; *b* 29 March 1905

1 (cont.) Traven Aitken *m* 2nd March 1912 Alleen, dau of George K Leeson, and *d* 1939, having had issue:

(3) *Annie Alleen; *b* 2 Aug 1915

2 (Joseph) Magnus ('Mauns'); *b* 26 Feb 1878; manager Roy Bank of Canada Toronto, Capt and Paymaster 208th Canadian Expeditionary Force WW I; *m* 1902 Katherine Margaret (*d* 2 March 1954), dau of John McAffee, and *d* Feb 1950, having had issue:

(1) William Traven (Sir), KBE (1963); *b* 10 June 1903; MP (C) Bury St Edmunds 1950-64; *m* 28 April 1938 *Hon Penelope Loader Maffey, MBE (1955), JP [The Hon Lady Aitken MBE JP, 2 North Court, Gt Peter St, London SW1P 3LL], dau of 1st Baron Rugby (*qv*), and *d* 19 Jan 1964, leaving issue:

1a *Jonathan William Patrick, PC (1994–97) [Jonathan Aitken Esq, 8 Lord North St, London SW1]; *b* 30 Aug 1942 (HM QUEEN JULIANA of the Netherlands stood sponsor); *educ* Eton and Ch Ch Oxford (MA hons law); Priv Sec to Rt Hon Selwyn Lloyd (later Baron Selwyn-Lloyd) 1964–66, MP (C) Thanet E Feb 1974–83 and Thanet S 1983–97, memb Select Ctee Employment 1979–82, Min of State (Procurement) Def 1992–94, Ch Sec to Treasury 1994–95, foreign correspondent *Evening Standard* 1966–71, md Slater Walker (Middle East) Ltd 1973–74, co-fndr Aitken Hume Internat plc 1981 (chm 1981–90, dep chm 1990–92), dir: TV-am plc 1981–88 (temp ch exec March-April 1983) and BMARC (British Manufacturer and Research Co) Sept 1988–June 1990, late dir Future Management Servs, advsr GEC-Marconi 1998–, late Special Constable E Suffolk Police, author: *A Short Walk on the Campus* (1966), *The Young Meteors* (1967), *Land of Fortune: a Study of Australia* (1969), *Officially Secret* (1970) and *Richard Nixon: a life* (1993); *m* 1979 *Lolicia Olivera, dau of O A Azucki, of Zürich, and has:

1b *William; *b* 7 Sept 1982

1b *Victoria; *b* 14 June 1980

2b *Alexandra; *b* 14 June 1980

1a *Maria Penelope Katharine [Miss Maria Aitken, c/o Michael Whitehall, 125 Gloucester Rd, London SW7 4TE]; *b* 12 Sept 1945; *educ* Riddlesworth Hall Norfolk, Sherborne Girls' Sch, St Anne's Coll Oxford; actress: (plays) *Travesties* (RSC 1974), *A Little Night Music* (1975), *Blithe Spirit* (1976), *Bedroom Farce* (1977), *Private Lives* (1980), *Design for Living* (1982), *Sister Mary Ignatius* (1983, which also directed), *Ambassadors* (1983), *Happy Family* (1983, which also directed), *Private Lives* (1984, which also directed), *After the Ball* (1985, which also directed), *The Rivals* (1985, which also directed) *Waste* (RSC, 1985), *The Women* (1986), *The Vortex* (1989), *Other People s Money* (1990), *As You Like It* (1992, which also directed), *Hay Fever* (1992) (films) *Some Girls Do* (1968) and *A Fish Called Wanda* (1988), author: *A Girdle Round the Earth* (1986); *m* 1st 19 Jan 1968 (*divorce* 1971) (Mark) Richard (Dick) Durden-Smith, yst s of A J Durden-Smith, FRCS, of Kensington; *m* 2nd May 1972 (*divorce* 1980) (Arthur) Nigel Davenport, the actor, and has:

1b *Jack; *b* 1973; *educ* UEA; actor in BBC2 TV series *This Life*

1a (cont.) Maria Aitken *m* 3rd 28 Dec 1991 *Patrick J McGrath, novelist, est s of Dr Patrick Gerard McGrath, CB, CBE, psychiatrist and sometime consultant at Broadmoor

(2) John Mauns; *b* 24 May 1904; *m* and *d* 3 Jan 1938, leaving:

1a *John

(1) *Margaret Annie, MP; *b* 3 July 1906

(2) Jane Katherine; *b* 9 Dec 1913; *d* unm

3 Max(well), **1st Baron** (but Anne Chisholm and Michael Davie, in *Beaverbrook – A Life*, 1992, state he was the fifth child, including the prematurely deceased Katie)

4 Arthur Noble; *b* 26 July 1883; BA, MD; Capt RAMC WW I; *m* 1921 Frances Emma Wargarel Hughes and *d* Canada 1969/70

5 Allan Anderson ('Bud'/'Buddie'), MC; *b* 15 Sept 1887; Maj HQ Staff 4th Canadian Div WW I (wounded at Gallipoli), stockbroker dealing in securities for his er bro Lord Beaverbrook; *m* 31 Oct 1929 *Phyllis, dau of Gordon Osler, of Toronto, and formerly w of — Dean, and *d* 23 Jan 1959, leaving issue:

(1) *Allan Osler; *b* 6 May 1932

(1) *Sarah Anne; *b* 25 Sept 1930; *m* 29 March 1958 *Richard Henry Stevenson, of Montreal

(2) *Margaret Jane; *m* 28 Sept 1957 *Lionel Arrington Bigelow Dodge, yr s of John Bigelow Dodge, of 35 Chester Row, SW1

1 Sarah Nob Margaret Jane;le ('Rahno'); *b* 1 March 1868; Superintendent Hosp of the Good Samaritan, Los Angeles; *m* 15 June 1907 Horatio Walker, MD, and *d* 1945

2 Annie Anderson ('Nan'); *b* 19 April 1870; Superintendent Rutland Hosp, Vt, USA; *d* 25 April 1942

3 Jean Noble ('Gyp'); *b* 11 Sept 1885; *educ* coll of librarianship in Pasadena, Calif; librarian, head Relief Div (London) Canadian Red Cross WW II; *m* 1919 William Stickney and *d* 20 Jan 1972

4 Laura Katherine; *b* 24 Feb 1892; *educ* Trafalgar Sch Montreal and U of Toronto; BA; *m* 9 Dec 1925 Douglas Monro Ramsay, DL (*d* 7 Aug 1951), of Bowland, Stow, Midlothian, and *d* 5 Aug 1954, leaving issue

The Rev WILLIAM AITKEN s 3rd s (and 5th child?),

Sir (William) Max(well) Aitken, 1st Bt, so *cr* 3 July 1916 and 2 Jan 1917 **1st Baron Beaverbrook**, of Beaverbrook, New Brunswick, and of Cherkley, Surrey (both UK), ED, CD, PC (4 March 1918); *b* 25 May 1879; *educ* Harkins Acad, Newcastle, New Brunswick; Pres Roy Securities Co (V-Pres 1906, Sec 1903), sometime dir Montreal Tst Co, MP (U) Ashton-under-Lyne 1910–16, ktd 20 June 1911, newspaper proprietor: *Canadian Century* 1910–11, *Globe* 1911–14, *Daily Express* 1916 to his death, *Sunday Express* 1918 to his death, *Evening Standard* 1923 to his death, *Scottish Daily Express* 1928 to his death and *Farming Express* 19– on, Chm Colonial Bank, WW I: Canadian Eye Witness (reporting post) on Western Front from 1914 with rank of Hon Lt-Col, Canadian Record Offr from May 1915, Canadian Govt Rep Expeditionary Force 1915–16 with rank of Hon Col, Lt-Col in charge of Canadian War Records 1916–18, head Pictorial Propaganda Ctee in Dept of Information and chm War Office Cinematographic Ctee 1917, Canadian Rep War Memorial Ctee, Chllr Duchy of Lancaster and Min of Information (1st holder ever of latter post) Coalition Govt Jan–Oct 1918, Min of Aircraft Production Coalition Govt 1940–41, Min of State 1941, Min of Supply 1941–42, Ld Privy Seal 1943–45, Memb War Cabinet 1940–42 (dep chm Def Ctee (Supply)), Tstee Br Museum 1943, Tstee Imperial War Museum, Order of Suvorov (USSR) 1944, Hon LLD: New Brunswick 1921, Toronto 1947, S Thomas U 1953, LitD Mt Allison 1948, DCL Bishops U (Quebec) 1950, Chllr U of New Brunswick 1947–53, Hon Life Chllr 1954, Hon Col Roy New Brunswick Regt, author: *Canada in Flanders* Vol I (1916),Vol II (1917) and Vol III (1919), *Success, Politicians and the Press* (1925), *Politicians and the War* Vol I (1928) and Vol II (1932), *Don't Trust to Luck, Three Keys to Success, Men and Power 1917–1918* (1956), *Friends: Sixty Years of Intimate Personal Relations with Richard Bedford Bennett* (1959), *Courage* (1961) and *My Early Life* (1964); *m* 1st 29 Jan 1906 Gladys Henderson (*d* 1 Dec 1927), 2nd dau of Maj-Gen Charles William Drury, CB, of Halifax, Nova Scotia, and had issue:

1 (JOHN WILLIAM) MAX(WELL) (Sir), **2nd Bt**, and briefly **2nd Baron**

2 Peter Rudyard (named Rudyard after Rudyard Kipling, his godfather); *b* 22 March 1912; *educ* Westminster; Capt Roy Fus WW II (wounded); *m* 1st 25 Jan 1934 (*divorce* 1939) Janet Ruth Murrenne, dau of Prof Murray Macneil, of Dalhousie U, Nova Scotia, and had issue:

(1) *Caroline Anne Christine [Mrs Conyers Baker, 28 Whitney Ave, Toronto 5, Canada]; *b* 4 April 1935; *m* 7 Sept 1957 *Lt Conyers Collingwood Massy Baker, RCNR, s of Massy Baker, of Ottawa, and has issue:

1a *William Hugh Massy; *b* 1958

2a *Philip Massy; *b* 1960

3a *Jonathan Piers Massy

2 (cont.) Peter Aitken *m* 2nd 28 Oct 1942, as her 1st husb, (Marie) Patricia (*m* 2nd 13 July 1948 (*divorce* 1956) Richard David Raft Lycett Green (*d* 17 Dec 1969), er s of Cdr David Cecil Lycett Green RN (*see* GREEN, Bt, of Wakefield), and *d* 27 Jan 1995), est dau of Michael Joseph Maguire, of Melbourne, Australia, by Mary Jane Carroll, and *d* 3 Aug 1947 following a fall from a yacht, having had:

(1) +Timothy ('Tim', named after his gf Lord Beaverbrook's friend Tim Healy, 1st Govr-Gen of the Irish Free State) Maxwell; *b* 28 Oct 1944; *educ* Repton, Sorbonne and McGill U Canada; sometime jnlst with *Evening Standard*, ch exec: TV-AM 1983–88 (chm 1988–), Aitken Hume International plc to 1986, Abbey Healthcare (California) 1987–95, chm National Securities & Research Corp and Omnicare (UK) 1995–, v-chm Apria Medical (US) 1995, chm Transworld Healthcare; *m* 1st 10 May 1966 Annete, dau of Claus Hansen, of Rogieriet, Thuro, Denmark; *m* 2nd 1972 *Julie Ruth, dau of Charles Filstead, and has:

1a *Theodore Maxwell; *b* 1976

2a *Charles; *b* 1979

(2) +Peter Michael [Peter Aitken Esq, Flat 1 121 Lansdowne Road, London W11]; *b* 20 Feb 1946; *educ* Malvern; *m* 1980 (*divorce* 1985), as her 3rd husb, Hon (Joan) Elizabeth Rees-Williams, only dau of 1st Baron Ogmore (*qv*)

1 Janet Gladys; *b* 9 July 1908; *m* 1st 12 Dec 1927 (*divorce* 1934) 11th Duke of Argyll (*qv*) and had issue; *m* 2nd 5 March 1935 Hon William Drogo Sturges Montagu (*kas* 26 Jan 1940), 2nd s of 9th Earl of Sandwich (*qv*), and had further issue; *m* 3rd 11 July 1942 Maj Thomas Edward Dealtry Kidd, MBE, Roy Canadian Airforce, of Slythehurst, Ewehurst, Surrey, er s of Hon Lt-Col Canon William Ennis Kidd, MC, MA, of Kingston, Ontario, and *d* 1988, having by him had:

(1) *John ('Johnny') Edward Aitken [John Kidd Esq, Holders House, St James, Barbados; Suite 1809, 745 5th Ave, New York City, NY, USA]; *b* 12 Dec 1944; *educ* Harrow; chm Columbia Laboratories Inc (USA) 1987–, dir: Careplus Inc (USA) 1987–, All England Jumping Course Hickstead 1989–, London United Investments 1977–81 and Aitken Hume 1982–86, jr European individual showjumping champion 1962, author: *Reins In Our Hands* (1966) and *Take Off* (1974); *m* 2 April 1973, as her 2nd husb, *Wendy Madeleine, dau of Sir John Rowland Hodge, 2nd Bt (*qv*), and has issue:

1a *Jack Edward; *b* 1973; *educ* Harrow

1a *Jemma Madeleine; *b* 1974

2a *Jodie Elizabeth; *b* 1978; model

(1) *Jane; *b* 1943; *m* 1972 (*divorce* 197–), as his 2nd w, Graham Morison Vere Nicoll, est s of Lt-Col Henry Vere Nicoll by his w Joan, herself dau of Adml of the Fleet Sir Charles Madden, 1st Bt (*qv*)

The **1st Baron** *m* 2nd 7 June 1963 Marcia ('Christofor') Anastasia, Hon LLD (1967) Dalhousie U and Chllr 1968–94 (*d* 28 Oct 1994), dau of John Christoforides, of Leyswood, Groombridge, Sussex, and widow of Sir James Hamet Dunn, 1st Bt (*qv*), and *d* 9 June 1964

His only surv s,

Sir (John William) Max(well) Aitken, 2nd Bt and briefly **2nd Baron Beaverbrook**, DSO (1942), DFC (1940), disclaimed his peerage for life 12 June 1964; *b* 15 Feb 1910; *educ* Westminster and Pembroke Coll Camb; G/Capt RAuxAF WW II (Czech War Cross), MP (C) Holborn 1945–50, chm Beaverbrook Newspapers Ltd, pres Newspaper Press Fund, dir Price Co Ltd and ATV, Chllr U of New Brunswick (Hon LLD 1966); *m* 1st 26 Aug 1939 (*divorce* 1944) Cynthia Helen Glencairn, dau of Col Hugh Glencairn Monteith, DSO, OBE; *m* 2nd 15 Aug 1946 (*divorce* 1950; she *m* 3rd 1951 Robert Compton, *see* NORTHAMPTON, M) (Ursula) Jane, yr dau of Capt Robert Orlando Rodolph Kenyon-Slaney, Gren Gds, of Hatton Grange, Shifnal, Salop (*see* KENYON, B), and formerly 1st w of Peter Lindsay, DSO (*see* CRAWFORD and BALCARRES, E), and had issue:

1 *Kirsty Jane Aitken [The Hon Mrs Smallwood, The Vineyard, Hurlingham Rd, London SW6 3NR]; *b* 22 June 1947; *m* 6 Sept 1966 (*divorce* 1973) Jonathan Derek Morley, yr s of Brig Michael Frederick Morley, MBE, of Biddlestone Manor, Chippenham, Wilts, and has issue:

(1) *Dominic Max Michael; *b* 1967

(2) *Sebastian Finch; *b* 1969; *m* 1993 *Victoria Clare Helen, only dau of Samuel Charles Whitbread, gs through his mother Helen of Hon Robert Henry Hepburn-Stuart-Forbes-Trefusis, 6th s of 20th Baron Clinton (*qv*)

1 (cont.) The Hon Mrs Kirsty Morley *m* 2nd 1975 *Christopher Marten Smallwood, s of Canon Graham Marten Smallwood, of Brook House, Childswickham, Hereford and Worcester, and has issue:

(1) *Eleanor Bluebell; *b* 1982

2 *Lynda Mary Kathleen [The Hon Mrs Dickson, 45 Broomwood Rd, London SW11]; *b* 30 Oct 1948; *m* 25 April 1969 (*divorce* 1974) Nicholas Saxton, s of Richard Saxton, of La Jolla, Calif, USA; *m* 2nd 1977 *Jonathan James Dickson and has issue:

(1) *Joshua James; *b* 20 Feb 1977

(2) *Leo Casper; *b* 1981

Sir Max *m* 3rd 1 Jan 1951 *Violet, Chllr U of New Brunswick 1981-92, Chllr Emeritus 1992– (Hon LLD 1990), chm Beaverbrook Canadian Fndn [Lady Aitken, Mickleham Downs House, Dorking, Surrey], 3rd dau of Sir Humphrey Edmund de Trafford, 4th Bt (*qv*), and *d* 1985, having had issue:

1 MAXWELL WILLIAM HUMPHREY AITKEN, **3rd and present Baron Beaverbrook**

3 *Laura [The Hon Mrs Levi, The Prospect, 83 High St, Cowes, Isle of Wight]; *b* 18 Nov 1953; jnlst, sometime on staff of the *Tatler*; *m* 1st 1984 (*divorce* 1989) David Victor Mark Mallet, s of Sir Victor Mallet, GCMG, CVO, Br Ambassador at Madrid 1945–46 and Rome 1947–53 (Sir Victor's mother being Marie, *née* Adeane, 1st cousin once removed of Sir Michael Adeane, *cr* Baron Adeane 1972 (LP, *extinct* 1984), while David Mallet's sis *m* 28th Baron Dunboyne (*qv*)), and has issue:

(1) *David Sonny Victor Maxwell; *b* 1984

3 (cont.) The Hon Laura Aitken, who had resumed her maiden name 1989, *m* 2nd 1992 *Martin K Levi, powerboat designer, s of R Levi, and has issue:

(2) *Louis Max Adam; *b* 1 Dec 1994

(1) *Lucci Violet; *b* 1993

BECKETT

Arms: Gu., a fess between three boar's heads couped erm., a crescent for difference. **Crest:** A boar's head couped or, pierced by a cross patée-fitchée erect gu. **Motto:** *Prodesse civibus* ('To benefit the state'). **Creation:** Bt (UK) 28 June 1921.

SIR MARTYN GERVASE BECKETT, 2ND BT, MC [Sir Martyn Beckett Bt MC, 3 St Alban's Grove, London W8 5PN; Kirkdale Farm, Nawton, Yorks]; *b* 6 Nov 1918; *s f* 1937; *educ* Eton and Trin Coll Cambridge (BA 1940); RIBA, Capt Welsh Gds, served WW II (MC); architect to King's Coll Cambridge 1960–, consulting architect: Gordonstoun 1954–58, Savoy Hotel Gp 1981–, Temple Bar Tst 1983–, Charterhouse 1983–, Ampleforth Coll 1984, Eton 1986–, Rank Labs 1987, BRCS 1994; tstee: The Wallace Collection 1972–92 (chm 1976–92), Br Museum 1978–88, CPRE Tst 1983–90, chm Yorks Regnl Ctee Nat Trust 1980–85; FRSA 1982, FAMS 1955, Freeman City of London 1986; *m* 22 Feb 1941 *Hon Priscilla Léonie Helen Brett, yst dau of 3rd Viscount Esher (*qv*), and has issue:

1+RICHARD GERVASE, QC (1988) [Richard Beckett Esq QC, 33 Groveway, London SW9 0AH]; *b* 30 March 1944; *educ* Eton and Oxford (Dip Ed); barrister Middle Temple 1965; *m* 17 Dec 1976 *Elizabeth (Libby) Ann, only dau of Major Charles Huguenot (Hugo) Waterhouse (*see* MARLBOROUGH, D), and has issue:

(1) +Walter Gervase; *b* 16 Jan 1987

(1) *Willa Marjorie; *b* 27 Aug 1977

(2) *Molly Rachel; *b* 1979

(3) *Catherine Rose; *b* 1983

2 +Jeremy Rupert [Jeremy Beckett Esq, Kirkdale Manor Farm, Nawton, Kirkbymoorside, Yorks]; *b* 5 July 1952; *educ* Eton; *m* 29 July 1978 *Perdita Rosemary, yst dau of Capt Hugo Francis Guy Charteris, MC (*see* WEMYSS and MARCH, E), and has had issue:

(1) +Joseph Hugo; *b* 1980

(2) Matthew Martyn; *b* 1984; *d* 1985

(3) +William Slingsby; *b* 1987

(1) *Lorna Elizabeth; *b* 1982

1 *Lucy Caroline [Mrs John Warrack, Beck House, Rievaulx, nr Helmsley, York YO6 5LB]; *b* 10 Aug 1942, *m* 1st 28 Jun 1962 (*divorce* 1969) Adrian Whitfield, of Holtby, Yorks, and has issue:

(1) *Teresa; *b* 3 June 1963; *m* 1996 *Jason Rosenbaum

(2) *Emily; *b* 13 May 1965

1 (cont.) Mrs Lucy Whitfield *m* 2nd 1970 *John Warrack, and has:

(1) *Benedict John; *b* 1971; Capt Light Dragoons

(2) *Christopher Martyn; *b* 1974

Lineage: The Hon **Sir (William) Gervase Beckett, 1st Bt** (UK), so *cr* 28 June 1921, of Kirkdale, Yorks, 2nd s of William Beckett-Denison and bro of 2nd Baron Grimthorpe (*qv*); granted rank 17 July 1905 of baron's yr s; MP (C) Whitby 1906–18, Scarborough and Whitby 1918–22 and Leeds N 1923–29, pncpl proprietor and ed-in-ch *Saturday Review*, dir Westminster Bank, Capt TFR, Capt Yorkshire Hus, Assist Mil Sec N Cmmd 1914–16, Assist Dir War Tde Dept 1918–19, *b* 14 Jan 1866, *m* 1st 12 Feb 1896 Hon Mabel Theresa Duncombe (*d* 2 April 1913), sis of 2nd Earl of Feversham (*see* FEVERSHAM, B), and had issue:

1 Marion Frances Theresa, *b* 8 Nov 1896, *m* 16 Oct 1919 V-Adml (Henry) Jack Egerton, CB, DL, JP (*see* 1956 edn EGERTON OF TATTON, B), 3rd son of Charles Augustus Egerton, DL, JP of Mountfield Court, Robertsbridge, Sussex, and *d* 2 Feb 1972, having had issue

2 Cynthia Maud, *b* 15 Dec 1900, *m* 1st 10 Nov 1919 (*divorce* 1928) Capt John Arthur Davison, MC, The Rifle Bde, only s of Major Arthur Pearson Davison, TD, of Carlton, Co Durham, and had issue; *m* 2nd 10 July 1929 (*divorce* 1952) Baron Kurt Hermann Paul Otto Valerio von Stutterheim, only son of Baron Richard Karl Ludwig von Stutterheim, of Coburg, and *d* 25 Dec 1969

3 Beatrice Helen, *b* 26 July 1905, *m* 5 Nov 1923 (*divorce* 1950) (Robert) Anthony Eden (later 1st Earl of Avon, KG; *see* 1970 edn), and *d* 29 June 1957, leaving issue

4 *Ann Prunella [Mrs Harry Norman, Flat 21, 27 Onslow Sq, London SW7]; *b* 16 Sep 1907, *m* 15 April 1936 Lt-Col Harry Rumbold Bathurst Norman, GM,

MD, MRCP, late RAMC (*d* Gulu, Uganda, 10 April 1966), son of Rev Harry Bathurst Norman, and has issue:

(1) *Paul Bathurst [Paul Norman Esq, Brandon Hall, Sudbury, Suffolk], *b* 23 April 1937, *educ* Harrow, *m* 15 Oct 1960 *Susan Mary, yr dau of Charles Lawrence Orbell, of The Hermitage, Clare, Suffolk, and has issue:

1a *Hal Charles; *b* 1 April 1969

1a *Arabella Harriet Bathurst; *b* 2 Aug 1961

2a *Teresa Prunella, *b* 2 May 1963

3a *Deborah Mary, *b* 11 Jan 1966

(1) *Harriet Rose, *b* 21 March 1939

(2) *Deirdre Nell [Mrs Nicholas Beresford-Jones, The Sett, Leavenheath, Colchester, Essex]; *b* 19 Oct 1946, *m* 1st 30 April 1964 (*divorce* 1970) Luciano Billi, of Florence, only son of Salvatore Billi, of Piazza Mercato Nuovo 1, Florence, and has issue:

1a *Selina Elizabeth; *b* 1964; *m* 1987 *Timothy Charles Kleingeld, and has:

1b *Oliver Max; *b* 1992

1b *Lydia Mary; *b* 1994

(2) (cont.) Mrs Deirdre Billi *m* 2nd 1971 *Nicholas Paul Beresford-Jones, and has issue:

2b *Alexandra Juliet; *b* 1973

Sir Gervase *m* 2nd 1 Nov 1917 Lady Marjorie Blanche Eva (*d* 25 July 1964), widow of 2nd Earl of Feversham (*see* FEVERSHAM, B) and dau of 5th Earl of Warwick (Isee WARWICK, BROOKE and, E), and *d* 24 Aug 1937, having by her had issue:

1 Sir MARTYN GERVASE BECKETT, **2nd and present Bt**

BEDINGFELD

see
(PASTON-)BEDINGFELD

BEDFORD

Arms: Arg. a lion rampant gu., on a chief sa. three escallops of the first. **Crest:** A goat statant arg., armed and unguled or. **Supporters:** Dexter, a lion rampant gu., gorged with a collar arg. charged with three escallops sa.; sinister, a goat arg., armed unguled and bearded or. **Motto:** *Che sara sara* ('What will be, will be'). **Badge:** A goat courant, the horns wreathed or and az. **Creations:** B. (E) 9 March 1538/9 (Russell), (E) 21 July 1603 (Russell of Thornhaugh) and (E) 13 June 1695 (Howland); E. (E) 19 Jan 1549/50; D. and M. (E) 11 May 1694.

THE 13TH DUKE OF BEDFORD, Marquess of Tavistock, Earl of Bedford, Baron Russell, Baron Russell of Thornhaugh, Northants, and **Baron Howland of Streatham**, Surrey (John (Ian) Robert Russell) [His Grace The Duke of Bedford, Les Ligures, 2 rue Honoré Labande, MC 98000, Monaco]; *b* 24 May 1917; *s f* 1953; served WW II 1939 Coldstream Gds, invalided 1940, author: *A Silver Plated Spoon* (1959), *The Duke of Bedford's Book of Snobs* (with George Mikes, 1965) and *How to Run a Stately Home* (1971); *m* 1st 6 April 1939 Claire Gwendolyn (*d* 1 Sept 1945), formerly w of Maj Kenneth Chamney Walpole Hollway, MC, and yst dau of John Bridgman, of Hoddesdon, Herts, and has:

1 +HENRY ROBIN IAN, *Marquess of Tavistock*, DL (Beds 1985) [Marquess of Tavistock DL, Woburn Abbey, Bedfordshire MK43 0TP]; dir Trafalgar House Ltd 1977–91, chm Cedar Investment Tst 1973–83, United Racecourses Ltd 1977–94 and Berkeley Govett & Co 1986– (now London Pacific), chm TR Property Investment Tst 1982–91, Berkeley Devpt Capital 1984–92, Tstees Kennedy Memorial Tst 1985–90, pres Woburn Golf Country Club 1976–, dir Woburn Enterprises Ltd 1996–; *b* 21 Jan 1940; *educ* Le Rosey and Harvard; *m* 20 June 1961 *Henrietta Joan, only dau by his 2nd w of Henry Frederick Tiarks (*see* also HEADFORT,M), of Casa Ina, Finca Torres, Marbella, Malaga, Spain, and has:

(1) +Andrew Ian Henry, *Lord Howland*; *b* 30 March 1962; *educ* Harrow and Harvard U; mktg dir Tattersall's

(2) +Robin Loel Hastings; *b* 12 Aug 1963; *m* 1994 *Stephanie, yst dau of Kurt Niklas, of Beverley Hills, Calif

(3) +James Edward Herband; *b* 11 Feb 1975

2 +Rudolf [The Lord Rudolf Russell, 2/3 Lyall St, London SW1X 8DW]; *b* 7 March 1944; *educ* Gordonstoun; *m* 1989 *Farah, yr dau of Gen R Mogaddam

The 13th DUKE *m* 2nd 12 Feb 1947 (*divorce* 1960) Hon Lydia, widow of Capt Ian Archibald de Hoghton Lyle, Black Watch (*see* LYLE, Bt), and 3rd dau of 3rd Baron Churston (*qv*), and by her has:

3 +Francis Hastings [The Lord Francis Russell, 13 George St, Milton Keynes MK17 9PX]; estate agent; *b* 27 Feb 1950; *educ* Eton; (BSc Land Admin), ARICS, ASVA; *m* 1st 29 March 1971 Faith Diane, formerly w of George Carrington and dau of Dr S I M Ibrahim, of Singapore, and has:

(1) *Czarina Lydia; *b* 14 July 1976

3 (cont.) Lord Francis *m* 2nd 1 Feb 1996 *Sarah, dau of Terence Clemence and by her has:

(1) +John Francis; *b* 5 June 1997

The 13th DUKE *m* 3rd 4 Sept 1960 *Nicole Charlotte Pierette, formerly w of Henri Milinaire and dau of Paul Schneider, War Cross with seven palms, Grand Offr Legn Hon, of Paris, late TV producer, author: *Nicole Nobody*, *The Joyful Guest* and *Superwoman*

Bedford, previous creations: KING STEPHEN created Hugh de Beaumont, known as 'Hugo Pauper', Earl of Bedford in 1138. Hugh was a younger son of Robert Count of Meulan, a Norman. As his sobriquet implies, he fell on hard times and may well have been deprived of his Earldom on that account. In any event the title appears to have expired on his death, if not before.

Over two hundred years later Enguerrand or Ingelram de Coucy, of a French family whose boast it was that they were neither Kings nor Princes nor Counts, just Sires de Coucy, suspended his ancestral fastidiousness long enough to accept the Earldom of Bedford from EDWARD III. This was in 1366. His mother was a Habsburg, great-granddaughter of the EMPEROR RUDOLF. He had come to England six years earlier as a hostage for KING JOHN OF FRANCE, who had been captured by the English early in the Hundred Years War. He married EDWARD's daughter Isabella in 1365 and was made a Knight of the Garter as well as ennobled. When RICHARD II came to the throne Lord Bedford threw up all his English honours and went back to France, where he became a Marshal of France, Governor of Brittany and a member of the Regency Council during CHARLES VI's minority.

The first Dukedom of Bedford was created in 1414, when HENRY V conferred it on his younger brother John. Bedford stayed behind to look after his brother's kingdom when the latter crossed over to France for the Agincourt Campaign in 1415, though he won a victory over a French fleet off Harfleur just as HENRY departed. After HENRY's death he acted as Regent of English-occupied France, though England claimed all France and he arrogated to himself several French titles as well as his English ones. He led an Anglo-Burgundian army to victory over a Franco-Scottish one at the Battle of Verneuil in 1424, crowned his nephew HENRY VI King of France in 1432 and died three years later without surviving issue, when the Dukedom expired.

It was revived for George Nevill(e) (*see* ABERGAVENNY, M) in January 1469/70 by EDWARD IV at a time when that king had it in mind to make George his son-in-law by marrying him to his daughter Elizabeth. But the new Duke's father was attainted after the Battle of Barnet a little over 15 months later and as a result Bedford lost his family estates, fell into poverty and was deprived of his peerage, a rare but not unprecedented occurrence. Indeed, as has been seen already, it may well have happened in the case of another holder of the Bedford title. (Elizabeth later made a much better match, marrying HENRY VII.) The removal of George's peerage was carried out by Act of Parliament in 1477.

The last pre-Russell Duke of Bedford was HENRY VII's uncle Jasper Tudor, so created two months after Bosworth. His wife's mother was widow of the Duke of Bedford created in 1414 and her family, the Luxembourg Counts of Pol, were at one time representatives of the De Coucys through the great-granddaughter of Ingelram created Earl of Bedford in 1366.

Lineage: STEPHEN RUSSELL; Bailiff Weymouth 1388/9; owned property in Dorchester, Weymouth and Maiden Newton; *m c* 1400 Alice, gdau and heir of Cecil de Blynchesfield, who held property in Shaftesbury and Stour Provost 1382, and heir general of Gregory de Turri or de la Tour, who held the Manor of Berwick in Dorset before 1221; in July 1427 STEPHEN successfully claimed this Manor in the name of his w; *d* between June and Oct 1438, leaving:

HENRY RUSSELL; *b c* 1401; MP Weymouth 1425, 1427 and 1441–42, Customs Offr Exeter and Dartmouth Nov 1440, Bailiff Weymouth 1440–41, Dep Butler Poole 1455; *m* Elizabeth, dau and coheir of John Herring, of Chaldon Herring, and *d* between Oct 1463 and Oct 1464, leaving issue:

JOHN RUSSELL; *b c* 1431; *m c* 1449 Alice /Elizabeth, dau of John Froxmere, probably of Droitwich, Worcs, and *d* 1505, leaving a s or n:

JAMES RUSSELL, of Kinston Russell, Dorset; *m* 1st Alice, dau of John Wyse, of Sydenham, Devon, and *d* 1509, leaving issue:

JOHN RUSSELL, **1st Earl of Bedford**, so *cr* 19 Jan 1549/50, as also earlier 9 March 1538/9 BARON RUSSELL (both E), KG (1539), PC (1538, 1547 and 1553); *b c* 1485; Gentleman Privy Chamber 1507 and (in new reign) 1509, accompanied HENRY VIII in French expdn 1513, was made Deputy Tournai 1514 and granted lands there 1517; ktd 1522 after capture of Morlaix, Brittany, during which he lost his right eye; envoy to Italy and Germany; Kt Marshal 1523, Sheriff Dorset and Somerset 1528, MP Bucks 1529–36, Comptroller Household 1537–39; granted the same year as his first step in the peerage the Amersham, Bucks, portion of the attainted Duke of Buckingham's estates and at the Dissolution of the Monasteries the Cistercian Abbey of Dunkeswell, Devon, and that of Tavistock (together with the town itself), as well as other estates in Bucks, Devon and Somerset, some of which had formed part of St Albans Abbey, but it was not until 1549 under EDWARD VI that he got possession of the lands of the Cistercian Abbey of Woburn, later the chief seat of the family, plus the Benedictine Abbey at Thorney, Cambs, and the Dominican Priory at Exeter; in 1552 he acquired seven acres in what is now the West Central part of London, called 'Long Acre', part of the estates of the disgraced Duke of Somerset, and the garden of a dissolved convent later corrupted to 'Covent Garden'; High Steward Cornwall and Warden Stannaries 1539, Lord High Adml 1540–42, Capt Gen Vanguard of the Army at Boulogne 1545; Jt Envoy to negotiate peace with France 1550, Ld Lt Cornwall, Devon, Dorset, Somerset 1552; Ld Privy Seal 1553; *m* 1526 Anne (*d* March 1558/9), dau and heiress of Sir Guy Sapcote (through whom the Russells acquired the Chenies estate, Bucks) and widow of (a) Sir Richard Jerningham and (b) John Broughton, and *d* 14 March 1554/5, leaving issue:

FRANCIS RUSSELL, **2nd Earl of Bedford**, KG (1564), KB (Feb 1546/7), PC (1558); *b* 1527; Sheriff Beds and Bucks 1547–48, MP Bucks 1547–52, Ld Lt Bucks 1552 and later Devon, Dorset and Cornwall; called up to Ho Lds 1 March 1552/3 *vp* in f's Barony; Warden Stannaries 1559–80, Amb France 1559 and 1561, Govr Berwick and Warden E Marches Feb 1563/4; *m* 1st Margaret (*d* 27 Aug 1562), sis of 1st Baron St John of Bletso (*qv*) and widow of Sir John Gostwick; *m* 2nd *c* 25 June 1566 Bridget, widow of (a) 2nd Earl of Rutland (*see* RUTLAND, D) and (b) Sir Richard Morrison and dau of 1st and last Lord (Baron) Hussey, and *d* of gangrene 28 July 1585, leaving by his 1st w, with three daus:

1 Edward, *Lord Russell*; *m c* 1571 Jane Sibella (*m* 2nd 14th Lord (Baron) Grey (of Wilton) (*see* GREY, B), and was *bur* 26 June 1580), dau of Sir Richard Morrison, of Cashiobury, Herts, and *dsp* & *vp* by 30 June 1572

2 JOHN RUSSELL, **3rd Baron Russell**, as which called up to Ho Lds Jan 1580/1 *vp*; MP Bridport 1572–80/1; *m c* 12 Dec 1574 Elizabeth, dau of Sir Anthony Cook, of Gidea Hall, Essex, and widow of Sir Thomas Hoby, of Bisham, Berks, and *dspms* & *vp* 1584, leaving, with another dau (Elizabeth, *d* unm):

(1) Anne; *m* 16 June 1600 Henry, Marquess of Worcester, and *d* 1 April 1639, leaving issue (*see* BEAUFORT, D)

3 Francis, *Lord Russell*; ktd 1570, MP Northumberland 1572–84; *m* 15 July 1571 Juliana, dau and coheir of Sir John Fo(r)ster, and *d* 27 July 1585 of wounds recd in a skirmish on the English-Scottish border, leaving issue:

(1) EDWARD RUSSELL, **3rd Earl of Bedford** and **4th Baron Russell** (which once more was now held with the Earldom); *b* 20 Dec 1572; *m* 12 Dec 1594 Lucy (*d* 26 May 1627), sis and heir of 2nd Baron Haryngton of Exton (*see* HARINGTON, Bt), and *dsps* 3 May 1627

4 WILLIAM RUSSELL, **1st Baron Russell of Thornhaugh**, Co Northampton (E), so *cr* 21 July 1603; *m* (by licence 13 Feb 1584/5) Elizabeth (*d* 12 June 1611), dau of Henry Long, of Shengay, Cambs, and *d* 9 Aug 1613, leaving issue:

(1) FRANCIS RUSSELL, **4th Earl of Bedford**, also **5th Baron Russell** and **2nd Baron Russell of Thornhaugh**, PC (1641); *b* 1593; ktd 1607, Ld Lt Devon 1623–41; from 1630 drained the Fens of Cambs, Hunts, Lincs, Norfolk and Northants (the so-called 'Bedford Level'); *m* 26 Feb 1608/9 Catharine Brydges (*d* 29 Jan 1656/7), dau and coheir of 3rd Baron Chandos of Sudeley (*see* BRAYE, B), and had issue, with four daus:

1a WILLIAM, **1st Duke**

2a Francis; *dsp*

3a John, Col 1st Foot, now Gren Gds

4a Edward; *m* Penelope, dau of Sir Moyses Hill, of Hillsborough, Ireland (*see* DOWNSHIRE, M), and widow of Sir William Brooke, KB, and had issue:

1b William, Standard-Bearer to CHARLES II; *d* unm

2b EDWARD RUSSELL, 1st EARL OF ORFORD, Co Suffolk, so *cr* 7 May 1697, as also BARON OF SHINGAY, Co Cambridge, with in this peerage's case only special remainder, failing heirs male of his body, to his sister's only s Edward Cheeke (*see* below), and VISCOUNT BARFLEUR (commemorating his victory of La Hogue, the latter being off the French coast at Barfleur), PC (Feb 1688/9, 1709 and 1714); *b* 1652; Lt RN 1671, Capt 1672, served Third Dutch War; Groom Bedchamber to JAMES II when Duke of York 1677 and 1682 but retired from Court life (and the RN) after his cousin's execution (*see* below); active supporter WILLIAM III at Glorious Revolution 1688; MP (Whig) Launceston 1689–90, Portsmouth 1690–95 and Cambs 1695–97; Treas Navy 1689–99, Adml Blue 1689, a Commr Admlty 1690–91, C-in-C Channel Fleet 1690, victor over the French Fleet at La Hogue 1692 (thanks of Parl, though criticised for want of despatch in following up victory and unemployed for a year afterwards), V-Adml of England, Capt-Gen Narrow Seas and Adml of the Fleet 1693, First Commr Admlty 1694–99, 1709–10 and 1714–17; C-in-C Mediterranean 1694–95, C-in-C Channel Feb-March 1695/6, Ld Lt Cambs 1714; *m* 12 Nov 1691 his cousin Lady Margaret Russell, yst dau of **1st Duke of Bedford** (*see* below), but *dsp* 26 Nov 1727, when all his titles expired

3b Francis; Col, Govr Barbados; *m c* 30 April 1691, as her 3rd husb, Catharine, dau of 1st Baron Grey of Warhe (*see* GREY, E) and widow of (a) Sir Edward Mosley, 2nd Bt (*see* RAVENSDALE, B), and (b) 5th Lord (Baron) North and 1st Lord (Baron) Grey (of Rolleston) (*see* GUILFORD, E); *d c* 1 Oct 1696

1b Laetitia; *m* Thomas Cheeke, of Pirgo, Essex, and *d* 9 Jan 1721/2, having had:

1c Edward; *dsps* 8 Oct 1707

1c Anne; *m* Sir Thomas Tipping, Bt 1st, and had:

1d Laetitia; inherited her great-uncle Lord Orford's Chippenham (Cambs) estate; *m* 9 June 1725 1st Lord Sandys, Baron of Ombersley, and *d* 26 May 1779, leaving issue

The 4th EARL *d* 9 May 1641; his est son,

WILLIAM RUSSELL, **1st Duke of Bedford**, so *cr* 11 May 1694, as also MARQUESS OF TAVISTOCK and 13 June 1695 BARON HOWLAND OF STREATHAM, Surrey (all E), with in the last case special remainder to his said gs and the heirs male of the latter's body begotten of the body of his w Elizabeth Howland, KG (1672), KB (1626), PC (Feb 1688/9); *b* Aug 1613; MP Tavistock 1640–41, Gen Horse Parly Army 1642 (fought Edgehill Oct), Ld Lt: Devon and Somerset 1642, Beds and Cambs 1689 and Middx 1692; changed over to CHARLES I 1643 and fought for royalists 1st Battle of Newbury 20 Sept 1643; *m* 11 July 1637 Anne Carr (*b* Tower of London 9 Dec 1615; *d* 10 May 1684), dau and sole heiress of 1st and last Earl of Somerset (*see* LOTHIAN, M), and had, with an est s (*d* young):

1 William, *Lord Russell*; *b* 29 Sept 1639, PC (April 1679–31 Jan 1679/80); MP Tavistock 1660–61 and 1661–79 and Beds 1679–81; led the 'Country' (Whig) party and the Exclusionists (those who wanted the future JAMES II excluded from the throne on CHARLES II's death as an RC); tried for involvement in Rye House Plot 13 June 1683 and beheaded (following attainder, which was reversed 16 March 1688/9) in Lincoln's Inn Fields 21 July 1683; *m* (by licence 31 July 1669) Lady Rachel Wriothesley (*d* 29 Sept 1723 aged 87), 2nd dau and eventual heir (bringing the Russells the Bloomsbury estate in London) of 4th Earl of Southampton (*see* SOUTHAMPTON, B, preliminary remarks), and widow of Francis, Lord Vaughan, and left, with two daus:

(1) WRIOTHESLEY, **2nd Duke**

2 James *m* Elizabeth Lloyd (*m* 2nd 14 April 1721 Sir Henry Hoghton, 5th Bt (*see* DE HOGHTON Bt), and *d* 1 Dec 1736), and *dsp* 22 June 1712

3 Edward; *m* as her 2nd husb Frances, dau of Sir Robert Williams, 2nd Bt (*see* WILLIAMS-BULKELEY, Bt), and widow of Robert Lloyd

1 Diana; *m* 1st 29 Aug 1667 Sir Greville Verney, *de jure* 9th Lord (Baron) Willoughby de Broke (*qv*); *m* 2nd 15 July 1675 3rd Baron Alington of Killard and *d* 13 Dec 1701

The 1st DUKE *d* 7 Sept 1700; his gs,

WRIOTHESLEY RUSSELL, **2nd Duke of Bedford**, KG (March 1701/2); *b* 1 Nov 1680; *m* 23 May 1695 Elizabeth, dau and heiress of John Howland, of Streatham (an estate in which part of what is now London she brought the Russells, who sold it 1811), by Elizabeth, dau of Sir Josiah Child, Bt, of Wanstead, Essex, and *d* 26 May 1711, leaving, with other issue:

1 WRIOTHESLEY RUSSELL, **3rd Duke of Bedford**; *b* 25 May 1708; *m* 22 April 1725 Anne (*m* 2nd 23 June 1733 3rd Earl of Jersey (*qv*) and *d* 16 June 1762), only dau of 1st Duke of Bridgwater (*see* GREY EGERTON, Bt), and *dsp* 23 Oct 1732

2 JOHN, **4th Duke**

1 Rachel; *m* 1st 4 Aug 1722 as his 2nd w 1st Duke of Bridgwater; *m* 2nd Sir Richard Lyttelton, KB (*see* COBHAM, V), and *d* 22 May 1777

2 Elizabeth; *m* 3 Feb 1726 3rd Earl of Essex (*qv*), and *d* 8 June 1784

The 3rd DUKE's bro,

JOHN RUSSELL, **4th Duke of Bedford**, KG (1749), PC (1744); *b* 30 Sept 1710; First Ld Admlty 1744–Feb 1747/8; Ld Lt: Beds 1745–71, Devon 1751–71 and Ireland 1756–61; Lt Gen 1759, Sec State Southern Dept Feb 1747/8–51, Ld Privy Seal 1761–63, Amb France 1762–63, Ld Pres Cncl 1763–65; *m* 1st 11 Oct 1731 Lady Diana Spencer (*d* 27 Sept 1735), yst dau of 3rd Earl of Sunderland (*see* MARLBOROUGH, D), and had a s (John, *b* and *d* 6 Nov 1732); *m* 2nd 2 April 1737 Lady Gertrude Leveson-Gower (*d* 1 July 1794), 3rd dau of 1st Earl Gower (*see* SUTHERLAND, D), and *d* 15 Jan 1771, leaving, with a dau (Caroline, *m* 4th Duke of Marlborough (*qv*)):

1 Francis, *Marquess of Tavistock*; *b* 27 Sept 1739; MP (Whig) Armagh I Parl 1759–60 and Beds (GB Parl) 1761–67; *m* 8 June 1764 Lady Elizabeth Keppel (*d* 2 Nov 1768), dau of 2nd Earl of Albemarle (*qv*), and was *k* by a fall from his horse 22 March 1767, leaving issue:

(1) FRANCIS RUSSELL, **5th Duke of Bedford**; *b* 23 July 1765; *d* unm 2 March 1802

(2) JOHN, **6th Duke**

(3) William; *b* postumously 20 Aug 1767; *m* 1789 Lady Charlotte Anne Villiers (*d* 31 Aug 1808), est dau of 4th Earl of Jersey (*qv*), and was murdered 6 May 1840 by his valet, Benjamin Francis Courvoisier, leaving, with other issue:

1a Francis, Lt-Col; *b* 7 March 1793; *d* unm 24 Nov 1832

2a George; *b* 7 April 1795; *d* 15 Sept 1825

3a John, Cdr RN; *b* 10 July 1796; *m* 21 Aug 1822 Sophia, Baroness de Clifford in her own right (*qv*) and *d* 27 April 1835, having had issue

4a William, Accountant-Gen Court of Chancery; *b* 15 July 1800; *m* 17 May 1828 Emma (*d* 14 Jan 1886), dau of Col John Campbell, of Shawfield, Argyllshire, by Charlotte, dau of 5th Duke of Argyll (*qv*), and *d* 5 Sept 1884, having had, with other issue:

1b George; *b* 21 Sept 1830; *m* 28 Oct 1862 Charlotte Isabella (*d* 24 April 1881), yr dau of 6th Duke of Roxburghe (*qv*), and *d* 1911, having had issue:

1c George William Henry; *b* 28 Oct 1864; *m* 12 April 1893 Mabel Mary (*d* 2 Dec 1941), est dau of W H Walker, of Ceylon, and *d* 21 July 1908, having had issue:

1d Odo George Henry, Maj Black Watch WW II 1939–40 (wounded, POW); *b* 10 Feb 1899; *m* 8 June 1927 Lisalie Maude, yst dau of Capt Marcus Beresford Armstrong, of Moyaliffe Castle, Thurles, Co Tipperary, by Rosalie, 2nd dau of Maurice Ceely Maude (*see* HAWARDEN, V)

2c John; *b* 12 Feb 1869; *m* Elsa — (*d* 12 Oct 1967), and *d* 19 May 1954

1c Lilian Emmeline; *b* 23 June 1874; *m* 1st 5 Nov 1895 Capt St John Halford Coventry, Gren Gds (*d* 9 June 1920), of Henbury Manor, Dorset, and The Knoll, Dorset, and had issue (*see* COVENTRY, E); *m* 2nd 30 May 1922 Charles Edwin Allen, and *d* 27 Oct 1948

2b Reginald; *b* 18 Dec 1839; *m* 21 July 1881 Nina, yst dau of Capt McGeachy Alleyne, 7th Dragoon Gds, and *d* 1897, leaving issue:

1c Muriel Elsie Augusta; *b* 28 Jan 1884; *m* — Greenfield (*d* 1928)

The 5th DUKE's bro,

JOHN RUSSELL, **6th Duke of Bedford**, KG (1830), PC (1806); *b* 6 July 1766; Ensign 3rd Foot 1783–85, MP (Whig) Tavistock 1788–90 and 1790–1802, Ld Lt Ireland 1806–07; *m* 1st 21 March 1786 Hon Georgina Elizabeth Byng (*d* 11 Oct 1801), 2nd dau of 4th Viscount Torrington (*qv*), and *d* 20 Oct 1839, having had, with other issue:

1 FRANCIS RUSSELL, **7th Duke of Bedford**, KG (1847), PC (1846); *b* 13 May 1788; *educ* Westminster and Trin Coll Cambridge; called up to Ho Lords 15 Jan 1833 *vp* in f's Barony of Howland of Streatham; Ld Lt Beds 1859–61; *m* 8 Aug 1808 Lady Anna Maria Stanhope (*d* 3 July 1857), day of 3rd Earl of Harrington (*qv*), and *d* 14 May 1861, leaving:

1 WILLIAM RUSSELL, **8th Duke of Bedford**; *b* 1 July 1809; *educ* Eton and Ch Ch Oxford; MP (Lib) Tavistock 1832–41; *d* unm 26 May 1872

2 George William, GCB (1838, CB 1831); *b* 8 May 1790; Cornet 1st Dragoons 1806, ADC to Sir G Ludlow Copenhagen Expdn 1807, Captain 23rd Dragoons 1808, served Peninsular War (wounded Talavera 1809, ADC to Gen Graham 1810, present Battle of Barrossa, ADC to Duke of Wellington 1812 and 1817

and on his Staff at Vittoria, Orthez and Toulouse 1814, Toulouse Gold Medal, Brevet-Lt-Col), MP Bedford 1818–30, cmded 8th Hus 1824–28, Min Lisbon Aug 1833 and Wurttemberg Nov 1833, Amb Berlin 1835, Order Leopold 1st Cl 1841, Maj-Gen Nov 1841; *m* 21 June 1817 Elizabeth Anne (*d* 10 Aug 1874), only child of Hon John Theophilus Rawdon, bro of 1st Marquess of Hastings, KG (*see* LOUDOUN, E), and *d* 16 July 1846, leaving issue:

(1) FRANCIS CHARLES HASTINGS, **9th Duke**

(2) Arthur John Edward, granted rank of duke's yr s; MP Tavistock 1857–85, Priv Sec to Lord John Russell 1849–54; *b* 13 June 1825; *m* 25 Sept 1865 Laura (*d* 27 Feb 1910), dau of Viscomte de Peyronnet and gdau of Count de Peyronnet, Min of CHARLES X OF FRANCE, and *d* 4 April 1892, leaving issue:

1a Harold John Hastings, barrister, Recorder Bedford 1912; *b* 23 Jan 1868; *m* 8 Sept 1896 Lady Victoria Alberta Leveson-Gower (*d* 11 Feb 1953), dau of 2nd Earl Granville (*see* SUTHERLAND, D), and *d* 22 Aug 1926, leaving issue:

1b Anthony Arthur; *b* 1904; *educ* Eton and Balliol Coll Oxford; *m* 22 Nov 1947 *Alicia Charlotte [Mrs Anthony Russell, The Ridgeway, Shere, Guildford, Susrrey], only dau of Seton Eustace, of Stoodwell, Merrow, Surrey, and *d* 7 April 1978, leaving issue:

1c +Francis Anthony; *b* 14 Oct 1948; *educ* Crookham Court, Newbury

2c +Hugo Eustace Arthur; *b* 5 Oct 1951; *educ* Milton Abbey; *m* 1991 *Caroline, est dau of Donald Grant, OBE, of Milino de la Hoz, Las Rozas de Madrid, Spain, and has issue:

1d +Arthur Donald Anthony; *b* 1994

1d *Catherine Lucy; *b* 1992

1c *Julia Alicia [Mrs Ian Sanderson, 6 Markham St, London SW3 3NP]; *b* 10 Feb 1950; *educ* Downe House, Newbury; *m* 1985 *Prof Ian Rutherford Sanderson and has:

1d *Vita Frances [Miss Vita Sanderson, 12 Cloudesdale Rd, London SW17 8ES; *b* 1988

2c *Victoria Evelyn Elizabeth]; *b* 27 Sept 1953; *educ* Downe House, Newbury

1b *Elizabeth Frances; *b* 6 July 1899; *m* 21 Dec 1925 (*divorce* 1943) Richard George Hubert Plunket Greene and has issue

2b Rachel Georgiana; *b* 28 Jan 1903; author: *Lord William Russell and His Wife* (1972) and *Woburn and the Russells* (1980); *m* 10 Oct 1929 Hugh Noel Blakiston (*d* 1984), writer, 2nd son of Rev Canon Felix Milburn Blakiston, of Kirkby-on-Bain, Lincs, and *d* by 1996, leaving:

1c *Rachel Castalia; *b* 1930; *m* 1951 (*divorce* 1968) James Gordon Akers Campbell and has:

1d *Julian James Noel; *b* 1953; *m* 1971 *Sandra Hale

2d *Marcus George Akers; *b* 1954

3d *Benedict Robert Gordon; *b* 1958; *m* 1986 *Lynnette Caicco

4d *Cosmo Thomas Aretas; *b* 1960; *m* 1989 *Brigite Gurke

2c *Caroline Georgiana [Mrs Caroline Blakiston, Flat 6, 19 Buckingham St, London WC2N 6EF]; *b* 1933; *m* 1970 (*divorce* 19–) Adam Russell Hunter and has:

1d *Adam Russell; *b* 1969

1d *Charlotte; *b* 1972

2a Claud Frederick William (Sir), KCMG, Envoy Extrdy and Min Plen Abyssinia 1920–25 and Berne 1925–31, Amb Portugal 1931–35; Grand Cross Order Christ Portugal, Maj Yeo WW I (three medals); *b* 9 Dec 1871; *educ* Balliol Coll Oxford (MA); *m* 4 Nov 1920 Athenais, er dau of Shirley Clifford Atchley, CMG, OBE, and *dsp* 9 Dec 1959

3a Gilbert Byng Alwyn, Maj Gren Gds, Maj Bedfordshire Yeo, served Egypt 1898 (present Khartoum; Queen's medal and Khedive's medal and clasp), Boer War 1899–1902 (two medals, seven clasps) and WW I (three medals, Order White Eagle Serbia 4th Cl); *b* 1 June 1875; *m* 14 March 1917 Maud (*d* 1982), er dau of Paul Nelke, and *d* 28 May 1942, leaving issue:

1b +Martin Basil Paul [Martin Russell Esq, Dungrove Farm House, Tarrant Gunville, Blandford, Dorset DT11 8JS], served in KRRC 1939–40, Assist Priv Sec to Min Info 1940–41, Priv Sec to Chllr Duchy Lancaster 1941–42, Capt General Staff 1943–46, with Br S Africa Co 1954–61, Minerals Separation 1961–63, Ionian Bank 1964–66, fndr MBP Russell & Co Ltd 1967, Memb Cncl Roy Soc for India, Pakistan and Ceylon, author: *The Art of George Keyt*; *b* 12 June 1918; *educ* Eton and King's Coll Cambridge (MA); FRAS; *m* 14 May 1954 *Anne Swinton, Croix de Guerre (served French Army 1944–46), dau of Brig Stanlake Swinton Lee, CBE, DSO, and has issue:

1c +Julian Hugh [Julian Russell Esq, 86 South Hill Park, London NW3 2SN]; *b* 17 Aug 1955; *educ* Harrow

2c +Stephen Raymond (twin); *b* 17 Aug 1955; *educ* Harrow

1c *Laura Diana; *b* 12 May 1959; *educ* Essex U (BA) and Ways Coll of Biblical Research, USA; *m* 1989 *Colin Beresford, and has issue:

1d *Helen Anne; *b* 1992

2c *Emily Esther; *b* 21 Jan 1962; *educ* Manchester U (BA)

2b Raymond Anthony, FSA, FRHistS, Capt Roy Fus 1945–47; *b* 27 May 1922; *educ* Eton and Downing Coll Cambridge; *d* unm 17 March 1964

4a Conrad George Edward, Beds Yeo, Assist Priv Sec to Colonial Sec 1903–07; *b* 3 April 1878; *d* unm 27 April 1947

1a Flora Magadalen Isabel; *b* 28 Sept 1869; *d* unm 23 Aug 1967

2a (Caroline) Diana Rosalind, MBE (1918); *b* 2 Jan 1874; *d* unm 31 Oct 1971

(3) ODO WILLIAM LEOPOLD RUSSELL, 1st BARON AMPTHILL (*qv*)

(1) Blanche; *b* 9 April, *d* 26 June 1818

3 JOHN RUSSELL, 1st EARL RUSSELL (*qv*)

The **6th Duke** *m* 2nd 23 June 1803 Lady Georgiana Gordon (*d* Nice 24 Feb 1853), 5th dau of 4th Duke of Gordon, and by her had further issue:

4 Wriothesley (Rev), Rector Chenies, Canon Windsor; *b* 11 May 1804; *m* 23 June 1829 his cousin Elizabeth Laura Henrietta (*d* 5 May 1886), yst dau of Lord William Russell (*see* above), and *d* 6 April 1886, having had issue

5 Edward, CB; Adml, Offr Legion Honour, Kt Medjidie; *b* 24 April 1805; *m* 8 Feb 1860 Mary Ann (*d* 16 Oct 1874), dau of Aaron Taylor, of Kensington, and *dsp* 21 May 1887

6 Charles James Fox, Lt-Col 52nd Regt and RHG, MP Beds 1832–48, Serjeant-at-Arms H of C 1848–75; *b* 10 Feb 1807; *m* 2 April 1834 Isabella Clarissa (*d* 19 June 1884), dau of William Davies, of Penylan, Carmarths, and gdau of Lord Robert Seymour, and *d* 29 June 1894, having had, with other issue:

(1) Henry Charles (Rev), Rector Wollaton, Notts; *b* 30 Oct 1842; *m* 10 Feb 1876 Hon Leila Louisa Millicent Willoughby (*d* 24 Feb 1886), dau of 8th Baron Middleton (*qv*), and *d* 20 July 1922, leaving issue:

1a Alexander Cosmo; *b* 13 Sep; *d* 30 Oct 1877

2a James Cosmo, DSO (1917), Maj IA and Lt-Col cmdg 6th Bn Cameron Highrs; *b* 18 Oct 1878; *m* 8 June 1916 Mary Katharine (*m* 2nd 23 Oct 1919 Lt-Col Cyril Frankland Mears, DSO, Roy Irish Fus, son of Col George Brooke Meares, Roy Fus, and *d* 1959), dau of Rev Edward Mansfield Clements, Rector Barkston, Lincs, and was *ka* 31 July 1917

3a Thomas Wentworth (Sir), KBE (1938), CMG (1926), OBE (1919), Cmdt Cairo City Police and Dir Narcotic Intell Bureau, Orders Crown Italy, Leopold II of Belgium, St Maurice and St Lazarus Italy, Sword Sweden, 3rd Cl Medjidie and 2nd Cl Order Nile, 3rd Cl Order Astaur Afghanistan, Cdr Crown Romania, Grand Offr Order Ismail, V-Pres League of Nations Advsy Ctee Opium Traffic 1939, Dir Egyptian Govt Anti-Narcotic Bureau 1929–46; *b* 22 Nov 1879; *m* 1 June 1911 Evelyn Dorothea Temple, MBE (*d* 25 April 1968), dau of Francis Moore, of 93 Sloane Street, London SW1, and *d* 10 April 1954, leaving issue:

1b John Wriothesley (Sir), GCVO (1968, KCVO 1965), CMG (1958); Amb Ethiopia 1962–66, Brazil 1966–69 and Spain 1969, Coronation Medal 1952, Grand Cross Star Ethiopia 1965, Grand Cross Southern Cross Brazil, Cdr Taj Iran; *b* 22 Aug 1914; *educ* Eton and Trin Coll Cambridge (BA 1935, MA 1956); *m* 15 Dec 1945 *Aliki [Lady Russell, The Vine Farm, Northbourne, nr Deal, Kent; Flat 1, 48 Queens Gate Gdns, London SW7 5ND], formerly w of Paul Louis Weiller (*d* 1993) and dau of George Diplarakos, of Athens, and *d* 1984, leaving issue:

1c +Alexander Charles Thomas Wriothesley [Alexander Russell Esq, 48 Chester Row, London SW1W 9DU]; *b* 28 June 1950; *educ* Eton and Trin Coll Cambridge; *m* 1986 *Elizabeth (Libby) Diana, er dau of Lord John Manners, of Knipton, Grantham, Lincs (*see* RUTLAND, D), and has issue:

1d *Sophie Camilla Mary; *b* 1989

2d *Rose Isobel Aliki; *b* 1991

1c *Georgiana Alexandra [Lady Boothby, Fonmon Castle, Barry, S Glamorgan CF6 23ZN]; *b* 24 Jan 1947; PR consultant and co dir; *m* 9 June 1976 *Sir Brooke Charles Boothby, 16th Bt (*qv*), and has issue

1b Camilla Georgiana; *b* 18 April 1912; *m* 25 Oct 1936 Christopher Hugh Sykes, FRLS (*d* 1986), 2nd son of Sir Mark Sykes, 6th Bt, of Sledmere (*qv*), and *d* 1983, leaving issue

1a Leila Elizma; *b* 8 Nov 1876; *m* 8 Aug 1899 Frank Evelyn Seely, DL (*d* 16 April 1928), 3rd son of Sir Charles Seely, 1st Bt (*qv*), and *d* 16 Feb 1903, leaving issue

2a Marjorie Violet; *b* 6 April 1881; *d* unm 11 May 1960

3a Olive Isobel; *b* 23 June 1882; *m* 29 April 1909 Maj Harry Lawrence Birkin, TD (*d* 6 Jan 1951), yst son of Sir Thomas Isaac Birkin, 1st Bt (*qv*), and *d* 22 April 1960, leaving issue

4a Sheila; *b* 8 Jan 1886; *d* unm 2 Dec 1951

7 Alexander George, GCB, Gen, Col Cmdg Rifle Brigade; *b* 16 Dec 1821; *m* 3 July 1844 Anne Emily Worsley (*d* 16 Oct 1906), yst dau of Sir Leonard Worsley Holmes, 9th and last Bt, and *d* 10 Jan 1907, leaving:

(1) Alexander Gordon, Capt Rifle Birgade; *b* 11 July 1854; *m* 22 Oct 1885 Ella Maude (*d* 4 Sept 1887), dau of Adml Sir Edmund Commerell, VC, GCB, and *d* 4 June 1917, leaving:

1a Ella Maude Emily; *b* 9 July 1886; *m* 1 Feb 1917 Thomas Bowman, of 2 Moreton Rd, S Croydon, Surrey, and *d* 26 March 1933, leaving issue

(2) Leonard George, Maj Rifle Brigade; *b* 6 June 1858; *m* 8 April 1890 Agnes Harriett (*d* 1 Nov 1934), est dau of Rev Godfrey Bollies Lee, MA, Warden Winchester Coll, and *d* following an accident 7 April 1946, having had:

1a Leonard Cosmo Boles, Capt Rifle Brigade; *b* 19 March 1895; *ka* 7 Oct 1916

1a Violet Agnes Mary; *b* 27 Jan 1891

2a Eileen Worsley; *b* 22 Oct 1906; *m* 22 Jan 1935 Jocelyn Walter Hoare, yst son of Walter Hoare, of Daneshill, Basingstoke, and had issue

1 Louisa Jane, VA; *m* 1832 1st Duke of Abercorn (*qv*)

2 Rachel Evelyn; *m* 3 April 1856 Lord James Wandesforde Butler, 2nd s of 1st Marquess of Ormonde (*see* MOUNTGARRET, V), and had issue

The 8th DUKE's cousin,

FRANCIS CHARLES HASTINGS RUSSELL, **9th Duke of Bedford**, KG (1880); *b* 16 Oct 1819; served Scots Fus Gds 1838–44, MP (Lib) Beds 1847–1872, Ld Lt and Custos Rotulorum Hunts 1884–91; *m* 18 Jan 1844 Lady Elizabeth Sackville-West, VA, Mistress Robes 1880–83, Extra Ldy Bedchamber 1883 (*d* 22 April 1897), est dau of 5th Earl De La Warr (*qv*), and shot himself dead while temporarily deranged during a bout of pneumonia 14 Jan 1891, leaving issue:

1 GEORGE WILLIAM FRANCIS SACKVILLE RUSSELL, **10th Duke of Bedford**, DL (Beds); *b* 16 April 1852, MP Beds (Lib) 1875–85; *m* 24 Oct 1876 Adeline Marie, GBE, LJStJ (*d* 12 April 1920), dau of 3rd Earl Somers (*see* SOMERS, B), and *dsp* 23 March 1893

2 HERBRAND ARTHUR, **11th Duke**

1 Ela Monica Sackville; *d* unm 2 Feb 1936

2 Ermyntrude Sackville; *m* 19 March 1885 Sir Edward Baldwin Malet, 4th Bt, PC, GCB, GCMG (*qv*), and *d* 22 March 1927

The 10th DUKE's yr bro,

HERBRAND ARTHUR RUSSELL, **11th Duke of Bedford**, KG (1902), KBE (1919), DL (Beds); *b* 19 Feb 1858; *educ* Balliol Coll Oxford; chm Beds CC 1895–1928, Ld Lt and Custos Rotulorum Middx 1898–1926, chm Lts of Counties Assoc 1910–26, 1st Mayor Holborn 1900, 1st Hon Freeman Holborn 1931, Col, Lt Gren Gds, served Egyptian Campaign 1882 (medal and clasp and Khedive's star), ADC to Viceroy India 1884–88, ADC to TM EDWARD VII and GEORGE V 1908–1920, Col cmdg 3rd Bn Beds Regt 1897–1908, served WW I (despatches),

KGStJ, FRS, Tstee Br Museum 1906–27, pres Imperial Cancer Research Fund and Zoological Society London 1899–1936 (gold medal 1936), Hon LLD Edinburgh 1906; *m* 30 Jan 1888 Mary du Caurroy, DBE (1928), FLS, RRC, DGStJ (*d* in an aeroplane accident 22 March 1937), dau of Ven Walter Harry Tribe, Archdeacon of Lahore, and *d* 27 Aug 1940, leaving:

HASTINGS WILLIAM SACKVILLE RUSSELL, **12th Duke of Bedford**; Lt Middx Regt, MA Balliol Coll Oxford; *b* 21 Dec 1888; *m* 21 Nov 1914 (Louisa) Crommelin Roberta Jowitt (*d* 2 Oct 1960), yr dau of Robert Jowitt Whitwell, of Thornbury Lodge, Oxford, and *d* following an accident 9 Oct 1953, leaving issue:

1 JOHN IAN ROBERT RUSSELL, **13th and present Duke of Bedford**

2 +Hugh Hastings [The Lord Hugh Russell, The Bell House, Dolau, Llandrindod Wells, Powys LD1 5UN]; *b* 29 March 1923; *educ* Christ's Coll Cambridge; ARICS; *m* 7 Sept 1957 *Rosemary, yr dau of Keith Freeling Markby, of Treworder, Blisland, Bodmin, Cornwall, by Violet Muriel, er dau of Maj William Croughton Peel, JP, of Trenant Park, Cronwall, and formerly of Peele Fold, Lancs, and has:

(1) +Mark Hugh [Mark Russell Esq, Churchtown Farm, Lanteglos-by-Fowey, Cornwall PL23 1NR]; *b* 29 July 1960; *m* 1987 *Charlotte E A , dau of J W D Stewart, of Kingston-upon-Thames, Surrey, and has:

1a +Laurie Stewart; *b* 1990

1a *Chloe Ruth; *b* 1988

2a *Hester Mae; *b* 1994

(1) *Karen Diana; *b* 16 Aug 1961; *m* 1991 *Hugh Yelverton Scott Barrett

1 *Daphne Crommelin; *b* 2 Sept 1920

Seat: Woburn Abbey, nr Leighton Buzzard, Beds. Although Woburn remained laid out in a rectangle vaguely reminiscent of a cloister until the early 1950s, when dry rot forced the demolition of the east wing, nothing could be less monastic in style. (The dry rot may have been a blessing since it opened up the west wing with its mid-18th-century pediment by Henry Flitcroft, who by coincidence was a predominantly ecclesiastical architect, to air, light and a view from a distance.) The oldest part of the present house dates from late in JAMES I's reign, when the **4th Earl** started transforming the religious foundation acquired by his great-grandfather into a nobleman's seat. The north wing was the first to be completed. The west wing followed between 1747 and 1761 and the southern and eastern ones were put up a generation later by Henry Holland, architect of that other temple of Whiggism Brooks's. The Far East provides a certain unifying influence, with both a Chinese room among Flitcroft's state apartments and a Dairy in the Chinese taste by Holland in the grounds. Holland's library is considered his best work in the actual house.

The present Duke is sometimes described as the first landed proprietor in Britain to go into the stately home business. That is not strictly accurate, since the Thynnes threw Longleat open to the public soon after the War. What the present Duke did grasp was that the public's appetite for boiseries, the classical orders and plastered ceilings was strictly limited, and that an ancestral estate's inmates, whether himself or his deer and hippopotami, were what really drew the crowds. Accordingly he developed something of a cult of personality in the 1950s and 1960s.

BEECHAM

Arms: Per fess gules and sable a fess nebuly plain cotised, in chief an escallop between two martlets and in base the like, all or. **Crest:** Between two escallops or a swan's head erased argent holding in the beak gules a like escallop gold. **Motto:** *Nil sine labore* ('Nothing without labour'). **Creation:** Bt (UK) 17 July 1914.

(SIR) JOHN STRATFORD ROLAND BEECHAM, 4TH BT, of Ewanville, Co Lancaster [John Beecham Esq, Shalow, Station Rd, Shipston-on Stour, Warwicks]; *b* 21 April 1940, *s f* 1982 but has declined to prove his claim and does not use the title; *educ* Winchester and Queen's Coll Oxford

Lineage: THOMAS BEECHAM, of St Helens and Southport, Lancashire, *b* 3 Dec 1820, founder of the pill making business at St Helens, son of JOSEPH BEECHAM, of Curbridge, nr Witney, Oxon, and his wife Sarah, *m* 26 May 1847 Jane (*d* 19 Aug 1872), dau of William Evans, of Bangor, and *d* 6 April 1907, LEAVING:

Sir Joseph Beecham, 1st Bt (UK), so *cr* 17 July 1914, of Ewanville, Huyton, Lancs, JP (Lancs); Mayor St Helens 1899, 1910 and 1911, Kt Order St Stanislaus Russia, *b* 8 June 1848, ktd 1912; *m* 12 April 1873 Josephine (*d* 3 Nov 1934), dau of William Burnett, of London, and *d* 23 Oct 1916, having had issue:

1 THOMAS (Sir), **2nd Bt**

2 Henry, Lt RASC, *b* 20 Aug 1888, *m* 25 Oct 1914 Ethel Anne (*d* 12 Oct 1951), dau of Herbert Baxter, of Keyham Hall, Leics, and *d* 10 Jan 1947, leaving issue:

(1) Joseph Michael, MBE (1944), Maj RA WW II, *b* 16 Jan 1917, *educ* Eton, *m* 25 Aug 1939 *Sylvia [Mrs Joseph Beecham, C7 Shirley Towers, Vane Hill Rd, Torquay, Devon TQ1 2BY], only child of Frank Benjamin Nathan, of 14 Charleville Mansions, London W14, and *d* 1994, having had issue:

1a *Valerie Anne [Mrs Julian Allan, 22 Westgate Terrace, London SW10 9BJ], *b* 1941, *m* 1st 3 Sept 1960 John Keenan, BA, MB, BChir, son of James Keenan; *m* 2nd 1978 *Julian Allan, s of Maj Alexander William Allan, and has issue by her 1st husb:

1b *Lucinda Jane, *b* 22 April 1964

2d *Katharine Victoria, *b* 13 July 1968

(2) (Henry Robert) Derrick, composer, *b* 11 April 1921, *educ* Eton; *m* 1st 8 Nov 1943 (*divorce* 1950) Annie Ellen, 2nd dau of Thomas John King, RM, of Birmingham; *m* 2nd 31 Oct 1951 (*divorce* 1961) Sheila, dau of Bertram John Martin, of Bushey Heath, Herts; *m* 3rd 26 Sept 1966 *Freda, dau of Rev David Railton, MC, MA, of Ard Rhu Onich, Inverness-shire and *d* 13 Sept 1988, having had by his 1st w:

1a *Jasmine Heather [Mrs David Heaps, Benington Bury, Walkern Rd, Benington, Herts SG2 7LN], *b* 17 Oct 1944, *m* 1963 *David George Heaps and has:

1b *Daniel Blue, *b* 1974

1b *Judith Ann, *b* 1971

2 *Priscilla Rosamunde, *b* 19 July 1947, *m* 1982 *Wilfred Staples

3a *Susan Jane, *b* 24 May 1949, adopted by W A Whithear, whose surname she assumed, *m* 1969 (*divorce* 1985) Roland Vaughan, and has issue:

1b *Rhianon Jane, *b* 1969

(3) Paul; *b* 15 March 1923, *educ* Charterhouse, *m* 6 Feb 1952 Mary (*d* 1990), dau of William Arthur, of Pill Lawn, Barnstaple, Devon, and *d* 1986, having had issue:

1a William Henry Mark, *b* 29 Nov 1954, *d* 1990

2a +Hugh Joseph, *b* 14 Oct 1957, *m* 1990 *Rachel Nelson and has issue:

1b *Celia Mary, *b* 1992

3a +Matthew Arthur, *b* 15 June 1965

1a *Sarah Caroline [Mrs Graham Howard, Wonston Barn, Wonston, nr Winchester, Hants], *b* 14 May 1953, *m* 1st 1971 Kevin Pigott (*d* 1974) and has issue:

1b Dominic Kingsley, *b* 1972

1a (cont.) Mrs Kevin Pigott *m* 2nd 1981 *Graham Jonathan Howard and has further issue:

1b *Freya Helewise, *b* 1982

2a *Hannah Charlotte [Mrs John O'Mahony, 8 Wolstonbury Rd, Hove, E Sussex BN3 6EJ], *b* 4 July 1956, *m* 1989 *John O'Mahony, s of Joseph O'Mahony, and has issue:

1b *Callum Paul Joseph, *b* 1993

1b *Catherine Holly Amber, *b* 1990

3a *Emma Ruth [Ms Emma Beecham, Y Wern, Llanfairfechan, Gwynedd], has resumed her maiden name, *b* 26 Feb 1960, *m* 1977 (*divorce* 1992) Peter Lloyd Edmondson and has issue:

1b *Richard Thomas Lloyd, *b* 1980

1b *Josephine Alice Mary, *b* 1978

(4) Christopher, *b* 11 Feb 1925, *educ* King's Sch Canterbury, *m* 27 Oct 1951 *Kathleen Elizabeth, dau of Major Bertie Orme Collis, of Pinner, Middlesex, and *d* 1970, having had issue:

1 +Philip Henry Orme, *b* 9 Sept 1962, *m* 1983 (*divorce* 1988) Suzanne, dau of William Wright, of London

1a *Diana Mary, *b* 23 Jan 1953, *m* 1974 *John Heap, of Southampton, and has issue:

1b *Jessica Amy, *b* 1989

2a *Honor June, *b* 7 June 1955, *m* 1984 *Michael William Johnson, of Lichfield, Staffs

3a *Jennifer Kate, *b* 27 Feb 1957, *m* 1986 *Peter Cook, of Faversham, Kent

4a *Penelope Carol, *b* 22 April 1960, *m* 1984 (*divorce* 1994) Philip William Gray

5a *Sally Helen, *b* 11 Nov 1965

(1) *Helen Audrey, BA (1937), MA (1949) Oxford, Senior Research Assist at Oxford Univ Agricultural Economics Research Institute 1940–50, Warden of Florence Nightingale Hall, and Lecturer in Economic History at Univ of Nottingham 1950 on, author, *b* 1915

1 Emily, taught operatic dancing as Madame Helena Dolli; *b* 7 April 1874; *d* unm aged 91

2 Josephine, *b* 27 June 1881, *m* 1st 31 Jan 1905 Charles Frederick Boston; *m* 2nd 1919 Thomas Lionel Scott, and *d* 12 Feb 1959, leaving issue

3 Edith, *b* 25 July 1884, *m* 10 Sept 1910 Frederick Duke Duke-Woolley, MRCS, and has issue. They added by deed poll 16 Nov 1925 the name DUKE. He *d* 11 Dec 1937

4 Jessie, *b* 30 Jan 1886, *m* 8 June 1909 Lt-Col Leonce Delphin, DSO, MC, RE (*d* 1932)

5 Elsie Olive, *b* 17 March 1889, *m* 9 Oct 1915 William Senior Ellis (*d* 16 March 1940), son of Joseph Ellis, of St Helens

6 Amy Christine, *b* 20 Feb 1894, *m* 1st 27 March 1917 Reginald John Wrathall, 2nd son of H Lonsdale Wrathall, of Huyton. He *das* 30 Oct 1918. She *m* 2nd Rex Walker (*d* 19–)

Sir JOSEPH's elder son,

Sir Thomas Beecham, 2nd Bt, CH (1957), conductor and composer, *educ* Rossall and Wadham Coll Oxford; Cr Orders of the Crown of Italy and Legion of Honour of France; hon DMus Oxford 1930 and Manchester 1937, hon Master of Music Birmingham 1939; hon FRCM 1934; Gold Medallist Royal Philharmonic Soc London; *b* 29 Apr 1879; ktd 1916; *m* 1st 27 July 1903 (*divorce* USA 1943) Utica (*d* 12 Oct 1977 aged 96), dau of Dr Charles J Stuart Welles, of New York (descended from Thomas Welles, 2nd Governor of Connecticut) by his wife Ella Celeste Miles, and had issue:

1 ADRIAN WELLES (Sir), **3rd Bt**

2 Thomas Welles, AMIStruct E, Capt RE WW II, *b* 19 June 1909, *m* 27 Jan 1937 Mozelle (*d* 1988), dau of Edward Cairn, and *d* 1988, having had issue:

(1) +Thomas Richard, *b* 31 May 1944

(2) +Henry John [Henry Beecham Esq, Tidmington Lodge, Tidmington, Shipston-on-Stour, Warwicks]; *b* 12 Nov 1947; *educ* Winchester and Wadham Coll Oxford; *m* 1978 *Carola Fiona, dau of Charles Ring, of The Green, Puddletown, Dorset

(1) *Ann Margaret [Mrs Charles Hetherington, Yew Tree, Donhead St Mary, nr Shaftesbury, Dorset]; *b* 11 Oct 1949; *m* 1978 *Charles Hoste Hetherington and has:

1a *Peter Hoste; *b* 1980

2a *John Gabriel; *b* 1982

1a *Rebecca Clare; *b* 1984

2a *Emma Sarah Elizabeth; *b* 1992

(2) *Elizabeth Marian (twin) [Mrs Christopher Hall, Hundalee Cottars Farm, by Jedburgh, Roxburghshire TD8 6PA]; *b* 11 Oct 1949; *m* 1st 25 Jan 1969 (*divorce* 1977) Andrew George Richard Birtwell, 2nd s of Rev Stanley Birtwell, and has:

1a *Emily Jane; *b* 18 March 1970

(2) (cont.) Mrs Elizabeth Birtwell *m* 2nd 1987 *Christopher Hall and by him has:

2a *Madeline Thomasina; *b* 1988

Sir Thomas *m* 2nd Feb 1943 Betty (*d* 2 Sept 1958), formerly wife of Rev H C Thomas and dau of Daniel Morgan Humby, MRCS, LRCP, of 16 Wellington Road, NW8; *m* 3rd 10 Aug 1959 *Shirley Jean [Shirley Lady Beecham, Denton House, Denton, Harleston, Norfolk IP20 0AA], dau of Albert George Hudson, of 69 Oakwood Park Road, London N14, and *d* 8 March 1961

Sir THOMAS's elder son,

Sir Adrian Welles Beecham, 3rd Bt, MusB Durham 1926, composer of songs and choral works; *b* 3 Sept 1904; *m* 9 Feb 1939 (Barbara) Joyce, dau of Edward Cohen by Emma, afterwards Hon Mrs Stratford Tollemache (*see* TOLLEMACHE, B), and had:

1 Sir JOHN STRATFORD ROLAND BEECHAM, **4th and present Bt**

2 +ROBERT ADRIAN [Robert Beecham Esq, 30 Church Rd, Barnes, London SW13 9HN]; *b* 6 Jan 1942; heir presumptive; *educ* Winchester and Clare Coll Cambridge; *m* 1969 *Daphne Mattinson and has:

(1) +Michael John; *b* 1972

(1) *Judith Mary; *b* 1970

1 *Jane [Mrs Jane Brabyn, Longdon Manor, Shipston-on-Stour, Warwicks CV36 4PW]; *b* 23 Nov 1945; *m* 1969 (*divorce* 1988) Frederick Charles Brabyn, and has:

(1) *Adrian Alexander Benjamin; *b* 1972

(1) *Lowdy; *b* 1978

BEEVOR

Arms: Per pale or and argent on a chief indented sable three lions rampant of the first. **Crest:** A beaver passant proper. **Motto:** *Suaviter in modo, fortiter in re* ('Gentle in manner, but vigorous in deed'). **Creation:** Bt (GB) 22 Jan 1784.

SIR THOMAS AGNEW BEEVOR, 7TH BT, of Hethel, Norfolk [Sir Thomas Beevor Bt, Hargham Hall, Hethel, Norfolk NR16 2JW]; *b* 6 Jan 1929; *s f* 1943; *educ* Eton and Magdalene Coll Cambridge; *m* 1st 27 April 1957 (*divorce* 1965) Barbara Clare, yst dau of Capt Robert Lionel Brooke Cunliffe, CBE, RN (ret), of Pakenham Lodge, Bury St Edmunds (*see* CUNLIFFE, Bt), and has issue:

1 +(THOMAS) HUGH CUNLIFFE; *b* 1 Oct 1962; *educ* Radley, Pembroke Coll Cambridge and RAC Cirencester; *m* 1988 *Charlotte Louise, er dau of Keith Ernest Harvey, of Nuthall, Nottingham, and has issue:

(1) +Thomas William Harvey; *b* 15 April 1990

(2) +Joshua Peter Hugh; *b* 1992

1 *Bridget Anastasia; *b* 6 April 1958; *m* 1984 *Matthew J Le Fanu Porteous, FRCS, est s of John Porteous, of London W1, and has issue:

(1) *Samuel Thomas Le Fanu; *b* 1986

(2) *Tancred John Octavian; *b* 1988

(1) *Anastasia Catherine Lucie; *b* 1991

(2) *Elizabeth Clare Mary; *b* 1993

2 *Juliana Clare; *b* 16 June 1960; *m* 1988 *Dr Roderick Peter Ross Marrs, s of Alan Ross Marrs, of Watchet, Somerset, and has issue:

(1) *Adam; *b* 1990

Sir THOMAS *m* 2nd 22 Feb 1966 (*divorce* 1975) Carola, er dau of His Honour Judge Jesse Basil Herbert, MC, QC, of 2 Crown Office Row, London EC4, by Hon Isabella Russell, er dau of 1st Baron Rea (*qv*); *m* 3rd 6 Aug 1976 *Mrs Sally Bouwens, only dau of Edward Madoc, of White Hall, Saham Toney, Thetford, Norfolk

Lineage: Sir Thomas Beevor, 1st Bt (GB), so *cr* 22 Jan 1784, of Hethel, Norfolk, son of Thomas Beevor, of Norwich (by his wife Hester, dau of John Sharpe, of the same place), grandson of Rev William Beevor, Rector of South Walsham, Norfolk (by his wife Elizabeth, dau and coheir of William Batt, of Okewell, Yorks), and great-grandson of Abraham Beevor, of Heckmondwike, Co York; Sir Thomas was *b* 25 Oct 1726, *m* 7 July 1750 Elizabeth (*d* 15 Jan 1794), dau and heir of Miles Branthwayt, of Hethel, and *d* 18 Feb 1814, having had, with other issue:

Sir Thomas Beevor, 2nd Bt, *b* 15 Nov 1753, *m* 24 Aug 1795 Anne, dau and sole heir of Hugh Hare, of Hargham Hall, Norfolk, and *d* 10 Dec 1820, leaving, with other issue:

Sir Thomas Branthwayt Beevor, 3rd Bt, *b* 7 April 1798, *m* 1st 9 Dec 1819 Elizabeth Bridget (*d* 2 Nov 1831), 2nd dau of Richard Lubbock, MD, of Norwich, and had, with a dau:

1 THOMAS (Sir), **4th Bt**

Sir Thomas *m* 2nd 4 Sept 1832 Martha (*d* 25 Oct 1843), dau of Archibald Herdiment, of Old Buckenham, Norfolk and by her had three s and four daus; *m* 3rd 15 March 1845 Mary (*d* 1878), dau of F Davies, and *d* 6 April 1879, having by her had another s and two daus

His eldest son,

Sir Thomas Beevor, 4th Bt, of Hargham Hall, and Hingham, Norfolk, JP, *b* 23 Aug 1823, *m* 10 Dec 1850 Sophia Jane (*d* 22 Feb 1890), widow of Isaac Jermy Jermy, of Stanfield Hall, Norfolk, and dau of Rev Clement Chevallier, Rector of Badingham, Suffolk, and *d* 18 Aug 1885, having had issue:

1 Thomas Edward, *b* 9 May 1854; *d* 6 Aug 1879

2 HUGH REEVE (Sir), **5th Bt**

3 Ralph Jermy, MA Trin Coll Camb, *b* 29 Dec 1859, *m* 26 Apr 1894 Sophia Mary (*d* 19 May 1948), er dau of Rev Joseph Preston by his wife Marian Anne, dau of William Atkinson Green, and *d* 1 Nov 1937, leaving issue:

(1) Ralph Branthwayt, ICS, late Lt RAF, had Croce di Guerra of Italy, *b* 29 April 1895, *educ* Felsted and Emmanuel Coll Camb, *m* 2 Dec 1921 Phyllis Margaret Ashburner (*d* 1972), eldest dau of Henry Oliver Minty, of St Albans, and *d* 21 Jan. 1970, leaving issue:

1a Ralph Vernon Ashburner, *b* 5 Jan 1924, *educ* Gresham's Sch Holt and Emmanuel Coll Camb

2a Michael Branthwayt, *b* 2 Sept 1935, *educ* Gresham's and Trin Coll Camb

1a *Ruth Margaret [Mrs Dennis Outwin, Curacao, Ray Park Rd, Maidenhead, Berks SL6 8NN], *b* 18 Sept 1929, *m* 15 Sept 1956 *Dennis, only son of William Leslie Outwin, and has issue:

1b *Christopher Dennis, *b* 25 April 1960

1b *Daphne Margaret, *b* 15 Aug 1958, *m* 1984 (*divorce* 1994) John Albert Benford, and has issue:

1c *Abigail Jane, *b* 1987

2b *Wendy Ruth, *b* 17 April 1964, *m* 1991 *Dr David John Ekbery and has:

1c *Benjamin William; *b* 21 Dec 1995

1c *Harriet Louise; *b* 30 May 1994

(2) Vernon Savile, MC, 2nd Lt 14th Bn Essex Regt, *b* 21 June 1897, *educ* Felsted, *ka* 10 March 1917

(3) Esmond Ayton, FCA, *b* 2 Dec 1902, *educ* Felsted, *m* 1 May 1953 Olive May, widow of William Henderson Gray and dau of Henry Joseph Beazley, of Bitterne, Southampton

(1) Irene Bedingfeld, *b* 10 July 1898, *d* unm 17 May 1979

(2) Nancy Clover, *b* 18 Sept 1899, *m* 6 Feb 1928 Robert Lawson Bennett (*d* 24 April 1967), s of Robert Buchanan Bennett, of Christchurch, NZ, and *d* 11 July 1988, leaving:

1a *Robert Graham Temple, MSc (1954), PhD (1958) U of NZ [Robert Bennett Esq, 60 Kirkwood Ave, Christchurch 4, New Zealand], *b* 7 Sept 1930, *m* 17 April 1958 *Helen Gertrude, only dau of Bruce Kirk Dawber, of St Albans, Christchurch, NZ, and has issue:

1b *Robert Hugh, *b* 12 April 1960

2b *Bruce Stephen, *b* 13 Aug 1962

1b *Alison Hilda, *b* 15 Dec 1967; *m* 18 April 1995 *Nigel Martin Wallis and has:

1c *Elizabeth Helen; *b* 28 Aug 1997

1a *Anne Moyna [Mrs Gavin Crew, 29A Little Barrier Ave, Whangaparaoa, Auckland, New Zealand], *b* 22 Oct 1928, *m* 22 July 1958 *Gavin Albert Loftus Crew, yr son of Albert Crew, of New Brighton, NZ, and has:

1b *Miles Gavin, *b* 5 April 1964

2b *Paul Thomas, *b* 26 Oct 1965

1b *Fiona Anne, *b* 9 Sept 1967; *m* 27 Jan 1996 *Bruce Sydney Barnett

(3) Averil Preston, *b* 1 April 1901; *d* unm 6 Sept 1988

4 John Hare (Rev), MA Camb, *b* 1 June 1861, *m* 22 Feb 1892 Susan Heard Oliver, OBE (1918) (*d* 20 Nov 1938), dau of Charles William Dabney, of Boston, USA, and *d* 27 Feb 1914

5 Cecil Nicholas, Lt RE, *b* 24 Jan 1863; *d* 15 Sept 1888

6 Rowland, slr, *b* 7 Feb 1866; *m* 13 Sept 1893 Margaret Frances (*d* 23 April 1954), yst dau of George Evans, of Nottingham, and *d* 7 Nov 1942, leaving issue:

(1) Cecil Thomas Ashworth, OBE (1957), TD, DL (1954) Norfolk, Solicitor, Lt.-Col RA (TA), served WWs I (wounded) and II, *b* 4 Jan 1898, *m* 10 Sept 1925 Violet Babington (*d* 1985), only child of Edward Babington Lenton, of Ivy House, Fritton, Great Yarmouth, and *d* 1989, having had issue:

1a *Elizabeth Bridget Babington [Mrs John Painter, Myrobella, Upton, Norwich, Norfolk], *b* 7 July 1928, *m* 6 Aug 1952 *John Clifford Painter, MA, son of A E Painter, of Kentisbeare, Devon, and has issue:

1b *Stephen Langman, *b* 23 Nov 1956

1b *Hilary Joanna, *b* 10 May 1953

2b *Philippa Jane, *b* 19 July 1961

(2) Miles, JP Herts, slr 1925, WW II 1941–43 as F/Lt RAFVR, Ch Legal Advsr LNER 1943, A/Chief Gen Manager June 1947, Chief Sec and Legal Adviser Br Tport Commn 1947–51, Brush Gp Ltd 1951–58 (md 1954); *b* 8 March 1900; *educ* Winchester and New Coll Oxford (BA 1921); *m* 1st 17 Sept 1924 Margaret Florence (*d* 15 Feb 1934), elder dau of Algernon John Frederick Platt, of Barnby Manor, Newark-on-Trent, and had:

1a +John Rowland [John Beevor Esq, 104 Defoe Ho, Barbican, London EC2]; *b* 26 June 1930; *educ* Winchester and Ch Ch Oxford (BA 1953), FCA, dir Midland Montagu Industrial Finance; *m* 5 Nov 1955 *Fenella Sybil, yr dau of Brig John Gordon Bedford-Roberts, CBE, of Park House, Bury St Edmunds, Suffolk, and has:

1b +Timothy James; *b* 18 Feb 1957

2b +Justin Miles; *b* 22 Sept 1961; *m* 1990 *Isobel Rose, of Cambridge

1b *Catrina Margaret; *b* 10 June 1958; *m* 1989 *Robert MacLean Mull, only s of Arthur Mull, of Whitwell Ho, Huntingdon, and has:

1c *Ishbel Mary; *b* 1990

2c *Olivia; *b* 1992

1a Susan Margaret; *b* 15 July 1927; *d* unm 12 July 1948

(2) (cont.) Miles Beevor *m* 2nd 23 April 1935 Sybil, JP Herts (*d* 1991), only dau of Lt-Col John Babington Gilliat, DSO, DL, JP, of The Manor House, Welwyn, Herts, and *d* 9 Sept 1994 leaving by her:

2a +Antony Romer [Antony Beevor Esq, 20 Radipole Rd, London SW6 5DL], slr, late Lt of Inns of Court and City Yeo, dir: Rugby PLC 1993– and Hambros plc 1990–, Gerrard Gp Plc 1995– and Croda Internat Plc 1996–, exec dir Hambros Bank 1985– (dir 1974), Dir-Gen Panel on Takeovers and Mergers 1987–89; *b* 18 May 1940; *educ* Winchester and New Coll Oxford (BA 1962); *m* 1970 *Cecilia, dau of John G Hopton, and has:

1b +Mark Andrew Antony; *b* 1975

1b *Karen Louise; *b* 1974

3a +Ronald Hugh [Ronald Beevor Esq, 35 Fairfax Rd, Bellevue Hill, NSW 2023, Australia]; *b* 9 Aug 1947; *educ* Winchester; *m* 1st 29 Jan 1972 (*divorce* 1977) Sabina Margaret Anne, only dau of Harman Joseph Grisewood, CBE, of Field House, Widford, Ware, Herts; *m* 2nd 1981 *Fiona Mary, dau of John Francis Partridge, of Toragay, Sollas, N Uist, and has by her:

1b *Harriet Clare; *b* 1984

2a *Helen [Mrs Jonathon Foster, Badger Farmhouse, Badger, Wolverhampton WV6 7JS]; *b* 8 Aug 1943; *m* 17 Sept 1966 *(Norman) Jonathon Dudley Foster, son of Kenneth Dudley Foster, of Claverley, Salop, and has:

1b *Peter; *b* 19 Dec 1972

1b *Charlotte Anne; *b* 30 June 1967; *m* 9 July 1994 *David Ian Bruce of Beckbury, Salop

2b *Caroline Jane; *b* 7 Nov 1968; *m* 7 Sept 1996 *Alexander Maximilian Michaelis, er s of Dominic Michaelis, of Rycote Park, Thame, Oxon

3b *Elizabeth Amy; *b* 27 Dec 1970

(3) Humphry (Rt Rev), formerly Chaplain of St John's Church, Montreux, Switzerland, Bp of Lebombo 1952–57, formerly Chaplain of Shrewsbury School, and Chaplain RNVR; *b* 24 Aug 1903; *educ* Winchester and Oriel Coll Oxford (BA 1926, MA 1929); *m* 15 Oct 1955 *Mrs Mary Elizabeth Seaton, dau of E Leonard Young, and *d* 12 June 1965

(1) Joan Hepworth; schs inspector; *b* 6 March 1895; *d* unm 6 June 1969

(2) Judith Chevallier; *b* 30 Jun 1896; *m* 29 Nov 1921 James Alister Pope, CIE, ICS (*d* 27 Oct 1954), s of Rev Arthur Frederick Pope, of The Furlong, Tring, Herts, and had:

1a *John Rose [John Pope Esq, Cromwell House, Court St, Tisbury, Wilts]; WW II in RE, Dep Dir Research BUSM Co Leicester; *b* 7 Oct 1924; *educ* Eton and Magdalene Coll Camb (BA 1949); *m* 9 June 1956 *Patricia Anne, eldest dau of Harry Stanley Squires, of 1 Wellington Rd, Hampton Hill, Middx, and has:

1b *Nicholas James Arend; *b* 26 April 1957

1b *Elizabeth Jane; *b* 29 March 1960

1a *Margaret Elizabeth [Mrs John Phillips, The Homestead, Hall Road, Wallington, Surrey SM6 0RT]; *b* 4 Sept 1922; *m* 11 Feb 1961 *Lt-Cdr John Gordon Phillips, RN (ret), elder son of Sydney Edwin Phillips, of Brynford, Horsell Rise, Woking, Surrey, and has:

1b *Richard Martin; *b* 24 Nov 1961

2b *Simon John; *b* 28 Oct 1963

1b *Catherine Bridget (twin); *b* 24 Nov 1961

7 Edmund, master Aldenham Sch Elstree; *b* 23 May 1867; *educ* Pembroke Coll Camb (MA); *m* 4 Aug 1896 Mary (*d* 4 Feb 1947), dau of Sir William Foster, 2nd Bt, and *dsp* 1 Nov 1948

8 Richard Temple; *b* 28 Aug 1869; *d* 22 July 1897

1 Sophy Elizabeth; *d* unm 8 Dec 1870

2 Amy; *d* unm 12 Feb 1918

3 Lucy Jane; *m* 23 Aug 1894 Charles Henry Delamain, of Mousehall, Tidebrook, Sussex, est s of Col Delamain, CB, 3rd Bombay Cav, and *d* 7 Jan 1946, leaving issue. He *d* 13 June 1928

4 Margaret; *m* 12 Sept 1891 Henry Penrice Frederick and *d* 17 July 1904, leaving issue (*see* FREDERICK, Bt)

5 Alice Franklin; *d* 13 July 1869

Sir THOMAS's 2nd son,

Sir Hugh Reeve Beevor, 5th Bt, MD Lond, FRCP, Fell King's Coll Lond, late Consulting Physician to King's Coll Hosp, Maj 4th Lond Gen Hosp RAMC; *b* 31 Oct 1858; *m* 29 June 1894 Emily Georgina (*d* 17 April 1909), dau of Sir William Foster, 2nd Bt, and *d* 24 Feb 1939, having had:

1 THOMAS LUBBOCK (Sir), **6th Bt**

1 Bridget Chevallier; *b* 5 May 1895; *m* 11 Feb 1920 Rev Henry Hibberd, MA Camb, rector Burnham Thorpe, Norfolk, s of Dr Henry Jukes Hibberd, of Holmwood, Brockenhurst, Hants, and *d* 28 April 1967, leaving a s and dau. He *d* 27 April 1952

Sir HUGH's only son,

Sir Thomas Lubbock Beevor, 6th Bt; Cdr RN, served WWs I and II; *b* 1 June 1897; *m* 19 Feb 1919 Edith Margaret (*m* 2nd 28 Aug 1944 R-Adml Robert Alexander Currie, CB, DSC, son of John Currie, and *d* 1985), dau of Frank Agnew, of Eccles Hall, Attleborough, Norfolk, and was *kas* April 1943, having had:

1 Sir THOMAS AGNEW BEEVOR , **7th and present Bt**

1 *Ina Margaret Anastasia; *b* 2 Oct 1920; *m* 9 May 1942 Capt John Lewis, RA, er s of Major Alfred Elliot Lewis, JP, of Danecroft, Stowmarket, and has:

(1) *Peter John Elliott; *b* 14 Feb 1943; *educ* Marlborough

(2) *William Beevor; *b* 21 Nov 1948; *educ* Marlborough.

(1) *Judith Margaret Anne; *b* 18 Oct 1946; *m* 3 Feb 1968 *David Isaac, Lt RA, son of W H Isaac, BSc, ARIC, of Brecon and Manningtree

2 *Jocelyn Mary [Lady Warner, The Grove, Southend Rd, Chelmsford, Essex CM2 7AB]; *b* 4 July 1927; *m* 8 Oct 1949 Sir (Edward Courtenay) Henry Warner, 3rd Bt (*qv*), and has issue

3 *Christian Chevallier; *b* 30 Oct 1934; *m* 14 Oct 1959 George Habib Homsi (*d* Nov 1996), er s of Habib George Homsi, of Beirut

BELHAVEN AND STENTON

Arms: Quarterly, 1st and 4th, gules, a mullet argent between three cinquefoils ermine (for HAMILTON of Udston); 2nd and 3rd, gules, a man's heart proper, shadowed or, between three cinquefoils ermine, all within a bordure argent (for HAMILTON of Raplock). **Crest:** A horse's head couped argent, bridled gules. **Supporters:** Two horses argent, bridled gules. **Motto:** Ride through. **Creation:** L. (S) 15 Dec 1647.

THE 13TH LORD BELHAVEN AND STENTON, Co Haddington (Robert Anthony Carmichael Hamilton) [The Rt Hon The Lord Belhaven and Stenton, 16 Broadwater Down, Tunbridge Wells, Kent TN2 5NR]; *b* 27 Feb 1927; *s* f 1961; *educ* Eton; late Lt The Cameronians; Cdr Cross Order of Merit (Poland) 1995; *m* 1st 27 Sept 1952 (*divorce* 1973) (Elizabeth) Ann, dau of Col Arthur Henry Moseley, DSO, MB, ChM, DPH, of 41 Hastings Rd, Warrawee, NSW, Australia, and has:

1 +FREDERICK CARMICHAEL ARTHUR, *Master of Belhaven*; *b* 27 Sept 1953; *educ* Eton; *m* 1st 11 July 1981 (*divorce*) (Elizabeth) Anne, only dau of S V Tredinnick, of Naldretts Court, Wisborough Green, W Sussex, and has:

(1) +William Richard; *b* 30 Dec 1982

(2) +James Frederick; *b* 1984

1 (cont.) The Master of Belhaven *m* 2nd 1991 *Philippa Martha Gausel, dau of Sir Rowland John Rathbone Whitehead, 5th Bt (*qv*), and formerly wife of Brian James Douglas Collins (*see* MORTON, E), and by her has:

(1) *Olivia Martha; *b* 9 Aug 1993

1 *Julia Elizabeth Heather [The Hon Julia Hamilton, 14 Westcroft Sq, London W6 0TD]; *b* 15 May 1956; resumed maiden name 1992; novelist: *The Idle Hill*, *A Pillar of Society* (1995), *The Good Catholic* (1995), *After Fiona* (1997); *m* 1st Dec 1975 (*divorce* 1979) Richard Newbury, est s of Roy Newbury, of Eleighwater House, Chard, Somerset; *m* 2nd 2 Nov 1979 (*divorce*) Stephen Hobbs of London W14, est s of Alan Percy Hobbs, of Holland Cottage, Great Holland,

Essex, and Mrs Hamish Macdougall, of Magnolia Cottage, Cookham Dean, Berks, and by him has:

(1) *Sophie Louise Ann; *b* 18 Feb 1981

(2) *Arabella Leonie; *b* 1983

The 13th LORD *m* 2nd 20 June 1973 (*divorce* 1986) Rosemary (*d* 1992), only dau of Sir Herbert Geraint Williams, 1st Bt (*qv*), and formerly wife of Sir Ian Auld Mactaggart, 3rd Bt (*qv*); *m* 3rd 1986 *Malgorzata Maria, dau of Tadeusz Pobog Hruzik-Mazurkiewicz, of Batorego 11/8, Krakow, Poland, and by her has further issue:

2 *Alexandra Maria; *b* 1987

Lineage (of 1st Lord): JAMES HAMILTON, 1st LORD HAMILTON of the 1445 *cr* (*see* ABERCORN, D) had an illegitimate s by Janet Calderwood:

JOHN HAMILTON of Broomhill; legitimated 20 Jan 1512/3; *m* 1st, as her 2nd husb, Elizabeth (who had *m* as her 1st husb John Hamilton of Neilsland and was by him great-grandmother of Margaret, w of Sir JAMES HAMILTON, 1st Bt (*see* below), also great-great-great-grandmother of **2nd Lord Belhaven and Stenton** (*see* below)), dau and heir of Patrick Hamilton, of Udston, and *d c* 1550, having had an er s:

CLAUD HAMILTON of Broomhill; *m* Margaret, dau of James Hamilton of Kilbrackmont, Fifeshire, and *d* 1605, leaving:

Sir JAMES HAMILTON, 1st Bt (NS), so *cr* 5 Jan 1635, of Broomhill; Sheriff Perthshire; *m* 1st Margaret, dau of William Hamilton, of Udston (*see* below), and had issue; *m* 2nd Jean Hamilton, heiress of Parkhead, and *d* probably by 1647; his s by his 1st w:

Sir JOHN HAMILTON, 2nd Bt, of Broomhill later of Beil, **1st Lord Belhaven and Stenton**, Co Haddington (S), so *cr* 15 Dec 1647, with remainder to heirs male of his body then heirs male whatsoever; since by 1661 his only son had died he surrendered the Lordship and obtained a regrant 10 Feb 1675 to himself for his life, with remainder to John Hamilton, husb of his gdau Margaret (for whom *see* below) and a distant cousin of his own, and the heirs male of John's body, whom failing to John's nearest heirs male whatsoever; went with a Scottish army to England to rescue CHARLES I (whose gratitude was reflected in the grant of a peerage) and fought Battle of Preston 1648; *m* Margaret, illegitimate dau of 2nd Marquess of Hamilton (*see* HAMILTON and BRANDON, D) out of Anne, dau of 1st Lord Blantyre and widow of 8th Lord Saltoun (*qv*) of Abernethy, and *dspms* 17 June 1679, when the btcy expired or became dormant, having had:

1 Margaret; *m* 1650 Sir Samuel Baillie, yr of Lamington (*d* 8 March 1668), and *d* 18 March 1674 leaving issue

2 ANNE; *m* Sir Robert HAMILTON, Bt, of Silvertonhill (*qv*), and had, with two s and three yr daus:

(1) MARGARET; *m* John HAMILTON, **2nd Lord Belhaven and Stenton**, for whom *see* below

3 Elizabeth; *m* Alexander Seton, 1st Viscount Kingston (*forfeited* 1715), and *dsp*

Lineage (of 2nd Lord): Sir JOHN HAMILTON, 4th of Cadzow (*see* ABERCORN, D); living 1390s; had a 3rd s:

WALTER HAMILTON; *m* Helen, dau of Sir Henry Douglas of Lochleven, and had issue:

JAMES HAMILTON of Raploch, Lanarks, which he was granted by charter 20 May 1441 by his cousin Sir James Hamilton, 6th of Cadzow, 1st Lord Hamilton (*see* above; also ABERCORN, D); had:

WILLIAM HAMILTON of Raploch; had an est s:

JAMES HAMILTON of Raploch; *m* Isabel, dau of Weir of Blackwood and had a 4th s:

JOHN HAMILTON of Neilsland, Lanarks; *m* as her 1st husb Elizabeth (*m* 2nd John Hamilton, 1st of Broomhill (*see* above)), only child of Patrick Hamilton of Udston, and had:

JOHN HAMILTON, of Udston; *m* Margaret, dau of Sir Robert Dalziel of that Ilk, and was *ka* 13 May 1568 fighting for MARY QUEEN OF SCOTS at the Battle of Langside, leaving:

WILLIAM HAMILTON of Udston ('Willie Wisehead'); *m* allegedly Margaret, dau of Hamilton of Loughermiston, and had, with a dau (Margaret, *m* Sir JAMES HAMILTON, 1st Bt, of Broomhill, of the 1635 *cr* (*see* above), and had issue):

JOHN HAMILTON, of Udston; living 20 April 1593; *m* Margaret, dau of James Muirhead of Lauchope, Lanarks, and had issue:

1 John, of Coltness; *m* Helen Whiteford, dau of — Milton, and had an er son:

(1) John, of Udston; Commr of Supply 1646; *m* a dau of Archibald Stewart, of Castlemilk, and had an est son:

1a John, of Udston; Sheriff Clydesdale; *m* Margaret, dau of Cleland of Cleland, and left:

1b John, of Udston; Collector of Customs Prestonpans; *m* Elizabeth, dau of Robert Brown, of Coalstown, and had an est s:

1c Alexander, of Udston; *m* Elizabeth, dau of William Cumming, of Drummine, and had:

1d William; Capt 22nd Foot, Maj, assumed as heir male whosoever the title LORD BELHAVEN AND STENTON, voted at the election of rep S peers 24 July 1790 but vote disallowed by Ho of Lds 25 Feb 1793; *d* 19 Jan 1796

2 James; *m* Margaret, dau and heir of Robert Hamilton of Barncleuch, Lanarks, which he acquired through her, and *d* by 21 May 1635, having had, with other issue:

(1) Quintin of Barncleuch; had:

1a John; *dsp* by 21 Feb 1705

(2) James; Minister Eaglesham; *m* 30 March 1652 Helen, dau of John Hamilton of Udston, Commr of Supply (*see* above), and *d* 1684, leaving issue, of which the issue male died out by 1777

(3) Sir Robert of Presmennan; Ld of Session as Lord Presmennan 1689–95; *m* Marion, dau of John Denholm of Muirhouse, and *d* 10 Nov 1695, having had, with other issue:

1a JOHN HAMILTON of Biel, **2nd Lord Belhaven and Stenton**; *b* 5 July 1658; a Ld of the Treasury 1704, opposed the Union 1706, committed to the Tower of London as a Jacobite 1708; *m* 1674 Margaret (*d* 4 Jan 1717; *see* above), dau of Sir Robert Hamilton, 1st Bt, of Silvertonhill (*qv*), by Anna, dau of **1st Lord Belhaven and Stenton**, and *d* 21 June 1708 soon after his release from the Tower, having had issue:

1b JOHN HAMILTON, **3rd Lord Belhaven and Stenton**; rep S peer 1715–21, Govr Barbados 1721; *m* Anne, dau of Andrew Bruce, merchant in Edinburgh, and *d* 17 Nov 1721 on his passage to Barbados, having had, with other issue:

1c JOHN HAMILTON, **4th Lord Belhaven and Stenton**; Gen of the Mint; *d* unm 28 Aug 1764

2c Andrew; offr in the Army; *d* unm 1736

3c JAMES HAMILTON, **5th Lord Belhaven and Stenton**; advocate 1728, Assist Slr Bd of Customs and Excise 1733, Sheriff Depute Haddington 1747; *d* unm 25 Jan 1777 when the peerage became *dormant* but the family estates passed to Mary, w of William Nisbet of Dirleton (*see* below), under an entail drawn up by the **2nd Lord** 17 Oct 1701 and confirmed by the **5th Lord** 14 May 1765

2b James; advocate, Assist Slr to Bd of Customs and Excise Scotland; *m* Anne, dau of John Walkinshaw of that Ilk, and *dsp* 28 June 1732

2a James, of Pencaitland; *bapt* 28 Aug 1659; Ld of Session as Lord Pencaitland 1712–26; *m* Catherine, dau of James Denholm of Westshires, and *d* 1729, having had issue:

1b John of Pencaitland; *m* Margaret (*m* 2nd Hon William Carmichael, 2nd son of 1st Earl of Hyndford), heiress of Alexander Menzies of Saltcoats, Haddington, and *dsps* 14 Feb 1724

2b Alexander of Pencaitland, Dechmont, Saltcoats and Barncleuch; *m* after 31 Jan 1847 Mary (*d* 24 Feb 1772), er dau of Sir Francis Kinloch, 3rd Bt, of Gilmerton (*qv*), and *d* 21 March 1758, having had an only child:

1c Mary of Pencaitland; *s f* in his estates and her cousin **5th Lord Belhaven and Stenton** as heir general in his estates of Beil and Presmennan 1777; *m* 2 Feb 1747 William Nisbet (*d* 1 March 1783) of Dirleton, and *d* 13 March 1797, leaving a s and two daus

(4) Sir ARCHIBALD HAMILTON, 1st Bt (NS), so *cr* 10 April 1703, of Rosehall; *m* 1st Catherine (*dspm*), dau of George Jardine of Applegarth, and had two daus; *m* 2nd Anne, dau of Murray of Deuchar, and *d* 1709, having by her had, with other issue (including a dau Euphemia, *see* below):

1a Sir JAMES HAMILTON, 2nd Bt; *bapt* 24 Nov 1682; MP Lanarks 1710–15 and 1735–50; *m* 2 March 1707 Hon Frances Stuart, dau of Alexander, 4th Lord Blantyre, and *dsp* 15 March 1750

2a Sir HUGH HAMILTON, 3rd Bt; *m* 23 June 1750 Margaret, dau of James Stirling of Keir, and *dspm* 29 Aug 1755, when the btcy became dormant, leaving:

1b Marion; *d* unm 28 July 1757

3 William, 1st of Wishaw; *m* Aug 1621 Beatrix, dau of James Douglas, of Morton, and *d c* 1642, leaving a 3rd s:

(1) William, 3rd of Wishaw; antiquary; *m* 1st 1660 his cousin Anne, dau of John Hamilton of Udston, and *d* 1726, having had, with other issue, including eight other sons:

1a Robert, yr of Wishaw; *b* 6 July 1664; *m* 1686 Jean, er dau and heir of Robert Hamilton of Brownmuir, and *dvp* by 21 Dec 1726, having had, with other issue:

1b William, 4th of Wishaw; *b* 2 Feb 1690; *m* 16 Dec 1726 his cousin Bethia (*d* 2 Oct 1785), er dau of Charles Hamilton, of Weatherley (*see* below), and had, with other issue:

1c Charles, 5th of Wishaw; *b* 19 Sept 1727; *d* unm 15 May 1763

2c William; *b* 25 Oct 1728; an officer in the Army; *dspm* by 1763

3c ROBERT HAMILTON, 6th of Wishaw, *de jure* 6th LORD BELHAVEN AND STENTON; *b* 3 May 1731; did not assume the title; *m* 11 Feb 1764 Susan (*d* 9 Jan 1789), 2nd dau of Sir Michael Balfour, Bt, and *d* 27 March 1784, having had, with at least two daus (Jean, *m* George Ramsay of Barnton, Edinburgh, and had a dau, Georgina, who *m* 4 March 1824, as his 1st w, Sir Thomas Woollaston White, 2nd Bt, of Wallingwells (*qv*), and *d* 2 Dec 1825; Bethia, *m* William Ramsay, of Gogal, Edinburgh, and by him was mother of Sir Thomas Woollaston White, 2nd Bt, of Wallingwells's 2nd w) an est s:

1d WILLIAM HAMILTON, **7th Lord Belhaven and Stenton**; *b* 13 Jan 1765; claimed title 1795, claim allowed by Ho of Lds 19 April 1799; *m* 2 March 1789 Penelope (*d* 5 May 1816), dau of Ronald Macdonald of Clanranald, and *d* 29 Oct 1814, leaving, with other issue:

1e ROBERT MONTOMERY HAMILTON, **8th Lord Belhaven and Stenton**, KT (1861); *b* 1793; Ld High Commr Gen Assembly Church of Scotland, Ld Lt Lanarks 1863–68, rep S peer 1819–31, *cr* 10 Sept 1831 BARON HAMILTON OF WISHAW, Co Lanark (UK; *m* 16 Dec 1815 Hamilton (*d* 8 Sept 1873), dau of Walter Frederick Campbell, of Shawfield and Islay, and *dsp* 22 Dec 1868, when the UK barony expired

2b James, 1st of Stevenston, Bothwell, Lanarks; *b* 25 Sept 1700; *m* 1st 10 Nov 1736 Helen (*bur* 22 April 1758), dau of Andrew Baillie, of Parbroath, and had, with other issue:

1c James, 2nd of Stevenston; *b* 10 June 1745; *m* Mary, dau of Archibald Nisbet, of Carfin, and *d* 30 March 1812, having had, with an est and yst s:

1d Archibald; *b* 19 Nov 1774; Surgn 92nd Regt; *m* 25 Feb 1810 Mary, dau of David Clarke, and *d* 23 Feb 1823 having had, with two daus:

1e JAMES HAMILTON, **9th Lord Belhaven and Stenton**; *b* 29 Aug 1822; claim to title allowed 2 Aug 1875; *m* 30 Oct 1877 Georgina (*d* 9 Nov 1940), dau of Sir John Watson, 1st Bt, of Earnock and Nielsand (*see* INGLEFIELD-WATSON, Bt), and *dspm* 6 Sept 1893, leaving:

1f Leonare Agnes Watson Nisbet; *b* 27 Aug 1878; *m* 24 March 1903 Robert Borras Whiteside, Capt RASC (*das* 20 April 1915), and *d* 25 Dec 1946 leaving issue

2f May Clarke Mary Nisbet; *b* 26 Nov 1879; *m* 29 April 1913 2nd Baron Hemphill (*qv*) and *dsp* 9 Jan 1970

3f Clarice Jessie Evelyn; *b* 10 Oct 1881; *m* 12 Dec 1899 12th Lord Napier and Ettrick (*qv*) and *d* 11 May 1951, leaving issue

4f Muriel Louise; *b* 1 Feb 1884; *m* 29 March 1910 Maj William Michael Jamieson Martin, RGA, son of John M Martin, of Craufurd, Midlothian, and *d* 26 Jan 1961 having had issue

5f Winifred Maude; *b* 13 Dec 1886; *d* unm 4 Aug 1932

6f Dorothy Henrietta; *b* 24 March 1888; *m* 29 Aug 1916 Maj Bertram Joseph Wakley, Loyal N Lancashire Regt (*d* of wounds received in action 11 Feb 1917), son of Henry Wakley, and *d* 7 July 1951, leaving issue

7f Georgina Violet; *b* 11 Aug 1889; *m* 1st 22 Nov 1913 her cousin James Cowie Simpson, ARSM, FGS, Lt RE (*ka* 4 Dec 1916), son of James Cowie Simpson, of The Avenue, Grange, Edinburgh, by his wife Margaret, dau of Sir John Watson, 1st Bt, of Earnock; *m* 2nd 19 April 1921 S/Ldr Alfred George Horsley-Carr, OBE, RAF (accidentally *k* flying 12 Feb 1926), est son of William Horsley-Carr, of Barnsley, Yorkshire, and had issue

2e Archibald, twin with his bro; *b* 29 Aug 1822; *d* at sea 30 Sept 1839

2b (cont.) James Hamilton, 1st of Stevenston, *m* 2nd Elizabeth, dau of William Cunningham, of Brownhill and was *bur* 28 Nov 1769

(1) William Hamilton, 3rd of Wishaw, *m* 2nd 31 Aug 1676 May, dau of Hon Sir Charles Erskine, of Alva, s of John, 18th/2nd Earl of Mar (*qv*), and by her had, with other issue:

2a Charles, of Weatherley; *b* 17 Dec 1678; *m* 1699 his cousin Euphemia, dau of Sir ARCHIBALD HAMILTON, 2nd Bt, of Rosehall (*see* above), and had issue:

1b A son; *b* 28 Dec 1700; *d* young

2b Archibald; *b* 7 Jan 1703; *d* young

1b Bethia; *b* 31 Jan 1702; *m* her cousin William Hamilton of Wishaw (*see* above)

2b Charlotte; *d* unm

3a Alexander; *b* 21 May 1693; slr in London; *m* 1st Frances (*dsp*), dau of Col Dalzell; *m* 2nd 23 Oct 1729 Barbara Lilley and *d* 1781, leaving a 3rd s:

1b Anthony (Ven); *b* 5 May 1739; DD; vicar St Martin-in-the-Fields, rector Hadham, Herts, Archdeacon Colchester; *m* 12 Feb 1767 Anne (*d* 3 Dec 1782), dau of Rt Rev Richard Terrick, Bp of London and *d* 4 Oct 1812, having had issue:

1c Terrick ; *b* 12 July 1778; *d* an infant

2c WILLIAM RICHARD, for whom *see* below

3c Anthony (Ven); *b* 12 July 1778; Rector Loughton, Essex, Archdeacon Taunton; *m* 13 July 1807 Charity Graeme (*d* 9 Nov 1869), dau of Sir Walter Farquhar, 1st Bt (*qv*), and *d* 10 Sept 1851, leaving issue:

1d Walter Kerr (Rt Rev); *b* 12 Nov 1808; DD; Bp of Salisbury; *m* 9 Jan 1845 Isabel, dau of Rev Francis Lear, Dean of Salisbury, and *d* 1 Aug 1869, leaving issue:

1e Edward Walter (Sir), PC, GCB, GCVO, ISO; *b* 7 July 1847; MusB; Treasury 1870–1907 (Jt Perm Sec); *d* unm 2 Sept 1908

2e Clement Edward; *b* 8 March 1854; *m* 21 April 1898 Fanny (*d* 28 May 1955), dau of James Winch, JP, of Rochester, and *d* 1923, leaving issue:

1f Ethel Isabel Roby; *b* 17 Dec 1900

2f Eleanor Clara Roby; *b* 24 March 1902

3f Marjorie Frances Roby; *b* 7 Sept 1907

3e Sydney William Henry; *b* 25 May 1865; *d* 4 Nov 1926

1e Ethel Linda; *d* unm

2e Alice Sidney; *m* 29 June 1880 Rev Robert Campbell Moberly, Canon Ch Ch Oxford (*d* 8 June 1903), *s* of Rt Rev George Moberly, DCL, Bp of Salisbury, and *d* 3 Aug 1939, leaving issue

3e Eleanor Frances; *m* 1887 Ernest Kingscote, MB, CM, of 31 Lower Seymour Street, London W, and had issue

4e Maude Isabel Mary; *m* 22 Jan 1884 Rev Edward Bickersteth Ottley, DD, Preb St Paul's and Canon Rochester (*d* 15 Dec 1910), and *d* 16 April 1942, leaving issue

5e Lucy Constance Farquhar; *m* 1890 Rev Francis George Anderson Phillips, vicar Bloxham, and *d* 19 July 1902 leaving issue

2d Edward William Terrick, of Charters, Berks; *b* 26 Nov 1809; JP and DL, MP Salisbury 1865–69; *m* 14 Aug 1844 Ann (*d* 1891), dau of John Thacker, of Ascot, Berks, and *d* 1898, leaving issue:

1e Terrick Alfred; *b* 5 Oct 1851; *m* Feb 1878 Alice, dau of Helenus John Scott, of Newcastle, NSW, and *d* 1925 leaving issue:

1f Terrick Elyston Scott; *b* 1881; JP; *m* Agnes (*d* 1 Oct 1944), dau of W Lynch, of Tambo, Queensland, and has issue:

1g +Anthony Elystan John, of Edward St, Tambo, Queensland, Australia; *b* 6 April 1905; *m* 23 June 1928 *Helen Margaret Doherty, and has issue:

1h +Patrick, of Edward St, Tambo, Queensland, Australia; *b* 25 Dec 1928; *m* 26 Feb 1952 *Dulcie Emily Hafey, and has issue:

1i +Patrick William; *b* 26 Dec 1954; *m* 1977 *Maree Helen Fitzgerald, formerly wife of — Ward, and has issue:

1j +Brendan James; *b* 1979

1j *Michelle Susan; *b* 1978

2i +Anthony John; *b* 16 June 1955; *m* 1977 *Suzanne Sylvia Heineman, and has issue:

1j *Alison Madalene Natasha; *b* 1975

2j *Janie Leigh; *b* 1978

3i +Terrick Daniel; *b* 12 Oct 1957; *m* 1979 *Heather-Anne Watson

4i +Dale Thomas; *b* 23 Jan 1959

2h +Elyston William, of Arthur St, Tambo, Queensland, Australia; *b* 12 Nov 1936; garage proprietor; *m* 24 Sept 1960 *Norma Merion Ilott, and has issue:

1i *Jeanette; *b* 17 June 1963

2i *Kathleen; *b* 8 Nov 1966

3h +Reginald John, of Barcoo St, Tambo, Queensland, Australia; *b* 6 May 1940; *m* 19 Dec 1962 *Thelda Rosemary, dau of Harold Henry Park, of Garden St, Tambo, Queensland, and has issue:

1i +Glenn; *b* 22 Sept 1963

2i +Bradley; *b* 17 Jan 1965

3i +Ashley Reginald; *b* 1969

4i +Steven; *b* 1971

1h *Margaret [Mrs Roy Carige, 351 Deplock St, Berserker Heights, North Rockhampton, Queensland, Australia]; *b* 20 March 1930; *m* 1st 18 Sept 1952 Brian George Denny (*d* 5 Oct 1959) and has issue:

1i *Annette Margaret; *b* 1 Oct 1953; *m* 1971 *Thomas William Kitchiner, and has issue:

1j *Kellie Maree; *b* 1974

2j *Necia Ann; *b* 1976

3j *Suzanne; *b* 1980

2i *Denise; *b* 5 April 1958; *m* 1975 *Mark William Owttrim, and has issue:

1j *Ryan Mark; *b* 1981

1h (cont.) Mrs Brian Denny *m* 2nd 17 Dec 1967 *Roy Carige, and had further issue:

2i *Toni Maree; *b* 1970

2h *Marjorie Jean; *b* 12 March 1935; *m* 16 Jan 1954 *Donald James McKnight, of Bungendore, NSW, Australia, son of Allan Donald Thomas McKnight, of Allamby Park, Chinchilla, Queensland, and has issue:

1i *Michael James; *b* 20 Nov 1957; *m* 1980 *Barbara Gascoigne

2i *Allan Donald Thomas; *b* 25 June 1967

1i *Teresa Margaret; *b* 15 April 1955

2i *Tracy Ann; *b* 1973

3h *Helen Margaret; *b* 4 Sept 1938; *m* 24 Dec 1957 *Russell Mcquie, of Edward St, Tambo, Queensland, Australia, and has issue:

1i *Russell Scott; *b* 19 Sept 1959; *m* 1981 *Dana Cheree Mills

2i *Larry; *b* 8 May 1964

1i *Wendy Ann; *b* 14 Jan 1961

4h *Rita Grace; *b* 29 Oct 1941; *m* 18 Aug 1962 *Allan Benjamin Park, of Edward St, Tambo, Queensland, Australia, and has issue:

1i *Jenny Lorraine; *b* 29 Jan 1964; *m* 1982 *Neville Allen, and has issue:

1j *Melissa Lorraine; *b* 1981

2i *Julie Maree; *b* 8 Sept 1965

3i *Alison Jane; *b* 3 Jan 1969

2g +Vernon Harvey, of Mount Enniskillen Station, Tambo, Queensland, Australia; *b* 13 Aug 1914; *m* 18 Oct 1943 *Gloria Volk, and has issue:

1h +Ian Vernon; *b* 16 Dec 1944; *m* 1976 *Patti Marie O'Neil and has issue:

1i +Roderick Joseph; *b* 1969

2i +Simon John; *b* 1974

3i +Ashley James; *b* 1980

1h *Joy Agnes; *b* 18 March 1947; *m* 1967 *Geoffrey Francis O'Neil, and has issue:

1i *Lindsay Francis Louis; *b* 1968

2i *Peter Sean; *b* 1973

1i *Renée Rose; *b* 1975

3g +John Edward, of Arthur St, Tambo, Queensland, Australia, JP; *b* 1917; *m* 1937 *Olive Amy Florence Hannah Russell, and has issue:

1h +Peter John, of Arthur St, Tambo, Queensland, Australia; *b* 1939; *m* 10 Sept 1960 *Joan Adele, dau of William Harold Kuhn, of Nobby, Queensland, and his issue:

1i +Geoffrey; *b* 5 May 1962

2i +Peter Scott; *b* 1966

2h +Alan Patrick; *b* 22 March 1952; *m* 1973 *Marilyn Ann Ward and has issue:

1i +John Alan; *b* 1976

2i +Michael Frederick; *b* 1981

1i *Rosalea Anne; *b* 1975

2i *Jantelle Maree; *b* 1978

1h *Margaret Evelyn; *b* 6 Jan 1938; *m* 1st 6 Jan 1957 (*divorce* 1969) Colin Leslie Miller, of Garden St, Tambo, Queensland, Australia, son of James Miller, of Tambo, Australia, and has:

1i *Kimberley Mark; *b* 18 Oct 1957

2i *Rodney John; *b* 11 July 1961

1i *Kara Lea; *b* 1 April 1964

1h (cont.) Mrs Margaret Miller *m* 2nd 1970 (*divorce* 19–) William John Dolgner, and has further issue:

3i *Jason Ashley; *b* 1970

2i *Clayton Scott; *b* 19—

2h *Mary Rose Hamilton; *b* 12 Jan 1948; *m* 1964 *William Eckel, of Mount Enniskillen Station, Tambo, Queensland, Australia, son of William Eckel, of Springsure, Queensland, Australia, and has issue:

1i *William John; *b* 28 March 1965

2i *Raymond Francis; *b* 4 July 1967

4g +William Robert, of Edward St, Tambo, Queensland, Australia; *b* 1921; *m* 1947 *Jean Elsie Higgins, and has issue:

1h *Diane Carol; *m* 1965 *Daniel Cameron, and has issue:

1i *Andreena Louise; *b* 1978

2h *Marie Estelle; *b* 1947; *m* 1966 (*divorce* 1978) Dale McDonald and has issue:

1i *Michael John; *b* 1967

3h *Lynda Agnes; *b* 1949; *m* 1969 *Robert Sing, and has issue:

1i *Sharlene Maree; *b* 1971

2i Bronwyn Anne; *b* 1981

4h *Mary Anne; *b* 1950; *m* 1978 *John King, and has issue:

1i *Aeron James; *b* 1971

5h *Charmaine Lee; *b* 1962; *m* 1983 *Steven Bailey

1g *Julia Agnes [Mrs John E Whitman, Hamilton, Rundle-Jardine St, Wandal, Rockhampton, Queensland, Australia]; *b* 5 March 1908; *m* 12 Dec 1938 *John Edward Whitman, JP, 2nd son of Charles Edward Whitman, and has issue:

1h *Barry John, of Kerrigan St, N Rockhampton, Queensland, Australia; *b* 9 Aug 1944; *m* 1969 *Margaret Collins, and has issue:

1i *Mark John; *b* 1975

1i *Joanne Maree; *b* 1970

2i *Louise Margaret; *b* 1977

2h *Michael John, of Houlihan St, N Rockhampton, Queensland, Australia; *b* 24 Jan 1948; *m* 1971 *Lynette Wallace, and has issue:

1i *Karl Anthony; *b* 1975

2i *Clint Andrew; *b* 1977

3i *Luke Philip; *b* 1980

1i *Emily May; *b* 1983

1h *Paulanne Mary [Mrs Edward Kelly, 49 Blenheim St, Chermside West, Brisbane, Queensland, Australia]; *b* 25 Nov 1939; *m* 13 May 1961 *Edward John Kelly, son of James Kelly, of 123 Crosby Rd, Albion, Brisbane, Australia, and has issue:

1i *Christopher James; *b* 6 July 1965

2i *Kim Edward; *b* 1967

3i *Lee Michael; *b* 1969

4i *Jason John; *b* 1974

1i *Julie Maree; *b* 1974

2h *Julie Anne, JP; *b* 23 April 1941; *m* 30 May 1964 *Philip John Walsh, of 129 Rundle St, Rockhampton, Queensland, Australia, and has issue:

1i *Anthony John; *b* 10 April 1965; *m* 1990 *Verena Finocchiaro

2i *Justin Philip; *b* 1966

3i *John Edward; *b* 1969

2g *Mary Alice; *b* 9 Dec 1911; *m* 1 Sept 1939 *Thorwald Harold Widt, of 22 Boowgala Rd, Florida Gdns, Gold Coast, Queensland, Australia, son of Thorwald Frederick Christensen Widt, and has issue:

1h *Peter Anthony; *b* 31 March 1945; *m* 1969 *Diane McCallum, and has issue:

1i *Stephen Anthony; *b* 1968

1h *Helen Margaret; *b* 26 May 1940

3g *Eileen Marjorie; *b* 10 Feb 1925; *m* 20 Sept 1947 Roland Mervyn Smith (*d* 1975), son of Harold Dale Smith, of Bolton St, Rockhampton, Queensland, and has issue:

1h *Terrick Elystan Scott; *b* 22 Feb 1953; *m* 1982 *Yasmine Hartmann

1h *Linda Ngaio; *b* 2 Feb 1949; *m* 1974 *S/Ldr Gordon Maxwell Bennett

2h *Ruth Bronwyn; *b* 18 June 1954; *m* 1973 *Capt Roland Francis Bagshawe, and has issue:

1i *Kristi Leanne; *b* 1973

2i *Alison Louise; *b* 1975

3i *Veronica Lauren; *b* 1978

2f Charles; *b* 19 Aug 1885; *m* 14 Aug 1911 Olivia Abbott Palmer and *d* 3 Aug 1961, leaving:

1g +Charles Clive; *b* 9 Sept 1919; *m* 19– *Nellie Olive Watson, and had issue:

1h +Noel Peter; *b* 25 Dec 1953

1h *Judith Helen; *b* 28 May 1945

2h *Lexie Mae; *b* 20 May 1949

1g *Olivia Jessie; *b* 5 Feb 1913; *m* 19– Edmund Rockett, and has:

1h *James Edmund; *b* 3 May 1947

2g *Margaret Jean; *b* 13 Aug 1915; *m* 1st Ernest Henry Bellingham, and had issue:

1h *Alan Ward; *b* 9 Oct 1940; *m* 1966 *Lynne Fawcett

2g (cont.) Mrs Margaret Bellingham *m* 2nd 1965 *William Edward McCulloch

3g *Kepple Osborne; *b* 16 Sept 1917; *m* *Dudley Halliwell Milton, and has issue:

1h *Raymond Charles; *b* 30 March 1945

3f John Helenus; *b* 1888

4f Reginald; *b* 1890

1f Annie Rose Scott, JP; memb Australian Red Cross; *m* May 1900 William Leonard Cowen (*d* Aug 1935), and *d*, having had issue:

1g Edward William Terrick; *b* 12 Dec 1905; *m* Edna Christine, dau of Frank Lionel Wilson, and *d*, having had issue:

1h *Alistair Edward [Alistair Cowen Esq, 87 Herston Rd, Kelvin Grove, Brisbane, Queensland, Australia]; *b* 9 July 1942; *m* 27 Oct 1965 *Mary Patfield Caffery

1h *Shirley Rose [Mrs Bruce McPherson, 7 Kirkdale Rd, Chapel Hill, Brisbane, Australia]; *b* 1 Oct 1934; *m* 19 Nov 1960 *Bruce H McPherson, BA, LLB, PhD, barrister, Brisbane, and has issue:

1i *Andrew William; *b* 1 July 1963

1i *Fiona Rose; *b* 23 Oct 1967

2h *Judith Craig [Mrs Edwin Hayne, 28 Aragon St, Indooroopilly, Brisbane, Australia]; *b* 15 March 1937; *m* 24 Aug 1963 *Edwyn Southwick Hayne, and has issue:

1i *Ian Edwin; *b* 3 Sept 1965

2e Clive Alexander [Clive Cowen Esq, Arc College, Cooce Bay, Yeppoon, Queensland, Australia]; *b* 15 April 1911

2f Alice May Scott Hamilton; *b* 1883; *m* Esmond Shadforth, and *d* 13 Dec 1968 aged 85, having had issue

2e Charles Gipps, OBE; *b* 27 June 1857; *educ* Trin Coll Cambridge (MA); barrister Inner Temple; *m* 28 Sept 1892 Anna Gertrude Montgomerie (*d* 21 Feb 1937), dau of Hugh Morris Lang, and *d* 8 June 1955, having had issue:

1f Edward William, TD; *b* 8 July 1893; *educ* Trin Coll Cambridge (MA); Lt-Col TAR, Queen Victoria's Rifles (KRRC), WW I and WW II as Maj The Buffs; *m* 15 Aug 1931 Alice May Cox (*d* 29 June 1989), dau of James Turner, and *dsp* 25 Aug 1949

1f Margaret Graham, MBE (1946); *b* Sept 1895

2f Katharine; *b* 12 June 1899; *m* 24 June 1927 Sebastian Louis Brunicardi, yr s of Sebastian Angelo Brunicardi, of Clonmel, Co Tipperary, and *d* Dec 1948

3f Winifred Anna, JP (Northumberland 1951); *b* 22 Nov 1905; *m* 23 June 1926 James Seymour Spencer (*d* 25 Sept 1967), s of Seymour Spencer, and *d* 9 Aug 1986, leaving:

1g Antony James; *b* 21 March 1927; *educ* Eton; BSc; *m* 6 April 1956 Felicity Jacqueline (*d* 26 Dec 1977), dau of C L C S Baines, of Coneygore House, Penselwood, Wincanton, Somerset, and *d* 26 April 1993, leaving:

1h *Martin Antony; *b* 28 March 1959

2h *Philip Mark; *b* 4 May 1961

1h *Josephine Claudia; *b* 6 June 1957

2g *Simon Charles [Simon Spencer Esq, Redesmouth Hall, Redesmouth, Hexham, Northumberland NE48 2ER]; *b* 22 March 1929; *educ* Eton; *m* 12 June 1965 *Nancy Loveday, 2nd dau of Edmund George Coryton, of Linkicorn House, Yelverton, S Devon, and has issue:

1h *Charles James; *b* 20 Aug 1966

2h *Andrew George; *b* 14 Aug 1968

3e Harvie Cavendish, of Charters, Melbourne, Australia; *b* 22 Oct 1861 *m* 13 Feb 1890 Edith (*d* 6 May 1917), dau of David Moore, of Charnwood, St Kilda, Melbourne, and *d* 4 March 1917, having had issue:

1f Clive; *b* 1896; *d* 1909

2f Anthony, of Lyncroft, Flinders, Victoria, Australia; *b* 1901

1f *Constance, of Lyncroft, Flinders, Victoria, Australia

2f *Sibyl, of Lyncroft, Flinders, Victoria, Australia

1e Frances Graeme; *d unm* 21 May 1915

2e Emily Ursula; *b* 29 Dec 1846; *m* 29 May 1877 Francis Carew Charles Barnett, 2nd son of Charles George Barnett, JP, of King's Beeches, Sunningdale, Berks (*d* 26 Nov 1924), and *d* 2 Oct 1942, having had issue

3e Julia Isabel; *d unm* 13 Feb 1943

4e Ann Sybella Jane; *d unm* 27 Dec 1944

5e Margaret Erica Harriet; *d unm* 25 Feb 1939

6e Mary Clive; *d unm* 15 May 1951

1d Jane; *m* 27 Dec 1838 Rev Thomas Hans Sotheby (*d* 1888), vicar Langford Budville, Somerset, and *d* 1842, leaving issue

4c Terrick; *b* 25 Sept 1781; Dip Serv; *d unm* 15 Sept 1876

The Ven ANTHONY HAMILTON's est surv son,

WILLIAM RICHARD HAMILTON; *b* 9 Jan 1777; Under Sec of State FO 1809–22, Min Naples 1822–25, Tstee Br Museum 1838–58, archaeologist; *m* 3 Sept 1804 Juliana, sis of Lt-Col Robert Udny, of Udny, Aberdeenshire, and *d* 11 July 1859, having had with other issue:

1 WILLIAM JOHN, for whom *see* below

2 Alexander Edmund; *b* 29 Oct 1806: *d unm* 30 June 1827

3 Henry George; *b* 22 Feb 1808; Capt RN; *m* 7 June 1845 Fanny Elizabeth (*d* 14 Dec 1875), est dau of Rev Charles Tower, MA, Perpetual Curate Brentwood, Essex, and *d* 25 March 1879, leaving issue:

(1) Edmund William; *b* 10 July 1853; *d* young

(2) Frederick Tower (Sir), GCVO, KCB, of Anmer Hall, King's Lynn; *b* 8 March 1856; Adml, ADC to HM EDWARD VII 1906–07, Zulu War 1879 (despatches, promotion, medal and clasp), Grand Cordon Legn of Honour; *m* 3 Dec 1889 Maria Walpole (*d* 20 Nov 1952), dau of Adml of the Fleet Hon Sir Henry Keppel, GCB (*see* ALBEMARLE, E), and *d* 4 Oct 1917, leaving issue:

1a Louis Henry Keppel (Sir), KCB (1944), DSO (1915) and bar (1940); *b* 31 Dec 1890; Adml, Cameroons and Niger River, WWs I and II, Flag Offr Malta 1943–45, Ch Naval Advsr Australian Govt, Russian Order of St Stanislas 3rd Cl with swords; *d* unm 27 June 1957

2a Henry; *b* 18 May 1892; Capt RN, WW I (despatches) and WW II; *m* 6 Feb 1932 Margaret Mary, dau of Maj Charles Henry Stilwell, of Lorton House, Broadwey, Weymouth

1a Alexandra Alberta Jean; *b* 1897; *m* 28 June 1920 Hon Ronald John Sholto Douglas, OBE (*d* 31 Jan 1922), yst son of 18th Earl of Morton (*qv*), and *d* 2 March 197, leaving issue

2a Jean; *b* 1899

(1) Henrietta Georgiana; *m* 13 Oct 1874 John Spooner Hardy (*d* 1901), of The Vale, Addington, West Malling, Kent, and *d* 29 June 1933, leaving issue

(2) Laura; *d* 2 March 1939

(3) Cecilia Martha; *m* 3 Oct 1878 Henry Rycroft Giffard (*d* 4 Sept 1934), of Lockeridge House, Marlborough, yr son of Capt Henry Wells Giffard, RN, and *d* 13 Sept 1908, leaving issue

4 Charles Anthony *b* 3 Oct 1809; Dep Clerk Privy Cncl; *d* unm 1860

5 Arthur Richard; *b* 4 Jan 1814; *m* 1st 7 Sept 1839 Charlotte Cox (*dsp* 26 March 1866); *m* 2nd 1872 Annie Steele, and *d* 1882, leaving issue:

(1) Arthur Henry; *b* 28 April 1872; *m* 30 May 1906 Mabel (*d* 1918), dau of John Harrower, of Baldur, Manitoba, and *d* 1930, leaving issue:

1a *Gladys Dorothy, of 126 Forest Avenue, Winnipeg, Canada; *b* 27 Nov 1908; *m* 1928 Walter Booth Jorgeson (*d* 1978), and has issue:

1b *Robert Arthur; *b* 1929

2b *Allen Edward; *b* 1932

1b *Lynda Dorothy; *b* 1940

2b *Ellen Jean; *b* 1942

(2) Charles Augustus; *b* 1874; *m* 1906 Alice May, dau of Benjamin Thorn, of Souris, Manitoba, and *d* 21 June 1960, leaving issue:

1a +Frederick William, MC (1943); *b* 1 June 1910; *educ* U of Manitoba (BSA 1932); WW II as Maj Roy Canadian Engrs (MC); ec advsr UN 1955 and 1968, economist Manitoba Pool Elevators 1946–68; *m* 1945 Alice Elizabeth (*d* 1969), dau of George A Stevenson, of Morris, Manitoba, and has issue:

1b *Mary Ellen [Mrs Michael Halligan, 119 Balliol St, Toronto, Ontario, Canada MHS 1C2]; *b* 12 Oct 1947; *m* 1st 1969 (*divorce* 1982) Donald Keith Truman, of Winnipeg, Canada, and has:

1c *Catherine Martha; *b* 1973

1b (cont.) Mrs Mary Truman *m* 2nd 1985 *Michael Anthony Halligan

2b *Catherine Alice; *b* 3 Dec 1949; *m* 1979 *Robert Webster, and has issue:

1c *Paul Robert; *b* 1981

2a +Richard Terrick, of Baldur, Manitoba, Canada; *b* 14 Jan 1912; *m* 1933 *Muriel, dau of John McLeod, of Belmont, Manitoba, and had issue:

1b *Betty Lorraine; *b* 1934; *m* 1961 *W Lexton Young, of Killarney, Manitoba, Canada, and has issue:

1c *Candis; *b* 1961

2c *Lana; *b* 1963

3c *Lisa; *b* 1964

4c *Jan; *b* 1966

2b *Margaret Rose; *b* 1935; *m* 1955 *Clare Vrooman, of Belmont, Manitoba, Canada, and has issue:

1c *Terry; *b* 1956

2c *Kevin; *b* 1957

3c *Dean; *b* 1960

1c *Patricia; *b* 1958

2c *Brenda; *b* 1961

3c *Kathy; *b* 1962

4c *Shelly; *b* 1965

3b *Gertrude Joan; *b* 1936; *m* 1955 *Neil Cline, of Wawanesa, Manitoba, Canada, and has:

1c *Bradley; *b* 1956

2c *Perry; *b* 1959

3c *Francis; *b* 1965

1c *Laurie; *b* 1955

2c *Pamela; *b* 1958

4b *Joyce Elaine; *b* 1938; *m* 1956 *Owen Vrooman, of Belmont, Manitoba, Canada, and has:

1c *Darrel; *b* 1956

2c *Gordon; *b* 1964

1c *Debbie; *b* 1957

2c *Vicki; *b* 1960

1a *Rose Aileen [Mrs William Crump, Bishopsthorpe, Box 1058, Prince Albert, Saskatchewan, Canada]; *b* 14 July 1908; *m* 1st 1954 George W Easter (*d* 1958); *m* 2nd 1964 Rt Rev William Henry Howes Crump, Bp Saskatchewan

WILLIAM HAMILTON's est son,

WILLIAM JOHN HAMILTON; *b* 5 July 1805; FRS, MP Newport; *m* 1st 26 April 1832 Martin (*d* March 1833), dau of John Trotter, of Dyrham Park, Herts, and *d* 27 June 1867, having had issue:

1 Robert William, of Holyfield Hall, Essex; *b* 12 March 1833; unsuccessfully claimed the title 1868; Lt-Col; *m* 10 July 1856 Charlotte Maria (*d* 2 Jan 1916), dau of Col George Palmer, of Nazing Park and *d* 3 Oct 1883, having had issue:

(1) William Ronald; *b* 17 July 1864; *d* 7 April 1873

(1) Mary Geraldine; *m* 21 May 1901 Henry Alfred Newton (*d* 18 Jan 1924) and *d* June 1942, leaving issue

(2) Edith Lilian; *m* 29 Jan 1898 Norman Alexander Sinclair (*d* 11 May 1904) and *d* 28 May 1951, leaving issue (*see* SINCLAIR, Bt)

(3) Helen Violet; *m* 25 March 1912 (*divorce* 1924) Joseph Forman and *d* 10 July 1962, leaving issue

WILLIAM JOHN HAMILTON *m* 2nd 26 July 1838 Hon Margaret Frances Florence (*d* 19 April 1885), dau of 13th Viscount Dillon (*qv*), and by her had, with four daus:

2 ALEXANDER CHARLES HAMILTON, **10th Lord Belhaven and Stenton**, TD, JP and DL (Lanarks); *b* 3 July 1840; Col RE, Hon Col Lanarks RE Vols and Lowland Divl Engrs RE, Brig Surrey Vol Inf Bde 1888–1902, rep S peer 1900–20; *m* 7 July 1880 Georgiana Katharine (Lily) (*d* 26 Sept 1932), dau of Legh Richmond, and *dsps* 31 Oct 1920, having had issue:

(1) Ralph Gerard Alexander, *Master of Belhaven*; *b* 22 Feb 1883; T/Lt-Col RFA, Maj cmdg Essex RHA, formerly Lt 3rd KO Hus, Hon Attaché Dip Serv, WW I cmdg a Bde Field Artillery (wounded twice, despatches three times, Croix de Guerre avec palme); *m* 1 March 1904 Lady Grizel Winifred Louisa Cochrane, est dau of 12th Earl of Dundonald (*qv*), and *dsp ka* France 31 March 1918

3 Constantine Henry; *b* 21 June 1843; Lt-Col RA; *d* unm 1885

4 Archibald William; *b* 4 April 1847; RN; *m* 1869 Elizabeth Ann (*d* 6 April 1912), dau of W Billyard, of Sydney, NSW, Australia, and *d* 5 Jan 1886, leaving issue:

(1) ROBERT EDWARD ARCHIBALD, **11th Lord**

(1) Margaret Elizabeth; *m* 21 June 1921 Col Hon Alfred Frederick William Harris (*see* MALMESBURY, E), and *d* 21 May 1965

The 10th LORD's nephew,

ROBERT EDWARD ARCHIBALD HAMILTON later UDNY HAMILTON (added with arms on *s* to the Udny estates 1934), **11th Lord Belhaven and Stenton**, CIE (1918), DL (Lanarkshire); *b* 8 April 1871; Lt-Col IA, Hon Col 52nd (Lowland) Div Engrs, Chitral Relief Force 1895 (medal and clasp), Br E Africa 1896 (medal), Tirah Expdn 1897–98 (two clasps), Mesopotamia 1915–18 (three medals, despatches), rep S peer, Kaisar-i-Hind Gold Medal, Kt Order of Charles XII of Sweden 1933, Grand Master Mason Scotland 1931–33; *m* 1st 15 Nov 1898 Kathleen Gonville (*d* 1 Dec 1935), and had issue:

1 ROBERT ALEXANDER BENJAMIN, **12th Lord**

1 Julia Hamilton, CStJ; *b* 1901; *m* 9 April 1923 4th Baron Raglan (*qv*) and *d* 17 April 1971, leaving issue

The **11th Lord** *m* 2nd 25 March 1938 Sheila de Hauteville (*d* 20 Sept 1962), only dau of Maj Algernon George Pearson, DSO, Roy Berks Regt, and *d* 26 Oct 1950, having by her had issue:

2 *Margaret de Hauteville [The Hon Mrs Williams, Udney Castle, Aberdeenshire]; *b* 3 July 1939; *m* 1st 5 May 1964 (*divorce* 1981) (Clifford) Keith Wain Schellenberg, son of Clifford Robertshaw Schellenberg, of The Grove, Morton-in-Cleveland, and has issue:

(1) *Nicholas Udny; *b* 6 April 1966

(1) *Amy Julia Udny; *b* 24 March 1971

(2) *Rose Camilla Udny; *b* 19 June 1973

2 (cont.) The Hon Mrs Margaret Schellenberg *m* 2nd 1983 *James Frank Williams, of Udny Castle, Aberdeenshire

3 *Victoria Edith [The Hon Mrs Tufnell, 990 Hanley Ave, Los Angeles, California 90049, USA]; *b* 17 April 1941; PhD; *m* 1976 *Nicholas Tufnell, of Los Angeles, and has issue:

(1) *Samuel; *b* 1978

The 11th LORD's only son,

ROBERT ALEXANDER BENJAMIN HAMILTON, **12th Lord Belhaven and Stenton**; *b* 16 Sept 1903; *educ* Eton and RMC Sandhurst; Hon Lt-Col, Roy Scots Fus 1924–31, seconded Aden P Levies 1931–34, Admin Colonial Serv Aden Protectorate 1934–46, WW II, ret 1946; FRGS, FRCAS; *m* 1st 4 Feb 1922 (*divorce* 1941) Heather Mildred Carmichael, dau of Lt-Col Richard Carmichael Bell, DSO, OBE, Central India Horse, by his wife Mildred Charlotte, 3rd dau of Rev Bennett Clear Davidson-Houston, Vicar St John's, Sandymount, Dublin, and had issue:

1 ROBERT ANTHONY CARMICHAEL HAMILTON, **13th and present Lord Belhaven and Stenton**

The **12th Lord** *m* 2nd 21 March 1942 *Cyrilla Mary [Mrs Cyrilla Vale, Copper Cottage, New Galloway, Castle Douglas, Kirkcudbrightshire] (*m* 2nd (*divorce* 19–) 25 June 1969 Dennis Beaumont Vale, OBE, of Brenta Lodge, Monkmead Lane, Pulborough, Sussex), dau of Raymund Louis Binns, and *d* 10 July 1961, having by her had:

1 Janet Cyrilla; *b* 19 Sept 1946; *d* 16 April 1955

Bell

Arms: Arg. on a fess between three hawk's lures az. as many hawk's bells of the first. **Crest:** A hawk or, holding in the beak a hawk's lure az. and resting the dexter claw on a sun in its splendour.
Motto: *Perseverantia* ('Perseverance').
Creation: Bt (UK) 21 July 1885.

SIR JOHN LOWTHIAN BELL, 5TH BT [Sir John Bell Bt, Arncliffe Hall, Ingleby Cross, Northallerton, N Yorks DL6 3PA]; *b* 14 June 1960; *s* f 1970; *educ* Trin Coll Glenalmond and RAC Cirencester; *m* 1985 *Venetia Mary Frances, 2nd dau of J A Perry, of Llanstefan, Taunton, Som, and has issue:

1 +JOHN HUGH; *b* 29 July 1988

1 *Sophia Amelia Bridget; *b* 1990

Lineage: THOMAS BELL, Alderman of Newcastle-on-Tyne, Northumberland; *b* 5 March 1784, *m* 25 March 1815 Katherine (*d* 11 Sept 1875), dau of Isaac Lowthian, of Newbiggin, Cumberland, and *d* 20 April 1845, leaving an est s:

Sir (Isaac) Lowthian Bell, 1st Bt (UK), so *cr* 21 July 1885, of Rounton Grange, Yorks, and Washington Hall, Co Durham, DL and JP Co Durham and High Sheriff 1884, JP N R Yorks and Newcastle-on-Tyne, DCL, LLD, FRS, ironmaster and coal owner, MP (Lib) Hartlepool 1875–1880, *b* 15 Feb 1816, *m* 20 July 1842 Margaret (*d* 18 Nov 1886), dau of Hugh Lee Pattinson, FRS, of Scots House, Co Durham, and *d* 20 Dec 1904, having had, with other issue:

Sir (Thomas) Hugh Bell, 2nd Bt, CB, Ld Lt N Riding Yorks, pres N Riding Yorks TA, DL and JP Co Durham and High Sheriff 1895, JP Middlesbrough, Mayor 1874, 1883 and 1911, Alderman N Riding CC, pres Iron and Steel Inst 1907–10, Memb Senate U of Durham, hon DCL Durham 1909, hon LLD Leeds 1910, hon DCL Oxford 1929 and Sheffield 1930, FSA, *b* 10 Feb 1844, *m* 1st 23 April 1867 Maria (*d* 19 April 1871), dau of John Shield, of Ashburn, Isle of Bute, and had issue:

1 **Sir Maurice Hugh Lowthian Bell, 3rd Bt,** CMG (1916), TD, DL and JP N Riding, Yorks, High Sheriff Co Durham 1921–22, memb N Riding Yorks TAA, Col 4th Bn Yorkshire Regt, hon Capt Army, served S Africa 1900–01 (medal with six clasps) and WW I 1914–16 (despatches twice), *b* 29 March 1871; *d* unm 17 Nov 1944

1 Gertrude Margaret Lowthian, CBE (1917), author and Arabic scholar, Oriental Sec to High Commr Mesopotamia, rendered services to BRCS during World War I, *d* unm 12 Jul 1926

Sir Hugh *m* 2nd 10 Aug 1876 Florence Eveleen Eleanor, DBE (1918), JP (*d* 16 May 1930), dau of Sir Joseph Olliffe, MD, and *d* 29 June 1931, having by her had issue:

2 Hugh Lowthian (Rev), *b* 21 Oct 1878, *educ* Trin Coll Oxford (MA), *m* 24 Nov 1921 Frances Helena, only dau of John William Morkill, DL, JP, of Newfield Hall, Bell Busk, Yorks, and *d* 2 Feb 1926, leaving issue:

(1) HUGH FRANCIS (Sir), **4th Bt**

(2) John Lowthian, Ordinary Seaman RNVR WW II; *b* Johannesburg 17 June 1925; *ka* in HMS *Warwick* Feb 1944

2 Florence Elsa; *m* 8 July 1907 Adml Sir Herbert William Richmond, KCB, 2nd son of Sir William Blake Richmond, KCB, RA, and *d* 3 May 1971 aged 91, leaving issue (*see* PLOWDEN,B). He *d* 15 Dec 1946

3 Mary Katharine, OBE (1963), *m* 6 Jan 1904 Sir Charles Philips Trevelyan, 3rd Bt (*qv*), and *d* 8 Oct 1966, leaving issue

The 3rd Bt's nephew,

Sir Hugh Francis Bell, 4th Bt, of Rounton Grange, Yorks; *educ* Bryanston, Lt RNVR WW II; *b* Johannesburg 7 Dec 1923; *m* 1st 17 Oct 1947 (*divorce* 1958) Mary Helen, dau of Archibald Mathieson, of 50 Clarendon Court, NW11; *m* 2nd 11 Aug 1959 *Mary, JP (Yorks), MB, ChB, DObst RCOG [Dr Mary Graham JP, The Hollins, E Rounton, Northallerton, Yorks DL6 2LG] (*m* 2nd 1991, as his 2nd w, Prof Dominick Stuart Graham, MC, late Maj RA (*see* GRAHAM, Bt)), 2nd dau of George Howson, MC, of The Hyde, Hambleden, Bucks, and *d* 6 Aug 1970, having by her had:

1 Sir JOHN LOWTHIAN BELL, **5th and present Bt**

2 +David Hugh; *b* 8 Oct 1961

3 +Andrew Mark Howson; *b* 8 Aug 1963

4 +Thomas Hugh; *b* 16 Jan 1965

Bellew

Arms: Sa. fretty or. **Supporters:** Dexter, a leopard or, gorged with a mural crown, az.; sinister, a wolf az., gorged with a ducal coronet or.
Crest: An arm embowed in armour, holding a sword ppr.
Motto: *Tout d'en haut* ('All from above').
Creations: Bt (I) 11 Dec 1688, B. (I) 10 July 1848.

THE 7TH BARON BELLEW OF BARMEATH, Co Louth, and a **Baronet** (Sir James Bryan Bellew, Bt) [The Rt Hon The Lord Bellew, c/o Royal Bank of Scotland, 45 The Promenade, Cheltenham, Glos GL50 1PY]; *b* 5 Jan 1920; *s* f 1981; late Lt Irish Gds; *m* 1st 1942 Mary Elizabeth (*d* 1978), est dau of Rev Edward Eustace Hill; *m* 2nd 1978 *Gwendoline, dau of Charles Redmond Clayton-Daubeny, of Bridgwater, Som, and Bihar, India, and formerly w of Maj P Hall, and has issue by his 1st w:

1 +BRYAN EDWARD; *b* 19 March 1943; *educ* Eton and RMA Sandhurst; Maj Irish Gds (ret); *m* 18 April 1968 *Rosemary Sarah, er dau of Maj Reginald Kilner Brasier Hitchcock, of Meers Court, Mayfield, Sussex, and has:

(1) +Patrick Edward; *b* 29 March 1969

(2) +Anthony Richard Brooke; *b* 9 Sept 1972

2 +Christopher James [The Hon Christopher Bellew, 56 Margravine Gdns, London W6]; *b* 3 April 1954; *educ* Eton and Durham U (BA 1976); *m* 1984 (*divorce* 1991) Hon Rose Griselda Eden, yst dau of 7th Baron Henley (*qv*) and formerly w of Stuart Ballin

1 *Angela Mary [The Hon Mrs Walford, Summerstown House, Trim, Co Meath, Ireland]; *b* 11 April 1944; *m* 2 May 1964 *Capt Simon Hugh Walford, 17th/21st Lancers, s of Lt-Col Hugh Carr Walford, and has:

(1) *Jeanie Anne; *b* 26 Oct 1966; *m* 1993 *Timothy Hugo Pollock (*see* LONDESBOROUGH, B)

(2) *Caroline Sarah; *b* 26 March 1968; *m* 17 May 1997 *Anthony Brockbank, s of Maj-Gen Robin Brockbank of Steeple Langford, Wilts

Lineage: Sir ADAM De BELLA AQUA (Bellew), living 1210, ancestor of:

JOHN BELLEW, of Bellewstown, Co Meath, fourth in descent from whom was:

Sir JOHN BELLEW, of Castle Roche, *fl* 1402; *m* Rosyn Byrtals de Verdon and had, with a yr twin s (John, of Bellewstown):

JOHN BELLEW, of The Roche; had:

Sir RICHARD BELLEW, of The Roche and Castletown, High Sheriff Uriel 1474; *m* Maud Plunkett, of Beaulieu, and left issue:

Sir WALTER BELLEW, of The Roche and Castletown *s* 1542 by his gs:

Sir JOHN BELLEW, of Bellewstown; *m* Margaret Plunkett, dau of Oliver, 1st Lord Louth, and had issue:

1 Christopher (Sir), of Bellewstown; *m* Alice, dau of Sir Thomas Cusack, Lord Chancellor of Ireland, and had:

(1) John (Sir), of Bellewstown, *m* Aminet, dau of John Barnewall, Recorder of Drogheda, and was f of:

1a Christopher (Sir), of Bellewstown; *m* Frances Plunkett, dau of Mathew, 5th Lord Louth, and had, with six daus:

1b JOHN BELLEW, 1st BARON BELLEW OF DULEEK (I), so *cr* 29 Oct 1686 (expired 1770 on death *sp* of 4th Baron)

2d Mathew, of Rogerstown, ancestor of the BELLEWs of Castle Martyr, Co Cork

3b Thomas, of Gaffney; left issue

2 JOHN, of Lisrany, of whom hereafter

3 Richard, of Stameen; *m* Margaret, dau of Nicholas Alcock, of Drogheda, and had:

(1) John; *m* Mary and had:

1a Richard

The 2nd s,

JOHN BELLEW, of Lisrany and Graftonstown, Co Louth; *m* Joan Lynam, of Adamstown, and had, with a yr s (Nicholas):

PATRICK BELLEW, of Lisrany and Graftonstown; *m* Mary, dau of James Warren, of Warrenstown, Co Louth, and had:

Sir JOHN BELLEW, of Lisrany and Willystown; MP Co Louth; *m* Mary, dau of Robert Dillon, of Clonbrock, and *d* between 17 Feb 1672 and 27 May 1679, having had, with four yr sons (including Christopher, of Corgarrowes, had issue; see GRATTAN-BELLEW, Bt):

Sir Patrick Bellew, 1st Bt (I), so *cr* 11 Dec 1688, of Barmeath or Bellew Mount, Co Louth, High Sheriff 1687, and of Castle Bellew, Co Galway; *m c* 1660 Elizabeth, dau of Sir Richard Barnewall, 2nd Bt (*qv*), of Crickstown Castle, and *d* Jan 1715/6, having had, with four yr s and six daus:

Sir John Bellew, 2nd Bt, of Barmeath and Castle Bellew; *m* 1st 1 Dec 1685 Mary Margaret (*d* 1708), dau of Edward Taylor and sister and heir of Nicholas Taylor, of Dublin, and had, with other issue (including an est s, Patrick, *m* 1st July 1713 Mary, dau of 8th Earl of Clanricarde (*see* SLIGO, M); *m* 2nd in or after 1714 Frances, dau of Sir George Hamilton, Count Hamilton in France (*see* ABERCORN, D), and widow of 8th Viscount Dillon (*qv*) of Costello-Gallen):

1 EDWARD (Sir), **3rd Bt**

Sir John *m* 2nd Elizabeth (*m* 2nd St Laurence Besford and *d* 3 Jan 1735), dau of Edward Curling, storekeeper of Londonderry during the siege, and *d* 23 July 1734, having by her had, with three daus:

2 Richard
3 William
4 Charles

His est s,

Sir Edward Bellew, 3rd Bt, *m c* 1728 Eleanor, est dau and coheir of Michael Moore, of Drogheda, and *d* Oct 1741, leaving, with other issue:

1 **Sir John Bellew, 4th Bt**; *b* 1728; *d* unm 2 Nov 1750

2 **Sir Patrick Bellew, 5th Bt**; *m* by licence 18 Aug 1756 Mary, dau and coheir of Matthew Hore, of Shandon, Co Waterford, and *d* 5 March 1795, having had, with two daus (Frances, *m* Malachy Donelan of Ballydonelan; Mary) nine sons (whose legitimate male issue would be in remainder to the baronetcy), of whom the est:

(1) **Sir Edward Bellew, 6th Bt**; *m* 13 Aug 1786 Mary Ann (*d* 14 May 1837), dau and heir of Richard Strange, of Rockwell Castle, Co Kilkenny, and *d* 15 March 1827, having had, with other issue:

1a PATRICK BELLEW, **1st Baron Bellew of Barmeath**, Co Louth (I), so *cr* 10 July 1848, PC, Ld Lt Co Louth, High Sheriff 1831, MP 1831–37, *b* 29 Jan 1798; *m* 19 Jan 1829 Anna Fermina (*d* 2 Aug 1857), dau of Adml Don José Maria de Mendoza y Rios, of Seville, and had, with other issue:

1b EDWARD JOSEPH, **2nd Baron**

The 1st BARON *d* 10 Dec 1866; his only son,

EDWARD JOSEPH BELLEW, **2nd Baron Bellew of Barmeath**, Maj Louth Militia, *b* 3 June 1830, *m* 7 Feb 1853 Auguste Mary (*d* 11 May 1904), only dau of Col George Bryan, MP, of Jenkinstown, Co Kilkenny, and *d* 28 July 1895, having had issue:

1 Patrick George, Lt 20th Regt, *b* 1 Dec 1853; *d* unm 25 May 1874, *vp*

2 CHARLES BERTRAM BELLEW, **3rd Baron Bellew of Barmeath**, rep I peer, Lt Co Louth, High Sheriff 1895, Capt 6th Bn Royal Irish Rifles, *b* 19 April 1855, *m* 8 Aug 1883 Mildred Mary Josephine (*d* 29 Dec 1934), dau of Sir Humphrey de Trafford, 2nd Bt (*qv*), and *dsp* 15 July 1911

3 GEORGE LEOPOLD BELLEW later BRYAN (taken by roy licence 13 Oct 1880 under terms of will of his unc George Leopold Bryan, of Jenkinstown Park, Co Kilkenny), **4th Baron Bellew of Barmeath**, rep I peer 1914, DL Co Kilkenny, High Sheriff 1902, Major 10th Hus, served Afghan War 1878–79, Nile Expdn 1884–85, Imp Yeo S Africa 1900–01, Territorial Force WW I; *b* 22 Jan 1857, *m* 9 April 1927 Elaine Carlisle (*d* 7 March 1973), Councillor for Kilkenny from 1955, served WW I 1914–15 with VAD (despatches), widow of Herbert Lloyd-Dodd, of Johannesburg, and dau of John Benjamin Leach, of Queenstown, S Africa, and *dsp* 15 June 1935

4 Richard Eustace, *b* 31 July 1858, *m* 1st 27 Oct 1887 Ada Kate (*d* 20 March 1893), 2nd dau of Henry Parry Gilbey, of Stansted, Essex (*see* GILBEY, Bt), and had issue:

(1) EDWARD HENRY BELLEW, **5th Baron Bellew of Barmeath**, MBE (1919), Capt RAF WW I, *b* 6 Feb 1889, *educ* Oratory School and Trin Hall Camb; *m* 20 July 1912 Barbara Helan Mary (*d* 23 Oct 1967), only dau of Sir Henry Farnham Burke, KCVO, CB, FSA, Garter King of Arms, and *d* 1975, having adopted 1918:

1a *Barbara Mary Corisande [Mrs Barbara Harrison, Elm Tree Cottage, Stradbally, Co Waterford, Ireland], *b* 14 July 1917, *m* 11 Feb 1936 (*divorce* 1948) Maj Cholmeley Dering Harrison, RM, only son of Col Cholmeley Harrison, CMG, CBE, of Barty House, Bearstead, Kent, and has issue

(2) BRYAN BERTRAM, **6th Baron**

(1) Guendaline Ada; granted with her siblings rank of baron's daus 19 Oct 1935; *m* 19 Oct 1916 Hugh Lloyd Thomas, CMG, CVO, Envoy Extrdy and Min Plen Paris, est s of William Lloyd Thomas, of Tredilion Park, Abergavenny, and *d* 25 Jan 1976, leaving issue. He was k whilst riding in a steeplechase, 22 Feb 1938

(2) Ada Kate; *b* 1893; *m* 1st 1 March 1917 (*divorce* 1936) Charles Barry Domvile (*d* 25 July 1936), of Loughlinstown, Co Dublin; *m* 2nd 1 July 1937 Lt-Col Hon Herbrand Charles Alexander, DSO (*d* 6 May 1965) (*see* CALEDON, E), and had by her 1st husb:

1a *Denys Barry Herbert [Denys Domvile Esq, Brook House, Sutton Courtney, Oxon]; 1921; *educ* Eton and Tin coll Oxford; Capt Life Gds and Maj Inns of Ct Regt; *m* 1958 *Mary Elise, only child of Lt-Col Rowland Morrow Byers, DL, of Birchwood, Virginia Water, Surrey, and has issue:

1b *Rowland Barry John; *b* 1960

1b *Katherine Lake; *b* 1959; *m* 1986 *Alexander Christie Stewart (*see* COCHRANE OF CULTS, B)

2b *(Rosamund) Lucy [Mrs Henry Forwood, 9A Bedford Rd, London SW4 7SH]; *b* 1965; *m* 1988 *W Henry A Forwood, son of William Forwood, of Woodstock, Newtownmountkennedy, Co Wicklow

4 (cont.) The Hon Richard Bellew *m* 2nd 30 Nov 1895 Gwendoline Marie Josephine (*d* 21 Feb 1940), dau of William Reginald Joseph FitzHerbert Herbert-Huddleston, of Clytha, and *d* 8 Feb 1933, having by her had issue:

(3) Richard Courtenay, 2nd Lt Irish Guards, *b* 16 July 1898, *educ* Wellington, *d* 21 Aug 1917 of wounds recd in action

(4) George Rothe (Hon Sir), KCB (1961), KCVO (1953, CVO 1950, MVO 4th Class 1935), ktd 1950, FSA, Garter King of Arms and Genealogist of the Order of the Bath and OStJ Dec 1950–July 1961; Portcullis Pursuivant 1922–26, Somerset Herald 1926–50, Register Coll of Arms 1935–45, hon Genealogist to the Royal Victorian Order 1945–61, Inspr of Regtal Colours 1957–61, Sec Order of Garter 1961–74, Kt Prin Imp Soc of Kts Bachelor 1957, Dep Kt Prin 1961, S/Ldr RAFVR, served WW II (despatches), KStJ, *b* 13 Dec 1899, *educ* Wellington and Ch Ch Oxford, *m* 24 Sept 1935 Ursula Kennard (*d* 1994), est dau of Anders Eric Knös Cull, KStJ, of Warfield House, Bracknell, Berks, and *d* 1993, having had issue:

1a +Richard George [Richard Bellew Esq, The Grange, Old Park Lane, Farnham, Surrey GU9 0AH], 2nd Lt Irish Gds, Res of Offrs, OStJ, *b* 29 Dec 1936, *educ* Eton, *m* 15 Jan 1965 *Shona Deirdre, formerly w of Roderic Marshall Knowles and only dau of Col John Edward Mercer Ewart Clarke Leask, MBE, IA, and Mrs Ivan Kaufman, of Delavor, Elton Park, Sandycove, Co Dublin, and has issue:

1b +Henry Edward Courtenay, *b* 14 Dec 1973
2b +Aidan Nicholas, *b* 1980
1b *Serena Leonie Georgia, *b* 13 Nov 1969

(5) Patrick Herbert, late Lt RNVR, *b* 2 April 1905, *m* 1st 16 April 1936 (*divorce* 1947) Hon Catherine Moya de la Poer Beresford (*d* 26 May 1967), yr dau of 5th Baron Decies (*qv*); *m* 2nd 7 Sept 1954 *Helen Carol, dau of Walter Clinton Louchheim, of New York, and *d* 1984, having had issue by his 1st w:

1a +Bellew, John Jeremy de la PoerJohn Jeremy de la Poer [Mr John Bellew, 42 Meadow Lane, Chappaqua, New York, USA]; *b* 19 Feb 1937, *educ* Princeton; *m* 8 Jan 1966 *Cynthia Annette, dau of Ernest J Saunders, of Johannesburg, S Africa, and has issue:

1b +John Patrick, *b* 12 Dec 1966
1b *Catherine Moyra, *b* 3 March 1969

The 5th BARON's bro,

BRYAN BERTRAM BELLEW, **6th Baron Bellew of Barmeath**, MC (1916), Lt South Irish Horse WW I, *b* 11 June 1890, *educ* Trin Hall Camb, *m* 17 Dec 1918 Jeannie Ellen Agnes (*d* 18 May 1973), only dau of James Ormsby Jameson, of Dolland, Clonsilla, and *d* 1981, leaving:

1 JAMES BRYAN BELLEW, **7th and Present Baron Bellew of Barmeath**

BELLINGHAM

Arms: Arg. three bugle horns sa., stringed and garnished or. **Crest:** A buck's head, couped or. **Mottoes:** *Amicus amico* ('A friend to a friend') and (over the crest) *Ainsi il est* ('So it is'). **Creation:** Bt. (GB) 19 April 1796.

SIR NOEL PETER ROGER BELLINGHAM, 7TH BT, of Castle Bellingham, Co Louth [Sir Noel Bellingham Bt, 20 Davenport Park Rd, Davenport, Cheshire SK2 6JS]; *b* 4 Sept 1943; *s* f 1973; *educ* Lindisfarne Coll; accountant; *m* 1977 *Jane, dau of Edwin William Taylor, of Sale, Cheshire

Lineage: WILLIAM de BELLINGHAM; Sheriff Tynedale, Northumberland, 1279, forester to ALEXANDER III of Scotland; probably f of:

RICHARD de BELLINGHAM; *m* Margaret, dau and heir of Sir Gilbert de Burnside, and moved to Burnside, nr Kendal, Westmorland; ancestor of:

ROBERT BELLINGHAM, of Burnside, living *temp* HENRY V; *m* Elizabeth, dau of Sir Richard Tunstall, KG, and had, with four other s:

1 Henry (Sir), of Burnside, KB (1460); had:

(1) Roger (Sir), of Burnside, KB (1487); *d* 1533, leaving:

1a Robert (Sir), of Burnside, captured Lambert Simnel at Battle of Stoke 1487, *dspm*, when Burnside was sold

2 Richard, ancestor of the BELLINGHAMs of Lincs, whose line seems to have ended with Richard Bellingham, Govr Massachussetts (*d* 1671)

3 Thomas, settled in Sussex, and was ancestor of the BELLINGHAMs of Erringham (one of whom was Sir Edward Bellingham, Ld Dep Ireland 1584) and the BELLINGHAMs of Hangleton, Lyminster and Newtimber, all in Sussex

4 Alan (8th s), of Bellingham, Northumberland; boughts Levens, nr Kendal, and built a mansion there which later became his successors' chief seat; Treasurer Berwick, Dep-Warden Marches; *m* Elizabeth, dau of William Gilpin, of Kentmore, and had:

(1) Thomas, of Levens; *m* Margery/Marion, dau of Thomas Beck, of Holbrink; his est s:

1a Alan, of Helsington and Levens; MP Westmorland, Bencher Inner Temple; *m* 1st Katherine (*dsp*), dau of Anthony Ducket; *m* 2nd Dorothy, dau of Thomas Sandford, of Askham, Westmorland, and *d* 7 May 1577, having had, with five daus (one of whom *m* Sir Gerard Lowther; *see* LONSDALE, E) and four er sons:

1b Robert, of Dublin; *educ* Middle Temple 1595, inherited from his f the lands of Gt Strickland and Milkinthorpe, which he probably sold before migrating to Ireland; Sheriff Co Longford 1611–12, Attorney to Second Remembrancer Exchequer Ireland between 1616 and 1622; *m* Margaret Whyte (*d* 11 Nov 1668), of Clongell, Co Meath, and *d* 1639, having had, with other issue:

1c Sir DANIEL BELLINGHAM, 1st Bt (I), so *cr* 18 March 1666/7, of Dubber, Co Dublin; Memb Goldsmiths' Guild 1644, Dublin: Sheriff 1655, Alderman 1656, Ld Mayor 1665–66, ktd 1662, Dep Receiver-Gen and V-Treas Ireland 1663–66; *m* Jane, dau of Richard Barlow, of Little Toghill, Cheshire, and *d* between 27 April and 12 July 1672, leaving, with other issue, including six sisters:

1d Sir RICHARD BELLINGHAM, 2nd and last Bt, of Dubber; High Sheriff 1684, *bapt* 21 Oct 1648; *educ* Trin Coll Dublin (BA); *d* unm between 13 June and 25 July 1699, when the btcy expired

2c Henry, of Gernonstown, Co Louth, which he bought together with other lands from a Cromwellian trooper who had been granted them in lieu of pay; memb Goldsmiths' Guild 1652, Cornet Army; *m* Lucy, dau of William Sibthorpe, of Dunany, and *d* 1676, having had, with a dau (Anne, *m* Robert Bickerton):

1d Thomas, of Gernonstown (Castle Bellingham), Co Louth; *b c* 1646; Col under WILLIAM III, who he guided on the march from Dundalk to the Boyne, before which battle (1690) JAMES II's troops burnt Castle Bellingham to the ground; Col Thomas rebuilt it by 1700 but his descendants sold it in the mid–1950s; *m* 1671 Abigail, dau of William Handcock, of Twyford, Co Westmeath, and *d* 15 Sept 1721, leaving an only s:

1e Henry; MP Dundalk; *m* Mary, dau and coheir of Thomas Moore, and had:

1f Henry; MP Co Louth; *m* Margaret, dau of Hugh Henry, of Straffan, Co Kildare, and *dsps* 1755

2f ALAN, for whom *see* further below

The yr s,

ALAN BELLINGHAM, of Castle Bellingham; *b* 1709; *m* 1738 Alice (*d* 6 Dec 1785), dau and coheir of Rev Hans Montgomery, of Grey Abbey, Co Down, and *d* 19 Jan 1796, having had, with another s and four daus:

1 Alan, of Kilsaran; *b* 1740; *m* 1st 14 Aug 1774 Anne (*d* 6 May 1789), dau of John Cairnes, of Killyfaddy, Co Tyrone, and had issue:

(1) ALAN (Sir), **2nd Bt**

(2) Henry, Maj 1st Bengal Native Inf; *b* 5 July 1778; *m* 25 March 1809 Henrietta Elizabeth (*d* 13 March 1872), dau of Capt William Cruden, RN, and *d* 26 May 1820, leaving issue:

1a Henrietta Anne; *m* 10 Jan 1833 Henry Shebbeare, MD

2a Mary

3a Jane; *m* 4 May 1841 her cousin William Stewart Bellingham (*d* 29 Dec 1869), and had issue (*see* below)

(3) John; *b* 17 March 1781; *m* 1st Elizabeth Jane (*d* 13 July 1820), dau of William Stewart, of Wilmont, Co Down, and had issue:

1a William Stewart; *b* 18 June 1805; *m* 4 May 1841 Jane, dau and coheir of his unc, Maj Henry Bellingham, and *d* 29 Dec 1869, having had issue:

1b William; *b* 13 April 1842; *m* 17 Aug 1865 Grace Burscoe (*d* 16 Feb 1931), dau of George Folliott, of Vicars Cross, Cheshire, and *dsp* 14 Jan 1875

2b Henry; *b* 30 Sept 1844; *m* 1st 1 June 1870 Harriet Eleanor Ingoldsby (*d* 5 Jan 1880), dau of Henry Smythe, of Stephenstown, Co Louth; *m* 2nd 24 Feb 1892 Josephine Maude (*d* 22 Jan 1934), dau of William Cotton Laming, of Rotterdam, and *d* 1906, having by his 1st w had issue:

1c William Guy Henry Stewart; *b* 5 Nov 1873; *d* unm 15 April 1904

2c Alan Somerset; *d* 26 March 1880 aged three

1c Frances Henrietta Jane; *m* 1906 Capt Thomas Carson Burnside (*d* 29 Sept 1931), of and *d* 25 Feb 1943, leaving issue

3b John; *b* 27 June 1847; BA Camb; *m* 27 Dec 1887 Alice Jane (*d* 27 March 1930), dau of Hon Bouverie Francis Primrose, CB (*see* ROSEBERY, E), and widow of George Mercer Henderson, of Fordell, and *dsp* 8 Feb 1911

4b Thomas Eudo; *b* 24 March 1849; *m* 15 March 1882 Grace (*d* 1 Oct 1905), dau of Rev William Harkness, of Garryfine, Co Limerick, and *d* 1923, leaving issue:

1c William Eudo; *b* 11 Dec 1882; *m* 28 July 1908 Louisa Bertha (*d* 21 April 1935), dau of William Arthur Krick, of Chicago, and *d* 2 March 1954, having had issue:

1d +William Arthur Eudo; *b* 4 April 1909; *m* 26 June 1932 *Myrna Arlene, dau of Edwin T Nester, and has issue:

1e +William Edwin [William Bellingham, 4506 Shadow Glen Dve, Colorado Springs, CO 80909, USA]; *b* 7 Jan 1938; *m* 1959 *Renee Anne, dau of Wayne McGrew, and has issue:

1f +William Keith [William Bellingham, 2915 Haystack Dve, Colorado Springs, CO 80922, USA]; *b* 1967; *m* 1990 *Clara Margi Hutchinson and has issue:

1g +William Clifton; *b* 1992

1f *Catherine Anne; *b* 1971

1e *Kay Arlene; *b* 5 March 1934; *m* 1st 1959 (*divorce* 1989) Thomas Huntington Taylor; *m* 2nd 1993 *Lewis Saxby and has had issue by 1st husb:

1f Thomas Huntington; *b* 1959; *d* 1993

1f *Jane Arlene [Mrs Peter Elfers, 777 N Macqueston Pky, Mt Vernon, NY 10552, USA]; *b* 1961; *m* 1994 *Peter Elfers

2e *Jean Carolyn [Mrs James Johnson, 3534 Edgevale, Toledo, Ohio 43606, USA]; *b* 16 Oct 1941; *m* 1967 *Patrick James Johnson, and has adopted:

*Jonathan Patrick; *b* 1971

*Jodi Jean; *b* 1973

3e *Linda Ann [Mrs Richard Allardyce, 11606 Helmont Dve, Oakton, VA 22124, USA]; *b* 15 July 1944; *m* 1970 *Richard Henry Allardyce and has issue:

1f *Kristin Lynn; *b* 1976

2f *Julie Anne; *b* 1979

4e *Gwen Frances [Mrs Richard Osenbaugh, 3543 Robin, Toledo, Ohio 43623, USA]; *b* 26 March 1946; *m* 1970 *Richard Osenbaugh

2d Jack Francis; *b* 27 Sept 1917; *d* unm 1935

3d Frederick Richard; *b* 6 Nov 1923; *m* 1st 1944 (*divorce* 1947) Mary Winifred, dau of Cary C Winans, and had issue:

1e *Patricia; *b* April 1945

2e *Kathleen; *b* 9 July 1947

3d (cont.) Frederick Bellingham *m* 2nd 1951 Elizabeth Hayes and by her had issue:

3e *Michelle; *b* 1952

3d (cont.) Frederick Bellingham *m* 3rd 1958 *Geraldine Helen Hermanson [Mrs Frederick Bellingham, 140 N Hilltop Dve, Titusville, Florida, USA] and *d* 1990, having had further issue:

1e +Timothy Shane; *b* 1959; *m* 1985 *Leslie Anne Fritz and has issue:

1f +Shane Patrick; *b* 1989

2f +Brian Lewis; *b* 1992

1d *Vesper Grace; *b* 4 Dec 1910; *m* 24 April 1941 *Roy Arthur Justofson and has issue:

1e *Lucy Christine; *b* 20 Jan 1942

2d *Louise Hazel [Mrs Conrad Nelson, 1023 S 72nd Ave W, Duluth, Minnesota, USA]; *b* 26 Feb 1913; *m* 1932 *Conrad Edward Nelson and has issue:

1e *Constance Paulette; *b* 5 Jan 1944; *m* March 1963 *Thomas Neil Nelson and has issue:

1f *Rodney Kirk; *b* Nov 1963

2f *Ryan Jay; *b* 1973

3d *Laurel Joyce [Mrs Thomas Telando, 568 Everett St, Duluth, Minn 55803, USA]; *b* 2 Dec 1925; *m* 7 June 1945 *Thomas Edward Telando and has issue:

1e *Thomas Michael; *b* 18 Aug 1946; helicopter pilot US Army, served Vietnam

2e John Francis; *b* and *d* 10 Jan 1950

1e *Charlotte Louisa; *b* 11 Oct 1947; *m* 21 Dec 1967 *Sgt Marcell R Merolli, s of Marcell Merolli, of Shickshinny, Pa., and has issue:

1f *Mark Thomas; *b* 10 Aug 1968

2c Thomas Francis Gordon; *b* 28 Feb 1885; *m* 29 Jan 1918 Iva Abigail, dau of A E Bridge, and had issue:

1d +Stewart [Stewart Bellingham Esq, Bawlf, Alberta, Canada]; *b* 4 March 1921; *m* 19– — and has issue:

1e +Roger, *b* 19–

1e *A dau; *b* 19 –

2d +William Milton; *b* 2 May 1922

3d +Stephen Ramsay; *b* 18 Jan 1924; *m* 19– — and has issue

1d *Frances; *b* Feb 1918

3c John Stewart; *b* 13 Dec 1889; *m* 28 Dec 1937 Doreen (*d* 1974), yst dau of Edward O'Brien, of Ambleside, Westmorland, and *d* 15 Dec 1965, leaving issue:

1d +Roger Graham [Roger Bellingham Esq, 13 Ridgeway Close, Lightwater, Surrey GU18 5XU]; *b* 9 Dec 1939; *m* 29 May 1965 *Pauline, only dau of David Rankine and Mrs Alan Smart, of W Byfleet, Surrey, and has:

1e +Alan Graham; *b* 1966; *m* 31 Aug 1991 *June Rose, dau of Harry Doran, and has:

1d *Tara Pauline Doran; *b* 1994

2e +John Terence; *b* 1969; *m* 22 April 1995 *Hazel Katherine, dau of Harding Derek Spencer

1c Hazel; *b* 21 June 1887; *m* 1 Nov 1915 Charles Wunabald Christen (*d* 1961), s of Wunabald Christen, of Louiscaine, Switzerland, and had issue:

1d *Charles Patrick Harkness; *b* 6 Oct 1918; *m* 21 March 1946 *Virginia Beane and has issue:

1e *Charles Patrick; *b* 28 Oct 1947

1e *Julia Hazel; *b* 26 Dec 1949

2e *Christina Helen; *b* 9 June 1953

2d *John Wunabald; *b* 2 Jan 1923; *m* 25 July 1946 *Theresa Lucille Lovich and has issue:

1e *John Hazel; *b* 1946

2e *Steven William; *b* 1948

3e *Daniel Thomas; *b* 1952

4e *David Paul; *b* 1953

1e *Patricia Terese; *b* 3 July 1944

1d *Hester Pansy; *b* 17 April 1917; *m* 8 Aug 1946 *Mathew Prestopic and has:
1e *Catherine Mary; *b* 16 Jan 1949
2d *Hazel Mary Franklin [Mrs William Harrison, 225 S Hackman Dve, Staunton, IL, 62088, USA]; *b* 11 May 1924; *m* 1st 1943 Albert Jackson, of Staunton, and has issue:
1e *Anthony Lee; *b* 1945
2d (cont.) Mrs Jackson *m* 2nd 1946 Lawrence Robert Hanstein; *m* 3rd 27 Nov 1968 *William Harrison, s of Prof William Parnell Franklin, of Edwardville, Ill., and has further issue by her 2nd husb:
2e *Lawrence Robert; *b* 1948
3e *David; *b* 1953
1e *Mary Lynn; *b* 1951
2c Juanita Maude; *b* 3 Dec 1891; *m* 24 June 1914 William Gordon Wright and *d* 6 Feb 1963, leaving issue
5b Arthur D'Arcy; *b* 27 Oct 1853; *m* 1892 Nannie (*d* 23 Oct 1938), dau of Addison Hone, and *d* 1 May 1903, leaving issue:
1c Arthur Stuart; *b* 30 July 1893; *educ* Radley; Lt-Col Res Offrs, late RA, WW I (twice wounded, 1914 Star, two medals), and WW II AQMG N Command; *m* 7 Aug 1923 Jean, RRC (*d* 7 May 1979), dau of Andrew Arthur, of Rosemount, Ayrshire (*see* GLENARTHUR, B), and *d* 6 Sept 1969, leaving issue:
1d Arthur Henry, Capt Leics Yeo (TA); *b* 8 Feb 1926; *educ* Radley and Corpus Christi Coll Cambridge (BA 1950); *m* 16 April 1953 *June Marion Cloudesley (*m* 2nd 29 March 1962 Maj Ian Bruce Baillie, Life Gds (*see* BURTON, B)), only dau of Arthur Cloudesley Smith and Mrs Christopher Edwards, and *d* following an accident on manoeuvres 3 June 1959, leaving issue:
1e +Henry Campbell; *b* 29 March 1955; *educ* Eton and Magdalene Coll Cambridge (BA 1977); barrister Middle Temple 1978; MP (C) Norfolk N W 1983–97, PPS to Sec of State: Tport 1990–92, Def 1992–95, For Affairs 1995–97; chm C Cncl E Europe 1989–94; *m* 1993 *Emma Louise, dau of Peter John Henry Whiteley (*see* GUILFORD, E)
1e *Elizabeth Alison; *b* 15 Sept 1956; *m* 1989 *Richard Charles Rowley, only s of Sir Charles Robert Rowley, 7th Bt (*qv*)
2d +John Stuart [John Bellingham Esq, The Cliffs, Baily, Dublin 13 Ireland; Flat 5, 87 Harcourt Terr, London SW10 9JP; 5 rue Paul-Louis-Courier, Paris VII, France]; *b* 24 Sept 1929; *educ* Eton and Magdalene Coll Cambridge (BA 1951); *m* 14 Feb 1989 *Fiona Aileen, er dau of Sir Peter Nugent, Bt (*qv*)
3d Andrew Michael; *b* 15 March 1943; *educ* Eton; 2nd Lt Irish Gds; *k* in an accident Belgium 13 Aug 1963
6b O'Bryen Cairnes; *b* 23 Jan 1859; *m* 1st 27 May 1892 Wilhelmina (*dsp* 3 July 1897), dau of William Vincent; *m* 2nd 1903 Maud Mary, dau of Maj Abbott, of Newport, Co Limerick, and *d* 1936
1d Hester Frances Mary; *m* 15 Oct 1885 Charles Page, of Durrant Ho, Rye, Sussex, and *dsp* 26 Dec 1935
2d Henrietta Anne; *m* 8 Nov 1887 John Henry Ryan, LLB, MICE, of Kilhefernan Ho, Co Tipperary (*d* 10 May 1929), and *d* 5 Nov 1918, leaving a dau
3b Jane Alice; *m* 20 March 1880 Alfred Edward Ruthven and *dsp* 1894
2a Alan; *d* unm 1835
1a Anne; *b* 1802; *m* 24 Sept 1822 John Peebles (originally de Peblys), physician of Dublin, and *d* 10 Oct 1847, leaving issue
3 (cont.) John Bellingham *m* 2nd Katherine Ann, dau of R Clarke, and *d* 1826, having by her had further issue:
3a Percy John; *d* young
(4) William Cairnes, Capt 64th Regt; *d* unm 1835
1 (cont.) Alan Bellingham *m* 2nd Mary (*dsp*), dau of Ralph Smith, of Drogheda, and *d* 5 Nov 1800
2 O'Bryen; *m* Anne, dau of Edward Tandy, of Dublin, and *d* 6 June 1798, having had:
(1) Alan O'Bryen
(1) Elizabeth
(2) Anne
3 Thomas, RN; *d* unm
4 **Sir William Bellingham, 1st Bt** (GB), so *cr* 19 April 1796 with special remainder to the heirs male of his f; Sec to Pitt the Younger, Commr Navy, MP Reigate; *m* 3 Dec 1783 Hester Frances (*d* 10 Jan 1844), yst dau of Rev Hon Robert Cholmondeley (*see* CHOLMONDELEY, M), and *dsp* 26 Oct 1826
His n,
Sir Alan Bellingham, 2nd Bt; *b* 2 Feb 1776; *m* 5 Nov 1799 Elizabeth (*d* 22 Jan 1822), 2nd dau of the Rev Edward Walls, of Boothby Hall, Lincs, and had, with other issue:
1 ALAN EDWARD (Sir), **3rd Bt**
2 Henry Richard; *b* 12 June 1804; barrister Lincoln's Inn; *d* unm 23 Nov 1836
3 O'Bryen, MD; *b* 12 Dec 1805; physician; *m* Matilda (*d* 2 June 1883), dau of Bryan Molloy, of Millicent Ho, Co Kildare, and *d* 11 Oct 1857
4 Sydney Robert; *b* 2 Aug 1808; *m* Arabella (*d* 5 May 1887), dau of William Holmes, of Quebec, and *dsp* 9 March 1900
5 William Johnstone; *b* 20 March 1818; Capt 50th Regt, Hon Col 6th Bn Roy Irish Rifles; *m* 15 April 1852 Felicia (*d* 17 Oct 1909), only dau of Rev John Short Hewett, DD, Rector Rotherhithe, and *d* 20 Jan 1903, having had issue:
(1) Sydney Edwin; *b* 5 April 1853; Maj Duke of Cambridge's Own; *m* 3 March 1880 Helen Mary (*d* 1950), dau of A A Dunlop, of Sutton, Co Dublin, and *d* 5 Nov 1893, leaving issue:
1a Alan Mure, MC (1918); *b* 21 Feb 1881; AMINA, Maj Res Offrs, Roy Ulster Rifles, Lt Middx Regt, Boer War 1900–02 (two medals, five clasps, wounded), WW I (twice wounded), N Russia 1919, Order St Vladimir 2nd Cl with swords and ribbons; *m* 1st 15 Aug 1941 (*divorce* 1930) Beatrix Laura (*d* 26 Aug 1962), 3rd dau of John Henry Harrison, ICS, and had issue:
1b *Beatrix Pamela BELLINGHAM-KIGGELL (took name by deed poll 1970); *b* 28 July 1918; *m* 1st 19 March 1938 (*divorce* 1946) Ronald Arthur Cleave, adopted s of Lt-Cdr John Raymond Cleave, RN, and has issue:
1c *Zenia Sophia SIM (took name by deed poll 1948); *b* 16 Nov 1938
1b (cont.) Mrs Beatrix Cleave *m* 2nd 12 Dec 1947 (*divorce* 1962) John Chatterton Coysgarne Sim, 2nd s of Alexander Chatterton Sim, and has further issue:
2c *Carol Ann; *b* 6 July 1950
1a (cont.) Maj Alan Bellingham *m* 2nd 3 July 1930 Mabel Theodora Lucy, WVS Long Service Medal (*d* 1981), 2nd dau of Theodore Seton Dury, Ch Master Supreme Court, and formerly w of Nestor Seppings Tirard, and *d* 19 Sept 1946, having by her had issue:
1b +Patrick Alan Sydney [Patrick Bellingham Esq, 22 Willow View, Straightway Head, Whimple, Devon]; *b* 20 March 1936; *educ* Christ's Hosp; *m* 1st 24 Oct 1958 (*divorce* 1981) Elizabeth Mary, dau of Harold Hall Bagnall, and has issue:
1c +Alan Hall [Alan Bellingham Esq, 22 Woodfield Crescent, London W5 1PD]; *b* 3 Feb 1960; *educ* Christ's Hosp and St Catharine's Coll Cambridge; *m* 1st 1984 (*divorce* 1991) Anne Crick; *m* 2nd 14 Dec 1996 *Colette Susan Reap
1c *Dorcas Elizabeth; *b* 11 March 1962; *m* 1984 (*divorce* 1994) Richard Puczynski
2c *Isobel Marie; *b* 11 March 1962; *m* 1982 *Philip Morgan and has:
1d *Charles Henry; *b* 1986
2d *Purdey Ashley; *b* 1988
1b (cont.) Patrick Bellingham *m* 2nd 1981 (*divorce* 1990) Elizabeth, dau of Maj Stanislas Lis, Polish Army, and widow of Arnold Derrick Workman; *m* 3rd 1991 *Brenda Mary Nixon, formerly w of Jack Hal Nixon, and has further issue by his 2nd w:
2c +Jasper Guy Patrick; *b* 1981
3c *Katharine Lucy Rose; *b* 1985
2b *Brigid Alaine [Mrs Gene Smith, K12 Forrest Place, 356 Blunder Rd, Durack, Qld 4077, Australia]; *b* 25 Sept 1933; *m* 1st 25 Sept 1954 (*divorce* 1969) Brian Deakin, est s of George Stanley Deakin, OBE; *m* 2nd 1970 (*divorce* 1978) Richard Barham; *m* 3rd 1978 Dr Gene Don Smith (*d* 1985) and has by her 1st husb:
1c *Charles Rupert Deakin [Charles Barham Esq, 14 Drury St, Hill End, Qld 4101, Australia]; *b* 23 April 1956; legally adopted by stepfather 1972 and took surname Barham but kept patronymic as forename; *m* 1985 *Cheryl Robyn Pearce and has:
1d *Courtney Rebecca; *b* 1993
2d *Brittany Louise; *b* 1996
2c *Timothy Graham [Timothy Deakin Esq, 14 Nearco St, Fig Tree Pocket, Qld 4069, Australia]; *b* 8 Dec 1959; *m* 1985 *Leith Gaye Perkins and has:
1d *Kiera Adele; *b* 1991
2d *Kezia Sinnet; *b* 1997
1c *Helena Judith [Mrs Joel Smith, 19599 E Belleview Place, Aurora, Colorado 80015, USA]; *b* 14 Aug 1959; has:
1d *Jessica Renee; *b* 1990
1c (cont.) Miss Helena Deakin *m* 1995 *Joel David Smith
1a Maud Alice; *m* 8 Feb 1910 Lt-Col Cecil Ford Anderson, DSO, RE (*d* 5 April 1946), er s of Dr Ford Anderson, and had issue
2a Helen Mary Dorothea (Helen Beauclerk, novelist, a name she took by deed poll, having been adopted by Maj Ferdinand Beauclerk; *see* SAINT ALBANS, D)
(2) Alan Hele; *b* 13 May 1857; *d* unm 12 July 1900
(3) William Edward Patrick; *b* 11 March 1864; *d* 23 Aug 1917
(1) Mary Louisa; *m* 7 Aug 1877 Arthur Maran, of Drumcashel, Co Louth (*d* 26 March 1938), and *d* 20 Dec 1950, leaving issue
(2) Alice Anna; *m* 18 Sept 1913 Lt-Col Henry Chamney, CMG (*d* 8 June 1947), s of Rev Joseph Chamney, DD, of Ard Ronan, Castle Bellingham, and *d* 19 Nov 1941
(3) Dorothea; *d* 27 Oct 1948
Sir ALAN *d* 26 Aug 1827; his est son,
Sir Alan Edward Bellingham, 3rd Bt, MA, DL; *b* 8 Oct 1800; *m* 12 Jan 1841 Elizabeth (*d* 11 April 1887 aged 77), only child of Henry Clarke, and had issue:
1 ALAN HENRY (Sir), **4th Bt**
2 William Claypon (Rev), MA; *b* 11 Nov 1847; Rector Kilsaran, Co Louth; *m* 22 Aug 1878 Susan Caroline (*d* 25 Oct 1928), dau of Ven Ambrose Power, Archdeacon Lismore (*see* POWER, Bt), and *d* 3 Oct 1892, leaving issue:
(1) Eudo William Alan; *b* 1884; *d* unm 24 Nov 1929
(1) Vera Susan; *d* unm 14 Dec 1966
(2) Alice Marian; *m* 22 Jan 1918 R-Adml Hugh Turnour England, CB, DSO and bar, 4th s of Capt William George England, RN, and *d* 10 Jan 1968, having had issue
(3) Hester Frances Zoe; *d* 9 April 1900
1 Hester Elizabeth; *m* 8 Sept 1864 Sir Thomas Pierce Butler, 10th Bt (*qv*), and *d* 5 Aug 1904, leaving issue
2 Alice Sophia; *m* 28 July 1864 Sir Victor Alexander Brooke, 3rd Bt (*see* BROOKEBOROUGH, V), and *d* 27 July 1920, leaving issue
3 Charlotte Mary; *m* 8 Feb 1872 Frederick Stringer Wrench, PC (*d* 7 June 1926), and *d* 14 May 1935, leaving issue
4 Frances Anne Jane; *m* 29 July 1869 Richard Altamont Smythe (*d* 1924), of Court-na-Farraga, Co Dublin, and *d* 23 July 1934, leaving issue
5 Agnes Matilda; *m* 3 Nov 1875 Montagu Yeats-Brown, CMG (*d* 22 Feb 1921), Br Consul Boston, and had issue
Sir ALAN *d* 19 April 1889; his son,
Sir (Alan) Henry Bellingham, 4th Bt; *b* 23 Aug 1846; Lt and Custos Rotulorum Co Louth 1911; *educ* Exeter Coll Oxford (MA); barrister Lincoln's Inn, Commr Nat Educn Ireland, Hon LLD and Senator Roy U 1909, MP Co Louth 1880–85,

Capt 6th Bn Roy Irish Rifles, Privy Chamberlain to TH Popes PIUS IX, LEO XIII and PIUS X; *m* 1st 13 Jan 1874 Lady Constance Julia Eleanor Georgiana Noel (*d* 8 April 1891), dau of 2nd Earl of Gainsborough (*qv*), and had issue:

1 **Sir Edward Henry Charles Patrick Bellingham, 5th Bt**, CMG (1918), DSO (1916); *b* 26 Jan 1879; Boer War 1899–1901 (two medals, three clasps), WW I (wounded, despatches three times), S/Ldr RAFR and CCG WW II, Brig-Gen Roy Scots, T/Brig-Gen and Bde Cdr 1917–18, Brevet Lt-Col 1919, Cnsllr Br Legation Guatemala, Lt and Custos Rotulorum Co Louth, peace commr Co Louth, Senator Irish Free State 1925–36; *m* 11 June 1904 Charlotte Elizabeth (*d* 20 May 1964), dau of Alfred Payne, of Greenheys, Manchester, and widow of Frederick Gough, and *dspm* 19 May 1956, leaving:

(1) Gertrude Mary; *m* 15 Feb 1927 Ronald Derwent Hawker, only surv s of Bertram Hawker, of Runton Old Hall, Cromer, by Constance Victoria, dau of Sir Thomas Fowell Buxton, 3rd Bt (*qv*), and had issue:

1a *Martin [Martin Hawker Esq, Claydon Hall, Ipswich, Suffolk]; *b* 10 Feb 1929; *educ* Stowe and Trin Coll Cambridge (BA 1952, MA 1962)

2 Roger Charles Noel; *b* 28 April 1884; ADC to Ld Lt Ireland 1912–14, Capt RFA SR; *m* 18 Jan 1910 Alice Ann (*d* 10 Jan 1949), dau of Richard Naish, of Ballycullen, Co Limerick, and was *ka* 4 March 1915, leaving issue:

(1) ROGER CARROLL PATRICK STEPHEN (Sir), **6th Bt**

1 Constance Catherine Mary Pia; *b* 21 Oct 1912; *m* 1st 23 April 1935 Brendan Russell (*d* 23 June 1956), est s of Charles McMahon Russell, of Dundalk; *m* 2nd 7 Jan 1963 *Oswald Shaw-Hamilton, s of Robert Cope Hardy Shaw-Hamilton, of Ard Ronan, Castle Bellingham, Co Louth, and had issue by 1st husb:

(1) Ida Mary Elizabeth Agnes; *b* 26 Jan 1876; nun Order Holy Child; *d* 28 Nov 1945

2 Augusta Mary Monica, DBE; *b* 19 Aug 1880; DJStJ, medal Queen Elisabeth Belgium; *m* 6 July 1905 4th Marquess of Bute (*qv*) and *d* 16 May 1947, leaving issue

Sir Henry *m* 2nd 11 June 1895 Hon Lelgarde Clifton, DGStJ (*d* 15 Oct 1939), yr dau of Augustus Wykeham Clifton and Baroness Grey (of Ruthin) (*see* GREY,B, and SAINT DAVIDS, V), and *d* 9 June 1921

Sir EDWARD's n,

Sir Roger Carroll Patrick Stephen, 6th Bt; *b* 23 April 1911; *educ* Oratory Sch, U Coll Dublin and Edin U (MB, ChB 1936), DA (Eng) 1956; memb: BMA, Assoc Anaesthetists GB and Ireland, Fell Manchester Med Soc, F/Lt RAFVR WW II, Kt SMO Malta; *m* 27 Dec 1941 *Mary, dau of William Norman, and *d* between 1 April and 1 July 1973, having had issue:

1 Sir NOEL PETER ROGER BELLINGHAM, **7th and present Bt**

2 +ANTHONY EDWARD NORMAN; *b* 24 March 1947; heir presumptive; *educ* Rossall

BELLWIN

Arms: Azure in chief two bellows argent garnished or and in base a rose argent, barbed and seeded proper, a border or fretty azure. **Crest:** Upon a wreath an owl guardant azure, beaked, legged, murally crowned and holding in the dexter claws a bell bendwise gold. **Supporters:** Dexter, a ram azure, armed, langued and tailed or; sinister, a lion rampant azure, armed, crined, langued and the tail tufted or, both with a collar argent, charged with triangles interlaced in pairs azure. **Motto:** *Suas quisque sciat felicitates* ('May each know his own idea of happiness'). **Creation:** B. (LP, UK) 1979.

THE BARON BELLWIN, of the City of Leeds (Irwin Norman Bellow, JP (Leeds 1969), DL (W Yorks 1991)) [The Rt Hon The Lord Bellwin JP DL, 6a Rodley Lane, Rodley, Leeds LS13 1HU]; *b* 7 Feb 1923; *educ* Leeds GS and Leeds U (LLB); Parly Under Sec Environment 1979–83, Min State Local Govt and Environmental Servs 1983–84; Leeds: City Council Leader 1975–79, Chm Housing Ctee 1967–72, Alderman 1968–73; memb New Towns Commn 1985–, v-pres Internat New Towns Assoc 1985–; dir: Lewis Gp 1993–, Stewart Title UK 1993–, Farr Brokers 1994–, Chm N Hull HAT 1993–; *m* 1948 *Doreen Barbara, dau of Myer Saperia, and has:

1 *Stephen Jeremy [The Hon Stephen Bellow, The Oval, 25a Bracken Park, Scarcroft, Leeds LS14 3HZ]; *b* 1953; *educ* Leeds GS and Leeds Poly; *m* 1974 *Marilyn Stern and has:

(1) *Adam; *b* 1989

(1) *Milena; *b* 1986

1 *Frances Rochelle [The Hon Mrs Taylor, (Balboa), 12 Fern Chase, Scarcroft, Leeds LS14 3JL]; *b* 1951; *m* 1971 *Stephen Taylor and has:

(1) *Daniel Mark; *b* 1973

(2) *Benjamin Paul; *b* 1974

(3) *Edward David; *b* 1976

2 *Linda Carol [The Hon Mrs Porter, 30 Ventnor Drive, London N20 8BP]; *b* 1956; *m* 1st 1976 (*divorce* 1988) Leslie Harris; *m* 2nd 1990 *Steven Porter and by him has:

(1) *Alexander; *b* 1993

(2) *Robert; *b* 1993

(1) *Eleanor; *b* 1992

Lineage: ABRAHAM BELLOW; *m* Leah — and had:

IRWIN NORMAN, *cr* a **Baron**

BELMORE

Arms: Quarterly, 1st and 4th, gu., a saltire arg., in chief a rose or (for CORRY); 2nd and 3rd, sa., a cup arg., with a garland between two laurel branches, all issuing out of the same, vert (for LOWRY). **Crests:** 1 A cock ppr. (for CORRY), 2 A garland of laurel between two branches of the same, ppr. (for LOWRY). **Supporters:** Two tiger cats, guardant, ppr., ducally gorged and chained or. **Motto:** *Virtus semper viridis* ('Virtue is always green'). **Creations:** B. (I) 6 Jan 1781; V. (I) 6 Dec 1789; E. (I) 20 Nov 1797.

THE 8TH EARL BELMORE, Viscount Belmore, and **Baron Belmore of Castlecoole**, Co Fermanagh (John Armar Lowry-Corry) [The Rt Hon The Earl Belmore, The Garden House, Castle Coole, Enniskillen, Co Fermanagh, N Ireland BT74 6JY]; *b* 4 Sept 1951; *s f* 1960; *educ* Lancing and RAC Cirencester; *m* 8 Sept 1984 *Lady Mary Jane Meade, 2nd dau of 6th Earl of Clanwilliam (*qv*), and has issue:

1 +JOHN ARMAR GALBRAITH, *Viscount Corry*; *b* 2 Nov 1985

2 +Montagu Gilford George; *b* 1989

1 *Martha Catherine; *b* 1992

Lineage: JOHN CORRY, of Belfast, a native of Scotland, bought Castlecoole, Co Fermanagh, 1656, High Sheriff Co Fermanagh 1666; *m* Blanch Johnston and *d c* 1683, leaving issue:

Col JAMES CORRY, of Castlecoole, MP Co Fermanagh 1692–1718, High Sheriff 1671, High Sheriff Co Monaghan 1677, *b c* 1634, *m* 1st Feb 1663 Sarah, dau of Oliver Anketell, of Anketell Grove, Co Monaghan, and had, with other issue:

1 JOHN

Col CORRY *m* 2nd 1683 Lucy, dau of Henry Mervyn, of Trillick; *m* 3rd 1692 Elizabeth Harryman, of London, and *d* 1 May 1718

Col JAMES CORRY's only s,

Col JOHN CORRY, of Castlecoole, MP Enniskillen 1711–13 and Co Fermanagh 1719–26, High Sheriff Co Fermanagh 1711, *b* 1666, *m* 7 Feb 1701/2 Sarah, 3rd dau and coheir of William Leslie, of Prospect, Co Antrim, and *d* 1726, leaving issue:

1 Leslie, of Castlecoole, Col Fermanagh Militia, High Sheriff Co Fermanagh 1737, MP Killybegs 1739–41, *b* 1712; *d* unm 1740/1

1 Martha; *b* 1704/5; *m* 1738 her 2nd cousin Capt Edmund LESLIE later CORRY; (took name on succeeding to part of the Corry estates), MP Newtown-Limavady, and *dsps c* 1764

2 SARAH CORRY, *b* 1709; *s* her sister Mary at Castlecoole 1774; *m* 26 July 1733 GALBRAITH LOWRY later LOWRY-CORRY, MP Co Tyrone 1748–68, and *d* 1779, leaving issue (with two er sons who *d* young):

(1) ARMAR, **1st Earl Belmore**

3 Mary; *b* 1710; *m* 1736 her cousin Col Margetson Armar, High Sheriff Co Fermanagh 1742, who *s* Col Leslie Corry at Castlecoole and *dsp* 1773. His widow *s* her husband there and *d* 1774

4 Elizabeth; b 1715; *m* 1st 1751 Archibald Hamilton; *m* 2nd 4 Dec 1754, as his 1st w, her cousin James Leslie, and *d* 1791

Lineage:

JAMES LOWRY or LAURIE (said to have been of the family of Laurie of Maxwelton), emigrated from Scotland in the 17th century, settled at Ballimagory, Co Tyrone, before 1641, and *d* intestate 1665, leaving issue:

JOHN LOWRY, of Ahenis, Co Tyrone, *m* 1st Mary, dau of James Buchanan, and by her had, with other issue:

1 ROBERT LOWRY, of Ahenis, a Commr for Cos Armagh and Tyrone 1698, High Sheriff Co Tyrone 1707–08 and 1719, *m* Anna, dau of Rev John Sinclair, of Holyhill, Co Tyrone, and *d* 1729, having had, with other issue, a 3rd s and eventual heir:

(1) GALBRAITH LOWRY later LOWRY-CORRY, of Ahenis, MP Co Tyrone 1747–68, High Sheriff 1733, High Sheriff Co Monaghan 1743; assumed 1764 on the death of his sister-in-law Martha, wife of Edmund Leslie-Corry, MP, the additional surname and arms of CORRY, *b* 11 July 1706, *m* 26 July 1733 Sarah (*d* 1779), 2nd dau and eventual coheir of John Corry, of Castlecoole (*see* above), and had, with other issue:

1a ARMAR, **1st Earl**

1 Janet; *m* John McLintock and had issue (*see* RATHDONNEL, B)

JOHN LOWRY *m* 2nd Jane, dau of William Hamilton, of Ballyfatton, and by her had further issue. He was present with his second wife at the Siege of Derry, where he *d* 1689

Mr LOWRY-CORRY *d* 28 Dec 1769; his son,

ARMAR LOWRY later LOWRY-CORRY, **1st Earl Belmore**, so *cr* 20 Nov 1797, as also earlier 6 Jan 1781 BARON BELMORE OF CASTLE COOLE, Co Fermanagh, and 6 Dec 1789 VISCOUNT BELMORE (all I); MP Co Tyrone 1769–81, High Sheriff of that Co 1769 and Co Fermanagh 1779, *b* 7 April 1740; *s* his mother at Castlecoole in 1779 and constructed the present house there between 1790 and 1798 to James Wyatt's designs, using Portland stone shipped at vast expense across the Irish Sea; Mark Bence-Jones calls it the most palatial Irish house of the entire late-18th century; from 1951 the NI National Trust has maintained the house, painting it a 'germolene pink' which attracted criticism some years ago from the current earl; *m* 1st 3 Oct 1772 Lady Margaret Butler (*d* April 1775), est dau of 1st Earl of Carrick, and had issue:

1 Galbraith; *b* 1772; *dvp* 1773

2 SOMERSET, **2nd Earl**

1 Juliana; *b* 1775; *d* young

The **1st Earl** *m* 2nd 2 March 1780 (*divorce* 1793) Lady Harriet or Henrietta Hobart, est dau and coheir of 2nd Earl of Buckinghamshire (*qv*), Lord Lt Ireland, and by her had issue an only dau:

2 Louisa Mary Ann Julia Harriet; *b* 1781; *m* 1804 6th Earl of Sandwich (*qv*) and *d* 19 April 1862

The **1st Earl** *m* 3rd 11 March 1794 Mary Anne (*d* 13 Dec 1841), est dau of Sir James Caldwell, 4th Bt, of Castle Caldwell, Co Fermanagh, and *d* 2 Feb 1802

His son,

SOMERSET LOWRY-CORRY, **2nd Earl Belmore**; *b* 11 July 1774; Govr and Custos Rotulorum Co Tyrone, MP 1798–1802, sometime Capt-Gen and Govr-in-Ch Jamaica, Col of the Tyrone Militia, rep I peer; *m* 20 Oct 1800 his cousin Lady Juliana Butler (*d* 22 July 1861), 2nd dau of Earl of Carrick (*qv*), and had issue:

1 ARMAR, **3rd Earl**

2 Henry Thomas, PC, MP Co Tyrone 1825–73, First Lord of the Admiralty; *b* 9 March 1803; *m* 18 March 1830 Lady Harriet Anne Ashley-Cooper (*d* 25 March 1868), 2nd dau of 6th Earl of Shaftesbury (*qv*), and *d* 5 March 1873, having had, with other issue:

(1) Armar Henry; *b* 14 March 1836; *m* 26 Feb 1867 Alice Margaret (*d* 20 June 1932), only dau of Thomas Greg, of Ballymenoch House, Co Down, and *d* 9 Sept 1893, leaving issue:

1a Noel Armar, DSO (1900), Col late cmdg 2nd Bn Gren Guards, hon Brig-Gen 1920, served S Africa 1899–1901 and WW I 1914–15, JP Brecon; *b* 25 Dec 1867; *m* 1st 14 Feb 1895 Rosalind Gertrude (*d* 2 June 1903), only dau of Col Robert Hamilton Lloyd Anstruther, of Hintlesham Hall, Suffolk (*see* ANSTRUTHER, Bt), and had:

1b Armar Valentine, MC, Lt Gren Gds WW I; *b* 25 March 1896; *ka* 12 Sept 1916

1b Rosemary Victoria; *b* 24 May 1897; *m* 24 July 1928 Capt Arthur Wyndham Louis Paget, MC, s of Gen Rt Hon Sir Arthur Henry Fitzroy Paget, PC, GCB, KCVO, of East Kennet Manor, Marlborough, Wilts, and *d* 5 May 1970, leaving issue (*see* ANGLESEY, M)

1a (cont.) Brig-Gen N A Lowry-Corry *m* 2nd 26 July 1904 Hon Clare O'Brien (*d* 21 Sept 1950), 2nd dau of 14th Baron Inchiquin (*qv*), and *d* 23 Aug 1935, having by her had:

2b Montagu William, Capt Gren Guards WW II (wounded), barrister Inner Temple 1933, mem LCC S Paddington 1958–65 and New Westminster CC 1964 (Dep Chm 1964–65); *b* 21 March 1907; *educ* Harrow,;*m* 1st 9 July 1929 (*divorce* 1938) Hon Mary Constance Biddulph, yr dau of 2nd Baron Biddulph (*qv*), and had:

1c *Josephine Clare [Princess Rupert zu Löwenstein, Petersham Lodge, River Lane, Richmond, Surrey TW10 7AG]; *b* 26 Jan 1931; *m* 18 July 1957 *Prince Rupert zu Löwenstein, only son of Prince Leopold zu Lowenstein-Wertheim-Freudenberg, of 209 Coleherne Court, London SW5, and has:

1d *Rudolf Amadeus Josef Karl Ludwig Emmanuel; *b* 17 Nov 1957

2d *Konrad Friedrich Ferdinand Johannes Ottakar Sylvester; *b* 26 Nov 1958

1d *Maria Theodora Marjorie; *b* 11 July 1966

2b (cont.) Capt Montagu Lowry-Corry *m* 2nd 30 Sept 1969 *Jean Trefusis [Mrs Montagu Lowry-Corry, Clover Farm, Shalden, Alton, Hants], widow of Lt-Col Eion James Henry Merry, MC, and dau of Hon Arthur Owen Crichton (*see* ERNE, E), and *d* 16 June 1977

2b *Patricia [Miss Patricia Lowry-Corry, 33 Wynnstay Gardens, Allen St, London W8]; *b* 7 May 1905

2a Oscar Henry; *b* 28 July 1869; *d* unm 24 Nov 1904

3a Sydney Richard; *b* 15 April 1871; *d* 18 April 1873

4a Reginald Charles; *b* 14 June 1875; *m* 9 Aug 1912 Dorothy Cecilia (*d* 10 Feb 1936), widow of Capt Christopher Egerton Balfour, DSO, and dau of Gerald Cecil Stewart Paget (*see* ANGLESEY, M), and *d* 15 Oct 1945, leaving issue:

1b *Faythe; *m* 1st 23 June 1933 (*divorce* 1941) Bernard Clifford Lee-Hutson and has issue; *m* 2nd 25 Jan 1951 *Gerald Rawson Coldstream, son of Francis Menzies Coldstream, of The Corner House, East Blatchington, Seaford, Sussex

2b *Nina Arlette

1a Berta Mary, twin with Oscar; *m* 2 May 1899 Sir Maurice William Ernest de Bunsen, 1st Bt, PC, GCMG, GCVO, CB, and *d* 21 Nov 1954, leaving issue. He *d* 21 Feb 1932

2a Violet Edith; *b* 18 July 1880; *m* 20 July 1904, as his 1st wife, Capt Robert Bingham Brassey, late 17th Lancers, of Heythrop, Chipping Norton, and *d* 9 March 1919, leaving issue (*see* BRASSEY OF APETHORPE, B)

1 Sarah; *d* an infant 1806

The 2nd EARL *d* 18 April 1841; his er s,

ARMAR LOWRY-CORRY, **3rd Earl Belmore**, MP Fermanagh 1823–30, High Sheriff 1832; *b* 28 Dec 1801; *m* 27 May 1834 Emily Louise (*d* 3 Jan 1904), yst dau and coheir of William Shepherd, of Brabourne, Kent, and *d* 17 Dec 1845, having had, with other issue:

1 SOMERSET RICHARD LOWRY-CORRY, **4th Earl Belmore**, PC Ireland (1867), GCMG (1890); Ld Lt and Custos Rotulorum Co Tyrone; JP Cos Fermanagh, Tyrone and Kent; Maj London Irish RV, Capt Fermanagh Militia; *educ* Trin Coll Camb (MA); MRIA; rep I peer 56 years; Parly Under-Sec Home Dept 1866–67, Govr and C-in-C NSW 1867–72; a Ld Justices I; *b* 9 April 1835; *m* 22 Aug 1861 Anne Elizabeth Honoria (*d* 5 Oct 1919), 2nd dau of Capt John Neilson Gladstone, RN, MP, and n of the PM W E Gladstone (*see* GLADSTONE, Bt), and *d* 6 April 1913, having had:

(1) ARMAR LOWRY-CORRY, **5th Earl Belmore**, barrister Inner Temple, DL and JP Co Fermanagh, High Sheriff 1895, JP Co Tyrone, High Sheriff 1901, formerly Capt 3rd Bn Royal Inniskilling Fus, Life Memb Court of Reading U, Memb Rep Body C of I; *b* 5 May 1870; *educ* Winchester and Trin Hall Camb (MA), *d* unm 12 Feb 1948

(2) CECIL LOWRY-CORRY, **6th Earl Belmore**, JP Co Tyrone, High Sheriff 1916, DL and JP Co Fermanagh, High Sheriff 1922, Memb Fermanagh CC, Chm 1943, Chm Enniskillen RDC, Memb Gen Synod C of I, hon Sec Clogher Diocesan Cncl; *b* 20 March 1873; *educ* Wellington, *d* unm 2 March 1949

(3) Ernest; *b* 23 Nov 1874; *educ* Wellington,;*d* 11 March 1912

(1) Theresa; *b* 24 Oct 1862; *d* unm 16 March 1938

(2) Florence; *b* 31 March 1864; *m* 12 Oct 1893 Lt-Col John Henry Eden, late Inspector Constabulary England and Wales, Maj Yorkshire Regt, and *d* 10 May 1943, leaving issue (*see* EDEN, Bt)

(3) Madeline; *b* 6 Nov 1865; *d* unm 30 March 1898

(4) Mary; *b* 5 Aug 1867; *d* unm 5 Oct 1928

(5) Winifred; *b* 19 Aug 1876; *d* unm 19 May 1959

(6) Edith; *b* 26 Aug 1878; *d* unm 25 Oct 1915

(7) Violet; *b* 15 Jun 1881; *d* unm 11 July, 1969

(8) Margaret; *b* 15 July 1883; *d* unm 16 Nov 1975

(9) Dorothy; *b* 6 June 1885; *d* unm 22 March 1967

(10) Kathleen; *b* 28 July 1887; *m* 7 May 1919, as his 2nd w, Brig-Gen Thomas Ward, CMG (*d* 16 Jan 1949), of Brynhir, Criccieth, Caernarvonshire, late Queen's Bays, 2nd son of Joseph Ward, JP, of St Peter's, Kent, and *d* 13 Oct 1972, having had issue:

1a Richard Thomas, MC, Lt The Queen's Bays WW II; *b* 10 Dec 1921; *ka* 20 Sept 1944

1a *Honoria Kathleen; *b* 15 March 1920

2 Armar, Adml; *b* 25 May 1836; *m* 8 Feb 1868 Geraldine (*d* 8 Jan 1905), 5th dau of James King King, MP, of Staunton Park, Hereford, and *d* 1 Aug 1919, having had issue:

(1) Arthur; *b* 21 Feb 1869; *m* 1st 7 Dec 1897 (*divorce* 1905) Kate Elizabeth, dau of Capt James Bullen; *m* 2nd 1913 Wilhelmina Amelia (*d* 24 Feb 1935), dau of August Johns, of Gardena, N Dakota, USA, and *dsp* 28 Nov 1946

(2) Lionel; *b* 9 Feb 1870; *d* 13 Jan 1871

(3) Gerald (Rev), RC priest, T/CF 1914–19, late Lt 2nd Bn Cheshire Regt, *b* 24 Aug 1871; *d* 7 March 1929

(4) Algernon Frederick, *b* 29 June 1874, *d* 15 June 1875

(5) Adrian, Maj RAOC, Lt Roy W Kent Regt, served S Africa 1901–02 and WW I; *b* 11 Feb 1876; *m* 11 Feb 1909 Geraldine (*d* 27 May 1944), 4th dau of William Thomas Hartcup, of Eastwood, Old Catton, and *d* 12 Feb 1921, leaving issue:

1a GALBRAITH ARMAR, **7th Earl**

1a *Doreen Stella; *b* 29 July 1916; 2nd Offr WRNS WW II, granted rank of earl's dau 1951; *m* 6 April 1948 Rev John Gwinnett, MC, BA, CF (*d* 1977), s of John Gwinnett, of Glos, and has:

1b *Adrian John; *b* 5 Jan 1949; *educ* Sherborne; *m* 4 Dec 1971 *Jane Elliot Allen, dau of Jack Allen, of Whetstone, London N3, and has:

1c *Giles Marcus; *b* 16 April 1974

1c *Verity Jano; *b* 8 May 1977

(6) Hubert Armar, Assist DC Uganda, *b* 22 May 1881; *d* 27 March 1927

(7) Bertram; *b* 13 Dec 1883; *d* 26 Feb 1884

(8) Walter, Maj Indian Cavalry, served Somaliland 1914–15 (wounded), WW I 1915–18 and NE Frontier India 1918–19; *b* 6 March 1885; *d* unm 15 Oct 1946

(1) Rosamund Florence; *b* 27 Jan 1873; *d* unm 17 Jan 1932

(2) Muriel; *b* 26 Dec 1877; *m* 4 March 1905 Alexander Wallace Gilmour, son of Capt Wallace Gilmour, RA, and *d* 5 June 1965, leaving issue. He *d* 5 Sept 1946

(3) Evelyn; *b* 12 Nov 1879; *m* 30 April 1907 Charles William O'Conor, only son of Denis O'Conor, MP, and *d* 12 Jul 1963, leaving issue. He *d* 13 May 1963

(4) Ethel Mary; *b* 20 Aug 1882; *d* 27 Jan 1883

3 Frederick Cecil George; *b* 24 June 1839; *d* 12 May 1855

4 Henry William, Col Coldstream Gds, DL, JP and CA Suffolk, Chm Suffolk TAA, MP Co Tyrone 1873–80, MA Trin Coll Camb; *b* 30 June 1845; *m* 21 Sept 1876 Hon Blanche Edith Wood (*d* 21 July 1921), dau of 1st Viscount Halifax (*see* HALIFAX, E), and *d* 6 May 1927, having had issue:

(1) Henry Charles (Sir), ktd 1954, MC, Lt-Col RA WWs I (wounded, MC) and II 1939–42 (prisoner), DL (1946), JP (1931) Suffolk, V-Lt 1957–65, CA W Suffolk, Chm W Suffolk CC 1950–57, Chm Suffolk T&AFA 1947–53; *b* 20 Feb 1887; *educ* Eton; *m* 27 April 1920 Betty Alice Adeline (*d* 1978), dau of Col Douglas James Proby (*see* ABERCORN, D), and *d* 23 Jan 1973, leaving:

1a +Frederick Henry [Frederick Lowry-Corry Esq, Edwardstone Hall, Boxford, Suffolk], memb stock exchange, Lt RN WW II 1945; *b* 23 Dec 1926; *educ* Eton; *m* 3 Dec 1949 *Hon Rosemary Diana Lavinia Plumer, yst dau of 2nd Viscount Plumer (*see* 1940 edn), and has:

1b +Charles Frederick Armar; *b* 29 April 1951; *educ* Eton; *m* 16 Feb 1980 *Elizabeth Jean, twin dau of J W A Andrews, of Alton, and has:

1c +Michael Henry Charles; *b* 24 Nov 1983

2c +Robert Galbraith; *b* 1990

1c *Joanna Elizabeth Louise; *b* 4 May 1982

2c *Angela Rosemary; *b* 1987

2b +James Leopold Vincent; *b* 19 March 1955; *educ* Harrow; *m* 18 Feb 1984 *Judith, yr dau of F A Lodge, of Overtrees, Foxhill, Leeds, Yorks, and has issue:

1c *Charlotte; *b* 1989

2a Armar Douglas (Rev), vicar All Saints' Oakham 1968, late assist curate Christ The Saviour Ealing; *b* 6 Jan 1929; *educ* Eton and Trin Coll Camb (MA)

1a *Elizabeth Margaret; *b* 1 May 1921

2a *Edith; *b* May 1923; *m* 22 Nov 1947 *FM Baron Carver (*qv*) and has issue

(2) Frederick Richard Henry, T/Lt RFA; *b* 13 May 1890; *educ* Trin Coll Camb (BA); *d* 30 Sept 1915 of wounds recd in action in France

(1) Emily Mary; *b* 14 Dec 1882; *m* 1 Feb 1911, as his 2nd wife, Sir Richard Nelson Rycroft, 5th Bt (*qv*), and had issue

(2) Alice Frances Louisa, JP Suffolk; *b* 22 May 1885; *d* unm 8 Aug 1978

The 6th EARL's cousin,

GALBRAITH ARMAR LOWRY-CORRY, **7th Earl Belmore**, DL, JP Co Fermanagh, Maj Roy Inniskilling Fus WW II (wounded); *b* 14 April 1913; *educ* Lancing and RMC Sandhurst; *m* 18 Feb 1939 *Gloria Anthea (*m* 2nd 23 Nov 1963 Col Robert James Thompson Irwin, MC (*d* 1984), Roy Inniskilling Fus, s of Benjamin Hugh Gray Irwin, of Johannesburg, S Africa), dau of Herbert Bryant Harker, of Melbourne, Australia, and *d* 20 July 1960, leaving:

1 JOHN ARMAR LOWRY-CORRY, **8th and present Earl Belmore**

1 *Anthea Geraldine [The Lady Anthea Forde, Seaforde, Co Down, N Ireland]; *b* 16 Feb 1942; *m* 24 April 1965 *Patrick Mathew Desmond Forde, JP, DL, only son of Lt-Col Desmond Charles Forde, DL, of Seaforde, Co Down (*see* BANGOR, V), and has:

(1) *Mathew Galbraith; *b* 8 June 1967

(2) *Charles Patrick; *b* 21 Aug 1972

(3) *Finnian Nicholas; *b* 11 March 1982

(1) *Emily Louise; *b* 1 Feb 1966; *m* 1 July 1995 *Peter Mackie, s of Dennis Mackie, of Lissanouve, Co Antrim

2 *Sarah Lilian; *b* 31 March 1945; *m* 1979 *Gary McNulty and has:

(1) *Katherine; *b* 24 Dec 1979

(2) *Margaret; *b* 13 April 1984

BELOFF

Creation: B. (UK, LP) 1981.

THE BARON BELOFF, of Wolvercote, Co Oxon (Max Beloff) [The Rt Hon The Lord Beloff, Flat 9, 22 Lewes Crescent, Brighton BN2 1GB]; *b* 2 July 1913; *educ* St Paul's and Corpus Christi Coll Oxford (MA, DLitt); assist lecturer history Manchester U 193946, Nuffield Reader Comparative Study Instns Oxford 194656, Gladstone Prof of Govt and Public Admin Oxford 1957–74, Pncpl U Coll Buckingham 1974–79, Fell All Souls 1957–74, Emeritus Fell 1980–, Supernumerary Fell St Antony's Coll Oxford 1975–84, Hon Prof St Andrews 1993–98, Govr Haifa U, Hon LLD: Pittsburgh 1962, Manchester 1989, Hon DCL Bishop's U Canada 1976, Hon Dlitt Bowdoin Coll USA 1976 and Buckingham 1984; served Roy Signals WW II, FBA 1973, FRHistS, FRSA, ktd 1980; author: *Public Order and Popular Disturbances 1660–1714* (1938), *The Foreign Policy of Soviet Russia* (vol I 1947, vol II 1949), *Thomas Jefferson and American Democracy* (1948), *Soviet Policy in the Far East 1944–1951* (1953), *The Age of Absolutism 1660–1815* (1954), *Foreign Policy and the Democratic Process* (1955), *Europe and the Europeans* (1957), *The Great Powers* (1959), *The American Federal Government* (1959), *New Dimensions in Foreign Policy* (1961), *The United States and the Unity of Europe* (1963), *The Balance of Power* (1967), *The Future of British Foreign Policy* (1969), *Imperial Sunset* (vol I 1969, vol II: *Dream of Commonealth 1921–1942*, 1989), *The Intellectual in Politics* (1970), *The Government of the United Kingdom* (with G R Peele, 1980), *Wars and Welfare 1914–1945* (1984), *An Historian in the Twentieth Century* (1992), *Britain and European Union* (1996); *m* 1938 *Helen, dau of Samuel Dobrin, and has:

1 *Michael Jacob, QC (1981) [The Hon Michael Beloff QC, President's Lodgings, Trinity College, Oxford OX1 3BH]; *b* 1942; *educ* Eton and Magdalen Coll Oxford; barrister Gray's Inn 1967 (Bencher 1988), Recorder 1985, Dep High Court Judge 1989–, Judge Court of Appeal Jersey and Guernsey 1996; author: *The Plateglass Universities* (1968), *The Sex Discrimination Act* (1976); *m* 1969 *Judith Mary Arkinstall and has:

(1) *Rupert; *b* 1973

(1) *Natasha; *b* 1976

2 *Jeremy Benjamin [The Hon Jeremy Beloff, Glenwood, Templewood Lane, Farnham Common, Bucks SL2 3HW]; *b* 1943; *educ* Rugby and Oxford; *m* 1973 *Carol Macdonald and has:

(1) *Nicholas; *b* 1975

(2) *Jonathan Max; *b* 1986

(1) *Catherine; *b* 1978

Lineage: SIMON BELOFF; *m* Mary — and had:

MAX, *cr* a **Baron**

BELPER

Arms: Per pale sa. and az. two chevronels engrailed between three cross crosslets fitchée or. **Crest:** In front of rays of the sun ppr. a cubit arm erect, vested bendy of six or and sa., cuffed arg., in the hand a roll of paper ppr. **Supporters:** On either side a leopard ppr., gorged with a collar gemel az., therefrom pendant an escutcheon also az., charged with a cross crosslet fitchée or. **Motto:** *Propositi tenax* ('Firm of purpose'). **Creation:** B. (UK) 29 Aug 1856.

THE 4TH BARON BELPER, of Belper, Co Derby ((Alexander) Ronald George Strutt) [The Rt Hon The Lord Belper, Kingston Hall, Nottingham NG11 0DH]; *b* 23 April 1912; *s* f 1956; *educ* Harrow and RMC Sandhurst, Maj Coldstream Gds WW II (wounded); *m* 15 Nov 1940 (*divorce* 1949) Zara Sophie Kathleen Mary, yr dau of Sir Harry Stapleton Mainwaring, 5th Bt (*qv*), and has issue:

1 +RICHARD HENRY [The Hon Richard Belper, Slaughter Farm, Bourton-on-the-Water, Glos]; *b* 24 Oct 1941; *educ* Harrow and RAC Cirencester; *m* 1st 22 Oct 1966 (*divorce* 1979) Jennifer Vivian, dau of Capt Peter Winser; *m* 2nd 12 May 1980 *Judith Mary, dau of James Rufus Twynam, of Kitemore Ho, Faringdon, Berks, and formerly w of Alexander de Jonge, and has issue by 1st w:

(1) +Michael Henry; *b* 5 Jan 1969

(1) *Henrietta Lavinia; *b* 28 Dec 1970

Lineage: JEDEDIAH STRUTT, of Derby, cotton spinner and inventor of improvements in the stocking frame, ptnr of Sir Richard Arkwright; *b* 1726; 3rd s of William Strutt, of South Normanton; *m* 24 Sept 1765 Elizabeth (*d* May 1774), dau of William Woollat, of Derby, and *d* 7 May 1797, leaving an est s:

WILLIAM STRUTT, of St Helen's House, Derby, DL; *b* 20 July 1756; *m* 12 Jan 1793 Barbara (*d* 18 May 1808), dau of Thomas Evans, of Derby, and *d* 30 Dec 1830, having had issue (with three daus, Elizabeth, Anne and Frances) an only s:

EDWARD STRUTT, **1st Baron Belper**, of Belper, Derby (UK), so *cr* 29 Aug 1856, FRS, Ld Lt Notts, High Sheriff 1850, MA, LLD Camb, PC 1846, Ch Commr Rlwys 1846–48, Chllr Duchy of Lancaster 1852–54, MP (Lib) Derby 1830–48, Arundel 1851–52 and Nottingham 1852–56; *b* 26 Oct 1801, *m* 28 March 1837 Emily (*d* 12 Dec 1890), yst dau of Rt Rev William Otter, DD, Bp Chichester, and had, with other issue:

1 William; *b* 7 May 1838; *d* 19 Jan 1856

2 HENRY, **2nd Baron**

3 Arthur, *b* 3 March 1842, *m* 22 April 1873 Alice Mary Elizabeth (*d* 31 March 1926), 2nd dau of Ambrose Lisle March Phillipps de Lisle, of Garendon Park and Grace Dieu Manor, and *d* 6 Feb 1877, leaving issue:

(1) Edward Lisle, CBE (1919), DSO (1918), Lt-Col Roy Scots, T/Lt-Col and GSO (1) 1916, served S African War 1900–02 (despatches, two medals, six clasps) and WW I 1914–19 (wounded, despatches four times, 1914 Star), Allied High Commr Danzig 1920, Chevalier Order of Leopold of Belgium, Officer Legion of Honour, Officer Star of Romania, Croix de Guerre France and Belgium with four palms, 2ic Mt Everest Expedition 1922, *b* 8 Feb 1874, *m* 10 Oct 1905 Florence Nina (*d* 6 Jan 1969), dau of John Robert Hollond, DL, JP, of Wonham, Bampton, Devon, MP Brighton, and *dsp* 7 July 1948

(1) Laura Mary, *b* 21 April 1875, *m* 15 Dec 1903 Adml Sir Edward Francis Benedict Charlton, KCB, KCMG, JP, and *d* 26 Feb 1909, leaving issue. He *d* 23 Oct 1937

1 Ellen; *m* 22 Oct 1885 George Murray Smith, DL, of Gumley Hall, Market Harborough, and *d* 31 Dec 1940, leaving issue. He *d* 18 April 1919

The 1st BARON *d* 30 June 1880; his eldest surv son,

HENRY STRUTT, **2nd Baron Belper**, JP and DL Notts, JP Leics and Derbys, hon Col, Lt-Col cmdg S Notts Yeo (TD), ADC to HM, Capt Gentlemen-at-Arms 1895–1906, Chm Notts CC and QS, MP E Derbys 1868–74 and Berwick-on-Tweed 1880, LLM Camb, *b* 20 May 1840, *m* 2 May 1874 Lady Margaret Coke (*d* 2 Aug 1922), 6th dau of 2nd Earl of Leicester (*qv*), and had issue:

1 William; *b* 8 Feb 1875; *d* unm 5 Oct 1898

2 Reginald Edward; *b* 12 July 1881; *d* 10 May 1888

3 ALGERNON HENRY, **3rd Baron**

1 Norah; *b* 17 June 1876; *m* 1st 20 Nov 1911 Maj Robert Lee Morris, IA, s of Gen Morris; *m* 2nd 1920 Rev Joseph David Samuel Parry-Evans, CMG, CBE, FKC, KHC, Commdt Roy Army Chaplain's Dept, s of Maj Samuel Evans, of Felixstowe, Suffolk, and *d* 14 Sept 1948. He *d* 29 March 1936

2 Lilian; *b* 31 Oct 1877; *m* 10 Jan 1901 Vernon Austen Malcolmson, MA, JP, of Aston Bury, Herts, and *d* 22 Feb 1956, leaving issue. He *d* 23 Nov 1947

3 Hilda; *b* 25 May 1879; *m* 23 Oct 1906 Charles Israel Loraine Allix, DL, MA, of Swaffham Prior, Cambs, and *d* 28 April 1923, leaving issue. He *d* 13 March 1960

4 Margaret; *b* 4 Feb 1886.

5 Muriel, Sr Commandant ATS; *b* 30 Oct 1890; *m* 30 Nov 1916 Maj Frank Haultain Hornsby, late RFA, er s of Lt-Col Henry Francis Hornsby, and *d* 8 Aug 1976, leaving issue. He *d* 22 May 1935

The 2nd BARON *d* 26 July 1914; his only surviving son,

ALGERNON HENRY STRUTT, **3rd Baron Belper**, DL Notts; *b* 6 May 1883; *m* 1st 26 April 1911 (*divorce* 1922) Hon Eva Isabel Marian Bruce, DBE (1955), JP, 3rd dau of 2nd Baron Aberdare (*qv*), and had issue:

1 (ALEXANDER) RONALD GEORGE STRUTT, **4th and present Baron Belper**

2 Michael, P/O RCAF; *b* 31 Oct 1914; *educ* Harrow and Trin Coll Cambridge; served WW II; *m* 15 July 1939 *Arielle (she *m* 2nd 1947 (*divorce* 1967) Eric Eweson), dau of Joseph Washington Frazer, of Newport, RI, and was *ka* 25 Aug 1942, leaving issue:

(1) +Joseph Raymond Arnold, USN 1962–64; *b* 20 March 1941; *educ* Groton, MIT and U of Illinois

1 Lavinia Mary, LG (1990), CBE (1971); *b* 22 March 1916; Steward at Goodwood 1975–95 (first woman to hold that position), bore the Queen's canopy at Coronation of KING GEORGE VI, Ld Lt W Sussex 1975–95; *m* 27 Jan 1937 16th Duke of Norfolk (*qv*), and *d* 10 Dec 1995, having had issue

The **3rd Baron** *m* 2nd 12 July 1923 *Angela Mariota [Mrs Norman Tollemache, Bentley House, Ipswich, Suffolk] (she *m* 2nd 2 Oct 1958 Rev (Harry) Norman Tollemache (formerly Wrigley), s of Joseph Henry Wrigley), yr dau of Hon Douglas Alfred Tollemache, of The Moat, Ipswich (*see* TOLLEMACHE, B), and *d* 20 March 1956, having by her had issue:

3 +Peter Algernon, MC (1945); *b* 18 June 1924; *educ* Eton; Lt Coldstream Gds 1943–45, chm Tollemache & Cobbold Breweries, dir Britannia Bldg Soc; *m* 10 Jan 1953 *Gay Mary, yr dau of Sir (Frank Guy) Clavering Fison, JP, of Crepping Hall, Stutton, Ipswich, Suffolk, and has issue:

(1) +Henry Clavering Tollemache [Henry Strutt Esq, Stutton Hall, Stutton, Ipswich, Suffolk]; *b* 22 Dec 1953; *educ* Eton; *m* 1979 *Athena, only dau of Jeremy Mas, of Suffolk Ho, Montpelier Row, Twickenham, and has issue:

1a +Algy Jeremy Valentine; *b* 1983

2a +Leo Edward Orlando; *b* 1988

3a +Sam Jedediah; *b* 1993

4a +Daniel; *b* 11May 1998

1a *Scarlett; *b* 1985

(2) +Martin Andrew [Martin Strutt Esq, 100 Woodwarde Rd, London SE22]; *b* 30 Nov 1958; *m* 1985 *Mrs Emma Lithgow, dau of Jeremy John Holt and Mrs Richard Cobbold, of Holbrook Lodge, nr Ipswich, Suffolk, and has issue:

1a +Laurence; *b* 1986

2a +Luke; *b* 1988

(1) *Jane Mariota; *b* 4 June 1956; *m* 19 May 1979 *Dr Murdoch Laing and has issue:

1a *Mungo Peter; *b* 1984

2a *Jash Murdoch; *b* 1987

1a *Tara; *b* 1981

2a *Alice Caitlin; *b* 1982

(2) *Elisabeth (Lizzie); *b* 14 May 1963; *m* 29 July 1995 *Jo(nathan) Burgo, 2nd s of Ian Burgo, of Glen Usk, Gwent, and has

1a *Jack Valentine; *b* 21 Feb 1997

4 (Desmond) Rupert, late Capt Coldstream Guards; *b* 17 June 1926; *educ* Eton; *m* 1st 10 July 1951 (*divorce* 1961) Jean Felicity (*d* 1984), yr dau of Capt Hon Francis Walter Erskine, of 5 Portman Mansions, London W1 (*see* MAR and KELLIE, E), and had issue:

(1) +Jeremy Bevil; *b* 5 Jan 1954; *educ* Eton; *m* 5 Feb 1979 *Petrina, MP, twin dau of Peter Neville Smith, DFC, of Fir Tree Cottage, Henbury, Macclesfield, Cheshire, and has issue:

1a +Toby Charles; *b* 20 Oct 1981

2a +Julian Rupert; *b* 16 July 1983

3a +Rupert Peter; *b* 1987

(2) +Christopher Charles; *b* 22 Aug 1955

4 (cont.) The Hon Rupert Strutt *m* 2nd 11 July 1964 Lucy Gwendolen (*d* 16 Sept 1993), only dau of Maj James William Stirling Home Drummond Moray, DL, JP, of Abercairny, Crieff, Perthshire, and *d* 27 Feb 1993, having by her had further issue:

(3) +Dominick James; *b* 3 May 1966

(4) +James Edward; *b* 8 Nov 1969

BELSTEAD

Arms: Per fess az. and arg. a gentian plant flowered and eradicated ppr., between in chief a mullet and an increscent both or.
Supporters: Two seahorses ppr., each gorged with a collar or, pendent therefrom a portcullis with chains of the last.
Crest: A demi-lion or, supporting a gentian plant as in the arms.
Motto: *Fidelitas vincit* ('Fidelity overcomes').
Creations: Bt. (UK) 22 March 1929, B. (UK) 27 Jan 1938.

THE 2ND BARON BELSTEAD, of Ipswich, Suffolk (Sir John Julian Ganzoni, Bt, PC (1983), JP (Ipswich 1962)) [The Rt Hon The Lord Belstead PC JP, House of Lords, London SW1A 0PW]; *b* 30 Sept 1932; *s* f 1958; *educ* Eton and Ch Ch Oxford (MA 1961); Parly Under-Sec: DES 1970–73, NI 1973–74, Home Office 1979–82, Min of State: FCO 1982–83, MAFF 1983–87, DoE 1987–88, Dep Ldr Ho of Lds 1983–87, Ldr Ho of Lds and Ld Privy Seal 1988–90, Min State NI and Paymaster Gen 1990–92, chm Parole Board 1992–, Ld Lt Suffolk 1994 (DL 1979), chm Asoc Governing Bodies Public Schs 1974–79

Lineage: JULIUS CHARLES GANZONI, formerly of 7 Prince's Gdns, London SW7; *m* Mary Frances, only dau of Maj James Childs, and *d* 20 Jan 1949, aged 96, leaving an only s:

Sir Francis John Childs Ganzoni, 1st Bt, so *cr* 22 March 1929, as also 27 Jan 1938 **1st Baron Belstead**, of Ipswich, Co Suffolk (both UK), ktd 1921, DL and JP Suffolk; *b* 19 Jan 1882; *educ* Tonbridge and Ch Ch Oxford (MA 1906); barrister Inner Temple 1906, MP (C) Ipswich 1914–23 and Oct 1924–37; PPS to PMG 1924; chm: Private Bills Ctee H of C 1923–37, Kitchen Ctee 1932–37, T/Chm Ctees whole Ho 1932–34, Private Bills Ctee Ho Lds 1940, Capt late 4th Bn Suffolk Regt TF WW I, WW II as Lt-Col (Welfare), FRGS; *m* 31 May 1930 Gwendoline Gertrude (*d* 23 Feb 1962), er dau of Arthur Turner, of Ipswich, and *d* 15 Aug 1958, leaving:

1 JOHN JULIAN GANZONI, **2nd and present Baron Belstead**

1 *(Mary) Jill, DL (Suffolk 1988) [The Hon Jill Ganzoni DL, Rivendell, Spring Meadow, Playford, nr Ipswich, Suffolk]; *b* 27 March 1931; memb Gen Synod C of E 1970–95, a Ch Commr 1978–93

Benn

Arms: Arg. two barrulets indented gu. between in chief as many dragon's heads erased and in base a pencil and a pen in saltire ppr. tied with a lace az., pendant therefrom a torteau charged with the figure 1914 or. **Crest:** On a rock a spear erect ppr., flowing therefrom a pennon az. charged with the word Onward, letters or.
Motto: *Deo favente* ('By God's favour').
Creation: Bt (UK) 15 July 1914.

SIR (JAMES) JONATHAN BENN, 4TH BT [Sir Jonathan Benn Bt, Fielden Lodge, Tonbridge Rd, Ightham, nr Sevenoaks, Kent TN15 9AN]; *b* 27 July 1933; *s* f 1984; *educ* Harrow and Clare Coll Cambridge (BA 1957, MA 1961), chm: SCA Pension Tsts 1988–, Reedpack Paper Gp 1988–90, (and ch exec) Reed Paper and Board (UK) 1977–90, J & J Maybank and Reed Tport, pres British Paper and Board Industries Fedn 1985–87; *m* 2 July 1960 *Jennifer Mary, est dau of Wilfred Vivian Howells, OBE, MA, MB, BCh, MRCS, LRCP, of The Ferns, Clun, Shropshire, and has:

1 +ROBERT (ROBIN) ERNEST [Robin Benn Esq, 22 Rue J B Fresez, L-1542 Luxembourg]; *b* 17 Oct 1963; *educ* Judd Sch Tonbridge and Corpus Christi Coll Cambridge (BA 1985, MA 1989); ACA 1989, Réviseur d'Entreprises 1996, pncpl Deloitte & Touche, Luxembourg; *m* 1985 *Sheila Margaret, 2nd dau of Dr Alastair Macleod Blain, of Braco Lodge, Elgin, Moray, and has:

(1) +Alastair Frederick; *b* 28 Feb 1995

(1) *Catriona Jennifer; *b* 8 Sept 1997

1 *Juliet Clare; *b* 2 Feb 1966; *m* 1993 *Simon M Erridge, yr s of Francis Erridge, of Goldhanger, Essex, and has:

(1) *Alison Ann; *b* 8 Sept 1996

Lineage: WILLIAM BENN, quilting mfr, of Hyde, Cheshire; had:

Rev JULIUS BENN; *b c* 1826, Congregational Minister, of London; *m* 13 Feb 1850 Ann (*d* 30 Dec 1890), dau of William Taylor, joiner, of Gerrards, Cheshire, and *d* 4 March 1883, leaving, with other issue:

Sir John Williams Benn, 1st Bt (UK), so *cr* 15 July 1914, JP Essex, JP and DL London; *b* 13 Nov 1850; MP (Lib) St George Div of Tower Hamlets 1892–95 and Devonport 1904–10, memb LCC E Finsbury and Kennington from 1889, Chm LCC 1904–05, dir Benn Bros, publishers, of London, ktd 1906; *m* 1 July 1874 Elizabeth (*d* 18 March 1928), yst dau of John Pickston, of Silver Hill, Hyde, Cheshire, and had:

1 ERNEST JOHN PICKSTONE (Sir), **2nd Bt**

2 WILLIAM WEDGWOOD BENN, *cr* VISCOUNT STANSGATE (*qv*)

3 Christopher Julius; *b* 27 Nov 1878; *d* 29 Dec 1879

4 Oliver Williams, Capt 9th Bn Somerset LI; *b* 11 July 1887; *ka* 6 June 1915

1 Lilian Margaret; *b* 7 Dec 1880; *m* 3 June 1905 Cecil Eldred Hughes, Lt RAF (*d* 19 July 1941), s of Eldred Augustus Hughes, of Lamarsh House, Richmond, and *d* 27 Sept 1953, leaving issue

2 Eliza Irene; *b* 26 Feb 1882; *m* 1st 7 Dec 1912 Arthur Richard Pain, Lt Somerset LI, 2nd s of Arthur Cadlick Pain, JP, of St Catherine's, Frimley (*d* 24 Dec 1940), and had issue; *m* 2nd 29 Dec 1956 Dr Theodore Craig (*d* 8 Nov 1960), s of Rev Dr Robert C Craig, of Edinburgh, and *d* 1974

Sir JOHN *d* 10 April 1922; his est s,

Sir Ernest John Pickstone Benn, 2nd Bt, CBE (1918), High Sheriff London 1932, publisher, dir (sometime chm) Benn Bros, Ernest Benn Ltd, dir (sometime chm) UK Provident Inst, pres Boys' Hostels Assoc and British Export Soc, *b* 25 June 1875, *m* 3 Jan 1903 Gwendolen Dorothy, JP Surrey (*d* 30 Dec 1966), yst dau of Frederick May Andrews, of Edgbaston, and had:

1 JOHN ANDREWS (Sir), **3rd Bt**

2 +(Edward) Glanvill [Maj Glanvill Benn, Crescent Cottage, Aldeburgh, Suffolk IP15 5HW]; *b* 31 Dec 1905; *educ* Harrow and Clare Coll Cambridge; Life Pres Benn Bros Ltd 1976– (chm 1945–75), Maj E Surrey Regt WW II (despatches), Master Stationers' Co 1977 and Newspaper Makers' Co; *m* 4 June 1931 *Beatrice Catherine, MBE, est dau of Claude Newbald, of Lyndhurst, Wallington, Surrey, and has:

(1) +James Glanvill [James Benn Esq, Bovey Cottage, Station Rd, Betchworth, Surrey, RH3 7DF]; *b* 26 July 1944; *educ* Harrow; *m* 1st 6 Oct 1967 Judith Gail, yr dau of Walter Herbert McMinn, of 15 Ingram House, Park Rd, Hampton Wick, Kingston, Surrey; *m* 2nd Susan Mary, yst dau of Vivian Beardsell, of Balcombe, Sussex; *m* 3rd 1990 *Claire Stephanie, dau of Eric Baverstock, of Southampton, and has by his 2nd w:

1a +Peter Glanvill; *b* 1974

2a +Alistair James; *b* 20 March 1975

1a *Suzanna Victoria; *b* 1979

(1) *Elizabeth [Mrs Kenneth Young, The Old Rectory, Buckland, nr Aylesbury, Bucks]; *b* 21 Dec 1936; *m* 16 Feb 1961 *Kenneth Charles Stewart Young, yr son of Andrew Blackwood Stewart Young, of Belhaven, Troon, Ayrshire, and has:

1a *Catherine Ann; *b* 20 Dec 1962

2a Miranda; *b* 1 Dec 1964; *d* 1988

3 (Frederick) Christopher; *b* 6 April 1912; *educ* Harrow and Clare Coll Cambridge (MA); barrister Middle Temple, Capt Intelligence Corps WW II; *m* 11 Sept 1937 *Phyllis, 2nd dau of Edwin Mumford Preston, of Slaugham Park, Sussex, and was *ka* M East 30 Nov 1941, leaving:

(1) +Oliver Preston [Oliver Benn Esq, Hackhurst Stud, Lower Dicker, Hailsham, Sussex]; *b* 13 July 1938; *educ* Eton and Clare Coll Cambridge; late 2nd Lt Intelligence Corps, barrister Middle Temple 1970; *m* 1st 1970 Clarissa Dorothy Jeannette, dau of Guillermo Sergio Santa Cruz y Zerrano, of Weybridge, Surrey, and has:

1a *Belinda Alice Irene; *b* 1970; *m* 1993 *Timothy Francis Farnfield (*see* WIGRAM, Bt)

(1) (cont.) Oliver Benn *m* 2nd July 1996 *Tran da Thao, yr dau of Tran van Trong and Mrs Le Thi Nhi, of Ho Chi Minh City, Vietnam

1 *Elizabeth; *b* 10 May 1907; *m* 30 July 1935 Paul Alfred Shinkman (*d* Dec 1975), 2nd s of Joseph Charles Shinkman, of Grand Rapids, Michigan, and has:

(1) *Paul Glanvill, Assist Prof U of N Carolina, late Capt US Army Medical Service Corps [Prof Paul Shinkman, 617 Shady Lawn Rd, Chapel Hill, NC 27514, USA]; *b* 18 June 1936; *educ* Landon Sch, Harvard (BA 1958) and U of Michigan (MA 1959, PhD 1962); *m* 18 Jan 1969 *Judith Kay, yst dau of Floyd Edwin Barnett, of Charlotte, North Carolina

(2) *Christopher Joseph, late US Marine Corp Res, assist to Dean Student Affrs Cornell; *b* 19 May 1940, *educ* St Albans Sch, Thiel Coll (BA 1962) and Westminster Coll (MA 1965, MEd), U of Pittsburgh (PhD); *m* 28 Aug 1965 *Marsha Ann, BA, est dau of Marshall Axel Friberg, of Jamestown, New York, and has issue

(3) *Bernard Francis [Mr Bernard Benn, 5600 Wood Way, Sumner, Bethesda, Maryland 20816, USA], Lt US Army Signals Corps, served with 1st Field Forces Vietnam, US Army in Vietnam 1967–68 (Bronze Star); *b* 19 Sept 1943; *educ* St Mark's Sch and Dartmouth Coll (BA 1966); *m* 25 May 1974 *Gillian Claire, yr dau of Daniel Crawley, of London SE, and has issue

2 *Julia Wedgwood; *b* 26 Nov 1916; *m* 19 July 1945 Albert Edward Louis Mash, OBE (*d* 1991), s of Thomas Edward Mash, of Mitcham, Surrey, and has:

(1) *John Martin; *b* 3 Aug 1948, *educ* Bradfield

(1) *Jennifer Dorothy; *b* 19 June 1946

Sir ERNEST *d* 1954; his est s,

Sir John Andrews Benn, 3rd Bt, of Old Knoll, Lewisham, *educ* Harrow, Princeton and Gonville and Caius Coll Camb, Chm: ESU 1969, Cincinnati Milling Machines, dir: UK Provident Inst, Technical Devpt Capital, Ernest Benn Ltd and Benn Bros, Maj KOYLI WW II; *b* 28 Jan 1904; *m* 23 July 1929 *Hon Ursula Helen Alers Hankey [The Hon Lady Benn, 15 The Waldrons, Oast Rd, Hurst Green, Oxted, Surrey RH8 9DY], only dau of 1st Baron Hankey (*qv*), and *d* 1984, leaving:

1 Sir JAMES JONATHAN BENN, **4th and present Bt**

2 +Timothy John; *b* 27 Oct 1936; *educ* Harrow, Princeton and Clare Coll Cambridge (MA); late Lt Scots Gds, formerly chm and md Benn Bros Ltd, chm Timothy Benn Publishing Ltd 1983–, Bouverie Publishing 1983–, SE Magazines Ltd, Buckley Press Ltd, Henry Greenwood & Co, Stone & Cox (Publications), Dalesman Publishing; *m* 1st 12 Sept 1959 (*divorce* 1973) Valerie Hamlyn, yr dau of Capt Peter Hamlyn Wilson Davie; *m* 2nd 1973 Mrs Susan Elizabeth Hardingham, only dau of George Hodges; *m* 3rd 1982 *Christina Grace Townsend, dau of W R Hughes, and has issue by 1st w:

(1) +Peter Quentin; *b* 26 Dec 1961

(2) +William Justin; *b* 4 April 1964

(3) +Thomas Hamlyn; *b* 15 Feb 1966; *m* 1988 *Yvette, yr dau of G B Wilson, of Buckfastleigh, Devon, and has:

1a *Louella; *b* 1986

2a *Charlotte; *b* 1989

3a *Jemima Jaye; *b* 1993

1 *Susan Paschal [Mrs Michael Compton, Michaelmas Lodge, Limpsfield, Surrey]; *b* 20 April 1930; *m* 4 Sept 1952 *Michael Graeme Compton, er s of Joseph Neild Compton, OBE, of Sheffield, and has:

(1) *Josephine; *b* 1953

(2) *Ann; *b* 1956

2 *Christina Frances; *b* 1948; *m* 1976 *J Andrew R Wilton and has:

(1) *Henry; *b* 1979

3 *Marigold Margaret; *b* 1950

BENNETT

Arms: Gu., a cross moline between three demi-lions rampant or. **Crest:** In front of a lion rampant gu., charged on the shoulder with a cross moline arg., a scaling ladder fesswise or. **Motto:** *Servir le roy* ('To serve the King'). **Creation:** Bt (UK) 31 July 1929.

SIR RONALD WILFRID MURDOCH BENNETT, 3RD BT, of Kirklington, Co Nottingham [Sir Ronald Bennett Bt, 23 rue de Rive, 1260 Nyon, Switzerland]; *b* 25 March 1930; *s f* 1952; *educ* Wellington and Trin Coll Oxford; Lt RA; *m* 1st 16 May 1953 (*divorce* 1964) Audrey Rose-Marie Patricia, only dau of Maj A L J H Aubépin, of Co Mayo; *m* 2nd 1968 *Anne, dau of Leslie George Tooker, and has issue by 1st w:

1 *Anne-Marie Julia; *b* 30 Oct 1954; *m* 1973 *Stephen Hickman
2 *Georgina Marion; *b* 16 May 1956

Lineage: EDWARD BENNETT; *b* Manchester 19 April 1840; *m* 15 Jan 1868 Eliza Ann, dau of John Chapple, and *d* 20 Dec 1888, leaving, with three daus:

Sir Albert James Bennett, 1st Bt (UK), so *cr* 31 July 1929, JP, MP (Lib) Mansfield 1922–23 and (U) Nottingham Central 1924–30, chm and dir of various industrial and mining cos, memb Mechanical Tport Bd War Office and Leather Control Bd, Controller Propaganda Centl and S America WW I 1914–19; *b* 17 Sept 1872; *m* 1st 15 Dec 1896 (*divorce* 1938) Caroline Carleton (*d* 17 June 1945), dau of Jacob Backus, of Lima, Peru, and had:

1 (CHARLES) WILFRID (Sir), **2nd Bt**
2 Frank Carleton, Lt RN; *b* 28 Sept 1900; *m* 20 March 1923 Mariella, dau of Algernon Douglas-Pennant (*see* PENRHYN, B), and had issue:
(1) Michael; *b* 15 Feb 1924; *m* 7 June 1952 *Janet Hazel Margaret [Mrs Michael Bennett, 70 Albert Hall Mansions, London SW7], est dau of Brig Edward Joseph Todhunter, TD, JP, of The Glebe House, Great Bedwyn, Wilts, and *d* 1987, having had issue:
1a +MARK EDWARD FRANCIS; *b* 5 April 1960; heir presumptive
1a *Caroline Mariella Carleton; *b* 20 March 1954
2a *Victoria Serena; *b* 1 Feb 1957
(2) David, Coldstream Gds 1945–57; *b* 14 Sept 1927; *educ* Radley; *m* 28 Aug 1959 *Hilary Sheridan [Mrs David Bennett, The Gate House, Wing, Leighton Buzzard, Beds], dau of Bernard F Clarke, and *d* 1988, having had issue:
1a +Algernon James; *b* 13 Jan 1962
1a *Sarah Elisabeth; *b* 11 Sept 1967
1 *(Margaret) Audrey; *b* 5 March 1904; *m* 22 June 1928 Douglas Haultain Phillips (*d* May 1965), 2nd son of Hon Sir William Watkin Phillips, and has issue:
(1) *Susan; *b* 1929; *m* 1954 *Timothy Ernle Gilpin and has issue:
1a *Joanna Clare; *b* 1955
2a *Henrietta Haultain; *b* 1957
(2) *Caroline Louise; *b* 1931

Sir Albert *m* 2nd 28 May 1938 *Leopoldine, dau of Leopold Armata, of Vienna, and *d* 14 Dec 1945, having by her had issue:

3 +Peter; *b* 18 Aug 1938; *educ* Charterhouse, Pembroke Coll Cambridge and Wharton Business Sch Philadelphia; late 2nd Lt The Green Howards; *m* 1 April 1966 *Monique Christine, est dau of Amade Monsempès, of St Maur, Des Fossés, Seine, France

His eldest son

Sir (Charles) Wilfrid Bennett, 2nd Bt, TD, Lt-Col Sherwood Rangers Yeo, Lt Res of Offrs 9th Lancers, served WWs I 1916–19 and II (despatches), barrister Inner Temple 1924, Metropolitan Police Court Magistrate 1946–52; *b* 15 March 1898; *m* 3 June 1927 (Agnes) Marion, OBE (1953), dau of James Somervell, DL, JP, of Sorn Castle, Ayrshire, and *d* 25 April 1952, leaving:

1 Sir RONALD WILFRED MURDOCH BENNETT, **3rd and present Bt**
1 *Anne MBE (1996) [Mrs Conrad Voss-Bark MBE, Lyd Cottage, Leat Rd, Lifton, Devon PL16 0AE]; *b* 7 Oct 1928; *m* 1st 21 Nov 1961 Gerald Norman Fox-Edwards, s of Norman Fox-Edwards, of High Meadow, nr Bridgnorth, Salop; *m* 2nd 1974 *Conrad Lyddon Voss-Bark and has by her 1st husb:
(1) *Adam; *b* 13 July 1962
(1) *Jane; *b* 23 April 1964

BERESFORD-PEIRSE

Arms: Quarterly, 1st and 4th, azure a ducal coronet between three cross-crosslets fitchée or (for PEIRSE); 2nd and 3rd, argent semée of cross-crosslets fitchée three fleurs-de-lys two and one sable within a bordure wavy ermines (for BERESFORD). **Crests:** 1 A cross-crosslet fitchée or surmounted with a mural crown gules (for PEIRSE), 2 Out of a naval crown or a dragon's head per fess wavy argent and gules, the lower part of the neck tranfixed by a broken tilting-spear in bend sinister, and in the mouth the remaining part of the spear, point upwards, or (for BERESFORD). **Mottoes:** *Non sine pulvere palma* ('The palm is not won without getting one's hands dirty') (for PEIRSE), *Nil nisi cruce* ('Nothing is achievable unless with the cross') (for BERESFORD). **Creation:** Bt. (UK) 21 May 1814.

SIR HENRY GRANT DE LA POER BERESFORD-PEIRSE, 6TH BT, of Bagnall, Co Waterford [Sir Henry Beresford-Peirse Bt, 34 Cadogan Sq, London SW1X 0JL]; *b* 7 Feb 1933; *s f* 1972; *educ* Eton and Ontario Ag Coll Canada; late Lt Scots Gds; *m* 13 Aug 1966 *Jadranka, dau of Ivan Njers, of Zagreb, Yugoslavia, and has issue:

1 +HENRY NJERS DE LA POER; *b* 25 March 1969; *educ* Harrow
2 +John; *b* 27 June 1973

Lineage: The 1st MARQUESS OF WATERFORD (*qv*) had an illegitimate s:

Sir John de la Poer Beresford, 1st Bt (UK), so *cr* 21 May 1814, KCB, GCH, KTS, cmded Portuguese Forces Peninsula War, Adml the White, MP; *m* 1st May 1809 Mary (*d* July 1813), dau of Capt Anthony James Pye Molloy, RN, and had issue:

1 **Sir George de la Poer Beresford, 2nd Bt**, Maj; *b* 1 March 1811; *m* 1 March 1846 Elizabeth (*d* 23 Dec 1898), 2nd dau of Davis Lucas, of Clontibret, Co Monaghan, and Glenalough, Co Galway, and had issue:
(1) John Edward Francis de la Poer; *b* 23 June 1851; *d* 1854
(2) William Carr de la Poer; *b* 1858; *d* 14 May 1880
(1) Mary; *d* 1847
(2) Marcia Mary Ann Harriet Wilhelmina de la Poer; *m* 23 June 1875 Capt Francis Colebrooke Beresford-Drummond (*d* 9 April 1926), 7th Dragoon Gds (*see* PERTH, E), and *dsp* 29 June 1908

Sir John *m* 2nd 17 Aug 1815 Harriet Elizabeth (*d* 28 Feb 1825), 3rd dau of Henry Peirse, of Bedale, and by her had issue:

2 Henry William de la Poer, of Bedale and Hutton Bonville, Yorks; *b* 27 Sept 1820; *m* 2 March 1848 Henrietta Anne Theodosia (*d* 28 Oct 1921), only dau of Rev Hon Thomas Monson (*see* MONSON, B), and *d* 24 July 1859, leaving, with other issue:
(1) HENRY MONSON DE LA POER (Sir), **3rd Bt**
(2) William John de la Poer, Lt-Col Berks Regt; *b* 8 Nov 1852; *m* 22 Feb 1887 Mary (*d* 27 Nov 1939), dau of Thomas Chambers, of Aberfoyle, Londonderry, and *d* 1 Sept 1917, having had issue:
1a Noel Monson de la Poer (Sir), KBE (1941), CB (1943), DSO (1918), Lt-Gen, Col Cmdt RA 1944, served WW I Mesopotamia, France and Belguim (despatches), Instr Sr Offrs Sch Belgium 1937–38, Brig cmdg RA Southern Command India 1938–39, Brig RAGHQ Middle East 1940, Maj-Gen cmdg 4th Indian Div 1940–41, Cdr Western Desert Force, GOC Sudan 1941, Lt-Gen cmdg 15th Indian Corps 1942, COC-in-C S Army India 1942–45, Welfare-Gen India Cmd 1945–46, ret 1947, ADC to HM GEORGE VI 1939–40; *b* 22 Dec 1887; *educ* Wellington and RMA Woolwich; *m* 1st 11 Dec 1912 (*divorce* 1925) Hazel Marjorie, dau of J A Cochrane; *m* 2nd 22 Dec 1925 Jean (*d* 10 May 1926), only child of Surg-Capt Robert Dundonald Jameson, CMG, RN; *m* 3rd 27 July 1929 Katherine Camilla, VAD, Kaisar-i-Hind medal, dau of Col James Morris Colquhoun Colvin, VC, and *dsp* 14 Jan 1953
2a Thomas Chambers de la Poer, Lt IA; *b* 9 Oct 1891; *d* unm 5 Nov 1911
(3) Windham de la Poer (Rev), Rector Bedale Yorks 1899–1931, Hon Canon Ripon 1921; *b* 1 Nov 1858; *educ* Keble Coll Oxford (MA); *m* 17 July Ethel Milman Proctor, Order Queen Elisabeth Belguim (*d* 1 Dec 1948), only dau of William Proctor Baker, and *d* 11 Sept 1940, having had issue:

1a Arthur Cecil Proctor de la Poer, MBE (1919), FLAS, Capt 7th Bn Northumberland Fus (TA) WW I (wounded), Head Agent Duke Northumberland 1929–62, FLAS; *b* 20 Oct 1890; *educ* Eton and BNC Oxford; *m* 29 June 1916 Gertrude Ann Ormonde (*d* 16 Jan 1974), yr dau of Maj Henry Wallis Prior Wandesforde, JP, of Kirklington Hall, Yorks, and *d* 12 June 1970, leaving:

1b +Michael Wandesforde de la Poer [Michael Beresford-Peirse Esq, Padgepool House, Wooler, Northumberland NE71 6BD]; *b* 19 April 1917; *educ* Lancing; farmer; *m* 10 June 1944 Joyce Franklin (*d* 1 March 1997), yr dau of Philip Hope Percival, of Kenya, and has:

1c *Judith Anne Vivian [Mrs James Kennedy, Dunlossit Estate, Ballygrant, Isle of Islay, Argyll PA45 7QL]; *b* 7 Oct 1948; *m* 1980 *James Stephen Bingham Kennedy and has:

1d *Thomas James Peirse; *b* 1984

1d *Clare Louise; *b* 1982

2c *Susan Alice Prior [Mrs Richard Margesson, 27 Bridge Rd, Welwyn Garden City, Herts AL8 6UG]; *b* 20 Aug 1950; *m* 1st 1975 (*divorce* 1982) Phillip Hamilton Newman; *m* 2nd 1983 *Richard William Margesson, s of Maj E C Margesson (*see* HAGART-ALEXANDER, Bt), and has:

1d *Lucy Emma Alexander; *b* 1986

2b +Robert Henry Windham de la Poer (Rev), OBE (1963) [The Rev Robert Beresford-Peirse OBE, 30 Burt St, Albany 6330, W Australia], Hon Assist St John's Ch Albany, Dist Offr, Colonial CS N Borneo, ret 1964, F/Lt RAF WW II; *b* 2 June 1922; *educ* Eton; *m* 1st 7 Aug 1943 Margaret (Peggy) (*d* 25 Nov 1972), yr dau of Edward Giles, and has issue:

1c +Ian Arthur de la Poer [Ian Beresford-Peirse Esq, 1/10 Quinton Road, Manly, NSW, Australia]; *b* 31 Oct 1944; *educ* Tabley Ho Sch; *m* 31 Aug 1968 *Janice Patricia, SRN, SCM, er dau of Lt-Cdr Lawrence Edward Murphy, RANR, and has issue:

1d +Giles Windham de la Poer; *b* 5 Nov 1969

2d +Angus Arthur de la Poer; *b* 1971

3d +Digby John de la Poer; *b* 1975

1c *Patricia Margaret; *b* 25 Aug 1950; *m* 1972 *Richard Stuart Callender, of Adelaide, S Australia, and has issue:

1d *Ian Stuart; *b* 1974

2d *Fiona Margaret; *b* 1978

2b (cont.) The Rev Robert Beresford-Peirse *m* 2nd 1974 *Dorothy Maud, dau of Percy Donald Beard, of Melbourne

1b *Anne Ethel Mary [Mrs Peter Lowe, Tamerton, Upton Lovell, Warminster, Wilts], Jr Cdr ATS WW II; *b* 3 Dec 1919; *m* 14 Jan 1942 *Col Peter Anthony Lowe, late RA, only s of Col Sydney Joseph Lowe, DSO, OBE, and has issue:

1c *David Michael Peirse, Capt RHA, Aden Protectorate 1965–67, Lt-Col RA; *b* 22 March 1944; *educ* Sherborne and RMA Sandhurst; *m* 1 Jan 1968 *Catherine Lily-Mare, widow of Capt John Alec Fleming, RA, and dau of Leonard Arthur Peek, and has issue:

1d *Peter David; *b* 1 March 1969

2c *Michael Peter; *b* 12 Aug 1949; *educ* Sherborne and U of Pennsylvania; *m* 1st 1971 (*divorce* 1984) Rorie, dau of G K Waters, of Wayman, Pa.; *m* 2nd 1984 *Sheila Zaha, of Bensalem, Pa.

1c *Elizabeth Anne; *b* 27 March 1948; *m* 1970 *Richard George Goodman and has issue:

1d *Thomas Richard; *b* 1978

2d *James Anthony (twin); *b* 1978

2a Raymond Windham de la Poer, Maj RAOC, Lt 2nd Life Gds Res Regt, WWs I and II; *b* 4 July 1896; *educ* Eton; *m* 1st 3 July 1923 Aileen Phyllis (*d* 2 April 1944), yst dau of Lt-Col Sir William Thomlinson, DL, JP, and had issue:

1b John Raymond de la Poer, 2nd Lt KRRC WW II; *b* 14 Aug 1924; accidentally *kas* March 1944

2a (cont.) Maj Raymond Beresford-Peirse *m* 2nd 28 Feb 1945 Suzanne Ashley (*d* 5 Oct 1967), widow of Sandys Stewart Macaskie (by whom she had previous issue; *see* STUART-FORBES, Bt) and yst dau of Lt-Col Samuel Fleming, and *d* 1 March 1971

1a Mary Ethel; *b* 10 June 1893; *m* 12 Oct 1921 Rev Ronald Hartley (*d* 21 Dec 1945), Rector Spennithorne, Yorks, s of Thomas Hartley, of Armathwaite Hall, nr Keswick, Cumberland

(1) Charlotte Grace; *m* 8 Oct 1874 Capt Maximillian Dudley Digges Dallson, Scots Gds. (*k* Sudan War 20 March 1885), and *d* 17 Feb 1928, having had issue

3 John George de la Poer (Rev), MA, Rector Bedale, Yorks; *b* 28 Sept 1821; *m* 3 Feb 1846 Hon Caroline Amelia (*d* 23 May 1911), yst dau of 1st Baron Denman (*qv*), and *d* 17 July 1899, leaving, with other issue:

(1) John Peirse de la Poer, Lt S Wales Bdrs; *b* 2 Dec 1846; *m* 25 Aug 1881 Mary Elizabeth Thomasina (*d* 24 March 1926), dau of Col Henry Stewart Beresford Bruce, of Ballyscullion House, Co Londonderry (*see* BRUCE, Bt, of Downhill), and *d* 30 Oct 1902, leaving issue:

1a George Wilfred Bruce de la Poer, Capt Roy Canadian Regt; *b* 1888; *m* 1921 Louisa Barbara (*m* 2nd 19– Ralph Jones Coles (*d* 1969)), er dau of Jacob Frederick Beck, and *d* 30 March 1931, leaving issue:

1b +John George; *b* 12 July 1923; *m* 1947 *Edith Joan, dau of Henry Thomas John Mellaby, and had issue:

1c +John Henry; *b* 1948; *m* 1971 *Meredith Jean, dau of Murray Victor Jones

2c +Peter Bruce; *b* 1950; *m* 1972 *Julianne La Far, dau of Julian La Far Smith

1c *Diane Louise; *b* 1949; *m* 1972 *Glen Churchill

2c *Cynthia Joan; *b* 1950

2b +James Francis; *b* 29 Sept 1925; *m* 19– *—

1b *Mary Isabel; *b* 1921; *m* 19– *Robert Campbell Moreland and has issue:

1c *George Alexander; *b* 1947; *m* 1969 *Marilyn Christine dau of William Reginald Lower

2c *David Beresford; *b* 1951; *m* 1973 *Leslie Michelle, dau of George Franklin Bowles

1a Mary Caroline Helen

2a Marion Evelyn Jane Alexander; *m* 21 Oct 1914 Alban Coore (*d* 31 March 1950), of Scruton Hall, Bedale, Yorks, er s of Rev Alfred Thomas Coore, and *d* 14 Feb 1953

(2) Charles Windham de la Poer, Lt RN, Capt Mexican Navy; *b* 2 June 1858; *m* 27 Aug 1891 Mary (*m* 2nd 27 June 1906 John Barton Hunt), dau of John Warrington Rogers, KC, of Brighton, Melbourne, and *d* 1896, leaving issue:

1a Charles Zaragoza de la Poer, Lt Northampton Regt WW I; *b* 28 March 1893; *ka* 9 May 1915

1a Mary Caroline Laura (Cara); *m* 20 Jan 1917 Capt Arthur Douglas McKinstry, Rifle Bde, s of Col A W McKinstry

(3) Henry William de la Poer (Rev), Indian Marine, served Egypt 1882 (medal and star), Sudan 1885 (clasp); *b* 27 April 1862; *m* 1916 Constance Grace (*d* 1961), dau of James McLaurin, JP, of Verulam, Natal, and *d* 12 Jan 1932 leaving issue:

1a +Alfred de la Poer [The Rev Canon Alfred Beresford, Braehead House, Auburn Rd, Kenilworth, 7700 Cape, S Africa]; *b* 18 Dec 1919; RN WW II, Hon Canon St John's Cathedral Umtata

1a Annie; *b* 10 March 1917; *m* 1942 Reginald Mactory of Durban (*d* 1994) and *d* 1961 leaving:

1b *Michael Denmon; *b* 1943; *m* 1977 *Isabella Emmerentia, dau of Gerrit Viviers, of Bonnievale, Cape, S Africa

1b Maureen Frances; *b* 1949; *m* 1974 *David Peter Donaldson and *d* 1980, leaving

1c *Warren David; *b* 1977

(4) Walter Vevers de la Poer (Rev), MA Oxon, A/Chaplain Forces Natal 1902–05; *b* 22 June 1864; *m* 3 Sept 1902 Eleanor Mary (*d* 17 March 1944), dau of William Robert Staveley of Harrogate, Yorks, and *d* 7 Dec 1908, leaving:

1a Charles Denman de la Poer; *b* 10 Aug 1906; *educ* Clifton and Worcester Coll Oxford (MA 1934); *m* 29 Dec 1950 *Pamela Croot [Mrs Charles Beresford, 50 Ryan Court, Whitecliff Mill St, Blandford Forum, Dorset DT11 7DQ], dau of Rev Frank Stone, MC, Vicar Waterloo, Liverpool, and *d* 29 Aug 1990, leaving:

1b +Marcus John de la Poer [Marcus Beresford Esq, 23 Temple St, Oxford]; *b* 5 Nov 1954; *educ* Clifton and Balliol Coll, Oxford (BA)

1b *Julia Caroline [Mrs Simon Amos, 27 Beckhampton Rd, Bath, Avon]; *b* 28 Oct 1951; *m* 1979 Simon Mark Amos (*d* 10 May 1987), s of Edward Amos of Blunham, Beds, and has:

1c *Rosemary Cecilia; *b* 1 July 1984

2a Marcus Walter de la Poer, assist master Rugby 1931–69, RNVR WW II; *b* 9 April 1909 (posthumous); *educ* Clifton and Merton Coll Oxford (BA 1932, BMus 1939, MA 1946); *m* 28 Aug 1942 *Patricia Muriel (*d* 14 Dec 1992), dau of Charles Reginald Fox, of Plymouth, and *d* 5 Oct 1995 leaving:

1b +Charles Richard de la Poer [Dr Charles Beresford, Barn Hall, The Rideaway, Hemingford Abbots, Cambs PE18 9AG]; *b* 17 Oct 1943; *educ* Clifton, Gonville and Caius Coll Cambridge (BA 1965, MA 1969), Reading U (Dip Ed 1966) and London U (PhD), Educ Devt Consultant; *m* 1 April 1967 *Tessa Rosemary, dau of Henry William Dean, of Cambridge, and has:

1c +John Charles de la Poer [John Beresford Esq, c/o Barn Hall, The Rideaway, Hemingford Abbots, Cambs PE18 9AG]; *b* 21 Sept 1973; *educ* The Leys Sch Cambridge

1c *Fiona Carolyn [Mrs Fiona Beardall, 2 Hall Court, Botley Rd, Shedfield, Hants SO32 2HL]; *b* 14 Sept 1969; *educ* Heriott Watt U, Edinburgh (BA 1993); *m* 9 Sept 1995 *Lt Cdr Michael John Dodson Beardall, RN, s of Kenneth Beardall, of Gerrards Cross, Bucks

2b +Peter Marcus de la Poer (Rev) [The Rev Peter Beresford, The Vicarage, Barby, Rugby, Warwicks]; *b* 20 April 1949; *educ* Cranmer Hall, Durham U; *m* 15 Sept 1979 *Charlotte Frances Hester, er dau of Rev John Grenfell McClintock, MC, and has:

1c *Helen Caroline; *b* 15 June 1981

2c *Elizabeth Joy; *b* 22 Sept 1985

1a Eleanor Caroline Frederica; *b* 19 June 1903; *d* Sept 1990

(1) Caroline Theodosia; *m* 3 Dec 1866 Thomas Hood Cockburn-Hood and *dsp* 7 June 1915, leaving issue. He *d* 1889

(2) Marion Harriet

(3) Gertrude Georgine; *m* 19 April 1876 Rev John Cockburn-Hood (*d* 13 Aug 1902), Vicar Kirkby Fleetham, Yorks, and *d* 1 Dec 1941, leaving issue

(4) Frances Anne; *m* 8 Aug 1888 Rev Edgar Carr (*d* 6 Jan 1911), Rector Kirby Wiske,Thirsk, and *d* 7 Feb 1936, leaving issue

(5) Elizabeth Margaret; *m* 31 Jan 1877 Rev Ernest Henry Kellett Long (*d* 17 May 1920), Rector Newton Flotman, Norwich, s of Robert Kellett Long, of Dunston Hall, Norfolk, and *d* Feb 1942, leaving issue

(6) Catherine Emily; *m* 1 Sept 1894 Rev Joseph Frederick Griffiths, Vicar Mears Ashby, Northants, and *d* 13 May 1925 leaving issue

1 Harriet Charlotte; *m* 12 June 1843 Rev Anthony Hammond and *d* 1893, leaving issue

2 Georgiana; *m* 23 July 1842 Rt Rev Reginald Courtenay (*d* 13 April 1906), Bp Kingston, n of 10th Earl of Devon (*qv*), and *d* 7 Sept 1870, leaving issue

3 Marianne Catherine Emily; *m* 1 March 1849 Lt- Gen Sir Charles Ash Windham (*d* 2 Feb 1870), KCB, and *d* 14 April 1865, leaving issue

Sir John *m* 3rd 26 May 1836 Amelia (*d* 17 Dec 1862), widow of Samuel Peach and 2nd dau of James Baille, and *d* 2 Oct 1844

Sir GEORGE *d* 11 Feb 1873; his nephew,

Sir Henry Monson de la Poer Beresford-Peirse, 3rd Bt, DL, JP, CC NR Yorks; *b* 25 Sept 1850; *m* 1st 11 Nov 1873 Lady Adelaide Mary Lucy Bernard (*d* 29 Sept 1884), 5th dau of 3rd Earl of Bandon (*see* 1970 edn), and had issue:

1 HENRY BERNARD De La POER (Sir), **4th Bt**

2 Richard Windham de la Poer (Rev), Vicar Christ Church, Lancaster Gate, Preb Portpool St Paul's, RD Paddington 1930, Vicar St John, Middlesbrough; *b*

6 Aug 1876; *educ* Eton and Trin Coll Oxford (BA 1899, MA 1903); *m* 1st 21 July 1910 Lady Lillian Katherine Campbell (*d* 2 Jan 1918), 3rd dau of 3rd Earl Cawdor (*qv*), and had issue:

(1) Francis Campbell de la Poer, G/Capt RAF WW II, dir Everett Edgecumbe & Co; *b* 26 April 1911; *educ* Eton, RAF Coll Cranwell and RAF Staff Coll; *m* 1st 1 Aug 1936 (*divorce* 1957) Lady Katharine Lillian Edgecumbe, dau of 6th Earl of Mount Edgecumbe (*qv*), and had issue:

1a Jeremy Edgecumbe de la Poer; *b* 7 Sept 1937; *d* 16 Feb 1940

1a *Susan Katherine; *b* 7 Sept 1940; *m* 1972 *John Miles Bird and has issue:

1b *Tiffany; *b* 1973

2a *Philippa Jane; *b* 4 April 1944; *m* 1970 *Nigel Hope

(1) (cont.) Francis Beresford-Peirse *m* 2nd 1958 *Kathleen Graham, dau of Charles Machattio, and *d* 1986

(2) James; *b* 11 Feb, *d* 12 Feb 1914

(1) *Sybil Adelaide, LRAM, OBE [Miss Sybil Beresford-Peirse OBE, 6 Queensdale Walk, London W11 4QQ]; *b* 9 Aug 1912

(2) *Barbara; *b* 30 Aug 1915; *m* 27 April 1942 (*divorce* 1956) Barry Martin Baker, RA, yr s of Harold John Baker, of Clevedon, and has issue:

1a *Janet Bridget; *b* 24 Feb 1943; *m* 19– *Thomas Banks

2a *Katherine Elizabeth; *b* 1 Dec 1946; *m* 19– *David Phillips

(3) *Lilian Bridget [Mrs Godfrey Mapplebeck, Bryher, West Broyle Drive, Chichester, Sussex]; *b* 1 Jan 1918; *m* 9 May 1945 Godfrey John Mapplebeck, OBE, MC (*d* 1991), yst s of William Mapplebeck, and has issue:

1a +Anthony Peirse; *b* 25 Oct 1946; *educ* Tonbridge and St Catharine's Coll Cambridge

1a *Althea Rosamund Louise; *b* 28 April 1951

2a *Selina Bridget Lucy; *b* 28 April 1960

2 (cont.) Richard Beresford-Peirse *m* 2nd 4 Sept 1924 Katherine Mabel Helen (*d* 25 Jan 1974), er dau of William James Yorke Scarlett, of Fyfield House, Andover, and *d* 13 March 1952

3 Evelyn Francis de la Poer, Capt Yorkshire Regt (T); *b* 3 Sept 1877; *educ* Eton and Downton Coll; *m* 1st 30 April 1912 Marian Annette Owen (*d* 29 Feb 1944), yst dau of Rev Walter Charles Edward Kynaston; *m* 2nd 10 Jan 1946 Elfa Oliver Kynaston, dau of James Loftus Owen, and *dsp* 9 March 1953

4 Ernest Arthur de la Poer; *b* 2 Oct 1879; *educ* Eton and Trin Coll Oxford; *d* unm 16 May 1961

5 John William de la Poer (Rev), Assist Priest St Augustine's Hull, Hon Chaplain to Bp Kimberley, Assist Priest Cathedral 1915–36, T/CF 4th Cl 1918; *b* 12 June 1883; *educ* Eton and Lichfield Theological Coll; *d* unm 31 Jan 1956

1 Sybil Georgiana Mary; *b* 13 Oct 1878; *d* 9 Dec 1893

2 Ethel Mary; *b* 18 May 1881

Sir Henry *m* 2nd 23 Jan 1886 Henrietta, OBE (*d* 1 Nov 1926), only dau of Sir Matthew Smith Dodsworth, 4th Bt (*see* SMITH-DODSWORTH, Bt, of Newland Park), and by her had issue:

3 Dorothy Harriet Julia; *b* 3 July 1894; *m* 8 June 1922 Cdr Geoffrey Thomas Wright, RN (ret), and had issue

Sir HENRY *d* 8 July 1926; his est son,

Sir Henry Bernard de la Poer Beresford-Peirse, 4th Bt, DSO (1900), JP NR Yorks; *educ* Eton and Magdalen Coll Oxford (BA 1899), Hon Maj, Lt Yorks Hus Imp Yeo Boer War 1900–01 (despatches twice); *b* 9 Jan 1875; *m* 7 July 1904 Lady Mabel Marjorie Campbell (*d* 13 Jan 1966 aged 89), JP NR Yorks, 2nd dau of 3rd Earl Cawdor (*qv*), and had issue:

1 HENRY CAMPBELL De La POER (Sir), **5th Bt**

2 Peter de la Poer (Rev), Vicar Overbury 1948–54, Rector Richmond Yorks 1954–62, Tilehurst Reading 1962; *b* 27 Aug 1907; *educ* Eton and Magdalen Coll Oxford (BA 1929, MA 1954); *m* 26 Nov 1940 *Muriel [Mrs Peter Beresford-Peirse, Stable Flat, Danby Hill, Northallerton, N Yorks], dau of Joseph Griffiths, and *d* 1984 leaving issue:

(1) +Hugh de la Poer [Hugh Beresford-Peirse Esq, 18 Southway, Carshalton Beeches, Surrey SM5 4HW]; *b* 21 Sept 1941; *m* 21 Sept 1963 *Carolyn Anne Elizabeth, er dau of Hubert George Frederick Barker, and has:

1a +Julian de la Poer; *b* 8 Aug 1966; *m* 1994 *Tracy Gates and has:

1b +Thomas de la Poer; *b* 1996

1a *Claire Elizabeth; *b* 1 May 1969; m 1995 *Iain Andrew Wilson

(2) +Mark de la Poer (Rev) [The Rev Mark Beresford-Peirse, 21 Crimple Meadows, Pannal, Harrogate, N Yorks HG3 1EL]; *b* 3 Feb 1945; *educ* Richmond Sch, Magdalen Coll Oxford and Coll of St Mark and St John, Chelsea; *m* 1976 *Margaret Joan Arnott and has:

1a Duncan de la Poer; *b* and *d* 1980

1a *Rachel Helen; *b* 1977

2a *Sophia Rosemary; *b* 1981

(1) *Mary; *b* 16 Jan 1948

(2) *Ruth (twin) [Mrs Hugh Wrigley, Danby Hill, Danby Wiske, Northallerton, N Yorks]; *b* 16 Jan 1948; *m* 1976 *Hugh Charles Wrigley, of Northallerton, and has issue:

1a *Elspeth Rosemary; *b* 1977

1a *Camilla Mary; *b* 1980

Sir HENRY *d* 14 May 1949; his er son,

Sir Henry Campbell De La Poer Beresford-Peirse, 5th Bt, CB (1957) *educ* Eton and Magdalen Coll Oxford (BA 1927, BSc Forestry 1929); FRSE, Maj Lovat Scouts WW II, dir Gen Forestry Commn 1962–68 (Dep Dir-Gen 1953–62); *b* 24 April 1905; *m* 19 April 1932 Margaret (*d* 1 Feb 1995), JP (NR Yorks 1956), 4th dau of Frank Morrison Seafield Grant, of Knockie, Whitebridge, Inverness-shire, and *d* 11 Aug 1972, leaving:

1 Sir HENRY GRANT De La POER BERESFORD-PEIRSE, **6th and present Bt**

2 John David de la Poer; *b* 10 Oct 1937; *educ* Eton; *d* unm 5 June 1961

Sir Henry adopted Jan 1965 his foster-dau:

*Mary Spiers [Mrs Andrew Gilmour, Pratis House, Leven, Fife KY8 5NX]; *b* 1947; SSStJ; *m* 1 May 1971 *Andrew Frank Gilmour, yr s of Sir John Edward Gilmour, 3rd Bt (*qv*), and has issue

BERKELEY

Creation: B. (E) by writ 20 Oct 1421.

THE 18TH LORD (Baron) **BERKELEY** (Anthony FitzHardinge Gueterbock, OBE (Civil 1989)) [The Rt Hon The Lord Berkeley OBE, House of Lords, London SW1]; *b* 20 Sept 1939; *s* aunt 1992; *educ* Eton and Trin Coll Cambridge (MA); MICE, engr: with Sir Alexander Gibb & Ptnrs 1961–65, George Wimpey PLC 1965–81, Channel Tunnel Gp/Eurotunnel 1981–, public affrs manager Eurotunnel 1987–, advsr Adtvanz 1995–, chm Rail Freight Gp 1996–; *m* 10 July 1965 (*separated* 1994) *Diana ('Dido') Christine, est dau of Eric William John Townsend, MRCS, LRCP, of Shaldon, Devon, and Mrs J B Murray and has:

1 +THOMAS FitzHARDINGE; *b* 5 Jan 1969; *educ* St Paul's; *m* 1995 *Helen Ruth, er dau of Lt-Cdr Brian Walsh, RN

2 +Robert William; *b* 22 Dec 1970; *educ* St Paul's and Kent U

1 +Philippa Louise; *b* 1975; *educ* Godolphin and Latymer

Lineage: EADNOTH (*k* 1068), Staller (an important royal official, though unspecified as to duties) to KINGs HAROLD GODWINSON and EDWARD THE CONFESSOR, had:

HARDING, living *c* 1125, had:

ROBERT Fitz HARDING, feudal Lord of Berkeley; *b c* 1095; granted by HENRY II 1153/4 the castle of Berkeley, Glos, fndr 1141 Abbey of St Augustine, Bristol; *m* Eve (*d* 12 March 1170) and *d* 5 Feb 1170/1, leaving:

1 MAURICE Fitz ROBERT Fitz HARDING, otherwise de BERKELEY, feudal Lord of Berkeley, for whom *see* further below

1 Helen; *m* Roger de Berkeley, feudal Lord of Dursley, s and heir of Roger de Berkeley, feudal Ld of Berkeley before the grant to Robert Fitz Harding, who had lost the manor of Berkeley *c* 1152 for temporising between STEPHEN and the EMPRESS MAUD, and had issue

ROBERT Fitz HARDING's s,

MAURICE Fitz ROBERT Fitz HARDING, otherwise de BERKELEY, feudal Lord of Berkeley; *b c* 1120; grant of Berkeley confirmed by HENRY II 1155 and 30 Oct 1189 by QUEEN ELEANOR (Regent for her s RICHARD I), Justice Itinerant Glos 1190; *m* 1153/4 Alice, 1st dau of Roger de Berkeley (*see* above), previous feudal Ld of Berkeley, and *d* 16 June 1190, leaving, with four other sons:

1 Robert, feudal Lord of Berkeley; *b c* 1165; Justice Itinerant 1208, joined the barons opposed to KING JOHN, pardoned 1214, rebelled again and regranted all his lands except Berkeley 1216/7; *m* 1st by 11 June 1200 Julian (*d* 15 Nov 1217), dau of Robert de Pont de l'Arche and n of William Marshal, Earl of Pembroke (*see* PEMBROKE and MONTGOMERY, E, preliminary remarks); *m* 2nd 1218 Lucy (*m* 2nd Hugh de Gurnay and *d* 18 Jan 1234), possibly dau of Sir Thomas Malesmains, and *dsp* 13 May 1220

2 Thomas, feudal Lord of Berkeley; *b c* 1170; *s* to all his bro's lands on latter's death, bar Berkeley Castle, which he did not obtain till 1223; *m c* 1217 Joan (living 1273/4), dau of Sir Ralph de Somery, of Dudley, Worcs, and possibly another n of William Marshal, Earl of Pembroke, and *d* 29 Nov 1243, leaving:

(1) Maurice, feudal Lord of Berkeley; *b* 1218; ktd by 1242, joined baronial rebellion against HENRY III; *m* by 12 July 1247 Isabel (*d* 7 July 1276/7), dau of Richard FitzRoy, illegitimate s of KING JOHN, and *d* 4 April 1281, having had:

1a Maurice; *kvp* 1279 in a tournament at Kenilworth

2a THOMAS de BERKELEY, feudal Lord of Berkeley and 1st LORD (Baron) BERKELEY (E) so *cr* by writ of summons to Parl 24 June 1295; *b* 1245; V-Constable England 1297, present at the victory over the Scots of Falkirk 22 July 1298 and at Siege of Carlaverock July 1300, taken prisoner at Scottish victory of Bannockburn 24 June 1314, Commr to examine claims to the crown of Scotland June 1292; *m* 1267 Joan de Ferrers (*d* 19 March 1309/10), dau of 7th Earl of Derby (*qv*, preliminary remarks) of the 1138 *cr*, and *d* 23 July 1321, having had:

1b MAURICE, 2nd LORD

2b Thomas, ancestor of the BERKELEYS of Wymondham, Leics, extinct in male line 1622

3b John; *dsp c* 1317

4b James

1b Isabel; *d* unm

2b Margaret; *m* 1st Thomas Fitz Maurice (*see* FitzGERALD, Bt, of Valencia) and had issue; *m* 2nd Reynald Rasel/Russel

The 1st LORD (Baron) BERKELEY's est s,

MAURICE de BERKELEY, 1st(?)/2nd LORD (Baron) BERKELEY; *b* April 1271; took part in Scottish Wars 1295–1318, at Siege of Carlaverock July 1300, called to Parl 1308 in his f's lifetime by a series of writs worded to him as 'Maurice de Berkeley', which by a later interpretation would have meant that he was made LORD (Baron) BERKELEY in a separate creation to that of his f, but in fact there is no record of his having taken his seat, Warden Gloucester 1312, Capt Berwick 1315, Commr to Scotland 1316, Ch Justiciar S Wales 1316, Seneschal Aquitaine 1320, joined the Earl of Lancaster's insurrection against EDWARD II and his favourites the Despensers 1321 but was captured and imprisoned in Wallingford Castle; *m* 1st 1289 Eva (*d* 5 Dec 1314), sis of 1st Lord (Baron) Zouche (*qv*) of the 1308 *cr*, *m* 2nd *c* 1316 Isabel de Clare (*dsp* 1333), dau of 7th Earl of Hertford (*cr temp* KING STEPHEN), and *d* 31 May 1326, having had by his 1st w:

1 THOMAS, 3rd LORD

2 Maurice (Sir); *m* Margaret, dau of Sir Maurice Berkeley, of Uley, Glos, and *d c* 1348 at Calais, and with her was ancestor of the Lords (Barons) Botetourt (*see* BEAUFORT, D), the Lords Berkeley of Stratton and the Berkeleys of Pylle, represented by Viscount Portman (*qv*)

3 John; Constable Bristol Castle, ancestor of the BERKELEYS of Salop

4 Eudo

5 Peter

1 Isabel; *m* 1st June 1328 3rd Lord (Baron) Clifford (*see* DE CLIFFORD, B); *m* 2nd *c* 9 June 1345 1st Lord (Baron) Musgrave (*see* MUSGRAVE, Bt, of Hartley Castle) and *d* 25 July 1362, leaving issue by her 1st husb

2 Milicent; *m* 1313, as his 1st w, 1st Lord (Baron) Mautravers (*see* NORFOLK, D)

The 2nd LORD (Baron) BERKELEY's est s,

THOMAS de BERKELEY, 3rd LORD (Baron) BERKELEY; *b c* 1296; ktd before 1322, joined with his f in Lancaster's insurrection, imprisoned until 16 Oct 1326, later Jt Custodian of EDWARD II 4 April 1327 but guessing what was in store for the deposed king left Berkeley Castle before the actual regicide, tried by jury of 12 knights 1330/1 as accessory to EDWARD's murder but acquitted, Ch Warden Glos, Worcs and Herefs, Marshal English Army in France 1342, Capt Scottish Marches, Warden and Ch Justice in Eyre S of Trent 1345–48; *m* 1st *c* 25 July 1320 Margaret Mortimer (*d* 5 May 1337), dau of 1st Earl of March of the 1328 *cr*, and had issue, with three s who *dsp:*

1 MAURICE de BERKELEY, 4th LORD (Baron) BERKELEY, for whom *see* further below

1 Joan; *m* 1st Lord (Baron) Cobham of the 1347 *cr* (*d* 5 Oct 1361) and *d* 2 Oct 1369, leaving issue

The 3rd LORD (Baron) BERKELEY *m* 2nd 30 May 1347 Katherine (*d* 13 March 1385), dau and heir of Sir John Clivedon, of Charfield, Glos, and widow of Sir Peter Le Veel, of Tortworth, Glos, and *d* 27 Oct 1361, leaving issue, with three s who *dsp*:

2 John, ancestor of the BERKELEYs of Beverstone

The 3rd LORD (Baron) BERKELEY's est s,

MAURICE de BERKELEY, 4th LORD (Baron) BERKELEY; *b* 1330; severely wounded and taken prisoner at Battle of Poitiers 19 Sept 1356; *m* 1338 Elizabeth le Despenser (*d* 13 July 1389), dau of 2nd Lord (Baron) Le Despenser (*see* FALMOUTH, V) by Alianore de Clare, gdau of EDWARD I, and *d* 8 June 1368 of wounds received at Battle of Poitiers, leaving, with daus who *d* unm:

1 THOMAS de BERKELEY, 5th LORD (Baron) BERKELEY, PC; *b* 5 Jan 1352/3; a Commr for deposition of RICHARD II 30 Sept 1399, Adml S and W 1403, Jt Warden Welsh Marches 1404, a Regent of the Kingdom April 1416; *m* Nov 1367 Margaret de Lisle (*d* 20 March 1391/2), dau and heir of 2nd Lord (Baron) Lisle of the 1347 *cr*, and on the latter's death in 1382 styled himself LORD LISLE by right of his w; *dspm* 13 July 1417, leaving an only child:

(1) Elizabeth; *b c* 1386; by later doctrine she would have inherited her f's Barony as a peeress in her own right (together indeed with her mother's Barony of Lisle) and it/they would then have fallen into abeyance on her death without male issue, but it is probable that according to the notions then prevailing the Barony of Berkeley was considered to go with physical and legal possession of Berkeley Castle (*see* also ABERGAVENNY, M, for a discussion of the concept of barony by tenure), so that by a combination of this, together with what was then considered good practice as regards inheritance of baronies by writ (topped up by the political influence wielded by Elizabeth's cousin James de Berkeley) and what later became the legal doctrine, her cousin James, who was called to Parl by writs from 1421, thereby became the grantee of a totally new creation; *m* by 5 Oct 1397, as his 1st w, Richard de Beauchamp, 13th Earl of Warwick (*qv*) of the 1088 *cr*, and had:

1a Margaret; *b* 1404; *m* 6 Sept 1425, as his 2nd w, 1st Earl of Shrewsbury and Waterford (*qv*) and *d* 14 June 1467

2a Eleanor; *m* 1st 8th Lord (Baron) de Ros (*qv*) of Helmsley; *m* 2nd by 1436 Edmund, Duke of Somerset (*see* BEAUFORT, D); (?)*m* 3rd(?) Walter Rokesley

3a Elizabeth; *b c* 1417; *m c* Feb 1436/7, as his 1st w, George Nevill(e), 1st(?) Lord (Baron) Latimer/Latymer of the putative Feb 1431/2 *cr* (*see* ABERGAVENNY, M) and had issue; *m* 2nd, as his 2nd w, Thomas Wake (*see* WAKE, Bt) and *d* by 2 Oct 1480

2 James (Sir), Ld Manor of Raglan, Mon; *m* Elizabeth, dau and heir of Sir John Bluet, of Raglan, and *dvf* 13 June 1405, leaving:

(1) JAMES, **1st Lord** (Baron) **Berkeley**

3 John; *dsp*

4 Maurice; *m* Joan — and had:

(1) Maurice; living 1371/2

The 5th LORD (Baron) BERKELEY's n,

JAMES de BERKELEY, **1st Lord** (Baron) **Berkeley** of the 1421 *cr*; *b c* 1394; *s* to the Castle of Berkeley and other estates under the entail executed by his ggf but was hindered in obtaining posession by his cousin the Countess of Warwick who was heir general of the 5th Lord (Baron) Berkeley; nevertheless (*see* above) called by writ to Parl 20 Oct 1421 thus being *cr* LORD (Baron) BERKELEY (E) (this Barony, being by writ, is by later doctrine held to be heritable by heirs general, which can include females, so that the + against each living female and her issue indicates that she is/they are in remainder to this peerage), ktd 1426; contracted to marry (and perhaps actually did so) 19 April 1410 —, dau of Sir John St John; *m* (?)2nd 1415 — (*dsp*), dau of Sir Humphrey Stafford, of Hooke, Dorset; *m* (?)3rd 1423/4 Isabel Mowbray (*d* 27 Sept 1452), est dau of 1st Duke of Norfolk (*qv*) of the 1396 *cr* and widow of Henry Ferrers (*dvp* 1394), s and heir of 5th Lord (Baron) Ferrers (of Groby); *m* (?)4th *c* 25 July 1457 Joan Talbot (*m* 2nd 1487 Edmund Hungerford), dau of 1st Earl of Shrewsbury and Waterford (*qv*), and *d* Nov 1463, having had by his 3rd w, with three daus:

1 WILLIAM de BERKELEY, **2nd Lord** (Baron) **Berkeley** and 1st and last MARQUESS OF BERKELEY, KB (1475), PC (1482/3); *b* 1426; involved in a family dispute with Margaret Countess of Shrewsbury and his great-uncle (the 5th) Lord Berkeley's other heirs general over the family estates, challenged by the Countess's gs Viscount Lisle to single combat 20 March 1469/70 to settle the claim and did so by killing Lord Lisle, *cr* 21 April 1481 VISCOUNT BERKELEY (E); on inheriting half the enormous estates of the Mowbray family he was further *cr* 28 June 1483 EARL OF NOTTINGHAM (E), Earl Marshal and Gt Marshal of England Feb 1485/6; settled 1487 Berkeley Castle and most of his other properties on himself in tail general with remainder to HENRY VII in tail male with further remainder to his own rightful heirs (it may well be the alienation of Berkeley Castle for several generations following his death that led to the failure of his immediate successors as Lord Berkeley to take their seats in Parl), *cr* 28 Jan 1488/9 MARQUESS OF BERKELEY (E), assumed between 1481 and 10 Feb 1484/5 the title of VISCOUNT OF CATHERLOUGH, Co Carlow (I); *m* 1st 1466 (*divorce* 1467) Elizabeth West, dau of 3rd Lord (Baron) West and 6th Lord (Baron) La Warre of the 1298/9 *cr*; *m* 2nd Nov 1468 Joan (*d* 24 Feb 1484/5), dau of Sir Thomas Strangeways by Katherine, dau of 1st Earl of Westmorland (*see* ABERGAVENNY, M), *m* 3rd *c* 1486 Anne (*m* 2nd Sir Thomas Brandon, KG, uncle of 1st Duke of Suffolk of the 1514 *cr*, and *d* 10 Sept 1497), dau of Sir Thomas Fiennes, and *dsps* 14 Feb 1491/2, when all his titles except the Barony of Berkeley expired, having had by his 2nd w:

1 Thomas (Sir), KB (1475); *b* March 1469/70; betrothed June 1475 to Mary Herbert, dau of 1st Earl of Pembroke of the 1468 *cr*; *dsp* shortly afterwards

(1) Katherine; *d* young

2 MAURICE, *de jure* 3rd LORD

3 James; *k* in France

4 Thomas, of Dursley, Glos; *m* Margaret, dau of Richard Guy, of Minsterworth, Glos, and *d* 1484, leaving issue:

(1) Richard, of Dursley; *m* Margaret Dyer and had issue:

1a William, MP; *m* Elizabeth Burghill and had issue:

1b Rowland, MP Worcester, bought from Philip Sheldon the estate of Spetchley, Worcs; *m* Catherine, dau of Thomas Heywood, and *d* 1611, having had issue, with five yr sons and nine daus:

1c William, of Cotheridge, Worcs, High Sheriff 1618; *m* Margaret, dau of Thomas Chettle, and *d* 1658, having had, with two daus:

1d Rowland (Sir), of Cotheridge; *b* 1613; MP Worcester; *m* Dorothy, dau of Sir Thomas Cave, of Stanford, Northants, and *d* 1696, having had, with four daus:

1e Thomas; *d* unm 1669 Megara, Greece

2c Robert (Sir), of Spetchley; *b* 1584; Judge Court of King's Bench; *m* Elizabeth, dau and coheir of Thomas Conyers, of E Barnet, and *d* 1656, leaving:

1d Thomas, of Spetchley; *m* Anne, dau of William Darell, of Scotney, Sussex, and had:

1e Robert, of Spetchley; *b* 1650; fndr the Berkeley Hosp in Worcester; *m* Elizabeth, dau of Sir Richard Blake, and *dsp* 1694

2e Thomas, of Spetchley; *b* 1652; *m* Elizabeth, dau of William Holyoake, of Morton Bagott, Warwicks, and *d* 1719, leaving:

1f John, of Spetchley; *b* 1683; *m* Judith Hagon and *d* 1741, leaving:

1g Thomas, of Spetchley; *m* Mary, dau of Edward Ferrars, of Baddesley Clinton, and *dsp* 1742

2f Thomas, of Spetchley; *b* 1681; *m* Mary, dau and heiress of Robert Davis, of Clytha, Mon, and *d* France, leaving:

1g Robert, of Spetchley; *m* 1st Anne, sis and coheir of John Wyborne, of Flixton, Norfolk; *m* 2nd Katherine, dau of Peter Parry, of Twysog, Denbigh, and *dsp* 1804

2g John, of Hindlip, Worcs; *m* 1st Catherine, dau of Charles Bodenham, of Rotherwas, Herefs, and had:

1h Robert of Spetchley; *m* 1792 Appollonia, 3rd dau of Richard Lee, of Llanfoist, Mon, and had:

1i Robert of Spetchley, JP, DL (Worcs); *b* 21 May 1794; *m* 24 Jan 1822 Henrietta Sophia (*d* 15 Dec 1857), est dau of Paul Benfield, MP, of Grosvenor Sq, by his w Mary Frances, gdau of Sir John Swinburne, 3rd Bt, of Capheaton, Northumberland (*see* 1970 edn), and *d* 26 Sept 1874, having had:

1j Robert of Spetchley Park, Worcs, JP, DL; *b* 9 Oct 1823; *m* 24 March 1851 Lady Mary Caroline Browne (*d* 26 Aug 1924), dau of 3rd Earl of Kenmare (*see* 1949 edn), and *d* 9 Sept 1897, having had:

1k Robert Valentine BERKELEY, of Spetchley, JP, DL (Worcs); *b* 29 April 1853; *educ* Beaumont and Oscott; High Sheriff 1909, late Maj Worcs Militia; *m* 20 Aug 1891 Rose (*d* 21 Aug 1922), yr dau of Frederick Wilmot, of Warley Place, Essex, and *d* 14 Aug 1940, having had:

1l Robert George Wilmot, of Spetchley Park and Berkeley Castle, DL (Worcs 1952); *b* 23 April 1898; *educ* Downside, Oratory Sch and Magdalen Coll Oxford; served with Westminster Dragoons in Palestine 1917–18, on W Front and with Army of Occupation 1918–19, Capt RA WW II, High Sheriff Worcs 1933, CC 1928–46, Dep MFH Berkeley 1923–28, Jt Master 1928–69; *m* 23 Nov 1927 Hon Myrtle Emmeline Theresa Dormer (*d* 1982), dau of 14th Baron Dormer (*qv*), and *d* 1969, leaving:

1m +Robert John Grantley, JP (Glos 1960), DL (Herefs, Worcs and Glos), TD [Maj Robert Berkeley, Berkeley Castle, Glos GL13 9BQ; Spetchley Park, Worcs]; *b* 24 July 1931; *educ* Oratory Sch and Magdalen Coll Oxford; High Sheriff Worcs 1967 and Glos 1982, Maj QO Warwicks and Worcs Yeo, Lt 10th Roy Hus (PWO), Jt MFH Berkeley 1960–84; *m* 25 Jan 1967 *Georgina Bridget, est dau of Maj Andrew Stirling Home Drummond Moray, of Easter Ross, Comrie, Perthshire, and has:

1n +Robert Charles; *b* 1968; *educ* Ampleforth

2n +Henry John Mowbray; *b* 1969; *educ* Ampleforth and RMA Sandhurst; commnd QO Hus 1992

1m +Rosalind Magdalen Ellen; *b* 14 Sept 1928; Nun Convent of Our Lady of Sion, Holloway

2m +Juliet Elizabeth Mary [Miss Juliet Berkeley, Spetchley Park, Worcs]; *b* 6 June 1930

1l Eleanor Mary; *b* 1892; *m* 5 Feb 1930 John Brennan (*d* 1961), of Barraghcore, Goverbridge, Co Kilkenny, and *d* 30 May 1930

2l Rosamund Mary; *d* 24 March 1894 an infant

3l Margaret Elizabeth; *b* 10 Jan 1902; nun Order of Our Lady of Sion; *d* 7 March 1998

2k Maurice Henry, JP, DL (Worcs); *b* 2 April 1856; Capt and Hon Maj 6th Bn Worcs Regt, Boer War 1901–02 (medal with clasps) and WW I; *d* 1 March 1921

3k Thomas Mowbray Martin; *b* 11 Nov 1859; Bde-Maj TF Inf, Memb Gentlemen-at-Arms, Maj and Brevet Lt-Col The Black Watch (Roy Highrs), served Egypt (medal with clasps, bronze star), S Africa (wounded at Magersfontein and Paardeburg, despatches, medal with clasps); *m* 12 June 1912 Helena, dau of T M Koecher, of Manchester, and widow of Capt George Henry Jackson, Bengal NI, and was *ka* 1916

4k Hubert, JP (Worcs 1927), ISO (1921); *b* 25 June 1864; late Malay States CS, Capt 6th Bn Worcs Regt and RNR, served WW I; *d* unm 27 April 1942

5k Oswald (Rev), MC; *b* 8 Dec 1866; Benedictine monk; *d* 29 April 1924

6k Wolstan Edward Francis; *b* 2 Nov 1870; *m* 2 July 1916 Alice, dau of Col Francis Baynham Vaughan, of Courtfield, and *d* 24 Oct 1943

1k Augusta; *m* 9 May 1878 3rd Earl of Gainsborough (*qv*) and *d* 5 Nov 1877, leaving issue a dau who *d* unm

2k Mary Ida; *m* 9 May 1876 William FitzHerbert Brockholes, CBE (*d* 21 Jan 1924), of Claughton Hall, Lancs, and *d* 14 Jan 1883, leaving issue

3k Maud Ellen; *d* 6 March 1944

4k Agnes Mary; Sister of Charity Shanghai; *d* 9 March 1944

5k Constance Mary; *d* 8 Feb 1946

6k Ethelreda Mary; *m* 27 July 1893 Maj Joseph Chichester (*d* 2 Feb 1924), Worcs Regt, of Claverleigh Court, nr Tiverton, Devon, and *d* 3 Dec 1924

2j John Edward; *b* 6 March 1827; *d* 1847

3j Henry William; *b* 24 Feb 1831; *educ* Stonyhurst; *m* 18 April 1872 Matilda Catherine (*d* 28 June 1916), dau of George Forde Copeland, of Bayshill, Glos, and *d* 30 Jan 1916, leaving:

1k Henry George; *b* 23 March 1873; *d* unm 13 Sept 1922

2k Christopher Robert, CMG (1917), DSO (1900), OBE (1919); *b* 18 Jan 1877; *educ* Oratory Sch and RMC Sandhurst; served S Africa 1899–1902 (severely wounded, despatches twice), WW I (wounded, despatches six times, Brevet Lt-Col), Waziristan 1922, AQMG Staff Coll 1921–22, Lt-Col cmdg 1st Bn Welch Regt 1922–26, Legion of Honour and Croix de Guerre of France with palms; *m* 8 May 1919 Nest, yr dau of Col Sir Joseph Alfred Bradney, CB, of Tai-y-Coed, Mon, and *d* 27 April 1959, leaving:

1l Maurice; *b* 12 Jan 1921; *educ* Beaumont; Lt-Col RA, served WW II; *m* 18 Nov 1950 *Sylvia Mary Close [Mrs Maurice Berkeley, 21 Chancellor House, Mt Ephraim, Tunbridge Wells, Kent TN4 8BT], only dau of John Tennant Maudsley, of Caton, Lancs, and *d* 1993, leaving:

1m +Hugh Christopher; *b* 28 July 1952; *educ* Stonyhurst

2m +John Henry; *b* 8 March 1956; *educ* Worth and LCP (BA); *m* 1980 *Nina Elaine, yr dau of A R S Pritchard-Davies, of Tudor Cottage, Burford, Oxon, and has:

1n +Luke Dominic; *b* 1981

2n +Milo Thomas; *b* 1983

3n +Benn Alexander; *b* 1986

3m +Michael Frederick [Michael Berkeley Esq, 14 Prebend Gdns, London W4 1TW]; *b* 25 Nov 1958; *educ* Worth, Magdalene Coll Cambridge (MA) and SDA Bocconi Milan (MBA); *m* 1989 *Caroline Jane, er dau of Sydney Riddell, of 31 Belmont Gdns, Edinburgh, and has:

1n +Oscar Frederick Robert; *b* 1991

2n +Thomas Bertram Maurizio; *b* 1993

2l Edward Henry; *b* 5 Feb 1923; *educ* Beaumont; served WW II RE (despatches); *m* 21 April 1951 *Joyce Louise [Mrs Charles Phillips, 63 Larkhall Rise, London SW4] (*m* 2nd 30 Dec 1965 Charles Michael Phillips, of Elston Hall, Newark, Notts), 2nd dau of D C Duncan, of Valparaiso, Chile, and *d* 6 Nov 1962, leaving:

1m Mowbray Thomas; *b* 15 Feb 1952; *educ* Stonyhurst; *d* 1970

2m +Grantley William Andrew; *b* 2 Oct 1954; *educ* Stonyhurst and Southampton U (LLB); *m* 1985 *Sally Ann Stenson, dau of C A S Webb, of Sutton Coldfield, Warwicks, and has:

1n +Edward Charles Mowbray; *b* 1986

1n +Alice Mary; *b* 1989

2n +Sophie Louise; *b* 1991

3m +Wulstan Herbert; *b* 17 July 1956; *educ* Stonyhurst and Worcester Coll Oxford

4m +Thurstan Timothy Edward [Thurstan Berkeley Esq, 26 Ashland Ave, Toronto, Ontario, Canada M4l 1 KJ]; *b* 20 Oct 1961; *educ* Stonyhurst and Hatfield Coll Durham; *m* 1992 *Karen Ann Theresa, est dau of Norman Goodale, of Beaconsfield, Quebec, Canada

5m +Fiona Maria Louise (twin); *b* 17 July 1956; *educ* St Mary's Ascot and Bristol U; *m* 1990 *Laurent Fauquex, of Geneva, Switzerland, and has:

1n +Zoe; *b* 1990

3l Basil Robert; *b* 8 Oct 1925; *educ* Beaumont; Capt Irish Gds WW II (wounded), memb Lloyd's, dir Anton Underwriting Agencies Ltd; *m* 8 April 1953 *Gillian Rosamund Wellesley [Mrs Basil Berkeley, Highmoor House, Mayfield, E Sussex TN20 6PW], yst dau of Richard Henry Spencer, MD, of Alcester, Warwicks, and *d* 1994, leaving:

1m +Giles Robert [Giles Berkeley Esq, Christmas Cottage, Upper Green, Hawkley, Liss, Hants GU33 6LX]; *b* 19 Jan 1959; *educ* Downside and Durham U; *m* 1990 *Alexandra Louise, yst dau of Anthony Love, of Beggars Bush, Wadhurst, Sussex, and has:

1n +Benedict Robert; *b* 1992

2n +Anthony Basil; *b* 1994

2m +Roger Maurice [Roger Berkeley Esq, Hoggeshaws, Milstead, Sittingbourne, Kent ME9 OSA]; *b* 6 May 1961; *educ* Downside; *m* 1986 *Victoria, only dau of John Russell Selmon, of Hemingfold Grange, Battle, E Sussex, and has:

1n +Rupert Charles; *b* 1988

2n +Robert Francis; *b* 1989

3k Frederick; *b* 8 June 1879; Capt Cheshire Regt; *d* unm 4 July 1949

4k Andrew Joseph; *b* 26 Aug 1880; slr; *d* unm 18 April 1949

1k Eva Mary; *b* 27 April 1873; *d* unm 24 Nov 1965

4j Frederick Charles; *b* Feb 1835; *d* 8 June 1866

5j Francis Rowland; *b* May 1840; *m* 26 June 1879 Frances (*d* 7 March 1925), dau of John Weld, JP, DL, of Leagram Park, Lancs, and *d* 7 March 1925, leaving:

1k John Joseph Francis BERKELEY later BERKELEY-WELD, JP Lancs (1906); *b* 1880; *educ* Stonyhurst and New Coll Oxford; Capt att 1st Bn King's Own Regt WW I (despatches), added surname WELD 1924, CC (1935); *d* unm 11 Aug 1960

2k Francis George, MC; *b* 9 June 1882; Capt Hampshire Regt; *d* unm 12 March 1935

1k Eleanor; Benedictine Nun; *d* 27 Sept 1949

1j Mary Frances; *b* 1841

2j Harriet Eliza; *d* 26 Nov 1878

3j Agnes Mary Caroline; Nun Order of St Dominic; *d* 16 July 1860

4j Emily Jane; *m* 31 Oct 1855 Simon Thomas Scrope (*d* 4 March 1896), of Danby Hall, Yorks, and *d* 20 Jan 1919, leaving issue

5j Mary; *m* 29 Sept 1857 8th Earl of Denbigh and (7th Earl of) Desmond (*qv*) and *d* 3 June 1901, leaving issue

2g (cont.) John Berkeley *m* 2nd Jane, dau of Sir William Compton, 3rd Bt, of Hartbury, Glos, of the 1686 *cr*, and had further issue:

1h Catherine; *m* Robert Canning, of Foxcote, Warwicks, and *dsp* 1823

2h Jane; *m* 14 May 1799 3rd Viscount Southwell (*qv*) and *d* 26 Oct 1853, leaving issue

The 1st and last MARQUESS OF BERKELEY's yr bro,

MAURICE BERKELEY, *de jure* 3rd LORD (Baron) BERKELEY; *b c* 1435; Kt of the Body to EDWARD IV, *m* 1465 Isabel (*d* after 29 May 1514), dau of Philip Mead, of Mead's Place, Wraxall, Somerset, Alderman and thrice Mayor Bristol, and *d* Sept 1506, leaving:

1 MAURICE BERKELEY, *de jure* 4th LORD (Baron) BERKELEY, KB (1509); *b* 1467; Keeper Kingswood Forest 1508, Sheriff Glos 1509–10 and 1515–16, Leics and Warwick 1516–17, Kt of the Body to HENRY VIII 1512, Marshal of Army for Spain 1512, Lt Calais 1520, called to Parl 15 April 1523 but never took his seat; *m c* 28 Jan 1484/5 Katherine (*d c* 1526), dau of Sir William Berkeley, of Stoke Gifford, Glos, and *dspl* 12 Sept 1523

2 THOMAS BERKELEY, *de jure* 5th LORD (Baron) BERKELEY; *b* 1472; ktd 9 Sept 1513 at Battle of Flodden, Constable Berkeley Castle 1514, Sheriff Glos Nov 1522–Nov 1523, called to Parl 9 Aug 1529 by writ worded as being to 'Thomas Berkley de Berkley'; *m* 1st 1504/5 Eleanor (*d* 1525), dau of Sir Marmaduke Constable, of Flamborough, Yorks, and widow of William Ingleby; *m* 2nd 1526 Cicely (*d* July/Nov 1558), dau and coheir of — Arnold and widow of Richard Rowdon, of Gloucester, and *d* 22 Jan 1532/3, leaving by his 1st w:

(1) THOMAS BERKELEY, **6th Lord** (Baron) **Berkeley**, KG (1533); *b* 1505; *educ* St Omer, France; called to Parl 5 Jan 1533/4, Constable and Porter Berkeley Castle and Keeper of the Park 8 March 1532/3; *m* 1st 1526 Lady Mary Hastings (*dsp* March 1532/3), dau of 1st Earl of Huntingdon (*qv*); *m* 2nd April 1533 Anne (*d* Oct 1564), dau of Sir John Savage, of Frodsham, Chester, and *d* 22 Sept 1534, leaving by her, together with at least one dau (Elizabeth, *m c* 1559, as his 1st w, 10th Earl of Ormonde and (2nd Earl of) Ossory; *see* MOUNTGARRET, V) a posthumous s:

1a HENRY BERKELEY, **7th Lord** (Baron) **Berkeley**, KB (1553); *b* 26 Nov 1534; on the death of EDWARD VI, the last male heir of HENRY VII, obtained possession (under the entail of 1488) of Berkeley Castle and many other estates, by roy warrant 13 May 1555 had special livery of his lands though under age, called to Parl 5 Nov 1558, Ld-Lt Glos 1603–13; *m* 1st Sept 1554 Lady Catherine Howard (*d* 7 April 1596), 3rd dau of Henry Howard, Earl of Surrey (*see* NORFOLK, D), *m* 2nd 9 March 1597/8 Jane (*d* 3 Jan 1617/8), dau of Sir Michael Stanhope, of Shelford, Notts (*see* 1967 edn,

CHESTERFIELD and STANHOPE, E), and widow of Sir Roger Townshend (*see* TOWNSHEND, M), and *d* 26 Nov 1613, leaving by his 1st w:

1b Thomas (Sir), KB; *b* 11 July 1575; *m* 19 Feb 1595/6 Elizabeth Carey (*d* 23 April 1635), dau and sole heir of 2nd Lord Hunsdon of the 1559 *cr*, and *dvp* 22 Nov 1611, having had:

1c GEORGE BERKELEY, **8th Lord** (Baron) **Berkeley**, KB (1616); *b* 7 Oct 1601; *educ* Ch Ch Oxford (MA 1623); *m* 13 April 1614 Elizabeth, 2nd dau and coheir of Sir Michael Stanhope, of Sudbury, Suffolk (*see* 1967 edn), and *d* 10 Aug 1658, having had:

1d Charles; *dvp* 27 Jan 1640/1, drowned in English Channel

2d GEORGE BERKELEY, **9th Lord** (Baron) **Berkeley** and 1st EARL OF BERKELEY, PC (1678–79, 1685–89); *b c* 1627; *educ* Ch Ch Oxford; one of the six peers deputed to invite CHARLES II to return from exile, custos rotulorum Glos 1660–89, FRS 1663, *cr* 11 Sept 1679 VISCOUNT DURSLEY and EARL OF BERKELEY, both Co Gloucester (E), Govr Levant Co 1673–96, Master Trin Ho 1681–82, Custos Rotulorum Surrey 1689–98; *m* 11 Aug 1646 Elizabeth (*bur* 10 Dec 1708), er dau and coheir of John Mas(s)ingberd, of London, merchant, Treasurer HEIC, and *d* 14 Oct 1698, having had, with other issue:

1e CHARLES BERKELEY, **10th Lord** (Baron) **Berkeley** and 2nd EARL OF BERKELEY, KB (1661), PC (1694); *b* 8 April 1649; *educ* Ch Ch Oxford (MA 1663); on ctee Levant Co 1678–79 and HEIC 1699–1705, MP (Whig) Gloucester 1679–81, Envoy Madrid 1689, called up to Ho of Lds *vp* 11 July 1689 in f's barony as LORD BERKELEY, Envoy States of Holland 1689–95, Custos Rotulorum 1689–1710 and Ld Lt Glos 1694–1710, High Steward Gloucester 1695, Custos Rotulorum 1699–1710 and Ld Lt Surrey 1702–10, Constable St Briavel's Castle and Warden Forest of Dean 1697–1710, a Ld Justice and Govr of Ireland 1699–1700; *m c* 16 Aug 1677 Hon Elizabeth Noel (*d* 30 July 1719), dau of 3rd Viscount Campden and sis of 1st Earl of Gainsborough (*qv*), and *d* 24 Sept 1710, having had, with other issue:

1f Charles, *Viscount Dursley*; *b* 17 June 1679; *dvp* unm and was *bur* 1 June 1699

2f JAMES BERKELEY, **11th Lord**

3f George; *m* 26 June 1735 Henrietta (*d* 26 July 1767), dau of Sir Henry Hobart, 4th Bt, of Blickling, Norfolk, sis of 1st Earl of Buckinghamshire (*qv*), and widow of 9th Earl of Suffolk (*see* SUFFOLK and BERKSHIRE, E), the celebrated mistress of GEORGE II, and *dsps* 29 Oct 1746

1f Elizabeth; *m* as his 2nd w Sir John Germaine, 1st and last Bt (*see* MORDAUNT, B), and *dsps* 1769

2f Mary; *m* Thomas Chambers, of Haworth Middx, and had issue (*see* SAINT ALBANS, D)

1e Theophila; *b* 1650; *m* 1st Sir Kingsmill Lucy, 2nd Bt (*see* RAMSAY-FAIRFAX-LUCY, Bt); *m* 2nd Robert Nelson, ecclesiastical author

1b Frances; *m c* 21 Feb 1586/7, as his 1st w, Sir George Shirley, 1st Bt, and *d* 29 Dec 1595, leaving issue (*see* FERRERS, E)

The 10th LORD/2nd EARL's 2nd s,

JAMES BERKELEY, **12th Lord** (Baron) **Berkeley** and 3rd EARL OF BERKELEY, KG (1718), PC (1717); Capt RN 1701, MP (Whig) Gloucester 1701–02, called up to Ho of Lds *vp* 5 March 1704/5 in his f's barony as LORD BERKELEY, V-Adml the Blue 1707/8 and the Red 1709, Ld Lt Glos, High Steward Gloucester, Warden Forest of Dean and Constable St Briavel's Castle 1710–12 and 1714–36, Custos Rotulorum Surrey 1710–36, 1st Ld Admlty 1717–27, Hon V-Adml Gt Britain 1717/8–1736, a Ld Justice Regent 1719, 1720, 1726 and 1727 during GEORGE I's absence from Britain; *m c* 13 Feb 1710/1 Lady Louisa Lennox (*d* 15 Jan 1716/7), er dau of 1st Duke of Richmond (*see* RICHMOND, GORDON and LENNOX, D), and *d* 24 Sept 1736, leaving:

AUGUSTUS BERKELEY, **13th Lord** (Baron) **Berkeley** and 4th EARL OF BERKELEY, KT (1739); *b* 18 Feb 1715/6; Ensign 1st Regt Foot Gds 1734, Lt-Col 2nd Regt Foot Gds 1737, Ld-Lt Glos and Constable St Briavel's Castle 1737–55; *m* 7 May 1744 Elizabeth (*m* 2nd 2 Jan 1757 1st Earl Nugent of the 1776 *cr* and *d* 29 June 1792), 1st dau of Henry Drax, of Ellerton, Abbey, Yorks, and *d* 9 Jan 1755, leaving, with other issue:

1 FREDERICK AUGUSTUS BERKELEY, **14th Lord**

2 George Cranfield (Sir), GCB; *b* 10 Aug 1753; Adml RN and sometime Ld High Adml of Portugal; *m* 23 Aug 1784 his cousin Emily Charlotte, dau of Lord George Lennox (*see* RICHMOND and GORDON, D), and *d* 25 Feb 1818, having had, with other issue (including Grenville Charles Lennox, *m* Mary, sis of 1st Baron Leigh, *qv*):

(1) George Henry Frederick (Sir), KCB; *b* 9 July 1785; Gen Army, Col 35th Regt; *m* March 1815 Lucy (*d* 13 Feb 1870), er dau and coheir of Sir Thomas Sutton, 1st and last Bt of the 1806 *cr*, of Molesey, Surrey, and *d* 25 Sept 1857, having had:

1a Charles Assheton FitzHardinge, CB; *b* 10 Oct 1818; Col Scots Fus Gds, cmded 32nd Regt; *d* unm 25 Sept 1858 on board the *Simla* off Socotra

2a Alexander Henry Hastings; *b* 19 Aug 1824; *d* unm 8 June 1854

3a GEORGE LENNOX RAWDON BERKELEY, 7th EARL OF BERKELEY; *b* 25 Feb 1827; *m* 22 Feb 1860 Cecile (*d* 1 Nov 1914), dau of Edward Drummond, Count de Melfort Drummond (*see* PERTH, E), previously w of Adml Hon Sir Fleetwood Broughton Reynolds Pellew, CB, KCH (*see* EXMOUTH, V), and *d* 27 Aug 1888, having had issue:

1b RANDAL THOMAS MOWBRAY BERKELEY, 8th EARL OF BERKELEY; *b* 31 Jan 1865; Lt RN 1887, FRS 1908; *m* 1st 9 Nov 1887 Kate (*dsp* 29 March 1898), yst dau of William Brand, and widow of Arthur Jackson; *m* 2nd 8 Nov 1924 Mary Lloyd (*d* Assisi, Italy, 11 Aug 1975 aged 91), dau of John Lowell, of Boston, Mass, USA, and *dsp* 15 Jan 1942, when all his titles became *extinct* or *dormant*

1a Caroline Mary; *b* 27 Dec 1815; *m* 30 Sept 1838 Gen Randal Rumley (*d* 13 Sept 1884), and *d* 29 Dec 1882

1 Georgiana Augusta; *b* 18 Sept 1749; *m* 1st 20 April 1766 5th Earl of Granard (*qv*) and had issue; *m* 2nd Jan 1781 Rev Samuel Little, DD, and *d* 24 Jan 1820

2 Elizabeth; *b* 17 Dec 1750; *m* 1st 10 May 1767 6th Baron Craven (*see* CRAVEN, E) and had issue; *m* 2nd 13 Oct 1791 HSH CHRISTIAN FREDERICK CHARLES ALEXANDER, MARGRAVE OF BRANDENBURG-ANSPACH-BAYREUTH (*d* 5 Jan 1806) and *d* 13 Jan 1828

The 13th LORD/4th EARL's est s,

FREDERICK AUGUSTUS BERKELEY, **14th Lord** (Baron) **Berkeley** and 5th EARL OF BERKELEY; *b* 24 May 1745; Ld Lt Glos, High Steward Gloucester, Constable St Briavel's Castle and Warden Forest of Dean 1766–1810; *m* 16 May 1796 (he alleged a previous marriage to the same lady on 30 March 1785 was claimed but this was not recognised by the Ho of Lds Ctee of Privileges) Mary (*d* 30 Oct 1844), dau of William Cole, of Wotton, nr Gloucester, publican and butcher, and *d* 8 Aug 1810, leaving issue *b* before1796:

1 WILLIAM FitzHARDINGE BERKELEY, 1st and last EARL FitzHARDINGE; *b* 26 Dec 1786; MP (Whig) Glos 1810–11; on his f's death *s* to the family's huge estates and unsuccessfully petitioned for a writ of summons to the Ho of Lds, his inability to prove his legitimacy undermining his case; *cr*: 10 Sept 1831 BARON SEGRAVE OF BERKELEY CASTLE, Co Gloucester, and 17 Aug 1841 EARL FitzHARDINGE (both UK), Ld Lt Glos 1836–57; *d* unm 10 Oct 1857

2 MAURICE FREDERICK FitzHARDINGE BERKELEY, 1st BARON FitzHARDINGE OF BRISTOL, GCB (1861, KCB 1855, CB 1840), PC (1855); *b* 3 Jan 1788; Capt RN, R-Adml 1849, V-Adml 1856, Adml the Blue 1862 and the White 1863, MP (Whig then Lib) Gloucester 1831–33 1835–37 1841–57, a Ld of Admlty 1833–34, 1837–39, 1846–52 and 1852–57, Naval ADC to HM QUEEN VICTORIA 1846–49, inherited his bro's estates, including Berkeley Castle, and unsuccessfully claimed the Barony of Berkeley as one by tenure of the Castle (claim disallowed 26 Feb 1861); *cr* 5 Aug 1861 BARON FitzHARDINGE of the city, and county of the city of BRISTOL; *m* 1st 4 Dec 1823 his cousin Lady Charlotte Lennox (*d* 20 Aug 1833), 6th dau of 4th Duke of Richmond (*see* RICHMOND and GORDON, D), *m* 2nd 30 Sept 1834 Lady Charlotte Reynolds-Moreton (*dsp* 2 July 1881), dau of 1st Earl of Ducie (*qv*), and *d* 17 Oct 1867, leaving by his 1st w:

(1) FRANCIS WILLIAM FitzHARDINGE BERKELEY, 2nd BARON FitzHARDINGE OF BRISTOL; *b* 16 Nov 1826; *educ* Rugby; Capt RHG 1853–57, MP (Lib) Cheltenham 1856–65, FSA 9 Dec 1886; *m* 24 Nov 1857 Georgina (*d* 30 July 1897), dau of William Holme-Summer, of Hatchlands, E Clandon, and *dsp* 29 June 1896

(2) CHARLES PAGET FitzHARDINGE BERKELEY, 3rd and last BARON FitzHARDINGE OF BRISTOL; *b* 19 April 1830; *educ* Rugby; MP (Lib) Gloucester 1862–65; *m* 6 Dec 1856 Louisa Elizabeth (*d* 15 Nov 1902), dau of Henry Lindow Lindow, formerly Rawlinson, of Gawcomb, Glos, and *dsp* 5 Dec 1916

(1) Swinburne Frederica Charlotte FitzHardinge; *b* 15 April 1825; *m* 2 April 1845 2nd Baron Gifford (*qv*) and *d* 1920, leaving issue

(2) Fenella FitzHardinge; *m* 12 April 1851 Lt-Col Henry Armytage (*see* ARMYTAGE, Bt) and *d* 20 Nov 1903, leaving issue

3 Augustus FitzHardinge; *b* 26 March 1789; 10th Hus; *m* Oct 1815 Mary, er dau of Sir John Dashwood-King, 3rd Bt, of West Wycombe (*see* DASHWOOD, Bt, of West Wycombe), and had:

(1) Emily Anna; *d* 13 Nov 1820

(2) Georgina Mary; *m* 1842 St Vincent William Ricketts (*see* RICKETTS, Bt) and had issue

4 Francis Henry FitzHardinge; *b* 7 Dec 1794

1 Maria FitzHardinge; *b* 2 April 1790

2 Henrietta FitzHardinge; *b* 13 June 1793

The 14th LORD/5th EARL, also had issue *b* after 1796:

5 THOMAS MORETON FitzHARDINGE BERKELEY, *de jure* 15th LORD (Baron) BERKELEY and 6th EARL OF BERKELEY, although he never himself assumed any of his titles, did not take his seat in the House of Lords and would have lost his small inheritance from his f under an explicit clause in the latter's will had he disputed his est bro's claim to the the title; *b* 19 Oct 1796; *educ* Corpus Christi Oxford; *d* unm 27 Aug 1882

6 George Charles Grantley FitzHardinge; *b* 10 Feb 1800; MP W Glos 1832–52; *m* 16 Aug 1824 Caroline Martha, yst dau of Paul Benfield, and *dsps* 20 Feb 1881, having had:

(1) A son; *b* 20 Oct 1825

7 Craven FitzHardinge; *b* May 1805; *m* 1st 10 Sep 1839 Augusta (*d* 25 May 1841), illegitimate dau of Sir Horace St Paul, Bt, and widow of George Henry Talbot (*see* SHREWSBURY and WATERFORD, E); *m* 2nd 27 Aug 1845 Charlotte (*d* 25 Jan 1897), dau of Gen Denzil Onslow and widow of George Newton, and *d* 1 July 1855, leaving by his 1st w:

(1) LOUISA MARY, **Baroness Berkeley** in her own right, for whom *see* further below

3 Mary Henrietta; *b* 4 Oct 1801; *d* unm 19 Nov 1873

4 Caroline FitzHardinge; *b* 12 April 1803; *m* 24 Dec 1829 James Maxse (*d* 3 March 1864) and *d* 20 Jan 1886, having had issue:

(1) Henry FitzHardinge Berkeley (Sir), KCMG; *b* 1832; Lt-Col, served Crimea, Govr Heligoland and Newfoundland; *m* 1859 Augusta (*d* 23 April 1915), dau of — von Rudloff, of Austria, and *d* 1883, leaving:

1a Ernest George Berkeley, CMG (1899); *b* 18 Nov 1863; V-Consul Algiers 1891–94, Consul: Continental Greece 1894–97, Samoa 1897–1900 (Dep Commr W Pacific 1897–1900) and Island of Reunion 1900–12 and 1913, Consul-Gen: Valparaiso 1912–13, Netherlands 1913, Zurich 1919 and Prinicipality of Liechtenstein 1921, served Naval Brig Samoa 1899, Admlty Convoy Offr and Mily Control Offr Holland WW I ret 1924, FRGS; *m* 1st 5 May 1888 Sarah Alice (*d* 25 May 1908), only dau of Thomas Nottage-Miller, of Bishop's Stortford; *m* 2nd 7 May 1914 Mary Louisa, dau of Arthur Turle, MRCS, of Avon, Swanage, and *d* 13 March 1943, having had by his 1st w:

1b Henry FitzHardinge Berkeley; *b* 3 Dec 1889; 1st Sec Diplomatic Serv, Cdr RN (ret); *dsp* 5 April 1936

1b Dame (Sarah Algeria) Marjorie, DBE (1952, CBE 1941, MBE 1918); V-Chmn WVS 1940–44, Dir Children's Overseas Reception Bd 1940–44, V-Chm Conservative Pty Orgn 1944–50; *d* 4 May 1975

2a Craven FitzHardinge Alexander; *b* 1865; *m* 1st Oct 1886 (*divorce* 1914) Clara, dau of E Basch, of Hanover; *m* 2nd 20 Jan 1916 Nellie Kate (*d* 19 May 1968 aged 90), yst dau of John Grout, of Hereford, and *d* 10 May 1926

3a Reginald Edgar; *b* 1869; DLitt Oxford, lecturer modern languages Brasenose Coll Oxford; *m* May 1909 Elizabeth Augusta, Baroness Fircks (*d* 23 Aug 1911), of Gross Wurzau, Courland, dau of Baron Hahn, and *dsp* 29 June 1945

(2) Frederick Augustus; *b* 13 April 1833; Adml RN; *m* 1861 Cecilia (*d* 7 Feb 1918), dau of Gen — Steel, and *d* 25 June 1900, leaving:

1a (Frederick) Ivor (Sir), KCB (1917), CVO (1907), DSO (1898), DL (Sussex 1932); *b* 22 Dec 1862; Gen late Col cmdg 2nd Bn and Regt Coldstream Gds 1904–10, 2nd Lt Roy Fus 1884, transferred to Coldstream Gds 1891, cmdg 1st Gds Bde 1910–14, 18th Div 1914 and 18th Corps 1917, Inspector Gen Trg 1918, GOC-in-C N Command 1919–23, Col Middlesex Regt 1921–32, served Sudan, S Africa and WW I, Croix de Guerre, Legion of Honour, Grand Offr Crown of Belgium; *m* 18 Dec 1899 Hon Mary Caroline Wyndham (*d* 21 Jan 1944), dau of 2nd Baron Leconfield (*see* EGREMONT, LECONFIELD and, B), and *d* 28 Jan 1958, leaving:

1b John Herbert; *b* 17 Oct 1901; *educ* Eton and RMC Sandhurst; Maj Coldstream Gds WW II; *m* 9 July 1931 Dorinda Mary JP (*d* 1988), dau of William Hobart Houghton Thorne, a Judge Mixed Courts of First Instance, Egypt, and *d* 1978, leaving:

1c +Anthony John [Anthony Maxse Esq, Homestead Farm, Galley Hill, Selborne, Hants GU34 3LN]; *b* 22 June 1932; *educ* Eton and RMA Sandhurst; ARICS, Chartered Surveyor, Capt Coldstream Gds 1952–62, ADC to Govr Cyprus 1959–60, MFH Hampshire 1975–83; *m* 7 July 1961 *Susan Jane, yst dau of Frederick James Emson, MC, and Mrs J Carmichael, of Battles Hall, Manuden, Bishop's Stortford, and has:

1d +John James Ivor; *b* 1 Jan 1968; *educ* Eton

1d +Georgina Anne; *b* 1 Aug 1962; *m* 1989 *Hugh S K Knowles, of London SW13, 2nd s of Keith Knowles, of Kensington, and has:

1e +Alicia Genevieve; *b* 1 Sept 1991

2e +Claudia Rose; *b* 6 March 1993

2d +Sarah Charlotte [Mrs George Bingham, Peak House, West Meon, Hants]; *b* 6 May 1964; *m* 1990 *George J C Bingham, only s of Cdr George Edward Bingham, of Grenville House, Droxford, Hants, and has:

1e +George Frederick; *b* 9 Dec 1992

1e *Charlotte Poppy; *b* 16 Aug 1994

2c +Martin William Frederick, LVO (1997) DL Devon (1995) [Col Martin Maxse LVO, DL, Gt Fisherton, Bishops Tawton, Barnstaple, N Devon EX32 0ER]; *b* 5 Jan 1935; *educ* Eton and RMA Sandhurst; Regtl Lt-Col Coldstream Gds 1981–84; *m* 19 Sept 1959 *Penelope Ann, est dau of Maj Charles Chichester, TD, JP, of Hall, Barnstaple, N Devon, Roy Devon Yeo (*see* FOWKE, Bt), and has:

1d +Charles John Chichester; *b* 12 Sept 1962; *educ* Harrow; *m* 8 April 1995 *Naomi Henrietta, dau of Michael Joseph Bennet Parker, of Gooderstone Manor, King's Lynn, Norfolk, and has:

1e *Katherine Penelope; *b* 1997

2d +Edward William; *b* 21 Aug 1969; *educ* Bradfield

1d +Clare Caroline; *b* 3 Aug 1960; *m* 1987 *Capt Michael Patrick Campbell-Lamerton, Scots Gds, 2nd s of Col Michael John Campbell-Lamerton, of Shipston-on-Stour, Warwicks, and has:

1e +Rory Patrick Chichester; *b* 1989

2e +William Michael John; *b* 1991

3e +Alexander Charles Martin; *b* 5 March 1996

3c +Christopher James Ivor [Christopher Maxse Esq, Kings Paddock, Meonstoke, Droxford, Hants]; *b* 19 June 1942; *educ* Eton and OU (BA)

2b Frederick Henry Joseph, TD (1947); *b* 21 Jan 1904; *educ* Eton and New Coll Oxford (BA); Capt Roy Sussex Regt (TA), served WW II, Assist Advsr to Monuments, Fine Arts and Archives of Allied Mily Govt and Allied Control Commn Sicily and Italy 1943–45, served BMA Eritrea 1946–48, Controller Customs and Excise to Govt of Cyrenaica 1948–50; *d* unm 11 April 1970

1b Violet Constance; *b* 18 Nov 1905; Jr Cdr ATS WW II; *d* 6 Feb 1984

2a Leopold James; *b* 11 Dec 1864; ed *National Review* 1893–1932; *m* 23 Dec 1890 Katherine (*d* 4 Oct 1922), est dau of His Honour Judge Vernon Lushington (*see* LUSHINGTON, Bt), and *d* 22 Jan 1932

1a Olive Hermione; *d* unm 16 March 1955

2a Violet Georgina, DGStJ, Chevalier Legion of Honour, ed *National Review* 1931–48, author: *My Picture Gallery*; *m* 1st 18 June 1894 Col Lord Edward Herbert Gascoyne-Cecil, KCMG, DSO (*d* 13 Dec 1918), s of 3rd Marquess of Salisbury (*qv*), and had issue; *m* 2nd 26 Feb 1921 1st Viscount Milner, KG, PC, GCB, GCMG (*d* 13 May 1925), and *d* 16 Oct 1958

(1) Ella Henrietta; *m* 18 Nov 1862 Lt-Gen Hon Edward Thomas Gage, CB (*d* 21 May 1889), and *d* June 1916, leaving issue (*see* GAGE V)

(2) Beatrice; *m* 9 Jan 1866 Maj-Gen Robert William Duff, RE (*d* 3 Dec 1913), and *d* 29 Jan 1928, leaving issue

5 Emily Elizabeth; *b* 30 April 1807; *m* 10 Aug 1839 Col Sydney Augustus Capel (*d* 1872) and *d* 30 March 1895, leaving issue:

(1) Capt Sydney Augustus Berkeley; *m* and had issue:

1a Winifred Laura; *b* 1875; *m* 1905 Dr Ernest Faber Fookes (*d* 1948) and *d* 1927, leaving issue:

1b Sydney Faber; *b* 1906; *m* 1939 *Lorna Kathleen Joblin and *d* 1983, leaving issue:

1c +Timothy Faber [Timothy Fookes Esq, 48 Messines Rd, Karori, Wellington, NZ]; *b* 1946; slr; *m* 1972 *Sandra Jane Field and has issue:

1d +Kate Faber; *b* 1974

2d +Jane Faber; *b* 1977

1c +Sally Faber [Mrs Barrie Owen, 10 Benjamin Place, Tauranga, NZ]; *b* 1941; *m* 1965 *Barrie Miles Owen and has:

1d +Simon John; *b* 1972

1d +Angela Jane [Mrs Wilson Mellow, MacVille Rd, Mt Maunganui, NZ]; *b* 1967; *m* 19–*Wilson George Mellow and has:

1e *Benjamin George; *b* 1992

2e *Matthew Barrie; *b* 1994

2d +Philippa Ann [Mrs Andrew Pollock, 1/43 Auld St, Torbay, Auckland, NZ]; *b* 1969; *m* 19– *Andrew Pollock

2b Kenneth Faber; *b* 1907; *m* 1936 *Constance Joyce Christian Boden and *d* 1984, leaving:

1c Patrick Faber; *b* 1937; *m* 1961 *Anna Maree Tracy and *d* 1982, leaving:

1d +John Faber; *b* 1962

2d +Paul Faber; *b* 1966

3d +Stephen Faber; *b* 1967

1d +Joanna Tracy; *b* 1970

2c +Alister Faber [Alister Fookes Esq, 4A Dunholme Rd, Remuera, Auckland, NZ]; *b* 1941

3c +Russell Faber [Russell Fookes Esq, 61 Dyers Pass Rd, Christchurch, NZ]; *b* 1947; *m* 1971 *Margaret Edith Wilson and has issue:

1d +Craig; *b* 1976

1d +Kerry; *b* 1975

2d +Megan Joy; *b* 1978

1c +Jennifer Faber [Mrs David Olsen, 71 Rangitane St, Palmerston N, NZ]; *b* 1942; *m* 1964 *David Aiken Olsen and has issue:

1d +Carl David; *b* 1966

2d +Dean William; *b* 1969

1b +Ernestine Emily Faber [Mrs Stuart Black, 31 Beach St, Fitzroy, New Plymouth, NZ]; *b* 1912; *m* 1940 *Stuart Alexander Black and has:

1c +Anna Catherine; *b* 1946; *m* 19— *— Orr

2a Maude Harold; *m* — Nolan and had issue:

1b David; *b* 1912; *m* 1940 *Elsa Isabel Mooney, and *d* 1975, leaving:

1c +Robert Leslie [Robert Nolan Esq, 11 Fairearth St, The Gap, Brisbane, Qld 4061, Australia]; *b* 1941; *m* 1967 *Maureen Anne Heffernan and has:

1d +Brent Robert; *b* 1972

1d +Kim Kathleen; *b* 1974

1c +Susanne Margaret [Mrs David Thorp, Mountain Rd, RD3, New Plymouth, NZ]; *b* 1944; *m* 1970 *David Thomas Thorp

2c +Elizabeth Mary [Mrs Charles Brown, 13 Konini St, Riccarton, Christchurch, NZ]; *b* 1945; *m* 1969 *Charles Miles Brown

3c +Catherine Ruth; *b* 1947; *m* 1971 *Ian James Robinson

1b Nina Leslie; *b* 1908; *m* 1935 *John Dixon Law [John Law Esq, 14 Takomaru St, New Plymouth, NZ] and *d* 1992, leaving:

1c Barry; *b* 1936; *m* 1961 *Faith Georgina Gordon Glassford and *d* 1980, leaving:

1d +Michael Barry [Michael Law Esq, 129 Fisher Parade, Pakuranga, Auckland, NZ]; *b* 1963

1d +Stephanie Jane; *b* 1968

2c +John Berkeley [John Law Esq, 8 Cracroft St, New Plymouth, NZ]; *b* 1941; *m* 1970 *Janet Elizabeth Slater and has:

1d +Richard Berkeley; *b* 1973

1d +Catherine Muriel; *b* 1975

1c +Janet Capel [Mrs Bryan Cleland, 450 Carrington, New Plymouth, NZ]; *b* 1947; *m* 1969 *Bryan Alexander Cleland and has:

1d +Scott Law; *b* 1971

1d +Sarah Jane Capel; *b* 1971

2d +Sarah Jane Capel; *b* 1974; m 19– *Dean Roy Garrod and has:

1e *Dylan Roy; *b* 1994

2e *Jacob Thomas; *b* 1996

The *de jure* 14th LORD/6th EARL's niece,

LOUISA MARY Berkeley, **Baroness Berkeley** in her own right; *b* 28 May 1840; *m* 3 April 1872 Maj-Gen Gustavus Hamilton Lockwood MILMAN, RA (*d* 28 March 1915), s of Lt-Gen Francis Miles Milman, Coldstream Gds, by his w Maria Margaretta, sis of 1st Baron Tredegar (*see* 1959 edn), and gs of Sir Francis Milman, 1st Bt (*qv*); Mrs Milman was as heir-general of the 1st Lord Berkeley of the 1421 *cr* by letters patent 12 June 1893 declared to have *s* to that dignity on the death of her unc the 6th Earl of Berkeley; she *d* 10 Dec 1899, leaving an only child:

EVA MARY FitzHARDINGE Milman, **Baroness Berkeley** in her own right, MBE (1920); *b* 4 March 1875; *m* 5 Aug 1903 Col Frank Wigram FOLEY, CBE, DSO, Roy Berkshire Regt, T/Lt-Col cmdg 5th Serv Bn 1914 (*d* 7 Oct 1949), 4th s of Capt Edward Foley, RN (*see* FOLEY, B), and *d* 4 Dec 1964, when the title fell into abeyance between her two daus until terminated in favour of the er 5 April 1967:

1 MARY LALLE FOLEY later FOLEY BERKELEY (deed poll Sept 1951), **Baroness Berkeley** in her own right; *b* 9 Oct 1905; *d* unm 1992

2 CYNTHIA ELLA Foley; *b* 31 Jan 1909; *m* 4 Aug 1937 Brig Ernest Adolphus Leopold GUETERBOCK, RE (*d* 1984), of The Plough, Terrick, nr Aylesbury, Bucks, yst s of Alfred Gueterbock, of Bowden, Cheshire, and *d* 1991, leaving:

(1) ANTHONY FitzHARDINGE GUETERBOCK, **18th and present Lord (Baron) Berkeley**

BERNARD

Arms: Sa. two greyhounds rampant and addorsed arg., in chief as many stag's heads cabossed or. **Crest:** On a wreath arg. and az. issuant from a circlet of bezants a demi-bear sa., muzzled or. **Motto:** Bear and forbear. **Badge:** Two stag's heads cabossed fesswise,attires entwined or. **Creation:** Bt (UK) 27 Jan 1954.

SIR DALLAS EDMUND BERNARD, 2ND BT, of Snakemoor, Southampton [Sir Dallas Bernard Bt, Stow, 106 Cheyne Walk, London SW10 0DG]; *b* 14 Dec 1926; *s* f 1975; *educ* Eton and Corpus Christi Coll Oxford (BA 1948, MA 1955); dir Morgan Grenfell & Co Ltd 1964–79, memb Monopolies and Mergers Commn 1973–79, Nat & Foreign Securities Tst Ltd 1982–86, chm Thames Tst Ltd 1983–86, dir Italian Int Bank plc 1978–89, memb Cncl Girls' Public Day Sch Tst 1988–93, FCIS; *m* 1st 3 July 1959 (*divorce* 1979) Sheila Mary, er dau of Arthur Gordon Robey, of 14 Waggon Rd, Beech Hill, Hadley Wood, Herts, and has had:

1 Juliet Mary; *b* 19 Oct 1961; *d* unm 10 Feb 1998

2 *Alicia Elizabeth; *b* 4 July 1964

3 *Sarah Jane; *b* 2 March 1968

Sir DALLAS *m* 2nd 31 Oct 1979 *Mrs Monica Joan Montford, dau of James Edward Hudson, and by her has:

4 *Olivia Louise; *b* 10 April 1981

Lineage: THOMAS BERNARD, of Huguenot descent; *m* Sybil Brackstone, and *d* 16 May 1680, leaving:

THOMAS BERNARD; *m* 1689 Elizabeth Colson, and *d* Dec 1709, leaving issue:

1 THOMAS, of whom presently,

2 Peter, of Bristol

1 Sarah; *m* Charles Adney, of Portsmouth

2 Elizabeth; *m* 1724 William Edwards, of Portsmouth

The er son,

THOMAS BERNARD of Durley, Hants; *b* 1699; *m* 1729 Christian (*d* 15 Jan 1797), dau of Rev William Houghton, Vicar of Romsey, and *d* Sept 1749, leaving issue:

1 Peter, surgeon; *d* unm 29 April 1805

2 COLSON, of whom presently

3 Thomas; *b* 1736; *dsp* 8 May 1820

4 William; *b* 1740; *d* unm 28 Feb 1812

5 Joseph; *b* 1741; *d* unm 25 Feb 1800

The 2nd son,

COLSON BERNARD, a yeoman farmer; *m* 1st 1761 Hannah Sharp, and had issue:

1 Thomas; *b* March 1764; *m* Harriet Cooke, and *d* 20 Aug 1819, leaving issue:

(1) Colson; *b* 11 March 1805; *d* 28 Dec 1855

(2) Thomas; *d* in infancy

2 PETER, of whom presently

3 Colson; *b* 17 July 1767; *d* unm 28 Feb 1808

He *m* 2nd Margaret Everett (*dsp*), and 3rd Mary Plyer (*dsp*), and *d* 8 Sept 1807

The 2nd son,

PETER BERNARD, a surgeon; *b* 29 Oct 1765; *m* 28 June 1797 Sophia (*d* 2 April 1808), dau of Duncan Dallas, of Murray, Forfarshire, and *d* 5 July 1932, leaving issue:

1 Peter, Capt Bt Col 68th Regt of Infantry; *b* 13 Sept 1801; *d* 12 Nov 1866

2 Joseph, JP, barrister, Mayor of Southampton 1838; *b* 6 Feb 1804; *m* 19 May 1841 Georgina Emily Abbot (*d* 10 April 1851), of Warnford Park, Hants, and *d* 8 April 1879, having had issue:

(1) William Joseph; *b* 28 Nov 1842; *d* 22 March 1851

(2) Charles Colson, BA; *b* 23 June 1848; *d* 21 Sept 1872

3 WILLIAM DALLAS, of whom presently

1 Christian; *b* 3 April 1798; *m* 3 Dec 1822 William De Foe Baker, MD, of Southampton, and *d* 30 Aug 1850, leaving issue, two sons and two daus

The yst son,

WILLIAM DALLAS BERNARD, of Durley, Hants, sometime Physician to King of Hanover, Priv Sec to Lord Torrington, Govr of Ceylon 1845–51, Dep Commissary Gen for Ceylon 1851–66; *b* 21 March 1808; *m* in Madras Cathedral 6 Oct 1849 Anne Dawson (*d* 10 Feb 1891), dau of Lt Francis Dawson, RA, by his w Margaret Mercer of Huntingtower, and *d* 1 Feb 1866, leaving issue:

1 William George; *b* 18 Sept 1853; *d* unm

2 EDMUND BOWEN, of whom presently

1 Maria Catherine Geraldine; *b* 20 Oct 1850; *m* 28 Nov 1878 Keith Francis George Anstruther, FRGS, son of Philip Anstruther, Colonial Sec for Ceylon, and *d* 23 Aug 1921, leaving issue (*see* CARMICHAEL-ANSTRUTHER, Bt). He *d* 24 July 1915

The yr son,

EDMUND BOWEN BERNARD, of Snakemoor, Durley, Hants, JP; *b* 25 Nov 1854; *m* 30 Jan 1883 Arabella Margaret (*d* 1 April 1949, aged 90), dau of Benjamin Piercy, JP, of Marchwiel Hall, Wrexham, Denbighshire, and *d* 4 April 1910, leaving issue:

1 Edmund Piercy; *b* 12 Feb 1886; *d* 3 Feb 1983

2 **Sir Dallas (Dan) Gerald Mercer Bernard, 1st Bt** (UK), so *cr* 27 Jan 1954, Lt City London, Midshipman RN 1903–06; md Jardine Matheson 1922–28; memb Exec Cncl Hong Kong 1927–28 and Legve Cncl 1926–28; chm: Hong Kong Gen Chamber Commerce 1923, 1926 and 1927 and Court Dirs Hong Kong and Shanghai Banking Corp 1924, 1926 and 1927; dir: Matheson & Co London 1928–42, Alliance Assur 1931–42, Br and Chinese Corp 1928–42, Chinese Centl Rlwys 1928–42, memb London Consulting Ctee Hong Kong and Shanghai Banking Corp 1929–42; Sheriff London 1942; Dir Bank England 1936–49 (Dep-Govr 1949–54); chm Br Bank of Middle East 1954–65 and Jordan Currency Bd 1954–57, dir Courtaulds 1954–56 (dep chm 1956–62, chm 1962–64, dir 1964–65); dir Proprietors of Hays Wharf; *b* 22 March 1888; *educ* Stubbington Ho Sch and HMS *Britannia*; *m* 16 Nov 1922 Betty (*d* 5 Oct 1980), est dau of Sir Charles Stewart Addis, KCMG, LLD, and *d* 26 Nov 1975, having had issue:

(1) Sir DALLAS EDMUND BERNARD, **2nd and present Bt**

(1) Elizabeth Piercy, served WW II as 3rd Offr WRNS; *b* 10 April 1924; *educ* Southover Manor Sch and London U; *m* 10 Sept 1949 Gordon William Strang, FCA, yst son of James Strang and Mrs K Jarvis, and *d* 29 Nov 1981, leaving three sons and a dau

(2) *Margaret Anne; *b* 6 June 1929; *educ* Southover Manor Sch, Lewes; resumed surname of Cleverly; *m* 1st 8 March 1952 (*divorce* 1974) Dr William Geoffrey Cleverly, MB, BS, yr s of Sir Osmund Somers Cleverly, CB, CVO, of Jesses Hill, Gomshall, Surrey and has had two sons (one *decd*); *m* 2nd 1975 (*divorce* 1980) Charles Bevan Meeres

1 Eveline Isabel; *b* 1 March 1884; *m* 1st 1910 Charles Henderson Ross (*d* 1919), of Rossie; *m* 2nd 1921 Capt George Bibby Hartford, DSO, RN (*d* 29 May 1941), and *dsp* 25 Sept 1945

2 Sybil Piercy; *b* 15 June 1889; *m* 26 Oct 1917 (*divorce* 1926) Gerald Rowley Sawrey-Cookson, Gordon Highrs, son of James Sawrey-Cookson, JP, of Broughton Tower, and Neasham Hall, Durham, and *d* 2 Nov 1963, leaving issue, one son and one dau. He *d* 19 May 1964

3 Enid Magdalen, served WW I in Women's Legion 1917–18, and WW II in FANY 1941; *b* 3 Sept 1895; *m* 16 Sept 1919 Capt Hubert Edward Goddard, E Yorks Regt (*d* 17 Sept 1935), of Haisthorpe Hall, Yorks, s of Col William Edward Goddard, VD, DL, JP, of Thwaite Ho, Cottingham, Yorks, and *d* 1 Jan 1986, leaving a s and dau

BERNERS

Arms: Quarterly of ten, 1st argent a chevron reversed per pale azure and gules per chevron reversed counterchanged (for WILLIAMS); 2nd grandquarter, quarterly 1st and 4th, gules three peewits two and one or (for TYRWHITT); 2nd and 3rd, argent a lion rampant vert vulned in the mouth proper (for JONES); 3rd, gules three peewits two and one or (for TYRWHITT); 4th, argent three boar's heads erect and erased sable (for BOOTH); 5th, sable a wolf salient or, in chief a fleur-de-lys argent between two bezants (for WILSON); 6th, argent a bend sable, a bordure engrailed sable (for KNYVETT); 7th, argent a cross engrailed gules between four water bougets sable; over all a label azure of three points charged with three lions rampant or (for BOURCHIER); 8th, gules a fess argent, between seven billets in chief, four and three, and seven in base; four and three or (for LOVAYNE); 9th grandquarter, quarterly of four, 1st and 4th, France modern; 2nd and 3rd, England, all within a bordure argent (for THOMAS of Woodstock); 10th, quarterly or and vert (for BERNERS). **Supporters:** Dexter, a falcon rising; wings elevated argent, jessed and belled or; sinister, a greyhound proper, gorged with a collar gules studded or. **Motto:** Time tryeth truth.
Creation: B. (E) 24 May 1455.

THE BARONESS BERNERS (Pamela Vivien Williams) [The Rt Hon The Lady Berners, Ashwellthorpe, 103 Charlton Lane, Cheltenham, Glos GL53 9EE]; *b* 30 Sept 1929; *s* mother on termination of abeyance in her favour 30 June 1995; *educ* Stonar Sch Wilts and Radcliffe Infirmary (SRN 1951); *m* 1 March 1952 *Capt Michael Joseph Sperry Kirkham, late Derbys Yeo, yr son of Joseph William Kirkham, of Parwich Lees, Derbys, and has:

1 +RUPERT WILLIAM TYRWHITT; *b* 18 Feb 1953; *m* 12 Feb 1994 *Lisa Carol, dau of Col Edward Gibson Lipsey, USAF (ret), of Phoenix, Arizona, and has:

(1) +Edward Michael Tyrwhitt; *b* 7 July 1994

2 +Robin Raymond Tyrwhitt; *b* 1 Dec 1958; *m* 16 Nov 1991 *Jennifer Anne, dau of Eric Gaynor Eller, of Johannesburg, and has:

(1) +Tess Natalie; *b* 27 Dec 1994

(2) +Annie Rose; *b* 25 March 1997

1 +Caroline Rosemary Tyrwhitt [The Hon Mrs Gordon, Swiss Cottage, Parwich Lees, Ashbourne, Derbys DE6 1QB]; *b* 6 May 1956; *m* 1 Aug 1981 *Robert Francis Gordon and has:

(1) +John Francis; *b* 30 July 1986

(1) +Sally Grace Tyrwhitt; *b* 30 May 1984

Lineage (of Tyrwhitt): Sir HERCULES TYRWHITT; ktd 1067; presumably f of:

Sir HERCULES TYRWHITT; living 1109; had:

Sir ROBERT TYRWHITT; *m* a dau of Sir John Witherington and had an est s:

Sir OLIVER TYRWHITT; *m* Jane, dau of Sir Thomas Umfreville, of Harbottle, Northumberland, and had an est s:

BRIAN TYRWHITT; *m* Anna, dau of Sir Stephen Lowther, and had an est s:

RICHARD TYRWHITT, of Tyrwhitt, Northumberland; *m* Jane, dau of Thomas Lawson, and had an est s:

ROBERT TYRWHITT, of Tyrwhitt; *m* Agnes, dau of William Wyckliff, and had a 2nd s:

Sir WILLIAM TYRWHITT, of Kettleby, Lincs; *m* the dau and heiress of John Groval, of Harpswell, Lincs, and had:

Sir ROBERT TYRWHITT, of Kettleby; *m* — Kelke and had an est s:

Sir WILLIAM TYRWHITT, of Kettleby; *m* — St Quintin and had:

ADAM TYRWHITT, of Kettleby; *m* a dau of 1st/2nd Lord (Baron) Lumley (*see* SCARBROUGH, E), and was presumably f of:

Sir WILLIAM TYRWHITT, of Kettleby; *m* Anne, dau of Sir Robert Constable, of Flamborough, and had a 2nd s:

Sir ROBERT TYRWHITT, of Kettleby; *m* Maud, dau of Sir Robert Talboys, of Goulton and Kyme, and had an est s:

Sir WILLIAM TYRWHITT, of Scotter, Lincs; *m* Isabella, dau of Sir William Ayscough and widow of (a) Christopher Kelk and (b) William Girlington, and *d* 19 March 1541, leaving, with at least one dau (Elizabeth, *m* as his 1st w Sir William Skipwith; *see* SKIPWITH, Bt), a 4th s:

MARMADUKE TYRWHITT, of Scotter; *b* 1533; *m* Ellen, dau of Lionel Reresby, of Thribergh, Yorks, and was *bur* 22 Jan 1599, leaving an est s:

ROBERT TYRWHITT, of Scotter; *bapt* 2 Sept 1562; *educ* St John's Coll Cambridge and Gray's Inn; Sheriff Lincs 1611; *m c* 1587 Anne (*d* Dec 1652 aged 88), dau of Edward Basset, of Fledborough, Notts, and was *bur* 24 Dec 1626, leaving an est s:

MARMADUKE TYRWHITT; *b c* 1588; *educ* St John's Coll Cambridge; Ld Manor of Cameringham, Lincs; *m c* 1623 Mary Haggerston (*bur* 24 Sept 1667) and *d* 1629, leaving an est s:

CECIL TYRWHITT; *b c* 1624; *educ* St John's Coll Cambridge; Ld Manor Cameringham; *m c* 1653 Anne Townshend (*bur* 8 July 1698) and was *bur* 9 March 1695, leaving an est s:

ROBERT TYRWHITT, of Cameringham; *b c* 1654; High Sheriff Lincs 1701; *m* Ellen (*bur* 31 Dec 1713), sis of Thomas Lister, of Coleby Hall, Lincs, and was *bur* 2 Nov 1703, leaving, with an er s (Thomas, of Cameringham (sold to Duke of Marlborough), *d* 1758):

Rev ROBERT TYRWHITT; *b* 1698; *educ* Magdalene Coll Cambridge (MA 1723, DD 1728), Rector Kensington and St James's Westminster 1729–33, Canon Residentiary St Paul's, Canon Windsor 1730; *m* 15 Aug 1728 Elizabeth (*d* 27 April 1748), dau of Rt Rev Edmund Gibson, DD, Bp London, and *d* 15 June 1742, leaving a yst s:

JOHN TYRWHITT, of Netherclay Ho, Somerset; *bapt* 5 July 1737; Capt RN; *m* 28 Oct 1764 Katherine (*d* 4 Dec 1800), only child and heir of Very Rev Penyston Booth, DD, Dean Windsor, and *d* 11 June 1812, having had, with two yr sons (*see* TYRWHITT, Bt):

Sir THOMAS TYRWHITT later JONES (took name and arms by roy licence 3 March 1790 after inheriting the estates of his maternal cousin, Sir Thomas Jones), 1st Bt (UK), so *cr* 2 Oct 1808; *b* 1 Sept 1765; MP Weymouth 1790–91, Denbigh 1797–1802, Athlone 1802–6 and Shrewsbury; *m* 25 April 1791 Harriet Rebecca (*d* 24 July 1824), dau of Edward Williams, of Eaton, Salop, and *d* 24 Nov 1811, leaving, with a 2nd s (Charles, *m* 28 Nov 1819 Emily, sis of 1st Baron Tollemache; *qv*) an est s:

Sir THOMAS JOHN TYRWHITT-JONES, 2nd Bt, High Sheriff Salop 1816, MP Bridgnorth 1818; *b* 12 July 1793; *m* 13 June 1821 Eliza Walwyn (*d* 24 June 1865, having reverted to surname TYRWHITT by roy licence 13 April 1841), yst dau of John Macnamara, of St Kitts, WI, and aunt of Louisa, 2nd w of Sir William Boothby, 8th Bt (*qv*) and had, with other issue:

1 HENRY (Sir), 3rd Bt

2 Edmund Thomas; *b* 16 Oct 1825; Maj-Gen Bengal Staff Corps, Dep Inspr-Gen Police Meerut 1864–80; *m* 10 Feb 1851 Mary Jane (*d* 11 April 1916), dau of Richard Ford, travel writer, by his 1st w Harriet, an illegitimate dau of 5th Earl of Essex (qv) and *d* 21 July 1899, leaving surv issue:

(1) Minnie; *m* 12 June 1878 Lt-Col Francis William Bromfield, Cheshire Regt, and *d* 19 Oct 1936, leaving issue

(2) Louisa Harriet; *m* 25 May 1880 (*annulled* 1882) Louis Alphonse Duperell and *dsp* 2 March 1920

(3) Lucy Marian; *d* unm 23 Aug 1935

3 George Booth; *b* 25 Oct 1830; Lt-Col Bombay SC; *m* 12 June 1874 Emma Matthews (*d* 12 Nov 1893) and *dsp* at sea off Aden 28 April 1875

Sir THOMAS *d* 5 Oct 1839; his est son,

Sir HENRY THOMAS TYRWHITT, 3rd Bt, Lt Rifle Bde; *b* 16 April 1824; *m* 3 Nov 1853 Emma Harriet, **Baroness Berners** in her own right (*d* 18 Aug 1917), only dau and heir of Rev Hon Robert Wilson, and *d* 26 Jan 1894, leaving an est surv s:

Sir RAYMOND ROBERT TYRWHITT later TYRWHITT-WILSON, 4th Bt, and **13th Baron** (*see* below)

Lineage (of Barons Berners): JOHN BOURCHIER/BOUSSER/BURGCHIER, of Stansted, Essex; Judge Common Pleas 1321; *m* Helen, dau of Walter of Colchester, of Stansted, and *d* 1329, leaving, with a yr s (John):

ROBERT BOURCHIER, 1st LORD (Baron) BOURCHIER or BURGCHIER (E), so *cr* by writ of summons to Parl 20 Nov 1348; MP Essex 1329, 1330, 1332 and 1339; fought Battles of Cadsant 1337 and Crécy 1346 in Hundred Years War (envoy conducting peace talks 1347 and 1349), Ld Chllr 1340–41; *m* Margaret, dau of Sir Thomas Prayers, of Sible Hedingham, Essex, and *d* of plague 1349, leaving, with a yr s (William):

1 JOHN BOURCHIER, 2nd LORD (Baron) BOURCHIER, KG (1392), KB by 1380; fought in Hundred Years War Battle of Auray 1364, Govr in Ch Flanders 1384; *m* Elizabeth, dau of Sir John Coggeshall, and *d* 21 May 1400, leaving:

(1) BARTHOLOMEW BOURCHIER, 3rd LORD (Baron) BOURCHIER; *b* 1374; *m* 1st by 5 July 1396 Margaret, widow of Sir John Sutton, but had no issue by her; *m* 2nd Idoine *née* Lovey, widow of (a) Edmund Brooksburn and (b) John Glevant and *dspm* 18 May 1409, leaving:

1a ELIZABETH Bourchier, BARONESS BOURCHIER in her own right according to later doctrine; *b c* 1399; *m* 1st by Sept 1410 Sir Hugh STAFFORD, KG (*see* STAFFORD, B); *m* 2nd Sir Lewis Robsart, KG (*ka sp* 26 Nov 1431) and *dsp* 1 July 1433

2 William (Sir); *m* 1359 Alianore (*d* 5 Oct 1397), yr dau and eventual sole heiress of Sir John de Lovayne (*see* MILFORD HAVEN, M), of Little Easton and Broxted, Essex, and Bildeston, Suffolk, and *d* 1375, leaving:

(1) Sir WILLIAM BOURG(H)CHIER, COUNT OF EU, in Normandy, so *cr* 10 June 1419 (one of six *comtés* in Normandy *cr* by HENRY V within a period of a single year to cement his power in France following the victory of Agincourt); *b c* 1374; *m c* 20 Nov 1405, as her 3rd husb, Anne, Countess of Buckingham, Hereford and Northampton, widow of 3rd and 5th Earls of Stafford

(*see* STAFFORD, B), and dau of Thomas of Woodstock, Duke of Gloucester (6th s of EDWARD III), and sis and eventually sole heir of her bro Humphrey, Earl of Buckingham, and *d* 28 May 1420, leaving, with three er sons (the 1st of whom, Henry, Count of Eu, was *cr* by 14 Dec 1446 Earl of Essex (*see* ESSEX, E, preliminary remarks)) and a dau:

1a Sir JOHN BOURCHIER, KG (1459), **1st Lord** (Baron) **Berners** (E), so *cr* by writ of summons 26 May 1455; ktd 1426, Constable Windsor Castle 1461–74; *m* Margery (*d* 18 Dec 1475), widow of John Ferreby (*dsp* 1441) and dau and heir of Sir Richard Berners, of W Horsley, Surrey (*see* PLYMOUTH, E), and *d* 16 or 21 May 1474, having had, with a yr s:

1b Humphrey (Sir); *m* Elizabeth (*m* 2nd 1472 2nd Duke of Norfolk; *qv*), dau and heiress of Frederick Tylney, of Boston, Lincs, and *dvp ka* as a Yorkist Battle of Barnet 14 April 1471, leaving, with another dau:

1c Sir JOHN BOURCHIER, **2nd Lord** (Baron) **Berners**, KB (Jan 1477/8); *b c* 1467; translator: Froissart's *Chronicles* (2 parts, 1523, 1525), *Huon of Bordeaux* (completed *c* 1530 but only published posthumously), *The History of the Most Noble and Valiant Knight Arthur of Little Brittain* (reprinted 1812), *The Golden Book of Marcus Aurelius* (1534) and *The Castle of Love* (*c* 1540), Chllr Exchequer 1516–27, envoy France and Spain, Deputy of Calais 1520; *m* Lady Katherine Howard, dau of 1st Duke of Norfolk (*qv*), and *dspml* 19 March 1532/3, when the Barony became dormant, having had:

1d Mary; *m* Alexander Unton, of Wadley, Berks, and *dvp* & *sp*

2d JANE Bourchier, of Ashwellthorpe, Norfolk, *de jure* BARONESS BERNERS; *m* Edmund KNYVETT, Sgt-Porter to HENRY VIII (*d* April 1539), and *d* 17 Feb 1561/2, having had, with other issue:

1e John, of Plumstead, Norfolk; *b c* 1518; *m* 1537 Agnes (*m* 2nd William Bowyer, of Wimbledon), dau of Sir John Harcourt, of Stanton Harcourt, Oxon, and *dvm*, leaving:

1f Thomas (Sir), *de jure* 4th LORD (Baron) BERNERS; *b c* 1539; ktd 1579, Sheriff Norfolk 1579–80, procured a certificate declaring that he was rightful Lord Berners but *d* 9 Feb 1617/8 before JAMES I had confirmed it, having *m* Muriel (*d* 25 April 1616), dau of Sir Thomas Parry, and having had:

1g Thomas (Sir); *m* 1592 Elizabeth, 2nd dau of Sir Nathaniel Bacon, KB, of Stiffkey, Norfolk, and *dvp* and was *bur* 20 Sept 1605, leaving:

1h Thomas, of Ashwellthorpe, *de jure* 5th LORD (Baron) BERNERS; *bapt* 10 June 1596; *m* 28 Feb 1619/20 Katherine (*bur* 1 May 1646), yst dau of 3rd Lord (Baron) Burgh (*qv*), and *d* 30 June 1658, leaving, with other issue:

1i John (Sir), KB, *de jure* 6th LORD (Baron) BERNERS, KB (1661); *m* 13 June 1655 Mary (*d* 13 April 1713), est dau of Sir Thomas Bedingfield, of Darsham, Suffolk, and *d* 28 July 1673, having had, with other issue:

1j THOMAS KNYVETT, *de jure* 7th LORD (Baron) BERNERS; *bapt* Feb 1655/6; MP (Tory) Dunwich 1685–87 and Eye 1689–90; *d* unm 28 Sept 1693, when the Barony fell into abeyance until 1711

1j Elizabeth; *m* Thomas Glemham, of Little Glemham, Suffolk, and left:

1k Thomas, Capt of Dragoons, *dsp* 1711

2j KATHARINE, **Baroness Berners**, so declared by Ho Lds 30 May 1720; *bapt* 13 Aug 1658; *m* 1st 2 Oct 1665 John Harris, of London (*dsp* Sept 1686); *m* 2nd 5 Jan 1696 Richard Bokenham, of Weston Market, Suffolk (*dsp* 2 Sept 1721), and *dsp* 29 Nov 1743, when the Barony again fell into abeyance

2i Thomas, of Mutford, Suffolk; *bapt* 22 Feb 1624; *m* Emme, dau of Thomas Haward and *d* 1656–58, leaving:

1j John, of Trowse, Norfolk; *m* Lucy, dau and coheir of Charles Suckling, and was *bur* Oct 1731, having had several children, of whom two daus only left issue:

1k ELIZABETH, of whom presently

2k Lucy; *m* 1st Thomas Holt, of Reading (*d* Nov 1728), s of Ld Ch Justice Holt, and had an only dau; *m* 2nd 1728/9 John Field, carpenter, of Reading, and was *bur* 11 April 1740, having had a further two daus

1c Anne; *m c* 1492 8th Lord (Baron) Dacre (*qv*)

1b Joanna; *m* Sir Henry Nevill(e), s of 1st Lord (Baron) Latymer (*qv*), and had issue (*see* also WARWICK, BROOKE and, E)

2b Elizabeth; *m* 1st 8th Lord (Baron) Willoughby de Eresby (*qv*); *m* 2nd 8th Lord (Baron) Welles

JOHN KNYVETT's er dau,

ELIZABETH Knyvett, of Ashwellthorpe; *b c* 1691/2; *m* 2 May 1720 Henry WILSON (*bur* 28 March 1741), of Didlington, Norfolk, son of Edward Wilson, of Didlington, by Judith, dau of Henry Webster, of Bungay, Suffolk, and gs of Robert Wilson, of Didlington (*d* 11 Nov 1660), and was *bur* 24 Aug 1757, leaving, with a dau (Harriet, *m* John Leighton):

HENRY WILLIAM WILSON, of Didlington and Ashwellthorpe, Norfolk; *bapt* 12 April 1728; *m* 20 May 1757 Mary (*d* 13 Aug 1772), dau of Sir John Miller, 4th Bt, of Chichester (*qv*), and *d* 6 Sept 1796, leaving, with four daus:

1 ROBERT WILSON, **9th Lord** (Baron) **Berners** (abeyance terminated 7 May 1832), of Didlington and Ashwellthorpe; *bapt* 20 Jan 1761; Col (ret by 1820); *d* unm 25 March 1838, when the Barony again fell into abeyance

2 HENRY, **10th Lord**

3 Knyvett; *bapt* 9 Oct 1763; Maj 21st Inniskillen Foot; *ka* against French in W Indies 21 May 1796; *d* unm

4 William; *bapt* 21 Dec 1766; *bur* 25 Oct 1772

5 George (Rev); *b* 27 Nov 1768; Rector Didlington; *m* 12 Sept 1797 Anna Maria (*d* 20 Jan 1846), est dau of Rev Charles Millard, Chllr of Norwich, and *d* 7 Aug 1837, having had 13 sons and a dau

6 Edward; *bapt* 18 June 1770; Maj 46th Foot; *d* unm 11 Dec 1796

The 9th BARON's bro,

Rev HENRY WILSON, **10th Lord** (Baron) **Berners**, as which recognised on termination of abeyance 27 April 1838; *b* 1 Oct 1762; *educ* Emmanuel Coll Cambridge; Rector Kir(k)by Cane, Norfolk, 1820–51 and Allexton, Leics, 1789–1845; *m* 1 May 1788 Elizabeth (*d* 15 Dec 1845), dau of Thomas Sumpter, of Histon Hall, Cambs, and *d* 26 Feb 1851, having had:

1 HENRY WILLIAM WILSON, **11th Lord** (Baron) **Berners**, JP (Leics, Norfolk and Rutland), DL (Leics); *b* 23 Feb 1797; *educ* Eton and Emmanuel Coll Cambridge; Pres Roy Ag Soc 1858; *m* 1st 24 Feb 1823 his cousin Mary Letitia (*d* 30 Sept 1856), er dau and coheir of Col George Crump, of Alexton Hall, Leics; *m* 2nd 21 July 1857 Henrietta Charlotte (*d* 13 Aug 1874), only dau of 1st Baron Delamere (*qv*), and *dsp* 27 June 1871

2 Robert (Rev); *b* 1 Sept 1801; *educ* Eton and Emmanuel Coll Cambridge; Rector Ashwellthorpe 1829–50, and Wreningham; *m* 1st 18 May 1826 Emma (*dsp* 6 Feb 1829), dau of Col Pigott, of Doddershall Park, Bucks; *m* 2nd 13 April 1832 his cousin Harriet (*m* 3rd 28 June 1859 Very Rev Edward Newenham Hoare, Dean of Waterford (*d* 1 Feb 1877), and *d* 3 Sept 1881), widow of John Sheppard and dau and coheir of Col George Crump, of Alexton Hall, and *d* 10 Dec 1850, having by her had:

(1) Harry William Pigott; *b* 11 Feb 1833; Cornet 6th Dragoons; *d* unm 28 April 1853

(1) EMMA HARRIET Wilson, **Baroness Berners**; *b* 18 Nov 1835; *m* 3 Nov 1853 Sir Henry Thomas TYRWHITT, 3rd Bt (*d* 26 Jan 1894; *see* above), and *d* 18 Aug 1917, having had:

1a Harry TYRWHITT later WILSON (roy licence 23 Feb 1876), Lt Gren Gds, 2nd Brig E Div RA, Equerry to HM EDWARD VII when PRINCE OF WALES; *b* 7 Aug 1854; *d* unm 9 Aug 1891

2a Sir RAYMOND ROBERT TYRWHITT later TYRWHITT-WILSON (roy licence 13 Sept 1892), 4th Bt (*s* f in btcy 1894), and **13th Lord** (Baron) **Berners**, BA Trin Coll Cambridge, High Sheriff Salop 1910; *b* 22 July 1855; *d* unm 5 Sept 1918

3a Hugh, CSI, CVO, Cdre (2nd Cl) RN, ADC to HM GEORGE V, Priv Sec to First Ld Admlty 1902–05; *b* 14 July 1856; *m* 10 Aug 1882 Julia Mary (*m* 2nd 18 Nov 1908 Col William Ward Bennitt, 5th Lancers (*d* 21 March 1931), of Stoke Green Ho, Slough), and *d* 15 Feb 1931), dau of William Orme Foster, MP, of Apley Park, Salop, and *d* 26 Oct 1907, leaving:

1b Sir GERALD HUGH TYRWHITT later TYRWHITT-WILSON (roy licence 31 March 1919), 5th and last Bt, and **14th Lord** (Baron) **Berners**; *b* 18 Sept 1883; *educ* Eton; Hon Attaché Dip Serv 1912–19 Constantinople and Rome, author: *First Childhood* (1934), *The Camel* (1936), *The Girls of Radcliffe Hall* (1937), *Far From the Madding War* (1941), *Percy Wallingford and Mr Pidger* (1941), *Count Omega* (1941), *The Romance of a Nose* (1942), *A Distant Prospect* (1945), composer (as Gerald Tyrwhitt; works include the opera *La Carosse du Saint Sacrement* (first performed Paris 1923) and ballets *Triumph of Neptune* (London, Paris and Monte Carlo 1926), *Luna Park* (London, 1930), *A Wedding Bouquet* (London 1937), *Cupid and Psyche* (London 1939) and *Les Sirènes* (1946), also music to film *The Half-Way House* (1944)) and painter; *d* unm 19 April 1950, when the btcy expired

4a Clement; *b* 21 Oct 1857; *m* 25 Nov 1884 Annie (*d* 1 Jan 1936), dau of John Webb, of Adelaide, S Australia, and *d* 28 Feb 1939, having had:

1b Hubert; *b* 9 April, *d* 16 April 1887

5a Rupert, Maj RA, rejoined 1914; *b* 25 May 1859; *m* 15 Nov 1900 Louise Isabel Frances (*d* 20 June 1964), est dau of Walter Fox Williamson Wells, ICS, and *d* 3 Aug 1940, having had issue:

1b Lionel Rupert Knyvett, DSO, DSC, Lt-Cdr RN WW II (despatches four times); *b* 9 Aug 1903; *m* 11 Sept 1936 *Kathleen Mary Pauline, er dau of Brig-Gen Paul Aloysius Kenna, VC, DSO, 21st (Empress of India) Lancers, and was *k* while in command of HMS *Jaguar* 26 March 1942

1b VERA RUBY, **Baroness Berners**

6a Philip Bourchier, Sub-Lt RN and 2nd Lt Inland Water Transport; *b* 28 Nov 1861; *m* 6 Dec 1905 Grace Agnes (*d* 1 Dec 1949), widow of Hugh Gallagher, of Co Donegal, and Westport, Co Mayo, and dau of John May, of Fitzwilliam St, Dublin, and *dsp* 14 April 1938

7a Leonard Francis (Rev), MVO (1906), OBE (1919), Vicar of Fenton, Staffs, and Rector of Rolleston, Staffs 1907, Chaplain-in-ordinary 1899, Canon St George's Chapel, Windsor 1910, CF WW I (wounded); *b* 29 Oct 1863; *educ* Magdalene Coll Cambridge (MA); *d* unm 7 July 1921

8a Thomas Knyvett; *b* 28 Dec 1864; *d* unm 8 Oct 1886

9a John; *b* 14 Sept 1876; *educ* Harrow; *m* 5 Aug 1905 Florence, dau of Richard Collins, of High Plain, Vict, Australia and *d* 14 March 1937, leaving:

1b Stanley Raymond; *b* 13 Aug 1905

1a Ardyn Mary; *b* 2 Sept 1860; *m* 11 April 1887 1st Viscount Knollys (*qv*) and *d* 26 Dec 1922, leaving issue

2a Sybil Grace; *b* 26 April 1866; DGStJ; *m* 14 Feb 1895 James Volant Wheeler, LLM, 2nd s of Edward Vincent Wheeler, DL, of Newnham Court, Worcs, and *d* 9 Feb 1962 aged 95, leaving issue. He *d* 15 April 1939

3a Hester Efa; *b* Feb 1869; *d* unm 4 March 1949

1 Charlotte; *b* 10 April 1790; *m* 3 April 1809 Abbot Upcher (*d* 11 Feb 1819), of Sheringham, Norfolk, and *d* 8 Feb 1857, leaving issue

2 Elizabeth; *b* 6 March 1792; *m* 8 Jan 1810 Rev William Chester and *d* 10 Feb 1865, leaving issue (*see* BAGOT, B)

3 Anne; *b* 13 Nov 1793; *d* an infant

4 Mary; *b* 16 June 1795; *d* unm 28 Jan 1874

5 Anne; *b* 1 May 1799; *m* 3 Jan 1833 Rev John Munnings Johnson (*d* 10 Nov 1886), Rector Scoulton, Norfolk, and *d* 17 Sept 1875

The 13th LORD (Baron) BERNERS's cousin,

VERA RUBY Tyrwhitt, **Baroness Berners**; *b* 25 Dec 1901; *educ* Ladies' Coll Eastbourne and St Agnes's Sch E Grinstead; *m* 2 Aug 1927 Harold WILLIAMS, JP, 2nd s of William Williams, of 59 Eaton Rise, Ealing, W5, and *d* 20 Feb 1992, when the Barony fell into abeyance, leaving:

1 PAMELA VIVIEN, **present Baroness Berners**

2 +Rosemary Tyrwhitt [The Hon Mrs Kelvin Pollock, The Malt House, Hollingbourne, Kent ME17 1VW]; *b* 20 July 1931; *m* 8 June 1959 *Kelvin Alexander Pollock, FCA , son of Kelvin Clayton Pollock, of St Helier, Rochester, Kent, and has issue:

(1) +Simon Kelvin Tyrwhitt; *b* 31 May 1962; *m* 16 May 1998 *Susan Lynne Elizabeth, only dau of Dr Alan Powell, of Christchurch, Dorset, and Mrs Jean Powell, of London

(2) +Alastair Michael Tannahill; *b* 24 April 1964

BERNEY

Arms: Quarterly; gu. and az., over all a cross engrailed, erm.
Crest: A plume of five ostrich feathers, alternately az. and gu.
Motto: *Nil temere, neque timore* ('Nothing with rashness or fear').
Creation: Bt (E) 5 May 1620.

SIR JULIAN REEDHAM STUART BERNEY, 11TH BT, of Park Hall, Reedham, Norfolk [Sir Julian Berney Bt, Reeds House, 40 London Rd, Maldon, Essex CM9 6HE]; *b* (posthumously) 26 Sept 1952; *s gf* 1975; *educ* Wellington and NE London Polytechnic; FRICS 1992; *m* 3 April 1976 *Sheena Mary, yr dau of Ralph Day, of Driftwood, Elm Green Lane, Danbury, Essex, and has:

1 +WILLIAM REEDHAM JOHN; *b* 29 June 1980
2 +Hugo Ralph; *b* 1987
1 *Jessica Mary; *b* 1982

Lineage: This family derived its name from the town of Berney in the hundred of North Greenhow in Norfolk.

Sir THOMAS de BERNEY; *m* Margaret, dau and heir of William de Reedham, through whom he acquired, with other lands, the Manor of Reedham, settling there from Witchingham, Norfolk, *temp* EDWARD III.

His descendant,

HENRY BERNEY moved the family seat, which stood near Reedham Church, and enclosed it in a park nearby, where he built the mansion called Reedham Hall or Park Hall (sold 1696, burnt down and the remains dismantled *c* 1750); *m* Alice, dau of Roger Apleton, of Comb, Essex, and *d* 1584, leaving an est s:

Sir THOMAS BERNEY; Sheriff Norfolk 1610; *m* Juliana, dau of Sir Thomas Gawdy, of Redenhall, Norfolk, Judge Court Common Pleas, and *d* 1616, having had, with other issue:

1 RICHARD (Sir), **1st Bt**
2 Thomas; High Sheriff Norfolk 1647, ancestor of the BERNEYs of Morton Hall, Norfolk

The est surv s,

Sir Richard Berney, 1st Bt (E), so *cr* 5 May 1620, of Park Hall; High Sheriff Norfolk 1622; *m* Anne, dau of Michael Smallpage, of Chichester, and *d* 1668, having had several children, leaving all his estates at Reedham and elsewhere to his 2nd s, Richard, but being *s* in the baronetcy by his est s:

Sir Thomas Berney, 2nd Bt; *m* Sarah, dau of Thomas Tyrell, of Essex, and *d* 1693, having had an est s:

Sir Richard Berney, 3rd Bt, of Kirby Bedon; *m* Dorothy, dau of William Branthwayte, of Hethel, Norfolk, and *d* May 1706, leaving an est s:

Sir Richard Berney, 4th Bt; Sheriff Norwich 1762; *d* unm 1710; *s* by his bro,

Sir Thomas Berney, 5th Bt; *m* Elizabeth, only dau and heir of Simon Folkes, of Suffolk, by Elizabeth, dau and coheir of Samuel Hanson, of Barbados, and *d* 1742, leaving, with a yr s (Richard, Rector Stokesby and Bramston, *d* 1794):

Sir Hanson Berney, 6th Bt; Sheriff Norwich 1762; *m* 8 April 1756 Catherine, dau and heir of William Woolball, of Walthamstow, Essex, and *d* 1778, having had, with two daus (Elizabeth, Catherine):

Sir John Berney, 7th Bt; *m* 9 Sept 1779 Lady Henrietta Nevill(e) (*d* 2 April 1833), dau of 1st Earl of Abergavenny (*see* ABERGAVENNY, M), and *d* 4 Sept 1825, having had, with other issue:

Sir Hanson Berney, 8th Bt; *b* 3 Dec 1780; *m* 1st April 1811 Anne (*dsp* 14 Jan 1838), est dau of Henry Tahourdin, of Sydenham, Kent; *m* 2nd 10 Oct 1843 Agnes (*d* 6 Oct 1870), dau of Thomas Peck, and *d* Sept 1870, having by her had:

Sir Henry Hanson Berney, 9th Bt; *b* 30 Nov 1843; LLB Cambridge; *m* 31 Jan 1866 Jane Dorothy (*d* 7 Dec 1921), dau of Rev Andrew Bloxam, Rector Harborough Magna, Warwicks, and had:

1 Thomas Hugh; Capt 2nd Bn Prince of Wales's Own West Yorks Regt, *b* 17 Oct 1866, *m* 2 July 1892 Fridzwede Katherine (*d* 1941), dau of Lt-Col F W Bell, of Fermoy, Co Cork, and was *ka* Monte Cristo, Natal, 18 Feb 1900, leaving:

(1) THOMAS REEDHAM (Sir), **10th Bt**

(2) (Richard) Geoffrey Gordon; *b* 19 Jan 1897; *m* 1st 1930 (*divorce* after 1937) Marjorie Vernon, dau of Lt-Col Vernon Urquhart, of Huntingfield, Suffolk, and adopted 29 Jan 1937:

*Mhairi Dolores; *b* 26 July 1936

(2) (cont.) Geoffrey Berney *m* 2nd *Doris Rosemary, dau of Cecil Dalziel Beckwith, of London and West Africa, and *d* 1962

2 Richard William; S African Constab, served Boer War 1901–02 and German SW Africa and German E Africa WW I; *b* 20 Dec 1867; *m* 25 June 1913 Maria Theresa, dau of Rev Leslie Carter, Rector Eglish, Co Armagh, and *d* 1945

3 John Hanson; *b* 22 Nov 1868; *m* April 1900 Margaret (*d* 1948), dau of Sinclair George, of New Zealand, and *d* 26 May 1959, leaving:

(1) Hugh Barton; *b* 11 Jan 1902; MB, ChB (NZ) 1925; *m* 18 March 1931 Lillian Irene, dau of Robert William Grigor, of Blenheim, NZ, and *d* 1977, having had:

1a *Helen, BA 1952 1 QSM [Mrs Edward Dashfield, 53 Miro St, Masterton, New Zealand]; *b* 26 Nov 1931; *m* 1955 *Rev Edward Maurice Dashfield, 2nd s of Edward Dashfield, of Wanganui, NZ, and has:

1b *Philip Berney; *b* 10 Aug 1958
2b *James Gilbert; *b* 4 Feb 1961
1b *Prudence Ann; *b* 27 April 1956

2a Ann; *b* 26 Nov 1931 (twin); *m* 1st 1955 Dr Peter Miller Denniss and had:

1b *Simon Hugh Miller; *b* 31 March 1959
1b *Charlotte Jane; *b* 16 May 1956
2b *Helen Clare; *b* 16 May 1956 (twin)
3b *Catherine Ann; *b* 19 Sept 1960

2a (cont.) Mrs Denniss *m* 2nd 1964 *William Edward Willmott [William Willmott, 3780 Point Grey Rd, Vancouver 8, BC, Canada], s of L Earl Willmott of Chengtu, China, and had further issue:

2b *Andrew Mark; *b* 24 Jan 1966

3a Janet Douglas, BA 1955; *b* 29 Aug 1935; *m* 1960 *Terence Daniel O'Leary, CMG, Dipl Serv (ret), 2nd s of Daniel O'Leary, and *d* 27 May 1997, leaving:

1b *John Terence; *b* 1960
2b *Daniel Hugh; *b* 1960 (twin); *m* *Nina –
1b *Helen Fiona; *b* 1964; *m* *Col –

(2) Sinclair Henry Hanson, 2nd NZEF WW II; *b* 31 Jan 1906; *m* 22 April 1936 *Barbara May [Mrs Sinclair Berney, 39A Opaki Rd, Lansdowne, Masterton, New Zealand], yst dau of Andrew Roby Bloxam, of Christchurch, NZ, and *d* 18 June 1967, leaving:

1a *Jenifer May [Mrs David Logan, 94 Titoki St, Lansdowne, Masterton, New Zealand]; *b* 4 June 1938; NZRN 1961, NZMN 1962; *m* 27 Feb 1965 *David Kennedy Logan LLB, only s of John Kennedy Logan, LLM, of Lansdowne, Masterton, NZ, and has:

1b *John Berney Kennedy; *b* 16 April 1968; B Forestry Sc 1989
1b *Helen Margaret; *b* 19 July 1966; B Horticultural Sc 1989
2b *Robyn Elizabeth; *b* 1971; NZRN 1993

2a *Diana Margaret (twin) [Mrs Arthur Grovely, 126A West St, Greytown, S Wairarapa, New Zealand]; *b* 4 June 1938; *m* 1st 6 Jan 1962 (*divorce* 1983) John Allan Burnett, only s of Allan R Burnett, of Featherston, NZ, and has:

1b *Andrew John Hanson; *b* 1971
1b *Margaret Jane [Mrs Stephen Daltrey, 86 Northcliffe Court, Kempton Walk, Shirley, Surrey CR0 7XF]; *b* 8 March 1967; *m* 12 Feb 1994 *Stephen David Daltrey, of Croydon, Surrey

2a (cont.) Mrs Diana Burnett *m* 2nd *Arthur Neill Cooper Grovely

(3) +John Reedham [John Berney Esq, PO Box 25, Rawene, Northland, New Zealand]; *b* 8 Nov 1911; RNZAF WW II; *m* 1937 *Joyce, dau of Donald Bennett, and has:

1a +John Reedham Donald; *b* 1944; *m* 1975 *Noralyne Maxine, dau of G Reid, of Hawaii, and has issue:

1b +Gareth Elijah; *b* 1977
1b *Nalani Kalua; *b* 1976
2b *Juana Marguerite; *b* 1979

2a +Richard Warwick; *b* 1946

1a *Jocelyn Margaret; *b* 1938; *m* 1960 *Thomas William Burgess, of Sydney, Australia, and has:

1b *Matthew Sinclair; *b* 1966
1b *Janette Joyce; *b* 1961

2a *Juliet Alice; *b* 19 Aug 1953

(4) Richard Bruce, DFM, AFC, DFC (USA); *b* 8 Dec 1916; F/Lt RNZAF WW II as Pathfinder RAF (despatches); *k* in a flying accident at Karachi 1947

(1) *Margaret Loraine; *m* 1937 Harold Arthur Roland Dunderdale, s of Harold Antonio Patrick Dunderdale, of Middlesbrough, and has:

1a *Francis John Berney; *b* 23 April 1939; *educ* Massey Coll (DipAg); *m* 1962 *Jennifer, dau of John Rutherford, of Middlewood, Feilding, N Z, and has:

1b *Craig John; *b* 1965

2a *David Bruce; *b* 1 June 1942; *m* 1964 *Jeanette Winifred, dau of John Hamilton Blair, of Masterton, NZ, and has:

1b *Michelle Claire; *b* 9 Sept 1966
2b *Gaye Maria; *b* 15 March 1969

1a *Antonia Margaret Berney; *b* 8 Aug 1944; ATCL, BA (1965)

(2) *Barbara Dorothy [Mrs Melvin Armstrong, 15 College Ave, Christchurch 5, New Zealand]; *b* 9 Dec 1916; *m* 1942 *Melvin Cooper Armstrong, BAgSc

(NZ), BVSc (Sydney), s of Thomas Armstrong, of New Plymouth, NZ, and has:

1a *David Warwick; *b* 27 Sept 1946

2a *Richard Thomas; *b* 30 June 1948

1a *Philippa Jane; *b* 2 Sept 1943; *m* 6 Oct 1967 *Ian George Hamilton, BAgSc, s of Robert Bell Hamilton, of Blenheim, NZ

4 Robert Henry; assist master Godstowe Sch and St George's, Harpenden, served WWs I and II; *b* 5 May 1871; *educ* Trin Hall Camb (MA); *m* 1st 24 Dec 1904 Edith Ann (*d* 19 Oct 1937), yst dau of Daniel Wilson, of The Old Hall, Sandal Magna, Yorks; *m* 2nd 20 Dec 1938 Salome Constance (*d* 20 July 1969), dau of Cdr Edwin Dawes, RIN, of Holmbury, Bedford, and *dsp* 9 Feb 1961

5 Matthew Cromwell; *b* Aug, *d* Sept 1872

6 Andrew James; *b* 23 Sept 1873; *educ* Trin Hall Camb (BA); DC Gold Coast Sierra Leone; *d* unm 28 Dec 1910

7 Alexander David; *b* 20 Sept 1877; *m* 19 March 1924 Alice Lizzie (*d* Oct 1939), 4th dau of A J Moore, of Lowestoft, and *d* 1942, leaving:

(1) Olive Maud; *b* 6 Jan 1925; *m* 1st 19– Paul Rafoth, of USA; *m* 2nd 19– *Rolf Merton and *d* 19–

1 Mary Agnes; *b* 30 March 1876; *d* unm 3 April 1958

2 Jane Dorothy Elizabeth; *b* 28 Nov 1878; *m* 3 July 1907 Henry Dubs Middleton, MA (Oxon), slr, est s of Arthur Middleton, of Far Headingley, Leeds, and *d* 15 Dec 1964, leaving two sons. He *d* 18 Sept 1932

3 Catherine Ann; *b* 19 June 1880; *m* 24 Aug 1904 Robert William Thomas Ewart, MD, of Sailfoot, Moffat, Dumfresshire, est s of Lt -Col Robert William Ewart, of Allershaw, Lanarkshire, and *d* 25 Dec 1918, leaving issue. He *d* 10 April 1939

Sir HENRY *d* 27 Feb 1907; his gs,

Sir Thomas Reedham Berney, 10th Bt, MC; *b* 6 July 1893; *educ* Wellington and Trin Hall Camb (BA 1915, MA 1919), Capt 5th Bn Norfolk Regt, ADC to Govr and C-in-C S Rhodesia 1925–26, served WWs I and II; *m* 1st 23 Aug 1921 (*divorce* 1927) Estelle Irene, yst dau of R Norton Dawson, of The Grange, Pakefield, Lowestoft, and had:

1 *Estelle Elaine [Mrs Mark Strutt, Crix, Hatfield, Peverel, Essex]; *b* 1922; *m* 1st 25 Sept 1940 Maj Kenneth William Bols, PAVO, IA (*ka* Italy 19 July 1944) (*see* STRICKLAND-CONSTABLE, Bt), yr s of Maj-Gen Sir Louis Jean Bols, KCB, KCMG, DSO, and has:

(1) *Andrew Nevile David; *b* 24 April 1943; *educ* Gordonstoun and McGill U; Maj The Blues and Roys; *m* 1st 22 May 1971 Sally Jane, only dau of ACM Sir John Alexander Carlisle Aiken, KCB; *m* 2nd 1980 *Mrs Anne Hard, yst dau of J A Meade, of London

(1) *Erica Sarah; *b* 27 Sept 1941; *m* 23 April 1966 *Capt Nigel Frederick D'Ewes Burch, RA, s of Maj-Gen Frederick Whitmore Burch CSI, CIE, MC, of The Wall Ho, Dedham, Essex

1 (cont.) Mrs Kenneth Bols *m* 2nd 1946 *Lt-Col Mark Frederic Strutt MC, RHA (TA), and has further issue (*see* RAYLEIGH, B)

Sir Thomas *m* 2nd 25 July 1927 (*divorce* 1947) Marjorie Agnew Erskine, yr dau of William Erskine Gill, of Salisbury, S Rhodesia, and by her had:

1 John Reedham Erskine; *b* 31 March 1929; *educ* St Andrews Coll Grahamstown, S Africa and RMA Sandhurst; Lt Roy Norfolk Regt, served Korea (despatches posthumously); *m* 27 July 1951 *Hon Jean Davina Stuart [The Hon Mrs Ritchie, Tannachie, Findhorn, Forres, Moray 1V36 0YJ], only dau of 1st Viscount Stuart of Findhorn (*qv*) (*m* 2nd 30 Jan 1954 Percy William, only s of Lt-Col Harold Jesson; *m* 3rd 1985 *Michael Denison Ritchie, only s of Maj-Gen W H D Ritchie, CB, CBE), and was *ka* in Korea 24 July 1952, leaving:

(1) Sir JULIAN REEDHAM STUART BERNEY, **11th and present Bt**

2 *Elizabeth Anne [Mrs Elizabeth Shepherd, Claydon House, Clare Rd, Hundon, Suffolk CO10 8DL]; *b* 1927; *m* 19 April 1952 (*annulled* 1960) Allan Eustace Shepherd

3 *Cláire [Mrs Richard Christie, 11 Akademie St, Franschhoek, 7690 Cape Town, S Africa]; *b* 1933; *m* 1st 20 Dec 1956 (*divorce* 19–) Lt Jeremy Michael Lynch, RN; *m* 2nd 1992 *Prof Richard Christie, and has by her 1st husb:

(1) *Lewis Reedham; *b* 1967

(1) *Nicole; *b* 2 Jan 1958

(2) *Tania; *b* 7 March 1962

Sir Thomas *m* 3rd 26 April 1947 Peggie (served WW II 1942–45 with BRC), yr dau of Howard M Page, and *d* 5 Jan 1975

BESSBOROUGH

Arms: Gu., a chevron between three combs arg. **Crest:** Out of a ducal coronet az., three arrows, one in pale, two in saltire, points downwards, entwined by a snake, ppr. **Supporters:** Two lions regardant, ppr. **Motto:** *Pro rege, lege, grege* ('For king, law and people'). **Creations:** B. (I) 11 Sept 1721, V. (I) 28 Feb 1722/3, E. (I) 6 Oct 1739, B. (GB) 12 June 1749 and (UK) 19 July 1834.

THE 11TH EARL OF BESSBOROUGH, Viscount Duncannon, of the Fort of Duncannon, Co Wexford, and **Baron Bessborough**, of Bessborough, Co Kilkenny, **Baron Ponsonby of Sysonby**, Co Leicester, and **Baron Duncannon of Bessborough**, Co Kilkenny (Arthur Mountifort Longfield Ponsonby) [The Rt Hon The Earl of Bessborough, Roche Court, Winterslow, Wilts SP5 1BG]; *b* 11 Dec 1912 (HRH THE DUKE OF CONNAUGHT stood sponsor); *s* cousin 1993; *educ* Harrow and Trin Coll Cambridge (BA); served WW II Capt Welsh Gds 1940–46; *m* 1st 28 July 1939 Patricia (*d* 12 Sept 1952), dau of Col Fitzhugh Lee Minnigerode, of Viginia, USA, and has issue:

1 +MYLES FITZHUGH LONGFIELD, *Viscount Duncannon* [Viscount Duncannon, Broadreed, Stansted Park, Rowlands Castle, Hants PO9 6DX]; *b* 16 Feb 1941; *educ* Harrow and Trin Coll Cambridge (MA); FCA; *m* 1972 *Alison Marjorie, 3rd dau of William Storey, OBE, of Playford Mount, Gt Bealings, Woodbridge, Suffolk, and has issue:

(1) +Frederick Arthur William; *b* 9 Aug 1974; *educ* Harrow and UEA

(2) +Henry Shakerley; *b* 1977; *educ* Harrow

(1) *Chloë Patricia; *b* 1975

1 *Sarah [The Lady Sarah Ponsonby, Le Manoir du Moulin de Marolles, 14100 Lisieux, Calvados, France]; *b* 1943; painter and sculptress

The 11th EARL *m* 2nd 20 Sept 1956 (*divorce* 1963) Anne Marie, dau of Lt-Gen Sir Rudolph Carl Slatin Pasha (Baron von Slatin), GCVO, KCMG, CB, and formerly w of Prince George Galitzine; *m* 3rd 17 Dec 1963 *Madeleine Lola Margaret, only dau of Maj-Gen Laurence Douglas Grand, CB, CIE, CBE, of Delaford Manor, Iver, and by her has issue:

2 +Matthew Douglas Longfield [The Hon Matthew Ponsonby, 281 New King's Rd, London SW6 4RD]; *b* 27 Jan 1965; *educ* Marlborough and Manchester U (BSc); *m* 1993 *Jamilie Emett, est dau of Graham Searle, of S Kensington, and has:

(1) +Douglas Arthur William; *b* 20 Feb 1998

3 +Charles Arthur Longfield [The Hon Charles Ponsonby, 36 St Maur Rd, London SW6 4DP]; *b* 12 July 1967; *educ* Marlborough and Downing Coll, Cambridge

Lineage: JOHN PONSONBY, of Haugh Heale, Cumberland; f of:

SIMON PONSONBY, of Hale; *m* Anne Englesfield, of Alenburgh Hall, Cumberland, and had issue:

HENRY PONSONBY, of Hale; *m* 14 May 1605 Dorothy, dau of Henry Sands, of Rottington, Cumberland, and had, with a yr s:

Sir JOHN PONSONBY, of Hale and Bessborough (formerly Kilda(l)ton), Co Kilkenny, Col Regt of Horse under CROMWELL; a commr for depositions by Irish Protestants concerning murders allegedly committed during CROMWELL's campaign in Ireland; Sheriff Cos Wicklow and Kilkenny 1654, MP (I Parl) Co Kilkenny in first parl called after Restoration; *b* 1608; *m* 1st Dorothy, dau of John Briscoe, of Crofton, Cumberland, and had issue:

1 JOHN, ancestor of the PONSONBYs of Hale

Sir JOHN *m* 2nd Elizabeth (after a shortened version of whose name he rechristened his new property of Kilda(l)ton 'Bess'-borough), dau of Henry, 1st Lord Folliott, of Ballyshannon, and widow of (a) Richard Wingfield, of Powerscourt (*see* POWERSCOURT, V), and (b) Edward Trevor, bro of Marcus Trevor, 1st Viscount Dungannon, and *d* 1678, having by her had issue:

2 Henry (Sir), of Bessborough; *m* 1 Oct 1674 Dorothy, dau of Capt Shaw, of Drogheda, and *dsp temp* WILLIAM III, when the estates devolved upon his brother

3 WILLIAM, **1st Viscount**

The 3rd s,

WILLIAM PONSONBY, **1st Viscount Duncannon**, of the fort of Duncannon, Co Wexford, so *cr* 28 Feb 1722/3, as also earlier 11 Sept 1721 BARON BESSBOROUGH, of Bessborough, Co Kilkenny (both I), PC (I 1715); *b* 1659; *educ* Trin Coll Dublin; MP Co Kilkenny 1692–93, 1695–99 and 1703–21; *m* Mary (*d* 26 May 1713), dau of Hon Randal Moore, of Ardee, Co Louth, son of 2nd Viscount Moore (*see* DROGHEDA, E), and had, with other issue:

1 BRABAZON, **1st Earl**

2 Henry, of Ashgrove, Maj-Gen; *m* Lady Frances Brabazon (*d* 4 Nov 1751), dau of 5th Earl of Meath (*qv*), and was *ka* Fontenoy 11 May 1745, leaving, with a dau (Juliana, *m* 1743 William Southwell):

(1) Chambré Brabazon, of Ashgrove, MP; *m* 1st 28 Sept 1746 Elizabeth, dau and heir of Edward Clarke, and had issue:

1a Frances; *m* 28 July 1767 Gorges Lowther, of Kilrue, Co Meath

(1) (cont.) Chambré Ponsonby *m* 2nd 23 Oct 1752 Louisa, dau of John Lyons of Belmont, Westmeath, Deputy Clerk Cncl and Dep Muster Master Gen, and by her had issue:

2a Sarah, of Plasnewydd, Llangollen; one of the two celebrated 'Ladies of Llangollen'; *d* unm 8 Dec 1831

(1) (cont.) Chambré Ponsonby *m* 3rd Mary (*m* 2nd Sir Robert Staples, Bt (*qv*)), dau of Sir William Barker, Bt, of Kilcooley, Co Tipperary, and *d* 20 Dec 1762, having by her had issue:

1a Chambré Brabazon PONSONBY-BARKER, of Kilcooley, *b* 12 June 1762, *m* 4 June 1791 Lady Henrietta Taylour (*d* 12 Jan 1838), dau of 1st Earl of Bective (*see* HEADFORT, M), and *d* 13 Dec 1834, leaving, with other issue:

1b William, of Kilcooley, DL; *b* 9 Nov 1795; *m* 8 Aug 1816 Elizabeth Selina (*d* 28 June 1878), dau of Rt Rev Hon William Knox, Bp Derry, and *dsp* 9 Jan 1877

2b Chambré Brabazon PONSONBY; *b* 14 Nov 1799; Capt 8th Hus; *m* 30 April 1834 Mary (*d* 10 Aug 1840), dau of Col David La Touche, of Marlay, and *dsp* 1 May 1863

3b Thomas Henry PONSONBY, of Kilcooley; *b* 21 Feb 1807; Capt 6th Dragoon Guards; *m* 21 Feb 1838 Fanny Mary, dau of Major R L Dickson, and *d* 10 Feb 1880, leaving, with other issue:

1c Chambré Brabazon, of Kilcooley; *b* 14 Dec 1839; Lt 10th Hus; *m* 22 Oct 1873 Hon Mary Eliza Sophia Plunkett (*d* 5 July 1921), dau of 16th Baron of Dunsany (*qv*), and *d* 9 Dec 1884, leaving issue:

1d Thomas Brabazon, of Kilcooley, DL Co Tipperary; *b* 29 Dec 1878; 10th Hus; *m* 25 Nov 1909 Frances May (*d* 1978), yr dau of Maj George Paynter, of Eaton Grange, Grantham, Lincs, and *d* 17 Nov 1946, leaving:

1e +Chambré Brabazon [Col Chambré Ponsonby, Low Port, Linlithgow, W Lothian, Scotland]; *b* 20 Jan 1911; *educ* Stowe; Hon Lt-Col 10th Hus, served WW II, ADC to Govr NSW 1935–36, Comptroller to Govr-Gen and C-in-C Australia 1936–37; *m* 1st 3 Jan 1941 (*divorce* 1953) Merelina (*d* 1993), only dau of Lt-Col James Tindal Ives Bosanquet, JP, of Bayfields, Headley, Hants, and has issue:

1f *Merelina Karen [Merelina Ponsonby, 10 Lansdowne Gdns, London SW8 2EG]; *b* 6 May 1946; *m* 27 Feb 1971 (*divorce* 1977) John Dymoke White (*d* 27 May 1998), and has:

1g *Merelina Rosanne; *b* 8 Feb 1973

1g *Lucinda Jane; *b* 16 Oct 1974

1e Col Ponsonby *m* 2nd 1954 *Diana Wray Hurt, of Reigate, Surrey, and by her has issue:

1f +Richard Brabazon; *b* Jan 1955; BSc Eng (Hons), Capt RE (ret) (despatches); *m* 1978 (*divorce* 19–) Diana Louise, dau of A R Moodie, of Bonnytown House, Linlithgow, and has:

1g +Tristan; *b* 1984

1g *Lorna Anne; *b* 1980

2g *Marianne Jane; *b* 1982

2f +Miles Chambré; *b* Aug 1958; *m* 1987 *Jane Elizabeth, yr dau of (Oliver) Barry Hopton, and has:

1g +Simon Chambré; *b* 1990

2g +Jason Chambré; *b* 1992

2e George Thomas, MC and bar; *b* 3 April 1913; *educ* Eton and RMC Sandhurst; Maj 17th/21st Lancers WW II (severely wounded); *m* 18 Sept 1948 *Elizabeth Penelope Melville [Mrs George Ponsonby, Kilcooley Abbey, Thurles, Co Tipperary, Ireland], er dau of (Walter) Douglas Melville Wills, CBE, JP, of Barley Wood, Wrington, Somerset, and *d* 1984, having had issue:

1f +Thomas Charles George [Thomas Ponsonby Esq, 31 Ladbroke Gdns, London W11 2PY]; *b* 23 Aug 1950; *educ* Eton and Trin Coll of Music London; *m* 1980 (*annulled* 1989) Elisabeth Marie Philippine, dau of Jean Jules Marie Masurel, of Paris, and has:

1g +Sebastian Jean; *b* 1983

2f +Henry Brabazon [Henry Ponsonby Esq, Ballynatray, Youghal, Co Cork, Ireland]; *b* 6 May 1952; *educ* Eton, Bristol U and RAC Cirencester; *m* 1977 *Elizabeth Fiona Mary, est dau of Peter Bedford Brotchie, and has:

1g +Thomas George Peter; *b* 22 Sept 1981; *educ* Glenstal Abbey

1g *Rose Elizabeth Mary; *b* 5 Feb 1988

3f +Peter Douglas [Peter Ponsonby Esq, Kilcooley Abbey, Thurles, Co Tipperary, Ireland]; *b* 24 June 1955; *educ* Eton; *m* 1982 *Faith Primrose Orr, only child of Rev Canon Ernest Arthur Brandon, of The Rectory, Foulksmills, Co Wexford, and has:

1g *Emma Rebecca Brandon; *b* 1984

2g *Sarah Georgina Brandon; *b* 1986

3g *Julia Nicola Brandon; *b* 1992

3e +Henry Jeffrey [Henry Ponsonby Esq, Grove, Fethard, Co Tipperary, Ireland]; *b* 30 Nov 1930; *educ* Canford; *m* 30 April 1960 *Rosemary Jane, est dau of Ernest Sydney Wells, of Little Potters, Buxted, Sussex, and has:

1f +Julian Henry; *b* 23 April 1963; *m* 1993 *Patricia Lynn, dau of Dr Robert Ingram, of Washington, USA, and has:

1g +George Thomas; *b* 22 March 1996

1f *Jane Frances; *b* 6 May 1965; *m* 1994 *Simon D Marsh, only s of Hugh Marsh, of Westmill, Buntingford, Herts, and has:

1g *Harry Duncan; *b* 9 Sept 1995

2g *Peter Nicholas; *b* 7 May 1997

2f *Rosanna; *b* 21 Dec 1966

1e *Noreen de Vere [Mrs Henry Young, End House, Pilton, Somerset]; *b* 14 Aug 1917; *m* 19 Sept 1939 *Brig Henry Lawrence Savill Young, DSO, (*see* YOUNG, Bt, of North Dean), and has issue

2d Henry Chambré, DSO (1918), MC; *b* 8 April 1883; Col late KRRC, GSO (1) 4th Div 1932–35, Cdr (T/Brig) 6th Inf Brigade 1935–39, hon Brig 1939, served WW I (despatches, Brevet), Greek Military Cross; *m* 5 July 1923 Beatrice Maud Cecil (*d* 4 Feb 1961), 2nd dau of Sir William Henry Levinge, 9th Bt (*qv*), and *d* 2 Jan 1953, leaving:

1e Eileen Dorothy; *b* 5 Jan 1925; *d* 198–

1f Dorothy Constance; *m* 5 Dec 1905 Col Bryan Henry Chetwynd-Stapylton, CBE, and *d* 23 Aug 1942, leaving issue (*see* CHETWYND, V)

2d Alice Isabel; *m* 21 April 1902 Capt Rowland Henry Tyssen Holroyd-Smyth, DL, of Ballynatray, Youghal, Co Cork, and *d* 1945, leaving issue

3a Mary; *m* Thomas Barton, of Grove

3 Folliott; *d* 1746

The 1st VISCOUNT *d* 17 Nov 1724; his eldest son,

BRABAZON PONSONBY, **1st Earl of Bessborough**, so *cr* 6 Oct 1739 (I), as also 12 June 1749 BARON PONSONBY OF SYSONBY, Co Leicester (GB); MP (Whig) Newtonards 1705–14 and Kildare 1715–24; *m* 1st Sarah (*d* 21 May 1733), widow of Hugh Colvill and dau of John Margetson, son and heir of Most Rev James Margetson, DD, Archbp Armagh, and had, with other issue:

1 WILLIAM, **2nd Earl**

2 John, PC; *b* 29 March 1713; Speaker I H of C; *m* 22 Sept 1743 Lady Elizabeth Cavendish (*d* 1796), dau of 3rd Duke of Devonshire (*qv*), and *d* 16 Aug 1787, leaving, with other issue:

(1) WILLIAM BRABAZON, 1st BARON PONSONBY OF IMOKILLY (UK), so *cr* 13 March 1806, PC (I 1789); *b* 15 Sept 1744; MP (I Parl) Cork 1764–76, Bandon 1776–83 and Co Kilkenny 1783–1800, also (UK Parl) 1801–06, Jt PMG Ireland 1784–89; *m* 26 Dec 1769 Hon Louisa Molesworth (*m* 2nd 21 July 1823 4th Earl Fitzwilliam (*see* 1970 edn) and *d* 1 Sept 1824), dau of 3rd Viscount Molesworth (*qv*), and *d* 5 Nov 1806, having had:

1a JOHN PONSONBY, 2nd BARON PONSONBY OF IMOKILLY and 1st and last VISCOUNT PONSONBY OF IMOKILLY, Co Cork (UK), so *cr* 20 April 1839, GCB (1834); *b c* 1770; when a young man in Paris his surpassing good looks allegedly saved him from lynching by a crowd during the French Revolution 1791; MP (I Parl) Tallagh(t) 1793–97, Dungarvan 1797–1800 and (UK Parl, Whig) Galway 1801–02, Envoy Extrdy and Min Buenos Aires 1826–28, Rio de Janeiro 1828–29, Brussels 1830–31 and Naples June–Nov 1832, Amb Constantinople 1832–41 and Vienna 1846–50; *m* 13 Jan 1803 Elizabeth Frances, dau of 4th Earl of Jersey (*qv*), and *dsp* 21 Feb 1855, when the Viscountcy expired

2a William (Sir), KCB; Maj-Gen; *m* 26 Jan 1807 Hon Georgiana FitzRoy, yst dau of 1st Baron Southampton (*qv*) and was *ka* Waterloo 18 June 1815, having had, with other issue:

1b WILLIAM PONSONBY, 3rd BARON PONSONBY OF IMOKILLY; *b* 6 Feb 1816; Cornet 3rd Light Dragoons 1834–36; *m* 12 April 1851 Maria Theresa Duerbeck, of Munich, and *dsp* 2 Oct 1861

1b Charlotte Georgiana; *m* 1st 8 July 1834 Lt-Col John Horace Thomas Stapleton (*see* 1970 edn STAPLETON, Bt); *m* 2nd 11 Dec 1838 R-Adml Sir Charles Talbot, KCB (*see* SHREWSBURY and WATERFORD, E), and had issue

2b Mary Elizabeth; *m* 1 Aug 1835 Rev Henry George Talbot (*see* SHREWSBURY and WATERFORD, E) and *d* 14 Sept 1838

3a Richard (Rt Rev); DD, Bp Derry and Raphoe; *m* 1804 Frances, 2nd dau of John Staples, PC (*see* STAPLES, Bt), and *d* 27 Oct 1853, having had, with other issue:

1b WILLIAM BRABAZON, 4th and last BARON PONSONBY OF IMOKILLY; *b* 21 Aug 1807; Ensign 7th Roy Fus 1827, Capt 1838, ret 1843; *d* unm 10 Sept 1866, when the Barony expired

4a George, of Woodbeding, W Sussex; *m* 1st 7 April 1807 —, dau of John Jacob Gladstanes, and had a s; *m* 2nd 1812 Diana Juliana Margaretta, dau of Hon Edward Bouverie (*see* RADNOR, E), and *d* 5 June 1863, leaving by her, with a s:

1b Diana; *m* 16 Aug 1842 1st and last Baron Lanerton of Lanerton (*see* CARLISLE, E)

1a Mary Elizabeth; *m* 18 Nov 1794 2nd Earl Grey (*qv*) and *d* 26 Nov 1861

(1) George; *b* 4 March 1755; MP (I Parl) Inistiogue 1784, Ld Chllr Ireland 1806; *m* 1781 Mary, dau of 2nd Earl of Lanesborough (*qv*), and *d* 1817, leaving:

1a Elizabeth; *m* 1803 Hon Francis Aldborough Prittie (*see* DUNALLEY, B) and *d* 11 Jan 1849

(1) Catharine; *m* 15 Dec 1763 2nd Earl of Shannon (*qv*) and had issue

(2) Frances; *m* 13 Dec 1774 1st Baron Lismore of Shanbally (*see* 1898 edn) and had issue

The **1st Earl** *m* 2nd 28 Nov 1733 Elizabeth (*dsp* 17 July 1738), widow of (a) Sir John King, 1st Bt, of Abbey Boyle, and (b) John, 1st Lord Moore of Tullamore, and est dau and coheir of John Sankey, of Tenelick, Co Longford, and *d* 4 July 1758

His elder son,

WILLIAM PONSONBY, **2nd Earl of Bessborough**; *b* 1704; a Ld Treasury, PMG; *m* 5 July 1739 Lady Caroline Cavendish (*d* 20 Jan 1760), est dau of 3rd Duke of Devonshire (*qv*), and *d* 11 March 1793, having had surv issue (with two daus):

FREDERICK PONSONBY, **3rd Earl of Bessborough**; *b* 24 Jan 1758; *m* 27 Nov 1780 Lady Henrietta Frances Spencer (*d* 14 Nov 1821), 2nd dau of 1st Earl Spencer (*qv*), and had issue:

1 JOHN WILLIAM, **4th Earl**

2 Frederick Cavendish (Sir), GCMG, KCB, KCH; *b* 6 July 1783; KMT, KSG, Maj-Gen, Govr Malta; *m* 16 March 1825 Lady Emily Charlotte Bathurst (*d* 1 Feb 1877), yst dau of 3rd Earl Bathurst (*qv*), and *d* 11 Jan 1837, leaving, with other issue:

(1) Henry Frederick (Sir), GCB, PC; *b* 10 Dec 1825; Gen, Col Gren Gds, Kt Medjidie, Priv Sec and Equerry to HM QUEEN VICTORIA and Keeper Privy Purse 1878–95, formerly Equerry to HRH THE PRINCE CONSORT, served Crimea (capture Sebastopol), previously Priv Sec to Ld Lt Ireland; *m* 30 April 1861 Hon Mary Elizabeth, VA, Maid-of-Honour to HM QUEEN VICTORIA, Extra Woman Bedchamber HM 1896–1901 (*d* 16 Oct 1916), est dau of John Crocker Bulteel, MP, of Pamflete, Devon, by Elizabeth, dau of 2nd Earl Grey (*qv*), and *d* 21 Nov 1895, leaving:

1a John (Sir), KCB, CMG, DSO; *b* 25 March 1866; Maj-Gen Coldstream Gds, Col Suffolk Regt 1925–39, served Matabeleland 1893–94 (medal), Uganda 1898 (medal), S Africa 1899–1902 (despatches, Queen's and King's medals, DSO) and WW I (wounded, despatches, CB, Brevet), Officer Legion of Honour, Cdr Order Leopold of Belgium, Croix de Guerre France and Belgium; *m* 21 Dec 1935 Mary, dau of Thomas Robley, of Ingleberg, Beckermet, Cumberland, and *dsp* 26 May 1952

2a FREDERICK EDWARD GREY, *cr* BARON SYSONBY (*qv*)

3a ARTHUR AUGUSTUS WILLIAM HARRY, *cr* BARON PONSONBY OF SHULBREDE (*qv*)

1a Alberta Victoria (HM QUEEN VICTORIA stood sponsor); *m* 22 June 1891 Maj-Gen William Edward Montgomery, late Scots Guards, of Grey Abbey, Co Down, and *dsp* 15 Oct 1945. He *d* 11 June 1927

2a Magdalen; *d* unm 1 July 1934

3 WILLIAM FRANCIS SPENCER, *cr* BARON DE MAULEY (*qv*)

1 Caroline; the notorious Lady Caroline Lamb; *m* 1805 2nd Viscount Melbourne and *d* 1828

The 3rd EARL *d* 3 Feb 1844; his eldest son,

JOHN WILLIAM PONSONBY, **4th Earl of Bessborough**, PC (1831); *b* 31 Aug 1781; MP (Whig) Knaresborough 1805–06, Higham Ferrers 1810–12, Malton 1812–26, Co Kilkenny 1826–32 and Nottingham 1832–34, Ld Lt Co Carlow 1831–38 and Co Kilkenny 1838–47, *cr* 19 July 1834 BARON DUNCANNON OF BESSBOROUGH, Co Kilkenny (UK); apptd Ld Lt Ireland 10 July 1846, *d* in office 16 May 1847; *m* 16 Nov 1805 Lady Maria Fane (*d* 19 March 1834), dau of 10th Earl of Westmorland (*qv*), and had, with other issue:

1 JOHN GEORGE BRABAZON PONSONBY, **5th Earl of Bessborough**, PC (1848); *b* 14 Oct 1809; *m* 1st 8 Sept 1835 Lady Francs Charlotte Lambton (*d* 18 Dec 1835), dau of 1st Earl of Durham (*qv*); *m* 2nd 4 Oct 1849 Lady Caroline Amelia Gordon Lennox (*d* 30 April 1890), dau of 5th Duke of Richmond (*see* RICHMOND and GORDON, D), Ld Lt and Custos Rotulorum Co Carlow, Master Queen's Staghounds 1848–52 and 1859–66, Ld Steward Household 1868–74; *dsp* 28 Jan 1880

2 William Wentworth Brabazon; *b* 1812; *d* 1831

3 FREDERICK GEORGE BRABAZON PONSONBY, **6th Earl of Bessborough**, DL; *b* 11 Sept 1815; barrister; *d* unm 11 March 1895

4 George Arthur Brabazon; *b* 17 May 1820; *d* 1841

5 WALTER WILLIAM BRABAZON, **7th Earl**

6 Spencer Cecil Brabazon PONSONBY later PONSONBY-FANE (roy licence 1875) (Sir), GCB, ISO, PC, of Brympton, Yeovil, Somerset, JP; *b* 14 March 1824; Kt Order St Ernestine of Saxe-Coburg, Comptroller Ld Chamberlain's Dept 1857–1901, Gentleman Usher to the Sovereign 1859–1915 and to Sword of State 1901–15, Bath King of Arms 1904–15; *m* 7 Oct 1847 Hon Louisa Anne Rose Lee Dillon (*d* 18 July 1902), 3rd dau of 13th Viscount Dillon (*qv*), and *d* 1 Dec 1915, having had, with other issue:

(1) John Henry, of Brympton, Yeovil, Somerset; *b* 21 July 1848; *m* 14 Oct 1875 Florence (*d* 30 April 1922), est dau of Harvie Morton Farquhar (*see* FARQUHAR, Bt), and *d* 11 Sept 1916, leaving issue:

1a Richard Arthur Brabazon, of Kyoto, Japan, and Brympton; Hon LLD Hong Kong 1925; *d* 10 Dec 1937

1a Violet Louisa; *b* 6 Oct 1876; *m* 11 Oct 1905 Capt Edward Archer Bolton Clive, Seaforth Highrs, s of Gen Edward Henry Clive, of Perrystone Court, Herefs, and *d* 2 March 1953, leaving issue. He *d* 3 July 1928

(2) George Richard; *b* 6 March 1850; Lt RA; *d* 5 Feb 1871

(3) Robert Charles; *b* 6 June 1854; *m* 17 July 1877 Mary (*d* 15 May 1935), est dau of George Maclachlan of Machlachlan, and *d* 16 Nov 1909, leaving:

1a George Arthur (Sir), KCVO (1939); *b* 8 April 1878; Lt Gren Gds, Comptroller and Priv Sec to HM QUEEN MAUD of Norway 1919–38, Grand Cross St Olav of Norway 1966, Extra Equerry to TM GEORGE VI 1939–52 and THE QUEEN 1952; *m* 1st 27 Feb 1906 Julia Winifred Maitland (Sheila) (*d* 23 Nov 1918), dau of Phineas A R Oldfield, and had:

1b Robert Martin Dominic; *b* 4 Aug 1911; Lt-Cdr RN WW II (despatches); *m* 1st 4 June 1941 (*divorce* 1962) Dorothy Edith Jane (*d* 1994), formerly w of Cholmeley Ranson Cuthbert and yst dau of Henry Hervey Vincent Lane, JP, DL, of King's Bromley Manor, Staffs, and had:

1c Hermione; *b* 23 Jan 1945; *m* 9 Oct 1975, as his 1st w, *Viscount Raynham, s and heir of 7th Marquess Townshend (*qv*), and *d* 1985 in a motor accident, leaving issue

1b (cont.) Lt-Cdr Robert Ponsonby *m* 2nd 12 July 1962 Jane Frances (*d* 1993), widow of (a) Capt William Morrice, Queen's Bays, and (b) Maj George Reginald Benson, formerly of Lutwyche Hall, Salop, and yr dau of Thomas Hood Henderson Walker, JP, LLD, of Tigh-na-muira, Monifieth, Angus, and *d* 11 Dec 1995

2b Frederick William; *b* 13 April 1917; Lt-Cdr RN WW II (despatches twice), accidentally drowned at Setubal, nr Lisbon, 20 Oct 1950

1b Rosamond Mary; *b* 17 Dec 1906; *m* 10 May 1930 (Oliver) Peter Haig, TD (*d* 13 May 1987), only s of Col Oliver Haig of Ramornie, and *d* 14 April 1985, having had:

1c *Anthony Oliver [Anthony Haig Esq, Laggan House, Scaniport, Inverness IV1 2DL]; *b* 29 Aug 1932; *m* 5 Oct 1957 *Belinda Valerie, dau of Maj Derek Hugo Burr, and has:

1d *Alexander Veitch; *b* 19 Nov 1960; *m* 24 Aug 1991 *Susan Anne Harriet, dau of Sir Anthony W A Campbell, of Co Down, and has:

1e *Kirsty Louise; *b* 27 Nov 1993

2e *Iona Frances; *b* 2 Jan 1995

2d *Hugo Peter; *b* 8 May 1962; *m* 23 July 1988 *Janey Fiona Maitland, dau of Sir Alexander Maitland Bt (*qv*) and has issue

1c *Iona Sheila [Mrs Anthony Wheatley, 2 Claridge Court, Munster Road, London SW6 4EY]; *b* 22 Aug 1941; *m* 17 Nov 1962 *R-Adml Anthony Wheatley, CB, RN, and has:

1d *Charlotte Emma; *b* 1 Oct 1963; *m* 7 Dec 1991 *Charles Edmund Magris Sylvester and has:

1e *Henry Magris Ransome; *b* 1996

1e *Hermione Emma Louise; *b* 1996

1a (cont.) Sir George Ponsonby *m* 2nd 26 July 1921 Elisa, Ldy-in-Waiting to HM QUEEN MAUD of Norway, dau of Capt Hendrick Andreas Broch, of Christiania, and *d* 12 Nov 1969, having by her had issue:

2b *Maud Elisabeth [Mrs William Hutton-Attenborough, 32 Maidenhead Rd, Stratford-upon-Avon, Warwicks]; *b* 29 April 1922; *m* 24 Aug 1957 *Lt-Cdr William Hutton-Attenborough, RN, yr s of Edwin Augustus Hutton-Attenborough, MB, BS, MRCS, LRCP, of Barklye House, Sylvan Way, Bognor Regis, Sussex, and has:

1c *George William; *b* 5 Sept 1958; *m* 1988 *Julie, er dau of J B Davidge, of The Bryn, Pontllanfraith, Gwent

2c *John Frederick; *b* 25 June 1960; *m* 1987 *Helen Louise, dau of John T Brewer, of Rickmansworth, Herts, and has issue:

1d *Matthew George; *b* 1993

2d *Robert William (twin); *b* 1993

1d *Emma Eileen Maud; *b* 1988

2d *Katherine Elisabeth; *b* 1991

3b Victoria; *b* 6 July 1926; *m* 25 Oct 1947 *Capt Rupert Mahaffy, Irish Guards, only surv s of Maj Robert Pentland Mahaffy (*see* DILLON, V), and *d* 1 April 1995, having had issue:

1c Dominic John; *b* 1955; *d* 1956

1c *Henrietta Clare Elisabeth [Mrs Henrietta Usherwood, Pine Cottage, Ealing Green, London W5 5EN]; *b* 1949; *m* 1979 (*divorce* 1990) Nicholas John Usherwood and has issue:

1d *Theodore Patrick John; *b* 1981

1d *Constance Hazel Kate; *b* 1985

2c *Sarah Georgiana [Mrs William Baker, The Old Rectory, Scremby, Lincs PE23 5RP]; *b* 1952; *m* 1977 *William Hugh Baker and has:

1d *Charles Frederick Benno; *b* 1988

1d *Sophia Victoria; *b* 1994

3c *Kate Alexandra Mary [Marquise de Fayet de Montjoye, 33 rue Georges Appay, 92150 Suresnes, France]; *b* 1959; *m* 1983 *Henry Melchior Marie Gerard, Marquis de Fayet de Montjoye, and has had:

1d *Alexander Jacques Rupert; *b* 1986

1d *Clementine Marie; *b* 1989

2d Emilie; *b* and *d* 1991

2d *Daisy Camille Marie; *b* 1993

4c *Susanna Victoria; *b* 1963

(4) Sydney Alexander; *b* 26 Feb 1863; *m* 10 June 1893 Hon Audrey St Aubyn (*d* 11 Sept 1936), 2nd dau of 1st Baron St Levan (*qv*), and *d* 27 Aug 1940, having had issue:

1a Patrick Spencer John; *b* 10 Sept 1894; Lt RN; *d* 10 July 1922

2a James Michael, MBE; *b* 7 Sept 1901; Frontier Control Force N Rhine Regn; *m* 5 Feb 1929 (*divorce* 1937) Lesley Maude Hamilton (drowned after being torpedoed *c* 1942), only child of James Kershaw, of Bridgefoot House, South Mimms, Herts, and *dsp* 21 Nov 1946

1a Eleanor Elizabeth Anne; *b* 28 Oct 1899; *d* unm Blantyre, Malawi, 23 March 1977

(5) Hugh Spencer, of Oporto; *b* 5 Dec 1865; *m* 8 Nov 1894 Anitha Magdalene (*d* 11 June 1938), eldest dau of Hermann Lorenz Feuerheerd, of Oporto, and *d* 13 May 1934, having had issue:

1a Spencer Lawrence; *b* 12 April 1896; T/Lt 12th Service Bn Middx Regt; *d* 12 Jan 1916 of wounds recd in action

2a David Brabazon; *b* 21 Dec 1901

1a Odeyne Anitha Rose; *b* 31 Dec 1907; *m* 2 July 1936 Cyrille Alexandrovitch Wolfman, yr s of Col Alexandre Wolfman, late of St Petersburg, and *d* 3 April 1966, leaving two daus

(6) Theobald Brabazon; *b* 24 Sept 1868; *m* 10 Aug 1892 Bertha (*d* 25 Nov 1934), dau of John Edwards, and *d* 14 May 1929

7 Gerald Henry Brabazon; *b* 17 July 1829; *m* 9 Feb 1858 Lady Maria Emma Catherine Coventry (*d* 7 Feb 1912), sis of 9th Earl of Coventry (*qv*), and *d* 30 Nov 1908, having had issue:

(1) Louis George de Hale; *b* 11 Nov 1858; *m* 9 Feb 1882 Elizabeth Susan (*d* 5 Aug 1935) (*m* 2nd 9 Sept 1899 George Augustus Bligh Livesay, of Ardmore, Parkstone, Dorset, who *d* 1916), dau of Francis Leyborne Popham, of Hunstrete and Littlecote, Wilts, and *d* 6 Nov 1887, leaving issue:

1a Mabel Elizabeth; *b* 27 April 1883; *m* 10 Oct 1907, as his 1st w, Lt-Col Douglas Stewart, DSO, RFA, s of Maj — Stewart, Inniskilling Dragoons, and *d* 1913, leaving issue

2a Eileen Cecilia; *b* 24 March 1885; *m* 1919, as his 2nd w, her bro-in-law Lt-Col Douglas Stewart and *d* 21 Jan 1931, leaving issue

3a Joan; *b* 3 July 1887; *m* 9 June 1914 Maurice Bevan, est s of David Augustus Bevan, of Rowney Priory, Ware, Herts, and had issue. He *d* 6 Jan 1925

(2) Cecil Edward George; *b* 18 Feb 1860; *d* 19 April 1877

(1) Geraldine Sarah; *m* 3 Nov 1885 7th Earl of Mayo (*qv*) and *d* 29 Nov 1944
(2) Adela Sophia Georgiana; *d* unm 27 March 1902
1 Kathleen Louisa Georgina; *m* 10 Aug 1858 Frederick Edward Banbury Tighe, of Woodstock, and *d* 9 July 1863. He *d* 6 Jan 1891

The 6th EARL's brother,

Rev WALTER WILLIAM BRABAZON PONSONBY, **7th Earl of Bessborough**; *b* 13 Aug 1821; MA Cantab; *m* 15 Jan 1850 Lady Louisa Susan Cornwallis Eliot (*d* 15 Jan 1911), only dau of 3rd Earl of St Germans (*qv*), and had:
1 EDWARD, **8th Earl**
2 Cyril Walter, OBE (1920); *b* 8 Sept 1853; a Lt City of London; *m* 19 Sept 1893 Emily H Eyre (*d* 10 Dec 1932), dau of Rev H Addington, of Henlow Grange, Beds, and *d* 29 Nov 1927, having had:
(1) Cyril Thomas; *b* 30 Oct 1894; Lt KRRC; *ka* 24 Aug 1916
(2) Michael Henry; *b* 22 June 1896; Lt Gren Gds; *d* 27 Aug 1918 of wounds recd in action
3 Granville; *b* 13 Sept 1854; Ch Police St Lucia; *m* 10 June 1879 Mabel (*d* 20 Jan 1922), dau of Hon Charles Jackson, of St Anne's, Jamaica, and *dsp* 24 Feb 1924
4 Arthur Cornwallis; *b* 8 Jan 1856; *m* 17 Aug 1892 Kathleen Eva (*d* 3 Nov 1944), dau of Henry Sillery, and *d* 25 April 1918, leaving issue:
(1) Guy Evelyn; *b* 11 Aug 1885; *educ* Sherborne; served BEF 1916–18 (wounded); *m* 16 Nov 1915 Irene Rodger, est dau of William Greig, and *d* 10 Jan 1960, leaving issue:
1a *David Arthur; *b* 14 Oct 1924; served USN WW II 1943–46, Stationary Fireman Dept Mental Hygiene, Met State Hosp; *m* 5 Sept 1952 *Vila R, est dau of Alma Christopher Mortenson, of Huntington, Utah, and has:
1b *Rodger Bruce; *b* 6 May 1956
2b *Christopher Greig; *b* 1 April 1960
1a *Evelyn Eirene [Mrs David Bliss Dekker, 1300–92nd Avenue NE, Bellevue, Washington 98004, USA]; *b* 18 Oct 1916; *m* 1942 *David Bliss Dekker, Ph D, v-pres Computer Center Corp, and has two sons
2a *Patricia Cornwallis; *b* 1921; *m* 1945 *John Harry Cummins and has two sons and a dau
3a *Judith Brabazon [Mrs Kenneth Ungermann, 3022 Sulivan Road, Sebastopol, California, USA]; *b* 17 March 1927; *m* 1951 *Kenneth Armistead Ungermann and has three sons
(2) Cecil Brabazon; *d* unm 1945
(1) Iris; *m* 29 Jan 1925 Thomas William Mitchell, s of Thomas William Mitchell, of John Street, New Shoreham, Sussex, and had two sons and two daus
(2) *Diana Louise Constance, MBE; *m* 5 Feb 1930 William Heywood Haslam, OBE, s of William Haslam of White Bank, Bolton, Lancs, and has:
1a *(Ralph) Michael [Michael Haslam Esq, The Orangery, Felix Hall, Kelvedon, Essex CO5 9DG]; *b* 4 Jan 1931; *m* 6 June 1958 *Hon Judith Browne, dau of 4th Baron Oranmore and Browne (*qv*), and has two sons and a dau
2a *William John Heywood; *b* 1 Aug 1933; *m* 18 April 1964 *Penelope Jane, only dau of Dr Peter Morrice, of Hayle, Cornwall, and has a s
3a *Nicholas (Nick) Ponsonby [Nicholas Haslam Esq, Brompton Lodge, London SW7 2JA]; *b* 27 Sept 1939; *educ* Eton
(3) *Judith Cornwallis
5 Walter Gerald; *b* 31 July 1859; barrister; *d* 28 April 1934
1 Maria; *d* unm 19 Nov 1949 aged 97
2 Ethel Jemima; *m* 28 Feb 1883 3rd Baron Raglan (*qv*) and *d* 22 June 1940, leaving issue
3 Sara Kathleen; *m* 26 June 1883 Maj Charles Lancelot Andrews Skinner, est s of Charles Binny Skinner, of The Chantry, Suffolk, and *d* 10 June 1936, leaving issue. He *d* 13 April 1934

The 7th EARL *d* 24 Feb 1906; his est s,

EDWARD PONSONBY, **8th Earl of Bessborough**, KP, CB, CVO, JP Cos Middlesex, Carlow and Kilkenny, DL Co Kilkenny; *b* 1 March 1851; KGStJ, Off Legn Hon, Lt RN 1874, barrister 1879, Sec to Lord R Grosvenor at the Treasury 1880–84, Sec to the Speaker 1884–95, High Sheriff Co Carlow 1898, CC Kilkenny 1897–1900, *m* 22 April 1875 Blanche Vere, CBE (1918) (*d* 11 Oct 1919), dau of Sir John Guest, 1st Bt, MP (*see* WIMBORNE, V), and *d* 1 Dec 1920, leaving:
1 VERE BRABAZON PONSONBY, **9th Earl of Bessborough** (I) and 1st EARL OF BESSBOROUGH, so *cr* 2 June 1937 (UK), GCMG (1931, CMG 1919), PC (1931); *b* 27 Oct 1880; *educ* Trin Col Camb (BA); Govr-Gen and C-in-C Canada 1931–35; Hon LLD McGill, Toronto and Ottawa Us, Hon Fell RIBA, DL Co Kilkenny, barrister, LCC 1907–10, MP (C) Cheltenham 1910 and Dover 1913–20, GSO (3) 1915, Capt late TF Reserve and T/Maj Special Service 1918, formerly Bucks IY; Pres Cncl Foreign Bondholders 1936, Chm League Loans Ctee 1937; KJStJ, Russian Order of St Anne 3rd Class with Swords and Bow, Order of St Maurice and St Lazarus Italy, Order Leopold Belgium, Order Redeemer Greece and Medaille de la Reconnaissance, Grand Cross Legion of Honour; *m* 25 June 1912 Roberte, JP (W Sussex 1943–56), GCSt J, Chevalier Legion Honour, Co Pres St John's Amb, chm St John Cncl Sussex (*d* 1979), only dau of Baron de Neuflize, CVO, of Paris, and *d* 10 March 1956, leaving:
(1) FREDERICK (ERIC) EDWARD NEUFLIZE PONSONBY, **10th Earl of Bessborough** (I) and 2nd and last EARL OF BESSBOROUGH (UK), DL Sussex (1977); *b* 29 March 1913; *educ* Eton and Trin Coll Cambridge (MA); 2nd Lt (Surrey and Sussex Yeo), Field Bde RA 1936–38, Sec High Commn for refugees 1936–39, served WW II, ADC to GOC 44 Div 1939–40 France and Flanders, ADC to GOC Canadian Corps 1940, GSO 2 (L) W and N Africa 1942–44, Maj 1942, For Serv 1944 (1st Sec 1948), Parly Sec Min Science Oct 1963–April 1964, Jt-Parly Under-Sec DES, chm Metrication Bd 1969, chm European Atlantic Gp, memb cncl for Atlantic Treaty Organization, MEP 1972–79, Dep Leader Conservative Delegn 1973, memb advsy ctee Science Policy Fndn 1977, chm govrs Br Soc for International Understanding, pres European-Atlantic Group, hon pres Atlantic Treaty Assoc, dir Assoc TV, English Stage Co, Planned Hldgs, Carlton Tower Ltd, pres Br Drama League, Chichester Festival Theatre Tst, Men of The Trees, OStJ, Chev Legion of Honour, playwright; *m* 29 Sept 1948 *Mary, still life painter [The Rt Hon Mary Countess of Bessborough, Stansted Park, Rowlands Castle, Hants PO9 6DY; 4 Westminster Gdns, London SW1], dau of Charles A Munn, of Washington, DC and Paris, and *d* 5 Dec 1993, leaving:
1a *Charlotte Mary Roberte Paul [The Lady Charlotte Petsopoulos, 43 Pembridge Villas, London W11]; *b* 28 Sept 1949; *m* 5 Sept 1974 *Yanni Petsopoulos and has issue:
1b *Alexis Anthony Frederick Ponsonby; *b* 1975; *educ* St Paul's
2b *Eric Demetri; *b* 1994
(2) Desmond Neuflize; *b* 4 Aug 1915; *d* 8 April 1925
(3) George St Lawrence Neuflize; *b* 14 Aug 1931 (HM GEORGE V stood sponsor); 2nd Lt 9th Lancers; *d* as the result of a traffic accident on military duty in Germany 16 May 1951
(1) *Moyra Blanche Madeleine, DBE (1977, OBE 1962) [The Lady Moyra Browne DBE, 16 Wilton St, London SW1X 7AX]; *b* 2 March 1918; SEN 1946, ENG 1997, chm Hospitality Ctee Victoria League 1956–62, v-chm Central Cncl Victoria League 1961–65, Dept Supt-in-Ch St John Ambulance Bde 1964–70 (Supt-in-Ch 1970–83), v-pres Roy Coll Nursing 1970–85, Nat Chm Support Gp Research into Ageing 1987–93 (Govr 1988), GCStJ; *m* 10 Dec 1945, as his 2nd w, Sir Denis John Wolko Browne, KCVO, FRCS (*d* 9 Jan 1967), and has:
1a *Desmond John Michael, QC (1990) [Desmond Browne Esq QC, 5 Raymond Buildings, Gray's Inn, London WC1R 5BP]; *b* 5 April 1947; *educ* Eton and New Coll Oxford (BA 1968); barrister Gray's Inn 1969, Recorder 1994; *m* 1 Sept 1973 *Jennifer Mary, dau of Frank Wilmore, of Brierfield, Lancs, and has:
1b *Natasha Clare; *b* 1974
2b *Harriet Francesca; *b* 1976
1a *Rosemary Anne Roberte [Countess Franco Lanza, 16 Wilton St, London SW1X 7AX]; *b* 18 April 1950; *m* 27 April 1974 *Count Franco Aleramo Lanza, of Dronero, Italy, and has:
1b *Aleramo Denis; *b* 1979
2b *Riccardo Vere (twin); *b* 1979
2 (Cyril) Myles Brabazon, MVO; *b* 16 Nov 1881; Maj Gren Gds, ADC to Govr Ceylon 1903–10 and HRH THE DUKE OF CONNAUGHT 1906–09, served S African War 1902 and WW I 1914–15; *m* 20 July 1911 Rita Narcissa (*m* 2nd 1 Jan 1918 Neville Alfred Cyril Flower, of Codicote Mill, Hitchin, Herts, who *d* 3 April 1931 as the result of a motor accident, son of Arthur Flower, of Prince's Gate, SW, and *d* 16 Sept 1977), est dau of Lt-Col Mountifort John Courtenay Longfield, of Castle Mary, and was *ka* France 28 Sept 1915, leaving issue:
(1) ARTHUR MOUNTIFORT LONGFIELD PONSONBY, **11th and present Earl of Bessborough**
3 Bertie Brabazon; *b* 10 Feb 1885; *educ* Harrow and Trin Coll Cambridge (BA 1907); barrister Inner Temple 1909, Lt (SR) Gren Gds, late Capt Roy Bucks Hus, WW I 1914–16 (wounded); *m* 7 Feb 1933 Constance Evelyn, only dau of Rev Canon Horace Rollo Meyer, rector Watton-at-Stone, Herts, and *dsp* 24 June 1967
1 Olwen Verena; *b* 9 Sept 1876; LGStJ; *m* 2 Jan 1901 3rd Baron Oranmore and Browne (*qv*) and *d* 7 June 1927, leaving issue
2 Helena Blanche Irene; *b* 16 June 1878; *m* 26 July 1904 John Congreve, of Mount Congreve, Co Waterford, and *d* 28 Jan 1962 leaving issue. He *d* 1957
3 Gweneth Frida, JP Kent; *b* 15 June 1888; Order of Mercy; *m* 1st 10 July 1913 Hon Windham Baring, Lt RNVR, 2nd s of 1st Earl of Cromer (*qv*), and had issue. He *d* 28 Dec 1922. She *m* 2nd 4 Feb 1926 Col Ralph Henry Voltelin Cavendish, CBE, MVO, DL, and had further issue (*see* DEVONSHIRE, D)

Best-Shaw

Arms: Quarterly, 1st and 4th, arg., a chevron between three fusils erm. (for SHAW); 2nd and 3rd, sa., a cinquefoil pierced, and in chief two cross crosslets fitchée or (for BEST). **Crest:** 1 Six arrows interlaced saltire-wise or, flighted, headed, tied together by a belt gu., buckle and pendant or (for SHAW). 2 On a wreath of the colours issuing out of a mural crown or a demi-ostrich arg., in the beak a cross crosslet fitchée or (for BEST). **Mottoes:** *Vincit qui patitur* ('He conquers who endures') (SHAW); *Sola cruce* ('With the Cross alone') (BEST). **Creation:** Bt. (E) 15 April 1665.

SIR JOHN MICHAEL ROBERT BEST-SHAW, 10TH BT, of Eltham, Co Kent [Sir John Best-Shaw Bt, Belmont, 104 High St, W Malling, Kent ME19 6NE]; *b* 28 Sept 1924; *s* f 1984; *educ* Lancing, Hertford Coll Oxford (BA 1950, MA 1955) and London U (PGCE); Capt late QO Roy W Kent Regt, served WW II 1943–45 (three medals), formerly Roy Fedn Malaya Police 1950–58, Church work 1959–71, advsr Christian Stewardship, Diocese Rochester, Assist Sec Additional Curates Soc, teacher 1972–82; *m* 13 Feb 1960 *Jane Gordon, 2nd dau of Alexander Gordon Guthrie, of Hampton Court Ho, Farningham, Kent, and has had:

1 Matthew John Guthrie; *b* 18 Dec 1962; *d* 11 April 1970

2 +THOMAS JOSHUA; *b* 7 March 1965; *educ* Maidstone GS and Reading U (BSc 1987); surveyor; *m* 1992 *Emily Susan, dau of Vivian Rubin, of Wateringbury, Kent, and has:

(1) +Joshua John Kirkland; *b* Jan 1995

(2) +William Vivian Guthrie; *b* 30 Oct 1997

3 +Samuel Stevenson; *b* 28 March 1971; *educ* Maidstone GS and Exeter Coll Oxford (BA 1992, MA 1997); teacher

1 *Lucy Ann; *b* 8 May 1961; *m* 1985 (*divorce* 1989) Terence Wentworth-Wood and has issue:

(1) *Alexander; *b* 1985

(1) *Christina Lily; *b* 1987

Lineage: (of SHAW) WILLIAM SHAW, living 1443; *m* Elizabeth Starkie, of Stretton, and had issue:

RANDALL SHAW, of Haslington, Cheshire; *m* Margery Vernon, of Haslington, and had issue:

ROGER SHAW, of Haslington; *m* Alice, dau of John Walker, of Leigh Green, and left issue:

ROBERT SHAW, of Haslington; *m* Alice, dau of Humphrey Perrott, of Haslington, and had issue:

ROBERT SHAW, of Southwark, living 1633; *m* Elizabeth, dau of John Domilawe, of Mincing Lane, and had issue, with an er and yr son and three daus:

Sir John Shaw, 1st Bt (E), so *cr* 15 April 1665, of London, MP Lyme Regis 1661–79, subsidised CHARLES II in exile, farmed the Customs after the Restoration, ktd 1660; *m* 1st 25 Oct 1649 Anne (*d* Dec 1662), dau of John Ashe, of Freshford, Somerset, and had issue, with a dau (*d* unm):

1 JOHN (Sir), **2nd Bt**

Sir John *m* 2nd 24 June 1663 Bridget (*m* 2nd 15 Feb 1680/1 Sir John Baber and was *bur* 11 July 1699), widow of 4th Viscount Kilmorey (*see* KILMOREY, E) and dau and coheir of Sir William Drury, and by her had issue:

2 Charles (CHARLES II stood sponsor); *m* Elizabeth, dau of Philip Harbord, of Besthorpe, and had issue:

(1) Charles; *m* Frances Lyford, of Hants, and left issue:

1a Elizabeth; *m* 28 March 1747 5th Baron Byron (*qv*) and *d* 5 Nov 1788, leaving issue. He *d* 19 May 1798

1 Elizabeth; *m* King Gould

Sir JOHN *d* 1 March 1679/80 and was *s* by his er son,

Sir John Shaw, 2nd Bt; *m* 1st c 12 May 1684 Margery (*d* 3 Aug 1690), dau and heiress of Sir John Peake, Ld Mayor London, and had issue:

1 JOHN (Sir), **3rd Bt**

2 William; *d* young

1 Sarah; *m* William Smith, one of the six Clerks in Chancery

2 Elizabeth; *m* Stephen, son of Sir Abel Ram, JP, of Ramsford, Co Wexford, Ld Mayor Dublin

Sir John *m* 2nd Sarah (*bur* 12 Jan 1724/5), dau and coheir of William Paggen, of London, and by her had three sons and six daus

Sir JOHN *d* 11 Dec 1721, and was *s* by his est son,

Sir John Shaw, 3rd Bt, MA Oxford; *m* Sept 1716 Anna Maria (*d* 30 Nov 1755), est dau and coheir of Sir Thomas Barnardiston, 3rd Bt, of Brightwell Hall, Suffolk (*extinct c* 1750), and by her had, with other issue (*d* in infancy):

1 JOHN (Sir), **4th Bt**

1 Anna Maria; *m* Peter Delme, son and heir of Sir Peter Delme, Ld Mayor London, and *d* 1740

Sir JOHN *d* 4 March 1738/9, and was *s* by his only surv son,

Sir John Shaw, 4th Bt, MA, DCL Oxford; *b* 22 Nov 1728; *m* 1st 4 Feb 1749/50 Elizabeth (*d* 3 Feb 1750/1), dau of William Hedges, of Alderton, Wilts, and had a son (*d* young); *m* 2nd 17 Feb 1752 Martha (*bur* 28 Oct 1794), dau and heiress of John Kenward, of Kenward, Yalding, Kent, and by her had issue:

1 JOHN GREGORY (Sir), **5th Bt**

2 John Kenward SHAW later BROOKE (Rev), MA, Vicar Eltham, Rector Hurstpierpoint; *b* 22 Dec 1758, Iinherited 1796 property of Joseph Brooke, of West Malling, and so took the name BROOKE; *d* 16 Dec 1840

Sir JOHN *d* 18 June 1779, and was *s* by his er son,

Sir John Gregory Shaw, 5th Bt; *b* 25 July 1756; *m* 9 March 1782 Theodosia Margaret (*d* 24 Oct 1847), dau of 2nd Baron Monson (*qv*), and *d* 28 Oct 1831, having had issue, with another son and four daus (*d* young or unm):

1 **Sir John Kenward Shaw, 6th Bt**; *b* 15 March 1783; *m* 1809 Charlotte (*d* Boulogne 12 Feb 1870), 2nd dau of William Lloyd, of Betchworth, Surrey, and *dsp* 17 March 1857

2 Charles, Capt RN; *b* 18 Aug 1785; *m* 13 April 1822 Frances Anne (*d* 11 Dec 1872), 4th dau of Sir Henry Hawley, 1st Bt (*qv*), and *d* 2 May 1829, leaving issue:

(1) **Sir Charles Kenward Shaw, 7th Bt**, JP Kent; *b* 8 June 1829; *m* 1st 19 June 1860 Maria (*d* 4 Sept 1863), only child of Henry Sparkes, of Summerberry, nr Guildford; *m* 2nd 15 Oct 1868 Sophia Emma Anna Maria (*d* 2 Aug 1911), est dau of Capt John William Finch, RN, of Knight's Place, Pembury, Kent, and *dsp* 7 Jan 1909

(2) Charles John Kenward (Rev), MA, Vicar Newington, Kent; *b* 8 June 1829; *m* 22 Nov 1859 Julia Elizabeth (*d* 18 May 1905), dau of Capt John Harvey Boteler, RN, and *d* 20 June 1875, having had issue:

1a CHARLES JOHN MONSON (Sir), **8th Bt**

2a Henry Hawley; *b* 4 Sept 1862; *m* 3 Jan 1893 Agneta Maud (*d* 8 Oct 1933), dau of Rev Robert Stammers Tabor, MA, and *d* 8 March 1897, leaving issue:

1b John Charles Hawley, civil servant, served Roy Signals; *b* 2 March 1895; *educ* Tonbridge; *m* 20 May 1948 Elsie Anne (*d* 12 Feb 1959), widow of H S Brown and dau of Frederick Walker, of Reading, and *d* 11 Nov 1990

1b Henrietta Frances Lilian SHAW (surname reassumed 1937); *m* 1st 7 Oct 1919 (*divorce* 1933) Rev Reginald Fleming Rynd; *m* 2nd 2 Feb 1933 Maj Arthur James Skey, MC, and *d* 15 Feb 1969. He *d* 12 Feb 1936

3a John Gregory; *b* 1866; *d* 1887

4a Barnardiston Edward Boteler, Nigerian CS; *b* 10 Sept 1873; *m* 21 Oct 1924 Beatrice Ellen (*d* Oct 1965), only dau of Charles O Leefe, and *d* 30 Aug 1927

1a Helen Catherine Teresa; *d* 14 April 1876

2a Lilian Adelaide; *m* 11 July 1893 Sir Charles Robert Tyser, Ch Justice Cyprus 1906–18, and *d* 17 Dec 1926. He *d* 23 Aug 1926

3a Julia Emma Frances; *m* 9 Aug 1894 Thomas Reginald Colquhoun Dill, barrister, and *d* 12 July 1937, leaving issue. He *d* 6 Nov 1934

4a Annie Maria; *m* 1 Nov 1906 Richard Mawdistly Best, 2nd son of William Mawdistly Best (*see* below), and *d* 27 Nov 1929, leaving issue. He *d* 14 March 1918

5a Dorothy Emily Augusta; *m* 14 Jan 1897 Sir Alexander Murray Ashmore, KCMG, Lt-Govr Ceylon 1904–06, and *d* 4 Jan 1952, leaving issue. He *d* 7 Dec 1906

(1) Alicia Frances; *m* Sept 1846 Charles Henry Woodgate, Madras CS, and *d* 5 March 1905, leaving issue

(2) Gertrude Anne; *m* 2 Dec 1847 Rupert Henry Warre, only child of Thomas Warre, and *d* 3 Dec 1899, leaving issue. He *d* 25 Dec 1855

(3) Harriet Augusta; *m* 2 April 1850 Rev John Beauvoir Dalison, Rector Upwell, Cambs, and *d* 1896

(4) Louisa Margaret; *m* 2 Dec 1847 Rev George Stephen Woodgate, Vicar Pembury, Kent, and *d* April 1916, leaving issue. He *d* 14 April 1871

3 Henry Thomas, Lt-Col; *b* 21 Feb 1788; *d* 20 June 1832

4 Robert William (Rev), Rector Cuxton, Kent, Hon Canon Rochester; *b* 4 Oct 1804; *educ* Eton and Ch Ch Oxford (MA); *m* 18 Feb 1830 Sophia (*d* 14 March 1875), yst dau of John Cornwall, of Hendon, Middx, and *d* 28 Dec 1873, having had issue, with a dau (*d* unm):

(1) Robert John (Rev), Vicar Danehill, Sussex, Madehurst, Sussex, and Wiggenhall, Norfolk; *b* 31 July 1831; *educ* Marlborough and St John's Coll Oxford; *m* 17 April 1860 Ella de Visme (*d* 17 July 1926), est dau of Richard Thomas, of Eythorne, Kent, and *d* 30 Oct 1903, having had issue:

1a Robert Reginald Monson; *b* 31 May 1861; *d* 1885

2a Lewis Hugh de Visme; *b* 26 Aug 1865; *m* 30 April 1901 Edith Mary (*d* 16 Sept 1929), only surv child of Capt John Smyth Nelson, 38th Staffs Regt, and *d* 11 June 1931, having had issue:

1b John Monson de Visme; *b* 20 Jan 1907; *m* 1940 *Helen Doreen, only dau of Charles O'Callaghan, 19th Hus, and *dsp* 15 Dec 1957

1b *Horatia Edith de Visme [Miss Horatia Shaw, Nazareth House, Queen Wilhelmina AV, Waterkloof, Pretoria 0002, S Africa]; *b* 14 March 1902

2b Theodosia Mary de Visme; *b* 2 Aug *d* 17 Nov 1903

3a John Gerard Cornwall; *b* 22 Feb 1868; *m* 6 July 1916 Mary, 2nd dau of Angus Macdonald, of the Falkland Islands, and *dsp* 9 April 1946

4a Henry Augustus Gregory; *b* 30 Aug 1876; *m* 17 June 1925 Eileen (*d* 1973), est dau of Charles William Howard, of Dorking, and *d* 25 Sept 1954, leaving issue:

1b +John Gregory Monson de Visme [John Shaw Esq, 22 Brunswick Terrace, Hove, Sussex]; *b* 3 July 1930; *m* 1st 24 Dec 1959 (*divorce* 1972) Helene Maud, dau of Cyril Ernest Kerslake Baker, of N Ireland; *m* 2nd 1976 *Joan Phyllis, er dau of Alfred Frank Elphick

2b +Robert Henry Barnardiston de Visme [Robert Shaw Esq, 9 Cranswick Rd, Willowild, Sandton, Transvaal, S Africa]; *b* 26 May 1932; *m* 6 Oct 1961 *Valerie Ann, only dau of Bernard Richard Lobb, of Johannesburg, and London, and has issue:

1c +Philip Gregory de Visme; *b* 1970

1c *Christine Ann de Visme; *b* 23 Aug 1965; *m* 1991 *Mark John Fraser-Valentine and has issue:

1d *Katelyn Ann; *b* 1991

2d *Emily Jo; *b* 1993

1b *Eileen Ann de Visme [Mrs Alan Baker, Tamway, 9 Bracken Rd, Seaford, Sussex]; *b* 9 Sept 1928; *m* 14 June 1952 *Alan Baker, son of Albert Godfrey Baker, of Seaford, and has issue:

1c *Robert Alan; *b* 16 Feb 1960

2c *James Paul; *b* 26 April 1963

1c *Catherine Ann; *b* 15 March 1953

1a Eleanor Marian; *m* 27 Jan 1904 Leopold Arthur Bingham Gipps, son of Maj Henry Gipps, 9th Regt, and *d* 30 Nov 1961 aged 91, leaving issue. He *d* 5 Feb 1959

2a Ella Florence; *d* unm 1 Jan 1952

(2) John Monson; *b* 1 Oct 1832; *educ* Eton; *m* 8 Feb 1872 Sarah Pain (*d* 1887), only dau of Thomas Francklyn, of Cobtree, Kent, and *dsp* 4 Sept 1912

(3) Hugh Cornwall; *b* 3 May 1837; *d* 14 Aug 1881

(1) Sophia Anna; *b* 27 Jan 1834; *m* 27 Nov 1857 Rev Harry Launcelot Wingfield, Rector Market Overton, Rutland, and *d* 25 Aug 1915, leaving issue. He *d* 1891

(2) Margaret Augusta; *b* 25 Feb 1842; *m* 1st 19 Feb 1867 Rev Spencer Philip Harvey and had issue. He *d* Jan 1869. She *m* 2nd 6 June 1877,her cousin William Shaw Brooke George, yst son of Edward George, MD, of Sandgate, Kent, and *d* Jan 1925, leaving issue

1 Catherine Elizabeth; *m* 29 Nov 1806 Sir Henry Hawley, 2nd Bt (*qv*), and *d* 15 March 1862, leaving issue. He *d* 29 March 1831

2 Anna Maria; *b* 12 Dec 1795; *m* 8 May 1819 Maximillian Dudley Digges Dalison, DL, JP, of Hamptons, Kent, and *d* 13 Oct 1871, having had issue. He *d* 11 May 1870

3 Horatia; *b* 19 May 1799; *m* 31 Jan 1825 19th Lord Forbes (*qv*) and *d* 24 Dec 1862, leaving issue. He *d* 2 May 1868

4 Charlotte Susan; *b* 23 Feb 1801; *m* 5 Dec 1822 R-Adml John Cornwall, of Elstead, Surrey, and *d* 22 Feb 1874

5 Caroline Alicia; *b* 22 March 1803; *m* Edward George, MD, of Sandgate, Kent, and *d* 4 Aug 1881, leaving issue

6 Harriet Grace; *b* 24 April 1806; *m* 30 March 1842 Rev Allen Cooper, MA, Minister St Mark's, N Audley Street, London W1, and *d* his widow 29 Oct 1872

Sir CHARLES's n,

Rev Sir Charles John Monson Shaw, 8th Bt, Rector Wrotham, Kent 1913–21; *b* 24 Nov 1860; *educ* Hertford Coll Oxford (MA); *m* 1 June 1893 Elizabeth Louisa Whatman Best (*d* 29 July 1961), dau of James Whatman Bosanquet, of Claysmore, Enfield, by Emily Dorothy, er dau of James Best, of Park House (*see* below), and *d* 11 Sept 1922, leaving issue:

1 Sir JOHN JAMES KENWARD SHAW later BEST-SHAW (roy licence 20 July 1956), **9th Bt**, High Sheriff Kent 1961; *educ* RNCs Osborne and Dartmouth, Cdr (E) RN, served WWs I and II, lay guardian Sanctuary Our Lady of Walsingham 1932, OStJ; *b* 11 June 1895; *m* 28 March 1921 Elizabeth Mary Theodora (*d* 5 July 1986), est dau of Sir Robert Heywood Hughes, 12th Bt, of East Bergholt (*qv*), and *d* 26 Feb 1984, leaving:

(1) Sir JOHN MICHAEL ROBERT BEST-SHAW, **10th and present Bt**

(2) +Charles John Hughes [Charles Best-Shaw Esq, Cornerfield House, Charing, Kent TN27 0LU]; *b* 23 Jan 1928; *educ* Lancing; *m* 12 Oct 1971 *Carol Mary, 2nd dau of Joseph Martin Drew, of Beckenham, Kent, and has:

1a *Helen Mary Elizabeth; *b* 7 Nov 1972; *educ* Ashford Sch and St Chad's Coll Durham (BSc, MA)

(3) +Stephen Bosanquet [Stephen Best-Shaw Esq, Boxley Abbey, Maidstone, Kent ME14 3BT], with Combined Insurance Co of America; *b* 9 Aug 1935; *educ* Lancing; *m* 11 April 1964 *(Elizabeth) Annette Freda, yst dau of Gerald Baldwin Hayward, MBE, of Athens, by Margaret Sarah, er dau of Lt-Col Owen Godfrey-Faussett, DSO, and has:

1a +James Robert Hawley; *b* 12 March 1965; *m* 1992 *Charlotte Louise, 2nd dau of Nigel Ashley, of Mijas, Spain, and has:

1b +Harold (Harry) Richard Gaussen; *b* 20 Nov 1996

2a +Hugh Edward Gerald; *b* 12 Feb 1975

1a *Louisa Margaret Aylmer; *b* 27 Jan 1967; *m* 15 Oct 1988 *Andrew Charles Robert Beale, s of Robert Beale, of Wellington Sq, London SW3, and has:

1b *Freddie James Robert; *b* 16 Sept 1993

1b *Roseanna Mary Elizabeth; *b* 26 Dec 1991

2b *Polly Theodora; *b* 15 Feb 1997

(1) *Mary Elizabeth Helen [Mrs John Adams-Beck, Jonstone West, Egerton, Ashford, Kent TN27 9DR], JP Kent; *b* 22 April 1922; *m* 1st 5 June 1943 Capt Patrick Henry Coates, RA (*d* 27 April 1949), only son of Cdr Henry Venner Coates, RN, of Barnscote, Old Compton Lane, Farnham, Surrey, and has:

1a *David Carlyon [David Coates Esq, Mark's Farmhouse, Bramshaw, Lyndhurst, Hants]; *b* 9 Sept 1944; *educ* Charterhouse and Coll of Estate Management; FRICS; *m* June 1970 *Lavinia Jane O'Connor-Fenton and has:

1b *Emma Mary; *b* 1973

2b *Alice Julia; *b* 1975

3b *Georgina Ruth; *b* 1980

2a *Simon Patrick, JP (Somerset) [Simon Coates Esq JP, Rectory Farm, Raddington, Somerset TA4 2QW]; *b* 8 Oct 1948; *educ* Charterhouse; *m* 1979 *Katherine Jane, 2nd dau of Maj Richard Hodgkinson Jessop, IA, and has:

1b *Thomas George Carlyon; *b* 1981

2b *Nicholas Henry Jessop; *b* 1983

(1) Mrs Patrick Coates *m* 2nd 12 Nov 1968 John Melliar Adams-Beck (*d* 1979), son of James Francis Adams-Beck, of Pantiles, Colchester, Essex

(2) *Julia Aylmer [Miss Julia Best-Shaw, Boxley Abbey, Maidstone, Kent], served WW II 1943–45 in WRNS; *b* 22 July 1923

(3) *Hermione Theodora [Miss Hermione Best-Shaw, Boxley Abbey, Maidstone, Kent]; *b* 10 May 1926

(4) *Martha Mary [Miss Martha Best-Shaw, Boxley Abbey, Maidstone, Kent]; *b* 6 April 1934

Lineage (of Best): RICHARD BEST, of Bibrooke, Kent; *m* Dorothy, dau and coheir of John Barrow, of Hinxhill, Kent, and left issue:

JOHN BEST, of Allington Castle, Kent, St Lawrence, nr Canterbury, and Wellcourt, Cosmusbleane, Kent, which he bought 1610; *m* 1st Anne, dau of Reginald Knatchbull, of Saltwood Castle, and had, with other issue:

RICHARD, of whom presently

He *m* 2nd 1598 Anne, gdau of Sir Reginald Scott, of Scott's Hall, Kent, and dau of Lawrence Rooke, of Horton Monachorum and later Christchurch, Kent, and had issue

His son and heir,

RICHARD BEST, described as of Wringleton, Winsborough, Kent, 1625 and St Lawrence, nr Canterbury, 1633; *b* 1597; *m* Elizabeth (*d* Oct 1662), dau of Andrew Hughes, of Wringleton, and *d* 1633, having had, with seven daus:

JOHN BEST, of St Lawrence, which estate he sold by 1654 to William Rooke; *m* Katherine, dau of John Allanson, of Norwood, Middx, and *d* 1666, having had issue, with three er sons:

THOMAS BEST, of Cowling Castle, Kent; *bapt* 2 June 1657; *m* 1st Elizabeth (*d* 1702), dau of John Mawdisty, of Chatham, where he settled, and had, with five daus, a son; *m* 2nd but *d* 22 Aug 1710 without further issue. His son:

MAWDISTLY BEST, of Park House, Boxley, Kent, High Sheriff 1730; *m* 1742 Elizabeth Fearne, and had, with other issue:

JAMES BEST, of Park House, High Sheriff Kent 1751; *m* Frances (*d* 30 Oct 1808), dau and coheir of Richard Shelley, of Michelgrove, Sussex, and *d* 29 Jan 1782, leaving issue:

1 THOMAS, of whom presently

2 James; *m* twice; *dsp* 1828

3 Richard; *b* 26 June 1757; *m* 1st Martha Boorman and *d* 4 April 1801, having had issue:

(1) Richard; *b* 29 April 1786; *m* Anna Maria Darke (an Austrian) and *d* 7 Aug 1850, leaving issue:

1a Richard Mawdistly, Gen, served Sikh campaigns 1842–43; *b* 1814; *m* Eliza Hastings, dau of Maj Alexander Macleod of Macleod, HEICS, and *d* 12 March 1892, leaving issue:

1b Richard William Mawdistly; *b* 1847; *m* 1865 Maria Anna (*d* 23 July 1891), dau of Maj Jones, Govr Cape Coast Castle, and *d* 3 March 1883, having had issue:

1c Mawdistly Rokeby, of Esmont, Albermarle Co, Virginia, USA; *b* 14 Nov 1867

2c Richard Mawdistly; *b* 5 Feb 1870; *m* 1 Nov 1906 Annie Marie Shaw (*d* 27 Nov 1929), 4th dau of Rev Charles John Kenward Shaw (*see* above), and *d* 14 March 1918, leaving issue

1d Lily Dorothy; *b* 28 May 1907

(1) Harriet; *b* 1Dec. 1784; *m* Capt Richard Lovelace, 1st Foot Gds, and *d* 27 Nov 1864, leaving a dau

4 George, of Chilston Park, Boughton Malherbe, Kent, DL, JP, MP Rochester 1790–96; *b* 10 Nov 1757; *m* 7 Dec 1784 Caroline,dau of Edward Scott, of Scott's Hall, Kent, and *d* 8 Sept 1818, having had issue:

(1) Thomas Fairfax, of Chilstone, and Wierton, Kent, Offr Gren Gds, served Corunna; *b* 15 Oct 1786; *m* Margaret Anna (*d* 24 Nov 1882), dau of Joseph George Brett, of Grove House, Old Brompton, Middx, and *d* London 30 June 1849, leaving issue:

1a Caroline Georgiana; *m* her cousin William Mawdistly Best (*see* below) and *d* 7 March 1900. He *d* 16 Nov 1860

2a Isabella Dorothy; *m* 18 July 1859 Edward Disbrowe Kortright, 2nd son of Lawrence Kortright, of Highlands, Essex, and had a dau

3a Margaret Anna; *b* 18 May 1821; *d* 5 Dec 1923

4a Frances; *m* William Henry Archer, Maj 16th Lancers, son of Col Archer, and had issue

(2) George, Offr 10th Foot, *dsp* 1814

(3) William Balliol; *dsp* 1822

(1) Caroline; *d* 17 March 1860

(2) Dorothy; *m* Rev Joseph George Brett

(3) Louisa; *m* George Matcham Tarlton, late 6th Foot

1 Elizabeth; *m* Rev Maurice Lloyd, Vicar Lenham

2 Frances; *m* 4 June 1779 Rev Henry Hardinge and *d* 27 Oct 1837, having had issue (*see* HARDINGE, Bt). He *d* 7 Sept 1820

3 Dorothy; *m* William Twopenny, of Woodstock Park, Kent,

His est son,

THOMAS BEST, of Park House; *b* 14 Nov 1753; *m* Elizabeth, dau of Dr Irwin, MD, and *d* 27 May 1815, leaving issue:

1 JAMES, of whom presently

2 Thomas, Capt 26th (Cameronian Regt) Foot; *m* Anne, est dau of William Kearney, of Tuam, Co Galway, and *d* Gibraltar 8 Oct 1813, leaving issue:

(1) William Mawdistly; *b* Dec 1809; *m* Dec 1854 Caroline Georgiana (*d* 7 March 1900), est dau of Thomas Fairfax Best, of Wierton (*see* above), and *d* 16 Nov 1869

(2) James John, Maj 34th Foot; *b* 1811; *d* 9 Nov 1844

1 Frances Julia; *d* 1842

2 Elizabeth Charlotte; *d* 1861

3 Dorothy; *d* 1871

The er son,

JAMES BEST, of Park House, JP, Lt-Col W Kent Militia; *b* 1781; *m* 1817 Harriet Susannah (*d* 21 Jan 1875), dau of Samuel Robert Gaussen, of Brookman's Park, Herts, and *d* 20 June 1849, having had issue:

1 James; *b* 27 Oct 1822; *dvp* 10 June 1845

2 Mawdistly Gaussen, of Park House, JP, High Sheriff 1881, served 34th Regt Crimea 1855, present Siege of Sebastopol and assault on the Redan (medal and clasp, Turkish medal), served Indian Mutiny 1857 (present Cawnpore and relief of Lucknow), Brevet Maj (medal and clasp); *b* 23 Aug 1826; *m* 14 April 1864 Katherine Annabella (*d* 18 June 1896), er surv dau of Rev Tatton Brockman, of Beachborough, nr Hythe, Kent, and *dsp* 14 July 1906, leaving his estates to his niece, Harriet Emily Hardinge Best, Mrs Best-Dalison (*see* below)

3 Thomas Charles Hardinge, served 72nd Highrs Indian Mutiny, present capture of Kotah 30 March 1858, pursuit of Gwalior Rebels at Rajputana and Battle of Bunass (medal and clasp); *b* 22 May 1828; *d* 21 Sept 1887

4 Thomas Henry; *d* young

5 John Aylmer; *d* young

1 EMILY DOROTHY, of whom presently

2 Elizabeth Caroline Ann; *b* 18 May 1836; *d* 17 Aug 1885

The er dau,

EMILY DOROTHY; *b* 15 Dec 1829; *m* 25 April 1864, as his 3rd w, James Whatman Bosanquet, JP, of Claysmore, Enfield, Middx. He *d* 22 Dec 1877. She *d* 23 Dec 1899, leaving issue:

1 Harriet Emily Hardinge Best, of Park House, Boxley, Kent (in which she *s* her uncle, Maj Mawdistly Gaussen Best 1906 (*see* above)), Order of Mercy and Queen Elisabeth Medal Belgium; *b* 23 April 1867; *m* 12 April 1899 Rev Charles Edmund Waller Dalison, 2nd son of Maximilian Hammond Dalison, JP, of Hamptons, Kent. He added by royal licence 21 June 1907 the name and arms of BEST quarterly with those of his own family, and *d* 20 Jan 1955, aged 96; she had:

(1) Thomas Maximillian, JP; *b* 18 Feb 1905; *d* 10 July 1947

2 ELIZABETH LOUISA WHATMAN BEST, of whom presently

3 Aylmer Adela Mawdistly Best; *b* 13 May 1870; *d* Pasadena, California, 8 Feb 1921

The 2nd dau,

ELIZABETH LOUISA WHATMAN BEST; *b* 27 June 1868; *m* 1 June 1893 **Rev Sir Charles John Shaw, 8th Bt**, MA, of Eltham, and *d* 29 July 1961, leaving issue (*see* above). He *d* 11 Sept 1922

BETHELL

Arms: Or, on a chevron az. an estoile of the first, in chief two boar's heads couped of the second. **Crest:** Upon a rock ppr. a boar's head couped azure. **Supporters:** Two wolves ppr., the dexter charged on the shoulder with an estoile and the sinister with a portcullis,or. **Motto:** *Servabo fidem* ('I will keep faith'). **Creations:** Bt (UK) 26 June 1911, B. (UK) 23 Nov 1922.

THE 4TH BARON BETHELL, of Romford, Essex, and a **Baronet** (Sir Nicholas William Bethell, Bt) [The Rt Hon The Lord Bethell, 73 Sussex Sq, London W2; Manor Farm, Brill, Bucks HP18 9SL]; *b* 19 July 1938; *s* cousin 1967; *educ* Harrow and Pembroke Coll Cambridge (PhD 1987); Ld in Waiting 1970–71, MEP (C) 1975–94, chm Friends of Cyprus 1981–, pres Friends of Gibraltar's Heritage 1992–, Cdr Order of Merit (Poland), publications: *Gomulka: His Poland and his Communism* (1969), *The War Hitler Won* (1972), *The Last Secret* (1974), *Russia Besieged* (1977), *The Palestine Triangle* (1979), *The Great Betrayal* (1984), *Spies and Other Secrets* (1994); *m* 1st 7 April 1964 (*divorce* 1971) Cecilia Mary Lothian (*d* 1977), er dau of Prof Alexander Mackie Honeyman, of Cowan's Rigg, St Andrews, and has issue:

1 +JAMES NICHOLAS; *b* 1 Oct 1967; *educ* Eton and Edinburgh U; fin jnlst with *Independent* to 1995, manager Ministry of Sound nightclub, Elephant and Castle, London, 1995–

2 +William Alexander; *b* 18 March 1969

The 4th BARON *m* 2nd 1992 *Bryony Lea Morgan, dau of Brian David Griffiths, of Llanrhystyd, Dyfed, and Arguignac, France, and has further issue:

3 +John Andrew Rowland; *b* 18 Aug 1995

Lineage: JOHN BETHELL, of Didsbury, Lancs; *m* 8 Nov 1828 Elizabeth Brundreth (*d* 10 Feb 1876) and *d* 28 April 1870, leaving issue:

GEORGE BETHELL, of The Firs, South Woodford, Essex, *b* 20 April 1833, *m* 23 Jan 1858 Frances (*d* 25 Jan 1894), dau of Robert Tipper, and *d* 26 Aug 1908, having had issue:

1 JOHN HENRY (Sir), **1st Baron**

2 Thomas Robert (Sir), *d* 23 Dec 1957

1 Elizabeth

The elder son,

Sir John Henry Bethell, 1st Bt, and **1st Baron Bethell**, of Romford, Essex (both UK), so *cr* 26 June 1911 and 23 Nov 1922 respectively, JP Essex, Lt City of London, twice Mayor W Ham and twice E Ham, MP Romford 1906–18 and E Ham (N) 1918–22, dir Barclays Bank and Roy Exchange Assur, *b* 23 Sept 1861, ktd 1906; *m* 30 May 1895 Florence (*d* 8 May 1957), dau of James Woolley Wyles, of Essex House, E Ham, and *d* 27 May 1945, having had issue:

1 Frank Harry, Lt 3rd Bn Connaught Rangers, *b* 18 May 1896; *ka* 25 Sept 1915

2 JOHN RAYMOND, **2nd Baron Bethell**; *b* 23 Oct 1902; *educ* Harrow and Jesus Coll Cambridge (MA 1934), served WW II as F/Lt AAF; *m* 1st 22 June 1927 (*divorce* 1948) Veronica Eileen, 2nd dau of Hon Sir James Daniel Connolly, and had issue:

(1) GUY ANTHONY JOHN, **3rd Baron Bethell**; *educ* Eton, Lt Roy Irish Fus, served Palestine 1947–48, *b* 17 March 1928; *d* unm 2 Dec 1967

(1) *Jennifer Mary [The Hon Mrs Brown, 48 Priors Acre, Boxgrove, Chichester, W Sussex PO18 0ER]; *b* 26 Aug 1930; *m* 14 Oct 1954 *Edward Peter Moncrieff Brown and has issue:

1a *Alistair Peter; *b* 5 Aug 1955; *m* 1977 *Eva Jacobsen, of Norway, and has issue:

1b *Alexander; *b* 1977

1b *Charlotte; *b* 1982

2a *Craig Edward; *b* 23 May 1957; *educ* Eton and Bristol U; newspaper columnist and humorous writer; *m* 1987 *Frances J M, dau of Colin Welch, of Aldbourne, Wilts, and has:

1b *Silas; *b* 1990

1b *Tallulah; *b* 1988

3a *James David; *b* 9 May 1959; *m* 1990 *Tracey, yr dau of John Gadd, of Torrington, Devon, and has issue:

1b *Daisy; *b* 1991

2b *Florence; *b* 1995

4a *David Francis; *b* 21 July 1960

(2) *Patricia Catherine [Mrs Michael Nesbitt, Rotherwood, Fittleworth, Pulborough, Sussex RH20 1EW]; *b* 20 May 1933; *m* 19 Aug 1956 *Michael William Nesbitt, DFC, and has issue:

1a *William Patrick [William Nesbitt Esq, The Bakehouse, Turkdean, nr Cheltenham, Glos]; *b* 15 Dec 1963; *m* 1989 *Caroline L, yr dau of Dr *d* Charlton-Smith, of Wellesbourne, Warwicks, and has issue:

1b *Frederick William; *b* 1993

1b *Clementine Rose; *b* 1991

1a *Anna Catherine [Mrs Kerry McDonagh, Manor Farmhouse, Wendlebury, nr Bicester, Oxon]; *b* 12 May 1957; *m* 19– *Kerry James McDonagh, er s of James McDonagh, of Runcorn, Cheshire, and has issue:

1b *Thomas; *b* 1988

2b *Edward; *b* 1989

2a *Caroline Mary; *b* 20 Aug 1959

2 (cont.) The **2nd Baron** *m* 2nd 6 Aug 1948 Joan (*d* 22 April 1966), widow of Lt-Cdr Henry Nevile Reid, RN, and only dau of Brig Gen Norman William Webber, CMG, DSO, of Lingwood, Camberley, and *d* 30 Sept 1965

3 William Gladstone, 2nd Lt RA (invalided 1941) WW II, *b* 11 April 1904, *educ* Harrow and Pembroke Coll Camb (MA 1934), *m* 19 Oct 1937 (*divorce* 1946) Ann Margaret Frances (*d* 17 Aug 1966), only dau of Lt-Col Robert George Barlow, of The Holt, Ledbury, Herefs (she *m* 2nd 1946 John Rupert Dupree (*see* DUPREE, Bt), who *d* 1965; *m* 3rd 1956 Roger Thornycroft, DSC (*d* 1983), s of Sir John Edward Thornycroft, KBE; *m* 4th 1984 Stuart Warren Don), and *d* 17 Oct 1964, leaving issue:

(1) NICHOLAS WILLIAM BETHELL, **4th and present Baron Bethell**

(1) *Sally Ann [Mrs Anthony Wigram, 16 Porchester Terr, London W2 3TL]; *b* 23 Dec 1943; *m* 25 Feb 1965 *Anthony Francis Wigram, s of Maj Lionel Wigram, and has issue:

1a *Maximilian John Lionel; *b* 2 March 1966

1a *Camilla Ann; *b* 3 Dec 1966; *m* 1989 *Rupert Alister Peter John Cordle (*see* POWERSCOURT, V) and has issue:

1b *Alexander Anthony; *b* 1993

2b *Hugo Andrew; *b* May 1995

2a *Lucy Olga (twin); *b* 3 Dec 1966; *m* 1990 *Benjamin V Sangster, s of Robert Sangster, the football pools millionaire and race horse-owner, of The Nunnery, Douglas, IOM, and Mrs Ian Strathearn Gordon, of River House, Bounton, nr Cirencester, Glos, and has had:

1b James Vernon; *b* Feb, *d* Dec 1995

2b *Oliver Robert James; *b* March 1997

1b *Eliza Camilla; *b* 1992

1 Dorothy Frances, *m* 3 Oct 1930 (*divorce* 1957 but remarried 21 Feb 1966) Col Ian Ferguson MacAlpine, only s of Francis Ferguson Macalpine, MA, of Guernsey. He *d* 22 Sept 1970.

2 Grace, *m* 1st 29 April 1927 (*divorce* 1957) Frederick Joseph Parsons, JP (*d* 4 Jan 1966), est s of Joseph Parsons, of Cumberland House, Hastings, and had issue,

(1) *Frank Joseph Timothy, *b* 9 Sept 1928, *m* 21 June 1957 *Mrs Elizabeth Wragg, dau of Gerald Wilkes, of Constantina, S Africa, and has issue,

1a *A son, *b* 21 Feb 1958

(1) *Sarah Penelope Ann, *b* 9 Dec 1933, *m* 3 April 1957 *Philip Macgregor Rue, s of Harry Rue, of Montrose, Hampton, and has issue,

1a *Leonora Louise, *b* 30 March 1960

2 (cont.) The Hon Mrs Grace Parsons *m* 2nd 1 Aug 1958 (*divorce* 1963) Henry Seton Middleditch, s of Henry Howard Middleditch, of Cromford, Derbys

3 Phyllis, *m* 2 March 1933 Capt Clive Harrison Martyn, MC, late RE, 3rd son of Charles Harrison Martyn, of Aspley Guise, Beds, and *d* 21 June 1955. He *d* 4 Jan 1959

BIBBY

Arms: Az. a saltire parted and fretty arg. surmounted in fess point by a lion rampant pean between two escallops in pale and as many mullets of six points in fess of the second. **Crest:** Upon a plate a cubit arm erect holding a sword in bend sinister proper pommel and hilt or. **Motto:** *Vi et virtute* ('By strength and courage').
Creation: Bt (UK) 8 July 1959.

SIR DEREK JAMES BIBBY, 2ND BT, of Tarporley, Co Palatine of Chester, MC (1945), DL (Cheshire 1987) [Sir Derek Bibby Bt MC DL, Willaston Grange, Willaston, S Wirral, Cheshire L64 2UN]; *b* 29 June 1922; *s* f 1986; *educ* Rugby and Trin Coll Oxford (MA 1941); Capt RA World War II 1942–46 (wounded), joined Bibby Bros 1946 (ptnr 1950, chm 1969–92, pres Bibby Line Gp 1992), past chm TS *Indefatigable* and Nat Sea Training Sch for Boys, also Britain Steamship Co, past dir: Charles Hill of Bristol, Bristol City Line of Steamships, Seabridge Shipping and Liverpool and London War Risks Insur Assoc, memb Gen Cncl Br Shipping; *m* 11 Jan 1961 *Christine Maud, yst dau of Rt Rev Frank Jackson Okell, MA, DD, Bp Stockport, and has issue:

1 +MICHAEL JAMES; *b* 2 Aug 1963; *educ* Rugby and Oxford; CA; *m* 1994 *Beverley, only dau of Donald Graham, and has:

(1) +Alexander James; *b* 24 Aug 1997

(2) +Christopher Graham; *b* 24 Aug 1997

2 +Geoffrey Frank Harold; *b* 18 Feb 1965; *educ* Rugby and Exeter U; *m* 1994 *Sarah, est dau of Frederick Robinson, of Huntington, Cheshire, and has:

(1) +Charles James; *b* 28 Dec 1995

3 +Peter John; *b* 26 March 1969; *educ* Rugby and Manchester U

4 +David Richard; *b* 1970; *educ* Rugby and Bath U

1 *Jennifer Margaret; *b* 3 March 1962; *educ* Howells and Oxford; CA; *m* 1995 *Peter Smith, and has:

(1) *Alice Louise; *b* 16 Oct 1996

Lineage: JAMES BIBBY, of Wrightington, Standish, Lancs, *m* 9 June 1765 Alice, dau of Jacob Gill, of Parbold, Eccleston, Lancs, and had, with other issue:

JOHN BIBBY, of Liverpool, and Mount Pleasant, Linacre, Lancs, merchant and shipowner, bapt 19 Feb 1775, *m* 17 Aug 1805 Mary (*d* 17 June 1819), est dau of Joseph Mellard, Mayor Newcastle-under-Lyme, Staffs, 1783, and *d* 17 July 1840, leaving issue:

1 Joseph Mellard; *b* 6 Aug 1806; *m* Ellen Lord (*d* 25 Oct 1904 aged 93) and *dsp* 22 Dec 1855

2 John, of Hart Hill, Allerton, Lancs, JP; *b* 14 Dec 1810; *m* 1st 5 June 1838 Fanny (*d* 13 Nov 1856), dau of Jesse Hartley, of Bootle, Lancs, ch engr and designer Liverpool Docks, and had issue:

(1) John, of Liverpool, and Fachwen, St Asaph; *b* 2 May 1839; *m* Frances Caroline Grundy (*d* 24 Feb 1884) and *d* 2 Aug 1898, having had issue:

1a John Hartley, of Plas-yn-Roe, nr Conway, Caernarvonshire, JP (1917), md John Bibby, Sons & Co, Garston, Lancs, dir Broughton Copper, Manchester, Tstee Blue Coat Hosp and Ctee Roy Infirmary, Liverpool, hon Sec Altcar Club and Waterloo Cup Coursing 17 years; *b* 1 June 1865; *educ* Eton; *m* 7 Jan 1890 Eugenie (*d* 25 Feb 1959 aged 95), 2nd dau of Capt Chesborough Claude Macdonald, of Ness Castle, Inverness-shire, and *d* 26 Nov 1938, leaving issue:

1b John Eric Hartley, W/Cdr RFC and with Roy Welch Fus WWs I and II (RCAF); *b* 30 Oct 1896; *educ* Eton; *d* 8 Jan 1962

2b Rupert Bernard Hartley; *b* 25 Sept 1903; *educ* RNC Dartmouth; *m* 19– (*divorce* 19–) Angela Van Scheylenburgh (*née* Cleaver) and *d* 22 June 1960

1b Noelle Francis Hartley; *b* 10 Jan 1891; *d* unm 12 Sept 1963

2b Eileen Evereld Hartley; *b* 17 Dec 1898; *m* 29 Sept 1934 Lt-Col Brian Maxwell Strang, 12th Roy Lancers, and had issue:

1c *Elfreda Eugenie Priscilla Maxwell; *b* 25 Dec 1935

2c *Xenia Vivienne Maxwell; *b* 1 June 1939; *m* 23 Nov 1968 *Oliver Rudston de Baer, s of Lt-Gen de Baer, legal advsr Belgian Govt in exile 1939–45, memb War Crimes Tbnl Nüremburg

3c *Erica Antoinette Maxwell (twin); *b* 1 June 1939; *m* 2 Oct 1965 *Martin Patrick Hotham, s of Lt-Cdr Hon (John) David Hotham, DSC, RN, and has issue (*see* HOTHAM, B)

2a Edmund Bernard; *d* 31 March 1902

3a William Cardwell

4a Hugh Grundy

5a Henry Leigh; *ka* 1916

6a Francis Jesse; *m* 12 Sept 1906 Lilian Gertrude Thomas and *d* 29 April 1954, leaving issue:

1b Violet Lillian; *b* 1909

7a Robert Gordon

1a Irene Frances; *d* 1946

2a Elizabeth Edna; *b* 25 Oct 1871; *m* 1897 Maj Albert Ernest Lees, of Rowton Castle, nr Shrewsbury, only s of Joseph Lees, JP, of Mannickfold, Holmwood, Surrey, and *d* 1939, leaving issue

3a Enid Dorothea; *d* unm 8 Dec 1960

4a Muriel Amy; *d* 1955

5a Alice Gladys Mabel; *d* Nov 1958

6a Helen Mary

7a Frances Caroline; *d* 1944

(2) Hartley; *b* 19 May 1842; *d* 2 July 1849

(3) Alfred; *b* 15 Mar 1847; *m* 3 June 1890 Hylda Frances Maryon (*d* 8 July 1953), er dau of Richard Battye, of Skelton Hall, York, by Frances, er dau of James Jenkinson Bibby, of Hardwicke Grange, Salop, and *d* 10 May 1920, having had issue:

1a James David, Lt-Col 4th QOH, served WWs I and Russia 1919 (despatches) and WW II; *b* 2 Oct 1891; *educ* Eton; *m* 21 Aug 1928 Lady Jean Douglas, er dau of Lt-Col Hon Douglas George Carnegie, of Fair Oak, Rogate, Sussex, and sister of 12th Earl of Northesk (*qv*), and *d* 23 June 1979, leaving issue:

1b *John Alfred James; *b* 25 July 1931; *m* 17 Aug 1957 *Gillian Frances, er dau of Col John Miller-Hallet, Gurkha Rifles, of Phoenix Cottage, Shirley Holms, Lymington, Hants, and has issue:

1c *Peter David; *b* 13 July 1967

1c *Elizabeth Anne; *b* 21 Dec 1958

2c *Susan Frances; *b* 20 March 1960

3c *Caroline Mary; *b* 16 Feb 1963

1b *Anne Mary Jean; *b* 9 April 1938

2a John Patrick; *b* 9 Nov 1892; *ka* March 1915

3a Richard Peter; *b* 27 May 1894; *d* 15 July 1901

4a Francis Stephen; *b* 10 July 1896; *ka* June 1916

1a Alice Hylda Mary; *b* 29 March 1898; *m* 1926 Lt-Col C P Moore, MC, King's Regt (*d* 1959), and had a s

2a Alfreda Constance Margaret; *b* 5 Oct 1899; *m* 29 July 1927 Lt-Col John Augustus Lawrence Powell, 4th Hus, s of Lt-Col Albert Laurence Powell, of The Crossways, Sheringham, Norfolk, and had issue:

1b *David, Maj Coldstream Gds [Maj David Powell, The Red Cottage, Finchampstead, Berks]; *b* 27 Oct 1931; *educ* Eton; *m* 29 June 1957 *Susanna Mary Stewart, dau of Brig Cynric Puleston Prescot, CBE, MA, AMICE, ACGI, of The Chantry, Bourton-on-the-Hill, Moreton-in-Marsh, Glos, and has issue:

1c *David; *b* 15 May 1960

2c *William Henry Algernon; *b* 19 Nov 1961

1c *Clare Susanna; *b* 12 May 1958

1b *Mary Ann; *b* 31 May 1928

(4) Edward; *b* 10 Feb 1848; *d* unm 25 Oct 1907

(1) Ellen; *b* 28 March 1841; *d* unm 12 Jan 1903

(2) Fanny; *b* 18 July 1843; *d* unm 29 July 1922

(3) Alice; *b* 28 Jan 1845; *m* 30 April 1873 William Samuel Graves and *d* 2 Nov 1879, leaving a dau

(4) Amy; *b* 15 Aug 1849; *d* 6 Sept 1852

2 (cont.) John Bibby *m* 2nd 19 April 1860 Anna Maria Emily Fleetwood (*d* 8 April 1899), est dau of Rev Charles Hesketh, of North Meols Hall, Lancs, and coheir of her bro Edward Fleetwood Hesketh, and *d* 4 April 1883, having by her had issue:

(5) Charles Hesketh BIBBY later BIBBY-HESKETH later still FLEETWOOD-HESKETH, of North Meols, Lancs, and Stocken Hall, Rutland, DL, JP Lancs, High Sheriff 1901, Mayor Southport 1905, barrister Inner Temple 1895, Maj Duke of Lancaster's Own Yeo, served S African War 1900 and WW I 1914–17, added by roy licence 6 Feb 1899 the name and arms of HESKETH; by roy licence 29 June 1907 discontinued the BIBBY and replaced it with FLEETWOOD and the arms of FLEETWOOD quarterly with those of HESKETH; *b* 13 Oct 1871; *educ* Eton and Trin Coll Camb (BA 1893, MA 1897); *m* 1st 4 Jan 1900 (*m* diss by div 1934) Anne Dorothea, est dau of Sir Thomas Brocklebank, 2nd Bt (*qv*), and had issue:

1a Roger BIBBY-HESKETH later FLEETWOOD-HESKETH later still Fleetwood HESKETH, OBE (1970), TD (1942), JP (Lancs 1947), Lancs: V-Lt 1972–77 (DL 1950), High Sheriff 1947, MP (C) Southport 1952–59, memb Southport Borough Cncl 1938–53, Mayor 1950, Freeman Southport 1966, barrister Inner Temple 1928, served with Duke of Lancaster's Own Yeo

1922–39 and WW II (despatches, Lt-Col 1944), hon Col Duke of Lancaster's Own Yeo 1956–67, chm Lancs Ag Exec Ctee 1965, US Bronze Star, took surname HESKETH only by deed poll 10 Aug 1956; *b* 28 July 1902; *educ* Eton and Ch Ch Oxford; *m* 23 Aug 1952 Lady Mary Constance Lumley, OBE (1974), DStJ (*d* 23 Jan 1998), est dau of 11th Earl of Scarbrough (*qv*), and *d* 1987, having had issue

2a (Charles) Peter Fleetwood BIBBY-HESKETH later FLEETWOOD-HESKETH later still Fleetwood HESKETH, TD (1943), DL (1961), High Sheriff Lancs 1960, served with Duke of Lancaster's Own Yeo 1926–39 and WW II, architect, author and illustrator, hon dist rep Nat Tst 1947–68, sec Victorian Soc 1960–63 (hon architectural advsr 1963), architectural correspondent *Daily Telegraph* 1964–67, Burgess Preston, govr Rossall Sch; *b* 5 Feb 1905; *educ* Eton; *m* 20 July 1940 (Mary) Monica (*d* 14 June 1982), JP (1951) Lancs, 2nd dau of Sir Ralph Cockayne Assheton, 1st Bt (*see* CLITHEROE, B), and *d c* 1985, leaving issue:

1b *Everilda Dorothea; *b* 2 June 1941

3a (Francis) Cuthbert Bold, TD, served Duke of Lancaster's Own Yeo 1936–39 and WW II; *b* 10 May 1910; *educ* Eton and Trin Coll Camb; *m* 28 Dec 1967 *Helen Margery, twin dau of Major Mowbray Louis Buller, MC, JP, and *dsp* 7 Feb 1970

1a Lucy; *b* 14 Oct 1900; *m* 23 Nov 1935 Franz Peter George Eberhard (*d* 31 Dec 1963), son of T Eberhard, of Portschach-am-Worthersee, Austria, and *d* 24 Oct 1970, leaving issue

1b *Anne Theresa; *b* 12 May 1937; *m* 28 Jan 1963 *John Sisson

2a (Margaret) Joan Mary; *b* 19 April 1912; *d* unm 31 Aug 1975

3a Elizabeth Dorothea Maud; *b* 14 June 1914; *m* 28 July 1936 Brian Boteler FitzGerald, 2nd s of Lord Henry FitzGerald (*see* LEINSTER, D)

(5) (cont.) Charles FLEETWOOD-HESKETH *m* 2nd 23 April 1935 Gladys Victoria (*d* 18 Nov 1963), yst dau of Capt Charles Howard McPherson, 2nd W India Regt, and *d* 13 April 1947

(5) Edith; *b* 16 Jan 1861; *m* 18 Sept 1890 Percy Richard Neville Palin (*d* 8 April 1933) and *d* 7 Oct 1948

(6) Maud; *b* 26 March 1864; *d* 7 Oct 1868

(7) Ethel; *b* 23 April 1866; *d* 12 Oct 1868

3 THOMAS (Rev), of whom presently

4 James Jenkinson, of Hardwicke Grange, Hadnall, and Sansaw, Clive, Salop, DL, JP, High Sheriff Salop 1882, bought Hardwicke Grange from 2nd Viscount Hill 1868 and Sansaw from Robert Gardner; *b* 24 June 1813; *m* 18 April 1844 Sarah (*d* 19 May 1892), dau of Thomas Cook, of Dewsbury, Yorks, and *d* 8 Jan 1897, having had issue,

(1) James; *b* 28 Feb 1852; *d* 11 Aug 1857

(2) Thomas Cook; *b* 20 Sept 1854; *d* 28 March 1855

(3) Frank, CBE (1920), of Hardwicke Grange and Sansaw, DL, JP Salop, High Sheriff 1900; *b* 4 Jan 1857; *educ* Eton; *m* 22 July 1890 Edith Mary (*d* 11 Jan 1933), est dau of Maj-Gen Sir Stanley de Astel Calvert Clarke, GCVO, CMG, of The Ranger's Lodge, Hyde Park, London W, Clerk Marshal and Ch Equerry to HM KING EDWARD VII, Serjeant-at-Arms Ho of Lds 1910–11, and *d* 12 Feb 1923, leaving issue:

1a Frank Brian Frederic, of Hardwicke Grange and Sansaw, High Sheriff Salop 1929, Capt Shropshire Yeo, formerly 1st Life Guards, MFH N Shropshire 1925–29; *b* 15 Dec 1893; *educ* Ch Ch Oxford (MA); *m* 2 Dec 1919 Ethel Mildred, MFH N Shropshire 1929–31, formerly of Hardwick Grange (demolished 1931) (who *m* 2nd 12 June 1935 Maj John Ronald Campbell, Coldstream Gds (*ka* in France, 30 May 1940), only s of Brig-Gen John Vaughan Campbell, VC, CMG, DSO (*see* CAWDOR, E), and *d* 17 May 1967), yst dau of Thomas Reginald Hague Cook, JP, of 46 Portman Sq, London W1, and *d* 21 July 1929, leaving issue:

1b Cynthia Joan; *b* 2 Oct 1921; *m* 26 Sept 1945 Capt Noel Dennis Thompson, Yorks Hus (*d* 17 Jan 1967), yr s of Claude William George Hugh Thompson, JP, of Red House, Escrick, Yorks, and *d* 5 Feb 1971 leaving issue:

1c *David Robin Bibby, Queen's Royal Irish Hus; *b* 23 July 1946; *educ* Uppingham

1c *Sarah Jane; *b* 14 Oct 1950

1a (Averil) Margaret Mary, Jt MFH S Dorset 1936; *b* 14 April 1905; *m* 1st 27 April 1925 (*m* diss by div 1951) Capt Charles Michael St Maur Wellesley-Wesley, Leics Yeo (ret), son of Rev L H Wellesley-Wesley, of Handford Hill, and had two s and a dau; *m* 2nd 22 Oct 1951 Count Stanislaw Thomas August Anton Krasicki, son of Count August Konstantin Krasicki, and *d* 13 Feb 1965

2a *Katherine Edith; *b* 11 March 1916; *m* 1st 1 Oct 1935 (*m* diss by div 1944) Maj-Gen George Erroll Prior-Palmer, CB, DSO (*d* 18 Aug 1977,) yr son of Prior Spunner Prior-Palmer, of 32 Merrion Sq, Dublin, and has issue:

1b *Karol Ann [The Hon Mrs Simon Maxwell, The Dower House, Westcote, Kingham, Oxon]; *b* 19 Dec 1938; *m* 5 May 1964 *Hon Simon Kenlis Maxwell, yr son of Lt-Col Hon Somerset Arthur Maxwell, MP, and bro of 12th Baron Farnham (*qv*), and has issue

2a (cont.) Mrs Katherine Prior-Palmer *m* 2nd Capt (Hesketh) Raoul le Jarderay Millais, 2nd s of John Guille Millais (*see* MILLAIS, Bt), and has further issue

(1) Frances; *b* 15 Dec 1845; *m* 6 Sept 1866 Richard Battye and had issue

(2) Sarah; *b* 26 April 1847

(3) Agnes Jessie; *b* 9 Jan 1849; *m* 21 Jan 1880 Edward Holmes Baldock and had issue

(4) Gertrude; *b* 10 Oct 1850; *m* 1 May 1880 Percy Wormald and *d* 23 Feb 1897, leaving issue

1 Mary Mellard; *b* 8 July 1809; *m* 5 Jan 1836 Henry Francis Penny and *d* 27 April 1887, leaving issue. He *d* 21 Dec 1881

The 3rd son,

Rev THOMAS BIBBY, MA Camb, rector/vicar various parishes Lancs and Warwicks; *b* 7 March 1812; *m* 21 Sept 1843 Elizabeth (*d* 2 Oct 1905), dau of Thomas Wilson, merchant, of Liverpool, and *d* 3 Sept 1883, leaving issue:

1 Herbert Kirkman, of 7 Hyde Park St, London; *b* 8 July 1844; *m* 27 Oct 1877 Julia, yst dau of John Carless, MD, of Stroud, Glos, and *d* 15 Nov 1927, having had issue:

(1) Thomas Frederick Allen; *b* Aug 1878; *m* 12 June 1918 *Dorothea Ruth Gilroy (*m* 2nd 6 Nov 1943 Henry Z Persons) and *d* 1 Jan 1940, leaving issue,

1a *Thomas Frederick Allen; *b* 9 April 1921; *m* 14 Nov 1953 *Joan Keefer and has issue:

1b *Thomas Frederick Allen; *b* 17 Feb 1955

2b *Christopher; *b* 4 June 1956

1a *Dorothy Audrey; *b* 19 March 1919; *m* 24 April 1948 *Willis P Donkin and has issue:

1b *Ellen; *b* 6 Aug 1949

2b *Kathleen; *b* 1 Dec 1952

3b *Rhoda; *b* 15 May 1954

2a *Rhoda Mary; *b* 19 Nov 1924; *m* 7 Dec 1944 *Alexis Painter Nason and has issue:

1b *Steven Everingham; *b* 10 Sept 1948

1b *Mary Sheridan; *b* 16 Sept 1946

2b *Dorothy Gilroy; *b* 6 Aug 1951

(2) Claude Bertram; *b* Aug 1880; *m* 1st (*divorce*) Doris Margaret Johnson; *m* 2nd 1923 Pamela Beatrice Chapman and *d* Dec 1928

(3) John Pengelly; *b* Oct 1890; *ka* 1917

(1) Lillian Julia; *b* 10 April 1883; *m* 11 March 1930 Henry Bramwell Withers, OBE, JP, and *dsp* 27 Jan 1957

(2) Brenda Agnes; *b* 9 Sept 1887; *m* 2 April 1919 Gordon Burrell and *d* 11 July 1959, leaving issue. He *d* 8 June 1949

2 ARTHUR WILSON, of whom presently

3 Ernest Vincent, of Throstles Nest, Gateacre, Lancs; *b* 9 July 1849; *m* 13 April 1875 Sarah, dau of John Carless, MD, of Stroud, Glos, and *d* 17 Sept 1899, leaving issue:

(1) Ernest Carless; *b* 12 Jan 1876; *d* 1 Sept 1922

(2) Herbert Carless; *b* 12 Jan 1876 (twin); *m* 11 June 1903 Katharine Mary Fairbairn Clarke (*d* Durban 24 July 1970 aged 88) and *d* 29 Nov 1953, leaving issue:

1a Arthur Herbert; *b* 19 July 1904; *m* 28 July 1925 Helen Jessie Booty (who *m* 2nd 28 June 1963 Alec Gerald Lindsay) and *d* 12 Jan 1954, leaving issue:

1b *Peter Lester; *b* 23 Aug 1928; *m* 23 Aug 1955 *Mornay Francesca Morphy-Morris and has issue:

1c *Andrew Lester; *b* 30 Nov 1956

1c *Sandra Josephine; *b* 15 May 1959

2c *A dau; *b* 1963

1b *June Valerie Fairbairn; *b* 14 Feb 1926; *m* 29 Oct 1956 *Philip John Maurice Wilson and has issue:

1c *Richard Peter Philip; *b* 9 May 1958

1c *Virginia Valerie; *b* 1 Feb 1960

(3) Kenneth; *b* 26 Aug 1878; *m* 12 June 1906 Evelyn Emily Greta Clover (*d* 3 Feb 1933) and *d* 20 May 1922, leaving issue,

1a Vivian Kenneth Clover; *b* 4 Dec 1907; *d* 9 May 1931

2a *Desmond Terence; *b* 24 June 1911; *m* 11 April 1935 *Patricia Kirkman Clover

1a *Doreen Greta; *b* 20 April 1909; *m* 14 Dec 1933 Percy Charles Brands Sheriffs

(1) Ethel Norah; *b* 10 Aug 1883; *m* 17 May 1912 William Frothingham Roach, MD, and *d* 2 Oct 1948

The 2nd son,

ARTHUR WILSON BIBBY, of Hill Foot, Woolton, Liverpool, ptnr Bibby Bros, shipowners and bankers, dir Canada Shipping, N and S Wales Bank of Maritime Insur, Warner Barnes & Co, Ledward Bibby & Co and English Coaling Co, Port Said, sometime chm Pacific Steam Navigation Co and Liverpool Steamship Owners Assoc, govt nominee memb Mersey Docks and Harbour Brd, chm ctee training ship *Indefatigable*; *b* 10 Feb 1846; *educ* Rugby; *m* 7 Oct 1885 Beatrice Eveline (*d* 14 Jan 1940), yr dau of Thomas Heald, of Greenfield House, Billinge, nr Wigan, Mayor and Clerk of the Peace of Wigan, and *d* 15 Dec 1935, leaving issue:

1 (ARTHUR) HAROLD (Sir), **1st Bt**

1 Beatrice Helen; *b* 28 July 1886; *m* 4 Jan 1910 John Robert Collie, est s of Rev A S Collie, and *d* 13 Dec 1926, leaving two sons and two daus

2 Constance Eveline; *b* 6 April 1891; *m* 20 Aug 1919 Maurice FitzGerald Sandes Magill, 7th s of Capt James McGillycuddy Magill, JP, of Churchtown, Beaufort, Co Kerry, and *d* 16 Aug 1970, leaving two s and a dau He *d* 1 March 1967

Arthur Bibby's s,

Sir (Arthur) Harold Bibby, 1st Bt (UK), so *cr* 8 July 1959, DSO (1917), DL (Cheshire 1937), High Sheriff 1934; *b* 18 Feb 1889; *educ* Rugby; Hon LLD Liverpool U 1959, served RFA (TA) 1908–19, served WW I 1914–19 France and Flanders (despatches twice), sr ptnr Bibby Bros, chm Bibby Line 1935–69, dir: Sea Insur 1922–68 (chm 1930–56), Martins Bank 1929–67 (chm 1947–62), Suez Canal Co 1939–57 and Liverpool and London Steamship Protection and Imdemnity Assoc 1921–68, memb Mersey Docks and Harbour Bd 1931–65, govr Rugby Sch 1932–67, chm Liverpool Steamship Owners' Assoc 1927–28, Centenary Chm 1958–59, Jt V-Chm Gen Cncl Br Shipping 1958–59, pres training ship *Indefatigable* (chm 1931–60), pres Liverpool Sailors Home (chm 1921–51), ktd 1956); *m* 26 May 1920 Marjorie Guthrie, eldest dau of Charles James Williamson, of Camp Hill, Woolton, Liverpool (*see* FORRES, B), and *d* 7 March 1986, having had issue:

1 Sir DEREK JAMES BIBBY, **2nd and present Bt**

2 John Christopher, Lt RA, jt md Executive and Commercial Travel Ltd 1965; *b* 7 June 1932; *educ* Rugby; *d* unm 1 Oct 1968

1 *Patricia Mary [Mrs Iain Macdonald, 100 Old Church St, London SW3 6EP]; *b* 1921; *m* 1st 1944 (*divorce* 1956) Ronald Stuart Kinsey; *m* 2nd 1962 Iain Hall Brookes Macdonald (*d* 1990) and has issue by 1st husb:

(1) *Anne Quenelda Stuart [Mrs Julian Avery, Bardown, Stonegate, Wadhurst, E Sussex TN5 7EL]; *b* 13 July 1947; *m* 1972 *Julian Ralph Avery

(2) *Hilary Jane Stuart [Mrs Simon Reed, 62 Streathbourne Rd, London SW17]; *b* 30 Jan 1951; *m* 1983 *Simon Francis Reed

2 *Joan Elizabeth; *b* 5 Jan 1926; *m* 1st 22 Dec 1951 Maj Reginald Francis Foster, IA (*d* 1974); *m* 2nd 1985 (*divorce* 1987) Clifford Haines and has issue by 1st husb:

(1) *Rachel Frances [Mrs Rachel Nicoll, Meonside, Workhouse Lane, E Meon, Hants GU32 1PD]; *b* 25 Aug 1955; *m* 1977 (*divorce* 1990) Gp-Capt Ian Thomas Nicoll, RAF

3 *Anne Marjorie; *b* 30 Oct 1928; *m* 1st 5 May 1951 Lt-Col John Hamilton Palairet (*d* 1969); *m* 2nd 1976 (*divorce* 1980) Denis Justin Beattie and has issue by 1st husb:

(1) *Sarah Lillias [Mrs Christopher Capper, Chedglow Manor, Crudwell, Malmesbury, Wilts SN16 9EZ]; *b* 13 Feb 1953; *m* 1977 *Christopher Neston Ord Capper

(2) *Joanna Vivian [Mrs Jeremy Hicks, Gaskells Farmhouse, Winstone, nr Cirencester, Glos GL7 7JZ]; *b* 25 Jan 1955; *m* 1979 *Jeremy William Hicks and has:

1a *William John Palairet; *b* 14 Aug 1983

1a *Eleanor Anne Hicks; *b* 8 June 1985

(3) *Ailsa Jane; *b* 30 Oct 1957; *m* 1980 *Stephen John Duyland Bush

Bicester

Arms: Or, a chevron cotised between two demi-gryphons couped, respecting each other, in chief, and a like demi-gryphon in base, sa. **Crest:** An elephant's head erased or, eared gu., charged on the neck with three fleurs-de-lys, two and one, az. **Supporters:** On either side a griffin sa., charged on the shoulder with a horseshoe inverted or. **Motto:** *Tenax in fide* ('Steadfast in the faith'). **Creation:** B. (UK) 29 June 1938.

THE 3RD BARON BICESTER, of Tusmore, Co Oxford (Angus Edward Vivian Smith) [The Rt Hon the Lord Bicester, House of Lords, London SW1A 0PW]; *b* 20 Feb 1932; *s* unc 1968; *educ* Eton

Lineage: JOHN SMITH, of Dale Park, Sussex, successively MP Wendover, Nottingham, Midhurst, Chichester and Bucks, 6th *s* of Abel Smith, of Nottingham, and yr bro of 1st Baron Carrington (*qv*); *b* 6 Sept 1767; *m* 1st 1 Dec 1793 Sarah (*dsp* 23 Sept 1794), dau of Thomas Boone; *m* 2nd 6 Jan 1800 Elizabeth (*d* 9 April 1809), dau of Lt-Col Tucker, and had two *s*; *m* 3rd 1 May 1811 Emma (*d* 15 March 1851), dau of Egerton Leigh, of West Hall, High Leigh, Cheshire, and *d* 20 Jan 1842, having by her had two daus; the er *s*:

JOHN ABEL SMITH, of Dale Park, Sussex, and 47 Belgrave Sq, London SW, MP Midhurst and Chichester; *b* 2 June 1802; *m* 26 Dec 1827 Anne (*d* 24 Jan 1858), widow of Ralph William Grey, of Backworth House, Northumberland, and est dau of Sir Samuel Clarke Jervoise, 1st Bt (*see* 1933 edn), and *d* 7 Jan 1871, leaving, with two er *s*:

HUGH COLIN SMITH, of Mount Clare, Roehampton, Surrey; Lt City of London, Govr Bank of England; *b* 31 Oct 1836; *m* 9 Aug 1865 Constance Maria Josepha (*d* 1 Dec 1918), dau of Henry John Adeane, of Babraham, Cambs, and *d* 8 March 1910, leaving, with other issue, an est *s*:

VIVIAN HUGH SMITH, **1st Baron Bicester**, of Tusmore, Co Oxford (UK), so *cr* 29 June 1938; Ld Lt Oxon 1934–54, Govr Roy Exchange Assur, chm Yule, Catto & Co, dir Morgan Grenfell, Assoc Electrical Industs, KStJ; *b* 9 Dec 1867; *m* 6 March 1897 Lady Sybil Mary McDonnell, CStJ (*d* 16 April 1959), dau of 6th Earl of Antrim (*qv*), and *d* 17 Feb 1956, having had issue:

1 RANDAL HUGH VIVIAN SMITH, **2nd Baron Bicester**; High Sheriff Oxon 1945, md Morgan Grenfell, a Dir Bank of England, dir Associated Electrical Industries, Shell Transport and Trading and Vickers Ltd, OStJ; *b* 9 Jan 1898; *educ* Eton and RMC Sandhurst; *m* 29 Nov 1922 Hon Dorothea Gwenllian James (*d* 20 Aug 1974), est dau of 3rd Baron Northbourne (*qv*), and was *k* in a motor accident 15 Jan 1968, leaving issue:

(1) Gillian Mary Randal; *b* 28 April 1924; *m* 20 Nov 1946 John Ernest Harley Collins, MBE, DSC, DL, High Sheriff Oxon 1975, CStJ 1975, dir Morgan Grenfell Hldgs, *s* of George William Collins, of Taynton House, Taynton, Glos, and had issue:

1a *John Randal Timothy [John Collins Esq, Combe House, Combe Fishacre, Devon TQ12 5 UQ]; *b* 21 Feb 1951; *educ* Eton; *m* 16 May 1974 *Catherine Anastasia, est dau of Christopher Petherick, of 83 Addison Rd, London W14

1a *Sarah Elizabeth; *b* 13 Nov 1948; *m* 25 May 1968 (*divorce* 1985) Denzil Robert Onslow How (*see* ONSLOW, E), and has issue

(2) *Jane Beatrix Randal [The Hon Mrs Jane Green, Taylors Mead, Sparsholt, Hants SO21 2NR]; *b* 12 Feb 1928; *m* 4 April 1949 (*divorce* 1991) John Richard Daniel Green, yr *s* of John Everard Green, of Chelsea, and has:

1a *John James Randal [John Green Esq, Foxboro Hall, Melton, Suffolk IP12 1ND]; *b* 9 Sept 1953; *m* 1980 *Hon Claerwen Gibson-Watt, dau of Baron Gibson-Watt (*qv*) and formerly *w* of Enrique Ulvert, and has issue:

1b *Toby James Ralph; *b* 1982

2b *Richard John Sebastian; *b* 1984

3b *David Peter Julian (twin); *b* 1984

1a *Elizabeth Jane; *b* 20 Nov 1950; *m* 1982 (*divorce* 1991) Ian Mackinnon, only *s* of Maj C N Mackinnon, of Old Garth, Bembridge, IoW

2a *Amanda Carol [Mrs Charles Bunbury, 22 Balham Pk Rd, London SW12 8DU]; *b* 9 July 1957; *m* 1986 *Charles Thomas Bunbury, 2nd *s* of Sir (John) William Napier Bunbury, 12th Bt (*qv*)

2 Stephen Edward Vivian, Lt-Col; *b* 1 Aug 1903; *m* 1st 15 May 1929 (*divorce* 1947) Elenor Anderson, dau of Edward Shepard Hewitt, of New York, and had issue:

(1) John Stephen Vivian; *b* 24 March 1930; *educ* Eton; *d* unm Calcutta 19 April 1957

(2) ANGUS EDWARD VIVIAN SMITH, **3rd and present Baron Bicester**

(3) +HUGH CHARLES VIVIAN; *b* 8 Nov 1934; heir presumptive; *educ* Eton and Worcester Coll Oxford; late 2nd Lt RAC

2 (cont.) Lt-Col the Hon Stephen Smith *m* 2nd 7 May 1948 *Mabel, MusB [The Hon Mrs Stephen Smith, 6 Ravenscar Lodge, 22 The Downs, London SW20 8HT], er dau of Albert William Rogers Lovering, of Balcombe, Sussex, and *d* 9 June 1952

3 Hugh Adeane Vivian, MBE (1945); Maj Irish Gds, served WW II (despatches); *b* 25 April 1910; *educ* Eton and Ch Ch Oxford; *m* 26 June 1933 *Lady Helen Dorothy Primrose [The Lady Helen Smith, the Old Rectory, Souldern, Bicester, Oxon], dau of 6th Earl of Rosebery (*qv*), and *d* 20 March 1978, leaving issue:

(1) +George Harry Vivian; *b* 13 July 1934; *educ* Michaelhouse Sch S Africa and Christ's Coll Cambridge; *m* 1st 31 Jan 1962 (*divorce* 1965) June Rose Jager, only dau of Basil William Foster-Towne, of S Africa, and Mrs Diana Beatrice Jager, and has issue:

1a +Charles James Vivian; *b* 7 Sept 1963

(1) (cont.) George Smith *m* 2nd 16 Feb 1966 *Susan Mary, dau of Frank Goodfellow, of Johannesburg, and by her has issue:

1a *Sarah Helen; *b* 1968

2a *Amanda Mary; *b* 1972

(1) *Sarah Vivian [Mrs James Macdonald-Buchanan, Strathconon, Muir of Ord, Ross-shire]; *b* 30 March 1939; *m* 26 April 1960 *(Alexander) James Macdonald-Buchanan, yr *s* of Maj Sir Reginald Narcissus Macdonald-Buchanan, KCVO, MBE, MC, of Cottesbrooke Hall, Northants, by Hon Catherine, only child of 1st and last Baron Woolavington, GCVO, and has issue:

1a *Hugh James; *b* 10 Sept 1961

2a *James Iain Harry; *b* 4 Feb 1963

3a *Nicholas Mark; *b* 26 April 1967

4a *Charles Alexander; *b* 1970

1 Victoria Alexandrina Vivian; *b* 21 Dec 1899 (HM QUEEN VICTORIA stood sponsor); *d* unm 5 Jan 1969

2 Mary Constance Vivian; *b* 5 Nov 1901; *m* 3 Aug 1928 2nd Baron Rennell (*qv*) and *d* 31 May 1981, having had issue

3 Joyce Sybil Vivian; *b* 6 Aug 1905; *m* 25 Feb 1926 Maj-Gen Gerald Lloyd-Verney, DSO, MVO, late Irish Gds, est *s* of Sir Harry Lloyd-Verney, GCVO, and had issue (*see* VERNEY, Bt). He *d* 3 April 1957

4 Honor Mildred Vivian, OBE (1962); *b* 13 Nov 1908; *educ* London (BSc, BS, MD) and Oxford U (MA); MRCS E and LRCP London 1940, MRCP 1954, FRCP 1965; *d* by 18 Jan 1995

BIDDULPH, Baron

Arms: Quarterly, 1st and 4th, vert an eagle displayed arg., armed and langued gu., a canton of the second (for BIDDULPH); 2nd and 3rd, or a lion rampant gu. Couped at all his joints of the field within a double tressure flory counterflory az. (for MAITLAND). **Crest:** A wolf salient arg., charged on the shoulder with a trefoil slipped gu. **Supporters:** Two wolves arg., semée of trefoils gu. **Motto:** *Sublimiora petamus* ('Let us aim for higher things'). **Creation:** *b* (UK) 1 Aug 1903.

THE 5TH BARON BIDDULPH, of Ledbury, Co Hereford ((Anthony) Nicholas Colin Maitland Biddulph) [The Rt Hon The Lord Biddulph, Makerstoun House, Kelso, Borders TD5 7PA]; *b* 8 April 1959; *s f* 1988; *educ* Cheltenham and RAC Cirencester; interior designer and sporting manager, Armourer and Liveryman City of London; added surname MAITLAND 1978; *m* 28 Aug 1993 *Hon Sián Diana Gibson-Watt, yr dau of Baron Gibson-Watt (*qv*), and has issue:

1 +ROBERT JULIAN WATT; *b* 8 July 1994

2 +David Michael William; *b* 20 Oct 1997

Lineage: ANTHONY BIDDULPH, s of Simon Biddulph, of Elmhurst, Staffs, and yr bro of Michael Biddulph, ancestor of the BIDDULPH Bts (*qv*); *b* 1584; *m* Elizabeth, dau of Robert Palmer, Alderman London. His er s:

ROBERT BIDDULPH; *m* Mary, dau of Sir William Cullen, Bt, of E Sheen, and *d* 1679, leaving issue:

ANTHONY BIDDULPH; settled at Ledbury, Herefs, High Sheriff Herefs 1694; *m* Constance, dau and coheir of Francis Hall, and *d* 1718, issue: with two yr sons:

ROBERT BIDDULPH, of Ledbury; *bapt* Oct 1682; *m* Anne, dau of Benjamin Joliffe, of Cofton Hall, Worcs, and *d* 1772, leaving issue:

1 MICHAEL

2 Benjamin; in Holy Orders; f of:

(1) Benjamin, of Burghill, Herefs

3 Francis; banker, of Charing Cross, *dsp* 1800

ROBERT BIDDULPH's est s,

MICHAEL BIDDULPH, of Ledbury and Cofton Hall; *m* Penelope, est dau of John Dandridge, of Balden's Green, Malvern, Worcs, and *d* 6 Dec 1800, having had a 2nd s:

JOHN BIDDULPH, of Ledbury; *b* 1768; *m* 9 Sept 1797 Augusta Roberts and had, with three yr sons and six daus:

ROBERT BIDDULPH, of Ledbury, DL and JP, MP Hereford; *b* 3 March 1801; *m* 25 Feb 1830 Elizabeth (*d* 26 Jan 1899), dau of George Palmer, MP, of Nazeing Park, Essex, and *d* 28 Feb 1864, leaving, with other issue:

1 MICHAEL, **1st Baron**

2 Robert (Sir), GCB, GCMG, Gen Army, Master-Gunner St James's Park, High Commr Cyprus 1879–86, QMG Forces 1887 and 1893, Dir-Gen Mil Educn 1888–93, Govr Gibraltar 1893–1900; *b* 26 Aug 1835; *m* 11 Aug 1864 Sophia (*d* 23 April 1905), widow of Richard Stuart Palmer and dau of Rev Anthony Lewis Lambert, rector Chilbolton, Hants, and *d* 18 Nov 1918, having had, with other issue:

(1) Hope, DSO (1918), Lt-Col RFA WW I; *b* 27 Oct 1866; *m* 1st 1889 (*divorce* 1910) Mabel Gordon, only child of William Henry Urquhart, of Cromarty, and had issue:

1a Geoffrey Hope Sandys; *b* 3 April 1893; *dsp* 20 July 1937

2a John, Maj Glos Regt, reemployed as Staff-Capt Bicester 1961; *b* 1 June 1905; *m* 1930 Dorothy, er dau of Frederick C Wakefield, of York, and Natal, S Africa

1a Hermione Mary; *m* Eric Vincent Poore (*d* 3 April 1953) and *d* 15 July 1969, leaving issue:

1b *Richard John Benvenuto Biddulph; *b* 19 Sept 1943; *educ* Charterhouse

1b *Mary Elizabeth Penelope; *b* 7 Jan 1935; *m* —

(1) (cont.) Lt-Col Hope Biddulph *m* 2nd 1911 Mabel Alice, dau of Col T Edmonds Holmes, Oxfordshire LI, and *d* 4 March 1940

(2) Michael, OBE (1919), Lt-Col APD WW I; *b* 5 April 1871; *m* 30 March 1904 Ruth Emma (*d* 10 Dec 1930), 2nd dau of George Frederic Trench, of Abbeylands, Co Kerry (*see* ASHTOWN, B), and *d* 8 April 1920

(3) Harry, CB (1927), CMG (1919), DSO (1917), Col RE WW I, Hon Brig-Gen 1929, Dir Works and Bldgs Air Ministry 1928; *b* 19 July 1872; *m* 13 Jan 1904 Constance Emily (*d* 2 July 1958), yr dau of Rowland Smith, DL, JP, of Duffield Hall, Derbys, and *d* 21 April 1952, having had issue:

1a Robert Granville, Nigerian Admin Serv; *b* 26 March 1905; *m* (Kathleen) Esmé (*d* 22 April 1992), dau of Dr Fletcher-Jones, of Alderney and China, and *d* 1 July 1957, leaving issue:

1b (Robert Arthur) John, OBE; MRCP Edin, Emeritus Prof Child Health UPNG; *b* 15 Jan 1935; *m* *Mary Ann Harper, of Boston, USA, and *d* 6 Jan 1998, leaving two adopted children:

*Michael John; *b* 13 Oct 1967

*Frances Ann; *b* 25 Dec 1968

1b *Mary Esmé [Mrs Davidson, 58 Sadleir Avenue, Ashcroft, NSW 2168, Australia]; *m* 19– Trevor Davidson, JP, RAR (ret), and has issue:

1c *Catherine Mary; *b* 19 Jan 1966

2c *Barbara; *b* 30 Jan 1974

2b *Jane, SRN; *b* 5 June 1937

3b *Sarah Antonia [Mrs Norman Bakker, 10 Praed Place, Garran, ACT 2605, Australia]; *m* 9 July 1966 *Dr Norman Adrianus Bakker, PRD, Fell Chem Engineering Harwell, s of Arie Bakker, of Holland, and has issue:

1c *Jeremy; *b* 31 March 1979

1c *Angela Kathleen; *b* 11 June 1967

2c *Vanessa; *b* 15 Nov 1971

2a Rowland; Lt-Col RA, served WW II France and Burma; *b* 2 Aug 1906; *m* Marion, dau of Lt-Col Burton, and had issue:

1b *Thomas Harry Symons; *b* 23 March 1948; *m* 1st 1974 (*divorce* 1982) Ingrid Wellham; *m* 2nd 12 Oct 1985 *Donna Lynne Wellham, has adopted her son (*Robert John; *b* 18 Aug 1982) and by her has:

1c *Michael; *b* 4 Sept 1986

1b *Elizabeth Ursula Constance; *b* 5 Dec 1949

3a Michael Anthony, BA, Capt RE, served WW II; *b* 5 April 1913; *das* 22 April 1943

1a *Constance Sophia; *b* 23 June 1917

(4) Lewis; manager overseas branch Barclays Bank, Mentone; *b* 27 June 1876; *m* 28 Jan 1907 Margaret (*d* 23 Dec 1946), er dau of John Forbes, of Westfield, Linlithgow, and *d* 28 Nov 1958, leaving issue:

1a *George Michael Rollo; *b* 28 Dec 1913; *m* 1st 5 June 1939 (*divorce* 1950) Rita Christian Kiernan and has issue:

1b *Desmond Rollo; *b* 9 June 1943

2b *Michael John Patrick; *b* 19 Sept 1944

1b *Ann Margaret; *b* 25 March 1940

1a (cont.) George Biddulph *m* 2nd 15 July 1950 *Francina Nutting Cameron, 3rd dau of W H Close, MC, of Hampstead, and by her has issue:

3b *Stephen Michael; *b* 13 March 1951

2b *Jessica Ruth; *b* 11 June 1957

1a Elizabeth; *b* 29 Oct 1907; *m* 7 June 1928 Brig Henry Neville Sowdon, MBE, late RA (*d* 17 May 1969), est s of Henry Lucy Sowdon, of Avon View, Leamington Spa, and *d* 7 Feb 1998, leaving:

1b *Neville Robert Best [Neville Sowdon Esq, The Old Rectory, Hampton Bishop, Hereford]; *b* 6 Jan 1931

2b * Henry Lewis Malcolm (Rev) [The Rev Henry Sowdon, 1 Ayala Croft, Birmingham B36 8SN]; *b* 20 Aug 1937, team vicar Hodge Hill, Birmingham, from 1986

2a *Leonora [Mrs Charles Duffett, Southdene, 15 Borough Lane, Saffron Walden, Essex CB11 4AG]; *b* 11 Nov 1911; *m* 1 June 1942 Capt Charles Henry Duffett, CBE, DSO, RN (*d* 1981), est s of Henry Allcroft Duffett, FRCS, of Withy Holt, Sidcup, and has:

1b *Christopher Charles Biddulph; *b* 23 Aug 1943; *m* 26 Jan 1973 *Jennifer Mary Edwards, only dau of Kenneth Edwards, of Silverton, and has:

1c *Samuel Owen Salisbury; *b* 2 April 1975

2c *Daniel Charles William Biddulph; *b* 14 July 1977

1b *Petronella Margaret Elizabeth [Mrs David Oelman, Southdene, 15 Borough Lane, Saffron Walden, Essex]; *b* 30 May 1947; *m* 8 Oct 1985 *David Oelman, only s of H H E Oelman, of Letchworth, and has:

1c *Sophia Rosamund; *b* 28 Aug 1987

2c *Camilla Louise; *b* 14 Dec 1990

3a Isobel Sophia; *b* 24 Aug 1916; *m* 24 June 1950 Roy Ian Hanson, BA, barrister (*d* 28 Nov 1988), s of G Hanson, of Altrincham, Cheshire, and *d* 21 Nov 1996, leaving:

1b *Margaret Susan Leonora [Mrs Craig Pickering, 29 Mayfield Ave, London W4]; *b* 1 Aug 1952; *m* *Craig Robert Pickering, PhD, s of Raymond Pickering, of S Shields, Tyne and Wear, and has:

1c *Hannah Louise; *b* 19 Feb 1990

2b *Georgina Elizabeth [Mrs Georgina Aschenbrenner, 2 Whitethorn Lane, Letchworth, Herts]; *b* 18 Jan 1956; *m* 1978 (*divorce* 1997) — and has:

1c *Michael Anthony; *b* 8 Nov 1980

(1) Eva; *m* 10 April 1893 Lt-Col Alexander Herbert Mason, CB, DSO, RE, and *d* 16 March 1947, leaving issue. He *d* 1896

(2) Constance; *m* 12 July 1888 Sir Charles Anthony King-Harman, KCMG, and *d* 24 Feb 1961, leaving issue (*see* KINGSTON, E). He *d* 17 April 1939

3 Jessie; *d* unm 25 Dec 1954

4 Helen; *d* unm 14 Nov 1961

5 Mabel; missionary NW Province India; *d* unm 12 May 1974 aged 96

6 Georgiana; *d* 8 June 1939

The er s,

MICHAEL BIDDULPH, **1st Baron Biddulph** (UK), *so cr* 1 Aug 1903, DL and JP Herefs, JP Glos, MP (Lib) Herefs 1865–85 and (Lib U) S Herefs 1885–1900; *b* 17

Feb 1834; *m* 1st 9 Aug 1864 Adelaide Georgiana (*d* 22 May 1872), dau of Gen Jonathan Peel, PC, DCL, MP (*see* PEEL, E), and had issue:

1 JOHN MICHAEL GORDON, **2nd Baron**

2 Claud William; *b* 8 Feb 1871; *m* 12 Dec 1906 Margaret (*d* 21 June 1970), only dau of Alfred John Howard (*see* CARLISLE, E), and *d* 6 Aug 1954, leaving issue:

(1) Anthony, TD; High Sheriff Glos 1960, Maj Roy Gloucester Hus (TA) WW II; *b* 18 Aug 1910; *educ* Eton and Ch Ch Oxford (MA); *m* 4 Aug 1938 Mary Dearman (*d* 1991), dau of Maj Sir John Dearman Birchall, TD, MP, of Cotswold Farm, Cirencester (*see* WESTMORLAND, E), and *d* 1984, leaving issue:

1a +Simon [Simon Biddulph Esq, Rodmarton Manor, Rodmarton, Cirencester, Glos]; *b* 23 Nov 1942; *educ* Eton and Ch Ch Oxford *m* 3 Dec 1970 *Christina, dau of George McCorquodale (*see* LUKE, B), and has issue:

1b +John; *b* 1 Sept 1971; *educ* Eton

2b +(Anthony) George; *b* 4 Dec 1973

1b *Sarah Rose; *b* 1980

2a +(Anthony) Jasper [Jasper Biddulph Esq, Manor Farm, Tarlton, Cirencester, Glos]; *b* 19 Aug 1946; *educ* Eton and RAC Cirencester; *m* 18 Oct 1975 *Louise Perrett, dau of William Sandeman Cox, of Coffs Harbour, NSW, Australia, and has issue:

1b *James Jasper; *b* 12 April 1977

1b *Emily Serena Mary; *b* 12 May 1979

1a *Clarissa Mary [Mrs James Ferard, 28 Laxford Ho, Cundy St, London SW1W 9JU]; *b* 16 July 1939; *m* 21 July 1962 *James Richard Ferard, only s of Lt-Col Richard Ferard, of Tredean, nr Chepstow, Mon, and has issue:

1b *Richard Anthony Agace; *b* 27 March 1963; *m* 1994 *Lucilla Fleur Scott, er dau of Hon (John) Granville Napier (*see* NAPIER and ETTRICK, L)

2b *Edward Charles Lawrence; *b* 14 March 1970

1b *Susan Mary; *b* 27 Aug 1965

(1) Marjory Mary; *b* 8 Jan 1915; *m* 1st 15 Feb 1938 (*divorce* 1962) Major Philip Wilfred Cripps (*d* 31 May 1965), 2nd s of Maj Sir Frederick William Beresford Cripps, DSO, DL, JP, of Ampney Park, Cirencester, and had:

1a *John Philip; *b* 12 Aug 1940; *educ* Eton; *m* 1975 *Aileen Elizabeth, dau of William Alexander Hamilton

1a Angela; *b* 26 June 1950; *d* 18 Sept 1959

2a *Diana Josephine [Mrs Richard Turner, Friskys Cottage, Gt Bowden, Market Harborough LE16 7HD]; *b* 27 Feb 1953; *m* 17 May 1984 *Richard P Turner, yr s of John Turner, of Lound, Retford, Notts

(1) (cont.) Mrs Marjory Cripps *m* 2nd 28 Oct 1964 Lt-Col Sir Roland Lewis Findlay, 3rd and last Bt (*d* 28 July 1979; *see* 1970 edn), and *d* 8 June 1995

1 Adela Margaret Mary; *d* young Sept 1876

2 Edith Mary; *m* 31 March 1891 Charles Wentworth Bell, DL, JP, of Bronsil, Eastnor, Herefs (*d* 20 Jan 1929), and *d* 1939, leaving issue

3 Violet Maud; *d* unm 7 March 1960

The 1st BARON *m* 2nd 16 July 1877 Lady Elizabeth Philippa, VA (*d* 13 Jan 1916), Woman of the Bedchamber to HM QUEEN VICTORIA, widow of Henry John Adeane, MP, of Babraham, and dau of 4th Earl of Hardwicke (*qv*) and *d* 6 April 1923

The 1st BARON's er s,

JOHN MICHAEL GORDON, **2nd Baron Biddulph**, DL, JP Herefs, Govr Guy's Hosp, dir Martins Bank; *b* 19 Nov 1869; *educ* Eton and Ch Ch Oxford; *m* 10 Nov 1896 Marjorie Caroline Susan (*d* 9 Nov 1961), dau of Col William Mure, of Caldwell, and had issue:

1 MICHAEL WILLIAM JOHN, **3rd Baron**

2 Rupert Arthur; *b* 1 July 1904; *educ* Eton and Ch Ch Oxford; *d* 26 Jan 1975

1 Adelaide ('Dig') Mary; *m* 25 July 1929 Henry Vincent Yorke, novelist (as Henry Green), s of Vincent Wodehouse Yorke, of Forthampton Court, Tewkesbury, and had issue (*see* HARDWICKE, E). He *d* 13 Dec 1973

2 Mary Constance; *m* 9 July 1929 (*divorce* 1938) Montagu William Lowry-Corry, Res of Offrs Gren Gds (*d* 16 June 1977), only s of Gen Noel Armar Lowry Corry, DSO, and had issue (*see* BELMORE, E)

The 2nd BARON *d* 17 Dec 1949; his er son,

MICHAEL WILLIAM JOHN BIDDULPH, **3rd Baron Biddulph**; Lt Coldstream Gds; *b* 6 March 1898; *educ* Eton and RMC Sandhurst; *m* 21 Oct 1925 Lady Amy Louise Agar, 6th dau of 4th Earl of Normanton (*qv*), and had:

1 ROBERT MICHAEL CHRISTIAN, **4th Baron**

2 +Edward Sidney [The Hon Edward Biddulph, Ribston Lawn, Much Marcle, Ledbury, Herefs HR8 2ND]; *b* 16 Nov 1934; *educ* Eton; Lt RHG (ret)

1 *Marjorie Amy (Molly); *b* 17 Dec 1927; *m* 15 Jan 1947 Thomas Ian Michael Walker-Munro (*d* 1965) (*see* MUNRO, Bt of Lindertis), and has issue

2 *Susan Louise [The Hon Susan Biddulph, Under Down, Ledbury, Herefs]; *b* 24 Aug 1929

The 3rd BARON *d* 20 July 1972; his er son,

ROBERT MICHAEL CHRISTIAN BIDDULPH, **4th Baron Biddulph**; *b* 6 Jan 1931; *educ* Canford and RMA Sandhurst; Lt 16th/5th Queen's Roy Lancers, memb Roxburgh CC 1961–70; underwriting memb Lloyd's; Liveryman Armourers' and Brassers' Co; *m* 9 April 1958 *Lady Mary Helena Maitland [The Lady Mary Biddulph, Gt Ridge Hall, Makerstoun, Kelso TD5 7PD], est dau of Ivor Colin James, Viscount Maitland, and gdau of 15th Earl of Lauderdale (*qv*), and *d* 1988, leaving:

1 (ANTHONY) NICHOLAS COLIN BIDDULPH later MAITLAND BIDDULPH, **5th and present Baron Biddulph**

2 +William Ian Robert BIDDULPH later MAITLAND BIDDULPH [The Hon William Maitland Biddulph, Fair Oak, Ashford Hill, Newbury, Berks RG15 8B]; *b* 27 March 1963; *educ* Loretto; Armourer and Freeman City of London; added surname MAITLAND 1978

1 *Fiona Mary Biddulph later Maitland Biddulph [The Hon Mrs Fraser, 4 Wilmington House, Highbury Crescent, London N5 1RU; Keeper's Cottage, Spanhoe Wood, nr Harringworth, Northants NN17 3AB]; *b* 28 Aug 1961; *educ* Courtauld Inst; co-author: *Metropolitan: A Portrait of Paris* (1994); added surname MAITLAND 1981; *m* 1994 *Anthony Henry Joseph Fraser and has issue (*see* LOVAT, L)

BIDDULPH, Bt

Arms: Vert, an eagle displayed arg. and a canton arg. **Crest:** A wolf salient arg, charged on the shoulder with a trefoil slipped gu. **Creation:** Bt. (E) 2 Nov 1664.

SIR (IAN) JACK D'OLIER BIDDULPH, 11TH BT, of Westcombe, Kent [Sir Jack Biddulph Bt, Christensens Rd, Mount Walker, M/S 23, via Rosewood Qld 4340, Australia]; *b* 28 Feb 1940; *s* f 1986; *m* 1967 *Margaret Eleanor, only dau of John Gablonski, of Oxley, Brisbane, and has issue:

1 +PAUL WILLIAM; *b* 30 Oct 1967

1 *Julie Denise; *b* 1969

2 *Roslyn Mary; *b* 1971

Lineage: RICHARD BUDDULPH, of Biddulph, Staffs, living 1598, left a 2nd s:

SIMON BIDDULPH, of Elmhurst, Staffs; f of:

SIMON BIDDULPH, of Elmhurst; *m* Joyce, dau of Sir Robert Weston, and had issue:

SIMON BIDDULPH, of Elmhurst; *m* Joyce, dau of Richard Floger, of Uttoxeter, and *d* 1632, leaving (with a 3rd s, Anthony, ancestor of the Barons Biddulph (*qv*)) an est s:

MICHAEL BIDDULPH, of Elmhurst; *m* Elizabeth (*d* 30 Aug 1657), dau of Sir William Skeffington, 1st Bt, of Fisherwick, Staffs, and *d* 20 Jan 1657, leaving issue; his 3rd s:

Sir Theophilus Biddulph, 1st Bt (E), so *cr* 2 Nov 1664, MP London 1656–59 and Lichfield 1661–79; memb New England Co 1662; *m* 10 May 1641 Susannah (*bur* 17 Nov 1702), dau of Zachary Highlord, Alderman London, and was *bur* 11 April 1683, having had, with other issue:

1 **Sir Michael Biddulph, 2nd Bt**; MP Lichfield; *m* 1st 31 Dec 1678 Henrietta Maria (*bur* 15 Oct 1689), dau of Col Roger Whitley, and had issue:

(1) **Sir Theophilus Biddulph, 3rd Bt**; *m* Carew (*d* 18 April 1741), dau of Sir Charles Lyttelton, 3rd Bt, of Frankley (*see* COBHAM, V), and *dsp* 16 May 1743

(1) Susannah

(2) Charlotte

1 (cont.) **Sir Michael** *m* 2nd 7 March 1697/8 Elizabeth (*d* April 1740), dau of William Doyley, and *d* 20 April 1718, having by her had issue:

(3) Arabella

(4) Sarah

(5) Bridget

2 Simon, of Birdingbury, Warwicks; *m* Jane (*bur* 15 Aug 1755), dau of Edmond Birch, barrister, and *d* 19 Oct 1736, having had issue:

(1) Edward, of Birdingbury; *m* his 1st cousin Anne, est dau of Edward Birch, and had issue:

1a **Sir Theophilus Biddulph, 4th Bt**; *m* Jane (*d* 14 Aug 1818), only child of his uncle, Rev Michael Biddulph, Preb Lichfield, and Sir Theophilus *d* 1801, having had, with other issue:

1b **Sir Theophilus Biddulph, 5th Bt**; *b* 28 March 1757; *m* 1784 Hannah (*d* 1824), dau of H Prestige, and *d* 30 July 1841, having had issue:

1c **Sir Theophilus Biddulph, 6th Bt**; *b* 28 March 1785; *m* 12 April 1825 Jane Rebecca (*d* 19 March 1843), dau of Robert Vyner, of Eathorpe, Warwicks, and *d* 15 July 1854, having had issue:

1d **Sir Theophilus William Biddulph, 7th Bt**, DL, JP Warwicks, Maj 2nd Warwickshire Militia; *b* 18 Jan 1830; *m* 18 June 1872 Mary Agnes (*d* 16 June 1889), 3rd dau of 16th Lord Somerville, and *d* 1 March 1883, leaving:

1e **Sir Theophilus George Biddulph, 8th Bt**; *b* 3 April 1874; *m* 21 Sept 1907 Eleanor, OBE (1920) (*d* 19 Aug 1969 aged 92), yst dau of Samuel Thompson, of Muckamore Abbey, Co Antrim, and *dsp* 31 Jan 1948

1e Mary; *b* 4 April 1873; *d* 8 Jan 1895

1d Laura; *d* young

2d Jane Constance; *m* 6 June 1855 Sir William Biddulph Parker, 2nd Bt, DL, JP (*qv*), and *dsp* 20 July 1879. He *d* 23 Jan 1902

2c Charles; Capt RN; *d* unm 24 April 1815

3c Edward, CB; Lt-Col HEIC's HA; *b* 1788; *m* 1st Louisa, dau of Col Kelly, and had issue:

1d Edward Theophilus Price; *d* Moodarabad, 20 Oct 1864

1d Louisa Theodosia; *m* 1865 Lt-Col George Harris, RE, and *d* 27 March 1926. He *d* 1899

2d Frances Sophia; *m* 1884 Rev Henry Deshon. He *d* 1905

3c (cont.) Lt-Col Edward Biddulph *m* 2nd Mary Anne Marriott and *d* 3 Dec 1858, having by her had further issue:

3d Mary Anne; *m* 9 April 1872 George Josiah Curtis and *d* May 1929, leaving issue. He *d* 1895

4d Laura Georgiana; *m* 20 Oct 1883 Charles Valance Cambridge and had issue. He *d* April 1893

5d Edith Mary; *d* unm July 1947

4c Simon; Capt 25th Regt; *m* Anne, dau of Francis Harrison Biddulph, of Annamore, Ireland, and *d* 25 April 1823, leaving issue Margaret, *d* unm

5c Henry (Rev), MA; rector Birdingbury, Warwicks; *m* 1 July 1834 Emma Susan (*d* 14 April 1873), only dau of John Nuttall, of Worley Bank, Worcs, and *d* 19 Sept 1867, leaving issue:

1d Adelaide Emma; *m* 26 Oct 1865 Rev Humberston Skipwith, 9th s of Sir Grey Skipwith, 8th Bt (*qv*), and *d* 27 March 1869, leaving issue. He *d* 7 Jan 1911

1c Charlotte; *d* unm 30 Sept 1853

2c Frances Anne; *m* 9 June 1810 Adml Sir William Parker, 1st Bt (*see* PARKER, Bt, of Shenstone), and *d* 9 Jan 1871, leaving issue. He *d* 13 Nov 1866

2b John (Rev); Rector Frankton, Warwicks; *m* Sophia (*d* 18 Feb 1863), dau of Rev Sir Charles William Wheler, 7th Bt (*qv*), and *d* 16 Jan 1826, leaving issue:

1c John (Rev); Rector Frankton; *m* Mary Frances (*m* 2nd 15 Nov 1838 Gen George Dixon (*d* 15 May 1874) and *d* 1839), dau of Edward Sacheverell Wilmot,and gdau of Sir Robert Meade Wilmot, 2nd Bt, of Chaddesden (*qv*), and *dsp* 20 Aug 1837

2c William; Capt Bengal Army; *b* 8 Jan 1805; *m* 17 April 1841 Hannah Sarah (*d* 1893), est dau of Dr Nathaniel Wallich, HEIC's Botanical Gdn, Calcutta, and *d* Jan 1852, leaving issue:

1d William Wallich; *b* 1 May 1842; *m* 11 July 1868 Annie, dau of William Hugh Barnikel, of Pembroke, and *d* 19 April 1891, leaving issue:

1e William Hugh, of Frankton Manor, Rugby, patron living of Frankton, Hon Col Ceylon Def Force, Hon Lt-Col, Col late Cmdg Ceylon Planters' Rifle Corps, JP Ceylon, DL, JP Warwicks; *b* 2 June 1869; *m* 1st 20 Feb 1892 Annette Louisa (*d* 17 Jan 1915), dau of Lt-Col Harcourt Master, 4th (Queen's Own) Light Dragoons, of Catton, Norwich; *m* 2nd 1915 Kathleen Anna (*d* 2 Feb 1948), dau of Harman Herring-Cooper, of Shrule Castle, Co Carlow, and *dsp* 7 Oct 1947

2e Alexander George Scale (Rev); *b* 18 Jan 1872; *m* 9 Aug 1899 Winifred Agnes (*d* 27 June 1958) (who *m* 2nd 4 Jan 1923 Rory Eric McLaren, MD, of Adelaide, S Australia, yst s of James Grieve McLaren, of Calcutta), est dau of Rev David Ardill Maxwell, of Broomholm, Langholm, and *d* 16 April 1900, leaving a posthumous child:

1f Ruth Sofia; *b* 30 Aug 1900; *m* 3 Oct 1922 Rev Alfred Lane-Davies, MA Oxon (*d* 6 Feb 1976), s of Rev J Lane-Davies, and *d* 4 July 1974, leaving:

1g *Hugh John, FRIBA [Hugh Lane-Davies Esq, White Rose Cottage, White Hill, Bletchingley, Surrey]; *b* 20 Dec 1927; *m* 30 April 1955 *Wendy Isabel, dau of John Pierce, of Cricklewood, and has:

1h *Mark; *b* 16 April 1963; *m* 8 Aug 1994 *Lori Ann, dau of Raymond Strolin, and has:

1j *Benjamin Strolin; *b* 17 Jan 1996

1g *Sylvia Anne [Mrs Reginald Ridgley, PO Box 96, Clarksburg, Ontario, Canada]; *b* 1 Feb 1931; *m* 16 Feb 1952 Reginald Charles Ridgley (*d* 19 Nov 1997), s of Ralph Ridgley, of Pye Corner, Speen, Bucks, and has:

1h *Martin Charles; *b* 4 April 1956

1h *Alison Katharine; *b* 13 April 1959; *m* 17 June 1995 *John Wallace Carey, s of Dr Lewis Stafford Carey and has:

1j *William Wallace Daniel; *b* 31 Oct 1996

2h *Elaine Suzanne; *b* 3 July 1960; *m* 22 Dec 1993 *Jim Beauchemin, s of Patrick Emil Beauchemin, and has:

1j *Reid Patrick; *b* 9 June 1996

1j *Tory Anne; *b* 12 Aug 1994

1e Dora Margaret Lucy; *m* 1st 31 July 1899 Reginald Thomson (*d* 26 Aug 1922); *m* 2nd 6 March 1923 Hablot John Moxon Browne, MD, s of Edgar Athelstan Browne, FRCS, and *d* 11 Oct 1927

1d Sophia; *d* unm 27 Nov 1927

3c Trevor; *d* unm

4c Francis; *d* unm

5c George, Col HEICS; *k* Lucknow 1857, unm

1c Sophia; *d* 1838

2c Jane; *d* unm 1896

3c Lucy (twin with Jane); *d* unm 12 July 1904

3b William; *d* unm

1b Jane

2b Susannah

3b Elizabeth

4b Charlotte Mabella

2a Edward

3a John

4a William

5a Charles

1a Jane

2a Anne; *m* Rev James Stafford, incumbent of Penkridge, Staffs

(2) John; *m* his 1st cousin Jane, dau of Thomas Birch, of Leacroft, Staffs

(3) Michael (Rev); Preb Lichfield, whose only dau, Jane *m* Sir Theophilus Biddulph, 4th Bt

(4) Charles, of London

(5) Walter, of Sutton-in-Ashfield, Notts, and Barton-under-Needwood, Staffs; *bapt* 18 Aug 1705; *m* 24 Sept 1745 Mary (*bur* 21 June 1779), dau of — Adcock, of Shenston, Staffs, and was *bur* 20 Aug 1775, leaving, with other issue, a 3rd s:

1a Simon, emigrated to S Africa 1820; *bapt* 17 May 1761; *m* 11 July 1785 Anne Burnet and *d* 5 Jan 1842, leaving, with other issue, a 3rd s:

1b Edward, of Hunter's River, NSW; Cdr RN; *b* 16 Jan 1790; *m* 10 Feb 1821 Mary Stewart Chase and *d* 28 Jan 1851, leaving, with other issue:

1c Walter John; *b* 25 Feb 1827; *m* 13 June 1865 Harriett Sophia (*d* 8 Sept 1940), dau of Theophilus Foot, of Springsure, Queensland, and *d* 27 June 1905, having had issue:

1d Walter Edward; *b* 16 March 1866; *d* 12 March 1867

2d Theophilus Burnet; *b* 19 Oct 1869; *dsp* 8 Oct 1896

3d FRANCIS HENRY (Sir), **9th Bt**

1d Mary Ellen; *b* 23 July 1867; *m* 10 Nov 1893 Henry John Bredhauer, of Springsure, Queensland, and *d* 22 July 1957, leaving four s and a dau

2d Anna Sophia; *b* 1 Aug 1871; *m* 3 Aug 1898 John Cunningham Wells and *d* 16 July 1964, leaving three s and two daus. He *d* 1935

3d Alice Caroline; *b* 27 Dec 1873; *m* 22 April 1904 Edward Dunbar Wells and *d* 25 Sept 1971, leaving two daus. He *d* 1954

4d Lucy Maud; *b* 29 Sept 1876; *m* 25 June 1902 James Henry Wells and *d* 24 June 1923, leaving four s and two days. He *d* 31 Jan 1941

5d Florence Frances; *b* 8 Feb 1879; *d* unm 5 May 1964

6d Ethel; *b* and *d* 1881

(1) Elizabeth; *m* Sir John Napier, Bt

(2) Susannah; *m* Sir Edward Littleton, Bt, of Pillaton Hall,

(3) Mary

(4) Rachel; *m* Sir William Bassett, of Claverton, Somerset

The 8th Bt's kinsman,

Sir Francis Henry Biddulph, 9th Bt, of Westcombe; grazier; *b* 8 June 1882; *m* 5 March 1907 Janet (*d* 19 July 1956), dau of Walter Bain Hannah, of Brisbane, Queensland, and had issue:

Sir Stuart Royden Biddulph, 10th Bt; *b* 24 June 1908; *m* 18 May 1939 Muriel Margaret (*d* 1995), 3rd dau of Angus Harkness, of Hamley Bridge, S Australia, and *d* 1986, leaving issue:

1 Sir (IAN) JACK D'OLIER BIDDULPH, **11th and present Bt**

(1) *Wendy Margaret [Mrs Huan Fraser, 10 El Rancho St, Daisy Hill, Qld 4127, Australia]; *b* 15 March 1946; *m* 1966 *Huan Donald John Fraser and has issue:

1a *Stuart Donald John; *b* 1974

1a *Gina Margaret; *b* 1969

2a *Jodie Maree; *b* 1972

(2) *Mary Estelle [Mrs Ian Sutherland, Edward St, Tambo Qld 4478, Australia]; *b* 3 July 1947; *m* 1968 *Ian Sutherland and has issue:

1a *Timothy Andrew; *b* 1969

1a *Lee-Anne; *b* 1970

2 Malcolm Francis; *b* 13 May 1910; *m* 14 Aug 1936 Inez Margaret, dau of James Donnelly, of Longreach, Queensland, and *d* 1993, having had issue:

(1) +Peter Michael; *b* 13 Feb 1939; *m* 28 Jan 1963 Beverley Marie (*d* 1987), only dau of Sgt-Maj Wilson Story, of St George's Heights, Sydney, and has:

1a +Michael Andrew; *b* 9 Jan 1964; *m* 1989 *Tamara, yst dau of Thomas Kelly, of Charleville, Qld

2a +Sean Gregory; *b* 1970

3a +Craig; *b* 1973

4a +Mark Sterling; *b* 1975

1a *Anne Marie; *b* 1971

(2) +David Francis [David Biddulph Esq, Blackall Motel, Blackall, Qld, Australia]; *b* 21 April 1942; *m* 1968 *Doreen Power and has issue:

1a +Dennis; *b* 1980

1a *Sally; *b* 1973

(1) *Janice Claire; *b* 17 Feb 1937; *m* 1958 *Lionel Garth Moody and has issue:

1a *Peter; *b* 1969

1a *Alison Marie; *b* 1959; *m* 1980 *Michael Stally

2a *Tanya Claire; *b* 1962

3a *Fiona Margaret; *b* 1963

1 Anita Lillian; *b* 1 Oct 1911; *d* unm 23 March 1961

BIFFEN

Creation: B. (LP, UK) 19 April 1997.

THE BARON BIFFEN, of Tanat, Co Salop ((William) John Biffen, PC (1979), DL (Salop 1993)) [The Rt Hon The Lord Biffen PC DL, House of Lords, London SW1A 0PW; Tanat House, Llanyblodwel, Oswestry, Shropshire SY10 8NQ]; *b* 3 Nov 1930; *educ* Dr Morgan's Sch Bridgewater and Jesus Coll Cambridge; with Tube Investments 1953–60, EIU 1960–61, MP (C) Oswestry 1961–83, Shropshire N 1983–97, Ch Sec Treasury 1979–81, Sec State DTI 1981–82, Ld Pres Cncl 1982–83, Leader H of C 1982–87, Ld Privy Seal 1983–87; dir: Glynwed Internat 1987–, J Bibby & Sons 1988–, Rockware Gp 1988–91; author: *Inside the House of Commons* (1989); *m* 1979 *Mrs Sarah Wood, *née* Drew

Lineage: VICTOR W BIFFEN; had:

JOHN, *cr* a **Baron**

BINGHAM OF CORNHILL

Creation: B. (LP, UK) 1996.

THE BARON BINGHAM OF CORNHILL (Sir Thomas Henry Bingham, PC (1986)) [The Rt Hon The Lord Bingham of Cornhill PC, House of Lords, London SW1A 0PW]; *b* 13 Oct 1933; *educ* Sedbergh (Govr 1978–88) and Balliol Coll Oxford (Visitor 1986–); 2nd Lt Roy Ulster Rifles 1952–54, London Irish Rifles (TA) 1954–59, barrister Gray's Inn 1959, Bencher 1979, Standing Jr Counsel Dept Employment 1968–72, QC 1972, Crown Court Recorder 1975–80, High Court Judge Queen's Bench and Judge Commercial Court 1980–86, Ld Justice Appeal 1986–92, Master of Rolls 1992–96, Ld Ch Justice of England 1996–; chm Advsy Cncl Public Records 1992–96, Magna Carta Tst 1992–96, Roy Commn Historical MSS 1994–, Pres: CIArb 1991–, Br Records Assoc 1992–, Visitor: RPMS 1989–, UCL 1992–, Nuffield Coll Oxford 1992–, London Business Sch 1992–, Tstee Pilgrim Tst 1991–, Hon Bencher NI Inn of Court 1993, assist ed *Chitty on Contracts* (22nd edn 1961); *m* 1963 *Elizabeth, only dau of Peter Loxley and has two sons and a dau

Lineage: Dr T H Bingham, of Reigate; *m* Dr C — and had:

THOMAS HENRY (Sir), *cr* a **Baron**

BIRD

Arms: Vert on a pale or two popinjays of the field, on a chief ermine three garbs of the second. **Crest:** A garb as in the arms, between two roses per pale gules and argent, barbed and seeded proper.
Motto: *Copia ex industria* ('Plenty arises out of hard work').
Creation: Bt. (UK) 27 Jan 1922.

SIR RICHARD GEOFFREY CHAPMAN BIRD, 4TH BT, of Solihull, Co Warwick [Sir Richard Bird Bt, 39 Ashleigh Rd, Solihull, W Midlands B91 1AF]; *b* 3 Nov 1935; *s f* 1963; *educ* Beaumont and St Peter's Coll Saltley; *m* 1st 2 Feb 1957 Gillian Frances (*d* 6 Nov 1966), 2nd dau of Bernard Haggett, of Iona, Ladbroke Rd, Solihull, and has issue:

1 +JOHN ANDREW; *b* 19 Jan 1964
2 +Mark Richard; *b* 27 Sept 1965
1 *Cecilia Mary; *b* 17 Nov 1957
2 *Frances Bernadette; *b* 11 Feb 1959
3 *Brigitte Anne; *b* 28 Sept 1960
4 *Rowena Clare; *b* 28 April 1962

He *m* 2nd 15 April 1968 *Helen Patricia, only dau of Frank C Beaumont, of Kimberley House, Ackworth Rd, Pontefract, Yorks, and has further issue:
4 *Catherine Veronica; *b* 1970
5 *Denise Helen; *b* 1972

Lineage: JOHN BIRD, of Windsor, Berks; f of:

ALFRED BIRD, FCS, of Edgbaston, Warwicks; *b* 1811; *m* Elizabeth Lavinia, dau of Richard Ragg, of Nottingham, and *d* 1878, leaving, with other issue:

Sir Alfred Frederic Bird, 1st Bt (UK), so *cr* 27 Jan 1922, DL and JP Warwicks, MP (Con U) W Wolverhampton 1910–22, chm Alfred Bird & Sons, mfrg chemists, of Derltrend, Birmingham; *b* 27 July 1849; ktd 1920; *m* 4 Dec 1875 Eleanor Frances (*d* 27 Nov 1943), dau of Robert Lloyd Evans, of Birchfields, Birmingham, and was accidentally *k* 7 Feb 1922, having had issue:

1 **Sir Robert Bland Bird, 2nd Bt**, KBE (1954), MP W Wolverhampton 1922–29 and 1931–45, chm Alfred Bird & Sons, pres Midland Union, v-pres Soc Model Aero Engrs, memb Roy Inst, sr tstee Roy Wolverhampton Sch; experimented in early types of bicycles and automobiles and with early colour photography, Kt Legion of Honour 1947, Offr Order of Leopold (Belgium) 1951; *b* 20 Sept 1876; *m* 23 July 1904 Edith Wilmhurst, OBE (1957) (*d* 1 June 1961), dau of Stephen William Challen, of Totehill, Solihull, and *d* 20 Nov 1960, leaving:

(1) *Pamela Stephanie Helen [Mrs Pamela Evans, Mille Fiori, 20217 St Florent, France]; *b* 1909; assumed by deed poll 1974 the surname of Evans; *m* 1st 26 July 1934 (*divorce* 1946) Reginald William Bell, er s of Randal Bell, of Deepdene, Dorking, and has issue:

1a *Robert Reginald; *b* 26 May 1935; *educ* Eton and McGill U Montreal
2a *Thomas Randal, RCMP [Thomas Bell Esq, 21 Katrine Rd, Rexdale, Ontario, Canada]; *b* 21 March 1937; *educ* Eton
3a *William Andrew, F/Lt RAF; *b* 6 April 1940; *educ* Eton and Exeter Coll Oxford

(1) (cont.) Mrs Pamela Bell *m* 2nd 24 May 1951 (*divorce* 1973) Vicomte Alain de Mauduit de Kervern, 3rd s of Robert de Mauduit, of Quimperlé, Finisterre, and has further issue:

1a *Françoise Hélène; *b* 1 Nov 1952

2 Geoffrey; High Sheriff Warwicks 1931; *b* 10 April 1878; *m* 16 April 1902 Elsie Hilda (*d* 22 June 1967), dau of Edward Suckling, and *d* 1 Aug 1937, leaving issue:

(1) DONALD GEOFFREY (Sir), **3rd Bt**

(1) Eileen Hilda; *m* 1st 17 Jan 1930 John Walter Jones (*d* 26 Feb 1934), only s of James Jones, of Parkfield, Hendon; *m* 2nd 24 April 1935 G/Capt Frank Grenville Argyle Robinson, DFC, RAF, DL, only s of Frank Sydney Robinson, and had issue:

1a *Ronald Geoffrey Argyle; *b* 21 Feb 1936
1a *Josephine Elsie; *b* 30 July 1949

(2) *Eleanore Marshall [Mrs Vernon Harms-Cooke, Monks Meadow, Iveley, Winchcombe, Glos]; *b* 30 July 1915; *m* 24 Nov 1932 Vernon Harms-Cooke (*d* 1987), s of Herbert Harms-Cooke, and has:

1a *Sylvia [Mrs Sylvia Harms-Cooke, Monks Meadow, Iveley, Winchcombe, Glos]; *b* 26 May 1934; resumed her maiden name; *m* 17 Sept 1959 *Peter John Smith, only s of C F Smith of Mickleton, Glos, and has:

1b *Nigel Peter; *b* 25 May 1961
2b *Charles Francis; *b* 30 April 1963
1b *Christabel; *b* 16 June 1964

1a *Annalova [Mrs David Faber, Monks Meadow, Iveley, Winchcombe, Glos]; *b* 4 March 1936; *m* 27 Oct 1953 David Stanley Faber (*d* 1981), s of Capt Frank Stanley Faber, and has:

1b *Geoffrey David; *b* 1 Sept 1961
1b *Rosanne; *b* 31 July 1955
2b *Colleen; *b* 30 Sept 1957
3b *Anita; *b* 16 Dec 1959

3a *Geoffrena; *b* 4 Feb 1938; *m* 6 June 1959 *Lt-Col James William Beachus, RA, only s of James H Beachus, of The Gardens, Old Rd, Shipton-on-Stour, Warwicks, and has:

1b *Timothy James; *b* 1962
2b *Simon Jeremy James; *b* 18 Dec 1964
3b *Justin Nicholas; *b* 21 Sept 1968
1b *Lucinda; *b* 3 June 1961
2b *Tanya; *b* 1966

4a *Eleanore; *b* 18 Oct 1940; *m* 4 July 1964 *James Thomas Askew, only s of James Thomas Askew, of Tolworth, Surrey

5a *Carol [Mrs Kenneth Rose, 6 Bibsworth Ave, Broadway, Hereford and Worcester]; *b* 28 Oct 1941; *m* 1st 8 Sept 1962 John Edmund Davies, yr s of Edward Gordon Davies, of Broom Court, Broom, nr Alcester, Warwicks; *m* 2nd 1990 *Kenneth Rose and has issue by her 1st husb:

1b *Anthony William Gordon; *b* 25 Sept 1968
1b *Tracey Anne; *b* 1971

(3) Oliver, MC, JP Warwicks, High Sheriff 1943, late Capt Welsh Gds, served WW II (Civil Defence); *b* 1880; *m* 1909 Gwendoline Heaton, dau of William Albert Upton, and *d* April 1963

(4) Christopher Alfred; *b* 20 May 1884; *m* 1910 Ethel Constance (*d* 1952), dau of Henry May, and *d* 1965, leaving issue:

1a Isobel Dorothy; *b* 1911

1 Dorothy Frances; *m* 27 July 1927 Edgar Bernard Attwood Rayner, barrister, s of Bernard Rayner, of Spalding, Lincs, and *d* 7 April 1960. He *d* Nov 1951

2 Eleanor Mary; *m* 1912 Cuthbert Hermon Bradley and *d* 14 March 1930, leaving issue

The 2nd Bt's nephew,

Sir Donald Geoffrey Bird, 3rd Bt; *educ* Uppingham and Ch Ch Oxford; *b* 3 July 1906; *m* 24 April 1930 (Anne) Rowena, dau of Charles Chapman, of Carlecote's Hall, Yorks, and *d* 18 Oct 1963, having had issue:

1 John Alfred Chapman; *b* 4 June 1932; *d* 29 Aug 1940
2 Sir RICHARD GEOFFREY CHAPMAN BIRD, **4th and present Bt**

3 +Peter Donald Chapman [Peter Bird Esq, The Gables, Whitecroft Rd, Bream, nr Lydney, Glos]; *b* 8 Jan 1938; *educ* Beaumont; *m* 22 Sept 1962 *Vera Mary, dau of Albert Seymoor, of Northfield, and has issue:

(1) +Anthony Donald; *b* 11 Aug 1964

(2) +Christopher Robert; *b* 17 Feb 1967

1 *Elizabeth Anne [Mrs John Brigg, The Soundings, Bosham Hoe, Chichester PO18 8ET]; *b* 16 June 1931; *m* 29 Jan 1955 *John Rodney Wilford Brigg, only *s* of John Edward Brigg, of 504 Rodney House, Dolphin Sq, London SW1, and has issue:

(1) David Lockwood John; *b* 28 March 1956; *m* 1982 *Carolyn Froy and *d* 1989, leaving issue:

1a *Joanna Louise; *b* 1986

(2) *Michael James; *b* 7 Aug 1957; BChir 1982; MB 1983; *m* 1991 *Fiona Anne Wheatcroft and has issue:

1a *Emma Charlotte; *b* 1992

(3) *Peter Donald (twin); *b* 7 April 1957; MB, BS 1980; *m* 1986 *Lynne Goulden and has issue:

1a *William James; *b* 1987

2a *Thomas David; *b* 1989

1a *Aimée Eleanore Beatrice; *b* 1992

BIRDWOOD

Arms: Az. five martlets, two, two and one, within an inescutcheon voided a representation of the Southern Cross, all arg. **Crest:** Out of a mural crown gu. a martlet arg. between two branches of laurel ppr. **Supporters:** Dexter, a Sergeant of the 12th (The Prince of Wales's Royal) Lancers mounted on a horse; sinister, a Sikh Daffadar of the 11th (The Prince of Wales's Own) Bengal Lancers, mounted on a chestnut horse, both habited and accoutred ppr. **Motto:** *In bello quies* ('Cool in action'). **Creations:** Bt. (UK) 6 Oct 1919, B. (UK) 25 Jan 1938.

THE 3RD BARON BIRDWOOD, of Anzac and Totnes, Devon (Sir Mark William Ogilvie Birdwood, Bt) [The Rt Hon The Lord Birdwood, 5 Holbein Mews, London SW1W 8NW; Russell House, Broadway, Worcs WR12 7BU]; *b* 23 Nov 1938, *s* f 1962; *educ* Radley and Trin Coll Cambridge (MA 1970); late 2nd Lt RHG, chm: Martlet Ltd 1986–, Worthington & Co 1994–; dir: Wrightson Wood 1979–86, Scientific Generics 1989–; Liveryman Glaziers' Co; *m* 27 April 1963 *Judith Helen, er dau of Reginald Gordon Seymour Roberts, of Newton Aycliffe, Co Durham, and has issue:

1 *Sophie Frederika; *b* 29 July 1964; *m* 1987 *3rd Earl of Woolton (*qv*) and has issue

Lineage: The name of this family, long resident in Devon and Cornwall, occurs as Brydewoode, Burdwood, Burwood, and as Bodgewood as early as 1314 among the Portreeves of Kingsbridge, and as Bridwould and Burhwold as that of one of the Saxon Bishops of St Germans (1016–35), to whom KING CANUTE granted a charter of lands in 1018; it occurs also in Subsidy Rolls. John Birdwood in 1356 was named co-feofee for Glebe Land at Thurlestone.

RICHARD BIRDWOOD, of Preston; *b* 1536, had:

RICHARD BIRDWOOD, of Preston; *b* 1561; *d* 1624, leaving:

1 JAMES

2 Richard; *b* 1585; *m* 1620 Elizabeth Hele, of Flete, and *d* 1645, leaving:

(1) Richard; *b* 1637; *m* 1655 Joan Polexfen, of Stancombe, and *d* 1668

The er son,

JAMES BIRDWOOD, of W Alvington; *b* 25 Oct 1582; *m* 1611 Elizabeth Harris (*d* 1652) and *d* 1643, leaving:

Rev JAMES BIRDWOOD, of Pembroke Coll Oxford, evicted from St Petrox, Dartmouth, for non-conformity 1662; *b* 9 Sept 1626; *m* 2nd 27 Aug 1654 Dorothy Chapman (*d* 4 Oct 1684), and *d* 21 Aug 1693, having by her had 14 children; the est s:

JOHN BIRDWOOD, of Kingsbridge; *b* 14 Sept 1665; *m* 19 Oct 1700 Elizabeth Bowen (*d* 1741), and was f of

ROGER BIRDWOOD, of Kingsbridge; *b* 1703; *m* 1736 Mary Sawle, of Penrice; *d* 19 July 1764, and had a yr s:

RICHARD BIRDWOOD, of Plymouth, Mayor Plymouth 1796, Freeman Totnes, Agent for HEIC; *b* 20 Jan 1745; *m* 1770 Anne Travers (*d* 1818) and *d* 1810. His son:

PETER BIRDWOOD, Maj Plymouth Vols, Freeman Plymouth and Totnes, Agent for HEIC; *b* 29 Jan 1773; *m* 12 Sept 1795 Mary Brodrick (*d* 1810), of Co Cork, and *d* 1839, having had, with other issue:

CHRISTOPHER BIRDWOOD, Gen IA; *b* 12 March 1807; *m* 12 Jan 1832 Lydia Juliana, est dau of Rev Joseph Taylor, HEICS Missionary, and *d* 1882, leaving, with other issue:

1 George Christopher Molesworth (Sir), KCIE, CSI, MD; *b* 8 Dec 1832; *m* 10 Feb 1856 Frances Anne (*d* Jan 1921), dau of Edward Tolcher, RN, of Harewood, Plympton, and *d* 28 June 1917, leaving issue:

(1) George Brodrick; *b* 27 Dec 1860; *d* 11 Dec 1921

(2) Alan Roger, formerly of HM The Khedive's Serv; *b* 27 Jan 1862; *m* Dec 1892 Anna C, dau of Rev S C Ewing, of Alexandria, and *d* 15 Oct 1944, leaving issue:

1a Katherine Frances; *d c* 1958

(3) Francis Travers, slr; *b* 6 Dec 1865; *m* 26 July 1893 Amy Segar (*d* 24 April 1951), and *d* 17 March 1936, leaving issue:

1a Christopher Travers, served WW I (wounded); *b* 25 Aug 1894; *educ* Westminster; *m* 3 Nov 1923 Martha M Brooks, and *d* 29 June 1968

2a Hubert Brodrick, MC, served WW I (wounded); *b* 10 Feb 1896; *educ* Westminster; *m* 18 July 1918 Brenda C F Fortune, and had issue:

1b *Nigel Fortune, served WW II in RE; *b* 18 Dec 1919; *educ* Marlborough; *m* 14 Nov 1947 *Charlotte Woods, and has issue:

1c *Anthony; *b* 1950

1c *June; *b* 1948

2b *George Fortune Brodrick, late Capt RAMC; *b* 23 April 1929; *educ* Radley, Clare Coll Cambridge (BA 1950, MA 1965) and St Bart's Hosp (MB 1954, BCh 1953); *m* 12 Sept 1953 *(Dorothy) Gaynor Hughes, dau of Capt Robert George Evans, MBE, JP, KStJ, of Fernyfield, Llay, N Wales, and has issue:

1c *James Gresford Brodrick; *b* 13 July 1955; *educ* Radley

2c *John Richard Gresford; *b* 3 May 1958

3a Felix Tolcher, OBE (1946), Col IA (ret), served WW I (wounded), and WW II; *b* 20 May 1897; *educ* Westminster; *m* 15 Jan 1926 Louise J H Lamond (*d* 19 Aug 1975), of Richmond, and had issue:

1b *Elizabeth Ursula; *b* 19 Aug 1927; *m* 16 July 1949 *Herbert Bernard Juby, son of L H Juby, of The Durdans, Stowmarket, Suffolk, and has issue:

1c *Jonathan Birdwood; *b* 18 Oct 1950; *educ* Culford Sch, Bury St Edmunds

2c *Nicholas Bernard; *b* 22 July 1960

1c *Penelope Jane; *b* 16 March 1953

2c *Heather Susan; *b* 23 March 1955

2b *Helen Sylvia; *b* 7 June 1930

1a Ursula Segar; *d* 1946

(1) Mary Brodrick; *d* unm 14 Nov 1955, aged 85

2 HERBERT MILLS, of whom below

3 William Spiller, of Colmer, Modbury, S Devon, Col IA (ret), and GOC Baroda State Army 1909–17; *b* 22 Oct 1854; *m* 1st 1881 Ellen Frances (*d* 1882), dau of Dr C Turner, of Bideford, and had issue:

(1) Christopher William Brodrick, Capt IA; *b* 1882; *m* Helen Bourdillon (*d* 14 April 1951), and *d* of wounds received in action, 7 June 1915, leaving issue:

1a *Christopher R Brodrick, OBE (1966), MA, MICE, served WW II in RE; *b* 1910; *m* 11 Feb 1939 *Sheila Kathleen, dau of W F Woodward, and has had issue:

1b Christopher William Brodrick; *b* 23 Aug 1949; *educ* Gordonstoun; *d* 5 April 1967, after an accident in Austria

1b *Amanda Jane; *b* 28 Sept 1947; *m* 4 April 1970 *Robert N T Honeybourne, er son of Brig C T Honeybourne, of 16 St Peter's Sq, London W6, and has issue:

1c *A son; *b* 15 May 1974

1c *Tamsin

1a *Elizabeth Frances Brodrick RUSSELL (former surname resumed 1958); *m* 1st 30 July 1935 (*divorce* 1946) John Eaton Nevill Russell, yr son of Maj Leonard Russell, E Lancs Regt, and has issue:

1b *Anthony John Nevill; *b* 4 Feb 1941; *m* 2 July 1965 *Julia Rosalind, est dau of William Whythead Boulton, CBE, TD, of Garth End, Little Braxted, Essex, and has issue:

1c *William Jonathan; *b* 24 April 1968

1a (cont.) Mrs Elizabeth Russell *m* 2nd 20 Dec 1952 (*annulled* 1958) Cdr Christopher Michael Jacob, DSC, RN, only son of Lt-Col Arthur Lawrence Baldwin Jacob, DSO, RA, of Woodcote, Great Bookham, Surrey. He *d* 2 Sept 1960

3 (cont.) William Birdwood *m* 2nd 1886 Evelyn Stuart (*d* 1910), dau of G F Sheppard, ICS, and by her had issue:

(2) George Brodrick, Lt Roy Sussex Regt; *b* 1888; *d* 1910

(3) Gordon Alic Brodrick, 2nd Lt S Lancs Regt, 1895; *ka* in France, 19 Sept 1914

(1) Elinor Brodrick; *m* 1912 Brig Edward George Hall, CB, CIE, late IA (*d* 20 Dec 1968), son of Rev Edward Stephenson Hall, MA, and *d* 20 Jan 1970, leaving issue:

1a *Edward Michael, MBE, Maj-Gen, late RE, Mil Dep to Head of Def Sales, Min of Def from 1966; *b* 16 July 1935; *educ* Sherborne, RMA Woolwich, and Peterhouse, Cambridge (BA); *m* 4 Dec 1948 *Nina Diana, er dau of V G McArthur, and has issue:

1b *Timothy Edward, Lt RTR, serving in BAOR; *b* 16 Nov 1949; *educ* Sherborne and RMA Sandhurst

2b *Jeremy John; *b* 25 July 1952
3b *Robin Michael; *b* 12 June 1958
2a *Eric Peter, MRCS, LRCP (1946)
1a *Evelyn Mollie; *b* 8 June 1913; *m* 12 Sept 1936 Maj-Gen Nigel John Buchanan Stuart, CBE (*d* 16 Aug 1966), son of Capt H H Stuart, and has issue:
1b *Edward John Buchanan; *b* 18 Oct 1937
2b *James Nigel Buchanan, Capt RE; *b* 28 Oct 1942; *m* 11 May 1968 *Susan Mary, est dau of Lt-Col Philip James Cornwallis, of Lisburn, Co Antrim, and has issue:
1c *A son; *b* 30 June 1970
2c *A son; *b* 29 Oct 1971
1b *Caroline Mary Buchanan; *b* 13 Oct 1940; *m* 23 May 1964 *Charles Shaun Harte, only son of Dr Robert William Harte, of Prestbury, Cheshire, and has issue:
1c *Charles Edward Robert; *b* 14 Feb 1966
2c *William Nigel Brett; *b* 14 Aug 1967
3c *Matthew; *b* 10 March 1971
(2) Gladys Brodrick; *m* Cecil H Bradbury, PWD India, and *d* 1918, leaving issue
3 (cont.) William Birdwood *m* 3rd 14 Feb 1917 Altha (*d* 11 Nov 1930), dau of J James Barlow Smythe, and widow of Cecil Edward Bewes, JP, of Devon, and *d* 26 Dec 1930

The 2nd son,
HERBERT MILLS BIRDWOOD, CSI, MA and LLD Camb, JP, Judge of the High Ct and Memb Cncl Bombay; *b* 29 Jan 1837; *m* 29 Jan 1861 Edith Marion Sidonie (*d* Aug 1912), er dau of Surg-Maj Elijah George Halhed Impey (*see* RIDDELL, Bt), and *d* 21 Feb 1907, having had:
1 WILLIAM RIDDELL (Sir), **1st Baron**
2 Herbert Christopher Impey, Capt RE; *b* 26 Dec 1863; *m* Nov 1892 Ethel Frances, dau of Lt-Gen C T Palin, and *d* 15 Oct 1894, leaving issue:
(1) Joan; *m* Cyril Norman, of Canada, and had issue
3 Gordon Travers, MD, MA, DPH, Lt-Col (ret) IMS, served in Abor Expdn (despatches) and Waziristan and Chitrai campaigns (medal, two clasps); *b* 24 Jan 1867; *educ* Clifton and Peterhouse, Cambridge; *m* 1st 1902 Dora (*d* 1905), dau of John Samuel Champion Davis, CBE, of Kingford, Devon, and had issue:
(1) Richard Douglas Davis, MC, JP (Devon 1964), DL (1964); *b* 5 Jan 1905; *educ* Peterhouse Cambridge (MA, MB, BCh); High Sheriff Devon 1962, Mayor Bideford 1963, Hon Freeman Bideford 1972, memb Bideford Borough Cncl 1959, MRCS, LRCP, Lt-Col IMS (ret 1947), served WW II 1939–45, ADMS Allied Land Forces, SE Asia 1943–45, cmd'd Mil Hosp Bannu, N W Frontier 1945–47; *m* 1930 Phyllis Rosa, JP (*d* 23 April 1997), er dau of Lt-Col Sir Thomas Bilbe Robinson, KCMG, KBE, and *d* 9 May 1995, leaving:
1a *Roger Halhed Bilbe; *b* 1932; *m* 1960 *Cherry, est dau of Christopher Harrison, and has had:
1b Richard Christopher; *b* 6 Oct 1961; *d* 3 April 1974
1b *Victoria Rose; *b* 22 April 1963
2a *Gordon Thomas Riddell [Lt-Col Gordon Birdwood, 31 Alexander St, London W2 5NU]; *b* 2 June 1948; *educ* Wellington; 2nd Lt RHG 1968, cmded Household Cavalry Mtd Regt 1992 (ret); consultant Workman and Ptnrs 1992–97, dir Defence Systems Ltd 1998–; Gentleman Usher to HM THE QUEEN 1997–; *m* 1st 29 April 1976 (*divorce* 1979) Anne Sheila, er dau of Capt D K Price, of Chiddingfold, Surrey; *m* 2nd 8 Dec 1984 *Arabella Katherine, dau of Gen Sir David Fraser, GCB (*see* SALTOUN, L), and has issue:
1b *Katie; *b* 9 Sept 1993
1a *Georgina Margaret; *b* 1 Nov 1935; *m* 22 Sept 1962 *John Charles Kirkland, of Lockbie, Duddenhoe End, Saffron Walden, Essex, only son of Maj John Wallace Cleland Kirkland, of Orchard Cottage, Hardington Moor, nr Yeovil, Somerset, and has issue:
1b *William John; *b* 9 June 1966
1b *Alexandra Georgina; *b* 8 Oct 1964
(1) *Mary Elizabeth; *b* 1904; *m* 1931 Col Joseph Cawley-Way, of Fox Warren, Withycombe, Minehead, Somerset, and has issue:
1a *Jane Elizabeth; *b* 17 May 1934; *m* 14 Nov 1959 John Reginald Morris-Eyton, of Berkside, Whicham, Millom, Cumberland, yr son of Robert Edward Morris-Eyton, JP, of Calvington, Newport, Salop, and has issue:
1b *Helen Elizabeth; *b* 11 Aug 1966
2b *Claire Louise; *b* 23 Dec 1967
2a *Rosalind Mary; *b* 16 July 1941
3 (cont.) Gordon Birdwood *m* 2nd *Alice Caroline, dau of Col Henry Thomas Finlay, DL, of Corkagh House, Co Dublin, and *d* 14 April 1945, having by her had issue:
(2) *Travers John Durand, Maj; *m* *Diana V Turner, and has had issue:
1a John Nicholas; *d* 19–
1a *Jennifer Alice; *b* 1952
(3) *Christopher Halhed Lovett (Rev), Maj IA (ret), ordained 1965, Rector of Little Berkhamsted from 1966; *b* Aug 1918; *educ* Clifton and RMC Sandhurst; *m* 19 June 1948 *Beatty Hamilton, only child of Capt Claud Scott, of 76 Walton St, London SW3, and had issue:
1a *William Halhed; *b* 13 May 1951; *educ* Haileybury
1a *Helen Hamilton; *b* 23 March 1949
2a *Elizabeth Jane; *b* 4 Nov 1952
(2) Ursula Jane; *b* 1911; *m* 1st Roderick Dilwyn Sims (*d* 24 April 1965); *m* 2nd *Charles Pursford Bailey and *d* 19 Feb 1998, leaving by her 1st husb:
1a *Caroline Mary Dilwyn; *b* 12 June 1935; *m* 29 March 1963 Surgn Cdr *Alan McEwan, RN, s of Norman McEwan, and has:
1b *Angus Norman; *b* 19 June 1964
2b *Alistair James; *b* 21 Nov 1967
(3) *Margaret Riddell; *b* Dec 1915; *m* 18 June 1938 Lt-Col Roderick Esmond Thomas Keelan, RA (*d* May 1965), and has issue:
1a *Gordon Douglas Birdwood, Capt RM, *b* 26 Nov 1942; *m* 18 Dec 1966 *Shandra Elizabeth, dau of Stanley Glasbrook, of Park Henri, Dryslwyn, Carmarthenshire
2a *Andrew Piers, Lt S Wales Borderers, Capt Roy Regt of Wales, serving in Ulster; *b* 27 Dec 1944; *m* Wendy Potter, of 5 Mellons, nr Cardiff
1a *Margaret Anne; *b* 28 Oct 1947; *m* Francis Archer Coulson, of 22 Regency Mews, Whitton Dene, Isleworth, Twickenham
4 Halhed Brodrick, Brig-Gen (ret) IA, late Central India Horse, served in Tirah Exped 1897–98 (medal, two clasps), in S African War 1901–2 (King's Medal, five clasps), in Persia 1911–13 (Brevet), and WW I 1914–19; *b* 29 May 1870; *educ* Clifton, Peterhouse Cambridge, and RMC Sandhurst; *m* 1906 Dorothy (*d* 4 May 1973), dau of Col C W Ravenshaw, of Nether Priors, Halstead, Essex, and *d* 20 Dec 1939, leaving issue:
(1) Dorothy; *m* 2 Jan 1933 Cdr Sir Richard Colville, KCVO, CB, DSC, RN, 3rd son of Admin Hon Sir Stanley Cecil James Colville, GCB, GCMG, GCVO; *d* 3 April 1972, leaving issue (*see* COLVILLE OF CULROSS, V)
5 Richard Lockington, Capt Political Dept IA; *b* 7 Sept 1879; *educ* Clifton and RMC Sandhurst, *ka* at Basra, Nov 1914
1 Edith Jane; *m* 1885 Gen Sir Robert Charles Ochiltree Stuart, KCSI, and *d* 6 Jan 1936 (*see* CASTLE STEWART, E). He *d* 14 Oct 1948

The est son,
Sir William Riddell Birdwood, 1st Bt, so *cr* 6 Oct 1919, and **1st Baron Birdwood**, of Anzac and of Totnes, Devon, so *cr* 25 Jan 1938 (both UK), with thanks of Parl and a grant of £10,000, GCB (1923, KCB 1917, CB 1911), GCSI (1930, KCSI 1915, CSI 1910), GCMG (1919, KCMG 1915), GCVO (1937), CIE (1908), DSO (1908)*educ* Clifton and RMC Sandhurst; Lt 4th Bn Roy Scots Fus 1883, 12th Lancers 1885 and 11th Bengal Lancers 1886, Capt 1896, Maj 1900, Lt-Col 1902, Col 1905, Brig-Gen 1909, Maj-Gen 1911, Lt-Gen 1915, Gen 1917, FM 1925; Adj 11th Bengal Lancers 1883–93, Viceroy's Bodyguard 1893, Bde-Maj S Africa 1899, DAAG 1900, Mil Sec to C-in-C S Africa 1902, AMS and interpreter to C-in-C India 1902, AAG India 1904, Mil Sec to C-in-C India 1905, ADC to TM EDWARD VII 1906–10 and GEORGE V 1910–11; Bde-Cdr Kohat 1909, QMG India 1912, Sec to Govt India, Army Dept and MLC the Govr-Gen 1912–14, GOC AIF 1915–20, GOC ANZAC 1914–18, GOC 5th Army France 1918–19, ADC Gen to HM GEORGE V 1917–22, GOC-in-C N Army India 1920–24, Actg C-in-C India, Memb Exec Cncl and Cncl State India 1924; C-in-C Army India, Memb Viceroy's Exec Cncl and Cncl State India 1925–30; served Hazara Expdn 1891 (medal and clasp), Isazai Expdn 1892, Tirah Campaign 1897–98 (despatches, medal, three clasps), Boer War 1899–1902 (severely wounded, despatches five times, Queen's medal and six clasps, King's Medal and two clasps, Brevets of Maj and Lt-Col), Ch Staff Offr Mohmand Expdn 1908 (despatches, medal and clasp), Grand Cross Legn Honour, Croix de Guerre with palm, Grand Offr Crown and Croix de Guerre Belgium, Grand Cordon Mil Order Avis and Grand Cross Tower and Sword Portugal, Order Nile 2nd Cl, Grand Cordon Rising Sun Japan 1st Cl, Star Nepal 1st Cl, Order Timsai Persia, American DSM; Fell Roy Empire Soc, pres Clifton Coll, v-pres Roy Soc St George, Overseas League and Devonian Assoc, Freeman Borough of Totnes;, Col RHG, 12th Lancers, KEO, Probyn's Horse and 6th Gurkha Rifles, Col Cmdt 13th F F Rifles, Col-in-C 1st NZ Mounted Rifles (Canterbury Yeo Cav), Col 16th Australian Light Horse (Hunter River Lancers) and 3rd Australian Infantry Bn; Hon FM Australian Mil Forces, Hon Col 75th AA Regt RA (1939); Hon LLD Cambridge, Melbourne (Victoria), Sydney (NSW) and Bristol, Hon DCL Durham, Hon DLitt Reading, MA Cambridge, Master Peterhouse Cambridge 1931–38 (Hon Fell 1938); Capt Deal Castle 1935, KGStJ; *b* 13 Sept 1865; *m* 5 April 1894 Janetta Hope Gonville, CI (*d* 14 Nov 1947), er dau of Col Sir Benjamin Parnell Bromhead, 4th Bt (*qv*), and had issue:
1 CHRISTOPHER BROMHEAD, **2nd Baron**
1 Constance Jean Gonville (Nancy); *m* 5 March 1919 Frank Colin Craig (*d* Sept 1951), sometime RAF, son of Frank Craig, of Perth, W Australia, and *d* 19 Oct 1975, leaving a s and two daus
2 *Judith Horatia; *m* 1st Sept 1939 (*divorce*1947) Roger William Colville-Wallis, only son of Rev William Colville-Wallis, of St Agnes Vicarage, Newmarket. He *d* 28 March 1959; *m* 2nd 23 Oct 1947 Rudolph Putnam Messel, only son of Harold George Messel. He *d* 3 May 1958

The 1st BARON *d* 17 May 1951; his only son,
CHRISTOPHER BROMHEAD BIRDWOOD, **2nd Baron Birdwood**, MVO (1939), Lt-Col 5th King Edward VII's Own Lancers (Probyn's Horse), IA, ADC to C-in-C India 1929–30, served WW I (despatches), Waziristan 1919–20 and 1937–38, WW II, memb UK Delegn UN 1959, Mil Order Aviz 5th Cl Portugal, FRCS, chm Anglo-German Assoc, E India Assoc, memb: RIIA and Exec Ctee Cwlth Migration Cncl; author: *A Continent Experiments*, *A Continent Decides*, *Nuri as Said, a study in Arab Leadership*, *Two Nations and Kashmir* and *A History of the Worcestershire Regiment*; *b* 22 May 1899; *educ* Clifton and RMC Sandhurst; *m* 1st 7 March 1931 (*divorce* 1954) (Elizabeth) Vere Drummond, CVO (1972, MVO 1958) (*d* 1 May 1997), only dau of Lt-Col Sir George Drummond Ogilvie, KCIE, CSI, late IPS, and had issue:
1 MARK WILLIAM OGILVIE BIRDWOOD, **3rd and present Baron Birdwood**
1 *Sonia Gina Ogilvie [The Hon Mrs Archer, Renson Mill, Ashwater, Devon EX21 5ER]; *b* 25 Nov 1933; *m* 21 July 1956 *Geoffrey Thynne Valentine Archer, yst son of Maj Gerald Valentine Archer, of High Salvington, Sussex, and has issue:
(1) *David Birdwood; *b* 18 June 1959; *m* 1984 *Gwenyth Daphne, dau of Ian Highley, of Standford Dingley, Berks, and has:
1a *Thomas Benjamin Highley; *b* 1988
2a *James Geoffrey Birdwood; *b* 1990
1a *Isabel Gwenyth
(1) *Sarah-Jane Birdwood; *b* 11 Aug 1957; *m* 1997 *Don Fernando Muñoz y Gomez, s of Fernando Muñoz Lopez and Regina Gomez Fernandez de Aranguiz, of Bilbao, Spain

The **2nd Baron** *m* 2nd 22 Feb 1954 *Joan Pollock, dau of Christopher Norman Graham, of Ealing, and *d* 5 Jan 1962

BIRKETT

Arms: Gu. three full-bottomed wigs arg. **Crest:** Between two wings gu. a viking ship ppr., charged on the sail with a raven close sa. **Supporters:** Dexter, a lion or semée of roses gu.; sinister, a wolf sa. semée of mullets gold. **Motto:** *Lex mea lux* ('The law is my light'). **Creation:** B. (UK) 31 Jan 1958.

THE 2ND BARON BIRKETT, of Ulverston, in the Co Palatine of Lancs (Michael Birkett) [The Rt Hon The Lord Birkett, The House of Lords, London SW1A 0PW]; *b* 22 Oct 1929; *s f* 1962; *educ* Stowe and Trin Coll Cambridge; film producer and theatre dir, Pres Sch for Performing Arts and Technology, Br Record Industry Tst 1990–, dep dir Nat Theatre 1975–77, Dir Recreation and Arts GLC 1979–86, chm: Children's Film and TV Fndn 1981–, Management Ctee Park Lane Gp 1991–, a v-pres Br Bd for Film Classification 1985–, Master Curriers' Co 1975–76; *m* 1st 13 Oct 1960 Mrs Junia Crawford (*d* 1973), dau of Harold Elliott; *m* 2nd 1978 *Gloria, dau of Thomas Taylor, of Queen's Gate, S Kensington, and by her has:

1 +THOMAS; *b* 25 July 1982

Lineage: THOMAS BIRKETT, of Nithsdale, Ulverston, Lancs; *m* Agnes Tyson (*d* 1886) and *d* Oct 1913, leaving:

(WILLIAM) NORMAN BIRKETT, **1st Baron Birkett**, of Ulverston, in the County Palatine o f Lancs (UK), so *cr* 31 Jan 1958, PC (1947), KC (1924); *b* 6 Sept 1883; *educ* Barrow-in-Furness GS and Emmanuel Coll (later Hon Fell) Cambridge (MA, LLB, pres Union 1910); barrister Inner Temple 1913, Bencher, Treasurer 1956, High Court Judge King's Bench 1941, ktd 1941, a Ld Justice of Appeal 1950, ret 1957, four times Master Curriers' Co, MP (Lib) Nottingham E Dec 1923–Oct 1924 and 1929–31, chm Court London U 1948 and Buckingham QS, pres: Nat Book League 1949, English Assoc 1952 and Friends of the Lake District, Hon LLD Us of London , Birmingham and Cambridge and Hull U Coll; *m* 25 Aug 1920 Ruth (*d* 1969), dau of Emil Nilsson, of Sweden and Glasgow, and *d* 10 Feb 1962, having had issue:

1 MICHAEL BIRKETT, **2nd and present Baron Birkett**

1 *Linnea Nilsson [The Hon Mrs Cliff Hodges, Willow Cottage, Stourton Caundle, Dorset DT10 2JW]; *b* 27 June 1923; *m* 25 June 1949 *Gavin Cliff Hodges, est s of Dr William Cliff Hodges, of Hascombe, Surrey, and has:

(1) *Marcus Birkett Adam; *b* 1959

(1) *Victoria Françoise; *b* 1951

(2) *Gabrielle; *b* 1953

(3) *Charmian Sophie [Mrs John Allwright, 17 East Common, Harpenden, Herts]; *b* 1957; *m* 1981 *Christopher John Allwright

BIRKIN

Arms: Arg., a cross raguly couped vert, in the first and fourth quarters a bee volant, in the second and third a birch tree eradicated, all ppr. **Crest:** A scorpion erect ppr. **Motto:** *Pace et bello paratus* ('Ready for both war and peace'). **Creation:** Bt. (UK) 25 July 1905.

SIR JOHN CHRISTIAN WILLIAM BIRKIN, 6TH BT, of Ruddington Grange, Nottingham [Sir John Birkin Bt, 23 St Luke's St, London SW3 3RP]; *b* 2 July 1953; *s f* 1985; *educ* Eton, Trin Coll Dublin and London Film Sch; freelance TV producer and director, dir Compound Eye Productions 1987–; *m* 1994 *Emma Louise, dau of Roger Leonard Gage, of Chantry House, Aveton Gifford, nr Kingsbridge, Devon, and has issue:

1 +BENJAMIN CHARLES; *b* 4 Nov 1995

Lineage: RICHARD BIRKIN, of Aspley Hall, Nottingham, JP; *b* 5 July 1805, s of RICHARD BIRKIN, of Belper, Derbys; *m* 30 Sept 1825 Mary Anne, dau of Thomas Walker, of Trowell, Notts, and *d* 9 Oct 1870, having had, with three daus (and an er s Richard, of Aspley Hall, JP, *b* 17 Dec 1828, *m* 20 Sept 1860 Annie Sophie, only dau of William Cliff, of St Quentin, Aisne, France, and *d* 14 March 1895, having had issue):

Sir Thomas Birkin, 1st Bt (UK), so *cr* 25 July 1905, DL and JP, High Sheriff 1892–93, dir GNR and Mercantile Steamship Co, Capt 3rd Vol Bn Notts and Derbyshire Regt (Robin Hood Rifles), of which he was an original offr and promoter on its formation 1859; *b* 15 Feb 1831; *m* 9 Oct 1856 Harriet (*d* 23 July 1921), yst dau of Matthew Terbutt, of Bluntisham, St Ives, Hunts, and *d* 16 Jan 1922, leaving issue:

1 **Sir Thomas Stanley Birkin, 2nd Bt**, JP Notts, High Sheriff 1915; *b* 18 Oct 1857; *m* 2 June 1894 Hon Margaret Diana Hopetoun Chetwynd (*d* 24 July 1927), sis of 8th Viscount Chetwynd (*qv*), and *d* 7 April 1931, having had issue:

(1) Thomas Richard Chetwynd, Lt 7th Dragoon Gds and RAF; *b* 5 March 1895; *ka* 12 June 1917

(2) **Sir Henry Ralph Stanley Birkin, 3rd Bt**, Lt 108th (Norfolk and Suffolk Yeo) Field Bde, formerly Roy Warwicks Regt and RAF; *b* 26 July 1896; racing motorist (held several records); *m* 12 July 1921 (*divorce* 1928) Audrey Clara Lilian, yr dau of Sir Thomas Paul Latham, 1st Bt (*qv*), and *d* 22 June 1933, leaving issue:

1a Pamela Mary; *m* 1st 6 Aug 1941 Maj Samuel Luckyn Buxton, MC, 17th/21st Lancers (*ka* May 1944), 3rd s of Cdr Bernard Buxton, DSO, RN (*see* BUXTON, Bt), and had issue; *m* 2nd 14 Nov 1946, as his 1st w, Baron Buxton of Alsa (*qv*) and *d* 1983, having had issue

2a Sara Margaret; *m* 1st 1 June 1950 (*divorce* 1961), as his 2nd w of three, Maj James Robert Hanbury (*d* 4 March 1971), late Roy Scots Greys, Jt MFH Belvoir 1947–64, of Burley-on-the-Hill, Rutland, s of Maj Robert Evan Hanbury, and had issue:

1b *Evan ('Joss') Robert [Joss Hanbury Esq, Burley on the Hill, Oakham, Rutland]; *b* 18 March 1951; *educ* Eton and RAC Cirencester; sometime MFH Quorn and Cottesmore; *m* 1st 22 July 1974 (*divorce* 19–) Rosalind Jeanette (*m* 2nd 22 Dec 1997 Rodney Portman, *see* PORTMAN), dau of Derrick Allix Pease (*see* PEASE, Bt, of Hummersknott), and has issue; *m* 2nd 15 Jan 1995 *Nicky Rawlinson, of Stody, Norfolk, and has further issue:

1c *Sophie Rose; *b* 2 Oct 1996

2b *Timothy James [Timothy Hanbury Esq, Wembury House, Wembury, Plymouth PL9 0EF]; *b* 26 Sept 1952; *educ* Eton

2a (cont.) Mrs Sara Hanbury *m* 2nd 17 Nov 1961 Lt-Col George Anthony Murray Smith, s of Arthur George Murray Smith, of Gumley, Market Harborough, and *d* 1976

(3) Charles Archibald Cecil; *b* 30 March 1905; *k* in a motor-cycle accident 7 June 1927

(1) Margaret Ida Maud; *b* 8 Feb 1901; *d* unm 26 June 1923

2 **Sir Alexander Russell Birkin, 4th Bt**; *b* 9 Sept 1861; *m* *Louie — and *d* 5 May 1942

3 Richard Leslie, DSO (1900), JP Notts, MFH, Lt-Col, Maj S Notts Hus Imp Yeo, served S Africa 1900–02 (despatches twice); *b* 2 Feb 1863; *m* 27 April 1929

Rizza (*d* 20 April 1968), dau of Aquilino Rizza Bianchi, of Vacallo, Switzerland, and *d* 22 July 1936

4 Charles Wilfred, CMG (1916), TD, DL, JP Notts, Lt-Col and Brevet Col cmdg 7th Bn Notts and Derbyshire Regt, served WW I (despatches); *b* 11 Feb 1865; *m* 2 July 1892 Clare Lloyd (LGStJ, Médaille de la Reine Elisabeth Belgium and Médaille de la Reconnaissance France), pres Women's Conservative Assoc Notts (*d* 27 Sept 1934), dau of Alexander Howe, of New York, and *d* 3 April 1932, leaving issue:

(1) **Sir Charles Lloyd Birkin, 5th Bt**; *b* 24 Sept 1907; *educ* Eton; Capt 112th Regt 9th Sherwood Foresters WW II; *m* 18 July 1940 Janet Ramsey (*d* 18 Dec 1983), dau of Peter Johnson, of Melbourne, Australia, and *d* 1985, leaving issue:

1a Sir JOHN CHRISTIAN WILLIAM BIRKIN, **6th and present Bt**

1a *Jennifer Claire Eleanor; *b* 26 July 1941; *m* 1971 *Charles de Clermont and has issue:

1b *Araminta; *b* 19–

2a *Amanda Jane Averill; *b* 16 Jan 1943; has issue:

1b *Luke TOYNE; *b* 19–

(1) Winifred May, chm Feathers Club Assoc 1934–64; *b* 28 July 1894; *m* 1st 9 July 1913 (*divorce* 1931) William Dudley Ward, PC, er s of Capt William Humble Dudley Ward, and had issue (*see* DUDLEY, E); *m* 2nd 20 Oct 1937 (*divorce* 1954) Pedro Jose Isidro Manuel Ricardo Mones Maury, Marques de Casa Maury (later Peter de Casa Maury), and *d* 16 March 1983, leaving issue. He *d* 27 June 1968

(2) Violet Hilda Margaret; *b* 19 March 1899; *m* 1st 17 Dec 1918 Maj Douglas Holden Blew-Jones, 1st Life Gds, s of Walter Bethune Blew-Jones, of Woodtown, Bideford, and had issue. He *d* 18 Sept 1947. She *m* 2nd 1949 Geoffrey Hoare and *d* 14 June 1953

(3) Vera Lilian; *b* 22 April 1903; *m* 5 Feb 1925 Maj (Frank) James (Wriothesley) Seely, er s of Col Frank Evelyn Seely, DL, JP, of Ramsdale Park, Notts (*see* 1967 edn, SHERWOOD, B), and *d* 30 Oct 1970, leaving issue. He *d* 15 Aug 1956

5 Philip Austen, OBE (1919), Maj 3rd Notts Yeo (Sherwood Rangers), TF Res, served WW I, JP, High Sheriff Notts 1931; *b* 24 Sept 1869; *m* 6 Nov 1900 Frances Emily (*d* 15 Nov 1953), 2nd dau of Joseph Littlewood, JP, of The Park, Nottingham, and *d* 12 Jan 1951, having had issue:

(1) Philip Gervaise, Maj RA (TA) WW II (despatches twice); *b* 29 May 1909; *ka* May 1942

(2) Geoffrey Ivor, TD, Maj RA (TA) WW II (despatches); *b* 17 Nov 1911; *educ* Harrow

(1) Philippa Effie; *b* 1 Sept 1902; *d* unm 14 Feb 1966

(2) *Frances Marjorie [Mrs Douglas Lockwood, La Adela, Vivorata, Argentina]; *b* 8 Oct 1905; *m* 1st 21 April 1928 Duncan William Grant (*d* 1933), est s of A D Grant, of Winkfield Manor, Ascot, and Rosario, Argentina, and has issue; *m* 2nd 1938 Douglas William Lockwood

(3) Beatrice Sylvia; *b* 26 April 1907; *d* 3 April 1969

6 Harry Laurence, TD, Maj S Notts Hus, Hon Lt, served S Africa 1900 (despatches, Queen's medal, three clasps) and WW I 1914–18 (despatches); *b* 17 March 1872; *m* 29 April 1909 Olive Isobel (*d* 22 April 1960), 3rd dau of Rev Henry Charles Russell (*see* BEDFORD, D), and *d* 6 Jan 1951, leaving issue:

(1) Peter Lawrence, OBE (1954), TD; Lt-Col and Brevet Col WW II (despatches twice, POW 1942–43), lace manufacturer, sec Notts, Lincs and Derbys RFU; *b* 17 March 1910; *educ* Harrow; *d* unm 27 Nov 1971

(2) (James) Michael, CB (1956), DSO (1944), OBE (1951), DFC (1944), AFC (1941), G/Capt RAuxAF, Insp 1952–62, Hon A/Cdre Notts Units and Middx FCU 1956–60, served WW II 1939–45, ADC to HM THE QUEEN 1957–63, High Sheriff IoW 1977, dir Birkin & Co; *b* 23 April 1912; *educ* Harrow and Trin Coll Cambridge (BA 1933, MA 1936); *m* 1st 26 April 1956 Antonia, only dau of Lt-Col Alexander Francis Stanley-Clarke; *m* 2nd 1980 *Susan [Mrs Michael Birkin, The Boathouse, Ashlake, Fishbourne, IoW], dau of Edward Mitchell, of Wellington, Salop, and *d* 1985, having had issue by his 1st w:

1a +James Francis Richard; *b* 27 Feb 1957

1a *Abigail Victoria Ann; *b* 6 March 1959

(3) David Leslie, DSC; Lt-Cdr RNVR WW II; *b* 12 Nov 1914; *educ* Harrow and Trin Coll Cambridge; *m* 9 Nov 1943 *Judy Mary (Judy Campbell, the actress), only dau of John Arthur Gamble, OBE (aka J A Campbell), of Summer End, Grantham, and *d* 1991, having had issue:

1a +Andrew Timothy; author: *The Lost Boys*; *b* 9 Dec 1945; *educ* Harrow; has issue:

1b *David Tristan; *b* 1977

2b *Alexander Kingdom; *b* 1980

3b *Edmund Xavier; *b* 1985

1a *Jane Mallory; actress; *b* 14 Dec 1946; *m* 16 Oct 1965 (*divorce* 1968) John Barry Prendergast, musician and composer, and has issue:

1b *Kate; *b* 8 April 1967; has issue by Pascal de Kermadec:

1c *Roman; *b* 1987

1a (cont.) Jane Birkin has further issue by Serge Gainsbourg (*d* 1991):

2b *Charlotte GAINSBOURG; *b* 1971; actress

1a (cont.) Jane Birkin has further issue by Jacques Doillon:

3b *Lou DOILLON; *b* 1982

2a *Linda Mary Deborah [Mrs Michael Jephson, Hawthorn Lodge, Bushey Park, Teddington, Middx TW11 0EW]; *b* 21 Feb 1950; *m* 1978 *Michael Charles William Norreys Jephson and has:

1b *Henry Denham Robert; *b* 1983

2b *George Mounteney David Aubrey; *b* 1984

3b *Jack Norreys William Orlando; *b* 1988

1 Harriet Maud; *m* 26 July 1883 Cecil Edward Willoughby, late RN (*d* 28 Jan 1930), of Willford, Notts, s of Rev Hon Charles James Willoughby, and *d* 16 June 1951, leaving issue (*see* MIDDLETON, B)

2 Hilda Mary; *d* unm 26 Nov 1926

3 Ethel Lilian, OBE (1917); Medal of Queen Elisabeth Belgium and Cross 'pro Ecclesia et Pontifice', served WWs I and II with BRCS (hon life memb); *m* 1 June 1922 Charles Arthur Carlin, Kt of St Gregory (*d* 1 Feb 1964), only s of Arthur Charles Carlin, of Barnes, and *d* 7 Nov 1972

BIRKMYRE

Arms: Per chevron arg. and sa. in chief two eagle's heads erased and in base a thistle, leaved and slipped, all ppr. **Crest:** In front of a rising sun ppr. an eagle displayed sa. **Motto:** *Avance* ('Advance'). **Creation:** Bt. (UK) 29 Jan 1921.

SIR ARCHIBALD BIRKMYRE, 3RD BT, of Dalmunzie, Co Perth [Sir Archibald Birkmyre Bt, The Old Presbytery, Buckland, Oxon SN7 8QW]; *b* 12 Feb 1923; *s* f 1992; *educ* Radley; Capt RA Burma WWII, memb London Stock Exchange 1954–88; *m* 2 May 1953 *Gillian Mary, only dau of Eric Mytton Downes, OBE, of Dordon Ho, Hurst, Berks, and has issue:

1 +JAMES [James Birkmyre Esq, Ashmore Green Cottage, Ashmore Green, Berks RG16 9EY]; *b* 29 Feb 1956; *educ* Radley; *m* 1990 *Leslie Amanda, er dau of Dr Richard Lyon, of Seal Beach, California, and has issue:

(1) +Alexander; *b* 24 May 1991

1 *Alison Mary [The Rt Hon The Lady De Ramsey, Abbots Ripton Hall, Huntingdon, Cambs]; *b* 5 Sept 1954; *m* 1984, as his 2nd w, *4th Baron De Ramsey (*qv*) and has issue

2 *Serena Jane [Mrs Hugo Jackson, c/o Sir Edward Jackson, KCMG, 17 Paulton's Sq, London SW3]; *b* 17 June 1960; *m* 1988 *Hugo Edward Stainton Jackson, yr s of Sir (John) Edward Jackson, KCMG, and has issue:

(1) *George Edward Stainton; *b* 1990

(2) *Thomas Archie Stainton; *b* 1994

(3) *James Hugo Stainton; *b* 1996

Lineage: Sir Archibald Birkmyre, 1st Bt, CBE (1918), of Dalmunzie, Co Perth, ktd 1917, sr ptnr Birkmyre Bros, of Calcutta, memb Viceroy of India's Legislative Cncl and Bengal Legislative Cncl, *cr* a Baronet 29 Jan 1921 (UK); *b* 28 June 1875; yst s of Henry Birkmyre, of Port Glasgow, Renfrewshire; *m* 8 Dec 1896 Anne (*d* 20 Feb 1959), est dau of Capt James K Black, of Arcot, Giffnock, Renfrewshire, and had issue,

1 HENRY **(Sir), 2nd Bt**

2 Archy; *b* 29 Nov 1904; served WW II with RAC (invalided 1943); *m* 3 April 1940 *Doreen [Mrs Archy Birkmyre, Dalchonzie Lower Cottage, by Comrie, Perthshire PH6 2LB], only child of Robert Barclay, of Glenpresen, Milton Road, Kilbirnie, Ayrshire, and *d* 1992, having had issue:

(1) +David; *b* 7 Dec 1941; *educ* Trin Coll Glenalmond and Edinburgh U; *m* 1976 *Mrs Margot Rogerson, dau of William Rogerson, of Rothesay, Isle of Bute, and has issue:

1a *Rebecca; *b* 1978

(1) *Adelaide [The Rt Hon The Lady Borthwick, The Neuk, by Heriot, Midlothian EH38 5YS]; *b* 10 Jan 1945; *educ* St Leonards Sch St Andrews, Fife; *m* 9 Feb 1974 *24th Lord Borthwick (*qv*)

Sir ARCHIBALD *d* 24 June 1935; his son,

Sir Henry Birkmyre, 2nd Bt; *educ* Wellington; RFA WW I 1916–18 Flanders, chm Malaya Gen Co, chm and dir Assam Consolidated Tea Estates; *b* 24 March 1898; *m* 7 March 1922 Doris Gertrude, er dau of Col Herbert Austen Smith, CIE, IMS, and *d* 1992, leaving:

1 Sir ARCHIBALD BIRKMYRE, **3rd and present Bt**

1 *Jane Henrietta [Mrs Russell Smallwood, Finches, Pembury, Kent TN2 4BA]; *b* 29 Oct 1929; *m* 23 Sept 1952 *Maj (Robert Evelyn) Russell Smallwood, yr s of Maj-Gen Gerald Russell Smallwood, CB, DSO, MC, of Kenya, and has:

(1) *Rosemary Jane [Mrs Andrew Holmes, 51 Doneraile St, London SW6 6EW]; *b* 18 Jan 1954; *m* 1977 *Andrew Peter Geoffrey Holmes and has issue

(2) *Susan Caroline [Mrs Peter Houston, Fair Dawn, Packhorse Lane, South Stoke, Bath BA2 7DJ]; *b* 1 Sept 1957; *m* 1979 *Peter Richard Vivian Houston (*see* SWANSEA, B)

BLACK

Arms: Argent, a saltire sable, between two crescents in pale and as many mullets in fess gules, on a chief of the second three trefoils slipped of the field. **Crest:** Issuant out of clouds a demi-lion rampant proper, charged on the shoulder with a trefoil vert, and holding in the paws a fylfot sable. **Motto:** *Non crux sed lux* ('Not the cross, but the light'). **Creation:** Bt. (UK) 19 June 1922

SIR (ROBERT) DAVID BLACK, 3RD BT, of Midgham, Co Berks, DL (Caithness 1991) [Sir David Black Bt DL, Beech Farm House, Woodcote, Berks RG8 0PX; Shurrery Lodge, Shebster, Thurso, Caithness]; *b* 29 March 1929; *s* f 1979; *educ* Eton; High Sheriff Oxon 1993, Maj RHG (ret 1961), Maj Berks and Westminster Dragoons (TA) 1963 and Berks TAVR III, v-chm (Berks) E Wessex TAVR Assoc 1985–92, Hon Col 94 (Berks Yeo) Signal Sqdn (V) 1988–, Jt MFH Garth and S Berks 1965; *m* 1st 22 Oct 1953 (*divorce* 1972) Rosemary Diana, only dau of Maj Sir Rupert John Hardy, 4th Bt (*qv*), and has issue:

1 *Diana Sarah [Mrs Mark Newton, The Old Rectory, Church Langton, Leics]; *b* 15 Oct 1955; *m* 1979 *Mark Robert Newton and has issue:
(1) *William David Rupert; *b* 1989
(2) *James Robert George; *b* 1993
2 Fiona Caroline; *b* 11 July 1957; *m* May 1982 *Christopher E J Jerram, only son of Col Edward Jenner Jerram, MC, of Poplars Farm, Evenlode, nr Moreton-in-Marsh, Glos, and *d* Dec 1982
3 *Joanna Rosemary Violet [Mrs Christopher Wild, Manor Farm House, Farmington, Glos GL54 3ND]; *b* 3 May 1966; *m* 8 June 1991 *Christopher Robert Caspar Wild, yr son of Robert Wild, of Slade Farm, Ockham, Surrey, and has:
(1) *Maximilian Robert David; *b* 14 May 1995
(2) *Luke Christopher Rupert; *b* 9 Feb 1997

Sir DAVID *m* 2nd 1973 *(Dorothy) Maureen, yst dau of Maj Charles Robert Eustace Radclyffe and widow of Alan Roger Douglas Pilkington

Lineage: ROBERT JOHN BLACK, MD; *b* 1828 (son of John Black, of Belfast); *m* 1853 Rosa Sinclair (*d* 1902), 2nd dau of William Neill Blow, of Belfast, and *d* 1879, leaving, with other issue:
1 William Neill; *b* 1855; *m* 1891 May (*d* 1950), 2nd dau of John Anderson, of London, and *d* 3 Nov 1926
2 ROBERT JAMES (Sir), **1st Bt**
3 Ernest Harry; *b* 1863; *m* 1889 Amy, dau of J Whitehorn, of London, and *d* 16 May 1926
4 Walter Clarence, CSI (1922), CIE (1919), Maj-Gen IA (ret 1922); *b* 1867; *m* 1899 Hope (*d* 15 July 1955) yst dau of John Anderson, of London, and *d* 17 Dec 1930, leaving:
(1) Walter Gordon; *educ* Oxford (BA 1923, MA 1929); pres Cochin Chamber of Commerce 1954–55; *m* 28 Nov 1933 *Kathleen Mary, dau of W W Alcock, of Perth, Australia, and *d* 26 Oct 1962, leaving issue:
1a *Rosemary Mary Gordon [Mrs Colin Porteous, 3 Cygnet Crescent, Dalkeith 6009, W Australia]; *b* 3 Feb 1936; *m* 21 Sept 1956 *Colin James Porteous, only son of F J Porteous, of Reigate, Surrey, and has issue:
1b *John James; *b* 17 April 1958
2b *Robert Gordon; *b* 27 July 1967
1b *Susan Mary; *b* 31 Dec 1963
1 Rosalinda St Clair; *m* 1886 Hugh Tulloch
2 Evelyn Agnes *m* 1889 John Carrick (*d* 1915), of Glasgow
3 Gertrude Alice; *m* 1889 W Whitehorn, of London
4 Lilian Annie; *d* 19 June 1939

The 2nd son,
Sir Robert James Black, 1st Bt (UK), so *cr* 19 June 1922; *b* 19 July 1860; chm Mercantile Bank of India, dir Shell Tport; *m* 26 Dec 1890 Ellen Cecilia (*d* 24 March 1958 aged 87), 2nd dau of Lt-Gen William Paget La Touche, IA, and had issue:
1 ROBERT ANDREW STRANSHAM (Sir), **2nd Bt**
1 Dorothy Rosalinda Frances; *m* 23 April 1914 Capt James Archibald Lochnell Campbell of Jura, Argyll and Sutherland Highrs (*ka* 19 March 1915), and *d* 21 July 1973, leaving issue
2 Muriel; *m* 13 Oct 1917 Jack E Addinsell, 3rd son of W A Addinsell, of Harrow Weald Lodge, Middx, and *dsp* 12 May 1948
3 *Marjorie Rhona Cecilia [Mrs Reginald Currie, Box Cottage, Donnington, Newbury]; *m* 6 Oct 1928 Reginald Michael Currie (*d* June 1962), only surv son of James Blyth Currie, of Woolhampton, Berks, and has issue:
(1) *James Michael Blyth; *b* 9 May 1932; *educ* Eton
(2) *John Robert Blyth; *b* 11 Aug 1933; *educ* Eton
(3) *Peter Thomas Blyth; *b* 5 June 1937
4 *Gladys Mary [Mrs Leonard Holmes, Headlams Well, Ipsden, Oxon]; *m* 6 April 1940 Brig Leonard Geoffrey Holmes, CBE, son of Leonard Holmes, of Brighton, and has issue:
(1) *Andrew Peter Geoffrey; *b* 16 May 1944; *educ* Radley and Magdalene Coll Cambridge

Sir ROBERT *d* 28 Sept 1925; his only son,
Sir Robert Andrew Stransham Black, 2nd Bt, JP (1934), High Sheriff 1934; *b* 17 Jan 1902; *educ* Eton; Maj 99th (Bucks and Berks Yeo) Field Bde, RA (TA); *m* 21 June 1927 Ivy, only dau of Brig-Gen Sir Samuel Herbert Wilson, GCMG, KCB, KBE, and *d* 1979, having had issue:
1 Sir (ROBERT) DAVID BLACK, **3rd and present Bt**

BLACKETT

Ams: Arg. on a chevron between three mullets pierced sa. as many escallops of the field. **Crest:** A hawk's head erased ppr. **Motto:** *Nous travaillerons en espérance* ('We will labour in hope'). **Creation:** Bt. (E) 12 Dec 1673.

SIR HUGH FRANCIS BLACKETT, 12TH BT, of Newcastle, Co Northumberland [Sir Hugh Blackett Bt, Halton Castle, Corbridge, Northumberland]; *b* 11 Feb 1955; *s* f 1995; *educ* Eton; *m* 1982 *Anna M, yr dau of J St G Coldwell, of Somerton, Oxon, and has issue:
(1) +HENRY DOUGLAS; *b* 2 Feb 1992
(1) *Amelia; *b* 1984
(2) *Isabella; *b* 1986
(3) *Flora; *b* 1988

Lineage: EDWARD BLACKETT, of Hoppyland, Co Durham; *b* 1557; *m* 1 July 1582 Jane Kirkhouse and *d* 1627, leaving:

WILLIAM BLACKETT, of Hoppyland; *b* 1588; *m* Isabella, dau of William Crook, of Wolsingham, Co Durham, and *d* 1648, having had, with two er s:
Sir William Blackett, 1st Bt (E), so *cr* 12 Dec 1673; MP Newcastle 1673–80; *m* lst 10 July 1645 Elizabeth (*d* 7 April 1674), dau of Michael Kirkley, of Newcastle, merchant, and had, with three daus:
1 EDWARD (Sir), **2nd Bt**
2 Michael, *dsp*
3 Sir WILLIAM BLACKETT, 1st Bt, so *cr* 23 Jan 1684/5, of Wallington, Northumberland; MP Newcastle 1685–1705; *m* 27 Jan 1684/5 Julia (*m* 2nd Sir William Thomson, and *d* 16 Aug 1722), dau of Sir Christopher Conyers, 2nd Bt, of Horden, Co Durham, and *d* Dec 1705, leaving, with other issue:
(1) Sir WILLIAM BLACKETT, 2nd Bt; MP Newcastle 1710–28; *m* 20 Sept 1725 Barbara, dau of 2nd Earl of Jersey (*qv*), and *dspl* 25 Sept 1728, when the btcy expired

Sir William *m* 2nd Margaret, dau of Ralph Cock and widow of Capt John Rogers, and *d* 16 May 1680

His est s,
Sir Edward Blackett, 2nd Bt; MP Ripon 1689–90 and Northumberland 1690–1700, Alderman and Mayor Newcastle-upon-Tyne; bought Newby Park, Yorks; *m* 1st Mary (*dsps*), only child of Thomas Norton, of Langthorne, Yorks; *m* 2nd Mary, only dau of Sir John Yorke, of Gowthwaite, and by her had, with other issue:
1 William; *m* Diana, dau of Sir Ralph Delaval, Bt, of Seaton Delaval, Northumberland, and *dvp* leaving:
(1) Diana; *m* 26 July 1725 Henry Mainwaring, of Over Peover, and had issue
2 **Sir Edward Blackett, 3rd Bt**, Capt RN; *m* Mary (*d* Dec 1756), dau of Rev Thomas Jekyll, DD, and widow of Nicholas Roberts, and *dsp* March 1756
3 John, of Newby; *m* Patience, dau of Henry Wise, and had with other issue:

(1) EDWARD (Sir), **4th Bt**

Sir Edward *m* 3rd 21 Oct 1699 Diana (*d* 7 Oct 1713), dau of 1st Baron Delamere of Dunham Massey and widow of Sir Ralph Delaval, Bt, and *d* 23 April 1718

The 3rd Bt's nephew,

Sir Edward Blackett, 4th Bt, MP Northumberland 1768–74; *m* Sept 1757 Anne (*d* 30 Dec 1805), dau and heir of Oley Douglas, of Matfen, Northumberland, and *d* 3 Feb 1804, leaving:

1 WILLIAM (Sir), **5th Bt**

1 Anne; *m* Lt-Gen Scott, son of Benjamin Scott

His son,

Sir William Blackett, 5th Bt; *b* 16 Feb 1759; *m* 6 Aug 1801 Mary Anne (*d* 7 Aug 1859), dau of Benjamin Keene, of Westoe Lodge, Cambs, and had, with other issue:

1 EDWARD (Sir), **6th Bt**

2 John Charles, RN, of Thorpe Lea, Egham; *b* 3 April 1813; *m* 1st 22 June 1845 Maria (*d* 23 Aug 1847), dau of Benjamin Berthon, of Woodlands, Tasmania, and had two daus; *m* 2nd 18 March 1852 Emily Jane (*d* 22 Dec 1899), 2nd dau of Col William Wild Cockcraft, 58th Regt, and *d* 8 Aug 1896, having had issue:

(1) Harold, Lt 4th Bn Prince of Wales' Own (W Yorks) Regt; *b* 27 Jan 1854; *m* 15 Sept 1881 Marion (*d* 24 Dec 1937), dau of Richard Gosling, of Ecclesfield, Ashford, Middx, and *d* 28 May 1923, leaving issue:

1a Henry Beaumont; *b* 20 June 1886; *educ* Radley; Capt 4th Bn Alexandra, Princess of Wales' Own Yorks Regt, served WW I (wounded, despatches); *m* 3 Aug 1916 Evelyn Nora Mary (*d* 22 May 1966), dau of John Booth Lazenby, of Newcastle, and *d* 16 March 1964, leaving issue:

1b John Harold Booth [John Blackett Esq, Seven Stars House, Whalton, Morpeth, Northumberland NE61 3XA]; *b* 20 Dec 1922; *educ* Radley and Jesus Coll Cambridge (BA 1945, MA 1948); late Lt 15th/19th King's Roy Hus, served in WW II (wounded and invalided 1945), slr 1949; *m* 20 April 1953 *Veronica Heath Stuart, dau of Henry Stuart Tegner, of West Manor Ho, Whalton, Northumberland, and has issue:

1c (John) Simon [Simon Blackett Esq, Clunie Cottge, Braemar, Aberdeenshire AB35 5XQ]; *b* 16 Sept 1954; *educ* Radley; *m* 1987 *Hon Geva Charlotte Caroline Winn, only dau of 5th Baron St Oswald (*qv*), and has issue:

1d *(Helena) Charlotte Rose; *b* 1988

2d *(Camilla Harriet) Eve; *b* 1989

3d *Letitia; *b* 1991

4d *Annabel; *b* 1993

2c +Rupert Beaumont [Rupert Blackett Esq, Merle Cottage, 89 High St, Westerham, Kent]; *b* 28 Oct 1957; *educ* Radley; *m* 1984 *Hendrika Theresa, dau of Wilhelmus Marinus Bouwman, of Utrecht, Netherlands, and has issue:

1d +James Henry; *b* 1988

2d +William Luke; *b* 1994

1d *Rebecca Anne; *b* 1985

2d *Kate Elizabeth; *b* 1990

3d *Lucia Georgia; *b* 1994 (twin)

1c *Caroline Rose; *b* 2 Aug 1960; *m* 1987 *Robert Murray-Brown, yst son of Lt-Col C R Murray-Brown, DSO, and of Lady Loyd, of Aldeburgh, Suffolk, and has issue:

1d *Francis William; *b* 1994

2d *John Frederick; *b* 1996

2c Juliet Evelyn; *b* 11 Nov 1965; *m* 1991 *Andrew Charles Pumphrey (*see* AYKROYD, Bt), and has:

1d *Oliver Jonathan; *b* 1997

1d *Kate Annabel; *b* 1995

1a Kathleen Marion; *d* unm 30 March 1955

(2) Arthur Vere; *b* 6 May 1857; *d* 1860

(3) John Charles (Rev), BA Durham, Rector of Compton and Shawford, Hants; *b* 23 Feb 1865; *d* 21 Dec 1927

(4) Henry, CBE (1919); *b* 28 Nov 1867; Adml (ret); a Lt for the City of London; *m* 14 July 1906 Hon Pamela Mary Fisher (*d* 22 Nov 1949), yst dau of 1st Baron Fisher, GCB (*qv*), and *d* 1 Dec 1952, leaving issue:

1a *Pamela [Mrs Clifford Bray, 8 Homedrive Ho, 95/97 The Drive, Hove, Sussex BN3 6GE]; *b* 3 July 1911; *m* 20 March 1957 Clifford Henry Bray (*d* 1980), est son of Tom Henry Bray, of Streatham

(1) Ida Frances; *d* unm 8 Dec 1941

(2) Louisa; *m* 22 June 1882 James Blenkinsop, and *d* 28 March 1900, leaving issue

(3) Emily; *d* unm 14 June 1944

(4) Florence; *m* 1883 Percival Septimus Hodgson (*d* 20 June 1895), and *d* 13 Feb 1885

(5) Edith; *d* unm 4 Dec 1950

(6) Nesta Mary; *m* 1st 15 Dec 1898 (*divorce* 1920) Lionel Charles Lane-Fox-Pitt, of Cliff Ho, Shaftesbury. He *d* 7 April 1937. She *m* 2nd 4 Dec 1920 Henry Francis Campbell Johnston, late 91st Argyll and Sutherland Highrs, 2nd son of Capt Frederick Erskine Johnston, RN, and *d* 25 Dec 1944. He *d* 24 Oct 1943

(7) Evelyn; *m* 24 Feb 1902 Maj Christopher Montagu Blackett, Rifle Brigade, JP, 3rd son of Edward Algernon Blackett, RN, of Wylam, Northumberland, and *d* 20 March 1963. He *d* 16 March 1940

Sir WILLIAM *d* 27 Oct 1816; his est surv son,

Sir Edward Blackett, 6th Bt, DL and JP, formerly the 1st Life Gds; *b* 23 Feb 1805; *m* 1st 1 May 1830 Julia (*d* 25 June 1846), last surv dau of Sir Charles Monck, 6th Bt, of Belsay Castle, and had, with five daus (including Louisa *m* Hon Sir Charles Elliot-Murray-Kynynmound, 3rd s of 2nd Earl of Minto, *qv*):

1 EDWARD WILLIAM (Sir), **7th Bt**

2 Charles Francis, Maj Rifle Brigade, served in Indian Mutiny 1859; *b* 6 Jan 1841; *m* 27 Nov 1886 Henrietta Louise Johanna Martha (*d* 24 Jan 1944), 2nd dau of Carl Friedrich Schmidt, of Dresden, and *d* 3 Feb 1919, leaving issue:

(1) Vera Katerina; *b* 19 Dec 1888; *m* 25 Sept 1911 Baron Octave George Lecca, Maj (ret) Romanian Roy Horse Gds, formerly Govr of Co Suceava, Kt of Star of Roumania and Kt Cdr of St Anne of Russia, and *d* 28 Oct 1960, leaving issue

3 Henry Wise Ridley, Lt-Col 19th Hus; *b* 24 June 1842; *d* 28 Dec 1935

4 Frederick Arthur, Lt RN; *b* 10 June 1846; lost at sea in HMS *Atalanta* Feb 1880

Sir Edward *m* 2nd 16 Oct 1851 Frances Vere (*dsp* 28 May 1874), dau of Sir William Loraine, 4th Bt, and widow of William Henry Ord, MP, of Whitfield, Northumberland; *m* 3rd 15 June 1875 Isabella Helen (*dsp* 28 Feb 1879), dau of John Richardson, of Kirklands, Roxburghshire; *m* 4th 5 Aug 1880 Alethea Rianette Anne (who *m* 2nd 5 Nov 1888 Capt Sir Henry Frederick Gisborne Holt, JP, 4th Bn Suffolk Regt, of Ropley Grove, Hants, and *d* 22 April 1920), 2nd dau of Maj-Gen William Henry Scott and Hon Mrs Scott, and *d* 23 Nov 1885

His est son,

Sir Edward William Blackett, 7th Bt, CB, Maj-Gen, Chevalier Legion of Honour; *b* 22 March 1831; *m* 23 Nov 1871 Hon Julia Frances Somerville (*d* 30 March 1913), yst dau of 17th Lord Somerville (*see* 1970 edn) and sis and co-heir of 18th Baron, and had issue:

1 HUGH DOUGLAS (Sir), **8th Bt**

2 Arthur Edward; *b* 14 May 1874; *m* 30 Oct 1917 Diana de Bonetto (*d* 19 Aug 1943), dau of Rudolph Goetz, Swiss Dip Serv, and *dsp* 24 Feb 1959

3 Ralph, Capt S Irish Horse (SR), late 14th Hus, served in S African War, and WW I; *b* 19 Sept 1877; *m* 2 April 1910 Evaleen Maud Mary (*d* 21 Nov 1952), dau of Maj-Gen Walter Weldon, 3rd son of Sir Anthony Weldon, 4th Bt (*qv*), and *dsp* 20 June 1964

1 Ethel; *b* 22 April 1876; *d* 1884

Sir EDWARD *d* 13 Sept 1909; his est son,

Sir Hugh Douglas Blackett, 8th Bt; JP Northumberland, High Sheriff 1914, Capt late Northumberland Yeo; *b* 24 March 1873; *m* 5 Feb 1903 Helen Katharine (*d* as the result of an accident 10 Jan 1943), 3rd dau of George William Lowther (*see* LOWTHER, Bt), and *d* 13 Nov 1960, leaving:

1 **Sir Charles Douglas Blackett, 9th Bt**, DL (Northumberland 1953), High Sheriff 1953; *educ* Eton and RMC Sandhurst; Maj The Queen's Bays, and Adj Northumberland Hus Yeo, served WW II 1939–42 (POW); *b* 15 Aug 1904; *m* 28 Sept 1935 Ursula Mary, yr dau of Maj Maurice Fearing Cely-Trevilian, DL, JP, of Midelney Manor, Taunton, and *d* 26 Dec 1968, having had issue:

(1) Edward Douglas; *b* 30 July, *d* 7 Oct 1938

(1) *Caroline Ann [Mrs Warren Fenwicke-Clennell, Kirk Hammerton House, York YO5 8DD]; *b* 22 June 1936; *m* 1 June 1957 *Capt (Geoffrey Thomas) Warren Fenwicke-Clennell, late 11th Hus (PAO), son of Lt-Col Geoffrey Edward Fenwicke-Clennell, DL, of Eland Hall, Ponteland, Northumberland, and has issue:

1a *Nicholas [Nicholas Fenwicke-Clennell Esq, Deans Hall, Little Maplestead, Halstead, Essex C09 2RT]; *b* 28 Feb 1959; *m* 1984 *Susan Elizabeth, dau of Peter Roy Herbert Gould, of Little Barn, Gt Chesterford, Saffron Walden, Essex, and has issue:

1b *Oliver Edward; *b* 1986

2b *Toby; *b* 1988

1b *Antonia Ursula; *b* 1991

2a Luke Thomas [Luke Fenwicke-Clennell Esq, 75 Rodenhurst Rd, London SW4 8AF]; *b* 18 Sept 1961; *m* 1996 *Emily Sorrel, dau of D P Ackroyd

1a Katharine Mary [Mrs James Boughey, The Manor House, Piddletrenthide, Dorset DT2 7QX]; *b* 14 June 1963; *m* 1989 *James Richard Boughey, yr son of Sir Richard James Boughey, 10th Bt (*qv*)

(2) Lucinda Mary; *b* 28 June 1940; *m* 1st 11 April 1964 (*divorce* 1971) Ewan Iain Macleod Hilleary, yst son of Iain Hilleary, of Tayinloan, Isle of Skye, and has issue:

1a Iain Douglas; *b* 28 April 1965

2a William James; *b* 19 Nov 1966

(2) (cont.) Mrs Lucinda Hilleary *m* 2nd 1971 *Sir Michael Henry Basil Peto, 4th Bt, and has further issue (*see* PETO, Bt, of Barnstaple)

2 **Sir George William Blackett, 10th Bt**, served WW II in CMP; *b* 26 April 1906; *m* 1st 26 July 1933 Euphemia Cicely (*d* 22 Oct 1960), yst dau of Maj Nicholas Robinson, of Frankton Grange, Salop; *m* 2nd 5 Nov 1964 Daphne Laing [Dowager Lady Blackett, Colwyn, Corbridge on Tyne, Northumberland], dau of Maj Guy Laing Bradley, TD, of Bridge End Ho, Hexham, Northumberland, and *d* 1994

3 FRANCIS HUGH (Sir), **11th Bt**

4 Rupert Henry ; *b* 13 Feb 1911; *educ* Eton and Lincoln Coll Oxford (BA 1932); Maj Durham LI WW II 1939–42 (wounded twice); *m* 11 Jan 1941 Felicity Mary Audley [Mrs Rupert Blackett, Errington Hill Head, Hexham, Northumberland], dau of Lt-Col William Alfred Scudamore-Smith, and formerly w of — Clapton, and *d* 1992, leaving issue:

(1) +Piers Rupert; *b* 3 Sept 1941; *educ* U of Cape Town Med Sch (MB, ChB)

(1) *(Rose) Miranda; *b* 6 May 1944; *m* 1975 (*divorce* 19–) Merlin Pearson-Rogers, and has:

1a *Jack Rupert; *b* 1977

The 10th Bt's bro,

Sir Francis Hugh Blackett, 11th Bt; *b* 16 Oct 1907; *educ* Eton; Maj The Roy Dragoons WW II; *m* 1st 11 July 1950 Mrs Elizabeth Elly Barrie (*d* 1982), 2nd dau of Howard Dennison, of Valparaiso, Chile; *m* 2nd 1985 *Mrs Joan Chowdry, and *d* 1995, having had issue by his 1st w:

1 Sir HUGH FRANCIS BLACKETT, **12th and present Bt**

2 +Marcus Henry [Marcus Blackett Esq, 11 Waverley Rd, Liverpool L17 8TY]; *b* 9 March 1961

1 *Angela Frances [Mrs Ewan Bell, Easter Coul, Auchterarder, Perthshire PH3 1DS]; *b* 19 July 1951; *m* 1979 *Ewan Follett Bell (*see* WYFOLD, B), and has issue

2 *Charlotte Elizabeth [Miss Charlotte Blackett, 30A Mount Ephraim Rd, London SW16]; *b* 6 Sept 1952; has issue:

(1) *Theophania Eve BLACKETT OGRAM; *b* 1990

BLACKSTONE

Creation: B. (LP, UK) 1987.

THE BARONESS BLACKSTONE, of Stoke Newington, Greater London (Tessa Ann Vosper Blackstone) [The Rt Hon The Baroness Blackstone, 2 Gower St, London WC1E 6DP]; *b* 27 Sept 1942; *educ* Ware GS and LSE (BSc Soc, PhD); associate lecturer Enfield Coll 1965–66, assist lect later lecturer Dept Social Admin LSE 1966–75, advsr CPRS Cabinet Office 1975–78, Prof Educnl Admin U of London Inst of Educn 1978–83, Dep Educn Offr (Resources) later Clerk and Dir Educn ILEA 1983–87, Master Birkbeck Coll 1987–97; dir ROH 1987–97, Chm ROH Ballet Bd 1991–97, fndr memb and chm Tstees Inst for Public Policy Research 1988–97; Tstee Natural History Museum 1992–97; Min State Educn and Employment 1997–; *m* 1963 (*divorce* 1975) Tom Evans (*d c* 1985) and has issue:

1 *Benedict Blackstone; *b* 1963; *m* 1987 *Suzi, dau of Donal Godson, and has:

(1) *Scarlet Eloise; *b* 1991

(2) *Amber; b 1994

(3) *Ruby; b 1994

1 *Liesel Morwenna; *b* 1966; with BBC

Lineage: GEOFFREY VAUGHAN BLACKSTONE; Ch Fire Offr Herts; *m* Joanna — and had, with two sons and another dau:

TESSA ANN VOSPER, *cr* a **Baroness**

BLACKWELL

Arms: Arms confirmed by the College of Arms, but blazon not available at time of going to press. **Motto:** Endeavour and integrity.
Creation: B. (LP, UK) 2 Aug 1997.

THE BARON BLACKWELL, of Woodcote, Co Surrey (Norman Roy Blackwell) [The Rt Hon The Lord Blackwell, House of Lords, London SW1A 0PW]; *b* 29 July 1952; *educ* Trin Coll Cambridge, Wharton Business Sch and Pennsylvania U; with Plessey 1976–78, McKinsey & Co 1978–95 (ptnr 1984); Head Policy Unit PM's Office 10 Downing St 1995–97 (special advsr 1986–87); dir Gp Development NatWest Gp 1997–; *m* *Brenda Clucas and has three sons and two daus

Lineage: ALBERT BLACKWELL; *m* Frances Luttman and has:

NORMAN ROY, *cr* a **Baron**

BLAKE

Creation: B. (LP, UK) 1971

THE BARON BLAKE, of Braydeston, Co Norfolk (Robert Norman William Blake, JP (Oxford)) [The Rt Hon The Lord Blake JP, Riverview House, Brundall, Norwich, Norfolk NR13 5LA]; *b* 23 Dec 1916; *educ* King Edward VI Sch Norwich and Magdalen Coll Oxford (MA, DLitt); Hon DLitt Glasgow, UEA, Westminster Coll, Fulton, Missouri, USA, and Buckingham; Capt RA WW II N Africa 1942, POW Italy 1942–44, escaped 1944, despatches 1944; memb Oxford City Cncl 1957–64, Oxford: lecturer politics 1946–47, Student and Tutor in Politics Ch Ch 1947–68, Censor 1950–55, Sr Proctor 1959–60, Ford's Lecturer in English History 1967–68, Provost Queen's Coll 1968–87, Pro-V-Chllr 1971–87; Memb Bd Channel 4 TV 1983–87; author: *The Private Papers of Douglas Haig* (1952), *The Unknown Prime Minister* (1955), *Disraeli* (1966), *The Conservative Party from Peel to Churchill* (1970), *The Office of Prime Minister* (1975), *The Conservative Opportunity* (ed, with John Patten (*see* PATTEN, B), 1976), *A History of Rhodesia* (1977), *Disraeli's Grand Tour* (1982), *The Decline of Power 1915-1964* (1985), *The Conservative Party from Peel to Major* (1997), Chm Roy Commn Historical MSS 1982– and Rhodes Tst 1983–87, Tstee Br Museum 1978–88, Prime Warden Dyers' Co 1976–77, High Steward Westminster Abbey 1989–; *m* 1953 *Patricia Mary, est dau of Thomas Richard Waters, of Great Plumstead, Norfolk, and has:

1 *Deborah Cicelie; *b* 1955

2 *Letitia Lindley; *b* 1960

3 *Victoria Mary; *b* 1963

Lineage: WILLIAM JOSEPH BLAKE, of Brundall, Norfolk; *m* Norah Lindley Daynes and had:

ROBERT NORMAN WILLIAM, *cr* a **Baron**

BLAKE, Bt, of Menlough

Arms: Arg., a fret gu. **Crest:** A cat passant-guardant ppr.
Motto: *Virtus sola nobilitat* ('Virtue alone ennobles').
Creation: Bt. (I) 10 July 1622.

SIR (THOMAS) RICHARD VALENTINE BLAKE, 17TH BT, of Menlough, Co Galway [Sir Richard Blake Bt, Old Janes, River, nr Petworth, W Sussex GU28 9AY]; *b* 7 Jan 1942; *s f* 1963; *educ* Bradfield; served RNR from 1963, memb Standing Cncl Baronetage; *m* 1st 1976 Jacqueline, dau of Desmond E Daroux and formerly w of Peter Alers Hankey; *m* 2nd 1982 (*divorce* 1986) Bertice Reading (*d* 1991), singer, formerly w of Eddie Meyer; *m* 3rd 1991 *Wendy, widow of Anthony Ronald Roberts

Lineage: THOMAS BLAKE, Mayor Galway 1545 and 1562, third s of Valentine Blake (*d* 1499), held the castle and lands of Ballimacroe (now Carnmore, nr Galway), granted 1277 to Richard Caddle, called Niger, his ancestor, and *d* 20 Jan 1574, leaving an est s:

WALTER BLAKE; *dvp* Nov 1573, leaving issue by his w Juliana, dau of James Browne or Fitz Stephen:

1 VALENTINE (Sir), **1st Bt**

2 James, Capt; *m* Margery, dau of Alderman Dominick Browne (*see* ORANMORE AND BROWNE, B), and *d* 20 Feb 1635, leaving issue. He was ancestor of the BLAKEs of Drum

3 Robert; Mayor Galway 1624; *m* Juliana Lynch and left four s, one of which was gf of Sir Francis Blake, of Twisel, Co Durham, *cr* a Bt 25 May 1714 (*extinct* 10 Sept 1860)

The eldest son,

Sir Valentine Blake, 1st Bt (I), so *cr* 10 July 1622, of Galway; MP 1613–15, Mayor Galway 1611 and 1630; *b* 1560; *m* 1st Margaret, dau of Robuck French, of Galway, and had, with other issue:

1 THOMAS (Sir), **2nd Bt**

Sir Valentine *m* 2nd Annabel (*dsp*), dau of James Lynch, and *d* 2 Jan 1634

His est s,

Sir Thomas Blake, 2nd Bt, of Menlough Castle, MP Galway (City) 1634–35, Mayor 1637; *m* Julliane, 2nd dau of Geoffrey Browne, of Carrowbrowne (*see* ORANMORE AND BROWNE, B), and *d* 1642, leaving, with several daus and three yr s:

Sir Valentine Blake, 3rd Bt, of Menlough Castle, MP Co Galway 1634–35 and Galway 1639–42, Mayor Galway 1643, ktd in his gf's lifetime; *m* (settlement dated 27 June 1632) Ellinor (*d* 1692), 3rd dau of Sir Henry Lynch, 1st Bt (*see* LYNCH-BLOSSE, Bt), and *d* 1652, having had issue:

1 **Sir Thomas Blake, 4th Bt**; *m* 1st 1649 Mary (*dsp*), dau of Richard Martin; *m* 2nd Ellinor Lynch (*dsp*); *m* 3rd (sett dated 6 Oct 1656) Mary (*d* 1694), dau of Marcus French (ancestor of the FRENCHes of Rahassane), and *d* Sept 1676, having had issue, with several daus:

(1) **Sir Valentine Blake, 5th Bt**, of Menlo; *b* 1664; *d* unm Oct 1686

(2) **Sir Walter Blake, 6th Bt**, MP Co Galway 1689, Capt Col Henry Dillon's Regt of Foot in JAMES II's Irish Army but benefited from Articles of Capitulation of Galway 1691, allegedly the first catholic gentleman of distinction to join WILLIAM III, maintaining and clothing a regiment at his own expense; *m* 1st 10 Aug 1687 Anne (*d* Aug 1705), dau of Sir John Kirwan, of Castlehacket, Co Galway, and had, with another s and two daus:

1a **Sir Thomas Blake, 7th Bt**, of Menlough, previously of Summerville, Co Galway; *m* 1716 Elizabeth, poetess, dau of Ulick Burke, of Tyaquin, and *d* March 1749, having had issue:

1b **Sir Ulick Blake, 8th Bt**, of Menlough; *m* Mary (*m* 2nd Peter Smith), dau of Robert Blake, of Ardfry (*see* 1917 edn WALLSCOURT, B), and *dspm* 22 June 1766, having had an only child:
1c Anstace; *m* 1769 Francis Foster, of Ashfield, Co Galway, and had issue
1b Anne; *m* 1757 Richard Kirwan, scientist, of Creg, Co Galway
(2) (cont.) **Sir Walter** *m* 2nd 1706 Agnes (*d* by 10 Sept 1748), dau of John Blake, and *d* May 1748, having by her had an only child:
1a Catherine; *m* 1st 10 April 1722 Denis Daly, of Carrownakilly (*see* 1911 edn DUNSANDLE AND CLANCONAL, B); *m* 2nd Sir John Browne, 5th Bt, of the Neale (*see* KILMAINE, B), and *dsp* 1775
2 Henry; *b* 1640; *m* Catherine Gibson, and left an only s:
(1) Thomas, of Brendrum, Co Galway; *m* Mary, dau of Peter Lynch, 2nd s of Sir Robuck Lynch, 2nd Bt (*see* LYNCH-BLOSSE, Bt), and *d* 1764, leaving issue:
1a **Sir Thomas Blake, 9th Bt**, of Menlough, formerly of Bordeaux; *m* 1730 Eleanor Lynch (*d* July 1791) and *dspm* 3 March 1787, having had an only dau, Mary, who *m* Edward Lynch
2a WALTER (Sir), **10th Bt**
3 Francis, allegedly a patentee of lands in Carolina; left issue:
(1) Joseph, a Ld Proprietor of Carolina; *dsp*
4 John, of Clooneen, Co Mayo, later of Muckinish, Co Clare; *m* (setts dated 10 Jan 1678) Mary, dau of Isidore Lynch, of Drimcong, and *d* June 1691, having had issue, with a yr s Patrick:
(1) Isidore, of Clooneen; *m* Mary, dau of Maurice Blake, of Ballinafad, and *d* April 1763, leaving, with other issue:
1a Maurice, of Clooneen; *m c* 25 Feb 1741 Ann, dau of Walter Blake, of Galway, and *d* 17 Jan 1789, leaving:
1b Isidore, of Towerhill, Clooneen; *m c* 6 July 1767 Frances (*d* 6 March 1824), dau and coheir of Thomas Ruttledge, of Cornfield, Co Mayo, and *d* 15 Dec 1818, having had, with other issue:
1c Maurice, of Towerhill, DL; *b* 1771; *m* 4 Aug 1803 Maria (*d* July 1810), dau of Valentine O'Connor, and *d* 7 May 1847, leaving, with other issue:
1d Valentine O'Connor, of Towerhill, JP, DL Co Mayo, High Sheriff 1839; *b* 1 Jan 1808; *m* 7 Jan 1836 Hon Margaret Mary ffrench (*d* 16 July 1869), only dau of 3rd Baron ffrench (*qv*), and *d* 9 Aug 1879, leaving, with other issue:
1e Maurice Charles Joseph, CB , of Towerhill; Col 3rd Bn Connaught Rangers, JP, DL Co Mayo, High Sheriff 1864, JP Co Galway; *b* 20 July 1837; *m* 24 Nov 1863 Jeanette (*d* 1916), dau of Richard Pearce O'Reilly, surgeon, of Sans Souci, Co Dublin, and *d* 29 April 1915, leaving issue:
1f Valentine Joseph, of Towerhill, High Sheriff Co Mayo 1916, Capt 3rd Bn Connaught Rangers; *b* 10 June 1866; *d* unm 29 July 1947
2f Charles Joseph; *b* 11 June 1867; *d* 1913
1f Olivia; *d* unm 24 May 1955
2f Georgina; *d* unm 2 Jan 1959
3f Cecilia; *d* 1886
4f Margaret; *d* umm 1938
5f Frances; *d* unm 8 Sept 1897
2e Charles Joseph, of Heath House, Queen's Co (now Co Laois), and Bunowen Castle, Clifden, Co Galway, JP Galway and Queen's Co, High Sheriff Queen's Co 1895, barrister; *b* 1839; *educ* Trin Coll Dublin (BA); *d* unm 27 Nov 1917
3e Valentine Joseph, of Cahir House, Loughglynn, Castlerea, Co Roscommon, JP Cos Mayo and Roscommon; *b* 4 Oct 1842; *m* 1 Sept 1880 Hon Mary Josephine French (*d* 20 Feb 1919), only dau of 3rd Baron De Freyne (*qv*), and *d* 2 Oct 1912, having had issue:
1f Arthur Joseph, MC and bar, LRCPI, LRCSI, Lt-Col RAMC, Croix de Guerre; *b* 1884; *educ* Stonyhurst; *m* 7 Nov 1938 Barbara, only dau of Raymond Stephenson, of Cranford, Stillorgan Rd, Dublin, and *d* 24 May 1974, having had issue:
1g +Martin Joseph [Martin Blake Esq, Castlewood House, Durrow, Co Laois, Ireland]; *b* 1952
1g *Anne Meriel Josephine [Mrs Patrick Leonard, Edmondstown Park, Dublin 16 Ireland]; *b* 16 Oct 1939; *m* 16 May 1964 *Patrick Benedict James Leonard, s of John S Leonard, of Balloy, Stamullen, Co Meath, and has:
1h *John (Sean) Arthur; *b* 13 Dec 1967
2h *Jeremy Charles; *b* 14 June 1973
3h *Dominic Stephen; *b* 23 July 1975
1h *Natasha Veronica; *b* 19 Oct 1965
2g *Erica Mary Josephine [Mrs Bernard Corbally, Gilspear, Kilmacanogue, Co Wicklow, Ireland]; *b* 22 Dec 1940; *m* 9 July 1966 *Bernard Humphreys Clement Corbally, BA, BAL, lecturer production engrg Strathclyde U, s of Herbert Corbally, of St Roch's, Ballymoney, Co Wexford, and has issue:
1h *Simon Herbert Arthur; *b* 23 Aug 1967
2h *Colin George Eric; *b* 13 Nov 1968
1h *Ruth Ida Mary *b* 11 Nov 1974
2h *Linda Clare Cecilia; *b* 4 Aug 1977
2f Valentine Charles, Capt 1st Bn Irish Guards; *b* 1885; *ka* 29 Jan 1916
3f Isidore, High Sheriff Queen's Co 1921; *b* 1887; *d* 6 Dec 1969
4f Lionel; *educ* Stonyhurst; *b* 1888; *d* unm 27 June 1961
5f Harold Martin Joseph, Lt Roy Munster Fus; *b* 1893; *d* 20 Nov 1917 of wounds recd in action
6f Gerald; *b* 12 Dec 1896; *m* 9 Feb 1943 *Ann Deegan and had issue:
1g +Valentine; *b* 20 Oct 1945; *m* 1971 *Madeleine, only dau of J Andrews, of Perivale, Middx
2g +Gerald [Gerald Blake Esq, 6 Campbell Court, Campbell Rd, Hanwell, London W7]; *b* 9 March 1947; *m* 1968 *Elaine Thomas, of Baglan, Glam, and has issue:
1h +Gervase; *b* 1969
1h *Emma Josephine; *b* 1972
3g +Arthur; *b* 2 Sept 1950
1f Kathleen; *b* 28 March 1882; *d* unm 2 Jan 1972
2f Gladys; *m* 3 Oct 1918 John Arthur Howard Gorges and *d* 30 Oct 1962
3f Mary; *d* 21 Nov 1904
2c Anthony, of Browneville, Co Galway; *m* Rebecca (*d* 12 April 1843), widow of Col Lines Fawcett and dau of — Skerrett, and *d* 1840, having had issue:
1d Isidore; *d* unm
2d Joseph, of Carrick, Co Galway; *m* his cousin Fanny (*d* Jan 1894), dau of Arthur Lynch, of Petersburgh, Co Galway, and *d* 2 March 1886, having had issue:
1e Anthony, MD, of The Grange, Cappaghgluff, Co Mayo, surgeon; *m* 21 Jan 1902 Winifred, dau of Michael Hopkins, and *d* 14 June 1916, leaving issue:
1f Joseph; *b* 21 Dec 1902
2e Arthur
3e Fawcett
1e Mary; *d* young
2e Frances; *m* Charles Crean, MD, and *d* Aug 1891, having had issue
1d Frances; *m* — Hickson and *d* 1891, leaving issue
2f Mary; *m* James Valentine Browne and had issue
2b Anthony, of Ross Lodge, Co Galway; *m* Katherine, dau of William Burke, of Keelogues, Co Galway, and was ancestor of the BLAKEs of Ross Lodge
2a Patrick; *m* 21 Feb 1761 Catherine, dau of John Foster, of Higham Dikes, Northumberland, and had issue
1 Juliane; *m* Alexander Kirwan, of Dalgan, Co Mayo
2 Elizabeth; *m* Andrew Blake, of Fartigar or Castlegrove, Co Galway, 7th s of Robert Blake, of Ardfry (*see* 1917 edn WALLSCOURT, B)
3 Annabel (Nell or Elena); *m* Thomas Fleming and *d* 1705, leaving issue

The 9th Bt's only brother,

Sir Walter Blake, 10th Bt; *m* 10 April 1751 Barbara (*d* 14 April 1802), dau of Myles Burke, of Ower, Co Galway, and had, with other issue:
1 JOHN (Sir), **11th Bt**
2 Dominick Joseph; *m* 1797 Mary, dau of George Yelverton, of Belleisle, Co Tipperary, by Letitia, dau of Sir Henry Burke, 7th Bt, of Glinsk, and *d* Sept 1843, leaving, with other issue:
(1) Walter, of Meelick, Whitegate, Co Galway; *b* 1799; *m* 1840 Mary, dau of Charles Blake, of Bridge House, Tuam, and *d* 1860, leaving issue:
1a Charles Anthony, of Meelick, JP, of NZ Military and Civil Service; *b* 1848; *m* 1896 Harriet Elizabeth (*d* Sept 1945), dau of Rev William Pender Roberts, MA (Camb), rector Trevalga, Cornwall, by Mary Elizabeth, dau of Hon William Henry Yelverton, of Whitland Abbey, Carmarthenshire (*see* 1910 edn AVONMORE, B), and *dsp* 12 Aug 1911
2a Walter, Surgn-Maj; *m* 1875 Ellen Gertrude, dau of Capt William Moriarty, and *d* 7 May 1881, leaving issue:
1b Luttrell Bruce, of Meelick and Pwllyhead, Whitland, Carmarths, JP; *m* 30 June 1904 Lucy Charlotte Ellen (*d* 5 July 1907), only dau of John Newall Moore, JP, and *d* 1919, leaving issue:
1c Walter William Yelverton Bruce BLAKE later BLAKE-YELVERTON (deed poll 19 May 1927); *b* 28 Sept 1905; *m* 23 Nov 1949 Ellen Ida (*d* 18 Dec 1964), er dau of David Holland, of The Genners, Northfield, Birmingham, and *dsp* 27 March 1971
2b Cecil Bruce, Maj RFA, served S African War 1901–02 (medal and three clasps) and WW I (wounded, 1914 star, two medals); *b* 4 Jan 1880; *m* 19 Nov 1909 Effie (*d* 12 Sept 1969), dau of S Earnshaw Howell, FSA, JP, of Beltwood, Sheffield, and *d* 22 June 1937, leaving issue:
1c Charles Anthony Howell Bruce, Lt-Col Roy Ulster Rifles, served WW II, American DSC and Polish and Czech MCs; *b* 1 Dec 1911; *m* 2 April 1948 *Elspeth Lilian, MBE, MA (*m* 2nd Maj Patrick Michael Gardner, MBS, MA, only s of Capt George Henry Gardner, 21st Lancers, of Sulby House, Sunninghill, Berks), er dau of Lt-Col Allan Maxwell Arnott, 4th Gurkha Rifles, of Holly Lodge, Carcolston, Notts, and was *ka* Korea 4 Jan 1951, leaving issue:
1d +ANTHONY TEILO BRUCE [Anthony Blake Esq, 42 High Lane, Lymm, Cheshire]; *b* posthumously 5 May 1951; heir presumptive; *educ* Wellington; *m* 1988 *Geraldine, dau of Cecil Shnaps, and has issue:
1e *Sarah Elizabeth Bruce; *b* 1990
2e *Rachel Louise Bruce; *b* 1991
1e *Caroline Bruce; *b* 16 Feb 1949
2c Valentine John Bruce, Lt IA WW II (POW); *b* 25 Nov 1914; *m* 2 Dec 1950 *Carla Maria Aida [Mrs Valentine Blake, Carnival, Spikle, Conna, Co Cork, Ireland], dau of Dr Helmut Wrinch-Schulz, of Gardens, Cape Town, and *d* 10 Aug 1993, leaving:
1d +Jonathan Luttrell [Jonathan Blake Esq, 82 Willow Ave, Rowville, 3178 VIC, Australia]; *b* 5 Feb 1953; *m* 1977 (*divorce* 19–) Eleanora Elizabeth Mostert, of Holland, and has:
1e *Suzanne May [Mrs Christopher Crocket, Flat 1, 70 Petra Ave, Tamworth, NSW 2340, Australia]; *b* 1978; *m* 6 Oct 1996 *Christopher Maxwell Crocket and has:
1f *Elijah Valentine; *b* 20 Aug 1997
2e *Tonya Carla; *b* 1982

3e *Rachel Marie; *b* 1984

1d (cont.) Jonathan Blake *m* 2nd 13 Jan 1990 *Valerie Anne, dau of Graeme James Boasman, of Geelong, Victoria, Australia, and by her has:

4e*Jessica Maisie; *b* 27 April 1993

5e *Lucinda Anne; *b* 14 Feb 1997

2d +Kerry Valentine [Kerry Blake, Carnival, Conna, Co Cork, Ireland]; *b* 21 Aug 1963; *m* 20 Aug 1988 *Ursula Susanne, dau of Hermann Josef Zieger, of Tübingen, Germany, and has:

1f *Jonathan Valentine Bruce; *b* 1 Nov 1996

1f *Catriona Elizabeth Bruce; *b* 1 Nov 1996

1d *Rosalie Julianne [Mrs Kevin Byrne, 2 Church Rd, Barford, Norfolk NR9 4AU]; *b* 8 Nov 1951; *m* June 1977 *Kevin Byrne, s of Prof Patrick S Byrne, CBE, MRCGP, of Milnthorpe, Cumbria and has:

1e *Anna Louise; *b* 1981

2e *Philippa Elizabeth; *b* 1984

2d *Noelle Claire Louise [Mrs Karl Böhm, Scart House, Castlegrove, Ring of Kerry, Ireland; *b* 23 Dec 1959; *m* 31 Dec 1991 Karlheinz Böhm, s of Bernhard Böhm, of Bad Aibling, Rosenheim, Germany, and has:

1e *Torsten Valentine Tobias; *b* 17 June 1992

1e *Andrea Visce; *b* 19 Nov 1993

1c *Elinor Joyce; *b* 1910; *m* 4 Oct 1933 *Cyril Hall Green, s of George Hall Green, of Wigmore Grange, Leintwardine, Salop, and has issue:

1d *Jeremy Dominic Blake [Jeremy Green Esq, Ballyvolane House, Ballyvolane, Castlelyons, Co Cork, Ireland]; *b* 28 Aug 1934; *educ* Harrow; *m* 24 April 1965 *Gabriel Meredith, only dau of Ian James Wishaw Benson, of Carrigane Lodge, Ballyduff, Co Waterford, and has issue:

1e *Justin Toby; *b* 12 Jan 1969

2e *Sebastian Dominic; *b* 30 April 1971

3e *Adam Matthew; *b* 28 March 1973

1d *Celia Elinor Vadyn; *b* 7 Feb 1936; *m* 2 June 1958 *Edward John Mansel Hugh Frampton Child-Villiers, er s of Hon Edward Mansel Child-Villiers (*see* JERSEY, E), and has issue

2c *Patricia Honora; *b* 2 June 1919; *m* 1st 1942 (*divorce* 1951) Samuel Francis Hewitt-Haughton, MB, BCh; *m* 2nd 8 June 1957 Joseph Gerald Caulfeild Kirby-Turner (*d* 29 Dec 1961), er s of Lloyd Caulfeild Kirby-Turner (*see* KILMAINE, B), and has issue:

1d *Belinda Shiralee Anne; *b* 29 Jan 1959; *m* 1990 *Jehanbaz Ali Khan

2d *Sharon Briar Rose; *b* 29 Dec 1960; *m* 1987 *David Andrew Wallace, 2nd s of Bruce Wallace, of Fruitlawn, Abbeyleix, Co Laois, and has issue:

1e *Timothy Caulfeild Daniel; *b* 1991

1e *Victoria Kirby; *b* 1989

1b Gwendoline Bruce; *m* her kinsman Robert Campbell Grey and *d* 31 Dec 1934

3a John Bruce; *b* 1852; *d* unm 1880

1a Mary Selina; *d* 1922

2a Elizabeth Campbell; *d* 1921

3a Rose Georgina; *m* 1880 Charles Blake, of Tuam, and had issue

3 Walter, Brig; *m* 1st 1794 Letitia, widow of Henry Bingham (*see* CLANMORRIS, B) and dau of Denis Daly, of Raford; *m* 2nd Martha, dau of John Kirwan

Sir WALTER *d* 14 April 1802 (on the same day as his wife); his eldest son,

Sir John Blake, 11th Bt; *b* 15 July 1753; *m* 1st 12 May 1779 his cousin Eleanor (*d* 1795), dau of Edward Lynch, and had issue:

1 VALENTINE JOHN (Sir), **12th Bt**

1 Barbara; *m* 1804 Thomas Turner, of Hales Hall, Staffs, and had issue

Sir John *m* 2nd 20 Oct Rose, dau of Edward Brice, of Kilroot, Co Antrim, by Hon Theodora, dau of 1st Baron Ventry (*qv*), and by her had another s and three other daus

Sir JOHN *d* 1834; his elder son,

Sir John Valentine Blake, 12th Bt, MP Galway 1812–20 and 1841–47; *b* 23 June 1780; *m* 1st 8 Aug 1803 Eliza (*d* 8 May 1836), est dau of Joseph Donelan, of Killagh, and had issue, with three daus (*d* unm):

1 THOMAS (Sir), **13th Bt**

2 John Francis; *b* 14 April 1809; *m* 21 Dec 1835 Frances (*d* 30 Sept 1868), 2nd dau of Bernard Mullins, of Ballyeigan, King's County (now Co Offaly), and *d* 9 July 1888, leaving issue:

(1) Bernard Valentine; *b* 24 Sept 1841; *m* 1868 Harriett, widow of Major Paul, and *d* 1875, leaving issue:

1a Bernard; *b* 1872

1a Elizabeth; *d* unm 1898

Sir John *m* 2nd 8 April 1843 Julia Sophia (*m* 2nd 10 Oct 1850 John Cuxson, yst s of John Cuxson, of Shifnal, Salop, and *d* 11 March 1883), dau of Robert MacDonnell, MD, and n of Rev Richard MacDonnell, DD, Provost Trin Coll Dublin, and by her had issue:

3 Valentine Charles; *b* 6 July 1844; *m* 1871 Isabella (*d* Aug 1882), dau of Rev John Dill, of Clonmel, Co Tipperary, and had issue:

(1) Valentine; *b* 6 Feb 1874; *d* unm

(1) Elizabeth

Sir VALENTINE *d* Jan 1847; his eldest son,

Sir Thomas Blake, 13th Bt; *b* 25 May 1805; *m* 29 May 1830 Letitia Maria (*d* 18 Jan 1879), only dau and heiress of Ulick O'Brien, of Waterview, Co Galway, and had issue:

1 VALENTINE (Sir), **14th Bt**

1 Louisa; *m* 1st 27 Oct 1862 Thomas Ulick Burke (*d* 1867), of Smythesdale, Victoria; *m* 2nd 1872 John King

2 Eliza Maria; *m* 4 June 1879 Thomas von Donop-Hardinge, late Madras Civil Service

Sir THOMAS *d* 2 Jan 1875; his only son,

Sir Valentine Blake, 14th Bt, of Menlough Castle, JP Co Galway, High Sheriff 1872; *b* 2 Dec 1836; *m* 25 June 1864 Camilla Eugenia (*d* 4 March 1929), yst dau of Harvey Combe, late Madras CS, and had issue:

1 THOMAS PATRICK ULICK JOHN HARVEY (Sir), **15th Bt**

2 Valentine Joseph; *b* 22 March 1871; *d* 6 Sept 1889

3 James Herbert; *b* 9 May 1874; *d* unm 1 Aug 1904

1 Eleanor Camilla Eliza; *b* 30 May 1865; *d* unm 26 July 1910

2 Florence Anne; *b* 10 Aug 1866; *m* 3 June 1896 Capt Norton Clowes Castle (*d c* 1930), Roy Irish Regt, est s of Charles Castle, DL, of Hawford, Worcester, and *d* 15 July 1899

3 Maude Julia; *b* 30 April 1868; *m* 6 June 1901 Maj Frederick Sheward Cartwright, JP, 4th Bn Connaught Rangers (*d* 12 Dec 1942), est surv s of William George Cartwright, JP, of Springfield, Newport, Mon, and Fairwater, Glam, and *d* 26 June 1939, having had issue

Sir VALENTINE *d* 24 July 1912; his eldest son,

Sir Thomas Patrick Ulick John Harvey Blake, 15th Bt, Capt RGA, JP Co Galway; *b* 18 March 1870; *m* 8 July 1903 Evelyn Winifred (*d* 15 Nov 1959), yst dau of Lewes Gower Stewart, RE, and *d* 15 Dec 1925, leaving:

Sir Ulick Temple Blake, 16th Bt; *educ* Wellington, 2nd Lt 4th/7th Dragoon Gds, Lt RA, served WW II; *b* 6 Aug 1904; *m* 23 Oct 1940 (*divorce* 1950) Betty, 2nd dau of Arthur Gordon, of Blundellsands, Lancs, and *d* 5 Oct 1963, leaving issue:

1 Sir THOMAS RICHARD VALENTINE BLAKE, **17th and present Bt**

BLAKE, Bt, of Tillmouth

Arms: Per chevron arg. and sa. a chevron per chevron between in chief two garbs and in base a fret, all counterchanged.
Crest: A morion ppr., thereon a martlet arg., holding in the beak a sprig of barley sa. **Motto:** *Resurgam* ('I shall rise again').
Creation: Bt. (UK) 22 July 1907.

SIR (FRANCIS) MICHAEL BLAKE, 3RD BT, of Tillmouth Park, Cornhill-on-Tweed, Co Northumberland [Sir Michael Blake Bt, The Dower House, Tillmouth Park, Cornhill-on-Tweed, Northumberland TD12 4UR]; *b* 11 July 1943; *s f* 1950; *educ* Rugby; *m* 6 July 1968 *Joan Ashbridge, only dau of Frederic Cecil Ashbridge Miller, of Ramsay Lodge, Kelso, and has issue:

1 +FRANCIS JULIAN; *b* 17 Feb 1971; *educ* Aysgarth Sch and Harrow

2 +Nicholas Winston; *b* 30 Dec 1974; *educ* Aysgarth Sch and Harrow

Lineage: FRANCIS BLAKE, of Tillmouth Park, Northumberland, Capt Northumberland Light Infantry Militia; *b* 1832, *s* to that estate by devise of Sir Francis Blake, 3rd and last Bt, of Twisel, who *dspl* 10 Sept 1860. Mr Blake *m* 21 June 1853 Mary, 2nd dau of Rev Roddam Douglas, of Thorganby, perpetual curate Trimdon, Co Durham, and *d* 1861, leaving issue:

1 FRANCIS DOUGLAS (Sir), **1st Bt**

2 Arthur Roddam Frederick; *b* 21 Dec 1860; *m* 24 Sept 1900 Annie Moreton (*d* 14 July 1964), dau of Rev E Shortt, vicar Woodhorn, and *d* 22 Sept 1933

1 Mary *b* 1854; *d* 1926

The elder son,

Sir Francis Douglas Blake, 1st Bt (UK), *so cr* 22 July 1907, CB (1919), JP, DL, chm: Northumberland CC, QS and TAA, V-Lt Northumberland 1920 and 1931; *educ* Univ Coll Oxford (BA); barrister Inner Temple, hon Col Tynemouth Heavy Bde RA (TA), Lt-Col and Hon Col cmdg Northumberland RGA (Militia), MP (Coalition Lib) Berwick 1916–22; *b* 27 Feb 1856; *m* 14 Dec 1886 Selina Colquhoun (*d* 12 Sept 1915), dau of James Cleland Burns, of Glenlee, Hamilton, and had issue:

1 FRANCIS EDWARD COLQUHOUN (Sir), **2nd Bt**

2 Patrick Delaval; *b* 27 March 1904; *educ* Marlborough and Univ Coll Oxford; *m* 1st 1 Sept 1927 (*divorce* 1944) Phyllis, dau of William Lee Ellison, of Vicars Cross, Chester, and had issue:

(1) +Ian Francis, Lt-Cdr RN [Lt-Cdr Ian Blake RN (ret), Nibelungengasse 1, A–1010 Vienna, Austria]; *b* 18 Aug 1929; *m* 1st 12 June 1954 (*divorce* 1977) Frances Jillian, dau of William Thomas Barton, of Shepherds Hurst, Out-

wood, Surrey; *m* 2nd 1979 *Elisabeth Maria Aloisia Theresa, dau of Prof Dr Gustav Ortner, of Vienna, and has issue by his 1st w:

1a +Philip Ian; *b* 31 March 1955; *m* 1986 *Rebecca, dau of Rev Bernard Marshall

1a *Carol Patricia; *b* 15 March 1957; *m* 1st 1980 (*divorce* 1982) Clive Richardson; *m* 2nd 19– *Hugh Campbell and by him has issue:

1b *Emma Mary Scott; *b* 1987

2b *Charlotte Fiona; *b* 1989

3b *Sarah Victoria; *b* 1992

(1) *Mary Douglas [Mrs Peter Branson, Oaklands Cottage, Wray Common, Reigate, Surrey]; *b* 29 June 1931; *m* 1965 *Dr Peter Branson and has 2 adopted children:

*Adam Robert; *b* 1969

*Sara Jane; *b* 1972

2 (cont.) Patrick Blake *m* 2nd 24 Aug 1944 *Ruby Hilda, formerly w of Alexander Holdsworth and dau of Arthur Pearson Crosland, of Huddersfield (she *m* 3rd 1973 W E Sweet, of 18 Spencer Close, Warsash, Southampton, Hants), and *d* 14 March 1961

1 Kathleen Selina Douglas; *b* 4 April 1888; *m* 14 Sept 1910 Maj George Henry Ivar Grey, JP, of Milfield, Northumberland, 2nd s of George Grey, JP, of Milfield, and *d* 11 Oct 1958, leaving issue. He *d* 7 Oct 1943

2 Marjory Frances; *b* 5 Jan 1890; *m* 1st 6 June 1917 Capt R N F Mills, RFC (*ka* 21 Sept 1917), s of Robert Fenwick Mills, of Tapton Grove, Derbys; *m* 2nd 24 Dec 1921 Maj Alfred Davis Welch, RMLI (*d* 21 May 1960), yr s of Col William Davis Welch, RMA

Sir FRANCIS *d* 5 Feb 1940; his er son,

Sir (Francis) Edward Colquhoun Blake, 2nd Bt; Capt Northumberland Hus; *b* 11 Aug 1893; served WWs I and II; *m* 1st 16 Feb 1924 Olive Mary (*k* in a car crash 23 Oct 1946), only dau of Charles Liddell Simpson, of Whiteside, Dunscore, Dumfriesshire, and had issue:

1 Sir FRANCIS MICHAEL BLAKE, **3rd and present Bt**

1 Pamela, served WRNS 1943–45; *b* 1925; *m* 1st 24 April 1944 (*divorce* 1947) Lt Richard Oliver Hosking, RNR, est s of Wilfred Hosking, of Yealmpton, S Devon; *m* 2nd 29 Nov 1947 Capt David Clayhills-Henderson, late KOSB, only s of Beckett Clayhills-Henderson, JP, of Invergowrie, Angus, Hallyards, Perthshire, and Loan End, Alnwick, Northumberland, and *d* Nov 1990, leaving:

(1) *Edward James; *b* 25 July 1952; *educ* Aysgarth Sch and Gordonstoun; *m* 1981 *Pamela Bradshaw and has:

1a *Gemma; *b* Sept 1984

2a *Christina; *b* July 1986

(2) *Christopher David; *b* 13 Dec 1963; *m* 19– *Pamela Bradshaw and has:

1a *Alexander; *b* Sept 1994

1a *Helena; *b* March 1997

(1) *Deborah; *b* 20 Sept 1948; *m* 1971 *Stephen Perepeczko Churchill and has:

1a *Jonathan; *b* Jan 1976

1a *Nicola; *b* March 1974

2a *Bryony; *b* June 1981

(2) *Joanna; *b* 1 Nov 1949; *m* 1975 *Anthony James Tweeddale Willoughby and has issue:

1a *James Lucas; *b* July 1978

2a *Nicholas; *b* Jan 1982

1a *Rachel Joanna; *b* June 1976

(3) *Olive; *b* 19 Jan 1954; *m* 1976 (*divorce* 1994) Edward Perepeczko, of Zimbabwe and has:

1a *Andrew; *b* May 1981

2a *Timothy; *b* Dec 1986

1a *Claire; *b* Sept 1979

(4) *Dinah; *b* 24 June 1960; *m* 19– *John Bentley and has:

1a *Edward; *b* Jan 1984

2a *William; *b* Aug 1985

Sir Edward *m* 2nd 4 Nov 1947 *Doreen Maud [Mrs John Grey, Oxendean Burn, Cornhill-on-Tweed, Northumberland TD12 4UW] (who *m* 2nd 24 July 1961 W/Cdr John Francis Grey, DSO, DFC, RAF (*d* 21 March 1964), er s of Maj George Henry Ivar Grey, JP, of Milfield, Northumberland, by his w Kathleen Selina Douglas, er dau of Col Sir Francis Douglas Blake, 1st Bt (*see above*)), yr dau of James Bertram Sample, of Stoneleigh, Elvaston Rd, Hexham-on-Tyne, and *d* 24 Nov 1950, leaving by her further issue:

2 *Caroline Anne Honey [Mrs Caroline Simonds, 31 Lauder Rd, Edinburgh EH9 2JG]; *b* 6 Oct 1948; *m* 1975 Adam Henville Simonds (*d* 1989) and has issue:

(1) *Alasdair David Henville; *b* 1977

(1) *Kim Shona; *b* 1980

BLAKENHAM

Arms: Gules, two bars and a chief indented or. **Crest:** A demi-lion rampant argent, ducally gorged or. **Supporters:** Dexter, a dragon ermine armed and langued gules; sinister, a Guernsey cow proper. **Motto:** *Odi profanum* ('I hate the profane'). **Creation:** V. (UK) 8 Nov 1963.

THE 2ND VISCOUNT BLAKENHAM, of Little Blakenham, Co Suffolk (Michael John Hare) [The Rt Hon The Viscount Blakenham, 12 St James's Sq, London SW1X 4LB]; *b* 25 Jan 1938; *s* f 1982; *educ* Eton and Harvard (AB Econ); late 2nd Lt Life Gds, chm S Pearson 1983–97 (ch exec 1978–90, joined 1977), chm MEPC 1993– (dir 1990–), ptnr Lazard Ptnrs 1984–, dir: Lazard Bros 1975–97, Sothebys Hldgs 1987–, UK-Japan 2000 Gp 1990–, chm Financial Times 1983–93, chm RSPB 1981–86 (v-pres 1986–), pres Sussex Wildlife Tst 1983–; *m* 12 Jan 1965 his cousin *Marcia Persephone, only dau of Maj Hon Alan Victor Hare, MC (*see* LISTOWEL, E), and has issue:

1 +CASPAR JOHN; *b* 8 April 1972

1 *Cressida; *b* 15 April 1966; commercial artist

2 *Emily; *b* 24 July 1967; commercial artist

Lineage: JOHN HUGH HARE, **1st Viscount Blakenham**, of Little Blakenham, Co Suffolk (UK), so *cr* 8 Nov 1963, OBE (1945, MBE 1943), PC (1955), DL (1968); *b* 22 Jan 1911, 3rd s of 4th Earl of Listowel (*qv*); *educ* Eton; Alderman LCC 1937–52, chm London Municipal Soc 1947–52, V-Chm Conservative Party 1952–55, Min State Colonial Affrs 1955–56, Sec State War 1956–58, Min: Ag Jan 1958–July 1960 and Labour 1960–63, Chllr Duchy Lancaster and Dep Ldr Ho of Lords 1963–64, Chm Conservative Party 1963–65, MP (C) Woodbridge 1945–Feb 1950 and Sudbury and Woodbridge Feb 1950–63, served Suffolk Yeo WW II (despatches), chm Cncl Toynbee Hall 1966–82, chm Peabody Donation Fund 1967–82, treas RHS 1971–82 (Victoria Medal Honour 1974), US Legion of Merit; *m* 31 Jan 1934 Hon (Beryl) Nancy Pearson (*d* 2 Nov 1994), 2nd dau of 2nd Viscount Cowdray (*qv*), and *d* 7 March 1982, leaving issue:

1 MICHAEL JOHN, **2nd and present Viscount**

1 *Mary Anne [The Hon Mrs Sergison-Brooke, Chipping Warden Manor, nr Banbury, Oxon]; *b* 9 April 1936; *m* 12 Nov 1964 *Timothy Mark Sergison-Brooke, only s of Sir Bertram Norman Sergison-Brooke, KCB, KCVO, CMG, DSO (*see* BROOKEBOROUGH, V), and has issue

2 *Joanna Freda [The Hon Mrs Breyer, 12 Dunstable Rd, Cambridge, Mass, USA]; *b* 27 July 1942; *m* 4 Sept 1967 *Judge Stephen Breyer, er s of Irving Breyer, of San Francisco

BLAKER, Baron

Arms: Per pale argent and or, on a chevron sable between three martlets volant azure each holding in the beak a rose slipped gules seeded or, two Blackamoor heads couped argent the ears ringed or between three ermine spots argent. **Crest:** A horse's head sable, maned or, bridled argent, reined ermine. **Supporters:** Dexter, a wildcat guardant or; sinister a Chinese Dragon also or. **Motto:** *Esto quod esse videris* ('Be what you seem to be'). **Creation:** B. (LP, UK) 20 Aug 1994.

THE BARON BLAKER, of Blackpool, Co Lancaster and of Lindfield, Co W Sussex (Sir Peter Allan Renshaw Blaker, KCMG (1983), PC (1983)) [The Rt Hon The Lord Blaker KCMG PC, House of Lords, London SW1A 0PW]; *b* 4 Oct 1922; *educ* Shrewsbury, Trin Coll Toronto and New Coll Oxford (Pres Union); Capt Argyll and Sutherland Highrs WW II (wounded), slr 1948, barrister 1952, Dip Serv 1953–64 (Cambodia 1955–57, Canada 1957–60, FO 1960–62, Priv Sec to Min State For Affrs 1962–64), MP (C) Blackpool S 1964–92, Oppn Whip 1966–67, PPS to Chllr Exchequer 1970–72, Parly U-Sec MOD 1972–74, FCO 1974, Min State FCO 1979–81, MOD 1981–83, memb: Intell and Security Ctee 1996–, Cncl for Arms Control 1983–, Freedom Assoc 1984–, V-Pres C For and Cwlth Cncl 1983–, Cncl Britain-Russia Centre 1974–79 and 1992– (V-Chm 1989–92); *m* 1953 *Jennifer, dau of Sir Pierson Dixon, GCMG, CB, and has a s and two daus

Lineage: CEDRIC BLAKER, CBE, MC; had:

PETER ALLAN RENSHAW, *cr* a **Baron**

BLAKER, Bt

Arms: Erm. three chevronels, and in chief two towers sa. **Crest:** A horse's head sa., charged with three chevronels arg. **Creation:** Bt. (UK) 5 Sept 1919.

SIR JOHN BLAKER, 3RD BT, of Brighton, Sussex [Sir John Blaker Bt, Stantons Farm, E Chiltington, E Sussex BN7 3BB]; *b* 22 March 1935; *s* f 1975; *m* 1st 3 Sept 1960 (*divorce* 1965) Catherine Ann, only dau of Francis John Anselon Thorold, of Tye Farm, Hartfield, Sussex (*see* THOROLD, Bt); *m* 2nd 24 Nov 1968 *Elizabeth Katherine, dau of Col John Tinsley Russell, DSO, of New Zealand

Lineage: JOHN BLAKER, of Church St, Brighton, Sussex; *m* 15 May 1830 Frances Stevens (*d* 1 Dec 1882), and *d* 15 Aug 1856 leaving:

JOHN GEORGE BLAKER, of St James's Terrace, Burgess Hill, Sussex; *b* 9 Aug 1833; *m* 13 Dec 1853 Margaret (*d* 19 June 1919), dau of Henry Cocks, of Sandgate, Kent, and had:

Sir John George Blaker, 1st Bt (UK), so *cr* 5 Sept 1919, OBE (1918), JP (Sussex); *b* 15 Oct 1854; Mayor Brighton 1895–98, Ch Mil Rep Brighton Area WW I, ktd 1897; *m* 16 Sept 1890 Eliza (*m* 2nd 3 Jan 1928 Arthur David Cutts; *d* 1 Oct 1945), dau of Samuel Cowell, of Brighton, and had issue:

1 REGINALD (Sir), **2nd Bt**

1 Jessie; *b* 29 May 1891; *m* 12 July 1921 Arthur Newington, s of George Newington

Sir JOHN *d* 11 June 1926; his son,

Sir Reginald Blaker, 2nd Bt, TD (1942); *educ* Charterhouse; Maj RA (TA), Coldstream Gds SR, barrister Inner Temple 1921, MP Spelthorne Middx 1931–45; *b* 27 April 1900; *m* 4 Nov 1930 *Sheila Kellas [Sheila Lady Blaker, 5 Oak Bank, Lindfield, Sussex], 3rd dau of Dr Alexander Cran, of Little Court, Merrow, nr Guildford, and *d* Jan 1975, having had issue:

1 Sir JOHN BLAKER, **3rd and present Bt**

1 *Anne [Mrs Edmund Crosby-Cockburn, Glebe Farm, Shuckburgh, Daventry, Northants]; *b* 29 Feb 1932; *m* 26 Aug 1953 *Edmund Crosby-Cockburn, son of Samuel Crosby-Cockburn, of Budbrook Lodge, Warwick, and has issue:

(1) *Bay Crosby *b* 18 May 1956

(2) *Kim Crosby; *b* 7 May 1958

(1) *Georgina Gay; *b* 11 April 1954

BLAKISTON

Arms: Arg. two bars gu., in chief three cocks of the last. **Crest:** A cock gu. **Motto:** Doe well and doubt not. **Creation:** Bt. (GB) 22 April 1763.

SIR FERGUSON ARTHUR JAMES BLAKISTON, 9TH BT, of London [Sir Ferguson Blakiston Bt, Cortington, 8 Waimi Terr, Geraldine, New Zealand]; *b* 19 Feb 1963; *s* f 1977; *educ* Lincoln Coll NZ (Dip Ag 1983), Auckland Inst Technology (Cert Mktg 1993); entrepreneur and writer; *m* 1993 *Linda Jane, dau of Robert John Key, farmer, of Queenstown, NZ

Lineage: This is a branch of the Blakistons of Blakiston, Co Durham. Two other Blakiston baronetcies existed (both E): 1615–30 and 1642–1713.

JOHN BLAKISTON, of Blakiston; *d* 1587; f of:

ROBERT BLAKISTON, of Durham; *d* 1637; f of:

GEORGE BLAKISTON, of Houghall, Co Durham, and Stapleton-on-Tees, Yorks; *b* 1633; *m* 1654 Mary, 6th dau of Sir John Bourchier, of Bendingborough, MP Ripon 1641, and had, with other issue (*dsp*):

1 Bourchier; *b* 1667; *d* 1709, leaving:

(1) Bourchier, *k* 1718 aboard HMS *Devonshire*

2 GEORGE BLAKISTON, of London; *bapt* 10 June 1675; *m* Elizabeth, dau of Matthew Kay, London merchant, and had (with a yr s George, *d* 1764):

(1) **Sir Matthew Blakiston, 1st Bt** (GB), so *cr* 22 April 1763; *b* 1702; City London: Alderman 1750, Sheriff 1753, Ld Mayor 1760, ktd 1759; *m* 1st Margaret, dau of Rev Charles Hall, of E Harsley, Yorks, and had:

1a Charles George; *d* unm 1758

(1) (cont.) **Sir Matthew** *m* 2nd Mrs Mary Blew, of Chelsea (*d* 8 Jan 1754); *m* 3rd 1760 Annabella, dau of Thomas Bayly, MP Derby, by Bridget (*m* 2nd 1776 Lt-Col Hugh Cane; *d* 1807), dau of Sir W Dixie, Bt (*see* 1970 edn), and *d* 1774, having by her had:

2a MATTHEW (Sir), **2nd Bt**

3a Charles; *b* 1762; *d* in infancy

The only surv son,

Sir Matthew Blakiston, 2nd Bt; *b* 6 July 1761; *m* Sept 1782 Anne (*d* 27 Nov 1862 in her 101st year), dau of John Rochfort, of Clogrenane, Co Carlow, and had, with other issue:

1 MATTHEW (Sir), **3rd Bt**

2 John, of Mobberley Hall, Cheshire, Maj 27th Regt; *b* 8 Feb 1785; *m* 26 Sept 1814 Jane (*d* 21 June 1874), dau of Rev Thomas Wright, Rector Market Bosworth, Leics, and *d* 4 June 1867, having had issue:

(1) Matthew, BA London, MICE; *b* 13 Jan 1821; *m* 26 Sept 1848 Anne (*d* 9 June 1917), dau of Richard Bayly Blakiston-Houston, of Orangefield (*see* below), and *dsp* 19 April 1907

(2) Thomas Wright, FRGS, FZS, Capt RA; *b* 27 Dec 1832; *m* 1885 Ann Mary (*d* 17 March 1937), dau of James Dunn, of Dundaff, Ohio, and *d* 15 Oct 1891, leaving issue:

1a Lawrence Wright, Capt lst Norfolk Regt; *b* 21 Jan 1889; *m* 1st 11 March 1918 Ileene (*d* 19 Oct 1918), dau of Edwin James Kelly, of Gungapore, Rajputana; *m* 2nd 28 April 1921 Marion (*d* 27 Dec 1958), dau of Thomas Edward Deacon, of London, and *dsp* 18 March 1947

1a Jessie Carmichael; *m* 4 April 1914 Francis Joseph O'Reilly, est s of Peter O'Reilly, of Point Ellice, Victoria, BC, and *d* 20 Feb 1963, leaving issue. He *d* 1941

(3) Lawrence, Lt 62nd Regt; *b* Oct 1834; *k* Sebastopol 8 Sept 1855

(4) John Rochfort; *b* 9 April 1840; *m* 14 Sept 1876 Georgina Helen (*d* 30 April 1928), dau of Rev Francis William Cubitt, Rector Fritton, and *d* 2 April 1921, leaving issue:

1a John Francis, CIE (1937); *b* 21 March 1882; *educ* Wellington; Dir-Gen Archaeological Survey India 1934–37, Capt Cav IARO, Maj HG WW II; *m* 1st 2 May 1918 (*divorce* 1930) Paula, dau of Edwin Allen Howard; barrister; *m* 2nd 20 July 1937 Margaret Dora (*d* 1991), er dau of Rev George Alan Ward-Jackson, Rector Rousham with Lower Heyford, Oxon, and *d* 8 Jan 1965, leaving by her:

1b +John Alan Cubitt [Lt-Col John Blakiston, Grove House, Lydiard Millicent, Wilts SN5 9LP]; *b* 15 July 1938; *educ* Wellington; Lt-Col 13th/18th R Hus; *m* 1975 *Sally Ann, dau of Lt-Col John David Logan Dickson, MC, RHA (*see* WESTMORLAND, E), and has issue:

1c +John William Matthew; *b* 1982

1c *Caroline Mary; *b* 1979

2c *Emma Elizabeth; *b* 1981

1b *Susan Anne Margaret; *b* 18 May 1940

2b *Jane Mary Dora Helen; *b* 28 Feb 1944; *m* 1st 2 March 1968 (*divorce* 1978) Richard Parker, s of Robert Parker, of Broadhempston, Devon; *m* 2nd 1991 *Edward Peter Jonathan Darmady and has by 1st husb:

1c *Nycolas Sebastian Robert Blakiston; *b* 1970

1c *Venetia Clare Rosalind; *b* 1969

1a Margaret

2a Catherine; *d* unm 11 Jan 1970 aged 83

3a Mary Helen; *m* 30 June 1921 Charles Summer Durst, OBE, and had issue. He *d* 1961

(1) Eleanor Frances; *d* unm 1 Aug 1879

(2) Mary; *d* unm 11 Jan 1895

(3) Dorothea; *d* unm 9 Nov 1911

3 Richard Bayly BLAKISTON later BLAKISTON-HOUSTON (roy licence 1843), of Orangefield and Roddens, Co Down; *b* 13 May 1793; *m* 11 July 1827 Mary Isabella (*d* 4 Nov 1873), dau of John Holmes Houston, of Orangefield, Co Down, and *d* 21 July 1857, having had, with other issue:

(1) John, of Orangefield, JP, V-Lt Co Down (previously DL), High Sheriff 1860, MP N Down 1898–1900; *b* 11 Sept 1829; *m* 16 Nov 1859 Marian Gertrude (*d* 8 Feb 1890), yr dau of Richard Shuttleworth Streatfeild, DL, JP, of The Rocks, Sussex, and *d* 27 Feb 1920, leaving issue:

1a Richard, of Orangefield and Roddens, DL and JP, High Sheriff 1922, late Capt Rifle Bde (Prince Consort's Own), Capt 5th Bn Roy Irish Rifles; *b* 8 Feb 1864; *m* 24 Feb 1897 Lilian Agnes (*d* 25 Jan 1952), dau of George Jardine Kidston, of Finlaystone, Renfrewshire, and *d* 21 May 1933, leaving issue:

1b John Matthew, DL (Co Down 1946); *b* 31 Aug 1898; *educ* Eton and RMC Sandhurst; High Sheriff Co Down 1944 and Co Tyrone 1954, Lt-Col 11th Hus, Capt Tank Corps WW I, Capt 11th Hus 1924, ADC to Govr-Gen and C-in-C Australia 1929–30, cmdg S Rhodesia Armoured Car Regt WW II; *m* 2 July 1931 Lettice Arden (*d* 1982), 3rd dau of Henry Gervas (Harry) Stobart, of Thornton Hall, Thornton-le-Dale, Yorks, and *d* 1984, having had issue:

1c +Richard Patrick, JP and DL (Co Down) [Richard Blakiston-Houston Esq JP DL, Beltrim Castle, Gortin, Omagh, Co Tyrone; Roddens, Ballywater, Co Down]; *b* 25 July 1948; *educ* Eton and RAC Cirencester; ARICS 1972; High Sheriff 1989; *m* 1988 *Lucinda Mary Lavinia, dau of Lt Cdr Theodore Bernard Peregrine Hubbard, RN, of Thurston Croft, Thurston, Bury St Edmunds, Suffolk (*see* NORFOLK, D), and has issue:

1d +Jack Peregrine; *b* 1989

2d +Christopher George; *b* 1991

3d +Harry Charles; *b* 7 Sept 1996

1d *Leticia Sadhbh Miriam; *b* 1993

2d *Felicia Grace Miriam; *b* 14 Aug 1994

1c *Mary Bridget [Mrs Gavin Rowan-Hamilton, The Horse Mill, Stenton, Dunbar, E Lothian]; *b* 8 Aug 1932; *m* 4 Sept 1956 *Gavin Rowan-Hamilton, 2nd s of Brig Gawain Basil Rowan-Hamilton, DSO, MC, of Killyleagh Castle, Co Down, and has issue:

1d *James (Hamish) John; *b* 5 May 1961; *m* 1990 *Venetia E, dau of John Carter, of Steel, Northumberland, and has issue:

1e *Frederick John; *b* 8 Sept 1993

2e *Tamara Mary Ann; *b* 17 Aug 1995

2d *Patrick Gawaine; *b* 1 Feb 1964

1d *Catherine Nicola Blanche; *b* 2 Aug 1957; *m* 1987 *Bartholomew Evan Eric Smith and has issue (*see* NORTHESK, E)

2c *Anne [Lady Hallifax, The Brew House, Englefield, Berks RG7 5EN]; *b* 8 Jan 1934; *m* 8 Dec 1962 Adml Sir David John Hallifax, KCB, KCVO, KBE (*see* HUGHES, Bt) (*d* 1992), only s of V-Adml Ronald Hamilton Curzon Hallifax, CB, CBE, of Longcroft, Shedfield, Hants, and has issue:

1d *Thomas Ronald; *b* 19 Sept 1965

2d Matthew William Hughes; *b* 17 Sept 1967; *educ* Edinburgh U; drowned in a boating accident 1989

1d *Louisa Kate; *b* 22 May 1964; *m* 1993 *Hugo Roderick Charles Burnand, s of Peter Vere Burnand, and has:

1e *Fergus Matthew Christian; *b* 2 Oct 1994

2e *Lily Susan Hallifax; *b* 9 March 1996

3c *Prudence [Mrs John Douglas-Menzies, Mounteagle, Fearn, Ross-shire]; *b* 27 July 1936; *m* 14 Nov 1964 *John Archibald Douglas-Menzies, 3rd s of Norman Edward Douglas-Menzies, of Newtownairds, Dumfries, and Mrs Vere Dashwood, of The Clachan, Newtonairds, Dumfries (*see* DASHWOOD, Bt, of Kirtlington Park), and has:

1d *John William; *b* 25 June 1966

2d *Andrew Edward; *b* 15 Feb 1968

3d *James; *b* 1970

4c *Elizabeth [Mrs Michael Haines, 82A Mortimer Rd, London N1 4LH]; *b* 31 Dec 1939; *m* 21 Dec 1973 *Michael Geoffrey Minton Haines, er s of G F M Haines, and has issue:

1d *Francis Christopher Minton; *b* 1975

2d *Richard Walter Minton; *b* 1977

1d *Rosalind Marion Minton; *b* 1979

5c *Patience Victoria [Mrs Ron Long, Twiglees, Boreland, Dumfries-shire]; *b* 9 Aug 1944; *m* 1979 *Ron Long and has issue:

1d *Joshua; *b* 1975

2d *Daniel; *b* 1977

2b George, 2nd Lt Irish Gds; *b* 17 May 1900; *d* unm 1 Aug 1925

1b Marian, OBE (1952), CStJ; *b* 26 Nov 1905; *m* 10 Aug 1929 Gen Sir Gordon Holmes Alexander MacMillan of MacMillan and Knap, KCB, KCVO, CBE, DSO, MC, DL, Hon LLD (Glasgow), KStJ, Argyll and Sutherland Highrs, only s of Dugald Alexander MacMillan, of Farnham, Surrey, and *d* 29 April 1991, having had issue:

1c *George MacMillan of MacMillan [George MacMillan of MacMillan and Knap, Finlaystone, Langbank, Renfrewshire PA14 6TJ]; *b* 20 June 1930; *educ* Eton and Trin Coll Cambridge (BA 1953, MA 1956); *m* 2 Sept 1961 *Cecilia Jane, only dau of Capt Arthur R Spurgin, IA, and has issue:

1d *Arthur Gordon; *b* 29 July 1962

2d Richard Anthony; *b* 30 Dec 1963; *d* 1984

3d *Malcolm James; *b* 30 June 1967; *m* 20 April 1996 *Amanda Taylor

2c *John Richard Alexander, KCB (1988), CBE (1978, OBE 1973) [Lt-Gen Sir John MacMillan KCB CBE, c/o Northern Bank, 9 Donegall Sq North, Belfast BT1 5GJ]; *b* 8 Feb 1932; *educ* Eton and Trin Coll Cambridge (BA 1953, MA 1955); Lt-Gen Argyll and Sutherland Highrs, cmded 1st Bn Gordon Highrs 1971–73, GOC E Dist 1982–84, ACGS MoD 1984–87, Col Gordon Highrs 1978–86, Col Cmdt Scottish Div 1986–91, GOC Scotland and Govr Edinburgh Castle 1988–91; fruit farmer 1991–; *m* 5 Sept 1964 *Belinda, dau of Lt-Col Richard Henry Lumley-Webb, of Tunstall House, Sittingbourne, Kent, and has issue:

1d *Gordon John; *b* 16 July 1967

1d *Elizabeth Mary; *b* 13 April 1966

3c *David [David MacMillan Esq, The White House, Finlaystone, Langbank, Renfrewshire]; *b* 15 Jan 1939; *educ* Eton; *m* 24 April 1962 *Liv Senstad, only dau of Rolf Anderson, of Oslo, and has issue:

1d *Alastair Thomas; *b* 30 July 1964; *m* 16 Sept 1989 *Alexandra Mary, dau of David John Delaforce, of Oporto, and has issue:

1e *Phoebe Alice; *b* 18 Aug 1994

2e *Freya Mary; *b* 18 July 1996

1d *Lilian Victoria; *b* 9 Aug 1968

4c *Andrew Allardice [Andrew MacMillan Esq, Via Ambrogio Traversari 80, Rome, Italy]; *b* 25 Sept 1942; *educ* Eton, Trin Coll Cambridge (BA 1964) and St Augustine U WI (PhD AgEcon 1968); *m* 19– *— and has issue:

1d *Harry Julius; *b* 5 April 1973

2d *Thomas; *b* 14 May 1977

1c *Elizabeth Judy; *b* 7 Aug 1935; *m* 16 April 1963 *Cdr John Robin Hutton, MBE, RN, 2nd s of R-Adml Reginald Maurice James Hutton, CB, CBE, DSO, of IoW, and has issue:

1d *James Rupert; *b* 1 Sept 1966; *m* 12 Feb 1994 *Penelope Alison Veronica Salvesen

1d *Alice; *b* 5 May 1964; *m* 29 Dec 1989 *Maj David John Harrison, Devon and Dorset Regt

2b Elizabeth Agnes; *b* 6 Oct 1911; *m* 31 July 1939 Lt-Col Michael Henry Colin Hughes-Young, MC, MP, Black Watch (*cr* BARON ST HELENS; *qv*), and *d* 2 Oct 1956, leaving issue

2a Thomas; *b* 12 Sept 1865; *d* unm 10 March 1919

3a Charles , DL and JP Co Down, Maj RASC WW I (despatches), MP (NI Parl) Belfast Dock 1929–33; *b* Aug 1868; *m* 27 July 1904 Norah Emily (*d* 1959), only dau of Edward Hickman Persse, of Mount Verner, Co Galway, and *d* 9 Oct 1935

4a James Edward, OBE, Maj and Brev Lt-Col 8th Hus WW I, Cdr Ulster Spec Constabulary Co Down 1936; *b* 18 Nov 1877; *m* 18 Oct 1913 Dorothy Irene (*d* 12 Nov 1962), dau of Col Frederic William Rea, 99th Inf, and *d* 27 Jan 1958, having had issue:

1b *Sheelah, Jr Cdr ATS WW II; *b* 7 March 1915; *m* 31 Jan 1942 Maj Robert Dempster Wilson, RASC (*d* 27 Jan 1957), s of Moses Wilson, of Craigavad, Co Down, and has had issue:

1c *James Dempster; *b* 19 Feb 1944; *educ* Portora Roy Sch

2c John Houston; *b* 19 Feb 1944; *d* 18 Sept 1961

2c Barbara Kathleen, Assist Section Offr WAAF WW II; *b* 24 Nov 1917; *kas* in flying accident 16 March 1942

4a John, CB (1936), DSO (1917), Maj-Gen, 3rd Bn Roy Irish Rifles 1899, tfd 11th Hus 1902, served Boer War 1899–1902, W African Frontier Force 1905–08, Adj Sussex Yeo 1911–15, served WW I (wounded, despatches), tfd 12th Roy Lancers 1923, cmdg 2 Cavalry Bde 1927–31, Brig i/c admin N Cmd 1931–34, Inspr-Gen Cav 1934, Maj-Gen 1935, ret 1938, re-employed 1939–42; *b* 18 April 1881; *m* 1st 22 Nov 1910 Louise Henrietta (*d* 11 Jan 1952), yst dau of Gustave Louis Leconte, of Port St Ouen, France; *m* 2nd 20 May 1954 Emma Millicent, dau of George Frederick Coles, of Shenington, Oxon, and *dsp* 14 Dec 1959

1a Mary Charlotte, Ldy League Mercy; *m* 6 Aug 1884 Harry Scarlett, LLB, of W Firle, Sussex, and *d* 9 Sept 1954, leaving issue. He *d* 28 Feb 1919

2a Annie Marian (Nina); *d* unm 15 May 1951

3a Dora; *m* 2 Feb 1905 AVM Francis Rowland Scarlett, CB, DSO, formerly Capt RN, 3rd s of Col William James Scarlett, of Gigha, and *d* 13 Feb 1954, leaving issue. He *d* 15 April 1934

4a Mabel; *m* 24 June 1896 George Hurst Fowler and *d* 30 Oct 1951, leaving issue. He *d* 17 April 1928

5a Isabel; *m* 5 Jan 1911 Brig-Gen David Ramsay Sladen, CMG, DSO, Lt-Col KOSB, and *d* 18 Nov 1956, leaving issue. He *d* 21 June 1923

6a Ethel Fanny; *m* 1st 20 Aug 1902 Capt James Robert Macalpine-Downie, of Appin, Argyllshire, and had issue. He *d* 21 March 1918 of wounds recd in action. She *m* 2nd 8 Jan 1929 Arthur George Florence McClintock, of Rathvinden, Co Carlow. He *d* 16 Nov 1930

7a Hilda; *m* 25 Sept 1907 Capt George James Bruce, DSO, MC, est s of Samuel Bruce, DL, of Norton Hall, Glos, and *d* 4 Nov 1936, leaving issue. He was *ka* 2 Oct 1918

4 Peyton (Rev), MA, MD, FRS, Dixie Fell Emmanuel Coll Cambridge; *b* 25 Sept 1801; *m* Aug 1825 Frances (*d* 23 Feb 1858), est dau of John Folliott Powell, 2nd s of Richard Powell, of Radnorshire, and *d* 17 Dec 1878, having had issue:

(1) John Richard, MA, Ch Inspr Schs; *b* 30 June 1829; *m* 1st 6 June 1854 Elizabeth (*dsp* Feb 1856), dau of Gen Sir Edward Nicolls; *m* 2nd 30 June 1857 Marie (*d* 7 March 1908), widow of Maj Hill, and dau of Pierre Simon, MD, FRS, and *d* 21 Sept 1917, leaving issue:

1a Ralph; *b* 1 April 1861; *m* 1st 18 April 1889 Ellen Ann Fell (*d* 25 Dec 1910), dau of Rev Robert Walker, Vicar Wymeswold, Leics, and had issue:

1b Rev Robert Ralph Christian; *b* 22 March 1890; *educ* U Coll Durham (LTh 1912, BA 1914, MA 1917); Rector Willian, Herts, vicar All Saints Newton-le-Willow, Lancs, Succentor Liverpool Cathedral 1920–24, Chaplain Sea Cadet Corps 1944; *m* 18 June 1929 Winifred Muriel (*d* 1988), yr dau of John Frost, and *d* 1983 leaving issue:

1c +John Robert [John Blakiston Esq, Wood Sorrel Cottage, Nutley, Sussex]; *b* 29 July 1931; *educ* Haileybury; *m* 6 Aug 1960 *Carol Helen, yst dau of John C Durham, of Haywards Heath, and has issue:

1d *Michéle Anne; *b* 30 June 1964

2d *Rachel Jane; *b* 8 March 1966

2b John Horace; *b* 27 June 1897; *educ* Merchant Taylors', Crosby, HMS *Conway* and Birmingham U (BSc); Lt RNR; *m* 17 Dec 1928 Winifred Kathleen Maybank (*d* 1988), dau of Archie William Webb, and *d* 1982 leaving issue:

1c +David [David Blakiston Esq, 65 Curley Hill Rd, Lightwater, Surrey GU18 5YH]; *b* 14 March 1934; *educ* Haileybury and Loughborough Coll (BSc, MIMechE, CEng); *m* 13 Oct 1962 *Joanna Averil, dau of Cecil Green, and has issue:

1d +John [John Blakiston Esq, 38 Warwards Lane, Selly Park, Birmingham B29 7RB]; *b* 30 April 1967; BCom, ACMA; ACA; *m* 12 Aug 1995 *Elizabeth Nina Edith, MB, ChB, dau of Ian Andrew Palmer

1d *Anne; *b* 1970; BA

2d *Carol Clare; *b* 1972

1b Anna Marie; *m* 14 May 1921 George Haistead Whitaker, AMICE, s of John Whitaker, MD, of Westhoughton, and had issue:

1c *Ellen Frances, actress as Elizabeth Regan; *b* 31 Dec 1933; *m* 31 May 1955 *Michael Manning Lawrence Watkins, s of C E L Watkins, of Hove, and has issue:

1d *Simon Michael; *b* 24 March 1956

2d *Stephen Benedict; *b* 4 Nov 1957

3d *Robert Francis; *b* 3 Jan 1961

1d *Mary Teresa; *b* 19 May 1964

2d *Tamsin; *b* 19 Nov 1966

1a (cont.) Ralph Blakiston *m* 2nd 1916 Rosemary (*d* 1972), dau of Edmund Gore, of Crosby, and *d* 27 Dec 1936

2a Aubrey, MFH Lamerton, Devon; *b* 26 Aug 1862; *m* 19 July 1881 Lelia Emily (*d* 4 June 1915), 2nd dau of Edmund Harris, of Rugby, and *d* 10 March 1935, leaving issue:

1b Eleanor Lelia Marie; *m* 26 Nov 1903 Anthony James Hasslacher, s of James Hasslacher, of Weybridge. He *d* 18 June 1950

2b Violet Audrey Mary

3b Dorothy Mary; *m* Newman Brown (*d* 6 June 1957) and had issue:

1c *Jack Blakiston [Jack Brown, 147 E Jackson Street, PO Box 58, Cannon Beach, Oregon 97110, USA] *b* 26 March 1919; *m* 1944 *Evelyn M Paulson and has issue:

1d *John Michael; *b* 18 May 1950

1d *Jacquelyn Marie; *b* 12 July 1948; *m* *— Martini and has issue:

1e *Dana Marte; *b* 4 Oct 1967

1c *Mary Teresa Lelia; *b* 19 March 1915; *m* 1st 1935 Frank A Mortimer; *m* 2nd 1952 *Edward H Libbey and by her 1st husb has issue:

1d *Bonnie Lynn; *b* 12 Aug 1945

2c *Frances Judith; *b* 22 March 1917; *m* 1st 1937 Thomas Adrian Sroufe; *m* 2nd 1953 *Eugene Norman Henderson and by her 1st husb has issue:

1d *Sally Anne; *b* 14 March 1942; *m* 2 Oct 1965 *Philip Cowell Webster, s of Charles S Webster, of Darien, Connecticut

2d *Carolyn Frances; *b* 27 March 1945

4b (Mary) Clare Josephine, PhD (Milan 1931); *b* 12 May 1889

3a Clarence; *b* 23 April 1864; *m* 1888 Clementine (*d* 13 Feb 1936), dau of J Lindsay, of Glasgow, and *d* 23 March 1943

1a Maud Douglas; *m* 29 July 1882 George Richard Green, MRCS, LRCP, of Portmadoc, and had issue. He *d* 1920

2a Minnie; *m* 1st 1893 Robert Ellis, s of Sir Adam Gibb Ellis, Ch Justice Jamaica, and had issue; *m* 2nd 1902 Maj Richard Francis Gunter, 3rd Bn S Wales Borderers. He *d* 1960

3a Hilda Marie; *b* 1869; *m* May 1895 Percy North Gleig, yst s of Maj H L Gleig, Bengal Staff Corps, and *d* 17 Oct 1900

(2) Peyton, Cdr RN; *b* 19 Feb 1831; *m* 1 Nov 1862 Annie (*d* 31 July 1897), 3rd dau of William Ford Bally, FRS, MD, of Bath, and *d* 20 Dec 1865, leaving issue:

1a William Graham, slr; *b* 13 Dec 1863; *m* 5 May 1909 Jessie Norton (*d* 1923), widow of Kinsley Mayoun, of New York, and dau of Gen Joseph T Torrence, of Chicago, and *d* 5 March 1919

2a Peyton, RN, Midshipman HMS *Audacious*; *b* 20 Dec 1865; accidentally shot Hong Kong 31 March 1883

1a Evelyn Frances; *d* unm 23 July 1929

(3) Douglas Yeoman (Rev), MA Cantab, Vicar E Grinstead 1871–1908; *b* 20 Nov 1832; *m* 11 July 1861 Sophia Matilda (*d* 12 May 1912), yst dau of Rev William Dent, of Crosby Hall, Yorks, and *d* 7 Sept 1914, leaving, with other issue:

1a Herbert Edward Douglas (Rev), MA, DD (Oxon), Pres Trin Coll Oxford 1907–38, V-Chllr Oxford 1917–20; *b* 5 Sept 1862

2a Charles Reginald; *b* 27 Sept 1863; accidentally shot 21 Oct 1887

3a John Lionel; *b* 24 June 1867; *k* on a relief party Mazoe, Mashonaland, 18 June 1896

4a William Peyton; *b* 14 March 1870; *d* 6 Oct 1889 following an accident at Charing Cross Station

(4) Matthew Folliott; *b* 22 Sept 1835; *m* 1st 23 Sept 1858 Elizabeth (*d* 10 Feb 1868), yst dau of John Mason, and had, with other issue:

1a Rochfort Folliott; *b* 25 Nov 1860; *educ* Oriel Coll Oxford (BA); barrister; *m* 1st 26 June 1907 Ellen Kate (*d* 29 Sept 1929), only dau of George Greenleaf; *m* 2nd 18 Dec 1930 Elizabeth Lilian Diane (*d* 1976), est dau of Rev David Jones, vicar Goodwick, Pembs, and *d* 12 June 1949, leaving by her:

1b +Digby Rochfort David [Lt Digby Blakiston RN (ret), Yet y Gors, Seleddau, Fishguard, Dyfed]; *b* 1 Dec 1931; Lt RN 1950–58; *m* 25 June 1959 *Dorothea Irene Louise Walser, WRNS, and has issue:

1c +Matthew Simon Rochfort; *b* 6 April 1964

1c *Louise [Mrs Andrew Jenkins, Gelliwernfawr, Felindre, nr Swansea]; *b* 16 May 1961; *m* 198– *Andrew P M Jenkins, yr s of Dr John Richard Everett

2c *Caroline; *b* 30 Dec 1962

2b +Michael Peyton Folliott [Michael Blakiston Esq, 90 York Mansions, Prince of Wales Drive, London SW11]; *b* 16 April 1933; *educ* Trin Coll Oxford (MA 1954); *m* 8 Sept 1973 *Mrs Fanny Marie Francis, est dau of Henri Roquette, of Lille, France

(4) (cont.) Matthew Blakiston *m* 2nd 11 April 1885 Charlotte Augusta (*d* 1896), widow of Isaac Spooner, and *d* 19 Aug 1906

1 Frances; *m* 26 April 1859 Prof Lionel Smith Beale MB, FRS, and *d* 15 Jan 1892, leaving issue. He *d* 28 March 1906

Sir MATTHEW *d* 20 Sept 1806; his est son,

Sir Matthew Blakiston, 3rd Bt; *b* 13 May 1783; *m* 12 April 1810 Lucy (*d* 29 Dec 1871), est dau of James Mann, of Linton Place, Kent, by Lucy, dau of Sir Horace Mann, Bt, and Lady Lucy Noel (*see* GAINSBOROUGH, E), and *d* 23 Dec 1862, having had, with other issue:

1 **Sir Matthew Blakiston, 4th Bt**; *b* 15 Jan 1811; *d* unm 3 Dec 1883

2 Henry James; *b* 19 Dec 1814; *d* 1836

3 John Edward; *b* 14 April 1818; *d* 22 Sept 1822

4 Horace Mann (Rev); *b* 10 Dec 1819; Vicar Benhall, Suffolk; *m* 26 June 1860 Charlotte (*d* 12 Feb 1918 aged 89), 2nd dau of Rev W H G Mann, Vicar Bowdon, Cheshire, and *d* 9 Feb 1878, having had issue:

(1) **Sir Horace Nevile Blakiston, 5th Bt**; *b* Aug 1861; *dsp* 12 Sept 1936

(2) **Sir Charles Blakiston, 6th Bt**; *b* 28 Dec 1862; *m* 1887 Harriett Eleanor (*d* 18 Feb 1953), dau of Robert Wills of Highbury, London N, and *dsp* 12 Aug 1941

(3) Frederick Turnly; *b* 22 April 1864; *m* 19 May 1888 Eleanor Isabella (*d* 29 March 1954), dau of John Richard Fitzgerald, and *d* 6 Dec 1894, having had issue:

1a **Sir Arthur Frederick Blakiston, 7th Bt**, MC (1918); *educ* Bedford Sch and Emmanuel Coll Cambridge (BA), Lt RFA WW I, MFH S Shropshire 1946–48, Wylye Valley 1948–52 and Hampshire 1952 on; *b* 16 June 1892; *m* 1st April 1915 (*divorce* 1954) May Walton, MB, ChB Manchester (1920), dau of Frederick Walton Fuller, of W Didsbury; *m* 2nd 18 May 1954 *Ann Hope Percival [Ann Lady Blakiston, 42A Corton, Warminster, Wilts], yr dau of Purcell Cooke Jeans, of Cortington Grange, Warminster, Wilts, and *dsp* 31 Jan 1974

1a Edith Mabel; *m* 25 Nov 1916 Col Sidney Walter Doyle, VD, s of James Doyle, of Liverpool, and *d* 24 Oct 1937, leaving issue. He *d* 7 Nov 1920

2a Lucy Eleanor, MA Oxon 1938, Fell and Bursar St Hilda's Coll Oxford; *m* 25 April 1912 George William Winckworth Wallace Milroy, s of Rev A W Milroy, of Carlisbrooke Vicarage IoW, and *d* 2 Dec 1960, leaving issue. He *d* 31 Aug 1929

(1) Lucy Charlotte; *d* 17 May 1874

5 Charles Robert; *b* 6 July 1825; MLC NZ; *m* 23 Sept 1858 Mary Anna (*d* 1924), 2nd dau of Rt Rev Dr H J C Harper, DD, Bp Christchurch, and *d* 1898, leaving issue:

(1) Henry Matthew, barrister; *b* 24 Aug 1860; *m* 1899 Julia, widow of L E H Corbett, and *d* 13 Dec 1925

(2) Arthur John, JP NZ, sheep farmer; *b* 25 June 1862; *m* 1897 Mabel Bohun (*d* 18 Sept 1946), dau of Henry Hayes Hennah, JP, of Christchurch, and *d* 23 Oct 1963 having had issue:
1a Mabel Rona, VAD WW II; *m* 20 Jan 1945 Charles Henry Cowan and *dsp* 23 Aug 1955. He *d* 18 Dec 1954
(3) Edward Nevile (Rev), Vicar Avonside Christchurch 1931–32; *b* 2 Oct 1864; *m* 1902 Theodora Mary (*d* 23 Nov 1940), dau of Lewis Prichard Moline, MICE, of Melbourne, and *dsp* 26 Jan 1952
(4) Reginald Norman, barrister; *b* 15 Aug 1866; *m* 22 Dec 1894 Annie Constance (*d* 1955), dau of William Henry Hunter, and *d* 11 April 1946, leaving issue:
1a (ARTHUR) NORMAN HUNTER (Sir), **8th Bt**
1a Hilda Mary; *b* 1896
2a Annie Constance Olive; *b* 1905; *m* 17 Sept 1935 Robert Norman Graham McNab and had issue:
1b *Graham Norman Anthony [Graham McNab Esq, RD Motueka, New Zealand]; *b* 1 May 1938; *m* 20 May 1961 *Jacqueline, dau of Eric C Tutbury, and has issue:
1c *Jack; *b* 2 Feb 1969
1c *Jody; *b* 1961; *m* 7 June 1997 *Murray Elford
2c *Mandy; *b* 1963; *m* 26 Nov 1988 *John Graham Haddock and has:
1d *Bradley Graham Geoffrey; *b* 26 Aug 1991
1d *Holly Rachelle; *b* 9 Sept 1994
1b *Janice Constance Agnes; *b* 13 Jan 1942; *m* 18 Dec 1965 *Brian Dennison Maurice
(5) Charles Douglas; *b* 26 June 1868; *m* 1908 Ethel Anne (*d* 1967), dau of John Henley Whishaw, of Featherston, NZ, and *d* 10 July 1950, leaving issue:
1a Peter Henley Douglas (Rev); *b* 18 March 1911; *m* Dec 1940 *Eileen, dau of Dr John C Bradshaw, of Christchurch, and *d* 29 Jan 1966
2a +Charles Michael Hardy [Charles Blakiston Esq, 7 Lighthouse Rd, Napier, New Zealand]; *b* 3 Feb 1919; *m* Sept 1945 *Nancy, dau of Charles E Holmes, of Wellington, and has issue:
1b +David Holmes [David Blakiston Esq, Bruce Rd, PO Box 1039, Levin, New Zealand]; *b* 21 Sept 1946; *m* 1982 *Susan Margaret, dau of Maj-Gen Robin Hugh Ferguson Holloway, CB, CBE, of Waikanae, NZ, and has issue:
1c +Matthew Robin; *b* 1983
2b +Roger Charles [Roger Blakiston Esq, 15 Rue Maurice Herzog, Magenta, New Caledonia]; *b* 29 Aug 1948; *m* 1st 1975 (*divorce* 1991) Victoria Jane, dau of Peter L Marshall, and has issue:
1b +Charles Rupert Hardy; *b* 1976
2b +Samuel James; *b* 1980
1b *Alice Jane; *b* 1977
2b (cont) Roger Blakiston *m* 2nd 1993 *Françoise Vallino and has further issue:
2b *Isaura; *b* 1993
3b +Simon Michael [Simon Blakiston Esq, 12 Highbury Cres, Highbury, Wellington, New Zealand]; *b* Oct 1952; *m* 1981 (*divorce* 1996) Nell, dau of Michael Pouajen, of Bipi Island, Papua New Guinea, and has issue:
1c +Manu Sangak; *b* 1983
1a Phyllis Anne Whishaw; *m* 11 Sept 1948 Frederick Harrison Beckett, ANZIA, ARIBA, FRSA, and *d* 11 Nov 1990, leaving:
1b *Anne Priscilla; *b* 14 June 1949; *m* 1968 (*divorced*) Graham Lester Pitts, BArch, of Timagu, and has:
1c *Jonathan Graham; *b* 15 Jan 1971
2b *Diana Pauline; *b* 18 Nov 1950; *m* 7 Dec 1970 (*divorce* 19–) Jeffrey Laurence Jamieson and has:
1c *Tessa Diane; *b* 1 June 1971; *m* 8 Aug 1992 *Mark Vander Klei and has:
1d *Jordan Lena Anne; *b* 24 Oct 1992
2a Patricia Elizabeth Harper; *m* 13 July 1938 John Abercrombie Bolton and *d* 7 June 1992, leaving:
1b *Peter David Cheyney; *b* 11 May 1939; *m* 1964 *Gael Macrae and *d* 7 Sept 1993, leaving:
1c *John Abercrombie Collyns; *b* 1965
2c *Michael McRae Cheyney; *b* 31 Oct 1966; *m* 8 Jan 1994 *Deborah Hall and has
1d *Jake; *b* 11 April 1996
1d *Jasmine; *b* 17 April 1993
3c *Ian Samuel; *b* 21 Sept 1969
2b *Timothy John; *b* 15 Nov 1946; *m* 12 Feb 1977 *Diana Margaret Grieve and has:
1c *Andrew William; *b* 29 Oct 1979
1c *Emma Patty; *b* 4 May 1978
2c *Penelope Diane; *b* 12 March 1982
1b *Belinda Anne; *b* 7 May 1941; *m* 1961 Hugo Ryland Johnston and has issue:
1c *Christopher Hugh; *b* 1963; *m* 24 Oct 1992 *Kathryn Jessica Buchanan and has:
1d *Oliver Hugo; *b* 4 Nov 1994
2c *David Moore; *b* 11 Oct 1966
1c *Sarah Elizabeth; *b* 1964; *m* 18 March 1995 *Steven Richard Harris
2b *Elizabeth Patsy; *b* 14 Feb 1944; *m* 10 May 1968 *Anthony Charles Everard White and has:
1c *Charles Henry Everard; *b* 11 June 1969
1c *Caroline Mary Harper; *b* 4 Nov 1970
2c *Patricia Sydney; *b* 3 Oct 1975
3b *Juliet Barbara; *b* 16 Aug 1949; *m* 30 Aug 1969 *Michael Gordon Neale and has:
1c *Simon Michael; *b* 22 Nov 1972
2c *Jonathon Harper; *b* 10 Oct 1974
3a *Barbara Helen Joan; *m* 1st Feb 1940 Henry Frank Seymour (*ka* Dec 1941) and has issue:
1b *Nicholas Charles [Nicholas Seymour Esq, Wensleydale Station, Priv Bag, Gisborne, New Zealand]; *b* 21 May 1941; *m* 11 April 1966 *Patricia Anne Ingram, of Auckland, and has issue:
1c *Howard Frank; 28 Feb 1970
2c *Patrick James; *b* 19 Feb 1974
1c *Andrea June; *b* 3 March 1972
3a (cont.) Mrs Barbara Seymour *m* 2nd Nov 1945 Allan Frederick Palairet (*d* 8 March 1990) and has further issue:
1b *Anthea Gay [Mrs Noel Kershaw, Koeko, Moutere, Nelson, New Zealand]; *b* 22 Jan 1949; *m* 19 April 1973 *Noel Morris Kershaw
2b Rosemary Jan; *b* 26 Aug 1950; *d* 6 Aug 1970
3b *Penelope Sue [Mrs Lindsay Everingham, Lot 1 Meryla St, Couridjah, NSW 2571, Australia]; *b* 2 Oct 1955; *m* 5 Oct 1974 *Lindsay Graeme Everingham and has issue:
1c *Nicholas James; *b* 8 July 1975
1c *Malika; *b* 25 Nov 1978
(1) Rosamond Mary; *m* June 1919 Rev Samuel Graves Compton, Vicar St Michael's Wandsworth Common, and *d* 26 April 1922
(2) Lucy Eleanor; *m* 24 Aug 1898 Arthur Granville Turner and *d* 6 Oct 1963, leaving issue. He *d* 15 April 1921

The 7th Bt's cousin,

Sir (Arthur) Norman Hunter Blakiston, 8th Bt, barrister, slr; *b* 26 April 1899; *m* 27 Feb 1962 Mary Ferguson (*d* 1982), dau of Alfred Ernest Gillingham, of Pleasant Point, S Canterbury, NZ, and *d* 1977, having had:
1 Sir FERGUSON ARTHUR JAMES BLAKISTON, **9th and present Bt**
2 +NORMAN JOHN BALFOUR; *b* 7 April 1964; heir presumptive

BLATCH

Creation: B. (LP, UK) 1987.

THE BARONESS BLATCH, of Hinchingbrooke, Co Cambridge (Emily May Triggs, CBE 1983, PC 1994) [The Rt Hon The Baroness Blatch CBE, PC, House of Lords, London SW1A 0PW]; *b* 24 July 1937; *educ* Prenton Secondary Sch for Girls Birkenhead and Huntingdonshire Coll; Air Traffic Control Assist WRAF 1955–59 and A&AEE Boscombe Down 1959–63, memb: Bd Peterborough Devpt Corp 1984–, Cambs CC 1977–89 (Leader 1981–85), ACC 1981–85, European Ec and Social Ctee 1986–87; Chm Anglo-American Community Relations Ctee RAF Alconbury 1985–91; Baroness in Waiting 1989–90, Parly U-Sec DOE 1990–91, Min State DOE 1991–92, Min State Educn 1992–94, Min State Home Office 1994–97, Min State DES 1992–; FRSA 1985; *m* 1963 *John Richard Blatch, AFC, and has, with another s (*d* young):
1 *James Richard; *b* 1967
2 *Andrew Edward; *b* 1968
1 *Elizabeth Anne; *b* (twin) 1968

Lineage: STEPHEN JOSEPH TRIGGS; had issue:
EMILY MAY, *cr* a **Baroness**

Blease

Creation: B. (LP, UK) 1978.

THE BARON BLEASE, of Cromac, City of Belfast (William John Blease, JP (Belfast 1976)) [The Rt Hon The Lord Blease JP, House of Lords, London SW1A 0PW]; *b* 28 May 1914; *educ* McClure Public Elementary Sch, New U of Ulster (Hon DLitt) and Queen's U Belfast (Hon LLD); MBIM, Hon Fell BIM, NI Offr ICTU 1959–76, Memb: Standing Advsy Commn Human Rights NI 1977–79, IBA 1974–79, NI Ec Cncl 1964–76; *m* 1939 Sarah Evelyn (*d* 1995), dau of William Caldwell, and has:

1 *William Victor; *b* 1942; *m* 1969 *Rose Mary, dau of Alan Seaton, and has issue

2 *Maurice Caldwell; *b* 1944; *m* 1967 *Mary, dau of Philip Carrol, and has issue

3 *Paul Charles; *b* 1953; *m* 1979 *Ann, dau of Howard Jennings, and has issue

1 *Gillian Sarah; *b* 1948; *m* 1972 *John Compton and has issue

Lineage: WILLIAM JOHN BLEASE; *m* Sarah — and had:
WILLIAM JOHN, *cr* a **Baron**

Bledisloe

Arms: Sa. two bars erm., in chief three crosses patée or. **Crest:** A dexter arm in mail embowed, holding in the hand all ppr. a club with spikes or. **Supporters:** On either side a bull guardant gu., ringed and a line therefrom reflexed over the back or. **Motto:** *Tien ta foy* ('Hold to thy faith'). **Creations:** V. (UK) 24 June 1935, B. (UK) 15 Oct 1918.

THE 3RD VISCOUNT BLEDISLOE and **Baron Bledisloe**, of Lydney, Co Gloucester (Christopher Hiley Ludlow Bathurst, QC (1978)) [The Rt Hon The Viscount Bledisloe QC, 14 Mulberry Walk, London SW3; Lydney Park, Glos GL15 6BT]; *b* 24 June 1934; *s f* 1979; *educ* Eton and Trin Coll Oxford; Verderer Forest of Dean, 2nd Lt 11th Hus 1954–55, barrister Gray's Inn 1959, bencher 1986, pres San Moritz Tobogganing Club 1991–; *m* 29 Aug 1962 (*divorce* 1986) Elizabeth Mary, 2nd dau of Sir Edward Walter Thompson, of Gatacre Park, Bridgnorth, Salop (*see* COVENTRY, E), and has issue:

1 +RUPERT EDWARD LUDLOW; *b* 13 March 1964

2 +Otto Benjamin Charles; *b* 16 June 1971

1 *Matilda Blanche; *b* 16 Feb 1967

Lineage: BENJAMIN BATHURST, of Lydney, Glos, and Mixbury, Oxon, FRS, MP Cirencester 1713–27, Gloucester 1727–54 and Monmouth 1754–67; *b* 1693, 3rd s of Sir Benjamin Bathurst, MP, and yr bro of 1st Earl Bathurst (*qv*); *m* 1st 1714 Finetta (*d* 27 Feb 1737/8), dau and coheir of Henry Poole, of Kemble, Wilts, and had 22 children; *m* 2nd 22 Oct 1741 Catharine (*d* 1795), dau of Rev Laurence Brodrick, DD, Preb Westminster and Chaplain to H of C, bro of 1st Viscount Midleton (*qv*), and *d* 5 Nov 1767, having by her had 14 children; by his 1st w he had:

1 Thomas, of Lydney; *b* 1725; *m* Anne, dau and heir of Thomas Fazakerly, and *dsp* 9 Nov 1791

2 Poole, of Lydney, *dsp* 5 May 1894

3 Anne; *m* Charles BRAGGE, of Cleve Hill, Glos, and had:

(1) Charles BRAGGE later BATHURST (roy licence 11 May 1804), PC (1801), of Lydney Park, DCL Oxford; Bencher Lincoln's Inn 1813, MP Monmouth 1790–96, Bristol 1796–1812, Bodmin 1812–18 and Harwich 1818–23, Treasurer Navy 1801–03, Sec at War 1803–04, Master of the Mint 1806–10, Pres Bd of Control 1812, Chllr Duchy Lancaster 1812–23; *m* 1 Aug 1788 Charlotte (*d* 27 May 1839), dau of Anthony Addington, MD (*see* SIDMOUTH, V), and *d* 13 Aug 1831, leaving:

1a Charles, of Lydney Park, JP; *b* 15 Jan 1790; *educ* Ch Ch Oxford (MA); *m* 27 Aug 1819 Mary, dau of William Fendall, of Hall Court, Marcke, Herefs, and *dsp* 30 Jan 1863

2a WILLIAM HILEY (Rev)

1a Charlotte; *d* unm 27 Aug 1866

2a Anne; *d* unm 18 Oct 1862

CHARLES BATHURST's bro,

Rev WILLIAM HILEY BATHURST, of Lydney Park; *b* 25 Aug 1796; *educ* Ch Ch Oxford (MA); *m* 1828 Mary Anne (*d* 1861), dau of Matthew Rhodes, of Leeds, and *d* 25 Nov 1877, having had issue:

1 CHARLES

2 William Addington (Rev), vicar Gerrard's Cross 1870–78 and Holy Trinity, Eastbourne, 1878–1906, rector Micheldean, Glos, 1907–10; *educ* Trin Coll Cambridge (MA); *m* 1st 23 Feb 1867 Anna Frances (*d* 10 April 1876), dau of Ven Richard Brindley Hone, Archdeacon Worcester, and had issue:

(1) Henry William; *b* 26 Dec 1871; *m* 15 June 1904 Sophia Emily, dau of Rev Edward Latham, vicar Matlock, Bath, and *d* 18 Jan 1947, leaving issue:

1a *William Nevile, AMIMechE; *b* 6 June 1908; *educ* Magdalene Coll Cambridge (MA); *m* 4 Aug 1933 *Ivy, dau of Harry Stevens, of Sheffield, and has issue:

1b *Elizabeth Jane; *b* 16 Nov 1939; *m* — Roberts

2b *Mary Ann Rose [Mrs Duckworth, 30 Ravenoak Park Rd, Cheadle Hulme, Cheshire SK8 7EH]; *b* 7 Sept 1943; *m* — Duckworth

1a *Sophia Eleanor Frances; *b* 10 June 1910

(2) Nevile Charles; *b* Nov 1874; *d* 22 April 1902

(1) Frances Mary; *m* 19 June 1900 Rev William Leeke Latham, MA, vicar St James's, Nottingham

2 (cont.) The Rev William Bathurst *m* 2nd 26 July 1877 Harriet Jesse (*d* 4 March 1932), dau of Canon Charles Dent Bell, DD, rector Cheltenham, and *d* 23 Jan 1922, having by her had issue:

(3) Charles Robert, Lt-Col 3rd Bn Northants Regt WW I (wounded, despatches); *b* 28 July 1879; *educ* St Lawrence Coll Ramsgate and Emmanuel Coll Cambridge (MA); *m* 5 Feb 1916 Felicite Esther Theophila (*d* 29 Oct 1960), dau of Charles Theophilus Metcalfe (*see* 1970 edn, METCALFE, Bt), and *d* 14 Feb 1967, leaving issue:

1a *Christopher Metcalfe Addington; Maj RA WW II (despatches), Bronze Star USA; *b* 4 Feb 1919; *educ* Beaumont and Queens' Coll Cambridge (BA); *m* 17 Jan 1952 *Sophie Mary Elizabeth, only dau of Lt-Gen Sir Colin Bishop Callander, KCB, KBE, MC, of Old Way House, Fordwich, Kent, and has issue:

1b *Charles Colin Addington; *b* 29 April 1955; *educ* Downside

1b *Jane Elizabeth; *b* 30 Jan 1960

2a *Philip Charles Metcalfe [Maj Philip Bathurst, Appletree Cottage, Box, Stroud, Glos GL6 9HH], Maj RE WW II; *b* 5 May 1922; *m* 14 May 1953 Winifrede Gillian (*d* 1977), er dau of Leonard Snowden Debenham, FRCS, of Lynwood, Scarborough, Yorks, and has issue:

1b *Nicholas Charles George; *b* 3 June 1954

2b *Robert Guy *b* 22 Feb 1957

1b *Charlotte Mary; *b* 23 Sept 1961

(4) Herbert Addington, Maj RGA; *b* 25 Feb 1882; *educ* Pembroke Coll Cambridge (BA); *d* unm 19 Dec 1956

(2) Elizabeth Harriet; *b* 4 Dec 1880; *d* unm 6 Feb 1962

1 Charlotte; *m* 8 Sept 1869 Rev Francis Thomas Bedford Willesford and *d* 1921, leaving issue

2 Eleanor; *m* 30 Oct 1872 Rev Canon Charles Trollope, rector Stibbington, and *d* 5 July 1929, leaving issue (*see* TROLLOPE, Bt)

The Rev WILLIAM HILEY BATHURST's er son,

CHARLES BATHURST, of Lydney Park, JP, barrister Inner Temple; *b* 27 Nov 1836; *educ* Ch Ch Oxford (MA); *m* 27 Jan 1864 Mary Elizabeth (*d* 28 Jan 1885), only dau of Col Thomas Pasley Hay (*see* HAY, Bt, of Alderston), and *d* 1907, leaving issue:

1 William Hay; *b* 17 Oct 1864; *d* 26 Jan 1883

2 CHARLES, **1st Viscount**

3 Arthur Henry, Maj Roy Berkshire Regt, served S African War and WW I; *b* 29 Aug 1872; *m* 7 Aug 1902 Margaret Cicely (*d* 24 Aug 1968), dau of Capt Walter Bentley Marling, of Clanna (*see* MARLING, Bt), and *d* 13 June 1936, having had issue:

(1) Arthur Marling; *b* 18 April 1904; *educ* Winchester; *d* unm 24 June 1950

(2) Ralph; *b* 4 July; *d* 19 Sept 1906

(3) William Henry, MA; *b* 4 Nov 1907; *educ* Oundle and St John's Coll Oxford; *m* 14 Jan 1941 Joan Ernestine Rose (*d* 10 Sept 1996), only dau of Henry Ernest Wyatt, of Castle Lodge, Broadstairs, and *d* 14 Aug 1992, leaving:

1a *Mark [Mark Bathurst Esq, 37 Kent Rd, Margate, Kent CT9 3SW]; *b* 16 June 1948; *educ* privately; *m* 1st 7 April 1969 (*divorce* 1978) Veronica, dau of Edwin Smith, and has:

1b *Rebecca Joan; *b* 19 Sept 1971; *m* 1990 *Kevin Stanworth, s of John Stanworth, and has:

1c *Kirstie Rebecca, *b* 7 Sept 1990

2c *Siân Ayesha; *b* 7 Jan 1991

1a (cont.) Mark Bathurst *m* 2nd 28 Oct 1978 *Pamela Rosemary Alice, 3rd dau of John Harold Stevenson, and by her has:

1b *Joseph John; *b* 24 March 1977

2b *Katherine Joan; *b* 1 July 1980

1a *Mary [Mrs Ivan Heanley, 21 Gloucester Rd, Whitstable, Kent CT5 2DS]; *b* 2 July 1942; *m* 25 Jan 1965 *Ivan Davey Warburton Heanley and has:

1b *Steven Warburton [Steven Heanley Esq, 69 Cranbrook Rd, London W4 2LJ]; *b* 5 Jan 1968; *m* 30 March 1996 *Sophia, dau of A Khalique, and has issue:

1b *Susan [Miss Susan Heanley, 24 Henry Ct, Gordon Rd, Canterbury, Kent CT1 3PL]; *b* 29 Nov 1969

2a *Ruth [Mrs George Hawkes, Falconwood, 170 Ramsgate Rd, Broadstairs, Kent CT10 2EW]; *b* 27 Aug 1945; *m* 1 April 1967 *George Harold Hawkes and has:

1b *Adam George; *b* 22 Oct 1971; *m* 16 July 1994 *Kirstie Frances, est dau of Alexander Keith Templeton Shannon

1b *Julia Ruth; *b* 25 April 1973

4 Robert; *b* 18 May 1875; *m* 1 June 1898 Geraldine Mimi Clere (*d* 16 Feb 1948), dau of Maynard Willoughby Colchester-Wemyss, CBE, DL, of Westbury Court, Glos, and *d* 7 March 1929, leaving issue:

(1) Finetta Dorothea; *b* 6 June 1899; *m* 6 April 1929 (*divorce* 1940, when she assumed by deed poll the surname Colchester) Henry Bristowe, only s of Hubert Carpenter Bristowe, MD, LRCP, of Wrington, Somerset

1 Mary Georgina; *m* 3 Aug 1905 Algernon Mainwaring Vaughan Hughes, of Mount Severn, Newnham, Glos, and *d* 25 Feb 1950. He *dsp* 22 May 1942

2 Margaret Frances; *d* young 28 July 1886

The 2nd son,

CHARLES BATHURST, **1st Viscount Bledisloe**, so *cr* 24 June 1935, as also earlier 15 Oct 1918 BARON BLEDISLOE, of Lydney, Co Gloucester (both UK), GCMG (1930), KBE (1917), PC (1926), JP Glos, Verderer Forest of Dean 1907; *educ* Univ Coll Oxford (MA 1892, hon fell 1935); barrister Inner Temple 1892, hon DSc Bristol 1925, Pro-Chllr Bristol U 1934, hon DCL Oxford 1935, hon LLD Edin 1935 MP (C) Wilton 1910–18, Parly Sec: Min Food 1916–17, Min Ag and Fisheries 1924–28, Govr-Gen and C-in-C New Zealand 1930–35, pres Nat Cncl Social Service, Capt Roy Monmouthshire RE (SR), Assist Mil Sec Salisbury Trg Centre and Southern Cmmd 1915–16, memb Cncl Duchy of Lancaster, chm Centl Chamber Ag 1915 and Roy Commn Sugar Supply 1917–19, Dir Sugar Distribution 1918–19, chm Lawes Ag Tst Ctee (Rothamsted) 1919–25, first sec (hon) CLA 1908–10 (pres 1921–22), pres Bath and W of England Ag Soc 1918–20, pres British Dairy Farmers' Assoc 1918–20, chm: Fedn Co (War) Ag Exec Ctees 1917–20, Roy Commn Land Drainage of England and Wales 1927 and Imp Ag Research Conf 1927, v-pres Br Science Guild, govr Imp Coll Science and Technology 1935–39; a Carnegie (UK) Tstee, dir: P&O Steamship Co, Australian Mutual Prov Soc and Lloyds Bank, FSA, Fell Chemical Soc, gold medal Roy Ag Coll, gold and silver medals Roy Ag Soc (pres 1946), Kt Grand Cross Order of Orange-Nassau (Netherlands), KGStJ, Coronation Medal 1937; *b* 21 Sept 1867; *m* 1st 17 Dec 1898 Hon Bertha Susan Lopes (*d* 6 May 1926), dau of 1st Baron Ludlow (*see* ROBOROUGH, B), and had issue:

1 BENJAMIN LUDLOW, **2nd Viscount**

2 (Henry Charles) Hiley, F/Lt RAF (SR); *b* 16 March 1904; *educ* Oundle and Trin Coll Cambridge; *m* 1st 30 April 1937 (*m* diss by div 1951) Mary Myrtle, yst dau of Maj-Gen Kenneth Marten Body, CB, CMG, OBE; *m* 2nd 3 Oct 1951 Lauretta Theresa (*d* 17 April 1957), widow of Reginald Evelyn Peter Southouse Cheyney (the writer Peter Cheyney), formerly w of Cecil Mortimer Singer and dau of William Frederick Groves, of Westchester Co, NY, and *dsp* 10 April 1969

1 Ursula Mary; *m* 14 May 1929 (*divorce* 1942) Horace Field Parshall, only s of Horace Field Parshall, DSc, and had issue:

(1) *John Field; *b* 3 Feb 1932; *educ* Eton and RAC Cirencester; *m* 1958 *Mary Elizabeth, dau of W R Whitney, of NSW, and has two s and a dau; *m* 2nd 19– *— and by her has a s

The **1st Viscount** *m* 2nd 16 April 1928 Hon Alina Kate Elaine, DGStJ, Offr Order of Orange-Nassau (*d* 6 Feb 1956), widow of Thomas Cooper-Smith and dau of 1st Baron Glantawe (*see* 1915 edn), and *d* 3 July 1958

His er son,

BENJAMIN LUDLOW BATHURST, **2nd Viscount Bledisloe**, QC (1952); *educ* Eton and Magdalen Coll Oxford (BA); barrister Inner Temple and Lincoln's Inn 1927, Bencher Lincoln's Inn 1956, 2nd Lt RA WW I, S/Ldr RAF and Sr Cdr ATA WW II, chm Salmon and Freshwater Fisheries Ctee, v-pres Br Light Aviation Centre, pres St Moritz Tobogganing Club; *b* 2 Oct 1899; *m* 2 June 1933 *Joan [The Rt Hon The Dowager Viscountess Bledisloe, 14 Mulberry Walk, London SW3], only dau of Otto Krishaber, of 113 Mount St, London W1, and *d* 1979, leaving:

1 CHRISTOPHER HILEY LUDLOW BATHURST, **3rd and present Viscount Bledisloe**

2 David Charles Lopes; 2nd Lt 12th Roy Lancers 1956–58, dir Christie's; *b* 15 Dec 1937; *educ* Eton and Magdalen Coll Oxford (BA 1961); *m* 25 Aug 1967 *(Mary) Cornelia (Nelly) [The Hon Mrs David Bathurst, South Lodge, East Heath Rd, London NW3], yst dau of Andrew Kirkwood McCosh, of Culter Allers, Biggar, Lanarks, and *d* 1992, leaving:

(1) *Arabella Rose; *b* 15 June 1969

(2) *Lucy Celeste; *b* 8 Aug 1974

(3) *Flora Elizabeth; *b* 1977

Seat: Lydney Park, Cirencester, Glos. The Manor of Lydney was granted to Sir William Wynter in gratitude for his part as one of the commanding officers who helped defeat the Armada in 1588. Unfortunately the residence he then proceeded to build, known as White Cross House, ended a couple of generations later right in the middle of one of the West of England's main battlegrounds, being between the royalists centred on Chepstow and the Parliamentary-held city of Gloucester. Sir William's grandson Sir John Winter lost it once to Col Massey, his local Roundhead opponent. He managed to regain it but in exasperation torched it so as to deny it to the enemy for ever.

He won back his estates at the Restoration but did not start on a new house till about 10 years later. The new building was sited further west than White Cross (though that too had stood on the westerly side of Lydney town). It was L-shaped under a hipped roof, the principal block being three storeys with seven windows to each storey. A wing of similar height and of only slightly less length (six windows) stretched at right angles to the rear. The elevations were apparently very sparsely ornamented. Lady Winter (the widow of Sir John's son Sir Charles) sold it in 1723 to Benjamin Bathurst (*see* above), who was probably responsible for the stable block. This is now virtually all that remains of the 17th-century buildings.

It was in the time of Benjamin's son Thomas that dormer windows and various ornamental structures in the park such as a Gothick temple were added. Thomas's great-nephew Charles, himself great-uncle of the **1st Viscount**, in the late 1830s asked Thomas Greenshields, an Oxford architect, to tack a new entrance onto the main front, also perhaps to replace the old mullion and transom windows with sash ones. This was the last major remodelling before the house was totally demolished and replaced in the late 1870s.

BLENNERHASSETT

Arms: Gu., a chevron ermine, between three dolphins embowed arg. **Crest:** A wolf sejant ppr. **Motto:** *Fortes fortuna juvat* ('Fortune favours the brave'). **Creation:** Bt. (UK) 22 Sept 1809.

SIR (MARMADUKE) ADRIAN FRANCIS WILLIAM BLENNERHASSETT, 7TH BT, of Blennerville, Co Kerry [Sir Adrian Blennerhassett Bt, 54 Staveley Rd, London W4 3ES]; *b* 25 May 1940; *s* f 1940; *educ* McGill U, Imperial Coll London (MSc) and Cranfield Business Sch (MBA); *m* 23 Sept 1972 *Carolyn (Cally) Margaret, yr dau of Gilbert Brown, of The Courthouse, Marston Magna, Somerset, and has issue:

1+CHARLES HENRY MARMADUKE; *b* 18 July 1975

1 *Celina Mary Charlotte; *b* 15 Oct 1973

Lineage: ALAN de BLENERHAYSET inherited property in Carlisle 1354 and 1362, Mayor Carlisle 1382; had issue, with a dau Maria (*m* 1391 William de Aglionby, MP Carlisle 1387):

ROBERT; sealed a deed 1395 with the arms still born by the family, which apparently included:

JOHN de BLENHERHAYSET; MP Carlisle 1381–84

RALPH de BLENERHAYSET; MP for Carlisle 1413; *m* the heiress of Staffol of Staffol in the reign of HENRY V

RICHARD de BLENERHAYSET; *m* one of the four daus and coheirs of Sir Clement de Skelton, MP Cumberland 1378, by Joan, dau and heir of Sir Gyles de Orton, MP Carlisle 1337 (gs of Sir Alan de Orton, living *temp* HENRY III and EDWARD I), and had issue:

1 JOHN, of whom presently

2 Ralph; *m* Joan (*d* 20 June 1501 aged 97), dau and heir of John Lowdham, of Lowdham, Suffolk, and Frense, Norfolk, by Joan, dau and heir of Sir William Kelvedon, of Kelvedon, Essex, and *d* 8 Nov 1475 (ancestor of the BLENNERHASSETTs of Lowdham, Frense, and Kelvedon, also of Barsham, Suffolk, who died out with John Blennerhassett (*d* 11 June 1704))

The er son,

JOHN BLENNERHAYSET, Mayor Carlisle 1430, MP Carlisle 1441, mentioned as among the Cumberland gentry 1433, owned a third part of the Manor of Orton and right of presentation to the living there; *d* 1472, being ancestor of:

THOMAS BLENNERHASSETT; mentioned 1543 as among the principal Cumberland gentlemen liable for service in defending the border; had issue (with a dau Jane; *m* Sir John Lamplugh, of Lamplugh):

JOHN BLENNERHASSETT; *m* Janet de Martindale, heir of — Newton, of West Newton, and acquired 1544 the manors of Newton, Ormesby and Allonby, bought 1547 the manor of Flimby (sold 1772 by William Blennerhassett to Sir James Lowther)

THOMAS BLENNERHASSET, of Flimby, MP Carlisle 1584–85, claimed 1578 right to present to living of Orton as coheir of Sir Gyles de Orton (*see* above), granted 1586 by Sir Edward Denny lands in Co Kerry 'to be held for ever, for one red rose to be rendered yearly at the feast of St John the Baptist'; f of:

ROBERT BLENNERHASSETT, settled in Co Kerry, granted further lands 1611–28, including Ballyseedy Castle, MP and first Provost Tralee; *m* Elisabeth, dau of Capt Jenkin Conway (descended from Conway of Bodrhyddran, Pembs), who was granted 1614 the lordship of Killorglin or Castle Conway, and had, with other issue, an est s:

JOHN BLENNERHASSET, MP Kerry; *m* Martha, dau of George Lynn, of Southwick Hall, by Isabel, dau of Sir Myles Forrest, of Morburn, and had issue, with three daus:

1 John, of Ballyseedy, Co Kerry, MP Tralee; *m* Elisabeth, dau of Sir Edward Denny, of Tralee Castle, by Ruth, est dau of Sir Thomas Roper, Viscount Baltinglass, and was ancestor of the BLENNERHASSETTs of Ballyseedy

2 ROBERT, of whom presently

3 Thomas; *m* Ellen, dau of Anthony Stoughton, of Rattoo, by Honora, dau of 5th Baron Inchiquin (*qv*)

The 2nd son,

ROBERT BLENNERHASSETT, MP Tralee 1634; *m* his cousin Avice, dau and coheir of Edward Conway, of Castle Conway, and had a yst s:

HENRY BLENNERHASSETT; *m* Dorcas, dau of Francis Crumpe, of Killarney, by Dorcas, dau of Robert Orpen, of Killowen, and had, with four daus:

1 Arthur; went to France, Dr of the Sorbonne

2 ROBERT, of whom presently

3 Samuel; *m* Catherine, dau of Ven Maurice Connor, Archdeacon Ardfert, and had issue

4 Richard; *m* Mary, dau of Edward Rice, and had issue

The 2nd son,

ROBERT BLENNERHASSET; *m* Frances, dau of Richard Yielding by Belinda, dau of Rowland Bateman, of Oak Park, Killeen, High Sheriff Co Kerry, and had, with four daus:

1 Henry; *d* young

2 ROWLAND (Sir), **1st Bt**

3 Arthur; *m* Catherine, dau of James Hickson, and had a son, Robert, and a dau, Rosanna (*m* Sir Robert Blennerhassett, 2nd Bt)

The er surv son,

Sir Rowland Blennerhassett, 1st Bt (UK), so *cr* 22 Sept 1809, of Blennerville, Co Kerry; *b* 1741; *m* Millicent Agnes, dau of Richard Yielding, of Belview, Co Limerick, and had issue:

1 ROBERT (Sir), **2nd Bt**

2 Richard Francis; *b* 23 May 1772; *m* Agnes (*d* 19 Dec 1842), est dau of Sir Barry Denny, 1st Bt (*see* DENNY, Bt, of Castle Moyle), and *dsp* Nov 1827

3 Arthur, of Blennerville; *b* 27 Oct 1776; *m* 1799 Helena Jane (*d* 24 Dec 1846), dau of 1st Baron Ventry (*qv*), and *d* 31 May 1839, leaving issue:

(1) Millicent Agnes; *m* Rev Edward Maynard Denny, MA Trin Coll Dublin, rector Listowel, and left issue

(2) Theodora; *m* 18 Oct 1836 Richard Chute, of Tullygaron, Co Kerry, and *d* 25 July 1845. He *d* 13 Sept 1862

4 Rowland, of Kells; *b* 26 Dec 1780; *m* Letitia, est dau of John Hurly, of Tralee, and *d* 12 April 1854, leaving:

(1) John; *b* 1812; *m* 1844 Annabella, dau of Richard Yielding, of Belview, and *dvp* 14 Dec 1847, leaving a dau Letitia

(2) Richard Francis, of Kells; *b* 1819; *m* 13 Oct 1849 Honoria (*d* 3 Dec 1883), dau of William Carrique Ponsonby, of Crotto, and *dvp* 16 Feb 1854, leaving issue:

1a Rowland Ponsonby, of Kells, Co Kerry, KC, Bencher Inner Temple, JP, MP Kerry 1872–85; *b* 22 July 1850; *m* 21 Sept 1876 Mary Beatrice (*d* 13 May 1928), dau of Walter Armstrong, of Ennismore Gardens, London SW, and *d* 7 April 1913, leaving issue:

1b Richard Francis Ponsonby; *b* 29 June 1879; *m* 10 July 1914 Sylvia (*d* 3 July 1957), only dau of Frederic William Henry Myers, of Leckhampton, Cambs, and *d* 17 June 1938, leaving issue:

1c *Diana Mary Ponsonby [Mrs Richard Goold-Adams, 33 Gt Pulteney St, Bath, Avon BA2 4BX]; *b* 26 Dec 1916; *m* 31 March 1939 *Richard John Moreton Goold-Adams, CBE, only *s* of Maj Sir Hamilton John Goold-Adams, GCMG, CB

(3) Rowland; *d* unm Sept 1840

(1) Millicent Agnes; *m* John Collis, of Barrow, and had issue

(2) Mary; *m* Rev George Purdon

(3) Letitia; *d* unm

(4) Lucy; *d* unm

(5) Alice; *m* Charles Chute and *dsp*

5 William (twin with Rowland); *m* Elizabeth (*d* 21 Dec 1857), dau of Richard Blennerhassett, of Ballymacprior, and *d* 1842, having had issue

Sir ROWLAND *d* 14 March 1821; his est son,

Sir Robert Blennerhassett, 2nd Bt, High Sheriff Co Kerry, 1823; *b* 26 Jan 1769; *m* 27 May 1790 his cousin, Rosanna (*d* 4 Feb 1828), only dau of Arthur Blennerhassett, of Fortfield, Co Kerry, and had issue:

1 ARTHUR (Sir), **3rd Bt**

2 Rowland, RN; *b* 6 Nov 1795; *d* unm

3 Robert; *b* 27 July 1797; *m* 4 Sept 1838 Sarah (*d* 2 Feb 1856), dau of Dr Alexander Eager, and *dsp* 2 July 1862

4 Richard; *b* 25 Aug 1799; *d* unm

5 William; *b* 2 Feb 1802; *d* unm

1 Catherine; *m* 16 May 1822 Rev Edward Fitzgerald Conyers, 2nd son of Charles Conyers, of Castletown Conyers, Co Limerick, and *d* Nov 1869, having had issue

Sir ROBERT *d* 21 Sept 1831; his son,

Sir Arthur Blennerhassett, 3rd Bt, High Sheriff Co Kerry 1820; *b* 30 July 1794; *m* 26 July 1826 Sarah (*m* 2nd 16 May 1850 Frederick Randall, of Highbury, and *d* 11 July 1866), dau of John Mahony, and *d* 22 April 1849, leaving issue:

1 ROWLAND (Sir), **4th Bt**

1 Rosanna; *d* unm 9 Oct 1907

The only son,

Sir Rowland Blennerhassett, 4th Bt, PC, DL and JP Co Kerry, High Sheriff 1866, LLD Roy U of Ireland, Commr Nat Educn Ireland, Inspector Reformatory and Industl Schs Ireland 1890–96, Pres Queen's Coll Cork 1897–1904, Senator Roy U Ireland and memb Standing Ctee; Visitor Queen's Coll Cork 1905–09, MP (Lib) Galway 1865–74 and Kerry 1880–85; *b* 5 Sept 1839; *m* 9 June 1870 Countess Charlotte de Leyden (*d* Feb 1917), only dau of Count de Leyden, and had issue:

1 ARTHUR CHARLES FRANCIS BERNARD (Sir), **5th Bt**

2 Paul Charles William Marmaduke Rowland; *b* 4 Dec 1877; *d* 25 Aug 1878

3 William Lewis Rowland Paul Sebastian, DSO (1920), OBE (1920), Capt late Intelligence Corps, Croix de Guerre; *b* 6 Oct 1882; *m* 14 July 1910 Olivia Frances (*d* 2 Jan 1953), yst dau of Sir Thomas Fraser Grove, 1st Bt (*qv*), and *d* 24 May 1958, leaving issue:

(1) (Casimir Paul Francis) Rowland; *b* 25 Aug 1911; Assist Comptroller Customs Nigeria, Maj Nigeria Regt; *m* 4 June 1945 Elizabeth Charlotte Josephine (*d* 1996), dau of Cdr Gregory Stapleton, RN (*see* NORFOLK, D), and widow of Maj Francis John Angus Skeet, of Stortford Park, Herts, and *d* 1993, leaving:

1a +John Rowland; *b* 14 July 1952

1a *Rosanna Frances; *b* 15 Oct 1946

1 Marie Carola Franciska Roselyne, CBE (1926), DGStJ; *b* 5 Jan 1876; *m* 1st 28 Nov 1894 Baron Raphael d'Erlanger, est son of Baron d'Erlanger, of Paris, and had issue. He *d* 1897. She *m* 2nd 26 Aug 1913 Lt-Col Sir Henry Lionel Galway (formerly Gallwey), KCMG, DSO, son of Lt-Gen Sir Thomas Lionel John Gallwey, KCMG, and *d* 29 June 1963. He *d* 17 June 1949

Sir ROWLAND *d* 22 March 1909; his est son,

Sir Arthur Charles Francis Bernard Blennerhassett, 5th Bt; *b* 14 April 1871; *educ* Balliol Coll Oxford (BA 1895); entered ICS 1895; Centl Provinces Commn: Dep Commr 1908, Ch Sec to Ch Commr 1912, JP; *m* 12 July 1899 Mary Frances (*d* 9 Sept 1950), only dau of Baron Ludwig von Aretin, of Haidenburg, Bavaria, by Mary Louisa, dau of Sir Henry Howard, GCMG, and *d* 29 Jan 1915, leaving issue:

1 **Sir Marmaduke Charles Henry Joseph Casimir Blennerhassett, 6th Bt**, served WW II as T/Lt RNVR; *b* 20 Nov 1902; *m* 2 July 1938 Gwenfra Mary (*d* 21 Dec 1956), er dau of Harington Morgan, Judge Civil Courts Justice Khartoum, by Lilian Elizabeth Lutley, only dau of Philip Lutley Sclater, MA, DSc, PhD, FRS (*see* BASING, B), and was *ka* 25 May 1940, leaving issue:

1 Sir (MARMADUKE) ADRIAN FRANCIS WILLIAM BLENNERHASSETT, **7th and present Bt**

BLOIS

Arms: Gu., a bend vair between two fleurs-de-lys arg. **Crest:** A gauntlet ppr., holding a fleur-de-lys arg. **Motto:** *Je me fie en Dieu* ('I trust in God'). **Creation:** Bt. (E) 15 April 1686.

SIR CHARLES NICHOLAS GERVASE BLOIS, 11TH BT, of Grundisburgh and Cockfield Hall, Suffolk [Sir Charles Blois Bt, Red House, Westleton, Saxmundham, Suffolk IP17 3EQ]; *b* 25 Dec 1939; *s* f 1968; *educ* Harrow, Trin Coll Dublin and RAC Cirencester; dir Access to Justice to 1997 and Introcom, farmer, FRGS; *m* 8 July 1967 *Celia Helen Mary, only dau of Cyril George Francis Pritchett, CBE, of Hill Top House, Five Ashes, Mayfield, Sussex, and has issue:

1 +ANDREW CHARLES DAVID; *b* 7 Feb 1971

1 *Helen Janet; *b* 1974

Lineage: THOMAS BLOIS, living at Norton, Suffolk, 1470; ggf of:

RICHARD BLOIS, of Grundisburgh Hall, Suffolk, where the family moved *temp* HENRY VII; ggf of:

WILLIAM BLOIS, of Grundisburgh Hall; *m* Cecily, dau of Thomas Wingfield, and *d* 1672, leaving an est surv son:

Sir WILLIAM BLOIS, of Grundisburgh Hall; *m* 1st Martha, dau of Sir Robert Brooke, of Cockfield Hall, Suffolk, and had an only surv son; *m* 2nd Jane, dau of Sir Nathaniel Barnadiston, and had an only dau (*m* Sir Andrew St John, Bt (*see* ST JOHN OF BLETSO, B), being *s* 1675 by:

Sir Charles Blois 1st Bt (E), so *cr* 15 April 1686; moved from Grundisburgh to Cockfield Hall 1693 on death of his aunt Mary, only surv child of Sir Robert Brooke; *bapt* 14 Sept 1657; *m* 1st 11 May 1680 Mary (*d* 18 Jan 1692/3), dau of Sir Robert Kemp, Bt, of Gissing, Norfolk (*see* 1933 edn), and had, with other issue:

1 Robert; *m* Amy, only dau of John Burrough, of Ipswich, and *dsp* & *vp* 21 March 1728

2 William; *m* Jane, 3rd dau of Sir Robert Kemp, 3rd Bt, and *dvp* 24 May 1734, leaving issue:

(1) **Sir Charles Blois, 2nd Bt**; *bapt* 25 June 1733; *d* unm 26 Feb 1760

3 **Sir Charles Blois, 3rd Bt**; *bapt* 3 April 1692; *d* unm, *bur* 27 Dec 1761

Sir Charles Blois, 1st Bt, *m* 2nd by licence 18 April 1694 Anne (*d* 29 Nov 1727), dau of Ralph Hawtrey, of Ruislip, Middx, and *d* 9 April 1738, having by her had issue:

4 John, of Gray's Inn; *d* unm 1745

5 RALPH (Sir), **4th Bt**

1 Anne; *m* Samuel Thompson, of Ufford

The 3rd Bt's half-bro,

Rev Sir Ralph Blois, 4th Bt, MA Cambridge; *bapt* 16 June 1706; *m* 24 Oct 1738 Elizabeth (*d* 7 Jan 1780) (who *m* 2nd 14 Oct 1767 Osborn Fuller), est dau of

Reginald Rabett, of Bramfield, Suffolk, and *d* 8 May 1762, having had issue an only surv son:

Sir John Blois, 5th Bt, MA Cambridge; *bapt* 21 Nov 1740; *m* 1st 3 Feb 1762 Sarah (*d* 17 May 1766), yr dau of George Thornhill, of Diddington, HuntS, and had issue:

1 CHARLES (Sir), **6th Bt**

1 Sarah

Sir John *m* 2nd 21 April 1772 Lucretia (*d* 11 July 1808), dau and heir of Thomas Offley, of St Kitts, and by her had issue:

2 Ralph John; *d* 1818

2 Lucretia Grace; *m* 1805 Dr Turner and *d* 1826

Sir JOHN *d* 17 Jan 1810; his son,

Sir Charles Blois, 6th Bt; *bapt* 4 March 1766; *m* 19 Jan 1789 Clara (*d* 22 Feb 1847), dau of Joycelyn Price, of Camblesworth Hall, Yorks, and *d* 20 Aug 1850, having had, with other issue:

1 **Sir Charles Blois, 7th Bt**, Maj 1st Dragoons, Lt-Col E Suffolk Militia; *b* April 1794; *d* unm 12 June 1855

2 John Ralph, Cdr RN; *b* 1795; *m* 15 Feb 1827 Eliza Knox (*d* 10 Sept 1886), 2nd dau of Rev John Barrett, rector Iniskeel, Co Donegal, and *d* 19 June 1853, leaving, with other issue:

(1) Charles Samuel, Lt 37th Regt; *b* 1 Aug 1828; *d* unm 31 July 1849

(2) JOHN RALPH (Sir), **8th Bt**

(3) George Vanneck; *b* 1838; *m* 9 June 1870 Claudine Frances (*d* 10 July 1928), dau of G Marshall, of St Leonards, and *dsp* 26 March 1872

(4) William Thornhill; *b* 1 Aug 1842; Lt-Col late 6th Roy Warwickshire Regt, JP Derbys; *m* 4 June 1874 Fanny Elizabeth (*d* 17 July 1912), est dau of William Arkwright, of Sutton Scarsdale, Derbys, and *d* 5 April 1889, leaving issue:

1a Eustace William, OBE (1919), T/Maj and Dep Assist Dir Remount Servs, formerly Lt Rifle Brigade; *b* 4 Dec 1877; *d* 16 May 1933, leaving issue:

1b *Susan; *m* 7 Aug 1930 (*divorce* 1947) Capt John Nash Edwards Vaughan, only son of Lt-Col John Edwards Vaughan, DL, JP, of Rheola, Glamorgan

2a Ernest Pierrepoint; *b* 10 March 1880; *m* 1900 Lilian Emily (*d* 1918), dau of J W Moore, and had issue:

1b +Trevor Galfridus; *b* 1904

1b *Esmé Ernestine; *b* 1901

2b *Agnes Mary; *b* 1903

3b *Fanny Elizabeth; *b* 1911

4b *Nancy Avril; *b* 1918

3a Basil Frederic; *b* 1881; *educ* Wellington; Capt late RFA (TF); *m* 19– Kathleen (*d* 4 Dec 1922), dau of Robert Overell

4a Geoffrey Stephen; *b* 1884

Sir CHARLES's nephew,

Sir John Ralph Blois, 8th Bt, DL, High Sheriff Suffolk 1862, sometime RN; *b* 18 Aug 1830; *m* 25 Jan 1865 Eliza Ellen (*d* 23 Oct 1924), yst dau of Capt Alfred Chapman, RN, and had issue:

1 RALPH BARRETT MACNAGHTEN (Sir), **9th Bt**

2 Charles Godfrey; *b* 27 Dec 1867; *d* unm 19 Dec 1900

3 Eardley Steuart BLOIS later BROOKE (roy licence 23 Feb 1931), TD; *b* 3 July 1869; Maj 1st Co London Middx Yeo; *m* 6 July 1916 Violet Mary Magdalene (*d* 15 Sept 1945), dau of Thomas Sproat, of Port Mary, Kirkcudbright, and Valparaiso, and *d* 13 Dec 1955, leaving issue:

(1) Thomas Eardley; *b* 27 June 1918; *educ* Wellington; FLAS, late Capt RA, served WW II; *m* 25 June 1948 *Joy Mary [Mrs Thomas Brooke, Cresborough, Rhos, Haverfordwest, Pembrokeshire], only dau of Maj-Gen Robert Stedman Lewis, CB, OBE, of Neuadd, Rhyader Radnorshire, and *d* 1986, leaving issue:

1a +Thomas Robin Eardley [Thomas Blois-Brooke Esq, Cresborough, Rhos, Haverfordwest, Dyfed]; *b* 15 March 1951; *educ* Wellington; added surname BLOIS to BROKE; *m* 1978 *Philippa de Courcy, dau of John Fryer, and has issue:

1b +Thomas Eardley; *b* 1982

2b +Edward Charles; *b* 1984

1a *Jennifer Mary [Mrs Guy Farmiloe, Heatherbank, Sheepsetting Lane, Heathfield, E Sussex TN21 0UY]; *b* 28 June 1949; *m* 1980 *Guy William Meakin Farmiloe, yr s of Leslie Farmiloe, and has issue:

1b *Toby Nicholas; *b* 1987

2a *Elizabeth Ann [Mrs Michael Read, 91 Camberwell Grove, London SE5 8JH]; *b* 21 Feb 1953; *m* 1986 *Michael John Read, er *s* of T H Read, of Northlands, Fishbourne, Sussex, and has issue:

1b *Harry Thomas; *b* 1987

1b *Alice Louise; *b* 1990

(2) Michael Steuart BROOKE later BLOIS-BROOKE (deed poll 24 March 1953), RD; *b* 13 Aug 1919; Lt-Cdr RNR WW II; *m* 20 Aug 1949 *Mary (Cherry), yr dau of Cecil Harvey Mead, of Oak House, Crawley Down, Sussex, and *d* 13 Nov 1995, leaving:

1a +Mark Harvey; *b* 12 June 1954; *educ* Felsted; *m* 1997 *Amanda, dau of Henry Wade, of Wargrave, Berks

1a *Susan Penelope [Mrs Nigel Clifford, PO Box 190, George Town, Grand Cayman, Cayman Is]; *b* 24 Sept 1950; *m* 8 Sept 1973 *Nigel Robert Clifford, barrister, only son of H M C Clifford, of Buxted, Sussex, and has:

1b *Joanna Mary; *b* 1976

2b *Louise Rosemary; *b* 18 July 1979

2a *Diana Mary; *b* 21 June 1959

(3) Robert John, BL; *b* 20 Oct 1923; *m* March 1949 *Ann Hamerton Gordon [Mrs Robert Brooke, St Aidan's, Morebattle, Kelso, Roxburghshire], er dau of Capt Francis Gordon Troup, of Dunbennan and of Oak Lodge, Malvern, and *d* 24 Feb 1963, leaving issue:

1a +Alastair John [Alastair Brooke Esq, Pen Hay, Bevington, nr Berkeley, Glos GL13 9RB]; *b* 2 Jan 1950; *educ* Wellington; *m* 1989 *Julia, dau of J A Burgess, of Bristol, and has issue:

1b +Alexander David; *b* 1991

2b +Christopher John; *b* 1993

2a +Ian Steuart BROOKE later BLOIS; *b* 16 Jan 1953; *educ* Wellington; *m* 1991 *Clare, dau of Peter Champkin, of Sussex, and has issue:

1b *Katharine Ann; *b* 1993

1a *(Katharine) Margaret; *b* 3 Nov 1961; *m* 1989 *Ian W Thomson, 2nd s of Lewis Thomson, of Canberra, Australia, and has issue:

1b *Robert Lewis; *b* 1994

1b *Amy Blois; *b* 1991

2b *Elizabeth Ann; *b* 28 Aug 1996

(1) Eileen Mary; *m* 1 Nov 1938 Lt-Col Edward Douglas Garnett, MC, RA (*d* 21 April 1964), son of Capt Douglas Gordon Knowles Garnett, of Kelsale Hall, Saxmundham, and had issue:

1a *Anthony Eardley Douglas [Anthony Garnett Esq, Redgate House, Wherstead, Ipswich, Suffolk]; *b* 16 Sept 1939; *educ* Charterhouse

4 Stephen Russell; *b* 6 Oct 1870; Lt 4th Bn E Surrey Regt; *m* 1st 17 Sept 1919 Emile Freeman (*d* 2 Dec 1925), dau of Martin Schultz, of Philadelphia, USA; *m* 2nd 15 Sept 1930 *Helen Hill-Trevor, widow of (a) Wilmot Johnson and (b) Edward Henry Packe and dau of Hill-Trevor Irwin, and *d* 13 Feb 1951

5 Dudley George, DSO (1916); *b* 12 Feb 1875; Lt-Col RFA, Boer War 1900–02 (despatches, two medals, six clasps) and WW I 1914–16 (despatches twice); *m* 28 July 1914 Georgiana Isabella Frances (*d* 23 Dec 1967), 2nd dau of Adml Sir Compton Edward Domville, GCB, GCVO, and was *ka* 14 July 1916 leaving:

(1) John Dudley; *b* 17 June 1915; *educ* Stowe and RMC Sandhurst; Maj Irish Gds, later W/Cdr RAF Regt; *m* 28 April 1948 Elizabeth Catharine (*d* 1993), only dau of R-Adml Sir Wellwood George Courtenay Maxwell, KBE, CMG (*see* CHESHAM, B), of Sudborough Manor, nr Kettering, and *d* 19 Jan 1954, leaving issue:

1a *(Elizabeth) Frances Moyra [Miss Frances Blois, 6 St Augustine's Mansions, Bloomburg St, London SW1V 2RG]; *b* 29 May 1949

2a *Sarah Jane [Mrs Miles Ward, Church Farm, East Woodhay, Berks RG20 0AL]; *b* 2 Oct 1951; *m* 1982 *Miles Tobias (Toby) Ward, yr s of P T Ward, and Mrs Mark Chaytor, of Aston Towers, Coal Aston, Derbys, and has:

1b *Lomax Blois; *b* 1984

2b *Sam Philip; *b* 1986

3b *Thomas Dudley; *b* 1990

(1) *Jane Elizabeth Georgiana Joan [Miss Jane Blois, 26 Manchester St, London W1]; *b* 1916; 3rd Offr WRNS WW II

6 Gervase Vanneck (Rev); *b* 25 Aug 1881; *educ* Wellington and Trin Coll Cambridge (BA 1903, MA 1907); Vicar Fretherne, Framilode and Whitminster, Glos, 1949–61, served WW II (CD); *m* 21 April 1914 Hon Hester Murray Pakington (*d* 14 Oct 1973), yst dau of 3rd Baron Hampton (*qv*), and *d* 22 Dec 1961, leaving issue:

(1) +Anthony Gervase, DFC [Anthony Blois Esq DFC, 19 Bilton Rd, Rugby]; *b* 11 July 1918; *educ* Wellington and Phillips Acad, Andover, Mass, USA; F/Lt RAFVR, formerly 2nd Lt Welsh Gds, served WW II; *m* 30 March 1957 Ivy Tucker (*d* 1983), yr dau of William Charles Bell, of Cinderford, Glos

(2) +David Pakington [David Blois Esq, 34 Strawberry Vale, Twickenham, Middx TW1 4RU]; *b* 27 June 1923; Capt MN; *m* 15 June 1951 *Joan Cecilia, yr dau of Capt Leopold R Brock, of Putney, and has issue:

1a +Michael David Stuart [Michael Blois Esq, PO Box 595, 2149 Riverclub, S Africa]; *b* 11 June 1955; *m* 1983 *Heather, dau of James W Davidson, of Buccleuch, nr Johannesburg, S Africa, and has issue:

1b +Stuart Murray; *b* 1992

1b *Fiona Claire; *b* 1994

1a *Angela Claire [Mrs Steven Tuhey, 2 River Lane, Randalls Rd, Leatherhead, Surrey]; *b* 20 Feb 1958; *m* 1982 *Steven Russell Tuhey

(1) *EVELYN HESTER, *cr* BARONESS MACLEOD OF BORVE (*qv*)

(2) Margaret Elaine; *b* 14 July 1916; *m* 14 June 1941 (David) Ian, s of David Charles Wilson, of Marne Lodge, Roehampton Vale, London SW15, and had:

1a *David Gervase Frederick; *b* 1 Nov 1954

1a *Fiona Margaret; *b* 12 April 1942; *m* 10 April 1965 *Rev David John Lawrence Agassiz, son of Dr Cuthbert Agassiz, and has issue:

1b *Michael Lewis; *b* 3 April 1967

1b *Christine Mary; *b* 2 Feb 1969

2a *Sheila Elizabeth; *b* 18 March 1944; *m* 12 Oct 1968 *David Watkins, of Hampton, Middx

3a *Ann Rosemary; *b* 27 Dec 1945

(3) *Elizabeth Mary [Mrs Francis Smith, 8681 Shepherd Way, Delta, BC, Canada]; *b* 20 Oct 1921; Subaltern ATS WW II; *m* 30 May 1953 *Francis George Smith, s of Capt Alexander Smith, of Lossiemouth, and has issue:

1a *Fiona Elizabeth; *b* 11 July 1956

2a *Gillian Hester; *b* 3 May 1958

3a *Jennifer Margaret; *b* 15 Dec 1962

1 Alice Clara; *m* 27 July 1929 James Henry Monk, MA, barrister Inner Temple, son of Charles James Monk, MP, and was *k* with her husband by enemy action Nov 1940

2 Maude Beatrice; *m* 18 Jan 1902 Rev Canon John Cossham Vawdrey, MA, rector Drayton with Hellesdon, Norwich, and Hon Canon Norwich Cathedral, and *dsp* 26 May 1961. He *d* 22 Dec 1931

3 Adeline Louisa; *m* 1 June 1905 Charles George Lumley Cator, Lt RNVR, only son of Charles Oliver Frederick Cator, of The Hall, Beckenham, Kent, and *d* 28 May 1941, leaving issue (*see* NAPIER OF MAGDALA, B); He *d* 1 Oct 1954

4 Constance Violet; *m* 26 Nov 1898 Edward James Heron-Maxwell and *d* 24 Aug 1915, leaving issue (*see* HERON-MAXWELL, Bt). He *d* 2 Feb 1949

5 Cecily Mabel; *d* unm 1 Oct 1945

6 Hylda Letitia Grace; *m* 11 June 1908 Roland Hugh Nelson, MA, barrister, son of John Henry Nelson, MA, of 41 Prince's Gardens, SW7, and *d* 17 April 1955, leaving issue. He *d* 19 Dec 1940

Sir JOHN *d* 31 Dec 1888; his est son,

Sir Ralph Barrett Macnaghten Blois, 9th Bt, DL Suffolk, High Sheriff 1905, Capt late Scots Gds; *b* 21 Nov 1866; *m* 30 April 1898 Winifred Grace Hegan (*d* 28

Nov 1963), yr dau of Col Edmund Hegan Kennard, of Great Tangley Manor, Guildford, Surrey (*see* KENNARD, Bt), and had issue:
1 GERVASE RALPH EDMUND (Sir), **10th Bt**
2 Carol Edward John; *b* 9 Nov 1906; *d* unm 9 Sept 1945
1 Iris Freda; *b* 21 Aug 1899; *d* unm 11 Aug 1962
2 *Christian Frances [Mrs Christian Bing, Orchard Cottage, Walpole, Suffolk]; *b* 21 Oct 1902; *m* 1st 18 Jan 1928 (*divorce* 1940) Edward Archibald Fraser Harding (*d* 25 Jan 1953), er s of Col Edward Harding, of Shroton, Blandford, Dorset, by his w Nina Maud, yr dau of Maj Charles Maxwell Ryves, Prince of Wales's Bombay Gren; *m* 2nd April 1940 (*divorce* 1955) Maj Geoffrey Henry Cecil Bing, CMG, QC, of Stanhope, Yoxford, Suffolk, only s of Geoffrey Bing, MA, of Rockport, Craigavad, Co Down, and has issue by 2nd husb:
(1) *Inigo Geoffrey; *b* 1 April 1944
(2) *Richard Daniel; *b* 5 April 1946
3 Flavia Ria Joan; *b* 26 Dec 1914; *m* 20 Aug 1948 Capt Julian Ward Snow, MP, son of Henry Martin Snow, CVO, of Eltham, Kent, and had issue:
(1) *Harriet Louise Julia; *b* 5 Nov 1950

Sir RALPH *d* 18 March 1950; his only surv son,

Sir Gervase Ralph Edmund Blois, 10th Bt, MC (1944), Capt late Scots Gds, served WW II, ADC to Govr Bengal 1925–28, with ICI 1929–53, Legion of Honour and Croix de Guerre; *b* 6 June 1901; *educ* Wellington and RMC Sandhurst; *m* 1st 20 Sept 1938 (*divorce* 1948) Audrey Winifred (*d* 18 July 1997), only dau of Col Harry Johnson, DSO, of Boden Hall, Cheshire, and had issue:
1 Sir CHARLES NICHOLAS GERVASE BLOIS, **11th and present Bt**
2 +Rodney John Derek [Rodney Blois Esq, Hill Farm, Yoxford, Suffolk]; *b* 12 Nov 1941; *educ* Harrow; High Sheriff Suffolk 1989; *m* 2 Nov 1968 (*divorce* 1992) Lady (Elizabeth) Caroline (Elinor Evelyn) Giffard, er dau of 3rd Earl of Halsbury (*qv*), and has issue:
(1) *Camilla Frances Elizabeth; *b* 5 June 1970
(2) *Susanna Gillian Caroline; *b* 11 Sept 1972; *m* 11 Oct 1997 *Christopher Lye, s of Raymond Lye, of Enstone, Oxon
1 *Gillian Frances Audrey [Mrs Gilbert Chalk, Foxcote Grange, Andoversford, Cheltenham, Glos]; *b* 5 Sept 1943; *m* 1st 9 June 1965 (*divorce* 1970) Hugh Christopher Riddle, only s of Joseph John Riddle; *m* 2nd *Gilbert John Chalk, s of R A Chalk (*see* SHREWSBURY and WATERFORD, E), of Loudwater Ho, Rickmansworth, Herts, and has issue by her 2nd husb:
(1) *Alexander John Gervase; *b* 8 Aug 1976
(2) *Christopher Harry Gilbert; *b* 1985
(1) *Nicola Elizabeth; *b* 1978

Sir Gervase *m* 2nd 24 April 1948 Margaret Lucia, only child of Maj Hon Charles James White (*see* ANNALY, B), and *d* 22 May 1968

BLOMEFIELD

Arms: Sa., on a chevron arg. a branch of laurel between two bomb shells fired ppr., and in a canton or a spear head embrued ppr.
Crest: Issuant from a mural crown arg. a heraldic demi-tiger az., armed and tufted or, collared arg., and holding a sword, broken in the middle, ppr. **Motto:** Zeal and honour.
Creation: Bt. (UK) 14 Nov 1807.

SIR (THOMAS) CHARLES PEREGRINE BLOMEFIELD, 6TH BT, of Attleborough, Co Norfolk [Sir Charles Blomefield Bt, Attlepin Farm, Chipping Campden, Glos GL55 6PP]; *b* 24 July 1948; *s* f 1984; *educ* Wellington and Mansfield Coll Oxford; fine art consultant, md Charles Blomefield & Co 1980–; *m* 26 April 1975 *Georgina Geraldine, dau of Cdr Charles Over, RN, of Lugger End, Portscatho, Cornwall, and has issue:
1 +THOMAS WILLIAM PEREGRINE; *b* 16 July 1983
1 *Emma Georgina; *b* 1980
2 *Harriet Elizabeth; *b* 1986

Lineage: Rev THOMAS BLOMEFIELD, MA, Rector Hartley and Chalk, Kent; *m* 1st —; *m* 2nd Mary, widow of William Branch and dau of John Matthews, and by her had issue:

Sir Thomas Blomefield, 1st Bt (UK), so *cr* 14 Nov 1807 on his return from cmdg artillery expdn to Copenhagen 1807 as Maj-Gen; *m* Elizabeth, 2nd dau of Sir John Eardley Wilmot, Ld Ch Justice Common Pleas (*see* EARDLEY-WILMOT, Bt), and *d* 24 Aug 1822, leaving issue:

Sir Thomas William Blomefield, 2nd Bt; *b* 24 March 1791; *m* 11 Nov 1819 Salome (*d* 22 Jan 1862), dau of Samuel Kekewich, of Peamore, Devon, and had issue:
1 THOMAS EARDLEY WILMOT (Sir), **3rd Bt**
2 William; *b* 19 Feb 1822; *d* 14 April 1829
3 Samuel Edward (Rev), BA Cambridge, Rector of Burnham Sutton, and Vicar of Overy, Norfolk; *b* 22 April 1823; *m* 23 April 1850 Jean Abigail (*d* 28 March 1907), yst dau of John Macwhirter, MD, and *d* 18 May 1903, having had issue:
(1) Allan Macwhirter Newnham; *b* 19 Feb 1851; *d* 18 Aug 1879
(2) Edward Hugh, MVO (1914), UK V-Consul Calais, Marine Supt cross-Channel Packets 1898–1914, Marine Supt Dover WW I; *b* 4 July 1852; *m* 10 April 1888 Lilian Emily (*d* 16 March 1946), dau of Rev Henry Augustus Marsh, Vicar of Tuxford, Notts, and *d* 12 Oct 1938, leaving issue:
1a Allan Herbert; *b* 31 Jan 1891; *educ* Charterhouse and King's Coll London; *m* 1935 Olive Nesfield Cookson (*d* 1980), and *d* 1978 leaving issue:
1b +Roger Stanley [Roger Blomefield Esq, 41 Forresters Rd, Burbage, Leics LE10 2RU]; *b* 9 June 1937; LBIPP, AMPA; *m* 17 Oct 1959 *Eve Kathleen, dau of S Bartlett, of Thorne, nr Doncaster, Yorks, and has issue:
1c +Adrian Paul; *b* 21 Nov 1964; *m* 1994 *Roseann Kane and has:
1d +Matthew; *b* 13 April 1997
1c *Dawn Lesley; *b* 17 Oct 1960
1a Edith Alicia; *m* 26 July 1913 Robert John Goldsmid Levien, son of Rev John Levien, formerly Rector Burnham Thorpe, Norfolk. He *d* 19 Feb 1937
(1) Georgina Elizabeth; *m* 1885 Rev James Henry Lamb, MA, and *d* 27 Sept 1925. He *d* 1914
(2) Alicia Jean; *d* unm 12 Feb 1909
(3) Frances Harriet Eardley; *d* unm 5 Dec 1914
4 John (Rev), MA Cambridge, Rector Pleasley, Derbys, 1884–1907; *b* 27 Oct 1824 *m* 3 April 1850 Sophia Elizabeth (*d* 1896), 2nd dau of Rev John D'Arcy Jervis Preston, of Askham Bryan, Yorks, and *d* 22 Feb 1908, having had issue:
(1) John D'Arcy; *b* 17 May 1851; *d* 1874
(2) Eardley Wilmot; *b* 7 Jan 1855; *d* 31 Oct 1927
(3) Lawrence Woodyeare; *b* 8 Oct 1870; late Lt 3rd Bn Yorks LI; *m* 1 June 1899 Celia Nora (*d* 5 Oct 1961), dau of Alexander Benjamin Caldwell, and *d* 2 Dec 1956, leaving issue:
1a John Woodyeare; *b* 11 Oct 1903; *m* 1 March 1927 Dorothea Mae (*d* 1981), dau of Arthur Farr, of Fairview, Somerset East, Cape Colony, and *d* 15 Oct 1967, leaving issue:
1b *Anne Shirley [Mrs Cecil Meyers, 5 Loerie Mews, Loerie Lane, Beacon Bay, E London 5241, S Africa]; *b* 24 Nov 1927; *m* 1st 23 June 1947 (*divorce* 1966) Pieter Barendse Botha Van Gend, and has issue:
1c *Nardi Anne; *b* 18 Aug 1949; *m* 1971 *William Henry Raubenheimer
2c *Cornelia Mae; *b* 7 March 1952; *m* 1983 *Terence Anthony Carroll, and has issue:
1d *Byron Terence Anthony; *b* 1986
1b (cont.) Mrs Anne Botha Van Gend *m* 2nd 1969 Cecil James Meyers (*d* 1992), and has further issue:
1c Donovan James; *b* 1972
2b *Elizabeth Jill [Mrs Elizabeth Davies, 31 Leadwood Place, Beacon Bay, E London 5241, S Africa]; *b* Sept 1931; *m* 1st 1 May 1954 John Charsley Meyer (*d* 1979); *m* 2nd 1989 (*divorce* 1990) David Edward Hugh Davies, and has issue by 1st husb:
1c *Mark William; *b* 5 March 1955; *m* 1977 *Noël Lynn Cotton, and has issue:
1d *Lindi Elaine; *b* 1979
2d *Julie Elizabeth; *b* 1981
3d *Kristy Lynn; *b* 1983
2c *Bruce Woodyeare; *b* 4 Aug 1957
3c *Colin John; *b* 1959; *m* 1982 *Rosemary Anne Sweeney, and has issue:
1d *Ross John; *b* 1984
2d *James Colin; *b* 1987
1a Sophia Emily; *b* 5 July 1900; *m* 5 July 1920 Dr George Frederick Faustmann, son of Rev George Frederick Faustmann, and *d* 3 May 1945, leaving issue
2a *Frances Celia; *b* 3 June 1901; *m* 3 July 1922 Dr Arnold Klosser Van Niekerk dental surgeon (SA) (*d* 1976), s of Jasper A Van Niekerk, of Constantia, Cape Town, and has issue:
1b *Olive Joan; *b* 16 March 1926; *m* 15 Feb 1947 *Kenneth Louis Clur, and has issue:
1c *Robert Louis; *b* 28 Dec 1955; *m* 1978 *Cheryl Lynn Randall, and has issue:
1d *Gregory Louis; *b* 1981
2d *Tarryn Lynn; *b* 1985
1c *Linda Ann; *b* 19 Dec 1947; *m* 1967 *Christian John Flemmer, and has issue:
1d *Wendy Ann; *b* 1970
2d *Caryn; *b* 1976
3d *Angela; *b* 1978
2c *Beverley Louise; *b* 24 Jan 1952; *m* 1978 *Richard Charles Bishop, and has issue:
1d *Russell Allan; *b* 1984
1d *Kristi-Lee; *b* 1981
2b *Valerie Ellen [Mrs Garth Latimer, 17 Greenfields, Pinewood Rd, Rondebosch, Cape 7700, S Africa]; *b* 13 Jan 1928; *m* 11 March 1948 Garth Cox Latimer (*d* 1966), and has issue:

1c *Dean Andrew; *b* 14 Oct 1949; *m* 1979 (*divorce* 1987) Susan Coetzee, and has issue:
1d *Tamara Anne; *b* 1980
2d *Carolyn Grace; *b* 1982
2c Michael Garth; *b* 18 Dec 1951; *m* 1977 *Jacqueline Barbara Forbes, and has issue:
1d *Gareth Ross; *b* 1982
1d *Kerry-Anne; *b* 1984
3c *Alan John; *b* 16 Sept 1953; *m* 1977 *Anne Muriel Sabberton, and has issue:
1d Gregg; *b* 1983; *d* 1986
2d *Brennan John; *b* 1987
1d *Peta Anne; *b* 1981
(1) Sophia Mary; *d* unm 9 Feb 1928
(2) Emily Louisa; *d* unm 8 March 1922
(3) Margaret Ellen; *d* unm 26 June 1927
(4) Annie Hamilla; *d* unm 2 March 1947
5 Rev Robert Allan, BA; *b* 22 March 1826; *m* 25 April 1851 Georgiana (*d* 6 Nov 1905), 4th dau of George Pinchin, of Hatt House, Wilts, and *d* 31 May 1877, leaving issue:
(1) Rev George Pinchin Allan; *b* 6 July 1854; *educ* St Catharine's Coll Cambridge (MA); vicar Abbots Bickington, Devon, 1889–1905; *m* 1st 26 June 1879 Madeleine Amelia (*d* 1896), dau of Rev Alfred Bligh Hill, MA, vicar of St Paul's, Tiverton; *m* 2nd 1898 Kathleen Ruth (*d* 1 April 1926), dau of Lewis Stephen Woodthorpe, of Glazenwood, Braintree, Essex, and *d* 29 June 1923, leaving issue:
1a May Dorothy Wilmot; *b* 12 April 1901; *d* Aug 1997
6 Charles David (Rev), Br Chaplain Munich, BA Cambridge; *b* 13 April 1836; *m* 22 Nov 1870 Marguerite (*d* 1 Feb 1923), dau of Henry Meyer, of Basle, and *d* 20 June 1907, having had issue:
(1) Charles Allan; *b* 15 Aug 1871; with Transvaal Educn Dept; *m* 18 March 1902 Minnie Otway (*d* 1964), est dau of Loftus Otway Burrowes, and *d* 1940, having had issue:
1a Allan Arthur; *b* 28 Feb 1903; *educ* Witwatersrand U (BSc 1925); Principal English Med Sch Lichtenburg, Transvaal; *m* 1930 Dorothy Jane, dau of A T Adams, and had issue:
1b *Justine; *b* 30 Sept 1931
2b *Jennifer; *b* 1934
2a Loftus Charles; *b* 26 May 1905; U of S Africa, Pretoria, BVSc 1928, DVSc (Courtesy) 1944, Assist Ch Veterinary Field Servs, Petermaritzburg (ret 1965); *m* 30 June 1937 *Una Innes [Mrs Loftus Blomefield, 214 Zwartkop Rd, Pietermaritzburg, Natal 3201, S Africa], dau of John Anand Munro, of Port St John, and *d* 1981, having had issue:
1b +John Alan [John Blomefield Esq, 214 Zwartkop Rd, Pietermaritzburg, Natal 3201, S Africa]; *b* 1942; *m* 1967 *Norma Ann, er dau of B A R Schefermann, and has issue:
1c +Peter Annand; *b* 1970
1c *Monica Ann; *b* 1968
2b +Thomas Loftus [Thomas Blomefield Esq, 24 Harewood Ave, Helderberg Estate, Somerset W, Cape Province, S Africa]; *b* 1944; *educ* U of Natal (MSc Agric 1980); *m* 1980 *Pamela Anne, 2nd dau of Dr J T Sonnenberg, and has issue:
1c +Stephen Lyle; *b* 1989
1c *Jessica Rosanne; *b* 1986
1b +Margaret Otway [Mrs Allan Nicol, 11 Moyeni Pk, Moyeni Rd, Gillitts 3610, Natal, S Africa]; *b* 1938; *m* 1962 Allan John Nicol (*d* 30 April 1993) and has:
1c *Deborah Margaret; *b* 1968; *m* 7 Nov 1991 *Wayne Smit and has:
1d *Michaela; *b* 28 Aug 1996
2c *Jacqueline Jennifer [Mrs Murray Kirkland, Kwambonambi, Zululand, Natal, S Africa]; *b* 1970; *m* 28 Nov 1992 *Murray Kirkland
(2) Julius Wilmot; *b* 5 Jan *d* 25 Jan 1873
(3) Henry Arthur Gilbert (Rev), Rector of Sherington, Bucks; *b* 16 June 1876; *educ* Corpus Christi Coll Cambridge (MA); *m* 1st 21 April 1903 Mary Lilian (*d* April 1936), only dau of S Wallis Frost, and had issue:
1a Lilian Margaret; *b* 3 March 1904; *m* 5 Nov 1932 E Harry G Vigor, yr son of Maj F G Vigor, DCLI, and *d* 4 June 1965. He *d* 26 June 1956
2a *Beatrice Leila; *b* 12 July 1911; *m* 10 Oct 1936 Alexander Johnstone Anderson, er son of Duncan Anderson, of Sanderstead, and has issue:
1b *Alexandra Gay; *b* 18 March 1942; *m* 17 Aug 1963 *John Pick, only son of Charles Leonard Pick, of Lewisham, Kent, and has issue:
1c *David Charles; *b* 27 Sept 1965
1c *Sarah Louise; *b* 12 June 1967
2b *Anne Penelope [Mrs Richard Bain, 5 Rokeby Close, Park Rd, Bracknell, Berks]; *b* 20 Aug 1946; *m* 4 Nov 1967 *Richard John Shenton Bain, ACA, 2nd son of Arthur Thomas Shenton Bain, of Ifield, Sussex
(3) (cont.) The Rev Henry Blomefield *m* 2nd 6 July 1937 Mildred Mary Elizabeth (*d* 9 March 1971), dau of John Marsh, of St Margaret's Dene, Shanklin, and *d* 1 Sept 1942
(1) Margaret Katherine Hermina; *b* 17 Feb, *d* 13 April 1884
1 Salome; *b* 19 Sept 1850 Rev Reginald Guy Bryan, MA, principal of the Coll, Monckton Combe, nr Bath, 3rd son of Rev Guy Bryan, Rector of Woodham Walter, Essex, and *d* 30 Dec 1894
2 Elizabeth Mary; *d* unm 13 June 1892, aged 52

Sir THOMAS *d* 30 June 1858; his est son,

Rev Sir Thomas Eardley Wilmot Blomefield, 3rd Bt, Master of Archbishop Holgate's Hosp, Hemsworth, Yorks; *b* 3 Aug 1820; *m* 1st 2 Jan 1844 Georgina Louisa (*d* 5 Jan 1852), 3rd dau of Gen Sir Peregrine Maitland, GCB, Govr Cape of Good Hope, and had issue:
1 THOMAS WILMOT PEREGRINE (Sir), **4th Bt**
2 Charles Edward; *d* an infant 1852
1 Caroline Sarah; *d* unm 22 Nov 1915
2 Louisa Charlotte Emily; *m* 11 April 1866 Capt Theodosius Stuart Russell, DL, Ch Constable W R Yorks, and *d* 7 Aug 1923, leaving issue. He *d* 2 Feb 1906
3 Georgina Salome; *m* 28 June 1870 Lt-Col Loftus Henry Martin, late Lt 69th Regt, and *d* 1939, leaving issue. He *d* 17 Dec 1906

Sir Thomas *m* 2nd 19 Oct 1853 Fanny (*d* 9 Jan 1906), est dau of Rev John D'Arcy Preston, of Askham Bryan Hall, York, and by her had issue:
3 D'Arcy William; *b* 31 July 1854; *d* 13 Dec 1859
4 Henry Eardley Edward; *d* an infant 1857
5 Malcolm; *b* 1 June 1858; *d* 24 April 1912
6 Arthur Hugh; *b* 1 Dec 1862; *m* —, and *d* 10 Oct 1924
7 Charles Preston; *d* an infant 1865
4 Laura Elizabeth; *m* 2 Aug 1882 Rev Alfred Ernest Jalland, late Vicar of Woolley, Wakefield, and *d* 18 May 1917, leaving issue. He *d* 20 Feb 1934
5 Charlotte Isabella; *d* young 1857
6 Margaret Edith; *d* unm 8 Jan 1943

Sir THOMAS *d* 21 Nov 1878; his son,

Sir Thomas Wilmot Peregrine Blomefield, 4th Bt, CB, JP (Staffs), a Govr of Repton Sch, late Bd of Trade, Priv Sec to Pres Bd Tde 1876–80, Assist Sec Bd Tde (Finance Div) 1901–08; *b* 31 Dec 1848; *m* 5 Aug 1874 Lilias (*d* 6 Aug 1933), dau of Maj Hon Charles Napier, of Woodlands, Taunton (*see* NAPIER and ETTRICK, L and B), and had issue:
1 Thomas Charles Alfred, Cdr RN; *b* 27 June 1875; *m* 27 June 1904 Margaret Josephine (*d* 16 Feb 1964), est dau of Edward Palmer Landon, of Wimbledon, Surrey, and *d* 14 Aug 1915 of wounds recd in action, leaving issue:
(1) THOMAS EDWARD PEREGRINE (Sir), **5th Bt**
(1) Angela Margaret; *b* 18 June 1905; *m* 26 Dec 1958 Cary Best, yst son of L Vans Best, of Montreux, Switzerland
2 Nigel Napier, late Lt RFA; *b* 15 March 1877; *m* 18 July 1930 Ida Clementina (*d* 11 March 1961), widow of Col Walter Gordon Neilson, CMG, DSO, and dau of Frederick Graham Lacon (*see* LACON, Bt), and *dsp* 5 Feb 1955
3 Wilmot, OBE (1919); *b* 26 Nov 1878; Lt-Col late RE, Chevalier Legion of Honour; *m* 5 Dec 1907 Jessie Leila (*d* 28 Sept 1976), only dau of William Abraham Hodges, JP, of E Bridgford, Notts, and *d* 5 July 1926, leaving issue:
(1) Wilmot Edward, MC, Capt RA, served WW II (despatches twice); *b* 16 June 1912; *educ* Repton; *ka* 3 July 1942
(2) Peregrine Maitland; *b* 25 Oct 1917; *educ* Repton and Trin Coll Oxford (MA 1944), barrister Middle Temple 1947, Bencher 1967, Dep Chm Berks QS 1967, Capt Roy Signals, served WW II (wounded); *m* 23 Aug 1941 *Angela Catherine, yst dau of Maj Geoffrey Hugh Shenley Crofton, and *d* 1988, having had issue:
1a +Adam Peregrine Horatio [Adam Blomefield Esq, Chaussée de Namur 73, B-1315 Incourt, Belgium]; *b* 14 Jan 1946; *educ* Repton and Trin Coll Oxford; *m* 1st 1970 (*divorce* 1976) Esther Margaret, dau of Vaughan Lewis, of Swansea, and has issue:
1b *Anna Claudia; *b* 1972
1a (cont) Adam Blomefield *m* 2nd 1981 *Gertraud Elisabeth, dau of Heinrich Tophinke, of Mörnsheim, and has further issue:
1b +Georges Peregrine; *b* 1982
2b *Nora Katharina; *b* 1976
(1) *Leila Winifred; *b* 2 Sept 1908; *m* 29 Dec 1934 Stephen Charles Hawtrey, CB, Clerk of the Journals, H of C, 2nd son of Edmond Charles Hawtrey, and has issue:
1a *Ralph Stephen Wilmot; *b* 8 May 1941; *educ* Eton and Trin Coll Cambridge (MA 1968); *m* 18 Jan 1969 *Eleanor Mary, er dau of Leo Mengasson Waterford, of Mosman, NSW, Australia
2a *Charles Francis Peregrine; *b* 8 Jan 1944; *educ* Eton, Trin Coll Cambridge and Northampton Coll of Advanced Technology; *m* 31 Dec 1967 *Veronica, dau of Dr L F Wiggins, of Wargrave, Berks
1a *Anne Leila; *b* 30 May 1937; *m* 25 Feb 1964 Patrick Jean-Bernard George Destenay, son of Bernard Destenay, of 126 Blvd Magenta, Paris X, and has issue
1b *Marc Stephane Henri; *b* 21 June 1968
(2) Rowan Lilias Augusta; *b* 16 Feb 1910
(3) *Rosemary Eardley [Lady Hayman, 3 Cherry Tree Close, Stoke Row, Henley-on-Thames, Oxon]; *b* 24 March 1914; *m* 6 June 1942 Sir Peter Telford Hayman, KCMG, CVO, MBE (*d* 1992), FCO, s of Charles Henry Telford Hayman, of The Manor House, Brackley, Northants, and has issue:
1a *Christopher Wilmot Arden [Christopher Hayman Esq, Kingsbury Farm House, Little Cornard, Sudbury, Suffolk CO10 0NZ]; *b* 30 Oct 1947; *educ* Eton; *m* 1 Aug 1979 *Joanna, dau of James O'Reilly, of Ballyfaskin, Ballylanders, Co Limerick, and has issue:
1b *Daniel Peter James; *b* 18 Sept 1980
2b *Oliver Christopher; *b* 19 Jan 1995
1b *Emily Rosemary Annabel; *b* 18 Aug 1997
1a *Virginia Rosemary; *b* 5 Sept 1944; *m* 27 April 1974 *Michael Jerrold Philipson, and has issue:
1b *Stephen Ralph Peter; *b* 10 Dec 1977
1b *Claire Leila; *b* 23 Aug 1980
1 Lilias Marrow; *b* 30 Sept 1880; *m* 8 Oct 1903 Maj Cedric Llewellyn Longstaff, CBE, DL, of Nearfield Ho, Lichfield, Staffs, 2nd son of Lt-Col Llewellyn W Longstaff, OBE, of Wimbledon, Surrey, and *d* 25 April 1942, leaving issue. He *d* 1 March 1950
2 Nancy; *b* 16 May 1883; *m* 1 June 1904 Francis Palmer Landon, Maj Res of Offrs RASC, est son of Edward Palmer Landon, of Wimbledon, and *d* 30 July 1953, leaving issue. He *d* 8 April 1963

Sir THOMAS *d* 20 July 1928; his grandson,

Sir Thomas Edward Peregrine Blomefield, 5th Bt; *educ* Wellington and Trin Coll Oxford (BA 1930, MA 1936) T/Lt-Cdr RNVR WW II, dir Whitehall Securities Corp; *b* 31 May 1907; *m* 10 April 1947 *Mme Ginette Harting [Ginette Lady Blomefield, 22 Campden House, 29 Sheffield Terrace, London W8], dau of Dr

Raphael Massart, Chev Legn Hon, of Paris, and formerly w of George Harting, and *d* 1984, leaving issue:
1 Sir (THOMAS) CHARLES PEREGRINE BLOMEFIELD, **6th and present Bt**

BLOUNT

Arms: Barry nebulée of six or and sa. **Crest:** An armed foot in the sun. **Motto:** *Lux tua via mea* ('Thy light, my path').
Creation: Bt. (E) 6 Oct 1642.

SIR WALTER EDWARD ALPIN BLOUNT, 12TH BT, of Sodington, Co Worcester, DSC (1943) and two bars (1945) [Sir Walter Blount Bt DSC, Tilkhurst, Imberhorne Lane, E Grinstead, Sussex RH19 1TY]; *b* 31 Oct 1917; *s* f 1978; *educ* Beaumont and Sidney Sussex Coll Cambridge (BA 1939, MA 1943); Lt RNVR in MTBs WW II, farmer, slr (ret), sr ptnr Underwood & Co; *m* 25 June 1954 *Eileen Audrey, only dau of Hugh Blasson Carritt, and has issue:
1 *Nicola Jane Eileen; *b* 17 Sept 1955; *m* 1990 *Charles Foster Glanville, son of John Foster Glanville, DSC, of Emsworth, Hants, and has issue:
(1) *Edward Foster Blount; *b* 24 March 1992
(2) *Robert Alexander Charles; *b* 20 Oct 1993
(3) *Oliver William John; *b* 1 April 1995

Lineage: Sir JOHN BLOUNT, of Sodington, Worcs, s of Sir Walter Blount, of The Rock, Worcs; *m* 1st Isolda, dau and heir of Sir Thomas Mountjoy, son and heir of Sir Ralph Mountjoy, and by her had issue:
1 Richard, of Sodington, *dsp* after 1359
2 JOHN, of whom we treat

Sir JOHN *m* 2nd Eleanor, dau of John Beauchamp, and by her was ancestor of the Blounts, Lords Mountjoy

Sir JOHN *d* 1357; his second son,
Sir JOHN BLOUNT, of Sodington; *m* 1st Juliana Foulhurst and had a son, who *dvp* leaving:

JOHN, heir to his gf

Sir JOHN *m* 2nd Isabel, dau and heir of Sir Bryan Cornwall, and by her was ancestor of the BLOUNTs of Kinlet; *m* 3rd Helen, who survived him

Sir JOHN *d* 1423; his gs,
JOHN BLOUNT, of Sodington; *m* Catherine, dau and heiress of Thomas Corbet, and had, with an est s (Edward, of Sodington, *m* Joan, widow of Sir Walter Devereux, and *dsp*) and a yst s (Humphrey):

PETER BLOUNT, of Sodington; *m* Anne, dau of Sir Edward Cornwall, of Burford, and had:

Sir THOMAS BLOUNT, of Sodington; *m* 1st Catherine, dau of Thomas Sandford, of Rowley, Staffs, and had issue:
1 Walter, of Sodington; *m* 1st Dorothy, dau of Sir T Talbot; *m* 2nd Catherine, dau of Thomas Gray, of Envile, but *dsp*
2 Henry, *dsp*
1 Dorothy; *m* Henry Heath, of Cobham, Surrey

Sir THOMAS *m* 2nd Joyce, dau and coheir of Thomas Shirley, of Envile, and by her had:
3 Peter; *dsp*
4 Sir GEORGE BLOUNT, of Sodington; *m* Eleanor, dau of William Norwood, of Leckhampton, Glos, and had an er s:
(1) **Sir Walter Blount, 1st Bt** (E), so *cr* 6 Oct 1642, ktd; *b c* 1594, Sheriff Worcs 1619–20, MP Droitwich 1624–5, royalist Civil War, imprisoned at Oxford and in Tower London, his estates confiscated by Parl 2 Nov 1652; *m* Elizabeth (*d* 23 April 1656), dau of George Wylde, of Droitwich, Worcs, Serjeant-at-Law, and *d* 27 Aug 1654, having had, with three yr surv s (all royalists) and four daus:
1a **Sir George Blount, 2nd Bt**; *m* Mary (*d* by 10 Feb 1667/8), dau and heir of Richard Kirkham, of Blagdon, Devon, and *d* 12 Nov 1667, having had, with other issue:
1b **Sir Walter Kirkham Blount, 3rd Bt**, Sheriff Worcs 1687–88; *m* 1st Alicia, dau of Sir Thomas Strickland, of Sizergh; *m* 2nd Mary, dau of Sir Caesar Cranmer, or Wood, and *dsp* 12 May 1717
2b George, of Mawley Hall; *m* 1st Mary, dau of 5th Earl of Thomond, and widow of Charles, Viscount Cullen; *m* 2nd Constantia, dau of Sir George Cary, of Tor Abbey, and *d* 20 May 1702, having by her had, with other issue:
1c EDWARD (Sir) **4th Bt**
1c Constantia; *m* 1719 Sir John Smythe, 3rd Bt, of Acton Burnell, and had issue. He *d* 17 Sept 1737
2c Mary; *m* 7 Feb 1722 Edward Dicconson, of Wrightington, Lancs, and *d* 17 Oct 1744, leaving issue
3b Edward, of Blagdon; *m* Anne, dau of Sir John Guise, 2nd Bt (*qv*), and *d* 1726, leaving, with two other daus:
1c Elizabeth; *m* 14 Oct 1725 3rd Baron Clifford of Chudleigh (*qv*) and had issue
2c Mary; *m* 26 Nov 1727 9th Duke of Norfolk (*qv*)
1b Anne; *m* 29 June 1675 Sir Francis Jerningham, 3rd Bt, and *d* 13 Feb 1734/5, leaving issue

The 3rd Bt's n,
Sir Edward Blount, 4th Bt, of Maurly Hall, Salop; *m c* 11 Aug 1722 Apollonia (*d* 19 Jan 1749), dau of Sir Robert Throckmorton, 3rd Bt, and *d* 16 Feb 1758, having had surv issue, with three daus:
1 **Sir Edward Blount, 5th Bt**; *m* 1752 Frances (*d* 18 Dec 1787), dau and heir of William Molineux, of Mosborough, Lancs, and *dsp* 19 Oct 1765
2 **Sir Walter Blount, 6th Bt**; *m* 21 Sept 1766 Mary (*d* 31 Jan 1805), dau and coheir of 5th Baron Aston of Forfar, and had issue:
(1) WALTER (Sir), **7th Bt**
(2) Edward, of Shablington, MP Steyning; *b* 18 July 1769; *m* 20 April 1803 Frances (*d* 2 May 1859), dau and coheir of Francis Wright, and *d* 20 March 1843, leaving issue:
1a Walter Aston Edward, Clarenceux King of Arms; *b* 17 Feb 1807; *d* unm 9 Feb 1894
2a Edward Charles (Sir), KCB, of Imberhorne, Sussex, Consul Paris 1871, Legn Honour; *b* 14 March 1809; *m* 18 Nov 1834 Gertrude Frances (*d* 9 Nov 1897), yst dau of William Charles Jerningham (*see* STAFFORD, B), and *d* 15 March 1905, having had:
1b Herbert Aston Edward; *b* 22 April 1837; *d* 21 July 1878
2b Henry Edmund, Chev Legn Honour; *b* 16 Dec 1844; *m* 5 July 1869 Marguerite Marie Hyacinthe de la Rochette (*d* 24 April 1898), dau of Charles Paul Marie Moreau, Baron de la Rochette, and *d* 10 Jan 1911, having had issue:
1c Edward Aston Charles Marie, OBE (1920), JP and CA Sussex, chm Queen Victoria Hosp E Grinstead 1940–51, Hon Attaché St Petersburg and Brussels; *b* 2 Jan 1874; *m* 27 Feb 1897 Clara Marie Anne Ghislaine, OBE (1919) (*d* 4 June 1953), dau of the Duke de Bassano, and *d* 4 Feb 1953, leaving issue:
1d Clare Gertrude Mary Ghislaine; *b* 28 Feb 1898; *d* unm 4 Aug 1988
2d Marguerite Pauline Mary, MBE (1946), CA E Sussex; *b* 5 July 1908; *d* unm 2 Aug 1992
1c Marie Charlotte Gertrude Louisa; *d* unm 28 April 1894
1b Alice Mary; *m* 9 June 1856 Edward, Baron Hainguerlot, and *d* 9 May 1873. He *d* 7 March 1889
2b Mary Frances Gertrude; *d* unm 13 June 1871
3b Nellie, twin with her sis; *d* 1860
3a Herbert James, Lt-Col; *b* 20 May 1811; *d* 10 May 1860
4a George Thomas; *b* 3 May 1819; *dsp*
5a Henry Joseph, a Benedictine monk; *b* 5 June 1821; *d* Feb 1865
1a Mary Frances; *m* 14 Sept 1830 Sir Edward Blount, 8th Bt, and *d* 26 May 1893, leaving issue (*see* below)
2a Constantia Catherine; *d* 19 Aug 1894, aged 89
3a Apollonia; a nun
4a Frances; *m* 11 Jan 1852 Henry William Pownal, of Isleworth, and *d* 28 Nov 1858
5a Laura Juliana; a nun
(3) George; *b* 5 Feb 1771; *m* 1st April 1799 Elizabeth Courtenay (*d* March 1820), dau of John Chichester, of Arlington; *m* 2nd Frances, dau of Count de Mansigny

Sir WALTER *d* 5 Oct 1785; his est son,
Sir Walter Blount, 7th Bt, DCL; *b* 3 Sept 1768; *m* 25 Nov 1792 Anne (*d* 15 Feb 1823), yst dau of Thomas Riddell, of Felton Park and Swinburne Castle, Northumberland, and *d* 31 Oct 1803, leaving an only surv s:
Sir Edward Blount, 8th Bt, High Sheriff Worcs 1835; *b* 3 March 1795; *m* 14 Sept 1830 his cousin Mary Frances (*d* 26 May 1893, aged 89), est dau of Edward Blount, MP, of Shablington, Bucks (*see* above), and had issue:
1 WALTER DE SODINGTON (Sir), **9th Bt**
2 Edward; *b* 11 Oct 1837; *d* 20 March 1843
3 Robert Joseph; *b* 20 June 1839; *d* 11 Dec 1876
4 Stephen, barrister; *b* 15 Nov 1840; *m* 18 Aug 1874 Elizabeth (*d* 20 Nov 1915), dau of William Worswick, of Normanton, and *dsp* 13 May 1917
5 Hugh Francis; *b* 1 June 1844; *m* 1883 Frances, dau of Samuel Johnston, MD, and *d* 24 March 1928
1 Mary Catherine; a nun; *d* 26 Sept 1907
2 Joan Frances; *d* unm 13 Nov 1903
3 Margaret Mary Teresa; *m* 1st 10 Jan 1878 George Edmund Wicksted (*dsp* 1895), of Betley Hall, Staffs; *m* 2nd 13 Aug 1901 Col John A Macdonald, CB, of Glenaladale, Inverness-shire, and *d* 1 Nov 1922. He *d* 23 Feb 1916

Sir EDWARD *d* 28 April 1881; his est son,
Sir Walter de Sodington Blount, 9th Bt, DL, JP Worcs; *b* 19 Dec 1833; *m* 1874 Elizabeth Anne Mould, FRSL, FSA (*m* 2nd 1923 Stephen Morgan; *d* Dec 1935), dau of James Zecharias Williams, of Cader Idris, and *d* 26 Oct 1915, leaving:
1 **Sir Walter Aston Blount, 10th Bt**, T/Capt, Actg Lt-Col Roy Fus WW I (wounded twice); *b* 9 Oct 1876; *m* 1 Feb 1929 Margaret (*d* 24 Feb 1959), dau of Charles Augustus Adames, and *dsp* 13 June 1958

2 **Sir (Edward) Robert Blount, 11th Bt**; *educ* Wimbledon Coll, RFC WW I, with Br Sugar Corpn 1924–50; *b* 2 Dec 1884; *m* 27 Aug 1914 Violet Ellen (*d* 25 June 1969), dau of Alpin Grant Fowler, FRAS, FRGS, MICE, and *d* 21 Jan 1978, having had issue:

(1) Sir WALTER EDWARD ALPIN BLOUNT, **12th and present Bt**

(1) *Diana Apollonia [Miss Diana Blount, South Heathercombe, nr Manaton, Newton Abbot, Devon TQ13 9XE]; *b* 17 March 1916

1 Mary Corisande; *d* 22 Aug 1938

2 Eva Apollonia; *d* 20 July 1982

Blunden

Arms: Quarterly, 1st and 4th, arg., ten billets, four, three, two and one, sa.; 2nd and 3rd, or a lion passant-guardant per pale gu. and sa.
Crests: 1 A demi-lion rampant per fess sa. and arg., armed and langued gu., 2 A griffin sejeant vert, armed, winged and beaked or.
Motto: *Cedamus amori* ('We must yield to love').
Creation: Bt. (I) 12 March 1766.

SIR PHILIP OVERINGTON BLUNDEN, 7TH BT, of Castle Blunden, Co Kilkenny [Sir Philip Blunden Bt, 60 The Drive, Castletown, Celbridge, Co Kildare, Ireland]; *b* 27 Jan 1922; *s* bro 1985; *educ* Repton; served WW II 1942–45 with RN, artist and art restorer; *m* 1945 *Jeanette Francesca Alexandra (WRNS), est dau of Capt D Macdonald, RNR, of Portree, Isle of Skye, and has issue:

1 +HUBERT CHISHOLM; *b* 9 Aug 1948; *educ* Avoca Sch, Blackrock; served 1st Bn Irish Gds; *m* 1975 *Ellish O'Brien and has issue:

(1) +Edmond; *b* 31 July 1982

(1) *Amelia; *b* 1977

2 +John Maurice Patrick; *b* 1955

1 *Marguerite Eugenie; *b* 1967

Lineage: OVERINGTON BLUNDEN, of Blunden's Castle, Co Kilkenny, granted Glanmore otherwise Clanmore 'to be for ever called Blunden's Castle' and other lands in Co Kilkenny, Queen's Co and Co Waterford 1667; *m* Elizabeth — and *d* by 16 Nov 1685, leaving, with a yr son and four daus:

JOHN BLUNDEN, of Castle Blunden; *d* intestate by 10 May 1717; f of:

JOHN BLUNDEN, of Castle Blunden, MP Co Kilkenny; *m* Martha (*d* 1726), dau of Agmondesham Cuffe, of Castle Inch, Co Kilkenny, and sis of 1st Baron Desart, and had, with a dau (*m* Samuel Waring, of Springfield, Co Kilkenny):

Sir John Blunden, 1st Bt (I), so *cr* 12 March 1766, of Castle Blunden; barrister, MP Kilkenny; *m* 25 Feb 1755 his cousin Lucy Susanna, dau of 1st Baron Desart (*see* 1934 edn), and *d* 1783, having had, with five daus:

1 **Sir John Blunden, 2nd Bt**; *m* 1st 1786 Frances (*d* 12 Jan 1808), dau and sole heir of John Robbins, of Ballyduff; *m* 2nd 1812 Hester, dau of John Helsham, of Leggetsrath, Co Kilkenny

2 William Pitt; *b* 22 Oct 1761; *m* 29 July 1813 Harriet (*m* 2nd Rev Henry Herbert), only dau of Thomas Pope, of Popefield, Queen's Co, and *d* 17 April 1817, leaving issue:

(1) JOHN (Sir), **3rd Bt**

(2) William Pitt, of Bonnettstown, Co Kilkenny, JP, High Sheriff 1884; *b* 15 Nov 1815; *m* 1 Sept 1846 Frances Maria (*d* 1899), 2nd dau of Maj John Knox, of Dublin, and *d* 1094, leaving issue:

1a Overington William; *b* 1852; *d* unm

2a Frederick Edward; *d* unm 3 June 1937

1a Catherine Elizabeth

(1) Harriet; *m* 21 July 1841 Rev Joseph Carson, DD, Sr Fell Trin Coll Dublin. He *d* Feb 1898

3 Overington, Gen; *b* 14 Aug 1767; *d* Feb 1838

Sir JOHN *dsp* 1 March 1818; his nephew,

Sir John Blunden, 3rd Bt, DL, barrister; *b* 21 Dec 1814; *m* 22 April 1839 Elizabeth, 3rd dau of John Knox, of Castlerea, Co Mayo, and had issue:

1 WILLIAM (Sir), **4th Bt**

2 John Overington, barrister; *b* 27 Nov 1842; *educ* Trin Coll Dublin (BA); *m* 1871 Frances, dau of Joseph Hone, of Dublin, and *dsp* 28 Oct 1915

3 Edward Herbert, barrister Sydney, NSW; *b* 21 Jan 1847; *d* unm 1932

4 Maurice Robert; *b* 28 March 1849; *m* 10 April 1875 Ellen Louisa (*d* 2 Dec 1930), dau of Edmund J Armstrong, DL, of Lismoher, Co Clare, and *dsp* 17 April 1876

5 Arthur Henry; *b* 21 Aug 1850; *d* unm 1 May 1904

6 Abraham, LRCS Edin; *b* 13 Oct 1852; *m* 30 June 1881 Mary Josephine (*d* 13 Feb 1946), dau of Col Richard J Magee, 5th Bn Roy Irish Regt, and *d* 1893, leaving issue:

(1) Abraham, Lt Waterford Res Art; *b* 1887

1 Kate; *m* 5 June 1872 Nicholas Gosselin Richardson, and had issue

2 Harriette; *m* James Egan and had issue

3 Nicola Sophia; *m* 22 June 1887 Ven John Richard Hedges Becher, and had issue. He *d c* 1948

Sir JOHN *d* 17 Jan 1890; his est son,

Sir William Blunden, 4th Bt, High Sheriff 1904; *educ* Trin Coll Dublin (BA), MB, LRCSI, LMKGCPI; *b* 25 July 1840; *m* 26 April 1879 Florence Caroline (*d* 10 Jan 1942), dau of Henry Shuttleworth, of New Zealand, and had issue:

1 JOHN (Sir), **5th Bt**

2 Eric Overington; *b* 15 Oct 1892; *educ* Trin Coll Dublin (BA, BAI); MICE, divnl rd engr N Midland Div Min Tport, Hon Lt RE, served WW I (despatches); *m* 30 April 1918 Bridget Constable (*d* 1980), only dau of Henry George Constable Curtis, MA, and *d* 28 April 1969, leaving issue:

(1) *Josephine Bridget Annette [Mrs George Kenyon, Highfields Lodge, Ware, Herts; Pier View, Dunmore E, Co Waterford, Ireland]; *b* 10 Nov 1926; *m* 24 Sept 1947 Col George Vicary Kenyon, CBE, TD (*d* 1990), *s* of Maj Harold Godfrey Kenyon, and has issue:

1a *Robin George Blunden; *b* 16 May 1950; *educ* Charterhouse; *m* 1984 *Marcia Joan, dau of Hon Mr Justice John T Ludeke, of Sydney, NSW, and has issue

2a *Crispin Simon Vicary; *b* 10 Nov 1955; *educ* Charterhouse; *m* 1983 *Carolyn Isabel, dau of Collingwood Peter Drinkwater, of Sacombe, Ware, Herts, and Bradden, IoM, and has issue

1a *Rowena Josette Caroline; *b* 13 June 1953

1 Muriel; *m* 1918 John E H Richardson, of Lane Rank, Poulner, Ringwood, Hants, late Dist Insp RIC, and *d* 24 June 1936. He *d* 1951

Sir WILLIAM *d* 25 Oct 1923; his est son,

Sir John Blunden 5th Bt; *b* 26 Feb 1880; *m* 4 June 1918 Phyllis Dorothy (*d* Oct 1967), dau of Philip Crampton Creaghe, RM Co Kilkenny, and *d* 28 Oct 1923, leaving issue:

1 **Sir William Blunden 6th Bt**; Lt-Cdr RN (ret 1958); *b* 26 April 1919; *educ* Repton; *m* 29 Sept 1945 *Pamela Mary [Pamela Lady Blunden, Castle Blunden, Kilkenny, Ireland] (formerly 2nd Offr WRNS), dau of John Purser, of Murton House, Dublin 6, Prof Civ Engrg Trin Coll Dublin, and *d* 1985, having had issue:

(1) *Sarah Vanessa [Mrs John Perceval Maxwell, Moore Hill, Tallows, Co Waterford, Ireland]; *b* 4 Sept 1946; *m* 11 July 1970 *John Edward Spencer Perceval Maxwell, only *s* of Maj Edward Napier Perceval Maxwell, of Ballyclement, Tallow, Co Waterford, and has issue

(2) *Griselda Jane; *b* 17 Oct 1948

(3) *Caroline Susan; *b* 17 Oct 1948

(4) *Rowena Mary Phillida [Mrs Gillies Macbain, Cranagh Castle, Templemore, Co Tipperary, Ireland]; *b* 13 Sept 1952; *m* 1985 *(Andrew) Gillies Macbain and has issue

(5) *Elizabeth Anne Gabrielle [Mrs Nicholas Marshall, 47 Smith St, Cairns, Queensland, Australia]; *b* 18 April 1955; *m* 1985 *Nicholas Bryan Marshall, er s of Bryan Marshall, of Compton House, Compton, Berks, and has issue

(6) *Fiona Christine; *b* 28 May 1958; *m* 1996 *John Fischer MacGovern

2 Sir PHILIP OVERINGTON BLUNDEN, **7th and present Bt**

Seat: Castle Blunden. Built in the mid-18th century with a lake either side. A wing added in the 1970s is by the distinguished Dublin architect Jeremy Williams.

BLUNT

Arms: Per pale or and sa., barry nebuly of six counterchanged. **Crest:** Issuing out of clouds a sun in splendour charged with an eye issuing tears, all ppr. **Motto:** *Lux tua vita mea* ('The light is my life'). **Creation:** Bt. (GB) 17 June 1720.

SIR DAVID RICHARD REGINALD BLUNT, 12TH BT, of London [Sir David Blunt Bt, 74 Kirkstall Rd, London SW2 4HF]; *b* 8 Nov 1938; *s* f 1975; *m* 1969 *Sonia Tudor Rosemary, dau of Albert Edward Day, and has:

1 *Davina Angela Rosemary; *b* 1972

Lineage: This family claims to be a branch of the Blounts of Sodington, Worcs (*see* BLOUNT, Bt).

Sir John Blunt, 1st Bt (GB), so *cr* 17 June 1720; 4th s of Thomas Blunt, a baptist cobbler, of Rochester, Kent; *m* 1st 16 July 1689 Elizabeth Court (*d* 22 March 1707/8) and had, with other issue:

1 HENRY (Sir), **2nd Bt**

2 Charles, army offr; *b* 4 Nov 1700; *m* Mary (*d* 12 Dec 1765), dau of Peter Short, of Tenterden, Kent, and *d* 18 June 1747, leaving an only surv son:

(1) Harry, of Ringmer, Sussex; *b* 23 May 1735; *m* 28 Dec 1768 Mary (*d* 17 Jan 1822), only child of Ferdinando Askew, of Liddiard Millicent, Wilts, and had issue:

1a Charles Burrell (Sir), of Ringmer; *m* 1st Elizabeth Anne, dau of John Wyche, of Salisbury, and had issue:

1b Henry Charles; *b* 19 Oct 1788; *d* unm 13 Feb 1810

2b William Oakes, Col; *b* 28 July 1791; *m* 2 April 1829 Frances Charlotte (*m* 2nd 21 Feb 1833 Capt John William Robe, of Tickford Abbey, Bucks, and *d* 1860), yst dau of Richard Orlebar, DL, JP, of Hinwick House, Northants, and *dsp* 24 April 1831

1a (cont.) Sir Charles Blunt *m* 2nd 10 Nov 1801 his second cousin, Elizabeth (*d* 1839), dau of Charles William Blunt, 3rd Bt (*see below*)

Sir John *m* 2nd 22 Dec 1713 Susannah, widow of Benjamin Tudman and dau of Richard Cradock, Govr Bengal, and *d* 24 Jan 1732/3

His est surv son,

Sir Henry Blunt, 2nd Bt; *m* March 1724 Dorothy, est dau of William Nutt, coheir with her bro, James Nutt, of Walthamstow, and had, with other issue:

1 CHARLES WILLIAM (Sir), **3rd Bt**

2 Walter, of Kensington, and Wallop House, Stockbridge, Hants; *b* 7 March 1735/6; *m* 1st 11 Nov 1762 Mary, dau of James Dandridge, and had an only child:

(1) James, of Wallop House; *m* 1st 8 Oct 1799 Henrietta (*d* 11 Sept 1807), dau of Robert Garden, and had:

1a Walter (Rev), of Wallop House; *b* 23 Jan 1802; *m* 16 Oct 1827 Marian (*d* 1886), dau of William Pearce, and *d* 13 May 1868, having had issue:

1b Rowland Pearce; *b* and *d* 1828

1b Emily Anna Maria; *m* Aug 1859 Thomas Edward Bidgood, of Rockbeare Court, Devon, and had issue

2b Agnes Rebecca; *m* 6 Jan 1859 Rev William FitzWilliam Wharton and *dsp* 30 Dec 1904. He *d* 9 March 1893

2a Edward Powlett (Rev), Rector Spetisbury, Dorset; *b* 24 April 1806; *m* 22 June 1831 Caroline Anne (*d* 1886), dau of Rev Roger Clavell, and *d* 24 Sept 1880, leaving issue:

1b Alfred James; *b* 10 July 1835; *dsp*

2b Francis Theophilus, Capt 12th Lancers and 7th Dragoon Gds, Ch Commr Seychelles Islands; *b* 7 July 1837; *m* 1st Marian Pierson and had issue:

1c Mary Anne; *m* 25 April 1881 Robert John Lepper, LRCP, and *d* 21 Ang 1947, leaving issue. He *d* 7 Jan 1893

2c Maud Fanny; *m* 1st 18 Sept 1883 Col Charles Arthur de Neufville Lucas, IA, and had issue. He *d* 1894. She *m* 2nd 1904 Vyell Vyvyan Williams, s of Charles Hussey Williams, and *d* 23 June 1960 aged 96

3c Emily Charlotte; *d* 28 April 1937

2b (cont.) Capt Francis Blunt *m* 2nd 21 Aug 1870 Emily Ellen Hobart (*d* 23 June 1911), 2nd dau of Bennington Robert Rainsford, of Carmarthen, and St Mâlo, France, and *d* 24 Feb 1881, having by her had further issue:

1c Edward Arthur Henry (Sir), KCIE, OBE; *b* 14 March 1877; *educ* Marlborough and Corpus Christ Coll Oxford (BA); ICS from 1901, served UP, U-Sec to Govt 1905–07, Supt Census Ops 1910–12, Settlement Offr Basti 1915–18, Revenue Sec 1919, Finance Sec 1920–31, memb Govr's Exec Cncl UP 1931–35, ret 1936; *m* 15 Oct 1901 Ada (*d* 26 Jan 1948), 3rd dau of Cdr Charles H Stone, RN, and *d* 29 May 1941, leaving issue:

1d John Edward Chicheley; *b* 8 Feb 1907; *educ* Marlborough; Lt-Col RA, served WW II; *m* 3 June 1936 *Margaret [Mrs John Blunt, Appletree Cottage, N Carr Farm, Terrington, York YO6 4PN], dau of R Whiteley, of Heath, Wakefield, and *d* 1988, having had issue:

1e +John Michael Chicheley [Maj John Blunt, Birdforth, Terrington, York YO6 4PX]; *b* 19 Dec 1937; *educ* Canford, RMA Sandhurst and RMCS Shrivenham (BEng); Capt RE, Maj RA; *m* 1964 *Pauline Susan, dau of M Oliver, of Market Harborough, and has:

1f +James William; *b* 1969; *educ* Canford and Portsmouth U (BA)

2f +Richard Michael; *b* 1971; *educ* Canford and RMA Sandhurst

1d May Frances; *b* 8 Oct 1902; *m* 1st 21 March 1922 Maurice Halifax Bates, Lt RA, yst son of Sir Edward Percy Bates, 2nd Bt (*qv*), and had issue. He *d* 23 Sept 1925. She *m* 2nd 24 Oct 1927 Brig Ralph Emerson Pickering, CBE, The Queen's Roy Regt, son of Thomas Pickering, of The Hill House, Gilsland, and *d* 25 Feb 1969, leaving further issue. He *d* 27 March 1962

2d Violet Constance; *b* 9 Aug 1904; *m* 23 March 1926 Brig Sydney Henry Persse, DSO, IA (*d* 14 July 1945), yr son of William Henry Persse, and had issue:

1e *Burton Richard Edward; *b* 21 Aug 1941

1e *Elizabeth Anne Audrey; *b* 10 Jan 1934; *m* 21 July 1956 George Marcus Telford, s of Thomas Telford, of 147 Dunluce Avenue, Belfast, and has issue:

1f *Peter Marcus; *b* 7 Nov 1957

2f *Andrew Richard Thomas; *b* 1962

1f *Alison Anne; *b* 1959

2f *Caroline Margaret Seymour; *b* 13 Nov 1937; *m* 25 July 1959 Capt Roderick Norman Alexander Macleod, RA, only son of Lt-Col R W Macleod, RA, of Littly Cottage, Nairn, and has issue

2c Alfred Walter Frank (Rt Rev), DD; *b* 24 Sept 1879; Bp Bradford 1931–55; *m* 20 Oct 1909 Margaret Catherine (*d* 1 Dec 1963), est dau of Lt-Col Joshua Duke, late IMS, and *d* 2 June 1957, having had issue:

1d +David Alfred Chicheley [David Blunt Esq, 7 The Coppice, Bishopthorpe, York YO2 1QP]; *b* 28 Oct 1915; *educ* St Catharine's Coll Cambridge (MA); Lay Chaplain to Archbp York; *m* 9 Nov 1940 *Dorothy Brailsford, yr dau of Richard T Booth, of Myrtle Bank, Heaton, Bradford, and has issue:

1e +Peter Robin Chicheley [Peter Blunt Esq, Home Farm, Newburgh, Coxwold, Yorks]; *b* 21 Sept 1946; *m* 1st 23 July 1969 Angela Shirley (*d* 1992), dau of Arthur Benjamin Drane, MA, of 33 Simbalk Lane, Bishopthorpe, York; *m* 2nd 1993 *Jane Clough and has by his 1st w:

1f +Michael Peter Chicheley; *b* 1975

1f *Jenny Elizabeth; *b* 1972

1e *Patricia Anne Brailsford [Mrs Timothy Piper, 4 St Nicholas Rd, Copmanthorpe, York YO2 3UX]; *b* 29 Sept 1941; *m* 11 April 1967 *Timothy Steuart Hallam Piper, er s of Donald Piper, of St Anselm's, Bakewell, Derbys, and has:

1f *Richard David Steuart; *b* 31 Jan 1969

2f *Nicholas James Steuart; *b* 1970

3f *James William Steuart; *b* 1976

1f *Sarah Catherine Brailsford; *b* 1982

2d Geoffrey Chicheley; *b* 3 April 1921; *d* unm 2 Feb 2 1941

1d Helen Amy; *b* 20 March 1911; *m* 1st 21 April 1934 (*divorce* 1941) Christopher Hodgson, est s of Malcolm Hodgson, of Scalby, Scarborough; *m* 2nd 29 Aug 1942 (*divorce* 1948) Geoffrey Hawkes Dawson, s of Robert Southworth Dawson, of Bradford, and had by her 2nd husb:

1e *Jane [Mrs John Glennie, Thatched Cottage, Widdington, Saffron Walden, Essex CB11 3SJ]; *b* 27 Dec 1943; *m* 1st 23 Jan 1965 (*divorce* 1983) Nigel Hartley Dryden Butterworth (*see* 1970 edn DRYDEN, Bt), son of Maj Hartley Butterworth, of Scotney Lodge, Fleet, Hants; *m* 2nd 1984 *Dr John Glennie and has by her 1st husb:

1f *Julian Richard Nigel [Julian Glennie Esq, 16 Brandon Mansions, Queens Club Gdns, London W14 9RE]; *b* 21 Nov 1970

1f *Fiona Catharine [Mrs Christopher Crace, Molens Cottage, Bures Rd, White Colne, Essex CO6 2QF]; *b* 1 Nov 1967; *m* 6 June 1992 *Christopher Gregory Crace and has:

1g *Jack Edward; *b* 19 April 1996

1g *Sasha Amy; *b* 14 March 1994

1d (cont.) Mrs Helen Dawson *m* 3rd 3 April 1962 *Richard Marshall Bond, son of Richard Bond, of Bryncliffe, Wilmslow Park, Wilmslow, Cheshire, and *d* 20 July 1994

2d *Margaret Dorothy [Mrs Rudolf Kirchem, Adlington Lodge, Albury Rd, Burwood Park, Walton on Thames, Surrey]; *b* 12 June 1913; *m* 12 Sept 1936 *Rudolf Paul Gerard Kirchem, s of Moritz S Kirchem, of High Barnet, Herts, late of Berlin-Grünewald, and has:

1e *Michael Hans Edward [Michael Kirchem Esq, 36 Southview Court, Guildford Rd, Woking, Surrey]; *b* 2 Nov 1937; *educ* Stowe and Exeter Coll Oxford (BA); slr 1965; *m* 3 April 1965 (*divorce* 1976) Jean Miriam, ACA, dau of Dr John McKenna, of Co Sligo, and has:

1f *Michael John Geoffrey; *b* 17 June 1966

1f *Catherine Marina; *b* 4 Oct 1967

2e *Anthony Peter Francis; *b* 8 June 1953; *educ* Cranleigh
1e *Elizabeth Jane [Mrs David Cross, 25 Cité Joseph Bech, Gonderange, Luxembourg]; *b* 15 March 1940; *m* 1971 *David George Cross and has issue:
1f *Andrew David Jonathan; *b* 1973
2f *Geoffrey Mark Timothy; *b* 1974
3f *Nicholas Edward Benjamin; *b* 1976
3b Grant, Maj-Gen RE, Govr St Helena 1882–87; *b* 6 March 1840; *m* 23 April 1867 Rachel Eliza (*d* 12 May 1942), dau of Conrad Pile, of Barbados, and *d* 26 March 1912, leaving issue:
1c Conrad Edward Grant, CBE (1919), DSO (1917); *b* 21 Feb 1868; Col ASC, attached Egyptian Army 1894, served Dongola Expdn 1896 (despatches), Nile Expdn 1898 (despatches), WW I 1915–19 (despatches), Order of Osmanieh (3rd Cl), Medjidie (4th Cl) and Order of Nile (2nd Cl); *m* 1st 19 Sept 1900 Aimée (*d* 24 Aug 1918), 2nd dau of Col Abel Straghan, CB, and had issue:
1d A son; *d* an infant 3 Oct 1902
2d Hugh Clavell; *b* 24 Sept 1908; *m* 22 July 1939 Elizabeth Marjorie (*d* Sept 1986), only dau of W S Campbell, and *d* May 1986, leaving issue:
1e *Susan Pamela [Mrs Susan Blunt, 751 Eden Place, W Vancouver, BC, Canada BCV 7T]; *b* 1940; uses her maiden name; *m* 1992 *Brian James Clayden and has issue:
1f *Kay Meredith BLUNT later BLUNT-CLAYDEN (son); *b* 1981
1d Marjorie Nina; *b* 14 Sept 1903; *m* 6 Nov 1930 George Douglas Laurie Pile, CBE (*d* 29 Jan 1965), only son of Sir George Laurie Pile, CBE, of Bulkeley, Barbados, and *d* 1982, leaving issue:
1e *Richard Edward Laurie [Richard Pile Esq, Ampney Knowle, nr Cirencester, Glos]; *b* 24 Oct 1934; *educ* Stowe and Trin Coll Cambridge (MA); *m* 1 Dec 1962 *Elizabeth Ann, yr dau of Charles Henry Lewis Bubb, of Brook House, Cricklade, Wilts, and has issue:
1f *Edward George Laurie; *b* 9 Jan 1965; *educ* Radley
2f *Hugo Richard Laurie; *b* 4 Nov 1967; *educ* Eton and Edinburgh U (MA)
1e *Celia Aimée Lorna Laurie [Princess Andrei Drutskoy-Sokolinsky, 36 Av Des Statuaires, 1180 Brussels, Belgium]; *b* 23 July 1937; *m* 20 June 1959 *Prince Andrei Drutskoy-Sokolinsky, only s of Prince Vladimir Drutskoy-Sokolinsky, of Rome, and has issue:
1f *Alexander [Prince Alexander Drutskoy-Sokolinsky, 9 Rue de Vervier, 1000 Brussels, Belgium]; *b* 29 June 1963; *educ* Brussels U (BAeq) and Darwin Coll Cambridge (LLM); *m* 1990 *Monique, dau of Dr François Debauche and has:
1g *Alexei; *b* 18 June 1991
2g *Ilya; *b* 20 May 1997
1g *Nikita; *b* 26 Aug 1993
2f *Nicolai; *b* 15 April 1966; *educ* Louvain U (MAeq)
1f *Ilyena [Mme Marc Ferrive, 53 Av du Cor de Chasse, 1170 Brussels, Belgium]; *b* 25 March 1961; *educ* Inst des Sciences Politique Paris (DEA) and Sorbonne; *m* 1990 *Marc Ferrive and has:
1g *Marie; *b* 25 Dec 1991
2g *Alexandre; *b* 25 Dec 1993
3g *Darya; *b* 25 Oct 1995
1c (cont.) Col Conrad Blunt *m* 2nd 22 June 1920 Beatrice (*d* 22 April 1946), widow of Frank Fullagar, and *d* 26 Dec 1948
2c Walter Theodore, Lt Roy Irish Regt; *b* 25 Nov 1870; *d* unm 3 Jan 1892
3c Charles Alfred; *b* 4 Nov 1873; *d* unm 4 April 1905
4c Arthur Powlett; *b* 13 July 1883; CMG (1923), Consul-Gen Canton 1937, WW I 1917–18 as Capt Chinese Labour Corps; *m* 11 Jan 1919 (*divorce* 1937) Winifred Grace (Freda) (*d* 1988), only dau of William Herbert Fawcett, MD, FRCS, of Bournemouth, and *d* 15 April 1946, leaving issue:
1d +Grant Anthony Clavell [Grant Blunt Esq, 12 Warwick Drive, London SW15]; *b* 8 Feb 1920; *educ* Bradfield; ACIS, Capt RM WW II; *m* 10 Jan 1942 *June Dorothy, er dau of J C Liddle, of 40 Bramley Rd, London N14, and has issue:
1e +Alistair Clavell; *b* 30 March 1946; *educ* Bradfield, Essex U (BA) and Heriot Watt U Edinburgh (MSc); *m* 1st 1973 (*divorce* 1980) Elizabeth Harden; *m* 2nd 19– *Ida, dau of Col Estioko, of Quezon City, Philippines, and has issue by 2nd w:
1f *Joachim Estioko Grant; *b* 1982
2f *Thomas Paul; *b* 1985
1e *Gene Carol [Mrs Bertrand Doger de Speville, 55 The Avenue, Richmond, Surrey]; *b* 24 April 1943; *educ* Cheltenham Ladies Coll and Bedford Coll London (BSc); *m* 1967 *Bertrand Edouard Doger de Speville, and has:
1f *Guy Rollo; *b* 1971; *educ* Ampleforth and R Holloway & Bedford New Coll, London (BSc)
1f *Claire Anne Maude; *b* 1974
2d +Evelyn Powlett Clavell, RD [Evelyn Blunt Esq RD, 45 Uplands Crt, Tallai, Queensland 4213, Australia]; *b* 29 Nov 1924; *educ* RNC Dartmouth; served WW II as Sub-Lt (Sp) RNVR 1942–46, Lt-Cdr (Sp) RNR 1964; *m* 19 May 1956 *Patricia Mary Elizabeth, only dau of Col William Joseph Gaunt Beach, MBE, of 2 The Mount, Market Drayton, Salop, and has issue:
1e +Jonathan Andrew Clavell [Jonathan Blunt Esq, 44 Pulsford Rd, Prospect, SA 5082, Australia]; *b* 2 March 1959; *m* 13 Sept 1997 *Sara Jane, only dau of James Crowe Davidson Mill, MB, BS, FRCS, FRACS, of Gould Creek, S Australia
1e *Sarah Virginia Clavell; *b* 10 Oct 1957; and has
1f *Elizabeth Marie; *b* 22 March 1983
2e *Philippa Mary Clavell; *b* 2 June 1960; *m* 22 March 1986 *Steven Peter Hunt and has issue:
1f *Rebecca Kate; *b* 26 March 1988
2f *Rachael Clare; *b* 16 Feb 1993
5c William Senhouse, MC, Lt-Col RE, served WWs I and II, 4th Cl Order of Nile; *b* 15 June 1885; *m* 3 Oct 1916 *Emmeline (*d* 18 Dec 1978), dau of Lt-Col Oswald Moseley Bradshaw, Madras Staff Corps, and *dsp* 29 March 1965
1c Caroline Elise; *m* 2 Sept 1919 Rev Charles Winwood Harnett, Vicar of Hatherden, Andover, Hants, son of Falkiner Minchin Harnett, Dist Insp RIC, of Cashel, Co Tipperary, and *d* 18 Aug 1958
2c Gertrude Amy; *d* unm April 1891
3c Isabel Maud; *d* unm 20 March 1890
1b Henrietta Laura; *m* 1 Jan 1859 Dr Hyde Salter, FRS, and had issue. He *d* 1871
2b Charlotte Anne; *m* 6 Jan 1853 Gen John Everett Thring, late RA, and *d* 1 April 1904, leaving issue. He *d* 1895
3b Mary Anne; *d* unm
(1) James Blunt *m* 2nd 9 April 1810 Sarah (*d* 5 April 1833), dau of Richard Little, and *d* 28 Sept 1832, having by her had, with other issue:
1a Harriet Louisa; *m* 24 June 1835 Hulbert Wathen, of Beckenham Lodge, Kent, yr son of Samuel Wathen, JP, of New House, Stroud, Glos, and *d* 1 Sept 1866, leaving issue. He *d* 2 Aug 1880
2a Caroline Arabella; *m* 4 July 1837 Rev Alfred Wilkinson, and *d* 13 July 1878. He *d* 16 July 1868
3a Sarah Selina; *m* 1840 Rev Alex Annand, and *d* 1899, leaving issue. He *d* 15 Sept 1853
2 Walter Blunt *m* 2nd 26 July 1774 Anna Maria (*d* 3 Dec 1829, aged 80), only dau of Sir Thomas Gatehouse, of Headley Park, Hants, and by her had, with other issue:
(2) Edward Walter, of Kempshott Park, Hants, DL and JP; *b* 28 Nov 1779; *m* 9 March 1813 Janet Shirley (*d* 23 April 1884), dau of James Allan, of The Hall, Stirling, and *d* 11 March 1860, having had, with other issue:
1a Charles Harris, CB, of Adderbury Manor, Oxon, Maj-Gen Roy Bengal Art; *b* 7 Sept 1825; *m* 1856 Mary Augusta (*d* 1892), dau of Col James Tod, and *d* 15 Aug 1900, having had issue:
1b Edward Walter BLUNT later BLUNT-MACKENZIE (added 1905), Maj RHA, T/Lt-Col RA 1915, served India, Egypt on Lord Kitchener's Staff, Ashanti and Sierra Leone Expdns and WW I, DL, JP Ross and Cromarty, planned one of the first hydro-electric schemes in Britain 1900; *b* 19 May 1869; *educ* Charterhouse,and RMA Woolwich; *m* 16 Dec 1899 Sibell Lilian, Countess of Cromartie in her own right (*see* CROMARTIE, E), and *d* 31 July 1949, leaving issue
2b Charles David McKinnon, Capt 4th Bn Seaforth Highlanders, TFR, served Riel Rebellion 1885 (medal), S African War 1899 (medal with three clasps) and WW I 1914; *b* 3 July 1865; *d* unm 30 Jan 1948
1b Janet Heatly; *d* unm 4 Aug 1950
2b Beatrice Marian; *d* unm 1 Dec 1900
2a James St John (Rev), Vicar Windsor, Berks, Chaplain in Ordinary to HM QUEEN VICTORIA, Master St Katherine's, Regent's Park; *b* 5 June 1827; *m* 1st 13 April 1863 Isabella Elizabeth (*d* 1866), dau of Rev John Stokes, Vicar of Cobham, Kent, and had issue:
1b Edward Henry, Capt Roy Berks Regt, Assist Embarkation Officer 1914; *b* 12 March 1865; *m* 20 Feb 1909 Constance, dau of Thomas Moore, and *dsp* 12 March 1943
2a (cont.) The Rev James Blunt *m* 2nd 23 July 1872 Lady Florence Catherine Seymour (*d* 7 May 1921), dau of 5th Marquess of Hertford (*qv*), and *d* 13 May 1889
3a Arthur, Col Roy Bombay Art; *b* 1 Jan 1829; *m* 3 Sept 1861 Frances Jemima (*d* 17 Nov 1910), dau of R S Roper, of Richmond, Yorks, and *d* 25 Dec 1904, having had issue:
1b Arthur Wharton; *b* 27 July 1866; India Forest Dept; *m* 19 April 1906 Mary (*d* 12 Dec 1936), dau of Col Arthur Edward Ward, Roy Welch Fus, and *d* 4 Feb 1939, leaving issue:
1c Arthur Roper Lascelles; *b* 29 June 1925
1c Frances Georgina Shirley; *b* 21 March 1907
2c Marjory Grace; *b* 17 Sept 1908
3c Joan Evelyn Mary; *b* 15 Sept 1914; *m* 6 June 1947 Cadet Offr Kazimierz Wysokinski, Polish Army, son of Andrzej Wysokinski, of 88 Starowiejska, Siedlec, Poland
4c *Joyce Cautley [Mrs Peter Presnail, 210 Coromandel Parade, Coromandel Valley, SA 5051, Australia]; *b* 1921; *m* 22 Feb 1946 *Peter James Presnail, son of James Presnail, of 5 The Ridgeway, Chatham, Kent, and has:
1d *Richard James; *b* 14 Aug 1947; *m* 1975 *Marilyn Rowan, and has issue:
1e *Catharine Louise; *b* 1980
2e *Elizabeth Anne; *b* 1982
1d *Shirley Jane; *b* 29 May 1951; *m* 1972 *Jeremy Cuthbertson, and has issue:
1e *Dayle Deanne Shirley; *b* 1986
2d *Hazel Jean; *b* 22 Feb 1954; *m* 1990 *Leon Marshall
2b Hugh Roper; *b* 21 Sept 1874; *m* 13 Oct 1915 Agnes Sara (*d* 13 March 1948), dau of Charles Gray, of Waiohika, Gisborne, NZ, and *d* 21 Jan 1931, leaving issue:
1c Michael Hugh; *b* 5 March 1920; PhD, MRCVS, served in Burma 1944–47 as Capt RAVC; *m* 15 Nov 1959 Susanne Mary (*d* 1983), dau of Lawson L C Field, of Gisborne, NZ, and *d* 1983, leaving issue:
1d +Gerald Hugh Lawson [Gerald Blunt Esq, 63 Barnard St, Wadestown, Wellington, New Zealand]; *b* 27 Dec 1959; *m* 1990 *Emma Tamsin Harcourt, dau of Phillip Armes, of Hurstpierpoint, W Sussex, and has issue:
1e *Isabella Rose Henrietta; *b* 1992

2c +Richard Mark [Richard Blunt Esq, 9 Highbridge Way, Karrinyup, WA 6018, Australia]; *b* 25 April 1924; Lt RN (ret), served WW II; *m* 1st 23 Aug 1952 (*divorce* 1963) Adrien Seldon, dau of Leslie Seldon Truss, of Dale Hill House, Ticehurst, Wadhurst, Sussex, and has issue:

1d *Teresa June; *b* 13 June 1953

2c (cont.) Richard Blunt *m* 2nd 18 Sept 1965 *Patricia Eileen, dau of Walter Stanley Lee, of Perth, W Australia, and by her has issue:

1d +David Mark; *b* 6 July 1967

1d *Georgia Alison; *b* 1969

1c Barbara Aldham; *b* 25 Nov 1918; *d* unm June 1967

3b Allan St John; *b* 27 Oct 1880; DSO (1915), Lt-Col and Brev Col late York and Lancaster Regt, served S African War 1899–1902 (two medals, eight clasps), and WW I 1914–18 (wounded despatches, brevet); *m* 4 March 1914 Doris Elizabeth (*d* 1 April 1948), dau of John George Stephen, of Douglas, IoM, and *d* 31 July 1931, leaving:

1c Arthur Colvin; *b* 3 Oct 1918; *d* 1925

1c Rosamund Audrey; *b* 5 Nov 1921; *m* 31 May 1947 Maj Ian Henry Whitworth, TD, FLAS, JP, land agent to the Earl of Leicester, only son of Capt John Whitworth, of Yaxham, Norfolk, and has issue:

1d *Robert St John; *b* 2 April 1949; *educ* Harrow

1d *Sally Judith Prudence; *b* 21 Sept 1952

2d *Lucinda; *b* 26 Jan 1957

2c *Elizabeth Shirley; *b* 1923; *m* 6 Sept 1944 *Harry Batten Poustie, DSC, RD, est son of Cdr William Taylor Poustie, RD, RNR, of Carnoustie, Scotland, and has issue:

1d Allan William; *b* 14 Dec 1946; *d* 19 Dec 1961

2d *John David; *b* 6 Feb 1948; *educ* Bedford Sch; *m* 1981 *Sandra Mason

3d *Michael Ian; *b* 28 July 1954; *educ* Bedford Sch; *m* 1977 *Coral Purton, and has issue:

1e *Simon Ian William; *b* 1978

2e *James Michael; *b* 1981

1e *Elizabeth Claire; *b* 1979

2e *Rosemary; *b* 1984

4d *Richard Hugh; *b* 9 March 1965; *m* 1989 *Sandra Cording

5d *Charles Christopher; *b* 9 March 1965; *m* 1993 *Heather Pinner

1d *Vivienne Mary; *b* 6 May 1951; *m* 1974 *Leslie Keast, and has issue:

1e *Christopher John; *b* 1978

1e *Deborah Jane; *b* 1977

2e *Katherine Louise; *b* 1983

2d *Louise Caroline; *b* 7 Jan 1964; *m* 1991 *Gary Castleton, and has issue:

1e *Joshua Allan; *b* 1993

1b Helen Shirley; *d* unm 19 March 1898

2b Dorothy; *m* 6 Feb 1926 Frederick Alcock, civil servant, son of Walter William Alcock, of Wellesley House, Twickenham, and *d* 15 Aug 1944

3b Marjory Armytage; *m* 18 April 1907 Lt-Col Arthur Eyre Beadon, late APD, son of Sir Cecil Beadon, KCSI, and *d* 10 June 1962. He *d* 28 Aug 1945

4b Sybil Allan; *d* unm 21 Oct 1952

4a Alexander Colvin (Rev), Rector Millbrook 1865–89 and Burghclere, Berks, 1899–1915, Hon Canon Winchester 1889; *b* 14 Nov 1831; *educ* Ch Ch Oxford (MA); *m* 27 June 1865 Lady Susanna Nelson (*d* 8 April 1900), dau of 2nd Earl Nelson (*qv*), and *dsp* 1 April 1920

1a Elizabeth Maria; *m* 8 May 1839 Rev Harris Jervoise Bigg Wither and had issue

2a Harriet; *m* 17 Aug 1841 Rev John Lawrell, and had issue

1 Eliza Maria; *m* 17 Nov 1804 John Greathead Harris

Sir HENRY *d* 12 Oct 1759; his est son,

Sir Charles William Blunt, 3rd Bt; *b* 4 Sept 1731; *m* 22 July 1764 Elizabeth (*d* 17 Jan 1836 aged 91), only dau of Alderman Richard Peers, of London, and sis and heiress of Sir Richard Peers Symons, Bt, and *d* 29 Aug 1802, having had, with other issue:

1 **Sir Charles Richard Blunt, 4th Bt**, HEICS; *b* 6 Dec 1775; *m* 20 March 1824 Sophia (*d* 14 Aug 1862), widow of Richard Auchmuty and dau of Richard Baker, MD, and *d* 29 Feb 1840, leaving issue:

(1) **Sir Walter Blunt, 5th Bt**; *b* 16 March 1826; *d* unm 13 July 1847

2 Richard Charles, of Bretlands, Chertsey; *b* 2 Jan 1777; *m* 15 Nov 1809 Eliza Forbes (*d* 23 April 1871), dau of Major William Forbes Mercer; *d* 16 Jan 1846, leaving, with other issue:

(1) **Sir Charles William Blunt, 6th Bt**, DL, barrister; *b* 22 Nov 1810; *d* unm 5 Nov 1890

(2) Richard John, of Bretlands, Chertsey, JP, Capt 25th Madras NI; *b* 23 Sept 1822; *d* 13 May 1874

3 William, Bengal Civil Service; *b* 7 Dec 1780; *m* 23 Jan 1822 Eliza, dau of Gen Goddard Richards, HEICS, and *d* 1859, leaving issue:

(1) Charles, civil servant Burma; *b* 1 Jan 1824; *dsp* 1884

(2) **Sir William Blunt, 7th Bt**, of Heathfield Park and Ringmer, Sussex, which estates he sold; Bengal Civil Service 1846–75; *b* 25 June 1826; *m* 1st 1852 Margaret (*dsp* 1854), dau of Capt Scott, RN; *m* 2nd 3 Nov 1857 Henrietta Georgina Josephine (*d* 6 Feb 1892), dau of Rev Robert Green Jeston, Rector Avon Dassett, Warwicks, and *dsp* 27 Dec 1902

(3) JOHN HARVEY (Sir), **8th Bt**

(1) Annie Eliza; *b* 9 Nov 1822; *m* Maj-Gen Charles Pulley, Madras Army, and had issue. He *d* 1888

(2) Charlotte Sophia; *b* 24 April 1825; *m* 1845 Mungo Smith Gilmore, late Bengal Civil Service, and *d* 1900, leaving issue. He *d* 1808

(3) Emily Louise; *b* 28 Dec 1836; *m* Capt Coape, 12th Lancers, and had issue

1 Louisa; *m* William Dent, of Brickendonbury, Herts, and *d* 9 March 1833

2 Maria Tryphena; *m* Sir C Cockrell, Bt, and *d* 1789

3 Elizabeth; *m* 10 Nov 1801, as his 2nd wife, her second cousin Sir Charles Burrell Blunt, of Ringmer, Sussex (*see above*), and *d* 1839

4 Charlotte; *m* Lt-Gen Sir Charles Imhoff

5 Lydia; *m* Sir Alexander Seton, Bt, of Abercorn (*qv*)

6 Anna Maria; *m* Hon Charles Andrew Bruce

Sir WILIAM's bro,

Sir John Harvey Blunt, 8th Bt, Capt 1st Bn Roy Dublin Fus and 4th Bn N Lancs Regt, served 1st Bn Roy Welch Fus Indian Mutiny 1857 (medal with clasp); *b* 1 Jan 1839; *m* 28 April 1870 Susan (*d* 1 April 1917), dau of Philip Hoad, and had issue:

1 JOHN HARVEY (Sir) **9th Bt**

2 Walter Cecil; *b* 1 March 1877; *d* 17 Nov 1936

3 Charles William Lockhart; *b* 2 June 1882; *m* 15 March 1913 Lillian (*d* 20 Jan 1958), dau of H Calcut, of Goudhurst, Kent, and *d* 18 Jan 1958, having had issue:

(1) Charles John Harvey, Sergt/Pilot RAF WW II; *b* 9 Dec 1920; *ka* over Hamburg 30 Dec 1941

(2) +ROBIN ANTHONY [Robin Blunt Esq, Little Paddock, Fairacre, Lea, Wilts SN16 9PA; 14 Allée du Chateau, 31770 Colomiers, France]; *b* 2 Feb 1926; heir presumptive; *educ* Wellington; CEng, MIMechE; *m* 1st 23 Nov 1949 (*divorce* 1962) Sheila Stuart, dau of C Stuart Brindley, of Duffield, Derbys, and has issue:

1a +Jonathan Stuart; *b* 10 April 1955

(2) (cont.) +ROBIN BLUNT *m* 2nd 31 Dec 1962 *June Elizabeth, dau of Charles Wigginton, of The Park, Duffield, Derbys, and by her has further issue:

2a +Mark Charles; *b* 28 Sept 1963

4 Henry Wilfrid; *b* 17 May 1887; *m* 10 May 1915 Maud Etta, dau of J Hyde, and *d* 13 Oct 1957, leaving issue:

(1) *Gabrielle Hilda [Mrs Gabrielle Bond, 3 Gingerbread Lane, Hawkhurst, Kent]; *b* 8 Jan 1919; *m* 1st 3 Aug 1941 (*divorce* 1950) Capt Tony Thawnton, 3rd King's Own Hus, and has issue:

1a *Paul John Anthony THAWNTON later BOND; *b* 1946; adopted 1955 by his stepfather, Julian Bond, whose surname he assumed, and has issue by Jenny Desmond:

1b *Laurence Jack; *b* 1983

1b *Alice Pearl Sweetpea; *b* 1981

2a *Nicholas Peter THAWNTON later BOND; *b* 1947; adopted 1955 by his stepfather, whose surname he assumed; W/Cdr RAF and RNZAF (ret 1994); *m* 1970 *Diane Christine Edwards, and has issue:

1b *Karen Kirsten; *b* 1972

2b *Alexis Alison; *b* 1977

(1) (cont.) Mrs Gabrielle Thawnton *m* 2nd 10 Nov 1955 (*divorce* 1972) Julian M Bond, only son of Maj-Gen John Arthur Mallock Bond, CB, CBE, of 15 Queen's Gate Terrace, London SW7, and has further issue:

1a *Stella Mary; *b* 30 Aug 1956

1 Cicely Mary Fanny; *d* unm 21 Jan 1908

2 Eliza Hilda; *d* unm 11 April 1951

Sir JOHN *d* 26 Jan 1922, and was *s* by his est son,

Sir John Harvey Blunt, 9th Bt, Capt Natal Border Police, served Imp Yeo S African War 1899–1902 (two medals and eight clasps) and RASC WW I 1914; *b* 30 July 1872; *m* 22 March 1906 Maud Julia (*d* 24 Dec 1935), est dau of Sir David Lionel Goldsmid-Stern-Salomons, 2nd Bt, and *d* 11 July 1938, having had issue:

1 **Sir John Lionel Reginald Blunt, 10th Bt**; *b* 28 May 1908; *educ* Harrow; 2nd Lt 10th Hus (SR); *m* 1st 31 March 1932 (*divorce* 1941) Heather Alice, yr dau of Capt John Broadley Harrison-Broadley, MFH, of Welton; *m* 2nd 1947 *Margaret Hunam, formerly wife of (a) 2nd Viscount Rothermere (*qv*) and (b) Capt Thomas Andrew Hussey, RN (ret), and dau of William L Redhead, of Carville Hall, Brentford, and Janet Lady Lacon, and *d* 29 Sept 1969

2 **Sir Richard David Harvey Blunt, 11th Bt**, Lt 4th/7th Dragoon Gds; *b* 22 Oct 1912; *m* 1st 20 Oct 1936 Elisabeth (Fif) Malvine, est dau of Cdr F H Fransen Van de Putte, Roy Netherlands Navy, and had issue:

(1) Sir DAVID RICHARD REGINALD BLUNT, **12th and present Bt**

2 (cont.) **Sir Richard** *m* 2nd 18 May 1943 Margaret (*d* 1 Sept 1995), est dau of John H Dean, of Duntisbourne Leer, Cirencester, and *d* 13 Feb 1975, leaving by her:

(1) *Georgina Lavinia [Mrs Martin Trotter, Winterwell Farm, Northleach, Glos GL54 3QD]; *b* 12 Oct 1945; *m* 1981 *Martin Frederick Trotter, yr son of Maj Frederick Liddell Trotter, JP, of Mells Park, Frome, Somerset, and has:

1a *James Martin; *b* 26 Jan 1982

1a *Camilla Julia Margaret; *b* 29 March 1983

(2) *Caroline Margaret; *b* 21 Nov 1947

3 Charles Henry David; *b* 18 Sept 1919

1 *Cecily Maud Helen [Mrs Robin Whitworth, 45 Plantation Rd, Oxford OX2 6JE]; *b* 12 May 1910; *m* 10 July 1934 Robin Aymer Whitworth (*d* 27 July 1996), only *s* of Geoffrey Arundel Whitworth, CBE, FRSL, of S Kensington, and has:

(1) *Anna Maureen Cecily; *b* 6 April 1945

2 Doris Ruth Julia Sybil; *b* 4 June 1916; *m* 9 April 1945 Maj Frederick William Kennedy, IA, Probyn's Horse (*d* 1972), yr son of Frederick William Kennedy, of Limerick, and *d* 10 June 1997, leaving:

(1) *Amber Julia [Mrs David Sinclair, 48 Cyril Mansions, Prince of Wales Dve, London SW11 4HW; Kilcurly Adare, Co Limerick, Ireland]; *b* 19 Oct 1946; *m* 1st 1972 (*divorce* 1984) Rodger A Brooks; *m* 2nd 1985 *David Sinclair

(2) *Susan Anne [Mrs Patrick McSwiney, 12 Macaulay Rd, London SW4 0QX]; *b* 18 July 1948; *m* 1976 *Patrick McSwiney and has issue:

1a *Luke Frederick Patrick; *b* 1984

1a *Zoe Julia; *b* 1980

BLYTH

Arms: Az., on a mount in base ppr. a bull statant arg., ringed ppr. and attached and fastened to the ground with a chain or, on a chief arched of the last a stag's head erased of the second between two annulets gu. **Crest:** In front of a stag's head erased and gorged with a wreath of vine ppr., three roses gu. **Supporters:** On either side a stag ppr. semée of annulets or and gorged with a wreath of vine, also ppr. **Motto:** *Spero meliora* ('I hope for better things'). **Creations:** Bt. (UK) 30 Aug 1895, B. (UK) 19 July 1907.

THE 4TH BARON BLYTH, of Blythwood, Stansted Mountfitchet, Essex, and a **Baronet** (Sir Anthony Audley Rupert Blyth, Bt) [The Rt Hon The Lord Blyth, Blythwood Estate, Athenry, Co Galway, Ireland]; *b* 3 June 1931; *s f* 1977; *educ* St Columba's Coll Dublin; *m* 1st 1954 (*divorce* 1962) Elizabeth Dorothea, dau of Robert T Sparrow, of Vancouver, BC, and has had issue:

1 Riley Audley John; *b* 4 March 1955; *educ* Portora Roy Sch; *m* 1979 (*divorce* 1984) Peggy, dau of John Scanlon, and *d* 23 June 1996

1 *Marcia Edna Dorothea; *b* 1956

2 *Alexandra; *b* 1957

The 4th BARON *m* 2nd 1963 *Oonagh Elizabeth Ann, yr dau of William Henry Conway, of Dundrum, Dublin, and by her has further issue:

2 +JAMES AUDLEY IAN; *b* 13 Nov 1970

3 *Lucinda Audley Jane; *b* 10 Nov 1966

Lineage: JAMES BLYTH, of Chelmsford, Essex; *b* 24 Dec 1803; *m* 15 April 1836 Caroline (*d* 2 July 1894), est dau of Henry Gilbey, of Bishop's Stortford, Herts (*see* GILBEY, Bt), and *d* 15 Jan 1862, leaving, with other issue:

1 JAMES, **1st Baron**

2 Henry Arthur, of Stansted Mountfitchet, Essex, and 45 Portland Place, London W; *b* 10 April 1843; *m* 15 Aug 1867 his er bro's sis-in-law Sarah (*d* 23 May 1914), dau of William Mooney, of Clontarf, Co Dublin, and *d* 4 Jan 1901, leaving issue

The er son,

Sir James Blyth, 1st Bt, and **1st Baron Blyth**, of Blythwood, Stansted Mountfitchet, Essex, so *cr* 30 Aug 1895 and 19 July 1907 respectively (both UK), JP (Herts and Essex), dir W & A Gilbey Ltd, v-pres RSA, govr, pres, v-pres or memb: Br Dairy Farmers' Assoc, English Jersey Cattle Soc, Southdown Sheep-Breeders' Assoc and Nat Poultry Organisn Soc, chm: Organising Ctee Franco-British Exhibition 1908, Japan-British Exhibition 1910 and Coronation Exhibition 1911, pres Latin-Br Exhibition 1912, Order: Leopold of Belgium, Medjidie and Grand Cross Portuguese Merito Agricola; *b* 10 Sept 1841; *m* 29 Aug 1865 Eliza (*d* 12 Dec 1894), dau of William Mooney, of Clontarf, Co Dublin, and *d* 8 Feb 1925, having had issue:

1 HERBERT WILLIAM BLYTH, **2nd Baron Blyth**; *educ* Rugby, JP (Essex), dir W & A Gilbey; *b* 1 March 1868; *m* 12 Jan 1927 Sylvia Mary (*m* 3rd 5 June 1947 Maj Chave Charles Nainby-Luxmoore and *d* 15 June 1974), formerly w of Ronald Lionel Fitzroy Cole and only dau of Edwin Edward Dennis, and *dsp* 27 Feb 1943

2 Audley James, Lt Essex Imp Yeo; *b* 20 Feb 1874; *m* 20 Jan 1903 Ethel Jane, MBE (1918) (*d* 17 Nov 1931), yst dau of Sir John Brunner, 1st Bt (*qv*), and *d* 21 March 1908, leaving issue:

(1) IAN AUDLEY JAMES BLYTH, **3rd Baron Blyth**; *b* 28 Oct 1905; *m* 30 May 1928 Edna Myrtle (*d* 1952), dau of Ernest Lewis, of Wellington, New Zealand, and *d* 1977, leaving issue:

1a ANTHONY AUDLEY RUPERT BLYTH, **4th and present Baron Blyth**

2a +Adrian Ulrick Christopher David [The Hon Adrian Blyth, Torwood, Maree, Oranmore, Co Galway, Ireland]; *b* 23 Oct 1944; *educ* Sebright Sch and Northants Coll of Ag; engine reconditioner, ag engr; *m* 22 Oct 1966 *Patricia Maureen, dau of Desmond C Southey, of Northampton, and has issue:

1b +Mark Terence; *b* 1969

2b +Ian Christopher; *b* 1975

1b *Sarah Ursula; *b* 20 Oct 1967

2b *Verena Rosemary; *b* 1971

3b *Natasha Rachael; *b* 1973; *m* 20 July 1996 *William, er s of Peter Hemmings, of Pasadena, Calif

1a *Tanya Ormond Audley [The Hon Tanya Blyth, Rockfield House, Athenry, Co Galway, Ireland]; *b* 1 Sept 1929; SRN, SCN; BA (1981) U Coll Galway

2a *Barbara Edna Patricia; *b* 20 Oct 1936; *m* 1966 Aidan William Doyle, MRCVS (*d* 1991), yst s of Martin E Doyle, of Hill View, Athy, Co Kildare, and has issue:

1b *Nicholas Richard; *b* 1968

1b *Fiona Sarah; *b* 1971

3a *Anne Shelagh Jennifer (twin) [The Hon Anne Blyth, Rockfield House, Athenry, Co Galway, Ireland]; *b* 1936

3 Rupert Alfred, Capt Essex Yeo; *b* 14 June 1877; *m* 6 Nov 1924 Charlotte May (*d* 1 Jan 1956), only dau of William Gibson and n of 1st Baron Glanely (*see* 1940 edn), and *d* 10 March 1951, having had issue:

(1) Louisa Juliet; *b* 22 March 1929; *d* unm 22 Sept 1942

1 Nora Beatrice; *m* 29 April 1885 Col Alan Coulston Gardner, DL, JP, of Clearwell Castle, Coleford, Glos, and *d* 5 Jan 1944, leaving issue (*see* RYCROFT, Bt)

2 Grace Loudenne; *m* 24 Oct 1905 Brig-Gen Claude Stuart Rome, CMG, DSO, late 2nd Dragoon Gds, est son of Thomas Rome, JP, of Charlton House, Charlton Kings, Glos, and *d* 11 July 1952, leaving issue. He *d* 17 May 1956

3 Gladys Ellen; *m* 17 Feb 1898 Gerald Gilbey Gold, son of Sir Charles Gold, of Birchanger, Essex, and *d* 22 Nov 1967, aged 88, leaving issue. He *d* 14 Jan 1939

4 Millicent Catherine; *d* unm 1940

BLYTH OF ROWINGTON

Arms: Gyronny of twelve gules and argent a horse rampant sable langued gules. **Crest:** upon a helm with a wreath argent and gules out of an Eastern crown gules a dexter arm embowed in armour the hand gauntletted proper grasping by its blade a sword pointing downwards all argent and holding to the blade by its stalk leaved vert a double rose argent upon gules, barbed and seeded proper. **Supporters:** On either side an Unicorn reguardant argent, armed and unguled or, in the mouth a double Rose argent upon gules, barbed, seeded and leaved proper. **Motto:** *Quod verum tutum* ('What is safe is true'). **Creation:** B. (LP, UK) 1995

THE BARON BLYTH OF ROWINGTON, of Rowington in the County of Warwickshire (Sir James Blyth) [The Rt Hon The Lord Blyth of Rowington, c/o The Boots Co, Nottingham NG2 3AA]; *b* 8 May 1940; *educ* Spiers Sch and Glasgow U; with Mobil Oil 1963–69, Gen Foods 1969–71, Mars 1971–74, gen manager Lucas Batteries 1974–77, Lucas Aerospace 1977–81, head def sales MOD 1981–85, md Plessey Electronic Systems 1985–86, The Plessey Co 1986–87; dir: Imperial Gp 1984–86, Cadbury-Schweppes 1986–90, Br Aerospace 1990–94 and NatWest 1998–, chm advsy panel Citizens' Charter 1991–97, Govr London Business Sch 1987–96, dir and ch exec The Boots Co 1987– (dep chm 1994–98, exec chm 1998–), ktd 1985, FRAeS 1994, Liveryman Coachmakers' and Coach Harness Makers' Co, Hon LLD Nottingham 1992, Hon Fell London Business School 1997; *m* 1967 *Pamela Anne Campbell Dixon and has a dau and a s decd

Lineage: DANIEL BLYTH; *m* Jane Power Carlton and had:

JAMES, *cr* a **Baron**

BOARDMAN

Arms: Azure, on a fess embattled, between in chief two horses salient and in base a boar's head couped argent, three roses gules, barbed and seeded proper. **Crest:** A demi-horse argent, maned, crined and hooved or, about its neck by the strings a purse azure tasselled gold, mantled azure doubled or. **Supporters:** Dexter, a lion reguardant or, head and mane gules, gorged with a collar sable bezanty; sinister, a horse rampant argent, maned, crined and hooved or, with a collar sable bezanty. **Creation:** B. (LP. UK) 1980

THE BARON BOARDMAN, of Welford, Co Northants (Thomas Gray Boardman, MC (1944), TD (1952), DL (Northants 1977)) [The Rt Hon The Lord Boardman MC TD DL, The Manor House, Welford, Northants NN6 6HX; 29 Tufton Court, Tufton St, London SWlP 3QH]; *b* 12 Jan 1919; *educ* Bromsgrove Sch; Lt-Col Comdg I Northants Yeo WW II NW Europe, slr 1947, MP (C) Leicester SW 1967–74 and Leicester S Feb-Sept 1974, Min for Industry DTI 1972–74, Ch Sec Treasury 1974; chm: Chamberlain Phipps Ltd 1958–72, Ctee of London and Scottish Bankers 1987–89 and Heron International NV 1993–95, dir: Allied Breweries 1968–72 and 1974–76 (v-chm 1975–76), Steetley Co Ltd 1975–83 (chm 1978–83), Nat West Bank 1979–89 (chm 1983–89) and MEPC Ltd 1980–89, Pres Assoc Br Chambers Commerce 1977–80, memb: advsy bd LEK Ptnrship 1990–97 and Exec Assoc C Peers 1981–84 and 1991–95, HM Lt City London 1989–; *m* 1948 *(Norah Mary) Deirdre, only dau of late Hubert Vincent Gough, of Pangbourne, Berks, and widow of John Henry Chaworth Musters, and has:

1 *Anthony Hubert Gray [The Hon Anthony Boardman, Lodge Farm, Hall Lane, Welford, Northants]; *b* 1949; *m* 1977 *Catherine, dau of W Penn, of Denton, Northants, and has three daus

2 *Nigel Patrick Gray; *b* 1950; *m* 1975 *Sarah, dau of T A Coslett, of Cambridge, and has had:

(1) *Hugo, *b* 1990
(1) *Tamsin, *b* 1980
(2) *Charlotte, *b* 1981
(3) *Rebecca, *b* 1984
(4) Victoria, *b* and *d* 1985
(5) *Cordelia, *b* 1987
(6) *Elizabeth, *b* 1992

1 *Grania Janet Gray, *b* 1955; *m* 1981 *Capt Hon Rupert Edward Henry Law, late Coldstream Gds, est s of 8th Baron Ellenborough (*qv*), and has issue

Lineage: JOHN CLAYTON BOARDMAN, of Daventry, Northants; *m* Janet Houston and had:

THOMAS GRAY, *cr* a **Baron**

BOILEAU

Arms: Az. a castle triple-towered or, masoned sa., in base a crescent of the second. **Crest:** A pelican in her piety ppr., charged on the breast with a saltire couped gu. **Motto:** *De tout mon coeur* ('With all my heart'). **Creation:** Bt. (UK) 24 July 1838.

SIR GUY FRANCIS BOILEAU, 8TH BT, of Tacolneston Hall, Norfolk [Sir Guy Boileau Bt, 14 Faircroft Ave, Glen Iris, Victoria 3146, Australia]; *b* 23 Feb 1935; *s* f 1980; *educ* Xavier Coll Melbourne and RMC Duntroon; antique dealer, Lt-Col, Lt Aust Staff Corps 1956, platoon cdr 3rd Bn Roy Aust Regt, Malaya, 1957–58, observer UN Mil Observer Gp India and Pakistan 1959–60, Instructor Australian Army Training Team Vietnam 1963–64, attached US Def Dept Washington, DC, 1966–68, Security Advsr Dept Administrator Territory of Papua-New Guinea 1970–71, cmdg offr Army Intell Centre 1972–74, Directing Staff (Instr) Australian Staff Coll 1975–76, SO1 Personnel HQ 3rd Mil Dist 1979; *m* 1962 *Judith Frances, dau of Senator George Conrad Hannan, of Glen Iris and Canberra, and has issue:

1 +NICHOLAS EDMOND GEORGE; *b* 17 Nov 1964
2 +Christopher Guy; *b* 1969
1 *Simone Teresa; *b* 1963
2 *Caroline Virginia; *b* 1968
3 *Antonia Josephine; *b* 1975

Lineage: CHARLES BOILEAU (descended from Etienne Boileau, Govr and first Grand-Provost Paris 1255), feudal lord of Castelnau and St Croix, Languedoc, France; *b* Nîmes 10 Feb 1673; as a Huguenot left France at the Revocation of the Edict of Nantes 1685, cmded a corps of French Gentlemen at Blenheim under the Duke of Marlborough; *m* 30 Dec 1703 Mary Magdalen (*d* Sept 1731), dau of Daniel Collot d'Escury, also a Huguenot émigré of noble family, and *d* 7 March 1733, leaving issue:

SIMEON BOILEAU, merchant in Dublin; *b* Southampton 4 Oct 1717; *m* 6 Aug 1741 Magdalen, dau of Theophilius La Cour Desbrisay, and *d* 1 Jan 1767, having had issue, with several daus:

1 SOLOMON; *b* 31 Jan 1744/5; *m* 1st 3 May 1766 Dorothea, dau of Francis Gradwell, of Dublin, and had issue; *m* 2nd 1792 Lucy, dau of John Slater, and *d* 21 Dec 1810; ggf of:

(1) Col Francis William Boileau, CB, IA, heir male of the BOILEAUx and rep of the Lds of Castelnau; *d* 14 Nov 1915, leaving issue:

1a Col Frank Ridley Farrer Boileau, RE; *dvp* 27 Aug 1914 of wounds recd in action, leaving issue, with two yr sons:

1b Capt Etienne Henry Tudor Boileau, Somerset LI

2 JOHN PETER, of whom presently

3 Thomas, of Calcutta; *b* 14 Dec 1754; *m* 24 March 1796 Leah (*d* 22 June 1845), dau of Lt-Col Ebenezer Jessop, of Albany, NY, USA, and *d* 11 June 1806, leaving issue

4 John Theophilus, of Dublin; *b* 28 Dec 1755; *m* Jane (*d* 20 Sept 1851), dau of H Wilson, and *d* 1817, leaving issue

The 2nd son,

JOHN PETER BOILEAU, of Tacolneston Hall; *b* 30 Nov 1747; *m* 25 Nov 1790 Henrietta (*d* 4 Nov 1817), est dau and coheir of Rev George Pollen, of Little Bookham, Surrey (*see* POLLEN, Bt), and *d* 10 March 1837, leaving issue:

1 JOHN PETER (Sir), **1st Bt**

2 George Pollen BOILEAU later BOILEAU-POLLEN (Rev), Rector Little Bookham, Surrey, an estate he inherited from his maternal gf, adding the name POLLEN; *b* 14 Aug 1798; *m* 13 Feb 1824 Elizabeth (*d* 26 Feb 1873), dau of Sir James Hall, Bt, of Dunglass (*qv*), and *d* 7 Nov 1847, having had issue

3 Charles Lestock, Maj Rifle Bde; *b* 8 Feb 1800; *m* 1st 27 Feb 1833 Amelia (*dsp* 2 Nov 1833), only child of Lt-Gen Sir Frederick Adam, GCB, GCMG, PC; *m* 2nd 16 Aug 1836 (*divorce* 1846) Margaret, widow of Claudius Kerr, HEICS, and dau of William Stirling, and had a dau; *m* 3rd 27 Nov 1848 Maria (*d* 26 Nov 1899), dau of Edward Wenham, of Hastings, and *d* 18 Jan 1889

1 Henrietta Maria; *m* 28 June 1828 John Scott, MD, and *d* 3 May 1837, leaving issue

The est son,

Sir John Peter Boileau, 1st Bt (UK), so *cr* 24 July 1838, of Tacolneston, DL, JP, FRS; *b* 2 Sept 1794; *m* 14 Nov 1825 Lady Catherine Sarah Elliot (*d* 25 June 1862), 3rd dau of 1st Earl of Minto (*qv*), and *d* 9 March 1869, having had issue:

1 John Elliot; *b* 28 Sept 1827; *dvp* unm 8 Oct 1861

2 **Sir Francis George Manningham Boileau, 2nd Bt**, of Kettringham and Tacolneston, Norfolk, VD, BA Oxford, DL, JP, CA Norfolk, FSA, FRSL, barrister, Lt-Col 3rd Norfolk Rifle Vols, KStJ; *b* 26 March 1830; *m* 2 Aug 1860 Lucy Henrietta (*d* 19 Nov 1925), est dau of Sir John Nugent, 2nd Bt, and *d* 2 Dec 1900, having had:

(1) Arthur John Vernon; *b* 18 June 1861; *d* 8 Aug 1863

(2) John Francis Elliot; *b* 30 Oct 1863; *d* unm 9 April 1894

(3) **Sir Maurice Colborne Boileau, 3rd Bt**, DL, JP Norfolk; *educ* Worcester Coll Oxford, (MA); *b* 3 Dec 1865; *d* unm 13 Sept 1937

(4) **Sir Raymond Frederic Boileau, 4th Bt**, DL and JP (Norfolk), Lt-Col RFA, formerly Lt Northants Regt, served WW I (despatches); *b* 6 Oct 1868; *m* 1 Nov 1905 Ethel Mary (*d* 16 Jan 1942), only child of Rev James Foster Young, and *dsp* 23 June 1942

(1) Margaret Lucy Augusta, MB, BS London; *b* 18 July 1867; *d* 17 Sept 1923

3 Edmund William Pollen; *b* 8 Aug 1831; *m* 1870 Bridget Mary (*d* 16 Aug 1912), dau of James Walsh, and was drowned in Corlo Bay 9 July 1883, leaving issue:

(1) **Sir Francis James Boileau, 5th Bt**, JP; *b* 6 Nov 1871; *m* 20 Nov 1895 Wilhelmina, dau of George Lyon, of Victoria, Australia, and *d* 20 Feb 1945 had issue:

1a **Sir Gilbert George Benson Boileau, 6th Bt**; *educ* Xavier Coll and Newman Coll Melbourne U (MB, BS 1923); MOH health Shire of Dandenong, Maj Australian AMC (Res); *b* 13 Feb 1898; *m* 1st 15 July 1924 (*divorce* 1933) Chica Patricia, dau of James Louis Edgworth-Somers, LRCSI, of Mornington, Victoria, Australia, and had issue:

1b *Prudence Despreaux [Mrs Anthony Harvey, 138 Napolean St, Eltham, Victoria, Australia]; *b* 12 May 1925; *m* 1954 *Anthony Harvey and has issue:

1c *Georgia; *b* 1955

2c *Tracey; *b* 1958

2b *Angela Mary; *b* 1 Aug 1927; *m* 1949 *John Stewart Milne and has issue:

1b *Anthony Stewart; *b* 1950

1b *Virginia; *b* 1951

2b *Sarah; *b* 1952

3b *Jane; *b* 1954

4b *Lisa; *b* 1956

5b *Elizabeth; *b* 1967

6b *Melanie; *b* 1967

1a **Sir Gilbert** *m* 2nd 28 July 1941 *Mary Catherine [Mary Lady Boileau, 146 Power St, Hawthorn, VIC, Australia], dau of Lawrence Riordan, of Cradock, S Australia, and *d* 1978, leaving further issue:

3b *Madelon Mary; *b* 12 May 1945; *m* 1970 *Geoffrey George Foletta, and has issue:

1b *Gregory George; *b* 1972

2b *Samuel George; *b* 1976

3b *Hamish; *b* 1978

1b *Monique Louise; *b* 1974

4b *Elizabeth Ann; *b* 7 June 1948; *m* 1974 *Simon John File, and has issue:

1b *Simon Charles; *b* 1977

1b *Trinity; *b* 1975

2b *Melody; *b* 1976

5b *Mary Ann Louise; *b* 11 Sept 1953; *m* 1976 *John Yeager Pye, and has issue:

1b *Benjamin; *b* 1977

2b *Angus; *b* 1978

3b *William James Boileau; *b* 1984

1b *Elizabeth Catherine; *b* 1987

2a **Sir Edmond Charles Boileau 7th Bt**; *b* 9 May 1903; Capt Australian ASC, served WW II; *m* 1934 *Marjorie [Marjorie Lady Boileau, 61 Erica Ave, Glen Iris, Victoria, Australia], dau of Claude Monteath D'Arcy, of Launceston, Tasmania, and *d* 1980, leaving issue:

1b Sir GUY FRANCIS BOILEAU, **8th and present Bt**

2b +Peter Linden; *b* 1937; *m* 1967 *Claudia, dau of Alan Edward Mills, of Wanganui, NZ, and has issue:

1c +Dominic Peter; *b* 1968

2c +James Edward; *b* 1971

3c +Simon Charles; *b* 1975

3a +Patrick Etienne; *b* 17 March 1912; *m* 20 July 1940 *Jean Frances, dau of John Jordan Moore, and has issue:

1b +Michael Donald; *b* 16 March 1949

1b *Patricia Ann; *b* 12 Nov 1943

1a Mina Lucy; *b* 1901; *m* 1937 Maj James Waring, IA, and *d* 1946

(2) Noel Gilbert Elliot; *b* 26 Dec 1874; *d* 1952

(3) John Peter; *b* 29 March 1876; *d* 1951

(4) Edmund Charles; *b* 5 Sept 1877; *m* 1902 Jean Ballantyne (*d* 19–), and *d* 1940, leaving issue:

1a +Maurice; *b* 1904

2a Eric; *b* 1906

1a *Catherine; *b* 1908

(1) Catherine Theresa; *m* Herbert Francis Russell, and has issue. He *d* 1906

4 Charles Augustus Penrhyn, Lt Rifle Bde; *b* 9 Aug 1835; *d* Malta 1 Aug 1855 of wounds recd at Siege of Sebastopol 18 June 1855 during Crimean War

1 Anna Maria; *m* 8 Sept 1852 Rev William Hay Gurney, MA, Rector of North Runcton, Norfolk, 2nd son of Daniel Gurney, of North Runcton Hall, Norfolk, and *d* 21 Nov 1897, leaving issue. He *d* 29 May 1898

2 Caroline Mary; *d* unm 2 April 1877

3 Agnes Lucy; *m* 8 May 1855 Hon William John Borlase-Warren-Venables-Vernon (*see* (VERNON, B), and *d* 30 Sept 1881, leaving issue

4 Mary Georgina; *d* unm 2 Oct 1910

5 Theresa Anne Catherine; *d* unm 1 July 1872

BOLES

Arms: Az. on a fess erm., between three standing bowls arg., out of each a boar's head or, a portcullis also or. **Crest:** In front of a rising sun or a demi-boar az., pierced in the left shoulder by an arrow ppr. **Motto:** *Ut tibi sic alteri* ('As I do to thee so will I do to others'). **Creation:** Bt. (UK) 17 June 1922.

SIR JEREMY JOHN FORTESCUE BOLES, 3RD BT, of Bishop's Lydeard, Somerset [Sir Jeremy Boles Bt, Buttys, Stogumber, Taunton TA4 3TD]; *b* 9 Jan 1932; *s* f 1945; *educ* Stowe; *m* 1st 16 April 1955 (*divorce* 1970) Dorothy Jane, yr dau of James Alexander Worswick, of Enmore, Somerset, and Singapore, and has issue:

1 +RICHARD FORTESCUE [Richard Boles Esq, 1 Oldbrook, Holbrook Rd, Lydbrook, Glos GL17 9PY]; *b* 12 Dec 1958; *m* 1990 *Allison Beverley, dau of Brian MacDonald, and has issue:

(1) +James Alexander Fortescue; *b* 25 May 1993

(1) *Samantha; *b* 1997

2 +David Hastings Fortescue; *b* 9 Nov 1967

1 *Sarah Jane; *b* 5 Aug 1956; *m* 1986 *Paul Bird, and has issue:

(1) *Simon Callum; *b* 1990

(1) *Georgina Jane; *b* 1988

Sir JEREMY *m* 2nd 1970 (*divorce* 1981) Elisabeth Gildroy, yr dau of Edward Phillip Shaw, of Englefield Green, Surrey, and widow of Oliver Simon Willis Fleming; *m* 3rd 1982 *Marigold, est dau of Donald Frank Seckington, of Clevedon, Avon, and widow of Laurence Frederick Aspey, and has further issue by 2nd w:

2 *Jessica Blanche Mary; *b* 1971

Lineage: The Rev JAMES THOMAS BOLES, of Ryll Court, Exmouth, and Moyge, Co Cork, had a yst s:

Sir Dennis Fortescue Boles, 1st Bt (UK), so *cr* 17 June 1922, CBE (1919), DL, JP, High Sheriff 1923, MP W Somerset 1911 and Taunton 1918–21, Lt-Col cmdg 3rd Bn Devonshire Regt; *b* 6 Sept 1861; *m* 26 July 1894 Beatrice Ringrose (*d* 30 April 1939), yst dau of John Lysaght, of Hengrave Hall, Suffolk, and had issue:

1 Hastings Fortescue, 2nd Lt 17th Lancers, attached RFC, served WW I 1915; *b* 21 June 1895; *d* of wounds, 24 May 1915

2 GERALD FORTESCUE (Sir), **2nd Bt**

1 Violet Beatrice; *m* 30 April 1932 Michael Allen Bucknall, 2nd son of Edgar Allen Bucknall, and had issue

2 Doreen Frances; *m* 26 Nov 1936 Cyril Alfred Anderson, only son of Rev A E Anderson, and had issue. He *d* 1958

3 Nesta Mary

Sir DENNIS *d* 26 July 1935; his son,

Sir Gerald Fortescue Boles, 2nd Bt, Capt 17th/21st Lancers WW II; *b* 19 June 1900; *m* 2 June 1927 Violet Blanche Hall (*m* 2nd 30 Oct 1945 S/Ldr David Dove Carver, OBE, RAFVR, son of Henry George Dove, of 62 Ellerton Rd, London SW18, and *d* 1974), est dau of Maj Reginald John Hall Parlby, of Manadon, and *d* 9 April 1945 from injuries recd in action in the Centl Mediterranean, leaving issue:

1 Sir JEREMY JOHN FORTESCUE, **3rd and present Bt**

BOLINGBROKE and SAINT JOHN

Arms: Arg. on a chief gu. two mullets or. **Crest:** A mount vert thereon a falcon rising or, ducally gorged gu. **Supporters:** Dexter, a falcon, wings displayed or, ducally gorged gu.; sinister, an eagle, wings displayed or, charged on the breast with the Hames. (The Hames is a badge of the family of Tregoze, *viz.*, on an antique shield, rimmed gold, party per pale, arg. and gu., a crescent sa., thereon a label of three points or.) **Motto:** *Nec quærere, nec spernere honorem* ('Neither seeking nor despising honour').

Creations: Bt (E) 22 May 1611, B. (GB) 7 July 1712 (St John of Lydiard Tregoze) and (GB) 2 July 1716, V. (GB) 7 July 1712 (Bolingbroke) and (GB) 2 July 1716.

THE 7TH VISCOUNT BOLINGBROKE and 8TH VISCOUNT SAINT JOHN, Baron St John of Lydiard Tregoze, Wilts, **Baron St John** of Battersea, Surrey, and a **Baronet** (Sir Kenneth Oliver Musgrave St John, Bt) [The Rt Hon the Viscount Bolingbroke and St John, PO Box 25.069, Christchurch, New Zealand]; *b* 22 March 1927; *s* kinsman 1974; *educ* Eton and Geneva U; chm A and P Gp of Cos 1958–75, dir: Shaw Savill Holidays Pty Ltd, Bolingbroke and Ptnrs Ltd, Italian importing Cos; Fell Australian Inst Travel, pres Travel Agents Assoc NZ 1966–68, dir World Assoc Travel Agencies 1966–75, chm Australian Cncl Tour Wholesalers 1972–74; *m* 1st 1953 (*divorce*1972) Patricia Mary, dau of B J McKenna, of Christchurch, NZ, and has issue:

1 +HENRY FITZROY; *b* 18 May 1957; *educ* Rudolf Steiner Sch, Christchurch, NZ

The 7th/8th VISCOUNT *m* 2nd 22 Dec 1972 (*divorce* 1987) Jainey Anne, dau of Alexander Duncan McRae, of S Canterbury, NZ, and by her has:

2 +Oliver John Beauchamp; *b* 1972

3 +Nicholas Alexander Mowbray; *b* 1974

Bolingbroke, other creations by the name of: Between 1624 and 1711 another branch of the St Johns held the Earldom of Bolingbroke (*see* SAINT JOHN OF BLETSO, B). The choice of title reflected their Beaufort (*see* also below) marriage connection. The Beauforts descended from the 14th- and early 15th-century Dukes of Lancaster, whose family name 'of Bolingbroke', made famous by Shakespeare, derived from a manor of the same name which was their chief seat. This had actually been acquired by the marriage of Thomas 2nd Earl of Lancaster (grandson of HENRY III) and a de Lacy heiress, last holder of the early medieval Earldom of Lincoln (*see* LINCOLN, E, preliminary remarks).

Lineage: Sir OLIVER ST JOHN, of Bletso; *m* by 1442, as her 1st husb, Margaret (*m* 2nd 1st Duke of Somerset of the 1443 *cr* (*see* BEAUFORT, D), and was grandmother of HENRY VII; *see* also SAINT JOHN OF BLETSO, B) and had, with an er s:

OLIVER ST JOHN, Ld Manors of Lydiard Tregoze and Deptford; *m* Elizabeth (*d* 12 June 1503), 2nd dau of 4th Lord (Baron) Scrope (of Bolton) and widow of (a) Sir John Bigod and (b) Henry Rochford, of Stoke Rochford, Lincs, and *d* Fonterabia, Spain, by 10 April 1497, leaving issue:

1 JOHN (Sir), his heir

1 Elizabeth; *m* 1st 8th Earl of Kildare (*d* 3 Sept 1513; *see* LEINSTER, D) and had issue; *m* 2nd Sir John Wallop, KG (*dsp* July 1551; *see* PORTSMOUTH, E), and *d* 28 June 1516

2 Eleanor; *m* Thomas Grey, Marquess of Dorset

3 Margaret, Abbess of Shaftesbury

The only son,

Sir JOHN ST JOHN, Chamberlain to Margaret, Countess of Richmond (mother of HENRY VII), and one of the executors of her will; *b* 1473; *m* Joan, dau and heir of Sir John Iwardby, of Quainton, Bucks, Hurley, Berks, and Farley Chamberlayne or Farley St John, Hants, and *d* 1 Sept 1512, leaving:

JOHN ST JOHN, of Lydiard Tregoze and Farley Chamberlayne; *b* 1504/5; *m* 1st Margaret, dau of Sir Richard Carew, of Beddington, Surrey, and had:

1 NICHOLAS, of Lydiard Tregoze

JOHN ST JOHN *m* 2nd Elizabeth, dau of Sir Richard Whettle/Whetehill, of Calais, and *d* 5 April 1576, having by her had:

2 William, of Farley Chamberlayne, ancestor in the female line of ST JOHN-MILDMAY, Bt (*qv*)

JOHN ST JOHN's er son,

NICHOLAS ST JOHN, of Lydiard Tregoze; *m* Elizabeth, dau of Sir Richard Blount, of Maple Durham, Oxon, and *d* 1589, having had, with a yst s (Richard) and at least one dau (Elizabeth, *m* Sir Richard St George; *see* ST GEORGE, Bt):

1 Sir JOHN, for whom *see* further below

2 OLIVER ST JOHN, 1st VISCOUNT GRANDISON OF LIMERICK, Co Leitrim (I) (the name being chosen to commemorate his connection with the medieval family of Grandison through his ggggf's w Margaret Beauchamp (*see* above)), so *cr* 3 Jan 1620/1 with special remainder to heirs male of his n Barbara by her husb Sir Edward Villiers (*see* JERSEY, E), as also 21 May 1626 BARON TREGOZ OF HIGHWORTH, Co Wilts (E), PC (I 1605, E 1622); *b* c 1560; *educ* Trin Coll Oxford; MP Cirencester 1592–93, Portsmouth 1604–06 and (I Parl) Co Roscommon 1613–15, ktd Feb 1599/1600, soldier in Low Countries and Ireland (fought Battle of Kinsale 1601), Master Gen Ordnance Ireland 1605–14, Pres Munster, V-Pres Connaught, Ld Dep Ireland 1616–22; granted 1627 the manor of Battersea, formerly the property of ANNE OF DENMARK, JAMES I's QUEEN; *dsp* 30 Dec 1630 when the Barony expired

The er bro,

Sir JOHN ST JOHN; *b* c 1552; *m* as her 1st husb Lucy, dau and heiress of Sir Walter Hungerford, of Farley, Wilts (*see* SAINT DAVIDS, V), and *d* 1594, having had surv issue:

1 Walter; *d* 1597

2 JOHN (Sir), **1st Bt**

3 Oliver; *d* young

1 Barbara; *m* Sir Edward Villiers (*d* 7 Sept 1626) and was *bur* 16 Sept 1672, having had issue (*see* JERSEY, E)

Sir JOHN's 2nd s,

Sir John St John, 1st Bt (E), so *cr* 22 May 1611, of Lydiard Tregoze; *b* c 1585; inherited Manors of Battersea and Wandsworth from his unc 1st Viscount Grandison, ktd 1609, MP Wilts, royalist Civil War (three of his sons were *k* fighting on the royalist side); *m* 1st Anne dau of Sir Thomas Leighton, of Feckenham, Worcs; *m* 2nd Margaret, widow of Sir Richard Grubham, and *d* 1648, having by his first w had, with six other sons and four daus:

1 Oliver; *m* Catherine Vere (*m* 2nd *c* 6 March 1640/1, as his 1st w, 2nd Baron Poulett of Hinton St George; *see* 1970 edn POULLETT, E), dau and coheir of 1st and last Baron Vere of Tilbury (*see* SAINT ALBANS, D), and *dvp* Nov 1641, having had issue:

(1) **Sir John St John, 2nd Bt**; *d* unm 1656

2 **Sir Walter St John, 3rd Bt**, MP Wilts; *m* his cousin Jo(h)anna, dau of Oliver St John (*see* SAINT JOHN OF BLETSO, B), and *d* 3 July 1708, leaving an only s:

(1) **Sir Henry St John, 4th Bt**, and **1st Viscount Saint John**, so *cr* 2 July 1716, as also BARON SAINT JOHN OF BATTERSEA, Co Surrey (both GB), with special remainder to his yr sons in order of their birth (since his est s, the statesman Henry, **1st Viscount Bolingbroke**, had by then been attainted) and the heirs male of their bodies and failing them with remainder to the heirs male of his own body, DL (Wilts 1683); *b* 17 Oct 1652; *educ* Eton and Caius Coll Cambridge; MP (Whig) Wootton Bassett 1679–81, 1685–87, Jan 1688/9–95 and 1698–1700 and Wilts 1695–98; *m* 1st 11 Dec 1673 Lady Mary Rich, 2nd dau and coheiress of 3rd Earl of Warwick (*see* WARWICK, BROOKE and, E), and had an only s:

1a HENRY ST JOHN, **1st Viscount Bolingbroke**, Co Lincoln, so *cr* during his f's lifetime 7 July 1712, as also BARON ST JOHN OF LYDIARD TREGOZE (both GB), with special remainder, failing his own male issue, to his f and half-bros, PC (171014); *bapt* 10 Oct 1678; *educ* Eton and (?)Ch Ch Oxford(?); MP (Tory) Wootton Bassett 1701–08, Berks 1710–12, Sec War 1704–08, Sec State the North 1710–13, the South 1713–14, dir South Sea Co 1711–15, Ld Lt Essex 1712–14, Amb Paris 1712; for the last five days of the reign of QUEEN ANNE he was her chief minister, as he had been the chief person at court for the last few months, but her death frustrated whatever plans he may have had to promote the Jacobite succession (for which he had scant personal enthusiasm) and he fled to France; attainted 10 Sept 1715, Sec State to titular James III (who *cr* him titular Earl of Bolingbroke) 1715–March 1716 (when dismissed), restored May 1725 to his estates and in blood though not peerages by GEORGE I; a considerable influence on FREDERICK PRINCE OF WALES (f of GEORGE III), author of various historical essays and polemical pieces to do with contemporary politics, also philosophy, chiefly political, the chief example of the latter being *The Patriot King* (1738); *m* 1st 1700 Frances (*dsp* 24 Oct 1718), dau and coheir of Sir Henry Winchcombe, 2nd Bt, of Bucklebury, Berks; *m* 2nd May 1720 Marie Claire (*dsp* 18 March 1750), widow of the Marquis de Vilette, dau of Armand des Champs, Seigneur de Marcilly, and n of Mme de Maintenon, and *dsp* 12 Dec 1751, when the special limitation in the patent creating the Viscountcy made the attainder inoperative as regarded his actual heirs' rights of succession, so that it revived and passed to his deceased half-bro's (*i.e.*, the **2nd Viscount St John's**) est surviving s, while the btcy *cr* 1611, having been inherited by him *after* his restoration in blood (and the remaining restrictions as to honours still in force after the restoration applying to peerages only), also passed to his n

(1) (cont.) The **1st Viscount Saint John** *m* 2nd 1 Jan 1686/7 Angelica Magdalena (*d* Aug 1736), dau of George Pelissary, Treas-Gen Marine France, and widow of — Wharton, and *d* 8 April 1742, having by her had:

2a George; Sec to English Plens Congress Utrecht; *d* unm *vp* Jan 1716

3a JOHN ST JOHN, **2nd Viscount Saint John**; *b* 1702; *m* 1st 17 April 1729 Anne (*d* 11 July 1747), dau and heiress of Sir Robert Furnese, Bt, and had surv issue:

1b FREDERICK, **3rd Viscount Saint John** and **2nd Viscount Bolingbroke**

2b Henry, Gen, MP Wootton Bassett; *m* 31 Aug 1771 Barbara, dau of Col Bladen, and sis of Harriet, Countess of Essex

3b John; *d* unm 8 Oct 1793

1b Louisa; *m* 20 Aug 1760 1st Baron Bagot (*qv*) and *d* 4 Feb 1820

3a (cont.) The **2nd Viscount Saint John** *m* 2nd 19 June 1748 Hester (*dsp* 8 March 1752), dau of James Clarke, of Wharton, Herefs, and *d* 26 Nov 1748

4a Holles; *d* unm *vp* 6 Oct 1738

1a Henrietta; *m* 10 June 1727 1st and last Earl of Catherlough (*d* 30 March 1772) and had issue

The 2nd VISCOUNT SAINT JOHN's est son,

FREDERICK ST JOHN, **3rd Viscount Saint John** and **2nd Viscount Bolingbroke** (*s* unc 1751); *b* 1734; *educ* Eton; sold 1763 the Battersea estate to Viscount Spencer; *m* 8 Sept 1757 (*divorce* 8 March 1768) Lady Diana Spencer, est dau of 3rd Duke of Marlborough (*qv*), and had:

1 GEORGE RICHARD, **3rd Viscount Bolingbroke** and **4th Viscount Saint John**

2 Frederick, of Chailey, Sussex; *b* 20 Dec 1765; Gen; *m* 1st 8 Dec 1788 Lady Mary Kerr (*d* 6 Feb 1791), 3rd dau of 5th Marquess of Lothian (*qv*), and had:

(1) Robert William, Consul-Gen Algiers; *b* 5 Feb 1792; *m* Elizabeth Maria, dau of John Barker, of Wakefield, Yorks, and *d* 19 Nov 1844, having had, with other issue:

1a Henry Thomas; *b* 1818; *d* 1847

2a Frederick Arthur, Maj; *b* 28 Feb 1827; *m* 28 March 1857 Elizabeth Depau (*d* 1 Jan 1888), dau of Samuel M Fox, of Philadelphia, and *dsps* 23 Jan 1861

3a Mark Kerr, Capt 8th Bengal Cav; *b* 9 May 1834; *m* 26 Sept 1862 Agnes Isabella (*d* 31 May 1904), est dau of T Fraser, of Calcutta, and *d* 28 Sept 1867, leaving issue:

1b Mary Caroline

2 (cont.) Gen Frederick St John *m* 2nd 6 April 1793 Arabella (*d* 9 June 1819), 3rd dau of 6th Baron Craven (*see* CRAVEN, E), and by her had further issue:

(2) George William (Rev), Rector Stanton Lacy, Salop; *b* 4 May 1796; *d* unm 5 June 1876

(3) George Frederick Berkeley, Maj 52nd Regt, Mil Kt Windsor; *b* 2 Oct 1797; *m* 18 Jan 1836 Henrietta Louisa Maria (*d* Feb 1887), 3rd dau of Rev John Jephson, and *d* 24 July 1866, leaving issue:

1a Frederick Edward Molyneux, Lt RMLI; *b* 28 Nov 1838; *m* 20 Jan 1862 Katherine (*d* 1903), est dau of James Ranoe, and *dsp* Jan 1904

2a Berkeley Craven; *b* 18 April 1842; *m* 10 March 1869 Florence Margaret (*d* 5 Aug 1924), est dau of William Molle Cadell, MCS, and *d* 22 Oct 1873, leaving issue:

1b Berkeley Charles; *b* 5 Jan 1870; *d* 10 April 1877

3a Aubrey Beauclerk Lennox; *b* 20 Oct 1846; *m* 12 Sept 1876 Clara Constance, only dau of James Wilson, MD, of Gt Malvern, and had issue:

1b James Frederick; *b* 20 Aug 1881; *d* May 1956

4a Henry Augustus Bolingbroke; *b* 29 Dec 1847; *m* Anna (*d* 22 April 1933), dau of Maj Henderson, HEICS, and *d* 9 March 1921 leaving issue:

1b Aubrey; *b* 1881; *d* 7 Nov 1955

1b Henrietta; *b* 1883; *d* unm 26 July 1957

2b Mary Constance; *b* 1889

3b Margaret; *b* 1896; *m* 7 July 1928 Fred Gordon Sweet, son of Fred John Sweet, of Plymouth, Devon

1a Louisa Diana; *m* 4 Feb 1869 Richard Bell, of Cobham, and *d* 12 Aug 1919, leaving issue

2a Arabella Cecilia Frances; *d* unm 19 April 1894

(4) Henry George; *b* 1798; *d* 1821

(5) Charles William George; *b* 3 Dec 1809; *m* 20 Nov 1834 Anne (*d* 25 Oct 1865), dau of T Gibson, and *d* 12 July 1856, leaving issue:

1a Frederick Charles, Col Indian Staff Corps; *b* 29 Aug 1835; *m* 7 June 1860 Jane, dau of Dep-Inspr-Gen Edmund Walter Eyre, and *d* 24 Nov 1900, leaving issue:

1b Charles William Pelly, Assist Commr of Excise Revenue, Madras; *b* 3 May 1861; *d* unm 7 Sept 1906

2b Henry Edmund; *b* 29 Dec 1865; *d* unm

3b Alexander Storey, MRCS, LRCP; *b* 16 April 1867; *m* 1 Aug 1906 Mabel Eleanor (*d* 4 June 1928), 3rd dau of Inspr-Gen Sir Henry Frederick Norbury, KCB, RN, and *d* 11 April 1923, leaving issue:

1c Alexander Bolingbroke; *b* 18 May 1910; *m* 1937 Gladys Spencer (*d* 1981), and *d* 17 Nov 1968, leaving issue:

1d +Stewart Bolingbroke [Stewart St John Esq, The Nursery, Main St, Kirby Bellars, Melton Mowbray, Leics]; *b* 1942

1d *Janet Eleanor [Mrs Michael Hall, 38 The Ridgeway, Tonbridge, Kent TN10 4NJ]; *b* 1938; *m* 1962 *Michael Stanley Hall and has:

1e *Stephen Philip St John; *b* 1969

1e *Wendy Deborah; *b* 1964; *m* 1990 *Malcolm William Forsyth

2e *Alison Judith; *b* 1967

1c Stella Swithina Legge; *b* 1907; MRCVS; *d* unm 19–

1b Annie Elphinstone; *m* 2 Aug 1881 Lt-Col John North

2b Emily Jane Georgina; *m* Col Hugh Thornton, and *d* 1940, leaving issue. He *d* 1920

3b Margaret Isabella; *b* 26 April 1869; *d* unm 2 May 1965

4b Florence Alicia; *d* unm 25 Feb 1951

2a Henry Craven, JP, Adml, Naval ADC to HM QUEEN VICTORIA 1887–89; *b* 5 Jan 1837; *m* 8 May 1860 Catherine Dora (*d* 18 May 1914), dau of John Stratford Rodney (*see* RODNEY, B), and *d* 21 May 1909, leaving issue:

1b Montagu Rodney; *b* 3 March 1861; *m* 4 June 1898 Theodora Mary Land (*d* 19 April 1958), dau of Dr Henry N Land James, AMD, and *d* 20 March 1944, leaving issue:

1c Theodore Henry Montagu; *b* 19 June 1908; *d* 24 Nov 1931

1c Henrietta Doreen; *b* 13 March 1900; *m* 27 April 1928 Lt-Col Douglas Graham Moncrieff of Kinmonth, MC and bar, DL, JP, FRGS, Cameronians, officially recognised by Ld Lyon King of Arms 1946 in the name of Moncrieff of Kinmonth, only child of John Moncrieff Wright, of Kinmonth, Bridge of Earn, Perthshire, and had issue:

1d *John Graham, of Kinmonth, Maj Black Watch Korea 1952–53 (despatches), Kenya 1953–54 (medal and clasp) and Aden 1962–63, memb Roy Co Archers; *b* 31 Aug 1929; *educ* Eton and RMA Sandhurst; *m* 30 July 1966 *Susan Mary, yr dau of Rupert Claude Martin

2d *Charles St John Graham, Capt (ret) Scots Gds, memb Roy Co Archers) [Capt Charles Moncrieff, Easter Elcho, Rhynd, Perthshire]; *b* 11 Jan 1931; *educ* Eton and RMA Sandhurst; *m* 15 June 1957 *Joanna Dava, 2nd dau of Maj John Peto (*see* PETO, Bt, of Barnstaple), and has issue

1d Alice Rosemary Graham; *b* 12 April 1935; *m* 27 April 1957 Capt David John Wemyss Anstice, 10th Royal Hus (PWO), yr son of V-Adml Sir Edmund Anstice, KCB, of Inverdunning Ho, Perthshire, and *dsp* 22 March 1960

2d *Dora Heather Graham; *b* 24 Oct 1938; *m* 14 Oct 1961 Donald John Harper Gow, yst son of Brig John Wesley Harper Gow, CBE, DL, JP, of Halhill, Howwood, Renfrewshire, and has issue:

1e *Alastair John Moncrieff; *b* 2 Aug 1963

2e *Jeremy Douglas Moncrieff; *b* 22 Feb 1965

3e *Colin Rodney Moncrieff; *b* 5 July 1968

2b Percy Stuart, Lt RN; *b* 29 April 1863; *m* 1896 Alice Cecilia Anna, dau of Rev A Williamson, and *dsp* 11 March 1900

3b Harry Lionel Rodney; *b* 11 June 1867; *d* unm 1 July 1941

4b Francis Gerald, CB (1917), MVO (1914); *b* 22 Dec 1869; V-Adml served in S African War (medal), China 1900 (medal) and WW I (despatches twice), ADC to HM 1920–21; *m* 1st 28 May 1893 Winifred Jessie (*dsp* 19 Dec 1898), er dau of Col George Howard Trollope, of Farmile Hatch, Cobham, Surrey; *m* 2nd 29 Dec 1902 Emily Frances Louise (*d* 27 Feb 1969, aged 93), er dau of Allan F Turner, of Bombay, and *d* 15 Feb 1947, leaving issue by 2nd w:

1c +Stratford Allen Gerald [Capt Stratford St John RN, Thornbury, Shamley Green, Guildford, Surrey]; *b* 5 June 1911; Capt RN, served WW II (despatches twice); *m* 25 April 1942 Honor Madeleine (*d* 6 Sept 1997), er dau of Philip Smiles, of Belfast, and adopted:

*Charles Alan; *b* 10 Oct 1952

*Anne Margaret; *b* 17 Feb 1950; *m* 7 March 1970 *Anthony Peter Montgomery, RA, only s of Maj David Montgomery, late The Buffs (Roy E Kent Regt), of Monk Down, Shamley Green, Guildford, Surrey, and has issue

1c Winifred Joan; *b* 26 Jan 1904; *m* 17 Oct 1934 Lt-Col Charles Cecil Mostyn Macleod-Carey, late RA, son of A E Macleod-Carey, of Ryde, IoW, and had issue:

1d *Adrian St John; *b* 22 Oct 1941

1d *Susan Joan; *b* 19 Feb 1950

2c Betty Allane; *b* 17 Dec 1905

3c *Peggy Katharine Mary [Mrs Colin Crickmay, 2 Lynchen's Close, Bembridge, Isle of Wight]; *b* 3 June 1908; *m* 1st 14 Oct 1939 (*divorce* 1948) Maj Leslie Fairfax d'Arch Smith, son of Col H d'Arch Smith, of Datchet, Bucks; *m* 2nd 1988 *Colin Rosser Crickmay, and has issue by 1st husb:

1d *Nicola Lesley [Mrs Charles James, Sandy Lane Farm, Parkmill, Swansea, W Glam]; *b* 13 Nov 1940; *m* 1 Sept 1962 *Charles Quentin James, only son of Thurstan James, of 23 Arundel Rd, Kingston-on-Thames, Surrey, and has issue:

1e *Andrew Thurstan Trewartha; *b* 17 May 1965

2e *Simon Charles Trewartha; *b* 1969

1d *Emma Charlotte; *b* 11 Oct 1963; *m* 1994 *Douglas Smith

2d *Sophie Louise; *b* 1971

1b Mabel Elinor Rowena; *m* 18 Feb 1890 Gen Sir Thomas Lethbridge Napier Morland, KCB, KCMG, DSO, KRRC, and *d* 27 Jan 1901, leaving issue. He *d* 21 May 1925

2b Violet Cecile Annie; *m* 31 Aug 1899 Lt-Col Charles Edwin Frederick Rich, DSO, and *d* 6 June 1957, leaving issue (*see* RICH, Bt)

3b Eleanor Dora; *m* 3 Jan 1899 Brig-Gen Arthur Uniacke Stockley, CMG, late RA, est son of Col George Watts Stockley, RE, and *d* 12 Aug 1954. He *d* 16 Oct 1939

4b Rosamond Aline; *m* 1st 2 Jan 1902 (*divorce* 1915) Cdr Henry Percy Valentine Hickman, RN, son of Maj Robert John Hickman, late 60th Rifles; *m* 2nd 18 Jan 1916 Capt Morgan Tindal, RN, son of Symonds Tindal, and *dsp* 3 Oct 1946

5b Muriel Geraldine; *b* Aug *d* Sept 1880

3a Edward George, late Capt 29th Regt; *b* 24 June 1840; *m* 25 Oct 1866 Isabel Mary Purdie, dau of Edgar Carpenter Grantham, of Nova Scotia, and *d* 1894, leaving issue:

1b Edward George; *b* 27 June 1870

1b Violet Boycott

1a Anne; *m* 11 June 1864 Maj Robert John Hickman, late 60th Rifles, and *d* 20 March 1919, leaving issue. He *d* 6 March 1908

(2) Louisa Diana; *m* 23 Jan 1846 Richard Vincent, of Stratford, and *d* 6 May 1855

(3) Elizabeth, 9 March 1841 Rev George Carter, MA, and *d* 27 Oct 1846

2 (cont.) Gen Frederick St John *m* 3rd 14 Nov 1821 Caroline (*d* 27 May 1869), dau of J Parsons, and *d* 19 Nov 1844, having by her had issue:

(6) Welbore William Oliver; *b* 12 April 1825; *d* at Madeira, Nov 1853

The 2nd and 3rd VISCOUNT *d* 5 May 1787; his er son,

GEORGE RICHARD ST JOHN, **3rd Viscount Bolingbroke** and **4th Viscount Saint John**; *b* 5 March 1761; *m* 1st 26 Feb 1783 Charlotte (*d* 11 Jan 1803), dau of Rev Thomas Collins, of Winchester, and had:

1 HENRY, **4th** and **5th Viscount**

HENRY ST JOHN, **4th Viscount Bolingbroke** and **5th Viscount Saint John**; *b* 6 March 1786; *m* 3 June 1812 Maria (*d* 31 Dec 1836), 2nd dau of Sir Henry Paulet St John-Mildmay, 3rd Bt (*qv*), and *d* 1 Oct 1851, having had:

(1) HENRY MILDMAY ST JOHN, **5th Viscount Bolingbroke** and **6th Viscount Saint John**, DL; *bapt* 30 March 1820; *m* 5 Jan 1893 Mary Emily Elizabeth (*d* 22 Feb 1940), dau of Robert Howard, and *d* 7 Nov 1899, having had:

1a VERNON HENRY ST JOHN, **6th Viscount Bolingbroke** and **7th Viscount Saint John**; *b* 15 March 1856; *m* 15 June 1950 (*annulled* 1952) Valezina, dau of Frederick William Frohawk, of Sutton, Surrey, and *dsp* 1 May 1974

(2) Spencer Mildmay; *b* 1822; EICS; *m* 1 Feb 1842 Dora (*d* 22 March 1847), only dau of Capt Clutterbuck, 59th Regt, and *dsp* 20 Aug 1849

(1) Maria Louisa; *m* 11 March 1839 John Lauriston Kneller, 2nd son of Godfrey John Kneller, of Donhead Hall, Wilts, and *d* 2 June 1861, leaving issue

(2) Anne Jane Charlotte; *m* 21 April 1838 Lawrence Robert Shawe, 5th Dragoon Gds, and *d* his widow 2 April 1881

(3) Isabella; *dsp*

(4) Emily Arabella Jane; *m* 1st June 1840 William Corbet Smith (*d* 9 March 1847), of Bitteswell Hall, Leics; *m* 2nd 14 Jan 1852 Frederick Geldart Webbe Horlock, of The Rocks Ho, Marshfield, Glos, and *d* 1855

The **3rd** and **4th Viscount** *m* 2nd 1 Aug 1804 Isabella Charlotte Antoinette Sophia, Baroness Hompesch (*d* 1848), and *d* 1824, having by her had:

2 Ferdinand; *b* 16 Oct 1804; *m* 8 Feb 1826 Selina Charlotte (*d* 23 March 1897), dau of Col Maurice St Leger Keatinge, of Narraghmore, Co Kildare, by his w Lady Martha, dau of 8th Earl of Meath (*qv*), and *d* 10 Oct 1865, having had issue:

(1) Maurice William Ferdinand (Rev), DD, MA Durham, Canon Glos, Vicar Kempsford, RD Fairford; *b* 14 Nov 1827; *m* 30 June 1853 Charlotte Lucy Hamilton (*d* 28 April 1902), dau of John Dalyell, of Lingo, and *d* 18 Feb 1914, having had issue:

1a Henry Percy, Pncpl Clerk Judicial Dept, Taxing Offr Ho of Lds; *b* 23 March 1854; *m* 12 Oct 1887 Maud Louisa (*d* 28 Oct 1938), dau of Hon Pascoe Charles Glyn (*see* WOLVERTON, B), and *d* 9 Sept 1921, leaving issue:

1b Geoffrey Robert, MC, late Capt Roy Fus, served WW I (despatches); *b* 4 Jan 1889; *m* 1st 10 Dec 1914 (*divorce* 1925) Gwendolen Isabel, only child of Herbert George Okeden, of Stutton Ho, Suffolk, and had issue:

1c Ralph Geoffrey Julian, Midshipman RN *b* 11 Feb 1917; *educ* RNC Dartmouth; *d* as result of a motor accident, 31 May 1937

1b (cont.) Geoffrey St John *m* 2nd 5 Dec 1925 (*divorce* 1940) Katharine Mary (*d* 22 April 1958), only dau of A S J Musgrave, of Abbeylands, Settle, Yorks, and by her had issue:

2c KENNETH OLIVER MUSGRAVE ST JOHN, **7th and present Viscount Bolingbroke** and **8th Viscount Saint John**

3c Henry Ferdinand Musgrave; *b* 5 May 1928; *educ* Eton; Lt LG; *m* 1 Nov 1956 *Patricia Margaret Mary [The Hon Mrs Henry St John, Newnham Corner, Newnham Green, Basingstoke, Hants], dau of Edward Ryan, of Exeter, Devon, and *d* 26 Oct 1995, having had:

1d Oliver Geoffrey; *b* 18 June 1958; *educ* Eton; *d* 1982

1c *Antonia Josephine [Mrs Peter Johnson, c/o Midland Bank, 799 Fulham Rd, London SW6]; *b* 19 Nov 1933; *m* 1st 1955 (*divorce* 1966) Henry Wilson; *m* 2nd 1 April 1967 *Peter Johnson, and has issue by 2nd husb:

1d *Melanie Joanne; *b* 20 Oct 1967

1b Geoffrey St John (cont.) *m* 3rd 4 March 1941 Mary Violet Handley (*d* 29 Aug 1951), niece and adopted dau of John Mills, of Maffra, Victoria, Australia; *m* 4th 1957 Brynhildr Archdall (*d* 14 May 1975), widow of W Bryant Purkis and dau of Harold Archdall Vicars, and *d* 4 Oct 1972

1b Margaret Oliva; *b* 3 June 1890; *m* 6 Aug 1914 Guy Melvil Gibbs, of Barro Court, Somerset (*see* ALDENHAM and HUNSDON OF HUNSDON, B), and *d* 29 Sept 1964, leaving issue. He *d* 14 March 1959

2b Ursula Mary; *b* 11 Oct 1891; *m* 10 July 1912 Capt Cyril Francis Hawley, 2nd son of Sir Henry Michael Hawley, 5th Bt (*qv*), and *d* 18 Feb 1971, leaving issue

2a Ferdinand John; late Capt Oxford Yeo, and Maj and Hon Lt-Col Surrey Imp Yeo, served in S Africa 1900 and WW I, as Maj KOYLI; *b* 25 Oct 1861; *m* 1924 Zulmée Marie Thérèse, dau of Théophile Lesoing, of Avesnes-le-Comte, France, and *d* 27 March 1930

1a Aline, twin with her bro Henry; *m* 11 April 1883 Robert Ingham Tidswell, of Haresfield Court, Glos, and *d* 29 March 1884, leaving issue

(2) John Henry; *b* 3 Jan 1829; Maj late 92nd Regt, served in Crimea and Indian Mutiny; *m* 6 April 1854 Margaret (*d* 29 Feb 1912), dau of Maj-Gen Sir Charles Warren, KCB, and *d* 18 Sept 1912, having had issue:

1a Charles Ferdinand; *b* 12 April 1855; *d* 1884

2a Normanby Hay; *b* 21 May 1857; *d* 12 Nov 1913

3a Henry Warren; *b* 13 Aug 1860; *m* 30 Nov 1916 Justina Margaret (*d* 1969), dau of Duncan Mackenzie, of Hill View, E Grinstead, and *d* 2 Feb 1931, leaving issue:

1b *Margaret Irene [Mrs Gerald Matthews, Ibstock, Rowplatt Lane, Felbridge, Sussex RH19 2NY]; *b* 4 July 1917; *m* 9 Aug 1939 (*divorce* 1947) Gerald William Francis Matthews, and has issue:

1c *Texicia [Mrs Tony Hodson, Scatwell, 41 Brook Rd, Horsham, W Sussex]; *b* 1940; *m* 1974 *Tony Hodson, and has issue:

1d *Caroline Rose; *b* 1975

2d *Sophie Louise; *b* 1977

2c *Wendy [Miss Wendy Matthews, Flat C, 11 The Goffs, Eastbourne, Sussex]; *b* 1941

4a Louis William; *b* 12 June 1862; *d* 12 Oct 1928

5a Frederick George; *b* 27 July 1866; *m* 12 Nov 1910 Edith Constance, dau of Claude Wilkin, and widow of James W Addyman, of Harrogate, and *d* 26 Jan 1924

6a Walter Cecil Hompesch; *b* 27 Sept 1867; *m* 3 Jan 1908 Maria Salome (*d* 1930), dau of — Rodriques, of Santiago del Estero, and *d* 1955, leaving issue:

1b +Walter Warren [Walter St John Esq, B° JM Paz-Ed 7-4° P-Dpto 27 (cp 1772), Villa Celina, Buenos Aires, Argentina]; *b* 14 Feb 1921; *m* 1949 *Lida Amelia Goicoechea, and has issue:

1c +Henry William [Henry St John Esq, Juan J Paso 30-CP 1832, Lomas de Zamora, Prov Buenos Aires, Argentina]; *b* 1952; *m* 1977 (*divorce* 1981) Silvia Mazzoni, and has issue:

1d +German Andres; *b* 1980

1c *Alice [Mrs Alejandro Lorea, Centenera 181, San Justo, Prov Buenos Aires, Argentina]; *b* 1950; *m* 1974 *Alejandro Funes Lorea, and has issue:

1d *Paulo; *b* 1978

1d *Clara; *b* 1976

2d *Maria Guadalupe; *b* 1980

3d *Marianna; *b* 1982

1b *Lila Romona del Rosario [Sra de Ernesto Christensen, Entre Rios 166, Santiago del Estero, Argentina]; *b* 1910; *m* 2 Jan 1935 *Dr Ernesto Christensen, and has issue:

1c *Eduardo Ernesto [Sr Eduardo Christensen, Entre Rios 166, Santiago del Estero, Argentina]; *b* 1936; advocate; *m* 1974 *Olga Vieyra, and has issue:

1d *Alexander; *b* 1976

2d *Edward; *b* 1979

1c *Lilian Margarita [Sra de Rodolfo Diedrich, INTA Los Cerrillos, Salta, Argentina]; *b* 1943; *m* 1965 *Rodolfo Diedrich, forest engr, and has issue:

1d *Rodolpho; *b* 1967

2d *Alejandro; *b* 1973

3d *Eduardo; *b* 1973 (twin)

1d *Constanza; *b* 1966

2d *Cristina; *b* 1971

2b *Fanny de Valle; *b* 1912; Medal of Merit, Red Cross of Argentina; *m* 1938 *Dr Ramon Bernardo Juarez, and has had issue:

1c Hugo Ramon; *b* 1939; *m* 1959 *Maria Cristina Rodriguez, and *d* 1974 leaving issue:

1d *Hugo Walter; *b* 1959

2d *Gustavo Alejandro; *b* 1963

1d *Monica Alicia; *b* 1961; *m* 1981 *Juan Failla, and has issue:

1e *Alicia Veronica; *b* 1982

2c *José Enrique [Sr Jose Juarez, Av Colón 4726-CP 5000, Córdoba, Argentina]; *b* 1944; *m* 1969 *Maria Virginia Espindola Araoz

1c *Fanny Celina [Sra de Roberto Vazquez, Las Retamas 427-CP 4400, Salta, Argentina]; *b* 1940; *m* 1965 *Roberto Varela Vazquez, forest engr, and has issue:

1d *Roberto Enrique; *b* 1968

2d *Sebastian Ernesto; *b* 1972

1d *Gabriela Celina; *b* 1966

3b *Margarita del Carmen [Sra de Luis Quade, Peru 161, Catamarca, Argentina]; *b* 1913; *m* 1941 Luis Frederico Quade, engr, and has issue:

1c *Josepha Margarita [Sra de José Cisneros, Caseros 537, 4700 Catamarca, Argentina]; *b* 1943; *m* 1965 *José Alberto Cisneros, Engr, and has issue:

1d *Luis Eduardo; *b* 1967

2d *Carlos Alberto; *b* 1975

3d *Marcela Inez; *b* 1968

1d *José Maria; *b* 1966

2d *Maria Laura; *b* 1971

2c *Luisa Celina [Sra de Raul Cardoso, Ayacucho 636, 4700 Catamarca, Argentina]; *b* 1949; *m* 1974 *Dr Raul Cardoso; lawyer, and has issue:

1d *Maria Constanza; *b* 1975

4b *Rosa Pastora [Sra de Ubaldo Garcia, Madero 755, CP 1408 Buenos Aires, Argentina]; *b* 1916; *m* 1940 *Ubaldo Casimiro Garcia, agron Engr, Inter-American Agric Medal of OAS, Croix de Mérite Agric, France, Hon Agric Economist Texas U, and has issue:

1c *Guillermo Ubaldo; *b* 1946; industrialist; *m* 1st (*divorce* 1985) Norma Isabel Diez; *m* 2nd 1985 *Patricia Mónica Casto, and has issue by 2nd w:

1d *Christian Guillermo; *b* 1989

1d *Cintia Analía; *b* 1986

1c *Graciela Salomé [Sra de Alfredo Pinto, Cochicó 781, CP 1408, Buenos Aires]; *b* 1941; *m* 1970 *Alfredo Pinto, and has issue:

1d *Paula Marcela; *b* 1971

2d *Maria Alejandra; *b* 1972

3d *Natalia Virginia; *b* 1973

4d *Maria Costanza; *b* 1979

2c *Maria Rosa del Carmen [Sra de Guillermo Teijo, Calle 16 No 785, Balcarce, Prov de Buenos Aires]; *b* 1942; *m* 1964 *Guillermo Teijo, and has issue:

1d *Alejandro; *b* 1966

2d *Esteban Guillermo; *b* 1977

3d *Alfonso Ezequiel; *b* 1978

1d *María Victoria; *b* 1971

3c *Teresa Pastora [Sra de Germán Aznar, Cantilo 155, Haedo, Prov de Buenos Aires]; *b* 1945; *m* 19– Germán Aznar, Capitan de Fragata, Argentine Navy (*d* 1986), and has issue:

1d *Germán Agustin; *b* 1971

2d *Federico; *b* 1972

1d *Maria Lidia; *b* 1970

2d *Maria Lucilla; *b* 1975

7a John Oliver; *b* 1874; *d* 1876

8a Edward Archibald; *b* 7 April 1876; *m* 12 July 1922 Clara Esmeralda Magno, and *d* 11 Nov 1949, having had issue:

1b George Edward; *b* 10 Oct 1923; *d* 25 Jan 1925

1b *Zelina Mabel Alice; *b* 1923 (twin)

2b *Gloria Alida; *b* 23 Nov 1924; *m* 19– *Prof Cesar Guerresi, and has issue:

1c *A son; *b* 19–
1a Sophia Rose Bethel; *d* unm 25 May 1953
2a Mary Lilian Muriel; *d* unm 17 May 1954
3a Margaret Zeline
(3) Charles Louis, consul for States of New Orleans; *b* 2 March 1831; *m* 1 July 1875 Aglaé, dau of Alexander de Jora, of Jassy, and *d* 8 June 1897, having had issue:
1a Alfred Henry Valentine; *b* 14 Feb 1883; *m* 1st 8 March 1907 (*divorce*) Catherine, dau of John Ciolaco, of Jassy, Romania
(4) Frederic Robert (Sir), KCMG (1901), joined Dip Serv 1855, Sec of Embassy at Constantinople 1879–81, Min Resident in C America 1881, and to Colombia 1884, Min Resident at Caracas 1884–88, Envoy Extrdy and Min Plen to King of Servia 1888–90, Consul Gen in Servia 1890–92, and Envoy Extrdy and Min Plen at Berne 1893–1901 (ret); *b* 2 March 1831 (twin with his bro); *m* 18 April 1882 Isabella Annie (*d* 29 Feb 1948), dau of Capt Hon James Terence FitzMaurice, RN (*see* ORKNEY, E), and *d* 27 Feb 1923, leaving:
1a (Frederick) Oliver, DSO (1917), MC; *b* 13 Oct 1886; Lt-Col late Roy Signals, formerly 1st Bn The Roy Scots, served WW I 1914; *m* 1st 8 Jan 1923 (*divorce* 1929) Dotie, er dau of Sydney Bernard Burney, CBE, of Bayswater; *m* 2nd 11 Nov 1931 *Elizabeth [Mrs Oliver St John, Journeys End, E Looe, Cornwall], dau of E H Pierce, of Peachland, BC, and *d* 10 Feb 1977, leaving by her:
1b +OLIVER PETER ST JOHN, 9th EARL OF ORKNEY (*qv*)
2a George Ronald, DSC, Capt late RAF; *b* 26 March 1888; *d* unm
3a Terence Alexander; *b* 24 March 1896; added by deed poll 1933 the particule 'de' to ST JOHN, later dropped it; Lt Roy Sussex Regt; *m* 1st 1923 (*divorce* 1933) Simone Suzanne Marie Anne, only dau of Jean Baptiste Guthmann of Paris; *m* 2nd 1947 *Winifred Gladys, dau of Charles Giles and formerly w of George Lewis Barry West, and *d* 1951, leaving issue by 1st w:
1b *Rosemary Anne; *b* 14 Aug 1927
1a Violet Rhoda; *m* 6 Nov 1914 Lt-Cdr George Thomas Wolfe Perkins, RN, and *d* May 1965
2a Dorothy Emily Olga; *m* 19 July 1906 Sir Henry Crofton Lowther, GCVO, KCMG (*d* 23 Nov 1939), yst son of Rev Brabazon Lowther, of Shrigley Park, Cheshire, and Brookside, Wineham, nr Henfield, and has issue:
1b *Oliver Peter; *b* 29 Nov 1910; *educ* Harrow and Balliol Coll, Oxford; *m* 2 Oct 1937 *Jean, dau of C J Inder, of NZ, and has issue:
1c *James Brabazon [James Lowther Esq, Brookside, Wineham, nr Henfield, Sussex]; *b* 28 Sept 1939; *educ* Harrow
1b *Esmée Katalin; *b* 18 Nov 1913; *m* 30 July 1936 Cdr (E) John Harry Roughton, RN, son of Capt John Roughton, RN, of Weymouth, and has issue:
1c *Jeremy John Lowther; *b* 8 Aug 1944
1c *Priscilla Dorothy; *b* 27 Nov 1937; *m* 22 March 1969 *John Paul
2c *Jacqueline Esmée; *b* 3 Feb 1951
3a Natalie Edith
3 Charles Robert; *b* 21 Nov 1807; *m* 20 April 1841 Jane (*m* 2nd 22 June 1848 Sir Percy Florence Shelley, 3rd Bt (*qv*), and *dsp* 24 June 1899), dau of Thomas Gibson, and *dsp* 21 Jan 1844
1 Isabella
2 Antonia

BOLTON

Arms: Sa., three swords in pile, points downwards arg., pommels and hilts or, on a canton of the second an escutcheon of the field, charged with a salmon hauriant ppr. **Crest:** A falcon rising or, charged on the breast with an estoile gu., gorged with a ducal coronet az. and holding in the beak a salmon ppr.
Supporters: Dexter, a hind ppr., gorged with a ducal coronet or and charged on the shoulder with a rose arg., barbed vert, seeded gold; sinister, a Cornish chough ppr., charged with a rose, as with the dexter. **Motto:** *Aymez loyaulté* ('Love loyalty').
Creation: B. (GB) 20 Oct 1797.

THE 7TH BARON BOLTON OF BOLTON CASTLE, Co York (Richard William Algar Orde-Powlett, JP (N RYorks 1959–78)) [The Rt Hon The Lord Bolton, JP, Bolton Hall, Leyburn, Yorks DL8 4UF]; *b* 11 July 1929; *s* f 1963; *educ* Eton and Trin Coll Cambridge (BA 1951); FLAS, FRICS, chm Richmond Conservative Assoc 1957–80, chm Yorks branch Roy Forestry Soc 1962–64, dir: Yorks Insur 1964–70, Gen Accident Life Insur 1970–, chm Waterers Gp, v-chm Farm Records Ltd, cncl memb: Timber Growers' Orgn and Yorks Ag Soc; *m* 1st 31 July 1951 (*divorce* 1981) Hon Christine Helena Weld-Forester, est dau of 7th Baron Forester (*qv*); *m* 2nd 1981 (*divorce* 1990) Masha Anne, only dau of Maj Francis Edward Hudson, TD, of Winterfield House, Bedale, Yorks; *m* 3rd 1991 *Mrs Lavinia Fenton, dau of William Edward Wright, and has issue by 1st w:
1 +HARRY ALGAR NIGEL [The Hon Harry Orde-Powlett, The Corner House, Wensley, Leyburn, N Yorks]; *b* 14 Feb 1954; *educ* Eton; *m* 1977 *Philippa A, dau of Maj Peter L Tapply, of Wanstead, Essex, and has issue:
(1) +Thomas; *b* 16 July 1979
(2) +William Benjamin; *b* 1981
(3) +Nicholas Mark; *b* 1985
2 +Michael Brooke [The Hon Michael Orde-Powlett, Hayes Barton, Jacobstowe, Okehampton, Devon]; *b* 21 April 1959; *m* 1985 *Kate Mary, dau of George William Laing, of Newsham, N Yorks, and has issue:
(1) +James Michael; *b* 1987
(1) *Emma Katherine; *b* 1988
1 *Rosemary Victoria [The Hon Mrs North, RMB 590 Boddington, WA 6390, Australia]; *b* 14 June 1952; *m* 14 Dec 1974 *(John) Richard Bentley North, son of W A North, of Salisbury, Rhodesia, and has issue:
(1) *Charles Richard; *b* 1975
(2) *James William; *b* 1981
(1) *Veronica Caroline; *b* 1977

Lineage: WILLIAM ORDE, of East Orde, Newbiggin, High Sheriff Northumberland 1638; *m* Mary — and had an est son:
WILLIAM ORDE, of East Orde; *m* —, dau of Sir William Selby, of Twizel Castle, and *d* 1678, leaving issue:
1 William, of East Orde, High Sheriff Northumberland 1711, MP Berwick 1713, *dsp*
2 THOMAS, of Felkington, Co Durham; *m* Mary (*d c* 1701), dau of William Strother and sis of Sir William Strother, of Fowberry Tower, and was *bur* 21 March 1737, having had:
(1) JOHN, of whom presently
(2) Thomas (Rev), ancestor of the ORDEs of Weetwood
The er son,
JOHN ORDE, DL, of Morpeth and later East Orde; *m* 1st 1734 Mary (*d* 1735), dau of Edward Ward, of Morpeth and Nunnykirk, and had issue:
1 WILLIAM, ancestor of the ORDEs of Nunnykirk
JOHN ORDE *m* 2nd Anne (*d* 26 Dec 1788), widow of Rev William Pye and dau of Ralph Marr, of Morpeth, and had issue:
2 THOMAS, **1st Baron**
3 John (Sir), 1st Bt, so *cr* 27 July 1790 (GB; *see* CAMPBELL-ORDE, Bt)
1 Anne *d* 1825
2 Mary; *m* Robert Lisle, of Acton House, Northumberland
JOHN ORDE *d* 1784. His est son by his 2nd marriage,
THOMAS ORDE later ORDE-POWLETT (added by sign manual name and arms of POWLETT 1795), **1st Baron Bolton of Bolton Castle**, Co York (GB), so *cr* 20 Oct 1797, PC (GB 1785, I 1784), of Hackwood Park, Hants; *b* 30 Aug 1740; *educ* Eton and King's Coll Cambridge; Auditor Duchy Lancaster 1772–74 (Receiver 1774–1807), MP (Tory) Aylesbury 1780–84 and Harwich 1775, also Rathcormick (I Parl) 1784–90, Under Sec Home Dept April-July 1782, Sec Treasury 1782–83, Sec to Duke of Rutland (*qv*) as Ld Lt Ireland 1784–87, Memb BOT 1786–1807, Ld Lt Hants 1800–07; *m* 7 April 1778 Jean Mary Powlett (*d* 14 Dec 1814), illegitimate dau and eventually pncpl heiress of 5th Duke of Bolton (*see* WINCHESTER, M) by Mrs Mary Browne Banks, and *d* 30 July 1807, leaving issue:
1 WILLIAM POWLETT ORDE later ORDE-POWLETT, **2nd Baron Bolton of Bolton Castle**; *b* 31 Oct 1782; *educ* King's Coll Cambridge; MP (Tory) Yarmouth 1807; *m* 8 May 1810 Maria (*d* 16 Nov 1863), est dau of 1st Baron Dorchester, KB (*see* 1963 edn), and *dsp* 13 July 1850
2 Thomas Powlett ORDE later ORDE-POWLETT; *b* 16 Oct 1787; *m* 7 Feb 1811 Letitia (*d* 9 March 1859), illegitimate dau of Henry O'Brien, of Blatherwick Park, Northants, and *d* 31 Jan 1843, having had issue (the two yr sons were granted precedence of a baron's yr son), with an est s who *d* young:
(1) WILLIAM, **3rd Baron**
(2) Thomas (Rev), Rector Wensley; *b* 24 Jan 1822; *educ* Trin Coll Cambridge (MA); *m* 19 Feb 1846 Elizabeth Jane (*d* 31 March 1906), 3rd dau of Marmaduke Wyvill, of Constable Burton, Yorks, JP, DL, and *d* 12 Sept 1894, leaving issue:
1a Thomas Charles, Col cmdg 48th Regtl Dist; *b* 3 Feb 1849; *m* 15 Sept 1886 Harriet Georgiana (*d* 25 Dec 1939), dau of Rev Plumer Pott Rooper, of Abbots Ripton, Hunts, and *d* 18 Jan 1926, having had issue:
1b Gladys Harriet Beryl; *b* 14 March 1888; *d* 15 Oct 1903
2b Beryl Georgina Louisa; *b* 19 Jan 1891; *m* 14 Sept 1921 Cdr Francis Wharton Darwin, RN, 2nd son of Col Charles Waring Darwin, CB, of Elston Hall, Newark, and *d* 18 Feb 1952
2a Ernest (Rev), Rector Wensley; *b* 27 July 1850; *educ* Trin Coll Cambridge (MA); *m* 19 June 1879 Ann Gertrude (*d* 12 Nov 1934), est dau of Rev Alexander Hunter, Rector Tanworth, Warwicks, and *d* 7 May 1926
1a Elizabeth Letitia; *m* 28 Nov 1877 Capt James Edward Hunter, RN, and *d* 19 Jan 1917, leaving issue. He *d* 18 Oct 1932
2a Louisa Rachel; *m* 18 Jan 1883 Capt Charles Michell, late 60th Rifles, of Forcett Park, Yorks, and Glassel, Aberdeenshire; and *d* 27 Oct 1921. He *dsp* 25 Jan 1900
3a Henrietta Maria; *m* 1st 29 Aug 1888 Rev Robert B M Chancellor, Vicar Otley. He *dsp* 1890. She *m* 2nd 3 Oct 1893 Rev Henry Milner Sharples, late Rector Fingall, Yorks, and *d* 16 Jan 1935, leaving issue. He *d* 14 Dec 1919

(3) Amias Charles, of Thorney Hall, Leyburn, Yorks, DL and JP; *b* 22 April 1828; *m* 14 July 1852 Anne Martha (*d* 21 Feb 1917), only child of Christopher Topham, of Middleham Hall, Yorks, and *d* 30 Sept 1899, leaving issue:

1a Amias Christopher Thomas, of Thorney Hall and Middleham Hall; Capt 4th Bn Roy Welch Fus, Lt 1st Bn Manchester Regt, Capt 7th Bn Yorkshire Regt WW I, JP N R Yorks; *b* 7 March 1862; *m* 1st 16 Oct 1886 Alice (*d* 1920), dau of Humphrey Brooke Firman, of Gateforth Hall, Selby; *m* 2nd 1920 Violet Mary (*d* 14 May 1960), er dau of Clervaux Darley Chaytor, DL, JP, of Spennithorne Hall, Leyburn, and *dsp* 18 Nov 1945

1a Florence Annie Letitia; *m* 26 Sept 1883 William Ferrand, DL, of St Ives, Bingley, Yorks; *d* 23 July 1926, leaving issue. He *d* 25 Feb 1927

2a Edith Blanche; *d* young 1856

3a Amy; *m* 14 Jan 1885 Robert Manners Howard Williams, 2nd son of Col Vincent Williams, of Northenby, and *d* 2 Feb 1948, leaving issue. He *d* 31 Oct 1916

4a Letitia; *m* 9 Oct 1889 Sir David Edward Durell Barclay, 12th Bt (*qv*), and *d* 5 April 1923. He *dsp* 2 Oct 1918

5a Georgina; *m* 18 Aug 1897 Sir Henry Allen William Johnson, 4th Bt (*see* JOHNSON, Bt, of Bath), and *d* 31 March 1954, leaving issue

The 2nd BARON's n,

WILLIAM HENRY ORDE-POWLETT, **3rd Baron Bolton of Bolton Castle**, DL; *b* 24 Feb 1818; *m* 12 March 1844 his cousin Letitia (*d* 4 Jan 1882), yst dau of Col Robert Crawfurd, of Newfield, Ayrshire, and had issue:

1 WILLIAM THOMAS, **4th Baron**

2 Henry Robert, barrister; *b* 20 Sept 1846; *educ* Trin Coll Cambridge (MA); *m* 2 Aug 1877 Henrietta Cathcart (*d* 14 Feb 1934), dau of John Randolphus de Trafford, of Croston Hall, Lancs (*see* DE TRAFFORD, Bt), and *d* 9 Feb 1915, leaving issue:

(1) Kathleen Mary; *b* 21 Nov 1878; *m* 16 April 1902 Sir Leslie Edmund Percy Riggs Falkiner, 7th Bt (*qv*), and *d* 7 Jan 1948, leaving issue

(2) Ivy; *b* 8 Jan 1882; *d* unm 2 Jan 1967

3 Frederick; *b* 8 Nov 1849; *d* 3 July 1858

4 Amias Lucien, MA Cambridge; *b* 7 Aug 1855; *d* unm 6 May 1905

1 Jean Mary *m* 28 Nov 1866 Col Hon Augustus Murrey Cathcart, 2nd son of 2nd Earl Cathcart (*qv*), and *d* 27 Jan 1931, leaving issue. He *d* 14 July 1914

His Lordship *d* 7 Nov 1895, and was *s* by his est son,

WILLIAM THOMAS ORDE-POWLETT, **4th Baron Bolton of Bolton Castle**, FSA, Hon Col (late Lt-Col cmdg) Yorkshire (Princess of Wales's Own) Hus Yeo, KGStJ; *b* 31 Jan 1845; *educ* Eton and Trin Coll Cambridge; *m* 13 Aug 1868 Lady Algitha Frederica Mary Lumley (*d* 22 June 1919), est dau of 9th Earl of Scarbrough (*qv*), and had issue:

1 WILLIAM GEORGE ALGAR, **5th Baron**

1 Algitha Alkenda Brenda; *b* 29 June, *d* 3 Nov 1871

2 Rhoda Lelia Alice; *b* 8 June 1875; *d* 15 July 1890

3 Myra Rowena Sibell, CStJ; *b* 22 Dec 1879; *m* 16 April 1901 5th Marquess of Exeter (*qv*) and *d* 27 Oct 1973, leaving issue

His Lordship *d* 14 Aug 1922, and was *s* by his only son,

WILLIAM GEORGE ALGAR ORDE-POWLETT, **5th Baron Bolton of Bolton Castle**, Lt-Col TFR, Maj 4th Bn Yorks Regt, Lt Yorks (Princess of Wales's Own) Hus IY and KRRC, JP, Ld Lt N R Yorks 1935–44, MP Richmond 1910–18, Coronation Medal 1937; *b* 21 Aug 1869; *m* 6 June 1893 Hon Elizabeth Mary Gibson (*d* 9 Dec 1943), est dau of 1st Baron Ashbourne (*qv*), and had issue:

1 William Percy, 2nd Lt 4th Bn Yorkshire Regt; *b* 7 April 1894; *ka* 17 May 1915

2 NIGEL AMYAS, **6th Baron**

1 Elaine Letitia Algitha; *b* 20 Feb 1895; *m* 10 Sept 1922 Rt Rev Percy Mark Herbert, KCVO, DD, Bp Norwich, and had issue (*see* POWIS, E.). He *d* 22 Jan 1968

His Lordship *d* 11 Dec 1944, and was *s* by his only surv son,

NIGEL AMYAS ORDE-POWLETT, **6th Baron Bolton of Bolton Castle**, DL (1952) and JP (N R Yorks); *b* 26 March 1900; *m* 11 June 1928 Victoria Mary (*d* 1 Nov 1933), est dau of Henry Montagu Villiers, MVO (*see* CLARENDON, E.), and *d* 15 June 1963, leaving issue:

1 RICHARD WILLIAM ALGAR ORDE-POWLETT, **7th and present Baron Bolton of Bolton Castle**

2 +(Patrick) Christopher [The Hon Christopher Orde-Powlett, Little Bordeaux, Little Chesterford, Essex CB10 1UA]; *b* 9 April 1931; *educ* Eton and Jesus Coll Cambridge (MA 1958); ARICS, cncl memb Timber Growers E England to 1993, ptnr J Rothschild Assur 1994–; *m* 29 Sept 1962 *Elizabeth Jane, dau of Arthur Spencer Kent, of The Thatched House, Worlington, Bury St Edmunds, Suffolk, and has issue:

(1) *Rosamund Jane; *b* 22 July 1964

(2) *Heather Victoria; *b* 5 Feb 1966

BONHAM

Arms: Sa., a chevron nebulée between three crosses patée-fitchée at the foot arg., on a canton of the last a squirrel sejant, gu. **Crest:** A mermaid, holding in the dexter hand a wreath of coral and in the sinister a mirror, ppr. **Motto:** *Esse quam videri* ('To be, rather than to seem to be'). **Creation:** Bt. (UK) 27 Nov 1852.

SIR ANTONY LIONEL THOMAS BONHAM, 4TH BT, DL (Glos 1983) [Major Sir Antony Bonham Bt DL, Ash House, Ampney Crucis, Cirencester, Glos GL7 5RY]; *b* 21 Oct 1916; *s* f 1937; *educ* Eton and RMC Sandhurst; served Roy Scots Greys 1937–49, retiring as Maj; *m* 19 Feb 1944 *Felicity, only dau of Col Frank Lionel Pardoe, DSO, of Bartonbury, Cirencester, and has issue:

1 +(GEORGE) MARTIN ANTONY [Martin Bonham Esq, 15 St James St, Castle Hedingham, Essex CO9 3EN]; *b* 18 Feb 1945; *educ* Eton and Aston U Birmingham; *m* 1979 (*divorce* 1992) Nenon Baillieu, er dau of Robert Ruttan Wilson, of Durford Knoll, Petersfield, Hants (*see* BERNERS, B), and has issue:

(1) +Michael Francis; *b* 24 May 1980

(1) *Lucie Nenon; *b* 15 July 1982

(2) *Camilla Felicity; *b* 1984

(3) *Sarah Yvette; *b* 1987

2 +Simon Philip [Simon Bonham Esq, Rectory House, Ogbourne St George, Wilts SN8 1SL]; *b* 5 April 1947; *educ* Eton and RAC Cirencester; *m* 20 Aug 1977 *(Elizabeth) Ann, yr dau of Robert Ducas, of Saratoga Springs, NY, and has issue:

(1) *Zoe Virginia; *b* 11 June 1979

(2) *Sophie Jean; *b* 1982

3 +Timothy Eric; *b* 21 June 1952; *educ* Eton; *m* March 1978 *Hester Suzette, yst dau of Sir James Arnold Stacey Cleminson, MC, DL, of Loddon Hall, Hales, Norfolk, and has issue:

(1) *Emma Claire; *b* 1981

(2) *Georgina Sarah; *b* 1983

Lineage: SAMUEL BONHAM, of Orsett House, Essex; *b* 1677 (descended from George Bonham, of Stanway Hall, Essex, who was ggs of Sir Thomas Bonham, of Stanway Hall, Sheriff Essex and Herts 1520 and 1526); Capt; *m* 9 Feb 1713 Jane, est dau of Andrew Pinson, and *d* 28 Feb 1745, leaving with other issue:

SAMUEL BONHAM, of Great Warley Place, Essex; *m* Sarah (*d* 24 July 1807), only dau of O Richardson, of London, merchant, and n of Sir G Richardson, Bt, and *d* 25 Jan 1821, leaving, with other issue:

1 Pinson, of Great Warley Place; Gen, Govr Surinam; *b* 1762; *m* Agnes, dau of John Bathwaite Skeete, Pres Barbados, and *d* 19 April 1855, leaving issue

2 Henry, of Titness Park, Berks, and Portland Place; MP Rye; *m* 8 Dec 1802 Charlotte Elizabeth (*d* 14 Oct 1878), dau of Rev James Morrice, of Betteshanger, Kent; *d* 9 April 1830, leaving issue

3 GEORGE, Capt HEICMS; *m* 1st 18 March 1797 (*divorce* June 1802) Paulina, dau and coheir of William Lushington, and had issue:

(1) George William, Maj HEICS

3 (cont.) Capt GEORGE BONHAM *m* 2nd 28 Oct 1802 Isabella Baines (*d* 18 June 1852), dau of Robert Woodgate, of Dedham, Essex, and sis of Col William Woodgate, CB, and *d* in a typhoon in the China seas 1810 when in command of the *True Briton*, East Indiaman, leaving issue:

(2) SAMUEL GEORGE (Sir), **1st Bt**

1 Isabella Charlotte; *m* Ferdinand, Count d'Oultremont, of Belgium

Capt BONHAM's yr son,

Sir Samuel George Bonham, 1st Bt (UK), so *cr* 27 Nov 1852, KCB (1850); *b* 7 Sept 1803; Govr Prince of Wales's Island, Singapore and Malacca, Govr and C-in-C Hong Kong 1847, Plen and Ch Supt Br trade in China, ret 1853; *m* 16 June 1846 Ellen Emelia (*d* 3 April 1859), est dau of Thomas Barnard, HEICS, and *d* 8 Oct 1863, leaving issue:

1 **Sir George Francis Bonham, 2nd Bt**, JP; *educ* Exeter Coll Oxford (MA); *b* 28 Aug 1847; Dip Serv 1869–90, Sec Legation Lisbon 1885–90 and The Hague 1890–93, Sec Embassy Madrid 1893–97 and Rome 1897–99, Envoy Extrdy and Min Plen Belgrade 1900–03 and Berne 1905–09; *m* 23 Aug 1871 Louisa (*d* 19 Jan 1923), 3rd dau of Sir Andrew Buchanan, 1st Bt (*qv*), and had issue:

(1) George Lionel, Maj Gren Gds, Staff Offr Macedonian Gendarmerie 1907–09, Col Turkish Gendarmerie Smyrna 1909–10; *b* 6 Aug 1873; *m* 11 June 1898 Amy (*d* 18 Feb 1910), dau of Capt Henry Brooks Gaskell, of Kiddington Hall, Woodstock, and *dsp* 23 Jan 1910
(2) ERIC HENRY (Sir), **3rd Bt**
(3) Cecil Maurice; *b* 7 Aug 1887; *d* unm 28 Sept 1908
(1) Edith Florence, CBE (1918), GCStJ; *b* 12 Jan 1877; *m* 27 March 1900 Sir Evelyn Mountstuart Grant Duff, KCMG, Envoy Extrdy and Min Plen Berne 1913–16, 2nd son of Sir Mountstuart Grant Duff, GCSI, PC, and *d* 30 May 1937. He *d* 19 Sept 1926
(2) Lilian Frances; *b* 23 May 1883; *m* 26 June 1911 George Jardine Kidston, CMG, Dip Serv, 2nd son of George Jardine Kidston, of Finlaystone, Renfrewshire, and *d* 9 May 1953, leaving issue. He *d* 26 Dec 1954
(3) Evelyn Mary; nun; *b* 2 July 1885; *d* unm 13 March 1965

Sir GEORGE *d* 31 July 1927; his son,

Sir Eric Henry Bonham, 3rd Bt, CVO (1926, MVO 1912), JP (Surrey), Maj Roy Scots Greys, Extra Equerry to HRH PRINCE ARTHUR OF CONNAUGHT 1909, Equerry 1911, Comptroller Household 1913–26, Hon Attaché Dip Serv 1898–99; served S Africa 1900–02 (two medals, four clasps) and WW I (despatches); Chevalier Legion Honour; *b* 3 July 1875; *m* 23 May 1910 Ethel (*d* 7 Sept 1962), yr dau of Lt-Col Leopold Richard Seymour (*see* HERTFORD, M), and *d* 14 Nov 1937, leaving issue:

1 Sir ANTONY LIONEL THOMAS BONHAM, **4th and present Bt**
1 Elizabeth Mary; *b* 10 July 1914; *m* 1 June 1939 Lt-Cdr Bryan William Richard Curling, VRD, RNVR, formerly of Conford Park, Liphook, Hants, er son of Brig-Gen Bryan James Curling, DSO, of Lyneham Lodge, Warsash, Hants and had issue:
(1) *David Anthony Bryan [David Curling Esq, Middle Oakshott, Hawkley, Hants GU33 6LP]; *b* 27 Jan 1943; *educ* Eton
(2) *Christopher Desmond [Christopher Curling Esq, 24 Colville Rd, London W11 2BS]; *b* 4 May 1947; *educ* Eton and Trin Coll Cambridge; *m* 1974 *Hon Melissa Llewelyn-Davies (*see* 1970 edn LLEWELYN-DAVIES OF HASTOE, B) and has:
1a *Richard William Samuel; *b* 1983
1a *Allegra Rose Elizabeth; *b* 1979
(3) *Jonathan James [Jonathan Curling Esq, 4 Victoria Rd, London N4 3SQ]; *b* 21 May 1951; *educ* Eton
(1) *Belinda Jane Mary; *b* 15 Oct 1940

BONSOR

Arms: Per fess az. and arg. a pale counterchanged, three lion's heads erased or, on a chief also or three roses gu., barbed and seeded ppr. **Crest:** A wolf passant sa., collared and chained gold, resting the dexter forepaw on a rose, as in the arms. **Motto:** *Omne bonum Dei donum* ('Every good is a gift from God'). **Creation:** Bt. (UK) 26 Jan 1925.

SIR NICHOLAS COSMO BONSOR, 4TH BT, of Kingswood, Epsom, Surrey [Sir Nicholas Bonsor Bt MP, Liscombe Park House, Soulbury, Leighton Buzzard, Beds]; *b* 9 Dec 1942; *s f* 1977; *educ* Eton and Keble Coll Oxford (MA); Lt Roy Bucks Yeo 1963–69, barrister Inner Temple 1967, DL 1973, MP (C) Nantwich 1979–83 and Upminster 1983–97, Min State FCO 1995–97, chm H of C Select Ctee Def 1992–95, v-chm Cons For Affrs Ctee 1981–83, Def Ctee 1987–90; chm: Cyclotron Tst for Cancer Treatment 1984–92, Food Hygiene Bureau 1987–, Br Field Sports Soc 1988–, Standing Cncl Baronetage 1990–93, memb Cncl Lloyd's 1987–, FRSA 1970; *m* 4 Sept 1969 *Hon Nadine Marisa Lampson, yr dau of 2nd Baron Killearn (*qv*), and has issue:

1 +(ALEXANDER) COSMO WALROND; *b* 8 Sept 1976
2 +James Charles; *b* 1983
1 *Sacha Henrietta; *b* 26 March 1975
2 *Elizabeth Nadine; *b* 1987
3 *Mary Catherine (twin); *b* 1987

Lineage: JOSEPH BONSOR, of Polesden Lacey, Dorking, Surrey; *b* 9 Jan 1768; *m* 19 March 1796 Jane, 2nd dau of Anthony Hartshorne, of Moorgate, Clarborough, Notts, and *d* 13 Nov 1835, leaving an only son:

JOSEPH BONSOR, of Polesden Lacey; *b* 15 Aug 1807; *m* 14 July 1836 Eliza Denne (*d* 5 March 1909), dau of Maj — Orme, and *d* 27 Nov 1873, having had, with other issue:

Sir Henry Cosmo Orme Bonsor, 1st Bt (UK), so *cr* 26 Jan 1925, DL, JP Surrey, CA, MP NE Surrey 1885–1900, a Lt City London, Chm Income Tax Commn for the City 1886–1925; *b* 2 Sept 1848; *m* 1st 18 April 1872 Emily Gertrude (*d* 18 July 1882), dau of James Fellowes, of Kingston, Dorset (*see* DE RAMSEY, B), and had issue:

1 Malcolm Cosmo, Capt Norfolk Yeo; *b* 2 Aug 1878; *m* 6 Dec 1906 Sybil Henrietta (*d* 7 Feb 1966) (who *m* 2nd 12 May 1920 Mervyn Adrian Touchet Ridley (*see* RIDLEY, V)), 2nd dau of Charles Robert Kennet Fergusson, late Capt Cameron Hghrs, of The Hill, Creetown, Kirkcudbrightshire (*see* FERGUSSON, Bt), and was *ka* 10 March 1918
2 REGINALD (Sir), **2nd Bt**
3 Robert Cecil, MC; *b* 20 Nov 1880; served WW I as Lt Welsh Gds; *m* 25 Nov 1922 Eugenie Constance Frances Pattinson (*d* 13 July 1958), dau of S Lawrence, and *d* 3 March 1932, leaving issue:
(1) +Michael Cosmo; *b* 10 May 1926; *educ* Eton; Lt Gren Gds 1944–47, chm St Helen's Securities 1973, dir Allied Investments 1974–75; *m* 17 July 1951 *Ann Marie, dau of Marc Wallenberg, of Stockholm, and Lady Hambro, and has issue:
1a +Robert Angus Cosmo; *b* 14 Feb 1963; *m* 1989 *Kasandra Noel, yst dau of Dr Joseph Patton, of Great Falls, Virginia
1a *Celia Jane [Mrs Nigel Pilkington, 11 Chester Sq, London SW1]; *b* 9 Feb 1954; *m* 1983 *Nigel Douglas Pilkington, yst *s* of Maj Thomas Douglas Pilkington, JP, of Hyde Mill, Stow-on-the-Wold, Glos, and has issue:
1b *Emma Douglas; *b* 1985
2b *Tessa Douglas; *b* 1987
2a *Charlotte Serena [Mrs Christopher Milln, Kelvedon Hall, Kelvedon, Colchester, Essex]; *b* 7 Oct 1956; *m* 1980 *Christopher J Milln, er *s* of John Milln, of Froglane Farm, Rotherwick, Hants, and has issue:
1b *Frederick John; *b* 1985
1b *Louise Emma; *b* 1983
3a *Camilla Ann [Miss Camilla Bonsor, 22 Queen's Gate Terrace, London SW7]; *b* 2 April 1961
(1) *Ann Elizabeth; *b* 22 Sept 1923
4 Arthur Charles, DL London, memb LCC, memb Westminster City Cncl, Maj W Kent Yeo (TF) WW I, Croix de Guerre with Palms; *b* 13 July 1882; *educ* Eton; *d* unm 25 July 1966
1 Edith Gertrude; *m* 18 June 1896 Henry Charles Thomas Hambro, JP (*see* HAMBRO, B), and *d* 4 June 1959, leaving issue. He *d* 14 Feb 1933
2 Mary Emily; *m* 9 Oct 1900 Sir Edward Hall Alderson, KCB, KBE, son of Francis John Alderson, and *d* 24 Oct 1935, leaving issue. He *d* 7 March 1951
3 Muriel Mary *m* 23 Nov 1911 Gen Sir Reginald John Thoroton Hildyard, KCB, CMG, DSO, Roy W Kent Regt, yst son of Gen Sir Henry Hildyard, GCB, and *d* 26 March 1975, leaving issue. He *d* 29 Sept 1965
4 Ethel; *d* unm Oct 1966

Sir Henry *m* 2nd 3 March 1886 Mabel Grace (*d* 11 April 1944), yr dau of James Brand, JP, of Sanderstead Court, Croydon, and *d* 4 Dec 1929

Sir HENRY's est surv son,

Sir Reginald Bonsor, 2nd Bt, JP Bucks, High Sheriff 1940–41; *educ* Eton; Maj Surrey Yeo (TF), served S African War 1900 and WW I 1914–19; *b* 9 Aug 1879; *m* 30 July 1914 Nancy Frances (*d* 8 June 1965), dau of Col Arthur Melville Hood Walrond and n of 1st Baron Waleran (*see* 1963 edn), and had issue:

1 BRYAN COSMO (Sir), **3rd Bt**
2 +David Victor, MC [Major David Bonsor MC, Little Stocks, Aldbury, nr Tring, Herts]; *b* 7 March 1918; *educ* Eton; Maj Gren Gds WW II; *m* 14 July 1945 his sis-in-law (Sheila) Valerie (*d* 9 Sept 1995), only dau of Maj-Gen Sir Miles William Arthur Peel Graham, KBE, CB, MC (*see* LOVELACE, E, and PEEL, E), of Wiverton Hall, Bingham, Nottingham, and has issue:
(1) +Anthony Miles [Anthony Bonsor Esq, 16 Pembroke Rd, London W8]; *b* 3 May 1948; *educ* Eton; *m* 1980 *Frances Elizabeth, only dau of David Lindsay Bankes, of 32 Holroyd Rd, London SW15 6LN, and has issue:
1a +Miles; *b* 1984
1a *Sophie; *b* 27 Aug 1982
2a *Laura; *b* 1988
(2) +Neil Reginald David [Neil Bonsor Esq, 9 Second Ave, London SW14 8QF]; *b* 11 Oct 1950; *educ* Eton; *m* 1992 *Sophie B, dau of Col Frederick Walter James, TD, DL, of Hopstone, Claverley, nr Wolverhampton
(1) *Caroline Sheila [Mrs Bruce Hodges, Fell Yard, Slapton, Towcester, Northants]; *b* 23 July 1946; *m* 1974 *Bruce Hodges and has issue:
1a *A dau; *b* 1978
2a *A dau; *b* 1980
1 *Daphne Marion [Mrs Alexander Stewart, North Green, Kelsale, Saxmundham, Suffolk]; *b* 1924; *m* 1st 25 May 1944 F/O Clyde Euan Miles Graham, RAF (*das* Sept 1944), only son of Maj-Gen Sir Miles William Arthur Peel Graham (*see* above); *m* 2nd 1 June 1948 Alexander David Stewart, MBE, TD (*d* 1985), er son of Lt-Col Walter Robert Stewart, DSO, MC (*see* GALLOWAY, E), and has issue

Sir REGINALD *d* 4 April 1959, and was *s* by his er son,

Sir Bryan Cosmo Bonsor, 3rd Bt, MC (1945), TD; *educ* Eton; Maj RA, served WW II with Bucks Yeo (despatches), dir: Watney's 1947–58, Watney Mann 1958–77; *b* 27 Sept 1916; *m* 7 March 1942 Elizabeth (*d* April 1995), 3rd dau of Capt Angus Valdimar Hambro (*see* HAMBRO, B), and *d* 1977, leaving issue:

1 Sir NICOLAS COSMO BONSOR, **4th and present Bt**
2 +Richard Angus [Richard Bonsor Esq, Cliddesden Down House, Basingstoke, Hants RG25 2JD]; *b* 3 Feb 1947; *educ* Eton and Keble Coll Oxford; dir Vantage Ltd; *m* 14 Jan 1971 *Susan Anne, dau of F/Lt David Henry Lewis Wigan, RAFVR (*see* 1935 edn TWEEDMOUTH, B), and has issue:
(1) +Rupert James; *b* 1974
(2) +Edward Richard; *b* 1976
(1) *Clare Lucinda; *b* 1981

BOORD

Arms: Per fess az. and gu. a goat's head erased within an orle of eight martlets arg. **Crest:** A goat arg. guttée de poix, resting the dexter leg on an escutcheon gu. charged with a martlet of the first. **Motto:** *Virtute et industria* ('By integrity and industry'). **Creation:** Bt. (UK) 18 Feb 1896.

SIR NICHOLAS JOHN CHARLES BOORD, 4TH BT, of Wakehurst Place, Ardingly, Sussex [Sir Nicholas Boord Bt, 61 Travers Le Mée, 13009 Marseilles, France]; *b* 10 June 1936; *s* f 1975; *educ* Eton, the Sorbonne, Società Dante Alighieri Italy, U of Santander Spain; scientific translator and English training specialist; *m* 1st 29 April 1960 (*divorce* 1965) Françoise, dau of Giuseppe Tempra, of Rue Etienne D'Orves, Berck Plage, Pas de Calais; *m* 2nd 9 Dec 1965 *Françoise Renée Louise, dau of Marcel Clovis Mouret, of 69 Travers de Carthage, Marseilles 8

Lineage: ROBERT BOURDE, of Batcombe, Somerset, *fl* 1327.

JOHN BORDE *fl* 1341

WILLIAM BORDE of Batcombe granted lands at Ilchester to the almshouses there 1429.

WILLIAM BORDE was Escheator (roy official implementing return of fedual lands to overlord on tenant's death) Oxon and Berks 1444.

But the Coll of Arms pedigree only begins with:

RICHARD BOORD, of Batcombe, Somerset; *d* 30 March 1630; f of:

ROBERT BOORD, of Batcombe; *m* 20 Dec 1595 Anne, dau of Alderman Biggs, of Bristol and Bath, and *d c* 1640, leaving, with other issue, a 2nd son:

WILLIAM BOORD, of Batcombe; *b* 1601; *m* 22 April 1630 Hester (*bur* 2 Aug 1680), yst dau of John Bond, of Lutton, Dorset, sis to Denis Bond, MP, memb Cncl of State 1648–52, and 5th in descent from Sir John Hody, Ch Justice England 1440, and was *bur* 12 April 1687, leaving issue, with three daus:

1 John, LLD, Sr Fell Trin Hall Cambridge, Regius Prof Law there 1673–84; *b* 1633; *d* unm, *bur* 23 Nov 1684

2 SAMUEL, of whom presently

3 James, of New Brentford, Middx; *b* 1639; *d* 1700, having had issue:

(1) Elizabeth; *m* Rev Samuel Packer, Vicar New Brentford

The 2nd son,

SAMUEL BOORD, of Batcombe; *b* 1635; *m* Joan Pitman (*bur* 29 Feb 1712), of Milborne Port, Dorset, and was *bur* 30 Jan 1713, leaving, with other issue:

1 Richard; *bapt* 4 Aug 1675; *m* Sarah — and *d* 1730, leaving three sons and three daus. His male line is extinct

2 SAMUEL, of Batcombe; *b* 26 Aug 1690; *m* 9 May 1717 Anne (*d* 12 Aug 1775), dau of Thomas Adams, of Poyntington, nr Sherborne, Dorset, and was *bur* 7 April 1769, having had issue, with three er sons:

(1) SAMUEL, of Batcombe; *bapt* 15 Nov 1722; *m* 21 July 1760 a cousin(?) Sarah (*d* 7 Dec 1807), dau of John Boord, of Batcombe, and *d* 11 Oct 1801, leaving, with other issue, a 2nd son:

1a SAMUEL, of Kingsdown, Glos, and Bristol; *b* 31 Oct 1764; *m* 22 Nov 1796 Ann (*d* 13 Aug 1833), dau of Edward Savage, of Netley, Salop, and *d* 2 May 1824, leaving, with other issue, a 3rd son:

1b JOSEPH, of Harefield Grove, Uxbridge, JP Bucks; *b* 15 July 1804; *m* 1st 12 Oct 1837 Mary Ann (*d* 17 Oct 1852), dau of Thomas Newstead, of Dunham, Notts, and had issue:

1c Sir (THOMAS) WILLIAM, **1st Bt**

2c Edward Henry; *b* 27 Dec 1846; *d* 14 May 1925

3c Arthur Charles; *b* 23 Feb 1852; *d* young

1c Mary Maude; *b* 14 Feb 1845; *m* 9 March 1872 Capt Thomas D'Almaine Mackinlay, 5th Fus, and *dsp* 27 April 1899. He *d* 25 May 1872

2c Kate; *b* 3 June 1849; *d* young

1b (cont.) JOSEPH BOORD *m* 2nd 1 March 1855 Frances Hester (*d* 4 Sept 1927), dau of Thomas Golding Cocke, of Chapel, Essex, and by her had further issue:

4c Francis Joseph; *b* 1864; *d* unm 1888

5c Oscar Philip, of Northwick Grange, Worcs, Capt 6th Bn 1st Garrison Bn Devonshire Regt; *b* 22 Feb 1866; *m* 5 Jan 1898 Amy Louisa (*d* 31 Aug 1959 aged 87), dau of Albert Harris, and *d* 9 Oct 1948, leaving issue:

1d (Oscar) Leslie, MC (1918), Lt-Col 10th Royal Hus, 2nd Lt RA 1917, served WW I, tfd to 10th Royal Hus 1930, served WW II; *b* 18 Nov 1898; *m* 20 Sept 1939 Julia Mary, er dau of Maj Geoffrey Edward Huth, Coldstream Gds, of Wan's Dyke End, Ham, Marlborough, Wilts, and *d* 12 Nov 1967, leaving issue:

1e *Gerald John William, of Wan's Dyke End, late Lt Roy Wilts Yeo, chartered accountant; *b* 11 Aug 1943; *educ* Eton; *m* 19– *Sarah Heyward and has issue:

1f *A dau; *b* 14 Feb 1982

1e *Veronica Mary; *b* 16 April 1941; *m* 25 April 1964 *Michael Francis Mostyn Owen Jodrell, only son of Col Herbert Louis Mostyn-Owen, of Via S Carlo1c, Bellosguardo, Florence, Italy, and has issue:

1f *Henry Francis; *b* 28 April 1967

2e *Rosemary Ann *b* 22 Oct 1946 *m* 5 Sept 1970 *Peter Thomas Baskerville Mynors, son of T H B Mynors (*see* MYNORS Bt), and has issue

2d Victor Francis, Capt RA; *b* 23 Jan 1900; *m* 26 Sept 1942 Gwendoline Alice (Ann) (*m* 2nd 5 May 1956 Lt-Col Edward James O'Brien Croker, OBE, MC, only son of Engr R-Adml Edward James O'Brien Croker, CBE), dau of Alexander Douglas Tyler, of Worcester, and *dsp* 22 March 1955

3d Sydney John Savage, Capt RN; *b* 29 April 1904; *m* 24 Nov 1928 Mary Ethel Margaret, dau of Sydney Arthur Monckton Copeman, MD, FRCP, FRS, and had issue:

1e *Mary Patricia; *b* 17 Aug 1931; *educ* Bristol Univ (BA 1954); *m* 8 June 1956 *Dr Humphrey Frederick Sassoon, MA, PhD, est son of Maj Frederick Sassoon, RA, of Milton Ho, Milton Abbas, Dorset, and has issue:

1f *Timothy John Frederick; *b* 2 May 1957

2f *Mark Richard Humphrey; *b* 1 April 1959

1f *Clare Penelope Mary; *b* 17 March 1961

2e *Margaret d'Almaine; *b* 10 July 1934; *m* 8 Sept 1956 *Capt William George David Greene, late RA, only son of Brig Howard Greene, CBE, DSO, MC, of Glebe Cottage, Bishopstrow, Warminster, Wilts, and has issue:

1f *Andrew Howard; *b* 6 Aug 1957

2f *Toby William; *b* 23 June 1961

1f *Jane Elizabeth; *b* 8 April 1959

2f *Lucinda Mary; *b* 3 March 1963

6c Walter Bertram; *b* 9 April 1870; *d* 31 May 1949

3c Eva Jessie; *b* 7 May 1859; *d* unm 20 April 1953

4c Hester Brenda; *m* 8 Sept 1888 Arthur Palliser and *d* 25 Jan 1905, leaving issue

5c Mabel Gertrude; *b* 2 Oct 1862; *m* 15 Aug 1901 Charles David Bowen, of Titcombe Manor, Kintbury, Berks, son of Sir Charles Bowen, KCMG, and *d* 7 March 1953. He *d* 4 Dec 1939

6c Hilda Edith; *b* 12 Oct 1867; *d* unm 11 May 1962

JOSEPH BOORD *d* 14 Dec 1875. His est son,

Sir (Thomas) William Boord, 1st Bt (UK), so *cr* 18 Feb 1896, of Wakehurst Place, Sussex, JP, FSA; Capt 1st Vol Bn KRRC, VD; MP Greenwich 1873–95; *b* 14 July 1838; *m* 18 July 1861 Margaret D'Almaine (*d* 22 Dec 1918), er dau of Thomas George Mackinlay, FSA, by Katherine, only dau of Dr Andrew Ure, FRS, and *d* 2 May 1912, having had issue:

1 **Sir William Arthur Boord, 2nd Bt,** FRGS; *b* 24 May 1862; *d* unm 26 May 1928

2 Harry Percy, of Batcombe, Somerset; *b* 10 April 1868; *educ* Clare Coll Cambridge (MA); *d* 22 Dec 1923

3 Alexander Edgar, of Batcombe, Somerset; *b* 13 Feb 1872; *m* 31 Oct 1901 Coralie Mary (*d* 10 Nov 1936), yst dau of Herman Hoskier, of Hayes, Kent, and *d* 6 June 1925, leaving issue:

(1) RICHARD WILLIAM (Sir), **3rd Bt**

(1) Ellinor Mary; *b* 23 Aug 1902; *m* 5 Sept 1931 Col Roland St George Tristram Harper, RA (TA), MA Lincoln Coll Oxford, only son of Lt-Col Tristram Harper, of Cranleigh, Surrey, and *d* 10 July 1968, leaving a son and two daus

(2) Helen Margaret; *b* 15 April 1904; *d* unm 23 Oct 1961

(3) Sybil Katherine; *b* 14 Jan 1906

1 Mary Lilian; *m* 30 Sept 1897 Capt Warren Frederick Caborne, CB, RD, RNR, and *d* 9 Sept 1937, leaving issue. He *d* 14 June 1924

2 Ethel Margaret; *m* 12 July 1899 Sydney Arthur Monckton Copeman, MA, MD Cambridge, FRCP, FRS, KGStJ, and *d* 24 April 1944, leaving issue. He *d* 11 April 1947

Sir WILLIAM's n,

Sir Richard William Boord, 3rd Bt; *educ* Marlborough and Lincoln Coll Oxford; S/Ldr RAFVR; *b* 9 Nov 1907; *m* 1st 9 March 1933 (*divorce* 1944) Yvonne Swingler, only dau of Joseph Arthur Hubert Bird, of 61 Melbury Ct, London W8; *m* 2nd 17 June 1944 Ethel El Marie (*d* 20 April 1973), dau of Herman A Moline, of Duluth, Minnesota, and *d* 12 Dec 1975, leaving issue by his 1st w:

1 Sir NICOLAS JOHN CHARLES BOORD, **4th and present Bt**

2 +ANTONY ANDREW [Antony Boord Esq, Darch House, Stogursey, Bridgewater, Somerset]; *b* 21 May 1938; heir presumptive; *educ* Charterhouse; *m* 9 July 1960 *Anna Christina, dau of Capt George F von Krogh, of Kulangsu, Amoy, China, and Horten, Norway, and has issue:

(1) +Andrew Richard; *b* 23 Oct 1962

(1) *Tamsin Katrina; *b* 28 Oct 1961

BOOTH

Arms: Per pale and per chevron arg., erm. and sa., in chief two boar's heads erased and erect of the last and in base a like boar's head of the first. **Crest:** A rose gu., barbed, seeded and encircled by two olive branches ppr., thereon a lion passant arg.
Motto: *Nec temere nec timide* ('Neither rashly nor timidly').
Creation: Bt. (UK) 24 Jan 1916.

SIR DOUGLAS ALLEN BOOTH, 3RD BT, of Allerton Beeches, City of Liverpool [Sir Douglas Booth Bt, 22933 Portage Circle Drive, Topanga, CA 90290, USA]; *b* 2 Dec 1949; *s f* 1960; *educ* Beverly Hills High Sch and Harvard (BA); writer and producer for television; *m* 1991 *Yolanda Marcela Scantlebury, and has issue:

1 *Zahra Jessica; *b* 1993

Lineage: THOMAS BOOTH, of Toxteth Lodge, Liverpool; *b* 15 May 1749; *m* 1784 Esther (*d* 1826), dau of James Noble, of Lancaster, and *d* 1832, having had, with other issue:

1 George; *b* 1793; *d* 1829
2 Thomas; *b* 1795; *d* 1855
3 Henry; *b* 1789; Liverpool rlwy projector and corn merchant, was Sec and Treas Liverpool and Manchester Rlwy 1826–46, first Sec LNWR 1846–8 (dir 1848–59); *m* 1812 Ellen Crompton (*d* 1871), and *d* 1869, having had issue:
(1) Crompton; *b* 1814; *m* Marianne Trimmer, and *d* 1892
(2) William; *b* 1819; *d* 1853
(1) Caroline; *m* Thomas Avison, and *d* 1870
(2) Emily; *m* C Boult, and *d* 1871
(3) Mary Anne; *b* 1822; *d* 1908
4 James; CB; *b* 1796; Counsel to Speaker H of C 1839, Sec BOT 1856–65; *d* 1880
5 CHARLES, of whom presently

The yst son,

CHARLES BOOTH, of Liverpool; *b* 2 July 1799; *m* 1st 20 Aug 1829 Emily (*d* 4 July 1853), dau of Thomas Fletcher, of Liverpool, and had, with other issue:

1 ALFRED, of whom presently
2 Thomas; *b* 1837; *d* 1863
3 Charles, PC; *b* 30 March 1840; FRS, Hon DSc Cambridge, Hon DCL Oxford, and LLD Liverpool, Pres Roy Statistical Soc 1892–94, ptnr Alfred Booth & Co of Liverpool 1862–1916, chm Booth Steamship Co to 1912, memb: Roy Commn on Aged Poor 1893, Tariff Commn 1903–04; *m* 29 April 1871 Mary (*d* 25 Sept 1939), only dau of Charles Zachary Macaulay, and *d* 23 Nov 1916, having had issue:
(1) Thomas Macaulay, DSO (1916) and bar (1917), JP Leics 1932; *b* 10 April 1874; *educ* Harrow; dir Alfred Booth & Co, Col Gordon Highrs, Bde-Major 174th Inf Bde BEF 1914–16, cmdg 7th Bn Gordon Highrs 1916, Assist Mil Attaché 1917, Offr Order Crown Belgium, served Boer War 1900–02 (medal with three clasps) and WW I 1914 (despatches twice); *m* 21 June 1902 Elizabeth Alice (*d* 1965), dau of Capt William Powell, and *d* 24 Feb 1970, leaving issue:
1a (Chambre) Thomas Macaulay; *b* 17 March 1906; *m* Anne Tucker, yr dau of Dr Hunter McGuire, of Winchester, Virginia, and *d* 19 June 1979, leaving issue:
1b *Jane
2a Patrick Arthur; *b* 5 March 1907; *d* 1938
3a *Colin Macaulay, OBE; *b* 7 Jan 1909
4a *George; *b* 9 March 1912
(2) George Macaulay, Dir Bank of England, Lt City London, High Sheriff 1936, Legn Honour; *b* 22 Sept 1877; *educ* Harrow; *m* 6 Oct 1906 Margaret (*d* 2 April 1959), 2nd dau of Daniel Meinertzhagen, of Mottisfont Abbey and Brockwood Park, Hants, and *d* 10 March 1971, having had issue:
1a Daniel; *b* 25 Sept 1907; *d* 1962
2a *John Sebastian Macaulay; *b* 26 April 1913; *educ* Harrow; *m* 25 April 1957 Juno (*d* 13 Nov 1968), 2nd dau of Guy Maynard Liddell, CB, CBE, MC (*see* RAVENSWORTH, B), and has issue:
1b *Georgina; *b* 24 July 1959
2b *Theresa; *b* 20 March 1961
3a *Charles Zachary Macaulay; *b* 5 April 1917
1a *Antonia; *b* 27 March 1909
2a *Georgiana; *b* 17 Feb 1912
3a *Paulina; *b* 6 March 1915
(3) Charles Zachary Macaulay, Coronation Medal 1953; *b* 2 Aug 1886; *m* 30 July 1919 Mary Honora, only dau of Stephen Edward Spring Rice, CB (*see* MONTEAGLE OF BRANDON, B), and *d* 7 Nov 1968, leaving issue:
1a *James Charles Macauley, Lt RN WW II (despatches twice, Croix de Guerre); *b* 9 July 1921; *educ* Eton and Trin Coll Cambridge; *m* 14 Nov 1951 *Bertha, 3rd dau of John Thomas Evans, of Felin, Mydroilyn, Cards, and has issue:
1b *Charles Robert Macauley; *b* 15 Jan 1953
2b *Stephen Richard; *b* 14 May 1958
1b *Antonia Mary; *b* 29 Aug 1956
2b *Victoria Anne; *b* 27 Aug 1961
1a Julia; *b* 20 Aug 1920; *d* 11 July 1921
2a *Cecilia Frances, FANY WW II; *b* 17 March 1924; *m* 23 Sept 1959 George Harold Champion, only son of George William James Champion, and has issue:
1b *Sara Jane; *b* 27 Dec 1960
2b *Mary Ann; *b* 12 July 1963
1 Antonia Mary; *b* 3 Feb 1873; *m* 4 Feb 1899 Sir Malcolm Martin Macnaghten, PC, KBE, QC, 4th s of Baron Macnaughten, and *d* 18 Jan 1952, leaving issue (*see* MACNAGHTEN, Bt)
(2) Paulina Mary; *b* 7 Oct 1875; *d* 18 March 1876
(3) Margaret Paulina; *b* 26 July 1879; *m* 8 Aug 1906 William Thackeray Denis Ritchie, son of Sir Richmond Thackeray Ritchie, KCB, and *d* 5 June 1970, leaving a s and three daus
(4) Mary Imogen; *m* 8 Aug 1912 Col Sir Eric Gore-Browne, DSO, OBE, TD, yr son of Spencer Gore-Browne, JP, of Rowledge, Farnham, Surrey, and *d* 31 July 1975, aged 92 leaving issue. He *d* 28 May 1964
1 Anna; *b* 1833; *m* 1857 Philip Henry Holt, of Liverpool, and *d* 9 March 1899. He *d* 1914
2 Hester Emily; *b* 1842; *d* unm 1906

CHARLES BOOTH *d* 2 Feb 1860; his est son,

ALFRED BOOTH, JP, of 46 Ullet Rd, Liverpool; *b* 3 Sept 1834; *m* 24 Oct 1867 Lydia Allen (*d* 30 Oct 1923), dau of Benjamin Franklin Butler, of New York, Attorney-Gen USA, and *d* 2 Nov 1914, leaving issue:

1 Charles, Hon Capt RNR, chm Alfred Booth & Co and Booth Steamship Co 1912, Midland Rlwy 1919–22, dir LMS Rlwy Co and Martins Bank, memb Mersey Docks and Harbour Bd; *b* 27 Oct 1868; *m* 2 Oct 1895 Grace Bryson, dau of John Wells, of New Brunswick, NJ, USA, and *d* 9 Dec 1938, leaving issue:
(1) Henry; *b* 25 July 1901; *m* 1st 7 April 1926 (*divorce* 1937) Grace Susan Lockhart, est dau of S J Lawry, of Hillside, Plympton, and had issue; *m* 2nd 10 July 1937 *Bertha Flora Ann, est dau of E Snelgrove, of Mavis Ho, Sunningwell Rd, Oxford
(2) *John Wells, Lt-Cdr RN (E List); *b* 19 May 1903; *m* 20 April 1929 *Agnes Margaret, 2nd dau of S J Lawry, of Hillside, Plympton, and has issue
(3) Alfred; *b* 23 May 1906; *d* unm 19 Aug 1932
(4) *Charles, added by deed poll 20 March 1931 the name ENFIELD between Charles and BOOTH; *b* 21 Jan 1910
(5) *Thomas Lawrence; *b* 3 April 1914
(1) *Lydia Grace; *b* 25 Sept 1899
2 ALFRED ALLEN (Sir), **1st Bt**
1 Mabel; *d* unm 1953
2 Hester Emily; *b* 27 Sept 1874; *m* 21 Dec 1893 Alfred Hughes, Prof Birmingham U, and *d* 1965, leaving two s and a dau. He *d* 29 Sept 1940
3 Constance Lydia Allen; *b* 25 Jan 1876; *m* 21 Dec 1904 Godfrey Isaac Howard Lloyd, Prof Toronto U, and *d* 1965, leaving a s and dau. He *d* 9 Feb 1939
4 Harriet Anna; *b* 9 Jan 1879; *m* 11 Nov 1909 Arthur Gregory Whitting, and *d* 19 Jan 1964. He *d* 20 Dec 1937

The yr son,

Sir Alfred Allen Booth, 1st Bt (UK), so *cr* 24 Jan 1916, Hon LLD Liverpool, dir Alfred Booth & Co, chm and dir Cunard Steamship Co; *b* 17 Sept 1872; *educ* Harrow and King's Coll Cambridge (MA); *m* 1st 15 Dec 1903 Mary Blake (*d* 6 Nov 1924), only child of Edmund Dwight, of New York, by Mary Flanagan, dau of Cdre Homer Blake, USN, and had issue:

1 PHILIP (Sir), **2nd Bt**
2 +Edmund; *b* 29 May 1908; *m* 28 July 1933 Henrietta Mary (*d* 1987), 4th dau of Sir Charles (Stewart) Addis, KCMG, of Woodside, Frant, Sussex, and has issue:
(1) +Anthony Edmund, FRCS, FRCSE; *b* 20 April 1934; *educ* Gordonstoun and King's Coll Cambridge (MB, BCh); *m* 1st 28 July 1957 Margaret Helen Elizabeth, dau of Maj A B Miller, and has issue:
1a +Edmund Stuart; *b* 2 July 1960
2a +Sam Andrew; *b* 19 May 1962
3a +Adam Piper; *b* 12 Dec 1963
(1) (cont.) Anthony Booth *m* 2nd 8 Nov 1969 *Susan Ailsa Letitia, dau of Lt R O'Neill Roe, RN, and has further issue:
1a *Harriet Ailsa; *b* 1971
2a *Emily Charlotte; *b* 1973
(2) +Martin Butler [Martin Booth Esq, 60 Elmbridge, Churchgate St, Old Harlow, Essex]; *b* 18 Dec 1936; *educ* Gordonstoun and King's Coll Cambridge (MA 1960); *m* 27 July 1968 *Margaret Hilary, MB, BS, dau of Clifford Birch, of 7 Ousecliffe Gdns, Clifton, York
(3) +Philip Addis; *b* 28 Jan 1946; *educ* King's Coll Sch Wimbledon and King's Coll Cambridge
(4) +Edmund Dwight; *b* 16 May 1948; *educ* King's Coll Sch Wimbledon and King's Coll Cambridge

(1) *(Mary) Rachel; *b* 22 Feb 1939; *educ* Cranborne Chase; *m* 4 Aug 1967 *James William Bruce Douglas, BM, BCh

1 Sylvia Emily; *b* 23 May 1905; *m* 30 April 1927 Ivan Amis, yr son of Henry Amis, of 28, Thornton Way, NW 11, and *d* 20 June 1968, leaving a s

Sir Alfred *m* 2nd 9 Nov 1925 Margaret Lucy (*d* 1 Dec 1943), dau of Charles Edward Brightwen, of Scarborough, and *d* 13 March 1948

His er son,

Sir Philip Booth, 2nd Bt; *b* 8 Feb 1907; *educ* Malvern, King's Coll Cambridge (BA) and Yale U Grad Sch; television dir and producer, memb Screen Dirs' Guild, served WW II with RCAF, Roy Fus and Pioneer Corps; *m* 1st 22 Aug 1935 (*divorce* 1946) Stella Fenton Wood, dau of I J Gerr, of Vredefort S Africa and NYC; *m* 2nd 20 Nov 1948 *Ethel [Mrs Ethel Booth, 1255 Daniels Drive, Los Angeles, CA 90035, USA] (*m* 2nd 1962 (*divorce* 1965) Prof Winston R Weisman, PhD, and resumed name BOOTH), dau of Joseph Greenfield, of NY, USA, and *d* 5 Jan 1960, having had issue by his 2nd w:

1 Sir DOUGLAS ALLEN BOOTH, **3rd and present Bt**

2 +DEREK BLAKE; *b* 7 April 1953; heir presumptive; *educ* Hants Coll and U of California (BA); *m* 1981 *Elizabeth Dreisbach, and has issue:

(1) +A son; *b* 19–

(1) *A dau; *b* 19–

BOOTHBY

Arms: Arg., on a canton sa. a lion's jamb, erased and erect or. **Crest:** A lion's jamb erased and erect or. **Motto:** *Mors Christi mors mortis mihi* ('The death of Christ is to me the death of death'). **Creations:** Bt. (E) 5 Nov 1644 and 13 July 1660.

SIR BROOKE CHARLES BOOTHBY, 15TH BT, of Broadlow Ash, Derbys [Sir Brooke Boothby Bt, Fonmon Castle, Barry, S Glamorgan CF62 3ZN]; *b* 6 April 1949; *s* f 1986; *educ* Eton and Trin Coll Cambridge (BA Econ); High Sheriff S Glam 1986–87; md: Fontygarry Leisure 1979–. chm: Tourism Quality Servs Ltd 1990–, Associated Quality Servs 1994–, HHA Inheritance Ctee 1984–86; High Sheriff S Glam 1986–87; *m* 9 June 1976 *Georgiana Alexandra, journalist, only dau of Sir John Wriothesley Russell, GCVO, CMG (*see* BEDFORD, D), of 86 Chester Sq, London SW1, and has issue:

1 *Aliki Ann Charlotte; *b* 8 July 1977

2 *Francesca Rafela Marina; *b* 1983

Lineage (of Boothby): THOMAS BOOTHBY, of Marchington, Staffs; *m* 2nd Joanne — and *d* between 17 Dec 1583 and 6 Nov 1584, leaving, with other issue, a 3rd son:

WILLIAM BOOTHBY, of London; *m* Judith (*m* 2nd William Basset, of Blore, Staffs, and had issue Elizabeth, w of (a) Henry Howard, who *d* 3 Oct 1616 (*see* SUFFOLK and BERKSHIRE, E), and (b) 1st Duke of Newcastle-upon-Tyne (*see* DEVONSHIRE, D)); *m* 3rd Sir Richard Corbett, of Moreton Corbett (*see* 1970 edn CORBET, Bt), and *d* 28 Aug 1640), dau of Sir Thomas Oesten or Austen, of Oxley, Staffs, and *d* Aug 1597, having had, with other issue:

(Sir) HENRY BOOTHBY 1st Bt, of Clater Clote, Oxon; *bapt* 24 June 1594, inherited from his mother the estates of Clater Clote, Oxon, Boddington, Northants, Broadlow Ash, Derbys, and lands in Cheadle, Staffs; *cr* 5 Nov 1644 a Baronet (E) by sign manual of CHARLES I but the letters patent did not pass the Gt Seal owing to the Civil War; *m c* 1638 Mary, dau of Sir Thomas Hayes, Ld Mayor London 1615, and *d* 3 Sept 1648, leaving issue:

Sir William Boothby, 1st Bt, of Broadlow Ash, *cr* 13 July 1660 a Baronet afresh, though his f's *cr* was noted in heraldic visitations of 1662 and 1663; Sheriff Derbys 1663–64; *m* 1st *c* 13 Aug 1653 Frances (*bur* 11 Sept 1654), dau of Col John Milward, of Snitterton, Staffs, and had issue:

1 FRANCIS, of Peterborough; *b* 1654; *m c* 25 Sept 1678 Anne, dau and coheir of Thomas Child, of Dogsthorpe, Northants, and *dvp* 1684, leaving issue:

(1) **Sir Henry Boothby, 2nd Bt**; *b* 1682; *d* unm; *bur* 25 Nov 1710

Sir William *m* 2nd *c* 25 Dec 1657 Hill Brooke (granted 19 May 1665 rank of a baron's dau; *d 14 May 1704), 2nd dau and eventually sole heiress of Sir William Brooke, KB, n and heir of 11th Lord (Baron) Cobham (abeyant 1951; see* 1970 edn COBHAM, B, and COBHAM, V, preliminary remarks), and *d* 24 March 1706/7, having by her had, with other issue:

2 **Sir William Boothby, 3rd Bt**; *bapt* 1 Jan 1663/4; *m* 1695 Frances, dau of Sir Trevor Williams, 1st Bt, of Llangibby, and *d* 1731, having had, with other issue:

(1) Gore; *bapt* 24 July 1698; *m* 11 June 1720 Elizabeth (*m* 2nd 7 April 1735 John Smith, of Nottingham), dau of John Bury, of Nottingham, and *dvp* (*bur* 10 Aug 1730), leaving issue:

1a **Sir William Boothby, 4th Bt**; Maj-Gen, Col 6th Regt Foot, Master of Horse to HRH THE DUKE OF YORK 1761; *bapt* 4 May 1721; *d* unm 15 April 1787

(1) Frances; *bapt* 22 Nov 1696; *m c* 1 Sept 1715 William Thorp, of Nottingham (*bur* 29 Dec 1746), and left issue (*see* also BRAYE, B, BURGH, B and STRABOLGI, B))

3 Brooke, of Ashbourne; *bapt* 8 Jan 1670; *m* 1st Anne (*dsps*), dau of Henry Cavendish, of Doveridge; *m* 2nd Elizabeth, dau of John Fitzherbert, of Somersall Herbert (*see* WATERPARK,B), and was *bur* 10 Oct 1727, having by her had an only son:

(1) **Sir Brooke Boothby, 5th Bt**; *bapt* 8 Nov 1710; *m* 1st 13 Oct 1737 Anne Byard, of Derby (*dsp* 4 Oct 1739); *m* 2nd 1742 Phoebe (*d* 5 May 1788), dau and heir of William Hollins, of Moseley, Staffs, and *d* 9 April 1789, having had issue:

1a **Sir Brooke Boothby, 6th Bt**, minor poet, one of the literary circle at Lichfield of which Miss Seward, Dr Eramus Darwin and Richard Lovell Edgeworth were also membs; *b* 3 June 1774; *m* 1784 Susanna, dau and sole heir of Robert Bristoe, of Hants, and *d* 23 Jan 1824, having had issue:

1b Penelope; *b* 11 April 1785; *d* 19 March 1791

2a **Sir William Boothby, 7th Bt**, FLS, of Ashburn Hall, Maj 51st Foot; *b* 4 March 1745/6; *m* 14 May 1781 Rafela (*bur* 30 March 1829), dau of Don Miguel Del Gardo, of Mahon, Minorca, and had issue:

1b WILLIAM (Sir), **8th Bt**

2b Brook (Rev), MA, Rector Kirkby-in-Ashfield, Preb Southwell, Notts; *b* 15 March 1784; *m* 4 Nov 1816 Louisa Henrietta (*d* 6 March 1861), dau of 3rd Baron Vernon (*qv*), and *d* 4 Jan 1829, leaving, with other issue:

1c Henry Brooke (Rev), BA, Rector Lissington, Lincs; *b* March 1818; *m* 5 July 1849 Frances Sarah (*d* 22 June 1877), est dau of Rt Rev John Bankes Jenkinson, DD, Bp St David's, and sis of Sir George Samuel Jenkinson, 11th Bt (*qv*), and *d* 30 April 1893, leaving:

1d Henry Vernon, Lt 24th Regt; *b* 2 June 1850; *m* 12 March 1878 Augusta Louisa (*d* 20 Nov 1933), only dau of Maj-Gen John George Boothby (see below), and *d* 24 April 1926, having had issue:

1e Cyril John; *b* 15 Dec 1878; *d* 17 April 1879

2e Ernest Brooke, 2nd/Lt Rifle Bde; *b* 30 May 1881; *m* 31 Dec 1910 Mary (Maeve) Susan Harriett (*d* 3 Dec 1961), er dau of Whitley Stokes, CSI, CIE, of Grenville Place, London SW, and was *ka* 11 July 1916

3e John Henry, Lt RHA; *b* 1 June 1893; *ka* 23 July 1916

1e Gwendolen Margaret Frances; *b* 24 June 1885; *d* unm 1959

2d Horace Brooke; *d* young

1d Gertrude Raffela Hill; *b* 22 Feb 1853; *d* 18 May 1908

2d Louisa Frances; *b* 22 June 1855; *d* unm 31 May 1930

2c George William, Cdr RN; *b* 25 Aug 1819; *m* 3 Sept 1850 Harriet (*m* 2nd 3 Jan 1871 Ven Angus Gunn, DD, of Dollar, Scotland; *d* 14 Nov 1911), dau of Edward Binney Glass, Bengal CS, and *d* 28 March 1868, leaving issue:

1d George; *b* 2 Feb 1867; *m* 1904 Mabel Gertrude (*d* Aug 1961), dau of Bernard Flanagan, and *d* 1921, leaving issue:

1e George William Bernard; *b* 3 Feb 1917; *m* 30 Dec 1942 Avril Alice (*d* 1993), dau of John Edward Innell, and *d* aboard his ship *Royston Grange* 11 May 1972, leaving issue:

1f +GEORGE WILLIAM [George Boothby Esq, Ivy Wall House, Back Lane, Batcombe, Shepton Mallet, Somerset]; *b* 18 June 1948; heir presumptive; Capt MN; *m* 1977 *Sally Louisa Thomas and has issue:

1g *Jane Penelope; *b* 1979

2g *Fenella Susan; *b* 1981

2g *Imogen Roberta; *b* 1982

2f +Richard Charles Brooke [Richard Boothby Esq, Y Garth Gwernogle, nr Brechfa, Dyfed SA32 7RN]; *b* 16 Dec 1955; *educ* Barry Boys' Comp Sch, Manchester U (MusB) and Salzburg Mozarteum; musician; *m* 1992 *Fiona Clare, dau of Peter Padfield, and has:

1g *Maximillian Brooke; *b* 31 Jan 1995

1e Irene Mabel; Anglican Nun

2e Hildred Annie; *d* in infancy

3e *Violet Dora [Mrs Ernest Evans, 11 Birch Grove, Barry, S Glamorgan CF6 8SX]; *b* 1908; *m* 23 April 1935 *Ernest Victor Evans and has issue:

1f *Geoffrey Boothby [Geoffrey Evans Esq, 44 Greenfield Rd, Brunton Park, Gosforth, Newcastle-upon-Tyne]; *b* 1937; MSc, PhD; *m* 1964 *Elizabeth Jane Furneaux Friend and has issue:

1g *Michael Meredith; *b* 1965

1g *Susan Sian; *b* 1967

4e *Edna Frances [Mrs Ronald Steele, Rangeworthy, 3 West Town Dve, Brislington, Bristol]; *b* 1910; *m* 1940 *Ronald George Henry Steele and has issue:

1f *Penelope; *b* 1944

1d Katherine; *m* 16 Jan 1886 Daniel Lehane, MD, and *d* 2 Jan 1939. He *d* 16 July 1907

2d Louisa; *m* 6 Aug 1880 Henry Casson Barnes Bazely, BCL Oxon, s of Rev Thomas Tyssen Bazely, of 8 Town Wall Street, Dover, and *d* 23 May 1918, leaving issue. He *d* 1 March 1883

3d Cora; *m* 1st 13 Sept 1881 Col George Duncan Wahab, late 2nd Lancs Fus, 2nd son of Gen Charles Wahab, Madras Army, and had issue. He *d* 23 March 1899. She *m* 2nd 30 April 1913 Thomas Hart-

Davies, late ICS, MP N Hackney 1906–10, s of Archdeacon Hart-Davies, and *d* March 1927. He *d* 3 Jan 1920

4d Frances; *m* 2 Jan 1891 Capt Robert James Charteris Tod and *d* 29 April 1941, leaving issue. He *d* Feb 1934

5d Rafella; *m* 28 June 1892 Rev John Talbot Godfrey, Vicar St Saviour's, Sunbury-on-Thames, s of William Percy Godfrey, of De Parys Avenue, Bedford, and *d* 9 Dec 1951, leaving issue. He *d* 14 June 1939

6d Ada Rundall; *d* unm 28 Feb 1958

3c John George, Maj-Gen RA; *b* 22 June 1824; *m* 1850 Margaret E F (*d* 10 April 1909), only dau of Capt Charles Henry Seale, RN (*see* SEALE, Bt), and *d* 27 April 1876, leaving issue:

1d Cecil George Frederick, Lt RN; *b* 27 April 1853; *d* unm 29 Jan 1899

2d Walter Herbert; *b* 28 Aug 1854; *dsp* 21 Oct 1899

1d Augusta Louisa; *m* 12 March 1878 Henry Vernon Boothby (*see* above) and *d* 20 Nov 1933. He *d* 24 April 1926

3b Charles (Rev), Capt Engrs, fought Battle of Talavera 1809 (where lost a leg, French POW), later Preb Southwell and Vicar Sutterton, Lincs; *b* 20 Feb 1786; *m* 24 Oct 1820 Marianne Catherine (*d* 1884), dau of Rev Basil Beridge, of Algarkirk, Lincs, and *d* 19 Aug 1846, leaving issue:

1c William Henry (Rev), Vicar Hawkesbury, Glos; *b* 23 May 1823; *m* 10 Sept 1851 Eleanor Jane (*d* 6 July 1907), yr dau of Rev John Thomas Fenwick, JP, Rector Northfield, Worcs, and *d* 1896, having had issue

2c Evelyn (Rev), MA, Rector Whitwell, Derbys; *b* 24 April 1825; *m* 1 June 1853 Margaretta Jane (*d* 5 Jan 1907), dau of John Carr, and *d* 24 May 1874, having had issue:

1d Reginald Evelyn, Lt-Col and Brev-Col RFA; *b* 18 Jan 1855; *d* unm 25 Feb 1915

2d William Osbert, CB, CVO; *b* 7 Jan 1866; Cdre 1st class RN, served Egypt 1882 and China 1900; *m* 17 Aug 1907 Hilda Lambert (*d* 30 July 1959), dau of Capt Henry Stephen Swiney, of Gensing Ho, St Leonards-on-Sea, and *d* 20 May 1913, leaving issue:

1e Osbert Stephen, Lt RN, served WW II 1939–40; *b* 24 Nov 1909; *m* 21 June 1938 *Phoebe Louise (*m* 2nd 17 Oct 1946 Herbert Trench Hart, son of Ansell Hart, of Saxthorpe, Constant Spring, Jamaica), dau of Robert Bagley Foster, and was lost in HMS *Glow-worm*, off Norway 8 April 1940

2e Christopher Evelyn; *b* 15 Sept 1912; *educ* Lancing; Maj RM, served WW II; *m* 25 May 1940 *Pamela Gertrude [Mrs Christopher Boothby, 26 Cwrt Deri, Heol-y-Felin, Rhiwbina, Cardiff CF4 6JB], er dau of Frederick Lewis Heriot-Maitland, of Buenos Aires (*see* LAUDERDALE, E), and *d* 1991, having had issue:

1f Marilyn Susan; *b* 16 June, *d* 26 June 1942

2f *Marilyn Susan [Mrs Stanley Le Blanc, 2301 Oakwood Drive, Carrollton, Texas 75006, USA]; *b* 15 Jan 1944; *m* 24 June 1967 *Stanley John LeBlanc Jr, er s of Stanley Leblanc and Mrs L Romero, of Jeanerette, Louisiana, and has:

1g *James Boothby; *b* 3 Aug 1971

1g *Sarah Maria; *b* 29 March 1968

3f *Diana Mary [Mrs John Spiller, 3 Clos Brynderi, Rhiwbina, Cardiff CF4 8NN]; *b* 4 Aug 1948; *m* 1969 *John Michael Spiller and has issue:

1g *Nicholas Michael; *b* 1979

1g *Christina Ruth; *b* 1976

1e Margaretta Laura; *b* 6 Aug 1908; *d* 4 June 1995

2e Alice Rafela; *b* 6 May 1911; *d* 28 March 1994

3d Frederick (Rev), Vicar Ellistown, Leics, 1903–18; *b* 5 Feb 1871; *d* 4 Aug 1931

4d Basil Tanfield Beridge; *b* 14 Jan 1873; Maj RE, MICE, FRGS, served France and Flanders 1916–19 (despatches twice); *m* 23 Oct 1909 Katharine Georgina (*d* 20 Feb 1938), only surv dau of Maj Francis Blake Knox, RA, and *d* 8 May 1948, leaving issue:

1e (Evelyn) Basil, CMG (1959); *b* 9 Sept 1910; *educ* Winchester and Corpus Christi Coll Cambridge (BA 1933); Consular Serv (China) 1933, V-Consul Boston 1940, Counsellor Rangoon 1951, FO 1953, Counsellor Brussels 1954–59, Head African Dept FO 1959–62, Amb Iceland 1962–65, Perm Rep Cncl Europe 1965–69, lecturer Morley Coll 1969–70, tutor London U Extra-Mural Studies 1970–90; *m* 18 Sept 1946 *Susan Penelope [Mrs Basil Boothby, 23 Holland Park Ave, London W11], 3rd dau of Brig-Gen Hon Arthur Melland Asquith, DSO, of Clovelly Court, Devon (*see* OXFORD AND ASQUITH, E), and *d* 9 Feb 1990 leaving issue:

1f +(John) Joseph [Joseph Boothby Esq, 19 Frithville Gdns, London W12]; *b* 18 June 1947; *educ* St Lawrence Coll Ramsgate and Lond U; *m* 1982 *Isabel Rose, est dau of John Paget Chancellor (*see* PAGET, Bt), and has issue:

1g +Roland Arthur; *b* 1984

2g +Francis George; *b* 1987

1g *Dolores Ann; *b* 1992

2f Philip Sebastian; *b* 13 Dec 1952; *d* 22 Dec 1974

3f +Henry Alexander [Henry Boothby Esq, 459 Latimer Rd, London W10 6RD]; *b* 1 Oct 1955; *educ* Trin Coll Dublin (MB, BS); *m* 1992 *Laura Frances Albinia, er dau of Richard St Clair de la Mare (*see* NORMANBY, M)

1f *Emily Albertine [Mrs Piers Read, 50 Portland Rd, London W11 4LG]; *b* 23 Dec 1948; *m* 29 June 1967 *Piers Paul Read, the writer, 3rd s of Sir Herbert Edward Read, DSO, MC, and has issue:

1g *Albert Nathaniel; *b* 5 Jan 1970

2g *William Edward; *b* 1978

1g *Martha Mariana; *b* 1972

2g *Beatrice Mary; *b* 1981

1e Jane Penelope; *b* 27 June 1914; *m* 22 July 1937 St John Bernard Vyvyan Harmsworth (*see* ROTHERMERE, V), and *d* 15 April 1994, leaving issue

2e (Katharine) Anne; *b* 11 June 1915; *m* 21 March 1939 Col Hubert Layard Chesshyre, MA, late RE, er s of Maj-Gen Hubert Isacke, CB, CSI, CMG, of Polhampton, Overton, Hants, by his w Ada Mildred, er dau of Sir Charles Peter Layard, of The Grey House, Langton Green, Kent, and *d* 9 Feb 1995, leaving:

1f *(David) Hubert Boothby, LVO (1988)[Hubert Chesshyre Esq LVO, Clarenceux King of Arms, Hawthorn Cottage, 1 Flamborough Walk, London E14 7LS]; *b* 22 June 1940; *educ* King's Sch Canterbury, Trin Coll Cambridge and Ch Ch Oxford (MA, DipEd); Rouge Croix Pursuivant 1970–78, Chester Herald 1978–95, Registrar Coll Arms 1992–, Norroy and Ulster King of Arms 1995–97, Clarenceux King of Arms 1997–, Sec Order Garter 1988–, memb Westminster Abbey Architectural Advsy Panel 1985–, hon genealogist Roy Victorian Order 1987–, FSA 1977, FHS 1990, author: *The Identification of Coats of Arms on British Silver* (1978), *The Green: a history of the heart of Bethnal Green* (with A J Robinson, 1978), *Heralds of Today* (1986, with Adrian Ailes) and *Dictionary of British Arms*, vol I (ed, with T Woodcock, 1992)

2f *William John; *b* 24 March 1943; *educ* King's Sch Canterbury, RMA Sandhurst and Trin Coll Cambridge (BA); Col late RE, Def Attaché Prague; *m* 26 April 1975 *Capt Bimala Bangdel, QARANC, of Kalimpong, W Bengal

3f *Matthew Henry [Dr Matthew Chesshyre Esq, 1 Grasmere Rd, London N10 2DH]; *b* 19 July 1944; *educ* King's Sch Canterbury, Trin Coll Cambridge (BA) and St Thomas's Hosp; MA, MB, BChir, MRCGP, FFARCS; *m* 21 Aug 1976 *Jennifer Diana, dau of Maj John Christopher Clapham Maude, MC, Croix de Guerre, and has:

1g *Emily Laura Diana; *b* 5 Sept 1977

2g *Lydia Katharine; *b* 17 Aug 1979

3g *Mary Elizabeth; *b* 18 Sept 1983

4f *John Francis; *b* 19 July 1948; *educ* King's Sch Canterbury and Trin Coll Cambridge; *m* 22 May 1982 *Mary Rebecca, er dau of Maj J F J Worth, of The Mount, Salisbury, and has issue:

1g *Joseph Hugo; *b* 6 May 1984

2g *Thomas Francis; *b* 9 Dec 1985

1g *Sarah Margaret; *b* 27 July 1990

2g *Rebecca Katharine; *b* 19 May 1992

1f *Katharine Mildred [Mrs Thomas Bryant, 26 Exeter Ho, London SW15 3SX]; *b* 8 May 1947; *educ* Sherborne and Newnham Coll Cambridge (BA); *m* 11 Oct 1969 *Thomas Peregrine Stansfeld Bryant, MA, DipArch, yr s of Richard Bryant, CB, of Marsh Farm, Brancaster, Norfolk, and has issue:

1g *William Hugh Chesshyre; *b* 24 Oct 1974

1g *Charlotte Rosemary Chesshyre; *b* 24 Oct 1974

2g *Jessica Katharine Chesshyre; *b* 30 Nov 1980

2f *Alice Jane; *b* 30 Nov 1956; *m* 1st 3 March 1984 (*divorce* 1989) Marc Mucha; *m* 2nd 23 July 1992 *Mark Timothy Swanston Sutton, Prof Guildhall Sch of Music and Drama

1d Mary; *d* 1874 aged 17

2d Laura Cecilia; *d* unm 7 Dec 1937

3d Louisa Jane; *m* 25 Oct 1892 Lt-Col Arthur Charles Jackson, The Buffs, Mil Kt Windsor, s of George Jackson, of Westhorfar, Marlow, and *d* 31 Jan 1940, leaving issue. He *d* 2 June 1936

4d Alice Evelyn; *m* 11 Nov 1884 Col Henry John Blagrove, CB, CBE, 13th Hus, and *d* 14 June 1897, leaving issue. He *d* 29 Nov 1925

5d Judith Letitia; *m* 25 July 1906 Adml James Clement Ley, CB, CVO, son of Rev Clement H Ley, of Sellack, Ross-on-Wye, and *d* 13 Nov 1961. He *d* 15 July 1946

3c Reginald FitzHenry; *d* unm 1849

4c Basil Charles, Capt 95th Regt, Col, severely wounded Battle of the Alma (leg amputated); *b* 13 Jan 1834; *m* 28 Jan 1860 Emily Sarah (*d* 28 Nov 1890), dau of Maj-Gen Sir Joshua Jebb, KCB, and *d* 9 Aug 1892, leaving issue:

1d Beridge Gladwyn; *d* 1864

2d Hubert Basil, DSO (1915), Cdr RNR, with Canadian Pacific Rlwy, served WW I (despatches); *b* 4 March 1863; *m* 1912 Frances Ann (*d* 4 Aug 1948), dau of John Carr Good, of Grimsby, and *dsp* 10 Nov 1941

3d Walter Ralph Jebb (Rev), Rector Thimbleby, Lincs; *b* 26 June 1865; *educ* Selwyn Coll Cambridge (MA); *m* 29 Sept 1900 Mary (*d* 1948), er dau of Rev G F Prescott, Vicar St Michael's and All Angels, Paddington, and *d* 10 Aug 1925, leaving issue:

1e Basil Frederick, MBE (1957); *b* 5 Jan 1904; *educ* Lancing and Selwyn Coll Cambridge (BA); served WW II 1942–45 as Capt RASC; *m* 27 Oct 1934 Dorothy (*d* 1990), dau of Frank Gould, of Ryde, IoW, and Calcutta, and had issue:

1f +Christopher Brooke [Dr Christopher Boothby, St Nicholas, Hollow Rd, Bury St Edmunds, Suffolk]; *b* 1930; *educ* Lancing; MB, BS, MRCS, MRCP Lond; Consultant Paediatrician W Suffolk Hosp, Hon Clinical Assist Hosp for Sick Children Gt Ormond St, memb Gen Nursing Cncl England and Wales 1978; *m* 22 Aug 1969 *Anne Barrow, dau of S B Dalston, of Torcross, Kingsbridge, Devon, and has issue:

1g +Hugo Thomas Brooke; *b* 12 March 1972

2g +William Jebb Dalston; *b* 12 March 1972

1g *Margaret Elizabeth Prescott; *b* 14 Feb 1974

4d Francis Stewart Evelyn, OBE (1918), DL (Lincs), Capt Lincs Regt; *b* 23 April 1867; *m* 1st 3 Aug 1893 Hannah Mildred (*d* 23 March 1932), 2nd dau of Robert Swan, JP, of The Quarry, Lincoln; *m* 2nd 21 Feb

1938 *Constance Ivy, dau of Harold Brackenbury, and *d* 16 June 1946, having had issue by his 1st w:

1e Basil Clayton; *b* 11 Oct 1894; *d* 13 Feb 1895

2e John Clayton, Lt Roy Tank Corps; *b* 19 Aug 1899; *d* 6 Dec 1928

3e William; *b* 7 March, *d* 26 March 1903

1e Joan Penelope; *b* 24 May 1897; *m* 22 April 1924 John Edwin Spickernell (*d* 1 March 1967), s of Frank Spickernell, of Little Roy-den, Kent, and *d* 28 Oct 1970, leaving issue:

1f *Richard Francis; *b* 29 Nov 1930; *educ* Gonville and Caius Coll Cambridge (BA 1952, LLB 1954, MA 1956); *m* 13 Feb 1960 *Elizabeth Charmian, yst dau of Maj Hon Richard Coke, of The White House, Weasenham, Norfolk (*see* LEICESTER, E), and has issue:

1g *Godfrey John Wenman; *b* 11 Jan 1962

2g *James William Richard; *b* 10 April 1965

2e Mildred Serena; *b* 19 Jan; *d* 22 Feb 1902

3e Betty; *b* 12 Nov 1905; *m* 3 June 1930 John Bellenden Alford, yst son of Robert Greenwood Alford, of 21 Cheyne Walk, Chelsea, and *d* 6 April 1944, leaving issue. He *d* 17 Nov 1947

5d Evelyn Leonard Beridge, DSO (1916); *b* 4 May 1876; Capt RN; *m* 1st 21 Nov 1905 Esmé Frances Nevill Augusta (*d* 2 Jan 1913), dau of Sir Edward Beauchamp, 1st Bt, of Grosvenor Place (*see* 1970 edn), and had issue:

1e Esmé Janet; *b* 14 Dec 1906; *d* unm 14 Dec 1977

2e Penelope Frances; *b* 13 Aug 1909; *m* 28 July 1934 Hugh Robert Macdonald Farmer, CB, Clerk/Administrator H of C, yst s of Charles Edward Farmer, of 18 Sloane Court, London SW, and *d* 5 April 1963, leaving issue

5d (cont.) Capt Evelyn Boothby *m* 2nd 1924 Lucy Margaret Amy (*d* 10 Jan 1948), widow of Capt F T Gardiner, HLI, and dau of Alfred Edward Gregory, MusB, and *d* 14 Jan 1937, having by her had further issue:

1e +Walter Evelyn Brooke [Walter Boothby Esq, 40 Calmore Gdns, Totton, Southampton]; *b* 9 Feb 1927; *m* 1st 29 Dec 1951 (*divorce* 1974) Yvonne, dau of J S Capewell, of Harlesden, London NW; *m* 2nd 1964 *Catherine Jane, dau of Ralph Forrester Stobart, of Newton Farm, Tregony, Cornwall, and has issue by 1st w:

1f +Martin William; *b* 19 Jan 1953; *m* 1982 *Stephanie Anne, dau of H G Mills, of Portstewart, Co Londonderry, and has issue:

1g +Bryn; *b* 1982

1g *Tara; *b* 1980

2f +Bruce Michael; *b* 1 Dec 1959; *m* 1984 *Trudy Frith, dau of Kenneth Frith Williams, of Sunbury, Middx

1d Marion Agnes Serena Penelope; *d* unm 8 Aug 1943

2d Mary Dorothy Cecilia; *d* 13 Feb 1921

1c Martha Serena; *m* 7 Sept 1852 Rev Sir Brooke William Robert Boothby, 10th Bt, and *d* 29 June 1909, leaving issue (*see* below)

2c Judith Agnes; *m* 1860 William Henry Millais and *d* 6 April 1862, leaving issue (*see* MILLAIS, Bt). He *d* 20 March 1899

3c Cecilia Elizabeth; *d* unm 15 March 1925

1b Louisa Rafela; *b* 1787; *d* 30 April 1870

Sir WILLIAM *d* 17 March 1824, and was *s* by his est son,

Sir William Boothby, 8th Bt, CB, Capt 15th Light Dragoons and ADC to DUKE OF CUMBERLAND; *b* 25 March 1782; Receiver-Gen Customs Port of London, Paymaster Gentlemen-at-Arms; *m* 1st 29 Jan 1805 Fanny (*d* 2 Jan 1838), only dau of Col John Jenkinson and n of 1st Earl of Liverpool (*see* JENKINSON, Bt), and had, with other issue:

1 BROOKE WILLIAM ROBERT (Sir), **9th Bt**

2 Cecil Brooke; *b* 18 Nov 1813; *d* 8 Jan 1883

Sir William *m* 2nd 15 Oct 1844 Louisa Cranstoun, actress (*d* 16 Jan 1858), widow of John Alexander Nisbett, of Brettenham Suffolk, and dau of Frederick Hayes Macnamara, Offr 52nd Foot (*see* BERNERS, B), and *d* 21 April 1846

His son,

Rev Sir Brooke William Robert Boothby, 9th Bt, BA, Fell All Souls' Oxford 1829, MA 1833, Rector Elmley, Kent, 1846–52, and Welwyn, Herts, 1852–65; *b* 29 Jan 1809; *m* 7 Sept 1852 his cousin Martha Serena (*d* 29 June 1909), dau of Rev Charles Boothby (*see* above), and *d* 21 Sept 1865, leaving issue:

1 **Sir Brooke Boothby, 10th Bt**, *b* 18 Nov 1856; Dip Serv 1881–1913: Sec Legn Rio de Janeiro 1898–1901, Tokyo 1901–02 and Brussels 1902–05, Counsellor Embassy Vienna 1905–07, Envoy Extrdy and Min Plen Santiago 1907–13; *d* unm 22 Jan 1913

2 **Sir Charles Francis Boothby, 11th Bt**, Lt N Mayo Militia; *b* 22 June 1858; *d* unm 4 April 1926

3 Hugo William Robert, Midshipman RN; *b* 12 Feb 1862; *d* unm 10 Aug 1881

4 **Rev Sir Herbert Cecil Boothby, 12th Bt**; *educ* Ch Ch Oxford (BA); Lt Derbyshire Regt; *b* 8 Dec 1863; *d* unm 27 March 1935

5 SEYMOUR WILLIAM BROOKE (Sir), **13th Bt**

1 Florence Emma; *d* unm 14 Nov 1931

2 Rosalind Louisa; *d* unm 29 Nov 1923

3 Beatrice Georgiana; *d* unm 13 Feb 1921

The 12th Bt's bro,

Sir Seymour William Boothby, 13th Bt; *b* posthumously 6 Feb 1866; *m* 30 Oct 1906 Clara Margaret (*d* 4 Nov 1969), dau of Robert Arthur Valpy, and had issue:

1 HUGO ROBERT BROOKE (Sir), **14th Bt**

1 *Serena Margaret [Mrs Herbert Homfray, The Church House, Penllyn, Cowbridge, Glam]; *b* 21 June 1914; *m* 19 Nov 1958 Herbert Charles Richards Homfray, JP, est son of Col Herbert Richards Homfray, DL, JP of Penllyn Castle, Cowbridge, Glam. He *d* 10 July 1960

Sir SEYMOUR *d* 17 March 1951; his only son,

Sir Hugo Robert Brooke, 14th Bt, JP (Glam 1950), High Sheriff 1953, Ld Lt S Glam 1974–86 (V-Lt Glam 1957–74, DL 1953), Capt RA 53rd (Welsh) Div 1942–44 WW II, Capt RA (TA), memb Cardiff RDC 1936–58 (chm 1948–49 and 1949–50), memb: Rep Body Church in Wales 1955–65, Nat Bdcasting Cncl Wales 1953–56 and cncl Nat Museum Wales 1955–86 (chm Art Ctee 1962), S Wales regnl dir Lloyds Bank 1963–78, Fell Woodard Corp 1961–86, dir Wales Tourist Bd 1965–70; *b* 10 Aug 1907; *educ* Lancing and Hertford Coll Oxford; *m* 11 June 1938 *Evelyn Ann, only dau of Herbert Charles Richards Homfray, JP, of Penllyn Castle, Glam, and had issue:

1 Sir BROOKE CHARLES BOOTHBY, **15th and present Bt**

1 *Penelope Ann; *b* 26 May 1939; *m* 29 Aug 1959 (*divorce* 1965) Cdr Timothy John Windham Hale, RN, AMINucE, est s of Bernard John Windham Hale and Mrs Alexander Craven Vicary, of Scarhill House, Chagford, Devon, and has issue:

(1) *Veronica Ann Leslie; *b* 29 March 1960

2 *Caroline Serena [Mrs Richard Parry, Manton Weir Farm, Manton, Wilts SN8 4HH]; *b* 15 June 1941; *m* 1st 7 July 1962 (*divorce* 1972) Ifor Morel Lewis, racehorse owner, only son of Ivor Llewellyn Lewis, of Upper Porthkerry, Barry, Glam, and has issue:

(1) *Vivienne Serena; *b* 14 March 1966

(2) *Carina Cecilia; *b* 21 Feb 1969

2 (cont) *Caroline Serena *m* 2nd *Richard Hugh Parry and has issue by 2nd husb:

(1) *James Hugo; *b* 1981

Lineage (of Jones, of Fonmon): RHYS HIR Ap DAFYDD, 11th in descent from Bleddyn ap Maenrych (*k* 1093), Lord of Brecon (not a peer, but ruler over his territory as a semi-independent princeling); *m* 1st Gwenllian, dau of John ap Thomas, of Bryscedwyn, Glam and had issue; *m* 2nd — (*dsp*), dau of Philip Mansel; one of his sons by his 1st w:

JOHN Ap RHYS HIR; *m* 1st —, dau of Thomas ap Hopkin, of Mynachlog, Glam; *m* 2nd Gwenllian, dau of Hywel Gwyn ap Llywelyn, and had, with an est s (Dafydd, *dsp*) and a yst s (Harry):

PHILIP Ap JOHN; *m* Jane, dau of Ieuan Powell Cyffyn, of Powys, and had:

DAVID JONES, of Llangyfelach, Glam; *m* Elizabeth, dau of William David Gruffudd, of Llangyfelach, Glam, and had, with two yr sons (Morgan; Richard) and three daus:

PHILIP JONES; *b* 1618; Col Parliamentary army Civil War; memb of CROMWELL's 'Other House'; bought Fonmon Castle; *m* Jane (*d* 23 Oct 1678), dau of William Price, of Gelli-hir, Ilston, Glam, and *d* 5 Sept 1674, having had, with five daus:

1 Samuel; *dsp* & *vp* 13 Jan 1671

2 Philip; *dsp*

3 John (Sir), of Fonmon Castle; ktd by 1677; *m* 1st Sarah (*d* 16 July 1675), dau of William Dashwood, and had two daus (*d* in infancy); *m* 2nd, as her 1st husb Ann (*m* 2nd, as his 2nd w, 1st Baron Jeffreys of Wem; *see* JEFFREYS, B), dau of Sir Thomas Bludworth, and *dspm* 15 Oct 1678

4 Oliver, of Fonmon Castle; *b c* 1654; *m* Mary (*d* 20 Oct 1688), dau of Martin Button, of Dyffryn St Nicholas, Glam, and *d* 23 May 1685, leaving:

(1) Philip; *d* shortly after his f

(2) ROBERT

(3) Oliver; *b c* 1684; *d* 1701

The 2nd s,

ROBERT JONES, of Fonmon Castle; MP Glam 1710, 1713 and 1715; *m* 1703 Mary, 2nd dau of Sir Humphrey Edwin, of Llanfihangel, Glam, and *d* 1715, having had, with a yr s (Oliver, *d* 1736) and three daus:

ROBERT JONES, of Fonmon Castle; *b c* 1706; High Sheriff Glam 1729; *m* 1732 Mary, dau of Richard Forrest, of Minehead, Somerset, and *d* 1742, having had, with four daus:

ROBERT JONES, of Fonmon Castle; *m* 1st *c* 1770 Jane, dau and heir of Evan Seys, clerk, of Boverton, Llantwit Major, Glam, and had two daus (*d* young); *m* 2nd Joanna, dau of Edmund Lloyd, of Cardiff, and had, with four other daus:

1 Robert, of Fonmon Castle; *b* 1773; *d* June 1834

2 Oliver Thomas; *b* 8 Sept 1776; Lt-Gen Peninsular War; *m* 1st Louisa (*d* 1810), dau of Col — Stanley, and had two daus; *m* 2nd Maria Antonia, dau of Henry Swinburne, of Hamsterley, Co Durham (*see* 1949 edn SWINBURNE, Bt), and *d* 15 Nov 1815, having had, with another dau:

(1) ROBERT OLIVER

(2) Oliver John; *b* 1813; Capt RN

The er s,

ROBERT OLIVER JONES, of Fonmon Castle, JP, DL Glam; High Sheriff 1838, chm QS; *b* 16 Dec 1811; *m* 1st 1843 Alicia (*d* 1 April 1851), dau of Evan Thomas, of Llwyn Madog, Abergwesyn, Breconshire, and had:

1 Oliver Evan; *b* and *d* May 1844

2 Oliver Henry; *b* 7 Jan 1846

3 Reginald Charles; *b* 17 Sept 1848; *d* 12 Jan 1854

4 Edith Alicia; *b* 2 Nov 1850; *m* 14 Jan 1874 Robert Arthur Valpy, JP Mon, barrister (*d* 11 Sept 1894), and had, with other issue:

(1) Clara Margaret; *b* 26 Oct 1877; *m* **Sir Seymour William Boothby, 13th Bt**, and had issue (*see* above)

BOREEL

Arms: Arg., on a chevron between three bugle horns sa. two whips thonged ppr., a chief gu., charged with a lion passant guardant or. **Crest:** A demi-man sa., wreathed about the head and loins, holding in his dexter hand an arrow in bend sinister, point upwards, ppr. **Creation:** Bt. (E) 21 March 1645.

SIR FRANCIS DAVID BOREEL, 13TH BT, of Amsterdam, Holland [Sir Francis Boreel Bt, Kapellstraat 25, 4351 A L Veere, Netherlands]; *b* 14 June 1926; *s f* 1964; *educ* Utrecht U; late F/Lt (Res) Regt Huzaren van Boreel, Counsellor Press and Cultural Affrs Netherlands Foreign Service 1966–87; *m* 14 Aug 1964 *Suzanne Julie, dau of Willy Campagne, of Paris, and has issue:

1 *Reiniera Adriana; *b* 22 Aug 1965

2 *Christina Wilhelmina; *b* 1966

3 *Titia Florence; *b* 1973

Lineage: This family lived in the 14th and 15th centuries at Ghent and Bruges.

PETER BOREEL; *b* Sluys 24 Dec 1524; settled Middleburg, Zeeland; as a Protestant, migrated 1567 to England; *m* 1551 Catherine Josse and *d* Norwich 9 Jan 1568, leaving, with other issue, an est son:

Sir JAMES BOREEL, of Duynbeke, West Hoven, Domburg and St Aegterskerke, Col, Burgomaster Middleburg, Deputy to the States-Gen, Envoy 1618 to JAMES I of England, by whom ktd 1623; *b* 28 Oct 1552; *m* 1st 18 Oct 1574 Mary Passchier and had, with other issue:

1 Sir John, Councillor-Pensionary Zeeland, Envoy to JAMES I, by whom ktd 1622; issue *extinct*

Sir JAMES *m* 2nd 19 Aug 1584 Mary Grimminck and *d* Dec 1636, having by her had, with an er son and other issue:

2 **Sir William Boreel, 1st Bt** (E), so *cr* 21 March 1644/5, of Amsterdam, Envoy to England, ktd by JAMES I 1619, Pensionary Amsterdam 1628, Amb Venice 1636, also in Sweden 1640, England 1642 and France 1648, allegedly recd from CHARLES II a roy warrant as a baron of England 28 June 1653 but no full peerage *cr* was ever effected; *b* 24 March 1591; *m* 22 Sept 1626 Jacoba Carels (*d* Paris 17 June 1657) and *d* Paris 29 Sept 1668, having had issue:

(1) **Sir John Boreel, 2nd Bt,** Marshal Court of Prince of Orange (later WILLIAM III of England, Scotland and Ireland), Lt-Col; *b* 29 Oct 1627; *m* 7 Nov 1666 Amaranthe van Vredenburgh (*d* 27 July 1715), and *d* 29 March 1691, having had, with other issue:

1a William; *b* 26 Feb, *d* 6 April 1671

2a **Sir William Boreel, 3rd Bt,** Capt; *b* 4 Oct 1672; *d* unm 23 Sept 1710

3a **Sir Adrian Boreel, 4th Bt,** Lt-Col Dutch Army, Capt Dutch Navy, Chief d'Escadra (i.e., Squadron, roughly equivalent therefore to Cdre) and Contra Adml (equivalent to R-Adml) Portuguese Navy; *b* 9 Dec 1674; *m* Margaret van den Bosch (*d* 14 April 1726) and *d* 15 July 1723

(2) James, Utd Provinces Amb Russia, France and peace preliminaries (with France) Nijmwegen and Ryswick 1697; *b* 21 March 1630; *m* 26 Feb 1667 Isabella Coymans (*d* 28 Jan 1705) and *d* 21 Aug 1697, having had issue:

1a William; *b* 20 Dec 1667; *d* 19 April 1668

2a **Sir Balthasar Boreel, 5th Bt,** Counsellor Deputy Holland; *b* 21 May 1673; *m* 17 Dec 1720 Apollonia Rendorp (*d* 28 Oct 1757) and *dsp* 28 June 1744

3a William, Utd Provinces Amb France; *b* 19 March 1675; *m* 3 Dec 1704 Catharina Clara Geelvinck (*d* 19 Nov 1729) and *dsp* 12 June 1727

4a James, Commissary of the Post; *b* 6 Jan 1679; *m* 25 May 1710 Sarah Samaer and *d* Amsterdam 28 March 1736, having had issue:

1b **Sir William Boreel, 6th Bt,** Master of the Vendution Amsterdam; *b* 1712; *d* unm 14 Feb 1787

2b James; *d* unm 2 Feb 1746

3b Balthasar; *d* before his brothers

5a John Hieronimus, Echevin (equivalent to Alderman) Amsterdam; *b* 14 Dec 1684; *m* 16 Dec 1709 Anne Mary Pels (*d* 1 Dec 1776) and *d* 9 Sept 1738, having had issue:

1b James, Utd Provinces Amb Gr Britain 1761; *b* 28 March 1711; *m* 28 Feb 1735 Agnes Margareta Munter (*d* 8 Dec 1761) and *d* 4 April 1778, having had, with other issue:

1c John; *b* 16 July 1741; *d* 26 Dec 1757

2c **Sir William Boreel, 7th Bt,** Echevin Amsterdam, Deputy to the States-Gen; *b* 20 June 1744; *m* 30 Dec 1766 Mary Trip (*d* 23 Jan 1813) and *d* 31 July 1796, having had issue:

1d **Sir James Boreel, 8th Bt,** Memb Equestrian Order and States of Holland; *b* 25 Oct 1768; cr 28 Aug 1814 Jonkheer in the nobility of The Netherlands; *m* 21 Aug 1791 June Margaret (*d* The Hague 1 Nov 1846), dau of William Munter, Echevin of Amsterdam, and *d* The Hague 12 April 1821, having had issue:

1e **Sir William Boreel, 9th Bt,** memb Netherlands Upper House, Min of State; *b* 23 March 1800; *m* 24 July 1833 his cousin Margaret Jaqueline Mary Pauline (*d* 9 Feb 1892), Ldy-in-Waiting to Queen of Holland, dau of Lt-Gen William Francis Boreel, and *d* 1883, having had issue:

1f **Sir Jacob Willem Gustaaf Boreel, 10th Bt,** Chamberlain to Queen of the Netherlands 1905–37, Burgomaster Haarlem; *b* 10 Sept 1852; *m* 1st 14 March 1878 Maria Cornelia (*d* 11 Dec 1891), dau of Baron William Assneer Jacob Schimmelpenninck van der Oye, Grand Master Ceremonies to King of Holland, and had issue:

1g Cornelia Maria, Mistress of the Robes to Queen of the Netherlands; *b* 4 April 1879; *m* 27 Nov 1902 Baron Frederick William van Tuyll van Serooskerken, yst son of Ernest Louis Leopold, Baron van Tuyll van Serooskerken, and *d* 4 April 1957, leaving issue. He *d* 1 April 1950

2g Agnes; *b* 14 April 1880; *m* 17 Oct 1907 Ernest Cremers, son of Epimachus Jacobus Johannes Baptista Cremers, and *d* 23 Nov 1961. He *d* 8 June 1944

3g Henrietta Sarah; *b* 27 Oct, *d* 2 Nov 1881

1f (cont.) **Sir Jacob** *m* 2nd 15 Feb 1898 Cornelia Maria (*d* 10 Oct 1927), dau of Hendrik Maurits van Weede, Chamberlain to King of Holland, and *dspm* 16 July 1937

1f Agnes Cornelie Hugonia; *b* 23 March 1839; *m* 12 Aug 1863 Baron William van Goltsein, Dutch Min Plen UK, and *d* 17 Dec 1924. He *d* 1901

2f Marie; *b* 24 March 1850; *m* 1874 Baron F W C H van Tuyll van Serooskerken, Chamberlain to Queen of the Netherlands, of Vilserbeek, Velsen, N Holland, and *d* 27 Jan 1919. He *d* 13 Feb 1924

1e Wendela Eleanora; *b* 11 July 1792; *m* 7 Sept 1814 William Gustaaf Frederik van Reede, 9th and last Earl of Athlone of the March 1691/2 cr, and *d* 30 Jan 1868. He *dsp* 21 May 1844

2e Mary; *m* 1 Sept 1815 James, Baron Fagel, Cllr of State Netherlands, and *d* 17 April 1858. He *d* 21 April 1835

3e Cornelie Adriane, Ldy-in-Waiting to QUEENS ANNA and SOPHIE (Consorts of WILLIAM II and WILLIAM III); *m* 12 March 1823 Hugo, Baron von Zuylende Nyevelt, Dutch Amb Sublime Porte, Min of State, and *d* 18 March 1853

4e Jaqueline Mary; *b* 23 June 1798; *d* 1812

2d Luc; *b* 11 Oct 1773; *d* 9 April 1779

3d William Francis, Lt-Gen, Grand Equerry to WILLIAM II of The Netherlands, Grand Master Household of WILLIAM III of The Netherlands; *b* 15 Sept 1775; *m* April 1803 Catherine Anne (*d* 18 April 1825), dau of Francis Fagel and Anne Mary Boreeel, and *d* Friederichschafen, Württemberg, 21 May 1851, having had, with other issue:

1e William James; *b* 2 Oct 1804; *d* 16 Sept 1824

2e Francis Robert, Memb Equestrian Order N Holland, Grand Master Ceremonies to King of The Netherlands; *b* 25 July 1806; *m* 2 April 1834 Sarah Astor (*d* 3 March 1895), Ldy-in-Waiting to QUEEN SOPHIE, and *d* 9 March 1869, leaving, with other issue:

1f William Walter Astor, Chamberlain to WILLIAM III; *b* 20 Nov 1838; *m* 19 April 1866 Mary Emily (*d* 18 May 1906), dau of Sir John Milbanke-Huskisson, 8th Bt, and *d* 24 Sept 1892, leaving issue:

1g Robert John Ralph; *b* 14 Jan 1867; *m* 17 Dec 1891 Edith Margaret (*m* 2nd 8 Nov 1905 Jacob Pieter Crommelin and *d* 17 June 1933), dau of Philo Lewis Ives, of Hartford, Connecticut, USA, and *d* 12 Feb 1904, leaving:

1h Helen Barbara Isabella; *b* 1894; *m* 27 Oct 1921 (*divorce* 1944) Sir Ralph Clarmont Skrine Stevenson, GCMG (*d* 23 June 1977), s of Surg-Gen Henry Wickham Stevenson, CSI, JP, of Balladoole, and had:

1i *Mark Boreel; *b* 1924

2h (Edith) Wendela Dorothy; *b* 1896; ARE; *m* 16 July 1924 Leslie George Wylde (*d* 29 May 1935), Lt Canterbury Regt (NZ Forces), s of George Rich Wylde, of Greymouth, NZ, and had:

1i *James Paxton de Eglesfield; *b* 1927

2f Alfred Montalto; *b* 11 May 1849; *m* 16 June 1881 Louise Antoinette Maximilienne (*d* 29 April 1950), dau of Daniel d'Hangest, Baron d'Yvoyde Mydecht, and *dsp* 2 May 1912

3f Robert Eugene; *b* 19 Dec 1850; *m* 26 Sept 1878 Florence (*d* 9 Dec 1928), dau of Francis Capper Brooke, of Ufford Place, Suffolk, and *d* 22 April 1896, leaving issue:

1g **Sir Francis William Robert Boreel, 11th Bt;** *b* 19 March 1882; *d* unm 1 June 1941

2g ALFRED (Sir), **12th Bt,** for whom *see* further below

1g (Florence Ida) Sophia; *b* 1 Nov 1879; *d* unm 10 Feb 1964

2g Christine Sybil Sarah; *b* 25 Dec 1880; *m* 17 Dec 1901 Maurits Johan Emanuel, Baron Huyssen van Kattendyke, son of Baron Frederik Johann Emanuel Huyssen van Kattendyke, and *d* 24 Jan 1903. He *d* 21 May 1961

3g Hélène Cécile; *b* 20 Sept 1886; *m* 19 Nov 1912 Ridder Hendrick Willem Gustaf Maurits Huyssen van Kattendyke, CMG,

Netherlands Dip Serv, s of Ridder Johan Willem Frederik Huyssen van Kattendyke, and *d* 23 Sept 1966, leaving issue. He *d* 19 March 1949

1e Margaret Jaqueline Mary Pauline; *m* 24 July 1833 Sir William Boreel, 9th Bt (*see* above)

4d Luc, memb Equestrian Order and States of Holland; *b* 1 Sept 1780; *m* 24 April 1811 Mary Jane Sarah, Countess van Limburg Stirum (*d* 3 Jan 1848), and *d* 23 Jan 1854, leaving issue, with two daus:

1e William, Chamberlain to WILLIAM III of The Netherlands; *b* 1 March 1812; *d* unm 14 Dec 1857

2e Jacob Otto Bernard, Chamberlain to WILLIAM II and WILLIAM III; *b* 5 March 1813; *m* 2 May 1850 Catherine Mary Ulrica (*d* 12 Sept 1900), dau of Salomon, Baron Dedel, and *d* 1888, leaving issue:

1f Luc Gerard; *b* 20 May 1852; *m* 26 Nov 1891 Anna (*d* 11 Aug 1925), dau of Jonkheer Volkert Barnaart, and *dsp* 30 March 1934

2f Gerard Salomon; *b* 30 April 1855; *m* 10 May 1882 Susanna Gertrude Françoise (*d* 15 Sept 1942), dau of Jonkheer Hugo Gevers, of Noordwyk, Holland, and *d* 1938, leaving issue:

1g James Lucas; *b* 1 April 1883; *m* 10 Oct 1911 Baroness Adriana Sophia (*d* 7 Aug 1958), dau of Baron Maurice Van Randwijck, and *d* 18 Dec 1939, leaving issue:

1h Gerard Lucas Cornelis; *b* 23 July 1913; *m* 15 Aug 1943 Virginia Rae (*d* 1972), dau of Frank Gervin Bright, of NY, USA, and *d* 1970 leaving issue:

1i +STEPHEN GERARD [Jonkheer Stephen Boreel, Elzenoord 30, 8172 AZ Vaassen, Netherlands]; *b* 9 Feb 1945; heir presumptive; *m* *Francien P Kooijman and has issue:

1j +Jacob Lucas Cornelis; *b* 29 Sept 1974

2i +Maurits [Jonkheer Maurits Boreel, Wieselseweg 102, 7345 CC Apeldoorn, Netherlands]; *b* 27 May 1946; *m* 1971 *Tilde Anna Eisma and has issue:

1j +Gerard Lucas; *b* 1973

2j +Joris Siebrand; *b* 1975

3j +Maurits Willem; *b* 1981

1i *Joan [Joan Boreel, Grentelsweg 70, 7345 CR Wenum Wiesel, Netherlands]; *b* 24 March 1949

2h +Maurits [Jonkheer Maurits Boreel, Oude Kleefsebaan 217, 6572 AM Bergen Dal, Netherlands]; *b* 23 July 1914; *m* 11 Aug 1942 (*divorce* 1980) Antoinette Johanna Charlotte, dau of Samuel Crommelin, and has issue:

1i +Lucas Jacob [Jonkheer Lucas Boreel, Beekmansdalseweg 9 6522 KC, Nijimegen, Netherlands]; *b* 20 July 1945; *m* 1st 1966 (*divorce* 1975) Henriette van Teunenbroek and has issue:

1j *Elsa-Bertha; *b* 1967; *m* 1992 *Emile R Lemoine, of USA

2j *Esther Nanette; *b* 1970

1i (cont.) Lucas Boreel *m* 2nd 1978 *Angeline Marie Sassen and has further issue:

3j *Sophie Mechteld; *b* 1980

3j *Maeke Willemijn; *b* 1982

2i +Paul Marinus [Jonkheer Paul Boreel, Rembrandtlaan 22, 3941 CH Doorn, Netherlands]; *b* 14 Oct 1949; *m* 1976 *Simone C Bouwman and has issue:

1j +David Gustaaf; *b* 1979

2j +Thomas Arthur; *b* 1982

3i +Willem [Jonkheer Willem Boreel, Beerse 112, 3961 HE Wijk bij Duurstende, Netherlands]; *b* 8 Oct 1952; *m* 1978 (*divorce* 1983) Louis G Peizel and has issue:

1j +Robert Jan; *b* 1981

1i *Jacoba Francina; *b* 12 June 1943; *m* 1968 *Arnold Hendrick Tieleman

1h *Henriette; *b* 12 Oct 1917; *m* 20 June 1947 *Dirk Jacobus Gerhard Buurman, s of Johannes Willem Buurman, and has issue:

1i *Johan Willem Godard; *b* 7 Feb 1949

2i *Jacob Lucas; *b* 11 Feb 1957

2g Hugo; *b* 5 Dec 1884; *m* 3 June 1930 Baroness Emilie Henriette Adele (*d* 1970), dau of Baron Cornelis J van Tuyll van Serooskerken, and *d* 26 Feb 1962, leaving issue:

1h +Lucas Gerard [Jonkheer Lucas Boreel, Eikenhorstlaan 19, 2245 BC Wassenaar, Netherlands]; *b* 16 Aug 1931; *m* 14 May 1960 *Marie Louise, dau of Pierre van Son by Margaretha Annie Teixeira de Mattos, and has 2 adopted daus:

*Marguerite Emilie; *b* 22 Oct 1968

*Stephanie Rosanne; *b* 1 Aug 1971

2h +Cornelis Jan [Jonkheer Cornelis Boreel, Pieter de Hooghlaan 23, 3723 GR Bilthoven, Netherlands]; *b* 1 Dec 1932; Capt (Res) Hus of Boreel, Sec Boreel Fndn; *m* 5 Sept 1959 *Claudine Wilhelmina Woltera, dau of Willem Jan Royaards by his w Baroness Claudina Maria Carolina Bentinck van Schoonheten, and has issue:

1i +Robert Jan Willem; *b* 2 July 1960; *m* 1993 *Sigrid, dau of S Karsten, and has:

1j +Pim Simon Jan; *b* 2 Aug 1994

1j *Noor Astrid; *b* 23 Sept 1995

2i +Lucas Wolter; *b* 26 April 1966; *m* 1994 *Jacqueline Nelly, dau of H A G Hofman, and has:

1j *Eliane Péronne; b 26 Aug 1995

1i *Claudine Emilie Amarante; *b* 30 Aug 1963; *m* 1992 *H M Hinloopen

3h +Geert Frans [Jonkheer Geert Boreel, Bruggenbosch, Blikkenweg 15, 7391 NA Twello, Netherlands]; *b* 29 June 1934; *educ* Leiden U (LLB); *m* 11 Oct 1958 *Henriette Nancy Leopoldine, dau of Jonkheer Barthold Willem Floris van Riemsdijk, of 5 Zwaluwenweg, Aerdenhout, by his w Countess Nancy Leopoldine Marie van Limburg Stirum, and has issue:

1i +Hugo Geert [Jonkheer Hugo Boreel, Van Wÿkplein 3, 2101 EL Heemstede, Netherlands]; *b* 26 March 1959; *educ* Lerden U and Fontainebleu (MBA); *m* 1986 *Alice Marie, dau of William Schwartz and has:

1j +Lucas William Geert; *b* 6 June 1994

1j *Frédérique Pauline; *b* 6 March 1996

2i +Barthold Willem Lucas [Jonkheer Barthold Boreel, Berkenlaan 33, 370 BB Zeist, Netherlands]; *b* 9 Aug 1960; *educ* Rotterdam U, Sch of Economics; *m* 1992 *Petra Martine, dau of Pieter Arie de Ruiter, and has issue:

1j *Daan Floris; *b* 6 Jan 1993

2j *Maud Martine Emilie; *b* 5 Feb 1995

1i *Pauline Danielle; *b* 14 May 1964; *educ* Leyden U; *m* 1 July 1996 Godfried Nicolaas Insinger (*d* 15 April 1997), s of Edward William Insinger

1h Pauline Johanna; *b* 13 Feb 1887; *d* unm 25 Jan 1961

2g Kathrine Maria Ulrica; *b* 11 Aug 1889; *d* unm 28 Feb 1960

3f Marius Willem; *b* 23 Aug 1856; Lt Ordnance Offr to King of Holland; *m* 24 June 1886 Cornelia (*d* 3 Sept 1939), dau of Theodor Prince van Westdorpe, of Haarlem, Holland, and *d* 10 Dec 1905, leaving issue:

1g William Constant; *b* 29 July 1890; *d* 2 June 1923

1g Catharina Margaretha; *b* 5 Dec 1891; *m* 4 April 1918 Henri Louis van Eeghen (*d* 1977), son of Samuel Pieter van Eeghen

4f James; *b* 25 Sept 1857; *d* 4 Feb 1858

5f Paulus James; *b* 18 Feb 1863; *m* 1 June 1892 Johanna Marie (*d* 4 Feb 1945), dau of Albert Suermondt, and *d* 18 July 1938, leaving issue:

1g Marie; *b* 27 Oct 1893; *m* 24 Dec 1925 James Skinner Mackenzie Eddison, OBE, MA (*d* 7 Sept 1965), son of William Eddison, and *d* 1971, leaving issue:

1h *John Michael; *b* 2 Sept 1930; BSc, FICE, FASCE, MIStructE, MEIC; *m* 11 Aug 1956 *Marjorie Joyce Halley

2g Anna; *b* 16 March 1896

3g Wendela; *b* 3 Aug 1898

1f Wendela Catherine Mary; *m* 1876 Reinhard, Baron van Lynden, and *d* 1930

2f Agnes; *m* 1878 Francis, Baron van Randwyck, and *d c* 1923

3f Catherine; *d* unm *c* 1935

4f Anne; *m* 1881 William Snouck Hurgronje, of 28 Princessegracht, The Hague, and *d c* 1927

1d Jaqueline Margaret Mary; *m* Aug 1785 André Adolf Deutz, memb Equestrian Order of Holland and Upper House of the Netherlands

2d Agnes Margaret Catharine, Mistress of the Robes to Princess of Orange; *m* Oct 1790 Henry, Baron Fagel, GCH, Dutch Amb to Britain, and *d* 8 July 1824. He *d* 22 March 1838

(3) William; *b* 22 April 1634; *m* 7 Aug 1672 Petronella Vlasvat

(1) Mary

The 11th Bt's yr bro,

Sir Alfred Boreel, 12th Bt, LD, Burgomaster; *b* 22 July 1883; *m* 1st 1 July 1911 Countess Aletta Cornelia Anna (*d* 3 June 1913), dau of Count Francis David Schimmelpenninck; *m* 2nd 28 March 1919 Countess Reiniera Adriana (*d* 9 Feb 1957), dau of Count Francis David Schimmelpenninck, and *d* 20 Aug 1964, leaving issue:

1 Sir FRANCIS DAVID BOREEL, **13th and present Bt**

1 Florence; *b* 14 April 1922; *m* 30 Sept 1955 Henri William van Lelyveld, son of Ludolf Alexander van Lelyveld

BORRIE

Creation: B. (LP, UK) 18 Nov 1995.

THE BARON BORRIE, of Abbots Morton in the County of Hereford and Worcester (Sir Gordon Johnson Borrie, QC (1986)) [The Rt Hon The Lord Borrie QC, Manor Farm, Abbots Morton, Worcs WR7 4NA]; *b* 13 March 1931; *educ* John Bright GS Llandudno and Manchester U (LLB, LLM); barrister Middle Temple 1952, Bencher 1980, served Army Legal Servs Korea 1952–54, lecturer and sr lecturer Coll of Law 1957–64, sr lecturer law Birmingham U 1965–68 (Prof English Law 1969–76, Hon Prof 1989–), memb: Parole Bd 1971–74, Cicrcuit Advsy Ctee Birmingham Courts 1972–74 and Equal Opportunities Commn 1975–76, chm Commn Social Justice 1992–94, fought (Lab) Croydon NE 1955 and Ilford 1959 gen elections, dir: Woolwich Bldg Soc 1992–, Three Valleys Water 1992–, Mirror Gp 1993– and TeleWest Communicns Gp 1994–, pres Inst Trading Standards Admin 1992–, Dir-Gen Fair Trading 1976–92, FCIArb 1992, FRSA 1982, Hon LLD City London Poly 1989, Manchester U 1990, Hull U 1991, Dundee U 1993, author: *Commerical Law* (6th edn 1988), *The Consumer, Society and the Law* (with A L Diamond, 4th edn 1981), *Law of Contempt* (with N V Lowe, 3rd end 1995) and *The Development of Consumer Law and Policy* (1984); *m* 1960 *Dorene, dau of Herbert Toland, of Toronto

Lineage: STANLEY BORRIE, slr; had:

GORDON JOHNSON (Sir), *cr* a **Baron**

BORTHWICK, Lord

Arms: Argent three cinquefoils sable. **Crest:** A moor's head couped proper, wreathed argent and sable. **Supporters:** Two angels proper, winged or. **Motto:** *Qui conducit* ('[He] who leads'). **Creation:** L. (S) 12 June 1452.

THE 24TH LORD BORTHWICK (John Hugh Borthwick of that Ilk) [The Rt Hon The Lord Borthwick, The Neuk, Heriot, Midlothian EH38 5YS]; *b* 14 Nov 1940; *s* f 1996; *educ* Gordonstoun and Edinburgh Sch of Ag (SDA, NDA); farmer and landowner; *m* 9 Feb 1974 *Adelaide, dau of Archy Birkmyre (*see* BIRKMYRE, Bt), of Overdale, Crieff, Perthshire, and has issue:

(1) *Georgina; *b* 18 Dec 1975; *educ* St Leonards and Newcastle U

(2) *Alexandra; *b* 25 Aug 1977; *educ* St Leonards and Bristol U

Lineage: Sir WILLIAM BORTHWICK of that Ilk, Amb to England 1398–1415, granted a charter of the lands of Borthwick, Selkirkshire, by the Regent Albany 1410, hostage for safe return from England of JAMES I 1421, commr to treat for the King's release 1423; *m* —, dau of Sir Thomas Hay of Lochorwart (*see* TWEEDDALE, M), and *d* by 1439, having had, with two daus (Janet, *m* as his 2nd w Sir James Douglas, putative 1st Lord Dalkeith (*see* MORTON, E); Margaret, *m* William Abernethy, Yr of Saltoun; *see* SALTOUN, L):

WILLIAM BORTHWICK, **1st Lord Borthwick** (S), so *cr* 12 June 1452, ktd *vp* 1430, one of the magnates who according to contemporary records habitually plundered the Customs; *m* 14– — and *d* 14–, leaving issue:

1 WILLIAM BORTHWICK, **2nd Lord Borthwick**; Amb England 1471 and 1473; *m* 1458 Mariot Hoppringle, widow, and *d* between 6 Oct 1483 and 7 Feb 1483/84, leaving issue:

(1) WILLIAM BORTHWICK, **3rd Lord Borthwick**, ktd *vp*; a guarantor treaty with England 20 Sept 1484, a conservator other treaties 1497 and 1499, Master Household to JAMES III 1485; *d* 20 May 1503, leaving issue:

1a WILLIAM BORTHWICK, **4th Lord Borthwick**; Govr Stirling Castle, Guardian infant JAMES V after Flodden 1513; sealed treaty with England 7 Oct 1517; settled 21 Aug 1538 his lands in tail male with remainder to heirs male whatsoever bearing the name and arms of Borthwick; *m* 1491 Margaret, dau of John Hay of Yester (*see* TWEEDDALE, M), and *d* 1543, having had issue:

1b Thomas or Arthur, *Master of Borthwick*; *m* (papal annulment by 1530 due to consanguinity) Mariot, dau of 3rd Lord Seton (*see* EGLINTON and WINTON, E), and *dsp* & *vp* by 21 Aug 1538

2b JOHN BORTHWICK, **5th Lord Borthwick**, PC (S 1545); present Battle of Ancrum Moor March 1544/5, opposed Reformation; *m* by 1544 Isobel (*m* 2nd George Preston of Cameron; *d* 15 Nov 1577), dau of 8th Earl of Crawford (*see* CRAWFORD and BALCARRES, E), and *d* March 1565/6, leaving:

1c WILLIAM BORTHWICK, **6th Lord Borthwick**; supported MARY QUEEN OF SCOTS; *m* by 1570 Grizel, dau of Sir Walter Scott of Buccleuch (*see* BUCCLEUCH and QUEENSBERRY, D), and *d* Oct 1582, having had issue:

1d William, *Master of Borthwick*; *dvp* unm 17 Mar 1570/1

2d JAMES BORTHWICK, **7th Lord Borthwick**, PC (S 1594 and 1595/6); *b* 1570; Protestant by early 1590s; *m* 1582 Margaret, dau of 5th Lord Hay of Yester (*see* TWEEDDALE, M), and *d* 1599, leaving issue:

1e JOHN BORTHWICK, **8th Lord Borthwick**; *m* by 1616 Lilias, dau of 1st Earl of Lothian of the 1606 *cr* (*see* LOTHIAN, M), and *d* Nov 1623, leaving issue:

1f JOHN BORTHWICK, **9th Lord Borthwick**; *b* 9 Feb 1616; held Borthwick Castle for royalists Civil War but capitulated to OLIVER CROMWELL18 Nov 1650; *m* 23 Aug 1649 Lady Elizabeth Ker, dau of 1st Earl of Lothian of the 1631 *cr* (*see* LOTHIAN, M), and *dsp* between 13 Mar 1673/4 and 26 Nov 1675, when the peerage became dormant until adjudicated 1762 as having passed to his cousin HENRY (*see* below)

1f A dau; *m* Robert Dundas of Harvieston and had issue:

1g John; inherited Borthwick Castle from his unc

(2) Alexander, of Nenthorn, Roxburghshire; *m* Margaret — and had issue:

1a William, of Soltray; *m* Janet — and *d* by May 1541, leaving issue:

1b William, of Soltray; *m* Katherine Crichton and *d* by 1564, leaving issue:

1c William, of Soltray and Johnstonburn; forfeited his estate 1603; *m* Barbara Lawson and *d* 1640, leaving issue:

1d William, of Soltray and Johnstonburn; *d* by 1669 leaving issue:

1e WILLIAM BORTHWICK, *de jure* 10th LORD BORTHWICK; Maj; *m* 28 April 1665 Marion Moorhead and *d* by 28 June 1690, having had issue:

1g WILLIAM BORTHWICK, *de jure* 11th LORD BORTHWICK; *bapt* 8 Feb 1666; Capt Cameronian Regt 1689, Col; *m* Jean, dau of Robert Ker of Kersland, *ka* Battle of Ramillies 12 May 1706

2g Robert; *bapt* 7 June 1687

1g Barbara; *m* William Borthwick of Falahill

2g Katherine; *m* William Stewart

2e Alexander; living 1668; *m* Sibilla, dau and heir of William Cairns of Pilmuir, and had issue:

1f William of Pilmuir and Mayshiel; *m* 1st Marion Borthwick and had issue:

1g Mary; *m* Sir Alexander Livingstone

2g Margaret; *m* John Campbell of Knockreoch

1f (cont.) William Borthwick of Pilmuir and Mayshiel *m* 2nd Marjory Stewart and by her had issue:

1g HENRY BORTHWICK of Pilmuir, *de jure* 12th LORD BORTHWICK; Capt Army, *m* Mary, dau of Sir Robert Pringle, 1st Bt (*qv*), was mortally wounded at Battle of Ramillies 12 May and *d* 16 May 1706, leaving:

1h WILLIAM BORTHWICK, *de jure* 13th LORD BORTHWICK; *dsp* by 28 Nov 1723

2h HENRY BORTHWICK, **14th Lord Borthwick**; served heir male general to **1st Lord** 1727, voted 1734–62 at elections for representative Scottish peers in Parl of GB (which he could only have done legally if a Scottish peer himself) but was then ordered by the Ho of Lds to abstain from voting until he had established his right, which he did 8 April 1762; *m* 5 March 1770 Margaret, dau of George Drummond of Brioch, Co Stirling, and *dsp* 6 Sept 1772, when the title again became dormant

2d Alexander, of Reidhall and Sauchnell; *m* Margaret Turnbull and had issue:

7e Andrew of Sauchnell; f of:

1f Archibald (Rev), Min Polwarth; *m* 17– — and *d* by Sept 1799, leaving issue:

1g PATRICK BORTHWICK, *de jure* 15th LORD BORTHWICK; merchant Leith; *m* Marion Scott and *d* 1772 , leaving issue:

1h ARCHIBALD BORTHWICK, *de jure* 16th LORD BORTHWICK; *b* 13 May 1732; merchant at Christiansund, Norway, later Edinburgh, claimed the peerage 1808 but claim undecided at his death; *m* Margaret Nicholson, dau of James Scott, Clerk to the Signet, and *d* 13 July 1815, leaving issue:

1i PATRICK BORTHWICK, *de jure* 17th LORD BORTHWICK; *b* 12 Sept 1779; manager Nat Bank Scotland Edinburgh, claimed the peerage 8 April 1816; *m* 13 Nov 1804 Ariana, dau of Cunninghame Corbet, of Tolcross and Glasgow, merchant, and *d* 12 April 1840, leaving issue:

1j ARCHIBALD BORTHWICK, *de jure* 18th LORD BORTHWICK; *b* 31 Aug 1811; *m* 1 Aug 1840 Mary Louisa, dau of John Home Home of Longformacus, and *dspms* 3 July 1863, having had:

1k Louisa Ramsay, *m* 3 June 1873 Lt Col Henry Philip Miles Wylie, KRRC

2k Mary Catherine, *m* 27 April 1870 William George Spens and had issue

2j CUNNINGHAME BORTHWICK, **19th Lord Borthwick**; *b* 16 June 1813; *educ*Edinburgh High Sch and U; memb London Stock Exchange 1853–77, bought estate of Ravenstone, Wigtownshire, 1870, claim to peerage allowed 5 May 1870, rep S peer 1880–85, FSA 1871; *m* 18 July 1865 Harriet Alice, dau of Thomas Hermitage Day, banker, of Frinsbury and Rochester, Kent, and *d* 24 Dec 1885, having had:

1k ARCHIBALD PATRICK THOMAS BORTHWICK, **20th Lord Borthwick**; *b* 3 Sept 1867; *educ* Trin Coll Glenalmond and Ch Ch Oxford; ptner Borthwick, Wark & Co, stockbrokers, rep S peer 1906–10; *m* 18 July 1901 Susanna Mary, dau of Sir Mark John McTaggart-Stewart, 1st Bt, and *dspm* 4 Oct 1910, when the title yet again became dormant, leaving issue:

1l Isolde Frances; *b* 2 Feb 1903

1k Gabrielle Margaret Ariana; *b* 30 June 1866

2k Alice Rachel Anne; *b* 17 Dec 1868; *m* 5 July 1893 Alexander Stratton Campbell, of Swaffham, Norfolk

3k Violet Dagmar Marion Aga; *b* 3 June 1871; *m* 22 Nov 1900 Capt Lewis G Freeland and had issue

4k Mary Frances Harriet; *b* 11 Feb 1876; *m* 1 July 1897 Harold Chaloner Dowdall, DCL, barrister Inner Temple, of Liverpool

1i Rachel; *d* 1876

2 JOHN, for whom *see* further below

The yr s,

JOHN BORTHWICK, 1st of Crookston, charter of which was granted him by Sir Alexander Ramsey of Dalwolsey 17 July 1446; mentioned as a bro of WIL-

LIAM, **Lord Borthwick**, in a document of 24 June 1456 (the authenticity of part of which was queried by the Ho of Lds Privileges Ctee 1808 but ruled genuine by the Lyon Court 26 July 1944); *m* Margaret — and *d c* 1459, leaving issue:

GEORGE BORTHWICK, 2nd of Crookston; *b* 1447; *d* 1473, leaving issue:

JOHN BORTHWICK, 3rd of Crookston, had Crown charter of confirmation 5 Nov 1484; *m* Margaret Wenlock and *d* 1 Dec 1508, leaving issue:

WILLIAM BORTHWICK, 4th of Crookston; *d* 1547, leaving issue:

JOHN BORTHWICK, 5th of Crookston; *k* Battle of Pinkie 9 Sept 1547, leaving issue:

JOHN BORTHWICK, 6th of Crookston, supported MARY QUEEN OF SCOTS; *m* Jean Blaikie (*m* 2nd James Hoppringle of Halheriot) and *d c*1556, leaving issue:

WILLIAM BORTHWICK, 7th of Crookston; *m* 1589 Elizabeth Hoppringle of Hoppringle (*m* 2nd George Pringle of Torwoodlee) and *d* 1618, leaving issue:

WILLIAM BORTHWICK, 8th of Crookston; *m* Eupham, dau of George Brown, of Coalston, and *d c* Jan 1673, leaving issue:

WILLIAM BORTHWICK, 9th of Crookston; matriculated arms 26 May 1693; *m* 1678 Janet, dau of Thomas Craig, of Riccarton, and *d* by 20 April 1681, leaving issue:

JOHN BORTHWICK, 10th of Crookston; advocate 1701; *m* 1705 Mary, dau of William Nairne, Baillie (magistrate) Dalkeith, and *d* 16 May 1743, leaving issue:

JOHN BORTHWICK, 11th of Crookston; unsuccessfully claimed Parly Ldship of Borthwick 1774; *m* Agnes Hunter, heiress of Glengelt, and had:

JOHN BORTHWICK, 12th of Crookston; *m* 1786 Grizel (*d* 1852), est dau of George Adinston, of Carcant, and *d* 1830, leaving issue:

JOHN BORTHWICK, 13th of Crookston, JP, DL; *b* 1787; bought 1812 Borthwick Castle, the seat of the Lords Borthwick which had been sold soon after the death of the **9th Lord** 1674/5; *m* 1st 16 March 1819 Anne (*d* 1832), est dau of Robert Dundas of Arniston, PC, and had:

1 John, 14th of Crookston, JP (Edinburgh and Berwick); *b* Sept 1824; *m* 1853 Elizabeth Mason, est dau of V-Adml James Pringle, of Torwoodlee, Selkirk, and *dsp* 11 Feb 1907

2 Robert; Lt 91st Regt; *d* unm

3 WILLIAM HENRY BORTHWICK, 15th of Crookston and *de jure* 21st LORD BORTHWICK; *b* 28 Nov 1832; *m* 31 Dec 1864 Rebecca (*d* 6 Dec 1887), dau of Robert Cathcart, and *d* 8 Oct 1928, having had issue:

(1) HENRY BORTHWICK OF BORTHWICK, 16th of Crookston and *de jure* 22nd LORD BORTHWICK; *b* 23 July 1868; *educ* Madras Coll and St Andrews U; Lt Fife and Forfar Yeo WW I; *m* 27 Nov 1902 Melena Florence (*d* 2 May 1962), 4th dau of Capt James Thomas Pringle, of Torwoodlee, RN, and *d* 27 May 1937, leaving issue:

1a JOHN HENRY STUART BORTHWICK OF BORTHWICK, **23rd Lord Borthwick**, TD (1943), JP (1938), DL (Lothian 1965); *b* 13 Sept 1905; claim to Lordship admitted by Lord Lyon 1986; *educ* Fettes and King's Coll Newcastle (Dip Ag 1926); Baron of Heriotmuir and Laird of Crookston, Midlothian; Hereditary Falconer of Scotland to the Sovereign; formerly RA (TA), re-employed 1939, served NW Europe, Allied Mil Govt Staff (Jr Staff Coll, SO2) 1944, CCG (SO1) Lt-Col 1946, Dept Ag Scotland 1948–50, farmer 1950–71, chm: Heriotmuir Properties Ltd 1965–96, Heriotmuir Exporters 1972–96; ptnr Crookston Farms 1971–79, NFU Scotland, Mid and W Lothian Ctee 1967–73 (pres 1970–72), memb cncl 1968–72, memb Lothian Area Ctee NFU Mutual Insur Soc 1969, Scottish S Regnl Ctee Wool Marketing Bd 1966–87, memb: Scottish Landowners Fedn 1937–96, Land Use Ctee 1972–83, Scottish Livestock Export Gp 1972–83, chm: Area Ctee S Scotland Electricity Bd Consultative Cncl 1972–76, Monitoring Ctee for Scottish Tartans 1976; dir Castles of Scotland Preservation Tst 1985–96, CC Midlothian 1937–48, memb: Local Appeal Tribunal (Edinburgh and Lothians) 1963–75, Midlothian Valuation Ctee 1966–78, Standing Cncl Scottish Chiefs, Ctee Baronage of Scotland (Int Delegate), Corresp Istituto Italiano di Genealogica e Araldica Rome and Madrid 1964, Hon Memb: Cncl Scottish Clans Assoc USA 1975, Roy Mil Inst Canada 1976; patron Normandy Veterans Assoc 1985–96, KLJ, GCLJ 1975, Cdr Rose of Lippé 1971, Niadh Nask 1982; *m* 8 Jan 1938 Margaret Frances (*d* 22 March 1976), dau of Alexander Campbell Cormack, of Edinburgh, and *d* 30 Dec 1996, leaving:

1b JOHN HUGH BORTHWICK OF THAT ILK, **24th and present Lord Borthwick**

2b +(JAMES) HENRY ALEXANDER OF GLENGELT, *Master of Borthwick* [The Master of Borthwick, Channelkirk Cottage, Oxton, Lauder, Berwicks TD2 6PT]; *b* 14 Nov 1940; heir presumptive; *educ* Gordonstoun and Heriot-Watt U; *m* 1972 *Elspeth, dau of Brig Allan Dunn MacConachie, of Lauder, Berwicks (*see* MOLESWORTH, V), and has issue:

1c +Malcolm Henry; *b* 1973; *educ* Loreto and Bristol U

(2) Alfred Edward, of Burnhouse; *b* 22 April 1871; Capt Scottish Sharpshooters, served Boer War, Staff Capt War Office WW I, Pres Roy Scottish Soc of Painters 1931, memb RSA, ARE, PRSW, six times Pres Soc of Scottish Artists; *m* 12 June 1907 Mary Simcoe Violet (*d* 20 Jan 1967), 5th dau of Capt James Thomas Pringle, of Torwoodlee, Selkirk, and *d* 7 Dec 1955, leaving issue:

1a Ann Violet; *educ* Edinburgh U (BSc 1930); *m* 4 Nov 1936 Alexander Charles Stephen, DSc, FRSE (*d* 19–), s of Rev William Stephen, BD, Min Galvock, and had issue

2a Grizel Rebecca; *b* 22 Feb 1910; *educ* Edinburgh U (BSc 1932, PhD 1935); *m* 25 Oct 1939 *James Alexander Barclay, MA, BSc, MB, ChB, s of Alexander Walker Barclay, and had issue:

1b *Alfred Donald Walker; *b* 2 Dec 1941

2b *Bruce James Walker; *b* 9 Feb 1946

3a Marjorie Elspeth

(3) Albert William, OBE, of Glengelt; *b* 16 Oct 1872; DSc, Prof Forestry Aberdeen U; *d* unm 19 April 1937

(4) Arthur Francis; *b* 4 April 1877; *d* 9 Jan 1911

1 Elizabeth Dundas; *b* 1819; *d* unm 21 March 1864

2 Grace Henrietta; *d* young 1828

3 Grace; *m* 16 April 1868 Rev Robert Brown, Vicar All Saints Scarborough (added the name BORTHWICK), and *d* 29 June 1884

JOHN BORTHWICK, 13th of Crookston, *m* 2nd 28 April 1838 Elizabeth Sutherland (*d* 1872), dau of Alexander Dallas, WS, of Ridockhill, and widow of Col Francis Simpson, of Plean, Stirlingshire, and *d* 18 Sept 1845, having by her had issue:

4 Alexander, MVO; *b* 28 Feb 1839; Lt-Col Rifle Bde, Ch Constable Lothians and Peebles; *m* 20 July 1876 Katherine (*d* 19 April 1941), dau of Thomas Thistlethwayte, of Southwick Park, Hants, by Elizabeth Catherine, dau of Lt-Gen Hon Sir Hercules Robert Pakenham, KCB (*see* LONGFORD, E), and *d* 6 Oct 1914, leaving issue:

(1) Frank Hugh Pakenham BORTHWICK later BORTHWICK-NORTON (28 April 1944 on succeeding his uncle in the Southwick estate), of Southwick House, Purbrook, Hants, and Borthwick Hall, Midlothian; *b* 23 July 1877; *m* 5 Jan 1944 Eva Sardinia, dau of George Burrows, of Burston, Norfolk and *dsp* 5 Oct 1959

(2) Arthur Sandilands; *b* 26 Dec 1879; Capt Boer War and WW I; *m* 14 July 1910 Vera Janet Hervey, yr dau of William Bethel-Hervey, and had issue:

1a Richard Quentin; *b* 10 May 1911; *educ* Cambridge; *m* 21 March 1942 Vivien, 3rd dau of Cdr Arthur Henry de Kantzow, DSO, RN

(3) Geoffrey Darnley; *b* 9 May 1881; *d* 20 Oct 1884

(1) Evelyn Grace Stanhope; *b* 27 Oct 1878; *m* 21 Oct 1922 Charles Morden Collett, ICS (*d* 31 Jan 1946), est s of Charles Collett, HEICS, and *d* 15 April 1959

5 Francis; *b* 10 Feb 1840; *m* 15 Sept 1864 Alice Ord (*d* 28 Aug 1935), dau of John Mackenzie of Dolphinton (*see* MACKENZIE, Bt, of Coul), and *d* 1934, leaving:

(1) Francis John Gordon; *b* 15 Jan 1871; WS; *m* 6 Aug 1912 Eugenie Helen Francklyn, dau of Edmund Stow Thompson, of Pelham House, Folkestone, and *d* 22 May 1948, leaving:

1a *Mary Alice [The Hon Mrs Douglas Vivian, Edington Cottage, Inmead, Edington, Wilts]; *m* 3 April 1943 Lt-Cdr Hon Douglas David Edward Vivian, DSC, RN (*d* 1973), yr s of 4th Baron Vivian (*qv*), and has issue

2a *Margaret Eugenie Borthwick [Mrs Ian Farquhar, Hamlyns, Chudleigh, S Devon]; *m* 18 March 1944 *Maj Ian Rupert Farquhar, Gren Gds, er s of Sir Harold Lister Farquhar, KCMG, MC (*see* FARQUHAR, Bt), and has a s

(1) Margaret Kirkpatrick; *m* 3 Aug 1900 Hon Sir John Carnegie Dove Wilson (*d* 18 April 1935), Pres Supreme Court Natal, 2nd s of Prof J Dove Wilson, and *d* 27 Jan 1947, leaving issue

(2) Alice; *d* unm July/Aug 1935

(3) Beatrice Eleanora Borthwick; *m* 27 July 1905 Rev Preb Philip Thomas Bainbrigg (*d* 1 Nov 1919), s of Maj-Gen Philip John Bainbrigg, of Woolwich, and *d* 10 July 1951, having had a s

(4) Harriette Mackenzie; *d* 26 Jan 1911

Seat: Borthwick Castle, Midlothian. Set in a position to guard the road south to the Borders from Edinburgh, Borthwick, a massive structure in ashlar towering some 80 feet high with low wings spread either side, has been called the 'greatest keep in Scotland'. It certainly has a good claim to be regarded as the completest example of its type. Sir William Borthwick of that Ilk was granted a licence to build a castle in 1430, but an earlier fortification on the site had existed called the Mote (*i.e.*, 'motte', as in motte and bailey, rather than 'moat') of Lochorwart. The new licensee set to with a will: a huge central block arose topped with a triple row of corbels under a parapet, its wall being deeply indented on one side between bartizans in a pattern similar to that of Bunratty Castle, Co Clare, probably the example best known to the average castle-spotter. One side no longer has the corbels, having been demolished by Cromwellian forces in 1650 and never fully restored.

A protective circumvallation was added studded with defensive bastions and towers. There was also a drawbridge, at the end of which a twin gate and portcullis further impeded unauthorised entry. The circular tower adjacent to this is still standing. As with many castles of the period the entrance to the keep was at first-floor level. The great hall has a splendid barrel-vaulted ceiling culminating in a blunt but discernibly ogival point. The fireplace here is of the canopy type, tapering upwards, more familiar in France than in the British Isles. It rests on double columns each side.

In early June 1567 MARY QUEEN OF SCOTS arrived at Borthwick with her new husband Lord Bothwell. Whether she actually slept there, as opposed to spending a sleepless night, is another matter, for her opponents laid siege to the place and Bothwell swiftly and rather ungallantly decamped. In order to follow him MARY was obliged to dress in a man's clothes before slipping out of the Castle.

BORTHWICK, Bt

Arms: Argent, a cinquefoil sable, on a chief invected of the last two cinquefoils of the first. **Crest:** A staff raguly fesswise sable, thereon a blackamoor's head in profile couped proper. **Motto:** *Qui conducit* ('[He] who leads'). **Creation:** Bt. (UK) 21 July 1908.

SIR JOHN THOMAS BORTHWICK, 3RD BT, of Whitburgh, Midlothian, MBE (1945) [Sir John Borthwick Bt MBE, 41 Mizzentop, Warwick, Bermuda]; *b* 5 Dec 1917, *s* unc 1967; *educ* Eton and Trin Coll Oxford; Maj Rifle Bde (TA) WW II; *m* 1st 4 Nov 1939 (*divorce* 1961) Irene Sophie (*d* 1978), only child of Joseph Heller, of 2 Buckingham Place, London SW1, and has issue:

1 +ANTONY THOMAS; *b* 12 Feb 1941; *educ* Eton; *m* 1st 30 July 1966 Gillian Deirdre Broke, twin dau of Lt Nigel Vere Broke Thurston, RN; *m* 2nd 1985 *Jenny, est dau of George Lanning, and has issue by 1st w:

(1) +Matthew Thomas Thurston; *b* 2 July 1968

(1) *Suzanna Claire Irene; *b* 20 Feb 1970

(2) *Camilla Fay Broke; *b* 23 March 1973

2 +Peter Richard John; *b* 22 May 1943; *educ* Eton; *m* 1970 *Helen, yr dau of T C Vogel, of Cudgewa, Victoria, Australia, and has issue:

(1) +Linton; *b* 1977

(1) *Maya Irene; *b* 1975

(2) *Iona Christine; *b* 1980

3 +(Patrick) James Joseph [James Borthwick Esq]; *b* 27 Dec 1945; *educ* Eton; *m* 1st 26 July 1969 Amanda Rosemary, yr dau of Richard Guy Arthur Wells, of Lines End, Winchelsea, Sussex, and has issue:

(1) +Alexander; *b* 18 Dec 1971

3 (cont.) James Borthwick *m* 2nd 3 April 1978 (*divorce* 19–) Sally A, dau of Geoffrey Chase Gardener, and has further issue:

(2) +Edward; *b* 21 April 1980

(3) +Timothy; *b* 18 Oct 1984

(1) *Sophie; *b* 7 March 1979

(2) *Annabel; *b* 3 March 1983

Sir JOHN *m* 2nd 23 Jan 1962 *Irene, dau of Leo Fink, of 26 Rue de Franqueville, Paris XVI, and by her has further issue:

4 +Mark George Alexander; *b* 18 Oct 1962; *m* 1988 *Maria Gornejo

5 +John Kelly Leo; *b* 22 Aug 1965

Lineage: THOMAS BORTHWICK, of Edinburgh; f of:

Sir Thomas Borthwick, 1st Bt (UK), so *cr* 21 July 1908, of Whitburgh House, Ford, Midlothian, JP; *b* 11 Jan 1835; dir Thomas Borthwick & Sons; his *cr* as a baron (UK) announced 14 June 1912 but no letters patent issued by time of his death soon afterwards; *m* 2 Jan 1872 Letitia Mary (allowed 8 Feb 1913 to use style and title Lady Whitburgh, as if her husb had lived to be *cr* a Baron fully, but not the precedence, privileges or rights of a baron's widow, as were in like manner *mutatis mutandis* her children by him; *d* 25 Dec 1935), dau of Thomas Banks, of West Derby, Liverpool, and *d* 31 July 1912, leaving issue:

1 **Sir Thomas Banks Borthwick, 2nd Bt**, and 1st and last BARON WHITBURGH, DL and JP Midlothian; *b* 21 Aug 1874; *cr* 10 Dec 1912 BARON WHITBURGH, of Whitburgh, Co Midlothian (UK); *d* unm 29 Sept 1967, when the barony expired and the baronetcy passed to his n

2 James Alexander; *b* 29 Jan 1876; *m* 15 June 1912 Irene Evangeline (*d* 1 Nov 1982 aged 97), dau of George Wise, JP, of Sydney, Australia, and *d* 20 Nov 1961, having had issue:

(1) Sir JOHN THOMAS BORTHWICK, **3rd and present Bt**

(2) Peter George Alexander, Capt Rifle Bde (attached Middx Regt) WW II; *b* 27 May 1922; *ka* W Europe 15 Nov 1944

3 William; *b* 14 June 1879; T/Capt KRRC WW I 1914–19 (wounded twice, POW), barrister Inner Temple 1919; *m* 10 June 1909 Ruth Margery (*d* 1971), only dau of Jason Rigby, MICE, of Wimbledon, and *d* 16 Dec 1956, leaving issue:

(1) (William) Jason Maxwell, DSC; *b* 1 Nov 1910; *educ* Winchester and Trin Coll Cambridge; barrister Inner Temple 1933, Cdr RNVR WW II; *m* 26 July 1937 Elizabeth Cleveland (*d* 28 Jan 1978), dau of Herbert Elworthy, of Timaru, NZ, and *d* 15 Jan 1998 leaving:

1a +Alister Jason [Alister Borthwick Esq, Deepdale Farm, Burnham Deepdale, King's Lynn, Norfolk]; *b* 23 July 1945; *educ* Winchester and Edin U; *m* 1970 *Verily Anne, dau of Albert Augur East, and has issue:

1b +Jason Matthew; *b* 11 Oct 1971

1b *Fiona Anne; *b* 12 April 1974

2b *Anna Elizabeth; *b* 24 Dec 1981

1a *Josephine Cleveland [Mrs John Luddington, Millhouse, Brancaster, King's Lynn, Norfolk]; *b* 28 Nov 1939; *m* 6 Feb 1960 *John James Luddington, 2nd son of Maj James Luddington, of Wallington Hall, King's Lynn, Norfolk, and has issue:

1b *Peter William; *b* 16 Feb 1966

1b *Julia Ruth; *b* 24 Aug 1961; *m* 1st 1983 (*divorce* 1987) Mark Eustace Landon; *m* 2nd 1995 *Barry Lang

2b *Mary Elizabeth; *b* 30 June 1963; *m* 1989 *Nigel Anthony Ward and has:

1c *Harry John; *b* 12 March 1993

1c *Megan Amy; *b* 25 Jan 1995

2a *Rosalind Cleveland [Mrs Andrew Spedding, The Manor, Sampford Spiney, Horrabridge, Devon]; *b* 31 Dec 1942; *m* 27 April 1968 *(Robert) Andrew Spedding, son of Cdr Horace Robinson Spedding, of The Old Lime House, Goudhurst, Kent, and has issue:

1b *Harry George William; *b* 1973

1b *Joanna Elizabeth; *b* 19 Nov 1970

3a *Celia Cleveland; *b* 10 Sept 1947

(2) Brian Thomas; *b* 28 June 1920; *educ* Eton; Lt RNVR, served WW II; *m* 15 March 1946 *Jennifer Ruth, JP (Norfolk 1960) [Mrs Brian Borthwick JP, Manor Farm, Brancaster, King's Lynn, Norfolk PE31 8AU], est dau of Maj Evelyn Ronald Moncreiff Fryer, MC, Gren Gds, of Nine Acres, Selborne, Hants (*see* PEEL, E), and *d* 1989 leaving issue:

1a +Simon William Frederick [Simon Borthwick Esq, 36 Kenilworth Rd, London W5]; *b* 2 June 1950; *educ* Eton; *m* 1974 *Bozena, dau of Alfons Edward Podwojski, of Poland, and has issue:

1b +Michael Edward Waclaw; *b* 4 June 1977

2b +Ian Philip Miroslaw; *b* 1979

3b +William Martin Stanislaw; *b* 1981

4b +Alexander Thomas Zdzislaw; *b* 1983

2a +Nicholas James; *b* 20 Sept 1953; *educ* Eton; *m* 1981 *Peng-Chin, dau of Lával Li Kwong In, of Mauritius, and has issue:

1b +Anthony Timothy William; *b* 1984

3a +Charles Thomas; *b* 10 Dec 1955; *educ* Eton; *m* 1984 *Jayne Alexandra, only dau of Donald Cooke, of Warmington, Peterborough, and has issue:

1b +Maximilian Thomas; *b* 1985

1b *Anna Georgina; *b* 1987

4a +Timothy Michael [Timothy Borthwick Esq, 10 St Ann's Villas, London W11]; *b* 17 Sept 1958; *educ* Eton and Magdalen Coll Oxford; *m* 1987 *Justin, yr dau of Jerry Rosenholtz, of Chicago, USA

1a *Sara Marjorie; *b* 16 Oct 1951

(1) *(Elinor) Valerie [Mrs Robert Fane, Hoo Lodge, Hoo, Woodbridge, Suffolk IP13 7QJ]; *b* 1915; *m* 15 Oct 1940 Maj Robert William Augustus Fane, MBE, late RA (*d* 1989), only son of Hubert William Fane, JP (*see* WESTMORLAND, E), and has issue

(2) *Margaret Ruth [Mrs Henry Hemsley, Langham Lodge, Oakham, Rutland LE15 7HZ); *b* 1926; *m* 26 Feb 1949 *Henry Neville Hemsley, only son of Neville Hemsley, of Jersey, CI, and has issue:

1a *John Neville; *b* 23 Feb 1956; *m* 2 June 1984 *Nicole Irene, dau of Rudolph Hans Walter, of Zürich, and has issue:

1b *Ralph Neville; *b* 1985

2b *Philip John; *b* 1989

3b *Timo Sean; *b* 1992

1b *Colette Irene; *b* 1987

2a *Oliver Charles; *b* 19 June 1960; *m* 29 Feb 1992 *Deborah Simone Michelle Warr, dau of Eric Blackbourn, of Nottingham

1a *Clare Margaret; *b* 3 June 1953; *m* 1980 *Charles Edward Spencer Atkins, and has issue:

1b *Edward Oliver; *b* 1982

2b *Nicholas Charles; *b* 1985

3b *Matthew Spencer; *b* 1988

1b *Katherine Margaret Lucy; *b* 1992

2a *Patricia Mary; *b* 6 March 1964; *m* 29 Sept 1990 *Giles Henry Matthew Martin and has:

1b *Christopher Giles; *b* 1994

4 Malcolm Algernon; *b* 27 April 1881; Lt Gren Gds (SR); *m* 9 March 1905 Blanche Buckland (*d* 10 March 1965 aged 82), dau of Henry Thomson Gorrie, of Auckland, NZ, and *d* 27 May 1941, leaving issue:

(1) Algernon Malcolm, MC, TD; *b* 22 March 1907; *educ* Harrow and Ch Ch Oxford (BA 1927, MA 1934); Lt-Col cmdg London Scottish Gordon Highrs, served WW II; *m* 20 Feb 1935 Edith Wylde (*d* with husband 6 Jan 1975), only dau of James Stanley Addison, of Wethersfield Place, Braintree, Essex, and was *k* in a motor accident caused by gales 6 Jan 1975, having had issue:

1a +Malcolm [Malcolm Borthwick Esq, Heriot, Midlothian]; *b* 8 Oct 1938; *educ* Winchester; late Lt Gordon Highrs, dir Thos Borthwick & Sons 1975; *m* 2 Aug 1966 *(Dorothy Mary) Prudence, 2nd dau of Alan M Barker, of 31 New St, Salisbury, and has issue:

1b +Benedict; *b* 1 Sept 1971

1b *Sophie Alexander; *b* 1967

2b *Kate Cecile; *b* 14 July 1969

2a William; *b* 22 May; *d* 20 June 1943

1a *Winifred Letitia, OBE (1992) [Lady Tumim, River House, 24 Upper Mall, London W4]; *b* 3 June 1936; *educ* Lady Margaret Hall Oxford (BA 1958); Tstee Nat Portrait Gallery since 1992; *m* 1 Feb 1962 *Sir (Stephen) Tumim, Ch Inspr Prisons 1987–95, Ktd 1996, Pncpl St Edmund Hall,

Oxford 1996–, yr son of Joseph Tumim, CBE, of Headington, Oxford, and has issue:

1b *Matilda Edith; *b* 7 Jan 1963

2b *Emma Renée; *b* 5 Jan 1964

3b *Olivia; *b* 11 Oct 1968

2a *Lucilla Blanche [Mrs Lucilla Borthwick, c/o Fisher Dowson and Wasbrough, 10 Gt James St, London WC1]; *b* 11 Feb 1942; *m* 24 June 1960 (*divorce* 1977) Hon Samuel James Butler, son of Baron Butler of Saffron Walden, KG, PC, CH (LP), and has:

1b *Malcolm James; *b* 11 June 1964; *m* 19– Carolyn Lambert, dau of Martin Lambert, and has:

1c *Callum James; *b* 1989

2c *Francis Xavier Butler; *b* 1994

1c *Lucilla Imogen Butler; *b* 24 March 1986

2c *Sarah Elizabeth Butler; *b* 10 Aug 1987

3c *Alexandra Hermione Mercedes Butler; *b* 13 Dec 1996

2b *George Victor (George Butler Esq, 18 Aynhoe Rd, London W11]; *b* 5 Sept 1969

1b *Sydney Louise; *b* 6 Sept 1962; *m* 24 May 1986 *Charles Peter David Sutcliffe, est s of David Sutcliffe, OBE, DL, of Kettlesing, Harrogate, and has:

1c *Jake Montague David James; *b* 30 July 1993

1c *Polly Louise Hannah; *b* 26 Nov 1987

2c *Phoebe Mary Samuel; *b* 2 May 1989

2b *Fleur Josephine [Mrs Richard Selwyn Sharpe, Lowfields, Exelby, Bedale, N Yorks DL8 2HE]; *b* 24 April 1967; *m* 8 Dec 1991 *Richard Charles Selwyn Sharpe, barrister, s of Rev Canon Roger Sharpe, Rector Warminster, Wilts, and has:

1c *Thomas Richard Gildart; *b* 7 Oct 1992

2c *George James Augustus; *b* 6 Jan 1994

3c *Jasper William; *b* 15 June 1995

3b *Lucilla Katherine Joan; *b* 29 Dec 1974

4b *Emily Rebecca; *b* 29 Dec 1974

(2) Patrick John; *b* 3 Oct 1908; *educ* Harrow; *m* 7 Nov 1931 Nancy Hope (*d* 1984), 2nd dau of Guy C Williams, of Te Parae, Masterton, NZ, and *d* 15 Dec 1994, leaving:

1a +Thomas Malcolm [Thomas Borthwick Esq, Rocklands, Redesdale, Victoria 3444, Australia]; *b* 30 Aug 1933; *educ* Harrow; *m* 23 Jan 1957 *Wendy Alison, dau of Linden Wood, of N Adelaide, Australia, and has issue:

1b +Thomas Linden; *b* 9 June 1958; *educ* Melbourne GS; *m* 19– *Margaret Mary, dau of Edward Ferncliffe Bartley, and has issue:

1c +Lachlan Thomas; *b* 1991

2c +Charles Patrick; *b* 1993

2b +Angus Patrick; *b* 13 Dec 1959; *educ* Geelong GS; *m* 1985 *Jane Amanda Louise, dau of Robin Ninian Paisley, and has issue:

1c +William James; *b* 1988

2c +Harry Robert; *b* 1991

3b +Nigel; *b* 29 May 1963; *educ* Scotch Coll; *m* 1994 *Susan Valentia, dau of Christopher James Stafford Morris

2a +Robin John [Robin Borthwick Esq, Te Whanga RD4, Masterton, New Zealand]; *b* 21 March 1938; *m* 19– *Robin Gay McGregor and has issue:

1c +Patrick Andrew; *b* 1967

2c +Shamus James [Shamus Borthwick Esq, Waitui RD10, Masterton, New Zealand]; *b* 1969

1c *Belinda Hope; *b* 1965; *m* 19– *Andrew Murry of The Tummil, blenheim, NZ]

3a +Hamish Charles [Hamish Borthwick Esq, Dakabin, McDonalds Rd, Palmwoods, Qld 4555, Australia]; *b* 31 Jan 1940; *educ* Christ's Coll NZ; *m* 5 June 1965 *Anne Florence, est dau of Edward Dixon Cameron, of Teebah, Hannaford, Qld, and has issue:

1b +Geoffrey Robert; *b* 29 May 1966

2b +Andrew Hamish; *b* 1968; *m* 1991 *Cindy-Anne, yst dau of James Lawson Storey, of Mooloolaba, Qld

3b +James Patrick; *b* 1971; *m* 1994 *Karen Maree, est dau of Noel Garth Hooper, of Buderim, Qld

1b *Fiona Anne Jeane; *b* 1969

3a *Patricia Mary [Mrs Michael Bell, Ngaiana, Masterton, New Zealand]; *b* 8 July 1936; *m* *Michael Dillon Bell, son of Cheviot Bell, of Masterton, and has issue:

1b *Henry Dillon [Henry Bell Esq, Ngaiana, Masterton, New Zealand]; *b* 1957; *educ* Christ's Coll NZ; *m* 19– *Rebecca Anne Lawrence, and has issue:

1c *Amelia; *b* 1988

2c *Emma; *b* 1990

2b *Jonathan Dillon; *b* 1960; *m* 1990 *Lady Lilias Catriona Maighearad Graham, dau of 7th Duke of Montrose (*qv*), and has issue:

1c *Charles; *b* 1993

1b *Sarah Mary [Mrs Roger Broughton, Pohatu RD 12, Masterton, New Zealand]; *b* 1959; *m* 1982 *Roger Broughton, and has issue:

1c *Thomas; *b* 1986

1c *Belinda; *b* 1985

2c *Rosie; *b* 1989

1b *Nicola Mary [Mrs Marcus Wilkins, 14 11th Avenue, Tauranga, New Zealand]; *b* 1962; *m* 1989 *Marcus Yardley Wilkins and has issue:

1c *Marcus George; *b* 1991

2c *Patrick James; *b* 1993

3c *Guy Michael; *b* 1995

(1) *Letitia Blanche [Mrs James Thomson, Stable Court, Walkern Hall, Stevenage, Herts]; *b* April 1913; *m* 1st 28 July 1934 Capt Michael Valentine Paul Fleming, Oxon and Bucks LI (*d* of wounds recd in action 1 Oct 1940), yst son of Maj Valentine Fleming, DSO, MP, and has issue:

1a *Valentine Patrick [Valentine Fleming Esq, Stonewall Park, Chiddingstone, Edenbridge, Kent TN8 7DG]; *b* 1 Aug 1935; *educ* Eton; late 2nd Lt Gren Gds; *m* 14 June 1963 *Elizabeth Helen, only dau of Hon Sir Geoffrey Cokayne Gibbs, KCMG, of The Manor House, Clifton Hampden, Abingdon-on-Thames, Berks (*see* ALDENHAM and HUNSDON OF HUNSDON, B), and has issue:

1b *Matthew Valentine [Matthew Fleming Esq, Great Woodland Farm, Lyminge, Kent]; *b* 12 Dec 1964; *m* 1989 *Caroline Mary, yst dau of John Joseph Buxton, of Horsley Hall, Gt Yarmouth, Norfolk (*see* BUXTON, B), and has issue:

1c *Hannah Elizabeth; *b* 1992

2b *Harry Geoffrey; *b* 14 March 1966

3b *Rupert Michael; *b* 9 June 1969

4b *Thomas Mungo; *b* 1971

2a *Christopher Michael [Christopher Fleming Esq, Briff Farm, Bucklebury Common, nr Reading, Berks]; *b* 8 May 1937; *educ* Eton; *m* 1975 *Judy, dau of Lt-Col Godfrey Jeans, of Broadchalke, Wilts, and has issue:

1b *Lucy; *b* 1976

2b *Nicola; *b* 1977

3a *David Algernon [David Fleming Esq, Soundess House, Nettlebed, Oxon]; *b* 24 Nov 1938; *educ* Eton; stockbroker; *m* 2 Feb 1967 Jocelyn Ishabel Ann (*m* 2nd 1978, as her 2nd husb, John Edmund Kincaid Floyd), 2nd dau of Sir John Macleod, TD, of Turkdean Manor, nr Northleach, Glos, by his w Rosemary Theodora Hamilton, est dau of Frederick Noel Hamilton Wills, yst brother of 1st Baron Dulverton (*qv*), and *d* 1975 leaving issue:

1b *Lara Kate; *b* 18 Jan 1968

2b *Annabel Theodora; *b* 28 Dec 1968

3b *Katrina Jane; *b* 1971

1a *Gillian [Mrs Nigel Newbery, Pudding Poke Barn, Mootthwaite Lane, Barbon, Kirkby Lonsdale, via Carnforth, Cumbria LA6 2LW]; *b* 28 Jan 1940; *m* 10 June 1966 *Nigel Colin Newbery, only son of Surg Cdr Douglas Arnold Newbery, RN, and Mrs Reginald Seymour Young, of Burks House, Sedbergh, Yorks, and has issue:

1b *Alexander Douglas; *b* 13 June 1970; *m* 2 Sept 1994 *Francesca McCarrey and has:

1c *Lucy Elizabeth; *b* 12 Sept 1996

1b *Georgina Blanche; *b* 28 April 1967

2b *Beatrice Laura; *b* 9 June 1968

(1) (cont.) Mrs Michael Fleming *m* 2nd 12 May 1945 *James Currie Thomson, MBE, TD, JP, DL, late Lt-Col The Queen's Own Cameron Highrs (cmded 2nd Bn 1944–45), er son of James Thomson, of 2 Rothesay Terrace, Edinburgh, and has further issue:

4a *James Borthwick [James Thomson Esq, Mains of Cairnies, Glenalmond, Perthshire PH1 3SE]; *b* 9 Feb 1946; *educ* Eton; *m* 1970 *Maureen Angela, yr dau of W G Scott, of Forres, and has issue:

1b *James Angus Wilfred [James Thomson Esq, Whiterow, Forres, Moray IV36 0SG]; *b* 1972; *m* 28 June 1997 *Oonah Davina Mordaunt, dau of Peter Snagg, of Roxby House, Thornton Le Dale, N Yorks

1b *Tanya Hilda; *b* 1974

2a *Clare Nell [The Hon Mrs Robin Denison-Pender, Jessups, Mark Beech, Edenbridge, Kent]; *b* 9 Feb 1946; *m* 7 May 1966 *Hon Robin Charles Denison-Pender, yr son of 2nd Baron Pender (*qv*), and has issue

(2) *Rachel Sybil, JP Wilts; *b* 7 Oct 1914; *m* 17 July 1937 Maj Peter Sturgis (*d* 1986), er son of Lt-Col Henry Russell Sturgis, of Moat Park Farm, Isfield, Sussex, and has issue:

1a *Julian Russell [Julian Sturgis Esq, Dauntsey Park, Chippenham, Wilts]; *b* 1938; *m* 1981 *Mrs Christine Sutherland, er dau of Patrick Butler-Henderson, RAFVR (*see* FARINGDON, B), and has issue:

1b *Hugh Russell; *b* 1983

2a *Toby Russell [Toby Sturgis Esq, Brook Farm, Gt Somerford, Chippenham, Wilts SN15 5JA]; *b* 1947; *m* 1972 *Gail Virginia, er dau of Brian Cole, and has issue:

1b *Rupert Tobias; *b* 1974

1b *Victoria Clare; *b* 1977

2b *Nicola; *b* 1982

1a *Ann Elisabeth [Miss Ann Sturgis, 24 S Eaton Place, London SW1; Garden Cottage, Dauntsey Park, Chippenham, Wilts]; *b* 1945

1 Elinor Colston; *m* 18 Oct 1902 John Brunton, MD, MRCS, of White House, Nettlebed, Oxford, only son of John Brunton, MA, MD, of London, and *dsp* 7 Jan 1949

2 Letitia Margaret; *m* 24 June 1905 Wilberforce Ernest Hazell, FRIBA, er surv son of Walter Hazell, JP, sometime MP, of Walton Grange, Aylesbury, and *d* 16 Feb 1963, having had issue. He *d* 4 March 1953

3 Sybil Mary; *m* 17 Nov 1937 Lt-Col Vernon Northwood Whitamore, OBE, FRCS, IMS (*d* 9 April 1959), and *d* 5 Feb 1977

Borwick

Arms: Arg., three escarbuncles fesswise sa. between as many bear's heads erased of the last, muzzled or. **Crest:** Upon a mount ppr., in front of a staff raguly erect az., a stag browsing or, attired sa. **Supporters:** On either side a bear sa., muzzled and charged on the shoulder with an escarbuncle or. **Motto:** *Fugit* ('It passes'). **Creations:** Bt. (UK) 1 July 1916, B. (UK) 20 July 1922.

THE 4TH BARON BORWICK, of Hawkshead, Co Lancaster, and a **Baronet** (Sir James Hugh Myles Borwick, Bt, MC (1945)) [The Rt Hon The Lord Borwick MC, Leys Farm, Bircher, Leominster, Herefs HR6 0AZ]; *b* 12 Dec 1917; *s* f 1961; *educ* Eton and RMC Sandhurst; Maj HLI WW II (wounded); *m* 14 Sept 1954 *Hyllarie Adalia Mary, yr dau of Lt-Col William Hamilton Hall Johnston, DSO, MC, DL, of Bryn-y-Groes, Bala, Merionethshire, and has issue:

1*(Angela) Jane [Miss Jane Borwick, The Cider Mill, Brrcher, Herefs HR6 0AU]; *b* 12 July 1955; *m* 1988 (*divorce* 1991; resumed maiden name) Charles William Heathcoat Amory, yr son of Lt-Col Sir William Heathcoat Amory, 5th Bt (*qv*)

2 *Mary Anne; *b* 11 July 1957

3 *Diana [Mrs Giles Newman, Newton Cottage, Newton lane, Whiteparish, wilts SP5 2QQ]; *b* 28 June 1959; *m* 30 Sept 1995 *Giles Newman, s of Lt-Col Nigel Newman, of Windsor

4 *Amanda Gwynneth Rosemary [Mrs Brian Parry, The Steppes, West Bank, Yarpole, Herefs HR6 0BU]; *b* 24 Jan 1965; *m* 1987 *Brian Wynn Parry, est son of P Owen Parry, of Llandderfel, and has issue:

(1) *Robert James William; *b* 21 Feb 1990

(1) *Caroline Hyllarie Wynne; *b* 8 Jan 1988

(2) *Helen Rebecca Louisa; *b* 11 April 1994

Lineage: GEORGE BORWICK, of Morven, Torquay, Devon; *b* 12 June 1806 (son of Myles Borwick); *m* 1st 31 March 1831 Jane (*d* 25 April 1868), dau of Rev John Hudson, of West Bromwich, Staffs, and had issue:

1 Alfred; *b* 17 June 1836; *m* 4 Oct 1859 Euphemia (*d* 14 June 1891), dau of William Lord, of Connecticut, USA, and *d* 24 Jan 1897, leaving issue:

(1) George Ernest; *b* 21 Sept 1864; *d* 1932

(2) William Heron; *b* 25 Nov 1865; *d* 1948

(3) Frank; *b* 16 Dec 1866; *m* 1924 Margaret Theresa Baker, JP (Devon 1935) (*d* 26 Feb 1969), dau of James Mark Heslop, of Newcastle-upon-Tyne, and *d* 1945, leaving issue:

1a Peter John; *b* 1927; *d* 13 Nov 1953

2a Andrew, MC, Capt KSLI; *m* 8 Jan 1955 *Susan (who *m* 2nd Jonathan J O Clennell, son of S/Ldr G J S Clennell, RAF, and Mrs R A B Howden), dau of Lt-Col Harry Owen Hughes, OBE, ED, of Coombe Hollow, Compton Dundon, Somerton, Somerset, and *d* as the result of an accident 5 Feb 1960, leaving issue:

1b *Richard Leonard; *b* 19 Aug 1956

1b *Catherine; *b* 13 Oct 1958

1a *Jane Margaret

2a *Mary; *m* 24 March 1956 *Jørgen Gammelgaard, of Kokkedal, Denmark

(4) Leonard; *b* 26 Feb 1868; *d* 15 Sept 1925

(5) Archibald; *b* 31 Jan 1870; *d* 25 Feb 1923

(1) Constance; *d* 12 Jan 1926

(2) Mabel; *d* 3 Dec 1916

2 ROBERT HUDSON (Sir), **1st Bt**, and **1st Baron**

3 Joseph Cooksey, of 27 Prince's Gate, London SW; *b* 30 Jan 1847; *m* 30 Aug 1876 Ellen Elizabeth (*d* 23 Oct 1934), dau of George Oldroyd, of Stonyhurst, Dewsbury, Yorks, and *d* 28 April 1913, leaving issue:

(1) George Oldroyd, DSO (1917), Lt-Col Surrey and Sussex Yeo RFA, MP N Croydon 1918–22, Legion Honour; *b* 7 March 1879; *educ* Harrow and Trin Coll Oxford; *m* 14 May 1915 Hon Mary Cavendish (*d* 15 May 1967), est dau of 4th Baron Waterpark (*qv*), and *dsp* 27 June 1964

(2) Malcolm, DSO (1918), Lt-Col Roy Scots Greys, Jt MFH Pytchley 1939 on, JP Northants; *b* 25 June 1882; *educ* Harrow; *m* 29 April 1909 Violet Georgina (*d* 20 Dec 1961), dau of William George Middleton, of Hazelbeech Hill, Northampton, and *d* 14 Dec 1957, leaving issue:

1a Peter Malise, MC, Maj The Greys WW II, ADC to Viceroy and Govr-Gen India 1936–37, CC, Jt MFH Pytchley 1949 on; *b* 21 Nov 1913; Ieduc Harrow; *m* 5 Feb 1947 *Cecily Sheppard Nickalls, dau of Col Cecil Patteson Nickalls, of Barby, Rugby, and *d* 23 Dec 1983, leaving issue:

1b *Luke Malise; *b* 19–; Capt Roy Scots Dragoon Gds (Carabiniers and Greys); *m* 1972 *Caroline Nancy, er dau of James Carlisle Stormonth Darling, MC, TD, WS, of The Harestones, Longniddry, East Lothian, and has issue:

1c *Malcolm Peter; *b* 2 Jan 1977

1c *Alexandra Sarah; *b* 9 July 1975

1b *Tessa Mary Cecily; *b* 21 Jan 1951

2a Michael George, CC Ayrshire 1959, V-Lt 1979– (DL 1960), Lt-Col cmdg Roy Scots Greys 1954–57, ret 1957, late Leicester Yeo (TA), served WW II (Middle East Commandos 1940–41, POW, despatches 1942), Jt MFH Eglinton 1960 on; *b* 27 March 1916; *educ* Harrow; *m* 17 Aug 1946 *Veronica June [Mrs Michael Borwick, Blair, Dalry, Ayshire KA24 4ER], dau of Lt-Col John Fenwick Harrison, of King's Walden Bury, Hitchin, Herts, and d 19– having had:

1b Frederick George; *b* 25 Feb 1948; *educ* Harrow; *d* following a car crash 1 Feb 1969

2b James Quinton; *b* 5 Nov 1950; *educ* Harrow; *d* in the same crash 1 Feb 1969

1a *Cecily Valentine Jane; *b* 14 Feb 1910; *m* 12 April 1939 5th Baron Hindlip (*qv*) and has issue

(1) Winifred Jane; *m* 18 Aug 1910 Brig-Gen Francis Lyon, CB, CMG, CVO, DSO, RA, 2nd son of Col Francis Lyon, RA, and *d* 13 Nov 1961, leaving issue. He *d* 21 Feb 1953

(2) Ethel Maud; *m* 20 Jan 1909 Lt-Col Harry Douglas Palmer and had issue

1 Mary; *m* 5 Oct 1860 Robert Newman Lloyd, of Denmark Hill, and *dsp* 16 June 1905

2 Sarah Jane; *m* 22 Aug 1872 Morris Jones Hudson, of St Cuthbert's, Bathampton, Somerset, and *d* 9 March 1923

3 Charlotte Elizabeth; *m* 24 Aug 1870 Arnold Thomas, of Newnham-on-Severn, Glos, and *d* 28 Jan 1933. He *d* 19 April 1908

GEORGE BORWICK *m* 2nd 16 Sept 1869 Eliza Pool Hester (*d* 10 March 1904) and *d* 20 Jan 1889

The 2nd son,

Sir Robert Hudson Borwick, 1st Bt, and **1st Baron Borwick**, of Hawkshead, Co Lancaster, so *cr* 1 July 1916 and 20 July 1922 respectively (both UK), JP (London), KGStJ, Chevalier Legion Honour; *b* 21 Jan 1845; ktd; *m* 6 March 1872 Caroline Smith (*d* 1 April 1936), 6th dau of Rev Richard Daniel Johnston, of Kurnool, Madras, and *d* 27 Jan 1936, having had issue:

1 GEORGE BORWICK, **2nd Baron Borwick**; *educ* Eton and New Coll Oxford (BA); T/Capt Beds Regt and RAF WW I, barrister Middle Temple 1905; *b* 22 May 1880; *m* 1st 7 Dec 1908 (*divorce* 1913) Mary Mason, dau of Lewis Cruger Hasell, of New York; *m* 2nd 8 June 1918 (*divorce* 1938) Dorothea Gertrude, 2nd dau of Charles Grey, of Anerley, and *dsp* 27 Jan 1941

2 ROBERT GEOFFREY, **3rd Baron**

1 Sybil Lloyd; *d* an infant,15 May 1873

2 Hilda; *m* 2 July 1896 Alexander Henry Morris, ICS, son of Sir John Morris, of Killundine, Argyll, and *d* 21 March 1908, leaving issue. He *d* 27 Aug 1941

3 Clarice May; *m* 6 Dec 1899 Brig-Gen William Ward Warner, CMG, late IA, son of Capt George Alves Warner, ISC, and *d* 23 Oct 1959, leaving issue. He *d* 21 March 1950

4 Helen Irene; *d* young 23 June 1881

5 Vanessa Margaret; *m* 24 June 1903 Capt Edward Henry Dormer and *d* 16 June 1962, leaving issue (*see* DORMER, B). He *d* 9 July 1943

6 Mary Dorothea; *m* 8 Feb 1904 Leonard Cecil Woodman, DC S Nigeria, son of L J Woodman, and *d* 2 April 1915, leaving issue. He *d* 2 April 1917

7 Nancy Beatrice, CStJ; *m* 10 July 1907 1st Baron Croft (*qv*) and *d* 24 Jan 1949, leaving issue

The 2nd BARON's bro,

ROBERT GEOFFREY BORWICK, **3rd Baron Borwick**; *b* 1 July 1886; Lt RFA and 20th Hus, Capt Herts Regt; *m* 1st 8 July 1913 (*divorce* 1920) Irene Phyllis, dau of Thomas Main Patterson, of Littlebourne Ho, Canterbury, and *d* 30 Jan 1961, leaving issue:

1 JAMES HUGH MYLES BORWICK, **4th and present Baron Borwick**

1 *Katharine Hilda; *b* 25 April 1914; *m* 17 Oct 1938 Ashton Jack Ulyate (*d* 19–), son of Raymond Robert Ulyate, of Moshi, Tanganyika, and has issue:

(1) *Stanley Robert Borwick; *b* 3 Sept 1939; *m* 1973 *Margaret Mary Anne Morling and has issue:

1a *William Robert; *b* 1975

2a *James Ashton; *b* 1976

(2) *Raymond Grant [Raymond Ulyate Esq, 23 Park Rd, Glenfield, Auckland, New Zealand]; *b* 2 Aug 1955; *m* 1979 *Shelley Diana, dau of Alfred Bryan Stent, of 34 Maygrane Dr, Orewa, Hibiscus Coast, NZ, and has issue:

1a *Angus Bryan; *b* 1985

1a *Genevieve Kathryn; *b* 1987

(1) Jacqueline Borwick; *b* 17 May 1942; *d* 30 Jan 1951

(2) *Sandra Irene Borwick [Mrs Peter Berry, 18 Phipson Rd, Scottsville, Pietermaritzburg 3201, Natal, South Africa]; *b* 6 July 1945; *m* 1972 *Peter Leslie Berry and has issue:

1a *Bruce Sidney; *b* 1975

1a *Cynthia Jacqueline; *b* 1972

2 *Phyllis Dorothy [The Hon Mrs Bergne, 16 Wood Lane, Falmouth, Cornwall]; *b* 24 Aug 1916; late F/O WAAF; *m* 26 July 1963 John A'Court Bergne (*d* 1978), son of Hervey A'Court Bergne, of Budleigh Salterton, Devon

The **3rd Baron** *m* 2nd 20 July 1920 Margaret Elizabeth (Betty) (*d* 4 Feb 1969), yst dau of Gilbert Robertson Sandbach, of Liverpool, and by her had:

2 George Sandbach; *b* 18 Oct 1922; *educ* Eton; *m* 1981 Esther (*d* 1985), dau of Clarence de Sola, of Montreal, Canada, and widow of Sir John Reeves Ellerman, 2nd Bt, and *dsp* 28 Nov 1994

3 +ROBIN SANDBACH [The Hon Robin Borwick, Neptune House, Newells Lane, Bosham, W Sussex PO18 8PS]; *b* 22 March 1927; heir presumptive; *educ* Eton; late Lt Life Gds; *m* 2 Dec 1950 *Patricia Garnett, only dau of Baron McAlpine of Moffat (*see* McALPINE, Bt), and has issue:

(1) +(Geoffrey Robert) James (Jamie) [James Borwick Esq, 1 Love Lane, London EC2]; *b* 7 March 1955; *educ* Eton; *m* 1981 *Victoria Lorne Peta, only dau of W/Cdr Roger Dennistoun Poore, of 33 Phillimore Gdns, London W8 (*see* POORE, Bt), and has issue:

1a +Edwin Dennis William; *b* 1984

2a +Thomas James Robert; *b* 1987

3a +William; *b* 9 April 1997

1a *Alexandra Victoria; *b* 1990

(2) +Richard David; *b* 24 July 1960; *educ* Eton; *m* 1983 *Nicole D, dau of S/Ldr Ronald M Kerr, MVO, of Westwinds, Moulsford, Oxon, and has issue:

1a +Christian Richard Sandbach; *b* 1985

2a +Fraser James Montgomery; *b* 2 May 1992

1a *Summer Louise Molly; *b* 24 June 1987

2a *Charlotte Alexandra Nicole; *b* 1989

3a *Skye Isabella Paula; *b* 16 March 1994

4a *Lily; *b* 3 March 1997

(1) *Judith Patricia [Mrs Padraic O'Hagan, 29 Barton Court Rd, London W14]; *b* 13 June 1952; *m* 27 Nov 1971 *Padraic Desmond Curry-Towneley-O'Hagan, only son of Capt Ian Desmond Curry-Towneley-O'Hagan (*see* O'HAGAN, B)

BOSSOM

Arms: Gu. a representation of a steel building column and three floor girders with wind bracing projecting therefrom to the sinister or, on a chief or an antique lamp inflamed sa. between on the dexter a rose gu., barbed and seeded ppr, and on the sinister a thistle leaved and slipped, also ppr. **Crest:** Upon a mount vert on oak tree fructed charged with an eye irradiated ppr. **Motto:** *Esto quod es* ('Be what thou art'). **Creations:** Bt. (UK) 4 July 1953.

SIR CLIVE BOSSOM, 2ND BT, of Maidstone, Kent [Major The Hon Sir Clive Bossom Bt, 97 Cadogan Lane, London SW1X 9DU; Rotherdown, Petworth, W Sussex GU28 0BT]; *b* 4 Feb 1918; *s* f 1965; *educ* Eton; Maj The Buffs (Roy E Kent Regt), served WW II, ret 1948, CC Kent 1949–52, MP (C) Leominster 1959–74, PPS to: Jt Parly Secs Min Pensions and Nat Insur 1960–61, Sec State Air 1962–64, MOD (RAF) 1964, Home Sec 1970–72, chm Europ Assistance 1973–88, pres: Anglo-Belgian Union 1970–73, 1983–85, Anglo-Netherlands Soc 1978–89, BARC 1985–91, v-pres: Int Automobile Fedn 1975–81, Int Social Serv 1989–, chm: RAC 1975–78, Iran Soc 1973–76, memb cncl RGS 1982–86, memb Chapter Gen OStJ, memb Jt Ctee OStJ and BRCS, Badge of Honour BRCS 1993, Liveryman Cos: Grocers' (Master 1979), Paviors' and Needlemakers', v-pres Urban DCs Assoc, chm Trans-Care Int 1973, dir Vosper 1973, KStJ 1961, Cdr Order Leopold II, Order Crown (Belgium), Kt Cdr Order Orange Nassau Netherlands, Order Homayoun III Iran, FRSA; *m* 28 Sept 1951 *Lady Barbara Joan North, sis of 9th Earl of Guilford (*qv*), and has issue:

1 +BRUCE CHARLES [Bruce Bossom Esq, Overbury Court, nr Tewkesbury, Glos GL20 7NP]; *b* 22 Aug 1952; *educ* Eton, Coll Estate Management and Harvard Business Sch; FRICS; *m* 1985 *Penelope Jane, only child of Edward (Ruby) Holland-Martin, of Overbury Court, nr Tewkesbury, Glos, and has:

(1) +George Edward Martin; *b* 21 Feb 1992

(1) *Rosanna Emily; *b* 1986

(2) *Amanda Lucy; *b* 1988

2 +Andrew Clive; *b* 19 Feb 1954; *educ* Eton and RMA Sandhurst; Lt Life Gds 1975; *m* 12 July 1997 *Amza Walbrook, dau of Lloyd Horton, of USA

3 +James Edward; *b* 24 Nov 1962

1 *Arabella Emily; *b* 27 May 1968

Lineage: CHARLES BOSSOM, of Twickenham, Middx; *m* 30 May 1786 Eleanor Lloyd (*d* 2 June 1844 aged 80) and *d* by 1837, leaving issue:

1 John; *bapt* 12 May 1793

2 EDWARD, of whom presently

3 George; *bapt* 11 Nov 1798; *d* 18 Nov 1821

1 Elizabeth; *bapt* 16 May 1790; *m* Thomas Wood

2 Frances; *bapt* 10 May 1821

3 Harriett; *bapt* 29 May 1803; *d* unm

The 2nd son,

EDWARD BOSSOM, of Twickenham; *bapt* 12 June 1796; *m* Mary — and left issue:

1 Charles; *b* 13, *bur* 16 Oct 1822

2 GEORGE, of whom presently

1 Mary Ann; *bapt* 9 April 1820

2 Eleanor Waterloo; *bapt* 24 July 1826

The 2nd son,

GEORGE BOSSOM, of Euston Rd, St Pancras; *bapt* 2 Sept 1821; *m* 11 Aug 1847 Mary Ann, dau of James Moffat, of Shadwell, Middx, and *d* 25 July 1876, leaving issue:

1 Edward; *b* 1849

2 Charles; *b* 1850

3 ALFRED HENRY, of whom presently

1 Lucy, of Whittington Rd, St Pancras; *m* — Walker; *d* in or after 1902

The 3rd son,

ALFRED HENRY BOSSOM, of Holloway; *b* 13 June 1854; *m* 18 May 1879 Amelia Jane (*d* 2 Jan 1920), dau of Edmund Hammond, of Finsbury, and *d* 27 May 1919, leaving issue:

Sir ALFRED CHARLES BOSSOM, **1st Bt** and BARON BOSSOM, of Maidstone, Kent (LP), so *cr* 4 July 1953 and 30 Jan 1960 respectively (both UK), JP; *b* 6 Oct 1881; *educ* St Thomas's Charterhouse London EC1 and Roy Acad Arts; architect: Carnegie Steel Mills workers' housing Pittsburgh 1903, restoration Fort Ticonderoga 1908, US Shipping Bd 1917–18, Magnolia Petroleum (Dallas), Seabord Nat Bank (NYC); Treas Architectural League NY 1923–26; fndr Co-operation in Govt Movement US, chm Exec Ctees American Mid-European Assoc, Hon Sec American Baltic League 1920–23; MP (C) Maidstone 1931–59, pres and fndr Anglo-Baltic Soc 1933, Ald LCC 1930–34; pres Assoc Public Health Insprs 1957–60; chm Slum Clearance Sub-Ctee LCC 1930–34; v-chm LCC Improvement Sub-Ctee and Housing Ctee, Leader Br Bldg Mission US 1943; chm: SE Provincial Area C and U Assocs 1949–52 and Kent C and U Assocs 1947–49; v-pres: Maidstone RDC, RDCs Assoc 1961; fndr Alfred C Bossom Travelling Scholarship RIBA; tstee Antarctic Film Tst; chm Roy Soc Arts 1957–59 (v-pres 1959); chm Anglo-Belgium and Anglo-Iranian Gps 1956; Sec HG Parl Ctee Lds and Commons 1942–44, memb Select Ctee on Nat Expenditure 1939–45, Hon LLD Pittsburgh 1952, Hon Fell UCL 1953, Liveryman Armourers', Brasiers' and Paviors' and Master Needlemakers' Cos 1959–60; Grand Prior Primrose League; Lloyd's underwriter, Hon Fell Faculty Bldg and Inst Quality Surveyors; Hon Freeman Maidstone; Maj HG WW II 1940–44; author: *Our House* (1948), FRIBA, GCStJ, Offr Legion Honour, Cdr Order Crown Belgium, Cavaliere Order Crown Italy, Real Academia de Nobles Artes de San Fernando Spain, Order Christ Portugal, Dip and Gold Medal Les Invalides Prevoyantes Belgium; Kt Order White Lion Czechoslovakia, Order Grand Duke Gediminas 2nd Cl Lithuania, Cdr Order Grand Cross Three Stars, Order Merit Latvia, Order Eagle Cross 2nd Cl Estonia, Cdr Order White Rose Finland, Order Merit Chile, Firdausi Medal Persia, Order Taj 2nd Grade Iran 1963,*m* 1st 26 April 1910 Emily (*k* air crash 27 July 1932), dau of Samuel Gamble Bayne, of New York, and had issue:

1 Bruce Bayne; *b* 25 March 1911; *educ* Harrow; *k* with mother 27 July 1932

2 Sir CLIVE BOSSOM, **2nd and present Bt**

3 Doric; *b* 3 May 1922; *educ* Eton and Trin Coll Cambridge (BA 1948); Capt Coldstream Gds WW II, underwriting memb Lloyd's, Liveryman Paviors' and Needlemakers' Cos; *m* 15 Dec 1949 *June [Mrs Kenneth Crawley, Flat 6, 89 Cadogan Gdns, London SW3 2RE] (*m* 2nd 25 Oct 1967 Kenneth Arnold Gibbs Crawley, TD (*d* 1988), yst son of Rev Arthur Stafford Crawley; *see* CRAWLEY-BOEVEY, Bt), er dau of Vernon Bertram Longworth, of Clevedon Court, Port Elizabeth, S Africa, and *d* 14 Oct 1959, leaving issue:

(1) +Doric Alfred Howard [Doric Bossom Esq, 9 Rumbold Rd, London SW6 2JA]; *b* posthumously 27 Feb 1960; *m* 1986 *Sara J, only dau of Lt-Col Derek Vaughan, and has issue:

1a +Theo Doric Alfred; *b* 1988

2a +Caspar Luke Sebastian; *b* 1991

3a +Barnaby David Vaughan; *b* 28 Dec 1995

He *m* 2nd 30 July 1934 (*divorce* 1947) Elinor, dau of Samuel Dittenhofer, of Minnesota, and *d* 4 Sept 1965, when the barony expired and the baronetcy passed to his only surv s

BOSTON

Arms: Arg. fretty sa., on a canton gu. a chaplet or. **Crest:** A Saracen's head in profile ppr., wreathed about the temples arg. and sa. **Supporters:** Two antelopes gu., each gorged with a chaplet or. **Motto:** *Honor fidelitatis præmium* ('Honour is the reward of fidelity'). **Creations:** Bt. (E) 13 April 1704, B. (GB) 10 April 1761.

THE 10TH BARON BOSTON of Boston, Co Lincoln, and a **Baronet** (Sir Timothy George Frank Boteler Irby, Bt) [The Rt Hon The Lord Boston, Cae'r Borth, Moelfre, Anglesey LL72 8NN]; *b* 27 March 1939; *s* f 1978; *educ* Clayesmore Sch Dorset and Southampton U (BSc Econ); *m* 1967 *Rhonda A, dau of Ronald Albert Bate, of Melbourne, Australia, and has issue:

1 +GEORGE WILLIAM EUSTACE BOTELER; *b* 1 Aug 1971

2 +Jonathan Charles Timothy; *b* 30 May 1975

1 *Rebecca Frances Anne; *b* 4 April 1970

Lineage: The IRBYs take their name from Irby on Humber, Lincs.

ANTHONY IRBY, of Gosberton, Lincs, *m* Alice (*d* 1557), dau of John Bunting, of Evedon, and *d* 21 June 1552, having had, with five daus, three er sons and three yr sons:

THOMAS IRBY, of Whaplode; *m* Isabel (*d* 1573), dau and coheir of Thomas Serjeant, of Moulton, and *d* April 1561, having had, with other issue, an only s:

ANTHONY IRBY, of Whaplode, MP Boston *temp* ELIZABETH I and JAMES I; Bencher and Autumn Reader Lincoln's Inn, Master Chancery *temp* JAMES I; *m* 22 Dec 1575 Alice (*d* April 1602), dau of Thomas Welbye, of Moulton, and widow of — Tash, and *d* Sept 1625, having had, with other issue:

1 ANTHONY (Sir), his heir

2 Thomas, of Lincoln's Inn; *bapt* 5 March 1579/80; *m* 30 May 1609 Anne, dau of Sir Daniel Dunn, Master Court Requests

1 Alice; *m* Robert Balamy

2 Anne; *m* Sir Francis South, of Kelstern

The est son,

Sir ANTHONY IRBY, MP, High Sheriff Lincs *temp* CHARLES I; *bapt* 9 Jan 1576/7; *m* Feb 1602/3 Elizabeth, dau of Sir John Peyton, Bt, of Isleham, Cambs, and *d* 1610, leaving an est s:

Sir ANTHONY IRBY, MP Boston, Recorder Boston, High Sheriff Lincs 1637; *m* 1st Frances, dau of Sir William Wray, Bt, of Glentworth, Lincs, and had a dau (Elizabeth, *m* 1645 Hon George Montague, s of 1st Earl of Manchester; *see* MANCHESTER, D); *m* 2nd Margaret, dau of Sir Richard Smyth, Bt, of Osterhanger, Kent; *m* 3rd Margaret, dau of Sir Edward Barkham; *m* 4th 19 Aug 1641 Catherine, dau of William, 6th Lord (Baron) Paget (*see* ANGLESEY, M), and *d* 1681, having had, with five daus:

ANTHONY IRBY; *m* Mary, dau and heir of John Stringer, of Ashford, Kent, and *d* 1684, leaving an er s:

Sir Edward Irby, 1st Bt (E), so *cr* 13 April 1704, MP Boston; *m* 1706 Dorothy (*bur* Oct 1784), gdau of Lord Paget (*see* ANGLESEY, M), and was *bur* 11 Nov 1718, leaving an only s:

Sir William Irby, 2nd Bt, and **1st Baron Boston** of Boston, Co Lincoln (GB), so *cr* 10 April 1761; *b* 8 March 1706/7; Page Honour to GEORGE I and GEORGE II, MP (Tory) Launceston 1735–47 and Bodmin 1747–61, Chm Ctees Ho Lds 1770–75; *m* 26 Aug 1746 Albinia (*d* 1 April 1769), Maid Honour to AUGUSTA, PRINCESS OF WALES, only dau of Henry Selwyn, of Westminster, and had, with a dau (Augusta Georgina Elizabeth, *m* 30 April 1772 2nd Baron Walsingham, *qv*):

1 FREDERICK, **2nd Baron**

2 William Henry; *b* 29 Aug 1750; *m* 1781 Mary, yst dau and coheir of Rowland Blackman, of Antigua, and *d* 1830, leaving issue:

(1) William Henry Rowland; *b* 13 March 1784; *d* 1842

(1) Augusta Priscilla; *m* 19 May 1810 Sir William Langham, Bt (*qv*)

The 1st BARON *d* 30 March 1775; his er son,

FREDERICK IRBY, **2nd Baron Boston**, FAS and DCL; *b* 9 June 1749; *m* 15 May 1775 Christian (*d* 9 May 1832), only dau of Paul Methuen, of Corsham Ho, Wilts, and had issue:

1 GEORGE, **3rd Baron**

2 Frederick Paul, CB, R-Adml the Red, of Boyland Hall, Long Stratton, Norfolk; *b* 18 April 1779; *m* 1st 1 Dec 1803 Emily Ives (*d* 7 Aug 1806), yst dau and coheir of William Drake, of Amersham, Bucks, and had issue:

(1) Frederick William, of Boyland Hall; *b* 28 July 1806; *m* 7 March 1846 Isabella Harriet (*d* 13 April 1906), only child of Robert Bruce, of Chester Square (*see* BRUCE, Bt, of Stenhouse), and *dsp* 1 June 1877

2 (cont.) R-Adml The Hon Frederick Irby *m* 2nd 23 Jan 1816 Frances (*d* 16 Jan 1852), 2nd dau of Ichabod Wright, of Mapperley Hall, Notts, and *d* 24 April 1844, having by her had:

(2) Charles Paul, RN; *b* 17 June 1818; accidentally shot 14 May 1836

(3) Montagu Henry John; *b* 18 May 1828; *d* 13 Dec 1893

(4) Leonard Howard Lloyd, Lt-Col 7th Regt, served in the Crimea and Indian Mutiny, Relief of Lucknow, etc; *b* 13 April 1836; *m* 1st 31 Aug 1864 Geraldine Alicia Mary (*d* 18 April 1882), dau of Rev J Magenis, and had issue:

1a Frederick Arthur, of Boyland Hall, JP, formerly Capt Rifle Bde, and Maj and Hon Lt-Col 7th Bn KRRC, served Burmese War 1885–87 and Boer War 1902; *b* 23 June 1865; *m* 9 April 1907 Louisa Christian (*d* 20 Jan 1942), 3rd dau of Col James Fellowes, RE, and *d* 19 Sept 1930, leaving issue:

1b Christian Geraldine Mary; *b* 6 Aug 1913; *m* 14 Sept 1939 Lt-Cdr Victor George Hargrave Ramsay-Fairfax, DSC, RN, yr son of William George Ramsay-Fairfax (*see* RAMSAY-FAIRFAX-LUCY, Bt), and *d* 21 April 1967, leaving issue

2a Leonard Paul, OBE (1919), late Lt-Col KRRC, and Capt and Hon Maj of its 6th Bn, Lt-Col cmdg 15th Bn Rifle Bde, 24th Bn KRRC and 16th Bn Training Reserve WW I; *b* 9 Jan 1871; *m* 11 Jan 1896 Ethel Maud (*d* 20 Sept 1957), er dau and coheir of Capt William John Casberd Boteler, RN, of The Elms, Taplow, and Brook Ho, Eastry, Kent, and heiress of that estate, and *d* 26 Nov 1936, leaving issue:

1b **GERALD HOWARD BOTELER, 9th Baron**

2b Anthony Paul, TD; *b* 21 March 1908; granted rank of baron's yr s 1976; *educ* Eton and Trin Coll Cambridge (BA 1930); barrister Lincoln's Inn 1932, Maj late The Rifle Bde, served WW II; *m* 1st 20 Sept 1934 Countess Mary Apponyi (*d* 1 April 1952), er dau of Count Anton Apponyi; *m* 2nd 8 June 1957 *Mrs Beryl Harrison [The Hon Mrs Anthony Irby, 44 Rosebank, Holyport Rd, London SW6 6LQ], yst dau of Harold Mayman, of Bramsgore, Hants and *d* 1986, leaving issue by his 1st w:

1c +Paul Anthony [Paul Irby Esq, Piercy House, 79 Copthall Ave, London EC2R 7NJ; Garth House, Highclere, Berks RG20 9RE]; *b* 7 Aug 1935; *educ* Eton; late 2nd Lt KRRC; *m* 29 Jan 1982 *Mrs Emma Aschan, dau of Robert Henderson and formerly w of (a) Hugh Leopold Seymour (*see* HERTFORD, M) and (b) John Laurence David Aschan (*see* LOWTHER, Bt), and has:

1d +Rupert Paul Anthony; *b* 1983

2d +Harry Robert Paul Anthony; *b* 1985

2c +(George Anthony) Peter [Peter Irby Esq, Hill House, 64 Honor Oak Rd, London SE23 3RZ]; *b* 3 June 1942; *educ* Eton; late Maj RGJ; *m* 1981 *Ginger Kay Patricia Wanda May, dau of Frank Edward Wallace, of Texas, USA, and has had issue:

1d +Edward Peter Anthony Wallace; *b* 1986

2d Richard Peter Anthony Wallace; *b* 1988; *d* 1989

1d Mary Charlotte Alexandra Wallace; *b* and *d* 1983

2d *Katharine Mary Louise Wallace; *b* 1984

3c +Charles Leonard Anthony [Charles Irby Esq, 125 Blenheim Crescent, London W11 2EQ]; *b* 5 June 1945; *educ* Eton; *m* 23 Sept 1971 *Sarah Jane, dau of David Sutherland, of 51 Victoria Rd, London W8, and has issue:

1d +Nicholas Charles Anthony; *b* 10 July 1975

1d *Caroline Sarah; *b* 21 May 1977

1b Frances Dorothy, VAD 1939–45; *b* 24 March 1901; *d* 21 Nov 1951

(4) (cont.) Col Leonard Irby *m* 2nd 22 Jan 1884 Mary (*d* July 1939), dau of Col John James Brandling, CB, RHA, and *d* 14 May 1905, having by her had issue:

1a Frances Margaret; *b* 1 Dec 1884; *m* 1st 12 Dec 1905 (*divorce* 1910) Sir Morgan George Crofton, 6th Bt, DSO, of Mohill (*qv*), and had issue; *m* 2nd 22 Oct 1910 (*divorce* 1921) James Fountayne Montagu, of Papplewick Hall, Notts, and Cold Overton Hall, Oakham, 2nd s of James Montagu, of Merton Park, Doncaster; *m* 3rd 5 May 1922 3rd Earl of Kimberley (*qv*) and *d* 4 Jan 1950, leaving further issue

(1) Frances Harriet; *m* 19 June 1845 Lewis Loyd, JP, of Monk's Orchard, Kent, est son of Edward Loyd, banker, of Coombe Ho, Surrey, and *d* 27 Jan 1902. He *dsp* 19 July 1891

(2) Margaret Amelia; *m* Feb 1843 Henry Kett Tompson, of Witchingham Hall, Norfolk, and *d* Dec 1873. He *d* Nov 1872

(3) Adelaide Paulina; *d* unm 15 Sept 1911

3 William Augustus (Rev); *b* 28 Nov 1780; *d* 10 March 1807

4 Henry Edward, Offr 2nd Life Gds, served Waterloo (medal), Lt-Col 1st W India Regt (ret 2 March 1820); *b* 27 Aug 1783; *d* 9 March 1821

5 Paul Anthony (Rev), Rector Cottesbrook, Northants; *b* 16 Dec 1784; *m* 1st 2 Dec 1814 Patience Anne (*d* 22 March 1831), est dau of Sir William Champion De Crespigny, 2nd Bt (*see* 1949 edn), and had issue:

(1) Claude Frederick, Maj, late Madras Army; *b* 19 Sept 1815; *d* 19 Aug 1898

(2) Thomas William (Rev), Rector Rushmere; *b* 2 April 1817; *d* 9 June 1892

(3) Augustus Henry, Lt-Col; *b* 12 May 1818; *d* in India, Sept 1861

(4) Edward; *b* 14 May 1821; *m* 3 Aug 1850 Mary (*d* 20 July 1885), dau of Archibald Windeyer, of NSW, and *d* 27 July 1900, leaving issue:

1a Edward de Crespigny, JP NSW; *b* 21 Sept 1851; *m* 1874 Edith (*d* 2 June 1946), dau of Dr Campbell, and *d* 10 Jan 1924, leaving issue:

1b Francis Edward; *b* 17 Oct 1877; *m* 10 June 1925 Katie Lorna, 2nd dau of W C Tibbits, of Gilgandra, NSW, and *d* 6 Dec 1960, having had issue:

1c *Edith Elizabeth; *b* 13 April 1927; *m* 1953 Richard E Wratten (*d* 1969), and has issue:

1d *Nigel Richard Irby; *b* 21 Jan 1955

2c Eunice Lorna; *b* 25 Nov 1928; *m* 1954 Thomas Henry Hocking, and had issue:

1d *Gregory Francis; *b* 11 June 1955

1d *Gwendalyn Jean; *b* 14 May 1963

3c *Isla Frances [Mrs Wildred Tibbits, Cottage Green, Gilgandra, NSW, Australia]; *b* 29 June 1930; *m* 6 Oct 1954 her cousin Wilfred Charles Tibbits (*d* 1985)

4c Alison Jean; *b* 31 Jan, *d* 2 Feb 1934

2b Paul Anthony; *b* 1881; *m* 5 Nov 1914 Mabel Clive (*d* 1960), of Casino, NSW, Australia, and *d* 26 Aug 1968, leaving issue:

1c +Paul Anthony [Paul Irby Esq, 2 Ray St, Bray Park, Murwillumbah, NSW 2484, Australia]; *b* Nov 1916; served New Guinea and Solomon Islands 1944–45 with AIF; *m* 1948 *Dorothy Mary, dau of R H Hogg of Wahroonga, Cecil Plains, Queensland, and has issue:

1d +Paul Anthony Richard; *b* 1949; BEcon

2d +Ross James; *b* 1959; BA

1b *Judith Jessie [Mrs Geoffrey Williams, 28 Carlton St, Highgate, Adelaide, S Australia]; *b* 1951; *m* 1982 *Geoffrey Robert Williams, and has issue:

1c *Benjamin Robert; *b* 1984

1c *Courtney Jayne; *b* 1987

2c Gordon Edward; *b* 1922; *m* 1950 *Beryl Margaret [Mrs Gordon Irby, Weerona, Mooball, NSW, Australia], dau of C D Mills, and *d* 1979 leaving issue:

1d +Leonard Edward [Leonard Irby Esq, 12 Opal Place, Golden Links Estate, Murwillumbah, NSW 2484, Australia]; *b* 1951; *m* 1981 *Judith Ann, dau of Robert B Noble, of Murwillumbah, NSW, and has issue:

1e +Mark Edward; *b* 1983

1e *Melissa Jan; *b* 1986

2e *Suzanne Marie; *b* 1988

2d +Kenneth Francis; *b* 1954; *m* 1973 *Robyn M Shillan, and has issue:

1e +Peter Richard; *b* 1978

1e *Felica Lea; *b* 1974

3d +Stephen Victor; *b* 1960; *m* 1989 *Robyn, dau of Horace Alfred Martin, of 4 Ewing St, Murwillumbah, NSW, and has issue:

1e +Benjamin Anthony; *b* 1992

1e *Jacinta Elizabeth; *b* 1990

1d *Robyn Joyce; *b* 1953

2d *Sharon Lea [Mrs Geoffrey Grace, Burringbar, NSW 2483, Australia]; *b* 1966; *m* 1989 *Geoffrey David Grace and has:

1e *Zachary James; 19 Oct 1995

3c +John Charles [John Irby Esq, Weerona, Mooball, NSW 2483, Australia]; *b* 1928; *m* 1952 *Orene Ethel, dau of W D Scott, of Burringbar, NSW, and has issue:

1d +Douglas John [Douglas Irby Esq, Greenvale Estate, Burringbar, NSW 2483, Australia]; *b* 1953; *m* 1975 *Barbara Anne, dau of W Murray, of Sydney, NSW, and has issue:

1e +David John; *b* 1978

1e *Joanne Louise; *b* 1977

2e *Rachael Elizabeth; *b* 1982

2d *Michael Anthony [Michael Irby Esq, 43 Guildford Rd, Guildford, NSW 2161, Australia]; *b* 1961; *m* 1994 *Carolina, dau of Manuel Baca, of Concord W, Sydney, NSW

1d *Delmay Orene [Mrs Terence Brady, 38 Sunbakers Drive, Forster, NSW 2428, Australia]; *b* 1955; *m* 1996 *Terence Brady

2d *Janelle May [Mrs John Butturini, Mooball, NSW 2483, Australia]; *b* 1957; *m* 1984 *John Butturini, and has issue:

1e *Matthew John; *b* 1987

2e *Nicholas James; *b* 1989

3e *Andrew Anthony; *b* 1993

3d *Elsie Maree; *b* 1959; *m* 1986 *Mark Clapham and has:

1e *Thomas Anthony; *b* 1991

1e *Melanie Alice; *b* 1988

4d *Shirley Ellen [Mrs Gregory King, Pottsville, NSW 2484, Australia]; *b* 1963; *m* 1987 *Gregory Craig King, and has issue:

1e *Lucas Scott; *b* 1990

1e *Stacey Mary; *b* 1992

1c *Florence Mabel, JP [Mrs Dalley Griffin JP, 15 Napier Cres, N Ryde, NSW 2113, Australia]; *b* 1919; *m* 1946 *Dalley Leslie Griffin, JP, and has issue:

1d *David Leslie Paul; *b* 1947; JP; *m* 1978 *Wendy, dau of E R Raynor, of Manly, NSW, and has issue:

1e *Jacqueline Lea; *b* 1982

2e *Lauren Jane; *b* 1986

2d *Brian Arthur Charles, JP; *b* 1948; BA; Aust Forces, 3rd Cav Regt, Vietnam; *m* 1972 *Cherly, dau of K Trescott, of Baulkham Hills, Sydney, NSW, and has issue:

1e *Fiona Leigh; *b* 1978

2e *Kate Michelle; *b* 1980

3e *Sara Louise; *b* 1984

1d *Elizabeth Ann; *b* 1951; SRN

2c *Nancy [Mrs Mervyn Carthy, Myponga, S Australia]; *b* 1926; *m* 1946 Mervyn James Carthy (*d* 1976), and has issue:

1d *Terry James; *b* 1947; *m* 1971 *Maxine, dau of K Hutchinson, of Myponga, S Australia, and has issue:

1e *Todd Lee; *b* 1978

1e *Lisa Jane; *b* 1975

2d *Peter; *b* 1949; served Australian Forces, Vietnam; *m* 1972 *Wendy, dau of Robert Rossiter, of Victor Harbour, S Australia, and has issue:

1e *Meagan Emma; *b* 1978

2e *Belinda Abbie; *b* 1980

3d *Graeme; *b* 1956

1d *Anne [Mrs Graham McKinley, Jerrramungup, W Australia]; *b* 1953; *m* 1973 *Graham McKinley, and has issue:

1e *Ryan James; *b* 1976

1e *Amie Louise; *b* 1978

3b Llewellyn George, Conservator of Forests, Tasmania; *b* 1883; *m* 15 Aug 1914 Mary Louisa, er dau of Rev Reginald Walter Stockdale, of Grafton, NSW (*see* STOCKDALE, Bt), and *d* 12 Jan 1964, having had issue:

1c +Kenneth Alan [Kenneth Irby Esq, 1 Gibbons St, Wynward, Tasmania, Australia]; *b* 5 Jan 1920; served WW II with RAAF; *m* 4 Dec 1948 *Mary Rushton, only dau of Rev Ernest Edward Johnson, Rector of Carrick, Tasmania, and has issue:

1d +Philip Anthony Kenelm; *b* 6 Aug 1951

1d *Judith Mary; *b* 18 Sept 1949; *m* 1971*Rev Ross Flint, and has issue:

1e *Andrew Mark; *b* 1979

1e *Janine Ruth; *b* 1974

2e *Natasha; *b* 1976

1c *Mary Edith (Rosemary) [Mrs George MacDonell, Pond Garth, RMB 2545, Greens Rd, Upper Lurg, via Benalla, Victoria, Australia]; *b* 24 June 1915; *m* 6 Nov 1943 George Philip MacDonell (*d* 1980), est s of George Macolm MacDonell, of Nairobi, Kenya

2c *Elspeth Douglas [Mrs Frederick Ingoldsby, 3 Ivanhoe Ct, Newcomb, Vic 3219, Australia]; *b* 27 Sept 1917; late Sister in Australian Army Nursing Serv; *m* 1 June 1948 Rev Frederick Searle Ingoldsby, ThL, DipRE (*d* 1976), 4th son of John Ingoldsby, of Merrylands, Sydney, NSW, and has had issue:

1d *James Douglas; *b* 28 Feb 1949; BA; *m* 1980 *Leonie Christine Praetz, and has issue:

1e *Sophie Sky; *b* 1981

2e *Liria Vida; *b* 1982

2d *David Llewellyn; *b* 2 March 1954; *m* 1987 *Rosemary Crosby, and has issue:

1e *Jonathan Dale; *b* 1990

1e *Clare Elizabeth; *b* 1988

3d Roger Glynne; *b* 10 Feb *d* 5 Dec 1957

1d *Marilyn Margaret; *b* 25 Sept 1950; BFA

2d *Pamela Jean; *b* 7 Sept 1952; BA; *m* 1974 *Rev M J Vercoe, and has issue:

1e *Stephen Philip; *b* 1980

1e *Alison Mary; *b* 1982

3d *Janet Elspeth Irby; *b* 7 Nov 1959; BA; *m* 1981 *Michael John Down, and has issue:

1e *John Philip Frederick; *b* 1982

1e *Elizabeth Winsome Mary; *b* 1984

2e *Deborah Lyn Emily; *b* 1986

3c Elfrida Margaret; *b* 7 March 1924; *m* 27 June 1947 Allan Archie Walker, only son of Vernon Edgar Walker, of Nugent, Tasmania, and was *k* in a car crash 5 Dec 1948, leaving a s

1b Florence Margaret *b* 1875; *d* unm 21 July 1964

2b Winifred Edith; *b* 1880

2a George Archibald; *b* 24 March 1855; *d* unm

3a Frederick William; *b* 21 April 1859; *d* unm

4a Charles Augustus; *b* 17 June 1861; *m* 1888 Eva Georgiana, dau of Richard Roberts, of Sydney, and *d* 1941, leaving issue:

1b Charles Edward; *b* 1889; *d* unm

2b Arthur Algernon; *b* 1890; *m* 1927 Mary Isabel Marsden, and *d* 1953 leaving issue:

1c John; *b* 1929; *m* 1949 *Peggy May White

2c +Brian Keith [Brian Irby Esq JP, 3 Banyeena Place, Belrose 2085, Sydney, NSW, Australia]; *b* 1931; JP; *m* 1952 *June Eve Hutton, and has issue:

1d +Peter Brian Edward; *b* 1956; *m* *Ruth Helen Goven, and has issue:

1e +Nicholas Roland; *b* 1989

2e +Cameron Peter; *b* 1993

1d *Donna Elizabeth; *b* 1953

3b Walter Leonard; *b* 1896

4b Beverley Keith; *b* 1899; *m* 1943 *Kathleen Pilley, of Mudgee

5b Richard Wilfred; *b* 1901; *m* 1939 Margery McMillan, of Bathurst, Australia, and had:

1c *Jenny Eva; *b* 1942; *m* 1964 *Raymond Connell

6b Roland Frank; *b* 1906; *m* 1938 Mary Brown

1b Mary Eva; *b* 1903; *m* 1940 Royston Maurice Greenshields (*ka* Tobruk 1941) and *d* 1959

5a Rowland John; *b* 20 Aug 1863; *d* unm

6a Walter Claude; *b* 22 Oct 1865; *d* unm

1a Mary Elizabeth; *m* 1876 Edward Priestly Carr, and had issue:

2a Fanny Australia; *m* 1886 Walter Windeyer Traill, of Wirepe, Turramurra, Sydney, NSW, and had issue. He *d* 1916

(5) Leonard; *b* 1822; *d* 1856

(6) Algernon; *b* 10 July 1825; *d* unm 23 Nov 1876

(1) Frances Anne; *m* 14 May 1850 John Cotton Powell, of Selsfield, Sussex, and *d* 21 Jan 1895

(2) Caroline; *m* 1st 27 Feb 1849 Rev Septimus Stockdale, Rector of Wilby (*see* STOCKDALE, Bt). He *d* 11 May 1849; *m* 2nd 5 May 1859 Rev Robert Gibbings, Vicar of Radley, and *d* 29 Jan 1894 leaving issue. He *d* 3 Jan 1865

(3) Emma; *d* unm 26 Feb 1890

5 (cont.) The Rev Hon Paul Irby *m* 2nd Sept 1836 Wilhelmina (*d* 28 July 1872), dau of David Powell, of Loughton, Essex, and by her had further issue:

(7) George Powell (Rev), Vicar of Weedon 1883–92, Chaplain at Nantes 1897–1903 and at Dinan 1903–10; *b* 26 Aug 1838; *m* 23 Sept 1869 Emma Sarah Bransby (*d* 13 Jan 1930), est dau of John Lewis Aubert, of Nunsbury, Herts, and *d* 20 April 1910, leaving issue:

1a Paul Aubert; *b* 1 Aug 1872; *m* 4 June 1907 Lucy Evelyn Deschamps, dau of Charles William Chalmers, of Cults, and widow of Richard Reichburg, and *d* 17 June 1952

2a Lewis Michael Aubert, sometime Lt RAOC; *b* 29 Sept 1882; *educ* Lancing and Hertford Coll Oxford (BA 1908); *m* 23 June 1914 Isabel Kate (*d* 12 Oct 1972 aged 91), only dau of G M Thornton, of Cheltenham, and *d* 17 July 1974, leaving issue:

1b *Audrey Cynthia Yvette [Mrs Christopher Chamberlin, Withybed Cottage, Butleigh Wootton, Glastonbury, Somerset BA6 8TX]; *b* 12 April 1915; *m* 3 Aug 1955 Christopher Lucian Chamberlin, TD, MA (*d* 21 Feb 1996), est s of Rev Charles Marshall Chamberlin, MA, of Witton Rectory, Norwich

2b *Beryl Diana Noël, BA [Mrs Henry Bunting, 5 Cambray Court, Cheltenham G50 1JU]; *b* 25 Dec 1919; served WW II 1940–45 as Subaltern ATS; *m* 30 June 1951 *Henry John Bunting, only son of H W Bunting, and has had issue:

1c *George Irby; *b* 17 July 1952; *educ* Wells Cathedral Sch; *m* 1974 *Julia Angela Davey, and has issue:

1d *Samuel Charles; *b* 1979

2d *Timothy George; *b* 1984

2c *James Walter Irby; *b* 8 Aug 1954; *educ* Wells Cathedral Sch; *m* 1982 *Hisaka Margaret Hiraoka, and has issue:

1d *Paul Shu; *b* 1985

2d *Mark Rhu; *b* 1990

1d *Sarah Mai; *b* 1992

3c Charles Irby; *b* 29 Jan, *d* 15 Nov 1957

4c *Edward Irby; *b* 9 Feb 1959; *educ* Wells Cathedral Sch and Cheltenham GS; *m* 1991 *Boika Spasova

5c *Richard Irby; *b* 15 March 1962; *educ* Dean Close; *m* 1995 *Karen Elizabeth Dowling, and has:

1d *William Richard; *b* 26 Feb 1998

1a Emma Wilhelmina; *b* 20 Aug 1870; *d* unm 27 Aug 1916

2a Mary Katharine, deaconess; *b* 13 Sept 1871; *d* unm 16 April 1955

3a Helen Elizabeth; *b* 21 Oct 1874; *d* unm 27 Oct 1918

4a Henrietta Margaret; *b* 15 July 1879; *m* 15 April 1913 Rev Basil Eversley Owen, BA, late Rector of Woodford, nr Kettering, Northants, yst son of Rev J W Owen, of Adelaide, and *d* 14 Aug 1965, leaving issue. He *d* 1963

5a Evelyn May, Librarian, Min of Labour, and Union of PO Workers 1931–32; *b* 28 May 1885; *d* unm 5 March 1959

(8) Paul Anthony; *b* 1840; *d* 1846

5 (cont.) The Rev Hon P A Irby *m* 3rd 9 Aug 1849 Augusta (*dsp* 25 Aug 1870), dau of John B Cowell, and *d* 10 Feb 1865

6 Edward Methuen, Offr 3rd Regt Foot Gds; *b* 21 March 1788; *ka* Talavera 27 July 1809

7 Charles Leonard, Capt RN; *b* 9 Oct 1789; *m* 8 Feb 1825 Frances, dau of John Mangles, and *d* 3 Dec 1845, having had issue:

(1) John James Charles, Maj, Adj Chelsea Hospital; *b* 16 Aug 1830; *m* 15 April 1856 Henrietta Elizabeth (*d* 17 Jan 1916), est dau of Rev Thomas Walpole (*see* WALPOLE, B), and *d* 20 May 1895, leaving issue:

1a Charles Leonard, Colonial Serv; *b* 4 April 1857; *m* 1898 Edwin (*d* 21 July 1928), widow of Charles Humphrey Philip Pedley, of Coonoor, Madras

2a Ernest John Frederick; *b* 30 March 1864; *d* 23 Aug 1913

3a Ralph Alexander; *b* 11 April 1866; *d* unm 29 Oct 1943

4a Alfred Spencer Christian; *b* 24 Aug 1863; *d* 3 May 1950

5a Augustus Horatio; *b* 11 Sept 1873; *m* 1st 3 June 1899 Florence Annie (*d* 24 May 1920), dau of Elijah Baker; *m* 2nd 19 July 1925 Dorothy Louise Thursfield (*d* 2 Sept 1934), and *dsp* 14 April 1940

1a Frances Rachel Gertrude; *d* 3 May 1950

2a Theresa Margaret; *d* young, 5 Jan 1869

3a Henrietta Dorothea; *d* unm 21 Aug 1912

4a Amicie Maud; *m* 3 March 1904 Frederick Clark Macdonald, est son of James Macdonald, of Edinburgh

(1) Frances Elizabeth; *m* 22 Nov 1855 Rev R J Howard Rice, MA, Vicar of Sutton Courtney, Berks, and *d* 13 Dec 1921, leaving issue

8 Adolphus Frederick (Rev); *b* 1797; *d* 29 April 1863

1 Charlotte; *d* unm 1848

2 Albinia; *d* 21 Aug 1839

3 Christian Elizabeth; *d* 5 Feb 1875

4 Augusta Matilda; *m* 20 Jan 1853 Rev William Holdsworth, MA, incumbent of Notting Hill, and *d* his widow, 4 April 1877

5 Anne Maria Louisa; *m* 21 Oct 1817 3rd and last Baron Selsey of Selsey and *d* 19 Dec 1870. He *d* 10 March 1839

The 2nd BARON *d* 23 March 1825; his son,

GEORGE IRBY, **3rd Baron Boston**, DCL; *b* 27 Dec 1777; *m* 17 Oct 1801 Rachel Ives (*d* 6 Sept 1830), est dau and coheir of William Drake, of Amersham, and had issue:

1 GEORGE IVES, **4th Baron**

2 William Drake; *b* 18 Sept 1808; *d* 18 Oct 1839

3 Augustus Anthony Frederick; *b* 13 Feb 1820; *m* 22 May 1866 Jessie Augusta (*d* 13 July 1908), est dau of Sir Thomas Montgomery Cuninghame, 8th Bt (*qv*), and *d* 5 April 1870, leaving issue:

(1) Charlotte Augusta, OBE; *m* 31 July 1888 Edward Neil Baynes, FSA, son of Sir William Baynes, 3rd Bt (*qv*), and *d* 8 July 1949, leaving issue

(2) Cecilia Constance, had Order of Mercy; *m* 13 March 1890 6th Baron Boston (*see* below), and *d* 10 Jan 1938

4 Llewellyn Charles Robert (Rev), MA Oxford, Rector of Whiston, Northants; *b* 14 Nov 1822; *m* 1 July 1845 Margaret Emily (*d* 13 March 1913), dau of Jonathan Bullock, of Faulkbourn, Essex, and *dsp* 11 Feb 1911

1 Rachel Emily; *m* 7 may 1840 Capt William Jones Prowse, RN, and *d* 9 July 1873. He *d* 1860

2 Charlotte Isabella; *m* 14 March 1826 5th Earl of Orkney (*qv*), and *d* 7 Sept 1883, leaving issue

3 Frances Matilda; *d* 25 Nov 1879

4 Frederica Maria Louisa; *m* 17 Dec 1840 Edward Horatio Hussey, of Rathkenny, styled Baron of Galtrim, only son of Edward Thomas Hussey, and *d* 13 July 1885, leaving issue. He *d* 1 May 1876

5 Georgina Albinia; *d* unm 20 June 1900

6 Catherine Cecilia; *m* 11 March 1852 Col Walter Caulfeild Pratt, DL, JP, late 67th Regt, 4th son of Col Joseph Pratt, of Cabra Castle, Co Cavan, and *d* 25 March 1894, leaving issue. He *d* 9 June 1900

The 3rd BARON *d* 12 March 1856; his est son,

GEORGE IVES IRBY, **4th Baron Boston**; *b* 14 Sept 1802; *m* 1st 25 Jan 1830 Fanny Elizabeth (*d* 1 April 1860), est dau of W R Hopkins-Northey, of Oving Ho, Bucks, and had issue:

1 FLORANCE GEORGE HENRY, **5th Baron**

1 Rachel Fanny Anne; *m* 26 May 1857 Augustus Arthur Vansittart, of Bisham Abbey, Berks, and *dsp* 27 May 1909. He *d* 17 April 1882

2 Alice Frederica; *m* 25 July 1861 1st Baron Malcolm of Poltalloch, CB, VD, DL, JP, and *dsp* 12 Oct 1896. He *d* 6 March 1902

The **4th Baron Boston** *m* 2nd 30 July 1861 Caroline Amelia (*d* 20 Dec 1927), est dau of 3rd Baron De Saumarez (*qv*), and *d* 22 Dec 1869, having by her had further issue:

3 Maud Caroline; *d* 1 Sept 1873

4 Dorothy Gwenddolen; *d* an infant, 1865

His son,

FLORANCE GEORGE HENRY IRBY, **5th Baron Boston**; *b* 9 March 1837; *m* 17 Oct 1859 Augusta Caroline (*m* 2nd 16 April 1883 Sir Henry Percy Anderson, KCB, KCMG (*d* 19 July 1896), and *d* 16 Feb 1929), 2nd dau of 3rd Baron De Saumarez (*qv*), and *d* 4 Jan 1877, having had issue:

1 GEORGE FLORANCE IRBY, **6th Baron Boston**, DL Anglesey; *b* 6 Sept 1860; *educ* Ch Ch Oxford (MA); FGS, FSA, Hon LLD Wales 1936, Ld-in-Waiting 1885–86; *m* 13 March 1890 his cousin Cecilia Constance (*d* 10 Jan 1938), dau of Hon Augustus Anthony Frederick Irby, of Hillingdon Grove, Uxbridge (*see* above), and *dsp* 16 Sept 1941

2 Cecil Saumarez, JP Bucks, late Capt 7th Bn KRRC; *b* 3 Feb 1862; *m* 31 Jan 1885 Florence Augusta (*d* 7 March 1947), dau of Clement Upton Cottrell Dormer, of Rousham, Oxon, and *d* 21 Feb 1935, leaving issue:

(1) GREVILLE NORTHEY IRBY, **7th Baron Boston**, Hon Capt Oxford and Bucks LI; *b* 24 Aug 1889; *m* 1st 29 Sept 1913 (*divorce* 1954) Constance Beryl (*d* 17 Jan 1969), er dau of William Richard Lester, of Alderley, Llandudno, and had issue:

1a *Rachel Elizabeth Cecily [The Hon Mrs Rawlins, 11 Framers Court, Lane End, High Wycombe HP14 3LL]; *b* 30 Aug 1914; *m* 15 June 1940 *Lt Darsie Rawlins, RNVR, ARBS, ARCA, son of George Edward Hawkes Rawlins, of King's Lane, Great Missenden, and has:

1b *Adrian Drake [Adrian Rawlins Esq, Worth Farm Cottage, The Street, Worth, Kent CT14 0DF]; *b* 29 Oct 1942; *educ* Sherborne; *m* 1st Jan 1968 (*divorce* 1975) Juliana, dau of Eugene Simon; *m* 2nd 1980 *Jill Catharine, dau of Charles William Pays, and has issue by 1st w:

1c *Titus Nicholas Gabriel; *b* 1968

2c *Alexander Francis Edward; *b* 1971

2b *Anthony Irby [Anthony Rawlins Esq, 14 Island Close, Staines, Middx TW18 4YZ]; *b* 12 Aug 1944; *educ* Sherborne

1b *Diana Caroline Zoë [Mrs Colin Ind, Langton Cottage, 78 Gretton Rd, Winchombe, Glos GL54 5EL]]; *b* 25 May 1949; *m* 1976 *Colin Cyril Ind, and has issue:

1c *Christopher Edward; *b* 1980

1c *Charlotte Emily; *b* 1984

1b *Christina Elizabeth [Mrs Seamus Mulvihill, 27 Ashmead Rd, London SE8 4DY]; *b* 1955; *m* 1st 1983 (*divorce* 1991) Graham Joseph Tayar; *m* 2nd 1992 *Seamus Mulvihill, and has issue by 2nd husb:

1c *Thomas James Irby; *b* 1992

2a *Isobel Caroline [The Hon Mrs Sales, 18 Fourth Ave, Hove, E Sussex BN3 2PJ]; *b* 4 May 1917; *m* 1st 3 Nov 1946 (*divorce* 1950) Maj Vernon Owain Roberts, E Kent Regt, only son of Rev Robert Owen Roberts, of Llantrisant Rectory, Anglesey; *m* 2nd 1950 S/Ldr Edward Horatio Sales (*d* 1988), only son of Joseph Edward Sales, of Chesney Hall, Madras, and has issue by 2nd husb:

1b *Christian Caroline [Mrs David Hughes, 18 The Crescent, Barnes, London SW13 0NN]; *b* 11 Oct 1950; *m* 1973 David Wyndham Hughes (*d* 1989), and has issue:

1c *Alexander Wyndham; *b* 1977

2c *Ben Cressall; *b* 1979

1c *Alice Irby; *b* 1982

2c *Holly Irby; *b* 1988

2b *Alexandra Josephine [Mrs Martin Doyle, 27 Rowan Ave, Hangleton, Hove, E Sussex]; *b* 30 Dec 1952; *m* 1st 1973 (*divorce* 1980) Daniel Sean Devaney; *m* 2nd 1991 Martin Paul Doyle (*d* 1993), and has issue by 1st husb:

1c *Damian Julian; *b* 1977

1c *Fleur Josephine; *b* 1978

3a *Christian Florance [The Hon Mrs Humblet, 2510 Ocean Court, 83–85 Spring St, Bondi Junction, NSW 2022, Australia]; *b* 27 Nov 1921; *m* 11 Oct

1947 Etienne Adolphe Joseph Humblet, Belgian Artillery (Res) (*d* 1971), 2nd son of Amedée Humblet, of 74 Rue St Bernard, Brussels, and adopted:
*Dominic; *b* 27 Dec 1956
*Charles Etienne; *b* 16 Jan 1960
*Laure Isabelle; *b* 13 May 1961

(1) (cont.) The **7th Baron** *m* 2nd 6 Feb 1954 Irene Frances (*d* 1987), only child of Francis Holt of Ewell, Surrey, and widow of Harry Mills, and *dspm* 16 Sept 1958

(2) CECIL EUSTACE IRBY, **8th Baron Boston**, MC (1917); *educ* Eton and RMC Sandhurst; Maj Gren Gds WW I and WW II (despatches); *b* 14 July 1897; *d* unm 12 Oct 1972

(1) Evelyn Augusta; *b* 25 Sept 1887

3 Gilbert Neville IRBY later SMYTH (roy licence 16 April 1915, quartered arms of SMYTH with those of IRBY), of Braeside, Bangor, N Wales; *b* 23 Oct 1864, Hon Attaché Dip Serv; *m* 1 Jan 1891 Esmé (*d* 1 May 1946), dau of George Odham Edwards by Emily Frances (*m* 2nd 24 April 1884 Sir J Henry Greville Smyth, Bt, of Ashton Court, and *d* 23 Nov 1914), est dau of Rev Henry Hugh Way, JP, of Alderbourne Manor, Gerrards Cross, Bucks, and *d* 13 Feb 1940, having had issue:

(1) Esmé Frances Sylvia; *b* 24 Feb 1901; *m* 25 Jan 1923 Capt Evan George Charles Cavendish, OBE, son of Brig-Gen Hon William Edwin Cavendish, MVO, and *d* 6 Oct 1959, leaving issue (*see* CHESHAM, B)

(2) A dau; *b* and *d* 12 Oct 1903

1 Alice Fanny Catherine; *m* 3 July 1890 Gordon Frederick Deedes, est son of Rev Canon G F Deedes, Vicar of Heydour, Lincs, and *d* 1953, leaving issue. He *d* 11 Nov 1933

2 Winifred Mary, OBE (1902), BRCS War Medal (1914–18); *m* 15 Oct 1896 Sir Harry Hamilton Johnston, GCMG, KCB, 3rd son of John Brookes Johnston, and *d* 8 July 1933. He *d* 31 July 1927

3 Evelyn Maud Mary; *b* 22 Oct 1875; *d* 2 April 1876

The 8th BARON's cousin,

GERALD HOWARD BOTELER IRBY, **9th Baron Boston**, MBE (1918); served WW I 1915–18 as Lt KRRC, and WW II as Maj RASC; *b* 29 Aug 1897; *m* 1st 14 Aug 1926 (*divorce* 1931) Katherine Gertrude, dau of Capt C M H Edwards, late RASC, and had issue:

1 *Anne Pauline [The Hon Mrs Crews, 86 Wentworth Rd, haiborne, Birmingham B17 9SY]; *b* 1927; *m* 1951 Sydney James Crews, MB, BChir, FRCSE (*d* 1994), and has issue:
(1) *Francis Robert; *b* 1953
(1) *Emma Rosemary Joanna; *b* 1956
(2) *Bridget Harriet; *b* 1963

The **9th Baron** *m* 2nd 8 Feb 1936 Erica Nelly (*d* 1990), dau of T H Hill, and *d* 17 Feb 1978, having by her had further issue:

1 TIMOTHY GEORGE FRANK BOTELER IRBY, **10th and present Baron Boston**

BOSTON OF FAVERSHAM

Arms: Per pale gules and azure a lion passant guardant dimidiated with a ship's hull or, on a chief argent a duck-billed platypus statant proper between two cat's faces sable. **Crest:** A chapeau gules doubled ermine, thereon a boar's head couped azure. **Supporters:** Dexter, a lion sejant erect guardant or; sinister, a kangaroo guardant proper, each resting the exterior foreleg on a fasces erect, the axe facing outwards sable, the whole upon a compartment comprising a grassy mount vert, growing therefrom roses gules and argent, barbed, seeded, slipped and leaved proper. **Motto:** Change with courtesy. **Creation:** B. (LP, UK) 1976

THE BARON BOSTON OF FAVERSHAM, of Faversham, Co Kent (Terence George Boston, QC (1981)) [The Rt Hon The Lord Boston of Faversham QC, House of Lords, London SW1A 0PW]; *b* 21 March 1930; *educ* Woolwich Poly and King's Coll London; F/Lt RAF 1950–52, BBC News sub-ed External Servs 1957–60, sr BBC producer current affrs 1960–64, barrister Inner Temple 1960 and Gray's Inn 1973, MP (Lab) Faversham 1964–70 (fought Wokingham 1955 and 1959), PPS to: Min Public Bldg and Works 1964–66, Min Power 1966–68 and Min Tport 1968–69, Assist Govt Whip 1969–70, UK Del UN Gen Assembly 1976–78, Min State Home Office 1979, Oppn Spokesman Home Office Affrs 1979–84 and Def 1984–86, chm: TVS (TVS Entertainment plc) 1980–90 and Sheppey Gp 1967–, Pncpl Dep Chm Ctees and Chm Select Ctee EC Ho Lds 1992–94, Chmn Ctees 1994–; *m* 1962 *Margaret Joyce, dau of Rowley Henry Jack Head and step-dau of Henry Fermin Winters, of Melbourne, Australia

Lineage: GEORGE THOMAS BOSTON *m* Kate Bellati and had a yr surv s:

TERENCE GEORGE, *cr* a **Baron**

BOSVILLE MACDONALD

Arms: Quarterly, 1st and 4th grand quarters counterquartered, 1st, argent a lion rampant gules, armed and langued azure; 2nd, or a hand in armour fesswise proper, holding a cross-crosslet fitchée gules; 3rd, argent a lymphad, sails furled and oars in action sable, flagged gules; 4th, vert a salmon naiant in fess proper (for MACDONALD); 2nd and 3rd grand quarters, argent five lozenges conjoined in fess gules, in chief three bear's heads erased at the neck sable, muzzled or, a canton ermine (for BOSVILLE). **Crests:** 1 A hand in armour fesswise, holding a cross-crosslet fitchée gules (for MACDONALD), 2 A bull passant argent, armed or, issuing from a hurst of oaks, charged on the shoulder with a rose proper (for BOSVILLE). **Supporters:** Two leopards proper, collared or. **Mottoes:** 1 *Per mare per terras* ('By sea and land'), 2 *Virtus propter se* ('Virtue for its own sake'). **Creation:** Bt. (NS) 14 July 1625 (with precedence of 28 May 1625).

SIR IAN GODFREY BOSVILLE MACDONALD OF SLEAT, 17TH BT, of Sleat, Isle of Skye, Co Inverness, DL Co of Hull and E R Yorks 1997– [Sir Ian Bosville Macdonald of Sleat Bt DL, Thorpe Hall, Rudston, E Yorks YO25 0JE]; *b* 18 July 1947; *s f* 1958 as Premier Bt of NS, also as 25th Chief of Sleat; *educ* Eton and RAC Cirencester (ARICS, FRICS 1986); memb Humberside CC 1981–84 and Cncl BRC 1996–97 (also Tstee, Pres Hull and E R Branch 1996–, Dep Chm N Regnl Cncl 1998–), Chm: CoSIRA Humberside 1988–, Humberside Co Ctee and Rural Devpt Commn 1988–95 and Rural Advsy Gp E R Yorks Cncl 1997–; Pres: Br Food and Farming Humberside 1989–, Humberside Young Farmers 1990–96; Humber and Wolds Rural Community Cncl 1996–; High Sheriff Humberside 1988; *m* 1 Aug 1970 *Juliet Fleury, only dau of Maj-Gen John Ward-Harrison, OBE, MC, of Hazel Bush House, Stockton-on-the-Forest, York, and has:

1 +SOMERLED ALEXANDER; *b* 30 Jan 1976
1 *Deborah Fleury; *b* 14 Jan 1973
2 *Isabel Mary; *b* 7 Jan 1983

Lineage: SOMERLED, KING OF ARGYLL; *m* Raghnild, dau of OLAF, KING OF MAN AND THE ISLES (a realm comprising the IOM, Hebrides and western islands off Scotland that flourished from the late 11th century to 1266), and was *k* Renfrew 1164 campaigning against MALCOLM IV KING OF SCOTS, leaving, with other issue, including an est s (Dougal, of Lorne; ancestor of the MACDOUGALs):

RANALD; Lord of Isla and Kintyre; had:

DONALD; Lord of Isla; *m* a dau of Walter Stewart, 3rd Gt Steward of Scotland (*d* 1241; *see* MORAY, E), and had:

ANGUS *Mor* ('The Elder') MACDONALD, Lord of Isla; became a vassal of the Scottish Crown by the 1266 treaty between MAGNUS IV KING OF NORWAY and ALEXANDER III KING OF SCOTS that ended Manx independence and brought the islands off Scotland's west coast under nominal suzerainty of the Scottish Crown; supported Robert Bruce (2nd cousin of ALEXANDER III and the latter's oral nominee for the succession) in his claim to the Scottish throne 1291–92 and *d c* 1296, leaving with other issue, including an er s (ALEXANDER, LORD OF THE ISLES; accepted the office of Adml of the Western Isles from the English Crown, opposed ROBERT I (THE BRUCE), hence him and and his seven sons expelled from Scotland, after which their whereabouts and very existence becomes uncertain):

ANGUS *Og* ('The Younger') MACDONALD, LORD OF THE ISLES; supported ROBERT I (THE BRUCE), cmdg the highrs at Scots victory over the English of Bannockburn 1314; *m* Agnes, dau of Guy O'Cathan, of Ulster, and *d* 1330, leaving:

IAIN MACDONALD, LORD OF THE ISLES; assumed the style of an independent sovereign but resumed his allegiance to ROBERT II KING OF SCOTS 1369; *m* 1st Amie, dau of Roderick MacRuari of Garmoran, and had three sons (Iain, *dvp*; Ranald, *d* Castle Tioram 1386, leaving, with other issue, Allan, ancestor of the MACDONALDs of Clanranald, and Donald, ancestor of the MACDONELLs of Glengarry; Godfrey; Lord of Uist); *m* 2nd MARGARET, dau of ROBERT II, and *d* Ardtornish Castle 1387, having had by her, with five yr sons (Ian *Mor* (*see* ANTRIM, E); Hugh, *dvp*; Alisdair *Carrach* ('Mangy'), ancestor of the MACDONALDs of Keppoch; Hugh, Thane of Glentilt; Marcus, ancestor of the MACDONALDs of Cnocanduith):

DONALD MACDONALD, LORD OF THE ISLES (so designated as successor by his f in preference to his er half-bros under the Celtic system called tanistry) and self-styled (9th) EARL OF ROSS in right of his w; either in support of his claim to the Earldom or as a sovereign ruler in alliance with England or France he invaded the Scottish mainland with an army made up of men of the Isles and Ross but was checked at Harlaw 24 July 1411 in a pyrrhic victory by the Regent of Scotland (JAMES I being a prisoner of the English 1406–24), whose side lost more men and who despite his 'victory' failed to prevent the MACDONALDs styling themselves Earls of Ross for at least two generations as well as promulgating charters from Dingwall Castle, the chief place of the territory over which the Earls of Ross were supposed to hold sway, though in the immediate aftermath of the Battle of Harlaw the Regent captured the Castle; *m* Mary (*d* probably *c* 1435), dau of Sir Walter Leslie (*see* ROTHES, E) by Eupheme, Countess of Ross (of the *c* Dec 1225 *cr*) in her own right, and *d* 1423, having had, with other issue:

ALEXANDER MACDONALD, 10th EARL OF ROSS and LORD OF THE ISLES, as both of which apparently recognised by JAMES I on latter's release by English 1424; nevertheless ordered by JAMES to attend a meeting with other Highland chiefs at Inverness 1427 and placed under virtual house arrest as a permanent 'guest' of JAMES's at latter's court; later fled or was let go, gathered an army of men of the Isles and Ross and put Inverness and its environs to fire and the sword, but was defeated by JAMES at Lochaber 23 June 1429; after pleading for mercy in penitential garb he was confined for a while in Tantallon Castle; recognised again as EARL OF ROSS by Jan 1435/6; Justiciar North of Forth 1438; *m* (as his 1st(?) of two ws?) Elizabeth Halyburton, probably of Dirletoun (*d* in or after Dec 1444), and *d* 8 May 1449, leaving:

1 JOHN MACDONALD, 11th and last EARL OF ROSS and (1st and last) LORD OF THE ISLES; *b* probably 1435; Warden Marches 1449–60, negotiated treaty with England 1461 as if an independent sovereign and launched an attack in alliance with EDWARD IV on the islands of Arran and Bute and, on the Scottish mainland, Inverness and Nairn, hence his life and lands forfeited following a summons (which he ignored) to appear before the Scottish Parliament 1 Dec 1475; he submitted in person to Parl 10 July 1476, when *cr* a Ld of Parl (S) (rather than a prescriptive Chief, as hitherto) as LORD OF THE ISLES, while the Earldom was appropriated by the Crown, with intended (though not in the event invariable) use for a s of the King (whereas the title Lord of the Isles has remained an exclusively royal subsidiary title, being borne by Princes of Wales to this day); *m* by 1464 Elizabeth Livingston, dau of 1st Lord Livingston, who apparently had no issue by him, and *d c* 1455, leaving illegitimate issue:

(1) John; *dsp* & *vp*

(2 Angus; styled 'Master of the Isles and Lord of Trotternish'; *m* Mary, dau of 1st Earl of Argyll (*see* ARGYLL, D), and was assassinated Inverness 1490, leaving:

1a Donald *Dubh* ('The Dark'); claimed 1545 title of Earl of Ross and Lord of the Isles, also power to make treaties, *e.g.*, with England; *d* Drogheda, Ireland, leaving:

1b A s, of whom no more is heard

1 Celestine, of Lochalsh; served heir of her bro 1515; *m* —, and had:

(1) Margaret; *m* Alisdair Macdonnell, 4th of Glengarry, and had:

1a Aeneas, 5th of Glengarry; *m* Janet, only dau of Hector *Mor* Maclean of Dowart (*see* MACLEAN, Bt, of Dowart), and had:

1b Donald, 6th of Glengarry; *m* his distant cousin Margaret, dau of Alexander Macdonald, Capt of Clanranald, and *d* 1630, leaving:

1c Alexander, 7th of Glengarry; *m* Jean, dau of Allan Cameron of Lochiel, and had:

1d AENEAS MACDONNELL, 8th of Glengarry, 1st and last LORD MACDONNELL AND ARRASS (S), so *cr* 20 Dec 1660, when also restored to Chiefship of Name and Arms of Macdonnell; royalist Civil War, captured in Ireland with other royalist offrs 1647, forfeited by OLIVER CROMWELL 1651; *m* 1646 his distant cousin Margaret, est dau of **Sir Donald Macdonald, 8th of Sleat, 1st Bt**, and *dspms* 6 Dec 1680, when the Ldship of Parl expired

2c Donald, of Scothouse; had:

1d Reginald, of Scothouse; had:

1e Aeneas, 9th of Glengarry

The 10th EARL had illegitimately by a dau of Gilpatrick Roy, s of the 'Green Abbot':

2 *Uisdean* (Hugh), 1st of Sleat in the Island of Skye, Co Inverness, of which, with the lands of Skirhough in S Uist and Benbecula in N Uist, had 28 June 1469 a charter (to him and his heirs male lawfully or unlawfully begotten or to be begotten; confirmation by the Crown 10 Nov 1495) from his half-bro the 11th EARL; *m* Fynvola, dau of MacIan of Ardnamurchan, and *d* 1498, leaving by her a s (John, 2nd of Sleat, *dsp* 1502) and by the dau of Gun, Cruineir Ghall (or Crowner of Caithness):

(1) Donald *Gallach* ('Foreigner', because educated in Caithness), 3rd of Sleat; *m* a dau of John of Islay and The Glens, and was *k* 1506 by his half-bro Archibald, leaving:

1a Donald *Gruamach* ('The Gloomy'), 4th of Sleat; besieged Eilean Donan Castle in support of his claim to the Lordship of the Isles 1539; *m* 1st his distant cousin Catherine Macdonald of Clanranald; *m* 2nd Margaret Macleod of Lewis and *d* 1539, having been shot from the battlements of Eilean Donan Castle, leaving by his 1st w:

1b Donald *Gorm* ('Blue-eyed'), 5th of Sleat; *m* Mary, dau of Roderick Macleod, of the MACLEODs of Harris, and *d* (probably in England) soon after 1546, having had, with a yr s:

1c Donald *Gormeson* (*i.e.*, s of his f, known as 'Blue'), 6th of Sleat; *m* Mary, dau of Hector *Mor* Maclean of Dowart (*see* MACLEAN, Bt, of Dowart), and *d* 1573, having had:

1d Donald *Gorm Mor* ('Big Blue-eyed'), 7th of Sleat; *m* 1st Margaret, dau of Norman Macleod of Harris; *m* 2nd Mary, sis of 1st Lord Mackenzie of Kintail (*see* CROMARTIE, E), and *dsp* Dec 1616

2d Archibald, called 'The Clerk'; *m* Margaret/Mary, dau of Angus Macdonald of Duniveg and The Glens, and had:

1e **Sir Donald Macdonald, 8th of Sleat, 1st Bt** (NS), so *cr* 14 July 1625, with remainder to his heirs male whatsoever and with precedence over the btcies of Douglas of Glenbervie, Strachan and Livingstone, the three creations otherwise next above him; royalist Civil War; *m* Janet, sis of 1st Earl of Seaforth (*see* CROMARTIE, E), and had, with four daus (*dsp*):

1f JAMES (Sir), 2nd Bt

2f Donald; ancestor of the MACDONALDs of Castleton (*see* below against **4th Bt**)

The 1st Bt *d* Oct 1643; his er s,

Sir James Macdonald, 9th of Sleat, 2nd Bt; joined royalists under Marquess of Montrose (*see* MONTROSE, D) 1645; sent men to help CHARLES II in invading England 1651; *m* 1st (contract 23 Feb 1633) his cousin Margaret, only dau of Sir Roderick Mackenzie of Castle Leod and Tarbat (*see* CROMARTIE, E), and had:

1 DONALD (Sir), 3rd Bt

2 Roderick; had issue

3 Hugh, of Glenmore

4 Somerled, of Sortie

1 Katherine; *m* as his 2nd w Sir Norman Macleod of Bernera, 3rd s of Sir Roderick Macleod of Macleod, 15th Chief

2 Florence; *m* Ian *Breac* ('The Spotted', probably from smallpox) Macleod, 18th Chief

Sir James *m* 2nd Mary, est dau of Ian *Mor* Macleod, 16th Chief (*see* CROMARTIE, E), and *d* 8 Dec 1678, having by her had:

5 John, of Backnay or Balconie

His est s,

Sir Donald Macdonald, 10th of Sleat, 3rd Bt; had the name and representation of the MACDONALDs restored 1660, Clan Donald having been treated as Chiefless (and its major branches treated as distinct tribes and families) since the forfeiture of the 11th EARL; the family lands (having been in Crown possession since the 11th EARL's forfeiture) were apparently erected into a territorial Barony of Macdonald by 1689; *m* 24 July 1662 Lady Mary Douglas, yr dau of 8th Earl of Morton (*qv*), and *d* 5 Feb 1695, having had:

1 Sir Donald Macdonald, 11th of Sleat, 4th Bt; called 'Sir Donald of the Wars'; led his f's clan at Battle of Killecrankie (presumably on behalf of the Jacobites) 1689, Jacobite 1715 and allegedly attainted, though no forfeiture recorded; *m* his cousin Mary, dau of Donald Macdonald of Castleton, and *d* 1718, leaving:

(1) Sir Donald Macdonald, 12th of Sleat, 5th Bt; *b c* 1697; *educ* Ch Ch Oxford; *d* unm 1720

(1) Mary; *m* 1712 John MacDougall of Dunoltie and *d* 1779

(2) Margaret; *m* Capt John McQueen and had issue

(3) Isabella; *m* Alexander Munro of Auchenbowie and had issue

(4) Janet; *m* Norman Macleod, 22nd Chief of Macleod, and had issue

2 JAMES (Sir), 6th Bt

3 William; ancestor of the MACDONALDs of Vallay

1 Isabella; *m* Sir Alexander Bannerman, 2nd Bt (*qv*)

2 Barbara; *m* Col Macdonald of Keppoch

The 5th Bt's unc,

Sir James Macdonald, 13th of Sleat, 6th Bt; *m* 1st Janet, dau of Alexander Macleod of Talisker and Greshornish, and had:

1 ALEXANDER (Sir), 7th Bt

1 Margaret; *m c* 1738 Sir Robert Douglas, 6th Bt, of Glenbervie, author: Peerage of Scotland (*d* 24 April 1770), and had issue

2 Isabel; *d* unm

3 Janet; *m* Sir Alexander Mackenzie, 5th Bt, of Coul (*qv*), and had issue

Sir James *m* 2nd his cousin Margaret, dau of John Macdonald of Castleton, and *d* 1723, having by her had:

2 John; *d* young

His est s,

Sir Alexander Macdonald, 14th of Sleat, 7th Bt; *b* 1711; supported Govt at time of 1745 Uprising; *m* 1st 5 April 1733 Anne (*d* 27 Nov 1735), dau of David Erskine of Dun, Forfar, and widow of James, Lord Ogilvy (*see* AIRLIE, E), and had a s (Donald, *b* 1734, *d* young); *m* 2nd 24 April 1739 Margaret (*d* 30 March 1799), dau of 9th Earl of Eglinto(u)n (*see* EGLINTON and WINTON, E), and *d* 23 Nov 1746, having by her had:

2 **Sir James Macdonald, 8th Bt**; *b c* 1742; *educ* Ch Ch Oxford; scholar and mathematician; *d* unm Rome 26 July 1766

3 **Sir Alexander Macdonald, 9th Bt**, and 1st BARON MACDONALD (*qv*) OF SLATE [*sic*], Co Antrim (I), so *cr* 17 July 1776, DL (Inverness-shire); raised Macdonald Highrs 1778 and another regt in the Highlands and the Islands for the Govt 1794–95; Brig-Gen Roy Co Archers; *m* 3 May 1768 Elizabeth Diana, est dau and in her issue coheir of Godfrey Bosville, of Gunthwaite, and had, with five other sons and three daus:

(1) **Sir Alexander Wentworth Macdonald, 10th Bt**, and 2nd BARON MACDONALD OF SLATE; *d* unm 19 June 1824

(2) Sir GODFREY MACDONALD later BOSVILLE (roy licence 11 April 1814 after inheriting 16 Dec 1813 his unc William Bosville's Thorpe and

Gunthwaite estates, Yorks, as life tenant, an entail of 7 Feb 1807 (date of the original will) directing that they should pass next to Godfrey's s Alexander William Robert (later *de jure* 12th Bt); by a codicil of 20 Jan 1812 William Bosville ordered that should Alexander prove his legitimacy and ever become entitled to the Scottish estates the Yorkshire property was to pass to the next surv bro Godfrey William Wentworth, later 4th Lord Macdonald of Slate) later still BOSVILLE MACDONALD (roy licence 20 July 1824 on inheriting the Barony), **11th Bt**, and 3rd BARON MACDONALD OF SLATE; according to some sources went through a form of marriage 1799 in Scotland but certainly *m* lawfully 29 Dec 1803 in the Parish of St Gregory, Norwich, Louisa Maria La Coast/Laccoast, illegitimate dau of THE DUKE OF GLOUCESTER (yr bro of GEORGE III) by Lady Almeria Carpenter (dau of 1st Earl of Tyrconnel of the 1761 *cr*; *see* 1853 edn), and *d* 13 Oct 1832, having had three children *b* before the (English) marriage and 10 *b* after it (*see* MACDONALD, B); as their f was of Scottish domicile the est three children were legimated under Scottish law by their parents' subsequent (English) marriage but not under the law of England or Ireland; the two sons thus legitimated could therefore inherit the NS btcy (though this was not the view then); accordingly the Bosville estates in Yorkshire were settled by private Act of Parl 22 July 1847 on the er s *b* before the English marriage, who thus became known as 'Bosville of Thorpe and Gunthwaite', while the est s *b* after the English marriage got the Scottish property (probably to ensure that it went with the peerage, which despite its nomenclature 'Macdonald of Slate' was an Irish creation hence governed by Irish law, so that only sons *b* after their parents' English marriage were in remainder); the three er children were:

1a ALEXANDER WILLIAM ROBERT MACDONALD later BOSVILLE (roy licence 26 Dec 1832), *de jure* 12th Bt (believed himself illegimate hence did not assume btcy); *b* 12 Dec 1800; *m* 10 July 1823 Matilda Eliza Moffat (*d* July 1859), dau of John Bayard, of an originally French Huguenot family, and *d* 22 Sept 1847, leaving:

1b GODFREY WENTWORTH BAYARD BOSVILLE, de jure 13th Bt (also did not assume btcy), of Thorpe and Gunthwaite; *b* 6 Jan 1826; *m* 5 July 1864 his sister's sister-in-law Hon Harriet Cassandra Willoughby (*d* 28 Sept 1903), sis of 8th Baron Middleton (*qv*) of Middleton, and *d* 11 Oct 1865, leaving:

1c Sir ALEXANDER WENTWORTH MACDONALD BOSVILLE later BOSVILLE MACDONALD OF THE ISLES (Lord Lyon decree 30 June 1910), **14th Bt**, which title he assumed following a Court of Session decree of 4 June 1910 declaring his male-line gf legitimate in Scottish law, also 22nd Chief of Sleat, JP, DL (E R Yorks); *b* 26 Sept 1865; E R Yorks: High Sheriff 1901, V-Chm CC 1918–31, Chm QS 1920–31; *m* 20 Oct 1886 Alice Edith (*d* 15 July 1935), dau of John Middleton, of Kinfauns Castle, Perthshire, and had:

1d GODFREY MIDDLETON (Sir), 15th Bt

1d Celia Violet, CBE (1937, OBE 1919); *b* 28 Jan 1889; Chm Dominions Fellowship Tst 1948–61, Hon MA Oxon 1960

1b Julia Louisa; *m* 3 Aug 1843 8th Baron Middleton (*qv*) of Middleton and *d* 11 Oct 1901, leaving issue

2a William; *d* young

1a Louisa; *b* 16 Sept 1802; *m* 4 June 1826 5th Earl of Hopetoun and *d* 1 Sept 1854, leaving issue (*see* LINLITHGOW, M)

4 Sir ARCHIBALD MACDONALD, 1st Bt, so *cr* 27 Nov 1813, of East Sheen; barrister, Slr-Gen 1784, Attorney-Gen 1788, Ch Baron Exchequer 1793; *m* 27 Nov 1777 Lady Louisa Leveson-Gower (*d* 29 Jan 1827), est dau of 1st Marquess of Stafford (*see* SUTHERLAND, D), and *d* 18 May 1826, leaving:

(1) Sir JAMES MACDONALD, 2nd Bt; *b* 14 Feb 1784; MP Hants, Clerk Privy Seal; *m* 1st 5 Sept 1805 Elizabeth (*dsp*), dau of John Sparrow, of Bishton, Staffs; *m* 2nd 10 Aug 1819 Lady Sophia Keppel (*d* 29 Sept 1824), est dau of 4th Earl of Albemarle (*qv*), and by her had:

1a Sir ARCHIBALD KEPPEL MACDONALD, 3rd Bt, JP, DL (Hants), JP (Surrey); *b* 15 Oct 1820; Capt Scots Fus Gds, Equerry to DUKE OF SUSSEX, High Sheriff Hants 1865; *m* 1st 1 May 1849 Lady Margaret Sophia Coke (*dsp* 4 Nov 1868), dau of 1st Earl of Leicester (*qv*); *m* 2nd 25 Nov 1869 Catherine Mary (*d* 27 Nov 1894), est dau of John Coulthurst, of Gargrave Hall, Yorks, and widow of Hon Thomas Edward Stonor (*see* CAMOYS, B), and *d* 28 March 1901, having by her had:

1b Sir ARCHIBALD JOHN MACDONALD, 4th and last Bt, JP (Hants); *b* 2 Feb 1871; *m* 10 Jan 1900 Constance Mary, yr dau of Rev Henry Martyn Burgess, of Bramshott, Hants, and *dsp* 11 Oct 1919, when the btcy expired

1b Mary Catherine; *b* 20 Aug 1874; *m* 11 May 1901 Leonard Labouchere Hillyer (*d* 1905)

2a Granville Southwell; *b* 1821; *d* 1831

(1) (cont.) Sir JAMES *m* 3rd 20 April 1826 Anne Charlotte (*dsp* 21 Sept 1886 aged 83), dau of Rev J Savile Ogle, of Kirkley Hall, Northumberland, and *d* 29 June 1832

(1) Louisa; *d* 15 April 1862

(2) Caroline Diana; *m* Rev Thomas Randolph, Preb St Paul's, Chaplain to HM QUEEN VICTORIA, Rector Hadham, Herts, s of Rt Rev Dr John Randolph, Bp London, and *d* 13 Dec 1867

The 15th Bt *d* 26 March 1933; his s,

Sir Godfrey Middleton Bosville Macdonald of the Isles, 15th Bt, MBE (1916), JP (E R Yorks); *b* 25 Sept 1887; *educ* Eton and Magdalen Coll Oxford; i/c BRCS Stores Tport Dept WW I; Clerk Peace and E R Yorks CC 1932–39; *m* 31 Jan 1917 Hon Rachel Audrey Campbell, yr dau of 1st Baron Colgrain (*qv*), and had:

1 ALEXANDER SOMERLED ANGUS (Sir), 16th Bt

2 +Nigel Donald Peter BOSVILLE MACDONALD later CHAMBERLAYNE-MACDONALD (deed poll 1958), CVO (1997, LVO 1960), OBE (1981), DL (Hants 1975) [Maj Nigel Chamberlayne-Macdonald CVO OBE DL, Cranbury Park, Winchester, Hants; 17 William Mews, Lowndes Sq, London SW1; Glaschoille House, Knoydart, Mallaig, Inverness-shire]; *b* 10 June 1927; *educ* Radley; late Maj Scots Gds, Equerry to HRH 1st DUKE OF GLOUCESTER 1954–55 and 1958–60, Assist Private Sec 1958–60, Extra Equerry 1964–74, Gentleman Usher to HM THE QUEEN 1979–97, Extra Gentleman Usher 1997–, memb Roy Co Archers, High Sheriff Hants 1974, V-Chm Nat Assoc Boys' Clubs 1969–90, Chm Hants and IoW Assoc Boys' Clubs 1967–83, Pres Coaching Club 1982–90, OStJ; *m* 15 April 1958 *Penelope Mary Alexandra, only child of Tankerville Chamberlayne, of Cranbury Park, and has had:

(1) +Alexander Nigel Bosville; *b* 2 March 1959; *m* 1991 *Shirley Irene, dau of George Cecil Pridmore, of Swayfield, Lincs

(2) +Thomas Somerled; *b* 24 Nov 1969

(1) *Diana Mary; *b* 12 Sept 1961; *m* 1982 *16th Earl of Lindsay (*qv*)

(2) Frances Penelope; *b* 8 March 1965; *d* 1985

1 *Jean Alice [Mrs Basil Ringrose, Royal Oak, Morby, nr Boston, Lincs]; *b* 30 July 1919; *m* 22 Nov 1952 *Lt-Col Basil John Ringrose, DSO, TD, s of Ernest Ringrose, JP, MD, of Balderton, Newark, Notts

2 *Angela Daphne Rachel [Mrs Michael Fell, 332 Cherry Lane, Wynnewood, PA 19096, USA]; *b* 4 Feb 1923; *m* 4 July 1957 *(James) Michael Gardner Fell, PhD, only s of Col James Pemberton Fell, OBE, RCE, of Lismore, Argyllshire, and Vancouver, and has:

(1) *Peter; *b* 5 Dec 1960

(1) *Rachel Mary; *b* 23 April 1959

The 15th Bt *d* 3 Aug 1951; his er s,

Sir (Alexander) Somerled Angus Bosville Macdonald of Sleat, 16th Bt, MC (1943), JP (Yorks); *b* 6 Nov 1917; *educ* Eton and Magdalen Coll Oxford (BA 1939); Capt 5th Bn E Yorks Regt (TA) WW II 1939–43 (wounded, ret ill-health 1944), ACA 1947, memb Roy Co Archers; *m* 6 June 1946 *Mary Elizabeth [Mary Lady Bosville Macdonald of Sleat, West Croft Farm, Rudston, E Yorks], est dau of Lt-Col Ralph Crawley-Boevey Gibbs (*see* ALDENHAM and HUNSDON OF HUNSDON, B), and *d* 21 Oct 1958, leaving:

1 Sir IAN GODFREY BOSVILLE MACDONALD OF SLEAT, **17th and present Bt**

2 +James Alexander [James Macdonald Esq, Rose Manor, Guilsborough, Northants NN6 8QB]; *b* 11 April 1949; *educ* Ardingly; *m* 21 Oct 1995 *Mary Lucinda, dau of Col Lionel Castletown Connolly, and has:

(1) +Robert James Bosville; *b* 7 July 1996

1 *Janet Elizabeth [Mrs John Trapp, Swann House, Swaffham Bulbeck, Cambs CB5 0NE]; *b* 27 May 1950; *m* 1980 *John Joseph Trapp, er s of R E Trapp and Mrs L Reynolds, and has:

(1) *Alexander John Nicolai; *b* 1984

2 *Annabel Celia Dorothy [Mrs Clive Evans,West Croft Farm, Rudston, E Yorks]; *b* 14 Sept 1953; *m* 1987 *Clive Duncan Evans, s of M R Evans, of Swansea, and has:

(1) *Benedict Ian; *b* 1989

(1) *Caitlin Mary; *b* 1993

BOUGHEY

Arms: Quarterly, 1st and 4th, sa. a cross wavy erm. between four plates, each charged with an arrow in bend of the first (for FLETCHER); 2nd and 3rd, arg. three buck's heads, erased and affrontée erm. (for BOUGHEY). **Crests:** 1 A plate charged with a pheon per pale erm. and sa. (for FLETCHER), 2 Out of an eastern crown gold, the points alternate or and arg., a buck's head erm. attired and collared of the first (for BOUGHEY). **Motto:** *Nec quærere, nec spernere honorem* ('Neither seeking nor despising distinction'). **Creation:** Bt. (GB) 24 Aug 1798.

SIR JOHN GEORGE FLETCHER BOUGHEY, 11TH BT, of Newcastle, Co Stafford [Sir John Boughey Bt, Bratton House, Westbury, Wilts BA13 4RN]; *b* 12 Aug 1959; *s* f 1978; *educ* Eton and U of Zimbabwe (MB, ChB 1984); LRCPE, LRCSE, LRCPS Glasgow 1990, MRCPI 1994; medical practitioner

Lineage: THOMAS FLETCHER, of Newcastle-under-Lyme; *b* 23 Jan 1717; *m* Elizabeth, dau and coheir of John Fenton (*d* Oct 1760), and *d* 4 Nov 1783, leaving issue:

Sir Thomas Fletcher, 1st Bt (GB), so *cr* 24 Aug 1798, of Betley Court, Staffs, DL and JP, High Sheriff 1783 and 1789; *b* 25 Nov 1747; *m* 8 May 1781 his cousin Anne (*d* 22 Oct 1821), dau and heiress of John Fenton, of Newcastle (*d* March

1782), by Anastasia, dau of John Cradock, of Betley, Staffs, and gs of Thomas Fenton, Recorder Newcastle, and *d* 14 July 1812, having had, with other issue:

Sir JOHN FENTON later BOUGHEY (taken by sign manual 16 May 1805 on inheriting the estates of his cousin George Boughey, of Audley, Staffs (barrister Inner Temple; *d* 15 Feb 1788)), **2nd Bt**; *b* 1 May 1784; MP Staffs1820–23; *m* 9 Feb 1808 Henrietta Dorothy (*d* 22 Jan 1849), est dau of Sir John Chetwode, of Oakley, Staffs, and had, with other issue:

1 THOMAS FLETCHER FENTON (Sir), **3rd Bt**

2 John Fenton Fletcher (Rev), Rector Forton, Staffs; *b* 6 June 1811; *d* 21 June 1853

3 George Fenton Fletcher, Lt-Col 59th Regt; *b* 9 Sept 1813; *m* 16 Dec 1842 Matilda Elwin (*d* 29 Feb 1904), dau of Hon George Weatherill Ottley, MLC Antigua, and *d* 20 July 1855, leaving issue:

(1) George Fletcher Ottley, CSI, Col RE, served Bhutan Expdn 1865–66 and Afghan War 1878–80; *b* 23 Jan 1844; *m* 2 April 1872 Harriet Rose Amy (*d* 23 Feb 1925), dau of Lt-Col William Stuart Menteth (*see* STUART-MENTETH, Bt), and *d* 17 Jan 1918, leaving issue:

1a GEORGE MENTETH (Sir), **9th Bt**

1a Amy Matilda; *m* 27 July 1892 William Arthur Briscoe, of Longstowe Hall, Cambs, and *d* 20 Jan 1950, leaving issue. He *d* 3 Feb 1934

2a Elizabeth Mabws; *m* 1 Oct 1898 Lt-Col Duncan Darroch, DL, Argyll and Sutherland Highrs, of Gourock, and *d* 18 May 1958, leaving issue. He *d* 22 May 1923

3a Gertrude Mary (Minta); *m* 1 June 1913 Alan Kenyon Smith, ICS, and *d* 24 July 1958, leaving issue. He *d* 3 Nov 1949

(2) John, Maj-Gen Wiltshire Regt; *b* 20 Jan 1845; *m* 21 Dec 1872 Constance Susan (*d* 4 Dec 1916), dau of John Penny, and *d* 20 Feb 1932, leaving issue:

1a Percy Fletcher (Rev), Vicar Soham with Barway, RD Fordham, non-residentiary Canon Ely; *b* 23 March 1882; *educ* Pembroke Coll Cambridge (MA); *m* 12 July 1911 Elsie le Strange (*d* 18 Feb 1964), 2nd dau of Lt-Col William Herring, JP, 27th Inniskillings, of Narborough House, W Norfolk, and *d* 26 Oct 1961, having had issue:

1b John William Fletcher (Rev Canon), Vicar Brackley with Halse, CF 1941–47, Hon CF 1947, RD Brackley, non-residentiary Canon Peterborough 1965; *b* 6 June 1912; *educ* Haileybury and Pembroke Coll Cambridge (BA 1934, MA 1938); *m* 25 April 1940 *Esme Eleanor, 3rd dau of Henry Eliot Howard, JP, of Clareland, Stourport-on-Severn, and *dsp* 6 Jan 1971

2b Thomas Fletcher; *b* 25 May 1914; *d* 28 Nov 1951

1b Elizabeth Margaret; *m* 26 March 1940 Maj Richard Quintin Gurney, City of London Yeo (Roughriders), of Bawdeswell Hall, Dereham, Norfolk, est son of Maj Quintin Edward Gurney, of Keswick Hall and Bawdeswell Hall, Norfolk, and had issue:

1c *David Quintin [David Gurney Esq, Hambleton Old Hall, Oakham, Rutland]; *b* 6 Feb 1941; *educ* Harrow, Trin Coll Cambridge and Grenoble U; *m* 1965 *Jacqueline McLeod, yr dau of John Rawle, of Estancia El Fortin, 9 Neochea, Argentina, and has issue:

1d *Elisabeth Anne; *b* 10 June 1966; *m* 1991 *Michael Francis Morley-Fletcher (*see* WINDLESHAM, B)

1c *Mary Elisabeth; *b* 5 Sept 1945; *m* 23 March 1968 *Stephen Dickenson, son of Rev Arthur Dickinson, of St Christopher, Caistor St Edmunds, Norfolk

2c *Sarah Carolyn; *b* 22 Nov 1949

3c *Nicola Ruth; *b* 25 June 1953

2b Mary Ursula, Jr Cdr ATS WW II; *das* unm 20 Jan 1945

1a Ethel Constance; *d* unm 15 June 1973 aged 96

(3) Rev Anchitel Harry Fletcher; *b* 14 Aug 1849; *educ* Trin Coll Cambridge (MA, Fell 1874); Vicar St Mary the Great Cambridge 1909–13, RD Cambridge 1912–16; *m* 9 Aug 1883 Katharine Annie (*d* 24 Aug 1935), dau of I S Lovell, of Thornby, Rugby, and *d* 22 Sept 1936, having had issue:

1a Charles Lovell Fletcher, headmaster Sherborne 1927–33, assist master Marlborough, Lt-Col OTC, Lt Gren Gds; *b* 10 May 1887; *educ* Trin Coll Cambridge (MA); *d* 16 Oct 1934

2a Anchitel Edward Fletcher, Lt Rifle Brigade; *b* 6 Nov 1891; lost at sea by enemy action 10 Oct 1918

1a Constance Evelyn Mary; *m* 5 Nov 1913 Arthur Pickett Scott, son of R P Scott, LLD, and *d* 12 Nov 1962. He *d* 3 June 1933

2a Katharine Clare (Beda); *m* 1st 8 April 1915 Robert Mervyn Powys Druce (*d* 28 Oct 1949), son of Robert Alexander Druce, of Hove, Sussex; *m* 2nd 8 Aug 1950 Lionel John Treleaven Polgreen, MC (*d* 1980), s of Henry Polgreen, and *d* 1990, leaving by her 1st husb:

1b *Pamela Matilda [Mrs Richard Stratton, Seagrams, Kingston Deverill, Warminster, Wilts BA12 7HD]; *b* 1918; *m* 1943 *Richard Stratton and has issue:

1c *David, OBE [David Stratton Esq, OBE, Manor Farm, Kingston Deverill, Warminster, Wilts BA12 7HB]; *b* 1944; *m* 1976 *Frances Alice, dau of Harry Hardwill, of Hurst Farm, Blackdown, Beaminster, Dorset, and has issue:

1d *Richard William; *b* 1977

2d *Henry Robert; *b* 1978

1d *Alice Louise; *b* 1980

2c *Peter William [Peter Stratton Esq, 37 Westbourne Park Rd, London W2 5QD]; *b* 1947; *m* 1973 *Caroline Claire, dau of George Michael Sparkes, of Paddock Wood, E Knoyle, Salisbury, Wilts, and has issue:

1d *Edward Alexander Boughey; *b* 1981

2d *George William Boughey; *b* 1984

3d *Jack Richard Michael; *b* 1988

1d *Emily Caroline McKechnie; *b* 1979

1c *Rosemary [Mrs Anthony Boardman, Nenstone House, Westbury, Brackley, Northants NN13 5JS]; *b* 1949; *m* 1976 *Anthony John Livesey Boardman, and has issue:

1d *Andrew Nicholas Livesey; *b* 1977

2d *Tom Christopher William; *b* 1979

3d *Simon David Richard; *b* 1982

2c *Hilary [Miss Hilary Stratton, Hillview Cottage, Wigginton, OX15 4JX]; *b* 1951

2b Evelyn Patricia; *b* 1922; *m* 1st 1942 (*divorce* 1949) Lt Richard D Deuchar, RNVR; *m* 2nd 1960 (*divorce* 1974) Philip Wayre and *d* 1995, leaving by 1st husb:

1c *Carol [Mrs William Alexander, The Old School House, Frampton-on-Severn, Glos]; *b* 1943; *m* 1967 *William Alexander, and has issue:

1d *Juliet Patricia; *b* 1968; *m* 1993 *Paul Atherton

2d *Fiona Catherine; *b* 1969

2c *Rosalind [Mrs Michael Banks, Manor Farm, Waresley, Beds]; *b* 1945; *m* 1972 *Michael Banks and has issue:

1d *Melanie Catherine; *b* 1974

2d *Nicola Claire; *b* 1977

3c *Juliet Lovell [Mrs Adrian Taunton, The Old Barn House, Kelling, Norfolk NR25 7EF]; *b* 1948; *m* 1969 *Adrian John Taunton and has:

1d *Dominic John; *b* 1976

1d *Harriet Lovell Rose; *b* 1979

4 William Fenton Fletcher, MA, barrister, Recorder Shrewsbury 1867–79, stipendiary magistrate S Staffs 1879–85; *b* 9 Nov 1814; *m* 30 April 1874 Caroline (*d* 22 March 1913), dau of Rev Benjamin Lucas Cubitt, Rector Catfield, and *d* 14 July 1890, leaving issue:

(1) William Charles Fletcher; *b* 5 Nov 1874; *d* 7 Feb 1928

(2) Edward Harry Fletcher, Cdr RN; *b* 25 Aug 1878; *m* 22 March 1902 Ethel Georgina Emily (*d* 21 Jan 1959), only dau of Capt George Alexander Harrison, Cameron Highrs, by Emily Jane, dau of Edward Henry Cradock Monckton, of Fineshade Abbey (*see* GALWAY, V), and *d* 20 Dec 1953, leaving issue:

1a (Edward) Peter Fletcher, OBE (1945), Lt-Col Gen List WW II; *b* 27 Nov 1911; *educ* ISC; *m* 1st 11 March 1945 (*divorce* 1949) Halina Anna, dau of Count Stanislaw Ambrozewicz, of Lodz, Poland; *m* 2nd 12 May 1949 Nina Gladys (*d* 8 May 1966), formerly w of Alexander Richard Glen and twin dau of Brinsley Nixon, of Seafield, Westward Ho!; *m* 3rd 7 Sept 1973 Emmeline Amy, widow of Lt-Col Francis David Eardley Fremantle, TD, DL, JP, of Brayford Ho, Herts (*see* COTTESLOE, B), and 2nd dau of Brig-Gen Vigant William de Falbe, CMG, DSO, DL, JP, of Whittingdon Ho, nr Lichfield, Staffs

1a Patience; *b* 9 March 1908; *m* 3 April 1943 Denys Vincent Douglas Gill, son of Rev Arthur John Gill, and had issue

(3) Richard Fletcher; *b* 30 March, *d* 14 Sept 1880

(4) John Fletcher, Roy W Surrey Regt; *b* 11 June 1882 (twin); *ka* 4 Oct 1917

(5) George Fletcher, cofndr and Hon Treas Queen Victoria Hosp Hanwell; *b* 11 June 1882 (twin); *d* unm 9 June 1962

(6) Alfred Fletcher BOUGHEY later COPLESTONE-BOUGHEY (added by deed poll 24 May 1910); *b* 29 June 1883; Cdr RN; *m* 11 May 1910 Mary Cliffe (*d* 24 April 1955), dau of Frederick Coplestone, CBE, JP, of Barrel Well Ho, Chester, and was *ka* Battle of Jutland 31 May 1916, leaving issue:

1a +John Fenton [His Honour John Coplestone-Boughey, 82 Oakley St, London SW3]; *b* 5 Feb 1912; *educ* Shrewsbury and BNC Oxford (BA 1934); barrister Inner Temple 1935, Co Court then Circuit Judge 1969–85, chm cncl Queen's Coll London 1976–, special tstee St George's Hosp 1974–; *m* 16 Dec 1944 *Gillian Beatrice, BA Oxon (1934), est dau of Hugh Alfred Counsell, of Appleby, Westmoreland, and has issue:

1b +William Fenton [William Coplestone-Boughey Esq, Ebworthy, Manaton, Devon TQ13 9UL]; *b* 19 April 1947; *educ* Winchester, BNC Oxford (MA) and King's Coll London (LLM); *m* 1978 *Clare Louise, only dau of Lester B Wilson, and has issue:

1c +Robert Fenton; *b* 1984

1c *Katharine Elizabeth; *b* 1987

1b *Mary [Miss Mary Coplestone-Boughey, 82 Oakley St, London SW3]; *b* 1 March 1946

(7) Cecil Fletcher; *b* 11 Sept 1884; *d* 1 June 1885

(1) Henrietta Emma; *b* 28 July 1876; *m* 3 Aug 1907 Reginald Arthur Wolseley Whitestone, s of Rev Arthur Wolseley Whitestone, Vicar Micheldever, and *d* 13 July 1952, leaving issue. He *d* Sept 1942

1 Anne Henrietta; *m* 21 June 1832 Rev Hon Everard Robert Bruce Feilding, bro of 7th Earl of Denbigh and Desmond (*qv*), and *d* 21 Aug 1879

2 Henrietta Dorothy; *m* 7 July 1836 Walter Peter Giffard, of Chillington, and *d* 7 Sept 1889, leaving issue. He *d* 6 March 1877

3 Anastasia Elizabeth; *m* 1st 28 April 1840 Edward Joseph Smythe, est son of Sir Edward Joseph Smythe, Bt (*d* 28 Aug 1841), of Acton Burnell, Shropshire; *m* 2nd 16 May 1848 Edward Henry, 2nd son of Sir Edward Mostyn, 7th Bt, of Talacre (*qv*), and *d* 23 Nov 1893

4 Elizabeth; *m* 8 June 1843 Rev Robert Dayrell, and *d* 8 Nov 1876. He *d* Nov 1904

Sir JOHN *d* 27 June 1823; his est son,

Sir Thomas Fletcher Fenton Boughey, 3rd Bt, High Sheriff Staffs 1832; *b* 22 Jan 1809; *m* 27 Dec 1832 Louisa Paulina (*d* 10 Dec 1879), yst dau of Thomas Giffard, of Chillington, and *d* 6 Oct 1880, having had, with other issue:

1 **Sir Thomas Fletcher Boughey, 4th Bt**, DL (Staffs), High Sheriff 1898, Capt 2nd Staffs Militia; *b* 5 April 1836; *m* 25 Aug 1864 Sarah Anabella (*d* 18 Feb 1914), only dau of Harold Littledale, of Liscard Hall, Cheshire, and *dsp* 30 Aug 1906

2 **Rev Sir George Boughey, 5th Bt**, MA Oxon, Rector Forton, Newport, Salop 1863–1908; *b* 2 May 1837; *m* 25 April 1875 Theodosia Mary (*d* 13 July 1923), est dau of Rev Charles Smith Royds, Rector Haughton, Staffs, and patron living of Heysham, Lancs, and *d* 4 Aug 1919, leaving issue:

(1) Ethel; *m* 9 Dec 1919 John Robert Morris, JP, of Dol-llys Hall, Llanidloes, late Capt 5th Vol Bn Roy Welch Fus, and *dsp* 16 Dec 1956. He *d* 26 Jan 1936

(2) Eva Pauline, JP, CA W Suffolk, Mayor Bury St Edmunds 1927–28 and 1932–33; *m* 30 July 1912 John Wollaston Greene, of The Panels, Bury St

Edmunds, son of John S Greene, and *d* 4 March 1973, having had issue. He *d* 30 April 1925

(3) Dorothy; *m* 3 April 1907 Hon Gerald Spencer Clegg-Hill, yst son of 3rd Viscount Hill (*qv*), and *d* 18 Jan 1978 aged 98, leaving issue. He *d* 4 April 1930

(4) Mary; *d* unm 2 Dec 1964, aged 84

3 John Fenton, Lt 2nd Foot; *b* 8 Aug 1839; *d* unm 12 July 1867

4 **Sir William Fletcher Boughey, 6th Bt**, Cdr RN (ret), served N Zealand War 1863 and Abyssinian War; *b* 3 Sept 1840; *m* 1 Aug 1891 Mary Ann Gundry, dau of Richard Pearce, and *dsp* 17 April 1912

5 **Rev Sir Robert Boughey, 7th Bt**, of Aqualate, Staffs, Vicar Betley, Staffs, 1876–1921; *b* 21 March 1843; *d* 22 May 1921

6 Walter; *b* 7 April 1844; *d* unm 3 July 1885

7 **Sir Francis Boughey, 8th Bt**; *b* 2 April 1848; *d* unm 6 March 1927

8 Henry, Col late York and Lancs Regt; *b* 29 April 1850; *m* 16 Jan 1882 Maria Loraine (*d* 30 Jan 1910), widow of Renton George Felix Poynter, late Capt 87th Regt, and dau of George Yeldham Wilkinson, and *dsp* 7 Dec 1912

Sir FRANCIS's cousin,

Sir George Menteth Boughey, 9th Bt, CBE (1928, OBE 1919); *educ* Trin Coll Cambridge (BA); ICS 1901–16; *b* 28 March 1879; *m* 1 Feb 1913 Noel Evelyn (*d* 14 Feb 1974), dau of James George Henry Glass, CIE, and had issue:

1 John Fletcher, 2nd Lt Coldstream Gds WW II; *b* 22 March 1919; *kas* Sept 1940

2 RICHARD JAMES (Sir), **10th Bt**

1 *(Mary) Hermia [Mrs Robert Priestley, The Manor, Church Oakley, Hants RG23 7ED]; *b* 14 April 1914; *m* 24 April 1935 *Robert Hugh Priestley, est son of Hugh William Priestley

2 Camilla; *b* 9 Dec 1916; *m* 29 Jan 1941 (*divorce* 1964) Maj Robert Charles Sanford Barclay, Intell Corps, yst son of Sir Colville Barclay, KCMG, CB, CBE, MVO, PC, and *d* 4 May 1997, leaving issue (*see* BARCLAY, Bt)

3 *Anne [Mrs Roddy Huff, 172 N Crest Rd, Chattanooga, Tennessee, USA]; *b* 23 Nov 1922; *m* 26 Jan 1946 *Lt (James) Roddy Huff, US Army, est son of C M Huff, of Chattanooga, and has issue:

(1) *James David [James Huff, 88 Whitehead Rd, Buford, Georgia, USA]; *b* 18 Nov 1947

(2) Richard John; *b* 28 March 1952; accidentally drowned 14 June 1958

(1) *Elizabeth Anne [Mrs David Rooks, 109 Winsome Lane, Chapel Hill, NC 27516, USA]; *b* 10 Feb 1949; *m* 1971 *David M Rooks III, and has issue:

1a *Kathryn Elizabeth; *b* 1979

2a *Adrienne Emily; *b* 1982

(2) *Celia Jane [Mrs Michael Mattingly, 304 Strasburg Pike, Lancaster, PA 17602, USA]; *b* 27 Aug 1958; *m* 1983 *Michael Mark Mattingly, and has issue:

1c *Emma Caitlin; *b* 1986

2c *Chloë Elizabeth; *b* 1989

Sir GEORGE *d* 28 June 1959; his only son,

Sir Richard James Boughey, 10th Bt, JP (E Sussex 1958), DL (E Sussex); *b* 30 July 1925; *educ* Eton; Lt Coldstream Gds WW II 1943–45, High Sheriff Sussex 1964, chm E Sussex Ag Exec Ctee 1958–67, Liaison Offr Min Ag 1965, chm Apple and Pear Development Cncl 1967, Lewis Award for Mktg (Fruiterers' Co) 1971, OStJ 1965; *m* 1st 10 Oct 1950 (*divorce* 1975) Davina Julia (*m* 2nd 1979, as his 2nd w, 4th Baron Loch, MC, who *d* 1991), 2nd dau of FitzHerbert Wright (*see* POWERSCOURT, V), and had:

1 Sir JOHN GEORGE FLETCHER BOUGHEY, **11th and present Bt**

2 +JAMES RICHARD [James Boughey Esq, The Manor House, Piddletrenthide, Dorset DT2 7QX; *b* 29 Aug 1960; heir presumptive; *educ* Eton, RMA Sandhurst and RAC Circencester; *m* 1989 *Katherine Mary, only dau of Capt (Geoffrey Thomas) Warren Fenwicke-Clennell (*see* BLACKETT, Bt), and has issue:

(1) +George Richard Douglas; *b* 27 March 1992

(2) +William James; *b* 1995

(1) *Victoria Rose; *b* 1990

1 *Julia Mary [Mrs Peregrine Chadwyck-Healey, Vern Leaze, Calne, Wilts]; *b* 1 Oct 1952; *m* 12 May 1973 *Peregrine James Chadwyck-Healey, yst son of Lt-Col Charles Arthur Chadwyck-Healey, OBE, of Old Middleton, Westmeston, Hassocks, Sussex (*see* CHADWYCK-HEALEY, Bt) and has issue

2 *Rosalind Jane [Mrs Richard Steele, Hazeldene, Highgate Rd, Forest Row, Sussex]; *b* 4 Nov 1954; *m* 1978 *Richard Herbert Dennis Steele

3 *Clare Anne [Miss Clare Boughey, Chestnut Cottage, Stubhampton, Blandford, Dorset]; *b* 19 Dec 1957

Sir Richard *m* 2nd 8 April 1976 *Gillian Claire [Gillian Lady Boughey, Alebank House, Ancrum, Jedburgh, Roxburghshire TD8 6XH], yst dau of Maj Robert Moubray, DL, (*see* MORRISON-BELL, Bt), and *d* 3 Oct 1978

BOULTON of Braxted Park

Arms: Arg., on a bend engrailed couped gu. three leopard's faces or.
Crest: Upon a holly bush fructed a falcon rising ppr., belled or.
Creation: Bt. (UK) 30 June 1944.

SIR WILLIAM WHYTEHEAD BOULTON, 3RD BT, of Braxted Park, Co Essex, CBE (1958), TD (1949) [Sir William Boulton Bt CBE TD, The Quarters House, Alresford, Essex CO7 8AY]; *b* 21 June 1912; *s* bro 1982; *educ* Eton and Trin Coll Cambridge (BA Hons 1934); barrister Inner Temple 1936, Sec: Gen Cncl Bar 1950–74, Senate Inns of Court 1974–75, Lt-Col Essex Yeo and 14th RHA WW II 1939–44, Staff Coll Camberley 1944 (Hon Lt-Col), served with CCG (Legal Div) 1945–50, ktd 1975, secretary general Cncl Bar 1950–74, Senate Inns of Court and Bar 1974–75, author: *A Guide to Conduct and Etiquette at the Bar of England and Wales* (1953); *m* 30 Sept 1944 *(Margaret) Elizabeth, only dau of Brig Henry Noel Alexander Hunter, DSO, of Chelsea, and has:

1 +(JOHN) GIBSON; *b* 18 Dec 1946; *educ* Stowe

1 *Julia Rosalind [Mrs Anthony Russell, Elm House, Elmdon, Saffron Walden, Essex]; *b* 17 July 1945; *m* 24 July 1965 *Anthony John Nevill Russell, son of John Francis Nevill Russell, of Fairstow, W Byfleet, Surrey, and has issue:

(1) *William Jonathan; *b* 24 April 1968

(1) *Jennifer Rosalind; *b* 1969

2 *Susan Elizabeth [Mrs Roger Harrison, The Pink House, Hedgerley Close, Cambs CB3 0EW]; *b* 28 Dec 1948; *m* 1985 *Roger Donald Harrison, yr son of Robert Harrison, of Stratford-upon-Avon, and has issue:

(1) *Alexander Barnaby; *b* 1986

(2) *Rupert Michael; *b* 1988

Lineage: CHRISTOPHER BOLTON [*sic*], of New Malton, Yorks; *m* Mary — and was *bur* 7 Jan 1681, leaving issue:

ROBERT BOLTON, of New Malton; *bapt* March 1653; *bur* 19 Feb 1700; his est s:

ROBERT BOLTON, of New Malton; *bapt* 19 Nov 1688; left an only s:

ROBERT BOLTON, of New Malton; slr; *m* Margaret (*d* 1781), dau of Thomas Smith, of York, by Mary, dau of William Atkinson, of York, and had an est s:

ROBERT BOULTON, of New Malton; slr; *bapt* 25 Nov 1774; *m* 19 April 1798 Margaret (*d* 28 Aug 1828; gggdau of Bridget Cromwell, er dau of OLIVER CROMWELL), dau of James Luccok, of New Malton, and *d* 13 Dec 1824, leaving a 2nd son:

ROBERT GEORGE BOULTON, of Beverley, Yorks, JP; *b* 3 July 1805; *m* Anne (*d* 20 Dec 1892), dau of Rev Henry Robert Whytehead, BA, of Thormanby, Yorks, by Hannah Diana, dau and heir of Rev Thomas Bowman, MA, Rector Crayke and Preb Durham, and *d* July 1877, leaving issue:

1 WILLIAM WHYTEHEAD, of whom presently

2 Barnard Robert; *b* 13 July 1837; *d* 23 Aug 1840

3 Percy; *b* 9 July 1840; *m* twice; *dsp* May 1910

4 Henry Yates; *b* 24 Oct 1842; *d* 9 July 1846

5 Frederic Conyers; *b* 21 Aug 1844; *m* Alice Rose, and had issue

6 Charles; *b* 10 Aug 1846; *m* Georgina Marchant

7 Harold; *d* an infant

1 Annie Sophia; *m* 7 Aug 1861 Rev Robert Codrington Collins, of Towcester, Northants, and *d* 18 Nov 1877

2 Emily; *d* unm 13 April 1892

3 Harriet Jane; *m* Sept 1867 Arthur Gibson Hill, of Welton Dale, Yorks, and *d* 12 June 1912

4 Fanny; *m* Maj Valentine Griffiths, and *d* 28 Dec 1930

5 Clementine Mary; *d* 1 July 1852

6 Adelaide Margaret; *m* 10 Oct 1871 Thomas John Thompson, of Beverley. He *d* Nov 1881

The est son,

WILLIAM WHYTEHEAD BOULTON, of Beverley, JP; *b* 15 Dec 1833; *m* 4 Nov 1858 Mary Hudleston (*d* 14 May 1909), dau of John Gibson, RN, of Norton, Durham, formerly of Quernmore Park, by Mary Hopper, of Chilton Hall, Durham, and *d* 17 Jan 1897, leaving issue:

1 Edward Gibson; *b* 16 Feb 1861; *d* 6 Sept 1890

2 John Whytehead; *b* 1862; *d* 1905

3 Gerald Bowman; *b* 31 May 1863; *m* 3 June 1892 Florence Emily Newbald (*d* Feb 1938), and *d* 28 May 1905, leaving issue:

(1) Dorothy Joane; *m* 8 June 1921 Capt William Mansel Shewen, KOSB, and *d* 6 March 1932

(2) Sybil Mary Willoughby; *m* 1st 9 Dec 1931 Lt-Col Ronald Steuart-Menzies of Menzies, The Menzies, late Scots Gds (*d* 2 Oct 1961), son of William George Steuart-Menzies of Culdares, and had issue:

1a *David Ronald, The Menzies, Capt late Scots Gds [The Menzies, Mundena, Walebing, WA 6510, Australia]; *b* 20 March 1935; *educ* Eton; *m* 17 Nov 1962 *Diana Winifred, dau of T F de Pledge, of Mandora Station, Port Hedland, W Australia, and has issue:

1b *A son; *b* 15 Sept 1965

2b *Simon Stewart; *b* 29 Dec 1966

3b *Andrew James; *b* 29 Dec 1966

1a *Susan; *b* 30 March 1933; *m* 30 April 1953 14th Earl of Leven and Melville (*qv*), and has issue

2a *Mariota; *b* 27 Feb 1938; *m* 1st 28 Nov 1959 (*divorce* 1967) William Henry Stirling, only son of Brig James Erskine Stirling, DSO, TD, DL, of Holme Rose, Croy, Inverness-shire; *m* 2nd 4 Aug 1967 Ewen John Brodie, er son of Maj David James Brodie of Lethen, OBE, DL

(2) (cont.) Mrs Ronald Menzies *m* 2nd 5 March 1963 Maurice Oliver Pease, yr son of Reginald Pease

4 Arthur Thomas; *b* 4 Jan 1868; *m* 25 Oct 1894 Catherine Edith (*d* 3 Nov 1950), 2nd dau of Alderman John William Owsley, ISO, barrister, and *d* 11 Aug 1921, leaving issue:

(1) Edward Newdigate, Cdr RN; *b* 21 July 1895; *educ* RNCs Osborne and Darmouth; *m* 1st 10 April 1928 (*divorce* 1951) Elizabeth Eleanor Lechmere, dau of Robert Bruce Harding, and had issue:

1a *Robert Bruce Lechmere, Maj RASC; *b* 22 Dec 1933; *educ* RMA Sandhurst; *m* 28 Jan 1961 (*divorce*) Jane Katherine, dau of Denis William Frederick Starkey, of Church Cottage, Southfleet, Kent, and has issue

1a *Elizabeth Anne Vane; *b* 29 Nov 1930; *m* 15 June 1957 George Henry Douglas Gaisford, of 84 Beaufort Mansions, Beaufort Street, London SW3, 2nd son of Brig John William Gaisford

2a *Rosemary Perdita Owsley; *b* 30 March 1935; *m* 14 July 1956 (*divorce* 1964) Robin de Lisle Green, son of Herbert Green, of Goodwood, Ilkley, Yorks, and has issue:

1b *Amanda Jane; *b* 1 July 1958

(1) (cont.) Cdr Edward Boulton *m* 2nd 2 May 1953 *Sheila Sybilla, only dau of Herbert Green, of Goodwood, Ilkley, Yorks, and *d* 10 March 1963, having by her had issue:

3a *Caroline Chetwode Owsley Dallewy Vane; *b* 4 June 1959

(2) Arthur Vane, Lt Glos Regt; *b* 15 June 1898; *educ* Marlborough and RMC Sandhurst; *d* of wounds recd in action 25 Feb 1917

(1) Catherine Elizabeth Louisa Owsley; *d* unm 12 Oct 1954

5 Robert George Hopper; *b* 28 Aug 1871; *d* unm 29 Oct 1953

6 WILLIAM WHYTEHEAD (Sir), **1st Bt**

7 Harold Mowbray; *b* 21 Aug, *d* 4 Oct 1874

1 Jessie; *m* 14 Aug 1889 William Wastell Whytehead and *d* 19–. He *d* 22 Feb 1920

2 Mabel Eleanor; *m* July 1890 Harry Ernest Craddock, JP, of Hartforth Hall, Richmond, Yorks, and *d* 27 Dec 1934, having had issue

3 Mary Dorothy Hopper; *m* 1894 Lt-Col Charles Edward Percy Fowler, OBE, AMS, and *d* 8 May 1942, leaving issue

4 Muriel Edith Mary; *m* 26 April 1897 Lt-Col William Maxwell Tress, TA, and had issue. He *d* May 1926

The 6th son,

Sir William Whytehead Boulton, 1st Bt (UK), so *cr* 30 June 1944, DL; *b* 10 Jan 1873; Ld Manors Gt Braxted and Kelvedon Hall, Maj 7th Vol Bn Essex Regt, Lt RHG, MP Centl Sheffield 1931–45, Ld Commr Treasury 1940–42, Govt Whip 1940–44; *m* 23 April 1903 Rosalind Mary (*d* 11 Dec 1969), only dau of Sir John Davison Milburn, 1st Bt (*qv*), and *d* 9 Jan 1949, having had issue:

1 **Sir Edward John Boulton, 2nd Bt**; *b* 11 April 1907; *educ* Eton and Trin Coll Cambridge (BA 1929); served WW II (despatches), stockbroker with Mitton, Butler, Priest & Co; *d* unm 10 Aug 1982

2 Ralph Milburn Gibson; *b* 19 May 1909; *d* Oct 1916

3 Sir WILLIAM WHYTEHEAD BOULTON, **3rd and present Bt**

4 Christopher Carmichael; *b* 30 May 1919; *educ* Eton and Trin Coll Cambridge; Capt Intell Corps WW II France, Middle East, Italy and Austria; ptnr Burn & Boulton; *d* May 1994

BOULTON of Copped Hall

Arms: Arg. on a bend gu. two leopard's faces of the first, on a chief enarched of the second two falcons close ppr. **Crest:** On a holly bush a falcon rising, holding in the dexter claw a birdbolt in pale, point downwards, and in the beak a sprig of holly, all ppr. **Supporters:** Dexter, a Knight of St John in armour, robed ppr.; sinister, a female figure representing charity, vested arg. with mantle gu., round the head a fillet arg. inscribed 'caritas' and holding in the exterior hand a heart or, inflamed ppr. **Motto:** I will never quit. **Creation:** Bt. (UK) 24 July 1905

SIR (HAROLD HUGH) CHRISTIAN BOULTON, 4TH, of Copped Hall [Sir Christian Boulton Bt, 37 Jay Ave, Nepean, Ont K2G 0C1, Canada]; *b* 29 Oct 1918; *s* f 1968; *educ* Ampleforth; Capt Irish Gds SR WW II; *m* 8 Sept 1944 *Patricia Mary, OBE, Subaltern ATS (resumed maiden name by deed poll 1951), er dau of Maj-Gen Sir Walter Joseph Constable Maxwell-Scott, 1st Bt, CB, DSO (*see* HERRIES OF TERREGLES, L)

Lineage: GEORGE BOULTON, of Ealing, Middx; *m* Mary — and had, with three yr s:

CHARLES BOULTON; *m* 1st 7 Aug 1759 Mary Tawlen (*d* March 1761) and had a s (Charles, *b* 21 May 1760); *m* 2nd 22 June 1765 Sarah Clark and by her had, with two er s:

JOHN BOULTON; *b* 7 Jan 1769; *m* Sarah Della (*d* 1 Dec 1841), and *d* 26 Sept 1824, leaving an est s:

Rev THOMAS BOULTON, of Cranbrook, Kent, and Grahamstown, S Africa; *b* 20 Dec 1791; *m* 10 Jan 1813 Rhoda (*d* 9 March 1860), dau of John Parker, of Ashwellthorpe, Norfolk, and *d* 6 Aug 1861, leaving, with other issue (including a dau Rhoda Elizabeth, *b* 9 April 1826, *m* 14 April 1848 Henry Ballard and *d* 1914 leaving issue):

Sir Samuel Bagster Boulton, 1st Bt (UK), so *cr* 24 July 1905, of Copped Hall, Totteridge, Herts, DL and JP Herts, JP Middx and W Ham, pres W Ham Chamber Commerce 1863–1902, V-Pres London Chamber Commerce 1893–98, fndr London Labour Conciliation Bd 1889 (chm 1889–1913), Ld Manor Totteridge, FRGS, AInstCE, received Telford Medal 1884, KGStJ; *b* 12 July 1830; *m* 19 April 1855 Sophia Louisa (*d* 25 Nov 1900), dau of Thomas Cooper, of Newbury, Berks, and had issue:

1 HAROLD EDWIN (Sir), **2nd Bt**

2 Oscar Evan, TD, Lt-Col late cmdg 2nd City of London (Rough Riders) Yeo, late Capt Ayrshire Yeo, served in S Africa (medal with three clasps) and WW I 1914 (despatches), chm Rochester Diocesan Bd of Finance, author: *The Way Out, Truth in a Nutshell*, etc, and several volumes of poetry, ed *The British Lion*, KJStJ; *b* 29 May 1866; *educ* Harrow and Balliol Coll Oxford (MA); *m* 2 June 1894 Barbara Marion, 4th dau of Maj-Gen Robert Adam Wauchope, IA, and *d* 17 Nov 1942, leaving issue:

(1) Hersey Barbara; *b* 26 June 1895; *m* 16 July 1921 Walter Cowan Forbes, yst son of Dr R E Forbes, of Bonavista, Newfoundland, and *d* 1 May 1961, leaving issue. He *d* 22 Sept 1951

1 Cora Burt; *b* 7 March 1856; *m* 16 Dec 1884 Richard Cowper, and *d* 24 Oct 1921, leaving issue. He *d* 1886

2 Hilda Louisa; *b* 30 Jan, *d* 8 March 1858

3 Mabel Anne, DGStJ; *b* 3 Feb 1862; *m* 1st 16 July 1884 St Clair Kelburn Mulholland Stobart, BA, of Mount Bagnall, Co Louth, and had issue. He *d* 9 April 1908; *m* 2nd 11 March 1911 John Stobart Greenhalgh, BA, barrister, Inner Temple, and *d* 7 Dec 1954. He *d* 2 March 1928

4 Enid Alice; *b* 20 March 1863; *m* 12 April 1883 Frederick Hugh Capron, BA, son of Rev George Halliley Capron, of Southwick Hall, Northants, and *d* Jan 1940, leaving issue. He *d* 28 Feb 1955

5 Eva Gertrude; *b* 10 Sept 1864; *m* 2 Sept 1915 Sir George Power, 7th Bt (*see* 1967 edn), and *d* 24 March 1952. He *dsp* 17 Oct 1928

6 Beatrice Amy; *b* 16 July 1867; *m* 1 June 1891 Sidney Clement Galpin, MA, of The Moorings, Meads, Eastbourne, and *d* 7 Oct 1945, leaving issue. He *d* 17 Jan 1939

Sir SAMUEL *d* 27 April 1918; his son,

Sir Harold Edwin Boulton, 2nd Bt, CVO, CBE, JP (W Ham); *educ* Balliol Coll Oxford (MA); Capt late TFR, formerly Capt Militia Bn QO Cameron Highrs and City of London Yeo, KJStJ, Ovate Bard of Wales, and chm and fndr of many Charitable Organizations, chm of Queen Victoria's Jubilee Inst for Nurses 1919–32, v-pres 1932; Dir RAM, dir Burt, Boulton, and Haywood Ltd, author *The Skye Boat Song, Glorious Devon*, and many other lyrics, ed *Songs of the North* and other works; *b* 7 Aug 1859; *m* 1st 26 Jan 1889 Adelaide Lucy, DGStJ (*d* 26 April 1926), 3rd dau of Duncan Henry Caithness Reay Davidson, of Tulloch Castle, Dingwall, and had issue:

1 (DENIS DUNCAN) HAROLD (OWEN) (Sir), **3rd Bt**

2 Christian Harold Ernest, Capt Cameron Highrs, ADC to Govr of NSW; *b* 17 Feb 1897; *ka* 1917

1 Louise Kythé Veronica; *b* 18 Sept 1890; *m* 30 April 1917 Gustavus Edward Huscared Yonge, IA Res of Offrs, son of Cdr G H Yonge, RN, and *d* 21 May 1934, leaving issue

Sir Harold *m* 2nd 29 Dec 1926 Margaret Cunningham (*d* 18 Oct 1938), dau of James Lennox Lyons, of Montreal, and *d* 1 June 1935

His son,

Sir (Denis Duncan) Harold (Owen) Boulton, 3rd Bt; *educ* Stonyhurst; formerly Lt 4th Bn Beds Regt, late Hon Equerry to HRH PRINCESS LOUISE, served WW II as F/Lt RAFVR 1940–42, seconded to FO and Home Security, Commandant Civ Defence Unit 1943–44, agent in UK for Grosvenor Properties, Canada 1953–55, ch rep in N America for BTA 1949–51, CStJ; *b* 10 Dec 1892; *m* 9 Feb 1918 Louise (*d* 1978), dau of Hugh J McGowan, of USA, and *d* 10 Aug 1968, having had:

1 Sir HAROLD HUGH CHRISTIAN BOULTON, **4th and present Bt**

2 Duncan Davidson, Lt Gren Gds WW II; *b* 5 April 1924; *ka* in Italy, Feb 1944

1 *Marie Louise [Mrs James Smith, 83 Bryant St, Buffalo, NY 14209, USA]; *b* 16 July 1921; *m* 22 May 1948 *James Russell Smith, son of Carlton M Smith, of Buffalo, NY, and has:

(1) *Carlton Michael; *b* 23 Oct 1949

(2) *Duncan Rumsey (twin); *b* 23 Oct 1949

(1) *Marie Louise; *b* 14 March 1952

BOWATER of Friston

Arms: Arg. on an inescutcheon sa. between eight martlets in orle gu. a crescent of the field. **Crest:** A rainbow issuant from water ppr. **Motto:** *Nec aspera terrent* ('Difficulties do not daunt'). **Creation:** Bt. (UK) 11 Oct 1939.

SIR EUAN DAVID VANSITTART BOWATER, 3RD BT, of Friston, Suffolk [Sir Euan Bowater Bt, Conifers, St George's Hill, Weybridge, Surrey; Riscombe, Exford, Somerset]; *b* 9 Sept 1935; *s f* 1984; *educ* Eton and Trin Coll Cambridge (BA); late 2nd Lt Scots Gds; *m* 17 Sept 1964 *Susan Mary Humphrey, dau of A R O Slater, FCA, and has issue:

1 +MORAY VANSITTART; *b* 24 April 1967

2 +Lucien Ross Thomas; *b* 29 April 1973

1 *Jacqueline (Jackie); *b* 17 Aug 1965

2 *Alexis; *b* 15 Aug 1969

Lineage: WILLIAM VANSITTART BOWATER, of Bury Hall, Middx, had, with other issue (*see* BOWATER, Bt, of Hill Crest) a 2nd s:

Sir Frank Henry Bowater, 1st Bt (UK), so *cr* 11 Oct 1939, TD; joined RA 1905, Maj 1908, 4th London Howitzer Bde RFA WW I, Maj RFA (TA), Lt City London 1914, Alderman Bridge Without Ward, memb Court Common Cncl, Sheriff London 1929–30, ktd 1930, Ld Mayor 1938–39, memb LCC 1934, Grand Offr Legion Honour, Order Crown Romania, CStJ; *b* 3 April 1866; *m* 8 Oct 1891 Ethel Anita, CStJ (*d* following an accident 19 Dec 1945), dau of Mark Lindsay Fryar, ICS, of Rangoon, and had issue:

1 NOEL VANSITTART (Sir), **2nd Bt**

2 Ian Frank (Sir), GBE (1970), DSO (1945), TD; *b* 16 Dec 1904; *educ* Eton and Magdalen Coll Oxford; Lt-Col RA (TA) WW II, Sheriff City London 1965, Lt City London 1939, Alderman 1960, ktd 1967, Ld Mayor 1969–70, pres City and Metropolitan Bldg Soc, chm Bowater Hotels, dep chm CGA, dir GKN Birfield Industs, Assist Court Haberdashers' Co (1st Warden 1966–67, Master 1967–68), govr Christ's Hosp, OStJ; *m* 20 Oct 1927 Hon Ursula Margaret Dawson, 2nd dau of 1st Viscount Dawson of Penn, GCVO, KCB, KCMG, PC, MD (*see* 1940 4en), and *d* 1 Oct 1982, leaving issue:

(1) +Michael Ian Vansittart [Michael Bowater Esq, 16 Rocky Point Rd, Rowayton, CT 06853, USA]; *b* 26 Nov 1934; *educ* Eton and RMA Sandhurst; late Maj Scots Gds; head communications Bowater Corp; *m* 22 June 1960 *Camilla Caroline, er dau of A/Cdre Whitney Willard Straight, CBE, MC, DFC, of The Aviary, Windmill Lane, Southall, Middx, by Lady Daphne Margarita, er dau of 14th Earl of Winchilsea and Nottingham (*qv*), and has issue:

1a *Arabella Charlotte; *b* 13 July 1961; *m* 1990 *Carl W Wend, Jr, son of Carl Wend, of White Plains, NY

2a *Katherine Elizabeth; *b* 2 March 1963; *m* 1988 *Mark Beaumont, son of Michael Beaumont, and has issue:

1b *James; *b* 1990

1b *Emma Camilla; *b* 1992

3a *Caroline Mary; *b* 2 Jan 1965

4a *Sophia Melissa; *b* 26 Nov 1970

(1) *Susan Vansittart [Mrs George Doughty, 60 Clonmel Rd, London SW6 5BJ]; *b* 26 Aug 1929; *m* 5 May 1956 *George Crofton Addison Doughty, yst son of Sir Charles Doughty, QC, and has issue:

1a *Caroline Susan; *b* 10 Jan 1958

(1) (cont.) Mr and Mrs George Doughty also adopted:

*John Addison; *b* 19 May 1961

(2) *Charlotte Mary [Mrs J Watcyn Lewis, 66 Clifton Hill, London NW8 0JT]; *b* 17 July 1937; *m* 1st 27 Sept 1961 (Denis) Anthony Russell (*d* 30 July 1966), er son of Maj Denis Leslie Russell, OBE, TD, of Burdenshot Ho, Burdenshot Hill, Guildford, Surrey (*see* RUSSELL, Bt, of Littleworth Corner), and has issue; *m* 2nd 1970 *J Watcyn Lewis, son of John Lewis, of Denison Ho, Little Goddesdon, Herts, and has further issue:

1a *Damian Watcyn; *b* 11 Feb 1971

2a *Gareth Hugh Bowater; *b* 25 Jan 1973

1 Ethel May; *b* 13 May 1896; *m* 5 Feb 1916 Capt William Olaus Charles Johnsen, DFC (*d* 20 April 1960), 2nd son of W M Johnsen, and has issue:

(1) *William Hugo Gilroy, MC, served RA WW II 1939–46; *b* 1 Sept 1917; *educ* Eton; *m* 10 May 1947 *Maisie, er dau of Henry S Frazier, of Fernhall Rock, Worcs, and has issue:

1a *William Martin; *b* 20 Nov 1947; *educ* Eton

2a *Graham Claridge; *b* 15 Aug 1960

1a *Marye Rose; *b* 19 April 1953

(2) John Martin Claridge, served WW II; *b* 9 Oct 1921; *educ* Harrow; *ka* 3/4 March 1943

(3) *Peter Bowater [Peter Johnsen Esq, The Mirrie, Denham, Bucks], served WW II (despatches, Croix de Guerre); *b* 12 Oct 1923; *educ* Eton; *m* 31 Aug 1954 *Birthe Nina, er dau of Baron Raben-Levetzau, of Aalholm Castle, Nysted, Denmark, and has issue:

1a *Hugo Anthony; *b* 23 May 1956

2a *James William *b* 7 May 1960

1a *Josephine Nina; *b* 10 June 1958

(4) *Richard, Lt Roy Sussex Regt WW II; *b* 17 July 1927; *educ* Eton; *m* 14 July 1960 *Patricia Nadejad (Nadia), formerly w of Capt-Engineer Jiri, of Florence, Italy, and only dau of Capt Frank Moxon, MC, of Little Chickney, Nazeing, Essex, and has issue:

1a *William Frank; *b* 22 Dec 1961

2a *Julian Richard; *b* 2 July 1963

1a *Arabella Charlotte; *b* 30 Dec 1966

(5) Graham Stuart; *b* 29 April 1930; *educ* Eton; *d* 27 May 1947

(6) *(Michael) Robin NANI-MOCENIGO JOHNSEN (added w's name 2 Aug 1968) [Robin Nani-Mocenigo Johnsen, Via Schaffer 28, Merano, Italy]; *b* 24 Feb 1941; *educ* Millfield; *m* 11 May 1966 *CountessVirginia, only dau of Count G B Nani Mocenigo, of Merano, Italy

(1) *Pamela May [Mrs Richard Tulk-Hart, The Cottage, Fairwarp, E Sussex TN22 3BU]; *b* 30 Oct 1918; *educ* Benenden; Pilot ATA 1941–45; *m* 11 March 1944 Richard Braddyll Tulk-Hart, MRCS, LRCP, DCH (*d* April 1996), yr s of Thomas John Tulk-Hart, of Tainters, Piltdown, Sussex, and has issue:

1a *Jeremy John Bowater; *b* 27 March 1947; *educ* Gordonstoun

1a *Nicola; *b* 6 Dec 1948; *m* 1978 *Thomas Colville

2a *Tessa Claridge; *b* 13 July 1953; *educ* Beneden; *m* 2 June 1979 Richard Youell, son of Canon George Youell, of Ely, and has:

1b *Robert George Braddyll; *b* 1985

1b *Alice Carbery; *b* 1988

(2) *Sheilagh Claridge [Mrs Peter Candler, 14 Bearemount Pk, Ryanford Rd, Pinetown, Natal, S Africa]; *b* 4 May 1920; *educ* Benenden; *m* 10 June 1939 Peter Lawrence Candler, MRCOG (*d* 1993), est son of Lawrence Candler, FRCS, of Exeter, Devon, and has issue:

1a *Peter Jonathan; *b* 1945; *educ* Sherborne and Rhodes U

1a *Rowena Ruth; *b* 1940; *m* 1963 *Maj Nigel Marry-Taylor, RA, and has issue:

1b *Henry Sebastian; *b* 1965

2 Beryl Stuart; *b* 11 Dec 1902; *m* 9 April 1931 Col Arthur Howard Eckford Howell, DSO, TD, DL, RA, only son of Lt-Col Ernest Alfred Russell Howell, and *d* 8 Oct 1972, leaving issue:

(1) *DAVID ARTHUR RUSSELL HOWELL, BARON HOWELL OF GUILDFORD (*qv*)

(1) *Jane Duncombe; *b* 25 May 1932; *m* 30 Jan 1957 (*divorce*) Maj Peter Evan Wyldbore Gibbs, Coldstream Gds (*see* ALDENHAM and HUNSDON OF HUNSDON, B), and has issue

Sir FRANK *d* 10 Nov 1947; his er son,

Sir Noël Vansittart Bowater, 2nd Bt, GBE (1954), Ld Mayor London 1953–54, Lt City London, Hon Burgess Coleraine 1962, Pres Bowater Paper Corp, Alderman City London 1948–49, Master Vintners' Co 1954–55, Govr Irish Soc 1961–63, served WW I 1914–19, KStJ, Kt Cdr: N Star Sweden, Order of Menelik II Ethiopia; *b* 25 Dec 1892; *educ* Rugby; *m* 1 Feb 1921 Constance (*d* 1993), dau of David Gordon Bett, of Woodbridge, Suffolk, and *d* 22 Jan 1984, leaving issue:

1 Sir EUAN DAVID VANSITTART BOWATER, **3rd and present Bt**

1 *Anne Patricia; *b* 3 July 1925; *educ* Westonbirt; *m* 21 April 1954 *G/Capt Randolph Stuart Mills, DFC, RAF, son of Capt Randolph Henry Mills, of Northampton, and has issue:

(1) *Philip Stuart; *b* 21 March 1956

(2) *William Stuart; *b* 12 Aug 1957

2 *Jane Gillian [Mrs Christopher Beeson, Ford Farm, Manaton, Devon]; *b* 10 April 1930; *educ* Benenden; *m* 25 April 1953 *Christopher William Restarick Beeson, yst son of G E W Beeson, of Gratnar, N Bovey, S Devon, and has issue:

(1) *Mark; *b* 31 May 1954

(2) *Peter; *b* 20 Jan 1956

(3) *David; *b* 30 Sept 1957

(1) *Oona; *b* 14 June 1960

BOWATER of Hill Crest

Arms: Arg. on an inescutcheon sa. between eight martlets in orle gu. a crescent of the field. **Motto:** *Omnia vincit labor* ('Toil overcomes all'). **Creation:** Bt. (UK) 16 July 1914.

SIR JOHN VANSITTART BOWATER, 4TH BT, of Hill Crest, Croydon [Sir John Bowater Bt, 214 Runnymede Ave, Bearwood, Bournemouth BH11 9SP]; *b* 6 April 1918; *s* unc 1972; *educ* Branksome Sch Godalming; served RA WW II; *m* 22 Oct 1943 Joan Kathleen (*d* 1982), dau of Wilfrid Ernest Henry Scullard, of 46 Darracott Rd, Boscombe, Bournemouth, and has issue:

1 +MICHAEL PATRICK [Michael Bowater Esq, The Anchorage, Quay W, Minehead, Somerset]; *b* 18 July 1949; *m* 1968 *Alison, dau of Edward Wall, of Knowle, and has issue:

(1) *Suzanne; *b* 1969

(2) *Juliette; *b* 1972

(3) *Jennifer; *b* 1973

(4) *Katherine; *b* 1980

1 *Penelope Ann [Mrs Martin Doughty, 16 Victoria Rd, Acocks Green, Birmingham B27 7YA]; *b* 31 July 1954; *m* 1973 *Martin Doughty, son of Geoffrey Doughty, and has issue:

(1) *Samantha; *b* 1976

(2) *Hannah; *b* 1978

(3) *Laura; *b* 1982

Lineage: JOHN BOWATER, of Whitley, Coventry, Warwicks, and City of London, living 1634; *m* Anne, dau of Stephen Cross, of Stafford, and had, with four yr s and three daus (of whom the yst Elizabeth *m* Sir Charles Lloyd, Bt, of Garth, Montgomeryshire (*d* 1678)):

THOMAS BOWATER, of Whitley, lawyer; *fl c* 1650; *m* Anne, dau of Deane Tindall, of Essex, and had (with a dau Amy; *m* Ralph Hartley, of Kingsbury, Middx):

JOHN BOWATER, of Whitley; *b c* 1650; *m* Ann, dau of Henry Cater, of London, and previously Coventry, and *d* between 13 March 1702 and 6 Dec 1703, having had, with a yr s and two daus:

JOHN BOWATER, of Whitley; *b c* 1676; *m* 4 April 1706 Bridget Murcott (*bur* as his widow 10 Sept 1751) and had:

RICHARD BOWATER, of Whitley; *bapt* 24 July 1715; *m* 15 March 1738/9 Mary (*d* 3 Dec 1790), dau of Thomas Bayly, MP Derby, and *d* 7 Nov 1772, having had, with six yr s:

WILLIAM BOWATER, RM, of Horsley Court; *b* 24 Aug 1755; Maj; *m* 23 Oct 1803 Maria (*m* 2nd 18 May 1830 William Thompson; *d* 24 Jan 1844), dau of Capt Thomas Cole, 53rd Regt, and *d* 15 March 1829, having had, with two yr s and six daus:

THOMAS VANSITTART BOWATER; *b* 2 Oct 1808; *m* 14 Feb 1837 Sarah, dau of John Davis, of Caerleon, Mon, and had, with a yr s and four daus:

WILLIAM VANSITTART BOWATER, of Bury Hall, Edmonton, Middx; *b* 15 March 1838; *m* 8 June 1861 Eliza Jane (*d* 23 June 1912), dau of Thomas Davey, of Bristol, and had issue:

1 THOMAS VANSITTART (Sir), **1st Bt**

2 FRANK HENRY (Sir), also *cr* a Bt (*see* BOWATER, Bt, of Friston)

3 Frederick William (Sir), KBE (1920); *b* 8 June 1867; *m* 25 Sept 1890 Alice Emily, dau of Joseph Sharp, of Bognor, Sussex, and *d* 16 May 1924, leaving issue:

(1) Eric Vansittart (Sir), ktd 1944, FRSA, chm Bowater Gp 1927, dir Lloyds Bank, Alliance Assur, Sun Alliance Insur, Br Newfoundland Corp, Dir-Gen Min Aircraft Prodn 1940–43, Dep Controller 1943–45, Controller 1945, RA WW I, Offr Legion Honour; *b* 16 Jan 1895; *educ* Charterhouse; *m* 1st Blanche Murre, dau of Charles de Ville, of Cheshire, and had issue:

1a Elizabeth Murre Vansittart; *m* 1939 Desmond Yorath, and had issue

(1) (cont.) Sir Eric *m* 2nd 23 June 1937 Margaret Vivian (*d* 4 March 1995), dau of Charles Perkins, of Toronto, Canada, and *d* 30 Aug 1962, having by her had issue:

1a *Nicolas Charles Vansittart [Nicolas Bowater Esq, Dundle Farm, Bells Yew Green, Tunbridge Wells, Kent]; *b* 6 April 1943; *educ* Eton; *m* 6 Oct 1964 *Jacqueline Mina Hartley, dau of Peter Armstrong Hartley Marriott, of Thyro Grove, London N9, and has issue:

1b *Brooke Eric Vansittart; *b* 31 March 1965

2b *Justin Nicolas Vansittart; *b* 29 Sept 1966;

2a *Sarah Vansittart; *b* 2 June 1939; *m* 12 July 1962 Peter William Talbot-Ponsonby, son of Lt-Col John Talbot-Ponsonby, of Todenham Manor, Moreton-in-Marsh, Glos (*see* SHREWSBURY and WATERFORD, E), and has issue

(1) Gladys; *m* 1913 Gerrard Masterman Loly

(2) Phyllis Irene; *m* 1st 1914 William Timmis and had issue; *m* 2nd Capt Cecil Mackintosh Boileau and *d* 26 April 1959

(3) Nina; *m* André Fillonneau, and *d* 1925

4 Herbert James; *b* 9 Nov 1869

5 Arthur Edward; *b* 18 Feb 1873

6 Sydney, of Bury Hall, Edmonton; *b* 29 Aug 1874; *m* Jeanette Lucille — (*d* 23 Dec 1967 aged 77) and *d* 14 May 1939

7 Norman Vansittart; *b* 1 July 1882; *m* 1st 1907 Jessie Selina Talbot (*d* 1925) and had:

(1) *Norman Knightley Vansittart [Major Norman Bowater, 4 Malvern Rd, Ashford, Kent]; *m* 1 Nov 1944 *Jessie, dau of John Barber Sproat, of Lennox Plunton, Borgue, Kirkcudbrightshire, and has issue:

1a *Jane Margaret; *b* 28 July 1950

7 (cont.) Norman Bowater *m* 2nd 1925 Jessie F (*m* 2nd 17 Dec 1948 Sir Dudley Bowater, 3rd Bt (*see* below)), dau of W J Frampton, of Stone, Kent, and *d* 6 May 1934, having by her had issue:

(2) *Michael Vansittart; *b* 7 Oct 1928; *educ* Ashford GS; served RAF; *m* 20 Aug 1955 *Joan Edith, est dau of Joseph Hughes, of Osterley, Middx, and has issue:

1a *David Vansittart; *b* 7 May 1957

2a *Nigel Vansittart; *b* 21 July 1961

3a *Michael Richard; *b* 12 Feb 1963

1a *Sara Ann; *b* 16 Jan 1959

(1) *Pamela Ann [Mrs Roger Burdge, 3 Sheafe Dr, Cranbrook, Kent TN17 2PH]; *m* Aug 1953 *Roger Derek Burdge, son of W D Burdge, of Hocker Edge, Cranbrook, Kent, and has issue:

1a *Nicholas Andrew; *b* 28 May 1955

1 Edith Annie; *b* 6 April 1864; *d* unm 7 Jan 1930

2 Mabel; *b* 3 Sept 1871; *m* 2 July 1896 Harold Greenwood, and *d* 16 June 1919

WILLIAM VANSITTART BOWATER *d* 28 April 1907. His est son,

Sir Thomas Vansittart Bowater, 1st Bt (UK), so *cr* 16 July 1914, DL; *b* 29 Oct 1862; MP City London 1924–38, Govr Roy Hosps, Treas Roy Masonic Inst for Boys, Chm Morden College Tstees, V-Pncpl Imp Soc Kts Bachelor, Hon Col 10th Roy Fus (City London Regt), Lt City; Hon Freeman Manchester, Alderman City London 1907, Sheriff 1905–06 and Ld Mayor 1913–14; Almoner Christ's Hosp, Govr Irish Society, ktd 1906, Kt 1st Cl Order St Olaf Norway; Grand Cdr Redeemer Greece, Cdr Legion Honour France, Cdr Order Leopold, Cdr 1st Cl Dannebrog, Palmes Académiques France, Offr Order Crown of Belgium; *m* 1st 8 June 1887 Emily Margaret, DGStJ (*d* 3 June 1924), dau of John Spencer, of Croydon, and had:

1 **Sir Rainald Vansittart Bowater, 2nd Bt**; *b* 27 Jan 1888; *m* 18 June 1914 Ethel Maud, 3rd dau of John Keeler-Grix, of Keith Lodge, Woodside, S Norwood, and *d* 2 March 1945, leaving issue:

(1) *Daphne Audrey; *b* 15 July 1919; *m* —

(2) *Rowena Maud; *b* 11 Oct 1926; *m* —

2 **Sir (Thomas) Dudley Blennerhassett Bowater, 3rd Bt**; *b* 29 Sept 1889; Capt TFR, formerly Capt Westminster Dragoons, Liveryman Gardeners' Co; *m* 1st 8 Jan 1916 Kathleen Mary (*d* 24 April 1921), only child of Albert A Frost, of Bayfield, Rugby; *m* 2nd 17 Dec 1948 Jessie F, dau of W J Frampton, of Stone, Kent, and widow of his unc Norman Vansittart Bowater, and *dspm* 3 March 1972, leaving issue by 1st w:

(1) Kathleen Stella Mary; *b* 25 March 1921; *m* 19 Sept 1945 Leslie Colling-Mudge, son of Percy Colling-Mudge, of Roxburgh Park, Harrow, Middx

3 Victor Spence, Capt 4th Bn London Roy Fus; *b* 24 May 1891; *m* 8 Feb 1917 Hilda Mary (*d* 11 Aug 1918), dau of W Henry Potter, of Croydon, and *d* 10 Sept 1967, leaving:

(1) Sir JOHN VANSITTART BOWATER, **4th and present Bt**

4 Leslie Frank; *b* 8 Jan 1898; Capt 3rd Dragoon Gds; *d* May 1933

1 Elsie Mary (Queenie); *b* 14 Oct 1893

2 Doris Margaret; *b* 20 June 1896; *m* 15 Nov 1916 Norman Gerald Kerr Salmon, MC, 3rd Bn Leics Regt, 2nd s of Hedley W Salmon, of Rearsby, Leics

Sir Thomas *m* 2nd 12 Aug 1925 Alice Mary (*d* 12 April 1949), dau of Samuel Hoskins and widow of Archibald Coysgarne-Sim, of Harrow Weald Park, and *d* 28 March 1938

BOWDEN

Arms: Quarterly, sa. and or, over all a bow in bend of the second, between two cycle wheels charged in the centre with a winged foot couped at the ankle, all ppr. **Crest:** A heron's head erased at the neck ppr. and gorged with a mural crown gold. **Motto:** *Fide et spe* ('With faith and hope'). **Creation:** Bt. (UK) 23 June 1915.

SIR FRANK HOUSTON BOWDEN, 3RD BT, of the City of Nottingham [Sir Frank Bowden Bt, The Old Vicarage, Winkfield, Windsor, Berks SL4 4SE]; *b* 10 Aug 1909; *s* f 1960; *educ* Rugby and Merton Coll Oxford (BA 1931, MA 1953); added forename Houston 1960, Lt (S) RNVR WW II, industrialist and landowner; *m* 1st 28 April 1934 (*divorce* 1936) Marie José Stiénon de Messey, only dau of Charles Stiénon, of Paris, and Countess Laure de Messey, and has issue:

1 +NICHOLAS RICHARD [Nicholas Bowden Esq, 4 Hensting Farm Cottages, Fishers Pond, Eastleigh, Hants SO5 7HH]; *b* 13 Aug 1935; *educ* Millfield

Sir FRANK *m* 2nd 3 March 1937 Lydia Eveline (*d* 1981), dau of Jean Manolovici, of Bucharest, Roumania; *m* 3rd 1989 *Oriol Annette Mary, only dau of Charles Hooper Bath, of London, and has further issue by his 2nd w:

2 Adrian Harold Houston; *b* 30 June 1938; *educ* Radley and Merton Coll Oxford (BA 1962, MA 1967); added forename Houston 1960; *m* 20 April 1968 *Marjorie Walter, est dau of John Dozier Gordan, of New York, and *d* Oct 1995, leaving issue:

(1) +Alexander Gordan; *b* 14 May 1972
(2) +Richard Waring Baylor; *b* 1979
(1) *Stephanie Florence; *b* 1975

3 +Aubrey Francis Houston [Aubrey Bowden Esq, The Old Vicarage, Winkfield, Windsor, Berks SL4 4SE]; *b* 16 Feb 1940; *educ* Eton and Merton Coll Oxford. (BA 1965, MA 1969); added forename Houston 1960; *m* 4 Oct 1969 *Mary Julia, dau of David Richard Colville (*see* COLVILLE OF CULROSS, V), and has had:

(1) James Edward Houston; *b* 1975; *d* 1994
(1) *Victoria Houston; *b* 1973

4 +Gregory Andrew Houston [Gregory Bowden Esq, Bucknell Manor, Bicester, Oxon]; *b* 1 July 1948; *educ* Eton and Mansfield Coll Oxford (MA 1970); added forename Houston 1960; *m* 1978 *Michaela, dau of Sir John Figgess, KBE, CMG, and has issue:

(1) +Charles John Houston; *b* 1986
(1) *Alexandra Frances Houston; *b* 1981
(2) *Georgina Houston; *b* 1983

Lineage: WILLIAM BOWDEN, of Bristol, gs of John Bowden, also of Bristol, had issue:

Sir Frank Bowden, 1st Bt (UK), so *cr* 23 June 1915, JP, FRGS; *b* 30 Jan 1848; fndr and chm Raleigh Cycle Co and Sturmey Archer Gears; *m* 17 Sept 1879 Amelia Frances (*d* 4 April 1937), dau of Col Alexander Houston, of California, and had issue:

1 HAROLD (Sir), **2nd Bt**
2 Claud; *b* 4 Aug 1890; *d* 21 Oct 1906
1 Helen; *m* 29 June 1910 John Davison Barnsdale (*d* 5 Aug 1960) and had two s
2 Winifred; *m* 6 June 1906 Capt Harold Mowat, MD, RAMC, of 51 Hanover Gate Mansions, London NW, and *d* 1 May 1915, leaving issue
3 (Caroline) Louise; *m* 31 July 1918 Edwin John Tanner (*d* 11 June 1939), son of Sir Henry Tanner, CB, ISO, and had issue:

(1) *Anne Elizabeth; *b* 14 Dec 1919; *m* 4 April 1945 *Thomas Robson Deighton, MA, BSc, and has issue:

1a *Rupert John Greenway, b, 17 Aug 1946
2a *Thomas Nicholas; *b* 3 May 1949

4 Sylvia; *m* 26 Jan 1916 Maj Leonard Owen Whitaker Taylor, MB, ChB, RAMC (SR)

Sir FRANK *d* 25 April 1921; his only surv son,

Sir Harold Bowden, 2nd Bt, GBE (1929); *b* 9 July 1880; *educ* Clifton, Lausanne and Clare Coll Camb; High Sheriff Notts 1933, pres Raleigh Industries, Rudge-Whitworth, Triumph Cycle, Raleigh Cycle and Sturmey-Archer Gears, Br Cycle and Motor Cycle Mfrs Union 1920–23 and 1937, Motor and Cycle Trades Benevolent Fund 1924–25, v-pres Fedn of Br Industries, chm Cncl Br Olympic Assoc 1931, Grand Cross Order Phoenix; *m* 1st 7 July 1908 (*divorce* 1919) Vera, dau of Joseph Whitaker, JP, FZS, of Rainworth Lodge, Mansfield, Notts, and had issue:

1 Sir FRANK HOUSTON BOWDEN, **3rd and present Bt**

1 *Ruth [Mrs Ernest Wittmann, Flat 3, Hale House, 34 De Vere Gdns, London W8 5AQ]; *b* 26 Feb 1911; *m* 1st 8 June 1932 (*divorce* 1947) Christopher Bourchier Wrey (*d* 1976), yr son of Edward Castell Wrey, of Oxton, Notts (*see* WREY, Bt); *m* 2nd 3 Sept 1947 Ernest Wittmann (*d* 2 Sept 1995), son of Armin Wittmann, of Zilina, Czechoslovakia

Sir Harold *m* 2nd 18 Jan 1920 Muriel Smythe (*d* 24 Oct 1952), dau of William Ker-Douglas, of Dalry, Ayrshire; *m* 3rd 4 Nov 1952 June Bowden (*d* 30 June 1953), dau of Thomas Henry MacKay, of Birmingham, and formerly w of George Karpeles Schenker; *m* 4th 11 Feb 1957 Valerie Raymont, dau of Richard Raymont Came, AIMM, FRGS, of 8 Weymouth St, London W1, and widow of Albert Renfew Porter, and *d* 24 Aug 1960

BOWEN

Arms: Az. a lion rampant within an orle, all within four roses or and as many bezants alternately. **Crest:** A lion sejant ppr., holding in the dexter paw a Bowen knot arg. **Motto:** *Audaces fortuna juvat* ('Fortune favours the brave'). **Creation:** Bt. (UK) 10 Jan 1921.

SIR MARK EDWARD MORTIMER BOWEN, 5TH BT, of Colworth, Co Bedford [Sir Mark Bowen Bt, 14 Pendarves Rd, London SW20 8TS]; *b* 17 Oct 1958; *s* f 1989; *educ* Wellington; *m* 1983 *Kerry Tessa, dau of Michael John Moriarty, of The Grey House, Links Rd, Worthing, Sussex, and has issue:

1 +GEORGE EDWARD MICHAEL; *b* 27 Dec 1987
1 *Grace Francesca; *b* 1989

Lineage: EDWARD BOWEN, of Hanley, Staffs, son of Edward T Bowen, of Hanley; *m* Clarissa, dau of Thomas Hackwood, and had issue:

Sir Albert Edward Bowen, 1st Bt (UK), so *cr* 10 Jan 1921, JP (Beds), High Sheriff 1910; *b* 1 Nov 1858; pres Buenos Aires Great S Rlwy Co; *m* 24 April 1884 Alice Anita (*d* 21 Nov 1943), dau of Frederick Crowther, of Buenos Aires, and had issue:

1 EDWARD CROWTHER (Sir), **2nd Bt**
2 Harold Cedric; *b* 4 Nov 1896; *m* 20 Aug 1921 Vera (*d* 1967), dau of Alexander Polianov, of Kharkov, Russia, and *d* 1959, leaving issue:

(1) +Nicholas Edward [W/Cdr Nicholas Bowen, Apartado 1301, Ctra Cala Llonga, 07849 St Eulalia, Ibiza, Spain]; *b* 30 April 1923; *educ* Harrow; W/Cdr RAF; served WW II; Mil and Air Attaché Oslo 1968–71; *m* 1944 *Evelyn, dau of Edward Batty, and has issue:

1a +Michael Edward [Michael Bowen Esq, Phoenix House, Beadlam, York]; *b* 14 Dec 1944; *educ* Harrow; *m* 1968 *Gillian Margaret, dau of Col B R D Garside, MC, and has issue:

1b *Nicola Emma; *b* 1969
2b *Victoria Margaret; *b* 1972
3b *Anabel Elizabeth; *b* 1974

2a +Christopher Anthony Richard [Christopher Bowen Esq, 71 Bolingbroke Grove, London SW11]; *b* 24 April 1947; *educ* Harrow; *m* 1975 *Mary Olivia, dau of Alexander Walcot Stewart, and has issue:

1b +Robert Alexander Edward; *b* 1978
1b *Katherine Olivia; *b* 1976
2b *Clare Rowena; *b* 1982

(1) *Clarissa [Mrs Mervyn Heald, Colhook Lodge, Ebernoe, W Sussex GU28 9LE]; *b* 24 April 1929; *m* 26 March 1954 *Mervyn Heald, QC, 2nd son of Sir Lionel Frederick Heald, PC, QC, MP, of Chilworth Manor, Guildford, Surrey, and has had:

1a Edward; *b* 8 March 1971; *d* 14 March 1971
2a *Robert Lionel; *b* 23 Feb 1974; *educ* Eton
1a *Henrietta Sara; *b* 26 Nov 1955; *m* 1981 *Adam Curtis, and has issue:

1b *James Nathaniel; *b* 1990
1b *Sophie Clarissa; *b* 1986

2a *Annabel Clare; *b* 22 Aug 1957; *m* 1989 *Timothy Peter Smith, and has issue:
1b *Harrison Oscar; *b* 1990
1b *Ottoline Amelia; *b* 1994
3a *Julia Elizabeth; *b* 8 Feb 1959; *m* 1979 *Charles Stewart Prescot, and has issue:
1b *Nicholas Hugh; *b* 1980
2b *Rupert James; *b* 1985
1b *Alexandra Constance; *b* 1990
1 Winifred Ada; *m* 1 Oct 1910 Gen Sir Alexander Stanhope Cobbe, VC, GCB, KCSI, DSO (*d* 29 June 1931), 2nd son of Lt-Gen Sir Alexander Hugh Cobbe, KCB, and *d* 11 Aug 1956, having had issue
2 Gertrude Dorothy; *m* 14 Oct 1911 (*divorce* 1925) Sir Kinahan Cornwallis, GCMG, CBE, DSO (*d* 3 June 1959), and *d* 15 Nov 1958, leaving issue
3 Evelyn Constance; *m* 29 July 1911 John Dale Read (*d* 19 March 1940), son of John Jervis Read, of High House, Brentwood, Essex, and *d* 25 Feb 1959, leaving issue

Sir ALBERT *d* 19 Sept 1924; his er son,

Sir Edward Crowther Bowen, 2nd Bt, MC; *b* 11 March 1885; Maj 12th Lancers, formerly Inniskilling Dragoons, WW I; *m* 2 June 1910 May Isobel (*d* 9 March 1972), dau of John Frederick Roberts, of Buenos Aires, and *d* 31 Oct 1937, leaving issue:

1 **Sir John Edward Mortimer Bowen, 3rd Bt**; *b* 2 June 1918; *k* while motor-racing 12 Aug 1939
2 **Sir Thomas Frederic Charles Bowen, 4th Bt**; *b* 11 Oct 1921; Ieduc Eton; Capt Wilts Regt; *m* 30 Aug 1947 *Jill Claude Murray [Jill Lady Bowen, 1 Barford Close, Fleet, Hants], dau of Cyril Lloyd Evans, of Prestea, Ghana, and *d* 1989, having had issue:
(1) Sir MARK EDWARD MORTIMER BOWEN, **5th and present Bt**
(1) *Julia Rosemary [Mrs Julia Fewings, 13 Barnet Close, Yeovil, Somerset]; *b* 10 July 1950; *m* 1970 (*divorce* 1983) Lt-Cdr Robert Andrew Fewings, RN, and has had issue:
1a Paul Stuart; *b* 1973; *d* 1993
2a *James Andrew Murray; *b* 1977
(2) *Margot Claire [Mrs Malcolm Kirkpatrick, 70 Netherby Park, Weybridge, Surrey]; *b* 30 March 1952; *m* 1974 *Malcolm Ivison Kirkpatrick and has issue:
1a *Joanna Claire; *b* 1978
2a *Verity Juliet Elizabeth; *b* 1986
(3) A dau; *b* and *d* 13 Jan 1954
1 Angela Betty Isobel; *m* 1st 1 June 1933 (*divorce* 1944) Ivan Francis Low, Capt KOYLI, er s of Maj Henry Francis Low, and had issue; *m* 2nd — Farris

BOWLBY

Arms: Per fess sa. and arg. a pale with three hind's heads erased two and one, and as many annulets one and two, all counterchanged. **Crest:** Three annulets interlaced, one and two or, between two thorn branches ppr. **Motto:** *Ne cede malis* ('Yield not to adversity'). **Creation:** Bt. (UK) 17 July 1923.

SIR RICHARD PEREGRINE LONGSTAFF BOWLBY, 3RD BT, of Manchester Square, Borough of St Marylebone [Sir Richard Bowlby Bt, Boundary House, Wyldes Close, London NW11 7JB]; *b* 11 Aug 1941; *s* unc 1993; *educ* Dauntsey's Sch; *m* 1963 *Xenia, dau of Roderick Paul Agnew Garrett, of 28 Southwood Lane, London N6, and has issue:

1 +BENJAMIN [Benjamin Bowlby Esq, 15 Highwood Ave, London N12 8QL]; *b* 2 Nov 1966; *educ* King Alfred Sch; *m* 1992 *Mylanna Sophia, er dau of Michael Case Colyer, of Harlech, Gwynedd, and has:
(1) +Roderick Peter Colyer; *b* 18 July 1996
1 *Sophia; *b* 1969

Lineage: Rev THOMAS BOWLBY (7th in descent from Richard Bowlby, of Helmsley, Yorks, who *d* 1553), MA Cantab, Rector Tudhoe, perpetual Curate Painshaw, Co Durham; *b* 1762; *m* 3 March 1786 Eleanora Elizabeth (*d* 15 Aug 1842), er dau of Anthony Salvin, of Sunderland Bridge Ho, Co Durham, and *d* 28 Jan 1835, having had a 2nd but est surv s:

THOMAS BOWLBY, RA, of Bishopwearmouth, Co Durham; *b* 19 Feb 1790; Capt; *m* 1st 1 Feb 1817 Williamina Martha Arnold (*d* 3 Feb 1834), dau of Maj-Gen William Balfour, of Pilrig, Pres Cncl and C-in-C New Brunswick, and had issue; *m* 2nd 24 Aug 1835 Margaret Matilda (*d* 23 April 1882), dau of Pulteney Mein, of Forge Lodge, Canonbie, Dumfriesshire, and *d* 11 Aug 1842, having by her had issue; the est s of the 1st w:

THOMAS WILLIAM BOWLBY; *b* 7 Jan 1818; *m* 23 Sept 1848 Frances Marion (*d* 11 May 1891), yr dau of Pulteney Mein, Surgeon 73rd Regt, of Forge Lodge, Canonbie, Dumfriesshire, and *d* Sept 1860, leaving a 3rd s:

Sir Anthony Alfred Bowlby, 1st Bt (UK), so *cr* 17 July 1923, KCB, KCMG, KCVO, FRCS, Hon Maj-Gen AMS, Hon DCL Durham 1923, Consultant Surg St Bartholomew's Hosp, Surgn to HM EDWARD VII's Household 1904–10, Hon Surgn-in-Ordinary to HM GEORGE V 1910, PRCS 1920–23, Sr Surgn-in-Charge Portland Hosp S African War 1899–1900 (despatches, medal), Consultant Surgn BEF WW I (despatches), American DSM; *b* 10 May 1855; *m* 12 April 1898 Maria Bridget (*d* 12 Sept 1957), est dau of Rev Canon Hon Hugh Wynne Mostyn (*see* MOSTYN, B), and *d* 7 April 1929, leaving:

1 **Sir Anthony Hugh Mostyn Bowlby, 2nd Bt**; *b* 13 Jan 1906; *educ* Wellington and New Coll Oxford; dir GKN; *m* 27 Jan 1930 *Dora Evelyn [Dowager Lady Bowlby, The Old Rectory, Ozleworth, Wotton-under-Edge, Glos GL12 7QA], only dau of John Charles Allen, of York, and *d* 1993, leaving issue:
(1) *Anthea [Mrs Jolyon Dromgoole, 13 Gladstone St, London SE1 6EY]; *b* 21 Aug 1930; *m* 10 March 1956 *Jolyon Dromgoole, 2nd son of Nicholas Arthur Dromgoole, of 167 Turney Rd, London SE21, and has issue:
1a *Emma; *b* 8 May 1957
2a *Julia; *b* 16 Sept 1961
3a *Rose; *b* 8 Jan 1964
4a *Susanna; *b* 8 Jan 1964
5a *Belinda; *b* 8 Jan 1964
(2) *Sophia; *b* 19 Oct 1944
2 (Edward) John Mostyn, MRCP 1960, FRCP 1964; *b* 26 Feb 1907; *educ* Trin Coll Cambridge (MA 1932, BCh 1933, MD 1939); Lt-Col RAMC WW II, consultant psychiatrist Tavistock Clinic (dep dir 1946–49), Consultant Mental Health WHO 1950; *m* 16 April 1938 *Ursula [Mrs John Bowlby, Wyldes Close Corner, Hampstead Way, London NW11 7JB], 3rd dau of Tom George Longstaff, MD, and *d* 1990 leaving issue:
(1) Sir RICHARD PEREGRINE LONGSTAFF BOWLBY, **3rd and present Bt**
(2) +Robert John Mostyn [Robert Bowlby Esq, Wyldes Close Corner, Wyldes Close, London NW11 7JB]; *b* 25 April 1948; *educ* Grenville Coll
(1) *Mary Hamilton Victoria Ignatia [Mrs Anthony Gatling, White Lodge, Berwick St James, Salisbury, Wilts]; *b* 26 Oct 1939; *m* 1st 28 March 1964 (*divorce* 1980) Capt Timothy Richard Holbrook Dawson, BScEng, RE, only s of Lt-Col Richard John Palliser Dawson, OBE; *m* 2nd 1980 *Anthony Gatling and has issue by 1st husb:
1a *Guy Philip Richard; *b* 18 Feb 1965; *educ* John Masefield GS and City U; *m* 1997 *Susan, dau of Allan Romero
2a *Patrick Timothy John; *b* 5 Sept 1969; *educ* Solihull Sch and UCL; *m* 1993 *Anna, dau of Rev Canon Richard Kingsbury, of The Rectory, Church Lane, Caversham, Reading
(2) *Pia Rose Whitworth [Mrs Carlos Durán, 70 Northway, London NW11 6PA]; *b* 9 Feb 1945; *m* 27 July 1968 *Carlos Durán-Rodriguez, only son of Don Bernardino Duran Barros, of Caracas, and Doña Dolores Rodriguez de Duran, of Vigo, Spain, and has issue:
1a *Xohan; *b* 22 Sept 1968; *educ* Oak Lodge
2a *Xavier; *b* 29 Dec 1973; *educ* King Alfred Sch
1a *Xulia Tareixa; *b* 9 Jan 1978; *educ* King Alfred Sch
3 +Charles James Mostyn, memb Br Soc Animal Prodn, Br Grassland Soc, Medical Cncl on Alcoholism, C of E Men's Soc, Br Inst Ag Botany and Farm Bldgs Assoc; *b* 8 Dec 1908; *educ* St Catharine's Coll Cambridge
1 (Frances) Winifred Mostyn
2 Marion Ellen Mostyn; *b* 1902/3; *d* unm following a riding accident 5 July 1973
3 *Dorothy Evelyn Mostyn [Lady Phelps Brown, 16 Bradmore Rd, Oxford]; *b* 1910; *m* 14 March 1932 *Sir Ernest Henry Phelps Brown, MBE, FBA, Fell New Coll Oxford, Prof Ec London U, only son of Ernest William Brown, of Calne, Wilts, and has issue:
(1) *Nicholas Anthony Phelps [Nicholas Brown Esq, 73 Fitzjohns Ave, London NW3]; *b* 5 May 1936; *educ* Westminster, Trin Coll Cambridge (MA) and Middx Hosp (MB, BChir); 2nd Lt RA 44th Regt HAA 1955–57; *m* 17 Dec 1960 *Heather Mary, only child of Ronald Hubert White, of 6 Baldock Way, Cambridge, and has issue:
1a *Emily Sarah Phelps; *b* 1 June 1967
(2) *Thomas Henry Phelps; *b* 21 Nov 1948; *educ* Westminster and New Coll Oxford
(1) *Juliet Virgina Phelps; *b* 19 Dec 1934; *educ* Newnham Coll Cambridge; *m* 1964 *Keith Hopkins, Prof Ancient History Cambridge

BOWMAN

Arms: Or on a chevron between three bows stringed palewise gu. two lions combatant of the first between as many escallops arg. **Crest:** Upon a mount vert the stump of a tree ppr., around the upper part a belt sa., pendent therefrom on the dexter side a quiver gu. filled with arrows arg. **Motto:** *Quondam his vicimus armis* ('We conquered formerly with these arms'). **Creation:** Bt. (UK) 23 Jan 1884.

SIR PAUL HUMPHREY ARMYTAGE BOWMAN, 5TH BT, of Holmbury St Mary, Co Surrey [Sir Paul Bowman Bt, Apt 3, 414 Edgecliff Rd, Woollahra, NSW 2028, Australia]; *b* 10 Aug 1921; *s* cousin 1994; *educ* Eton; Maj Coldstream Gds WW II, dir Hill Samuel 1962–78; *m* 1st 15 June 1943 (*divorce* 1947) Felicité Ann Araminta, er dau of Sir Harold Alfred MacMichael, GCMG, DSO (*see* LEVEN and MELVILLE, E); *m* 2nd 12 Feb 1946 (*divorce* 1974) Gabrielle May, dau of Thomas Hapgood Hudson, of Sydney, Australia, and formerly w of Lt-Col Walter Currie, US Army; *m* 3rd 1974 Elizabeth Deirdre (*d* 19–), yr dau of Bruce R Campbell, of Goorianawa, NSW, and formerly w of Maj-Gen Thomas Bell Lindsay Churchill, CB, CBE, MC, and has issue by 2nd w:

1 *Amanda Caroline; *b* 30 Dec 1946

Lineage: JOHN EDDOWES BOWMAN, of Welshpool, Montgomeryshire; *m* 6 July 1809 Elizabeth, dau of William Eddowes, of Shrewsbury, and had, with other issue:

1 WILLIAM (Sir), **1st Bt**

2 John Eddowes; *b* 7 July 1819; Prof Pract Chem King's Coll London; *m* Ellen, dau of Thomas Paget, of Leicester, and *d* Feb 1856, leaving issue:

(1) John Herbert; *b* 27 Sept 1846; *m* Katharine (*d* 1874), dau of John S Lister, and *d* 5 Sept 1932, leaving issue:

1a Herbert Lister, DSc, Fell Magdalen Coll Oxford, Waynflete Prof Mineralogy; *b* 15 March 1874; *m* 28 Dec 1921 Pleasance Edith (*d* 9 April 1965), dau of James Walker, MA, of Kempsey, Worcs, and *d* 22 April 1942

(2) George Cyril; *m* 1st Frederica Merriman; *m* 2nd Margaret Percival Clark and *d* 6 March 1915, having had issue by his 1st w:

1a Paget John Merriman; *m* 3 May 1905 Sybil Mary, yr dau of Capt Norcliffe Gilpin, 84th Regt, and *d* 23 Feb 1928 following a car crash

1a Ethel Mary; *m* 10 April 1907 Guy Eddowes Paget Bowman, MA (*d* 17 March 1933; *see* below)

The er son,

Sir William Bowman, 1st Bt (UK), so *cr* 23 Jan 1884, MD, LLD, FRS, FRCS(E); *b* 20 July 1816; consulting surgn, V-Pres Roy London Ophthalmic Hosp, Prof Physiology King's Coll Lond (Hon Fell, memb Cncl), original memb Court Victoria U; *m* 28 Dec 1842 Harriet (*d* 25 Oct 1900), 5th dau of Thomas Paget, of Leicester, and had issue:

1 WILLIAM PAGET (Sir), **2nd Bt**

2 John Frederick; *b* 1 Nov 1850; *m* 8 July 1875 Cecilia (*d* 14 Oct 1926), dau of Edward Charrington, of Bury's Court, nr Reigate, and *d* 21 Dec 1914, leaving issue:

(1) Humphrey Ernest, CMG (1936), CBE (1919); *b* 26 July 1879; *educ* Eton and New Coll Oxford (MA 1905); T/Maj Roy Fus WW I, Egyptian CS, Dir Educn Palestine 1920–36, Min Info 1939, FO 1941–45, KStJ, Cdr Order Nile; *m* 1st 2 Dec 1916 Frances Guinevere (*d* 13 Feb 1923), dau of Lt-Col Arthur Henry Armytage, RHA (*see* ARMYTAGE, Bt); *m* 2nd 20 Aug 1925 Elinor Marion (*d* 5 Feb 1957), widow of Arthur William Bowman (*see* below), and *d* 23 March 1965, having had issue:

1a Sir PAUL HUMPHREY ARMYTAGE BOWMAN, **5th and present Bt**

1a *Cynthia Pamela Mary [Lady Macdonald, Ollach, Braes, Isle of Skye]; *b* 22 Oct 1918; *m* 1st 19 Nov 1943 (*divorce* 1969) R-Adml Josef Czeslaw Bartosik, CB, DSC, RN, s of Thomas Bartosik, of Poznan, Poland; *m* 2nd 17 Oct 1980 *V-Adml Sir Roderick Douglas Macdonald, KBE, and has issue by 1st husb:

1b *Jan Joseph [Jan Bartosik Esq, 11 Morpeth Mansions, London SW1]; *b* 2 Aug 1946; *educ* Downside; *m* 1978 *Lesley Anne, dau of Dr J Meehan, and has issue:

1c *James; *b* 1980

1c *Lucy Olivia; *b* 1983

2b *Conrad Joseph (Sam) [Conrad Bartosik Esq, 4 Beauclerc Rd, London W6]; *b* 2 March 1948; *m* 1978 *Claudia, dau of Maj R Pitman, and has issue:

1c *Luke; *b* 1982

2c *Daniel; *b* 1985

3c *Humphrey; *b* 1989

3b *Mathew Timothy [Mathew Bartosik Esq, 9 Lansdown Crescent, Cheltenham, Glos]; *b* 28 March 1954; *m* 1980 *Catherine, dau of J McDonnell, and has issue:

1c *Robert; *b* 1982

1b *Kristina Cynthia [Mrs Christopher Thomasson, 2 Hill Close, Pershore, Worcs]; *b* 5 May 1945; *m* 1969 *Christopher Lucas Thomasson, of Somerton Castle, nr Lincoln, s of Franklin Thomasson, and has issue:

1c *Thomas; *b* 3 July 1970

2c *Charles; *b* 1976

1c *Sophy; *b* 20 April 1969

2c *Clare; *b* 1977

(2) Clive Frederick, MC, JP (Berks 1928–46); *b* 3 Feb 1884; *educ* Eton and New Coll Oxford (BA 1905); Maj RASC, Bursar Wellington 1920–46; *m* 10 April 1920 Erica Violet (*d* 1972), yr dau of Col Robert George Wardlaw-Ramsay, DL, of Whitehall and Tillicoultry, and *d* 11 Feb 1972, leaving issue:

1a Martin Ramsay; *b* 10 Nov 1928; *educ* Ampleforth and Ch Ch Oxford (BA 1952, MA 1957); barrister Inner Temple 1953, 2nd Lt The King's Regt, CC Inverness-shire 1973–75; *d* 8 Sept 1996

1a *Erica Rosemary [Mrs Douglas Law, Redfriars, E Linton, E Lothian EH40 3DS]; *m* 18 Sept 1948 *Douglas Burch Law, late Maj Seaforth Highrs, s of S/Ldr George Frederick Law, OBE, of Ipswich, and has issue:

1b *Nicholas Simon; *b* 26 May 1954; *educ* Wellington; *m* 1979 *Virginia Halliday and has issue:

1c *Hamish; *b* 1982

1c *Sarah Catherine; *b* 1980

2b *James Christopher; *b* 30 May 1956; *educ* Wellington

2a *Heather Mary [Mrs Trevor Cairns, 4 Ashmore Terrace, Sunderland, Co Durham SR2 7DE]; *b* 1922; *m* 3 March 1956 *Trevor Cairns, s of John Thomas Cairns, and has issue:

1b *Conrad Thomas; *b* 28 Dec 1957; *educ* Dublin and Edinburgh Us

2b *Edmund Frederick; *b* 17 Sept 1960; *educ* Peterhouse Cambridge; *m* 1987 *Alison Margery Anna Court

3a *Dorothea Vivien; *b* 1924; nun Order Sacred Heart

(1) Dorothea Percy; *m* 4 April 1899 Hubert Brinton (*d* 5 April 1941), s of William Brinton, MD, FRCP, FRCS, and *d* 25 March 1951, leaving issue

3 Arthur Gerald (Rev), MA Oxon, Vicar St Mark's Kennington; *b* 1854; *m* 1879 Edith (*m* 2nd 20 July 1905 Robert Harold Paget, s of Arthur Paget, of Loughborough; *d* 18 Jan 1908), dau of William Paget, of St Anne's Manor, Notts, and *d* 8 Sept 1904, leaving issue:

(1) Arthur William; *b* 1887; *m* 24 Jan 1911 Elinor Marion (*m* 2nd 20 Aug 1925 Humphrey Ernest Bowman, CMG, CBE (*d* 23 March 1965; *see* above); *d* 5 Feb 1957), est dau of Rev Charles Conybeare, Vicar Privett, Hants, and *d* 17 April 1918 of wounds recd in action, leaving issue:

1a *Barbara Paget [Mrs Douglas Sender, L'Espine, Millbrook, Jersey, CI]; *b* 3 Jan 1912; *m* 30 April 1932 W/Cdr Douglas Sender, RAF (*d* 1987), yr s of Harry Sender, and has issue:

1b *Michael Conybeare [Maj Michael Sender, 5 Rivermount Gdns, Portsmouth Rd, Guildford, Surrey GU2 5DN]; *b* 5 Sept 1933; *educ* Wellington and RMA Sandhurst; Maj RA; *m* 1st 26 May 1962 (*divorce* 1984) Judy Olivia, dau of Edward Prescott Hedley, and has issue:

1c *Richard Paget; *b* 23 Feb 1964

1c *Katherine Elizabeth; *b* 10 May 1966

1b (cont.) Maj Michael Sender *m* 2nd 19– *Carla Raffaella, dau of Gregorio Barogi, of Misano Monte, Italy

1b *Penelope Markland [Mrs Anthony Wells, Wirrabara, Lot 62, Devon Rd, Exeter, NSW 2579, Australia]; *b* 13 May 1936; *m* 20 June 1959 *Lt-Col Anthony John Carter Wells, RA (ret), RAA (ret), s of John Carter Wells, and has:

1c *Pandora Markland; *b* 21 Jan 1965; has issue:

1d *Samantha Markland JOBBINS WELLS; *b* 1986

1c (cont.) Pandora Wells *m* 1991 *Gregory John Bailey and has further issue:

2d *Jasmine; *b* 1993

2b *Joanna Paget [Mrs Christopher Askham, 10 Frogmore Village, St Albans, Herts]; *b* 18 Jan 1953; *m* 1982 *Christopher John Askham and has issue:

1c *Jonathan Piers; *b* 1986

4 Harry Ernest, MRCSF; *b* 1855; *d* 5 April 1938

1 Eliza; *d* unm 16 Sept 1917 aged 73

2 Mary; *m* 1877 Sir Alfred Bray Kempe, MA, DCL, FRS (*d* 21 April 1921), 3rd s of Rev John Edward Kempe, MA, Vicar St James's Piccadilly, and *d* 4 June 1893

3 Agnes; *m* 1st 1876 John Conyers Merrion, MRCS (*d* 1888); *m* 2nd 14 May 1892 Rev Earle Augustus Langston, Vicar Hebburn, Co Durham, and *d* 30 Aug 1893

Sir WILLIAM *d* 29 March 1892; his est son,

Sir WILLIAM BOWMAN later PAGET-BOWMAN, **2nd Bt**; *b* 25 Sept 1845; *educ* Univ Coll Oxford (MA); barrister, Registrar Corpn Sons of Clergy, Treas Cholmondeley Charities, Dir Clergy Mutual Assur Soc; *m* 9 Aug 1870 Emily Frances (*d* 13 Jan 1927), dau of William Swabey, DL, of Wavendon Ho, Bucks, Capt RHA, and had issue:

1 PAGET MERVYN (Sir), **3rd Bt**

2 Guy Eddowes Paget; *b* 1878; barrister Lincoln's Inn, Actuary Lower Ho Convocation (Canterbury Prov), Treas Cholmondeley Charities; *educ* Univ Coll Oxford (MA); *m* 10 April 1907 Ethel Mary (*d* 11 Feb 1943), only dau of George Cyril Bowman (*see* above), and *d* 17 March 1933, leaving issue:

(1) *Nancy Freda; *b* 31 Aug 1913; *m* 1st 5 June 1937 Vernon Dalziel Riddell Pakenham Gilbert, F/Lt RAF (ret) (*d* 17 May 1965), s of Rev Frederick William

Pakenham Gilbert; *m* 2nd 1966 *James Henry Guy Burney and has issue by her 1st husb:

1a *Anthony Guy Pakenham; *b* 27 May 1939; *educ* Tonbridge and Durham U (BA 1966); *m* 23 July 1966 *Brenda Constance Mary, dau of John Anthony Hazelbrock, and has issue:

1b *Christopher Guy; *b* 24 Feb 1968

2a *Richard John Michael; *b* 26 Aug 1942; *educ* Lancing and Coll Estate Management London; *m* 26 March 1966 *Patricia Jean, dau of Lionel W Butt

1 Muriel Paget; *m* 22 Jan 1896 Samuel Forde Ridley, JP, MP Rochester (*d* 17 Nov 1944), only s of Samuel Edwin Ridley, and *d* 25 July 1928, leaving issue

Sir WILLIAM *d* 7 Jan 1917; his er son,

Rev Sir Paget Mervyn Bowman, 3rd Bt; *educ* Magdalen Coll Oxford (MA), Vicar Newington Kent 1907–11, St Luke Woodside S Norwood 1911–19, Rector Shere, Surrey 1919–50, Surrogate Commissary for Bp Trinidad 1918, RD Cranleigh 1928–48; *b* 1 Sept 1873; *m* 1st 12 Feb 1901 Rachel Katherine (*d* 26 Sept 1936), yst dau of James Hanning, of Kilcrone, Co Cork; *m* 2nd 11 Sept 1946 Evelyn Florence, MBE (1919), dau of Col William Pott and widow of Sir John Murray Ewart, CIE, Indian Police, and *d* 2 Dec 1955, leaving by his 1st w:

1 **Sir John Paget Bowman, 4th Bt**; *b* 12 Feb 1904; *educ* Eton; 2nd Lt 98th Surrey and Sussex Yeo, Queen Mary's Army Field Bde, RA (TA), industrial strategist, fin manager and Dir Centl Europe Western Electric, company sec Decca Records, gen manager Brymbo, gen manager Carter & Co Poole 1947–52, dir 1951–52, proprietor Purbeck Decorative Tile Co 1952; *m* 1st 7 Feb 1931 Countess Cajetana Hoyos (*d* 1 Feb 1948), dau of Count Edgar Hoyos, of Schloss Sooss, Lower Austria, and had issue:

(1) David Anthony Paget; *b* 16 Oct 1935; *educ* Bradfield; *m* 22 June 1968 *Valerie Winifred (*m* 2nd *Greig Barr) [Mrs Greig Barr, Sherwood, Boar's Hill, Oxford], only dau of Reginald Cyril Tatham, FRCS, and *d* 9 April 1985

(1) *Rachael Elinor [Mrs Gerald Clarkson, Manor Farm House, Ryme Intrinseca, Dorset, DT9 6JX]; *b* 5 Oct 1938; SRN; *m* 8 July 1967 *Gerald William Wensley Clarkson, er s of Patrick Wensley Clarkson, MBE, FRC, and has issue (*see* LANE, Bt)

1 (cont.) The **4th Bt** *m* 2nd 14 July 1948 Frances Edith Marian (*d* 1992), dau of Sir (James) Beethom Whitehead, KCMG, of Efford Park, Lymington, Hants (*see* MIDLETON, V); *m* 3rd 1993 *Christian, yst dau of Col Sir Arthur Grant, 10th Bt, CBE, DSO, of Monymusk and Cullen (*qv*), and widow of John Gordon Ogston Miller, and *d* 16 Aug 1994

1 Frances Rachel *b* 2 Jan 1902; *d* unm 17 Jan 1970

BOWNESS

Arms: Four pallets sable overall within a cross flory nowy round pierced and parted a roundel or. **Crest:** A demi-bull argent armed and unguled and holding in the mouth a sword point downwards in bend or. **Supporters:** Dexter a dachshund reguardent sableholding in the mouth a daffodil slipped and leaved or; sinister a dachshund reguardent tenné holding in the mouth a daffodil slipped and leaved or. **Motto:** *N'Esperdre ja mes* ('Never give up'). **Creation:** B. (LP. UK) 18 Nov 1995.

THE BARON BOWNESS, of Warlingham in the County of Surrey and of Croydon in the London Borough of Croydon (Sir Peter Spencer Bowness, CBE (1981), DL Gtr London (1981)) [The Rt Hon The Lord Bowness CBE DL, Three Gables, 10 Westview Rd, Warlingham, Surrey CR6 9JD]; *b* 19 May 1943; *educ* Whitgift (Govr Whitgift Fndn 1982–96); slr 1966 (ptnr Weightman, Sadler 1970–), memb (C) Croydon Cncl 1968 (Leader 1976–94, Mayor Croydon 1979–80), chm London Boroughs Assoc 1978–94, dep chm Assoc Metropolitan Authorities 1978–80, memb: Audit Commn 1983–95, UK Delegn Cncl Europe 1990– and (for UK) Bureau and Transportn and Telecommunicns Commn EC Ctee Regns 1994–, Freeman City London 1984, ktd 1987; *m* 1st 1969 (divorce) Marianne Hall and has a dau; *m* 2nd 1984 *Mrs Patricia Jane Cook

Lineage: HUBERT SPENCER BOWNESS; *m* Doreen (Peggy) — and had:

PETER SPENCER (Sir), *cr* a **Baron**

BOWYER-SMYTH

Arms: Quarterly, 1st and 4th, sa. a fess dancettée arg. billettée sa., between three lioncels rampant guardant of the 2nd, each supporting an altar or, flaming ppr. (for SMYTH); 2nd and 3rd, or a bend vair, cotised gu. (for BOWYER). **Crests:** 1 A salamander in flames ppr. (for SMYTH); 2 On a ducal coronet or a heraldic tiger sejant arg. (for BOWYER). **Motto:** *Qua pote lucet* ('He shines in every way possible'). **Creation:** Bt (E) 28 Nov 1661.

SIR THOMAS WEYLAND BOWYER-SMYTH, 15TH BT, of Hill Hall, Essex [Sir Thomas Bowyer-Smyth Bt, c/o Stour House, Fordwich, Canterbury, Kent CT2 0DA]; *b* 25 June 1960; *s f* 1978; *m* 14 Aug 1992 (*divorce* 1997) Sara Louise, dau of Kurt Breinlinger, of Hong Kong

Lineage: JOHN SMITH, of Saffron Walden, Essex (allegedly descended from Sir Roger de Clarendon, illegitimate s of the Black Prince), Sheriff Essex and Herts *c* 1539; *m c* 1508, as his 1st w, Agnes, dau and heiress of Charnocks, of Lancs, and *d c* 1556/7, having had, with other issue:

1 Sir Thomas, of Hill Hall, Essex, MP Essex, Chllr Order Garter, Sec of State *temp* EDWARD VI and ELIZABETH I, Amb to France under the latter; *b* 28 March 1514; *m* 1st 15 April 1549 Elizabeth (*d* 3 Aug 1553), dau of William Karkeck; *m* 2nd 23 July 1554 Philippa (*d* 13 June 1578), widow of Sir John Hampden and dau of John Wilford, and *dsp* 12 Aug 1577

2 GEORGE

3 John, of Walden; *m* Elizabeth and *d* between 27 Feb 1557 and 16 Feb 1557/8, leaving, with two daus:

(1) William; *m* 25 Oct 1574 Jane Cawode and *dsp* 23 Jan 1577

The 2nd s,

GEORGE SMITH, of Ankerwycke Priory, Wraysbury, Bucks; *m* Isabella (*d* 1584) and *d* by 9 March 1584, leaving, with four yr sons:

Sir WILLIAM SMITH, of Hill Hall, Sheriff Essex 1615, inherited his unc's estates, Col in Ireland; *m* 1590 Bridget, dau of Thomas Fleetwood, of The Vache, Chalfont St Giles, Bucks, and *d* 12 Dec 1626, having had, with other issue:

1 Sir William, of Ankerwycke; *m* 1st 9 April 1627 his cousin Helegonway (*bur* 25 Aug 1629), 3rd dau of 1st Viscount Conway (*extinct*), and had:

(1) Edward; *d* unm, *bur* 24 Jan 1652

1 (cont.) Sir William *m* 2nd 1631 Anne (*m* 2nd 1632 Sir William Salter; *bur* 25 Dec 1675), dau of Edward Croft, and *d* 5 March 1631, having by her had no issue

2 THOMAS (Sir), **1st Bt**

1 Elizabeth; *m* 1 Nov 1610 Sir William Spring and had issue. He *d* 1637

2 Bridget; *m* Sir Robert Jocelyn and was *bur* 24 Jan 1662/3 leaving issue. He was *bur* 3 May 1664

The 2nd s,

Sir Thomas Smith, 1st Bt (E), so *cr* 28 Nov 1661, of Hill Hall, Essex, High Sheriff 1633; *m* 1st 1632 Johan (*d* 14 July 1658), dau of Sir Edward Altham, of Mark Hall, Essex, and had issue; *m* 2nd 1664 Beatrice (*dsp, bur* 26 March 1668), widow of Sir John Lloyd, 1st Bt, and dau of Francis Annesley, Viscount Valentia (*qv*), and *d* 5 May 1668, having by his 1st w had, with other issue (*d* young):

1 EDWARD (Sir), **2nd Bt**

2 Charles (Ven), Archdeacon Colchester; *dsp, bur* 12 Sept 1678

3 William; *bapt* 20 April 1639; *m* Ann, dau of R Lynch, and *dsp*

4 James; *bapt* 13 Aug 1640; *m* Elizabeth (*d* 3 April 1705), dau of Sir Robert Parkhurst, and *dsp* 16 June 1711

5 John, of Langley Lawn, Essex; *m* Anne Linde and had a dau

6 Altham, barrister; *m* 1st after 19 Oct 1682 Susanna, *née* Gore, widow of Sir Richard Munden, of Bromley, and had issue:

(1) Althamina; *m* 7 March 1699 Nathaniel Parkhurst and had issue

6 (cont.) Altham Smith *m* 2nd 18 Oct 1691 Lucy Gardon, widow, and by her had:

(2) Lucy

The est surv son,

Sir Edward Smyth, 2nd Bt; *bapt* 28 Sept 1637; *m* 6 May 1674 Jane (*d* 28 July 1720), sis of Sir Peter Vandeput, and *d* 24 June 1713, leaving, with other issue (*d* young):

Sir Edward Smyth, 3rd Bt; *b* 1686; *m* 1st 16 Jan 1709/10 Anne (*d* 18 Oct 1719), dau of Sir Charles Hedges, PC, Sec State *temp* WILLIAM III and ANNE, and had, with other issue:

1 **Sir Edward Smyth, 4th Bt**; *b* 12 Nov 1710; *m* 11 June 1747 Elizabeth Mayse (*d* 22 June 1770), of Milton Bryant, Beds, and *dsp* 4 March 1760

2 **Sir Charles Smyth, 5th Bt**, High Sheriff Essex 1761; *bapt* 12 Oct 1711; *m* 11 April 1760 Elizabeth (*d* 2 Feb 1776), dau of John Burgess, of London, and *dspm* 24 March 1773, leaving:

(1) Ann; *m* 13 Jan 1778 Rev Robert Willan, Vicar Cardington, Beds, and *d* 24 April 1833, leaving issue. He *d* 31 Jan 1796

3 WILLIAM (Sir), **6th Bt**

Sir Edward *m* 2nd Elizabeth, (*dsp* 23 May 1748), dau of John Wood, of London, and *d* 16 Aug 1744

Sir CHARLES's bro,

Sir William Smyth, 6th Bt, of Hill Hall and Horham Hall, Essex, LLB, Rector Theydon Mount and Stapleford Tawney; *m* Abigail (*d* 28 Feb 1787), dau of Andrew Wood, of Shrewsbury, and eventually heiress of her bro, Richard Wood, and had issue:

1 WILLIAM (Sir), **7th Bt**

2 Charles; *b* April 1752; *m* 14 Dec 1779 Philadelphia, dau of Sir George Vandeput, 2nd and last Bt, and *d* May 1792, leaving two daus

3 Richard (Rev), Rector Gt Warley; *b* 4 March 1756; *m* Charlotte, dau of James Montagu, of Lackham Ho, Wilts, and *dsp* Nov 1811

1 Elizabeth; *m* 1776 Capt George Handfield, 40th Regt, of Serlby Hall, Notts, and had issue

Sir WILLIAM *d* 25 Jan 1777; his est son,

Sir William Smijth, 7th Bt, Col W Essex Militia; *b* 23 April 1746; *m* 22 March 1779 Anne (*d* 20 Dec 1815), only dau of John Windham, of Waghen, Yorks, and Camberwell, Surrey, who took the name BOWYER, and *d* 1 May 1823, having had issue:

1 **Sir Thomas Smijth, 8th Bt**; *b* 6 Feb 1781; *d* unm 5 Oct 1833

2 **Sir John Smijth, 9th Bt**, Cdr RN; *b* 8 June 1782; *d* unm 9 Dec 1838

3 EDWARD (Sir), **10th Bt**

4 Joseph SMIJTH later SMIJTH-WINDHAM (added by roy licence 22 May 1823 name and arms of WINDHAM), of Waghen Hall, Yorks, DL and JP, Capt 10th Hus and 17th Lancers Peninsular War; *b* 19 May 1792; *educ* Eton; *m* 10 Aug 1824 Katherine (*d* 29 Sept 1865), dau of John Trotter, of Dyrham Park, Herts, and *d* 3 Feb 1857, leaving issue:

(1) William George SMIJTH-WINDHAM later WINDHAM (dropped SMIJTH by roy licence 1861), of Wawne/Waghen Hall, Hull, Yorks, DL (Yorks), Capt E Yorks Militia; *b* 26 April 1828; *educ* Eton and Downing Coll Cambridge (MA); *d* unm 26 Dec 1887

(2) Ashe SMIJTH-WINDHAM later WINDHAM (dropped SMIJTH by roy licence 1888), of Wawne/Waghen Hall, RM Natal 1857–67, Judge Native High Court Natal 1879–84; *b* 18 March 1830; *educ* Eton and Trin Coll Cambridge (MA); *m* 19 Aug 1859 Juliet Alexa (*d* 8 Dec 1909), dau of Col Hugh Maclean, Scots Gds, of Coll, Argyll, and *d* 7 Sept 1909, leaving issue:

1a Ashe, JP (E R Yorks), of Wawne/Waghen Hall, Natal and Zululand CS 1881–90, Capt and Hon Maj 3rd Bn E Yorks Regt Boer War 1900–02 (two medals, five clasps); *b* 16 March 1863; *educ* Diocesan Coll Cape Town and U of Cape of Good Hope (BA 1881); *m* 3 Feb 1903 Cora Ellen Sowerby (*d* 30 Dec 1948), dau of Capt Henry Sowerby Middleton, Oxford LI, and *d* 18 Nov 1937, leaving issue:

1b Ralph (Sir), ktd 1960, barrister Lincoln's Inn 1930 (Buchanan Law Prize 1930), legal draftsman Govt Palestine 1935, Judge District Ct Palestine 1942, Puisne Judge Supreme Ct Ceylon 1947, Judge Supreme Ct Kenya 1950, Ch Justice Zanzibar 1955, Ct Appeal E Africa 1959, Ch Justice Tanganyika (later Tanzania) 1960–65, Commr For Compensn Commn 1965 (v-chm 1969, chm 1972), Order Brilliant Star Zanzibar 1959; *b* 25 March 1905; *educ* Wellington and Trin Coll Cambridge (MA 1930, LLB 1928); *m* 11 Sept 1946 *Kathleen Mary [Lady Windham, Hook's Cottage, Kingscote, Tetbury, Glos], only dau of Capt Cecil Henry FitzHerbert, DSC, RN, of Millbrook, Abbeyleix, Co Laois, and *d* 6 July 1980, leaving issue:

1c +JOHN JEREMY [John Windham Esq, The Hyde, Woolhope, Herefs HR1 4RE]; *b* 22 Nov 1948; heir presumptive; *educ* Wellington; Capt (ret) Irish Gds and 22nd SAS Regt; *m* 24 July 1976 *(Rachel) Mary, dau of Lt-Col (Walter) George Finney (*see* PERTH, E), and has:

1d +(Thomas) Ralph; *b* 5 Aug 1985

1d *Katharine Anne; *b* 5 Nov 1981

2d *Emma Georgina; *b* 3 Dec 1983

2c +Andrew Guy [Andrew Windham Esq, Shobdon Farm, Newton St Margaret's, Vowchurch, Herefs HR2 0QW]; *b* 8 Dec 1949; *educ* Wellington and Trin Coll Cambridge (MA); slr, dir Clyde Petroleum plc 1996–; *m* 1976 *Diana Susan, yr dau of Hon Norman Dunlop Galloway Galbraith (*see* STRATHCLYDE, B), and has issue:

1d +Rory Michael; *b* 27 May 1978; *educ* Malvern and Newcastle U

1d *Ruth Emily; *b* 18 Sept 1980

2d *Lydia Mary; *b* 28 May 1982

3d *Harriet Rachel; *b* 28 Feb 1984

1c *Penelope Susan; *b* 6 June 1952

2c *Belinda Mary Victoria; *b* 2 July 1955; *m* 1989 *Mark Baxter, 2nd s of David Baxter, and has:

1d *Thomas; *b* 22 May 1990

1d *Luke; *b* 22 May 1993

2b +Ashe [Maj Ashe Windham, 16 Severnside South, Bewdley, Worcs], Maj E Yorks Regt, ADC to Govr Assam 1938–40, Intell Staff Control Commn Germany 1945–48, BAOR 1961–70, Br Consulate Stuttgart 1970; *b* 29 Sept 1916; *educ* Radley and RMC Sandhurst; *m* 8 June 1940 *Iris Daphne, yr dau of Col Edward Selby Phipson, CIE, DSO, MD, FRCP, IMS, and has issue:

1c +Ashe Adrian [Ashe Windham Esq, Rectory Lodge, The Fairland, Hingham, Norfolk NR9 4HW], Capt RA (ret), Dip Serv; *b* 28 Nov 1941; *educ* Woodbridge Sch and RMA Sandhurst; Priv Sec to UK Perm Rep NATO Brussels 1973, V-Consul: Hamburg 1976, Johannesburg 1979, Consul: Kuala Lumpur 1987, Düsseldorf 1991; *m* 29 March 1969 *Daphne Anne, dau of Maj Albert Adolphus Pyne Cotton Thomas, TD, and has:

1d *Philippa Mary; *b* 1977; *educ* St Felix Southwold and UEA

2c +Daniel Harry [Daniel Windham Esq, Willow Cottage, Hackford, Wymondham, Norfolk NR18 9HS]; *b* 1 Nov 1948; *educ* Radley and Magdalene Coll Cambridge; late Roy Irish Rangers and Muscat Regt SAF; *m* 1975 *Caroline Mary, dau of Richard Pelham Warren, FRCS, and has issue:

1d +William; *b* 23 Nov 1978; *educ* Norwich Sch and Magdalene Coll Cambridge

1d *Alexa; *b* 29 Oct 1980

1b Joan; *b* 13 April 1904; MCSP; *m* 1st 8 May 1959 Brig Ord Henderson Tidbury, MC (*d* 14 July 1961), only s of Col James Tidbury, OBE; *m* 2nd 20 Sept 1964 Maj Hugh D'Oyly Lyle, Roy Welch Fus (*d* 1977), s of Col Hugh Thomas Lyle, DSO, OBE, DL, of Knocktarana, Coleraine, and *d* 19 Dec 1990

2b Anne, MBE (1942); *b* 17 Aug 1906; For Serv 1928–66; *d* 27 Jan 1991

3b Mève; *b* 20 Sept 1909; *d* 24 Sept 1990

4b *Ruth [Mrs John Woodroffe, Little Beechford, Childe Okeford, Dorset]; *b* 1912; *m* 1st 21 Jan 1938 (*divorce* 1962) Robert Bellord (*d* 5 Nov 1970), yst s of Edmund Joseph Bellord; *m* 2nd 1972 Brig John Henry Patrick Woodroffe, DSO (*d* 199–), and by her 1st husb has:

1c Robert WINDHAM later WINDHAM-BELLORD (added 1963), Capt RGJ; *b* 27 Aug 1943; *educ* Downside, RMA Sandhurst and Univ Coll Oxford; *m* 26 Oct 1968 *Jane Eleanor, 2nd dau of Carleton John Richard Tufnell, and had issue:

1d *Charles Robert Carleton; *b* 16 Feb 1971

2c *Edward James [Edward Windham-Bellord Esq, The Cottage, Cucklington, Somerset]; *b* 25 July 1947; *educ* Downside and Wadham Coll Oxford; added BELLORD 1965; *m* 1972 (*divorce* 1976) Caroline Irene (*d* 1979), only dau of Robert Grenville Plantagenet Morgan-Grenville (*see* KINLOSS, L), and has issue:

1d *James Robert Grenville; *b* 29 Aug 1973; *educ* Downside and King's Coll London

3c *Richard Valentine; *b* 22 Feb 1949; *educ* Downside; added BELLORD 1966; *m* 1st 1974 (*divorce* 1982) Cheung Wai Lan and has issue:

1d *Richard Valentine (Siddha); *b* 1975

1d *Satya; *b* 1976

2d *Subhadra; *b* 1977

3c (cont.) Richard Windham-Bellord *m* 2nd 1982 *Julieta Estina Bisco and has further issue:

3d *Jamuna; *b* 1983

1c *Ellen Mary; *b* 5 Nov 1938

2c *Alice Mary; *b* 14 Dec 1939

5b Grace; *b* 1914; *m* 1st 12 Jan 1937 (*divorce* 1955) Wilfred Gerard Sidney, 7th Baron Grand d'Hauteville, only s of Paul, Baron Grand d'Hauteville, of Vaud, Switzerland; *m* 2nd 19– *Dr Galli and by her 1st husb had:

1c *Philip Anthony Ashe; *b* 1 July 1938; *m* 8 May 1965 *Tania, only dau of Gerald Cramer, of Mies, Switzerland, and has issue:

1d *Henry; *b* 27 March 1967

2d *Eric (twin); *b* 27 March 1967

1d *Diane Cora; *b* 1971

2c *Jacques Pierre; *b* 16 Sept 1943; *m* 1st 1968 (*divorce* 1973) Françoise Mayer and has issue:

1d *Marc Serge; *b* 1969

2c (cont.) Jacques Grand d'Hauteville *m* 2nd 1973 *Marie-Claire Chappuis and has further issue:

1d *Muriel; *b* 1977

1c *Elisabeth Suzanne; *b* 15 Nov 1940; *m* 1st 1 June 1963 (*divorce*) Baron Aymon G L R de Blonay, only s of Baron Remi de Blonay and Mme M du Pasquier, of Geneva; *m* 2nd 1976 (*divorce* 1984) Serge du Buis and by her 1st husb has issue:

1d *Nicolas Aymon Pierre Henri; *b* 1967

1d *Marie-Hélène Blanche Renée; *b* 1964

2d *Sophie Caroline Elizabeth Grace; *b* 1970

2a William (Sir), ktd 1923, CBE (1917), MRES, Govt Serv Zululand 1882–97, Registrar-Gen Natal 1901, Sec Native Affairs Transvaal 1901–10, Commr 1904–05, MLC 1905–07, with BOT UK 1912–17, Min Labour 1917–22; *b* 12 Nov 1864; *educ* Diocesan Coll Cape Town; *m* 10 April 1894 Blanche Marie (*d* 25 Aug 1933), dau of Achille Erneste Titren, RM Durban, and *d* 21 March 1961, leaving issue:

1b William Evan, barrister Gray's Inn 1936, Sr RM N Rhodesia 1952, Puisne Judge 1956–62 Colonial Admin Fiji and W Pacific 1930–34, S/Ldr RAF WW II (despatches); *b* 1 May 1904; *educ* Wellington; *m* 1st 1 March 1932 Constance (*d* 17 July 1939), formerly w of Capt Humphrey Clifford Lloyd, MVO, MC, and er dau of James Hope Loudon, OBE, and had:

1c *Elisabeth Aylva; *b* 26 March 1935; *m* 17 Dec 1955 (*divorce* 1974) George Alfred Bakewell, only s of Dr G V Bakewell, and has issue:

1d *Constance Louise; *b* 1957

2d *Charlotte Alice; *b* 1959

2c *Juliet Alexa [Mrs Juliet Windham Hackett, 54 Wimpole St, London W1]; *b* 7 Oct 1938; *m* 17 July 1962 (*divorce* 1971) Raymond Bingham Hackett, s of Philip Douglas Vernon Hackett, and added WINDHAM 1978

1b (cont.) William Windham *m* 2nd 16 April 1962 *Dorothy Muir, widow of Carl Raymond Davis and dau of Robert Deans Johnston, and *d* 1977

1b Alba, OBE (1942), Ch Cdr ATS WW II; *b* 20 Oct 1898; *educ* St Hugh's Coll Oxford (BA 1922)

3a John, Registrar Zululand High Ct 1895–97, RM Zululand 1897–1902; *b* 14 July 1867; *educ* Diocesan Coll Cape Town; *d* unm 16 March 1951

1a Katharine Jane; *b* 3 Oct 1861; *m* 18 June 1889 Maj-Gen Hon George Talbot Devereux and *d* 5 June 1934, having had issue (*see* HEREFORD, V)

(3) George SMIJTH-WINDHAM, Maj Rifle Bde Crimea and Indian Mutiny (three medals and four clasps); *b* 15 Feb 1833; *educ* Eton; *m* 19 April 1865 Clarissa Elizabeth (*d* 21 Feb 1908), dau of Lord Charles James Fox-Russell (*see* BEDFORD, D), and *d* 7 March 1921, having had issue:

1a Charles Joseph WINDHAM, CIE (1915), Lt-Col IA, Res Jodhpur and Bikaner and Baroda and Kashmir; v-pres Cncl Jodhpur State 1927–31; *b* 7 Aug 1867; *m* 1893 Mildred Bayntun (*d* 11 Feb 1947), dau of John Bayntun Starkey, of Spye Park, Wilts, and *d* 28 Dec 1941, having had issue:

1b Ashe Wadham George, MC (1918), Capt Res Offrs 5th Lancers, Lt 6th Inniskilling Dragoons, served WW I (despatches); *b* 14 Aug 1894; *educ* Wellington; *d* 17 April 1922 accidentally while pig-sticking in India

2b John Bayntun Russell, Capt 18th KGO Lancers, F/O, RAF; *b* 27 Aug 1897; *educ* Eton; *m* 25 Oct 1938 Mrs Monica Vicary (*d* 1952), dau of Rev Harry James Oliver, and *dsp* 5 May 1965

2a Walter George WINDHAM (Sir), ktd 1923, Cdr RIN, King's Messenger 1901–09, fndr: Air Mail and Aeroplane Club, Freeman City of London, Roy Humane Soc silver and bronze medals, Lloyd's silver medal; *b* 15 Sept 1868; *m* 26 July 1916 Helene Adeline Blanche (*d* 2 Sept 1957), widow of Capt Archibald Glen Kidston, JP, 3rd Bn Black Watch, and 2nd dau of Spencer Chapman, and *d* 5 July 1942

3a Claude Seymour, Intell Dept S Africa (medal with five clasps); *b* 21 Oct 1869; *d* 20 Dec 1934

4a Edwards John WINDHAM; *b* 3 March 1871; *m* 13 Feb 1914 Muriel (*d* 24 Feb 1958), widow of Frederick Stanley Brewer Walters and dau of Frank Harry Goulding, of Plymouth, and *d* 26 June 1945

5a James Ashe; *b* 5 Oct 1873; *d* 5 June 1912

6a Henry Steuart WINDHAM, twin, Lt-Col 3rd Bn Beds Regt Boer War 1900–02, Strathcona's Horse and Remount Dept WW I; *b* 5 Oct 1873; *m* 9 June 1915 Marjory Russell (*d* 1971), dau of Henry McClean Dymock, and *d* 20 Oct 1958, leaving issue:

1b James Steuart, Maj RA WW II (despatches); *b* 7 Nov 1917; *educ* Bedford Sch and RMA Woolwich; *m* 20 July 1957 *Annette de Mèstre [Mrs James Windham, Wainbayvil, Felindre Farchog, Crymych SA41 3XH], er dau of William John Wilkins, FRCS, and *d* 1989, leaving issue:

1c +Mark Hastings Wriothesley; *b* 17 Dec 1959

2c +Tobias Cosmo Russell; *b* 16 May 1962

1c *Sophia Louise de Mestre; *b* 24 April 1958; *m* 1982 *Bruce Robinson and has issue:

1d *Willoughby; *b* 1993

1d *Lily India; *b* 1986

2b +William Ashe Dymoke [William Windham Esq, Parc Gwynne, Glasbury-on-Wye, Powys HR3 5LL]; *b* 2 April 1926; *educ* Bedford Sch (scholar) and Christ's Coll Cambridge (BA 1947, MA 1951); chm Guinness Brewing 1947–84, Skelmersdale Devpt Corp 1979–85, Steward Henley Regatta 1953–, Pres Leander Club 1993, High Sheriff Powys 1996–97; *m* 9 June 1956 *Alison Audrey Primrose, 2nd dau of Maj Philip Pinckney Curtis (*see* CURTIS, Bt), and has:

1c +Ashe George Russell, LVO (1982); *b* 11 July 1957; *educ* Eton and RMA Sandhurst, Capt Irish Gds, T/Equerry to HM QUEEN ELIZABETH THE QUEEN MOTHER 1980–82, Extra Equerry 1993–; *m* 17 Oct 1997 *Arabella, dau of Francis Hoare

2c +(Charles) William Fitz-Roy; *b* 1 March 1960; *educ* Gordonstoun and Surrey U

1c *Emma Rose Dymock [Mrs Simon Phillpotts, The White House, White St, Market Lavington, Wilts SN10 4DP]; *b* 6 March 1959; *m* 1991 *Simon Vivian Surtees Phillpotts, s of Christopher Phillpotts, CMG, and has issue:

1d *Archie Christopher Louis; *b* 29 Dec 1992

1d *Lara Georgina Windham; *b* 21 April 1995

1b *Rachel Russell [Mrs George Sheppard, 2 Chancery Court, Hay-on-Wye, Herefs HR3 5BP]; *b* 19 May 1916; *m* 15 July 1963 Lt-Col George Kinloch Sheppard, Rajputana Rifles (*d* 23 Dec 1963), est s of Sir William Didsbury Sheppard, KCIE, JP, of North Place, Great Bardfield, Essex

7a Arthur Russell SMIJTH-WINDHAM, Sudan CS, 3rd Cl Order Medjidie; *b* 27 Nov 1874; *m* 21 Nov 1901 Brenda Helen (*d* 15 June 1947), 2nd dau of Gerald Hall, JP, of Anstey Manor, Alton, Hants, and was lost in the sinking of the *Persia* 30 Dec 1915, leaving issue:

1b William Russell, CBE (1946), DSO (1942), Brig Roy Sigs WW II (despatches), ADC to HM THE QUEEN 1957–60, FIEE, Mt Everest Expdns 1933 and 1936; *b* 21 Oct 1907; *educ* Wellington and RMA Woolwich; *m* 5 Sept 1934 *Helen Teresa [Mrs William Smijth-Windham, Estate Corner, Pitney, Langport, Somerset], 2nd dau of Brig Hubert Clementi Smith, DSO, and *d* 12 Nov 1994, leaving:

1c +Simon William [Simon Smijth-Windham Esq, Middle Lodge, Hughenden Estate, High Wycombe, Bucks MP14 4LA]; *b* 7 July 1937; *educ* St Paul's; *m* 16 July 1960 *Wendy Myra, dau of Edgar William John Albrow, and has issue:

1d +Alastair William; *b* 6 May 1966

1d *Tanya Myra; *b* 6 May 1961

1c *Joanna Felicity [Mrs Peter Lazarus, Fairseat Farm, Chew Stoke, nr Bristol]; *b* 2 Oct 1938; *m* 1st 28 July 1963 Peter Anthony Lazarus (*d* 1980), Headmaster Downs Sch, Wraxall, s of George Louis Lazarus, of Langley Park, Bucks; *m* 2nd 1984 *Alan Robert Brown and by 1st husb has issue:

1d *George William; *b* 26 Sept 1969

1d *Mary Helen; *b* 27 Sept 1966

2c *Prudence Helen [Mrs Prudence Murdoch, Keele House Cottage, 33 St Mary's Rd, Harborne, Birmingham 17]; *b* 13 April 1945; *educ* St Hugh's Coll Oxford (MA); slr; *m* 9 Sept 1967 (*divorce* 1985) John Derek Walter Murdoch, yr s of Duncan Murdoch, and has issue:

1d *Thomas; *b* 15 March 1970

1d *Clarissa Helen; *b* 1972

2d *Rosamond Elsie; *b* 1977

3c *Rachel Beatrice [Mrs John Santer, 78 Enborne Rd, Newbury, Berks]; *b* 13 Dec 1946; *m* 1970 *John Santer and has issue:

1d *William Robert Clive; *b* 1976

2d *Harry Joseph; *b* 1978

1d *Evelyn Margaret; *b* 1973

2d *Ann Dorothy Sarah; *b* 1981

1b *Diana Elizabeth [Mrs E Paul, Maysleith, Milland, Hants GU30 7JN], FO 1939–47; *b* 19 Sept 1911; *m* 1947 *E M W Paul and has issue

1c *Isabella Brenda Windham; *b* 14 Aug 1948; *m* 1972 *Michael Braine Morton-Smith and has issue

1a Evelyn; *b* 15 March 1866; *m* 29 April 1903 Maj Francis Hooper Rawlins, MA, FRGS, er s of Rev Francis John Rawlins, MA, FSA, Rector Fiddington, and *d* 11 Oct 1945, leaving issue. He *d* 14 Oct 1925

2a Rachel Isabella; *d* unm 18 Nov 1897

(4) Joseph Charles SMIJTH-WINDHAM, Lt-Col RA; *b* 14 March 1838; *m* 1st 25 Oct 1876 Emily Harriet (*d* 8 Dec 1878), dau of Sir Claude William de Crespigny, 3rd Bt (*see* 1953 edn), and had issue:

1a Katharine Emily; *b* 15 Aug 1877; *m* 9 Feb 1907 Thomas Bonhôte Henderson, MB, FRCS, of Salisbury, est s of John Henderson, of Lincoln's Inn, and *d* 16 Jan 1926, leaving issue. He *d* 19 April 1920

2a Mary; *b* 3 Dec 1878; *d* unm 12 June 1963

(4) (cont.) Lt-Col J C Smijth-Windham *m* 2nd 11 May 1886 Frances Helen (*d* 20 July 1921), widow of G Fordati and est dau of William Currey, and *d* 16 April 1915, leaving issue:

3a Violet Agnes; *b* 13 April 1889; *m* 15 Aug 1912 Lt-Col John Wright, OBE, Roy Surrey Regt, and *d* 14 Jan 1959, leaving issue. He *das* 19 Feb 1919, having added on marriage the name WINDHAM to WRIGHT

(5) Francis Wentworth WINDHAM, Civil Engr; *b* 12 Jan 1847; *educ* Wellington; *m* 1st 14 Aug 1869 Edith Mary (*d* 21 July 1876), dau of Frederick Boss, and had issue:

1a William Steuart; *b* 3 May 1874; *d* 19–

1a Edith Constance; *b* 17 Nov 1871; *d* 21 Feb 1872

(5) (cont.) Francis Windham *m* 2nd 1912 Mary Frances (*d* 27 March 1947), dau of William Allin Moore, of Lyme Regis, and *d* 29 Jan 1926

(1) Anne; *b* 26 June 1836; *m* 31 Aug 1875 Col Sheffield Hamilton-Grace, of Knole Ho, Frant, Sussex, and *d* 20 July 1898, leaving issue (*see* GRACE, Bt). He *d* 7 Jan 1915

1 Caroline; *b* 12 April 1796; *m* 1st 29 Aug 1817 Augustus James Champion de Crespigny, est surv s of Sir William Champion de Crespigny, 2nd Bt (*see* 1953 edn), and had issue. He *d* 24 Oct 1825. She *m* 2nd his younger brother Herbert and *d* 25 Jan 1876. He *d* 1 July 1881

Sir JOHN's bro,

Rev Sir EDWARD SMIJTH later BOWYER-SMIJTH (added name and arms of BOWYER by roy licence 10 June 1839), **10th Bt**, MA Cantab; *b* 1 March 1785; *m* 29 May 1813 Letitia Cicely (*d* 3 March 1868), dau of John Weyland, of Woodeaton, Oxon, and Woodrising Hall, Norfolk, and had issue:

1 WILLIAM (Sir), **11th Bt**

2 Alfred John Edward (Rev), MA, Rector Attleborough, Norfolk; *b* 20 Aug 1825; *m* 17 June 1847 Mary Constantia (*d* 24 Sept 1898), only dau of Maj-Gen Sir John Rolt, KCB, and *d* 19 Jan 1887, leaving issue:

(1) Sir ALFRED JOHN BOWYER-SMIJTH later BOWYER-SMYTH (resumed spelling SMYTH on inheriting title), **13th Bt**, Maj and Hon Lt-Col 3rd Bn Hampshire Regt; *b* 12 Sept 1850; *dsp* 4 Aug 1927

(2) Clement Weyland; *b* 23 Nov 1851; *m* 1891 Edith Maude (*d* 29 July 1938), dau of W Gray, and *d* 22 Feb 1910, leaving issue:

1a PHILIP WEYLAND (Sir), **14th Bt**

1a Alice Mary

2a Lily Marcia; *b* 1905

(3) Edmund Caswell; *b* 20 July 1853; *m* 1884 Annie Elizabeth (*d* 8 Aug 1957), dau of S W Gray, of Sydney, NSW, and *d* 20 July 1921, leaving issue:

1a Cedric Gray, Capt Glos Regt; *b* 10 June 1888; *ka* Cameroons 4 Nov 1915

1a Gladys Mary; *m* 1915 Capt (S) Bernard Carter, CBE, RN, s of Charles Carter, and *d* 10 Jan 1970, leaving issue. He *d* 28 March 1954

2a Gwendoline Cicely; *m* 1914 Edward McKenzie de Mestre and *d* 17 May 1929, leaving issue

3a Doris Maude; *d* 14 July 1925

(1) Etheldreda Frances; *m* 3 Nov 1880 Maj Reginald Edward Pole and *d* 9 Dec 1935, having had issue (*see* POLE, Bt). He *d* 13 Nov 1926

(2) Ada Cicely; *m* 15 Jan 1880 Capt William Boyle Moore, 37th Regt, and *d* 6 Dec 1880, leaving issue (*see* DROGHEDA, E)

(3) Helen Mary; *m* 1876 Gerald Hall, of Anstey Manor, Alton, Hants, 2nd s of Henry Hall, of Alton Manor, and *d* 23 May 1933, leaving issue

1 Cicely Abigail; *m* 1st 18 Aug 1840 Henry Bullock, of Faulkbourne Hall; *m* 2nd 4 April 1861 Edgar Bury; *m* 3rd 5 Feb 1874 Maj James H McEwen, 4th (King's Own) Regt, and *d* 4 Feb 1880

2 Anne Elizabeth; *m* 20 Aug 1839 Gordon Willoughby Gyll, of Wraysbury, Bucks, and *d* 25 Feb 1888, leaving issue. He *d* 6 April 1880

3 Adela Moncton; *m* 4 July 1843 Capt Edward Jodrell, 16th Regt, n of Sir Richard Paul Jodrell, 2nd Bt, of Sall Park, and *d* 23 Sept 1896, having had issue. He *d* 1868

4 Marianne Weyland; *m* 4 May 1847 Col Sir Samuel Brise Ruggles-Brise, KCB, of Spains Hall, Essex (*see* RUGGLES-BRISE, Bt), and *d* 12 Dec 1900, leaving issue

Sir EDWARD *d* 15 Aug 1850; his er son,

Sir William Bowyer-Smijth, 11th Bt, DL and JP, MP S Essex 1852–57; *b* 22 April 1814; *m* 1st 2 April 1839 Marianne Frances (*d* 11 March 1875), 2nd dau of Sir Henry Meux, 1st Bt, of Theobalds Park, Herts (*see* 1900 edn), and had, with a s and dau (*d* unm):

1 **Sir William Bowyer-Smijth, 12th Bt**, Dip Serv 1858–81, High Sheriff Essex 1889; *b* 1 Sept 1840; *d* unm 22 July 1916

The **11th Bt**, *m* 2nd 19 March 1875 Eliza Fechnie (*m* 2nd 2 Sept 1890 William Herbert Edward Stanford; *d* 20 Oct 1926), only dau of David Baird Malcolm, of Crieff, Perthshire, and gdau of Capt W Malcolm, Roy Ceylon Rifle Regt, having by her had five other s and seven daus born before the marriage (plus two daus born after it), for 11 of whom (except the 2nd s Henry, who had d), together with the 11th Bt's two grandchildren in the male line, a declaration of legitimacy was granted in Scotland 1918, though this did not entitle them to inherit the baronetcy, and *d* 20 Nov 1883:

2 William Baird; *b* 9 Aug 1859; *m* C V Sweeny (*d* 1892) and *d* 1940, having had issue:

(1) William; *b* 1889; *m* 1913 Janie Isabel Norman, of NSW, and *d* 1937, leaving issue:

1a William; *b* 1915; *m* 1941 *Eileen May Peterson [Mrs William Bowyer-Smijth, 9/601 Wyse St, Albury, NSW, Australia] and *d* 1989, leaving issue:

1b *Ian William [Ian Bowyer-Smijth, 16 Yattenden Crescent, Baulkham Hills, NSW 2153, Australia]; *b* 1942; *m* 1964 *Jennifer Shepard and has issue:

1c *Stuart *b* 1965; has issue:

1d *Fiona; *b* 1987

2c *Mark; *b* 1968

2b *Keith Raymond [Keith Bowyer-Smijth, 823 Burrows St, Albury, NSW 2640, Australia]; *b* 1945; *m* 1973 *Lorraine Campbell and has issue:

1c *Bruce; *b* 1977

2c *Louise; *b* 1975

2a *Henry; *b* 1916

3a *Edward; *b* 1930

1a Jean; *b* 1919

2a *Betty; *b* 1921

(2) Henry; *b* 1891; *ka* 1917

3 Edward; *b* 20 Oct 1867; *d* 22 Jan 1899

4 David Malcolm; *b* 26 March 1869; *m* 1900 (*divorce* 1910) Miriam McCheyne (*d* Dec 1942), er dau of Maj Legh Richmond Battye, and *d* 8 March 1930, leaving issue:

(1) Basil Malcolm, of BC, Canada; *b* 10 Nov 1901; *m* 1924 Mabel Henrietta, dau of James Samuel Tetlock, and had issue:

1a *Barrie Malcolm [Barrie Bowyer-Smyth Esq, 1090 Keith Rd, W Vancouver, BC, Canada]; *b* 1925; *m* 1959 *Margaret, dau of George Kilpatrick Morrison, and has issue:

1b *John Barrie; *b* 1962

1b *Jane Catherine; *b* 1965

2b *Elizabeth Margaret; *b* 1968

2a *James Brian [James Bowyer-Smyth Esq, 8366 Victoria Dve, Vancouver, BC, Canada]; *b* 1929; *m* 1965 *Marianne, dau of Max Bruno Schwaerzler, and has issue:

1b *Marc; *b* 1967

1b *Simone; *b* 1969

3a *David Anthony; *b* 1931; *m* 1953 (*divorce* 1972) Lee Smith and has issue:

1b *David; *b* 1954

2b *Michael; *b* 1956

1b *Kathie; *b* 1955

2b *Lisa; *b* 1958

(2) *Brian Thomson; *b* 1909

(1) *Evangeline; *b* 9 Feb 1904; *m* 1928 *Jack Veale and has issue:

1a *Robert; *b* 1929

2a *Douglas; *b* 1933

1a *Joan; *b* 1931

2a *Nellie; *b* 1935

3a *Beverley; *b* 1937

5 Henry; *b* 25 April 1870; *d* 13 Nov 1933

6 Frederick; *b* 3 Aug 1871; *d* 9 July 1930

1 Catherine; *b* 2 Feb 1861; *m* 1890 Alfred Albert Tindall and *d* 7 July 1935, leaving issue. He *d* 21 Aug 1931

2 Jessie; *b* 19 Jan 1862; *m* 9 Aug 1886 Edward Tidswell and *d* 28 Nov 1940, having had issue

3 Mary; *b* 24 July 1863; *m* (*divorce* 1916) William Thomas Hastings and *d* 23 Dec 1947, leaving issue

4 Eliza; *b* 14 July 1864; *m* 1895 Arthur Godfrey Howlett and *d* 21 April 1947, leaving issue. He *d* 9 Jan 1937

5 Leila; *b* 11 March 1866; *m* 1916 Rev Raymond Hammersley and *d* July 1942

6 Beatrice, *b* 20 Oct 1867; *d* unm 28 Nov 1937

7 Cicely; *b* 8 Nov 1872; *m* 1900 Alfred Victor Mason and *d* 21 Oct 1963, leaving issue. He *d* 1950

8 Wilhelmina; *m* 2 July 1904 Lt-Col Arthur Baldwyn Battye, 6th King Edward's Own Cav, IA, s of Maj Legh Richmond Battye, IA, and *d* 13 March 1946

9 Adela; *m* 6 Jan 1903 Cyril Charles Stafford Northcote, 2nd s of Stafford Charles Northcote, and *d* 31 Oct 1963, leaving issue (*see* IDDESLEIGH, E)

The 13th Bt's n,

Sir PHILIP WEYLAND BOWYER-SMIJTH later BOWYER-SMYTH (resumed spelling SMYTH on inheriting title), **14th Bt**, RN WW I and WW II (wounded, despatches), Naval Attaché Rome 1938–40, Capt HMAS *Perth* 1940–41, Dir Radio Equipment Admlty 1943–44, Cdre E Africa 1945–46, ADC to HM GEORGE VI 1946; *b* 4 Feb 1894; *m* 1st 24 June 1922 (*divorce* 1951) (Margaret) Joan, OBE (1952), Lt-Col WRAC (TA) (*d* 2 July 1976), only dau of Samuel McCall McCowan, of Sydney, NSW; *m* 2nd 9 June 1951 *Veronica Mary [Veronica Lady Bowyer-Smyth, Stour House, Fordwich, Kent CT2 0DA], 2nd dau of Capt Cyril Whichelo Bower, DSC, RN, of Fordwich, Kent, and *d* 1978, leaving issue:

1 A son; *b* and *d* 19 April 1955

2 Sir THOMAS WEYLAND BOWYER-SMYTH, **15th and present Bt**

1 *Amelia Anne [Mrs James Gracie, Le Moulin de Gillebert, Montjean, 16240 Villefagnan, France]; *b* 27 May 1958; *m* 1982 *James Duncan Johnstone Gracie, s of Rev Anthony Johnstone Gracie, and has issue:

(1) *Luke; *b* 1986

(1) *Leah; *b* 1989

BOYCE

Arms: Or, on a chevron gu. an open book ppr., edges and clasps of the first, on a chief of the second a portcullis chained, also of the first, between two swords erect, also ppr., pomels and hilts gold.
Crest: A demi-lion gu., grasping in the dexter paw a pen or.
Motto: Do it with thy might. **Creation:** Bt. (UK) 24 Nov 1952.

SIR ROBERT CHARLES LESLIE BOYCE, 3RD BT, of Badgeworth, Co Glos [Dr Sir Robert Boyce Bt, The Barn House, Ascott Earl, Ascott-under-Wychwood, Oxon OX7 6AG]; *b* 2 May 1962; *s* f 1968; *educ* Cheltenham, Salford U (BSc 1984) and Nottingham U (BMedSci 1991, BM, BS 1993); demonstrator anatomy Manchester U Med Sch 1994–95, Sr House Offr Ophthamology Manchester Roy Eye Hosp 1995–; *m* 1985 *Fiona Margaret, 2nd dau of John Savage, of Whitmore Park, Coventry, and has issue:

1 +THOMAS LESLIE; *b* 3 Sept 1993

Lineage: CHARLES BOYCE, of London, later Taree, NSW; *b* 22 Dec 1835; *m* 18 June 1860 Elizabeth Pinchin (*d* 26 Dec 1914), of London, and *d* 19 March 1917, leaving issue:

CHARLES MACLEAY BOYCE, of Sydney, NSW; *b* 12 Jan 1868; *m* 18 Sept 1890 Ethel May (*d* 14 Feb 1943), er dau of Charles Thorne, of Sydney, by Sophia, and *d* 14 Dec 1936, leaving issue:

Sir (Harold) Leslie Boyce, 1st Bt (UK), so *cr* 24 Nov 1952; barrister Inner Temple 1922, chm and md Gloucester Rlwy Carriage and Wagon Co, chm Wagon Repairs Ltd, Ld Mayor London 1951–52, AIF WW I, legal advsr League Nations 1922, technical advsr to Australian Rep Perm Mandates Commn 1922, MP Gloucester 1929–45, memb Empire Parly Delegn N Rhodesia 1930, Leader UK Mission China 1946, High Sheriff Glos 1941–42, Sheriff City London 1947–48, memb Court Assistants Loriners' (Master 1951–52) and Carpenters' Cos, KStJ; *b* 9 July 1895; *educ* Sydney GS and Balliol Coll Oxford (BA 1920, MA 1924); *m* 16 July 1926 Maybery Browse, DStJ (*d* 12 March 1978), only dau of Edward Philip Bevan, of Melbourne, and had issue:

1 RICHARD LESLIE (Sir), **2nd Bt**

2 +John Leslie [John Boyce Esq, 182 Huntingdale Rd, Mt Waverley, Victoria 3149, Australia]; *b* 16 Nov 1934; *educ* Cheltenham; missile design engr Sir W G Armstrong-Whitworth Aircraft 1956–73; *m* 1st 19 Jan 1957 (*divorce* 1975) Finola Mary, dau of James Patrick Maxwell, of Bansha, Co Tipperary, and has issue:

(1) +Richard Alan; *b* 1968

(1) *Elizabeth Jane Leslie; *b* 16 Oct 1958

(2) *Evelyn Mary; *b* 17 Aug 1961

(3) *Suzanne Caroline; *b* 13 Dec 1963

Sir Leslie *m* 2nd 1980 *Fusako, dau of Yonesaku Ishibashi, of Sinagawa-ku, Tokyo, and had further issue:

(4) *Miyo Maybery; *b* 1981

(5) *Kyoko Jacqueline; *b* 1983

3 Charles Francis Leslie; *b* 26 Feb 1936; *educ* Cheltenham; Glos Regt: 2nd Lt 1st Bn, Maj 5th Bn (TA); *m* 19 Jan 1963 *Elizabeth, only dau of William Todd, of 130 Meadoway, Bishop's Cleave, Cheltenham, Glos, and *d* 1985, leaving issue:

(1) +Edward Neal Leslie; *b* 17 Jan 1965

(2) +PhilipWilliam James; *b* 1971

(1) *Kathryn Maybery; *b* 9 April 1966; *m* 1990 *Alistair Cone, and has issue:

1a *Megan Louise; *b* 1993

(2) *Victoria Claire Alexandra; *b* 6 June 1973

Sir LESLIE *d* 30 May 1955; his est son,

Sir Richard Leslie Boyce, 2nd Bt; *b* 5 July 1929; *educ* Cheltenham; Lt Glos Regt (TARO), engr, OStJ; *m* 20 Sept 1958 *Jacqueline Anne [Mrs Christopher Boyce-Dennis, The Barn House, Ascott Earl, Ascott-under-Wychwood, Oxon] (*m* 2nd 1974 *Christopher Richard Boyce-Dennis), only dau of Ronald Aubrey Hill, of Threeways, Brimscombe, Glos, and *d* 12 Oct 1968, leaving issue:

1 Sir ROBERT CHARLES LESLIE BOYCE, **3rd and present Bt**

1 *Sarah Jane Leslie; *b* 12 Sept 1960

BOYD

Arms: Az. a fess chequy arg. and gu. between three estoiles or. **Crest:** Out of a crest coronet or charged with three erm. spots a dexter hand erect having the two last fingers turned in and the rest pointing upwards ppr. **Motto:** *Confido* ('I trust'). **Creation:** Bt. (UK) 29 June 1916.

SIR ALEXANDER WALTER BOYD, 3RD BT, of Howth House, Howth, Co Dublin; *b* 16 June 1934; *s* unc 1948; *m* 3 May 1958 *Molly Madeline, only dau of Ernest Arthur Rendell, of RR3, Vernon, BC, and has issue:

1 +IAN WALTER RENDELL; *b* 14 March 1964; *m* 1986 *Lee-Ann Dillon, and has issue:

(1) +Kyle Robert Rendell; *b* 1987

(2) +Cameron Rendell Ian; *b* 1991

(3) +Dawson Alexander Cecil; *b* 1992

2 +Robert Alexander; *b* 15 Feb 1966

1 *Heather Lynn; *b* 7 March 1959; *m* 1st 1986 (*divorce* 1992) Francis J McAnally; *m* 2nd 19– *Peter E McLennan, and has issue by 1st husb:

(1) *Matthew Alexander; *b* 1986

(1) *Erin Christine; *b* 1989

2 *Susan Christine; *b* 3 March 1961; *m* 1985 (*divorce* 1990) Paul H Saarinen and has:

(1) *Tory (son); *b* 1988

(1) *Melissa Jenna; *b* 1990

3 *Sandra Molly; *b* 1967; *m* 1992 *Eric A Bay

Lineage: WALTER BOYD, of Walworth, Dublin, and West Pier House, Howth, Co Dublin; *m* 1st Jane Stephens, stepdau of Samuel Warren, Ld Mayor Dublin, and had issue:

1 Alexander; *d* unm

2 Samuel; left issue

WALTER BOYD *m* 2nd Jane (*d* 8 Oct 1869), dau of Robert Macrory, of Castledawson, Co Londonderry, and by her had issue:

3 Robert Macrory, of East Pier Ho, Howth; *b* 7 Jan 1831; *m* 16 Feb 1856 Julia Emma, dau of James Stapleton, of Riverside Ho, Drumcondra, and *d* 16 June 1894, having had issue:

4 WALTER (Sir), **1st Bt**

1 Margaret Helen; *d* unm

WALTER BOYD *d* Jan 1866. His yst son,

Sir Walter Boyd, 1st Bt (UK), so *cr* 29 June 1916, PC (I 1916), QC (1877), JP, of Howth House, Howth; *b* 28 Jan 1833; *educ* Trin Coll Dublin (BA 1855, LLD 1864); barrister King's Inns 1856, Queen's Advocate Ireland 1878–85, Judge Court Bankruptcy Ireland 1885–97, High Court King's Bench 1897–1916 and Admlty 1910–16; *m* 4 Sept 1862 Annie Catherine (*d* 7 Jan 1920), dau of Matthew Anderson, Crown Slr, and *d* 25 June 1918, leaving:

1 **Sir Walter Herbert Boyd, 2nd Bt**, KC 1918; barrister 1891, Ch Registrar Bankruptcy Ireland 1912–37; *b* 31 March 1867; *educ* Trin Coll Dublin (BA); *m* 19 Dec 1901 Ruth, dau of Sir William Fry, of Nevin, Hook Heath, Woking, Surrey, and *dspm* 17 April 1948, leaving issue:

(1) Marjorie Ruth Elizabeth, MD, MSc, MCOG, FRCS (Edin); *b* 15 Oct 1902

2 Cecil Anderson, MC, T/Maj RAMC WW I (despatches); *b* 27 June 1875; *educ* Trin Coll Dublin (MD); *m* 1st 20 June 1923 Kathleen Mary Gwendolyn (*d* 25 Feb 1929), dau of Arthur D Hardie, of Port Essington, BC, and had issue:

(1) *Deirdre Anna [Mrs Walter V Dunham, 532 11th St, New Westminster, BC, Canada]; *b* 25 Jan 1925; *m* 8 Aug 1944 *Walter V Dunham, and has issue:

1a *David; *b* July 1964

1a *Ruth Aideen; *b* 12 Dec 1946

2a *Patricia Anne; *b* 16 Jan 1948

3a *Beverley Jean; *b* 3 May 1951

4a *Mary Elizabeth; *b* 12 April 1953

(2) *Aideen Gwendolyn [Mrs Robert Russell, 3022 S 253rd St, Kent, Washington, USA]; *b* 11 Aug 1926; *m* 27 Dec 1947 *Robert Laird Russell, son of Thomas William Russell, of Tugaske, Saskatchewan, and has issue:

1a *Heather Joanne; *b* 31 Jan 1959

(3) *Ruth Mary [Mrs Anthony Weisgarber, 1154 Tolmie Ave, Victoria, BC, Canada]; *b* 20 Oct 1927; *m* 27 Jan 1951 *Anthony Weisgarber, son of Adam Weisgarber, of Sea Island, Vancouver, and has issue:

1a *Kathleen Mary; *b* 20 March 1957

2a *Tracy Ann; *b* 20 March 1962

2 (cont.) Dr Cecil Boyd *m* 2nd 6 May 1932 Marjorie Catherine, formerly w of — Allan and dau of Francis Kinloch, JP (*see* KINLOCH, Bt, of Gilmerton), and *d* 27 Feb 1942, having by her had issue:

(1) Sir ALEXANDER WALTER BOYD, **3rd and present Bt**

3 Henry Alexander, CMG (1919), DSO (1916); *b* 11 July 1877; Lt-Col RFA S African War 1901–02 (Queen's medal, four clasps) and WW I (despatches four times, Legion Honour); *m* 22 July 1908 Moya (*d* 26 March 1959), dau of John Shaw Exham, JP, of Worlington, Suffolk, and *d* 1 Nov 1943, leaving issue:

(1) Ronald Walter; MC (1944); *b* 29 Jan 1914; Maj Roy Ulster Rifles WW II; *m* 8 June 1939 *Constance Virginia [Mrs Humphrey Walter, Courthay, 47 Gatton Rd, Reigate, Surrey RH2 0HJ] (*m* 2nd 29 Oct 1949 Humphrey Allen Walter, ERD, MA (*d* 1979), son of Frank Edward Walter, AISA), dau of John Freeman, of Bexleyheath, Kent, and was *ka* Italy 23 Oct 1944, leaving issue:

1a +Noel Alexander; *b* 18 July 1940; *educ* Canford; *m* 5 Oct 1968 *Sarah Caroline, er dau of Michael F Sherwin, OBE, of Langridge, West Hoathly, Sussex

2a +Nigel Cecil John; *b* 27 Feb 1943; *educ* Seaford Coll

(1) *Heather [Miss Heather Boyd, 82 Foster Ave, Blackrock, Co Dublin, Ireland]; *b* 17 Jan 1910

4 Robert Reginald; *b* 11 July 1880; Indian Police; *m* 11 Jan 1922 Agnes Maria Dorothea (*d* 9 Jan 1964), dau of Lt-Col Charles Harrison, of Ross, Herefs, and *d* 10 Feb 1959, leaving issue:

(1) +Walter Michael Stewart [Walter Boyd Esq, 3 Glenarm Court, Flagstaff Hill 5159, S Australia]; *b* 19 Sept 1924; *m* 15 Sept 1951 *Janet Ethelwyn, dau of Harold Mallows Brown, of Potters Bar, Herts, and has issue:

1a +Nicholas Michael [Nicholas Boyd Esq, 20 Kenny Dve, Duncraig, WA 6023, Australia]; *b* 12 Oct 1954; *m* and has issue:

2a +Jonathan Peter; *b* 27 March 1956

1a *Emma Jane; *b* 29 May 1960

(2) +Robert Stanley, CB (1982) [Robert Boyd Esq CB, Great Beere, N Tawton, Devon EX20 2BR]; *b* 6 March 1927; *educ* Wellington and Trin Coll Dublin (BA, LLB); barrister Inner Temple 1954, slr Inland Revenue 1979–86; *m* 30 April 1965 *Ann, dau of Daniel Hopkin, MC, MP, Metropolitan Magistrate

1 Alice Mary; *d* unm 22 Jan 1959

2 Ida Jane; *d* unm Oct 1954

BOYD OF MERTON

Arms: Az. a fess chequy arg. and gu. between an abbatical mitre, simplex arg. filleted gu., in chief and in base a rose arg., seeded vert and barbed gu. **Crest:** A dexter hand erect in pale, having two fingers turned in and the rest pointing upwards ppr., the wrist habited in a close sleeve az. with cuff chequy arg. and gu. **Supporters:** Two squirrels ppr. having collars chequy arg. and gu. **Motto:** (above the crest) *Confidas* ('Thou dost confide'). **Creation:** V. (UK) 8 Sept 1960.

THE 2ND VISCOUNT BOYD OF MERTON, of Merton-in-Penninghame, Co Wigtown (Simon Donald Rupert Neville Lennox-Boyd) [The Rt Hon The Viscount Boyd of Merton, 9 Warwick Sq, London SW1V 2AA; Ince Castle, Saltash, Cornwall PL12 4QZ]; *b* 7 Dec 1939; *s* f 1983; *educ* Eton and Ch Ch Oxford (BA 1962, MA 1966); dep chm Arthur Guinness & Sons plc 1981–86, chm: Save the Children 1987–92, Stonham Housing 1992–, Scottish Licensed Trade Assoc; *m* 24 July 1962 *Alice Mary, DL Cornwall 1995– (High Sheriff 1987–88), memb cncl RHS 1996–, only dau of Maj Meysey George Dallas Clive, Gren Gds, of Whitfield, Herefs, and Lady Mary Pakenham, dau of 5th Earl of Longford (*qv*), and has issue:

1 +BENJAMIN ALAN [The Hon Benjamin Lennox-Boyd, South Broadmoor, Saltash, Cornwall]; *b* 21 Oct 1964; *educ* Millfield; *m* 1993 *Mrs Sheila Mary Margaret Carroll, dau of Harold Emmanuel George Williams, of 343 North Rd, W Plymouth, and formerly w of Michael Carroll, of Saltash, Cornwall, and has issue:

(1) +Alan George Simon; *b* 11 March 1993

(1) *Mary Alice; *b* 14 Feb 1994

2 +Edward George [The Hon Edward Lennox-Boyd, 43 Brunswick Gdns, London W8]; *b* 30 March 1968; *educ* Eton and Ch Ch Oxford (BA 1989); *m* 1994 *Tamsin, dau of Antony Hichens, of Slape Manor, Bridport, Dorset, and has:

(1) +Jago George Antony; *b* 19 Jan 1997

1 *Charlotte Mary [The Hon Mrs Mitchell, 10 Essex Villas, London W8]; *b* 16 April 1963; *educ* Cheltenham Ladies' Coll and UCL (BA 1984, PhD 1989); *m* 1992 *Charles C J Mitchell, est son of James Mitchell, of Wilsford-cum-Lake, Wilts, and has issue:

(1) *Albert James Edward; *b* 3 Oct 1996

(1) *Gwendolen Charlotte Julia; *b* 18 April 1994

2 *Philippa Patricia [The Hon Philippa Lennox-Boyd, 38 Charlwood St, London SW1]; *b* 12 March 1970; *educ* St Mary's Calne

Boyd (other peerage titles): *See* KILMARNOCK, B.

Lineage: The Rev WILLIAM BOYD, Min Dalry, Kirkcudbrightshire; *educ* U of Glasgow, Licentiate Cameronians, admitted Ch of Scotland 1690, ordained to Dalry 1690; *b* 1658; *m* 1st 11 March 1691 Isobel Anderson and had issue:

1 William; *bapt* 2 Dec 1694

2 ANDREW (Rev), of whom presently

3 John, mercer in London; *d* by Sept 1773

The Rev WILLIAM *m* 2nd 26 Nov 1701 Jean, widow of Rev John Sinclair, Minister of Kirkpatrick-Irongray, and sis of Edward Maxwell, of Hills, and *d* 13 April 1741, having by her had issue:

4 Edward, Min Wigton Parish, MA Glasgow; *b* 1702; *m* Elizabeth Agnew, and *dsp* 14 Aug 1763

5 Robert

6 David

1 Isobel

2 Barbara

The 2nd son,

Rev ANDREW BOYD, MA Glasgow, Min Tynholm 1726; *b* 1697; *m* 3 Nov 1720 Margaret (*d* 4 Feb 1780), dau of Walter Boyd, maltster Glasgow, and *d* 16 April 1761, having had issue:

1 Walter

2 WILLIAM (Rev), of whom presently

3 Basil; *d* at St Helena, 1750

4 Edward; *b* 19 Feb 1741

5 John, of Milton; *b* 13 Nov 1742; living 29 July 1783

6 Robert; *b* 27 Aug 1745

1 Jean; *b* 26 May 1730; *m* 17 Aug 1768 Rev John Scott, Minister of Tynholm, son of Rev John Scott, Minister of the New Church, Dumfries, and *d* 21 June 1819, leaving issue:

(1) Margaret; *m* Rev John Maitland of Fairgirth, Minister of Minnigaff, bro of Joanna Maitland, who *m* her uncle Dr William Boyd (*see* below)

2 Elizabeth; *b* 17 May 1737 Henry Home, WS, est son of Alexander Home, writer, in Duns, Berwickshire

3 Isobella; *m* Alexander Broun, Portioner of Newtown, Dumfries, and later of Langlands

The 2nd son,

Rev Dr WILLIAM BOYD, MA Edinburgh, MA Glasgow, DD Edinburgh 1785, bought lands and barony of Myrton (Mertonhall), Wigtownshire, from Charles Gordon, WS, 1772; Min Penninghame Parish, where Merton situated; *m* 16 Aug 1762 Joanna (*b* 19 Jan 1740; *d* 31 July 1802), only child of Rev James Maitland, Min Sorbie, by his 1st w, and *d* 17 June 1794, having had issue:

1 Andrew; *b* 21 Aug 1763; *d* before July 1787

2 John; *b* 21 July 1765; *dspvp*

3 James; *b* 12 March 1767; *d* in infancy

4 EDWARD, of whom presently

5 William, merchant Charleston, SC; *b* 21 Aug 1773; *d* New York 1814, leaving issue:

(1) Maitland Wilson; *b* 1814; *d* London 12 May 1877

6 James, merchant London; *b* 5 Jan 1776; *dsp* under full age

The est surv son,

EDWARD BOYD, of Mertonhall, DL; *b* 3 Sept 1770; *m* 15 Nov 1797 Janet, est dau of Benjamin Yule, of Wheatfield, Edinburgh, and *d* 27 Aug 1846, leaving issue:

1 William Sprot, HEIC, Political Commr Gujerat, Resident Baroda; *b* 16 Dec 1799; *dspvp* 18 Aug 1844

2 Benjamin, of Mertonhall, banker; *b* 1803; *k* Oct 1851 Guadalcanal, Solomon Islands, on landing from his yacht *The Wanderer*

3 Mark, of Mertonhall, JP; *b* 14 April 1805; *m* 1848 Emma Anne (*d* 15 Sept 1872), widow of Robert Coates, of Montagu Sq, London, and *dsp* 13 Sept 1879

4 John Christian Curwen, of Mertonhall, Wigtownshire (*s* his bro Mark, through concession of property 16 Oct 1874), and 33 Champs Elysées; *b* 1811; *m* 1841 Margaret Roberta, only surv dau of Robert Campbell, DL, JP, and *d* 3 June 1882, leaving issue:

(1) Campbell, of Mertonhall, and Villa Cardon, Deauville, JP, Lt RA; *b* 1842; *m* Josephine, dau of Lewis Livingstone, of New York, and had issue:

1a Aubrey Paget Livingstone Curwen, of Mertonhall and Rue Boccador, Paris; sold the estate 1899

(2) William Arthur Edward, 2nd Life Gds; *b* 6 April 1885; *m* 17 Jan 1893 Lady Lillian Adelaide Katherine Mary FitzClarence (*d* 15 July 1948), dau of 2nd Earl of Munster (*qv*), and *d* 6 Dec 1931, having had issue:

1a Benjamin Harold Alan; *b* 26 July 1912; *dvp* 22 Nov 1930

1a Phyllis Meeta; *b* 1894; *m* 17 Jan 1922 (*divorce*) Vicomte Henri Louis Leon de Janzé, son of Vicomte François Louis Leon de Janzé, and *dsp* 19 March 1943

(1) Edith Marion; *m* N Coquelin, of Paris

(2) Caroline Augusta; *b* 1848; *m* 30 April 1867 Reginald Beauchamp Yorke (*d* 15 May 1881), 3rd son of Ven Hon Henry Reginald Yorke, Archdeacon Huntingdon (*see* HARDWICK, E), and *dsp* 8 Nov 1878

(3) Leila Jessie; *b* 11 March 1849; *m* 27 Oct 1875 Count Oscar Gustav von Heidenstam, son of Chargé d'Affaires Count Carl Peter von Heidenstam, and *d* leaving issue

(4) Blanche Mary; *m* 2 Feb 1874 4th Marquess of Anglesey (*qv*) and *d* 14 Aug 1877, leaving issue

(5) Bertha Margaret Mabel; *m* Robert Lancaster Johnstone

5 EDWARD LENNOX, of whom presently

6 James; *b* 25 Dec 1819; *m* Elizabeth Gray, and *d* 4 March 1852, leaving issue:

(1) Marion Gray; *m* Edward William Sprot, of Drygrange (*d* 1 Feb 1898), son of Mark Sprot of Riddell, and *d* 27 June 1916, leaving issue

1 Marion; *b* 1803; *d* unm 23 Jan 1892

2 Mary; *b* 7 Nov 1808; *d* unm 28 Dec 1878

3 Jane Stewart; *b* 4 July 1810; *d* unm 7 March 1868

4 Janet; *b* 20 Feb 1814; *d* unm 6 March 1834

The 2nd surv son,

EDWARD LENNOX BOYD, of Burnham Priory, and 35 Cleveland Sq, London; *b* 1819; *m* 1 June 1848 Georgiana Hannah (*d* 25 Nov 1901), dau of Col Barnard Hague, of Kelfield Hall, Selby, Yorks, and *d* 9 Feb 1905, leaving issue:

1 ALAN WALTER, of whom presently

1 Elizabeth Barnard Evelyn; *b* 15 Oct 1851; *m* 29 April 1874 Lt-Col Charles William Kennaway, RA (*d* 28 July 1914), 2nd son of Sir John Kennaway, 2nd Bt (*qv*), and *d* 17 Jan 1917, leaving issue

2 Georgiana Gordon Lennox; *b* 10 Nov 1852; *d* unm 23 July 1892

3 Jessie; *m* Thomas William Tindal, barrister, son of Thomas Tindal, and *dsp* 1919. He *d* 6 Nov 1903

4 Mary Gertrude Lennox; *b* 8 Aug 1858; *m* 3 Jan 1885 Daniel Breay Ledsam, son of Rev Daniel Ledsam, Vicar Hollington, Sussex, and had issue

5 Helen Stewart Lennox; *b* 12 April 1860; *d* unm

The only son,

ALAN WALTER BOYD later LENNOX-BOYD (added by deed poll 8 Sept 1925); *b* 7 Aug 1855; *m* 1st 6 March 1886 Clementina Louisa (*d* 23 Jan 1896), dau of Gen Samford Wittingham, CB, and had issue:

1 Phyllis Georgie; *b* 30 July 1890; *d* unm 31 Jan 1964

He *m* 2nd 29 Oct 1901 Florence Anne (*d* 10 Nov 1949), dau of James Warburton Begbie, MD, of Charlotte Sq, Edinburgh, and by her had further issue:

1 George Edward, Maj HLI WW II; *b* 20 Aug 1902; *educ* Ch Ch Oxford; *das* 9 Nov 1943

2 ALAN TINDAL, **1st Viscount**

3 Donald Breay Hague, Capt Scots Greys; *b* 23 Nov 1906; *educ* Sherborne and Ch Ch Oxford; *d* unm Germany 5 April 1939

4 Francis Gordon, CC Beds 1939–44, Maj Roy Scots Greys WW II; *b* 23 Feb 1909; *educ* Ch Ch Oxford; *ka* leading 22nd Ind Para Co, Normandy, 6 June 1944

ALAN LENNOX-BOYD *d* 23 Nov 1934; his 2nd son,

ALAN TINDAL LENNOX-BOYD, PC (1951), CH (1960), DL (Beds 1954–60, Cornwall 1965), **1st Viscount Boyd of Merton**, of Merton-in-Penninghame, Co Wigtown (UK), so *cr* 8 Sept 1960; *b* 18 Nov 1904; *educ* Sherborne and Ch Ch Oxford (Hon Student 1968, Beit Prize, MA, pres Oxford Union 1926); MP (C) Mid-Beds 1931–60, Parly Sec to: Min Labour 1938–39, Min Home Security 1939, Min Food 1939–40 and Min Aircraft Prodn 1943–45, Min State Colonial Affs 1951–52, Min Tport and Civil Aviation 1952–54, Sec State Colonies 1954–59, Lt RNVR WW II 1940–43, barrister Inner Temple 1941, md Arthur Guinness & Sons 1959–67, jt v-chm 1967, chm Brewers Soc 1965, chm VSO 1962–64, memb Court Dirs Roy Exchange Assur, pres Overseas Employers Fedn 1962, pres: Save the Children Fund 1960–69 and Br Leprosy Relief Assoc 1960, chm Roy Cwlth Soc 1960–63 (pres 1966), tstee: Br Museum 1962 and Nat History Museum 1963–76, Prime Warden Goldsmith's Co 1964, pres RNVR Assoc 1964–72, chm Govrs Sherborne Sch 1962–73, Messel Medal Soc Chemical Industry 1966; *m* 29 Dec 1938 *Lady Patricia Florence Susan Guinness [Patricia Viscountess Boyd of Merton, Ince Castle, Saltash, Cornwall], 2nd dau of 2nd Earl of Iveagh (*qv*), and *d* 8 March 1983, leaving issue:

1 +SIMON DONALD RUPERT NEVILLE LENNOX-BOYD, **2nd and present Viscount Boyd of Merton**

2 +Christopher Alan [The Hon Christopher Lennox-Boyd, 42 Upper Brook St, London W1]; *b* 22 July 1941; *educ* Eton and Ch Ch Oxford (BA 1963, MA 1971)

3 +Mark Alexander [The Hon Sir Mark Lennox-Boyd, 3 Bloomfield Terr, London SW1; Gresgarth Hall, Caton, Lancs]; *b* 4 May 1943; *educ* Eton and Ch Ch Oxford (BA 1964, MA 1965); barrister Inner Temple 1968, MP (C): Morecambe and Lonsdale 1979–83 and Morecambe and Lunesdale 1983–97, PPS to: Chllr Exchequer 1983–84, Sec State Energy 1981–84 and PM 1988–90, Assist Govt Whip 1984–86, Govt Whip 1986–88, Parly Under-Sec FCO 1990–94, ktd 1994, Fifth and Renter Warden Fishmongers' Co 1995–96; *m* 29 June 1974 *Mrs Arabella Lacloche, only dau of Piero Parisi, of Rome, and formerly w of Philippe Lacloche, and has issue:

(1) *Patricia Irene; *b* 13 Aug 1980

BOYD-CARPENTER

Creation: B. (LP, UK) 1972.

THE BARON BOYD-CARPENTER, of Crux Easton, Co Southampton (John Archibald Boyd-Carpenter, PC (1954), DL (Gtr London 1973)) [The Rt Hon The Lord Boyd-Carpenter PC DL, House of Lords, London SW1A 0PW]; *b* 2 June 1908; *educ* Stowe and Balliol Coll Oxford (BA, Dip Econ, Pres Union 1930); barrister Middle Temple 1934; Maj Scots Gds WW II, Kingston-upon-Thames: MP (C) 1945–72 and High Steward 1973–, Fin Sec Treasury 1951–54, Min Tport and Civ Aviation 1954–55, Min Pensions and NI 1955–62, Ch Sec Treasury and Paymaster Gen 1962–64, Oppn Spokesman Housing and Land 1964–66, Chm Public Accounts Ctee 1964–70, chm: Orion Insur 1968–72, CLRP Investment Tst 1969–72, CAA 1972–77, Rugby Portland Cement 1976–84 and Carlton Club 1980–86, dir TR Far East Income Tst 1977–, memb cncl THF 1977–; *m* 1937 *Margaret Mary, dau of Lt-Col George Leslie Hall, OBE, RE (*see* COVENTRY, E), and has:

1 *Sir Thomas Patrick John, KBE (1993, MBE 1973) [Lt-Gen The Hon Sir Thomas Boyd-Carpenter KBE, c/o Barclays Bank, 6 Market Place, Newbury, Berks RG14 5AY], *b* 1938; *educ* Stowe; Lt-Gen, Dep Ch Staff (Programmes and Personnel) MOD 1992–; *m* 1972 *Mary Jean, da of John Elwes Duffield, BM, BCh, of The Tithe House, Church St Marcham, Berks, and has issue
1 *Anne Mary, *b* 1942
2 *SARAH ELIZABETH MARY BOYD-CARPENTER, BARONESS HOGG (*qv*)

Lineage: Rt Rev WILLIAM BOYD CARPENTER, KCVO; Bp Ripon; *m* 1st Harriet Peers, of Chiselhampton, Oxon, and had, with an est s (Henry, *m* 1902 Ethel dau of Sir Francis Ley, 1st Bt, *qv*), a 4th s:

Sir ARCHIBALD BOYD BOYD-CARPENTER, JP (Surrey), of River House, Walton-on-Thames; *b* 26 March 1873; *educ* Harrow and Balliol Coll Oxford; Maj Highland LI Boer War and WW I, MP (U) Bradford N 1918–23, Coventry 1924–29 and Chertsey 1931–37, ktd 1926, Parly Sec Min Labour 1922–23, Fin Sec Treasury 1923, Paymaster Gen 1923, Fin Sec Admlty and Paymaster-Gen 1923–24; *m* A Dugdale, of Moor Park, Harrogate, and *d* 27 May 1937, leaving an only s:

JOHN ARCHIBALD, *cr* a **Baron**

BOYLE

Arms: Per bend raguly gu. and arg. two staves raguly bendwise, one in chief and one in base, counterchanged. **Crest:** In front of a lion's head arg. a staff raguly fesswise gu. **Motto:** God's providence is my inheritance. **Creation:** Bt. (UK) 14 Dec 1904.

SIR STEPHEN GURNEY BOYLE, 5TH BT, of Ockham, Salehurst, Sussex [Sir Stephen Boyle Bt, 19 Gibb Croft, Harlow, Essex CM18 7JL]; *b* 15 Jan 1962; *s* f 1983; *educ* Mark Hall Comprehensive Harlow

Lineage: RICHARD O'BOYLE, of Lisnakirka, nr Castlebar, Co Mayo, of a family long resident in the barony of Carra, Co Mayo, had issue:

PATRICK ROBERT O'BOYLE, of Grove House, Highgate, Middx, Lt RA; *b* 23 July 1780; *m* Celia — and *d* 8 Nov 1827, leaving issue:

EDWARD O'BOYLE, CE, of London; *m* 26 Jan 1842 Eliza (*d* 24 Feb 1888), dau of James Gurney, of Culloden, Norfolk, and *d* 31 Jan 1865, having had issue (with a yr s James; *d* unm):

Sir Edward Boyle, 1st Bt (UK), so *cr* 14 Dec 1904, KC, FSI, FRGS, dir London and India Docks, dep chm Imp Life Off, MP Taunton 1906–09; *b* 6 Sept 1848; *m* 18 March 1874 Constance Jane (Bulgarian Order Civil Merit 1st Cl, Grand Offr Order St Sava Serbia, Cdr Order Skanderbeg Albania, Serbian Red Cross Decoration 1st Cl; *d* 27 May 1944), yr dau of William Knight, JP, of Kensington Pk Gdns, London W, and had issue:

1 EDWARD (Sir), **2nd Bt**
1 Constance Beryl Bertha; *b* 31 March 1882; *m* 4 Oct 1905 Capt George Crosby Halahan, JP, Lincs Regt, s of Col Samuel Handy Halahan, The Buffs, E Kent Regt, and *d* 8 Feb 1965, leaving a s and dau. He *d* 29 July 1929

Sir EDWARD *d* 19 March 1909; his only son,

Sir Edward Boyle, 2nd Bt, JP, High Sheriff 1927, FRGS, Hon LLD Sofia 1939; *educ* Eton and Balliol Coll Oxford (MA); barrister Inner Temple 1902, Associate Surveyors' Instn, chm Balkan Ctee, actg Br Commr Serbia 1915, Grand Cordon Order: Civil Merit Bulgaria and Skanderbeg Albania, Grand Offr Order St Sava Serbia, Serbian Red Cross decn 1st Cl, Croix de Charité, dir Richard Thomas & Co, Properties Investment Tst, pres Br Legion Hurst Green Branch; *b* 12 June 1878; *m* 29 April 1920 Beatrice (Order St Sava Serbia 3rd Cl; *d* 2 Nov 1961), er dau of Henry Greig, of Belvedere Ho, Kent, and *d* 31 March 1945, leaving issue:

1 **Sir Edward Charles Gurney Boyle, 3rd Bt** and BARON BOYLE OF HANDSWORTH, of Salehurst, Sussex (LP, UK), so *cr* 3 July 1970, PC (1962), CH (1981); *b* 31 Aug 1923; *educ* Eton and Ch Ch Oxford (BA 1949, MA 1959, pres Union 1949); t/jr admin offr FO 1942–45, MP (C) Handsworth 1950–70, PPS to Parly Under-Sec Air 1951–52 and Min Def 1952, Parly Sec Min Supply 1954–55, Ec Sec Treasury 1955–56, Parly Sec Educn 1957–59, Fin Sec Treasury 1959–62, Min Educn 1962–64, Min State Educn and Sci Apr-Oct 1964, V-Chllr Leeds U 1970, Tstee Br Museum 1970–81, chm ctee of V-Chllrs and Pncpls UK Us 1977–78, Hon LLD: Leeds and Southampton 1965, Bath 1968, Sussex 1972, Liverpool 1981; *d* unm 28 Sept 1981, when the life barony expired
2 RICHARD GURNEY BOYLE (Sir), **4th Bt**
1 *Ann Constance Beatrice [Mrs Jack Gold, 123 St George's Rd, London SE1]; *b* 8 Nov 1926; *m* 19 Aug 1948 *Jack Brunner Gold, est son of Maj Guy Gilbey Gold, TD, DL, JP, of Abbots Hall, Shalford, Braintree, Essex, and has issue:
(1) *Jason; *b* 13 Sept 1950; *educ* St Paul's; *m* 1972 *Ann Elizabeth Stewart and has:
1a *Matthew Guy; *b* 1981
2a *James Alexander; *b* 1991
(1) *Georgina Beatrice; *b* 10 Nov 1952; *m* 1981 *Kenneth Neil Burney Dunlop and has:
1a *Kenneth Edward George; *b* 1984
2a *Richard Nicholas; *b* 1985

BARON BOYLE OF HANDSWORTH's bro,

Sir Richard Gurney Boyle, 4th Bt; *b* 14 May 1930; *educ* Millfield; private gardener at Pans Hall and Hastingwood House; *m* 27 May 1961 (*divorce* 1974) Elizabeth Ann, yr dau of Norman Dennes, of Middle Green, Poulshot, Devizes, Wilts, and *d* 1983, leaving issue:

1 Sir STEPHEN GURNEY BOYLE, **5th and present Bt**
2 +MICHAEL DESMOND; *b* 16 Sept 1963; heir presumptive
3 +Roger Edward Bartholemew; *b* 1966

BOYNE

Arms: Quarterly, 1st and 4th, argent, between two chevronels a cinquefoil, all between three cross crosslets fitchée sable (for RUSSELL); 2nd and 3rd, gules, three cinquefoils pierced ermine (for HAMILTON). **Crests:** 1 A goat passant argent, collared gemell, charged on the body with an escallop sable (for RUSSELL), 2 Out of a ducal coronet or an oak fructed of the first and penetrated transversely in the main stem by a frame-saw, all proper (for HAMILTON). **Supporters:** Two mermaids proper, hair dishevelled or, each holding in the exterior hand a mirror of the last. **Mottoes:** *Nec timeo, nec sperno* ('I neither fear nor despise') and above HAMILTON crest 'Through'. **Creations:** B. (I) 20 Oct 1715 (Hamilton) and (UK) 31 Aug 1866 (Brancepeth), V. (I) 20 Aug 1717.

THE 11TH VISCOUNT BOYNE in the province of Leinster, **Baron Hamilton of Stackallan** and **Baron Brancepeth** of Brancepeth, Co Durham (Gustavus Michael Stucley Hamilton-Russell) [The Rt Hon The Viscount Boyne, Dingle Leys, Burwarton, Bridgnorth, Salop WV16 6QG]; *b* 27 May 1965; *s* f 1995; *educ* Harrow and RAC Cirencester; ARICS; *m* 1 June 1991 *Lucy, dau of George Potter, of Foxdale, Bunbury, Cheshire, and has issue:

1 +Frederick Gustavus George; *b* 23 March 1997
1*Emelia Rose; *b* 25 Jan 1994

Lineage: Sir FREDERICK HAMILTON, of Manor Hamilton, Dromahaire, Co Leitrim, yst s of 1st Lord Paisley and bro of 1st Earl of Abercorn (*see* ABERCORN, D), served under GUSTAVUS ADOLPHUS, King of Sweden, in Thirty Years War (1618–48), later Govr Ulster; *m* 1st Sidney, dau and heiress of Sir John Vaughan, Govr Londonderry; *m* 2nd Agnes — (*m* 2nd John Maxwell) and *d* 31 March 1646, having by his 1st w had, with other issue (including another s older than the **1st Viscount Boyne**):

1 James, of Manor Hamilton; *m* 1647 his cousin Catherine (*m* 2nd Owen Wynne; *m* 3rd John Bingham, of Castlebar, Co Mayo), dau of 2nd Lord Hamilton, Baron of Strabane (*see* ABERCORN, D), and *d* 27 Dec 1652, leaving issue:

(1) Sidney; *b* 1648; *m* Sir John Hume, 2nd Bt (*d* 1695), of Castle Hume, and *d* 10 Jan 1685/6, leaving issue

(2) Hannah; *b* 1651; *m* Sir William Gore, 3rd Bt, of Manor Gore (*see* ARRAN, E), and *d* 16 May 1733, leaving issue

2 GUSTAVUS, **1st Viscount**

1 Christian; *m* Sir George Munro, (*see* MUNRO, Bt, of Foulis-Obsdale), and *d* by 1700, leaving issue

Sir FREDERICK HAMILTON's 3rd s,

GUSTAVUS HAMILTON, **1st Viscount Boyne** in the province of Leinster, so *cr* 20 Aug 1717, as also earlier BARON HAMILTON OF STACKALLAN 20 Oct 1715 (both I), PC (I 1710); *b* 1642; served under WILLIAM III in Ireland at Siege of Londonderry 1689, Battle of the Boyne 1690 and storming of Athlone, granted lands forfeited by supporters of JAMES II, Maj-Gen 1704, MP (I Parl) Donegal 1692–93, 1695–99 and 1703–13 and Strabane 1713–14, Lt-Gen; *m* Elizabeth (*d* 28 Dec 1721), dau of Sir Henry Brooke, MP, of Brooke's Borough, Co Fermanagh (*see* BROOKEBOROUGH, V), and *d* 16 Sept 1723, having had:

1 FREDERICK; *m* 1 Sept 1707 Sophia (*d* 6 May 1748), sis of 1st Earl of Clanbrassil and dau of James Hamilton, of Tollymore, and *dvp* 10 Dec 1715, leaving issue:

(1) GUSTAVUS HAMILTON, **2nd Viscount Boyne**, PC (I); *b* 1710; MP (Whig) Newport (IoW) 1736–41; *d* unm 18 April 1746

2 Gustavus, of Redwood, King's Co (now Co Offaly), MP Co Donegal (I Parl); *m* Jan 1717 Dorothea Bellew (*m* 2nd David Dickson), only dau of 3rd Baron Bellew of Duleek (*qv*), and *d* 26 Feb 1733/4, having had, with other issue:

(1) FREDERICK HAMILTON, **3rd Viscount Boyne**; *bapt* 9 Nov 1718; *m* 1737 Elizabeth, dau of Benjamin Hadley, and *dsp* 2 Jan 1772

(2) RICHARD, **4th Viscount**, for whom *see* further below

(1) Caroline; *m* 1744 Edward Lovibond (*d* 27 Sept 1775), poet, of Kingston, Surrey, and had issue

3 Henry; *b* Feb 1692; MP Donegal (I Parl), Collector Port of Cork; *m* 27 Oct 1722 Mary (*d* 1770), est dau of Joshua Dawson, of Castle Dawson, Co Derry, and *d* 3 June 1743, leaving, with other issue:

(1) Joshua; *m* 1750 Mary (*d* April 1764), dau of Sir Richard Cox, 2nd Bt (*see* 1873 edn), of Dunmanway, Co Cork, and *d* 1784, having had, with other issue:

1a Henry HAMILTON later HAMILTON-COX (added on inheriting Dunmanway on the death of his 1st cousin once-removed Sir Richard Cox, 4th Bt, 1784); *m* Letitia, dau of David Wilson Hutcheson, of Dublin, and *d* 1821, having had, with other issue:

1b William John; *m* 16 April 1837 Rebecca Armstrong and had issue:

1c Henry Augustus; *b* 28 April 1841; *m* 1878 Rose Josephine (*d* 1922), dau of Johann Hofmarksrichter, and *d* 1890, having had issue:

1d William; *b* 1884; *m* 1910 Caroline (*d* 1977), dau of William Colling, and *d* 1970, leaving issue:

1e Walter; *b* 1915; horologist; *m* 1938 *Lola, dau of Clarence Bradley, and *d* 1993, leaving issue:

1f *Carolyn Jane; *b* 1940; *m* 1964 *Francis Donovan and has issue:

1g *Michael William; *b* 1970

2f *Linda Jean; *b* 1947; *m* 1st 1967 (*divorce* 19–) Charles Entwistle and has issue:

1g *Scott Alan; *b* 1972

1g *Melissa Ann; *b* 1969

2f (cont.) Mrs Linda Entwistle *m* 2nd 1981 *James Krysiak

1e *Louise Rose [Mrs Clinton C King, 1115 Herbert Street, Peru, Ill, USA]; *b* 1916; *m* 1942 *Clinton Carlton King, horologist, and has issue:

1f *James Hamilton [Dr James King, 93 Victoria Av, Galesburg, Ill 61401, USA]; *b* 1944; MD, FACP; *m* 1968 *Mary, dau of Kenneth Gibson, and has issue:

1g *John Hamilton; *b* 1971

2g *James Thaddeus; *b* 1973

1d Teresa Rebecca; *b* 1880; *m* 1906 Dr Arthur Stanley Bayne (*d* 1951) and had issue

1c Arabella Dorothea; *m* Jasper E Lucas, of Richfordstown, Co Cork

1a Mary; *m* Rev Samuel Beamish, MA, of Mount Beamish, Co Cork, and had issue

2a Catherine; *m* 25 Sept 1785 Capt Bent Ball (*d* 12 Oct 1832), 63rd Regt (*see* BALL, Bt), and had issue

(2) Sackville HAMILTON, PC; *b* 14 March 1732; Ch Sec for Ireland; *m* Arabella, dau of Rev Robert Berkeley, a yr bro of Dr George Berkeley, Bp Cloyne, and *d* 29 Jan 1818, leaving, with other issue:

1a Sackville Robert (Rev); Rector Mallow, Co Cork; *m* Jane, dau of Edward Deane Freeman, of Castle Cor, Co Cork, and *d* 20 Feb 1853, leaving, with other issue:

1b Sackville Deane; *b* 1808; *m* 1845 Eleanor (*d* 19 June 1870), est dau of Matthew Sankey, and *d* 30 July1878, leaving, with other issue:

1c Sackville Berkeley; *b* 26 Oct 1846; AIG RIC; *m* 10 July 1880 Eva Maria Eleanor (*d* 2 June1926), dau of Gen Charles Annesley Benson, and *d* 4 May 1913, leaving issue:

1d Sackville William Sackville, DSO (1916) and bar (1917), MBE (1946); *b* 3 Nov 1882; Col RE, Dir Survey of India, Assist Supt Survey of India 1906–12, served WW I, Ch Instructor RMA Woolwich 1917–19, Co ARP Offr Dorset 1938–46; *m* 18 March 1920 Margaret Dowell (*d* 1993), only dau of Samuel Charles Hester, MA, of North-down-in-Thanet, and *d* 11 May 1956, having had issue:

1e Sackville Charles Sackville; *b* 15 March 1921; *d* 22 July 1929

2e +James Berkeley [Lt-Col James Sackville Hamilton, Acklam Grange, Malton, Yorks YO17 9RG]; *b* 28 May 1923; *educ* Wellington and King's Coll Cambridge (MA); Lt-Col RE, served WW II 1943–46 with QVO Madras Sappers and Miners in India, Burma and Malaya (despatches), Staff Coll Camberley 1953, Br Jt Services Mission Washington DC 1954–57, OC 4th Field Sqdn RE BAOR 1957–9, HQ 1st Div BAOR 1959–61, 2nd in Command 4th Div Engrs BAOR 1961–63, MOD Directorate of Army Trg 1963–5, CO Cambridge U OTC 1965–7, HQ Engr-in-Ch 1967; Bursar Pocklington Sch nr York 1972–88; *m* 10 Dec 1947 *Mary Grizel, er dau of Col Cecil Alexander Boyle, CIE, DSO (*see* GLASGOW, E), and has issue:

1f +Charles Patrick [Charles Sackville Hamilton Esq, Thrussendale Farm, Acklam, Malton, N Yorks]; *b* 10 Dec 1949; *educ* Wellington and St Catharine's Coll Cambridge (MA); *m* 29 Sept 1980 *Heather, dau of Thomas Goodwin, of Mow Cop, Staffs

2f +Andrew James Sackville; *b* 17 Nov 1951; *educ* Wellington and Oxford (MA), Liverpool U (MSc), London U (MSc), Virginia U (USA) (PhD); FRAS; *m* 25 Feb 1978 *Catherine Clare, dau of Dr R A Davidson, of Mombasa, Kenya, and has issue:

1g +Jamie Wildrose; *b* 27 Dec 1988

1g *Jessica Liberty; *b* 24 May 1984

3f +Nigel Ruaraidh [Dr Nigel Sackville Hamilton, Bronwydd, Cross St Bow St, Dyfed]; *b* 23 July 1953; *educ* Wellington and Cambridge (MA, PhD); *m* 11 June 1983 *Dr Charmian, dau of Col J J G Hunter, and has issue:

1g *Henry James; *b* 3 June 1989

1g *Alice Charlotte; *b* 8 May 1991

1f *Patricia Margaret [Mrs Richard Hall, Old Manor Farm, Helperthorpe, nr Malton, N Yorks YO17 8TQ]; *b* 1 Feb 1956; *educ* Tudor Hall; *m* 12 June 1982 *Richard Hall, s of W W L Hall, of Burythorpe, N Yorks, and has issue:

1g *Jonathan; *b* 19 March 1983

2g *Nicholas; *b* 26 Nov 1984

3e Henry Sackville; *b* 28 May 1929; Lt RN; *k* in a flying accident at RN Air Station Lossiemouth 26 May 1952

1e *Anne Margaret Sackville [Mrs David MacEwen, Stuckeridge House, Oakford, nr Tiverton, Devon]; *b* 2 May 1925; *educ* Newnham Coll Cambridge (MA); *m* 9 Sept 1950 *David MacEwen, MA (Cambridge), only s of Ewyn Alastair MacEwen, and has issue:

1f *Diana Cushla; *b* 15 Sept 1951

2f *Helen Margaret; *b* 17 Feb 1953

3f *Penelope Anne Georgina; *b* 8 July 1965

2d Charles Sackville; *b* 4 Dec 1885; *educ* St Columba's Coll; Maj E Lancs Regt, in Leinster Regt 1907–22, employed with W African Frontier Force 1910–4, served WW I and II; *m* 25 Nov 1918 Averina Jane (Reena) (*d* 1973), est dau of William Richardson Oliver, of Kil-na-mulla, Buttevant, Co Cork, and *d* 1971, leaving issue:

1e *Averina Rachel Grace Sackville [Mrs Colin Hargreave, The Willows, 10 Clifton Drive, Lytham, Lancs]; *b* 30 Jan 1923; *m* 29 Jan 1951 *Colin Oliver Hargreave, 2nd s of Oliver Hargreave, and has issue:

1f *Jeremy David Hamilton; *b* 26 Aug 1955; *educ* Eton

2f Nicholas Peter; *b* 15 Nov and *d* 19 Nov 1957

2e *Patricia May Sackville [Mrs Derek Spooner, The Garden Cottage, Fritham Court, Lyndhurst, Hants SO43 7HH]; *b* 27 Oct 1924; ARCA 1948; *m* 28 Aug 1948 Lt Derek Richard Spooner, RN (ret) (*d* 1978), er s of Capt Lancelot Arthur Wetherell Spooner, OBE, RN, and has issue:

1f *Richard Hamilton [Richard Spooner Esq, 3 Green Hill, High Wycombe, Bucks]; *b* 17 Feb 1952; *educ* King's Sch Ely; BA, ACA; *m* 1978 *Susan Elizabeth Ann, yr dau of John Rowntree, and has issue:

1g *Victoria Emily Barbara; *b* 1985

2g *Catherine Esmé Averina; *b* 1987

3g *Elizabeth Sackville; *b* 1990

1f *Jane Rosemary Eleanor; *b* 23 June 1955; *m* 1979 *Lt-Col John Malcolm Carmichael Watson, QOH, er s of John Watson, of Northallerton, Yorks, and has issue:

1g *Anna Patricia Louise; *b* 1983

2g *Edwina Rose Jane; *b* 1986

3g *Fenella Margaret Grace; *b* 1990

1d Grace Arabella Sackville; *m* 24 July1915 Lt-Col Thomas Charles McCombie Young (*d* 25 Jan 1959), late IMS, only s of Rev Dr Young, rector Ellon, Aberdeenshire, and *d* 17 March 1962

1c Eleanor Mary; *m* 27 July 1880 Lt-Col William Augustus Riall, DL (*d* 25 Oct 1918), late RA, of Heywood, Clonmel, Co Tipperary, and *d* 13 Oct 1913, leaving issue

2b Henry, CB; *b* 1812; Gen, Col Leinster Regt; *m* 15 March 1842 Isabella (*d* 16 Oct 1889), dau of Joseph Deane Freeman, of Castle Cor, Co Cork, and *d* 25 Aug 1891, leaving, with other issue:

1c Henry Claud; *b* 23 Jan 1850; *m* 9 March 1880 Henrietta Elmina (*d* March1929), dau of James Wise, and *d* 25 April 1923

(1) Mary; *m* by licence 4 Oct 1763 Rev Nathaniel Preston (*d* 1796), of Swainston, Meath, and had issue

1 Elizabeth; *m* Charles Lambart, of Painstown, MP (I Parl), gs of 1st Earl of Cavan (*qv*), and had issue

The 3rd VISCOUNT's yr bro,

RICHARD HAMILTON, **4th Viscount Boyne**; *b* 24 March 1724; MP (I Parl) Navan 1755–60, Sheriff Co Meath; *m* Georgiana, 2nd dau of William Bury, of Shannon Grove, Co Limerick, by his w Hon Jane Moore, dau of 1st Baron Moore of Tullamore and sis and heiress of 1st and last Earl of Charleville of the 1758 *cr*, and *d* 30 July 1789, leaving, with other issue, an est s:

1 GUSTAVUS HAMILTON, **5th Viscount Boyne**; *b* 20 Dec 1749; Sheriff Co Meath 1774; *m* 1 April 1773 Martha Matilda (*m* 2nd 11 July 1821 Sir Thomas Webb, Bt, and *d* 16 Sept 1826), only dau of Sir Quaile Somerville, Bt, of Somerville, Meath (*see* 1929 edn, ATHLUMNEY, B), and *d* 29 Feb 1816, leaving, with other issue, an est s:

(1) GUSTAVUS HAMILTON, **6th Viscount Boyne**; *b* 12 April 1777; *m* 4 Aug 1796 Harriet (*d* 1 Nov 1854), only dau of Benjamin Baugh, of Burwarton House, Salop, and *d* 30 March 1855, leaving issue an only surv s:

1a GUSTAVUS FREDERICK HAMILTON later HAMILTON-RUSSELL (added by roy licence 26 Feb 1850 name and arms of RUSSELL on his w's inheriting Brancepeth 1850 from her bro), **7th Viscount Boyne**; *b* 11 May 1797; Sheriff Salop 1841, *cr* 31 Aug 1866 BARON BRANCEPETH OF BRANCEPETH, Co Durham (UK); *m* 9 Sept 1828 Emma Maria (*d* 29 April 1870), dau of Matthew Russell, MP, of Brancepeth Castle, Co Durham, and *d* 27 Oct 1872, leaving, with other issue, an only s:

1b GUSTAVUS RUSSELL HAMILTON later HAMILTON-RUSSELL, **8th Viscount Boyne**, JP (Cos Meath and Durham), DL (Salop); *b* 28 May 1830; *m* 2 Sept 1858 Lady Katherine Frances Scott (*d* 19 May 1903), 3rd dau of 2nd Earl of Eldon (*qv*), and *d* 30 Dec 1907, having had issue:

1c Gustavus Claud; *b* 29 Dec 1861; *d* 9 Feb 1862

2c GUSTAVUS WILLIAM, **9th Viscount**

3c Frederick Gustavus, JP (Salop and Co Durham), DL (Co Durham); *b* 12 June 1867; *m* 27 April 1897 Lady Margaret Rachel Scott (*d* 27 Jan 1938), dau of 3rd Earl of Eldon (*qv*), and *dsp* 3 Oct 1941

4c Claud Eustace, JP, DL (both Co Durham); *b* 4 March 1871; Lt 4th Bn Cheshire Regt; *m* 11 April 1899 Maria Lindsay, JP (*d* 26 Jan 1963), est dau of Sir Lindsay Wood, 1st Bt (*see* 1940 edn), and *d* 7 May 1948, having had issue:

1d Arthur Gustavus Lindsay; *b* 30 April 1900; Maj Rifle Bde, served WW II 1939–40; *ka* May 1940 France

2d Edric Claud; *b* 24 Nov 1904; *educ* Eton and Trin Coll Cambridge (BA 1926); mining engr, chartered surveyor; *m* 11 April 1932 (Helen) Rosa, JP (Northumberland) (*d* 4 March 1996), only dau of William Humble, of Skellow Grange, Doncaster, and *d* 1984, having had issue:

1e Christopher Claud; *b* 23 April 1936; *d* unm 17 Dec 1957

1e *Ann Katharine [Mrs William Currie, Rollington House, Redlynch, Salisbury, Wilts SP5 2HF]; *b* 10 Feb 1933; *m* 6 July 1953 *Lt-Col William Frank Philip Currie, QRIH, only s of Maj Philip John Reginald Currie, OBE, MC, and has issue:

1f *Richard William; *b* 13 Sept 1955; *educ* Radley; Lt-Col QRH

1f *Joanna; *b* 12 Nov 1959

1d *Jean Katharine [Mrs Arthur Heywood-Lonsdale, Shavington Grange, Market Drayton, Shropshire]; *b* 18 July 1907; *m* 1 June 1931 Lt-Col Arthur Heywood-Lonsdale, CBE, MC, JP (*d* 14 March 1976), Gren Gds Res of Offrs, est s of Col Henry Heywood Lonsdale, DSO (*see* HAMILTON OF DALZELL, B), and has issue:

1e *Timothy Claud [Timothy Heywood-Lonsdale Esq, The Old Laundry, Shavington, Market Drayton, Shropshire]; *b* 1937; *m* 1964 *Jennifer Elizabeth, only dau of William Beck, of Tabley Grange, Knutsford, Cheshire, and has issue:

1f *William Pemberton; *b* 1970

1f *Nichola Caroline; *b* 1966

5c Arthur; *b* 8 Sept 1872; Maj N Irish Horse, Maj 1st Dragoons, served S Africa 1899–1902 (despatches, wounded) and BEF France and Flanders 1915–8 (despatches); *m* 14 June 1905 Marion Lilias (*d* 15 Jan 1934), yst dau of Henry Harris, of Steventon, Whitchurch, and *d* 6 Feb 1951, leaving issue:

1d David Henry Gustavus; *b* 4 May 1911; *m* 26 April 1950 *Pauline Albinia [Mrs David Hamilton-Russell, 103 Rowan Ho, Greycoat St, London SW1P 2QD], dau of George Penkivil Slade, KC, of St Michael's, Painswick, Glos, and *d* 1988, leaving issue:

1e *Marion Albinia [Mrs Simon Armson, Broad Oak, Hurley, Maidenhead, Berks SL6 5LW]; *b* 16 Jan 1952; *m* 8 Feb 1975 *Frederick Simon Arden Armson, only s of Dr Gerald Armson, of The Moat, Yoxall, Staffs, and has issue:

1f *Patrick David Arden; *b* 8 May 1982

1f *Meriel Albinia; *b* 31 May 1979

2f *Katherine Geraldine; *b* 9 Dec 1984

2e *Georgiana Mary [Mrs John Hayward, 4 Herondale Ave, London SW18 3JL]; *b* 31 May 1955; *m* 1983 *John Kenrick Hayward, s of Surg-Col Edwin William Hayward, OBE, and has issue:

1f *Cicely Albinia; *b* 1985

2f *Edwina Mary; *b* 1987

3e *Annette Katharine [Mrs Brian Lanaghan, 100 Huron Rd, London SW17 8RD]; *b* 1 Nov 1958; *m* 1989 *Brian Lanaghan, s of Richard Lanaghan, of Bath, and has issue:

1f *James Henry David; *b* 1993

1f *Marina Katharine Albinia; *b* 1991

4e *Margaret Louisa; *b* 23 May 1960

6c Eustace Scott, OBE (1919), JP (Salop); *b* 7 Feb 1878; *educ* Eton and Magdalen Coll Oxford; Lt 3rd Bn Northumberland Fus, OStJ; *m* 27 June 1906 Olive Mary (*d* 6 Oct 1951), yr dau of Col Francis Alexander Woolryche-Whitmore, JP, of Dudmaston, Salop, and *d* 3 Nov 1962, leaving issue:

1d Rachel Katharine; *b* 31 Aug 1908; *m* 1st 14 June 1930 (*divorce* 1940) Malcolm Findanus MacGregor, est s of Alasdair MacGregor, of Cardney, Dunkeld, Perthshire (*see* MacGREGOR of MacGREGOR, Bt); *m* 2nd 10 May 1943 *Sir George Peter Labouchere, GBE, KCMG, only s of Francis Anthony Labouchere, by his w Evelyn Mary, only dau of Sir Walter George Stirling, 3rd Bt, of Faskine (*see* 1934 edn), and *d* 22 March 1996

7c Hubert; *b* 13 Feb, *d* 7 March 1886

1c Louisa; *d* 23 May 1861

2c Emma Maria; *d* 30 May 1861

3c Alice Katharine; *m* 27 July 1888 Capt Wyndham Paulet St John-Mildmay (*d* 2 March 1934), Rifle Bde (*see* 1970 edn ST JOHN-MILDMAY, Bt), and *dsp* 17 Nov 1959 aged 96

4c Maud Harriet; *d* unm 19 April 1951

5c Constance Elizabeth; *m* 9 Aug 1898 Very Rev Albert Victor Baillie, KCVO, DD (*d* 3 Nov 1955), Dean Windsor, and *d* 27 Sept 1924, leaving issue (*see* BURTON, B)

6c Florence Rachel; *d* unm 3 April 1957

The 8th VISCOUNT's est surv s,

GUSTAVUS WILLIAM HAMILTON-RUSSELL, **9th Viscount Boyne**, JP (Salop 1942 and Co Durham), DL (Salop and Co Durham); *b* 11 Jan 1864; Capt 3rd Bn Northumberland Fus, Hon Col 7th Bn Durham LI, KGStJ; *m* 4 Oct 1906 Lady Margaret Selina Lascelles, CBE (1920), DGStJ, memb RDC and Salop Ag Exec Ctee 1939–50, CA (Salop 1941), JP (Salop 1942), Hon LLD (Leeds 1951) (*d* Dec 1978), dau of 5th Earl of Harewood (*qv*), and *d* 18 Jan 1942, having had issue:

1 Gustavus Lascelles; *b* 18 Oct 1907; *educ* Eton and Magdalene Coll Cambridge (BA); Lt Gren Gds Res of Offrs; *m* 20 Jan 1931 Joan Verena (*d* 1 April 1938), dau of Sir Henry Lloyd Verney, GCVO (*see* VERNEY, Bt), and was *ka* June1940 France, having had issue:

(1) GUSTAVUS MICHAEL GEORGE, **10th Viscount**

(1) Charmian Joan; *b* 8 April 1933; *d* 12 May 1937

2 +RICHARD GUSTAVUS, DSO (1943) and bar (1944), LVO (1977), DL (N Riding Yorks 1973) [Brig The Hon Richard Hamilton-Russell DSO LVO DL, The Old Prebendal House, Shipton-under-Wychwood, OX7 6BQ]; *b* 4 Feb 1909; heir presumptive; *educ* Eton; High Sheriff Yorks 1968, Brig late17th/21st Lancers (Col 1957–65), served WW II (despatches), memb Gentlemen-at-Arms 1956– (Standard Bearer 1977–); *m* 17 July 1939 Hon Pamela Penelope Cayzer (*d* 1987), er dau of 1st Baron Rotherwick (*qv*), and has issue:

(1) +Brian Gustavus [Col Brian Hamilton-Russell, Hardwick Forge, Stottesdon, Kidderminster, Worcs DY14 8TL]; *b* 8 May 1940; *educ* Eton and RMA Sandhurst; Col 17th/21st Lancers; *m* 1st 17 Oct 1967 Lea (*m* 2nd 18 Nov 1982 5th Baron Leigh (*qv*)), only child of Col Henry Noël Havelock Wild, OBE, 11th Hus, by Violet Nina, yst dau of Henry William Selby-Lowndes, and has issue:

1a +Henry William Gustavus; *b* 28 Feb 1969

1a *Victoria Essex Lea; *b* 9 March 1976

(1) (cont.) Col Brian Hamilton-Russell *m* 2nd 1982 *Sarah Julianne, dau of Reginald Waugh Harris, formerly w of Jeremy Colebrook-Robjent

(2) +Richard Desmond [Richard Hamilton-Russell Esq, Mincinbury Manor, Barley, Royston, Herts]; *b* 30 May 1943; *educ* Eton; commd 17th/21st Lancers; *m* 2 Sept 1965 *Prudence Sophia, only dau of Maj Ronald Penrhyn Pockney, of The Old Barn, Bishopthorpe, York, and has issue:

1a +Charles Richard; *b* 1965; Maj Queen's Roy Lancers; *m* 1993 *Claire Fiona, dau of Ian Dussek, of Little Allens, Plaxtol, Kent

1a *Emma Sophia [Mrs Jonathan Bray, 14 Trewint St, London SW18 4HA]; *b* 28 July 1968; *m* 11 May 1996 *Jonathan Charles Bray, s of Geoffrey Bray, of Lilbourne, Warwicks

2a *Katharine Roseanna; *b* 6 Jan 1972

(1) *Veronica Anne [Mrs Nicholas Jones, 12 Paultons St, London SW3 5DR]; *b* 8 Nov 1949; *m* 25 March 1971 *Nicholas Houssemayne Jones, son of Henry Jones, of Kitsbury Orchard, Addington, Moreton-in-Marsh, Glos, and has:

1a *Oliver Mark; *b* 1977

1a *Rowena Rose; *b* 1975

3 John, MC; *b* 22 April 1911; Maj The Royals WW II; *m* 27 Sept 1937 Lady Diana Legge, CStJ (1965) (*m* 2nd 1 June 1946 Brig Adrian Lewis Matthews, OBE, MC, RA, s of Maj Bertram Henry Matthews, and *d* 25 Feb 1970), 3rd dau of 7th Earl of Dartmouth (*qv*), and was accidentally *kas* Aug 1943 Sicily, leaving issue:

(1) +James Gustavus, MBE (1976); *b* 11 Sept 1938; *educ* Eton; Col Household Cavalry (ret); FIMgt; *m* 30 Oct 1965 *Alison Mary, yr dau of Sydney Haydn Heard, MBE, MRCS, LRCP, CStJ, Lt-Col IMS (ret), Lt Bailiff and Jurat of R Court of Albecq, Guernsey, of La Giffardiere, Albecq, Guernsey, CI, and has issue:

1a +Mark John Gustavus; *b* 17 May 1969; *educ* Stowe and RMA Sandhurst; commd RHG/D 1989

2a +Edward Haydn James; *b* 17 May 1969; commd Life Gds 1990

1a *Julia Mary; *b* 14 Sept 1967

4 Michael Gustavus; *b* 26 Oct 1912; *d* 20 Nov 1918

5 Desmond Claud; *b* 11 Aug 1917; Capt Roy Dragoons WW II; *ka* Africa 19 April 1943

1 *Rosemary Katharine [The Rt Hon The Lady Forbes, Balforbes, Alford, Aberdeenshire AB33 8DR]; *b* 1 April 1921; *m* 23 May 1942 *Maj 22nd Lord Forbes, KBE, late Gren Gds (*qv*), and has issue

The 9th VISCOUNT's gs,

GUSTAVUS MICHAEL GEORGE HAMILTON-RUSSELL, **10th Viscount Boyne**, KCVO (1995), JP (Salop 1961); *b* 10 Dec 1931 (HM GEORGE V stood sponsor); *educ* Eton, RMA Sandhurst and RAC Cirencester; Lt Gren Gds, Ld-in-Waiting 1981–95, Ld Lt Salop (DL 1965), KStJ, bd memb Telford New Town Devpt Corp 1963–83 (dep chm 1975–82), dir: Nat West Bank (chm W Midlands and Wales Reg Bd) 1976–90, Private Patients Plan 1986–95, Priplan Investments 1987–95, chm: Ludlow Race Club Ltd 1987–95, Harper Adams Ag Coll 1990–95, pres St John's Ambulance Bde, govr Wrekin Coll 1965–86; *m* 11 April 1956 *Rosemary Anne, 2nd dau of Maj Sir Dennis Frederic Bankes Stucley, 5th Bt, JP, DL (*qv*), and *d* 14 Dec 1995, having had issue:

1 +GUSTAVUS MICHAEL STUCLEY HAMILTON-RUSSELL, **11th and present Viscount Boyne**

1 *Caroline Veronica [The Hon Mrs Cotterell, Upper Norton, Bromyard, Herefs]; *b* 15 Feb 1957; *m* 25 Oct 1975 (*divorce* 1990) David George Fothergill Banks, FRICS, est s of Thomas Herbert Fothergill Banks, of Laugherne Hill, Wichenford, Worcester, m 2nd 11 April 1997 *Maj R C R Cotterell and has by her 1st husb:

(1) *Richard George Fothergill; *b* 21 May 1977

(1) *Georgina Emma; *b* 26 April 1980

2 Sara Emma; *b* 15 July1959; *m* 24 Oct 1981 (*divorce* 1987) Nigel Anthony Twiston-Davies (*see* ARCHDALE, Bt), yr s of William Anthony Twiston-Davies, of The Mynde, Much Dewchurch, Hereford, and *d* as result of an accident 1989

3 *Lucy Jane [The Hon Mrs Sherwood, Sheepdrove House, Lambourn, Berks RG17 7UN]; *b* 18 Sept 1961; *m* 1st 6 Aug 1983 (*divorce* 1986) Patrick James Bailey, yst s of Sir Derrick Bailey, 3rd Bt, DFC (*qv*); *m* 2nd 1989 *Simon E H Sherwood, s of Nathaniel Edward Carwardine Sherwood, of Easthorpe Hall, Colchester, Essex, and has issue:

(1) *Jack Edward; *b* 1992

(1) *Anna; *b* 1993

Seat: Burwarton, Salop. The original house was built in the early 19th century to Salvin's designs. Over the next century it was added to, though unsystematically, until it contained 40 bedrooms and was costing the equivalent today of some £50,000 a year just to heat. So by the mid-1950s the 10th Viscount engaged the firm of Philip Skelcher & Partners to carry out some badly needed pruning. The huge north and northwest chunks, which included a water tower, were pulled down, as were also the easterly-aspect drawing and billards rooms. The round bay of the dining room was converted into a canted one and the sitting room then became the drawing room. The spacious library, which measured 32 feet by 57, alone of the major internal features was preserved. The latter, though itself only dating back to the early 20th century, contains a mid-18th-century marble fireplace from Brancepth Castle, Co Durham, once a Hamilton-Russell property too. The down-sized dining room was also fitted out with materials from Brancepeth. The result, still a commodious mansion with between nine and 11 bedrooms and five bathrooms, had cost the late-1990s equivalent of just over £450,000.

BRABAZON OF TARA

Arms: Quarterly, 1st and 4th, gules on a bend or three martlets sable (for BRABAZON); 2nd and 3rd, azure on a chief per pale argent and or three mullets gules (for MOORE). **Crest:** 1 On a mount vert a falcon rising, belled or (for BRABAZON), 2 Issuant from a crown composed of eight mullets set upon a rim or, a Moor's head and shoulders proper wreathed about the temples argent and azure (for MOORE). **Supporters:** On either side a gull volant over water supporting the shield with its beak, all proper. **Motto:** *Vota vita mea* ('My life is dedicated'). **Creation:** B. (UK) 27 April 1942.

THE 3RD BARON BRABAZON OF TARA, of Sandwich, Kent (Ivon Anthony Moore-Brabazon, DL (IoW 1993)) [The Rt Hon The Lord Brabazon DL, House of Lords, London SW1A 0PW]; *b* 20 Dec 1946; *s* f 1974; *educ* Harrow; memb London Stock Exchange 1972–84, Govt Whip 1984–86, Parly Under-Sec Tport 1986–89, Min State: FCO 1989–90, Dept of Tport 1990–92, Hon Treas Assoc of C Peers; dep chm Fndn Sport and Arts 1992–, pres: UK Warehousing Assoc 1992–, Natural Gas Vehicles Assoc 1994–; *m* 8 Sept 1979 *Harriet Frances, only dau of Mervyn Peter de Courcy Hamilton, of Harare, Zimbabwe, and has issue:

1 +BENJAMIN RALPH; *b* 15 March 1983

1 *Anabel Mary; *b* 1985

Lineage: JOHN MOORE, of Dublin, bought 1721 lands in the barony of Mellifont, Co Louth, in a sale of the estates of William Graham decreed by Act of Parl; *m* a sis of Charles Campbell, PC, MP, of New Grange, Co Meath, and had issue (with a dau Alice; *m* Gen Sir John Whiteford, Bt):

1 Charles; barrister; *dsp*

2 JOHN MOORE, of Tullyhallen, Co Meath, MD; *m* 26 Aug 1752 Frideswide, dau of Dixie Coddington, of Athlumney Castle, Co Meath, and had issue:

(1) JOHN

(1) Alice; *m* Thomas Achmuty, of Madeira

(2) Jane; *m* July 1799 John Hewitt, Dean Cloyne (*see* LIFFORD, V), and *d* 22 May 1848, leaving issue

3 Frideswide; *m* 1786 Col Hon Robert Henry Southwell, son of 1st Viscount Southwell (*qv*), and had issue

Dr JOHN MOORE *d* 29 Aug 1817; his son,

JOHN MOORE, of New Lodge, Herts; *b* 20 Sept 1763; *m* 1st 24 May 1788 Barbara, dau of Hon William Brabazon (2nd son of 7th Earl of Meath (*qv*; one of the earldom's subsidiary titles being the barony of Brabazon)), of Tara House, Co Meath, by Katherine, only dau of Arthur Gifford, of Aghern, Co Cork; *m* 2nd 26 April 1839 Charlotte, dau of George Samuel Collyer, and *d* 1842, having had issue by his 1st w:

1 William John MOORE later MOORE-BRABAZON (added by sign manual July 1845 with arms on inheriting mother's estates) (Rev), of Tara House, Co Meath; *b* 29 April 1789; *dsp* 1866

2 John Arthur, CIE, Maj, offr RN, Dir HEIC; *b* 24 Sept 1791; *m* 31 July 1827 Sophia Stewart (*d* July 1905), dau of Col Yates, and had issue:

(1) JOHN ARTHUR HENRY; his unc's heir

(2) William Richard, BCS, Jt Magistrate Mirzapore; *k* Indian Mutiny

(3) Charles William, BCS; left issue

(4) Adolphus Warburton, India Office

(1) Frances Stewart; *m* Capt Richard Charles Acton Throckmorton, late 87th Foot (later 10th Bt (*see* 1970 edn THROCKMORTON, Bt), and *d* 21 Feb 1895, leaving issue

3 Charles Henry; *b* 21 March 1798

The Rev WILIAM MOORE-BRABAZON's nephew,

JOHN ARTHUR HENRY MOORE later MOORE-BRABAZON (added 1866), of Tara House and Tallyallen, Co Louth; *educ* Addiscombe; High Sheriff Co Louth 1872, Hon Lt-Col, Maj Bengal Staff Corps; *b* 13 June 1828; *m* Feb 1879 Emma Sophia (*d* 11 Feb 1937), dau of Alfred Richards, of Tewkesbury Lodge, Forest Hill, Kent, and *d* 11 Jan 1908, leaving issue:

1 William Lockhart Chambré, Lt Coldstream Gds; *b* 3 Jan 1880; *m* Alice —, and *dsp* 7 April 1953

2 JOHN THEODORE CUTHBERT, **1st Baron**

1 Kathleen Barbara Sophia; *b* 26 March 1882; *m* 13 Sept 1911 Sir Gustavus Francis William Lambart, 1st Bt (*see* 1970 edn), and had issue. He *d* 16 June 1926

2 (Hebe) Crystabel Frideswide; *d* unm 26 April 1962

The yr son,

JOHN THEODORE CUTHBERT MOORE-BRABAZON, **1st Baron Brabazon of Tara**, of Sandwich, Co Kent (UK), so *cr* 27 April 1942, GBE (1953), MC, PC (1940); *educ* Harrow and Trin Coll Camb; Hon LLD St Andrews 1959, MP Chatham 1918–29 and Wallasey 1931–42, PPS to Sec State Air 1919–21, Parly Sec Tport 1923–27, Min: Tport 1940–41 and Aircraft Prodn 1941–42; pres: Roy Instn 1948, Internat Aeronautical Federation 1946 and Roy Aero Club 1943, chm Air Registrn Bd 1946, Capt Roy and Ancient St Andrews 1952, pres PGA 1954, Lt-Col and Head Photographic Interpretn RFC WW I (despatches three times, Legion Honour), chm Associated Commercial Vehicles, dir: Kodak, EMI, Thomas Tilling and David Brown Corp, author: *The Brabazon Story* (1956); *b* 8 Feb 1884; *m* 27 Nov 1906 Hilda Mary (*d* 23 July 1977 aged 100), only dau of Charles Henry Krabbé, of Colina, Buenos Aires, Argentina, and had issue:

1 DEREK CHARLES, **2nd Baron**

2 Michael Jaques, RAF and RNVR WW II; *b* 8 July 1913; *educ* Harrow; *d* unm 16 Aug 1950

The 1st BARON *d* 17 May 1964; his only surv son,

DEREK CHARLES MOORE-BRABAZON, **2nd Baron Brabazon of Tara**, CBE (1960); *b* 24 Dec 1910; *educ* Harrow and Trin Coll Cambridge (BA 1931), served NFS WW II, memb London Stock Exchange 1937, ptnr Read, Hurst, Brown & Co, dir Bowden Hldgs, memb Kensington Borough Cncl 1948–56, chm S Kensington Cons Assoc 1952–54, chm London Cons Union 1957–58, pres St Moritz Tobogganing Club 1964–68; *m* 1 Sept 1939 Henrietta Mary (*d* 1985), formerly w of Iver Frederick Jardine Krabbé and dau of Sir (Alfred) Rowland Clegg, of Llanidan Hall, Brynsiencyn, Anglesey, and *d* 11 Dec 1974, leaving issue:

1 IVON ANTHONY MOORE-BRABAZON, **3rd and present Baron Brabazon of Tara**

BRABOURNE

Arms: Quarterly, 1st and 4th, arg., on a mount vert two boars erect, respecting each other, sa., their forelegs resting against an oak tree ppr. (for HUGESSEN); 2nd and 3rd, az., three cross crosslets fitchée between two bendlets or (for KNATCHBULL). **Crests:** 1 An oak tree ppr. between two wings elevated, pinions az., feathered or (for HUGESSEN); 2 On a chapeau az., doubled erm., an ounce statant arg., spotted sa. (for KNATCHBULL). **Supporters:** On either side a leopard arg. pellety, gorged with a wreath of oak vert, fructed gold, holding in the mouth a cross crosslet fitchée or. **Motto:** *In crucifixa gloria mea* ('My glory is in the Cross'). **Creation:** Bt. (E) 4 Aug 1641, B. (UK) 26 May 1880.

THE 7TH BARON BRABOURNE OF BRABOURNE, Kent, and a **Baronet** (Sir John Ulick Knatchbull, Bt, CBE (1993)) [The Rt Hon The Lord Brabourne CBE, Newhouse, Mersham, Ashford, Kent TN25 6NQ; 39 Montpelier Walk, SW7 1JH]; *b* 9 Nov 1924, *s* bro 1943; *educ* Eton and BNC Oxford; Capt Coldstream Gds WW II (wounded), film producer: *Sink The Bismarck!* (1959), *Othello* (1965), *Up the Junction*, *Romeo and Juliet* (1967), *Dance of Death* (1968), *Tales of Beatrix Potter* (1971), *Murder on the Orient Express* (1974), *Death on the Nile* (1978), *A Passage to India* (1984), *Little Dorrit* (1987), TV producer, chm Mersham Productions Ltd 1970–, dir Thames TV 1978–95 (chm 1991–93), Euston Films 1978–95, Thorn EMI 1981–86, v-chm Copyright Promotions Gp 1987– (dir 1974–), Pro-Chllr U of Kent 1993– (memb cncl 1968–); Chm Govrs Norton Knatchbull Sch 1955–95 (govr 1947–), Wye Coll 1994– (Provost Govr 1955–), Govr Gordonstoun 1964–94, Utd World Coll of the Atlantic 1965–96, Nat Film & TV Sch 1981–96, Tstee BAFTA 1988–, Sci Museum 1983–94, Museum of Photography, Film & TV 1983–94; Memb Br Screen Advsy Ctee 1985–, Advsy Ctee Br Library Nat Sound Archive 1990–; Patron London Internat Film Sch 1977–; Fell BFI 1979 (Govr 1979–94), Pres Kent Wildlife Tst 1958–, V-Pres Roy Soc Nature Conservation 1988–, Liveryman Fishmongers Co; *m* 26 Oct 1946 *Patricia Edwina Victoria, Countess Mountbatten of Burma (*qv*), and has had issue

Lineage: One JOHN KNATCHBULL held land in Lympne, Kent, *temp* EDWARD III. Any connection between him and the Knatchbulls below, however, would seem to be conjectural.

THOMAS KNATCHBULL; f of:

RICHARD KNATCHBULL; bought 1487 from the Edwards family an estate at Mersham (Le) Hatch, Kent; *m* Catherine, dau of Sir Thomas Lewknor, and had issue:

RICHARD KNATCHBULL, of Mersham Hatch; *m* Agnes, dau of Robert Brent, and *d* 1523, leaving an est s:

JOHN KNATCHBULL, of Mersham Hatch; *m* Alice Fowle, of Tenterden, and *d* 1540, leaving, with three yr s and a dau:

RICHARD KNATCHBULL, of Mersham Hatch; *b c* 1525; *m* 1st Joan Sheaf, and had, with other issue:

1 Richard; *b c* 1554; *m* Nov 1584 Anne (*m* 2nd Sir Henry Bromley, of Upton, Worcs, s of Sir Thomas Bromley, Ld Chllr), 2nd dau of Sir Thomas Scot, of Scot's Hall, Kent, and *d* 20 Jan 1590, leaving issue:

(1) Thomas; *dsp*

2 John; *m* his sis-in-law Elizabeth (*m* 2nd Sir Richard Smythe), 4th dau of Sir Thomas Scot; *dsp*

1 Anne; *m* Sir Edward Boys, of Fridville

RICHARD KNATCHBULL *m* 2nd Susan, dau of Thomas Green, of Bobbing, Essex, and *d* 22 Aug 1582, having by her had, with other issue:

3 Sir Norton, of Mersham Hatch, High Sheriff Kent *c* 1608, MP Hythe; *m* 1st Anne, dau of Paul Wentworth; *m* 2nd Bridget (*d* 4 Nov 1625), dau of John Astley, of Maidstone, Kent, Master of the Jewel House, and sis and coheir of Sir John Astley, of Allington; *m* 3rd Mary, dau of John Aldersea, of Spurgrove, Cheshire, and widow of Thomas Westrow, and *dsp* 1636

4 THOMAS; *m* his sis-in-law Eleanor, dau of John Astley (*see above*) by Margaret, dau and heir of Lord Thomas Grey, bro of Henry, Duke of Suffolk, and *d* 1623, having had, with other issue:

(1) **Sir Norton Knatchbull, 1st Bt** (E), so *cr* 4 Aug 1641; MP Kent 1640 and New Romney 1640–48; *m* 1st *c* 22 Oct 1630 Dorothy, dau of Thomas Westrow, Sheriff London, and had surv issue:

1a **Sir John Knatchbull, 2nd Bt**, MP New Romney 1660 and Kent 1685–95; *m* 17 Jan 1659 Jane (*d* 7 June 1699), dau of Sir Edward Monins, 2nd Bt, of Waldershare, Kent, and *dspms* 15 Dec 1696, having had issue, with two other daus:

1b Jane; *m* 1st Sir George Herbert, Bt; *m* 2nd Richard Whitshed

2a THOMAS (Sir), **3rd Bt**

3a Norton; *d* unm

(1) **Sir Norton** *m* 2nd 27 Nov 1662 Dorothy (*bur* 2 May 1694), dau of Sir Robert Honeywood and widow of Sir Edward Steward, and *d* 5 Feb 1684/5

Sir JOHN's bro,

Sir Thomas Knatchbull, 3rd Bt; *m* Mary (*bur* 24 June 1724), dau of Sir Edward Dering, Bt, and had, with other issue:

1 EDWARD (Sir), **4th Bt**

1 Catharine; *m* 1st 18 Jan 1705/6 V-Adml Sir George Rooke; *m* 2nd Rev Hon Henry Moore (*see* DROGHEDA, E), and *d* 1755

Sir THOMAS *d* after 12 Dec 1711 and was *s* by his est son,

Sir Edward Knatchbull, 4th Bt, MP Rochester 1702–05, Kent 1713–15 and 1722–27 and Lostwithiel 1728–30; *m* 22 Dec 1698 Alice (*d* 15 April 1723), dau of John Wyndham, of Norrington, Wilts, and sis of Thomas, Lord Wyndham, Ld Chllr Ireland, and *d* 3 April 1730, having had, with other issue:

1 Sir WYNDHAM KNATCHBULL later KNATCHBULL-WYNDHAM (Act of Parl 1746), **5th Bt**; *b* 26 Nov 1699; *m* 23 June 1730 Catharine (*d* 6 Jan 1740/41), dau of James Harris, of Salisbury (*see* MALMESBURY, E), and *d* 3 July 1749, leaving issue:

(1) Sir WYNDHAM KNATCHBULL later KNATCHBULL-WYNDHAM, **6th Bt**, MP Kent 1760–63; *b* 16 Feb 1737; *d* unm 26 Sept 1763

2 EDWARD (Sir), **7th Bt**

3 Wadham (Rev), LLD, Chllr and Preb Durham; *b* 28 April 1707; *m* 8 July 1743 Harriet, dau of Charles Parry, and *d* 27 Dec 1760, leaving issue:

(1) Charles, Capt RN; *b* 23 May 1747; *m* 31 July 1785 Frances (*d* 18 March 1818), dau and heir of Maj Norton Knatchbull (*see below*), and *dsp* 25 Dec 1826

(2) Wyndham; *b* 11 Sept 1750; *m* 12 June 1790 his cousin Catherine Maria (*d* 30 Jan 1807), dau of Sir Edward Knatchbull, 7th Bt, and *d* 29 June 1833, leaving, with other issue:

1a Wadham (Rev), of Cholderton Lodge, Hants, Preb Wells; *b* 9 Aug 1794; *m* 5 July 1825 Louisa Elizabeth (*d* 25 June 1845), 2nd dau of William Wyndham, of Dinton, Wilts, and *d* 9 Jan 1876, leaving, with other issue:

1b Wyndham, of Babington, Bath, JP, Capt 3rd Dragoon Gds; *b* 27 Nov 1829; *m* 22 March 1892 Dora Estella (*d* 16 Nov 1951), dau of Augustus Bright, of Sheffield, and *dsp* 3 Feb 1900

2b Wadham, JP (Cornwall); *b* 7 April 1831; *educ* Magdalene Coll Cambridge (MA); *m* Aug 1862 Maria Helena (*d* 8 Nov 1930), dau of Rev Bryan Faussett, of Heppington, Kent, and *d* 18 April 1914, leaving issue:

1c Edward Wadham, JP (Wilts); *b* 8 July 1863; *m* 5 July 1894 Gertrude Louise (*d* 25 April 1958), 4th dau of Rev Thomas Sellwood Stephens, Rector St Erme, Truro, and *d* 28 April 1937, having had issue:

1d Eleanor Gertrude; *m* 2 Sept 1924 Capt Richard Glyn Griffith, Wilts Regt (*d* Sept 1944), s of Surgn Col Richard Glyn-Griffith, MRCS, of Portledge Ho, Newbridge Hill, Bath, and *d* 6 March 1931, leaving issue:

2d Dorothea Wyndham; *m* 27 June 1927 W/Cdr Richard Maelor Thomas, RAF (*d* 5 Aug 1966), s of Daniel Thomas, of Balthalan, London Rd, Corwen, Merionethshire, and had issue:

1e *Pamela Trevelyan; *b* 1930; *m* *D Gosling

2e *Diana Margaret; *b* 1933; *m* *J F Hawkins

3d *Beatrice Wadham

3b Francis, Col 1st Bn Norfolk Regt, served Crimea 1854–55 (medal with clasp, Turkish medal); *b* 25 July 1832; *m* 25 July 1870 Sarah Belinda (*d* 9 Feb 1947), dau of Thomas Moore Persse, of Mount Vernon, Co Galway, and *d* 2 Dec 1920 leaving issue:

1c Wyndham Persse; *b* 20 Oct 1873; Maj RA WW I; *m* 30 May 1911 Sybil Mathilde (*d* 5 Aug 1957), yst dau of Ulick Ralph Burke, MA, and *d* 28 Jan 1967, leaving issue:

1d Charles Norton; *b* 11 Feb 1918; *educ* Sherborne; ERA Submarine Serv WW II; *m* 1 June 1940 *Jacqueline Nora [Mrs Charles Knatchbull, Batch Farm, Kilmersdon, Bath, Somerset], dau of Henry Presland Veall, of Netley, Hants, and *d* 1980 leaving issue:

1e +Henry Norton [Henry Knatchbull Esq, 19 Riverside Rd, Westmoors, Ferndown, Dorset BH22 0LG]; *b* 23 Sept 1942; *educ* Stanbridge Earls Sch Romsey; *m* 1988 (*divorce* 1994) 1st Jenny Elizabeth, yst dau of Roy Brown, of Ferndown, Dorset; *m* 2nd 9 Aug 1996 *Annette, dau of Ernest John Dudley, of Bournemouth

2e +Richard Wyndham [Richard Knatchbull Esq, Batch Farm, Kilmersdon, Bath]; *b* 23 April 1947; *educ* Hurn Court Christchurch; *m* 7 Feb 1970 *Susan Ann Russell, dau of Arthur John Candy, of Mells, Somerset, and has issue:

1f +Paul Wyndham; *b* 15 July 1973

2f +James Wyndham; *b* 1975

1d *Angela Alice; *b* 9 Nov 1912; *m* 3 April 1948 Reginald Cyril Neville Owbridge, MA (*d* 1975), son of Cyril Smith Owbridge, of Seagarth, 336 Sandbanks Rd, Parkstone, Dorset, and has issue:

1e *Anthony Wyndham [Anthony Owbridge Esq, 112 Grenville Rd, Aylesbury, Bucks HP21 8EZ]; *b* 18 Aug 1949; *educ* Taunton Sch; *m* 1972 (*divorce* 19–) Barbara Jean, only dau of Lawrence Lacy, of Chesham, Bucks

2d *Zara Eleanor [Mrs Christopher Lapage, 93 Livermore Green, Werrington, Peterborough PE4 5DQ]; *b* 2 Aug 1920; ATS WW II in; *m* 1st 27 July 1942 (*divorce* 1953) John Mackay, son of John Mackay, of

Wick, Scotland; *m* 2nd 3rd Dec 1953 Christopher Jocelyn Lapage (*d* 1990), son of John Clement Lapage, of Nantwich, Cheshire, and has issue by 2nd husb:

1e *Fiona Anne; *b* 3 Sept 1954; *m* 1976 *Hamdy Taha and has:

1f *Geoffrey Eric; *b* 1984

2f *Robin Michael; *b* 1986

1c Maud Frances; *d* unm 27 Sept 1959 aged 88

2c Eileen Louisa; *m* 28 Sept 1912 Capt Hugh Storer Bowen, Essex Regt, son of Henry Storer Bowen, barrister, of Little Howletts, Littlebourne, Kent, and *d* 11 June 1928, leaving issue

4b Norton, Col Sherwood Foresters, served Crimea 1855 (medal with clasps, Turkish medal) and Indian Mutiny 1858 (despatches, medal with clasp); *b* 16 Jan 1834; *m* 16 Feb 1871 Elizabeth Florence Paxton (*d* 17 May 1923), dau of Maj-Gen Arthur Goodall Wavell (*see* 1953 edn, WAVELL, E), and *d* 14 Dec 1921, leaving issue:

1c Reginald Norton, DSO, Lt-Col Leics Regt, served S Africa 1899–1900 and WW I; *b* 7 Feb 1872; *m* 17 March 1906 Winifred (*d* 25 March 1910), dau of William Felton Peel, of Blackwater, Hants, and *das* 24 July 1917, leaving issue:

1d Ida Winifred; *b* 20 July 1907; *m* 29 April 1930 Walter Francis George Kingsbury, 2nd son of Gerald Francis Kingsbury, of Potters Cross Ho, Iver Heath, Bucks, and had issue:

1e *Richard Norton Orlando [Richard Kingsbury Esq, Hamsell Farm, Eridge Green, Sussex TN3 9LL]; *b* 31 Dec 1932; *m* 1 Jan 1971 *Heather Jacqueline Malcolm, dau of Malcolm Melville (*see* 1970 edn CAMPBELL, Bt, of Ardnamurchan), and has:

1f *Nicholas James Melville; *b* 26 Nov 1971; *educ* Harrow

2f *Benjamin Francis Knatchbull; *b* 18 Oct 1978; *educ* Harrow

2e *Hugh Wyndham Evelyn KNATCHBULL later KNATCHBULL-KINGSBURY (deed poll 7 Feb 1958); *b* 22 Nov 1936; *m* 20 April 1968 *Emily Sofia, dau of Robert Thorburn, of Gothenburg, Sweden

1c Ethel Mary; *m* 1 June 1895 Lt-Col Cecil Du Pré Penton Powney, OBE, OStJ, JP (*d* 18 April 1936), and *d* 3 July 1963, leaving issue

2c Muriel Wyndham; *m* 4 Dec 1902 16th and last Earl of Carnwath (*see* 1940 edn), and *d* 5 July 1958, leaving issue. He *d* 9 March 1941

3c Eleanor Gladys Annie Wyndham; *d* unm 16 Jan 1949

1b Catherine; *m* 22 June 1854 Rev John Wilkinson Peacock (*d* 8 Nov 1857) and *d* 28 April 1909, leaving issue

2b Eleanor; *m* 3 Oct 1861 Maj Francis John Slade Gully (*d* 12 Nov 1864), of Trevennen, Cornwall, and *d* 30 Oct 1900, leaving issue

4 Norton, Maj; *b* 28 May 1711; *m* 1758 Judith (*d* 18 May 1772), dau and coheir of William Long, and *d* 10 May 1782, leaving issue:

(1) Frances; *m* 31 July 1785 her cousin Capt Charles Knatchbull, RN (*see* above) and *dsp* 18 March 1818

1 Catharine *b* 3 Feb 1709/10; *m* 11 June 1754 Thomas Harris, a Master in Chancery (*see* MALMESBURY, E), and *dsp* 8 June 1796

Sir WYNDHAM's uncle,

Sir Edward Knatchbull, 7th Bt; *b* 12 Dec 1704; MP Armagh 1727–60, *m* Grace 2nd dau of William Legge, of Salisbury, and *d* 21 Nov 1789, having had, with other issue (including an est dau Anne Eliza; *m* Lt-Col Newton, of Southover), an only surv s:

Sir Edward Knatchbull, 8th Bt, DCL Oxford, Sheriff Kent 1785, MP Kent 1785–86, 1790–1802 and 1806–19; *m* July 1780 Mary (*d* 24 May 1784), dau and coheir (with her sis Dorothea, w of Rt Hon Sir Joseph Banks, Bt), of William Western Hugessen, of Provender, Kent, by his w Thomazine, dau of Sir John Honywood, Bt, and had issue, with another son:

1 EDWARD (Sir), **9th Bt**

Sir Edward *m* 2nd 4 June 1785 Frances (*d* 23 Nov 1799), dau of Govr John Graham of Georgia, and by her had, with other issue:

2 Thomas, Capt RA; *m* 30 April 1825 Jane, dau of Sir John Connell, Judge Admlty, of Edinburgh, and *dsp* 1855

Sir Edward *m* 3rd 13 April 1801 Mary (*d* 19 Dec 1850), dau and coheir of Thomas Hawkins, of Nash Court, Kent, by Mary Theresa, only dau of John Bradshaw, and by her had, with other issue:

3 Reginald Edward, of Claremont Court, Jersey; Lt-Gen RA; *b* 11 May 1812; *m* 1st 11 July 1845 Lucy Eleanor (*d* 20 Sept 1846), 2nd dau of Capt William Bowen, and had issue:

(1) Reginald Edward; *b* and *d* 20 Sept 1846

3 (cont.) Reginald Knatchbull *m* 2nd 21 Oct 1852 Sarah Emma (*d* 23 Nov 1907), est dau of Capt Owen Lomer, Bengal Native Inf, and *d* 15 April 1885, having by her had, with other issue:

(2) George Wyndham Chichester, CMG (1916), Hon Brig-Gen, Lt-Col IA, served Burmese Expdn 1885–87 (despatches, medal with clasp), China 1900 (medal) and WW I 1914 (despatches); *b* 3 March 1862; *m* 21 April 1900 Constance (*d* 22 March 1913), 2nd dau of Alexander Marsden, MD, and *d* 2 June 1943, leaving issue:

1a Wyndham Marsden; *b* 15 Feb 1901; *educ* Marlborough; Lt-Col Queen's Own W Kent Regt WW II; *m* 21 June 1934 Eileen Mary (*d* 1986), er dau of Lt-Col William Chapman Croly, DSO, RAMC, of Ardvarna, The Spa, Tralee, Co Kerry, and *d* 1977 leaving issue:

1b +Patrick Wyndham, RD [Cdr Patrick Knatchbull RD RNR, 16 Seafront Rd, Cultra, Co Down BT18 0BB]; *b* 26 April 1936; *educ* Marlborough and Queen's U Belfast; Cdr RNR; *m* 28 May 1966 *(Una) Mary Bernadette, dau of Leo Francis Kelly, of Tile Hatch, Bishops Down Park Rd, Tunbridge Wells, Kent, and has issue:

1c +Simon Marsden; *b* 16 Dec 1967; *m* 24 Feb 1996 *Jane Spolton

2c +Andrew Wyndham; *b* 20 Dec 1969; *m* 19 April 1997 *Sandra Jeffreys

1c *Felicity Jane; *b* 1972

2b +Michael Walter [Michael Knatchbull Esq, Gambles Lodge, Upper Mountain, Dun Laoghaire, Co Dublin, Ireland] (twin); *b* 26 April 1936; *educ* Marborough; Lt NI Horse (TA); *m* 9 Sept 1959 *Rhona Dorothy, yr dau of John Sinclair Gunning, of Owena, Demesne Park, Holywood, Co Down, and has issue:

1c +Richard Edward Walter; *b* 23 July 1971

2c +Mark Wyndham John; *b* 1978

1c *Fiona Bridgid; *b* 25 April 1962; *m* 1987 *David Holmes, and has issue:

1d *Philip Edward Knatchbull; *b* 1993

2d *Michael John Wyndham; *b* 1995

1d *Polly Amanda; *b* 1991

2c *Lucy Rhona; *b* 2 May 1964; *m* 1988 *Robert O'Riordan and has issue:

1d *Samson Robert; *b* 1992

2d *Andrew James; *b* 1994

1d *Rosie Katharine; *b* 1997

3c *Gillian Mary; *b* 18 Nov 1966; *m* 1996 *William Paul McChesney

1b *Bridget Eileen Mary [Mrs Robert Somekh, 6 Lyndewode Rd, Cambridge CB1 2HL]; *b* 8 Oct 1943; *m* 1st 16 June 1964 (*divorce* 1971) James Seymour Emerson, only son of Donald George Emerson, of Primrose Hill, Utkinton, Tarporley, Cheshire (*see* KEANE, Bt); *m* 2nd 1974 *Robert Ernest Somekh

2a Walter Dalrymple, Lt The Buffs; *b* 21 March 1905; *d* 31 Oct 1927

(3) Henry Dalrymple (Rev), Rector Hill Croome, Worcs, 1922–24; *b* 11 June 1864; *educ* St John's Coll Oxford (MA); *m* 16 Sept 1902 Cecilia Maud (*d* 21 Jan 1947), yst dau of Samuel Woodhouse, DL, of Norley Hall, Cheshire, and *d* 6 March 1932, leaving issue:

1a Mary; *b* 17 Nov 1903; *d* unm 21 July 1978

2a Ursula; *b* 1 July 1906

(4) Owen Edward; *b* 21 Feb 1868; *m* 14 Sept 1892 Amy Elizabeth (*d* 11 Dec 1942), dau of Edward Bingley Wright, of Bingley, and *d* 8 Nov 1946, leaving issue:

1a +Reginald Edward, Capt IARO; *b* 8 Aug 1893

1a Daphne Mary Knatchbull; *b* 10 June 1902; *m* Clifton Edmond Lamb, and *d* 7 April 1968

(1) Eliza Inna; *m* 13 April 1884 Lt-Col Piers Richard Legh, IA, and *d* 17 May 1910

1 Eleanor; *m* 4th Baron Sondes (*see* MONSON, B) and *d* 30 Oct 1883

Sir EDWARD *d* 1 Sept 1819; his est son,

Sir Edward Knatchbull, 9th Bt, PC; *b* 20 Dec 1781; inherited the Hugessen estates through his mother and willed them ultimately to his issue by his 2nd w; MP Kent 1819–31 and E Kent 1833–45, Paymaster-Gen 1834–35 and 1841–45; *m* 1st 25 Aug 1806 Annabella Christiana (*d* 4 April 1814), dau of Sir John Honywood, 4th Bt (*qv*), and *d* 24 May 1849, having had, with other issue:

1 **Sir Norton Joseph Knatchbull, 10th Bt**; *b* 10 July 1808; *m* 31 May 1831 Mary (*d* 3 Sept 1874), est dau of Jesse Watts-Russell, of Ilam Hall, Staffs, and *d* 2 Feb 1868, having had, with other issue:

(1) **Sir Edward Knatchbull, 11th Bt**; *b* 26 April 1838; barrister; *d* unm 30 May 1871

(2) **Sir Wyndham Knatchbull, 12th Bt**, JP (Kent); *b* 9 June 1844; MP E Kent 1875–76; *m* 18 March 1902 Margaret Elizabeth (*d* 5 Nov 1921), dau of Charles Taylor, of Frensham Hill, Surrey, and widow of John Dillon Browne, late 100th Regt, and *d* 30 July 1917

1 Mary Louisa; *m* 29 March 1856 Maj-Gen Charles Stirling Dundas, Bengal Artillery, s of James Dundas, of Dundas Castle, Linlithgow, and *d* 30 Jan 1923, leaving issue

2 Eleanor Grace; *m* 29 Aug 1857 Robert John O'Reilly, of Mill Castle, Co Westmeath (*d* 18 Dec 1879), son of James O'Reilly, of Baltrasna, Meath, and *d* 20 April 1913, leaving issue

3 Beatrice Joanna; *m* 1 Dec 1874 3rd Baron Ellenborough (*qv*), and *d* 17 May 1932

1 Mary Dorothea; *m* May 1826 Edward Knight, DL (*d* 5 Nov 1879), of Godmersham Park, Kent and *d* 22 Feb 1838, leaving issue

Sir Edward *m* 2nd 24 Oct 1820 Fanny Catherine (*d* 24 Dec 1882), est dau of Edward Knight, of Godmersham Park, Kent, and by her had further issue (who all took the additional surname of HUGESSEN, though the living descendants of all but EDWARD are in remainder to the baronetcy only):

2 EDWARD HUGESSEN KNATCHBULL later KNATCHBULL-HUGESSEN (added 1849 on f's death), **1st Baron Brabourne of Brabourne**, Kent (UK), so *cr* 26 May 1880, PC (1873), DL, JP; *b* 29 April 1829; *educ* Eton and Magdalen Coll Oxford; chm E Kent QS, MP (Lib) Sandwich 1857–80 (C thereafter), Ld of Treasury 1859–66, Under-Sec Home Dept 1866 and 1868–71 and Colonies 1871–74, children's author; *m* 1st 19 Oct 1852 Anna Maria Elizabeth (*d* 26 May 1889), dau of Rev Marcus Richard Southwell, Vicar St Stephen's, St Albans, and *d* 6 Feb 1893, having had issue:

(1) EDWARD KNATCHBULL-HUGESSEN, **2nd Baron Brabourne of Brabourne**, JP and DL (Kent); *b* 5 April 1857; *educ* Eton and Magdalen Coll Oxford; Lt Coldstream Gds, MP (Lib) Rochester 1889–92; *m* 2 Nov 1880 Amy Virginia (*d* 19 May 1949), 2nd dau of 1st Baron Allendale (*qv*), and *d* 29 Dec 1909, having had issue:

1a Richard Edward Wentworth; *b* 24 Aug 1881; *dvp* 3 May 1883

2a WYNDHAM WENTWORTH KNATCHBULL-HUGESSEN, **3rd Baron Brabourne of Brabourne**, Lt Gren Gds (SR); *b* 21 Sept 1885; *ka* 11 March 1915

1a Margaret Eva de Burgh; *m* 15 July 1905 6th Earl of Mexborough (*qv*) and *d* 26 Jan 1957, leaving issue

2a Bettine Henrietta; *m* 11 May 1912 William Lewis Brownlow Loyd (*d* 27 Oct 1947), est son of Edward Henry Loyd, DL, of Langleybury, Herts, and *d* 9 Aug 1967, leaving issue

(2) Sir CECIL MARCUS KNATCHBULL-HUGESSEN, **13th Bt**, and **4th Baron Brabourne of Brabourne**; *b* 27 Nov 1863; *s* n in barony 1915 and cousin in baronetcy 1917; *educ* King's Coll Cambridge (BA); barrister Inner Temple 1890; *m* 8 Nov 1893 Helena Regina Frederica (*d* 15 Nov 1919), dau of

Hermann von Flesch Brunningen, Imperial Cllr, of Vienna, and *d* 15 Feb 1933, leaving issue:

1a MICHAEL HERBERT RUDOLF KNATCHBULL-HUGESSEN later KNATCHBULL (deed poll 29 June 1919), **5th Baron Brabourne of Brabourne**, GCSI (1937), GCIE (1933), MC, JP, MP Ashford 1931–33, PPS Sec State India 1932–33, Govr Bombay Dec 1933–37 and Bengal 1937–39, Actg Govr-Gen India 1938, Capt RAF, Lt RA, served WW I (despatches three times); *b* 8 May 1895; *m* 22 Jan 1919 Lady Doreen Geraldine Browne, CI, DStJ (*d* 27 Aug 1979), 3rd dau of 6th Marquess of Sligo (*qv*), and *d* 23 Feb 1939, leaving issue:

1b NORTON CECIL MICHAEL KNATCHBULL, **6th Baron Brabourne of Brabourne**; *b* 11 Feb 1922; *educ* Eton and RMA Sandhurst, Lt Gren Gds WW II (wounded, POW); *kas* 15 Sept 1943 (shot by Germans after recapture following his escape from a prison train N Italy)

2b JOHN ULICK KNATCHBULL, **7th and present Baron Brabourne of Brabourne**

(1) Katharine Cecilia; *m* 17 Oct 1883 Col Charles Robert Prideaux-Brune, late Rifle Bde, of Prideaux Place, Cornwall (*d* 11 Dec 1936), and *d* 21 March 1926, leaving issue

(2) Eva Mary; *d* 23 Oct 1895

2 The **1st Baron** *m* 2nd 3 June 1890 Ethel Mary (*d* 7 Jan 1929), 3rd dau of Col Sir George Gustavus Walker, KCB, of Crawfordton, Dumfriesshire, and by her had further issue:

(3) Adrian Norton, KC (1932); *b* 5 July 1891; *educ* Eton and McGill U Montreal; OC, LLD, barrister Canada 1914, Senator Canadian Parl 1937, Canadian Artillery WW I; *m* 7 Sept 1922 Margaret Cecilia (*d* 1980), only dau of George Herrick Duggan, of 3636 McTavish St, Montreal, and *d* 30 March 1976, having had issue:

1a Edward Herrick; *b* 4 June 1923; *educ* Eton; *m* 1947 Mary Louise (*d* Sept 1964), dau of Walter Asahel Newton, of Montreal, and *d* 1955, leaving issue:

1b +Kenneth Norton [Kenneth Knatchbull-Hugessen Esq, 31 Russell Hill, Toronto, Ontario M4V 2S9, Canada]; *b* 1949; *m* 1969 *Karen, dau of Olaf Wolff, of Montreal, and has issue:

1c +Arlo Edward; *b* 1970

1b *Kathleen Mary; *b* 1950

2b *Patricia Mary; *b* 1952; *m* 19– *— Osgoode

2a Kenneth Wyndham; *b* 18 Feb 1925; *d* 19 Dec 1942

3a +Andrew John [Andrew Knatchbull-Hugessen Esq, 5 Beacon Rd, Kirkland, Quebec, Canada]; *b* 30 June 1926; *m* 1952 *Jane Frances, dau of Douglas Gilfillan Currie, of Montreal, Canada, and has issue:

1b +Brian Andrew; *b* 1954

2b +John; *b* 1958

1b *Wendy Jane (twin); *b* 1954

2b *Martha; *b* 1960

4a +James Cornelius [The Hon James Knatchbull-Hugessen, 31 Elmdale Ave, Ottawa, Canada K1M 1A1]; *b* 26 July 1933; *educ* Balliol Coll Oxford and McGill U Montreal; barrister Quebec 1958, V-Chllr Diocese of Montreal 1968, Puisne Judge Superior Court and Court of Queen's Bench Quebec 1972–73, Assoc Ch Justice Superior Court Quebec 1973–83, Puisne Justice Fedl Court of Appeal 1983–; *m* 12 Sept 1958 *Mary Rosamond, dau of Ruben Ewart Stavert, of 3250 Cedar Ave, Montreal, Canada, and has issue:

1b +James William; *b* 24 July 1959

2b +Alexander Ewart; *b* 26 Oct 1965

3b +Ross Adrian; *b* 10 Jan 1969

1b *Kathleen Jill; *b* 27 Oct 1960

2b *Alicia Mary; *b* 23 Jan 1962

1a *Mary Cecilia [Mrs Stephen Keynes, 37 Roundhay Ave, Leeds LS8 4DN]; *b* 30 Nov 1929; *m* 22 April 1955 *Stephen John Keynes, yst son of Sir Geoffrey Langdon Keynes, MA, MD, FRCS, of Lammas Ho, Brinkley, Newmarket, by Margaret Elizabeth, yr dau of Sir George Howard Darwin, KCB, FRS, LLD, DSc, of Newnham Grange, Cambs, and has issue:

1b *Gregory Robert Edward; *b* 3 June 1956

2b *Toby William; *b* 2 Nov 1959

3b *Zachary Edmund; *b* 18 Oct 1962

1b *Elizabeth Harriet; *b* 15 Dec 1957

2b *Martha Paganel; *b* 25 April 1961

(3) Alicia Mary Dorothea; *b* (posthumously) 18 Feb 1893; *m* 14 Oct 1915 Hon (Bernard) Clive Pearson, Maj Sussex Yeo, 2nd s of 1st Viscount Cowdray (*qv*), and *d* 15 Jan 1974, leaving issue

3 Reginald Bridges (Rev), Rector W Grinstead, Sussex; *b* 19 Feb 1831; *educ* Balliol Coll Oxford (BA); *m* 1st 23 Aug 1866 Maria (*d* 28 Dec 1880), 2nd dau of Rev Tatton Brockman, MA, of Beachborough, nr Hythe, Rector Otham, Kent, and had, with other issue:

(1) Everard; *b* 17 April 1871; JP (Kent); Maj Northants Regt S African War 1899–1901 (despatches, medal with five clasps) and WW I; *m* 23 Sept 1908 Grace Marshall (*d* 11 Aug 1937), est dau of James Arthur Hindmarsh, of Ayr, and *d* 13 Oct 1946, having had issue:

1a John Sancroft; *b* 21 July 1917; *d* 13 Dec 1928

1a *Mary, OBE (Civil 1946) [Mrs William Keith OBE, Leylands, Coleman's Hatch, Sussex]; *b* 22 Sept 1909; served WW II in NFS, SSStJ; *m* 22 March 1932 William Paterson Keith, MVO (*d* 6 March 1963), yst son of Samuel Paterson Keith, of Edinburgh

2a *Pleasance Anne [Mrs John Comery, Home Farm, Upper Hayesden, Tonbridge, Kent]; *b* 7 Sept 1920; F/O WAAF WW II; *m* 16 Feb 1948 *John Stuart Comery, MC, son of William Comery, of 20 W Parade, Worthing, Sussex, and has issue:

1b *William Knatchbull; *b* 13 Feb 1952; *educ* Sherborne

1b *Patricia Mary,b 26 April 1950

(1) Mabel Katharine; *b* 26 June 1868; *m* 19 June 1902 Rev Harry de Vitre Watson, Rector Belbroughton, Stourbridge, Worcs (*d* 4 Feb 1947), yst son of Gen Watson, Bengal Army, and *d* 4 Aug 1944, leaving issue

(2) Violet; *b* 24 Dec 1869; *d* unm 20 Nov 1953

(3) Winifred Martina; *b* 12 May 1873; *m* 3 May 1905 Rev Henry Edward St John Macdonald, Rector Hurstmonceux, Sussex, son of Rev J L Macdonald, and *d* 19 May 1921, leaving issue

(4) Margaret Amy; *b* 2 Nov 1880; *m* 25 June 1913 Albert Edmund Gyngell, Dir Johannesburg Art Gallery, and *d* leaving issue

3 (cont.) Reginald Knatchbull-Hugessen *m* 2nd 26 May 1885 Rachel Mary (*d* 2 Oct 1929), dau of Adml Sir Alexander Leslie Montgomery, 3rd Bt, of The Hall, Co Donegal, and *d* 28 Jan 1911, having by her had issue:

(2) Hughe Montgomery (Sir), KCMG (1936); *b* 26 March 1886; *educ* Eton and Balliol Coll Oxford (BA 1907); Amb China 1936–37, Turkey 1939–44, Amb Berlin and Min Luxemburg 1944–47, ret 1947, author: *Diplomat in Peace and War* (1949) and *Kentish Family* (1960); *m* 16 July 1912 Mary (*d* 14 July 1978), dau of Brig-Gen Sir Robert Gordon Gilmour, 1st Bt (*see* GILMOUR OF CRAIGMILLAR, B), and *d* 21 March 1971, having had issue:

1a Norton Reginald; *b* 14 April 1913; *educ* Balliol Coll Oxford (BLitt); *d* unm 26 March 1941

1a Elisabeth; *b* 17 March 1915; *m* 14 Feb 1939 Sir George Peregrine Young, 5th Bt (*see* YOUNG, Bt, of Formosa Place), and *d* 15 Aug 1957, leaving issue

2a *Alethea [Miss Knatchbull-Hugessen, 23 Emden Ho, Barton Lane, Old Headington, Oxford]; *b* 15 March 1918; joined Br Cncl 1946

(3) Maurice Astley, MC, Lt Gren Gds SR; *b* 18 May 1888; *ka* 25 Sept 1916

(5) Rachel Joyse; *b* 17 May 1893; *m* 16 July 1917 Rev Hugh Henry Molesworth Bevan, MA, Archdeacon Emeritus Ludlow, Preb Hereford (*d* 15 Jan 1970), er son of Ven Henry Edward James Bevan, Archdeacon Middx, and had issue

4 Herbert Thomas, MP Faversham 1885–95; *b* 1 Dec 1835; *m* 20 Sept 1883 Elizabeth Lewis, dau of Moses Burton, and *d* 15 May 1922, leaving, with other issue:

(1) Edwin Llewellyn; *b* 2 Aug, *d* 31 Aug 1873

(2) Paul Lionel; *b* 28 July 1874; *m* 1906 Marie Blanche (*d* 9 Dec 1945), yst dau of Rémi Poullin, of St Boniface, Manitoba, and *d* 1958, leaving issue:

1a +Herbert Clifford; *b* 28 July 1907; Canadian Army WW II; *m* 6 July 1936 *Violet, er dau of Samuel Oliver Emily Sutherland, of Edson, Alberta, and has issue:

1b *Darolyn Gail; *b* 7 Nov 1941

(3) Edward; *b* 13 April 1877; *m* 9 Feb 1920 Edith Elizabeth (*d* 13 Oct 1957), dau of Charles Edward Chatfield, of Bloomsbury, and *d* 30 Dec 1969, leaving issue:

1a Maurice Knatchbull; *b* 11 March 1921; *d* 15 April 1928

2a Denis Norton; *b* 7 March 1923; *m* 26 July 1947 Mavis Josephine (*d* 1980), er dau of Henry Albert Peard, of Bath, and *d* 1982, leaving issue:

1b +Mark Wyndham [Mark Knatchbull-Hugessen Esq, 11 Frayslea, Cowley Rd, Uxbridge, Middx]; *b* 21 May 1953

1b *Bernice Simone [Mrs Raymond Morley, 112 Springdale Rd, Corfe Mullen, Wimborne, Dorset]; *b* 14 June 1949; *m* 1975 *Raymond Charles Morley, and has issue:

1c *Joseph Ronan Charles; *b* 1983

1c *Jessica Natasha; *b* 1985

2b *Teresa Frances [Mrs Donald Pooley, 145 Cowley Rd, Uxbridge, Middx]; *b* 19 Nov 1951; *m* 1971 *Donald Pooley, and has issue:

1c *Matthew Lee; *b* 1970

2c *Damon Ross; *b* 1972

1a *Christina Pauline [Miss Christina Knatchbull-Hugessen, 11 Greville Lodge, Highgate, London N6 5DP]; *b* 12 April 1931

(4) Algernon Albert; *b* 25 Dec 1879; 28 Aug 1949

(5) George Arthur; *b* 1 Feb 1883; *m* 26 Dec 1910 Jessie (*d* 24 April 1961), dau of John Downie Kay, of Brinkley, Newmarket, and *d* 24 Feb 1966, leaving issue:

1a +Peter Merrick [Peter Knatchbull-Hugessen Esq, Ropley House, Ropley, Hants]; *b* 5 June 1915; *educ* Wadham Coll Oxford (MA 1952); late Capt RA, served WW II with 111th Field Regt RA and 6th Indian Field Regt, Headmaster Papplewick Sch Ascot 1950; *m* 1992 *Anna-Rose, dau of Maj H Bramwell, of The White House, Mallow, Co Cork, and widow of Lord James Charles Crichton-Stuart (*see* BUTE, M)

2a Robin John Kay; *b* 5 Oct 1921; served WW II as Capt 8th King George V's Own Light Cav (Viceroy's Body Guard 1943–45), transferred to 3rd Dragoon Gds 1945, ret 1952; *m* 1st 29 Oct 1945 (*divorce* 1956) Enid Mabel, dau of Edward Thomas Marlow, of Highgate, N6, and had issue:

1b +Peter Wyndham [Peter Knatchbull-Hugessen Esq, Grove Barn, Beckley, Oxon OX3 9US]; *b* 4 Sept 1947; *m* 1975 (*divorce* 1988) Henrietta Frances, dau of Col John Ellis Spencer, of Hill Farm, Swalcliffe, Oxon; *m* 2nd 10 Dec 1994 *Marilyn Freda Barrett, neé Higgs, and by his 1st w has:

1c +Thomas Michael; *b* 1977

2c +William Peter; *b* 1979

3c James; *b* and *d* 1981

1c *Lydia Victoria; *b* 1982

2c *Holly Frances; *b* 1984

2a (cont.) Robin Knatchbull-Hugessen *m* 2nd 23 May 1958 *Barbara Anne Wilcox [Mrs Robin Knatchbull-Hugessen, Cilwern, Talley, Llandeilo, Dyfed Sa19 7YH], and *d* 1986, having by her had:

2b +Simon Stephen [Simon Knatchbull-Hugessen Esq, 25 The Topiary, Lychpit, Basingstoke, Hants]; *b* 17 Nov 1960; *m* 1990 (*divorce* 1995) Tracy Helen, est dau of G Burns, of Hook, Hants

1b *Sally Anne, MVO (1989) [Mrs Thomas O'Brien MVO, 103 Ridgewood Rd, Baltimore, 21210, USA]; *b* 15 March 1959; *m* 1987 *Dr Thomas P O'Brien, and has:

1c *William Thomas Robin; *b* 1991

2b *Jane Elizabeth; *b* 21 Nov 1962

(6) Robin Herbert; *b* 22 Sept 1885; *d* 4 May 1921

(1) Mary Mabel; *b* 20 Oct 1887; *d* unm 25 March 1944

(2) Mabel Thomasine; *b* 30 Nov 1890; *m* 26 March 1921 John Tilsley Wright, son of Daniel Wright, of Blackheath, Birmingham, and had issue

BRADBURY

Arms: Sa. a chevron erm., between in chief two buckles and in base a fleur-de-lis arg. **Crest:** In front of two ostrich feathers in saltire arg. a boar's head erect ppr. **Supporters:** Dexter, a raven ppr.; sinister, a dove ppr. **Motto:** *Justitia æquitas fides* ('Justice, equity, and good faith'). **Creation:** B. (UK) 28 Jan 1925.

THE 3RD BARON BRADBURY, of Winsford, Co Chester (John Bradbury) [The Rt Hon The Lord Bradbury, 10 Clifton Hill, London NW8 0QG]; *b* 17 March 1940, *s* f 1994; *educ* Gresham's and Bristol U; *m* 1968 *Susan Anne, dau of William Liddiard, of E Shefford, Berks, and has issue:

1 +JOHN TIMOTHY; *b* 16 Jan 1973
2 +Benjamin Edward; *b* 14 March 1975

Lineage: WILLIAM BRADBURY, of Cliff Grange, Drayton-in-Hales, Salop; *b* 1722; *d* 9 Jan 1779; *m* and had seven sons and a dau; the 3rd s:

GEORGE BRADBURY, of Cliff Grange; *b* 5 Sept 1760; *m* 1st 8 Oct 1783 Elizabeth Preston, of Almington, and had four sons and two daus; *m* 2nd 30 June 1800 Ann (*d* 1852), widow of — Warrington and dau of — Swanwick, and *d* 16 Oct 1819, having by her had issue, with two other sons and two other daus, a 7th son:

JOHN BRADBURY, of Winsford, Cheshire; *b* 23 Jan 1811; *m* 8 Jan 1870 Sarah (*d* 14 Jan 1901), 3rd dau of William Cross, of the Dockyard, Winsford, Cheshire, and *d* 1 June 1889, having had issue:

1 JOHN SWANWICK, **1st Baron**
2 Rupert; *b* 23 May 1875; *d* 25 March 1878

The er son,

JOHN SWANWICK BRADBURY, **1st Baron Bradbury**, of Winsford, Co Chester (UK), so *cr* 28 Jan 1925, GCB (1920, KCB 1913, CB 1909), Hon LLD Cantab and Manchester; *educ* BNC Oxford (MA, Hon Fell 1926), Pncpl Clerk Treasury 1908–13, Insur Commr and Memb Nat Insur Jt Ctee 1911–13, Jt Perm Sec Treasury 1913–19, Pncpl Br Del Reparations Commn 1919–25, chm Nat Food Cncl 1925–29, *ex officio* dir Anglo-Iranian Oil 1925–27, Prime Warden Goldsmiths' Co 1938–39; *b* 23 Sept 1872; *m* 9 March 1911 Hilda Maude (*d* 6 June 1949), 2nd dau of William Arthur Kirby, of Hampstead, and had issue:

1 JOHN, **2nd Baron**
2 +Paul; *b* 28 Nov 1915; *educ* Westminster and BNC Oxford; *m* 25 March 1940 *Margaret Amy, only dau of John William Stammers, of Purley, Surrey, and has issue:
(1) +Richard [Richard Bradbury Esq, Milcote House, Long Wood Dve, Jordans, Bucks]; *b* 19 Jan 1941; *educ* Radley and BNC Oxford (BA 1963); *m* 27 Aug 1966 *Elizabeth Mary Auchinleck, yr dau of Douglas Christopher Lewis Love, of 3 Glenmore Ho, Richmond, Surrey, and has issue:
1a *Clare; *b* 26 Aug 1967
2a *Jane; *b* 26 Aug 1967
3a Philippa; *b* 1972
(2) +James [James Bradbury Esq, Barnford, Holy Cross, Clent, West Midlands DY9 9QD]; *b* 13 Oct 1945; *educ* Radley and BNC Oxford (BA); *m* 1967 *Patricia Mary, dau of Hedley Arthur Charles Funnell, and has issue:
1a +Anthony James; *b* 2 April 1969
2a +Jonathan Paul; *b* 1971
1a *Charlotte Ann; *b* 1973
(3) +David [David Bradbury Esq, Pencot, Tresham, Wotton-under-Edge, Glos]; *b* 6 June 1950; *educ* Radley; *m* 1973 *Janet Ann Salier, dau of David H Davidson, of Battramsley Cottage, Boldre, Lymington, Hants, and has:
1a *Caroline Salier; *b* 1978
2a *Anna Sarah; *b* 1980
1 *Margaret; *m* 16 Oct 1937 (*divorce* 1950) Sir Stanley George Hooker, CBE, DPh, yst son of William Harry Hooker, of Sheerness, Kent, and has issue:
(1) *Jane Margaret; *b* 22 Feb 1940; *m* 7 Sept 1965 *Sir John Napoleon Ruthven Barran, 4th Bt (*qv*), and has issue

The 1st BARON *d* 3 May 1950; his er son,

JOHN BRADBURY, **2nd Baron Bradbury**; *b* 7 Jan 1914; *educ* Westminster and BNC Oxford; *m* 1st 19 Aug 1939 (*divorce* 1946) Joan, only dau of Walter Dingle Knight, of Darley, Addlestone, Surrey, and had issue:

1 JOHN BRADBURY, **3rd and present Baron Bradbury**
1 *Elizabeth Joan (twin) [The Hon Mrs Hansen, 2 Sargent Place, Waxahachie, Texas 75165, USA]; *b* 17 March 1940; *m* 27 Feb 1965 *Warren Gustin Hansen, s of Joseph Harrison Hansen, of Dallas, and has issue:
(1) *Karl Geoffrey; *b* 18 Jan 1971
(1) *Christine Joan; *b* 17 Dec 1967

The **2nd Baron** *m* 2nd 2 Dec 1946 *Gwerfyl [The Rt Hon The Dowager Lady Bradbury, 1 Iraki St, Engomi, Nicosia, Cyprus], dau of Edward Stanton Roberts, of Gellifor, nr Ruthin, Denbighshire, and *d* 1994, having by her had issue:

2 *Anne [Mrs Alastair Ker-Lindsay, 15 Grosvenor Sq, London W1]; *b* 19 Sept 1947; *m* 1 June 1970 *Alastair James Ker-Lindsay, son of Ronald Ker-Lindsay, of Dormer Cottage, Hundon, Sudbury, Suffolk, and has issue:
(1) *James; *b* 4 May 1972
(2) *Mark; *b* 21 June 1973
(3) *John Alexander; *b* 10 Aug 1977
(4) *Adam Ronald; *b* 28 Feb 1979
(1) *Laura; *b* 1985

BRADFORD, Earl

Arms: Sa. ten plates, four, three, two and one, on a chief arg. a lion passant erm. **Crest:** A demi-lion rampant arg. holding between the paws a wreath of laurel ppr. **Supporters:** Two leopards guardant gu. pellety. **Motto:** *Nec temere, nec timide* ('Neither rashly nor timidly'). **Creations:** Bt. (E) 7 June 1660, B. (GB) 13 Aug 1794, E. and V. (UK) 30 Nov 1815.

THE 7TH EARL OF BRADFORD, Viscount Newport, both Co Salop, **Baron Bradford of Bradford**, Co Salop, and a **Baronet** (Sir Richard Thomas Orlando Bridgeman, Bt) [The Rt Hon The Earl of Bradford, Woodlands House, Weston-under-Lizard, Shifnal, Shropshire TF11 8PX]; *b* 3 Oct 1947 (HRH THE DUCHESS OF GLOUCESTER stood sponsor); *s* f 1981; *educ* Harrow and Trin Coll Cambridge (BA 1969, MA 1973); restaurateur, chm, Weston Park Enterprises; *m* 1979 *(Joanne) Elizabeth, er dau of Benjamin Miller, turf accountant, of 42 Pembroke Rd, London W8, and sis of Mrs Sholto Douglas Home (*see* HOME, E), and has issue:

1 +ALEXANDER MICHAEL ORLANDO, *Viscount Newport*; *b* 6 Sept 1980; *educ* Shrewsbury
2 +Henry Gerald Orlando; *b* 18 April 1982
3 +Benjamin Thomas Orlando; *b* 1987
1 *Alicia Rose; *b* 1990

Lineage (of Newport): The Newports were originally from the Shropshire town of that name.

THOMAS NEWPORT, of High Ercall, Salop (held as a tenant-in-chief of the Crown); *d* by 1401, leaving issue:

THOMAS NEWPORT, of High Ercall, Sheriff Salop 1403; gf of:

WILLIAM NEWPORT, of High Ercall, Sheriff Salop 1473; *m* Elizabeth, dau and coheir of Sir John Burgh, of Mowthwy, and had issue:

JOHN NEWPORT, of High Ercall, Sheriff Salop 1491; *m* Alice, dau of Sir Thomas Swynerton, and *d* 1512, leaving issue:

THOMAS NEWPORT, of High Ercall, Sheriff Salop 1542; *m* Ann, dau of Sir Robert Corbet, of Moreton Corbet (*see* 1970 edn CORBET, Bt), and had an er son:

Sir RICHARD NEWPORT, of High Ercall, several times Sheriff Salop, memb Cncl Welsh Marches of Wales; *m* Margaret, dau and heiress of Sir Thomas Bromley, Ld Ch Justice, and *d* 1570, leaving an est s:

Sir FRANCIS NEWPORT, of High Ercall, several times Sheriff Salop; *m* Beatrix, dau of Roland Lacon, of Willey, Salop, and *d* 1623, leaving issue:

Sir RICHARD NEWPORT, 1st BARON NEWPORT OF HIGH ERCALL (E), so *cr* 14 Oct 1642, nominally for his loyalty to CHARLES I at the start of the Civil War but actually in consideration of a present of £6,000 (just under £430,000 in late-1990s terms); *b* 7 May 1587; *educ* BNC Oxford; MP Salop 1614, 1624–26 and 1626–29 and Shrewsbury 1620–22, ktd 1615; *m* by 1615 Rachel, dau of Sir John

Leveson, of Haling, Kent (*see* SUTHERLAND, D), and *d* 8 Feb 1650/1, leaving issue:

FRANCIS NEWPORT, 2nd BARON NEWPORT OF HIGH ERCALL and 1st EARL OF BRADFORD, Co Salop, so *cr* 11 May 1694, as also earlier 11 March 1674/5 VISCOUNT NEWPORT OF BRADFORD, Co Salop (both E), PC (1668–79 and Feb 1688/9–1708); *b* 23 Feb 1619/20; *educ* Ch Ch Oxford; MP Shrewsbury 1640–Jan 1643/4, royalist Civil War, Ld Lt Salop 1660–87 and 1689–1704, Roy Household: Comptroller 1668–72, Treasurer 1672–87 and 1689–1708 and Cofferer 1691–1702; *m* 28 April 1642 Lady Diana Russell (*d* 3 Jan 1695), dau of 4th Earl of Bedford (*see* BEDFORD, D), and had issue, with several daus:

1 RICHARD, 2nd EARL

2 THOMAS NEWPORT, 1st and last BARON TORRINGTON, Co Devon (E), so *cr* 20 June 1716, PC (1717); *b* 1654/5; *educ* Ch Ch Oxford; barrister Inner Temple 1678, MP (Whig) Ludlow 1695–98 and 1699–1700, Winchelsea Jan-Feb 1700/1 and Gt Wenlock 1715–16, Commr Customs 1699–Jan 1711/12, a Ld Treasury 1715–18, Teller Exchequer 1718–19; (?)*m*(?) 1st(?) Lucy (*d c* 1696), dau of Sir Edward Atkyns, Ld Ch Baron Exchequer; *m* 2nd(?) 22 July 1700 Penelope (*d* 1705), dau of Sir Orlando Bridgeman, 1st Bt; *m* 2nd or 3rd Anne, dau of Henry Murray, and *dsp* 27 May 1719, when the barony expired

The 1st EARL *d* 19 Sept 1708; his er son,

RICHARD NEWPORT, 2nd EARL OF BRADFORD, PC (Feb 1709/10); *b* 3 Sept 1644; *educ* Ch Ch Oxford; MP (Whig) Salop 1670–81 and 1689–98, Ld Lt: Salop 1704–12 and 1714–23 and Montgomeryshire to 1723; *m c* 7 Oct 1680 Mary (*d* 3 Dec 1737), dau and coheir of Sir Thomas Wilbraham, Bt, of Woodhey, Cheshire, and Weston-under-Lizard, Staffs, thus acquiring the Manor of Weston, and *d* 14 June 1723, having had, with other issue:

1 HENRY NEWPORT, 3rd EARL OF BRADFORD; *b* 1683; *educ* Ch Ch Oxford; MP (Whig) Bishop's Castle 1706–08 and Salop 1708–10 and 1713–22, Ld Lt Staffs 1715–25 and Salop and Montgomeryshire 1724–34; *dspl* 25 Dec 1734, leaving by Mrs Ann Smyth, of Hammersmith:

(1) John HARRISON later NEWPORT; inherited his f's estates; insane by 1742; *d* insane 29 April 1783

2 THOMAS NEWPORT, 4th and last EARL OF BRADFORD; *d* unm and insane 18 April 1762, when the barony, viscountcy and earldom expired

1 Ann Newport; *m* 9 April 1719 **Sir Orlando Bridgeman, 4th Bt**, of Great Lever, Lancs, and Castle Bromwich, Warwicks (*see* below), and *d* 19 Aug 1752, leaving an er s:

(1) HENRY (Sir), **5th Bt**, and **1st Baron**

2 Diana; *m* 28 Nov 1721 6th Earl of Mountrath (*see* COOTE, Bt) and had issue

Lineage (of Bridgeman): EDWARD BRIDGEMAN, Sheriff Exeter and Devon 1563; had, with other issue (including an est s Michael; *dspm*):

THOMAS BRIDGEMAN, of Greenway, Devon; had an est s:

Rt Rev JOHN BRIDGEMAN, DD, Bp Chester 1619, Rector Wigan, Lancs, 1615; *b* 2 Nov 1577; *m* 29 April 1606 Elizabeth, dau of Rev William Helyar, DD, Canon Exeter and Archdeacon Barnstaple, and had, with other surv issue:

1 ORLANDO (Sir), **1st Bt**

2 James (Sir); *m* Anne Allen, of Chester, and had, with other issue:

(1) Frances; *m* 3rd Baron Howard of Escrick (*see* SUFFOLK and BERKSHIRE, E)

3 Richard, of Combs Hall, Suffolk; *m* Katherine Watson, and had issue:

(1) William, of Combs Hall, Sec Admlty and Clerk PC; *m* Diana Vernatti, an Italian, and had issue:

1a Orlando, whose only surv son, William, *d* unm 1637

1a Katherine; *m* her cousin Orlando Bridgeman, 4th s of 2nd Bt, and *dsps*

Bishop BRIDGEMAN *d* 11 Nov 1652. His est son,

Sir Orlando Bridgeman, 1st Bt (E), so *cr* 7 June 1660, of Great Lever, Lancs, memb New England Co 1668; *b* 30 Jan 1609; Ld Ch Baron Exchequer 1660, Ld Ch Justice Common Pleas 1660, Ld Keeper Gt Seal 1667–74; *m* 1st 30 Jan 1627/8 Judith (*d* 12 July 1644), dau and heir of John Kynaston, of Morton, Salop, and had an only son:

1 **Sir John Bridgeman, 2nd Bt**; *b* 16 Aug 1631; *m* 1663 his stepmother's dau Mary (*d* 30 Dec 1713), dau and coheir of George Cradock, of Caverswell Castle, Staffs, and *d* 24 Aug 1710, having had, with other issue:

(1) **Sir John Bridgeman, 3rd Bt**; *b* 9 Aug 1667; *m* 19 June 1694 Ursula (*d* 31 Jan 1719/20), dau and sole heir of Roger Matthews, of Blodwell, Salop, and had, with other issue:

1a ORLANDO (Sir), **4th Bt**

1a Ursula; *m* as his 1st w Hugh Williams (*see* WILLIAMS-WYNN, Bt)

(2) Orlando; *m* his cousin, Katherine, dau of William Bridgeman, of Westminster, and *dsps*

1 Mary; *m* 1st Sir Edward Morgan; *m* 2nd Richard Hanbury (*see* SUDELEY, B)

Sir Orlando *m* 2nd 1648 Dorothy (*bur* 12 Jan 1696/7), widow of George Cradock, of Caverswell Castle, and dau of John Saunders, Provost Oriel Coll Oxford, and *d* 25 June 1674, having by her had further issue:

2 Sir ORLANDO BRIDGEMAN, 1st Bt (E) of the 12 Nov 1673 *cr*, of Ridley, Cheshire; *b c* 1650; barrister Inner Temple 1669, MP Horsham 1669–79; *m c* 28 Sept 1670 Mary (*d* 8 June 1701), dau of Sir Thomas Cave, 1st Bt, of Stamford (*see* CAVE-BROWNE-CAVE, Bt), and *d* 20 April 1701, having had, with other issue:

(1) Sir ORLANDO BRIDGEMAN, 2nd Bt; *b c* 1679; *educ* Rugby and Trin Coll Oxford; MP Coventry 1707–10, Calne 1715–22, Lostwithiel 1724–27, Bletchingley 1727–34 and Dunwich 1734–38, Auditor-Gen PRINCE OF WALES (later GEORGE II), Commr Trade 1727–38, nominated Govr Barbados 1737 but never resided there; *m c* 15 April 1702 Susanna (*d* 4 Sept 1747), dau of Sir Francis Dashwood, 1st Bt, of Wycombe, Bucks (*qv*), and *d* by 10 June 1738, leaving issue:

1a Sir FRANCIS BRIDGEMAN, 3rd and last Bt; *b* Aug 1713; *d* unm at sea Nov or Dec 1740, when the baronetcy expired

(1) Penelope Mary; *m* her cousin 1st and last Baron Torrington (*see* above)

3 Francis (Sir); *m* Susan, dau and heir of Sir Richard Barker, of London, MD, and *dsp*

1 Charlotte; *m*, as his 2nd w, Sir Thomas Myddleton, 2nd Bt, of Chirk, and had issue. He *d* 5 Feb 1683

Sir JOHN *d* 23 July 1747; his est son,

Sir Orlando Bridgeman, 4th Bt, MP Shrewsbury; *b* 2 July 1695; *m* 9 April 1719 Lady Ann Newport (*d* 19 Aug 1752), dau of 2nd Earl of Bradford of the 1694 *cr* (*see* above), and *d* 25 July 1764, having had issue, with three other sons and two daus:

Sir Henry Bridgeman, 5th Bt, and **1st Baron Bradford of Bradford** (GB), so *cr* 13 Aug 1794; *b* 7 Sept 1725; MP Ludlow 1748–68 and Wenlock 1768–94; *m* 12 July 1755 Elizabeth (*d* 6 March 1806), dau and heir of Rev John Simpson, of Stoke Hall, Derbys, and had, with other issue:

1 ORLANDO, **2nd Baron** and **1st Earl**

2 John BRIDGEMAN later SIMPSON, of Babworth Hall, Notts; *b* 13 May 1763; took by Act of Parl name and arms of SIMPSON only; *m* 1st 3 June 1784 Henrietta Frances (*d* 25 July 1791), only dau of Sir Thomas Worsley, 6th Bt, of Appuldercombe, and had, with other issue:

(1) Henrietta Anna Maria Charlotte Bridgeman; inherited the estates of her unc, Sir Richard Worsley, 7th Bt; *m* 11 Aug 1806 1st Earl of Yarborough (*qv*) and *d* 1813, leaving issue

2 (cont.) John SIMPSON *m* 2nd 27 Nov 1793 Grace (*d* 1 Jan 1839), dau of Samuel Estwicke, and *d* 5 June 1850, having by her had, with other issue:

(1) William Bridgeman SIMPSON (Rev), MA, Rector Babworth, nr Retford; *b* 9 Sept 1813; *m* 23 June 1837 Lady Frances Laura Wentworth Fitzwilliam (*d* 25 March 1887), dau of 5th Earl Fitzwilliam (*see* 1970 edn), and *d* 1 April 1895, leaving, with other issue:

1a Orlando John George Bridgeman BRIDGEMAN-SIMPSON; *b* 27 Aug 1838; *educ* Harrow; *m* 30 April 1873 Catherine Maria (*d* 29 May 1918), 2nd dau of John Cotes, of Woodcote, Salop, and *d* 5 July 1907, leaving issue:

1b Lillian France; *m* 17 Dec 1903 Maj Henry Percy Thurnall, York and Lancaster Regt, and *d* 9 Dec 1957, leaving issue. He *d* 17 April 1909

2b Evelyn Mary; *m* 30 Sept 1902 Henry Grenville Barnett, 3rd son of Charles Edward Barnett, of Edge Grove, Aldenham, and *d* 23 Nov 1954, leaving issue. He *d* 15 Sept 1952

3b Olga Florence; *m* 1st 18 June 1908 Cuthbert Edmund Arnold Huddart, LRCP (*d* 29 Jan 1917), of 226 Gloucester Terrace, London W, son of Dr C H C Huddart, of Shayswell Manor, Etchingham, Sussex, and had issue; *m* 2nd 22 Dec 1920 George Ernest Harrison, son of W Harrison, of Woods Farm, Beckingham, Notts. He *d* 8 Aug 1943

2a George Arthur Bridgeman BRIDGEMAN, of W Retford House, Retford, Notts; *b* 14 Nov 1846; *m* 26 Nov 1896 Lady Mary Eleanor (*d* 12 Oct 1938), dau of 3rd Earl Fortesue (*qv*), and *dsp* 16 Nov 1913

3a Francis Charles Bridgeman BRIDGEMAN (Sir), GCB (1912), GCVO (1911), of Copgrove Hall, near Leeds, Adml, V-Adml UK, Lt Admlty UK 1920, C-in-C Home Fleet 1907–09 and 1911, 2nd Sea Ld 1909–11, 1st Sea Ld 1911–12, ADC to HM EDWARD VII 1901–03, Cdr: Legion of Honour 2nd Cl and Saviour Greece; *b* 7 Dec 1848; *m* 6 Nov 1889 Emily Charlotte (*d* 25 Nov 1922), dau of Thomas Shiffner, DL, of Westgate, Sussex (*see* SHIFFNER, Bt), and *dsp* 17 Feb 1929

1a Mary Bridgeman; *m* 22 Feb 1876 Maj Walter Pleydell Bouverie, JP, son of Edward Pleydell Bouverie, PC, FRS, of East Lavington, Wilts (*see* RADNOR, E), and *d* 18 Jan 1880, leaving issue

2a Beatrice Dorothy Mary Bridgeman; *m* 7 Dec 1881 Adolphus Montagu Duncombe (*see* FEVERSHAM, B), and *d* 8 July 1936

4 George (Rev), Rector Wigan and Weston; *b* 11 Aug 1765; *m* 1st 28 July 1792 Lady Lucy Boyle (*d* 7 Sept 1801), dau of 7th Earl of Cork (*see* CORK and ORRERY, E), and had issue; *m* 2nd 16 Aug 1809 Charlotte Louisa (*dsp* 26 Jan 1840), 2nd dau of William Poyntz, of Midgham Ho, Berks, and *d* 27 Oct 1832

1 Elizabeth; *m* Sir George William Gunning, 2nd Bt (*qv*), and *d* 1810, leaving issue

The 1st BARON *d* 5 June 1800; his son,

ORLANDO BRIDGEMAN, **2nd Baron Bradford of Bradford** and **1st Earl of Bradford**, so *cr* 30 Nov 1815, as also VISCOUNT NEWPORT, both Co Salop (both UK); *b* 19 March 1762; *educ* Harrow and Trin Coll Cambridge; MP Wigan 1784–1800; *m* 29 May 1788 Hon Lucy Elizabeth Byng (*d* 20 Sept 1844), dau and coheir of 4th Viscount Torrington (*qv*), and had, with other issue:

1 GEORGE AUGUSTUS FREDERICK HENRY, **2nd Earl**

2 Charles Orlando, V-Adml; *b* 5 Feb 1791; *educ* Harrow; *m* 2 Jan 1819 Eliza Caroline (*d* 11 Dec 1887 aged 88), est dau of Sir Henry Chamberlain, 1st Bt, and *d* 13 April 1860, having had, with other issue:

(1) Ursula Lucy Grace; *m* 1st 21 Dec 1847 1st Baron Londesborough (*qv*) and had issue; *m* 2nd 14 Dec 1861 Lord Otho FitzGerald, 3rd son of 3rd Duke of Leinster (*qv*), and *d* 13 Nov 1883, leaving issue

(2) Caroline Elizabeth Anne Agnes; *m* 9 May 1854 Sir Vincent Rowland Corbet, 3rd Bt (*see* 1970 edn), and *d* 13 Aug 1914, leaving issue. He *d* 22 May 1891

(3) Charlotte Sobieski Isabel, VA; *m* 16 May 1863 Sir Leopold Cust, 2nd Bt, and *d* 13 June 1914, leaving issue. He *d* 3 March 1878

3 Orlando Henry, Capt Army; *b* 6 May 1794; *educ* Harrow; *m* 5 July 1817 Lady Selina Needham (*d* 10 Jan 1876), dau of 1st Earl of Kilmorey (*qv*), and *d* 28 Aug 1827, leaving with other issue:

(1) Francis Orlando Henry, Capt 10th Hus; *b* 10 Sept 1819; *educ* Harrow; *m* 30 June 1846 Countess Josephine Wilhelmina Francesca (*d* 27 June 1908), est dau of Anthony Joseph Clement, Count von Torring Minucci, of Bavaria, and *d* 4 Oct 1895, leaving issue:

1a Lucy Selina Frances; *b* 29 June 1847; *m* 21 Sept 1868 Count Albrecht Seinsheim, Chamberlain to Prince Regent of Bavaria, and *dsp* 30 April 1932. He *d* 23 Feb 1915

2a Selina; *m* 2 April 1850 Sir Henry Fox Bristowe, QC, V-Chllr Duchy Lancaster, 2nd s of Samuel Ellis Bristowe, of Beesthorpe, Notts, and *d* 15 May 1886, leaving issue. He *d* 20 Feb 1893

4 Henry Edmund (Rev), Rector Blymhill, Staffs; *b* 18 Oct 1795; *educ* Harrow and Trin Coll Cambridge; *m* 25 Aug 1820 Louisa Elizabeth (*d* 23 March 1880), dau of Hon John Simpson, of Babworth, Notts (*see* above), and *d* 15 Nov 1872, having had, with other issue:

(1) Caroline Louisa Sophia Georgiana; *m* 29 Dec 1879 William Joseph Kingsbury (*d* 9 Jan 1904), 2nd son of Thomas Kingsbury, of Bathwick Priory, Somerset, and *d* 19 March 1920, leaving issue

The 1st EARL *d* 7 Sept 1825; his est son,

GEORGE AUGUSTUS FREDERICK HENRY BRIDGEMAN, **2nd Earl of Bradford**; *educ* Harrow and Trin Coll Camb; *b* 23 Oct 1789; *m* 1st 5 March 1818 Georgina Elizabeth (*d* 12 Oct 1842), only dau of Sir Thomas Moncreiffe, 5th Bt (*see* ERROLL, E), and had, with other issue:

1 ORLANDO GEORGE CHARLES, **3rd Earl**

2 George Thomas Orlando (Rev), Rector Wigan, RD, Hon Canon Liverpool, Chaplain in Ordinary to HM QUEEN VICTORIA; *b* 21 Aug 1823; *educ* Harrow and Trin Coll Cambridge (MA); *m* 25 June 1850 Emily Mary (*d* 13 Dec 1853), dau of Rt Rev Hon Richard Bagot, DD, Bp Bath and Wells (*see* BAGOT, B), and *d* 25 Nov 1895, leaving issue:

(1) Ernest Richard Orlando (Rev), Rector Blymhill, RD Penkridge, Preb Lichfield, Proctor in Convocation 1924–31; *b* 9 May 1851; *educ* Harrow and Trin Coll Cambridge (MA); *d* unm 9 Oct 1940

(2) Charles George Orlando, barrister; *b* 13 July 1852; *educ* Harrow and Trin Coll Cambridge (MA); *m* 26 July 1888 Sidney (*d* 8 April 1936), dau and coheir of Gen Sir Henry Lynedoch Gardiner, KCVO, CB, and *d* 19 Dec 1933, leaving issue:

1a Roger Orlando, Capt and Brevet Maj Rifle Bde, Prison Govr, Head Prison Section Br Police and Prison Mission to Greece, served WW I (wounded); *b* 4 Oct 1889; *educ* Harrow and Trin Coll Cambridge (BA 1911, MA 1919); *m* 6 Feb 1929 Marjorie Susan, only dau of Lt-Gen Hon Sir Alan Richard Montagu-Stuart-Wortley, KCB, KCMG, DSO, of Home Close, Highclere, Newbury (*see* WHARNCLIFFE, E), and *d* 10 May 1975, leaving issue:

1b Richard Lynedoch Orlando; *b* 23 June 1931; *educ* Harrow; Lt Rifle Bde, dir Justerini and Brooks 1958; *m* 23 June 1965 Romayne Georgette Ord (*d* 1985), only dau of Ingram Ord Capper, of The Mill, Polstead, Suffolk, and *d* 22 Sept 1982, leaving issue:

1c +(Leopold) Orlando [Orlando Bridgeman Esq, 8 Cranbourne Crt, Albert Bridge Rd, London SW11 4PE]; *b* 20 April 1968; *educ* Harrow

2c +Constantine Orlando [Constantine Bridgeman Esq, 52 Ebury Mews, London SW1]; *b* 2 Jan 1970

1c *Celestine Victoria [Mrs Roger Bramley, 40 Anhalt Rd, London SW11 4NX; Chedglow Barn Cottage, Crudwell, Malmesbury, Wilts]; *b* 5 March 1966; *m* 1988 *Roger D Bramley, son of Richard Bramley, of Unstone, Derbys, and has issue:

1b *Edward Orlando; *b* 28 July 1995

1b *Cressida Romayne; *b* 1994

1a Victoria Alexandrina Leopoldine; *b* 19 July 1894 (HM QUEEN VICTORIA stood sponsor); *d* unm 15 Jan 1961

(1) Harriet Georgiana Isabel; *b* 7 Dec 1853; *m* 22 April 1879 Rev Douglas Stuart Murray, Rector Blithfield, Staffs, and *d* 11 Nov 1921, leaving issue (*see* ATHOLL, D)

3 John Robert Orlando (Rev), Rector Weston-under-Lizard, RD Brewood; *b* 18 Aug 1831; *educ* Eton and Trin Coll Cambridge (MA); *m* 5 June 1862 Marianne Caroline (*d* 19 Feb 1930), only dau of Ven William Clive, Archdeacon Montgomery, and *d* 26 Nov 1897, leaving issue, with a dau:

(1) WILLIAM CLIVE, 1st VISCOUNT BRIDGEMAN (*qv*)

1 Mary Selina; *b c* 1830; *m* 20 Oct 1852 Hon Robert Windsor-Clive, MP (*see* PLYMOUTH, E), and *d* 12 July 1889, leaving issue

The **2nd Earl** *m* 2nd 30 Oct 1849 Helen (*d* 25 April 1869), widow of Sir David Moncrieffe, 6th Bt (*see* ERROLL, E), and dau of Capt Aeneas MacKay, of Scotstoun, and *d* 22 March 1865

His son,

ORLANDO GEORGE CHARLES BRIDGEMAN, **3rd Earl of Bradford**, PC (1852); *educ* Harrow and Trin Coll Cambridge; Ld Chamberlain 1866–68, Master of the Horse 1874–80 and 1885–86, Ld Lt Salop, MP S Shropshire 1842–65, Hon Col 1st Vol Bn Shropshire LI; *b* 24 April 1819; *m* 30 April 1844 Hon Selina Louisa, yst dau of 1st Baron Forester (*qv*), and had, with other issue:

1 GEORGE CECIL ORLANDO, **4th Earl**

2 Francis Charles, JP (Staffs and Salop), Brig-Gen cmdg Central Gp London Regt Vol Training Corps, MP Bolton 1885–95, Col Scots Gds, cmded Staffs Inf Bde 1892–99, Kt of Isabella Catolica; *b* 4 July 1846; *educ* Harrow; *m* 1st 26 July 1883 Gertrude Cecilia (*d* 11 March 1911), est dau of George Hanbury, JP, of Blythewood, nr Maidenhead, Berks; *m* 2nd 27 Nov 1913 Agnes Florence (*d* 3 Dec 1946), dau of Richard Holt Briscoe, and *d* 14 Sept 1917, having had issue by his 1st w:

(1) Reginald Francis Orlando, CMG (1917), MVO (1914); *b* 14 Oct 1884; *educ* Harrow; Counsellor Dip Serv; *m* 4 June 1923 Olwen Elizabeth (*d* 1985), only dau of Maurice Jones, MPS, and *d* 11 Dec 1968, having had issue:

1a Humphrey Reginald, Lt Scots Gds WW II; *b* 15 Aug 1924; *educ* Harrow; *ka* Italy 28 May 1944

2a +(Henry) Clive Orlando [Clive Bridgeman Esq, 10 Waxwell Close, Waxwell Lane, Pinner, Middx HA5 3ET]; *b* 12 June 1946; *educ* Harrow and Trin Coll Cambridge (BA)

1a *Victoria Mary [Miss Victoria Bridgeman, 71 Lauderdale Mansions, Lauderdale Rd, London W9 1LX]; *b* 24 Feb 1926; WRNS WW II

2a *(Olwen) Valery [Mrs Anthony Golding, 12 Clifton Hill, London W8; Keepers Cottage, Byworth, Petworth, Sussex]; *b* 7 Feb 1928; *educ* Birkbeck Coll London (BA 1956); psychologist Tavistock Inst and Clinic; *m* 29 Aug 1962 *Dr Anthony Mark Barrington Golding, MA, MB, BChir, FFPHM, yr s of Dr Mark Golding, of 29 Dawson Place, London W2, and has:

1b *Richard Mark Orlando; *b* 30 June 1965; MEng and Man; *m* 1990 (*divorce* 1992) Sarah Dolman and has:

1c *Leo Dolman; *b* 1 July 1991

1b *Rosemary Victoria Anne; *b* 20 July 1963; LLB, slr; *m* 26 April 1996 *Christopher Chilton, BSc, and has:

1c *Jasmine Rebecca Anne; b 24 May 1997

2b *Catherine Elizabeth Marian; *b* 22 Jan 1967; BMedSc, MB, BS, MRCP; *m* 19 July 1997 *Sean James Connell, BA, slr, est s of Sir Michael Connell

3b *Charlotte Valery Patricia; *b* 28 March 1970; *educ* Bristol U (BA 1994)

(2) Francis Paul Orlando; *b* 25 July 1888; Cdr RN; *m* 11 May 1922 Alice Dorothy (*d* 22 Jan 1979), 5th dau of Herman Greverus Kleinwort, of 45 Belgrave Sq, London SW, and Wierton Place, nr Maidstone, Kent (*see* KLEINWORT, Bt), and *d* 30 Oct 1930, leaving issue:

1a +Gerald William Paul Orlando [Gerald Bridgeman Esq, Dowdeswell Manor, Andoversford, nr Cheltenham, Glos; 43 Cheval Place, London SW7; 51 Maxnam's Lane, Chertsey, Surrey]; *b* 3 Dec 1929; *educ* Eton; *m* 31 March 1965 *Mrs Rosemarie Ingrams, dau of S/Ldr Willis Tomlinson, RAF, of Hillingdon, Middx, and formerly w of Michael Ingrams

1a *Jeannine Patricia, MBE [Mrs Josef Bartosik MBE, Well House, Donnington, Moreton-in-Marsh, Glos GL56 0XZ; 33 Cheval Place, London SW7]; *b* 5 June 1923; *m* 1st 5 May 1951 (*divorce* 1955) Alan Forde Scott, DCTanganyika, yr son of N W Scott, of Blackhill, Transvaal; *m* 2nd 18 Oct 1969, as his 2nd w, *R-Adml Josef Czeslaw Bartosik, CB, DSC, son of T Bartosik, of Warsaw, Poland

2a *Marigold Helen [Miss Marigold Bridgeman, Never End, Foxcote, Cheltenham Glos GL54 4LP]; *b* 29 Oct 1925

(3) Humphrey Herbert Orlando, Lt RHG (Res) WW I; *b* 22 July 1891; *educ* Cheltenham; *ka* 11 May 1917

(4) Orlando Clive, MC (1918), Capt RAF (SR); *b* 29 Nov 1898; *educ* Harrow and Trin Coll Cambridge (MA); *m* 30 April 1924 Nancye Newzam (*d* 14 Sept 1967), yr dau of Arthur Beresford Nicholson, of Hove, and *d* 21 Dec 1931

(1) Selina Adine; *b* 24 June 1886; *m* 1st 1 Feb 1913 Capt Hon Lawrence Ughtred Kay-Shuttleworth, barrister, er son of 1st Baron Shuttleworth (*qv*), and had issue. He was *ka* at Vimy, 30 March 1917. She *m* 2nd 31 Jan 1920 Maj-Gen William Birchall Macaulay King, CMG, DSO, and had further issue. He *d* 22 June 1950

1 Mabel Selina; *m* 22 Feb 1887 Col William Slaney Kenyon-Slaney, PC, DL, MP, of Hatton Grange, Salop, and *d* 28 Jan 1933 leaving issue (*see* KENYON, B)

2 Florence Katharine, DJStJ; *m* 5 Nov 1881 5th Earl of Harewood (*qv*), and *d* 5 May 1943, having had issue

The 3rd EARL *d* 9 March 1898; his son,

GEORGE CECIL ORLANDO BRIDGEMAN, **4th Earl of Bradford**, DL and JP Salop and Warwicks, JP Staffs; *educ* Harrow; MP N Salop 1867–85, Lt 1st Life Gds, Capt Shropshire Yeo Cav; *b* 3 Feb 1845; *m* 7 Sept 1869 Lady Ida Frances Annabella Lumley, DGStJ (*d* 22 Aug 1936), 2nd dau of 9th Earl of Scarbrough (*qv*), and had issue:

1 ORLANDO, **5th Earl**

2 Richard Orlando Beaconsfield, DSO, Cdr RN WW I; *b* 28 Feb 1879; *kas* E Africa 9 Jan 1917

3 Henry George Orlando, DSO (1918), MC (1916), DL (1946), JP (Northumberland 1945); *b* 15 Aug 1882; *educ* Harrow; Lt-Col RFA, ADC to GOC Ireland, served WW I, Order Danilo Montenegro; *m* 30 Dec 1930 Joan (*d* 1991), 4th dau of Hon Bernard Constable-Maxwell, of Farlie House, Beauly, Scotland (*see* HERRIES, L), and *d* 19 May 1972, leaving issue:

(1) +Peter Orlando Ronald, TD (1968), DL (Northumberland 1983) [Lt-Col Peter Bridgeman TD DL, Fallodon, Embleton, Alnwick, Northumberland]; *b* 9 May 1933; *educ* Ampleforth; High Sheriff Northumberland 1975, Lt-Col 7th Bn Roy Northumberland Fus (TA), Lt (Res) Scots Gds, Kt SMO Malta; *m* 4 May 1967 *Sarah Jane Davina, only dau of Patrick Geoffrey Corbett, of Silverlands, Boar's Head, Crowborough, Sussex, and has:

1a +Mark George Orlando; *b* 29 May 1968

1a *Emma Virginia; *b* 18 Oct 1969

2a *Davina Sacha; *b* 1972

(2) +John Henry Orlando [John Bridgeman Esq, Boreland House, Lockerbie, Dumfriesshire, Scotland]; *b* 11 Oct 1938; *educ* Ampleforth; Lt (Res) Scots Gds, Kt SMO Malta; *m* 9 Feb 1970 *Susan Gay, dau of A Leonard Hill, of Boreland of Dryfe, Lockerbie, Dumfriesshire, and has issue:

1a *Camilla Jane; *b* 1971

2a *Alexandra Mary; *b* 1973

(1) *Mary Helena; *b* 9 March 1932; *m* 26 May 1960 *(William) Simon Rodolph Kenyon-Slaney, yr son of Maj Robert Orlando Rodolph Kenyon-Slaney, DL, JP, of Hatton Grange, Shifnal, Salop (*see* KENYON, B), and has issue

(2) *(Alice) Christina [Mrs Bruce McKenzie, Haselbech Hall, Northants NN6 9LG; PO Box 52, Ukunda, Kenya]; *b* 27 April 1936 (HRH THE DUCHESS OF GLOUCESTER stood sponsor); *m* 19 July 1967 *Bruce McKenzie, DSO, DFC, Min Ag Kenya, s of Roy Douglas McKenzie, of Durban, Natal, and has issue:

1a *Kim Alexander; *b* 29 May 1969

2a *James Malcolm; *b* 28 Dec 1971

1 Beatrice Adine, OBE (1919); *b* 2 Dec 1870; *m* 28 June 1894 Col Ernest George Pretyman, PC, DL, of Orwell Park, Suffolk, and *d* 27 June 1952, leaving issue. He *d* 26 Nov 1931

2 Margaret Alice; *b* 20 Jan 1872; *m* 20 Jan 1893 7th Duke of Buccleuch and Queensberry (*qv*) and *d* 7 Aug 1954, leaving issue

3 Helena Mary, OStJ; *b* 16 July 1875 (HRH PRINCESS CHRISTIAN stood sponsor); *m* 8 Jan 1898 6th Earl of Sefton (*see* 1967 edn) and *d* 27 Aug 1947, leaving issue

4 Florence Sibell; *b* 24 March 1877; *m* 10 Feb 1904 Ronald Collet Norman, of Moor Place, Much Hadham, Herts, 2nd son of Frederick Henry Norman, of Moor Place, Much Hadham, and *d* 16 June 1936, leaving issue. He *d* 5 Dec 1963

The 4th EARL *d* 2 Jan 1915; his est son,

ORLANDO BRIDGEMAN, **5th Earl of Bradford**, DL, JP (Warwicks and Salop); *educ* Harrow and Trin Coll Cambridge (BA 1896, MA 1903), Priv Sec to PM 1898–1900, 1902 and 1902–05, Govt Whip 1919–24, Lt-Col 3rd Bn Roy Scots, served S Africa 1900–02 and WW I 1915–17, Hon Col 4th Bn KSLI 1939; *b* 6 Oct 1873; *m* 21 July 1904 Hon Margaret Cecilia Bruce (*d* 16 April 1949), est dau of 2nd Baron Aberdare (*qv*), and had issue:

1 GERALD MICHAEL ORLANDO, **6th Earl**

1 (Helen) Diana; *b* 22 June 1907; *m* 10 Feb 1930 (*divorce* 1962) Sir Robert Henry Edward Abdy, 5th Bt (*qv*), and *d* 7 May 1967, leaving issue

2 Ursula Mary; *b* 12 July 1909; *d* 6 May 1912

3 *Anne Pamela [The Lady Anne Cowdray, Broadleas, Devizes, Wilts SN10 5JQ]; *b* 12 June 1913; *m* 19 July 1939 (*divorce* 1950) 3rd Viscount Cowdray (*qv*) and has issue

4 Joan Serena; *b* 29 May 1916; *d* unm 23 July 1935

The 5th EARL *d* 21 March 1957; his only son,

GERALD MICHAEL ORLANDO BRIDGEMAN, **6th Earl of Bradford**, TD, DL (1951), JP (Salop 1949); *educ* Harrow and Trin Coll Cambridge (BA 1932, MA 1961); Capt Shropshire Yeo RAC (TARO) WW II (despatches), pres CLA 1955–57, pres Timber Growers' Orgn 1962–64, chm Forestry Ctee GB 1964–66, Crown Estate Commr 1956–67, chm W Midlands Regn Nat Tst 1973, Freeman Shrewsbury 1957; *b* 29 Sept 1911; *m* 31 Oct 1946 Mary Willoughby (*d* 1986), er dau of Lt-Col Thomas Hassard Montgomery, DSO, of Cadogan Ho, Shrewsbury, and *d* 30 Aug 1981, leaving issue:

1 RICHARD THOMAS ORLANDO BRIDGEMAN, **7th and present Earl of Bradford**

2 +Charles Gerald Orlando [The Hon Charles Bridgeman, Albion Hayes Farm, Bomere Heath, Salop SY4 3PW]; *b* 25 June 1954; *educ* Harrow, Warwick U and RAC Circencester; ARICS 1993; *m* 17 Jan 1982 *Nicola Marie-Thérèse, only dau of Brian Sales, of Congleton, Cheshire, and has issue:

(1) +James Edward Charles Orlando; *b* 22 March 1978

(2) +Robert Gerald Orlando; *b* 19 May 1983

(3) +Nicholas Francis Orlando; *b* 2 June 1991

1 *Serena Mary [The Lady Serena Bridgeman, Dell House, Whitebridge, Inverness-shire IV1 2UP; Flat 1, 3 Westgate Terr, London SW10 9BT]; *b* 1 July 1949; has resumed her maiden name; *m* 27 April 1978 (*divorce* 1989) Richard Arnold Andrew, yr son of John Ramsay Andrew, of St Saviours, Guernsey

2 *Caroline Louise [The Lady Caroline Garnell, 16 Holland Park Ave, London W11 3QU]; *b* 18 April 1952; *m* 5 Oct 1974 *Brian Martin Garnell, only son of Henry Joseph Garnell, of Woodhay, Manaden, nr Bishop's Stortford, Herts, and has issue:

(1) *Thomas Henry Michael; *b* 1986

(2) *Benedict Charles Orlando; *b* 1990

(3) *Daniel Gerald Orlando; *b* 1993

(1) *Tara Serena Clare; *b* 21 Oct 1983

BRADFORD, Bt

Arms: Arg., on a fess embattled counter-embattled, between three mural crowns sa., as many stag's heads erased or. **Crest:** A stag's head erased or, charged on the neck with a mural crown and suspended from the mouth a bugle horn stringed sa. **Motto:** *Humani nihil alienum* ('Nothing human is indifferent to me'). **Creation:** Bt. (UK) 24 July 1902.

SIR EDWARD ALEXANDER SLADE BRADFORD, 5TH BT; *b* (posthumously) 18 June 1952; *s* half-bro 1954 but does not use title

Lineage: Rev WILLIAM MUSSAGE BRADFORD, of Hall Place, Beaconsfield, Bucks, JP, MA Oxon, Rector Hedsor; *b* 1773; *m* 21 Sept 1803 Mary Wharton (*d* 11 March 1835), of Bray, Co Wicklow, and *d* 19 Aug 1840; their est s:

Rev WILLIAM MUSSAGE KIRKWALL BRADFORD, Rector W Meon, Hants; *b* 7 May 1806; *educ* Magdalon Hall Oxford (MA); *m* 1 July 1834 Mary (*d* 4 Aug 1894), er dau of Rev Henry Colborne Ridley, Rector Hambleden, Bucks, 3rd s of Sir Matthew White Ridley, 2nd Bt (*see* RIDLEY, V), and *d* April 1872, having had, with an est and yst s and five daus:

Sir Edward Ridley Colborne Bradford, 1st Bt (UK), so *cr* 24 July 1902, of S Audley Street, Westminster, GCB (1897, KCB 1890), GCVO (1902), KCSI (1885, CSI 1876), JP (London); *b* 27 July 1836; Col Indian Staff Corps, served Persian War 1857 and NW Provinces India 1858–59, Gen Superintendent Ops for Suppression Thuggee and Dacoitee 1874; Resident 1st Cl and Govr-Gen's Agent Rajputana, Ch Commr Ajmere and Mhairwarra 1878–87; Sec Political and Secret Dept India Office 1887–90; ADC to HM QUEEN VICTORIA 1889–93; Ch Commr Met Police 1890–1903, Extra Equerry to TM EDWARD VII 1903–10 and GEORGE V 1910–11; *m* 1st 17 June 1866 Elizabeth Adela (*d* 21 May 1896), 3rd dau of Edward Knight, DL, of Chawton Ho, Hants, and had:

1 Montagu Edward, ICS; *b* 9 June 1867; *dvp* unm 22 Aug 1890

2 EVELYN RIDLEY (Sir), **2nd Bt**

3 Daryl Colborne; *b* 25 Jan 1872; *d* 30 May 1874

4 Herbert Lewkenor; *b* 25 Sept 1873; *d* 19 March 1874

5 Edward Austen, DSO (1917); *b* 8 Dec 1879; *educ* Eton; Lt-Col KRRC S African War and WW I; *m* 1 Jan 1908 Margaret Louisa (*d* 1972), 3rd dau of Herbert Carey Hardy, of Danehurst, Sussex, and *d* 5 June 1958, leaving:

(1) Berenger Colborne, DSO (1944) and bar (1945), MBE (1942), MC; *b* 15 Oct 1912; *educ* Eton; Brig, joined Black Watch 1932, served WW II (wounded, despatches), cmded 5th Bn Black Watch 1944–46 and 2nd Bn 1953–56, ret 1959, Memb Roy Co Archers; *m* 30 Oct 1951 *Susan [Mrs Berenger Bradford, The Flat, Kincardine, Kincardine O'Neil, Aberdeenshire], yr dau of Col Arthur Hanning Vaughan-Lee, of Dillington Park, Ilminster, Somerset, and *d* 4 March 1996, leaving:

1a +Robert Berenger Pickering [Robert Bradford Esq, Holestone Lodge, Pool O'Muckart, Clackmannanshire]; *b* 12 Aug 1952; *educ* Eton

2a +Andrew Edward Hanning [Andrew Bradford Esq, Kincardine, Kincardine O'Neil, Aboyne, Aberdeenshire, Scotland]; *b* 6 Jan 1955; *educ* Eton and Aberdeen U (BSc); memb Roy Co Archers; *m* 1978 *Nicola Barbara, dau of David Philip Smythe, and has issue:

1b +Edward Austen Philip; *b* 1980

2b +Charles Graham Knight; *b* 1988

1b *Louisa Aimée Felicity; *b* 1982

3a +Ronald James Knight; *b* 30 March 1958; *educ* Aberdeen U (BSc); Maj Black Watch NI (despatches); *m* 1986 *Katherine Ferguson, yr dau of Sir Ian Denholm, CBE, of Newton of Belltrees, Lochwinnoch, Renfrewshire, and has issue:

1b *Victoria Jane Ferguson; *b* 1989

2b *Kirstin Elizabeth Hardy; *b* 1992

1a *Margaret Jane [Mrs Robert Gladstone, Capanoch, Thornhill, Dumfriesshire]; *b* 6 Dec 1953; *educ* Glasgow U (BMus); *m* 16 Jan 1982 *Robert Hamilton Gladstone and has issue:

1b *John Berenger; *b* 3 March 1983

2b *Harry William (twin); *b* 3 March 1983

1b *Catherine Susan; *b* 13 April 1986

(1) Adela Evelyn; *b* 20 Sept 1909; *m* 4 Sept 1933 (*divorce* 1945) Lt-Col Fergus Gleeson, IA (*d* 1962), yst son of Denis Gleeson, of London, and had issue

(2) Cassandra Felicity, MBE (1946), Capt ATA WW II, WAAF (VR) (Flying) Corps 1947; *b* 22 Sept 1915; *m* 9 July 1941 G/Capt Peter Hugh Bragg, RAF (*d* 1966), only son of Rev Tom Bragg, of Bournemouth, and has issue:

1a *Ronald Wakefield; *b* 27 Jan 1948; *educ* Haileybury

(3) *Diana Elizabeth [Mrs Rupert Shervington, The Villa Ware, Ware Lane, Lyme Regis, Dorset DT7 3EJ]; *b* 10 Jan 1919; WAAF WW II 1939–41; *m* 8 Feb 1941 *Rupert Patrick Shervington, late Capt RE, son of Arthur Peter Shervington, of Wembley, and has issue:

1a *Evelyn Arthur; *b* 8 Feb 1942; *educ* Trin Coll Dublin (BA)

1a *Diana Clare; *b* 23 Sept 1943

2a *Caroline Faith; *b* 4 Jan 1954

1 Beryl Adela; *d* unm 1957

Sir Edward *m* 2nd 25 Oct 1898 Edith Mary (*d* 28 March 1951), 2nd dau of William Nicholson, DL (*see* NICHOLSON OF WINTERBOURNE, Bt), and *d* 13 May 1911

His er surv son,

Sir Evelyn Ridley Bradford, 2nd Bt, Lt-Col Seaforth Highrs, served Nile Expdn 1898, S African War 1899–1902 (despatches, Brevet Maj, Queen's and King's Medals with clasps) and WW I 1914; *b* 16 April 1869; *m* 25 Nov 1909 Elsie Clifton (*d* 2 Dec 1958), 3rd dau of Col James Clifton Brown (*see* BROWN, Bt), and was *ka* cmdg his Regt France 14 Sept 1914, leaving issue:

1 EDWARD MONTAGU ANDREW (Sir), **3rd Bt**

2 Ridley Lewkenor, S/Ldr RAF WW II; *b* 11 April 1912; *ka* 1 May 1940

3 +DONALD CLIFTON [Donald Bradford Esq, The Barns, Tapnell, Yarmouth, IoW PO41 0YJ]; *b* 22 May 1914; heir presumptive; *educ* Eton and Ch Ch Oxford; Capt Seaforth Highrs WW II; *m* 10 June 1949 *Constance Mary, yr dau of Richard Thomas Morgan, of Glyncorrwg, S Wales, and has issue:

(1) *Susan Jane; *b* 18 March 1950

(2) *Katherine Anne; *b* 16 Oct 1952

(3) *Joanna Mary; *b* 17 April 1957

Sir EVELYN's est son,

Sir Edward Montagu Andrew Bradford, 3rd Bt, Maj Cameronians WW II (despatches); *b* 30 Nov 1910; *m* 1st 24 June 1937 (*divorce* 1947) Alison (*m* 2nd 1951 John Owen Fisher Davies, CBE, MD, MRCP (*d* 1978)), er dau of John Lawson, of Borrobol, Sutherland, and *d* as result of a riding accident 1 April 1952, leaving issue:

1 **Sir John Ridley Evelyn Bradford, 4th Bt**; *b* 14 Sept 1941; *k* in a tractor accident 23 Dec 1954

1 *Alison Rose [Mrs James Adams, Riverside House, N Manchester, Indiana, USA]; *b* 30 April 1939; *educ* Manchester Coll (BA 1960); *m* 19 June 1957 *James Ronald Creighton Adams, MFA, BA, son of Arnold Adams, of 35 Joharry Dve, Fairmont, W Virginia, USA, and has issue:

(1) *John Evelyn Creighton; *b* 15 April 1959

(2) *Bradford Michael; *b* 7 July 1965

Sir Edward *m* 2nd 2 March 1950 *Marjorie Edith [Marjorie Lady Bradford, Faith Cottage, Pett, Sussex], dau of Samuel Bere, of Addiscombe, Surrey, and formerly w of Stephen Chapman, and by her had further issue:

2 Sir EDWARD ALEXANDER SLADE BRADFORD, **5th and present Bt**

BRAIN

Arms: Per pale or and arg. three cat's heads erased gu. **Crest:** A falcon sa., armed and belled or, supporting with the dexter claw a representation of the silver staff of office of the President of the Royal College of Physicians of London ppr. **Supporters:** Dexter, a lion statant, guardant or, gorged with a coronet composed of fleurs-de-lys arg., set upon a rim gobony silver and az., holding in the interior paw a pomegranate slipped ppr.; sinister, a griffin gold beaked gu., gorged with a like coronet, holding in the interior claw a poppy slipped, also ppr. **Motto:** (above the crest) *Sum ergo cogito* ('I am, therefore I think'); (below the crest) *Mens stella cerebri* ('The mind is the star of the brain'). **Creations:** B. (UK) 26 Jan 1962, Bt. (UK) 29 June 1954.

THE 2ND BARON BRAIN, of Eynsham, Oxon, (Sir Christopher Langdon Brain, Bt) and a **Baronet** [The Rt Hon The Lord Brain, The Old Rectory, 34 Cross St, Moretonhampstead, Devon TQ13 8NL]; *b* 30 Aug 1926; *s* f 1966; *educ* Leighton Pk and New Coll Oxford (BA 1952, MA 1956); ARPS 1970, served RN 1946–48, chm: Rhone Alps Regnl Cncl, Br Chamber Commerce (France), Liveryman Weavers' Co 1955 (Upper Warden 1974–75, Renter Bailiff 1983–84, Upper Bailiff 1984–85), dir Keirman & Co 1973; *m* 11 April 1953 *Susan Mary, 2nd dau of George Philip Morris, of Clifton Cottage, Over, Cambs, and has issue:

1 *Nicola Dorothy; *b* 26 Oct 1955; *educ* Edinburgh U (MB, ChB, MRCP); *m* 1994 *Dr Stephen Bashforth, er son of G P Bashforth, of Norton, Sheffield

2 *Fiona Janice [Mrs Andrew Proud, The Rectory, 136 Church Hill Rd, E Barnet, Herts EN4 8XD]; *b* 25 June 1958; BSc; *m* 2 July 1977 *Rev Andrew John Proud, BD, est son of J G Proud, of Colchester, and has issue:

(1) *Justin Dominic Edward; *b* 1979

(1) *Emma Jane Chrysogen; *b* 16 Dec 1977

3 *Naomi Melicent; *b* 27 May 1960; MA, MB, BS; *m* 1990 *Malcolm Hugh David Kemp, er son of Prof C D Kemp, of St Andrews, Fife

Lineage: The family of Brayne/Braine/Brain lived at Over Norton, parish of Chipping Norton, Oxon, from at least the mid-16th century.

THOMAS BRAYNE, of Ascott-under-Wychwood, Oxon; *b c* 1570; *m* 29 Nov 1593 Elliner Hicks (*bur* 4 March 1640/1) and was *bur* 28 Feb 1635/6, leaving issue:

1 WILLIAM, of whom presently

2 Edward; *d* after his mother

3 Thomas; *bapt* 30 May 1613; f of:

(1) Edward; *bur* 7 July 1638

1 Ann; *bapt* 14 Oct 1594

2 Elizabeth

3 Mary; *bapt* 15 April 1599; *m* Henry Berkes and had a dau

4 Martha; *bapt* 21 Feb 1600/1; *d* by 1637

5 Frances; *bapt* 7 Sept 1603

6 Priscilla; *bapt* 30 Nov 1605

7 Mary; *bapt* 16 Oct 1608

The est son,

WILLIAM BRAYNE, of Ascott-under-Wychwood; *m* 1st — (*bur* 3 Oct 1683) and had a s (*bur* 13 July 1629); *m* 2nd 17 Nov 1639 Elizabeth Hicks and by her had issue:

1 William, of Finstock, Charlbury; *b c* 1625; *dspm* 1713

2 Edward BRAYNE, of Finstock; juryman Manor of Charlbury 1712; *b c* 1628; *m* and *d* in or after 1715, leaving issue:

(1) William BRAINE, of Charlbury; *m* 8 May 1677 Elizabeth Hancocke (*bur* 6 Dec 1764) and was *bur* 3 Jan 1729/30, leaving, with another s and three daus:

1a William; *bapt* 7 April 1678; *m* 1 Aug 1708 Martha Gardener (*bur* 24 May 1710) and was *bur* 3 Jan 1729/30, leaving issue:

1b Elizabeth; *bapt* 8 March 1709/10

2a Edward, of Finstock, yeoman; *bapt* 22 Feb 1679/80; *bur* 25 May 1743

3a John BRAINE, of Church Hanborough; *bapt* 30 Aug 1685; *m* 1 Oct 1715 Susannah Bell (*d* 25 Feb 1768 aged 80), and was *bur* 29 Sept 1728, leaving, with two er s and a dau:

1b John BRAIN, of Church Hanborough; *bapt* 31 July 1726; *m* 15 March 1756 Jane Dell (*bur* 15 March 1790) and was *bur* 25 March 1798, having had issue (with two er sons, a yst s and two daus):

1c Thomas, of Reading; musician, in Berks Militia at Reading; *bapt* 22 Nov 1762; *m c* 18 Feb 1794 Ann Burnham and *d* 1835, having had issue (with three yr sons and four daus):

1d John, of Reading; bapt 3 Nov 1799; *m c* 1822 Ann Badcock (*d* 30 Oct 1852) and *d* 1 Jan 1865, having had, with two daus:

1e John Alfred, of Reading, JP (1894), Cllr 1875–78; *b* 8 Dec 1827; *m* 26 May 1853 Ann Catherine (*d* 13 Sept 1892), dau of Thomas Cottrell, of Portland Place, Reading, and *d* 12 April 1901, having had, with two yst s and three daus:

1f WALTER JOHN, of whom presently

2f Sydney, of Reading, slr, Clerk to Reading Justices 1918–38; *b* 15 Nov 1860; *educ* Christ's Hosp; *m* 9 April 1891 Gertrude Mary (*d* 4 Feb 1939), dau of John Atkins, of Windsor, and *d* 21 Oct 1939, having had issue:

1g John Atkins, slr, Clerk to Berks Magistrates 1934–42, 2nd Lt Roy Berks Regt WW I (wounded 1918); *b* 22 Jan 1892; *educ* Leighton Park; *m* 3 Sept 1919 Doris May, dau of Edward Oliver Farrer, of Reading, and *d* 11 March 1954, leaving issue:

1h *Geoffrey John Farrer, slr and notary public, Capt RA WW II 1942–45; *b* 2 June 1922; *educ* Leighton Park and St Edmund Hall Oxford (MA 1947); *m* 19 Aug 1950 *Pamela Martyn, dau of William Martyn Green, of New York, and has issue:

1i *Joanna Elizabeth; *b* 10 March 1953

2i *Philippa Carol; *b* 2 May 1956

2h *David Francis, ARIBA 1951, AADip 1951, DesRCA 1953, Sub-Lt RNVR WW II; *b* 9 June 1925; *educ* Leighton Park, Reading U, Architectural Assoc Sch and RCA London; *m* 1st 3 Aug 1957 (*divorce* 1968) Patricia Valerie, dau of Ewart Walter West James; *m* 2nd 2 March 1968 *Jennifer Anne-Mary, dau of Rev John Dickson Dalgleish, of Edinburgh, and by her had issue:

1i *Benedict John; *b* 10 June 1968

3h *Ronald Sydney; *b* 27 Oct 1927; *educ* privately

2g Francis Sydney, Capt 1st Bn Dorset Regt WW I (despatches); *b* 22 Dec 1893; *educ* Leighton Park and Trin Hall Cambridge (BA 1915); *ka* France 3 Oct 1918

3g Ernest Walter, slr, pres Berks, Bucks and Oxon Law Soc 1949–50; *b* 7 Sept 1903; *educ* Leighton Park; *m* 25 Sept 1929 Constance Hilary, dau of Alexander Hall Downes, of Totteridge, Herts, and had issue:

1h Anthony; *b* 3 April 1933; *educ* Leighton Park and St Edmund Hall Oxford (BA 1956); *m* 30 Dec 1958 *Ann Treasure, dau Dr William Bowen Owen, of Glam, and *d* 2 Jan 1971, leaving issue:

1i *Nicholas David; *b* 13 March 1960

2i *Guy William; *b* 28 Nov 1963

1i *Rachel Catherine; *b* 24 Dec 1961

1h *Anne; *b* 24 Aug 1930

1g Katharine Gertrude; *b* 9 Nov 1897

2g Helen Mary; *b* 8 Aug 1906; *m* 30 Dec 1933 Leslie Henry Stevens, son of Thomas Richard Stevens, of Reading, and had issue. He *d* 12 Oct 1962

The est son,

WALTER JOHN BRAIN, slr; *b* 7 Sept 1854; *educ* Christ's Hosp; *m* 1 Sept 1886 Edith Alice (*d* 23 April 1947, aged 83), dau of Charles Smith, JP, of Reading, and *d* 17 Oct 1927, leaving issue (with a dau Edith Dorothy, FLS; *b* 16 May 1899):

Sir (Walter) Russell Brain, 1st Bt, and **1st Baron Brain**, of Eynsham, Co Oxford, so *cr* 29 June 1954 and 26 Jan 1962 respectively (both UK); *educ* Mill Hill, New Coll Oxford (BA 1922, BM 1922, BCh 1922, MA 1925, DM 1925, Hon Fellow 1952) and London Hosp (FRCP Lond 1931, Hon FRCP Edin 1953, Ireland 1952, FACP 1954); Hon FRCS 1958, Hon DCL Durham, Hon LLD Wales, Belfast, Hon DSc Oxon, Manchester and Southampton, Hon MD Cairo, PRCP 1950–57, Physician London Hosp and Maida Vale Hosp for Nervous Diseases; Red Cross (Ambulance Unit) WW I, ktd 1952, FRS 1964; *b* 23 Oct 1895; *m* 8 Sept 1920 Stella (*d* 1993), er dau of Reginald Langdon Langdon-Down, MA, MB, ChB, of Broom Close, Teddington, Middx, and *d* 29 Dec 1966, leaving issue:

1 CHRISTOPHER LANGDON BRAIN, **2nd and present Baron Brain**

2 +MICHAEL COTTRELL [The Hon Michael Brain, 131 N Shore, Blvd E, Burlington, Ontario L7T4A4, Canada]; *b* 6 Aug 1928; heir presumptive; *educ* Leighton Pk and New Coll Oxford (BA 1950, BM, BCh, 1953, MA 1955, DM 1963); MRCP Lond 1955, FRCP Lond 1968, FRCP Canada, DTM and HEng 1958, DM 1963; Capt RAMC, Physician Hammersmith Hosp 1966–69, Assist Prof Medicine McMaster U Ontario 1969 (Prof 1976); *m* 10 Dec 1960 *Dr Hon Elizabeth Ann Herbert, MA, BM, BCh, est dau of Baron Tangley (LP), and has:

(1) +Thomas Russell; *b* 23 Oct 1965

(1) *Hilary Catherine; *b* 5 Sept 1961; *m* 1986 *Guido Dino de Luca

(2) *Philippa Harriet; *b* 1 Oct 1963; *m* 1991 *Armando Teves

1 *Janet Stella [The Hon Mrs Arthur, Royal Oak Cottage, Church Broughton, Derby]; *b* 30 Jan 1931; *educ* Surbiton High Sch; BA; *m* 27 Feb 1954 Leonard John Henry Arthur, MB, ChB (*d* 1983), only s of Rev John Sigismund Arthur (*see* ARTHUR, Bt), and has issue

Braine of Wheatley

Creation: B. (LP, UK) 1992.

THE BARON BRAINE OF WHEATLEY, of Rayleigh, Co Essex (Sir Bernard Richard Braine, PC (1985), DL (Essex 1978)) [The Rt Hon The Lord Braine of Wheatley PC DL, King's Wood, 67 Great Wheatley Rd, Rayleigh, Essex SS6 7AW]; *b* 24 June 1914; *educ* Hendon County GS; N Staffs Regt WW II Africa, NW Europe and SE Asia, Camberley Staff Coll, T/Lt-Col SEAC; MP (C) Billericay 1950–55, SE Essex 1955–83 and Castle Point 1983–92 (Father H of C 1987–92), Parly Sec Pensions and NI 1960–61, Parly Under-Sec Cwlth Rels 1961–62, Parly Sec Health 1962–64, Chm Parly Ctee Overseas Aid 1970–74, Dep-Chm Cwlth Parly Assoc 1963–64 and 1970–74, Chm Nat Cncl Alcohol 1974–82, Br-German Parly Gp 1970–92, Br-Greek Parly Group 1979–92, UK Chapter Soc Internat Devpt; Tstee 1981– and Govr Cwlth Inst 1968–81, Visiting Prof Baylor U Texas 1987–91; KStJ 1985, European Peace Medal 1979, Cdr Polonia Restituta (Polish Govt in Exile) 1983 (Grand Cross 1991), Kt Cdr Order Merit W Germany 1984, FRSA 1971, Kt Cdr St Gregory 1987, Grand Cdr Order Honour Greece 1987, ktd 1972; *m* 1935 Kathleen Mary (*d* 1982), dau of Herbert William Faun, of E Sheen, Surrey, and has:

1 *Richard Laurence; *b* 1939
2 *Michael Rodney; *b* 1942
3 *Brendan Timothy; *b* 1945

Lineage: ARTHUR ERNEST BRAINE, of Kew Gdns, Surrey; had:

BERNARD RICHARD, *cr* a **Baron**

Bramall

Creation: B. (LP, UK) 1987.

THE BARON BRAMALL, of Bushfield, Hants (Sir Edwin Noel Westby Bramall, KG (1990), GCB (1979, KCB 1974), OBE (1965), MC (1945), JP (London 1986)) [Field Marshal The Rt Hon The Lord Bramall KG GCB OBE MC JP, House of Lords, London SW1A 0PW]; *b* 18 Dec 1923; *educ* Eton; commnd KRRC 1943, served WW II NW Europe 1944-45, occupation of Japan 1946-47, Instr Sch of Inf 1949–51, psc 1952, Middle East 1953–58, Instr Army Staff Coll 1958–61, on Lord Mountbatten's staff with responsibility for reorganization MOD 1963–64, CO 2nd Green Jackets KRRC Malaysia 1965–66 and 5th Airportable Bde 1967–69, IDC 1970, GOC 1st Div BAOR 1971–73, Lt-Gen 1973, Cmdr Br Forces Hong Kong 1973–76, Gen 1976, C-in-C UK Land Forces 1976–78, V-Ch Def Staff 1978–79, CGS 1979–82, CDS 1982–85, ADC (Gen) to HM 1979–82, Col Comdt 3rd Bn RGJ 1973–84, Col 2nd Goorkhas 1976–, FM 1982, Ld Lt Gtr London 1986–, Tstee Imp War Museum 1983– (Chm 1989–), Pres: MCC 1988–89, London Playing Fields Assoc 1990–, OStJ London and Not Forgotten Assoc, KstJ 1986, jt author: *The Chiefs* (1993); *m* 1949 *Dorothy Avril Wentworth, only dau of Brig-Gen Henry Albemarle Vernon, DSO, of Stoke Bruerne Park, Northants, and has:

1 *Nicolas; *b* 1952; *m* 1976 (*divorce* 1986) Janet Livingston and has a s and dau
1 *Sara; *b* 1951; *m* 1987 *Dr Edwin R Bickerstaff

Lineage: Maj EDMUND HASELDON BRAMALL, RA, of 2 Symons St, Sloane Sq, SW3; *m* Katherine Bridget Westby and had:

EDWIN NOEL WESTBY, *cr* a **Baron**

Brandon of Oakbrook

Creation: B. (LP, UK) 1981.

THE BARON BRANDON OF OAKBROOK, of Hammersmith, Greater London (Henry Vivian Brandon, MC (1942), PC (1978)) [The Rt Hon The Lord Brandon of Oakbrook MC PC, 6 Thackeray Close, London SW19 4JL]; *b* 3 June 1920; *educ* Winchester and King's Coll Cambridge; served RA WW II UK, Madagascar, India and Burma (Maj 1944), barrister Inner Temple 1946, memb Bar Cncl 1951–53, QC 1961, High Court Judge Probate, Divorce and Admlty Div 1966–71, Judge Family Div and Admlty Court 1971–78, Judge Commercial Court 1977–78, Ld Justice of Appeal 1978–81, Ld of Appeal in Ordinary 1981–91, member panel Lloyd's arbitrators in salvage cases 1961–66 and panel Wreck Commrs 1963–66, ktd 1966; *m* 1955 *Jeanette Rosemary, dau of Julian Vivian Breeze Janvrin, and has:

1 *James Roderick Vivian [The Hon James Brandon, 50 Richmond Rd, London SW20 0PQ]; *b* 1956; LLB, ACA; *m* 1991 *Amelia Mary Hungerford, er dau of Maj Peter Hungerford Jackson (*see* JACKSON, Bt, of Arlsey)
2 *Richard Henry; *b* 1961; *m* 1988 *Jean Patricia, 2nd dau of R B Horsfield, of Eccles, Manchester
3 *William Roland; *b* 1964; *m* 1991 *Polly Jennifer, dau of Janos Nyiri
1 *Juliet Mary; *b* 1958; *m* 1978 *William Patrick Neill-Hall

Lineage: Capt VIVIAN RONALD BRANDON, CBE, RN, of Kensington, W8; *m* Joan Elizabeth Maud Simpson and had:

HENRY VIVIAN, *cr* a **Baron**

Brassey of Apethorpe

Arms: Quarterly, 1st, quarterly per fess indented sa. and arg., in the first quarter a mallard of the second, beaked and legged gu; 2nd, gu., in chief three mullets arg. and in base a dexter hand appaumée, couped at the wrist of the last; 3rd, sa. a chevron between three bull's heads cabossed arg.; 4th, arg. on a chevron gu. three trefoils, slipped of the field. **Crest:** A mallard as in the arms. **Supporters:** On either side a mallard, holding in the beak an ear of wheat, slipped and leaved ppr. **Motto:** *Arduis sæpe, metu nunquam* ('Often in difficulties, never in fear'). **Creations:** Bt. (UK) 22 Nov 1922, B. (UK) 26 Jan 1938.

THE 3RD BARON BRASSEY OF APETHORPE, of Apethorpe, Co Northampton, and a **Baronet** (Sir David Henry Brassey, Bt, OBE (1994), JP (Northants 1970), DL (Northants 1972)) [The Rt Hon The Lord Brassey OBE JP DL, The Manor House, Apethorpe, Peterborough PE8 5DL]; *b* 16 Sept 1932; *s f* 1967; *educ* Stowe; Maj Gren Gds (ret 1967); *m* 1st 15 Oct 1958 Myrna Elizabeth (*d* Nov 1974), only dau of Lt-Col John Baskervyle-Glegg, of 9 The Gateways, Chelsea, London SW3, and Withington Hall, Cheshire, and has issue:

1 +EDWARD; *b* 9 March 1964; *educ* Eton

The 3rd BARON *m* 2nd 17 Oct 1978 *Caroline, dau of Lt-Col Godfrey Ariel Evill, of Brynderwen, Chepstow, Gwent, and Dowager Lady Duntze (*qv*), of 55 Elm Park Gdns, London SW10, and has further issue:

1 *Zara; *b* 29 Feb 1980
2 *Chloe; *b* 26 Feb 1982

Lineage: RICHARD BRASSEY, of Brassey, Cheshire, descended from a Brassey who had married the heiress of the Bulkeley estates; *b c* 1595; *d* in or after 1663; ancestor through a cadet branch of:

JOHN BRASSEY, of Buerton, Cheshire; had an est s:

THOMAS BRASSEY, of Bulkeley and Lowndes Sq, London; *b* 7 Nov 1805; one of the most successful railway contractors of the 19th century; *m* 20 Dec 1831 Marie Farrington (*d* 3 Jan 1877), dau of Joseph Harrison, of Liverpool, and had issue:

1 THOMAS BRASSEY, 1st EARL BRASSEY, so *cr* 5 July 1911, as also VISCOUNT HYTHE OF HYTHE, Co Kent, and earlier 16 Aug 1886 BARON BRASSEY OF BULKELEY, Co Chester (all UK), GCB (1906, KCB 1881), DL, JP (Sussex), TD; *b* 11 Feb 1836; *educ* Rugby and Univ Coll Oxford (MA), Hon DCL Oxford, Hon LLD Dublin, barrister Lincoln's Inn 1864, MP (Lib) Devonport June-July 1865 and Hastings 1868–86, a Ld Admlty 1880–84, Govr Victoria 1895–1901, Hon Col 2nd Home Counties Bde RFA, 5th Bn Roy Sussex Regt, KStJ, Cdr Legion Honour, Grand Cross Order Crown Italy; *m* 1st 9 Oct 1860 Anna (*d* 14 Sept 1887), only child of John Allnutt, of Charles Street, London W, and had issue:

(1) THOMAS ALLNUTT BRASSEY, 2nd and last EARL BRASSEY, DL, JP (Sussex), TD; *b* 7 March 1863; *educ* Balliol Coll Oxford (MA, Hon Fell 1907), Hon DCL Oxford 1911, AMICE, MInstNA, Lt-Col W Kent Yeo, KStJ, Cdr Order Crown Italy; *m* 28 Feb 1889 Lady Idina Mary Nevill (*d* 21 Feb 1951), dau of 1st Marquess of Abergavenny (*qv*), and *dsp* 12 Nov 1919, when his titles expired

(1) Mabelle Annie, CBE (1918), LJStJ; *m* 17 April 1888 Charles Augustus Egerton, DL, JP, of Mountfield Court, Robertsbridge, Sussex, er son of Edward Christopher Egerton, MP (*see* 1956 edn EGERTON OF TATTON, B), and *d* 18 Feb 1927, leaving issue. He *d* 13 Oct 1912

(2) Constance Alberta; *d* 24 Jan 1873

(3) Muriel Agnes; *m* 4 Aug 1891 (*divorce* 1902) 8th Earl de la Warr (*qv*), and *d* 8 Aug 1930, leaving issue

(4) Marie Adelaide, CI (1917), GBE (1924), DJStJ, Order of Mercy, Kaisar-i-Hind Gold Medal; *m* 20 July 1892 1st Marquess of Willingdon, PC, GCSI, GCMG, GCIE, GBE (*see* 1970 edn), and *d* 30 Jan 1960, leaving issue. He *d* 12 Aug 1941

1 (cont.) The 1st EARL *m* 2nd 18 Sept 1890 Hon Sybil de Vere Capell (*d* 20 Feb 1934), dau of Viscount Malden (*see* ESSEX, E), and *d* 23 Feb 1918, having by her had issue:

(5) Helen de Vere; *b* 4 Sept 1892; *m* 16 Aug 1916 Lt-Col Sir John Murray, KCVO, DSO, TD, DL, of Folla, Rothienorman, Aberdeenshire, son of Sir John Murray, KCVO, DL, JP, FSA, and *d* 30 June 1971. He *d* 6 Oct 1967

2 John; *b* 1 June, *d* 16 June 1839

3 HENRY ARTHUR, of whom presently

4 Albert, of Heythrop, Oxon, and Charlton Park, Glos, JP, High Sheriff 1878, MP Banbury 1895–1906, Col QO Oxfordshire Yeo, formerly Lt 14th Hus; *b* 22 Feb 1844; *educ* Eton and Univ Coll Oxford; *m* 12 Jan 1871 Hon Matilda Maria Helena Bingham, OBE (*d* 16 July 1943), dau of 4th Baron Clanmorris (*qv*), and *d* 7 Jan 1918, having had issue:

(1) Robert Bingham, of Cottesbrooke Hall, Northants, DL, JP (Oxon 1919), Capt Res of Offrs 17th Lancers, MP Banbury Jan-Nov 1910; *b* 18 Oct 1875; *educ* Eton; *m* 1st 20 July 1904 Violet (*d* 9 March 1919), 2nd dau of Armar Henry Lowry-Corry (*see* BELMORE, E), and had issue:

1a Thomas; *b* 10, *d* 23 July 1905

2a Hugo Bulkely, Cdr RANVR WW II; *b* 5 March 1910, *educ* Eton and RMC Sandhurst; *m* 1st 27 July 1935 (*divorce* 1938) Baroness Christa von Bodenhausen; *m* 2nd Barbara (Bubbles) Frederica de Roll Peacocke (*m* 2nd 30 June 1965 Nicholas Francis Hirsch) and *d* 24 Dec 1963, leaving issue:

1b *Thomas Noel Bingham; *b* 21 April 1952

1b *Sarah Jane; *b* 11 March 1951; *m* 24 July 1975 *Timothy Christopher Hewitt, of 71 Cambridge St, SW1, son of Maj O D S Hewitt, RA, and has issue:

1c *Hugo George; *b* 10 Jan 1977

1a Moira Violet; *b* 23 Dec 1906; *m* 27 July 1928 (*divorce* 1940) John Edward O'Brien, later Sir John O'Brien, 5th Bt (*qv*), and *dsp* 10 Jan 1970

2a *Pamela Rachael; *b* 4 Dec 1911; *m* 20 Jan 1932 Capt Duncan Mackinnon, s of William Mackinnon, of Ballinakill, Argyllshire, and has issue (*see* ROCKLEY, B)

3a *Diana; *b* 7 July 1914; *m* 18 Jan 1938 Lt-Col Humphrey William Lloyd, JP, 2nd son of Brig-Gen Arthur Henry Orlando Lloyd, CB, CMG, MVO, TD, of Leaton Knolls, Shrewsbury, and has issue:

1b *John Humphrey; *b* 21 July 1940 *m* 11 July 1970 *Lucy Jane, 2nd dau of Keith Cameron, of Fifield House, Oxon

2b *David Arthur; *b* 25 Feb 1945; *m* 24 Aug 1968 *Jessica Jane, only dau of Brig Bryan John Fowler, DSO, of Rahinston, Enfield, Co Meath, and has issue:

1c *A son; *b* 17 July 1970

(1) (cont.) Robert Brassey *m* 2nd 16 March 1920 (*divorce* 1927) Dorothy Alice Margaret Augusta (*d* 11 Jan 1966), formerly w of 6th Earl of Rosebery (*qv*) and dau of Lord Henry George Grosvenor (*see* WESTMINSTER, D); *m* 3rd 8 Nov 1927 Mrs Constance Marion Bennett, dau of Thomas Britten, of Johannesburg, S Africa, and *d* 14 Nov 1946

(2) Percy Frederick, Lt 9th Lancers S African War; *b* 10 Dec 1876; *educ* Eton and New Coll Oxford, *ka* Kimberley 16 Feb 1901

(3) Ralph Albert; *b* 2 Oct 1883; *educ* Eton and New Coll Oxford; *d* unm 4 Dec 1905

(1) Lilian Maude; *b* 20 Oct 1871; *m* 6 Dec 1899 Maj Richard Alexander Scott, Queen's Bays, 2nd s of Capt William Scott, of Charlton Place, Bishopsbourne, and *d* 31 Aug 1952, leaving issue. He *d* 20 Sept 1942

(2) Rose Zara Maria; *m* 2 May 1896 Maj Denis St George Daly, DL, JP, of Over Norton Park, Chipping Norton, Oxon, and *d* 21 Jan 1949, leaving issue. He *d* 16 April 1942

(3) May Eleanor Annie; *m* 2 March 1905 Robert Kenrick Price, DL, JP, of Rhiwlas and Rhiwaedog, Merionethshire, and *d* May 1941, leaving issue. He *d* 19 July 1927

(4) Violet Catherine, MBE (1949); *m* 18 Oct 1906 John Peter Arkwright, JP, 2nd son of John Thomas Arkwright, DL, JP, of Hatton House, Warwicks, and *d* 20 Feb 1963, leaving issue. He *d* 18 Nov 1931

(5) Iris Hermione; *b* 10 Nov 1880; *m* 7 July 1903 Brig-Gen Malcolm Orme Little, CB, CBE, 9th Lancers, 2nd s of Gen Sir Archibald Little, GCB, and *d* 6 Aug 1970, leaving issue. He *d* 1 Feb 1931

THOMAS BRASSEY *d* 8 Dec 1870. His 3rd son,

HENRY ARTHUR BRASSEY, of Preston Hall, DL, JP, MA Oxon, MP Sandwich 1868–85, High Sheriff 1890; *b* 14 July 1840; *m* 24 June 1866 Anna Harriet (*d* 15 July 1898), dau of Maj George Robert Stevenson, of Tongswood, Hawkhurst, Kent, late 7th Dragoon Gds, and *d* 13 May 1891, having had issue:

1 Arthur Albert; *b* 4 March 1868; *d* 1 Jan 1869

2 (HENRY) LEONARD CAMPBELL (Sir), **1st Bt**, and **1st Baron**

3 Harold Ernest, Maj, T/Lt-Col RHG; *b* 29 March 1877; *m* 25 July 1906 Lady Norah Hely-Hutchinson (*m* 2nd 27 Aug 1917 (*divorce* 1934) Maj Alan Charles Douglas Graham, MC; *m* 3rd 9 Oct 1935 Geoffrey Wilfred Melson Smith (*d* 1 Jan 1949); *d* 2 Aug 1964), 3rd dau of 5th Earl of Donoughmore (*qv*), and was *ka* 16 July 1916, leaving issue:

(1) Oonagh Evelyn; *m* 1st 14 Jan 1929 (*divorce* 1948) Lt-Col Hon Michael Thomas Henderson, 16/15th Lancers (Reserve), 2nd son of Lt-Col Hon Harold Greenwood Henderson, CVO, and had issue (*see* FARINGDON, B); *m* 2nd 21 Dec 1949 (*divorce* 1962) Vernon Motion

(2) *Honora Mary, BEM (1943)

(3) *Nancy Elizabeth; *m* 1st 16 July 1935 S/Ldr Reginald Frederick Stuart Leslie, DSC, DFC, AFC, RAF (*ka* 1943); *m* 2nd 25 July 1945 William Anthony Younger, er son of Sir William Robert Younger, 2nd Bt (*qv*)

4 Edgar Hugh, MVO, Lt-Col 1st Life Gds, High Sheriff Wilts 1927; *b* 6 April 1878; *m* 26 Jan 1911 Margaret Harriet (*d* 2 Nov 1966), yst of dau of Col Hon Walter Trefusis, CB (*see* CLINTON, B), and *d* 11 April 1946, leaving:

(1) *Hugh Trefusis (Sir), KCVO (1985), OBE (1959), MC (1944), JP (Wilts 1951), Wilts: High Sheriff 1959, Ld Lt 1981 (V-Lt 1968–81, DL 1955–68), Lt-Col Roy Wilts Yeo 1955–58, Brevet Col formerly Maj The Scots Greys, served WW II (Croix de Guerre), Yeomen of the Guard: Exon 1964–70, Ensign 1970–79, Lt 1979–85 and Adj and Clerk Cheque 1971, ADC (TA) to HM THE QUEEN 1964–69, chm Chippenham Cons Assoc 1951–53 and 1966–68, pres 1968, pres Wilts Assoc Boys' Clubs; *b* 5 Oct 1915; *educ* Eton and RMC; *m* 18 July 1939 *Joyce Patricia, dau of Capt Maurice John Kingscote, Berks Yeo, of Kingscote, Tetbury, Glos, and *d* 199–, having had issue:

1a *Antony Hugh Owen [Antony Brassey Esq, The Manor Farm, Little Somerford, Chippenham, Wilts], served Roy Scots Greys 1964–67; *b* 5 Jan 1945; *educ* Eton

2a *Kim Maurice; *b* 27 March 1955

1a Fiona Gillian; *b* 31 Jan 1942; *d* 26 Feb 1958

2a *Jane Margaret [Mrs John Rogers, Riverhill, Sevenoaks, Kent]; *b* 8 May 1946; *m* 5 May 1971 *John Morrison Rogers, and has issue:

1b *A son; *b* 10 May 1974

2b *A son; *b* 2 July 1976

3a *Sarah Patricia; *b* 20 July 1949; *m* 15 Sept 1973 *Walon Charles Green, son of Walon Wilbur Green, of Hot Springs, Arkansas, USA

(1) *Marjorie Eva; *m* 22 Feb 1933 Hugh Myddelton Peacock, only dau of Hugh Peacock, of Greatford, Lincs, and has issue:

1a *Michael Hugh, late 2nd Lt Coldstream Gds; *b* 2 Aug 1946; *educ* Eton

1a *Idina Caroline; *b* 23 Nov 1933; *m* 27 Sept 1957 Capt James William Gordon Pirie, late 60th Rifles, son of Lt-Col G M Pirie, and has issue:

1b *James Hugh; *b* 15 Dec 1959

1b *Amanda Caroline; *b* 10 June 1962

2a *Susan Margaret; *b* 14 June 1938; *m* 15 Sept 1964 Michael Andrieus Jones, and has issue:

1b *Philip Andrieus; *b* 19 Jan 1966

1b *Idina Maria; *b* 8 Jan 1968

5 Edwin Perceval, DSO (1919), MC, DL (Glos 1956), High Sheriff Glos 1946, Lt-Col Coldstream Gds (SR), Capt 7th Queen's Own Hus, Jt MFH Heythrop 1925–36; *b* 2 Oct 1882; *educ* Eton and RMC Sandhurst; *d* unm 15 March 1973

1 Ethel Anna Maria; *d* 23 April 1880

2 Florence Maud; *d* 15 June 1875

3 Hilda Madeline, DBE (1946, CBE), JP Sussex and Morayshire, v-pres SSAFA; *b* 16 June 1872; *m* 8 June 1893 8th Duke of Richmond and Gordon (*qv*) and *d* 29 Dec 1971, leaving issue

4 Evelyn Mildred; *m* 3 Feb 1894 Granville Charles Gresham Leveson-Gower, DL, JP, of Titsey Place, Limpsfield, and *d* 18 April 1957, leaving issue (*see* SUTHERLAND, D)

5 Gwendoline; *m* 27 May 1902 Col Philip Blencowe Cookson, CMG, OBE, of Meldon Park, Morpeth, and *d* 26 July 1947, leaving issue. He *d* 27 Feb 1928

6 Beatrice Mary; *b* 20 April 1899 Thomas Stacey, JP, yr son of John Thomas Cyril Stacey, of Southam-de-la-Bere, Cheltenham, and *d* 24 March 1951, leaving issue. He *d* 2 April 1940

7 Ruby Mabelle; *m* 22 July 1911 Lt-Col William Gibbs, CVO, late 7th Hus, son of Antony Gibbs, of Tyntesfield, Somerset (*see* ALDENHAM and HUNSDON OF HUNSDON, B), and had issue

The est surv son,

Sir Henry Leonard Campbell Brassey, 1st Bt, and **1st Baron Brassey of Apethorpe**, of Apethorpe, Co Northampton, so *cr* 29 Nov 1922 and 26 Jan 1938 respectively (both UK), DL (Northants), JP (Kent and Northants), High Sheriff 1907, MP N Northampton 1910–18 and Peterborough 1918–29, Maj Northants Yeo and W Kent Yeo Cav; *b* 7 March 1870; *m* 30 June 1894 Lady Violet Mary Gordon-Lennox (*d* 19 Nov 1946), 2nd dau of 7th Duke of Richmond and Gordon (*qv*), and had issue:

1 Ronald Henry; *b* 21, *d* 29 May 1895

2 Cecil Henry, JP (Wilts), Capt Res Offrs Life Gds; *b* 3 Oct 1896; *m* 10 Nov 1920 Hon Victoria Ivy Louise Spencer, est dau of 1st Viscount Churchill (*qv*), and *dsp* 11 Sept 1949

3 Gerard Charles, Lt Coldstream Gds; *b* 28 Dec 1898; *ka* 27 Aug 1918

4 John Leonard; *b* 1903; *d* 9 March 1903

5 BERNARD THOMAS, **2nd Baron**

6 Peter Esmé, JP (Peterborough 1947), DL (Northants 1961–67, Hunts and Peterborough 1965); *b* 5 Dec 1907; *educ* Eton and Magdalene Coll Cambridge; High Sheriff Hunts and Peterborough 1966, barrister Inner Temple 1930, Lt-Col Northants Yeo, Ld Lt Cambs 1975–81, served WW II (wounded), chm Southend Waterworks Co; *m* 12 Dec 1944 *Lady Romayne Elizabeth Algitha Cecil, yr dau of 5th Marquess of Exeter (*qv*), and *d* 14 March 1995, leaving:

(1) +Henry Charles [Henry Brassey Esq, Close House, Barnack, Stamford, Lincs PE9 3DY]; *b* 22 July 1947; *educ* Milton Abbey; *m* 1972 *Linda, dau of Geoffrey C Pinnock, of Fern Cottage, Ripley, Surrey, and has issue:

1a +Thomas Charles; *b* 1974

1a *Elizabeth Jane; *b* 1978

(2) +Richard Edwin [Richard Brassey Esq, 116 Lots Rd, London SW6]; *b* 8 Oct 1949; *educ* Eton; *m* 1st 4 June 1971 (*divorce* 1979) Tania Duckworth, dau of Norman William Duckworth, and has issue:

1a *Pikka (a dau); *b* 1973

(2) Richard Brassey *m* 2nd 1986 *Pamina, dau of Robert Caruso, of New York, and has further issue:

1a +George Peter; *b* 1987

(1) *Rowena Jane, LVO (1974) [Mrs Andrew Feilden LVO, The Old Manor House, Minster Lovell, Oxon]; *b* 6 Nov 1945; Ldy-in-Waiting to HRH THE PRINCESS ROYAL 1970–; *m* 16 April 1977 *Andrew James Feilden, yr surv son of Maj-Gen Sir Randle Guy Feilden, KCVO, CBE, DL (*see* HAMPDEN, V)

The 1st BARON *d* 22 Oct 1958; his er surv son,

BERNARD THOMAS BRASSEY, **2nd Baron Brassey of Apethorpe**, MC (1945), TD (1945), DL (Northants 1958); *educ* Eton; Lt-Col Leics Yeo (TA), formerly RHG, WW II (wounded), Hon Col Leicester and Derbyshire Yeo; *b* 15 Feb 1905; *m* 1st 14 April 1931 Crystal Gloria (*d* 15 March 1962), yr dau of Lt-Col Francis William George Gore (*see* TEMPLE OF STOWE, E), and had issue:

1 DAVID HENRY BRASSEY, **3rd and present Baron Brassey of Apethorpe**

2 +Thomas Ian [The Hon Thomas Brassey, The Coach House, Duncote, Northants NN12 8AQ]; *b* 14 June 1934; *educ* Stowe; Lt Gren Gds 1952–57; *m* 28 Sept 1960 *Valerie Christine, only dau of Alan David Finlason, and of Mrs

Frederick Francis Powell, of Pennymarsh, Abbotts Ann, Andover, Hants, and has issue:

(1) +(Thomas) Hugh; *b* 20 Oct 1971; *m* 2 May 1998 *Leonie, dau of Allan Boardman, of NSW

(1) *Miranda; *b* 25 Feb 1963; *m* 4 June 1988 *Andrew Robinson Rawlin, est son of Dr Michael Rawlin, of N Anston, Sheffield, Yorks, and has issue:

1a *William Bradbury; *b* 1994

1a *Alexandra Catherine; *b* 25 Aug 1996

(2) *Louise; *b* 27 Oct 1964; *m* 19 Dec 1995 *Jeremy Wilkins, s of Denis Wilkins, of Amsbury Croft, Hunton, Kent

(3) *Davina Christine; *b* 24 Sept 1969; *m* 30 April 1994 *Christopher Robert Merriman, yst son of Patrick Merriman, of Rearsby House, Rearsby, Leics, and has:

1a *Harriet Charlotte Nell; *b* 13 May 1997

The **2nd Baron** *m* 2nd 4 April 1963 *Barbara [The Rt Hon Barbara Lady Brassey of Apethorpe, 23 Bull Lane, Ketton, Stamford, Lincs], yr dau of Leonard Jorgensen, of W Tytherley, and formerly w of Lt-Col Herbert Campbell Westmorland, DSO, MC, and *d* 28 June 1967

BRAYBROOKE

Arms: Quarterly, 1st and 4th, gu., on a saltire arg. a rose of the field, seeded and barbed ppr.; 2nd and 3rd, or fretty gu., on a canton of the first a lymphad sa. **Crest:** A bull statant arg., pied sa., collared and chained or. **Supporters:** Two lions rampant regardant arg., maned and tufted sa., gorged with a chaplet of olive vert. **Motto:** *Ne vile velis* ('Incline to nothing base'). **Creation:** B. (GB) 5 Sept 1788.

THE 10TH LORD BRAYBROOKE, BARON OF BRAYBROOKE, Co Northampton (Robin Henry Charles Neville) [The Rt Hon The Lord Braybrooke, Abbey House, Audley End, Saffron Walden, Essex CB11 4JB]; *b* 29 Jan 1932; *s f* 1990; *educ* Eton, Magdalene Coll Cambridge (BA 1955, MA 1961) and RAC Cirencester; farmer and landowner, Ld Lt Essex 1992– (DL 1980–92), commnd Rifle Bde 1951 (served 3rd Bn KAR Kenya and Malaya 1951–52), dir Essex and Suffolk Insur, memb Saffron Walden RDC 1959–69, CC Essex 1969–72, memb cncl CLA 1965–83, chm: Price Tst 1983–95, Rural Devpt Commn Essex 1984–90, Hereditary Visitor Magdalene Coll Cambridge; *m* 1st 29 July 1955 (*divorce* 1974) Robin Helen, dau of Thomas Adolph Brockhoff, of Rose Bay, Sydney, NSW, and has had issue:

1 *Amanda Muriel Mary; *b* 8 April 1962; *m* 14 Oct 1989 *Stephen Christopher Jerningham Murray, only s of Christopher Mark Henry Murray, of La Glinette, St Aubin, Jersey, and Mrs Michael P Wyndham, and has issue:

(1) *Alexander Henry Jerningham; *b* 24 May 1992

(1) *Isabella Henrietta Laura; *b* 20 June 1994

2 *Caroline Emma; *b* 28 Dec 1963; *m* 21 Oct 1995 *19th Earl of Derby (*qv*) and has issue

3 Henrietta Jane; *b* 21 July 1965; *d* 16 Dec 1980

4 *Victoria; *b* 20 May 1970; *m* 6 May 1995 *Edward Bromet, s of John Bromet, of Wighill, N Yorks

5 *Arabella (twin); *b* 20 May 1970

The 10th BARON *m* 2nd 19 March 1974 (*divorce* April 1998) Linda, dau of Arthur Norman, barber, of Saffron Walden, and by her has:

6 *Sara Lucy; *b* 1 April 1975

7 *Emma Charlotte; *b* 9 June 1979

8 *Lucinda Octavia; *b* 2 Aug 1984

Lineage: RICHARD NEVILL(E), of Billingbere (*see* ABERGAVENNY, M); *m* Anne, dau of Sir John Heydon, and *d* 1676, having had, with other issue:

1 RICHARD; *m* Katherine, dau of 2nd Baron Grey of Warke, and had issue (with an er son, *dsp*):

(1) Henry NEVILL(E) later GREY, *m* his cousin Elizabeth (*m* 2nd 1st Earl of Portsmouth (*qv*)), sis and coheir of 3rd Baron Griffin of Braybrooke (*see* below), and *dsp* 1740

(1) CATHERINE; *m* Richard Aldworth and *d* 1720, leaving issue:

1a RICHARD ALDWORTH later NEVILLE; *m* Magdalen, dau of Francis Calendrini, of Geneva, and *d* 1793, leaving issue:

1b RICHARD ALDWORTH later NEVILLE, **2nd Baron**

1 Anne; *b* 14 Feb 1647; *m* Richard Raynsford, est s of Sir Richard Raynsford, of Dallington, Northants, Ld Ch Justice Court King's Bench 1676–78, and *d* 1700, leaving an only dau and heiress:

(1) ANN; *m* 1684 2nd Baron Griffin of Braybrooke (*b* 1667; *d* 1715) and *d* 1707, having had issue:

1a EDWARD GRIFFIN, 3rd BARON GRIFFIN OF BRAYBROOKE; *b* 1693; *dsp* 1742 when the Barony expired and his property passed to his sisters as coheirs

1a Elizabeth; *m* 1st her cousin Henry NEVILLE/GREY (*see* above); *m* 2nd 1st Earl of Portsmouth; *dsp* 1762

2a Anne; *m* 1717 William Whitwell, of Oundle, Northants, and eventually became sole heiress of the Barons Griffin of Braybrooke; *d* 1770, leaving:

1b JOHN GRIFFIN WHITWELL later GRIFFIN, **1st Lord Braybrooke, Baron of Braybrooke** Co Northampton; so *cr* 5 Sept 1788, with remainder in default of his own male issue to his 3rd cousin Richard (Aldworth later Neville; *see* above) and 4th Baron Howard de Walden (*qv*), KB (1761); *b* 1719; on inheriting his aunt the Countess of Portsmouth's share in the Saffron Walden estate took by Act of Parl 1749 the surname and arms of GRIFFIN, LORD BRAYBROOKE, BARON OF BRAYBROOKE; *dsp* 25 May 1797, when the Barony of Howard de Walden fell into abeyance and that of Braybrooke passed to:

RICHARD ALDWORTH later NEVILLE, alternatively ALDWORTH-NEVILLE, later GRIFFIN, **2nd Lord Braybrooke, Baron of Braybrooke**; *b* 3 July 1750; *educ* Merton Coll Oxford; MP (Tory to 1780, pro-Grenville or Pittite 1780–1797) Grampound 1774–80, Buckingham 1780–82 and Reading 1782–97, took 27 July 1797 surname and arms of GRIFFIN for himself and his successors in the Griffin estate (from the ownership of which the Lords Braybrooke derive their position as Hereditary Visitors of Magdalene Coll Cambridge), Ld Lt and V-Adml Essex, Provost-Marshal Jamaica, Recorder Saffron Walden, High Steward Wokingham; *m* 19 June 1780 Catharine (*d* 6 Nov 1796), yst dau of Rt Hon George Grenville, and sis of 1st Marquess of Buckingham, and had, with other issue:

1 RICHARD, **3rd Baron**

2 Henry, Capt Dragoons; *d* Spain 1809 after Battle of Talavera

3 George NEVILLE later NEVILLE GRENVILLE (Very Rev), of Butleigh Court, Somerset, MA, Master Magdalene Coll Cambridge, Dean Windsor, Chaplain-in-Ordinary to HM QUEEN VICTORIA; *b* 17 Aug 1789; added name GRENVILLE 1825 under the will of his kinsman Lord Glastonbury; *m* 9 May 1816 Lady Charlotte Legge (*d* 15 June 1877), dau of 3rd Earl of Dartmouth (*qv*), and *d* 10 June 1854, leaving with other issue (*see* ST- JOHN-MILDMAY, Bt):

(1) Ralph, of Butleigh Court, MP Mid-Somerset 1868–78; *b* 27 Feb 1917; *m* 18 Sept 1845 Julia Roberta (*d* 17 Oct 1892), dau of Sir Robert Frankland Russell, 7th Bt, and *d* 20 Aug 1886, leaving issue:

1a Robert, of Butleigh Court, DL, JP, CA Somerset, High Sheriff 1900, CE; *b* 16 Dec 1846; *educ* Magdalene Coll Cambridge (MA); *m* 24 April 1879 Gertrude Agnes (*d* 18 Aug 1936), 6th dau of Rev Fitzhardinge Berkeley Portman, Rector Staple Fitzpaine (*see* PORTMAN, V), and *d* 13 Sept 1936

2a George NEVILLE (Sir), KCB (1909), CVO (1905), Adml cmdg 3rd and 4th Divs Home Fleet 1909–11, ADC to HM EDWARD VII 1903–04, Offr Legion Honour, 2nd Cl Rising Sun Japan, Orange Nassau Order; *b* 18 March 1850; *m* 9 Nov 1886 Fairlie Florence (*d* 3 Sept 1960), dau of David Lloyd-Jones, of Llandovery, Carmarths, and Victoria, Australia, and *d* 5Feb 1923, leaving issue:

1b Ralph, Cdr RN; *b* 4 Sept 1887; *m* 6 June 1918 Hon Lettice Cary (*d* 19 Dec 1963) (who *m* 2nd 26 Jan 1937 Maj Philip John Sherwin Pearson-Gregory, MC (*d* 12 June 1955)), dau of 12th Viscount Falkland (*qv*), and *d* 4 Aug 1936, leaving issue:

1c +Richard; *b* 14 March 1922; *m* 21 Oct 1960 *Pauline, formerly w of Michael Forrester and only dau of Rev Canon James Atherton Fisher, MA, JP, of 36 Leonard Court, London W8

1c Monica; *m* 1st 11 Jan 1939 (*divorce* 1946) Maj Peter Holdsworth Hunt, MC, Coldstream Gds, s of Holdsworth Hunt, of Little Berkhamsted, Herts, and had issue; *m* 2nd 29 April 1948 (*divorce* 1955) Robert Maxtone Inglis; *m* 3rd 12 May 1955 Lt-Col Viscount Anson, Gren Gds (*d* 18 March 1958), er son of 4th Earl of Lichfield (*qv*); *m* 4th 29 July 1959 (*divorce* 1967) Lt-Col Eric Astley Cooper-Key, MBE, MC, Roy Norfolk Regt, only son of Capt Astley Dundas Cooper Cooper-Key, DSO, RN, and *d* 8 Nov 1969

2b Philip Lloyd, CVO (1954); *b* 7 Oct 1888; Capt RN, Gentleman Usher to TM GEORGE VI 1937–52 and THE QUEEN 1952–67, Extra Gentleman Usher 1967–76, served WWs I and II; *m* 25 April 1942 Eleanor (*d* 1972), dau of Duncan Campbell Fellowes, of Toronto, Canada, and *d* 23 Aug 1976, leaving issue:

1c +GEORGE [George Neville Esq, 4A Belvedere Grove, London SW19 7RL]; *b* 23 March 1943; heir presumptive; *educ* Eton; *m* 1972 *Patricia Quinn, dau of Patrick Quinn, and has issue:

1d +Richard Ralph; *b* 1977

1d *Eleanor Anne; *b* 1975

2c +John [John Neville Esq, Welgoer, Poyntington, Sherborne, Dorset]; *b* 26 Sept 1944; *educ* Eton and McGill U (MBA 1971); *m* 1980 *Frances Jane, dau of John Stuart Lomax, and has issue:

1d +Edward Grey; *b* 1982

1d *Cicely Georgia; *b* 1984

3b Alfred Geoffrey, CBE (1944), MC, JP, DL; *b* 27 Jan 1891; Brig RA, Mil Assist to CIGS, Assist Mil Attaché Paris; *m* 1 May 1922 Philippa (*d* 1981), only dau of V-Adml Sir George Hope, KCB, KCMG (*see* LINITHGOW, M), and *d* 3 March 1955, leaving issue:

1c *Caroline Philippa [Mrs Andrew Crawshaw, The Manor House, Fowlmere, Herts SG8 7SJ; Belvedere, La Haule, St Brelade, Jersey JE3 8BY]; *b* 25 July 1935; *m* 1st 15 Dec 1960 Sir Gerard Robert Henry Sigismund Newman, 3rd Bt, of Cecil Lodge, Newmarket (*qv*), and has issue; *m* 2nd 17 July 1996 *Andrew F B Crawshaw

3a Hugh, barrister; *b* 9 June 1851; *educ* Magdalene Coll Cambridge (MA); *d* 30 June 1938

4a Louis; *b* 29 July 1852; *m* 25 Feb 1879 Ada Isabel (*m* 2nd 27 Oct 1924 Capt William Henry Darley Livingstone, DL, JP, s of Henry Darley Livingstone, JP, of Belclare, Westport, Co Mayo, and *d* 18 Aug 1929), est dau of J T Rouse, of Lyttelton, NZ, and *d* 7 May 1919, leaving issue:

1b Bertram; *b* 20 Jan 1880; Lt RMLI, Cape Mounted Rifles and RFA, served S African War and WW I; *m* 11 Oct 1919 Gertrude, dau of Matthew Thompson, of Newport, Mon, and *d* 5 April 1950, leaving issue:

1c *Edith Beryl [Mrs Derek Rands, 51 Wychwood Ave, Luton, Beds]; *b* 16 March 1925; *m* 30 Oct 1954 *Derek George Rands and has issue:

1d *Margaret Elizabeth; *b* 1957

2d *Pauline Jane; *b* 1961

2c *Margaret Roberta

5a Claud; *b* 6 June 1858; *educ* Eton; *m* 12 June 1897 Frances Cromwell (*d* 9 April 1959 aged 93), dau of Col Sir William Adolphus Frankland, 9th Bt (*see* ZOUCHE, B), and *d* 15 Jan 1944, leaving issue:

1b +Edward, JP (Somerset 1952), Cdr RN WW II, Naval Attaché The Hague and Brussels 1947–49; *b* 1 Nov 1904; *educ* RNCs Osborne and Darmouth; *m* 30 Jan 1960 *Gabrielle Naomi Helen, formerly w of Kenneth William Vandy and 2nd dau of Ellis Taylor Collins, of Chislehurst, Kent

6a Percy; *b* 24 Aug 1868; *d* unm 23 Aug 1917

1a Agnes Magdalene; *m* 7 Aug 1878 William James Maitland, CIE, and *d* 30 Oct 1908, leaving issue (*see* MAITLAND, Bt)

2a Beatrice; *d* unm 10 April 1926

3a Etheldreda; *m* 23 Sept 1885 Adml Robert Wilbraham Stopford and *d* 20 June 1938, leaving issue (*see* COURTOWN, E)

(2) William Frederick (Rev), Vicar Butleigh, Somerset, Preb Wells, RD; *b* 3 July 1818; *m* 26 Jan 1847 Fanny Grace (*d* 27 Sept 1908), dau of William Blackwood, and *d* 18 April 1882, having had, with other issue:

1a William (Rev), Rector E Knoyle, Wilts, 1912–32; *b* 11 July 1850; *educ* Magdalen Coll Oxford (MA); *m* 7 Nov 1894 Muriel (*d* 25 Nov 1951), dau of Gen Edward Arthur Somerset, CB (*see* BEAUFORT D), and *d* 27 June 1939

The 2nd BARON *d* 28 Feb 1825; his son,

RICHARD GRIFFIN, **3rd Lord Braybrooke Baron of Braybrooke**, DCL, FSA, High Steward Wokingham; *b* 26 Sept 1783; *educ* Eton and Ch Ch Oxford; MP (Whig) Thirsk 1805–06, Saltash Feb-April 1807, Buckingham 1807–12 and Berks 1812–25, ed *Pepys' Diary* (1825), author: *The History of Audley End and Saffron Walden* (1835) and *The Life of Jane, Lady Cornwallis* (1842); *m* 13 May 1819 Jane (*d* 23 Sept 1856), dau of 2nd Marquess Cornwallis, and *d* 13 March 1858, having had issue (who all took the surname NEVILLE only), with three daus:

1 RICHARD CORNWALLIS GRIFFIN later NEVILLE, **4th Lord Braybrooke Baron of Braybrooke**; *b* 17 March 1820; *educ* Eton; army offr, antiquarian author; *m* 27 Jan 1852 Lady Charlotte Sarah Graham-Toler (*m* 2nd 6 Nov 1862 Frederick Hetley, MD, of Upper Norwood, and *d* 4 Feb 1867), dau of 2nd Earl of Norbury (*qv*), and dspm 21 Feb 1861, having had two daus

2 CHARLES CORNWALLIS GRIFFIN later NEVILLE, **5th Lord Braybrooke, Baron of Braybrooke**, High Steward Wokingham, V-Lt and DL and JP Essex; *b* 29 Aug 1823; *educ* Magdalene Coll Cambridge (MA); *m* 9 Oct 1849 Hon Florence Priscilla Alicia Maude (*d* March 1914), 3rd dau of 3rd Viscount Hawarden (*qv*), and had:

(1) Augusta; *b* 19 Jan 1850; *m* 24 April 1879 Hon Richard Strutt, 2nd surv son of 2nd Baron Rayleigh (*qv*), and *d* 23 Jan 1903, leaving issue

3 Henry Aldworth, Capt Gren Gds; *b* 26 Oct 1824; *ka* Inkerman 5 Nov 1854

4 LATIMER, **6th Baron**

5 Grey, 5th Dragoon Gds; *b* 15 Oct 1830; *d* 11 Nov 1854 of wounds recd at Balaclava

The 5th BARON *d* 7 June 1902; his bro,

LATIMER GRIFFIN later NEVILLE, **6th Lord Braybrooke, Baron of Braybrooke**, MA Cantab, Master Magdalene Coll Cambridge, Rector Heydon with Little Chisall, Hon Canon St Albans; *b* 22 April 1827; *m* 2 June 1853 Lucy Frances Le Marchant (*d* 4 Dec 1918), dau of John Le Marchant Thomas Le Marchant, and *d* 12 Jan 1904, leaving:

1 HENRY NEVILLE, **7th Lord Braybrooke, Baron of Braybrooke**, DL (Cambs), JP (Cambs, Essex and Herts); *educ* Magdalene Coll Cambridge (MA); *b* 11 July 1855; *m* 1st 3 Nov 1898 Emilie Pauline (*dsp* 20 Oct 1912), yst dau of Antoine Gonin, of Macon, France; *m* 2nd 18 Sept 1917 Dorothy Edith, JP (Saffron Walden 1931, Essex 1934; *d* 10 Oct 1973), yst dau of Sir George Lawson, KCB, and *d* 9 March 1941, having by her had issue:

(1) RICHARD HENRY CORNWALLIS NEVILLE, **8th Lord Braybrooke, Baron of Braybrooke**, Lt Gren Gds WW II; *b* 13 July 1918; *ka* 23 Jan 1943

(2) George Robert Latimer, Ordinary Seaman RN WW II; *b* 20 June 1920; *kas* 12 Aug 1941

(1) *Catherine Dorothy [The Hon Mrs Ruck, Asherne, Strete, Dartmouth, Devon]; *b* 21 Jan 1922; *m* 19 June 1954 Gordon Alexander Egerton Ruck (*d* 1977), only s of Maj John Egerton Ruck, Gloucestershire Regt, of The Delles, Gt Chesterford, Essex, and has issue:

1a *Louise Dorothy Catherine; *b* 21 Dec 1959; *m* 1992 *Richard Claude Newman (*see* NEWMAN, Bt, of Mamhead)

2 Grey (Rev), Rector Bluntisham, Hunts, 1917–20; *b* 4 Dec 1857; *educ* Magdalene Coll Cambridge (MA); *m* 4 Sept 1889 Mary Peele (*d* 30 April 1943), dau of Rev Canon Francis Slater, Vicar St Giles's, Cambridge, and *d* 28 Dec 1920, leaving issue (the yr s and daus being granted rank of a baron's dau/yr s March 1944):

(1) HENRY SEYMOUR, **9th Baron**

(2) Grey Aldworth, Cdr RN, served WWs I and II; *b* 20 Sept 1900; *educ* RNC Dartmouth; *m* 8 Feb 1930 Margaret Emily Cortlandt, er dau of Rev Henry Cortlandt Stokes, of Elmdene, Sandown, IoW

(1) Magdalene Grace; *b* 15 Aug 1890; *d* unm 13 Dec 1960

(2) Evelyn; *b* 5 Sept 1891 *d* unm 7 Feb 1975

(3) Mirabel Mary; *b* 28 Aug 1893; *d* unm 20 May 1958

(4) Audrey; *b* 15 Jan 1895

(5) Cicely; *b* 18 June 1898

1 Alice Mirabel Cornwallis; *b* 25 Dec 1869; *d* 23 Sept 1937

The 8th BARON's cousin,

HENRY SEYMOUR NEVILLE, **9th Lord Braybrooke, Baron of Braybrooke**, DL (Essex 1950), JP (Essex 1953), Staff Capt RAF, served WW I in RNAS and RAF; *b* 5 Feb 1897; *educ* Shrewsbury, Magdalene Coll Cambridge (Hon MA 1948); *m* 1st 1 March 1930 Muriel Evelyn (*d* 16 June 1962), dau of William Charles Manning, of Newmarket, and widow of Euan Curle Cartwright; *m* 2nd 2 Sept 1963 Angela Mary (*d* 1985), dau of William Herbert Hollis, of Wadhurst, Sussex, and widow of John Ree, and *d* 1990, having had issue by his 1st w:

1 ROBIN HENRY CHARLES NEVILLE, **10th and present Lord Braybrooke, Baron of Braybrooke**

BRAYE

Arms: Quarterly, 1st and 4th, az. fretty arg. (for CAVE); 2nd and 3rd, az., on a cross arg. five mullets gu. (for VERNEY). **Supporters:** On either side a lion guardant or, winged vair az. and arg. **Motto:** *Gardez* ('Beware'). **Creation:** B. (E) 9 Aug 1529.

BARONESS BRAYE ((Mary) Penelope Verney-Cave, JP (S Northants 1981)) [The Rt Hon The Lady Braye JP, Stanford Hall, Lutterworth, Leics LE17 6DH]; *b* 28 Sept 1941; *s f* 1985; *educ* Assumption Convent, Hengrave Hall and Warwick U; High Sheriff Northants 1983; govr: St Andrew's Hosp Northampton 1978–, Three Shires Hosp Northampton 1983–; chm sch ctee St Andrew's Occupational Therapy Sch 1988–93; *m* 1981, as his 2nd w, *Lt-Col Edward Henry Lancelot Aubrey-Fletcher, Gren Gds (*see* AUBREY-FLETCHER, Bt)

Lineage: Sir RICHARD BRAY(E)/BREY; *m* 1st Margaret, dau of John Sandes, of Furnes Felles, Lancs, and had:

1 John (Sir); f of:

(1) Margaret, *m* by 26 Aug 1496 1st Baron Sandys, of The Vyne, Hants, and *d* March 1538/9, leaving issue

Sir RICHARD *m* 2nd Joan — and by her had:

2 Sir Reginald, KG, Ld High Treas to HENRY VII, for whom he had fought at Bosworth 1485, and for whom in Jan 1503 he helped lay the fndn stone of Henry VII's Chapel Westminster as well as building most of St George's, Windsor, where he is *bur* in the Braye Chapel

3 JOHN BRAY, of Eaton Bray, Beds; had, with a dau (*m* Sir John Norris):

(1) EDMUND, **1st Baron**

(2) Edward (Sir), ancestor of the BRAYs of Shere, Surrey

(3) Reginald, of Barrington, Glos, ancestor of the BRAYs of Barrington

The est son,

EDMUND BRAY, **1st Lord** (Baron) **Bray(e)**, so *cr* by writ 9 Aug 1529; *b c* 1484; ktd 1513, Sheriff Beds 1514–15 and Surrey and Sussex 1522; *m* Jane (*d* 24 Oct 1558), dau and heir of Sir Richard Halighwell/Halywell, and *d* 18 Oct 1539, having had issue:

1 JOHN BRAY, **2nd Baron Bray(e)**; *b c* 1523; *m* Lady Anne Talbot (*m* 2nd 18 Nov 1561 Thomas, Lord Wharton (*d* 23 Aug 1568), and *d* 3 Feb 1584), dau of 5th Earl of Shrewsbury and Waterford (*qv*), but *dsp* 19 Nov 1557 of wounds recd at the Siege of St Quintin 1556, when the barony fell into abeyance between his sisters and their descendants

1 Anne; *m* by 1526 9th Lord (Baron) Cobham (of Kent), KG, and *d* 1 Nov 1558, leaving issue (*see* BOOTHBY, Bt)

2 ELIZABETH Bray; *b c* 1513; *m* 1st 1528 Sir Ralph VERNEY (*d* 1546), of Pendley and Middle Claydon, Bucks; *m* 2nd Sir Richard Catesby; *m* 3rd William Clark; *m* 4th Henry Phillips and was a widow by 1573; by her 1st husb she had, with other issue (*see* WILLOUGHBY DE BROKE, B):

(1) Edmund (Sir); *m* 1st Frances (*dsp*), dau of John Hastings, of Elford, Oxon; *m* 2nd Audrey, dau of William Gardner, of Fulmer, Bucks, and widow of Sir Peter Carew, and had an only child:

1a Francis (Sir), of Penley; *m* Ursula, dau and coheir of William St Barbe, and *dsp* abroad, having sold the estate

(1) (cont.) Sir Edmund *m* 3rd Mary, dau of John Blakeney, of Sparham, Norfolk, and widow of Geffrey Turvile, of Leics, and *d* 1599/1600, having by her had issue:

2a Edmund (Sir), Kt Marshal and Standard-Bearer to CHARLES I; *b* 7 April 1596; *m* Margaret, dau of Sir Thomas Denton, and was *k* at Edgehill 23 Oct 1642, leaving an est s:

1b Sir RALPH VERNEY, 1st Bt (E), so *cr* 16 March 1660/1; *m* Mary, dau and heir of John Blacknall, of Abingdon and Wasing, Berks, and *d* 24 Sept 1696, having had issue:

1c Sir JOHN VERNEY, 2nd Bt, and 1st VISCOUNT OF THE COUNTY OF FERMANAGH, so *cr* 16 June 1703, as also BARON VERNEY OF BELTURBET, Co Cavan (both I); *b* 5 Nov 1640; MP (Tory) Bucks 1710–15 and Amersham 1715–17; *m* 1st 27 May 1680 Elizabeth (*d* 20 May 1686), dau of Ralph Palmer; *m* 2nd 10 July 1692 Mary (*d* 24 Aug 1694), dau of Sir Francis Lawley, 2nd Bt; *m* 3rd 8 April 1696 Elizabeth (*dsp* 12 Dec 1736), dau of Daniel Baker, of Little Chelsea, and *d* 23 June 1717, having by his 1st w had, with other issue:

1d Sir RALPH VERNEY, 3rd Bt, 2nd VISCOUNT and 1st EARL VERNEY in the province of Leinster (I), so *cr* 22 March 1742/3; *bapt* 18 March 1683; MP (Tory) Amersham 1717–27 and Wendover (Whig) 1741–52; *m* 24 Feb 1707/8 Catherine, est dau and coheir of Henry Paschall, and *d* 4 Oct 1752, when he was *s* by his only surv son Ralph, 2nd and last Earl Verney, who *dsp* 31 March 1791. The 1st Earl's line entirely failed on the death of his gdau Mary Verney, who was *cr* 13 June 1792 BARONESS FERMANAGH and *d* unm 15 Nov 1810, having alienated the Verney estates

1d MARGARET Verney; *m* 20 Feb 1703 Sir Thomas CAVE, 3rd Bt (*qv*), of Stanford Hall, Leics, and was great-grandmother (*see* CAVE-BROWNE-CAVE, Bt) of Sarah, eventually **Baroness Braye** (*see* below)

3 Frideswide; *b* c 1516; *m* Sir Percival Hart, of Lullington, Kent (*d* 1580; *see* DYKE, Bt)

4 Mary; *b* c 1518; *m* Sir Robert Peckham and *d* 1569; by 1839 her issue was presumed *extinct*

5 Dorothy; *b* c 1530; *m* Edmund Brydges, Lord Chandos; her gdau Catherine Brydges *m* 4th Earl of Bedford (*see* BEDFORD, D)

6 Frances; *b* c 1535; *m* Thomas Lyfield, of Stoke d'Abernon, Surrey, and *d* 1592, leaving a dau and heiress:

(1) Jane; *m* Thomas Vincent and was ancestor of Sir Francis Vincent, Bt (*see* 1941 edn D'ABERNON, V); Sir Francis's only child, Blanche, *m* 1871 John Raymond Trevilian

The 1st BARON's seven times-great-granddaughter,

SARAH Cave later OTWAY-CAVE (added maiden name after her husb's by roy licence 12 March 1818), **Baroness Braye** in her own right, so declared by letters patent terminating the abeyance in her favour 13 Oct 1839; *b* 2 July 1768; *m* 25 Feb 1790 Henry OTWAY (*d* 13 Sept 1815), of Castle Otway, Co Tipperary, High Sheriff Leics, er bro of Adml Sir Robert Otway, Bt (*see* 1912 edn), and *dspms* 21 Feb 1862, when the barony again fell into abeyance betwee her daus, having had, with other issue:

1 Robert, of Castle Otway and Stanford Hall, MP Leics; *m* 23 Oct 1833 Sophia (*d* 30 Dec 1849), er dau of Sir Francis Burdett, 5th Bt, and *dsp* & *vm* 30 Nov 1844

1 Maria, of Stanford Hall; *d* unm 13 May 1879, when the 2nd abeyance in the barony was terminated and it passed to her surv sis Henrietta (*see* below)

2 Anne, of Stanford Hall; *m* 1st 28 Feb 1828 John Arthur Arnold (*dsp* 1844), of Lutterworth; *m* 2nd 2 Dec 1847 Rev Henry Kemp Richardson, Rector of Leire, Leics, and *dsp* 22 May 1871

3 Catherine, of Stanford Hall; *m* 1st 19 Oct 1826 Henry Murray (*dsp* 26 Nov 1830), yst son of Lord George Murray (*see* ATHOLL, D); *m* 2nd 11 Feb 1850 3rd Earl Beauchamp (*see* 1970 edn) and *dsp* 4 Nov 1875. He *d* 21 Jan 1853

4 HENRIETTA Otway later Otway-Cave, **Baroness Braye** in her own right; *b* 3 Nov 1809; *m* 24 Sept 1844 Edgell WYATT-EDGELL (*d* 26 Sept 1888 aged 87), 2nd son of Edgell Wyatt-Edgell, of Milton Place, Egham, Surrey, and had issue:

(1) Edmund Verney, of Stanford Hall, Leics, Capt 17th Lancers; *b* 16 Aug 1845; *ka* at Ulundi, Zululand, 4 July 1879. His sword is in the Braye Chapel, Windsor

(2) Henry Adrian, 13th Regt; *b* 17 May 1847; *d* unm 6 Nov 1866

(3) ALFRED THOMAS TOWNSHEND, **5th Baron**

(1) Frances Catherine Sarah (twin with Edmund Verney); nun; *d* 23 Feb 1884

BARONESS BRAYE *d* 14 Nov 1879; her only surv s,

ALFRED THOMAS TOWNSHEND WYATT-EDGELL later VERNEY-CAVE (roy licence 5 Feb 1880, also quartered arms of CAVE with those of VERNEY), **5th Baron Braye**, DL and JP Leics, JP Warwick and Northants, Kt SMO Malta, Lt-Col and Hon Col 3rd Bn Leics Regt (S African medal with clasp); *b* 23 July 1849; *educ* Eton and Ch Ch Oxford; RC 1870; *m* 9 Sept 1873 Cecilia Harriet (*d* 25 Nov 1935), dau of William Gerard Walmesley, of Westwood Hall, Lancs, and had issue:

1 ADRIAN VERNEY, **6th Baron**

2 Thomas Florian; *b* 11 April 1885; *d* unm 4 April 1909

1 Cecilia Violet; *b* 4 Aug 1876; *m* 2 May 1903 Maj — von Gratzy, and *d* 21 Nov 1950, having had issue:

(1) Verney Kurt; *b* 1904; *d* Jan 1909

(1) Vera Cecilia; *b* 1906; *m* 20 April 1929 Claude Henry Browne, of Foresters, Keeper's Walk, Virginia Water, Surrey, er son of Claude M Browne, of 10 Queensberry Pl, SW7, and *d* 1981 leaving issue:

1a +LINDA KATHLEEN [Mrs Christopher Fothergill, Otway House, Chobham, Surrey]; *b* 2 May 1930; co-heiress presumptive; *m* 6 Feb 1965 *Cdr Christopher Henry Fothergill, RN, son of Capt Henry Maclean Fothergill, RN, of Fairway, Camberley, Surrey, by Lucy, dau of Capt Edward Bouverie-Pusey, RN (*see* RADNOR, E), and has:

1b +Nicholas Henry; *b* 29 Nov 1965

2b +Alexander Verney Edmund; *b* 17 Nov 1967

2a +THERESA BEATRICE; *b* 9 Aug 1934; co-heiress presumptive

2 Ianthe Mary Dolores; *b* 12 July 1880; *d* 5 Jan 1881

3 Vera Angela; *b* 14 Aug 1881; *m* 22 July 1905 Maj Charles Hillary Wild, JP, late Roy W Kent Regt (*d* 10 Oct 1954), only surv son of Charles Augustus Wild, of Longdown Lodge, Berks, and South Ash Manor, Kent, and *d* 21 Nov 1952, having had issue:

(1) Charles Edric Verney, Capt Green Howards WW II; *b* 29 May 1906; *educ* Ampleforth

(2) Reginald Hillary; *b* 4 Oct 1910; *d* 3 Sept 1938

The 5th BARON *d* 1 July 1928; his son,

ADRIAN VERNEY WYATT-EDGELL later VERNEY-CAVE, **6th Baron Braye**, Cdr RNVR; *b* 11 Oct 1874; *m* 28 Aug 1900 Ethel Mary (*d* 7 July 1955), dau of Capt Edward Bouverie-Pusey, RN (*see* RADNOR, E), and had issue:

1 THOMAS ADRIAN, **7th Baron**

2 Ambrose Jordan; *b* 23 Oct 1906; *educ* Ampleforth; F/Lt RAFVR WW II

1 Lucy Agnes Vera, Ferry Pilot ATA WW II; *b* 1 Jan 1905; *m* 10 May 1935 Capt Lucien Leslie Falkiner (*ka* nr Cassel *c* 30 May 1940), 43rd LI, 2nd son of Sir Leslie Falkiner, 7th Bt (*qv*)

The 6th BARON *d* 12 Feb 1952; his er son,

THOMAS ADRIAN VERNEY-CAVE, **7th Baron Braye**, DL (1954), JP (Leics 1953), CC Northants; *educ* The Oratory; Maj 13th/8th Roy Hus, F/O RAF WW II, on personal staff of HRH The Prince of the Netherlands 1945–46, Order of Orange Nassau (Netherlands); *b* 26 July 1902; *m* 3 Feb 1934 Dorothea (*d* May 1994), dau of Daniel Charles Donoghue, of Philadelphia, USA, and *d* 1985, having had issue:

1 (MARY) PENELOPE, **present Baroness Braye**

Seat: Stanford Hall, Lutterworth, Leics. Before the 1690s the family seat of the CAVEs had stood on lower ground and nearer the village church, indeed in a different county altogether, being across the Avon in Northamptonshire. The site of the present building is more elevated, though it still commands a view out over the river, which at one point has been widened to create a lake. Some materials from the old house were used in its construction, notably stone and wainscotting. It also retains among other examples of fine furniture a medieval refectory table that is thought to have started life in the old house.

A regular mansion of hipped roof covering a south-facing front facade of sandstone (the other three sides being brick with stone dressing), Stanford can be dated fairly precisely, to 1697. It has two wings jutting ever so slightly forward, each of two bays, with unfussy rectangular panels below the windows. This style, which derives from the Dutch taste of the time, is appropriate for a building erected in WILLIAM III's reign.

The central part, however, is more ornate, being of five bays on the second storey over four bays divided by a door on the raised ground floor, the two principal rows of sash windows (a novelty at the time outside London) being separated by balustrades and the central second-storey window being garlanded on either side with a decorative motif that swells to a scroll at the base. The door, flanked by pilasters, has a D-shape pediment and steps up to it. It is no longer the main entrance, however, even though it is approached by a generously proportioned avenue. That honour falls to the eastern flank, where a a door approached by twin steps that turn in on themselves half-way up looks across to the stable-block, an elegant building of 1737 surmounted by a central pediment under a belvedere.

The top storey on the south face is of dormer windows, the semi-basement of truncated lights. The original architects were brothers from Warwick, Francis and William Smith, who had built up the most extensive practice in the Midlands. William died in 1724, some 30 years after embarking on the project. Francis then continued alone, though he became more adventurous, creating an extremely elegant Grand Staircase, for instance. Work on the house continued in the family, for his son, another William, was carrying out internal decoration by the 1740s. The Saloon's coved ceiling contains a series of idealised hunting scenes of 1880 by Félix Joubert, a tour de force given that era's less successful pastiches of 18th-century work generally. The moveables include a collection of Jacobite memorabilia amassed in Rome by the Lady Braye of the day in 1842.

BRENTFORD

Arms: Gu., on a fess wavy between three fleurs-de-lys or a portcullis sa., all within a bordure of the second. **Crest:** A stag's head ppr., gorged with a collar or, thereon five roses gu., and charged on the neck with a fleur-de-lys gold. **Supporters:** On either side a stag ppr., gorged with a collar or, thereon five roses gu., and charged on the neck with a fleur-de-lys gold. **Motto:** *Cassis tutissima virtus* ('Virtue is the safest helmet'). **Creations:** Bt. (UK) 20 Sept 1919 and (UK) 21 Jan 1956, V. (UK) 5 July 1929.

THE 4TH VISCOUNT BRENTFORD, of Newick, Sussex, and a **Baronet** (Sir Crispin William Joynson-Hicks, 2nd and 4th Bt) [The Rt Hon The Viscount Brentford, Cousley Place, Wadhurst, E Sussex TN5 6HF]; *b* 7 April 1933; *s* f 1983; *educ* Eton and New Coll Oxford (BA 1956, MA 1961); late Lt 9th Queen's Roy Lancers, slr 1960, ptnr Taylor Joynson Garrett (formerly Joynson-Hicks) 1961–95, Master Girdlers' Co 1983–84; *m* 21 March 1964 *Gillian Evelyn OBE (1996), High Sheriff E Sussex 1998–9, er dau of Gerald Edward Schluter, OBE, of Nairobi, Kenya, and has issue:

1 +PAUL WILLIAM; *b* 18 April 1971

1 *Emma Rosalie; *b* 11 Feb 1966

2 *Rowena Phyllis; *b* 23 Oct 1967; *m* 1989 *Simon J Banks, yr son of M J Banks, of Bishop's Stortford, Herts

3 *Amy Gillian; *b* 29 Nov 1978

Lineage: RICHARD HICKS, of Weybridge, Surrey; had:

HENRY HICKS, of Bexhill, Sussex; *b* 15 July 1840; *m* 5 Sept 1864 Harriett (*d* 21 Jan 1931), dau of William Watts, of Oadby, Leics, by Sarah Ann Johnson, and had issue:

Sir WILLIAM HICKS later JOYNSON-HICKS, **1st Bt**, so *cr* 20 Sept 1919, also **1st Viscount Brentford**, of Newick, Co Sussex (both UK), so *cr* 5 July 1929, PC (GB 1923, NI 1928), DL (Norfolk), sometime of Tradnorton Hall, Norwich (formerly the seat of the Boileau, Bts); *b* 23 June 1865; FRGS, slr, MP NW Manchester 1908–10, Brentford 1911–18 and Twickenham 1918–29, Parly Sec Overseas Trade Dept 1922–23, Postmaster-Gen and Paymaster-Gen 1923, Fin Sec Treasury 1923, Min Health 1923–24, Home Sec 1924–29, Ecclesiastical Commr England 1924, Freedom of Portsmouth and Twickenham; *m* 12 June 1895 Grace Lynn (*d* 17 Jan 1952), only child of Richard Hampson Joynson, JP, of Chasefield, Bowdon, Cheshire, and *d* 8 June 1932, leaving issue:

1 RICHARD CECIL JOYNSON-HICKS, **2nd Viscount Brentford**, Lt Res of Offrs Queen's Roy Regt, RFC and RAF, Staff Offr W Indies and 17th Div BEF WW I (wounded 1915), Staff Offr (invalided) WW II 1939–44; *b* 15 Nov 1896; *m* 1st 28 Oct 1920 Evelyn Mary Rothery (*d* 27 Nov 1954), dau of John Francis McNellan, of Dollar, Clackmannanshire; *m* 2nd 16 Sept 1955 Grace Esther Amelia, widow of Danald Sinclair Tait McNellan, of Johannesburg, and dau of Arthur Ernest Alfred Tothill, of Cape Town, and *dsp* 27 June 1958

2 **Sir Lancelot William Joynson-Hicks, 3rd Bt** of the 1919 *cr*, **3rd Viscount Brentford** and **1st Bt** (UK), so *cr* 21 Jan 1956; *b* 10 April 1902; *educ* Winchester and Trin Coll Oxford (BA 1923, MA 1926); slr 1926, sr ptnr Joynson-Hicks & Co, Pres Church Soc, memb Nat Assembly C of E, Lt-Cdr RNVR WW II 1941–44, MP Chichester 1942–58, Parly Sec Min Fuel and Power 1951–55, Chm AA 1957, Master Girdlers' Co, pres S Regnl Assoc Blind 1972; *m* 15 July 1931 Phyllis (*d* 1979), only dau of Maj Herbert Cyril Allfrey, of Newnton Ho, Tetbury, Glos, and *d* 25 Feb 1983, leaving issue:

(1) Sir CRISPIN WILLIAM JOYNSON-HICKS, **2nd** and **4th Bt** and **4th and present Viscount Brentford**

1 Helen Grace; *b* 2 June 1899; *d* unm 14 Dec 1969

BRICKWOOD

Arms: Arg. a pale checky az. and or between two oak trees couped vert, on a chief gu. three ears of barley, slipped and leaved of the third, and a sprig of hop, slipped and leaved ppr., in saltire between two billets gold. **Crest:** A demi-savage wreathed about the temples with a chaplet of oak holding in the dexter hand a sprig of hop, slipped and leaved ppr., and resting the sinster hand upon a billet or. **Motto:** *Nil arduum* ('Nothing arduous'). **Creation:** Bt. (UK) 29 June 1927.

SIR BASIL GREAME BRICKWOOD, 3RD BT, of Portsmouth [Sir Basil Brickwood Bt, c/o RAF Club, Piccadilly, London W1]; *b* 21 May 1923; *s* half-bro 1974; *educ* King Edward's GS Stratford and Clifton; RAF WW II; *m* 1st 1947 Betty Cooper and had:

1 A dau; *b* 6 Dec 1948; *d* 1956

Sir BASIL *m* 2nd 1956 *Shirley Anne, dau of Richard Wallace Brown, and by her has:

2 *Tessa Anne; *b* 3 Sept 1959; *m* July 1991 *Roger Frederick Norgrove and has:

(1) *Oliver Nicholas Richard; *b* Sept 1992

(1) *Abigail Jane; *b* Nov 1993

3 *Gail Anne; *b* 10 Nov 1963; *m* 1984 (*divorce* 19– resumed maiden name) Michael Horsnell, er s of R N Horsnell, of Thorvington, Essex

Lineage: WILLIAM BRICKWOOD, of Guildford; *m* 12 Jan 1706 and was *bur* 30 Nov 1749, leaving:

WILLIAM BRICKWOOD; *bapt* 26 Sept 1707; *bur* Stoke-cum-Guildford 20 June 1782, leaving:

THOMAS BRICKWOOD; *bapt* 7 Aug 1737; *bur* 4 Sept 1781, leaving:

THOMAS BRICKWOOD; *bapt* at Shelford 12 Dec 1767; *d* 3 Jan 1836, leaving a son,

THOMAS BRICKWOOD; *b* 16 July 1796; *d* 3 Nov 1848, leaving:

HARRY BRICKWOOD, of Cleveland Ho, Southsea, Hants; *b* 6 Feb 1828; *m* 20 Aug 1851 Rosetta Ann (*d* 25 Aug 1859), dau of William Frederick Schneegans, and *d* 8 Dec 1862, having had, with other issue:

Sir John Brickwood, 1st Bt (UK), so *cr* 29 June 1927, chm and md Brickwood & Co, brewers, of Portsmouth, chm Portsmouth Chamber Commerce; *b* 23 June 1852; ktd 1904; *m* 1st 10 Jan 1881 Eliza (*d* 27 Feb 1889), dau of William Miller, and had issue:

1 Madeline Mary; *m* 2 Feb 1907 Franz Wachendorff and was drowned in the Elbe with her est son 7 July 1923

Sir John *m* 2nd 30 Sept 1893 Jessie Eliza (*d* 17 April 1917), dau of John Cooper, of Burghfield, and by her had issue:

1 Arthur Cyril, 2nd Lt York and Lancaster Regt; *b* 2 Nov 1896; *d* unm 15 April 1915

2 **Sir Rupert Redvers Brickwood, 2nd Bt**; *educ* Cheltenham, S/Ldr RAuxAF WW II, dir Portsmouth Brewery (Brickwoods Ltd); *b* 18 Feb 1900; *m* 30 April 1932 Rachel Neale (*d* 27 Jan 1972), only dau of Dr Malcolm Winifred Shutte, MRCS, LRCP, of Newnham, Weybridge, Surrey, and *d* 29 April 1974, leaving issue:

(1) *Sally Neale [Mrs Nigel Yonge, Homefields, Bulls Lane, Cowfold, Sussex RH13 8AP]; *b* 30 March 1933; *m* 2 June 1956 *Nigel William Seville Yonge, 2nd surv s of Maj Edward Yonge, of Bexley Hill, nr Lodsworth, Sussex, and has:

1a *William Jonathan Michael; *b* 26 Jan 1961

2a *Andrew James Neale; *b* 16 Sept 1964; *m* 3 Nov 1990 *Kate, dau of John Jamieson, of Laghead, Gatehouse of Fleet, and has:

1b *Jack William Alexander; *b* 17 Aug 1995

1b *Philippa Mary; *b* 26 June 1997

1a *Susannah Mary; *b* 30 July 1957; *m* 21 July 1987 *Nicholas Broome, 2nd s of Maj Richard Broome, MC, OBE, of Corfe Castle, and has:

1b *Phoebe; *b* 19 May 1990

2b *Ionie; *b* 8 April 1993

2a *Annabel Mary; *b* 3 Aug 1959; has:

1b *Matthew Dudek; *b* 2 Dec 1994

(2) *Ann Neale; *b* 29 March 1934; *m* 1st 12 Sept 1959 (John) Colin Caldecott Bauer, yr son of Douglas Niel Bauer, of Place Farm Ho, Nether Wallop, Hants; *m* 2nd 1986 *Peter A Van den Bergh, and has by her 1st husb:

1a *John William Neale; *b* 10 Nov 1960; *m* 19– *Claire Katy, dau of Frederick Jennett, OBE, and has:

1b *George William Frederick; *b* 9 Aug 1992

1b *Katy Louisa; *b* 29 June 1990

1a *Nicola Ann; *b* 16 April 1962; *m* 11 March 1989 *Graham Trevor Brooks, s of Trevor Brooks, of Dublin, and has:

1b *Benjamin Edward; *b* 5 May 1991

1b *Hannah Rachel; *b* 6 Dec 1995

2b *Serena Jane Marigold; *b* 23 April 1997

Sir John *m* 3rd 8 Jan 1922 Isabella Janet Gibson (*m* 2nd — Davis; *d* 1967), dau of James Gordon, of Castle Douglas, Kirkcudbright, and *d* 12 Feb 1932, having by her had further issue:

3 Sir BASIL GREAME BRICKWOOD, **3rd and present Bt**

BRIDGE OF HARWICH

Arms: Azure, issuant from the centre of a bar wavy of water proper in the nombril point of a bridge of three arches, embattled argent, masoned sable, the whole between as many sealions naiant guardant, each crowned with a mural crown gold. **Crest:** An eagle rising proper, the beak or, holding therein a sprig of lilac, also proper. **Supporters:** Dexter, a winged horse in trian aspect argent, hooved or, resting the dexter hoof upon a portcullis, chained also or; sinister, a sealion in trian aspect all argent, resting the sinister forepaw on a portcullis, chained gold, the compartment comprising a grassy mount growing therefrom on a rose gules, barbed, stalked and leaved proper, another rose argent, barbed and seeded also proper, between on the dexter a rose argent and on the sinister a rose gules, both barbed, seeded, stalked and leaved proper, on the sinister side of the mount a flat rock proper.

Motto: *Me juvat ire per altum* ('I rejoice in trading the high path')

Creation: B. (LP, UK) 1980.

THE BARON BRIDGE OF HARWICH, of Harwich, Co Essex (Sir Nigel Cyprian Bridge, PC (1975)) [The Rt Hon The Lord Bridge of Harwich PC, House of Lords, London SW1A 0PW]; *b* 26 Feb 1917; *educ* Marlborough; Capt KRRC WW II Italy, France and Germany; barrister Inner Temple 1947, Bencher 1964, Jr Counsel Treasury 1964–68, High Court Judge Queen's Bench 1968–75, Presiding Judge Western Circuit 1972–74, Ld Justice of Appeal 1975–80, Ld of Appeal in Ordinary 1980–92, Member Security Commn 1977–82 (Chm 1982–85), Treas Inner Temple 1986; ktd 1968; *m* 1944 *Margaret, dau of Leonard Heseltine Swinbank, of Weybridge, Surrey, and has:

1 *Charles Cyprian; *b* 1951; *m* 1971 *Sheila Marie Street

1 *Jane Elizabeth; *b* 1944; *m* 1978 *Prof J M Kister

2 *Rachel Ann; *b* 1946; *m* 1975 *Martin Pick

Lineage: Cdr CYPRIAN DUNSCOMB CHARLES BRIDGE, RN; had:

NIGEL CYPRIAN, *cr* a **Baron**

BRIDGEMAN

Arms: Sa., ten plates, four, three, two and one on a chief arg., a lion passant erm. **Crest:** A demi-lion rampant arg., holding between the paws a wreath of laurel ppr. **Supporters:** On either side a leopard guardant gu. pellety, charged on the shoulder with a portcullis or.

Motto: *Nec temere, nec timide* ('Neither rashly nor timidly').

Creation: V. (UK) 18 June 1929.

THE 3RD VISCOUNT BRIDGEMAN, of Leigh, Salop (Robin John Orlando Bridgeman) [The Rt Hon The Viscount Bridgeman, Watley House, Sparsholt, Winchester, Hants SO21 2LU; 19 Chepstow Rd, London W2 5BP]; *b* 5 Dec 1930; *s* unc 1982; *educ* Eton; 2nd Lt Rifle Bde 1950–51, Lt Roy Greenjackets RARO, CA 1958, ptnr: Fenn and Crosthwaite 1973, Henderson Crosthwaite & Co 1975–86, dir: Nester-BNA 1988–, Guiness Mahon 1988–90, Bridgeman Art Library 1972–, Special Tstee Hammersmith Hosp 1986–, govr Reeds Sch 1994–; *m* 10 Dec 1966 *(Victoria) Harriet Lucy, 3rd dau of Ralph Meredyth Turton, TD, of Kildale Hall, Whitby, Yorks (*see* CHETWYND, V), and has issue:

1 +WILLIAM ORLANDO CASPAR; *b* 15 Aug 1968; *educ* Eton and Bristol U

2 +Luke Robinson Orlando; *b* 1 May 1971; *educ* Eton and New Coll Oxford; *m* 25 May 1996 *Victoria, yst dau of Henry Frost and Mrs William Mellen, of Moor Farm, W Farndon, Northants

3 +Esmond Francis Ralph Orlando; *b* 3 Oct 1974; *educ* Bryanston and Bristol U

4 +Orlando Henry Geoffrey; *b* 11 April 1983; *educ* Eton

Lineage: The Rev and Hon JOHN ROBERT ORLANDO BRIDGEMAN, MA, s of 2nd Earl of Bradford (*qv*); had an only s:

WILLIAM CLIVE BRIDGEMAN, **1st Viscount Bridgeman**, of Leigh, Salop (UK), so *cr* 18 June 1929, PC (1920), DL and JP; *educ* Trin Coll Cambridge (MA), Fellow Eton Coll 1929, LLD Cambridge 1930, Er Bro Trinity House, MP Oswestry 1906–29, Priv Sec to Sec State Colonies 1889–1892 and Chllr Exchequer 1895–1902, a Ld Treasury, Assist Dir War Trade Dept 1915–16; Parly Sec to: Min Labour 1916–19, BOT 1919–20, First Sec Mines 1920–22, Home Sec 1922–24, First Ld Admlty 1924–29; *b* 31 Dec 1864; *m* 30 April 1895 Caroline Beatrix, DBE (1924), JP, V-Chm Ho of Laity Church Assembly, Govr BBC 1935–39 (*d* 26 Dec 1961), er dau of Hon Cecil Thomas Parker (*see* MACCLESFIELD, E), and *d* 14 Aug 1935, leaving:

1 ROBERT CLIVE BRIDGEMAN, **2nd Viscount Bridgeman**, KBE (1954), CB (1944), DSO (1940), MC, JP (1951), DL (Salop 1951); *b* 1 April 1896; *educ* Eton; Col and Hon Maj-Gen Rifle Brigade, Bde Maj 7th Inf Bde 1932–34, GSO(2) War Office 1935–37, Dir-Gen HG 1941–44, Dep Adj-Gen War Office 1944–45, CA 1951, dir Australia and New Zealand Banks, Hon Col 4th Bn KSLI (TA) 1954–59, pres Army Cadet Force to 1974, served WW I 1915–18 (wounded) and WW II 1939–44 (despatches); *m* 12 June 1930 *Hon Mary Kathleen Lane Fox, JP (Salop 1942), 2nd dau of 1st and last Baron Bingley (*see* 1940 edn), and *d* 17 Nov 1982, leaving issue:

(1) *Anne Caroline Mary [The Hon Mrs Stacey, The Old Vicarage, Selling, Faversham, Kent ME13 9RD]; *b* 30 July 1932; *educ* Reading U (BSc Ag 1953); *m* 19 July 1955 *Rev Nicholas David Stacey, er son of David Henry Stacey, of 54 Egerton Crescent, London SW3, and has issue:

1a *David Robert; *b* 10 May 1958; *m* 1992 *Annabel M E, dau of Maj Michael Edwards, of Norwood Farm, Corscombe, Dorset

1a *Caroline Jill; *b* 20 Sept 1956

2a *Mary Elizabeth; *b* 15 May 1961

(2) *Susan Elizabeth [The Hon Mrs Foster, The Spicer's House, 101 Corve St, Ludlow, Salop SY8 1EB]; *b* 19 Oct 1935; JP; Ldy-in-Waiting to Lady May Abel Smith, w of Govr Queensland 1958–60; *m* 1 Aug 1962 *David Kenneth Dudley Foster, est son of Kenneth Dudley Foster, of The Lodge, Claverley, Salop, and has issue:

1a *Robert Peter Dudley; *b* 14 July 1966

2a *Edward Kenneth Clive; *b* 3 Nov 1967

3a *Simon David Thomas; *b* 10 Dec 1969

(3) *Mary Selina, JP [The Hon Mrs Bayliss JP, Sheepbridge Court, Swallowfield, nr Reading, Berks RG7 1PT]; *b* 14 Jan 1940; *m* 14 July 1962 *Jeremy David Bagot Bayliss, only son of Edmund Bayliss, of Guernsey, and has:

1a *Jonathan Andrew Bagot [Jonathan Bayliss Esq, 6 Netheravon Rd, London W4 2NA]; *b* 2 Jan 1964; *educ* Wellington; *m* 1992 *Sarah E, er dau of Richard Bowes, and has issue:

1b *Walter Richard Bridgeman; *b* 6 May 1993

2b *Caispar Jeremy Lyle; *b* 11 Jan 1995

3b *Charles Robert Bowes; *b* 18 Oct 1996

2a *Richard Charles; *b* 11 Dec 1965; *educ* Wellington; *m* 1996 *Anna M, only dau of Maurice Lidstone

3a *Patrick Thomas Clive; *b* 6 March 1968; *educ* Wellington; *m* 1995 *Rebecca, only dau of Jeremy Woodhouse

2 Geoffrey John Orlando, MC, of Watley House, Sparsholt, Winchester, Hants, formerly Brig RAMC, Lt late RFA (SR), FRCS, LRCP, Consultant Ophthalmic Surgn St George's Hosp and W Ophthalmic Hosp, served WWs I 1917–19 and II; *b* 3 July 1898; *educ* Eton and Trin Coll Cambridge (BA 1920, MA 1926, MB, BCh 1928); *m* 3 July 1929 Mary Meriel Gertrude (*d* 5 July 1974), only dau of Sir George John Talbot, PC, Judge High Court (*see* SHREWSBURY and WATERFORD, E), and *d* 15 Oct 1974, leaving issue:

(1) ROBIN JOHN ORLANDO BRIDGEMAN, **3rd and present Viscount Bridgeman**

(1) *Helena Mary [Mrs James Bayley, Wassall House, Rolvenden, nr Cranbrook, Kent]; *b* 2 Nov 1932; *m* 1st 18 July 1953 (*divorce* 1963) Hon Paul Asquith (*d* 1984), yr son of Baron Asquith of Bishopstone, PC, and has issue (*see* OXFORD AND ASQUITH, E); *m* 2nd 15 July 1963 *James Francis Leslie Bayley, son of Thomas Eliot Bayley, of Edinburgh, and has further issue:

1a *Thomas Francis; *b* 18 July 1966

1a *Rachel Helena; *b* 16 July 1964

(2) *Daphne [Mrs William Montgomery, Grey Abbey, Newtownards, Co Down, Ireland BT22 2QA]; *b* 9 April 1940; *m* 4 Dec 1965, as his 2nd w, *William Howard Clive Montgomery, er son of Maj Hugh Edward Montgomery, DL, of Grey Abbey, Co Down, and has issue:

1a *Hugh Geoffrey Clive; *b* 27 Sept 1966

1a *Rose Evelyn; *b* 26 May 1968; *m* 3 Sept 1994 *Mark Henry Leo Adams, s of Col N Adams, of Hollies Farm, Crowland, Lincs

2a *Frances Mary; *b* 29 May 1970

3a *Flora Anne Selina; *b* 1974

3 Maurice Richard (Sir), KBE (1964), CBE (1946); *b* 26 Jan 1904; *educ* Eton and Trin Coll Cambridge; Chm BP 1960–69, Petroleum Advsr Min Ec Warfare 1939, Pncpl Assist Sec Min Fuel and Power (Petroleum Div) 1944–46, Pres Middle East Assoc, KStJ; *m* 23 Feb 1933 Diana Mary Erica (*d* in a motor accident 20 May 1979), yr dau of Humphrey Minto Wilson, of 9 S Audley St, London W1, and *d* 18 June 1980, leaving:

(1) *Erica Jane [Lady Harman, Brook House, Highclere, Newbury, Berks]; *b* 20 April 1934; *m* 15 Sept 1960 (*divorce* 1987) Sir Jeremiah Le Roy Harman, QC, er s of Sir Charles Eustace Harman, PC, and has:

1a *Charles Richard Le Roy; *b* 30 May 1963

2a *Toby John; *b* 23 Jan 1967; *m* 1992 *Joanne L, dau of Neville Boxer, of Farnham Royal, Bucks

1a *Sarah Jane; *b* 15 April 1962; *m* 1993 *Hugh Lewis Evans, only son of Maj-Gen John Alan Maurice Evans, CB, of Littletown, Co Durham

(2) *Teresa Anne [Mrs Peter Baring, 29 Ladbroke Sq, London W11]; *b* 25 Oct 1937; *m* 9 Nov 1960 *Peter Baring (*see* REVELSTOKE, B), and has issue

1a *Augusta Daisy Elizabeth; *b* 1974

(3) *Elizabeth Caroline [Mrs Martin Drury, 3 Victoria Rise, London SW4 0PB]; *b* 15 March 1944; *m* 5 Jan 1971 *Martin Dru Drury, er s of Walter Neville Dru Drury, TD, of Little Brook St, Edenbridge, Kent, and has:

1a *Matthew Orlando Dru; *b* 1972

2a *Joseph Walter Richard Minto Dru; *b* 1977

1a *Augusta Daisy Elizabeth; *b* 1974

(4) *Rachel Diana [Mrs Ben Hay, Plummer, Tenterden, Kent TN30 6TU]; *b* 9 March 1947; *m* 18 Nov 1972 *(Philip) Benjamin Hay, s of Alexander Hay, of Lodge House, Brabourne Lees, Kent, and has:

1a *Thomas Alexander; *b* 18 Jan 1974

1a *Tara Caroline; *b* 20 Feb 1976

1 Anne; *b* 23; *d* 24 July 1900

BRIDGES

Arms: Arg., a cross sa. charged with a wreath of laurel fructed arg., a chief chequy also sa. and arg. **Crest:** A man's head and shoulders couped ppr., wreathed about the temples arg., the ribands gu. vested paly of six sa. and arg. **Supporters:** On either side a swan, wings elevated and addorsed ppr., gorged with a collar chequy sa. and arg. **Motto:** *Faire sans dire* ('To act without speaking'). **Creation:** B. (UK) 4 Feb 1957.

THE 2ND BARON BRIDGES, of Headley, Surrey, and St Nicholas-at-Wade, Kent (Sir Thomas Edward Bridges, GCMG (1988, KCMG 1983, CMG 1975)) [The Rt Hon The Lord Bridges, GCMG, Great House, Orford, Suffolk IP12 2NT]; *b* 27 Nov 1927; *s f* 1969; *educ* Eton and New Coll Oxford; Dip Serv 1951–87, Assist Priv Sec to For Sec 1963–66, Head Chancery Athens 1966–68, Counsellor Moscow 1969–71, Priv Sec (Overseas Affairs) to PM 1972–74, Min (Commercial) Washington 1976–79, Dep Under Sec FCO 1979–82, Amb Italy 1983–87; *m* 1 Sept 1953 *Rachel Mary, yst dau of Sir Henry Nöel Bunbury, KCB, of 8 Church St, Ewell, Surrey, and has issue:

1 +MARK THOMAS [The Hon Mark Bridges, 66 Lincoln Inn Fields, London WC2A 3LH]; *b* 25 July 1954; *educ* Eton and Corpus Christi Coll Cambridge (BA 1976, MA 1980); ptnr Farrer & Co; *m* 13 May 1978 *Angela Margaret, er dau of J L Collinson, of Mansfield, Notts, and has issue:

(1) +Miles Edmund Farrer; *b* 1 July 1992

(1) *Venetia Rachel Lucy; *b* 21 Feb 1982

(2) *Camilla Frances Iona; *b* 22 June 1985

(3) *Drusilla Katharine Anne; *b* 12 July 1988

2 +Nicholas Edward [The Hon Nicholas Bridges, 6 Oakhill Park Mews, London NW3 7LH]; *b* 29 March 1956; *educ* Eton and U of Bath (BSc 1979), BArch (1981); ARIBA; ptnr Blee Ettwein Bridges; *m* 1985 *Susan, est dau of Peter Guggenheim, of Woodbury Salterton, Devon, and has issue:

(1) +Matthew Orlando; *b* 31 Dec 1988

(1) *Alice Clementine; *b* 13 Dec 1986

1 *Harriet Elizabeth [The Hon Harriet Bridges, 20 Highland Ave, Beverly, MA 01905–4911, USA]; *b* 28 Nov 1958; *educ* Bryanston and York U (BA 1980); resumed her maiden name 1983; *m* 4 July 1981 (*divorce* 1983) John Charles Eells

Lineage: Rev JOHN BRIDGE or BRIDGES, Vicar: Herne 1562, Monkton 1574–90, Harbledown 1579 (all Kent), Rector Snare 1590; *m* 18 Dec 1568 Margaretta Leycester and *d* 14 Feb 1590, having had issue, with three other s and two daus, a yst s:

JOHN BRIDGES, of Harbledown, Kent; *m* 7 Oct 1595 Maria Clocys (*bur* 1 May 1650) and was *bur* 11 July 1646, leaving with other issue:

THOMAS BRIDGES, moved to St Nicholas-at-Wade, Kent, *c* 1660, where the family continued for 200 years; *bapt* 31 Jan 1612; *m* 1635 Elizabeth Hart, and had, with other issue:

EDWARD BRIDGES; *b* 2 Jan 1647; *m* 2nd Margaret Kennett and *d* 11 Nov 1688, having by her had issue:

1 Robert; *d* 14 Oct 1737

2 EDWARD, of whom presently

3 John; *d* 4 Aug 1708

The 2nd son,

EDWARD BRIDGES, of St Nicholas-at-Wade; *b* Nov 1685; *m* Elizabeth Wood and was *bur* 26 July 1759, leaving issue:

1 Thomas, of St Nicholas-at-Wade

2 EDWARD, of whom presently

3 Ezekiel

The 2nd son,

EDWARD BRIDGES; *m* Mary Sankey and *d* 1765, leaving issue:

1 JOHN, of whom presently

2 Edward; *d* 25 April 1789 aged 28

The er son,

JOHN BRIDGES; *b* 1759; *m* 1789 Elizabeth Denne (*d* 1841) and *d* 1823, leaving issue:

JOHN THOMAS BRIDGES, of St Nicholas Court, Isle of Thanet, JP Kent; *b* 1805; *m* 23 April 1829 Harriett Elizabeth (*m* 2nd 31 Oct 1854 Rev J E N Molesworth, DD, Vicar Rochdale; *d* 1897), 3rd dau of the Rev Sir Robert Affleck, 4th Bt (*see* 1939 edn), and *d* 10 May 1853, leaving issue:

1 John Affleck; *b* 1832; *m* Henrietta Philippa and had two sons

2 George, *dsp* 1860

3 Thomas Walker, Maj RA; *b* 1839; *m* Mary Ann Philippa and *d* 1880, leaving three s

4 ROBERT SEYMOUR, of whom presently

5 Edward, *dsp* 1866

The 4th son,

ROBERT SEYMOUR BRIDGES, OM (1929), MA, MB, Hon DLitt Oxford, Hon LLD St Andrews, FRCP, Poet Laureate 1913–30; *b* 23 Oct 1844; *educ* Eton and Corpus Christi Coll Oxford; *m* 3 Sept 1884 Mary Monica (*d* 9 Nov 1949), er dau of Alfred Waterhouse, RA, of Yattendon Court, Berks, and *d* 21 April 1930, leaving:

1 EDWARD ETTINGDENE, **1st Baron**

1 Elizabeth; *b* 5 Dec 1887; *m* 29 Dec 1923 A A Daryush and *dsp* 7 April 1977

2 Margaret; *b* 10 Oct 1889; *m* 3 July 1919 Horace William Brindley Joseph, Fell New Coll Oxford, and *d* 24 April 1926

ROBERT BRIDGES's only s,

EDWARD ETTINGDENE BRIDGES, **1st Baron Bridges**, of Headley, Co Surrey, and St Nicholas-at-Wade, Co Kent (UK), so *cr* 4 Feb 1957, KG (1965), PC, GCB (1944), GCVO (1946), MC; Perm Sec Treasury 1945–56, Capt and Adjt 4th Bn Oxford and Bucks LI WW I, Treasury 1919, Sec Cabinet 1938–46, Fell Eton 1945–65, Hon Fell Magdalen Coll Oxford, All Souls' Coll Oxford and LSE, Hon DCL Oxford, Hon LLD Bristol, Cambridge, London, Leicester, Hong Kong and Liverpool, Hon DLitt Reading, Hon FRIBA, Chllr Reading U 1959, chm Roy Fine Art Commn 1957–68, chm Br Cncl 1959–67, FRS; *b* 4 Aug 1892; *educ* Eton and Magdalen Coll Oxford; *m* 1 June 1922 Hon Katharine Dianthe Farrer, 2nd dau of 2nd Baron Farrer (*see* 1963 edn), and *d* 27 Aug 1969, leaving:

1 THOMAS EDWARD BRIDGES, **2nd and present Baron Bridges**

2 +Robert Oliver [The Hon Robert Bridges, Goodmans Furze, Headley, Epsom, Surrey]; *b* 18 Aug 1930; *educ* Eton, Magdalen Coll Oxford (MA) and AA Sch of Architecture (AA Dip); ARIBA, architect; *m* 12 Jan 1963 *Rosamund Theresa, yr dau of Roger C Vaughan de Wesselow, of 3 York House, London W8, and has issue:

(1) +John Edward [John Bridges Esq, 44 Primrose Mansions, Prince of Wales Drive, London SW11]; *b* 22 Aug 1968; *educ* Eton and Edinburgh U (MA Hons); antique dealer, with Carlton Hobbs Ltd

(2) +James George Robert, MBE [James Bridges Esq MBE, 110 Cambridge St, London SW1V 4QF]; *b* 15 July 1970; *educ* Eton and Exeter Coll Oxford (Stapledon Scholar, 1st Class MA); Assist Political Sec to PM 1994–97

1 *Shirley Frances [The Hon Mrs Corke, Eversheds, Abinger Hammer, Surrey RH5 6QA]; *b* 23 Oct 1924; *m* 15 June 1957 *Hilary Topham Corke, s of Alfred Topham Corke, of Malvern, Worcs, and has:

(1) *William Edward Orlando; *b* 5 Nov 1961; *m* 21 June 1995 *Sophie, dau of Michael Wigram, and has:

1a *Madeleine Olga; *b* 20 Dec 1996

(1) *Emma Lucy; *b* 13 Dec 1958

(2) *Cicely Catharine; *b* 26 May 1960

(3) *Georgiana Phoebe; *b* 23 Dec 1963

2 *Margaret Evelyn [The Hon Mrs Buxton, Castle House, Chipping Ongar, Essex]; *b* 9 Oct 1932; *m* 1st 7 Aug 1954 (*divorce* 1969) Trevor Henry Aston, FSA, Fell and Librarian Corpus Christi Coll Oxford, only s of Oliver John Aston, of Old House, Woolbeding, Midhurst; *m* 2nd 17 Sept 1971, as his 2nd w, *Paul William Jex Buxton, only son of W/Cdr Denis Alfred Jex Buxton, JP, DL, FSA, RAF, and has issue by 2nd husb (*see* BUXTON, Bt)

BRIDPORT

Arms: Quarterly, 1st and 4th, azure a fret argent, on a chief or three crescents sable (for HOOD), 2nd and 3rd, or a cross patonce sable, a bend gules surmounted of another engrailed of the field charged with three bombs fired proper, on a chief undulated argent, waves of the sea from which a palm tree issuant between a disabled ship on the dexter, and a battery in ruins on the sinister all proper, over all a fess wavy azure, thereon inscribed the word 'Trafalgar' or (for NELSON). **Crest:** A Cornish chough proper, resting the dexter claw on the fluke of an anchor in bend sinister or. **Supporters:** Dexter, Neptune proper, mantled vert, supporting with the sinister arm a trident, and resting the right upon an anchor or; sinister, a sealion argent, the back fin and end of the tail gules, supporting with the sinister paw an anchor, or. **Motto:** Steady. **Creation:** B. (I) 14 Nov 1794, V. (UK) 6 July 1868, D. (Kingdom of Two Sicilies) 1799.

THE 4TH VISCOUNT BRIDPORT OF CRICKET ST THOMAS, Co Somerset, **AND OF BRONTE** in the Kingdom of Italy, **Baron Bridport**, and **Duke of Brontë**, in Sicily (Alexander Nelson Hood) [The Rt Hon The Viscount Bridport, 1 Place Longemalle, 1204 Geneva, Switzerland]; *b* 17 March 1948; *s* f 1969; *educ* Eton and Sorbonne; managing ptnr Bridport et Cie SA 1991–; *m* 1st 5 Jan 1972 (*divorce* 1979) Linda Jacqueline, dau of Lt-Col Vincent Paravicini, of Nutley Manor, Basingstoke, Hants, and has issue:

1 +PEREGRINE ALEXANDER NELSON; *b* 30 Aug 1974

The 4th VISCOUNT *m* 2nd 5 Dec 1979 *Nina, dau of Curt Lincoln, of Helsinki, and formerly w of (a) Philip Martyn and (b) Jochen Rindt, racing driver, and by her has issue:

2 +Anthony Nelson; *b* 7 Jan 1983

Lineage: ALEXANDER HOOD, 1st VISCOUNT BRIDPORT OF CRICKET ST THOMAS (GB), so *cr* 16 June 1800, as also earlier 14 Nov 1794 BARON BRIDPORT (I), with special remainder to his g-nephew Samuel and subsequently to the heirs male of his unc Alexander (*see* 1970 edn ST AUDRIES), and 13 June 1796 BARON BRIDPORT OF CRICKET ST THOMAS, Co Somerset (GB), KB (1788); *b* 2 Dec 1726, s of Rev Samuel Hood and bro of 1st Viscount Hood (*qv*); RN: Lt 1746, Cdr and Post Capt 1756, Treasurer Greenwich Hosp 1766–99, Rear-Adml 1780, V-Adml 1787, Rear-Adml GB 1790–96, Adml of the Blue 1794, White 1795, V-Adml GB 1796 and UK 1801–14, C-in-C Channel Fleet 1797–1800, Lt-Gen 1799–1800, Gen Marines 1800–14, Adml the Red 1805, MP (Tory) Bridgwater 1784–90 and Buckingham 1790–96, took two French warships Hyères Bay 1757, retook *The Warwick* 1761, R-Adml under 1st Earl Howe (*qv*) relief of Gibraltar 1782, 2nd in command aboard *The Royal George* The Glorious First of June (1794); defeated a French fleet of 12 ships of the line and 10 frigates near Port l'Orient 23 June 1795; dispersed a French Fleet which had landed troops in Wales 1796, helped quell the Mutiny at the Nore 1797; *m* 1st 1761(?) or more probably soon after April 1763 Maria (*d* 12 Sept 1786), dau of Rev Richard West, DD, Preb Winchester, and Mary, dau of Sir Richard Temple, 3rd Bt (*see* TEMPLE OF STOWE, E); *m* 2nd 26 June 1788 Maria Sophia (*d* 18 Feb 1831 aged 85), dau and heiress of Thomas Bray, of Edmonton, and *dsp* 3 May 1814, when his GB titles expired while the Irish barony passed to his great-nephew

The 1st BARON BRIDPORT's g-nephew,

SAMUEL HOOD, **2nd Baron Bridport**; *b* 7 Dec 1788; *m* 3 July 1810 Charlotte Mary Duchess of Brontë in her own right (*d* 29 Jan 1873), only surv dau and heir of 1st Earl Nelson (*qv*), and *d* 6 Jan 1868, having had issue:

1 ALEXANDER NELSON, **1st Viscount**

2 Horatio Nelson; *b* 24 April 1826; *d* 1832

1 Mary Sophia; *m* 17 Aug 1841 John Lee-Lee, of Dillington, Somerset, and Orleigh Court, Devon, and *d* 29 Jan 1888, leaving issue

2 Charlotte; *m* 4 Sept 1845 Horace W N Rochfort (*d* 16 May 1891), of Clogrenane, Co Carlow, and *d* 21 Aug 1906, leaving issue

3 Jane Sarah; *m* 1st 4 Jan 1838 Hugh Holbech (*d* 8 June 1849), of Farnborough, Warwicks; *m* 2nd 10 Dec 1853 Capt Sir Charles Hotham, KCB, RN (*see* HOTHAM, B; he *d* 31 Dec 1855); *m* 3rd 30 Aug 1860 Capt William Armytage, RN (*see* ARMYTAGE, Bt), and *dsp* 28 April 1907

4 Catherine Louisa; *m* 18 April 1837 Henry Hall (*d* 17 Nov 1862), of Holbrook House, Somerset, and *d* 6 Oct 1893 aged 75, leaving issue

5 Fanny Caroline; *m* 20 May 1845 Sir John Walrond Walrond, 1st Bt (*d* 23 April 1889), and *d* 1 Oct 1903, leaving issue (*see* 1963 edn WALERAN, B)

The 2nd BARON BRIDPORT's er son,

ALEXANDER NELSON HOOD, **1st Viscount Bridport of Cricket St Thomas**, Co Somerset, **and of Brontë** in the Kingdom of Italy (UK), so *cr* 6 July 1868, GCB (1891, KCB 1885), DL Somerset, Devon and Dorset, *s* mother 1873 as **Duke of Brontë**; *b* 23 Dec 1814; Gen, Col Scots Gds, Groom-in-Waiting to HM QUEEN VICTORIA 1841–58, Equerry 1858–84, Extra Equerry and Ld-in-Waiting 1884–1901, Clerk Marshal to HRH THE PRINCE CONSORT 1853–61, Hon Equerry to HM EDWARD VII 1901–04; *m* 2 Aug 1838 Lady Mary Hill (*d* 15 July 1884), 2nd dau of 3rd Marquess of Downshire, KP (*qv*), and *d* 4 June 1904, having had issue:

1 ARTHUR WELLINGTON ALEXANDER NELSON HOOD, **2nd Viscount**

2 Horatio Nelson Sandys; *b* 24 March 1843; Cdr RN; *m* 28 Sept 1872 Isabella Emily (*m* 2nd 7 Aug 1888 Percy Edward James Leveson (*d* March 1896) and *d* 22 Dec 1939), 3rd dau of Lt-Col Sir Robert Mundy, KCMG, JP, RHA, and *dsp* 3 Feb 1881

3 William Nelson; *b* 6 Jan 1848; Lt RN; *d* 25 Oct 1921

4 Alexander Nelson (Sir), KCVO (1917); *b* 28 June 1854; Comptroller Household and Equerry to HRH THE DUCHESS OF TECK 1892–97, Extra Gentleman Usher Privy Chambers to HM QUEEN VICTORIA 1892–1901, Priv Sec to HM QUEEN MARY when PRINCESS OF WALES 1901–10, Treasurer to HM 1910–19, Grand Offr Crown of Italy, KGStJ; *d* unm 1 June 1937

5 Alfred Nelson; *b* 1 Oct 1858; *m* 29 Sept 1910 Ada Louisa (*d* 13 Oct 1959), er dau of Lt-Col Francis Charles Gavegan, Roy Berks Regt, and *dsp* 1 Dec 1918

6 Victor Albert Nelson, CMG (1916), JP (Qld and Vict, Australia); *b* 14 Nov 1862 (HM QUEEN VICTORIA stood sponsor); Priv Sec to Govrs S Australia 1903–05, Victoria 1906–20, W Australia 1912–13 and NSW 1913, Chamberlain to Govr-Gen Australia 1911; *m* 3 July 1928 Violet Annie (*d* 29 July 1942), widow of Alec McBean, of Kirndean, NSW, and *dsp* 1 May 1929

1 Nina Maria, VA; Woman of Bedchamber to HM QUEEN VICTORIA 1877–1901; *m* 7 Feb 1861 Lt-Col George Arthur Ferguson, DL, of Pitfour (*d* 15 Dec 1924), late Gren Gds, and *d* 5 June 1923, leaving issue

2 Mary; *m* 16 April 1868 6th Marquess of Hertford (*qv*) and *d* 6 April 1909, leaving issue

3 Adelaide Fanny; *m* 16 Sept 1879 Capt Herbert F Gye, MVO, RN (*d* 26 April 1906), Offr Legion of Honour, HM Consul Brest, and *d* 17 Jan 1927, leaving issue

4 Rosa Penelope; Maid of Honour to HM QUEEN VICTORIA 1886–94; *m* 31 July 1894 William Herbert Evans, DL (*dsp* 18 Sept 1900), of Forde Abbey, Dorset, and *d* 17 March 1922

The 1st VISCOUNT's est s,

ARTHUR WELLINGTON ALEXANDER NELSON HOOD, **2nd Viscount Bridport of Cricket St Thomas and of Brontë**, CB (1892), JP (Somerset); *b* 15 Dec 1839; MP (C) W Somerset 1868–80, Capt 25th Foot 1857–70, Col cmdg W Somerset Yeo Cav 1872–95; *m* 4 April 1872 Lady Maria Georgiana Julia Fox-Strangways (*d* 12 Oct 1922), sis of 5th Earl of Ilchester (*qv*), and *d* 28 March 1924, having had issue:

1 Alexander John Nelson; *b* 13 Aug 1876; *d* 31 Aug 1877

2 Maurice Henry Nelson; *b* 16 Jan 1881; Lt RN; *m* 19 Nov 1908 Ethel Rose (*d* 17 April 1931) (granted by roy warrant 11 March 1925 the title and precedence of widow of a Viscount), est dau of Charles Kendall, of Wokingham, and was *ka* 4 June 1915, leaving:

(1) ROWLAND ARTHUR HERBERT NELSON, **3rd Viscount**

(1) Eileen Sybil Mary Nelson; *b* 25 Jan 1910; granted by roy warrant 11 March 1925 rank of viscount's dau; *m* 11 July 1933 David Lawrence Baker, est s of Charles J Baker, formerly of Letcombe Manor, Wantage, and *d* 26 May 1936, leaving issue

1 Mary; *b* 19 Jan 1873; *m* 21 April 1898 Sir Herbert Frederick Cook, 3rd Bt (*qv*), and *d* 28 Nov 1934, leaving issue

2 Sybil Amy; *b* 10 Aug 1874; *d* unm 8 March 1956

The 2nd VISCOUNT's gs,

ROWLAND ARTHUR HERBERT NELSON HOOD, **3rd Viscount Bridport of Cricket St Thomas and of Brontë**; *b* 22 May 1911; *educ* RNC Dartmouth; Cadet RN 1924–29, Midshipman HMS *Nelson*, Home Fleet 1928–31, Sub Lt Courses 1931–32, HMS *Daring*, Mediterranean Fleet, 1933, transferred to Emerg List RN, Ld-in-Waiting to HM KING GEORGE VI 1939–40, served WW II (campaign stars Atlantic, Africa and Burma), Lt RN 1940, Lt-Cdr 1943, HMS *Newcastle* 1939–44, Pres Div Admlty 1944–45, Emerg List 1946, Coronation Medal 1953; *m* 1st 11 July 1934 (*divorce* 1945) Pamela Aline Mary, only dau of Charles J Baker, formerly of Letcombe Manor, Wantage, and had issue:

1 Peter Peregrine Nelson; *b* and *d* 6 May 1938

The **3rd Viscount** *m* 2nd 2 Jan 1946 Sheila Jeanne Agatha (*m* 3rd 1988 Alexei V Haieff and *d* 24 May 1996), only dau of Johan Hendrik van Meurs, of London, and widow of W/Cdr James Hayward Little, DFC, RAuxAF, and *d* 1969, leaving issue by her:

2 ALEXANDER NELSON HOOD, **4th and present Viscount of Cricket St Thomas and of Brontë**

BRIGGS

Creation: B. (LP, UK) 1976.

THE BARON BRIGGS, of Lewes, Co of E Sussex (Asa Briggs) [The Rt Hon The Lord Briggs, The Caprons, Keere St, Lewes, Sussex BN7 1TY]; *b* 7 May 1921; *educ* Keighley GS and Sidney Sussex Coll Cambridge (MA); MA Oxford; BSc (Econ) London; served Intelligence Corps 1942–45; Fell Worcester Coll Oxford 1945–55, Reader Oxford U 1950–55; Dep Pres WEA 1954–58 (Pres 1958–67); Prof Modern History: Leeds U 1955–61, Sussex U 1961–76 (V-Chllr 67–76); memb UGC 1959–67; Tstee: Glyndebourne Arts Tst 1966–91, Internat Broadcasting Inst 1968–87; Chm: Bd Govrs Inst Devpt Studies 1967–76, Standing Conf Study of Local History 1969–76, Ctee on Nursing 1970–72, Cncl European Inst of Educn 1975, Heritage Educn Gp 1976–86, Civic Tst 1976–86; Govr BFI 1970–77; V-Chm Cncl UN U 1974–80; Provost Worcester Coll Oxford 1976–91, Chllr OU 1979–; Pres: Social History Soc 1976–, Victorian Soc 1983–, Ephemera Soc 1984–, Br Assoc for Local History 1984–86, Assoc of Research Assocs 1986–88; V-Pres Historical Assoc 1986–; Chm: Advsy Bd Redundant Churches 1983–89, Commonwealth of Learning 1988–93; Hon LLD York, Canada, New England, OU; Hon DLitt UEA 1966, Strathclyde 1973, Leeds 1974, Liverpool 1977, OU 1979, Bradford, Sussex, Birmingham 1989, Missouri 1993, Cincinnati, George Washington; FBA; Fell American Academy; Hon Fellow: Sidney Sussex Coll Cambridge 1968, Worcester Coll Oxford 1969, St Catharine's Coll Cambridge 1977; author: *Patterns of Peace-making* (with D Thomson and E Meyer 1945), *History of Birmingham 1865–1938* (1952), *Victorian People* (1954), *Friends of the People* (1956), *The Age of Improvement* (1959), *Chartist Studies* (ed, 1959), *Essays in Labout History* (ed with John Saville, vol 1 1960, vol 2 1971, vol 3 1977), *They Saw it Happen 1897–1940* (ed, 1961), *Seebohm Rowntree 1871–1954* (1961), *History of Broadcasting in the United Kingdom* (vol 1 1961, vol 2 1965, vol 3 1970, vol 4 1979, vol 5 1995), *Victorian Cities* (1963), *William Cobbett* (1967), *How They Lived 1700–1815* (1969), *The Nineteenth Century* (1970), *Cap and Bell* (with Susan Briggs, 1971), *Essays in the History of Publishing* (1974), *Iron Bridge to Crystal Palace* (1979), *Governing the BBC* (1979), *The Power of Steam* (1982), *Marx in London* (1982), *A Social History of England* (1983, rev edn 1994), *Toynbee Hall* (1984), *Collected Essays* (vols1 and 2 1985, vol 3 1991), *The BBC: The First 50 Years* (1985), *TheFranchise Affair* (with Joanna Spicer 1986), *Victorian Things* (1988), *Haut Brion* (1994), *The Channel Islands: Occupation and Liberation 1940–1945* (1995), *Fins de Siecle: How Centuries End* (with Daniel Snowman, 1996), *Modern Europe 1789–1989* (with Patricia Calvin, 1996); *m* 1955 *Susan Anne, dau of Donald William Banwell, of Keevil, Wilts, and has:

1 *Daniel Nicholas; *b* 1958; *m* 1989 *Anabel E M, yst dau of Harvey Ziegler, of Chiddingfold, Surrey, and has:

(1) *Henry Nathaniel; *b* 1994

(2) *William Wilkie; *b* 1995

(3) *Arthur Asa; *b* 1997

2 *Matthew William Banwell; *b* 1964

1 *Katharine Jane [The Hon Mrs Wheeler, 30 Alexandra Rd, Epsom, Surrey]; *b* 1956; *m* 1980 *David Robert Wheeler, and has:

(1) *Timothy Robert; *b* 1985

(1) *Caroline Jane; *b* 1982

(2) *Charlotte Rose; *b* 1987

(3) *Georgina May; *b* 1991

2 *Judith Susanna; *b* 1961; *m* 1985 *Philip G F Preston, only s of W Preston, of Folkestone, Kent, and has issue:

(1) *Jonathan; *b* 1989

(2) *Samuel; *b* 1993

(3) *Thomas (twin); *b* 1993

Lineage: WILLIAM WALKER BRIGGS; *m* Jane — and had:

ASA, *cr* a **Baron**

BRIGHTMAN

Arms: Per fess wavy azure and argent, in chief two dolphins naiant or and in base the stern of a man of war of *c* 1805 proper. **Crest:** Upon a wreath argent and gules a herring gull statant, wings elevated and addorsed proper, supporting with the dexter claw a rose gules, barbed and seeded proper. **Supporters:** Two otters, each on a grassy mount encircled by water proper and collared with a crown rayonny gold. **Motto:** Steer a true course. **Creation:** B. (LP, UK) 1982.

THE BARON BRIGHTMAN, of Ibthorpe, Co Southampton (Sir John Anson Brightman, PC (1979)) [The Rt Hon The Lord Brightman PC, House of Lords, London SW1A 0PW; Ibthorpe, Hants SP11 0BY; 30 Onslow Gardens London SW7 3AH]; *b* 20 June 1911; *educ* Marlborough and St John's Coll Cambridge; barrister Lincoln's Inn 1932; Able Seaman Merchant Navy 1939–40, Lt-Cdr RNVR 1940–46, RNSC 1944, Assist Naval Attaché Ankara 1944; Memb Gen Cncl of the Bar 1955–60 and 1966–70, QC 1961, Bencher 1966, Attorney-Gen Duchy Lancaster and Attorney and Serjeant within the County Palatine of Lancaster 1969–70, Judge Nat Industl Rels Court 1971–74, Judge High Court Chancery 1970–79, ktd 1970, Ld Justice Appeal 1979–1982, Ld Appeal in Ordinary 1982–86; Chm: Tancred's Charities 1982–96, Ho Lds Select Ctees on: charities 1983–84, Abortion Law 1987–88, City of Bristol Devpt 1988, Spitalfield Mkt 1989, Br Waterways 1991, Property Law 1994, Private International Law 1994–95, Family Homes and Domestic Violence 1995; memb Ctee on Tax Law Simplification 1996; Hon Fellow St John's Coll Cambridge 1982; FRGS 1992; *m* 1945 *Roxane, dau of Gerasimo Ambatielo, of Kephalonia, and has issue:

1 *Christopher Anthony John; *b* 1948; *educ* Marlborough and St John's Coll Cambridge (MB, BChir, MSc); *m* 1975 *Elisabeth, yr dau of Jonkheer Willem de Beyer, and has issue:

(1) *Louisa; *b* 1978

(2) *Justina; *b* 1980

(3) *Eugénie; *b* 1982

Lineage: WILLIAM HENRY BRIGHTMAN, of St Alban's, Herts, had a 2nd son:

JOHN ANSON, *cr* a **Baron**

BRIGSTOCKE

Creation: B. (LP, UK) 1990.

THE BARONESS BRIGSTOCKE, of Kensington, Royal Borough of Kensington and Chelsea (Heather Renwick Brown) [The Rt Hon The Baroness Brigstocke, House of Lords, London SW1A 0PA]; *b* 2 Sept 1929; *educ* Abbey Sch Reading and Girton Coll Cambridge; Hon Bencher Inner Temple 1992, classics mistress Francis Holland Sch London 1951–53 and (part-time) Godolphin and Latymer Sch 1954–60, Latin teacher Nat Cathedral Sch Washington DC 1962–4, headmistress Francis Holland Sch 1965–74, High Mistress St Paul's Girls' Sch 1974–89, memb cncl: London Ho Overseas Grads 1965–91 (V-Chm 1975–80), Middx Hosp Medical Sch 1971–80, Roy Holloway Coll 1977–85, City U 1978–83, memb Cncl RSA 1983–87, St George's House Windsor 1984–90, Modern For Languages Working Gp 1989–90, Museums and Galleries Commn 1992– and Health Educn Authority 1989–; Tstee Nat Gallery 1975–82, Kennedy Meml Tst 1980–85 and Tech Colls Tst 1987–; Pres Bp Creighton House Settlement Fulham 1977– and Girls' Schs Assoc 1980–81, Govr Wellington 1975–87, Roy Ballet Sch 1977–92, Forest Sch 1982–90, Museum of London 1986–92 and Gordonstoun 1991–93, Chm ESU 1993–, non-exec dir LWT 1982–90, memb Programme Advsy Bd LWT 1990–93, chm Autistic Care & Training Devpt Appeal 1990, Tstees Geffrye Museum 1990–, Thames LWT Telethon Tst 1990 and Minerva Educnl Tst 1991–93; independent nat dir Times Newspaper Hldgs 1991–, memb governing body Imp Coll 1991–, chm Landau Forte City Tech Coll Derby 1993– (Govr 1992–), assoc dir GUS 1993–96, V-Pres City & Guilds London Inst 1993–, non-exec dir Burberrys 1993–96, ctee memb AA 1975–90, special advsr Kays 1989–90 and Burberrys 1989–92; Tstee G B Sasa Kawa Fndn 1994–; *m* 1952 Geoffrey Brigstocke (*d* 1974) and has issue:

1 *David Hugh Charles; *b* 1953

2 *Julian Renwick; *b* 1955

3 *Thomas James Jefferson; *b* 1961

1 *Emma Persephone; *b* 1957

Lineage: JOHN RENWICK BROWN had issue:

HEATHER RENWICK, *cr* a **Baroness**

BRINCKMAN

Arms: Quarterly, 1st and 4th, arg. three hills az. (for BRINCKMAN); 2nd and 3rd, erm., two eagles displayed in chief gu. and a lion rampant in base ppr., collared and chained or (for BROADHEAD). **Crest:** A pair of wings, quarterly arg. and az. **Motto:** *Perseverando* ('By persevering'). **Creation:** Bt. (UK) 30 Sept 1831.

SIR THEODORE GEORGE RODERICK BRINCKMAN, 6TH BT, of Monk Bretton, Co York [Sir Theodore Brinckman Bt, Hazleton Manor, Cirencester, Glos GL7 6PG]; *b* 20 March 1932; *s* f 1985; *educ* Millfield, Trin Coll Sch Port Hope Ontario, Millfield, Ch Ch Oxford and Trin Coll Toronto (BA); publisher and antiquarian bookseller; *m* 1st 11 June 1958 (*divorce* 1983) (Helen) Mary Anne, er dau of Arnold Elliot Cook, of 14 Cluny Dve, Rosedale, Toronto; *m* 2nd 1983 *Hon Greta Sheira Bernadette Grant-Ferris, dau of Baron Harvington (LP; *d* 1 Jan 1997) and formerly w of (a) John Frederick Edward Trehearne and (b) Christopher Mark Henry Murray, and has issue by 1st w:

1 +THEODORE JONATHAN [Theodore Brinckman Esq, 93 Roxborough St W, Toronto, Ontario M5R 1T9, Canada]; *b* 19 Feb 1960; *educ* Lakefield Coll Sch Ontario, Yale U (BA) and Columbia Graduate Sch of Journalism (MSc)

2 +(Roderick) Nicholas [Nicholas Brinckman Esq, 54 Astley Ave, Toronto, Canada]; *b* 16 Sept 1964; *educ* Lakefield Coll Sch, Toronto U (BA) and U of Victoria Law Sch (LLB)

1 *Sophia Theresa [Miss Sophia Brinckman, 74 Abdale Rd, London W12 7EU]; *b* 16 April 1963; *educ* Bishop's Coll Sch Quebec

Lineage: JOHN BROADHEAD, one of the chief freeholders of Bretton, Burton or Monk Bretton, Yorks, was granted as a tstee by JAMES I *c* 1612 the Manor of Bretton etc. His gs:

JOHN BROADHEAD, of Monk Bretton; *fl temp* CHARLES II; f of:

1 Henry, of Monk Bretton and St Giles-in-the-Fields, Middx, brewer; *b* 1682/3; *m* twice but *dsp* 14 Nov 1754

1 Margaret; *m* John Bingley, of Bolton-upon-Dearne, and *d* 1706, having had issue:

(1) William; *dsp*

(2) Henry; *dsp*

(1) ANNE; *m* John Richard Brinckman, 2nd s of Theodore, Baron Brinckman (who migrated to England from Hanover with GEORGE I) by his w Elizabeth Ducheros, and had issue:

1a THEODORE HENRY BRINCKMAN later BROADHEAD, of Bretton, later Doncaster, later Carshalton House, Surrey, later still Holly Grove, Windsor Pk, High Sheriff Surrey 1786; *b* Sept 1741; took by Act of Parl in compliance with the will of his unc Henry (whose heir he was) the name and arms of BROADHEAD; *m* 1767 his cousin Mary, dau and heir of John Bingley, of Goldthorpe, Bolton-upon-Dearne (the estate of Sir John Bingley, Auditor Exchequer *temp* JAMES I), and *d* 20 March 1810, leaving an est s:

1b THEODORE HENRY BROADHEAD, of Holly Grove, Windsor Pk; MP Wareham and Yarmouth; *b* 3 Dec 1767; *m* 11 May 1797 Elizabeth, dau of William Gordon Macdougall, descended from the Macdougalls of Lorn, and *d* 12 Dec 1820, having had, with other issue, an est son:

1c Sir THEODORE HENRY LAVINGTON BROADHEAD later BRINCKMAN (roy licence July 1842), **1st Bt** (UK), so *cr* 30 Sept 1831 of St Leonards, Windsor; *b* 17 Jan 1798; MP Yarmouth 1820–26; *m* 1st 29 Aug 1829 Charlotte (*d* 1838), only dau of 1st Baron Godolphin and sis of 8th Duke of Leeds (*see* 1963 edn), and had issue:

1d THEODORE HENRY (Sir), **2nd Bt**

2d Frederick John, 2nd W India Regt; *b* 17 Feb 1832; *d* 19 Feb 1855

3d William Edward, RN; *b* 25 Nov 1833; *m* 13 Sept 1859 Mary Alice (*d* 27 Jan 1901), est dau of Rowland Eyles Egerton-Warburton, DL, JP, of Arley Hall, Cheshire (*see* GREY EGERTON, Bt), and *d* 10 Jan 1872, leaving:

1e William Henry, AMICE; *b* 21 June 1860; *m* 7 June 1894 Winifred Blanche Victoria (*d* 18 Feb 1969), dau of Caleb Cox, Customs and Excise Offr, and *d* 10 April 1920, leaving issue:

1f William Brian; *b* 10 May 1904; served WW II 1942–45 in RAFVR (despatches); *m* 6 March 1937 *Marjorie, dau of John Ashbrook Hughes, and *d* 1975 leaving issue:

1g *Hilary Anne; *b* 26 April 1937

1f Winifred Peris, MB, ChB, MRCS, LRCP; *b* 26 Feb 1895; *d* unm 29 April 1969

2f Rosemary; *b* 15 July 1900; *m* 6 Sept 1941 Col Harold Alonzo Bazley, RE, BA, FRICS, son of James Bazley, of Whitchurch, Tavistock, and *d* 19–

2e Rowland, OBE (1919); *b* 19 Nov 1861; Maj Roy Irish Fus, GSO 1914; *m* 1st 26 Aug 1891 Anna Alexander (*d* 11 Sept 1910), dau of Prof John Elliot Cairnes; *m* 2nd 18 Oct 1911 Marian (*d* 7 April 1941), dau of Richard Baxter, and *d* 4 Jan 1948, leaving issue by his 1st w:

1f Rowland Egerton; *b* 24 Feb 1894; *d* 9 April 1936

2f Denys; *b* 15 March 1896; Lt Roy Irish Fus; *ka* 10 June 1915

1f Doris Audrey; *b* 30 Sept 1892; *d* 1893

2f Christine Phyllida; *b* 25 Dec 1907; *m* 25 Nov 1931 Sir Hugo Frank Marshall KBE, CMG, JP Nigerian Admin Serv (*d* 10 June 1986), son of Henry Mieres Marshall, of The Manor Ho, Limpley Stoke, and *d* 15 Jan 1996, leaving:

1g *Robert Rowland [Robert Marshall Esq, 194 Richmond Rd, Kingston-on-Thames, Surrey]; *b* 6 Aug 1942; *educ* Bryanston and Exeter Coll Oxford; *m* 24 Sept 1966 *Joan Monica Theresa, dau of Rev Canon Henry Leach, of Johannesburg, S Africa

2g *David William; *b* 25 Nov 1945; *educ* Bryanston and Exeter Coll Oxford; *m* 1969 *Lorraine June, dau of C W Robbins, of Miami Beach, Florida, and has issue:

1h *William Denys; *b* 1970

2h *Reuben Grey; *b* 1972

3h *Henry Balfour; *b* 1977

4h *Alexander Rowland; *b* 1988

1h *Danae Gwyneth; *b* 1980

1g *Janet Mary [Mrs David Cunliffe-Jones, 9 Elson Rd, Formby, Lancs L37 2EG]; *b* 16 Sept 1937; *educ* Godolphin Sch and St Hilda's Coll Oxford; *m* 3 Sept 1960 *David Brian Cunliffe-Jones, son of Dr Hubert Cunliffe-Jones, of 5 Wood Rd, Manchester 16, and has issue:

1h *Andrew Robert; *b* 3 Aug 1962

2h *Peter David; *b* 17 Dec 1964

1h *Judith Elizabeth; *b* 21 Aug 1961

2h *Rosemary Janet Helen; *b* 28 Jan 1968

1e Gwynnedd; *m* 1st 31 July 1888 Maj-Gen Charles William Campbell, late 2nd Bengal Cav (*d* 1894), and had issue (*see* 1970 edn BREADALBANE, E); *m* 2nd 28 Oct 1925 Rev Walter D Williams, MA (*d* 13 Jan 1931), vicar Bodelwyddan, Flints, and *d* 24 Feb 1948

4d Arthur (Rev), Lt 94th Foot; *b* 6 Jan 1838; *m* 19 April 1864 Louisa Georgiana Edith (*d* 22 Aug 1867), est dau of Rev Henry Hutchinson Swinny, Vicar Cuddesdon, and *d* 28 Jan 1913, leaving issue:

1e Helen Louisa; *d* 2 June 1921

1d Frances Grace; *m* 16 Sept 1856 George John Johnson, DL, MP, of Winkleigh Court, Devon, only son of Rev P Johnson (*d* 1896), Rector Wembworthy, N Devon, and *d* 16 March 1908, leaving issue

1c (cont.) Sir THEODORE *m* 2nd 18 Feb 1841 Annabella (*d* 23 Jan 1864), dau of John Corbet, of Sundorne Castle, Salop

Sir THEODORE *d* 9 Feb 1880; his est son,

Sir Theodore Henry Brinckman, 2nd Bt of Holly Grove and St Leonards, DL (Yorks), MP Canterbury 1868–74, Capt 17th Regt; *b* 12 Sept 1830; *m* 18 July 1861 Lady Cecilia Augusta (*d* 16 Aug 1877), yst dau of 2nd Marquess Conyngham (*qv*), and had:

1 THEODORE FRANCIS (Sir), **3rd Bt**

2 Claude Ernest William; *b* 31 May 1871; *m* 6 June 1895 Mary (*d* 2 Aug 1906), only dau of Col Sydenham Malthus, CB, of Albury, Surrey, and *dsp* 2 April 1938

Sir THEODORE *d* 7 May 1905; his er son,

Sir Theodore Francis Brinckman, 3rd Bt; *b* 26 May 1862; Hon Col, Lt-Col cmdg 3rd Bn The Buffs (Roy E Kent Regt), Lt-Col TF, served S Africa 1899–1902 (despatches, two medals, six clasps) and WW I 1914, Order Dannebrog; *m* 1st 3 Sept 1883 (*divorce* 1895) Fanny Lucy, DBE (*d* 29 Dec 1936), 4th dau of Thomas Radmall, of St Margaret's, Twickenham; *m* 2nd 27 April 1895 (*divorce* 1912) Mary Frances (*d* 11 March 1948), dau of Capt James Wingfield Linton, of Hemingford, Hunts, by Ella Victoria, afterwards Countess of Aylesford (*qv*); *m* 3rd 30 April 1913 Elizabeth Marie Jeanne (*d* 12 May 1956), dau of Denis M A A Bergerand, of Roanne, France, and *d* 8 Sept 1937, having had issue by his 2nd w:

1 **Sir Theodore Ernest Warren Brinckman, 4th Bt**; *b* 21 May 1898; *educ* Eton and RMC Sandhurst, Maj Res Offrs Life Gds WW I 1916–18; *m* 1st 12 Jan 1921 (*annulled* 1922) Gretta Frances Florence, dau of John Russell Bedford Cameron by Frances (formerly Marchioness Conyngham); *m* 2nd 19 July 1926 (*divorce* 1929) Anne Margrethe (Grete), dau of E T A Wennerwald, of Copenhagen, and formerly w of Count Eggert Christopher Knuth; *m* 3rd 5 June 1939 (*divorce* 1952) Ethel Jean, dau of Wilson Mills Southam, of Rockcliffe, Ottawa, Canada, and formerly w of Paul E V Peters, and *dsp* 26 July 1954

2 RODERICK NAPOLEON (Sir), **5th Bt**

1 Daphne Cecilia; *b* 9 Dec 1899; *m* 25 Nov 1946 (*annulled* 1949) Maj Thomas Leefe, RASC (*d* 1968), er son of Oswald Leefe, of Malton, Yorks, and *dsp* 22 Jan 1953

Sir THEODORE's bro,

Sir Roderick Napoleon Brinckman, 5th Bt, DSO, MC; *b* 27 Dec 1902; *educ* RN Cs Osborne and Dartmouth; Col Gren Gds, ADC to Govr Victoria 1926–27, Capt and ADC to Govr-Gen Canada 1930–31, served WW II (wounded, despatches, POW, escaped), Ch Staff to Br Mil Mission Russia 1944–45, Head Br Mil Mission Netherlands Govt 1945–46; *m* 1st 10 Jan 1931 (*divorce* 1943) Margaret Wilson, dau of Wilson Mills Southam, of Rockcliffe, Ottawa, and had issue:

1 Sir THEODORE GEORGE RODERICK BRINCKMAN, **6th and present Bt**

2 +John Francis [John Brinckman Esq, 191 St George St, Toronto, Ontario M5R 2M6, Canada]; *b* 14 Sept 1933; *educ* TCS Ontario and McGill U Montreal (BA); *m* 1st 2 March 1963 (*divorce* 1973) Susan Jennifer, er dau of Peter Woodburn Blaylock, of Toad's Tooting, Ile Bizard, Quebec, and has issue:

(1) +Adam Blaylock; *b* 24 May 1965

(1) *Theodora Southam; *b* 29 March 1966

2 (cont.) John Brinckman *m* 2nd 7 Dec 1983 (*divorce* 1989) Eve Napier Murray and has further issue:

(2) +John Christian Napoleon; *b* 13 April 1985

2 (cont.) John Brinckman has by Kerry, dau of Thomas Bingham, of Victoria, BC:

(3) *Nigel Thomas Bingham; *b* 1988

Sir Roderick *m* 2nd 1943 Rosemary Marguerite, yr dau of Lt-Col James Charles Hope Vere, of Blackwood, Lanarkshire (*see* LINLITHGOW, M), and formerly w of Quintin Holland Gilbey, and *d* 1985, having by her had further issue:

1 *Theadora Elizabeth [Mrs Theadora Lavarack, 491 Fulham Rd, London SW6]; *b* 11 Nov 1943; *m* 19 May 1964 (*divorce* 1976) Gerard Francis Campbell, er son of Capt Robin Francis Campbell, DSO, and Hon Mrs Lees Mayall, est dau of 4th Baron Harlech (*qv*), and has issue; *m* 2nd 1978 (*divorce* 1994) Dennis Cordell Lavarack and by him has:

(3) *Milo Napoleon; *b* 10 Nov 1978

(1) *Emerald Clare; *b* 19 Feb1981

BRISCO

Arms: Arg. three greyhounds courant in pale sa. **Crest:** A greyhound courant sa., seizing a hare ppr. **Motto:** *Grata sume manu* ('Take with a grateful hand'). **Creation:** Bt. (GB) 11 July 1782.

SIR CAMPBELL HOWARD BRISCO, 9TH BT, of Crofton Place, Cumberland [Sir Campbell Brisco Bt, Kawariri, 134 Park St, Winton, Southland, New Zealand]; *b* 1944; *s* cousin 1995; livestock farmer and manager; *m* 1969 *Kay Janette, dau of Ewan W McFadzien, of Winton, and has issue:

1 +KENT RIMINGTON; *b* 1972

2 +Shannon Gregory; *b* 1974

1 *Rebecca Kaye; *b* 1978

Lineage: The BRISCOs take their name from Brisco, Cumberland.

ISOLD BRISCO; *m c* 1390 Margaret, dau and heiress of Sir John Crofton, of Crofton, Cumberland, through whom Crofton passed to the BRISCOs, and was ancestor of:

JOHN BRISCO, of Crofton Hall, Cumberland; *m* Catherine, dau of Sir Richard Musgrave, Bt, of Hayton Castle, and *d* 1760, leaving, with other issue (including Musgrave Brisco, ancestor of the BRISCOs of Coghurst, nr Hastings):

Rev JOHN BRISCO, DD, of Crofton Hall, Rector Orton, Vicar Aspatria; *b* 19 Dec 1701; *m* Catherine, dau and coheir of 'Baron' (a form of address somewhere between a sobriquet and a family forename, used for generations by the Hyltons, who were of ancient albeit provincial importance in Co Durham; *see* HYLTON, B) Hylton, of Hylton Castle, Co Durham, and had an est s:

Sir John Brisco, 1st Bt (GB), so *cr* 11 July 1782, of Crofton Hall; *b* 15 May 1739; *m* 8 July 1776 Caroline Alicia (*d* 27 Dec 1822), dau of Gilbert Fane Fleming by Lady Camilla Bennet, dau of 2nd Earl of Tankerville (*qv*), and *d* 27 Dec 1806, leaving an er s:

Sir Wastel Brisco, 2nd Bt; *b* 17 May 1778; *m* 18 Nov 1806 Sarah Lester (*d* 28 Aug 1861), dau of Robert Ladbrook, and had, with other issue:

1 ROBERT (Sir), **3rd Bt**

2 Hylton, Lt-Col 2nd Dragoon Gds; *b* 24 March 1810; *d* 8 Jan 1896

3 Wastel; *b* 26 Oct 1812; *d* 11 June 1835

Sir WASTEL *d* 1 Oct 1862; his est son,

Sir Robert Brisco, 3rd Bt; *b* 17 Sept 1808; *m* 10 July 1832 Annie Drewry (*d* 14 Aug 1875), 3rd dau of George Rimington, of Tyne Field House, Cumberland, and *d* 23 Dec 1884, having had issue:

1 **Sir Musgrave Horton Brisco, 4th Bt**, DL, JP, and CA for Cumberland; *b* 11 Aug 1833; *m* 27 June 1867 Mary Elizabeth (*d* 31 July 1922), widow of Capt Richard Newsham Pedder, 10th Hus, and est dau of Sir William Henry Feilden, 2nd Bt (*qv*), and *d* 19 Dec 1909, having had issue:

(1) **Sir Hylton Ralph Brisco, 5th Bt**; *b* 24 Sept 1871; *m* 1st 20 April 1904 (*divorce* 1916) Lilian Mabel, dau of James King, and n and adopted dau of Lucy, Countess of Egmont (*see* EGMONT, E); *m* 2nd 1916 (*divorce* 1922) Grace, dau of Henry Vaughan, and *d* lost at sea 29 Jan 1922

(1) Hilda Cunningham, *s* to the Crofton estate; *d* unm 19 May 1946

(2) Violet; *m* 1904 William Cheesman and *dsp* 13 Aug 1907

2 Robert George; *b* 7 Sept 1836; *m* 24 July 1860 Lydia (*d* 1896), dau of John Spencer, and *d* 19 Oct 1873, leaving issue:

(1) Hylton Tankerville; *b* 23 Feb 1863; *d* 11 Jan 1881

(2) John Spencer; *b* 6 Jan 1866; *d* unm 25 Aug 1898

(1) Helen Mary; *m* 1 June 1895 William Francis Cochrane, of Nelson, BC (*d* 1924)

(2) Ada Louisa

(3) Henrietta; *d* 17 Nov 1882

3 Wastel, 11th Hus; *b* 26 Sept 1838; *d* 10 Feb 1866

4 Fleming; *b* 20 April 1845; *m* 13 April 1871 Fanny Aubrey, est dau of Rev Bulkeley O Jones, Chllr St Asaph, and *d* 17 March 1901, leaving issue:

(1) **Sir Aubrey Hylton Brisco, 6th Bt**; *b* 11 Dec 1873; *m* 1st 14 Feb 1904 Anna Victoria (*d* 9 May 1929), 2nd dau of James Doyle, of San Francisco; *m* 2nd 26 March 1938 Ruby Pearl, dau of John Jacob Runck, and *dsp* 16 June 1957

(2) Cecil Fleming; *b* 31 Jan 1876; *d* 1931

(3) Musgrave Wynne; *b* 14 Feb 1886; *m* and *d* 1945, leaving issue

1a Phyllis; *m* — Anderson

(1) Gwendolen Constance; *m* 1906 William Clay Baker, of Virginia, and had issue

5 Arthur Hylton; *b* 18 Sept 1847; *m* 1885 Jessie Mary (*d* 24 Oct 1932), dau of Capt Francis Eastwood Campbell, Roy Welch Fus, and *d* 1927, leaving issue:

(1) **Sir Hylton Musgrave Campbell Brisco, 7th Bt**; *b* 1886; *m* 1914 Kathleen, dau of W Fenwick McAllum, and *d* 1968, having had:

1a Robert Hylton; *b* 1916; *ka* 1943

2a **Sir Donald Gilfrid Brisco, 8th Bt**; JP (Hawke's Bay 1967); *b* 15 Sept 1920; *educ* Wairapa Coll NZ; P/O RNZAF and RAF WW II (POW 1942–45), sheep farmer; *m* 5 Aug 1945 *Irene [Irene Lady Brisco, 27a Chambers St, PO Box 8165, Havelock N, Hawke's Bay, New Zealand], only dau of Henry John Gage, of Ermine Park, Brockworth, Glos, and *d* 1995, leaving:

1b *Barbara Ann [Mrs William Wilson, Lot 56, Melaleuca Dve, Lamb Island, Qld 4184, Australia]; *b* 14 Nov 1946; *m* 1983 *William Ian Wilson

2b *Penny Christine [Miss Penny Brisco, 1/448 Marine Parade, Biggera Waters, Qld 4216, Australia]; *b* 28 Jan 1949

3b *Jill Kathleen [Mrs Wayne Brunton, 97 Awanui St, New Plymouth, New Zealand]; *b* 6 Sept 1952; *m* 1974 *Wayne George Brunton

1a Kathleen Margaret; *b* 1915; *m* 1943 Arvin R Murphy and *d* 16 Nov 1959

2a Barbara Grace (twin); *b* 1916; *d* 1937

3a Estelle Mary; *b* 1917; *m* Harold Dowrick (*d* 18 Dec 1955)

4a *Joan Elsie [Mrs F McTague, 33 Kennedy Rd, Napier, Hawke's Bay, NZ]; *b* 1923; *m* 1953 *F J A McTague and has issue:

1b *Robert Howard; *b* 1953

2b *Richard Patrick; *b* 1957

3b *Steven Francis; *b* 1965

5a *Oriel Patricia [Mrs Oriel Spicer, 2/211 Windsor Ave, Hastings, Hawke's Bay, New Zealand]; *b* 8 Dec 1926; *m* 1st 1950 (*divorce* 1974) James C Waldren; *m* 2nd 1975 Lt-Col Reginald Henry Spicer, MC (*d* 19–), and has by her 1st husb:

1b *Murray David; *b* 1951

1b *Christine Lesley; *b* 1953

(2) Wastel; *b* 1888; *ka* 1915

(3) Oriel Arthur, served NZ Forces WW I Egypt, Gallipoli and France, Home Def Forces WW II; *b* 26 June 1892; *m* 1st 1921 Lilian Frederica, dau of Francis Ernest Dominic Saunderson, of Christchurch, NZ; *m* 2nd Dec 1960 Sarah Louisa, dau of Rice Owen Clark, of Hobsonville, NZ

(4) Gilfrid Rimington; *b* 1895; served WW I; *m* 1941 Constance Freda (*d* 1980), 2nd dau of Charles John Polson, of Masterton, NZ, and *d* 1981 leaving:

1a Sir CAMPBELL HOWARD BRISCO, **9th and present Bt**

1a *Rosemary Robyn [Mrs Peter Neale, 24 Newcastle St, Rose Bay, Sydney 2029, Australia]; *b* 1943; *m* 3 Feb 1966 *Peter Colin Neale, est s of K Neale, of Auckland, NZ, and has issue:

1b *Adam Hylton; *b* 20 Dec 1968

(5) Bertram Isold; *b* 1896

BRISCOE

Arms: Argent two greyhounds courant sable, on a chief arched of the last two roses of the first, barbed and seeded proper. **Crest:** Upon a mount of heather proper a greyhound courant paly of twelve argent and sable. **Motto:** *Præsto et persisto* ('I perform and persevere'). **Creation:** Bt. (UK) 12 July 1910.

SIR JOHN GEOFFREY JAMES BRISCOE, 6TH BT, of Bourn Hall, Bourn, Co Cambridge [Sir John Briscoe Bt, Hall Barn, Swainsthorpe, Norwich, Norfolk NR14 8QA]; *b* posthumously 4 Nov 1994; *s* f at birth

Lineage: JOHN BRISCOE, of Penley Hall, Flints, and Northwood, Salop; *b* 1699; *m c* 1735 Mary Turner and was *bur* 4 Feb 1782, leaving issue:

JOHN BRISCOE, of Penley Hall; *bapt* 14 July 1739; *m* 10 Feb 1763 Deborah (*bur* 20 Dec 1820 aged 79), dau of Thomas Beddow, of Ellesmere, and was *bur* 16 Jan 1826, having had issue:

1 Thomas; *bapt* 7 Nov 1769; *m* Frances (*bur* 16 Dec 1831) and *d* Feb 1855, having had issue:

(1) John; *bapt* 6 Jan 1798

(1) Mary; *bapt* 19 May 1793

(2) Sarah; *bapt* 13 Apr 1795

(3) Jane; *bapt* 8 Jan 1800

2 JAMES

3 John, of Gwalia, Knowlton, Flints; *bapt* 31 Oct 1772; *m* Mary, dau of Hugh Birch, of Lancaster, and *dsp* 28 Jul 1840

4 Edward, of Wem, Salop; *bapt* 15 May 1780; *bur* 23 Jul 1838

5 Richard, of Wrexham; *bapt* 21 Apr 1783; *m* 26 Nov 1807 Margaret (*b* 1783; *d* 18 Sept 1850), dau of Rev Thomas Owen, MA, rector Llangelynin, Merioneths, and *d* 28 Jan 1848, having had, with other issue:

(1) Rev Richard, JP (Flints); *b* 4 Jan 1808; MA, DD, Fell Jesus Coll Oxford, rector Nutfield, Surrey, 1865–80, vicar Whitford, Flints, 1839–65; *m* 3 Apr 1866 Jane Eliza Anne Pollexfen (*b* 2 Nov 1834; *d* 27 Dec 1900), er dau and eventual sole heir of Capt Rose Henry Fuller, RN (yr bro of Sir Thomas Trayton Fuller-Elliott-Drake, Bt), and *d* 17 Oct 1880, having had issue:

1a Theodore Francis Heathfield; *b* 15 Oct 1867; *educ* Jesus Coll Oxford (MA); *m* 30 Aug 1898 Lilian Maude Sophia (*d* 1934), dau of H H Gain, Fleet Paymaster, of Johannesburg, and *d* Dec 1935

2a Rev Henry Meyrick Eliott-Drake; *b* 12 Sep 1870; *educ* Jesus Coll Oxford (MA 1896), rector Burnham Thorpe, Norfolk, and Rural Dean Burnham; *m* 24 Aug 1896 Louise Mary (*d* 25 April 1959), dau of Isaac Robinson, of Guildford, Surrey, and *d* 25 Apr 1935, leaving issue:

1b Francis Meyrick Eliott-Drake BRISCOE later DRAKE-BRISCOE; *b* 5 Oct 1898; Lt-Col Roy Norfolk Regt; added by deed poll 1937 the name DRAKE; *m* 18 Feb 1928 Rosalind Gertrude, est dau of Thomas F Adshead, of Wimbledon and Ewell, and *d* 15 Sept 1985, having had issue:

1c John; *b* and *d* 9 Feb 1931

2c Francis Eliott-Drake BRISCOE later DRAKE-BRISCOE; *b* 18 Oct 1934; *educ* Leys Sch and RMA Sandhurst; *m* 19– *Carol Clarke and *d* 14 March 1990, having had issue:

1d *Mark; *b* 19 Dec 1964

1d *Joanna; *b* 7 Jan 1963

2d *Holly; *b* 1970

1c Elizabeth Angela; *b* 24 Apr 1932; *m* 18 Mar 1964 Geoffrey Gorton Horrocks, MA (*d* 8 Feb 1996), slr, yr s of G Horrocks, of Southport, Lancs, and *d* 27 Oct 1965, leaving issue:

1d Clive; *b* 27 Aug 1965; *d* 29 Oct 1995

2b George Augustus Eliott-Drake; *b* 22 March 1903; *m* 1935 Mary, 4th dau of Edward William Bands, of Christiana, Transvaal, and Co Galway, and *d* 19–, having had issue:

1c *Gilbert Eliott-Drake [Gilbert Briscoe Esq, 52 Anreith St, Roosevelt Park 2195, Johannesburg, S Africa]; *b* 27 Dec 1936; dir ops S African Landscape Inst, Johannesburg ; *m* 15 Jan 1964 *Patricia Elizabeth Southey and has issue:

1d *Richard Eliott-Drake; *b* 10 Oct 1964; *m* 19 Feb 1994 *Vivienne Plank and has issue:

1e *Matthew Robert; *b* 7 April 1995

1d *Louise Eliott-Drake; *b* 15 Nov 1965; *m* 14 Nov 1993 *Mark Guy Shuter and has:

1e *Gavin Michael; *b* 16 April 1993

1e *Kerry Louise; *b* 23 July 1995

2d *Jane Eliott-Drake; *b* 11 Aug 1969; *m* 25 Feb 1995 *Anthony Robert Walsh

3d *Mary Lilian Eliott-Drake; *b* 9 May 1971; *m* 13 April 1996 *Jason Sinclair Drever

1c *Margaret Eliott-Drake [Mrs Stephen Elkington, Ade House, Taddington, Derbys SK1 9TY]; *b* 24 Oct 1938; *m* 7 Nov 1959 Rev Stephen Lumsden Elkington (*d* 12 Feb 1992), er s of S H Elkington, of Fox House, Stanningfield, Suffolk, and has issue:

1d *Thomas Sydney; *b* 16 Sept 1960

1d *Sarah Felicity; *b* 8 Dec 1961; *m* 1990 *Jean Pascal Aubergé and has issue:

1e *Siobhan Pascal; *b* 29 June 1991

2e *Salomé Jade; *b* 15 Feb 1994

2d *Katherine Mary; *b* 16 July 1965

3b *Horatio Eliott-Drake; *b* 7 Sep 1904; *m* 26 Jun 1940 *(Dorothea) Felicity, only child of Alan Barclay Vanderplank, of Samarang, Eshowe, Zululand, and has issue:

1c *Peter Alan Eliott-Drake; *b* 7 Jun 1946; *m* 19– *Christina Luck and has issue:

1d *Alan Eliott-Drake; *b* 15 Jun 1979

2d *Andrew Peter Eliott-Drake; *b* 20 Sept 1983

1d *Jeannette Cicely Louise; *b* 11 Nov 1980

2c *Timothy Horace Eliott-Drake; *b* 5 Oct 1948; *m* 19– *Ann Scott and has issue:

1d *Craig Eliott-Drake; *b* 24 Feb 1977

2d *James Eliott-Drake; *b* 24 Jan 1980

1d *Jillian Pamela; *b* 12 June 1975

1c *Alannah Jane Eliott-Drake [Mrs Graham McDougall, Scafell, PO Box 301, Underberg, Kzn 3257, S Africa]; *b* 5 Aug 1941; *m* 7 July 1962 *Graham McDougall, est s of Michael Henry McDougall, of Scafell, and has issue:

1d *Michael Graham; *b* 30 Jan 1965; *m* 24 Sept 1993 *Bunty, dau of Hugh Workman, of Cape Town

2d *Richard Charles; *b* 9 May 1969; *m* 27 April 1996 *Maryke, dau of Joop Brouwer, of Cape Town

1d *Felicity Jane; *b* 19 July 1963; *m* 27 May 1989 *Hans Schmotzer, s of Walter Schmotzer, of Germany

2d *Alison Hélène; *b* 2 Feb 1968

2c *Shareen Mary Eliott-Drake [Mrs Richard Beswick, 13 Coldharbour Court, Micheldever Rd, Andover, Hants SP10 2BL]; *b* 18 Mar 1943; *m* 24 Sep 1966 *Bryan Rex Beswick (assumed by deed poll 1994 the Christian name Richard), est s of Bryan Gerard Beswick, of Queenstown, S Africa, and has issue:

1d *Rex Eliott; *b* 2 May 1969

1d Lisa Eileen; *b* 21 Oct 1967; *d* 28 Oct 1981

2d *Kathleen Felicity; *b* 3 Feb 1971

3c *Rosanne Felicity Eliott-Drake; *b* 5 Oct 1948; *m* 19– *Michael Clark and has issue:

1d *Gordon Eric; *b* 25 Sept 1977

1d *Margaret Ellanor; *b* 10 July 1975

1b Beatrice Eliott-Drake; *m* 1st 21 Feb 1925 (*divorce* 1950) Ivor Herbert McClure, DSO and bar (*d* 25 April 1981), 2nd s of Rev Canon Edmund McClure, MA, and had issue; *m* 2nd 27 Oct 1951 Alan Colin Campbell-Orde, CBE, AFC (*d* 18 April 1992), 2nd s of Colin Ridley Campbell-Orde, JP (*see* CAMPBELL-ORDE, Bt), and *d* 20 Nov 1989

2b Margaret Eliott-Drake; *m* 26 Apr 1924 Matthew Hackforth-Jones, JP (*d* 17 March 1959), of Arkley House, Barnet, and *dsp* 21 June 1968

3b Ellen Eliott-Drake; *m* 12 Dec 1938 Wilfred Vincent Millar Koch, JP, MD, MCh (*d* 28 Jan 1939), s of Edwin L Koch, MD, CM, of Ceylon, and *d* 19–

4b Mary Louise Eliott-Drake; *m* 12 Jun 1930 Maj (John) Geoffrey Steward, Norfolk Regt (*d* 30 April 1980), only surv s of Maj John H Steward, of East Carlton Manor, Norfolk, and *d* 22 Dec 1984, having had issue

5b *Grace Eliott-Drake [Mrs Alan Edelsten, The Dower House, Glanvilles Wootton, Sherborne, Dorset DT9 5QR]; *m* 20 Jul 1929 Dr Alan John Ernest Edelsten, MA, MB (*d* 18 Feb 1968), 2nd s of Dr E A Edelsten, of Streatham, and has issue

6b *Elizabeth Rose Eliott-Drake; *m* April 1939 Capt Otto Solomon, rep S Africa at Polo, 2nd s of Col Owen Solomon, of Thong, Kent, and has issue

1a Rhoda Louisa Beatrice; *b* 24 July 1872; *d* 2 Jan 1874.

(2) (Rev) Thomas; *b* 30 Jun 1813; MA, DD, Fell esus Coll 1834–59, Tutor 1835–39 and 1843–57, V-Pncpl, Proctor for Dean and Chapter Bangor 1880–85, vicar Holyhead 1857–95, Chllr Bangor Cathedral; *d* unm 15 Feb 1895

(3) William Kyffin Bostock; MA, Fell Jesus Coll Oxford, V-Pncpl, Sr Tutor, Master Schools Oxford 1858–59, rector Shipston-on-Stour 1873–83, rector Nutfield, Surrey, 1883–92; *m* 7 Jan 1876 Anne Elizabeth Ellis (*d* 20 Jan 1898), dau of John Ellis Lloyd, of Trallwyn Hall, Caernarvs, and *d* 6 Sep 1892, leaving issue:

1a Eleanor Lucy Ellis-Lloyd; *m* 10 Aug 1904 Norman Dennison Barcroft, er s of William Greer Barcroft, JP (*d* 15 Jun 1937), of Coverhill, Claughton, Cheshire, and *dsp c* 1948

JOHN BRISCOE's 2nd s,

JAMES BRISCOE, of Pentretycham Hall, Wrexham; *bapt* 8 Apr 1770; *m c* 1800 Anne — and *d* by 6 Apr 1837, leaving, with other issue, a 2nd s:

JOHN BRISCOE, of Radbrook, Salop; *bapt* 6 Apr 1804; *m* 1828 Elizabeth (*d* 26 Jul 1886 aged 79), dau of Leigh Burroughes, and *d* 2 Oct 1877, having had issue:

Sir John James Briscoe, 1st Bt (UK), so *cr* 12 July 1910, JP, DL, of Bourn Hall, Cambs; *b* 8 Dec 1835; CA, High Sheriff 1888; *m* 11 Jun 1863 Ellen (*d* 18 April 1910), only surv dau of Alfred Charlton, of Oak House, Altrincham, Cheshire, and *d* 1 May 1919, leaving issue:

1 **Sir Alfred Leigh Briscoe, 2nd Bt**, JP; *b* 26 April 1870; *educ* Corpus Christi Coll Oxford (MA); barrister; *m* 14 Sep 1910 Margaret Mackie (*d* 18 April 1946), dau of Thomas Blythe Sinclair, of Conair, Harray, Orkney, and Greenbank, New Brighton, Cheshire, and *d* 13 May 1921

2 JOHN CHARLTON (Sir), **3rd Bt**, for whom *see* further below

3 Robert Charlton; *b* 26 Oct 1877; *d* 18 Apr 1942

4 Hugh Kynaston, CSI (1931), CIE, (1921); *b* 29 Sep 1879; *educ* Bedford Sch and Pembroke Coll Oxford (MA); ICS from 1903, Ch Sec to Govt Bihar and Orissa 1927–30, Acting Memb Exec Cncl 1930, ret 1933; *m* 4 Nov 1919 Noel (*d* 1 Jan 1971), 2nd dau of John Edward Worrall, of Langstones, Oxton, Cheshire, and *d* 6 Jul 1956, leaving issue:

(1) John Arthur; *b* 16 Apr 1925; *educ* Marlborough and Corpus Christi Coll Oxford (BA 1949, MA 1953), Lt KRRC WW II; *m* 27 Aug 1955 *Hilary Mary [Mrs John Willis, Wressle House, nr Brigg, S Humberside DN20 0RU], yr dau of Sidney Kay Shaw, of Lynbank, Mill Gap Road, Eastbourne (who *m* 2nd 1990 *John Willis), and *d* 1983, having had issue:

1a +Neil David; *b* 11 Jul 1956; *m* 1981 *Bryony Virginia Jane, dau of S/Ldr Clifford Basil Warwick-Spaul, of St Vincents, Tilstock, Salop, and has issue:

1b +Peter; *b* 19–

1b *Jenny Louise; *b* 19–

2a +Andrew Mark; *b* 20 Mar 1960; *m* 1990 *Clare —

1a *Lindsay Ann; *b* 6 Mar 1958; *m* 1983 *Timothy Fell

(1) *Ellen Kathleen [Mrs Anthony Jeans, Testaway, Chilbolton, nr Stockbridge, Hants]; *b* 14 Aug 1920; *m* 27 Sep 1945 *Maj Anthony Stanley Purcell Jeans, TD, The Wilts Regt, only s of Purcell Cooke Jeans, of Cortington Grange, Warminster, Wilts, and has issue:

1a *Michael Anthony Purcell; *b* 13 March 1947; *educ* Marlborough; *m* 1975 *Christine Anne Woodley

1a *Jennifer Rosemary Ellen; *b* 1 March 1950; *m* 1982 *Maj Peter McComas, RA

(2) *Nancy Charlton [Miss Nancy Briscoe, Yew Box, Penton Mewsey, Andover, Hants]; *b* 15 Nov 1921

(3) *Mary Clare [Mrs James Farrer-Halls, 4 Framers Ct, Ellis Way, Lane End, High Wycombe, Bucks HP14 3LL]; *b* 10 Feb 1928; MCSP; *m* 12 June 1954 *James Antony Farrer-Halls, MA, AMIMechE, only child of Arthur James Halls, and has issue:

1a *Alan Anthony; *b* 21 Feb 1961; *m* 1983 *Linda Sturgess

1a *Barbara Mary; *b* 14 Aug 1955; *m* 1983 *Gary William Taylor

2a *Gillian Clare; *b* 7 Feb 1958

1 Ellen; CC Cambridge; *d* unm 29 Nov 1945

2 Esther Mary; *m* 18 June 1902 Rev Canon Herbert Henry Baker Ayles, DD (*d* 18 July 1940), rector Barrow, Examining Chaplain to Bp St Edmundsbury, s of P W Ayles, and *d* 24 Dec 1930, leaving issue

3 Elizabeth Charlton; *d* unm 3 June 1955

The 2nd Bt's bro,

Sir (John) Charlton Briscoe, 3rd Bt; *b* 8 April 1874; *educ* Harrow, King's Coll London (Fell, Scholar and Prizeman) and U of Göttingen; MD London, FRCP, MRCS, Arris and Gale Lecturer 1919, T/Maj RAMC, Consulting Physician King's Coll Hosp and Evelina Hosp for Sick Children, Lumleian Lecturer RCP 1927, author articles in text books and journals, memb exec ctee Gt Ouse Catchment Bd; *m* 7 July 1909 Grace Maud, JP (Suffolk 1937), MB, BS (Lond), FSA (*d* 30 Oct 1973 aged 92), dau of Rev Samuel William Stagg, of Waveney House, Weybread, and *d* 28 Feb 1960, leaving issue:

1 **Sir John Leigh Charlton Briscoe, 4th Bt**, DFC (1945); *b* 3 Dec 1911; *educ* Harrow and Magdalen Coll Oxford (BA 1933, MA 1950); ACA (1937), F/Lt RAFVR WW II, Dir Aerodromes Min Aviation 1961–66, Dir Ops BAA 1966; *m* 8 Apr 1948 Teresa Mary Violet, OBE (1972) (*d* 23 Nov 1995), archaeologist, pres Bucks branch BRCS, yr dau of Brig-Gen Sir Archibald Fraser Home, KCVO, CB, CMG, DSO, of 9 Montpelier Sq, London SW7, and *d* 1993, leaving issue:

1 **Sir (John) James Briscoe, 5th Bt**; *b* 15 July 1951; *educ* The Oratory Sch and U Coll London; *m* 1985 *Felicity Mary [Lady Briscoe, Hall Barn, Swainsthorpe, Norwich, Norfolk NR14 8QA], est dau of David Melville Watkinson, of Gowthorpe Manor, Swardeston, Norwich, and *d* 2 July 1994 following a car crash, leaving issue:

(1) Sir JOHN GEOFFREY JAMES BRISCOE, **6th and present Bt**

(1) *Amanda Mary Louise; *b* 1993

2 +EDWARD HOME; *b* 27 March 1955; heir presumptive; *educ* Ampleforth; *m* 1st 1979 (*divorce* 1987) Anne Mary, dau of Peter Vincent Lister, of Southside, Kingsash, The Lee, Gt Missenden, Bucks; *m* 2nd 1994 *Sandy Elizabeth King, 2nd dau of Victor Lloyd, of 1a Orchard Mews, Seer Green, Bucks, and has issue by his 1st w:

(1) +Guy Home Sebastian; *b* 1983

(1) *Fay D'Arcy; *b* 1981

1 *Diana Clare; *b* 26 July 1949

2 +Richard Kynaston [Richard Briscoe Esq, Maple House, Higher Combe Rd, Haslemere, Surrey GU27 2LQ]; *b* 10 Apr 1914; *educ* Charterhouse and Balliol Coll Oxford (BA 1936, MA 1947); FCA, served WW II 1940–45 as Capt RA; *m* 12 Jul 1951 *Margaret Hamilton, er dau of Sir Hugh Mallinson Rigby, 1st Bt (*qv*)

BRISTOL

Arms: Gu. on a bend arg. three trefoils slipped vert. **Crest:** An ounce passant sa. bezanté, ducally collared and chain reflexed over the back or, holding in the dexter paw a trefoil slipped vert. **Supporters:** On either side an ounce sa. bezanté, ducally collared and chain reflexed over the back or. **Motto:** *Je n'oublieray jamais* ('I shall never forget'). **Creations:** B. (E) 23 March 1702/3, E. (GB) 19 Oct 1714 (Bristol), E. and M. (UK) 30 June 1826.

THE 7TH MARQUESS OF BRISTOL, Earl of Bristol, Earl Jermyn of Horningsheath, Suffolk, and **Baron Hervey of Ickworth**, Suffolk ((Frederick William) John Augustus Hervey) [The Most Hon The Marquess of Bristol, House of Lords, London SW1 0PW]; *b* 15 Sept 1954; *s f* 1985; *educ* Harrow and Neuchâtel U; Hereditary High Steward Bury St Edmunds, governing ptnr Jermyn Shipping, chm Estate Associates Ltd, MInst D; *m* 1984 (*divorce* 1987) Francesca, dau of Douglas H Fisher, of Marbella, and formerly w of Phillip Jones, of USA

Earldom of Bristol: A previous creation under this title was conferred on John Digby (*see* DIGBY, B) in 1622.

Lineage: JOHN HERVEY; *b c* 1290; *m* Joan, dau and coheir of John, s of Hamo de la Leye, and Isobel, of Thurleigh, Beds, thus acquiring the Thurleigh estate, and had an est s:

JOHN HERVEY; *m* Joan Dengayne, and *d c* 1384, leaving:

JOHN HERVEY, of Thurleigh; *b c* 1353; *m* Marjery, dau of Ralph Parles, and *d c* 1410, having had (with Thomas, *m* Christian, dau of John Chicheley, n of Henry Chicheley, Archbp Canterbury; *d* 1468):

JOHN HERVEY, of Thurleigh; *m* Joan, dau and coheir of Sir John Neyrnuit, of Burnham and Fleetmarston, Bucks, and had:

JOHN HERVEY, of Thurleigh; *m* Jane/Joan, dau of William Paston, of Norfolk, and had:

1 John, of Thurleigh; *m* Agnes, dau of Nicholas Morley, of Glynde, Sussex, and *d* 23 Sept 1474, having had, with a dau:

(1) Sir George, mil offr *temp* HENRY VIII; had issue Nicholas and Elizabeth but bequeathed most of his estates to his illegitimate s by Margaret Smart (née Page):

1a Gerard, inherited the manor of Thurleigh and took name HERVEY. His male line continued at Thurleigh till it was sold under the will of John Hervey (*d* 1715)

2 Thomas; *m c* 1457 Jane, dau and heir of Henry Drury, of Hawstead, Suffolk, thus acquiring the manor of Wordwell and for his s that of Ickworth; *d* by 1470, leaving:

(1) William, of Ickworth; *m* Joan, dau of John Cochett, of Ampton, Suffolk, and *d* 1538, leaving, with other issue:

1a JOHN, his successor, of whom presently

2a Sir Nicholas; Amb to EMPEROR CHARLES V; ancestor of the HERVEYs of Marks, Essex, and f of:

1b Henry, of Kidbrooke, Kent; *m* Jane, dau of James Thomas, of Llanvihangell, and had:

1c Sir WILLIAM HERVEY, 1st and last Bt (E), so *cr* 31 May 1619, 1st and last BARON HERVEY OF ROSSE, Co Wexford (I), so *cr* 5 Aug 1620, and 1st and last BARON HERVEY OF KIDBROOKE, Co Kent (E), so *cr* 27 Feb 1627/8; involved in defeat of the Armada 1588, *kt* 1596, served expdn against Cadiz 1597, fought in Ireland, MP Horsham 1601 and Petersfield 1604–11, a contender for the identity of Shakespeare's Mr WH; *m* 1st by 31 Jan 1598/9 Mary (*d* 1607), dau of Anthony Browne, 1st Viscount Montagu, and widow of (a) 2nd Earl of Southampton and (b) Sir Thomas Heneage, but by her had no issue; *m* 2nd 5 Feb 1607/8 Cordell/Cordelia, dau of Brian Annesley, of Kidbrooke and Lee, Kent, *dspms* and was *bur* 8 July 1642 when all his titles expired, leaving:

1d Elizabeth; *m* her cousin John (*see* below)

WILLIAM's er son,

JOHN HERVEY, of Ickworth; *m* Elizabeth, dau of Henry Pope, of Mildenhall, Suffolk, and *d* 11 June 1556, leaving an est s:

WILLIAM HERVEY, of Ickworth; *m* Elizabeth, dau of John Poley, and *d* 2 Nov 1592, leaving an est s:

JOHN HERVEY, of Ickworth; *m* Frances, dau and coheir of Edmund Bocking, of Bocking, Essex, and *d* 1630, leaving:

Sir WILLIAM HERVEY; *m* 1st 1612 Susan, dau of Sir Robert Jermyn, of Rushbrook, Suffolk; *m* 2nd 1642 Lady Penelope Gage, widow of Sir John Gage, Bt (*see* GAGE, V), and dau of Thomas, Earl Rivers, and *d* 1660, leaving by his 1st w:

1 John, of Ickworth; *b* 18 Aug 1616; Treasurer Household CATHERINE OF BRAGANZA, MP; *m* his cousin Elizabeth, only surv child and sole heiress of 1st and last Baron Hervey of Kidbrooke, and *dsp* 18 Jan 1679

2 Thomas (Sir), MP; *m* Isabella, dau of Sir Humphrey May, V-Chamberlain to CHARLES I; *d* 27 May 1694, leaving an est surv s:

(1) JOHN HERVEY, **1st Earl of Bristol** (GB), so *cr* 19 Oct 1714, as also previously 23 March 1702/3 BARON HERVEY OF ICKWORTH (E); *b* 27 Aug 1665; *educ* Clare Hall Cambridge; MP (Whig) Bury St Edmunds 1694–1703, Hereditary High Steward Bury St Edmunds; *m* 1st 1 Nov 1688 Isabella (*d* 7 March 1692/3), dau and sole heir of Sir Robert Carr, Bt, PC, of Sleaford, Lincs, Chllr Duchy Lancaster, and maternal n of Lord Arlington (*see* GRAFTON, D), and had, with two daus:

1a Carr, *Lord Hervey*, MP (Whig) Bury St Edmunds 1713–22, Gentleman Bedchamber to Prince of Wales; *b* 17 Sept 1691; *dvp* unm 15 Nov 1723

(1) The **1st Earl** *m* 2nd 25 July 1695 Elizabeth (*d* 2 May 1741), dau and coheir of Sir Thomas Felton, Bt, of Playford, Suffolk, by Lady Elizabeth Howard, dau and coheir of 3rd Earl of Suffolk (*see* SUFFOLK and BERKSHIRE, E), and *d* 20 Jan 1750/1, having had, with seven other sons and six daus (including Elizabeth, *m* 4th and last Baron Mansell of Murgam; *see* MANSEL, Bt):

2a JOHN HERVEY, **2nd Baron Hervey of Ickworth**, called up to Ho of Lds *vp* 11 June 1733, PC (1730); *b* 15 Oct 1696; *educ* Clare Hall Cantab; MP (Whig) Bury St Edmunds 1725–33, Ld Privy Seal 1740–42, Pope's Sporus, author: *Memoirs* (1848); *m* 21 April 1720 Mary (*d* 2 Sept 1768), dau of Brig-Gen Nicholas Lepell, and *dvp* 5 Aug 1743, leaving, with other issue:

1b GEORGE WILLIAM HERVEY, **2nd Earl of Bristol**, PC (1766); *b* 3 Aug 1721; *s f* as **3rd Baron Hervey of Ickworth** 1743, Envoy Turin 1755–58, Amb Madrid 1758–61, Ld Lt Ireland 1766–67, Ld Privy Seal 1768–70, Groom Stole and 1st Ld Bedchamber 1770–75; *d* unm 18 March 1775

2b AUGUSTUS JOHN HERVEY, **3rd Earl of Bristol**, PC (I 1766); *b* 19 May 1724; RN: joined 1740, Lt 1740, Cdr 1746, Post Capt 1746/7, Col Marines 1762–75, C-in-C Mediterranean 1763, R-Adml 1775, V-Adml of the Blue 1778, MP (Whig) Bury St Edmunds 1757–63 and 1768–75 and Saltash 1763–68, Ch Sec to Ld Lt Ireland 1766–67, a Ld of Admlty 1771–75; *m* privately 4 Aug 1744 Elizabeth (*b* 1720; *m* 2nd bigamously and illegally 8 March 1769 Evelyn Pierrepont, Duke of Kingston (*dsp* 1773), for which tried before Ho of Lds 15–22 April 1776 and found guilty, whereupon she lived abroad at St Petersburg and elsewhere, being nevertheless known as the Duchess of Kingston; *d* 26 Aug 1788), dau of Col Thomas Chudleigh and gdau of Sir George Chudleigh, Bt, of Ashton, and *dspmsl* 22 Sept 1779

3b FREDERICK AUGUSTUS, **4th Earl**

3a Thomas, MP Bury St Edmunds, Equerry to QUEEN CAROLINE; *b* 20 Jan 1698/9; *m* 1744 Anne, dau and coheir of Francis Coghlan, and *d* Jan 1775, leaving issue:

1b William Thomas, Col Gds; *m* Elizabeth, only child of Francis Marsh

4a William; *b* 25 Dec 1699; Capt RN; *m* 27 Nov 1729 Elizabeth (*d* 13 July 1730), dau of Thomas Ridge, of Kilmiston Ho, Hants, and had issue:

1b Elizabeth; *d* unm 30 April 1803

5a Henry (Rev), DD; *b* 5 Jan 1700; assumed the name of ASTON on his marriage; *m* 2 March 1730 Catherine, sis and heir of Sir Thomas Aston, of Aston Hall, Cheshire, and had issue:

1b Henry Hervey, of Aston; *m* 1758 Catherine, yst dau of Edward Dicconson, of Wrightington, Lancs, and *d* 1785, having had issue:

1c Henry Hervey, of Aston, Col; *m* 16 Sept 1789 Hon Harriet Ingram Shepherd, dau of 9th Viscount Irvine, and was *k* in a duel 23 Dec 1798, leaving, with other issue:

1d Henry Charles, of Aston; *m* Margaret, dau of William Barron, and *d* 1820, leaving issue:

1e Arthur Wellington, of Aston; *b* 1815; Lt 1st Life Gds; *d* unm 28 Aug 1839

1e Harriet; *m* 17 July 1832 Rev Hon Arthur Talbot and *d* 6 Feb 1845, leaving issue (*see* SHREWSBURY and WATERFORD, E)

The 3rd EARL's yr bro,

FREDERICK AUGUSTUS HERVEY, **4th Earl of Bristol**; *b* 1 Aug 1730; *educ* Westminster and Corpus Christi Coll Cambridge; Bp Cloyne 1767–68 and Derry 1768–1803; *m* 10 Aug 1752 Elizabeth (*d* 15 Dec 1800), dau of Sir Jermyn Davers, Bt, and *d* 8 July 1803, having had issue, with three daus:

1 John Augustus, *Lord Hervey*; *b* 1 Jan 1757; Capt RN; *m* 4 Oct 1779 Elizabeth (*d* 4 Sept 1818), dau of Colin Drummond, of Quebec, and *dvp* 10 Jan 1796, leaving:

(1) Elizabeth Catherine Caroline; *m* 2 Aug 1798 1st Baron Seaford (*see* HOWARD DE WALDEN, B) and had issue

2 FREDERICK WILLIAM HERVEY, **1st Marquess of Bristol**, so *cr* 30 June 1826, as also EARL JERMYN OF HORNINGSHEATH, Suffolk (both UK); *b* 2 Oct 1769; FRS, FSA, MA, LLD Cambridge, MP (Whig) Bury St Edmunds 1796–1803, Under Sec For Affrs 1801–03; *m* 20 Feb 1798 Elizabeth Albana (*d* 25 May 1844), 2nd dau of 1st Baron Templetown (*see* 1970 edn TEMPLETOWN, V), and had issue, with three daus:

(1) FREDERICK WILLIAM, **2nd Marquess**

(2) George; *b* 25 Jan 1803; Maj; *d* 1838

(3) William, CB; *b* 27 Sept 1805; *m* 7 Sept 1844 Cecilia Mary (*d* 24 Nov 1871), yst dau of V-Adml Sir Thomas Fremantle, GCB, and *d* 6 May 1850, leaving, with other issue:

1a George William (Sir), KCB, Sec and Comptroller-Gen Nat Debt 1894–1910; *b* 16 June 1845; *m* 9 Feb 1881 Emily Dora (*d* 30 Sept 1921), est dau of Lord Charles Pelham Clinton (*see* LINCOLN, E), and *d* 17 Aug 1915, leaving issue:

1b Gerald Edward William, Lt Suffolk Regt; *b* 5 Dec 1881; *m* 23 Sept 1914 Elizabeth Margaret (*d* June 1964), dau of Stephen John du Toit, of Johannesburg, and *d* 21 Aug 1934, leaving issue:

1c Alexander George; *b* 26 May 1920; Pte 1st Rand LI WW II (POW)

1c Hazel Lily; *b* 20 Dec 1915; *m* 13 Feb 1937 William Christian Bouwer (*das* 29 Sept 1944), s of William Christian Bouwer, of S Africa, and had issue:

1d *Kenneth William; *b* 10 Jan 1940; *educ* Witwatersrand U (BCom)

2b Philip Henry Charles; *b* 13 Jan 1883; Lt RASC; *d* unm 4 Aug 1963

3b Eric George; *b* 6 Dec 1884; served WW I and II; *d* unm 8 Oct 1953

4b Claude Arthur; *b* 16 March 1891; Capt RNAS; *m* 14 Feb 1920 Edith Kathleen (*d* 1972), dau of Humphrey B Lamb, of Penn, Staffs, and *d* 25 Dec 1927, leaving issue:

1c *Cecilia Dora [Mrs John Quay, 48 Garden Wood Rd, E Grinstead, Sussex RH19 1NL]; *b* 12 April 1923; *m* 19 Dec 1945 *John Quay, s of James Quay, of Worcester, and has issue:

1d *Jacqueline Teressa; *b* 7 Oct 1950

2a Francis Arthur; *b* 11 March 1849; *m* 1 June 1876 Louisa Maude (*d* 8 July 1923), dau of Rice Richard Clayton (*see* CLAYTON, Bt), and *d* 13 Jan 1905, having had issue:

1b Cecil Edward; *b* 12 March 1877; *d* 13 Dec 1889

2b Richard George, OBE (1919); *b* 17 July 1879; Capt RN, served WWs I and II, Orders St Stanislas Russia and White Eagle Serbia; *d* unm 18 Nov 1964

3b Alec Francis; *b* 8 Oct 1885; T/Lt Roy Sussex Regt; *m* 1st 16 Nov 1912 (*divorce* 1924) Winifred Victoria (*d* 18 Jan 1963), dau of Frederick George Cosens, of Kensington and Bacton, Norfolk; *m* 2nd 1925 Edyth Cecilia (*d* 1987), dau of Lt-Col John Charles Cowan and formerly w of Alexander Lockington, and *d* 28 May 1949, leaving by his 1st w:

1c Ronald Frederick William; *b* 4 Oct 1919; RNR, RA and REME WW II, Capt 1947; *m* 1st 10 June 1943 (*divorce* 1948) Constance Mary, dau of James David Bunce, of Torquay, and widow of F/O Alexander Zatonski, RAF; *m* 2nd 6 Sept 1958 *Jeanne Patricia, dau of Rev Archibald Wynne Esmonde Dowse, MA, of Bexhill, and *d* 4 June 1997, leaving:

1d +Timothy Hugh [Timothy Hervey Esq, Brambledown, Friston Hill, East Dean, E Sussex BN20 0EB]; *b* 5 Feb 1960; *m* 10 Oct 1992 *Susan Mary, dau of Sidney Arthur Peacham, of Bexhill, and has issue:

1e +Benjamin James William Peacham; *b* 29 Jan 1997

1e *Rebecca Maria; *b* 18 Dec 1992

2e *Hannah Rachel Louisa; *b* 29 Nov 1994

1d *Jennifer Charlotte [Mrs Kevin Moon, Church Farm Barn, Ninfield, E Sussex TN33 9JX]; *b* 14 March 1962; *m* 1987 *Kevin Allen Moon

1c Patricia Leila; *b* 15 Jan 1914; *m* 8 March 1940 Capt Martain Edward Scobell Boissier, DSO, RN (*d* 1964), s of Rev Frederick Scobell Boissier, MA, and *d* 29 Sept 1995

4b Lionel Arthur; *b* 24 June 1889; Maj RAF; *m* 12 Aug 1929 Dora Lambert, dau of Michael Thomas Gillender and formerly w of H Havercroft, and *dsp* 18 June 1940

(4) Arthur Charles (Rt Rev), DD; *b* 20 Aug 1808; Bp Bath and Wells 1869, Rector Ickworth and Horningsheath, Archdeacon Sudbury; *m* 30 July 1839 Patience (*d* 14 Dec 1904), dau of John Singleton, and *d* 9 June 1894, leaving, with other issue:

1a John Frederick Arthur (Rev); *b* 11 Nov 1840; *educ* Trin Coll Cambridge (MA); Rector Shotley Suffolk 1866–1922; *m* 22 April 1885 Emily (*d* 9 June 1940), dau of Thomas Ely, and *d* 25 April 1926, leaving issue:

1b Arthur Charles Constantine; *b* 18 Dec 1886; *educ* Marlborough and King's Coll Cambridge (BA 1909, MA 1921); Indian Educn Serv, Kaisar-i-Hind Gold Medal; *m* 8 Oct 1930 Ernestine Apolonia, dau of Emil Stix, of Vienna, and *dsp* Jan 1968

1b Margaret Caroline; *b* 7 Aug 1888; memb Felixstowe UDC 1946–65 (chm 1956–57); *d* unm 30 Sept 1965

2b Mary Edith Emily; *b* 24 Feb 1891; BSc(Econ) London 1939; *m* 9 Sept 1929 Rev John Francis Langton Durham, s of Ferdinand Durham

3b Patience Gertrude; *b* 2 July 1896; *m* 25 May 1927 (*divorce* 1938) Ronald Lepel Griffin (*d* 5 Sept 1955), er s of Sir Lepel Griffin, KCSI, and *d* 19 Aug 1953, leaving issue

2a George Henry William; *b* 17 Feb 1843; *m* 1st 13 July 1876 Emma (*d* 29 April 1877), 2nd dau of William Arkwright, and had issue:

1b Gwendolen Emma

2a (cont.) George Hervey *m* 2nd 3 July 1879 Mary (*d* 21 Aug 1900), dau of William Wells Cole, and *d* 10 Feb 1933, having by her had issue:

1b Douglas George; *b* 3 April 1880; *educ* Marlborough; Inspr Min Ag and Fisheries; *m* 18 June 1913 Ida Constance (*d* 1972), yst dau of Rev Edward Clowes, and *d* 13 Dec 1965, having had issue:

1c Edward George, Maj; *b* 13 Jan 1917; *m* 31 July 1956 *Sheila Mary Howard (*m* 2nd 7 Jan 1965 Sir Hugo Giles Edmund Sebright, 14th Bt (*qv*)), dau of Walter Howard Rocke, of Salisbury, S Rhodesia, and *d* 14 April 1959, leaving issue:

1d *Elizabeth Lepel Howard; *b* 27 May 1957

1c Mollie Gwendolen; *b* 12 Feb 1915; *m* 26 Nov 1949 Walker Hylton Jessop (*d* 25 Dec 1960), s of Hylton Jessop, of Cheltenham

2c *Constance Mary Valentine [Mrs Constance Lamsdale, 51 Priory Rd, Hastings, E Sussex]; *b* 14 Feb 1920; *m* 17 Sept 1951 Duncan C Lamsdale (*d* 1993) and has issue:

1d *Judith Susan; *b* 18 June 1952

2d *Susan Sarah; *b* 1956

3c *Margery, MBE [Mrs Arthur Hingle MBE, PO Box 1067, Wimberley, Texas, USA]; *b* 18 Dec 1921; *m* 3 Oct 1945 *Arthur Thomas Hingle and has had issue:

1d Michael George; *b* 15 Jan 1949; *d* 1978

2d *Peter John Benedict; *b* 27 Oct 1956

1d *Margery Jane; *b* 2 April 1947

2d *Gillian Mary; *b* 10 Nov 1950

3d *Veronica Anne; *b* 2 Jan 1954

4d *Margaret Mary Bridget; *b* 24 Aug 1959

2b Gerald Arthur; *b* 1881; *educ* Pembroke Coll Cambridge (BA); Lt RGA (TF); *m* 14 Aug 1912 Dorothy (*d* 17 Oct 1949), dau of Alfred Symes, of Frinton-on-Sea, and was *ka* Flanders 8 Aug 1917, leaving issue:

1c +Anthony Gerald [Anthony Hervey Esq, 3825 Sarasota Golf Club Blvd, Sarasota, Florida, USA]; *b* 28 April 1915; *educ* Marlborough and Pembroke Coll Cambridge (MA); *m* 3 April 1948 *Aileen Margaret, er dau of Dr Leonard Robert Pickett, MRCS, LRCP, LDS, of Bexhill, and has issue:

1d +Gerald Edward [Gerald Hervey Esq, 12 Bucknalls Lane, Garston, Watford, Herts]; *b* 22 Dec 1949; *m* 1974 *Mary Agnes, dau of Michael Dore, of Co Limerick, and has issue:

1e +Simon Anthony; *b* 1985

2d +Christopher Symes [Christopher Hervey Esq, 5 Burlington Gdns, London W4]; *b* 20 Oct 1952; *m* 1st 1977 (*divorce* 1984) Christina Ann, dau of Watson Failes; *m* 2nd 1984 (*divorce* 1989) Nicole, dau of Colin Charters; *m* 3rd 1992 *Lesley, dau of John Exley, and by 2nd w has:

1e +Toby James Symes; *b* 1987

1e *Tanya Maria; *b* 1985

1c *Elizabeth Mary; *b* 10 June 1913; *m* 2 March 1948 John Charles Jones, MBE (*d* 1969), s of Frederick William Jones, of Manchester

2b Geraldine Mary; *d* unm 11 Nov 1954

3b Eveline Victoria; *b* 7 March 1887; *m* 1 June 1915 Edward Bertram Parker, RN (*d* 28 Dec 1926), and had:

1c *Robin [Robin Parker Esq, c/o Zavallis Press, Ledia Street, Nicosia, Cyprus]; *b* 7 Dec 1918

1c *Thelma [Miss Thelma Parker, Coolinge, Smoke Lane, Reigate, Surrey]; *b* 1 March 1916

2c Sylvia; *b* 9 Sept 1917; *d* unm 17 Sept 1940

3c *Pamela; *b* 3 Jan 1921; Jr Cdr ATS; *m* 1955 Charles R Reid-Seith, DSM (*d* 1962)

3a Sydenham Henry Augustus (Rev); *b* 20 Dec 1846; Vicar Wedmore; *d* unm 4 Feb 1946

4a Constantine Rodney William; *b* 6 Dec 1850; Col RA, JP Suffolk; *m* 12 Aug 1886 Mary Frances (*d* 9 July 1937), dau of William Hanford Flood, of Farmley, Co Kilkenny, and Wollas Hall, Pershore, Worcs, and *d* 19 July 1949, leaving issue:

1b Alice Lucy Patience; *b* 9 July 1887; *m* 21 Dec 1912 Aymer William Whitworth, s of William Whitworth, JP, of Ouse Manor, Sharnbrook, Beds, and had issue

5a Arthur Henry Wriothesley; *b* 3 Nov 1851; Capt Rifle Bde; *d* unm 20 Aug 1889

6a James Arthur (Rev); *b* 26 Sept 1854; Rector Chipstead 1902–13; *m* 15 July 1886 Margaret Augusta (*d* 8 Feb 1924), dau of Sir Robert Percy Douglas, 4th Bt, of Carr, and *d* 19 Oct 1948, having had issue:

1b Thomas Percy Arthur; *b* 1887; Lt 15th Bn KRRC, attd to Govt Fiji Islands, Lt 5th Bn Notts and Derby Regt; *ka* 15 Sept 1916

2b Peter John Berkeley; *b* 1889; *d* 1890

1a Caroline Augusta; *b* 7 July 1857; *d* unm 13 Nov 1949

(5) Charles Amelius (Rev), DD, MA; *b* 1 Nov 1814, Rector Chesterford Essex; *m* 15 Aug 1839 Lady Harriet Charlotte Sophia Ryder (*d* 26 Sept 1899), 4th dau of 1st Earl of Harrowby (*qv*), and *d* 11 April 1880, having had with other issue:

1a Dudley Francis Amelius, CMG, JP, MRAS, FRGS; *b* 7 Jan 1849; Res Cnsllr Malacca; *m* 7 June 1894 Griselda Mary Theophila (*d* 1 April 1929), yst dau of Col Sir Edward Fitzgerald Campbell, 2nd Bt (*see* Campbell, Bt, of 1815 cr), and *d* 1 June 1911, leaving issue:

1b Dudley Edward Francis Cyril; *b* 12 May 1895; Lt Seaforth Highrs WW I; *m* 2 Jan 1926 Ruth, dau of Henry John Wellesley Williamson, barrister, of Grahamstown, S Africa

2b Ambrose Colin Campbell; *b* 31 Aug, *d* 14 Sept 1899

1b Griselda Harriet Violet Finetta Georgina; *b* 1 Oct 1901; *m* 12 Sept 1957 3rd Baron Aberdare (*qv*)

2a William George Edward; *b* 11 Oct 1850; V-Consul Ostend, Sec to Br Resident Perak; *m* 16 Oct 1886 Eva Florence (*d* 10 Nov 1942), 2nd dau of Judge Henry West, QC, of Loughlinstown Ho, Co Dublin, and *d* 24 April 1913, leaving issue:

1b Charles Granville *b* 1 Nov 1888; *d* 1 Sept 1932

1b Venetia Harriet Lepel; *b* 4 Aug 1887; *m* 1 July 1926 (*divorce* 1952) Cdr Duncan Alexander Irvine, DSC, RN, s of Hugh Alexander Irvine, and had issue:

1c *Elizabeth Hervey (Sally); *b* 24 Sept 1928; *m* 24 Jan 1953 Robert Angus (Robin) Clay, s of Robert Angus Clay, of Kenya, and has issue:

1d *Robert Angus Hervey; *b* 25 April 1954

2d *Jonathan; *b* 8 Jan 1960

1d *Susan Lynda; *b* 5 April 1956

2b Osyth Christina Frederica; *b* 18 Dec 1897; *m* 2 April 1918 Frank Pilkington Scott, Maj RAF, s of Albert Harold Scott, and had issue:

1c *Rae Hervey, MB, ChB; *b* 14 July 1922; *m* 29 Jan 1946 *Thomas Straton, MB, ChB, 3rd s of Alexander Walter Keith Straton MRCS, LRCP, of Drummond Lodge, Fordingbridge, Hants, and has had issue:

1d *David; *b* 30 March 1949; *educ* Sherborne and Bristol U; *m* *Elizabeth, dau of —Turner, of Bristol

2d *Peter; *b* 1 Feb 1956
3d Keith; *b* 17 Sept; *d* 21 Sept 1954
1d *Nicola; *b* 18 Feb 1951; *m* *David Simon Crump
2c *Pauline Hervey; *b* 2 Jan 1924; *m* 1948 *Maj Raymond Charles Crossley Dodd, MC, TD, RA, s of Albert Crossley Dodd, ISO, MBE, and has issue:
1d *Andrew Harvey Crossley; *b* 3 March 1951; *educ* Rugby
2d *James Scott Crossley; *b* 3 April 1953; *educ* Bryanston
3c *Veronica Hervey; *b* 24 Oct 1930; *m* 27 Oct 1951 *Maj William Wemyss Ker, RE, only s of Alan William Wemyss Ker, of Singapore, and has issue:
1d *Alan Wemyss; *b* 31 Aug 1955
1d *Shelia Hilary; *b* 26 Nov 1956
(6) Alfred; *b* 25 June 1816; Receiver-Gen Inland Revenue, MP and Ld Treasury, Ld Bedchamber to Prince of Wales; *m* 5 Aug 1845 Sophia Elizabeth (*d* 20 Sept 1892), est dau of Lt-Gen John Chester (*see* BAGOT, B), and *d* 15 April 1875, leaving, with other issue:
1a Frederick Alfred John (Rev), CVO, Chaplain in Ordinary to HM QUEEN VICTORIA 1886–1901, Domestic Chaplain Sandringham to HM EDWARD VII 1878–1910, Canon Residentiary Norwich 1897–1910, Rector Sandringham 1878–1907; *b* 18 May 1846; *m* 13 Oct 1881 Mabel Elizabeth (*d* 25 Dec 1939), est dau of Maj-Gen Augustus Frederick Francis Lennox (*see* RICHMOND and GORDON, D), and *d* 8 Aug 1910, leaving:
1b Alexandra Leila; *b* 1 Nov 1883 (HM QUEEN ALEXANDRA stood sponsor); *m* 1st 7 Jan 1909 Sir Walter Clervaux Chaytor, 5th Bt (*qv*); *m* 2nd 15 Sept 1914 George Pym Gore (*d* 25 June 1959), er s of Spencer William Gore, and *d* 9 Dec 1970, leaving issue (*see* ARRAN, E)
2a Algernon Charles George; *b* 28 Sept 1851; *m* 18 Oct 1910 Maud (*d* 24 July 1930), 2nd dau of Hamon le Strange, DL, of Hunstanton Hall, Norfolk, and *d* 24 Feb 1934
3a Herbert John Antony; *b* 19 May 1859; *d* of wounds recd in action Rhodesia 6 Aug 1896

The 1st MARQUESS *d* 15 Feb 1859, and was *s* by his est son,

FREDERICK WILLIAM HERVEY, **2nd Marquess of Bristol**, PC, MA, LLD Cantab, MP Bury St Edmunds 1826–59, Treasurer Household 1841–46, Col W Suffolk Militia; *b* 15 July 1800; *m* 9 Oct 1830 Lady Katherine Isabella Manners (*d* 20 April 1848), 4th dau of 6th Duke of Rutland (*qv*), and *d* 30 Oct 1864, having had issue:

1 FREDERICK WILLIAM JOHN HERVEY, **3rd Marquess of Bristol**; *b* 28 June 1834; Ld Lt Suffolk, MP W Suffolk 1859–1864, Hon Col 3rd Bn Suffolk Regt, MA Cambridge; *m* 4 March 1862 Geraldine Georgiana Mary, DGStJ (*d* 25 Jan 1927), yst dau of Gen Hon George Anson (*see* LICHFIELD, E), and *d* 7 Aug 1907, leaving:
(1) Katherine Adine Geraldine; *m* 4 March 1886 Allan Harvey Drummond, of Sherborne Ho, Warwick (*see* PERTH, E), and *d* 1 Nov 1948, leaving issue
(2) Alice Adeliza; *m* 29 Aug 1896 3rd Baron Hylton (*qv*) and *d* 27 Aug 1962, leaving issue
2 Augustus Henry Charles, MP W Suffolk; *b* 2 Aug 1837; *m* 30 July 1861 Mariana (*d* 30 Jan 1920), yst dau of William P Hodnett and widow of Ashton Benyon, of Stetchworth Park, Cambs, and *d* 28 May 1875, leaving issue:
(1) Charles Henry Augustus; *b* 30 June 1862; Capt and Adj RA; *d* unm 11 Nov 1893
(2) FREDERICK WILLIAM FANE HERVEY, **4th Marquess of Bristol**, MVO, Chm W Suffolk CC 1914–35, R-Adml, Bury St Edmunds: MP 1906–07 and Hon Freeman 1943, pres Inst Naval Architects 1911–16, White Cross Spanish Naval Order Merit; *b* 8 Nov 1863; *educ* Tonbridge GS; *m* 6 Dec 1896 Alice Frances Theodora (*d* 15 Sept 1957), dau of George Edward Wythes, of Copped Hall, Epping, and had issue:
1a Marjorie; *b* 16 Oct 1898; CStJ, Kaisar-i-Hind Gold Medal; *m* 2 Dec 1919 Lord Erskine (*d* 3 May 1953), s of 12th Earl of Mar and Kellie (*qv*), and *d* 22 Nov 1967, leaving issue
2a Phyllis; *b* 30 Nov 1899; *m* 9 Nov 1921 Capt John Duncan George MacRae, Seaforth Highrs, of Ballimore, Otter Ferry (*d* 11 March 1966), s of Lt-Col John MacRae-Gilstrap, of Eilean Donan and Ballimore, Argyllshire, and had issue
(3) Walter John, JP (Notts and Wilts), CC Wilts, Maj Army Remount Serv 1915–19, Lt Suffolk Imp Yeo; *b* 29 Jan 1865; granted 15 Nov 1907 with his siblings rank of marquess's yr s/dau; *m* 20 Oct 1903 Hon Hilda Gough-Calthorpe (pres BRCS Wilts 1930; *d* 25 Sept 1972 aged 91), 3rd dau and coheir of 6th Baron Calthorpe (*qv*), and *dsp* 13 July 1948
(4) Manners William (Rev); *b* 10 June 1866; *educ* Trin Coll Cambridge (BA); Rector Ickworth-cum-Horringer; *d* unm 10 Dec 1944
(5) HERBERT ARTHUR ROBERT, **5th Marquess**
(1) Maria Louisa Helen; *m* 24 Nov 1887 Sir Charles Glynne Earle Welby, 5th Bt (*qv*), and *d* 11 July 1920, leaving issue
(2) Geraldine Mariana; *m* 28 Dec 1898 Henry Hoare (*d* 29 July 1956), of Ellisfield Manor, Basingstoke, Hants, and *d* 3 June 1955, leaving issue
3 John William Nicholas; *b* 15 Nov 1841; Maj 3rd Bn Suffolk Regt; BA Cambridge, JP Suffolk; *d* unm 25 Feb 1902
4 Francis; *b* 16 Oct 1846; *educ* Balliol Coll Oxford (MA), Hon Fell Hertford Coll; barrister, JP (Suffolk), MP Bury St Edmunds 1874–80 and 1885–92, Civil Serv Commr 1892–1907, 1st Civil Serv Commr 1907–09; *d* 10 Jan 1931
1 Elizabeth Frederica; *d* unm 1 June 1856
2 Adeliza Georgiana; *m* 29 Nov 1866 4th Earl of Clancarty (*qv*) and *d* 7 Nov 1911, leaving issue
3 Mary Katharine Isabella; *d* unm 1 Aug 1928

The 4th MARQUESS *d* 24 Oct 1951, and was *s* by his bro,

HERBERT ARTHUR ROBERT HERVEY, **5th Marquess of Bristol**, Dip Serv, Envoy Extrdy and Min Plen Colombia 1919–23, and Peru and Ecuador 1919–28, ret 1929, Grand Cross Sun Peru; *b* 10 Oct 1870; *educ* Clifton; *m* 1st 29 Oct 1914 (*divorce* 1933) Lady Jean Alice Elaine Cochrane (*d* 5 Jan 1955), dau of 12th Earl of Dundonald (*qv*), and had issue; *m* 2nd 15 Dec 1952 Dora Frances Emblin (*d* 27 March 1953), only dau of George Marshall and widow of Don Pedro de Zulueta, and *d* 5 April 1960, leaving by his 1st w:

VICTOR FREDERICK COCHRANE HERVEY, **6th Marquess of Bristol**; *educ* Eton and RMC Sandhurst; chm Marquis of Bristol and Co, Eastern Caravan Parks Ltd, The Bristol Publishing Co, Radio Marina, British Int Airways Ltd, Dominica Enterprises Co, owner Ickworth Stud and Emerald Hillside Estates, Dominica, WI, v-pres Tax Payers Union, cncl memb Nat Yacht Harbour Assoc, GCLJ; *b* 6 Oct 1915 (HM QUEEN VICTORIA EUGENIE of Spain stood sponsor); *m* 1st 6 Oct 1949 (*divorce* 1959) Pauline Mary (*m* 2nd 1959, as his 2nd w, Capt Edward George Lambton, RHG (*see* DURHAM, E); *d* 2 Sept 1996), dau of Herbert Coxon Bolton, and had:

1 FREDERICK WILLIAM JOHN AUGUSTUS HERVEY, **7th and present Marquess of Bristol**

The **6th Marquess** *m* 2nd 23 April 1960 (*divorce* 1972) Lady (Anne) Juliet Dorothea Maud Wentworth Fitzwilliam, MA Oxford (*m* 2nd, as his 4th w, Somerset de Chair), only child of 8th Earl Fitzwilliam, DSC (*see* 1970 edn), and by her had issue:

2 (Frederick William Charles) Nicholas Wentworth; *b* 26 Nov 1961; *educ* Eton and Yale; *d* by his own hand 26 Jan 1998
1 Ann; *b* and *d* 24 Feb 1966

The **6th Marquess** *m* 3rd 12 July 1974 *Yvonne Marie, only dau of Anthony Sutton, of Woodstock, The Glen, Farnborough Park, Kent, and *d* 1985, having by her had issue:

3 +FREDERICK WILLIAM AUGUSTUS; *b* 19 Oct 1979; heir presumptive; *educ* Eton
2 *Victoria Frederica Isabella; *b* 6 Oct 1976; *educ* Bristol U
3 *Isabella Frederica Louisa; *b* 9 March 1982

BROADBENT

Arms: Per pale erm. and az, a fess nebuly counterchanged, in the dexter chief quarter a caduceus erect ppr. **Crest:** In front of a pheon, the staff rompu, a serpent nowed, all ppr. **Motto:** 'Αιεν αριστευειν ('To excel always'). **Creation:** Bt. (UK) 10 Aug 1893.

SIR ANDREW GEORGE BROADBENT, 5TH BT, of Brook St, London, and Longwood, Yorkshire; *b* 26 Jan 1963; *s* f 1992; *educ* Monkton Combe and RMA Sandhurst; Capt POW's Own Regt of Yorks to 1994

Lineage: JOHN BROADBENT, of Longwood, Huddersfield, Yorks; *m* 17 May 1832 Esther (*d* 11 Oct 1879), dau of Benjamin Butterworth, of Hillhouse, Holmfirth, Yorks, and had:

1 WILLIAM HENRY (Sir), **1st Bt**
2 Butterworth; *b* 19 Jan 1837; *m* 1863 Julia Minerva, dau of John Harpin, and *d* 10 July 1873, leaving issue
3 John Edward, CB, JP Berks, Col RE Malakand FF 1897 and Tirah Expdn 1897–98; *b* 14 April 1845; *m* 1st 1870 Dora (*d* 7 July 1897), dau of Thomas Nicholson, and had issue; *m* 2nd 1 Feb 1900 Hon Alexandra Caroline Frances (*d* 3 Feb 1938), dau of 17th Baron Saye and Sele (*qv*), and *d* 7 Jan 1931
4 Benjamin; *b* 7 May 1850; *m* 15 April 1880 Louisa Ann (*d* 3 Feb 1938), dau of William Keighley, and *d* 25 June 1925, leaving issue
5 Arthur; *b* 24 March 1855; *m* June 1897 Mary Ellen, dau of E Mallinson, and had issue
1 Sarah Anne
2 Eliza; *m* Aug 1881 John Burnley Walker, MD

JOHN BROADBENT *d* 11 Sept 1880. His est son,

Sir William Henry Broadbent, 1st Bt (UK), so *cr* 10 Aug 1893, KCVO, of Longwood and Brook St, London, MD, FRCP, Hon LLD: Edin, St Andrews, McGill and Toronto, Hon DSc Leeds, FRS, Physician Extrdy to HM QUEEN VICTORIA, Physician in Ordinary to HM EDWARD VII and HRH THE PRINCE OF WALES, Cdr Legn Honour; *b* 23 Jan 1835; *m* 5 Aug 1863 Eliza (*d* 9 Feb 1919), dau of John Harpin, of Birks Ho, Holmfirth, and *d* 10 July 1907, having had issue:

1 **Sir John Francis Harpin Broadbent, 2nd Bt**, MA and MD Oxfon, MRCS Eng, FRCP Lond, Consultg Physician St Mary's Hosp and King Edward VII San Midhurst; *b* 16 Oct 1865; *m* 12 Feb 1895 Margaret Elizabeth (*d* 15 Aug 1958), dau of George P Field, MRCS, and *d* 27 Jan 1946, having had issue:

(1) **Sir William Francis Broadbent, 3rd Bt**; *b* 29 Nov 1904; *educ* Winchester and Trin Coll Oxford (MA); slr 1933; *m* 24 April 1935 Veronica Pearl (*d* 8 Nov 1951), dau of Benjamin Fawcett Eustace, JP, of Dublin; *m* 2nd 18 Nov 1982 *Miranda Hamilton, 2nd dau of Donald George Pilcher-Clark, of Port St Mary, IoM, and *d* 1987

(1) Phyllis Margaret; *b* 4 July 1896; *m* 2 June 1923 Capt Arthur Henry Parsons, RN, s of R M P Parsons, of The Manor Ho, Misterton, Somerset, and had issue:

1a *Alan John Maurice [Alan Parsons Esq, 23 Tanson St, Attadale, WA 6156, Australia]; *b* 27 June 1928; *m* 6 Aug 1960 *Jillian Sidney Fergus, dau of Maj W Prain and Mrs Vida Turner, and has issue:

1b *Giles Henry William; *b* 20 July 1961

1b *Penelope Barbara; *b* 15 March 1963

1a *Cynthia Margaret; *b* 25 Jan 1926; *m* 5 March 1955 *Paul Bertram Baker and has issue:

1b *John Paul Philip; *b* 17 June 1957

1b *Janet Cynthia; *b* 18 Aug 1959

(2) Sylvia Mary; *b* 18 Feb 1898; *m* 15 Sept 1931 William George Dawson, s of William Dawson, and had issue:

1a *Richard William [Richard Dawson Esq, Green End Farm, Pegsdon, Hitchin, Herts]; *b* 20 Aug 1932; *m* 31 Aug 1958 *Mary, dau of Arthur Heath, and has issue:

1b *Paul Richard; *b* 15 Dec 1958

2b *Timothy Charles; *b* 28 Nov 1963

1a *Rosemary Katharine; *b* 22 Aug 1935; *m* 19 Jan 1959 *James Martin Stewart Caldwell, s of J S M Caldwell, and has issue:

1b *Marcus Stewart; *b* 17 Jan 1968

1b *Hazel Katharine; *b* 9 June 1962

(3) Katherine Mabel; *b* 3 Dec 1899; *m* 4 July 1953 Philip Lander Birley, est s of Philip Arthur Birley, JP

(4) Irene; *b* 2 June 1902; *d* 30 March 1919

2 William Herbert; *b* 10 April; *d* 17 May 1867

3 Walter, MD, FRCP, MRCS Lond, Consulng Physician Roy Sussex Co Hosp and Roy Alexandra Hosp Children Brighton, Maj RAMC (TF); *b* 4 Aug 1868; *educ* Trin Coll Cambridge (MA); *m* 16 Oct 1896 Edith, OBE (*d* 25 June 1952), dau of John Monroe, PC, Judge High Court Ireland, and *d* 17 Oct 1951, leaving issue:

(1) John Graham Monroe; *b* 19 Jan 1901; *educ* Charterhouse and Trin Coll Cambridge (BA 1922); *m* 21 Oct 1933 Elizabeth Mary Beatrice, only dau of Robert Arthur Dendy, of Hove, and *d* 1967, leaving issue:

1a **Sir George Walter Broadbent, 4th Bt**, AFC; *b* 23 April 1935; *educ* Stamford Sch; S/Ldr; *m* 17 March 1962 *Valerie Anne [Lady Broadbent, La Maison Neuve, 85390 Bazoges en Pareds, France], only dau of Capt (Cecil) Frank Ward, of Horncastle, Lincs, and *d* 1992, leaving issue:

1b Sir ANDREW GEORGE BROADBENT, **5th and present Bt**

1b *Ione Charlotte Elizabeth; *b* 1967

2a +ROBERT JOHN DENDY [Robert Broadbent Esq, 19 Aplin Way, Lightwater, Surrey GU18 5TT]; *b* 4 Nov 1938; heir presumptive; *educ* Stamford Sch; late RAF

(2) Hubert William Lonsdale; *b* 19 Feb 1908; *educ* Charterhouse and Trin Coll Cambridge (MA, MB, BCh); *m* 21 April 1934 *Marjorie, dau of Sir Arthur Kirwan Agar, Ch Justice Br Honduras, and *d* 1988 leaving issue:

1a +Graham Agar [Graham Broadbent Esq, 17 Heathgate, London NW11 7AR]; *b* 12 May 1938; *educ* Charterhouse and Pembroke Coll Cambridge (BA); *m* 4 April 1964 *(Valerie) Suzanne, er dau of Charles Edward Henry Mytton, and has issue:

1b +Charles Richard; *b* 18 Feb 1968

2b +Philip David; *b* 1972

1b *Juliet Fiona; *b* 1977

1a *Judith Anne [Mrs Robin Scoones, Bessells Cottage, Iwerne Courtney, Blandford Forum, Dorset]; *b* 6 July 1935; *m* 2 April 1960 *Robin Scoones, s of Douglas Leonard Scoones, and has issue:

1b *Ian Christopher; *b* 8 May 1962

2b *Simon Richard; *b* 17 Nov 1964

3b *Timothy Graham; *b* 16 June 1967

(1) Elizabeth Ione; *m* 23 Sept 1922 (John) Eric Whittome, s of John Whittome, and *d* 9 June 1966, leaving three s

(2) Moira Edith; *m* 20 April 1927 Maj Colin Davenport, OBE, FRCVS, RAVC, and had:

1a *Doreen; *b* March 1928; *m* 18 Jan 1958 Capt John Eric Sheldon Ellis, RTR, and has issue

2a Wendy Moira; *b* 24 Feb 1931; *d* 17 Aug 1933

3a *Cicely; *b* 11 July 1934

1 Mary Ethel; *d* unm 10 March 1954

2 Gertrude; *m* 23 April 1895 Ven Henry Pownall Mains Lafone, MA, Archdeacon Westmorland, Vicar Kendal (*d* 23 March 1955), est s of Henry Lafone, and *d* 2 Aug 1905, having had issue

3 Eliza Madeleine; *m* 17 April 1903 Louis Arthur Hamand, DMus Oxon, FSA (*d* 18 July 1955), s of Arthur Hamand, and *d* 17 Dec 1949, leaving issue

BROADBRIDGE

Arms: Gu. in chief two pens in saltire or, and in base over water a stone bridge of a single span, embattled ppr. **Crest:** A dolphin haurient arg. between two gilly flowers gu., slipped and leaved vert. **Supporters:** On either side a dolphin ppr. charged with a sword erect gu. **Motto:** *Industria et perseverantia* ('By industry and perseverance'). **Creations:** Bt. (UK) 22 Nov 1937, B. (UK) 14 Sept 1945.

THE 3RD BARON BROADBRIDGE, of Brighton, Co Sussex and a **Baronet** (Sir Peter Hewett Broadbridge, Bt) [The Rt Hon The Lord Broadbridge, House of Lords, London SW1A 0PW]; *b* 19 Aug 1938; *s* f 1972; *educ* Hurstpierpoint and St Catherine's Coll Oxford (BA 1961, BSc 1962, MA); Dep Speaker Ho Lds 1994–, with Unilever 1963–65, Colgate Palmolive 1966, Gallaher 1967–70, management consultant: Peat Marwick Mitchell 1970–78, Coopers and Lybrand 1979–80; dir London Venture Capital Mkt 1980–86, manager Guild Master Craftsmen 1993–, Freeman City London 1980, Liveryman Goldsmiths' Co 1980; *m* 1st 1 April 1967 (*divorce* 1980) Mary, only dau of W O Busch, of Ditterhausen, Kassel, W Germany; *m* 2nd 1989 *Sally Frances Finn and has issue by 1st w:

1 *Jemima Louise; *b* 7 July 1970

2 *Sophie Mary; *b* 25 Aug 1972

Lineage: HENRY BROADBRIDGE, of Brighton, Sussex, had issue:

Sir George Thomas Broadbridge, 1st Bt, so *cr* 22 Nov 1937, as also 14 Sept 1945 **(1st) Baron Broadbridge**, of Brighton, Co Sussex (both UK), KCVO (1937), FCIS (Pres 1939), FRGS, KStJ, Lt City London, Alderman Candlewick Ward, Sheriff 1933–34, Ld Mayor 1936, MP City London 1938–45, Master Gardeners' Co 1934, dep chm Nigerian Chamber Mines, ktd 1929; *b* 13 Feb 1869; *m* 1st Dec 1894 Fanny Kathleen (*d* 8 March 1928), dau of Richard Brigden, of Brighton, and had:

1 ERIC WILBERFORCE BROADBRIDGE, **2nd Baron Broadbridge**; *b* 22 Dec 1895; *educ* Hurstpierpoint; MGC WW I(despatches), mech engr, md A J Barton & Co; *m* 2 June 1924 Mabel Daisy (*d* 14 Feb 1966), only dau of Arthur Edward Clarke, of Carshalton, and *d* Nov 1972, leaving:

(1) PETER HEWETT BROADBRIDGE, **3rd and present Baron Broadbridge**

2 Ralph George Cameron, LDS, RCS 1924; *b* 20 Nov 1901; *educ* Shoreham GS; *m* 14 March 1925 Emma Rose Hancock (*d* 22 Oct 1965), dau of Harry van der Weyden, and *d* 1983, leaving issue:

(1) *Enid Rose; *b* 5 Jan 1926; *m* 14 July 1948 *Alexander Rolland, s of Thomas Carmichael Rolland, and has issue:

1a *Andrew; *b* 20 Oct 1949; *educ* Caterham Sch

2a *Martin; *b* 27 Sept 1951; *educ* Caterham Sch

3a *Nigel; *b* 9 Oct 1955; *educ* Caterham Sch

(2) *June; *b* 3 July 1927

(3) *Anita; *b* 14 Dec 1928; *m* 19 Nov 1949 *Denis Robert Hutchins, s of Capt Robert Hutchins, and has issue:

1a *Anthony David; *b* 15 Aug 1953; *educ* Andrew Cairns Sch and Southdown Tutors

1a *Lucy Jane; *b* 16 May 1955; *m* 16 Jan 1981 *Daniel Leroy Spanburg, s of James H Spanburg, of Clearwater, Florida

3 Hugh Trevor; *b* 22 July 1903; *educ* Shoreham GS; *m* 18 June 1927 *Anne Marjorie, dau of J Locke Elfick, and *d* 1979 leaving issue:

(1) +MARTIN HUGH; *b* 29 Nov 1929; heir presumptive; *m* 1st 31 July 1954 Norma, dau of Maj Herbert Sheffield, MC; *m* 2nd 1968 *Elizabeth, dau of J E Trotman, and has issue by 1st w:

1a +Richard; *b* 1959

1a *Katherine; *b* 1956

(1) *Jill Margaret [Mrs John Damment, c/o Lloyds Bank, 6 Pall Mall, SW1 5NH]; *b* 17 Jan 1932; *m* 23 Jan 1954 *John F Damment, s of F G Damment, and has issue:

1a *Stephen; *b* 1957

1a *Helen; *b* 1956

2a *Deborah; *b* 1958

3a *Louise; *b* 1959

4a *Susan; b 1962

4 +Howard Eustace [The Hon Howard Broadbridge, 12 Texel, Alexandra Rd, Pietermaritzburg, Natal, S Africa]; b 17 Nov 1904; m 21 May 1935 *Margaret Ada Marion, dau of Capt H H Witherington, and has had issue:

(1) George Witherington; b 7 March 1939; BSc; m 10 Oct 1962 *Joan Margaret, dau of Cyril Ridge, of Pietermaritzburg, and d 8 Jan 1968, leaving issue:

1a *Ann Margaret; b 22 Jan 1967

(1) *Sally Kathleen [Mrs Peter Horne, Opondweni, 1 Springdale Rd, Kloof, 3610 Natal, S Africa]; b 23 July 1937; m 30 Sept 1966 *Peter Jeremy Chadwick Horne, s of G L Horne, of Jersey, CI, and has issue:

1a *Lance Chadwick; b 26 March 1969

2a *Timothy George Chadwick; b 1971

5 Rupert Guy; b 1907; served WW II in Abyssinia, Libya and Tripoli; m 7 Aug 1948 *Margaret Anne, dau of George S Cumming, of Bloemfontein, and d 19– leaving issue:

(1) *Beverley; b 13 Dec 1949; m 19– *Maurice Roger Descroizilles,and has issue:

1a *Lee; b 1975

2a *Andrew Vivian; b 1977

1a *Corinne; b 1980

The **1st Baron** m 2nd 1929 Clara Maud (d 17 May 1949), dau of John Swansbourne, of Bognor, Sussex, and d 17 April 1952

BROCKET

Arms: Quarterly, 1st and 4th, arg. three salmon haurient gu., in chief an oak tree eradicated ppr. (for CAIN); 2nd and 3rd, per chevron barry of six gu. and or and of the first, in chief two stag's heads cabossed ppr., and in base a lion rampant guardant of the second (for NALL). **Crest:** 1 A cat salient guardant erminois, holding between the paws a dexter hand couped gu. (for CAIN), 2 Within a leathern garter buckled gu. a bee or (for NALL). **Supporters:** On either side a cat guardant erminois. **Motto:** *Felis demulcta mitis* ('The stroked cat is gentle'). The salmon in the Cain arms signify the fishing rights to the three rivers of Bann, Foyle and Roe which were held by the O'Cahans. The wild cat crest and supporters were reputedly used on the O'Cahan battle shield in the mid–9th century (though this was several centuries before a system of true heraldry originated), a time when Cathan first took the surname O'Cahan.

Creation: Bt. (UK) 1 July 1921, B. (UK) 19 Jan 1933.

THE 3RD BARON BROCKET, of Brocket Hall, Co Hertford, and a **Baronet** (Sir Charles Ronald George Nall-Cain, Bt) [The Rt Hon The Lord Brocket, House of Lords, London SW1A 0PW]; b 12 Feb 1952; s gf 1967; educ Eton; Lt 14th/20th King's Hus 1970–75, pres Herts Chamber Commerce and Industry 1992–96, chm Br motor Centenary Tst 1990–96, dir De Havilland Museum Tst 1992–96; m Sept 1982 (*divorce* 1994) Isa(bell) Maria, former *Vogue* model, only dau of Gustavo Lorenzo, of Whaleneck Dve, Merrick, Long Island, NY, and has issue:

1 +ALEXANDER CHRISTOPHER CHARLES; b 30 Sept 1984; educ Eton

2 +William Thomas Anthony; b 1991

1 *Antalya Stephanie Lauren; b 1987

Lineage: The O'Cahans held a large territory called O'Cahan's County in Ulster and claimed descent from Niall of the Nine Hostages, King of Ulster in the 5th century. They were Lords (that is perhaps to say, Celtic chiefs rather than feudal lords) of the Ronte and Princes (again a loose translation of a word for chief, as in the Prince of Coolavin, rather than any formal title) of Limavady before the early 17th-century Plantation of Ulster.

MANUS CATHAN Au DUIN, PRINCE OF LIMAVADY was k at the Battle of Down 1260.

Sir DONELL O'CAHAN of Limavady; ktd 1607; d Tower of London; gf of:

ENAGH, robbed of his lands at time of Plantation of Ulster, settled Co Galway 1631; ggf of:

JOSEPH O'CAHAN; d Ballybane, Co Galway, 1756; his 2nd s:

WILLIAM; m Catherine O'Malley and had issue:

JAMES O'CAHAN, later CAIN (changed name on joining 88th Foot (afterwards Connaught Rangers); b Galway, 1787; fought Peninsular War; m 1824 Mary (d 2 Sept 1864), dau of Alexander Deane, of Cork, and sis of Sir Thomas Deane, Ld Mayor Cork, and d 26 Dec 1871, having had:

ROBERT CAIN; b Co Cork 29 April 1826; migrated to England 1844, fndr Robert Cain & Sons 1848; m 4 April 1847 Ann (d 12 March 1896), dau of James Newall, of Lowton, and d 19 June 1907, leaving, with other issue:

1 Robert James

2 Alfred Deane

3 Sir WILLIAM ERNST CAIN, 1st Bt (UK), so cr 29 Jan 1920, JP (Berks); b 7 May 1864; ktd, Govr Liverpool U; m 8 April 1886 Florence (d 9 June 1936), dau of Joseph Oakes Roberts, of Manchester, and d 5 May 1924, having had issue:

(2) Sir ERNEST CAIN, 2nd and last Bt; b 25 Sept 1891; educ privately and Trin Hall Cambridge (BA 1914); barrister Gray's Inn 1920; m 17 July 1923 Enid Bertha Willoughby, only dau of George Glasgow, of Liverpool, and d 1969, when the btcy expired, having had:

1a Michael Ernest; b 18 July 1929; accidentally drowned nr Alexandria, Egypt, 11 March 1955

1a *Ann, b 13 June 1925

2a *Joan [Mrs Ian Hill, Windsor House, Gotham, Cranborne, Wimborne, Dorset BH21 5QY]; b 13 June 1925; m 17 April 1952 *Ian Merrick Cuthbertson Hill, OBE, yr s of Thomas Cuthbertson Hill, of Warkworth, Northumberland, and has issue:

1b *Christopher Michael Ian; b 3 Nov 1957

1b *Susan Elizabeth; b 23 March 1955; m 1979 *Norman Allen Bradley

3a *Vivien Elizabeth [Mrs Vivien Wilson, Mais de Pan, Les Stes Maries de la Mer, 13460 Camargue, France]; b 24 May 1932; m 1st 26 Aug 1954 (*divorce* 1959) Charles William Munro Wilson, s of Charles Skinner Wilson, of Hampstead; m 2nd 14 June 1961 (*divorce* 1966) Baron Pierre Cervello, er s of Baron Michel Cervello, and has issue by her 1st husb:

1b *Amanda Louise; b 25 March 1956

4 Sir CHARLES ALEXANDER CAIN later NALL-CAIN (deed poll 14 July 1921), **1st Bt**, so cr 1 July 1921, as also 19 Jan 1933 (**1st**) **Baron Brocket**, of Brocket Hall, Co Hertford (both UK), DL and JP Herts, High Sheriff 1925, patron living Lemsford, Herts, KGStJ; b 29 May 1866; m 1st 13 Sept 1888 Florence (d 21 Oct 1923), yst dau of William Nall, of Kegworth, Derbys (*see* NALL, Bt), and had issue; m 2nd 27 Oct 1928 Anne Page, JP, CStJ, pres Herts BRCS 1938–47, govr Ware GS for Girls (d 18 Oct 1949), dau of Richard Benyon Croft, DL, JP, of Fanhams Hall, Ware (*see* CROFT, Bt, of Croft Castle), and d 21 Nov 1934, leaving by his 1st w:

(1) ARTHUR RONALD NALL CAIN later NALL-CAIN, **2nd Baron Brocket**, JP (Herts); b 4 Aug 1904; educ Eton and Magdalen Coll Oxford (BA 1925, MA 1930), barrister Inner Temple 1927, MP Liverpool Wavertree Div of 1931–34, memb Herts CC and TAA 1931–46, chm: Herts Soc 1936 and Land Union 1936–51, v-chm Allied Breweries, pres: Herts Ag Soc 1935 and 1956, Clun Forest Sheep Soc 1943–44, Nat Sheep Breeders Assoc 1945–47, Assoc Land and Property Owners 1960–67, Suffolk Sheep Soc 1961–62, Ryeland Flock Book Soc 1962–63, memb Nat Tst Historic Bldgs Ctee 1937–67 and exec CPRE 1936–67, KStJ; m 1 Nov 1927 Angela Beatrix (d 22 Aug 1975), yr dau of Rev William Geoffrey Pennyman, Preb St Paul's, and d 24 March 1967, having had issue:

1a Ronald Charles Manus; b 15 Aug 1928; educ Eton, RMA Sandhurst and RAC Cirencester; m 15 Dec 1950 *Elizabeth Mary [Mrs Colin Trotter, Attingdon Stud, Tetsworth, Oxon] (m 2nd 10 July 1964 *Colin John Richard Trotter, er s of Maj Frederick Liddell Trotter, JP, of Mells Park, Frome, Somerset), 2nd dau of Richard John Stallard, of Monte Carlo, and d 15 March 1961, leaving issue:

1b CHARLES RONALD GEORGE NALL-CAIN, **3rd and present Baron Brocket**

2b +Richard Philip Christopher [The Hon Richard Nall-Cain, Potters Hall, Dane End, Herts SG12 0JU]; b 5 April 1953; educ Eton, RMC Sandhurst and U of Herts (LLB Hons 1996); late Lt 2nd Bn RGJ, barrister Inner Temple 1997, Govr The Princess Helena Coll, granted rank of baron's yr s 1969; m 9 Dec 1978 *Juliet, dau of J E V Forester, of Jersey, CI, and has had:

1c Sam Christopher; b and d 1987

1c *Rebecca Elizabeth Emily; b 1981

2c *Claire Antonia Louise; b 1982

3b +David Michael Anthony [The Hon David Nall-Cain, 39 Pembridge Rd, London W11 3HG]; b 17 Dec 1955; educ Harrow; m 1992 *Albertine Hungerbühler

2a +David Lawrence Robert, JP (Cheshire 1964) [The Hon David Nall-Cain JP, Ballacleator, St Judes, IOM IM7 2EP]; b 1 Sept 1930; educ Eton and Magdalene Coll Cambridge (BA 1953, MA 1957); late 2nd Lt 12th Roy Lancers, FRICS, Govr St Patrick's Hosp Dublin 1973–77, m 10 June 1958 *Katherine Elizabeth, sis of 4th Earl of Selborne (*qv*), and has:

1b +James Alexander; b 22 April 1961; m 1992 *Sarah-Jane, er dau of Anthony Bremner, of Llorts, Andorra, and has:

1c +Andrew David Bremner; b 18 March 1995

1c *Susan Beatrix Eloise, b 19 April 1998

1b *Caroline Davina; b 17 Nov 1959; m 1986 *Paul David Cherry, yr s of Peter Harold Cherry, of Weston Manor, Hitchin, and has:

1c *Alexander David; b 17 Feb 1988

1c *Harriet Alice; b 18 Oct 1989

2b *Annabel Priscilla Angela; b 7 Dec 1965; m 1992 *Lord Anthony Hill, yr s of 8th Marquess of Downshire (*qv*)

1a *Elizabeth Angela Veronica Rose [The Hon Mrs Elizabeth Knight, Thoodyn, Bay View, Ramsey, IOM IM8 3EQ]; b 3 May 1938 (HM QUEEN

ELIZABETH THE QUEEN MOTHER stood sponsor); *m* 1st 2 May 1958 (*divorce* 1969) 6th Marquess of Headfort and has issue (*qv*); *m* 2nd 7 April 1970 (*divorce* 1987) William Murless Knight (*d* 12 Sept 1993), of Horsley Hall, Eccleshall, Staffs, and by him has:

1b *Peregrine Robert Christian Murless; *b* 1971

BROCKLEBANK

Arms: Arg. three brocks ppr., each upon a mount vert, on a chief az. as many escallops of the field. **Crest:** An anchor fesswise sa., thereon a cock arg., combed and wattled gu., charged on the breast with an escallop also sa. **Motto:** God send grace.
Creation: Bt. (UK) 22 July 1885.

SIR AUBREY THOMAS BROCKLEBANK, 6TH BT, of Greenlands, Cumberland and Springwood, Co Lancaster [Sir Aubrey Thomas Brocklebank Bt, 120 B Gloucester Terrace, London W2 6HP]; *b* 29 Jan 1952; *s* f 1974; *educ* Eton and Univ Coll Durham (BSc); ACA, chm Sanctuary Leisure Plc, Cafe Inns Plc 1996– and Scotswood Industries Plc; *m* 1979 (*divorce* 1990) Dr Anna-Marie, dau of Dr William Dunnet, of Woldingham, Surrey, and has:

1 +AUBREY WILLIAM THOMAS; *b* 15 Dec 1980
2 +Hamish John; *b* 1987

Lineage: RALPH BROCKLEBANK, of Roebeck, Cumberland; *bapt* 6 June 1659; *m* 1st Jane — (*d* 1699) and had:

1 Joseph; *b* 1693
2 William; *b* 1697
1 Mary; *b* 1691

RALPH BROCKLEBANK *m* 2nd 3 May 1703 Elinor Jackson, of Bridekirk (*bur* 22 Dec 1761) and was *bur* 20 Nov 1727, having by her had issue:

3 DANIEL, of whom presently
4 Ralph; *b* 1716
5 Aaron; *b* 1718
2 Grace; *b* 1704
3 Anne; *b* 1713

The 3rd son,

Rev DANIEL BROCKLEBANK, Curate of Torpenhow, Cumberland 1735–57, Vicar of Morland Westmorland 1757–73; *b* 1705; *m* 13 June 1734 Sarah Slack, of Ireby (*d* 18 Nov 1773 aged 71) and was *bur* 25 April 1773, leaving issue:

1 John; *b* 1734; *m* — Burnyeat and *d* 18 June 1782, leaving issue:
(1) John; *b* 1769; *m* 7 April 1766 Mary Priestman, and *d* 10 Feb 1814, leaving:
1a Mary; *b* 1796; *m* 13 Jan 1820 John Kewley, and *d* 1865, leaving issue
(2) Ralph; *m* Sarah — (*d* 30 Jan 1845 aged 75) and had issue:
1a Daniel; *dsp* 23 March 1847 aged 37
1a Mary; *m* — and *d* 21 Aug 1874 aged 74, leaving issue
(1) Eleanor; *m* John Lawrence
(2) Sarah; *m* Joseph Poole
2 Thomas, of London; *b* 1735; *d* unm 1783
3 Ralph (Rev)
4 DANIEL, of whom presently
1 Margaret; *bapt* 3 Jan 1739; *m* Rev Christopher Bird, and *d* 20 Aug 1822, leaving issue
2 Eleanor; *b* 1744; *m* Col John Hebson, of Kendal, and had issue

The yst son,

DANIEL BROCKLEBANK, fndr Brocklebank Shipping Line 1770; *b* 1741; *m* 7 March 1769 Anne (*d* 7 March 1825), dau of Isaac Cuppage, of Greenlands, Irton, Cumberland, and *d* 7 March 1801, leaving issue:

1 Daniel, of Montego Bay, Capt; *b* 1773; *d* unm 1790 Jamaica in cmd of the ship *Alfred*
2 Thomas, of Greenland, Cumberland, and Standfield, Lancs; ptnr with his bro John in firm of Thos & Jho Brocklebank, Merchants and Ship-Owners, of Liverpool 1801; *b* 1774; *d* unm 1848
3 John, of Greenland, Cumberland, and Standfield, Lancs; *b* 1779; *d* unm 1831
1 Sarah; *b* 1770; *d* 1853
2 ANNE, of whom presently
3 Margaret; *b* 1782; *d* 1849

The yst dau

ANNE Brocklebank; *b* 1777; *m* 15 April 1812 Wilson FISHER, of Keekle, Cumberland (*bapt* 10 Dec 1774; *d* 7 Oct 1844), s of Thomas Fisher, of Whitehaven, by Mary Wilson, and *d* 16 Oct 1835, leaving:

1 THOMAS, of whom presently
1 Mary Anne; *b* 1815; *d* 1860
2 Sarah; *b* 1817; *m* Robert Gordon, of Cheltenham, and *d* 1855, leaving issue. He *d* 1883
3 Jane; *b* 1819; *d* 1904

The son,

Sir THOMAS FISHER later BROCKLEBANK (roy licence with arms 5 Dec 1845 on inheriting maternal uncle's estate), **1st Bt** (UK), so *cr* 22 July 1885, of Greenlands and Irton Hall, Cumberland, and Springwood, Lancs, DL, JP, High Sheriff Cumberland 1864; *b* 24 Nov 1814;; *m* 4 June 1844 Anne (*d* 7 Jan 1883), dau and heiress of Joseph Robinson, of Bolton Hall, Cumberland, and *d* 8 June 1906, having had issue:

1 THOMAS (Sir), **2nd Bt**
2 John; *b* 24 July 1860; *d* 22 Jan 1851
3 Harold, JP Lancs; *b* 24 Nov 1853; *m* 1878 Mary Ellen (*d* 20 Nov 1929), dau of John Brogden, of Ulverstone, and *d* 1 Dec 1936, having had issue:
(1) Thomas Geoffrey, Capt 4th W Lancs (Howitzer) Bde RFA; *b* 3 Nov 1882; *ka* 5 Aug 1916
(2) Harold Arthur, Capt late 4th Bn Roy Lancaster Regt; *b* 1889; *m* 15 Jan 1920 Morwenna, only dau of John Athelstan Riley, and *d* 12 June 1944
(1) Katharine Mary; *m* 25 July 1911 Alfred Geoffrey Turner, yr son of Alfred Morrison Turner, of Broughton, West Derby, Liverpool, and *d* 18 Aug 1955, leaving issue. He *d* 7 April 1956
(2) Ruth Leonide; *m* 7 Aug 1919 Brig Frank Hole Witts, DSO, MC, Irish Gds, son of Rev Francis Edward Broome Witts, Canon of Gloucester. He *d* 9 May 1941
(3) Eleanor Hilda; *m* 18 Sept 1923 Brig Edward Rigby Kewley, DSO and Bar, MC, only surv son of Edward Kewley, of Oran, Catterick, Yorks
4 Charles Henry (Rev), of Westwood Park, West Bergholt, Essex, JP, late Vicar of Pampisford, Cambs; *b* 27 June 1864; *educ* Trin Coll Cambridge (MA); *m* 25 June 1889 Isabel Katherine (*d* l6 Oct 1940) (who *m* 2nd 17 Nov 1936 Lt-Col Robert James Leslie Ogilby, DSO (*d* 27 Jan 1964), only son of Capt Robert Alexander Ogilby, DL, JP, of Ardnargle, Co Londonderry), dau of Capt P C G Webster, 8th Hus, and *d* 6 Dec 1935, leaving issue:
(1) Charles Gerald, MC, Capt RE (SR) WW I (despatches, Médaille Militaire); *b* 21 March 1893; *m* 22 April 1925 Beatrice Gresley (*d* 1992), yr dau of Falconer Madan, and *d* 28 May 1940, leaving issue:
1a +Charles William [Charles Brocklebank Esq, Giffords Hall, Stoke-by-Nayland, Suffolk; 17 Grosvenor Sq, London W1]; *b* 11 March 1930; *educ* Eton and Ch Ch Oxford; *m* 24 July 1965 *Marcia Andrea, AB Smith Coll, MA New York U, only dau of Arthur Early, of Kalamazoo, Mich, USA, and has issue:
1b +James Gerald; *b* 1970
2b +Willaim Falconer; *b* 1976
1b *Diana Lasswell; *b* 25 May 1968
1a *Mary [Mrs Michael Bevan, Longstowe Hall, Longstowe, nr Cambridge CB3 7UH]; *b* 27 May 1926; *m* 22 May 1948 Michael Guy Molesworth Bevan (*d* 1992), son of Lt-Col Temple Percy Molesworth Bevan, of Longstowe Hall, Cambs, and has issue:
1b *Roger Anthony Briscoe [Roger Bevan Esq, 29 Connaught Sq, London W2]; *b* 23 Dec 1951; *educ* Eton; *m* 1st 1980 (*divorce* 198–) Marion Casey, dau of Theodore Donahue, of Litchfield, Conn, USA; *m* 2nd 1994 *Beverly D Anastopolis
2b *William George Briscoe [William Bevan Esq, Longstowe Hall, Longstowe, nr Cambridge CB3 7UH]; *b* 18 April 1958; *m* 1985 *Annabel Jane, dau of William Bertram Weatherall, of Shorndown, Mursley, Bucks (*see* RUSSELL, Bt), and has issue:
1c *George Michael Briscoe; *b* 1988
1c *Lucy Clare; *b* 1990
2c *Victoria Mary; *b* 1993
3b *James Edward Briscoe [James Bevan Esq, Bulby Hall, Bulby, Lincs]; *b* 6 Dec 1960; *m* 1986 *Susan Fiona, dau of Victor Parker, of Appleton, Cheshire, and has:
1c *Diana Mary; *b* 31 July 1997
1b *Penelope Anne [Mrs Geoffrey Probert, Grounds Farm, Hook Norton, Banbury, Oxon]; *b* 2 March 1955; *m* 1982 *Geoffrey Thomas Carwardine Probert, s of Lt-Col Richard Harlackenden Probert, OBE, DL, of Bevills, Bures, Suffolk, and has issue:
1c *Thomas Henry Carwardine; *b* 1985
2c *Jack Michael Harlackenden; *b* 1993
1c *Rebecca Mary; *b* 1988
2c *Isobel Loveday; *b* 1991
2a *Ann; *b* 28 May 1928
(1) Edith Katherine, JP Herts; *m* 15 May 1915 Charles Sidney Bowen Wentworth-Stanley, CBE, MA, formerly Capt W Kent Yeo, of High Wych Grange, Sawbridgeworth, Herts, only s of Maj Sir Charles Wentworth Stanley, DL, of Bentley Corner, Trumpington Rd, Cambridge, and *d* 1 Aug 1948, leaving issue. He *d* 13 Feb 1960
1 Jane; *b* 30 Sept 1846; *m* 13 Sept 1871 Frederick Dresser, MInstCE, of Maryton Grange, Allerton, Lancs, s of Henry Dresser, of Topcliffe, and Thirsk, Yorks, and *d* 29 Sept 1901 leaving issue. He *d* 31 March 1903
2 Anne Margaret; *b* 29 Aug 1856; *d* 14 April 1873
3 Edith Mary; *b* 31 Jan 1859; *m* 8 May 1886 Edward Kewley, of Oran, Catterick, Yorks, and *d* 2 Dec 1921, leaving issue

4 Katherine Leonide; *b* 25 April 1869; *m* 7 Feb 1893 Maj Henry Holt Beever, late RA, of Littleton Ho, Blandford, Dorset, 2nd s of Rev William Holt Beever, of Pencraig Court, Hereford, and had issue

The est son,

Sir Thomas Brocklebank, 2nd Bt, JP Cumberland and High Sheriff Co Palatine of Lancaster 1908, MA Cambridge; *b* 1 March 1848; *m* 9 July 1872 Agnes Lydia (*d* 1 Dec 1913), dau of Sir James Joseph Allport, of Littleover, Derbys, and had issue:

1 AUBREY (Sir), **3rd Bt**

2 John Jasper, DSO (1900), Maj late Scottish Horse, formerly Capt 1st Dragoon Gds, Bde-Maj 1916, served in S African War 1899–1901, and WW I 1914; *b* 5 Sept 1875; *educ* Eton; *m* 21 April 1914 Constance Mary (*d* 10 July 1965), est dau of Sir Robert Leonard Powell, JP, of Stratton, Gt Marlow, Bucks, and *d* 26 Feb 1942, having had issue:

(1) John Maurice, Lt-Cdr (S) RNVR, served WW II; *b* 9 Aug 1917; *educ* Eton; *m* 18 Nov 1944 Evelyn Margaret (*d* 1985), widow of 2nd Lt Thomas Leigh Stephenson, 1st Punjab Regt IA, and dau of Gordon Pyper, of Ceylon, and *das* 1 June 1945, leaving issue:

1a +John Daniel [John Brocklebank Esq, 8 Grange Rd, Barnes, London SW13 9RE]; *b* posthumously, 29 Sept 1945; *educ* Eton and Keble Coll Oxford; *m* 1971 *Donna Jean, dau of Maj Clixby Fitzwilliams, of Hazeldene, Healing, nr Grimsby, and has issue:

1b *Daniel Maurice; *b* 1975

2b *Edward John; *b* 1982

(2) +Thomas Gordon [Thomas Brocklebank Esq, PO Box 75, Breyten, Transvaal 2330, S Africa], served WW II as Lt RNVR (FAA); *b* 4 Dec 1921; *educ* Eton; *m* 1st 23 April 1952 Gillian Chester (*d* 1 Sept 1967), only child of William Francis Cardew, of Lanteglos, Eiffel Flats, S Rhodesia; *m* 2nd 1970 *Edith Josephine, dau of William Geoffrey Ward, and widow of Neville Wells Abbott, and by 1st w has issue:

1a +Robin John; *b* 18 Nov 1954

2a +Geoffrey Cardew; *b* 29 Aug 1959

3a +Christopher Philip; *b* 14 Oct 1963

1a *Anne Frances; *b* 16 Aug 1962

(1) Constance Eirene *b* 11, *d* 13 Jan 1916

(2) Margaret Anne; *b* 12 Jan 1920; *d* 8 May 1931

3 Robert Allport, T/Lt RE; *b* 25 Oct 1878; *m* 21 Jan 1903 Frances (*d* 11 Dec 1942), yr dau of John H Walker, JP, of Newport, Fife, and *d* 18 Feb 1946, having had issue:

(1) Christopher; *b* 31 Jan, *d* 24 April 1907

(2) +Oliver [Lt-Cdr Oliver Brocklebank RN (ret), Redbourne, Lowestoft Rd, Gorleston-on-Sea, Norfolk]; *b* 17 Aug 1908; *m* 1st 20 April 1931 (*divorce* 1947) Diana (*d* 1994), dau of Col Wilford Boteler, DSO, RA; *m* 2nd 10 Sept 1947 *Marjorie Joan, dau of Horace Snowling, of Gt Yarmouth, and has issue:

1a *Alison Philippa; *b* 21 Dec 1948

2a *Elizabeth Joanna; *b* 5 March 1950

3a *Edwina Jane; *b* 21 Oct 1952

4 Stephen; *b* 4, *d* 26 May 1880

1 Anne Dorothea; *b* 29 July 1877; *m* 4 Jan 1900 (*divorce* 1935) Charles Hesketh Fleetwood-Hesketh, DL, J P, of Meols Hall, N Meols, Lancs, and *d* by enemy action at sea 17 Sept 1940, leaving issue (*see* BIBBY, Bt)

2 Agnes Sylvia, OBE (1920), JP Rutland; *b* 23 Feb 1882; *d* 27 Nov 1962

3 Evelyn Violet, twin with her sis Agnes Sylvia; *m* 4 March 1909 George Westinghouse, of Victoria, BC, Canada, only son of George Westinghouse, of Pittsburg, Pennsylvania, and *d* 9 June 1943, leaving issue

Sir THOMAS *d* 12 Jan 1911; his est son,

Sir Aubrey Brocklebank, 3rd Bt, JP and High Sheriff, Cumberland 1921; *b* 12 July 1873; *educ* Trin Coll Cambridge (BA), chm T and J Brocklebank Ltd, dir: GWR, Suez Canal Co, Cunard Steamship Co; *m* 15 Oct 1898 Hon Grace Mary Jackson (*d* 5 April 1940), dau of 1st Baron Allerton (*see* 1970 edn), and *d* 19 April 1929, leaving:

1 **Sir Thomas Aubrey Lawies Brocklebank, 4th Bt**; *b* 23 Oct 1899; *educ* Eton and Trin Coll Cambridge; chm Mersey Docks and Harbour Bd, dir: T and J Brocklebank Ltd, Midland Bank Ltd and Roy Insur Co; *d* unm 15 Sept 1953

2 JOHN MONTAGUE (Sir), **5th Bt**

1 Angela Grace; *m* 11 June 1931 John Vincent Wrigley, MBE, only son of Vincent Shiers Wrigley, MBE, of Delbury Hall, Craven Arms, Salop, and had issue:

(1) *John Patrick, late 2nd Lt The Roy Dragoons; *b* 3 Nov 1946; *educ* Eton

(1) *Leila Virginia Grace; *b* 11 April 1934; *m* 19 June 1954 Ross Kearsley Pigot, yr son of Col Arthur Percival Vernon Pigot, of Spy Hill, Mouldsworth, Cheshire, and has issue:

1a *David Kearsley; *b* 18 Dec 1956

1a *Carolyn Jane; *b* 31 March 1955

2a *Fenella Clare; *b* 11 July 1958

(2) *Rosamond Catherine; *b* 1 May 1945; *m* 16 July 1966 *Christopher Robert Dunbar Woodward, only son of Maj Peter Robert Egerton Woodward, of Hopton Court, Cleobury Mortimer, Salop, and has issue:

1a *Nicholas Robert; *b* 27 Jan 1969

1a *Charlotte Jane; *b* 5 June 1967

2 Helen Venetia; *b* 19 Aug 1912; *d* 3 Feb 1913

The 4th Bt's bro,

Sir John Montague Brocklebank, 5th Bt, TD; *b* 3 Sept 1915; *educ* Eton and Trin Coll Cambridge; Maj RA (TA) WW II (POW 1943–45), chm T and J Brocklebank, Cunard Ltd and Cunard White Star Ltd 1959–65, dep chm Martin's Bank; *m* 15 Feb 1950 *Pamela Sue, formerly w of Maj Leslie Forshaw-Wilson and est dau of William Harold Pierce, OBE, JP, of Bidston, Cheshire, and *d* 1974, leaving issue:

1 Sir AUBREY THOMAS BROCKLEBANK, **6th and present Bt**

BRODIE

Arms: Az. on a chevron between three mullets arg. three civic wreaths vert. **Crest:** A dexter cubit arm erect, holding a civic wreath, as in the arms, with three arrows, one in fess and two in saltire, points towards the dexter arg. **Motto:** Unite.
Creation: Bt. (UK) 30 Aug 1834.

SIR BENJAMIN DAVID ROSS BRODIE, 5TH BT, of Boxford, Suffolk [Sir Benjamin Brodie Bt, Betchworth Lodge, Betchworth, Surrey]; *b* 29 May 1925; *s* f 1971; served Royal Signals; *educ* Eton; *m* and has issue:

1 +ALAN; *b* 19–

1 *A dau; *b* 19–

Lineage: ALEXANDER BRODIE, of Glassaugh, Banffshire; *b* by 1680; had (with James *b* 1706, migrated to Strabane, Co Tyrone, and Isabel, *b* 1704, *m* 1724 Alexander Duff and had issue):

ALEXANDER BRODIE; *b* Glassaugh, 1701; left for London (settled Brewer Street, St James's) by 1740, allegedly after involvement in political troubles (Jacobitism?); *m* Margaret, dau of Dr Samuel Shaw, master Tamworth Sch, by Anne Antrobus, and *d* Jan 1772, having had, with other issue (including Elizabeth, *b* 12 Jan 1746/7, *m* 1770 Thomas Denman, MD, of Mount St, Mayfair, and had issue (*see* DENMAN, B)):

Rev PETER BELLINGER BRODIE; *b* 17 Nov 1742; DL, JP, MA Oxon 1768, Rector Winterslow, Wilts; *m* 1 Nov 1775 Sarah (*d* 1847), 3rd dau of Benjamin Collins, banker and publisher, of Salisbury, and *d* 19 March 1804, leaving, with other issue:

1 Peter Bellinger; *b* 30 Aug 1778, barrister Lincoln's Inn, conveyancer; *m* 1st Elizabeth Mary (*d* 9 May 1823), dau of Sutton Thomas Wood, and had issue; *m* 2nd 1 June 1826 Susan Mary, dau of John Morgan, and had further issue

2 William Bird; *b* 26 Sept 1780; MP Salisbury; *m* 1st 18 Oct 1810 Louisa (*d* 28 March 1816), dau of Thomas Hussey, of Salisbury, and had issue; *m* 2nd 5 March 1826 Frances, dau of Rev Richard Huntley, of Boxwell Court, Glos, and *d* 1863, having had further issue

3 **Sir Benjamin Collins Brodie, 1st Bt** (UK), so *cr* 30 Aug 1834; *b* 9 June 1783; FRS, DCL, Corresponding Memb Inst of France, Serjeant-Surgn to WILLIAM IV and QUEEN VICTORIA, PRS; *m* 21 May 1816 Anne (*d* 10 July 1861), 3rd dau of Mr Serjeant Sellon by Charlotte Dickinson, and had issue:

(1) BENJAMIN COLLINS (Sir), **2nd Bt**

(2) William (Rev); *b* 8 Oct 1821, Vicar E Meon, Hants; *m* 2 Oct 1844 Lady Maria Waldegrave, 3rd dau of 8th Earl Waldegrave (*qv*), and *d* 5 June 1882, having had issue, with three daus:

1a William Waldegrave; *d* an infant 1849

2a Alfred Waldegrave; *b* 13 Nov 1851; *m* 26 Sept 1878 Catherine Eliza (*d* 25 April 1935), est dau of Maj-Gen Francis Applegarth, and *d* 1916

3a Edgar Waldegrave; *b* 19 Nov 1857; Capt 60th Rifles, Adj Queen's Westminster Vols 1886–91, JP Co Clare; *m* 28 April 1886 Nora Kathleen (*d* 19 May 1936), yr dau of Capt Charles George Martin O'Callaghan, DL, JP, of Ballinahinch, Co Clare, and *d* 15 June 1929, leaving issue:

1b Malcolm William O'Callaghan; *b* 30 Jan 1887; Capt London Regt WW I (despatches); *m* 1st 1 Nov 1922 Phyllis Gwavas (*d* 12 Jan 1940), dau of Henry Tredenham Carlyon, of Opoutama, Hawkes Bay, NZ; *m* 2nd 28 Nov 1948 *Sybil Barbara, dau of Henry Shearburn Clark, of Fernhill, Hawkes Bay, and *d* 2 Nov 1966, leaving by his 1st w:

1c +Mark Donald Carlyon William; *b* 1 Jan 1928; *m* 23 July 1955 *Patricia Isobel, only child of Judge Arnold Admiral Whitehead, of NZ, and has:

1d +Malcolm Robert; *b* 6 May 1956

2d +Douglas William; *b* 5 Jan 1958

3d +Christopher Mark; *b* 22 Sept 1961

4d +Philip John Edgar; *b* 12 Aug 1964

2b Donald Francis O'Callaghan; *b* 1 April 1888; Lt RN; lost in HM Submarine D5 3 Nov 1914

3b Angus George O'Callaghan; *b* 11 July 1902; *d* 11 Nov 1948

4a Wilfred Leslie Waldegrave; *b* 5 Jan 1866; *m* 1 June 1892 Sidonie Anna Franziska (*m* 2nd 5 Feb 1935 Richard Arabin Shore; *d* 23 Sept 1945), dau of Field-Marshal Von Neuber, Austrian Army, and *d* 2 Aug 1929, leaving issue:

1b Franziska Maria Sidonie; *b* 7 Nov 1900; *d* unm 23 Dec 1968

(1) Maria Eliza; *m* 20 July 1839 Rev Edward Hoare (*d* 7 July 1894) and *d* 27 July 1863, leaving issue

Sir BENJAMIN *d* 19 Oct 1862; his er son,

Sir Benjamin Collins Brodie, 2nd Bt; *b* 5 Feb 1817; FRS, Waynflete Prof Chemistry Oxford; *educ* Harrow and Balliol Coll Oxford (MA, DCL); *m* 11 April 1848 Philothea Margaret (*d* 27 Jan 1882), dau of John Vincent Thompson, Serjeant-at-law, and had issue:

1 BENJAMIN VINCENT SELLON (Sir), **3rd Bt**

1 Margaret Ann; *m* 16 Dec 1882 James Usher Huxley, MD, of Charlbury Lodge, Oxford (*d* 24 June 1917), and *d* March 1944, leaving issue

2 Ida Philothea; *d* unm 22 April 1917

3 Lilian; *m* 19 Sept 1872 Lt-Col William Alexander Cardwell, of Eastbourne (*d* 30 Aug 1916), and *d* 9 Aug 1916, leaving issue

4 Ethel; *m* 29 July 1880 Rev Michael George Glazebrook, DD, Canon Ely, Head Master Clifton (*d* 1 May 1926), s of M G Glazebrook, and *d* 16 May 1926

5 Mary Isabel; *m* 16 Dec 1886 Sir Thomas Herbert Warren, KCVO, DCL (*d* 9 June 1930), 2nd s of Algernon William Warren, JP, and *d* 17 Feb 1940

The 2nd Bt *d* 24 Nov 1880; his son,

Sir Benjamin Vincent Sellon Brodie, 3rd Bt; *b* 19 June 1862; DL, JP and CA Surrey, CC Surrey Betchworth 1895–1908, High Sheriff Surrey 1912; *educ* Magdalen Coll Oxford (MA); FSA, barrister Lincoln's Inn, Lt TF; *m* 4 May 1887 Caroline Eliza (*d* 13 Jan 1895), yst dau of Capt John R Woodriff, RN, Serjeant-at-Arms to HM QUEEN VICTORIA, and *d* 20 Jan 1938, leaving issue:

1 **Sir Benjamin Collins Brodie, 4th Bt**, MC and bar; *b* 6 March 1888; *educ* Eton and Magdalen Coll Oxford (BA 1911); served 1914–19 with Surrey Yeo and Gordon Highrs WW I (despatches twice), Master Skinner's Co 1944–45 and 1950–51, Assist Cmmdnt Cards Spec Constabulary 1940–45, Spec Constabulary Long Service Medal, Govr Tonbridge Sch; *m* 9 Jan 1924 Mary (*d* 1940), est dau of Ross Palmer, of Ballyheigue, Co Kerry, and *d* 2 Aug 1971, leaving issue:

(1) Sir BENJAMIN DAVID ROSS BRODIE, **5th and present Bt**

(2) +Colin Alexander, QC 1980 [Colin Brodie Esq QC, The Granary, Chadhurst Farm, Coldharbour Lane, Dorking, Surrey RH4 3JH]; *b* 19 April 1929; *educ* Eton and Magdalen Coll Oxford; late 8th (King's Irish) Hus, barrister Middle Temple 1953, Bencher Lincoln's Inn 1988; *m* 29 Oct 1955 *Julia Anne Irene, yr dau of Norman Edward Wates, of Elmore, Chipstead, Surrey, and has issue:

1a +Christian Norman; *b* 10 Feb 1957

2a +Alexander Colin; *b* 16 Nov 1959

(1) *Angela Mary [Miss Angela Brodie, Betchworth Lodge, Betchworth, Surrey]; *b* 30 March 1933; *educ* St Andrews (MA Econ)

1 Phoebe, Mary; *b* 23 Nov 1889

2 Olive Marjory; *b* 11 May 1892

BROMHEAD

Arms: Az. on a bend arg. between two leopard's faces or a mural crown gu. between two fleurs-de-lys sa. **Crest:** Out of a mural crown gu. a unicorn's head arg., horned or, in the mouth a rose gu., slipped and leaved ppr. **Motto:** *Concordia res crescunt* ('Possessions increase with concord'). **Creation:** Bt. (UK) 19 Feb 1806.

(SIR) JOHN DESMOND GONVILLE BROMHEAD, 6TH BT, of Thurlby Hall, Co Lincoln [John Bromhead Esq, Thurlby Hall, Aubourn, Lincs]; *b* 21 Dec 1943; *s* f 1981 but does not use title; *educ* Wellington and privately

Lineage: HENRY BROMHEAD owned large estates at Bole and N Wheatley, Notts, 1612.

EDWARD BROMHEAD, of Thurlby Hall, Lincs; *m* Anne, dau, and coheir of Anthony Eyre, and had:

BENJAMIN BROMHEAD, of Lincoln; *m* Margaret, dau and coheir of James Bordman, of Lynn, and *d* 21 Jan 1782, leaving:

1 Edward, Dragoons offr; *k* Falkirk aged 19

2 BORDMAN, of whom presently

3 Benjamin, Col 21/24th and 69th Foot; *dsp* 20 May 1803

4 James, Capt 5th and 34th Foot Battle of Minden 1759; *b* 21 May 1738; *m* Elizabeth Matthews (*d* 13 Jan 1804) and *dsp* 7 Jan 1804

5 John; *b* 15 Oct 1742; Capt 69th Regt, served with Adml Boscawen against the French Fleet 1762; *m* Anne (*d* 25 Feb 1837), dau of Dr Darwin, and *d* 5 Jan 1818, leaving issue

6 Edward (Rev); *b* 30 Oct 1746; Rector Rephem, Lincs; *m* 11 June 1776 Catherine (*d* 10 Feb 1837), dau of Thomas Ayre, and *d* 16 Jan 1835, leaving two daus

1 Anne; *m* 3 May 1761 Richard Gardiner, of Aldborough, Suffolk (*d* 14 Sept 1781), and *d* 31 Jan 1802, leaving issue

The 2nd son,

BORDMAN BROMHEAD, of Thurlby, Col in the Army, served with his bro under Adml Boscawen against the French Fleet 1762; *m* 1756 Frances (*d* 26 Jan 1801), only child of William Gonville (the last male heir of the GONVILLEs of Lincs, whose ancestor Edmund de Gonville founded Gonville Hall (now Gonville and Caius Coll), Cambridge, 1348), and *d* 7 Dec 1804, leaving, with a dau (Frances, *m* Rev James Wood, DD):

Sir Gonville Bromhead, 1st Bt (UK), so *cr* 19 Feb 1806; *b* 20 Sept 1758; Lt-Gen , served War American Independence 1777 (wounded, captured at Saratoga); *m* 18 July 1787 Jane (*d* 2 Sept 1837), yst dau of Sir Charles ffrench, 1st Bt, of Castle ffrench, by Rose, Baroness ffrench in her own right (*see* FFRENCH, B), and *d* 18 May 1822, leaving issue:

1 **Sir Edward ffrench Bromhead, 2nd Bt**, MA, FRS, High Steward Lincoln; *b* 26 March 1789; *d* unm 14 March 1855

2 EDMUND GONVILLE (Sir), **3rd Bt**

3 Charles ffrench (Rev); *b* 18 May 1795; MA, Vicar Cardington, Beds; *d* unm 2 Aug 1855

Sir EDWARD's bro,

Sir Edmund Gonville Bromhead, 3rd Bt; *b* 22 Jan 1791; Maj, fought Waterloo; *m* 15 Sept 1823 Judith Christine (*d* 12 June 1873), yst dau of James Wood, of Woodville, Co Sligo, and had, with other issue:

1 Edward; *b* 21 March 1832; Capt 4th Regt Crimea 1855; *d* unm 9 Jan 1869

2 BENJAMIN PARNELL (Sir), **4th Bt**

3 Charles James, CB (1898), JP (Denbighs); *b* 15 Sept 1840; Col S Wales Borderers Ashanti War 1873–74, Zulu War 1870, Burma 1887–89; *m* 5 Oct 1876 Alice Marie (*d* 19 Oct 1932), only dau of Thomas Freckleton, and *d* 24 Dec 1922, having had issue:

(1) Richard Freckleton Gonville; *b* 6 Nov 1877; Maj Lincs Regt Boer War 1900–02 (two medals, five claps) and WW I (star with bar, two medals); *m* 15 June 1927 Lydia (*d* 30 Oct 1935), yst dau of W J Davey, and *d* 16 Dec 1949

(2) Charles Edward Gonville; *b* 23 Dec 1882; *d* 1891

4 Gonville; *b* 29 Aug 1845; VC (for defence of Rorke's Drift 1879), Lt-Col 2nd Bn S Wales Borderers ; *d* unm 10 Feb 1891

1 Frances Judith; *m* 5 April 1847 Rev Arthur Coates, Rector Pemberton, Lancs (*d* 1906), and *d* 20 Feb 1917, leaving issue

2 Victoria Gonville; *m* 15 Sept 1863 Warren Hastings Diamond, MD, and *d* 8 June 1909, leaving issue

3 Elizabeth Frances; *m* 5 Sept 1870 Evelyn Pocklington, MRCS, of Wimbledon (*d* 1911), yst surv s of Rev Roger Pocklington, of Walesby, Notts, and *d* 10 Oct 1921, leaving issue

Sir EDMUND *d* 25 Oct 1870; his est surv son,

Sir Benjamin Parnell Bromhead, 4th Bt, CB; *b* 22 Oct 1838; Col Indian Staff Corps, Cmdt 32nd Sikh Pioneers, Govr Aitchison Coll Lahore; *m* 24 Oct 1866 Hannah (*d* 8 Feb 1902), dau of Rev James Smith, and had issue:

1 Edward Gonville; *b* 2 Sept 1869; Maj 2nd KEO Goorkhas, IA; *m* 8 Nov 1897 Emily May (*d* 22 Nov 1956), est dau of Edward Hosking, ICS, and *d* 18 Dec 1910, leaving issue:

(1) BENJAMIN DENIS GONVILLE (Sir), **5th Bt**

(2) Edmund de Gonville Hosking; *b* 23 Aug 1903; *educ* Wellington; Lt-Col IA NW Frontier 1930 (medal) and WW II; *m* 24 Aug 1938 *Joan Winifred [Mrs Edmund Bromhead, 12 Market Sq, Bicester, Oxon OX6 7AW], er dau of Brig Sir Henry Lawrence Scott, CB, DSO, MC, IA, and *d* 1976 leaving issue:

1a +JOHN EDMUND DE GONVILLE [John Bromhead Esq, 17 Turnstone Green, Langford Village, Bicester OX6 0TT]; *b* 10 Oct 1939; heir presumptive; *educ* St Andrew's Coll Grahamstown and RAF Coll Cranwell; P/O RAF (ret 1964), with BEA 1964, Capt BA; *m* 17 April 1965 *Janet Frances, est dau of Harry Vernon Brotherton, of Moreton-in-Marsh, and has issue:

1b +Alistair John de Gonville; *b* 1969; *educ* St Edward's Oxford, Birmingham U, Manchester Met U and U of Surrey; BA (Hons), PG Dipl, MSc, AMIEMgt

1b *Amanda-Jane de Gonville; *b* 1965

2a +David de Gonville, CBE (1994, OBE 1988), LVO (1984); *b* 16 Sept 1944; *educ* St Andrew's Coll Grahamstown and RMA Sandhurst; Lt-Col Roy Regt Wales, Brig 1991, Gen Serv Medal (clasps), S Arabia and NI, Equerry to HRH THE PRINCE OF WALES 1982–84, Freeman Bezirk of Wilmersdorf 1993; *m* 10 Oct 1970 *Susan, dau of Lt Cdr Richard Furley Fyson, DSC, JP, RN, of Manor Farm, Kencot, Lechlade, and has issue:

1b +James Henry de Gonville; *b* 1974

1b *Annabel Suzanne de Gonville; *b* 1973

2b *Antonia Diana de Gonville; *b* 1978

1a *Jacqueline Anne Gonville [Mrs James Boonzaier, 7 Ngaio Rd, Kelburn, Wellington 5, NZ]; *b* 16 Feb 1942; *m* 1971 *James Boonzaier and has issue:

1b *Ann Marie Gonville; *b* 1977

2b *Julia Gonville; *b* 1979

(1) Dorothea Janetta Gonville; *b* 1898; *m* 18 Dec 1919 Maj Roland William Wrigley Grimshaw, IA (*d* 22 Feb 1933), s of Thomas Wrigley Grimshaw, CB, MD, and had issue:

1a Desmond Kenneth Bromhead; *b* 22 Nov 1920; Capt RE, served WW II; *ka* N Africa 12 April 1943

1a *Kathleen Vera Anne; *b* 17 Feb 1924, WRNS WW II

(2) Annie Marie Gonville; *b* 1905; *m* 20 Feb 1928 Brig Keith Cyril Darlington Dawson, OBE, IA, s of Peter Dawson

2 Benjamin Gonville; *b* 19 Aug 1876; Maj Roy Berks Regt Boer War 1900–02 and WW I; *m* 30 April 1912 Edith Maud (*d* 1975), est dau of Lt-Col Robert Charles Andrews, IA, and *d* 13 May 1939, leaving issue:

(1) Robert ('George') Benjamin Gonville, CBE (1966, OBE 1958, MBE 1943); *b* 26 Dec 1913; Col Roy Berks (DERR), serv advsr to HC Nigeria 1960–63, Col Duke of Edinburgh's Roy Regt (Berks and Wilts) 1965–70, served WW II and Cyprus 1958 (despatches); *m* 7 Jan 1947 *Mary Traill [Mrs Robert Bromhead CBE, Brownshill Court, Wick St, Stroud, Glos GL6 7QN], est dau of Harold McMeekin, of Bearsden, Dunbartonshire, and *d* 22 Nov 1995

(1) *Kathleen Constance [Mrs Cyril Walter, 5 St Mary's Close, Chitterne, Warminster, Wilts]; *b* 1915; *m* 23 Aug 1941 *Lt-Col Cyril Frederick Hembrough Walter, 11th Sikh Regt, IA, s of Capt Arthur Edward Hill Walter, of Bedford, and has had issue:

1a Stephen Benjamin; *b* 9 June 1942; *d* 4 April 1949

2a +Jonathan Benedict; *b* 29 Nov 1944

1 Janetta Hope Gonville, CI; *b* 5 April 1894 1st Baron Birdwood (*qv*) and *d* 14 Nov 1947, leaving issue

2 Dorothy Judith Gonville; *m* 15 Nov 1898 Col Percy Gerald Walker, IA (*d* 17 Nov 1934), yst s of George James Walker, and *d* 24 March 1957, leaving issue

3 Kathleen Gonville; *m* 15 Nov 1898 11th Lord Belhaven and Stenton (*qv*) and *d* 1 Dec 1935, leaving issue

Sir BENJAMIN *d* 31 July 1935; his gs,

Sir Benjamin Denis Gonville Bromhead, 5th Bt, OBE (1943); *educ* Wellington; Lt-Col Frontier Force Regt IA Iraq 1920 (medal with clasp), Waziristan 1922–24 (wounded, medal with clasp) and 1937 (despatches), NW Frontier 1930 (despatches, medal with clasp), Cmdt Zhob Militia Baluchistan 1940–43, Political Agent N Waziristan Feb 1945–April 1947; *b* 7 May 1900; *m* 6 Aug 1938 *Nancy Mary [Lady Bromhead, Thurlby Hall, Aubourn, Lincs], only dau of Thomas Seon Lough, of Buenos Aires, and *d* 1981, leaving issue:

1 Sir JOHN DESMOND GONVILLE BROMHEAD, **6th and present Bt**

1 *Diana Jane Gonville [Mrs Paul Sherwood, 2 Devonshire Place, London W1]; *b* 20 Jan 1940; *m* 17 March 1966 *Dr Paul Sherwood, s of Martin Sherwood, and has issue:

(1) *Robin Paul Austen; *b* 22 March 1969

(2) *Julian George; *b* 1974

2 *Anne Kathleen Gonville [Mrs Robin German, Thurlby Hall, Aubourn, Lincs]; *b* 1 Sept 1942; *m* 1 May 1965 *Robin James German, s of Maurice German, and has issue:

(1) *Patrick Benjamin James; *b* 15 Jan 1967

(2) *Robin Piers Gonville; *b* 15 March 1969

(3) *Alexander Henry Bromhead; *b* 1971

BROMLEY

Arms: Quarterly, per fess indented gu. and or. **Crest:** A pheasant sitting, ppr. **Motto:** *Pensez fort* ('Think firmly'). **Creation:** Bt. (GB) 31 Oct 1757.

SIR RUPERT CHARLES BROMLEY, 10TH BT, of East Stoke, Co Nottingham [Sir Rupert Bromley Bt, PO Box 249, Rivonia 2128, Transvaal, S Africa]; *b* 2 April 1936; *s f* 1966; *educ* Michaelhouse Natal, Rhodes U Grahamstown (BA, Rhodes Scholar 1956) and Ch Ch Oxford (MA); barrister Inner Temple 1959; *m* 26 April 1962 *Priscilla Hazel, only dau of Maj Howard Bourne, HAC, and Mrs Jack Warren Pollock, of Bridge House, Shoreham, Kent, and has issue:

1 +CHARLES HOWARD; *b* 31 July 1963

2 +Philip Anthony; *b* 21 Sept 1964; *m* 11 June 1994 *Carole Frances, yr dau of Gerard Damp, of Malmesbury, CP, S Africa

3 +Henry Walford; *b* 5 March 1970

Lineage (of Wilson): THOMAS WILSON, of Kendal; *d c* 1624, leaving:

THOMAS WILSON, of Kendal; *m* Dorothy, dau of Henry Fisher, of Bradleyfield, and had:

EDWARD WILSON, of Heversham Hall, Nether Levins, Westmorland; *b* 1618; *m* 1st Jane, dau of Gawen Braithwaite, of Ambleside, and had issue:

1 EDWARD, of whom we treat

1 Elizabeth; *m* Philip Swetenham, only s of Edward Swetenham, of Somerford, Cheshire

EDWARD WILSON *m* 2nd Dorothy, dau of Richard Kirkby, of Kirkby Hall, Furness, and *d* 2 July 1707, having by her had issue:

2 Roger, ancestor of CARUS-WILSON of Casterton Hall

The er son,

EDWARD WILSON, of Dallam Tower, Westmorland; *m* Catherine, dau and coheir of Sir Daniel Fleming (*see* Le FLEMING, Bt), and *d* 5 Feb 1719/20, leaving:

DANIEL WILSON, of Dallam Tower, MP Westmorland, High Sheriff Lancs 1727; *b* 1680; *m* Elizabeth, dau of William Crowle, of Hull, and *d* 31 May 1754, having had issue:

1 EDWARD, his heir

2 George; *b* 1723; Col 1st Foot Gds; *m* Anne Sybil, dau and heiress of Allan Harrison, and had a dau

3 Thomas, ancestor of WILSON of Redgrave

1 Dorothy; *m* 27 Dec 1739 Ven William Fleming (*see* Le FLEMING, Bt), Archdeacon Carlisle, only s of Sir George Fleming, 2nd Bt, Bp Carlisle, and *dvp* 12 March 1742, leaving a dau

The est son,

EDWARD WILSON, of Dallam Tower; *m* 19 June 1746 Dorothy, est dau and coheir of Sir William Fleming, 1st Bt, of Rydal, and *d* 1764, leaving an est s:

DANIEL WILSON, of Dallam Tower; *m* 1st Beatrix (*dsp* 1779), only dau of Samuel Egerton, of Tatton Park, Cheshire; *m* 2nd 17 July 1782 Sarah, only dau and heiress of Samuel Harper, of Heath, Yorks, and *d* 11 Nov 1824 aged 78, leaving:

1 Sarah, of Dallam Tower; *m* 1811 Lt-Col George Smyth (took the name and arms of WILSON; *d* 3 March 1853), of the Gds, 2nd s of John Smyth, PC, of Heath Hall, Yorks, and *d* 29 May 1831, having had, with five daus:

(1) GEORGE EDWARD WILSON, of Dallam Tower; *b* 17 Nov 1814; DL and JP, High Sheriff 1849; *m* 3 March 1842 Gertrude Mary (*d* 1892), dau of William Hulton, of Hulton Park, Lancs (*see* 1970 edn, HULTON, Bt), and *d* 1879, having had, with three daus and two other sons (*d* unm):

1a EDWARD HUGH WILSON, of Dallam Tower; *b* 3 Feb 1849; DL and JP, High Sheriff 1886; *dsp* 8 Dec 1886; on the death 1892 of his last surv sis the estates passed to his cousin, who took the name and arms of WILSON (*see* below)

(2) Charles Henry (Rev); *b* 8 Dec 1817; MA Cantab; Rector Cuberley, Glos

(3) Frederick John; *dsp* 23 Sept 1906

2 Anne; *m* 8 June 1812 Sir Robert Howe Bromley, 3rd Bt, and had issue (*see* below)

Lineage (of Smith): JOHN SMITH, of Cropwell Boteler, Titheby, Notts; *d* 1641, leaving:

THOMAS SMITH, of Nottingham, and Gadesby, Leics; *bapt* 1 Nov 1631; *m* 1st Mary, dau of John Hooper, and had two daus; *m* 2nd 27 Feb 1681 Fortune (*d* March 1716), dau of Laurence Collin, and *d* 14 July 1699, having by her had:

1 Thomas, of Broxtowe, Notts (which he bought 1717), High Sheriff Leics 1717–18; *m* Mary (*m* 2nd William Standfast, of Clifton, Notts; *d* 1744), dau of Thomas Manley, and *d* 8 Jan 1727/8, leaving five daus

2 Samuel, ancestor of the DORRIEN-SMITHs of Tresco Abbey

3 ABEL SMITH, of E Stoke, Notts, banker; *m* 1713 Jane (*d* 1743), dau of George Beaumont, of Chapelthorpe, Yorks, and *d* Dec 1756, having had (with yr sons John, ancestor of the extinct Barons Pauncefote, and Abel, ancestor of the Barons Carrington (*qv*)):

(1) **Sir George Smith, 1st Bt** (GB), so *cr* 31 Oct 1757, of E Stoke, Notts, High Sheriff 1758–9; *m* 1st 18 Aug 1747 Mary (*d* 18 May 1761), only dau and heiress of Maj William Howe (*see* HOWE, E) by Elizabeth, dau and coheir of William Pauncefote, of Carswalls, Glos, and had issue; *m* 2nd 23 Feb 1768 Catherine (*dsp* 21 Feb 1786), est dau of Rev William Vyse, Canon Lichfield, and *d* 5 Sept 1769, having had by his 1st w an only surv s:

1a Sir GEORGE SMITH later BROMLEY later still PAUNCEFOTE-BROMLEY, **2nd Bt** (took name BROMLEY by sign manual 7 Feb 1778, added name and arms of PAUNCEFOTE by roy licence 6 April 1803); *b* 18 Aug 1753; *m* 8 Jan 1778 Hon Esther Curzon (*d* 7 Nov 1839), est dau of 1st Viscount Curzon of Penn (*see* HOWE, E), and *d* 17 Aug 1808, leaving:

1b **Sir Robert Howe Bromley, 3rd Bt**; *b* 28 Nov 1778; Adml of the White; *m* 8 June 1812 Anne (*d* 6 March 1873), 2nd dau and coheir of Daniel Wilson, of Dallam Tower, Westmorland (*see* above), and had, with two daus (*d* unm):

1c Robert; *b* 13 Nov 1815; MP; *d* unm 30 Dec 1850

2c HENRY (Sir), **4th Bt**

3c Charles; *b* Feb 1820; Capt RN; *d* 21 Feb 1892

4c William; *b* July 1821; *d* 23 Dec 1836

5c Thomas; *b* 3 Nov 1822; HEIC's Bombay Army; *m* 1st 3 Nov 1843 Lucie (*d* 10 Jan 1852), 2nd dau of Gen Henry Webber, of Buckland, Devon, and had, with other issue:

1d Adela Helena Elizabeth Maude

2d Constance Geraldine (twin); *m* 23 Nov 1875 Rev Reginald Hay Hill, Vicar Weathersfield, Essex, 3rd s of John David Hay Hill, of Cressenhall, Norfolk, and *d* 23 Sept 1917

5c (cont.) Thomas Bromley *m* 2nd 19 Sept 1855 Clara FitzRoy (*d* 16 July 1869), only child of Ld Ch Baron Sir FitzRoy Kelly and widow of Capt John Green Paley, 10th Foot, and *d* 28 April 1903, having by her had issue, with a dau (*d* unm):

1d Rupert FitzRoy; *b* 28 Aug 1862; Lt RN; *m* 26 July 1904 Emilye (*d* 4 July 1936), dau of Capt Rennie, CB, RIN, and *d* 27 June 1933, leaving issue:

1e *Rosemary Sylvia; *b* 8 April 1906; *m* 18 Feb 1939 (Alfred) John Owston, CStJ, MA Cantab, S/Ldr RAFVR (*d* 3 May 1961), only s of John Charles Owston, and has had issue:

1f Anthony John Wyndham; *b* 24 June 1940; *educ* Eton; barrister Inner Temple 1965; *m* 1967 *Vivien Patricia, only dau of Brig Robert Hugh Bellamy, CBE, DSO and bar, 1st Parachute Bde, of 7 Eaton Place, London SW1, by Kathleen Louisa Isabel, 2nd dau of Sir Alfred George Lascelles (*see* HAREWOOD, E), and *d* 1992, leaving issue:

1g *Vanessa Rosemary; *b* 4 Dec 1968

2f *Nicholas Adrian Fenton [Nicholas Owston Esq, 4 Coniger Rd, London SW6]; *b* 21 June 1947; *educ* Stowe

2e Daphne Louise; *b* 29 May 1909; *m* 29 Sept 1936 Maj Frederick Warburton Davies, RA and RFC (*d* 27 Jan 1964), and *d* 29 May 1956

3d Beatrice Ruperta; *m* 1 July 1880 Adml Sir Hilary Gustavus Andoe, KCB (*d* 11 Feb 1905), s of William Andoe, and *d* 4 April 1945, leaving issue

6c Arthur; *b* 28 March 1828; Maj Notts Mil; *m* 1865 Harriet, dau of R Meyrick, and *dsp*

7c Edward, JP Middx; barrister; *b* 1 March 1831; *m* 1st 21 Nov 1868 Emma Georgina (*dsp* 1891), dau of William Hanmer, of Bodnod (*see* HANMER, Bt); *m* 2nd 28 March 1895 Edith Mary Thoroton (*d* 1 July 1928), dau of Thomas Blackborne Thoroton Hildyard, MP, of Flintham Hall, Newark, Notts, and *dsp* 13 March 1908

1c Caroline; *m* 28 July 1840 Sir James Campbell, 5th Bt (*d* 27 March 1903), and *d* 9 Dec 1900, leaving issue

2c Elizabeth; *m* 4 Jan 1869 Sir Thomas Frederick Elliot, KCMG (*see* MINTO, E), and *d* 8 Feb 1880

3c Mary; *m* 23 April 1844 John Henry Elwes, DL, JP, of Colesbourne, Glos (*d* 29 April 1891), and *d* 25 June 1913, leaving issue

Sir ROBERT *d* 8 July 1857; his est surv son,

Sir Henry Bromley, 4th Bt; *b* 25 Dec 1816; DL and JP; Capt 48th Regt; *m* 1st 1848 Charlotte Frances (*d* 29 Jan 1853), yst dau of Col Lancelot Rolleston, MP, of Watnall, and had issue; *m* 2nd 3 Feb 1856 Georgiana Ellen (*d* 17 June 1906), 3rd dau of Vere Fane, MP, of Little Ponton Hall, Lincs, gs of 8th Earl of Westmorland (*qv*), and *d* 21 Sept 1895, leaving by his 1st w:

Sir Henry Bromley, 5th Bt; *b* 6 Aug 1849; Capt Notts Yeo Cav, formerly 27th Foot; *m* 23 Jan 1873 Adela Augusta (*d* 23 Sept 1926), only child of Westley Richards, of Archwell Rattand, by Emma, 2nd dau of Vere Fane, MP, of Little Ponton Hall, Lincs (*see* WESTMORLAND, E), and *d* 11 March 1905, having had:

1 **Sir Robert Bromley, 6th Bt**, JP; *b* 4 Jan 1874; Adminr St Christopher and Nevis 1904–06, Hon Attaché Washington 1897–1901, Assist Priv Sec to Sec State Colonies 1901–03; *m* 24 Feb 1900 his cousin Hon Lilian Pauncefote (*d* 1 July 1963), 3rd dau of 1st and last Baron Pauncefote, and *d* 13 May 1906, leaving:

(1) Ruperta Sibyl; *b* 15 Oct 1901; *m* 3 June 1924 (*divorce* 1933) John Lister Shand (*das* June 1941), only s of Sir Charles Lister Shand, of Banshee, Newport, Salop, and *d* 6 Sept 1984

(2) Esther Lilian; *b* 11 Feb 1905; *m* 1st 5 July 1927 (*divorce* 1943) 12th Viscount of Oxfuird (*qv*); *m* 2nd 5 Feb 1946 James J A Murray, LLB, Capt 1st/10th Gurkha Rifles (*d* 30 April 1964), est s of Francis Edward Murray, of Coney Island, and *d* 1 Nov 1996, leaving issue

2 Sir MAURICE BROMLEY later BROMLEY-WILSON, **7th Bt** (added with arms of WILSON by roy licence 4 Feb 1897), DL and JP (Westmoreland); *b* 27 June 1875; High Sheriff 1901; *educ* Eton; Maj TAR and S Notts Yeo; *m* 1st 16 Dec 1916 Elizabeth Ann (*d* 27 July 1936), dau of W Turner, of Over Hall, Winsford, Cheshire, and widow of Godfrey Armitage; *m* 2nd 1 Sept 1942 Violet Dorothea (*d* 2 Feb 1953), 2nd dau of Lord Francis Horace Cecil (*see* EXETER, M) and widow of Lt-Col Oswald Henry Ames, and *dsp* 7 Nov 1957

3 ARTHUR (Sir), **8th Bt**

4 Herbert Assheton; *b* 16 Oct 1879; Lt 7th Canadian Inf, BC Regt; *ka* 24 April 1915

1 Esther; *m* 9 May 1905 Charles Robert Tryon (*d* 21 Oct 1916), 2nd son of Adml Robert Tryon, and *d* 21 July 1958, leaving issue (*see* TRYON, B)

Sir MAURICE's bro,

Sir Arthur Bromley, 8th Bt, KCMG (1941, CMG 1919), KCVO (1953, CVO 1935); *b* 8 Aug 1876; *educ* Farnborough Sch and HMS *Britannia*; R-Adml, WW I: Flag Capt HMS *Courageous* 1916–19, Flag Capt to V-Adml Napier cmdg Light Cruiser Force, ret 1926, Gentleman Usher-in-Ordinary to HM GEORGE V 1927, Ceremonial and Reception Sec Dominion and Colonial Office 1931–52, Gentleman Usher to TM EDWARD VIII 1936, GEORGE VI 1937–52 and THE QUEEN 1952–61; *m* 24 June 1904 Laura Mary (Maye) (*d* 19 Sept 1959), 3rd dau of Hon James Dunsmuir, of Hatley Park, Victoria, BC (sometime Govr), and had issue:

1 RUPERT HOWE (Sir), **9th Bt**

1 Marion Victoria; *b* 15 May 1908; *d* unm 11 Aug 1983

2 Anne; *b* 3 Feb 1915; *m* 7 Sept 1939 Thomas Henry Perceval Lloyd (*d* 1992), yr s of Maj Thomas Henry Lloyd, of Padua House, Wimbledon, and *d* 11 Sept 1996, leaving:

(1) *David Anthony Henry [David Lloyd Esq, 20 Afghan Rd, Broadstairs, Kent]; *b* 1945; has issue:

1a *Emma Louise; *b* 1979

(1) *Mary-Anne [Mrs William Hurn, Top Flat, 21 Trinity Sq, Margate, Kent CT9 1HR]; *b* 1941; *m* 1962 William Dennis Hurn (*d* 1989) and has issue:

1a *Michael John; *b* 1966

1a *Belinda Ann; *b* 1963

2a *Tania Brigitta; *b* 1968

3a *Chantal Anne; *b* 1978

(2) *Arabella Patricia [Mrs Arabella Andrup, 10 Britannia Ct, Brighton Marina, Sussex]; *b* 1954; *m* 1972 (*divorce* 1989) Claus Andrup and has issue:

1a *Daniel Lloyd; *b* 1973

1a *Georgina Kirsten; *b* 1978

3 *Elizabeth Mary [Lady Collins, Kirkman Bank, Knaresborough, Yorks]; *b* 13 May 1919; *m* 1st 30 Nov 1940 6th Baron Sudeley (*qv*); *m* 2nd 27 Oct 1965 *Maj Sir Arthur James Robert Collins, KCVO, late RHG, only s of Col William Fellowes Collins, DSO, of Knaresborough

4 Patricia Sophia; *b* 17 March 1922; *m* 23 July 1956 John Richard Franco, Jr, s of Hon John Richard Franco, of Detroit, and *d* 29 April 1991

Sir ARTHUR *d* 12 Jan 1961; his only son,

Sir Rupert Howe Bromley, 9th Bt, MC (1944); *educ* Eton and Radley; WW II: Gren Gds 3rd Bn 1939–40 and Armoured Div 1941–44, Maj 1940, Mil Sec's Branch GHQ MELF 1946–47; *b* 31 Dec 1910; *m* 1st 6 June 1935 (*divorce* 1960) Dorothy Vera (*d* 1982), only dau of Sir Walford Harmood Montague Selby, KCMG, CB, CVO, of Lucas Green House, Greendale, Salisbury, S Rhodesia, and had issue:

1 Sir RUPERT CHARLES BROMLEY, **10th and present Bt**

2 +Maurice David [Maurice Bromley Esq, 50/1 Tambon Sanna Maeng, Amphur Sansai, Chiangmai 50200, Thailand]; *b* 20 Nov 1941; *educ* Michaelhouse Natal and Natal U; *m* 1st 20 Feb 1965 (*divorce* 1984) Heather Mary Estcourt-Cutter, and has issue:

(1) *Caroline Margaret; *b* 13 Jan 1966; *m* 19– *G Ramirez and has issue

(2) *Jennifer Mary; *b* 20 Dec 1968; *m* 19– (*divorce* 19–); m 2nd 19– *R Aguirre and has issue

2 (cont.) Maurice Bromley *m* 2nd 1985 *Renita Lopez Amador and has further issue:

(2) +Robert Howe; *b* 1986

Sir Rupert *m* 2nd 11 Aug 1960 Ethel Maud, formerly w of C Schofield and dau of Francis Richard Stephens, of Killarney, Co Cork, and *d* 14 June 1966

BROOKE, Bt, of Almondbury

Arms: Arg. a cross nebuly per pale gu. and sa., in the first and fourth quarters a boar's head erased of the last. **Crest:** In front of a sword erect, the blade entwined by two serpents respecting each other ppr., a boar's head erased sa. **Motto:** *Est nec astu* ('And it is not by cunning'). **Creation:** Bt. (UK) 13 Sept 1919.

SIR ALISTAIR WESTON BROOKE, 4TH BT, of Almondbury, Co York [Sir Alistair Brooke Bt, Wootton Farm, Pencombe, Hereford]; *b* 12 Sept 1947; *s* f 1983; *educ* Repton and RAC Cirencester; *m* 6 Nov 1982 *Susan Mary, only dau of Barry Charles Roger Griffiths, MRCVS, of Orchards End, Norton, Powys, and has:

1 *Lorna Rosemary Weston; *b* 1983

Lineage: WILLIAM BROOKE, of Northgate House, Honley, Yorks; *b* 30 June 1763; *m* 4 Sept 1788 Hannah (*d* 24 March 1840), dau of William Clapham, of Leeds, and *d* 21 April 1846, having had a 4th s:

THOMAS BROOKE, of Northgate House; *b* 26 Feb 1798; *m* 23 Oct 1828 Ann (*d* 10 Aug 1889), dau of Joseph Ingham, of Hunslet, Yorks, and *d* 31 Aug 1859, having had:

1 Sir THOMAS BROOKE, 1st and last Bt (UK), so *cr* 4 Aug 1899, of Armitage Bridge, Huddersfield, Yorks, DL, JP, FSA; *b* 31 May 1830; *m* 1st 20 Sept 1854 Eliza (*d* 5 Sept 1855), dau of Enoch Vickerman, and had issue; *m* 2nd 3 July 1860 Amelia (*dsp* 10 May 1901), dau of David Dewar, of Dunfermline, Scotland; *m* 3rd 30 Sept 1902 Mary (*d* 12 March 1938), dau of James Priestley, JP, of Bankfield, Huddersfield, and widow of Rev Charles Farrar Forster, Vicar Beckwithshaw, Yorks, and *dsps* 16 July 1908, when the btcy expired, leaving by his 1st w:

(1) Francis Thomas; *b* 25 Aug 1855; *dsp* 27 Aug 1872

2 **Sir John Arthur Brooke, 1st Bt** (UK), so *cr* 13 Sept 1919, JP Ross-shire and W R Yorks; MA Oxford; *b* 22 March 1844; dir John Brooke & Sons, chm York Ho of Laymen; *m* 7 Jan 1873 Blanche (*d* 27 Nov 1924), dau of Maj Charles Samuel Weston, 36th Native Inf, IA, of Morvich, Sutherland, and had issue:

(1) John Weston; *b* 2 July 1880; FRGS; *k* Tibet 24 Dec 1908

(2) ROBERT WESTON (Sir), **2nd Bt**

(1) Blanche; *m* 30 July 1907 Rev Charles Dixon Hoste (*d* 4 April 1957), s of Maj-Gen Dixon Edward Hoste, CB, RA, and *d* Aug 1964

(2) Dorothy, JP (Middx 1922–38); *m* 12 Dec 1905 Col Walter Henry Patrick Law, DSO, RASC, Chev Order Leopold (*d* 8 Aug 1956), s of Patrick Francis Law, and *d* 13 Aug 1948, leaving issue

Sir JOHN *d* 12 July 1920; his only surv son,

Sir Robert Weston Brooke, 2nd Bt, DSO (1918), MC (1916), DL and JP Ross and Cromarty, Maj QO Yorks Dragoons WW I (despatches four times); *b* 10 Aug 1885; *m* 1 June 1909 Margery Jean, MBE (1920) (*d* 2 May 1975), dau of Alexander Geddes, of Blairmore, Aberdeenshire, and had issue:

1 JOHN WESTON (Sir), **3rd Bt**

2 Richard Weston; *b* 29 April 1921; Maj Seaforth Highrs, attd IA; drowned at sea 19 April 1958

1 *Elizabeth Jean [Mrs Malcolm Buist, Katewell, Evanton, Ross-shire]; *b* 10 April 1910; *m* 8 Dec 1939 Lt-Cdr Malcolm Buist, RN, Chev Legion d'Honneur (*d* 20 April 1965), yst s of Col Frederick Braid Buist, of Scone, Perthshire, and has issue:

(1) *Elizabeth Mary; *b* 10 Feb 1944; *m* 19–

(2) *Jane Christine; *b* 14 Feb 1947

2 Edith Frances; *b* 16 July 1914; *d* unm 6 Dec 1941

3 *Hazel Mary [Mrs John Lochore, Burgie Mains House, Forres, Moray]; *b* 16 June 1918; *m* 21 Feb 1942 Maj John Alexander Lochore, Seaforth Highrs (*ka* Normandy 30 June 1944), est s of Sir James Lochore, and has issue:

(1) *Hamish John, DL (Moray) [Hamish Lochore Esq DL, Burgie House, Forres, Moray]; *b* 29 July 1943; *educ* Strathallan Sch Perthshire and RMA Sandhurst; late Capt RSG; *m* 6 June 1970 *Pollyann Elise, dau of Lt-Col Hon David Edward Hely-Hutchinson (*see* DONOUGHMORE, E), and has issue:

1a *Alexander David; *b* 1971

2a *Hugh Mark; *b* 1974

1a *Clare Hermione; *b* 1977

(1) *Fiona Margery [Mrs Ian Meiklejohn, Burgie Mains, Forres, Moray]; *b* 18 Jan 1945; *m* 1971 *Lt-Cdr Ian Patrick Forbes Meiklejohn, RN, and has issue:

1a *James Forbes; *b* 1976

1a *Clodagh Kirsteen; *b* 1974

Sir ROBERT *d* 24 Aug 1942; his er son,

Sir John Weston Brooke, 3rd Bt, TD, DL (1963), JP (1960 Ross-shire); *b* 26 Sept 1911; *educ* Repton and Trin Coll Cambridge (BA); Maj Lovat Scouts WW II; *m* 1st 17 Nov 1945 (*divorce* 1963) Rosemary, dau of Percy Nevill (*see* ABERGAVENNY, M), and had issue:

1 Sir ALISTAIR WESTON BROOKE, **4th and present Bt**

2 +CHARLES WESTON [Charles Brooke Esq, Midfearn, Ardgay, Ross-shire IV24 3DL]; *b* 27 Jan 1951; heir presumptive; *educ* Repton; *m* 1984 *Tanya Elizabeth, dau of Antony Thelwell Maurice, and has issue:

(1) +John Weston; *b* 23 Feb 1992

(1) *Nicola Margery; *b* 1985

(2) *Emily Grace; *b* 1988

Sir John *m* 2nd 1 March 1966 Phoebe Napier, MB, FFARCS, DA (*d* 16 May 1977), dau of G A Harvey and widow of Sir Peter Drummond Macdonald, KBE, FRS, and *d* 19 July 1983

BROOKE, Bt, of Norton Priory

Arms: Or a cross engr. per pale gu. and sa. **Crest:** A brock or badger ppr. **Motto:** Faste without fraude. **Creation:** Bt. (E) 12 Dec 1662.

SIR RICHARD NEVILLE BROOKE, 10TH BT, of Norton Priory, Chester [Sir Richard Brooke Bt, Pond Cottage, Crawley, Hants SO21 2PR]; *b* 1 May 1915; *s f* 1981; *educ* Eton; Lt Scots Gds WW II (wounded, POW, escaped), FCA, sr ptnr Price Waterhouse 1969–75; *m* 1st 21 July 1937 (*divorce* 1959) Lady Mabel Kathleen Jocelyn (*d* 27 June 1985), yr dau of 8th Earl of Roden (*qv*), and has issue:

1 +(RICHARD) DAVID CHRISTOPHER [David Brooke Esq, The Manor House, Cholderton, Wilts]; *b* 23 Oct 1938; *educ* Eton; late Lt Scots Gds; *m* 1st 16 Nov 1963 (*divorce* 1976) Carola Marion, er dau of Sir Robert Erskine-Hill, 2nd Bt (*qv*); *m* 2nd 1979 *Lucinda Barlow, only dau of John Frederick Voelcker, of Natal, and formerly w of William Barlow, and has by his 1st w:

(1) +Richard Christopher; *b* 10 July 1966

(2) +Edward Marcus; *b* 24 March 1970

2 +Piers Leighton [Piers Brooke Esq, 37 Yeomans Row, London SW3 2AL]; *b* 29 Dec 1940; *educ* Eton; late Lt Scots Gds; *m* July 1967 *Susan Wheeler, dau of John Davenport, of New York, and has issue:

(1) +Sebastian Piers; *b* 5 Nov 1974

(1) *Arabella Elinor; *b* 14 Sept 1973

Sir RICHARD *m* 2nd 26 April 1960 *Jean Evison, dau of Lt-Col Arthur Cecil Corfe, DSO, and formerly w of Sir Nicolas John Alexander Cheetham, KCMG

Lineage: THOMAS BROKE, of Leighton, Cheshire; *m* the dau and heir of John Parker, of Cuerden Hall, Lincs, and had issue:

1 JOHN, of whom presently

2 Robert, of Nantwich, Govr Calais

3 Richard (Sir), Ch Baron Exchequer *temp* HENRY VIII

4 Henry, Pncpl Clerk Bd Green Cloth

The est son,

JOHN BROKE, of Leighton; had:

THOMAS BROKE, of Leighton; had, with an er s, Thomas, of Leighton:

RICHARD BROOKE, of Norton, Cheshire (bought from HENRY VIII 1545), Kt of Rhodes/St John of Jerusalem, Sheriff Cheshire 1563; *d* 1569, leaving:

THOMAS BROOKE, Sheriff Cheshire 1578 and 1592; *m* 1st Anne, dau of 10th Lord (Baron) Audley (*qv*), and was ancestor of the BROOKEs of Norton; *m* 2nd Elizabeth, sis of Thomas Merbury, of Merbury, and was ancestor of the BROOKES of Dromavana; *m* 3rd Elinore Gerard, and was ancestor of the BROOKEs of Mere; *d* 1622, leaving an est s:

Sir RICHARD BROOKE, of Norton; *m* 1st Jane, dau of William Chaderton, Bp Chester; *m* 2nd Catherine, dau of Sir Henry Nevill (*see* ABERGAVENNY, M), of Billingbere, Berks, and *d* 10 April 1632, leaving by her an est s:

Sir Henry Brooke, 1st Bt (E), so *cr* 12 Dec 1662 ; *b* 1611; Sheriff Cheshire 1644–47, MP Cheshire 1654–56; *m* Mary, dau of Timothy Pusey, of Selston, Notts, and *d* 1664, leaving an est s:

Sir Richard Brooke, 2nd Bt, Sheriff Cheshire 1667–68; *m* April 1656 Francisca Posthuma, sis of Richard Legh, of Lyme, and *d* Feb 1709/10, having had, with four yr sons and four daus (Mary, *m* Randle Wilbraham (*see* SKELMERSDALE, B) and had issue; Letitia, *m* 17 Oct 1701 Henry Legh (*see* GREY, B)):

Sir Thomas Brooke, 3rd Bt, Govr Chester Castle *temp* QUEEN ANNE; *m* 12 July 1688 Grace, dau of Roger Wilbraham, of Townsend, nr Nantwich, and *d* 1739, having had, with five other s (all dv) and two daus:

RICHARD; *m* Margaret, dau of John Hill, of Hawkstone, and *dvp* 1720, leaving:

Sir Richard Brooke, 4th Bt; *m* 1752 Frances (*d* 12 Feb 1778), only dau of Thomas Patten, DL, JP, of Bank Hall, Lancs, and had, with other issue:

1 RICHARD (Sir), **5th Bt**

2 Thomas, of Church Minshull, Cheshire; *b* 1760; *m* 2 May 1780 Margaret (*d* 16 Dec 1826), yst dau of Sir Robert Cunliffe, 2nd Bt (*qv*), and *d* 1825, leaving, with other issue:

(1) Emily; *m* 9 July 1825 V-Adml Sir Henry Shiffner, 2nd Bt (*qv*), and *d* 9 March 1878

Sir RICHARD *d* 6 July 1781; his est s,

Sir Richard Brooke, 5th Bt, MA Oxon; *m* 4 May 1780 Mary (*d* 13 April 1825), 2nd dau of Sir Robert Cunliffe, 2nd Bt (*qv*), and *d* 6 March 1795, having had (with Mary, *m* 27 March 1822 Sir James M Riddell, Bt, and *d* his widow 30 Jan 1866) an est s:

Sir Richard Brooke, 6th Bt; *b* 18 Aug 1785; *m* 4 Dec 1809 his first cousin Harriot (*d* 13 April 1825), 2nd dau of Sir Foster Cunliffe, 3rd Bt (*qv*), and had, with other issue:

1 RICHARD (Sir), **7th Bt**

2 Thomas, Gen, Col 28th Regt, Lt-Col cmdg 12th Foot; *b* 2 April 1816; *m* 8 Dec 1840 Catherine Marie Diana (*d* 24 Jan 1907), only dau of Col Draper, Scots Fus Gds, and *d* 4 Nov 1880, having had, with other issue:

(1) Alured de Vere, Col RE; *b* 10 Nov 1841; *m* 14 July 1874 Mary Augustus (*d* 4 Mar 1947), dau of Bonamy Dobrée, and *d* 19 April 1926, leaving issue:

1a Maye Amélie Lucile; *m* 20 April 1904 R-Adml Archibald Cochrane, CMG (*d* 15 July 1952), er s of Adml Basil Edward Cochrane, and *d* 10 Aug 1954, leaving issue (*see* DUNDONALD, E)

3 Arthur; *b* 24 April 1819; *m* 19 Feb 1852 Susan (*d* 25 Nov 1852), est dau of Rev Alexander Buchanan, of Hales, Staffs, and *d* 7 June 1903, having had twins:

(1) Susan Alice; *d* young 22 April 1862

(2) Helen Maude; *m* 26 June 1878 Rev William Wentworth Wodehouse, Rector Distington, Cumberland (*d* 26 Mar 1888; *see* KIMBERLEY, E), and *d* 1 Aug 1932, leaving issue

1 Mary; *b* 1810; *m* 7 May 1831 Rowland Eyles Egerton Warburton, DL, JP, of Arley, Cheshire (*d* 6 Dec 1891; *see* GREY EGERTON, Bt), and *d* 21 April 1881, leaving issue

2 Harriot; *m* 24 Nov 1837 11th Earl of Meath (*qv*) and *d* 16 July 1898, leaving issue

3 Jessy; *m* 22 May 1832 Hon Richard Bootle-Wilbraham, est s of 1st Baron Skelmersdale (*qv*), and *d* 18 July 1892, leaving issue

4 Caroline Frances; *m* 18 Nov 1834 Hon Arthur Lascelles, 5th s of 2nd Earl of Harewood (*qv*), and *d* 8 Jan 1895, leaving issue

5 Clare Emily; *m* 23 Sept 1845 Sir Frederick Hervey-Bathurst, 3rd Bt (*qv*), and *d* 24 Jan 1867, leaving issue

Sir RICHARD *d* 11 Nov 1865; his est son,

Sir Robert Brooke, 7th Bt, 1st Life Gds, High Sheriff Chester 1870; *b* 13 Dec 1814; *m* 1st 12 Dec 1848 Lady Louisa Duff (*d* 23 Sept 1864), sis of 5th Earl of Fife (*see* FIFE, D), and had, with other issue:

1 RICHARD MARCUS (Sir), **8th Bt**

2 Basil Poynings; *b* 28 Sept 1853; *d* unm 6 May 1939
3 Joscelyn James Pusey; *b* 21 Jan 1855; *d* 29 Jan 1935
4 Victor Alexander; *b* 20 April 1857; *m* 15 Aug 1893 Nora (*d* 8 Nov 1957), dau of James Linton, of Palmerston N, NZ, and *d* 20 April 1937, leaving issue:
(1) Victor James, JP 1934; *b* 29 May 1899; Alderman Tamworth 1931–48; *m* 15 Jan 1927 Doris Isabella (*d* 1971), dau of John Bull Ware, of Tamworth, NSW, and *d* 31 Dec 1976, leaving issue:
1a +Bladen James, JP [Bladen Brooke Esq, JP, 107 Hillvue Rd, Tamworth, NSW 2340, Australia]; *b* 30 Dec 1928; Alderman Tamworth City Cncl 1987; *m* 15 Feb 1958 *Adeline Ruth, er dau of Kenneth Field Clemson, JP, of NSW, and has issue:
1b +Daron James Clemson; *b* 8 Mar 1964; *m* 1993 *Cherelle Kay, dau of Phillip Corbett, of Sydney
1b *Kim Anabel; *b* 15 Mar 1959; *m* 1979 *John Francis Mannion, JP, est s of William Mannion, of Tamworth, NSW, and has issue:
1c *Elissa Jane; *b* 1982
2c *Rebekah Anne; *b* 1983
2b *Anthea Kay [Mrs Scott Hamilton, 1/347A Livingstone Rd, Marrickville, Cammiray, NSW 2204, Australia]; *b* 21 Oct 1960; *m* 1989 *Scott Robert Hamilton, only s of William Robert Hamilton, of Melbourne, and has issue:
1c *Luke Bladen William; *b* 1994
1c *Samantha Nichole Brooke; *b* 1991
(2) Reginald Marcus; *b* 18 Jan 1905; *m* 1st 5 Oct 1927 Beth Allender (*d* 14 June 1957), dau of Andrew John Telfer; *m* 2nd 5 May 1960 Dulcie Louise (*d* 6 Jan 1994), and *d* 2 March 1980, leaving by his 1st w:
1a +Peter Brabazon, JP [Peter Brooke Esq JP, PO Box 3258, Weston Creek, ACT 2611, Australia]; *b* 2 Feb 1929; *m* 20 March 1954 *Beverley Elizabeth, only dau of Francis William George Vincent, and has issue:
1b +Victor Garry; *b* 3 Jan 1956
2a +Donald John Allender; *b* 17 May 1932
3a +Lynton Marcus [Lynton Brooke Esq, 21 Maxwell Brown Dve, Southport, Qld, Australia]; *b* 23 June 1933; *m* 1st 1956 (*divorce* 1960) Wendy Vida, only dau of David Arthur Kenneth Miller; *m* 2nd 11 June 1960 *Eileen Adele, dau of William Henry Humphreys, and has by her:
1b +Stephen Mark; *b* 14 March 1963
1b *Lynda Kay; *b* 17 July 1961; *m* 1st 12 Oct 1980 Stephen Williams; *m* 2nd 22 June 1985 *Allan Hector McEwan McKay and by her 1st husb has:
1c *Danielle Anita Virginia; *b* 14 April 1981
2b *Stacey Anne (twin); *b* 14 March 1963
4a +Richard Michael [Richard Brooke Esq, Alexandria Ave, Bayview, Sydney, NSW, Australia]; *b* 25 July 1937; *m* 17 Oct 1959 *Lena Hazel Maureen, dau of George Alfred Childs, and has issue:
1b +Richard George; *b* 12 Dec 1968
1b *Louise Kate; *b* 19 Jan 1965
1a *Pamela Elizabeth [Mrs Grahame Baillie, 6 Ebony Drive, Warnevale, NSW 2259, Australia]; *b* 19 June 1935; *m* 1st 11 Nov 1953 (*divorce* 19–) Anthony John Glasgow; *m* 2nd 22 Sept 1962 *Grahame Vance Baillie and by her 1st husb has:
1b *Peter John; *b* 1 June 1954; *m* 21 Dec 1972 *Carol Anne Gulliver and has:
1c *Malcolm Ian; *b* 7 Nov 1981
1c *Cathryn Jane; *b* 8 Oct 1978
2c *Rebecca Anne; *b* 31 Jan 1980
1b *Denise Beth; *b* 8 Aug 1957; *m* 3 Dec 1988 *Geoffrey John Reeve-Parker and has:
1c *Camilla Brooke; *b* 24 Dec 1982
2c *Parissa; *b* 11 April 1986
(1) Lilian; *b* 7 May 1894; *d* unm 19 Sept 1955
5 Octavius George; *b* 19 June 1858; *d* unm 26 Sept 1944
6 Lionel; *b* 17 Nov 1859; *educ* BNC Oxford (BA); *d* unm 12 Jan 1939
1 Winifred Agnes Emily; *d* unm 17 Aug 1946

Sir Richard *m* 2nd 21 Dec 1871 Henrietta Elizabeth (*d* 20 Aug 1911), 2nd dau of Sir Harry Mainwaring, 2nd Bt (*see* 1934 edn), and *d* 3 March 1888, having by her had, with other issue:
2 Rosalind Hester; *m* 11 July 1925 Lt-Col Denis Erskine Knollys, DSO, IA (*d* 8 Dec 1952), s of Canon E W Knollys, and *dsp* 31 Jan 1954

His est s,

Sir Richard Marcus Brooke, 8th Bt, DL and JP, 1st Life Gds; *b* 28 Oct 1850; *m* 16 Jan 1883 Alice (*d* 21 Jan 1933), dau of John Sambrooke Crawley, of Stockwood, Beds, and *d* 30 Sept 1920, leaving:

Sir Richard Christopher Brooke, 9th Bt, DL (1931–46), JP (1929) and CC (1928–46) Worcs, High Sheriff 1931, v-chm Worcs War Emergency Ctee 1939–45, chm Bewdley Div U Assoc 1945–46; *educ* Eton and Ch Ch Oxford (MA 1923), Lt Scots Gds; *b* 8 Aug 1888; *m* 1st 12 Sept 1912 Marian Dorothea (*d* 13 Feb 1965), only dau of Arthur Charles Innes-Cross, DL, MP, of Dromantine, Co Down (*see* ROXBURGHE, D), and had issue:
1 Sir RICHARD NEVILLE BROOKE, **10th and present Bt**
1 *Audley Marian [Mrs Kurt Seebohm, 45 Hartäckerstrasse, 1190 Vienna, Austria]; *b* 1913; *m* 18 Aug 1937 Dr Kurt Adolf Seebohm, Commercial Sec German Embassy Vienna (*d* 1981), est surv s of Gen-Direktor Kurt Seebohm, and has issue:
(1) *Kurt Florian; *b* 30 May 1939; DEcon Vienna; *m* 1967 *Karin Schaeffer, of Salzburg, and has issue:
1a *Katja; *b* 1972
(1) *Andrea Gabrielle; *b* 20 Dec 1941

Sir Richard *m* 2nd 29 March 1967 Kathleen Edna (*d* 21 March 1995), yr dau of Francis John Gildea, of The Windsor Hotel, Dun Laoghaire, Co Dublin, and *d* 1981

BROOKE, Bt, of Summerton

Arms: Or a cross engrailed per pale gu. and sa., in the dexter canton a crescent of the second, and in the sinister canton a martlet of the third, both for difference. **Crest:** A badger passant ppr., charged with a crescent and a martlet gu. **Motto:** *Gloria finis* ('Glory is the aim'). **Creation:** Bt. (UK) 12 Oct 1903.

SIR FRANCIS GEORGE WINDHAM BROOKE, 4TH BT, of Summerton, Co Dublin [Sir Francis Brooke Bt, 65 Sterndale Rd, London W14 0HU]; *b* 15 Oct 1963; *s* f 1982; *educ* Eton and Edinburgh U (MA); AIIMR, dir Foreign and Colonial Management Ltd; *m* 1989 *Hon Katharine Elizabeth, only dau of Baron Hussey of North Bradley *qv*; (*see* also WALDEGRAVE, E), and has issue:
1 +GEORGE FRANCIS GEOFFREY; *b* 10 Sept 1991
1 *Olivia Nancy; *b* 12 Jan 1994
2 *Sarah; *b* 20 March 1996

Lineage: FRANCIS BROOKE, of Colebrooke, Co Fermanagh (*see* BROOKEBROUGH, V), had a 6th s:

GEORGE FREDERICK BROOKE, of Summerton, Co Dublin, and Coolgreany, Co Wexford, High Sheriff Co Dublin; *b* 1779; *m* 1814 Jane (*d* 28 Dec 1835), dau of Richard Grace, MP, of Boley, Queen's Co (by Jane, dau of Hon John Evans, of Bulgaden Hall, and gdau of 1st Baron Carbery (*qv*)), and sis of Sir William Grace, 2nd Bt, of Grace Castle (*see* 1970 edn), and *d* 5 Nov 1865, leaving, with other issue (including Louisa Caroline, *m* 21 May 1839 Charles Cobbe, DL, of Newbridge House, Co Dublin (*d* 5 July 1886); *dsp* 2 June 1882):

FRANCIS RICHARD BROOKE, of Summerton and Coolgreany, High Sheriff 1860; *b* 24 Aug 1817; *m* 18 Nov 1848 Hon Henrietta Monck (*d* 6 May 1911), dau of 3rd Viscount Monck (*qv*), and *d* 2 March 1867, leaving issue:
1 GEORGE FREDERICK (Sir), **1st Bt**
2 Gerald Richard; *b* 29 April 1852; *m* 10 April 1875 Kathleen Maude (*m* 2nd Seymour Coghill Hort Bushe, KC (*d* 27 Jan 1922); *d* 25 Jan 1939), dau of 1st Earl de Montalt (*see* HAWARDEN, V), and *d* 26 April 1891, having had issue
3 John Monck; *b* 23 Aug 1853; *m* 23 July 1878 Edwina Johanna (*m* 2nd 1892 Lt-Col Guy Percy Wyndham, 16th Lancers (*see* EGREMONT and LECONFIELD, B), dau of Rev Frederick Fitzpatrick, Rector Cloone, Co Leitrim, by Lady Olivia Taylour, dau of 2nd Marquess of Headfort (*qv*), and *d* 14 Aug 1887, having had issue
1 Louisa Caroline Elizabeth; *m* 10 Sept 1874 Charles Robert Hamilton (*d* 26 Oct 1913), est s of Charles William Hamilton, of Hamwood, Co Meath, and *d* 4 Jan 1922, leaving issue
2 Eva Henrietta; *m* 1st 28 Feb 1878 Capt Hon Cornwallis Maude, Gren Gds (*k* Majuba *vp* 27 Feb 1881), s of 1st Earl de Montalt (*see* HAWARDEN, V), and had issue; *m* 2nd 9 June 1883 Col George Holden Hutton, DL, 23rd Roy Welch Fus, of Thorney Hall, Notts (*d* 17 Oct 1908), and *d* 8 Nov 1940, leaving further issue
3 Grace Agnes; *m* 1st 29 July 1884 Col Henry L'Estrange Malone, 16th Lancers (*d* 1894); *m* 2nd 25 July 1908 Heremon John Francis Headfort Lindsey Fitzpatrick, of Hollymount, Co Mayo (*d* 1 July 1929), and *d* 12 Jan 1937

The est son,

Sir George Frederick Brooke, 1st Bt (UK), so *cr* 12 Oct 1903, JP Wexford and Dublin, DL Dublin, High Sheriff Co Wexford 1882 and Co Dublin 1898; *educ* Eton and Trin Coll Cambridge; *b* 13 Aug 1849; *m* 1st 4 April 1875 Anna Maria (*d* 13 June 1877), dau of Geoffrey Joseph Shakerley (*see* SHAKERLEY, Bt), and had, with other issue:
1 George; *b* 10 June 1877; Lt Irish Gds, Gentleman-in-Waiting to Ld Lt Ireland, served Boer War (medal with 3 clasps) and WW I; *m* 25 June 1907 Nina (*d* 3 Sept 1970), dau of Lord Arthur William Hill (*see* DOWNSHIRE, M), and *d* 5 Oct 1914 of wounds recd in action, having had issue:
(1) Arthur Basil; *b* 28 Oct; *d* 23 Dec 1908
(1) *Nancy Myra [Mrs Michael Stratton, 48 High St, Croughton, Brackley, Northants]; *b* 22 Aug 1911; *m* 1st 24 June 1931 (*divorce* 1934) John Hollingworth Roberts, 2nd s of Ralph Montagu Cook, of Roydon Hall, Kent; *m* 2nd 15 Feb 1941 Capt (Charles) Michael Stratton (*d* 1991), s of Charles John Stratton, of Heathfield Ho, Bletchington, and by him has:

1a *Patrick Michael [Patrick Stratton Esq, 5 Maple Close, Alresford, Hants SO24 9JF]; *b* 13 Sept 1945; *educ* Stowe; *m* 1992 *Miriam, dau of David Anderson, and has:

1b *Luke Nicholas; *b* 1994

2b *Adam Neil; *b* 1996

1a *Juliet Nina [Mrs William Clark-Maxwell, Speddoch, Dumfries-shire DG2 GU8]; *b* 5 June 1942; *m* 1973 *(John) William Clark-Maxwell and has issue:

1 b *James Michael Gilchrist; *b* 1975; added forename Gilchrist by deed poll 1990

1 b *Alice Louise; *b* 1979

Sir George *m* 2nd 21 April 1881 Emily Alma (*d* 28 Sept 1910), er dau of Augustine Hugh Barton, of Rochestown, Co Tipperary, and by her had issue:

2 FRANCIS HUGH (Sir), **2nd Bt**

3 Augustine Henry, MC; *b* 25 Feb 1884; *educ* Winchester and RMC Sandhurst; Lt-Col 19th King George V's Own Lancers IA WW I (1915 star); *d* unm 27 July 1958

4 Raymond Frederick; *b* 2 June 1885; *educ* Winchester; Grand Master Grand Lodge I Freemasons 1948–64 (Dep 1930–48); *d* unm 13 June 1964

5 Arthur Charles, DSO (1917); *b* Sept 1886; Maj and brevet Lt-Col RA WW I (despatches three times, wounded, Legion Honour), DAAG 1916, cmdg Oxf Yeo WW II; *d* unm 27 April 1954

6 John; *b* 2 Oct 1887; DSC, Capt RN WW I (despatches, Legion Honour) and Baltic 1919–20, Ch Constable RM Police 1936–46; *m* 4 June 1918 Margaret (Midge) Winifred, MBE (1971), only dau of Col Francis Tothill, RA, and *d* 13 March 1974, leaving issue:

(1) +Geoffrey Arthur George, DSC [Lt-Cdr Geoffrey Brooke DSC RN (ret), Beech House, Handcross Rd, Balcombe, Sussex RH17 6PS]; *b* 25 April 1920; *educ* RNC Dartmouth; Lt-Cdr RN WW II; *m* 25 Oct 1956 *Venetia Mabel, only dau of Capt Hon Oswald Wykeham Cornwallis, OBE, RN (ret) (*see* CORNWALLIS, B), and has issue:

1a *Caroline Jane; *b* 26 Aug 1957; *m* 1989 (*divorce* 1992) Barry Rudolf, of Santa Fé, New Mexico

2a *Venetia Anne Margaret; *b* 6 Feb 1959

3a *Georgina Emily Rose; *b* 10 Nov 1963; *m* 1st 1986 Lanto Millington Synge, est s of John Samuel Synge, of Mill Grange, Ballinglen, Co Wicklow; *m* 2nd 1993 *Michael Paul Boulter Bochmann, s of Paul Martin Bochmann

7 Basil Gerald; *b* 10 March 1894; *educ* Winchester; Capt 17th Lancers, Maj Roy Pioneer Corps, WWs I and II; *m* 23 Sept 1919 Essex Vere (*d* 16 Dec 1996), only child of Brig-Gen Sir Charles Vere Gunning, 7th Bt (*qv*), and *d* 12 Sept 1969, leaving:

(1) +Henry Arthur Gunning, MC (1944) [Henry Brooke Esq MC, 23 Halsey St, London SW3]; *b* 17 Sept 1923; *educ* Winchester; served WW II Tunisia and Italy, Lt-Col cmdg 16th/5th Queen's Roy Lancers 1966–69 (Col 1980–85)

(1) Mary Essex Gunning; *b* 2 Dec 1928; *m* 8 June 1960 Col Graham Chatfield Chatfield-Roberts, TD, City London Yeo Rough Riders (Rifle Bde), yr s of William Lionel Lloyd Roberts, and had issue:

1a *John Henry; *b* 26 July 1962

1a *Essex Jane; *b* 28 Nov 1963

8 Geoffrey Thomas; *b* 19 Oct 1896; *educ* Winchester; Lt 16th Lancers WW I (1914 star and Croix de Guerre); *m* 1942 Millicent Bettine, formerly w of — Stewart and dau of Maj H H D Seaton, of Mount Coote, Co Limerick

1 Emily Henrietta; *m* 18 June 1921 Henry Seymour Persse (*d* 5 Sept 1960), s of Henry Sadleir Persse, and *d* 2 Aug 1953, having had issue

2 Rose Dorothy

Sir GEORGE *d* 21 Aug 1926; his est surv s,

Sir Francis Hugh Brooke, 2nd Bt ; *b* Nov 1882, Capt and Adj S Irish Horse, Lt KRRC, WW I (1914 star); *m* 5 May 1915 Mary Louisa Mabel, yst dau of Sir John Arnott, 1st Bt (*qv*), and *d* 4 Nov 1954, leaving issue:

Sir George Francis Cecil Brooke, 3rd Bt, MBE (1949); *b* 30 March 1916; *educ* Stowe; Maj 17th/21st Lancers WW II (wounded, despatches), ret 1958; *m* 25 June 1959 *Lady Melissa Eva Caroline Wyndham-Quin [The Lady Melissa Brooke, Glenbevan, Croom, Co Limerick, Ireland], er dau of 6th Earl of Dunraven and Mount Earl (*qv*), and *d* 1982, leaving issue:

(1) Sir FRANCIS GEORGE WINDHAM BROOKE, **4th and present Bt**

(1) *Emma Nancy [Mrs Charles Thompson, 28 Irene Rd, London SW6 4AP]; *b* 10 Feb 1965; *m* 1993 *Charles C Thompson, only s of S/Ldr James Thompson, of Mijas, Spain

1 Emily Alma; *b* 3 Nov 1918

BROOKE OF ALVERTHORPE

Creation: B. (LP, UK) 2 Aug 1997.

THE BARON BROOKE OF ALVERTHORPE, of Alverthorpe, Co W Yorks (Clive Brooke) [The Rt Hon The Lord Brooke of Alverthorpe, House of Lords, London SW1A 0PW]; *b* 21 June 1942; *educ* Thornes House Sch Wakefield; Assist Sec Inland Revenue Staff Fedn 1964–82 (Dep Gen Sec 1982–88), Jt Gen Sec Public Services Tax and Commerce Union 1988–; memb: Lab Party, Fabian Soc, Inland Revenue Departmental Whitley Cncl TUS 1976–88 (Chm 1986–88), H of C Speaker's Commn Citizenship 1988–, Gen Cncl TUC 1989–, Exec Ctee Involvement and Participation Assoc 1991–, Exec Ctee TUC 1993, Cncl Civil Servs Unions; Tstee: Community Servs Volunteers 1989–, Duke of Edinburgh Study Conf 1993–; *m* 1967 *Lorna Hopkin Roberts

Lineage: JOHN BROOKE; *m* Mary Colbeck and has:

CLIVE, *cr* a **Baron**

BROOKE OF YSTRADFELLTE

Creation: B. (LP) (UK) 7 Dec 1964.

THE BARONESS BROOKE OF YSTRADFELLTE, of Ystradfellte, Brecknock (Dame Barbara Muriel Brooke DBE (1960)) [The Rt Hon The Baroness Brooke of Ystradfellte DBE, Roman's Halt, Mildenhall, Wilts SN8 2LX]; *b* 14 Jan 1908; *educ* Queen Anne's Caversham and Gloucester Trng Coll Domestic Sci; memb Hampstead Cncl 1948–65, chm exec ctee Queen's Inst District Nursing 1961–71, jt v-chm C Pty Orgn 1954–64, memb NW Met Regnl Hosp Bd 1954–66, chm: N London Hosp Management Ctee 1963–66, Govrs Godolphin, and Latymer Girls' Sch 1966–78, Hon Fell Queen Mary and Westfield Colls London U 1968; *m* 22 April 1933 Baron Brooke of Cumnor, PC, CH (LP; *d* 29 March 1984, *see* 1970 edn), and has issue:

1 *Peter Leonard, CH (1992), PC (1988) [The Rt Hon Peter Brooke CH PC MP, House of Commons, London SW1A 0AA]; *b* 3 March 1934; *educ* Marlborough, Balliol Coll Oxford (BA 1957, MA 1960) and Harvard Business Sch (MBA 1959); MP (C) Cities London and Westminster 1977–, Assist Govt Whip 1979–81, a Ld Commr Treasury 1981–83, Parly Under-Sec DES 1983–85, Min State Treasury 1985–87, Paymaster Gen 1987–89, chm C Party 1987–89, Sec State: NI 1989–92, Nat Heritage 1992–94; Chm H of C Select Ctee NI 1997–; V-Pres NUS 1955–56, Chm Nat Conf Student Christian Movement 1956, Pres Oxford Union 1957, memb Camden Cncl 1968–69, Chm St Pancras N C Assoc 1976–77, pres IAPS 1980–95, Govr Marlborough 1977–83, 1992–, lay adviser St Pauls Cathedral 1980–; *m* 17 March 1964 Joan Margaret (*d* 1985), dau of Frederick George Smith, of São Paulo; *m* 2nd 1991 *Mrs Lindsay Allinson and by his 1st w has issue:

(1) *Jonathan Keith Lawrence; *b* 8 May 1965

(2) *Daniel Roderick Villaret; *b* 1 June 1967

(3) *Sebastian Henry; *b* 6 Sept 1968

2 *Henry (Sir) PC (1996) [The Rt Hon Lord Justice Brooke, Royal Courts of Justice, Strand, London WC2A 2LL]; *b* 19 July 1936; *educ* Marlborough and Balliol Coll Oxford (BA 1961, MA 1964); barrister Inner Temple 1963, QC 1981, ktd 1988, High Court Judge (Queen's Bench) 1988–96, Chm Law Commn 1993–95, Ld Justice Appeal 1996–; *m* 16 April 1966 *Bridget Mary, 2nd dau of Wilfrid George Kalaugher, MA, BSc, and has:

(1) *Michael John; *b* 1 June 1967

(2) *Nicholas George; *b* 5 Oct 1968

(3) *Christopher Robert; *b* 23 Jan 1973

(1) *Caroline Mary (twin); *b* 23 Jan 1973

1 *Honor Leslie, SRN, *b* 2 April 1941; *educ* St Mary's Sch Calne, Grenoble U and St Thomas's Hosp; *m* 6 Aug 1966 *Dr Thomas Nigel Miller, MA, MRCP, er s of Nathaniel Allan Miller, FRCS, and has issue:

(1) *Matthew Thomas Vivian; *b* 14 Oct 1968

(2) *David Edward Benyon; *b* 20 April 1978

(3) *Alexander Henry Julian (twin); *b* 20 April 1978

(1) *Auriol Jane Verona; *b* 7 Jan 1971

(2) *Elena Frances Loveday; *b* 1975

2 *Margaret Hilary Diana; *b* 16 Jan 1944; *educ* St Mary's Sch Calne and Sussex U (BSc 1966); *m* 6 March 1971 *Dr James Pulfer, PhD, s of Max Pulfer, of Saskatchewan, and has issue:

(1) *Mark Douglas; *b* 10 Aug 1973

(1) *Rachael Barbara; *b* 15 June 1975

Lineage: JENKIN MATHEWS, of Rhymney, Mon, JP; *m* Elizabeth Hughes and had:

Rev ALFRED AUGUSTUS MATHEWS, of Gt Milton, Llanwern, Mon, deacon 1887, priest 1888, Curate Holy Trin Swansea 1887–92, Vicar 1892–97, Vicar Blaenavon with Capel Newydd 1897–1904, Vicar St Paul's Newport 1904–33, Vicar Caerwent with Dinham 1933–39, Canon Monmouth 1930–41; *b* 7 Feb 1864; *educ* Christ's Hosp, Llandovery Sch and St David's Coll Lampeter (BA 1886); *m* 4 Oct 1898 Ethel Frances (*d* 24 Sept 1951), dau of Dr Edward Beynon Evans, of Swansea, and *d* 13 Aug 1946, leaving issue:

1 Arthur Kenneth (Rev), OBE (1942), DSC (1944), deacon 1932, priest 1933, Chaplain RNVR 1939–44, Dean and Rector St Albans 1955–63, Rector St Peter's Peebles 1963–68, Vicar Thursley 1968; *b* 11 May 1906; *educ* Monkton Combe Sch and Balliol Coll Oxford (BA 1932, MA 1936); *m* 19 Sept 1936 *(Agnes) Elisabeth, dau of Edward Montagu Butler, JP, of Beach Ho, Bitton, Glos

1 Evelyn Mary; *b* 23 July 1899; *m* 1 Feb 1931 Rev Vernon Harold Jenkyn

2 Averil Charlotte, Carmelite Nun (Sister Mary of the Trinity)

3 Isobel Frances; *b* 3 July 1902; *m* 1 Dec 1945 Charles Richard Leoline Phillips

4 BARBARA MURIEL, *cr* a **Baroness**

BROOKEBOROUGH

Arms: Or a cross engrailed per pale gu. and sa., a crescent for difference. **Crest:** A brock or badger passant arg. **Supporters:** Dexter, a dolphin sa.; sinister, a lion double-queued gu., langued az. **Motto:** *Gloria finis* ('Glory is the end'). **Creations:** Bt. (UK) 7 Jan 1822, V. (UK) 4 July 1952.

THE 3RD VISCOUNT BROOKEBOROUGH, of Colebrooke, Co Fermanagh, and a **Baronet** (Sir Alan Henry Brooke, Bt, DL (Fermanagh 1987)) [The Rt Hon The Viscount Brookeborough DL, Colebrook Park, Brookeborough, Co Fermanagh BT94 4 DW]; *b* 30 June 1952; *s* f 1987; *educ* Harrow and Millfield; High Sheriff Co Fermanagh 1995, commnd 17th/21st Lancers 1971, served 4th Bn UDR and Roy Irish Regt, Lt-Col 1993, tfd RARO, memb Ho of Lds EEC Ag Ctee 1988, Ld in Waiting 1997–, Hon Col 4th/5th Rangers 1997–; *m* 1980 *Janet Elizabeth, only dau of John P Cooke, of Ballyvoy Lodge, Doagh, Co Antrim

Lineage: Sir BASIL BROOKE; *b* 1567, Capt English Army sent as reinforcement to Ireland 1598, served Munster and conquest of Ulster, Commr settlement C of I, Govr Co Donegal, granted extensive lands, including Borough and Castle of Donegal, both of which he rebuilt, ktd 1616; *m* Anne (*d* 1656), dau of Laurence Leycester, of Chester, and gdau of Sir Ralph Leycester, of Toft, and *d* 1633, having had (with Anne, *m* Richard Crofton, of Lisnaderne, Co Roscommon, and Elizabeth, *m* Thomas Chambers, of Ardgreagh, MP):

Sir HENRY BROOKE, MP Donegal Borough, Govr Co Donegal, granted land at Brookeborough, Co Fermanagh, for services during the 1641 Uprising, Parliamentarian in Civil War, when Donegal Castle was temporarily captured by Royalists, High Sheriff Co Fermanagh 1669, ktd 1664; *m* 1st Elizabeth, dau of Capt John Wynter, of Dyrham, Glos, and had, with other issue:

1 Basil, LLD Oxon, ancestor of the BROOKEs of Donegal; attainted by JAMES II, successfully defended Donegal against Jacobite army under Sarsfield; *d* 1692

Sir HENRY *m* 2nd Elizabeth, dau of Henry, Baron Docwra, and by her had further issue:

2 George; Williamite in 1690s wars, Staff Offr of Maynard, Duke of Schomberg; *m* 1667 Elizabeth Whitechurch and had issue

Sir HENRY *m* 3rd 1652 Anne (*d* 1685), dau of Sir George St George, MP, of Carrickdrumruisk, Co Leitrim, and *d* 1671, having by her had issue:

3 Thomas, MP, of Colebrooke, Maj Williamite Regt of Foot, estates declared forfeit by JAMES II; *m* Catherine (*d* 1699), dau of Sir John Cole, Bt, and sis and coheir of Arthur, Viscount Ranelagh, and was *bur* 23 Feb 1696, leaving an er s:

(1) HENRY

1 Elizabeth; *m* 1st Viscount Boyne

2 Anne; *m* Col Hon Kilner Brasier and had issue. He *d* 1725

THOMAS BROOKE's er son,

HENRY BROOKE, of Colebrooke, MP Dundalk 1713–17 and Co Fermanagh 1727–61, High Sheriff and Govr Co Fermanagh 1709; *m* 29 March 1711 Lettice (*d* 1763), dau of Benjamin Burton, Ld Mayor Dublin, and was *bur* 17 July 1761, leaving, with other issue:

1 Sir ARTHUR BROOKE, 1st and last Bt (I), so *cr* 1764, PC, MP Fermanagh; *m* 6 Aug 1751 Margaret (*d* 22 Sept 1756), only dau of Thomas Fortescue, of Reynold's Town, Co Louth, and sis of 1st Lord Clermont, and *d* 7 March 1785, when the btcy expired, having had, with other issue:

(1) Selina; *m* 24 April 1769 1st Viscount de Vesci (*qv*) and had issue

(2) Letitia Charlotte; *m* 19 July 1774 Sir John Parnell, 2nd Bt, PC, and had issue (*see* CONGLETON, B)

2 FRANCIS

1 Lettice; *m* Robert Gore, of Woodford, and was ancestor of the Barons Harlech (*qv*)

The 2nd son,

FRANCIS BROOKE, of Whibrooke; *m* 24 June 1765 Hannah (*d* June 1819), dau of Henry Prittie, of Dunalley, Co Tipperary, and sis of 1st Baron Dunalley (*qv*), and had, with other issue (*see* VIVIAN, B):

1 HENRY (Sir), **1st Bt**

2 Arthur (Sir) KCB, Lt-Gen, Col 86th Foot; *m* Marianne (*d* 14 Nov 1846), dau of Rev William Sneyd, of New Church, IoW, and *d* 26 July 1843, leaving issue:

3 Richard Prittie, Maj-Gen; *m* Elizabeth (*d* Dec 1832), dau of Col Thomas Call, 1st cousin of Sir John Call, Bt, and *d* 12 Dec 1836, leaving issue

4 George Frederick, of Summerton House, ancestor of BROOKE, Bt, of Summerton (*qv*)

1 Caroline; *m* John Trant, n of 1st Earl of Clare, Ld Chllr of Ireland, and est s of Dominick Trant, of Dovea, Co Tipperary, and had issue (*see* HOLMPATRICK, B)

2 Harriet; *m* 1834 Hon Robert Leeson (*see* 1970 edn MILLTOWN, E) and *d* his widow Jan 1858

FRANCIS BROOKE *d* 1800; his est son,

Sir HENRY BROOKE, 1st Bt (UK), so *cr* 7 Jan 1822, of Colebrooke, Co Fermanagh; *b* 10 May 1770; *m* 1792 Harriet, dau of Hon John Butler and gdau of 1st Viscount Lanesborough (*see* LANESBOROUGH, E), and had, with other issue:

1 ARTHUR BRINSLEY (Sir), **2nd Bt**

2 Richard BROOKE later HOWARD-BROOKE (added with quartered arms of HOWARD by sign manual 3 Jan 1835), of Castle Howard, Co Wicklow, and Rockleton, Queen's Co, barrister; *b* 1801; *m* 3 June 1837 Frances Caroline (*d* 18 Sept 1876), aunt of 1st Baron Holmpatrick (*qv*), and *d* 6 April 1877, leaving, with other issue:

(1) Robert, of Castle Howard, High Sheriff Co Wicklow 1880, Lt-Col N Irish Div RA; *b* 25 Sept 1840; *m* 25 July 1878 Florence Elizabeth (*d* May 1893), dau of William Johnston, of Kinlough, Co Leitrim, and *dsp* 18 Dec 1902

(2) Hans Hamilton, Lt RN; *b* 1 April 1852; *m* 30 March 1880 Lina Mary (*m* 2nd 14 July 1892 Maj Hubert Richard Lovett, KRRC), only child of Lauderdale Maitland, of Eccles, Dumfriesshire, and *dsp* 16 June 1890

(1) Caroline Harriett; *m* 7 Aug 1866 Sir John Robert Heron Heron-Maxwell, 7th Bt (*qv*), and *d* 20 Feb 1900, leaving issue

(2) Edith Georgina; *m* 19 Feb 1879 Lamplugh Frescheville Ballantine Dykes, of Dovenby, Cumberland (*d* 5 Feb 1893), and *d* 1 Nov 1912, leaving issue

3 George Augustus Frederick, of Ashbrooke, Co Fermanagh, DL; *b* 1805; *m* 25 April 1833 Lady Arabella Georgina Hastings (*d* 29 Jan 1899), dau of 11th Earl of Huntingdon (*qv*), and *d* 20 Feb 1874, leaving, with other issue:

(1) Henry Francis, Brig-Gen cmdg 2nd Inf Bde Kandahar, Col, Adj-Gen Bombay; *b* 3 Aug 1836; *m* 11 March 1865 Ann Isabella (*d* 26 Aug 1927), dau of Maj-Gen Leonard Raisbeck Christopher, Ind Staff Corps; *ka* in the sortie against Deh Khojah 16 Aug 1880, leaving, with other issue:

1a George Cecil; *b* 30 Dec 1870; Maj Border Regt Waziristan Expdn 1895 (medal with clasp), Malakand Field Force 1897–98 (medal with clasp), China Expdny Force 1900 (medal with clasp) and WW I; *m* 23 May 1912 Barbara Hampton (*d* 1979), only child of Capt William Henry Allen, of Dhuarigle Castle, Co Cork, and was *ka* 28 April 1915, leaving issue:

1b +Henry John Allen, MBE (1974), DSC (1945) [Cdr Henry Brooke MBE DSC RN, Benbow, Bosham, Chichester, W Sussex PO18 8QL]; *b* 21 Oct 1913; *educ* Wellington; Cdr RN, Nyon Patrol Spanish Civil War 1937–38, WW II (despatches) Mediterranean, N African Landings, Arctic Convoys Ops Norway and Pacific, Actg Capt while Sr Offr Reserve Ships Portsmouth 1960–61, ret 1963, Assist Dir Marine Servs MOD (Navy Dept) 1961–74 (ret from Active List 1963); *m* 21 Dec 1946 *Lesley Mary, 2nd dau of Capt Eric Noble, of Harpsden Court, Henley-on-Thames, and has:

1c +Michael Henry Hastings, OBE (1991); *b* 10 March 1948; *educ* Pangbourne Nautical Coll; Col late RE; *m* 16 Oct 1971 *Philippa Wendy, yst dau of Brig R C Crowdy, OBE, and has issue:

1d +Simon Mark Hastings; *b* 1974

2d +James Matthew Crowdy; *b* 1976

2c +George John [Prof George Brooke, 45 Brookfield Ave, Poynton, Cheshire SK12 1JE]; *b* 27 April 1952; *educ* Wellington and St Peter's Coll Oxford (MA), St John's Coll Cambridge and Claremont Graduate Sch USA (PhD); staff Salisbury and Wells Theological Coll 1978–84, V-Pncpl 1982, lecturer theology Manchester U 1984–94, sr lecturer 1994–97, Prof Biblical Studies 1997–; *m* 1976 *Rev Rosemary Jane, dau of Rev Dr Arthur R Peacocke, MBE, DSc, DD, and has issue:

1d +Peter George; *b* 1979

2d +David John; *b* 1981

1d *Rachel Mary; *b* 1982

1c *Sarah Lesley [Mrs John Pointing, 81 Spitalfield Lane, Chichester PO19 4SJ]; *b* 1949; *m* 1973 *John Nigel Pointing, s of Leslie Arthur Pointing, and has issue:

1d *Edward Hugh; *b* 1983

2d *Toby Richard; *b* 1990

1d *Clare Isabel; *b* 1985

1c (cont.) Mr and Mrs Pointing also adopted:

*Benjamin John; *b* 1980

*Jane Louise; *b* 1978

2c *Mary Barbara; *b* 31 March 1954; BEd

1a Mabel Alice; *m* 27 May 1890 Maj-Gen Alister Grant Dallas, CB, CMG, 2nd s of Alexander Grant Dallas, DL, JP, of Dunain, Inverness-shire (*d* 2 Feb 1931), and *d* 18 Dec 1954, leaving issue

2a Violet Florence; *m* 15 July 1919, as his 1st w, Col Frank Hall, RA (*d* 20 April 1964), yst s of Maj William James Hall, DL, JP, of Narrow Water, Co Down, and *d* 28 April 1936

3a Sybil Mary; *d unm* 5 July 1898

(2) Arthur Thomas CB, Capt RN; *m* 1st 2 Sept 1880 Alice Marianne (*d* 1882), dau of Clement Archer, of Hill House, Hampton; *m* 2nd 17 March 1892 Rosalie Blanche (*d* 26 Jan 1940), dau of Sir James Vaughan, and *dsp* 5 April 1893

(3) George Hastings, late Capt 48th Regt, Hon Col, Maj and Adj 4th Bn POW's Leinster Regt; *b* 21 June 1842; *m* 1st 12 Sept 1868 Beatrice Georgina (*dsp* 20 March 1898), 2nd dau of Sir John Craven Carden, 4th Bt, of Templemore (*qv*); *m* 2nd 24 Feb 1903 Adela Harriett (*dsp* 21 May 1915), dau of Lord Charles Pelham Clinton (*see* 1970 edn NEWCASTLE, D) and widow of John Campbell, of Stonefield, and *d* 5 April 1922

(4) Lionel Godolphin, CB (1900); *b* 19 May 1849; Brig-Gen, Col Connaught Rangers, cmdg Brigade TF 1908–10, served Zulu War 1879 and Boer War 1899–1900; *m* 1st 28 Nov 1881 Emma Adelaide Christina (*dsp* 2 July 1882), dau of Lord John Henry Taylour (*see* HEADFORT, M); *m* 2nd 30 April 1895 Gertrude Isabella (*d* 24 Oct 1930), est dau of Col Henry Mills Goodeve, RA, and *d* 10 June 1931, leaving issue by 2nd w:

1a Ruth Isa Patricia; *b* 21 Feb 1896

2a Gertrude Vera; *b* 12 Oct 1899; *m* 1st 30 April 1917 (*divorce* 1944) Nigel Augustus Kennedy, Capt Argyll and Sutherland Highrs (*d* 1 Sept 1957), s of Capt John Gilbert Kennedy, and gs of Lord Gilbert Kennedy (*see* AILSA, M); *m* 2nd 1944 Sidney Simon Van Den Bergh (*d* 14 Aug 1967 aged 90)

3a Amy Dorothy; *b* 21 Sept 1901

(5) Francis Theophilus, PC (I 1918), DL, JP Co Fermanagh and Wicklow; *b* 1851; Lt RN; *m* 1st 20 June 1877 Alice Mary (*d* 16 April 1909), dau of Very Rev William Ogle Moore, Dean Clogher, and had issue:

1a George Frank, DSO (1917) with two bars (1918); *b* 30 Oct 1878; Lt-Col Connaught Rangers Boer War 1899–1900 (wounded) and WW I (despatches four times); *m* 12 June 1907 Theodora Olivia (*d* 5 May 1967 aged 89), dau of Richard Meredith Jackson, of Natal, and *d* 20 Nov 1966, leaving issue:

1b Frank Hastings, CB (1958), CBE (1956), DSO (1944); *b* 18 March 1909; *educ* RMC Sandhurst; Maj-Gen cmdg Fedn Army Malaya, Hon ADC to Govr NI 1937–38, served NW Frontier 1935 (medal and clasp), WW II, Dep Cdr Br Servs Mission Burma 1948, Col Welch Regt 1965–69, US Bronze Star; *m* 1st 23 Oct 1935 Helen Edith Mary (*d* 1973), dau of Maj Rupert Berkeley; *m* 2nd 1974 *Mrs Sheila N Carson and *d* 1982, leaving issue by 1st w:

1c +George Hugo Hastings [Maj George Brooke TD, Hawthorne Cottage, Biddestone, Wilts SN14 7DG]; *b* 26 July 1936; *educ* Blundell's and RMA Sandhurst; Maj RTR (ret), ADC to GOC(1) Div 1959–61; *m* 1st 3 Nov 1962 (*divorce* 1978) Sarah, yr dau of Robert Blackburn, of Bowcliffe Hall, Boston Spa, Yorks, and has had issue:

1d A son; *b* and *d* 30 Jan 1968

2d +Andrew Robert Hastings; *b* 26 April 1969

1d *Belinda Jane; *b* 24 Feb 1955

1c (cont.) Maj George Brooke *m* 2nd 1983 *Mrs Elizabeth Paula Minty, dau of Herbert Edwin Foxwell Morris, and had further issue:

2d *Emily; *b* 1985

3d *Rebecca; *b* 1987

2c +Nigel Francis; *b* 20 Aug 1937; *educ* Blundell's

2b Oliver George, CBE (1958, MBE 1944), DSO (1945); *b* 3 July 1911; *educ* Wrekin Coll and RMC Sandhurst; Brig Welch Regt, Col Cmdt Somaliland Scouts 1959–60, served WW II; *m* 22 July 1961 *Gillian Leonora, only dau of Edward Jolliffe Strutt (*see* RAYLEIGH, B), and formerly w of Sir Anthony Nutting, 3rd Bt, PC (*qv*)

2a Henry Hastings; *b* 28 April 1882; Capt 4th Bn Connaught Rangers Boer War 1902 (medal with two clasps) and WW I (wounded); *m* 28 Sept 1916 Frances Mary (*d* 3 March 1970 aged 89), dau of Percy Broderick Bernard (*see* 1970 edn, BANDON, E), and formerly w of George Arthur Paley, of Ampton Hall, Bury St Edmunds, and *d* 19 Feb 1920

1a Alice Gertrude; *m* 26 April 1905 Dermot Henry Doyne, DL, of Arden, Shillelagh, Co Wicklow (*d* 3 July 1942), yr s of Charles Mervyn Doyne, of Wells, and *d* 7 March 1964, leaving issue

5 (cont.) Mr F T Brooke *m* 2nd 3 May 1913 Agnes Letitia (*d* 18 March 1943), 2nd dau of Frederick Drummond Hibbert, JP, of Chalfont Park, Bucks and Bucknell Manor, Oxon, and was murdered in his office in Dublin 30 July 1920

1 Florence Selina; *m* 28 April 1875 as his 2nd w William James Hall, of Marrow Woods, Co Down (*d* 21 May 1896), and *d* 25 March 1915, leaving issue

Sir HENRY *d* 24 March 1834; his son,

Sir Arthur Brinsley Brooke, 2nd Bt, MP; *b* 1797; *m* 15 Dec 1841 Hon Julia Henrietta Anson (*d* 27 Dec 1886), Maid-of-Honour to QUEEN VICTORIA, yst dau of Gen Sir George Anson, GCB (*see* LICHFIELD, E), and had issue:

1 VICTOR ALEXANDER (Sir), **3rd Bt**

2 Harry Vesey (Sir), KBE (1920), DL, JP, of Fairley, Countesswells, Aberdeenshire, Capt 92nd Gordon Highrs; *b* 23 Sept 1845; *m* 9 Dec 1879 Patricia (*d* 25 Dec 1951 aged 92), only child of James Gregory Moir Byres, of Tonley, Aberdeenshire, and *d* 11 June 1921, having had, with other issue:

(1) James Anson Otho, VC; *b* 3 Feb 1884; Capt Gordon Highlanders; *ka* Ypres 29 Oct 1914

(2) Arthur; *b* 13 Feb 1886; Col IA, DL, JP, Durbar Medal 1911, served WW I (severely wounded), Zone Cdr HG WW II; *m* 15 July 1913 Aimée Isabella, dau of Richard Charles Brooman White, of Arddarroch, Dunbartonshire, and *d* 13 April 1952, having had issue:

1a Victor Harry; *b* 3 Aug 1914; Colonial Police Force; *kas* 18 Nov 1939

2a Basil Arthur, MC; *b* 27 Aug 1917; *educ* Trin Coll Glenalmond; Maj 15th/19th King's Roy Hus, Lt Gordon Highrs, served WW II; *m* 1st 2 Feb 1946 Moira Allison, dau of Col James Alexander Stewart Balmain, 15th Hus, of Alford House, Somerset; *m* 2nd 1968 *Jane, dau of — Lane and widow of Howard Samuel, and *d* 1992, leaving issue by 1st w:

1b *Patricia Alison; *b* 26 Dec 1946

2b Sheelah Anne; *b* 6 Aug 1949; *m* 22 Aug 1972 Peter Geoffrey Lowndes, yr s of (William) Geoffrey Lowndes Lowndes

3b *Diana Eva *b* 22 Jan 1951

(3) Henry Brian; *b* 9 Dec 1889; Capt 2nd Bn Gordon Highrs; *d* 24 July 1916 of wounds recd in action

(4) Patrick Harry; *b* 21 May 1895; Sub-Lt RN; *ka* 1917

(1) Constance Geraldine; *m* 4 Nov 1913 Capt Napier Charles Gordon Cameron, 1st Bn Cameron Highrs (*ka* 25 Dec 1914), s of Gen Sir William Gordon Cameron, GCB, and *d* 9 July 1973, leaving issue

(2) (Alice) Irene; *m* 7 Aug 1926 Lt-Col Richard Gilbert Lees, MBE, Gordon Highrs, est s of Capt Gilbert Lees

3 Arthur Basil; *b* 1847; RN; *m* 11 Sept 1869 Alice Georgina (*d* 1 Feb 1915), dau of Rev William Norton, Rector Baltinglas, Co Wicklow (*see* RATHCREEDAN, B), and widow of Thomas Shirley Ball, 10th Hus, of Abbeyland, Co Longford, and *d* 3 Aug 1884, having had, with other issue:

(1) Harry Brinsley; *b* 30 June 1872; 2nd Sec Dip Serv Berne to 1915; *m* 10 Jan 1907 Hilda Gertrude (*d* 15 Dec 1938), yst dau of Henry Tootal Broadhurst, and *dsp* 21 March 1916

(2) Basil Vernon (Sir), GCVO; *b* 9 March 1876; R-Adml, Grand Fleet WW I, cmded Roy Yacht *Alexandra* to 1922, Treasurer Household, Groom-in-Waiting and Extra Equerry to HM GEORGE VI 1937–45; *m* 26 Aug 1915 Olave Barbara Clementina, Cllr Paddington (*d* 16 Dec 1966), dau of Cdr Charles Elphinstone Fleming Cunninghame Graham, MVO, and *d* 11 Dec 1945, having had issue:

1a Basil Malise; *b* 4 May 1921; Lt 11th Hus (PAO) WW II; *m* 5 Sept 1941 *Ann Mary (*m* 2nd 21 June 1947 (*divorce*) Robert H Angell; *m* 3rd A E Dyke), only dau of Cecil W Bateson, and *das* 4 March 1944

(3) Bertram Norman BROOKE later SERGISON-BROOKE (roy licence 30 Sept 1915), Sir; KCB (1942), KCVO (1937), CMG (1919), DSO; *b* 20 July 1880; Lt-Gen, Gren Gds, T/Brig Cmdg 1st Inf Bde 1928–31, T/Brig-Gen Staff E Cmd India 1931–34, GOC London Dist 1934–38 and 1939–42, ADC to HM 1933–34, served Boer War 1899–1902 (medals with five clasps) and WW I (wounded, despatches), Legn Honour, Order Crown Belgium, KStJ; *m* 1st 8 July 1915 Prudence Ida Evelyn (*d* 23 Oct 1918), er dau and coheir of Capt Charles Warden Sergison, DL, of Cuckfield Park, Sussex, and had issue:

1a Patience Ann; *b* 5 June 1916; *m* 29 March 1939 Sir Edward Henry Windley, KCMG, KCVO (*k* air crash Brisbane 5 Jan 1972), s of Edward Crosland Windley, of S Rhodesia, and Florence, Vicomtesse de Toustain, and had issue (*see* PORTARLINGTON, E)

(3) Gen Sir Bertram Sergison-Brooke *m* 2nd 2 June 1923 Hilda (*d* 23 July 1954), dau of Mark Fenwick, and *d* 26 March 1967, having by her had issue:

1a +Timothy Mark [Timothy Sergison-Brooke Esq, Chipping Warden, Banbury, Oxon]; *b* 30 March 1924; *educ* Eton; High Sheriff 1975, Lt (Hon Capt) Gren Gds (Res of Offrs) WW II; *m* 12 Nov 1964 *Mary Anne Hare, er dau of 1st Viscount Blakenham (*qv*), and has issue:

1b +Nicholas Mark; *b* 1966

1b *Kate Constantia; *b* 1 June 1968

(1) Norah Mary; *d unm* 27 April 1930

1 Constance Henrietta; *m* 1st 3 Oct 1872 Colin John Campbell, Roy Scots Greys (*d* 6 Aug 1880), est s of Colin Campbell, and had issue; *m* 2nd 24 Sept 1883 Col Robert Henry Patrick Doran, QOR W Kent Regt (*d* 9 April 1924), and *d* 21 Feb 1920

Sir ARTHUR *d* 21 Nov 1854; his est son,

Sir Victor Alexander Brooke, 3rd Bt, DL; *b* 5 Jan 1843 (QUEEN VICTORIA stood sponsor); *m* 28 July 1864 Alice Sophia (*d* 27 July 1920), 2nd dau of Sir Alan Edward Bellingham, 3rd Bt (*qv*), and had, with other issue:

1 ARTHUR DOUGLAS (Sir), **4th Bt**

2 Ronald George, CBE (1919), DSO (1898), Lt-Col, Brevet-Col, 11th and 7th Hus, GSO2 1914, cmdg 12th Res Cav and 3rd Res Hus 1914–19, Roy Humane Soc silver medal, Chev Legn Honour, served Chitrai 1895 (despatches, medal with clasp), Matabeland 1896, Tirah 1897–98 (two clasps), Nile Expdn 1898 (despatches twice, medal with two clasps, Egyptian medal), S Africa 1899–1902 (severely wounded, despatches thrice, two medals with nine clasps, Brevet-Maj), Somaliland 1903–04 (despatches twice, medal with two clasps, Brevet Lt-Col) and WW I (despatches, Brevet); *b* 25 Sept 1866; *m* 6 May 1908 Haller (*d* 2 Feb 1932), yst dau of Orville Horwitz, of Baltimore, Md, USA, and formerly w of C A C Ponsonby, and *d* 28 Nov 1930

3 Butler; *b* 2 May 1870; T/Capt, 1st Assist Supt Remount Serv; *m* 2 June 1910 Mary Viva Francesca (*d* 5 Dec 1944), dau of Cyril Earle Johnston, of Pau, France, and *d* 11 March 1924, leaving issue:

(1) Cyril; *b* 3 April 1911; *educ* Eton and New Coll Oxford; *d unm*

(2) Victor Butler (Rev); *b* 1919; *educ* Eton and New Coll Oxford; monk OSB, RC priest 1954; *d* 12 Jan 1971

4 Victor Reginald, CIE, DSO, Maj 9th Lancers Boer War 1899–1902 (wounded, despatches twice, Queen's medal with four clasps, King's medal with two clasps), Kabul Mission 1904 (Brevet) and BEF WW I; *b* 22 Jan 1873; *ka* 29 Aug 1914

5 ALAN FRANCIS BROOKE, 1st VISCOUNT ALANBROOKE (*qv*)

1 Alice Mildred; *b* 4 March 1875; *m* 28 Sept 1896 Lt-Col James Ramsay Campbell, of Ardachie, Fort Augustus (*see* CAMPBELL, Bt, of Succoth) (*d* 12 Jan 1924), and *d* 13 Nov 1914

2 Hylda Henrietta, CBE (1918); *b* 22 Feb 1879; *m* 1st 5 July 1899 Sir Frederick Henry Arthur Des Voeux, 7th Bt (*d* 4 Jan 1937; *see* 1940 edn), and had issue; *m* 2nd 18 May 1937 Sir (John) Evelyn Leslie Wrench, KCMG, LLD (*d* 11 Nov 1966), yr s of Frederick Stringer Wrench, PC, DL, JP, of Killacoona, Ballybrack, Co Dublin, and *d* 7 Oct 1955

Sir VICTOR *d* 23 Nov 1891; his est son,

Sir Arthur Douglas Brooke, 4th Bt, DL and JP Co Fermanagh, High Sheriff 1896; *b* 7 Oct 1865; *m* 28 July 1887 Gertrude Isabella (*d* 29 Sept 1918), only dau of Stanlake Batson, of Horseheath, Cambs, and *d* 27 Nov 1907, having had, with other issue:

1 Sir BASIL STANLAKE (Sir), **5th Bt**, and **1st Viscount**

2 Victor Morvyn; *b* 8 June 1093; *d* 29 March 1919

3 Arthur Francis, Lt 10th Hus, S/Ldr RAF WW I (wounded), Waziristan 1920 (medal with clasp); *b* 24 Sept 1896; *m* 9 Oct 1919 Lilian Maude, er dau of Charles Butler Irwin, of Drumglass, Co Tyrone, and *dsp* 17 Nov 1949

1 Sylvia Henrietta; *b* 17 Feb 1890; *m* 26 Feb 1920 Capt Hon Charles Mulholland, CBE, DSO (later 3rd Baron Dunleath; *qv*), and *d* 19 May 1921

2 Sheelah; *b* 9 Jan 1895; *m* 16 April 1914 Sir Henry George Hill Mulholland, 1st Bt, PC (*d* 5 March 1971), and had issue

Sir ARTHUR *d* 27 Nov 1907; his est son,

BASIL STANLAKE BROOKE, **1st Viscount Brookeborough**, of Colebrooke, Co Fermanagh (UK), so *cr* 4 July 1952, KG (1965), PC (NI 1933), CBE (1921), MC (1961), HM Lt and Custos Rotulorum Co Fermanagh 1963–69, V-Adml Ulster 1961–73, CC, Hon LLD Queen's U Belfast, KStJ, Capt 10th Hus, MP (NI) Lisnaskea 1933, Min Commerce and Prodn 1941–45, PM NI 1943–63, Assist Parly Sec Min Finance, Hon A/Cdre Ulster Maritime Support Unit RAuxAF

1960–73, Hon Cmdt Ulster Special Constab, Hon ADC to Govr NI, chm Carreras NI 1964, served WW I (despatches), Croix de Guerre); *b* 9 June 1888; *m* 3 June 1919 Cynthia Mary, DBE (1959; Sr Cmdt ATS WW II; *d* 2 March 1970), 2nd dau and coheir of Capt Charles Warden Sergison, DL, of Cuckfield Park, Sussex, and had issue:

1 Basil Julian David,; *b* 18 April 1920; *educ* Eton; Lt Gren Gds WW II; *ka* March 1943

2 JOHN WARDEN, **2nd Viscount**

3 Henry Alan, MC; *b* 29 Oct 1923; *educ* Eton; Lt 10th Hus WW II; *ka* Italy April 1945

The **1st Viscount** *m* 2nd 25 March 1971 Sarah Eileen Bell (*d* 1989), dau of Henry Healey, of Belfast, and widow of Cecil A Calvert, FRCS, Dir Neuro-surgery Roy Victoria Hosp Belfast, and *d* 18 Aug 1973

The 1st VISCOUNT's only surv s,

JOHN WARDEN BROOKE, **2nd Viscount Brookeborough**, PC (NI 1971); memb Fermanagh CC 1947 (chm 1961–87), High Sheriff 1955, MP (NI) Lisaskea 1968–72, Parly Sec Min Commerce (NI) 1969, Memb: (Down) Ulster Assembly 1973, N Ireland Constitutional Convention 1975–76 Min State Finance and Govt Ch Whip, Capt 10th Hus WW II (wounded), ADC to Viceroy India 1946, Cdr Fermanagh HG 1952; *b* 9 Nov 1922; *m* 4 March 1949 *Rosemary Hilda [The Rt Hon Rosemary Viscountess Brookeborough, Ashbrooke, Brookeborough, Co Fermanagh, N Ireland], est dau of Lt-Col Arthur O'Neill Cubitt Chichester, OBE, MC, of Galgorm Castle, Ballymena, Co Antrim (*see* O'NEILL, B), and *d* 1987, leaving issue:

1 ALAN HENRY BROOKE, **3rd and present Viscount Brookeborough**

2 +CHRISTOPHER ARTHUR [The Hon Christopher Brooke, Galgorm Castle, Ballymena, Co Antrim BT42 1HL]; *b* 16 May 1954; heir presumptive; *educ* Gordonstoun; Lt 5th Inniskilling Dragoon Gds; *m* 1990 *Amanda M, dau of G N R Hodges, of Lowlands, Trinity, Jersey, CI, and has issue:

(1) +Archie Alan John; *b* 17 Dec 1991

(2) +Henry Arthur Oliver; *b* 8 Sept 1993

(3) +Mathew Victor Francis; *b* 29 June 1995

1 *(Rosalind) Juliana [The Hon Mrs Grose, The Old Bakery, Aldsworth, Cheltenham, Glos; Ashbrooke, Brookeborough, Co Fermanagh]; *b* 4 Feb 1950; *m* 1st 2 March 1973 Maj Nigel Hugh Alexander Cowie, 16th/5th Queen's Roy Lancers (*d* 1991), 2nd s of Lt-Col Howard Elphinstone Cowie, of S Poorton, Powerstock; *m* 2nd 2nd 1994 *Christopher James Grose, only s of Brig James Grose, of Bicknoller, Somerset, and has by her 1st husb:

(1) *Alexander John; *b* 29 June 1975

(1) *Rosalind Mary; *b* 14 June 1977

2 *Melinda Charlotte [The Hon Mrs Taylor, Bradley Fields Farm, Lillingstone Lovell, Buckingham MK18 5BH]; *b* 13 April 1958; *m* 11 Sept 1982 *Nicholas R Taylor, est s of Ronald Taylor, and has issue:

(1) *Christopher Martin John; *b* 1990

(1) *Alice Melinda; *b* 1988

3 *Susanna Cynthia [The Hon Mrs Hamilton Stubber, Foley Hill, Aghalee, Co Antrim BT67 0DZ]; *b* 17 April 1962; *m* 1989 *Richard John Hamilton Stubber, 2nd s of Col John Henry Hamilton Stubber, of Aughentaine, Fivemiletown, Co Tyrone, and has issue:

(1) *Thomas Richard; *b* 1991

(1) *Iona Rose; *b* 1993

Seat: Colebrooke, Brookeborough, Co Fermanagh. The 1st Baronet commissioned William Farrell to design the house, which was erected in the 1820s in the neo-classical style.

BROOKES

Arms: Or on a pale sable between in chief two crosses crosslet gules a sword, the point upwards and enfiling a Stafford knot, the blade charged above with guard with a sun in splendour over all, all or. **Crest:** a demi-bear rampant proper beside and resting its sinister paw on an anvil sable. **Supporters:** Dexter, a dragon sable, armed gules; sinister, a figure habited as Vulcan standing in front of an anvil resting his exterior hand on a hammer, all proper. **Motto:** *Ignis indurat animum* ('Fire toughens the spirit') **Creation:** B. (LP, UK) 1975.

THE BARON BROOKES, of W Bromwich, Co of W Midlands (Sir Raymond Percival Brookes) [The Rt Hon The Lord Brooks, Mallards, Santon, Isle of Man]; *b* 10 April 1909; *educ* Kenrick Tech Coll W Bromwich; chm and ch exec GKN 1965–74, pt-time memb BSC 1967–68, V-Pres Engrg Employers' Fedn 1967–75, Pres Br Mechanical Engrg Confedn 1968–70, Memb: Cncl UK-S Africa Trade Assoc Ltd 1967–74, Cncl CBI 1968–75, BNEC 1969–71, ktd 1971, Wilberforce Inquiry into electricity supply industry dispute Jan 1971, Industl Devpt Advsy Bd 1972–75 (memb Exec Ctee 1970–, Cncl 1969–, Pres 1974–75), Soc of Motor Manufacturers and Traders, Birmingham U Court of Govrs 1966–75 (Cncl 1968–75), Pres Motor Industry Research Assoc 1973–75, Life Pres GKN 1975–, chm Rea Bros (IoM) Ltd 1976–89, dir Plessey 1974–79, AMF Inc 1975–78; *m* 1937 *Florence Edna, dau of Isaac William Sharman, and has issue:

1 *John David [The Hon John Brookes, 30425 S Greenbriar, Franklin, Mich 48025, USA]; *b* 1940; *m* 1st 1970 Faith, dau of John Rees Redman, of Blythe, Bidford on Avon, Warwicks; *m* 2nd 1986 *Susan Nemeth and has issue

Lineage: WILLIAM PERCIVAL BROOKES; *m* Ursula — and had:

RAYMOND PERCIVAL, *cr* a **Baron**

BROOKS OF TREMORFA

Creation: B. (LP, UK) 1979.

THE BARON BROOKS OF TREMORFA, of Tremorfa in the County of Glamorgan (John Edward Brooks, DL (S Glam 1994)) [The Rt Hon The Lord Brooks of Tremorfa DL, 46 Kennerleigh Rd, Rumney, Cardiff, S Glam CF3 9BJ]; *b* 12 April 1927; *educ* Coleg Harlech and U Coll Cardiff; Field Offr Cncl of Social Servs Wales, Sec Cardiff SE Constituency Lab Party 1966–84, memb S Glamorgan CC 1973–93 (Leader 1973–77, 1986–92, Chm 1981–82), Chm Lab Party Wales 1978–79, Ho Lds opposition def spokesman 1980–81; Steward Br Boxing Bd of Control 1986–; *m* 1st 1948 — (*divorce* 1956) and has a s and dau; *m* 2nd 1958 *Margaret Pringle and has by her two sons

Lineage: EDWARD GEORGE BROOKS; *m* Rachel White and had:

JOHN EDWARD, *cr* a **Baron**

BROOKSBANK

Arms: Az. two bars wavy arg. within a bordure or. **Crest:** A hart's head couped arg., attired or, charged on the neck with two bars wavy az. **Creation:** Bt. (UK) 15 Sept 1919.

SIR (EDWARD) NICHOLAS BROOKSBANK, 3RD BT, of Healaugh Manor, Co York [Sir Nicholas Brooksbank Bt, Ryton Grange, Malton, N Yorks]; *b* 4 Oct 1944; *s f* 1983; *educ* Eton; Roy Dragoons 1963–69, Capt Blues and Royals 1969–73 (Adj 1971–73), Christie's 1974–; *m* 17 Dec 1970 *Hon Emma Myrtle Mary Anne, only dau of Baron Holderness (LP; *qv*), and has issue:

1 +(FLORIAN) TOM CHARLES; *b* 9 Aug 1982

1 *Victoria Mary Grania; *b* 1985

Lineage: WILLIAM BROOKSBANK/BROOKBANK, of Alford, Lincs (s of John Brookbank and gs of another John Brookbank, living *temp* HENRY VII); *m* Elizabeth, dau and heiress of Francis Forset, and had:

JOHN BROOKSBANK, of Elland, Yorks; *m* Grace — and had, with other issue:

JOHN BROOKSBANK, of Elland; *m* Judith Thornhill and *d* 1685 aged over 70, having had, with other issue:

JOSEPH BROOKSBANK, of Healaugh Manor, Yorks (which he bought *c* 1702) and Elland; *m* 1679 Mary (*d* 1727), dau and heir of Richard Stamp, of Reading, er bro of Sir Thomas Stamp, Ld Mayor London 1691, and *d* 1726; his only surv s:

STAMP BROOKSBANK, of Healaugh; *b* 1694, MP Colchester and Saltash, Govr Bank England, memb New England Co 1726; *m* Elizabeth, yst dau and coheir of Joseph Thomson, of Nonsuch Park, Surrey, and had, with other issue:

1 JOSEPH

2 Stamp; *b* 1726; *m* 1771 Anne, dau of Thomas Gataker, of Mildenhall, and *d* 1802, leaving, with other issue:

(1) Anne; *m* 10 Dec 1795 Rev William Villiers Robinson, Rector Grafton, Northants, 2nd s of Sir George Robinson, Bt, MP (*see* ROBINSON, Bt, of London)

3 William; *b* 1741; had:

(1) Anne; *m* 17 July 1810 Sir Edward Hardinge John Stracey, 2nd Bt (*qv*), and *dsp* 1832

1 Sophia; *m* Hardinge Stracey, of Denne Hall, and Nethersole House, Kent, est s of Sir John Stracey, Recorder London, and bro of Sir Edward Stracey, 1st Bt (*qv*)

The est son,

JOSEPH BROOKSBANK, of Healaugh; *b* 1725; *m* Jan 1752 Elizabeth (*m* 2nd William Snell, Dir Bank England and HEIC, s of William Snell by Cecilia (dau and coheir of Sir Edmund Harrison by Mary Fiennes, n of Viscount Saye and Sele; *qv*)), dau and coheir of Benjamin Bond, of London, and *d* 1759, having had (with a dau Catherine, *m* Thomas Page, of Poynters, Surrey) an only surv s:

BENJAMIN BROOKSBANK, of Healaugh, JP; *b* 30 July 1757; *m* 27 Feb 1782 Philippa (*d* 3 May 1849), 2nd dau and coheir of Col James Clitherow, LLD, of Boston House, Middx, by Anne, dau and coheir of Reginald Kemeys, of Persholly, Mon, and *d* 21 Sept 1842, having had, with other issue:

1 Stamp, of Healaugh; *b* 31 Mar 1784; *educ* Trin Coll Cambridge (MA); *m* Anne (*d* 15 Jan 1853), dau and coheir of John Hunter, of Medomsley, Durham, and Hermitage, Northumberland, and *dsp* 28 Oct 1856

2 James, JP, of The Bailey, Durham; *b* 21 Sept 1786; *m* 19 July 1815 Ann (*d* 19 Dec 1857), only dau of John Raper, of Abberford and Lotherton, Yorks, and *d* 27 Feb 1870, leaving issue:

(1) James; *b* 27 Sept 1816; barrister; *m* 4 Feb 1844 Marianne (*d* 11 Oct 1852), dau of Thomas Edmonds, of London, and *d* 27 March 1863, having had issue:

1a James; *b* 26 April 1845; *d* an inf

2a Walter Lamplugh, of Lamplugh Hall

1a Marianne Elizabeth Annie; *m* 28 Jan 1875 William Delisle Powles and had issue

(2) John; *b* 12 Aug 1818; *d* unm 22 Feb 1899

(3) Henry; *b* 16 Mar 1824; *d* an inf

(4) Walter (Rev), MA, of Thornbarrow, Westmorland, Rector Lamplugh; *b* 5 Aug 1830; *m* 29 May 1855 Elizabeth Jane, dau of Stephen Poyntz Denning, and *d* 20 Oct 1908, leaving, with other issue:

1a Hugh Lamplugh; *b* 25 Feb 1867; *m* 27 Dec 1900 Sybil Lavallin (*d* 26 Nov 1945), est dau of Herbert Lavallin Puxley, and *d* 2 March 1943

1a Ethel; *m* 13 June 1882 Rev Ernest Edward Stock, Vicar Rockcliffe, Carlisle (*d* Oct 1910), and *d* leaving issue

2a Gertrude; *m* 29 Nov 1883 Samuel Taylor, of Eccleston Hall, Lancs, and Birkdault, Ulverston (*d* 9 July 1935), and *d* 14 June 1949, leaving issue

3a Phillipa Beatrice; *m* 28 July 1892 Anthony Gerard Salvin (*d* 5 Sept 1929) and had issue

3 Joseph, Maj 24th Regt, of The Beach, Cheshire, which he inherited from his cousin Anne Lady Stracey; *m* 7 June 1832 Susan, 2nd dau of William James, of Otterburn Tower, Northumberland, and *dsp* 8 April 1853

4 EDWARD HAWKE

1 Philippa; *m* Sept 1828 Cher Giuseppi Pecchio, of Milan, Italy *(dsp* 1835), and *d* 24 Jan 1869

2 Jane; *m* 25 Oct 1813 John Lamplugh Lamplugh-Raper, of Lamplugh Hall, Cumberland and Lotherton, Yorks, and *d* 12 April 1878

STAMP's yst bro,

Rev EDWARD HAWKE BROOKSBANK, of Healaugh, MA Cantab, JP W R Yorks; *b* 19 Dec 1789; *m* 1st 3 May 1825 Hannah (*d* 29 Dec 1846), dau of Benjamin Heywood, of Stanley Hall, Yorks, and had issue:

1 EDWARD, of whom presently

2 Benjamin Heywood, of Sandrock, Tickill, Rotherham; *b* 26 Feb 1828; JP W R Yorks

3 Arthur, JP, of Middleton Hall, Beverley; *b* 19 May 1831; Hon Col Yorks Art Unit, Capt 38th Regt; *m* 27 Nov 1855 Anna Maria, dau of Rev Henry Gylby Lonsdale, of Shark Island, Yorks, and had issue:

(1) Arthur Heywood, JP W R Yorks; *b* 19 Dec 1857; Capt 19th Hus; *m* 10 Dec 1890 Dora Helen, dau of Sir Richard Baggallay, PC

(2) John Lonsdale; *b* April 1862

The Rev EDWARD *m* 2nd 5 Dec 1848 Mary (*dsp* 29 Dec 1877), est dau of Hugh Parker, of Woodthorpe, Derby, and Tickhill, Yorks, and *d* 5 Aug 1883

His est son,

EDWARD BROOKSBANK, of Healaugh, JP W R Yorks; *b* 22 July 1826; LLB Cantab, barrister; *m* 1st 16 April 1857 Lucy Mary (*d* 21 Feb 1893), est dau of Edward York, of Wighill Park, Yorks, and had, with five other sons and another dau:

1 EDWARD CLITHEROW (Sir), **1st Bt**

1 Laura Sophia; *m* 18 June 1885 Frederick William Slingsby, of Slingsby Hall, Malton, Yorks (*d* 13 Dec 1923), and *d* 29 June 1887, leaving issue

2 Lucy Hilda; *d* unm 10 Feb 1951

He *m* 2nd 19 April 1894 Ethel Margaret (*d* 7 Jan 1929), est dau of Marmaduke Constable, and *d* 2 Dec 1916, having by her had issue:

2 William Edward Constable; *b* 6 Aug 1899; Lt Rifle Bde; *m* 27 July 1929 Alison Stirling, MBE (1945), Capt WRAC, dau of Brig-Gen James Bruce Gregorie Tulloch, CB, CMG, JP, DL, of Hill Court, Abergavenny, and had issue:

(1) Christopher Stamp Constable; *b* 30 June 1930; F/Lt RAF; *k* in a flying accident 1 Sept 1959

The er son,

Sir Edward Clitherow Brooksbank, 1st Bt (UK), so *cr* 15 Sept 1919, JP W Riding and DL; *b* 24 Nov 1858; *educ* Trin Hall Cambridge (BA); chm W R QS 1936, Maj cmdg 8th Vol Bn W Yorks Regt, Hon Maj Yorks Art, OStJ; *m* 8 April 1885 Katherine Graham (*d* 22 April 1939), dau of Hugh Morris Lang, of Selkirk, and *d* 24 Nov 1943, having had issue:

1 Stamp; *b* 16 Jan 1887; Capt 2nd Bn Yorks Regt, barrister Inner Temple; *ka* 25 Sept 1915

2 Edward York; *b* 16 Dec 1888; Lt-Col 73rd Northumbrian Field Bde RA (TA), 5th Lancers; *m* 30 July 1912 Hazel (*d* 1968), dau of Henry Brockholes Thomas, of Scaftworth Hall, Yorks, and *d* 21 Oct 1935 following a motor accident, leaving issue:

(1) **Sir (Edward) William Brooksbank, 2nd Bt**, TD (1953), DL (1959), JP (1962) E R Yorks and Kingston-upon-Hull; *b* 15 June 1915; *educ* Eton; High Sheriff Yorks 1967, Col Yorks Yeo WW II; *m* 21 Dec 1943 *Ann, 2nd dau of Lt-Col Thomas Claud Clitherow, DSO, of Hotham Hall, Yorks, and *d* 1983, leaving issue:

1a Sir (EDWARD) NICHOLAS BROOKSBANK, **3rd and present Bt**

(2) Benjamin John; *b* 27 Sept 1918

(3) +Stamp Godfrey [Stamp Brooksbank Esq, 45 Cedar Lodge, Lythe Hill Park, Haslemere, Surrey]; *b* 14 April 1922; *educ* Eton; Capt Coldstream Gds WW II; *m* 30 May 1942 *Celia Dorothy, yr dau of Maj Hon Sir John Spencer Coke, KCVO, of Toy House, Toys Hill, Kent (*see* LEICESTER, E), and has issue:

1a +David William [David Brooksbank Esq, Rock Hill House, Hambledon, Surrey]; *b* 29 May 1946; *educ* Eton; *m* 6 Sept 1972 *Vanessa (Tessa), er dau of Kenneth A Whittome, and has issue:

1b +Scott William; *b* 21 Oct 1976

2b +Charles Henry; *b* 12 May 1979

1b *Anna Louise; *b* 1984

2a +George Edward Hugh; *b* 8 Feb 1949; *educ* Eton; *m* 1985 *Nicola, yr dau of Michael Newton, of Balcombe, Sussex, and has issue:

1b +Jack; *b* 1986

2b +Thomas; *b* 1988

(1) *Diana Hazel; *b* 1914; *m* 1st 11 Jan 1936 Robert Froude Norton (*d* 13 May 1967), only s of Lt-Col Harry Egerton Norton, 15th King's Hus, of Birdingbury Hall, nr Rugby; *m* 2nd *G Milford-Cottam

(2) *Crystal Elizabeth; *b* 1924; *m* 1st 14 Sept 1946 (*divorce* 1960) Henry Desmond Verner Pakenham, CBE, yst s of Hamilton Richard Pakenham, and has issue (*see* LONGFORD, E); *m* 2nd 8 Nov 1960 Ivor George Salmond, OBE (*d* 1981), s of Maj George Salmond; *m* 3rd *Vere Tweedie and has further issue by 2nd husb:

1a *Felicity Diana; *b* 11 Dec 1962

3 Hugh Godfrey; *b* 24 Nov 1893; Lt 2nd Bn Yorks Regt; *d* of wounds recd in action Ypres 16 Dec 1914

1 Margaret Graham; *b* 9 June 1890; *d* unm 15 Jan 1926

BROUGHAM AND VAUX

Arms: Quarterly, 1st, gu. a chevron between three luces hauriant arg. (for BROUGHAM); 2nd, or a fess chequy gold and gu. between three garbs of the third banded of the first, in chief a label of three points az. (for VAUX of Catterlen); 3rd, arg. a bend chequy or and gu. (for VAUX of Tryermayne); 4th, gu. a cross fleury or (for DELAMORE). **Crest:** A hand and arm in armour, holding a lucy fesswise arg., on the elbow a rose gules. **Supporters:** Dexter, a lion vert, armed and langued gules, collared with a Vaux collar, chequy or and of the second; sinister, a white hart, antlers and hoofs or, in his mouth a rose gu., barbed and seeded vert. **Motto:** *Pro rege, lege, grege* ('For king, law and people'). **Creation:** B. (UK) 22 March 1860.

THE 5TH BARON BROUGHAM AND VAUX OF BROUGHAM, Westmorland, **AND OF HIGHHEAD CASTLE**, Cumberland (Michael John Brougham, CBE (1995)) [The Rt Hon The Lord Brougham and Vaux CBE, 11 Westminster Gdns, Marsham St, London SW1P 4JA]; *b* 2 Aug 1938; *s* f 1967; *educ* Lycée Jaccard Lausanne, Millfield and Northampton Inst of Ag; Pres RoSPA 1986–89 (V-Pres 1990–), Chm Tax Payers' Soc 1989–91 and European Secure Vehicle Alliance 1992–, Co-Pres Nat Health & Safety Gps Cncl 1994–, Dep Chm Ctees Ho Lds 1993–, Dep Speaker 1995–; *m* 1st 20 July 1963 (*divorce* 1968) Olivia Susan (*d* 1986), only dau of R-Adml Gordon Thomas Seccombe Gray, DSC, by Sonia, 4th dau of Maj Joseph Gwyn Moore-Gwyn, JP, of Clayton Court, Liss, Hants, and has issue:

1 *Henrietta Louise; *b* 23 Feb 1965

The 5th BARON *m* 2nd 17 Jan 1969 (*divorce* 9 Dec 1981) Catherine Jill, er dau of William Gulliver, of London, and by her has:

1 +CHARLES WILLIAM; *b* 9 Nov 1971

Lineage: THOMAS BURGHAM, of Burgham, living 1553; *m* Jane, dau and heiress of John Vaux, of Catterlen and Tryermayne (*see* VAUX OF HARROWDEN, B), and had:

1 Henry Burgham, of Burgham *temp* ELIZABETH; *m* Catherine, dau and heir of Sir Ralph Nevill, of Thornton Briggs, Yorks, and widow of Sir Walter Stirkland/Strickland, and had, with three daus (Elizabeth, Margaret, Katherine):

(1) Thomas Brougham, JP (Cumberland); m Agnes — and *dsp* 1607

2 Peter BROUGHAM, of Blackhall, Cumberland; *m* Anne, dau and heir of John Southaic, of Scales Hall, Cumberland, and *d* 1570, leaving:

(1) Henry, of Scales and Blackhall, Sheriff Cumberland; *m* 1st Jane, dau of John Wharton, of Kirby-Thore, and had a dau (Jane, *m* Edward Aglionby (*d* 1648) and had issue); *m* 2nd Catherine, dau of Thomas Fallowfield, of Melkinthorpe Hall, Westmorland, and *d* 1622, leaving:

1a Thomas, of Scales, Sheriff Cumberland; *m* Mary, dau of Daniel Fleming, of Skirwith (ancestor of the FLEMING Bts of Rydal, so *cr* 1705), and had, with five other s and two daus:

1b Henry, of Scales; m 1st — and had two s and two daus (including Anne, *b* 1683, *d* Feb 1789); *m* 2nd Elizabeth, dau of Col John Lamplugh, 24th of Lamplugh, Cumberland, and by her had, with two other s and two daus:

1c John, of Scales, bought Brougham Hall from one James Bird; entailed his property on his four nephews in succession and their heirs male

2c Peter; *m* Elizabeth, dau and heiress of Christopher Richmond, of Highhead Castle, Cumberland, gs and heir of John Vaux, of Catterlen, and had issue:

1d Henry Richmond, *s* his mother in Highhead Castle and Catterlen and his unc in Scales Hall and Brougham; *dsp* 1749

2d John; *dsp* by 1749

3c Samuel; had:

1d John, Bencher Gray's Inn, *s* his cousin Henry Richmond in Brougham, Scales Hall and Highhead Castle, and *d* 1756, leaving two daus (both *dsp*)

2d Henry, *s* his bro; agent for Duke of Norfolk's Cumberland estates; *m* Mary (*d* 1807 aged 93), dau of William Freeman, DD, and *d* 21 Dec 1782, leaving issue:

1e HENRY; *s* his great unc (*see* below)

2e John (Rev), Rector Ballyhaise and Bailieborough, Ireland; *bapt* 2 July 1748; *educ* Eton and King's Coll Cambridge (MA 1775, Fell 1770–78); *m* 17 Oct 1785 Sarah (*d* 24 March 1843), dau of James Scanlan, of Ballyshannon, Co Donegal, by Anne, dau of Richard Babington, of Marble Hill, Co Donegal, and *d* 22 May 1811, leaving issue

The ultimate heir,

HENRY BROUGHAM, of Brougham and Scales Halls and Highhead Castle; *b* 18 June 1742; *m* 22 May 1777 Eleanora (*d* 31 Dec 1839 aged 89), only child of Rev James Syme, DD, by Mary, sis of Rev William Robertson, DD, Pncpl Edin U, historian, and *d* 19 Feb 1810, having had issue:

1 HENRY BROUGHAM, **1st Baron Brougham and Vaux of Brougham**, Westmorland, **and of Highhead Castle**, Cumberland, so *cr* 22 March 1860, as also earlier 22 Nov 1830 BARON BROUGHAM AND VAUX OF BROUGHAM, Westmorland (both UK), but in the former case with special remainder to his bro, PC (1830), KC (1827); *b* 19 Sept 1778; *educ* Edin High Sch and U (Chllr 1859–68); advocate (S) 1800, FRS 1803, barrister (E) 1808, advsr 1811 and Attorney-Gen 1820 to QUEEN CAROLINE, who he defended at her celebrated trial before the Ho of Lds 1820; MP (Whig) Camelford 1810–12, Winchelsea 1815–30, Knaresborough Feb-Aug 1830 and Yorkshire Aug-Nov 1830, Ld Chllr 1830–34, Rector Glasgow U 1824–26 and Marischal Coll Aberdeen 1838–39, Pres UCL 1836–68, DCL Oxon 1860, LLD Cantab 1862, fndr Soc for Diffusion of Useful Knowledge, gave his name to the brougham coach; *m* 1 April 1819 Mary Anne (*d* 12 Jan 1865), est dau of Thomas Eden, 4th s of Sir Robert Eden, 3rd Bt (*see* EDEN OF WINTERTON, B), and widow of John Spalding, of The Holme, and *d* 7 May 1868, having had:

(1) Sarah Eleanor; *b* 1820; *d* an infant

(2) Eleanor Louisa; b Oct 1822; *d* 30 Nov 1839

2 James, MP Tregony 1826, Downton 1829, Winchelsea 1831 and Kendal 1832, Registrar Affidavits, Clerk Letters Patent; *b* 16 Jan 1780; *dsp* 24 Dec 1833

3 Peter; Army Offr; *k* in a duel in San Salvador 11 July 1800

4 John Waugh, of Edinburgh; *b* 8 Feb 1785; *m* 18 Sept 1809 Margaret (*d* 26 Oct 1866), 3rd dau of Patrick Rigg, of Downfield, Tarvit, and Morton, Fife, and *d* 22 Sept 1829, leaving with other issue:

(1) Patrick; *b* 18 June 1819; *m* Mary, 4th dau of John Kennedy, of Keswycke, NSW, and had a s and dau

(2) James Rigg (4th s), of Bridge, House, Riverhead, Surrey, and Beathwaite, Milathorpe, Westmorland; *b* 5 May 1826; barrister, Registrar Bankruptcy 1848–91, Sr Registrar 1891–1917; *m* 4 Oct 1854 Isabella Eliza (*d* 1926), 5th dau of John Cropper, of Dingle Bank, Liverpool, and *d* 5 March 1919, leaving, with three other daus:

1a John Cropper, of Elmwood, Hackbridge, Surrey; *b* 2 Feb 1857; *m* 26 Jan 1882 Ursula Harriet Mary (*d* 16 March 1916), only dau of Sir Henry Orlando Chamberlain, 3rd Bt (*see* 1970 edn), and had issue:

1b Murielle; *m* 20 July 1912 Oswald Henry Wells, Lt RNVR (*d* 2 May 1935), 4th s of Adml Sir Richard Wells, KCB, and *dsp* 1956

2a Harold de Vaux; *b* 17 Aug 1858; *educ* Malvern; barrister, Sr Official Receiver 1906–20; *m* Elizabeth Dorothea, dau of T B —, of Woodcote Grove, Carshalton, Surrey, and *d* 26 March 1930, leaving a s

1a Margaret Lindesay; *m* 21 March 1877 Samuel Logan Johnston, est s of Carruthers Charles Johnston, of Liverpool

2a Annie Wakefield; *m* 27 April 1887 her 2nd cousin Jacob Wakefield, DL, JP (*d* 15 Nov 1948), of Sedgewick Ho, Kendal, Westmorland, and *d* 8 April 1951, leaving issue

(1) Margaret; *m* 6 May 1841 her 1st cousin Patrick Rigg, yr s of James Home Rigg, of Downfield, Tarvit, and Morton, Fife, and had a s (*see* LAUDERDALE, E) and three daus

(2) Eleanora; *m* 4 Sept 1845 Henry Mowbray, 3rd s of John Mowbray, of Hartwood, Scotland, and had issue

(3) Katherine; *m* 21 June 1875 John Monteith Douglas, s of Rev Robert Douglas, of Kilbrackan, Scotland

(4) Mary; *m* Aug 1855 Rev Walter Davidson (*d* Nov 1874) and *d* 11 May 1876, leaving two s

5 WILLIAM, **2nd Baron**

1 Mary

The 1st BARON's only surv bro,

WILLIAM BROUGHAM, **2nd Baron Brougham and Vaux of Brougham and of Highhead Castle**, JP, DL; *b* 26 Sept 1795; *educ* Edin High Sch and Jesus Coll Cambridge (MA 1822, Fell 1821–34); barrister Lincoln's Inn 1823, Master in Chancery 1835–52, MP (Whig) Southwark 1831–35, Lt-Col Cumberland Vol; *m* 12 Aug 1834 Emily Frances (*d* 8 April 1884), dau of Sir Charles William Taylor, 1st Bt, and had issue:

1 HENRY CHARLES, **3rd Baron**

2 Wilfrid; *b* 22 Jan 1842; Maj Westmorland and Cumberland Yeo, 10th Hus and 17th Lancers; *m* 1st 4 June 1863 Francesca (*d* 4 March 1901), only child of Gaetano Vignati; *m* 2nd 1901 Maria Sophia (*d* 20 June 1936), dau of Col Faunce, 4th King's Own Regt, and *d* 2 Nov 1904, having by his 1st w had issue:

(1) Wilfrid Francis; *b* 25 Nov 1864; *educ* Charterhouse and Pembroke Coll Cambridge (BA 1888); Slr Supreme Court BC; *m* 27 Nov 1889 Matilda Caroline (*d* 26 Feb 1928), dau of Alexander Donald Macgregor, of Melrose, Guernsey, and *d* Jan 1938, leaving issue:

1a Francis St John Macgregor; *b* 18 Sept 1890

1a Mary Monica Anita; *b* 24 July 1893; *m* 20 June 1925 Frederick George Metcalf

(1) Mabel Ellen; *m* 16 Dec 1890 Laurence MacBrayne, OBE, yr s of David MacBrayne, and *d* 8 Jan 1911, having had issue

(2) Evelyn Albinia; *m* 6 Aug 1890 Rev George Lowes Dickinson, MA, Vicar Sourton Bridestowe, Devon (*d* 1952), s of Gilbert Dickinson, and had issue

3 Reginald Thomas Dudley; *b* 2 Dec 1853; *m* 1st 25 Feb 1884 (*divorce* 1900) Augusta Louisa (*d* May 1902), dau of Arthur Wellesley Ward, of Calverly Manor, Tunbridge Wells, Kent; *m* 2nd 1 Dec 1900 Isabella Augusta (*d* 24 July 1945), dau of Samuel Leo Schuster by Lady Isabella FitzMaurice, dau of 5th Earl of Orkney (*qv*), and *d* 1 June 1925

1 Alice Eleanora; *m* 30 Nov 1863 Rev Hon Thomas Edwardes, bro of 3rd Baron Kensington (*qv*), and *d* 19 Oct 1924, leaving issue

2 Emily Evelyn; *m* 23 April 1867 Capt Francis Sandys Dugmore (*d* 10 Nov 1898), 2nd s of William Dugmore, QC, and *d* 13 Nov 1919, leaving issue

3 Adela Mary Grenville; *m* 20 April 1885 Sir Charles Archer Cook, KCB, barrister (*d* 14 Dec 1934), 2nd s of Silas Kemball Cook, and *d* 29 June 1933

The 2nd BARON *d* 3 Jan 1886; his est son,

HENRY CHARLES BROUGHAM, **3rd Baron Brougham and Vaux of Brougham and of Highhead Castle**, KCVO (1905), DL and JP; *b* 2 Sept 1836; *educ* Eton and Trin Coll Camb; *m* 18 April 1882 Adora Frances Olga (*d* 17 Dec 1925), dau of Peter Wells, of Forest Farm, Windsor Forest, Berks, by Julia, est dau of Gen Sir Robert John Harvey, CB, JP, DL (*see* HARVEY OF TASBURGH, B), and widow of Sir Richard Courtenay Musgrave, 11th Bt (*qv*), and had issue:

1 Henry; *b* 26 May 1887; Capt Coldstream Gds (SR); *m* 1st 13 July 1908 (*divorce* 1919) Hon Diana Isabel Sturt, OBE (1919), er dau of 2nd Baron Alington (see 1940 edn); *m* 2nd 24 April 1923 Baroness Hengelmuller, dau of Baron von Hengervar, sometime Austro-Hungarian Amb USA, and *d* 4 May 1927, having by his 1st w had issue:

(1) VICTOR HENRY PETER, **4th Baron**

(2) Anthony Charles; *b* 8 Sept 1915; *educ* Oundle; Lt S Lancs Regt; *m* 1st 21 Feb 1940 (*divorce* 1961) Sonya (*d* 17 March 1970), dau of Ivan Salzman; *m* 2nd 17 March 1961 Doreen Margaret (d 1972), dau of Roland Billington and formerly w of Richard Francis Warren, and had issue by his 1st w:

1a +Christopher Anthony; *b* 30 April 1941; *educ* priv and Univ Coll of Rhodesia (BSc Econ); *m* 30 Dec 1967 *Ann Elizabeth, er dau of Cecil Goldridge, and has issue:

1b +Benjamin Paul; *b* 1972

2b +Guy Christopher; *b* 27 May 1975

2a +Adrian Charles; *b* 4 Nov 1945; *educ* Downside; *m* 14 Oct 1967 Jan, dau of R J Westhope

(1) Eileen Cynthia Millicent Eva; *b* 6 Sept 1912; *m* 17 Aug 1940 Col Francis Thomas Davies, Gren Gds, 2nd s of Gen Sir Francis Davies, KCB, KCMG, KCVO, of Elmley Castle, Worcs, and had issue

1 Eleanor Mabel Valentine, Ldy-in-Waiting to HM QUEEN VICTORIA EUGENIE; *b* 14 Feb 1883; *d* unm 1 Feb 1966

The 3rd BARON *d* 24 May 1927; his gs,

VICTOR HENRY PETER BROUGHAM, **4th Baron Brougham and Vaux of Brougham and of Highhead Castle**; *b* 23 Oct 1909; Maj Middx Regt (TA), 2nd Lt Scots Gds, WW II (despatches); *m* 1st 21 April 1931 (*divorce* 1934) Violet Valerie, yr dau of Maj Hon Gerald French, DSO (*see* 1970 edn, YPRES, E), and had issue:

1 Julian Henry Peter; *b* 5 Oct 1932; 12th Roy Lancers; *das* Malaya 8 May 1952

The **4th Baron** *m* 2nd 3 June 1935 (*divorce* 1942) Jean (*d* 1992), dau of Brig-Gen Gilbert Burrell Spencer Follett, DSO, MVO, and by her had issue:

2 MICHAEL JOHN BROUGHAM, **5th and present Baron Brougham and Vaux of Brougham and of Highhead Castle**

3 +David Peter [The Hon David Brougham, Folly House, Bampton, Oxon]; *b* 22 Aug 1940; *educ* Sedbergh; *m* 1st 19 April 1969 (*divorce* 1976) (Moussie) Christina Margareta (*m* 2nd 12 March 1976 Michael P Sayers, of 31 S Eaton Place, SW1), dau of Sven Hornblad, of Stockholm, and has issue:

(1) +Henry Peter; *b* 12 Nov 1971

3 (cont.) The Hon David Brougham *m* 2nd *Caroline Susan, dau of Maj James Michael Heigham Royce Tomkin, MC (*see* BUNBURY, Bt), and formerly w of Julian Dixon, and by her has further issue:

(2) +Oliver Michael; *b* 14 Oct 1978

The **4th Baron** *m* 3rd 4 June 1942 *Edith Ellaline, dau of Leonard Teichman and formerly w of Richard Vaughan Hart-Davis, and *d* 20 June 1967

BROUGHSHANE

Arms: Gules a stag trippant and in chief a celestial crown and a fleur-de-lys or. **Crest:** Upon a billet fesswise a stag's head between two wings or. **Supporters:** On either side a stag or gorged with a chain gules and pendent therefrom a torteau, the dexter charged with a portcullis and the sinister with a grenade fired or. **Motto:** *Virtus in actione consistit* ('Strength consists in action'). **Creation:** B. (UK) 19 Sept 1945.

THE 3RD BARON BROUGHSHANE, of Kensington, London ((William) Kensington Davison, DSO (1945), DFC)) [The Rt Hon The Lord Broughshane DSO DFC, 3 Godfrey St, London SW3 3TA]; *b* 25 Nov 1914; *s* bro 1995; *educ* Shrewsbury and Magdalen Coll Oxford; barrister Inner Temple 1939, W/Cdr RAFVR WW II

Lineage: ALEXANDER DAVISON, of Knockboy, Broughshane, Co Antrim; *b* 1799; *m* Anne Disney (*d* 17 Sept 1897) and *d* Jan 1874, leaving:

RICHARD DAVISON, of Beachfield, Ballymena, Co Antrim (formerly of Knockboy, Broughshane); *b* 1846; *m* 1 March 1871 Annie (*d* 22 March 1927), yst dau of John Patrick, JP, of Dunminning, Co Antrim, and *d* 25 Dec 1929, leaving issue:

WILLIAM HENRY DAVISON, **1st Baron Broughshane** (UK), of Kensington, London, so *cr* 19 Sept 1945, KBE (1918), JP (Kensington), DL (Co London); *b* 1872; *educ* Shrewsbury and Keble Coll Oxford (BA 1893, MA 1898); barrister Inner Temple 1895; Alderman Kensington (Mayor 1913–19); MP (C) S Kensington 1918–45, FSA, v-pres RSA, Freeman City London, Memb Court Assists Clothworkers' Co (Master 1941–43); *m* 1st 1898 (*divorce* 1929) Beatrice Mary, 2nd dau of Sir Owen Roberts, DL, DCL, LLD, FSA, of Henley Park, Surrey, and Plas Dinas, Caernarvon; *m* 2nd 6 June 1929 Louisa Mary Constance (*d* 22 July 1971, aged 89), dau of Maj Charles Frederick Marriott, 6th Dragoon Gds, and *d* 19 Jan 1953, having by his 1st w had issue:

1 PATRICK OWEN ALEXANDER DAVISON, **2nd Baron Broughshane**; *b* 18 June 1903; *educ* Winchester and Magdalen Coll Oxford; barrister Inner Temple 1926, chm Greencoat Properties, Maj Irish Gds WW II, Assist Sec (Mil) War Cabinet 1942–45, US Legn Merit; *m* 9 Oct 1929 Bettine (*d* 20 Nov 1994), only dau of Sir Arthur Edward Ian Montagu Russell, 6th Bt (*see* RUSSELL, Bt, of Swallowfield), and d 22 Sept 1995, having had issue:

(1) Alexander; *b* 11 Jan 1936; *educ* Eton; *m* 1st 15 July 1961 (*divorce* 1966) Teresa Clare, only dau of James Guy Bramwell, of Mas Castaly, St Jacques-de-Grasse, AM, France (*see* SMITH-MARRIOTT, Bt), and had issue:

1a *Emma Bettine; *b* 26 Dec 1961

2a *Harriet Laura; *b* 7 June 1964

(1) (cont.) The Hon Alexander Davison *m* 2nd 4 Sept 1970 (*divorce* 1977) Cecilia Ann (*d* 1977), only dau of John William Ingrams, of Furlong, Patching, Sussex; *m* 3rd 1988 *(Daphne) Bridget [The Hon Mrs Alexander Davison, 29 Queen St, King's Lynn, Norfolk PE30 1HT], only dau of Thomas Walter Jones, of Cawston, Norfolk, and formerly w of Anthony John Nelson-Sullivan, and *d* 1988, leaving by her:

3a *Arundell; *b* 12 July 1972

2 (WILLIAM) KENSINGTON DAVISON, **3rd and present Baron Broughshane**

1 *Joyce Margaret; *b* 7 July 1900; *m* 12 Dec 1922 Humphrey Bowstead Wilson, OBE, MA, MB (*d* 1 Jan 1962), s of Joseph Bowstead Wilson, of Knightwick, Worcs, and has issue:

(1) *Michael; *b* 1923

(1) *Diana June; *b* 1926

2 *Sheila Beatrice [The Hon Mrs Gordon-Duff, 10 Jameson St, London W8]; *b* 14 June 1907; *m* 14 Dec 1936 G/Capt George Edward Gordon-Duff, CBE, RAFVR (*d* 10 Nov 1966), 2nd s of Thomas Duff Gordon-Duff, of Drummuir and Park, and has issue:

(1) *Roderick; *b* 1940; *m* 1965 *Patricia Anne, dau of Bruce Watson, of Fishing Cottage, Littleton Panell, Wilts

BROUGHTON

Arms: Arg. two bars gu., on a canton of the second a cross of the field. **Crest:** A sea-dog's head couped gu. and finned arg. **Motto:** *Haud muto factum* ('Not done by muteness'). **Creation:** Bt. (E) 10 March 1660/1.

SIR DAVID DELVES BROUGHTON, 13TH BT, of Broughton, Staffordshire [Sir David Broughton Bt, 31 Mayfield Court, Sandy, Beds SG19 1NF]; *b* 7 May 1942; *s* kinsman 1993; craftsman; *m* 1969 *Diane, dau of Ronald Lindsay Nicol, of Victoria, Australia, and has by Hildegard Weitzel:

1 *Jennifer Zoë Weitzel; *b* 1977

Lineage: JOHN; feudal Ld of Broughton and Charlton, Staffs, *temp* HENRY VI; gf of:

RICHARD BROUGHTON, living *c* 1490; *m* Margaret, dau of Hugh Sandford, of Sandford, and had:

RICHARD BROUGHTON, living *c* 1533; *m* Catharine, dau of Richard Aston, of Aston, and had:

THOMAS BROUGHTON, living 1583; *m* Mary, dau of Francis Roos, of Swinshed and Laxton, Notts, and had:

FRANCIS BROUGHTON, living *c* 1590; *m* Ellen Kinnersely, widow, and had:

THOMAS BROUGHTON, fined £3,200 for royalism after Civil War; *m* Frances, dau of Sir Hervey Bagot, 1st Bt (*qv*), of Blithfield, Staffs, and *d* 24 July 1648, having had, with a yr s (Peter, of Lowdham, Notts, ancestor of the BROUGHTONs of Tunstall Hall, Salop) and three daus (including Dorothy, *m* as his 2nd w Francis Cavendish; *see* WATERPARK, B):

Sir Brian Broughton, 1st Bt (E), so *cr* 10 March 1660/1, of Broughton, High Sheriff 1660–61; *b* 23 May 1618; ktd; *m* Bridget (*d* 1 Sept 1692), 2nd dau of Sir Thomas Lucy, of Charlecote (*see* RAMSAY-FAIRFAX-LUCY, Bt), and had, with other issue:

1 THOMAS (Sir), **2nd Bt**

2 Charles, Hamburg merchant, memb Co of Merchant Adventurers; *m* Hannah Margaret, dau of Thomas Adamson, of Ashton, Cheshire, and had issue:

(1) Charles, Hamburg merchant, memb Co of Merchant Adventurers; *b* 15 June 1692; *m* 28 Dec 1734 Anne-Elisabeth, dau of Baron William de Hertoghe, and had issue:

1a Charles, Hamburg merchant; *m* Elizabeth Young (*d* 16 Aug 1782) and *d* 7 Sept 1820, leaving, with other issue:

1b Charles, of the Auditor's Office; *d* unm

2b William Robert, CB, Capt RN; *b* 22 March 1762; *m* his cousin Jemina (*d* 15 Jan 1863), dau of Sir Thomas Broughton, 6th Bt, and *d* 12 March 1821, leaving with other issue:

1c Jemina; *m* 11 Jan 1827 Thomas de Moleyns, QC (*d* 5 March 1900; *see* VENTRY, B), and *d* 7 April 1883, leaving issue

2c Lucia; *m* 1826 Frederick William de Moleyns, MP, of Beauford Castle, Kerry (*d* 17 March 1854), s of Hon Frederick de Moleyns (*see* VENTRY, B), and *dsp* 1 Feb 1889

3b Bryan; *bapt* 29 June 1766; Rector Long Ditton, Surrey 1811, poet and artist; *m* — and *d* 8 Jan 1838, leaving a dau

2a William; *b* 3 March 1737; *m* 6 May 1794 Anna-Catharine Ravens

Sir THOMAS *d* 30 July 1708; his est son,

Sir Thomas Broughton, 2nd Bt; *m* 10 July 1672 Rhoda, dau of John Amcotts, of Aystrop, Lincs, and d 1710, having had, with three other sons and two daus (including Rhoda, *m* Sir J Huband, Bt, of Ipsley):

Sir Brian Broughton, 3rd Bt, MP Newcastle 1715–24; *m* Elizabeth (*d* 2 Jan 1746), only dau of Sir Thomas Delves, Bt, of Doddington, Cheshire (descended from Sir Henry Delves, of Delves Hall, bro and heir of Sir John Delves, who fought Battle of Poitiers 1356), and *d* 12 Sept 1724, having had, with two daus (Jane, *m* Sir Rowland Hill, Bt; Elizabeth, *d* unm 1725):

Sir BRIAN BROUGHTON later BROUGHTON-DELVES (added under terms of gf's will on inheriting latter's Cheshire estate), **4th Bt**; *b* 6 Jan 1717/8; MP Wenlock 1741–44; *m* 21 May 1738 Mary (*m* 2nd Jan 1746 William Mackworth Praed), dau of William Forrester, MP, and *d* 11 Aug 1744, having had:

1 **Sir Brian Broughton-Delves, 5th Bt**; *b* 1740; MA Oxon; *m* Mary, dau of Thomas Hill, of Tern, Salop, and *dsp* 16 Jan 1766

2 **Sir Thomas Broughton, 6th Bt**, High Sheriff Staffs 1772; *m* 1st 31 March 1768 Mary (*d* 7 June 1785), dau of John Wicker, of Horsham, Sussex, and had, with other issue:

(1) **Sir John Delves Broughton, 7th Bt**; *bapt* 17 Aug 1769; Gen; *m* 5 June 1792 Elizabeth (*d* 27 Jan 1857), sis of Sir John Egerton, Bt (see WILTON, E), and *dsp* 9 Aug 1847

(2) HENRY DELVES (Sir), **8th Bt**

(3) Thomas Delves; *b* 26 Aug 1778; *m* 28 March 1800 Elizabeth Hester Rowlls (*d* 15 Nov 1821), dau and heir of John Rowlls Legh, of Adlington Hall, Cheshire, and *d* 24 Jan 1846, leaving, with other issue:

1a Thomas Delves (Rev), Rector Bletchley; *b* 18 Feb 1801; *m* 2 April 1834 Frances, dau of Lewis Corkran, memb Cncl Bombay, and *d* 10 Aug 1859, leaving, with other issue:

1b Vernon Delves; *b* 6 Dec 1834; Dep Master Roy Mint Melbourne, Australia; *m* 4 July 1861 Augusta Mary Anne (*d* 6 Dec 1919), dau of George Arbuthnot, and *d* 25 Feb 1886, leaving issue:

1c Vernon Warburton; *b* 25 Nov 1864; *m* 1899 Frangiski (*d* 1957), dau of Epamenondas da Ponte, of Cephalonia, Greece, and *d* 1937, leaving issue:

1d John Francis; *b* 1901; *d* 25 Aug 1996

2d +James Epamenondas [James Delves-Broughton Esq, Moynes Court, Mathern, Chepstow, Gwent NP6 6HZ]; *b* 1916; BScEng; *m* 1st 1945 Iris Evelyn Grace (*d* 1959), dau of Joseph Jameson, of Wembley, and has:

1e +Roger Vernon [Roger Delves-Broughton Esq, Plâs Cottage, Llanarmon-yn-Ial, Mold, Clwyd]; *b* 1949

1e *Evelyn Rosemary [Mrs Anthony Symes, 10 Hanover St, Bath, Avon]; *b* 1947; *m* 1975 *Anthony Dacres Syme and has issue:

1f *David Matthew Trenchard; *b* 1976

1f *Anna Louise Trenchard; *b* 1979

2d (cont.) James Delves-Broughton *m* 2nd 1962 *Jean Margaret, dau of Arthur Williams, of Caerleon, and had further issue:

2e +Nicolas Charles Warburton [Nicolas Delves-Broughton Esq, 42 St Kildas Rd, Bath]; *b* 1969; *m* 9 Aug 1997 *Emma Maria, yst dau of Paul Anthony Botor

2e *Sonia Francesca; *b* 1967; *m* 1992 *Alistair McLay and has:

1f *Fiona Margaret; *b* 1989

2f *Shona Catherine; *b* 1992

3d +Paul Nicholas [Paul Delves-Broughton Esq, 1 College View, Fore St, Kingswear, Devon]; (twin) *b* 1916; *m* 1948 Joyce (*d* 1984), dau of Eric Francis Duckham, and has issue:

1e +Jonathan [Jonathan Delves-Broughton Esq, The Dairy House, Ryme Intrinseca, Dorset DT9 6JX]; *b* 1949; *m* 1972 *Susan Elizabeth, dau of Donald Marston, and has issue:

1f +Alexander Paul; *b* 1981

1f *Kathryne Alice; *b* 1978

2f *Anne Elizabeth; *b* 1984

1d Rachael da Ponte; *b* 1907; *m* 1942 James Thomas Currie (*d* 1985) and *d* 1993, leaving issue:

1e *Lyn Maria da Ponte [Mrs Alan Storey, 6A Mainston Rd, Remuera, Auckland, New Zealand]; *b* 1942; *m* 1964 *Alan Roylance Storey and has issue:

1f *Peter Douglas; *b* 1976

1f *Rachael Christina da Ponte; *b* 1967; *m* 1997 *Greig Terence Duncan

2f *Alana Maria da Ponte; *b* 1968

2d Janetta Patricia da Ponte; *b* 1945; *m* 1970 *John Hemus Griffiths, of Auckland, NZ, and *d* 1982, having had:

1e Mark James Hemus; *b* and *d* 1975

1e *Athena Elizabeth da Ponte; *b* 1971

2e *Maria Francesca da Ponte; *b* 1973

3d *Lynda Yvonne da Ponte; *b* 1947; *m* 19– Nicholas Dimitri Benveniste (*d* 1992)

2b Lewis Pryce Delves; *b* 10 May 1836; BA Cantab; Puisne Judge High Court Judicature Calcutta 1878–82, Adminr-Gen Bengal; *m* 26 Dec 1867 Mary Elizabeth Randall (*d* 9 Sept 1890), est dau of Gen Sir Frank Turner, KCB, Bengal Art, and *d* 3 Jan 1902, leaving, with other issue:

1c Cicely; *m* 30 Jan 1894 William Barrow-Simonds, barrister (*d* 15 May 1955), only s of William Barrow-Simonds, and *d* 23 Oct 1938, leaving issue

2c Margaret; *m* 16 April 1904 Robert Dabney Heinemann (*d* 12 Aug 1944), 3rd s of Emil Heinemann, and *d* 25 March 1956

3b Cecil Delves; *b* 19 June 1837; Cdr RN, V-Consul Ostend; *m* 1 June 1871 Marion Honora (*d* 20 May 1933), dau of Rev Theodore Bouwens, and *d* 1 May 1899, leaving, with other issue:

1c Theodore Delves; *b* 25 Dec 1872; Col RE, T/Brig, Ch Engr India 1925–29, WW I Mesopotamia and Persia (despatches twice, two medals), Malabar 1921–22 (medal with clasp); *m* 1st 1897 Marion Julia (*d* 14 July 1905), dau of Charles Augustus Theodore Bouwens, and had issue:

1d Brian Charles Delves; *b* 12 April 1903; *educ* Marlborough; *m* 14 Sept 1931 Margaret Gwenda (*d* 1991), 4th dau of Edmund Law, and *d* 29 Nov 1976, leaving issue:

1e +Simon Brian Hugo (Rev) [The Rev Simon Delves-Broughton, Christ Church Vicarage, 3 Christ Church Rd, Northampton]; *b* 17 Feb 1933; *educ* Marlborough and Exeter Coll Oxford (BA 1956, MA 1964); Priest 1960, Oxford Mission Calcutta 1960–64, Assist Priest St Nicholas Skirbeck, Lincs; *m* 2 Feb 1971 *Tin Tin Mar Marcia Patricia, dau of U Ni, of Burma, and has issue:

1f +Philip Andrew; *b* 29 July 1972; *educ* Eton and New Coll Oxford; jnlst *The Times*

1e Ann Marion; *b* 6 Feb 1939; SRN

1d Ruth Marion; *b* 29 Oct 1898

1c (cont.) Col Theodore Broughton *m* 2nd 28 Oct 1908 Eva Joanna (*d* 24 Feb 1959), dau of Col John Warre Sill, RE, and *d* 1 Feb 1944, having by her had, with other issue:

2d Kathleen Winifred Eva; *b* 29 Oct 1909; JP (Salop 1956); *m* 10 Sept 1936 Lt-Col Rupert Claude Nicholas, 3rd/15th Punjab Regt, s of Capt John Nicholas, and had issue:

1e *Rupert David; *b* 25 May 1939; *educ* Cheltenham and RMA Sandhurst; Capt KSLI

1e *Sarah Joanna Kathleen; *b* 19 Feb 1944

3d *Diana Sill; *b* 3 Dec 1920

2c Hugo Delves; *b* 25 Aug 1878; Capt 8th Bt, Lt 1st Bn Cheshire Regt; *m* 8 July 1914 Jessie Wingate (*d* 10 Nov 1957), dau of John Matthews, of Walmer, and was *ka* 4–5 April 1916

1c Marjorie Frances Delves; *m* 14 March 1905 Charles Holmes Harrison, ICS, of Algars Manor, Iron Acton, Glos, and *d* 17 June 1946

2c Ruth Delves; *m* 14 Aug 1907 Francis Maxwell Iremonger, Colonial CS, and *d* 28 Aug 1923, leaving a s and two daus

3c Dorothy Julia Delves; *m* 6 Dec 1914 Hugh Babington Blogg (*d* 3 Dec 1964), s of Rev Fowler Babington Blogg, Rector Gt Mongeham, Kent, and *d* 21 March 1957

4b Francis Sullivan Delves; *b* 6 Sept 1838; Cdr RN; *m* 14 Aug 1872 Josephine Harriet (*m* 2nd 17 Feb 1881 Cressett Thursby Pelham (*d* Dec 1884); *d* 23 Feb 1935), dau of William W Billyard, and *d* 27 Feb 1878, leaving, with other issue:

1c Marion Ida; *d* unm 7 Sept 1941

1b Frances Katharine Josepha; *m* 4 April 1866 1st Baron Fisher (*qv*) and *d* 18 July 1918, leaving issue

2a William Edward Delves; *b* 30 April 1802; Gen RE; *m* 15 Sept 1830 Anne Nugent (*d* 17 Jan 1879) and *d* 5 April 1880, leaving, with other issue:

1b John Delves; *b* 15 Aug 1836; Col RMLI; *m* 15 April 1876 Lucy (*d* 1887), dau of W H Roots, and *d* 1890, leaving issue:

1c Brian Delves; *b* 22 June 1879; *m* 13 Sept 1912 Elizabeth Annie (Bessie) (*d* 1922), dau of H K Osborn, of Ladysmith, Natal, and *d* 5 March 1926, leaving issue:

1d *Cecilia Dorothy [Mrs Guise Beaumont, Brushwood, PO Box 93, Grahamstown, Cape, S Africa]; *b* 1913; *m* 18 April 1938 Maj Guise Montgomery Foxton Beaumont, ED, est s of Frank Foxton Beaumont, and has issue:

1e *Michael Foxton [Michael Beaumont Esq, 9 Leicester St, Grahamstown, Cape, S Africa]; *b* 1939; *m* 16 April 1966 *Marion Egerton, dau of B E B White, and has issue:

1f *Warrick Foxton; *b* 15 Dec 1967

2f *Bruce Egerton; *b* 1969

2e *Keith Alan [Keith Beaumont Esq, PO Box 152, Alice 5700, S Africa]; *b* 1945; *m* 1969 *Lynda Jean, yst dau of C W Giles, of Pietermaritzburg, Natal, and has issue:

1f *Gavin Guise; *b* 1970

2f *Stephen John; *b* 1972

2d Lucy Margaret; *b* 1914; *m* 1940 Francis Alfred Heritage and had issue

3d *Joan Christine; *b* 1916; *m* 19 Dec 1942 Leonard Newnham Malyon (*d* 1983) and has issue:

1e Brian Alexander; *b* 28 Sept 1946; d 19–

2e *Rodney Charles; *b* 19 June 1956

1e *Sandra Ellen; *b* 13 Jan 1944; *m* 1st 1969 Sinclair Stanley Blunden (*d* April 1980); *m* 2nd Oct 1980 *Herbert Graham Roslyn Smith and has issue by 1st husb:

1f *Merle Iris; *b* 1970

2f *Fional Joan; *b* 1973

2f *Lynda Joy; *b* 1975

2c Alfred William Delves; *b* 16 Dec 1880; Capt RMLI; *m* 26 Dec 1914 Effie Christina (*d* 28 Dec 1963), dau of Herbert Hill Mackenzie, and was *ka* Battle of Jutland 31 May 1916, leaving issue:

1d Josephine Delves; *b* (posthumously) 6 Sept 1916; authoress; *d* unm 4 June 1975

1c Cecilia Mary Delves; *m* 7 June 1904 Ferdinand William Smallpiece, only s of Ferdinand Smallpiece, and *d* 26 Oct 1950, leaving issue

2b William Edward Delves; *b* 3 Jan 1837; Maj-Gen Bengal Army; *m* 28 April 1870 Laura Margaret (*d* 16 March 1906), dau of Stephen Lawson, and *d* 1895, leaving, with other issue:

1c Legh Harley Delves, DSO (1919); *b* 28 Oct 1873; Lt-Col RA Boer War 1900–02, WW I (despatches); *m* 3 June 1903 Constance (*d* 3 Jan 1965 aged 90), 2nd dau of George Randall Johnson, of Feniton Court, Devon, and *d* 15 May 1942, leaving issue:

1d Legh Randall Delves; *b* 29 April 1904; *educ* Eton and Univ Coll Oxford (BA); Nigerian CS; *m* 6 July 1944 Esse Maria (*d* 28 Aug 1971), dau of C J Petersen, of Durban, S Africa

2d William Edward; *b* 3 Oct 1908; *educ* Univ Coll Oxford (BA); Ord Seaman RN WW II; *d* unm 13 June 1968

3d John Rowlls; *b* 23 Sept 1910; *educ* Marlborough; *m* 1942 Ellen du Toit

1d Agnes Laura Margret; *b* 14 July 1906; *m* 27 Jan 1934 Cdr Christopher Mildmay Hall, RN, er s of Canon Mildmay Francis Hall, Rector Monkton Farleigh, Wilts, and had issue:

1e *Jocelyn Daphne Margaret; *b* 29 Mar 1935; *m* 10 Feb 1964 *Sir Ian Critchett, 3rd Bt (*qv*), and has issue

2e *Judith Anne; *b* 10 April 1936; *m* 1964 Jonathan Arundell Coode, s of Maj Perceval Edward Gott Coode, and has issue:

1f *Victoria Arundell; *b* 3 Feb 1967

2f *Claire Alexandra Margret; *b* 22 March 1968

3e *Catherine Elizabeth; *b* 13 Aug 1941; *m* 9 Dec 1967 S/Ldr Philip George Pinney, s of R Pinney, of NZ

2c William Edward Delves, MC; *b* 13 Aug 1879; Maj RA WW I (despatches, wounded); *m* 23 Oct 1912 Dorothy Grace (*m* 2nd 14 May 1968 Henry Franklin Young (*d* 1969)), yst dau of Edward Fairfax Studd, MA, JP, and *d* 20 April 1947, having had issue:

1d William Harley Fairfax; *b* 8 Oct 1913; *d* 6 May 1935

1c Louisa Fanny; *m* 26 Jan 1899 Arthur Buckwald Edgar Gibson (*d* 11 March 1932) and *d* 23 April 1941, leaving issue

2c Ethel Georgiana; *m* 3 Oct 1908 Robert Stoughton (*d* 26 Feb 1925), s of Clarke Stoughton, of Bardeswell Hall, Norfolk, and had issue

3c Florence Lucy; *m* 7 April 1904 Col Roger Gordon Thomson, CMG, DSO, RFA, s of Maj-Gen David Thomson, RE, and *d* 21 May 1949, leaving issue (*see* RICHARDSON-BUNBURY, Bt)

3b Francis Delves; *b* 6 March 1847; Capt 68th Regt; *m* Edith Mary (*d* 21 Jan 1957), dau of George Hall, of Wellington, NZ, and *d* 11 Jan 1922

4b Frederick Spencer Delves; *b* 16 March 1850; *m* 29 Sept 1874 Susan Reaves, dau of Rev Horatio Hewitt, and *d* 10 June 1896, leaving issue:

1c Horatio Delves; *m* 1st Lesley Jackson and had issue:

1d Lesley Elizabeth Delves; *b* 1 March 1912; *m* — Wilson

1c (cont.) Horatio Broughton *m* 2nd Anna M and *d* 19 Aug 1972, having had issue:

1d Frederick Spencer Delves; *b* 15 April 1922; *d* 10 Sept 1928

1c Anne Elizabeth Delves; *m* her cousin John Everett Hewitt, Maj Med Corps, US Army, and *d* 30 Aug 1962, leaving issue

2c Magdalene Reaves Delves; *m* David Herbert Woodward and had issue

1a Mary Magdalene; *m* 10 April 1834 Archibald William Blane (*d* 2 Nov 1852), n of Sir Gilbert Blane, 1st Bt (see 1916 edn), and had issue

(4) Edward Delves; *b* 11 Dec 1782; *m* 25 Oct 1808 Elizabeth (*d* 13 March 1857), dau of John Batt, of Moditonham Hall, Cornwall, and *d* 24 April 1825, leaving issue:

1a Edward Delves, of Wistaston Hall, Cheshire; *b* 6 Oct 1816; *m* 22 Sept 1847 Penelope (*d* 5 July 1883), sis and sole heir of James Walthall Hammond, of Wistaston Hall, and *d* 6 Oct 1889, leaving:

1b Edward Walthall Delves BROUGHTON later WALTHALL (took name by roy licence 1887), DL (Flints), of Wistaston Hall; *b* 20 Oct 1848; *m* 8 Sept 1870 Caroline Marion (*d* 5 July 1940), yst dau of Charles A Stewart, of West Hall, High Legh, Cheshire, and *d* 11 Sept 1897, leaving issue:

1c Edward Charles Walthall Delves, CMG (1918), DSO (1900), JP Derbys, of Alton Manor, Idridgehay, Derbys; *b* 24 April 1874; *educ* Charterhouse and RMA Woolwich; Col RA, T/Brig-Gen RA 1917–19, Hon Brig-Gen 1921, Boer War 1899–1901, WW I (despatches six times), Zone Cdr Derbys HG WW II, Order Danilo Montenegro 3rd Cl, Legn Honour and Croix de Guerre; *m* 11 Nov 1902 Isabel Sybil (*d* 14 Feb 1956), yr dau of Lt-Gen Sir James Bevan Edwards, KCB, KCMG, and *dsp* 22 Oct 1961

2c Brian James Delves; *b* 17 May 1876; Capt RM WW I (wounded); *d* unm 23 Jan 1948

3c Henry Douglas Delves, OBE (1919); *b* 7 Feb 1880; Capt RASC, Lt Denbighs Imp Yeo, Boer War 1900–01, WW I; *m* 11 Oct 1911 Hilda Maud (*d* 19–), dau of Frederick Leigh Hancock, JP (Flints), High Sheriff 1910, and *d* 21 March 1931, leaving issue:

1d Leigh Edward Delves, CBE (1961), DSC; *b* 21 Aug 1914; Capt RN WW II, Dir Air Equipment Admlty 1959–61, cmded HMS *Delight* 1956–58; *m* 7 April 1951 *Dorothy Margaret, er dau of Hugh Robert Leonard, and *d* 6 Sept 1996, leaving:

1e *Fiona Anne OBE; *b* 8 July 1953; CoL

2e *Louisa Delves; *b* 11 April 1956; *m* 1977 * Rodney Crisp, and has issue:

1f *Dominic John Delves; *b* 1981

2f *Charles Edward Delves; *b* 1986

1f *Joanna Margaret Delves; *b* 1984

3e *Theodora Serena Delves [Mrs David Jones, 4 Montroy Close, Henleaze, Bristol BS9 4RS]; *b* 4 July 1959; *m* 1990 *David Ian Jones and has:

1f *Kimberley Florence Delves; *b* 1994

1d Daphne; *b* 19 July 1912; *d* 22 Dec 1993

1c Helen Louisa Delves; *d* unm 15 Jan 1942

2c Rhoda Janet Delves; *d* unm 30 Dec 1933

3c Alice Dorothy Delves; *d* unm 4 May 1940

Sir Thomas *m* 2nd 6 June 1787 Lady Anne Windsor (*dsp* 10 Aug 1793), dau of 4th Earl of Plymouth (*qv*); *m* 3rd 2 July 1794 Mary (*d* 17 Nov 1813), dau of Michael Keating, of Co Cork, and widow of T Scott Jackson, and *d* 23 July 1813

His bro,

Rev Sir Henry Delves Broughton, 8th Bt; *b* 10 Jan 1777; *m* 15 June 1807 Mary (*d* 26 Dec 1863), only dau of John Pigott, of Capard, and *d* 3 Nov 1851 having had, with other issue:

1 **Sir Henry Delves Broughton, 9th Bt**, of Broughton; *b* 22 June 1808; High Sheriff Staffs 1859 and Cheshire 1871; *m* 24 Feb 1857 Eliza Florence (*d* 14 Nov 1882), dau of Louis Rosenzweig, and *d* 26 Feb 1899, leaving:

(1) **Sir Delves Louis Broughton, 10th Bt**, JP (Cheshire); *b* 1 June 1857; Lt 4th Bn POW' (N Staffs) Regt; *m* 1st 26 April 1881 Rosamond (*d* 11 Oct 1885), est dau of John Lambert Broughton, of Tunstall Hall, Market Drayton, Salop, and *d* 15 April 1914, having had, with other issue:

1a Delves; *b* and *d* 1882

2a **Sir (Henry John) Delves ('Jock') Broughton, 11th Bt**, DL (Cheshire); *b* 10 Sept 1883; Maj Irish Gds WW I; *m* 1st 8 July 1913 (*divorce* 1940) Vera Edyth (*d* 21 Aug 1968), yr dau of Boscawen Trevor Griffith-Boscawen, of Trevalyn, Denbighs, and had issue:

1b **Sir Evelyn Delves Broughton, 12th Bt**; *b* 2 Oct 1915; *educ* Eton and Trin Coll Cambridge; Maj RASC and Irish Gds WW II; *m* 1st 28 Jan 1947 (*divorce* 1953) Hon Elizabeth Florence Marion Cholmondeley, er dau of 4th Baron Delamere (*qv*); *m* 2nd 3 March 1955 (*divorce* 1974) Helen Mary, JP (Cheshire 1959), barrister Inner Temple 1951, only dau of John Shore, of Wilmslow, Cheshire, and had:

1c John Evelyn Delves; *b* 2 July 1962; *d* following an accident 12 Sept 1964

1c *Isabella Delves [Mrs Detmar Blow, Hilles, Edge, Glos GL6 6NW; 5 Theed St, London SE1 8ST]; *b* 19 Nov 1958; *educ* Heathfield and Columbia U NY; ed *American Vogue*, style ed *Tatler* 1987–90, British *Vogue* 1990–94, Fashion Dir *Sunday Times* 1997, memb Rare Breeds Soc and Farming Wildlife Advsy Gp Glos; *m* 1st 1981 (*divorce* 1983) Nicholas Taylor, of USA; *m* 2nd 1989 *Detmar Hamilton Lorenz Arthur Blow (*see* TOLLEMACHE, B)

2c *Julia Helen; *b* 11 Feb 1961; project manager to Sarah Duchess of York

3c *Lavinia Mary Delves [Mrs Harry Verney, Kimsbury Farmhouse, Upton Hill, Glos]; *b* 14 Feb 1965; *m* 1st 1985 Douglas Gerald Dawes (*d* 1989), yst s of Cdr Michael Dawes, RN, and has issue:

1d *Frederick Evelyn; *b* 1988

1d *Rosamond Esmé; *b* 1985

3c (cont.) Mrs Douglas Dawes *m* 2nd 1992, as his 2nd w, *Harry George Vivian Verney (*see* VERNEY, Bt, of Claydon), and has further issue

1b (cont.) **Sir Evelyn** *m* 3rd 14 May 1974 *Rona [Dowager Lady Delves Broughton, 37 Kensington Sq, London W8; Doddington Hall, Nantwich, Cheshire], memb Ruling Cncl Lloyd's 1991–, Lloyd's regulatory bd 1993–, Tstee Lloyd's Charities Tst 1991–, dau of Ernest Clifford Johns, of Wargrave, and formerly w of Donald Ian Crammond, and *d* Jan 1993

1b *Rosamund [The Rt Hon The Lady Lovat, Ballair House, Beauly, Inverness-shire]; *b* 20 May 1917; *m* 10 Oct 1938 15th Lord Lovat (*qv*) and has issue

2a (cont.) **Sir Delves ('Jock')** *m* 2nd 5 Nov 1940 Diana (*m* 3rd 1943 (*divorce* 1955) Gilbert de Préville Colvile, only s of Maj-Gen Sir Henry Edward Colvile, KCMG, CB, of Lullington Hall, Derbys (*see* DE CLIFFORD, B); m 4th 26 March 1955 4th Baron Delamere (*qv*); *d* 1987), formerly w of Vernon Motion and yr dau of Seymour Caldwell, of The Red House, Hove, and *d* by his own hand 5 Dec 1942, having been acquitted of the murder of 22nd Earl of Erroll (*qv*)

(1) (cont.) **Sir Delves** *m* 2nd 21 Dec 1887 Mary Evelyn (*d* 13 May 1915), 2nd dau of Rowland Hugh Cotton, of Etwall Hall, Derbys, and by her had issue:

3a Rowland Delves; *d* young 25 May 1890

4a Brian Evelyn Delves; *b* 16 April 1898; *educ* Eton; *m* 27 Feb 1943 Maud Alexandra, dau of H A Dickinson, and *dsp* 27 March 1966

1a Violet Evelyn Delves; *b* 10 April 1894; *m* 12 March 1918 Lt A Pike, IARO, and had issue:

1b *Audley Gareth; *b* 1 Dec 1931

1b *Delves Evelyn Mary; *b* 7 Nov 1919

2b *Pamela Amice; *b* 15 Aug 1925

2a Amice Ivy Delves; *b* 23 Oct 1902; *m* 5 Oct 1925 Sir Frank Todd Spickernell, KBE, CB, CVO, DSO, Capt (S) RN (*d* 31 March 1956), s of Frank Spickernell, and had issue

(2) Brian Delves; *b* 16 April 1865; *m* 26 July 1886 Minnie Elizabeth, dau of George Rowe, and *d* 20 Oct 1923

(1) Zoë Angelique; *b* 9 April 1859; *m* 1881 Neville Thursby, of Harleston, Northants (*d* 1916), s of Rev M W F Thursby, Rector Abington, Northants, and *d* 13 Dec 1932, leaving issue

(2) Rhoda Delves; *b* 28 Sept 1860; *m* 7 Nov 1885 her cousin Lt-Cdr Vernon Lamonnerie Delves Broughton, DSC, RNR, and *d* 7 March 1945, having had issue (*see above*)

(3) Saba Maud; *b* 25 June 1874; *m* 10 Nov 1896 Lionel Charles Molesworth (*d* 23 Dec 1916) and *d* 25 April 1956, leaving issue (*see* MOLESWORTH, V)

2 Delves (Rev), of Broughton Hall, Staffs; *b* 23 Jan 1812; *m* 22 June 1835 Jane (*d* 22 Sept 1860), dau of George Bennett, QC, and *d* May 1863, having had, with other issue:

(1) Delves; *b* 17 May 1846; Lt-Col 1st Bn E Yorks Regt; *m* 16 Oct 1872 Edith May Marion (*d* 9 Dec 1916), yst dau of Phineas Riall, of Old Connâ Hill, Bray, Co Wicklow, and *d* 4 Nov 1929, having had issue:

1a Brian Delves; *b* 14 Sept 1873; Maj 13th Rajputs IA, formerly E Yorks Regt; *d* 17 March 1919

2a Geoffrey Delves, OBE (1919); *b* 10 May 1880; Lt-Col Welch Regt WW I (wounded); *m* 1 Sept 1913 Violet Carnegie (*d* 14 Oct 1938), dau of H Anstey, and widow of Talbot Dean-Pitt, and *d* 24 Oct 1957, leaving issue:

1b Peter John Delves; *b* 22 June 1915; Lt-Cdr RN WW II; *m* 1st 28 Dec 1940 (*divorce*) Nancy Rosemary, yr dau of J E Paterson, and had issue:

1c Sir DAVID DELVES BROUGHTON, **13th and present Bt**

1b (cont.) Lt-Cdr Peter Broughton *m* 2nd 27 Aug 1948 *Evelyn Gunn [Mrs Peter Broughton, 6061 Yonge St, Suite 1504, Willowdale, Ontario, Canada], dau of J G Sutherland, and *d* 1963, having by her had further issue:

2c +GEOFFREY [Geoffrey Delves Broughton Esq, 140 Claremont Ave, Scarborough, Ontario, Canada M1N 3S4]; *b* 1962; heir presumptive; *m* 1986 *Karen Louise, dau of Thomas Wright, of Toronto, Ontario, and has issue:

1d +Peter Thomas Delves; *b* 16 Aug 1991

1d *Kathryn Louise Delves; *b* 1988

2d *Jennifer Anne Delves; *b* 1989

1c *Susan Delves [Mrs Clyde Dimmell, 60 Manning Cres, Newmarket, Ontario, Canada]; *b* 30 May 1950; *m* 1970 *Clyde Charles Victor Dimmell

2c *Patricia Delves; *b* 4 Feb 1956; *m* 1982 *William Henry Mair

3c *Shelagh Delves; *b* 1959

1b *Elizabeth Jane Delves; *b* 15 Oct 1918; *m* 1st 14 July 1940 Lt Bernard Willoughby, RN (*ka* over Java March 1942), yst s of Rev Nesbit Edward Willoughby (*see* MIDDLETON, B), formerly Vicar Bickington, Newton Abbot; *m* 2nd Anthony Pimand has issue; *m* 3rd 1948 Kenneth Phillips (*d* 1950); *m* 4th Bruce Clark

2b *Ann Joan Delves; *b* 13 Feb 1922; *m* 1942 (*divorce*) Lt F P Landsell, RA

1a Mary Edith; *m* 29 Jan 1931 George Simon Arthur Watson-Taylor (*d* 4 Oct 1942) and *d* 5 Jan 1951

3 Alfred Delves; *b* 20 Nov 1826; *m* 16 March 1858 Clemence, dau of C Fattorini, MD, of Sydney, and *d* 10 March 1895, leaving issue:

(1) Vernon Lamonnerie Delves, DSC; *b* 27 Oct 1859; Lt-Cdr RNR WW I (despatches); *m* 7 Nov 1885 his cousin Rhoda Delves, dau of Sir Henry Delves Broughton, 9th Bt, and *d* 18 Oct 1935, having had issue:

1a Rhoda Mary Delves; *b* 27 Jan 1894; *m* 12 June 1913 George Ralph Cox, MRCS, s of William Cox, MRCS, of Stone Ho, Winchcombe, and had issue

2a Nancy Delves; *b* 15 Jan 1896; *d* 25 Sept 1906

(2) Ernest Clement Vernon; *b* 29 Jan 1865; JP NSW, Victoria, Qld and S Australia, MLA King Div NSW; *m* 15 Feb 1890 Amelia Lockyer (*d* 18 May 1831), dau of William Newcombe, JP, of NSW, and *dsp* 15 Aug 1917

BROUN

Arms: Gules a chevron between three fleurs-de-lys or. **Crest:** A lion rampant gules, holding in the dexter forepaw a fleur-de-lys or. **Motto:** *Floreat majestas* ('Let majesty flourish'). **Creation:** Bt. (NS) 16 Feb 1685/6.

SIR WILLIAM WINDSOR BROUN OF COLSTOUN, 13TH BT [Sir William Broun Bt, Tamarisk Gdns, 12/2 Reed St, Cremorne, NSW 2090, Australia]; *b* 1917; *s* cousin 1995; Lt AIF WW II, FCA Australia 1991, V-Pres Scottish Australian Heritage Cncl; *m* 4 March 1952 *D'Hrie, dau of Frank King, of Bingara, NSW, and has:

1 *D'Hrie Sheree; *b* 16 July 1956; *educ* U of NSW (B Com); *m* 1988 *Rev Zachery Veron and has:

(1) *Désirée D'Hrie Marie; *b* 1991

(2) *Anne Grace; *b* 1993

(3) *Larissa Victoria; *b* 1995

2 *Rani Beverley; *b* 26 June 1959; *educ* Sydney U (LLB); *m* 1985 *Richard Patrick Morrison, and has issue:

(1) *Silas Patrick Broun; *b* 1987

(2) *Jasper William; *b* 1989

(3) *Isaac Richard; *b* 1991

(1) *Savannah Rose; *b* 1994

Lineage: PATRICK BROUN of Colstoun, Haddington, E Lothian, which his ancestors had held for some three hundred years; *d* 17 Oct 1603, leaving:

GEORGE BROUN of Colstoun; *m* 1599 Euphemia, dau of James Hoppringle of that Ilk, and had:

1 James, of Colstoun; *m* 1625 Anna, dau and heir of Robert Heriot of Trabroun, and *d* 1668/9, leaving:

(1) George, of Colstoun; *m* Margaret, dau of Sir David Murray of Stanhope, and *d* 1657, leaving issue:

1a Lilias; *m* James Bannatyne of Newhall

(2) **Sir Patrick Broun, 1st Bt** (NS), so *cr* 16 Feb 1685/6, with remainder to his heirs male for ever (*i.e.*, heirs male whomsoever), of Colstoun; Sheriff Depute of Haddington; *m* 1st Alison, dau of James Sinclair, of the Stevenson family; *m* 2nd Jean, dau of John Ramsay of Edington and widow of Rev Robert Ker, Minister of Haddington, and *d* 1688, having had issue:

1a **Sir George Broun, 2nd Bt**, of Colstoun; *m* 1692 Lady Elizabeth Mackenzie, dau of 1st Earl of Cromarty (*see* CROMARTIE, E), and *dsp* 1718

2a Robert; *m* Margaret, dau and heir of James Bannatyne of Newhall, Haddington; drowned with his sons Patrick and George in a stream on the Colstoun estate 31 May 1708, leaving, with three yr daus:

1b Jean; inherited Colstoun; *m* Charles Broun of Cleghornie and had issue:

1c George Broun; Ld of Session as Lord Colstoun; *m* Elizabeth, dau of Hew Dalrymple of Drunmmore, and had:

1d Charles Broun of Colstoun; advocate; had:

1e Christian; *m* 14 May 1805 9th Earl of Dalhousie (*qv*) and had issue

2 George, of Thornydikes, Berwickshire; *m* Marion Turnbull, and had issue:

(1) Alexander, of Bassendean, Berwickshire; *m* 1st Catherine, dau of Sir Alexander Swinton of Swinton; *m* 2nd Mary, dau of Robert Bruce of Kinnaird and widow of John Macpherson, and had issue:

1a **Sir George Broun, 3rd Bt**, of Thornydikes; *m* Janet, dau of Alexander Spottiswoode of Warristown, and *dsp* 15 Aug 1734

2a **Sir Alexander Broun, 4th Bt**, of Bassendean; *m* Beatrix, dau of Alexander Swinton of Mersington, a Ld of Session, and *d* 1750, leaving an only s:

1b **Sir Alexander Broun, 5th Bt**; *m* 1755 Molly, dau of Adam Colquhoun of Glins, and *d* 1775, leaving two daus (Agnes, living 1826; Beatrix)

(2) George; had:

1a Alexander, tenant of Hume Castle, Berwickshire had an est s:

1b George, tenant of Hume Castle; had an est s:

1c James, tenant of Hume Castle; *m* Alison, dau of William Brodie, and had an est s:

1d (Sir) RICHARD BROUN, **6th Bt** (Rev); Min of Kingarth and Lochmaben; never used the title; *m* 1765 Robina (*d* 5 Feb 1819), dau of Col Hugh McBryde of Beadland, and *d* 13 Dec 1781, having had, with several daus:

1e JAMES (Sir), **7th Bt**

2e William, of Newmains; *m* Nancy, dau of Col Peter Mainguy, of Guernsey, and *d* 1831, leaving issue:

1f William James; Lt-Col Guernsey Militia, Govt Sec Guernsey; *m* July 1824 his cousin Susan, 2nd dau of James Mainguy

2f Peter Nicholas; *b* 1797; Colonial Sec of Swan River; *m* 1824 Caroline, dau of James Simpson, and *d* 1846, leaving three s (McBryde, James and Charles) and five daus

3f Richard McBryde; *b* 1801; *m* 1st 1837 Anne, only child of G Leake, and had, with other issue:

1g William Luke; *b* 18 Sept 1850; Lt-Cdr RNR, Capt P&O; *m* 1st 25 March 1886 Harriet Louisa (*d* 13 Feb 1906), dau of William Boodle, slr, of Cheltenham, and had, with other issue:

1h Douglas George McBryde; *b* 24 April 1896; *m* 24 April 1936 Josephine Minna, dau of Joseph Arthur Burrell, of Lincoln's Inn, and *d* 14 Aug 1971

1g (cont.) William Broun *m* 2nd 1909 Alice Glen (*d* 19 June 1959), widow of Charles Wilson, of Melbourne, Australia, and *d* 2 March 1935, having by her had issue:

1h *Edith Elizabeth McBryde [Mrs Douglas Raper, Bourne House, Knotty Green, Beaconsfield, Bucks]; *b* 18 Nov 1911; *m* 23 March 1940 Douglas Matthew Duder Raper (*d* 1981), son of Charles Franklin Raper, and has issue:

1i *Rosemary Elizabeth Broun; *b* 7 Jan 1949; *m* 1972 *George Antony Alexander Johnson, and has issue:

1j *Matthew Alexander; *b* 1979

2j *Antony Christopher; *b* 1983

1j *Elizabeth Alice; *b* 1977

2i *Sarah Christian Broun; *b* 3 July 1952; *m* 1983 *Keith Raphael Briffa, and has issue:

1j *Amy Katherine Raper; *b* 1984

2j *Kirsten Fay Broun; *b* 1986

3f (cont.) Richard Broun *m* 2nd Charlotte (*d* 17 July 1898), dau of Gen Herbert, and *d* 1857

The 6th Bt's er son,

Sir James Broun, 7th Bt, of Mayfield; *b* 12 March 1768; *m* 1st 31 July 1798 Marion (*d* 20 Aug 1825), est dau of Robert Henderson of Cloughheads by Janet Carruthers, heiress of Whitecroft, and had, with other issue:

1 **Sir Richard Broun, 8th Bt**; *b* 22 April 1801; *d* unm 10 Dec 1858

2 WILLIAM (Sir), **9th Bt**

Sir James *m* 2nd 29 April 1835 Janet (*d* 17 June 1868), dau of R Watson, of Edinburgh, and *d* 30 Nov 1844

The 8th Bt's bro,

Sir William Broun, 9th Bt; *b* July 1804; *m* 18 July 1843 Elizabeth (*d* 19 Aug 1899), 2nd dau of John Smith, of Drongan, and *d* 10 June 1882, having had, with other issue:

1 WILLIAM (Sir), **10th Bt**

2 David Limond; *b* 1855; *m* 1877 Margaret (*d* 1928), dau of Martin Kelly, of NSW, and *d* 1934, leaving issue:

(1) William James; *b* 1882; *m* 1st 1914 Miriam Rheta, dau of Sydney T Peryman, of Mosman, NSW, and had:

1a +William James Peryman [William Broun Esq, 6 Epacris Ave, Forestville, NSW, Australia]; *b* 1922; *educ* Sydney U (BE 1944); Lt RAN 1944–48; *m* 1956 *Penelope Jane, dau of W T Horn, of Canberra, and has:

1b +William James Harvey; *b* 1958; *m* 1980 *Margaret Anne, dau of A W Quinn, of Roseville, NSW, and has:

1c +William James Christopher; *b* 1983

1c *Jacqueline Ann; *b* 1986

2b +Anthony Fraser Cameron; *b* 1960

2a +Malcolm David, QC (1982) [Malcolm Broun Esq QC, 61 Greenwich Rd, Greenwich, NSW 2065, Australia]; *b* 25 April 1935; *educ* Sydney U (BA 1957, LLB 1958); barrister NSW 1959; *m* 1st 1962 (*divorce* 1971) Janet Patricia, only dau of Alan Douglas Edwards, of Wagga Wagga, and has:

1b +Alexander Alan Hercules; *b* 16 March 1965

1b *Charlotte Doriam [*sic*]; *b* 11 Dec 1963; *m* 1989 (*divorce* 1996) Olivier Jean Jacques Eugène dit Rochesson, of Clamecy, France; by *Arthur Simpson has:

1c *Brigitte Lavinia Broun SIMPSON; *b* 24 Feb 1997

2b *Sophie Amelia; *b* 24 Feb 1969
2a (cont.) Malcolm Broun *m* 2nd 1972 *Wendy Sue, dau of W J Hannelly, and has issue:
1b +Nicholas Malcolm; *b* 1975
1b *Virginia Barbara; *b* 1976
1a *Wilga Joan [Mrs Ian Dutton, PO Box 153, Manilla, NSW 2346, Australia]; *b* 1917; *m* 1937 Ian Cecil de Courcy Dutton (*d* 6 Oct 1996), and has issue:
1b *Ian Herbert; *b* 1941; *m* 1963 *Irene Elizabeth Mary Archer and has:
1c *Anthony Ian de Courcy; *b* 1970; *m* 1992 *Donna Michele Sharpe and has:
1d *Joshua Robert de Courcy; *b* 1990
1d *Jade Louise de Courcy; *b* 1993
2c *Michael Leslie de Courcy; *b* 1974
1c *Jennifer de Courcy; *b* 1966; m 1990 *David Peter Porter and has:
1d *Teagan Emma; *b* 1992
2b *Peter James; *b* 1952; *m* 1975 *Judith Margaret Atherton, and has issue:
1c *Grant Peter de Courcy; *b* 1977
2c *Peter Jaye de Courcy; *b* 1979
3c *Thomas Arthur de Courcy; *b* 1984
1c *Lee Jane de Courcy; *b* 1976
3b *Christopher Cecil; *b* 1955; *m* 1978 *Vicki Janelle Beard, and has issue:
1c *Casey John de Courcy; *b* 1980
1c *Rachael Marie de Courcy; *b* 1982
2c *Melanie Louise de Courcy; *b* 1984
1b *Anne Wilga; *b* 1938; *m* 1957 *William Arthur Jones, and has issue:
1c *Wayne William Dutton; *b* 1958; *m* 1980 *Kerry Therese Weaver, and has issue:
1d *Scott Jeremy; *b* 1983
1d *Tara Leigh; *b* 1986
2c *Robert Hugh Dutton; *b* 1967; by *Cheryl Anne Miller has:
1d *Alex William; *b* 1993
1d *Taylah Marie; *b* 1990
1c *Debra Anne Dutton; *b* 1959; *m* 1979 *David John Oliphant, and has issue:
1d *Joshua Luke; *b* 1983
2d *Beau Jacob; *b* 1985
1d *Zoe Aleesha; *b* 1981
2c *Rebekah Letitia; *b* 1970; *m* 19– *Michael Chapman
2b *Melissa Judith; *b* 1945; *m* 1969 *Kenneth Beresford Abberfield and has:
1c *Derk Beresford; *b* 1973
1c *Natalie Terese; *b* 1969; *m* 1993 *Barnaby Joyce and has:
1d *Bridgette Maree; *b* 1996
2c *Stephanie Marie; *b* 1971; *m* 1993 *Thomas Andrew Ryan and has:
1d *Fergus James; *b* 1997
3b *Pauline; *b* 1946; *m* 1st 1967 (*divorce* 1974) David Ross Medway and has:
1c *Shayne David; *b* 1968
2c *Allyn Ross; *b* 1969
3c *Jarrod Barrington; *b* 1971
3b (cont.) Mrs Pauline Medway *m* 2nd 1974 (*divorce* 1990) John Allan Phoo, and has:
1c *Jayson John; *b* 1975
2c *Matthew James; *b* 1983
1c *Suzanne Lillian; *b* 1976
3b (cont.) Mrs Pauline Phoo *m* 3rd 1993 *John Malcolm Young
4b *Miriam Lillian; *b* 1953; *m* 1975 (*divorce* 1983) Paul Christopher Thomas and has issue:
1c *Darren Paul de Courcy Dutton
4b (cont.) Mrs Miriam Thomas *m* 2nd 1984 *Petrus Johannes-Valk and by him has:
1c *Myran Petrus de Courcy Dutton; *b* 1985
2c *Ashley Ian de Courcy Dutton; *b* 1987
3c *Lysander Maurhys de Courcy Dutton; *b* 1990
2a *Mario Rheta, OAM [Mrs Martin Hardie OAM, 7 Kurrajong Village, Barton lane, Tamworth, NSW 2340, Australia]; *b* 1918; *m* 1st 1943 (*divorce* 1970) Capt Maxwell Charles Halliday, AIF, DDS, MDS (Chicago); *m* 2nd 1970 Hon Mr Justice (Martin Francis) Hardie (*d* 1974) and has by her 1st husb:
1b *Miriam Victoria [Mrs Adam Hudson, 14 McRae Place, Turramurra, NSW, Australia]; *b* 1948; *m* 1973 *Adam Cowper Hudson, BE, BSc, and has:
1c *David Adam Halliday; *b* 1976
1c *Emma Victoria Gillett; *b* 1978
2c *Alice Rheta Broun; *b* 1980
2b *Catherine Eleanor Broun [Mrs Philip Brown, Subiaco Walcha, NSW 2354, Australia]; *b* 1952; *m* 1973 *Philip MacArthur Brown and has:
1c *Hamish Ross MacArthur; *b* 1980
3a *Dorothy Lenglen [Mrs Dorothy Woods, RMB 290B, Moore Creek, Tamworth, NSW 2340, Australia]; *b* 1919; *m* 1947 (*divorce* 1975) Walter W Woods and has:
1b *Michael William Frank [Michael Woods Esq, Tregarthen, Dunoon Rd, Tamworth, NSW, Australia]; *b* 1954; *m* 1983 *Helen Lynette Trythall and has:
1c *Timothy Michael; *b* 1989
1c *Jessica Margaret; *b* 1992
2b *Adam Lindsay Broun; *b* 1956
3b *Justin Thomas; *b* 1957; has issue by Nicola Griffin:
1c *Ashlea GRIFFIN WOODS; *b* 1986
1b *Margarita Henry; *b* 1959
2b *Sarah Dorothy Broun; *b* 1962; has by *Glenn Atkinson:
1c *Caitlin Hayley; *b* 1993
4a *June Joy OAM (1997) [Mrs Ross Hayes OAM, 98 Balfour Rd, Rose Bay, NSW 2029, Australia]; *b* 1921; *educ* NSW U (BA); *m* 1949 *Ross Abbott Hayes, MB, BS, FRCPA, FRC (Path), JP, and has had issue:
1b *Clive Broun Abbott [Clive Hayes Esq, 1 Genders Ave, Burwood, NSW 2134, Australia]; *b* 1950; *m* 1985 *Jennifer Anne McLean and has issue:
1c *Rebecca Mclean; *b* 1987
2c *Michaela McLean; *b* 1990
2b *Jamie Abbott Broun [Jamie Hayes Esq, 2 Royal St, Chatswood, NSW, Australia]; *b* 1953; *m* 1986 *Ellen Armstrong and has issue:
1c *Ryan Armstrong; *b* 1987
2c *Taylor Broun; *b* 1991
1c *Dakoda; *b* 1992
3b *David Broun Abbott [David Hayes Esq, 17 Kaboda St, Dover Heights, NSW, Australia]; *b* 1954; *m* 1981 *Jackie Ann Ryba and has issue:
1c *Kobe Ryba; *b* 1984
2c *Billi Ryba; *b* 1987
1c *Zoe Ryba; *b* 1992
4b Matthew George Broun; *b* 1964; *d* 1987
(1) (cont.) William Broun *m* 2nd 1947 Dorothea Esther (*d* 1968), dau of David A Strahley, of Sandy Knowe, Inverell, NSW, and *d* 1963
(1) Kate Mary Emily
(2) Sarah Honora; *m* 20 Aug 1904 William Bissett Whightman Knowles and *d* 1963, leaving issue
(3) Eleanor Gale; *m* 1915 Hercules Christian McIntyre, son of W McIntyre of Sydney
(4) Elizabeth Smith (Elsie); *m* 31 Jan 1914 Rumney Gibbons, only son of Benjamin Gibbons, of Manchester and Bowdon, and had issue
1 Elizabeth Smith; *m* 22 July 1886 Rev John Mackie, DD (*d* 3 July 1929), of St Andrew's Church, Kingston, Canada, and had issue

The 9th Bt's est surv son,

Sir William Broun, 10th Bt; *b* 18 Dec 1848; *m* 12 April 1871 Alice Jane (*d* 1921), 2nd dau of James Cornelius Peters, of NSW, and *d* 23 Oct 1918, having had issue:

1 **Sir (James) Lionel Broun, 11th Bt**; *b* 1875; *m* 3 June 1925 Georgie, yr dau of Henry Law, of Sydney, NSW, and *d* 1962, leaving:
(1) **Sir Lionel John Law Broun, 12th Bt**; *b* 25 April 1927; *d* 10 Aug 1995
2 William Arthur; *b* 12 Oct 1876; *m* 1916 Marie Victoria (*d* 1964), dau of William McIntyre, of Sydney, NSW, and *d* 31 July 1925, leaving, with other issue:
(1) Sir WILLIAM WINDSOR BROUN, **13th and present Bt**
(2) +HULANCE HADDINGTON [Hulance Broun Esq, 462 Pittwater Road, N Manly, NSW 2100, Australia]; *b* 1919; heir presumptive; WW II with AIF and Sgt/Pilot RAAF, Middle East 1940–42; *m* 21 March 1947 Joy Maud (*d* 1995), dau of A L Stack, of Mosman, NSW, and has issue:
1a +Wayne Hercules [Wayne Broun Esq, 7 Hasey Road, Kenthurst, NSW 2154, Australia]; *b* 23 Jan 1952; *educ* Sydney GS; Lt 5th Bn RAR; *m* 1976 *Anna Marie Paolucci, and has issue:
1b +Richard Haddington; *b* 1984
1b *Samantha Louise; *b* 1981
1a *Robyn Joy; *b* 19 July 1948; *m* 1974 *Cedric Hoare, and has issue:
1b *Timothy James; *b* 1976
2b *Jeremy Lachlan; *b* 1981
1b *Nicole Suzanne; *b* 1978
2a *Julie Christine; *b* 3 Dec 1955; *m* 1978 *William Lyons, and has issue:
1b *Tamara Suzanne; *b* 1982
2b *Eleanor Amy; *b* 1985
3b *Georgia Anne; *b* 1988
(3) Lionel McIntyre; *b* 1921; WW II with RAAF; *m* 1955 Shirley (*d* 1990), dau of A L Stack (*see* above), and *d* 1990, leaving issue:
1a +Walter Leslie [Walter Broun Esq, Mt Monopoly, Uralla, NSW 2441, Australia]; *b* 9 June 1961; *educ* New England U
2a +Steven McIntyre; *b* 12 Nov 1963; *educ* New England U; *m* 1992 *Helen McRae-Smith
1a *Lucinda Marie; *b* 1 Nov 1957; *educ* Sydney U (LLB); *m* 1981 *Russell Anthony Aboud, MB, and has issue:
1b *Angus Alfred McIntyre; *b* 1985
1b *Annabelle Louise; *b* 1988
2b *Jacqueline Lucinda; *b* 1994
(4) +John Hercules August [John Broun Esq, 5 Daniel Keane Cres, Gunnedah, NSW, Australia]; *b* 1923; *m* 1st 1953 Patricia Johnson and has issue:
1a +Richard; *b* 1954
(4) (cont.) John Broun *m* 2nd 1963 *Marjorie, dau of Reginald Chapman, of Dubbo, NSW, and by her has issue:
1a *Tracey Lee; *b* 1964
2a *Phoebe Margaret; *b* 1968; *m* 1992 *Andrew Beniac
3 Reginald Augustus; *b* 1878; *m* 1910 Alice Maude (*d* 1983), 2nd dau of W B Wilkinson, of Mosman, Sydney, NSW, and *d* 20 Jan 1948, leaving issue:
(1) Reginald William Wilkinson; *b* 1912; *d* 1997
(1) Nancy Alice; *m* 1st 13 Feb 1933 Cyril Richard Doyle, s of James Carton Doyle (*d* 1953), and had issue; *m* 2nd 1956 Eric Hill
(2) *Noël Marian; *b* 1918; *m* 1944 Charles Edward Robinson, and has issue:
1a *Bernard James; *b* 24 Oct 1946; *m* 5 July 1968 *Annie Kernihan, and has issue:

1b *Nicole Marie; *b* 1973
2b *Emma Jane; *b* 1975
4 Claude McBride; *b* 1882
1 Elizabeth Eleanor Maude; *m* 1896 Ernest Frederick Doyle, of Werris Creek, NSW, Australia, and had issue
2 Alice Marion Blanche; *m* 1907 Leslie Sprague (*d* 1942), and had issue
3 Linda Isabella; *m* 1910 William Shubrick Martin, of NSW, Australia, and had issue

BROWN

Arms: Quarterly, 1st and 4th, gu. a chevron or between two bear's paws erased in chief arg. and four hands conjoined in saltire of the second in base, on a chief engrailed or an eagle displayed sa. (for BROWN); 2nd and 3rd, arg. a chevron nebuly sa. between two moorhens close in chief ppr. and a fleur de lys in base az. (for LUXMOORE). **Crest:** A bear's paw erased arg. issuant out of a wreath of oak vert, holding a sinister hand ppr. **Motto:** *Est concordia fratrum* ('There is unity among brothers'). **Creation:** Bt. (UK) 24 Jan 1863.

SIR GEORGE FRANCIS RICHMOND BROWN, 5TH BT, of Richmond Hill, Lancs [Maj Sir George Brown Bt, Mas de Sudre, 81600 Gaillac, France]; *b* 3 Feb 1938; *s* f 1995; Maj Welsh Gds, Extra Equerry to HRH THE DUKE OF EDINBURGH 1961–63, ADC to Govr Qld 1963–65, Adj Welsh Gds 1966–68; *m* 1978 *Philippa Jane, dau of Capt E J Wilcox, RE, and has:
1 +SAM GEORGE RICHMOND; *b* 27 Dec 1979
2 +Harry Richmond; *b* 1982
3 +Edward Richmond; *b* 1987

Lineage: WILLIAM BROWN; *b* Cairnkirn, N Antrim, 1715; *m* 19 Nov 1745 Margaret (*d* 2 Jan 1805), dau of John Davison, of Knockboy, Co Antrim, and *d* 26 Jan 1778, leaving issue:
1 Patrick later John; *b* 21 July 1753, insur broker London; *m* and *d* 1836, leaving issue
2 ALEXANDER, of whom presently
2 Stewart, of Baltimore; *b* 2 July 1769; *m* 1st 18 April 1797 Sarah Harman (*d* 23 Aug 1811), and had, with other issue:
(1) Stewart; *b* 4 Jan 1802; *m* 6 May 1830 Mary Ann (*d* 28 Nov 1874), dau of Henry Robert Abbott, and *d* 30 Jan 1880, having had, with other issue:
1a Stewart Henry, of Quarry Bank, Allerton, Lancs, JP; *b* 5 April 1831; *educ* Columbia U USA (BA); *m* 27 Dec 1860 Emily Frances Sarah, DGStJ (*d* 22 March 1921), dau and coheir of James Birkett, of Liverpool, and *d* 17 March 1905, having had, with other issue:
1b Egerton Stewart-Brown (formerly Egerton Stewart Brown), of The Lawn, Ullet Rd, Liverpool, and Lleiniog Castle, Penmon, Anglesey, barrister Inner Temple and Northern Circuit; *b* 31 Jan 1862; *educ* Trin Coll Cambridge (MA); *m* 12 Sept 1888 Nessie (*d* 7 April 1958), dau of Edmund Knowles Muspratt, of Seaforth Hall, Liverpool (*see* MUSPRATT, Bt), and *d* 11 Aug 1938
2b Henry Stewart-Brown (formerly Henry Stewart Brown), of The Pole, Antrobus, Cheshire; *b* 19 June 1863; *m* 28 Aug 1890 Ellen Sophia (*d* 1 June 1956), dau of Thomas Sutton Timmis, of Cleveley, Allerton, and *d* 9 Dec 1947, having had, with other issue:
1c William Sutton, DSO (1943), Lt-Col Coldstream Gds, served WW II; *b* 23 March 1900; *educ* Harrow and RMC Sandhurst; *ka* July 1944
1c Mary; *m* 12 Jan 1921 Philip Boddington, JP, of Mere Court, Chelford, Cheshire, and has issue. He *d* 8 Nov 1952
2c Catherine; *m* 23 Nov 1926 Sir John Richard Hobhouse, MC, JP, son of Henry Hobhouse, PC, and has issue. He *d* 9 May 1961
3b Hamilton Stewart-Brown (formerly Hamilton Stewart Brown), Maj King's Liverpool Regt (TF) WW I; *b* 15 March 1870; *m* 11 Aug 1897 Cesarine (*d* 2 May 1961 aged 87), er dau of Capt D A Alson, of Cork, and *d* 10 March 1934, leaving issue:
1c Leslie, Maj Roy Pioneer Corps, formerly Lt Res of Offrs 19th Hus, served WWs I and II; *b* 6 March 1899; *educ* Harrow; *m* 1 Oct 1926 Barbara Hamilton, dau of Charles Kennedy Scott, of Addison Rd, Kensington
2c Dennis; *b* 6 Feb 1908; *educ* Harrow; *m* 14 Nov 1934 *Glenys, dau of Owen Trevor-Williams, of Glan Aber, Llangefni, Anglesey, and *d* 26 May 1978, leaving issue:
1d *Ian Hamilton, late 2nd Lt Welsh Gds; *b* 10 Nov 1936; *educ* Harrow; *m* 8 Oct 1963 *Jane, yr dau of Jonathan Brudenell Fenwick, of Larkhall, Six Mile Bottom, Newmarket, Suffolk, and has issue:
1e *William; *b* 22 June 1965
2e *James; *b* 1 June 1967
1e *Fiona; *b* 17 Sept 1971
2d *Brian Trevor; *b* 7 June 1945; *educ* Harrow
1d *Tonia Marion; *b* 25 Feb 1941; *m* 30 March 1971 *W Simpson RE, only son of Col Frank W Simpson, of Crabtree Ho, Byfleet, Surrey
3c *Patrick Abbott, TD (1948), Capt RA (TA) WW II; *b* 20 Jan 1916; *educ* Harrow; *m* 7 Jan 1939 Margaret (*d* 10 July 1979), only dau of Dan Calverley, of Dalton, Huddersfield, and has issue:
1d *Hamilton; *b* 30 Jan 1945
1d *Victoria Emily Ida; *b* 31 July 1949; *m* Geoffrey — and has issue
1c Aileen Maud; *m* 11 Aug 1925 Sir James Chadwick, FRS, PhD, Master Gonville and Caius Coll Cambridge 1948–58, s of J J Chadwick, and had issue:
1d *Joanna Stewart; *b* 1 Feb 1927; *m* 30 June 1966 John Frederic Hugh Batterham, 2nd s of James Nathaniel Batterham, of Tilney St Lawrence, Norfolk
2d *Judith; *b* 1 Feb 1927
2c Winifred Marian; *m* 7 July 1927 Jean Paravicini, JP, and *d* 10 May 1965, leaving a s. He *d* 16 Jan 1961
4b Ronald Stewart-Brown (formerly Ronald Stewart Brown), of Bryn-y-Grog, Marchwiel, Wrexham, High Sheriff Denbighshire 1934, FSA, Capt Duke of Lancaster's Own Yeo WW I; *b* 2 Oct 1872; *educ* Trin Coll Cambridge (MA); *m* 20 June 1903 Olga Sophia (*d* 4 Aug 1962), dau of George Theodore von Heyder (afterwards George Theodore St George), of Stone Ho, Allerton, and *d* 11 Jan 1940, leaving issue:
1c Philip Harman, served WW II as T/Maj RM, memb Lloyd's; *b* 30 April 1904; *educ* Harrow; *m* 24 Feb 1944 *Mavis, formerly w of Capt Charles Finch Farley, MC, and est dau of Lt-Col Robert Loftus Tottenham (*see* ELY, M), and *dsp* 21 Dec 1960
2c (Ronald) David, QC (1957); barrister Inner Temple 1934, Maj Welsh Gds WW II (despatches); *b* 5 Dec 1911; *educ* Harrow and Trin Coll Cambridge (MA); *m* 19 Feb 1946 (Esther) Lynette Sutherland, VAD (*m* 2nd 15 Sept 1969 Mervyn Talbot Rice), dau of Maj James Reay Sutherland Mackay, RAMC, of Calcutta and Balkerach, Doune, Perthshire, and widow of Capt Michael Hamish Alistair Stuart-Hamilton (*see* HAMILTON, Bt, of Silverton Hill), and *d* 10 Oct 1963, leaving issue:
1d *Ronald Reay; *b* 15 Aug 1948; *educ* Harrow and Trin Coll Cambridge
2d *Andrew Philip; *b* 20 March 1953; *educ* Harrow
1d *Sarah Lynette; *b* 24 March 1950; *educ* Lady Margaret Hall Oxford
1c *Cynthia Birkett; *m* 14 Feb 1930 Col David Taunton Raikes, DSO, MC (*d* 8 July 1966), yst son of Robert Taunton Raikes, JP, of Treberfydd, Breconshire, and has issue:
1d *Robin David Taunton [Robin Raikes Esq, Woodhouse, Middleton Tyas, Richmond, Yorks]; *b* 9 June 1935; *educ* Merton Coll Oxford; *m* 18 June 1960 *Sarah Elizabeth, yr dau of W/Cdr Robert Cecil Talbot Speir, OBE, DL, of Linkside, Nairn, and has issue:
1e *Emma Jane; *b* 16 April 1961
2e *Victoria Caroline; *b* 23 May 1963
3e *Joanna Elisabeth; *b* 10 March 1965
1d *Rosanne Margaret; *b* 17 Feb 1932; *m* 23 July 1960 her cousin *Roger Melville Taunton Raikes, 3rd s of Lt-Col Wilfrid Taunton Raikes, DSO, MC, of The Copyhold, Redhill, Surrey, and has issue:
1e *Roderick Melville; *b* 16 April 1964
2e *Antony Kennedy; *b* 16 April 1964
3e *Jonathan Paul; *b* 28 March 1969
2c *Virginia Susan; *m* 19 Jan 1938 *Ian Edward Hargreave, BA, est s of Oliver Hargreave, of The Willows, Lytham, and has issue:
1d *Ronald Hume Marsden [Ronald Hargreave Esq, Rosebank, Appletree Lane, Corbridge, Northumberland NE45 5LL]; *b* 24 Sept 1940; *educ* Shrewsbury and Merton Coll Oxford; *m* 25 July 1965 *Catherine Maxsted, only dau of Edward Johnson, of Holly Ho, Hornby, Lancaster, and has issue:
1e *Nicholas Edward Hume; *b* 17 Dec 1968
2d *Simon Oliver; *b* 11 Dec 1942; *educ* Shrewsbury
3d *Giles St George; *b* 2 Sept 1948; *educ* Harrow
1d *Cynthia Mary Caroline; *b* 11 Dec 1942; *m* 12 Feb 1966 *William Geoffrey Seddon-Brown, only s of Maj J G Seddon-Brown, OBE, of Tarn Beck, Brookhouse, Lancs
5b Brian Stewart-Brown (formerly Brian Stewart Brown); *b* 28 July 1877; *d* 8 June 1932
1b Emily; *b* 7 Oct 1865; *d* unm Oct 1939
2b Henrietta; *b* 2 Dec 1867; *m* 8 Sept 1892 James Heald, MA, and *d* 11 Dec 1961, leaving issue. He *d* 14 Feb 1921

The 2nd son,

ALEXANDER BROWN; *b* 17 Nov 1764; emigrated to USA 1799; *m* 17 June 1783 Grace (*d* 12 Jan 1843), dau of John Davison, of Drumnasole, and *d* Baltimore 4 March 1934, having had, with other issue:

Sir William Brown, 1st Bt (UK), so *cr* 24 Jan 1863, of Richmond Hill, Lancs, DL, JP, High Sheriff 1963, JP and Alderman Liverpool, MP S Lancs 1846–59, Hon Col 1st Bde Lancs Art Vols, fndr Brown, Shipley & Co, Liverpool, gave Liverpool 1860 a public library and museum costing over £42,000, author: *Letters on the Advantages of Free Trade to the Landed Interest*; *b* 30 May 1784; *m* 1 Jan 1810

Sarah (*d* 5 March 1858), dau of Andrew Gihon, JP, of Ballymena, Co Antrim, and had, with other issue:

1 Alexander, of Beilby Grange, Yorks, MA Oxford; *b* 17 May 1817; *m* 19 Dec 1838 his cousin Sarah Benedict, est child of James Brown, of New York, and *dvp* 8 Oct 1849, having had, with other issue:

(1) WILLIAM RICHMOND (Sir), **2nd Bt**

(2) James Clifton, of Holmbush, Sussex, JP, MP Horsham 1876–80, Hon Col cmdg 2nd Bde Lancs Div RA; *b* 13 Feb 1841; *educ* Trin Hall Cambridge (MA); *m* 21 March 1866 Amelia (*d* 17 Dec 1922), dau of Charles Rowe, of Elm Ho, Liverpool, and *d* 5 Jan 1917, leaving, with other issue:

1a Howard Clifton; *b* 13 April 1868; *educ* Eton; Hon Brig-Gen 12th Lancers, JP Sussex, MP Newbury 1922–23 and 1924–45; *m* 14 July 1903 Mary Eirene (*d* 11 Dec 1951), er dau of Sir Henry Edward Agincourt Hodges, and *d* 11 Sept 1946, leaving issue:

1b Elizabeth Clifton; *b* 20 Jan 1914; Co Assist ATS; *m* 24 Jan 1944 *Maj Edmund Archibald Calvert, DL, The Royals [Maj Edmund Calvert, Rose Cottage Farm House, Faygate, Horsham, Sussex RH12 4SE], er s of Col Charles Archibald Calvert, DSO, DL, JP, of Beare Green, Surrey, and *d* March 1995, leaving:

1c *Henry Clifton [Henry Calvert Esq, Holmbush, Faygate, Horsham]; *b* 19 Dec 1948; *educ* Stowe; *m* 1976 *Ruth Margaret, dau of Col Geoffrey Russell Armstrong, DSO, MC, TD (*see* ENNISKILLEN, E), and has:

1d *Piers Henry; *b* 1977

1d *Henrietta Amelia; *b* 1980

1c *Jennifer Clifton [Mrs Josceline Grove, 34 Stevenage Rd, London SW6 6ET; Fasnakyle, Cannich, Inverness-shire]; *b* 1 Jan 1947; *educ* Benenden; *m* 1970 *Josceline Philip Grove (*see* LIVERPOOL, E) and has had:

1d Evelyn Clifton; *b* 26 Nov 1972; *d* 12 March 1973

1d *Miranda Clifton; *b* 6 July 1974

2d *Venetia Mary; *b* 17 Dec 1976

2b *Katharine Clifton [Mrs Ion Garnett-Orme, Cheriton Cottage, Cheriton, Alresford, Hants SO24 0PR]; *b* 19 June 1917; *m* 23 Feb 1946 Ion Hunter Touchet Garnett-Orme (*d* 1991), er s of George Hunter Garnett-Orme, of Hill Lodge, Pangbourne, Berks

3b *Margaret Eirene Clifton [The Rt Hon Margaret Lady Amherst of Hackney, 138 Cranmer Court, Sloane Ave, London SW3]; *b* 23 Feb 1921; *m* 14 Sept 1939 3rd Baron Amherst of Hackney (*qv*) and has issue

2a Edward Clifton BROWN later CLIFTON-BROWN (deed poll 1 Feb 1923), of Burnham Grove, Burnham, Bucks, JP Bucks, High Sheriff 1936; *b* 10 Feb 1870; *m* 21 July 1897 Dora Winifred (*d* 21 July 1962), dau of George Hanbury, of Blythewood, Bucks, and *d* 1 Nov 1944, leaving issue:

1b Geoffrey Benedict; *b* 25 July 1899; *educ* Eton; Lt-Col 12th Lancers WW II, MP Bury St Edmunds 1945–50; *m* 14 July 1927 Mrs Robina Margaret Hill Miller, CA (*d* 1978), dau of Rowland Sutton (*see* SUTTON, Bt), and *d* 1983, leaving issue:

1c +Edward Geoffrey [Edward Clifton-Brown Esq, W Bradley House, Glastonbury, Somerset BA6 8LT]; *b* 22 July 1928; *educ* Eton; formerly dir Lloyds & Bolsa Interest Bank; *m* 1st 17 Oct 1953 (*divorce* 1958) Jillian Mary, only dau of David Walkinshaw, of Bishopton, Half Moon Hall, Haslemere, and has:

1d +James Benedict; *b* 1 May 1956; *educ* Marlborough; *m* 11 Oct 1980 *Priscilla Sarah, dau of Sir John Valentine Jardine Paterson, and has issue:

1e *Emma Victoria; *b* 8 Oct 1983

2e *Holly Rebecca; *b* 30 May 1985

3e *Laura Serena; *b* 22 Aug 1987

1d *(Margaret) Joanna; *b* 25 Sept 1957

1c (cont.) Edward Clifton-Brown *m* 2nd 17 Sept 1960 *Sarah Simonetta, yr dau of Roger Herbert Francis, OBE and by her has:

2d *Louisa; *b* 17 Sept 1961; *m* 1991 *Alexander Penrose Gordon Cumming, s of Sir William Gordon Gordon Cumming, 6th Bt (*qv*)

3d *Sarah; *b* 27 Oct 1964

2c +Robert Lawrence [Robert Clifton-Brown Esq, Maltings Farmhouse, Little Bradley House, nr Haverhill, Suffolk]; *b* 25 Sept 1929; *educ* Bryanston; *m* 26 April 1952 *Florence Elizabeth Lindsay, est dau of Ronald Arthur Vestey, of Great Thurlow Hall, Suffolk (*see* VESTEY, Bt), and has:

1d +Geoffrey Robert; *b* 23 March 1953; *educ* Eton; *m* 1979 *Alexandra Mary, yst dau of W/Cdr Denis Peto-Shepherd, of Gt Durnford, Salisbury, Wilts, and has issue:

1e *Jacqueline Florence; *b* 13 Oct 1983

2d +Ronald Colin; *b* 1963; *m* 1987 *Emily Joan, yr dau of Laver John Morgan Oliver, of Bury St Edmunds, Suffolk, and has issue:

1e +George; *b* 1992

1e *A dau; *b* 1993

1d *Jane Elizabeth; *b* 31 Oct 1954; *m* 25 April 1978 *Mark Corner Bailey, er s of L C Bailey, of Brinkley, Newmarket:

1e *Peter Robert Corner; *b* 1983

2e *A son; *b* 1993

1e *Rosemary Catherine; *b* 1980

2e *Florence; *b* 1989

2d *Angela Florence [Mrs Timothy Sills, Whites Farm, Helions Bumpstead, Haverhill, Suffolk]; *b* 7 Dec 1956; *m* 1984 *Timothy Sills and has issue:

1e *James; *b* 1987

2e *Robert Marett; *b* 1990

3e *Michael; *b* 1993

1c Margaret Winifred; *b* 7 Jan 1932; *m* 8 Oct 1955 Patrick Bury Buchanan, er surv son of Col Edmund Pullar Buchanan, OBE, MC, DL, late Argyll and Sutherland Highrs, of Touch, by Stirling, and *d* following a car crash 10 Dec 1955

2b Anthony George, TD, DL; *b* 11 Feb 1903; *educ* Eton and Trin Coll Cambridge (BA); served WW II (wounded), memb Court Assists Merchant Taylors' Co (Master 1945–46), Alderman Broad St Ward 1950–60, Lt City London, Sheriff 1957–58; *m* 1st 20 Feb 1930 Delia Charlotte Gordon (*d* 16 May 1947), yr dau of George Edward Wade, sculptor, of 30 Hyde Park St, W2, and *d* 1984 leaving issue:

1c *Georgiana Elmira [Mrs Anthony Bailey, 6/129 The Parade, Ascot Vale, VIC 3032, Australia]; *b* 27 Dec 1934; *m* 7 Sept 1962 *Prof Anthony Charles Bailey, MA, LLM, barrister, s of Hugh Somerville Bailey, of 4 Eton Villas, Hampstead, NW3, and has issue:

1d *Edward Hugh Clifton [Edward Bailey Esq, 58 Bank St, Ascot Vale, VIC 3032, Australia]; *b* 5 May 1966; *m* 1996 *Yasuko, dau of Dr Mazaki Kawahara, of Nagano, Japan

1d *Jane Delia [Mrs Robin Redgrave, 7 Westbrook Close, Oakley, Hants RG23 7HW]; *b* 4 July 1964; *m* 1990 *Robin Arthur Wellesley Redgrave, yr s of Maj-Gen Sir Roy Redgrave, KBE, MC, of Chelsea, and has issue:

1e *Thomas Roy Philip; *b* 1993

1e *Catherine Georgiana Wellesley; *b* 3 Nov 1995

2d *Felicity [Mrs Mark Lewis, 135 Maribyrnong Rd, Ascot Vale, VIC 3032, Australia]; *b* 16 Jan 1970; *m* 1994 *Mark Julian Lewis, s of Hywel Lewis, of Bribie Is, Queensland, and has:

1e *Julia Elizabeth; *b* Feb 1995

2c *Mora Delia [Mrs John Abell, Whittonditch House, Ramsbury, Wilts SN8 2PZ]; *b* 11 April 1936; *m* 16 Nov 1957 *John Norman Abell, yr son of Sir George Edmond Brackenbury Abell, KCIE, OBE, and has issue:

1d *Martin George [Martin Abell Esq, Foxcote Farm, Hillsburgh, Ontario N0B 1Z0, Canada]; *b* 16 June 1962; *m* 16 July 1994 *Nazare Albuquerque

2d *Anthony Philip Norman [Anthony Abell Esq, 41 Afghan Rd, London SW11]; *b* 17 Jan 1964; *m* 27 April 1996 *Alexandra, adopted dau of Sir John Richard Woodman Burbidge, 4th Bt (*qv*)

1d *Sarah Elizabeth [Mrs William Evans, 60 Portland Rd, London W11]; *b* 2 March 1959; *m* 1984 *William Mark Evans and has issue:

1e *Matthew George; *b* 1987

2e *Michael Timothy; *b* 1990

3e *Jonathan; *b* 1997

1e *Stephanie Susan; *b* 1989

3c *Julia Mary [Mrs Brian Leaver, 44 Ardross St, Applecross, WA 6153, Australia]; *b* 19 July 1942; *m* 1985 *Brian Edward Leaver

2b (cont.) Anthony Clifton-Brown *m* 2nd 16 Feb 1949 *Phyllis Adrienne (Bridget) (*d* 1977), 2nd dau of Francis Harvey, of Kyle, Co Wexford, and formerly w of Capt Alexander McGowan McCulloch, RN

1b Rhona; *b* 14 July 1901; *m* 23 June 1927 Lt-Col Sir Weston Cracroft-Amcotts, MC, DL, RE (*d* 1975), er s of Maj Frederick Augustus Cracroft-Amcotts, and *d* 25 Aug 1997, leaving:

1c *Rosemary Grace; *b* 17 April 1928; *m* 24 May 1952 Lt-Cdr Gervis Hugh Frere Frere-Cook, RN (ret) (*d* 1974), only s of R M O Cook and Mrs H A Hartley, of 62 Latymer Court, W6, and has issue:

1d *Simon Aubrey Cracroft; *b* 21 Feb 1955; *m* 1981 *Jennifer Jane Greenwood and has:

1e *Joanna Christine; *b* 1984

2e *Sarah Jane; *b* 1986

2d *David Bartle Cracroft; *b* 24 Jan 1957; *m* 1986 *Christine Margaret Strong and has:

1e *Hugh Leonard; *b* 1987

2e *Guy Weston; *b* 1989

3e *Piers Gervis; *b* 1993

1d *Jane Elizabeth Cracroft; *b* 17 Feb 1954; *m* 1979 *Charles Richard Ekin Pepys and has issue (*see* COTTENHAM, E)

2c *Marian Cicely [Mrs Thomas Micklem, Foxbridge Farm, Kirdford, W Sussex RH14 0LB]; *b* 13 Sept 1931; *m* 15 June 1957 *Thomas Charles Weguelin Micklem, only surv s of Maj Charles Micklem, DSO, JP, of Long Cross Ho, Chertsey, Surrey, and has issue:

1d *Jeremy Charles Cracroft; *b* 6 Feb 1961

1d *Philippa Rhona; *b* 24 Sept 1958; *m* 1986 (*divorce* 1992) Gary Maxwell Weiley

2d *Sylvia Diana; *b* 9 July 1964; *m* 1986 *Andrew Alistair Gavin Gow and has issue:

1e *Simeon Nathaniel Benjamin; *b* 1990

2e *Christopher Gavin Thomas; *b* 1996

3c *Bridget Katherine [Mrs Robert Cracroft-Eley, Hackthorn Hall, Lincoln LN2 3PQ]; *b* 29 Oct 1933; Ld Lt Lincs; *m* 31 Oct 1959 Robert Peel Charles Cracroft-Eley, DL (*d* 1996), er s of Charles Ryves Maxwell-Eley, OBE, of East Bergholt Place, East Bergholt, Suffolk, and has issue:

1d *Charles William Amcotts [Charles Cracroft-Eley Esq, Cliff House, Hackthorn, Lincs LN2 3PQ]; *b* 1963; *m* 1991 *Margaret E, only dau of Roger Lole, of Hermitage Farm, Wadborough, Worcs

1d *Annabel Louise Cracroft [Mrs Ross Jones, 153 Portland Rd, London W11]; *b* 1961; *m* 1987 *(Andrew Stewart) Ross Jones, est s of R H Jones, of London, and has issue:

1e *Felix Maxwell; *b* 1990

1e *Imogen Margaux; *b* 1993

4c *Penelope Sylvia; *b* 20 May 1938

3a Francis Clifton, CB (1919), CMG (1917), JP and DL Berks, V-Adml WW I (despatches), Order Redeemer and Mil Merit Greece, High Sheriff Berks 1931; *b* 10 July 1874; *m* 1st 14 Aug 1913 Violet (*d* 10 Feb 1952), dau of William Pitcairn Galton; *m* 2nd 2 July 1952 *Margaret Maud, dau of Samuel Crosby Halahan, of Littlecroft, Chiddingfold, Surrey, and formerly w of Philip Wood, and *dsp* 6 Sept 1963

4a DOUGLAS CLIFTON BROWN, 1st and last VISCOUNT RUFFSIDE (UK), of Hexham, Northumberland, so *cr* 14 Dec 1951, PC (1941), DL and JP Co Durham, Hon DCL Cambridge and Durham 1945, Hon Dr Caen 1948, Hon Col Northumberland Hus 1949, Maj 1st King's Dragoon Gds and Lt-Col and Brevet Col Northumberland Hus Yeo (TA), MP Hexham 1918–23 and 1924–51, Dep Chm Ways and Means Ctee 1938–43, Chm 1943–51, Dep Speaker H of C 1938–43, Speaker 1943–51, Hon Freeman and Liveryman Vintners' Co; Grand Cross Legn Honour; *b* 16 Aug 1879; *educ* Eton and Trin Coll Cambridge (BA 1901, MA 1905); *m* 24 June 1907 Violet Cicely Kathleen (*d* 17 Nov 1969), only dau of Frederick Eustace Arbuthnott Wollaston, DL, of Shenton Hall, Leics, and *dspm* 5 May 1958, when the Viscountcy expired, having had issue:

1b *AUDREY PELLEW, BARONESS HYLTON-FOSTER (*qv*)

5a Cedric Clifton; *b* 10 Dec 1887; *educ* Eton and Trin Coll Cambridge (BA 1909); Capt Sussex Yeo, Worcs Yeo and Gren Gds, JP Norfolk, High Sheriff 1941, Alderman Norfolk CC 1952, served WW I; *m* 30 April 1938 Mary Aymée Lilian, OBE (1960), JP (1968), CA 1958 Norfolk, Chm Dorking RDC 1968 and King's Lynn Dist Divnl Exec Educn 1965 (*d* 1980), dau of Rev John Arthur Labouchere, MA, and *d* 22 Oct 1968, leaving issue:

1b +Peter Cedric Clifton [Peter Brown Esq, Ballinamona, Cashel, Co Tipperary, Ireland]; *b* 20 Sept 1939; *educ* Eton; *m* 3 Aug 1968 *Petronelle Amy Mary, yr dau of Samuel Louis Grubb, of Beechmount, Fethard, Co Tipperary, and has issue:

1c +John Cedric Clifton; *b* 21 March 1970

2c +Louis Peter; *b* 21 Nov 1971

3c +Henry Samuel Clifton; *b* 21 March 1974

2b +Anthony John Clifton [Anthony Brown Esq, Perces, Greenstead Green, Halstead, Essex CO0 1RB]; *b* 11 Sept 1942; *educ* Eton; BSc; *m* 1st 2 Oct 1967 (*divorce* 1988) Françoise, dau of Meinrad Mooser, of Switzerland; m 2nd 1989 *Veronica Jane, est dau of Reginald Eric Stevens, of Willingdon, E Sussex, and has issue by 1st w:

1c +Douglas Alexander Clifton; *b* 3 July 1968

2c +Philippe Anthony Clifton; *b* 1975

1b *Ursula Mary Clifton; *b* 5 Jan 1941

1a Louisa Clifton; *b* 10 March 1871; *m* 24 April 1901 Alexander Balfour Williamson, 3rd s of Stephen Williamson, of Copley, Cheshire (*see* FORBES, L), and *d* 18 Nov 1956

2a Mildred Clifton; *b* 19 Feb 1876; *m* 8 Nov 1905 Charles George Ashburner Nix, of Free Chase, Warninglid, Sussex, only surv s of John Hennings Nix, of Tilgate, Crawley, Sussex, and *d* 4 April 1949, leaving issue. He *d* 8 March 1956

3a Elsie Clifton; *b* 9 Sept 1881; *m* 25 Nov 1909 Lt-Col Sir Evelyn Ridley Bradford, 2nd Bt (*qv*), and *d* 2 Dec 1958, leaving issue

4a Isla Clifton *b* 19 Dec 1883; *m* 1st 9 May 1911 Reginald George Henderson, 3rd s of Robert Henderson, of Sedgwick Park, Horsham. He *d* 29 March 1917 following war injuries. She *m* 2nd 31 Aug 1920 Col Charles Hemsley, DSO, late IA, son of Rev Charles Hemsley, of Bedford and Thurleigh, and *d* 5 Feb 1971. He *d* 23 Nov 1961

(3) ALEXANDER HARGREAVES (Sir), *cr* a Bt 1903 (*see* PIGOTT-BROWN, Bt)

(1) Louisa; *m* 18 Sept 1862 Alexander William Cobham, of Shinfield, Berks, Capt 44th and 24th Regts, est s of Alexander Cobham Cobham, of Shinfield, Berks, and *d* 18 Sept 1863. He *d* 13 May 1913

1 Grace; *m* 15 Feb 1831 John Hargreaves, of Broad Oak, Lancs, and Hall Barn, Bucks, and *d* 5 Jan 1849

Sir WILLIAM *d* 3 March 1864; his gs,

Sir William Richmond Brown, 2nd Bt, of Astrop, Northants, DL, High Sheriff 1873, Col 1st Bde Lancs Art Vol; *b* 16 Jan 1840; *m* 28 May 1862 Emily (*d* 8 July 1928), 2nd dau of Gen William T B Mountsteven, and *d* 10 May 1906, having had, with other issue:

1 **Sir Melville Richmond Brown, 3rd Bt**, Capt and Hon Maj 3rd Bn Devonshire Regt; *b* 13 Oct 1866; *m* 27 Feb 1906 (*divorce* 1931) Lilian Alice (Mabel), FLS, FRGS, FZS, FRAI 1923 (*d* 4 Oct 1946), est dau of Robert Roussel, of Rohais, Guernsey, and *dsp* 20 Feb 1944

2 Frederick Richmond, of Astrop and Llanfair, Caenarvs; *b* 28 Jan 1868; *m* 22 Nov 1900 Anne Luxmoore (*d* 30 Oct1943), dau of George John Dumville Lees, of Woodhill, Salop, and Okehampton Park, Devon, and *d* 29 Aug 1933, leaving issue:

(1) **Sir Charles Frederick Richmond Brown, 4th Bt**, TD, DL (N R Yorks 1962); *b* 6 Dec 1902; *educ* Eton; Capt Welsh Gds, Lt-Col cmdg 7th Bn Green Howards (TA) WW II; CA N R and N Yorks CC; *m* 1st 29 Nov 1933 (*divorce* 1948) Audrey (*d* 1996), 2nd dau of Hon Everard Baring (*see* REVELSTOKE, B), and had:

1a Sir GEORGE FRANCIS RICHMOND BROWN, **5th and present Bt**

1a *Jennifer Richmond; *b* 24 Dec 1934

2a *(Elizabeth) Maud Richmond [Mrs Guy Crawford, St Blanes, Dunblane, Perthshire]; *b* 7 Oct 1943; *m* 10 Nov 1970 *Guy M A Crawford, yst son of Col Mervyn Crawford, DSO, JP, of Dalgonar, Dunscore, Dumfries-shire, and has:

1b *George; *b* 1974

1b *Alice; *b* 1975

(1) (cont.) **Sir Charles** *m* 2nd 20 Nov 1951 (*divorce* 1968) Hon Gwendolen Carlis Meysey-Thompson (*d* 1989), yst dau of 1st and last Baron Knaresborough (*see* MEYSEY-THOMPSON, Bt); *m* 3rd 27 March 1969 Pauline Emily Gwyneth Mansel (*d* 1994), widow of Edward John Westgarth Hildyard, FSA, FRES, of Middleton Hall, Pickering, Yorks, and dau of Arden Henry William Llewelyn Morgan, and *d* July 1995

(2) Ralph Richmond, FSA (1953), F/Lt RAF WW II; *b* 18 March 1904; *educ* Eton and Trin Hall Cambridge; *d* unm 28 Feb 1975

(1) *Diana Sybil Richmond [Mrs Christopher Bacon, Ramsden Farm, Ebony, Tenterden, Kent]; *b* 4 Jan 1913; *m* 15 June 1940 Christopher Henry Bacon, 3rd s of Thomas Walter Bacon, of Ramsden Hall, Billericay (*see* BACON, Bt), and has issue

1 Alice Richmond, DGStJ; *m* 23 Nov 1904 George Hunter Garnett Garnett-Orme, of Hill Lodge, Pangbourne, Berks, and Greenfield, Buckden, nr Skipton-in-Craven, Yorks, and *d* 21 Jan 1933, leaving issue. He *d* 6 April 1957

2 Margaret Richmond; *b* 1876; *d* unm 7 Sept 1963

3 Dora Richmond; *m* 7 Jan 1913 Lt -Col Julian Lawrence Fisher, CMG, DSO, Roy Fus, s of Walter Fisher, of Amington Hall, Tamworth, and *d* 14 April 1971 aged 91, leaving issue. He *d* 1 May 1953

BROWNE-WILKINSON

Creation: B. (LP, UK) 1991.

THE BARON BROWNE-WILKINSON, of Camden in the London Borough of Camden (Sir Nicolas Christopher Henry Browne-Wilkinson, PC 1983) [The Rt Hon The Lord Browne-Wilkinson PC, House of Lords, London SW1A 0PW]; *b* 30 March 1930; *educ* Lancing and Magdalen Coll Oxford (BA); barrister Lincoln's Inn 1953, QC 1972, Bencher 1977, Jr Counsel to: Registrar of Restrictive Trading Agreements 1964–66, Attorney Gen in Charity matters 1966–72, DTI in bankruptcy 1966–72; Judge Courts of Appeal Jersey and Guernsey 1976–77, High Court Judge Chancery Div 1977–83, ktd 1977, Ld Justice of Appeal 1983–85, V-Chllr Supreme Court 1985–91, Ld of Appeal in Ordinary 1991–; Pres: Employment Appeal Tbnl 1981–83, Senate Inns of Court and the Bar 1984–86; Hon Fell: St Edmund Hall Oxford 1987, Magdalen Coll Oxford 1993; *m* 1st 1955 Ursula (*d* 1987), dau of Cedric de Lacy Bacon, and has issue:

1 *Adam; *b* 1957

2 *Simon; *b* (twin)1957

3 *Oliver; *b* 1962; *m* 1991*Carla R, dau of Charles Smith, of Hong Kong

1 *Henrietta; *b* 1960

2 *Martha; *b* 1964

The BARON BROWNE-WILKINSON *m* 2nd 1990 *Mrs Hilary Isabella Jane Tuckwell, dau of Prof James Wilfred Warburton

Lineage: Canon ARTHUR R BROWNE-WILKINSON; *m* Molly — and had:

NICOLAS CHRISTOPHER HENRY, *cr* a **Baron**

BROWNLOW

Arms: Erm. on a chevron sa. three fountains ppr. **Crest:** A lion's head erased sa., gorged with a collar paly wavy of six arg. and az. **Supporters:** Two lions regardant arg., gorged with collars paly wavy of six arg and az. **Motto:** *Esse quam videri* ('To be, rather than to seem'). **Creations:** Bt. (E) 29 Sept 1677, B. (GB) 20 May 1776.

THE 7TH BARON BROWNLOW OF BELTON, Co Lincoln, and a **Baronet** (Sir Edward John Peregrine Cust, Bt) [The Rt Hon The Lord Brownlow, La Maison des Prés, St Peter, Jersey JE3 7EL, CI]; *b* 25 March 1936 (HM EDWARD VIII stood sponsor); *s f* 1978; *educ* Eton; Lt Gren Gds 1954–56, High Sheriff Lincs 1978–79, memb Lloyd's 1962–88 and 1993–96, chm and md Harris and Dixon (Underwriting Agencies) 1976–82, dir Hand-in-Hand Fire and Life Insur Soc 1962–82, Ermitage Internat 1988–, Chm Cncl St J Jersey 1996–, OStJ 1997; *m* 31 Dec 1964 *Shirlie Edith, 2nd dau of John Paske Yeomans, of Manor Farm, Hill Croome, Upton-on-Severn, Worcs, and has issue:

1 +PEREGRINE EDWARD QUINTIN; *b* 9 July 1974

Lineage (of Cust): ROBERT CUST owned land at Pinchbeck, Lincs, 1479. His presumed descendant:

SAMUEL CUST, of Boston, Lincs; *m* Ann, dau of Richard Burrell, of Dowsby, Lincs, and *d* 5 March 1662/3, leaving:

Sir Richard Cust, 1st Bt (E), so *cr* 29 Sept 1677, of Pinchbeck; barrister, MP Lincs 1653 and Stamford 1679–81; *bapt* 23 June 1622; *m* 29 Dec 1644 Beatrice (*d* 1 April 1715), dau and heir of William Pury, of Kirton, Lincs, and had, with other surv issue:

1 Sir Pury Cust; *m* 1st 21 Aug 1678 Ursula, dau and heir of Edward Woodcock, of Newtimber, Sussex, and had, with other issue:

(1) RICHARD (Sir), **2nd Bt**

1 (cont.) Sir Pury Cust *m* 2nd Alice, dau and coheir of William Savile, of Newton, Lincs, and *dvp* 21 Feb 1698/9, having by her had issue:

(2) Savile Cockayne, of Cockayne Hatley, Beds; *dsp* 1772

Sir RICHARD *d* 30 Aug 1700; his gs,

Sir Richard Cust, 2nd Bt; *bapt* 30 Oct 1680; *m* 1717 Anne (*d* 29 Dec 1779), dau of Sir William Brownlow, 4th Bt (*see* below), and had, with other issue:

1 JOHN (Sir), **3rd Bt**

2 Francis Cockayne, KC, Counsel to Admlty and RN, also Cambridge U, MP Helston, Recorder Grantham; *dsp* 30 Nov 1791

3 Peregrine, London merchant, MP Bishopscastle 1761, Shoreham 1768 and Grantham 1774; *dsp* 2 Jan 1785

4 Richard (Very Rev), Chaplain H of C, Canon Ch Ch Oxford 1765, Dean Rochester 1779, Dean Lincoln; *m* 1767 Mary (*d* March 1791), dau of George Harris, DD, and *dsp* Oct 1783

Sir RICHARD *d* 25 July 1734; his est son,

Sir John Cust, 3rd Bt, PC (1768); *b* 29 Aug 1718, MP Grantham, Speaker H of C 1761–70; *m* 8 Dec 1743 Etheldred, dau and coheir of Thomas Payne, of Hough-on-the-Hill, Lincs, by Elizabeth, only dau of Martin Folkes, barrister, by Dorothy, dau and coheir of Sir William Hovel, and *d* 24 Jan 1770, leaving, with two daus (Anne, *m* 1777 Jacob Reynardson, of Holywell; Elizabeth, *m* 1770 Philip Yorke, of Erddig):

Sir Brownlow Cust, 4th Bt, and 1st Baron Brownlow of Belton, Co Lincoln (GB), so *cr* 20 May 1776 in recognition of his f's public service; *b* 3 Dec 1744; *educ* Eton and Corpus Christi Cambridge; MP (Tory) Ilchester 1768–74 and Grantham 1774–76, DCL Oxon 1773; *m* 1st 16 Oct 1770 Jocosa Katherina (*d* 11 Feb 1772), yst dau and coheir of Sir Thomas Drury, Bt, of Overstone, Northants, and had a dau (Ethelred Anne, *d* unm 7 Dec 1788); *m* 2nd 31 Aug 1775 Frances (*d* 13 April 1847), only child of Sir Henry Bankes, London Alderman, and *d* 25 Dec 1807, having by her had, with other issue:

1 JOHN CUST, **2nd Baron Brownlow of Belton** and 1st EARL BROWNLOW, also VISCOUNT ALFORD OF ALFORD, Co Lincoln (both UK), so *cr* 17 Nov 1815; *b* 19 Aug 1779; *educ* Eton and Trin Coll Cambridge (LLD 1835); MP (Tory) Clitheroe 1802–07, Ld Lt Lincs 1809–52, Recorder Boston 1820, DCL Oxon 1834, GCH 1834, Govr King's Coll London, Pres Roy Archaeological Inst 1841–49, FSA 1801, FRS 1805; *m* 1st 24 July 1810 Sophia (*d* 1814), 2nd dau and coheir of Sir Abraham Hume, 2nd Bt, and had issue:

(1) JOHN HUME CUST later HOME-CUST (by roy licence 12 Sept 1839 at request of his ggf Sir Abraham Hume, 1st Bt's cousin Mrs Elizabeth Home [sic]) later still EGERTON (roy licence 15 March 1849 on inheriting the huge estates of that family from the Dowager Countess of Bridgwater, whose late husb the 7th Earl had been his great-uncle), *Viscount Alford*; *b* 15 Oct 1812; *educ* Eton, Ch Ch Oxford and Magdalen Coll Cambridge; MP (C) Beds 1835–51, Col N Lincs Militia; *m* 10 Feb 1841 Lady Marian Margaret Compton, dau of 2nd Marquess of Northampton (*qv*), and *d* 3 Jan 1851, leaving issue:

1a JOHN WILLIAM SPENCER BROWNLOW (HOME-)CUST later EGERTON (roy licence 5 Sept 1853) later still EGERTON-CUST (roy licence 6 July 1863), **3rd Baron Brownlow of Belton** and 2nd EARL BROWNLOW; *b* 28 March 1842; *educ* Eton and Ch Ch Oxford; *d* unm 20 Feb 1867

2a ADELBERT WELLINGTON BROWNLOW (HOME-)CUST, **4th Baron Brownlow of Belton** and 3rd and last EARL BROWNLOW, GCVO (1921), VD, PC (1887), JP Salop, DL and JP Herts; *b* 19 Aug 1844; *educ* Eton; Lt Foot Gds 1836–66, MP (C) N Salop 1866–67, Parly Sec Local Govt Bd 1885–86, Paymaster-Gen 1887–89, Under-Sec War 1889–92, Pres Lincs TFA, Hon Col: Lincs Yeo, 4th Bn Lincs Regt and Herts Bn Beds Regt, cmdg Beds Vol Inf Bde 1892–1906, ADC to TM QUEEN VICTORIA 1897, EDWARD VII and GEORGE V, Ecclesiastical Commr 1872–1921, Tstee Nat Gallery; *m* 22 June 1868 Lady Adelaide Talbot (*d* 16 March 1917), yst dau of 18th Earl of Shrewsbury (*see* SHREWSBURY and WATERFORD, E), and *dsp* 17 March 1921, when the Earldom expired but the Barony and btcy passed to his cousin

(2) Charles Henry; *b* 27 Sept 1813; MP N Salop, Capt RHG; *m* 8 Sept 1842 Caroline Sophia (*d* 16 Oct 1887), est dau of Reginald George Macdonald, Ch of Clanranald, by Lady Caroline, dau of 2nd Earl of Mount Edgcumbe (*qv*), and *d* 23 May 1875, having had, with other issue:

1a Alice Marian CUST later PORCELLI-CUST; *b* 1 Dec 1845; *m* 9 Sept 1876 her first cousin Lt-Col Allan Roger Charles Porcelli, joined their names by roy licence 2 Dec 1893 and *d* 23 Oct 1919, leaving issue

(1) Sophia Frances; *b* 14 April 1811; *m* 10 Feb 1836 Christopher Tower, JP, DL, of Huntsmoor Park and Delaford Park, Iver, Bucks (*d* 3 March 1884), and *d* 21 Dec 1882, leaving issue

1 (cont.) **The 2nd Baron** (and 1st Earl) *m* 2nd 22 Sept 1818 Caroline (*d* 4 July 1824), 2nd dau of George Fludyer, of Ayston, Rutland, and by her had, with two other daus:

(2) Caroline Mary; *b* 25 Nov 1819, Ldy-in-Waiting to GRAND DUCHESS OF MECKLENBERG-STRELITZ; *d* unm 29 Aug 1898

(3) Katherine Anne; *b* 18 Nov 1822; *m* 1 Aug 1850 Viscount Cranley (*see* ONSLOW, E) and *d* 18 Oct 1885 aged 62, leaving issue

1 (cont.) The **2nd Baron** *m* 3rd 17 July 1828 Lady Emma Sophia Edgcumbe (*dsp* 28 Jan 1872), est dau of 2nd Earl of Mount Edgcumbe (*qv*), and *d* 15 Sept 1853

2 Henry Cockayne (Rev), of Cockayne Hatley, Beds; *b* 28 Sept 1780; MA, Canon Windsor; *m* 20 June 1816 Lady Anna Maria Needham (*d* 29 May 1866), est dau of 1st Earl of Kilmorey (*qv*), and *d* 19 May 1861, having had, with other issue:

(1) Henry Francis CUST later COCKAYNE-CUST (added with arms of COCKAYNE by roy licence), of Cockayne Hatley, Beds; *b* 15 Sept 1819; MP Grantham, Maj Shropshire Yeo, Capt 8th Hus; *m* 5 Aug 1852 Sara Jane (*d* 14 Sept 1867), 4th dau of Isaac Cookson, JP, of Meldon Park, Northumberland, and widow of Maj Sidney Robert Streatfeild, and *d* 5 April 1884, leaving:

1a Henry (Harry) John (COCKAYNE-)CUST, JP Lincs and Beds, DL Beds; *b* 10 Oct 1861; *educ* Trin Coll Cambridge (BA); MP Stamford 1890–95 and Bermondsey 1900–06, chm Centl Ctee Nat Patriotic Orgnsns 1914, ed *Pall Mall Gazette* 1892–96; *m* 11 Oct 1893 Emmeline Mary Elizabeth (*d* 29 Sept 1955), only dau of Sir William Welby-Gregory, 4th Bt (*see* WELBY, Bt), and *dspl* (*see* RUTLAND, D, for his supposititious issue) 2 March 1917

2a ADELBERT SALUSBURY, **5th Baron**

1a Lucy Anna Maria; *b* 6 July 1853; granted 24 Aug 1921 with her sisters rank of baron's daus; *m* 21 Feb 1881 Very Rev John Storrs, DD, Dean Rochester (*d* 29 Feb 1928), and *d* 26 May 1923, leaving issue

2a Marion Isabella; *b* 20 Aug 1854; *m* 20 April 1881 Brownlow Richard Christopher Tower, JP, of Ellesmere, Salop (*d* 18 May 1932), 2nd s of Christopher Tower, JP, DL, of Huntsmoor Park and Delaford Park, Iver, Bucks, and *d* 4 May 1939, having had issue

3a Violet Emily; *b* 22 July 1858; *d* unm 16 July 1941

4a Annette Katherine; *b* 17 April 1860; *m* 21 Feb 1887 Lt-Col William Frank Wheatley, VD (*d* 20 May 1923), of The Manor House, Little Gaddesden, Herts, and *d* 3 Oct 1932, leaving issue

(2) Robert Needham, JP London and Middx; *b* 24 Feb 1821; Hon LLD Edin, ICS, barrister; *m* 1st 10 May 1856 Maria Adelaide (*d* 17 Jan 1864), dau of Very Rev Hon Henry Lewis Hobart (*see* BUCKINGHAMSHIRE, E), and had, with other issue:

1a Robert Henry Hobart, JP London; *b* 13 May 1861; *educ* Magdalen Coll Oxford (MA); Alderman Hampstead BC 1935, YMCA WW I (medal); *m* 25 Oct 1906 Cornelia Octavia (*d* 4 March 1928), dau of William Henry Haggerty, of St Louis, Mo., and widow of John Roscoe Peacock, of St Louis, and *dsp* 19 July 1940

1a Albinia Lucy; *b* 18 Oct 1857; *m* 2 April 1881 George Edward Wherry, MA, MCh Camb, FRCS; Lt-Col RAMC (*d* 12 Aug 1928), and *d* 4 March 1929, leaving issue

2a Maria Eleanor Vere; *b* 30 Sept 1862; FRGS; *d* unm 2 Jan 1958

(2) (cont.) Robert Cust *m* 2nd 28 Dec 1865 Emma (*d* 20 Aug 1867), est dau of Rev Edward Carlyon, Rector Dibden, Hants, and by her had issue:

3a Emma Carlyon; *b* 20 Aug 1867; *d* 27 Aug 1868

(2) (cont.) Robert Cust *m* 3rd 11 Nov 1868 Elizabeth Dewar (*d* 3 May 1910), only dau of J Mathews, and *d* 27 Oct 1909, having by her had issue:

4a Anna Maria Elizabeth; *b* 10 June 1870; *m* 11 Dec 1917 Maj Henry Meredith Leaf, DSO, RMA (*d* 23 April 1931), s of Frederick Leaf, and *dsp* 20 Oct 1959

(3) Reginald John (Sir); *b* 25 Sept 1828; MA Cantab, barrister, Ch Commr WI Incumbered Estates Court 1887–92; *m* 13 Dec 1855 Lady Elizabeth Caroline Bligh (*d* 10 April 1914), er dau of 5th Earl of Darnley (*qv*), and *d* 11 June 1913, having had, with other issue:

1a Lionel Henry (Sir), KCVO (1927, CVO 1914); *b* 25 Jan 1859; *educ* Trin Coll Cambridge (Litt D); FSA, Surveyor King's Pictures, Life Tstee Shakespeare's Birthplace, Keeper, Dir and Sec Nat Portrait Gallery 1895–1909, Gentleman Usher to TM EDWARD VII and GEORGE V 1901–27, Extra Gentleman Usher 1928, KGStJ; *m* 16 July 1895 Hon Sybil Lyttelton (*d* 2 Oct 1934), dau of 4th Baron Lyttelton (*see* COBHAM, V), and *d* 12 Oct 1929, leaving issue:

1b (Lionel George) Archer (Sir), ktd 1959, CBE (1954, OBE 1939); *b* 6 June 1896; *educ* Eton; Col RA, WW I (despatches), WW II (despatches), ADC to HC Palestine 1921–23, Dist Offr Jerusalem and Jaffa 1920–28, Priv Sec to HC 1928–32, Assist Sec Govt Palestine 1929, Priv Sec to Govr N Rhodesia 1932–34, Sec-Gen Roy Cwlth Soc 1938–58, OStJ; *m* 16 July 1925 Margaret Violet Louisa (*m* 2nd 6 Jan 1975, as his 2nd w, 5th Viscount Templeton (*see* 1970 edn); *d* 1988), est dau of Lt-Col Henry Arthur Clowes, 1st Life Gds, and *d* 22 May 1962, leaving issue:

1c Christopher Ivo Henry; *b* 17 July 1930; *educ* Eton and Trin Coll Cambridge (BA); slr 1958; *d* 1980

1c *Elizabeth Jemima Mary [Mrs Jack Benn, 28 St Mary's Mead, Witan Way, Witney, Oxon OX8 6EZ]; *b* 10 May 1926; *m* 8 Dec 1947 Jack Musson Benn (*d* 1992), s of Hugh Benn, and has issue:

1d *Anthony Christopher; *b* 19 Sept 1948

2d *Michael Robert; *b* 10 March 1950; *m* 1st 1977 (*divorce* 1986) Zvia Silverman, of Israel, and has issue:

1e *Shandy; *b* 1977

2d (cont.) Michael Benn *m* 2nd 1992 *Bridene Forest, of Melbourne, Australia, and has further issue:

2e *James Edward; *b* 1993

1e *Samantha; *b* 1996

1d *Elizabeth Philippa [Mrs Istvan de Ujfalussy, Greenacres, New Rd, Shiplake, Henley, Oxon, RG9 3LA]; *b* 1 Sept 1952; *m* 1970 *Istvan Benedek de Ujfalussy and has issue:

1e *Nicholas; *b* 1981

1e *Catherine; *b* 1970; *m* 1996 *Gareth Griffiths

2e *Louisa; *b* 1972

3e *Andrea; *b* 1984

2c *Margaret Sybil [Mrs Oliver Ziegler, Hightown Farm, Hightown Hill, Ringwood, Hants BH24 3HE]; *b* 27 Jan 1928; *m* 19 July 1950 *(Paul) Oliver Ziegler, er s of Maj Colin Louis Ziegler, DSO, JP, DL, RA, and has issue:

1d *Adam Charles [Adam Ziegler Esq, The Corner House, Forest Edge Rd, Crow Hill, Ringwood, Hants]; *b* 26 Oct 1952; *educ* Eton; *m* 1st 1974 (*divorce* 1979) Christine Margaret Codling, of Ibsley, Hants, and has issue:

1e *Nathaniel Oliver; *b* 7 May 1977

1d (cont.) Adam Ziegler *m* 2nd 1984 *Trudi Lynette, dau of Clayton William John Burt, and by her has:

1e *Amy Louise; *b* 23 Dec 1983

2e *Joanna Margaret; *b* 8 Feb 1986

2d *William James Archer [William Ziegler Esq, Lords Oak Cottage, Landford, Salisbury, Wilts]; *b* 5 Aug 1956; *m* 1979 *Sarah Elizabeth, er dau of Cdr Ian Rochfort Johnston, RN (*see* VERNON, B), and has:

1e *Polly Laura; *b* 23 March 1983

2e *Daisy Alice; *b* 15 March 1985

3e *Harriet Louise; *b* 3 Feb 1988

1a Evelyn Georgiana; *b* 24 Sept 1857; *m* 30 April 1879 Hon Arthur Lowther Pelham, yst s of 3rd Earl of Chichester (*qv*), and *d* 21 Jan 1937

2a Beatrice Frances; *b* 22 May 1861; *d* unm 11 July 1948

(1) Eleanor Katherine; *b* 29 Jan 1823; *m* 19 Aug 1856 Walter Scott Seton-Karr, ICS (*d* 22 Nov 1910), and *d* 5 June 1903, leaving issue

(2) Georgiana Anne; *b* 8 Feb 1825; *m* 31 July 1865 Rev Isaac Taylor, LLD, Rector Settrington, Canon York (*d* 18 Oct 1901), and *d* 14 March 1907, leaving issue

3 William; *b* 23 Jan 1787; barrister, Commr Customs; *m* 8 July 1819 Sophia (*d* 18 Jan 1884 aged 94), dau of Thomas Newnham, and *d* 3 March 1845, having had, with other issue:

(1) William Purey; *b* 8 Aug 1821; Capt IA, Equerry to HRH THE DUCHESS OF CAMBRIDGE; *m* 9 May 1844 Emma Matilda (*d* 30 March 1852), only child of William Chaplin, Commr Deccan, and *d* 11 Feb 1865, having had issue:

1a Emma Sophia Ada; *d* 1849

(2) Arthur Perceval CUST later PUREY-CUST (Very Rev); *b* 21 Feb 1828; DD, Dean York 1880–1916, Precentor 1908–16; *m* 6 June 1854 Lady Emma Bess Bligh (*d* 27 July 1917), yr dau of 5th Earl of Darnley (*qv*), and *d* 23 Dec 1916, leaving issue:

1a William Arthur (Rev); *b* 25 March 1855; *educ* Eton and Ch Ch Oxford (BA 1878, MA 1892); Preb Lincoln 1917; *m* 14 Feb 1882 Lucy Caroline (*d* 3 Oct 1916), dau of Lt-Gen Sir William Francis Drummond Jervois, GCMG, CB, and *d* 28 Sept 1938, leaving issue:

1b Richard Brownlow, CBE (1942), DSO (1918), MC; *b* 22 April 1888; *educ* Eton; Col RA, T/Brig cmdg 35th AA Group TA 1938, WW I (wounded, despatches); *m* 27 Sept 1928 Gertrude Patricia Zoë (*d* 1993), only dau of Francis Julian Laurence Birch, and *d* 6 Feb 1958, leaving issue:

1c +John Richard [John Purey-Cust Esq, Campion Rd, 4 RDGore, New Zealand 9700]; *b* 30 June 1934; *educ* Eton and Edin U (BSc Forestry)

1c *Veronica Caroline [Mrs Hermann Portmann, C12, Site 3, RR7, Vernon, BC V1T 7Z3, Canada]; *b* 16 April 1937; *m* 14 June 1969 *Hermann Portmann, of Vancouver, and has issue:

1d *Robert Purey; *b* 1974

1d *Heidi Patricia; *b* 1976

1b Alice Margaret; *b* 15 Dec 1882; *d* unm 28 June 1962

2b Mary Adeilade; *b* 28 Aug 1884; *d* unm 19 Dec 1959

3b Gwendolen Ellora; *b* 25 Oct 1886; *m* 4 May 1927 Brig-Gen Arthur David Musgrave, DSO, RFA (*d* 12 Sept 1931), s of Sir Anthony Musgrave, GCMG

4b Honoria Katharine; *b* 2 Dec 1892

2a Herbert Edward (Sir), KBE (1919), CB (1911); *b* 26 Feb 1857; Adml, Hydrographer Navy 1909–14, Cdre RNR 1914–19, E Sudan 1884–5, Boer War 1899–1900, WW I; *m* 29 May 1895 Alice Ella (*d* 12 June 1949), est dau of George Stuart Hepburn, of Smeaton, Australia, and *d* 11 Nov 1938, having had issue:

1b Arthur John, Sub-Lt RN WW I (despatches); *b* 8 Aug 1897; *ka* 17 Oct 1917

1b Marjorie (Peggy); *b* 12 Oct 1905; celebrated as the childhood sweetheart of Sir John Betjeman through his mention of her in his autobiography *Summoned By Bells*; *d* 22 March 1995

1a Ella Margaret; *m* 21 July 1891 Col Wilford Neville Lloyd, CB, CVO, TD, JP, Standard Bearer Gentlemen-at-Arms, RA (*d* 15 Feb 1935), s of Col Robert Clifford Lloyd, of Lossett, Co Cavan, and *d* 22 Dec 1937, leaving issue

4 Peregrine Francis, Lt-Col; *b* 13 Aug 1791; *m* 1st 9 Oct 1823 Lady Isabella Mary Montagu Scott, 3rd dau of 4th Duke of Buccleuch and Queensberry (*qv*), and had with other issue:

(1) John Francis; *b* 17 June 1825; Lt-Col Gren Gds; *m* 31 Jan 1861 Lady Florence Harriet Lascelles, 4th dau of 3rd Earl of Harewood (*qv*), and *d* 24 Oct 1903

(1) Charlotte Isabella; *m* 8 Sept 1859 Col John Clark Kennedy, CB, of Knockgray (*d* 18 Dec 1867), and *d* 24 Nov 1914, leaving issue

4 (cont.) Lt-Col The Hon Peregrine Cust *m* 2nd 15 Jan 1833 Hon Sophia Townshend (*dsp* 6 Dec 1852), dau of 2nd Viscount Sydney; *m* 3rd 20 Aug 1860 Frances (*d* 16 May 1869), dau of Charles Steer and widow of 5th Earl of Albemarle (*qv*), and *d* 15 Sept 1873

5 Sir EDWARD CUST, 1st Bt (UK), so *cr* 26 Feb 1876, of Leasowe Castle, Cheshire (*see* 1931 edn)

1 Anne; *m* 1825 Sir William Fowle Middleton, Bt, and *d* his widow 8 May 1867

The 4th BARON's cousin,

ALDELBERT SALUSBURY COCKAYNE CUST, **5th Baron Brownlow of Belton**, JP, DL (Lincs); *b* 14 Sept 1867; Mayor Grantham 1924–25, Somerset LI 1888–1908, Hon Col 4th Bn Lincs Regt, Maj Res Offrs, WW I; *m* 5 Oct 1895 Maud (*d* 19 Sept 1936), dau of Capt S Buckle, RE, and had issue:

1 PEREGRINE FRANCIS ADELBERT, **6th Baron**

1 Elizabeth Barbara; *b* 24 Aug 1896; *d* 22 Feb 1913

2 Sarah Marie Adelaide; *b* 3 Jan 1906; *m* 20 Sept 1930 Edward Jan Hoos (*d* 22 Sept 1962), only s of Marten Hoos, of The Hague, and Manton, Rutland, and had issue:

(1) *Peter Hendrik Peregrine; *b* 8 Nov 1937; *educ* Stowe; *m* 30 March 1968 (*divorce* 1975) Caroline Fleur (*m* 3rd 1975, as his 2nd w, Lt-Cdr Sir Robert Hobart, Bt; *qv*), yr dau of Col Henry Monckton Vatcher, MC, by Beryl Methwold, est dau of Francis Arthur Walrond, of Thorne Court, Bury St Edmunds, Suffolk, and widow of 11th Duke of Leeds (*see* 1963 edn)

(1) *Henrietta Sarah Angenis; *b* 10 Jan 1933; *m* 23 April 1955 David Ralph Davies-Cooke, BA, yr s of Lt-Col Philip Ralph Davies-Cooke, CB, TD, JP, DL, of Gwysaney, Mold, and Owston Hall, Doncaster (*see* COOKE, Bt), and has issue

The 5th BARON *d* 19 April 1927; his son,

PEREGRINE FRANCIS ADELBERT CUST, **6th Baron Brownlow of Belton**, JP (1924), DL (Lincs 1929); *b* 27 April 1899; *educ* Eton and RMC Sandhurst; Ld Lt and Custos Rotulorum Lincs 1936–50, Mayor Grantham 1934, Ld-in-Waiting to HM EDWARD VIII 1936, Lt Res Offrs, Gren Gds, WW I, ADC to GOC London Dist 1922–23, Adj 3rd Bn Gren Gds 1923–26, S/Ldr RAFVR WW II, PPS to Min Aircraft Prodn 1940–41; *m* 1st 18 Oct 1927 Katherine Hariot (*d* 27 Nov 1952), yr dau of Brig-Gen Sir David Alexander Kinloch, 11th Bt, CB, MVO (*see* KINLOCH, Bt, of Gilmerton), and had issue:

1 David Peregrine Henry; *b* 9 March 1930; *d* 15 March 1931

2 EDWARD JOHN PEREGRINE CUST, **7th and present Baron Brownlow of Belton**

1*Caroline Elizabeth Maud [The Hon Mrs Partridge, Welland House, Weston by Welland, Market Harborough LE16 8HS]; *b* 5 Oct 1928; Mayoress Grantham 1950–51; *m* 15 May 1954 (*divorce* 1973) John Arthur Partridge, only s of Claude Partridge, and has issue:

(1) *Frank David Peregrine [Frank Partridge Esq, 7 Thurloe Sq, SW7 2TA]; *b* 14 Sept 1955; *m* 1982 *Susan Anne, yr dau of Brig Charles Hince, of Stretton Ho, Benington, Herts, and has issue:

1a *Charlotte Iris; *b* 1985

2a *Annabel Lucy; *b* 1987

3a *Lucy Marie; *b* 1989

(2) *Claude Edward; *b* 20 Aug 1962

(1) *Sophia Josephine; *b* 12 May 1969; *m* 1993 *Anthony John Waltham, er s of Donald Waltham, of Fleet, Lincs, and has:

1a *Helen Sarah; *b* 1995

The **6th Baron** *m* 2nd 10 Dec 1954 Dorothy (*d* 11 May 1966), yr dau of Thomas Sarsfield Kent Power, of Norfolk, Va., and formerly w of (a) Harry Ester Reynolds Hall, (b) 2nd Earl Beatty (qv) and (c) John Gordon Baragwanath; *m* 3rd 14 May 1969 Leila Joan (*d* 5 May 1983), dau of Maj Philip Guy Reynolds, DSO, 3rd Dragoon Gds, widow of 2nd Baron Manton (*qv*) and previously w of John Dane Player, and *d* 28 July 1978

Lineage (of Brownlow): RICHARD BROWNLOW, of Kirby Underwood, Lincs; Prothonotary Court Common Pleas *temp* ELIZABETH I and JAMES I; *m* Katharine, dau of John Page, of Wembley, and *d* 1638, leaving:

1 Sir JOHN BROWNLOW(E), 1st and last Bt (E), so *cr* 26 July 1641, of Belton; *b c* 1594; *educ* St Mary Hall Oxford; Sheriff Lincs 1639–40 and 1665, indicted for high treason Grantham 1643 from which it can be inferred he was a royalist in the Civil War; *m* Alice, 2nd dau and eventual heir of Sir John Pulteney, of Misterton, Leics, and *dsp* 23 Nov 1679 when the btcy expired

2 Sir WILLIAM BROWNLOW(E), 1st Bt (E), so *cr* 27 July 1641, of Gt Humby, Lincs; *b c* 1595; *educ* St Mary Hall Oxford; Parliamentarian Civil War, MP Lincs 1653; *m* by 1624 Elizabeth, dau and coheir of William Duncombe, London haberdasher, and *d* 1666, leaving, with a dau (Elizabeth, *m* Sir Charles Hussey Bt):

(1) Sir RICHARD BROWNLOW, 2nd Bt, of Gt Humby; *m* Elizabeth, dau of John Freke, of Ewern Courtney, Dorset, and *d* 30 Aug 1668, leaving:

1a Sir JOHN BROWNLOW, 3rd Bt, of Gt Humby; b 26 June 1659; inheritd the Belton estates of his great-unc Sir John, 1st and last Bt of the 26 July 1641 *cr*, Sheriff Lincs 1688–89, MP Grantham 1689–90, 1690–95 and 1695–97; *m* 27 March 1676 Alice, dau of Richard Sherard, of Lobthorpe, Lincs, and sis of Sir John Sherard, 1st Bt, and *dspm* 16 July 1697, leaving:

1b Elizabeth; b 18 May 1681; *m* 19 Sept 1699, as his 2nd w, 6th Earl of Exeter (*see* EXETER, M) and *d* 28 Nov 1723, leaving issue

2b Alicia; *b* 1684; *m c* 8 July 1703, as his 2nd w, 2nd Earl of Guilford (*qv*) and *d* 22 Aug 1727, leaving issue

3b Jane; *m* June 1711 2nd Duke of Ancaster (*see* WILLOUGHBY DE ERESBY, B) and *d* 26 Aug 1736, leaving issue

4b Eleanor; *m* her cousin 1st and last Viscount Tyrconnel (*see* below) and *dsp* 11 Sept 1730

2a Sir WILLIAM BROWNLOW, 4th Bt, of Belton and Gt Humby; *b* 5 Nov 1665; MP Peterborough 1689–90, 1690–95 and 1695–98 and Bishop's Castle 1698–1700; *m* 1st Dorothy (*d* by May 1700), est dau and coheir of Sir Richard Mason, of Sutton, Surrey; *m* 2nd Henrietta — and *d* 6 March 1700/1, having by his 1st w had, with other issue:

1b Sir JOHN BROWNLOW, 5th and last Bt, and 1st and last VISCOUNT TYRCONNEL, so *cr* 23 June 1718, as also BARON CHARLEVILLE, Co Cork (both I), KB (1725), of Belton and Humby; MP Grantham 1713–15 and 1722–41 and Lincs 1715–22; *m* 1st his cousin Eleanor, dau of Sir John Brownlow, 3rd Bt; *m* 2nd 24 Jan 1731/2 Elizabeth, dau of William Cartwright, of Marnham, Notts, and *dsp* 27 Feb 1754 when all his titles expired

1b ANNE; *m* **Sir Richard Cust, 2nd Bt** (*see* above)

BROWNRIGG

Arms: Arg. a lion rampant-guardant sa., grasping in the dexter paw a sword, pommel and hilt or, thereon a serpent entwined ppr., between three crescents gu., and as an honourable augmentation (granted by GEORGE IV 23 March 1822) a chief embattled vert, thereon a representation of the sceptre of the King of Kandy or, and the banner of the said king, being gu. within a bordure, with a ray of the sun issuing from each angle, a lion passant gold, holding a sword ppr. in saltire, the whole ensigned with a representation of the crown of the kingdom of Kandy, also ppr. **Crest:** 1 (of honourable augmentation) A demi-Kandian ppr., the body vested arg. and belted or, cap gold, in the dexter hand a sword and in the sinister a representation of the Kandian crown also ppr., 2 A mural crown or, theron a sword erect, entwined by a serpent vert. **Motto:** *Virescat vulnere virtus* ('Valour strengthens from a wound'). **Creation:** Bt (UK) 9 March 1816.

SIR NICHOLAS GAWEN BROWNRIGG, 5TH BT [Sir Nicholas Brownrigg Bt, PO Box 548, Ukiah, CA 95482, USA]; *b* 22 Dec 1932; *s* gf 1939; *educ* Stanford U California (BA 1957); USNR 1953–55, Chase-Manhatten Bank New York 1957–59; *m* 1st 4 April 1959 (*divorce* 1965) Linda Louise, dau of Jonathan B Lovelace, of Beverly Hills, and has issue:

1 +MICHAEL GAWEN [Michael Brownrigg, c/o US Dept of State, 2100 C St NW, Washington, DC 20520, USA]; *b* 11 Oct 1961; US For Serv 1985–; *m* 19– *Dr Margaret Dillon, dau of Dr Clay Burchell, and has issue:

(1) +Nicholas James; *b* 7 July 1993

1 *Sylvia Alderyn; *b* 16 Dec 1964

Sir NICHOLAS *m* 2nd 1971 *Valerie Ann, dau of Julian A Arden, of Livonia, Michigan

Lineage: HENRY BROWNRIGG, of Yerton, Cumberland; had:

THOMAS BROWNRIGG, of Loggan, Manor of Wingfield, Co Wexford; *d* Oct 1696, leaving, with a dau (Alice, *m* Thomas Constable, of Loggan):

HENRY BROWNRIGG, of Wingfield; *m* Joan (*d* 1740), dau of Jeremiah Symes, of Middleton, Co Wexford, and *d* 1723, having had, with seven daus and two other sons:

1 Thomas, of Wingfield; *m* Mary, dau of Benjamin Bennett, of Inch, Co Kildare, and had two daus and six sons, of whom:

(1) Henry, of Wingfield; *m* Katherine, dau of Jeremiah Walsh, of Torney, Co Dublin, and was ancestor of the BROWNRIGGs of Wingfield, now *extinct*

(2) John, ancestor of the BROWNRIGGs of Moneylawn and Tomgar, Co Wexford; *b* 1729; *educ* Trin Coll Dublin (BA 1750)

2 John, of Tubberpatrick, Co Wicklow; *m* Mary, dau of — Eliakim, of Studholme, Co Dublin, and had, with a yr s:

(1) Henry, of Rockingham, Co Wicklow; *m* 5 Oct 1753 Mary (*d* 1819), dau of Michael Alcock, of Norwich, and had, with other issue:

1a ROBERT (Sir), **1st Bt**

2a Thomas, Gen; *m* 16 July 1794 Anne, dau of Robert Shearman, of Kilcrean, Co Kilkenny, and *d* May 1826, leaving, with other issue:

1b Henry John (Sir), KB, CB, Inspr-Gen RIC; *b* 18 June 1798; *m* 1822 Elizabeth (*d* 23 Jan 1880), dau of Rev Thomas Cooke, and *d* 26 Nov 1873, having had, with other issue:

1c Quin John; *b* 20 Jan 1832; Co Inspr RIC; *m* 24 April 1861 Anne (*d* 9 Oct 1905), dau of William Chaine, and *d* 2 Sept 1907, having had, with other issue:

1d Herbert George; *b* 3 May 1864; Dist Inspr RIC; *m* 6 April 1906 Letitia Bedella (*d* 3 Sept 1967), dau of Thomas Hope and widow of Dr A Johnson, of Westport, Co Mayo, and *d* 31 Oct 1953, leaving issue:

1e Mildred Ann; *m* 14 Dec 1946 Matthew Righton Webb, est s of Matthew Righton Webb, JP, DL, FSA

2e Edith Dorothy; *m* 21 Oct 1935 William Geoffrey Iliffe (*d* 1958), only s of William Coker Iliffe (*see* ILIFFE, B), and *d* 28 June 1956, leaving issue

HENRY BROWNRIGG *d* 4 Dec 1793; his 2nd son,

Sir Robert Brownrigg, 1st Bt (UK), so *cr* 9 March 1816, GCB; *b* 8 Feb 1758; Gen, Col 9th Foot, Govr Landguard Fort, Govr Ceylon 1812; *m* 1st 8 April 1783 Elizabeth Catherine (*d* 14 April 1804), 5th dau of William Lewis, of Cornwall, Jamaica, and had issue:

1 Robert James; *b* 23 Dec 1790; Lt-Col; *m* 9 July 1816 Emma, dau of Maj-Gen Colebrooke Nisbet, and *d* 10 May 1822, leaving, with other issue:

(1) **Sir Robert William Colebrook Brownrigg, 2nd Bt**; *b* 29 July 1817; *d* 6 Aug 1882

(2) HENRY MOORE (Sir), **3rd Bt**

1 Katherine; *m* 2 Oct 1811 Maj-Gen Sir John Ross, KCB, and *d* 1 Aug 1834

Sir Robert *m* 2nd 27 June 1818 Sophia (*d* 25 April 1937), dau of Rev Alexander Bissett, DD, and *d* 27 May 1833

The 2nd Bt's bro,

Sir Henry Moore Brownrigg, 3rd Bt; *b* 17 Oct 1819; 52nd Regt; *m* 12 Feb 1863 Ada Cicely Georgiana (*d* 17 Feb 1911), dau of Sir John Hesketh Lethbridge, 3rd Bt (*qv*), of Sandhill Park, and had issue:

1 Henry Ernest; *b* 28 Aug 1863; *d* unm 20 Oct 1882

2 DOUGLAS EGREMONT ROBERT (Sir), **4th Bt**

1 Ada; *m* 14 Jan 1892 M Drury Lavin, of Heatherden, Bucks (*d* 24 Nov 1902), and *d* 26 Oct 1931, leaving issue

2 Beatrice Evans; *m* 18 March 1885 Charles Evan Davies Morgan-Richardson, of Morgenau, Rhoshil, Pembs (*d* 27 Sept 1913), and *d* 15 May 1927, leaving issue

Sir HENRY *d* 28 Jan 1900; his 2nd son,

Sir Douglas Egremont Robert Brownrigg, 4th Bt, CB (1918); *b* 25 July 1867; R-Adml, Hon V-Pres INA, Naval Attaché Tokyo 1910–12, Ch Naval Censor Admlty 1914–19, Offr Legn Honour, American DSM; *m* 18 Nov 1896 Beatrice (*d* 17 Jan 1952), dau of Sir Cecil Clementi-Smith, PC, GCMG, and *d* 14 Feb 1939, having had:

1 Robert Cecil; *b* 8 Aug 1903; *d* 19 Jan 1907

2 Gawen Egremont; *b* 15 Jan 1911; *m* 10 Sept 1931 (*divorce* 1936) Baroness Lucia von Borosini (*m* 2nd 1936 (*divorce* 1941) John Burnham; *m* 3rd 1941 (*divorce* 1957) Cdr Edmund Lyford Engel, USNR; *m* 4th 19– Harry Albert Batten (*d* 1966)), only dau of Baron Victor von Borosini, and *d* 8 Aug 1938, leaving issue:

(1) Sir NICHOLAS GAWEN BROWNRIGG, **5th and present Bt**

1 Juliet Teresa; *b* 9 April 1908; *m* 1st 12 Nov 1929 (*divorce*1936) Kenneth George Lampson, 2nd s of Alfred Curtis Lampson; *m* 2nd 24 Oct 1936 Sydney Victor Hine, only s of Victor Hine, and *d* 30 Jan 1947

BRUCE, Bt, of Downhill

Arms: Or on a saltire gu. a harp of the field, stringed arg., on a chief of the 2nd a canton arg., charged with a lion rampant az. **Crest:** A lion passant az., holding in his dexter paw a trefoil slipped vert. **Motto:** *Fuimus* ('We have been'). **Creation:** Bt. (UK) 29 June 1804.

SIR HERVEY JAMES HUGH BRUCE, 7TH BT, of Downhill, Co Londonderry [Maj Sir Hervey Bruce Bt, PO Box 19, Van Reenen 3372, Natal, S Africa]; *b* 4 Sept 1952; *s* f 1971; *educ* Eton and Mons OCS; Maj Gren Gds; *m* 1st 1979 (*divorce* 1991) Charlotte Sara Jane, er dau of John Temple Gore, of Bridgefoot, Spedham, Midhurst, W Sussex (*see* EGLINTON and WINTON, E), and has issue:

1 +HERVEY HAMISH PETER; *b* 20 Nov 1986

1 *Laura Crista; *b* 1984

Sir HERVEY *m* 2nd 1992 *Joanna, yst dau of Frank Pope, of Tavistock, Devon, and by her has:

2 +A son

Lineage: PATRICK BRUCE, of Newton, yr bro of Sir William Bruce of Stenhouse, 1st Bt (*qv*), left, with an er s (William, of Newton; f of Alexander; f of William Bruce of Newton, MD, who *m* Janet, dau of Col Henry Bruce, 13th of Clackmannan, and had a ggdau who *m* 4th Earl of Airlie, *qv*)

Rev MICHAEL BRUCE, Min of Killinchy, Co Down; *m* 1659 Jean, dau of Robert Bruce, of Kinnaird (*k* Naseby 1645) and sis of Col Robert Bruce, Life Gds, and had:

Rev JAMES BRUCE, Min of Killeleagh; *m* 1685 Margaret, dau of Lt-Col James Trail, of Tolychin, by Mary, dau of James Hamilton, Viscount Clandeboye (*see* DUFFERIN AND CLANEBOYE, B), and *d* 1726, leaving, with nine other children (including an er s, Michael, ancestor of the BRUCEs of Benburb, Co Tyrone, and Norton Hall, Glos):

Rev PATRICK BRUCE, Min of Killeleagh; *b* 11 April 1692; *m* 1718 Margaret, dau of James Hamilton, of Ladyland, Ayrshire (ancestor of the HAMILTONs of Craiglaw), and had an est s:

JAMES BRUCE, of Killeleagh; *b* 1720; *m* 1762 Henrietta, yst dau of Rev Hon H Hervey Aston, DD (4th s of 1st Earl of Bristol (*see* BRISTOL, M), by Catherine, sis and heiress of Sir T Aston, Bt), and had issue:

1 HENRY HERVEY ASTON (Sir), **1st Bt**

2 Sir STEWART BRUCE, 1st and last Bt (UK), so *cr* 24 Dec 1812; Gentleman Usher Dublin Castle, Genealogist Order of St Patrick; *m* 18 Oct 1838 Emma (*m* 2nd 18 Oct 1849 Bernard Ernest Jules de Koetteritz, Col Russian Imperial Gd, s of Gen de Koetteritz, of Leipsig), dau of James Ramsbottom, of Clewer Lodge, Windsor, and *dsp* 19 March 1841

1 Frideswid; *m* 1781 Daniel Mussenden, of Larchfield, Co Down, and *d* 1785, leaving issue

The er son,

Rev Sir Henry Hervey Aston Bruce, 1st Bt, so *cr* 29 June 1804, of Down Hill (UK); *m* 10 Nov 1786 Letitia (*d* 11 April 1816), dau of Rev Dr Henry Barnard and gdau of William Barnard, Bp Derry, by Mary, dau of Stratford Canning, of Garvagh, and had, with two other s and six daus:

1 JAMES ROBERTSON (Sir), **2nd Bt**

2 Henry William (Sir), KCB, of Ballyscullion, Co Londonderry, Adml; *b* 2 Feb 1792; *m* 1st 9 Feb 1822 Jane (*d* 22 June 1830), 2nd dau of Adml Hon Sir Alexander Forester Cochrane, GCB (*see* DUNDONALD, E), and had, with other issue:

(1) Henry Stewart Beresford; *b* 1824; DL, JP, Lt-Col 2nd Lancs Militia; *m* 1st 1846 Marriette (*d* 18 Nov 1886), dau of John Hill, JP, of Bellaghy Castle, Co Londonderry, and had, with other issue:

1a Henry Dalrymple; *b* 1848; *m* 1st 1878 Emma (*d* 1885), dau of W Whitcher, of Ottawa, and had issue:

1b Henry William Harvey; *b* 1881; *d* 1924

1b Mariette Frances; *m* 1904 Charles Elvin Bleakney and had issue

1a (cont.) Henry Bruce *m* 2nd 1889 Georgina Amelia (*d* 22 Aug 1928), dau of Arthur Dale, and *d* 1896, having by her had further issue:

2b Arthur Bonnycastle Dalrymple; *b* 1890; *m* 1916 Marguerite Heloise (*d* 1976), dau of Frederick Edward Neale, of Chatham, New Brunswick, Canada, and *d* 26 Dec 1934, leaving issue:

1c Frederick later Arthur Blair Dalrymple; *b* 5 July 1924; *m* 12 May 1951 *Patricia [Mrs Arthur Bruce, 258 S Taylor Mills Dve, Richmond Hill, Ontario, Canada], dau of Richard Raymond Jarvis, of Ottawa, and *d* 1985 leaving issue:

1d +Richard Neale Dalrymple; *b* 5 March 1954

1d *Susan Elizabeth; *b* 22 Nov 1955; *m* 1984 *Jefferson Scott Reade, and has issue:

1e *Shannon Kathleen; *b* 1986

2e *Kirstin Alexandra; *b* 1988

1c *Heloise Patricia [Mrs Robert McLaughlin, 85 Clifton Rd, Toronto, Canada]; *b* 11 Dec 1918; *m* 28 April 1945 Capt Robert John McLaughlin, Toronto Scottish Regt (*d* 6 Aug 1949), and has issue:

1d *Robert Bruce; *b* 15 Oct 1949; *m* 1991 Janora Catherine Thorpe of Chapeltown, Sheffield

2b Adeline Gladys

3b Emily Kathleen Cochrane; *m* Lt Basil Greene, RN

2a Arthur Hill Nunn; *b* 1854; *m* 1900 Rose (*d* 18 May 1947), dau of John Steen, and *d* 1918, leaving issue:

1b Arthur James Henry; *b* 2 Sept 1901; *m* 1931 *Gladys, dau of Edward Bearinger, of Waterloo, Ontario, and *d* 1992, leaving issue:

1c Arthur Michael Edward; *b* 14 Nov 1938; *m* 1st 1962 (*divorce* 19–) Holly, dau of Carl F Cunningham, of Toronto, Canada; *m* 2nd 1993 *(Dorothy) Ferne Lancaster, and *d* 1993, leaving by his 1st w:

1d *Wendy Raina; *b* 1968

2d *Susan Ann; *b* 1969

1c *Patricia Mary Jane [Mrs Robert Davey, 64 Lockart Rd, Collingwood, Ont L9Y 2L3, Canada]; *b* 17 Sept 1934; *m* 1956 *Robert Arthur Davey, son of Clayton James George Davey, and has issue:

1d *Robert Bruce; *b* 11 Sept 1958; has issue living:

1e *Ryan; *b* 1992

2d *Steven Michael; *b* 18 June 1967; *m* 1990 *Linda Diane Godwin

1d *Susan Patricia; *b* 12 April 1960

2d *Karen Elizabeth; *b* 25 July 1962; *m* 1993 *Gregory Willison, and has issue:

1e *Brendan Gregory Bruce; *b* 1993

2b Reginald Alexander Steen; *b* 10 Jan 1904; *m* 1933 *Marie Leona, dau of George Albert Blouin, of Ottawa Canada, and *d* 1993, leaving issue:

1c +Robert Arthur Stewart; *b* 15 April 1936; *m* 1963 *Karen, dau of James Dunn, of Old Chelsea, Quebec, and has issue:

1d +Reginald Arthur Spencer *b* 19 Sept 1964

2d +Alexander James Robert; *b* 1967

3d +D'Arcy Stewart Anthony; *b* 1968

4d *Justin Martin Maynard; *b* 1971

1c *Marie Elizabeth Claire [Mrs Frederick Anfossie, 2771 Salina St, Ottawa, Ont K2B 6PS, Canada]; *b* 30 July 1934; *m* 1956 *Frederick Reginald Anfossie, and has issue:

1d *Frederick Bruce; *b* 20 Nov 1957; *m* 19– *Maryann Helen, dau of Andrew Stasko, of Odessa, Ont, and has issue:

1e *Frederick Andrew; *b* 1985

2e *Matthew Alexander; *b* 1990

1e *Mackenzie Elizabeth Irene; *b* 1992

1d *Christine Elodie; *b* 11 June 1959

2d *Janet Marie; *b* 1 July 1961; *m* 1988 *Michael Ernest Peiffer, and has issue:

1e *Emily Claire; *b* 1989

2e *Katherine Marie; *b* 1991

3d *Heather Claire; *b* 25 March 1963

4d *Margo Elizabeth; *b* 1968

2c *Sandra Margo Ann [Mrs Grant McDonald, 16 Tadoussac Drive, Aylmer, PQ J9J 1G2, Canada]; *b* 7 Jan 1938; *educ* McGill U (BSc); *m* 9 July 1960 *Grant Pereigo McDonald, son of Stroud McDonald, of 3 Leonard Ave, Ottawa, and has issue:

1d *Reginald Albert Stroud; *b* 24 Feb 1962

2d *Robert Bruce Reid; *b* 21 June 1963; *m* 29 July 1995 *Josée Marie Pierrette, dau of Robert Le Brun, and has:

1e *Steven Alexander Grant; *b* 16 April 1993

1e *Lea Christine Margo; *b* 16 May 1995

3d *Adam Alfred Grant; *b* 9 Aug 1964; has:

1e *Jake Adam Michael; *b* 13 Aug 1994

4d *John Arthur Steen; *b* 2 Nov 1968; *m* 16 Aug 1997 *Marie Claire Genevieve Katherine, dau of Craig P Gaston

3b Stewart Frederick Dundonald; *b* 1904; *m* 1940 *Kathleen Edna [Mrs Stewart Bruce, 513 Westminster Ave, Ottawa, Ont, Canada], dau of Charles Cooke of Ottawa, Canada, and *d* 1982, leaving issue:

1c *Nona Frances Evelyn [Mrs John Argue, 19 Maplehill Way, Nepean, Ont, Canada]; *b* 7 April 1944; *m* 1970 *John Douglas Argue and has:

1d *Bruce Dugan; *b* 1975

1d *Sally; *b* 1973

2c *Joan Kathleen Susan [Mrs Walter Bruce Nibogie, PO Box 69, Victoria St, Metcalfe, Ontario K0A 2PO, Canada]; *b* 10 Dec 1947; *m* 1972 *Walter William Nibogie, and has issue:

1d *Jeremy Ryan Bruce; *b* 1977

1d *Krista Kathleen Andra; *b* 1974

3c *Nancy Elizabeth Ann; *b* 1949; *m* 1975 *Myles Julien Kowalyshen, and has issue:

1d *Bryan Mikael; *b* 1977

1d *Kara Anne; *b* 1979

4b Allan Ernest Hill; *b* 1906; *m* 1930 (*divorce* 1946) Maria Ann, dau of Elidore Sauvé, of Ottawa, and *d* 1973, leaving issue:

1c +Allan Alexander Dundonald [Allan Bruce Esq, 18 Lynhar Rd, Nepean, Ont K2H 6L9, Canada]; *b* 18 July 1931; *m* 1956 *Patricia Anne Leeks, and has issue:

1d +Stewart Allan Robert; *b* 1957

2d +Steven Christopher David; *b* 1961

3d +Donald Andrew James; *b* 1964; *m* 1988 *Deborah Lynn Boright, and has issue:

1e *Jessica Dawn; *b* 1989

2c +Hervey William Beresford [Hervey Bruce Esq, 5 Ashford Dve, Ottawa, Ont, Canada]; *b* 30 Dec 1932; *m* 1966 *Molly Margaret MacLaurin, and has issue:

1d +Cameron Allan Beresford; *b* 1972

2c (cont.) Mr and Mrs Hervey Bruce also adopted:

*Todd Roy; *b* 1961

*Scott Rodrick; *b* 1962

1c *Marie Lorraine Caroline [Mrs Patrick Timlin, 78 Harris Place, Nepean, Ont K2G 2P8, Canada]; *b* 24 Oct 1934; *m* 1957 *Patrick Francis Timlin and has had:

1d Michael Allan; *b* 1961; *d* 5 July 1992

2d *Robert Patrick; *b* 1966

1d *Brenda Marion; *b* 1958

1b Eileen Frances Mariette; *b* 1900; *m* 1924 David Pattee Kirby (*d* 21 May 1953), and has issue:

1c *David Arthur Sidney; *b* 12 Aug 1927; *m* 1953 *Grace Elizabeth MacNeill, and has issue:

1d *David Donald Neill; *b* 10 July 1954

1d *Leslie Grace Elizabeth; *b* 2 Dec 1956

2d *Susan Marjorie May *b* 2 Oct 1961

3d *Janet Lois Eileen; *b* 2 Feb 1964

2c *Bruce Robert William; *b* 2 Jan 1929; *m* 1956 *Margo Alma Dancey, and has issue:

1d *Margo Janice; *b* 3 Dec 1958

2d *Kelly June *b* 13 April 1960

1c *Beverley Eileen Rosemary; *b* 18 March 1935; *m* 27 May 1961 *David Bruce Brown, s of David Alexander Brown, and has issue:

1d *David Alexander; *b* 12 Oct 1966

1d *Pattee Allison; *b* 17 Aug 1963

2d *Karen Elizabeth; *b* 15 Jan 1969

3a Stewart Armit Macdonald, JP, of Ballyscullion Park, Co Antrim; *b* 1858; *m* 6 March 1891 Helen (*d* 26 June 1938), 2nd dau of John McGregor, of Balmanach, Strathspey, and *d* 6 April 1937, leaving issue:

1b Jean Mariette Isabel Otway; *b* 1892; fndr/ed *The Rambler* 1907–30; *m* 1916 (*divorce* 1932) Cyril Gordon Taylor, and *d* 14 Sept 1973

4a Dundonald Alexander Crawford; *b* 1860; *m* 1914 *Amy Constance, dau of Joseph Milton, of Bromsgrove, Worcs

5a Robert Frederick Hervey; *b* 1863; *m* 1899 Helen Bonfield, and *d* 1926, leaving issue:

1b George Robert Antony; *b* 1902; *m* 1928 Mary Lillian Stafford, and *d* 1931

6a Ernest Douglas Beresford; *b* 1869; *m* 3 Aug 1905 Lydia Mary, only dau of Rev John Lloyd-Jones, MA, of Bala, Merionethshire

7a Reginald Archibald Kenneth; *b* 1874; *m* 1908 Julia Vivian Keown Boyd, and *d* 1932, leaving issue:

1b William Reginald Richard Stewart; *b* 1910; Capt Irish Gds WW II; *m* 1934 *Mirabel Melville Gray (*m* 2nd 1946 *J M Hawkes, of Midwood, Clochan, by Buckie, Banffshire), dau of J D Walker, formerly of Balgownie Lodge, Aberdeenshire, and was *ka* 1944, leaving issue:

1c *Mirabel Hermione [Mrs James Simpson, 116 Brighton Place, Aberdeen]; *b* 1941; *m* 1st 1964 (*divorce* 1972) Alan Hamill, MN; *m* 2nd 197– *James G Simpson and has issue by 2nd husb:

1d *James Alexander Bruce; *b* 1976

1a Mary Elizabeth Thomasina; *m* 25 Aug 1881 John Peirse de la Poer Beresford (*d* 30 Oct 1902; *see* BERESFORD-PEIRSE, Bt), and *d* 24 March 1926, leaving issue

2a Adeline Henrietta Caroline Penelope; *m* 20 Dec 1887 William Moore (*dsp* 21 Jan 1910), Lt RN, of Moore Fort, Co Antrim, and *d* 1916

3a Emmeline Frances Maria; *m* Edward Box

4a Geraldine Beatrice Molyneux; *m* 6 June 1903 John Alexander Clark, DL, BA (*d* 23 Jan 1948), of Gravesend, Castledawson, Co Londonderry, and *d* 20 Oct 1955, leaving issue

(1) (cont.) Lt-Col Henry Bruce *m* 2nd Oct 1894 Frances Jane Augusta, widow of Edward Moran, and yst dau of John Hill, of Bellaghy, Co Londonerry, and *d* 17 May 1908

(2) Alexander Hervey, Lt-Col BSC; *m* Elizabeth Julia Mackinnon, and *d* 1874, leaving issue:

1a Elizabeth Julia Mackinnon; *m* 3 June 1876 Lt-Col St George Corbet Gore, CSI, RE (*see* GORE, Bt), and *d* 23 Oct 1902, leaving issue

2 (cont.) Adml Sir Henry Bruce *m* 2nd Louisa Mary Minchin (*d* 1834), dau of Col George Dalrymple, and *d* 14 Dec 1863, having by her had issue:

(3) James Minchin, R-Adml; *b* 24 Jan 1833; *m* 14 Oct 1856 Elizabeth Lucas (*d* 26 March 1913), dau of John Hill, of Bellaghy, and *d* 30 March 1901, leaving, with other issue:

1a James Minchin; *b* May 1859; *m* 1888 Ethelwynne, dau of Rev James Powell, and d 19–, leaving issue:

1b Minnie; *b* 1889

1a Emma Alexandra; *m* 20 Feb 1895 Hugh Lecky, est son of Maj Lecky, RMLI (*d* 2 March 1898), and had issue

2a Mary Minchin; *m* 27 March 1894 Thomas James Watson (*d* 21 Dec 1936), only son of Rev James Harrison Watson, MA, Vicar of Saxthorpe, Norfolk, and had issue

3a Frances Dalrymple; *m* 10 Jan 1900 William Hammond, est son of James Alfred Hammond, and had issue

4a Violet; *m* 7 Feb 1901 Maj Arthur Richmond, RA (SR), of Nottingham, only son of Arthur Richmond, and had issue

(4) Stewart Crawford; *b* 20 Jan 1801, JP and DL Co Londonderry; *m* 6 Dec 1828 Helen Baillie (*d* 23 Sept 1873), dau of William Alves, of Enham Place, Hants, and *d* 18 Feb 1878, having had, with other issue:

1a Stewart Hervey; *b* 10 July 1834, Maj 102nd Foot, JP Co Londonderry; *m* 19 Jan 1864 Frances Anna Maria (*d* 30 May 1927), dau of H C R Becher, QC, of Canada, and *d* 1899, leaving, with other issue:

1b Henry Becher; *b* 17 Feb 1866; *m* 28 Oct 1904 Marian Evelyn, dau of James MacFadden, JP, of Carleton Ho, Portadown, and *d* 14 May 1944

2b Stewart Alexander (Rev); *b* 2 June 1870, Rector of Pitney Lortie, nr Langport, Somerset 1930–54, formerly Rector of Kilmore, Erris, Co Mayo; *m* 19 Sept 1911 Ada Frances (*d* 20 July 1945), er dau of Dr R E MacDowell, MD, of Greenfield, Sandymount, and *d* 24 March 1956, leaving issue:

1c *Maire Frances Patricia [Mrs Reginald Cracknell, 4 Ashcroft, Cedar Dve, Hatch End, Middlesex]; *b* 10 Oct 1913; *m* 11 Nov 1939 S/Ldr Reginald Maurice Cracknell, MBE, RAFVR (*d* 1970), and has issue:

1d *Andrew Alexander Leon; *b* 24 Nov 1943; *educ* King's Sch Rochester and Brunel U (BTech 1967)

2d *Peter Bruce; *b* 19 July 1947; *educ* St John's Leatherhead

1b Helen Stewart; *m* 1890 Joseph Ewing Miller, MD (*d* 12 July 1923), and *d* 19 Sept 1939, leaving issue

2b Ethel Caroline; *d* unm 17 June 1949

Sir HENRY *d* 1822; his est son,

Sir James Robertson Bruce, 2nd Bt; *b* 4 Sept 1788; *m* 20 Sept 1819 Ellen (*d* 14 July 1864), yst dau of Robert Bamford Hesketh, of Gwyrch Castle, Denbighs, and had with other issue:

1 HENRY HERVEY (Sir), **3rd Bt**

2 Robert, CB; *b* 17 Feb 1825; Col 23rd Fus (Crimean medal with clasp and Turkish medal, Indian Mutiny medal with clasp), Inspr-Gen RIC 1882–85; *m* 1 Feb 1859 Mary Caroline (*d* 16 April 1893), only dau of Sir John Montagu Burgoyne, 9th Bt, of Sutton Park, and *d* 1 Sept 1899, leaving issue:

(1) Lilian Amy; *m* 3 Jan 1894 Lt-Gen Sir Gerald Francis Ellison, KCB, KCMG, Roy Warwicks Regt (*d* 27 Oct 1947), 2nd son of Canon Ellison, Rector of Haseley, Oxon, and *d* 6 Nov 1948, leaving issue

3 Lloyd Stewart (Rev); *b* 1 Aug 1829; MA, Canon of York, Rector of Stokesley, Northallerton, and Chaplain to Archbp York; *m* 1st 6 Oct 1863 Jane (*d* 30 Sept 1880), dau of James H Skene, Consul at Aleppo, and gdau of James Skene, of Rubislaw, and had, with other issue:

(1) Robert Douglas (Rev); *b* 30 March 1867; *educ* Worcester Coll Oxford (MA); Rector St Anne's, Dunbar; *m* 9 Oct 1894 Alice Margaret (*d* 7 April 1955), dau of Henry William Lord, barrister, and *d* 3 Sept 1944, having had issue:

1a Robert Lloyd; *b* 18 Nov 1895; Lt 11th Bn Cameronians, Scottish Rifles; *ka* 18 Nov 1916

2a Henry Douglas (Rev), Priest-in-Charge Andros Bahamas 1931–34, Curate St Margaret's Aberdeen 1935–37, Novice SSJE Oxford Aug 1937, professed as a Cowley Father July 1940, Scotland, Joppa 1946, Oxford 1947, Joppa 1951, Oxford 1954; *b* 15 June 1900; *educ* Keble Coll Oxford (BA 1922)

3a +Nigel Patrick; *b* 27 Feb 1905; *educ* Keble Coll Oxford (BA, BM, BCh); i/c Hosp of the Epiphany, Kamdara, Ranchi, Bihar, India 1934–40, Capt RAMC WW II; *m* 1 Aug 1934 *Audrey Patricia Villiers, only child of Rev Owen Samuel Edward Clarendon, Vicar of Iffley, Oxford, and has issue:

1b *Clare; *b* 16 July 1935; *m* 7 Aug 1956 (*divorce* 1972) Capt Peter Colpoys Paley Johnson, RA, son of Lt-Col Sir John Paley Johnson, 6th Bt (*see* JOHNSON, Bt, of New York), and has issue

4a Michael (Rev); *b* 21 July 1908; *educ* Edin U (BSc 1932), Rector Chiddingfold 1940–61, Vicar St Mark's N Audley St 1961, Proctor in Convocation for Guildford 1945–61, author: *The Science of Prayer* and *No Empty Creed*; *m* 2 Feb 1935 *Jean Stuart [Mrs Michael Bruce, 29 Grange Rd, Edinburgh EH9 1UQ], MA Edin, dau of Ian Campbell, LRCP, LRCS, of Hereford Rd, Harrogate, and *d* 5 Feb 1968, leaving issue:

1b +Robert John [Robert Bruce Esq, 19 Grange Rd, Edinburgh EH9 1UQ]; *b* 14 Feb 1936

1b *Elspeth Mary [Mrs Stuart Semple, Mounthooly, Winchburgh, Broxburn, W Lothian EH52 6PY]; *b* 21 April 1942; *educ* Edin U (MA 1964); *m* 9 Oct 1965 *Stuart Mackenzie Semple, MB, ChB Edin, and has issue:

1c *Jean; *b* 8 March 1968

2c *Sheila; *b* 1970

3c *Mairi; *b* 1971

4c *Elspeth; *b* 1975

(2) Francis Rosslyn Courtenay (Rev); *b* 14 Aug 1871; *educ* Worcester Coll Oxford (MA, DD); FLS, Rector Herstmonceux Sussex 1923, Chaplain RA (TA), Grand Chaplain of Grand Lodge of Freemasons; *m* 20 Oct 1908 Rachel (*d* 1971), er dau of Richard Hanbury Joseph Gurney, JP, DL, of Northrepps Hall, Norwich, and *d* 19 Jan 1956, leaving issue:

1a +Merlin, OBE (1959) [Cdr Merlin Bruce OBE RN (ret), 50 Tumbling Bay Court, Henry Rd, Oxford OX2 0PE]; *b* 3 Aug 1909; RN 1923–59 (Actg Capt) and RAF (F/Lt) 1931–39, served WW II and in Korea (despatches), memb Hemel Hempstead RDC 1961, Bursar Abbot's Hill Sch 1962–68; *m* 1932 Marjorie Joan (*d* 1991), only dau of William Percy Hitchcock, of Kettlewells Farm, St Albans, and has had issue:

1b Euslin; *b* 26 July 1933; *educ* RNC Dartmouth; late Sub-Lt RN; design artist; *m* 1957 *Enid Winifred, yr dau of Eric Woodward Pedley, of 20 Becketts Ave, St Albans, Herts and *d* 11 Aug 1997, leaving:

1c +Quinton Rosslyn; *b* 28 Dec 1959

2c +Roderick Hulme; *b* 11 Jan 1962; *m* 1997 *Rebecca Mary Christina Hanlon and has issue

3c +Damian Trispen; *b* 31 July 1970

4c +Jeremy Larick; *b* 19 May 1974

1c *Nicola Jane; *b* 21 May 1958; *m* 1988 (*divorce* 19–) Paul Darby and has issue

2c *Caroline Fiona; *b* 28 Feb 1964

2b +Rollo [Rollo Bruce Esq, 28 West End Grove, Horsforth, Leeds LS18 5JJ]; *b* 29 May 1939; *educ* St Edward's Sch Oxford and St Catharine's Coll Cambridge (BA Mech Sc); ed *AEI Engineering* 1967–68, Wool Industs Research Assoc 1968; *m* 17 July 1965 *Katharine Margaret, BA Leeds, 2nd dau of Ronald Hill, of Princethorpe, Warwicks, and has issue:

1c +Rory James; *b* 26 Aug 1968; has issue:

1d *Jack Merlin; *b* 13 July 1993

1c *Lucy Helen; *b* 21 March 1966; *m* 2 June 1995 *Warren Squire and has:

1d *Toby Montague; *b* 16 Oct 1996

3b Doriel; *b* 9 Oct, *d* 11 Oct 1937

2a +Erroll [Cdr Erroll Bruce RN, Lofts, Lower Pennington, Lymington, Hants]; *b* 4 Nov 1913; *m* 12 April 1939 *Silvia Daphne, only dau of Col Charles Reginald Sylvester Bradley, of Langton Herring Manor, Dorset, and has issue:

1b +Peregrine Erroll [Peregrine Bruce Esq, Pilgrims, Broadmead, Sway, Lymington, Hants]; *b* 13 May 1940; late Capt Roy Sigs; *m* 1974 *Fiona Anne, dau of Gp-Capt Reginald Bryson Wardman, OBE, AFC, and has issue:

1c *Rachael; *b* 1974

2c *Anna; *b* 1976

2b +Peter [Cdr Peter Bruce RN, Kestrel Cottage, Shirley Holms, Lymington, Hants]; *b* 26 Sept 1941; Cdr RN

1b *Rosamund [Mrs Jeremy Holmes, The Old Rectory, Stoke Rivers, Devon EX32 7LB]; *b* 16 Feb 1943; *m* 1st 1962 Terence Patrick Griffin and has had:

1c *Benedict James; *b* 1963

1c Tabitha Rose; *b* 15 April 1964; *d* 1980

2c *Polly Bridget; *b* 1966; has issue:

1d *Marcus; *b* 1991

1d *Rosy; *b* 1986

2d *Zenta Esther; *b* 1987

2c *Matilda Victoria; *b* 1968; has:

1d *Céleste; *b* 1997

3c *Flora Rhalou; *b* 1972; *m* 1997 *Mike Harlu Gebreyohanes and has:

1d *Axumawi; *b* 1997

1b (cont.) Mrs Griffin *m* 2nd 1978 *Jeremy Alan Holmes, MA, MB, BCh, MRCP, FRCPsych, and by him has:

2c *Joshua Thomas Cecil; *b* 1983

2b *Errollyn Daphne [Mrs Richard Lindley, Hainworth, Keighley, W Yorks]; *b* 20 March 1950; *m* 19– *Richard Charles Lindley, MA, DPhil, and has issue:

1c *Samuel James; *b* 1977

2c *Joseph Galen; *b* 1983

1c *Emma Rosamund; *b* 1978

3b *Chlöe Siola; *b* 28 June 1965

1a Rhalou; *b* 21 March 1911; *m* 19 Oct 1935 George Hugh Kirkby Peace, MRCVS, s of Hubert Kirkby Peace, and had issue:

1b *Colin Kirkby; *b* 23 July 1936; *educ* St John's Sch Leatherhead, Pembroke Coll Cambridge (MA, Vet MB) and Sch of Vet Med Cambridge; MRCVS, vet; *m* 14 Feb 1967 *Stephanie Anne, est dau of John Rawle, of Necochea, Argentina, and has issue:

1c *Rosslyn Lucas Kirkby; *b* 23 Aug 1968

2b *Hubert Kirkby; *b* 21 Nov 1937, NDA, MRAC; *m* 8 Feb 1964 *Penelope-Claire, only dau of Maj Patrick Brady, of Shotesham, Norfolk, and has issue:

1c *Henry Kirkby; *b* 6 Dec 1964

1c *Anne Maria Claire; *b* 13 Feb 1966

3b *Peter Kirkby; *b* 26 March 1941; *educ* St John's Leatherhead and Guy's (BSc 1963, MB, BS); LRCP, MRCS; *m* 15 Feb 1969 *Jane Andrea, BA, dau of Cedric Escort Knight, of Orpington, Kent

4b *Thomas Kirkby; *b* 9 July 1943; *m* 10 June 1967 *Judith Jane, dau of — Champion, and has issue:

1c *Emily Mary Delia; *b* 30 March 1968

5b *Benjamin Kirkby; *b* 9 July 1943; *m* 1967 *Kathleen Rosemary Denise Cornagh and has issue:

1c *Simon Kirkby; *b* 1 Dec 1968

6b *James Kirkby; *b* 23 Aug 1947

2a *Verily [Mrs Paul Paget, Templewood Gatehouse, Northrepps, Cromer, Norfolk NR27 0LJ]; *b* 12 Jan 1915; *m* 1st 2 Aug 1940 Capt Donald Clive Anderson, IA (*d* 2 Jan 1957); *m* 2nd 1971 Paul Edward Paget, CVO, FSA, FRIBA (*see* PAGET, Bt, of Harewood), and has issue by 1st husb:

1b *Edward [Edward Anderson Esq, Templewood, Northrepps, Cromer, Norfolk]; *b* 9 Sept 1948; *m* 1973 *Mrs Christina Bolt, yr dau of F G Raymond, and has issue:

1c *Evelyn; *b* 1973

2c *Beatrice; *b* 1978

1b *Marian [Mrs James O'Hare, 33 Frogshall, Northrepps, Cromer, Norfolk NR27 0LJ]; *b* 7 May 1941; *m* 1964 *James Haldane O'Hare, s of James O'Hare, of Edinburgh, and has issue:

1c *Justin; *b* 7 Feb 1966; *m* 1991 *Janet Robb, of Whale Beach, Sydney, NSW, and has:

1d *Lillian; *b* 1996

2d *Elspeth; *b* 1997

1c *Christina [Mrs Simon Evans, Sally Beans House, Northrepps, Norfolk]; *b* 2 Jan 1965; *m* 1989 *Simon Gerredd Evans and has:

1d *Botticelli Verily Boadicea; *b* 1990

2d *Piranesi Vita Lolita; *b* 1992

2c Eloise; *b* 1970

2b *Rachel [Mrs David Bradby, Lower Damsels, Northrepps, Norfolk]; *b* 18 March 1943; *m* 19 June 1965 *Prof David Henry Bradby, MA, PhD, est s of Edward Bradby, Principal of St Paul's Coll, Cheltenham, and has issue:

1c *Lawrence; *b* 23 Dec 1968

*Nguyen Thanh Sang; *b* 1970; adopted 1980

2c *Donald; *b* 1973

1c *Hannah; *b* 4 Dec 1966; has:

1d *Nguyea Edward Robinson; *b* 1996

3b *Janie [Mrs Charles Hampton, 80 Temple Rd, Temple Cowley, Oxford OX4 2EZ]; *b* 14 March 1952; *m* 1971 *Charles Hampton and has issue:

1c *Orlando; *b* 1975

2c *Joseph; *b* 1978

1c *Daisy Maya; *b* 1973

3b (cont.) Mr and Mrs Charles Hampton also adopted 1992

*Pamela Nyabadza; *b* 1978

4b *Alexandra [Mrs Gray Walker, 21 Humberstone Rd, Cambridge]; *b* 16 May 1953; MA (Cantab); *m* 1st 1972 (*divorce* 1989) Michael Holgreaves Allerhand; *m* 2nd 1993 *Gray Innis Walker, yr son of Rev Colin Walker, and has by her 1st husb:

1c *Taffeta Annie; *b* 1976

2c *Rhalou Gladys; *b* 1979

3a *Lorema [Mrs Alan Goolden, 31 West St, Osney Island, Oxford]; *b* 15 Feb 1920; *m* 7 Feb 1942 *Alan Wilfrid Gough Goolden, MB, BS, MRCS, FRCR, only s of R-Adml Francis Hugh Walter Goolden, CB, and has issue:

1b *Adrian French; *b* 16 April 1945; *m* 1st 1971 (*divorce* 1979) Penelope, dau of John Goober, and has issue:

1c *Jack Malago; *b* 1973

1c *Amy Apple Louise; *b* 1976

2c *Rosemary Alice; *b* 1978

1b (cont.) Adrian Goolden *m* 2nd 19– *Sally, dau of Malcolm Lower, MB, and has further issue:

2c *Leo Samson; *b* 1989

2b *Robin Massy; *b* 12 Feb 1948; *m* 1976 *Mrs Madelaine Mulholland, dau of George Nation, and has issue:

1c *Oliver Nation; *b* 1978

1c *Rachel Bruce; *b* 1980

(3) Wilfrid Montagu, CBE (1919), RD, Capt RNR; *b* 26 Oct 1874; Polar Medal 1913 for Scott Expedn; *m* 25 Nov 1913 Hon Dorothy Florence Boot (*d* 1980), dau of 1st Baron Trent (*see* 1956 edn), and *d* 21 Sept 1953, leaving issue:

1a *Nancy Jessica; *b* 1 April 1915; *m* 1940 Adriano Guarnieri (*d* 1983), yr son of Francesco Guarnieri, of Feltre and Venice, and has issue:

1b *Giovanni Bruce; *b* 16 Feb 1947; *m* 1973 *Cristina Ongania, and has issue:

1c *Gaia; *b* 1973

2c *Valentina; *b* 1978

3c *Isotta; *b* 1982

2b *Antonio Wilfred; *b* 24 June 1949; *m* 1981 *Anna Lisa Sacerdoti and has issue:

1c *Matteo; *b* 1981

1c *Ambra; *b* 1983

3b *Andrea; *b* 13 Jan 1953; *m* 1981 *Luisa Gamba and has issue:

1c *Lorenzo; *b* 1983

1c *Matilde; *b* 1981

1b *Francesca Flora; *b* 17 Feb 1941; *m* 1968 *Giuliano Ferrari-Brasso, PhD (Cantab), and has issue:

1c *Nicolo; *b* 1968

2c *Jacopo; *b* 1970

3c *Martino; *b* 1974

1c Nicolo Brutus; *b* Sept 1968

2a Charity Florence; *b* 3 Jan 1917; *m* 1st 8 June 1940 Edward Bruce Noel Mitchell, yr son of F G Mitchell, of Clapton Manor, Northants and had two daus; *m* 2nd Geoffrey Rigby, and *d* 2 Nov 1963

3a *Rosemary June; *b* 4 June 1919; *m* 11 Nov 1939 *Alan Burrough, MA, late Capt RHA, 3rd son of Ernest J Burrough, of Rowallan, Epsom, Surrey, and adopted:

*Bryan Robert Hardy; *b* 3 Feb 1960

*Alan Christopher Clive; *b* 26 March 1961

*Marianne Primrose Florence; *b* 13 April 1962

(1) Ellen Mary; *m* 16 Aug 1892 Rev Canon John Fitz Stephen Keating, DD (*d* 11 Feb 1911), and *d* 18 July 1951, leaving issue

(2) Zoe Mary (twin with Ellen); *m* 14 Feb 1885 Rev Charles Spencer Newham, Vicar of Prestlee, Manchester (*d* 3 June 1924), son of Henry Keating, of Mallow, Co Cork, and *d* 1957, leaving issue

(3) Irene Mary; *d* unm 1940

(4) Grace Guendolen, *d* unm 2 Jan 1950

(5) Rosamond Hilda; *d* unm 26 Oct 1963

(6) Edith Agnes Kathleen; *m* 1st 2 Sept 1908 Capt Robert Falcon Scott, CVO, RN (d c 29 March 1912), Antarctic explorer 1910–12, and had issue. She was granted by roy warrant 1913 the rank of widow of a KCB; *m* 2nd 3 March 1922 1st Baron Kennet (*qv*) and *d* 25 July 1947, leaving issue

3 (cont.) Canon Bruce *m* 2nd 1 June 1881 Anne (*d* 1893), widow of Samuel Parker, FRCS, and *d* 19 March 1886

1 Louisa Elizabeth Margaret; *m* 30 Oct 1860 Rev John Baghot De La Bere, MA (*d* 7 April 1909), Vicar of St Mary's, Buxted, and *d* 10 Oct 1907 leaving issue

Sir JAMES *d* 22 April 1836; his est son,

Sir Henry Hervey Bruce, 3rd Bt, PC; *b* 22 Sept 1820, MP Coleraine 1862–74 and 1880–85, Lt and Custos Rotulorum Co Londonderry, High Sheriff 1846; Hon Col 9th Bde NI Div RA, formerly 1st LG; *m* 12 July 1842 Marianne Margaret (*d* 28 July 1891), only dau of Sir Juckes Granville Juckes Clifton, 8th Bt, of Clifton, Notts, and had issue:

1 HERVEY JUCKES LLOYD (Sir), **4th Bt**

2 James Andrew Thomas (Sir), KCMG (1900); *b* 15 July 1846; Adml, served on Niger 1876 and in China 1900; *m* 27 June 1877 Catherine Mary Philippa (*d* 18 April 1924), er dau of Col Edwin Wodehouse, CB, RA (*see* KIMBERLEY, E), and *d* 25 May 1921

Sir HENRY *d* 8 Dec 1909; his er son,

Sir Hervey Juckes Lloyd Bruce, 4th Bt; *b* 5 Oct 1843, JP, DL Co Londonderry, High Sheriff 1903, JP Notts, Lt-Col Coldstream Gds, Hon Col Londonderry RFA (Res); *m* 15 Jan 1872 Ellen Maud, OBE (1918) (*d* 30 June 1924), yst dau of Percy Ricardo, of Bramley Park, Guildford, and had issue:

1 HERVEY RONALD (Sir), **5th Bt**

2 Percy Robert BRUCE later CLIFTON (roy licence 1 Nov 1919), CMG (1918), DSO (1916), TD, of Clifton Hall, Notts; *b* 9 Dec; Lt-Col TFR, Assist Dir Rlwy Tport 1916–19, WW I in Gallipoli, Egypt and Palestine, DL Notts, High Sheriff 1929; *m* 1st 19 Jan 1898 Alethea Georgina (*d* 14 Nov 1904), dau of Sir Richard Horner Paget, 1st Bt (*see* PAGET, Bt, of Cranmore), and had issue:

(1) Gervase Ronald, Midshipman RN; *b* 19 Jan 1899; *ka* in HMS *Monmouth* off coast of Chile 1 Nov 1914

(1) Marjory Sheila; *b* 11 Dec 1903; JP Leics; *m* 4 March 1930 3rd Baron Crawshaw (*qv*) and *d* 5 Sept 1964, leaving issue

2 (cont.) Lt-Col Percy Clifton *m* 2nd 27 Nov 1909 Evelyn Mary Amelia (*d* 6 Jan 1969 aged 93), er dau of Maj Thomas Leith, DL, of Petmathen, Aberdeenshire (*see* BURGH, B), and *d* 10 Nov 1944, having by her had issue:

(2) +Peter Thomas, DSO (1945), DL (1954), JP (Notts 1952–59 and Hants 1964) [Lt-Col Peter Clifton CVO DSO JP DL, Dummer House, Dummer, Basingstoke, Hants]; *b* 24 Jan 1911; *educ* Eton; Lt-Col Gren Gds WW II, memb Gentlemen-at-Arms 1960 (Clerk Cheque and Adj 1973, Standard Bearer 1979–81); *m* 1st 2 June 1934 (*annulled* 1936) Ursula Sybil, yr dau of Sir Edward Hussey Packe, KBE, of Prestwold Hall, Leics; *m* 2nd 28 April 1948 *Patricia Mary Adela, DStJ, yr dau of Maj James Miller Gibson-Watt, of Doldowlod, Radnorshire, and widow of Maj Robert Nevill Cobbold, Welsh Gds, and by her has:

1a *Georgina Anne; *b* 1 Sept 1949; *m* 1st 6 Nov 1967 Hon Richard Gerard Wrottesley (*d* 1970), 2nd s of 5th Baron Wrottesley (*qv*); *m* 2nd 1982 *Lt-Col Jonathan Lovett Seddon-Brown, Scots Gds

2a *Rose Amelia [The Hon Mrs Mark Vestey, Dummer House, Dummer, Basingstoke, Hants]; *b* 19 Nov 1952; *m* 6 Feb 1975 *Hon Mark William Vestey, yr s of Capt Hon William Howarth Vestey (*see* VESTEY, B)

3 William; *b* 12 July 1876; Capt E Yorks Regt, late RN, served S Africa 1899–1902, Zululand 1906 and WW I 1915–16 (wounded twice); *m* 9 Aug 1900 Constance Mary, 2nd dau of Col Richard Charles William Mansergh, and formerly w of T A R Purchas; *d* 19–

4 Henry James, CMG (1917), MVO (1907); *b* 1 Nov 1880; 1st Sec Dip Serv, Br Delegate Inter-Allied Commn Bulgaria 1925, Adviser Nat Bank Hungary 1931–39, author: *Silken Dalliance* and *Thirty Dozen Moons*; *m* 1915 Tamara Karsavina, the ballerina (*d* 1991), dau of Platon Karsavin, of St Petersburg, and *d* 10 Sept 1951, leaving issue:

(1) +Nikita [Nikita Bruce Esq, 38 Longfield Dve, Amersham, Bucks HP6 5HE]; *b* 5 Jan 1916; *educ* Eton; advtsg exec Schweppes, Sherwood Foresters and Intell Corps WW II; *m* 1st March 1940 (*divorce* 1945) Kay (Kay Bannerman, actress and playwright; *d* 1991), dau of Capt Robert George Bannerman, of 34 Dorset House, NW1; *m* 2nd 30 March 1957 *Dorothy Mary Norah Mostyn, dau of William Mostyn Bell, of Vienna, and by her has:

1a +Nicholas Henry William; *b* 19 July 1960

1a *Caroline Mary Tamara; *b* 4 April 1958; *m* 1984 *Keith Douglas Crampton, s of Douglas Crampton, and has:

1b *James Nicholas Douglas; *b* 18 Oct 1992

Sir HERVEY *d* 8 May 1919; his est son,

Sir Henry Ronald Bruce, 5th Bt, JP, DL; *b* 9 Dec 1872; Maj 14th Serv Bn RIR and Capt Irish Gds; *m* 1st 3 Nov 1903 Ruth Isabel (*dsp* 27 Sept 1915), 3rd dau of Haughton Charles Okeover (*see* WALKER-OKEOVER, Bt); *m* 2nd 11 July 1916 Margaret Florence (*d* 25 Feb 1954) (who *m* 2nd 3 June 1925 Lt-Col Charles Oxley Morris, DSO, IA, who *d* 1950), dau of Rev Robert Jackson, MA, Rector of Little Thurlow, Newmarket, and had:

1 HERVEY JOHN WILLIAM (Sir), **6th Bt**

2 +Ronald Cecil Juckes; *b* 22 Aug 1921; *m* 20 Aug 1960 *Jean, dau of Lewis James William Murfitt, of 5 Florence Wright Ave, Kenwick Rd, Lincs, and has issue:

(1) +Alan James; *b* 22 Dec 1964

1 Beryl Margaret Gwladys; *b* 27 Nov 1917

Sir HERVEY *d* 18 May 1924; his er son,

Sir Hervey John William Bruce, 6th Bt; *b* 29 June 1919; *educ* Eton and RMC Sandhurst, Capt RSG WW II; *m* 21 Feb 1949 Crista Irene Valentine (*d* 1984), yr dau of Lt-Col Chandos de Paravicini, OBE, of Birkholme Manor, Corby, Lincs, and formerly w of Maj David Charles Innes-Ker (*see* ROXBURGHE, D), and *d* 1971 as a result of a motor accident, having had issue:

1 Sir HERVEY JAMES HUGH BRUCE, **7th and present Bt**

1 *Lauretta Chinty [Mrs Nicholas Ridley, 150 Walton St, London SW3]; *b* 24 Sept 1950; *m* 1st 10 May 1971 Capt David Ralph Foster Harbord, 15th/19th Kings Roy Hus (*d* as result of an accident 22 July 1974), yr s of William Edward Harbord, of 11 Granby Rd, Harrogate, Yorks (*see* SUFFIELD, B); *m* 2nd 4 April 1978 *Nicholas Charles Wetherill Ridley, er s of Harold Ridley, of 53 Harley St, W1

BRUCE, Bt, of Stenhouse

Arms: Or a saltire and chief gules, in the dexter canton an escutcheon argent, charged with a chief sable. **Crest:** On a cap of dignity an arm from the shoulder couped fesswise holding a sceptre ensigned on the point with an open crown as that worn by Robert I of Scotland, all proper. **Supporters:** Dexter, a knight in armour, the vizor open and a plume of feathers in his helmet, holding a sceptre in his right hand, all proper; sinister, a lion rampant azure, armed and langued gules, crowned with the crown of Robert I and gorged with that of David II, chained with an antique chain, or. **Mottoes:** (over the crest) *Fuimus* ('We have been'); (under the shield) 'Do well and doubt not'. **Creation:** Bt. (NS) 29 Sept 1628.

SIR (FRANCIS) MICHAEL IAN BRUCE 12TH BT of Stenhouse, [Sir Michael Bruce Bt, 3424 Via Oporto #204, Newport Beach, California 92663, USA]; *b* 3 April 1926; *s f* 1957; *educ* Forman Sch, Litchfield, Conn., and Pomfret Conn.; served US Marine Corps amphibius forces WW II, Master Mariner 1968, ptnr Gossard-Bruce Co 1953–, Pres Newport Sailing Club Inc 1978– and Newport Acad of Sail Inc 1979–, owner American Maritime Co and The Eye Witness (legal photograph service) 1956–; has dropped forename Francis; *m* 1st 21 Aug 1947 (*divorce* 1957) Barbara Stevens, dau of Francis J Lynch, and has issue:

1 +MICHAEL IAN RICHARD; *b* 10 Dec 1950

2 +Robert Dudley; *b* 1 Aug 1952

Sir MICHAEL *m* 2nd 1961 (*divorce* 1963) Frances Keegan; *m* 3rd 1966 (*divorce* 1975) Marilyn Ann, dau of Carter Mulally; *m* 4th (*divorce* 1991) Patricia Gail, dau of Frederich Root; *m* 5th 1994 *Alessandro Conforto, MD

Lineage: Sir EDWARD BRUCE, yr s of the 1st Robert Bruce, of Clackmannan (*see* ELGIN and KINCARDINE, E); *m c* 1417 Agnes, dau and coheir of Sir William Airth of Airth, Stirling; Stenhouse, also in Stirling, also belonged to this branch of the BRUCEs, who were for a time styled either 'of Stenhouse' or 'of Airth'; their s:

Sir ROBERT BRUCE of Airth; *m* a dau of Sir Alexander Livingston, of Callendar, and had:

Sir ALEXANDER BRUCE of Airth and Stenhouse; *m* Margaret, dau of Sir Malcolm Forrester, of Torwoodhead, and *d* 1488, having had an est s:

JOHN BRUCE of Stenhouse; *m* Elizabeth, dau of Sir William Menteith of Kerse, and *dvp* 1483, leaving:

Sir ROBERT BRUCE; *m* Euphemia, dau of Alexander, Lord Montgomery, and had:

ROBERT BRUCE of Airth; *m* 1st Janet, dau of Sir Walter Forrester of Carden; *m* 2nd Marion, dau of Sir David Bruce of Clackmannan; his s by his 1st w:

Sir ALEXANDER BRUCE of Airth; *m* Janet, dau of Alexander, 5th Lord of Livingston, and had:

1 William; *m* 1582 Jane, dau of 5th Lord Fleming, and *dvp*, having had:

(1) John; *m* 1601 Margaret, dau of 4th Lord Elphinstone (*qv*), and had:

1a Alexander; gf of:

1b Alexander (Sir), last male rep of his branch; had:

1c A dau and heir; *m* Richard Elphinstone of Calderhall

(2) WILLIAM (Sir), **1st Bt**, of Stenhouse

(3) Patrick, of Newton, ancestor of the Bruce Bts, of Downhill, Co Londonderry (*qv*)

2 Robert (Rev), of Kinnaird; Presbyterian Minister; gtf of :

(1) Helen; *m* David Hay of Woodcockdale but kept the name BRUCE; grandparents of :

1a James; African explorer; gf of:

1b A gdau; *m* Charles Lennox Cumming Bruce of Roseisle and had an only child:

1c Mary Elizabeth; *m* 8th Earl of Elgin and Kincardine (*qv*)

Sir ALEXANDER's gs,

Sir William Bruce, 1st Bt (NS), so *cr* 29 Sept 1628, with remainder to his heirs male whomsoever; *m* 1st —, the dau (*dspm*) of Gen Middleton, of Letham; *m* 2nd Rachel, dau of Joseph Johnston, of Hilton, and widow of John Jackson, and *d* Feb 1630, leaving, with a yr s (Charles):

Sir William Bruce, 2nd Bt, of Stenhouse; *b* 19 Aug 1621; *m* Helen, dau of Sir William Douglas, of Cavers, hereditary Sheriff Teviotdale, and had, with a dau:

Sir William Bruce, 3rd Bt; *m* 1st 16 Sept 1665 Jean Fortune; *m* 2nd 17 April 1679 Alison Turnbull and *d* March 1682; his est s (by his 1st w(?)):

Sir William Bruce, 4th Bt; *m* Margaret, dau of John Boyde of Trochrigg, and *d* March 1721, having had three s and several daus; the 2nd but est surv s:

1 **Sir Robert Bruce, 5th Bt**; *d* unm

2 **Sir Michael Bruce, 6th Bt**; *m* Mary, est dau of Gen Sir Andrew Agnew, 5th Bt, of Lochnaw (*qv*), and *d* 1 Nov 1795, having had seven daus and six s, of whom:

1 WILLIAM (Sir), **7th Bt**

5 Patrick Craufurd; *b* 24 Jan 1748; banker, HEICS; *m* 22 Jan 1785 Jane (*d* 1840), dau of Edmund Smith, and *d* 1820, having had, with other issue:

(1) Michael; *b* 28 May 1787; *m* 15 Aug 1818 Marianne (*d* 20 Feb 1851), dau of Sir George Dallas, 1st Bt, and widow of Capt Sir Peter Parker, 2nd Bt, RN, and *d* 5 Nov 1861, leaving an only s:

1a Michael; *b* 8 May 1823; Gen, Col cmdg Gren Gds; *m* 1847 Anna Maria Frances (*d* 7 Nov 1885), dau of James Stuart, MP, and *d* 29 Sept 1883, leaving issue:

1b Eric Henry Stuart; *b* 20 Aug 1855; *educ* Exeter Coll Oxford (MA); Hon Sec RAerS; *m* 19 Aug 1884 Helen Florence Mary Auxilium, V-Pres Women's Aerial League (*d* 7 Aug 1941), dau of John Daniel King by Caroline Georgiana, 3rd dau of Sir Frederick William Slade, 2nd Bt (*qv*), and *d* 28 Feb 1935, leaving issue:

1c Michael Mary Victor Stuart (Very Rev Canon); *b* 24 Nov 1886; *educ* Corpus Christi Coll Cambridge and Scots Coll Rome; RC priest, Canon Diocesan Chapter 1939; *d* 19 June 1948

2c Ian Robert Craufurd George Mary, DSO (1941), MBE (1918); *b* 22 June 1890; *educ* Beaumont and RMC Sandhurst; Brig (ret) QO Cameron Highrs, WW I (despatches twice, 1914 star), Staff Capt Asia Minor 1919–22, DAQMG Br Forces Turkey 1922–23, Palestine 1936, WW II, cmded 1st Bn Gold Coast Regt E Africa and Inf Bde, Fighting French Troops in French Somaliland; Coronation medal 1937, Offr Order of Leopold I of Belgium with Palm, Belgian Croix de Guerre with Palm, Haile Selassie Mil Medal with palm Ethiopia; *m* 1 June 1926 Joan Mary (*d* 1991), est dau of Lt-Col Rowland Charles Feilding, DSO (*see* DENBIGH and DESMOND, E), and *d* 16 Jan 1956, leaving issue:

1d *Anne Mary [Mrs Patrick Reyntiens, Ilford Bridges Farm, Close Stocklinch, nr Ilminster, Somerset]; *b* 8 March 1927; *m* 9 Sept 1953 *Nicholas Patrick Reyntiens, yr s of Nicholas S Reyntiens, OBE, of Odiham, Hants, and has issue:

1e *Dominick Percival Ian [Dominick Reyntiens Esq, 5 Crastor Rd, London SW2]; *b* 8 Jan 1957; dancer and actor; *m* 1988 *Caroline Sophie, yr dau of William Adrian Liddell

2e *John Patrick Martin; *b* 23 June 1964

1e *Edith Mary Isabel [Mrs Edith Reyntiens, 62A Tyrwhitt Rd, London SE4]; *b* 3 Oct 1954; *m* 4 Aug 1989 (*divorce* 1993) Devon Arthur Hamil and has:

1f *Nicholas Laurence; *b* 2 Nov 1992

1f *Ervinie Anne Sophia; *b* 2 Oct 1987

2e *Lucy Mary Anne [Mrs Nicholas Durnan, Compton Farmhouse, Compton Durville, S Petherton, Somerset TA13 5ET]; *b* 17 July 1959; *m* Sept 1982 *Nicholas Gerrard Joseph Durnan and has:

1f *Sophie-Bell; *b* 7 March 1984

2f *Grace Louise; *b* 6 Nov 1987

2d *Janet Mary [Mrs Peter Ward, Waterdell House, Croxley Green, Herts WD3 3JH]; *b* 6 April 1928; *m* 16 Sept 1950 *Peter Michaeljohn Ward, only son of Lt-Col Francis Ward, OBE, MC, Scots Gds, and has issue:

1e *Jonathan Francis Bruce [Jonathan Ward Esq, 2 Olive Hill, Wyck Rissington, Glos GL54 2PW]; *b* 6 Oct 1954; *m* 1979 *Sarah Elizabeth Sophia, dau of Maj Mark Winton Slane Fleming (*see* RENNELL, B), and has issue:

1f *Christopher Luke; *b* 1980

2f *Hugh Basil; *b* 1982

2e *Robert Richard Craufurd; *b* 29 July 1959; *m* 19 Oct 1996 *Angeline Malaba

3e *Edmund Giles William [Edmund Ward Esq, 115 Exchange Rd, W Bridgford, Nottingham NG2 6BX]; *b* 15 May 1962; *m* 1991 *Gillian Elizabeth McCord

4e *Damian Peter Michael; *b* 29 Jan 1966

1e *Clare Dorothy [Mrs Christopher Thomson, 28 Gordonbrock Rd, London SE4 1JB]; *b* 27 Aug 1951; *m* 1976 *Christopher James Thomson, and has adopted:

*Edmund Christopher; *b* 1985

*Lucy Stephanie; *b* 1981

2e *Catharine Joan [Mrs Henry Thompson, 11 Douglas Crescent, Edinburgh EH12 5BB]; *b* 5 Dec 1952; *m* 1983 *Henry Swift Thompson Jr, and has issue:

1f *James Edwin Jerome; *b* 1987

1f *Emma Joan Douglas; *b* 1985

2f *Joanna Janet Henrietta; *b* 1991

3e *Magdalan Mary [Mrs Axel Goodbody, 2 First Ave, Bath, Avon BA2 3NW]; *b* 6 Dec 1955; *m* 1989 *Axel Howarth Goodbody and has:

1f *Roland Benedict; *b* 1993

1f *Laura Brigid; *b* 1990

3e (cont.) Mr and Mrs Axel Goodbody also adopted:

*Brendan Christian; *b* 1987

4e *Hester Janet Teresa [Mrs James Innes, 7 Warriston Crescent, Edinburgh EH5 1AF]; *b* 30 March 1964; MB, BS, MFPHM; *m* 1992 *James Alastair Innes, PhD, FRCPE, and has:

1f *Hamish Ian; *b* 1997

1f *Ailsa Helen; *b* 1994

2f *Mairi Catriona; *b* 1994

3d *Helen Mary [Mrs Edward Todd, 55 Tallai Rd, Mudgeeraba, Qld 4213, Australia]; *b* 14 Sept 1929; *m* 1st 6 Dec 1956 (*divorce* 1980) Stephen Edward Francis Bally (*d* 198–), s of Maj Edward Downes Bally, OBE of Newbury, Berks; *m* 2nd 25 June 1983 *Edward Louis Todd and by her 1st husb has:

1e *Ian Stephen Edward [Ian Bally Esq, 25 Denis St, Ayr, Qld 4807, Australia]; *b* 8 Sept 1959; *m* 1983 *Kay Louise Moffitt (*née* Lewis), and has issue:

1f *Sarah Ann Frances; *b* 1992

1e (cont.) Ian Bally also adopted:

*Mark William; *b* 1976

*Tabitha Louise; *b* 1978

*Jodie Marie (twin); *b* 1978

2e *Alexander St John; *b* 18 June 1963; *m* 1993 *Kay Therese Halley

3e *David Anthony; *b* 26 March 1968

1e *Louise Frances Joan [Ms Louise Bally, 6 Sean St, River View, Qld 4303, Australia]; *b* 24 Oct 1957; *m* 1977 (*divorce* 1987, resumed maiden name) David Bain and has issue:

1f *Aaron Ian; *b* 10 Oct 1987

1f *Madonna Anne; *b* 21 Aug 1976; has:

1g *Shanti-Marie; *b* 24 May 1997

2f *Michelle Helen; *b* 11 Sept 1978

1e (cont.) Ms Louise Bally also has:

3f *Madelaine Marie; *b* 19 May 1994

4d *Eynor Mary [Mrs Alfred Bell, Hillside Farm, Salisbury Rd, Shaftesbury, Dorset SP7 8BX]; *b* 6 April 1933; *m* 13 April 1957 Alfred Edwin Bell (*d* 1987), 2nd s of George Henry Bell, OBE, and has issue:

1e *Christopher Michael Ian [Christopher Bell Esq, 32 Alderney St, London SW1]; *b* 20 Dec 1958; *educ* Eton and UCL; slr, investment banker

2e *Julian Sebastian [Julian Bell Esq, 45 Island Rd, House No 1, Deepwater Bay, Hong Kong]; *b* 6 May 1962; *m* 15 April 1989 *Justin Chappell Day and has:

1f *Tatiana Victoria; *b* 21 Jan 1995

3e *Theodore Richard John; *b* 19 May 1972; *educ* Eton and Edinburgh U

5d *Philena Mary Edith [Miss Philena Bruce, Flat 4, 36 Russell Rd, London W14]; *b* 2 Nov 1949

3c Alastair Lavallette Eric Mary; *b* 4 May 1898; *educ* Cheltenham and RMC Sandhurst; late Lond Scottish and RAF, WW I; *m* 26 Aug 1923 Winifred Moultrie, dau of J A E Wren, of Southsea, and *d* 1950, leaving issue:

1d Anthony Crawford John; *b* 29 April 1925; late RAMC; *d* 1988

1c Mary Auxilium Maud Montagu, BRCS; *b* 8 March 1894; *d* 1973

1b Ethel Maude; *b* 7 May 1853; *m* 6 Aug 1878 Rev Henry Morden Bennett, of Bournemouth, and *d* 12 Jan 1921

(2) Robert Nicholson; *b* 5 April 1795; *m* 1822 Harriet Elizabeth, dau of Richard Williams, of Eaton Hall, Salop, and *d* 24 June 1867, leaving issue:

1a Isabella Harriet; *m* 7 March 1846 Frederick William Irby, of Norfolk (*dsp* 1 June 1877), s of Adml Hon Frederick Paul Irby, CB (*see* BOSTON, B), and *d* 13 April 1906

(1) Jane; *m* 8 July 1811 3rd Viscount Hawarden (*qv*) and *d* 24 March 1852, leaving issue

The 6th Bt's est surv son,

Sir William Bruce, 7th Bt; *m* June 1795 Anne Colquhoun, dau of Sir William Cunningham Fairlie, 6th Bt, of Robertland and Fairlie, and *d* 17 Nov 1827, having had, with other issue:

1 **Sir Michael Bruce, 8th Bt**; *b* 31 March 1798; *m* 10 June 1822 Isabella (*d* 19 Nov 1867), only child of Alexander Moir, of Scotstoun, by Margaret, dau of James Gordon, of Banff, and *dsp* 14 Dec 1862

2 William Cunningham; *b* 24 Nov 1798; Bombay CS; *m* 1820 Jane Catherine, dau of William Clark, of London, and *d* 11 Nov 1842, having had, with other issue:

(1) WILLIAM CUNNINGHAM (Sir), **9th Bt**

(2) Michael Robert; *b* 14 Dec 1832; Maj-Gen; *m* 5 March 1858 (*divorce* 1883) Lorina Mary Anne (*d* 1897), dau of Col George Wilson, Bombay Army (*see* BERNERS, B), and *d* 1893, leaving, with other issue:

1a Amy Eveleen; *m* 3 April 1894 Charles Montague Duncan Stewart, of Achnacone, Argyll (*d* 3 April 1924), and *d* 6 June 1954

(3) Arthur Neil; *b* 27 Jan 1838; Capt Bombay Army; *m* 28 March 1863 Marian Katherine (*m* 2nd 29 Aug 1876 Thomas Collet Sandars (*d* 1894) and *d* 2 Dec 1919), est dau of Surgn-Gen J Murray, Bengal Army, and *d* 8 June 1869, having had issue:

1a Arthur Francis; *b* 23 Dec 1863; Maj IA; *m* 22 Nov 1892 Rose Goleborn (*d* 22 Oct 1946, having *m* 2nd 1 Sept 1909 Arthur Philips Hoskyns (*d* 11 Feb 1935), yr son of Henry William Hoskyns, MA), dau of Rev Henry Swabey, MA, and *dsp* 20 May 1908

2a William Cunningham; *b* 1866; Cmdt Police Port Moresby, Papua, Br New Guinea; *m* 1897 Ellen, dau of John Scott, and *d* 30 May 1924, having had, with other issue:

1b +Robert Neil; *b* 3 May 1904

2b +William Cunningham; *b* 24 Nov 1907

3b +Colin Cadell; *b* 24 Nov 1914

1b *Corinna Joan; *b* 15 Aug 1916

2b *Lornas Dorothy; *b* 23 May 1919

(1) Ada Catherine; *m* 21 Jan 1865 James Waller O'Grady (*d* 23 May 1898), Lt RN, son of Hon Walter O'Grady (*see* 1953 edn GUILLAMORE, V), and *d* Jan 1902

3 Alexander Fairlie; *b* 31 Aug 1799; Madras CS; *m* 1st 26 Dec 1820 Mary Anne (*d* 12 June 1825), dau of Robert Cathcart, WS; *m* 2nd 7 Feb 1827 his sis-in-law Marion Harriet (*d* 29 Nov 1852), dau of Robert Cathcart, and by her had, with other issue:

(1) Alexander James; *b* 24 Dec 1828; Maj-Gen Madras Army; *m* 16 Dec 1853 Marianne (*d* 8 Jan 1925), dau of J F Thomas HEICS, and *d* 9 May 1906, leaving, with other issue:

1a Alexander Fairlie; *b* 3 Nov 1854; *m* 11 Sept 1902 Emily Louisa, dau of E D Carver, and *d* 27 June 1939, having had, with other issue:

1b Emily Hester; *b* 9 Sept 1903; *m* 29 Dec 1928 Maj John Donald de Wilton, RIASC, son of Capt D de Wilton, KOYLI, and *d* 3 May 1932, leaving issue

2a Robert Cathcart; *b* 8 Sept 1859; MD Edinburgh; *m* 7 Nov 1882 Grizelda Wilson (*d* 24 Aug 1940), est dau of Rev Alexander Rodger, MA, and *d* 24 Nov 1955, leaving issue:

1b Alexander Cathcart; *b* 8 Dec 1894; *educ* Bradfield; Maj HLI (ret), Staff Offr Local Forces and Adj Constabulary Trinidad 1933–34, WW I (wounded, star, two medals), Mohmand Operations 1935, Silver Jubilee Medal 1935, in Min Home Security 1937–43, Br Cncl Rep Malta 1945–50, Dir Trg and Ops CD for BC Canada 1950–58; *m* 18 April 1958 Betty, est dau of John Malcolm Aitken, of Lockerbie, Dumfriesshire, and widow of William Echin Grayburn, and *dsp* Sept 1966

2b Robert Cathcart; *b* 24 July 1898; *educ* Bradfield and New Coll Oxford; late 2nd Lt HLI, WW I in France and Belgium (two medals); *m* 2 June 1927 Christian Adeline (*d* 1990), yst dau of William Henderson, of Berkeley House, nr Frome, and *d* 14 April 1966, having had issue:

1c *Fairlie Cathcart [Mrs Charles Hutton, Brook House, Sampford Brett, Taunton, Som TA4 4LE]; *b* 13 April 1928; *m* 1951 Charles William Hutton, BArch, FRIBA (*d* 11 Sept 1995), and has issue:

1d *Fairlie Elizabeth [Mrs Philip Moore, 150 Sutton Court Rd, London W4]; *b* 10 March 1952; *m* 1977 *Philip Julian Moore, ARICS, and has:

1e *Alastair Philip; *b* 1980

2e *Dominic William; *b* 1983

2d *Julia Frances; *b* 28 Feb 1954; has by *Darrell Martin Whittaker:

1e *Luke Hutton WHITTAKER; *b* 1981

2e *Tom Hutton WHITTAKER; *b* 1983

3d *Anina Mary [Ms Anina Hutton, 37 St James' Sq, Bath, Somerset]; *b* 14 Jan 1955; has issue by *Martin Bruce Robertson:

1e *Walter Douglas HUTTON; *b* 1982

1e *Zoë Bruce HUTTON; *b* 1979

2e *Rose Matilda HUTTON; *b* 1986

2c Marianne Christian Cathcart; *b* 12 Feb 1932; *d* unm at Gibraltar, 1 May 1957

1a Diana Harriet; *m* 4 Sept 1879 William Bremner (*d* 7 June 1935), of Edinburgh, and *d* 30 July 1953, leaving issue

(2) George Cadell; *b* 23 Jan 1830; *m* 16 June 1855 Roberta (*d* 1900), dau of R Cadell, and *d* 1909, leaving, with other issue:

1a Alexander Fairlie, MICE; *b* 7 Sept 1857; late Capt RAF, WW I; *m* 26 Dec 1882 Katherine Elizabeth (*d* 14 Jan 1931), dau of William Freebairn, of Drummilling, Ayrshire, and *d* 1944, having had issue:

1b Alan Cathcart Fairlie; *b* 2 March 1894; Lt-Cdr RN; *m* 28 June 1919 Barbara Clarributt (*d* 1992), dau of E Clarributt Skinner, and *d* 10 Oct 1927, leaving issue:

1c +Colin Michael Fairlie [Colin Bruce Esq, Airth House, South Drive, Littleton, Winchester, Hants SO22 6PY]; *b* 16 Feb 1925; *educ* Christ's Hosp, Wadham Coll Oxford (MA), and Edinburgh U; WW II as Sub-Lt RNVR; lecturer economics Natal U 1950–53, ec advsr Maltese Govt 1956–57 and Dowty Gp 1957–58, Sec Malta Industl Devpt Bd and London Manager Malta Aids to Industs Bd 1959–61, ec advsr Uganda Devpt Corp 1962–63, Dir Ec Planning and Devpt Buganda 1963–65, economist African Dept IBRD 1965, World Bank 1965–84; *m* 1st 7 Oct 1946 (*divorce* 1962) Patricia Mary Platt, and has issue:

1d +Timothy Michael Fairlie [Timothy Bruce Esq, 400 Knecht Drive, Dayton, Ohio 45405, USA]; *b* 17 Feb 1948; *m* 1978 *Kate Ella Armpriester

2d +Alan Simon Fairlie [Alan Bruce Esq, HC Box 41, Elm Rd, Bolinas, Calif 94924, USA]; *b* 30 May 1950; *educ* Kingston Poly (Dip Arch), RIBA; V-Pres Stone, Marraccinni and Patterson, San Francisco; *m* *Mary Jan Alstad, and has issue:

1e *Abigail Emily Fairlie; *b* 1969

2e *Sarah Alison Fairlie; *b* 1981

3d +Jonathan Neil Fairlie [Jonathan Bruce Esq, 33 Henley Rd, Iffley, Oxford]; *b* 2 July 1958; *m* *Carrie Marie Gomm, and has issue:

1e +Joshua Thomas Fairlie; *b* 1983

1e *Lauren Fairlie; *b* 1980

2e *Sian Katie Fairlie; *b* 1981

3e *Jessica Fairlie; *b* 19–

1d *Lindsay Madeleine Fairlie [Mrs Barry Shapland, Dene Cliff, Palace House Rd, Hebden Bridge, W Yorks]; *b* 26 June 1953; *m* 1970 *Barry Shapland, and has issue:

1e *Fionn; *b* 19–

2e *Ruari; *b* 19–

3e *Megan; *b* 19–

2d *Jenny Catriona Fairlie; *b* 9 Sept 1960; *educ* Nottingham U; *m* 19– *Andrew Harker and has:

1e *Thomas; *b* 19–

1e *Grace Catriona; *b* 1993

1c (cont.) Colin Fairlie *m* 2nd 31 Jan 1963 *Georgina Morrison Baker, and by her had issue:

3d *Fiona Elspeth; *b* 23 May 1965

2c +John Alan Fairlie [John Bruce Esq, Beechbrook, 16 Colebrook St, Winchester, Hants SO23 9LH]; *b* 13 May 1926; *educ* Christ's Hosp, and Wadham Coll Oxford; late Lt RA; FIPD, MIPM, industl rels supervisor Roy Dutch Shell Gp Colombia 1948–49, Venezuela 1951–59, Assist Personnel Manager Shell Chemical 1959–62, Personnel Superintendent Stanlow Refinery, Shell Refining Co Ltd 1962–69, manager personnel and trg Carrington Works Shell Chemicals 1969; *m* 12 April 1950 *Joyce Edna Soffe and has issue:

1d +Iain Alasdair Fairlie; *b* 30 May 1954; *educ* Cambridge (BA), RCA (Dip Film making); *m* 6 July 1994 *Maria Esperanza Sanchez and has:

1e +David Malcolm; *b* 1993

1e *Hannah Eileen Jones; *b* 1987

2e *Alexandra Kathleen Jones; *b* 1991

2d +Andrew Stuart Cathcart [Andrew Bruce Esq, 14 Hastings Close, Polegate, E Sussex]; *b* 30 May 1954; *educ* Manchester Poly (BA), Bristol Poly (DPA); *m* 1988 *Maureen Hull

1d *Alison Jean [Mrs Paul Moore, Triffeny, 13a Stoney Lane, Winchester, Hants]; *b* 24 June 1951; *m* 1977 *Paul Richard Moore and has:

1e *Jonathan Paul Bruce; *b* 1980

1e *Nicola Jane Bruce; *b* 1982

1c *Barbara Jean [Mrs Robert Hornby, 38A The Broad Walk, Imperial Sq, Cheltenham, Glos GL50 1QG]; *b* 29 April 1921; *m* 27 Feb 1941 *Col Robert John Augustine Hornby, OBE, MIPR, Queen's Roy Surrey Regt (ret), son of Robert Hornby, of Ashtead, Surrey, and has issue:

1d *Vivien Sheena [Deaconess The Hon Mrs Edward Northcote, 96 Otho Ct, Augustus Cl, Brentford Dock, Middx]; *b* 18 Nov 1942; *m* 29 June 1963 (*divorce* 1980) Hon Edward Frederic Northcote, TD, yr s of 3rd Earl of Iddesleigh (*qv*), and has issue

2d *Louise Panette [Mrs Kenneth Bootes-Johns, GPO Box 4701, Sydney, NSW 2001, Australia]; *b* 6 July 1947; *m* 29 April 1967 (*divorce* 1993) Kenneth Dudley Johns Bootes-Johns, s of Roland Kenneth Bootes-Johns, of Dublin

1b Dorothy Morris Fairlie; *b* 20 May 1885; author: *The King's Curate, Mistress-Mariner, The Dimsie Books*; *d* 21 Sept 1970

2a Robert Cathcart; *b* 1804

1a Emelia Gardine; *d* unm 1946

(3) Charles Chesney; *b* 15 July 1837; *m* 1 Oct 1873 Emily Anne O'Callaghan, and *d* 21 May 1904, leaving issue:

1a Alexander Fairlie; *b* 1877

1a Marion Harriet

2a Elizabeth Mary Ann

3a Jacoba Helena Cathcart

4a Abriana Maria

(4) Elliott Armstrong; *b* 9 Aug 1840; Col IA, Afghanistan 1878–80 (medals), Burma 1885–88 (despatches, Brevet, medal with clasp); *m* 1st 9 Aug 1861 Mary Rebecca (*d* 12 Sept 1910), dau of Rev W Dawson, and had, with other issue:

1a William Alexander Macdonald; *b* 10 July 1866; Lt-Col (ret) IA, China 1900–01; *m* 1st 8 Dec 1892 Frances Alice (*d* 24 Sept 1933), dau of J T Lingard, of Cooga, Co Claire; *m* 2nd 19 Jan 1935 Mary Ellen (*d* 1956), widow of Dr William T St Stephens, and *d* 10 March 1939

2a John Elliott Lidderdale; *b* 10 Jan 1870; Maj RA, cmdg 26th Jacob's Mountain Bn; *m* 12 Sept 1900 Charlotte Mabel (*m* 2nd 1920 Ernest Neele, who *d* 24 June 1937), dau of T J G Johnstone, Ceylon, CS, and was *ka* 29 May 1915, leaving issue:

1b John Charles Douglas; *b* 2 Aug 1902; Brig Gurkha Rifles, Lt Somerset LI, WW II; *m* 12 Sept 1934 *Dorothy Barbara, er dau of Robert Thomas Dundas, CIE, Indian Police (ret)

2b Henry Malcolm; *b* 28 Feb 1904; *d* 15 Nov 1954

3a Malcolm Edward Lloyd; *b* 12 Feb 1872; Lt-Col (ret) IA; *m* 21 Oct 1903 Clementina Blyth (*d* 1958), yst dau of W F B Dalzel, MD, Surgn-Maj Bengal Army, and *d* 15 March 1952, leaving with other issue:

1b Robert Graham Dalzel; *b* 2 Oct 1910; Maj (ret) E Surrey Regt, WW II (POW); *m* 1956 Joan Mary Price

1b *Elizabeth Mary Dalzel (twin) [Mrs Neville Govett, 13 Clydesdale Gdns, Richmond, Surrey]; *b* 2 Oct 1910; *m* 1 July 1933 Neville Eugene Govett (*d* 1972), 3rd s of Lionel Arthur Govett, of Richmond, Surrey, and has issue:

1c *Bryan; *b* 1934; *educ* St Paul's

2c *Richard; *b* 1937; *educ* St Paul's

3c *Robert John; *b* 1944

4a Elliott Henry Rochford; *b* 17 Sept 1874; with Anglo-Saxon Petroleum Co; *m* 8 April 1905 Frances Maude (*d* 1949), dau of A McDonald, and *d* 1 July 1933, leaving issue:

1b +Elliott McDonald; *b* 19 June 1906; *m* 1932 *Kathleen Clarke, and has issue:

1c +Michael; *b* 1939

1c *Josephine; *b* 1945

2c *Heather; *b* 1949

2b Charles Cathcart; *b* 2 Jan 1909

3b +Malcolm Alexander; *b* 28 May 1912; *m* 1942 (*divorce* 19–) Doris Gwynnith, and has issue:

1c +Donald Malcolm; *b* 1944

2c +Geoffrey; *b* 1946

3c +Richard (twin); *b* 1946

1b Helen Doreen (twin with Malcolm); *d* unm 20 Feb 1960

2b *Beryl Brenda; *b* 1919; *m* 1947 *Herbert Winston Eaton, and has issue:

1c *Geoffrey Winston; *b* 1949

1c *Linda Christine; *b* 1952

5a Charles Mathewes, CB (1933), OBE (1918); *b* 14 Dec 1875; *educ* Emmanuel Coll Cambridge (MA); Pncpl Assist Sec Admlty; *m* 20 Feb 1929 Emily Violet, yst dau of George Taylor, and *d* 22 Sept 1940

1a Mary Anne Sophia; *m* 20 Sept 1900 William E Fenton-Wingate (*d* 4 Aug 1914)

(4) (cont.) Col Elliott Bruce *m* 2nd 21 March 1911 Emily Mary Goodall yst dau of George Goodall Dainty, of Rugby, and *d* 29 May 1919

(5) Michael McCubbin; *b* 15 Nov 1844; *m* 1878 Margaret, dau of Robert Kerr, and *d* 19 Dec 1909, leaving issue:

1a Robert Cathcart; *b* 1878; *m* 1916 Emma Dorothy (*d* 1983), dau of John Croce, and *d* 1968, leaving issue:

1b +Vivian Richard, MB, FRCGP [Dr Vivian Bruce, Lindavanally, 25A George Douglas Dve, Ryedale, Dumfries DG2 7ES]; *b* 1919; *m* 1st 1942 Norah Maeve Yates (*d* 1960) and has:

1c +Robert James, OBE [Maj Robert Bruce OBE, AHMIBAH Farm Estate, No 4 The Polo Centre, London Rd, Sunninghill, Berks SL5 7SE]; *b* 1946; Maj RM (ret); *m* 1969 *Elizabeth Jane Moira, dau of David Clement Burgess, and has issue:

1d +Robert David Cathcart; *b* 1977

2d +James Herbert William; *b* 1985

1d *(Elizabeth) Maeve [Mrs Maeve Bruce, 307 Banbury Rd, Summertown, Oxford]; *b* 1970; *m* 19– (*divorce* 1995) Adrian BRUCE-PURCHASE (formerly PURCHASE), and has:

1e *Jake Hamilton; *b* 1993

2d *(Laura) Christian; *b* 1971; has:

1e *Patrick Joseph BRUCE; *b* 1997

2c +Michael Alexander [Michael Bruce Esq, Welshmill Lodge, Welshmill Rd, Frome, Somerset BA11 2LA]; *b* 1949; FCA; Ch Accountant and Adminr Hall-Houston Malaysia Ltd, Kuala Lumpur; *m* 1983 *Patricia Sheila, dau of Col Peter Johnson, and has issue:

1d +Alexander Peter; *b* 1987

2d +David; *b* 1990

1d *Natasha; *b* 1985

2d *Diana (twin); *b* 1990

3c +Richard Hubert [Richard Bruce Esq, 17 Danvers Rd, Mountsorrel, Loughborough, Leics LE12 7JG]; *b* 1956

1b (cont.) Dr Vivian Bruce *m* 2nd 1962 (*divorce* 1983) Bernadette Yates and by her has:

4c +Paul Cathcart [Paul Bruce Esq, 26 Templars Close, Wheatley, Oxford OX33 1PA]; *b* 1963; BSc; *m* 1989 *Louise, dau of Hari Ratan Ker, and has:

1d +Benjamin Hamish; *b* 1995

1d *Hannah Amy; *b* 1992

5c +Angus Peter; *b* 1964; *m* 1990 (*divorce* 1993) Jennifer Tatum; *m* 2nd 1995 *Paola, dau of Santo Zanotti and by her has:

1d *Emma Frances; *b* 1997

6c +Joseph Douglas [Joseph Bruce Esq, 3 Julian Rd, Ludlow, Salop SY8 1HA]; *b* 1970; BA

1b (cont.) Dr Vivian Bruce *m* 3rd 1983 *Valerie Florence May Bruce, dau of Nelson Fitzroy Baylis

2a Charles Kerr; *b* 1880; *m* 1928 Lily (*d* 1959), dau of Charles Leonard, and *d* 10 Feb 1955, leaving issue:

1b +Ian Robert [Ian Bruce Esq, Weston Down Cottages, Weston Colley, Micheldever, Hants SO21 3AQ]; *b* 1931; *m* 1st 1956 (*divorce* 1980) Dorothy Evelyn Knight; *m* 2nd 1994 *Elizabeth Joan, dau of Col Harry Lacy and widow of Richard Swanwick, and by his 1st w has:

1c *Anne; *b* 1960

2c *Caroline Jane; *b* 1963

1b *Margaret [Mrs Norman Whight, The Cherries, 15 Fairfield Way, Hildenborough, Kent TN11 9ET]; *b* 1930; *m* 1956 *Norman Terence Whight, and has had issue:

1c Charles Bruce; *b* 1963; *d* 1980

1c *Fiona Margaret; *b* 1960

2b *Audrey Mary [Mrs George Morgan, 16 Heslop Rd, London SW12 8EG]; *b* 1935; *m* 1958 *George David James Morgan, and has issue:

1c *Christopher David *b* 1962

1c *Felicity Claire; *b* 1960

1a Harriet Jane Margaret; *m* 2 June 1904 James Harold Skilton (*d* 1949) and had:

1b Aubrey Bruce; *b* 24 Feb 1908; *m* May 1929 Della Cootes, and *d* 1995, leaving:

1c *Maria; *b* 21 Feb 1947; *m* 27 Nov 1965 *Robert John Brame, of New Lynn, Auckland, NZ, and has issue:

1d *Susan Maree; *b* 12 June 1966

2d *Jenny Lynaire; *b* 17 April 1969

1b Margaret Rose Bruce; *b* 9 Sept 1909; *m* 22 May 1939 Ronald James Thorp Collier (*d* 1963), and had issue:

1c *Maxine; *b* 13 June 1940; *m* 15 April 1966 *Donald Gordon Blake

3 (cont) Alexander Bruce *m* 3rd 16 Aug 1860 Janette Dickie, 2nd dau of Robert Perry, MD, of Glasgow, and *d* 26 June 1875, having by her had issue:

(6) Robert Perry; *b* 1 Aug 1861; *m* 1st 1886 (*divorce* 1899) Ethel Blanche (*d* 1911), dau of John Russell; *m* 2nd 19 Aug 1903 Olive Maud (*d* 1968), dau of Joseph Babington Macaulay, of Devon, and *d* 10 June 1914, having by her had:

1a Michael Macaulay; *b* 4 Sept 1904; Nat Coal Bd; *m* 20 Dec 1937 *Louise [Mrs Michael Bruce, 62 Bolton Rd, Windsor, Berks], dau of Professor Van der Pot, of The Netherlands, and *d* 1964, leaving issue:

1b +Robert William; *b* 28 June 1940; *m* 1964 *Jennifer Patricia Guilfoyle Brown, and has issue:

1c +Michael Gregory Macaulay; *b* 1968

1c *Rosalind Ellen Macaulay; *b* 1966

2c *Miranda Jane Macaulay; *b* 1970

2b +Michael Zachary [Michael Bruce Esq, 62 Bolton Rd, Windsor, Berks]; *b* 11 Oct 1951; *m* 1981 *Ellen, dau of Sigbert Leuchthold, of Switzerland, and has issue:

1c +Edgar; *b* 1989

1c *Catherine; *b* 1984

2c *Leanne; *b* 1986

1b *Mary Louise [Mrs Colin Prince, 19 Alexandra Rd, Kingston upon Thames]; *b* 1 Dec 1938; *m* 1961 *Colin Hugh Prince, and has issue:

1c *Hamish Robin John; *b* 1966

1c *Anna Louise; *b* 1964

2b *Vanessa Bertha Jane [Mrs Christopher Ryle, Upland Cottage, Holt Hill, Holt End, Bealey, Worcs]; *b* 12 Dec 1942; *m* 1968 *Christopher Ryle, and has issue:

1c *Deborah Louise; *b* 1968

2c *Xanthe; *b* 1969

3c *Octavia Georgina; *b* 1979

3b *Barbara Lucy [Mrs Paul Henderson, The Beeches, Boston Spa, W Yorks]; *b* 19 June 1945; *m* 27 Dec 1969 *Paul Lewis Henderson, est s of Dr James Henderson, of Chiswick, and has issue:

1c *James; *b* 1974

2c *Barnaby; *b* 1981

1c *Juliet; *b* 1972

2a Robert Macaulay; *b* 6 Feb 1906; *d* 11 Oct 1928

3a +Nigel Macaulay; *b* 6 Feb 1906 (twin); late Maj RA, ADC to GOC-in-C 14th Army, Burma, WW II; *m* 7 Dec 1940 *Helen Woodhall, dau of Charles Edward Kayler, of Mixbury Manor, Oxon

4a Edward Macaulay; *b* 9 Feb 1908; Maj Middx Regt WW II (despatches); gen manager Unilever; *m* 1939 *Nancy Elinor [Mrs Edward Bruce, Horseshoe Cottage, Arlington, Bilbury, Glos], dau of Lt-Col F G C Humfrey, late 12th Bengal Cav, and *d* 1986, having had issue:

1b Michael Alistair; *b* 1941; *d* 1948

2b +David Nigel Macauley [David Bruce Esq, 15 St Helena Rd, Bristol BS6 7NR]; *b* 8 Nov 1947; *educ* Gresham's, St Andrews (MA) and Edinburgh U (MPhil); lecturer Bristol Poly; *m* 1972 *Diana, dau of Cluny Dale, and has issue:

1c +James; *b* 1974

1c *Rebecca; *b* 1977

1b *Elizabeth Mary; *b* 1942; *m* 1966 (*divorce* 1978) Dirk Detert, PhD, and has issue:

1c *Niels Bruce; *b* 1970

2c *Jan Bruce; *b* 1974

1a Olive; *m* 10 Feb 1934 Gabriel Thomas Grisewood, yst son of Lt-Col Harman Mary Joseph Grisewood, of Gatwick House, Billericay, Essex, and had issue

1 Mary Agnew; *m* 1828 George C Moir, of Denmore, Aberdeenshire, and had two daus

The 8th Bt's nephew,

Sir William Cunningham Bruce, 9th Bt, DL; *b* 20 Sept 1825; Capt 74th Regt; *m* 21 Aug 1850 Charlotte (*d* 16 Oct 1873), dau of Hon Waller O'Grady (*see* 1953 edn GUILLAMORE, V), and *d* 29 May 1906, having had, with other issue, including two daus (Grace Katherine, *d* unm 19 July 1934; Corinna Maria, *d* unm 9 Sept 1929):

Sir William Waller Bruce, 10th Bt; *b* 27 Sept 1856; *m* 12 March 1892 Angelica Mary (*d* 16 Dec 1917), dau of Gen George Selby, RA, and *d* 22 March 1912, having had issue:

1 MICHAEL WILLIAM SELBY (Sir), **11th Bt**

2 (William) Nigel Ernle; *b* 4 Feb 1895; Lt 10th Serv Bn Somerset LI and HAC WW I (severely wounded); actor, chiefly famous for portrayals of Dr Watson; *m* 19 May 1921 Violet Pauline (*d* 10 Jan 1970), dau of Col Willington Augustus David Shelton, DSO, of Bruree House, Co Limerick, and *d* 8 Oct 1953, leaving issue:

(1) *Pauline Margaret; *b* 27 Dec 1922; *m* 1 Sept 1946 *W/Cdr A Geoffrey Page, DSO, DFC and bar, RAF, yr s of A J Page, ICS, and has issue:

1a *Nigel Geoffrey; *b* 28 Nov 1953

2a *Jamie Douglas; *b* 16 June 1958

1a *Pauline Shelley; *b* 9 June 1948

(2) Jennifer Beryl; *b* 19 Sept 1924; *m* 1st 17 Sept 1944 (*divorce* 1946) Lt Jay Gould III, US Army, and has issue; *m* 2nd 22 Oct 1947 Arthur Sebastian Gilbey (*d* 25 May 1964), est s of Sebastian Gilbey, of Croft House, Summerford-Keynes, Glos (*see* GILBEY, Bt), and has further issue

1 Grace Degla Mary; *d* an infant 1895

The 10th Bt's er son,

Sir Michael William Selby Bruce, 11th Bt; *b* 27 March 1894; Lt 8th Bn Middx Regt, Br SA Police, Capt RFA, F/Lt RAF, Dardanelles, Egypt and France WW I (wounded), and S/Ldr RAF Regt WW II (wounded); author: *Songs from the Saddle, Peaks of Hazard, Hunters' Yarns, Saddles and Sail, The Royal House of Bruce, The Romantic Journey of Prince Charles Edward, Sir William Wallace, Headlines 1837 to 1937, Tramp Royal*; *m* 1st 8 Aug 1925 (*divorce* 1928) Doreen Dalziel, dau of W F Greenwell, of Glos, and had issue:

1 Sir (FRANCIS) MICHAEL IAN BRUCE OF STENHOUSE, **12th and present Bt**

Sir Michael *m* 2nd 28 Oct 1933 Elizabeth Constance (*d* 26 Feb 1943), yr dau of Frank Plummer, of Toronto, by Fanny, yst dau of Francis Fetherstonhaugh, of Carrick, Mullingar, Co Westmeath, and by her had further issue:

1 *Corinna Mary Constance; *b* 20 March 1940

Sir Michael *m* 3rd 11 Jan 1945 (*annulled* 1946) Anne, WRNS, dau of Maj Gervase Percy Disney; *m* 4th 3 Oct 1946 *Margaret Helen, late Section Offr WAAF, dau of Sir Arthur Lennon Binns, CBE, MC, of Lytham St Annes, Dir Educn Lancs, and *d* 20 May 1957, leaving by her:

2 +Michael David Lennon; *b* 27 March 1948

BRUCE OF DONINGTON

Creation: B. (LP, UK) 1974.

THE BARON BRUCE OF DONINGTON, of Rickmansworth, Co Hertfordshire (Donald William Trevor Bruce) [The Rt Hon The Lord Bruce of Donington, 155 Gower St, London WC1E 6BH]; *b* 3 Oct 1912; *educ* Donington GS Lincs; FCA 1947; WWII: commissioned TA 1939, Maj Roy Signals (despatches)1942; MP (Lab) N Portsmouth 1945–50, PPS to Min Health 1945–50, Memb: Min Health Delegn to Sweden and Denmark 1946, H of C Select Ctee Public Accounts 1948–50, MEP 1975–79, Ho Lds oppn spokesman Treasury, trade, ec and industl matters 1979–90; *m* 1st 1939 (*divorce* 1980) Joan Letitia, dau of Hamilton Claude Butcher, of Maida Vale, and has had, with another s (*d* young):

1 *Michael Gordon; *b* 1952

1 *Ann; *b* 1942; *m* 19– *T Samuels

2 *Mary Trevor; *b* 1945; *m* 1968 *Shuhada Hilmi

The BARON BRUCE OF DONINGTON *m* 2nd 1981 *Mrs Cyrena Heard (*née* Shaw)

Lineage: WILLIAM TREVOR BRUCE, of Norbury, Surrey, had issue:

DONALD WILLIAM TREVOR, *cr* a **Baron**

BRUCE-GARDNER

Arms: Or, a saltire couped gules charged with five bezants, on a chief of the second a bee volant proper between two roses argent, barbed and seeded also proper. **Crest:** In front of a miner's pick and gad saltire a thistle leaved and slipped all proper. **Motto:** *Labore et virtute* ('By work and strength'). **Creation:** Bt. (UK) 12 Feb 1945.

SIR ROBERT HENRY BRUCE-GARDNER, 3RD BT, of Frilford, Berks [Sir Robert Bruce-Gardner, 121 Brackenbury Rd, London W6 0BQ]; *b* 10 June 1943; *s* f 1997; *educ* Uppingham and Reading U; *m* 1979 *Veronica Ann Hand-Oxborrow, dau of Rev W E Hand and Mrs R G Oxborrow, of Caterham, and has:

1 +THOMAS EDWARD PETER; *b* 28 Jan 1982

2 +Richard Tyndall Jowett; *b* 1983

Lineage: HENRY GARDNER, of Stanstead Lodge, Forest Hill, London SE23; *b* 20 May 1859; *educ* Glasgow Acad; fndr Henry Gardner & Co, steel merchants; *m* 24 May 1883 Florence (*d* 5 Sept 1947), dau of Walter J Arliss, and *d* 27 April 1941, leaving, with a yr s (Walter):

Sir CHARLES (BRUCE) GARDNER later BRUCE-GARDNER (deed poll 21 Dec 1937), **1st Bt** (UK), so *cr* 12 Feb 1945; *b* 6 Nov 1887; *educ* St Dunstan's Coll and Battersea Tech Coll; MIMechE; v-chm Crompton Parkinson Ltd, chm: John Lysaght Gp, Flintshire Coal Owners Assoc 1920–30, Iron and Steel Industrial Res Cncl 1929–30, London Iron and Steel Exchange 1936 and 1937, Soc Br Aircraft Constructors 1939–43, Br Iron and Steel Corp, dep chm The Steel Co of Wales, dir Consett Iron Co and GKN, dir John Summers & Sons 1913–20, memb: Sheet Trade Bd 1914–30, Sheetmakers Conf 1915–30, Centl Cncl Mining Assoc 1920–30, Advsy Ctee Dept Overseas Trade 1928–30, Sec State Air's Industl Advsy Panel 1938–39, Air Supply Bd 1939–41, Nat Prodn Advsy Cncl 1942–43, Flintshire CC 1913–17, exec ctee Br Iron and Steel Fedn, American Soc for Metals, industl advsr Govrs Bank of England 1930–38, md Securities Management Tst 1930–38, Air Cncl Ctee on Supply 1938–39, Civil Aviation Planning Ctee 1939, controller Labour Allocation and Supply Min Aircraft Prodn 1943–44, ch exec Industrial Reconversion BOT 1944–46, pres Iron and Steel Inst, hon life memb American Inst Mining and Metallurgical Engrs, ktd 1938; *m* 1 Feb 1911 Gertrude Amy (*d* 4 Oct 1978), dau of Charles Rivington Shill, and *d* 1 Oct 1960, leaving issue:

1 **Sir Douglas Bruce-Gardner, 2nd Bt**, *b* 27 Jan 1917; *educ* Uppingham and Trin Coll Cambridge (MA); dir GKN 1960–82 (v-chm 1972–74), chm GKN Rolled and Bright Steel 1968–72, GKN (S Wales) 1968–72, dir Henry Gardner & Co 1952–68, pres Iron and Steel Inst 1966–67, dep chm 1974–77, chm Rolled & Bright Steel 1968–72, pres Iron and Steel Employer's Assoc 1963–64; *m* 1st 27 July 1940 (*divorce* 1964) Monica Flummerfelt, only dau of Prof Sir Geoffrey Jefferson, CBE, FRS, of Didsbury, Manchester, and had:

(1) *(Erica) Judith [Mrs Paul Blackburn, 4 Hilbrow Cottages, Old Horsham Rd, Beare Green, Dorking, Surrey RH5 4RB]; *b* 8 Dec 1941; *m* 29 Sept 1962 *Paul Hamer Blackburn, 2nd s of William Blackburn, of Hustdale, Devisdale Rd, Bowdon, Cheshire, and has issue:

1a *Richard Martin; *b* 18 Nov 1965

2a *Robert Paul; *b* 12 June 1967

1a *Katherine Mary; *b* 1 Aug 1963; *m* 1986 *Guy Mark Larkin

2a *Emma Louise; *b* 18 Nov 1965; *m* 1984 (*divorce* 1988) Simon David Hamblin and has issue:

1b *Kirsty Alexandra; *b* 1985

(2) *(Sarah) Tanis; *b* 1 Oct 1952; *m* 1987 *Richard William Towse, s of John Towse, of London, and has issue:

1a *Benjamin William; *b* 1988

1 (cont.) **Sir Douglas** *m* 2nd 18 March 1964 *Sheila Jane [Sheila Lady Bruce-Gardner, Stocklands, Lewstone, Ganarew, nr Monmouth NP5 3SS], dau of Roger Stilliard, of Seer Green, Bucks, and *d* 25 Nov 1997, leaving by her:

(2) +(James) Graham; *b* 5 Sept 1969

(3) *Joanna Margaret; *b* 20 Feb 1966

2 +Bryan Charles [Bryan Bruce-Gardner Esq, Stedefield, Church Lane, Flyford Flavell, Worcs WR7 4BZ]; *b* 4 July 1924; *educ* Uppingham and Trin Coll Cambridge (MA); F/Lt RAFVR WW II 1942–46; *m* 16 Aug 1952 *Helen Rosemary, only dau of Digby B Sowerby, of Kirmington House, Ulceby, Lincs, and has:

(1) +Edwin Charles; *b* 17 Jan 1954; *educ* Uppingham

(2) +Robin Digby [Robin Bruce-Gardner Esq, 60 Cumberland St, London SW1V 4LZ]; *b* 7 Sept 1955; *educ* Uppingham; BA, ACIB; *m* 1987 *Caroline Stuart, dau of Peter S Wright, of Thurlstone, Devon

(3) +Stephen Bryan [Stephen Bruce-Gardner Esq, Eaton Lodge, Pulford, Cheshire]; *b* 21 Nov 1957; *m* 1990 *Karen, yst dau of Harry Spencer, of Mold, Clwyd

(4) +Ian Douglas [Ian Bruce-Gardner Esq, Greenspot Farm, Oldmeldrum, Inverurie, Aberdeenshire AB51 0AG]; *b* 15 May 1963; *m* 1990 *(Elisa)Beth Mary, dau of R D White and Mrs D H McLellan, of Ollerton, Cheshire, and has:

1a +Angus Ramsay; *b* 10 Feb 1995

1a *Rosannah Charlotte; *b* 27 April 1992

3 *Gertrude Doreen; *b* 14 May 1913; *m* 22 March 1941 *Paul de Kantzow Dykes, Fell King's Coll Cambridge, Maj RA, er s of F J Dykes, of Cambridge, and has issue:

(1) *Daphne Jane; *b* 6 Nov 1942

(2) *Sheila Rosemary; *b* 29 May 1946

BRUNNER

Arms: Gu. on the base of a stone hexagon fountain ppr. a rose of the first, in chief two mullets of six points, or. **Crest:** In front of a wing erect gu. a fountain charged with a rose as in the arms. **Motto:** *Bibe si sapis* ('If thou art wise, drink'). **Creation:** Bt. (UK) 27 July 1895.

SIR JOHN HENRY KILIAN BRUNNER, 4TH BT [Sir John Brunner Bt, 138 Victoria Ave, Dalkeith, WA 6009, Australia]; *b* 1 June 1927; *s* f 1982; *educ* Eton and Trin Coll Oxford (BA 1950); late Lt RA, with PEP (later became PSI) 1950–53, talks producer 1953, ec advsr Treasury 1958–61, assist manager *Observer* 1961; *m* 22 Dec 1955 *Jasmine Cecily, er dau of John Wardrop Moore, MA, by Janet Monteith, only dau of Sir James Malcolm Monteith Erskine, JP (*see* ERSKINE, Bt), and has issue:

1 +NICHOLAS FELIX MINTURN; *b* 16 Jan 1960

2 +(Mark) Jonathan Irving; *b* 28 June 1962

1 *Claire Eliza; *b* 14 Oct 1958

Lineage: Rev JOHN BRUNNER, of Zurich; *b* 20 June 1800; moved to Liverpool 1832; *m* 27 June 1835 Margaret Catherine (*d* 8 Sept 1847), dau of Thomas Curphey, of Balldroma, IOM, by Margaret Leece, of Ballamona, IOM, and had a 2nd s:

Sir John Tomlinson Brunner, 1st Bt (UK), so *cr* 27 July 1895, PC (1906), DL (Lancs), of Druids Cross, Lancs, and Winnington Old Hall, Cheshire; *b* 8 Feb 1842; fndr Brunner Mond & Co, alkali mfrs, MP (Lib) Northwich 1885–86 and 1887–1910, Pro-Chllr Liverpool U 1909–19, Hon LLD Liverpool 1909; *m* 1st 14 June 1864 Salome (*d* 29 Jan 1874), dau of James Davies, of Liverpool, and had, with other issue:

1 JOHN FOWLER (Sir), **2nd Bt**

2 Harold Roscoe, DL, JP Cheshire; barrister Inner Temple, Weaver Tstee, dir Brunner Mond & Co; *b* 22 Jan 1871; *m* 17 Dec 1898 Ethel (*d* 3 Nov 1926), est dau of Arthur Houston, LLD, KC, of Dublin, and *d* 3 Nov 1926, leaving issue:

(1) Anthony; *b* 21 May 1901; by deed poll 18 Oct 1919 dropped forenames Egbert Sidney Houston and took Anthony; *educ* Cheltenham and Pembroke Coll Cambridge (BA 1924); 2nd Lt RA (TA); *m* 5 March 1934 Amy Phyllis Ivy (Felicity) Whittaker (*d* 10 July 1994), and *d* 1970, leaving:

1a John Kilian Houston; *b* 14 Sept 1934; *educ* Cheltenham; author and poet; *m* 1st 12 July 1958 Marjorie Rosamond (*d* 1986), only dau of Edwin Charles Sauer; *m* 2nd 1991 *Li Yi Tan [Mrs John Brunner, The Square House, Palmer St, S Petherton, Somerset TA13 5DB], 3rd dau of Tan Quan, of Guangzhou, Guangdong, China, and *d* 28 Aug 1995

1a *Verena Hilda May [Mrs Arthur Thornton, 24 Mannerston Holdings, Linlithgow, W Lothian EH49 7ND]; *b* 17 Nov 1937; MA, DipEd Edin; *m* 2 Dec 1967 *Arthur Edward William Thornton, only s of Arthur Edmund Thornton II, 2nd Lt USAF, and has issue:

1b *Amabel Celia; *b* 1976

2b *Felicity May; *b* 1977

2a *Jennifer Margaret Felicity; *b* 30 July 1939; *m* *John Marchant and has issue

(2) Oswald Patrick O'Brien; *b* 21 Sept 1908; *educ* Cheltenham and Clare Coll Cambridge; W/Cdr RAFVR; *m* 10 July 1933 *Elaine [Mrs Oswald Brunner, Wotton House, Wotton Underwood, Bucks], only dau of Richard Howlett, of Ambassadors' Court, St James's Palace, SW1, and *d* 7 Oct 1966, leaving issue:

1a *(Mary Elizabeth) April [Mrs David Gladstone, 1 Mountfort Terrace, London N1 1JJ]; *b* 2 April 1936 (HM QUEEN MARY stood sponsor); *m* 29 July 1961 *David Arthur Steuart Gladstone, CMG, s of Thomas Steuart Gladstone, and has issue:

1b *Patrick; *b* 31 Jan 1969

1b *Perdita [Mrs Mark Williams, 85 Richmond Rd, London E8 3AA]; *b* 7 Jan 1965; *m* 1 Nov 1986 *Mark Williams and has issue:

1c *Christopher James; *b* 24 March 1989

2c *Michael Stuart; *b* 30 Jan 1992

3c *Thomas Alexander; *b* 23 Oct 1993

(1) Shelagh Salome Houston; *b* 6 Feb 1902; *m* 1st 14 Jan 1925 (*divorce* 1934, annulled in ecclesiastical courts 1939, the marriage not having met the lawful requirements of the ruling dynsty of Liechtenstein; she subsequently had conferred on her the title Countess von Rietberg) HSH Prince Ferdinand Andreas Josef Maria von und zu Liechtenstein, s of HSH Prince Eduard Viktor Maria von und zu Liechtenstein, and had issue:

1a *Christopher Richard Francis [Christopher Count von Rietberg, The Bays, Chapel Lane, Crawley Down, Sussex]; *b* 8 May 1926; *m* 17 Sept 1955 *Kathleen Hamilton, dau of Alfred Thayer Mahan, of Blauvelt, NY, USA, and has issue:

1b *Mark Andreas; *b* 30 June 1959

1b *Gabrielle Catherine; *b* 13 Jan 1957

1a *Ethel Elisabeth Olga Mary; *b* 11 Sept 1928; *m* 1st 16 March 1953 (*divorce* 1961, resumed maiden name by deed poll 11 May 1962) Klaus Bruno von Brehm; *m* 2nd 4 Nov 196– (*divorce* 1968), as his 2nd w, Richard Douglas Loftus Onslow (*see* ONSLOW,E)

(1) Countess von Rietberg *m* 2nd 1934 (*divorce* 1952) Georg Otto Suppancic

1 Grace; *b* 31 Jan 1869; *m* 22 April 1890 Thomas William Buckley, JP, MD, MRCS (*d* 8 Aug 1929), of Clopton Manor, Thrapston, Northants, 3rd s of Thomas William Buckley, and *d* 24 Sept 1940, having had issue

2 Mabel Alicia; *b* 14 Oct 1872; *m* 6 Feb 1894 Henry Parker Lowe, BCL (*d* 2 Sept 1940), barrister, and *d* 16 Dec 1949, leaving issue

3 Hilda; *b* 22 Jan 1874; *m* 1st 28 April 1897 Charles Harold Broadbent, JP (*d* 29 Nov 1905); *m* 2nd 5 Jan 1907 18th Viscount Dillon (*qv*) and *d* 23 May 1966

Sir John *m* 2nd 29 July 1875 Jane (*d* 4 April 1910), yst dau of William Sanderson Wyman, MRCS, of Kettering, Northants, and by her had, with other issue:

4 Maud Mary, MBE (1918); *b* 1 Sept 1879; *m* 12 Nov 1903 Maj Guy Gilbey Gold, TD, JP, DL (*d* 6 March 1968), of Abbot's Hall, Shalford, Braintree, yst s of Sir Charles Gold, and *d* 31 March 1965, leaving issue

5 Ethel Jane, MBE (1918); *b* 16 April 1881; *m* 20 Jan 1903 Hon Audley James Blyth, 2nd s of 1st Baron Blyth (*qv*), and *d* 17 Nov 1931, leaving issue

Sir JOHN *d* 1 July 1919; his est son,

Sir John Fowler Brunner, 2nd Bt, JP Cheshire, MP Leigh SW Lancs 1906–10, Northwich 1910–18 and Southport 1923–24; *educ* Cheltenham (Life Govr), Zurich Poly and Trin Hall Cambridge; *b* 24 May 1865; *m* 17 April 1894 Lucy Marianne Vaughan (*d* 10 Dec 1941), dau of Octavius Vaughan Morgan, JP, MP Battersea (*see* 1970 edn VAUGHAN-MORGAN, Bt), and *d* 16 Jan 1929, having had, with other issue:

1 **Sir Felix John Morgan Brunner, 3rd Bt**, *b* 13 Oct 1897; *educ* Cheltenham and Trin Coll Oxford (BA 1921, MA 1925); chm: Henley RDC 1954–57, Brunner Investment Tst to 1972, Pres Lib Pty Orgn 1962–63, Lt RFA (SR) WW I; *m* 8 July 1926 *(Dorothea) Elizabeth, OBE (1965), JP (Oxon 1946), Chm Nat Fedn WIs 1951–56, dau of Henry Brodribb Irving, and *d* 1982, having had issue:

(1) Sir JOHN HENRY KILIAN BRUNNER, **4th and present Bt**

(2) Nicholas Laurence Brodribb; *b* 1 Jan 1929; *d* 3 March 1931

(3) +(Timothy) Barnabas Hans [Barnabas Brunner Esq, 24 Bedford Gdns, London W8]; *b* 28 Feb 1932; *educ* Eton and Trin Coll Oxford (BA 1954); late Lt Irish Gds; *m* 16 Dec 1960 *Helen Ursula, 4th dau of Norris Marshall, and has issue:

1a +Jacob Sebastian; *b* 19 Dec 1961

2a +Conrad Orlando; *b* 28 July 1966

1a *Francesca Laura; *b* 13 March 1963

2a *Imogen Charlotte; *b* 29 Jan 1965

(4) Daniel Felix Brodribb; *b* 30 July 1933; *educ* St Edward's Sch Oxford; *m* 5 June 1959 *Helen Elizabeth (*m* 2nd 1981 Douglas Mitchell), only dau of James Alan Price, MD, FRCP, and *d* 28 Nov 1976, having adopted:

*Rupert James Brodribb; *b* May 1961

*Piers Daniel Carlyle; *b* 1967

*Rachel Elizabeth; *b* May 1962; *m* 1983 *Raymond Talbot

*Lucy Charlotte [Mrs James Anderson, 42 Clifton Gdns, London W9 1AU]; *b* March 1964; *m* 1992 *James R Anderson, s of Robin Anderson, of Quainton, Bucks

(5) +Hugo Laurence Joseph, JP (Oxon) [Hugo Brunner Esq JP, 26 Norham Rd, Oxford OX2 6SF]; *b* 17 Aug 1935; *educ* Eton and Trin Coll Oxford (BA 1957, MA 1959, Hon Fell 1994); High Sheriff Oxon 1988, Ld Lt 1996– (formerly DL), dir The Press 1975; *m* 7 Jan 1967 *Mary Rose Catherine, 3rd dau of Arthur Joseph Lawrence Pollen (*see* POLLEN, Bt), and has issue:

1a +Joseph Gabriel; *b* 9 Dec 1967

2a +Samuel Felix; *b* 26 March 1972

3a +Magnus Gregory Nathaniel; *b* 2 Jan 1974

4a +Philip James Daniel; *b* 26 July 1977

5a +Francis John Michael; *b* 6 May 1982

1a *Isabel Mary; *b* 19 May 1969

1 Joyce Morgan; *m* 20 May 1924 Sir William Arthington Worsley, 4th Bt (*qv*), and had issue

BRUNTISFIELD

Arms: Quarterly, 1st and 4th, arg. on a bend wavy between six roses gu. three plates (for WARRENDER); 2nd, or a lion rampant gu. couped at all joints of the field, within a double tressure flory-counter-flory az. (for MAITLAND); 3rd, grand quarter counterquartered, 1st quarter, 1st and 4th, vert a lion rampant arg., 2nd and 3rd, arg. three papingoes vert, beaked and membered gu. (for HUME), 2nd quarter, gyronny of eight or and sa. within a bordure gu. charged with eight escallops of the 1st and a canton also gyronny of eight gu. and erm. (for CAMPBELL of Cessnock), 3rd quarter, az. on a fess between three mascles arg. as many cinquefoils of the 1st (for PURVES of Purves), 4th quarter, 1st and 4th, gu. three piles engrailed arg. (for POLWARTH of that Ilk), 2nd and 3rd, arg. a cross engrailed az. (for SINCLAIR of Hermiston), en surtout of the grand quarter an inescutcheon arg. charged with an orange imperially crowned and slipped, all ppr. **Crest:** A hare sejant ppr. **Supporters:** Two lions reguardant arg. **Motto:** *Industria evehit* ('Industry promotes'). **Creation:** Bt. (GB) 2 June 1715, B. (UK) 10 March 1942.

THE 2ND BARON BRUNTISFIELD, of Boroughmuir, and a **Baronet** (Sir John Robert Warrender, Bt, OBE (1963), MC (1943), TD (1967), DL (Somerset 1965)) [The Rt Hon The Lord Bruntisfield OBE MC TD DL, 18 Warriston Crescent, Edinburgh EH3 5BL]; *b* 7 Feb 1921; *s* f 1993; *educ* Eton and RMC Sandhurst; Col RARO, Lt-Col cmdg N Somerset Yeo/44th RTR (TA) 1957–62, Dep Brig RAC (TA) S and E Cmds 1962–67, Roy Scots Greys (2nd Dragoons) WW II, ADC to Govr Madras 1946–48, v-chm Somerset TAAFA, memb Roy Co Archers (Brig 1973–85), chm Thistle Industl Hldgs 1973, memb cncl Nat Tst Scotland 1972; *m* 1st 15 April 1948 (Anne) Moireen (*d* 30 Dec 1976), 2nd dau of Lt-Col Sir Walter Fendall Campbell, KCIE; *m* 2nd 1977 Shirley (*d* 1981), dau of E J L Ross and formerly w of Jonathan James Crawley; *m* 3rd 1985 *Joanna (Jan) Kathleen, dau of David Chancellor, of Pencaitland, E Lothian, and formerly w of Capt Colin Hugh Campbell Graham (*see* GRAHAM, Bt, of Larbert), and has issue by 1st w:

1 +MICHAEL JOHN VICTOR [The Hon Michael Warrender, 21 St Petersburgh Place, London W2 4LA]; *b* 9 Jan 1949; *educ* Downside, RMA Sandhurst and Durham U (BA 1972); Capt Irish Gds 1967–86, dir Jardine Fleming Fund Management 1993– and Investment Management 1997–; *m* 18 Aug 1978 *Baroness Walburga, yr dau of Baron Johannes von Twickel, of Schloss Lembeck, Lembeck, Germany, and has:

(1) +John Michael Patrick Caspar; *b* 1 June 1996

2 +Jonathan James [The Hon Jonathan Warrender, Minuntion, Pinmore, Girvan, Ayrshire KA26 0TE]; *b* 11 May 1954; *educ* Downside and Camberwell Sch Art (BA 1976); artist; *m* *Fiona Mary, yr dau of Alexander Grant Laing, MC (*see* STAIR, E), and has issue:

(1) +George Alexander; *b* 9 July 1981

(2) +Jonathan Hew; *b* 1985

(1) *Alice Julian; *b* 4 Jan 1983

1 *Julian Mary [The Hon Julian Warrender, Barnham Farmhouse, E Hoathly, Lewes, Sussex BN8 6QL]; *b* 22 June 1950; *m* 4 Oct 1974 (*divorce* 1997, resumed maiden name) Francis Alexander Morton Akers-Douglas and has issue (*see* CHILSTON, V)

2 *Sarah Jane [The Hon Mrs Bune, PO Box 467, 60 Chapel Rd, Waccabuc, NY 10597, USA]; *b* 4 June 1952; *m* 9 Dec 1971 *Anthony David Bune, only s of David Bune, of Chelsea, and has:

(1) *Delius Jonathan; *b* 25 Aug 1976

(2) *Tertius Alexander; *b* 1 Nov 1978

(1) *Eloise Anne Moireen; *b* 26 Aug 1977

Lineage: GEORGE WARRENDER; had:

Sir George Warrender, 1st Bt (GB), so *cr* 2 June 1715, of Lochend; merchant, MP 1715–22 and Ld Provost Edinburgh; *m* 1st Margaret Lawrie and had issue:

1 JOHN (Sir), **2nd Bt**

Sir George *m* 2nd Grisell, dau of Hugh Blair, Edinburgh merchant and magistrate, and by her had, with other issue:

2 George, of Bruntisfield, nr Edinburgh, f of Hugh, Dep Keeper Signet (*dsp* 1820, his estate of Bruntisfield passing to his cousin Sir George Warrender, 4th Bt)

3 Hugh, of the Temple, barrister, took holy orders, Rector Aston, Yorks

Sir GEORGE *d* 4 March 1721/2; his s by his 1st w,

Sir John Warrender, 2nd Bt; *m* 1720 Henrietta, dau of Sir Patrick Johnston, MP, Ld Provost Edinburgh, and *d* 13 Jan 1772, having had, with five daus (including Grizel, *m* 19 Dec 1763 Hon Charles Napier (*see* NAPIER and ETTRICK, L); *dsp* 15 Nov 1774):

1 George, Maj RHG Seven Years' War; *d* Germany

2 **Sir Patrick Warrender, 3rd Bt**, Lt-Col 11th Dragoons Battle Minden 1759, MP Haddington Burghs 1768–74, King's Remembrancer Court Exchequer 1771–9; *b* 7 March 1731; *m* 1780 — Blair (*d* 8 May 1838) and *d* 14 June 1799, leaving, with a dau (Charlotte, *m* 30 July 1806 Sir John Dalrymple, 5th Bt (*d* 26 May 1835); *d* 14 April 1871, leaving issue):

1 **Sir George Warrender, 4th Bt**, PC, FRS, MA Camb, Lt-Col Berwickshire Militia, MP 1807–32, Ld Admlty 1812–22 and Bd Control 1822–28; *b* 5 Dec 1782; *m* 10 Oct 1810 Anne Evelyn (*d* 5 March 1871), yst dau of 3rd Viscount Falmouth (*qv*), and *dsp* 21 Feb 1849

2 **Sir John Warrender, 5th Bt**, Capt Gren Gds Peninsular War; *b* March 1786; *m* 1st 10 April 1823 Lady Julian Jane Maitland (*d* 19 May 1827), dau of 8th Earl of Lauderdale (*qv*), and had issue:

(1) GEORGE (Sir), **6th Bt**

(1) Julian Jane Jemima Maitland, Sister Community Epiphany Truro, *d* unm 17 Sept 1911

2 (cont.) **Sir John** *m* 2nd 25 June 1831 Frances Henrietta Arden (*d* 20 Feb 1852), dau of 1st Baron Alvanley, and by her had issue:

(2) Helen Catherine: *m* 17 Oct 1854 11th Earl of Haddington (*qv*) and *d* 29 May 1889, leaving issue

Sir JOHN *d* 21 Jan 1867; his only son,

Sir George Warrender, 6th Bt, DL and JP Haddington, DL Edinburgh, Capt Coldstream Gds; *b* 7 Oct 1825; *m* 13 July 1854 Helen (*d* 11 March 1875), only child of Sir Hugh Hume Campbell, 7th Bt, of Marchmont, and had, with other issue:

1 GEORGE JOHN SCOTT (Sir), **7th Bt**

2 Hugh Valdave, DSO, JP Middx; *b* 14 Sept 1868; Capt Gren Gds, Lt-Col cmdg 15th Bn London Regt WW I (despatches four times); *d* unm 8 March 1926

1 Julian Margaret Maitland; *d* unm 5 April 1950 in her 95th year

2 Alice Helen, OBE (1936); *d* unm 23 Sept 1947

3 Eleanor Charles, DGStJ, French War Cross with Palm; *d* unm Sept 1949

Sir GEORGE *d* 13 June 1901; his er surv son,

Sir George John Scott Warrender, 7th Bt, KCB, KCVO, JP Edin; *b* 31 July 1860; V-Adml, ADC to HM EDWARD VII 1907–08, C-in-C E Indies Station 1907–9, cmded 2nd Cruiser Sqdn 1910–12, 2nd Battle Sqdn 1912–15, C-in-C Devonport 1916; *m* 6 Feb 1894 Lady Maud Ashley (*d* 3 Sept 1945), dau of 8th Earl of Shaftesbury (*qv*), and had issue:

1 Sir VICTOR ALEXANDER GEORGE ANTHONY, **8th Bt**, and **1st Baron**

2 Harold John, actor, Lt RNVSR WW II; *b* 15 Nov 1903; *educ* Oundle and Magdalene Coll Cambridge (BA); *m* 27 June 1942 Constance Elizabeth, yr dau of Preb John Fowles, and *dsp* 6 May 1953

1 Violet Helen Marie; *b* 20 Nov 1896; *m* 4 Aug 1921 Maj Alexander Ruthven Pym (*see* PYM, B) and had issue

Sir GEORGE *d* 8 Jan 1917; his son,

Sir Victor Alexander George Anthony Warrender, 8th Bt and **1st Baron Bruntisfield**, of Boroughmuir in the City of Edinburgh (UK), so *cr* 10 March 1942, MC; *b* 23 June 1899 (HM QUEEN VICTORIA stood sponsor); *educ* Eton; MP (C) Grantham 1923–42, Lt Gren Gds (Gen Res Offrs), Orders St Stanislas Russia 3rd Cl with swords, St Anne Russia with swords, Star Romania, PPS to Parly Under-Sec State India 1924–28, Ld Commr Treasury 1931, V-Chamberlain Household 1932–35, Comptroller Household 1935, Parly and Fin Sec Admlty 1935 and 1940–42, Fin Sec War Office, Fin Memb Army Cncl 1935–40, Parly Sec Admlty 1942–45; *m* 1st 1 June 1920 (*divorce* 1945) Dorothy, OStJ (*d* 1 July 1975), dau of Col Richard Hamilton Rawson, MP, by Lady Beatrice Anson, dau of 2nd Earl of Lichfield (*qv*), and *d* 1993, having had issue:

1 JOHN ROBERT WARRENDER, **2nd and present Baron Bruntisfield**

2 +Simon George, DSC (1944) [The Hon Simon Warrender DSC, 57 Dixon St, Malvern, Victoria 3144, Australia]; *b* 11 Aug 1922; *educ* Eton; FAIB (UK), CRAeS, Hon Consul Uruguay, Lt RNVR WW II, Star Russia, Life Govr Prince Henry's Hosp Melbourne; aviation consultant, fndr and chm Australian World Airways; *m* 22 June 1950 *Pamela, only dau of Sir Norman Myer, of Toorak, Victoria, and has had issue:

(1) Alexander Victor Simon; *b* 14 June 1955; *k* in a car crash 23 Aug 1976

(2) +Simon Hamilton Angus Norman; *b* 13 June 1962; *educ* Melbourne C of E GS

(1) *Edwina Jane Maitland; *b* 11 Dec 1952

(2) *Alicia Gizelle; *b* 5 March 1953

3 +Robin Hugh [The Hon Robin Warrender, Capps Lodge House, Fulbrook, Burford, Oxon OX18 4DB]; *b* 24 Dec 1927; *educ* Eton and Trin Coll Oxford; chm: Bain Dawes plc 1973–85, London Wall Hldgs Ltd 1986–94, non-exec dir Bain Hogg Ltd 1994–; *m* 16 Oct 1951 *Gillian Elizabeth, only dau of Leonard Lewis Rossiter by Elsie Rose, dau of Sir Bernard Oppenheimer, 1st Bt (*qv*), and has issue:

(1) +Hugh Mark; *b* 19 Feb 1968; *educ* Eton and Brown U USA (BA)

(1) *Carolyn Robin [The Hon Mrs Hazeel, 54 Alderney St, London SW1V 4EX]; *b* 19 June 1953; *m* 1985 *Francis I M Hazeel, yr s of Capt Harry Hazeel, and has issue:

1a *James Albert Victor; *b* 1989

2a *Geordie Alexander Robin; *b* 1993

(2) *Annabel Rose [The Hon Mrs Alastair Campbell, The Stables, Everlands, Sevenoaks, Kent TN14 6HU]; *b* 17 Jan 1956; *m* 14 July 1979 *Hon Alastair Colin Leckie Campbell, only s of 3rd Baron Colgrain (*qv*), and has issue

The **1st Baron** *m* 2nd 22 June 1948 *Tania Vjekoslava [The Rt Hon The Dowager Lady Bruntisfield, Résidence le Village B1, CH-1837, Château-d'Oex, Switzerland], yr dau of Dr Michael Kolin, of Dubrovnik, and by her had issue:

4 +Anthony Michael [The Hon Anthony Warrender, Little Cotland Farm, PO Box 1431, Middleburg, VA 20118, USA]; *b* 17 July 1950; *educ* Eton and Ch Ch Oxford (FCA); *m* 1st 24 July 1976 Christine, dau of Serge Semeneko, of Boston, Mass.; *m* 2nd 21 Oct 1983 *Mrs Patricia Connors Kelly, dau of Philip Connors, of Middleburg, and by her has issue:

(1) +Patrick Victor Anthony; *b* 9 April 1984

(1) *Victoria Isabella [The Rt Hon Lady Reay, Kasteel Ophemert, Ophemert in Gelderland, Netherlands; 98 Oakley St, London SW3]; *b* 27 March 1952; *m* 20 June 1980, as his 2nd w, *14th Lord Reay (*qv*)

BRUNTON

Arms: Or a caduceus erect sa. on a chief az. three pallets arg. **Crest:** Upon a mount vert a beacon fired between two sprigs of laurel ppr. **Mottoes:** 1 *Fax mentis incendium gloriæ* ('The incitement of glory is the torch of the mind'), 2 *Deus noster refugium et virtus* ('God is our refuge and strength'). **Creation:** Bt. (UK) 17 July 1908.

SIR (EDWARD FRANCIS) LAUDER BRUNTON, 3RD BT, of Stratford Place, St Marylebone [Sir Lauder Brunton Bt, PO Box 140, Guysborough, NS B0H 1N0, Canada]; *b* 10 Nov 1916; *s f* 1943; *educ* Trin Coll Sch Port Hope, Bryanston and McGill U Montreal (BSc, MD, CM); Capt RCAMC, FACP, Fell Internat Soc of Haematology, Hon Attending Physician Roy Victoria Hosp Montreal, Assoc Prof Medicine McGill U, life govr Art Gallery Nova Scotia; *m* 30 Dec 1946 *Marjorie Grant, only dau of David Sclater Lewis, MSc, MD, CM, FRCP Canada, and has issue:

1 +JAMES LAUDER [Dr James Brunton, 7 Blaine Dve, Don Mills, Ontario M3B 2G3 Canada]; *b* 24 Sept 1947; *educ* Bishop's Coll Sch Montreal and McGill U (BSc 1968, MDCM 1972); MD, FRCP Canada; Prof Medicine Toronto U, Head Div Infectious Diseases Dept Medicine U of Toronto, Microbiologist in Ch Toronto Hosp; *m* 1st 1967 (*divorce* 1983) Susan Elizabeth, only dau of Charles Hons, and has issue:

(1) +Douglas Lauder; *b* 1968

(1) *Jennifer Anne; *b* 1971

1 (cont.) Dr JAMES BRUNTON *m* 2nd 1984 *Beverly Anne Freedman and has further issue:

(2) +Robert James; *b* 1987

1 *Nancy Elizabeth; *b* 5 April 1949; *m* 1977 *Ian Wilson

Lineage: JAMES BRUNTON, of Hilstonshill, Roxburghshire; *b* 10 March 1781; *m* as his 2nd w 3 Dec 1831 Agnes (*d* 16 April 1848 aged 42), dau of John Stenhouse, and *d* 19 May 1863; their 3rd s:

Sir Thomas Lauder Brunton, 1st Bt (UK), so *cr* 17 July 1908, of Stratford Place, London W1; MB Edin 1866, BSc 1867, MD 1868, ScD Edin 1870, FRCP Lond 1876, FRS, Hon MD Dublin 1908, Hon LLD Edin 1898 and Aberdeen 1889, Consultant Physician Bart's, ktd 1900; *b* 14 March 1844; *m* 20 Sept 1879 Louisa Jane (*d* 10 April 1909), dau of Ven Edward Adderley Stopford, LLD, of Kells, Archdeacon Meath, and had issue:

1 JAMES STOPFORD LAUDER (Sir), **2nd Bt**

2 Edward Henry Pollock, BA Camb, MRCS Eng, LRCP Lond, T/Lt RAMC, attd 4th Bn Gren Gds; *b* 2 Jan 1890; *ka* 8 Oct 1915

1 Alice Helen, OBE (1918), Offr de l'Instruction Publique (France) 1907, Hon Memb Soc Irish Foresters; *b* 12 Aug 1881; *m* 17 March 1908 Augustine Henry (*d* 23 March 1930), China explorer, Prof Forestry Roy Coll Sci Dublin, and *d* March 1956

2 Anne Stopford Agnes, added by deed poll 1916 surname LAUDER; *b* 12 Feb 1888; *m* 31 Dec 1928 Adolf Oscar Kruming, of Kiev

Sir THOMAS *d* 16 Sept 1916; his son,

Sir (James) Stopford Lauder Brunton, 2nd Bt, mining geologist, with Canadian Geological Survey 1912–13, WW I France; *b* 11 Oct 1884; *educ* Cheltenham, RMA Woolwich, McGill U Montreal (BSc 1910, Res Fell 1911–12, MSc 1913) and Columbia U, NY (MA 1912); *m* 30 April 1915 *Elizabeth (*m* 2nd 1948 Francis Hankin, of Guysborough, Canada), only dau of John Bonsall Porter, PhD, DSc, Prof Engrg McGill, and *d* 25 July 1943, having had issue:

1 Sir (EDWARD FRANCIS) LAUDER BRUNTON, **3rd and present Bt**

1 *Ethel Alice Bonsall; *b* 13 Dec 1918; *m* 6 June 1942 *Ralph Ferland H Hoskins, s of Ralph W Hoskins, of Toronto, and has had issue

BUCCLEUCH and QUEENSBERRY

Arms: Quarterly, 1st grandquarter (EARLDOM OF DONCASTER), quarterly 1st and 4th, quarterly (i) and (iv) azure three fleur-de-lys or; (ii) and (iii) gules, three lions passant guardant in pale or; 2nd, or a lion rampant gules within a double tressure flory-counter-flory of the second; 3rd, azure, a harp or; all debruised by a baton sinister argent; 2nd grandquarter (Dukedom of Argyll), quarterly, 1st and 4th, gyronny of eight or and sable (for CAMPBELL); 2nd and 3rd, argent a lymphad, sails furled sable, flags and pennons flying gules and oars in action of the second (for LORNE); 3rd grandquarter (Dukedom of Queensberry), quarterly, 1st and 4th, argent a human heart gules, crowned with an imperial crown or, on a chief azure three mullets of the field (for DOUGLAS); 2nd and 3rd, azure a bend between six cross crosslets fitchée or (for MAR); the whole of this grandquarter within a border or, charged with a double tressure flory-counter-flory gules; 4th grandquarter (for DUKEDOM OF MONTAGU), quarterly, 1st, argent three fusils conjoined in fess gules, a bordure sable (for MONTAGU); 2nd, or a griffin displayed vert, beaked and membered gules (for MONTHERMER); 3rd, sable a lion rampant argent, on a canton of the last a cross gules (for CHURCHILL); 4th, argent a chevron gules between three caps-of-maintenance, their fronts turned to the sinister azure, furred ermine (for BRUDENELL); over the grandquarters at the fess point an inescutcheon or, a bend azure mullet of six points between two crescents of the field (for SCOTT). **Crest:** A stag trippant proper, attired and unguled or. **Supporters:** Two female figures proper, habited from the waist downwards in kirtles azure gathered up at the knees, the arms and bosoms uncovered, around the shoulders flowing mantles as before suspended by the exterior hand, girdles and sandles gules, and their heads adorned with a plume of three ostrich feathers argent. **Motto:** *Amo* ('I love'). **Creations:** L. (S) 18 March 1605/6 (Scott of Buccleuch), 16 March 1618/9 (Scott of Quhitchester and Eskdaill), 20 April 1663 (Scott of Whitchester and Eskdale) and 3 Nov 1684 (regrant 17 June 1706) (Douglas of Kinmont, Midlebie and Dornock); B. (E) 14 Feb 1662/3 (Scott of Tindall); V. 3 Nov 1684 (regrant 17 June 1706) (Nith, Torthorwald and Ross); E. (S) 16 March 1618/9 (Buccleuch), (E) 14 Feb 1662/3 (Doncaster), (S) 20 April 1663 (Dalkeith) and 3 Nov 1684 (regrant 17 June 1706) (Drumlanrig and Sanquhar); M. (S) 3 Nov 1684 (regrant 17 June 1706) (Dumfriesshire), D. (S) 20 April 1663 (Buccleuch) and 3 Nov 1684 (regrant 17 June 1706) (Queensberry).

THE 9TH DUKE OF BUCCLEUCH, Duke of Queensberry, Marquess of Dumfriesshire, Earl of Buccleuch, Earl of Doncaster, Earl of Dalkeith, Earl of Drumlanrig and Sanquhar, Viscount of Nith, Torthorwald and Ross, Lord Scott of Buccleuch, Lord Scott of Quhitchester and Eskdaill, Lord Scott of Whitchester and Eskdale, Baron Scott of Tindall and **Lord Douglas, of Kinmont, Midlebie and Dornock** (Sir Walter Francis John MONTAGU-DOUGLAS-SCOTT later SCOTT (adopted for self and est s only) KT (1978), VRD (1959), JP (Roxburgh 1975), DL (Selkirkshire 1955, Roxburghshire 1962, Dumfriesshire 1974)) [His Grace The Duke of Buccleuch and Queensberry KT VRD JP DL, Bowhill, Selkirk TD7 5ET; Boughton House, Kettering, Northants; Drumlanrig Castle, Dumfriesshire]; *b* 28 Sept 1923; *s* f 1973; *educ* Eton and Ch Ch Oxford; Lt-Cdr RNVR and RNR 1942–71, WW II 1942–45, Hon Capt RNR 1988; MP (C) Edinburgh N 1960–73, PPS to Sec State Scotland 1962–64; Ld Lt Roxburghshire 1974–75, Selkirk 1975, Roxburgh, Ettrick and Lauderdale 1975–; Chllr Order Thistle 1992–, Capt Roy Co Archers, Ld Pres Cncl and Silver Stick for Scotland, Chm: Buccleuch Heritage Tst 1985–, Living Landscape Tst 1986–, Assoc of Ld-Lts 1990–, Pres: Roy Highland and Ag Soc Scotland 1969, St Andrew's Ambulance Assoc, Roy Scottish Ag Benevolent Inst, Scottish Nat Inst for War Blinded, Roy Blind Asylum and Sch, Galloway Cattle Soc, E of England Ag Soc 1976, Cwlth Forestry Assoc, V-Pres RSSPCC, Roy Scottish Forestry Soc, Hon Pres Animal Diseases Research Assoc, Scottish Ag Organisation Soc, Countryside Award, Countryside Commn and CLA 1983, Bledisloe Gold Medal 1992; Hon memb Co of Merchants of City of Edinburgh 1981, FRAgS 1996; *m* 10 Jan 1953 *Jane, only child of John McNeill, QC, MA, of Drumavuic, Appin, Argyll, and has issue:

1 +RICHARD JOHN WALTER, *Earl of Dalkeith*, DL (Nithsdale and Annandale and Eskdale 1987) [Earl of Dalkeith DL, Dabton, Thornhill, Dumfriesshire DG3 5AR; 24 Lansdowne Rd, London W11 3LL]; *b* 14 Feb 1954 (HRH PRINCESS MARGARET COUNTESS OF SNOWDON stood sponsor); *educ* Eton and Ch Ch Oxford (BA 1976); Page of Honour to HM QUEEN ELIZABETH THE QUEEN MOTHER 1967–69; Dir Border TV 1989–90, memb Nature Conservancy Cncl 1989–91, Scottish Nat Heritage 1992–95, Chm SW Region 1992–95, IBA 1990, ITC 1991, Millenium Commn 1994–95, Dist Cncllr Nithsdale 1984–90, memb Roy Co Archers; *m* 31 Oct 1981 *Lady Elizabeth Marian Frances Kerr, 4th dau of 12th Marquess of Lothian (*qv*), and has:

(1) +Walter John Francis, *Lord Eskdaill*; *b* 2 Aug 1984; Page of Honour to HM THE QUEEN 1996–

(2) +Charles David Peter; *b* 1987

(1) *Louisa Jane Theresa; *b* 1982

(2) *Amabel Clare Alice; *b* 1992

2 +(William Henry) John [The Lord John Montague-Douglas-Scott, Valikoma i Cad 62, Ni antä i, Istanbul, Turkey]; *b* 9 Jan 1957; *educ* Eton and Courtauld Inst (London U and Istanbul); *m* 1990 *Mrs (Hafize) Berrin Torolsan, only dau of Halil Torolsan, of Istanbul

3 +Damian Torquil Francis Charles; *b* 8 Oct 1970

1 *Charlotte-Anne; *b* 9 Jan 1966; *m* 1991 *Count Bernard de Castellane, son of Count Albert de Castellane, of Brussels, and has issue:

(1) *Boniface Louis Albert Charles; *b* 1993

Lineage: Sir RICHARD le SCOT, of Rankilburn and Murthockston; swore fealty to EDWARD I 1296; allegedly *m* —, dau and heiress of Murthockston of that Ilk, and had:

ROBERT SCOTT, of Rankilburn and Murthockston; *d c* 1389, leaving:

Sir WALTER SCOTT, of Rankilburn and Murthockston; granted charter of territorial Barony of Kirkurd by ROBERT II 7 Dec 1389; *ka* Battle of Homildon Hill 11 Sept 1402, leaving:

ROBERT SCOTT, of Rankilburn and Murthockston; *b* by 18 Feb 1406/7; acquired part of the lands of Branxholme, Roxburghshire; *d* 1426, having had issue, with a yr s (Stephen, of Castlelaw):

Sir WALTER SCOTT, of Branxholme; helped suppress 1455 the rebellious DOUGLASes, some of whose lands he was granted by charter 22 Feb 1453, also the other half of the lands of Branxholme; *d* 9 Feb 1469, leaving, with a yr s (Alexander, ancestor of the SCOTT Bts of Thirlestane; *see* NAPIER and ETTRICK, L) an est son:

DAVID SCOTT; feudal Ld of Buccleuch (a name derived from a legendary rescue of the then King of Scots by a member of the Scott family who held back an aggressive buck in a 'cleuch', or ravine); sat in Parl 1481 and 1487; Branxholme erected into a Barony by charter 21 May 1488; *d* March 1492, having had, with a dau (Janet, *m* James Douglas Stn of Drumlanrig; *see* QUEENSBERRY, M):

DAVID, Yr of Buccleuch; *m* Janet, dau of 4th Earl of Angus (*see* HAMILTON and BRANDON, D), and *dvp*, leaving:

Sir WALTER SCOTT of Buccleuch; *m* Elizabeth (*d* 19 Oct 1548), dau of Walter Kerr of Cessford (*see* LOTHIAN, M) and widow of Philip Rutherford, and *d* by 15 April 1504, leaving an er s:

Sir WALTER SCOTT of Buccleuch; Warden Middle March, ktd at Flodden 9 Sept 1513; tried to free the young JAMES V but defeated at Darnick, nr Melrose, by Earl of Angus 25 July 1526; fought Battle of Pinkie 10 Sept 1547; *m* 1st *c* 1523 Elizabeth Carmichael and had issue; *m* 2nd *c* 1530 Janet, dau of Sir Andrew Kerr of Ferniehurst (*see* LOTHIAN, M) and widow of George Turnbull of Bedrule; *m* 3rd *c* 1544 Janet (*d* 1569), dau of John Betoun of Creich (*see* below) and widow of Sir James Crichton, and was *k* by the KERRs in the High Street of Edinburgh 4 Oct 1552, having had a further two sons and three daus (one of whom, presumably by the 3rd w, was Grizel, *m* by 1570 6th Lord Borthwick; *qv*); his s by his 1st w:

Sir WILLIAM SCOTT of Kirkurd, Yr of Buccleuch; fought Battle of Pinkie 10 Sept 1547; *m* his stepmother's sis Grisel (*m* 2nd Sir Andrew Murray of Blackbarony), 2nd dau of John Betoun of Creich (*see* above), and *dvp* by 19 May 1552, having had, with three daus (including Margaret, *m* Sir John Johnstone of Johnstone; *see* ANNANDALE AND HARTFELL, E):

Sir WALTER SCOTT of Buccleuch; *b c* 1549; Capt Newark Castle 1566–79; *m* (contract 19 Jan 1567/8) Lady Margaret Douglas (*m* 2nd Francis Stewart, 1st Earl of Bothwell (*see* MORAY, E), and *d* 1640), dau of 7th Earl of Angus (*see* HAMILTON and BRANDON, D), and *d* 17 April 1574, leaving an only son:

Sir WALTER SCOTT, **1st Lord Scott of Buccleuch** (S), so *cr* 18 March 1606, PC (S 1611); *b* 1565 ; ktd 1590, Warden West March 1590; after carrying out many raids into England was delivered up as a hostage during an outbreak of peace 1579; helped quell Borders turbulence following JAMES I's accession; served in Low Countries against Spain; *m* (contract 1 Oct 1586) Mary, sis of 1st Earl of Roxburghe (*see* ROXBURGHE, D), and *d* 15 Dec 1611, having had, with other issue:

1 WALTER, **1st Earl**

1 Margaret; *m* 1st 1615 6th Lord Ross (*d* 1633; extinct 1754) and had issue; *m* 2nd 6th Earl of Eglinto(u)n (*see* EGLINTON and WINTON, E) and *d* 5 Oct 1652

2 Elizabeth; *m* 1616 2nd Lord Cranstoun (dormant or extinct 1689) and *dsp*

The only son,

WALTER SCOTT, **1st Earl of Buccleuch**, so *cr* 16 March 1618/9, as also LORD SCOTT OF QUHITCHESTER (*i.e.*, Whitchester) AND ESKDAILL, both it would seem with remainder ultimately to heirs gen (the titles as granted with the original remainder were apparently to heirs male but can only have been surrendered and regranted if the titles were to become heritable by females; given that females did inherit, it may well be that all female issue and issue through females of the 1st Earl are in remainder to that title and the Lordship of Scott of Quhitchester; pending irrefutable proof of such a remainder, however, it has been thought more convenient to the reader to treat such issue as being in the same position towards the aforesaid titles as they are to the numerous other titles that are held by the Dukes of Buccleuch and Queensberry); cmded a regt under the States of Holland against the Spaniards 1627; *m* (contract 11 and 15 Oct 1616) Lady Mary Hay (*d* 1631), dau of 9th Earl of Erroll (*qv*), and *d* 20 Nov 1633, having had, with other issue (including an illegitimate dau Margaret, *m* John Pringle of Bartingbush; *see* PRINGLE, Bt):

1 Walter, *Lord Scott*; *d* an infant

2 FRANCIS, **2nd Earl**

1 Elizabeth; *m* 1641, as his 1st w, 20th/4th Earl of Mar (*qv*) and *dsp*

2 Jean; *m* 1644 1st Marquess of Tweeddale (*qv*) and *d* 1688, leaving issue

The 1st EARL's only surv son,

FRANCIS SCOTT, **2nd Earl of Buccleuch**; *b* 21 Dec 1626; *m* (contract 25 July 1646) Lady Margaret Leslie (*m* 3rd 13 Jan 1653 2nd Earl of Wemyss; *see* WEMYSS and MARCH, E), dau of 6th Earl of Rothes (*qv*) and widow of Alexander, Lord Balgonie (*see* LEVEN and MELVILLE, E), and *d* 22 Nov 1651, having had, with other issue:

1 Walter, *Lord Scott*; *b* 5 Nov 1648; *d* an infant

1 MARY Scott, **Countess of Buccleuch** in her own right; *b* 31 Aug 1647; *m* 9 Feb 1659, as his 1st w, Walter SCOTT, of Highchester (*b* 25 Dec 1644; *cr* 4 Sept 1660 Earl of Tarras for life; *d* 9 April 1693; *see* POLWARTH, L); the marriage aroused controversy due to the youth (11 and 14 respectively) of the parties but was held good under an act of the Gen Assembly allowing such marriages if there were grounds for fearing the bride might be abducted; she *dsp* 11 March 1661

2 ANNE Scott, **Countess of Buccleuch** in her own right; *b* 11 Feb 1651; *m* 20 April 1663 Sir James SCOTT previously CROFTS, KG, 1st DUKE OF MONMOUTH, so *cr* 14 Feb 1663, as also **Earl of Doncaster**, Co York, and BARON SCOTT OF TINDALL, Northumberland (all E, forfeited 15 July 1685 following his failed uprising in favour of a Protestant succession and the consequent attainder), illegitimate son of CHARLES II by Lucy, dau of William Walters, of Haverfordwest, Pembs; on their marriage day he was also *cr* **Duke of Buccleuch**, EARL OF DALKEITH and LORD SCOTT OF WHITCHESTER AND ESKDALE (all S), with remainder to the heirs male of his body by his then w Anne, failing whom, to the heirs of his body who should succeed to the estates and Earldom of Buccleuch; these latter titles, together with the Earldom of Buccleuch possessed by Anne in her own right, were unaffected by his attainder; they had, with other issue:

(1) Charles, *Earl of Doncaster*; *b* 24 Aug 1672; *d* 9 Feb 1673/4

(2) James, *Earl of Doncaster* to 1685, subsequently *Earl of Dalkeith*, KT (1704); *b* 23 May 1674; *m* 2 Jan 1693/4 Lady Henrietta Hyde (*d* 30 May 1730), dau of 1st Earl of Rochester (*see* CLARENDON, E), and *dvm* 14 March 1704/5, having had, with other issue:

1a FRANCIS, **2nd Duke**

(3) HENRY SCOTT, 1st EARL OF DELORAIN, so *cr* 29 March 1706, as also VISCOUNT OF HERMITAGE and LORD GOLDIELANDS (all S), KB (1725); *b* 1676; Col 2nd Horse Gren Gds 1715–17, 16th Foot 1724–30, 7th Horse July-Dec 1730, Maj Gen 1727, rep S peer 1715–30; *m* 1st 1693 Anne, dau of William Duncombe, of Battlesden, Beds, Ld Justice Ireland; *m* 2nd 14 March 1726 Mary, dau of Charles Howard (gs of 1st Earl of Berkshire; *see* SUFFOLK and BERKSHIRE, E), and *d* 25 Dec 1730, leaving by his 1st w:

1a FRANCIS SCOTT, 2nd EARL OF DELORAIN; *b* 5 Oct 1710; *m* 1st 29 Oct 1732 Mary, widow of Thomas Heardson and dau of Matthew Lister; *m* 2nd 6 July 1737 Mary, est dau of Gervase Scrope, of Cockerington, Lincs, and *dsp* 11 May 1739

2a HENRY SCOTT, 3rd EARL OF DELORAIN; *b* 11 Feb 1712; Capt RN; *m* Elizabeth, dau of John Fenwick, and *d* 31 Jan 1739/40, leaving:

1b HENRY SCOTT, 4th and last EARL OF DELORAIN; *b* 8 Feb 1737; *m* 16 Nov 1763 Frances, widow of Hon Henry Knight and dau of Thomas Heath, of Stansted, Essex, and *dsp* 10 Sept 1807, when his titles expired

2 (cont.) The **Countess/Duchess of Buccleuch** *m* 2nd 6 May 1688 3rd Baron Cornwallis (*see* CORNWALLIS, B, preliminary remarks) and *d* 6 Feb 1732, having had further issue:

(1) Isabella; *d* unm 18 Feb 1748

The gs,

FRANCIS SCOTT, **2nd Duke of Buccleuch**, KT (1725); *b* 11 Jan 1694; rep S peer 1734–41; restored by Act of Parl 22 March 1742/3 as EARL OF DONCASTER and BARON SCOTT OF TINDALL only; *m* 1st 5 April 1720 Lady Jean Douglas (*d* 31 Aug 1729), 2nd dau of 2nd Duke of Queensberry (*see* QUEENSBERRY, M), and had, with other issue:

1 Francis, *Earl of Dalkeith*; *b* 19 Feb 1720/1; MP (Whig) Boroughbridge 1746–50; *m* 2 Oct 1742 Lady Caroline Campbell (*m* 2nd 15 Aug 1755 Rt Hon Charles Townsend, bro of 1st Marquess Townsend (*qv*), was *cr* 28 Aug 1767 Baroness Greenwich and *d* 11 Jan 1794, when her Barony expired), est dau of 2nd Duke of Argyll (*qv*), and *dvp* 1 April 1750, having had, with two other sons and another dau:

(1) John, *Lord (Scott of) Whitchester*; *b* 3 Jan 1745; *d* 31 Jan 1748/9

(2) HENRY, **3rd Duke**

(1) Frances; *b* posthumously 26 July 1750; *m* 13 May 1783, as his 2nd w, 1st Baron Douglas of Douglas (*see* 1857 edn), and *d* 31 March 1817, leaving issue

The **2nd Duke** *m* 2nd 4 Sept 1744 Alice (*dsp* 31 Dec 1765), allegedly a Windsor washerwoman, dau of Joseph Powell, and *d* 22 April 1751

His gs,

HENRY SCOTT, **3rd Duke of Buccleuch**, KG (1794), KT (1767–94); *b* 2 Sept 1746; *educ* Eton; Govr Roy Bank Scotland 1777–1812, Capt Gen Roy Co Archers 1778–1812, Ld Lt Midlothian and Haddington 1794–1812 and Roxburghshire 1804–12; inherited estates of Dukes of Argyll through his mother 1794 and those of his cousin 4th Duke of Queensberry 23 Dec 1810, simultaneously becoming, in accordance with the limitation of a regrant of 17 June 1706, **5th Duke of Queensberry**, MARQUESS OF DUMFRIESSHIRE, EARL OF DRUMLANRIG AND SANQUHAR, VISCOUNT OF NITH, TORTHORWALD AND ROSS and LORD DOUGLAS OF KINMONT, MIDLEBIE AND DORNOCK (all S); *m* 2 May 1767 Elizabeth (*d* 21 Nov 1827), est dau and eventual heiress of 1st Duke of Montagu (*see* AILESBURY, M, and MANCHESTER, D), and *d* 11 Jan 1812, having had:

1 George, *Earl of Dalkeith*; *b* 25 March, *d* 29 May 1768

2 CHARLES WILLIAM HENRY, **4th/6th Duke**

3 HENRY JAMES SCOTT later MONTAGU-SCOTT, 2nd and last BARON MONTAGU OF BOUGHTON, Co Northampton (GB), as which he *s* his maternal gf 23 May 1790 according to the special remainder in the creation of 21 Aug 1786, which was to the 2nd and every other yr s of his (the grantee's) dau Elizabeth Duchess of Buccleuch and their issue in tail male successively; *b* 16 Dec 1776; *educ* Eton and St John's Coll Cambridge; Ld Lt Selkirkshire 1823; *m* 22 Nov 1804 Hon Jane Margaret (*d* 10 Jan 1859), dau of 1st Baron Douglas of Douglas (*see* above, also 1857 edn), by his 1st w Lady Lucy Graham, dau of 2nd Duke of Montrose (*qv*), and *d* 30 Oct 1845, when the Barony expired, having had, with other issue:

(1) Lucy Elizabeth; *m* 4 Dec 1832 11th Earl of Home (*qv*) and *d* 15 May 1877, leaving issue

1 Mary; *m* 29 Jan 1791 3rd Earl of Courtown (*qv*) and *d* 21 April 1823, leaving issue

2 Elizabeth; *m* 6 Nov 1798 10th Earl of Home (*qv*) and *d* 29 June 1837, leaving issue

3 Caroline; *m* 13 Aug 1803 6th Marquess of Queensberry (*qv*) and *d* 29 April 1854, leaving issue

4 Harriet; *m* 1 Dec 1806 6th Marquess of Lothian (*qv*) and *d* 18 April 1833, leaving issue

The 3rd/5th DUKE's est surv son,

CHARLES WILLIAM HENRY MONTAGU-SCOTT, **4th Duke of Buccleuch** and **6th Duke of Queensberry**, KT (1812); *b* 24 May 1772; *educ* Eton and Christ's Coll Cambridge; Ld Lt Selkirkshire 1794–98, Dumfriesshire 1798–1819 and Midlothian 1812–19, MP (Tory) Marlborough 1793–96 and 1806–07, Ludgershall 1796–1804 and St Michael's 1805–06; called up to Ho Lds *vp* 11 April 1807 in f's Barony of Tynedale [*sic*]; Capt Gen Roy Co Archers 1812–19; *m* 24 March 1795 his cousin Harriet Catharine (*d* 24 Aug 1814), yst dau of 1st Viscount Sydney of St Leonards (*see* TOWNSHEND, M), and *d* 20 April 1819, having had, with other issue:

1 George Henry, *Lord (Scott of) Whitchester*; *b* 2 Jan 1798; *d* 1 March 1803

2 WALTER FRANCIS, **5th/7th Duke**

3 John Douglas; *b* 13 July 1809; Gren Gds Offr; MP Roxburghshire; *m* 10 March 1836 Alicia Anne (resumed maiden name and *d* 12 March 1900), composer of *Annie Laurie*, est dau of John Spottiswoode, of Spottiswoode, Berwickshire, and *d* 3 Jan 1860

1 Charlotte Albinia; *m* 4 July 1822 4th Earl of Courtown (*qv*) and *d* 29 Feb 1828, leaving issue

2 Isabella; *m* 9 Oct 1823 Hon Peregrine Francis Cust and *d* 9 Oct 1829, leaving issue (*see* BROWNLOW, B)

3 Margaret Harriet; *m* 7 Feb 1832 3rd Earl of Romney (*qv*) and *d* 5 June 1846, leaving issue

4 Harriet Janet Sarah; *m* 29 March 1842 Rev Edward Moore, Rector Frittenden, Kent, s of Rev G Moore, Preb Canterbury, and *d* 16 Feb 1870, having had issue

The 4th/6th DUKE's est surv son,

WALTER FRANCIS MONTAGU-DOUGLAS-SCOTT, **5th Duke of Buccleuch** and **7th Duke of Queensberry**, KG (1835), KT (1830–35), PC (1842); *b* 25 Nov 1806; *educ* Eton and St John's Coll Cambridge; DCL; ADC to HM QUEEN VICTORIA, Capt-Gen Roy Co Archers 1838–84, Ld Lt and Sheriff Pncpl Midlothian 1828–84 and Roxburghshire 1841–84, Hon Col 3rd Bn Roy Scots Lothian Regt, High Steward Westminster, Chllr U of Glasgow, Ld Privy Seal 1842–46, Ld Pres Cncl Jan-July 1846; *m* 13 Aug 1829 Lady Charlotte Anne Thynne, VA (*d* 28 March 1895), yst dau of 2nd Marquess of Bath (*qv*), and *d* 16 April 1884, having had, with other issue:

1 WILLIAM HENRY, **6th/8th Duke**

2 HENRY JOHN DOUGLAS-SCOTT-MONTAGU, 1st BARON MONTAGU OF BEAULIEU (*qv*)

3 Walter; *b* 2 March 1834; Capt 15th Hus; *m* 7 Oct 1858 Anna Maria (*d* 29 May 1886), 4th dau of Sir William Edmund Cradock Hartopp, 3rd Bt (*qv*), and *d* 3 March 1895, having had with other issue:

(1) Francis Walter; *b* 5 March 1860; Capt 3rd Bn Worcs Regt, formerly Lt 52nd LI; *m* 1st 16 April 1896 Katherine Charlotte (*d* 12 Nov 1917), dau of Melville Portal (*see* PORTAL, Bt); *m* 2nd 25 May 1929 Ethelreda Marjory (*d* 4 Nov 1961), 2nd dau of Rev Thomas Lane Coulson Bridges (*see* below), and widow of Gilbert Neville Hodson (*see* HODSON, Bt), and *dsp* 5 Jan 1942

(2) Walter George Leon; *b* 12 Oct 1870; *educ* Eton; Capt 1st Lovat Scouts and F/Lt RAF, Egyptian Army in Sudan 1914–19 (medals with clasps); *m* 31 May 1897 Alison Primrose Ralouka (*d* 8 Aug 1935), dau of Col Warner Heriot, of Spital House, Berwickshire, and *dsp* 27 March 1969

(1) Evelyn Mary; *b* 4 Aug 1865; *m* 16 Nov 1898 Rev Thomas Lane Coulson Bridges (*d* 11 Oct 1932), Rector Warkton Northants 1888–1909 and Barton Seagrave, Kettering, Northants, 1909–23 (*see* above), s of Henry Thomas Bridges, of Camp House, Clifton, nr Bristol, and *d* 19 Dec 1948, leaving issue

4 Charles Thomas (Sir), GCB; *b* 20 Oct 1839; Adml, C-in-C Australian Station 1888–92, Plymouth Station 1900–03, Baltic 1854 (medal), Black Sea 1855–56 (Crimean and Turkish medals), China War 1857 (medal with clasp), Pearl's Naval Bde 1857–58 (Indian medal); *m* 23 Feb 1883 Ada Mary (*d* 21 Nov 1943), dau of Charles Ryan, of Derriweit Heights, Macedon, Victoria, Australia, and *d* 21 Aug 1911, having had issue:

(1) Charles William; *b* 17 April 1884; *educ* Eton; FSI; *m* 4 April 1918 Hope Janet, only dau of Lt-Col William Johnston Younger, of Harmeny, Balerno, Midlothian, and *dsp* 18 Oct 1967

(2) David John (Sir), KCMG (1941), OBE (1919); *b* 7 March 1887; *educ* Eton; clerk FO 1911; Capt 3rd Bn Roy Scots (Lothian Regt), WW I (wounded, des-

patches), Chev Legn Hon, Hon Maj 1937; Cnsllr Embassy 1933, Assist U-Sec State 1938, Dep U-Sec of State For Aff 1944; *m* 1st 14 June 1918 Dorothy Charlotte (*d* 3 Dec 1965), 6th dau of Cecil George Assheton Drummond (*see* PERTH, E); *m* 2nd 31 July 1970 *Valerie Finnis, horticulturalist, and had by his 1st w:

1a Merlin; *b* 8 April 1919; 2nd Lt Rifle Bde WW II; *ka* Middle East May 1941

1 Victoria; *m* 1st 23 Feb 1865 9th Marquess of Lothian (*qv*) and had issue; *m* 2nd 21 Feb 1903 Bertram Chetwynd Talbot (*see* SHREWSBURY and WATERFORD, E) and *d* 19 June 1938

2 Margaret Elizabeth; *m* 9 Dec 1875 Donald Cameron of Lochiel, 24th Chief (*d* 30 Nov 1905), and *d* 5 Feb 1918, leaving issue

3 Mary Charlotte; *m* 24 July 1877 Col Hon Walter Randolph Trefusis and *d* 13 Dec 1908, leaving issue (*see* CLINTON, B)

The 5th/7th DUKE's est son,

WILLIAM HENRY MONTAGU-DOUGLAS-SCOTT, **6th Duke of Buccleuch** and **8th Duke of Queensberry**, KG (1897), KT (1875–97), PC (1901), JP (Selkirkshire), DL (Selkirkshire and Roxburghshire); *b* 9 Sept 1831; MP (C) Midlothian 1853–68 and 1874–80; Ld Lt and Pres TFA Dumfriesshire, Capt-Gen Roy Co Archers; *m* 22 Nov 1859 Lady Lousia Jane Hamilton, VA (*d* 17 March 1912), 3rd dau of 1st Duke of Abercorn (*qv*), and *d* 5 Nov 1914, having had issue:

1 Walter Henry, *Earl of Dalkeith*; *b* 17 Jan 1861; accidentally *k* while deer-stalking 18 Sept 1886

2 JOHN CHARLES, **7th/9th Duke**

3 George William, OBE (1919), JP, DL (Roxburghshire); *b* 31 Aug 1866; Lt-Col Lothians and Border Horse Yeo, Capt 10th Hus, Boer War, WW I; memb Roy Co Archers; *m* 30 April 1903 Lady Elizabeth Emily Manners (*d* 22 July 1924), yst dau of 7th Duke of Rutland (*qv*), and *d* 23 Feb 1947, leaving:

(1) John Henry, MC (1940), JP, DL (Roxburghshire); *b* 12 April 1911; *educ* Eton; Lt-Col 9th Lancers WW II (wounded); memb Roy Co Archers; *m* 3 Feb 1954 *Ann Peace Arabella (Arbell) [Mrs John Montagu-Douglas-Scott, Kirklands, Ancrum, Roxburghshire], only child of Capt Angus Alexander Mackintosh, Yr of Mackintosh, RHG (Blues), and formerly w of Maj John Anthony Warre, MC, 12th Roy Lancers, and *d* 1991, having had issue:

1a +James George; *b* 2 Oct 1959

1a *(Elizabeth) Arabella [Mrs Peregrine Lewis, Cotfield, Lilliesleaf, Melrose, Borders TD6 9JW]; *b* 16 Feb 1956; *m* 1987 *Peregrine J Lewis, son of Maj Raymond Lewis, 12th Roy Lancers, and has issue:

1b *Merlin John; *b* 1991

1b *Arbell Eleanora; *b* 1993

(2) Claud Everard Walter, MC (1943), TD; *b* 12 Oct 1915; *educ* Eton and Ch Ch Oxford; Lt-Col Lothians and Border Horse WW II N Africa and Italy, memb Roy Co of Archers; *m* 23 Aug 1941 *Margaret Frances [Mrs Claud Montagu-Douglas-Scott, Bourton Hill House, Moreton-in-Marsh, Glos], yr dau of Brig-Gen Lewis Francis Philips, CB, CBE, DSO, of Bembridge, IoW, and *d* 4 Nov 1994, leaving:

1a +Thomas Walter; *b* 1 July 1943; *educ* Eton; *m* 1973 (*divorce* 1985) (Marion) Miranda, dau of Hon Claud Stephen Phillimore (*see* PHILLIMORE, B), and has issue:

1b *Alice; *b* 1978

1a *Katharine Margaret [Mrs Robert Bernard, Bourton Hill House, Moreton-in-Marsh, Glos]; *b* 12 Jan 1946; *m* 12 April 1975 Robert Vere Spencer Bernard, son of John Gray Churchill Spencer Bernard (*see* MARLBOROUGH, D)

(1) Phyllis Anne; *b* 3 March 1904; *m* 14 June 1924 (*divorce* 1944) 4th Baron Delamere (*qv*) and *d* 1978, leaving issue

(2) Jeanetta Ruth; *b* 19 Nov 1906; *m* 20 Jan 1937 Maj James William Stirling Home Drummond Moray, JP, DL, late Scots Gds (*d* 4 Aug 1968), er son of Capt William Augustus Stirling Home Drummond Moray, 20th of Abercairny, JP, DL, of Crieff, Perthshire, and *d* 6 Sept 1997, having had:

1a Henry Alastair; *b* 29 Oct 1937; *d* 21 March 1942

2a *William George [William Stirling Home Drummond Moray of Abercairny, Abercairny, Crieff, Perthshire]; *b* 22 Aug 1940; *educ* Eton and RAC Cirencester; *m* 1st 7 Jan 1969 (*divorce* 1991) Angela Jane, dau of Lt-Cdr Michael John Baring, RN (*see* NORTHBROOK, B), and has issue:

1b *Anna Christian; *b* 1971

2b *Frances Tara; *b* 1974

3b *Georgina Jane; *b* 1979

2a (cont.) William Stirling Home Drummond Moray *m* 2nd 1991 *Emma Moyra, er dau of Capt James Silvester Rattray, 28th Chief, and has further issue:

4b *Caroline; *b* 1992

3a *John Robert [John Stirling Home Drummond Moray Esq, Seggiebank Farm House, Milnathort, Kinross KY13 7RP]; *b* 14 Oct 1943; *educ* Eton; Capt Scots Gds, Kenya 1963–64, ADC to Govr Tasmania 1966–68, Atholl Highers; *m* 1971 (*divorce* 1979) Meriel Frances, er dau of Peter Douglas Miller Stirling-Aird, of Kippendavie, TD; *m* 2nd 1981 (*divorce* 1997) Carole Anne, er dau of John N Peniston, of Geneva, and by her has:

1b *Andrew James George; *b* 1987

1b *Susannah Laura; *b* 1984

4a *David Maurice [David Stirling Home Drummond Moray Esq, Abercairny Cottage, Crieff, Perthshire]; *b* 6 March 1945; *educ* Eton; Capt Scots Gds, Malaysia and Borneo 1966–67, Atholl Highers; *m* 1st 1976 (*divorce* 1987) Amanda Mary, dau of Ian Bayles, of Victoria, Australia (*see* 1970 edn SHERBORNE, B), and has:

1b *Edwina Alice; *b* 1980

4a (cont.) David Stirling Home Drummond Moray *m* 2nd 1989 *Iona, dau of John Barber, of Majorca, and by her has:

1b *James Oliver; *b* 1992

1b *Hermione Rose; *b* 1995

1a Lucy Gwendolen; *b* 20 Feb 1939; *m* 11 July 1964, as his 2nd w, Capt Hon (Desmond) Rupert Strutt (*d* 27 Feb 1993), yst s of 3rd Baron Belper (*qv*), and *d* 16 Sept 1993, leaving issue

(3) Marjorie Katherine; *b* 19 Nov 1906; *m* 1st 21 March 1935 Maj Thomas Archibald Hacket-Pain, Irish Gds (*ka* 15 May 1940), er s of Brig-Gen Sir William Hacket-Pain, KBE, CB; *m* 2nd 4 Dec 1943 Adam Bell (*d* 24 Aug 1966), est s of Frank Bell, of Winston, Co Durham, and *d* 1994, leaving by him:

1a *Charles James; *b* 14 Nov 1944; *educ* Eton; memb Roy Co Archers; *m* 1969 *Caroline Jane, dau of Maj Peter Daniel Highton Fox, DSO, Green Howards, and has issue:

1b *Jonathan George; *b* 1972; *educ* Eton and Cambridge

1b *Susannah Katherine Janet; *b* 1975

1a *Louisa; *b* 23 Jan 1947

4 Henry, JP (Dumfriesshire, Roxburghshire and Berwickshire); *b* 15 Jan 1868; *educ* Ch Ch Oxford (MA); Hon Col 3rd Bn Roy Scots (Lothian Regt), cmdg 3rd Bn Roy Scots 1907–12, Boer War, WW I (despatches five times); Lt Roy Co Archers; *d* unm 19 April 1945

5 Herbert Andrew, CMG (1916), DSO (1901), DL (London); *b* 30 Nov 1872; Lt-Col Irish Gds and TF, formerly Capt 3rd Bn Roy Scots, commissioned 1st/23rd London Regt France, Assist Mil Sec 1st and 3rd Armies France, Med Expdny Force, Dep Asst Mily Sec WO, Boer War (Queen's Medal, eight clasps), WW I (despatches, Offr Legn Hon); memb Roy Co Archers, KJStJ; memb Gentlemen-at-Arms 1922–35, Chm Rolls-Royce and London Chamber of Commerce Educn Ctee 1934, Pres: Lond Chamber Commerce 1928–31, V-Pres: Br Assoc Chambers Commerce 1931, Pres: Fedn Br Industries 1934–35, memb Advsy Cncl BOT 1934–37, Pres: Roy Warrant Holders' Assoc 1936–37, Silver Jubilee Medal 1935 and Coronation Medals 1911 and 1937; *m* 26 April 1905 Marie Josephine (*d* 15 Feb 1965), yr dau of James Edwards, of Dovercourt, Essex, and *d* 17 June 1944, leaving issue:

(1) (Claud) Andrew, DSO (1943) and bar (1944); *b* 13 July 1906; *educ* Eton; Col formerly cmdg Irish Gds, WW II as Brig cmdg 1st Gds Bde (despatches); OStJ, memb London Stock Exchange; *m* 1st 10 Aug 1929 (*divorce* 1951) Lady Victoria Doris Rachel Haig (*d* 1993), 2nd dau of FM 1st Earl Haig (*qv*), and had issue:

1a +Douglas Andrew, OBE [Capt Douglas Montagu-Douglas-Scott OBE, Halford House, Halford, nr Shipston-on-Stour, Warwicks]; *b* 21 June 1930; *educ* Eton; late Capt Irish Gds, formerly ADC Govr S Australia; *m* 1st 12 Oct 1954 (*divorce* 1977) Bridget Elizabeth, only dau of AVM Sir Robert Allingham George, KCMG, KCVO, KBE, CB, MC, and adopted:

Adam; *b* 12 Nov 1961; *d* 1969

*Emily; *b* 1970

*Lucy Rosemary; *b* 1972

1a (cont.) Capt Douglas Montagu-Douglas-Scott *m* 2nd 1977 *Daphne Maureen, only dau of Dr Cyril de Vere Shortt, of Winchcombe, Glos, and formerly w of William George Fearnley-Whittingstall

1a *Henrietta [Lady Griffin, Barton's Cottage, Bushey Park, Teddington, Middx TW12 0EA]; *b* 9 Dec 1934; *m* 1 May 1962 *Maj Sir (Arthur) John Stewart Griffin, KCVO, Press Sec to HM QUEEN ELIZABETH THE QUEEN MOTHER, son of Arthur Wilfred Michael Stewart Griffin, of Greathed Manor, Lingfield, Surrey and has issue:

1b *Andrew Michael Stewart; *b* 27 April 1963; *m* 1989 *Maria Diane Cordelia, dau of Royston James Vavasseur-Williams, of Childwall, Liverpool, and has issue:

1c *Alexander William Michael Stewart; *b* 1992

2c *(Henry) Edward (Ralph) Stewart; *b* 8 Aug 1995

2b *Philip Anthony Stewart; *b* 23 May 1965; *m* 1992 *Heather, er dau of Gerald Kent by Mrs Malcolm Prescott, of Polstead, Suffolk and has:

1c *Hamish Andrew Lewis Stewart; *b* 4 June 1994

(1) (cont.) Brig Andrew Montagu-Douglas-Scott *m* 2nd 4 May 1951 Zalia (*d* 1986), yst (twin) dau of Sir Harold Edward Snagge, KBE, by Inez Alfreda, yr dau of Alfred Lubbock (*see* AVEBURY, B), and formerly w of Lt-Col Esmond Charles Baring, OBE (*see* ASHBURTON, B), and *d* 24 Jan 1971, leaving by her:

2a +Nicholas Herbert; *b* 17 Nov 1954; *educ* Eton

(1) Marian Louisa; *b* 16 June 1908; *m* 1st 1 Nov 1927 Col Andrew Henry Ferguson, Life Gds (*d* 4 Aug 1966), son of Brig-Gen Algernon Ferguson, of Polebrook Hall, Oundle, Peterborough, and had issue (*see* HAMPDEN, V, and ROYAL FAMILY); *m* 2nd 30 Oct 1968 Air Marshal Sir Thomas Walker Elmhirst, KBE, CB, AFC, DL, RAF (ret) (*d* 1982), 4th s of Rev William Heaton Elmhirst, of Barnsley, Yorks, and *d* 11 Dec 1996

(2) *Patricia Katharine [The Rt Hon Dowager Countess of Dundee, Coultra Farm House, Newport-on-Tay, Fife]; *b* 9 Oct 1910; *m* 1st 8 July 1931 Lt-Col Walter Douglas Faulkner, MC, Irish Gds (*ka* May 1940), only surv s of James Faulkner, and has had issue:

1a David James; *b* 8 Nov 1932; *educ* Eton; Maj Irish Gds; *m* 26 April 1958 *Victoria Mary Rose [Mrs David Faulkner, Haugh House, Longworth, Abingdon, Berks], est dau of Robert James Buxton (*see* BUXTON, Bt), and *d* 1993, leaving:

1b *John Douglas; *b* 29 May 1959

2b *Thomas Patrick; *b* 21 March 1965

3b *Matthew James; *b* 1 March 1968

4b *Robert David; *b* 27 Feb 1970

1b *Katherine Rose; *b* 7 Sept 1960

1a *Hermione Patricia; *b* 14 Jan 1937; *m* 1 May 1966, as his 2nd w, Sir (Rupert) Iain Kay Moncreiffe of that Ilk, 11th Bt (*see* ERROLL, E)

(2) (cont.) Mrs Walter Faulkner *m* 2nd 9 Sept 1940 Lt-Col David Scrymgeour Wedderburn, DSO, Scots Gds (*das* March 1944), and has further issue (*see* DUNDEE, E); *m* 3rd 30 Oct 1946 11th Earl of Dundee (*qv*) and has further issue

6 Francis George (Sir), KCMG (1937), DSO (1914); *b* 1 Nov 1879; Lt-Col Gren Gds Boer War, ADC to Viceroy India 1905–11, WW I (wounded, despatches, brevet), WW II with E African Forces 1941–45 (despatches); MLC Kenya 1925–52, Unofficial Memb Exec Cncl 1932–36 and 1937–44; *m* 11 Feb 1915 Lady Eileen Nina Evelyn Sibell Elliot (*d* 29 May 1938), dau of 4th Earl of Minto (*qv*), and *d* 26 July 1952, leaving issue:

(1) Pamela Violet, of Deloraine, Rongai, Kenya

(2) *Moyra Eileen [Mrs David Smiley, 30 Kensington Mansions, Trebovir Rd, London SW5 9TQ]; *b* 15 March 1919; WW II with ATS (FANY) (despatches); *m* 1st 28 Feb 1942 Maj Hugo Douglas Tweedie, Scots Gds (*ka* NE Europe April 1945), er son of John Tweedie, and has issue:

1a *Gavin Hugo [Maj Gavin Tweedie, Butterhall, Minto, Hawick, Roxburghshire TD9 8SD]; *b* 2 Aug 1944; *educ* Eton, Ch Ch Oxford (MA) and RMA Sandhurst; Maj RHG (Blues); *m* 25 April 1974 *Phillippa Mary, dau of Maj Michael Andrews, of Quarry House, Shepton Mallet, Somerset, and has issue:

1b *Esmond Michael Xan; *b* 7 June 1976

2b *Alexander; *b* 11 April 1978

1a *Anna Bridget Eileen [Mrs Anna McFerran, Muthaiga Country Club, Nairobi, Kenya]; *b* 18 Dec 1942; MCSP; *m* 30 April 1971 (*divorce* 1986) Peter Robert McFerran, son of Ian McFerran, of Karen, Kenya, and has issue:

1b *Hugo; *b* 1975

1b *Lucinda; *b* 1972

(2) (cont.) Mrs Hugo Tweedie *m* 2nd 28 April 1947 *Col David de Crespigny Smiley, LVO, OBE, MC, RHG (Blues), 3rd s of Sir John Smiley, 2nd Bt (*qv*), and has further issue

1 Katharine Mary; *b* 25 March 1875; *m* 29 April 1899 3rd Viscount Hampden (*qv*), and *d* 7 March 1951, leaving issue

2 Constance Anne; *b* 10 March 1877; Pres Nairnshire Nursing Assoc; *m* 21 Jan 1908 Hon Douglas Halyburton Cairns, yst s of 1st Earl Cairns (*qv*), and *d* 7 May 1970, leaving issue

The 6th/8th DUKE's est son,

JOHN CHARLES MONTAGU-DOUGLAS-SCOTT, **7th Duke of Buccleuch** and **9th Duke of Queensberry**, KT, GCVO, JP and DL (Selkirk and Roxburghshire), DL (Edinburgh); *b* 30 March 1864; Lt RN; MP (C) Roxburghshire 1895–1906; Ld Clerk Register Scotland 1926–35, Hon Col 78th (Lowland) Field Bde RA (TA) 1929–34, Capt-Gen Roy Co Archers, Ld Lt Dumfriesshire; *m* 30 Jan 1893 Lady Margaret Alice Bridgeman (*d* 7 Aug 1954), 2nd dau of 4th Earl of Bradford (*qv*), and *d* 19 Oct 1935, leaving:

1 WALTER JOHN, **8th/10th Duke**

2 William Walter, MC (1918); *b* 17 Jan 1896; *educ* Eton; Capt Res Offrs 10th Hus, ADC to Govr-Gen and C-in-C Canada 1925–26, WW II as Lt-Col (despatches), memb Roy Co Archers, MP Roxburgh and Selkirk 1935–50; *m* 27 April 1937 Lady Rachel Douglas-Home (*d* 4 April 1996), yr dau of 13th Earl of Home (*qv*), and *d* 30 Jan 1958, leaving issue:

(1) +Walter William; *b* 24 June 1946; *educ* Eton and Keble Coll, Oxford; *m* 1991 *Mrs Teresa Fisher, only dau of Anatole Urbaniak, of Cape Town

(1) *Margaret Elizabeth; *b* 19 April 1938

(2) *Frances Henrietta; *b* 3 Aug 1940; *m* 18 Jan 1968 *3rd Baron Cranworth (*qv*) and has issue

(3) *Rosemary Alice; *b* 3 Aug 1940; *m* 22 Feb 1978 *Mark Collins, s of Sir William Collins, and has issue:

1a *Sampson William Francis; *b* 1982

2a *Benjamin Mark Timothy; *b* 1984

(4) *Jean Louise; *b* 6 June 1943; *m* 14 March 1968 *Sir George Tapps-Gervis-Meyrick, 7th Bt (*qv*), and has issue

3 +George Francis John [Lt-Col The Lord George Montagu-Douglas-Scott, The Old Almshouse, Weekley, Kettering, Northants; 60 Glebe Pl, London SW3]; *b* 8 July 1911 (TM GEORGE V and QUEEN MARY stood sponsors); *educ* Eton and Ch Ch Oxford (BA); Brevet-Col TARO, formerly Maj 10th Hus and 23rd Hus, Lt-Col Northants Yeo in Europe WW II (despatches); memb Roy Co Archers; *m* 16 Dec 1938 *Mary Wina Mannin (Molly), portrait painter, only dau of Lt-Col Harry Oswald Bishop, of Harewood, Andover, Hants, and has issue:

(1) +David Henry George [David Montagu-Douglas-Scott Esq, 19 Petworth St, London SW11]; *b* 29 Jan 1945 (HRH THE DUKE OF GLOUCESTER stood sponsor); *educ* Eton; *m* 10 June 1967 *Laura Jane, yst dau of St John Bernard Vyvyan Harmsworth (*see* ROTHERMERE, V), and has:

1a *Lucy Rose; *b* 18 May 1969

2a *Harriet Mary; *b* 1972

(1) *Georgina Mary [The Rt Hon The Lady O'Neill, Shane's Castle, County Antrim, N Ireland]; *b* 28 Nov 1940; *m* 10 June 1963 *4th Baron O'Neill (*qv*) and has issue

(2) *Charmian Rachel [Mrs Colin Campbell, 23 Lansdowne Gdns, London SW8]; *b* 18 July 1942; *m* 11 Nov 1964 (*divorce* 1977) Archibald Hugh Stirling, Yr of Keir (*see* HERON-MAXWELL, Bt); *m* 2nd 1987 *Colin Guy Napier Campbell and has issue by 1st husb

1 Margaret Ida; *b* 13 Nov 1893; *m* 16 Feb 1926 Adml Sir Geoffrey Alan Brooke Hawkins, KBE, CB, MVO, DSC, son of Capt Herbert Reginald Montgomery Hawkins, of St Fenton's, Co Dublin, and *d* 17 Dec 1976, leaving issue

2 Sybil Anne; *b* 14 July 1899; *m* 14 May 1919 Charles Bathurst Hele Phipps, 1st Life Gds, of Chalcot, Wilts (*d* 12 Jan 1960), and had issue

3 *Alice Cristabel, GCB, CI, GCVO, GBE [HRH PRINCESS ALICE DUCHESS OF GLOUCESTER GCB CI GCVO GBE, 1 Kensington Palace, London W8]; *b* 25 Dec 1901; Air Ch Marshal RAF, Col-in-Ch KOSB, Dep Col-in-Ch Roy Anglian Regt and King's Roy Hus, Memb Cncl Br Red Cross, Dep Cmdt-in-Ch Nursing Corps and Div St John's Ambulance Bde; Pres RAM 1942–, Freedom Edinburgh 1937, Gloucester 1939, and Belfast 1952, GCStJ; *m* 6 Nov 1935 HRH PRINCE HENRY WILLIAM FREDERICK ALBERT, 1st DUKE OF GLOUCESTER (*d* 10 June 1974), and has issue (*see* ROYAL FAMILY)

4 Mary Theresa, CStJ; *b* 4 March 1904; *m* 10 Jan 1929 (*divorce* 1946) 6th Marquess of Exeter (*qv*) and *d* 1984, having had issue

5 *Angela Christine Rose [The Lady Angela Dawnay, The Old Post Cottage, Wield, Alresford, Hants]; *b* 26 Dec 1906; *m* 28 April 1936 V-Adml Sir Peter Dawnay, KCVO, CB, DSC, and has issue (*see* DOWNE, V)

The 7th/9th DUKE's est son,

WALTER JOHN MONTAGU-DOUGLAS-SCOTT, **8th Duke of Buccleuch** and **10th Duke of Queensberry**, KT (1949), GCVO (1935), TD, PC (1937), JP (Dumfriesshire and Roxburghshire), DL (Selkirkshire); *b* 30 Dec 1894; *educ* Eton and Ch Ch Oxford; Col TA, formerly Capt Gren Gds, cmded 4th Bn KOSB 1923–30, ADC to Govr-Gen Canada; MP Roxburghshire and Selkirk 1923–35; Ld Lt Roxburghshire 1932, Govr RBS 1935–68, Capt-Gen Roy Co Archers and Gold Stick Scotland, Ld Steward Household 1937–40, Hon LLD Edinburgh 1953 and St Andrews 1956, Pres: Roy Scottish Foresters Soc 1941–46, Roxburghshire TAA, St Andrews Amb Assoc, Cwlth Forestry Assoc; *m* 21 April 1921 Vreda Esther Mary (*d* 1993), er dau of Maj William Frank Lascelles (*see* HAREWOOD, E), and *d* 4 Oct 1973, leaving:

1 (WALTER FRANCIS) JOHN SCOTT, **9th and present Duke of Buccleuch and 11th and present Duke of Queensberry**

1 *Elizabeth Diana [Her Grace The Dowager Duchess of Northumberland, Friar's Well, Alnwick, Northumberland NE66 2LJ; Clive Lodge, Albury, Surrey GU5 9AB]; *b* 1922; WW II as 3rd Offr WRNS; Hon D U Newcastle Polytechnic (Northumbria U); Hon Col 6th Bn Northumberland Fus; *m* 12 June 1946 10th Duke of Northumberland (*qv*), and has issue

2 *Caroline Margaret [The Rt Hon The Lady Gilmour of Craigmillar, The Ferry House, Old Isleworth, Middx]; *b* 1927; a bridesmaid to HRH THE PRINCESS ELIZABETH (now HM THE QUEEN) 20 Nov 1947; *m* 10 July 1951 Baron Gilmour of Craigmillar (*qv*) and has issue

Seats: Boughton House, Kettering, Northants; Bowhill, Selkirk, Borders Region; Drumlanrig, Thornhill, Dumfriesshire. Boughton is the work of the 1st Duke of Montagu of the 1705 creation (*see* MANCHESTER, D), who was Ambassador to France in the 1660s and 1670s. He seems to have acquired a taste for the native civilisation while *en poste* and back home in England added to what had originally been a 15th-century monastery a wholly French-looking mansion, complete with mansard roof, high rectangular windows and an arcade on the park side. The work was not complete by the Duke's death in 1709 but much of it had been laid out by 1695. The old monastery had already been extended in a somewhat haphazard way (the Montagus had owned the property since the late 1520s) and the result was a series of no fewer than seven courtyards. Inside, particularly in the state apartments, Boughton is a monument to the age it was enlarged in, with parquet floors, ceilings and friezes by Louis Cheron, panelling, murals, Restoration and William-and-Mary furnitureand Mortlake tapestries. The collection of paintings is of the first importance. The property came to the Buccleuchs through the daughter of the 2nd and last Duke of Montagu of the 1705 creation.

Bowhill is more obviously the centre of an estate than the other two seats. Indeed architecturally it is not terribly distinguished, even though the Victorian alterations which so enlarged it were carried out very much with one respectful eye on its classical origins. The estate was a Scott property from some way back but passed into the ownership of a branch of the MURRAYs between 1690 and 1745. It was under these alien proprietors that the house itself was begun, probably as an intended hunting lodge. The **2nd Duke** bought back the place as a residence for his younger son in 1745, a year which saw not just a piece of real estate change hands but very nearly the Crown. His plans, like Bonnie Prince Charlie's, were frustrated: the younger son soon died, as did the **Duke** himself, and Bowhill passed to the next holder of the title, who lived elsewhere. It was not till the **4th Duke**'s time that Bowhill came to be occupied by the family, though even now it was only as a summer retreat to begin with.

The surrounding landscape must have cast a spell, however, for on succeeding to the title the **4th Duke** adopted Bowhill as one of his main homes, commissioning William Atkinson to tack on a villa-style extension to the south side and throwing out east and west wings a few years afterwards, in the case of the former so as to accommodate a dining room. Just over a decade later another architect, William Burn, shifted the main entrance round to the north face, allowing the southerly one to be used for private access. He also shook up Bowhill's internal organs, repositioning the principal staircase in the westerly part of the building and knocking down intervening walls to create a larger saloon and drawing room at the expense of what had been self-contained hallways contiguous to them. Burn continued to be occupied remodelling Bowhill for just about the rest of his life. Indeed his position seems to have been looked on not just as that of estate master builder but as almost hereditary, since after his death in 1870 further work continued under his nephew J MacVicar Anderson. It was the latter who erected the billiard room, the chapel, which nowadays shelters relics of the Duke of Monmouth, and — perhaps as a profane counterweight — the smoking room.

Bowhill's contents are of the first importance, including works by such distinguished portraitists as Gainsborough, Kneller, Lely, Reynolds and Van Dyck and such leading landscape artists as Lorrain and Ruysdael, tapestries from the Mortlake works and examples of the finest boulle, Sevres and Meissen. The gem of the collection for many is the Louis Quatorze looking glass presented to Monmouth by his fond father CHARLES II. It was a dangerous gift: had the admittedly godlike youth been less beguiled by his own attractiveness he might not have fallen victim to the hubris that led him ultimately to the block.

Drumlanrig dates from approximately the same period as Boughton but on the whole looks backwards rather than to contemporary influences. It is usually regarded as the last of the pre-classical mansions in Scotland but even here there are decorative features such as the balustrade surmounting the elevation, the steps up to the front door and the mouldings round the door itself which would never have appeared on a castle built for defence alone, as the previous castle on the site had been. Even the pink colour of the sandstone is hardly warlike. Constructed by the Douglases shortly after the Restoration, Drumlanrig passed to the Scott Buccleuchs along with the Douglas Dukedom of Queensberry. It too contains superb paintings.

BUCHAN

Arms: Quarterly, 1st, azure, a barrulet en crancelin of four strawberry leaves between three garbs or (for EARLDOM OF BUCHAN); 2nd, argent a pale sable, in the dexter canton a rose gules, barbed and seeded vert (for ERSKINE); 3rd, or a lymphad sable, sails furled and oars in action and at the mast-head a beacon, all proper, surmounted of a fess chequy azure and argent charged with a mullet of the second (for STEWART OF BUCHAN); 4th, argent a lion passant guardant gules, crowned with an imperial and gorged with an open crown or, a label of three points of the second, the centre point charged with a crescent of the third (for OGILVIE OF AUCHTERHOUSE); on an inescutcheon en surtout gules, an eagle displayed or, armed and membered azure, looking towards the sun in his splendour in dexter chief (for LORDSHIP OF CARDROSS). **Crest:** A dexter arm issuant from the wreath attired in a manche gules doubled ermine, the hand proper and grasping a club or. **Supporters:** Two ostriches proper, armed, beaked and membered or. **Motto** (above crest): Judge nocht. **Creations:** L. (S) 1469 (Auchterhouse) and 10 June 1610 (Cardross), E. (S) 1469, B. (UK) 10 Feb 1806.

THE 17TH EARL OF BUCHAN, Lord Auchterhouse, Lord (of) Cardross and **Baron Erskine of Restormel Castle**, Co Cornwall (Malcolm Harry Erskine, JP (Westminster)) [The Rt Hon The Earl of Buchan JP, Newnham House, Newnham, nr Basingstoke, Hants RG27 9AS]; *b* 4 July 1930; *s* f 1984; *educ* Eton; *m* 21 Feb 1957 *Hilary Diana Cecil, only dau of Sir Ivan McLannahan Cecil Power, 2nd Bt (*qv*), and has issue:

1 +HENRY THOMAS ALEXANDER, *Lord Cardross*; *b* 31 May 1960; *educ* Eton; *m* 1987 *Charlotte Catherine Lucinda, dau of Hon Matthew Henry Beaumont (*see* ALLENDALE, V), and has issue:

(1) +Alexander; *b* 26 April 1990

(2) +Frederick Alastair; *b* 1992

2 +Montagu John; *b* 17 Jan 1966; *educ* Eton; *m* 17 May 1997 *Rachel, dau of Stephen Pryor

1 *Seraphina Mary; *b* 14 July 1961; *educ* Edin U; *m* 1990 *Stephen K Berry, er son of Maj Roy Berry, of Witham, Essex, and has issue:

(1) *Katherine Aphra; *b* 1990

(2) *Eleanor India; *b* 1994

2 *Arabella Fleur; *b* 27 Aug 1969; *m* 1st 1992 Francis Robin Charles Salvesen, est son of Robin Salvesen, of Eaglescairnie House, Haddington; *m* 2nd 30 Nov 1996 *Mark A Biddle, yr s of Donald Biddle

Buchan, Earldom of: From the 10th century to the beginning of the 12th Scotland was divided into seven Mormaerships (*Mor* meaning 'great' and *Maer* 'steward'). The holders of these Mormaerships had originally wielded almost sovereign powers as rulers of what were in effect provinces. Indeed they were known at one time as Kings, though subject to a High King.

At that time the Mormaership of Mar (*see* MAR, E) and Buchan was a single entity. It covered the later counties of Aberdeenshire and Banffshire. By the 12th century Buchan and Mar had become separated and under the feudalising policy of DAVID I and his successors the Mormaerships were converted to earldoms whose possessors held land with them, both deriving from the Crown.

Gartnach, Mormaer of Buchan, is first mentioned as Earl of Buchan when witnessing a charter in 1115. It is thought that he acquired his Mormaership through his wife. Certainly the new earldom passed to his son-in-law Colban in right of the latter's wife, Gartnach's daughter Eve. It continued with Colban and Eve's male issue till the end of the 12th century, when an heiress, Margaret, became Countess of Buchan in her own right.

Margaret's second husband, William Comyn, whom she married in 1210, became Earl of Buchan through her. Their son Alexander, 6th Earl of Buchan, was a leading figure in the Scotland of his day, being one of the guarantors who undertook to protect the succession to the throne of MARGARET during her father ALEXANDER III's lifetime in Feb 1283/4, then one of the Guardians of the Realm (effectively Regents) after ALEXANDER died in 1285. The 6th Earl of Buchan's wife was a daughter of Roger de Quincy, Earl of Winchester (*see* WINCHESTER, M, preliminary remarks) and the two succeeding Earls of Buchan had property interests in England. It was in the latter kingdom that John Comyn, 7th Earl of Buchan, settled after his opposition to ROBERT I (THE BRUCE) had caused his Scottish lands, and even perhaps his titles, to be forfeited.

Henry Beaumont, the last of this line (and by marriage with the 7th Earl's niece rather than direct descent), continued to be recognised as Earl of Buchan after his political eclipse in Scotland. Following his death in 1340 the title Earl of Buchan ceased for a while to be used either in Scotland or England.

In or about 1382 ROBERT II conferred the Earldom of Buchan on his fourth son Sir Alexander Stewart, known from his ferocity as the 'Wolf of Badenoch'. The day before his first official recognition as Earl (or at any rate the first known official recognition) the Wolf had married the heiress of a moiety of the old Buchan estates, her great-uncle Sir John Ross having married Margaret Comyn, sister of Alice, the wife of Henry Beaumont (*see* above). Doubtless this accounted for the choice of title. The Earldom passed after the Wolf's death to his elder brother, thence to the latter's son, but after that it fell into disuse till conferred by JAMES I of Scotland on his daughter Mary, apparently on the occasion of her marriage to another Wolf, Wolfart van Borssele, son and heir of the Count of Grandpré in Champagne. He became Earl of Buchan in right of his wife and died without surviving male issue in 1487, his wife having predeceased him more than twenty years earlier.

Lineage (of Stewart): Sir JAMES STEWART of Lorn, known as 'the Black Knight of Lorn'; *m* 1439, as her 2nd husb, JANE/JOAN, QUEEN DOWAGER OF SCOTLAND (widow of JAMES I), and had, with other issue (*see* MORAY, E) :

Sir JAMES STEWART, **1st Earl of Buchan**, so *cr* 1469(?), as also LORD AUCHTERHOUSE (both S); High Chamberlain Scotland 1471–73 and 1478–84, Amb France 1473, Warden E Marches 1479; *m* by 1 March 1466/7 Margaret, dau and heir of Sir Alexander Ogilvy of Auchterhouse, through whom he became Hereditary Sheriff of Forfar, and *d* between Jan 1497 and Jan 1499/1500, leaving, with a dau (*m* 11th Lord Saltoun (*qv*) of Abernethy) and by an unknown woman an illegitimate dau who *m* 2nd Earl of Bothwell; *see* BUCHAN-HEPBURN, Bt):

ALEXANDER STEWART, **2nd Earl of Buchan**; *m* 1st by 20 May 1491 Isabel Ogilvy; *m* 2nd by 1499 Margaret (*m* 2nd by 21 June 1508 Sir John Erskine; Yr of Dun (either *k* Battle of Flodden 9 Sept 1513 or *d* 7 Sept 1563); (?)*m*(?) 3rd by 23 Dec 1518 James Stewart of Ryland (*k* by 11 March 1524/5); (?)*m*(?) 4th (*annulled* 18 Dec 1534) William Wood of Bonnyton and *d* 1548), dau of 1st Lord Ruthven of the Jan 1487/8 *cr* (*see* CARLISLE, E), and *d* 1505, leaving by her:

JOHN STEWART, **3rd Earl of Buchan**; *b c* 1498; *m* Margaret, dau of James Scrymgeour of Dudhope (*see* DUNDEE, E), and *d* after 14 July 1551, leaving an er s:

JOHN STEWART, *Master of Buchan*; *m* 1st Lady Mary Stewart (*dsp*), dau of James, Earl of Moray, illegitimate s of JAMES IV; *m* 2nd by 15 May 1547 Margaret, dau of Walter Ogilvy of Boyne (*see* SEAFIELD, E), and was *ka vp* Battle of Pinkie 10 Sept 1547, leaving by her:

CHRISTIAN Stewart, **Countess of Buchan** in her own right; *m* Robert DOUGLAS, **4th Earl of Buchan** in right of his w (*see* MORTON, E), and *d* 20 Sept 1580, leaving, with three daus (including Elizabeth, *m* 1st Lord Fraser, *see* SALTOUN, L):

JAMES DOUGLAS, **5th Earl of Buchan**; *m* 1598 Margaret (*m* 2nd 7th Lord Gray; *qv*), dau of 1st Lord Ogilvy of Deskford (*see* SEAFIELD, E), and *d* 26 Aug 1601, leaving:

MARY Douglas, **Countess of Buchan** in her own right; *m* by 1617 James ERSKINE, **6th Earl of Buchan** in right of his w (*m* 2nd Dorothy, dau of Sir Phillip Knyvett, of Buckenham, Norfolk, and *d* Jan 1639/40, having by her had a dau), 2nd s of 18th/2nd Earl of Mar (*qv*); on 22 March 1617 they were granted a charter conferring the Earldom to both of them and to whoever outlived the other, with remainder to the heir male of their marriage, which failing to James's nearest heir male; the limitation was repeated in a new charter of 26 Nov 1625; by a decree of the Court of Session 28 July 1628 the Earldom was granted higher precedence than at the 'Decreet of Ranking' of 1606, when the unmarried Countess as a minor had been unrepresented, the new decree effectively recognising the Buchan creation as dating from 1469; the Countess *d* 1628, leaving, with other issue (including Mary, *m* 2nd Lord Forbes of Pitsligo (*see* FORBES, Bt of Newe) and had issue; Margaret, *m* Sir James Graham, s of 7th Earl of Airth, and had issue):

JAMES ERSKINE, **7th Earl of Buchan**

Lineage (of Erskine): JOHN ERSKINE, 18th/2nd EARL OF MAR (*qv* for further biographical details) and **1st Lord Cardross** (S), so *cr* 10 June 1610, KG (1603), PC (S 1577, E 1603); granted by JAMES VI and I 27 March 1604 the lands of the Priory of Inchmahome and Abbeys of Dryburgh and Cambuskenneth together with the Lordship of Cardross (invalid, hence confirmed by Act of Parl 9 July 1606, which in addition erected the lands into a Barony, that of Cardross; however even this legal instrument appears to have lacked the validity of the charter of 1610 in creating the Lordship of Parliament of Cardross, hence the necessity for the latter instrument); the **1st Lord Cardross** on 31 Jan 1617 nominated as heir to the Lordship Henry, his 2nd s (by his 2nd w), and the heirs male of the latter's body; *m* 1st between 29 Oct and 1 Nov 1580 Agnes/Anne Drummond, 3rd dau of 2nd Lord Drummond (*see* PERTH, E), and had:

1 JOHN ERSKINE, 19th/3rd EARL OF MAR (*qv*)

The **1st Lord Cardross** *m* 2nd 7 Dec 1592 Lady Mary Stewart/Stuart, dau of 1st Duke of Lennox (*see* RICHMOND and GORDON, D), and *d* 14 Dec 1634, leaving by her, with other issue:

2 JAMES ERSKINE; **6th Earl of Buchan** (*see* above); had:

(1) JAMES ERSKINE, **7th Earl of Buchan**; *m* Lady Marjory Ramsay, dau of 1st Earl of Dalhousie (*qv*), and *d* Oct 1664, leaving, with other issue:

1a WILLIAM ERSKINE, **8th Earl of Buchan**; *d* unm 1695

1a Marjory Mary; *m* 1st 1669 Simon Fraser of Inverallochy and had issue (*see* LOVAT, L); *m* 2nd 1683 4th Lord Fraser (*see* SALTOUN, L) and had further issue

2a Margaret; *m* 23 Feb 1671 William Grey of Invereightie and had issue

3 Henry, *Master of Cardross*; *m* a little while after 14 Dec 1625 Margaret, sis of 1st Lord Bellenden of Broughton (*see* ROXBURGHE, D), and *dvp* 1628, leaving:

DAVID ERSKINE, **2nd Lord**

The 1st LORD CARDROSS's gs,

DAVID ERSKINE, **2nd Lord Cardross**; *bapt* 6 Feb 1626/7; granted 10 Feb 1663/4 a new charter of the Lordship of Cardross with power to nominate his heir, which failing with remainder to heirs male of his body, then to his heirs and assignees; *m* 1st after 9 Aug 1645 Anne, dau of Sir Thomas Hope, 1st Bt, of Craighall, and had, with other issue:

1 HENRY ERSKINE, **3rd Lord Cardross**, PC (S); *b* 1650; opposed the administration in Scotland of the Earl of Lauderdale (*qv*), being imprisoned 1675–79, migrated to Carolina in N America in 1680 and set up a colony there, later supported WILLIAM III and accompanied him from Holland to England 1688, Col 1689 and Govr the Mint; *m* 3 March 1671 Catherine (*d* 1725), yr sis and coheir of Sir Lewis Stewart of Kirkhill, and *d* 21 May 1693, leaving, with other issue:

(1) DAVID, **4th Lord Cardross** and **9th Earl of Buchan**

(2) Charles; advocate 1704; *m* —, dau and heir of Walter Scott, of Edenshead, Fife, yst s of Sir John Scott of Scotstarvel, and *dsps* 25 Feb 1763

(3) William; Dep Govr Blackness Castle; *m* Margaret, dau of Col John Erskine, and had, with other issue:

1a John; *m* Helen, dau of Sir William Douglas of Kelhead, Bt, and *d* 1741, leaving a s who *d* young

1a Catherine; *m* 1st Sir William Denholm of Westheels, Bt; *m* 2nd 1714 Daniel Campbell of Shawfield

The **2nd Lord Cardross** *m* 2nd 1655 Mary, dau of Sir George Bruce, of Carnock, Fife (*see* ELGIN and KINCARDINE, E), and *d* 1671, having by her had:

2 William, of Torry, Fife; Col, Dep Govr Blackness Castle; *m* Magdalen, dau of Sir James Lumsdain of Invergelly, and had issue:

(1) William; Col; *m* Henrietta, dau of Sir William Baillie of Lamington and widow of Robert Watson, of Muirhouse, and *d* 1754, leaving (with a dau, *m* 1755 Archibald Stirling of Keir):

1a Sir WILLIAM ERSKINE, 1st Bt (GB), so *cr* 21 June 1791, of Torry; Gen; *m* 1st Magdalen (*dsp*), dau of Sir Robert Myrton of Gogar; *m* 2nd 1767 Frances, dau of James Moray of Abercairny and widow of George Drummond of Blair Drummond, and *d* 1797, leaving by her:

1b Sir WILLIAM ERSKINE, 2nd Bt; *b* 1776; Gen; *dsp* 1813

2b Sir JAMES ERSKINE, 3rd Bt; Lt-Gen; *m* Lady Louisa Paget, dau of Henry, Earl of Uxbridge (*see* ANGLESEY, M), and *dsp* 1825

3b Sir JOHN ERSKINE, 4th Bt; *d* unm 30 July 1836, when the btcy expired

3 John, of Carnock, Fife, which he bought from his 1st cousin, 1st Earl of Kincardine; *b* 30 March 1662; Lt-Col, accompanied WILLIAM III from Holland, Lt-Govr Stirling, Govr Dumbarton Castle, MP (S and GB Parls) Stirling; *m* 1st 14 March 1690 Jane (*dsp* May 1690), dau and heir of William Mure of Caldwell; *m* 2nd 5 Jan 1691 Anna (*d* 29 June 1723), er dau and coheir (with her sis the Countess of Bute) of William Dundas of Kincavel, and by her had, with other issue:

(1) John, of Carnock and Cardross; *b* 4 Nov 1695; *m* 1st March 1719 Margaret, dau of Hon James Melville (*see* LEVEN and MELVILLE, E), and had an only son:

1a John (Rev), of Carnock; *b* 2 June 1719; DD; *m* 15 June 1746 Hon Christian Mackay (*d* 20 May 1800), dau of 3rd Lord Reay (*qv*), and *d* 19 Jan 1803, leaving a s and four daus

(1) (cont.) John Erskine *m* 2nd 1729 Anne, dau of James Stirling of Keir, and *d* 1 March 1768, leaving by her, with other issue:

2a James, of Cardross; *b* 1732; *m* 28 April 1762 Lady Christian Bruce (*d* 20 May 1810), dau of 8th Earl of Kincardine (*see* ELGIN and KINCARDINE, E), and *d* 27 March 1802, leaving, with other issue:

1b John; HEICS; *m* Jane Coleman, and *d* 1792, leaving issue

2b David, of Cardross; *b* 10 Jan 1772; Ceylon CS; *m* 5 Sept 1803 Hon Keith Elphinstone (*d* 4 Aug 1941), dau of 11th Lord Elphinstone (*qv*), and *d* 28 Nov 1847, leaving, with other issue:

1c James, of Cardross; *b* 21 Aug 1804; *m* 27 Feb 1836 Mary Eliza (*d* 26 June 1843), dau of Lt-Gen Christopher Fagan, and *d* Feb 1844, leaving issue:

1d (Henry) David (Sir), of Cardross, KCVO (1911), JP (Perthshire and Stirlingshire), DL (Port of Menteith, Perthshire); *b* 5 Jan 1838; Capt Scots Gds; Dep Serjeant-at-Arms H of C 1875–85, Serjeant-at-Arms 1885–1915, Groom of the Robes to HM QUEEN VICTORIA 1870–1901, Gentleman Usher of the Robes to TM EDWARD VII 1901–10 and GEORGE V 1910–19, Extra Gentleman Usher 1919; *m* 26 June 1861 Lady Horatia Elizabeth Seymour (*d* 16 April 1922), dau of 5th Marquess of Hertford (*qv*), and *d* 7 Sept 1921, leaving, with other issue:

1e James Francis, CB (1917), CMG (1916), MVO (1907), DL (Berwickshire); *b* 4 June 1862; Hon Brig-Gen Scots Gds, Sudan, S Africa, WW I; *m* 10 Dec 1896 Margaret Beatrix (*d* 17 July 1952), dau of Henry Lambton, of Redfield, Winslow, and *d* 26 June 1936, leaving, with other issue:

1f Malcolm David, CBE (posthumous 1949), DSO (1943); *b* 31 Aug 1903; Brig Scots Gds, WW II (despatches); disappeared on flight over Malayan Jungle, 27 Oct 1949

1f Christian; *b* 17 March 1901; *m* 26 July 1926 Capt Hugh Salvin Bowlby (*d* 15 June 1977), RN, s of Edward Salvin Bowlby, JP, DL, and had issue:

2e Seymour Elphinstone, CB, (1918); *b* 23 June 1863; Adml RN, ADC to HM GEORGE V 1911–13, Benin Expdn 1897 (medal), China 1900 (medal), WW I (medals); *m* 20 July 1912 Florence Laetitia, dau of Rev Sir Talbot Hastings Bendall Baker, 3rd Bt, and *dsp* 23 Feb 1945

3e Walter Hugh, CBE (1936, MBE 1920); *b* 27 April 1870; Assist Serjeant-at-Arms H of C 1900–29, Dep Serjeant-at-Arms 1929–40; *m* 1 June 1929 Violet Emily, dau of Rev R S Gregory, Rector of Much Hadham, and *d* 15 Feb 1948

4e Alan David, OBE (1929); *b* 26 Aug 1872; *educ* Magdalen Coll Oxford (BA); with Min Tport; *m* 1 June 1897 Enid (*d* 7 April 1931), dau of Lachlan Mackintosh Rate, MA, JP, of Milton Court, Dorking, and *d* 26 Oct 1947, leaving issue:

1f Ian David, CB (1949), CBE (1947), DSO (1941); *b* 17 March 1898; *educ* Winchester; Maj-Gen Scots Gds, former Regtl Adj, cmdg 22nd Gds Bde, Brig-Gen Staff Sudan, cmded 148 OCTU Training Est, Provost Marshall, WWs I & II (despatches twice); *m* 1 March 1945 Mariora Beatrice Evelyn Rochfort, only dau of Col Cecil George Herbert Alers Hankey, of Binderton House, Chichester, and formerly w of Brig Alan Henry Campbell Swinton, MC

1f Patience Lina; *b* 18 March 1901

5e Arthur Edward (Sir), GCVO, DSO; *b* 1 Sept 1881; *educ* Charterhouse; Col RA, WW I (despatches, brevet Lt-Col 1918); Equerry-in-Ordinary to HM GEORGE V 1919–24, Crown Equerry 1924–41 to TM GEORGE V, EDWARD VIII and GEORGE VI 1937–41, Extra Equerry 1941–63, Sec and Registrar Order of Merit 1939–63, Clerk of Course and Sec to Ascot Auth 1941–46; *m* 28 Nov 1921 Rosemary Freda (*d* 5 Jan 1970), est dau of Brig-Gen Edward William David Baird, of Kellow, Duns, Berwickshire, and *d* 24 July 1963, having had issue:

1f Keith George David; *b* 12 Oct 1922 (HM GEORGE V stood sponsor); *d* 2 July 1923

2f Donald Seymour, of Cleish House, Cleish, Kinross; *b* 28 May 1925; *educ* Wellington; Capt RA WW II 1943–45; memb Roy Co Archers, FLAS 1956, Ch Land Agt Nat Tst Scotland 1961; *m* 15 April 1953 *Catherine Annandale, only dau of Kenneth Thomas McLelland, of Wester Housebyres, Melrose, Roxburghshire, and has issue:

1g +James Malcolm Kenneth; *b* 22 Nov 1957; *educ* Wellington; Maj Black Watch (Roy Highr Regt); memb Roy Co Archers; *m* 1987 *Jennifer, er dau of Donald MacLellan, of Stockbridge, Symington, Ayrshire, and has issue:

1h +Harry Charles David; *b* 1988

2h +Geordie James Donald; *b* 1990

1g *Caroline Janet; *b* 15 Sept 1954; *m* 1982 *Lt-Col Alan Keith McCullock Miller, OBE, Argyll & Sutherland Highrs, and has issue:

1h *Kirsty Araminta Jane; *b* 1983

2h *Jennifer Catharine Susanne; *b* 1985

3h *Iona Caroline; *b* 1988

2g *Fiona Catharine; *b* 25 Jan 1956; *m* 1991 *Christopher Brendan Still, of Australia, and has issue:

1h *Alexander Christopher; *b* 1992

1h *Harriet Angela; *b* 1994

3g *Julia Rosemary; *b* 23 Jan 1962

4g *Joanna Christian; *b* 6 July 1968

3f +Angus Bruce [Cdr Angus Erskine RN (ret), 16 Braid Farm Rd, Edinburgh EH10 6LF]; *b* 11 May 1928; *m* 5 Aug 1961 *Alison Gillian, yr dau of Dr Comyn Duthie, of Welkom, OFS, S Africa, and has issue:

1g +Alexander David; *b* 27 Feb 1964

2g +Keith Malcolm; *b* 15 Sept 1967

1e Rachel Augusta; *b* 30 Dec 1875; *m* 13 May 1918 Allan Cyprian Bourne Webb (*d* 11 Jan 1955), barrister, est s of Rt Rev Alan Beecher Webb, DD, former Bp of Grahamstown, S Africa and Dean of Salisbury, and *dsp* 30 Nov 1953

2d James Elphinstone (Sir), KCB, JP, DL, of Venlaw, Peebles; *b* 2 Dec 1838; Adml of the Fleet, 1st and Pncpl Naval ADC to HM QUEEN VICTORIA, a Ld of Admlty 1886, C-in-C N American Station 1895–97; *m* 21 May 1885 Margaret Eliza (*d* 5 April 1939), dau of Rev John Constable, Rector of Marston Bigott, Somerset, and *d* 25 July 1911, leaving issue:

1e David Victor Fairfax; *b* 4 March 1886; Cdr RN; *m* 26 Oct 1915 Mabel (Dorothy) Webb (*d* 7 Dec 1960), and *dsp* 10 Feb 1959

1e Izme Veronica Doreen; *b* 16 June 1890; *d* unm 17 Nov 1935

2c John Elphinstone; *b* 13 July 1806; Adml; MP Stirling 1865–74; *d* unm 28 June 1887

3c George Keith; *b* 19 Feb 1809; Capt Bombay Light Cav; *m* 1837 Selina (*d* 14 April 1875), dau of Lt-Col Chambers, and *d* 12 Jan 1849, leaving, with other issue:

1d George Elphinstone, JP; *b* 20 Jan 1841; Maj-Gen IA, late Bombay Cav (US list); *m* 1st 26 Sept 1861 Blanche (*d* 27 Dec 1879), dau of George Cates, and had, with other issue:

1e Keith, CIE; *b* 12 June 1863; Lt-Col IA, Political Dept, Consul-Gen Baghdad 1914; *m* 3 Nov 1892 Mabel Seabrook (*d* 11 Sept 1950), dau of John Dyson, of Moorlands, nr Crewkerne, Somerset, and *dsp* 19 Oct 1914

2e Charles Ellis Hay; *b* 24 June 1866; Capt ISC; *m* 19 Nov 1897 Gertrude de Bary (*d* 18 Aug 1970 aged 98), dau of Gilbert Saunders, and *dsp* 3 Oct 1902

1d (cont.) Maj-Gen George Erskine *m* 2nd 3 July 1895 Eva Constance Sarah (*d* 20 Jan 1940), dau of Canon Ebenezer Wood Edwards, and *d* 12 Sept 1912, having by her had further issue:

3e George Watkin Eben James (Sir), GCB (1955, KCB 1952, CB 1943), KBE (1950), DSO (1942); *b* 23 Aug 1899; ADC Gen to HM THE QUEEN 1955–65, KRRC, DAQMG E Comd 1937–39, WW II (despatches three times), GOC Hong Kong 1947–48, Dir TA 1948–49, GOC Br Troops Egypt 1949–52, GOC-in-C Eastern Cmd 1952–53, GOC-in-C E Africa 1953–55, Gen 1953, GOC-in-C Southern Cmd 1955–58, Lt-Govr and C-in-C Jersey 1958–64, V-Chm

Securicor Ltd, Fell IOD, Govr Millfield, KStJ 1959, Cdr US Legion of Merit, Grand Cross Order Leopold II Belgium, Médaille Militaire Belgium, Ordre du Chêne Luxembourg; *m* 7 Jan 1930 Ruby (CStJ 1959; *d* 19 Jan 1974), est dau of Sir Evelyn Andros De La Rue, 2nd Bt (*qv*), and *d* 29 Aug 1965, leaving issue:

1f +Philip Neil [Maj Philip Erskine, Ida's Valley Homestead, PO Box 132, Stellenbosch, Western Cape, South Africa]; *b* 20 Aug 1933; *educ* Charterhouse and RMA Sandhurst; Maj Scots Gds, ADC to Govr-Gen NZ 1959–60, Equerry to HRH THE DUKE OF GLOUCESTER 1962–64; *m* 25 Nov 1960 *Alice Fiona, only dau of Capt Edward Copleston Radcliffe, 9th Lancers, of Derriford, Devon, and has:

1g +Rupert Alexander [Rupert Erskine Esq, The Auld House, Swellendam, Western Cape, S Africa]; *b* 5 Aug 1961; *m* 17 May 1986 *Alice Maria, yr dau of Gabriel Fagan, of Cape Town; and adopted:

*Malcolm John; *b* 11 May 1997

2g +(George) Edward [Edward Erskine Esq, Ridley Hall, Kenilworth, Cape Town, Western Cape, S Africa]; *b* 29 May 1966; *educ* Diocesan Coll Cape Town, RMA Sandhurst, Natal U; Lt RGJ; *m* 20 Dec 1992 *Deborah Jane, only dau of Paul Bennett, of Hilton, Natal

1g *Lucy Rose [Mrs Patrick Caruth, 62 Crescent Lane, London SW4 9PU]; *b* 10 Nov 1962; *m* 29 Oct 1994 *Patrick James Lumley Caruth and has:

1h *Catherine Alice; *b* 25 Sept 1996

2f +Robert Keith; *b* 24 June 1936; *educ* Charterhouse and King's Coll Cambridge; *m* 27 June 1964 *Susan Morag, 3rd dau of Sir Archibald Charles Edmonstone, 6th Bt (*qv*), and has issue:

1g +Hamish Robert Coll Charles; *b* 27 March 1967; *m* 1991 *Anne Nicola Parsons, and has issue:

1h +Jonathan; *b* 1994

2g *Alexander William Ian Marshall; *b* 14 March 1970; *m* 1991 *Carina Gustafsson, and has issue:

1h *Carl; *b* 1994

1g *Iona Mary; *b* 25 April 1965; *m* 1990 *John Hunter Andrews, and has issue:

1h *Morna; *b* 1993

1f *Polly Elizabeth; *b* 3 Dec 1945 (HRH PRINCE CHARLES of Belgium stood sponsor); *m* 30 March 1967 *Paul Lanfear Harold Bristol, of La Metairie, Fabas 31230, Toulouse, France, yr son of Arnold Charles Verity Bristol, of The Forester's Cottage, Wotton, Surrey, and has issue:

1g *Pollyanna; *b* 24 Feb 1969

2g *Sophy Louisa; *b* 1972

3g *Georgiana; *b* 1982

2d Charles Mountstuart; *b* 27 Aug 1843; Lt-Col Bombay SC; *m* 9 Jan 1875 Nellie (*d* June 1922), dau of Maj-Gen W Ashburner, and *d* 25 July 1898, leaving, with other issue:

1e Emily Olive; *m* 27 Dec 1906 Sir Charles William Charteris Carson, CIE, OBE, (*d* 10 May 1945), and *d* 22 June 1935, leaving issue

3b William; *b* 1780; Maj 71st Foot; *m* 15 Sept 1801 Elizabeth, dau of Gen Sir William Myers, Bt, and *dsp* 1 April 1805

3a Archibald, of Venlaw, Peebles; Maj; *m* 7 April 1781 Margaret (*m* 3rd 1822 1st Baron Amesbury and *d* 21 April 1841), dau of Hon Charles Maitland Barclay (*see* LAUDERDALE, E) and widow of Charles Ogilvy, and *d* 1 Aug 1804, having had issue

1a Christian; *m* 17 April 1762 Sir William Stirling, Bt (*d* 26 July 1799), and *d* 1 Feb 1788

(1) Mary; *m* 23 Feb 1721 Alexander, Earl of Leven and Melville (*qv*)

3 (cont.) Col John Erskine *m* 3rd 28 April 1725 Lilias (*dsp* 27 March 1729), est dau of Sir George Stirling of Keir, and widow of John Murray of Polmaisey; *m* 4th 25 Nov 1729 Mary (*d* 12 Sept 1772), dau of Charles Stuart of Duncarn, and *d* Jan 1743, having by her had:

(1) Charles; *b* 1731; *d* unm 1771

The 3rd LORD CARDROSS's est son,

DAVID ERSKINE, **4th Lord Cardross** and **9th Earl of Buchan** (*s* cousin 1695), PC (1697); *b* 1672; Govr Blackness Castle 1702–07 and 1710–14, opposed Union of Scottish and English Parls, Ld-Lt Stirlingshire and Clackmannanshire 1715–34, rep S peer 1715–34; *m* 1st 11 Feb 1697 Frances, dau and heir of Henry Fairfax, of Hurst, Berks, by Frances, dau of the author Sir Thomas Browne, and had, with other issue:

1 HENRY, **10th Earl**

1 Katherine; *m* 1724 William Fraser of Fraserfield (*see* SALTOUN, L) and *d* 1733

The **9th Earl** *m* 2nd 15 Sept 1743 Isabella (*dsp* 14 May 1763), dau of Sir William Blackett, Bt, of Wallington, Northumberland, and *d* 14 Oct 1745

His est surv son,

HENRY DAVID ERSKINE, **10th Earl of Buchan**; *b* 17 April 1710; *m* 31 Jan 1739 Agnes (*d* 17 Dec 1778), 2nd dau of Sir James Stewart, Bt, of Goodtrees, and *d* 1 Dec 1767, leaving:

1 DAVID STEUART ERSKINE, **11th Earl of Buchan**; *b* 1 June 1742; *educ* Foulis Acad, Glasgow, and Glasgow and Leiden Us; FRS 1765, FSA 1766, Sec Br Embassy Spain 1766–67, Grand Master Scottish Freemasons 1782–84, literary patron, a fndr Soc of Antiquaries of Scotland; *m* 15 Oct 1771 Margaret (*d* 12 May 1819), est dau of William Fraser of Fraserfield (*see* SALTOUN, L), and *dsp* 19 April 1829

2 Henry (Harry), of Amondell, Co Linlithgow; *b* 1 Nov 1746; advocate 1768, King's Advocate 1783 and 1806, Dean Faculty of Advocates 1786; *m* 1st 30 March 1772 Christian (*d* 1804), only child and heiress of George Fullerton, of Broughton Hall, and had, with another s and two daus:

(1) HENRY DAVID ERSKINE, **12th Earl of Buchan**; *b* July 1783; *m* 1st 28 Sept 1809 Elizabeth Cole (*d* 5 Oct 1828), yst dau and coheir of Maj-Gen Sir Charles Shipley, Col Engrs and Govr Grenada, and had, with two other sons and two other daus:

1a Henry, *Lord Cardross*; *b* 22 Oct 1812; *m* 15 May 1832 Jane Halliday (*d* 11 Sept 1886), 2nd dau of Archibald Torrie, of Gorgie and Edinburgh, and *dvp* 21 Dec 1836, leaving, with other issue:

1b Joan Berry; inherited the her Dryburgh Abbey estate, Berwicks, and the Holmes estate, Roxburghshire; *b* 16 Feb 1833; *m* 8 April 1856 Rev George Eden Biber, later Biber-Erskine (*d* 25 July 1866), and *d* 16 March 1870, having had issue

2a DAVID STUART ERSKINE, **13th Earl of Buchan**, DL (Linlithgow); *b* 6 Nov 1815; jockey; made bankrupt 1894 in the sum of £388, having 1872 made over his Linlithgow estates to his son for £500 pa; an RC by the time of his death; *m* 1st 27 April 1849 Agnes Graham (*d* 2 Sept 1875), yst dau of James Smith Esq, of Craigend, Stirlingshire, and had issue:

1b SHIPLEY GORDON STUART ERSKINE, **14th Earl of Buchan**, JP (Cambs); *b* 27 Feb 1850; *educ* Harrow; *m* 9 Nov 1876 Rosalie Louisa (*d* in an accident 29 Jan 1943), yst dau of Capt Jules Alexandre Sartoris, of Hopsford Hall, Coventry, and *d* 16 April 1934, leaving, with other issue:

1c RONALD DOUGLAS STUART MAR ERSKINE, **15th Earl of Buchan**; *b* 6 April 1878; Lt Argyll & Sutherland Highrs (militia) and E R Yorks Yeo, 2nd Bn Scots Gds S Africa 1900–02, WW I 1915–17 as Tport Offr London Mounted Bde and Camel Transport Corps; *d* unm 18 Dec 1960

1c Muriel Agnes Stuart; *b* 15 April 1879; *m* 7 Jan 1903 Brig-Gen Hon Charles Strathavon Heathcote-Drummond-Willoughby, CB, CMG (*d* 15 Dec 1949), 2nd s of 1st Earl of Ancaster (*see* WILLOUGHBY DE ERESBY, B), and *d* 23 Oct 1967, leaving issue

2 Evelyn Hilda Stuart; *b* 21 March 1883; *m* 24 June 1903 1st Baron Moyne (*qv*) and *d* 21 July 1939, leaving issue

2b Albany Mar Stuart; *b* 24 Feb 1852; Capt 3rd Bn Duke of Wellington's W R Regt; *m* 1st 16 May 1878 (*divorce* 1900) Alice Ellen (*dsp* 19 Sept 1902), dau of Alfred Keyser, of Cross Oak, Herts; *m* 2nd 2 Sept 1909 Elizabeth Kate (*d* 6 Oct 1965), only surv dau of George Samuel Craddock, of Melbourne, Australia, and *d* 9 June 1933, leaving issue:

1c *Rose Agnes Jessie Stuart; *b* 25 June 1910

2c *Gladys Evelyn Stuart; *b* 5 Sept 1916; *m* 1949 Johannes Adalbert Hopmann, of The Golliwogs, Windmill Road, Mortimer Common, Berks

3c Nancy Elizabeth Stuart; *b* 2 Oct 1921; *m* 19 July 1941 Frank Stonely Stone, of 38 College Piece, Mortimer, Berks, s of Frank Stone, of Glebe Farm, Kenn, Exeter, and had issue

2a (cont.) The **13th Earl** *m* 2nd 17 July 1876 Maria (*d* 17 Aug 1899), dau of William James and widow of Jervois Collas, of St Martin's House, Jersey, and *d* 3 Dec 1898

(1) (cont.) The **12th Earl** *m* 2nd 26 June 1830 Elizabeth (*d* 17 Dec 1838), yst dau of John Harvey, of Castle Semple, Renfrewshire, and by her had further issue:

1a Margaret Erskine; *m* 24 April 1860 Sir William Vincent, 12th Bt (*d* 16 Feb 1914), Rector of Postwick, Norfolk, and *d* 22 Nov 1872, leaving issue

(1) The **12th Earl** *m* 3rd 26 June 1839 Caroline Rose (*d* 22 April 1893), yst dau of James Primrose Maxwell, of Tuppendean, Kent, and *d* 13 Sept 1857

2 (cont.) Henry Erskine *m* 2nd 7 Jan 1805 Erskine, dau of Alexander Munro (*see* MUNRO, Bt, of Lindertis), and widow of Sir James Turnbull, of Edinburgh, and *d* 8 Oct 1817

3 THOMAS ERSKINE, **1st Baron Erskine of Restormel Castle**, Co Cornwall (UK), *so cr* 10 Feb 1806, KT (1815), PC (1806), KC (1783); *b* 10 Jan 1750; *educ* Edinburgh GS, St Andrews and Trin Coll Cambridge (MA 1778); joined RN 1764, joined Arms 1768, Lt 1st Foot 1773, barrister Lincoln's Inn 1778, MP (Whig) Portsmouth 1783–84 and 1790–1806, Attorney-Gen to PRINCE OF WALES 1783–92, Chllr Duchy of Cornwall 1802, Ld Chllr 1806; *m* 1st 29 March 1770 Frances (*d* 22 Dec 1805), dau of Daniel Moore, MP, and had, with other issue:

(1) DAVID MONTAGU ERSKINE, **2nd Baron Erskine of Restormel Castle**; *b* 1777; *educ* Winchester and Trinc Coll Cambridge; barrister Lincoln's Inn 1802, MP (Whig) Portsmouth Feb-Oct 1806, Envoy Washington 1806–10, Stuttgart 1824–28 and Munich 1828–43; *m* 1st 6 Dec 1799 Frances (*d* 25 March 1843), dau of Gen John Cadwallader, of Philadelphia, and had:

1a THOMAS AMERICUS ERSKINE, **3rd Baron Erskine of Restormel Castle**; *b* 3 May 1802; attaché Turin, Naples and Lisbon 1824–27; *m* 12 May 1830 Louisa (*d* 10 March 1867), dau of George Lewis Newnham, of New Timber Place, Sussex, and widow of Thomas Legh, of Adlington, and *dsp* 10 May 1877

2a JOHN CADWALLADER ERSKINE, **4th Baron Erskine of Restormel Castle**; *b* 1804; Bengal CS; *m* 1st 30 April 1829 Margaret (*d* 21 June 1862), dau of John Martyn, of Co Tyrone, and had issue:

1b WILLIAM MACNAGHTEN ERSKINE, **5th Baron Erskine of Restormel Castle**, JP, DL (Northants); *b* 7 Jan 1841; *educ* Eton; Capt 9th Lancers, barrister Lincoln's Inn 1873; *m* 2 July 1864 Caroline Alice Martha (*d* 2 March 1922), dau of William Grimble, and *d* 8 Dec 1913, leaving:

1c MONTAGU ERSKINE, **6th Baron Erskine of Restormel Castle**; *b* 13 April 1865; *educ* Eton; Lt-Cdr RNVR WW I; *m* 16 Jan 1895 Florence (*d* 3 Dec 1936), 4th dau of Edgar Flower, JP, of The Hill, Stratford-on-Avon, and Middlehill Park, Broadway, Worcs, and *d* 9 Feb 1957, leaving issue:

1d DONALD CARDROSS FLOWER, **7th Baron** and **16th Earl**

2d (Richard) Alastair; *b* 8 Jan 1901; *educ* Charterhouse; *m* 20 Oct 1933 Patricia (*d* 1989), dau of Maj Paul FitzGerald Norbury, DSO, of The Lench House, Stratford-on-Avon, and *d* 1987, leaving issue:

1e +Duncan FitzGerald [Duncan Erskine Esq, Little Cheesecombe, Hawkley, Liss, Hants, GU33 6NB]; *b* 20 May 1936; *educ* Malvern; *m* 1st 3 Dec 1964 (*divorce* 1984) Jillian Lavinia Mary, yr dau of Brig Vincent Alexander Prideaux Budge, CBE, MVO, and has had quadruplets:

1f *Roy Alistair; *b* 1972

2f *Alexander Fitzgerald; 1972
1f *Charlotte Louise Annabelle; b 1972
1e (cont.) Duncan Erskine m 2nd 1986 *Susan, dau of Maj Leslie Frederick Buckholt
2e Niall Stuart; b 4 Feb 1939; d 8 Aug 1941
2d (cont.) The Hon Alastair and Mrs Erskine adopted:
1e *Melanie; b 14 April 1938; m 19 Oct 1957 (divorce 1967) Sir John Patrick McLannahan Power, 3rd Bt (d 1984), and has issue
1f Victoria Esmée; b 3 Jan 1897; m 5 Oct 1932 A/Cdre Harry Aitken Hewat, CBE, MB, ChB, RAF (d 4 April 1970), s of Richard George Hewat, of Edinburgh
2c (Stuart) Ruaraidh Joseph, of Mar; b 15 Jan 1869; m 1st 18 July 1891 Muriel Lillas Colquhoun (d 27 April 1895), est dau of Maj-Gen G Irving Graham; m 2nd 6 Aug 1902 Doña Maria Guadalupe Zaara Cecilia Heaven v Ramirez de Arellano, Dama de la Gran Placa de Honor y Mérito (d 25 May 1956), only dau of Joseph Robert Heaven, of The Forest of Birse, Aberdeenshire, and d 5 Jan 1960, having had by his 1st w:
1d Alison Colquhoun; b 20 Aug 1893; d 1894
3c Esmé Standish; b 5 March 1873; Sub-Lt RNVR; d 13 Jan 1924
1c Margaret; b 27 April 1866; m 1st 23 Oct 1890 Capt Henry Edmund Lacon (d 18 March 1924), of the Lodge, Bramford, Ipswich, 71st Highrs (see LACON, Bt); m 2nd 10 Sept 1928 Maj Robert C Carr (d 6 Feb 1945), RA, and d 12 July 1947
1b Fanny Macnaghten; m 12 Jan 1861 Standish G Rowley, of Sylvan Park, Co Meath, and d 5 May 1872, leaving issue
2b Margaret Catherine; m 1st 30 April 1878 (divorce 1886) Rev Evelyn Henry Villebois Burnaby (d 15 Feb 1924), Rector of Burrough-on-the-Hill, yr s of Rev Canon Gustavus Andrew Burnaby, of Somerby Hall, Leics, and had issue; m 2nd 7 June 1887 Sydney Beaumont Willoughby (d 5 Aug 1921) and d 25 July 1940, having had further issue (see MIDDLETON, B)
2a (cont.) The **4th Baron** m 2nd 25 Jan 1865 Maria Louisa Cullen (m 2nd 20 Oct 1886 Philip Henry Egerton (see GREY EGERTON, Bt) and d 12 April 1889), dau of Col Alexander Campbell, CB, KH, of Blackburn House, Ayrshire, and d 28 March 1882
3a David; b 1816; Maj 21st Fus, Lt-Col Natal Carabiniers, Colonial Sec Natal; m 1st 12 Nov 1839 Anne Maria (d 3 Nov 1860), est dau of Josiah Spode, and had, with other issue:
1b Steuart Townsend; b 23 Nov 1844; m 17 Jan 1866 Jessie Smith, 3rd dau of David Dale Buchanan, of Natal, and dsp 11 July 1918
2b St Vincent Whitshed; b 22 Feb 1846; discovered source of River Limpopo 1868, later surveyor-Gen to S African Govt; m 1870 Alice, dau of David Dale Buchanan, of Natal, and had:
1c Charles Howard; b 1871; m 1900 Charlotte Mildred (d 1947), dau of William Wright Greathead, and d 1918, leaving issue:
1d +George St Vincent [George Erskine Esq, 961 Pershing Ave, San José, California 95126, USA]; b 1905; m 1936 Ruth Genevieve (d 1992), dau of Iver Nelson, and has issue:
1e +Charles Nelson [Charles Erskine Esq, 9205 Jura Rd, Sidney, BC, Canada V8L 5GI]; b 1938; m 1969 (divorce 18 June 1990) Linda Ruth, dau of Thomas G McReynolds, and has issue:
1f +George Lindley; b 1973
1f *Gyneth Alice; b 1971
1e (cont.) Charles Erskine m 2nd 23 July 1994 *Lona Diane, dau of Arthur Henry Cook
2c Esmé, CMG, MC; b 1884; m 1909 Elizabeth Susan Matilda (d 1973), dau of Herman Reinders, and d 1962 leaving issue:
1d Esmé Stephenson; b 1914; m 1941 *Jean Meriel [Mrs Esmé Erskine, Kingsclifffe Farm, PO Glenside 3477, Natal, South Africa], dau of Henry Crawford Boyd, of Chobham, Surrey, and d 1982, leaving issue:
1e +Stephen St Vincent [Stephen Erskine Esq, Kingsclifffe Farm, PO Glenside 3477, Natal, South Africa]; b 1947; m 1975 *Bridget Grey, dau of Derrick G Norton, of Pietermaritzburg, Natal, and has issue:
1f +Byron Thomas; b 1977
1f *Angela Jane; b 1979
2f *Paula Swanzie; b 1982
2e +Andrew Stuart [Andrew Erskine Esq, Bosch Hoek, Balgowan, Natal, South Africa]; b 1949; m 1972 *Margaret Ann, dau of Austin V Johnson of Howick, Natal, and has issue:
1f +Stuart Graeme; b 1974
2f +Chad Esmé; b 1980
1f *Sarah Margaret; b 1976
3e +David Boyd [David B Erskine Esq, 335 Cowey Rd, Durban, Natal, South Africa]; b 1954; m 1981 *Marilyn-Gene, dau of Harold Dodd, of Australia, and has issue:
1f *Catherine Ann; b 1983
2f *Jennifer Lynn; b 1986
1d *Swanzie; b 1916; m 1937 Sir Fulque Agnew of Lochnaw, 10th Bt (d 1975)
1c Renira Erskine; m 1 Jan 1910 Percy George Grant-Dalton, of Rustenburg, Transvaal, and had issue
3b Robert Henry; b 26 July 1848; k during a native rising in S Africa 5 Nov 1873
1b Frances Cadwallader; m 22 Aug 1862 Sir Michael Henry Gallwey, KCMG (d 24 July 1912), Ch Justice Natal 1890–1901, and d leaving issue
2b Annie Barton; m 14 Aug 1872 Maj Arthur H Pain, 1st Bn Gordon Highrs
3a (cont.) Maj The Hon David Erskine m 2nd 26 Sept 1870 Emma Florence Mary (d 5 April 1927), est dau of Capt Charles Joseph Harford, JP, 12th Lancers, of Frenchay Lodge, Bristol, and d 21 June 1903, having by her had further issue:
4b Herman Harford; b 21 Sept 1871; S African CS; m 3 May 1899 Adela Eva, dau of Richard Fielding Nevins, and d 2 Dec 1939, having had issue:
1c Angela Augusta; m 1st 1921 Barry H Howe and had issue; m 2nd Ronald Hayne
5b Robert Henry; b 31 Dec 1874; Consul-Gen Zurich 1930–33; m 1914 Clara Gudrun, dau of Christian Howden-Runnenkamp, Chamberlain Roy Court of Denmark, and d 12 Oct 1933
3b Sevilla Florence; b 7 May 1875; m 1 Aug 1908 George Glass Hooper, CE (d 5 July 1932), and d 25 Nov 1967, leaving issue
4b Gwladis Kathleen; b 1878; m 1st 15 April 1903 Fleet Paymaster Percy John Ling, RN (k at sea in HMS *Formidable* Jan 1915); m 2nd 1924 Aubrey George Erskine Shaw (d 1938), and d 22 Dec 1960, leaving issue by her 1st husb
4a Edward Morris, CB; b 28 March 1817; Envoy Extrdy and Min Plen Greece 1864–72, Min Stockholm 1872–81; m 24 July 1847 Caroline (d 23 Oct 1877), dau of Robert Hamilton Vaughan, and widow of Andrew Loughnan, and d 19 April 1883, leaving issue:
1b Mary Maud; m 1st 16 April 1872 William John Percy Lawton (d 1883), of Lawton Hall, Cheshire, and had issue; m 2nd 8 Sept 1885 Rev George William Charles Skene, MA, Rector of Barthomley, Cheshire, and d 1892
2b Elizabeth Steuarta; m 2 March 1875 Lt-Col Offley John Crewe-Read, JP (d Oct 1902), of Plas Dinam, Llandinam, Montgomeryshire, and d 9 Aug 1905, leaving issue
3b Evelyn Constance; m 1 June 1876 Francis William White, FRGS, Commr of Customs, China, yst s of Rev J White, Vicar of Barnet-by-the-Wold, Lincs, and d 13 Dec 1926, leaving issue
4b Christian Edith Eleanor
5a James Stuart; b 4 Sept 1821; cr 18 Jan 1872 Baron Erskine (Bavaria); m 27 Feb 1849 Wilhelmina (d 23 Feb 1880), dau of Anton Joseph Clemens, Count Toerring Minucci, of Munich, and d 4 June 1904, leaving, with other issue:
1b Hermann David Montagu, 2nd Baron Erskine; b 12 Feb 1854; Lt Bavarian Army; m and d 1 March 1934
1b Hermine Maria; m 18 Aug 1884 Prof Hermann von Sicherer (d 21 Sept 1901)
1a Frances; m 1824 Gabriel Shawe and d 7 June 1876
2a Mary; m 16 June 1832 Herman, Count von Paumgarten, of Bavaria (d 11 Jan 1846), and d 15 March 1874
3a Sevilla; m 23 Dec 1830 Sir Henry Francis Howard, GCB (see NORFOLK, D), and d 12 March 1835, leaving issue
4a Steuarta; m 6 Oct 1828 Yeats Brown, of Stuppington, Kent, Consul Genoa, and d 17 Sept 1863
5a Elizabeth; m 1 April 1832 Sir St Vincent Keene Hawkins-Whitshed, Bt (d 13 Sept 1870; see 1871 edn), and d 19 July 1886 aged 74
6a Harriett; m 29 Aug 1833 Charles Woomass, of Alveston, Warwicks, and d 19 Nov 1855
7a Jane Plumer; m 29 Aug 1837 James Henry Callander (d 31 Jan 1851), of Craigforth, Stirling, and d 30 March 1846
(1) The **2nd Baron** m 2nd 29 July 1843 his 1st w's 1st cousin Anne Bond (d 18 April 1851), dau of John Travis, of Lancs; m 3rd 21 Dec 1852 Anna (m 3rd 3 April 1856 Ven J Sandford, BD, Archdeacon of Coventry), widow of Thomas Calderwood Durham, of Largo, and dau of William Cunningham-Graham, of Gartmore, Peeblesshire, and d 19 March 1855
(2) Henry David (Very Rev); b 1786; Dean of Ripon; m 4 May 1813 Mary Harriet, 3rd dau of 1st Earl of Portarlington (qv), and d 27 July 1859, leaving, with other issue:
1a George David; b 2 June 1820; m 22 Jan 1845 Eleanor Elizabeth (d 1892), dau of Rev Henry Wintle, of Cheltenham, and dsp 12 Sept 1897
1a Louisa Lucy; m 21 May 1845 Rev T F Rudston Read, Rector of Winteringham, and d 1865
2a Fanny Louisa; m 16 Sept 1847 Henry Linwood Strong (d 1886), barrister, and d 13 Dec 1908, leaving issue
3a Anne Agnes; m 29 Aug 1859 Robinson Fowler (d 1895), barrister, Stipendiary Magistrate at Manchester, and d 26 May 1912
4a Julia Henrietta; m 17 Feb 1856 Lt-Gen Broadley Harrison, 11th Hus (d 30 June 1890), and d 20 Feb 1891, leaving issue
(3) Thomas (Rt Hon); b 12 March 1788; Judge Court Common Pleas; m 10 Dec 1814 Henrietta Eliza (d 21 Aug 1865), only dau of Henry Trail, and d 9 Nov 1864, leaving, with two daus (d unm):
1a Henry Trail; b 25 Dec 1815; m 18 Dec 1856 Eliza Sarah (d Feb 1899), only dau of Cdr Herbert William Hore, RN, of Pole Hore, Co Wexford, and dsp 21 May 1865
2a Thomas (Rev); b 12 Nov 1828; Rector of Alderley, Cheshire; m 8 April 1856 Emmeline Augusta (d 27 Nov 1930), 3rd dau of Henry John Adeane, of Babraham, Cambridgeshire, and d 28 Feb 1878, leaving, with other issue:
1b Henry Adeane, CB (1911), CMG (1915), CBE (1919), VD, TD; b 1 March 1857; Hon Col RASC, Cdr 6th Bn Northumberland Fus and Northumbrian Div Trg Col and Dep Dir Supplies 1917, Order Leopold Belgium, agent of Bank of England at Newcastle-on-Tyne; m 8 July 1891 Florence Eliza Palmer (d 11 Dec 1943), yr dau of Ven Robert Chapman, Archdeacon of Sudbury and Canon of Ely, and d 9 Feb 1953, having had:
1c Henry David; b 17 Oct 1897; Midshipman RN; ka on HMS *Minotaur* 31 March 1915
1c Margaret Helen; d 1974
2c Christian Mary; d 1987
3c Griselda Beatrice; m 7 Sept 1921 Canon George David Archer (d 13 Jan 1971), s of Rev Canon George Frederick Archer, MA, and d 1995, leaving:
1d *Henry David, DFC [W/Cdr Henry Archer DFC, 30 Ivinghoe Rd, Bushey Heath, Herts]; b 10 July 1922; W/Cdr RAF WW II; m 3 Aug

1957 Valda Mildred (*d* 1978), dau of John Smart, of Wimbledon, and has:

1e *John David [John Archer Esq, 6 The Brambles, Stone Close, Middle Winterslow, Wilts]; *b* 1 Aug 1958; *m* 1987 *Alexandra Hickish and has:

1f *Harry Thomas David; *b* 16 April 1996

1f *Emily Elizabeth; *b* 16 June 198–

2f *Catherine Harriet; *b* 9 May 1990

2e *Matthew George [Mathew Archer Esq, The Cottage, 6 Ellastone Gdns, Alverstone, Derbys]; *b* 3 Dec 1962; *m* 18 July 1987 *Sally Birch and has:

1f *William; b 3 Nov 1992

1f *Ruth; *b* 31 Dec 1994

1e *Margaret Elizabeth; *b* 30 Dec 1959; *m* 6 June 1992 *Jeremy Davy

2e *Charlotte Christian; *b* 14 Aug 1961; *m* 7 May 1988 *David Irwin and has:

1f *George Henry; *b* 27 Oct 1989

1f *Alice Catherine; *b* 22 Sept 1991

2d *Richard George [Richard Archer Esq, Park Corner, Old Hollow, Crawley, Sussex RH10 4SZ]; *b* 4 June 1925; late Lt REME; *m* 14 April 1956 *Elizabeth Rosemary, dau of Kingsley Dykes, OBE, MC, of Ottinge Court, nr Canterbury, and has issue:

1e *Caroline Griselda Erskine; *b* 12 April 1959; *m* 1991 *Charles Sussex, barrister

2e *Elizabeth Georgiana; *b* 3 June 1964

1d *Elizabeth Margaret Griselda [Mrs Robert Montgomery, Selwood House, Salisbury St, Mere, Wilts BA12 6HF]; *b* 6 Dec 1923; *m* 28 Nov 1946 *Lt-Col Robert Kerr Montgomery, MC, BSc Eng, RE (ret), s of Lt-Col R V Montgomery, Roy Signals, of Bennett Road, Hove, Sussex, and has:

1e *Robert Michael; *b* 4 Nov 1947; *educ* Wellington and Imp Coll London; *m* 1979 *Elizabeth Miles, of Stockbridge, Mass.

2e *David Richard; *b* 3 Feb 1949; *educ* Wellington and Southampton U; *m* 1979 *Gwynneth Owen, of Catcott, Somerset, and has:

1f *Alexander Owen; *b* 25 July 1984

1f *Huw Thomas; *b* June 1986

2d *Alethea Mary; *b* 21 Oct 1926; *m* 23 Oct 1947 Cdr Christian Peter Evensen, DSO and bar, RNVR (*d* 1996), of Staplehay, Somerset, s of Christian Martin Evensen, of Hull, and has:

1e *James Peter; *b* 11 Oct 1951; *m* 1987 *Robeena Holton, of Melbourne, Australia, and has:

1f *Christian James; *b* 1987

2f *Nicholas Robin; *b* 1989

1e *Patricia Christian; *b* 14 March 1948; *m* 1974 *Alan Tucker, of Taunton, Somerset

2e *Susan Alethea; *b* 15 Feb 1950; *m* 1974 *Donald Francis Heather Bent, of The Corner House, Sandy Lane, Tilford, Farnham, Surrey, and has issue:

1f *Simon Francis; *b* 1979

1f *Sarah Heather; *b* 1976

3e *Fiona Mary; *b* 28 Nov 1952; *m* 1972 *David Perratt, of Clavengers, E Nynehead, Wellington, Somerset, and has issue:

1f *James Michael; *b*1976

1f *Diana; *b*1974

3d *Mary Pamela; *b* 26 March 1929; *m* 18 Aug 1951 *Capt Richard Ewen Hartley, RN, of 3 Newton Rd, Canford Cliffs, Poole, Dorset, s of Dr Frank Hartley, of Tyne Dene, Canford Cliffs, Bournemouth, and has issue:

1e *Christopher Richard [Christopher R Hartley Esq, 5 Bentley Close, Matlock, Derbys]; *b* 15 June 1952; *m* 1976 *Julia, dau of Grenville Ball, of Sutton Ashfield, and has issue:

1f *David Richard; *b* 1985

1f *Katherine Mary; *b* 1983

2e *Michael Peter [Michael Hartley Esq, 4 Ashley Close, Charlton Kings, Cheltenham, Glos]; *b* 3 April 1956; *m* 1985 *Alison Mary, dau of William Jacobs, of Ipswich, Suffolk, and has issue:

1f *Caroline Alison; *b* 1987

2f *Charlotte Helen; *b* 1990

1e *Helen Mary; *b* 9 Feb 1955; *m* 1979 *Andrew George Alexander Wigmore, of 24 Chalfont Rd, Oxford, and has issue:

1f *George Alexander; *b* 1987

2f *Hugh Richard; *b* 1990

4d *Helen Christian; *b* 1 March 1935; *m* 1970 *Alastair Nigel Courtney Bruce, of The Barn, Great Durnford, Salisbury, Wilts, and has issue:

1e *Rowena Christian Bruce; *b* 1970

2e *Mary Courtney Bruce; *b* 1972

2b Thomas Edward; *b* 24 June 1859; Consul-Gen New Orleans; *m* 17 Nov 1888 Amy Getrude (*d* 10 Oct 1939), dau of Lt-Gen Robert Bruce, bro of 1st Baron Aberdare (*qv*), and *d* 29 Oct 1916, leaving issue:

1c Thomas; *b* 20 Feb 1898; Pte 42nd Highrs; *d* April 1967

2c John Steuart; *b* 8 Nov 1900; *educ* McGill U (MA 1942); 4th Bn King's Own Regt WW I; *m* 19 April 1928 *Rachel Diana Mary [Mrs John Steuart Erskine, 30 Tantramar Residences, Sackville, New Brunswick, Canada], dau of Lt-Col Arthur Wilmot Rickman, and *d* 16 Sept 1981, leaving:

1d +David Stuart [David Erskine Esq, 71 Green Bush Rd, Willowdale, Ontario, Canada]; *b* 24 Dec 1929; *educ* Acadia U (MA 1952, BSc 1948); *m* 10 May 1957 *Elizabeth (Elizavete Fyodorovna), dau of Fyodor Ivanovitch Kramarev, of Vrsac, Yugoslavia, formerly of Peterhof, Russia, and has issue:

1e +John David; *b* 23 Sept 1958

1e *Maria (Mary); *b* 6 July 1960; *m* 1981 (*divorce* 1990) Brian Clow, of Pickering, Ontario

2d +Anthony John [Anthony Erskine Esq, 16 Richardson St, Sackville, NB E4L 4H6, Canada]; *b* 25 June 1931; *educ* Acadia U (BSc 1952), Queen's U (MA 1955, Phd 1957), U of BC (MA 1960); wildlife biologist, Dept Indian Affairs N Development Canada 1960–91 Research Scientist Emeritus 1991–; *m* 11 June 1955 *Janet Madeline, dau of L H Clarke, of Canning, King's Co, Nova Scotia, and has issue:

1e +Thomas Edward; *b* 27 Feb 1957; *m* 11 May 1981 (*divorce* July 1994) Judith Rosemary, dau of James Reynolds, of Woodstock, Ontario; *m* 2nd *Leslie Clark, and by his 1st w has:

1f *Sarah Laurel; *b* 13 May 1982

2f *Bronwyn Rebecca; *b* 19 Nov 1985

1e *Rachel Julia Andrée; *b* 30 Nov 1958; *m* 8 Dec 1988 *Frank Collins, of Toronto, and has:

1f *Julia Erskine; *b* 1 Feb 1991

2e *Sally Eileen; *b* 7 Jan 1961; *m* 13 Sept 1980 *Glenn Doucette, formerly of Hubbards Point, Nova Scotia, and has issue:

1f *John Anthony Erskine; *b* 12 Oct 1988

1f *Madeleine Zoe; *b* 1 March 1991

2f *Clara Frances; *b* 11 Feb 1993

3d Roger Thomas; *b* 9 Nov 1933; *educ* Queen's U, Kingston, Ontario (MSc 1962); *m* 2 June 1956 *Florence Elizabeth [Mrs Roger Erskine, RR3 Box 809, Bathurst, New Brunswick, Canada], dau of C P Taylor, of Windsor, Nova Scotia, and *d* 12 Oct 1975, leaving issue:

1e +Gerald Conrad; *b* 4 Sept 1957; *m* 28 Aug 1978 *Carolyn, dau Clifford White, of Bathurst, New Brunswick, and has issue:

1f +John Andrew; *b* 1981

2f +Ian Ross; *b* 1985

2e +Neil Steuart; *b* 15 Dec 1960; *m* 13 March 1989 *Ava, dau of Stephen Czapaly, of Barrington, Nova Scotia, and has issue:

1f +Julian Benedict; *b* 15 Feb 1993

1f *Rachel Joanna; *b* 25 Feb 1995

3e +Joseph Christian; *b* 13 March 1962; *m* 1992 (*separated* 1997) *Donna MacDonald

1e *Jane Elizabeth; *b* 29 Oct 1966; *m* 1994 *Shawn Branch

1c Marjory Rachel Helen; *b* 12 Sept 1889; nun at Maryville Coll, St Louis Mo; *d* 23 Sept 1981

2c Diana Isobel; *b* 2 Feb 1892; *m* 15 June 1920 (*divorce* 1930) Sir Hugo Meynell FitzHerbert, 6th Bt (*qv*); *d* 3 Sept 1986

3c Violet Amy; *b* 22 March 1894; Sec Br Emb Washington; *m* 9 April 1917 Sir Horace James Seymour, GCMG, CVO (*see* HERTFORD, M), and *d* 11 Aug 1996, leaving issue

3b Robert Steuart; *b* 15 Dec 1880; *m* 7 March 1899 Beatrice Caroline (*d* 10 Sept 1948), dau of H Linwood Strong, and *d* 14 June 1913

4b Edward John; *b* 18 April 1864; *m* 1888 Gertrude (*d* March 1956), dau of J Harding, of NSW, and *d* 9 May 1917, leaving issue:

1c Steuart Edward; *b* 1902; *m* 1930 Marjory Luxton Clendening (*d* 1991) and *d* 1992, leaving:

1d +John Steuart [F/Lt John Erskine RCAF, 9448 Olympia Fields Dve, San Ramon, California 94583, USA]; *b* 1937; *educ* U of Toronto and U of BC (BSc); F/Lt RCAF (ret 1964); *m* 1967 *Sharyl LeAnn Tomes, of Omaha, Nebraska, and has:

1e *Karen Lynn; *b* 1968

1d (cont.) F/Lt John Steuart Erskine also adopted 1968:

*LeAnn; *b* 1965

1d *Patricia Louise Erskine [Mrs Stanley Falle, Le Petit Dixcart, Sark, CI]; *b* 24 May 1934; *educ* U of BC Vancouver (BA 1955) and Toronto U of BLS (1956); *m* 24 May 1968 *Stanley Philip David Falle, 2nd s and heir of Edmund Stanley Falle, Tenant of Le Grand Beau Regard and Dep Seigneur of Sark, and has issue:

1e *Marie Clare Erskine; *b* 1971

1c Sybil Gertrude; *b* 1892; *m* 1919 Capt John Joseph Power, OBE (*d* 1959), and *d* 1985, having had issue

2c Oona Maudi; *b* 1894; *m* 23 Jan 1924 John Eynon Wood, s of John Riggs Wood, of Wallasey, Cheshire, and *d* 1985

(4) Esmé Stewart; *b* 1789; Lt-Col DAG Battle of Waterloo (where he lost an arm); *m* 1809 Eliza Blane (*m* 2nd 3 Nov 1819 James Norton), dau of Lt-Col Smith, and had issue (*d* unm)

(1) Frances; *m* 20 June 1802 Rev Dr Samuel Holland (*d* 16 April 1857), Precentor and Preb Chichester, Rector Poynings, Sussex, and *d* 25 March 1859

(2) Elizabeth; *m* 17 Nov 1798 Sir David Erskine, illegitimate s of **11th Earl of Buchan**, and *d* 2 Aug 1800

(3) Mary; *m* 29 Jan 1805 Edward Morris (*d* 1815), Master in Chancery, and *d* 1864

The **1st Baron** *m* 2nd 12 Oct 1818 (*separated* 21 June 1821) Sarah Buck (*d* 25 Oct 1825), and *d* 17 Nov 1823, leaving by her a son:

(5) Hampden; *b* 5 Dec 1821

1 Isabella; *m* 1st 1770 William Leslie Hamilton (*d* 1780), Attorney-Gen Leeward Islands; *m* 2nd John, Earl of Glencairn, and *dsp* 1824

The 6th BARON's est son,

DONALD CARDROSS FLOWER ERSKINE, **16th Earl of Buchan** (*s* cousin 1960) and **7th Baron Erskine of Restormel Castle**; *b* 3 June 1899; *educ* Charterhouse and RMC Sandhurst; Lt-Col 9th Lancers WW II; *m* 5 Jan 1927 Christina, dau of Hugh Woolner and adopted dau of Lloyd Harry Baxendale, JP, of Greenham Lodge, Newbury, Berks, and *d* 1984, having had:

1 David Stuart; *b* 20 June 1928; *d* 1 Feb 1933

2 MALCOLM HARRY ERSKINE, **17th and present Earl of Buchan**

1 *Sarah Louise [The Lady Sarah Neill-Fraser, Redlands Row Cottage, Little Compton, Moreton-in-Marsh, Glos]; *b* 14 July 1931; *m* 12 June 1957 (*divorce* 1972) Maj Norman Neill-Fraser, of Willow Cottage, South Hay, Kingsley, Bordon, Hants, est s of Maj William Neill-Fraser, of 3 Joppa Rd, Portobello, Midlothian, and has issue:

(1) *James Montagu Nicholas; *b* 19 Jan 1959; *educ* Winchester and King's Coll London

2 *Caroline Flower [The Lady Caroline Lingard, Burnt Oak House, East Bergholt, Colchester, Essex]; *b* 29 June 1935; *m* 26 Feb 1963 *(John) Robin William Lingard, of Semley Grange, Shaftesbury, Dorset, son of Capt Henry Lingard, MC, of Bradford, Yorks, and Mrs C A Feely, of Peasenhall, Saxmundham, Suffolk, and has issue:

(1) *Christina Helen; *b* 31 Jan 1964; *m* 1st 1981 Murad Teja, *s* of M P Teja, and has issue:

1a *Alexandra Sophie; *b* 1985

(1) (cont.) Mrs Christina Teja *m* 2nd 19– *Gawaine Maxwell and has further issue:

2a *Jessica; *b* 19–

3a *Eloise Jane; *b* 1990

(2) *Victoria Margaret; *b* 6 March 1966

BUCHAN-HEPBURN

Arms: Quarterly, 1st and 4th, gu. on a chevron arg. a rose between two lions rampant of the first (for HEPBURN); 2nd, arg. three lion's heads erased gu. (for BUCHAN); 3rd, arg. an anchor in bend az., on a chief of the last three cranes or (for BECK). **Crests:** 1 A horse arg., furnished gu., tied to and in front of a yew-tree ppr. (for HEPBURN), 2 The sun in the dexter chief with a sunflower in full blow open to it ppr. (for BUCHAN). **Supporters:** Dexter, a lion gu.; sinister, a heron with an eel in its beak ppr. **Mottoes:** (over 1st crest) Keep traist; (over 2nd crest) *Non inferiora secutus* ('Having followed no mean pursuits') 3 (under shield) *Domum antiquam redintegrare* ('Restoring an ancient house'). **Creation:** Bt. (UK) 6 May 1815.

SIR (JOHN) ALASTAIR TRANT KIDD BUCHAN-HEPBURN, 7th Bt, of Smeaton Hepburn, Co Haddington [Sir Alastair Buchan-Hepburn Bt, Chagford, 60 Argyle St, St Andrews, Fife KY16 9BU]; *b* 27 June 1931; *s* 3rd cousin 1992; *educ* Charterhouse, St Andrews U and RMA Sandhurst; late Capt King's Dragoon Gds 1954, att Household Cav 1953, att Swiss Cav 1954, ADC to GOC Malaya 1956–57, memb: Inst of Brewing and Bts' Tst; *m* 21 Sept 1957 *Georgina Elizabeth, SRN, only dau of Oswald Morris Turner, MC, of Armathwaite, Cumberland, and has issue:

1 +(JOHN) CHRISTOPHER ALASTAIR [Christopher Buchan-Hepburn Esq, 18 Queen's Terr, St Andrews, Fife KY16 9QF]; *b* 9 March 1963; *educ* Cheltenham Coll and Portsmouth U (BA, DipArch), Laird of (territorial) Barony of Logan, Port Logan, Wigtownshire 1992–96, pncpl offr Performance Unit Dundee City Cnc 1994–; *m* 1990 *Andrea, dau of Kenneth Frederick Unwin, of Elmview, Ryarsh, Kent, and has issue:

(1) +(John) James Christopher Thomas; *b* 1 December 1992

(2) +Henry Robert; *b* 8 June 1997

1 *Caroline Georgina [Mrs Andrew Thomson, Ard Gowan, 37 Deeview Rd Sth, Cults, Aberdeen AB15 9NA]; *b* 30 May 1958; *educ* Grays' Sch of Art Aberdeen (BA); *m* 1987 *Andrew William Pollard Thomson and has issue:

(1) *Hamish Andrew Buchan; *b* 1993

2 *Sarah Elizabeth [Mrs David Cox, Kettins House, Kettins, Blairgowrie, Perthshire PH13 9JL]; *b* 17 April 1960; *educ* U Coll of N Wales Bangor (BA); *m* 1988 *David Arthur Cox and has:

(1) *Nicholas David Maurice; *b* 1990

(2) *Frederick Alastair; *b* 1992

3 *Louise Mary [Mrs David Kinnear, New Easter Delfour, Alvie Estate, Kincraig, by Kingussie, Inverness-shire PH21 1ND]; *b* 17 Nov 1966; *educ* Dollar Acad; *m* 1989 *(Alexander) David Stewart Kinnear and has:

(1) *(Alexander) Christopher Stewart; *b* 16 Oct 1995

(1) *Joanna Georgina Stewart; *b* 9 March 1998

Lineage (of Hepburn): The HEPBURNs/HEBBURNs are of Northumbrian origin, accordingly were often forced to choose between Scots and English in their loyalties.

Sir ROBERT de HYBURNE, 1st Ld of the manor of Newton; *fl* 1245; had, with an er s (John):

NICHOLAS de HIBBURNE; *m* Emme and left:

ADAM de HIBBURNE/HYLBURNE; sided with the Scots in 1317; he and his wife were in 1343 granted the lands of Ha(i)les, Traprain and other lands in E Lothian and elsewhere by Patrick de Dunbar Earl of March; *m* Mariota Fourbour and had, with other issue:

Sir PATRICK HEPBURN of Ha(i)les; had a safe conduct from RICHARD II in 1381 to pass through England to the Holy Land; *b* by 1322; *m* 1st Agnes — and had issue; *m* 2nd (dispensation granted 18 March 1376), as her 5th husb, Eleanor, only sis of 1st Earl of Douglas (*see* QUEENSBERRY, M), and *d* in or after 1402; his s by his 1st w:

PATRICK HEPBURN, Yr. of Ha(i)les; received safe conducts from EDWARD III in 1363 to visit the tomb of St Thomas of Canterbury and in 1364 to study at Oxford; he and his f contributed greatly to the Scottish victory at Otterburn 1388; *m* 1st — Vaux, dau and coheir of the family of that name who were feudal Lds of Dirleton, and had, with two other sons:

1 ADAM (Sir) of Ha(i)les; one of the Commrs sent to England in 1423 to treat for the release of JAMES I of Scotland; *m* (papal dispensation 2Nov 1411) Janet, dau of Sir William Borthwick, and *d c* 1446, leaving (with a dau Agnes, *m* Alexander, Master of Home, *see* HOME, E):

(1) Sir PATRICK HEPBURN, 1st LORD HAILES (S), so *cr* between 31 Oct 1452 and 14 June 1453; *b c* 1412; (?)*m* 1st(?) —; *m* (?)2nd(?) Ellen Wallace and *d* shortly after 6 Dec 1482, having had:

1a Adam, *Master of Ha(i)les*; *b c* 1435; said in 1462 to have been lover of MARIE, widow of JAMES II (*d* 1460), involved in a plot against JAMES III but pardoned; *m c* 2 Feb 1448/9 Helen (*m* 2nd by 15 July 1480, as his 2nd w, 3rd Lord Erskine (*see* MAR and KELLIE, E)), sis of 1st Lord Home (*see* HOME, E), and *dvp* 1479, leaving, with other issue:

1b PATRICK HEPBURN, 2nd LORD HAILES and 1st EARL OF BOTHWELL (S), so *cr* 17 Oct 1488, when the Lordship of Bothwell (previously held by an ancestor of the RAMSAY Bts of Balmain, *qv*) was erected into the superior honour and granted him by the new king JAMES IV following Hepburn's prominent part in the victory of Sauchieburn over JAMES III, against whom JAMES IV, although JAMES III's own son, had nevertheless contended; ktd 1480/1, High Admiral of Scotland, Master of the King's Household and Warden West and Middle Marches; in March 1491/2 he resigned the lordship of Bothwell to the Douglas who was then Earl of Angus, getting in recompense the important Lordship of Liddisdale together with the Castle of Hermitage and other like properties, a ploy of JAMES IV's to weaken the Douglas power; *m* 1st *c* 1 Feb 1480/1 Lady Janet/Joanna Douglas (*dspm*), dau of 1st Earl of Morton (*qv*), and had:

1c Jane/Janet; *m* 3rd Lord Seton (*see* EGLINTON and WINTON, E)

1b The 1st EARL *m* 2nd (contract 21 Feb 1490/1) Lady Margaret Gordon, dau of 1st Earl of Huntly (*see* HUNTLY, M), and *d* 18 Oct 1508, leaving, with other issue (*see* HAMILTON and BRANDON, D):

1c ADAM HEPBURN, 2nd EARL OF BOTHWELL, High Admiral of Scotland; *b c* 1492; *m* Agnes (before her marriage mistress of JAMES IV; she *m* 2nd 3 June 1514 3rd Lord Home (*see* HOME, E); *m* 3rd between 1520 and 15 Nov 1525 4th Lord Maxwell (*see* MAXWELL, Bt); *m* 4th by 13 Dec 1549 Cuthbert Ramsay; *d* Feb 1557), illegitimate dau of James Stewart, 1st Earl of Buchan (*qv*) of the (*c*) 1369 *cr*, and was *ka* in the disastrous defeat of the Scots by the English at the Battle of Flodden 9 Sept 1513, leaving:

1d PATRICK HEPBURN, 3rd EARL OF BOTHWELL, High Admiral of Scotland; made to resign the Lordship of Liddisdale 1538 because he had plotted against JAMES V, though it was restored to him 1543, imprisoned between 1545 and 1547 for intrigues on behalf of the English; *m* 1st(?) 1533/4 his cousin Agnes (*divorce c* Oct 1543), dau of 3rd Lord Sinclair and Margaret, dau of Adam Hepburn, Master of Hailes (*see* below); allegedly *m* 2nd Margaret Home and *d* Sept 1566, leaving issue:

1e JAMES HEPBURN, 4th and last EARL OF BOTHWELL, also 1st and last DUKE OF ORKNEY (S), so *cr* 12 May 1567, High Admiral of Scotland; *b c* 1535; *m* 1st 24 Feb 1565/6 (*divorce* 3 May 1567 for his adultery with one of his w's maids, annulment 7 May 1567 on grounds of consanguinity) Lady Jean Gordon (*m* 2nd 13 Dec 1573 12th Earl of Sutherland; *see* SUTHERLAND, E), dau of 4th Earl of Huntly (*see* HUNTLY, M); *m* 2nd 15 May 1567 MARY QUEEN OF SCOTS, whose previous husband the Earl of Darnley (*see* DARNLEY, E, preliminary remarks) he had undoubtedly helped murder, though he was never found guilty of the crime, and *dspl* 14 April 1578 in the Castle of Draxholm, Denmark, where he had been a prisoner for the last eight years, all his honours having been forfeited by Act of Parl 29 Dec 1567

1e Jean; *m* 1st 4 Jan 1561/2 John Stewart, Prior of Coldinghame, illegitimate son of JAMES V, and had issue; *m* 2nd 16 Jan 1566/7 (*divorce* 17 July 1575) John, Master of Caithness (*dvp c* 1578), and had issue (*see* CAITHNESS, E); *m* 3rd Archibald Douglas, Rector of Douglas, and *d* by 27 July 1599

2b Adam (Sir), of Craigs; *m* and had issue:

1c Helen; *m* her cousin Sir Patrick Hepburn of Waughton (*see* below)

1b Margaret; *m* 3rd Lord Sinclair (*qv*) and had issue (*see* above)

1a Margaret, *m* Andrew Kerr (*see* LOTHIAN, M)

PATRICK HEPBURN, Yr of Ha(i)les, *m* 2nd Christian, heiress possessed of the manor of Waughton (*m* 2nd Sir William Lindsay of the Byres), dau of William de Gourlay, maternal gs of Sir William of Erth, feudal Ld of Waughton, and was *k* 1402 at Nisbet Moor, having by her had issue:

2 Patrick (Sir), *dsp* by 1473

3 Alexander; *d* by 1469, leaving issue:

(1) David of Waughton; *m* Christian, dau of Sir James Sandilands of Calder (*see* TORPHICHEN, L), and *d* by 1513, leaving, with other issue:

1a Kentigern or Mungo, of Waughton and Luffness; *m* Margaret, dau of Robert Lauder of Bass, and *d* 1519, leaving, with other issue:

1b PATRICK (Sir)

2b John of Kirklandhill, ancestor of the HEPBURNs of Humble (*see* POLWARTH, L)

The er son,

Sir PATRICK HEPBURN of Waughton and Luffness; *m* his cousin Helen, dau of Sir Adam Hepburn of Craigs, yr brother of 1st Earl of Bothwell (*see* above), and *d* by 10 April 1549, leaving:

1 Patrick of Waughton and Luffness; had issue

2 George, Rector of Haugh or Prestonkirk, ancestor of the HEPBURNs of Monkrig

3 ADAM, of whom presently

4 William of Gilmerton, to whom, as 'my chosen cousin William', the 4th Earl of Bothwell (*see* above) in 1558 entailed his heritable honours (reserving only his own life rent of the same), passing over all closer relatives

5 John

1 Margaret

The 3rd son,

ADAM HEPBURN of Smeaton Hepburn; granted by his f in 1538 the lands of Smeaton and other lands; supported MARY QUEEN OF SCOTS, whom he joined after her escape from Loch Leven; present Battle of Langside 1568 and with other of his relatives was indicted for treason; *m* Isabella, dau of John Preston of Craigmillar, and had with other issue:

1 PATRICK, of whom presently

1 Helen; *m* her cousin George Hepburn of Athelstaneford and was mother of Sir John Hepburn, Marshal of France and fndr and 1st Col Roy Scots Regt

His est son,

PATRICK HEPBURN of Smeaton Hepburn; *m* Marion, dau of James Adamson of Tytwood, Ayrshire, and had, with other issue:

1 JOHN, of whom presently

2 Francis, ancestor of the HEPBURNs of Beanston

His est son,

JOHN HEPBURN of Smeaton Hepburn; *m* 1626 Helen, dau of Robert Swinton of Swinton, and had with other issue:

1 Patrick of Smeaton Hepburn; *m* 1656 Sarah, er dau of Sir Walter Riddell, 2nd Bt, of Riddell (*qv*), and *dsp* 1696

2 Alexander; *m* Janet, dau of William Little of Liberton, and had:

(1) PATRICK HEPBURN of Smeaton Hepburn; *b* 1685; *m* June 1710 Marion, 3rd dau of Sir George Suttie, 1st Bt, of Balgone (*see* GRANT-SUTTIE, Bt), and *d* 1726, leaving issue:

1a Patrick, *dsp*

2a GEORGE HEPBURN of Smeaton Hepburn, *dsp* 1764, when the representation of the family and the estates devolved upon his n George, later **Sir George Buchan-Hepburn, 1st Bt**

3a Alexander, *dsp*

1a Marion, *dsp*

2a Elizabeth; *m* John Buchan of Letham (*see* below) and *d* 14 Oct 1742

Lineage (of Buchan): GEORGE BUCHAN of Kelloe; *b* 1682 (descended from the BUCHANs of Auchmacoy through George, 2nd s of Alexander Buchan of Auchmacoy (*d* 1625) by Agnes, daughter of Thomas Fraser of Durris); Clerk to the Lords of Session; acquired much property in E Lothian and Berwickshire; *m* 1st Ann, dau of Alexander Hay of Balbythan, and had, with other issue:

1 JOHN, of whom presently

GEORGE BUCHAN *m* 2nd 1734 Christian (*d* 1784), dau of Sir Francis Grant, 1st Bt, of Cullen, Lord Cullen (*see* GRANT, Bt, of Cullen), and by her had:

2 George of Kelloe, ancestor of the FORDYCE-BUCHANs of Kelloe

1 Helen; *m* John McDouall of Logan and had issue

GEORGE BUCHAN *d* 5 March 1760; his est son,

JOHN BUCHAN of Letham; *m* 1st Elizabeth (*d* 1742), dau of Patrick Hepburn of Smeaton-Hepburn (*see* above) and had, with other issue:

1 George (Sir), **1st Bt**

JOHN BUCHAN *m* 2nd Anne (*d* 1790), dau of Charles Broun of Cleghornie and sis of George Broun of Colstoun, Lord Coulston, by whom he had numerous children including Francis Buchan-Sydserff of Ruchlaw

JOHN BUCHAN of Letham *d* 21 Nov 1792; his est son,

Sir GEORGE BUCHAN later BUCHAN-HEPBURN (added name and arms of his maternal uncle George Hepburn of Smeaton-Hepburn on latter's death in 1764), **1st Bt** (UK), so *cr* 6 May 1815, of Smeaton-Hepburn; advocate 1763, Slr to the Lords of Session 1767–90, Judge Admlty Court 1790–91, Baron of the Exchequer Scotland 1791–1814; *b* 1738; *m* 1st Jean, est dau of Alexander Leith of Glenkindie and afterwards of Freefield (*see* BURGH, B), and had:

1 JOHN (Sir), **2nd Bt**

Sir GEORGE *m* 2nd 19 April 1781 Margaretta Henrietta, formerly w of (a) Capt Alexander Grant, HEICS, and (b) Brig-Gen Simon Frazer (*ka* Battle of Saratoga 1777), and dau of John Zacharias Beck, of Saxe Gotha, and *d* 26 June 1819

His est son,

Sir John Buchan-Hepburn, 2nd Bt, Advocate 1790; *b* 17 June 1776; *m* 29 Aug 1800 Mary Turner (*d* 20 Feb 1854), only dau of Thomas Hog, of Newliston, Linlithgow, by his 1st wife Lady Mary Julian Maitland, 2nd dau of 7th Earl of Lauderdale (*qv*), and *d* 8 Oct 1833, having had, with other issue:

1 **Sir Thomas Buchan-Hepburn, 3rd Bt**, DL and JP, MP Haddington 1838–47; *b* 30 Sept 1804; *m* 28 July 1835 Helen (*d* 19 Jan 1910), dau of Archibald Little, of Shabden Park, Surrey, and *d* 17 Dec 1893, having had issue:

(1) John George, Lt 9th Lancers; *b* 24 Sept 1841; *k* by a party of miners at Pinos Altos, Mexico, Feb 1883

(2) **Sir Archibald Buchan-Hepburn, 4th Bt**, barrister Inner Temple; *educ* Trin Coll Glenalmond and Trin Coll Cambridge (BA 1875), DL and JP Co Haddington and Chm of CC; *b* 12 March 1852; *m* 7 Oct 1890 Edith Agnes (*d* 4 March 1923), only child of Edward Kent Karslake, QC, and *d* 17 May 1929, having had issue:

1a Thomas Edward Archibald, Capt Royal Scots; *b* 20 July 1892; *m* 27 Sept 1921 Janet, dau of E Steer, of Orpington, Kent, and *d* 12 April 1923

2a **Sir John Karslake Thomas Buchan-Hepburn, 5th Bt**; *b* 20 March 1894; *educ* Dulwich; *m* 24 June 1916 Jessie Lawrence (*d* 8 March 1961), yr dau of Francis William Smith, MD, and *d* 8 Feb 1961, leaving issue:

1b **Sir Ninian Buchan Archibald John Buchan-Hepburn, 6th Bt**; *educ* Canford; served WW II in QO Cameron Highrs in India and Burma; *b* 8 Oct 1922; *m* 1st 7 Oct 1958 Bridget, er dau of G/Capt Sir Louis Greig, KBE, CVO, of Binsness, Forres, Morayshire; *m* 2nd 1991 *(Mary) Angela [Mary Dowager Lady Buchan-Hepburn, Kailzie, by Peebles, Tweeddale EH45 9HT], dau of Thomas Ian Scott, of Balfunning, Balfron, Stirlingshire, formerly w of John Miller Richard, and widow of Jack Walch Lyne, and *d* 1992

1b *Primrose Eda [Mrs Ulick Roche, Ynysfor, Penrhyndeudraeth, Gwynedd LI48 6BJ], served WW II in VAD and FANY; *b* 3 April 1917; *m* 27 Oct 1949 Maj Ulick Edmund Burke Roche (*d* 1990), S Wales Borderers, only s of Col Hon Ulick Burke Roche, and has issue (*see* FERMOY, B)

2b Francesca Helen Claire; *b* 4 July 1919; *d* 29 April 1922

3a PATRICK GEORGE THOMAS BUCHAN-HEPBURN, 1st and last BARON HAILES, of Prestonkirk, East Lothian (UK), so *cr* 15 Feb 1957, GBE (1957), CH (1962), PC (1951); *b* 2 April 1901; *educ* Harrow and Trin Coll Cambridge; Hon Attaché Constantinople 1925–27, memb LCC N Kensington 1930–31, MP (C) E Toxteth 1931–50 and Beckenham 1950–57, PPS to Rt Hon Oliver Stanley 1931, Jr Ld Treasury 1939, Dep C Ch Whip 1945, C Ch Whip 1948, Parly Sec Treasury and Govt Ch Whip 1955–57, Govr Gen WI 1957–62, KstJ; *m* 7 June 1945 Diana *d* 7 June 1980), widow of William Hedworth Williamson (*see* WILLIAMSON, Bt) and only dau of Brig-Gen Hon Charles Lambton (*see* DURHAM, E), and *dsp* 1974 when the barony expired

1a Loelia Helen; *b* 1 July 1897; *m* 29 July 1933 Baron Somervell of Harrow, PC, OBE, QC, Lord of Appeal in Ordinary, and *d* 18 July 1945. He *d* 18 Nov 1960

(1) Agnes; *m* 16 Sept 1869 James M'Douall, of Logan, Stranraer, and *d* 15 March 1926, leaving issue. He *d* 1896

(2) Mary Turner, *d* unm 2 April 1937

(3) Jane; *m* 13 Aug 1867 Lt-Col David Milne Holme, RHG, of Paxton, Berwickshire, and *d* 26 Dec 1881, leaving issue. He *d* 19 Nov 1901

(4) Emily; *d* 8 July 1935

2 John Buchan, of Clune, Fife; *b* 29 May 1806; *m* 31 May 1837 Margaret Sophia (*d* 13 Feb 1873), dau of Archibald Henry Swinton, of Warsash, Hants, and *d* 12 Dec 1874, having had, with other issue:

(1) John, Capt 6th Dragoon Gds; *b* 30 April 1840; *m* 1888 Mary Caroline Margaret (*d* 6 Nov 1940), est dau of Gen John Fischer, RE, and *d* 18 July 1898, leaving issue:

1a John Trant, rubber planter, served WW I with Ceylon Planters' Rifle Corps and Australian Artillery; *b* 1890; *m* 7 Sept 1927 Edith Margaret Mitchell (*d* 1980), dau of William Robb, and *d* 20 April 1953, leaving issue:

1b Sir (JOHN) ALASTAIR TRANT KIDD BUCHAN-HEPBURN, **7th and present Bt**

1b *Elizabeth Joyce Agnes [Mrs James Scott, 38 Queen's Crescent, Edinburgh EH9 2BA]; *b* 22 Feb 1933; *educ* St Leonard's Sch St Andrews and St Andrews U (MB, ChB 1956); *m* 26 Aug 1957 *James Archibald Scott, CB, LVO, FRSE, and has issue:

1c *Thomas James Buchan; *b* 11 May 1962

2c *Robert Alastair Howie; *b* 24 July 1964

3c *Hector Michael Hepburn; *b* 21 May 1969

1c *Rachel Elizabeth Frances; *b* 17 Aug 1960

2a Thomas Swinton, Lt RFA WW I; *b* 1894; *d* 1919

1a Mary Margaret Lydia; *b* 1888; *m* 4 Sept 1915 Capt Nelson Guy O'Meara Deane, of the Abkarrie and Salt Dept, Madras, and had issue. He *d* 30 Oct 1936

2a Cecilia Mary Louisa Clare; *m* 29 Oct 1917 George Edwin Lloyd, of Bangalore, and *d* 28 Aug 1928, leaving issue

2 Archibald, Lt-Col Bengal SC; *b* 7 Aug 1841; *m* 31 July 1874 Janet Linning (*d* 12 Nov 1920), dau of Randal Callander, and *dsp* 1885

3 Thomas; *b* 24 May 1846; left issue

4 Roger; *b* 18 May 1852; *m* 1893 Lilian Gray, dau of Christopher T Winter, of Winterton, Birtle, Manitoba, Canada, and *d* 26 Jan 1907

5 Walter Scott; *b* 10 Sept 1856

1 Louisa; *m* 7 Nov 1866 Maj-Gen Thomas Ignatius M Hog, RA (*dsp* 19 Feb 1899)

2 Mary Turner; *m* 13 Dec 1866 William Waller Hooper

3 Harriet; *m* 26 Oct 1881 Edward A Ranken

BUCHANAN

Arms: Or, a lion rampant sa. between two otter's heads erased in chief ppr. and a cinquefoil in base of the second, all within the royal tressure of the last. **Crest:** An armed dexter hand holding a cap of dignity purpure, facing erm. **Supporters:** Dexter, a falcon, wings elevated and addorsed ppr., belled, beaked and charged on the breast with two branches of laurel conjoined or; sinister, a gryphon sa., charged in like manner with two branches of laurel. **Motto:** *Nunquam victus* ('Never conquered'). **Creation:** Bt. (UK) 14 Dec 1878.

SIR ANDREW GEORGE BUCHANAN, 5TH BT, of Dunburgh, Co [Sir Andrew Buchanan Bt, Hodsock Priory, Blyth, Worksop, Notts S81 0TY]; *b* 21 July 1937; *s f* 1984; *educ* Eton, Trin Coll Cambridge and Wye Coll London (Dip Farm Business Admin); late 2nd Lt Coldstream Gds; farmer, Notts: High Sheriff 1976, Ld Lt 1991– (DL 1985–91), KStJ 1991; *m* 26 April 1966 *Belinda Jane Virginia, JP (Notts), DL (Notts 1998), er dau of Donald Colquhoun Maclean and widow of Gresham Neilus Vaughan, and has issue:

1 +GEORGE CHARLES MELLISH; *b* 27 Jan 1975

1 *Laura Evelyn; *b* 13 Jan 1967; *m* 1992 *A James Mayes, yr s of Brig Andrew Mayes, of Kensington

Lineage: GEORGE BUCHANAN, of Buchanan House, Glasgow; had:

ARCHIBALD BUCHANAN, of Auchintorlie, Dunbartonshire (bought from one bro Andrew), and Hillington, Renfrewshire (inherited from another bro Neil); *m* Martha, dau of Peter Murdoch, of Rosehill, Renfrew, Provost Glasgow, and had, with a dau (Mary, *m* Alexander Speirs, of Elderslie, Renfrewshire):

1 Peter, of Auchintorlie; *m* Catherine Maxwell (*m* 2nd Sir Ewen Cameron, Bt, of Fassifern, Inverness-shire) and *dsp*

2 George, of Auchintorlie; *dsp*

3 Andrew, of Ardinconnal, Dunbartonshire, and Auchingray, Lanarkshire, DL, JP; *b* 12 July 1745; *m* 3 July 1769 Jane (*d* 15 Sept 1832), est dau of James Dennistoun, of Colgrain and Dennistoun, and *d* 14 July 1833, having had, with other issue:

(1) Archibald, of Auchintorlie and Hillington, DL, JP; *b* 13 April 1773; *m* 3 June 1816 Mary (*d* 30 June 1868), 2nd dau of Richard Dennistoun, of Kelvin Grove, Lanarks, and *dvp* 16 Dec 1832, having had, with other issue:

1a Andrew, of Auchintorlie, DL, JP; *b* 14 March 1817; *m* 20 Nov 1845 Mary Jemima Dundas Adamina, yr dau of Sir James Fergusson, of Kilkerran, 4th Bt (*qv*), and *dsp* 1886

1a Georgina Grace; *m* 28 July 1857 George Hermand Fergusson (*d* 27 April 1870), 3rd s of Sir James Fergusson, 4th Bt (*qv*), and *d* 4 May 1862 leaving issue

(2) James, of Blairvadock, Ardinconnal, DL, JP Caithness-shire; *b* 26 Jan 1776; *m* 10 May 1805 Lady Janet Sinclair (*d* 24 Feb 1867), dau of 12th Earl of Caithness (*qv*), and *d* 21 Dec 1860, having had, with other issue:

1a ANDREW (Sir), **1st Bt**

1a Camilla; *m* 2 Oct 1829 Richard Fox, of Awbawn, Co Cavan (*d* 12 July 1864), and had issue

2a Mathilda Frances Harriet; *m* 23 Oct 1844 Patrick Maitland, of Freugh (*d* 8 April 1859), and *d* 27 March 1894, leaving issue (*see* LAUDERDALE, E)

The only son,

Sir Andrew Buchanan, 1st Bt (UK), so *cr* 14 Dec 1878, GCB (1866, KCB 1860), PC (1863), DL Stirlingshire; *b* 7 May 1807; Min Switzerland 1852, Amb: Prussia 1862, Russia 1864 and Austria 1871 (ret 1877); *m* 1st 4 April 1839 Frances Katharine (*d* 1 Dec 1854), dau of Very Rev Edward Mellish, Dean Hereford, and had, with other issue:

1 **Sir James Buchanan, 2nd Bt**, DL and JP; *b* 7 Aug 1840; Cdr RN; *m* 19 Feb 1873 Arabella Catherine (*d* 25 Oct 1935), yst dau of Goodwin Charles Colquitt-Craven, of Brockhampton Park, Glos, and *dsp* 16 Oct 1901

2 ERIC ALEXANDER (Sir), **3rd Bt**

3 Andrew Archibald; *b* 16 Jan 1850; *m* 10 Jan 1882 Ellen Maria (*d* 6 May 1919), dau of Philip Edward Blakeway, and *d* 5 Oct 1932 leaving issue:

(1) Andrew Sinclair, MVO 5th Cl (1933), WW I; *b* 1882; *m* 24 June 1915 Violet Nita, dau of Sir Anderson Critchett, 1st Bt (*qv*), and *dsp* 10 April 1957

4 George William (Sir), PC (1910), GCB (1915), GCMG (1913), GCVO (1909), Dip Serv 1876, Envoy Extrdy and Min Plen The Hague 1908–10, Amb Petrograd 1910–18 and Rome 1919–21; *b* 25 Nov 1854; *m* 25 Feb 1885 Lady Georgina Meriel Bathurst (*d* 25 April 1922), dau of 6th Earl Bathurst (*qv*), and *d* 20 Dec 1924, leaving issue:

(1) Meriel, authoress; *b* 5 Sept 1886; *m* 30 May 1925 Maj Harold Wilfred Knowling, Welsh Gds (*d* 15 Sept 1954), s of Arthur Knowling, of Hereford, and *d* 6 Feb 1959, leaving issue

1 Frances Matilda; *m* 9 Dec 1873 John Willis Clark, MA Camb, Hon LittD Oxon, Registrar Cambridge U (*d* 10 Oct 1910), and *d* 13 Dec 1908, leaving issue

2 Louisa; *m* 23 Aug 1871 Sir George Francis Bonham, 2nd Bt (*qv*), and *d* 19 Jan 1923, leaving issue

Sir Andrew *m* 2nd 27 May 1857 Hon Georgina Elizabeth Stuart (*d* 21 March 1904), dau of 11th Lord Blantyre (*see* 1900 edn), and *d* 13 Nov 1882

The 2nd Bt's bro,

Sir Eric Alexander Buchanan, 3rd Bt; *b* 19 Aug 1848; *educ* Wellington; *m* 27 June 1898 Constance Augusta (*d* 26 Dec 1914), dau of Capt Charles Edmund Tennant, RN, of Needwood Ho, Burton-on-Trent, and *d* 29 July 1928, leaving:

1 **Sir Charles James Buchanan, 4th Bt**, DL (Notts 1954), JP (Notts 1952); *b* 16 April 1899; *educ* Harrow and RMC Sandhurst; Maj HLI N Russian Relief Force 1919 and WW II, ADC to Govr Madras 1928–32, memb Roy Co Archers 1930–84, High Sheriff Notts 1962; *m* 23 Feb 1932 Barbara Helen (*d* 1986), only child of Lt-Col Sir George Stanley, PC, GCSI, GCIE, CMG (*see* DERBY, E), and *d* 1984, having had:

(1) Sir ANDREW GEORGE BUCHANAN, **5th and present Bt**

(2) +Hugh Charles Stanley [Hugh Buchanan Esq, The Manor House, Little Milton, Oxon]; *b* 26 Aug 1942; *educ* Eton and McGill U Canada; slr, memb Oxon CC 1985–89; *m* 10 Dec 1969 *Nony Caroline Vatcher, dau of Lt-Col John Johnston Dingwall, DSO, of Lyford Grange, Lyford, Oxon (*see* GALWAY, V), and has issue:

1a +James Iain Stanley; *b* 6 March 1974

1a *Clarissa Victoria Rosamund; *b* 9 Oct 1972

2a *Arabella Patricia Dingwall; *b* 1981

(1) *Georgina Mary Gabrielle [Mrs Michael Clayton, 6 Cobden Cres, Edinburgh]; *b* 15 Dec 1932; *m* 16 April 1966 Michael Denzil Grierson Clayton (*d* 1991), s of D G Clayton, of Hampstead, and has issue:

1a *Roger Lancelot; *b* 25 Feb 1969; Capt Roy Scots Dragoon Gds

1a *Harriet Beatrix Evelyn; *b* 31 March 1971

(2) *Constance Carolyn [Mrs Hugh Lindsay, The Old Rectory, Litton Cheney, nr Dorchester, Dorset DT2 9AH]; *b* 31 Dec 1934; *m* 7 Oct 1961 *Hugh John Alexander Lindsay, est s of Hon James Louis Lindsay, and has issue (*see* CRAWFORD and BALCARRES, E)

1 Mary Constance Victoria; *b* 22 Jan 1901; *m* 27 April 1921 Maj Thomas Garrett Mayhew, DL, JP, E Yorks Regt (*d* 12 Dec 1965), s of Thomas Mayhew, of The Lodge, Hythe, Kent, and *d* 26 Oct 1982, leaving issue

BUCHANAN-JARDINE

Arms: Quarterly, 1st and 4th, per pale argent and or a saltire gules, on a chief engrailed of the third three mullets of the first (for JARDINE); 2nd, or a lion rampant gules within a double tressure flory counterflory sable (for BUCHANAN); 3rd, sable a chevron between three bear's heads argent muzzled gules (for LENY). **Crests:** 1 A spur rowel of six points gules (for JARDINE), 2 A sword erect in pale proper, hilted and pommelled or (for BUCHANAN). **Mottoes:** *Nobilis est ira leonis* ('Noble is the wrath of the lion'), (over the crest) *Cave adsum* ('Beware; I am present') and *Virtute gladii pari* ('With equal strength of sword'). **Creation:** Bt. (UK) 20 July 1885.

SIR (ANDREW) RUPERT JOHN BUCHANAN-JARDINE, 4TH BT, of Castle Milk, Co Dumfries, MC (1944), JP (Dumfriesshire 1957), DL (Dumfriesshire 1978) [Sir Rupert Buchanan-Jardine Bt MC JP DL, Dixons, Lockerbie, Dumfriesshire DG11 2PR]; *b* 2 Feb 1923; *s f* 1969; *educ* Harrow and RAC Cirencester; served RHG WW

II (Maj 1948), Jt MFH Dumfriesshire 1950–, Bronze Lion of Netherlands 1944; *m* 4 Oct 1950 (*divorce* 1975) (Jane) Fiona (*m* 2nd 5 Jan 1976 Hugh Alastair Cameron-Rose), 2nd dau of Sir Archibald Charles Edmonstone, 6th Bt (*qv*), and has:

1 +JOHN CHRISTOPHER RUPERT [John Buchanan-Jardine Esq, Castle Milk, Lockerbie, Dumfriesshire]; *b* 20 March 1952; *educ* Harrow and RAC Cirencester; *m* 29 May 1975 *Pandora Lavinia, yr dau of Peter Murray Lee, of 69 Eaton Terrace Mews, London SW1, and Eastleigh, Devon, and has issue:

(1) +Jamie Rupert; *b* 28 July 1994

(1) *Tessa Mary; *b* 24 June 1979

(2) *Katie Luella; *b* 1980

(3) *Lorna Jane; *b* 1984

(4) *Juliet Marina; *b* 1986

(5) *Alice Fiona; *b* 1988

1 *Diana Gwendolyn Jean [Miss Diana Buchanan-Jardine, 27 Pier House, Cheyne Walk, London SW3]; *b* 21 Dec 1955

Lineage: DAVID JARDINE, of Muirhousehead, in the parish of Applegarth, Dumfriesshire; *b* 1780; *m* 8 Feb 1806 Rachel (*d* 10 Sept 1860), dau of William Johnstone, of Linns, Dumfriesshire, and *d* 22 Oct 1827, having had, with other issue:

1 JAMES JARDINE, of Dryfeholm, Dumfriesshire, and Larriston, Roxburghshire; *b* 17 March 1816; *m* 27 April 1846 Jessie, dau of William Johnstone, and *d* 14 July 1893, having had, with other issue (*d* young or unm):

(1) DAVID JARDINE, of Jardine Hall, Lockerbie, Dumfriesshire; *b* 4 Aug 1847; *educ* Trin Coll Cambridge (MA); barrister; *m* 14 Jan 1886 Mary Angela (*d* 1 April 1924), 2nd dau of Sir Charles Tilston Bright, and *d* 23 Aug 1922, leaving issue

2 **Sir Robert Jardine, 1st Bt** (UK), so *cr* 20 July 1885, JP, DL (Perthshire); *b* 24 May 1825; head firm of Jardine, Matheson, China merchants, as were his two next successors in the btcy, MP (Lib) Ashburton 1865–68, Dumfries Burghs 1868–74 and Dumfriesshire 1880–92; *m* April 1867 Margaret Seton (*d* 7 March 1868), dau of John Buchanan Hamilton, of Leny, Perthshire, and sis of John Hamilton-Buchanan, Chief of Clan Buchanan, and *d* 17 Feb 1905, leaving issue:

(1) **Sir Robert William Buchanan Jardine, 2nd Bt**; *b* 21 Jan 1868; *educ* Eton and Magdalene Coll Cambridge; Maj 1st Bn Dumfriesshire Vol Regt, Lt-Col 3rd Vol Bn KOSB; *m* 4 July 1894 Ethel Mary, OBE (1920), JP (*d* 13 Sept 1952), 5th dau of Benjamin Piercy, of Marchwiel Hall, Denbighshire, and Macomer, Sardinia, and *d* 30 Jan 1927, having had issue:

1a Robert Buchanan; *b* 9 April 1895; *d* 14 Sept 1895

2a Sir JOHN WILLIAM, **3rd Bt**

1a Violet Margaret Florence; *m* 1st 18 Nov 1919 (*divorce* 1927) Capt Edmund Owen Ethelston Peel, MC (*d* 21 March 1935), 5th Dragoon Gds, only s of Maj Hugh Edmund Ethelston Peel, of Bryn-y-Pys, Ellesmere, Salop, and had issue; *m* 2nd 8 Feb 1928 15th Baron Strange (of Knokyn) (*qv*) and *d* Oct 1975, leaving further issue

Sir ROBERT's only surv s,

Sir JOHN WILLIAM JARDINE later BUCHANAN-JARDINE, **3rd Bt**, JP (1934); *b* 7 March 1900; *educ* Eton, RMC Sandhurst and Trin Coll Cambridge; Capt late RHG (2nd Lt 1940), memb Roy Co of Archers, MFH Dumfriesshire 1921, Jt Master New Forest Buckhounds 1936–38, author: *Hounds of the World* (1937); *m* 1st 8 June 1921 (*divorce* 1944) Jean Barbara, yr dau of Lord Ernest William Hamilton (*see* ABERCORN, D), and had issue:

1 Sir (ANDREW) RUPERT JOHN BUCHANAN-JARDINE, **4th and present Bt**

Sir JOHN *m* 2nd 12 Dec 1944 *Prudence Audrey [Lady Buchanan-Jardine, Moulin de la Mourachonne, 06370 Mouans Sartoux, France AM], dau of William Haggie, of Knayton, Thirsk, Yorks, and *d* 5 Nov 1969, having by her had issue:

2 +(Charles) James [James Buchanan-Jardine Esq, 27 Queen's Gate Place Mews, London SW7]; *b* 30 April 1946; *educ* Stowe and Trin Coll Cambridge; ARIBA; *m* 1st 9 Sept 1967 (*divorce* 1978) Lady Susan Ankaret Howard, yr dau of 11th Earl of Carlisle (*qv*), and has issue:

(1) *Flora Jane; *b* 15 July 1971

2 (cont.) James Buchanan-Jardine *m* 2nd 1978 *Irmgard Margarethe, dau of Maj Rudolf Bormann, and has further issue:

(2) *Claire Isabel; *b* 1980

(3) *Olivia Rose; *b* Hong Kong 6 Sept 1982

1 *Caroline Anne; *b* 8 Sept 1952

BUCKINGHAMSHIRE

Arms: Quarterly, 1st and 4th, arg. a saltire gu. between four eagles displayed az. (for HAMPDEN); 2nd and 3rd, sa., an estoile of six rays or between two flaunches erm. (for HOBART). **Crests:** 1 A talbot statant erm., collared, ringed and lined gu., the end of the line tied in a knot over his back (for HAMPDEN), 2 A bull passant per pale sa. and gu. bezantée, in the nose a ring or (for HOBART). **Supporters:** Dexter, a stag; sinister, a talbot, both ppr. and regardant, each gorged with a radiant collar and lined or. **Mottoes:** *Auctor preciosa facit* ('It is the giver who makes things valuable'), and *Vestigia nulla retrorsum* ('No steps backwards'). **Creations:** Bt. (E) 22 May 1611, B. (GB) 28 May 1728, E. (GB) 5 Sept 1746.

THE 10TH EARL OF BUCKINGHAMSHIRE, Baron Hobart of Blicking, Norfolk, and a **Baronet** (Sir George Miles Hobart-Hampden, Bt,) [The Rt Hon The Earl of Buckinghamshire, House of Lords, London SW1A 0PW]; *b* 15 Dec 1944; *s* cousin 1983; *educ* Clifton, Exeter U (BA 1967), Birkbeck Coll London and Inst of Cwlth Studies London (MA 1968); with Noble Lowndes and ptnrs 1970–81, dir: Scottish Pension Tstees 1979–81, various cos of Hong Kong Bank Gp 1981–91, The Wyatt Co (UK) Ltd 1991–95, ptnr Watson Wyatt Worldwide 1995–, memb Ho Lds Select Ctees 1985–93, pres John Hampden Soc 1993–, Patron Hobart Town (1804) First Settlers Assoc, FInstD 1983; *m* 1st 27 July 1968 (*divorce* 1975) Susan Jennifer, dau of R W Adams of Halesowen, Birmingham; *m* 2nd 5 July 1975 *Alison Wightman JP (Bucks 1990), DL (Bucks 1995), dau of William Forrest, of Edinburgh, and previously w of D A (Tim) Wishart, of Edinburgh

Lineage: THOMAS HOBART, of Layham, Suffolk, *d* by 8 April 1517, leaving descendants in Suffolk who died out in 1676, a descendant by a s other than Sir JAMES (*see* below) called Sir Miles Hobart, of Halford, Bucks (MP Gt Marlow, ktd 1623; opponent of CHARLES I 1628; *dsp* 29 June 1632) and yet other descendants who emigrated to Massachusetts 1633 (and who provided a V-Pres of the USA); his 2nd s:

Sir JAMES HOBART, of Hales Hall, Norfolk, PC; Attorney-Gen *temp* HENRY VII; *d* Feb 1517; gf of:

THOMAS HOBART, of Plumstead, Norfolk; *m* Audrey, dau of William Hare, of Beeston, Norfolk, and *d* 28 March 1560, leaving:

Sir Henry Hobart, 1st Bt (E), so *cr* 22 May 1611, of Blickling Hall, Norfolk; Ch Justice Common Pleas, ktd; *m* 21 April 1590 Dorothy (*d* April 1641), dau of Sir Robert Bell, of Beaupré Hall, Ch Baron Exchequer, and *d* 26 Dec 1625, having had, with other issue:

1 **Sir John Hobart, 2nd Bt**, MP, ktd 1611; *b* 19 April 1593; *m* 1st Philippa (*d* 24 Sept 1620), dau of Robert Sidney, Earl of Leicester (*see* DE L'ISLE, V), and had an only dau Dorothy; *m* 2nd Feb 1621 Lady Frances Egerton (*d* 27 Nov 1664), est dau of 1st Earl of Bridgwater, and by her had a surv child Philippa (*see* below); *dspm* 20 April 1647

2 Miles (Sir), of Plumstead, Norfolk, ktd 1 Feb 1625/6; *b* 12 April 1595; *m* Frances, dau of Sir John Peyton, 1st Bt, of Isleham, Cambs, and was *bur* 6 Dec 1639, leaving, with other issue:

(1) **Sir John Hobart, 3rd Bt**, MP; *bapt* 20 March 1627/8; *m* 1st his cousin Philippa (*dsp*, *bur* 19 Jan 1654/5), dau of **Sir John Hobart, 2nd Bt**; *m* 2nd June 1656 Mary (*d* by 2 May 1689), widow of Col Robert Hammond and dau and in her issue coheir of John Hampden, the leading opponent of CHARLES I's tax for national defence called 'Ship Money', nevertheless by some accounted 'the Patriot', of Hampden, Bucks, and had, with other issue:

1a HENRY (Sir), **4th Bt**

2a John, Brig-Gen, Govr Pendennis Castle, Cornwall; *d* 7 Nov 1734

1a Philippa; *m* *c* 28 April 1680 Sir Charles Pye, 2nd Bt, of Howe, Derbys, and *dsp*

Sir JOHN *d* 22 Aug 1683; his est son,

Sir Henry Hobart, 4th Bt, ktd 29 Sept 1671; Equerry to WILLIAM III Battle of the Boyne 1690; *m* 9 July 1684 Elizabeth (*d* 22 Aug 1701), er dau and coheir of Joseph Maynard (*see* RAVENSDALE, B), and had, with other issue:

1 JOHN, **1st Earl**

1 Henrietta, Lady Bedchamber to the consort of GEORGE II and the latter's mistress, she being allegedly instrumental in procuring an earldom for her bro; *m* 1st 2 March 1705/6 9th Earl of Suffolk (*d* 28 Sept 1733; *see* SUFFOLK and BERKSHIRE, E); *m* 2nd 26 June 1735 Hon George Berkeley, MP (*dsps* 29 Oct 1746; *see* BERKELEY, B), and *d* 26 July 1767

2 Catherine; *m* George Churchill, illegitimate s of Adml George Churchill, MP (*see* MARLBOROUGH, D), and *d* 2 June 1725. He *d* 1745

Sir HENRY was *k* in a duel with Oliver Le Neve 21 Aug 1698; his son,

Sir John Hobart, 5th Bt, and **1st Earl of Buckinghamshire** (GB), so *cr* 5 Sept 1746, as also earlier 28 May 1728 BARON HOBART OF BLICKLING, KB (1725), PC (Jan 1744/5); V-Adml and Ld Lt Norfolk; *b* 11 Oct 1693; *m* 1st 8 Nov 1717 Judith (*d* 7 Feb 1727), dau and coheir of Robert Britiffe, of Baconsthorpe, Norfolk, and *d* 22 Sept 1756, having had, with other issue:

1 JOHN HOBART, **2nd Earl of Buckinghamshire**, Amb Russia 1762, Ld Lt Ireland 1777; *b* Aug 1723; *m* 1st 14 July 1761 Mary Anne (*d* 30 Dec 1769), dau and coheir of Sir Thomas Drury, Bt, and had issue:

(1) Harriet; *m* 1st (*divorce*) 1st Earl Belmore (*qv*); *m* 2nd 6th Marquess of Lothian (*qv*) and *d* 14 July 1805, leaving issue

(2) Caroline; *m* 4 June 1792 2nd Baron Suffield (*qv*) and *dsp* 27 Oct 1850

(3) Sophia; *m* 21 Feb 1789 2nd Earl of Mount Edgcumbe (*qv*) and *d* 17 Aug 1806, leaving issue

1 (cont.) The **2nd Earl** *m* 2nd 24 Sept 1770 Caroline (*d* 26 Jan 1817), dau of William Conolly, of Stratton Hall, Staffs, by Lady Anne Wentworth, dau of 2nd Earl of Strafford of the 1711 *cr* (*see* STRAFFORD, E, preliminary remarks), and *d* 3 Aug 1793, having by her had an only surv child:

(4) Amelia Anne; *b* 20 Feb 1772; *m* 9 June 1794 2nd Marquess of Londonderry (*qv*), better known as the statesman Lord Castlereagh, and *dsp* 12 Feb 1829

1 Dorothy; *m* 21 Oct 1752 Sir Charles Hotham-Thompson, Bt, and *dspm* 1 June 1798

The **1st Earl** *m* 2nd 10 Feb 1728 Elizabeth (*d* 12 Sept 1762), dau of Robert Bristow, MP, and by her had issue:

2 GEORGE, **3rd Earl**

3 Henry, MP Norwich, Chm H of C Ctee Ways and Means; *b* 1738; *m* 22 July 1761 Anne Margaret (*d* 12 July 1788), dau of John Bristow, of Quiddenham Hall, Norfolk and *d* 10 May 1799, leaving, with other issue:

(1) Henry Charles (Rev), Canon of Hereford; *b* 30 Nov 1773; *m* 5 May 1800 Mary (*d* 5 May 1854), dau of Sir Thomas Beauchamp-Proctor, 2nd Bt (*see* PROCTOR-BEAUCHAMP, Bt), and *d* 17 Jan 1844, having had, with another s:

1a Charles Robert, Lt-Col 16th Regt Madras Army; *b* 4 March 1808; *m* 11 Feb 1840 Maria (*d* 14 Oct 1895), dau of Lt-Col Hodson, and *d* 28 Jan 1886, leaving issue:

1b Charles Beauchamp; *b* 18 Oct 1842; *m* 20 Jan 1864 Rhoda (*d* 18 April 1932), 5th dau of Rev Harry Jervoise Bigg Wither, Rector of Worthing, Hants, and *d* 16 Sept 1893, leaving with other issue:

1c Charles Guy Reginald Beauchamp; *b* 24 May 1881; *m* 21 April 1905 Maria Anna, dau of Thomas Frederick Hammond, of NSW, and *d* 9 April 1944, leaving issue:

1d Guy Verna; *b* 31 Jan 1906; *m* 24 March 1934 *Louise Gertrude Menzies

2d John Bertram; *b* 21 Jan 1911; *m* 26 Feb 1944 (*divorce* 1971) June Mary Barnes; *m* 2nd 1972 *Leone, dau of —, and *d* 1982, having had issue by his 1st w:

1e Roger John; *b* 25 Sept 1956; *d* as result of a motor accident 1978

1e *Hilary Rosamond; *b* 15 Feb 1958; *m* 1988 *Carl Bethridge Topp, and has issue:

1f *Matthew HOBART-TOPP; *b* 1987

1f *Annika Alexandra HOBART-TOPP; *b* 1990

3d Wallace Elliot; *b* 28 March 1922; *educ* Melbourne U (MB, BS); *m* 1st 18 April 1946 (*divorce* 1956) Joyce Stella Hussey; *m* 2nd 31 Jan 1957 *Halina Zofia, MB, ChB Edin, dau of W/Cdr Ferdinand Leliwa Bobinski, and *d* 1972, having had issue:

1e +Mark Michael [Dr Mark Hobart, 3 Derry St, Essendon, Vict 3040, Australia]; *b* 12 June 1958; *educ* Melbourne U (MB, BS); *m* 19– *Patricia Mildred Blair, and has issue:

1f +Michael Wallace; *b* 1991

2f +Benedict Conrad William; *b* 1993

1e *Pauline Ann; *b* 3 May 1960; *m* 1982 *Bruce Twite, and has issue

1d *Phyllis Marion Rhoda; *b* 14 March 1920

1c Mary Florence Leonora Aileen; *b* 17 Nov 1864; *d* unm 28 Oct 1944

2c Mabel Beatrice; *b* 6 Aug 1872; *d* unm 1926

3c Ethel Beatrice; *b* 9 Sept 1874

4c Mary Gladys; *b* 27 Aug 1884

2b George, Lt-Col RM; *b* 10 July 1847; *m* 12 Sept 1876 Louisa (*d* 19 May 1934), yst dau of William Douglas, ICS, of Landsdown Ho, Bath, and *d* 29 Dec 1920, having had, with other issue:

1c Noel, T/Lt Army Ord Dept; *b* 25 Dec 1885; *m* Iris Florence Daniel, and *d* 17 April 1968, leaving issue:

1d *Heather Iris; *b* 19 July 1923; *m* 22 Sept 1950 *Edgar William Boyles, Under-Sec Inland Revenue, and has issue:

1e *John Christopher; *b* 1 Sept 1951

2e *Peter James; *b* 4 July 1957

3e *Stephen Robert; *b* 29 Aug 1961

1e *Janet Elizabeth; *b* 1 May 1953

1c May; *b* 3 June 1877; *d* unm 1939

2c Irene; *b* 6 Aug 1878; *m* 17 April 1901 Rev Canon George Henry Round-Turner, JP, Rector of Great Bealings, Suffolk 1936–45, er son of Capt Henry Lewis Round-Turner, JP, RN, of Grundisburgh Ho, Woodbridge, Suffolk, and *d* 18 March 1960, leaving issue. He *d* 10 Jan 1951

3b William Henry (Rev), Vicar of Highbridge Somerset 1895–1918; *b* 17 Dec 1855; *educ* Exeter Coll Oxford (BA); *m* 3 Nov 1881 Margaret Emily (*d* 3 April 1940), only dau of Gen Edward Dayot Watson, Bengal Army, and *d* 23 Sept 1918, leaving, with other issue:

1c Vere Edward, Capt Canadian Expdny Force 1916–19, Lt 4th Bn RWF; *b* 19 Oct 1882; *m* 1903 Katherine Elizabeth (*d* 21 Aug 1964), est dau of Beaumont F Hitchcock, of Elmhurst, Compton, PQ, Canada

2c Charles Hampden (Rev), Chaplain Community of St Katharine, Parmoor, Henley-on-Thames, Vicar of St Matthew's Norwich 1943–56, mission priest Labrador, Canada, 1914–17; *b* 6 July 1886; *m* 29 April 1924 Alice (*d* 15 Jan 1960), est dau of Samuel Plumbly, of Findon Valley, Worthing, and *d* 21 Oct 1961, leaving issue:

1d +John Hampden, late Maj 5th Roy Inniskilling Dragoon Gds [Major John Hobart, Brandon, Buckland, Oxon SN7 8QW]; *b* 20 May 1925; *educ* St John's Leatherhead and RMA Sandhurst; *m* 25 Nov 1961 *Maureen, dau of Alfred Clowes, of 85 Cavour St, Etruria, Stoke-on-Trent, and has issue:

1e +Andrew Hampden; *b* 23 July 1962

2e +Jeremy Charles; *b* 3 July 1963

2d +Christopher Beauchamp, MBE [Christopher Hobart Esq MBE, The Old Stables, The Coppice, Clifton Hampden, Oxon OX14 3DF]; *b* 20 Sept 1927; *educ* St John's Leatherhead and New Coll Oxford (MA); *m* 1st 3 Jan 1953 (*divorce* 1970) Margaret, dau of Gibert Reed, of Lingfield, Surrey, and has issue:

1e +Richard Hampden; *b* 20 April 1960

2e +Simon Vere; *b* 24 Sept 1964

2d (cont.) Christopher Hobart *m* 2nd 21 Nov 1970 *Joanna Margaret, er dau of R-Adml Anthony Davies, CB, CVO, of Aldbourne, Wilts, and by her has:

3e +Edward Andrew Beauchamp; *b* 30 Nov 1971

4e +Robert Anthony; *b* in Holland 15 May 1973

5e +John Henry; *b* 4 April 1976

1c Mary Dorothea; *b* 29 March 1888; *d* unm 16 Nov 1975

2c Margaret Adelaide; *b* 10 Oct 1890; *d* unm 27 July 1983

3c Ruth Awdry; *b* 18 April 1894; *m* 1923 George Edwin Oxenham (*d* 15 March 1963), yr son of Henry Oxenham, of Bampton, Devon, and had issue:

1d *David George Henry; *b* 16 Aug 1925; *m* 14 July 1956 *Sharalee, dau of Frank Chandler, of Battle Creek, Nebraska, and has had issue:

1e Gregory David; *b* 21 March 1958; *d* 22 Oct 1967

1e *Gabrielle Ruth; *b* 17 Nov 1963

2d *Anthony Sydenham Charles; *b* 21 July 1928; *m* 1st 19 Nov 1949 *Diana Margaret, only child of Alfred Willey, of Canterbury, and has issue:

1e *Mar David; *b* 14 Sept 1953

1e *Adèle Margaret; *b* 12 May 1951

2e *Madeleine Ruth; *b* 26 March 1957

2d (cont.) Anthony Oxenham *m* 2nd 6 Nov 1971 *Juliet, dau of Frank Anderson Holme, and by her has:

2e *James; *b* 1 Aug 1973

3e *Anabel; *b* 1 Aug 1973

The 2nd EARL's bro,

GEORGE HOBART, **3rd Earl of Buckinghamshire**; *b* Oct 1731; *m* 16 May 1757 Albinia (*d* 11 March 1816), dau and coheir of Lord Vere Bertie and gdau of 1st Duke of Ancaster (*see* WILLOUGHBY DE ERESBY, B), and *d* 14 Oct 1804, having had, with other issue:

1 ROBERT HOBART, **4th Earl of Buckinghamshire**, PC, served army 1776–84, MP I and GB Parls 1784–96, called up *vp* to Ho Lds in f's barony of Hobart 1798, Ch Sec to Ld Lt Ireland 1789–93, Govr Madras 1793–98, Sec State War and Colonies 1801–04 (the capital of Tasmania is called after him), Chllr Duchy Lancaster 1805 and 1812, PMG 1806–07; *b* May 1760; *m* 1st 4 Jan 1792 Margaretta (*d* 9 Aug 1796), dau and coheir of Edmund Bourke, of Surrey, and widow of Thomas Adderley, of Innishannon, Co Cork, and had, with John (*d* an infant):

(1) Sarah Albinia Louisa; *m* 1 Sept 1814 1st Earl of Ripon (*see* 1923 edn RIPON, M) and *d* 9 April 1867 leaving issue. He *d* 28 Jan 1859

1 (cont.) The **4th Earl** *m* 2nd 1 June 1799 Eleanor Agnes (*dsp* 15 Oct 1851), dau of 1st Baron Auckland (*qv*), and *d* 4 Feb 1816

2 George Vere, Lt-Govr Canada; *b* 1761; *m* 1st Jane, dau of Horace Cataneo, of Leeds, Yorks, and had, with other issue (his daus were granted rank of earl's daus 9 Sept 1832):

(1) GEORGE ROBERT HOBART later HAMPDEN (roy licence 5 Oct 1824), **5th Earl of Buckinghamshire**, MP St Michael's 1812–13; *b* 1 May 1789; *m* 3 May 1819 Anne Glover (*m* 2nd 14 Sept 1854 David Wilson, of Brook St, Mayfair, and *d* 23 May 1878), dau of Sir Arthur Pigot, and *dsp* 1 Feb 1849

(2) AUGUSTUS EDWARD, **6th Earl**

(1) Albinia Jane; *m* 18 March 1815 Sir Augustus John Foster, 1st Bt, and *d* 28 May 1867, leaving issue. He *d* 1 Aug 1848

2 (cont.) The Hon George Hobart *m* 2nd 26 April 1802 Janet, dau of Col Alexander Maclean, of Coll, and *d* 5 Dec 1802, having by her had issue:

(2) Vere Catherine Louisa; *m* 31 July 1832 Donald Cameron of Lochiel, DL, 23rd Chief, and *d* 15 Nov 1888, leaving issue. He *d* 4 Jan 1859

3 Henry Lewis (Very Rev), DD, Dean of Windsor, Registrar Order of the Garter; *b* 1774; *m* 5 Oct 1824 Charlotte Selina (*d* 12 Jan 1867), dau of Richard Moore, ggs of Sir Thomas Moore, of Sayes Court, Surrey (gn of John Milton, the poet), and *d* 8 May 1846, having had, with other issue:

(1) Sir ROBERT HENRY HOBART, Bt, so *cr* 1914 (*see* HOBART, Bt), whose descendant is heir presumptive to the Earldom of Buckinghamshire

(2) George Bertie Benjamin, Col cmdg RA, DL, JP (E R Yorks and London), Mil Sec and Priv Sec to successive Govrs Madras; *b* 3 Feb 1838; *m* 19 June 1889 Rose Armatrude Frances (took 1912 name HOBART-GRIMSTON; *d* 20 Nov 1927), yr dau and coheir of Col Marmaduke Gerard Grimston, of Grimston Garth, Holderness, and Kilnwick Hall, Yorks, and *d* 27 Oct 1907, leaving issue:

1a Armatrude Bertie Sophia Effie, JP; *b* 20 May 1890; *m* 16 Sept 1912 Sir Max Leonard Waechter, DL (*d* 3 Oct 1924); took by deed poll 9 Dec 1927 name WAECHTER DE GRIMSTON

(1) Maria Adelaide; *m* 10 May 1856 Robert Needham Cust, 2nd son of Rev Hon Henry Cust, and *d* 17 Jan 1804, leaving issue (*see* BROWNLOW, B)

(2) Sophia Anne Eleanor; *m* 25 Oct 1864 Maj-Gen Algernon Augustus Stewart, RA, and *d* 20 Oct 1919, leaving issue (*see* GALLOWAY, E)

1 Maria Frances; *m* 30 Sept 1785 3rd Earl of Guilford (*qv*), and *d* 23 April 1794, leaving issue

The 5th EARL's bro,

AUGUSTUS EDWARD HOBART later HOBART-HAMPDEN (added with arms by roy licence 5 Aug 1878), **6th Earl of Buckinghamshire**, MA Oxford, Rector and Preb of Wolverhampton; *b* 1 Nov 1793; *m* 1st 12 Sept 1816 Mary (*d* 25 Jan 1825), est dau of John Williams, King's Serjeant, and had issue:

1 Vere Henry, *Lord Hobart*, Govr Madras 1872–75; *b* 8 Dec 1818; *m* 4 Aug 1853 Mary Catherine, CI (*m* 2nd 2 Sept 1879 Charles Coates, FRCP (*d* 23 March 1909), of 10 Circus, Bath, and *d* 24 Oct 1814), dau of Rt Rev Thomas Carr, Bishop of Bombay, and *dsp* 27 April 1875

2 Frederick John, *Lord Hobart*, Assist Sec in the Indian Dept; *b* 6 March 1821; *m* 27 March 1856 Catherine Annesley (*d* 2 Oct 1886), yst dau of Rt Rev Thomas Carr, Bishop of Bombay, and *dvp* 24 July 1875, having had, with other issue (his daus were granted rank of earl's daus 1886):

(1) SIDNEY CARR HOBART-HAMPDEN later HOBART-HAMPDEN-MERCER-HENDERSON (added by roy licence 12 Jan 1903, his w replacing HOBART-HAMPDEN with MERCER-HENDERSON the same date), **7th Earl of Buckinghamshire**, OBE (1919), DL Bucks, Hon Lt-Col cmdg 4th Vol Bn Oxford and Bucks LI, Ld-in-Waiting 1895; *b* 14 March 1860; *m* 13 June 1888 Georgiana Wilhelmina (*d* 26 March 1937), only child of Hon Hew Adam Dalrymple Hamilton Haldane-Duncan-Mercer-Henderson, DL (*d* 11 June 1900), by Edith Isabella (*d* 24 Feb 1902), yr dau of Lt-Gen Douglas Mercer Henderson, CB, of Fordell (3rd s of Lt-Col George Mercer and Jean, sis of Sir John Henderson, 6th and last Bt of Fordell), and *d* 15 Jan 1930, leaving:

1a JOHN HAMPDEN HOBART-HAMPDEN-MERCER-HENDERSON later MERCER-HENDERSON (roy licence 5 April 1938), **8th Earl of Buckinghamshire**, JP (Bucks 1952); *b* 16 April 1906; *educ* Eton; Dep Chm Ctees Ho Lds 1952–63, Dep Speaker Ho Lds 1954–63, Capt Oxfordshire and Bucks LI WW II; *d* unm 2 Jan 1963

1a Dorothy Edith Isabel; *b* 11 April 1891; *m* 6 July 1911 Hon Claude Hope-Morley, yr s of 1st Baron Hollenden (*qv*), and *d* 15 Dec 1972, leaving issue

2a Sidney Mary Catherine Anne, MBE (1941), Maj Women's Territorial Serv (EA) WW II (despatches), MLC Kenya Colony 1937–42; *b* 17 April 1900; *m* 14 Jan 1924 Capt Thomas Innis Farrar, MC, 5th Bn Devonshire Regt and MGC, s of Rt Rev Walter Farrar, DD, and had issue. He *d* 21 Oct 1934

(1) Catherine Mary Valentia; *m* 10 July 1886 Rev Barton Reginald Vaughan Mills, est son of Arthur Mills, DL, JP, MP, of Budehaven, Cornwall, and *d* 25 Sept 1889, leaving issue. He *d* 21 Jan 1932

(2) Albinia Frederica; *m* 2 Aug 1900 Rev Stuart Alexander Donaldson, DD, Master of Magdalene Coll Cambridge, est son of Sir Stuart Donaldson, and *d* 24 July 1932, leaving issue (*see* 1970 edn DONALDSON OF KINGSBRIDGE, B). He *d* 29 Oct 1915

(3) Isabel Augusta; *m* 10 Nov 1886 Sir Mortimer Reginald Margesson, est son of Rev Reginald Whitehall Margesson, Rector of Blendworth, Southampton, and *d* 1 July 1946, leaving issue (*see* MARGESSON, V)

(4) Henrietta Vere; *m* 1st 17 July 1889 James Ford Hughes; (*d* 9 June 1914); *m* 2nd 27 Aug 1915 Rev Arthur Danvers Melancthon Bidlake, MA, son of Alfred Danvers Bidlake, of Stroud, Glos, and *d* 10 Feb 1957. He *d* 4 July 1956

3 Augustus Charles, V-Adml, Adml Turkish Serv as Hobart Pasha, 2nd Cl Order Osmanieh, 2nd Cl Medjidie, Grand Cross of Franz Josef Austria, Cdr Legn Honour; *b* 1 April 1822; *m* 1st 1848 Mary Anne (*d* 13 April 1877), 2nd dau of Colquhoun Grant; *m* 2nd 5 May 1879 Edith Katherine (*d* 14 April 1823), dau of Herbert Francis Hore, of Pole Hore, Co Wexford, and *dsp* 19 June 1886

4 Charles Edward, Capt Bombay army; *b* 6 Jan 1825; *m* 1st Dec 1853 Catherine (*d* 22 Feb 1859), est dau of Dr A Cooke, and had issue:

(1) Augustus Edward; *b* 1856; *d* 1877

4 (cont.) The Hon Charles Hobart-Hampden *m* 2nd 6 Aug 1863 Lucy Pauline (*d* 25 July 1913), dau of John Wright, of Lenton Hall, Notts, and *d* 25 Sept 1913, having by her had issue:

(2) Arthur Ernest; *b* 20 June 1864; *m* 1st 26 July 1892 Henrietta Louisa (*d* 6 Dec 1916), only dau of Rev Thomas Orme Fetherstonhaugh, Rector of Moyne, Co Wicklow, and had issue

1a Arthur Edward Orme, served WW I with RFC; *b* 8 Nov 1893; *educ* Charterhouse; *m* 16 Feb 1942 *Gladys, dau of Arthur David Mitchell, and *dsp* 9 April 1950

2a VERE FREDERICK CECIL HOBART-HAMPDEN, **9th Earl of Buckinghamshire**; *educ* St Lawrence Coll Ramsgate and Switzerland; RAF WW II; *b* 17 May 1901; *m* 9 Aug 1972 *Mrs Margot Macrae, dau of John Storey Rodger, of NSW, Australia, and widow of Frederick Cecil Bruce Hittman, MD, FRACS, of Sydney, Australia, and *d* 1983

1a Aileen Mary Lorna; *b* 8 April 1895; *d* unm 30 July 1936

2a Lucy Sybil; *b* 18 Jan 1898; *m* 3 Dec 1923 William Terence Webb McCarthy, MM (*das* Italy 6 Jan 1944), 3rd s of Frank McCarthy, of Chefoo, N China, and had issue:

1b *Patrick Duniam, MD 1952; *b* 28 Dec 1924; *m* 23 Aug 1952 *Patricia, est dau of Archibald J Stewart, of Toronto, Canada

2b *Christopher Frank Renwick; *b* 9 Aug 1926; *m* 2 April 1953 *Ola Roma, 2nd dau of — Britlaff, of Ladysmith, Quebec, Canada

1b *Elizabeth Sybil Ai-mai, Reg Nurse of Ontario, Canada 1952; *b* 15 Feb 1928

2 (cont.) Arthur Hobart-Hampden *m* 2nd 18 March 1920 Cecilia Grace (*d* 18 March 1929), dau of Sir Arthur Blackwood, KCB (*see* DUFFERIN AND CLANEBOYE, B); *m* 3rd 18 April 1929 Bessie (Betty), RRC (*d* 2 Sept 1960), dau of John West Stephenson, and *d* 18 June 1952

The **6th Earl** *m* 2nd 15 Aug 1826 Maria Isabella (*d* 20 March 1873), est dau of Rev Godfrey Egremont, and *d* 29 Oct 1885, having by her had, with other issue:

5 George Augustus, Bombay CS; *b* 2 June 1827; *m* 9 June 1857 Jane (*d* 24 Dec 1874), est dau of Sir John Wither Awdry, DL, JP, of Notton Ho, Wilts, and *d* 8 Dec 1899, having had:

(1) Awdry George, India Forest Serv; *b* 29 March 1858; *m* 18 Feb 1893 Elsie Angel Heath (*d* 6 May 1958), 3rd dau of Col Duncan George Pitcher, IA, and *d* 28 March 1937 having had, with other issue:

1a George Miles Awdry, Lt Oxf and Bucks LI and RFC; *b* 1896; *ka* 1917

1a Alison Elizabeth; *b* 25 June 1899; *m* 3 June 1922 Lt-Cdr Michael Robert Cross, RNVR, 2nd son of Francis John Kynaston Cross, of Aston Tirrold Manor, Berks, and had issue. He *d* 23 March 1969

(2) Alfred Bertie (Rev), Rector of Cottered, Buntingford, Herts 1907–15; *educ* Lincoln Coll Oxford (MA); *m* 1 Oct 1902 Constance (*d* 2 Aug 1927), only surv child of Sir Henry Mervin Vavasour, 3rd Bt (*qv*), of Spaldington, and *d* 28 Dec 1923

(3) Ernest Miles, CMG (1914), entered Consular Serv in China 1888, tfd to Japan 1889, V-Consul Yokohama 1904–09, Japanese Sec Br Embassy Tokyo 1909–19 (local rank of 1st Sec 1916); *b* 11 Nov 1864; *educ* Clifton and BNC Oxford (BA 1888); *m* 20 Nov 1901 Marie Hélène (*d* 8 July 1938), est dau of Rev Louis Langel, and *d* 1 May 1949, having had issue:

1a Cyril Langel; *b* 31 Oct 1902; *educ* Clifton; *m* 6 June 1936 Margaret (*d* 1985), only dau of George Hilborne Jolliffe, formerly of Forrester, Govinna, Ceylon, and *d* 22 May 1972, leaving issue:

1b GEORGE MILES HOBART-HAMPDEN, **10th and present Earl of Buckinghamshire**

1b *Helen Moncrieff [Lady Helen Motteux, c/o Fallscroft Estates, Private Bag V7410, Mutare, Zimbabwe]; *b* 18 June 1937; granted 11 Jan 1986 rank of earl's dau; *m* 1962 *Hugues Renier Motteux, and has:

1c *Thierry; *b* 28 May 1968

2c *Jean-Paul; *b* 1973

1c *Nicole; *b* 1970

2a Harold Baldwin; *b* 13 May 1905; *d* unm 14 Sept 1926

(1) Sarah Maria; *d* unm 15 March 1939

(2) Frances Jane; *m* 30 Sept 1898 Maj-Gen Sir John Henry Keith Stewart, KCB, DSO, DL, IA, of Cairnsmore, Newton Stewart, Wigtownshire, and *d* 3 Dec 1952, leaving issue. He *d* 30 May 1955

(3) Edith Augusta; *d* unm 16 Jan 1939

6 William Arthur (Rev), Vicar of Wellesbourne, Warwicks; *b* 11 Oct 1828; *m* 1 June 1857 Marianne (*d* 1 March 1892), dau of Richard Kennet-Dawson, of Frickley Hall, Yorks, and *dvp* 7 Sept 1874, leaving issue:

(1) Arthur Kennet (Rev), Vicar St Anne, Boden Hill, Chippenham 1910–16; *b* 28 Nov 1858; *educ* New Coll Oxford (MA); *m* 1 Jan 1907 Isabella Thérèse (*d* 30 April 1955), dau of Rev Canon Henry Blagden, of Peverel Court, Aylesbury, and *d* 11 Dec 1932

7 Horace Miles, Maj 103rd Foot (Bombay Fus); *b* 5 Nov 1835; *m* 1st 14 Sept 1864 Gertrude (*dsp* 26 May 1875), 7th dau of George Bawtree, of Colchester; *m* 2nd 4 Nov 1880 Isabella (*d* 26 April 1932), est dau of Robert Druitt, MD, of Kensington, and *d* 12 Aug 1928, leaving issue:

(1) Isabella Gertrude; *b* 16 Aug 1882; *d* unm 19 Oct 1960

BUCKMASTER

Arms: Or semée of fleurs-de-lys az., a lion rampant of the last, on a chief of the second a portcullis of the first. **Crest:** A demi-lion az., holding in the dexter paw a fleur-de-lys and charged on the shoulder with a portcullis, both or. **Supporters:** On either side a buck ppr., each gorged with a chain, pendent therefrom a portcullis or. **Motto:** *Equanimitas magnanimitas* ('Equanimity, magnanimity'). **Creation:** B. (UK) 14 June 1915, V. (UK) 24 Feb 1933.

THE 3RD VISCOUNT BUCKMASTER and **Baron Buckmaster**, of Cheddington, Co Buckingham (Martin Stanley Buckmaster, OBE (1979)) [The Rt Hon The Viscount Buckmaster, 90 Cornwall Gdns, London SW7 4AX]; *b* 11 April 1921; *s* f 1974; *educ* Stowe; Capt Roy Sussex Regt (TA) 1939–46, F(C)O 1946–81: Political Offr Abu Dhabi 1955–58, 1st Sec (Info) Benghazi 1958–62, Tripoli 1962–63, 1st

Sec (Political) Bahrain 1963–67, FO 1967–69, 1st Sec Kampala 1969–71, Beirut 1971–73, FCO 1973–77, Chargé d'Affaires and Head Chancery Yemen Arab Republic 1977–81 (ret), FRGS

Lineage: JOHN CHARLES BUCKMASTER, JP, of Teddington, Middx, and the Science and Art Dept S Kensington; *b* 23 Feb 1823, s of Thomas Buckmaster, of Slapton, Bucks; *m* 9 Aug 1853 Emily Anne (*d* 30 June 1890), er dau of George Goodliffe, of Trumpington, Cambs, and *d* 20 July 1908, having had, with other issue:

1 Charles Alexander, JP (Middx), FIC, FPS, FCS, assist master Magdalen Coll Sch 1874, Llandovery Coll 1876–80, examiner science and art dept 1880, Inspr 1882, Sr Inspr 1890, Ch Inspr 1900, Assist Sec Bd Educn 1908–14, Memb Appeal Tbnl Middx 1916; *b* 16 May 1854; *educ* Lincoln Coll Oxford (MA); *m* 28 Dec 1887 Lucy Ormerod (*d* 27 Sept 1943), only dau of Henry Colley Mar, JP, MD, FSA, and *d* 24 May 1949, having had a s and four daus (all *d* unm or sp)

2 George Alfred, Prof Physiology Bristol, MA, MD, DPH Oxon, FRCS, LRCP Lond; *b* 7 Feb 1859; *m c* 1890 Amy Elizabeth, dau of Charles Brookes, of Milton Green, Cheshire, and *d* 21 Dec 1937, having had issue:

(1) Charles Oliver Brooks, Lt DCLI; *d* 16 March 1919

(2) Dorothy Emily Brooks, MB, BS Lond, MRCS, LRCP, Assist MO GPO; *m* 6 May 1931 Ronald Henry Tasker, MRCS, LRCP (*k* by enemy action 6 Nov 1942), er s of H G Tasker, of Clifton, Bristol, and *d* 23 Dec 1961, leaving issue

3 STANLEY OWEN, **1st Viscount**

4 Martin Arnold, ARCA, Hon ARIBA, art master and examiner; *b* 2 Aug 1862; *m* 4 Feb 1910 Dorothy Mary, MBE (*d* 5 Oct 1969), 3rd dau of William John Dyer, and *d* 14 Aug 1960, leaving issue:

(1) Dorothy Annette, BEM; *b* 12 Feb 1911; *m* 27 July 1946 Guy Frederick Sims Williams, 2nd s of Frederick Sims Williams, KC

The 3rd son,

STANLEY OWEN BUCKMASTER, **1st Viscount Buckmaster**, so *cr* 24 Feb 1933, as also earlier 14 June 1915 BARON BUCKMASTER, of Cheddington, Co Buckingham (both UK), GCVO (1930), PC (1915), KC (1902), JP Herts; *b* 9 Jan 1861; *educ* Ch Ch Oxford (BA 1882, MA 1886), Hon LLD Edin U, Hon LLD Toronto, Hon DCL Oxford, barrister Inner Temple 1884, Memb Cncl Duchy Lancaster 1912, Counsel to Oxford U 1911–13, Slr-Gen 1913–15, dir Press Bureau 1914–15, Ld Chllr 1915–16, MP (Lib) Cambridge Borough 1906–10 and Keighley 1911–15, ktd 1913; *m* 29 Dec 1889 Edith Augusta (*d* 23 Oct 1935), dau of Spencer Robert Lewin, and had issue:

1 OWEN STANLEY, **2nd Viscount**

1 Margaret Anna; *b* 8 March 1893; *m* 22 Dec 1921 Dighton Nicolas Pollock, barrister (*d* 9 March 1927), s of Maj-Gen Sir Frederick Richard Pollock, KCSI (*see* POLLOCK, Bt), and *d* 4 June 1929, leaving issue

2 Barbara; *b* 21 Oct 1903; *educ* Somerville Coll Oxford; *m* 22 Dec 1926 (*divorce* 1944) Lt-Cdr John Bryan Miller, GC, RNVR, er s of Brian Stothert Miller, JP, and *d* Sept 1966, leaving issue

The 1st VISCOUNT *d* 5 Dec 1934; his son,

OWEN STANLEY BUCKMASTER, **2nd Viscount Buckmaster**; *b* 24 Sept 1890; *educ* Winchester and Ch Ch Oxford (BA 1912); Capt 7th Bn DCLI, barrister Inner Temple 1913, memb Ctee London Stock Exchange 1938–42, pres: Nat Fedn Property Owners 1946–50, Assoc Land and Property Owners 1946–57, Arundel and Shoreham C Assoc 1951–60; WW I (wounded), Maj HG WW II; *m* 1st 21 Dec 1916 (*divorce* 1944) Joan (*d* 22 Dec 1976), 2nd dau of George Augustus Garry Simpson, MRCS, and had issue:

1 MARTIN STANLEY BUCKMASTER, **3rd and present Viscount Buckmaster**

2 +COLIN JOHN [The Hon Colin Buckmaster, Ryece Hall, Brettenham, nr Ipswich, Suffolk]; *b* 17 April 1923; heir presumptive; *educ* Winchester; late F/Lt RAFVR; *m* 12 Oct 1946 *May, only dau of Charles Henry Gibbon, and has issue:

(1) +Adrian Charles [Adrian Buckmaster Esq, The Close, Holdfast, Upton-on-Severn, Worcs]; *b* 2 Feb 1949; *educ* Charterhouse and Clare Coll Cambridge (BA 1970, MA 1974); md Dowty Mining 1980; *m* 26 July 1975 *Elizabeth Mary, MB, only dau of Norman Mark, MB, ChB, and has issue:

1a +Andrew Nicholas; *b* 1980

1a *Clare May; *b* 1 June 1979

2a *Nicola Mary; *b* 1986

(2) +Simon John; *b* 1 April 1956; *educ* Charterhouse and Exeter U (BA 1979); *m* 12 March 1983 *Emma Elizabeth, er dau of FM Sir John Wilfred Stanier, KCB, MBE, and has issue:

1a +George John; *b* 1984

2a +Hugo Denis; *b* 1987

3a +Toby Colin; *b* 1991

1a *Rachel May; *b* 1988

(3) +Michael Anthony Stanley; *b* 19 Oct 1959; *educ* Nautical Coll Pangbourne

(1) *Ann Susan [Mrs Nicholas Tavener, The Grange, Brettenham, Ipswich, Suffolk IP7 7PA]; *b* 28 Sept 1950; *m* 3 July 1976 *Nicholas J W Tavener, s of E A Tavener, and has issue:

1a *Thomas Henry; *b* 1980

2a *Geoffrey John; *b* 1985

1a *Sarah Georgina *b* 14 March 1979

(2) *Sarah Janet; *b* 6 Dec 1952; *educ* Durham U (BA 1975)

The **2nd Viscount** *m* 2nd 23 Jan 1961 *Diana Constance [Mrs Roderick Faure Walker, Ringwold House, Middle Wallop, nr Stockbridge, Hants] (*m* 3rd 1982, as his 2nd w, Roderick Edward Faure Walker), only dau of Maj Kenneth Arthur Seth-Smith, of Chesterwood Grange, Haydon Bridge, Northumberland, and formerly w of Charles Stewart M'Donnell Vane-Tempest (*see* LONDONDERRY, M), and *d* 25 Sept 1974

BUCKWORTH-HERNE-SOAME

Arms: Quarterly, 1st and 4th, gu. a chevron between three mallets or, a canton arg. for difference (for SOAME); 2nd and 3rd, sa. a chevron, between three cross-crosslets fitchée arg. an ermine spot (for BUCKWORTH). **Crests:** 1 A lure gu., garnished and stringed arg., thereon a falcon or, beaked and legged of the second (for SOAME), 2 A man's head, full-faced, armed with a helmet, the beaver up, all ppr. (for BUCKWORTH). **Creation:** Bt. (E) 1 April 1697.

SIR CHARLES JOHN BUCKWORTH-HERNE-SOAME, 12TH BT, of Sheen, Surrey [Sir Charles Buckworth-Herne-Soame Bt, Sheen Cottage, Coalbrookdale, Telford, Salop TF8 7EQ]; *b* 28 May 1932; *s f* 1977; *m* 22 March 1958 *Eileen Margaret Mary, dau of Leonard Minton, of Caughley, Salop, and has issue:

1 +RICHARD JOHN; *b* 17 Aug 1970

Lineage: RICHARD BUCKWORTH, of Wisbech, Cambs; *m* Grace, dau of Bartholomew Everard, of White Hall Manor, Wisbech, and had:

RICHARD BUCKWORTH, of White Hall and Fitton, Cambs; *m* 17 Aug 1593 Rose, dau and coheir of — Skegness, and had an est s:

EVERARD BUCKWORTH, of White Hall; *bapt* 4 Sept 1595; *m* Anne, dau of Thomas Oxburgh, of Lynn, Norfolk, and was *bur* 1 Oct 1641, leaving a 3rd s:

Sir JOHN BUCKWORTH, Alderman London, Dep Govr Turkey Merchants; *m* as his 2nd w *c* 4 Jan 1661/2 Hester, widow of Moses Goodyear, of London, and *d* Dec 1687, having had, with three daus:

Sir John Buckworth, 1st Bt (E), so *cr* 1 April 1697, of Sheen, Surrey, Sheriff London 1704; *b* 18 Oct 1662; *m* 27 Oct 1687 Elizabeth (*m* 2nd 13 Aug 1712 John Hiccocks, Master in Chancery; *d* 20 May 1737), dau of John Hall, Yarmouth merchant, and *d* 12 June 1709, having had, with a dau (*d* unm):

1 **Sir John Buckworth, 2nd Bt**, MP Weobley; *bapt* 5 April 1704; *m* Mary Jane (*d* 26 Jan 1775), sis of Angelique Faicho Clermont, and *dsp* 3 Jan 1759

2 **Sir Everard Buckworth, 3rd Bt**, Assist Gentleman Usher to GEORGE II; *bapt* 23 April 1704; *m* Mary (*d* 29 Nov 1767), dau of William Dobel, of Worcester, and *d* 2 Feb 1779, having had, with four daus:

(1) **Sir John Buckworth, 4th Bt**; *bapt* 8 July 1726; *d* unm 10 June 1801

(2) Sir EVERARD BUCKWORTH later BUCKWORTH-HERNE, **5th Bt**; *bapt* 12 Nov 1732, memb GEORGE II's household, Gentleman Pensioner and Exon Gd *temp* GEORGE III; *bapt* 12 Nov 1732; *m* 1st Anne (*d* 1806), illegitimate dau of Paston Herne, of Haviland Hall, Norfolk, consequently adding the name of HERNE; *m* 2nd — and *d* 15 July 1814, having by his 1st w had:

1a BUCKWORTH (Sir), **6th Bt**

2a John (Rev), Vicar W Hendred, Berks; *m* 1st Mary Anne (*d* 1823), dau and heiress of Sir Charles Price, of Blount's Court, Oxon; *m* 2nd Elizabeth, widow of Rev Dr Finch, and *dsp* 1854

1a Mary Elizabeth; *m* 1st James Vaughan, of Leicester; *m* 2nd Rev Calverley Bewicke; *m* 3rd Capt John Buckworth and *d* 1855

2a Charlotte; *m* Henry Lucas and had issue

The 5th Bt's er son,

Sir BUCKWORTH BUCKWORTH-HERNE later BUCKWORTH-HERNE-SOAME (added with arms of SOAME by roy licence 12 Dec 1806 under terms of will (which also bequeathed him the estates) of Sir Peter Soame, 4th and last Bt, of Heydon House, Essex, who was no relation whatsoever), **6th Bt**; *b* 17 April 1762; *m* 17 April 1792 Susan (*d* 6 Dec 1819), dau of Stephen Simperingham, of Cambridge, and *d* 21 Jan 1822, leaving issue:

1 **Sir Peter Buckworth-Herne-Soame, 7th Bt**; *b* 24 April 1793; *m* 13 Oct 1830 Mary (*d* 17 Oct 1888), dau of William Bradshaw, and *dsp* 25 Feb 1860

2 **Sir John Buckworth-Herne-Soame, 8th Bt**; *b* 21 June 1794; *m* 17 Jan 1833 Lydia (*d* 6 April 1863), dau of H Hagger, and had, with a dau (*d* an infant):

(1) Charles; *d* unm *vp* at Boston, USA, 9 Dec 1878

3 Charles; *b* 23 April 1798; *m* 20 June 1829 Hannah, dau of Richard Procter, of Hay, Brecknock, and *d* 6 Dec 1863, leaving issue:
(1) CHARLES (Sir), **9th Bt**
(2) Richard; *b* 29 Oct 1833; *d* 1893
(1) Hannah; *b* 8 Nov 1831; *m* 25 July 1864 John Richards, and *d* 1892

Sir JOHN *dsps* 1 Feb 1888; his n,

Sir Charles Buckworth-Herne-Soame, 9th Bt, JP Surrey, CC Salop, MRCSE, LSA; *b* 29 May 1830; *m* 29 March 1855 his cousin Mary (*d* 24 Dec 1893), dau of Richard Fellows Proctor, of Iron Bridge, Salop, and had:
1 Richard Everard; *b* 15 May 1863; *d* unm 1884
2 CHARLES (Sir), **10th Bt**
1 Mary Hannah; *b* 23 Aug 1856; *m* 1st 16 Oct 1878 Arthur Marcy, of Wellington, Salop. He *d* 1883. She *m* 2nd 24 July 1889 Rev Richard Herbert Snape (*d* 1918), Vicar St Bees, Cumberland
2 Evelyn; *b* 11 May 1861; *m* 7 June 1881 George Day Harrison later Buckworth-Herne-Soame (adopted together with the arms for himself and his issue by roy licence 26 Nov 1906; *d* 1912), of Radford Ho, Stone, Staffs, and had issue

Sir CHARLES *d* 25 March 1906; his only surv son,

Sir Charles Buckworth-Herne-Soame, 10th Bt; *b* 18 Sept 1864; *m* 1891 Mary (*d* 1926), widow of Peter Burnett Pring, MRCS, and dau of John Edge, and *d* 25 Aug 1931, having had issue:
1 Richard Everard, Lt King's Shropshire LI; *b* 21 Nov 1891; *d* 30 July 1916 of wounds recd in action
2 **Sir Charles Burnett Buckworth-Herne-Soame, 11th Bt**, Shropshire LI WW I (wounded); *b* 26 Sept 1894; *m* 1 Nov 1924 Elsie May dau of Walter Alfred Lloyd, of Coalbrookdale, Salop, and *d* 20 April 1977, leaving issue:
1 Sir CHARLES JOHN BUCKWORTH-HERNE-SOAME, **12th and present Bt**
1 *Mary [Mrs Keith Edwards, 27 Woodside, Coalbrookdale, Salop]; *b* 6 Jan 1936; *m* 27 Sept 1958 *Keith Howard Edwards, s of Frank Edwards, of Madeley, Salop, and has issue:
(1) *Robert John Edwards; *b* 1971
(1) *Carol Jane; *b* 4 Sept 1964

BULL

Arms: Sa., three astronomical signs of Taurus or. **Crest:** A bull's head cabossed sa., charged on the forehead with the sign of Taurus as in the arms. **Motto:** Hitherto. **Creation:** Bt. (UK) 25 Nov 1922.

SIR SIMEON GEORGE BULL, 4TH BT [Sir Simeon Bull Bt, Beech Hanger, Beech Rd, Shepherd's Hill, Merstham, Surrey RH1 3AE; Pen Enex, Pont l'Abbé, Tremeoc, Finisterre, France]; *b* 1 Aug 1934; *s* f 1986; *educ* Eton, Innsbruck and Paris; slr 1959, sr ptnr Bull and Bull, Liveryman Fishmongers' Co, Freeman City London, Hon Slr Standing Cncl Baronetage, memb Cncl RYA; *m* 17 June 1961 *Annick Elisabeth Renée Geneviève, yr dau of Louis Bresson, of Château des Masselins, Chandai, Orne, France, and has issue:
1 +STEPHEN LOUIS; *b* 5 April 1966; *educ* Downside and Crawley Coll of Technology; *m* 19 March 1994 *Maria Brampton and has issue:
(1) *Elizabeth Victoria; *b* 21 Jan 1995
1 *Jacqueline-Hester [Mrs David Burton, 20 Smithies Rd, Abbey Wood, London SE2]; *b* 15 Oct 1964; *m* 31 Dec 1993 *David Burton, and has issue:
(1) *Patrick Anthony; *b* 2 Nov 1985
(1) *Emma Patricia; *b* 24 Nov 1995
2 *Sophia Ann [Miss Sophia-Ann Bull, 24 Albert Square, Stratford, London E15]; *b* 2 March 1971

Lineage: EDWARD BULL, of Bulls, now the Brook Farm, Cowfold, Sussex; *b c* 1540; *d* Nov 1577, leaving:

RALPH BULL, of Cowfold; *b* 1570; *m* 8 July 1600 Elizabeth (*d* 1652), dau of Peter Marten, of Dragon's, Cowfold, and *d* 1640, leaving:

THOMAS BULL, of Kings, Cowfold; *b* 1601; *m* 8 July 1630 Joan (*d* 1641), dau of Thomas Parsons, of Ockenden, Cowfold, and *d* April 1652, leaving, with other issue:

THOMAS BULL, of Bull's Bridge, Cowfold, and Henfield, Sussex; *b* 1639; *m* 23 Sep 1662 Catherine Mose, of Horsham, and had, with other issue:

THOMAS BULL, of Bulls, Wivelsfield, Sussex; *b* 1663; *m* 2 April 1700 his cousin Mary (*d* April 1732), dau of Ralph Bull, of Clarke's and Hazelcroft, Henfield, and *d* 1746, leaving, with other issue:

THOMAS BULL, of Keymer, Sussex; *m* 1st 10 May 1722 Sarah Nye (*d* Dec 1725); *m* 2nd 12 April 1726 Jane, widow of Josia Turner, of Wivelsfield, and *d* Feb 1780, leaving, with other issue:

JOSEPH BULL, of Lewes, Sussex; *m* 10 April 1749 Sarah (*d* 1769), sis of Simeon Buckman, of Wivelsfield, and *d* Nov 1793, leaving, with other issue:

SIMEON BULL, of Holles St, Cavendish Sq, London, and Arundel Ho, Fulham; *b* 1750; *m* 23 Dec 1786 Sarah Leonard (*d* 4 July 1837) and *d* 24 Oct 1818, having had, with other issue:

HENRY WILLIAM BULL, of Knowle Green Ho, Staines, Middx; slr; *b* 5 Nov 1792; *m* 27 Dec 1826 Charlotte Susannah (*d* 2 March 1868), dau of William Swales, and *d* 8 Aug 1872, leaving, with other issue:

HENRY BULL, of Westbourne Park, London; slr; *b* 18 Sept 1829; *m* 24 April 1861 Cecilia Ann (*d* 29 March 1898), dau of James Peter Howard, of Whithed Wood, Shirley, Hants, and *d* 15 July 1878, leaving a 2nd s:

Sir William James Bull, 1st Bt (UK), so *cr* 25 Nov 1922, PC (1918), MP (C) Hammersmith 1900–18 and S Hammersmith 1918–29; Freeman Borough of Hammersmith 1930; FSA, Pres of Roy Albert Hall; slr 1889; Pncpl Imp Soc Kts Bachelor, Maltravers Herald of Arms Extrdy 14 Feb 1922, memb LCC for Hammersmith 1892–1901; *b* 29 Sept 1863; ktd 1905; *m* 5 Jan 1904 Lillian Hester (*d* 3 Sept 1963), 2nd dau of Gabriel Samuel Brandon, of Oakbrook, Ravenscourt Park, Hammersmith, and Heene, Worthing, and *d* 23 Jan 1931, leaving:
1 **Sir Stephen John Bull, 2nd Bt**; *b* 11 Oct 1904; *educ* New Coll Oxford (MA); slr 1928, F/Lt RAFVR WW II, ptnr Bull and Bull, dir London United Launderies Ltd, Liveryman Mercers' Co, Freeman City London, Hon Slr to League of Mercy and RLSS, v-pres Hammersmith (S) C Assoc; *das* unm Java 9 March 1942
2 GEORGE (Sir), **3rd Bt**
3 +Anthony, CBE (1968, OBE 1943) [Col Anthony CBE, 35 Clareville Grove, London SW7 5AU]; *b* 18 July 1908; *educ* Gresham's and Magdalene Coll Cambridge (BA 1929, MA 1933); Col RE WW II (American Bronze Star), Tport Div CCG (Br element), Berlin 1945–46, memb: LTE 1955–62, LTB 1962–65; v-chm LTE 1965–71, Pres of Inst of Transport 1969–70, transpt consultant: Kennedy and Donkin 1971–85, Freeman Fox and Ptnrs 1971–87, CStJ; *m* 5 Oct 1946 Barbara (*d* 18 Oct 1947), er dau of Peter Donovan, of Great Banks, Rye, Sussex, and has issue:
(1) *Caroline [Lady Chichester-Clark, 35 Ellerby St, London SW6]; *b* 11 July 1947; barrister (Inner Temple) 1974; *m* 1974, as his 2nd w, *Sir Robert (Robin) Chichester-Clark, MP, and has issue:
1a *Adam Tamniarn; *b* 1973
2a *Thomas Finn; *b* 1976
4 Peter Cecil, DSC; *b* 21 March 1912; *educ* Winchester; Lt-Cdr RNVR WW II, actor, author: *To Sea in a Sieve, Bulls in the Meadows, I know the Face, But, Not on your Telly!*, and *It isn't all Greek to Me*; *d* May 1984

The 2nd Bt's bro,

Sir George Bull, 3rd Bt, of Hammersmith, London; *b* 19 June 1906; *educ* RNCs Osborne and Dartmouth; late RN, slr 1929, WW II as Cdr RNVR, sr ptnr Bull and Bull, Cncllr London Borough of Hammersmith 1961–71, Liveryman Fishmongers' Co, Freeman City London, Chm Standing Cncl Baronetage 1977–1980; Hon Slr Roy Society of St George, V-Chm Govrs Goldolphin and Latymer Sch, Govr Latymer Upper Sch, Tstee Hammersmith United Charities, chm London Rent Assessment Panel; *m* 23 Sept 1933 Gabrielle, 2nd dau of Bramwell Jackson, MC, of Raw Hall, Bradfield St George, Bury St Edmunds, Suffolk, and *d* 1986, having had issue:
1 Sir SIMEON GEORGE BULL, **4th and present Bt**
1 *Charlotte Sophia [Mrs Christopher Gibbons, 48 Ravenscourt Gdns, London W6 0TU]; *b* 1 Feb 1938; *educ* Roedean and Emma Willard Sch, NY, USA; *m* 11 Sept 1964 *Christopher Adney Walter Gibbons, son of Adney Walter Gibbons and Lady Taylor, of Ratton Wood, Eastbourne, Sussex, and has issue:
(1) *Sybil Jemima; *b* 30 Aug 1965
(2) *Georgina Loveday; *b* 8 Nov 1967

BULLOCK

Creation: B. (LP, UK) 1974.

THE BARON BULLOCK, of Leafield, Oxon (Sir Alan Louis Charles Bullock) [The Rt Hon The Lord Bullock, Gable End, 30 Godstow Rd, Oxford OX2 8AJ]; *b* 13 Dec 1914; *educ* Bradford GS and Wadham Coll Oxford (MD DLitt); Fellow, Dean and Tutor New Coll Oxford 1945–52, Censor St Catherine's Soc Oxford 1952–62, Founding Master St Catherine's Coll Oxford 1960–80, V-Chllr Oxford U 1969–73; Chm: Research Ctee RIIA 1954–78, Nat Advsy Cncl on Training and Supply of Teachers 1963–65, Schools Cncl 1966–69, Ctee on Reading and Other Uses of English Language 1972–74, Tstees Tate Gallery 1973–80, Friends of Ashmolean Museum, Ctee of Enquiry on Indus Democracy 1976; memb: Arts Cncl GB 1961–64, SSRC 1966, Advsy Cncl on Public Records 1965–77, Organising Ctee Br Library 1971–72; Tstee *The Observer* 1957–69 (dir 1977–81), ktd 1972, Hon Fell: St Catherine's Coll 1980, New Coll, Merton Coll, Wadham Coll, Linacre Coll, Wolfson Coll, St Antony's (1996), all Oxford; Sr Fell Aspen Inst USA; Tstee Aspen Inst Berlin; memb Academia Europaea 1990; Foreign Memb American Acad Arts and Sciences; Hon FRIBA; FBA; Chev Legion Honour 1970; Hon Dr U Aix-Marseilles; Hon DLitt Bradford, Reading, Leicester, Sussex, Essex, Warwick, Newfoundland, OU; author: *Hitler, A Study in Tyranny* (1952), *The Liberal Tradition* (1956), *The Life and Times of Ernest Bevin* (vol I 1960, vol II 1967, vol III *Ernest Bevin-Foreign Secretary*, 1983), *The Humanist Tradition in the West* (1985), *Hitler and Stalin: Parallel Lives* 1991 (revised edn 1993), *The Twentieth Century* (1970), *Fontana Dictionary of Modern Thought* 1977 (co-editor, 2nd edn 1988), *Fontana Biographical Companion to Modern Thought* (1983); *m* 1940 *Hilda Yates, dau of Edwin Handy, of Bradford, and has issue:

1 *(Oliver) Nicholas Alan [The Hon Nicholas Bullock, King's College, Cambridge]; *b* 1942; *m* 1st 1967 (*divorce* 1972) —; *m* 2nd 1972 (*divorce* 1984) Ellen J Blatt; *m* 3rd 1984 *Sally Todd, dau of Sinclair Holmes, of Bolden

2 *Adrian Charles Sebastian [The Hon Adrian Bullock, 9 Wylie Close, Headington, Oxford OX3 7NH]; *b* 1944; *m* 1st 1970 (*divorce* 1984) Susan Elizabeth Swindlehurst; *m* 2nd 1992 *Bernadette Lucia Maria, dau of James Ferry, of Glasgow

3 *Matthew Peter Dominic; *b* 1949; *m* 1970 *Anna-Llena Margareta, dau of Sven Hansson, of Uppsala, Sweden

Lineage: Rev FRANK ALLEN BULLOCK; had:

ALAN LOUIS CHARLES, *cr* a **Baron**

BUNBURY

Arms: Arg. on a bend sa. three chess rooks of the field. **Crest:** Two swords saltirewise passing through the mouth of a leopard's face or, the blades ppr., hilted gold. **Mottoes:** *Firmum in vita nihil* ('Nothing in life is certain') and *Esse quam videri* ('To be rather than to seem').
Creation: Bt. (E) 29 June 1681.

SIR MICHAEL WILLIAM BUNBURY, 13TH BT, of Stanney Hall, Cheshire [Sir Michael Bunbury Bt, Naunton Hall, Rendlesham, Woodbridge, Suffolk IP12 2RD]; *b* 29 Dec 1946; *s* f 1985; *educ* Eton and Trin Coll Cambridge (MA 1968); ptnr Smith and Williamson, memb Cncl Duchy Lancaster 1993–; *m* 20 Nov 1976 *Caroline Anne, dau of Col Anthony Derek Swift Mangnall, OBE, of The Old Vicarage, Little Bedwyn, Wilts, and has issue:

1 +HENRY MICHAEL NAPIER; *b* 4 March 1980

2 +Edward Peter; *b* 1986

1 *Katherine Rosemary; *b* 1978

Lineage: HENRY de BONEBERI (*ie*, Bunbury, nr Nantwich, Cheshire); lived *temp* STEPHEN; alleged ancestor of:

THOMAS BUNBURY, of Bunbury and Stanney, Cheshire; *m* Bridget, dau of John Aston, of Aston, Cheshire, and had, with other issue:

Sir HENRY BUNBURY, of Stanney; ktd 1603; *m* 1st Anne, dau of Geoffrey Shakerley, of Shakerley, Lancs, and had issue: *m* 2nd Martha, dau of Edward Norris, of Speke, Lancs, and *d* 1634, having by her had another s (Thomas, ancestor of the BUNBURYs of Lisnevagh and Moyle, Co Carlow, and Kilfeacle, Co Tipperary; *see* RICHARDSON-BUNBURY, Bt); a dau by one of his wives *m* George Holland, of Newhall (*see* ZOUCHE, B); his s by his 1st w:

HENRY BUNBURY, of Stanney; fined and imprisoned five years for royalism in Civil War period; *m* Ursula, dau of Sir John Bayley, of Hoddesdon, Salop, and *d* 1 Feb 1664, leaving:

Sir Thomas Bunbury, 1st Bt (E), so *cr* 29 June 1681, of Stanney and Bunbury; *m* 1st Sarah (*d* 1671), dau of John Chetwode, of Oakley, Staffs, and had issue; *m* 2nd Mary, dau of Humphrey Kelsall, of Heathside, Cheshire, and *d* 22 Aug 1682, leaving by his 1st w:

Sir Henry Bunbury, 2nd Bt; *b* 1657; *m* Mary, dau of Sir Kendrick Eyton, and *d* 20 Dec 1687, leaving an er surv s:

Sir Henry Bunbury, 3rd Bt, MP Chester 1700–27; *m* Susannah (*d* 23 Sept 1744), dau of William Hanmer, and *d* 12 Feb 1732/3, having had, with two other s and five daus:

1 **Sir Charles Bunbury, 4th Bt**, MP Chester 1733–42; *bapt* 9 Feb 1707/8; *d* unm 10 April 1742

2 **Rev Sir William Bunbury, 5th Bt**, DD Oxon, MA Cantab, Vicar Mildenhall, *s* to the Barton and Mildenhall properties on the death *sp* 1746 of his unc Sir Thomas Hanmer, Bt (*qv*); *m* Eleanor (*d* 14 Feb 1764), dau and coheir of Vere Graham, of Wix Abbey, Essex, and *d* 11 June 1764, having had, with another dau:

(1) **Sir (Thomas) Charles Bunbury, 6th Bt**, of Barton, Suffolk; MP Suffolk; *b* May 1740; *m* 1st 2 June 1762 (*divorce* 1776) Lady Sarah Lennox, dau of 2nd Duke of Richmond (*see* RICHMOND and GORDON, D); *m* 2nd Margaret — (*d* 6 Feb 1822) and *dsp* 31 March 1821

(2) Henry William, artist and caricaturist; *b* 1750; *m* 1771 Catherine, dau of Kane William Horneck, Capt RE, and *d* 7 May 1811, having had, with another s:

1a HENRY EDWARD (Sir), **7th Bt**

(1) Annabella; *m* 1st Sir Patrick Blake Bt (*see* 1970 edn BLAKE, Bt, of Langham); *m* 2nd George Boscawen, of St Peter, Isle of Thanet

The 6th Bt's n,

Sir Edward Henry Bunbury, 7th, KCB; Lt-Gen, MP Suffolk, U-Sec War 1809–16, FAS; *b* 4 May 1778; *m* 1st 4 April 1807 Louisa Emilia (*d* Sept 1828), dau of Gen Hon Henry Edward Fox, 3rd s of 1st Baron Holland (*see* ILCHESTER, E), and had issue:

1 **Sir Charles James Fox Bunbury, 8th Bt**, High Sheriff Suffolk 1868; *b* 4 Feb 1809; *m* 31 May 1844 Frances Joanna (*d* 21 July 1894), dau of Leonard Horner, FRS, and *dsp* 18 June 1886

2 **Sir Edward Herbert Bunbury, 9th Bt**, MA, barrister, MP Bury St Edmunds 1847–52; *b* 8 July 1811; *d* unm 5 March 1895

3 Henry William St Pierre, CB, Col; *b* 2 Sept 1812; *m* 30 Nov 1852 Cecilia, dau of Lt-Gen Sir George Napier, KCB, and *d* 18 Sept 1875, having had, with other issue:

(1) HENRY CHARLES JOHN (Sir), **10th Bt**

(2) George Edward, Lt Norfolk Regt; *b* 17 Oct 1856; *m* 30 Oct 1884 Beatrice Dora (*d* 10 July 1940), dau of Thomas J Cottle, of Ontario, and *d* 1943, leaving issue:

1a Noreen Winifred Cecilia Napier; *d* 27 May 1973

(3) William St Pierre, T/Lt-Col RFA, Maj RA, Afghan War 1880, WW I; *b* 17 Jan 1859; *m* 13 April 1882 Lilian (*d* 12 June 1936), dau of Gen Hon Sir Henry Ramsay, KSCI, CB, bro of 12th Earl of Dalhousie (*qv*), and *d* 9 March 1942, leaving, with other issue:

1a Gerald Bruce St Pierre, Lt-Col IA WW I (wounded), Waziristan 1919; *b* 21 March 1883; *m* 10 Aug 1909 Frances Mary Olivia (*d* 31 Dec 1952), only dau of Francis Peter Dixon, JP, of Blackwell Lodge, Cumberland, and *d* 19 June 1954, leaving issue:

1b Francis Ramsay St Pierre, CBE (1958), DSO (1945) and bar (1953); *b* 16 June 1910; *educ* Rugby and RMC Sandhurst; Brig Duke of Wellington's Regt, NW Frontier 1935, WW II (despatches), Korea 1952–53, Cyprus 1958–59 (despatches); *m* 27 April 1933 Elizabeth Pamela Somers (*d* 12 Sept 1969), dau of Francis Reginald Liscombe, and *d* 1990 leaving:

1c +Charles Napier St Pierre, MBE (1974) [Maj Charles Bunbury MBE, HQ Berlin and Signals Regt, BFPO 45]; *b* 13 Feb 1941; *educ* Rugby and RMA Sandhurst; Maj Duke of Wellington's Regt NI 1974; *m* 10 Dec 1978 *Veronica Evelyn, only dau of Capt Peter Evelyn Fanshawe, CBE, DSC, RN (*see* LINDSEY and ABINGDON, E), and has issue:

1d +William Francis St Pierre; *b* 12 Nov 1982

1d *Victoria Elizabeth St Pierre; *b* 1979

1c *Ann Geraldine St Pierre [Mrs Roland Bird, 505 Duncan House, Dolphin Sq, London SW1V 3PP]; *b* 28 March 1934; *m* 1978 *Roland Ernest Bird, CBE

2a Noël Louis St Pierre, DSO (1937); *b* 25 Dec 1890; *educ* Bedford Sch and RMC Sandhurst; Brig IA WW I, Siberia 1919, Waziristan 1920, 1930 and 1936–37, cmded Area and Bde India 1941–44, ADC to HM GEORGE VI 1943–44, cmded 12th Co London HG Bn 1952–55; *m* 29 Nov 1923 Iris Graham (*d* 29 Dec 1965), er dau of James Baird Whitelaw, of North Berwick, and *d* 31 Jan 1971, leaving issue:

1b +David St Pierre [Dr David Bunbury, 1 Hazelwood Rd, Hale, Cheshire]; *b* 22 July 1926; *educ* privately and Imp Coll Sci and Technology, London; PhD, BSc

1a Marjorie Ellinor; *b* 28 Jan 1887; *d* unm 2 March 1971

4 Richard Hanmer, Capt RN; *b* 18 Dec 1813; *m* 19 Dec 1838 Sarah Susanna, dau of Robert Clement Sconce, and *d* 23 Dec 1857, having had, with other issue:

(1) Henry Fox, Capt 35th Native Inf India; *b* Oct 1839; *m* 1863 Elizabeth (*d* 1875), dau of J Kelsey, and *d* 16 Oct 1870, having had issue:

1a Cecil Edward Francis, CSI (1910), ICS, Resident and Judicial Commr NWFP India 1901–10; *b* 1 Dec 1864; *m* Jan 1893 May Valerie, dau of Edward de Visme, and *d* 12 April 1932

2a William Clement Hanmer, Capt Res Offrs, 3rd Bn W R Regt, Roy Scots and IA; *b* 17 Feb 1868; *m* 9 Dec 1903 (*divorce* 1930) Lilian Maude, only child of William Fox Tomson, and *d* 19 July 1952

(2) Cecil Hanmer, Col 2nd Bn Connaught Rangers; *b* 12 Feb 1845; *m* 1st 12 Feb 1873 Susan Frances (*d* 6 Nov 1878), dau of Gen William Craig Emilius Napier (*see* NAPIER AND ETTRICK, L); *m* 2nd 9 Sept 1897 May Lennox (*d* 15 April 1914), dau of Thomas Atkins, of Chepstow, and *dsp* 22 Dec 1909

(3) Robert Clement Sconce, BA Cantab, barrister; *b* 19 Jan 1847; *m* 9 Aug 1888 Elizabeth Anne (*d* 5 April 1933), er dau of John Henry Barnes, and *d* 10 Dec 1930, leaving issue:

1a May Marjorie; *b* 12 Feb 1892

2a Cecily Mary; *b* 2 March 1901

(4) Herbert Napier (Sir), KCB (1911), Maj-Gen RA Boer War 1899–1900; *b* 15 Feb 1851; *m* 8 Aug 1878 Mary Louisa (*d* 13 Oct 1938), dau of Maj Donald Patrick Campbell, of Balliveolan, Argyll, and *d* 18 Jan 1922, having had issue:

1a Patrick Stanley St Pierre, Lt Suffolk Regt; *b* 1879; *ka* 19 Dec 1916

2a Richard Seymour, DSO (1918), Lt-Col RA WW I (despatches thrice); *b* 19 Sept 1880; *m* 23 Jan 1928 Edith Beatrice Craufurd, syt dau of Col W Craufurd Kennedy, Roy Scots, and *dsp* 3 Sept 1955

3a Evan Campbell, Cdr RN WW I (despatches twice, Croix de Guerre with Palms, Order SS. Maurice and Lazarus Italy); *b* 1881; drowned on active service 16 Oct 1918

(1) Louisa Harriet Cometina; *m* 26 March 1874 Dr Max Marckwald, of Heidelberg and Berlin, and had issue

Sir Henry *m* 2nd 22 Sept 1830 Emily Louisa Augusta (*d* 18 March 1863), dau of Col Hon George Napier by Lady Sarah Lennox (*see* above), dau of 2nd Duke of Richmond, and *d* 13 April 1860

The 9th Bt's n,

Sir Henry Charles John Bunbury, 10th Bt, DL Suffolk, High Sheriff 1908, RN; *b* 9 Jan 1855; *educ* Magdalene Coll Cambridge (BA); *m* 11 March 1884 Laura Lavinia (*d* 14 Aug 1938), 3rd dau of Gen Thomas Wood, MP, of Littleton, Middx, and Gwernyfed Park, Brecon, and had issue:

1 CHARLES HENRY NAPIER (Sir), **11th Bt**

2 Henry William, WW I: Capt Suffolk Regt (SR), attd RAF 1918–19; *b* 1889; *educ* Eton and Trin Hall Cambridge; *m* 24 Aug 1918 Katherine Margaret (*d* 9 July 1951), only dau of R A Murray, and *dsp* 26 June 1956

1 Cecilia Frances Laura; *m* 19 April 1904 Hugh Sydney Marsham-Townshend, er s of Hon Robert Marsham-Townshend, DL, and *d* 30 Nov 1912, leaving issue (*see* ROMNEY, E)

2 Laura Constance Elinor, OBE (1945), Sr Cmdt ATS WW II; *m* 1913, as his 2nd w, her bro-in-law Hugh Sydney Marsham-Townshend, and *d* 26 June 1950, leaving issue (*see* ROMNEY, E)

Sir HENRY *d* 18 Dec 1930; his er son,

Sir Charles Henry Napier Bunbury, 11th Bt, DL, JP Suffolk, High Sheriff 1936, chm E Suffolk QS, Lt Coldstream Gds (SR) and Roy Wilts Yeo WW I; *b* 19 Jan 1886; *m* 12 Aug 1914 Katherine (*d* 25 Sept 1965), yst dau of Herbert Edward Reid, and had issue:

1 JOHN WILLIAM NAPIER (Sir), **12th Bt**

1 *Margaret Elinor [Mrs James Tomkin, The Red House, Wissett, Halesworth, Suffolk]; *b* 1918; *m* 11 Sept 1945 *Lt-Col James Michael Heigham Royce Tomkin, MC, DL, 5th Roy Inniskilling Dragoon Gds, s of Lt-Col Royce Tomkin, and has issue:

(1) *Alastair Peter Royce; *b* 1949

(2) *Richard James Royce; *b* 1951

(1) *Caroline Susan; *b* 1947; *m* 1st 1967 (*divorce* 1976) Julian Dixon, of Grantham, Lincs; *m* 2nd 1977 *Hon David Peter Brougham (*see* BROUGHAM AND VAUX, B)

2 Pamela; *d* unm 9 Dec 1941

Sir CHARLES *d* 24 June 1963; his only son,

Sir (John) William Napier Bunbury, 12th Bt; *b* 3 July 1915; *educ* Eton and Jesus Coll Cambridge; High Sheriff Suffolk 1972, Capt 60th Rifles WW II; *m* 28 Nov 1940 *Margaret Pamela [Margaret Lady Bunbury, 9 Lee Rd, Aldeburgh, Suffolk IP15 5HG], er dau of Thomas Alexander Sutton, of Westlecott Manor, Swindon, Wilts (*see* SUTTON, Bt), and *d* 1985, having had issue:

1 Peter Charles Napier; *b* 26 Nov 1941; *educ* Eton and RMA Sandhurst; *d* following a car crash 26 Aug 1964

2 Sir MICHAEL WILLIAM BUNBURY, **13th and present Bt**

3 Charles Thomas; *b* 4 May 1950; *educ* Radley and RAC Cirencester; *m* 1st 1971 (*divorce* 1985) Sarah Elizabeth, er dau of William Hancock, of Sherborne Hall, King's Lynn, Norfolk, and has issue:

(1) *Emma Sarah; *b* 24 May 1973

(2) *Rebecca Louise; *b* 14 May 1974

(3) *Venetia Alice; *b* 1978

3 (cont.) Charles Bunbury *m* 2nd 1986 *Amanda Carol [Mrs Charles Bunbury, 22 Balham Park Rd, London SW12 8DU], yr dau of John Richard Daniel Green (*see* BICESTER, B), and *d* 4 Nov 1997 leaving by her:

(1) +James William Rufus; *b* 1989

(2) +Dominic John Frederick; *b* 1990

(4) *Augusta Jane; *b* 1991

4 +Christopher Henry (twin) [Christopher Bunbury Esq, 5 The Benthills, Thorpness, Suffolk]; *b* 4 May 1950; *educ* Radley; *m* 1988 *Mrs Amanda M B Greenwell, er dau of H E R Stewart, MC, of Paulton's Sq, SW3, and formerly w of Timothy Smallwood

BURBIDGE

Arms: Arg. a chevron sa. between in chief two gads ppr. and in base a unicorn of the second. **Crest:** A stag's scalp, between the attires a boar's head erased and erect, all ppr. **Motto:** *Labor omnia vincit* ('Labour conquers all things'). **Creation:** Bt. (UK) 25 Jan 1916.

SIR HERBERT DUDLEY BURBIDGE, 5TH BT, of Littleton Park, Co Middlesex [Sir Herbert Burbidge Bt, 3809 W 24th Ave, Vancouver, BC V6S 1LD, Canada]; *b* 13 Nov 1904; *s* kinsman 1974; *educ* University Sch Victoria BC; with Harrods 1929–31, R P Clarke (stock brokers) Vancouver BC 1929–31, merchandising manager Silverwood Industries of Vancouver BC 1931–70, pres: Vancouver Exec Club 1942, Vancouver Sales Exec Club 1948, memb bd referees Workmen's Compensation Bd 1943–61; *m* 1933 Ruby Bly (*d* 1994), dau of Charles Ethelbert Taylor, of Vancouver, and has issue:

1 +PETER DUDLEY [Peter Burbidge Esq, 3809 W 24th Ave, Vancouver, BC, Canada]; *b* 20 June 1942; *m* 16 June 1967 *Peggy Marilyn, dau of Kenneth Anderson, of Ladner, BC, and has issue:

(1) +John Peter; *b* 1975

(1) *Kathleen Jean; *b* 1973

Lineage: JOHN BURBAGE, of Milton, E Knoyle, Wilts, living 1507–08, held land at Goodrigg; had:

JOHN BURBAGE, of Milton, living *c* 1529; *m* Ellen, dau of John Goddard, of Sedghill, Wilts (*bur* 7 April 1578) and *d* between 30 Aug and 6 Oct 1558, having had, with five yr sons and two daus:

JOHN BURBAGE, of Sherrington, Wilts; *m* Joane and *d* by 3 May 1599, leaving, with two other sons and two daus:

JOHN BURBIDGE, of Keevil, Wilts; *m* 25 May 1603 Mary Jeffery, of Keevil (*bur* 5 Oct 1658) and was *bur* 8 Aug 1637, having had, with four yr sons and three daus:

JOHN BURBIDGE, of Bulkington, Keevil; *bapt* 27 Jan 1603/4; *m* 1st 27 Sept 1629 Agnes Harroll (*bur* 3 Jan 1654/5) and had four sons and two daus; *m* 2nd 24 May 1655 Alice Jeffery, of Bulkington, and by her had, with an est and yst s:

ELIAS BURBIDGE, of Bulkington; *b* 24 Oct 1657; *m* Anne — (*bur* 22 Dec 1714) and was *bur* 30 Sept 1720, having had, with two er and four yr sons and three daus:

ROGER BURBIDGE, of Bulkington; *bapt* 28 July 1689; *m* Grace — (*bur* 16 Feb 1759) and was *bur* 15 Aug 1759, having had, with six er sons and three daus:

ELIAS BURBIDGE, of Bulkington; *bapt* 4 April 1732; *m* Sarah — (*d* 24 March 1775) and *d* 18 Jan 1789, having had, with an er s and four daus:

ANDREW BURBIDGE, of Bulkington; *bapt* 30 Nov 1765; *m* 19 Jan 1792 Sarah Stiles (*bur* 6 Aug 1840 aged 70) and *d* 18 Oct 1829, having had, with an est and two yr sons:

GEORGE BISHOP BURBIDGE, of S Wraxall and Hinton, Wilts; *bapt* 22 Sept 1795; *m* 1st 29 Sept 1830 Sarah Porter, of Seend, Wilts (*dsp* 26 Feb 1832 aged 41); *m* 2nd 29 Aug 1839 Elizabeth (*d* 1 March 1873 aged 62), dau of Richard Clarke, of Monkton Farleigh, Wilts, and had, with other issue:

1 Charles; *b* 2 June 1840; *m* 12 Jan 1868 Sarah Cape (*d* 23 June 1927), dau of George Cuff, of Rushall, Wilts, and *d* 10 Sept 1894, leaving three sons and four daus

2 Edward, of Wraxall, Wilts; *b* 29 June 1845; *m* 12 June 1878 Eliza, dau of John Spencer, of W Lavington, Wilts, and *d* 12 July 1906, leaving an only child (Jane Spencer, *m* 6 Feb 1907 her cousin, Henry James Burbidge, of Good Hall, Ardleigh, Essex, and had issue)

3 RICHARD (Sir), **1st Bt**

4 Thomas, of Good Hall; *b* 12 Dec 1848; *m* 2 July 1874 Louisa (*d* 25 March 1909), dau of Charles Osborne, of Newlands Farm, Grittleton, Wilts, and had seven sons and a dau

1 Mary; *b* 15 Nov 1843; *m* 8 Nov 1876 Edward James Jolly Kingdom, of Bristol, and had issue

GEORGE BURBIDGE *d* 12 July 1861; his 4th son,

Sir Richard Burbidge, 1st Bt (UK), so *cr* 25 Jan 1916, of Littleton, Middx, JP Co London, Ld Manors Littleton and Astlam, Tstee Crystal Palace, dir Hudson's Bay Co, md Harrods 1890–1917; *b* 2 March 1847; *m* 1st 9 May 1868 Emily (*d* 31 Aug 1905), yst dau of Jeremiah Woodman, of Melksham, Wilts, and had issue:

1 **Sir (Richard) Woodman Burbidge, 2nd Bt**, CBE (1919), chm: Harrods Ltd London, Harrods Ltd (Buenos Aires), S American Stores (Gath and Chaves) Dickins and Jones, D H Evans, memb Ctee Br Empire Mktg Bd, pres Incorporated Assoc Retail Distbrs 1928, Hon Treas Tariff Commn 1917–22, Cdr Order Leopold Belgium, Cross Romania; *b* 7 Dec 1872; *m* 2 Sept 1896 Catherine Jemina (*d* 15 Jan 1964 aged 91), dau of Henry Grant, of Sodbury Ho, Gt Clacton, Essex, and *d* 3 June 1945, leaving:

(1) **Sir Richard Grant Woodman Burbidge, 3rd Bt**, CBE (1946); *educ* Rugby; chm and md Harrods and Kendal Milne & Co (Manchester), chm: Dickins and Jones, D H Evans, John Walsh (Sheffield), Wm Henderson & Sons (Liverpool), J F Rockhey (Torquay), Rackhams (Birmingham) 1945–61, BHS; dir Maples, 3rd Civilian Memb Bd NAAFI 1941–52, pt-time memb LTE Br Tpt Commn 1947–49, Capt RASC WW I; *b* 23 June 1897; *m* 1st 14 Oct 1925 (*divorce* 1946) Gladys (*d* 1 Feb 1967), est dau of Charles Frederick Kearsley, and had:

1a **Sir John Richard Woodman Burbidge, 4th Bt**; *educ* Rugby; *b* 5 Oct 1930; *m* 12 June 1956 *Benita Roxane [Benita Lady Burbidge, Albury Farmhouse, Draycot, Oxon OX9 2LY], yst dau of Adriaan Willem Mosselmans, and *d* 1974, having adopted:

*Alexandra Louise; *b* 1970; *m* 27 April 1996 *Antony, yr s of John Abell (*see* BROWN, Bt), and has:

*Athena Madeline; *b* 30 Oct 1997

1a *Susan Woodman [Mrs Michael Pearson, Coach Hill Cottages, Burley St, Ringwood, Hants BH24 4HL]; *b* 15 May 1927; *m* 24 Sept 1949 *Michael Deric Lloyd Pearson, s of Deric Ernest William Pearson, and has:

1b *Robert Lloyd [Robert Pearson Esq, 1 Stoney Path, Shaftesbury, Dorset SP7 8HR]; *b* 10 May 1954

1b *Teresa Ann; *b* 5 Sept 1951; *m* 15 Dec 1973 *Derek Wakefield and has:

1c *Richard; *b* 17 April 1976

2c *Andrew; *b* 26 March 1978

3c *David; *b* 15 Jan 1981

2b *Kate Alexandra; *b* 6 June 1959; *m* 11 Aug 1995 *Marcus Peter Lowther Mortimer and has:

1c *Madeline Rose Pearson; *b* 3 Jan 1996

(1) (cont.) **Sir Richard** *m* 2nd 6 Dec 1946 Joan Elizabeth, dau of Ernest Reginald Moxey, of London, and formerly w of Leslie Montagu (Jack) Hamilton, and *d* 2 Feb 1966

(1) Enid Catherine Woodman; *b* 30 Nov 1902; *m* 21 April 1926 Capt Albert John Vernon Venables (*d* 27 Dec 1958), yr s of Frederick John Venables, and had issue:

1a *John Anthony Woodman, Capt RASC; *b* 24 Jan 1928; *educ* Bradfield and RMA Sandhurst; *m* 24 March 1956 *Hazel Margaret, dau of Ronald Leslie Harward, MB, BS, and has issue:

1b *Anthony Mark; *b* 20 Nov 1960

2b *Peter John Vernon; *b* 7 March 1964

1b *Margaret Anne Woodman; *b* 8 May 1962

1a *Jane Carol Woodman; *b* 29 May 1930

2a *Catherine Dawn Woodman; *b* 23 Jan 1933; *m* 1963 *H James Petherick and has issue

(2) Sylvia Emily Woodman; *b* 18 Oct 1906; *m* 1st 1 Feb 1934 (*divorce* 1948) Eric Macleod Mitchell, s of W H Mitchell; *m* 2nd 9 Sept 1948 Sir Roland Evelyn Turnbull, KCMG, s of George Turnbull, of Berwick-on-Tweed. He *d* 23 Dec 1960

(3) *Alva Grace Woodman [Mrs Gerald Holman, White Lodge, Elmstead Rd, W Byfleet, Surrey KT14 6JB]; *b* 28 Jan 1913; *m* 1 Oct 1935 Gerald Rudall Holman (*d* 4 Sept 1969), er s of Dr F Kay Holman, and has had issue:

1a Rodney Woodman; *b* 28 Jan 1942; *educ* Uppingham; *m* 1973 *Jill Andrew and *d* 1976

1a *Carol Woodman [Mrs John Beattie, Willow House, Blundel Lane, Cobham, Surrey KT11 2SP]; *b* 3 Dec 1938; *m* 3 June 1961 *John Humphrey Beattie, only s of Maj Walter Albert Beattie MC, and Mrs F J E Houghton, and has issue:

1b *Fiona Ann; *b* 25 May 1962; *m* 1987 *Philip Blood

2b *Nicola Jane; *b* 23 Jan 1966

2 Herbert Edward; *b* 13 March 1880; *m* 30 Sept 1902 Harriet Georgina (*d* 13 June 1952), dau of Henry Stewart Hamilton, of Castlerock, Londonderry, and *d* 25 April 1945, leaving:

(1) Sir HERBERT DUDLEY BURBIDGE, **5th and present Bt**

1 Emily Gertrude; *m* 3 Oct 1903 Allan Francis Hamilton, of Londonderry, and *d* Feb 1959. He *dsp* 2 June 1914

2 Marian; *m* 1 Nov 1902 Charles William Bracher and *d* 31 Dec 1939, leaving issue. He *d* 27 Sept 1933

3 Elizabeth Janet; *m* 7 Aug 1909 Robert Everett, of Barnes, SW, and *d* 14 Jan 1928. He *d* 31 July 1934

4 Edith Mary; *d* unm 20 Jan 1951

Sir Richard *m* 2nd 23 Aug 1910 Lilian (*d* 8 March 1955), yst dau of John Ambrose Precce, of Bartestree Court, Herefs, and *d* 31 May 1917

BURDEN

Creation: B. (UK) 1 Feb 1950.

THE 3RD BARON BURDEN, of Hazlebarrow, Co Derby (AndrewPhilip Burden) [The Rt Hon The Lord Burden, 13 Langham Drive, Taunton, Somerset TA1 4LJ]; *b* 20 July 1959; *s* f 1995

Lineage: THOMAS BURDEN, of Mile End, E London, Alderman Et Ham (Mayor 1935), had:

THOMAS WILLIAM BURDEN, **1st Baron Burden**, of Hazlebarrow, Co Derby (UK), so *cr* 1 Feb 1950, CBE (1948), JP (Essex); *b* 29 Jan 1885; *educ* LSE; memb Exec Ctee Rlwy Clerks Assoc 1916–32 and 1934–41, 2nd Church Estates Commr 1945–50, Ld-in-Waiting 1950–51, memb Ho Laity Church Assembly 1947, Church Commr and memb Bd of Govrs 1948, MP (Lab) Sheffield Park 1942–50; *m* 11 July 1910 Augusta, dau of David Sime, of Aberdeen, and *d* 27 May 1970, leaving issue:

1 PHILIP WILLIAM BURDEN, **2nd Baron Burden**, *b* 21 June 1916; *educ* Raines Fndn Sch; *m* 8 Sept 1951 *Audrey Elsworth [The Rt Hon The Lady Burden, 13 Langham Drive, Taunton, Domerset TA1 4LJ], dau of Maj Wilfred Elsworth Sykes, of Kirk Ella, Hull, and *d* 1995, leaving:

(1) ANDREW PHILIP BURDEN, **3rd and present Baron Burden**

(2) +Fraser William Elsworth; *b* 6 Nov 1964

(3) +Ian Stuart; *b* 24 Oct 1967

(1) *Carol Mary; *b* 30 June 1952

(2) *Corynne Lesley [The Hon Mrs Peters, Greenland, Royston Water, Churchinford, Taunton, Somerset TA3]; *b* 1 April 1955; *m* 1977 *William D-Day Peters, s of Leonard Thomas Peters, and has issue:

1a *Alexander; *b* 1983

1a *Lindsey Jane; *b* 1988

(3) *Adrienne Gail; *b* 22 Jan 1957

BURDETT

Arms: Paly of six arg and sa., on a bend gu. three martlets arg.
Crest: On a tower arg. a martlet rising or.
Creation: Bt. (E) 25 July 1665.

SIR SAVILE AYLMER BURDETT, 11TH BT, of Burthwaite, Co York [Sir Savile Burdett Bt, Farthings, 35 Park Ave, Solihull, W Midlands B91 3EJ]; *b* 24 Sept 1931; *s* f 1943; *educ* Wellington and Imperial Coll London (BSc Eng); late T/Sub Lt (E) RNVR, md Rapaway Energy Ltd; *m* 21 July 1962 *June Elizabeth Campbell, only dau of Dr James Mackay Rutherford, of Woking, and has issue:

1 +CRISPIN PETER; *b* 8 Feb 1967; *m* 1988 *Julia Winifred Gresham, yr dau of John Gresham Copeland, of Church Lawton, Cheshire

1 *Felicity Susan; *b* 30 Dec 1963

Lineage: FRANCIS BURDETT; *m* Elizabeth, dau of Sir Ferdinando Leigh, of Middleton, Yorks, and had:

Sir Francis Burdett, 1st Bt (E), so *cr* 25 July 1665; *bapt* 29 Sept 1642; *m* 21 Oct 1669 Frances Stephenson, of Lincs (*bur* 11 June 1679), and *d* 1719, leaving:

Sir Francis Burdett, 2nd Bt; *b* 2 Aug 1675; *m* 1st 31 July 1710 Elizabeth, dau and coheir of Charles Wyndham, of Stokesby, Norfolk, and widow of William Barnham, and was *bur* 11 Sept 1747, having had, with 13 other children:

1 **Rev Sir Hugh Burdett, 3rd Bt**, Rector Newington, Kent; *b* 18 Nov 1715; *dsp* 8 Sept 1760

2 **Sir Charles Burdett, 4th Bt**; *b* 22 May 1728; *m* 1st 29 Nov 1756 Jane (*d* 3 Sept 1764), dau of John Harrison, and had issue; *m* 2nd 26 Sept 1770 Sarah (*d* 1812), dau of Joseph Halsey and widow of — Phillips, of Boston, Mass., and *d* 19 July 1803, having by her had, with other issue:

(1) **Sir Charles Wyndham Burdett, 5th Bt**, Lt-Col; *b* 19 July 1771; *d* unm Colombo Ceylon Dec 1839

(2) George Saville, Maj; *b* 18 Aug 1774; *m* Sophia, dau of Col Wilkins, and was *k* with her and their child in the collapse of barracks during a hurricane on St Lucia 21 Oct 1817

3 Jerome, Army Capt; *b* 27 Sept 1778; *m* Elizabeth Bulleyn and *d* March 1817, leaving, with a dau:

1a **Sir Charles Wentworth Burdett, 6th Bt**, Offr HEIC's Militia; *b* 26 Dec 1806; *m* 31 Dec 1834 his cousin Harriet (*d* 21 July 1851), dau of William Hugh Burgess, and *d* 25 Aug 1848, having had, with two daus:

1b **Sir Charles Wentworth Burdett, 7th Bt**, Lt 52nd Regt; *b* 4 Nov 1835; *m* 4 April 1871 Grace, dau of Rev A Grant, of Napier, NZ, and *d* March 1890, leaving:

1c **Sir Charles Grant Burdett, 8th Bt**; *m* Annie, dau of R Hay, of Dunedin, NZ, and *d* 20 Nov 1918, leaving:

1d **Sir Charles Coventry Burdett, 9th Bt**; *b* 1902; *d* unm 2 June 1940

1d Frances; *b* 1904; *m* 1931 Anthony Lovat

2d *Constance Hay [Mrs Constance Burdett, 7 Kensington Heights, Campden Hill Rd, London W8 7BA]; *b* 1908; *m* 1938 (*divorce* 1952 resumed maiden name 1953) Albert Charles Blau, Swiss Dip Serv, and has issue:

1e *Charles Albert [Charles Burdett Esq, Roncal 7, 28002 Madrid, Spain]; *b* 1942; *m* 1977 *Christina L, dau of Jost E von Kursell, and has issue.

1f *(Charles) Nicholas Wentworth; *b* 28 Nov 1978

2f *Andrew James Hay; *b* 9 Jan 1983

1f *Alexandra Christina Coutts; *b* 10 June 1981

2e *John Coventry [John Burdett Esq, 11 Lawn Crescent, Kew, Surrey TW9 3N12]; *b* 1945; *m* 1970 *Judith Lisle Folkes and has issue:

1f *Edward Charles Coventry; *b* 13 July 1974

1f *Camilla Rose Sanderson; *b* 28 Oct 1984

1c Angelina Coutts; *b* 8 June 1873; *d* unm 1 Aug 1967

2b William Jerome (Rev), MA Oxon, Mil Chaplain Bengal Ecclesiastical Estab 1870–91, Rector W Wolverton Bath 1894–97; *b* 10 Dec 1841; *m* 20 Nov 1871 Eliza Katharine (*d* 24 Jan 1926), dau of Rev Joseph Theophilus Toye, MA, Vicar St David's, Exeter, and *d* 15 Oct 1899, leaving, with other issue:

1c HENRY AYLMER (Sir), **10th Bt**

2c Ernest Wyndham, DSO, MC; *b* 5 Sept 1887; *educ* King's Sch Bruton; Lt-Col IA WW I (despatches); *m* 17 Nov 1919 Hebe Etheldreda Ellen Curwen (*d* 18 March 1967), only dau of Lt-Col Gilbert Robert Henry Collis, and *d* 13 Sept 1962, leaving issue:

1d Arlingham Jerome D'Arcy; *b* 22 Dec 1922; *m* 17 April 1948 *Elizabeth Alix [Mrs Elizabeth Burdett, Birch Piece, Milland, Liphook, Hants], er dau of Sir Charles Holditch Bristow, CIE, of Brinton Grange, Melton Constable, Norfolk, and *d* 29 Nov 1995, leaving:

1e +Jeremy Francis D'Arcy; *b* 11 Jan 1951; *educ* Uppingham; *m* 1976 *Jacqueline Elizabeth Mary, dau of Ian Corner, and has issue:

1f +Daniel Ian Jerome; *b* 1977

1f *Lucy Joanna; *b* 1979

2f *Jenny Alix; *b* 1983

2e +Richard Wyndham; *b* 10 March 1962; *educ* Uppingham; Lt Cdr RN; *m* 1994 *Ann Marie Margaret, dau of James Buchanan Wellwood, and has had:

1f Matthew; *b* and *d* 1996

1e *Susan Priscilla [Mrs John Manley, 10 Loughborough Rd, Bunny, Nottingham NG11 6QA]; *b* 2 March 1949; *m* 1973 *John Patrick Manley and has had issue:

1f Robert George; *b* and *d* 1980

2f *Edward John; *b* 1981

1f *Anna Louise; *b* 1976

2f *Katherine Elizabeth; *b* 1984

2e *Marion Elizabeth; *b* 26 Nov 1953; *educ* RNS Haslemere and Bristol U

1d Elizabeth Sylvia; *b* 23 Jan 1921; *m* 2 Jan 1964 John L Duffus, est s of Capt J L L Duffus, and *d* 1984

1c Beatrice Mary; *m* 7 Aug 1902 Rev Charles Robert Loraine McDowall, Vicar Brabourne, Headmaster King's Sch Canterbury, Assist Master Eton, est s of Rev Charles McDowall, DD, Headmaster Highgate Sch, Preb St Paul's, and *d* 3 Dec 1961, leaving issue. He *d* 14 Oct 1950

2c Katherine Hilda; *d* 19–

3c Marion Edith; *d* unm 27 Sept 1971 aged 87

The 9th Bt's cousin,

Sir Henry Aylmer Burdett, 10th Bt, MC, Capt 11th Bn Essex Regt WW I (wounded); *b* 28 Nov 1881; *m* 17 Feb 1928 Audrey Grace Chichester, only dau of George Cutliffe, and *d* 23 Aug 1943, having had issue:

1 Sir SAVILE AYLMER BURDETT, **11th and present Bt**

1 Anne Margaret; *b* 4 April 1929; *d* 19–

2 *Jennifer Joyce [Mrs Donald Wise, 304 Bexhill Rd, St Leonards-on-Sea, Sussex]; *b* 15 Feb 1934; *m* 1st 30 March 1957 Marian Stachowiak; *m* 2nd 1970 Gordon Skinner; *m* 3rd 19– *Donald Wise and has by her 1st husb:

(1) *Nicholas John; *b* 1959

(2) *Martin Allen; *b* 1961

(1) *Sarah Margaret; *b* 1957

BURGH

Arms: Quarterly, 1st and 4th grand quarters, or a cross-crosslet fitchée sa. between three crescents in chief and as many fusils in base barways gu., all within a bordure az. (for LEITH); 2nd, az. three fleurs-de-lys erm. (for BURGH); 3rd, quarterly, 1st and 4th, or a lion rampant az., armed and langued gu. (for PERCY), 2nd and 3rd, paly of six or and sa. (for STRABOLGI). **Crests:** 1 A cross-crosslet fitchée sa. (for LEITH), 2 A falcon arg., beaked, legged and ducally gorged or (for BURGH). **Supporters:** On either side a stag az., charged with three fleurs-de-lys erm. in pale. **Mottoes:** 1 (over the crest) Trustie to the end, 2 With God's help. **Creation:** B. (E) 2 Dec 1529.

THE 7TH BARON BURGH (Alexander Peter Willoughby Leith) [The Rt Hon The Lord Burgh, House of Lords, London SW1A 0PW]; *b* 20 March 1935; *s f* 1959; *educ* Harrow and Magdalene Coll Cambridge (BA 1958, MA 1966, MSc 1966); RAF 1953–55; *m* 1st 29 Aug 1957 (*divorce* 1982) Anita Lorna, novelist (as Anita Burgh), dau of Frederick Clements Eldridge, of Gillingham, Kent; *m* 2nd 1984 *Wilma —, and by his 1st w has:

1 +(ALEXANDER) GREGORY DISNEY; *b* 16 March 1958; *educ* St Catherine's Athens, St John's Coll Cambridge and Brockwood Pk Hants; *m* 1984 *Catherine Mary, dau of David Parkes, of The Old Rectory, Wrighton, Bristol, and has:

(1) +Alexander James Strachan; *b* 11 Oct 1986

2 +Patrick Simon Vincent; *b* 16 April 1964; *educ* Comberton Village Coll Cambridge

1 *Rebecca Moraigh Eveleigh [The Hon Rebecca Leith, 66 Cumberland Rd, Spike Island, Bristol BS1 6UF]; *b* 17 Dec 1959; has resumed maiden name; *m* 9 Dec 1979 (*divorce* 1983) David K O Brandler, est s of J L Brandler

Barony of Burgh: A subsidiary title to the Earldom of Lonsdale (*qv*; preliminary remarks) of the 1784 creation was that of 'Baron of the Barony of Burgh'. It expired with the Earldom in 1802 (the current Earldom of Lonsdale is a revival, made five years later). An assertion by the peerage antiquary Sir William Dugdale that Ulick Bourke or de Burgh, only son of the 4th Earl of Clanricarde (*see* SLIGO, M), was called up to the House of Lords in his father's lifetime as Baron Bourke or Burgh has been shown to be false.

Lineage (of Burgh): THOMAS BOROUGH/BURGH; *m*, as her 1st husb, Elizabeth, dau and coheir of Sir Henry Percy (*see* NORTHUMBERLAND, D, and STRABOLGI, B), through whom he acquired the manor of Gainsborough, Lincs, and had:

Sir THOMAS BURGH, KG (*c* 1484); *b c* 1431; MP Lincs 1467 and 1478, called 1 Sept 1487 to Parl by writ such that he has been deemed to have been *cr* LORD (Baron) BURGH, though in other contemporary records he is not referred to as a peer; *m* May 1462–64 Margaret (*d* 10 Dec 1488), dau of 6th Lord (Baron) De Ros (*qv*) of Helmsley, and widow of 3rd Lord (Baron) Botreaux (*see* LOUDOUN, E), and had, with other issue:

1 EDWARD

1 Elizabeth; *m* 1st by 21 May 1481 7th Lord (Baron) FitzHugh (*d* 20 Nov 1487); *m* 2nd, as his 2nd w, Sir Henry Willoughby (*d* 1528), of Wollaton, Notts, and Middleton, Warwicks, and *d* 1 Aug 1507

2 Margaret; *m* as his 1st w Sir George Tailboys, *de jure* 9th Lord (Baron) Kyme, and *d* by April 1493

Sir THOMAS (LORD(?)) BURGH *d* 18 March 1495/6; his s,

Sir EDWARD BURGH, (?)2nd LORD (Baron) BURGH(?); *b c* 1463; MP Lincs 1492; a lunatic who was never called to Parl; *m* 1477 Anne, deemed by later doctrine to have been *de jure* Baroness Cobham, widow of 2nd Lord (Baron) Mountjoy and dau of Sir Thomas Cobham, of Sterborough, Surrey, and *d* 26 June 1526), dau and heir of Sir Thomas Cobham, of Sterborough, deemed by the same later doctrine to have been *de jure* Lord Cobham (*see* COBHAM, V, preliminary remarks), and *d* 20 Aug 1528, leaving, with a yr s (Henry, *m* Catherine, dau of Sir Ralph Nevill(e), and had a dau Anne, *m* Richard Vaughan):

THOMAS BURGH, **1st Lord** (Baron) **Burgh** (E), so *cr* by writ 2 Dec 1529, though made out to LORD BOROUGH DE GAYNESBORO (a later writ of 26 April 1539 was, however, to 'Thomas Bourgh' and the slight variation of this brought about by dropping the 'o' is the version in use today); *b c* 1488; ktd 1513, Sheriff Lincs 1518–19 and 1524–25; *m* 1st 1496 Agnes, dau of Sir William Tyrwhitt (*see* BERNERS, B); *m* 2nd Alice (*d* betwen 25 March 1558 and 1559), dau of William London and widow of (a) Sir Thomas Bedingfeld and (b) Edmund Rokewood, and *d* 28 Feb 1549/50, having had, with a yst s (Henry, of Stowe, Lincs, *m* Elizabeth, dau of Richard Constantine, of Bewdley, Salop, and was ancestor of the BURGHs of Stowe) and several daus:

1 Edward (Sir); *m c* 1529 Katharine (*m* 2nd 1533 John Nevill, Lord (Baron) Latymer (*d* 2 March 1542/3; *qv*); *m* 3rd 12 July 1543 HENRY VIII; *m* 4th 3 March 1546/7 Thomas, Lord Seymour of Sudeley, KG, and *d* 5 Sept 1584), dau of Sir Thomas Parr, of Kendal, and *dsp* & *vp*

2 Thomas (Sir); *m* Elizabeth, dau of Sir David Owen, and left issue, bastardised by Act of Parl 1542/3 since they were born well after Sir Thomas's death

3 WILLIAM BURGH, **2nd Lord** (Baron) **Burgh**; *b c* 1522; *m* Katharine (*bur* 14 Aug 1621), dau of 1st Earl of Lincoln (*qv*), and *d* 10 Sept 1584, having had, with other issue (including a yr s John (Sir), Adml, ktd 1586, *k* in a duel by John Gilbert 7 March 1594 aged 52):

(1) Henry; *dsp k* in a duel by — Holcroft Jan 1578

(2) THOMAS BURGH, **3rd Lord** (Baron) **Burgh**, KG (1593); *b c* 1558; Govr Brill, Flanders, 1587–97, Ld Dep Ireland 1597; *m* Frances (*bur* 19 July 1647), dau of John Vaughan, of Sutton-on-Derwent, Yorks, and *d* 14 Oct 1597, having had:

1a ROBERT BURGH, **4th Lord** (Baron) **Burgh**; *b c* 1594; *d* 26 Feb 1601/2, when the barony fell into abeyance between his sisters and coheirs

1a ELIZABETH, of whom presently

2a Anne; *m* 11 Oct 1604 Sir Drew Drury (*dsp* between 10 July 1618 and 7 Feb 1624/5) and *d* after 1 June 1641

3a Frances; *m* Francis Coppinger and had a descendant of W Drayton, Middx, who assumed the name De BURGH

4a Katherine; *m* 28 Feb 1619/20 Sir Thomas Knyvett and had issue (*see* BERNERS, B)

The est sis,

ELIZABETH Burgh, *m* 1st after 17 Jan 1598/9 George BROOKE, MA King's Coll Cambridge, Preb York (attainted and executed for high treason; *bur* 5 Dec 1603), 4th s of William, 10th Lord (Baron) Cobham (*see* 1970 edn); *m* 2nd by 24 Oct 1605 Francis Reade, 2nd s of Sir William Reade, of Osterleigh, Middx, and by her 1st husb had, with two daus (Frances, Elizabeth):

Sir WILLIAM BROOKE, KB (Feb 1625/6), of Sterborough and Cooling, Kent; *bapt* 1 Dec 1601; restored in blood 1609–10 but not to the barony of Cobham, MP Rochester 1628–29; *m* 1st Pembroke, dau of Henry, Lord (Baron) Dacre (*see* HAMPDEN, V), and had issue:

1 Pembroke; *bapt* 1 Oct 1626; *m* Sir Matthew Tomlinson, one of the regicides and a member of OLIVER CROMWELL's Ho of Lords, and *d* 10 June 1683, leaving two daus and coheirs. He *d* 5 Nov 1681

Sir WILLIAM *m* 2nd Penelope (*m* 3rd Edward Russell, bro of 1st Duke of Bedford (*qv*); *bur* 12 July 1694), dau of Sir Moyses Hill, of Hillsborough, Co Down (*see* DOWNSHIRE, M), and widow of Arthur Wilmot, and *d* 20 Sept 1643, when the barony of Cobham (already under attainder) fell into abeyance between his four daus and coheirs, having by her had:

2 HILL, of whom presently

3 Margaret; granted 19 May 1665 with her full sisters only rank of baron's daus; *m* 25 May 1665 Sir John Denham, KB (*d* 1669), the poet, Govr Farnham Castle 1642, and *dsp* 6 Jan 1666/7

4 Frances; *m* 1st by May 1665 Sir Thomas Whitmore (*bur* 21 May 1682), of Bueldas, Salop, s of Sir Thomas Whitmore, of Apley, and had three daus (including Frances, *b* 7 Nov 1666, *m* 2nd 1685 Sir Richard Middleton, 3rd Bt, of Chirk Castle); *m* 2nd Matthew Harvey (*dsp bur* 19 Jan 1693/4), of Twickenham, and was *bur* 1690

On the death of Mary Middleton in 1747 the issue of three of these coheirs expired and the representation of Sir WILLIAM BROOKE passed to the descendants of his 2nd dau,

HILL Brooke; *m c* 27 Dec 1657, as his 2nd w, Sir William BOOTHBY, 1st Bt (*qv*; *d* 24 March 1706/7), and had:

Sir WILLIAM BOOTHBY, 3rd Bt; had:

FRANCES Boothby; *bapt* 22 Nov 1693; *m c* 1 Sept 1715, as his 3rd w, William THORP, of St Peter's, Nottingham (*bur* 29 Dec 1746), and had:

MARY Thorp; *b* 25 Oct 1716; *m* 20 May 1736 Gervase DISNEY, BPh, of Nottingham and Pontefract (*d* 14 Nov 1786), and had, with other issue:

1 MARTHA, of whom presently

2 Harriot; *b* 4 Sept 1744; *m* 12 May 1768 Robert Alexander, of Halifax, Surgn, and was ancestor of 16th Lord (Baron) Cobham (*see* 1970 edn)

3 Lucy; *b* 19 April 1754; *m* 24 Feb 1787 Rev Thomas Lund, MA, Rector Barton-le-Street, and was ancestor of 11th Baron Strabolgi (*qv*)

Mrs GERVASE DISNEY *d* 17 Feb 1789; her est dau,

MARTHA Disney; *b* 7 March 1737; *m* 12 July 1763 Rev Robert Thorp (*d c* Aug 1815 aged 72), of Buxton, Derbys, and *d* 7 June 1806, leaving an est s:

ROBERT (William) DISNEY THORP, MD, of Headingley, Leeds; *bapt* 12 Nov 1766; *m* 7 Oct 1789 Ann Catherine (*d* 24 Jan 1827), dau of Gregory Grant, MD, of Edinburgh, by Maria, dau of Sir Archibald Grant, Bt (*see* GRANT, Bt, of Cullen), and was *bur* 5 July 1849, having had, with other issue:

1 Ven Thomas, Archdeacon Bristol, Rector Kemerton, Dean, Sr Tutor and Fell Trin Coll Cambridge; *b* 4 March 1797; *bur* 2 March 1877

2 Disney Launder, of Prestbury and Cheltenham, Glos, MD Cantab; *b* 8 June 1805; *m* 11 Nov 1835 Eleanor, dau of Francis Chorley, of Woodhouse, Leeds, and *dsp* 20 Dec 1888

1 MARIA, of whom presently

2 Mary Ann; *b* 25 Aug 1792; *m* 14 Feb 1820 Maj-Gen Henry Charles Russell, RA (*d* between 3 Jan 1857 and 19 March 1860), and *d* 15 May 1828, having had, with other issue:

(1) Thomas Francis Jeken, Capt 43rd Madras NI; *b* 1 May 1828; *m* 28 Feb 1861 Emma Louisa, dau of R J P Byde, Vicar Bengeo, Herts, and was *bur* 22 Dec 1865, leaving, with a dau:

1a John Francis Byde; *b* 17 Dec 1863; living 1915

The er dau,

MARIA Thorp; *b* 7 June 1791; *m* 13 Feb 1816 Gen Sir Alexander LEITH, KCB (*m* 2nd March 1841 Mary (*d* 20 Dec 1883), dau and coheir of Roderick Mackenzie, of Glack, and *d* 19 Feb 1859), of Freefield and Glenkindie, Aberdeenshire, Col 31st Foot, and *d* 2 Aug 1834, having had, with other issue:

1 Alexander, of Freefield and Glenkindie, DL, JP, memb Roy Co Archers, advocate Scotland; *b* 19 Dec 1817; *educ* Trin Coll Cambridge (MA); *m* 17 Aug 1843 Mary Anna (*d* 17 Nov 1900), only dau of Gen Sir Alexander Halkett, KH, s of Sir John Wedderburn Halkett, 4th Bt, and *d* 14 July 1886, leaving:

(1) Georgiana, of Freefield by Insch, Aberdeenshire; *b* 29 June 1844; *d* unm 21 April 1907

2 ROBERT WILLIAM DISNEY, of Glenkindie, *s* his bro

3 James, VC, Maj Scots Greys and 14th Hus; *b* 26 May 1826; *m* 8 Sept 1863 Isabella (*m* 2nd 6 April 1876 Col Hon John Scott Napier, CMG (*d* 9 March 1938), 2nd son of 10th Lord Napier and Ettrick (*qv*); *d* 12 Nov 1928), yr dau of Thomas Shaw, of Ditton, Lancs, and *d* 13 May 1869, leaving:

(1) Isabella Mary; *d* unm 6 April 1955

(2) Maria Caroline; *m* 28 July 1894 Brig James Dayrolles Crosbie, CMG, DSO, DL, of Ballyheigue Castle, Co Kerry, and *d* 17 March 1960, leaving issue. He *d* 18 Dec 1947

(3) Elizabeth Ann; *m* 5 Aug 1891 Walter Garden Duff, 4th s of Garden William Duff, of Hatton, and *d* 1943, having had issue. He *d* 1945

4 Thomas, of Pitmathen, Aberdeenshire, DL, JP, Maj Bombay Staff Corps, served Multan 1848–49, Persia 1857, Indian Mutiny 1858; *b* 1830; *m* 30 July 1874 Lady Mary Isabella Dalzell (*d* 5 Feb 1936), sis of 14th Earl of Carnwath (*see* 1940 edn), and *d* 30 Feb 1920, leaving issue:

(1) Alexander Robert, OBE (1919), DL, JP Aberdeenshire, Maj KRRC, Boer War 1899–1902, WW I (wounded), Croix de Guerre with palms, White Eagle of Serbia 4th Cl with Swords, Legn Honour, Sacred Treasure Japan, Wen Hu China; *b* 22 Feb 1878; *m* 7 Jan 1905 Hon Alexandra Gladys Vivian (*d* 17 July 1966), dau of 1st Baron Swansea (*qv*), and *d* 13 May 1950, leaving issue:

1a Patrick Thomas Vivian, Maj KRRC WW II, UN: NYC 1945–59, Dep Ch Personnel Div European Off Geneva 1959–67; *b* 18 April 1910; *educ* Eton; *m* 18 Oct 1943 Anne Rosemary Louise (*d* 11 Aug 1959), only dau of Col Henry William Mirehouse, MBE, and *d* 21 Sept 1967, leaving issue:

1b +Alexander Richard; *b* 13 May 1950; *educ* Millfield

1b +Meryan Patricia Louise; *b* 16 Sept 1944; *m* Charles B Lee, of 26 Chester St, SW1,

1a +Alba Gladys Ivy, MBE (1953); *b* 31 Oct 1905; *m* 1 March 1934 Capt Patrick Maynard Colchester-Wemyss, TD, RE (TA), yr s of Sir Maynard Francis Colchester-Wemyss, KBE. He *d* 7 Dec 1963

(2) Thomas Jeffrey, OBE, Maj; *b* 7 Nov 1883; *m* 1st 1913 Olga Renfrew, only dau of Edward Schwartz, of Drammen, Norway; *m* 2nd — and *d* 24 July 1969, leaving by his 1st w:

1a +Philip Edward Meric, DFC (1942), S/Ldr RCAF WW II; *b* 19 June 1914; *educ* Eton, U of BC (BSA and B Com 1949) and U of Alberta (MSc 1952)

1a +Thelma Olga, Subaltern ATS (MT) 1939–46; *b* 14 March 1916; *m* 4 May 1946 Capt Jack Murray Wall, RTR, only s of Frederick Murray Wall, of London, and has issue:

1b +Richard Murray; *b* 17 Oct 1948

2b +Thomas Ian Michael; *b* 20 Oct 1954

1b +Elizabeth Jane; *b* 23 March 1947; *m* 1 March 1969 Brian George Townsend, of 41 Rossal Rd, Greendale, Zimbabwe, only s of George Townsend

2b +Susan Margaret; *b* 10 Aug 1951

(1) Evelyn Mary Amelia; *m* 27 Nov 1909 Lt-Col Percy Robert Clifton, CMG, DSO, 2nd s of Sir Hervey Juckes Lloyd Bruce, 4th Bt, of Downhill (*qv*), and *d* 6 Jan 1969 aged 92, leaving issue

(2) Marjorie Edith, CBE; *m* 23 June 1906 Maj Charles Legge Eustace Robertson-Eustace, DSO, of Robertstown, and *d* 19 Oct 1957. He *d* 4 Oct 1908

1 Ann Katherine; *m* 5 April 1842 Alexander Innes of Raemoir and Cowie, Kincardineshire, and *d* 9 Jan 1908, leaving issue (*see* INNES, Bt, of Balvenie)

2 Mary Sarah; *m* 1857 Robert Francis Ogilvie Farquharson, DL (*d* 3 May 1890), of Haughton and Balfluig, Aberdeenshire, and *d* 1880, leaving issue

Lady LEITH's 2nd s,

Gen ROBERT WILLIAM DISNEY LEITH, CB, of Glenkindie and Westhall, Aberdeenshire, served Persian Gulf 1838–41, Multan 1849 (lost arm), Indian Mutiny 1857–58; *b* 28 Feb 1819; *m* 14 June 1865 Mary Charlotte Julia (*d* 21 Feb 1926), dau and heir of Sir Henry Percy Gordon, 2nd Bt, of Northcourt, by Lady Mary Agnes Blanche, dau of 3rd Earl of Ashburnham, and had issue:

1 ALEXANDER HENRY, **5th Lord**

1 Mary Levina; *d* unm 12 April 1964

2 Maria Alice; *m* 11 Oct 1898 Capt Sir Maynard Francis Colchester Wemyss, KBE, DL, JP, of Wendover, Cheltenham, Glos, and *d* 7 Dec 1940, leaving issue. He *d* 28 Feb 1954

3 Edith; *m* 20 April 1901 Col Sir Thomas Algernon Earle, 4th Bt (*qv*), and *d* 20 July 1963, leaving issue

4 Elizabeth Charlotte; *d* 10 Feb 1939

Gen ROBERT LEITH *d* 20 June 1892; his est son,

ALEXANDER HENRY LEITH, **5th Lord** (Baron) **Burgh** (found sr coheir 1915, abeyance in barony terminated in his favour 1916, called to Ho of Lds by writ 5 May 1916), JP (Aberdeenshire and Hants), DL (Aberdeenshire and IoW), Lt-Col cmdg 3rd Bn Gordon Highrs, Garrison Cdr Aberdeen WW I, Lt Welch Regt Nile 1888–89; *b* 27 July 1866; *m* 1st 1893 Mildred Katherine (*d* 6 April 1894), dau of Maj-Gen Stuart James Nicholson, CB, RA, and had issue:

1 Mildred Katherine

The **5th Lord** *m* 2nd 15 Oct 1902 Phyllis (*d* 6 Oct 1972), yst dau of Col Mark Henry George Goldie, RE, and by her had issue:

1 ALEXANDER LEIGH HENRY, **6th Lord**

2 John Disney; *b* 10 Aug 1909; *educ* Wellington; *m* 2 June 1938 *Mona, dau of C R Simpson, and was *k* in a car crash 15 Dec 1968, having had issue:

(1) James Alexander John; *b* 8 Oct, *d* 19 Dec 1942

2 Eveleigh Julia

The 5th LORD *d* 19 Aug 1926; his er son,

ALEXANDER LEIGH HENRY LEITH, **6th Lord** (Baron) **Burgh**, 2nd Lt 1st Bn Black Watch; *b* 16 May 1906; *m* 1st 6 June 1934 (*divorce* 1943) Elizabeth Rose, dau of Arthur Ross Vincent CBE, and *d* 26 May 1959, having had:

1 ALEXANDER PETER WILLOUGHBY LEITH, **7th and present Lord** (Baron) **Burgh**

The **6th Lord** *m* 2nd 19 May 1947 *Joyce Watts [Mrs Rupert Westmacott, Little Roding, 35 Combeland Rd, Alcombe, Minehead, Somerset] (*m* 2nd 14 June 1960 Rupert Walter Westmacott, s of Rev Canon Walter Westmacott), 2nd dau of William Wilson Wilson, of Hoylake, Cheshire, and by her had issue:

2 +John Barnabas [The Hon John Leith, 24 Gardiner Close, Abingdon, Oxon OX14 3YA]; *b* 27 Dec 1947; *educ* Wellington and Exeter U; *m* 18 July 1970 *Erica Jane, dau of David M Lewis, of Winchester, and has issue:

(1) +Alexander David Kalimat; *b* 13 July 1973

(2) +Thomas Magnus Abad; *b* 11 March 1976

(1) +Angharad Jane; *b* 21 Sept 1977

3 Thomas Disney; *b* 15 July 1951; *d* 16 March 1961

Lineage (of Leith): JAMES LEITH, of New Leslie; *m* Margaret, dau of Alexander Strachan, of Glenkindie, and had:

1 John, of Leith Hall

2 ALEXANDER, of Freefield and Glenkindie, Aberdeenshire; acquired dated 26 Jan 1702 the lands of Freefield and Bonnytoun from George Leith, of Freefield, and by a charter 26 Jan 1705 these and other lands were erected into the free Barony of Freefield; bought 1738 from his cousin Sir Patrick Strachan the lands and Barony of Glenkindie; *m* Christian, dau of Alexander Davidson, and *d* 1754 aged 90, leaving:

ALEXANDER LEITH, of Glenkindie, later Freefield; *m* 1st Jean, est dau of Alexander Gordon of Troup by Jean, dau of Sir Francis Grant, 1st Bt, of Moneymusk (*qv*), and had issue; *m* 2nd 7 Nov 1775 Martha (*d* 9 Oct 1777), dau and coheir of John Ross, of Arnage, and was ancestor of the LEITH-ROSSes of Arnage; his er son by his 1st w:

ALEXANDER LEITH, of Freefield and Glenkindie; *m* 1774 Mary Elizabeth, dau of James Gordon, of Cobairdy, by Mary, dau of 15th Lord Forbes (*qv*), and *d* 1828, having had issue:

Gen Sir Alexander LEITH, KCB (*see above*)

BURKE

Arms: Erminois a cross gu., in the first quarter a lion rampant sa. **Crest:** A cat-a-mountain sejant guardant ppr., collared and chained or. **Motto:** *Ung roy, ung foy, ung loy* ('One king, one faith, one law'). **Creation:** Bt. (I) 5 Dec 1797.

SIR JAMES STANLEY GILBERT BURKE, 9TH BT, of Marble Hill, Galway [Sir James Burke Bt, Lindenbergstrasse 231, CH-5618 Bettwil, Switzerland]; *b* 1 July 1956; *s* f 1980; *m* 1980 *Laura, dau of Domingo Branzuela, of Catmon, Cebu, Philippines, and has issue:

1 +MARTIN JAMES; *b* 22 July 1980

1 *Catherine Elizabeth; *b* 1982

Lineage: THOMAS BURKE McJONACK and RICHARD McEDMUND BURKE held lands in Creggeenmore by Sept 1617.

JONACK OGE McTHOMAS BURKE, who had also held lands there, was deprived of them 1641 following the Uprising of that year against the English.

THOMAS McJONACK BURKE; held lands in Creggeenmore and Gorteenagapoge; *k* (presumably fighting for JAMES II) during the Williamite wars Aug 1689, leaving, with two yr s:

THOMAS BURKE; was in 1747 leasing the lands forfeited by his f; *m* 1st *c* 1710 Julia, dau of James Tulley, of Gurnane, Co Galway, and had:

JOHN; *m* — (*d* 1768), widow of — Bodkin and 2nd dau of — Maughan, and *d* 1756; his only s:

JOHN BURKE, of Grallough; *b* 1713; renamed Creggeen Marble Hill; *m* by 16 Jan 1747/8 Mary, er dau and heir of Michael Carroll, of Killoran, Co Galway, and so acquired that estate; *d* 1793, leaving:

Sir Thomas Burke, 1st Bt (I), so *cr* 5 Dec 1797, of Marble Hill, Co Galway, JP; *m* April 1774 Christian (*d* 24 June 1833), dau of James Browne, of Limerick, and had, with other issue:

1 JOHN (Sir), **2nd Bt**

1 Maria; *m* 3 May 1794 Maurice Nugent O'Connor, of Mount Pleasant, King's Co, and had issue

2 Julia; *m* June 1797 Malachy Daly, of Raford, Co Galway, and had issue (*see* WESTMEATH, E)

3 Elizabeth; *m* 17 March 1799 13th Earl of Clanricarde (*see* SLIGO, M) and *d* 26 March 1854, leaving issue

4 Anne; *m* 23 April 1806 Sir Henry Tichborne, 8th Bt, and *d* 12 Aug 1853, leaving issue (*see* 1967 edn DOUGHTY-TICHBORNE, Bt)

5 Ellen; *m* 1st Feb 1804 Nicholas Browne (*d* 1816), of Mount Hazel, Co Galway, and had issue; *m* 2nd 17 July 1817 6th Viscount Strangford (*d* 29 May 1855) and *d* 26 Jan 1826, leaving issue (including the Young England-er George Smythe)

Sir THOMAS *d* 22 May 1813; his er son,

Sir John Burke, 2nd Bt, Col 98th Foot (raised by his f), MP Galway 1830–32, V-Lt Co Galway, High Sheriff 1838; *b* 1782; *m* 18 May 1812 Elizabeth Mary (*d* 27 Jan 1859), est dau of John Calcraft, PC, MP, of Remstone Hall, Dorset, and had, with other issue:

1 THOMAS JOHN (Sir), **3rd Bt**

2 Charles Granby, Master Court Common Pleas (I) 1852–82; *b* 14 Nov 1814; *m* 1st 20 June 1843 Emma Jane (*d* 8 April 1869), dau of Ralph Creyke, of Marton and Rawcliffe, Yorks, and had issue:

(1) Ulick Ralph, barrister, MA, Clerk Peace Co Dublin, author: *A History of Spain*; *b* 21 Oct 1845; *m* 9 July 1868 Katharine (*m* 2nd 11 Nov 1906 Rev John Richard Baldwin, Indian Chaplain (*d* 18 June 1912); *d* 24 June 1933), only dau of James Bateman, FRS, of Biddulph Grange and Knypersley Hall, Staffs, and *d* 18 July 1895, leaving issue:

1a Henry Ulick; *b* 6 Jan 1874; *m* 1st 4 Nov 1902 Rose Ellen Marian Antoinette Uvedale (*d* 4 June 1931), 3rd dau of Lt-Col Uvedale Edward Parry Parry-Okeden, of Turnworth, Dorset, and had issue:

1b Ulick Richard Samuel; *b* 11 Sept 1907; *educ* Sherborne; Lt-Col RM WW II; *m* 15 Feb 1930 *Cynthia Moya [Mrs Ulick Burke, 11 Ham Meadow, Marnhull, Sturminster Newton, Dorset, DT10 1LR], only dau of H Darling of Golders Green, and *d* 1963, leaving:

1c +Jeremy Ulick [Jeremy Burke Esq, 11 Ham Meadow, Marnhull, Sturminster Newton, Dorset, DT10 1LR]; *b* 17 Jan 1931; *educ* Univ Coll Wales; CEng, FICE, FIArb; *m* 1st 21 Sept 1954 (*divorce* 1962) Anne, est dau of J E Chinneck, of the Preparatory Ho, Berkhamsted Sch, Herts, and has issue:

1d +Ulick Simon; *b* 8 Feb 1957

1c (cont.) Jeremy Burke *m* 2nd 12 Jan 1963 *Prudence Mary, est dau of H P Stride, of Olveston, Bristol, and by her has issue:

1d *Ulick Jacquelyn; *b* 1964; *m* 2 Sept 1995 *James Shepherd and has:

1e *Matthew; *b* 28 Jan 1997

2d *Ulick Karen; *b* 1966; *m* 1 April 1995 *Robert Rose and has:

1e *Harry; *b* 16 June 1997

1e *Jenifer Karen Ulick; *b* 18 April 1996

2b John Okeden Ulick; *b* 5 May 1912; *d* 27 Dec 1920

1b Katrina Marian; *b* 20 Feb 1904; *m* 1st 13 Oct 1927 (*divorce* 1949) Guy Louis Beachim Beauchamp (*d* 1969), s of Louis Beachim Beauchamp; *m* 2nd 9 Jan 1950 Surgn-Cdr Francis William Armytage Fosbery, RN (*d* 1973), s of Dr Francis Clifford Fosbery, Freshford, nr Bath, and *d* July 1994, leaving by her 1st husb:

1c *John Louis; *b* 1930

1a (cont.) Henry Burke *m* 2nd 26 June 1934 Eva Mary (*d* 2 Sept 1964), dau of Thomas Foster, Priv Sec Admlty, and formerly w of Basil Hugh Stride, and *d* 22 Dec 1960

1a Mabel Emma; *m* 14 March 1901 Lt John Humphreys, RNR, and *d* 1954, leaving issue. He *d* 1954

2a Hope Katharine; *d* unm 29 June 1960

3a Sybil Mathilde; *m* 30 May 1911 Maj Wyndham Persse Knatchbull, RHA, only s of Col Francis Knatchbull, Norfolk Regt, and 5 Aug 1957, leaving issue (*see* BRABOURNE, B)

(2) Granby James, Priv Sec to Ld Chllr I, Assist-Examiner and Registrar High Court Justice I; *b* 19 Dec 1850; *educ* Trin Coll Dublin (MA); *m* 30 Nov 1888 Agnes Mary, dau of Very Rev A K H Boyd, DD, LLD, and *dsp* 25 Aug 1935

(1) Philippa Elizabeth; *m* 24 Jan 1871 Rev Franc Sadleir, Rector Newcastle Lyons, Hazlehatch, Co Dublin, s of Rev Ralph Sadleir, DD, and *d* 7 March 1922, leaving issue. He *d* 4 July 1915

(2) Emma Frances; *d* unm 24 Dec 1943

2 (cont.) Charles Burke *m* 2nd 9 Feb 1871 Anna Everilda (*dsp* 3 Jan 1909), 2nd dau of George Legard, of Easthorpe, Hall, Yorks (*see* LEGARD, Bt), and *d* 15 May 1898

3 James Henry, Maj-Gen Bombay Engrs; *b* 27 Feb 1816; *m* 18 May 1852 Marion Eliza (*d* 15 April 1892), dau of Maj-Gen B Crispin, and *d* 27 June 1882, leaving, with other issue:

(1) James Henry Thomas Joseph FitzGerald, CB, Capt RN; *b* 28 March 1853; *m* 4 Sept 1878 Edith (*d* 13 May 1935), dau of Capt Powell John Comyn, and *d* 12 May 1902, having had issue:

1a James Howe Campbell Ulick; *b* 4 Jan 1880; Lt RASC; *m* 1st 12 Aug 1912 (*divorce* 1928) Lilian Maud, dau of William John Whenmouth; *m* 2nd 31 May 1930 Annie Amelia (*d* 13 Sept 1967), dau of James Adolphus Granville, and *d* 1946, leaving issue by 2nd w:

1b +James Ulick Hubert [Maj James Burke, 6 Churchfield Rd, London W13]; *b* 6 Sept 1932; *educ* Cranleigh; Maj Para Regt, Assist Mil Attaché Moscow and Helsinki; *m* 30 Nov 1957 *Jean, only dau of Arthur Robert Murray, of Aldershot, and has issue:

1c +Martin James; *b* 20 Jan 1960

1c *Karen Jane; *b* 15 Oct 1958

1a Mary Edith Elizabeth; *b* 17 July 1881; *d* 27 Jan 1887

(2) Hubert William Austin, Fleet-Surgn RN, LRCP, LRCS; *b* 26 Aug 1858; *m* 10 April 1905 Florence Mary Elizabeth, 2nd dau of William Henry Bishop, of Kensington, and *d* 23 Feb 1933

(1) Catherine Mary Caroline; *m* 9 Feb 1893 her cousin Sir Thomas Malachy Burke, 6th Bt, and *d* 17 Jan 1922, leaving issue (*see* below)

(2) Elizabeth Mary Clare; *m* 24 Aug 1891 Jerome John MacMahon, MD, of Cork, and *d* July 1910

1 Elizabeth Anne; *m* 10 Jan 1850 David O'Connor Henchy (*d* 1 Dec 1876), of Stonebrook, MP Co Kildare, and *d* 31 Dec 1890, leaving issue (*see* KILLANIN, B)

Sir JOHN *d* 14 Sept 1847; his est son,

Sir Thomas John Burke, 3rd Bt, MP Galway 1847–65, DL, JP, Capt 1st Dragoons; *b* 7 June 1813; *m* 21 Feb 1857 Lady Mary Frances Nugent (*d* 1 Sept 1892), dau of 9th Earl of Westmeath (*qv*), and *d* 9 Dec 1875, having had, with other issue:

1 **Sir John Charles Burke, 4th Bt,** Lt 20th Hus; *b* 7 Feb 1858; *d* unm 16 Aug 1880,

2 **Sir Henry George Burke, 5th Bt,** DL, JP Galway; *educ* Trin Coll Dublin (BA), High Sheriff Co Galway 1883, Lt 4th Bn Connaught Rangers; *b* 30 Nov 1859; *d* unm 19 Jan 1910

3 THOMAS MALACHY (Sir), **6th Bt**

4 William Anthony, barrister; *b* 2 April 1866; *m* 2 Jan 1889 Caroline Evelyn (*d* 9 Feb 1910), yst dau of Capt Edmond James Power-Lalor, of Longorchard, Co Tipperary, and *d* 8 Feb 1939, leaving issue:

(1) Wilfred Maurice; *b* 14 Jan 1900; *educ* Downside; *m* 5 Sept 1933 Dorothea Sefton (*d* 20 Oct 1956), dau of William Sinclair, of Dublin, and *dsp* 1 Dec 1945

1 Julia Catherine Anne; *m* 16 Aug 1893 William Daly, DL, of Dunsandle, Co Galway, and *d* 25 April 1928, leaving issue. He *d* 27 Dec 1910

2 Mary Clare Theresa; *m* 7 Aug 1894 John James Smyth, of Masonbrook, Co Galway, and *d* 17 March 1913, leaving issue. He *d* 24 Feb 1933

The 5th Bt's bro,

Sir Thomas Malachy Burke, 6th Bt, JP Co Galway; *b* 8 Jan 1864; *m* 9 Feb 1893 his cousin Catherine Mary Caroline (*d* 17 Jan 1922), dau of Maj-Gen James Henry Burke, RE (*see* above), and *d* 19 Dec 1913, leaving:

Sir Gerald Howe Burke, 7th Bt, DL Galway, Capt Irish Gds WW I (wounded twice), ADC 1919–21; *b* 17 Nov 1893; *m* 1st 23 Dec 1914 Elizabeth Mary (*d* 27 June 1918), only dau of Patrick Mathews, of Mount Hanover, Drogheda, Co Meath, and had issue:

1 **Sir Thomas Stanley Burke, 8th Bt**; *b* 20 July 1916; *educ* Harrow and Trin Coll Cambridge; *m* 17 Aug 1955 Suzanne Margarete, er dau of Otto Theodor Salvisberg, of Thun, Switzerland, and *d* 1989, having had issue:

(1) Sir JAMES STANLEY GILBERT BURKE, **9th and present Bt**

(1) *Caroline Elizabeth; *b* 19 Aug 1959

Sir Gerald *m* 2nd 26 May 1920 Merrial Alison, only dau of Edward Christie, and *d* 30 Dec 1954, having by her had issue:

1 Bridget Alison; *b* 10 March 1921; *m* 6 Jan 1944 Lt-Col Eugene Dechelette, OBE, Compagnon da la Liberation, Offr Legn Honour, French Army Res, and had issue:

(1) *Edward Henry Charles; *b* 26 Aug 1950

(1) *Elizabeth Alison; *b* 20 Feb 1947

(2) *Anne Marie; *b* 16 March 1949

2 Elizabeth Anne; *b* 21 Aug 1924

BURLISON

Creation: B. (LP, UK) 2 Aug 1997.

THE BARON BURLISON, of Rowlands Gill, Co Tyne and Wear (Tom Burlison) [The Rt Hon The Lord Burlison, House of Lords, London SW1A 0PW]; *b* 23 May 1936; *educ* Edmondsley Co Durham; panel beater 1951–57; professional footballer 1953–65; RAF 1959–61; Regnl Offr GMBWU 1965–78 (Regnl Sec 1978–91, Dep Gen Sec 1991–); Treas Lab Party 1992; exec memb GMB Br North American Ctee 1994–; *m* 1981 *Valerie Stephenson and has two sons and a dau

Lineage: ROBERT BURLISON; *m* Georgina Doige and had:

TOM, *cr* a **Baron**

BURNETT

Arms: Per chevron or and sa. two holly leaves in chief vert, and in base a hunting horn of the first stringed arg. **Crest:** Issuing from flames a branch of holly erect ppr. **Motto:** *In arduis fortitudo* ('Fortitude in hardship'). **Creation:** Bt. (UK) 17 Oct 1913.

SIR (DAVID) HUMPHREY BURNETT, 3RD BT, of Selborne House, in the Borough of Croydon, MBE (1945), TD [Sir Humphrey Burnett Bt MBE TD, Tandridge Hall, nr Oxted, Surrey RH8 9NJ; Twizel Millhouse, Cornhill-on-Tweed, Northumberland TD12 4UX]; *b* 27 Jan 1918; *s* f 1955; *educ* Harrow and St John's Coll Cambridge (MA); FRICS 1970, ARICS 1948, FIMgt, FLS, Lt City London, Maj RA (TA) WW II (T/Lt-Col, despatches), ptnr David Burnett & Sons chartered surveyors 1947–50, dir: The Proprietors of Hay's Wharf Ltd 1950–80 (chm 1965–80), GRE Assur 1967–88, London and Thames Haven Oil Wharves, memb PLA, chm: S London Botanical Inst 1964–80, The London Wharfingers Assoc 1964–71, Master Watermen's and Lightermen's Co 1964–65 and Girdlers' Co 1970, memb cncl Brighton Coll 1971–93; *m* 21 July 1948 *Geraldine Elizabeth Mortimer, yr dau of Sir Godfrey Arthur Fisher, KCMG, and has had:

1 Robert Leslie Fisher; *b* 24 May 1949; *educ* privately; *d* unm 18 April 1977

2 +CHARLES DAVID [Charles Burnett Esq, 1 Queen's Gate Place, London SW7]; *b* 18 May 1951; *educ* Harrow and Lincoln Coll Oxford; *m* 1989 *Victoria Joan, er dau of James Simpson, of Rye, Sussex, and has issue:

(1) *Roberta Elizabeth; *b* 1992

3 +John Godfrey; *b* 29 March 1954; *educ* Harrow

Lineage: DAVID BURNETT, of Dalston; *b* 1 Aug 1815; *d* 28 March 1873, leaving:

Sir David Burnett, 1st Bt (UK), so *cr* 17 Oct 1913; *b* 22 Aug 1851, Hon Col 1st City London RFA (TF), Grand Warden Freemasonry, City London: Lt, Alderman Candlewick Ward 1902, Sheriff 1907–08, Ld Mayor 1912–13 (when he bought the Crystal Palace for the nation), ktd 1908, Grand Offr Legn Honour, Kt Cdr Crown Belgium; *m* 28 Aug 1875 Emily (*d* 19 May 1917), est dau of Thomas Sleap, of Dalston, and had, with other issue:

1 LESLIE TREW (Sir), **2nd Bt**

1 Ethel Emily; *m* 31 July 1900 Bernard Beresford Baddeley, 3rd s of Sir John James Baddeley, 1st Bt (*qv*), and *d* 9 June 1955, leaving issue

2 Gertrude Alice; *d* unm 17 Dec 1943

3 Maude Agnes; *m* 6 June 1907 Emil Stanley Franklin, of Bexhill, 3rd s of Alfred Walter Franklin, and *d* 19 Nov 1966

4 Marquerite Ida; *m* 9 April 1910 Basil Thomas Parsons-Smith, MRCS (Eng), FRCP, MD, BSc (Lond), 2nd s of Dr S H Parsons-Smith, and *d* 25 March 1963, leaving issue. He *d* 3 Sept 1954

5 Dorothy Gladys

Sir DAVID *d* 7 July 1930; his only surv son,

Sir Leslie Trew Burnett, 2nd Bt, CBE (1944), TD, DL Surrey, Lt-Col 4th Bn Roy Fus WW I (despatches), Hon Col 1936–51, Lt City London, Master Coopers' Co 1947, dir The Propietors of Hays Wharf Ltd, and Denny, Mott and Dickson Ltd; *b* 22 Sept 1884; *m* 21 April 1917 Joan (*d* 1994), 2nd dau of Lt-Col Sir John Humphrey, and *d* 17 July 1955, having had issue:

1 Sir (DAVID) HUMPHREY BURNETT, **3rd and present Bt**

2 +Richard Leslie [Richard Burnett Esq, 3 Macaulay Rd, London SW4]; *b* 23 June 1932; *educ* Eton and King's Coll Cambridge (BA); ARCM (1951), LRAM (1952), formerly 2nd Lt Roy Leics Regt; *m* 20 Nov 1969 *Katrina Eveline, only dau of W Graeme Hendrey

1 Mary; *b* 15 April 1919; *m* 9 Oct 1948 Richard Gilbert Dawson, MBE, MA, 2nd s of Richard Cecil Dawson, of Ball Hill, Newbury, and Cloghran, Dublin, and has issue. He *d* following an accident 5 June 1971

2 *Joan Dorothy [Mrs John Taylor, Braydells, Haywards Heath, Sussex]; *b* 29 June 1920; *m* 14 Nov 1953 John Clement Herbert Taylor, yst s of Edward Augustus Taylor, of Westerham, Kent, and has issue:

(1) Geoffrey; *b* 1958; *d* 1980

(2) *Thomas; *b* 1960

(1) *Marian Joan; *b* 1956

3 *Nancy [Mrs A Gerrard, Leyswood, Groombridge, Sussex]; *b* 14 April 1926; *m* 1st 30 Oct 1948 (*divorce* 1959) Capt Ian Alastair Sinclair, yst s of John Alexander Sinclair, of Highgate and Kirkcudbrightshire; *m* 2nd 1972 *Prof A H Gerrard and has issue by 1st husb:

(1) *Guy Alastair Burnett; *b* 31 May 1951; *educ* Eton

(1) *Josephine Anne; *b* 23 Dec 1949

(2) *Karen Lesley; *b* 18 April 1954

BURNEY

Arms: Az. a pale arg., two bars counter-embattled counter-changed, between in chief and in base a fountain ppr. **Crest:** Out of a naval crown gold a bull's head az., armed or. **Supporters:** On either side a sea-bull az., armed or. **Motto:** *Recte quod honeste* ('What is done honourably is right'). **Creaton:** Bt. (UK) 27 Jan 1921.

SIR CECIL DENNISTOUN BURNEY, 3RD BT, of Preston Candover, Co Southampton [Sir Cecil Burney Bt, 5 Lyall St, London SW1X 8DW]; *b* 8 Jan 1923; *s* f 1968; *educ* Eton and Trin Coll Cambridge; RNVR WW II, md 1951–68 and chm 1968–72 Northern Motors, pres N Rhodesia Motor Traders Assoc 1956–59, MLC N Rhodesia 1959–64, MP Zambia 1964–68, chm Public Accts Ctee Zambia 1963–67, chm: Hampton Tst 1975–87, JMD Gp 1986–92; dir: Security Bldg Soc 1959–71, Mount Martin Gold Mines 1985–87; *m* 5 Sept 1957 *Hazel Marguerite, formerly w of Trevor Etienne Bruno de Hamel and yr dau of Thurman Coleman, of Weymouth, Dorset, and has:

1 +NIGEL DENNISTOUN; *b* 6 Sept 1959; *educ* Eton and Trin Coll Cambridge; *m* 26 Sept 1992 *Lucy Vanessa Brooks and has:

(1) +Max; *b* 15 Sept 1994

(2) +Otto; *b* 1 Dec 1995

2 +(Philip) Julian Gerard; *b* 28 March 1961

Lineage: Lt WILLIAM VINCENT BURNEY, RN; *m* Elizabeth, dau of John Webster, of Plymouth, and had:

Capt CHARLES BURNEY, CB, RN, *b* 9 Oct 1825; Supt Greenwich Hosp Sch; *m* 7 Dec 1849 Catherine Elizabeth (*d* 11 May 1883), dau of Charles Jones, of London and La Ferrière, Jersey, and *d* 19 June 1887, having had, with other issue:

Sir Cecil Burney, 1st Bt (UK), so *cr* 27 Jan 1921, GCB (1922, KCB 1913), GCMG (1916, KCMG 1913), JP, DL Hants; *b* 15 May 1858; RN: Egypt 1882, E Sudan 1884, cmded Internat Sqdn blockading Montenegro 1913, Sr Offr Internat Commn administering Scutari and outlying Albania 1913, WW I: cmdg 1st Battle Sqdn, 2ic Grand Fleet 1914–16 (despatches), 2nd Sea Ld 1916–17, C-in-C coast Scotland 1917, C-in-C Portsmouth 1919–20, Adml of the Fleet 1920, ret 1925, ADC to HM EDWARD VII 1906–07; *m* 10 Sept 1884 Lucinda Marion (*d* 31 Jan 1944), 2nd dau of George Richards Burnett, of S Kensington, and *d* 5 June 1929, leaving:

1 **Sir (Charles) Dennistoun Burney, 2nd Bt**, CMG (1917), *b* 28 Dec 1888; Cdr RN, MP Uxbridge 1922–29, inventor explosive paravane and protector paravane; designed and built R100 airship 1923–29, built first rear-engine streamlined car 1929–30, designed first recoil-less rifle WW II, initiated stern trawling and refrigeration in fishing vessels 1946–50; *m* 15 March 1921 Gladys, yst dau of George Henry High, of Lake Shore Dve, Chicago, and *d* 11 Nov 1968, leaving:

(1) Sir CECIL DENNISTON BURNEY, **3rd and present Bt**

1 Sybil Katherine, OBE; *m* 1st 29 Dec 1905 Lt Arthur Corry Gotto, RN (*d* 18 Sept 1906), s of Arthur Gotto, CE, of Belfast; *m* 2nd 24 March 1917 Cdr Clive Neville-Rolfe, DSO, RN (*d* 27 Oct 1953), and *d* 3 Aug 1955, leaving issue

2 Violet Hazel; *m* 15 July 1913 Cdr Charles Frederick Ballard, RN (drowned sinking of HMS *Formidable* 31 Dec 1914), s of Col Ballard, of Watlington, Oxon, and *d* 25 July 1969, leaving by her 1st husb:

(1) *Margaret; *b* 29 Dec 1914; *m* 15 Sept 1939 her cousin *Arthur Charles Corry Gotto, est s of Charles Corry Gotto, of Bangor, Co Down, and has had:

1a *Charles Corry; *b* 8 Dec 1943; *educ* Dauntseys; *m* 13 July 1968 *Linda Carolyn, dau of David Brian Heath, of Gatton Manor, Ockley, Surrey

1a Margaret Mavis; *b* 15 Sept 1940; *d* 23 June 1992

BURNHAM

Arms: Quarterly, 1st and 4th, az. three bars gemel arg., over all a winged morion or; 2nd and 3rd, gu. a saltire double parted and fretted or between two ram's heads couped in fess arg. **Crests:** 1 In front of a terrestial globe ppr. a winged morion or, 2 A ram arg. holding in the mouth a trefoil slipped vert and resting the dexter foreleg on a quartrefoil or. **Supporters:** Dexter, the figure of Clio, the muse of history, ppr.; sinister, the figure of Hermes, vested arg. mantled az., on the head a winged morion, on his heels wings and in his exterior hand a caduceus or. **Motto:** Of old I hold.
Creations: Bt. (UK) 13 Oct 1892, B. (UK) 31 July 1903, V. (UK) 16 May 1919.

THE 6TH BARON BURNHAM, of Hall Barn, Beaconsfield, Co Bucks, and **a Baronet** (Sir Hugh John Frederick Lawson, Bt) [The Rt Hon the Lord Burnham, Woodlands Farm, Beaconsfield, Bucks HP9 2SF]; *b* 15 Aug 1931; *s* bro 1993; *educ* Eton and Balliol Coll Oxford (MA); late Lt Scots Gds, with *Daily Telegraph* 1955–86 (dep md 1984–86), dir-gen King George's Fund for Sailors 1988–93, Dep C Ch Whip Ho Lords 1997–; *m* 31 Dec 1955 *Hilary Margaret, yr dau of Alan Hunter, of Huntingtowerfield Ho, Almondbank, Perth, and has issue:

1 +HARRY FREDERICK ALAN; *b* 22 Feb 1968; *educ* Eton

1 *Charlotte Ann; *b* 12 Jan 1960

2 *Emma Lucia; *b* 8 Aug 1961

Lineage: MOSES LIONEL LEVY; *b c* 1765; London merchant; *m* Leah — (*d* 1861 aged 71) and had:

JOSEPH MOSES LEVY, of 51 Grosvenor St, London W, and Florence Cottage, Ramsgate, JP; *b* 15 Dec 1811; fndr *Daily Telegraph*, forwarded cheap press in UK; *m* 1830 Esther (*d* 2 March 1884), 2nd dau of Godfrey Alexander Cohen, of London, and *d* 13 Oct 1888, having had, with other issue:

1 EDWARD, **1st Baron**

1 Emily; *m* 5 June 1882 Col Edward Brydges Willyams, DL, of Carnanton, Cornwall, and *dsp* 5 Feb 1902. He *d* 10 Oct 1916

2 Matilda; *d* 5 May 1920

3 Helen; *m* 17 April 1867 Sir George Faudel Faudel-Phillips, 1st Bt, GCIE, and *d* 6 Aug 1916, leaving issue. He *d* 28 Dec 1922 (*see* 1940 edn)

4 Annie; *m* 15 Aug 1870 Sir Campbell Clarke and *d* 8 Aug 1909. He *d* 26 Aug 1902

5 Florence; *m* 2 Aug 1882 Col Sir William Owen Lanyon, KCMG, CB, and *d* 6 May 1883. He *d* 6 April 1887

JOSEPH LEVY's s,

Sir EDWARD LEVY later LEVY-LAWSON (roy licence 11 Dec 1875 under terms of will of his unc, Lionel Lawson), **1st Bt** (UK), so *cr* 13 Oct 1892, as also 31 July 1903 **(1st) Baron Burnham**, of Hall Barn, Beaconsfield, Bucks, KCVO (1904), DL, JP Bucks; *b* 28 Dec 1833; *educ* London U Sch; pncpl prop *Daily Telegraph*, pres IoJ 1891–92, CA Bucks, High Sheriff 1886, Lt City London, Cdr Rising Sun Japan; *m* 20 Feb 1862 Harriette Georgiana (*d* 25 May 1897), only dau of Benjamin Nottingham Webster, of Pen-y-Craig, Denbighs, and *d* 9 Jan 1916, leaving:

1 HARRY LAWSON WEBSTER LEVY later LEVY-LAWSON, **2nd Baron Burnham** and 1st and last VISCOUNT BURNHAM (UK), so *cr* 16 May 1919, GCMG (1927), CH (1917), TD, DL, JP Bucks; *b* 18 Dec 1862; *educ* Eton and Balliol Coll Oxford (MA 1888), MP W St Pancras 1885–92, Cirencester 1893–95 and Mile End 1905–06 and 1910–16, memb LCC 1889–92 and 1897–1904, Mayor Stepney 1907–09, barrister Inner Temple 1891, Lt City London, owner/manager *Daily Telegraph* to 1928 when sold it to the Berrys (*see* CAMROSE, V, and KEMSLEY, V), pres: IoJ 1910, Empire Press Union, Imp Press Conf Canada 1920, Australia and NZ 1925, Internat Labour 1921, 1922 and 1926, v-chm Empire Parly Assoc, memb Indian Statutory Commn 1927, Pres Birkbeck Coll Lond and Epsom Coll 1929, Hon Col 99th (Bucks and Berks Yeo) Bde RA (RA), Lt-Col TFR, cmded Roy Bucks Yeo (2nd Res Regt) WW I (despatches), LLD: Cantab, McGill 1920, Athens 1924, Perth W Australia 1925, Ghent 1927; Hon DLitt Durham 1921, Hon Fell RIBA, FRSL, GC: Leopold II Belgium, Crown Italy, Redeemer Greece, Star of North Sweden, Cdr: Legn Honour, Leopold, Grand Offr Star Romania; *m* 2 Jan 1884 Olive (*d* 20 Dec 1939), dau of Gen Sir Henry de Bathe, 4th Bt, KCB (*see* 1940 edn), and *dspm* 20 July 1933, when the viscountcy expired, leaving:

(1) Dorothy Olive; *b* 26 Jan 1885; *m* 15 Jan 1907 Maj Hon Sir John Spencer Coke, KCVO, Scots Gds, s of 2nd Earl of Leicester (*qv*), and *d* 22 Dec 1937, leaving issue

2 WILLIAM ARNOLD WEBSTER LEVY later LEVY-LAWSON, **3rd Baron Burnham**, DSO; *b* 19 March 1864, Lt-Col and Brev-Col 2nd Bucks Yeo, Maj Res Offrs, Hon Lt-Col 1904, Scots Gds, Boer War 1900 and 1901 (despatches twice) and WW I (despatches 1917); *m* 1887 (*divorce* 1912) Sybil Mary (*d* 3 May 1933), est dau of Lt-Gen Sir Frederick Marshall, KCMG, and *d* 14 June 1943, having had:

(1) EDWARD FREDERICK, **4th Baron**

(2) William Bernard Webster, Lt Scots Gds; *b* 22 Aug 1893; *ka* 22 Oct 1914

(1) Margaret Olive Edith; *m* 14 April 1910 Lt-Col John Fenwick Harrison, RHG (*d* 25 Oct 1966), s of Thomas Fenwick Harrison, of King's Walden Bury, Herts, and *d* 21 March 1969, leaving issue (*see* MILBORNE-SWINNERTON-PILKINGTON, Bt)

(2) Olive Emily, Sectn Offr WAAF WW II; *m* 6 Sept 1916 Maj John Edward Murray Smith, RHG (*d* 4 April 1928), s of George Murray Smith, DL, of Grumley Hall, Market Harborough, by Ellen, dau of 1st Baron Belper (*qv*), and *d* 2 July 1955, leaving issue.

1 Edith Maude Webster; *m* 1 Nov 1888 Sir Edward Henry Hulse, 6th Bt (*qv*), and *d* 1 Nov 1937, leaving issue

The 4th BARON's only surv son,

EDWARD FREDERICK LEVY-LAWSON, **4th Baron Burnham**, CB, DSO, MC, TD, DL Bucks, Maj-Gen TA cmdg RA 48th Div (TA) 1938–41, Yorks Div 1942, 99th (Bucks and Berks Yeo) Field Bde RA (TA); *b* 16 June 1890; *educ* Eton and Balliol Coll Oxford (BA 1914, MA 1920); served WW I (despatches three times), Sr Mil Advsr Min Info, Dir PR War Office 1943–45, md *Daily Telegraph* and *Morning Post*, chm Ld Mayor Treloar Coll; *m* 28 Jan 1920 (Marie) Enid, CBE (1957), JP (Bucks 1943) (*b* 27 May 1894; *d* 29 July 1979), only dau of Hugh Scott Robson, of Buenos Aires, and *d* 4 July 1963, leaving:

1 WILLIAM EDWARD HARRY (LEVY-)LAWSON, **5th Baron Burnham**, DL Bucks 1977, JP 1970; *b* 22 Oct 1920; *educ* Eton; Roy Bucks Yeo and Scots Gds WW II and thereafter to 1968 (Lt-Col), Malaya 1950–51 (despatches), chm Sail Training Assoc; *m* 27 June 1942 *Anne [The Rt Hon The Dowager Lady Burnham, West Flat, Hall Barn, Beaconsfield, Bucks HP9 2SG], 2nd dau of Maj George Gerald Petherick, of Porthpean Ho, St Austell, Cornwall, and The Mill Ho, St Cross, Winchester, Hants, by Lady Jeane, est dau of 6th Earl of Radnor (*qv*), and *d* 1993, having had:

(1) Edward Webster; *b* 6 March, *d* 8 March 1952

(1) *Jenefer Anne [The Hon Mrs Farncombe, Hall Barn, Windsor End, Beaconsfield, Bucks HP9 2SG]; *b* 17 Dec 1949; *educ* Heathfield; *m* 20 April 1985 *Andrew David Farncombe, s of George Frank Farncombe, of Ipswich, and has issue:

1a *Frederick Alexander Edward; *b* 10 Aug 1987

1a *Joanna Abigail; *b* 5 May 1990

(2) *Harriet Mary [The Hon Mrs Sain, via Ciamician 10, Trieste 34124, Italy]; *b* 5 March 1954; *educ* Cobham Hall and RCM; *m* 1984 *Marino Sain, only s of Silvano Sain, of Trieste, and has issue:

1a *Thomas Andrea; *b* 7 Dec 1987

2a *Giacomo Julian Lawson; *b* 23 Sept 1991

3a *Harry Benjamin; *b* 16 March 1994

1a *Teresa Anna (twin); *b* 16 March 1994

(3) *Sarah Jane [The Hon Mrs Maher, Newtown Park, Wicklow, Co Wicklow, Ireland]; *b* 7 Oct 1955; *educ* Heathfield; *m* 1st 11 Sept 1982 (*divorce* 1991) Michael Ian Grade (*see* GRADE, B); *m* 2nd 1992 *David Patrick Maher and by him has:

1a *Edward James Lawson; *b* 16 June 1997

2 HUGH JOHN FREDERICK LAWSON, **6th and present Baron Burnham**

1 *Lucia Edith [The Hon Mrs Whitehead, Hallin, 18 Burnham Ave, Beaconsfield, Bucks HP9 2JA]; *b* 29 Aug 1922; CSM ATS WW II (despatches); *m* 1st 9 Nov 1946 (*divorce* 1953) F/Lt Hon Roger David Marquis, RAFVR (later 2nd Earl of Woolton (*d* 7 Jan 1969); *qv*); *m* 2nd 25 Nov 1966 John William Whitehead (*d* 1982), er s of Charles Parkin Whitehead

BURRELL

Arms: Vert three plain shields two and one arg., each having a bordure engrailed or. **Crest:** A naked arm, embowed ppr., the hand grasping a sprig of laurel vert. **Motto:** *Per fluctas ad oram* ('Through the waves to the shore'). **Creation:** Bt. (GB) 31 May 1774.

SIR (JOHN) RAYMOND BURRELL, 9TH BT, of Valentine House, Essex [Sir Raymond Burrell Bt, Baynton House, Coulston, Westbury, Wilts BA13 4NY]; *b* 20 Feb 1934; *s* f 1985; *educ* Eton and RAC Cirencester; *m* 1st 3 Jan 1959 (*divorce* 1971) Rowena Frances, er dau of Michael H Pearce, of Brackenhills, Inyanga, Rhodesia, and has had:

1 +CHARLES RAYMOND [Charles Burrell Esq, Knepp Castle, W Grinstead, W Sussex RH13 8LJ]; *b* 27 Aug 1962; *educ* Millfield and RAC Cirencester; *m* 1 Dec 1993 *Isabella Elizabeth Nancy, er adopted dau of Michael Lambert Tree (*see* DEVONSHIRE, D), and has:

(1) +Edward Lambert; *b* 10 Oct 1996

(1) *Nancy Catherine; *b* 29 May 1995

1 Joanna Susan; *b* 23 July 1960; *d* 1 Jan 1976

Sir RAYMOND *m* 2nd 11 July 1971 *Margot Lucy, dau of F E Thatcher, of Sydney, NSW, and has further issue:

2 +Andrew John; *b* 15 July 1974

2 *Catherine Anne Lucy; *b* 29 May 1977

Lineage: NINIAN BURRELL, of Cuckfield, Sussex, son of Thomas Burrell, of Cuckfield, by Dorothy Weston, and gs of Ralph Burrell, of Cuckfield; *m* Jane, dau of Henry Smith, of Pepper Harrow, Surrey, and *d* 4 Sept 1614, having had, with four yr s:

WALTER BURRELL, of Cuckfield; *b* 1600; *m* Frances, dau of John Hooper, of Stockbury, Kent, and *d* 1671, having had, with eight er sons:

PETER BURRELL, of Langley Park, Beckenham, Kent; *b* 3 Jan 1639; settled in Kent 1684; *m* 1687 Isabella (*d* 15 Feb 1724), dau of John Merrik, of Stubbers, Essex, and *d* 13 Sept 1718, having had, with other issue:

1 PETER, his heir

2 Sir MERRIK BURRELL, 1st Bt (E), so *cr* 15 July 1766 (with remainder, failing heirs male of his body, to his n Peter Burrell), of W Grinstead Park, Sussex; *bapt* 5 Nov 1699; Govr of the Bank of England, MP Marlow 1747–54, Grampound 1754–68, Haslemere 1774–80 and Bedwyn 1780–84; *d* unm 6 April 1787

1 Anne; *m* Richard Acland and had issue (*see* ACLAND, Bt, of Columb John)

His er s,

PETER BURRELL, of Langley Park, Kent, MP Haslemere 1722–54 and Dover 1755–56, Sub-Govr of the South Sea Co; *b* 1692; *m* 14 March 1723 Amy (*d* 16 Aug 1789), dau of Hugh Raymond, of Saling Hall, Essex, and *d* 16 April 1756, having had, with other issue:

1 Peter, of Langley Park, MA, FRS, Surveyor-Gen of Crown Lands, MP Launceston 1759–68 and Totnes 1768–74; *b* 27 Aug 1724; *m* 28 Feb 1748 Elizabeth (*d* 8 June 1795), dau and heir of John Lewis, of Hackney, and *d* 6 Nov 1775, having had, with other issue:

(1) Sir PETER BURRELL, 2nd Bt, of Langley Park, and 1st BARON GWYDIR, Co Carnarvon (*see* WILLOUGHBY DE ERESBY, B), so *cr* 16 June 1796; *m* and had issue

(1) Susan Isabella; *m* 8 June 1775 1st Earl of Beverley and *d* 24 Jan 1812, leaving issue (*see* NORTHUMBERLAND, D)

(2) Francis Julia; *m* 23 May 1779 2nd Duke of Northumberland (*qv*) and *d* 28 April 1820, leaving issue

(3) Elizabeth; *m* 1st 5 April 1778 8th Duke of Hamilton (*see* HAMILTON and BRANDON, D); *m* 2nd 10 Aug 1800 1st Marquess of Exeter (*qv*) and *dsp* 17 Jan 1837

2 WILLIAM (Sir), **2nd Bt**

1 Amelia; *m* Tobias Frere

Lineage (of Raymond): Sir Charles Raymond, 1st Bt (GB), so *cr* 31 May 1774, with remainder, failing male issue, to his son-in-law, William Burrell, of Valentine Ho, Barking, Essex, High Sheriff 1771, son of John Raymond, of Marple, Devon, by his w Anna Maria, dau of Samuel Tanner; *bapt* 22 April 1713; *m* Sarah (*d* 15 April 1778), dau of Thomas Webster, of Bromley, and *d* 24 Aug 1788, having had, with other issue:

SOPHIA; *m* 1st 13 April 1773 **Sir William Burrell, 2nd Bt** (who *s* his father-in-law; *b* 10 Oct 1732; LLD, FSA, MP Haslemere 1768–74, Commr Excise; *d* 20 Jan 1796), 2nd s of Peter Burrell, of Langley Park, Beckenham (*see* above); *m* 2nd 23 May 1797 Rev William Clay and *d* 20 June 1802, having had, with other issue:

Sir Charles Merrik Burrell, 3rd Bt; MP (C) New Shoreham 1806–62; *b* 24 May 1774; at the time of his death he was Father of the Ho of Commons; *m* 4 July 1808 Frances Wyndham (*d* 25 Sept 1848), sis of 1st Baron Leconfield (*see* EGREMONT, LECONFIELD and, B), and *d* 4 Jan 1862, having had, with other issue:

1 **Sir Percy Burrell, 4th Bt**; MP (C) New Shoreham 1862–76; *b* 10 Feb 1812; *m* 26 Aug 1856 Henrietta Katherine (*d* 4 March 1880), dau of V-Adml Sir George Brooke Perchell, and *dsp* 19 July 1876

2 **Sir Walter Wyndham Burrell, 5th Bt**, barrister, MP (C) Shoreham 1876–86; *b* 26 Oct 1814; *m* 10 June 1847 Dorothea (*d* 8 Feb 1891), dau of Rev John A Jones, Rector of Burley-on-the-Hill, and had, with other issue:

(1) CHARLES RAYMOND (Sir), **6th Bt**

(2) Robert Merrick Raymond; *b* 30 Aug 1863; *d* unm 30 Jan 1905

(1) Frances Louisa; *m* 3 Jan 1884 Philip Alexander Palli, est son of Professor Alexis Palli, of the U of Athens, and *d* 1925, leaving issue. He *d* 1892

(2) Dorothea Mary Augusta; *m* 25 July 1878 Francis William Otter, of W Grinstead Lodge, Horsham, 2nd son of Ven William Bruère Otter, Archdeacon of Lewes, and *d* 21 Sept 1930, leaving issue. He *d* 1885

(3) Emily Charlotte Edrica; *m* 17 Aug 1876 Ernest Baggallay, of 19 Egerton Gardens, SW, late Metropolitan Police Magistrate, 2nd son of Rt Hon Sir Richard Baggallay, and *d* 28 Sept 1935, leaving issue. He *d* 9 Sept 1931

(4) Edith Henrietta; *m* 5 June 1888 Rev William Robert Pearson Strange, late Rector of Holford, Somerset, and *d* 8 Oct 1911, leaving issue

Sir WALTER *d* 24 Jan 1886; his son,

Sir Charles Raymond Burrell, 6th Bt, JP, DL Sussex, late Capt Roy Sussex Militia; *b* 29 March 1848; *m* 22 July 1872 Etheldreda Mary (*d* 25 Sept 1921), est dau of Sir Robert Loder, 1st Bt, MP (*qv*), and had issue:

1 MERRIK RAYMOND (Sir), **7th Bt**

1 Sybil Dorothy; *d* unm 22 Sept 1955

2 Mary Emma; *m* 2 March 1905 Capt Alan Cecil Lupton, only son of Alan Lupton, JP, of Highfield, Ripon, and *d* 2 Aug 1934, leaving issue. He *d* 11 July 1949

Sir CHARLES *d* 6 Sept 1899; his only son,

Sir Merrik Raymond Burrell, 7th Bt, CBE (1919), JP W Sussex, High Sheriff Sussex 1918, CA, Lt-Col late Inspr Remounts 1918, formerly Lt 1st Roy Dragoons, served in S African War 1899–1901, chm Bd of Govrs Roy Vet Coll 1929–46, tstee Roy Agric Soc of England (pres 1936), Gold Medallist for distinguished servs to agric; *b* 14 May 1877; *m* 11 Feb 1902 (*divorce* 1907) Wilhelmina Louisa (*d* 29 Nov 1916), dau of Walter Winans, of Surrenden Park, Kent, and Baltimore, Maryland, and had issue:

1 WALTER RAYMOND (Sir), **8th Bt**

2 +Peter Eustace, CBE (1957) [Peter Burrell Esq CBE, Long Hill, Moulton Rd, Newmarket, Suffolk CB8 8QQ]; *b* 9 May 1905; *educ* Eton and RAC Cirencester; Gold Medallist, RAC 1926, dir National Stud 1937–71, served WW II 1940–44 as S/Ldr RAF; *m* 1st 26 July 1929 (*divorce* 1940) (Margaret Edith) Pamela (*d* 1984), er dau of Lt-Col Stephen Hungerford Pollen, CMG (*see* POLLEN, Bt), and has issue;

(1) (Peter) Timothy, Lt Cdr RN (ret); *b* 5 March 1930; *m* 17 Nov 1955 *Patricia Clarice Marion [Mrs Timothy Burrell, The Dower House, Tacolneston, Norfolk], dau of Capt Arthur Thomas Thompson, of Morcott, Rutland, and formerly w of Ralph John Hamilton Pollock (*see* POLLOCK, Bt), and *d* 1975, having had issue:

1a *Nicola Pamela Jane; *b* 19 Feb 1957; *m* 21 Jan 1989 *James Donald McGregor Reevely, yr son of Desmond Reevely, of Mill Corner, W Chiltington, Sussex, and has issue:

1b *Timothy James McGregor; *b* 1997

1b *Lucy Elizabeth Constance; *b* 10 May 1991

(2) +Merrik Kay [Merrik Burrell Esq, Casa del Hilario, Yaiza 35570, Lanzarote, Canary Islands]; *b* 17 Feb 1937; *educ* Harrow; *m* 4 July 1962 (*divorce* 1968) Julian Sarah, est dau of David Hugo Burr, of Mombasa, Kenya; *m* 2nd 14 Nov 1968 *Molli Cecily Lalla, dau of Stanley Cooke, of Knysna, Cape, S Africa, and has issue by 1st w:

1a +Peter Merrik; *b* 18 Feb 1963; *m* 1st 25 June 1988 (*divorce* 1994) Sally, dau of Michael Wallis; *m* 2nd 17 Oct 1995 *Lucinda, dau of Charles Clifford-Kingsmill

2 (cont.) Peter Burrell *m* 2nd 1 July 1971 *Mrs Constance Prosser Mellon (*d* 1980), widow of Gen Richard King Mellon

1 Joan Louise; *b* 2 Dec 1902; *m* 1st 9 June 1927 Maj Lord North (*k* in an accident 25 Aug 1940), est son of 8th Earl of Guilford (*qv*), and had issue; *m* 2nd 25 June 1947 Charles Harman Hunt (*d* 1984), chartered surveyor, son of Charles Henry Hunt, of High Wycombe, Bucks, and *d* Dec 1993

Sir Merrik *m* 2nd 14 Aug 1908 (*divorce* 1927) Coralie Adelaide Mervyn (*d* 10 Feb 1966), dau of John Porter Porter, DL, of Belle Isle, Co Fermanagh, and Clonbalt, Co Longford, and by her had further issue:

2 *Etheldreda Josephine; *b* 20 June 1909; *m* 3 Aug 1939 2nd Baron Tryon (*qv*) and has issue

Sir MERRIK *d* 22 Dec 1957; his er son,

Sir Walter Raymond Burrell, 8th Bt, CBE (1956, MBE 1945), TD (1943); *b* 11 Dec 1903; *educ* Eton; DL 1937 and V-Ld Lt 1975 Sussex, CA W Sussex, Maj 98 Fd Regt (Surrey and Sussex Yeo) RA (TA) 1938, Lt-Col (Ch Instr) 123 OCTU 1942, Lt-Col BAS (Washington) 1943, cmded 3 Super Heavy Regt, RA 1945, WW II, Pres: CLA 1951, Roy Ag Soc 1964; *m* 6 Aug 1931 Hon Anne Judith Denman, OBE (1947) (*d* 1987), only dau of 3rd Baron Denman (*qv*), and *d* 4 May 1985, having had issue:

1 Sir (JOHN) RAYMOND BURRELL, **9th and present Bt**

2 +Mark William [Mark Burrell Esq, Bakers Farm, Shipley, Horsham, Sussex RH13 7JJ; 43a Reeves Mews, South Audley St, W1Y 3PA]; *b* 9 April 1937; *educ* Eton and Pembroke Coll Cambridge (BA); dir Pearson plc 1977–; *m* 20 April 1966 *Margot Rosemary, yr dau of Westray Pearce, of Killara, NSW, Australia, and formerly w of Mackenzie Munro, and has:

(1) +William Westray; *b* 17 April 1967; *educ* Eton; *m* Feb 1994 *Celia Ann, only dau of Peter Shelmerdine, of Toorak, Melbourne, Australia

(2) +Anthony Merrik; *b* 10 Jan 1969; *educ* Eton; *m* 18 April 1998 *Lady Louise Iona Campbell, only dau of Duke of Argyll (*qv*)

(1) *Sophia Judith; *b* 18 July 1974

1 *Penelope Anne [Mrs Richard Greenwood, Stone Hall, Balcombe, Sussex RH17 6QN]; *b* 21 March 1932; *m* 25 July 1953 *(John) Richard Greenwood, JP, DL, only s of John Eric Greenwood, of The Priory of Lady St Mary, Wareham, Dorset, and has issue:

(1) *(John) Simon; *b* 18 May 1955; *educ* Eton

(2) *James Anthony; *b* 20 April 1959; *educ* Millfield; *m* 1985 *(Julia) Anne, yr dau of Edward Maynard Denny, and has issue:

1 a *(Jennifer) Adelaide; *b* 1987

(1) *(Anne) Lucinda; *b* 14 March 1957; *m* 4 June 1994 *Patrick James Auchinleck Darling, s of Gerald Ralph Auchinleck Darling, and has:

1a *Etheldreda Anne; *b* 1997

(2) *Fiona Mary; *b* 3 Sept 1962; *m* 1987 *Charles John Martin, 3rd s of Cyril Patrick John Martin, and has:

1a *Michael George; *b* 1990

1a *Charlotte Emma; *b* 1988

2a *Susanna Tara; *b* 1993

2 *(Julia Mary) Rona [Mrs Jeremy Smith,The Old Rectory, Slaugham, W Sussex RH17 6AG]; *b* 20 Feb 1934; *m* 21 Feb 1953 *Jeremy Fox Eric Smith, DL, 2nd s of Capt Evan Cadogan Eric Smith, MC, LLD, of Ashfold, Sussex, and has issue:

(1) *Julian Raymond Eric [Julian Smith Esq, Balcombe House, W Sussex RH17 6PB]; *b* 13 April 1956; *educ* Eton and New Coll Oxford; *m* 8 May 1982 *(Caroline) Fiona, er dau of W/Cdr Gordon Leonard Sinclair, DFC (*see* FORTESCUE, E), and has issue:

1a *Oliver George Eric; *b* 10 March 1983

2a *Henry Thomas Eric; *b* 9 Sept 1986

1a *Lucy Alexandra; *b* 18 Dec 1984

(2) *Hugo Jeremy Eric [Hugo Smith Esq, Ley Farm House, Dullingham, Newmarket, Suffolk CB8 9XG]; *b* 22 Oct 1957; *educ* Eton and Exeter U; *m* 24 Oct 1992 *Sophie Diana, dau of Jeffrey Hernu, and has issue:

1a *Milo Thomas Eric; *b* 1 April 1996

1a *Arabella Diana; *b* 6 July 1994

(1) *Dione Angela; *b* 19 July 1954; *m* 12 Sept 1976 *7th Earl of Verulam (*qv*) and has issue

(2) *Sarah Helen [Mrs Ashley Preston, The Mill House, Gibbons Mill, The Haven, Billingshurst, W Sussex]; *b* 18 Dec 1962; *m* 10 Oct 1987 *Ashley Charles Preston, and has issue:

1a *Frederick Charles Fox; *b* 9 Dec 1989

2a *Rupert Merrik Arthur; *b* 19 Sept 1993

BURTON

Arms: Quarterly, 1st and 4th, az. nine stars, three, three, two and one, arg. within a border engrailed or, charged with six cinquefoils of the field (for BAILLIE); 2nd and 3rd, gu. on a chevron cotised arg. between three plates, each charged with a fleur-de-lys az., a demi-lion couped of the first (for BASS). **Supporters:** On either side a lion regardant sa., each charged on the shoulder with a plate, thereon a fleur-de-lys az., and resting the inner hind leg on a stag's head cabossed ppr. **Crest:** A boar's head couped arg., armed or, langued gu. **Motto:** *Quid clarius astris* ('What is brighter than the stars'.) **Creation:** B. (UK) 29 Nov 1897.

THE 3RD BARON BURTON OF BURTON-ON-TRENT AND OF RANGEMORE, Co Stafford (Michael Evan Victor Baillie, JP (1961), DL (Inverness-shire 1963) [The Rt Hon The Lord Burton JP, DL, Dochfour, Inverness IV3 6JY; The Gables, Rangemore, Burton-on-Trent, Staffs]; *b* 27 June 1924; *s* grandmother 1962; *educ* Eton; late Lt Scots Gds and Lt Lovat Scouts (TA); CC 1949–75 Inverness-shire; *m* 1st 28 April 1948 (*divorce* 1977) Elizabeth Ursula Forster (*d* 1993), er dau of Capt Anthony Forster Wise, of 89 Winchester Court, W8; *m* 2nd 1978 *Coralie Denise, dau of Claud R Cliffe, and has had by his 1st w:

1 +EVAN MICHAEL RONALD; *b* 19 March 1949; *educ* Harrow and RAC Cirencester; *m* 17 Oct 1970 (*divorce* 19–) Lucinda, est dau of Robert Law, of Turnpike Ho, Withersfield, Haverhill, Suffolk, and has issue:

(1) +James Evan; *b* 3 Dec 1975

(2) +Hamish Michael; *b* 20 March 1979

(1) *Emma Elizabeth; *b* 3 June 1977

2 +Alexander James; *b* 1 July 1963; *educ* Eton

1 Elizabeth Victoria; *b* 9 March 1950; *m* 8 Aug 1970 *Hon Angus Grenfell Maclay, yst s of 2nd Baron Maclay (*qv*), and *d* 1986, leaving issue:

(1) *Robert Michael; *b* 24 Sept 1972

(2) *Fergus; *b* 31 Dec 1981

(1) *Sara Elizabeth; *b* 30 Aug 1977

2 *Philippa Ursula Maud [The Hon Mrs McCowen, Polwarth Manse, Greenlaw, Berwickshire]; *b* 30 Aug 1951; *m* 17 Dec 1980 *(Richard) Ian McCowen, son of Donald Henry Ewan McCowen, of Bighton Manor, Alresford, Hants and has issue:

(1) *Ewan; *b* 1981

(2) *Christopher Richard; *b* 14 June 1983

3 *Georgina Frances; *b* 11 May 1955

4 *Fiona Mary [The Hon Mrs Hilleary, Greenhill House, Redcastle, Muir of Ord, Killearnan, Ross-shire IV6 7SG]; *b* 31 Oct 1957; *m* 1982 *Alasdair Malcolm Douglas Macleod Hilleary, cartoonist (*see* HAMILTON and BRANDON, D), and has issue:

(1) *Geordie; *b* 1991

(1) *Flora Elizabeth Macleod; *b* 1985

(2) *Rosannagh Catriona; *b* 1988

Other titles under name Burton: A Barony of Burton was conferred in Jan 1711/2 on the 1st Earl of Uxbridge of the 1714 *cr* (*see* ANGLESEY, M) before his promotion to the higher rank. A subsidiary title of the Earls of Egmont (*qv*) is Baron Perceval of Burton. In addition the name Burton appears as a place name in the full recital of titles connected with the Monson Barony of 1728 (*qv*) and the Oxenbridge Viscountcy of 1886 briefly held with it. Lastly, Pitt the Elder was created Baron Pitt of Burton Pynsent, though he is of course better known under his superior peerage title Earl of Chatham.

Lineage (of Bass): WILLIAM BASS, of Leicester; *m* 23 May 1717 Hannah Fish, of Quarn (?, Leics, or Quarndon, Derbys), and had:

WILLIAM BASS; *b* 1717; fndr 1777 brewery at Burton, Staffs; *m* Mary Gibbons (*d* 2 March 1786), of London, and *d* 2 March 1787, leaving:

MICHAEL THOMAS BASS, of Burton; *b* 23 July 1760; *m* 14 June 1793 Sarah, dau of Abram Hoskyns, of Newton Solney, Derbys, and *d* 9 March 1827, having had an est s:

MICHAEL THOMAS BASS, of Rangemore Hall, Tatenhill, Staffs, JP, DL; *b* 6 July 1799; MP Derby 1848–83; *m* 8 Dec 1835 Eliza Jane (*d* 7 Aug 1897), dau of Maj Samuel Arden, of Longcroft, Staffs, and *d* 29 April 1884, having had, with other issue (*see* 1934 edn BASS, Bt):

1 Sir MICHAEL ARTHUR BASS, 1st Bt (UK), so *cr* 17 May 1882, with remainder, in default of heirs male of his own body, to his yr bro and the heirs male of the latter's body, also 13 Aug 1886 (1st and last) BARON BURTON OF RANGEMORE AND OF BURTON-ON-TRENT, Co Stafford, with ordinary remainder to the heirs male of his body, and finally 29 Nov 1897, since he had no male issue, **Baron Burton of Burton-on-Trent and of Rangemore**, Co Stafford, with special remainder to his dau, KCVO (1904), VD, DL, JP Staffs, Hon Col 6th Bn N Staffs Regt, MP (Lib) Stafford 1865–68, E Staffs 1868–85 and Burton 1885–86, chm Bass and dep chm SE Rlwy; *b* 12 Nov 1837; *educ* Harrow and Trin Coll Cambridge U (MA); *m* 28 Oct 1869 Harriet Georgina (*d* 21 Jan 1931), 4th dau of Edward Thornewill, of Dove Cliff, Staffs, and *d* 1 Feb 1909, when the btcy passed to his n, the 1886 Barony expired and the 1897 one passed to his dau, leaving:

(1) NELLIE LISA, **Baroness Burton**

2 Hamar Alfred, DL, of Byrkley Lodge, Burton-on-Trent; *b* 30 July 1842; MP Tamworth 1878–85 and W Staffs 1885–98, Hon Col 4th Bn N Staffs Regt; *m* 22 Feb 1879 Hon Louisa Bagot (*d* as result of an accident 18 May 1942), dau of 3rd Baron Bagot (*qv*), and *d* 8 April 1898, having had, with other issue:

(1) Sir WILLIAM ARTHUR HAMAR BASS, 2nd and last Bt, JP (Staffs); *b* 24 Dec 1879; Maj 10th Hus Boer War 1899–1902 and WW I; *m* 9 June 1903 Lady Wilmot Ida Noreen Hastings, yst dau of 13th Earl of Huntingdon (*qv*), and *dsp* 1952, when the btcy expired

The 1st BARON's dau,

NELLIE LISA Bass, **Baroness Burton of Burton-on-Trent and of Rangemore**; *b* 27 Dec 1873; *m* 1st 31 Jan 1894 Col James Evan Bruce BAILLIE, MVO, VD, of Dochfour, Inverness-shire, DL, JP, MP Inverness-shire 1895–1900, V-Chm Inverness TFA, Maj and Hon Col Inverness-shire Bn RHA, Capt 3rd Bn Northumberland Fus (*d* 6 May 1931), and had issue:

1 George Evan Michael, MC, TD, DL (Derbys and Ross and Cromarty), Brig RA (and 51st AA Bde), Lt-Col 4th Bn Cameron Highrs TA, Maj 24th (Derbys Yeo) Armd Car Co (TA), served WWs I and II; *b* 19 Dec 1894; *educ* Eton; *m* 15 Nov 1923 Lady Maud, *née* Cavendish, CBE (1945), JP (*d* 30 March 1975), est dau of 9th Duke of Devonshire (*qv*) and widow of Capt Angus Alexander Mackintosh, RHG, and *das* 6 June 1941, leaving issue:

(1) MICHAEL EVAN VICTOR BAILLIE, **3rd and present Baron Burton of Burton-on-Trent and of Rangemore**

(2) +Peter Charles, JP (Hants 1968) [Maj The Hon Peter Baillie JP, Wootton Hall, Wootton, New Milton, Hants BH25 5SJ]; *b* 26 June 1927; granted 1964 with sis rank of baron's dau/yr s; *educ* Eton; Maj Life Gds (ret); *m* 15 Nov 1955 *Jennifer Priscilla, yr dau of Cdr Harold Reginald Newgass, GC, of Winterbourne, W Stafford, Dorset, and has issue:

1a *Catriona Margaret; *b* 10 Sept 1956

2a *Elizabeth Mary Eilidh [Mrs Philip Clabburn, Oddfellows Cottage, Setley, Brockenhurst, Hants]; *b* 21 March 1959; *m* 1st 1982 Michael Halstead-Morton (*d* 1995); *m* 2nd 4 Oct 1997 *Philip Clabburn and by her 1st husb has:

1b *Hannah Elizabeth; *b* 1983

2b *Emily Victoria; *b* 1985

3a *Susan Jennifer [Mrs Christopher Rushworth, Orchard Farm Ho, Long Load, Nr Landport, Somerset]; *b* 10 Dec 1960; *m* 1989 *Capt Christopher Rushworth, RAOC (ret), and has issue:

1b *William Christopher; *b* 1993
4a *Rachel Emma; *b* 26 April 1963
(1) *Judith Evelyn Maud [The Hon Mrs Cameron, Aldourie Castle, Inverness IV1 2DL]; *b* 1925; ATS 1944–47; *m* 5 Sept 1949 *Lt-Col Angus Ewen Cameron, MC, Scots Gds, only son of Capt Allan George Cameron, 1st Bn QO Cameron Highrs, and has issue:
1a *(Angus) Iain [Iain Cameron Esq, Drummond, Dores, by Inverness]; *b* 10 June 1952; *educ* Eton; *m* 1973 *Candida, dau of Ronald T Fryer Smith, of 8 Fulwood Park, Liverpool 17, and has issue:
1b *Lorien; *b* 1975
1b *Fiona; *b* 1978
1a *Hester Caroline; *b* 22 June 1950
2 Arthur Malcolm Augustus BAILLIE, Maj Life Gds, served WWs I and II; *b* 4 July 1896; *educ* Eton; *m* 17 March 1927 Rosemary, er dau of Brig-Gen Sir Joseph Frederick Laycock, KCMG, DSO, of Wiseton, Doncaster, and *d* 14 Feb 1963, leaving issue:
(1) Ian Bruce; *b* 18 Jan 1928; *educ* Eton; Col Lt-Col cmdg Household Cavalry and Silver Stick in Waiting 1969–78; *m* 29 March 1962 *June Marion Cloudesley [Mrs Ian Baillie, Congham Lodge, Hillington, King's Lynn, Norfolk PE31 6BZ], only dau of Arthur Cloudesley Smith and widow of Arthur Henry Bellingham (*see* BELLINGHAM, Bt), and *d* 1978, having had issue:
1a *Katherine Victoria Harriet [Mrs Benjamin Wallace, Old Farm, Potsgrove, Milton Keynes, MK17 9HQ]; *b* 5 Nov 1962; *m* 1990 *(John) Benjamin Agnew Wallace, only son of (John) Malcolm Agnew Wallace, of Lochryan, Stranraer, Wigtownshire (*see* BAGOT, B), and has issue:
1b *Alexander Ian Agnew; *b* 1992
2b *Hewie Mâlcolm Agnew; *b* 1993
1b *Lara Mary Agnes; *b* 1996
2a *Sarah Rosemary Caroline; *b* 3 June 1964
1 Victoria Frances Maud; *b* 14 March 1899; *m* 2 Nov 1922 Sir Digby Lawson, 2nd Bt (*see* LAWSON, Bt, of Weetwood), and *d* 10 Jan 1931, leaving issue

The **Baroness** *m* 2nd 25 July 1932 Maj William Eugene Melles (*d* 20 Feb 1953), est son of Joseph William Melles, MA, DL, JP, of Gruline, Isle of Mull, and *d* 28 May 1962

Lineage (of Baillie): Sir WILLIAM BAILLIE of Hoprig, Penston and Carnbrue; gf of:

Sir WILLIAM BAILLIE of Lamington; *m c* 1430 Marian, dau of Sir John Seton of Seton, and had mortally maimed their tutor, a clergyman, and fearing the power of the Church, fled the country,
1 ALEXANDER, of whom presently
2 David; ancestor of the BAILLIEs of Innishargie and Ringdufferin, Ireland
3 John, settled in the Isle of Anglesey
4 William, ancestor of the BAILLIEs of Lamington (*see* 1949 edn LAMINGTON, B)
1 Margaret; *m* John, Earl of Sutherland

The est son,

ALEXANDER BAILLIE, of Dunain; with his two yr bros killed their clergyman tutor and fled abroad; later returned and fought Battle of Brechin 1452 under his maternal cousin 1st Earl of Huntly (*qv*), being rewarded by the grant of Dunain, Dochfour, Leys and Torbreck and made Constable Inverness Castle; *m* Catherine, dau of Sir William Grant of Treucky, and had:

WILLIAM BAILLIE of Dunain, Sheriff Inverness, Constable Inverness Castle; *m* 1534 —, dau of Ross of Balnagown, and had:

ALEXANDER BAILLIE of Dunain; Sheriff Inverness 1547–48; had issue, with a yr s:

DAVID BAILLIE of Dunain and Shuglie, Glen-Urquhart, Constable Inverness Castle 1548; *m* Margaret, dau of Rose of Kilravock, and *d* 1558, leaving, with an er s:

WILLIAM BAILLIE of Dunain Mor, Dunain Croy and Balrepart; *m* 10 Jan 1577 Catherine, 3rd dau of Robert More Munro, Chief of the Munros, by Margaret, dau of Sir James Ogilvie of Finlater, and had, with a yr s (John, Provost Inverness 1583, ancestor of the BAILLIEs of Leys):

ALEXANDER BAILLIE of Dunain; Sheriff Inverness 1585–93; *m* Catherine, dau of Munro of Milltown, and had, with an er s (William of Dunain, ancestor of the BAILLIEs of Dunain, also of PRESIDENT THEODORE ROOSEVELT of the USA, *see* AMERICAN PRESIDENTIAL FAMILIES, 1994, Morris Genealogical Books SA):

DAVID BAILLIE 1st of Dochfour and Easter and Wester Dockairn; excommunicated as RC by Presbyterian Church 28 May 1673; *m* 1669 Margaret Fraser, dau of 8th Lord Lovat (*qv*), and had and est s:

ALEXANDER BAILLIE of Dochfour; *m* 1709 Hannah, dau of Fraser of Reelig and widow of James Grant of Shuglie, and had issue:
1 HUGH of Dochfour
2 William of Rosehall, Sutherland; f of Gen Sir Ewan Baillie, Bt
3 Evan, of Abriachan
4 David, ancestor of the BAILLIEs of Leics
1 Isabella; *m* 1723 John Grant, of London

The est son,

HUGH BAILLIE of Dochfour; *m* 10 June 1730 Emilia, dau of Fraser of Reelig, and had, with other issue:
1 Alexander of Dochfour; *d* 1798
2 James, MP, of Ealing Grove, Middx; *b* 1737; *m* Colin, dau and coheir of Colin Campbell of Glenure by Janet, dau and coheir of Col Hon Hugh Mackay of Bighouse, and *d* 7 Sept 1793, being ancestor of the BAILLIEs of Glenure Ho, Glos, and BAILLIEs of Filleigh, Devon
3 EVAN of Dochfour; W India merchant, MP Bristol, Col Bristol Regt Vol Inf; *m* Mary, dau of Peter Gurley, of St Vincent, WI, and *d* 1885, having had, with other issue (including a yr s Hugh Duncan, of Redcastle, ancestor of the BAILLIEs of Loch Loy):

PETER of Dochfour, MP; *m* 9 March 1797 Elizabeth, dau of John Pinney, of Somerton, Erleigh, Somerset, and *dvp* 1812, leaving, with other issue:
(1) EVAN
(1) Jane; *m* 17 Oct 1826 Rev Hon Baptist Wriothesley Noel, bro of 1st Earl of Gainsborough (*qv*), and *d* 18 May 1889, leaving issue
(2) Mary; *m* 1st John Morritt, Jr, of Rokeby; *m* 2nd 28 April 1832 Capt George William St John-Mildmay, RN, 4th son of Sir Henry Paulet St John-Mildmay, 3rd Bt, MP (*qv*), *and d* 17 Jan 1892, leaving issue. He *d* 14 Feb 1851

The est son,

EVAN BAILLIE of Dochfour; *b* 1 April 1798; *m* 1st 9 Aug 1821 Charlotte Augusta (*dsp*), dau of Ven Charles Baillie-Hamilton, Archdeacon of Cleveland (*see* HADDINGTON, E); *m* 2nd 11 Oct 1823 Lady Georgina Frederica Montagu (*d* 30 July 1892), 4th dau of 5th Duke of Manchester (*qv*), and *d* April 1883, having by her had issue:
1 EVAN PETER MONTAGU, of whom presently
2 William Montagu, JP Inverness, High Sheriff Bristol 1860; *b* 11 Oct 1827; MA Cambridge; *m* 10 Sept 1859 Lady Theodosia Gertrude Proby (*d* 21 Oct 1902), yst dau of 3rd Earl of Carysfort (*see* PROBY, Bt), and *d* 11 Sept 1902, leaving issue
1 Caroline Eliza Montagu; *m* 17 Dec 1857 3rd Baron Wynford (*qv*), and *d* 16 Jan 1913, having had issue
2 Georgiana Mary Montagu; *m* 20 Jan 1857 Col Hon Sir William James Colville (*see* COLVILLE OF CULROSS, V), and *d* 29 March 1918, leaving issue
3 Mary Emily; *m* 1 July 1856 Francis Henry Beaumont, DL, of Buckland Court, Surrey, and *d* 11 Jan 1923, leaving issue (*see* BEAUMONT, Bt)

The est son,

EVAN PETER MONTAGU BAILLIE; *b* 27 Aug 1824; *m* 15 Feb 1855 Lady Frances Anna Bruce (*d* 16 Aug 1894), dau of 7th Earl of Elgin and Kincardine (*qv*), and *dvp* 9 Nov 1874, having had issue:
1 JAMES EVAN BRUCE of Dochfour; *m* 31 Jan 1894 Nellie Lisa, **Baroness Burton of Burton-on-Trent and of Rangemore** in her own right (*see* above)
2 Augustus Charles, DSO (1900), Lt-Col and Brev-Col late cmdg Lovat Scouts, Lt RHA Boer War 1900–02; *b* 25 March 1861; *m* 26 Jan 1905 Meta (*d* 23 April 1944), only dau of Maj-Gen Sir Henry Trotter, GCVO, of Morton Hall, and *d* 8 Jan 1939, leaving issue
3 Albert Victor (Very Rev), KCVO (1932), Domestic Chaplain to Bp Rochester 1891–95, Vicar St Margaret's Plumstead Kent 1895–98, Hon Canon Worcester 1905–08, Canon Coventry 1908–12, Rector and RD Rugby 1898–1912, Vicar and Sub-Dean St Michael's Collegiate Church Coventry 1912–17, Vicar Styvechale Coventry 1915–17, Chaplain-in-Ordinary to HM GEORGE V 1917, Dean of Windsor and Registrar Order Garter 1917–44, Domestic Chaplain to TM EDWARD VIII 1936 and GEORGE VI 1937–44; *b* 5 Aug 1864; *educ* Marlborough and Trin Coll Cambridge (MA 1891, Hon DD 1918); *m* 9 Aug 1898 Hon Constance Elizabeth Hamilton-Russell (*d* 27 Sept 1924), 5th dau of 8th Viscount Boyne (*qv*), and *d* 3 Nov 1955, leaving issue
1 Victoria Mathilda Susan (Hon), VA, Maid of Honour and Extra Bedchamber Woman to HM QUEEN VICTORIA; *m* 6 May 1884 Cdr Alaric Frederick Grant, RN, and *d* 4 Nov 1938. He *dsp* 21 Dec 1918

BURTON-CHADWICK

Arms: Az. on water barry wavy arg. and vert in base a lymphad or, the sail of the second charged with a martlet of the first, flying at the masthead a pennon gu. fimbriated also of the second, and at the stern a banner as the sail, in chief a lion passant between two mullets also arg. **Crest:** A demi-seahorse ppr., gorged with a naval crown and holding between the fins a portcullis chained or.
Motto: *In candore decus* ('Honour is purity').
Creation: Bt. (UK) 3 July 1935.

SIR JOSHUA KENNETH BURTON CHADWICK, 3RD BT; *b* 1 Feb 1954; *s f* 1983; sales manager/trainer Joshua Chadwick Marketing Developers

Lineage: JOSEPH CHADWICK, of Bidston, Cheshire; had:

Sir ROBERT CHADWICK later BURTON-CHADWICK (deed poll 30 Sept 1936), **1st Bt** (UK), so cr 3 July 1935, of Bidston; *b* 20 June 1869; head of shipping firm of Chadwick and Askew, of London and Liverpool, dir Chadwick, Weir and Co, London; Hon Capt RNR, fndr Master Mariners' Co, fndr and hon treas Liverpool Merchants' Mobile Hosp 1915, Dir Munitions Overseas Dept and Dir-Gen Stores and Tport Min Munitions 1915–19, MP (C) Barrow-in-Furness 1918–22 and

Wallasey 1922–31, Parly Sec BOT 1924–28, Counsellor Br Emb Buenos Aires 1940–47 (Rep Min of War Tport), served Boer War 1900–01 with Duke of Lancaster's Yeo, Roy Humane Soc's cert for saving life; *m* 1st 8 Feb 1903 Catherine Barbara (*d* 6 Oct 1935), dau of Thomas Williams; *m* 2nd 27 Oct 1936 Mrs Norah Irene Lessing (*d* 11 March 1965), 2nd dau of Alfred John Gibbs, and by his 1st w had issue:

1 Noel Kenneth Burton, F/Lt RAFVR WW II; *b* 14 Sept 1904; *m* 18 Aug 1933 Beatrice May (WAAF 1943–46), dau of Reginald Booth, of San Juan, Uruguay, and was *ka* 6 June 1941

2 ROBERT BURTON (Sir), **2nd Bt**

1 *Gwynfa Burton [Mrs Gwynfa Edmondson, 40 Ovington St, London SW3]; *b* 1906; *m* 15 June 1935 (*divorce* 1955) George D'Arcy Edmondson, CMG, CVO, OBE, er son of George D'Arcy Edmondson, of 193 Ashley Gardens, SW1

Sir ROBERT *d* 21 May 1951; his only surv son,

Sir Robert Peter Burton Burton-Chadwick, 2nd Bt, served WW II 1942–45 with NZ Mil Force in N Africa and Italy; *b* 22 June 1911; *educ* St George's Sch, Harpenden, Herts; *m* 1st 1937 (*divorce* 1949) Rosalind Mary, dau of Harry John Stott, and had issue:

1 *Diana [Mrs Andrew Gemmill, 18 Lyndhurst St, Richmond, Melbourne, VIC 3121, Australia]; *b* 1938; *m* 1965 *Andrew William Neilson Gemmill, and has issue:

(1) *Tristan John; *b* 1967

(2) *Giles William; *b* 1968

(1) *Lucinda Harriet; *b* 1972

2 *Sally Virginia [Mrs Grahame Hadwen, Stradbroke Towers, 2/90 Goodwin St, Kangaroo Point, Brisbane, QLD 4169, Australia]; *b* 1940; *m* 1961 *Grahame Robert Hadwen, and has issue:

(1) *Michael Robert; *b* 1970

(1) *Debbie Anne; *b* 1963

(2) *Susan Jane; *b* 1965

Sir Robert *m* 2nd 1950 *(Beryl) Joan, dau of Stanley Frederick James Brailsford, and *d* 1983, having by her had:

1 Sir JOSHUA KENNETH BURTON-CHADWICK, **3rd and present Bt**

3 *Wendy Lorraine [Mrs Andrew Palmer, 4 Douglas St, Kensington, Whangarei, New Zealand]; *b* 12 Dec 1951; *m* 1978 *Andrew Haig Palmer

BUTE

Arms: Quarterly, 1st and 4th, or a fess chequy azure and argent within a double tressure flory-counterflory gules (for STUART); 2nd and 3rd, argent a lion rampant azure (for CRICHTON). **Crests:** 1 A demi-lion rampant gules (for STUART), 2 A wyvern, fire issuant from the mouth, all proper (for CRICHTON), 3 A wyvern proper, holding in the mouth a sinister hand couped gules (for HERBERT). **Supporters:** Dexter, a horse argent, bridled gules; sinister, a stag proper, attired or. **Mottoes:** 1 (over the 1st crest) *Nobilis est ira leonis* ('The wrath of the lion is noble'), 2 (over the dexter crest) God send grace, 3 *Avito viret honore* ('He flourishes in ancestral honour'). **Creations:** Bt. (NS) 28 March 1627; L. (S) 29 Jan 1487/8 (Crichton of Sanquhar), 2 Feb 1622 (Sanquhar), 22 June 1633 (Crichton of Sanquhar and Cumnock), 14 April 1703 (Mountstuart); B. (GB) 3 April 1761 (Mount Stuart of Wortley), 20 May 1776 (Cardiff of Cardiff Castle); V. (S) 2 Feb 1621/2 and 12 June 1633 (both Air), also (S) 14 April 1703 (Kingarth) and (GB 21 March 1796 (Mountjoy); E. (S) 12 June 1633 (Dumfries), 14 April 1703 (Bute) and 21 March 1796 (Windsor); M. (GB) 21 March 1796.

THE 7TH MARQUESS OF THE COUNTY OF BUTE, Earl of Dumfries, Earl of Bute, Earl of Windsor, Viscount of Air (twice), **Viscount Kingarth, Viscount Mountjoy**, of the Isle of Wight, **Lord Crichton of Sanquhar, Lord of Sanquhar, Lord Crichton of Sanquhar and Cumnock, Lord Mountstuart, Cumrae and Inchmarnock, Baron Mount Stuart of Wortley**, Co York, **Baron Cardiff of Cardiff Castle**, and a **Baronet** (Sir John Colum Crichton-Stuart, Bt [The Most Hon The Marquess of Bute, Mount Stuart, Rothesay, Isle of Bute; Dumfries House, Cumnock, Ayrshire]; *b* 26 April 1958; *s* f 1993; *educ* Ampleforth; Hereditary Sheriff and Coroner Bute, Hereditary Keeper Rothesay Castle; former racing driver (as Johnny Dumfries), Br Formula 3 Champion 1984, jt winner Le Mans 1988; *m* 1984 (*divorce* 1993) Carolyn ('Freddy'), dau of Bryson Waddell, and has:

1 +JOHN BRYSON, *Lord Mount Stuart*; *b* 21 Dec 1989

1 +Caroline; *b* 1984

2 +Cathleen; *b* 1986

Lineage (of Crichton): Sir ROBERT CRICHTON of Sanquhar; *m* Elizabeth, dau of Sir John/William Erskine of Kinnoull, and *d* 1478/9, leaving, with a dau (Christian, *m* 1st Sir Robert Colville of Oxnam, *m* 2nd *de jure* 14th Earl of Mar, *qv*):

Sir ROBERT CRICHTON, **1st Lord Crichton of Sanquhar** (S), so *cr* 29 Jan 1487/8; defended Lochmaben against the Douglases 1484; *m* 1st Margaret Hay; *m* 2nd by 1457 Christian, dau of Sir John Erskine of Kinnoull and widow of John Crichton, and *d* between July 1494 and Feb 1494/5, having had an only son:

ROBERT CRICHTON of Kinnoull; *m* 1472 Marion , dau of 1st Earl of Lennox (*see* MORAY, E), and *dvp* between Feb 1483/4 and Feb 1491/2, leaving:

ROBERT CRICHTON, **2nd Lord Crichton of Sanquhar**; *m c* 1491 Marion Maxwell and *d* after 13 July but before 6 Nov 1513 (probably *k* at the English victory over the Scots of Flodden 9 Sept), leaving issue:

ROBERT CRICHTON, **3rd Lord Crichton of Sanquhar**; *m* Elizabeth, dau of Sir John Murray of Cockpool, and *d* between 12 July 1516 and 16 Oct 1520, having had issue:

1 ROBERT CRICHTON, **4th Lord Crichton of Sanquhar**; *m* by 1 Dec 1534 Elizabeth, dau and heir of John Campbell of W Loudoun and widow of William Wallace the er, and *dsp* a minor by 7 Jan 1535/6

2 WILLIAM, **5th Lord**

3 John, of Ryhill

4 Herbert

The **3rd Lord** had illegitimately by Margaret, dau of JAMES III:

1 Margaret; *m* 1517, as his 1st w, 4th Earl of Rotnes (*qv*)

The 4th LORD's bro,

WILLIAM CRICHTON, **5th Lord Crichton of Sanquhar**; *m* by 24 May 1540 Elizabeth, yst dau of Malcolm, Lord Fleming, and was fatally stabbed by 3rd Lord Sempill (*qv*), in a quarrel in the Edinburgh house of the Regent Chatelherault 11 June 1550, having had, with other issue:

1 John; *dvp* a minor on or after 26 July 1549

2 ROBERT CRICHTON, **6th Lord Crichton of Sanquhar**; *m* Margaret, dau of John Cunningham of Caprington and widow of Gilbert Kennedy, and *dsp* 1561

3 EDWARD CRICHTON, **7th Lord Crichton of Sanquhar**; *m c* 4 June 1561 Margaret (*m* 2nd *c* 16 May 1571 5th Earl of Menteith; *see* MONTROSE, D), dau of Sir James Douglas of Drumlanrig (*see* QUEENSBERRY, M), and *d* 23 May 1569, leaving:

(1) ROBERT CRICHTON, **8th Lord Crichton of Sanquhar**; *b c* 1568; RC; lost an eye *c* 1605 in a bout with a fencing master, John Turner, at Lord Norris's house of Rycote in Oxfordshire; in revenge plotted Turner's murder for seven years, effecting it through the agency of one Carlyle, who killed Turner by a pistol-shot 11 May 1612; Carlyle and several other accomplices were hanged by a hemp rope but the **8th Lord** was granted a peer's privilege of being hanged by a silk one, despite having as a Scottish peer been turned down for trial in the High Steward's Court (instead being tried in the King's Bench Court as plain Robert Crichton); *m* 16 April 1608 Anne (*m* 2nd 17 July 1615 6th Earl of Thomond (*see* INCHIQUIN, B) and was *bur* 13 April 1675), dau of Sir George Fermer (*see* HESKETH, B), and *dspl* on the scaffold in Great Palace Yard, Westminster, 29 June 1612, leaving:

1a William; *b* France; legitimated 8 Aug 1609 but his claim to the title and other estates failed 1614, though served heir to territorial Barony of Sanquhar 15 July 1619

4 Andrew

5 William; *m* Katherine Carmichael and had issue:

(1) WILLIAM CRICHTON, **1st Earl of Dumfries**, so *cr* 12 June 1633, as also VISCOUNT OF AIR [*i.e.*, Ayr] and LORD CRICHTON OF SANQUHAR AND CUMNOCK, with special remainder to his heirs male bearing the name and arms of Crichton, as also earlier 2 Feb 1621/2 VISCOUNT OF AIR and LORD OF SANQUHAR; *m* 1st Eupheme, dau of James Seton of Touch (*see* SETON, Bt, of Abercorn) and widow of Patrick Hamilton of Peel of Livingston; *m* 2nd by 16 July 1630 Ursula, dau of Stephen Barnham and widow of Sir Robert Swift, of Rotherham, and *d* after 15 Aug 1642 but before 24 March 1642/3, having by his 1st w had, with other issue:

1a WILLIAM, **2nd Earl**

1a Mary; *m* 29 Aug 1618 Edward Swift, 1st Viscount Carlingford

2a Catherine; *m* Sir John Charteris of Amisfield (*see* WEMYSS and MARCH, E)

The 1st EARL's est son,

WILLIAM CRICHTON, **2nd Earl of Dumfries**; resigned his honours 10 Sept 1690 and got a regrant 3 Nov 1690 with the old precedence but a new remainder to his gs and heir apparent in tail male, failing whom, to the four daus of his dead son Charles and the heirs of their bodies respectively who inherited the family estates, then to Charles's nearest heirs; *m* 29 Aug 1618 Penelope, sis of his bro-in-law 1st Viscount Carlingford, and *d* 1691, having had, with three daus:

1 Robert, *Lord Crichton*; *bapt* 19 Dec 1641; *dvp* an infant

2 Charles, *Lord Crichton*; settled his estates 1686, failing sons and heir male issue, on his four daus successively; *m c* autumn 1679 Sarah, dau of 1st Viscount Stair (*see* STAIR, E), and *dvp* after 4 Oct 1686 but before 11 March 1689/90, leaving, with other issue:

(1) WILLIAM CRICHTON, **3rd Earl of Dumfries**; *d* unm 28 Feb 1693/4

(1) Elizabeth; *m* 1658 8th Earl of Eglinto(u)n (*see* EGLINTON and WINTON, E)

(2) PENELOPE, **Countess of Dumfries**

The 3rd EARL's sis,

PENELOPE Crichton, **Countess of Dumfries** in her own right; *m* 26 Feb 1697/8 her cousin Col Hon William Dalrymple, of Glenmure, MP Ayrshire (*d* 3 Dec

1744), 2nd son of 1st Earl of Stair (*qv*), and *d* 6 March 1741/2, having had, with other issue:

1 WILLIAM DALRYMPLE later DALRYMPLE-CRICHTON, **5th Earl of Dumfries** and 4th EARL OF STAIR (in which *s* yr bro 1760), KT (March 1751/2); served Army 1721–47, ADC to unc 2nd Earl of Stair at Battle of Dettingen 1743; *m* 1st 2 April 1731 Lady Anne Gordon (*d* 15 April 1755), dau of 2nd Earl of Aberdeen (*see* ABERDEEN AND TEMAIR, M), and had:

(1) William, *Lord Crichton*; *b* 12 Dec 1734; *dvp* 9 Sept 1744

1 (cont.) The **5th Earl** *m* 2nd 19 June 1762 Anne (*m* 2nd Hon Alexander Gordon, Ld of Session as Lord Rockville), dau of William Duff, of Crombie, and *dsps* 27 July 1768

2 JAMES DALRYMPLE, 3rd EARL OF STAIR (*qv*); *dsp* 13 Nov 1760

1 Elizabeth; *m* John Macdowall or McDouall, of Freugh, Wigtonshire, and had, with other issue:

(1) PATRICK, **6th Earl**

(2) John, of Glasgow; *m* 9 Dec 1767 Mary Isabel, dau of Ebenezer MacCulloch, of Glasgow, and *d* 22 Dec 1803, leaving, with other issue:

1a William (Rev); *b* 1775; Preb Peterborough; *m* 15 Feb 1815 Euphemia, dau of Jean Gaudin, and *d* 15 Dec 1849, leaving issue:

1b John Crichton Stuart, of New Freugh, NSW, Australia; *b* 5 July 1818; *m* 1st 23 Feb 1841 Ellen Maria (*d* 10 Sept 1861), dau of Robert Appleyard Fitzgerald; *m* 2nd 28 March 1864 Susan Mary (*d* 1906), dau of Rev Edward Hartigan, and *d* Jan 1891, having had by his 1st w, with other issue:

1c John Crichton Stuart; *b* 23 Oct 1844; *m* 20 Sept 1905 Isabella (*d* 5 Dec 1944), widow of John Gollan, and *d* 19 Dec 1923

2c Patrick James Crichton; *b* 20 June 1848; *m* 1883 Laura May (*d* 4 Jan 1941), est dau of Charles Swanston, of Victoria, and *d* 9 Sept 1943, leaving issue:

1d Crichton; *b* 7 Feb 1890; *d* 14 Jan 1952

1d Jessie; *b* 1886; *m* 1905 James Lockie Wilson, CBE (*d* 13 Nov 1956), and *d* 15 July 1953, leaving issue

2d Lorna; *b* 1888; *m* 1910 Henry Ernest Elliott (*d* 1934), and had issue

3d May; *b* 1892

4d Gwendolen; *b* 1894; *m* 12 Jan 1951 John Mountford Adnam

5d Elizabeth; *b* 1899

6d Noora Freugh; *b* 1903; *d* 1 April 1944

3c Willoughby Crichton; *b* 7 May 1852; *m* 1875 Mary Edith Emily (*d* 1943), dau of P H McArdell, and *d* 28 May 1914, leaving issue:

1d John Crichton Stuart, OBE (1929); *b* 1878; MRCS Eng, LRCP Lond; W African Med Staff, DMSS Sierra Leone; *m* 18 Feb 1914 Marguerite Lavinia (Madge) (*d* 1950), 2nd dau of Frank Garrett, of Highgate, and *d* 1941, leaving issue:

1e John Crichton Stuart; *b* 14 May 1920; Maj Roy Signals WW II; *m* 20 Jan 1945 *Dorothy Anne [Mrs John Bryden, 61 Swanston Ave, Edinburgh EB10 7BZ] (*m* 2nd 2 Feb 1954 Maj John Hewgill Anderson Bryden, RAPC, s of Col Ronald Anderson Bryden, DSO, RAMC), yst dau of Rev Claude Arthur Hedley Going, MA, of Shrewsbury, and *d* 17 Nov 1951, leaving issue:

1f +John Crichton Stuart; *b* 27 May 1950 (twin); *educ* Haileybury; Insp Roy Hong Kong Police; *m* 1975 *Susanna Sze Wing-Lai, and has issue:

1g +John Crichton Stuart; *b* 1976

2g +Patrick; *b* 1978

2f +Philip Lewis [Philip McDouall Esq, Box 580, RR2, Woodlawn, Ontario, K0A 3M0, Canada]; *b* 27 May 1950 (twin); *educ* Haileybury; 2nd Lt Roy Signals; mktg dir Newbridge Networks Corp, Canada; *m* 1976 (*separated* 1996) *Marlis Bartels and has issue:

1g +Andrew Philip; *b* 1977

2g +James Stephen; *b* 1979

1g +Joanna Marie; *b* 1984

1f +Patricia Anne; *b* 30 Oct 1945; *m* 1971 *James A Downing, son of S Downing, of Wharncliffeside, Sheffield, and has issue:

1g +Frederick James; *b* 1972

2g +Timothy John; *b* 1979

1g +Sarah Frances; *b* 1975

2f +Elizabeth Jean [Mrs Elizabeth Labaye, 4 Impasse Tarentaise 69300, Caluire, France]; *b* 9 Oct 1947; *m* 1971 (*divorce* 1994) Jean Labaye, and has:

1g +Jean Simon; *b* 1972

2g +Georges-Antoine; *b* 1982

1g +Victoria Ann; *b* 1974

2e +Lewis Willoughby [Lewis McDouall Esq, PO Box 194, Umtentweni, Natal 4235, S Africa]; *b* 25 Dec 1924; *m* 29 Feb 1964 *Madeline, dau of George Hall, of Yorks, and has:

1f +Francis John Stephen; *b* 29 May 1969

1e +Mary Crichton [Mrs Charles Parsons, Hillside, 62 Brattle Wood, Sevenoaks, Kent]; *b* 8 May 1917; *m* 1950 *Charles Grenville Parsons, DSC, and has issue:

1f +Susan Mary; *b* 5 June 1952

2f +Jane Elizabeth; *b* 7 June 1955

2e +Marguerite Lavinia [Mrs Ian McCormick, 19 Durham Gdns, Lower Largo, Leven, Fife YB6 DU]; *m* 1941 *Capt Ian Sibbald McCormick, MB, RAMC, and has issue:

1f +John Sibbald; *b* 1943; *m* 1975 *Irene Marilyn and has issue:

1g +John Steven; *b* 1981

2g +David Charles; *b* 1983

1g +Jill Elaine; *b* 1976

1f +Jennifer Anne; *b* 1943; *m* 1969 *Kenneth Anthony Fleming and has:

1g +Stuart Kenneth; *b* 1972

2g +Andrew Michael; *b* 1978

1g +Anne Margaret; *b* 1970

2f +Marguerite Lavinia; *b* 1948; *m* 1975 *John Glen Abercromby and has issue:

1g +Andrew Frank; *b* 1980

1g +Jane; *b* 1977

2g +Carol Marguerite; *b* 1983

2d Crichton Willoughby (Rev); *b* 1881; *educ* New Zealand U (BA); Missionary China 1909–48, rector Plymtree, Devon, 1948–53; *m* 1st 10 May 1911 Florence Charlotte (*d* Oct 1923), dau of William Bampfield Cogan, of Clifton, Bristol, and had issue:

1e John Crichton, CMG (1966); *b* 26 April 1912; *educ* Monkton Combe and Jesus Coll Cambridge (MA); Ch Social Welfare Offr Malaya 1952–57, Sec Chinese Affairs Hong Kong 1957–67; *m* 5 March 1946 *Kathleen Glover [Mrs John McDouall, 4 Bicester House, King's End, Bicester, Oxon OX6 7DT], dau of Archibald Black Moir, IoW, and *d* 1979, leaving issue:

1f +Brian John [Brian McDouall Esq, King George V School, 2 Tin Kwong Rd, Kowloon, Hong Kong]; *b* 26 June 1952; *educ* King's Canterbury; *m* 1st 1978 (*divorce* 1989) Barbara May, dau of Arnold Worth, of Manchester; *m* 2nd 1998 *Clare Louise Stern

1f +Anne Glover [Mrs Anne James, 26 Barrett St, Oxford OX2 OAT]; *b* 3 April 1948; *m* 18 Oct 1968 (*divorce* 1982) David Thomas Douglas James, PhD, son of Dr Alan George James, of Castleford, Yorks, and has issue:

1g +Simon Alan; *b* 1969; *m* 19 Oct 1996 *Michelle Louise Marcar

1g +Annabel Louise; *b* 1971

2f +Heather Crichton; *b* 11 Aug 1949; D Phil; *m* 1979 *Robert Norman Swanson, PhD, of 106 Northfield Rd, Kings Norton, Birmingham, and has issue:

1g +John Crichton Norman; *b* 1981

1g +Elizabeth Eleanor; *b* 1983

2e Kenneth Willoughby; *b* 9 July 1914; *educ* Monkton Combe, Christ's Coll Cambridge (MA); *m* 16 Sept 1958 *Edith Joan [Mrs Kenneth McDouall, 3 Mill Lane, Chinnor, Oxon OX9 4QU], dau of Henry George Sears, of Surrey, and *d* 16 March 1995, leaving:

1f +Rhoda Mary; *b* 20 July 1959; *m* 1st (*divorce* 1984) her 2nd cousin Jeremy Stuart Stevenson, Lt RNZN; *m* 2nd 1992 *Andrew Neil David Eagles and by him has:

1g +Ellen Joanna; *b* 14 July 1996

2d (cont.) The Rev Crichton McDouall *m* 2nd 23 April 1935 Jessie Kentish (*d* 1979), dau of George Rudolf Cole, of Sheffield, and *d* 14 Nov 1966, leaving by her:

3e +David Christopher; *b* 30 Aug 1936; *educ* Radley and Jesus Coll Cambridge (MA); *m* 4 Jan 1969 *Veronica Mary, yr dau of Harry Earl Heighway, of Hagley, Worcs, and has issue:

1f +Jonathan Crichton Stuart; *b* 1976

1f +Sara Frances; *b* 18 April 1972

2f +Fiona Mary; *b* 1974

3d Philip Hastings; *b* 1884; *educ* New Zealand U (BSc Eng); *m* 1917 Ivy Harriet, dau of Henry Charles Sanders, late PWD India, and *d* 1978, leaving issue:

1e +Philip John [Philip McDouall Esq, Blue Gentians, St George's Well, Cullompton, Devon]; *b* 1924; *m* 19 May 1950 Hazel Rosemary (*d* 1992), dau of Charles Frederick Bowring, late RN, and has issue:

1f +Andrew Crichton; *b* 22 Feb 1951; *m* 1977 *Katherine, dau of Rev G Hardy

1f +Janet Mary; *b* 18 Nov 1953

2f +Ellen Margaret Rosemary; *b* 8 Feb 1963

2e Willoughby Roy Crichton; *b* 1930

1e +Margaret Heather [Sra Leonardo de Castro Freire, Rua do Rio da Bica 7, S Pedro de Sintra, Portugal]; *b* 1920; *m* 11 Nov 1946 Leonardo Rey Calaco de Castro Freire (*d* 1970), son of Leonardo de Castro Freire, of Lisbon, and has issue:

1f +Martin Anthony [Sr Martin de Castro Freire, Rua Alexandro Herculano 91, Tomar, Portugal]; *b* 8 Jan 1952; *m* 1982 *Filipa Macedo, and has issue:

1g +Manuel Filipe; *b* 1984

2g +Martin Afonso; *b* 1986

2f +Jorge Leonardo [Sr Jorge de Castro Freire, Rua Garcia de Orta 70–3°, Lisbon, Portugal]; *b* 17 March 1956; *m* 1979 *Ana Simões Pinto, and has issue:

1g +Diego; *b* 1986

3f +Alexander Anthony [Sr Alexander de Castro Freire, Rua Garcia de Orta 70, Lisbon, Portugal]; *b* 2 March 1959; *m* 1984 *Paula Vieira, and has issue:

1g +Carolina; *b* 1986

1f +Philippa Mary; *b* 4 Sept 1949; *m* 1972 *João Manuel Rocheta, of Rua Garcia de Orta 70–2°, Lisbon, Portugal, and has issue:

1g +Gonçalo; *b* 1975

1g +Rita; *b* 1978

2f +Catherine Maria; *b* 30 Aug 1954

2e +Mabel Frances Harriet [Mrs Peter Haynes, 1 Woodlands, Budleigh Salterton, Devon]; *b* 1926; *m* 1985 *Peter Haynes

4d Eric Oldfield; *b* 2 June 1886; *m* 1 Jan 1913 Elizabeth Carpenter (*d* Jan 1954), dau of Richard Morrish, of Lincoln, Canterbury, New Zealand, and *d* 28 Oct 1918, leaving issue:

1e +Ella Barbara [Mrs Jack Eaton, 72 Wiggins St, Sumner, Christchurch 8, NZ]; *b* 25 March 1914; *m* 1937 Rev Henry Jackson Eaton (*d* 1991), and had issue:

1f +Michael McDouall [Michael Eaton Esq, Mountford, Wapara, N Canterbury, NZ]; *b* 1937; *educ* U of NZ (Dip Fine Arts); FRSA; *m* 1st 1962 Lynne Eleanor (*d* 1986), dau of Lester Leyward; *m* 2nd 1993 *Elizabeth Savill, and has issue by 1st wife:

1g +Jonathan Heyward McDouall; *b* 1964; LLB; *m* 1994 *Fiona Smith

2g +Benjamin Herriot McDouall Eaton; *b* 1967

1g +Penelope Jane Eaton; *b* 1962; *m* 1985 *William David Thomas, and has issue:

1h +James William Grigg; *b* 1986

1h +Georgina Lynne; *b* 1988

2h +Rosa Virginia; *b* 1990

3g +Sarah Lynne; *b* 1969

2f +Derek Lionel (Rt Rev), QSM; *b* 1941; QSM NZ 1985; MA Dip Theol, TTC, Bp of Nelson, NZ; *m* 1964 *Alice Janice, dau of George Maslin, and has issue:

1g +Simeon Michael; *b* 1968

2g +Stephen Daniel; *b* 1969

1g +Rebecca Ann; *b* 1971; *m* 1992 *Andrew Robert Burgess

2e Kathleen Oldfield; *b* 2 July 1916; *m* William Enright, and had issue

5d Gerald William; *b* 1887; *m* 10 Nov 1920 Dora Olive (*d* 1975), dau of Arthur Alexander McKinnon, of Oamaru, NZ, and *d* 12 April 1969, leaving issue:

1e +Eric Willoughby [Eric McDouall Esq, 22 Greendale Rd, Glen Hills, Leicester]; *b* 27 Dec 1921; *m* 5 Aug 1944 *Marion Maud, dau of J Holder, of Tetbury, Glos, and has issue:

1f +Maurice Willoughby [Mr Maurice McDouall, PO Box 388, Caledon, Ontario, Canada]; *b* 2 Aug 1945; RN; *m* 22 July 1967 *Bernice Towers, dau of Lindon Towers Cunliffe, of Fareham, Hants, and has issue:

1g +Fiona Bernice; *b* 30 Nov 1968

2g +Rebecca Jane; *b* 1972

1f +Geraldine Ann; *b* 10 Feb 1950; *m* 1976 *Martin Rex Challis, and has issue:

1g +Christopher Martin; *b* 1986

1g +Kirsty Ann; *b* 1983

2e +Gerald Ian Crichton OBE, JP [Mr Gerald McDouall OBE JP, Freugh, 54 Oakland Ave, Wanganui, NZ]; *b* 18 Nov 1929; *m* 27 July 1963 *Shirley Maureen, dau of Thomas Sanson, of Wanganui, NZ, and has issue:

1f +Gerald Andrew; *b* 27 Nov 1964; BCA; *m* 1992 *Denys Ann, dau of John Fotheringham, of Auckland, and has:

1g +Alice Jane Timpany; *b* 1995

2f +Hamish Crichton; *b* 1968; MA

1f +Rachael Deborah; *b* 1963; BPharm; *m* 1994 *Michael Patrick Hay, PhD, of Napier

1e +Patricia Ellen; *b* 31 Oct 1923; *m* 22 Nov 1947 W/Cdr George Stuart Alexander Stevenson (*d* 1993), DFC, RNZAF, and has issue:

1f +Hugh William; *b* 10 Nov 1951; *m* 1978 *Jillian Margaret, dau of Melville James Pitt Glasgow, and has issue:

1g +David James; *b* 1985

1g +Sarah Jane; *b* 1983

2f +Jeremy Stuart [Lt Jeremy Stevenson, 27 Rodney St, Howick, Auckland, NZ]; *b* 27 Nov 1956; Lt RNZN; *m* 1st 1982 (*divorce* 1984) his 2nd cousin Rhoda Mary, dau of Kenneth Willoughby; *m* 2nd 1990 *Melinda Jane Ferguson, of Auckland, and by her has:

1g +Timothy Alexander Stuart; *b* 1992

1f +Helen Patricia; *b* 1 March 1953; *m* 1st 1982 (*divorce* 1984) Michael John Fowler, of Wellington, NZ; *m* 2nd 1986 *Robert Stephen Schaffel, of NJ, USA

2e +Alison Crichton [Mrs Philip Wells, 14b Broadshard Lane, Ringwood, Hants BH24 1RR]; *b* 31 Aug 1926; *m* 2 Nov 1957 *Philip John Poulett Wells, er s of Dr Philip H Wells, MC, MRCP, of Stratford-on-Avon, and has issue:

1f +Philip David Crichton [Philip Wells Esq, 5 Collins Lane, Ringwood, Hants BH24 1LD]; *b* 19 Jan 1961; *m* 1990 *Sally Henrietta, dau of Peter Collings, of Denham, Middx and has:

1g +Oliver Philip Collings; *b* 1994

1g +Millie; *b* 1988

1f +Diana Jane [Mrs Richard Trinick, 3 Bucklands Drive, Nailsea, Somerset BS48 4PH]; *b* 20 Dec 1958; *m* 1984 *Richard David Trinick, and has issue:

1g +Chester Michael; *b* 1987

2g +Robert John; *b* 1989

3g +Laurence James; *b* 1990

2f +Elizabeth Joanna; *b* 2 Dec 1966

6d Alan Edward Crichton; *b* 1895; *m* 1922 Doris Annie (*d* 1984), dau of Joseph Preston, of Oamaru, NZ, and *d* Aug 1964, leaving issue:

1e +Stuart Preston [Stuart McDouall Esq, 28 Ure Street, Oamaru, New Zealand]; *b* 1922; *m* 1951 Winifred Edith (*d* 1985), dau of Maj Howard Rewa Jones, of Oamaru, NZ, and has issue:

1f +Philip Stuart; *b* 1955; *m* 1978 *Alison Nicholas, and has had issue:

1g +Daniel Stuart; *b* 1980

2g +James Murray; *b* 1984

3g +Timothy Philip; *b* 1987

1g +Melissa; *b* 1982; *d* 1983

1f +Patricia Mary; *b* 1952; *m* 1973 *Atholl Campbell, and has issue:

1g +Hamish Iain; *b* 1979

1g +Sarah Leigh; *b* 1976

2f +Judith Anne; *b* 1954; *m* 1976 *Rex Ormandy, and has issue:

1g +Michael Stuart; *b* 1987 (twin)

1g +Haylee Jan; *b* 1984

2g +Lisa Jane; *b* 1987 (twin)

3f +Heather; *b* 1959; *m* 1981 *Bruce Reilly, and has issue:

1g +Megan Jayne; *b* 1983

2g +Anna Marie; *b* 1985

3g +Rachel Dawn; *b* 1988

2e +Willoughby Alan [Mr Willoughby McDouall, PO Box 114, Kurow, N Otago, New Zealand]; *b* 26 Aug 1935; *m* 26 Jan 1963 *Pamela Ann, dau of Alan H Ruddick, of Oamaru, NZ, and has issue:

1f +John Alan Crichton; *b* 1971

1f +Fiona Mary; *b* 1969

2f +Joanna Louise; *b* 1974

1e +Doris Mary; *b* 1924; *m* 1947 *Ernest Benjamin Lyons, of Woodbury RD21, Geraldine, NZ, son of Clarence Mark Lyons, and has issue:

1f +Alan Mark; *b* 1950; *m* 1973 *Vivienne Lorna McPhail, of Wellington, NZ, and has issue:

1g +Nathan John; *b* 1979

1g +Valerie Anne; *b* 1976

2f John McDouall; *b* 1952; *m* 1982 *Sue Hodgson, of Christchurch, NZ, and *d* 1991, leaving issue:

1g +Jai Douglas; *b* 1985

2g +Charlie John; *b* 1987

3f +David Wayne; *b* 1954; *m* 1st 1974 (*divorce* 1982) Frances Margaret O'Connell, of Invercargill, NZ, and has issue:

1g +Jeremy Rhys; *b* 1974

1g +Rachel Jane; *b* 1978

2g +Megan Aimee; *b* 1980

3f (cont.) David Lyons *m* 2nd 1986 *Margaret Shirley Bain, of Kawerau, NZ, and has further issue:

3g +Vanessa Lee; *b* 1987

4g +Samantha Renee; *b* 19–

5g +Amanda Kay; *b* 1992

4f +Anthony Bruce; *b* 1956; *m* 1979 (*divorce* 1982) Gwen Haigh, of Perth

5f +Kenneth Brett; *b* 1957; *m* 1981 (*divorce* 1990) Jill Fowler, of Perth

1f +Susan Mary; *b* 1948; *m* 1972 Graeme Norris Sherwood (*d* 1985), of Palmerston, NZ, and has issue:

1g +Jacalyn Anne; *b* 1979

2g +Joanna Lisa; *b* 1982

2e +Josephine Anne [Miss Josephine McDouall, 16 Holly Road, Christchurch, New Zealand]; *b* 1926

3e +Ellen Coverdale [Mrs James Anderson, Monuina, Tripp Settlement Road, RD 21, Geraldine, S Canterbury, New Zealand]; *b* 1928; *m* 6 Sept 1952 *James Bruce Anderson, and has issue:

1f +Duncan Bruce; *b* 23 Sept 1955

2f +Ian James; *b* 19 Aug 1959; *m* 1st 1980 (*divorce* 1986) Carol Ruth Lynette Williams, of Geraldine, NZ; *m* 2nd 1989 *Rose Marie Anne Birnie, of Oamaru, NZ, and has issue by his 1st w:

1g +Steven Ian; *b* 1981

1g +Karen Lynette; *b* 1984

2g +Katherine Ruth (twin); *b* 1984

1f +Helen Mary [Mrs Halene Magatogia, Alofi, Box 87, Niue Island, New Zealand]; *b* 16 Jan 1954; *m* 1975 *Halene Kupa Magatogia, and has issue:

1g +James Kupa; *b* 1977

2g +Charles Bruce Tali; *b* 1979

1g +Tani Mary Pua; *b* 1981

2f +Barbara Ellen [Mrs Gerard Scott, Kerrytown, RD4, Timaru, New Zealand]; *b* 6 May 1958; *m* 1981 *Gerard Patrick Scott, and has issue:

1g +Finian Patrick; *b* 1990

1g +Lucy Bridget; *b* 1984

2g +Ingrid Jane; *b* 1989

3f +Susan Grace; *b* 8 Oct 1960; *m* 1st 1981 Geoffrey Ronald Taylor, of Taieri NZ, and has issue:

1g +Scott James; *b* 1981

2g +Mark Ronald; *b* 1984

3f (cont.) Mrs Susan Taylor *m* 2nd 1989 *Brian John Close, of Oamaru, NZ, and has further issue:

1g +Catherine Grace; *b* 1990

1d Mary Coverdale

2d Ellen Fitzgerald

4c Gerald Hastings Crichton; *b* 1 Oct 1855; *m* 1889 Florence Isabel (*d* 16 June 1912), dau of H P Stacey, of Singleton, NSW, and *dsp* 1909

5c Herbert Crichton; *b* 19 Feb 1860; MRCSE, LRCPL, DPH Cambridge, Silver Jubilee Medal (1935); *m* 1899 Hester Maria Corry (*d* 1942), dau of C S Hartigan, and *d* 3 Feb 1947, leaving issue:

1d Edith Isabella Stewart; *b* 1900; *m* 1926 Lindsey Fraser Single (*d* 1988), and *d* 1997 having had:

1e +Mark McDouall [Mr Mark Single, 61 View St, Wooloowin 4030, Queensland, Australia]; *b* 20 Aug 1930; *m* 30 Aug 1963 *Jean Margaret, dau of J M Vicars, of Lindfield, NSW, and has issue:

1f +Jane Margaret McDouall; *b* 4 Feb 1965; *m* 1985 *Peter Kessler and has had:

1g +Maxwell Peter; *b* 1995

2g +Edwin Thomas; *b* 1997

1g +Sophie Maria; *b* 1990

2g Claire Susan; *b* 1994; *d* 1995

2f +Claire Susan McDouall; *b* 1967

3f +Anne Noreen Vicars; *b* 1969

1e +Marion Elizabeth McDouall; *b* 5 Sept 1928; *m* 1st 12 April 1950 Douglas Lascelles Ryrie (*d* 2 April 1959); *m* 2nd 1966 *Peter Cowper, of 180 Queen Street, Woolahra, NSW, and has had by her 1st husb:

1f Mark Douglas; *b* 2 Sept 1957; *d* 6 Nov 1977

2e Lindsay McDouall; *b* 8 Aug 1939; *d* 17 March 1952

2d Barbara Crichton; *b* 1902; *m* 1930 John Jeffreys Ralph (*d* 1996), est son of Lionel Nethersole Ralph, of Tauranga, NZ, and *d* 1979, leaving:

1e +Richard Nethersole [Mr Richard Ralph, Box 663, PO Malanda 4885, Queensland, Australia]; *b* 24 July 1937; *m* 23 April 1965 (*divorce* 199–) Pamela, only dau of J Dunphy, of Duaringa, Qld, Australia, and has issue:

1f +Vanessa; *b* 1969

2f +Melinda; *b* 1971

3f +Samantha; *b* 1974

3d Penelope Crichton; *b* 1903; *d* 1995

4d Janet Hester Crichton; *b* 1905; *m* 1954 Frederick Tooth, MRCSE, LRCPL, DPH, DTM, OStJ (*d* 1963), of Balgreggan, Fox Valley Rd, Wahroonga, NSW, Australia and *d* 1993

5d +Margaret Ellen Crichton [Mrs William Leslie, 4 Redleaf Apartments, 1630 Pacific Highway, Wahroonga, NSW 2076, Australia]; *m* 1st 19 Nov 1938 Harry Granville Doyle, of Solomon Islands (*d* as POW Japan 1 July 1942); *m* 2nd 14 Dec 1951 William Stanley Leslie, MA (*d* 15 April 1957) Headmaster Barker Coll, Hornsby, NSW, s of A S Leslie, of Brisbane

6d +Mary Crichton Stuart [Mrs Alexander Bain, 74 Ruth Place, Dalmeny, NSW 2546, Australia]; *b* 1909; *m* 18 May 1938 Alexander Bain (*d* 3 April 1996), Master Mariner, and has issue:

1e +Roderick Alexander Crichton [Mr Roderick Bain, 19 Williams St, Watson, ACT 2602, Australia]; *b* 7 Oct 1940

2e +John Herbert Crichton [Mr John Bain, 28 Stapylton Street, Holder, ACT 2611, Australia]; *b* 13 Sept 1944; BSc (New England), MSc (James Cook U, Qld); *m* *Peta Jane Holdsworth, of Adelaide, Australia, and has issue:

1f +Scott James; *b* 1971

2f +Timothy Ross; *b* 1974

1c Maria Caroline; *m* 14 Sept 1903 Rev Preb Frederick Arthur Sanders (*d* 14 Aug 1930), Archdeacon and Canon of Exeter 1909–24, rector Woodleigh, S Devon, and *d* 24 April 1934

2b William Sutherland (Rev); *b* 27 June 1820; Rector Ousden, Suffolk; *m* 8 June 1854 Grace Maria (*d* 3 April 1923), dau of Sir James Dalrymple Hay, 2nd Bt (*qv*), and *d* 9 Aug 1902, leaving, with other issue:

1c William, of Khaniqin, Iraq; *b* 13 April 1855; Levant Consular Serv; *d* 2 Nov 1924

2c Claud Hay; *b* 8 July 1864; *m* 23 April 1904 Alice May (*d* 1955), dau of George Redding, and *d* 21 Aug 1905, leaving issue:

1d +Joan Alma [Mrs Brian Miller, Witches Moon, Stony Lane, Little Kingshill, Great Missenden, Bucks HP16 ODS]; *b* 1 Aug 1905; *m* 18 June 1931 Brian Miller (*d* 1992), and has issue:

1e +Ian Claud [Ian Miller Esq, 4 Fryer Close, Chesham, Bucks HP5 1RD]; *b* 1932; *m* 1st 1955 Violet Grace Waters (*d* 1987); *m* 2nd 1994 *Hazel Gwendolyn Wray, and has by his 1st w:

1f +Nicola Anne; *b* 1960; DPhil

2e +Peter Gerald [Peter Miller Esq, 3 Nicolas Ave, Glen Eden, Auckland 8, New Zealand]; *b* 1934; *m* 1955 *Patricia Ann Collins, and has issue:

1f +Rogan Edward Oliver; *b* 1966

2f +Cameron Peter; *b* 1970

1f +Carolyn Jane; *b* 1959

2f +Philippa Jane; *b* 1961

3c Kenneth Gilbert; *b* 22 Feb 1867; MA; *m* 18 May 1904 Evelyn Caroline Locke (*d* 1948), er dau of Ferdinand Marshall Huth, DL, of Fawley, Hants, and *d* 7 April 1939, leaving issue:

1d Ferdinand Huth; *b* 10 March 1905; 1st Offr ATA; *m* 10 March 1931 *Lilian Hall [Mrs Ferdinand McDouall, Wensley House, Wensley Rd, Richmond, Nelson, New Zealand], yr dau of W J Saville, of Rugby, and *d* 1990, leaving:

1e +Kenneth Hugh [Kenneth McDouall Esq, 2 West Street, Denbury, Newton Abbot, S Devon TQ12 6DP]; *b* 24 July 1935; *m* 28 Oct 1964 *Jean, only dau of Leonard Crouch, and has issue:

1f +Duncan Hugh; *b* 1969

2f +Justin Ian; *b* 1972

2e +Sid(ney) Morris [Sid McDouall Esq, 75 Hill St, Richmond, Nelson, New Zealand]; *b* 1 Feb 1944; *m* 1974 *Virginia Helen, est dau of M Charters, of NZ, and has issue:

1f +Michael Guy; *b* 1977

2f +Simon Geoffrey; *b* 1981

1e +Evelyn Susan [Mrs Andrew Barr-Sim, Blair House, 3 New St, Henley-on-Thames, Oxon]; *b* 12 Aug 1937; *m* 1st 1962 (*divorce* 1968) Stuart Wallace MacGregor; *m* 2nd 1977 *Andrew John Barr-Sim, of Blair House, and has issue by 1st husb:

1f +Fiona Judith; *b* 27 Feb 1964

2f +Alison Catherine; *b* 7 Jan 1966

1d Penelope; *b* 20 June 1909

4c Alan Patrick, MIEE; *b* 18 May 1872; *m* 1 Nov 1902 Frances Ethel (*d* 17 July 1968), dau of Edward Reeves, of NZ, and *d* 6 Jan 1947, leaving issue:

1d Patrick Sutherland; *b* 29 March 1904; *m* 9 June 1941 Esther Mary (*m* 2nd 1952 George Black, of Ferryhill, Co Durham), dau of Jack William Albutt, of Newcastle, and *d* 19 June 1950, leaving issue:

1e +Alan Sutherland; *b* 16 June 1946; *m* 1970 *Jennifer Ann Lingard, dau of Kenneth John Jarvis, and has issue:

1f +Alec Douglas Sutherland; *b* 1971

1f +Morwenna Jane; *b* 1973

1e +Joy Mary [Mrs John Wilson, 1 Tythe Place, Fenstanton, Huntingdon, Cambs]; *b* 16 March 1942; *m* 1963 *John Wilson, and has issue:

1f +Anthony John; *b* 15 April 1966

2f +Ian Patrick; *b* 10 March 1969

2d Alan Reeves; *b* 30 June 1906; *m* 1930 Helma Hornfelt (*d* 1994), of Saskatchewan, Canada, and *d* 1971, leaving issue:

1e +Katherine Anne [Mrs Royden Young, 956 Quadling Ave, Coquitlam, New Westminster, BC V3K 2A7, Canada]; *b* 1931; *m* 1st 6 Sept 1947 (*divorce* 1961) Raymond Frederick Flood, s of Frederick Ernest Flood, of Plymouth, Devon; *m* 2nd 1 Sept 1962 Royden Gilbert Young, s of George Charles Young, of New Westminster, BC, and by him has issue:

1f +Robert James; *b* 10 May 1967

2f +Douglas Alan; *b* 20 Nov 1968

2e +Audrey Ethel [Mrs Audrey Charlton, 105, 9295 122nd St, Surrey, BC, Canada V3V 4L4]; *b* 1933; *m* 1st 1955 (*divorce* 1969) Ronald O'Day; *m* 2nd 1971 (*divorce* 1992) Fred Charlton, and has issue by 1st husb:

1f +Frederick Alan; *b* 1955

2f +Ronald Patrick; *b* 1957; *m* 1st 1977 (*divorce* 1980) Shelley Mackenzie, and has issue:

1g +Shane Ronald; *b* 1979

2g +Lucas; *b* 1983

2f (cont.) Ronald O'Day *m* 2nd 1989 *Cheryl Eaglestad, and has further issue:

1g +Cody Reeves; *b* 1989

1f +Kathryn Rosanne [Mrs Kathryn Yaciw, Camp 37, Site 16, Kamloops, BC, Canada V2C 2J3]; *b* 1958; *m* 1977 *Steven Joseph Yaciw, and has issue:

1g +Angela Kristy; *b* 1958

2g +Lisa Marie; *b* 1981

2f +Lorraine Janet [Mrs Derek Dawe, 11352 Glenavon Drive, Surrey, BC, Canada V3R 4V5]; *b* 1960; *m* 1st 1983 (*divorce* 1986) —; *m* 2nd 1994 *Dereck Ross Dawe, and by him has issue:

1g +Colton Frederick; *b* 1990

2g +Levi Dereck Ron; *b* 1992

1g +Kaileigh Andra; *b* 1989

2g +Alison Mary Barbara; *b* 1993

1d Barbara; *b* 26 Jan 1905

2d +Mary Grace [Miss Mary McDouall, Flat 5, Joan Nightingale House, Bolnore Rd, Haywards Heath, Sussex RH16 4AB]; *b* 4 Jan 1908

1c Anne Euphenia; *d* unm 17 Jan 1931

2c Flora Isabella; *d* unm 1946

3c Mary Winifred; *d* unm 1942

4c Alice Kathleen; *m* 16 Jan 1901 Rev Canon Ernest William Carile Hayes (*d* 25 Nov 1950), MA (Camb), rector St Mark's Strandtown, Belfast, and *d* 5 June 1962

3b Patrick George (Rev); *b* 10 Sept 1822; rector Cosgrove, Northants; *m* 4 June 1851 Caroline Jane (*d* 28 Dec 1884), dau of John Fisher, and *d* 6 Oct 1904 having had, with other issue:

1c Caroline Elizabeth; *m* 6 May 1874 John Leonard Bolden, CVO (*d* 24 April 1929), of Hyning, Carnforth, and had issue

2c Anna Isabella

3c Florence Euphemia; *m* 1890 Henry William Gates (*d* 1902), of Peterborough

4b Hastings; *b* 20 Sept 1823; *m* 18 Aug 1853 Susan (*d* 8 May 1911), dau of Sir James Dalrymple Hay, 2nd Bt, and *d* 19 June 1869, leaving issue:

1c Hastings Boswell; *b* 21 Oct 1857; *d* unm 22 June 1929

5b Rawdon; *b* 20 Sept 1823; *m* 20 July 1847 Charlotte Shawford (*d* 1916), dau of Richard King, and *d* 1884, leaving, with other issue:

1c Rawdon George Herbert; *b* 10 April 1852; *m* 1906 Mary Somerville Townshend (*d* 1968), and *d* 18 Dec 1919, having had, with other issue:

1d +Rawdon Townshend, OAM (1983), JP [Rawdon McDouall Esq OAM JP, Doorah, Upper Horton 2347, NSW, Australia]; *b* 7 Sept 1907; *m* 12 Oct 1933 Elizabeth (*d* 1983), dau of A Cameron, of Glencoe, Narrabri, NSW, and has issue:

1e +David Rawdon [David McDouall Esq, Dunbeacon, Upper Horton, NSW 2347, Australia]; *b* 18 March 1937; *m* 1 Feb 1962 *Margaret Joan, dau of L Keith McDonald, of Strathallan, Warialda, NSW, and has issue:

1f +Rawdon Angus [Rawdon McDouall Esq, White Gates, Cooks Rd, Armidale, NSW 2350, Australia]; *b* 27 May 1963; *m* 1987 *Melinda Mary, dau of Watkin Williams, of Wattombri, Garah, NSW, and has issue:

1g +Thomas Rawdon; *b* 26 Feb 1991

2g +Henry Angus; *b* 27 July 1995

1g +Polly Gwendolene; *b* 23 July 1993

2f +Ian Alexander [Ian McDouall Esq, Dunbeacon, Upper Horton, NSW 2347, Australia]; *b* 28 Aug 1968

1f +Helen Annette [Mrs Stephen Ninnes, Doorah, Upper Horton, via Barraba, NSW, Australia]; *b* 6 Oct 1964; *m* 1st 1988 (*divorce* 1990) Timothy James Ross, of St Ives, NSW; *m* 2nd 1992 *Stephen Andrew Ninnes, of Ipswich, Qld

1d +Lucy Katherine Shawford [Mrs Thomas Capel, The Oaks, Narrabri, NSW, Australia]; *b* 1913; *m* 14 Feb 1946 Thomas Clark Capel (*d* 1986), 3rd s of Daniel George Capel, of The Oak's, Narrabri, NSW, and has issue:

1e +Donald Gilbert; *b* 20 April 1949; *m* 19– *Jennifer Anne, dau of Eric Bone, and has issue:

1f +Angus Donald; *b* 1985

1f +Louise Anne; *b* 1983

1e +Katherine Shawford [The Hon Mrs Alexander Erskine, 34 Awaba St, Mosman, NSW 2088, Australia]; *b* 15 Dec 1950; *m* 1977 *Hon Alexander David Erskine, 2nd s of 13th Earl of Mar and Kellie (*qv*)

2e +Nancy Patricia; *b* 5 Dec 1953

2d +Patricia Hastings [Mrs Eric Limburg, Windi, Bingara 2404, NSW, Australia]; *b* 20 Dec 1916; *m* 2 Oct 1954 Eric Gordon Limburg (*d* 10 June 1996), 4th son of Louis Limburg, of Gateshead, and has issue:

1e +Richard Eric; *b* 7 Oct 1955; *m* 1988 *Ann Margaret Simpson

2e David Patrick Rawdon; *b* 11 Sept 1957; *m* 1981 *Lea Ellen, dau of Brian Forth, of Telarah, NSW, and *d* 18 Oct 1986, leaving:

1f +Nicole Ellen; *b* 1983

2f +Katrina Lea (twin); *b* 1983

3f +Alyce Patricia; *b* 1986

1e +Elizabeth Mary; *b* 22 April 1960; *m* 1981 *Steven Mark Adams, of Gawler, S Australia, and has issue:

1f +Kris; *b* 1987

2f +Matthew; *b* 28 Feb 1992

1f +Naomi; *b* 1984

3d +Margaret Somerville [Mrs Jack Lattimore, 21 Trelawney St, Thornleigh 2120, Sydney, NSW, Australia]; *b* 25 Oct 1918; *m* 24 Feb 1951 Jack Lattimore (*d* 1988), only s of John Lattimore, of Parramatta, NSW, and has issue:

1e +Andrew Stuart; *b* 28 June 1958; *m* 1989 *Bronwyn Gay Macpherson, dau of Brig Brian Edwards, of Canberra, ACT, and has issue:

1f +Jack Edward Macpherson; *b* 1992

1e +Mary-Anne Elizabeth; *b* 27 June 1954; *m* 1979 *Hugh Geoffrey Beecher, of Narrandera, NSW, and has issue:

1f +Nicholas Hugh Lattimore; *b* 1991

1f +Emma Louise Lattimore; *b* 1988

2e +Margaret Louise; *b* 29 Dec 1960; *m* 1991 Christopher Allan Murphy (*d* 1992)

2c William Edward; *b* 29 Aug 1865; *m* 1904 May Edna (*d* 1961), dau of Robert Scoles, and *d* 11 June 1936, leaving issue:

1d Daniel Crichton Stuart; *b* 1905; *m* 14 March 1930 *Jean, dau of P A M'Alister, of Narrabri, NSW, and *d* 30 July 1961, leaving issue:

1e Peter Crichton Stuart; *b* 23 May 1933; *m* 23 April 1959 *Kay Margaret, yr dau of Kenneth Field Clemson, of Gurley, NSW, and *d* 1988 leaving issue:

1f +Sandra Anne; *b* 31 March 1961; *m* 19 Feb 1988 *Richard Alexander Dillon, 5th s of Bill Dillon, of Moree, NSW and has:

1g +Stephanie Alison; *b* 16 May 1991

2g +Georgia Caroline; *b* 13 Sept 1993

3g +Netia Louisa; *b* 4 Jan 1998

2f +Victoria Jane; *b* 16 May 1963; *m* 15 Feb 1997 *Angus John Cooke, er s of John Cooke, of Stony Ridge, Northam, W Australia

3f +Angela Susan; *b* 6 April 1967; *m* 5 Nov 1994 *Raphael Pierre Gaston Alkombre, er s of Jackie Alkombre, of Paimpol, Brittany, France

1e +Judith [Mrs Allan McMaster, Violet Downs, Narrabri 2390, NSW, Australia]; *b* 27 Aug 1931; *m* 5 March 1954 *Allan Richard McMaster, s of S B McMaster, of Narrabri, NSW, and has issue:

1f +Stuart Allan; *b* 6 Oct 1955; *m* 1979 *Deborah, dau of David Mackay of Brisbane, and has issue:

1g +Richard Stuart; *b* 1982

2g +Alec Bruce; *b* 1985

1g +Abby Jane; *b* 1981

1f +Margaret Jean; *b* 3 April 1957; *m* 1st 1979 (*divorce* 1989) Stephen Leslie Frost, of Toowoomba, NSW; *m* 2nd 1994 *Christopher Graden Lloyd and by her 1st husb has:

1g +Samuel Allan; *b* 1986

1g +Melanie Alaire; *b* 1980

2g +Angela Judith; *b* 1982

2f +Cathryn Mary; *b* 30 June 1960; *m* 1984 *John Charles Edmondson, of Sydney, NSW, and has issue:

1g +Allan Gordon; *b* 1988

2g +Andrew John; *b* 24 June 1990

1g +Sahy Louise; *b* 21 April 1992

2d Hastings Uchrid; *b* 1907; *m* 20 April 1938 *Nancy May [Mrs Hastings McDouall, Lowana, Upper Horton, via Barraba, NSW 2347, Australia], dau of Ernest Capel, of Burren Junction, NSW, and *d* 1992, leaving issue:

1e +Richard Hastings [Mr Richard McDouall, Kildare, Upper Horton, NSW 2347, Australia]; *b* 12 Nov 1940 (twin); *m* 1966 *Susan Anne Etheridge and has issue:

1f +Stuart John; *b* 12 Aug 1966; *m* 24 Oct 1992 *Jane Vickery and has:

1g *Toby Mathew; *b* 23 June 1994

1g *Samantha Vickery; *b* 11 April 1996

2g *Tabatha Vickery (twin); *b* 11 April 1996

2f +Graham Richard; *b* 21 Oct 1968; *m* 4 Oct 1997 *Lisa Maree and has:

1g *Alexis Jessica; *b* 27 March 1997

2e +Donald Hastings [Mr Donald McDouall, Boundary Creek, Bingara, NSW 2404, Australia]; *b* 2 March 1946; *m* 1973 *Bronwyn Lee, dau of W Cupitt of Bowral, NSW, and has issue:

1f +Benjamin Donald; *b* 1975

2f +Samuel Hastings; *b* 1977

1f +Serena Lee; *b* 1981

1e +Pamela Hastings [Mrs Fergus Fysh, 4 Breimba St, Grafton, NSW 2460, Australia]; *b* 12 Nov 1940 (twin); *m* 1st 1963 Dr Roderick Warren Scotton, MB, BS (*d* 1981); *m* 2nd 1983 *Fergus McMaster Fysh, and has issue by 1st husb:

1f +Richard Stuart; *b* 26 Nov 1966; *m* 2 May 1992 *Melissa Gail Simpson and has:

1g +Thomas Warren; *b* 27 March 1995

1g +Alysse Marie; *b* 4 Jan 1994

2f +Peter Roderick; *b* 1969

1f +Sandra Louise; *b* 4 April 1965; *m* 29 Sept 1994 *Benjamin Wellington Bundock and has:

1g +Henry Wellington; *b* 21 March 1994

2g +George McBean; *b* 25 March 1997

3d +Robert William [Mr Robert McDouall, Eungai, Upper Horton, Barraba, NSW 2347, Australia]; *b* 1909; *m* 14 Nov 1934 *Nancy Lamprell Spencer, and has had issue:

1e +William Robert; *b* 1939; *m* 1963 *Louise, dau of Eric Lauric, of Walcha, NSW, and has issue:

1f +James William; *b* 1965

2f +Andrew Alexander (twin); *b* 1965

3f +Jonathan Laurie; *b* 1967

2e +Arthur Frank; *b* 1942; *m* 1963 *Beverley Ann, dau of Clive Pyke, of NSW, and has issue:

1f +Baden Robert; *b* 1964

2f +Gavin John; *b* 1966

1e Jennette Ann; *b* 19 Nov 1935; *d* 19–

2e +Philippa May; *b* 10 Jan 1937; *m* 1957 *Andrew Ellis Wauch, of NSW, and has issue:

1f +John Andrew Robert; *b* 1958

1f +Wendy Ann; *b* 1959

2f +Sally May; *b* 1966

4d +Noel Edward [Mr Noel McDouall, Peri, Caroda, NSW, Australia]; *b* 1911; *m* 1942 Amy Patricia Hawke (*d* 1996), and has issue:

1e +Malcolm Noel [Mr Malcolm McDouall, 17 Blacks Rd, Arcadia, NSW 2159, Australia]; *b* 1943; *m* 7 Dec 1968 (*divorce* 1975) Louise, dau of Richard Albert Pedlingham, of NSW, and has issue:

1f +Matthew Richard Stuart; *b* 1970

1e +Jillian May [Mrs Jillian McDouall, 66 Liverpool St, Paddington, NSW 2021, Australia]; *b* 29 July 1946; *m* 27 March 1967 (*divorce* 1978 resumed maiden name 1997) Michael Mahony, s of Lloyd Thomas Mahony, of NSW, and has issue:

1f +Jake Thomas; *b* 1975

1f +Camilla; *b* 1972

5d +Harold Stuart [Mr Harold McDouall, Ulumbarella, Upper Horton, NSW 2347, Australia]; *b* 3 March 1920; F/Lt RAAF (ret); *m* 1st 25 Jan 1947 Doris Marion (*d* 1970), dau of Maj William Squires, of N Manly, NSW; *m* 2nd 1974 *Gloria Geraldine, dau of Capt W G Leadbeater, and has issue by 1st w:

1e +Garry Stuart [Mr Garry McDouall, Yarraman, Bingara, NSW 2404, Australia]; *b* 1947; *m* 1971 *Linda Anne, dau of Richard Littlejohn, of NSW, and has issue:

1f +Scott Stuart; *b* 1978

2f +Hamish Richard; *b* 1981

2e +Michael William; *b* 1953; *m* 1982 *Julie Kay, dau of Dr E Hughson, and has issue:

1f +Cameron Stuart; *b* 1983

2f +Mich William; *b* 1985

1f +Jenna Marion; *b* 1986

1e +Diane Marion [Mrs Philip Kelly, Blue Nobby, Cobbadah, NSW 2347, Australia]; *b* 1950; *m* 1st 1971 (*divorce* 1977) Peter Russell Jones, and has issue:

1f +Heulwen; *b* 1973

1e (cont.) Diane Marion Jones *m* 2nd 1983 Philip Arthur Kelly (*d* 1996), and by him has:

2f +Dustin Philip; *b* 1986

1f +Alana Mae; *b* 1984

2f +Kylie Elizabeth; *b* 1988

1d +Edna May [Mrs John Bowman, Tarpoly, Upper Manilla, NSW 2346, Australia]; *b* 7 Feb 1918; *m* 1941 *John Murray Bowman, and has issue:

1e +Roger Murray; *b* 11 Feb 1943; *m* 1973 *Sarah Wilkin Smith, and has issue:

1f +Thomas Murray; *b* 1976

1f +Katherine Sara; *b* 1974

2f +Susan Wilkin; *b* 1979

2e +Graham Edward; *b* 19 March 1945; *m* 1972 *Nanette Mary Mahony, and has issue:
1f +Luke Edward; *b* 1974
2f +Jonathan Graham; *b* 1980
1f +Anna Nanette; *b* 1977
3e +Christopher George; *b* 9 Dec 1953; *m* 1978 *Sharon Hubbard, and has issue:
1f +Samuel James; *b* 1984
1f +Laura Emily (twin); *b* 1984
2f +Angela Jane; *b* 1986
1e +Julie May; *b* 6 Aug 1950
3c Frederick Crichton; *b* 3 Jan 1871; *m* 1908 Florence Ethel Jackson (*d* 16 Sept 1961), and *d* 15 Jan 1932, leaving issue:
1d John Stuart Crichton; *b* 5 Dec 1908; AIF and Pacific Campaign, EM 1945; *m* 1935 Patricia (*d* 1997), est dau of T Mitchele-Moore, of Mile Station, Qld, and *d* 1951
1d Joan Shawford; *b* 15 March 1910; *m* 1936 Noel Peter Dawson (*d* 1981), Maj AIF, and *d* 1997, leaving:
1e +Suzanne Jane [Mrs Anthony Wadey, 45 Congewoi Rd, Mosman 2088, NSW, Australia]; *b* 1943; *m* 1970 *Anthony Keith Wadey
2d Gwendolen Melville; *b* 17 Aug 1918; *m* 1936 Frederick Neville Griffiths (*d* 1981), yst s of Dr Guy Griffiths, of Killara, Sydney, NSW, and *d* 31 Aug 1997 leaving:
1e +Frederick Ronald Neville; *b* 1936
2e +Richard Neville; *b* 1941; *m* 1971 *Margaret Ryan, of Sydney, and has issue:
1f +Philip Andrew; *b* 1974
2f +Matthew David; *b* 1976
1f +Kathryn Louise; *b* 1979
3e +Hugh Douglas [Hugh Griffiths Esq, 4 Wentworth St, S Hobart, Tasmania 7004]; *b* 11 Feb 1951; *m* 1990 *Sheila Mary Connell and has:
1f +Julia Elizabeth; *b* 14 Feb 1992
2f +Rosemary Helen; *b* 16 Aug 1993
1e +Elizabeth Joan [Mrs Geoffrey Scarlett, 2/73 Lauderdale Ave, Fairlight, NSW 2094, Australia; PO Box 301, Balgowlah, NSW 2093, Australia]; *b* 29 March 1943; *m* 1st 1972 (*divorce* 1983) Ray Johnson, MB, BS; *m* 2nd 1991 Dr Geoffrey Anthony Scarlett (*d* 1992) and by her 1st husb has:
1f +Victoria Yvonne; *b* 11 April 1972
2f +Kathleen Elizabeth; *b* 25 Feb 1974
1c Laura Amelia; *m* 1887 Edward Stanley Tresidder, MRCS, LRCP (*d* 1926), and had issue
2c Mary Penelope
3c Florence Christmas; *m* 1896 Austin J G Mack, of Luton Hoo, Bingara, NSW, and had three sons

The 5th EARL's nephew,

PATRICK MACDOWALL-CRICHTON, **6th Earl of Dumfries**; *b* 15 Oct 1726; offr 3rd Foot Gds 1762, rep S peer 1790–1803; *m* 12 Sept 1771 Margaret (*d* 5 May 1799), dau of Ronald Crauford, of Restalrig, Edinburgh, and *d* 7 April 1803, leaving an only surv child:

Elizabeth Penelope; *m* 12 Oct 1792 John Stuart, Lord Mount Stuart (*dvp* 22 Jan 1794), est son of **1st Marquess of Bute** (*see* below), and *dvp* 25 July 1797, leaving, with another son:

JOHN, **7th Earl** and **2nd Marquess** (*see* below)

Lineage (of Stuart): ROBERT II (*see* MORAY, E); had an illegitimate s:

JOHN STEWART; had *c* 1385 the islands of Arane (Arran), Bute and Cambrae erected into a county for him by his f and was constituted Hereditary Sheriff of the new entity; *d* between 1445 and July 1449, leaving, with an er s (James; *d* apparently *sp* or *sps* between 1454 and 1464):

WILLIAM STEWART; recd charter of lands of Fennock from his parents 28 Jan 1444/5, Keeper Brodick Castle, Arran, 1444–53; *m* Margaret Stewart (living 28 June 1485) and *d c* 1465, leaving, with two yr sons (William; *s* to Fennock; Alexander):

JAMES STEWART, Sheriff of Bute; *s* to that office probably in 1468; obtained a Crown Charter of an acre of the lands of Kilcattan 3 Nov 1474; *d* 1477, leaving, with a dau, an est s (James, *d c* 1488) and two yst ones (James (*secundus*), Robert):

NINIAN STEWART; Sheriff Bute and Arran, retoured heir of Ardmaleish, Greenan, Mill of Kilcattan and Corrigillis estates 28 May 1490, Hereditary Capt and Keeper Rothesay Castle 1498; *m* 1st — Campbell; *m* 2nd *c* 10 Aug 1506 Janet Dunlop; *m* 3rd *c* 15 Oct 1516 Elizabeth (living 30 July 1529), dau of John Blair, and *d* by 1539, having had, with seven yr s:

Sir JAMES STEWART; Sheriff and Chamberlain Bute, Sheriff Bute, Capt Rothesay Castle, ktd 1561; *m* 1st Mary, dau of Archibald, Earl of Argyll (*see* ARGYLL, D), by whom he had no male issue; *m* 2nd Marion, dau of John Fairlie of that Ilk and widow of Thomas Boyd of Linn, bro of Thomas, Lord Boyd (*see* KILMARNOCK, B), and *d* 1570, leaving, with two yr s:

JOHN STEWART of Ardmaleish; Sheriff Bute; Commr Buteshire in S Parl 20 Oct 1579; *m* 1st Mary, dau of John Campbell of Skipnish, and had issue; *m* 2nd *c* 23 Jan 1590 Fynegella of Finevole Nik Donald, dau of Sir James MacDonald, of Duniveg, Islay, and Glenns, and widow of Dugal Campbell of Auchinbreck; *m* 3rd *c* 15 Sept 1595 Jean, dau of John Blair of that Ilk and widow of Alexander Cunningham, Commendator of Kilwinning, and *d c* 10 Oct 1612, having by her had a dau (Grissell) and another son (Jaems, of Ardinho); his s by his 1st w:

Sir JOHN STUART of Ardmaleish; Sheriff Bute; living 1615; *m* Elizabeth (*m* 2nd Sir Alexander Foulis of Colinton), dau and coheir of Robert Hepburn of Fuird, by whom he acquired Fuird and several other lands in Haddington, and *d* 31 March 1618/9, leaving:

Sir James Stuart, 1st Bt (NS), so *cr* 28 March 1627, of Ardmaleish; Sheriff Bute, MP Bute 1644/5 royalist Civil War; *m* Grizel, dau of Sir Dugald Campbell of Auchinbreck, 2nd Bt (*qv*), and *d* 1662, having had, with other issue:
1 DUGALD (Sir), **2nd Bt**
2 Sir ROBERT STUART, 1st Bt (NS), so *cr* 29 April 1707, of Tillcoultry, Clackmannanshire; *b c* 1655; advocate 1681, MP Rothesay 1689–93, Dingwall 1698–1702 and Bute 1702–07, Sheriff Pncpl Clackmannanshire, a Ld of Session as Lord Tillicoultry 1701–09, Commr for Union S and E Parls; *m* 1st 20 Oct 1685 Violet, dau of Archibald Hamilton of Rosehall; *m* 2nd 25 Aug 1693 Cecil, sis of 2nd Lord Belhaven and Stenton (*qv*), and *d* 1 Oct 1710, leaving by her, with two other s (who are thought to have *dsp* or unm):
(1) Sir ROBERT STUART, 2nd Bt; *b c* 1700; *m* Jean, dau of Sir William Calderwood of Polton, a Ld of Session, and *dsp* 4 March 1767, when the btcy became dormant

Sir JAMES's est son,

Sir Dugald Stuart, 2nd Bt; *m* 1658 Elizabeth, dau of Sir John Ruthven of Dunglass and gdau maternally of 1st Earl of Leven (*see* LEVEN and MELVILLE, E), and *d* 1670, having had, with daus and a yr s (Dugald, of Blairhall; *see* 1949 edn):

Sir James Stuart, 3rd Bt, and **1st Earl of Bute**, so *cr* 14 April 1703, as also VISCOUNT KINGARTH, LORD MOUNTSTUART, CUMRA AND INCHMARNOCK (all S), PC (S temp QUEEN ANNE); Sheriff Tarbet 1684 and Argyllshire 1686, advocate 1685, MP Bute 1685–93 and 1702–03, Commr to negotiate (at that time abortive) Parly Union with England 1702; opposed Union of 1707; *m* 1st *c* 24 July 1680 Agnes, est dau of Sir George Mackenzie of Rosehaugh, Lord Advocate, and had issue; *m* 2nd Christian, dau of Sir William Dundas of Kincavel, and *d* 4 June 1710; his only son by his 1st w:

JAMES STUART, **2nd Earl of Bute**; inherited the Rosehaugh estate from his maternal unc but only after much litigation; rep S peer and Ld Lt Bute 1715–23; *m c* 19 Feb 1711 Anne (*m* 2nd 19 Sept 1731 Alexander Fraser of Strichen, Aberdeenshire, a Ld of Session, and *d* 20 Oct 1736), dau of 1st Duke of Argyll (*qv*), and *d* 28 Jan 1723, having had, with daus:
1 JOHN, **3rd Earl**
2 James STUART later STUART-MACKENZIE (on inheriting the Mackenzie estates), PC; MP 1742–84, Keeper Privy Seal Scotland 1763; *m* 16 Feb 1749 his cousin Lady Elizabeth Campbell (*d* 16 July 1799), 4th dau of 2nd Duke of Argyll (*qv*), but *dsps* nine months later, leaving the estates subject to litigation, which was decided 4 March 1803 in favour of Hon James Archibald Stuart-Wortley (*see* below, also WHARNCLIFFE, E)

The 2nd EARL's er son,

JOHN STUART, **3rd Earl of Bute**, KG (1762), KT (1738–62), PC (1760); *b* 25 May 1713; *educ* Eton; rep S peer 1737–41 and 1761–80, later Hereditary Sheriff Bute (till 1747, when heritable jurisdictions were abolished), Sec State for the North 1761–62, PM and First Ld Treasury 1762–63, V-Adml the Blue 1764–76; *m* 13/24 Aug 1736 Mary (*cr* 3 April 1761 **Baroness Mount Stuart of Wortley**, Co York (GB), with remainder to her male issue by her then husb, and *d* 6 Nov 1794), only dau of Edward Wortley-Montagu, of Wortley, Yorks, and ggdau of 1st Earl of Sandwich (*qv*), and *d* 10 March 1792, having had, with other surv issue:
1 JOHN, **1st Marquess**
2 James Archibald STUART later STUART-WORTLEY (on inheriting the Wortley estates through his mother); *b* 19 Sept 1747; *m* 8 June 1767 Margaret, dau of Sir David Conynghame, Bt, and *d* 1 March 1818, leaving issue (*see* WHARNCLIFFE, E)
3 Charles (Sir), KB; *b* Jan 1753; Lt-Gen, Govr Island of Minorca, which he had taken 1798; *m* 19 April 1778 Louisa, 2nd dau and coheir of Lord Vere Bertie, 3rd son of 1st Duke of Ancaster (*see* WILLOUGHBY DE ERESBY, B, and LINDSEY and ABINGDON, E), and *d* 25 May 1801, leaving issue:
(1) Sir CHARLES STUART, 1st and last BARON STUART DE ROTHESAY, of the Isle of Bute (UK), so *cr* 22 Jan 1828, GCB (1815), KB (1812), PC (1814); *b* 2 Jan 1779; *educ* Eton and Ch Ch Oxford; Dip Serv: Sec Legation Vienna 180104 (Chargé d'Affaires 1803–04 and 1805–06), Sec Embassy St Petersburg 1804–08 (Min Plen *ad interim* 1806–07), special missions Spain 1808–09 and Vienna April-May 1809, Envoy Extrdy and Min Plen Lisbon 1810–14, *cr* Count of Machico and Marquis of Angra in Portugal and Kt Grand Cross Tower and Sword, Envoy Extrdy and Min Plen *ad interim* Paris June-Aug 1814, Amb The Hague Feb-May 1815, Paris 1815–24 and 1828–31, Portugal and Brazil 1825–26 and St Petersburg 1841–44; *m* 6 Feb 1818 Elizabeth Margaret (*d* 23 June 1867), dau of 3rd Earl of Hardwicke (*qv*), and *d* 6 Nov 1845, when the barony expired, leaving:
1a Charlotte; *m* 5 Sept 1835 Charles John, Earl Canning (*d* 17 June 1862; *see* GARVAGH, B), and *dsp* Calcutta 18 Nov 1861
2a Louisa; *m* 8 June 1842 3rd Marquess of Waterford (*qv*) and *dsp* 12 May 1891
(2) John James; *b* 29 Aug 1782; Capt RN; *m* 26 Sept 1807 Albinia (*m* 2nd 1825 Rev Marmaduke Thompson and *d* 3 June 1827), est dau of Rt Hon John Sullivan, and *d* 19 March 1811, leaving:
1a Charles, of Hoburne, Christchurch, Hants, JP (Bute); *b* 16 March 1810; Gen, Col 2nd Bn DCLI; V-Lt Bute; *m* 1st 4 Sept 1830 Georgiana Stuart (Maid of Honour to QUEEN ADELAIDE; *d* 18 July 1877), dau of V-Adml Sir John Gore, KCH; *m* 2nd 24 Sept 1878 Louisa Gambier, dau of James Gordon Murdoch, and *dsp* 7 Sept 1892
4 William (Most Rev), DD; *b* March 1755; Archbp Armagh; *m* 3 May 1796 Sophia Margaret Juliana (*d* April 1847), dau of Thomas Penn, of Stoke Poges, and *d* 6 March 1822, leaving, with other issue:
(1) William, of Tempsford Hall, Beds, and Aldenham Abbey, Herts, JP, DL; *b* 31 Oct 1798; *m* 1st 8 Aug 1821 Henrietta Maria Sarah (*d* 26 July 1853), est dau of Adml Sir Charles Morice Pole, Bt, GCB, and had, with other issue:
1a William, of Tempsford and Aldenham Abbey, JP (Beds, Herts, Hunts), DL (Beds); *b* 7 March 1825; Hon Col 3rd Bn Beds Regt, MP Bedford 1851, High Sheriff Beds 1875; *m* 13 Sept 1859 Katherine (*d* 16 Oct 1881), est dau of John Armytage Nicholson, of Bairath, Co Meath, and *d* 21 Dec 1893, having had, with other issue:
1b William Dugald, of Tempsford Hall, JP; *b* 18 Oct 1860; Maj and Hon Lt-Col 3rd Bn Beds Regt, formerly Capt KRRC, WW I as T/Maj 14th KRRC;

m 11 July 1893 Millicent Helen Olivia (*d* 2 Feb 1933), est dau of Capt George William Bulkeley Hughes, JP, and *d* 2 April 1922, having had issue:

1c William Esmé Montague; *b* 22 Nov 1895; 2nd Lt Roy W Kent Regt; *ka* 7 Oct 1916

2b Henry Esmé; *b* 15 July 1865; *m* 16 Feb 1899 May Evelyn (*m* 2nd 1911 Leonard Just and *d* 28 May 1927), dau of James Cornwell, and *d* 21 Aug 1905, leaving issue:

1c Margaret Esmé Sylvia; *b* 17 Nov 1902; *m* 1928 James Douglas Lyle

2c Winifred Hilda Muriel; *b* 17 Nov 1902; *m* Laurence Desjardins

3c Dorothea France Irma; *b* 3 June 1904; *m* 11 June 1930 Clifford Frank Butcher, and had issue

2a Charles Pole, JP; *b* 7 May 1826; barrister; *m* 20 March 1860 Anne (*d* 19 Oct 1918), est dau of Robert Smyth, of Gaybrook, Co Westmeath, and *d* 26 Aug 1896, leaving, with other issue:

1b Robert Alexander; *b* 5 July 1862; *m* 6 Jan 1897 Edith Margaret Nina (*m* 2nd 20 Nov 1924 Maj Ernest Dawson, IARO, who *d* 1949), dau of Rev H E Stoker, and *d* 1899, leaving issue:

1c Enid Frances Anne; *b* 28 Nov 1897

2b Reginald Pole; *b* 22 July 1863; Lt-Col N Staffs Regt; *m* 1895 Hester Elizabeth (*d* 20 March 1940), dau of Gerhard Myburgh, Consul-Gen Netherlands in S Africa, and *d* 20 April 1934, leaving issue:

1c Kathleen Anne Pole; *m* 7 July 1926 G/Capt Frederick Robert Wynne, MBE, RAF (*d* 20 Aug 1988), est s of Frederick Edward Wynne, MB, DPH, of Sheffield, and had issue:

1d *Frederick Owen Stuart [Frederick Wynne Esq, The Estate Office, Tempsford, Sandy, Beds]; *b* 17 June 1933; *educ* Lancing; *m* 6 Sept 1955 *Susan Sheilah, dau of Jack Reginald Bushell, DFM, and has:

1e *Owen Christopher Robert; *b* 30 Aug 1959; *m* 25 July 1981 *Susan Jennifer, dau of J R Tuckett, and has:

1f *Andrew Owen Robert; *b* 4 May 1983

1d *Lucy Elizabeth Anne [Mrs Alan Turner, 62 Northchurch Rd, London N1 3NY]; *b* 7 May 1930; *m* 14 Jan 1961 *Alan Turner, ARIBA

2d *Althea Kathleen [Mrs Anthony Barrington-Brown, 26c Upton Lovell, Warminster, Wilts BA12 0JW]; *b* 6 Oct 1936; *m* 1st 1 Sept 1960 (*divorce* 19–) Philip Dresman and has:

1e *Philip Barnabas John; *b* 5 March 1966

1e *Ruth Kathleen; *b* 11 Dec 1961; *m* 1990 *Alasdair Donn

2e *Rebekah; *b* 12 Jan 1963; *m* 1986 *Stephen Braun

2d (cont.) Mrs Althea Dresman *m* 2nd 1982 *Anthony Charles Barrington-Brown

2c Rosalind Esmé Pole Stuart; JP; Lond U, BA, PhD; *d* 1986

3b Ralph Esmé; *b* 9 April 1869; Maj RGA; *m* 1st 30 April 1907 Beatrice (*d* 28 Aug 1913), est dau of John Kitchin, JP, of Scarborough; *m* 2nd 25 Feb 1919 Elizabeth (*d* 30 July 1962), dau of Samuel Thompson, of Muckamore Abbey, Co Antrim, and *d* 27 Oct 1927

1b Grace Henrietta; *b* 30 June 1872; *d* unm 8 June 1955

1a Mary Pole; *m* 1 Aug 1843 Jonathan Rashleigh (*d* 12 April 1905), of Menabilly, Cornwall, and *d* 25 Jan 1852, leaving issue

2a Louisa Pole; *m* 3 Aug 1852 Rev Oliver Matthew Ridley (*see* RIDLEY, V) and *d* 7 Jan 1858

(1) (cont.) William Stuart *m* 2nd 31 Aug 1854 Georgina Adelaide Forestier (*m* 2nd 15 Dec 1875 9th Earl of Seafield (*qv*) and *d* 7 Sept 1903), dau of Gen Frederick Nathaniel Walker, KCH (*see* FORESTIER-WALKER, Bt), and *d* 7 July 1874

(1) Mary Juliana; *m* 28 Feb 1815 2nd Earl of Ranfurly (*d* 21 March 1858), and *d* 11 July 1866, leaving issue

1 Mary; *m* 7 Sept 1761 1st and last Earl of Lonsdale of the 1784 *cr* (*see* LONSDALE, E) and *d* 5 April 1824

2 Jane; *m* 1 Feb 1768 George Macartney, 1st and last Earl Macartney (*dsp* 31 March 1806), and *d* 28 Feb 1828

3 Anne; *m* 2 July 1764 2nd Duke of Northumberland (*qv*) and *dsp*

4 Caroline; *m* 1 Jan 1778 1st Earl of Portarlington (*qv*) and *d* 20 Jan 1813, leaving issue

The 3rd EARL's er son,

JOHN STUART, **1st Marquess of the County of Bute**, so *cr* 27 Feb 1796, as also VISCOUNT MOUNTJOY of the Isle of Wight and EARL OF WINDSOR (the last two titles commemorating his 1st w's parentage), as also previously 20 May 1776 BARON CARDIFF OF CARDIFF CASTLE (all GB), the last title being conferred on him *vp* in recognition of his position as proprietor of vast (and, once they had been developed industrially in the next century by the **2nd** and **3rd Marquesses**, still more vastly valuable) South Walian properties which had come to him through his 1st wife, descendant of the Herberts (*see* PEMBROKE and MONTGOMERY, E), PC (1779); *b* 30 June 1744; *educ* Winchester and Oxford; MP (Tory) Bossiney 1766–76, Ld Lt: Glam 1772–93 and 1794–1814 and Bute 1794–1814; Envoy Turin 1779–83, Amb Spain March-Dec 1783 and 1795–96; *m* 1st 12 Nov 1766 Charlotte Jane (*d* 28 Jan 1800), est dau and coheir of Herbert Hickman-Windsor, 2nd and last Viscount Windsor of Blackcastle and 2nd Baron Mountjoy (both I), and had, with other issue:

1 John, styled (incorrectly) *Viscount Mount Stuart*; *b* 25 Sept 1767; MP (Tory) Cardiff 1790–94, Ld Lt Glam 1793–94; *m* 12 Oct 1792 Lady Elizabeth Penelope Mackdowal-Crichton (*d* 25 July 1797), dau and sole heir of **6th Earl of Dumfries** (*see* above, all her descendants, of either sex, being in remainder to that Earldom and its associated lesser titles), and *d* 22 Jan 1794, leaving issue:

(1) JOHN, **2nd Marquess**

(2) Patrick James Herbert STUART later CRICHTON-STUART (sign-manual March 1817, also granted rank of marquess's yr s); *b* posthumously 25 Aug 1794; MP, Ld Lt Bute; *m* 13 July 1818 Hannah (*d* 5 June 1872), dau of William Tighe, MP, of Woodstock, Kilkenny, and *d* 7 Sept 1859, having had, with other issue:

1a James Frederick Dudley; *b* 17 Feb 1824; Lt-Col Gren Gds, MP Cardiff 1857–80, Ld Lt Bute; *m* 28 July 1864 Gertrude Frances (*d* 2 Dec 1909), dau of Rt Hon Sir George Hamilton Seymour, GCB (*see* HERTFORD, M), and *d* 24 Oct 1891, leaving issue:

1b Patrick James; *b* 6 Jan 1868; Gren Gds, Hon Capt, JP and V-Lt Bute; *m* 1st 23 July 1894 Sophia Matilda (Cecil) (*d* 13 June 1895), yr dau of John Kirk, DL, of Annevale, Co Armagh, and had issue:

1c Cecilia; *m* 23 April 1936 James Alexander Stewart, formerly Lt RIT (SR) (*d* 18 Jan 1959), est son of Patrick Stewart, of Dublin, and *d* 3 May 1959

1b (cont.) Patrick Crichton-Stuart *m* 2nd 6 Oct 1904 Helen Katherine (Lady Pres of League Mercy Ayrshire and Chm Ayrshire County Nursing Assoc, who *d* 10 March 1948), dau of John J C Phillips, of Kingston, Jamaica, and widow of Hon Arthur James Dudley Stuart St Aubyn, 4th son of 1st Baron St Levan (*qv*), and *d* 25 Oct 1935, having by her had further issue:

1c Patrick Dudley; *b* 15 May 1909; *educ* Downside and Balliol Coll Oxford (BA 1931); WW II as Maj Intell Corps (despatches); *m* 22 July 1948 *Sheila Mary [Mrs Patrick Crichton-Stuart, 1 Sloane Gdns, London SW1], only dau of Lt-Col James Douglas Kendall Restler, OBE, MInstCE, and *d* 29 July 1978, leaving issue:

1d +Patrick James [Patrick Crichton-Stuart Esq, 1 Sloane Gdns, London SW1]; *b* 4 June 1954; *educ* Downside and RMA Sandhurst; Lt Scots Gds; *m* 1st 10 Jan 1978 (*divorce* 1982) Amanda Mary Howel, er dau of Michael Williams, of Surrey, and has issue by his 1st w:

1e +Frederick James; *b* 1981

1e +Katherine Rose; *b* 1979

1d (cont.) Patrick Crichton-Stuart *m* 2nd 1991 *Lady Rowena Katherine Meade, er dau of 7th Earl of Clanwilliam (*qv*), and by her has:

2e +Rory Torquil; *b* 25 March 1995

1d +Caroline Mary Katherine, MVO (1990); *b* 3 Nov 1949; *m* 1993 *Anthony Frederick Gandolfi Hornyold, 4th Duke Gandolfi (*see* MOWBRAY, SEGRAVE and STOURTON, B)

2c (Constance) Penelope; *b* 5 Nov 1907; *d* unm 3 Nov 1969

2b Dudley; *b* 4 March 1871; *d* 18 July 1939

1b Constance; *d* unm 14 Dec 1933

2b Audrey; *m* 25 June 1907 William Harris Best, MRCP, Capt RAMC (*d* 7 May 1946), son of William Harris Best, JP, of St Ives, and *d* 24 Sept 1962, leaving issue

2a Herbert, DL (Bute); *b* 5 Aug 1827; *m* 28 Aug 1860 Fanny Adelaide (*d* 31 May 1919), 3rd dau of John Labouchere, of Broom Hall, Surrey, bro of 1st Baron Taunton (extinct 1869), and *d* 29 Dec 1891, leaving, with other issue:

1b James Fortescue; *b* 3 March 1864; *m* 29 Sept 1894 Lilian Louisa (*d* 27 April 1950), est dau of Thomas Holdsworth Newman, of Coryton, Devon (*see* NEWMAN, Bt), and *d* 10 May 1932, leaving issue:

1c Joan Evelyn; *m* 26 April 1922 Richard John Vereker Astell (*see* GORT, V) and *d* Oct 1993

1b Margaret Adelaide; *m* 7 May 1892 Rev Harry Percy Grubb, MA (*d* 12 Sept 1925), 4th son of Richard Grubb, of Cahir Abbey, Co Tipperary, and *d* 20 Jan 1958, leaving issue

2 Henry; *b* 7 June 1777; *m* 15 July 1802 Lady Gertrude Amelia Mason-Villiers (*d* 30 Aug 1809), dau and sole heir of 2nd and last Earl of Grandison (*d* 1800), and *d* 19 Aug 1809, having had, with other issue:

(1) Henry STUART later VILLIERS-STUART (roy licence 17 Nov 1822 on inheriting Lord Grandison's estates), 1st BARON STUART DE DECIES, of Dromana, within the Decies, Co Waterford (UK), so *cr* 10 May 1839, PC (I 1837); *b* 8 June 1803; *educ* Eton and Ch Ch Oxford; MP (Tory) Co Waterford 1826–30 and Banbury (Tory to 1831, when resigned seat on becoming a Lib) 1830–31; Col Waterford Militia; Ld Lt Co Waterford 1831–74; went through a form of marriage 1826 at St James's, Spanish Place, London W1, and (under Scottish law) in Scotland with Theresia Pauline Ott (*d* 7 Aug 1867), of Vienna, who cohabited with him and was widely recognised as his w, and *d* 23 Jan 1874, when the Barony either expired or became dormant, leaving:

1a Henry Windsor; *b* 1827; claimed the barony 1876 but could not furnish proof of his parents' marriage prior to his birth; *d* 23 Jan 1874

(2) William STUART later VILLIERS-STUART; *b* 21 Aug 1804; Capt 12th Lancers; MP Waterford; *m* 1 June 1833 Catherine (*d* 14 Sept 1879), dau and eventual heir of Michael Cox, of Castletown, Co Kilkenny, and *d* 7 Nov 1873, having had, with other issue:

1a Henry John Richard, DL; *b* 3 March 1837; Capt 68th LI, afterwards Lt-Col Waterford Artillery; *m* 4 May 1870 Jane Rigby (*d* 12 March 1933), est dau of B Rigby Murray, of Parton, and *d* 10 March 1914, having had issue:

1b William Desmond, CBE (1917), DSO (1925); *b* 11 April 1872; Brig-Gen, Col cmdg 1st Bn 5th Roy Gurkhas, T/Lt-Col cmdg 9th (Service) Bn Rifle Bde 1914–16, Cmdt Mountain Warfare Sch India 1917–18 and 1920, i/c Nepalese Allied Contingent 1916–17, raised and cmded 3rd Bn QVO Corps of Guides Inf 1917–18, Inspr Infantry India as Brig-Gen 1918–20, Cmdt Mountain Warfare Sch India 1921 (two Brevets), NWF India 1897–98 (medal with two clasps), Tirah 1897 (dangerously wounded, clasp), Waziristan 1901–02 (clasp), WW I (1915 Star, two medals, despatches three times), Waziristan 1920 (medal and two clasps) and 1922–23 (despatches, clasp), 2nd Cl Order Star of Nepal; *m* 25 June 1926 Erica Cecil, yr dau of Robert Shepley Shepley, of Troquhain, Belmaclellan, Kirkcudbrightshire, and *dsp* 25 Jan 1961

2b Charles Herbert; *b* 2 Sept 1874; Maj 56th Punjabi Rifles FF, NWF India 1897–98 (medal, two clasps), Tirah Expdn 1898 (clasp), Waziristan 1901–02 (clasp), WW I; *m* 10 Sept 1913 Joan Lascelles (*d* 30 July 1950), dau of Robert Shepley Shepley, of Troquhain, and was *ka* Gallipoli May 1915, leaving posthumous issue:

1c +Charles Henry; *b* 9 June 1915; *educ* Eton and Wye Ag Coll; WW II with Oxon and Bucks LI and as Capt RIASC

3b John Patrick, CB (1924), DSO (1915), OBE (1920); *b* 1 March 1879; Col late 1st/13th FFR, DAAG 1914, AA&QMG 1916–17, GSO(1) 1917, China 1900 (medal), Waziristan 1901–02 (medal with clasp), E Africa 1903–04 (medal with clasp), NWF India (despatches, medal with clasp), WW I (despatches five times, Legion of Honour), Afghan War 1919 (despatches twice); *m* 1st 6 Dec 1914 Phyllis Mary (*d* 26 Jan 1933), dau of James C Read, of Darjeeling; *m* 2nd 22 Dec 1933 *Eileen Nora [Mrs John Villiers-Stuart, The Beeches, Catsfield, Battle, Sussex], dau of Col Alexander John Maunsell MacLaughlin, CIE, of Woking and Assam, and *d* 22 Oct 1958, having had issue by his 1st w:

1c John Michael; *b* 13 April 1927; Maj QO Highrs; *m* 23 July 1960 *Bridget Mary [Mrs John Villiers-Stuart, 11 East St, Wareham, Dorset BH20 4NN], only dau of Lt-Col Patrick Francis Grant, of Knockie, RA, and has issue:

1d +Michael Patrick [Michael Villiers-Stuart Esq, Gothic Cottage, 393 Harborne Rd, Birmingham BR15 3LB]; *b* 3 June 1961; *m* 1986 *Caroline Mary, er dau of David Richard Marsh, of Middleton-by-Youlgreave, Derbys, and has issue:

1e +Archie James; *b* 1992

2e +Angus Theodore; *b* 7 Aug 1994

1e *Katherine Amelia; *b* 1990

1d *Marianne Serena; *b* 10 Dec 1963; *m* 1st 1986 (*divorce* 1993) Oliver John Nicholson; *m* 2nd 1994 *Michael Thomas Donnelly, and has issue by 1st husb:

1e *Natasha Elizabeth; *b* 1986

1c Claire Marie; *b* 15 Jan 1917; *m* 5 June 1948 Col Basil Nevill Leslie Ditmas, OBE, MA Oxford, late RA, yr son of Lt-Col Francis Ivan Leslie Ditmas, DSO, MC, FGS, MInstME, of Cottingham, Yorks, and *d* 11 Oct 1966, leaving issue

2c *Stella [Mrs Anthony Barton, Manesty Cottage, The Green, Fernhurst, Haslemere, Surrey]; *b* 25 March 1918; formerly Assist SO, WAAF; *m* 1st 6 Sept 1941 S/Ldr Donald Maitland Wellings, DFC (*ka* 9 Oct 1944), yr son of Evelyn Valentine Wellings, of Walton-on-the-Hill, Surrey, and has issue:

1d *Donald James; *b* 19 Aug 1942; *educ* Sherborne

2c (cont.) Mrs Donald Wellings *m* 2nd 19 Sept 1949 *Lt-Col Anthony Hamilton Gerald Barton, MC, RA (ret), est son of Lt-Col Richard Lionel Barton, DSO, of Shoebury, Norfolk, and has further issue:

1d *Patrick Anthony Richard; *b* 15 July 1956; *m* 1980 *Jennifer Ann, dau of Anthony Lucas of Haslemere, Surrey, and has issue:

1e *Hamish Anthony; *b* 1987

2e *Angus Patrick; *b* 1990

1e *Sophie Caroline; *b* 1993

1d *Julia Penelope Susan; *b* 17 Sept 1950

1b Kathleen Jane; *m* 6 May 1903 Brig-Gen Henry Richmond Gale, CMG (*d* 29 July 1930), of Bardsea Hall, Lancs, son of H R H Gale, 48th Foot, and *d* 28 Dec 1958, leaving issue

2b Gertrude Elsie; *d* unm 8 June 1965

3b Marie Violet; *m* 26 Oct 1918 James William Henry Jellett (*d* 14 April 1943), est surv son of Very Rev Henry Jellett, DD, Dean of St Patricks, and *dsp* 4 Sept 1967

1a Geraldine; *m* 25 Aug 1874 Arthur J Chichester, and *d* his widow, 7 Jan 1931

3 William; *b* 18 Nov 1778; Capt RN; *m* June 1806 Hon Georgiana Maude (*d* 31 Aug 1807), 5th dau of 1st Viscount Hawarden (*qv*), and *d* 28 July 1814, leaving an only dau:

(1) Georgiana; *d* unm 1833

4 George, CB; *b* 1 March 1780; R-Adml; *m* 7 Oct 1800 Jane (*d* 1 Feb 1862), dau of Maj-Gen James Stewart, and *d* 19 Feb 1841, having had issue:

(1) Henry, of Montford, Isle of Bute; *b* 1 Jan 1808; *m* 9 Nov 1840 Cecilia (*d* 28 Feb 1890), 4th dau of Charles Hammersley, and *d* 19 May 1880, leaving, with other issue:

1a Dudley Charles; *b* 20 Nov 1844; Cdr RN; *m* 31 March 1875 Amy Clara (*d* 31 Jan 1943), only surv child of Lt-Col Charles Harrison Page, JP, of Dulwich House, Llandaff, Glamorgan, and *d* 21 Feb 1906, leaving issue:

1b Evelyn Charles Henry; *b* 21 Dec 1875; Cmdr RN; *m* 25 Sept 1906 Anna Knutzen Grane (*d* 1944), and *d* Dec 1944, leaving issue:

1c +Dudley Evelyn; *b* 1 July 1907

1c *Amy Ingeborg Sybil Eda; *b* 1911

2b James Martin; *b* 15 Jan 1877; Supt Sao Paulo and Minas Rlwy Co Ltd Brazil; *m* 1928 (*divorce* 1950) Beatrice Doreen, dau of John Hugo Walter Fussell, and *d* 10 Aug 1963

3b Dudley; *b* 8 Nov 1883; Lt-Cdr RN; *ka* battle of Horn Reef, 1 June 1916

4b Henry; *b* 30 July 1886; *m* 15 Aug 1919 Jane Elizabeth, dau of William Fraser Simpson Henderson, of Melkie Camalown, Fyvie, Aberdeenshire, and *d* 12 Feb 1936, leaving issue:

1c *Muriel Mary Henderson; *b* 23 Feb 1926; *m* 1st 18 Nov 1946 (*divorced*) Frederick Aloysius Santi, and has had issue:

1d *Stuart Nicholas; *b* 18 July 1947

2d Christian Francis; *b* 14 Feb 1951; *d* June 1953

1c (cont.) Mrs Muriel Santi *m* 2nd March 1962 *Robert Burties

5b Eric Hoy; *b* 1 Sept 1890; *m* 31 Aug 1918 Dorothie Primrose (*d* 1982, having *m* 2nd 12 Aug 1958 Hon Michael Scott, OBE (*d* 9 Jan 1959), yst son of 3rd Earl of Eldon (*qv*), and 3rd Surgn V-Adml Sir Edward Greeson, KBE, CB, who *d* 10 June 1979), dau of Maj C Murray Stewart, and *d* 20 Jan 1950, leaving issue:

1c *(Patricia) Elizabeth; *b* 28 Jan 1923; *m* 1st 5 Jan 1946 (*divorce* 1950) Thomas Daniel, and has issue:

1d *Timothy Hugh; *b* 6 Nov 1946; *m* 1973 *Sarah Nancy Hood-Daniel and has issue:

1e *Hugo Charles; *b* 1983

1e *Emily Sarah; *b* 1975

2e *Josephine Polly; *b* 1977

3e *Olive Zoe; *b* 1984

1c (cont.) Mrs Elizabeth Daniel *m* 2nd 23 Sept 1972 Lt-Cdr Philip Lionel Salisbury Baxendale, OBE, RD, of Alderney, CI (*d* 1986)

6b Kenneth Freemantle; *b* 4 June 1895; Pt, Black Watch; *ka* 1917

1b Mary Cecilia; *b* 9 Aug 1879; *m* 12 Sept 1906 Hon Osmund Scott, 3rd son of 3rd Earl of Eldon (*qv*), and *d* 20 Nov 1941, leaving issue

2b Lillias Amy; *b* 19 Nov 1881; *m* 19 June 1907 Hon Denys Scott, 4th son of 3rd Earl of Eldon (*qv*), and had issue

3b Heather Sybil; *b* 7 Feb 1900; *m* 2 Sept 1930 Alfred Mutlow Grosvenor Herd, of Carlisle, Cumberland, and had issue:

1c *Brenda Amy Grosvenor; *b* 24 May 1932; *m* 5 April 1969 *Christopher Patrick Cavendish Pelly, er son of Nigel Cavendish Pelly, OBE (*see* PELLY, Bt)

2a John Windsor, VD; *b* 3 Dec 1846; Lt-Col and Hon Col Argyll and Bute Vol Art, Hon Sheriff Substitute; *m* 30 April 1873 Flora (*d* 27 Sept 1934), only dau of Capt William C J Campbell, of Snettisham Hall, Norfolk, and *d* 8 Dec 1905, leaving issue:

1b Henry Campbell; *b* 2 March 1874; WW I, Capt Black Watch; *m* 20 April 1904 Eileen Barbara (*d* 1969), yr dau of Maj Henry Gerard Fenton Newall, JP, of Hare Hill, Lancs, and *d* 1953, leaving issue:

1c Mary Barbara; *b* 13 Jan 1905; *m* 12 Nov 1934 Kenneth Robertson, of London, son of Henry Robertson, and *d* 7 Aug 1938

2c Margaret Windsor; *b* 15 Oct 1908; *m* 5 April 1934 George Thomas Balfour-Kinear, only son of George William Balfour-Kinnear, WS (*d* in an accident 20 Sept 1945), of Teddington, and had issue

3c *Flora Emily Windsor; *b* 26 Feb 1910; *m* 4 Feb 1932 G/Capt Cyril Henry William Boldero (*d* 1979), RAF (ret), son of Rev John Herbert formerly of Rattlesden, Suffolk, and has issue:

1d *Ann Barbara; *b* 12 June 1933; *m* 1st 5 June 1954 (*divorce* 1963) Peter Ingoldby, yr son of Eric Ingoldby, CIE, of Holmbury St Mary, Dorking, Surrey, and has issue:

1e *Christopher Henry; *b* 6 March 1955

1e *Jane Patricia; *b* 19 April 1957

1d (cont.) Mrs Ann Ingoldby *m* 2nd 22 May 1968 (*divorce* 1975) John Harris-Burland, est son of William Malcolm Harris-Burland, CBE, of Buckinghamshire, and has further issue:

2e *James William; *b* 13 Dec 1968

1d (cont.) Mrs Ann Harris-Burland *m* 3rd 1982 *Gwynne Douglas James, of Killiemore, Wigtownshire

2d *Helen Cecilia [Mrs Robin Howard, West Glen, Newton Stewart, Wigtownshire]; *b* 12 Feb 1936; *m* Aug 1968 *Robin Malcolm Anderson Howard, son of H A Howard, OBE, and has issue:

1e *Alastair Charles Henry; *b* 1969

1e *Sarah Flora Margaret; *b* 1970

4c (Eileen) Sybil Windsor; *b* 21 July 1917; *m* 1953 *George Oswald Younghusband, 2nd son of Cdr Frank Charles Robert Romer Younghusband, RN (ret), of Oakhill Lodge, Isle of Man, and *d* in a climbing accident Scotland 26 Aug 1973, leaving issue:

1d *Andrew George Albert; *b* 19 Nov 1957

2d *John William; *b* 15 Jan 1959

1d *Victoria Mary; *b* 14 July 1954

2b John Dudley; *b* 1 Sept 1875; CE; Maj late 7th (Cyclist) Bn Welsh Regt; *m* 1st 30 April 1902 (*divorce* 1913) Florence Emily, yst dau of Charles E Hunter, Ch Engr Cardiff Rlwy Co; *m* 2nd 3 Feb 1915 Noelle Mary, only dau of James Phillip Goddard, and *d* 4 Nov 1954

1b Elizabeth Ada Mary; *b* 25 May 1878; *m* 20 Oct 1908 Francis Gerald Cradock-Hartopp (*d* 27 Aug 1946), of Barbrook, Bakewell, Derbyshire, and *d* 23 April 1955, leaving issue (*see* CRADOCK-HARTOPP, Bt)

1a Evelyn; *m* 2 Aug 1860 Charles Hallyburton Campbell, BCS (*d* 30 Jan 1911), 2nd son of Sir George Campbell, of Edenwood, and nephew of Ld Chllr Campbell (*see* STRATHEDEN AND CAMPBELL, B), and *d* 3 Jan 1867, leaving issue (*see* NORFOLK, D)

2a Emily Catherine; *m* 5 Nov 1861 Martin Ridley Smith (*d* 8 Nov 1908), of Hayes Common, Kent, and *d* 6 May 1882, leaving issue

3a Gertrude Mary; *m* 23 Oct 1866 Sir Everard Alexander Hambro (*d* 26 Feb 1925), of Hayes Place, Kent, and Milton Abbey, Dorset, and *d* 3 June 1905, leaving issue

4a Elizabeth Charlotte; *m* 21 Sept 1880 George Edward Sneyd (*d* 14 Jan 1894), and *d* 24 Dec 1931, leaving issue

5a Cecilia; *m* 1884 Martin Ridley Smith (*d* 8 Nov 1908), of Hayes Common, Kent, and *d* March 1939, leaving issue

6a Frederica; *m* 22 March 1877 Col Michael Rowand Gray Buchanan, OBE (*d* 16 Dec 1933), of Ettrickdale, Bute, and Wellshot, Lanarkshire, and *d* 18 June 1936, leaving issue

7a Octavia Henrietta Mary; *d* unm 30 March 1940

(1) Elizabeth Jane; *m* 18 Aug 1825 4th Marquess Townshend (*d* 10 Sept 1863; *qv*), and *d* 27 Jan 1877, leaving issue

(2) Emily Frances; *m* 9 Jan 1834 Hon Charles Abbott (*d* 17 Dec 1838), son of 1st Baron Tenterden (*see* 1939 edn), and *d* 16 June 1886, leaving issue

1 Charlotte; *m* 1797 Sir William Jackson Homan, Bt, and *d* his widow, 5 Sept 1847

The **1st Marquess** *m* 2nd 17 Sept 1800 Frances (*d* 12 Nov 1832), 2nd dau of Thomas Coutts, banker, of The Strand, by his 1st w (and bro's maid) Susan, dau of — Starkie, yeoman, of Lancs, and *d* Geneva 16 Nov 1814, having by her had issue:

5 Dudley Coutts; *b* 11 Jan 1803; MA (Camb) 1823; MP Arundel 1830–37 and Marylebone 1847–54; *m* 1824 Christiana Alexandrine Egypta (*d* Rome 19 May 1847), dau of Lucien Bonaparte, Prince of Canino, and *d* 17 Nov 1854, leaving issue:

(1) Paul Amadeus Francis Coutts; Capt 68th Regt; *d* unm 1 Aug 1889

2 Frances; *m* 15 Sept 1823 2nd Earl of Harrowby (*qv*) and *d* 29 March 1859, leaving issue

The 1st MARQUESS's gs,

JOHN STUART later CRICHTON-STUART (roy licence 26 Aug 1805), **2nd Marquess of the County of Bute** and **7th Earl of Dumfries** (as which he *s* his maternal gf 7 April 1803; *see* above, **Lineage (of Crichton)**; his descendants of both sexes being in remainder to that Earldom and its associated lesser titles), KT (1843); *b* 10 Aug 1793; *educ* Eton and Christ's Coll Cambridge; Ld Lt Glam and Bute 1815–48, Recorder Banbury and Keeper Rothsay Castle; *m* 1st 29 July 1818 Lady Maria North (*d* 11 Sept 1841), est dau of 3rd Earl of Guilford (*qv*); *m* 2nd 10 April 1845 Sophia (*d* 28 Dec 1859), dau of 1st Marquess of Hastings (*see* LOUDOUN, E), and *d* 18 March 1848, leaving by her:

JOHN PATRICK CRICHTON-STUART, **3rd Marquess of the County of Bute**, KT (1875); *b* 12 Sept 1847; Hereditary Keeper Rothsay Castle, Ld Lt Bute, Ld Rector St Andrews 892 and 1898, LLD, Mayor Cardiff 1891, Provost Rothsay 1896–99, a celebrated RC convert; *m* 16 April 1872 Hon Gwendolen Mary Anne Fitzalan-Howard (*d* 15 Jan 1932), est dau of 1st Baron Howard of Glossop (*see* NORFOLK, D), and *d* 9 Oct 1900, leaving:

1 JOHN, **4th Marquess**

2 Ninian Edward, JP (Fife); *b* 15 May 1883; MP Cardiff 1910–15, Lt-Col 6th Bn Welsh Regt, late Lt Scots Gds; *m* 16 June 1906 Hon Ismay Lucretia Mary Preston (who *m* 2nd 30 April 1917 Capt Archibald Henry Maule Ramsay, late Coldm Gds, who *d* 11 March 1955 (*see* DALHOUSIE, E), and *d* 16 Feb 1975), only dau of 14th Viscount Gormanston, GCMG (*qv*), and was *ka* 2 Oct 1915, having had issue:

(1) Ninian Patrick; *b* 31 March 1907; *d* 4 Feb 1910

(2) Michael Duncan David, of Falkland, MC (1943), JP (Fife 1951), DL (Fife 1953); *b* 14 March 1915; *educ* Eton and Ch Ch Oxford (MA); Maj Scots Gds WW II (wounded twice); Hereditary Keeper Falkland Palace, memb Scottish Nat Portrait Gallery Advsy Ctee 1959, V-Pres Nat Trust Scotland (Chm Exec Ctee 1967–69), Chm Red Deer Commn 1959–63, Provost Roy Burgh of Falkland 1964, OStJ, Kt SMO Malta; *m* 1 March 1941 Barbara (*d* 1985), only dau of Lt-Col Sir (George) Stewart Symes, KCMG, CBE, DSO, and *d* 1981, having had issue:

1a +Ninian John [Ninian Crichton-Stuart Esq, Moncreiff House, High St, Falkland, Fife KY7 7BP]; *b* 16 March 1957; *educ* Ampleforth and U of Stirling; Hereditary Keeper Falkland Palace; *m* 1982 *Anne Marie, dau of Neil O'Donnell, of Glasgow, and has issue:

1b +Francis Paul; *b* 1984

1b +Christina Marie; *b* 1983

1a +Elspeth Ann; *b* 26 July 1954; *m* 1981 *Prof Thomas Puttfarken, of Wivenhoe, nr Colchester, Essex

(2) (cont.) Maj Michael Crichton-Stuart also adopted:

*Mary (Marietta) Frances [Miss Mary Crichton-Stuart, 4 Fitzwilliam Rd, London SW4]; *b* 19 Oct 1951

*Frances Elizabeth [Miss Frances Crichton-Stuart, 6 Cadogan House, Beaufort St, London SW3]; *b* 25 Oct 1951; painter

(1) Ismay Catherine; *b* 23 Dec 1909; *m* 1st 1 Oct 1930 (*divorce* 1936) Viscount Tiverton (later 3rd Earl of Halsbury; *qv*), and by him had issue; *m* 2nd 30 Aug 1937 *Donald Walter Munro Ross, yr son of Brig-Gen Sir Walter Charteris Ross, of Cromarty, KBE, CB, CMG, and by him had issue:

1a +Ismay Victoria; *b* 19 Sept 1944

(2) +Claudia Miriam Joanna; *b* 24 June 1913

3 Colum Edmund, JP; *b* 3 April 1886; *educ* Ch Ch Oxford; 2nd Lt Scots Gds (SR); 2nd Sec Dip Serv, MP Northwich 1922–45, Ld Lt Bute 1953–57, Kt SMO Malta; *m* 14 Feb 1940 Elizabeth Caroline (*d* 25 March 1964), only dau of Sir Edward Stanlety Hope, KCB (*see* LINLITHGOW, M), and widow of 6th Marquess of Lansdowne (*qv*), and *d* 18 Aug 1957

1 Margaret, OBE (1920), JP Bute; *b* 24 Dec 1875; Co Commr Girl Guides (Bute), Pres Catholic Women's League Scotland, DJStJ, Order Holy Sepulchre, Medal of Queen Elisabeth of Belgium, Order Pro Ecclesia et Pontifice, Gold Cross Order Sacri Itineris Hierosylimitano; King's Serv Red Cross medal and clasps; Silver Jubilee Medal 1935; *m* 26 Oct 1909 Col Sir Colin William MacRae, CVO, CBE, JP, DL (*d* 10 Oct 1952), yst son of Duncan MacRae, JP, DL, of Conchra, and *d* 6 June 1954, leaving issue

The 3rd MARQUESS's est son,

JOHN CRICHTON-STUART, **4th Marquess of the County of Bute**, KT; *b* 20 June 1881; Pres Bute TAA, Hon Col 4th Highland Bde RGA, Ld Lt Bute; *m* 6 July 1905 Augusta Mary Monica, DBE (1909), DJStJ (*d* 16 May 1947), yr dau of Sir Henry Bellingham, 4th Bt (*qv*), and *d* 25 April 1947, having had issue:

1 JOHN, **5th Marquess**

2 Robert; *b* 12 Dec 1909; *educ* Downside and Trin Coll Cambridge (BA 1933); Capt Scots Gds; Ld Lt Bute 1958–63, Pres Br Assoc SMO Malta 1960–68, KStJ; *m* 18 April 1934 *Lady Janet Egidia Montgomerie [The Lady Robert Crichton-Stuart, Wards Cottage, Gartocharn, Dunbartonshire], 2nd dau of 16th Earl of Eglinton and Winton (*qv*), and *d* 1976, leaving issue:

(1) Ninian; *b* 31 Oct 1935; *educ* Eton; *d* 1992

(2) +Henry Colum [Henry Crichton-Stuart Esq, Kirkview, Duns Rd, Gifford, E Lothian EH41 4QW]; *b* 1 April 1938; *educ* Eton; Lt Scots Gds (RARO); *m* 20 July 1963 (*divorce*) Patricia Margaret (Tita), only dau of Brig Hugh Ronald Norman, DSO, of St Clere, Kemsing, Kent, and has issue:

1a +Alexander Colum; *b* 4 Feb 1967

1a +Camilla; *b* 15 April 1964

2a +Serena; *b* 9 July 1965

3a +Teresa Clare; *b* 1971

3 David CRICHTON-STUART later STUART (decree of Lord Lyon 1934); *b* 8 Feb 1911; *educ* Downside and Ch Ch Oxford; 2nd Lt 51st AT Regt RA; *m* 24 May 1940 Ursula Sybil Clifton (*d* 1989), yr dau of Sir Edward Hussey Packe, KBE, of Prestwold Hall, Leics, and formerly w of Peter Thomas Clifton (*see* BRUCE, Bt, of Downhill), and *d* 1970, leaving issue:

(1) +Flora; *b* Aug 1941

(2) Rose; *b* 6 April 1946; *k* in a car crash 5 Jan 1962

4 Patrick; *b* 1 Feb 1913; Hon Capt 11th Hus; *m* 1st 14 Oct 1937 Jane (*d* 18 Dec 1944), dau of Capt von Bahr, of Stockholm; *m* 2nd 16 April 1947 Linda Irene (*d* 1974), only dau of William Evans, of Monmouth, and *d* 5 Feb 1956, leaving issue by his 1st w:

(1) +Charles Patrick Colum Henry [Charles Crichton-Stuart Esq, 16 Douglas Court, W End Lane, London NW6]; *b* 10 March 1939; *educ* Ampleforth; RAF pilot instructor, former racing driver; *m* 1st 7 July 1967 (*divorce*) Shirley Ann Field, actress, and has issue:

1a +Nicola Jane; *b* 1967

(1) (cont.) Charles Crichton-Stuart *m* 2nd 1980 *Jennifer A Collie, and has further issue:

1a +Patrick James; *b* 1982

2a +Sophie; *b* 1980

(1) +Angela Mary Monica; *b* 25 March 1940; *m* 19 Feb 1963 (*divorce* 19–) Simon Mark Pilkington, only s of Capt Mark Leslie Pilkington, MC, Life Gds, and has issue:

1a +Rupert Charles; *b* 21 Feb 1964

2a +Mark Patrick; *b* 6 Oct 1965

1a +Janey Susan; *b* 7 Nov 1966

5 Rhidian; *b* 4 June 1917; *educ* Ampleforth and Magdalene Coll Cambridge; Capt RA (RARO); memb Roy Co of Archers 1948, Kt of Obedience SMO Malta 1964, Br Del Internat Legislative Assembly Tangier 1953–57; *m* 20 July 1939 Selina (*d* 1985), dau of Frederick Gerth van Wijk, Dutch Envoy Extrdy and Min Plen Paris, and *d* 25 June 1969, leaving issue:

(1) +Frederick John Patrick, TD [Fra Frederick Crichton-Stuart TD, 6 Huntly St, Edinburgh EH3 5HB]; *b* 6 Sept 1940; *educ* Ampleforth; Kt of Justice SMO Malta; *m* 3 Oct 1964 *Elizabeth Jane Douglas, er dau of Ernest James Whitson, and has issue:

1a +Rhidian Colum; *b* 3 Aug 1967; *m* 16 Sept 1997 *Claire F Short and has:

1b +Isabelle Alexandra; *b* 2 Feb 1997

2a +Edward Neil James; *b* 1974

1a +Ione Jane; *b* 22 Nov 1965

2a +Amanda Mary; *b* 31 Oct 1968

(2) +(Jerome) Niall Anthony [Niall Crichton-Stuart Esq, Oake Court, Portinscale Rd, London SW15 2HU]; *b* 1 Jan 1948; *educ* Ampleforth; 2nd Lt Scots Gds; Kt of Honour and Devotion SMO Malta, Chevalier du Wissam Alouite Morocco; *m* 1971 *Susan, est dau of Prof Patrick Dwyer-Joyce, of Dublin, and has issue:

1a +Rhidian Charles Patrick; *b* 1974

2a +Niall Rollo Robert; *b* 1977

3a +Archie Michael John; *b* 1984

(1) +(Mary) Margot Patricia [Mrs Edward Lovell, 62 Bramfield Rd, London SW11 6RB]; *b* 18 March 1942; *m* 20 June 1962 *Edward Henry Lovell, yst s of Col H O Lovell, and has issue:

1a +Peter Henry James; *b* 21 Feb 1965; *educ* Ampleforth; *m* — and has issue

1a +Nicola Mary; *b* 23 Aug 1963; *m* — and has issue

2a +Henrietta Margaret; *b* 1971

1 Mary Stuart-Walker (deed poll); *b* 8 May 1906; *m* 8 May 1933 Edward Alan Walker, Dip Serv (ret), er son of Arthur Walker, and had issue:

(1) +Ione Mary Stuart [Baroness Christian von Oppenheim, Vallehermoso 32, 28015 Madrid, Spain]; *b* 3 Aug 1934; *m* 27 July 1955 Baron Christian von Oppenheim Rivera (*k* air accident nr Lagos, Nigeria, 8 Oct 1967), s of Baron Harold von Oppenheim, of Cologne, and has issue:

1a +Edward Harold Manuel Maria Rodrigo; *b* 13 March 1958

1a +Corinna Maria del Rocio Pimpinella Fernanda; *b* 30 May 1956

2a +Flora Claudia Mari Del Mar Monica; *b* 4 May 1960

3a +Maria-Gabriella Isabel; *b* 22 Feb 1963

(2) +Hella Immaculate; *b* 8 Dec 1935; *m* 3 June 1957 *Frederick Villenueve Nicolle, MB, BCh, FRCS (Can), er s of Arthur Villeneuve Nicolle, of St Peter's House, Jersey, CI, and has issue:

1a +Hugo Arthur Villeneuve; *b* 12 Jan 1963

1a +Miranda Camilla; *b* 29 Oct 1958

2a +Edwina Mary; *b* 2 Feb 1961

2 Jean; *b* 28 Oct 1908; Dame Grand Cross of Honour and Devotion of SMO Malta (1959); *m* 12 June 1928 Lt-Cdr Hon James Willoughby Bertie, RN (*see* LINDSEY and ABINGDON, E) and *d* 23 Oct 1995, leaving issue

The 4th MARQUESS's est son,

JOHN CRICHTON-STUART, **5th Marquess of the County of Bute**; JP (Bute); *b* 4 Aug 1907; 2nd Lt RA (TAR), WW II in HG and RNVR; V-Lt and Hon Sheriff Substitute Bute, CStJ; *m* 26 April 1932 Lady Eileen Beatrice Forbes, yr dau of 8th Earl of Granard (*qv*), and *d* 14 Aug 1956, having had issue:

1 JOHN, **6th Marquess**

2 David Ogden; *b* 27 Feb 1933; *educ* Ampleforth and Trin Coll Cambridge; Lt RAC; *m* 24 Feb 1972 *Lady Helen [The Lady David Crichton-Stuart, Kames Court, Cronkbourne, Braddan, IOM IM4 4QH], dau of William Kerr McColl, and *d* 1977, leaving issue:

(1) +Kenneth Edward David; *b* 27 June 1975; *educ* Ampleforth

(1) +Elizabeth Rose; *b* 10 March 1973; *educ* St George's, Vevey, Switzerland

3 James Charles; *b* 17 Sept 1935; *educ* Ampleforth and Trin Coll Cambridge; Lt Scots Gds (Res), ADC to Govr-Gen Fedn of Rhodesia and Nysaland 1957 –58, Dir Coutts & Co; *m* 25 June 1959 (*divorce* 1968) Sarah (Sally) Frances (*m* 2nd (*divorce* 1995) HH The Aga Khan; *see* CHURSTON, B), only dau of Lt-Col Arthur Edward Croker Poole; *m* 2nd 1970 Anna Rose (*m* 2nd Peter Merrick Knatchbull-Hugessen; *see* BRABOURNE, B), dau of Maj H Bramwell, and *d* 1982, leaving by her:

(1) +William Henry; *b* 1971

(2) +Hugh Bertram; *b* 1973

(3) +Alexander Blain; *b* 1982

1 +(Caroline Moira) Fiona [The Lady Fiona Lowsley-Williams, Guadacorte, Estacion de San Roque, Cadiz, Spain]; *b* 7 Jan 1941; *m* 4 April 1959 Capt Michael Lowsley-Williams, late 16th/5th Queen's Roy Lancers, est son of Maj Frances Saville Hoole Lowsley-Williams, 16th/15th Lancers, and Lady Greene, and has issue:

(1) +Patrick David Edward; *b* 10 Feb 1960

(2) +Mark Ogden Francis; *b* 26 Feb 1961

(3) +Paul John Fermin; *b* 22 March 1964

(4) +Michael Charles Javier; *b* 1967

The 5th MARQUESS's est son,

JOHN CRICHTON-STUART, **6th Marquess of the County of Bute**; KBE, JP (Bute); *b* 27 Feb 1933; *educ* Ampleforth and Trin Coll Cambridge; Hereditary Keeper Rothesay Castle; Ld Lt Bute 1967–75, CC Bute, Convener Bute CC 1967–70, Hon LLD Glasgow, FSA Scotland 1972, Lt Scots Gds (RARO), Chm Scottish Ctee Nat Fund Research into Crippling Diseases 1966–93, Pres Scottish Standing Ctee Vol Internat Aid 1968–75, memb Cncl Nat Trust Scotland 1964 (Chm Cncl and Exec Ctee 1969–93, Dir Devpt Ctee 1973–78), memb Countryside Commn Scotland 1970–78, Chm Historic Bldgs Cncl Scotland; *m* 1st 19 April 1955 (*divorce* 1977) (Beatrice) Nicola Grace, only dau of Lt-Cdr Wolstan Beaumont Charles Weld-Forester, RN (ret) (*see* FORESTER, B), and had issue:

1 JOHN COLUM CRICHTON-STUART, **7th and present Marquess of the County of Bute**

2 +Anthony; *b* 14 May 1961; *educ* Ampleforth; *m* 1990 *Alison, yr dau of Keith Bruce, of Highgate, and has:

(1) +Flora Grace; *b* 10 Nov 1994

(2) +Eliza Rose; *b* 7 March 1996

1 +Sophia Anne; *b* 27 Feb 1956; *m* 1st 23 June 1979 (*divorce* 1988, resumed maiden name) James Stewart Bain, son of Alistair Roberson Bain, of BC, Canada, and has issue:

(1) +Ella Samantha; *b* 25 Jan 1981

1 (cont.) Lady Sophia Crichton-Stuart *m* 2nd 1990, as his 2nd w, *Alexius John Benedict Fenwick (*see* LILFORD, B), and has further issue:

(2) +Georgia Jessie; *b* 1990

2 Eileen Caroline; *b* 21 Feb 1957; *k* in motor accident 1984

The **6th Marquess** *m* 2nd 12 Nov 1978 *Jennifer, proprietor Bute Wines, Mount Stuart, only dau of John Brougham Home-Rigg, of Plaston, E Transvaal, S Africa, and formerly w of Gerald Percy, gs of 7th Duke of Northumberland (*qv*), and *d* 1993

Seat: Mount Stuart, Isle of Bute. An early Georgian house of 1716 designed by Alexander McGill was altered a couple of generations later by George Paterson. It is doubtful whether the **3rd Marquess**, who came into his patrimony seventy years still further on, would have left this rather unexciting inheritance untouched anyway, especially given his precociously acquired wealth and Romish fervour, all the stronger for his being a convert. As it was, a fire in 1877 destroyed the main part of the McGill-Paterson building.

To Lord Bute the flames may well have seemed divinely inspired. He commissioned Sir Robert Anderson, a pupil of Gilbert Scott's, and a gigantic edifice in marble, murals and stained glass arose from the ashes of the old house.

It is usual with Mount Stuart to exclaim at the rich Christian decorative motifs which infuse it. Certainly the plethora of lanterns resembling altar lamps, the mosaic on an outer wall showing Madonna and Child, the virginal white of the William Burges-designed Chapel, the six days of the Creation depicted in H W Lonsdale's murals in the curved triangular spaces between the groins of the ceiling on the staircase and the conventual ogives of the external elevations suggest a pious householder.

But the wealth of heraldry strikes a more profane note. The picture collection, mostly assembled by the **3rd Earl** at Luton Hoo, which he had bought in 1762 (and which like Mount Stuart burned down, doing so in 1843), is the hobby of a cultivated man of the Age of Reason. And the Horoscope Room whose ceiling depicts the exact aspect of the heavens at the **3rd Marquess**'s nativity suggests he had imperfectly absorbed the Christian theology pressed on him during instruction. The Marble Hall has a ceiling with a star motif too, the background being green and studded with glass that, when illuminated, shimmers like a galaxy. There is something Alhambra-like about the Drawing Room, with its screen of marble columns and window alcoves giving the impression almost of a courtyard.

The process of creation at Mount Stuart suffered some interruptions. Anderson was dismissed. His successor, a bibulous disciple of Burges's called William Frame, had to be let go too. Anderson returned, but on the **3rd Marquess**'s death in 1900 the Chapel and the western gallery were still unfinished. The crumbling of Victorian Age prestige thereafter was swifter than anything the Atlantic gales might wreak on Mount Stuart, for all its exposed position off the western coast of Scotland, and by the end of World War II the family was looking to sell. But Victorian architecture came back into fashion, and the **6th Marquess** undertook a heavy restoration programme, which fortunately was completed by the time of his death in 1993.

BUTLER of Cloughgrenan

Arms: Or, a chief indented az., a border erm. **Crest:** Out of a ducal coronet or a plume of five ostrich feathers, therefrom a falcon rising arg. **Motto:** *Comme je trouve* ('As I find'). **Creation:** Bt. (I) 16 Aug 1628.

SIR RICHARD PIERCE BUTLER, 13TH BT, of Cloughgrenan, Co Carlow [Sir Richard Butler Bt, 51 Thurloe Sq, SW7 2SX]; *b* 22 July 1940; *s* f 1994; *educ* Eton, New York U and Inst of Chartered Accountants in England and Wales; MBA, FCA; ptnr Charles Wakeling and Co 1964–66, dir: First Boston Corp (NY) 1967–68, Paine Webber Inc (NY) 1978–88, Paine Webber Internat Bank 1986–89, Emesco Industrial Equity Co SA 1987–, Ibercapital SA 1990–, R Pond C Internat 1992–; memb cncl Pestalozzi Children's Village Tst 1983– (chm 1985–94); *m* 21 Oct 1965 *Diana, yr dau of Col Stephen John Borg, of The Palms, St Julians, Malta, and has:

1 +THOMAS PIERCE [Thomas Butler Esq, Sriratana Mansions II, 59 Sukhumvit 23, Bangkok]; *b* 9 Oct 1966; *educ* Eton and Us of Pennsylvania and IMD; MBA, BSc; *m* 17 July 1993 *(Lucinda) Pamela, est dau of Edward Joseph Murphy, of Ste Foy, Quebec, and has:

(1) *Tymandra Grace; *b* 6 April 1995

(1) * Antonia Margaret; *b* 28 Aug 1996

2 +Stephen Patrick; *b* 18 May 1968; *educ* Eton and UEA (BSc); *m* 1994 *Keeley Wilson

3 +Rupert Dudley; *b* 1971; *educ* Eton and Trinity Coll Dublin (BSc)

1 *Anne Virginia; *b* 11 Sept 1973

Lineage: Sir Thomas Butler, 1st Bt (I), so *cr* 16 Aug 1628, of Cloughgrenan, Co Carlow; MP Co Carlow 1639; *m* Anne, widow of Nicholas Bagenal and dau of Sir Thomas Colclough, of Tintern Abbey, Co Wexford, and had, with three yr sons and three daus:

Sir Edmund Butler, 2nd Bt; *m* Juliana, dau of Bernard Hyde, of Shinfield, Berks, and had an est s:

Sir Thomas Butler, 3rd Bt; MP Co Carlow 1692; *m* 1st Jane, dau of Rt Rev Richard Boyle, DD, Bp Leighlin and Ferns, and had, with other issue:

1 **Sir Pierce Butler, 4th Bt**; MP Co Carlow 1713; *m* Anne, dau of Joshua Galliard, of Edmonton Berry, Middx

2 James; *m* 1st *c* 23 March 1696 Frances, dau of Sir Edward Abney and widow of Sir John Parker, of Fermoyle, Co Longford, and had a s (Thomas, *b* 1699, *dvp*); *m* 2nd Eleanor (*d* 13 Aug 1748), dau of Sir Nicholas Loftus, of Fethard, Co Wexford, and by her had an only s:

(1) RICHARD (Sir), **5th Bt**

Sir Thomas *m* 2nd July 1700 Jane (*m* 3rd Agmondisham Vesey), dau of Capt Edward Pottinger and widow of John Reynolds

The 4th Bt's nephew,

Sir Richard Butler, 5th Bt, MP Co Carlow 1729–61; *m* Henrietta (*d* 14 Jan 1794), dau and coheir of Henry Percy, of Seskin, Co Wicklow, and had, with other issue:

1 THOMAS (Sir), **6th Bt**

2 Pierce; *b* 1810; Maj 29th Regt, went to USA; ancestor of Pierce Butler, of Philadelphia; *m* 7 June 1834 Frances Anne, dau of Charles Kemble, and *d* 1867 leaving, with another dau:

(1) Frances; *m* 29 June 1871 Very Rev Hon James Wentworth Leigh, Dean Hereford, 3rd s of 1st Baron Leigh (*qv*), and *d* 18 Dec 1910, leaving issue

3 William Paul, of Broomville, Co Carlow; *m* Henrietta, dau of Abraham Nixon, of Munny, Co Wicklow, and had issue:

(1) James, of Broomville, JP Co Carlow; *m* Maria (*d* 18 Sept 1873), dau of Rev Charles Charlton, and *d* 2 Feb 1856, leaving, with other issue:

1a William Paul; *b* 13 April 1817; *m* 28 Oct 1846 Letitia Maria, dau of John Gray, of Upton, Co Carlow, and *d* Aug 1861, leaving, with other issue:

1b Charles James John, Capt late 1st Bn Beds Regt; *b* 24 Oct 1852; *m* 16 March 1893 Elizabeth Frances Massy (*d* 30 Nov 1933), dau of George Lethem Bennett, and widow of D W M Testro, Bengal CS, and *d* 6 Feb 1938

1b Elizabeth Anne; *m* 1879 Trevor Overend, and *d* 21 Jan 1945, leaving issue. He *d* 8 April 1919
2b Helen Williamina; *d* unm 8 March 1947
2a James Thomas, RM Co Kilkenny, JP Carlow; *b* 6 June 1825; *m* 2 Aug 1859 Adelaide Maria (*d* 3 Dec 1911), dau of G R Keogh, of Kilbride, Co Carlow, and *d* 20 July 1910, leaving issue:
1b Charles Richard, High Sheriff Co Carlow 1920; *b* 21 June 1860; *m* 1895 Ethel Elizabeth Jane (*d* 1 April 1943), dau of Capt Philip Charles Newton, JP, of Mount Leinster, Co Carlow, and sis and heir of H P Newton, of Mount Leinster, and *d* 20 Oct 1932, leaving issue:
1c James Humphrey; *b* 30 June 1897; G/Capt RAF, served WW I (wounded twice), NW Frontier India 1919–20 (medal, 3 clasps), WW II; *m* 1st 12 Aug 1925 Marguerite Kathleen Louise (*d* 3 June 1938), only dau of John Hale, of Donacloney Ho, Donacloney, Co Down, and had issue:
1d +Charles Humphrey John [Lt-Col John C Butler, 11210 Thomlar Dve, Fairfax Station, VA 22039, USA]; *b* 9 April 1927; *educ* Wellington and U of Virginia (AB 1953); Lt-Col US Army Res; *m* 29 June 1957 Elizabeth Ann (*d* 1990), twin dau of Harry F Mett, of Schenectady, NY, USA, and has issue:
1e +Bradford Frederick; *b* 1962; *educ* U of Oregon (BS 1984); Capt US Army (Res); *m* 1992 *Kyong-Oh (Kim), of S Korea
1c (cont.) Gp Capt James Butler *m* 2nd 3 Aug 1939 Freda Mary (*d* 1993), yst dau of F E Peto, of Alverstoke, Hants, and *d* 1979, having had further issue:
1d *Barbara Ann Somerset; *b* 10 April 1941; late 2nd Offr WRNS; *m* 1971 *Godwin Scerri, of Malta, and has issue:
1e *Fiona Somerset Paula; *b* 1973
2e *Eleanor Margaret Louise; *b* 1978
2d *Isobel Louise [Miss Isobel Butler, 13 Northcote Rd, St Margaret's, Twickenham, Middx TW1 1PB]; *b* 7 Nov 1945; Tech Co-ordinator RoH
2c Edward Walter Charles; *b* 30 May 1900; late 4th Dragoon Gds, served WW I 1918–19; *m* 6 Dec 1939 *Iris Courtenay, dau of Rev G Moriarty, Rector of Erganagh, Co Tyrone, and *d* 1988 leaving issue:
1d +Walter Richard Courtenay [Walter Butler Esq, 160 Drum Rd, Cookstown, Co Tyrone]; *b* 23 Aug 1944; late 3rd Offr Blue Funnel Line; *m* 19– *Alexandra McQueen, and has issue:
1e *Gavin; *b* 1980
2e *Corrin; *b* 1982
3e *Ewan; *b* 1984
1d *Maeve Geraldine Audley [Mrs Brian Hannon, The See House, Fivemiletown, Co Tyrone BT75 0QP]; *b* 11 Oct 1940; *m* 10 Sept 1964 *Rt Rev Brian Desmond Anthony Hannon, Bishop of Clogher since 1986, son of Ven Arthur Gordon Hannon, of Ramoan Lodge, Ballycastle, Co Antrim, and has issue:
1e *Desmond Pierce O'Brien; *b* 17 July 1965
2e *Brendan Gerald; *b* 23 Jan 1968
3e *Edward Neil Anthony; *b* 1970
3c Beauchamp Henry, DSO; *b* 1902; Lt-Col 1st Bn Roy Inniskilling Fus, served WW II; *b* 7 Jan 1902; *m* 8 June 1938 Vera Mary (*m* 2nd 17 Dec 1946 Maj Charles Patrick FitzGerald, of Turlough Park, Castlebar, Co Mayo, and *d* 1986), dau of Maj William Stewart, MC, JP, of Daisy Hill, Clogher, Co Tyrone, and was *ka* 27 Oct 1943, leaving issue:
1d +Michael Henry; *b* 30 Aug 1939; formerly in Roy Signals
2d +Patrick Beauchamp Rupert [Patrick Butler Esq, Turlough Park, Castlebar, Co Mayo, Ireland]; *b* 31 March 1943; *m* 1982 *Deirdre Anne, dau of Very Rev John Ernest Leeman, Dean of Killala, and has issue:
1e *Andrew John Beauchamp; *b* 1990
2e *Nicola Ann Leeman; *b* 1985
2e *Susannah May Frances; *b* 1987
1c Blanche Adelaide; *d* 1975
2b James Henry, Pasha in Egypt, Govr White Nile Province, Sudan to 1913, served Bechuanaland Expdn 1885, Sudan 1896–99 (two medals, six claps, despatches), had 2nd Cl Medjidie and 4th Cl Osmanieh; *b* 20 April 1863; *d* unm 7 Dec 1927
3b Somerset Edward Molyneux, LRCSI, LRCPI; *b* 13 Aug 1867; *m* 7 Jan 1902 Elsie Jessie (*d* 9 April 1942), only child of Reginald Bearcroft, and *d* 6 Nov 1914, leaving issue:
1c Reginald James Somerset, Lt-Cdr RN; *b* 4 June 1904
1c *Margaret Elsie; *b* 1908; *m* 18 June 1928 Maj Philip Anderson, late Argyll and Sutherland Highrs (*d* 4 Feb 1968), yst s of George Anderson, of Little Harle Tower, Northumberland, and has issue:
1d *Oliver George Bearcroft [Oliver Anderson Esq, Orchard Farm, Kirkmichael, Ayshire]; *b* 3 April 1943; *educ* Fettes; Argyll and Sutherland Highrs Reserve; *m* 1969 *Philippa Kate, dau of Maj C L Stephenson, and has:
1e *Philip George; *b* 1970
1e *Emily Mary; *b* 1971
2e *Nancy Rose; *b* 1983
2c Nancy Adelaide; *d* unm 2 Aug 1951
4b George Fitzwalter, served in Canadian Forces; *b* 4 Aug 1868; *m* 1899 Laura Jane (*d* 1945), dau of Daniel Teer, and *d* 1947, having had issue:
1c James Somerset; *b* 4 Nov 1901; *d* 2 Aug 1902
1c Adelaide Florence
1b Mary, 11 Feb 1903 John Molyneux Keogh, S African Heavy Art, of Kilbride, Co Carlow, and *d* 20 June 1938. He *d* 31 March 1946
2b Emily Blanche; *d* unm 15 June 1951

Sir RICHARD *d* 25 Dec 1771; his est son,

Sir Thomas Butler, 6th Bt, MP Co Carlow 1761; *m* 19 June 1759 Dorothea (*d* 1824), only dau of Edward Bayly, DD, of Ardfert and Archdeacon of Dublin, 2nd son of Sir Edward Bayly, 1st Bt, of Plas Newydd (*see* ANGLESEY, M), and *d* 7 Oct 1772, having had, with three yr s and four daus (the est, Dorothea, *m* Charles Lionel Fitzgerald, of Turlough Park, Co Mayo):

Sir Richard Butler, 7th Bt, MP Co Carlow 1783–1800; *b* 4 July 1761; *m* 23 Aug 1782 Sarah Maria, only dau of Thomas Worth Newenham, of Coolmore, Co Cork, and had, with other issue:
1 THOMAS (Sir), **8th Bt**
2 James, of Ballybar, Co Carlow; *b* 9 Nov 1788; *m* Eliza (*d* 27 Nov 1827), dau of Beauchamp B Hill, and *d* 1 March 1865, leaving, with other issue:
(1) James, of Ballybar; *b* 4 March 1826; *m* 10 April 1860 Henrietta Clara (*d* 31 July 1914), dau of Capt Charles George Butler, RN (*see* below), and *d* 28 Feb 1907, leaving issue:
1a James Walter; *b* 12 June 1864; *m* 25 July 1905 Charlotte Margaret, dau of Charles Messenger Major, of Cromwell Ho, Croydon, and *d* 21 Jan 1929
2a Beauchamp Charles; *b* 30 Sept 1865; *m* 1896 Elizabeth (who *m* 2nd — Hamilton), dau of Finlay Muirhead, of Natal, and *d* 1919, leaving issue:
1b Eileen Doris; *b* 8 Dec 1901; *m* 19– — Jones, and had issue
3a William Arthur; *b* 21 May 1868; *d* 22 Nov 1921
4a Henry Claude, Lt Irish Horse, served in S African War (Queen's medal with two clasps) and WW I (1914 star, three medals); *b* 10 Feb 1875; *m* 7 Feb 1921 Alice, 3rd dau of Michael Darcy, of Kingstown
1a Amy Sarah
3 Charles George, Capt RN; *b* 15 Oct 1793; *m* 28 Sept 1830 Emily (*d* 1876), dau of John Heseltine Bayford, and *d* 1 March 1867, leaving with other issue:
(1) John Bayford, Capt RN; *b* 27 Aug 1832; *m* 10 Jan 1867 Hon Sybil Catherine Devereux (*d* 19 July 1930), dau of 15th Viscount Hereford (*qv*), and *d* 3 Oct 1888, leaving issue:
1a Francis Algernon; *b* 26 Jan 1878; late Lt 5th Bn Middx Regt; *m* 31 July 1909 Dorothy Jean, est dau of Douglas James Chester, of Bedford, and *d* 1935, leaving issue:
1b Brian George; *b* 21 May 1910
1b Doreen Marjorie; *b* 1912; *m* 1st 1932 Frank Clear, of Victoria, BC (*d* 1989), and had issue:
1c *Donald Lloyd Francis; *b* 1937; *m* 1956 *Anne Dolores Barne, and has:
1d *Raymond Lloyd; *b* 1957
2d *Charles Patrick; *b* 1958
1d *Sharon Ann; *b* 1966
1c *Marjorie Butler; *b* 1932; *m* 1951 *Raymond Marquette, RCAF, and has:
1d *Gregory Dean; *b* 1952
2d *Matthew Perry; *b* 1958
3d *Kevin Anthony; *b* 1960
4d *Christopher Adam; *b* 1964
2c *Barbara Joan; *b* 1934; *m* 1957 *Denis Joseph Beaulac and has:
1d *Michael Brian; *b* 1951
2d *Joseph Denis; *b* 1958
3d *Daniel Mark; *b* 1962
1d *Delvina Marie; *b* 1959
2d *Doreen Marie; *b* 1959 (twin)
3d *Jacqueline Marie; *b* 1960
4d *Joni Marie; *b* 19–
3c *Frances Rhoda; *b* 1935; *m* 1954 *Kenneth Roy Suddaby and has:
1d *Michelle Lynn; *b* 1962
2d *Liana Marie; *b* 1965
1b (cont.) Mrs Doreen Clear *m* 2nd 1945 Charles Emil Burgess, of Victoria, BC (*d* 1971); *m* 3rd 1955 Lawrence George Alexander, of Victoria, BC (*d* 1990), and *d* 1976, having had further issue by 2nd husb:
4c *Helaine Charlotte [Mrs Lisle Frank, Westholme, BC, Canada]; *b* 1944; *m* 1st 19– Kenneth Donald Charters; *m* 2nd 1987 *Lisle Darwin Frank, of Westholme, BC, and has issue by 1st husb:
1d *Wayne Kenneth; *b* 1964
2d *Douglas Allan; *b* 1965
1d *Debra Lynn; *b* 1962
2b *Eileen Mary Paget; *b* 1914; WW II with CWAC in UK, Holland and France 1940–44; *d* unm 1979
3b *Vivienne Frances [Mrs Sydney Beswick, 411–1433 Faircliff Lane, Victoria, BC V8S 3J6, Canada]; *b* 1920; *m* 1939 *Sidney Bryan Beswick, and has issue:
1c *Kenneth Bryan [Kenneth Beswick Esq, 216 Linden Ave, Victoria, BC]; *b* 1941; *m* 19– *Sonja Georgette, dau of George Yakimovich, of Victoria, BC, and has issue:
1d *Gary Bryan; *b* 1966
1d *Laura Sonja; *b* 1970
2c *Gary Chester [Gary Beswick Esq, 5347 Kenwill Dr, Nanaimo, BC V9T 5Z8, Canada]; *b* 1954; *m* 1976 *Laura Rose, dau of Gordon Barne, of Port Alberni, BC, and has issue;
1d *Bryan Samuel Butler; *b* 1981
2a Humphrey Charles; *b* 19 Oct 1880; *m* 1st 27 Nov 1903 Emily Laura (*d* 1916), 2nd dau of Alexander J Baxter, and had issue:
1b Charles Humphrey de Bohun Bayford; *b* 2 Sept 1904; *educ* Haileybury and Stanford U California (AB 1928); *m* 1930 Mildred (*d* 1986), dau of William Erskine Duncan, of Oroville, Calif., and *d* 1991 leaving:
1c +Bayford Duncan [Bayford Butler, PO Box 380, Penryn, CA 95663, USA]; *b* 1938; *educ* Stanford U California (AB); U of California at Davis (MS Ag Econ 1962); *m* 27 June 1964 (*divorce* 1986) Nancy Jean, dau of James F Grandin, and has issue:
1d +Bayford Duncan; *b* 18 April 1965
2d +James Devereux; *b* 26 Aug 1969
3d *Cortlandt Pierce; *b* 15 July 1974

2a (cont.) Humphrey Butler *m* 2nd Helen Howard (*d* 1919); *m* 3rd 1920 Sheila Gertrude Edith Mary, dau of William Bernard Blackwell, of Mitre Court, Temple, EC4, and *d* 5 Jan 1969, having by her had issue:

2b Greville Humphrey; *b* 1921; *ka* WW II 1945

3b +Anthony Bernard; *b* 1929; Maj, late RTR; *m* 1st 1969 (*divorce* 1972) Amanda McBlain, dau of Lt-Col W McBlain Stephen; *m* 2nd 1973 *Mrs Harriet Eileen Harland

1a Nora; *b* 1870; *m* 1st 1894 Arthur L Macnamara, Lt RN (*d* 1895); *m* 2nd 1898 Capt W G Harding (*d* 1905), late Lincoln Regt, and *d* 1935, leaving issue

(2) William Charles, JP Cumberland, Registrar Probate Div High Court of Justice, late Capt 3rd Border Regt; *b* 17 Jan 1844; *m* July 1877 Emily (*d* 19 April 1922), dau of H S Chadwick, and *d* 6 Dec 1914, leaving issue:

1a Henry Beauchamp, slr, Resident Nigeria Political Serv, served Egba Expdn 1918 (medal and clasp); *b* 1 Dec 1878; *d* unm 1952

2a Charles Walter, OBE (1920); *b* 17 Feb 1880; Lt-Col late IA, served in S African War 1899–1900 (wounded, Queen's medal with two clasps), WW I 1914–19 (despatches twice), and in Afghan War 1919; *m* 1905 Vivien Eleanor (*d* 28 Dec 1943), dau of Rev Thomas Bowen, Canon of Bristol, late Vicar of St Nicholas, Bristol, and *d* 1941, leaving issue:

1b Richard Shirley; *b* 28 May 1907; *educ* Charterhouse; Col Glos Regt, served WW II and in Korea; *m* 30 April 1940 *Auriol Lilian Evelyn [Mrs Richard Butler, Long Ham House, Cornwood, S Devon], dau of Rev Alexander Ross Biddle, BA, of Temple Hill, E Budleigh, Devon, and *d* 1988, leaving issue:

1c +Patrick James Richard; *b* 12 June 1944; *educ* Wellington and Auckland U NZ

1c *Penelope Eve [Mrs Penelope Brooke, Southwood Hayes, Chilmark, Salisbury, Wilts]; *b* 6 July 1942; *educ* Ruskin Sch of Drawing and Fine Art; *m* 14 Dec 1968 (*divorce* 1988) Lt-Col Thomas Christopher Peter Brooke, Irish Gds, son of Peter Maurice Hewlett Brooke, of Gifford Hall, Broughton Gifford, Wilts, and has issue:

1d *James Richard Henry Ormonde; *b* 1972; *educ* Eton and Newcastle U

2b Walter George Ormonde, DSO (1951), MC; *b* 1917; *educ* Charterhouse and RMC Sandhurst; Brig Guides Cavalry IA and Queen's Roy Irish Hus, served WW II, and in Korea; *m* 5 Jan 1945 *Pamela Winsome Muriel (*m* 2nd 1970 *Brig Cuthbert Grafton Moore, OBE, of Patches, On the Green, Amport, Andover), dau of Sydney Owen, MD, FRCP, of Thornbury Court, Isleworth, Middx, and was *k* in a helicopter crash 6 June 1967, leaving:

1c +David Simon Ormonde [David Butler Esq, Britty Hill Cottage, Britty Hill, Elstead, Surrey]; *b* 17 May 1947; *educ* Milton Abbey; *m* 1971 *Vivienne Claire, er dau of Cdr R P FitzGerald, RN, of Petworth, Sussex, and has issue:

1d *Toby George Ormonde; *b* 1974

1d *Alice Chia; *b* 1979

3a William Bayford, MC, Capt late 3rd Bn Border Regt, served WW I; *b* 1888; *m* 1918 Beatrice Mary Nancy, dau of Col John Arthur Jackson, DL, JP, of Broomlands, Lorton, Cumberland, and *d* 30 Aug 1937

1a Eleanor Elizabeth Mary; *m* 1918 Gilbert Hudson, of Elm Croft, Berkhamsted, Herts, and *d* 9 Oct 1960. He *d* 31 Jan 1952

2a Sybil Emily; *d* unm 1961

3a Dorothy Clara; *d* unm 1963

(1) Henrietta Clara; *m* 10 April 1860 her cousin James Butler, son of James Butler, of Ballybar, Co Carlow, and *d* 31 July 1914, leaving issue (*see* above)

1 Louisa; *m* Peter Low, and had issue

Sir RICHARD *d* 16 Jan 1817; his est son,

Sir Thomas Butler, 8th Bt; *b* 23 Oct 1783; *m* 30 Jan 1812 Frances (*d* 30 Aug 1868), 4th dau of John Graham Clarke, of Sutton, Yorks, and had, with other issue:

1 RICHARD PIERCE (Sir), **9th Bt**

2 Thomas, 7th Fus; *b* 23 May 1814; *m* 1st 5 May 1840 Mary (*d* 13 April 1859), dau and heir of Henry Tulip, of Brunton and Walwick Hall, Northumberland, and had issue; *m* 2nd 15 Jan 1861 Emma Elizabeth Bertie (*d* 2 May 1905), dau of V-Adml Bertie Cator, and *d* 9 Oct 1893, having by her had issue:

(1) Laura; *m* 11 Feb 1884 Cdr Francis Fitzpatrick Tower, OBE, RNVR, of Upper Holmwood, Cowes, IoW, and *d* 30 May 1945, leaving issue (*see* HERVEY-BATHURST, Bt)

3 Antoine Sloet, CB, Divisional Magistrate in Ireland 1883–88, Capt 7th Dragoon Gds; *b* 11 Oct 1823; *m* 1st Sept 1854 Mary Matilda (*d* 22 Nov 1862), est dau of Rev George Hamilton Le Poer Beresford, and had issue:

(1) George Beresford (Sir), ktd 1922, RM Queen's Co 1889–1921; *b* 31 Jan 1857; *m* 9 July 1896 Georgina Rose Mary (*m* 2nd 22 April 1932 Thomas Percy Butler (*see* below), and *d* 1954), only dau of Capt Charles Walker, 21st Fus, and *d* 1 Sept 1924

(1) Frances Antoinette; *m* 10 Dec 1878 George Cosby Lendrum, DL, of Magheracross, and *d* 4 Feb 1945, leaving issue. He *d* 5 Feb 1933

(2) Laura Mary; *m* 5 Sept 1882 Capt James Sinclair Cramsie, of O'Harabrook, Ballymoney, Co Antrim, and *d* 7 April 1951, leaving issue. He *d* 29 Jan 1903

3 (cont.) Antoine Butler *m* 2nd 29 April 1875 Eliza (*d* 3 Dec 1914), est dau of Rev J Stevenson, and widow of Arthur Beresford Cane, and *d* 25 Dec 1901

4 Henry William Paget, JP (Cos Clare, Wicklow, and Kildare), Capt 7th Fus, in household of Ld Lt Ireland; *b* 28 April 1831; *educ* Trin Coll Dublin (BA); *m* 2 Oct 1855 Geraldine Sydney (*d* 1896), only dau of Lord William FitzGerald (*see* LEINSTER, D), and *d* 14 Aug 1913, leaving issue:

(1) Frederick Francis Baron; *b* 25 Jan 1861; *m* 15 Dec 1891 Bertha Florence (*d* 4 April 1928), 2nd dau of P J Dunne, of Rockhampton, Queensland, and *d* 29 Sept 1926, leaving issue:

1a Frederick Paget BUTLER later BUTLER-FitzGERALD (roy licence 13 July 1914); *b* 10 Dec 1892; *d* unm May 1945

2a Reginald Percy FitzGerald BUTLER later Reginald Percy BUTLER-FitzGERALD (deed poll 1946); *b* 10 April 1896; *m* 23 Sept 1930 Muriel (*d* 1971), yst dau of Frederick John Benjamin Martin, of New Farm, Brisbane, Qld, and *d* 1983 leaving:

1b +Frederick FitzGerald [Frederick Butler-FitzGerald Esq, PO Box 6054, Gold Coast Mail Centre, Qld 4217, Australia]; *b* 28 Oct 1933

1b +Geraldine [Miss Geraldine Butler-FitzGerald, PO Box 2103, Ascot, Brisbane, Qld 4007, Australia]; *b* 28 May 1946; resumed maiden name 1990; *m* 1972 (*divorce* 1988) John Conoplia, and has issue:

1c *Rebecca Frances; *b* 1973

2c *Jessica Jane; *b* 1976

1a Constance Geraldine; *b* 18 March 1903; *d* unm 8 April 1951

2a *Mabel Florence; *b* 27 March 1905

(2) Thomas Percy; *b* 9 June 1862; *m* 1st 23 April 1905 Harriette Gwendoline (*d* 21 March 1931), dau of Col John Henry Graham Holroyd-Smyth, CMG, by Lady Harriette Moore, dau of 5th Earl Mountcashell (*see* 1915 edn); *m* 2nd 22 April 1932 Georgina Rose Mary (*d* 1954), only dau of Capt Charles Walker, 21st Fus, and widow of Sir George Beresford Butler, of Island View, Clifden, Co Galway (*see* above), and *d* 12 Sept 1933, leaving by his 1st w:

1a +Tyssen Desmond; *b* 1906; Maj (ret) RWF; *m* 28 Nov 1940 *Dorothy, est dau of George Saltonstall West, of Chestnut Hill, Mass, USA, and has issue:

1b +George Tyssen [George Butler, True Farm, Holderness, NH 03245, USA]; *b* 12 Oct 1943

2b +Richard Percy [Richard Butler, 300 McKinstry Rd, Gardiner, NY 12525, USA]; *b* 14 Dec 1944

(1) Mabel Howard; *m* 28 April 1887 Brig-Gen James Alfred Coxhead, CB, DL, JP, late RA, 6th son of John Coxhead, of Russell Sq, WC, and *d* 7 May 1950, leaving issue. He *d* 27 Sept 1929

1 Arabella Sarah; *m* 31 May 1835 Sir Ralph Allen Gossett, KCB, Sereantj-at-Arms H of C, only s of Sir William Gosset, and *d* 29 Jan 1900, leaving issue. He *d* 1885

2 Louisa Charlotte; *m* 1841 Sir James Robert Carmichael, 2nd Bt, and *d* 9 March 1899, leaving issue. He *d* 1883

Sir THOMAS *d* 9 Nov 1861; his est son,

Sir Richard Pierce Butler, 9th Bt; *b* 4 March 1813; *m* 28 May 1835 Matilda (*d* 18 Sept 1893), 2nd dau of Thomas Cookson, of Hermitage, Co Durham, and had, with other issue:

1 THOMAS PIERCE (Sir), **10th Bt**

2 Richard Pierce; *b* 30 April 1839, late Lt 78th Highrs; *m* 15 Nov 1864 Florence Isabel (*d* 15 June 1924), dau of Hans Henry Hamilton, QC, and *d* 21 March 1912, having had, with other issue:

(1) Hans Pierce; *b* March 1880; *m* 1st 30 Dec 1908 Lenora Agnes Selina (*d* 14 Feb 1931), dau of William Edward Spurstow Moulson, of Solsgirth, Manitoba, and had issue:

1a Richard Pierce; *b* 1911; *m* 1st 1933 Vida McDonald (*d* 1968); *m* 2nd 1970 *Elsa Butler (now Lee) [Mrs Elsa Lee, 196 Plainsview, Regina, SK SR3 6LZ, Canada], and *d* 1976, leaving issue:

1b +Arthur Hans Richard Pierce [Arthur Butler Esq, Box 29, Erickson, Manitoba R0J 0P0, Canada]; *b* 1934; BSA (Hons), MSc, BEd, CBA; *m* 1955 *Elsie Elaine Laycock, and has:

1c +Walter Richard Pierce; *b* 14 Dec 1964; *m* 1989 *Leah Jane Findlater

1c *Kerrie Lee; *b* 1966; BGS

1b *Catherine Enid Selena [Mrs John Lochhead, Box 1495 Minnedosa, Manitoba R0J 1E0, Canada]; *b* 1935; B Comm (Hons), CA; *m* 1956 *John Francis Lochhead and has:

1c *Richard Francis [Richard Lochhead, Box 546, Melita, Manitoba, Canada]; *b* 6 April 1959; *m* 1982 *Judy Loucks and has:

1d *Andrew Francis; *b* 1990

1d *Catherine Jean; *b* 1985

2c *George Walter [George Lochhead, 51 Somercrest Close, Calgary, Alberta T2Y 3H8, Canada]; *b* 1967

1c *Phyllis Marie; *b* 16 May 1961; *m* 1986 *John Adam Land and has:

1d *Dylan Adam; *b* 1993

1d *Nicole Marie; *b* 1989

2b Sheila Margaret Eva; *b* 1939; *m* 1958 *John Richard Fawcett [John Fawcett Esq, Box 515, Swan River, Manitoba, Canada] and *d* 1984 leaving:

1c *Cherylyn Sheila; *b* 1961; *m* 1980 *Dennis Watts and has:

1d *Jeremy Steven; *b* 1983

1d *Amanda Marie; *b* 1981

2c *Kimberly Dawn; *b* 1963; *m* 1983 *Dennis Napady and has issue:

1d *Stephanie Eva Rose; *b* 1984

2d *Lynette Dennisa; *b* 1986

3d *Raylene Johnelle; *b* 1991

4d *Tamara; *b* 1993

3c *Lorilee Faye; *b* 1967; *m* 1988 *Curtiss Barrett and has issue:

1d *Tyler Richard Joseph; *b* 1991

2d *Taran John; *b* 1993

2a +John Edward; *b* 1916; *m* 1940 *Kathleen Wilson and has issue:

1b +Walter; *b* 1941; *m* 1968 *Elaine Prowse and has issue:

1c *Karen; *b* 1974

2c *Susan; *b* 1977

2b +Melvin; *b* 1943; *m* 1970 *Patricia Bolduc and has issue:

1c +Val; *b* 1970

2c +Melvin; *b* 1973

3b +Donald; *b* 1945; *m* 19— and has issue:

1c +Ryan; *b* 1981

1c *Lynn; *b* 1966

2c *Tami ; *b* 1973

3b (cont.) Donald Butler also adopted:

*Mandy; *b* 1972

4b +Gordon; *b* 1949; *m* 1st 19– — and has issue:
1c +Curt; *b* 1976
1c *Kim; *b* 1974
4b (cont.) Gordon Butler *m* 2nd 1985 *Lee Ann Johnston and by her has:
2c +Matthew; *b* 1986
3c +Timothy; *b* 1988
3a +Arthur Cecil [Arthur Butler Esq, Box 26D, RR2, Winnipeg, MB R3C 2E6, Canada]; *b* 1919; *m* 1st 1942 Joan Goodings (*d* 1951) and has:
1b +Leslie Grant; *b* 1947
1b *Barbara; *b* 1944; *m* 1964 *Gary McRindle and has issue:
1c *Joan Louise; *b* 1965
2c *Judy Lynn; *b* 1970
3a (cont.) Arthur Butler *m* 2nd 1956 *Isabelle Panting and by her has:
2b +James Arthur George; *b* 1957
3b +Thomas David; *b* 1964
2b *Valerie Louise; *b* 1960; *m* 1981 *James Roger Merkl and has issue:
1c *James Roger; *b* 1993
1c *Ashley Dawn Valene; *b* 1987
2c *Selina Alynn; *b* 1993
4a +William Hans [William Butler Esq, Foxwarren, Manitoba, Canada]; *b* 1922; *m* 1943 *Betty Attwell and has issue:
1b +Alan David; *b* 1944; *m* 1965 *Linda Stewart, and has issue:
1c +David Pearce; *b* 1969; *m* 1992 *Kirstine Miller
2c +Mark; *b* 1978
1c *Tanis Dawn; *b* 1975
2b +Garth Charles Butler; *b* 1946; *m* 1966 *Gwenyth Dodge and has:
1c +William Neal; *b* 1969; *m* 1992 *Bonnie Allen and has issue:
1d +Brendan; *b* 1989
1d *Nicole Randi; *b* 1992
1c *Kathleen Audrey; *b* 1967
3b +William Grant; *b* 1947; *m* 1978 *Mary Dalton and has issue:
1c +Jeremy Hans; *b* 1987
2c +Cory Grant; *b* 1990
5a +Charles Edwin [Charles Butler Esq, Solsgirth, Manitoba, Canada]; *b* 1926; *m* 1948 *Marian MacKay and has issue:
1b +Morley; *b* 1951; *m* 1973 *Lexie Hodgson and has issue:
1c +Jared Chane; *b* 1977
1c *Mandie Leigh; *b* 1975
2c *Shanda; *b* 1984
2b +Barry; *b* 1953; *m* 1974 *Karen Pizzey and has issue:
1c +Jack Heath; *b* 1976
1c *Vicki Lynn; *b* 1978
2c *Charla Ann; *b* 1979
3c *Kari Dayle; *b* 1981
6a Sidney Cyril; *b* 1928; *m* 1952 *Joan Murray
1a *Agnes Gertrude [Mrs Walter Taylor, 3262 Clive Ave, Vancouver, BC, Canada]; *b* 1913; *m* 1932 *Walter Taylor and has issue:
1b *William; *b* 1942
1b *Constance Lena; *b* 1934; *m* 1952 *Mike Rooney
2a *Eva Constance; *b* 1915; *m* 1936 *Walter McTavish and has issue:
1b *Walter Lloyd; *b* 1936
1b *Corinne Gertrude; *b* 1938; *m* 1957 *Edward James Perrin
2b *Selina Elsie; *b* 1944
3b *Wynona May; *b* 1952
(1) (cont.) Hans Butler *m* 2nd Nov 1932 Mrs Maude Adderson (*d* 1973) and *d* 1940, leaving by her:
7a +Home Pierce; *b* 11 Oct 1938; *m* 1962 *Robin Carol Boaden and had:
1b +Robert Pierce; *b* 1967
1b Katy-Jo; *b* 1964; *d* 1997
3a *Kathleen Frances Marina [Mrs Garry Chaloner, 15479-93rd Ave, Surrey, BC V3R 9B6, Canada]; *b* 1935; *m* 1956 *Garry Neil Chaloner and has:
1b *Neil Garry; *b* 1962
1b *Susan Leslee Anne; *b* 1960
4a *Maude Brenwyn [Mrs Klassen, 414, 7 Ave NW, Calgary, Alberta T2N 0Y7, Canada]; *b* 1937; *m* 10 Oct 1952 — Klassen and has:
1b *Linda Darlene [Mrs Nigel Kellett, 1092 Bellevue Rd, Parksville, BC V9P 2C5, Canada]; *b* 9 Nov 1954; *m* 19– *Nigel John Kellett and has:
1c *Christopher John [Christopher Kellett Esq, 444 12 St NW, Calgary, ALB T2N 1Y8, Canada]; *b* 13 Jan 1978
1c *Katerina Deanne; *b* 13 May 1982
2c *Patricia Anne; *b* 20 Dec 1983
(1) Violet; *m* 1891 John Francis, CE, of Winnipeg. He *d* 1929
(2) Eva; *m* 1893 Charles E Hall, of Belcourt, Manitoba. He *d* 1912
(3) Mildred; *m* 24 Sept 1924 Home Popham Vialoux, of 10 Dorchester Apts, Winnipeg, Canada, and *d* 27 Oct 1949
(4) Kathleen; *m* 1908 William Hadland, of Lavinia, Manitoba. He *d* Feb 1950
3 Walter Selby, Lt-Col late 8th Bn KRRC; *b* 14 Oct 1845 *m* 6 May 1885 Alice Lucy (*d* 20 March 1939), dau of Edmund Fowler, of Abberley, Edgbaston, Warwicks, and *d* 20 March 1939, having had issue:
(1) Edmund Pierce, TD, Lt-Col cmdg Roy Glos Hus 1936–40, Hon Sec Berkeley Hunt 1947–58, served WW I and WW II; *b* 20 May 1886; *educ* Harrow and Pembroke Coll Cambridge (BA 1908); *m* 27 Oct 1948 Mrs Mary Diana Eyre (*d* 18 Sept 1963), only dau of Lawrence Gardner Williams, of Bonvilston, nr Cardiff, and *dsp* 9 April 1964
(1)Vivienne Tilla; *m* 26 Nov 1913 Kenneth Cookson, OBE (*d* 6 March 1963), son of Norman Cookson, of Oakwood Hall, Northumberland, and had issue:
1a Christopher, F/O RAF, served WW II; *b* 6 Oct 1917; *educ* Harrow and Trin Coll Cambridge; *ka* 23 July 1941
2a *John Butler; served WW II as Lt Fleet Air Arm; *b* 6 Aug 1924; *educ* Harrow; *m* 12 Sept 1951 *Adene, dau of John Brady, and has issue:
1b *Christopher Alexander Kenneth; *b* 1954
1b *Elizabeth Julia; *b* 1953
1a *Mary; *b* 10 May 1916; *m* 1st 20 May 1941 (*divorce* 1953) Maj John George Spencer-Churchill, er son of Maj John Strange Spencer-Churchill, DSO (*see* MARLBOROUGH, D); *m* 2nd 25 March 1954 *Jacob Herman Huizinga, son of Prof Johan Huizinga, of Leiden, Holland
1 Emma; *m* 3 Oct 1867 Capt Geoffrey Joseph Shakerley, RA, est son of Geoffrey Joseph Shakerley, of Whatcroft Hall, Cheshire (*see* SHAKERLEY, Bt) and *d* 2 Feb 1894

Sir RICHARD *d* 22 Nov 1862; his est son,

Sir Thomas Pierce Butler, 10th Bt; JP, High Sheriff 1866 and V-Lt Co Carlow, Lt 56th and 24th Regts, served Crimea 1854–55 (medal and clasp, Turkish medal), Hon Col 8th Bn KRRC; *b* 16 Dec 1836; *m* 8 Sept 1864 Hester Elizabeth (*d* 5 Aug 1904), est dau of Sir Alan Edward Bellingham, 3rd Bt (*qv*), and had issue:
1 RICHARD PIERCE (Sir), **11th Bt**
2 Thomas Edmond; *b* 6 April 1875
3 Walter Alan; *b* 14 March 1877; *d* 25 Feb 1878
1 Edith Alice; *b* 4 Jan 1867; *m* 28 April 1921 Col Frederick Beauchamp Lecky, DSO, of Ballykealey, Co Carlow, and *dsp* 9 March 1950. He *d* 15 Nov 1928
2 Maude Isobel; *b* 29 Jan 1871; *d* unm 19 Dec 1958
3 Dorothea Hester; *b* 28 Dec 1874; *m* 7 July 1904 Most Rev Hon Benjamin John Plunket, DD, Bishop of Meath 1919–26, 2nd son of 4th Baron Plunket (*qv*), and *d* 8 July 1936, leaving issue. He *d* 26 Jan 1947
4 Eleanor Frances; *b* 19 Feb 1880; *d* unm 20 Aug 1965

Sir THOMAS *d* 8 March 1909; his er surv son,

Sir Richard Pierce Butler, 11th Bt, OBE (1919), DL Co Carlow, High Sheriff 1905, Hon Lt-Col late Remount Serv, formerly Capt and Hon Maj 8th Bn KRRC served in S African War 1901–02 (medal with five clasps), and WW I 1914 (despatches twice, star, two medals); *educ* Harrow and Downton Agric Coll (Diploma); *b* 28 Sept 1872; *m* 2 June 1906, his cousin Alice Dudley (*d* 13 July 1965, aged 91), only dau of Very Rev Hon James Wentworth Leigh, DD, late Dean of Hereford (*see* LEIGH, B), and had issue:
1 THOMAS PIERCE (Sir), **12th Bt**
1 *Joan [Mrs Robert Brunt, The Lodge, Cox's Hill, Twyford, Hants]; *b* 15 March 1908; *m* 1 Oct 1943 Robert Nigel Bright Brunt, CBE (*d* 1982), son of Henry Robert Brunt, of Belle Isle, Co Fermanagh, and has issue:
(1) *Nicholas John Pierce [Lt-Col Nicholas Brunt, 118 Elm Grove Rd, Barnes, London SW13 0BS]; *b* 17 April 1946; *educ* Marlborough; Lt-Col Roy Fus
(2) *(Nigel Richard) Pierce JP (Hants) [Pierce Brunt Esq JP, Mildmay House, Twyford, Winchester, Hants SO21 1NT]; *b* 1948; *educ* Harrow
(1) *Rosemary Helen [Mrs Anthony Hawley, The Rectory, Old Hall Lane, Kirkby, Liverpool L32 5TH]; *b* 20 Oct 1944; *educ* Lady Eleanor Holles Sch Hampton and King's Coll London U (BA); *m* 1971 *Canon Anthony Broughton Hawley
2 Doreen Frances; *b* 3 Sept 1913; *m* 5 July 1934 Denis William Powlett Milbank (*see* MILLBANK Bt,) and *d* 1991, leaving issue

Sir RICHARD *d* 25 March 1955; his only son,

Sir Thomas Pierce Butler, 12th Bt, CVO (1970), DSO (1944), OBE (1954), JP, FRGS; *educ* Harrow and Trin Coll Cambridge (BA), Col Cmdg The Grenadier Gds 1955–58, served WW II (despatches), Mil Adviser to UK High Commr in New Zealand 1959–61, Maj and Resident Govr of the Tower of London 1961, Keeper Jewel House at Tower 1968, CStJ; *b* 18 Sept 1910; *m* 21 Oct 1937 Rosemary Liège Woodgate (*d* 29 Oct 1997), dau of Maj James Hamilton Davidson-Houston, of Pembury Hall, Kent, and S Kensington, and *d* 1994, leaving:
1 Sir RICHARD PIERCE BUTLER, **13th and present Bt**
1 *Caroline Rosemary [Mrs Richard Keightley, Kennels Cottage, Tarrant Gunville, Blandford, Dorset DT11 8JQ]; *b* 20 Jan 1939; *m* 21 Oct 1958 *Maj-Gen Richard Charles Keightley, CB, 5th Roy Inniskilling Dragoon Gds, er son of Gen Sir Charles Frederic Keightley, GCB, GBE, DSO, and has issue:
(1) *Charlotte Joan [Mrs Howard Jenkinson, The Rectory, Willey, Salop TF12 5JJ]; *b* 24 March 1961; *m* 1985 *Howard Stephen Buchanan Jenkinson, er son of Barry Jenkinson, of Chetton Grange, Bridgnorth, Salop, and has:
1a *Alistair Charles Buchanan; *b* 1988
2a *William Howard Thomas; *b* 1990
3a *Benjamin Christopher Patrick; *b* 1994
1a *Sophia Elizabeth Rosemary; *b* 1992
(2) *Arabella Caroline; *b* 31 July 1962; *m* 1989 *Peter J O'Connell, of Australia, est son of T O'Connell, of Dorset
(3) *Victoria Rosemary; *b* 3 Dec 1965
2 *Virginia Pamela Liège [Mrs Michael Cunningham, Dolhyfryd, Denbigh, Clwyd]; *b* 28 July 1949; *m* 1970 *Capt Michael Cunningham, The Queen's Own Hussars, and has issue:
(1) *Charles Alexander Clunie; *b* 1978
(2) *Rupert Jasper Clunie; *b* 1984
(1) *Sophia Louisa Caroline; *b* 1973
(2) *Henrietta Maria Charlotte; *b* 1975

BUTLER of Old Park

Arms: Az. three covered cups in pale between two flaunches or, each charged with a cross-crosslet sa. **Crest:** A demi-horse sa. charged on the shoulder with a covered cup, and resting the sinister hoof upon a cross-crosslet or. **Creation:** Bt. (UK) 28 Jan 1922.

SIR (REGINALD) MICHAEL THOMAS BUTLER, 3RD BT, of Old Park, Devizes, Wilts, QC (1967) [Sir Michael Butler Bt QC, Old Park Cottage, 634 Avalon St, Victoria, BC V8V 1N7, Canada]; *b* 22 April 1928; *s* f 1959; *educ* Brentwood Coll Victoria, U of BC (BA) and Osgoode Hall Sch of Law Toronto; admitted Bar Ontario Province 1954, slr Upper Canada, dir Teck Corp; *m* 1st 27 Dec 1952 (*divorce* 1967) Marjà Margaret Elizabeth, only dau of Ewen Holmes McLean, of Toronto; *m* 2nd 1968 (divorce 1974) Barbara Anne, dau of Kevin Cahill, of Dublin; *m* 3rd 1980 *Judith Ann, dau of Harold Blackwell, of London, Ontario, and has issue by his 1st w:

1 +(REGINALD) RICHARD MICHAEL; *b* 3 Oct 1953; *m* 1982 *Dale Karen, only dau of Frederick William Piner, of Vancouver, BC, and has issue:
(1) +(Reginald) Paul; *b* 26 June 1988
(2) +Andrew; *b* 1991
(3) +Nicholas; *b* 1993
2 +Geoffrey McLean; *b* 30 June 1956
3 +Thomas David; *b* 1960
*Patrick Colman; *b* 1958 (adopted 1971)

Lineage: FREDERICK JAMES BUTLER, of Poulshot Lodge, Devizes; *m* Susan, dau of Robert Swanton, and *d* March 1881, leaving issue:

Sir (Robert) Reginald Frederick Butler, 1st Bt (UK), so *cr* 28 Jan 1922; *b* 19 June 1866; *m* 12 June 1895 Rose (*d* 26 Aug 1945), est dau of Thomas Goodwin Rich, of Rodbourne, Wilts, and had issue:
1 REGINALD THOMAS (Sir), **2nd Bt**
1 Gladys Marjorie; *m* 7 June 1922 Richard Wayland-Smith, MB, FRCS, only s of Richard Smith, of Bacchus, Glos, and had issue:
(1) *Anne Elizabeth; *b* 1 Dec 1923; *m* 19 Sept 1953 Capt Humphry Platt, son of Col Ernest Henderson Rowley Cook Richard Platt, The Somerset LI, of Lorraine Ho, Marle Hill, Cheltenham, Glos, and has issue:
1a *Caroline Elizabeth; *b* 6 May 1956
2a *Louisa; *b* 2 Sept 1959

Sir REGINALD *d* 19 Nov 1933; his son,

Sir (Reginald) Thomas Butler, 2nd Bt, Cdr RN; *b* 27 April 1901; *m* 1st 1 June 1927 (*divorce* 1949) Marjorie Brown, est dau of Sidney Brown Woods, KC, of Stirlingswood, Edmonton, Alberta, Canada, and had issue:
1 Sir REGINALD MICHAEL THOMAS BUTLER, **3rd and present Bt**
2 +Peter Woods, QC; *b* 16 Feb 1933; *m* 1959 *Lucia, yr dau of Michael Harris, of Winnipeg, Canada, and has issue:
(1) +Hugh Clifford Carson; *b* 21 June 1960
(2) +Thomas Woods; *b* 12 June 1963
(3) +Peter James Sydney; *b* 13 May 1965
(1) *Andrea Adaire Carroll; *b* 3 Nov 1961
(2) *Theresa; *b* 1967
1 *Patricia Carroll; *b* 6 Dec 1935; *m* 1 June 1957 *William Milburn, yr son of Maj William Hewlins Milburn (*see* MILBURN, Bt), and has issue

Sir Thomas *m* 2nd 1 Dec 1950 Kathleen Phyllis (Diane), dau of William Aubrey Southerton, of Chester, and formerly w of (a) Eric Graham-Scott and (b) Zephaniah Donald Berry, and *d* 22 March 1959

BUTLER OF BROCKWELL

Creation: B. (LP, UK) 31 Dec 1997.

THE BARON BUTLER OF BROCKWELL, of Herne Hill, London Borough of Lambeth (Sir (Frederick Edward) Robin Butler, GCB (1992, KCB 1988), CVO (1986) [The Rt Hon The Lord Butler of Brockwell GCB CVO, Cabinet Office, London SW1A 2AS]; *b* 3 Jan 1938; *educ* Harrow (Govr 1975–91, Chm Govrs 1988–91) and Univ Coll Oxford (Master 1998–); Treasury: joined 1961, Priv Sec to Fin Sec 1964–65, Sec Budget Ctee 1965–69, (seconded Cabinet Office 1971–75: memb CPRS Cabinet Off 1971–72, Priv Sec to PM 1972–75), Assist Sec i/c Gen Expenditure Intell Div 1975, U-Sec Gen Expenditure Policy Gp 1977–80, Pncpl Establishments Offr 1980–82, Pncpl Priv Sec to PM 1982–85, 2nd Perm Sec Public Expenditure 1985–87, Cabinet Sec and Head Home Civ Serv 1988–98, Hon LLD London 1998; *m* 1962 *Gillian Lois Galley and has a s and two daus

Lineage: BERNARD BUTLER; *m* Nora — and had:
1 (FREDERICK EDWARD) ROBIN, *cr* a **Baron**
1 Diana; *b* 12 Jan 1942; *d* unm 12 Jan 1982

BUTT

Arms: Arg. on a chevron engrailed gu., between in chief two torteaux and in base a trefoil vert, a portcullis or. **Crest:** A lion sejant ppr., gorged with a collar gemel or and supporting with the dexter forepaw a spear, the head fracted and dependent also ppr. **Motto:** *Sum quod sum* ('I am what I am'). **Creation:** Bt. (UK) 25 July 1929.

SIR (ALFRED) KENNETH DUDLEY BUTT, 2ND BT, of Westminster, London [Sir Kenneth Butt Bt, Wheat Hill, Sandon, Buntingford, Herts SG9 0RB]; *b* 7 July 1908; *s* f 1962; *educ* Rugby and BNC Oxford; Maj RA (TA) WW II; underwriting memb Lloyd's 1931–74, farmer and bloodstock breeder, chm Parker Wakeling & Co 1946–54, chm and md of Brook Stud Co 1962–81, pres Aberdeen-Angus Cattle Soc 1968–69, chm Thoroughbred Breeders Assoc 1973; *m* 1st 3 Oct 1938 (*divorce* 1948) Kathleen Breen, est dau of Edward Farmar, Shanklin, IoW; *m* 2nd 5 Aug 1948 *Marie Josephine, 2nd dau of John Bain, of Bestbeech St Mary, Wadhurst, Sussex, and widow of Lt-Col Ivor Watkins Birts (*kas*)

Lineage: Sir Alfred Butt, 1st Bt (UK), so *cr* 25 July 1929, MP (U) Wandsworth, Balham and Tooting 1922–36 (resigned from H of C on being found to have used information from the then Cllr Exchequer, J H Thomas, for private gain, *viz.*, insuring against a rise in the duty on tea on being told by Thomas, with whom he was playing golf just before the Budget, 'Tee Up!', the remark being accompanied by a wink), Dir Rationing Min Food 1917–18, breeder bloodstock (Brook Stud), chm and md Theatre Royal Drury Lane Ltd 1925–31; only son of F Butt, of Hampshire; ktd 1918; *b* 20 March 1878; *m* 1st 16 April 1902 Georgina Mary (*d* 7 Jan 1960), only dau of Frederick Say, of Norwich, and had issue:
1 Sir (ALFRED) KENNETH DUDLEY BUTT, **2nd and present Bt**

Sir Alfred *m* 2nd 23 Aug 1960 *Wilhelmine (Vilma) (*m* 2nd 1978 *10th Viscount Harberton (*qv*)), dau of Heinrich Wahl, of Gelsenkirchen-Buer, and *d* 8 Dec 1962

BUTTERFIELD

Arms: Azure a pale ermine per fess counterchanged on a fess gules, between three lozenges or, a lion passant in trian aspect also or and between on the dexter a domed tower proper ensigned by an increscent argent and on the sinister a like tower ensigned by an estoile gold. **Crest:** A cubit arm vested azure semy of pentacles or, the hand proper, holding a pair of keys fesswise, the bows interlaced gold. **Supporters:** Dexter, a greyhound statant erect argent, gorged with an open crown or; sinister, a griffin also statant erect gold. **Motto:** *Perseverantia* ('Perseverance') **Creation:** B. (LP, UK) 1988.

THE BARON BUTTERFIELD, of Stechford, W Midlands (Sir (William) John Hughes Butterfield, OBE (1953)) [The Rt Hon The Lord Butterfield OBE, 39 Clarendon St, Cambridge CB1 1JX]; *b* 28 March 1920; *educ* Solihull Sch, Exeter Coll Oxford (DM 1968) and Johns Hopkins U (MD 1951), MA, MD Cantab 1975; Maj RAMC 1947–50; memb MRC 1946–58; Research Fell Med Coll VA 1950–52; Prof: Experimental Medicine Guy's Hosp 1958–63, Medicine Guy's Hosp Med Sch 1963–71; V-Chllr Nottingham U 1971–75; V-Pres Cncl Br Diabetic Assoc 1974– (memb 1963–74, chm 1967–74); Master Downing Coll Cambridge 1978–87 (Professorial Fell 1975–78); V-Chllr Cambridge U 1983–85; Pres: Cncl St George's Ho 1987–92, Br U Sports Fedn; Chm: Croucher Fndn Hong Kong 1979– (Tstee 1985–92), Jardine Educnl Tst 1982–, Health Promotion Research Tst 1983–, GB-Sasakawa Fndn 1992– (Tstee 1985–92); Tstee Ely Cathedral 1986; Visitor King Edward's Hosp Fund 1964–71; Examiner in Medicine Oxford U 1960–66, E Africa U 1966, Cambridge U 1967–75; Visiting Prof Yale 1966, Harvard 1978; Rock Carling Fell Roy Coll Physicians 1968; FRSA 1971, FRCP, Hon Fell: NY Acad Science 1962, Exeter Coll Oxford 1978, NY Acad of Medicine 1987; Hon LLD Nottingham 1977, Hon DMedSci Keio U Tokyo 1983, Hon DSc Florida Internat U Miami 1985; Hon LLD Bristol 1994; ktd 1978; author: *On Burns* (jt author, 1953), *Tolbutamide After 10 Years* (1967), *Priorities in Medicine* (1968), *Health and Sickness — the choice of treatment* (1971), *International Dictionary of Medicine and Biology* (ed, 1986); *m* 1st 1946 Ann (*d* 1948), dau of Robert Sanders, of New York, and has:

1 *Jonathan West Sanders; *b* 1948; BA; has two sons and a dau

BARON BUTTERFIELD *m* 2nd 1950 *Isabel-Ann, dau of Dr Foster Kennedy, of New York, and by her has:

2 *Jeremy John Nicholas [The Hon Jeremy Butterfield, Jesus Coll, Cambridge]; *b* 1954; PhD, MA; has a s and dau

3 *Toby Michael John; *b* 1965; BA; barrister Lincoln's Inn

1 *Sarah Harriet Ann; *b* 1953; BSc, ARIBA, artist; *m* 1986 *David Lindsay Willetts, MP (C) Havant 1992–, C employment spokesman 1997– and Dep Chm CPS, and has:

(1) *Matthew John Foster; *b* 19–

(1) *Imogen Anna Kennedy; *b* 19–

Lineage: WILLIAM HUGHES BUTTERFIELD; *m* Mrs Doris North,and had:

(WILLIAM) JOHN HUGHES, *cr* a **Baron**

BUTTERWORTH

Arms: Sable on a fess argent a representation of a DNA double helix spirals azure, lined gules, with connecting lines or and in chief two bears erect argent, muzzled gules, and in base an elephant also erect, each standing against a ragged staff argent, and collared and chained or, the chain reflexed over the back round the foot of the staff and ending in a ring gold. **Crest:** Rising from a tree stock couped sable a phoenix or in flames proper, grasping in the dexter claw a millrind sable. **Supporters:** Upon a compartment comprising a grassy mount strewn with buttercups proper on either side a little owl proper, charged on the neck with a representation of a DNA double helix as in the arms. **Motto:** The fear of the Lord is the beginning of Wisdom. **Creation:** B. (LP, UK) 1985.

THE BARON BUTTERWORTH, of Warwick , Co Warwick (John Blackstock Butterworth, CBE 1982, JP (Oxford 1962 and Coventry 1963), DL (Warwicks 1967–74 and W Midlands 1974–) [The Rt Hon The Lord Butterworth CBE JP DL, The Barn, Guiting Power, Glos GL54 5US]; *b* 13 March 1918; *educ* Queen Elizabeth's GS Mansfield and Queen's Coll Oxford; WWII RA; barrister Lincoln's Inn 1947 (Hon Bencher 1989); Fell New Coll Oxford 1946–63 (Jr Proctor 1950–51, Dean 1952–56, Bursar 1956–63, Sub-Warden 1957–58); memb Hebdomadal Cncl Oxford U 1953–63; Faculty Fell Nuffield Coll 1953–58; Managing Tstee Nuffield Fndn 1964–85 (Tstee 1985–); Chm: Inter U Cncl for Higher Educn Overseas 1968–77, Us Ctee for Non-teaching Staffs 1970–85, Inquiry into Work of Probation Offrs and Social Workers in Local Authorities and Nat Serv 1971–73, Standing Ctee Internat Co-opn Higher Educn Br Cncl 1981–85, Inter-U and Poly Cncl 1981–85, Chm Fndn for Science and Tech 1990– (Pres 1997–); V-Chllr Warwick U 1963–85; Govr Roy Shakespeare Theatre 1964–; memb: Roy Commn Law of Contempt re Tbnls of Inquiry 1968, Jarratt Ctee on U Efficiency 1986–, Croham Ctee on review of U Grants 1987–, Noise Advsy Cncl 1974–81; memb Bd Br Cncl 1981–86; Br Del to Cwlth Educn Confs 1968, 1971, 1974, 1977 and 1980; U Commr (under Educn Reform Act 1988) 1988–; Hon DCL Sierra Leone 1976, Hon DSc Aston 1985, Hon LLD Warwick 1986; *m* 1948 *Doris Crawford, dau of George Elder, of Edinburgh, and has issue:

1 *John William Blackstock [The Hon John Butterworth, 5a Montpellier Grove, London NW5]; *b* 1952; *educ* Winchester and New Coll Oxford

1 *Anna Elizabeth Blackstock [The Hon Mrs Walker, 24 Old Park Ave, London SW12 8RH]; *b* 1951; *educ* Benenden and LMH Oxford; *m* 1983 *Timothy Edward Hanson Walker

2 *Laura Blackstock [The Hon Mrs Burley, College Farm House, Millington, Pocklington, Yorks]; *b* 1959; *educ* Benenden, Dean Close Sch Cheltenham and Westfield Coll London; *m* 1985 *John Laughton Burley, s of John Burley, of Pocklington

Lineage: JOHN WILLIAM BUTTERWORTH; *m* Florence Blackstock and had:

JOHN BLACKSTOCK, *cr* a **Baron**

BUXTON

Arms: Arg. a lion rampant, tail elevated and turned over the head sa., between two mullets of the second. **Crest:** A buck's head, couped gu., attired or, gorged with a collar of the last, therefrom pendant an escutcheon arg., charged with an African's head sa. **Supporters:** Dexter, an African sa., wreathed about the head and loins vert; sinister, a buck gu. attired or. **Motto:** Do it with thy might. **Creation:** Bt. (UK) 30 July 1840.

SIR JOCELYN CHARLES RODEN BUXTON, 7TH BT, of Belfield [Sir Jocelyn Buxton Bt VRD, Rodwell House, Loddon, Norfolk NR14 6QJ]; *b* 8 Aug 1924; *s* cousin 1996; WW II (despatches) and Korea 1952, Lt-Cdr RNVR; *m* 3 June 1960 *Ann Frances, dau of Frank Smitherman, MBE, For Serv, and has issue:

1 *Frances Dorothy; *b* 28 Nov 1960; *m* 1st 1981 (*divorce* 1989) Oliver P St John, est s of Lt-Col A R L St John; *m* 2nd *Henry Ellis Jones-Davies, son of Col T E Jones-Davies, JP, DL, and has issue

2 *Harriet Lucy; *b* 29 Dec 1962; *m* 1991 *Hon Michael Colin Dalrymple, yst s of 13th Earl of Stair (*qv*), and has issue

3 *Caroline Sarah; *b* 14 May 1964; *m* 1987 *Nicholas M Jarrett, s of Lt-Col Michael Jarrett, and has issue

Lineage: WILLIAM BUXTON, of Gt Coggeshall, Essex; *m* Anne — and was *bur* 22 Dec 1625, leaving:

THOMAS BUXTON, of Gt Coggeshall; *bapt* 3 July 1608; *m* 1636 Susan Sudbury and *d* 1646, leaving:

THOMAS BUXTON, of Gt Coggeshall; *bapt* 19 Oct 1643; *m* 1668 Judith Gunton, and *d* 16 Oct 1713, leaving:

ISAAC BUXTON, of Gt Coggeshall; *m* Elizabeth Arwaker, and had, with three daus:

1 Thomas, of Gt Coggeshall; *m* thrice and *d* 1777, leaving issue

2 Isaac, *dsp* 1766

3 John, of Gt Coggeshall; *m* twice and *d* 1751, leaving issue

4 CHARLES, of whom presently

5 William

6 Samuel, of Gt Coggeshall, *dsp* 1737

The 4th son,

CHARLES BUXTON, of Braxted, Essex; *b* 5 Feb 1703/4; *m* 29 Feb 1727/8 Hannah, dau of George Read, of London, and had, with an er s and three daus:

ISAAC BUXTON, of Bellfield, Dorset; *b* 22 Jan 1733; *m* 5 March 1755 Sarah, only dau of Thomas Fowell, and had, with a yr s (Charles, *m* Hannah, dau of Samuel Enderby) and a dau (Sarah, *m* 1777 Charles Dumbleton, of Horsley, nr Epsom):

THOMAS FOWELL BUXTON, of Earl's Colne, Essex, High Sheriff; *b* 1 Sept 1756; *m* 12 Feb 1782 Anna, est dau of Osgood Hanbury, of The Grange, Coggeshall, Essex, and *d* 3 Dec 1793, having had, with other issue:

1 THOMAS FOWELL (Sir), **1st Bt**

2 Charles; *b* 16 Dec 1787; *m* 19 Dec 1811 Martha, est dau of Edmund Henning, of Melcombe Regis, Dorset, and *d* 4 July 1817, having had, with other issue:

(1) Edmund Charles, of Daresbury Hall, Warrington and Buxton Ho, Essex; *b* 2 Sept 1813; *m* 3 Sept 1834 Charlotte Mary (*d* 16 Nov 1892), est dau of Abbot Upcher, of Sheringham, Norfolk, and *d* 1878, leaving issue, with two other daus:

1a Edmund Charles, of Coed Derw, Bettws-y-Coed, Caernarvonshire, JP; *b* 24 Jan 1839; *m* 18 June 1873 Gertrude (*d* 2 Sept 1932), dau of Richard Sykes, of Edgeley, Cheshire, and *d* 11 July 1925

(1) Anna; *m* 15 July 1836 Joseph Hoare, 4th son of Samuel Hoare, of Hampstead (*see* 1956 edn TEMPLEWOOD, V), and *dsp* 19 July 1843

1 Anna; *m* 3 Oct 1816 William Forster, of Bradpole, and had issue. He *d* 27 Jan 1854

The est son,

Sir Thomas Fowell Buxton, 1st Bt (UK), so *cr* 30 July 1840, of Bellfield and Runton; *b* 7 April 1786; anti-slavery campaigner; *m* 13 May 1807 Hannah (*d* 20 March 1872), 5th dau of John Gurney, of Earlham, Norfolk, and had, with other issue:

1 EDWARD NORTH (Sir), **2nd Bt**

2 Thomas Fowell, of Easneye, Ware, Herts, and Upton Ho, Cromer, JP Herts, High Sheriff 1878, MA Cambridge; *b* 29 Aug 1822; *m* 4 Feb 1845 Rachel Jane (*d* 6 Jan 1905), 5th dau of Samuel Gurney, of Ham Ho, Essex, and *d* 27 Jan 1908, leaving, with other issue:

(1) John Henry, of Easneye, and Upton Ho, DL Herts, High Sheriff 1897; *b* 15 Aug 1849; *educ* Trin Coll Cambridge (MA); *m* 19 Nov 1874 Emma Maria (*d* 22 Oct 1924), dau of Capt Richard Wilson Pelly, RN (*see* PELLY, Bt), and *d* 21 March 1934, having had, with other issue:

1a Henry Fowell, of Easneye and Smoo Lodge, Durness, Sutherland, High Sheriff Herts 1938, Capt 4th Bn Suffolk Regt WW I, dir Truman, Hanbury, Buxton & Co, Memb Ctee London Hosp; *b* 23 Jan 1876 1876; *educ* Harrow and Trin Coll Cambridge (BA); *m* 1st 24 July 1900 Katharine Tayspel (*d* 4 July 1945), dau of James Round, PC, of Birch Hall, Essex; *m* 2nd 25 Aug 1945 Mairi (*d* 29 July 1962), dau of James Milne and widow of Norman Clark Neill, of Home Close, Hursley, Hants, and *d* 16 Jan 1949, having by his 1st w had issue:

1b John Fowell, TD, High Sheriff Herts 1958, Maj 86th (Herts Yeo) Field Regt RA (TA), CC Herts 1946–57, dir Truman's Brewery, Master Brewers' Co 1946; *b* 21 June 1902; *educ* Harrow and Trin Coll Cambridge (BA 1924); *m* 22 July 1930 *Katharine Mary, yst dau of Sir Nicholas Henry Bacon, 13th Bt (*qv*), of Raveningham Hall, Norwich, and *d* 1970, having had issue:

1c +Henry Alexander Fowell [Henry Buxton Esq, Mardocks Mill, Ware, Herts SG12 7QN]; *b* 21 May 1937; *educ* Eton; late 2nd Lt 16th/5th The Queen's Roy Lancers, High Sheriff Herts 1992; *m* 10 Oct 1964 *Victoria, only dau of (Edward John) Ronald Bennett, of Hartwell Farm, Cirencester, Glos, by Rachel Constance, sis of Sir Thomas Stafford Bazley, 3rd Bt (*qv*), and has issue:

1d +Nicholas Fowell; *b* 17 March 1966; *m* 1994 *Henrietta Louise, est dau of Richard Wilson Jewson, of Dades Farm, Barnham Broom, Norfolk, and has:

1e +Edward; *b* 199–

2e +Thomas Archie; *b* 20 Oct 1997

2d +Anthony John; *b* 3 April 1968

1d *Katherine Louise; *b* 1971

1c *Bridget Jane; *b* 13 Aug 1931; *m* 28 Jan 1956 *Hon Reuben Pleydell-Bouverie, 2nd son of 7th Earl of Radnor (*qv*), and has issue

2c *Anna Katharine [Mrs George Myrddin-Evans, Church House, Llandefalle, Llyswen, Powys]; *b* 31 Jan 1934; *m* 23 April 1966 *George Watkin Myrddin-Evans, yr s of Sir Guildhaume Myrddin-Evans, KCMG, CB, and has:

1d *David Guildhaume; *b* 14 April 1967

3c *Penelope Mary Albinia, JP; *b* 28 March 1939; *m* 27 Jan 1966 *Richard Christopher Naylor, er son of Thomas Humphrey Naylor, of The Grange, Ashton, nr Chester, and has:

1d *Thomas Murray; *b* 1 March 1967

1d *Harriet Albinia; *b* 1970

4c *Elizabeth Priscilla; *b* 12 Sept 1947; *m* 1976 *Maj Thomas Tudor Riversdale Lort-Phillips, Gren Gds, and has issue:

1d *Hugh Thomas; *b* 1981

1d *Frances Katherine; *b* 1977

2d *Anna Elizabeth (twin); *b* 1977

5c *Teresa Constance (twin); *b* 12 Sept 1947

2b Robert James, MRCS, LRCP, DOMS, Maj RAMC 1942–46; *b* 29 April 1908; *educ* Harrow and Trin Coll Cambridge (BA 1929, MA 1934, MB, BCh 1937); *m* 12 June 1935 Lilla Mary Alyson (*d* 1979), er dau of Charles Ernest Pumphrey, of W Bitchfield, Belsay, Northumberland, and *d* 5 June 1968, leaving issue:

1c +James Anthony Fowell (twin) [James Buxton Esq, Galhampton Manor, Yeovil, Somerset BA22 7AL]; *b* 14 March 1948; *educ* Harrow and Trin Coll Cambridge (BA); barrister Inner Temple 1971, slr 1984; *m* 4 Nov 1975 *Margaret Elizabeth, only dau of Adml Hon Sir Guy Russell, GBE (*see* AMPTHILL, B), and has issue:

1d +Edward Guy Fowell; *b* 24 March 1978

2d +Charles Robert James; *b* 12 Dec 1986

1d *Harriet Faith Alyson; *b* 8 Aug 1976

2d *Meriel Lavinia Margaret; *b* 26 July 1980

2c +Richard Moberly [Richard Buxton Esq, 40 Clarendon St, Cambridge CB1 1JX]; *b* 30 June 1953; *educ* Harrow, Trin Coll Cambridge (BA, MA) and Yale (Master of Environmental Studies); slr 1978; *m* 1979 *Julia Grace, dau of Cdre Frank Dudley Elcock, RCN, of Ottawa, and has issue:

1d +David Mark Reford; *b* 1983

2d +Simon Cosmo Robert; *b* 1985

1d *Elinor Grace Alyson; *b* 1988

1c *Victoria Mary Rose; *b* 16 Jan 1937; *m* 26 April 1958 Maj David James Faulkner, Irish Gds (*d* 1993), s of Lt-Col Walter Douglas Faulkner, MC (*see* BUCCLEUCH and QUEENSBERRY, D), and has issue

2c *Lavinia Hermione [Lady Thorpe, Brooklands, Wheal Butson, St Agnes, Cornwall]; 29 Oct 1938; *m* 29 Dec 1966 (*divorce* 1989) Hon Mr Justice (Sir Matthew Alexander) Thorpe, s of Mathew Alexander Thorpe, of Rectory Gate Ho, Petworth, Sussex, and has:

1d *Gervase James Doncaster; *b* 12 Oct 1967

2d *Alexander Lambert; *b* 1969

3d *Marcus Somerled; *b* 1971

3c *Lettice Katharine; *b* 15 Feb 1941

4c *Rosamond Mary Alyson [Mrs Anthony Foottit, Ivy House, Whitwell St, Reepham, Norwich, Norfolk NR10 4RA]; *b* 14 March 1948; *m* 1977 *Ven Anthony C Foottit, and has:

1d *James Hugh Percival; *b* 1978

1d *Caroline Mary Alyson; *b* 1980
2d *Georgina Rose; *b* 1983
3b Joseph Gurney Fowell, Capt Gren Gds WW II; *b* 5 July 1913; *educ* Harrow; *m* 22 April 1938 *Elizabeth Langley (*m* 2nd 9 April 1946 Alexander Ludovic Grant, son of John Peter Grant of Rothiemurchus), er dau of Maj Robert Barbour, of Bolesworth Castle, Tattenhall, Chester, and was *ka* Tunisia May 1943, leaving issue:
1c +Andrew Robert Fowell [Andrew Buxton Esq, Bentley Park, Ipswich, Suffolk], late 2nd Lt Gren Gds; *b* 5 April 1939; *educ* Winchester and Pembroke Coll Oxford; Barclays Bank: joined 1963, dir 1978, gen manager 1980, v-chm 1984–91, md 1988–92, dep chm 1991–92, ch exec 1992–93, chm 1992–; *m* 1 May 1965 *Jane Margery, only dau of Lt-Col John Peter Grant, of Rothiemurchus, Aviemore, Inverness-shire, and has issue:
1d *Tessa Rosa; *b* 19 April 1966
2d *Veronica Mary; *b* 1970; *m* 23 Aug 1997 *Michael Barlow, 3rd s of Sir John Barlow, 3rd Bt, of Bradwell Hall (*qv*)
2c +Joseph William Henry [Capt Joseph Buxton, Rockstowes Hill, Uley, Dursley, Glos GL11 5AS] ; *b* 30 March 1943; *educ* Harrow and RMA Sandhurst; Capt Gren Gds; *m* 1st 1972 Sarah Louise (*d* 1974), er dau of Lt-Col Richard Patrick Pilkington Smyly, MC, of Eccleston Garden Ho, Eccleston, Cheshire; *m* 2nd 1981 *Ann, dau of Paul Boggis-Rolfe, of Martens Ho, Wargrave-on-Thames, and has issue:
1d +William Paul; *b* 1983
2d +Robert; *b* 1984
1d *Laura Elizabeth Verena; *b* 1990
1c *Meriel Rose [Mrs Peter Afia, 1 Hatton Grange, Shifnal, Salop TF11 9HS]; *b* 16 April 1940; Extra Lady in Waiting to HRH PRINCESS ALEXANDRA; *m* 1st 7 Jan 1964 Robert Ivan Kenyon-Slaney (*d* 1984) and has issue (*see* KENYON, B); *m* 2nd 1985 *Peter Maurice Afia
4b Michael Auriol, High Sheriff Rutland 1953, Lt-Cdr RNVR WW II; *b* 4 Sept 1914; *educ* Harrow; *m* 5 Feb 1938 *Elizabeth Edith Millicent, 2nd dau of Robert Hammond Arthur Elwes, JP, of Congham Ho, King's Lynn, Norfolk, and *d* 1990, leaving:
1c +Gervase Michael [Gervase Buxton Esq, 22 Chipstead St, London SW3]; *b* 2 Jan 1939; *educ* Harrow and Trin Coll Cambridge (BA 1962); late 2nd Lt Roy Scots Greys; *m* 2 March 1965 *Susan Margaret, er dau of Kenneth Malcolm McKenzie, of 40 Hans Place, SW1 and has issue:
1d +Matthew Thomas Gervase; *b* 28 Sept 1967
2d +Jocelyn David; *b* 1972
1d *Lucy Jane; *b* 23 Aug 1966
2d *Caragh Susan; *b* 1969
2c +Christopher Robert [Christopher Buxton Esq, Mulberry House, Little Wilbraham, Cambridge CB1 5LE]; *b* 1 Oct 1940; *educ* Harrow; QALAS 1965, FRICS; *m* 1st 4 Jan 1965 (*divorce* 1970) *Judy Frances, est dau of Gordon Hollingsworth Dixon, of Somerton Ho, Winkfield Row, Berks and has issue:
1d +Timothy James; *b* 21 April 1967
2d +Richard Antony; *b* 21 April 1967
2c (cont.) Christopher Buxton *m* 2nd 1973 *Priscilla, dau of Maj John Gardner, and has further issue:
3d +Edward Robert; *b* 1977
4d +Thomas Michael; *b* 1980
1d *Alexandra Mary; *b* 1975
3c +Jonathan James [Maj Jonathan Buxton, 62 Endlesham Rd, London SW12 8JL]; *b* 2 July 1943; *educ* Harrow; late Maj 17th/21st Lancers; *m* 4 April 1972 *Rosaleen Pleasance, dau of Sir John Bagge, 6th Bt (*qv*), and has:
1d *Georgina Elizabeth; *b* 28 Aug 1973
2d *Victoria Rose; *b* 24 July 1975
3d *Rosaleen Poppy; *b* 1 June 1979
4c +Charles Joseph; *b* 28 Dec 1951; *educ* Harrow; Lt-Col 17th/21st Lancers; *m* 1978 *Veronica Juliet Mary, yr dau of Francis David Paterson-Morgan, of Hospital of St Cross, Winchester, and has issue:
1d *Leonie Carinna Rose; *b* 1979
2d *Katriona Topaz Mary; *b* 1985
3d *Sophie; *b* 1990
5b +Henry Adrian, formerly 2nd Lt Rifle Bde SR Offrs; *b* 27 April 1916; *educ* Chillon Coll
2a Leonard (Rev), Vicar of North Mymms 1930; *b* 10 Oct 1877; *educ* Harrow and Ch Ch Oxford (M A); *m* 27 July 1903 Kathleen Lydia (*d* 24 March 1958), dau of Capt John Digby Wingfield-Digby, of Sherborne Castle, and *d* 7 Jan 1946, leaving issue:
1b +Edmund Digby (Rev) [The Rev Edmund Buxton, Pilgrims, 10 Pound Hill, Alresford, Hants SO24 9BW], Vicar of St Mary's Peckham 1939–44, Vicar of Wembley 1944–54, Vicar of Milborne Port, Somerset from 1954, Rural Dean of Merston 1957–67, Preb of Wells Cathedral 1964; *b* 1 March 1908; *educ* Charterhouse and Trin Coll Cambridge (BA 1929, MA 1933); *m* 30 July 1940 *Katharine Monsarrat, er dau of John Arthur Hargreaves, of Neston, Cheshire, and has issue:
1c +Francis (Rev) [The Rev Francis Buxton, 362 Franklin Rd, Kings Norton, Birmingham B30 1NE]; *b* 1 Jan 1942; *educ* Sherborne and Trin Coll Cambridge (MA), Birmingham U (DPS), Sheffield U and Lincoln Theol Coll; *m* 7 June 1969 *Jane Mary, only dau of Rev Arthur Leslie Jones, of Upwey Rectory, Weymouth, Dorset, and has:
1d +Nicholas Andrew; *b* 1972
2d +Thomas Mark; *b* 1974
1c (cont.) The Rev and Mrs Francis Buxton adopted 1979:
*Asha Theresa; *b* 1976
2c +Antony Leonard; *b* 14 March 1950; *educ* Sherborne and Trin Coll Cambridge; *m* 1977 *Heather Morwenna Marie, dau of Surgn-R-Adml Leslie B Osborne, and has:
1d *Laura Rose; *b* 1978
1c *Mary Ethel, SRN, SCM [Mrs David Grundy, The Old Post Office, Besomers Drove, Lower Redlynch, Salisbury, Wilts SP5 2PN]; *b* 8 Sept 1944; *educ* St George's Hosp; *m* 1972 *David James Grundy, MB, BS, FRCS, and has:
1d *Katharine Mary; *b* 1973
2d *Joanna Lucy; *b* 1976
2c *Lucy Jane; *b* 9 June 1947; *educ* UEA
2b +Kenneth Leonard, FRCS, LRCP, DTM and H, MB and BCh, Medical Supt and Consultant Mildmay Mission Hosp E2; *b* 19 July 1909; *educ* Charterhouse and Trin Coll Cambridge (BA 1930, MA 1935); *m* 1 June 1935 *Agnes Josephine, dau of Rev Dr Tom Bragg, and has:
1c +Paul Kenneth, MRCS, FRCP, MB, BChir [Paul Buxton Esq, Old Inzievar House, by Dunfermline, Fife KY12 8HA]; *b* 28 Feb 1936; *educ* St Lawrence Coll, Ramsgate and Trin Coll Cambridge (BA 1958, MA 1962); *m* 22 Dec 1962 *Heather Clive, only dau of Lt-Col Joseph Campbell Edlmann, of Whitegates, Tattonhall, Cheshire, and has issue:
1d +Jonathan Charles Fowell [Jonathan Buxton Esq, 43 Thorparch Rd, London SW8]; *b* 30 June 1965; *educ* Shrewsbury and Pembroke Coll Oxford; *m* 1990 *Victoria, only dau of Seth Bottom, of Killuney, Co Armagh and has:
1e *Thaddeus Alexander Wolf; *b* 21 Nov 1996
1d *Joanna Rachel; *b* 12 April 1967; *m* 199– *Maj Francis Hobbs, Gren Gds
2c +Andrew Wakefield; *b* 31 Jan 1939; *educ* St Lawrence Coll, Ramsgate
1c *Angela Josephine; *b* 4 March 1944; *m* 1974 *Simon Christopher Edward Kendall, of Liss, Hants, and has:
1d *Benjamin Edward Buxton; *b* 27 Oct 1976
2d *Matthew Simon Digby; *b* 4 Jan 1979
3d *Andrew Christopher Barclay; *b* 7 July 1984
2c *Susanna Rachel; *b* 4 Nov 1945; *m* 5 April 1969 *Terry Hookway, only son of C M Hookway, of Bedport Farm, Umberleigh, Devon, and has issue
3b +Daniel Richard [Daniel Buxton Esq, 240 Devonport Rd, Tauranga, New Zealand]; *b* 4 March 1913; *educ* Bryanston and Trin Coll Cambridge; *m* 17 Aug 1940 *Josephine Blake, dau of Hugh Burdekin, of Levin, NZ, and has issue:
1c +Timothy Richard Blake [Timothy Buxton Esq, 308 Fencourt Rd, RD1 Cambridge, New Zealand]; *b* 13 April 1942; *m* 1964 *Juliette Gaye, dau of Charles William Laurence Jex-Blake, of Hamilton, NZ, and has issue:
1d +Darren Richard Blake [Darren Buxton Esq, 11 Hilliard Place, Cambridge, New Zealand]; *b* 7 June 1966
2d +Shane Laurence Blake [Shane Buxton Esq, 11 Hulme Pl, Cambridge, New Zealand]; *b* 27 May 1968; *m* 1994 *Regina Yuet Mei; dau of Yuen Song Wong, and has:
1e +Blake Mark Chee-Meng; *b* 199–
2e +Jaeden Laurence Chee-Kan; *b* 199–
2c +David Adrian Leonard [David Buxton Esq, Ballantrae, 35 Silverdale Rd, Hamilton, New Zealand]; *b* 6 Nov 1945; *educ* Massey U (BAgSc); *m* 1970 *Lynley Anne, dau of J O'Connor, and has issue:
1d +Adrian David [Adrian Buxton Esq, 27 Rose St, Tirau, New Zealand]; *b* 1973; by *Jody Pederson has:
1e *Jessica Anne; *b* 9 June 1996
2d +Bruce John; *b* 1975
3d +Greig Daniel; *b* 1978
4b Digby Hugh (Rev); *b* 27 Jan 1916; *educ* Stowe and Trin Coll Cambridge (BA 1938, MA 1941); Curate All Saints', Queensbury, Edgware, 1946–50, and St Mary's St John's Newfoundland 1950, Rector Hantsport, NS 1952–54, Priest-in-charge Saguenay Mission, PQ, Canada, and Lake St John Mission, Quebec 1954–64, Rector St Barnabas N Hatley, PQ, 1964; *d* unm 9 Nov 1997
1b *Kathleen Hannah; *b* 6 Nov 1905
2b *Ruth Lydia; *b* 2 Oct 1906; *m* 29 Oct 1941 *John Willoughby Harris and has issue:
1c *Patrick John; *b* 10 Aug 1946; *educ* Wanganui Collegiate Sch and Canterbury U (BE); *m* 1972 *Diana, dau of Ian McW Harkness, and has issue
1c *Elizabeth Hannah; *b* 15 March 1943; *m* 1st 5 Oct 1963 Alfred Rudolf Bernd Ehrhardt and has issue; *m* 2nd 1980 *Frank Marlow, and has further issue
3a Arthur (Rev); *b* 7 Aug 1882; *educ* Harrow and Trin Coll Cambridge (BA 1904, MA 1908); Rector All Souls Langham Pl 1920–36, Vicar All Saints Southport, CF 4th Cl WW I; *m* 14 Jan 1908 Esme Caroline (*d* 1971), 2nd dau of Col Francis William Pixley, VD, JP, DL, FSA, of Wooburn Green, Bucks, and *d* 6 Jan 1958, leaving issue:
1b +Nigel Arthur [Dr Nigel Buxton, Eagle Lake Rd, South River, Ont P0A 1X0, Canada]; *b* 28 Jan 1909; *educ* Harrow and Trin Coll Cambridge (BA 1930, MB, BCh 1934), MRCS, LRCP; Capt RAMC WW II, medical missionary India to 1962; *m* 23 March 1948 *Elmira Mary, MD, dau of William Richli, MD, of Mariposa, Calif., and has:
1c +David Edson [David Buxton, 32201 Ne Dial Rd, Camas, WN 98607, USA]; *b* 10 Feb 1949; *m* 1974 *Terri, dau of Gerald Snyder, of Oregon, and has issue:
1d +Daniel Elliot; *b* 1976
2d +Douglas Edward; *b* 1979
2c +John Arthur, MD, FACS; *b* 14 Aug 1950; *m* 1983 *Susan, dau of Paul Smith, of Pennsylvania, and has issue:
1d +Ashley; *b* 1987
1d *Sara; *b* 1985
1c *Louise Elizabeth; *b* 5 Feb 1952; Dr of Health Sci; *m* 1978 *Kimber Schneider, MD, and has issue

1b Richenda Dorothy; *b* 30 Nov 1911; *m* 1 June 1938 George Blaker Blaker, CMG, Under-Sec DES, only s of Col William Frederick Blaker, DSO, OBE, and *d* 1987, having had:

1c *Richenda Jennifer; *b* 2 Jan 1955

2b *Mary; *b* 10 June 1913

3b *Priscilla Peronne, LRAM, Detachment Offr BRCS; *b* 9 Sept 1916

1a Dorothy Rachel; *m* 14 July 1903 1st Baron Hazlerigg (*qv*), and *d* 1972, having had issue

2a Margaret Katharine; *m* 9 July 1912 Rev Edward Louis Longfield McClintock, Hon CF, son of Lt-Col Charles Edward McClintock, JP, of Glendaragh, Co Antrim, and has issue. He *d* 25 May 1961

3a Lilian Rosamond; *d* unm 18 Feb 1969

(2) Geoffrey Fowell, CB (1919), VD, of Hoveton Hall, Norwich, DL, JP Norfolk, Sheriff 1890, Mayor Norwich 1903, Maj and Hon Lt-Col Norfolk Yeo, Lt-Col 1st Vol Bn Norfolk Regt; *b* 21 June 1852; *m* 3 Sept 1878 Mary (*d* 18 Nov 1940), est dau of Rev Hon John Harbord (*see* SUFFIELD, B), and *d* 11 April 1929, leaving issue:

1a Geoffrey Charles, TD, Maj Coldstream Gds (SR), formerly Norfolk Yeo; *b* 4 June 1879; *m* 9 April 1902 (*divorce* 1913) Clare Florence Mary (*d* in a fire 8 May 1949), only child of Sir Francis George Stapleton, 8th Bt (*qv*), and *d* 8 March 1958, having had issue:

1b Peter Stapleton, Maj Leics Yeo (TA) WW II; *b* 14 Oct 1904; *m* 15 Sept 1934 *Julia Victoria [Mrs Peter Buxton, Mansion House, Gainford, nr Darlington, Co Durham], yst dau of Claud Edward Pease, (*see* PEASE, Bt, of Hammersknott), and was *ka* July 1944, leaving:

1c +James Geoffrey Pease [James Buxton Esq, Manor Farm House, Lubenham, Market Harborough, Leics LE16 9TD]; *b* 24 Oct 1939; *educ* Eton and Trin Coll Cambridge; *m* 1970 *Meriel Jessica, dau of Maj Denis Cowen of E Farndon Manor, Market Harborough, and has:

1d +Hugh David; *b* 1975

1d *Rose Emma; *b* 1973

1c *Anne Victoria [Mrs Robin Pease, Hill House, Gainford, Co Durham]; *b* 17 Feb 1936; *m* 25 April 1959 *Robin Slingsby Pease, yr son of Maurice Pease, of Manchester, and has:

1d *Peter Gordon Charles; *b* 6 Feb 1965

1d *Victoria Julia Diana; *b* 19 March 1962

2d *Annabel Primrose Robin; *b* 1971

2a Bernard, DSO (1917), Cdr RN WW I (despatches), Order Sacred Treasure Japan; *b* 21 Oct 1882; *m* 28 Sept 1904 Lady Hermione Grimston (*d* 3 April 1924), 2nd dau of 3rd Earl of Verulam (*qv*), and *d* 29 Dec 1923, leaving issue:

1b Geoffrey Mungo, OBE (1946), FRAeS, G/Capt RAF WW II; *b* 26 May 1906; *educ* Harrow and Peterhouse Cambridge (MA); *m* 21 Dec 1929 *Horatia Mary [Mrs Geoffrey Buxton, Wiveton Green, Holt, Norfolk], yr dau of Adml Sir William Wordsworth Fisher, GCB, GCVO, and *d* 1979, having had issue:

1c Gabriel Hermione; *b* 27 May 1931; *d* 21 Feb 1944

2c *Carolyn Viola; *b* 29 March 1934

3c *Juliet Horatia; *b* 16 April 1937

4c *Rose Vivian; *b* 11 Jan 1951

2b Simon Fowell TD, Maj Intell Corps; *b* 22 Nov 1908; *educ* Harrow and Magdalene Coll Cambridge (MA); *m* 28 Feb 1947 *Belinda Margaret, OBE, only dau of Capt Hon James Boyle (*see* GLASGOW, E), and *d* 1974, leaving adopted children

3b Samuel Luckyn, MC, Maj 17th/21st Lancers WW II; *b* 10 March 1914; *m* 6 Aug 1941 Pamela Mary (*m* 2nd 14 Nov 1946 Baron Buxton of Alsa (*qv*), son of Leland Buxton (*see* below), and *d* 1983), er dau of Sir Henry Ralph Stanley Birkin, 3rd Bt (*qv*), and was *ka* Italy May 1944, leaving:

1c *Christina Hermione; *b* 13 May 1944; *m* 29 March 1967 *John David Millard Barnes, er s of James Millard Barnes, of Ethorpe Crescent, Gerrards Cross, Bucks, and has issue

1b Jane Hermione; *b* 6 Jan 1913; *m* 27 June 1934 Col Hon William Sigismund Patrick Alexander, DSO, DL, 4th s of 4th Earl of Caledon (*qv*), and *d* 13 Dec 1967, leaving issue

3a Ivor, DSO, TD (1919), Maj KO Norfolk Yeo WW I (despatches); *b* 28 Aug 1884; *educ* Eton and Trin Coll Cambridge (BA 1907); *m* 10 July 1918 Phyllis Dorothy (*d* 1976), 2nd dau of Hugh Gurney Barclay, MVO, JP, of Coloney Hall, Norwich, and widow of Maj Henry Cecil Johnson, DSO, KRRC, and *d* 23 April 1969, leaving issue:

1b *Nancy; *b* 3 April 1919; *m* 1st 1 June 1940 Lt-Col John Noel Ronald Loveday, 16th/5th Lancers (*kas* 15 May 1944), s of Arthur Frederick Loveday, OBE, of Aynhoe, Banbury, Oxon, and has issue:

1c *Tessa; *b* 8 Feb 1942; *m* 1972 *Andrew Henry Scott, and has issue

1b (cont.) Mrs John Loveday *m* 2nd 3 Feb 1947 Maj John Hallifax Weller-Poley, MC, JP (*d* 1976), s of Capt Edward Hallifax Weller-Poley, MVO, of Boxted Hall, Bury St Edmunds, and has further issue:

1c *Richard Hallifax [Richard Weller Poley Esq, Keeper's Cottage, Boxted, Bury St Edmunds, Suffolk IP29 4LN]; *b* 11 Aug 1949; *educ* Milton Abbey; *m* 1st 1970 (*divorce* 1991) Sarah Francesca, er dau of John Valentine Gosling, of The Claw, Brushford, Dulverton, Somerset; *m* 2nd 1992 *Isobel Muriel, dau of Maj Douglas Wade Reader, of Halvergate Ho, Halvergate, Norfolk, and has issue by 1st and 2nd w

2c *(Nicholas) Toby; *b* 6 Jan 1951; *educ* Eton; *m* 1992 *P Sue Bond

2b *Felicity Mary [Lady Blacker, Cowpasture Farm, Hook Norton, Banbury, Oxon]; *b* 22 Aug 1921; *m* 1st Aug 1942 Maj John Rew, 16th/5th Lancers (*ka* 4 March 1943), only son of John Rew, of Whitchurch Ho, Aylesbury; *m* 2nd 26 Feb 1947 *Gen Sir Cecil Hugh Blacker, GCB, OBE, MC, 5th Roy Inniskilling Dragoon Gds, only son of Col Norman Valentine Blacker, DSO, MC, of Fen Ho, S Walsham, Norwich, by Olive Georgina, dau of Lewis Austruther Hope, CB (*see* HOPE, Bt), and by him has:

1c *Terence; *b* 5 Feb 1948; *educ* Wellington and Trin Coll Cambridge; author; *m* 1975 *Hon Caroline Susan Dean Soper, dau of Baron Soper (LP, *qv*), and has issue

2c *Philip; *b* 27 Sept 1949; *educ* Milton Abbey; sculptor and former Nat Hunt jockey; *m* 1979 *Susan, dau of Colin Davies, of Oakgrove, Chepstow, and has issue

4a Guy; *b* 19 Jan 1888; *d* unm 1 July 1907

1a Joan; *b* 8 April 1881; *m* 15 May 1901 Sir John Frecheville Ramsden, 6th Bt (*qv*), and has issue

2a Olive; *b* 3 May 1886; *m* 14 Sept 1904 Lt-Col Miles Roland Charles Backhouse, DSO, 4th s of Sir Jonathan Backhouse, 1st Bt (*qv*), and *d* 16 Sept 1954, leaving issue

3a Avery; *b* 3 July 1889; *m* 22 May 1911 Col Hon Guy Greville Wilson, CMG, DSO, 2nd s of 1st Baron Nunburnholme (*qv*), and had issue

4a Hazel Mary; *b* 19 Jan 1893; *m* 10 Aug 1914 Capt Winchester St George Clowes, late 19th Hus, of Hitchin, Herts, and *dsp* 3 March 1967. He *d* 25 Feb 1940

5a Rose; *b* 25 Feb 1898; *m* 12 June 1923 Algernon Richard Aubrey Cartwright, Lt late Coldstream Gds (SR) (*d* 27 Sept 1947), 4th s of Aubrey Thomas Carter Cartwright, of Edgecote, Banbury, and had issue:

1b *Giles Aubrey; *b* 22 April 1924; *educ* Eton; *m* 20 May 1954 *Helen Celia, yr dau of John Arthur Pryor, of Bentworth Hall, Hants, and formerly w of Lt-Col Maurice Edward Cator Smart

1b *Prudence Tobina; *b* 19 April 1928; *m* 5 Feb 1949 *Arthur Gerald Cole, yr son of Hon Galbraith Lowry Egerton Cole (*see* ENNISKILLEN, E), and has issue

(3) Alfred Fowell, of Fairhill, Tonbridge, Alderman LCC 1892–95 and 1904–22, chm 1916–17, dir (extrdy) Nat Prov Bank and Alliance Assur, Govr Rugby Sch, memb: Ho of Laity and PLA; *b* 28 March 1854; *educ* Trin Coll Cambridge (BA); *m* 6 Jan 1885 Violet, OBE (1920) (*d* 6 June 1936), dau of Very Rev Thomas William Jex-Blake, DD, of Bunwell, Norfolk, Headmaster Rugby , and *d* 5 May 1952, leaving issue:

1a Patrick Alfred, CMG (1947), FRS, MRCS, LRCP, Dir Dept of Entomology London Sch of Hygiene and Trop Med, Prof Entomology London U; *b* 24 March 1892; *educ* Trin Coll Cambridge (MA, sometime Fell); *m* 16 Jan 1917 Muryell Gladys (*d* 1989), 4th dau of Rev Hon Canon William Talbot Rice, formerly Vicar of St Paul's Onslow Square (*see* DYNEVOR, B), and *d* 13 Dec 1955, having had issue:

1b Martin Patrick, 1st Sec For Serv, Capt Roy Sigs; *b* 22 Sept 1920; *educ* Rugby and Trin Coll Cambridge (BA); *m* 16 May 1949 Jacqueline Marcelle (*d* 17 Feb 1968), dau of Percival James Stokes, of S Somercotes, Lincs, and *d* 16 Oct 1966, leaving issue:

1c +James Patrick; *b* 25 Feb 1957; *m* 1993 *Liane Frances Jones, and has issue:

1d *Angharad Grace Jones; *b* 1993

1c *Eleanor Ruth; *b* 14 Aug 1950; *m* 1970 *Paul Hudson Stanford

2c *Rachel Phyllida; *b* 16 July 1952; *m* 1973 (*divorce* 1995) Leslie William Huson, and has issue

3c *Alice Richenda; *b* 6 May 1954; *m* 1974 *Charles Walsh, and has issue

2b Andrew Patrick, DFC, F/Lt RAF WW II; *b* 6 July 1923; *educ* Rugby and Trin Coll Cambridge (BA); *m* 23 July 1949 *Kathleen Audrey, MA [Lady Wood, The Manor House, Little Wittenham, Oxon OX14 4RA] (*m* 2nd 26 May 1955 *Sir Martin Francis Wood, OBE, DL, FRS, and has further issue), yst dau of Rev John Howard Stanfield, of Cathay, Colyford Rd, Seaton, Devon, and *d* 7 Jan 1952, leaving issue:

1c +Robin David; *b* 3 May 1950; *educ* Bradfield; *m* 1986 *Elizabeth Holmes and has:

1d +Andrew; *b* 1986

2d +Christopher; *b* 1992

1c *Sarah Margaret; *b* 17 Nov 1951

1b *Helen Muryell [Mrs Donald Wright, Mill Barn, Coulston, Westbury, Wilts BA13 4NY]; *b* 27 Feb 1925; *educ* Cambridge (BA 1948); *m* 26 June 1948 *(Arthur Robert) Donald Wright, OBE, yst s of Charles North Wright, of Tettenhall, Wolverhampton, and has issue:

1c *Simon Nicholas; *b* 16 Feb 1949; *educ* Bryanston; *m* 1989 *Margaret Woodliff

2c *Patrick Stephen; *b* 23 Jan 1951; *educ* Bryanston; has issue

1c *Hannah Elizabeth; *b* 14 Dec 1953; *m* 1995 *Ian Downie and has issue

2c *Charlotte Helen; *b* 23 Feb 1956; *m* 1979 George Reynolds Cannon (*d* 1992), of Denver, Colorado, USA, and has issue

3c *Lesley Rachel; *b* 7 July 1961; *m* 1993 Nicholas Knight (*d* 1993)

2b *Marian Elizabeth; *b* 26 Dec 1927; *m* 24 June 1950 *Michael Nicholson, s of Archibald Frederick Nicolson, of Bucknell, Bicester, and has:

1c *Catherine Muryell; *b* 27 March 1952

2c *Elizabeth Frances *b* 23 July 1953

3c *Rosamond Lillian; *b* 16 June 1956

4c *Teresa Marian; *b* 23 April 1958

3b *Rachel Katharine [Mrs Peter Gray, 13A The Causeway, Horsham, W Sussex]; *b* 9 Jan 1930; *educ* Cambridge (BA 1951); *m* 1st 19 July 1952 Christopher Herzig, CBE (*d* 1993), yr s of Leopold Adolph Herzig, of Enfield, Middx; *m* 2nd 1996 *Peter Gray and by her 1st husb has:

1c *Stephen Christopher; *b* 12 April 1954; *m* 1977 *Anita, dau of Johan Mostert, of Pretoria, S Africa, and has issue

2c *Francis Patrick; *b* 15 Dec 1955; *m* 1980 *Petra, dau of Prof Ambrose Rogers, of UCL, and has issue

3c *Edmund Martin; *b* 14 Feb 1958; *m* 1990 *Ana Novakovic, and has issue

4c *Hugh John; *b* 28 April 1961; *m* 1992 *Isobel Oriane Clare, est dau of Maj Count Charles John de Salis, DL, and has issue (*see* HERRIES OF TERREGLES, L)

1c *Harriet Elizabeth; *b* 8 March 1963; *m* 1995 *Peter Carty and has issue

4b *Lucy Bertha [Lady Chandler, 46 Hyde Vale, Greenwich, London SE 10 8HP]; *b* 30 Oct 1932; *educ* Cambridge (MA 1958); *m* 12 Aug 1955 *Sir Geoffrey Chandler, CBE, son of Dr Frederick George Chandler, MD, FRCP, of Newdigate, Surrey, and has issue:

1c *Hilary Jane [Mrs James Otter, 3 Horseshoes Farmhouse, Woodlands, Bramdean, Hants SO24 0HW]; *b* 8 May 1957; *m* 1981 *James A Otter, s of John Otter, of Pilton, Northants, and has issue

2c *Sarah Elizabeth [Mrs Sarah Armstrong, Ivy Cottage, 2 Mills Lane, Chipping Warden, Oxon OX17 1JX]; *b* 22 March 1959; *m* 1991 (*divorce* 19–) Richard A Armstrong, est s of Dr Alan Armstrong, of Bladon, Oxon, and has issue

3c *Clare Marjorie [Mrs John Walker, Ranfold Barn, Slinfold, W Sussex RG13 7RL]; *b* 4 Sept 1961; *m* 1991 *John Walker

4c *Susan Anne; *b* 12 March 1964; *m* 1997 *Edmund de Waal

2a Denis Alfred Jex, DL, JP Essex, High Sheriff, FSA, W/Cdr RAF, raised and cmded No 909 (Balloon) Sqdn AAF, late Lt W Riding Regt; *b* 26 March 1895; *educ* Rugby and Balliol Coll Oxford (BA 1924, MA 1926); *m* 27 Sept 1923 Emily Mary (*d* 1970), est dau of William Hollins, JP, of Berry Hill, Mansfield, Notts, and *d* 2 Sept 1964, leaving issue:

1b +Paul William Jex [Paul Buxton Esq, Castle House, Chipping Ongar, Essex CM5 9JT]; *b* 20 Sept 1925; *educ* Rugby and Balliol Coll Oxford (BA 1951, MA 1987); Dip Serv 1954–71, Counsellor Washington, Capt Coldstream Gds (RARO) WW II (wounded), banking 1972–74, NI Office 1974–85 (U-Sec 1981–85); *m* 1st 29 April 1950 (*divorce* 1971) Katharine (*d* 1977), 3rd dau of Sir Hubert Hull, CBE, of Kensington, and has:

1c +Charles Hubert Jex; *b* 17 June 1951; *educ* Ampleforth; *m* 1976 *Cecile Moss and has:

1d +Sam; *b* 1977

1d *Amy; *b* 1980

2c +Tobias Richard Valentine; *b* 25 Nov 1953; *educ* Ampleforth; has:

1d +Oliver; *b* 1982

2d +Xavier; *b* 1990

3d +Yvo (twin); *b* 1990

1d *Joe Grace; *b* 1993

1c *Mary Katharine; *b* 18 Aug 1956; has issue

1b (cont.) Paul Buxton *m* 2nd 1971 *Hon Margaret Evelyn Bridges, dau of 1st Baron Bridges (*qv*) and formerly w of Trevor Henry Aston, and by her has:

2c *Sophia Frances; *b* 1972

3c *Hero Elizabeth; *b* 1974

1b *Mary Violet; *b* 11 July 1924; ATS 1945–47; *m* 9 Dec 1950 +David Roden Buxton (*see below*) and has issue

2b Cecilia Rachel; *b* 26 July 1927; *educ* LMH Oxford (BA 1949); Fell Wolfson Coll Oxford; *m* 6 July 1951 (*divorce* 1968) Marcus William Dick (*d* 1971), s of Dr James Reid Dick, of Scarborough, Yorks, and *d* 1995, leaving:

1c *Jasper Henry; *b* 30 Dec 1956; *m* 1988 *Louise Blum

1c *Catherine Sophia; *b* 8 Feb 1953

2c *Cressida Rose; *b* 16 Oct 1960

3b *Elizabeth Rosalind [Mrs Elizabeth Yelin, 89 Brain Ave, Norwich NR1 2PD]; *b* 12 April 1929; *m* 8 April 1953 (*divorce* 1964) Tristram Yelin (*d* 1982), s of Walter Yelin and Baroness Hubert Khnopff, of Chateau de et à Bodeghen, St Martin, Belgium, and has issue:

1c *Francis North Hunter Buxton; *b* 18 Feb 1957

1c *Cecilia Mary; *b* 5 May 1954

2c *Natasha Vera; *b* 31 Oct 1959

1a Violet Elizabeth, MA Oxford; *b* 13 Feb 1900; *d* unm 16 March 1950

(4) Barclay Fowell (Rev); *b* 16 Aug 1860; *educ* Trin Coll Cambridge (MA); Vicar Holy Trinity Tunbridge Wells 1921–35, Hon Missionary Japan 1890–1917; *m* 22 July 1886 Margaret Maria Amelia (*d* 21 April 1947), dau of William Railton, of 65 Onslow Sq, SW, and *d* 5 Feb 1946, leaving issue:

1a Murray Barclay, MC, Capt Norfolk Regt WW I (severely wounded); *b* 30 July 1889; *educ* Trin Coll Cambridge (MA); *m* 30 June 1920 Janet Mary Muriel (*d* 21 Nov 1942), 3rd dau of Sir Hildred Carlile, 1st Bt, CBE (*see* 1935 edn), and *d* as a result of enemy action, 14 Oct 1940, leaving issue:

1b +Ronald Carlile [Ronald Buxton Esq, Kimberley Hall, Wymondham, Norfolk NR18 0RT; 67 Ashley Gdns, London SW1 1QG]; *b* 20 Aug 1923; *educ* Eton and Trin Coll Cambridge (BA 1943, MA 1950); late Capt REME, attd IA, chartered structural engr, MP Leyton 1965–66; *m* 20 June 1959 *Phyllida Dorothy Roden, yst dau of Capt Roden Henry Victor Buxton, CBE, RN (*see below*), and has issue:

1c +Peter Hildred; *b* 19 June 1960; *m* 1987 *Eleanor Charlotte, dau of Richard Anthony Brooke Winch, of Swannington Manor, Norfolk, and has:

1d *Laura Juliet; *b* 1990

2c +Robert Victor; *b* 22 Nov 1966

1c *Camilla Jane St John [Mrs Edward Baxter, Gilston, Leven, Fife]; *b* 19 June 1960; *m* 1992 *Edward Thomas Baxter, s of Alan G L Baxter, WS

2c *Vanessa Ann Carlile; *b* 12 April 1962

1b *Jean Carlile; *b* 10 June 1921; B Litt (1954), D Phil (1958) Oxford; social anthropologist and writer, formerly Jr Cdr ATS

2a Alfred Barclay, missionary Africa; *b* 3 Nov 1891; *educ* Trin Coll Cambridge (MA); *m* 27 Dec 1916 Edith Mary Crossley (*d* 1977), 3rd dau of Charles Thomas Studd, of Norwood, and *d* as a result of enemy action 14 Oct 1940, leaving issue:

1b Lionel Studd; *b* 4 May 1920; *educ* Stowe; Lt Coldstream Gds WW II; *d* of wounds recd in action 30 Sept 1943

1b *Susan Studd, MBE (1990) [Lady Wood MBE, Box 24277, Nairobi, Kenya]; *b* 19 Oct 1918; *m* 6 Nov 1943 Sir Arthur Michael Wood, CBE, MB, BS, FRCS (*d* 1987), fndr and dir gen AMREF ('The Flying Doctor'), est surv son of Athur Henry Wood, CB, of Dene Court, Shipbourne, Kent, and has issue:

1c *Mark Lionel; *b* 7 Jan 1945; *educ* Eton and London U (MB, BS); FRCS

2c *Hugo Charles; *b* 13 May 1948; *educ* Stanbridge Earls Sch Romsey and Wye Ag Coll (BSc)

1c *Janet Mary; *b* 8 Dec 1946; *m* 19 April 1969 Robin Ulyate, of Tanzania

2c *Katrina Susan; *b* 6 July 1951

3a George Barclay, 2nd Lt 5th Bn Norfolk Regt, ADC 54th Div, and RFC, served in Br E Africa, Egypt and France WW I; *b* 16 Oct 1892; *k* flying, 28 July 1917

4a Barclay Godfrey, MC and bar (1917), Capt Duke of Wellington's Regt WW I (severely wounded); *b* 7 Jan 1895; *educ* Repton and Trin Coll Cambridge (MA); *m* 24 Oct 1922 Dorothea Reader (*d* 26 April 1967), 2nd dau of Reader Harris, KC, of 51 North Side, Clapham Common, SW, and *d* 1986, leaving issue:

1b +Christopher Godfrey Reader, OBE (1982) [Christopher Buxton Esq OBE, Kirtlington Park, Oxon; 61 Harcourt Terrace, London SW10 9JP], late 2nd Lt RA, chm Windlesham Park Ltd; *b* 22 May 1929; *educ* Charterhouse, Trin Coll Cambridge (MA) and Dartmouth Coll, USA (MBA); *m* 25 April 1964 (*divorce* 1969) Margaret Isabel, yr dau of Col Hubert Bromley Watkins, OBE, MC, DL, of Shirley, Knighton, Radnorshire

1b *Joanna Margaret Reader, MBE (1993) [Miss Joanna Buxton MBE, 21a Portchester Terrace, London W2], market research consultant; *b* 17 July 1927; *educ* Sherborne Sch for Girls and Edin U

1a *Rachel Jane [Miss Rachel Buxton, Wayside, Stanway, Colchester, Essex]; *b* 11 June 1905

(1) Elizabeth Ellen; *m* 12 Feb 1868 Robert Barclay, of High Leigh, Hoddesdon, Herts, and *d* 20 Sept 1919, leaving issue. He *d* 19 July 1921

(2) Catherine Emily; *m* 9 Sept 1891 Thomas Morris MacKnight, and *d* 9 Jan 1925. He *d* April 1906

(3) Margaret Jane; *m* 26 April 1882 Rev Canon Richard Arnold Pelly, and *d* 23 Nov 1903, leaving issue (*see* PELLY, Bt)

(4) Effie Priscilla; *m* 1 Aug 1893 Rev Thomas Lancaster, Rector of Little Leighs, Chelmsford, and *d* Dec 1940, leaving issue

3 Charles, of Foxwarren, Cobham, MP E Surrey; *b* 18 Nov 1823; *m* 7 Feb 1850 Emily Mary (*d* 19 June 1908), est dau of Sir Henry Holland, 1st Bt (*see* KNUTSFORD, B), and *d* 10 Aug 1871, leaving issue:

(1) Bertram Henry; *b* 31 July 1852; *d* 5 Dec 1934

(2) SYDNEY CHARLES BUXTON, 1st and last EARL BUXTON, so *cr* 8 Nov 1920, as also earlier 11 May 1914 VISCOUNT BUXTON, of Newtimber, Co Sussex, PC, GCMG, Hon LLD Cape Town, Hon DCL Oxford, MP Peterborough 1883–85, and Tower Hamlets (Poplar Div) 1886–1914, Under-Sec for the Colonies 1892–95, Postmaster-Gen 1905–10, Pres Bd of Trade 1910–14, Govr-Gen and C-in-C Union of S Africa and High Commr of S Africa 1914–20, Chllr of Order of St Michael and St George 1920; *b* 25 Oct 1853; *m* 1st 5 Feb 1882 Constance Mary (*d* 3 Nov 1892), 2nd dau of 1st Baron Avebury (*qv*), and had issue:

1a Charles Sydney, BA Oxford, V-Pres Ruskin Coll 1907–08, priv sec to his f when Pres BOT 1910–11; *b* 26 May 1884; *d* unm 31 Aug 1911

2a Kenneth Sydney; *b* 4 Sept 1886; *d* 27 Aug 1894

1a Phyllis Sydney, OBE (1918); *b* 17 April 1888; *m* 23 Sept 1918 Rev Canon Maurice George Jesser Ponsonby, MC, MA, 2nd son of Hon Edwin Charles William Ponsonby, DL, JP (*see* DE MAULEY, B), and *d* 27 Jan 1942, leaving issue

(2) (cont.) The 1st and last EARL BUXTON *m* 2nd 7 July 1896 Mildred Anne, GBE (1919), JP (*d* 7 Dec 1955), dau of Hugh Colin Smith, of Mount Clare, Roehampton, and *d* 15 Oct 1934, when his titles expired, having by her had issue:

3a Denis Bertram Sydney, 2nd Lt Coldstream Gds; *b* 29 Nov 1897; *ka* 9 Oct 1917

2a Doreen Maria Josepha Sydney (twin with Denis); *m* 24 Jan 1918 10th Duke of Grafton (*qv*) and *d* 28 July 1923, leaving issue

3a *Alethea Constance Dorothy Sydney; *b* 2 Aug 1910; *m* 12 July 1934 *Ven Peter Charles Eliot, MBE, TD, (*d* 1995) (*see* SAINT GERMANS, E)

1 Eleanor Margaret; *m* 7 Feb 1877 Cecil William Boyle, and *d* 28 May 1922, leaving issue (*see* CORK and ORRERY, E). He was *ka* in S Africa, 5 April 1900

2 Mary Emma; *m* 27 Oct 1887 Albert Osliff Rutson and *d* 16 Dec 1942, leaving issue. He *d* 21 April 1890

3 Richenda; *m* 3 Jan 1907 Hon Reginald Gilbert Murray Talbot, CBE, 2nd s of 4th Baron Talbot of Malahide (*qv*), and *d* 29 Oct 1952

4 Sybil de Gournay; *m* 16 Aug 1887 Sir George Stapylton Barnes, KCB, KCSI, er s of George Carnac Barnes, CB, and *d* 19 June 1955, having had issue. He *d* 9 Dec 1946

Sir THOMAS *d* 19 Feb 1845; his est son,

Sir Edward North Buxton, 2nd Bt, MP; *b* 16 Sept 1812; *m* 12 April 1836 Catherine (*d* 11 Aug 1911 aged 97), 2nd dau of Samuel Gurney, of Ham Ho, Essex, and had, with other issue:

1 (THOMAS) FOWELL (Sir), **3rd Bt**

2 Samuel Gurney, of Catton Hall, Norfolk, DL, JP, Sheriff 1891; *b* 1 Nov 1838; *m* 1st 3 Sept 1861 Louisa Caroline (*d* 1 March 1879), yst dau of John Gurney Hoare, and had issue:

(1) Edward Gurney, of Catton Hall, Norwich, JP, Norfolk and Norwich, High Sheriff Norfolk 1922; *b* 4 Aug 1865; *educ* Trin Coll Cambridge (BA); *m* 24 Oct 1895 Laura, MBE (1919) (*d* 15 Dec 1957), yr dau of John Gurney, JP, of Sprowston Hall, Norwich, and *d* 19 April 1929, leaving issue:

1a Desmond Gurney, DL (1961), CC (Norfolk 1958), High Sheriff Norfolk 1960, Sheriff Norwich 1936, Maj KRRC, served WWs I and II; *b* 4 Jan 1898; *educ* Eton and RMC Sandhurst; *m* 9 Jan 1930 Rachel Mary (*d* 11 March 1994), yr dau of Lt-Col Arthur Francis Morse, DL, of Coltishall Mead, Norwich, and *d* 29 Sept 1987, having had issue:

1b +Andrew Edward; *b* 3 March 1935; *educ* Eton and Magdalene Coll Cambridge (BA 1957, MA 1962); High Sheriff Norfolk 1998–99; *m* 30 March 1967 *Barbara Anne, yr dau of Capt Cyril Gascoigne Loyd, of Sowber Gate, Northallerton, Yorks, and has issue:
1c +Harry Desmond Gascoigne; *b* 23 Oct 1972
1c *Laura Catherine; *b* 31 May 1968; *m* 5 Oct 1996 *Charles R Erith, est s of Robert Erith and has:
1d *Jemima Barbara; *b* 24 Aug 1997
2c *Nicola Rachel Anne; *b* 1971
2b +James Desmond; *b* 20 Aug 1947; *educ* Eton and Magdalene Coll Cambridge; *m* 26 July 1975 *Annabella, dau of Douglas Raymond Collins (*see* BACKHOUSE, Bt), and has:
1c +Jasper Francis; *b* 10 April 1979
2c +Oliver Desmond; *b* 10 Sept 1980
1b Gillian Mary; *b* 19 Sept 1931; *d* Nov 1969
2b *Annabel Audrey; *b* 19 Jan 1938; *m* 5 Oct 1979 *Iain Francis Wauchope Buchan
3b *Rosalinde Rachel; *b* 18 Oct 1939; *m* 20 Jan 1965 *John Raoul Wilmot Stansfeld, er s of Capt John de Bourbel Stansfeld, MC, DL, JP, of Dunninald, Montrose, Angus, and has issue (*see* EARDLEY-WILMOT, Bt)
4b *Elizabeth Laura; *b* 25 Feb 1941; *m* 27 Oct 1962 *William Lister Archibald Pryor, 2nd son of Rev Archibald Selwyn Pryor, of The Rectory, Upper Broughton, Leics, and has had:
1c Thomas William; *b* 2 June 1964; *d* 20 April 1967
2c *Alexander Timothy William; *b* 11 July 1968
3c *Hugh William Archibald; *b* 7 Oct 1974
1c *Victoria Elizabeth *b* 31 Dec 1965
2a Eric; *b* 30 June 1899; *d* 26 March 1979
3a Hubert Edward, chm Nakuru CC 1958–61, Maj late E African Pioneer Corps; *b* 15 Aug 1901; *educ* Eton and Trin Coll Cambridge; *m* 18 June 1932 (*divorce* 1948) Anne Hawise Colleton, dau of Lt-Col Arthur Hautayne Bowring, and *d* 1973, having had issue:
1b +Robert Hugh [Robert Buxton Esq, 60a Ladbroke Grove, London W11 2PB]; *b* 27 Nov 1933; *educ* Eton; *m* 25 Oct 1963 (*divorce* 1972) Helen Loveday, yr dau of D M R Plesse, of St Helena, and has issue:
1c +David Colleton; *b* 10 Sept 1964
2c +Henry Gurney; *b* 26 Sept 1966
1b (cont.) Robert Buxton *m* 2nd 1973 (*divorce* 1991) Mrs Judith Serena Lourenço; *m* 3rd 1992 *Mrs Anne Gamble and by his 2nd w has:
3c +Jonathan Hugh; *b* 1978
1b *Sara Carolyn Colleton; *b* 23 Nov 1937; *m* 17 Oct 1964 *Peter James Foot, son of J A Foot, of Eastbourne, Sussex, formerly of Kampala, Uganda, and has issue:
1c *Lorna Alice; *b* 26 July 1965
2c *Elizabeth Angela; *b* 1967
4a Mervyn, Lt RAPC WW II; *b* 5 May 1903; *m* 25 Oct 1932 *Carmela Mary Beatrice, only dau of George Herbert Lyon, of 50 Tregunter Rd, SW, and *das* 12 May 1944, leaving:
1b +Simon Lyon [Simon Buxton Esq, 104 Cameron St, Edgecliff, NSW 2027, Australia]; *b* 14 Nov 1935; *educ* Wellington and Magdalene Coll Cambridge (BA 1959, MA 1985); *m* 1971 *Janet Susan Paine and has issue:
1c +Thomas Lyon; *b* 6 Aug 1973
2c +Bennington Haille; *b* 26 Dec 1975
2b +Ian Lyon [Dr Ian Buxton, 12 Grand Parade, Tynemouth, Tyne and Wear NE30 4JS]; *b* 15 April 1937; *educ* Wellington and Glasgow U (BSc 1959, PhD 1965); CEng, Reader Marine Tport Newcastle U; *m* 19 Sept 1966 *Jean Mary, only dau of William Cochrane, of E Lothian, and has:
1c +Keith Mervyn Lyon; *b* 1974; *educ* Leeds U (BEng)
1c *Fiona Anne; *b* 1969; *educ* Sheffield Hallam U (BSc)
5a Mark, Lt RIASC WW II; *b* 23 Nov 1909; *educ* Charterhouse and Pembroke Coll Cambridge; *m* 11 July 1949 *Penelope Ann Cecil, widow of P/O O K Fisher, RAAF, and only dau of Edmund C Clifton, of Perth, W Australia, and *d* 1972, leaving:
1b +Jeremy Clifton Gurney; *b* 26 Aug 1952; *educ* Ch Ch GS Perth and U of W Australia (BA, MA)
1a Valerie Isabel; *d* May 1934
2a Daphne, MBE (1974); *m* 10 Oct 1929 Capt Russell Thomas Harmer, late RE (*d* 31 Oct 1940), son of Sir Sidney Harmer, KBE, FRS, of The Old Manor Ho, Melbourn, nr Royston, and had issue:
1b Thomas Edward; *b* 4 June 1932; *educ* Uppingham and Magdalene Coll Cambridge (BA 1955); *m* 5 Nov 1960 *Ruth Macmillan, dau of David L Walker, of Aylsham, Norfolk, and has issue:
1c *Charles Russell; *b* 16 Jan 1962
2c *Edward David; *b* 6 June 1967
3c *Nicholas John; *b* 1974
1c *Mary Elizabeth; *b* 6 Sept 1963; *m* 1989 *Neil Fraser Robertson
2c *Ann Catherine; *b* 23 Oct 1965
2b *Daniel Sidney; *b* 15 Oct 1936; *educ* Uppingham; *m* 17 Aug 1962 (*divorce* 1980) Jacqueline Erwin, yst dau of R J Moore, of Halifax, NS, and has had issue:
1c *Stephen Russell; *b* 20 Nov 1963
2c Philip Reginald; *b* 6 Oct 1965; *d* 15 Feb 1966
3c *Colin John; *b* Dec 1966
1b *Jean Laura; *b* 15 Nov 1930; *m* 11 April 1953 *David Ian Hird, er son of W F Hird, of Canford Cliffs, Bournemouth, and has issue:
1c *Alison Daphne; *b* 12 April 1954; *m* 1980 *Edward Evans
2c *Claire Laura; *b* 27 May 1955; *m* 1978 *Peter Pearson
3c *Isobel Rosalie; *b* 23 June 1957; *m* 1981 *Nigel Cooper
4c *Vivien Anne; *b* 25 Feb 1959; *m* 1984 *Ian Plummer
5c *Penelope; *b* 13 Oct 1961; *m* 1982 *John White
3a Phyllis; *b* 12 Feb 1907; *m* 22 April 1931 Lt-Col Cecil Townley MITFORD later MITFORD-SLADE (deed poll 1941) (*d* 13 Aug 1986), Ld Lt Somerset 1968 (*d* 1985), 2nd s of Col William Kenyon Mitford, CMG, of Pitshill, Petworth, Sussex, and *d* 26 April 1985, leaving:
1b *Anthony Cecil Wyndham, Maj SCLI [Maj Anthony Mitford-Slade, Montys Court, Norton Fitzwarren, Taunton, Somerset]; *b* 13 March 1932; *educ* Eton and RMC Sandhurst; *m* 9 May 1959 *Mary Dawn Rogers, and has issue:
1c *Christopher Neave; *b* 2 June 1962
2c *Richard Cecil; *b* 27 July 1965;m 199– *Fiona Pearson
3c *Timothy Clive; *b* 9 March 1976
1c *Rosemary Anne; *b* 25 Feb 1960; *m* 1992 *Michael Vacher, RA, and has issue
2b *Patrick Buxton; *b* 7 Sept 1936; *educ* Eton and RMA Sandhurst; *m* 7 March 1964 *Anne Catharine, est dau of Arthur Holbrow Stanton, MBE, TD, of Hatfield Peverel, Essex, and has:
1c *James Patrick; *b* 30 Aug 1973
1c *Nicola Claire; *b* 24 May 1967; *m* 1995 *Michael Rollason
2c *Fiona Dawn; *b* 27 Dec 1970
1b *Carolyn Noel [Mrs Peter Moore, Wheddons Farmhouse, Bagborough, Taunton, Somerset]; *b* 11 Dec 1949; *m* 9 July 1978 *Peter Alec Charles Moore and has:
1c *Alice Hermione; *b* 13 Nov 1987
4a Enid Laura; *m* 3 July 1937 Laurence Frederick York (*d* 13 May 1967), yr s of Col Edward York, TD, DL, JP, of Hutton Hall, York, and had issue:
1b *Sonia Elisabeth [Mrs John Coode-Adams, Feeringbury Manor, Feering, Essex]; *b* 24 Aug 1940; *m* 30 April 1960 *John Giles Selby Coode-Adams, only s of Geoffrey Coode-Adams, of Little Sampford Grange, Saffron Walden, Essex, and has issue (*see* WIMBORNE, V)
2b *Bridget Laura [Mrs William Stevenson, 2 Flanchford Rd, London W12]; *b* 28 Sept 1944; *m* 31 May 1969 *William Stevenson, est son of Arthur John Stevenson, and has issue
3b *Katherine Diana; *b* 24 Feb 1947
5a Monica [Mrs Monica Calvert, Picts House, Horsham, Sussex]; *b* 1916; *m* 22 April 1937 *Maj Robert Henry Calvert, Middx Yeo, yr s of Lt-Col Charles Archibald Calvert, DSO, DL, JP (*see* CHOLMELEY, Bt) and has had:
1b *(Monica) Julia; *b* 3 Feb 1939; *educ* Benenden; *m* 1st 23 June 1964 Maj John Dominic Morrogh Bernard, Irish Gds (*d* as result of a skiing accident Austria 11 March 1968), est son of Lt-Col Joseph Morrogh Bernard, of Fair Oak Lodge, Fair Oak, Hants, and has issue:
1c *Alexander Dominic Calvert; *b* 22 Aug 1966
1c *Katherine Mary; *b* 29 March 1965; *m* 1994 *Keith Bryant
1b (cont.) Mrs John Morrogh Bernard *m* 2nd 16 June 1969 *Maj Sir Shane Blewitt, KCVO, IG, son of Col Basil Blewitt, of Cathay Cottage, Willaston, Cheshire, and has further issue:
2c *Piers Shane Basil Calvert; *b* 1972
2c *Davina Henrietta; *b* 1970; jnlst on 'Londoner's Diary' *Evening Standard*
2b *Diana; *b* 7 Oct 1941; *m* *Richard Makepeace Martineau
3b *Patricia Rohays; *b* 19 Oct 1943; *m* 19 Oct 1968 *Michael Charles Richardson, CA, er son of S/Ldr Douglas Courtenay Richardson, of Cleverly's Farm, W Meon, Hants, and has issue
4b Richenda Henrietta; *b* 5 Aug 1946; *d* 2 Oct 1947
5b *Georgina Sophia; *b* 23 Aug 1949; *m* 1973 *John Richard Hill Moore, and has issue
6a *Louise Jacinth; *m* 9 April 1946 *Benjamin Whittaker, son of Benjamin Whittaker, of Ashton Old Rd, nr Openshaw, Manchester, and has issue:
1b *Edward Benjamin Buxton; *b* 4 Jan 1948; *educ* King Edward VI GS Bury St Edmunds and Chelsea Sch of Art
2b *Nigel Buxton; *b* 20 Sept 1950; *educ* King Edward VI GS Bury St Edmunds and CCAT
3b *Clive Buxton; *b* 16 May 1953; *educ* Ipswich Sch
(2) Harry Gurney, DL Norfolk, T/Capt 9th Bn Norfolk Regt, BA Trin Coll Cambridge, served Boer War 1900–01 and WW I; *b* 23 June 1871; *m* 30 April 1910 Evelyn Musgrave (*d* 24 Dec 1953), dau of Richard Musgrave Harvey, and *d* 6 Aug 1936, leaving issue:
1a *Grizell Evelyn, Jr Cdr ATS WW II; *b* 18 July 1919; *m* 4 Sept 1946 Ven Edwin James Greenfield Ward, MVO, MA, Archdeacon of Sherborne, Chaplain to HM THE QUEEN 1955, er son of Rev Frederick Greenfield Ward, MC, of N Elmham, Norfolk, and has issue:
1b *Simon Andrew Buxton; *b* 11 June 1952; *educ* Marlborough
1b *Joanna Grizelda; *b* 6 Oct 1947
2b *Alison Bridget; *b* 25 Jan 1950; *m* 1985, as his 2nd w, *Baron Wakeham (*qv*)
(3) Lionel Gurney, MVO (1905), MC, Maj RA, DAA and QMG 1917, Boer War 1901–02 and WW I (despatches, Legion of Honour); *b* 6 Sept 1876; *educ* Harrow and Trin Coll Cambridge; *d* unm 25 April 1962
(1) Margaret Caroline; *m* 13 Dec 1888 Richard Gurney Hoare, 2nd s of Francis Hoare, of Weylands, Cromer, Norfolk (*see* 1959 edn TEMPLEWOOD, V), and *d* 26 July 1943, leaving issue. He *d* 23 Feb 1945
(2) Anna Mildred; *m* 4 Sept 1889 Lt-Col William Douglas Whatman, CMG, late 20th Hus, of Beech Ho, Sturminster Newton, Dorset, yr s of William Godfrey Whatman, of Kitlands, Holmwood, Surrey, and *d* 29 March 1934. He *d* 28 June 1929
(3) Isabel Louisa; *m* 28 Aug 1894 Capt Edward Hay Gurney, of Stone Lodge, Ipswich, and *d* 21 April 1962 aged 92, leaving issue. He *d* 25 July 1935
(4) Victoria Catherine Audrey; *d* unm 1 Jan 1952
(5) Carolyn Gurney; *d* unm 30 July 1936
2 (cont.) Samuel Buxton *m* 2nd 7 June 1886 Mary Anne (*d* April 1938), est dau of Henry Birkbeck, JP, of Stoke Holy Cross, Norfolk, and *d* 12 Feb 1909, having by her had issue:

(4) Richard Gurney, Capt Norfolk Yeo, JP (Norfolk); *b* 1887; *educ* Eton and Trin Coll Cambridge; *m* 16 July 1914 Mary Primrose (*d* 1972), dau of Maj Antonio Stephen Ralli (*see* RALLI, Bt), and *d* 1972, leaving:

1a *Pamela Chloë [Mrs Michael MacCarthy, Wiveton Hall, Holt, Norfolk]; *b* 1915; *m* 24 May 1948 Michael Desmond MacCarthy (*d* 1973), er s of Sir Desmond MacCarthy (*see* SALISBURY, M), of Garrick's Villas, Hampton, Middx, and has:

1b *Desmond James; *b* 1 Oct 1956; *m* 1993 *Hon Christina Anne Loder, dau of 3rd Baron Wakehurst (*qv*); and has:

1c *Edmund Michael; *b* 1 Sept 1995

1c *Isabel Inge; *b* 22 Nov 1997

1b *Mary Lisa; *b* 1950

2a *Marian Camilla; *b* 1919; *m* 18 Dec 1946 *Maj Richard Peyton, late RHA, and has issue:

1b *Robin Derek; *b* 25 Jan 1950

2b *Nigel Richard; *b* 23 Oct 1951

(6) Minna Alice; *m* 17 Nov 1914 Maj Arthur Thomas MacMorrough Kavanagh, MC, late 7th Hus, of Borris, Co Carlow, and had issue. He *d* 9 Dec 1953

3 Edward North, of Knighton, Buckhurst Hill, Essex, DL, JP, chm of London Sch Bd 1881–85, MP Walthamstow 1885–86, CA and Chm QS Essex, High Sheriff 1889; *b* 1 Sept 1840; *m* 23 Jan 1862 Emily (*d* 26 Oct 1929), yst dau of Rev Hon Kenelm Henry Digby (*see* DIGBY, B), and *d* 9 Jan 1924, having had, with other issue:

(1) Gerald, JP Essex; *b* 30 Oct 1862; *educ* Trin Coll Cambridge (BA); *m* 3 Dec 1890 Lucy Ethel, OBE (1918) (*d* 24 July 1940), dau of Sir Joseph Pease, 1st Bt, of Hutton Lowcross (*qv*), and *d* 2 March 1928, having had, with other issue:

1a Edward North, MC, DL, JP Essex, High Sheriff 1934, Lt Col RA (TAR) WW I (despatches), WW II, Verderer Epping Forest; *b* 7 Feb 1894; *educ* Harrow and Trin Coll Cambridge (BA); *m* 1st 6 June 1924 Hon Sibyl O'Neill, MBE (*d* 26 July 1946), est dau of Hon Arthur O'Neill (*see* O'NEILL, B); *m* 2nd 21 July 1951 *Daphne Rosemary, only child of Lt Henry Noel Munro, RNVR, of Rushall, Norfolk, and *d* 10 Sept 1957, having had issue by his 1st w:

1b +Mark Gerald Edward North [Mark Buxton Esq, Coffyns, Spreyton, Crediton, Devon], Verderer Epping Forest 1962–67; *b* 30 April 1929; *educ* Harrow and Trin Coll Cambridge (BA 1952); *m* 19 July 1962 *Leucha Daphne Mary, yr dau of Col Sir Edward Courtenay Thomas Warner, 2nd Bt (*qv*), and has issue:

1c +Edward North; *b* 10 April 1963; *educ* Harrow and Edinburgh U (BSc 1985); *m* 1992 *Fiona Helen, er dau of E Nicholas Shaw, of Sheriffston, Elgin, Moray, and has:

1d +Nicholas Edward North; *b* 17 Dec 1996

2c +Terence Mark; *b* 25 May 1965

1b *Morna Annabel; *b* 19 Jan 1926; *m* 3 Feb 1951 Clive Ernest Arkle, MB, ChB (*d* 1991), yst son of Dr Alexander Septimus Arkle, of Marfield, W Derby, Liverpool, and has:

1c *Alexander Edward Buxton; *b* 9 March 1953; *educ* Shrewsbury

2c *Alwyn Gerald Buxton; *b* 10 Nov 1957

1c *Bridget Ayliffe Buxton; *b* 20 Sept 1955

2c *Anne Daphne Buxton; *b* 7 March 1959; *m* 1988 *Stephen Derek Pitts

1a Blanche Emily, ARRC, OStJ; *b* 15 Nov 1891

2a Rebekah Mary; *b* 21 Jan 1900; *m* 15 Dec 1921 Col Sir Ralph Stephenson Clarke, KBE, TD, DL, MA, MP E Grinstead Div 1936–55, est son of Col Stephenson Clarke, CB, of Borde Hill, Haywards Heath, Sussex, and had issue:

1b *Robert Nunn Stephenson, RNVR WW II; *b* 17 April 1925; *educ* Eton; *m* 23 April 1940 (*divorce* 1967) Juana Nidia Gereth, only dau of Lt-Col John Bickersteth-Wheeler, MC, 15th Hus, and has issue:

1c *Ralph Roland Bickersteth Stephenson; *b* 7 Aug 1953

2c *Andrew John Patrick Stephenson; *b* 26 Nov 1955

1c *Marylynn Jane Stephenson; *b* 5 July 1950

2b *Simon Edward Stephenson; *b* 5 Sept 1926; *educ* Eton; *m* 21 Oct 1952 *Jill Maureen, er dau of Harry Vos, of Kenwards, Lindfield, Sussex, and has issue:

1c *Christopher Stephenson; *b* 7 Dec 1954

2c *Rupert Stephenson; *b* 20 Nov 1959

1c *Caroline Stephenson; *b* 19 Sept 1956

2c *Alison Stephenson; *b* 8 Nov 1957

1b Anne Stephenson; *b* 1 March 1923; *d* unm 13 Oct 1967

(2) Anthony, DSO (1916), DL (1920), JP (Essex 1913), JP (Norfolk 1934), High Sheriff Norfolk 1945, Maj Essex Yeo WW I (despatches, wounded), OStJ; *b* 2 Sept 1881; *educ* Harrow and Trin Coll Cambridge (BA 1904); *m* 9 Feb 1926 Mary Philomena (*d* 16 March 1953), est dau of Hon Bernard Constable-Maxwell (*see* HERRIES OF TERREGLES, L), and *d* 1970, having had:

1a +John Joseph, DL (Norfolk 1989) [John Buxton Esq DL, Horsey Hall, Great Yarmouth, Suffolk], served in Roy Norfolk Regt 1946–48; *b* 9 Dec 1927; *educ* Ampleforth and Trin Coll Cambridge (BA 1951); *m* 11 Aug 1958 *Bridget, est dau of Charles de Bunsen, of 13 Porchester Terr, W2, and has issue:

1b +Robin Anthony; *b* 21 Feb 1963

1b *Jane Mary; *b* 10 June 1959; *m* 1986 *Timothy James Sheldon, yst son of Rev J G Sheldon and has issue

2b *Clare Margaret; *b* 9 Aug 1960; *m* 1993 *Theodore Thomas More Agnew (*see* AGNEW, Bt, of Gt Stanhope St)

3b *Caroline Mary; *b* 15 March 1965; *m* 1989 *Matthew Valentine Fleming and has issue (*see* BORTHWICK, Bt)

1a *Elizabeth Mary, JP (E Sussex 1965); *b* 16 Dec 1926; *m* 16 June 1951 *Michael Walter Bonn, son of Maj Walter Bonn, DSO, MC, of St Peters, Jersey, and has issue:

1b *Simon Michael Joseph; *b* 6 July 1953; *m* 1981 *Melissa Ann, dau of Lt-Col Daniel Patrick Cadoux-Hudson, and has issue

1b *Sara Mary Philomena; *b* 24 Aug 1952; *m* 1978 *Charles George Lacy Hulbert-Powell (*see* SAINT LEVAN, B)

2b *Mary Elizabeth; *b* 8 Aug 1956

3b *Theresa Mary; *b* 27 Feb 1959

2a *Jean Mary; *b* 29 April 1930; *m* 11 Feb 1956 *Christopher Richard Miles, er son of Maj Walter Harold Miles, MBE, of North Park Farm, Godstone, Surrey, and has issue (*see* GREENWELL, Bt)

3a *Judith Mary [Sister Mary Pia IBVM, 47 Fitzjohn's Ave, London NW3 6PG]; *b* 18 Dec 1932; nun

(1) Geraldine, twin with Gerald; *m* 21 Nov 1888 Francis Dent, barrister, 2nd son of John Dent, DL, JP, of Ribston Hall, Yorks, and *d* 30 Oct 1938, leaving issue. He *d* 11 Dec 1943

(2) Ella; *b* 17 Oct 1863; *d* unm 15 April 1945

(3) Hannah Maud, MBE (1920); *b* 23 March 1872; *m* 25 Jan 1900 Francis Hubert Barclay, of The Warren, Cromer, and *d* 19 Dec 1931, leaving issue. He *d* 28 Jan 1935

(4) Clare Emily, JP Essex; *b* 28 March 1873; *m* 9 April 1918 John Gurney Richard Pelly, of Theydon Place, Essex (*see* PELLY, Bt), and *dsp* 2 July 1959

(5) Theresa; *b* 17 May 1874; *d* unm 27 April 1961

4 Henry Edmund, VD, of Fritton Hall, Gt Yarmouth, JP (Norfolk and Suffolk), MA Cambridge, Hon Col 2nd Vol Bn Norfolk Regt, Mayor of Gt Yarmouth 1896, High Sheriff of Suffolk 1902; *b* 22 Jan 1844; *m* 16 Oct 1867 Mary Rosalind (*d* 4 July 1918), only dau of Rev Abbot Upcher, of Kirby Cane, Norfolk, and *d* 2 Nov 1905, leaving, with other issue:

(1) Abbot Redmond, of Fritton Hall, Gt Yarmouth, Maj Norfolk Yeo, Hon Capt Army, Boer War 1900–01, WW I; *b* 31 Aug 1868; *d* unm 7 March 1944

(2) Edward Hugh, Capt Suffolk Hus Yeo WW I, Order Crown Italy; *b* 27 Sept 1880; *d* unm 20 Nov 1955

(1) Winifred; *m* 28 Nov 1901 Col Arthur Charles Malleson Waterfield, MVO, late IA, of Attlebridge, Norwich, Norfolk, son of Col W G Waterfield, CSI, and *d* 21 Sept 1954, leaving issue. He *d* 25 Oct 1943

(2) Violet; *d* unm 3 Feb 1961, aged 89

(3) Rosalind Upcher; *m* 13 Sept 1911 Brig-Gen Philip Howell, CMG, 4th Hus, son of Lt-Col Horace Howell, and *d* 22 Sept 1968, aged 89, leaving issue. He was *ka* 7 Oct 1916

5 Charles Louis, Lt Norfolk Art Militia, JP and CC Buxton Div of Norfolk; *b* 1 Feb 1846; *educ* Trin Coll Cambridge (BA); *m* 3 July 1873 Maria (*d* 18 Aug 1830), 3rd dau of Rev Henry James Lee-Warner, of Thorpland Hall, Norfolk, and *d* 23 April 1906, leaving, with other issue:

(1) Walter Louis; JP Norfolk, Capt KO Norfolk Imp Yeo; *b* 6 May 1875; *educ* Trin Coll Cambridge (BA); *d* unm 4 Sept 1960

(1) Norah Louis; *b* 14 April 1874; *m* 22 Nov 1904 W Done Bushell, Inspr Local Govt Bd, and *d* 17 April 1907, leaving issue

(2) Amy Louis; *b* 18 Jan 1877; *d* 14 Oct 1937

(3) Melicent Louis; *b* 19 March 1883; *m* 16 Nov 1909 Gerald Anstruther Wathen, CIE, MA, yst son of William Hulbert Wathen, of Westerham, Kent, and had issue. He *d* 9 Aug 1958

6 Francis William, JP Co London and Hertford, MP Andover 1880–85, Public Wks Loan Commr 1893, memb London Sch Bd 1899–1904, MA Camb, barrister; *b* 5 Aug 1847; *m* 27 Feb 1872 Hon Mary Lawrence, OBE (1918) (*d* 21 Feb 1939), dau of 1st Baron Lawrence, GCB (*qv*), and *d* 14 Nov 1911, leaving issue:

(1) John Lawrence, CMG (1919), DSO (1916), Col 2nd Bn Rifle Bde, AAG, Aldershot 1929–30, Local Brig cmdg Troops Gibraltar 1930–31, Cdr 14th Gloucs and Worcs Inf Bde 1931–34, ADC to HM GEORGE V 1933–34, served Boer War 1899–1902 (severely wounded, despatches, two medals, six clasps) and WW I (despatches, Brevet Lt-Col), Equerry to HRH THE DUKE OF CONNAUGHT 1939–40; *b* 1 Dec 1877; *educ* Eton and Univ Coll Oxford; *m* 5 Feb 1916 Evelyne Elsye (*d* 19 Oct 1961), dau of Rev J W Rynd, and *d* 17 Jan 1951

(2) Hugh Forster, Lt Rifle Bde; *b* 9 April 1882; *m* 6 Sept 1904 Blanche Juliana (*d* 21 March 1907), 3rd dau of Maj W J St Aubyn, 24th Regt, and was *ka* 3 Nov 1916, having had:

1a Philip Olaf, JP (Oxon 1965), v-chm Witney RDC 1963 (chm 1965), with Kassala Cotton Co 1930–46; *b* 22 May 1906; *m* 15 Dec 1934 Ruth Christian, JP (*d* 1976), dau of Aubrey Trevor Lawrence, MBE, KC (*see* LAWRENCE, Bt, of Ealing Park), and *d* 1978, having had issue:

1b +Hugh Lawrence, JP [Hugh Buxton Esq JP, Widford Manor, Burford, Oxon OX18 4DU]; *b* 18 June 1936; *educ* Eton and Ch Ch Oxford; *m* 9 Oct 1965 *Elizabeth Caroline Tilden Whitelocke, only dau of Douglas Allan Abernethy, of Bampton, Oxon, and has issue:

1c +Guy Lawrence; *b* 1969

1c *Belinda Ruth; *b* 1967

2c *Anne Caroline; *b* 1975

1a Peggy; *b* 17 June 1905; *d* Nov 1905

(3) Robert Vere, DSO (1919), Sudan CS 1907–11, Capt W Kent Yeo, T/Lt-Col cmdg 2nd Bn Imp Camel Corps, served WW I (despatches twice), Order Nile, Crown of Italy; *b* 1883; *educ* Trin Coll Oxford (MA); *m* 31 Aug 1916 Irene Marguerite, dau of J H C Pix, of Bradford, widow of Sir Richard William Levinge, 10th Bt (*qv*), and *dsp* 1 Oct 1953

(1) Ruth; *m* 17 May 1898 6th Earl of Chichester (*qv*) and *d* 8 Feb 1965, leaving issue

(2) Madeline; *m* 26 March 1901 Lt-Gen Sir George Sidney Clive, GCVO, KCB, CMG, DSO, DL, JP, Hon FRAM, Gren Gds, of Perrystone Court, Herefs, and *d* 24 April 1957, leaving issue. He *d* 7 Oct 1959

(3) Hilda; *d* unm 28 Nov 1948

(4) Frances Mary, OBE (1919); *d* unm 13 Jan 1967

(5) Cecil; *m* 12 July 1906 Maj-Gen Guy Payan Dawnay, CB, CMG, DSO, MVO, Coldstream Gds and had issue (*see* DOWNE, V)

1 Laura Priscilla; *m* 30 July 1873 Prof Henry Francis Pelham, est s of Rt Rev Hon John Thomas Pelham, Bp of Norwich, and *d* 2 Nov 1918, having had issue (*see* CHICHESTER, E)

2 Sarah Evelyn; *m* 25 Aug 1881 Richard Hanbury Joseph Gurney, DL, JP, of Northrepps, Norfolk, and *d* 5 April 1926, leaving issue. He *d* 6 May 1899

Sir EDWARD *d* 11 June 1858; his est son,

Sir (Thomas) Fowell Buxton, 3rd Bt, GCMG, VD, DL and JP Norfolk and Essex, High Sheriff Norfolk 1876, Col 2nd Tower Hamlets RV 1864–83 and Hon Col 1884–1903, Govr and C-in-C S Australia 1895–98, MP Lyme Regis 1865–68; *educ* Trin Coll Cambridge (MA); *b* 26 Jan 1837; *m* 21 June 1862 Lady Victoria Noel (*d* 8 Aug 1916), yst dau of 1st Earl of Gainsborough (*qv*), and had issue:

1 THOMAS FOWELL VICTOR (Sir), **4th Bt**

2 NOEL EDWARD, *cr* BARON NOEL-BUXTON (*qv*)

3 Charles Roden, barrister, MP Ashburton 1910, Accrington 1922–23 and Elland 1929–31; *b* 27 Nov 1875; *educ* Trin Coll Cambridge (MA); *m* 11 Aug 1904 Dorothy Frances (*d* 8 April 1963), dau of Arthur Trevor Jebb, of The Lyth, Ellesmere, Salop, and *d* 16 Dec 1942, leaving issue:

(1) +David Roden, in service of Br Cncl 1946–67; *b* 26 Feb 1910; *educ* Trin Coll Cambridge (BA 1931, MA 1936); *m* 1st 24 Sept 1939 (*divorce* 1948) Annelore, dau of Arnold Gerstl, and has issue:

1a +Roden Arnold [Roden Buxton Esq, 15 Henleaze Gdns, Bristol BS9 4HH]; *b* 24 July 1942; *educ* St Christopher Sch and Trin Coll Cambridge (MA 1965); DArch, RIBA; *m* 1971 *Linda Jane, dau of Richard Miller, MRO, and has issue:

1b +Samuel Roden; *b* 1972

2b +Oliver Silas; *b* 1976

(1) (cont.) David Buxton *m* 2nd 9 Dec 1950 *Mary Violet, dau of Denis Alfred Jex Buxton (*see* above), and by her has:

2a +Charles Benedict; *b* 27 Aug 1958; *m* 1985 *Caroline Mavis Beadle and has issue:

1b +Toby Finbarr; *b* 1990

2b +Richard Ronan; *b* 1992

3b +Martin Patrick Mingulay; *b* 1994

3a +James Andrew Denis; *b* 5 May 1964

1a Elizabeth Eglantyne; *b* 13 Sept 1951; *m* 1976 *John Waterfield and *d* 1985

2a *Richenda Mary; *b* 14 Jan 1953; *m* 1987 *Michael Desmond Tennyson Barley, and has issue

3a *Francesca; *b* 3 March 1956

(1) Eglantyne Roden; *b* 4 Aug 1906; *educ* Somerville Coll Oxford (MA)

4 Harold Jocelyn (Rt Rev), Vicar of Horley, Oxon 1914–18, Sec Ld Mayor's Armenian Relief Fund 1918–26, Chaplain St George's Cathedral Jerusalem 1926–27 and St Paul's Nicosia 1927–31, Archdeacon Cyprus 1928–33, Bp Gibraltar 1933–47, Rector Lauton 1949–53, Sub-Prelate OStJ, 1st Cl Order Star Romania, Order St Sava Yugoslavia and George I of Greeece; *b* 20 June 1880; *educ* Harrow and Trin Coll Cambridge (BA 1901, MA 1905)

5 Leland William Wilberforce, JP Essex, barrister Inner Temple 1914, Egyptian CS 1907–09, Priv Sec to Govr Br Guiana 1909, S African Def Force and temp Staff Capt Hejaz Operations, Order Star Ethopia, served WW I; *b* 3 July 1884; *educ* Harrow and Trin Coll Cambridge (BA 1905, MA 1911); *m* 9 April 1912 Ada Mary (*d* 1979), est dau of Rev Thomas Henry Royal Oakes, BD, and *d* 12 March 1967, leaving issue

(1) +Julian Wilberforce, TD, Maj RA (TA) WW II; *b* 20 Aug 1913; *educ* Ampleforth and Trin Coll Cambridge (BA 1934); *m* 18 Dec 1939 (*divorce* 1948) Maria Iseult, only child of Walter Frederick Dunsterville, of Lushill, Stock, Essex

(2) +AUBREY LELAND OAKES BUXTON, *cr* BARON BUXTON OF ALSA (*qv*)

(1) *Diana Elizabeth; *b* 20 Nov 1915; *m* 27 March 1939 *Cdr Adrian James Dent, RN, CEng, FIEE, yst s of Sir Francis Henry Dent, CVO, and has issue:

1a *Simon Adrian Noel; *b* 10 July 1949; *educ* Winchester and Mozarteum Akademia Salzburg; *m* 1972 (*divorce* 1985) Brigitte Englehart and has issue

2a *Jeremy Francis; *b* 24 Jan 1951; *educ* Bradfield; *m* 1971 (*divorce* 1988) Penelope Linton, and has issue

1a *Henrietta Gladys; *b* 17 March 1940; *m* 25 May 1963 (*divorce* 1989) Simon Aldan Reynolds, s of Lt-Col Guy Franklin Reynolds, MC, 9th Lancers, of Penpergwm Lodge, Abergavenny, Mon, and has issue

2a *Janet Sylvia; *b* 28 March 1947; *m* 1976 *Maj Michael Robjohn, MBE, Roy Irish Rangers, and has issue

(2) *Mary Judith, ATS WW II; *b* 29 April 1922; *m* 1st 6 June 1942 Lt Philip Arthur Leo Gompertz, RA (*kas* 19 Aug 1942), yr s of Lt-Col A V Gompertz, MC, RE, of Barton-on-Sea, Hants; *m* 2nd 18 Aug 1945 *Maj Clement Wynter Lister, RA, yr son of Edmund Lister, and has issue:

1a Patrick Thomas Buxton; *b* 7 Aug 1948; *d* 1989

1a *Philippa Judith; *b* 31 May 1946; *m* 1971 (*divorce* 1980) David John Lloyd Watkins, MA

1 Edith Frances; *b* 30 Aug 1867; *m* 23 Nov 1888 7th Lord Polwarth (*qv*) and *d* 25 March 1930, leaving issue

2 Mary Catherine; *b* 29 July 1870; *m* 27 Nov 1889 Rev Stewart Gordon Ponsonby, MA Trin Coll Cambridge, Rector of St Mary-le-Bow, Cheapside, Hon CF 1st Cl, Preb and Chllr of Exeter Cathedral, s of Capt Charles Ponsonby, IA, and *d* 6 Jan 1960, leaving issue. He *d* 11 July 1938

3 Constance Victoria; *b* 5 June 1872; *m* 23 July 1896 Bertram Robert Hawker, and *d* 22 Sept 1957, leaving issue. He *d* 1952

4 Victoria Alexandrina; *b* 5 Jan 1874; *m* 25 June 1904 Lothar Henry George de Bunsen, and *d* 30 May 1953, leaving issue. He *d* 16 Feb 1950

5 Mabel Frances Evelyn; *b* 29 Jan 1878; *m* 21 Dec 1920 Maj William Morse Crowdy, MA Oxford, barrister, late Devonshire Regt, s of Alfred Southby Crowdy, of Tor Newton Ho, Denbury, Devon, and *d* 25 Oct 1966, leaving issue. He *d* 1949

Sir FOWELL *d* 28 Oct 1915; his est son,

Sir (Thomas Fowell) Victor Buxton, 4th Bt, JP Essex; *b* 8 April 1865; *educ* Trin Coll Cambridge (MA); High Sheriff 1905, T/Maj 2nd Bn Essex Vol Regt; *m* 10 Oct 1888 Anne Louisa Matilda (*d* 12 Jan 1956), 2nd dau of Rev Henry Thomas O'Rorke, MA, Rector of Feltwell, and *d* 31 May 1919, having had:

1 **Sir Thomas Fowell Buxton, 5th Bt**; *educ* Trin Coll Cambridge (MA), barrister Inner Temple, DL, JP Essex, High Sheriff 1928, Lt Essex Yeo WW I (despatches); *b* 8 Nov 1889; *m* 1st 21 July 1923 Hon Dorothy Agnes Cochrane (*d* 17 Sept 1927), yr dau of 1st Baron Cochrane of Cults (*qv*); *m* 2nd 10 Nov 1931 Eva Katharine, dau of Edward Balfour of Balbirnie, and *d* 28 Oct 1945, having by his 1st w had issue:

(1) **Sir Thomas Fowell Victor Buxton, 6th Bt**; *b* 18 Aug 1925; *educ* Eton and Trin Coll Cambridge; Scots Gds 1943–48; *m* 6 July 1955 Mrs Doris Mary Chisenhale-Marsh (*d* 28 Jan 1965), dau of Peter Randall Johnson, of 14 Warwick Sq, SW1, and formerly w of Maj Hugo Atherton Chisenhale-Marsh, and *d* 14 Nov 1996

(1) *Montagu Lucy [Mrs John Rose, Eveleghs, High St, Long Wittenham, nr Abingdon, Oxon OX14 4QH]; *b* 28 Aug 1927; *m* 29 May 1965 John Harold Rose (*d* 24 Oct 1996), s of H V Rose, of St George's Close, Jerusalem

2 Roden Henry Victor, CBE (1942), Capt RN, served WW I and WW II, 3rd Cl Order Polonia Restituta; *b* 17 Dec 1890; *m* 1st 7 Dec 1917 Dorothy Alina (*d* 11 Dec 1956), dau of Col Charles William Peter St John, late RE, and had issue:

(1) Sir JOCELYN CHARLES RODEN BUXTON, **7th and present Bt**

(2) +GERARD ST JOHN RODEN [Lt-Cdr Gerard Buxton RN, Pitteadie House, by Kirkcaldy, Fife KY2 5UN]; *b* 28 Sept 1927; heir presumptive; Lt-Cdr RN WW II; *m* 16 Dec 1954 *Judith Averil, est dau of Hon Angus Dudley Campbell, CBE, JP, of Doddington Cottage, Nantwich, Cheshire (*see* COLGRAIN, B), and has issue:

1a +Crispin Charles Gerard; *b* 29 March 1958

1a *Charlotte Anne Gerard; *b* 25 Sept 1955; *m* 1981 *Sardar Mandhir Singh Sethi, and has issue

2a *Laura Joan Gerard; *b* 31 Oct 1961

(1) Victoria Lilian Roden, WRNS WW II; *b* 25 Oct 1919; *m* 1st 1 May 1943 (*divorce* 1951) Cdr Arthur Walter Beeton, RIN, only s of A H Beeton, of Spilsby, Lincs, and had:

1a *Dorothy Anna; *b* 24 Jan 1947; *educ* Bristol U (BA); *m* 16 July 1966 *John Saunsbury, BSc, s of Dr Saunsbury, of Lichfield, Staffs, and has issue:

1b *Mark David; *b* 24 Nov 1966

1b *Laura Rebecca; *b* 21 Sept 1968

(1) Mrs Victoria Beeton *m* 2nd 15 July 1955 Aribert H W R A von Vollmar auf Veltheim, son of Mrs Elisabeth Grimble, and had further issue:

1a *Rudolf Jocelyn Heinrich William Oscar; *b* 20 March 1956

(2) *Anne Francis Roden; *b* 7 Dec 1920; *m* 1st 8 May 1945 (*divorce* 1978) Hans Henry Winterstein Gillespie, MD, son of Prof Hans Winterstein von Bronneck, of Munich; *m* 2nd 1979 *Hon Thomas Heron Hazlerigg (*see* HAZLERIGG, B), and has issue by 1st husb:

1a *Nicola Henrietta St John; *b* 22 Feb 1946; *m* 1st 20 Feb 1965 (*divorce*) Charles Rupert Raw, son of Rupert Raw, of 12 Cadogan Sq, SW1, *m* 2nd 1975 *John Latimer Smith, and has issue by 2nd husb

2a *Richenda Antoinette de Winterstein; *b* 30 March 1949

(3) *Elisabeth Lucy Roden; *b* 15 April 1922; *m* 30 July 1951 Maj Thomas Arnett Hughes-Ross, MBE, RCT (*d* 1981), son of G T Hughes, of Ferryhill, Darlington, and has:

1a *Timothy Arnett Ross; *b* 19 March 1954; *m* 1985 *Sally Ann Roe, and has issue

1a *Joanna Elisabeth Ross; *b* 20 March 1952; *m* *Anver Jamal Rizvi, and has issue

2a *Penelope Jane Ross; *b* 19 May 1956

(4) *Phyllida Dorothy Roden; *b* 9 July 1932; *m* 20 June 1959 +Ronald Carlile Buxton, only son of Capt Murray Barclay Buxton, MC, MA, and has issue (*see* above)

2 (cont.) Capt Roden Buxton *m* 2nd 2 Nov 1957 *Hilda, MBE (1956), dau of Charles Alfred Meadows, of Rainham, Kent

3 Clarence Edward Victor, MC, Maj RFA (SR) WW I (despatches); *b* 14 Jan 1892; *educ* Eton and Trin Coll Cambridge (MA); *m* 1st 13 Dec 1917 (*divorce*) Mary Aline, MBE (*d* 8 June 1954), est dau of Lt-Col Frederick Ewart Bradshaw, DSO, s of Sir Alexander Frederick Bradshaw, KCB, and *d* 1967, leaving:

(1) +Maurice [Maurice Buxton Esq, 4 Westmoreland Place, London SW1V 4AD], Capt Coldstream Gds WW II; *b* 28 Sept 1919; *educ* Eton; *m* 10 May 1941 (*divorce* 1978) Mary Alison Lydall, yst dau of Laurence Lydall Savill, of Camenden Manor, Cranbrook, Kent; *m* 2nd 1979 *Susan Whiteway, dau of A H Alexander, of Halifax, NS

(2) Rupert, Lt RNVR WW II; *b* 3 Aug 1923; *educ* Eton and Trin Coll Cambridge; *m* 12 Feb 1949 (*divorce*) Frances Ann, yst dau of Prof Frank Debenham, OBE, MA, DSc, of 19 Millington Rd, Cambridge, and had issue:

1a +Jonathan; *b* 27 Feb 1950

2a Terence Rupert; *b* 16 July 1952

3a +Paul Stephen; *b* 21 Aug 1954

4a +Colin; *b* 1957

(2) (cont.) Rupert Buxton *m* 2nd 1972 *Betty Webb, of S Africa, and *d* 1994, leaving further issue:

1a *Sarah Jane; *b* 1976

(1) *Gwendolen; *b* 28 March 1921; *m* 10 Dec 1960 Terence Leland Bowles (*d* 21 Sept 1968), s of Henry Branson Bowles, of 68 Kingsbury Rd, Erdington, Birmingham 24, and has issue:

1a *Katherine; *b* 25 Feb 1963

(2) *Rosemary; *b* 9 March 1927; *m* 10 Sept 1955 *Francis Henry Alastair Julian Lochrane , er s of Charles Damien Lochrane, MD, FRCS (E), FRCOG, of Ach-na-Greine, Nairn, Scotland

3 (cont.) Maj Clarence Buxton *m* 2nd 1945 *Mavis Jean, est dau of Walter Sydney Bromhead and formerly w of Maurice Fox, and *d* 10 Oct 1967, having by her had issue:

(3) *Rowena Clarence; *b* 25 May 1945; *m* 1st 1970 (*divorce* 1978) Colin Woods; *m* 2nd 1984 *Fredrik Louis Tauber

(4) *Rosalind Clarence; *b* 21 July 1946; *m* 1974 *Peter Ray Nightingale, and has issue

4 Jocelyn Murray Victor, 2nd Lt The Rifle Bde; *b* 1 April 1896; *ka* 1 July 1916

5 Maurice Victor, MC (1919), Lt Coldstream Gds; *b* 22 Oct 1898; *d* 8 Aug 1919
6 Rupert Erroll Victor; *b* 10 May 1900; *d* 19 May 1921
1 Lucy Victoria; *b* 20 April 1893; *m* 9 May 1922 Rev Sir Charles Henry Bentinck, KCMG, 2nd son of 5th Count Bentinck (*see* PORTLAND, E)

BUXTON OF ALSA

Arms: Argent a lion rampant, the tail elevated and turned over the head, between two mullets in fess sable. **Crest:** A stag's head couped gules, attired or, gorged with a collar of the last, pendant therefrom an escutcheon argent charged with a negro's head, couped at the shoulders in profile proper. **Supporters:** Dexter, a crowned crane (*balearica pavonina*); sinister, a flamingo proper. **Motto:** Do it with thy might. **Creation:** B. (LP, UK) 1978.

THE BARON BUXTON OF ALSA, of Stiffkey, Co Norfolk (Aubrey Leland Oakes Buxton, KCVO (1996) MC (1943), DL (Essex 1975–85)) [The Rt Hon The Lord Buxton of Alsa KCVO MC DL, Old Hall Farm, Stiffkey, Norfolk NR23 1QJ]; *b* 15 July 1918; *educ* Ampleforth and Trin Coll Cambridge; WWII RA (despatches 1944); Dir Anglia TV 1958–88 (Chm 1986–88, Ch Exec); Extra Equerry to HRH THE DUKE OF EDINBURGH 1964–; Br V-Pres World Wildlife Fund 1968–; Memb: Countryside Commn 1968–72, Roy Commn on Environmental Pollution 1970–74; Tstee: Br Mus Nat Hist 1971–73, Wildfowl Trust; High Sheriff Essex 1972; Pres Roy Television Soc 1973–77; Treas London Zoological Soc 1978–83; Chm: Ind TV Cos Assoc 1972–73, Chm UPITN Inc USA 1981–83, ITN 1981–86, Survival Anglia 1986–91; author: *The Birds of Arakan* (with Sir Philip Christison, 1946), *The King in his Country* (1955); *m* 1st 1946 Pamela Mary (*d* 1983), dau of Sir Henry Ralph Stanley Birkin, 3rd Bt (*qv*), and widow of Maj Samuel Luclyn Buxton, MC, 17th/21st Lancers (*see* BUXTON, Bt), and has issue:

1 *Timothy Leland [The Hon Timothy Buxton, The Dairy, Castle Howard, Yorks YO4 7BY]; *b* 1948; *educ* Ampleforth; *m* 1st 1972 (*divorce* 1986) Julie Mary, dau of Lt-Cdr (John) Michael Avison Parker, CVO, and has issue:
(1) *Edward Leland; *b* 1976
(1) *Alexandra (Zanna) Louise; *b* 1973; *m* 9 May 1998 *James Scrimgeour, s of Simon Scrimgeour, of Rozel, Jersey
1 (cont.) The Hon Timothy Buxton *m* 2nd 1994 *Mrs Amanda Dickinson, dau of A/Cdre Anthony Walkinshaw Fraser
2 *(Aubrey) James Francis [The Hon James Buxton, Church Farm, Carlton, Suffolk]; *b* 1956; *educ* Ampleforth and RAC Cirencester; *m* 1981 *Melinda, dau of Peter Henry Samuelson, of Ugley Hall, Ugley, Essex, and has issue:
(1) *Henry James Aubrey; *b* 1988
(1) *Emma Lucie Maria; *b* 1984
(2) *Olivia Louise; *b* 1986
1 *Nicola Mary Caroline [The Hon Mrs Sykes, Cook's Mill, Fordham Heath, Essex CO3 5TF]; *b* 1947; *m* 1970 *Adrian William Guy Sykes and has had:
(1) *Samuel Adrian Aubrey; *b* 1974
(1) *Eleanor Mary Fiona; *b* 1972
(2) *Miranda Pamma Lucinda; *b* 1982
(3) Daisy Maria Hester; *b* and *d* 1985
(4) *Pandora India Nicola; *b* 1987
2 *Lucinda (Cindy) Catherine [The Hon Lucinda Buxton, The Old House, Langham, Holt, Norfolk]; *b* 1950; wildlife photographer; FRGS
3 *Veronica Frances [The Hon Mrs Williams-Wynne, Talybont, Tywyn, Gwynedd]; *b* 1953; *m* 1975 *William Robert Charles Williams-Wynne and has issue (*see* WILLIAMS-WYNN, Bt)
4 *Victoria Jane; *b* 1960

The BARON BUXTON *m* 2nd 1988 *Mrs Kathleen Peterson, of Maine, USA

Lineage: *See* BUXTON, Bt

BUZZARD

Arms: Per chevron az. and arg., in chief two covered cups of the second, and in base a rod of Æsculapius ppr. **Crest:** Rising from clouds an eagle ppr., gorged with an eastern crown or. **Motto:** *Esto quod esse videris* ('Be what you seem to be'). **Creation:** Bt. (UK) 25 June 1929.

SIR ANTHONY FARQUHAR BUZZARD, 3RD BT, of Munstead Grange, in the parish of Godalming, Co Surrey [Sir Anthony Buzzard Bt, 185 Summerville Drive, Brooks, GA 30205, USA]; *b* 28 June 1935; *s* f 1972; *educ* Charterhouse, Ch Ch Oxford (BA 1960, MA 1968), Ambassador Coll Pasadena Calif (BA 1963) and Bethany Theological Seminary (MA Th); ARCM, freelance educnl Consultant and Tutor, lecturer Atlanta Bible Coll, Ga., 1982–; *m* 1970 *Barbara Jean, dau of Gordon Earl Arnold, of Mendon, Michigan, and has issue:
1 *Sarah Jane; *b* 1971
2 *Claire Judith; *b* 1974
3 *Heather Elizabeth; *b* 1988

Lineage: GEORGE BUZZARD, of Grove End Rd, St John's Wood, London, had:
THOMAS BUZZARD, MD, FRCP, of 74 Grosvenor St, London; *b* 24 Aug 1831; *m* Sept 1869 Isabel (*d* 1 July 1901), dau of Joseph Wass, and *d* 1 Jan 1919, leaving, with two daus:
1 (EDWARD) FARQUHAR (Sir), **1st Bt**
2 Charles Norman, CMG (1919), DSO (1918), Lt-Col RA (ret), served WW I 1914–19, Chev Legion of Honour, Mil Order of Savoy and Order of Crown of Italy; *b* 29 April 1873; *m* 1st 11 Feb 1902 Isabel May D'Aguilar (*d* 1922), dau of Maj-Gen George D'Aguilar Jackson (*see* JACKSON, Bt, of Arlsey); *m* 2nd 19 Dec 1922 Baroness Elizabeth Wrangell, dau of Baron Hoyningen Huene of Nawwast and Petrograd, and *d* April 1961, leaving two daus
3 Frank Anstie, DSO (1917) and bar (1919), Brig-Gen RA WW I (despatches); *b* 9 Nov 1875; *m* 2 Aug 1911 Joan, 2nd dau of Hon John Collier (*see* MONKSWELL, B), and *d* 28 Feb 1950, leaving issue:
(1) John Huxley; *b* 12 Aug 1912; *educ* Wellington and New Coll Oxford; barrister Inner Temple 1937 (Master Bench 1965), RAFVR WW II (despatches), Recorder Gt Yarmouth 1958–68, Dover 1968–71, Circuit Judge Centl Criminal Court 1974; *m* 1946 Hilary Ann Courtney Antrobus and *d* 28 Jan 1984, having had issue
(2) Richard Bethune, BM, BCh, Dir Inst Industl Psychology; *m* 4 Aug 1948 *Hon Ann Sophia Madeline Whitfield, only dau of 1st Baron Kenswood (*qv*), and *d* 1980, having had:
1a *Nicholas John; *b* 10 March 1952
1a *Jacqueline Frances; *b* 10 May 1950
2a *Jennifer Ann; *b* 17 Feb 1954
3a *Angela Caroline; *b* 22 June 1956
4 Archibald Dougan, Capt late Norfolk Regt; *b* 13 June 1879; *d* 4 Nov 1945

THOMAS BUZZARD's est son,

Sir (Edward) Farquhar Buzzard, 1st Bt (UK), so *cr* 25 June 1929, KCVO (1927), MA, MD, BCh, FRCP, Hon LLD, Regius Prof Medicine Oxford, Hon Fell Magdalen Coll Oxford; Consultant Physician St Thomas's Hosp, Hon Col RAMC (TA), Physician Belgrave Hosp for Children, Roy Free Hosp and Nat Hosp Paralysed and Epileptic, Goulstonian Lecturer RCP 1907, Lettsomian Lecturer Medical Soc London 1926, Pres Neurological Section RSM 1924, Physician-in-Ordinary to TM GEORGE V 1932–36 and EDWARD VIII 1936, Extra Physician to HM GEORGE VI 1937, Pres BMA 1936–37; *b* 20 Dec 1871; *m* 21 March 1899 May (*d* 22 March 1951), dau of Edward Bliss, JP, and had issue:
1 ANTHONY WASS (Sir), **2nd Bt**
2 Edward Miller, MRCP 1937, FRCP 1949; *b* 13 March 1909; *educ* Charterhouse and Magdalen Coll Oxford; Physician Utd Oxford Hosps, Oxford Regnl Hosp Bd, Lecturer Medicine Oxford U, Examiner Medicine Oxford, Cambridge and London Us; *m* 11 Aug 1937 *Sylvia Bevan [Mrs Edward Buzzard, The Barn, Oakley Park, Frilford Heath, Abingdon, Oxon], yst dau of Dr John William Fordham, of Hughenden, Loughborough Rd, Leicester, and *d* 1976 having had issue:
(1) David Miller; *b* 16 Sept 1950; *educ* Rugby; *d* 1985

(1) *Sarah [Mrs Michael Gear, Samscotts, Sheepscombe, nr Stroud, Glos]; *b* 31 Aug 1941; *m* 1962 *Michael Leishman Gear, and has issue:

1a *Susan Anne Buzzard; *b* 1965

2a *Nicola Leishman; *b* 1967

(2) *Judy Miller [Mrs Sydney Scammell, 5 Courtfield, 1 Castlebar Hill, London W5]; *b* 26 June 1944; *m* 1968 *Sydney Guy Anthony Scammell and has:

1a *Anthony Charles Miller; *b* 1974

1a *Louise Jane; *b* 1975

(3) *Sylvia Anne [Mrs Rupert Bowen, 83 Montholme Rd, Battersea, London SW11 6HX]; *b* 28 July 1947; *m* 1973 *Rupert Grenside Bowen and has:

1a *Miranda Juanita; *b* 1975

2a *Henrietta Alice; *b* 1977

1 Margaret Helen; *m* 6 June 1925 Harold Gardiner-Hill, MBE, MD, FRCP, s of Dr Hugh Gardiner-Hill, of Wimbledon, and has issue

2 Sylvia Marian; *b* 1900

3 Isabel May; *b* 1910; *m* 10 Oct 1933 Cdr Herbert William Acworth, RN (*d* 1987), est son of William Acworth, of Little Donnystone, Chobham, Surrey, and has issue:

(1) *William Farquhar; *b* 1934; *m* 1964 *Susan Henrietta, yr dau of Capt Roddie Casement, OBE, RN (*see* GREENWELL, Bt), and has issue:

1a *William Bernard; *b* 1965; *m* 1993 *Julia Beale

2a *James Michael; *b* 1966

1a *Anna Claire; *b* 1970

(2) *Adam Buzzard; *b* 1943

(1) *Susan Esmé; *b* 1936

(2) *Jane Marion; *b* 1941

The 1st Bt *d* 17 Dec 1945; his er son,

Sir Anthony Wass Buzzard, 2nd Bt, CB (1953), DSO (1940), OBE (1941); *educ* RNCs Osborne and Dartmouth; served WW II (despatches), R-Adml 1941, Dir Naval Intell 1951–54; *b* 28 April 1902; *m* 2 April 1932 Margaret Elfreda (*d* 1989), only dau of Sir Arthur Rowland Knapp, KCIE, CSI, CBE, and *d* 1972, leaving:

1 Sir ANTHONY FARQUHAR BUZZARD, **3rd and present Bt**

2 +TIMOTHY MACDONNELL [Timothy Buzzard Esq, Kennel Cottage, Lindfield, Haywards Heath, Sussex RH16 2QN]; *b* 28 Jan 1939; heir presumptive; *educ* Michael Hall and RAM; GRSM, LRAM; *m* 1970 *Jennifer Mary, dau of Peter Patching, and has issue

(1) +Jonathan Mark; *b* 1977

(1) +Rachel Mary *b* 1974

1 *Gillian Margaret [Mrs William Blenkinsop, 46 Melrose Rd, London SW18 1LY]; *b* 3 Oct 1944; BSc; *m* 1979 *William John Oates Blenkinsop

BYFORD

Creation: B. (LP, UK) 21 Aug 1996.

THE BARONESS BYFORD, of Rothley, Co Leicester (Dame Hazel Byford, DBE (1994)) [The Rt Hon The Baroness Byford DBE, House of Lords, London SW1A 0PW]; *b* 14 Jan 1941; *educ* St Leonard's Sch St Andrews and Moulton Ag Coll Northampton; WRVS Leics 1961– (Co Organiser 1972–76), Chm Nat Ctee C Women 1990–93, Pres Nat Union C and U Assocs 1996–97 (V-Pres 1993–96); *m* 1962 *C Barrie Byford, CBE, and has a s and dau

Lineage: Sir CYRIL OSBORNE; MP; had:

HAZEL, *cr* a **Baroness**

BYRON

Arms: Arg. three bendlets enhanced gu. **Crest:** A mermaid with her comb and mirror, all ppr. **Supporters:** Two horses of a chestnut colour ppr., hoofs or. **Motto:** *Crede Byron* ('Trust Byron').
Creation: B. (E) 24 Oct 1643.

THE 13TH BARON BYRON OF ROCHDALE, Co Lancaster (Robert James Byron) [The Rt Hon The Lord Byron, Marlow House, Lloyds Ave, London EC3N 3AL]; *b* 5 April 1950; *s* f 1989; *educ* Wellington and Trin Coll Cambridge (MA); barrister Inner Temple 1974, slr 1978, ptnr Holman, Fenwick & Willan 1984–, Pres Byron Soc; *m* 1979 *Robyn Margaret, dau of John McLean, of Hamilton, NZ, and has issue:

1 +CHARLES RICHARD GORDON; *b* 28 July 1990

1 *Caroline Anne Victoria; *b* 1981

2 *Emily Clare; *b* 1984

3 *Sophie Georgina; *b* 1986

Lineage: Sir RICHARD BYRON, of Byron and Clayton, Lancs; had:

Sir JOHN BYRON, of Clayton; *m* Margery, dau of John Booth, of Barton, Lancs, and had, with at least one dau (Margaret, *m* Sir Robert Harcourt, KG; *see* VERNON, B):

Sir NICHOLAS BYRON; *m* Alice, dau of Sir John Butler, of Bewsey, Lancs, and had:

Sir NICHOLAS BYRON, of Clayton; *m* Jane, dau of Sir John Bussey, of Haugham, Lincs, and had:

Sir JOHN BYRON, of Clayton; acquired Newstead Abbey, Notts, at the Dissolution of the Monasteries; *m* as his 2nd w Elizabeth, dau of William Casterden, and had (*b* before their marriage):

JOHN BYRON, of Newstead and Popplewick, Notts; *m* Alice, dau of Sir Nicholas Strelley, of Strelley, Notts, and had:

Sir JOHN BYRON, of Newstead; *m* Margaret, dau of Sir William Fitzwilliams, and had:

Sir JOHN BYRON, KB, of Newstead; living 1614; *m* Anne, est dau of Sir Richard Molyneux, 1st Bt, and *d* 28 Sept 1625, having had, with five other sons:

1 Sir JOHN BYRON, **1st Baron Byron of Rochdale**, Co Lancaster (E), so cr 24 Oct 1643 with limitation (possibly the earliest such ever), in default of his own male issue, to each of his bros, KB (Feb 1625/6); *b* c 1599; MP Nottingham 1624–25 and 1626 Notts 1628–29, High Sheriff Notts 1634–35, Gent Bedchamber, Lt Tower London 1641, commanded royalist reserve Battle of Edgehill 1642, FM Gen royalist forces Cheshire, Salop, Worcs and N Wales, Govr Chester till its capture by Parl Feb 1645/6, capitulated as royalist cdr Carnarvon Castle June 1646, Govr to JAMES DUKE OF YORK (later JAMES II) 1646–52; *m* 1st Cecilia (*d* Feb 1638), dau of 3rd Baron De La Warr (*see* DE LA WARR, E) and widow of Sir Francis Byndlose, of Barwick Hall; *m* 2nd 1644 Eleanor (*d* 26 Jan 1663), dau of Robert, Viscount Kilmorey (*see* KILMOREY, E), and widow of Peter Warburton, of Arley, Cheshire, and *dsp* Aug 1652

2 RICHARD, **2nd Baron**

3 Robert (Sir); royalist inf Col Civil War, Govr Liverpool; *m* Lucy, dau of 3rd Baron De La Warr (*see* DE LA WARR, E), and had, with other issue (*dsp*):

(1) Cicely; *m* 1665 Charles Balfour, of Castle Balfour, Co Fermanagh, and had:

1a Lucy; *m* 1st Hugh McGill; *m* 2nd Blayney Townley, of Townley Hall

4 Philip (Sir), Col, killed storming of York by Parly army 1644

5 Thomas (Sir), cdr Prince of Wales's Regt Battle of Hopton Heath 19 March 1642/3; *d* 9 Dec 1643

1 Mary; *m* Sir Thomas Lucas

The 1st BARON's bro,

RICHARD BYRON, **2nd Baron Byron of Rochdale**; ktd 1642, royalist Govr Appleby Castle, Westmorland, and Newark, Notts, in Civil War; *m* 1st Elizabeth, dau of Gervase Rossell, of Ratcliffe, Notts, and widow of Nicholas Strelley; *m* 2nd Elizabeth, dau of Sir George Booth, Bt, and *d* 4 Oct 1679, leaving an only surv s:

WILLIAM BYRON, **3rd Baron Byron of Rochdale**; *b* 1636; poetaster; *m* 1st 1660 Elizabeth (*d* 1683), dau of 2nd Viscount Chaworth, and had issue; *m* 2nd 25 June 1685 Elizabeth (*d* 28 Dec 1703), dau of Sir George Stonhouse, 3rd Bt (*qv*), and widow of Sir Richard Stydolph, Bt, and *d* 13 Nov 1695, leaving:

WILLIAM BYRON, **4th Baron Byron of Rochdale**; *b* 4 Jan 1669; *m* 1st Feb 1702/3 Lady Mary Egerton (*d* 11 April 1703), dau of 3rd Earl of Bridgewater (*see* BOLTON, B); *m* 2nd 19 Dec 1706 Lady Frances Williamina Bentinck (*d* 31 March 1712), 3rd dau of 1st Earl of Portland (*qv*), and by her had three sons and a dau (all *d* unm); *m* 3rd 3 Dec 1720 Frances Berkeley (*m* 2nd 31 July 1740 Sir Thomas Hay, 2nd Bt, of Alderston (*qv*)), 2nd dau of 4th Baron Berkeley of Stratton, and *d* 8 Aug 1736, having by her had, with other issue:

1 WILLIAM BYRON, **5th Baron Byron of Rochdale**; *b* 5 Nov 1722; killed his cousin William Chaworth 26 Jan 1765, either in a duel or during a less formal fight in a room the two men had occupied alone for a time following a dinner among a club of gentlemen of the county at which a quarrel had flared up; tried by his peers 16–17 April 1765, found guilty of manslaughter but was merely fined and formally discharged, benefitting from the privileges conferred on peers in certain criminal cases by a statute of EDWARD VI; *m* 28 March 1747 Elizabeth (*d* 5 Nov 1788), dau of Charles Shaw, of Besthorpe Hall, Norfolk, and *d* 19 May 1798, having had issue:

(1) William, MP Morpeth; *b* 27 Oct 1749; *m* his cousin Juliana Elizabeth, dau of Adml John Byron (*see* below), and *dvp* 22 June 1776, leaving issue:

1a William, *k* Corsica 1794

(1) Henrietta Diana; *d* unm

(2) Caroline; *d* unm

2 John; *b* 8 Nov 1723; served RN: as Midshipman aboard the *Wager* in Lord Anson's Circumnavigating Sqdn (*see* LICHFIELD, E) was a castaway on a desert island in the S Seas for five years (about which he published 1768 a *Narrative*), returned to England 1748, Adml; *m* 8 Sept 1748 Sophia, dau of John Trevannion, of Carhays, Cornwall, and *d* 10 April 1786, leaving issue:

(1) John ('Mad Jack'); *b* 7 Feb 1756; *educ* Westminster; Capt Gds; *m* 1st 1 June 1779, as her 2nd w, Amelia, *de jure* Baroness Conyers and Baroness D'Arcy de Knayth (*d* 26 Jan 1784; *see* DARCY DE KNAYTH, B), dau of 4th and last Earl of Holdernesse, and had issue:

1a Augusta; *m* 17 Aug 1807 Lt-Col Leigh, 10th Dragoons, and *d* 18 Oct 1851 aged 67, leaving issue

(1) John Byron *m* 2nd 12 May 1785 Catherine (*d* 1 Aug 1811), dau of George Gordon, of Gight, Aberdeenshire, and *d* 2 Aug 1791, perhaps by suicide, having by her had:

1a GEORGE GORDON BYRON later (following his w's inheritance from her maternal unc 2nd and last Viscount Wentworth of Wellesborough April 1815) NOEL-BYRON, **6th Baron Byron of Rochdale**; *b* 22 Jan 1788; *educ* Aberdeen GS, Harrow and Trin Coll Cambridge; poet (and latterly, with changing literary tastes, increasingly noteworthy as a letter-writer): *Poems on Various Occasions* (1807), *Hours of Idleness* (1807), *English Bards and Scotch Reviewers* (1809), *Hints from Horace* (1811), *Childe Harold's Pilgrimage* (1812–18), *The Curse of Minerva* (1812), *The Giaour* (1813), *The Bride of Abydos* (1813), *The Corsair* (1814), *Lara* (1814), *Hebrew Melodies* (1815), *The Siege of Corinth* (1816), *Parisina* (1816), *The Prisoner of Chillon* (1816), *The Lament of Tasso* (1817), *Manfred* (1817), *Beppo* (1818), *Mazeppa* (1819), *Don Juan* (1819–24), *The Prophecy of Dante* (1821), *Marino Faliero* (1821), *Sardanapalus* (1821), *The Two Foscari* (1821), *Cain* (1821), *Heaven and Earth* (1821), *The Vision of Judgement* (1822), *The Island* (1823), *The Age of Bronze* (1823), also playwright: *Werner* (1823) and *The Deformed Transformed* (1824); involved with Carbonarist nationalists in Italy *c* 1821 and the Greek Committe for the liberation of Greece from the Ottoman Empire thereafter, FRS 1816; *m* 2 Jan 1815 Anne Isabella (Annabella) Baroness Wentworth (*see* LYTTON, E)in her own right following the death 1856 of her cousin 3rd Baron Scarsdale (*see* SCARSDALE, V), also *de jure* Baroness le Despenser in her own right, only child of Sir Ralph Milbanke later Noel, 6th Bt, and *d* of rheumatic fever Missolonghi Greece 19 April 1824, having had legitimate issue:

1b Ada Augusta; *b* 10 Dec 1815; *m* 8 July 1835 1st Earl of Lovelace (*qv*) and *d* 29 Nov 1852, leaving issue (*see* LYTTON, E)

1a (cont.) By Claire Clairmont, step-sis of Mary Shelley (*see* DE LISLE, V) the **6th Baron** had:

2b Allegra; *b* Jan 1817; *d* 20 April 1822

1a (cont.) It has been suggested that the **6th Baron** also had a child by his half-sis Augusta

(2) George Anson; *b* 30 Nov 1758; Capt RN; *m* Charlotte Henrietta (*d* 26 Feb 1793), dau of Robert Dallas, of Dallas Castle, Jamaica, and *d* 11 June 1793, leaving:

1a GEORGE ANSON, **7th Baron**

1a Julia Maria; *m* 27 May 1816 Rev Robert Heath, Fell St John's Coll Oxford, and *d* 1858

(1) Frances; *m* Gen Charles Leigh and *d* 19 Oct 1823

(2) Juliana Elizabeth; *m* 1st Hon William Byron, est s of **5th Baron Bryon** (*see* above); *m* 2nd 23 Sept 1783 Sir Robert Wilmot, 2nd Bt (*see* 1931 edn WILMOT-HORTON, Bt), and *d* 15 March 1788

(3) Augusta Barbara Charlotte; *m* V-Adml Christopher Parker and *d* 1824

3 Richard (Rev); *b* 28 Oct 1724; Rector Haughton le Skerne, Co Durham; *m* 1768 Mary (*d* 9 May 1827), dau of Richard Farmer, and *d* 5 Nov 1811, having had, with other issue:

(1) Richard, CB; *b* 30 July 1769; R-Adml; *m* 23 Sept 1801 Sarah (*d* 11 Aug 1861), dau of James Sykes, and *d* 2 Sept 1837, leaving issue:

1a Richard; *b* 1802; Cdr RN; *d* at sea in cmd of HM Sloop *Champion* 23 Feb 1843

2a James, Army Capt; *b* 1803; *d* May 1858

3a John (Rev); *b* 21 Sept 1804; Vicar Elmstone-Hardwick, Glos, Chaplain to Duke of Sutherland; *m* 8 Dec 1830 Mary (*d* 30 Dec 1842), dau of William Richardson, of Leatherhead, and *d* 6 Dec 1878, having had, with other issue:

1b John; *b* 14 Sept 1832; Maj-Gen cmdg 10th Foot; *m* 24 Oct 1865 Susan Amelia Graves (*d* 15 May 1871), dau of Edward Chiappini, of Capetown, and *d* 13 Aug 1895, leaving issue:

1c Richard, DSO (1900); *b* 19 Feb 1870; Col KRRC, served in Hazara Expdn 1891, Miranzai Expdn 1891, Isazai Expdn 1892, Chitral 1895, S Africa 1899–1901, WW I (despatches); *m* 18 Nov 1896 Mabel Mackenzie (*d* 22 Feb 1962), dau of Charles Albert Winter, JP, of 33 Hyde Park Sq, W, and *d* 1 Aug 1939, leaving issue:

1d RICHARD GEOFFREY GORDON, **12th Baron**

1d *Sheila Margaret [Mrs George Kerr, 52 Eresby Ho, Rutland Gate, London SW7 1BG]; *b* 30 Oct 1903; *m* 1st 7 June 1923 (*divorce* 1929) James Roy Notter Garton, Lt KRRC (*d* 1937), only surv son of William Garton, of Brixdone, Bursledon, Hants; *m* 2nd 31 Jan 1929 Edward William Standish (*d* 30 Nov 1933), late of Marwell Hall, nr Winchester; *m* 3rd 7 Dec 1935 George Munro Kerr, of 8 Ennismore Gdns, SW7, only son of Professor J M Munro Kerr, of Starr's Ho, Canterbury, and has by her 2nd husb:

1e *Anthony Edward Byron [Anthony Standish Esq, Paternoster House, Ipplepen, S Devon]; *b* 1931; *educ* Eton; *m* 1956 *Diana Huguette, only dau of Dr Hugh Gordon, of 3 High St, Kirkcudbright, and has issue:

1f *Miles Anthony; *b* 1958

2f *Alexander Hugh; *b* 1959

3f *Edward Pery; *b* 1968; *m* 1992 *Ann Margaret, yr dau of John Raymond Perring, TD (*see* PERRING, Bt)

1e *Susan Felicity [Mrs Derek Trasenster, Compton House, Upton Grey, Basingstoke, Hants RG25 2RH]; *b* 1929; *m* 1949 *Capt Derek Russell de Courcy Trasenster, 4th/7th Roy Dragoon Gds, and has issue:

1f *Mark William de Courcy; *b* 1954; *m* 1983 *Elizabeth Ross and has issue:

1g *Sophie Georgina; *b* 1984

2g *Georgina Sarah; *b* 1986

3g *Sara Elizabeth; *b* 1989

4g *Cordelia Camilla de Courcy; *b* 1991

1f *Camilla de Courcy; *b* 1951; *m* 1974 *Brig Clendon Daukes, late 4th/7th Roy Dragoon Gds, and has issue:

1g *Anthony Clendon; *b* 1976

2g *Thomas Clendon; *b* 1978

1g *Rose-Anna; *b* 1981

1c Ada Mary; *m* 9 June 1894 Adml Charles Gauntlett Dicken, of The Hermitage, Weeke, Winchester, yst s of Rev Alldersey Dicken, DD, Fell and Tutor of Peterhouse Camb, and *d* 15 Dec 1938, leaving issue. He *d* 7 Sept 1937

2c Amy Helena; *d* an infant 31 Aug 1868

(2) Henry (Rev), Rector Muston, Leics; *m* 18 June 1803 Margaret (*d* 14 Sept 1813), est dau of Thomas Powditch, and *d* 1821, leaving, with other issue:

1a Henry, Consul Haiti; *b* 17 April 1804; *m* 1st April 1834 Elizabeth Josephine (*d* 18 Sept 1856), only dau of James Byron Bradley, MD, and had:

1b Henry James; *b* 8 Jan 1835; dramatist; *m* 1st Martha (*d* 25 Sept 1876), dau of John Foulkes, of Ashfield, and had issue:

1c Alfred; *b* 1858; *m* 5 Feb 1885 Annie Elizabeth, dau of George Boulton, and *d* 8 July 1891

2c John; *b* 1859; *d* 27 May 1931

3c George Frederick; *b* 1862; *m* 27 Aug 1892 Mary Clarissa (*d* 5 Nov 1936), dau of Rev John Maurice Gillington, and *d* 6 July 1939, having had issue:

1d James George; *b* 23 Oct 1894; *d* young

2d Charles, W/Cdr RAF; *b* 18 June 1897; *m* 25 May 1929 Joyce Evelyn, 4th dau of Thomas Godwin Chance, of Cambridge

1c Elizabeth; *m* 6 Dec 1888 Maj Henry James Seton (*see* SETON, Bt) and *dsp* 2 Sept 1897

1b (cont.) Henry James Byron *m* 2nd 17 Oct 1876 Eleanor Mary (*d* 18 Sept 1889), dau of Edward Joy, and 12 April 1884, having by her had issue:

2c Margaret Ada; *b* 13 Jan 1878

1a (cont.) Henry Byron *m* 2nd 1859 Josephine (*d* 19 June 1900), widow of Gen — du Frène and dau of — Berthomieux, and *d* 4 May 1884, having by her had, with other issue:

2b Manneville Henry; *b* 9 Dec 1867

1b Margaret; *m* 21 July 1897 Walter Henry Gayford and *d* Jan 1922, leaving issue

2a George; *b* 12 Aug 1805; Lt 48th Native Inf; *m* 16 Nov 1831 Georgiana Caroline (*m* 2nd Gen Edward Philipson Mainwaring), dau of Col Meiselback, and *d* 23 May 1834, leaving:

1b George Rochfort; *b* 9 Nov 1832; Lt 63rd Regt; *m* 8 Sept 1866 Rose (*d* 29 Aug 1923), dau of Frederick Templeton, and *d* 19 Nov 1911, leaving:

1c Frederick Rochfort; *b* 23 Dec 1867; Matabele Campaign 1896–97 (medal); *m* 30 Aug 1910 Maude Rose, only dau of Lt-Col A Cockburn McBarnet, DL, 79th Cameron Highrs, and *dsp* 1 March 1939

2c George Rochfort; *b* 17 Jan 1875; served WW I; *d* 23 Aug 1927

3c Richard Rochfort; *b* 28 March 1876; Indian State Rlwys, Govt Inspr Rlwys Burma 1929–31

1c Helena; *d* unm 4 Aug 1944

2c Frances Templeton; *m* 23 Oct 1918 Rev Walter Lilley Pritchatt-Shaw, MA, and *d* 16 Aug 1947. He *d* 15 Sept 1941

4 George; *b* 22 April 1730; *m* Frances, dau of Elton Levett, of Nottingham, and had issue:

(1) John, Maj; *dsp*

(1) Isabella; *m* Count Paravicini Capelli and *d* 1834

1 Isabella; *m* 1st 8 June 1743 4th Earl of Carlisle (*qv*); *m* 2nd 10 Dec 1759 Sir William Musgrave, Bt, of Hayton Castle; and *d* 22 Jan 1795, leaving issue

The 6th BARON's cousin,

GEORGE ANSON BYRON, **7th Baron Byron of Rochdale**; *b* 8 March 1789; Adml, Extra Ld-in-Waiting to HM QUEEN VICTORIA; *m* 18 March 1816 Elizabeth Mary (*d* 20 Aug 1873), dau of Sacheverell Chandos-Pole, of Radborne, Derbys, and *d* 1 March 1868, having had issue:

1 GEORGE ANSON BYRON, **8th Baron Byron of Rochdale**; *b* 30 June 1818; *m* 3 Aug 1843 Lucy Elizabeth Jane (*m* 2nd 17 Jan 1878 Rev Philip Henry Douglas, Vicar Thrumpton, Derbys; *d* 28 May 1912), est dau of Rev William Wescombe, of Thrumpton Hall, Notts, Rector Langford, Essex, and *dsp* 28 Nov 1870

2 Frederick; *b* 3 Feb 1822; MA, barrister, Fell All Souls Oxford; *m* 19 Aug 1851 Mary Jane (*d* 1 Sept 1909), dau of Rev William Wescomb, Rector of Langford, Essex, and *d* 4 April 1861, having had, with other issue:

(1) GEORGE FREDERICK WILLIAM BYRON, **9th Baron Byron of Rochdale**; *b* 27 Dec 1855; *educ* Ch Ch Oxford (BA); Lt 4th Bn Essex Regt; *m* 1 March 1901 Fanny Lucy, DBE (1917) (*m* 3rd 12 Dec 1924 Sir Robert Paterson Houston, 1st Bt (*d* 14 April 1926), and *d* 29 Dec 1936), 4th dau of Thomas Radmall, of St Margaret's, Twickenham, and formerly w of Sir Theodore Francis Brinckman, 3rd Bt (*qv*), and *dsp* 30 March 1917

(2) FREDERICK ERNEST CHARLES BYRON, **10th Baron Byron of Rochdale**; *b* 26 March 1861; *educ* Exeter Coll Oxford (MA); Deacon 1888, Priest 1889, Curate Royston Herts 1888–90, Rector Langford Essex 1891–1914, Vicar Thrumpton Notts 1914–42, Rector Barton-in-Fabis 1941–42; *m* 31 Jan 1921 Lady Anna Ismay Ethel FitzRoy (*d* 14 April 1966), sis of 10th Duke of Grafton (*qv*), and *dsp* 6 June 1949

(1) Eva Lucy Mary; granted rank of baron's dau; *m* 29 April 1879 Col Henry Robert Eyre, Coldstream Gds, and *d* 8 Feb 1895, leaving issue. He *d* 12 March 1904

3 Augustus (Rev); JP (Leics); *b* 8 June 1828; MA Oxon, Rector Kirkby Mallory, Leics, CA Leics; *m* 8 July 1852 Frederica (*d* 29 March 1903), yst dau of Lt-Gen Sir Thomas McMahon, 2nd Bt, KCB (*qv*), and *d* 17 July 1907, having had issue:

(1) Augustus William, Lt Leics Imp Yeo, Hon Capt; *b* 23 Feb 1856; *m* 5 Aug 1885 Constance Caroline (*d* 13 Aug 1941), dau of Edward Clough Taylor, of Firby, Yorks, and *d* 27 July 1939, leaving issue:

1a Nora Hermione Wentworth; *b* 11 Oct 1886

2a Ada Constance Frederica; *b* 23 Feb 1891; *d* unm 22 Dec 1950

(2) Claud Gordon; *b* 10 Jan 1861; *d* 4 Oct 1863

1 Mabel Charlotte; *m* 7 Jan 1880 Rev Charles Thomas Moore, Rector Appleby, Leics, 1877–1922, and *d* Dec 1929, leaving issue:

(2) Ethel Maud; *m* 9 Jan 1889 Horace George Clough Taylor, of Firby, Yorks, and *d* 2 June 1940. He *dsp* 14 Feb 1916

(3) Mary Beatrice; *m* 18 Aug 1886 Francis Curzon NEWTON later CURZON, DL, of Mickleover Manor and Lockington, Derbys, and *d* 16 Feb 1911, leaving issue. He *d* 3 March 1918

4 William (Rev); *b* 11 Oct 1831; MA Oxon, Rector Trowell, Notts; *m* 1st 4 Feb 1857 Mary Elizabeth (*d* 26 April 1877), dau of V-Chllr Sir Richard Torin Kindersley, and had, with other issue:

(1) George Anson, JP (Notts); barrister; *b* 3 March 1858; *educ* Ch Ch Oxford (MA); *m* 22 Aug 1891 Georgiana Maie, DGStJ (*d* 14 March 1941), dau of Sir Francis Burdett, 7th Bt, of Bramcote (*see* 1949 edn), and *d* 25 Sept 1941, leaving, with other issue:

1a Margaret Dorothy, OBE (1919); *b* 30 June 1892; *m* 2 June 1921 Capt Sir William Evelyn Houstoun-Boswall, KCMG, MC (*see* HOUSTON-BOSWALL, Bt), and *d* 15 Feb 1957, leaving issue

2a Rhona Mary; *b* 8 Aug 1893

(2) Wilfrid; *b* 31 Jan 1871; Col cmdg Leics Yeo, Boer War 1900–01 with Imp Yeo, WW I; *m* 25 Sept 1901 his cousin Sylvia Mary (*d* 27 Dec 1952), dau of Rev Charles Thomas Moore, Rector Appleby, Leics (*see* above), and *d* Nov 1936, leaving issue:

1a RUPERT FREDERICK GEORGE BYRON, **11th Baron Byron of Rochdale**; *b* 13 Aug 1903; RN WW II, 2nd Lt Leics Yeo TA; *m* 29 July 1931 Pauline Augusta (*d* 1993), dau of T J Cornwall, of Wagin, W Australia, and *d* 1983, leaving:

1b *(Isobel) Ann [The Hon Mrs Woods, 55A Mayfair St, Mount Claremont, W Australia 6010]; *b* 23 May 1932; *m* 1st 22 Sept 1951 Robert Reford Corr (*d* 1980), s of Ivan Reford Corr, of Perth, W Australia; *m* 2nd 1983 *Norman James Woods, son of James Park Woods, VC, of W Australia, and has by her 1st husb:

1c *John Byron Reford; *b* 8 Aug 1953; *m* 1982 *Suzette Margaret Brackenridge and has:

1d *Alexandra Isobel; *b* 28 March 1987

2d *Georgina Elizabeth; *b* 21 Feb 1992

2c *Anthony Byron Reford; *b* 12 Sept 1956; *m* 19– (*divorce* 19–) — and has:

1d *Louisa Ann; *b* 1988

2d *Alana May; *b* 1991

1c *Helen Jane (Rev); *b* 20 Oct 1961

2a Maurice Augustus William (Rev); *b* 12 March 1907; RC priest Sacred Heart Ch Goudhurst, Kent; *d* 14 March 1949

1a Daphne Mary; *b* 13 June 1909; *m* 24 Feb 1930 Leo Forbes O'Connor and had issue (*see* STAFFORD, B). He *d* 23 Jan 1958

(1) Eleanor Mary; *m* 21 Jan 1885 Henry Seymour Hoare, of Knoyle Ho, Salisbury, s of Henry James Hoare, of Morden, and *d* 25 April 1913, leaving issue. He *d* 16 June 1930

(2) Edith Mary; *m* 19 Jan 1888 Maj Gerard Thomas Noel, Durham LI, and *d* 29 May 1917, leaving issue (*see* GAINSBOROUGH, E)

(3) Katherine Mary; *m* 5 July 1894 Col Sir William Robert Campion, KCMG, DSO, DL, of Danny Park, Hurstpierpoint, Sussex, son of William Henry Campion, CB, and *d* 21 April 1951, leaving issue. He *d* 2 Jan 1951

4 (cont.) The Rev Hon William Byron *m* 2nd 23 Nov 1878 Mary (*d* 2 Oct 1888 aged 57), dau of Rev John Burnside, and *d* 17 May 1907

1 Mary Anne; *m* 4 June 1834 John Blenkinsopp Coulson, of Blenkinsopp Castle, Northumberland, and *d* 1 Aug 1885 aged 68, leaving issue. He *d* 12 June 1868

2 Georgiana; *m* 9 June 1842 Charles Rowland Palmer Morewood, of Alfreton Park, Derbys, and *d* 3 Jan 1893, leaving issue. He *d* 1873

The 11th BARON's second cousin three times removed,

RICHARD GEOFFREY GORDON BYRON, **12th Baron Byron of Rochdale**, DSO (1944), *b* 3 Nov 1899; *educ* Eton; ADC to Govr Bombay 1921–22, Mil Sec to Govr-Gen and C-in-C NZ 1937, WW II; Lt-Col 4th/7th Roy Dragoon Gds (cmdg 1941–44); *m* 1st 8 June 1926 (*divorce* 1946) Margaret Mary, only dau of Francis Gerald Steuart, of Fyfhyde, Winchester, Hants; *m* 2nd 8 Aug 1946 Dorigen Margaret (*d* 1985), only dau of Percival Kennedy Esdaile, and *d* 1989, having by her had issue:

1 Richard Noel; *b* 5 Jan 1948; *educ* Wellington; *d* unm, *k* air accident W Africa 1985

2 ROBERT JAMES BYRON, **13th and present Baron Byron of Rochdale**

CABLE-ALEXANDER

Arms: Per pale argent and sable a chevron, in base a crescent counterchanged; on a canton azure a harp or, stringed argent, in the sinister chief point a mullet of the last.
Crest: An armed arm embowed holding a sword proper, charged on the wrist with a mullet or.
Motto: *Per mare, per terras* ('By sea and land').
Creation: Bt. (UK) 11 Dec 1809.

SIR PATRICK DESMOND WILLIAM CABLE-ALEXANDER, 8TH BT, of Dublin [Sir Patrick Cable-Alexander Bt, Windrush House, Hoe Court, Lancing, W Sussex BN15 0QX]; *b* 19 April 1936; *s f* 1988; *educ* Downside and RMA Sandhurst; late Lt-Col Roy Scots Dragoon Gds (Carabiniers and Greys), Germany and Aden, psc 1967, Assist Mily Attaché Br Emb Saigon 1968; Bursar and Clerk Cncl Lancing Coll 1984–; *m* 1st 9 Dec 1961 (*divorce* 1976) Diana Frances, est dau of Col Paul Heberden Rogers, of Bushey, and has issue:

1 *Melanie Jane [Miss Melanie Cable-Alexander, Country Life, King's Reach Tower, Stamford St, London SE1 9LS]; *b* 14 Sept 1963; features ed *Country Life*; author: *Tottering-By-Gently* (ed, 1996), *Living National Treasures* (ed, 1997)

2 *Louise Fenella; *b* 17 Feb 1967; *m* 22 April 1995 *Massimo A, er s of G Reina, of Milan

Sir PATRICK *m* 2nd 1976 *Jane Mary, dau of Anthony Arthur Gough Lewis, MD, FRCP, of Oxford, and has further issue:

1 +FERGUS WILLIAM ANTONY; *b* 18 June 1981

Lineage: WILLIAM ALEXANDER, of Dublin, 3rd s of John Alexander, of Ballyclose and Gunsland, and yr bro of Nathaniel Alexander, ancestor of the Earls of Caledon (*qv*); *m* Mary Porter, of Vicardale, Co Monaghan, and *d* 1788, leaving an er s:

Sir William Alexander, 1st Bt (UK), so *cr* 11 Dec 1809, of Belcamp, Co Dublin; *b* 3 March 1743; Lt-Col Roy Dublin Militia, Ld Mayor Dublin; *m* 20 July 1764 Catherine, dau and heiress of John Folie Malpas, of Rochestown, Co Dublin, and *d c* 1820, leaving:

1 **Sir Robert Alexander, 2nd Bt**; *b* 16 Dec 1769; *m* 17 June 1796 Elisa (*d* 1844), dau and heir of John Wallis, and *d* 1 Dec 1859, having had, with other issue:

(1) **Sir William John, 3rd Bt**, QC; *b* 1 April 1797; Attorney-General to HRH THE PRINCE OF WALES; *d* unm 31 March 1873

(2) **Sir John Wallis Alexander, 4th Bt**; *b* 1 Oct 1800; *m* 1st 18 May 1857 Lady Lepel Charlotte Phipps (*d* 29 Jan 1869), sis of 1st Marquess of Normanby (*qv*); *m* 2nd 22 Aug 1877 Mary Kathleen (*d* 29 May 1934), 2nd dau of Rev John Dreaper, of Northampton, and *dsp* 25 Oct 1888

2 William John ALEXANDER later ALEXANDER-SHAW (added with arms by roy licence 4 May 1846); *m* 1 March 1815 his cousin Isabella (*d* 19 May 1834), dau of Robert Alexander, of Seamount, and *d* 14 May 1856, leaving issue:

(1) William ALEXANDER-SHAW later ALEXANDER (dropped SHAW by roy licence 17 June 1876), of Cruisetown, Co Meath, and Stoke Old Rectory, Guildford, Surrey; *b* 12 May 1817; Maj IA; *m* 10 Sept 1839 Mary (*d* 3 Sept 1897), 3rd dau of Rt Rev Hon Edward Grey (*see* GREY, E), Bp Hereford, and *d* 11 July 1885, leaving issue:

1a WILLIAM FERDINAND (Sir), **5th Bt**

1a Charlotte Elizabeth; *m* 22 April 1862 Rev Thomas Borlase Coulson (*d* 1895), Vicar Bramley, Hon Canon Truro, and *d* 25 Jan 1922

2a Anne Isabella; *m* 10 July 1871 Charles Forbes Calland, 98th Regt (*d* 5 July 1907), and *d* 3 Nov 1924, leaving issue

3a Mary; *m* 15 June 1869 Henry John Goodwin Robinson, 98th Regt (*d* 1916), and *d* 16 Dec 1925, leaving issue

4a Fanny Jane; *m* 9 March 1882 Cdr Aston Edward McMurdo, RN (*d* 21 April 1904), and *d* 28 July 1942, leaving issue

5a Lucy; *m* 2 June 1881 Frank Theodore Bagshawe (*d* 27 June 1923) and *d* 5 June 1932, leaving issue

(2) Robert Henry; *k* in the retreat from Kabul

(3) Henry; *d* 1856

(4) Richard ALEXANDER-SHAW; *d* 1867, leaving issue:

1b Kathleen; *b* 1892

2a Charles Henry ALEXANDER; *b* 1866; *m* 14 Aug 1890 Susie Macaulay, dau of Robert Alexander, and *d* 2 Dec 1898, leaving issue:

1b Robert Godrey; *b* 10 Nov 1894

1a Harriet; *m* 1st 19 April 1887 Arthur John Childe-Freeman, JP (*d* 9 June 1892), and had issue; *m* 2nd 14 April 1904 Col Richard Prescott-Decie, DL (*d* 23 Dec 1927), and *d* 4 April 1907

(1) Harriet; *m* 10 Oct 1850 her cousin Rev Godfrey Edward Alexander (*d* 1900), Rector Stoke Bliss, Herefs

(2) Elizabeth

(3) Anne Catherine; *m* 6 July 1834 Capt Edward Barnes and *d* 11 May 1876, leaving issue

1 Catherine; *m* Robert Hamilton, of Clonsilla (*see* HOLMPATRICK, B)

2 Eliza; *m* John Hamilton, of Hacketstown (*see* HOLMPATRICK)

The 4th Bt's cousin,

Sir William Ferdinand Alexander, 5th Bt; *b* 15 Oct 1845; *m* 27 Nov 1884 Edith (*m* 2nd 1897 Rev Frederick William Thurlow; *d* 6 Jan 1925), 2nd dau of George Frederick Heriot La Fargue, of Bosworth Hall, Leics, and *d* 13 Feb 1896, leaving:

1 **Sir Lionel Cecil William Alexander, 6th Bt**, DSO (1916); *b* 23 Sept 1885; Maj 23rd Bn London Regt, formerly Lt Gren Gds, Croix de Guerre, High Sheriff Hunts 1929; *m* 1st 5 Dec 1908 (*divorce* 1924) Hon Dawn Noorouz Weston Cable (*d* 17 Sept 1969), est dau of 1st and last Baron Cable (see 1927 edn), and had issue:

(1) DESMOND WILLIAM LIONEL (Sir), **7th Bt**

1 (cont.) **Sir Lionel** *m* 2nd 17 July 1924 Hopeful Merrison Rose, dau of Capt George William Hurrell, of Aberdeen, and by her had:

(2) +Nigel William [Maj Nigel Alexander, Rose Cottage, Underhill Lane, Lower Bourne, Surrey GU10 3NF]; *b* 27 July 1925; *educ* Haileybury; Maj Gren Gds WW II; *m* 5 Dec 1964 *Anne, yr dau of Bernard Ambrose Wheatley and Mrs Beer, of Palma, Majorca, and has issue:

1a +Hugh William; *b* 23 June 1967; *educ* Haileybury

1a *Charlotte Anne; *b* 1971

(3) Derek Malcolm; *b* 7 July 1932; *d* 2 March 1934

1 Eileen Edith Caledon; *m* 1st 8 Dec 1908 (*divorce* 1918) Lt-Col Donald Cuthbertson Dennistoun Sword, DSO, Scottish Rifles (*d* 11 May 1954), s of Alexander Bruce Dennistoun Sword, of Endon Hall, Staffs, and had issue; *m* 2nd 1919 Lt-Col Clifford Cyril Scott, MC

Sir LIONEL *d* 6 Aug 1956; his er surv son,

Sir DESMOND WILLIAM LIONEL ALEXANDER later CABLE-ALEXANDER (deed poll 30 Oct 1931), **7th Bt**; *b* 4 Oct 1910; *educ* Harrow and Magdalen Coll Oxford; *m* 1st 20 June 1935 (*divorce* 1941) Mary Jane (*d* 15 Sept 1994), dau of James O'Brien, JP, of Enniskillen, Co Fermanagh, and had issue:

1 Sir PATRICK DESMOND WILLIAM CABLE-ALEXANDER, **8th and present Bt**

Sir DESMOND *m* 2nd 1941 *Margaret Mabel [Margaret Lady Cable-Alexander, 1 Denne Park House, Horsham, W Sussex], dau of John Burnett, of Dublin, and *d* 1988, having had further issue:

1 *Jacqueline [Mrs Dillon Welchman, 11 Holmbush Rd, London SW15 3LE]; *b* 16 Dec 1941; *m* 15 May 1962 *Dillon Godfrey Welchman, 2nd s of Brig Godfrey de Vere Welchman, CBE, DSO, and has issue:

(1) *James Dillon; *b* 5 Feb 1969; *educ* Sherborne and Exeter and Reading Us

(1) *Sara Dawn; *b* 15 Dec 1964; *m* 1990 *Gregory Sebastian Porter and has:

1a *William Edward; *b* 1992

2a *Archie Jocelyn; *b* 1997

3a *Jake Rollo (twin); *b* 1997

2 *Susan; *b* 28 May 1948; *m* 30 May 1970 *Richard Humphrey, yr s of John Hardwicke, and has issue:

(1) *Humphrey Richard; *b* 1978

(1) *Caroline Amelia; *b* 12 April 1977

CADMAN

Arms: Az. three fleur-de-lys in pale between four endorses indented arg. **Crest:** A stork's head, holding in the beak a sprig of columbine ppr. **Supporters:** Dexter, a stork; sinister, a peacock arg., beaked gu., each gorged with a collar az. charged with a fleur-de-lys also arg. **Motto:** *Semper paratus* ('Ever ready'). **Creation:** B. (UK) 7 June 1937.

THE 3RD BARON CADMAN, of Silverdale, Co Stafford (John Anthony Cadman) [The Rt Hon The Lord Cadman, Heathcourt House, Ironmould Lane, Brislington, Bristol BS4 5RS]; *b* 3 July 1938; *s* f 1966; *educ* Harrow, Selwyn Coll Cambridge and RAC Cirencester; farmer; *m* 26 Dec 1975 *Janet Valerie, dau of Arthur Hayes, of Morecombe, Lancs, and has issue:

1 +NICHOLAS ANTHONY JAMES; *b* 18 Nov 1977

2 +Giles Oliver Richard; *b* 5 Feb 1979

Lineage: JOHN FURNIVAL CADMAN, of Field Ho, Chesterton, Staffs; *d* 24 Dec 1872, leaving:

JAMES COPE CADMAN, MICE, of Bryncliffe, Llandudno; Pres IME; *b* 24 May 1851; *m* 19 Oct 1874 Betty (*d* 4 Dec 1924), dau of Joseph Keeling, and *d* 1 Jan 1914, having had issue:

1 JOHN, **1st Baron**

2 James, DSC (1915), of Walton Hall, Staffs, DL Staffs, High Sheriff 1933, JP Newcastle-under-Lyme, T/Sub-Lt RNVR 1914, Lt attd 3rd Cavalry Div 1915, memb Staffs TAA, MFH N Staffs, dir Nat Prov Bank; *b* 11 Dec 1878; *m* 1900 Una Mildred (*d* 8 March 1919), 2nd dau of Simon Tate, MICE, and *d* car crash 8 Sept 1947, leaving issue:

(1) James Simon; *b* 2 March 1909; *m* 1st 17 Oct 1934 (*divorce* 1967) Kathleen Diana Cecilia Patricia, dau of Sir John Ferguson, KBE, MP; *m* 2nd 8 Sept 1976 his cousin *Hon Sybil Mary, yr dau of 1st Baron Cadman (*see below*) and widow of Maj-Gen William Pat Arthur Bradshaw, CB, DSO, Scots Gds, and *d* 1986

(1) Una Nancy; *b* 20 April 1911; *m* 17 Sept 1936 Reginald Colin Russell Clarke (*d* 22 July 1942), son of E E Clarke, and had:

1a *Peter James Colin; *b* 25 Aug 1938

1a *Una Janet; *b* 28 Aug 1941

(2) *Cynthia; *b* 24 Feb 1919; *m* 1 June 1939 Lt-Col Ian Arthur Marriott, RE, s of Hugh Frederick Marriot, of Newnham Hall, Newnham, Northants, and has had issue:

1a *Simon Hugh Cadman [Simon Marriott Esq, Higher End Farm, Hale, Hants SP6 2RA]; *b* 7 March 1941; *educ* Rugby and RMA Sandhurst; Maj 3rd Green Jackets, The Rifle Bde; *m* 27 April 1985 *Ann Davida Helen McMonnies and has:

1b *Annabel; *b* 11 Feb 1986

2b *Alexandra; *b* 5 Aug 1988

2a *Hugh William; *b* 4 March 1942; *educ* Rugby and Southampton U (BA 1963); *m* 1 Oct 1966 *Catherine Julia Marshall and has issue:

1b *Tamsin Caroline; *b* 17 Oct 1968

3a Charles Luke; *b* 16 April 1946; *d* 26 March 1949

3 William Henry, MBE (1946), FRIC, MIChemE, FCS, BSc, MRI Silver Medallist, RSA 1945–46, Capt 1st/6th Manchester Regt TF, seconded RE Special Bde, served WW I (despatches), Maj HG WW II, Lt-Col Technical Force; *b* 12 Aug 1880; *m* Lucy Lloyd (*d* 25 March 1973), dau of A H Whitworth, Sec Manchester Ship Canal, and *d* 20 Feb 1960, having had issue:

(1) (William) Guy, DFC (1944), F/O RAFVR WW II; *b* 19 Aug 1922; *ka* over Germany 7 Feb 1945

(2) *Martin Henry; *b* 26 Sept 1924; *educ* Selwyn Coll Cambridge (BA 1950, MA 1958); F/Lt RAFVR WW II; *m* 13 April 1950 and has issue:

1a *William Martin; *b* 10 Sep 1956

2a *Richard James Allen; *b* 5 Oct 1959

1a *Marion Lloyd; *b* 9 June 1951

2a *Julia Mary; *b* 21 April 1954

(1) *Evelyn Lloyd; *b* 5 Nov 1926

(2) *Jane Shireen [Mrs George Lissimore, Clarence House, Clarence Rd, Malvern, Hereford and Worcester]; *b* 18 April 1929; *m* 17 July 1954 George Ronald Lissimore, son of Edwin Lissimore, of Malvern, Worcs, and has issue:

1a *Mark Guy; *b* 31 Dec 1955

2a *John Ronald; *b* 19 June 1985

1a *Valerie Ann; *b* 29 Dec 1963

4 Frank; *b* 21 Sept 1883; *d* 27 March 1901

5 Herbert; *b* 24 Dec 1888; *m* 15 March 1919 Phyllis, dau of Sir Samuel William Knaggs, KCMG, and *d* 4 May 1957, leaving issue:

(1) *Kenneth John; *b* 31 Aug 1925; *educ* Berkhamsted and Queen's U Belfast (BSc (Civil Eng) 1951); F/O 208 Sqdn RAF WW II; *m* 12 March 1953 *Marie, dau of David R Bates, JP, of Ballygowan, Co Down, and has issue:

1a *James Patrick David; *b* 15 Feb 1964

1a *Janet Patricia; *b* 17 Aug 1960

(1) *Jean Phyllis; *b* 6 Oct 1921; *m* 25 June 1945 Capt Harry Oliver John Carter Jonas, est son of H Carter Jonas, and has issue:

1a *Peter John; *b* 18 May 1950

1a *Maralyn; *b* 5 Jan 1948

2a *Juliet; *b* 17 Dec 1956

6 Charles Joseph, MC, T/Lt RE WW I, Special Bde Signalling (despatches); *b* 1 Aug 1882; *ka* 26 Jan 1917

7 Richard, CBE (1951), DL (Glam), A/Cdre AAF, late Capt RFC, WW I (despatches), S/Ldr 614 Sqdn RAuxAF WW II; *b* 1 Nov 1894; *m* 1st Eileen Mary, dau of E W Johnson, of Llandudno, and had issue:

(1) *Richard Edward Charles, OBE, AIIA; W/Cdr RAuxAF WW II (despatches twice); v-pres and md Wire Rope Industs Canada; *b* 16 March 1919; *m* 26 Oct 1940 *Constance St Clair, dau of Capt Charles Fergie Carrol, of 12 Morningside Terrace, Edinburgh, and has issue:

1a *Carrol St Clair; *b* 3 Sept 1941; *m* 8 Jan 1962 *John Oscar Edward Lundell, son of Oscar Lundell, QC, of Vancouver, BC, Canada, and has issue

2a *Angela Muir; *b* 22 Dec 1943

3a *Susan Lesley; *b* 16 Aug 1948

4a *Elizabeth Jane; *b* 6 June 1952

7 (cont.) Richard Cadman *m* 2nd (*divorce*) Amy, dau of George Howson, of Stoke-on-Trent, and *d* 6 Nov 1957, having by her had issue:

1a *Robert Andrew; *b* 16 May 1931; *educ* Corpus Christi Coll Cambridge (BA 1954, MA)

1 Amy Bettina; *b* 10 Dec 1875; *m* John Nixon Watts, slr, and *d* 11 Dec 1932, leaving issue

2 Maude; *b* 7 March 1882; *m* 15 July 1933 Ven Charles Frederic Roberts, MA, FSA, Archdeacon St Asaph, only surv son of Rev David Roberts, MA, Rector of Llanelidan, Ruthin, and *dsp* 12 July 1967. He *d* 23 March 1942

3 Beatrice Ida; *b* 1 Aug 1885; *d* 9 May 1893

4 Ella Cope; *b* 2 Feb 1887; *m* Dr Isaac Lloyd Johnstone, and had issue:

(1) Margaret, BSc; *b* 16 Jan 1928

5 Dora; *b* 9 Sept 1890; *d* 17 Jan 1907

6 Betty; *b* 10 Jan 1898; *d* 18 July 1900

The est son,

JOHN CADMAN, **1st Baron Cadman**, of Silverdale, Co Stafford (UK), so *cr* 7 June 1937, GCMG (1929, KCMG 1918, CMG 1916), FRS, DSc, and Hon DCL Durham, Hon LLD Birmingham, Hon DEng Melbourne, Hon Assoc Coll Tech Manchester; Chm Anglo-Iranian Oil and Iraq Petroleum, dir: Suez Canal Co and GWR, memb: PM's Ec Advsy Cncl, Post Office Advsy Cncl and Advsy Cncl Dept Sci and Industl Research; Inspr Mines E Scotland 1902 and Stafford Dist 1903, Govt Mining Engr Trinidad and Tobago 1904, Inspr Mines Trinidad 1907; Prof Mining Birmingham U 1908–20, Memb Admlty Commn Investigate Iranian Oilfields 1913, technical advsr Govt Nigeria 1915, consulting petroleum advsr Colonial Off and Govt Trinidad 1917, memb Industl Transference Bd 1928 and Ctee Enquiry Post Office 1932, chm Ctee Enquiry Civil Aviation 1937–38, pres: IME, IPT, Inst of Fuel, Soc Br Gas Industs 1934–35, Emeritus Prof Birmingham U, freedom Newcastle-under-Lyme 1938, Pasha 1st Cl Transjordan, Gd Cordon Legn Honour, Crown Italy, Order Rafidain 1st Cl Iraq, chm Television Advsy Ctee 1939, visiting Fell Nuffield Coll Oxford 1939; *b* 7 Sept 1877; *m* 27 July 1907 Lilian (*d* 9 Nov 1963), dau of John Harragin, Stipendiary Magistrate, Trinidad, and had issue:

1 JOHN BASIL COPE, **2nd Baron**

2 +(Arthur) Denys [The Hon Denys Cadman, 4100 Jackson Apt 503, Austin, Texas 78731, USA]; *b* 1 June 1911; *educ* Harrow and Harvard; *m* 28 Dec 1933 *Cary, dau of Burke Baker, of Texas, and has issue:

(1) +John Denys [John Cadman Esq, QL, 26 Conj 6 Casa 1, Lago Sul, Brasilia, Brazil 74665–165]; *b* 28 Jan 1941; *educ* Princeton (BSE) and U of California (MS, PhD), MSc 1967; US Peace Corps NE Brazil 1962–64; *m* 1st 29 Aug 1964 Judith Ann, dau of Warren Cummings Whittaker, of Miami; *m* 2nd 1984 *Lais Moreira de Castro, of Rio de Janeiro, and has issue by 1st w:

1a *Cynthia; *b* 4 Aug 1965

2a *Cary Anne; *b* 4 June 1968

(2) +David BAKER [David Baker Esq, 1732 McSpadden, Vancouver, BC V5N 1L4, Canada]; *b* 13 Nov 1948; *educ* U of The South, Tenn. (BA); *m* 1980 *Marie, dau of Henrick C Orth-Pallavicini, of New York, and has issue:

1a *Darcy Eryn; *b* 1984

(1) *Anne [Mrs John Lawrence, 98 Ruskin, Ottawa, Canada]; *b* 24 June 1935; *m* 14 Sept 1957 *John Edward McCrea Lawrence and has issue:

1a *Edward Burke; *b* 7 April 1959; *m* 1995*Lori Hickling

2a *John Cadman; *b* 20 Aug 1960; *m* 1980 *Robyn Mooney and has:

1b *Jy Maya; *b* 1989

2b *Rohja Raina; *b* 1991

3b *Beniya Lalo; *b* 1996

3a *Denys McCrea; *b* 21 May 1962; *m* 1988 *Mona Stiffler, and has issue:

1b *Noah Denys; *b* 1989

1a *Cary Edwina; *b* 28 May 1964; *m* 1992 *Thomas Christopher Paul LaPierre and has:

1b *Paige Beryl Polly; *b* 1997

(2) *Mary Betty [Mrs Robert Calvin, 464 Oriole Parkway, Toronto, Ontario, Canada]; *b* 31 Aug 1937; *educ* Smith Coll (BA), Trin Coll Toronto U (MDiv); *m* 2 Sept 1958 *Robert Alexander Calvin and has issue:

1a *Robert Denys; *b* 3 Jan 1960; *m* 1986 *Barbara Patricia Lee, and has issue:

1b *Graham Denys; *b* 1992

1b *Sarah Emily; *b* 1990

2a *John Collamer; *b* 12 May 1962

1a *Isobel Anne; *b* 24 June 1965; *m* 1990 *Justin Gray Bonar

(3) *Cary; *b* 11 March 1945; *educ* Chatham Coll Pittsburgh USA (BA); *m* 1984 *Robert A Johnson, and has issue:

1a *Marlana Rose; *b* 1988

1 (Marguerite) Betty; *m* 15 Jan 1940 Maj Rev John Joseph Tatum (*d* 4 March 1966), son of T W Tatum, and had issue:

(1) *Michael Jon; *b* 15 April 1941; *educ* Whitgift Sch Croydon and Southampton Sch of Navigation; *m* 26 Sept 1963 *Marcia, dau of Gordon and has issue:

1a *Nicholas Benjamin; *b* 15 Jan 1969

1a *Sarah Louise; *b* 14 March 1965

(2) *Denys Jon; *b* 8 May 1948; *educ* Lewes GS Sussex

(1) *Frances Jane; *b* 6 Aug 1943; *m* 26 Sept 1968 *Jon David Levine, son of Maurice Levine, of 3388 Wayne Ave, Bronx 67, NY, USA

2 *Sybil Mary [Hon Mrs Cadman, Bryn-Dedwydd, Maerdy, Corwen, Clwyd LL21 9NY]; *b* 1916; *m* 1st 10 June 1938 Maj-Gen William Pat Arthur Bradshaw, CB, DSO, late Scots Gds (*d* 9 April 1966), son of Arthur Bradshaw; *m* 2nd 1968 James Simon Cadman (*see* above), and has had issue by 1st husb:

(1) *Christopher Patrick Cadman [Christopher Bradshaw Esq, Blackbrook House, Dorking, Surrey]; *b* 7 Jan 1941; *educ* Eton and St Andrews U (BSc); Project Leader BP Chemicals; *m* 1973 *Susan Elizabeth, dau of D W Vasey, of Downways, Old Bosham, Sussex, and has issue:

1a *Benjamin Patrick; *b* 1975; *educ* Ardingly

1a *Philippa Mary; *b* 1977

2a *Emma Judith; *b* 1979

(2) *(Francis) John Cadman, LVO (1984) [Cdr John Bradshaw LVO RN, Rhagatt Hall, Carrog, Corwen, Clwyd LL21 9NY]; *b* 30 July 1946; *educ* Pangbourne Nautical Coll and RNC Dartmouth; *m* 1981 *Frances Mary Christine, only dau of Col Robert Hugh Cuming, MBE (*see* ROBERTSON, B), and has issue:

1a *Anna Mary Christine; *b* 1983

2a *Juliet Frances; *b* 1985

3a *Isobel Fiona; *b* 1987

(3) Richard; *b* 24 Nov, *d* 26 Nov 1950

(1) *Caroline [Mrs Francis Black, The Old Vicarage, Wing, Beds LU7 0NU]; *b* 24 March 1939; *m* 23 April 1959 *Francis Rokeby Black, FCA, only son of Capt Alan Francis Black, DSC, RN, of Blackheath, and has:

1a *James Pat Rokeby; *b* 28 Nov 1963; *educ* Eton and Exeter U (BSc); *m* 1990 *Susan Elizabeth Bone and has:

1b *Charles Joshua Rokeby; *b* 9 April 1995

2a *Alexander William Francis; *b* 19 April 1967; *educ* Harrow and Exeter U (BSc); ACA

1a *Lucinda Rosalie; *b* 11 April 1960; *educ* Exeter U (BA); *m* 1985 *Philip Latham Baillieu (*see* BAILLIEU, B)

2a *Natasha Caroline; *b* 4 May 1976; *educ* Oxford Brookes U (BEd)

(2) *Rosalie Annette [Mrs David Adams, The Old Rectory, Holtby, York YO1 3UD]; *b* 30 June 1944; *m* 9 June 1965 *David Bernard Butler Adams, er son of Derek Butler Adams, TD, MA, of Great Cozens, Ware, Herts, and has issue:

1a *William David; *b* 1974; *educ* Rubgy

1a *Sophie Anne; *b* 21 May 1966

2a *Amanda Jane; *b* 8 March 1968

3a *Fiona Mary; *b* 1972

The 1st BARON *d* 31 May 1941; his er son,

JOHN BASIL COPE CADMAN, **2nd Baron Cadman**; *educ* Harrow and Grenoble U; *b* 23 March 1909; *m* 3 Dec 1936 *Marjorie Elizabeth [The Rt Hon Marjorie Lady Cadman, Overlands, 157 Church Rd, Combe Down, Bath], dau of Byron William Bunnis, of Middlesbrough, and *d* 5 April 1966, having had issue:

1 JOHN ANTHONY CADMAN, **3rd and present Baron Cadman**

2 +James Rupert [The Hon James Cadman, Overlands, 157 Church Rd, Combe Down, Bath]; *b* 9 June 1944; *educ* Harrow

CADOGAN

Arms: Quarterly, 1st and 4th, gu. a lion rampant regardant or; 2nd and 3rd, arg. three boar's heads couped sa. **Crest:** Out of a ducal coronet or a dragon's head vert. **Supporters:** Dexter, a lion regardant or, gorged with a collar gemel flory counterflory gu.; sinister, an eagle, wings elevated, sa., beaked, membered and navally crowned or, gorged with a riband arg., fimbriated gu., pendent therefrom a representation of the cross of the Imperial Austrian military order of Maria Theresa (conferred on 3rd Earl 1814 after combined UK/Austrian ops on Adriatic coast). **Motto:** *Qui invidet minor est* ('He who envies is the inferior'). **Creations:** B. (GB) 8 May 1718 (Cadogan of Oakley), E. and V. (GB) 27 Dec 1800, B. (UK) 10 Sept 1831.

THE 8TH EARL CADOGAN, Viscount Chelsea, Baron Cadogan of Oakley, Co Buckingham, and **Baron Oakley of Caversham,** Co Oxford (Charles Gerald John Cadogan, DL (Gtr London 1996)) [The Rt Hon The Earl Cadogan DL, 7 Smith St, London SW3 4EE; Marwdhill, Ardington, Wantage, Oxon OX12 8PN]; *b* 24 March 1937; *s f* 1997; *educ* Eton; late 2nd Lt Coldstream Gds, Liveryman Air Pilots' and Navigators' Guild, Freeman City London, Hon Fell Roy Vet Coll and ISVA, Dep Sr Steward Jockey Club 1985–89, dir Jockey Club Estates Ltd Newmarket, London Bd Eagle Star, chm Chelsea FC 1963–82; *m* 1st 6 June 1963 Lady Philippa Dorothy Bluett Wallop (*d* 1984), 2nd dau of 9th Earl of Portsmouth (*qv*); *m* 2nd 1989 Jennifer Jane Greig, dau of J E K Rae and Mrs S Z de Ferranti; *m* 3rd 25 July 1994 *Dorothy (Dot) Ann, MVO, matron King Edward VII Hosp for Offrs, yr dau of Dr W E Shipsey, and has by his 1st w:

1 +Edward Charles; *b* 10 May 1966; *educ* St David's Coll Llandudno; *m* 1990 *Katharina Johanna Ingeborg, dau of R-Adml Diether P H Hülsemann, German Navy, and has issue:

(1) +George Edward Charles Diether; *b* 24 Sept 1995

(1) *Philippa Katharina; *b* 1992

2 +William John; *b* 9 Nov 1973

1 *Anna-Karina; *b* 4 Feb 1964; *m* 1992 *Gary Andrew Thomson and has:

(1) *Alexander Rory; *b* 29 Jan 1998

Lineage: REES Ap Griffith Ap Llewelyn Ap Meredith Bengoch Ap Howell (Ld of Penbualit), Ap Sitsylt (Ld of Builth), Ap Llewelyn (Ld of Builth), Ap Cadwgan, Ap Elystan; of Dolygaer, Breconshire; had, with another s (Ieuan, ancestor of the GWYNs, formerly of Garth):

WILLIAM Ap REES; *m* Jane, dau of William Parry, and had:

WILLIAM Ap WILLIAM, of Llwyn Cadogan; *m* Lucy, dau and heir of John Gunter, and had:

GRIFFITH CADWGAN; *m* Jane, dau of William Kemeys, and had:

PHILIP CADWGAN; *m* Alice, dau of John Glandon, of Glanddewis, and had:

WILLIAM CADWGAN; *m* Jenet, dau of John Evan Meredith, and had:

THOMAS CADWGAN, of Trostrey, Mon; *m* Christian, dau of Howell of Kemeys, and *d* between 12 June and 12 July 1511, leaving:

WILLIAM CADWGAN, of Trostrey and Croftney; *m* Anne, dau of John Arnold, and had, with an er s (William, of Croftney):

HENRY CADOGAN, of Trostrey and later Llanbedr, Pembs; *m* Catherine, dau of Thomas Stradling, and had:

WILLIAM CADOGAN, of Liscartan, Co Meath, High Sheriff 1658, MP Co Monaghan 1639–49, Sec to Ld Deputy Ireland, Maj, defended Trim Castle, Co Meath, in Civil War; *b* 5 Feb 1600/1; *m* 1st Elizabeth (*dsp* 25 Jan 1641), only dau of Tremer Thring, of Drogheda; *m* 2nd Elizabeth (*d* 20 Feb 1664/5), dau of — Roberts, of Carnarvon, and *d* 14 March 1660/1, leaving by his 2nd w:

HENRY CADOGAN, of Liscartan, High Sheriff Co Meath 1700, barrister; *b* 1642; *educ* Trin Coll Dublin; *m c* 31 July 1671 Bridget (*d* Dec 1721), dau of Sir Hardress Waller, and *d* 13 Jan 1713/4 had:

1 WILLIAM CADOGAN, **1st Baron Cadogan of Oakley,** Co Buckingham, so *cr* 8 May 1718, as also VISCOUNT CAVERSHAM, Co Oxford, and EARL CADOGAN, Co Denbigh (with special remainder of the barony only to his bro Charles), as well as 21 June 1716 BARON CADOGAN OF READING, Co Berks (all GB), KT (1716), PC (1717); *b* 1672; *educ* Westminster and Trin Coll Dublin; Col 1694, Col 7th ('Cadogan's') Horse 1703–12, Brig-Gen 1704, Maj Gen 1706, Lt Gen 1709 (fought Battles of Blenheim 1704, Ramillies 1706, Oudenarde 1708 and Malplaquet 1709), Gen all Foot 1717, MP (Whig) Woodstock 1705–16, and served with distinction under Marlborough at; Envoy Hanover 1706 and The Hague 1707–10 (Amb 1714–20), Lt Tower London 1706–12, Master Robes 1714–26, Govr IoW 1715–26, C-in-C Scotland Feb-May 1716, Master Gen Ordnance 1722–25; *m* Margaretta Cecilia (*d* 22 Oct 1749), dau of John/William Munter, Cncllr Court of Holland, and dspm 17 July 1726, when the earldom, viscountcy and earlier barony expired, leaving:

(1) Sarah; *m* 4 Dec 1719 2nd Duke of Richmond (*see* RICHMOND and GORDON, D), and had issue

(2) Margaret; *m* 11 Jan 1738 Charles John Bentinck, 4th s of 1st Earl of Portland (*qv*)

2 Ambrose, Lt Killigrew's marines; *d* unm 11 Sept 1693

3 CHARLES, **2nd Baron**

1 Frances; *d* aged 9

2 Penelope; *m c* 10 Aug 1697 Sir Thomas Prendergast, Bt (*see* GORT, V)

The 1st BARON's bro,

CHARLES CADOGAN, **2nd Baron Cadogan of Oakley;** *b* 1685; MP (Whig) Reading 1716–22 and Newport IoW 1722–26, Gen 1761, Col 2nd Horse Gds; *m* 25 July 1717 Elizabeth (*d* 20 May 1768), dau and coheir of the physician Sir Hans Sloane, Bt, through whom the Cadogans acquired their London property, and *d* 24 Sept 1776, leaving:

CHARLES SLOANE CADOGAN, **3rd Baron Cadogan of Oakley** and **1st Earl Cadogan,** so *cr* 27 Dec 1800, as also VISCOUNT CHELSEA, Co Middx (both GB); *b* 29 Sept 1728; MP (Whig) Cambridge 1749–54 and 1755–76, Master Mint 1769–84; *m* 1st 30 May 1747 Hon Frances Bromley (*d* 25 May 1768), dau of 1st Baron Montfort, and had issue:

1 CHARLES HENRY SLOANE CADOGAN, **2nd Earl Cadogan;** *b* 29 Nov 1749; a lunatic; *d* unm 23 Dec 1832

2 William Bromley; Vicar Chelsea; *b* 22 Jan 1751; *m* 4 Dec 1782 Jane Bradshaw (*d* 19 March 1827) and *d* 18 Jan 1797

3 Thomas, RN; *b* 7 Feb 1752; lost in HMS *Glorieux* 1782

4 George; offr HEICS army; *b* 1 Dec 1754; *k* India 1780

5 Edward, army offr; *b* 12 Dec 1758; *d* 1779

6 Henry William; *b* 25 March 1761; *d* 4 Aug 1774

The **1st Earl** *m* 2nd 10 May 1777 (*divorce* 1796) Mary, dau of Col Charles Churchill by Mary, legitimated dau of 1st Earl of Orford (*see* WALPOLE, B), and *d* 3 April 1807, having by her had, with other issue:

7 Henry, Lt-Col 71st Regt; *b* 26 Feb 1780; *k* Battle of Vittoria 21 June 1813

8 GEORGE CADOGAN, **3rd Earl Cadogan** and **1st Baron Oakley of Caversham,** Co Oxford (UK), so *cr* 10 Sept 1831, CB (1815), Kt Maria Theresa 1815 (*see* **Supporters** above), Adml of the Red; *b* 5 May 1783; *m* 4 April 1810 Honoria Louisa (*d* 12 Sept 1845), dau of Joseph Blake, of Ardfry, Co Galway, and sis of 1st Baron Wallscourt (*see* 1917 edn), and had issue:

(1) HENRY CHARLES, **4th Earl**

(2) George (Sir), KCB, Gen, Col 71st Foot, Kt Medjidie, Cdr 1st Cl SS. Maurice and Lazarus; *b* 2 Dec 1814; *m* 1st 19 Feb 1846 Sophia (*d* 26 Jan 1852), dau of Col Thomas Armstrong, Coldstream Gds, and had issue:

1a Mary; *b* 8 Dec 1847; *d* unm 15 April 1882

2a Honoria Frances; *b* 15 June 1849; *d* unm *c* 1895

3a Olivia Georgiana; *b* 3 Sept 1850; *m* 6 Sept 1877 Lippo Neri, Count Palagi del Palagio, a Florentine patrician, and *d* 19 July 1910, leaving issue. He *d* 13 May 1893

4a Sophia Isabella Harriet; *b* 7 Jan 1853; *m* 24 Dec 1879 Marchese Augusto Brichieri Colombi, of Villa Bellosguardo, Florence, Capt Italian Army, s of Marchese Stanislao Giovanni Brichieri Colombi, and *d* 3 Feb 1928, leaving issue. He *d* 15 Dec 1922

(2) (cont.) Sir George *m* 2nd 23 July 1857 Emily (*d* 4 March 1891), dau of Gen Sir Frederick Ashworth, KCB, and *d* 27 Jan 1880, having by her had issue:

1a Horace James Henry; *b* 25 May 1862; *d* 28 April 1932

(3) Horace William; *d* an infant 21 Feb 1820

(4) Frederick William, MP Cricklade 1868–74, DL, JP Middx; *b* 16 Dec 1821; *m* 29 Nov 1851 Lady Adelaide Paget (*d* 21 Aug 1890), dau of 1st Marquess of Anglesey (*qv*), and *d* 30 Nov 1904, having had issue:

1a Henry George Gerald, Sec Legation Teheran; *b* 25 April 1859; *d* unm 21 Aug 1893

1a Charlotte Louisa Emily; *m* 9 Jan 1883 Rev Henry Montagu Villiers, MA, Vicar St Paul's Knightsbridge, Preb St Paul's Cathedral, and *d* 3 June 1947, leaving issue (*see* CLARENDON, E)

2a Ethel Henrietta Maria (Hon), VA, Extra Maid-of-Hon 1876–80, Maid-of-Hon 1880–97, Woman Bedchamber 1897–1901 to HM QUEEN VICTORIA; *d* unm 30 Dec 1930

3a Margaret Jane Caroline; *m* 6 Feb 1892 Maj Hon Walter Lewis Bagot, DSO, Gren Gds, s of 3rd Baron Bagot (*qv*), and *d* 14 June 1941, leaving issue

(1) Augusta Sarah, Ldy-in-Waiting to HRH THE DUCHESS OF CAMBRIDGE, *d* unm 28 Nov 1882

(2) Honoria Louisa; *b* 1813; *d* unm 19 July 1904

The 3rd EARL *d* 15 Sept 1864; his est son,

HENRY CHARLES CADOGAN, **4th Earl Cadogan,** PC (1866); *educ* Oriel Coll Oxford (BA), MP (C) Reading 1841–47 and Dover 1852–57, Capt Yeoman Gd, Col Roy Westminster Middx Mil; *b* 15 Feb 1812; *m* 13 July 1936 his cousin Mary Sarah (*d* 11 Feb 1873), 3rd dau of Rev Hon Gerald Valerian Wellesley, DD (*see* COWLEY, E), and had issue:

1 GEORGE HENRY, **5th Earl**

2 Arthur Charles Lewin, Capt 3rd Middx Mil, formerly Lt RN; *b* 23 June 1841; *m* 1st 9 April 1870 Alice Charlotte (*dsp* 16 Sept 1877), yst dau of Richard Arabin; *m* 2nd 25 Jan 1888 Mary (*d* 6 Jan 1914), yr dau of Rev George Livingstone

Fenton, MA, and widow of George W Schofield, of Buckley Hall, Rochdale, and *dsp* 20 Nov 1918

3 Cecil James George, Cdr RN; *b* 27 March 1846; *d* unm 5 June 1918

4 Charles George Henry, Capt Gren Gds; *b* 14 June 1850; *m* 20 June 1874 Henriette Wilhelmina (*m* 2nd 25 Nov 1903 Harry Hinton, of Funchal, Madeira, who *d* 16 April 1948 aged 91, and *d* 24 Sept 1913), 3rd dau of Henry Montgomery, of Gothenburg, and *d* 30 Sept 1901, leaving issue:

(1) Victor Henry Arnold; *b* 14 July 1879; *m* 5 Oct 1905 Lily (*d* 21 May 1956) (who *m* 2nd 27 April 1912 Geoffrey MacLaren, 4th son of James MacLaren, of Manchester), 2nd dau of Henry Charles Nelson Suter, and *dsp* 14 Feb 1910

(2) John Cecil, Lt Scots Gds; *b* 15 March 1883; *educ* Haileybury; *m* 25 Oct 1911 Ella (*d* 18 April 1971 aged 90) dau of Gustav Krafft, of Gothenburg, and Särö, Sweden, and *d* 24 Jan 1970, leaving issue:

1a Erik, JP (Warwicks 1959); *b* 22 May 1913; *educ* Stowe; *m* 23 March 1939 *Caroline, dau of Count Hans Wachtmeister, of Malmö, Sweden, and *d* 1990, leaving issue:

1b +Charles John; *b* 23 June 1954; *educ* Stowe

1b *(Caroline) Monica; *b* 15 March 1942; *m* 1974 *Maj Hon Peter Herbert Lewis and has issue (*see* MERTHYR, B)

2b *Patricia Elisabeth; *b* 6 Aug 1945; *m* 1974 *Simon Mark Corbett, and has issue:

1b *Camilla Louise; *b* 1978

2b *Lucy Miranda; *b* 1980

2a Peter; *b* 23 Feb 1918; *educ* Merton Coll Oxford; served WW II with SHAEF; *m* 1st 30 July 1940 (*divorce* 1955) Joan (*d* 1979), only dau of R-Adml (S) Frederick Arthur Frith Banbury, of Buddington, Midhurst, Sussex, and had issue:

1b +Gerald [Gerald Cadogan Esq, Culworth, Banbury, Oxon OX17 2AT]; *b* 26 Feb 1942; *educ* Harrow, Merton Coll Oxford (BA 1964, MA 1967) and Br Sch Athens; research lecturer Ch Ch Oxford 1968; *m* 6 April 1968 *Lucy Dodd, yr dau of Walter Ramberg, of Washington, DC, and has issue:

1c +Leo; *b* 11 Jan 1975

1c *Nancy; *b* 1979

1b *Sarah [Lady Burns JP, c/o FCO, King Charles St, London SW1A 2AH]; *b* 30 May 1944; *m* 1st 17 Sept 1966 (*divorce* 1971) Geoffrey Hugh Kenion, actor, s of Maj H G H Kenion, RA (ret), and Mrs D Rennie; *m* 2nd 1973 *Sir Robert Andrew Burns, KCMG, and has by her 1st husb:

1c *Robert Duncan; *b* 29 May 1975

2c *Thomas Alexander Luckwell; *b* 15 March 1977

1c *Ella Jane; *b* 23 Nov 1968; *m* 1997 *Andrew Curtis

2a (cont.) Peter Cadogan *m* 2nd 25 July 1955 *Pamela Mary, only dau of Alexander Henry Burman, OBE, of Abax, Bolney, Sussex, and *d* 24 June 1962

(3) Francis Charles; *b* 1 Jan 1885; *educ* HMS *Britannia*; Cdr RN, FZS, FRGS, served in S African War and WW I, Anzac Landing, Dover Patrol, and Black and Caspian Seas and WW II (Sea Transport Offr, London 1939–40, RNO Buckie 1941–44); *m* 2 Sept 1913 Ruth Evelyn (*d* 14 March 1962), dau of Sir Edward Stafford Howard, KCB (see NORFOLK, D), and widow of Gardner Sebastian Bazley, of Hatherop Castle, Glos, (*see* BAZLEY, Bt), and *d* 15 March 1970, having had issue:

1a Christopher Michael; *b* 4 Feb 1917; *educ* Eton and Magdalen Coll Oxford (BA 1938); Capt Roy Berks Regt WW II; *m* 11 July 1940 Stella Irena (*d* 2 Feb 1998 having *m* 2nd 6 Nov 1943 (*divorce* 1955) Lt-Col David Rhys Ellias, Intell Corps, only son of Rhys Ellias, of Sketty, Swansea; *m* 3rd 6 June 1958 Sir Geoffrey Arnold Wallinger, GBE, GCMG (*d* 5 July 1979), s of Capt William Arnold Wallinger, OBE, of Geneva), dau of Konni Zilliacus, MP, and was drowned on active service off Cyprus June 1941, leaving:

1b *Catharine Anne [Miss Catharine Cadogan, 32 Tierney Rd, London SW2 4QR]; *b* 23 April 1941

1a *Henriette Alice, DCVO (1977), JP [Lady Abel Smith DCVO JP, The Garden House, Quenington, Glos] *b* 6 June 1914; Extra Woman of the Bedchamber to HM THE QUEEN; *m* 1st 4 Sept 1939 Maj Sir Anthony Frederick Mark Palmer, 4th Bt (*ka* 18 May 1941; *see* PALMER, Bt, of Grinkle); *m* 2nd 17 Feb 1953 Brig Sir Alexander Abel Smith, TD, JP (*d* 1980), yst s of Lt-Col Francis Abel Smith, DL, of Wilford Ho, nr Nottingham, and Cole Orton Hall, nr Ashby, Leics, and has further issue:

1b *Christopher; *b* 28 June 1954 (HM THE QUEEN stood sponsor); *educ* Eton; *m* 19– *Catherine, dau of Paul Berger, of Nancy, France, and has:

1c *Lyam Paul Alexander; *b* 1988

1c *A dau; *b* 1985

1b *Juliet Sarah; *b* 26 Aug 1955; *m* 1979 *Christoher Graham Stainforth, s of Maj-Gen Charles Herbert Stainforth, CB, OBE, of Powderham Ho, Dippenhall, Farnham, Surrey, and has issue:

1c *Charles Alexander; *b* 1989

1 Emily Frances; *d* young 5 Oct 1843

2 Charlotte Georgiana Mary; *m* 14 July 1874 Rev Maynard Wodehouse Currie, 3rd son of Raikes Currie, of Minley Manor, Hants, and *d* 16 Nov 1908. He *dsp* 1887

The 4th EARL *d* 8 June 1873; his est son,

GEORGE HENRY CADOGAN, **5th Earl Cadogan**, KG, PC, JP (London, Middx, Cambs, Suffolk, and Norfolk), Under-Sec: War 1875–78, Colonies 1878–80, Ld Privy Seal 1886–92, Ld Lt Ireland 1895–1902, MP (C) Bath May-June 1873, Hon LLD Dublin, 1st Mayor Chelsea 1900, Hereditary Tstee Br Museum, Hon Col 3rd Bn Roy Fus and 2nd Middx Roy Vols; *b* 12 May 1840; *m* 1st 16 May 1865 Lady Beatrix Jane Craven, VA, LGStJ (*d* 9 Feb 1907), 4th dau of 2nd Earl of Craven (*qv*), and had issue:

1 Albert Edward George Henry, *Viscount Chelsea*; *b* 29 Dec 1866 (HRH THE PRINCE OF WALES later HM EDWARD VII stood sponsor); *d* 2 Aug 1878

2 Henry Arthur, *Viscount Chelsea*, DL (Co London), Capt 3rd Bn Roy Fus, Priv Sec to 1st Ld Treasury, MP (C) Bury St Edmunds 1892–1900; *b* 13 June 1868; *m* 30 April 1892 Hon Mildred Cecilia Harriet Sturt (*m* 2nd 18 April 1910 Adml of the Fleet Hon Sir Hedworth Lambton later Meux, GCB (*d* 20 Sept 1929), 3rd s of 2nd Earl of Durham (*qv*); *m* 3rd 4 Dec 1930 Lord Charles Montagu, CVO (*d* 10 Nov 1939), s of 7th Duke of Manchester (*qv*), and *d* 17 Sept 1942), dau of 1st Baron Alington (*see* 1940 edn), and *dvp* 2 July 1908, having had:

(1) Edward George John Humphrey, *Viscount Chelsea*; *b* 20 March 1903 (TH EDWARD VII and GEORGE V stood sponsor); *d* 2 June 1910

(1) Sibyl Louise Beatrix (Hon), Extra Maid of Hon to HM QUEEN MARY 1914–17; *b* 7 Jan 1893 (HRH THE DUCHESS of FIFE stood sponsor); *m* 17 July 1917 Lord Stanley, PC, MC, MP, er son of 17th Earl of Derby (*qv*), and *d* 21 June 1969, leaving issue

(2) Edith Mary Winifred, DBE (1939), chm of Central Women's Advsy Ctee C Party 1935; *b* 1 Aug 1895; *m* 8 Aug 1916 3rd Baron Hillingdon (see 1970 edn) and *d* 4 June 1969, leaving issue

(3) Cynthia Hilda Evelyn; *b* 8 Oct 1896; *m* 2 Oct 1917 Capt Sir Humphrey Edmund de Trafford, 4th Bt (*qv*), and *d* 13 March 1966, leaving issue

(4) Alexandra Mary, CBE (1953); *b* 22 Feb 1900 (HM QUEEN ALEXANDRA stood sponsor), Ch Cmdt ATS; *m* 17 Feb 1920 10th Duke of Marlborough (*qv*) and *d* 23 May 1961, leaving issue

(5) Victoria Laura, OBE (1927), TD, Controller ATS; *b* 22 Oct 1901; *m* 22 July 1922 (*divorce* 1929) Sir John Gilmour, 2nd Bt (*see* GILMOUR OF CRAIGMILLAR, B) and had issue

3 GERALD OAKLEY, **6th Earl**

4 Lewin Edward; *b* 9 Oct 1872; *d* unm 12 Aug 1917

5 William George Sydney, MVO, Maj 10th Hus, GSO (3) 1914, Equerry to HRH THE PRINCE OF WALES 1912–14, served Boer War 1899–1902 and WW I; *b* 31 Jan 1879; *ka* 12 Nov 1914

6 Edward Cecil George (Sir), KBE (1939), CB (1921), DL, JP and V-Lt Co London, barrister, MP Reading 1922–23, Finchley 1924–35 and Bolton 1940–45, Sec to Speaker H of C 1911–21, memb Indian Statutory Commn 1927–30, Maj Suffolk Yeo WW I (despatches) and RAF WW II, Order Al Rafidain Iraq 1st Cl 1956; *b* 15 Nov 1880; *educ* Eton and Balliol Coll Oxford (BA 1902); *d* unm 13 Sept 1962

7 Alexander George Montagu (Sir), PC (1946), OM (1951), GCMG (1939), KCB (1941); *b* 25 Nov 1884; *educ* Eton and Balliol Coll Oxford (BA 1908, Hon Fell 1960); entered Dip Serv 1908, Counsellor 1929, Envoy Extrdy and Min Plen Peking 1933, Amb Extrdy 1935, Dep Under-Sec For Affairs 1936–38 (PUS 1938), Perm UK Rep UN Security Cncl 1946, ret 1950, govt dir Suez Canal Co 1951, dir: Nat Prov Bank and Phoenix Assur 1951, chm Bd Govrs BBC 1952, Hon DCL Toronto 1947, McGill and Princeton 1950; *m* 3 Aug 1912 Lady Theodosia Louisa Augusta Acheson (*d* 1912), dau of 4th Earl of Gosford (*qv*), and *d* 9 July 1968, leaving issue:

(1) +Ambrose Alec Patrick George [Ambrose Cadogan Esq, 8 Wilton Rd, Reading, Berks]; *b* 19 March 1914; *educ* Le Rosey and Wye Ag Coll Kent; HG and RM WW II (invalided); *m* 7 Dec 1955 (*divorce* 1961) Pamela Maud, er dau of Lt-Col Ivan Murray Cobbold, DL, Scots Gds, of Glemham Hall, Woodbridge, Suffolk, and formerly w of Maj William Vernon Hope-Johnstone, late Gren Gds

(1) *Patricia; *b* 30 Jan 1916; *m* 2 Sept 1939 Lt-Col Gerald Edward Coke, Scots Gds, s of Maj Hon Sir John Spencer Coke, KCVO, late Scots Gds, and has had issue (*see* LEICESTER, E)

(2) *Cynthia JP (Berks 1957), Co Assist ATS; *b* 28 July 1918; *m* 6 Dec 1946 *Maj Sir Edward Christian Goschen, 3rd Bt (*qv*), and has issue

(3) *Gillian Moyra; *b* 4 Feb 1922; *m* 1 Oct 1948 *Patrick Henry Douglas Crichton (*see* ERNE, E), and has issue

1 Emily Julia; *b* 11 April 1871; *m* 7 Feb 1893 3rd Baron Lurgan (*see* 1970 edn) and *d* 12 Dec 1909, leaving issue. He *d* 9 Feb 1937

2 Sophie Beatrix Mary, CBE (1918); *b* 6 April 1874; *m* 29 June 1896 Sir Samuel Scott, 6th Bt , and *d* 8 Nov 1937, having had issue. He *d* 20 Feb 1943

The **5th Earl** *m* 2nd 12 Jan 1911 his cousin Adele (*d* 23 Feb 1960), dau of Lippo Meri, Count Palagi del Palagio by Olivia Georgiana, dau of Gen Hon Sir George Cadogan (*see* above), and *d* 6 March 1915

His 3rd but est surv son,

GERALD OAKLEY CADOGAN, **6th Earl Cadogan**, CBE (1919), DL Suffolk, hereditary Tstee Br Museum, Hon Lt-Col Suffolk Vol Regt, Lt 1st Life Gds, Capt 3rd Bn Suffolk Regt, ADC to Ld Lt Ireland 1895–1905, Boer War 1900; *b* 28 May 1869; *m* 7 June 1911 Lilian Eleanor Marie (*d* 24 Nov 1973) (*m* 2nd 31 March 1941 Lt-Col Harold Everard Hambro, CBE (*see* HAMBRO, B), only dau of George Stewart Coxon, of Craigleith, Cheltenham, and *d* 4 Oct 1933, leaving:

1 WILLIAM GERALD CHARLES CADOGAN, **7th Earl Cadogan**, MC (1943), DL (Co London 1958); *b* 13 Feb 1914; *educ* Eton and RMC Sandhurst; Lt-Col Roy Wilts Yeo TA, Capt (Hon Lt-Col) Coldstream Gds Res Offrs WW II, Hereditary Tstee Br Museum, memb Chelsea Borough Cncl 1953–59, Utd Grand Lodge England: Sr Grand Warden 1954–55, Dep Gd Master 1960–97, pres Chelsea FC 1934, Sr Steward Nat Hunt Ctee 1963, Mayor Chelsea 1964, pres Chelsea Soc; *m* 1st 11 June 1936 (*divorce* 1959) Hon Primrose Lilian Yarde-Buller (*d* 6 Dec 1970), yst dau of 3rd Baron Churston (*qv*); *m* 2nd 13 Jan 1961 *Cecilia Margaret [The Rt Hon Cecilia Countess Cadogan, Snaigow, Dunkeld, Perthshire; 28 Cadogan Square, London SW1X 0JH], yst dau of Maj Henry Kellerman Hamilton-Wedderburn, OBE, and *d* 4 July 1997, leaving by his 1st w:

(1) CHARLES GERALD JOHN CADOGAN, **8th and present Earl Cadogan**

(1) *Sarah Primrose Beatrix [The Rt Hon The Lady Rockley, Lytchett Heath, Poole, Dorset BH16 6AE]; *b* 23 Feb 1938; *m* 18 Nov 1958 *3rd Baron Rockley (*qv*), and has issue

(2) *Daphne Magdalen [The Lady Daphne Bailey, The Manor House, Dry Sandford, Abingdon, Oxon OX13 6JP]; *b* 23 Oct 1939; *m* 19 Dec 1961 *David Malcolm Graham Bailey, yr s of Ronald Graham Bailey, of 7 Lansdowne Crescent, W11, and has issue:

1a *Alexander Graham [Alexander Bailey Esq, 34 Twining Ave, Twickenham, Middx TW2 5UR]; *b* 21 Sept 1962; *educ* Eton; *m* 1986 *Mariam Atsede Ambaye and has issue:

1b *Antony Francis Christopher Graham; *b* 1987

1b *Antoinette Catonia Mia Lydia Alga; *b* 1987 (twin)

2a *Kevin David; *b* 6 April 1964; *educ* Eton

1a *Leonie Daphne; *b* 21 Aug 1965; *m* 1988 *Brian Sharrock, est s of Kevin Sharrock, of MacArthur, Victoria, Australia

(3) *Caroline Ann [The Lady Caroline Tahany, 11 Oakley Gardens, London SW3]; *b* 4 Feb 1946; assumed name TAHANY 1981; *m* 22 April 1965 (*divorce*

1975) Euan Woodroffe Foster, only s of Sir Peter Harry Baston Woodroffe Foster, MBE, TD, QC, BA, LLB, of 70 Elizabeth St, SW11 and Otley Hall, Suffolk and has:

1a *Guy Peter Woodroffe; *b* 10 May 1968

2a *Hugo Woodroffe; *b* 16 May 1971

1 *Beatrix Lilian Ethel [The Lady Beatrix Fanshawe, 74 Cranmer Court, Sloane Ave, London SW3 3HF] ; *b* 12 May 1912; *m* 1st 22 Jan 1931 (*divorce* 1941) Henry Peregrine Rennie Hoare (*d* 1981), er s of Henry Hoare, of Ellisfield, Hants, and has issue:

(1) *Henry Cadogan; *b* 1931; *educ* Eton and Trin Coll Camb (MA); *m* 1st 1959 (*divorce* 1970) Pamela Saxon, dau of Col George Francis Bunbury, OBE; *m* 2nd 1977 *Caromy, dau of Robert Jenkins, CBE, and formerly w of Donald Maxwell Macdonald (*see* DUCIE, E), and has issue by 1st w:

1a *Henry Timothy; *b* 1960

2a *Nicholas Colt; *b* 1964

1s *Arabella S; *b* 1968

(1) *Melanie Beatrix; *b* 1937; *m* 1963 *Charles Henry Petre (*see* PETRE, B)

1 (cont.) Lady Beatrix Hoare *m* 2nd 22 Aug 1942 Col Edward Leighton Fanshawe (*d* 1982), est s of Lt-Gen Sir Edward Arthur Fanshawe, KCB, and has further issue:

(2) *Ann Erika; *b* 1943

(3) *Clodagh Frances; *b* 1945

2 Alexandra Mary; *b* 10 March 1920; *m* 1st 21 Aug 1940 (*divorce* 1949) Maj Robert Gilliam Buchanan, KOSB, 1st Airborne Div, 2nd s of Lt-Col Arthur Louis Hamilton Buchanan, OBE; *m* 2nd 25 July 1951 Norman Hutchison Smith, and had issue:

(1) *Adam Gerald Norman; *b* 7 Dec 1959

(1) *Alexandra (Aleca) Josephine; *b* 5 July 1952; *m* 16 March 1978 *Charles Robson, er s of William Robbson, of Lincoln Old Rectory, Midhurst, Sussex

(2) *Andrula Mary; *b* 26 June 1954

CAHN

Arms: Gu. a cross raguly erm., between in the second and third quarters a fleur-de-lys or. **Crest:** In front of a fox's head erased two branches of willow in saltire ppr. **Motto:** *Possunt quia posse videntur* ('They are able because they seem able'). **Creation:** Bt. (UK) 27 June 1934.

SIR ALBERT JONAS CAHN, 2ND BT, of Stanford-upon-Soar, Co Nottingham [Sir Albert Cahn Bt, 10 Edgecoombe Close, Warren Rd, Kensington upon Thames, Surrey KT2 7HP]; *b* 27 June 1924; *s* f 1944; *educ* Harrow; company director; *m* 16 March 1948 *Malka, only dau of Reuben Bluestone, of Springfield Close, Angmering, Sussex, and has issue:

1 +JULIEN MICHAEL [Julien Cahn Esq, 1 Court Hope Villas, Wimbledon, London SW19]; *b* 15 Jan 1951; *educ* Harrow; *m* 1987 *Marilynne Janelle, dau of Frank Owen Blyth, and has issue:

(1) +Benjamin Albert; *b* 28 Feb 1988

(1) *Jessie Laura; *b* 1985

2 +Edward John; *b* 27 July 1959

1 *Madeleine Jane [Mrs David Waller, 52 Cascade Rd, London N10]; *b* March 1949; *m* 1st 1979 (*divorce* 1987) Richard Albert Smith; *m* 2nd 9 Aug 1997 *David Thomas Waller and by her 1st husb has:

(1) *Charles Joseph; *b* 13 July 1982

(1) *Mariza Joanna Phyllis; *b* 5 Aug 1980

2 *Valerie Janet [Mrs Peregrine Crosthwaite, 30 Larpent Ave, London SW15 6UU]; *b* 3 March 1954; *m* 1982 *Peregrine Kenneth Oughton Crosthwaite, and has issue:

(1) *Nicholas Anthony; *b* 1985

(2) *Thomas William; *b* 1986

(1) *Sally-Anne Claire; *b* 1989

Lineage: ALBERT CAHN; *m* Matilda, dau of Dr S Lewes, of Liverpool, and had:

Sir Julien Cahn, 1st Bt (UK), so *cr* 27 June 1934, JP, Ld Manor of Stanford-on-Soar, MFH Burton 1926–35, Woodland Pytchley 1935–37 and the Fernie 1937–39; captained cricket teams to Jamaica 1929, Argentine 1930, Denmark and Jutland 1932, Canada, USA and Bermuda 1933 and Ceylon and Singapore 1937, Kt Cdr George I Greece, Chevalier Legn Honour, ktd 1929; *b* 21 Oct 1882; *m* 11 July 1916 Phyllis Muriel, dau of A Wolfe, of Bournemouth, and *d* 26 Sept 1944, having had issue:

1 Sir ALBERT JONAS CAHN, **2nd and present Bt**

2 +Richard Ian [Richard Cahn Esq, Crispa, Bashurst Copse, Itchingfield, Horsham, Sussex RH13 7NZ]; *b* 15 Dec 1927; *m* 3 Sept 1964 *Marietta, only dau of Joseph Seidler, of 8 Strathearn Place, W2

1 Patience; *b* 10 Feb 1922; *m* 1st 24 July 1945 (*divorce* 1957) F/Lt Jules V Silverston, RAF, son of Bertram Silverston, of Birmingham, and had issue; *m* 2nd 1957 Edward Wynne-Jones, MB, ChB, MRCS, LRCP (*d* 1958); *m* 3rd Aug 1960 (*annulled* 1963) — Pratt (Garnet-Smith) and *d* 19–

CAIRNS

Arms: Gu. three martlets arg., a bordure of the last charged with as many trefoils, slipped vert. **Crest:** A martlet arg., charged on the breast with a trefoil slipped vert. **Supporters:** On either side a hawk ppr., chained and belled or, holding in the beak a trefoil vert. **Motto:** *Effloresco* ('I flourish'). **Creations:** B. (UK) 27 Feb 1867; V. and E. (UK) 27 Sept 1878.

THE 6TH EARL CAIRNS, Viscount Garmoyle, Co Antrim, and **Baron Cairns of Garmoyle**, Co Antrim (Simon Dallas Cairns, CBE (1992)) [The Rt Hon The Earl Cairns CBE, Windsor House, 50 Victoria St, London SW1H 0NL]; *b* 27 May 1939; *s* f 1989; *educ* Eton and Trin Coll Cambridge; former chm S G Warburg, chm BAT 1995– and Cwlth Devpt Corp 1995–, Receiver-Gen Duchy Cornwall 1990–; *m* 4 Feb 1964 *Amanda Mary, only dau of Maj Edward Fitzgerald Heathcoat-Amory, RA (*see* HEATHCOAT-AMORY, Bt), and has issue:

1 +HUGH SEBASTIAN FREDERICK, *Viscount Garmoyle*; *b* 26 March 1965; *educ* Eton and Edinburgh U; *m* 19 Dec 1991 *Juliet, only dau of Andrew Eustace Palmer, CMG, CVO (*see* PALMER,B), of Little Missenden, Bucks, and has issue:

(1) +Oliver David Andrew; *b* 7 March 1993

(1) *Tara Davina Amanda; *b* 3 April 1995

(2) *Harriet; *b* 3 March 1998

2 +(David) Patrick; *b* 27 May 1967; *educ* Eton and Bristol U; *m* 1993 *Francesca ('Fresci') L, dau of Oliver Rena, of Little Venice, W2, and has:

(1) +Oscar; *b* 23 Feb 1996

(2) +Felix Timothy; *b* 18 Feb 1998

3 +Alistair Benedict; *b* 16 May 1969; *educ* Eton and LSE

Lineage: WILLIAM CAIRNS, a cadet of the CAIRNESes of Orchardton (*see* ROSSMORE, B), leased 1716 from the Marquess of Downshire (*qv*) lands at Magheraconluce, Co Down; had:

WILLIAM CAIRNS, of Magheraconluce; *m* 1st — (*d* 1754) and had, with six daus (*dsp*):

1 John, of Parkmount, Co Antrim; *b* 1732; *dsp* 1794

2 Hugh, of Parkmount and Belfast, banker; *b* 1735; *dsp* 1808

3 William, of Magheraconluce; *b* 1737

WILLIAM CAIRNS *m* 2nd Agnes (*d* 1785), dau of William Gregg, of Parkmount, and *d* 1775, having by her had issue:

4 Nathan, of Dublin and Parkmount, merchant; *b* 1759; *m* 1st 20 June 1778 Sarah Hutchinson, of Dublin; *m* 2nd 9 March 1787 Margaret Keine, of Dublin, and *d* 1819, having had, with an er s (Daniel, offr 28th and 62nd Regts, *b* 1784, *d* unm 1802) and a dau (*d* young):

(1) William, of Parkmount, Capt 47th Regt; *b* 1789; *m* 1st 1806 Rosanna (*d* 1822), dau of Hugh Johnston, of Belfast, and had issue:

1a Nathan Daniel; *b* 1807; *m* 1839 Mary, dau of Thomas Miller, of Preston, and *d* 1844, leaving, with four daus:

1b William MacNeile, Capt 43rd LI; *b* 1843; *m* 1 July 1873 Josephine Percy, dau of Rev Charles Bushe, Rector Castlehaven, Co Cork. He *d* 29 Jan 1913

1b Katharine Maria; *d* unm 19 Aug 1908

2b Rosanna; *m* 1866 W H Coddington

2a HUGH McCALMONT, **1st Earl**

(1) (cont.) William Cairns *m* 2nd Matilda, dau of Francis Beggs, of The Grange, Malahide, Co Dublin, and by her had further issue, with five daus:

3a William Wellington (Sir), KCMG, Govr S Australia 1876; *d* unm 7 June 1888

The 2nd son,

HUGH McCALMONT CAIRNS, **1st Earl Cairns**, so *cr* 27 Sept 1878, as also VISCOUNT GARMOYLE, Co Antrim, and earlier 27 Feb 1867 BARON CAIRNS OF GARMOYLE, Co Antrim (all UK), PC (1866), QC (1856); *b* 27 Dec 1819; *educ* Trin Coll Dublin; barrister Middle Temple 1844, MP (C) Belfast 1852–66, Slr-Gen 1858–59, Attorney-Gen July-Oct 1866, Ld Justice Appeal Chancery 1866–68, Ld Chllr Feb-Dec 1868 and 1874–80, LLD Dublin and Cambridge, DCL Oxford, ktd 1858; *m* 9 May 1856 Mary Harriet (*d* 29 Oct 1919), est dau of John MacNeile, of Parkmount, and *d* 2 April 1885, having had:

1 Hugh; *d* an infant 22 July 1858

2 ARTHUR WILLIAM CAIRNS, **2nd Earl Cairns**; *b* 21 Dec 1861; *m* 19 Dec 1887 Olivia Elizabeth, OBE (1920) (who *m* 2nd 1 June 1899 Maj Roger Cyril Hans Sloane-Stanley, DL (*d* 18 Nov 1944), of Paultons, Romsey, Hants, and Roundhill, Lyndhurst, and *d* 20 June 1951, having had further issue), 2nd dau of Alexander Augustus Berens, and *d* 14 Jan 1890, leaving:

(1) Louise Rosemary Kathleen Virginia, MBE (1919), JP, CA Hants; *b* 10 March 1889; *m* 20 April 1909 1st Viscount Portal (*see* PORTAL, Bt) and *dsp* 17 May 1962

3 HERBERT JOHN CAIRNS, **3rd Earl Cairns**; *b* 17 July 1863; *d* unm 14 Jan 1905

4 WILFRID DALLAS, **4th Earl**

5 Douglas Halyburton; *b* 5 Sept 1867; *educ* New Coll Oxford (BA); *m* 21 Jan 1908 Lady Constance Anne Montagu-Douglas-Scott (*d* 7 May 1970), yst dau of 6th Duke of Buccleuch and Queensberry (*qv*), and *d* 6 March 1936, leaving issue:

(1) Hugh William, MC (1944); *b* 27 Jan 1911; Lt-Col Cameron Highrs WW II (wounded); *m* 28 Sept 1939 Diana (Dido) Katherine (*d* 4 Feb 1997), yr dau of Capt Arthur Granville Soames, OBE, of Hayes Lodge, Chesterfield Hill, W1, and had issue:

1a +Peter Granville [Peter Cairns Esq, 11 St Mary Abbot's Court, London W14]; *b* 3 Sept 1940; *educ* Eton; late The Roy Scots Greys; *m* 1991 *Mrs Ann Camilla Carlton, dau of J B Leworthy, of Beacon Hill, Westerham, Kent

2a +Francis John Hugh; *b* 1 Aug 1942; *educ* Eton and Trin Coll Cambridge; *m* 1983 *Ulla Agneta, yr dau of Sten Bylander, of Gothenberg, Sweden, and has issue:

1b *Catriona Helen; *b* 1984

1a *Celia Helen (Cherry) [Mrs David Barclay, Higham, Bury St Edmunds, Suffolk]; *b* 8 May 1944; *m* 4 May 1968 *David William Barclay, er son of Theodore David Barclay, and has issue:

1b *Robin David; *b* 25 July 1969

1b *Katharine Elizabeth; *b* 1971

(1) Helen Christina; *b* 23 Feb 1909; *m* 15 Aug 1935 Maj Hon Andrew Charles Campbell, Queen's Own Cameron Highrs, yr son of 4th Earl Cawdor (*qv*)

1 Lilias Charlotte; *b* 3 Feb 1860; *m* 5 March 1878 Rev Henry Neville Sherbrooke, son of Henry Porter Sherbrooke, DL, JP, of Oxton Hall, Notts, and *d* 5 Sept 1889, leaving issue (*see* WESTMORLAND, E)

2 Kathleen Mary; *b* 30 July 1870; *m* 30 July 1896 Rev Edward Francis Whateley Eliot, Canon of Gibraltar, Archdeacon in Italy, Chaplain of St Michael's Ch, Beaulieu-sur-Mer, France, 3rd son of Rev Canon William Eliot, and *d* 17 Feb 1939. He *d* 29 June 1943

The 3rd EARL's bro,

WILFRID DALLAS CAIRNS, **4th Earl Cairns**, CMG (1915), DL Somerset, Lt-Col London Rifle Bde, formerly The Rifle Bde, Prince Consort's Own, served in S African War 1902 (Queen's medal with three clasps) and WW I (despatches); *b* 28 Nov 1865; *m* 12 July 1894 Olive (*d* 19 Sept 1952), dau of John Patteson Cobbold, JP, MP, of The Cliffe, Ipswich, and had issue:

1 Hugh Wilfred John, *Viscount Garmoyle*, DSO and bar, Brig The Rifle Bde, ADC to GOC-in-C S Cmd 1937–38, served WW II; *b* 9 June 1907; *m* 2 June 1936 *Barbara Elizabeth [Lady Hogg, The Red House, Shedfield, Southampton, Hants; 11 Melton Court, SW7] (who *m* 2nd 28 Oct 1948 *Sir John Nicholson Hogg, only son of Sir Malcom Nicholson Hogg (*see* HOGG Bt)), yr dau of Capt Arden Franklyn, of New Place, Shedfield, Hants, and 33 Bryanston Sq, W1, and *d* of wounds received in action in Egypt July 1942

2 DAVID CHARLES, **5th Earl**

1 Hester Margaret, v-chm C Party Orgn and Pres Nat Soc C and Unionist Women Organisers 1939–43; *b* 3 Aug 1895; *m* 7 June 1917 Capt Robert Croft Bourne, PC, JP, MP, MA, Herefs Regt, only son of Col Gilbert Charles Bourne, FRS, of Cowarne Court, Herefs, and had issue. He *d* 7 Aug 1938

2 Ursula Helen; *b* 14 June 1899; *m* 7 June 1921 Capt John Roland Abbey, late Rifle Bde, est s of William Henry Abbey, of Sedgwick Park, Horsham, Sussex, and had issue

3 *Sheila Mary [The Lady Sheila Holroyd, Providence Cottage, Chute Cadley, Andover, Hants]; *b* 9 April 1905; *m* 26 Nov 1930 Maj Charles Ivor Patrick Holroyd, late The Rifle Bde (*d* 20 Jan 1976), only son of Maj Charles Patrick Holroyd, of Langton Ho, Blandford, and has issue:

(1) *(Charles) John [Lt-Col John Holroyd, Providence Cottage, Chute Cadley, Andover, Hants]; *b* 1933; Lt-Col RGJ (ret); *m* 1969 *Amanda Jane, dau of Col Sir Richard Hamilton Glyn, 9th Bt (*see* GLYN, Bt, of Ewell), and has:

1a *Charles Wilfrid; *b* 1970; *educ* Eton and New Coll Oxford

2a *George Alexander James; *b* 1974; *educ* Eton and Durham U

1a *Joanna Mary Ursula; *b* 1972; *educ* Sherborne and Exeter U

(2) *Richard Norton [Richard Holroyd Esq, Les Lausiers, Condillac, Montelimar, France]; *b* 1946; *m* 1977 *Karine, dau of Raymond Phèlip, and has issue:

1a *Wilfrid Andrew; *b* 1980

2a *Alistair Hugo; *b* 1985

3a *Alexander Ivor; *b* 1987

1a *Annabel Juliette; *b* 1983

(1) *Alice Elizabeth [Mrs Ronald Lilburne, 6c Battys Rd, Blenheim, New Zealand]; *b* 1936; *m* 1961 *Ronald L Lilburne, and has issue:

1a *David Milton; *b* 1964

1a *Linda Robyn; *b* 1962

(2) *Serena Jane [Mrs Thomas Gledhill, 5 Oakwood Rd, Henleaze, Bristol BS9 4NP]; *b* 1939; *m* 1978 *Dr Thomas D Gledhill, and has issue:

1a *Stephen Mark; *b* 1981; *educ* Clifton

1a *Sheona Grace; *b* 1979; *educ* Badminton

(3) *Susan Virginia; *b* 1943

4 Katharine Olive, Sr Cdr ATS; *b* 14 March 1912; *educ* St Hilda's Coll Oxford (BA); *d* unm 18 March 1955

The 4th EARL *d* 23 Oct 1946; his only surv son,

DAVID CHARLES CAIRNS, **5th Earl Cairns**, GCVO (1972, KCVO 1961), CB 1960, DL (Suffolk 1973), R-Adml 1961, served WW II (despatches), Pres RNC Greenwich 1958–61, Marshal Dip Corps 1962–71, Extra Equerry to HM THE QUEEN 1972, Pres Navy League 1966–77, Prime Warden Fishmongers' Co 1972; *b* 3 July 1909; *m* 16 April 1936 *Barbara Jeanne Harrisson [The Rt Hon Barbara Countess Cairns, The Red House, Clopton, Woodbridge, Suffolk], yst dau of Sydney Harrisson Burgess, of Altrincham, Cheshire, and *d* 1989, having had issue:

1 SIMON DALLAS CAIRNS, **6th and present Earl Cairns**

2 +(Hugh) Andrew David [The Hon Andrew Cairns, Knowle Hill Farm, Ulcombe, Maidstone, Kent]; *b* 27 Aug 1942; *educ* Wellington and Dublin U; *m* 22 Oct 1966 *Elizabeth, dau of Lt-Col Francis Cecil Leonard Bell, DSO, MC, TD, of Cross Glades, Chiddingfold, Surrey, and has issue:

(1) +Bertram Wilfrid Arthur; *b* 28 Jan 1972

(1) *Katherine Frances; *b* 27 June 1974

1 *Elisabeth Olive; *b* 12 July 1944; *m* 27 May 1965 *Capt Martin Ralph Lowe, 9th/12th Roy Lancers (ret), only son of Maj Ralph Mason Lowe, of Castle End, Ross-on-Wye, Herefs, and has issue:

(1) *Alexander Charles; *b* 3 Sept 1970

Seat: Bolehyde Manor, Allington, Wilts. Moated and of medieval origin, Bolehyde was probably part of Glastonbury Abbey's vast possessions before the Dissolution of the Monasteries. Richard Snell, Glastonbury's last reeve, seems to have carried out some rebuilding at Bolehyde, having acquired the manor of Kingston, of which it was a part, with money embezzled from the monks. Truly an unjust steward. One John Gale, who seems to have been of yeoman status, bought Bolehyde in 1635, but tenants of the same name had occupied the place as far back as 1539. The GALEs lived there till 1927, when they sold it to the Du Cros baronet family (*qv*). Had they been grander during their 400-year occupancy they would probably have torn it down and put up something more pretentious to reflect their elevated status. There are occasions when one must applaud social immobility. As it was they carried out modest but charming alterations in the 17th century, paying especial attention to the entrance, the major part of which is thought to date from *c* 1700.

The main entrance is from the south across the moat and runs between a pair of summer house-like structures or gazebos. Another approach is between gate houses, which lie east of the main building.

CAITHNESS

Arms: Quarterly, 1st, azure a lymphad at anchor or, flagged gules, sails furled argent, oars erect sable, within a double tressure-flory-counter-flory of the second (for Earldom of ORKNEY); 2nd and 3rd, or, a lion rampant gules, armed and langued azure (for SPARR-NITHSDALE); 4th, azure a three-masted ship or, flagged gules, under sail argent (for Earldom of CAITHNESS); over all a cross engrailed and counterchanged argent and sable (for SINCLAIR). **Crest:** A cock proper, armed and beaked or. **Supporters:** Two griffins gules, wings elevated, armed, beaked and winged or. **Motto:** Commit thy work to God. **Creations:** L. (S) 1449, E. (S) 28 Aug 1455, Bt. (NS) 2 June 1631.

THE 20TH EARL OF CAITHNESS, Lord Berridale and a Baronet (Sir Malcolm Ian Sinclair, Bt, PC (1990)) [The Rt Hon The Earl of Caithness PC, House of Lords, London SW1A 0PW]; *b* 3 Nov 1948; *s* f 1965; *educ* Marlborough and RAC Cirencester; FRICS; Ld-in-Waiting 1984–85, Parly Under Sec Tport 1985–86, Min State: Home Off 1986–88, Environment 1988–89, Treasury 1989–90 (also

Paymaster Gen), FCO 1990–92, Tport 1992–94; estate agent 1995– (formerly with Savill's); *m* 9 Jan 1975 Diana Caroline (*d* by her own hand 1994), only dau of Maj Richard Lovel Coke, DSO, MC, DL, Scots Gds, of Weasenham Hall, King's Lynn, Norfolk (*see* LEICESTER, E), and has issue:

1 +ALEXANDER JAMES RICHARD, *Lord Berriedale*; *b* 26 March 1981

1 *Iona Alexandra; *b* 18 Feb 1978

Caithness, Earldom of: Around the close of the first millennium the territory in the northernmost part of Scotland over which the Earls of Caithness later held sway was frequently divided in two, each part being in the possession of different Norse Jarls or Earls of Orkney, though each Jarl (or Earl) seems to have been a member of the same extended family. The Earldom (as it came to be called) of Orkney and that of Caithness differed to a certain extent in that the former was held of the Kings of Norway while the latter was held of the Kings of Scots. This meant that different customs were observed in each territory, specifically in the case of the Earldoms that the Orkney one was held jointly while the Caithness one was only sometimes so held. The Earldom of Caithness could be (and frequently was) disposed of by the KINGS OF SCOTS to different persons in the lifetime of the original grantee or grantee's heir, either jointly or solely, which makes it pointless, however tempting, to assign any ordinal numbering to the Earldom at this time.

SIGURD II, JARL OF ORKNEY; *m* a dau of MALCOLM II KING OF SCOTS (1005–34) and *d* 1014, leaving:

THORFINN II ('The Black'), JARL OF ORKNEY and 1st EARL OF (the entire territory of) CAITHNESS, so *cr* 1014 by his gf MALCOLM II; *b c* 1009; *m* by 1038 Ingebiorge/Ingibiorg (*m* 2nd as his 1st w MALCOLM III KING OF SCOTS), dau of Finn Arnason/Arnesson, Jarl of Halland, by Bergliot, n of HARALD III HARDRADI OF NORWAY, and *d c* 1056, leaving:

1 PAUL, JARL OF ORKNEY and apparently (Jt) EARL OF CAITHNESS; *m* —, dau of Hakon Ivarsson (ggs through his grandmother of JARL HAKON THE GREAT, who ruled Norway 976–995) by Ragnhild, dau of MAGNUS I THE GOOD OF NORWAY, and had:

(1) HA(A)KO(N), Jt EARL OF ORKNEY and apparently Jt EARL OF CAITHNESS till his cousin MAGNUS's death *sp*, when he became sole EARL; *m* 1st — and had:

1a PAUL, Jt JARL OF ORKNEY; *s* bro as EARL (entire) OF CAITHNESS but resigned the latter position to his n (*see* below)

(1) (cont.) HA(A)KO(N) *m* 2nd Helga, dau of Moddan of Dalr in Caithness, and had:

2a HARALD I *Slettmali* ('The Smooth-Spoken'), Jt JARL OF ORKNEY and apparently EARL (entire) OF CAITHNESS; had:

1b ERLEND *Ugni*; Jt EARL OF CAITHNESS during his cousin ROGNVALD's pilgrimage (*see* below)

1a Ingibiorg; *m* as his 2nd w OLAF BITLING, KING OF (the Isle of) MAN and had issue

2a MARGARET; *m* 1st *c* 1133, apparently as his 2nd w, MADACH, EARL OF ATHOLL (*see* STRABOLGI, B), s of DUNCAN I KING OF SCOTS (1034–40) and bro of MALCOLM III (1058–93), and had a 2nd son:

1b HARALD, Jt JARL OF ORKNEY with his cousin ROGNVALD (*see* below) and perhaps Jt EARL OF CAITHNESS too; *b* 1130; *k* his cousin HARALD *Ugni* 1198 and so became sole EARL OF CAITHNESS; *m* 1st Afrika/Alfreka, sis of Duncan Earl of Fife; *m* 2nd Gorm(f)la(e)th/Hvafleda/Hvarlod/Hvorflod, dau of Malcolm MacHeth, 1st Earl of Ross, supposedly himself s of Angus Earl of Moray (*see* MORAY, E, preliminary remarks), and had (presumably by her), with an est s (*d* young):

1c DAVID, JARL OF ORKNEY and EARL OF CAITHNESS; *d* 1214

2c JOHN, JARL OF ORKNEY and EARL OF CAITHNESS; *dspm* 1231, murdered by his servants in revenge for his supposed implication in the murder of the Bp of Caithness, for which latter unlawful killing his territory was confiscated by ALEXANDER II OF SCOTS though restored on JOHN's payment of a huge fine; possibly f of:

1d JOAN; *m* FRESKIN, Lord of Duffus and apparently Jt EARL OF CAITHNESS in right of his w; *d* by 1269, leaving by her:

1e MARY; *m* Sir REYNALD CHEYNE, apparently EARL OF CAITHNESS in the late 13th–early 14th century in right of his w

2e Christian; *m* William of Fedrett

2a (cont.) MARGARET is said to have *m* 2nd Erlend *Ugni*, Jarl of Orkney, presumably a different person from her great-uncle mentioned below since quite apart from their consanguinity he is said to have been *k* 1156

2 ERLEND, JARL OF ORKNEY and apparently (Jt) EARL OF CAITHNESS; had:

(1) St MAGNUS, Jt EARL OF ORKNEY and apparently Jt EARL OF CAITHNESS; *dsp* 1117

(1) GUNHILD; *m* Kol, a Norseman, and had:

1a KALI later renamed ROGNVALD by the KING OF NORWAY, who also made him Jt EARL OF ORKNEY; made a pilgrimage to Jerusalem; presumably on his return, and certainly following his cousin ERLEND UGNI's death, was made (or remade) EARL OF CAITHNESS; *dspm* 1158, leaving an only dau:

1b INGIGERD; *m* 1156 ERIK *Stagbrellr* and had, with two other sons:

1c HARALD *Ugni*, EARL OF CAITHNESS; *k* 1198 by his cousin HARALD (*see* above)

1c A dau; *m* as his 2nd w Gillebride Earl of Angus, who was by her f, gf or even ggf of:

1d MAGNUS or MALCOLM, JARL OF ORKNEY and Jt EARL OF CAITHNESS, also possibly EARL OF ANGUS; living as EARL of both the latter entities 1232; *d* 1239 and seems to have been f of:

1e MALCOLM, JARL OF ORKNEY and EARL OF CAITHNESS; had:

1f JOHN, JARL OF ORKNEY and EARL OF CAITHNESS; swore fealty to EDWARD I of England 1297; *d* by 28 Oct 1312 (*see* also LOVAT, L)

Two other descendants of ERLEND, 2nd s of THORFINN, 1st EARL OF CAITHNESS, were MAGNUS, JARL OF ORKNEY and EARL OF CAITHNESS, described as the last of his line, who *m* Katharine — and *d* after 6 April 1320 but before 1329 and:

MALISE (s of another Malise, Earl of Strathearn, who *d* by 1320, and his w Agnes (*d* in or after 1311), through the latter of whom the son may have *s* to the Caithness Earldom), self-styled in 1334 EARL OF THE EARLDOMS OF STRATHERN [*sic*], CAITHNESS and ORKNEY; *b c* 1290; seems to have enjoyed revenues of a quarter of the Earldom of Caithness 1331; *m* 1st by 1320 Mary —; *m* 2nd by 1334 Maud, dau of Hugh 4th Earl of Ross, by Maud, sis of ROBERT I (THE BRUCE) KING OF SCOTS, and *dspm* between 1344 and 1350, having been attainted 1332 and his honours forfeited, leaving, apparently by his 1st w:

1 Maud; mother of:

(1) Alexander de la Arde; *b* by 1357; resigned his right to the Earldom of Caithness 1375 to ROBERT II KING OF SCOTS, who *cr* David Stewart, his yr s, EARL OF CAITHNESS by Nov 1375, the title remaining with first David's dau then bro Walter (apart from a brief period between 1430 and 1431 when Walter resigned it in favour of his son Alan) till 1437, when it was forfeited by Walter for treason; the title was subsequently conferred on George Crichton, a favourite of JAMES II, in 1452 but resigned by him shortly afterwards

2 Eupheme of Strathern; living 1364

3 Agnes; *m* by 1353 Erngils, made Earl of Orkney 1353 by King of Norway, but in right of his (Erngils's) w; the Earldom of Orkney forfeited 1375

MALISE had by his 2nd w:

4 Isabel; decreed heir to Earldom of Caithness by her f, although the title was already forfeited, in the event of his having no heirs male of the body; *m* Sir William St Clair or Sinclair, of Roslin (*see* below)

Lineage (of Sinclair): ROBERT de Saint Clair, in Normandy; *m* Eleanor, dau of the Count of Dreux and thus cousin of Yolande de Dreux, 2nd w of ALEXANDER III OF SCOTS, and had a 2nd s:

Sir WILLIAM SINCLAIR of Roslin, of the territorial Barony of which he was granted a charter by ALEXANDER II 14 Sept 1280 on the resignation of Henry de Roskelyn (probably Sir WILLIAM's f-in-law); opposed EDWARD I's invasion of Scotland 1296–99; *m* Amicia, (probably) dau of Henry de Roskelyn, and *d* (probably as a prisoner in the Tower of London), leaving:

Sir HENRY SINCLAIR of Roslin; supported ROBERT I (THE BRUCE); signatory to the Scottish Barons' letter to the Pope 1320; *m* Alice de Fenton and *d* by 1335/6, having had, with a yr s (John, *k vp* Spain 25 April 1330) and either a dau or gdau (if the latter, by his er s WILLIAM; *see* below), Margaret, *m* Sir John St Clair of Herdmanston and had issue, who over three centuries later intermarried with the dau of the 9th Lord Sinclair (*qv*):

Sir WILLIAM SINCLAIR; *k vp* with his bro 25 April 1330 on their way to the East with the heart of ROBERT I (THE BRUCE), leaving issue:

Sir WILLIAM SINCLAIR of Roslin; *m* Isabel (*see* above), heiress-designate of the Earldom of Caithness, and *d c* 1358, having had issue:

HENRY SINCLAIR, 1st EARL OF ORKNEY, so *cr* 2 Aug 1379 by the HAAKON KING OF NORWAY; apparently discovered Greenland; *m* Jean, dau of Sir William Halyburton of Dirletoun, and was *k* in an attack on Orkney, possibly by English seamen, *c* 1400, leaving an est s:

HENRY SINCLAIR, 2nd EARL OF ORKNEY (under the reinvestiture of 1379); Guardian to Prince James, afterwards JAMES I OF SCOTS; *m* by 17 Nov 1407 Algidia/Egidia/Jill (*m* 2nd Sir Alexander Stewart, 3rd s of 2nd Duke of Albany of the 1398 *cr*; *see* MORAY, E), dau and heiress of Sir William Douglas of Nithsdale by his w Jill, dau of ROBERT II, and *d c* 1 Feb 1420/1, having had, with a dau (Beatrix, *m* 7th Earl of Douglas; *see* QUEENSBERRY, M):

WILLIAM SINCLAIR **1st Earl of Caithness** (S), so *cr* 28 Aug 1455 in settlement of a claim to the Lordship of Nithsdale through his mother, as also earlier 1449 LORD SINCLAIR (both S), and 3rd EARL OF ORKNEY till 1470, when he resigned the Earldom to JAMES III as Orkney had been part of the latter's w's dowry on her marriage with JAMES, receiving in exchange Ravenscraig Castle, Fife, and its lands 16 Sept 1470; fndr Collegiate Ch of Rosslyn, Midlothian, 1453; High Chllr Scotland 1454–58; Amb England 1471–73; made over the Earldom of Caithness to his s WILLIAM 2 Dec 1476 but reserved life rent; *m* 1st Elizabeth (*d c* 1451), dau of Archibald, 4th Earl of Douglas, and widow of (a) John Stewart, Earl of Buchan, and (b) Sir Thomas Stewart (*see* MAR, E), and had:

1 WILLIAM SINCLAIR, 2nd LORD SINCLAIR; ancestor of the succeeding Lords (*qv*)

1 Katherine; *m* 1469 (*divorce* on grounds of consanguinity March 1478) Alexander Stewart, Duke of Albany, 2nd s of JAMES II

The **1st Earl** *m* 2nd by 15 Nov 1456 Marjory, dau of Alexander Sutherland of Dunbeath, and by her had, with other issue:

2 Oliver (Sir); ancestor of the extinct St CLAIRs of Rosslyn

3 WILLIAM, **2nd Earl**

2 Eleanor; *m c* 27 April 1475, as his 2nd w, 1st Earl of Atholl of the 1457 *cr* (*see* MORAY, E) and had issue

The **1st Earl** *m* 3rd Janet Yeman and *d c* early 1480, having also had by one of his ws a dau (Elizabeth, *m* Andrew Master of Rothes; (*see* ROTHES, E)

The 1st EARL's 3rd son,

WILLIAM SINCLAIR, **2nd Earl of Caithness**; *m* Mary, dau of Sir William Keith of Inverugie, and was *k* 9 Sept 1513 at the English victory over the Scots of Flodden, leaving:

1 JOHN, **3rd Earl**

2 Alexander, of Dunbeath and Stemster; *m* Elizabeth Innes, dau of Alexander Innes, 13th of that Ilk (*see* ROXBURGHE, D), and had issue (including at least two daus: Helen, *m* Donald Mackay, (*see* REAY, L); Isabel, *m* Gilbert Gordon of Garty; *see* SUTHERLAND, E); also was ancestor of the SINCLAIRs of Dunbeath, apparently extinct in the male line

The 2nd EARL's er s,

JOHN SINCLAIR, **3rd Earl of Caithness**; *m* by 1527 Elizabeth, dau of William Sutherland of Duffus, and was *k* at Stenness, Orkney, 18 May 1529 in an attempt to recover the islands there, leaving, with an er s (William, *dvp* & *sp* on or after 14 July 1527):

GEORGE SINCLAIR, **4th Earl of Caithness;** *b* by 14 July 1527; resigned Earldom, receiving a regrant with remainder to his s and h John and the latter's male heirs and assigns, failing whom to the (re)grantee himself and his heirs male whatsoever; Justiciar Caithness 1566; memb jury trial 1567 of James, Earl of Bothwell, for murdering Earl of Darnley; *m* Elizabeth (*d* by 4 April 1576), dau of 2nd Earl of Montrose (*see* MONTROSE, D), and *d* 9 Sept 1582, having had, with a 4th s (David) and four daus (the 2nd of whom *m* 1st William Sutherland of Duffus (*see* DUNBAR, Bt, of Hempriggs) and 2nd Huistean Dy Mackay (*see* REAY, L), while another *m* 1st 13th Earl of Sutherland (*qv*) and 2nd Alexander Innes, 16th of that Ilk; *see* ROXBURGHE, D):

1 John, *Master of Caithness*; imprisoned by his f in Girnigo Castle 1567–73 following a quarrel; *m* between 10 Dec 1565 and 16 Jan 1566/7 Jean (*m* 3rd Archibald Douglas, Rector of Douglas, and *d* by 27 July 1599), only dau of Patrick Hepburn, 3rd Earl of Bothwell, and widow of John Stewart, Lord Darnley (*see* MORAY, E), and *dvp* in captivity 1573, having had issue:

(1) GEORGE SINCLAIR, **5th Earl of Caithness;** *b* 1566; resigned the Earldom but was regranted it 3 April 1592 with remainder to his est son William and the latter's heirs male and assigns whatsoever; *m* just after 29 July 1585 Lady Jean Gordon, only dau of 5th Earl of Huntly (*see* HUNTLY, M), and *d* Feb 1642/3, having had (with possibly another dau, Isabel, *m* 2nd Lord Reay, *qv*):

1a William, *Lord Berriedale*; *m* his cousin Margaret, sis of 6th, 7th and 8th Lords Sinclair (*qv*), and *dvp* after 27 July 1633, having had:

1b John, *Master of Berriedale*; had a charter of regrant of the the Earldom 27 July 1633, with remainder to himself and the heirs male of his body, failing whom to his f and the latter's heirs male and assigns whatsoever; *m* between May 1633 and Oct 1634 Jean (*m* 2nd Alexander, 1st Lord Duffus), yr dau and coheir of 1st Earl of Seaforth (*see* CROMARTIE, E), and *d* in the lifetime of his gf Sept 1639, having had issue:

1c GEORGE SINCLAIR, **6th Earl of Caithness;** *m* 22 Sept 1657 Mary (*m* 2nd 7 April 1678, as his 2nd w, Sir John Campbell of Glenurchy, to whom the **6th Earl of Caithness** was heavily in debt, so that he granted Campbell in 1672 a lien on the lands and title of the Earldom of Caithness which the latter could take up in six years on his rights to them becoming absolute; Campbell accordingly did so and got from CHARLES II on 28 June 1677 a charter creating him EARL OF CAITHNESS, VISCOUNT OF BREADALBANE and LORD ST CLAIR OF BERRIEDALE AND GLENURCHY; susbsequently, though he retained the lands, his right to assume the title was held invalid and he was compensated with the Earldom of Breadalbane and Holland; *see* 1970 edn), dau of Archibald, Marquess of Argyll (*see* ARGYLL, D), and *dsp* May 1676

2c James; *d* young

3c William; *d* young

2a Francis, of Keiss and Northfield; *m* Elizabeth, dau of Andrew Lord Fraser, and had issue:

1b GEORGE SINCLAIR, **7th Earl of Caithness,** so declared by PC 15 July 1681; *d* unm 1698

1b Jane; *m* her cousin Sir James Sinclair, 3rd Bt, of Mey (*see* below)

3a John; Lt-Col Munro's Regt Swedish serv; *k sp* Newmarket 1632

1a Elizabeth; *m* 1621 14th Earl of Crawford (*see* CRAWFORD and BALCARRES, E)

(2) James, of Murchil, which lands his er bro made over to him 19 April 1613; *m* 1st Elizabeth, dau of Robert Stewart, Earl of Orkney, illegitimate s of JAMES V, and had issue:

1a James (Sir), of Murchil; *m* 1st Margaret Dundas (*dsp*); *m* 2nd Jean (*d* by 22 Oct 1662), dau of William Stewart of Burray, bro of 1st Earl of Galloway (*qv*), and had, with five daus:

1b JOHN SINCLAIR, **8th Earl of Caithness;** *m* Jean Carmichael and *d* 1705, having had:

1c ALEXANDER SINCLAIR, **9th Earl of Caithness;** *b c* 1684; the last surv peer to have sat in the Parl of Scotland before the Union with the English Parl of 1707; *m* 15 Feb 1738 Lady Margaret Primrose (*d* 7 Oct 1785), dau of 1st Earl of Rosebery (*qv*), and *d* 9 Dec 1765, leaving:

1d Dorothea; *m* 5 June 1766 2nd Earl Fife (*see* FIFE, D) and *dspm* 24 Jan 1809

2c John; a Lord of Session as Lord Murkle; *m* Anne (*d* 21 Oct 1740), dau of George, 1st Earl of Cromartie (*qv*), and *dsp* 5 June 1755

3c Francis, of Forse; *m* Janet Morrison and *dsp* 2 March 1762

4c Archibald; *dsp*

1c Janet; *m* 1714 David Sinclair of Southdon and *d* 1720, leaving issue

2b David, of Broynach; *m* 1st —, dau of William Sinclair of Dun, and had issue:

1c James; *dsp c* 1754

1c Elizabeth

2b (cont.) David Sinclair of Broynach *m* 2nd June 1700 Janet Ewing and *d* by 1716, having by her had, with another s (*b* before the marriage, *d* an infant):

2c David; *b* Feb 1701; *m* 21 Oct 1744 Margaret More (or McKay) and *d c* 1760, having had issue:

1d James; Capt HEICS; unsuccessfully claimed the Earldom of Caithness 1765 and 1779; *dsp* 11 Jan 1788

2a Francis; soldier in Germany; *m* (contract 19 July 1621) Janet, dau of Alexander Sutherland of Forse, and had issue:

1b James; *dsp*

1a Agnes; *m* John Mackay of Diriot and Strathy

2a Elizabeth; *m* 1613 Sir John Lucas of Cromby (*m* 2nd Grizel Crichton, widow of Thomas Dunbar, Dean of Moray), bro to the Laird of Innes

(3) John (Sir), of Greenland and Ratter, charter of the latter of which he was granted by his er bro the **5th Earl of Caithness** 7 April 1613; *m* Janet Sutherland and *d* by 21 Dec 1627, having had a 4th s:

1a James (Sir), of Reaster and from 1634 of Ratter; *m* Janet, dau of William Bruce of Stanstill, and had issue:

1b William, of Ratter; *m* 1st (contract 24 March 1642) Elizabeth, only dau of John Sinclair of Ulbster (*see* THURSO, V), and had issue:

1c John, of Ratter; had a charter of his lands from his father 30 March 1650; *m* Elizabeth, dau of Sir William Sinclair, 2nd Bt, of Mey (*see* below), and *d* 1714, having had, with at least two daus (Frances, *m* 1728 her cousin James Sinclair of Latheron (*see* SINCLAIR, Bt); Margaret, *m* her cousin Alexander Sinclair of Brabster; *see* SINCLAIR, Bt) an er son:

1d John, of Ratter; *m* Janet, dau of Patrick Sinclair of Southdun, and *d* 3 Dec 1733, having had issue:

1e John, of Ratter; *d* unm 1734

2e WILLIAM SINCLAIR, **10th Earl of Caithness,** of Ratter; *b* 2 April 1727; served heir 28 Nov 1768 though an unsuccessful counter-claim was advanced by a ggs of David Sinclair of Broinach, bro of the **8th Earl** (it appeared that the latter's line was illegitimate, however) and his claim to the Earldom allowed 2 May 1772; *m* Barbara (*d* 20 Feb 1793), dau of John Sinclair of Scotscalder, and *d* 29 Nov 1779, having had, with other issue:

1f JOHN SINCLAIR, **11th Earl;** Lt-Col 76th Foot War American Independence (wounded Charlestown); *d* unm 8 April 1789

2f Isabella; *d* unm

2f Janet; *m* 31 July 1784 James Trail, of Hobbister, and *d* 29 March 1806, leaving issue

1e Jacobina; *bapt* 9 April 1717

1b (cont.) William Sinclair of Ratter *m* 2nd Jean, dau of John Cunningham of Geise and Bronhill and widow of Alexander Sinclair of Latheron, and *d* on or after 4 May 1663, having by her had three other sons and two daus

2b John; *dsp*

1b Janet; *m* Walter Bruce of Ham

2b Margaret; *m* 1655 John Smith

3b Elizabeth; *m* 1652 her cousin William Bruce of Stanstill

(1) Marie; living 20 Feb 1582

2 William, of Mey; *dvp* unm (strangled by his bro the Master) but left by Margaret, dau of James Mowat of Balguholly, two sons Patrick and John, legitimated 1607 (*see* 1949 edn SINCLAIR, Bt, of Ulbster)

3 George, of Mey; Chllr Diocese of Caithness 1572; *m* by 1583 Margaret, dau of 7th Lord Forbes (*qv*), and *d* 1616, having had issue:

(1) William (Sir), of Mey and Canisbay, Caithness, and Cadoll, Ross-shire; *m* (contract 23 April 1600) Katherine (*d* 5 July 1603), dau of George Ross of Balnagown, and *d c* 1643, having had:

1a **Sir James Sinclair, 1st Bt** (NS), so *cr* 2 June 1631, with remainder to heirs male whatsoever, of Canisbay and later of Mey; *m* (contract 26 July 1628) Elizabeth, dau of Sir Patrick Leslie of Lindores, and *d* 20 April 1662, having had issue:

1b **Sir William Sinclair, 2nd Bt;** *m* (contract 4 Oct 1643) Margaret (*d* 1692), dau of 2nd Earl of Seaforth (*see* CROMARTIE, E), and had issue:

1c **Sir James Sinclair, 3rd Bt;** *m* Jean, dau of Francis Sinclair of Keiss and Northfield and sis of **7th Earl of Caithness,** and had, with a dau (Margaret, *m* Francis Sinclair of Stiroke):

1d **Sir James Sinclair, 4th Bt;** *m* Mary, dau of James Sutherland, 2nd Lord Duffus, and *d* 26 March 1732, leaving an only son:

1e **Sir James Sinclair, 5th Bt;** *b* 26 April 1715; *m* Nov 1735 Margaret, dau of John Sinclair of Barrock, and *d* 4 Oct 1760, having had issue:

1f **Sir John Sinclair, 6th Bt;** *m* Charlotte, 2nd dau of Eric Sutherland (but for the attainder 4th Lord Duffus), and *d* 26 March 1774, having had, with a dau (Margaret, *m* 1 Sept 1782 Rev William Leslie, of Darkland, and had issue):

1g **Sir James Sinclair, 7th Bt,** of Mey, and **12th Earl of Caithness;** *b* 31 Oct 1766; found rightful Earl 4 May 1793, rep S peer 1807–18, Ld Lt Caithness 1794–1823, Postmaster-Gen 1811–23; *m* 2 Jan 1784 Jean (*d* 2 April 1853), 2nd dau of Gen Alexander Campbell of Barcaldine (*see* CAMPBELL, Bt, of Barcaldine), and *d* 16 July 1823, having had, with three daus (of whom the est, Janet, *m* James Buchanan and had issue, *see* LAUDERDALE, E, while another, Charlotte, *m* Maj-Gen Alexander MacGregor (*see* MacGREGORof MacGREGOR, Bt) and had issue)

1h John, *Lord Berriedale*; *b* 20 July 1788; *d* unm 1 June 1802

2h ALEXANDER CAMPBELL SINCLAIR, **13th Earl of Caithness;** *b* 24 July 1790; Ld Lt Caithness 1823–55; *m* 22 Nov 1813 Frances Harriet (*d* 23 Aug 1854), dau and coheir of the Very Rev William Leigh, of Rushall Hall, Staffs, Dean of Hereford, and *d* 24 Dec 1855, having had issue:

1i JAMES SINCLAIR, **14th Earl of Caithness;** *b* 16 Dec 1821; inventor of a steam carriage and compass, FRS, rep S peer 1858–66, Ld Lt and V-Adml Caithness, Ld-in-Waiting 1856–58 and 1859–66, *cr* 1 May 1866 BARON BARROGILL of Barrogill Castle, Co Caithness (UK); *m* 1st 17 July 1847 Louisa Georgiana (*d* 31 July 1870), yst dau of Sir George Richard Philips, 2nd and last Bt, of Weston, Warwicks, and had issue:

1j GEORGE PHILIPS ALEXANDER SINCLAIR, **15th Earl of Caithness;** *b* 30 Nov 1858; Ld Lt Caithness 1881–89, Lt-Col Caithness Artillery Vols; *d* unm 25 May 1889, when the UK Barony of BARROGILL expired, leaving Barrogill Castle to Frederick Granville Heathcote later Sinclair, JP, DL, FLS (*see* HEATHCOTE, Bt, of London)

1j Fanny Georgiana Elizabeth; *d* unm 11 Oct 1883

1i The **14th Earl** *m* 2nd 6 March 1872 Marie (*d* 3 Nov 1895), Duchess of Pomar (so *cr* 1879 by HH LEO XIII), dau of Senor Don José de Mariategui and widow of Gen Cunt of Medina Pomar, and *d* 28 March 1881

2i William Leigh Canning; *d* young 3 Jan 1834
3i Alexander Eric George; *b* 20 May 1827; 91st Regt; *d* unm 21 Aug 1857
3h James; *b* 24 Oct 1797; Lt-Col; *m* 1818 Elizabeth, yst dau of George Tritton, of Westhill, Wandsworth, and *dsp* 18 Jan 1856
4h Patrick Campbell; *b* 14 July 1800; *m* Isabella (*d* 13 March 1853), dau of Maj-Gen McGregor, and *d* 13 March 1834
5h Eric George; *b* 19 Aug 1801; RN; *d* 26 Sept 1829
6h John; *b* 4 July 1808; Army Offr; *m* 22 Oct 1833 Maria Petronella (*d* 26 Feb 1878), yst dau of John Church, and *d* 8 Jan 1861
2f William; *m* Elizabeth, dau of Richard Sinclair, 2nd son of Alexander Sinclair of Dun, and had:
1g John; Capt 79th Foot; *k* unm at Waterloo 18 June 1815
1g Williamina; *d* unm
2c George; *b* 2 Aug 1653; in the Army; *m* Margaret Moncrieff, and had issue:
1d Margaret; *b* 15 Nov 1687
1c Elizabeth; *m* John Sinclair of Ratter
2c Barbara; *m* David Sinclair of Feswick
3c Mary; *b* 29 March 1660
2b John, of Stangegill; *dspl*
3b Robert, of Durran; *m* (contract 1 March 1678) his cousin Anne, dau of William Sinclair of Ratter, and *d c* 1709, having had, with a dau (Anne, *m* James Sutherland and had issue):
1c John, of Durran; *m* Elizabeth, dau of George Sinclair of Barrock, and *d* 1728, having had an est surv son:
1d James, of Durran; *m* 1st 1744 Elizabeth, dau of Sir Patrick Dunbar, Bt, of Northfield, and had issue:
1e James; *bapt* 19 July 1745; *d* young
2e Patrick, of Durran; *bapt* 26 June 1747; Capt RN; *m* Anne, dau of Robert Sutherland of Langwell, and *d* 1794, having had issue:
1f Patrick; *d* young
2f James; Lt RN; *d* unm; *ka* 21 July 1801
1f Catherine; *s* to Durran, which she sold; *m* Capt John Worth, RN, of Oakley, Suffolk, and *d* 1849, leaving issue (*see* WALKER, Bt, of Oakley Horsey)
3e George; *bapt* 11 Feb 1749; WS; *m* 19 Sept 1775 Elizabeth, dau of John Sutherland, 13th Laird of Forse, and *d* 6 Dec 1779, having had an only child:
1f John Sutherland; *b* 1778; Lt-Col RA; *m* 1st 22 June 1802 Marianne, dau of John Gamble, MD, and had issue (*d* unm); *m* 2nd 23 Jan 1817 Frances (*d* 20 Jan 1823), dau of Capt David Ramsay, RN, and by her had three daus; *m* 3rd 13 Oct 1824 Euphemia (*d* 19 Dec 1872), dau of Thomas Buchan of Auchmacoy, Aberdeenshire, by Euphemia, dau of Robert Turner of Menie, Aberdeenshire, and sis (and in her issue heir) of James Buchan of Auchmacoy, and *d* 12 April 1841, having by her had issue:
1g JAMES AUGUSTUS SINCLAIR, **16th Earl**
2g Thomas Buchan; *b* 21 Feb 1829; *d* 30 April 1838
3g Charles Home; *b* 4 March 1837; Pncpl Clerk Exchequer and Audit Dept; *m* 23 April 1868 Mary Louisa (*d* 11 Jan 1917), dau of Col John Paton, of Grandholm, Aberdeenshire, and *d* 12 Aug 1910, leaving issue:
1h Euphemia Helen; *m* 7 Feb 1907 Lt-Col Horace Adrian Duncan, DSO, late Argyll and Sutherland Highrs, son of Andrew Duncan, of The Middle Temple, London, and *d* 9 April 1945, leaving issue
2h Mary Esmé; *m* 27 Aug 1921 Thomas Edward Holman (*d* 16 Nov 1942), son of Thomas Holman,MD, of Gate House, East Hoathly, Sussex, and *d* 7 Dec 1949
1g Euphemia Margaret; *d* 12 Oct 1836
2g Nicola Helen Meredith; *d* unm 24 Nov 1855
4e Robert; Maj HEICS; *d* unm Bombay 1793
1e Margaret; *bapt* 19 May 1744; *m* Patrick Honyman, of Graemsay and Armadale
2e Catherine; *m* 1788 Alexander Robertson (*bapt* 1747; *d* 1791), Offr RN, of Jamaica, son of James Robertson, of Bishopmiln, and was *bur* 1820
3e Elizabeth; *m* 1775 William Robertson, of Auchinroath
1d (cont.) James Sinclair of Durran *m* 2nd Dorothea Bruce and *d* 1793, having had by her:
5e John; *dsp* by 1789
4b George, of Olrig; *m* Elizabeth, dau of Alexander Sinclair, of Latheron, and widow of Walter Bruce, of Ham, and had:
1c Alexander, of Olrig; *m* Katherine, dau of Donald Budge, of Toftingall, and was *k* in a duel 1710, leaving:
1d Donald, of Olrig; *m* Finella, dau and heir of Charles Sinclair of Ulbster (see 1949 edn SINCLAIR, Bt, of Ulbster), and had:
1e Charles, of Olrig; *m* Elizabeth, dau of Eric Sutherland of Duffus, and had:
1f Donald, of Olrig; *dsp* 9 March 1772 (when the male line of SINCLAIR of Olrig expired)
1f Finella; *s* to Olrig; *m* Archibald Cullen, barrister, and had issue
1b Anne; *m* Sir George Mackenzie, of Tarbat, Earl of Cromartie (*qv*), and had issue
2b Elizabeth; *m* her cousin Sir William Sinclair of Dunbeath (*see* SINCLAIR, Bt)

(2) John (Sir), of Dunbeath; MP Caithness 1649; *m* 1st by 31 July 1634 Christian, dau of Magnus Mowat, of Balquholile; *m* 2nd Catherine, dau of 7th Lord Lovat (*qv*), and by his 1st w had, with two other daus:
1a Margaret; *m* Hugh Ross of Kilravock, and had issue
(3) Alexander, of Latheron; ancestor of SINCLAIR, Bt, of Dunbeath (*qv*)
(1) Janet; *m* Walter Innes of Inverbraekie
(2) Margaret; *m* 1618 Alexander Sinclair of Forse
(3) Barbara; *m* 1610 Alexander Keith of Pittendrum
(4) Elizabeth; *m* William Dunbar of Hempriggs (*see* DUNBAR, Bt, of Hempriggs)
(5) Anne

The 15th EARL's cousin,

JAMES AUGUSTUS SINCLAIR, **16th Earl of Caithness**; *b* 31 May 1827; banker and charetered accountant Aberdeen; claim recognised by Scottish authorities sufficiently for him to be enabled to vote at election of rep S peers Jan 1890; *m* 27 April 1855 Janet (*d* 5 Feb 1906), dau of Roderick MacLeod, MD, gggs of Donald MacLeod, 3rd of Talisker, and *d* 20 Jan 1891, having had issue:

1 JOHN SUTHERLAND SINCLAIR, **17th Earl of Caithness**; *b* 17 Sept 1857; *d* unm 30 May 1914
2 NORMAN MacLEOD SINCLAIR later BUCHAN (1911 after inheriting 19 April 1910 the Auchmacoy estate, Aberdeenshire, from his cousin Louisa Buchan, 15th of Auchmacoy), **18th Earl of Caithness**, CBE (1919), JP, DL (both Aberdeenshire); *b I*4 April 1862*; *educ* Uppingham, Trin Hall Cambridge (BA) and Aberdeen U (LLD); Lt-Col 5th Bn Gordon Highrs; rep S peer 1918–29; *m* 21 Dec 1893 Lilian (*d* 11 Aug 1933), 2nd dau of Higford Higford, of Aldermaston Court, Berks, and Eaton Pl, London SW1, and *d* 25 March 1947, having had issue:
(1) Olivia; *b* 15 Oct 1894; *m* 6 Oct 1920 Capt Stephen Lloyd Trevor, MA (*d* 22 Jan 1959), Beds Yeo, son of William Trevor, of Lathbury Pk, Newport Pagnell, Bucks, and *d* 13 Dec 1973, leaving issue
(2) Diana; *b* 21 April 1898; *d* unm 27 April 1963
(3) *Lucy; *b* 27 Feb 1902; *m* 27 Feb 1928 Sir Thomas Innes of Learney, GCVO, FSA (*d* 16 Oct 1971), Ld Lyon King of Arms, and has issue (*see* INNES, Bt, of Balvenie)
(4) Teresa; *b* 27 Feb 1902; *d* 22 Nov 1904
(5) Augusta Lilian, MBE (1943); *b* 29 Jan 1910; *d* unm 17 April 1988
3 Charles Augustus (Rev); *b* 11 May 1865; *educ* Trin Coll Oxford (MA) and Aberdeen U (MA); Rector Hempstead, Glos, Hon Canon Gloucester Cathedral; *m* 25 Oct 1899 Mary Ann (*d* 22 Nov 1938), 2nd dau of Rev Edward Harman, Rector Pickwell, Leics, and *d* 9 March 1944, leaving issue:
(1) JAMES RODERICK SINCLAIR, **19th Earl**
(1) Janet; *b* 14 Oct 1900; *m* 29 April 1931 Rev Noel Braithwaite Chard, Vicar Harlow, Essex (*d* 28 Nov 1936), only s of C E Chard, of St Albans, and had:
1a *Elisabeth Marianne [Mrs Cyril Costley-White, 129A Ashley Gdns, London SW1]; *b* 2 April 1932; *m* 30 April 1955, as his 2nd w, Cyril Grove Costley-White, CMG, only s of Very Rev Harold Costley-White, DD, of Little Fountains, Dulcote, Wells, Somerset, and has issue:
1b *David Richard; *b* 31 Dec 1956
2b *Patrick Charles Robert; *b* 5 Aug 1961
(2) Nicola Marianne; *b* 5 April 1904; *m* 27 Sept 1928 John Vernon Morley, MBE, slr, Clerk Severn River Authority, yst s of Edward Herbert Morley, of Warwick, and had issue:
1a *Hugh Sinclair [Hugh Morley Esq, Claremont End, 1 Milbourne Lane, Esher, Surrey]; *b* 23 Aug 1930; *educ* St Edward's Sch, Oxford; FCA; *m* 11 April 1959 *Hilary Ann, yr dau of Frank L Smith, of 16 Tantallon Place, Edinburgh 9, and has issue:
1b *Jennifer Margaret; *b* 26 April 1962
2b *Alison Jane; *b* 26 April 1965
2a *John Streatfield [John Morley Esq, Longford Lodge, 109 Tewkesbury Rd, Longford, Glos]; *b* 18 Aug 1934; *educ* St Edward's Sch Oxford; FCA; *m* 8 Aug 1959 *Anne Freeland, dau of G W White, of Malvern Coll, Worcs, and has issue:
1b *Charles Sinclair; *b* 26 Feb 1965
1b *Jane Woodgate; *b* 22 May 1960
2b *Lucinda Sarah; *b* 30 May 1962
(3) (Margaret) Alison; *b* 29 Nov 1910; granted with her sis rank of earl's dau 1948; *d* unm 23 Sept 1997
(4) *(Euphemia) Meredith [The Lady Meredith Sinclair, 5a Mulberry Dve, Wheatley, Oxon]; *b* 22 Oct 1915
4 George Arthur; *b* 28 April 1874; Ch Clerk Legal Dept BOT; *m* 30 March 1921 Gerda Andren (*d* 28 Nov 1965 aged 92) and *d* 29 July 1934
1 Margaret Helen; *d* unm 13 May 1926
2 Euphemia Wilhelmina; *d* unm 11 Jan 1941
3 Meredith Isabel; *d* unm 11 Dec 1959
4 Mary Jessie; *d* unm 22 Jan 1945

The 18th EARL's nephew,

JAMES RODERICK SINCLAIR, **19th Earl of Caithness**, CVO, CBE, DSO, JP (1956), DL (1963) (both Aberdeenshire); *b* 29 Sept 1906; *educ* Marlborough; rep S peer 1950–58, Bde Col Gordon Highlanders 1958–65, served WW II, Sr Advsr Br Serv Min Burma 1948–49, Cmdt Ceylon Army 1949–52, Cdr 51st Indep Inf Bde 1952, Dep Cdr Highland Dist 1955, HM's Resident Factor Balmoral Estates 1955–65; memb Roy Co Archers, Belgian Croix de Guerre (avec palme), Legion of Honour; *m* 1st 29 April 1933 Grizel Margaret (*d* 2 Sept 1943), only dau of Sir George Miller-Cunningham, KBE, CB, of Leithenhopes, Peeblesshire, and had issue:

1 *Jean Elizabeth [The Lady Jean Williams-Freeman, Glendean Farm, Box 42, Nottingham Rd, Natal 3280, S Africa]; *b* 11 Feb 1936; *m* 3 June 1961 *David Peere Williams-Freeman, only s of Cdr Frederick Arthur Peere Williams-Freeman, DSO, RN, of Constantia Rise, Cape Town, and has:
(1) *Andrew Frederick Peere; *b* 18 March 1962; *m* 1991 *Fiona, dau of Walter Hinds, of Nairobi
(1) *Juliet Margaret; *b* 2 June 1964; *m* 1994 *Clive King, of Natal, S Africa

(2) *Theresa Jean; *b* 21 April 1966; *m* 1991 *Robert Wilson, of Howick, Natal
(3) *Kim Janette; *b* 21 April 1966; *m* 1993 *Neil Roberts, of Zimbabwe

2 *Margaret Nicola Sinclair [The Lady Margaret Glasse, The Old Rectory, Milton Bryant, Beds]; *b* 11 Sept 1937; *m* 1st 29 Aug 1959 Capt David Colin Kirkwood Brown, The Gordon Highrs, yr son of G/Capt Hugh Mitchell Kirkwood Brown, of Crofts Butts, Kingsbarns, Fife, and has issue:

(1) *Nicola Jane; *b* 15 Aug 1960; *m* 1983 *Duncan A Clark, son of Michael Clark, CBE, of Braxted Park, Witham, Essex
(2) *Olivia Grizel; *b* 15 Oct 1962; *m* 1990 *Hon Rupert Timothy Guy Edwards, only son of Baron Crickhowell, PC (*qv*)

2 (cont.) Lady Margaret Brown *m* 2nd 9 July 1983 *John James Maxwell Glasse, son of J M Glasse, of Corsham, Wilts

3 *Fiona Catharine [The Lady Fiona Whitfield, PO Box 721, Marondera, Zimbabwe]; *b* 27 Oct 1941; *m* 10 Jan 1969 *Capt Michael Stephen Whitfield, 3rd Carabiniers (Prince of Wales's Dragoon Gds), er son of Maj Edward William Whitfield (*see* RENSHAW, Bt), and has issue

The **19th Earl** *m* 2nd 17 Aug 1946 (Madeleine) Gabrielle (*m* 3rd 1977 David Frederick Ewen, CBE (*d* 1986), and *d* 1990), 3rd dau of Herman Edward de Pury and widow of Capt George Wareing Drewery Ormerod, RA, of Tyldesley, Lancs, and *d* 8 May 1965, having by her had:

1 MALCOLM IAN SINCLAIR, **20th and present Earl of Caithness**

4 *Bridget Sarah [The Lady Bridget Oppenheim, 46 Lysia St, London SW6 6NG]; *b* 18 May 1947; *m* 1976 *Nicholas Anthony Oppenheim, son of Sir Duncan Oppenheim, and has issue:

(1) *Christopher Duncan; *b* 1981
(1) *Leonora Emily; *b* 1977
(2) *Zerlina Gabrielle; *b* 1979

CALDECOTE

Arms: Per chevron az. and arg. in chief two crosses paté or and in base an eagle displayed of the first. **Crest:** Upon the battlements of a tower a grouse's leg erased ppr. **Supporters:** Dexter, a talbot; sinister, a pegasus ppr., each charged on the shoulder with a garb or. **Motto:** Be careful. **Creation:** V. (UK) 6 Sept 1939.

THE 2ND VISCOUNT CALDECOTE, of Bristol, Co Glos (Sir Robert Andrew Inskip, KBE (1987), DSC (1941), DL (Hants 1991)) [The Rt Hon The Viscount Caldecote KBE DSC DL, Orchard Cottage, S Harting, Petersfield, Hants GU31 5NR]; *b* 8 Oct 1917; *s f* 1947; *educ* Eton (Fell 1953–72) and King's Coll Cambridge (MA 1944, Fell 1948–55); FEng, Lt-Cdr RNVR WW II, with Vickers Armstrong's Naval Yard Walker-on-Tyne from May 1947, Assist Manager 1947–48, lecturer engrg Cambridge 1948–55, dir: English Electric 1953–69, md English Electric Aviation 1960–63, dep md BAC 1961–67 (dir 1960–69), chm Legal and General Gp 1977–80, pres: Soc Br Aerospace Cos 1965–66, Int Assoc Aeronautical and Space Mfrs 1966–68, RINA 1987–90 (FRINA 1987); dir: Consolidated Gold Fields 1969–78, Lloyds Bank 1975–88, Lloyds Bank Int 1979–85; chm: Delta Gp plc (formerly Delta Metal Co) 1972–82, Investors in Industry (formerly Finance for Industry) 1980–87, Design Cncl 1972–80, BBC Gen Advsy Cncl 1982–85; memb BR Bd 1979–85; Pro-Chllr Cranfield Inst Technology 1976–84, memb Ch Assembly 1950–55, pres Dean Close Sch 1960–90; Hon: FICE, FIMechE, FIEE, FIM, FCSD (FSIAD); Hon DSc: Cranfield 1976, Aston 1979, City 1982, Bristol 1982; Hon LLD: London 1981, Cambridge 1985; *m* 22 July 1942 *Jean Hamilla, only dau of R-Adml Hugh Dundas Hamilton, of Limes, Haddenham, Bucks, and has issue:

1 +PIERS JAMES HAMPDEN; *b* 20 May 1947; *educ* Eton and Magdalene Coll Cambridge; *m* 1st 18 Feb 1970 Susan Bridget, only dau of William Palmer Mellen, of Hill Farm, Gt Sampford, Essex; *m* 2nd 1984 *Kristine Elizabeth, dau of Harvey Holbrooke-Jackson, of 12 Abbots Close, Ramsey, Cambs, and has issue by 2nd w:

(1) +Thomas James; *b* 22 March 1985

1 *Serena Helen Christian; *b* 12 June 1943; *m* 13 Nov 1965 (*divorce* 1979) John Andrew Brodie Armit, son of Capt Cecil Brodie Armit, RAMC, and Mrs A Guyader of 12 The Drive, NW11, and has issue:

(1) *Jerome Nathan; *b* 1971
(2) *Vashti Imogen; *b* 22 June 1969

2 *Antonia Jane Hamilla; *b* 12 Aug 1952; *m* 1972 *Piers Rowlandson, son of Richard Rowlandson, FRCS, of Broad Oak Milford, Godalming, Surrey, and has issue:

(1) *Titus Edmund; *b* 8 May 1973

Lineage: THOMAS FLINT INSKIP, of Caldecote, Baldock, Herts; *b* 28 April 1810; *m* 1829 Louisa Bowman, of The Mill, Stotfold, Beds, and *d* 14 July 1882, having had:

JAMES INSKIP, slr, of Clifton Park Ho, Clifton, Bristol; *b* 21 Jan 1839; *m* 1st July 1865 Elizabeth (*d* 27 Aug 1869), dau of Edward Thomas Inskip, and had issue:

1 James Theodore (Rt Rev), Bp Suffragan Barking, 1919–48, DD Cambridge 1919, Vicar St Paul's Penzance 1894–1900, Leyton Essex 1900–07, Jesmond Newcastle-on-Tyne 1907–16 and Ch Ch Southport 1916–19, Hon Canon: Newcastle-on-Tyne 1914–17, Liverpool 1917–19, Archdeacon W Ham 1920; *b* 6 April 1868; *educ* Clifton, Corpus Christi Coll Cambridge (BA 1889, MA 1893) and Ridley Hall Cambridge; *m* 2 Jan 1894 Lillian Hamilton (*d* 2 May 1940), 3rd dau of Charles Buchanan Ker, of Clifton, and *d* 4 Aug 1949, having had:

(1) James Sandys Ker; *b* 10 Feb 1901; *educ* Clifton and Trin Hall Cambridge; *m* 5 July 1950 *Pamela, yr dau of Oswald Mason, of The Moat Cottage, Flemings Hall, Bedingfield, Suffolk, and *d* 3 Feb 1977
(1) Lillian Alice Ker; *b* 26 June 1896; *d* unm 20 April 1975
(2) Norah Buchanan; *b* 14 April 1899; *m* 31 July 1926 Geoffrey Leonard Heawood
(3) Constance Elizabeth Hamilton; *b* 3 Nov 1905; *m* 20 April 1940 Dr Ernst Fellner, and *d* 4 Aug 1945

1 Elizabeth; *m* — Thomas and *d* 1946, leaving issue

JAMES INSKIP *m* 2nd 25 April 1872 Constance Sophia Louisa (*d* 1 Feb 1914), dau of John Hampden, and *d* 25 Oct 1909, having by her had further issue:

2 THOMAS WALKER HOBART (Sir), **1st Viscount**

3 John Hampden (Sir), KBE (1937), slr, Ld Mayor Bristol 1931, Alderman from 1932, dir Western Newspapers and Bristol Utd Press, Lt RFC and RAF WW I; *b* 16 Dec 1879; *educ* Clifton and King's Coll Cambridge (BA); *m* 18 April 1923 Hon Janet Maclay (*d* 4 April 1974), 2nd dau of 1st Baron Maclay (*qv*), and *d* 8 April 1960, leaving issue:

(1) John Hampden, QC (1966), Scots Gds WW II, barrister Inner Temple 1949, Master Bench 1975, dep chm Hants QS 1967, memb Criminal Law Revision Ctee 1973; *b* 1 Feb 1924; *educ* Clifton; *m* 26 June 1947 *Ann Howell, yr dau of Lt-Col Owen Stanley Davies, DSO, MC, TD, RE, and Lady (Paul) Gueterbock, and had issue:

1a *Owen Hampden; *b* 24 May 1953; *educ* Bryanston; *m* 8 Oct 1977 *Hon Clare Elizabeth Anne, only dau of 2nd Baron Noel-Buxton (*qv*), and has issue:

1b *Thomas Hampden; *b* 4 Sept 1986
1b *Victoria Ann; *b* 2 May 1983

1a *Diana Ann; *b* 1 April 1950

(2) *Joseph Maclay, late Lt RA; *b* 27 April 1930; *educ* Clifton and King's Coll Cambridge (BA)

(1) *Marta Maclay; *b* 10 May 1925; *m* 11 March 1953 (*divorce* 1968) John Philip Farquharson Oliver, 2nd son of Maj John Farquharson Oliver, and has issue:

1a *Janet Farquharson; *b* 19 Sept 1955

(2) *Constance Wiltshire; *b* 3 Aug 1927; *educ* Westonbirt; *m* 19 Nov 1966 *John Desmond Ware, son of Ralph Ernest Ware, of Exmouth, Devon, and has issue:

1a *Nicholas John; *b* 29 Nov 1967

(3) *Janet Fiona; *b* 21 Nov 1933; *m* 5 March 1960 *John Maurice Gray, MB, BS (Lond), MRCP(G), DObstRCOG, son of Oliver M Gray, of W Bridgford, Notts, and has issue:

1a *Christopher John; *b* 30 Jan 1963
2a *Andrew Peter; *b* 22 Feb 1966
3a *David; *b* 7 March 1968
1a *Angela Ruth; *b* 20 Feb 1961

2 Constance Katharine; *b* 12 May 1873; *m* 12 Aug 1907 Edward Luther Poulden, son of Capt Edward Poulden, RA, and *d* 17 March 1947, leaving issue

3 Ruth Emily Louisa; *b* 25 April 1874; *d* unm 6 Sept 1928

4 Grace Hampden, CBE; *b* 2 Aug 1877; *m* 18 Aug 1922 Charles Hay Walker, son of Charles Walker, and *d* 1951. He *d* 1941

5 Hilda Wake; *b* 5 June 1881; *d* unm 1957

6 Constance Nora Barne; *b* 14 April 1883; *m* 1 Dec 1909 Francis Edward Douglas, son of Rev Robert Douglas (*see* 1967 edn DOUGLAS OF KIRTLESIDE, B), and *d* 31 May 1945, leaving issue. He *d* 1 April 1951

7 Cicely Anne Churchill; *b* 25 March 1886; *m* 3 July 1916 Col Quentin Graham Kinnaird Agnew, DSO, MVO, 4th son of Sir Andrew Agnew, 8th Bt, of Lochnaw (*qv*), and *d* 1 May 1964, having had issue

The est son by the 2nd marriage,

THOMAS WALKER HOBART INSKIP, **1st Viscount Caldecote**, of Bristol, Co Glos (UK), so *cr* 6 Sept 1939, PC (1932), CBE (1920), JP Co Wigtown, KC (1914), Hon LLD Bristol U 1933; *educ* Clifton and King's Coll Cambridge (MA); barrister Inner Temple 1899, Bencher 1922, Treas 1943; MP Bristol Centl 1918–29 and Fareham 1931–39, Slr-Gen 1922–24, Nov 1924–28 and 1931–32, Attorney-Gen 1928–29 and 1932–36, Min Co-ordination Def 1936–39, Sec State Dominion Affrs Jan-Sept 1939 and May-Oct 1940 (when also Ldr Ho Lds), Ld Chllr 1939–40, Ld Ch Justice 1940–46, chm Cncl Legal Educn 1942–47, Recorder Kingston-on-Thames 1928–39, High Steward 1943–47, memb Naval Intell Dept Admlty 1915–17, Head Naval Law Branch Admlty 1917–19, Admlty Rep War Crimes Ctee 1919, Chllr Diocese Truro 1920–22, memb Ch Assembly, ktd 1922; *b* 5 March 1876; *m* 30 July 1914 Lady Augusta Helen Elizabeth (*d* 12 May 1967), est dau of 7th Earl of Glasgow (*qv*) and widow of Charles Lindsay Orr Ewing, MP (*see* ORR EWING, Bt), and *d* 11 Oct 1947, having had issue:

1 ROBERT ANDREW INSKIP, **2nd and present Viscount Caldecote**

CALEDON

Arms: Per pale arg. and sa. a chevron and in base a crescent, all counterchanged; on a canton az. a harp or, stringed arg. **Crest:** An arm in armour, embowed ppr., holding a sword of the last, hilt and pommel or. **Supporters:** Dexter, a mermaid with her mirror, all ppr.; sinister, an elephant arg. **Motto:** *Per mare, per terras* ('By sea and land'). **Creations:** B. (I) 6 June 1790, V. (I) 23 Nov 1797, E. (I) 29 Dec 1800.

THE 7TH EARL OF CALEDON, Co Tyrone, **Viscount Caledon**, of Caledon, Co Tyrone, and **Baron Caledon**, of Caledon, Co Tyrone (Nicholas (Nicky) James Alexander) [The Rt Hon The Earl of Caledon, Caledon Castle, Co Tyrone, Ireland; 3 Petyt Place, London SW3 5DJ]; *b* 6 May 1955; *s* f 1980; *educ* Gordonstoun; Ld Lt Co Armagh 1989; *m* 1st 15 Nov 1979 (*divorce* 1985) Wendy, yr dau of Spiro Nicholas Coumantaros, of Athens, and Mrs Suzanne Dayton; *m* 2nd 1989 (*divorce* 1997) Henrietta (Hetty) Mary Alison, er dau of John Francis Newman (*see* NEWMAN, Bt), and by her has:

1 +FREDERICK JAMES, *Viscount Alexander*; *b* 15 Oct 1990

1 *Leonora Jane; *b* 1993

Lineage: JOHN ALEXANDER, of Eridy, Co Donegal, living 1613; had a yst s:

Capt ANDREW ALEXANDER, of Gannochy, in Errigal, Co Londonderry; granted 1666 lands of Ballyclose, nr Newtown Limavaddy, Co Londonderry, by Sir Thomas Phillips, Govr Culmore Fort, Londonderry; attainted by JAMES II's Dublin Parl 1689; *m* 1st 51 Philips and was ancestor of the ALEXANDERs of Ahilly; *m* 2nd — Hillhouse and by her had:

JOHN ALEXANDER, of Ballyclose, bought 1717 the lands of Gunsland, Co Donegal; *m* Anne, dau of John White, of Cady Hill, Co Londonderry, and *d* 12 March 1747, having had:

1 John, of Ballyclose; ancestor of the ALEXANDERs of Milford, Co Carlow

2 NATHANIEL, of whom hereafter

3 William, ancestor of the ALEXANDER Bts of Dublin

1 Martha; *m* Alexander Kellie

The 2nd son,

NATHANIEL ALEXANDER, of Gunsland; *b* 1689; Alderman Londonderry 1755; *m* Elizabeth, 2nd dau of William McClintock, of Dunmore, Co Donegal (*see* RATHDONNELL, B), and *d* 22 Sept 1761, having had a 3rd s:

JAMES ALEXANDER, **1st Earl of Caledon**, Co Tyrone, so *cr* 29 Dec 1800, as also previously 23 Nov 1797 VISCOUNT CALEDON, of Caledon, Co Tyrone, and 6 June 1790 BARON CALEDON, of Caledon, Co Tyrone (all I); *b* 1730; with HEICS (where made enough money to buy for £600,000 estates at Caledon and other parts of Ireland), MP (I Parl) Londonderry 1775–90, Sheriff Cos Tyrone 1780 and Armagh 1781, Tory and pro-Union of I and GB Parls; *m* 28 Nov 1774 Anne (*d* 21 Dec 1777), 2nd dau of James Craufurd, of Craufurdsburn, Co Down, and *d* 22 March 1802, having had, with two daus:

DU PRE ALEXANDER, **2nd Earl of Caledon**, KP (1821), MP (Tory, I Parl) Newtownards Jan-Dec 1800, rep I peer 1804, Ld Lt Co Tyrone 1831–39, Col Tyrone Militia, 1st Govr Cape Good Hope 1806–11 on its cession to UK (the Caledon River and District of Caledon there are named after him); *b* 14 Dec 1777; *m* 16 Oct 1811 Lady Catherine Freeman Yorke (*d* 8 July 1863), 2nd dau and coheir of 3rd Earl of Hardwicke (*qv*), and *d* 8 April 1839, having had:

JAMES DU PRE ALEXANDER, **3rd Earl of Caledon**, MP (C) Tyrone 1837–39, rep I peer 1841, Capt Coldstream Gds, Col Tyrone Militia; *b* 27 July 1812; *m* 4 Sept 1845 Lady Jane Frederica Harriot Mary Grimston, VA 3rd Cl, Ldy Bedchamber to HM QUEEN VICTORIA (*d* 30 March 1888), 4th dau of 1st Earl of Verulam (*qv*), and had issue:

1 JAMES, **4th Earl**

2 Walter Philip, Lt-Col and Brevet Col cmdg 2nd Dragoons (Roy Scots Greys) Boer War 1899–1900 (Queen's medal, five clasps); *b* 9 Feb 1849; *m* 13 April 1882 Margaret Katherine, MBE (*d* 12 Sept 1929), dau of Rev Hon Francis Sylvester Grimston (*see* VERULAM, E), and *d* 30 Oct 1934, having had issue:

(1) Philip Sylvester; *b* 6 Feb 1883; Capt 8th KRI Hus WW I (despatches, wounded); *m* 31 Dec 1925 Violet Lucy (*d* 1979), yr dau of Hans Hendrick Aylmer, of Kerdiffstown, Sallins, Co Kildare, and *d* 22 Oct 1952, having had issue:

1a Charles Godfrey, Lt 8th Hus; *b* 22 Jan 1928; *ka* Korea 3 Jan 1951

1a *Patricia Margaret [The Rt Hon The Lady Gray, Airds Bay House, Taynuilt, Argyll]; *b* 29 Dec 1929; *m* 5 Sept 1959 *22nd Lord Gray (*qv*) and has issue

(1) Mary Catherine, JP Wilts; *b* 1885; *d* unm 25 Nov 1963

3 Charles, Maj and Hon Lt-Col 3rd Bn Roy Inniskilling Fus; *b* 26 Jan 1854; *m* 1880 Kate (*d* 4 Feb 1946), dau of Charles Stayner, of Halifax, NS, and *d* 27 Oct 1909, having had issue:

(1) Conn; *b* 2 Jan 1883; *educ* Harrow; Capt 3rd Bn Roy Inniskilling Fus, Lt Gren Gds, Boer War 1900–02, WW I, WW II (Pioneer Corps and CMP); *m* 1st 26 March 1906 Gladys Constance (*d* 31 Jan 1944), yr dau of Thomas Wrigley Grimshaw, CB, MD, and *d* 1970, leaving issue:

1a James Conn; *b* 11 June 1907; *m* 27 Feb 1939 *Beatrice Mary, dau of George Herbert Stringer, of 41 Lexden Rd, Colchester, Essex

1a *Mona; *m* 26 Jan 1939 Col Richard Michael Aylmer, RASC (*d* 1975), son of Algernon Ambrose Michael Aylmer, of Rathmore and Kerdiffstown, Co Kildare, and has issue:

1b *Justin Michael; *b* 3 Jan 1940; *educ* Wellington; *m* 1981 *Bridget Frances Georgina, er dau of Rev Canon George Alfred Salter, of St Luke's Rectory, Cork, and Lakka Ho, Castletownshend, Co Cork, and has issue:

1c *William George Algernon; *b* 1984

2c *Christopher Fenton Alexander; *b* 1987

2b *Dennis Fenton [Dennis Aylmer Esq, Valley House, Enniskerry, Co Wicklow, Ireland]; *b* 21 May 1942; *educ* Wellington; dir Lyons & Co (Ireland) Ltd; *m* 1976 *Dorothy Margaret, dau of Thomas Anthony Fleming, and has issue:

1c *Richard Thomas; *b* 1978

1c *Elizabeth Mona; *b* 1982

2a *Marjorie; *b* 30 Jan 1912; *m* 19 June 1931 Brig Richard Francis O'Donnell Gage, CBE, MC, RE (*d* 1973), yr son of Capt Richard Stewart Gage, and has issue:

1b *Ezekiel Conn; *b* 15 March 1933; *educ* Wellington; Lt-Col RA; *m* 7 Aug 1965 *Frances Elizabeth, er dau of Maj Frederick George Bolam, and has issue:

1c *Matthew James George; *b* 9 Jan 1967

2c *Alexander Richard; *b* 1972

1c *Victoria Louise; *b* 17 Oct 1968

2b *Patrick Richard; *b* 21 Sept 1938; *educ* Wellington; Cdr RN; *m* 6 Oct 1962 *Annette Daphne, only dau of John Charles Staveley, of Gloyns Ho, Yealmpton, Devon, and has issue:

1c *Rory James; *b* 11 Aug 1965

1c *Nicola Jane; *b* 17 April 1964

2c *Lucinda Georgina; *b* 1970

1b Patricia Ruth; *b* 19 Sept 1935; *d* Aug 1936

(1) (cont.) Capt Conn Alexander *m* 2nd 9 Dec 1944 Doris Minnie (*d* 1983), yst dau of Robert Pacey, of 24 Wolstonbury Rd, Hove, Sussex

(1) Ughna; *d* young 18 May 1893

(2) Sheelagh Jane

(3) Cethlyn Sarah Mohred; *m* 27 June 1925 Cdr Bredin Delap, RN, est son of Rev Canon Alexander Henry Delap, MA, of Strabane Rectory, Co Tyrone, and had two daus. He *d* 28 Sept 1970

1 Jane Charlotte Elizabeth; *b* 1 May 1850; *m* 1 Sept 1887 Capt Edmund Barker Van Koughnet, CMG, RN, JP, 2nd son of Hon Philip Michael Scott Van Koughnet, QC, Chllr Ontario, and *d* 23 June 1941. He *dsp* 27 March 1905

The 3rd EARL *d* 30 June 1855; his son,

JAMES ALEXANDER, **4th Earl of Caledon**, KP (1896), DL, rep I peer, Capt 1st Life Gds, Maj 4th Bn Roy Inniskilling Fus Egyptian Campaign 1882 (medal and clasp and Khedive's bronze star); *b* 11 July 1846; *m* 9 Oct 1884 Lady Elizabeth Graham Toler (*d* 6 Oct 1939), 2nd dau of 3rd Earl of Norbury (*qv*), and *d* 27 April 1898, having had issue:

1 ERIC JAMES DESMOND ALEXANDER, **5th Earl of Caledon**; *b* 9 Aug 1885; *educ* Eton and Trin Coll Cambridge; Maj Reserve of Offrs, late Life Gds, served WW I (wounded), and in Baltic on staff 1919–21; *d* unm 10 July 1968

2 Herbrand Charles, DSO (1915), Maj 5th Lancers WW I (despatches three times), WW II Lt-Col Pioneer Corps; *b* 28 Nov 1888; *educ* Harrow and RMC Sandhurst; *m* 1st 11 Feb 1919 (*divorce* 1927) Millicent Valla, only dau of Sir Henry Bayly Meredyth, 5th Bt; *m* 2nd 1 July 1937 Ada Kate (*d* 19–), dau of Hon Richard Eustace Bellew (*see* BELLEW, B) and formerly w of Charles Barry Domvile, and *d* 6 May 1965, having had:

(1) DENIS JAMES, **6th Earl**

3 HAROLD RUPERT LEOFRIC GEORGE, *cr* EARL ALEXANDER OF TUNIS (*qv*)

4 William Sigismund Patrick, DSO (1917), DL (Essex 1956–67); *b* 16 Nov 1895; *educ* Harrow; Col Irish Gds, formerly Maj HAC (TA), served in WW II (wounded, despatches); *m* 27 June 1934 Jane Hermione (*d* 13 Dec 1967), only dau of Cdr Bernard Buxton, DSO, RN (*see* BUXTON, Bt), and *d* 24 Dec 1972, leaving issue:

(1) +Alastair Patrick Lindsay [Alastair Alexander, 2665 Laguna St, San Francisco, CA 94123, USA]; *b* 27 July 1935; *educ* Eton; v-pres and gen manager Delli Silver Plate San Francisco, 2nd Lt Irish Gds 1953–55; *m* 19 Oct 1961 *Evelyn, dau of Massimo Forte, of 28 Via San Sebastiano, Rome, and has issue:

1a *Simone Eugenia; *b* 6 May 1962

(2) +Desmond Charles Bernard; *b* 7 April 1938; *educ* Eton, U of BC (BCom 1960) and Lancaster U (MA 1968)

(1) *Annabella Elizabeth Hero; *b* 10 March 1943

The 5th EARL's nephew,

DENIS JAMES ALEXANDER, **6th Earl of Caledon**; *b* 10 Nov 1920; *educ* Eton and RMC Sandhurst; Maj Irish Gds; *m* 1st 6 April 1943 (*divorce* 1948) Ghislaine, only dau of Cornelius Willem Dresselhuys, of Long Island, USA, and Edith Viscountess Kemsley (*qv*), and had issue:

1 *Tana Marie [The Lady Tana Focke, 7 Cheyne Walk, London SW3 5QZ]; *b* 2 March 1945; *m* 1973 *Paul Everard Justus Focke, QC, and has issue:

(1) *Diana Natasha; *b* 1974

(2) *Victoria Justine; *b* 1976

The **6th Earl** *m* 2nd 31 Dec 1952 Baroness Anne Louise (*d* 20 July 1963), only child of Baron Nicholas Werner Alexander de Graevenitz, and by her had issue:

1 NICHOLAS JAMES ALEXANDER, **7th and present Earl of Caledon**

2 *(Elizabeth) Jane [The Lady Jane Dobbs, The Farm, Castle Dobbs, Carrickfergus, Co Antrim]; *b* 28 March 1962; *m* 1st 1981 (*divorce* 1987; resumed maiden name by deed poll 1987) Rory F A Peck, war cameraman (*k* Moscow riots 1993), son of Julian Peck, of Prehen Ho, Co Londonderry, and has issue:

(1) *James Julian; *b* 1982

(2) *Alexander Nicolas de Graevenitz; *b* 1984

2 (cont.) Lady Jane Alexander *m* 2nd 1990 *Richard Francis Andrew Dobbs, est son of Richard Arthur Frederick Dobbs, of Castle Dobbs, Co Antrim, and has further issue:

(1) *Louisa Valla Joan; *b* 1992

(2) *Elizabeth Calixta Leslie; *b* 27 Sept 1994

(3) *Victoria Natasha Jane; *b* 12 March 1996

The **6th Earl** *m* 3rd 4 Aug 1964 *Marie Elisabeth Burton, dau of Maj Richard Burton Allen, late 3rd Dragoon Gds, of Benvheir Ho, Ballachulish, Argyll, and formerly w of Maj Hon Iain Maxwell Erskine, Gren Gds (*see* 1970 edn ERSKINE OF RERRICK, B), and *d* 20 May 1980

Seat: Caledon Castle, Co Tyrone. The present structure was put up in 1779 by the **1st Earl**, who had bought the estate from the 5th Earl of Orrery (*see* CORK and ORRERY, E). The previous house there had been in a different position altogether. Caledon employed Thomas Cooley, whose designs included a hall with doric columns (in scagliola) together with a frieze of the same order. When the **2nd Earl** remodelled the house in 1812 he employed John Nash, who added to the front a colonnade of ionic columns. From a purist point of view these rather clash with the doric ones internally. Nash rounded this colonnade off with domed end-pieces along the lines of pavilions. It has been suggested that this large and (for the climate) intolerably airy addition was in some sense a reworking of the stoep so common in South Africa, where Lord Caledon had served as Governor. Further changes were made in 1835.

CALLAGHAN OF CARDIFF

Arms: Quarterly vert and azure, in the former a portcullis or, in the latter a lymphad with an anchor at its prow and masted or, the sail set argent and pennants flying gules, overall a fess or, to the sinister thereof a grassy mount with a hurst of oak trees and issuing therefrom passant to the dexter a wolf proper. **Crest:** A sea-dragon sejant gules, langued and scaled or, its tail of the last and scaled gules, the dorsal fin also gules, about the neck a mural crown or, masoned gules, and supporting to the front with the fin of the dexter foreleg a portcullis gold. **Motto:** *Malo laborare quam languere* ('I had rather labour than be idle'). **Creation:** B. (LP, UK) 1987.

THE BARON CALLAGHAN OF CARDIFF, of the City of Cardiff, Co S Glamorgan (Sir (Leonard) James Callaghan, KG (1987), PC (1964)) [The Rt Hon The Lord Callaghan of Cardiff KG PC, House of Lords, London SW1A 0PW]; *b* 27 March 1912; *educ* Portsmouth Northern Secondary Sch; Civil Service Tax Officer 1929, Assist Sec Inland Revenue Staff Fedn 1936–47; WWII RN; MP (Lab) S Cardiff 1945–50, SE Cardiff 1950–83 and Cardiff S and Penarth 1983–87; Delegate to Cncl of Europe Strasbourg 1948–50 and 1954; consultant to Police Fedn Eng and Wales and Scottish Police Fedn 1955–64, Parly Sec Min Tport 1947–50, Parly and Fin Sec Admlty 1950–51, oppn spokesman: Tport 1951–53, Fuel and Power 1953–55, Colonial Affairs 1956–61, Shadow Chllr 1961–64, Chllr Exchequer 1964–67, Home Sec 1967–70, Shadow Home Sec 1970–71, oppn spokesman employment 1971–72, Shadow For Sec 1972–74, For Sec 1974–76, Min Overseas Devpt 1975–76, PM and First Ld Treasury 1976–79; Visiting Fellow Nuffield Coll Oxford 1959–67; Treasurer Lab Party 1967–76 (V-Chm 1973, Chm 1974); memb Lab Party NEC 1957–80, Treas Lab Party 1967–76 (V-chm 1973, Chm 1974), Leader Lab Party 1976–80, Leader Opposition 1979–80, Father H of C 1983–87; Pres: Advsy Ctee on Pollution of Sea 1963– (Chm 1952–63), UK Pilots Assoc 1963–76; Jt Pres RIIA 1983–; Hon Pres Internat Maritime Pilots Assoc 1971–76; Pres U of Wales Swansea 1986–; Hon Bencher Inner Temple 1976, Hon Freeman: Cardiff 1974, Sheffield 1979, Portsmouth 1991, Swansea 1993; Grand Cross 1st Cl Order of Merit Federal Republic of Germany 1979, Hon Life Fell Nuffield Coll Oxford 1967, Hon Fell U Coll Cardiff 1978, Portsmouth U 1981, Cardiff Inst of Higher Educn 1991, U of Wales Swansea 1993, Hon LLD Wales U 1976, Sardar Patel U India 1978, Birmingham U 1981, Meisei U Japan 1984, Sussex U 1989, Westminster 1993, Hon DLL Liverpool 1996; author: *A House Divided: the dilemma of Northern Ireland* (1973), *Time and Chance* (1987); *m* 1938 *Audrey Elizabeth, dau of Frank Moulton, of Loose, Kent, and has issue:

1 *Michael James [The Hon Michael Callaghan, 18 Brentwood Rd, Ingrave, Brentwood, Essex CM13 3QZ]; *b* 1945; *educ* Dulwich, U of Wales Cardiff and Manchester Business Sch; *m* 1968 *Jennifer Mary Morris, and has issue:

(1) *Joseph Edwin James; *b* 1981

(1) *Kate Elizabeth; *b* 1970

(2) *Sarah Jane; *b* 1972

1 *MARGARET ANN, BARONESS JAY OF PADDINGTON, *qv*

2 *Julia Elizabeth [The Hon Mrs Hubbard, Nettleslack Farm, Lowick Green, Ulveston, Cumbria]; *b* 1942; *m* 1967 *Ian Hamilton Hubbard, and has issue living:

(1) *Tobin James Hamilton; *b* 1970

(2) *Tom Ian; *b* 1975

(3) *Sam Jonathan; *b* 1976

(1) *Joanna Jane; *b* 1971

Lineage: — CALLAGHAN; *m* — Bernstein, of Sheffield, and had:

JAMES CALLAGHAN, Chief Petty Offr, RN, had:

(LEONARD) JAMES, *cr* a **Baron**

CALVERLEY

Arms: Azure, within two barrulets wavy argent between in chief a rose of the second barbed and seeded proper, and in base a fleece or, three ducal coronets of the last. **Crest:** In front of two miner's picks in saltire, a miner's safety lamp, all proper. **Supporters:** On either side a calf proper. **Motto:** *Labor omina vincit* ('Labour conquers all'). **Creation:** B. (UK) 17 Nov 1945.

THE 3RD BARON CALVERLEY, of the City of Bradford, in the West Riding of Yorks ((Charles) Rodney Muff) [The Rt Hon The Lord Calverley, 110 Buttershaw Lane, Wibsey, Bradford BD6 2DA]; *b* 2 Oct 1946; *s* f 1971; *educ* Moravian Sch for Boys, Fulneck, Pudsey; Detective Constable W Yorks Metropolitan Police; *m* 7 Oct 1972 *Barbara Ann, dau of Jonathan Brown, of Kelbrook, Colne, Lancs, and has issue:

1 +JONATHAN EDWARD; *b* 16 April 1975

2 +Andrew Raymond; *b* 25 Jan 1978

Lineage: GEORGE MUFF, miner, of Bradford; *b* 1841; *m* Sarah Jane Hodgson (*d* Nov 1913), and *d* 11 Feb 1877, leaving:

GEORGE MUFF, **1st Baron Calverley**, of the City of Bradford, in the W Riding of Yorks (UK), so *cr* 17 Nov 1945, DL, JP W R Yorks; *b* 10 Feb 1877; textile worker aged 10, Army Welfare Offr N Command 1940–47, City Cncllr Bradford 1923–29 and 1933–36, MP (Lab) Hull E 1929–31 and 1935–45, v-pres Br Boys Bde Movement and Leeds Prison Visiting Magistrates, memb Roy Commn on Jps 1946–55; *m* 27 July 1909 Ellen Eliza (*d* 1965), est dau of Charles William Orford, of Bath, and *d* 20 Sept 1955, leaving:

GEORGE RAYMOND ORFORD MUFF, **2nd Baron Calverley**, served WW II 1940–45 as Capt Roy IA Ord Corps; *b* 1 May 1914; *educ* Bradford GS; *m* 21 Dec 1940 *Mary, dau of Arthur Farrer, of Halifax, and *d* 24 June 1971, having had issue:

1 (CHARLES) RODNEY MUFF, **3rd and present Baron Calverley**

2 +Peter Raymond [The Hon Peter Muff, Oakhurst, 377 Shadwell Lane, Leeds LS17 8AH]; *b* 12 Aug 1953

CAMDEN

Arms: Quarterly, 1st and 4th, sa., on a fess between three elephant's heads erased arg., as many mullets of the first (for PRATT); 2nd, sa., a chevron between three spear heads arg., the points embrued (for JEFFREYS); 3rd, gu., an inescutcheon vair between eight cross crosslets or (for MOLESWORTH). **Crests:** 1 An elephant's head erased arg. (for PRATT), 2 A dragon's head erased vert, holding in the mouth a sinister hand couped at the wrist gu., and about the neck a chain, pendent therefrom a portcullis or (for JEFFREYS). **Supporters:** Dexter, a griffin sa., beak and claws gu.; sinister, a lion rampant or, each gorged with a collar arg., charged with three mullets sa. **Motto:** *Judicium parium aut lex terræ* ('The judgment of my peers, or the law of the land'). **Creations:** B. (GB) 17 July 1765, E. (Camden) and V. (GB) 13 May 1786, M. and E. (County of Brecknock) (UK) 7 Sept 1812.

THE 6TH MARQUESS CAMDEN, Earl Camden, Earl of the County of Brecknock, Viscount Bayham of Bayham Abbey, Kent, and **Baron Camden of Camden Place**, Kent (David George Edward Henry Pratt) [The Most Hon The Marquess Camden, Wherwell House, Andover, Hants SP11 7JP]; *b* 13 Aug 1930; *s f* 1983; *educ* Eton; late Lt Scots Gds, dir Clive Discount Co 1958–69; *m* 20 April 1961 (*divorce* 1984) Virginia Ann, only dau of Francis Harry Hume Finlaison, MA, MB, FRCS, LRCP, FRCOG, of Arklow Cottage, King's Rd, Windsor, Berks, and has had:

1 +JAMES WILLIAM JOHN, *Earl of Brecknock*; *b* 11 Dec 1965; *educ* Eton

2 Jonathan Bruce Charles; *b* 19 April 1970; *d* 30 May 1976

1 *Samantha Caroline; *b* 5 Oct 1964

Lineage: JOHN PRATT, of Dulford, Broadhembury, and of Plymtree, Devon; *b c* 1520; *m* Anstice — (*d* 1576) and *d* April 1573, leaving a 3rd s:

RICHARD PRATT, of The Priory, Broadhembury; *b* 1549; *m* Mary — (*d* 1646) and *d* Oct 1633, leaving, with four daus and five other s, a 5th s:

JOHN PRATT, of The Priory; *b* 1594; *m* Frances, dau of Henry Marker, of Woodford, Ottery St Mary, and *d* 1656, leaving, with four daus and three other s:

1 RICHARD, of whom later

2 Bernard, of Collumpton; *b* 1643; *m* 1st 21 Oct 1672 Dorothy Wood, of Culmstock; *m* 2nd 4 Sept 1677 Joan Glanville and *d* 1695

The er son,

RICHARD PRATT, of St Martin's, Oxford; *b* 1629; *m* 1st 7 Dec 1656 Elizabeth Skay and by her had issue:

1 JOHN (Sir), of whom later

2 Richard, of Oxford; living 1674

RICHARD PRATT *m* 2nd 25 Dec 1662 Anne (*d* Aug 1682), dau of Robert Wyatt, of Stanlake, Oxon, and *d* Aug 1692, having had further issue, with several daus:

3 Wyatt (Rev), Rector of Norton Fitzwarren, Somerset; *b* Dec 1670; *educ* New Inn Hall, Oxford (BA); *m* 30 April 1723 Anne Smith, of Creech St Michael, Somerset, and *dsp* 1723

4 Robert; *b* 1672

His est son,

Sir JOHN PRATT, of the Wilderness, Seale, Kent; MP Midhurst 1700–12, Ld Ch Justice King's Bench 1712–25; *m* 1st Elizabeth, dau and coheir of Rev Henry Gregory, Rector of Middleton Stonye, Staffs, and had, with other issue:

1 John, of The Wilderness, MP; *m* 1st Elizabeth, dau of Sir Geoffrey Jeffreys, of Brecknock Priory, Brecknockshire, and had, with a dau (*d* 1807):

(1) John, of Bayham Abbey, Sussex; *dsp* 1797, leaving the Marquess Camden his estates

1 (cont.) John Pratt *m* 2nd Dorothy, dau of Hon Robert Tracy, of Coscomb, Glos, Judge Court Common Pleas, and had:

(2) Robert, MP, of Coscomb, Master in Chancery; *dsp* 1775

Sir JOHN *m* 2nd Elizabeth (*d* 20 July 1728), dau of Rev Hugh Wilson, Rector of Llandinam and Canon of Bangor, and by her had, with other issue:

2 Thomas, Keeper Treasury Papers

3 William, Offr South Sea Co, lost at sea

4 CHARLES, **1st Earl**

5 Robert, Capt of Horse in the Earl of Albermarle's Regt; *d* unm in Germany

1 Caroline; *m* Herbert, Baron de Munster, Kt of the Teutonic Order, Lt-Col Roy American Regt

2 Jane; *m* Nicholas Hardinge, of Canbury, Surrey, Sec Treasury to GEORGE II

3 Anna Maria; *m* 17th Lord (Baron) Dacre (*see* HAMPDEN, V)

Lord Ch Justice PRATT *d* 24 Feb 1724; his third son by his 2nd w,

CHARLES PRATT, **1st Earl Camden**, so *cr* 13 May 1786, as also VISCOUNT BAYHAM OF BAYHAM ABBEY, Sussex, and earlier 17 July 1765 BARON CAMDEN OF CAMDEN PLACE, (Chislehurst), Kent, PC (1762); *bapt* 21 March 1714; *educ* Eton and King's Coll Cambridge; barrister 1738, KC 1755, Attorney-Gen to PRINCE OF WALES 1756–57, Attorney-Gen July 1757, MP (Whig) Downton 1757–61, Recorder Bath 1759, Ch Justice Common Pleas 1761–66, ktd 1761, Ld Chllr 1766–70, Ld Pres Cncl 1784–94; *m* 4 Oct 1749 Elizabeth (*d* 10 Dec 1779), dau and sole heir of Nicholas Jeffreys, of the Priory, Brecknockshire, and *d* 18 April 1794, having had, with five other daus (including Sarah, *m* 2 Nov 1779 Nicholas Price (*d* 4 June 1847), of Saintfield, Co Down, and *d* 7 April 1817, leaving issue):

JOHN JEFFREYS PRATT, **2nd Earl** and **1st Marquess Camden**, so *cr* 7 Sept 1812, as also EARL OF THE COUNTY OF BRECKNOCK (both UK), KG (1799), PC (1793); *b* 11 Feb 1759; *educ* Trin Coll Cambridge; MP (Tory) Bath 1780–89, a Teller Exchequer 1780–1834 (when the post was abolished), a Ld of Admlty 1782–April 83 and Dec 17823–89, a Ld of Treasury 1789–92, Ld Lt Ireland 1795–98, Sec State War and Colonies 1804–05, Ld Pres Cncl 1805–06 and 1807–12, Ld Lt and custos rotulorum Kent 1808–40, Chllr Cambridge U 1834–40; *m* 31 Dec 1785 Frances (*d* 7 July 1829), dau and heir of William Molesworth, of Wembury, Devon (*see* MOLESWORTH-ST AUBYN, Bt), and had issue:

1 GEORGE CHARLES, **2nd Marquess**

1 Frances Anne; *b* 21 Nov 1787; *d* 9 July 1822

2 Georgiana Elizabeth

3 Caroline; *m* 28 July 1825 Alexander Robert Stewart, of Ards House, Co Donegal, nephew of 1st Marquess of Londonderry (*qv*), and *d* 7 Oct 1827

The 1st MARQUESS *d* 8 Oct 1840; his son,

GEORGE CHARLES PRATT, **2nd Marquess Camden**, KG (1846), MP (Tory) Ludgershall 1821–26, Bath 1826–30 and Dunwich 1831–32, a Ld of Admlty 1822–29, called up *vp* to Ho Lds 8 Jan 1835 in f's Barony of Camden of Camden Place, Ld Lt Brecknockshire 1865–66; *b* 2 May 1799; *educ* Eton and Trin Coll Cambridge; *m* 27 Aug 1835 Harriet (*d* 22 Dec 1854), est dau of Rt Rev George Murray, DD, Bishop of Rochester (*see* ATHOLL, D), and had, with eight daus:

1 JOHN CHARLES, **3rd Marquess**

2 George Murray, Lt-Col 3rd Bn Berks Regt, formerly Capt W Kent YC, and Gren Gds; *b* 14 Jan 1843; *m* 2 July 1879 Hon Charlotte Harman Eaton (*d* 14 May 1928), est dau of 1st Baron Cheylesmore (*see* 1970 edn), and *d* 14 Oct 1922

3 Charles Robert, Lt-Col Oxfordshire LI; *b* 31 July 1847; *m* 5 Oct 1881 Florence Maria (*d* 10 April 1930), dau of Maj George Robert Stevenson, formerly 7th Dragoon Gds, and *d* Aug 1905, having had issue:

(1) Cecil John Charles (Rev), Priest-in-Charge, New Hythe, nr Maidstone, 1943; *b* 27 Aug 1886; *educ* Tonbridge and Gonville and Caius Coll Cambridge (BA 1908, MA 1912)

(2) Ronald Arthur Frederick (Ven), Chaplain of Kent and Canterbury Hosp, Canterbury, Archdeacon of Belize and Priest-in-Charge of St John's Cathedral, Belize, Br Honduras 1935–46, T/Chaplain RN 1917–19; *b* 27 Aug 1886; *educ* Tonbridge and Gonville and Caius Coll Cambridge (BA 1909, MA 1913); *m* 10 Jan 1925 Margaret, er dau of George Elam, MD, of Beckenham, Kent

(1) Gladys Florence; *d* an infant, 1 Aug 1882

(2) Sybil Madeline Georgina, MRCS Eng, LRCP Lond; *b* 11 Aug 1883; *d* unm 5 Jan 1951

The 2nd MARQUESS *d* 6 Aug 1866; his est son,

JOHN CHARLES PRATT, **3rd Marquess Camden**, DL, MP (Lib) Brecon Boroughs Feb-Aug 1866, Maj W Kent Yeo Cav; *b* 30 June 1840; *m* 12 July 1866 Lady Clementine Augusta Spencer-Churchill (*m* 2nd 28 Dec 1876 Capt Philip Green, late 9th Lancers (*d* 18 Nov 1904), and *d* 27 March 1886), yr dau of 6th Duke of Marlborough (*qv*), and had issue:

1 A son; *b* and *d* 11 Aug 1868

2 John Francis Charles; *b* and *d* 30 Aug 1869

3 JOHN CHARLES, **4th Marquess**

1 Clementine Frances Anne; *b* 2 Aug 1870; *m* 26 July 1890 3rd Baron Ormathwaite (*see* 1970 edn), and *d* 13 Jan 1921. He *d* 13 March 1937

The 3rd MARQUESS *d* 4 May 1872; his only surv son,

JOHN CHARLES PRATT, **4th Marquess Camden**, GCVO (1933), TD, JP Kent and Sussex, Ld Lt and custos rotulorum Kent 1905, Pres TAA 1908, Maj TFR, Maj W Kent Yeo WW I, Yr Bro Trin Ho, Cdre RYS 1942–3, KGStJ; *b* 9 Feb 1872; *m* 2 June 1898 Lady Joan Marion Nevill, CBE, OStJ (*d* 4 July 1952), dau of 3rd Marquess of Abergavenny (*qv*), and had:

1 JOHN CHARLES HENRY, **5th Marquess**

2 Roderic Arthur Nevill; *b* 13 Feb 1915; *educ* Eton and Trin Coll Cambridge (BA 1936); Maj Life Gds WW II Middle E, Italy and Germany (wounded); chm and md Roderic Pratt and Co; *m* 17 Jan 1945 Ursula Eva (*d* 1993), est dau of Capt Hon Valentine Maurice Wyndham-Quin, RN (*see* DUNRAVEN AND MOUNT-EARL, E), and *d* 30 May 1997, leaving:

(1) +Adrian John Charles; *b* 8 Nov 1952; *educ* Eton and RMA Sandhurst; late Capt Blues and Royals; md Br Equestrian Insur Brokers 1985–, dir Fontwell Pk and Plumpton Racecourses 1995–, memb cncl Racehorse Owners Assoc 1996–, pres Equisure Inc of Colorado USA 1996–, Steward Ascot, Goodwood and Plumpton racecourses, memb Lloyd's 1977–; *m* 1984 *Leanora R, dau of Maj Peter Murray Lee

(1) *Zara Elizabeth [Mrs John Johnstone, The Old Rectory, Lidgate, Newmarket, Suffolk]; *b* 11 March 1955; *m* 1988 *John Weir Johnstone, son of Andrew Johnstone, of Bonshaw Mains, Kirtlebridge, Lockerbie, Dumfriesshire, and has issue:

1a *Harry Andrew; *b* 1989

1 Irene Helen; *b* 23 Dec 1906; *m* 1st 9 Nov 1926 (*divorce* 1933) Hon Archibald Edward Cubitt, 2nd surv son of 2nd Baron Ashcombe (*qv*), and had issue; *m* 2nd 9 Feb 1933 (*divorce* 1937) James Cameron Clark, of New Jersey, USA; *m* 3rd 22 April 1937 Charles Claud Jervis Crawfurd, son of Lt-Col Reginald Crawfurd, DSO, and *d* 1976, having had further issue

2 Fiona; *b* 4 March 1911; *m* 1st 20 July 1931 (*divorce* 1944) Sir (John) Gerard Henry Fleetwood Fuller, 2nd Bt (*qv*), and had issue; *m* 2nd 30 Oct 1944 5th Earl of Normanton (*qv*), and *d* 1985, having had further issue

The 4th MARQUESS *d* 14 Dec 1943; his er son,

JOHN CHARLES HENRY PRATT, **5th Marquess Camden**, JP (1945), DL (1957); *b* 12 April 1899; *educ* Eton and RMC Sandhurst; Maj Reserve Offrs Scots Gds, ADC to GOC London Dist 1920–24, Hon Col 516 LAA Regt (RA), Yr Bro Trin Ho, Tstee Kent Playing Fields Assoc 1937–40, a Govr and memb Management Ctee RNLI, V-Cdre Roy Yacht Sqdn 1954–65 and Ho Lds Yacht Club, Hon Pres RAC Motor Sport Cncl 1975–83, Pres: SE Counties Agric Soc 1948, Kent & Sussex Hosp, St Pancras Alms Houses, RSPCA (Tunbridge Wells), Br Motor Cycle Club; V-Pres: RAC 1978–83, RNLI, Roy Northern Hosp, Marine Motoring Assoc; dir: Darracq Motor Engrg Co Ltd, Pogjoy Aircraft & Airmotors Ltd, Bayard Cars Ltd, Golf Club & Country House Ltd, RAC Travel Serv; *m* 1st 19 Oct 1920 (*divorce* 1941) Marjorie, DBE (1967) CStJ (*d* 24 Aug 1989), Supt-in-Ch, St John Ambulance Bde 1960–89, Ldy-in-Waiting to HRH PRINCESS MARINA, DUCHESS OF KENT, Hon Maj WRAC (TA), Sr Cdr ATS, Order of Mercy, only child of Col Atherton Edward Jenkins, JP, of Wherwell Priory, Andover, by his w Anna Isabella Cassel, and had issue:

1 DAVID GEORGE EDWARD HENRY PRATT, **6th and present Marquess Camden**

1 *Mary Clementine [The Lady Mary Pawle, Trehiven House, Madron, Penzance, Cornwall]; *b* 5 Aug 1921; DStJ (1975, CStJ 1965); *m* 1st 28 Sept 1940 F/Lt Hon (Herbert) Oswald Berry (*dsp* 8 June 1952), 5th son of 1st Viscount Kemsley (*qv*); *m* 2nd 10 Sept 1953 (Shafto) Gerald Strachan Pawle (*d* 1991), er son of Capt John Pawle, JP, of Little Havers, Bishops Stortford, Herts

The **5th Marquess** *m* 2nd 31 Jan 1942 Averil (*d* 4 June 1977), er dau of Col Henry Sidney John Streatfeild, DSO, TD, and formerly w of John Prescott Hallett; *m* 3rd 12 Jan 1978 (Cecil) Rosemary, artist, yr dau of Brig Hanbury Pawle, CBE, TD, DL, of The Priory Farm, Widford, Ware Herts, and formerly w of (a) G/Capt Peter Wooldridge Townsend, CVO, DSO, DFC, and (b) John Adolphus De Laszlo, and *d* 22 March 1983, having by his 2nd w had further issue:

2 +Michael John Henry [The Lord Michael Pratt, 16 Coulson St, London, SW3]; *b* 15 Aug 1946; *educ* Eton and Balliol Coll Oxford; author: *Britain's Greek Empire*

CAMERON OF LOCHBROOM

Arms: Gules three bars or, overall two flanches ermine, at the honour point also overall a fleur-de-lys sable. **Crest:** A kittiwake alighting, wings expanded proper. **Motto:** *Et regi et legi servire* ('Serving both the sovereign and the law').
Creation: B. (LP, UK) 1984.

THE BARON CAMERON OF LOCHBROOM, of Lochbroom, in the District of Ross and Cromarty (Rt Hon Kenneth John Cameron, PC 1984) [The Rt Hon The Lord Cameron of Lochbroom PC, Stoneyhill House, Musselburgh, EH21 6RP]; *b* 11 June 1931; *educ* Edinburgh Acad, Corpus Christi Coll Oxford (MA) and Edinburgh U (LLB); served RN 1950–52, Lt RNVR 1951; admitted Faculty of Advocates 1958; QC (Scot) 1972; Standing Jr Counsel to: Dept Tport 1964–71, DOE 1971–72; Chm Industl Tbnls Scotland 1966–81; Advocate Depute 1981–84, Ld Advocate 1984–89, Chm: Pensions Appeal Tbnl Scotland 1975 (Pres 1976–84), Ctee Investigation Scotland Ag Mktg Schemes 1980–84, Scottish Civic Tst 1989–95, Edinburgh New Town Conservn Ctee 1991–, Roy Fine Art Commn Scotland 1995–; Ld of Session 1989–; Pres Scottish Cncl for Vol Orgnsns 1989–; Hon Bencher Lincoln's Inn 1984; Hon Fell Corpus Christi Coll Oxford 1989; Hon FRIAS 1994; Hon FRSE 1990; *m* 1964 *Jean Pamela, dau of Col Granville Murray, and has issue:

1 *Victoria Christian; *b* 1965; *m* 1991 *James Annand Fraser, s of Sir Charles Annand Fraser, KCVO, DL, WS, of Shepherd House, Inveresk, Midlothian, and has:

(1) *Tabitha Christian Annand; *b* 1993

2 *Camilla Louise; *b* 1967

Lineage: LORD (JOHN) CAMERON (Scottish Lord of Session), KT, DSC, LLD; *m* 1st Eileen Dorothea — (*d* 1943) and had:

KENNETH JOHN, *cr* a **Baron**

CAMOYS

Arms: Quarterly, 1st and 4th, azure two bars dancettée or, a chief argent (for STONOR); 2nd and 3rd, or on a chief gules three bezants (for CAMOYS). **Crest:** On a rock argent charged with spots gules and azure a dove proper pecking thereat, with a stone gules in its beak. **Supporters:** Dexter, a lion rampant or; sinister, a lion rampant sable.
Creation: B. (E) 20 Aug 1383.

THE 7TH LORD (BARON) **CAMOYS** (Sir Ralph Thomas Campion George Sherman Stonor, GCVO (1998) DL (Oxon)) [The Rt Hon The Lord Camoys GCVO DL, Stonor Park, Henley-on-Thames, Oxon RG9 6HF]; *b* 16 April 1940; *s* f 1976; *educ* Eton and Balliol Coll Oxford; Ld in Waiting 1992–98, Ld Chamberlain and Chllr Roy Victorian Order 1998–, dir: Nat Provident Instn 1982–, Admin Staff Coll 1989–, 3i Gp 1991–, Perpetual 1994–, gen manager and dir Nat Prov & Rothschild Ltd 1968, md: Rothschild Inter-Continental Bank 1969, ch exec offr and md Amex Bank Ltd 1975–77 (chm 1977–78), Barclays Merchant Bank 1978–84, pres: Mail User's Assoc 1977–84, Henley Soc 1979–, memb: Ho Lds Select Ctee EEC 1979–81 and Roy Commission Historical MSS 1987–94, dep chm Barclays de Zoete Wedd Hldgs 1987– (ch exec 1986–88) and Sotheby's 1993–, chm Robert Jackson & Co 1968–85, dir Barclays Bank plc 1984–94, Consultor Patrimony of Holy See 1991–, Order of Gorkha Dakshina Bahu 1st Class Nepal, 3rd Warden Fishmongers' Co 1995–96 (memb Court 1980–, Prime Warden 1992–93); *m* 11 June 1966 *(Elisa)Beth Mary Hyde, only dau of Sir William Stephen Hyde Parker, 11th Bt, of Melford Hall, Suffolk (*qv*), and has:

1 +(RALPH) WILLIAM ROBERT THOMAS; *b* 10 Sept 1974 (HRH THE DUKE OF GLOUCESTER stood sponsor); *educ* Eton and Manchester U

1 +Alina Mary Stonor [The Hon Mrs Barrowcliff, 38 Abinger Rd, London W4 1EX]; *b* 15 May 1967; *educ* St Mary's Convent Ascot and Balliol Coll Oxford; ACA; *m* 1994 *Simon Derek Barrowcliff, ARICS, yst s of Dr Derek Barrowcliff, and has issue:

(1) +Thomas Simon Marmaduke; *b* 2 May 1994

(2) +Louis Edmund Ford; *b* 23 Sept 1995

2 +Emily Mary Julia; *b* 6 Oct 1969; *educ* St Mary's Convent Ascot and Durham U

3 +Sophia Ulla [The Hon Mrs Stourton, Stonor Park, Henley-on-Thames, Oxon RG9 6HF]; *b* 29 Sept 1971; interior designer, Freeman: Fishmongers' Co City London; *m* 1993 (*divorce* 1997) Hon James Alastair Stourton (*see* MOWBRAY, SEGRAVE and STOURTON, B)

Lineage: RALPH de CAMOYS; *m* Asceline, heiress of Torpel, Northants, and *d* 1259, leaving issue:

RALPH de CAMOYS; *b c* 1214; Constable Pevensey Castle 18 July 1264, called by writ to Simon de Montfort's assembly 24 Dec 1264 (now not recognised as a *bona fide* Parl, although the Ho of Lds on two occasions validated peerage claims based on writs of summons to it); *d* by 11 March 1276/7, leaving issue:

Sir JOHN de CAMOYS; *b c* 1247; *m c* 1279 Margaret (*m* 2nd before July 1301 Sir William Paynel and *d c* Jan 1311), dau and heir of Sir John de Gatesden, and *d* by 4 June 1298, leaving:

RALPH de CAMOYS, 1st LORD (Baron) CAMOYS, so *cr* by writ of summons to Parl 26 Nov 1313 according to later doctrine, Constable Windsor Castle 1319/20–23; *m* 1st by 25 June 1303 Margaret, dau of 1st Lord (Baron) Brewes of the 1290 *cr*, and had issue:

1 THOMAS de CAMOYS, 2nd(?) LORD (Baron) CAMOYS(?); never called to Parl; fought with barons opposed to EDWARD II's favourites at Battle of Boroughbridge 16 March 1321/2, also during Hundred Years War at Battle of Crécy 1346; *m c* 1327 Margaret — and *dsps* 11 April 1372

The 1st LORD (Baron) CAMOYS *m* 2nd by 1319 Elizabeth, probably dau or sis of William de Rogate, and *d* 1336, leaving further issue:

2 Sir JOHN de CAMOYS; *m* (?1st?) Margaret, sis and coheir of Richard Foliot, and had issue (but not necessarily of this w):

(1) THOMAS de CAMOYS, **1st Lord** (Baron) **Camoys** of the 1383 *cr*, for whom *see* further below

The 1st LORD (Baron) CAMOYS's gs,

THOMAS de CAMOYS, **1st Lord** (Baron) **Camoys** (E), so *cr* by writ of summons to Parl 20 Aug 1383 (such a *cr* was by a later doctrine held heritable by heirs general, which can include females, so that the + against each living female and her issue indicates that she is/they are in remainder to this peerage), KG (1415); cmded left wing English Army at Battle of Agincourt 25 Oct 1415; *m* 1st Elizabeth, dau of William Louches, of Milton, Oxon, and had issue:

1 Sir RICHARD de CAMOYS; *m* Joan, dau of Sir Richard Poynings, and *dvp* leaving issue:

(1) HUGH de CAMOYS, **2nd Lord** (Baron) **Camoys**; *b c* 1414; *d* 18 June 1426, when according to later doctrine the barony fell into abeyance between his sisters and their descendants, an abeyance not terminated for 413 years

(1) MARGARET, for whom *see* further below

(2) Alianora; *b c* 1408; *m* Sir Roger Lewknor, of Horsted Keynes, Sussex, and *d* by 1485, leaving issue; great-grandmother of Jane/Joan Lewknor, w of Sir Arthur Pole, s of Margaret, Countess of Salisbury (*see* ABERGAVENNY, M)

The 1st LORD (Baron) CAMOYS of the 1383 *cr m* 2nd Elizabeth Mortimer (*d* 20 April 1417), dau of 3rd Earl of March of the 1328 *cr* by his w Philippa, gdau of EDWARD III, and widow of Sir Henry ('Harry Hotspur') Percy, KG (*d* 21 July 1403) (*see* NORTHUMBERLAND, D), and *d* 28 March 1421, leaving issue, including a s who *dvp* an infant:

2 Sir Roger CAMOYS; *b c* 1406; in 1428 in possession of his f's estates in various counties including Hunts, described April 1429 as 'Roger lord de Camoys' but never summoned to Parl, although this description and similar others in numerous documents suggest he was recognized as a lord (of Parl?); Seneschal Guienne, France, July 1453; *m* 1st Isabel — (*d* by 26 Nov 1444; *m* 2nd (papal licence 1448) Isabel de Beaunoy

The 2nd LORD (Baron) CAMOYS's er sis,

MARGARET (de) Camoys; *b c* 1402; *m* Ralph RADMYLDE (*d* 3 Aug 1443), of Sussex, and had issue:

1 ROBERT; *m* and had issue:

(1) Sir WILLIAM; *dsp* 1499

1 MARGARET, for whom *see* further below

2 Isabella; *m* Nicholas Lewknor and was great-grandmother of Edward Lewknor, of Kingston Bowsey, bro of Sir Roger Lewknor (*see* above), who was attainted of high treason

MARGARET RADMYLDE (*née* de CAMOYS)'s er dau,

MARGARET Radmylde; *m* as his 1st w John GORING (*d* 1495), of Burton, Sussex (*see* GORING, Bt), and had issue:

1 JOHN GORING, of Burton; *m* Joan, dau and heir of Humphrey Hewster, and *d* after 1495, leaving issue:

(1) JOHN GORING, of Burton; *m* Constance, dau of Henry Dyke, and *d* 16 Oct 1520, leaving, with other issue:

1a Sir WILLIAM GORING, of Burton; Master of the Horse to HENRY VIII, Gent Privy Chamber to EDWARD VI, MP Sussex 1547, Sheriff Sussex and Surrey 1531, 1536 and 1550; *m* Elizabeth (*d* 16 Nov 1558), 2nd dau of John Covert, of Slaugham, Sussex, and *d* 2 March 1553, leaving, with other issue:

1b Sir HENRY GORING, of Burton; *b* 1521; ktd 21 Aug 1591, Sheriff Sussex and Surrey 1562 and Sussex 1569; *m* Dorothy, 2nd dau of William Everard, of Alborne, Sussex, and *d* 16 Dec 1594, leaving, with other issue:

1c WILLIAM GORING, of Burton; *m* 1st 1563 Ann, dau of Robert Burbridge, of Hayes, Middx, and *d* 1601, leaving issue:

1d Sir HENRY GORING, for whom *see* further below

1c (cont.) WILLIAM GORING *m* 2nd Margaret, dau of Thomas Chaloner, of Kenwards, Sussex, and widow of (a) William Courthope, of Hartfield, and (b) Richard Mill, of Greatham, both Sussex, and by her had further issue:

2d George GORING, ancestor of the GORINGs of Barcombe and Chailey, Sussex, extinct in the male line 1735

WILLIAM GORING's est s,

Sir HENRY GORING, of Burton; *m* 1st Eleanor, dau of Sir William Kingsmill, and *d* 16 July 1626, leaving issue:

1 Sir WILLIAM GORING, 1st Bt (E), so *cr* 14 May 1622, of Burton; *m* Eleanor/Bridget, dau of Sir Edward Francis, and was *bur* 25 Feb 1657/8, leaving issue:

(1) Sir HENRY GORING, 2nd Bt; *m* Mary, dau of John Chamberlaine, of Sherborne Castle, Oxon, and widow of Sir Thomas Gage, 2nd Bt, of Firle, Sussex (*see* GAGE, V), and *d* 8 June 1671, leaving with other issue:

1a ANN Goring; *m* Richard BIDDULPH, of Biddulph Castle, Staffs, and had with other issue:

1c JOHN BIDDULPH, of Biddulph; *m* Mary, dau of Charles Arundell, of Horningsham, and had issue:

1d Richard, of Burton; *d* unm 1767

2d Charles, of Burton; *m* Elizabeth, dau of Sir Henry Bedingfeld, Bt (*see* (PASTON-)BEDINGFELD, Bt), and *d* 1784, leaving, with other issue:

1e John, of Burton; *d* unm 2 Aug 1835

1d MARY Biddulph; *m* 19 April 1732 Thomas STONOR (*d* 2 Feb 1772), of Stonor, Oxon, and *d* 14 June 1778, leaving issue (*see* STONOR family below)

2d Ann; *m* Anthony Wright, of Wealside, and was by him great-grandmother of Anthony John Wright Biddulph, of Burton

Lineage (of Stonor): ROBERT de STONORE, of Stonor, Oxon; mentioned Pipe Rolls 1177–85

RICHARD de STONORE, of Stonor, mentioned Pipe Roll of 1204

RICHARD de STONOR, of Stonor, mentioned Oxon Placets of 1241 and 1273

Sir RICHARD de STONORE, of Stonor; *b* 1250; *m* Margaret, dau and heiress of Sir John Harnhull, of Harnhull, Glos, and *d* 1315, leaving issue:

Sir JOHN de STONORE; *b* 1280; Ld Ch Justice Court of Common Pleas 1329, granted roy licence for the sojourn and dwelling of six chaplains to celebrate divine service in a chapel founded at Stonor in honour of the Most Holy Trinity; *m* Maud — and *d* 1354, having had, with 12 other children:

Sir JOHN de STONORE; *b* 1310; fought Battle of Crécy 1346; *m* Margery Winard, of Devon, and *d* 1361, leaving issue:

Sir EDMUND de STONORE; *b* 1344; *m* Elizabeth, dau of Sir Gerard de l'Isle, of Shirburn Castle, Oxon, and *d* 1382, leaving, with other issue:

Sir RALPH de STONORE; *b* 1370; *m* Joan, dau of Sir Robert Belknap, Ch Justice Common Pleas, and *d* 1394 while accompanying RICHARD II to Ireland, leaving issue:

THOMAS STONORE, of Stonor; *b* 1394; Ld of 31 manors, Sheriff and MP Oxon; *m* Alice, dau of Sir John Kirkby, of Hornton Kirkby, Kent, and *d* 3 May 1440, leaving issue:

THOMAS STONOR, of Stonor; *b* 1424; *m* Jeanne, illegitimate dau of 2nd Duke of Suffolk of the 1448 *cr* and half sis of John de la Pole, Earl of Lincoln, Ld-Lt Ireland (*k* 16 June 1487 Battle of Stoke), n of EDWARD IV and RICHARD III, and *d* 23 April 1474, leaving issue:

1 William (Sir), of Stonor, KB; High Steward Oxford 1492; *m* 1st Elizabeth Ryche; *m* 2nd Agnes Wydeslade; *m* 3rd Lady Ann Nevill(e) (*d* by 1486), dau of 1st and last Marquess of Montagu of the 1470 *cr* (*see* ABERGAVENNY, M), and *d* 1494, having had:

(1) John; *d* young

(1) Anne; *m* Sir Adrian Fortescue and had issue (*see* LYTTON, E)

2 Edward

3 THOMAS, for whom *see* further below

THOMAS STONOR's 3rd s,

THOMAS STONOR, of Stonor; *b* 1450; *m* 1st Sibilla, dau and coheir of Sir David Brecknock, and had issue, with three daus:

1 Walter (Sir); *b* 1477; High Sheriff and MP Oxon, Lt Tower of London; *m* 1st Anne, dau of Sir Nicholas Folliot, of Worcester; *m* 2nd Elizabeth Chambers

2 John; *m* Isabel, dau of Sir Clement Agard, of Stafford, and had issue:

(1) FRANCIS (Sir), for whom *see* further below

THOMAS STONOR *m* 2nd Catherine, sis of Sir Robert Harcourt, of Stanton Harcourt, Oxon (*see* 1970 edn HARCOURT, V)

THOMAS STONOR's gs,

Sir FRANCIS STONOR, of Stonor; ktd 1553; *m* Cecily, dau of Sir Leonard Chamberlain, of Shirburn, Oxon, and *d* 1575, leaving issue:

1 Francis (Sir), of Stonor; *b* 1553; High Sheriff Oxon 1622; *m* Martha, dau of Sir John Southcote, Judge King's Bench, and *d* 1637, leaving issue, with another s and two daus:

(1) Henry (Sir); ktd 1603; *m* Elizabeth, dau of Sir Henry Wodehouse, of Waxham, and *dsp*

(2) William (Sir), of Stonor; *b* 1594; *m* Elizabeth, dau of Sir Thomas Lake, Sec of State, and *d* 1651, leaving with four other s and three daus:

1a William; *k* 1645 at Siege of Basing House (*see* WINCHESTER, M)

2a Thomas, of Stonor; *b* 1626; *m* 1651 Elizabeth Nevill(e), yst dau of 7th Lord (Baron) Abergavenny (*see* ABERGAVENNY, M), and *d* 1683, leaving, with three other s:

1b John, of Stonor; *b* 22 March 1656; *m* 8 July 1675 Mary Talbot, sis of 1st and last Duke of Shrewsbury of the 1694 *cr* (*see* SHREWSBURY and WATERFORD, E), and *d* 1687, leaving issue:

1c THOMAS, for whom *see* further below

2c John Talbot; *b* 1678; RC Bp Thespia, Vicar Apostolic Midland District; *d* 1756

3c Charles; *d* 1705

1c Mary; *m* as his 2nd w William Plowden (*see* PLOWDEN, B) and had issue

2c Anne; *m* Charles Bodenham, of Rotherwas

JOHN STONOR's est s,

THOMAS STONOR, of Stonor; *b* 20 June 1677; *m* 1st 16 March 1696 Isabel Belasyse (*dsp*), dau of 1st Baron Belasyse of Worlaby of the 1644 *cr*; *m* 2nd 14 July 1705 Winifred Roper, dau of 5th Baron Teynham (*qv*), and *d* 10 Aug 1724, leaving, with three other s and five other daus:

1 THOMAS, for whom *see* further below

1 Winifred; *m* 7 Jan 1723/4 as his 1st w Philip Howard, of Buckenham, Norfolk (*see* NORFOLK, D), and *d* 3 Feb 1730/1, leaving issue

THOMAS STONOR's est s,

THOMAS STONOR, of Stonor; *b* 18 April 1710; *m* 19 April 1732 Mary (*d* 14 June 1778), er dau of John Biddulph, of Biddulph (*see* above), and *d* 2 Feb 1772, leaving issue:

1 CHARLES, for whom *see* further below

2 Henry, of San Lucar; *b* 5 March 1741; *m* 1 July 1773 Elizabeth, dau of Norris Gardiner Browne, of Hinstock, and had three s

THOMAS STONOR's er s,

CHARLES STONOR, of Stonor; *b* 20 Jan 1737; *m* 15 Nov 1765 Mary Eugenia (*m* 2nd Thomas Canning), dau of Michael Blount, of Mapledurham, and *d* 31 Oct 1781, leaving, with other issue:

1 THOMAS, of Stonor; *b* 9 Dec 1766; *m* 7 Oct 1795 Catherine (*d* 31 Aug 1834), sis and coheir of Charles Robert Blundell, of Ince Blundell, and *d* 16 Aug 1831, leaving issue:

(1) THOMAS STONOR, **3rd Lord** (Baron) **Camoys** of the 1383 *cr*, for whom *see* further below

(2) Charles Henry, of Lostock, Lancs; *b* 1 Dec 1798; *m* 15 Aug 1828 Sophia (*d* 1883), dau of John Cary, 2nd s of George Cary, of Torre Abbey, Devon, and *d* 7 Feb 1840, leaving:

1a Charles Joseph, of Llanvair, Ascot, Berks, JP (Lancs); *b* 4 Aug 1837; *m* 3 Oct 1865 Maude Mary (*d* 26 April 1921), 3rd dau of Charles Noel Welman, of Norton Manor, Somerset, and *d* 8 Jan 1919, leaving issue:

1b Edmund Charles Joseph; *b* 14 Sept 1866; Capt 1st Garrison Bn Lincolnshire Regt, Lt 3rd Bn E Lancashire Regt; *m* 30 June 1896 Mary Louisa Catherine (*d* 21 May 1943), dau of Thomas William Charles Riddell, of Felton Park, Northumberland, and *d* 18 Oct 1929, leaving:

1c Winefride Mary Angela; *b* 2 Aug 1897

2b Maurice Aloysius; *b* 7 Jan 1869; *m* 1 Oct 1925 Helen (*d* 4 March 1945), only dau of Richard McNabb, of Hemsworth, Torquay and widow of Maj Francis Bowring, 22nd Punjabis, and *d* 12 March 1940

3b Oswald Francis Gerard, CMG (1925); *b* 3 June 1872; Br Resident Selangor, FMS 1921, Perak FMS 1926–27; *m* 24 Oct 1906 Florence Mary Josephine (*d* 3 June 1956), only dau of Edward Talbot Wolseley, of Maryland, Ascot (*see* WOLSELEY Bt), and *d* 22 June 1940, leaving issue:

1c Robert Joseph; *b* 28 Aug 1909; *educ* Christ's Coll Cambridge (MA); RC priest, CF WW II; *d* unm 12 Feb 1963

1c Joan Florence Mary; *b* 11 Nov 1907; *m* 1st 10 Nov 1927 (*divorce* 1948) John Colburn-Bennett, CMG, CBE (*d* 25 Aug 1969); *m* 2nd 18 April 1948 John Keith Macara, 2nd s of Sir William Cowper Macara, 2nd Bt (*qv*), and *d* 19 June 1956, leaving issue by her 1st husb:

1d +Jill Mary [Mrs Jill Scott, 48 Peel St, London W8 7PD]; *b* 1929; *m* 1954 (*divorce* 1967) David Noel Templer Scott (*d* 1989) and has:

1e +(John) Andrew Templer [Andrew Scott Esq, 49 Telford Ave, London SW2 4XL]; *b* 1960; *m* 1984 *Catherine Frances, dau of Cdr William John Macnamara Faulkner, RN (*see* DE TRAFFORD, Bt), and has issue:

1f +Rory David Templer; *b* 1993

1f +Alice Emily Cecilia; *b* 1989

1e +Virginia Jane [Mrs Charles Temple-Richards, 92 Huron Rd, London SW17 8RD]; *b* 1957; *m* 1985 *Charles Leofric Thomas Temple-Richards (*see* TEMPLE, Bt) and has issue:

1f +Alec Thomas Leofric; *b* 1995

1f +Cornelia Florence; *b* 1989

2f +Juliana Virginia; *b* 1991

2d +Veronica Anne [Mrs Veronica Rudman, Old House, Llanigon, Hay-on-Wye, Herefs HR3 5RH]; *b* 7 April 1942; *m* 3 April 1964 (*divorce* 1981) Michael Edward Rudman and has issue:

1e +Amanda Joan [Mrs Amanda Rudman, 50 Elsworthy Rd, London NW3 3BU]; *b* 13 Nov 1967

2e +Katherine Rose [Mrs Katherine Rudman, 15c Swains Lane, London N6 6QX]; *b* 20 July 1970

2c +Evelyn Mary; *b* 24 Sept 1911; *m* 17 Aug 1935 (*divorce* 1954) *Cdr Denis Hugh Bryan Barrett, CB, DSC, RN, only s of Maj Frederick Whitfield Barrett, of Wroughton Hall, Wroughton, Wilts, by his w Hon Isobel Edwardes, yst dau of 4th Baron Kensington (*qv*), and has issue:

1d +Michael Patrick Denis; *b* 11 Feb 1937; *educ* Downside and Trin Coll Cambridge; *m* 1951 (*divorce* 19–) Kytia Buchs

2d +Bryan Nicholas; *b* 4 Dec 1940; *educ* Downside; Lt-Cdr RN; *m* 28 Nov 1964 (*divorce* 19–) Sally Lois, yr dau of Arthur Maxwell Hankin, CMG, of 21 Montpelier Mews, London SW7, and has issue:

1e +Claire Fiona; *b* 3 July 1966

2e +Georgina Mary; *b* 8 Feb 1968

4b Charles Henry Joseph; *b* 17 March 1874; Lt 6th Bn Roy Welch Fus; *m* 21 Dec 1912 Hylda (*d* 23 Feb 1968), er dau of Henry Lloyd Carter, of Bryn Seiont, Caernarvon, and *d* 4 Feb 1930, leaving issue:

1c +Henry Anthony [Henry Stonor Esq, 10 The Green, Marlborough, Wilts; *b* 11 May 1926; *educ* Downside and Shrewsbury; Lt Roy Welch Fus

1c Beatrice Maude; *b* 3 Oct 1913; *m* 8 Jan 1949, as his 2nd w, Capt Ralph Aldersey, JP (*d* 12 Dec 1976), only surv s of Hugh Aldersey, of Aldersey and Spurstow, and *d* 1 Jan 1997, leaving:

1d +William Ralph; *b* 1950; *educ* Oswestry Sch

2c +Pamela Mary [Miss Pamela Stonor, Flat B, Ardle Bank, Kingsbury Street, Marlborough, Wilts SN8 1HU]; *b* 2 June 1915; Ch Welfare Offr, OStJ, BRCS WW II Italy (despatches), St John and Red Cross Service Hosps Welfare 1946–67, SSStJ 1967

3c Sheila Mary; *b* 8 Nov 1916; *m* 19 Oct 1946 *Brig Ernest James Cholmeley Harrison, OBE, Roy Signals, yst s of Sir Charlton Scott Cholmeley Harrison, CIE, of Prospect, Morant Bay, Jamaica, and *d* 16 July 1994, leaving issue:

1d +(James) Hugh Cholmeley; *b* 27 Nov 1947

2d Robert Mark Cholmeley; *b* 9 June 1950; *d* 20 June 1987

1d +Sally Ann Monamie; *b* 28 July 1950

4c Stella Frances Ursula; *b* 6 March 1922; *d* 10 Nov 1982

5c Anne; *b* 4 March 1929; *m* 29 Oct 1955 Peter Bryan Sawdy, s of Alfred Eustace Cholmondeley Sawdy, of Green Gables, London Rd, Wokingham, Berks, and *d* 12 Oct 1995, leaving:

1d +Caroline Ann; *b* 30 Sept 1957

2d +Susan Angela Lumley; *b* 1963

5b Wilfrid Thomas; *b* 8 April 1876; *m* 19 June 1923 Bertha (*d* 21 Feb 1953), dau of Col Lucius Cary, of Torre Abbey, Devon, and *dsp* 3 Jan 1962

6b Ambrose Francis; *b* 7 Dec 1877; Capt 3rd Bn Roy Inniskilling Fus; *d* unm 21 April 1941

7b Francis Cyril; *b* 15 Feb 1880; Lt 3rd Bn D of Wellington's Regt; *m* 20 March 1909 Juliana Tindal (*d* 16 Nov 1963), 2nd dau of Lt-Col Bernard Tindal Bosanquet, DL, of Claysmore, Enfield, and *d* 21 Jan 1955, having had issue:

1c Bernard Francis; *b* 13 Dec 1909; *m* 1935 *Elsie Graham and *d* 1982, leaving issue:

1d +Mortimer (Bernie); *b* 1941; *m* 19– *Erika, dau of — and has issue:

1e +Jamus; *b* 19–

2e +Brendon: *b* 19–

1e +Emily; *b* 19–

1d +Pride Cynthia (dropped original name Anne) Stonor [Mrs Douglas Maclean, PO Box 92 Margaret River, W Australia 6285]; *b* 1935; *m* 1st 1957 *C Killa, of Perth, Australia; *m* 2nd 1969 *Douglas G Maclean and has issue by her 1st husb:

1e +Deborah Anne; *b* 1958; *m* 1981 *Bruce Wishart Smith, of Bressay, Shetland Isles, and has issue:

1f +Jody Kimberley; *b* 1985

2d +Juliana [Mrs Colin Pember, 18 Tropicana Way, Safety Bay, W Australia 6169]; *b* 1938; *m* 1st 1960 (*divorce* 1978) Michael Carter; *m* 2nd 1981 *Colin Keith Pember and has issue by her 1st husb:

1e +David Michael [David Carter Esq, 14 Chadwin Place, Padbury, W Australia 6025]; *b* 1961

2e +Brian John CARTER later STONOR (deed poll 1986); *b* 1964; *m* 1989 *Leah, only dau of John Gadenne

1e +Jennifer Dawn; *b* 1962; *m* 1981 *Allan Burke and has issue:

1f +Zara Sheree; *b* 1982

2f +Karleah Marie; *b* 1985

2e +Tania Gaye; *b* 1971

3d +Virginia; *b* 1946; *m* 19– *Desmond — and has issue:

1e +Stephen; *b* 19–

1e +Raelene; *b* 19–

2c Charles Robert, of Brooklands N, Sarisbury Green, Hants; *b* 20 May 1912; *d* 19–

1c Cynthia Juliana; *d* 29 June 1932

8b Bernard James; *b* 14 Dec 1882; served RN; *d* unm 11 Oct 1901

9b Cuthbert Mary Anthony; *b* 13 Aug 1887; 2nd Lt Roy Inniskilling Fus; *ka* 1 July 1916

1b Blanche Mary Frederica; *m* 6 Sept 1904 Hubert Wheler Marsham (*d* 6 June 1952), 4th s of Rev Hon John Marsham, rector Barton Seagrave, Northants, and *d* 31 March 1963, leaving issue (*see* ROMNEY E)

2b Mary Clare; *b* 4 Oct 1890; *d* unm 9 Oct 1973 Kelowna, Canada

1a Mary; *d* 3 Sept 1882

2a Emily; nun; *d* 22 April 1917

3a Frances; *d* 1850

4a Clare; *d* unm 1904

5a Eugenia Mary; *m* 26 Nov 1862 Charles Welman (*d* 3 Feb 1914), 49th Regt, est surv s of Charles Noel Welman, of Norton Manor, Somerset, and *d* 27 April 1917, leaving issue

CHARLES STONOR's gs,

THOMAS STONOR, **3rd Lord** (Baron) **Camoys**; *b* 22 Oct 1797; MP (Whig) Oxford 1832–33, as heir general of his great-grandmother Mary Biddulph became a coheir of Hugh, 2nd Lord Camoys, and on 27 Aug 1839 the abeyance in this barony was terminated in his favour, called to Parl 14 Sept 1839 as LORD (Baron) CAMOYS, Ld in Waiting 1846–52, 1853–58, 1859–66 and 1868–74; *m* 25 July 1821 Frances (*d* 5 April 1880), dau of Peregrine Edward Towneley, (*see* O'HAGAN, B) and *d* 18 Jan 1881, having had issue:

1 Thomas Edward; *b* 29 Oct 1824; *m* 22 Apr 1863 Catherine (*m* 2nd 25 Nov 1869 Sir Archibald Keppel Macdonald, 3rd Bt (*see* BOSVILLE MACDONALD, Bt), and *d* 27 Nov 1894), est dau of John Coulthurst, of Gargrave Hall, Yorks, and *dsp* 28 May 1865

2 Francis, JP, DL; *b* 5 Jan 1829; Clerk Ho of Lds; *m* 25 Sept 1855 Elsie (Woman of the Bedchamber to HM QUEEN ALEXANDRA when Princess of Wales) (*d* April 1883), yst dau of Sir Robert Peel, 2nd Bt (*see* PEEL, E), and *d* 10 Jan 1881, leaving issue:

(1) FRANCIS ROBERT, **4th Lord**

(2) Harry Julian (Sir), GCVO; *b* 17 Nov 1859; granted precedence with his siblings as baron's dau/yr s May 1881, Gent Usher and Quarterly Waiter in Ordinary to HM QUEEN VICTORIA 1883–1901, Gent Usher and Groom-in-Waiting to TM EDWARD VII 1901–10 and GEORGE V 1910–36, Extra Groom-in-Waiting to TM EDWARD VIII 1936 and GEORGE VI 1937, Dep Master Household 1918–21, Sec and Registrar Order of Merit 1924–39, Chevalier Legion of Honour; *d* unm 5 May 1939

(3) Edward Alexander; *b* 16 Oct 1867; Pncpl Clerk and Taxing Master Private Bills Ho Lds, Sec Anti-Socialist and Anti-Communist Union, Maj RAF 1914–19, Lt Oxfordshire Yeo Cav, Orders of Legn Honour, Leopold of Belgium, SS. Maurice and Lazarus Italy, Crown Romania, St Anne Russia and St Sava Yugoslavia; *m* 16 Jan 1899 Christine Alexandra (*d* 9 Dec 1958), dau of Richard Ralli and widow of Ambrose Ralli (*see* RALLI, Bt), and *d* 12 May 1940, leaving issue:

1a Francis Edward; *b* 4 Aug 1900; *educ* Eton and Trin Coll Oxford (MA 1949); Page of Honour to HM GEORGE V 1915–17; *d* unm 22 March 1968

(1) Julia Caroline; *m* 18 July 1891 Marquis d'Hautpoul de Syre (*d* 11 March 1934) and *d* 4 Feb 1950, leaving issue

3 (Most Rev) Edmund; *b* 2 April 1831; RC priest, Canon St John Lateran, Archbp Trebizond; *d* 28 Feb 1912

1 Charlotte; *b* 15 May 1822; nun; *d* 28 Feb 1875

2 Catherine Frances; *b* 29 Aug 1823; *d* unm 25 March 1907

3 Eliza; *b* 23 July 1830; *m* 24 Aug 1852 Henry Charles Silvertop (*d* 3 Dec 1887), of Minister Acres, Northumberland, and *d* 24 July 1860, leaving issue

4 Maria; *b* 2 April 1832; *m* 17 Oct 1855 Sir Charles Frederick Smythe, 7th Bt (*d* 14 Nov 1897; *see* 1928 edn), and *d* 20 Jan 1914, leaving issue

5 Agnes; *b* 8 Oct 1833; Prioress St Mary's Rugby; *d* 6 Sep 1887

6 Harriet; *b* 5 April 1836; *m* 8 Feb 1864 5th Viscount Clifden (*see* 1970 edn) and *d* 17 May 1914, leaving issue

7 Caroline; *b* 24 May 1837; nun

8 Margaret Ann; *b* 8 Aug 1839; *m* 29 July 1862 Edward Pereira (*d* 5 Nov 1872), of 30 Grosvenor Sq, London, 5th s of Antonio Vincente Pereira, and *d* 7 July 1894, leaving issue

9 Eleanor Lucy; *b* 16 Jan 1842; nun; *d* June 1886

The 3rd LORD (Baron) STONOR's gs,

FRANCIS ROBERT STONOR, **4th Lord** (Baron) **Camoys**; *b* 9 Dec 1856; Ld-in-Waiting (Lib) to HM QUEEN VICTORIA 1886 and 1892–95, Lt Oxfordshire Yeo Cav; *m* 14 Sept 1881 Jessie Philippa (*m* 2nd 3 Sept 1914 Sir Evelyn Ruggles-Brise, KCB (*see* RUGGLES-BRIE, Bt), and *d* 29 Nov 1928), dau of Robert Russell Carew, of Carpenders Park, Watford, Herts, formerly of Province of Rohilkhund, India, merchant, and *d* 14 July 1897, leaving issue:

1 RALPH FRANCIS JULIAN, **5th Lord**

2 Edward Maurice; *b* 2 May 1885; Maj 4th Bn Bedfordshire Regt, formerly Northumberland Fus; *m* 1st 1909 (*divorce* 1921) Bertha, dau of John Oliver, of Manchester; *m* 2nd 1 Dec 1925 Florence Hilda (*d* 10 Oct 1965), 3rd dau of Thomas William Rothschild, of Pretoria, S Africa, and *d* 20 June 1931, leaving issue by his 1st w:

(1) Betty Joyce; *m* 23 July 1938 Benjamin Rudolf Bonas (*d* 31 Dec 1965), of Mutton Farm House, Abinger Hammer, Surrey, and 8 Lowndes Lodge, Cadogan Place, London SW1, only s of Ben Bonas, of Rosmary, Chiddingfold, Surrey, and *d* 1982, leaving issue:

1a +Benjamin Reginald Francis Stonor [Benjamin Bonas Esq, 16 Hereford Square, London SW7 4TS]; *b* 15 April 1940; *educ* Marlborough and Worcester Coll Oxford; *m* 10 June 1967 (*divorce* 1994) Jacqueline A J, est dau of Jacques de Brabant, of Torcy, Seine-et-Marne, France, and has issue:

1b +Charles Benjamin; *b* 29 April 1969

2b +Oliver Henry; *b* 28 Feb 1971

(2) Marjorie (Jessica); sculptress; *m* 1st 23 April 1935 (*divorce* 1940) Valentine Dyall, s of Franklin Dyall, of 57 Glebe Place, London SW3; *m* 2nd 23 Nov 1940 Jacob Herman Huizinga, of 14 St Leonards Terrace, London SW3, s of Prof Dr Johan Huizinga, of Leiden, Holland, and *dsp* 22 April 1948

3 Hugo Robert William; *b* 5 Oct 1887; 2nd Lt ASC, Hon Attaché Dip Serv; *m* 13 Dec 1917 Esther (*d* 11 July 1971 aged 92), dau of Mark Gilbert, of Hammersmith, and *dsp* 8 Aug 1941

4 Howard Carew; *b* 2 April 1893; Lt 4th Bn Bedfordshire Regt; *ka* 10 March 1915

The 4th LORD (Baron) CAMOY's est s,

RALPH FRANCIS JULIAN STONOR, **5th Lord** (Baron) **Camoys**; *b* 26 Jan 1884; *educ* Oratory Sch and Balliol Coll Oxford; Hon Attaché Madrid, Capt Oxfordshire Yeo and RFC, Capt Bucks Home Gd 1940–45; *m* 25 Nov 1911 Mildred (*d* 21 Nov 1961), dau of William Watts Sherman, of NYC and Rhode Island, and *d* 3 Aug 1968, leaving issue:

1 (RALPH ROBERT WATTS) SHERMAN, **6th Lord**

1 +(Pamela Sophia) Nadine Stonor [The Hon Mrs Pepys, 30 Lyefield Court, Kidmore End Rd, Emmer Green, nr Reading, Berks]; *m* 3 Feb 1941 *Lt-Col Charles Donald Leslie Pepys, KOYLI, est s of Col Gerald Leslie Pepys, of 1 Hurlingham Gardens, London SW6 (*see* COTTENHAM, E)

2 +(Mildred Sophia) Noreen Stonor [The Hon Mrs Drexel, Stonor Lodge, Bellevue Avenue, Newport, Rhode Island, USA; 960 Fifth Avenue, NY]; *m* 11 Jan 1941 *John R Drexel III, only s of John R Drexel, Jr, of NYC and Philadelphia, and has issue:

(1) +John Nicholas; *b* 14 April 1945; *m* 1st 1969 (*divorce* 1976) Pamela, dau of Bernardo Rionda Braga; *m* 2nd 1984 *M Jacqueline, dau of John Jacob Astor

(1) +Pamela Sandra Noreen [Mrs Pamela Walker, 3685 Upton St NW, Washington DC 20008, USA]; *b* 14 Jan 1943; *m* 1966 (*divorce* 1977) Bradford Hastings Walker and has issue:

1a +Andrew; *b* 1968

2a +James Drexel; *b* 1971

2a +Noreen Elizabeth Mildred; *b* 8 Feb 1961

The 5th LORD (Baron) CAMOYS's est s,

(RALPH ROBERT WATTS) SHERMAN STONOR, **6th Lord** (Baron) **Camoys**, DL Oxon (1953); *b* 5 July 1913; *educ* privately; Maj Oxford and Bucks LI (TA) WW II; *m* 14 July 1938 (Mary) Jeanne (*d* 1987), yst dau of Capt Herbert Marmaduke Joseph Stourton, OBE (*see* MOWBRAY, SEGRAVE and STOURTON, B), and *d* 9 March 1976, leaving issue:

1 (RALPH) THOMAS CAMPION GEORGE SHERMAN STONOR, **7th and present Lord** (Baron) **Stonor**

2 (John Edmund) Robert (Bobby), of Oscott College, Sutton Coldfield, Warwicks; *b* 8 May 1946; *educ* Beaumont; *d* 19–

1 +Julia Maria Christina Mildred Stonor [The Hon Julia Stonor, 90 Burnthwaite Rd, London SW6]; *b* 19 April 1939 (HRH THE INFANTA MARIA CHRISTINA stood sponsor); *educ* St Mary's Convent Ascot and Reading Tech; *m* 4 May 1963 (*divorce* 1977, *annulled* 1978) Donald Robin Slomnicki Saunders, er s of Joseph George Slomnicki, of 38 Brunswick Gardens, London W8, resumed by deed poll 1979 name STONOR and has issue:

(1) +Alexander William Joseph STONOR SAUNDERS; *b* 1 April 1964 (HRH PRINCE WILLIAM OF GLOUCESTER stood sponsor); *educ* Worth and St Andrews

(1) +Frances Hélène Jeanne STONOR SAUNDERS; *b* 14 April 1966; *educ* St Mary's Convent Ascot and St Anne's Coll Oxford

2 +Georgina Mary Hope, OStJ [The Hon Georgina Stonor, 112 West St, Henley-on-Thames, Oxon RG9 2EA]; *b* 8 Nov 1941 (HM KING GEORGE II OF THE HELLENES stood sponsor)

3 +Harriet Pauline Sophia [The Hon Mrs Cotterell, Steeple Manor, Steeple, nr Wareham, Dorset]; *b* 6 Jan 1943; *m* 24 July 1965 *(Jonathan) Julian Cotterell, only s of Maj Leonard Evelyn Cotterell, and has issue:

(1) +Edmund Julian Francis; *b* 29 Oct 1967; *m* 1993 *Angelica I L, est dau of Humphrey Stone, of Lower Lawn House, Tisbury, Wilts

(2) +Rupert Sherman John; *b* 18 June 1969

(1) +Alice Ellinor Mary; *b* 23 May 1966; *m* 1992 *Thomas Bernard Constable Maxwell (*see* HERRIES, L)

Seat: Stonor Park, Henley-on-Thames, Oxon. The origins of the house are claimed to date from around the last decade of the 12th century. Certainly the layout of the place is fundamentally medieval, the buttery, chapel, old hall and solar all dating from between the last two decades of the 13th century and the end of the first third of the 14th. They were joined up in the 16th century to form a Tudor seat in the usual E shape. It has been suggested that persecution of the Stonors as recusants (St Edmund Campion found refuge here in 1581) was architecturally a blessing in disguise, since it preserved the house as a hybrid gem of late medieval-high Tudor style. Possibly this was so of the Stuart period but the late Elizabethan one, well after the Reformation had estabished a Protestant ascendancy in England, saw substantial building activity. As late as 1600 Sir Francis Stonor could throw out wings at either end of the main block to form three sides of a rectangle and enclose the fourth side with a wall and gatehouse.

In the more tolerant 18th century the Stonors were able to lead less furtive lives and the house was again fairly heavily remodelled. The architect John Aitkins added a corniced roof and Georgian sash windows and stripped the front elevation of all but the central gable over the front door. He gothicised the hall and for a time this was used to hear mass in. The present structure is virtually a single long block, though its exquisite setting in the Chiltern Hills, mellow brick and medley of styles in the best tradition of English organic architectural growth prevent it appearing as anything so intrinsically dull.

CAMPBELL, Bt

Arms: Quarterly, 1st and 4th, gyronny of eight, or and sa.; 2nd arg., a lymphad sa., sails furled and oars in action; 3rd, or, a fess chequy az. and arg., all within a bordure embattled erm. **Crest:** A boar's head arraché or, langued gules. **Motto:** Follow me. **Creation:** Bt. (UK) 22 May 1815.

SIR LACHLAN PHILIP KEMEYS CAMPBELL, 6TH BT [Sir Lachlan Campbell Bt, 20 Rush Hill Rd, London SW11 5NW]; *b* 9 Oct 1958; *s* f 1993; *educ* Lyc33e Français, Temple Grove, Eton and RMA Sandhurst; commnd RGJ, served N Ireland, Queen Victoria's Rifles (TA); *m* 1986 *Harriet Jane Sarah, only dau of Frank Edward Jex Girling, of W Malvern, and has issue:

1 +ARCHIBALD EDWARD FitzGERALD; *b* 13 June 1990

Lineage: JOHN CAMPBELL, of The Citadel, Cashier Roy Bank Scotland, descended from the Earls of Breadalbane and Holland (*qv*); had a yr s :

COLIN CAMPBELL, Lt-Govr of Gibraltar, Col 55th Regt, Lt-Gen; *m* Mary (*d* 1832), est dau and coheir of Col Guy Johnstone and Mary, dau of Sir William Johnson, 1st Bt (*see* JOHNSON, Bt, of New York), and *d* 2 April 1814, having had, with five yr sons and five daus:

Sir Guy Campbell, 1st Bt (UK), so *cr* 22 May 1815 in compensation for the btcy intended for his f but of which the latter's illness prevented the conferring, CB, Maj-Gen, Col 3rd W India Regt; *m* 1st 17 Jan 1817 Frances Elizabeth (*d* 8 May 1818), est dau and coheir of Montagu Burgoyne, of Marks Hall, and had an only child:

1 Frances Elizabeth; *m* 7 March 1840 Col Henry Boys Harvey, and *d* 26 April 1893 aged 75. He *d* 1883

Sir Guy *m* 2nd 21 Nov 1820 Pamela (*d* 25 Nov 1869), est dau of Lord Edward FitzGerald (*see* LEINSTER, D), and by her had issue:

1 EDWARD FitzGERALD (Sir), **2nd Bt**

2 Guy Colin, Lt RN; *b* 18 May 1824; *d* unm at Singapore, 23 April 1853

3 John; *d* an infant

4 Frederick Augustus, Capt 60th Rifles, ADC to Ld Lt Ireland, Equerry to HRH PRINCESS LOUISE, Gentleman Usher to HM QUEEN VICTORIA; *b* 15 March 1839; *m* Aug 1862 Emma Mary (*d* 5 July 1914), 3rd dau of Maj Hugh Brabazon, of Brabazon Park, Co Mayo, and *d* 20 Dec 1916, having had issue:

(1) John St Clair CAMPBELL later CAMPBELL-BRABAZON (added by roy licence on inheriting estates of his unc Gen Sir John Brabazon, KCB), OBE (1920); *b* 23 May 1865; *m* 3 April 1900 Caroline Leavett and *d* 21 Aug 1942, leaving issue:

1a *Pamela Francis; *b* 1903; *m* 1st 1921 (*divorce* 1930) Francis Baer; *m* 2nd 1931 F/Lt Herbert Jeffery Brookman, RAF (*d* 1936); *m* 3rd 1937 (*divorce* 1956) Robert Walter Guy Grindlay

2a *Geraldine; *b* 23 June 1904; *m* 19 July 1928 Brig Edward Hamilton Grant, late Argyll and Sutherland Highrs, son of Capt Edward Chetwode Hamilton Grant, Argyll and Sutherland Highrs, and has issue:

1b *Rosemary Ann; *b* 3 Aug 1930; *m* 1st 1952 (*divorce* 1959) William Whitehead; *m* 2nd 1961 *Francis Buck

(2) Guy Edward Spencer; *b* 27 April 1873; *m* 6 Sept 1922 Nathalie, dau of John Holmes Magruder, of Washington, and *d* 4 July 1937

(1) Florence Frances Augusta; *m* 1 July 1903 William Henry Dudley Ryder, late RN, and *d* 6 Aug 1930, leaving issue (*see* HARROWBY, E)

(2) Pamela; *m* 2 June 1891 Lord Ernest William Hamilton, 7th son of 1st Duke of Abercorn (*qv*), and *d* 11 May 1931, leaving issue

2 Pamela Louisa; *m* 20 July 1841 Rev Charles Stuart Stanford, DD, Rector of St Thomas's, Dublin, and *d* 1 Feb 1859

3 Georgina Geneviève Louisa; *m* 29 April 1847 Capt Thomas Henry Preston, of Moreby Hall, Yorks, and *d* 6th April 1899, leaving issue. He *d* 3 Feb 1906

4 Lucy Sophia Julia; *m* 1848 Gen Sir Edward Selby Smyth, KCMG, and *d* 1898, leaving issue. He *d* 1896

5 Mary Louisa; *m* 8 July 1867 Maj William Frederick Carleton, 60th Rifles, and *d* 1897, leaving issue. He *d* 1887

6 Emily; *m* 17 Nov 1859 Maj Charles David Cunynghame Ellis, 60th Rifles, of Branksome Chine Ho, nr Bournemouth (*see* HOWARD DE WALDEN, B), and *d* 19 Nov 1924, leaving issue. He *d* 5 Dec 1906

7 Madeline Caroline Frances Eden; *m* 16 Oct 1860 Hon Percy Scawen Wyndham, 2nd surv son of 1st Baron Leconfield, and *d* 8 March 1920, leaving issue (*see* EGREMONT and LECONFIELD, B)

8 Julia Elizabeth Henrietta; *m* 25 Sept 1862 Maj-Gen Fitzroy William Fremantle, CB (*see* COTTESLOE, B), and *d* 27 June 1910, leaving issue

Sir GUY *d* 26 Jan 1849; his est son,

Sir Edward FitzGerald Campbell, 2nd Bt; *b* 25 Oct 1822; Lt-Col 60th Foot, ADC to C-in-C India and Viceroy India; medal and two clasps for the Punjab 1849, expdn against Afridis 1850, Siege of Delhi 1858; *m* 25 Oct 1853 Georgiana Charlotte Theophila (*d* 17 Oct 1872), 2nd dau of Sir Theophilus Metcalfe, 4th Bt (*see* 1970 edn), and had issue:

1 GUY THEOPHILUS (Sir), **3rd Bt**

2 Edward FitzGerald Frederick; *b* 5 Feb 1856; *m* 4 Feb 1889 Helen Emily, dau of Rev Charles Stuart Stanford, DD, and *dsp* 11 June 1902

3 Charles James Napier; *b* 5 Feb 1856; *m* 18 Feb 1889 Geraldine Harriette (*d* 23 Nov 1920), dau of Rev Charles Stuart Stanford, DD, Rector of St Thomas's, Dublin, and *d* 31 May 1924, having had issue:

(1) Edward FitzGerald; *b* 28 Sept 1890; Maj RTR, served WW I and WW II; *m* 15 Sept 1915 Agnes Catherine (*d* 1977), 3rd dau of Henry Templer Prior, Master of the Supreme Courts of Justice, and *d* 6 July 1950, leaving issue:

1a +Charles Colin [Charles Campbell Esq, Woolpit Farm, Ewhurst, Cranleigh, Surrey]; *b* 19 Nov 1923; *educ* Loretto and Pembroke Coll Cambridge (Fndn Scholar) (BA 1950, MA 1961); Capt RE WW II; *m* 1970 *Julia Margaret Rachel, dau of Anthony Smithson Russell, and has issue:

1b +James Charles Anthony; *b* 1971

1b *Lucy Catherine Isabel; *b* 1974

1a *Geraldine Mary [Mrs Neville Williams, 11 Culverwell Gdns, Winchester, Hants]; *b* 18 April 1917; *m* 26 June 1941 Maj Neville Glyn Williams, MC, 14th Punjab Regt, IA (*ka* in Burma March 1945), only son of Lt-Col Stanley Price Williams, CIE, late IA, and has issue:

1b *Fiona Glyn [Mrs Julian Smith, Bishopsway, Twyford, nr Winchester, Hants]; *b* 13 Jan 1944; *m* 27 July 1963 *Julian John Hamling Smith, and has issue:

1c *Colin Nigel Neville; *b* 13 May 1965; *educ* Winchester

1c *Emma Mary Glyn; *b* 27 May 1968; *m* 29 June 1996 *Robert William Middleton Brook

2c *Frances Margaret [Mrs Denys Squarey, Brigge House, Broughton, Stockbridge, Hants]; *b* 13 July 1919; *m* 28 July 1954 Denys Newell Pitts Squarey (*d* 1983), est son of Newell Pitts Squarey, of Bemerton, Salisbury

4 Gerald FitzGerald, CBE (1920), served WW I (Legion of Honour and Crown of Belgium); *b* 25 April 1862; *educ* Fettes and Clare Coll Cambridge (B A); *d* unm 4 July 1933

5 Francis Bunbury FitzGerald (Rev), with Br Museum Reading Room 1884–1900, Priv Sec to Bp Calcutta 1900–02, Curate of St Margaret's, Westminster 1902–05; *b* 17 June 1863; *d* unm 4 Dec 1905

6 Colin Arthur FitzGerald (Ven), MA, 1st Archdeacon of Wisbech and Rector of Feltwell, Brandon, Norfolk, Priv Sec to Govr of S Australia, Clerk Exec Cncl; *b* 17 June 1863 (twin); *d* unm 6 Jan 1916

7 Percy FitzGerald; *b* 12 June 1865; *m* 1889 Isabel Annie (*m* 2nd 30 July 1907 Gerald Cecil Dudgeon, CBE, who *d* 4 May 1930), dau of R Ballard, of Palumpur, Kangra Valley, Punjab, and *d* 2 April 1907, leaving issue:

(1) Ion Percy FitzGerald, OBE (1919); *b* Nov 1890; *educ* Repton and Hertford Coll Oxford (BA); Capt 9th Bn Hants Regt WW I (despatches); *m* 21 Dec 1923 Gwladys Mary, MBE (1942), 2nd dau of the Lewis Pugh Evans Pugh, KC, and *d* 25 Dec 1963, having had:

1a Ion Lewis FitzGerald, Capt Black Watch 1943–48 and in Malayan Police 1948–50, CPM; *b* 28 Sept 1925; *ka* Malaya 17 Feb 1950

1a *(Graeme) Diana [Mrs Louis ffrench-Constant, Silozwe, Pill Creek, St Feock, Truro, Cornwall TR3 6SE]; *b* 26 Dec 1929; *m* 16 July 1954 Louis Paul Humphrey ffrench-Constant, MA, BM, BCh (*d* 1990), er son of Charles Frederick ffrench-Constant, MRCS, LRCP, DMR, and has issue:

1b *Edward Paul Simon [Edward ffrench-Constant Esq, Tregew, Grenna Lane, Perranwell Station, Truro, Cornwall]; *b* 9 Jan 1958; BM, BCh; *m* 1987 *Elizabeth Frances Maitland, dau of Malcolm Sydney Maitland Adams, MB, ChB, and has issue:

1c *Matthew Paul; *b* 1994

1c *Katharine Anne Louis; *b* 1987

2c *Anna Elizabeth; *b* 1989

3c *Sophie Isabel; *b* 1992

1b *Rosamunde Sally; *b* 16 Jan 1956; *m* 1981 *Justin Wynn, and has issue:

1c *Kieran; *b* 1986

1c *Melissa; *b* 1989

2b *Tanya Mary Louise; *b* 4 Oct 1963

3b *Juliet Patricia; *b* 9 July 1967

(2) Gerald Arthur FitzGerald; *b* May 1893; *d* 21 April 1919

(1) Madeline Georgina Annie; *b* March 1896; *m* 1918 Capt Eric Rawlinson Wood, CIE, MC, ICS, son of A Rawlinson Wood, of Streatham, SW16, and *d* 8 Nov 1964, leaving issue

(2) Joan; *b* March 1904; *m* 11 Feb 1928 (*m annulled* 1929) Evelyn Bingham Baring, son of William Bingham Baring (*see* NORTHBROOK, B)

8 Ion Douglas FitzGerald; *b* 12 March 1868; Supt Terai and Bhaber Estates, India; *m* 8 May 1891 Mabel Unsworth (*d* 3 Feb 1931), est dau of Col Unsworth Quin, JP, of Shanganah, Bray, and *d* in India, Dec 1915, having had issue:

(1) Colin Douglas FitzGerald; *b* Sept *d* Oct 1893

(2) Robert Ion FitzGerald; *b* Nov 1894; *d* Aug 1895

(3) Ion Edward FitzGerald ; *b* 12 March 1897; Maj DCLI, served WW I 1914–19 (wounded); *m* 9 Nov 1933 Evelyn Julia (who *d* 1992, having *m* 2nd 16 May 1952, as his 2nd w, 11th Earl of Southesk (*see* FIFE, D), dau of Lt-Col Arthur Peere Williams-Freeman, DSO, OBE, and *d* 12 April 1936, leaving issue:

1a +Ion Edward FitzGerald [Ion Campbell Esq, Feathercombe, Hambledon, Godalming, Surrey GU8 4DP]; *b* posthumously 3 May 1936; served in DCLI; *m* 4 May 1963 *Muriel Elisabeth, only dau of Brig Leslie Frederic Ethelbert Wieler, CB, CBE, KOYLI, of Feathercombe, Hambledon, Surrey, and has issue:

1b +John Edward FitzGerald; *b* 13 July 1964; *m* 1990 *Patricia, dau of James O'Brien, and has issue:

1c +Christopher; *b* 1995

1c *Laura; *b* 1992

2b +Leslie James FitzGerald; *b* 17 Oct 1965; *m* 1995 *Christine, dau of Ronald Laurens, and has:

1c +Thomas; *b* 1996

3b +Robert Christopher FitzGerald; *b* 11 Sept 1967

4b +Peter Michael FitzGerald; *b* 12 June 1972

(1) Nina Mary Mabel; *b* 29 Dec 1892; *m* 1919 Maj Richard William Maxwell St Maur, 14th Hus, and *d* 10 Nov 1931 leaving issue

(2) Pamela Geraldine Theophila; *b* 25 April 1899; *m* 1919 Rudolph Agnew, and had issue

1a *Peter Douglas; *b* 7 March 1922; served WW II 1941–46 as Capt Irish Gds (wounded, despatches); *m* 1946 *Margaret Tawse, and has issue

2a Patrick John Alexander; *b* 4 May 1930; *m* 1950 *Lucia Murdock, and has issue

3a *Rudolph Ion Joseph; *b* 12 March 1934; *educ* Downside; served in 8th KRI Hus 1952–57; *m* 1st 1 June 1957 (*divorce* 1964) Tessa Eiluned, est dau of S/Ldr John Molony Longley, of The Old Rectory, W Knoyle, Wilts, and has had issue:

1b Charles Edward Molony; *b* 29 April 1961

3a (cont.) Rudolph Agnew *m* 2nd 29 March 1965 (*divorce* 1980) Hon Clare Rosalind Dixon, only dau of 2nd Baron Glentoran (*qv*); *m* 3rd 1980 *Whitney, dau of Chester Ingersoll Warren, and has further issue by his 2nd w:

2b *James Ion Daniel; *b* 23 April 1968; *m* 1992 *Sarah K, only dau of Peter Newman, of Frensham, Surrey

1b *Charlotte Diana Pamela Geraldine; *b* 17 Oct 1970

1a Mary Geraldine; *b* 13 June 1920; *m* 1943 Francis James Nichol

2a *Pamela Joan; *b* 1 June 1923; *m* 1941 Lt-Cdr Peter Piggford, RN, and has issue:

1b *Andrew Donovan; *b* 1956

1b *Sybil Jane; *b* 1941

9 George Theophilus; *b* 17 Oct 1872; Lt late Argyll and Sutherland Highrs; *m* 6 Oct 1917 Winifred Edna Boyd, dau of James FitzGibbon Black, of Montreal, Canada, and *d* 28 March 1924, leaving issue:

(1) Georgina Winifred Grant; *b* 22 Aug 1918; *m* 12 Dec 1945 Thomas Franklyn Manville, Jr, of Bon Repos, New Rochelle, NY, USA, and was *k* in a motor accident, 26 April 1952. He *d* 8 Oct 1967

(2) *Elspeth Griselda Theophila; *b* Nov 1919; *m* 15 Oct 1946 *Robin John Patrick Flynn, MC, DFC, and has issue:

1a *Michael George Alexander Robin Fitzgerald Campbell; *b* 1949

1a *Reidy Georgina Campbell; *b* 1948

1 Pamela Georgina; *d* July 1857

2 Annie Charlotte; *m* 26 Nov 1896 Stratford Hely-Hutchinson Keightley, and *d* 21 March 1947. He *d* 30 Aug 1930

3 Finetta Madeline Julia, MBE (1919); *m* Sept 1894 Brig Gen Hon Charles Granville Bruce, CB, MVO, late IA, 3rd son of 1st Baron Aberdare (*qv*), and *d* 16 June 1932

4 Griselda Mary Theophila; *m* 7 June 1894 Dudley Francis Amelius Hervey, CMG, son of Rev Lord Charles Hervey, and *d* 1 April 1929, leaving issue (*see* BRISTOL, M)

The 2nd Bt *d* 23 Nov 1882; his est son,

Sir Guy Theophilus Campbell, 3rd Bt, Lt-Col Res of Offrs, formerly Maj 60th Rifles, sometime ADC to Lt-Govr of Bengal, served in Afghan War 1878–80; *b* 16 Oct 1854; *m* 30 April 1884 Nina (*d* 7 Dec 1933), dau of Frederick Lehmann, by his w Nina, dau of Robert Chambers, LLD, of Edinburgh and St Andrews, and had issue:

1 GUY COLIN (Sir), **4th Bt**

2 Ronald Ian (Sir), PC (1950), GCMG (1947, KCMG 1941, CMG 1932), CB (1937); *b* 7 June 1890; *educ* Eton and Magdalen Coll Oxford (BA 1912); Dip Serv: Envoy Extrdy and Min Plen Paris, 1938–39 (Grand Offr Legion of Honour) and Belgrade 1939–41, Washington 1941–44, Assist Under-Sec FO 1945, Amb Extrdy and Plen Egypt 1946, ret 1950

3 Edward FitzGerald, DSO (1918), JP (1952), DL (1958) Argyllshire, Maj and Brevet Lt-Col late 60th Rifles, served WW I 1914–19 (wounded, despatches), and WW II; *b* 7 Oct 1893; *educ* Eton and RMC Sandhurst; *m* 8 Dec 1917 (*divorce* 1936) Enid Leyland, only dau of Maj Francis Elmer Speed, of Knowlton Court, Kent, and *dsp* 1 Dec 1958

4 (John) Archibald; *b* 16 Feb 1898; *educ* Eton; Col late 60th Rifles, served WW I 1914–19, and WW II; *m* 1st 29 July 1925 (*divorce* 1940) Dorothy, dau of John Field, of Perthi, Ruthin, and had issue:

(1) +Colin Guy Napier [Colin Campbell Esq, 23 Lansdowne Gdns, London SW8]; *b* 14 July 1930; Capt (ret) Res of Offrs 60th Rifles, served in Kenya Regt 1955–57, ADC to Govr of Kenya 1957–59; *m* 1st 17 July 1965 Lucy, dau of James A Barnett, of Bel Air, Los Angeles, USA, and formerly w of Clifford Smith, Jr; *m* 2nd 1987 *Charmian Rachel, yr dau of Col Lord George Francis John Montagu-Douglas-Scott (*see* BUCCLEUCH and QUEENSBERRY, D), and formerly w of Archibald Hugh Stirling, yr of Keir (*see* 1967 edn STIRLING-MAXWELL, Bt), and has issue by first w:

1a *Georgina Dorothy; *b* 1969

2a *Tessa Sylvia; *b* 1971

4 (cont.) Col Archibald Campbell *m* 2nd 8 Aug 1944 (*divorce* 1960) Elizabeth, dau of Reynard Pearth, of Pittsburgh, USA, and *d* 27 March 1974, having by her had issue:

(1) *(Henrietta) Nina Sylvia [Mrs Andrew Konig, 6 Molyneux St, London W1]; *b* 9 May 1945; *m* 1971 *Andrew Guy Louis de Chappuis Konig, and has issue

1 Pamela Madeline; *b* 11 Jan, *d* 11 Sept 1886

2 Sylvia Nina; *b* 18 March 1888; *m* 12 Jan 1916 Maj Rhys Clavell Mansel, DL, late Rifle Bde, of Smedmore, Dorset, and *d* 11 May 1944, leaving issue (*see* MANSEL, Bt)

The 3rd Bt *d* 12 Sept 1931; his est son,

Sir Guy Colin Campbell, 4th Bt; *educ* Eton and St Andrews U, late Maj 60th Rifles, served WW I 1914–19 and WW II; *b* 31 Jan 1885; *m* 1st 21 April 1909 Mary Arabella Swinnerton (*d* 1 July 1948), only dau of Halswell Milborne Kemeys-Tynte, JP, DL, of Halswell, Somerset, and Cefn Mably, Glamorgan, and sis of 18th Baron Wharton (*qv*), and had issue:

1 GUY THEOPHILUS HALSWELL (Sir), **5th Bt**

2 (Edward FitzGerald) David, MC, ERD, Maj (Res of Offrs) Black Watch (RHR), and Bimbashi, Sudan Def Force, served WW II, 8th Argyllshire Bn, The Argyll and Sutherland Highrs (TA) 1949–51, served in Korea 1952–54, served in 4th (Uganda) Bn The King's African Rifles and 2nd i/c Kenya Regt, Mau Mau Operations 1954–56; *b* 18 Jan 1910 (twin); *educ* Eton and St Andrews U

Sir Guy *m* 2nd 17 March 1955 *Alida Virginie (Lilian), only child of August Peeters van Nienwenrode, of Pachtof Nieuwenrode, Belgium, and widow of F A S Allan, and *d* 2 Oct 1960

His er twin son,

Sir Guy Theophilus Halswell Campbell, 5th Bt, OBE (1954), MC (1941); *b* 18 Jan 1910; *educ* Eton and St Andrews U, Col (Res of Offrs) 60th Rifles, served in Camel Corps, Sudan Defence Force 1939–47, operations in Sudan, Eritrea, Abyssinia and N Africa, cmded 2nd/7th and 7th Nuba Bns, Camel Corps WW II (wounded), served in Palestine 1948, and on staff of Count Bernadotte, UN Mediator June-Nov 1948, on Mil Mission to Ethiopia 1948–51, cmded Kenya Regt (TF) 1952–56 in operations against Mau Mau, head of Br Mil Mission to Libya 1956–60, ret 1960, life memb Anglo-Sudanese Assoc; *m* 17 Aug 1956 *Elizabeth [Elizabeth Lady Campbell, 18 Lansdown Terrace, Malvern Rd, Cheltenham, Glos GL50 2JT] (Lizbeth Webb, the actress), dau of Frederick Holton, of Reading, and formerly w of D H Parker, and *d* 1993, having had issue:

1 Sir LACHLAN PHILIP KEMEYS CAMPBELL, **6th and present Bt**

2 +Rory Charles FitzGerald [Rory Campbell Esq, Flat C, 103 Gloucester Rd, London SW7 4SF]; *b* 17 Aug 1961; *educ* Lycée Français, Temple Grove, Amersham Art Coll and RCM; actor; *m* 1985 (*divorce* 1991) Angela Victoria, dau of Victor Orman Phillis, of Pacific Highway, Killara, NSW, Australia

CAMPBELL, Bt, of Aberuchill

Arms: Quarterly, 1st and 4th, gyronny of eight or and sa.; 2nd, arg. a lymphad, her oars in action sa.; 3rd, or a fess chequy az. and arg., all within a bordure erm. **Crest:** A lion guardant gu., crowned with laurel and holding in his dexter paw a sword ppr., hilted and pommelled or, and in the sinister a dag or Highland pistol. **Supporters:** Two bloodhounds guardant ppr., collared and leashed or. **Motto:** *Sequitur victoria fortes* ('Victory follows the brave'). **Creation:** Bt. (NS) between 23 Jan 1667 and 16 May 1668.

SIR JAMES ALEXANDER MOFFAT BAIN CAMPBELL, 9TH BT, of Aberuchill, and Kilbryde, Dunblane, Co Perth [Sir James Campbell Bt, Kilbryde Castle, Dunblane, Perthshire FK15 9NF]; *b* 23 Sept 1956; *s* f 1997; *educ* Stowe; Capt Scots Gds, motorcycle dispatch rider 1983–84 London, with Bain Dawes, Bain Clarkson, Bain Hogg London 1984–95, Bain Hogg, Aon Risk Services Edinburgh 1995–97, Penrose Forbes Ltd Dunblane 1997–; *m* 6 Feb 1993 *Carola Jane, 2nd dau of George Denman (*see* DENMAN B) and has:

1 *Catherine Janet Denman; *b* 10 Nov 1994

2 *May Alexandra Landale; *b* 16 May 1996

Lineage: JOHN CAMPBELL, of Lawers, Perthshire (only surv s by his 4th w of Sir Colin Campbell, 1st of Glenorchy; *see* 1970 edn BREADALBANE, E); had an est son:

JAMES CAMPBELL, of Lawers; had a charter of the territorial Barony of Lawers from JAMES V 16 June 1525; *m* 1st Marion (*d* 31 Oct 1527), dau of Sir Walter Forrester and widow of Sir Henry Shaw of Camburmore; *m* 2nd *c* 1530 Janet (*d* Oct 1539), dau of 2nd Lord Gray (qv) and widow of (a) John Charters, (b) Alexander Keith and (c) Sir David Wemyss; *m* 3rd Isobel Hay, widow of Alexander Robertson, of Fasclay, and *d* 12 Feb 1561/2; his est son by his 1st w:

ARCHIBALD CAMPBELL, Yr., of Lawers; *m c* 29 May 1542 Agnes, dau of John Ross of Craigie, and *dvp c* 1546, leaving:

Sir JOHN CAMPBELL, of Lawers; ktd 1590, acquired Aberuchill and other lands from the Morays of Abercairny 1594, making them over to his 2nd son 1595; *m* his cousin Beatrix, dau of Sir Colin Campbell of Glenorchy, and *d* 1611, leaving, with other issue:

1 James (Sir), of Lawers; *m* (contract 23 June 1595) Jean, dau of 1st Lord Colville of Culross (*see* COLVILLE OF CULROSS, V), and *d* Jan 1645, leaving an est son:

(1) JOHN CAMPBELL, *cr* EARL OF LOUDOUN (*qv*)

2 COLIN, of Aberuchill

3 Archibald Campbell; Prior Strathfillan

Sir JOHN CAMPBELL's 2nd son,

COLIN CAMPBELL, of Aberuchill, for which he had a crown charter of confirmation 12 July 1596; also acquired Craiginch, Leonards and other lands; apparently *m* — Colville and had issue:

1 JAMES

2 John, of Foordie; memb Cctee of War 1647; *d c* 1683, leaving:

(1) Mary; *m* Henry Stewart, advocate, 4th son of Sir William Stewart of Grandtally, and was ancestor of Sir Archibald D Stewart, 8th and last Bt

COLIN CAMPBELL *d* 1618; his er son,

JAMES CAMPBELL, of Aberuchill; royalist Civil War; *m* Ann, dau of Patrick Hepburn of Woolling by w Janet Napier, and *d* Nov 1640, leaving issue:

Sir Colin Campbell, of Aberuchill, 1st Bt (NS), so *cr* between 23 Jan 1667 and 16 May 1668 (the patent was apparently not registered, like many NS btcies at the time), PC (S 1690); Sheriff Depute Argyllshire 1668, Ld of Session as Lord Aberuchill 1689, Ld of Justiciary, MP Perthshire 1690–1702, bought the territorial Barony of Kilbryde 1669; all his lands erected into a free Barony of Aberuchill; *m* 1st Margaret (*bur* 5 June 1666), dau of Alexander Foulis of Ratho, and had a son (Archibald, *dvp* unm); *m* 2nd (contract 9 Aug 1667) Catherine, sis of 1st Earl of Cromarty (*see* CROMARTIE, E), and *d* 16 Feb 1704, having by her had:

2 JAMES (Sir), **2nd Bt**

3 Colin; Commr of Customs; had:
(1) Colin
(1) Jean; *m* 6th Lord Lindores (*see* ROTHES, E)
1 Anna; *m* Sir Kenneth Mackenzie, Bt, of Cromartie, and had issue

Sir COLIN's est son,

Sir James Campbell, 2nd Bt; *m* 1st Jean, dau and heir of Sir John Dempster, of Pitliver, Fife; *m* 2nd his cousin Lady Jane Campbell, dau of 1st Earl of Loudoun (*qv*), and *d* 10 May 1754, having by his 1st w had:
1 Colin; sold Pitliver; advocate; *m* 1722 Catherine, dau of William Nisbet of Dirleton, E Lothian, and *dvp c* 1738, leaving issue:
(1) JAMES (Sir), **3rd Bt**
(1) Catherine
(2) Colina; *m* Thomas Hogg, Edinburgh banker, and had issue
1 Catherine; *m* 1721 George Drummond, Commr of Excise, Ld Provost Edinburgh, and had issue

Sir JAMES's gs,

Sir James Campbell, 3rd Bt; *b* 1723; sold Aberuchill 1772, executed an entail of the territorial Barony and estate of Kilbryde 1800; served Scots Greys Battle of Fontenoy 1745; *m* 1st 4 March 1754 Margaret (*d* 19 Sept 1766), dau and heir of Capt William Conductor Ball, of Hatton Garden, London, and had, with other issue:
1 Colin; Capt 19th Foot, Lt-Col Perthshire Militia; *d* unm 1811
2 ALEXANDER (Sir), **4th Bt**
1 Jane; *m* William Pearson of Kippenross, Perthshire, and had issue
Sir James *m* 2nd Mary Ann, dau of Joseph Burn, and *d* March 1812, having by her had, with other issue:
3 Thomas; *b* 1769; *d* unm 1799
4 William, WS; *b* 1774; *m* 1st 1804 Eliza, dau of William Hunter, of Glenormiston, Peeblesshire; *m* 2nd 1820 Jane, dau of H Cleghorn, of Stravithie, Fife, and *d* 1849, having had issue:
(1) James; *b* 1806; Col; *m* 1st Rebecca, dau of Rev John Stuart; *m* 2nd Margaret Alexina (*d* 25 March 1906), dau of John Boyd, and *d* 1884, leaving issue:
1a Colin; *b* 1864
2a Archibald James; *b* 1865; *d* 22 April 1919
1a Eleanor Margaret
(2) William Hunter, LLD; *b* 1814; *m* 1st 1848 Emily, dau of Anthony Lyons, of Demerara; *m* 2nd Anna, widow of Dr Nicholson, and *d* 1883, leaving issue:
1a Walter Frederick; *b* 1855; marine engr
1a Edith Mary Anne
2a Mildred Emily
(3) Robert Stuart; *b* 1815; *d* 1879, leaving issue
5 Frederick; *b* 22 April 1779; Capt 42nd Highrs; *m* Cordelia, dau of Capt Stephen P Mouat, RN, and *d* 29 Dec 1816, having had issue:
(1) James Colin; *b* 1810; *d* 1 June 1826
(1) Frances Sophia; *b* 1808; *m* 13 Jan 1834 Nicholas Whitaker Greene, of Basingstoke, and *d* 30 Jan 1856
(2) Marion; *b* 30 July 1814; *m* 24 Sept 1834 Jacob Wood, of Harve, and *d* 19 April 1897, having had issue
6 John, MD, FRCS (Edin); *b* 1785; *m* 1808 Catherine (*d* 1865), dau of John Logan, of Knockshinnoch, Ayrshire, and *d* 1867, leaving surv issue:
(1) John Logan (Sir), MD (Edin), FRCS; *b* 3 Nov 1817; *m* 23 Feb 1858 Emma (*d* 1912), dau of Sir John Cracroft Wilson, KCSI, CB, Judge Moradabad, and *d* 21 June 1912, having had issue:
1a John Logan; *b* 26 May 1864; *d* an infant
1a Ida; *b* 22 Dec 1859; *d* unm 8 Oct 1880
2a Winifred; *b* 26 May 1864; *m* 1st 10 Dec 1889 Maj Herbert Cyril Orde Murray (*d* 1910), Black Watch; *m* 2nd -Humphries

Sir JAMES's est surv son,

Sir Alexander Campbell, 4th Bt; *b* 16 Aug 1757; *m* 31 July 1816 Margaret (*d* 1871), dau of Alexander Coldstream, of Crieff, and *d* 13 Dec 1824, having had issue:
1 JAMES (Sir), **5th Bt**
2 Alexander Le Grand; *b* 18 July 18 19; *m* 26 July 1853 Hester Anne (*d* 17 Aug 1894), yst dau of Edward B Copeman, of Coltishall, Norfolk, and *d* 1890, leaving issue:
(1) Alexander Bulwer; *b* 2 Oct 1855; barrister; *m* 8th May 1894 Maude, dau of James Knight, and *d* 21 Oct 1938, leaving issue:
1a Alexander Colin Le Grand; *b* 16 March 1898; *m* 1922 Mavis Macdonald (*d* 1937), and *d* 1980, leaving issue:
1b David John
1b *Janet Glenn [Mrs Neil Lester, 551 South Titirangi Rd, Auckland 7, New Zealand]; *b* 1926; *m* 1953 *Neil Lester, and has issue:
1c *Mark Robert Alexander; *b* 1954
2a Clyde Coldstream; *b* 19 Sept 1904; *m* 1st 1936 Mary Fisher; *m* 2nd 1943 Eleanor Lorna Curnow (*d* 1982), of Auckland, and by her had issue:
1b +Alexander Edward Lindsay; *b* 1948; *m* 1977 *Mary Lesley Griffin and has:
1c *Elizabeth Mary; *b* 1978
2c *Joanna Margaret; *b* 1980
3c *Katherine Laura; *b* 1982
1b *Margaret Alison; *b* 1945
1a Marjory Jean Alison; *b* 31 Oct 1895; *m* 3 Dec 1935 Edward Bristow Waddington
2a Eleanor Margaret; *b* 19 July 1897; *m* 1925 Charles Dalrymple Watt, of Edinburgh, and had issue
3a Hester Joan; *b* 19 Sept 1910; *m* 15 July 1933 Bernard George Matheson Canning, and had issue
(2) George Frederic Colin, CMG (1919) VD; *b* 2 June 1858; Col NZ Forces cmdg Coast Defences, Wellington, WW I, Hon ADC to Govr-Gen NZ 1912–20, Sec NZ Treasury 1913–20; Controller and Auditor Gen NZ 1921; *m* 1896 Amabel Caroline, dau of Bayly Pike, of Elephant Hill Station, NZ, and *d* 3 March 1937, leaving issue:
1a Alan Le Grand; *b* 3 Dec 1896; Capt Highland LI, RAF, WW I, Kurdistan 1919–20; *m* 1928 *Barbara Alison, dau of James Marchbanks, of Wellington, NZ, and *d* 1960, leaving issue:
1b +John Graham Colin; *b* 1929; *m* 1957 *Anna Margaret, dau of Bertram Kay, of London, and has issue:
1c +Alexander James Le Grand; *b* 1958
2c +Robert Neil; *b* 1960
2b +Donald James [Donald Campbell Esq, Campbell St, Karori, Wellington, New Zealand]; *b* 1930; *m* 1963 *Barbara Mary Grear
(1) Margaret Jane; *m* 1884 Walter Edward Hacon, MRCS, LRCP (*d* 22 Sept 1898), of Christchurch, NZ, and *d* 1945, leaving issue
(2) Caroline Hester Mary; *d* unm
(3) Catharine Coldstream; *d* unm 24 Oct 1948
3 John Coldstream; *b* 1 Dec 1821; *d* unm 1872
4 Frederick Hugh Pearson; *b* 3 Sept 1823; Ceylon CS; *m* 17 April 1848 Mary Spencer (*d* 17 July 1880), est dau of Joseph Price, Ceylon CS, and *d* 27 May 1892, leaving issue:
(1) Alexander Henry Price; *b* 13 Dec 1850; *m* 4 Dec 1875 Frieda, dau of Dr Lothe, of Edinburgh
(2) Frederick William Burleigh; *b* 1 Jan 1854; Ceylon CS; *m* 28 June 1876 Mary Gertrude (*d* 4 Jan 1901), est dau of J Thomas, of Newport, Mon, and *d* 17 March 1903, leaving issue:
1a Richard Henry Burleigh (Rev); *b* 29 March 1877; MA Oxford; rector Baverstock, Wilts, vicar Worton, Wilts 1907–28; *m* 29 June 1909 Emily Gertrude (*d* 3 Sept 1954), only dau of George Parker, and *dsp* 15 April 1955
2a Fuller Alfred Bromley; *b* 29 July 1880; BA Oxford; Lt 3rd Bn Wilts Regt (SR); *m* Katharine Charlotte Corbould, and *dsp* 5 Sept 1953
1a Mary Caroline Langton; *b* 29 Nov 1882; nun; *d* 16 April 1966
2a Alice Dillon Malcolm; *b* 1 July 1884; *m* 20 Dec 1911 George Norman Longbotham (*d* 26 Jan 1949), yr son of Jonathan Longbotham, of Northwood, Middx, and had issue
(3) Richard Burleigh; *b* 3 June 1856; Ceylon CS; *m* 31 Dec 1877 Elizabeth Graham, dau of Dr Richard Thomas, of Tiverton, Devon, and *d* 22 Oct 1914
1 Caroline Emily Margaret; *m* 23 Jan 1872 John Tyler Taylor (*d* 1917), of Monmouth, and had issue

Sir ALEXANDER's est son,

Sir James Campbell, 5th Bt; *b* 5 May 1818; CA Glos, Mon and Perths; Col Glos Rifle Vols; *m* 28 July 1840 Caroline (*d* 9 Dec 1900), 2nd dau of Adml Sir Robert Howe Bromley, 3rd Bt (*qv*), and *d* 27 March 1903, leaving:

Sir Alexander Campbell, 6th Bt; *b* 10 Aug 1841; Col RA; *m* 1st 6 Feb 1871 Edith Frances Arabella (*d* 29 Jan 1884), only dau of Capt Alexander Sidney Godolphin Jauncey (*see* JAUNCEY OF TULLICHETTLE, B), and had:
1 James Colin; *b* 25 Nov 1875; Lt Cape Garrison Artillery; *ka* S Africa 5 May 1902
2 JOHN ALEXANDER COLDSTREAM (Sir), **7th Bt**
1 Caroline Sophia; *m* 7 July 1908 Rev Alexander Wintle Blanch (*d* 1941), Rector Colby, Norfolk, and *d* 16 Feb 1952
2 Edith Maud; *d* unm 31 Dec 1948
3 Helen May; *m* 7 June 1900 Henry Kenyon Daniel, yst son of Owen Fisher Daniel, of Ramsgate, and *d* 17 Jan 1964, leaving issue
4 Evelyn; *m* 8 July 1899 Francis John Cleverly Lake, and *d* 19 Feb 1953, leaving issue
Sir Alexander *m* 2nd 4 Oct 1893 Annie Augusta (*d* 10 March 1927), dau of Robert Henry Mitford, of Hampstead, and widow of Walter James, of Ryton-on-Tyne, and *d* 23 May 1914

His only surv son,

Sir John Alexander Coldstream Campbell, 7th Bt; *b* 27 June 1877; Capt Scottish Horse, Gallipoli WW I; *m* 24 Jan 1921 Janet Thomson Hood (*d* 27 May 1975), only dau of James Moffat, of Hamilton, Lanarks, and *d* 21 Jan 1960, having had issue:
1 **Sir Colin Moffat Campbell, 8th Bt**, MC (1945); *b* 4 Aug 1925; *educ* Stowe; Capt Scots Gds WW II (wounded), with James Finlay & Co Calcutta 1948–58, Nairobi 1958–71 (dep chm 1973–75, chm 1975–90), Chm Tea Bd Kenya 1961–71, Pres Fedn Kenya Employers 1962–70, dir James Finlay plc 1971–92, Pres E African Tea Trade Assoc 1960–61, 1962–63, 1966–67, memb Scottish Cncl CBI 1979–85, Cncl CBI 1981–92, Cwlth Devpt Corp 1981–89 (Dep Chm 1983–89), CIMgt, CBIM 1980, FRSA 1982; *m* 21 May 1952 *Mary Anne Chichester [Mary Lady Campbell, Kilbryde Castle, Dunblane, Perthshire FK15 9NF], er dau of Brig George Alexander Bain, OBE (*see* O'NEILL, B), and *d* 1 Dec 1997, having had:
(1) Sir JAMES ALEXANDER MOFFAT BAIN CAMPBELL, **9th and present Bt**
(2) +JOHN ALISTAIR CHICHESTER; *b* 20 April 1960; heir presumptive; *educ* Fettes; *m* 1987 (*divorce*) Carole Lesley, yr dau of Geoffrey Knowles, of Cornton, Stirling, and has:
1a *Louise Mary Walton; *b* 26 March 1989
(1) Janet Mary Bain; *b* 12 June 1953; *m* 1975 *Nicholas John Muir (*see* MUIR Bt), and *d* 1978
2 Alistair Bromley, OBE (1976) [Alistair Campbell Esq OBE, Grainston, Kilbryde, Dunblane, Perthshire FK15 9NF]; *b* 23 June 1927; *educ* Tonbridge; V-Chm Countryside Commn for Scotland 1972–81, memb Scottish Land Court 1981–; *m* 30 April 1952 *Rosemary, dau of J Lindsay Pullar, of Glenfarg House, by Perth, and has issue:
(1) +Christopher John; *b* 15 Oct 1954
(1) *Caroline Margaret; *b* 17 Nov 1956; *m* 1980 *Andrew J Fraser, son of John C Fraser, and has issue:
1a *John Campbell; *b* 1987
1a *Alice Margaret; *b* 1986
2a *Rosamund Mary; *b* 1990
(2) *Colina Mary; *b* 30 Dec 1964; *m* 1989 *Jonathan Humphrey, son of David Humphrey

Seat: Kilbryde Castle, Dunblane, Perths. Abandoned by the family for two generations before the **8th Bt** restored it following his return from East Africa in the early 1970s, Kilbryde was at one time occupied by a girls' school. The gardens have been particularly well tended in recent years.

CAMPBELL, Bt, of Auchinbreck

Arms: Gyronny of eight or and sa., a bordure chequy erm. and purpure. **Crest:** A dexter hand ppr., holding a spur or. **Motto:** Forget not. **Creation:** Bt. (NS) 12 or 24 Jan 1627/8.

SIR ROBIN AUCHINBRECK CAMPBELL, 15TH BT, of Auchinbreck [Sir Robin Campbell Bt, 287A Waikawa Rd, Picton, New Zealand]; *b* 7 June 1922; *s f* 1970; *educ* Eton; Lt (A) RNVR; *m* 1st 11 Dec 1948 Rosemary (Sally) Colin (*d* 1978), yr dau of Ashley Dean, of Christchurch, NZ, and has issue:

1 +LOUIS AUCHINBRECK; *b* 17 Jan 1953; *m* 1976 *Fiona Mary St Clair, dau of Gordon King, of Middlehill, Marlborough, NZ, and has issue:

(1) *Lucinda Louise; *b* 1982

(2) *Charlotte Virginia; *b* 1985

1 *Rosemary Fiona; *b* 23 Sept 1955

2 *Sophia Louise; *b* 25 Oct 1960; *m* 1984 *Philip Michael Darcey Pinniger, son of T K Pinniger, of Hunters, Lincoln's Inn, and has issue:

(1) *Rhiannon Louise

Sir ROBIN *m* 2nd 4 Nov 1978 *Elizabeth Mary, dau of Sir Arthur Colegate, MP (*see* WORSLEY Bt), of Bembridge, IoW, and former w of Richard Wellesley Gunston (*see* GUNSTON Bt)

Lineage: DUNCAN CAMPBELL of Kilmichael, in Glassary (son of 1st Lord Campbell; *see* ARGYLL, D); had a considerable estate confirmed to him by charter 19 June 1452; his son:

DUGALD CAMPBELL of Auchinbreck and Kilmichael; *m* Agnes, only dau of Sir John Lamont/Lawmond of Inverreyne, and *d* 1497, leaving:

ARCHIBALD CAMPBELL of Auchinbreck and Kilmichael; *m* 1st a dau of Campbell of Ardinglas and *d c* 1546, having had issue (including a 4th s Archibald, ancestor of the CAMPBELLs of Danna and Kilberry); *m* 2nd Catherine/Elizabeth, dau of 2nd Earl of Argyll (*see* ARGYLL, D) and widow of Lachlan Maclean of Dowart (*see* MACLEAN, Bt, of Dowart), and allegedly by her had a son (Alexander, ancestor of the CAMPBELLs of Strondour); his issue by his 1st w:

1 Dugald, of Auchinbreck and Kilmichael; had a charter of his lands 1543; *m* Fynewald (*m* 2nd John Stewart, Sheriff Bute), dau of Sir James Macdonald of Dunyveg and The Glen, Co Antrim, and *dsp*

2 Duncan, of Auchinbreck; Capt of Castleswene; had a charter of the lands 1546; *m* a dau of Patrick Buchanan of that Ilk, and was *k* Glenlivet 1594, leaving:

(1) Duncan; Capt of Castleswene; *m* 1573 Mary (living his widow 1602), dau and heir of William Macleod, of Dunvegan in Skye, and was possibly *k* with his f at Glenlivet, having had:

1a **Sir Dugald Campbell, of Auchinbreck, 1st Bt** (NS), so *cr* 12 or 24 Jan 1627/8 (sealed 23 Dec following); *s* to Auchinbreck *c* 26 Jan 1599; ktd 1617; *m* 1st (contract 23 April 1590) Catherine, est dau of Sir James Scrimgeour of Glassarie, Constable of Dundee, and had at least one dau (Margaret, *m* Sir John Graham, 2nd Bt, of Braco; *see* MONTROSE, D); *m* 2nd Mary, sis of 1st Earl of Kellie (*see* MAR and KELLIE, E); *m* 3rd Isabella, dau of Bp Boyd of Argyll, and *d* 1641, having had issue:

1b Archibald; *dsp* & *vp c* 1630

2b **Sir Duncan Campbell, 2nd Bt**; MP Argyllshire 1628–43, cmded Argyll's troops in Ireland 1641, taking Dunluce Castle, Co Antrim; Govr Rathlin Is; *m* 1st 1620 Margaret (*dsp*), dau of Brice Blair of Blair; *m* 2nd 1628 a dau of Maxwell of Newark, by whom he had issue:

1c **Sir Dugald Campbell, 3rd Bt**; granted 10,000 marks in recognition of his f's services and compensation for the destruction of his lands; MP Argyllshire 1649; *d* unm *c* 1662

2b (cont.) **Sir Duncan** *m* 3rd Jean (*m* 3rd Hon Sir William Hamilton), dau of Sir Alexander Colquhoun of Luss (*see* COLQUHOUN, Bt), and widow of 5th Lord Cathcart (*see* CATHCART, E), and was taken prisoner and murdered with Argyll's troops at Inverlochy 1645, having by her had further issue:

2c Archibald, of Knockemellie; *m* Margaret, dau of Colin Campbell, tutor (guardian) of Calder, and had, with other issue:

1d **Sir Duncan Campbell, 4th Bt**, his title and estates forfeited 1686 and the latter given to 1st Earl of Melfort (*see* PERTH, E), but forfeiture rescinded 1690; MP Argyllshire 1689–98, but resigned his seat and turned RC; *m c* 28 Feb 1679/80 Harriet, dau of 1st Earl of Balcarres (*see* CRAWFORD and BALCARRES, E), and *d c* 1700, leaving issue:

1e **Sir James Campbell, 5th Bt**; MP 1702–07 and 1707–08; *m* 1st Janet, yr dau of Ian Breac MacLeod of MacLeod, 18th Chief, and had issue:

1f Duncan; *m* Jean, dau of Alexander Clerk, of Glendoik, and *dvp*, leaving issue:

1g **Sir James Campbell, 6th Bt**; *b* 1721; Capt 49th Regt; *dsp* 1 Jan 1814

1g Janet

2f Dugald, of whom nothing is known

1f Jane; *m* Alexander McAlister, of Loup

2f Anne; *m* Donald Cameron of Lochiel (*d* 1748)

1e (cont.) **Sir James** *m* 2nd Susan, dau of Sir Archibald Campbell of Calder, and by her had:

3f James

4f Gilbert

5f Alexander; he or one of his two er bros was allegedly f of Pryce Campbell, who *dsp*

6f William; offr French serv; *m* Marie Angelique Robart, and had a son:

1g **Sir Jean Baptiste Guillaume Edouard Charles Campbell, 7th Bt**; *dsp c* 1838

3f Susanna

4f Elizabeth

5f Mary

6f Anne

1e (cont.) **Sir James** *m* 3rd Margaret, dau of Campbell, of Carradale, and *d* 14 Oct 1756, having by her had issue:

7f James; went to Jamaica

8f Donald; went to Jamaica and had a dau

1g Mary; *m* —Bailey, of Co Wexford, and was served heir to her gf 1836

7f Margaret; *m* Dr Thomas Campbell and had issue

8f Camerona; *d* unm

3c Alexander, of Strondour; *m* Jean (living 1710), dau of Campbell of Otter, and was murdered at Carnassary Castle 1685, having by her had issue

1b Grizel; *m* Sir James Stewart, 1st Bt, of Bute (*see* BUTE, M)

2b Anne; *m* John Campbell of Lochneil

3b Florence; *m* John Grave Maclean of Coll

4b Mary; *m* John Chalmers of Gadgirth, Ayrshire

2a Donald; living 11 May 1603

1a Elizabeth; *m* Neil McNeil of Taynish

2a Mary; *m* Ninian Bannatyne, of Kames, Bute

3 Donald, 1st of Kilmory; *m* Elspeth/Grizel Stewart, of Kildonnan, and *d* on or after 7 Nov 1593, having had (order of seniority uncertain):

(1) Dugald, of Kilmory, of which estate he had a charter 27 July 1593; *m* Elspeth Lamont and had:

1a Dugald; *d* unm

2a Duncan; *m* a dau of Lamont of Silvercraigs

3a Patrick, of Kilmory; *m* 1st Katherine McLachlan (*dsp*); *m* 2nd Guirnal, dau of Donald Campbell, of Kilmichael, Bute, and had:

1b Donald, of Kilmory; *dsp*; *s* by Dugald Campbell of Torblaron, of the CAMPBELLs of Stuck (*see* below)

4a Ian/John; had:

1b Donald; had:

1c Archibald

2b Patrick; had issue

(2) Archibald, of Kilmory; living 1620

(3) DUNCAN (Rev)

(4) Colin, of Kilmichael

(5) Patrick, of Stuck; *m* Elizabeth, dau of Cameron, of Callart, and was ancestor of:

1a Archibald Young Gipps Campbell (Sir), KCIE, CSI, CBE, VD; ICS; *m* 15 Dec 1910 Frances Irene (*d* 30 Dec 1967), dau of Rev H Savill Young, of Mallards Court, Stokenchurch (*see* YOUNG, Bt, of North Dean), and *d* 30 Oct 1957, leaving issue:

1b Archibald Hugh; *b* 1914; Lt-Col Roy Signals; *m* 1940 *Mary Alison [Mrs Archibald Campbell, 24 Langside Drive, Comrie, Perthshire PH6 2HR], dau of Lt-Col Herbert Nugent Young, DSO, RIF, and *d* 1981, having had issue:

1c +Archibald James [Archibald Campbell Esq, 2 Parrs Head Mews, George Lane, Rochester, Kent ME1 1NP]; *b* 1943; *m* 1976 (*divorce* 1996) Lorna Isobel, dau of John Scott, of Elderslie, Renfrewshire, and has issue:

1d +Archibald Malcolm Scott; *b* 1979

2d +Ewan Anton Hugh; *b* 1983

1d *Iona Lenor; *b* 1980

2d *Isla Rowena; *b* 1985

1c *Alison Margaret; *b* 1941; *m* 1966 *Robert John Michael, and has issue:

1d *Anthony Richard; *b* 1967

2d *Geraint Philip; *b* 1977
1d *Isobel Margaret; *b* 1969
2c *Christian Jean Mary; *b* 1948
2b +Colin Alan George [Colin Campbell Esq, The Old Manse, Lochgair, by Lochgilphead, Argyll PA31 8SB]; *b* 1917; Capt (ret) Black Watch, For Serv; *m* 1st 1945 (*divorce* 1961) Mary Cosser, dau of Ramsay Young; *m* 2nd 1966 *Joanna Frances, dau of George Falconer Ball, MC, and by his 1st w has issue:
1c *Mary Irene Young [Mrs Patrick Barwise, 6 Grange House, Highbury Grange, London N5 2QD]; *b* 1946; *m* 1973 *Patrick Barwise, and has issue:
1d *Alexander Mark Colin; *b* 1976
1d *Katherine Mary; *b* 1979
2c *Claire Elizabeth [Mrs Michael Bastian, 10 Riverside, Swallowfields, Totnes, Devon TQ9 5JB]; *b* 1949; *m* 1983 *Michael Anthony Bastian
3c *Fiona Penelope [Mrs Peter Rice, Oak Lodge, Laverstock Park, Laverstock, Salisbury, Wilts SP1 1QJ]; *b* 1955; *m* 1980 *Lt-Cdr Peter Langford Rice, RN, and has issue:
1d *Eleanor Young Rowley Campbell; *b* 1985
2d *Alice Camilla Campbell; *b* 1987
3b Niall Patrick; *b* 1925; Lt RE; *m* 1st 1953 (*divorce* 1965) Gillian Margaret Elizabeth, dau of Arthur John Morris, and had issue:
1c *Sarah Caroline [Mrs David Woodward, Rookery Cott, Clay Lane, Marton-over-Winsford, Cheshire]; *b* 1954; *m* 1985 *David Thomas Woodward, and has issue:
1d *Lucy Elizabeth Campbell; *b* 1988
2d *Stephanie Jane Campbell; *b* 1990
2c *Julia Anne; *b* 1956; *m* 1980 (*divorce* 1995) David Jon Slym, and has issue:
1d *Jessica Elizabeth; *b* 1982
2d *Katherine Margaret; *b* 1985
3b (cont.) Niall Patrick *m* 2nd 1967 *Peta Caroline [Mrs Niall Campbell, Westbrook, 5 Leadhall Cres, Harrogate, HG2 9NG], dau of William Kelso Paul, and *d* 1988, leaving issue:
1c +James William Patrick; *b* 1968
2c +Malcolm Niall Kelso; *b* 1978
1c *Rebecca Louise; *b* 1971

DONALD CAMPBELL's 3rd named son,
Rev DUNCAN CAMPBELL; Vicar Kilfinnan, Cowall, 1574; *m* the dau of McAlister of Loup, and had issue:
1 DUGALD (Rev), for whom *see* below
2 Donald; had a dau (Fingua, *m* Neil Malcolm, Parson Lochow)
3 Duncan; Maj; allegedly *dsp*
4 Colin; allegedly *dsp*

The Rev DUNCAN CAMPBELL's est son,
Rev DUGALD CAMPBELL; went to Ireland with Andrew Knox, Bp Raphoe, 1611; Incumbent Letterkenny, Co Donegal; *m* Annabella, dau of Robert Hamilton, of Barncleugh and Torrens, Ayrshire, and had, with other issue:
1 JOHN, for whom *see* below
2 Alexander, of Donegal; had a son (Patrick, mentioned in his will of 1664)
3 George; Army Capt; *m* Ann Melvill; *dsp*
4 Duncan, of Inverary; settled Ulster 1612; *m* Mary McCoy and had a son:
(1) Patrick, of Moyris and Magherahubber; *d* 1661, leaving a yst son:
1a John; settled Virginia 1726 and had issue
5 William; *m* 1st the dau of Lamont; *m* 2nd Mary, widow of Archibald Campbell, of Ormsary, and had issue

The Rev DUGALD CAMPBELL's son,
JOHN CAMPBELL, of Kildalloig, Argyllshire; Chamberlain Kintyre; *m* 1660 Elizabeth/Elspeth, dau of Lachlan McNeil of Losset, and *d c* 1706, having had issue:
1 Duncan, of Kildalloig; *m* (contract 29 April 1704) Margaret Hamilton, of Brownmuir, and had issue:
(1) James, of Kildalloig; *dsp* 12 Aug 1738
(1) Elspeth; *m* Patrick Campbell, of North Knapdale
2 DUGALD, for whom *see* below
3 Lachlan (Rev); Min Campbeltown, later of Capel Street, Dublin; *d* unm
4 William; *d* Darien Expdn
5 Archibald, of Danna in Knapdale; left issue

JOHN CAMPBELL's 2nd son,
Rev DUGALD CAMPBELL; *s* his nephew James in the estate of Kildalloig; Min Southend, Argyllshire, 1696; *m* 1st Grizel (*dsps* 18 Oct 1706), dau of Baillie Angus Campbell; *m* 2nd Ann (*d* 8 Jan 1786), dau of Archibald Macdonald, of Sanda, and *d* 16 Oct 1741, having by her had:
JOHN CAMPBELL, of Kildalloig; *m* Mary, dau of Rev David Campell, Min Southend, Kintyre, and *d* 3 Feb 1796, leaving issue:
1 DUGALD, for whom *see* below
2 Peter, of Askomell, Argyllshire; Capt HEICNS; *m* Catherine Williamson Ramsay, of Maxtone, and left issue:
(1) Elizabeth Jane; *m* July 1847 W D H Campbell-Davys (*d* 11 Sept 1885), and *d* May 1861, leaving issue
3 David, of Kildalloig; *m* Hetty (*d* 4th June 1864), dau of Peregrine Treves
1 Elizabeth Binning; *m* 6 March 1808 Norman Shairp (*d* 7 April 1864)

JOHN CAMPBELL's est son,
DUGALD CAMPBELL, of Kildalloig; Day Keeper Privy Seal Ireland; *m* Catherine Kingsley (*d* 29 Dec 1832), and *d* April 1834, leaving:
Sir John Eyton Campbell, 8th Bt0; claimed title 1841 and served nearest and lawful heir male to **Sir Dugald Campbell, 1st Bt**, 20 Sept 1847; *b* 22 May 1809; *m* 29 April 1841 Charlotte (*m* 2nd 16 Oct 1855 James Gardiner and *d* 17 Sept 1903), yst dau of Louis Henry Ferrier, of Belsyde, Linlithgow, and *d* 9 Dec 1853, having had issue:
1 **Sir Louis Henry Dugald Campbell, 9th Bt**; *b* 2 March 1844; Offr RN; *m* 5 Feb 1870 Mary Ellen Edith (*d* 28 Sept 1879), only child of Henry G Austin, and *d* 18 June 1875, leaving:
(1) Katherine Mary Edith; *b* 8 Sept 1874; *d* unm 22 Aug 1906
2 **Sir Norman Montgomery Abercrombie Campbell, 10th Bt**; *b* 2 March 1846; *m* 19 May 1886 Isabella Sara (*d* 3 Sept 1934), 3rd dau of Girolamo Carandini, 10th Marquis of Sarzano, and widow of George Cotterell, and *d* 25 Dec 1901, having had issue:
(1) Moira Constance
(2) Ida Cerise; *m* 18 Nov 1918 G W Kells, and had issue
3 John Ilay Shairp; *b* 7 Jan 1848; *d* unm 1882
4 **Sir Charles Ralph Campbell, 11th Bt**; *b* 24 Sept 1850; *m* 12 June 1878 Sara (*d* 25 June 1927), 2nd dau of Hon William Robinson, MLC, of Cheviot Hills, NZ, and *d* 4 Oct 1919, having had issue:
(1) William Robinson, DSO; *b* 26 Nov 1879; Maj 14th Hus Boer War 1899–1902 (despatches); *m* 11 Sept 1907 Maud Kathleen (*m* 2nd 7 Nov 1933 Adml Sir Edwyn Sinclair Alexander-Sinclair, GCB, MVO (*d* 13 Nov 1945), and *d* 12 Jan 1969), yr dau of Capt S Y H Davenport, 47th Loyal N Lancs Regt, and was *ka vp* Ypres 13 May 1915
(2) **Sir Charles Ralph Campbell, 12th Bt**; *b* 14 Dec 1881; Capt Reserve Regt 2nd Life Gds, ADC Personal Staff, served WW II (Adj East Wight HG); *m* 6 Oct 1915 Nancy Sarah, only dau of Edward Chapman, of Canterbury, NZ, and *d* 19 April 1948, having had issue:
1a Mary Sara, TD; *b* 1917; Jr Cdr ATS WW II, CStJ; *m* 22 April 1944 Lt-Gen Sir (Geoffrey Richard) Desmond Fitzpatrick, GCB, GCVO, DSO, MBE, MC, Col Blues & Roys, son of Brig-Gen Sir (Ernest) Richard Fitzpatrick, CBE, DSO, and *d* July 1996, leaving issue:
1b *Brian Richard Charles [Brian Fitzpatrick Esq, 11 Warwick Square, London SW1V 2AA]; *b* 13 April 1950; *educ* Eton
1b *Sara Georgina [Mrs Stewart Whittington, 109 Beaufort St, London SW3]; *b* 7 March 1948; *m* 1976 *R Stewart Whittington
(3) **Sir Norman Dugald Ferrier Campbell, 13th Bt**; *b* 19 Oct 1883; *educ* Eton; served WW II 1940–43 Truro 10th Bn HG, on HQ Staff as OC Signals (Capt); sheep farmer and stud breeder; *d* unm 20 Jan 1968
(4) **Sir Louis Hamilton Campbell, 14th Bt**; *b* 29 Sept 1885; *educ* Eton and Oriel Coll Oxford; served WW I in RNVR and WW II in RNR; *m* 7 Dec 1920 Margaret Elizabeth Patricia, dau of Patrick Campbell, and *d* 1970, having had issue:
1a Sir ROBIN AUCHINBRECK CAMPBELL, **15th and present Bt**
1a Elspeth Louise; *b* 11 May 1925; served WW II in WRNS; *d* unm 3 March 1958
(5) Ilay; *b* 1887; *dvp* Eton 30 Oct 1904
(6) Henry Auchinbreck; *b* 1893, *dvp* 1897

CAMPBELL, Bt, of Barcaldine

Arms: Quarterly, 1st, gyronny of eight or and sa. (for CAMPBELL), on a dexter canton arg. a bend sa. between a unicorn's head erased in chief and a cross crosslet fitchée in base gu. (for DENNISTOUN); 2nd, or a fess chequy az. and arg. (for STEWART); 3rd, arg. a galley sa., oars in action (for LORN); 4th, gyronny of eight or and sa. (for CAMPBELL), on a dexter canton gu. two bars of the first (for CAMERON); all within a bordure quarterly or and sa. **Crest:** A man in full highland garb, holding in his dexter hand a claymore and on his sinister arm a targe, all ppr. **Supporters:** A leopard and a stag, both ppr. **Motto:** *Paratus sum* ('I am prepared'). **Creation:** Bt. (UK) 30 Sept 1831.

SIR NIALL ALEXANDER HAMILTON CAMPBELL, 8TH BT, of Barcaldine, Co Argyll [Sir Niall Campbell Bt, The Old Mill, Milltown, Muddiford, Barnstaple, Devon EX31 4HG]; *b* 7 Jan 1925; *s f* 1978; *educ* Cheltenham and Corpus Christi Coll, Oxford; Hereditary Keeper of Barcaldine Castle; served WW II 1943–46 as T/Lt RM, barrister Inner Temple 1951, Assist Sec St Mary's Hosp Paddington

1955–60, Sec W Middx Hosp Isleworth 1960, Dep House Govr London Clinic 1960–69, Sec to Bd of Management Roy Home and Hosp for Incurables Putney 1969–70, Dep Clerk Inner London Magistrates' Courts 1970–76, Clerk to Justices of N Devon Divs of Barnstaple, Bideford and Gt Torrington and S Molton 1976–90; *m* 1st 1949 (*divorce* 1956) Patricia Mary, dau of R G Turner; *m* 2nd 17 Sept 1957 *Norma Joyce, dau of W N Wiggin, of Albrighton, and by her has issue:

1 +RODERICK DUNCAN HAMILTON [Roderick Campbell Esq, East Almer Farmhouse, Almer, Blandford, Dorset DT11 9 EL]; *b* 24 Feb 1961; *m* 1989 *Jean Caroline, dau of Laurence Bicknell, of Tom's Hill, Lobb, Braunton, Devon, and has issue:

(1) *Kate Emily Dennistoun; *b* 1990

(2) *Anna Iona Hamilton; *b* 1993

2 +Angus Charles Dundas; *b* 27 Oct 1967

1 *Fiona Madeline Hamilton; *b* 30 Sept 1958

2 *Lucy Catriona Margarette (twin with Angus); *b* 27 Oct 1967

Lineage: Sir DUNCAN CAMPBELL, 1st Bt, of Glenorchy (*see* BREADALBANE, E), had an illegitimate s:

PATRICK CAMPBELL, known as 'Para Dubh Beag', 1st of Barcaldine; *b* 1592; legitimated with his bro James 27 Dec 1614; obtained from his f Innerzeldies, and other lands in Perthshire; *m* 1st 1620 Annabel, dau of Campbell of Dunstaffnage, and had issue:

1 JOHN, his heir

1 Jean; *m* Archibald Campbell of Lix

2 Giles; *m* Colin Campbell of Bragleen

3 Annabella/Margaret; *m* 1648 John Campbell of Kinloch

PATRICK CAMPBELL *m* 2nd Bethia, dau of Murray of Ochertyre, and *d* 25 March 1678, having by her had, with other issue:

2 Colin, Minister of Ardchattan Parish from 1667, mathematician and astronomer who corresponded with Sir Isaac Newton *d* 13 March 1726, being ancestor of the CAMPBELLs of Achnaba and Capt John Campbell of Achnaba, who cmded a company of the Argyll Militia at Culloden 1746

3 William, Min of Balquhidder; *m* 1st Anna Campbell (*d* 1725), and by her had:

(1) Mary, *m* John Campbell, of Auchachanna

(2) Elizabeth

3 William Campbell *m* 2nd Mary, dau of Rev Donald Lindsay, last Episcopal Min of Balquhidder, and by her had a dau (*m* Campbell of Bragleen)

The est son,

JOHN CAMPBELL of Innerzeldies; *m* 1st 1647 Margaret, dau of Campbell of Clathic, and had:

1 ALEXANDER, his heir

JOHN CAMPBELL *m* 2nd a sis of Sir Ewan Cameron, 17th of Lochiel, by whom he had, with other issue:

2 Colin, ancestor of the CAMPBELLs of Balliveolan

3 Duncan, ancestor of:

(1) *Ewan Alexander; F/Lt RNZAF WW II; *b* 8 July 1915; *educ* Wanganui Coll; *m* 10 April 1948 *June Masson, dau of Eric Alexander Baddeley, of Kakathai, Wanganui, NZ, and has:

1a *Robert Ewan; *b* 1 June 1949

2a *John Alexander; *b* 8 Dec 1950

3a *Neil Colin; *b* 17 June 1953

1a *Katherine June *b* 3 Aug 1957)

The est son,

ALEXANDER CAMPBELL of Barcaldine; 2nd Lt Earl of Caithness' Highland Company 1678, Chamberlain to 1st Earl of Breadalbane (*qv*); *m* 1676 Mary, dau of Colin Campbell of Lochneil, and *d* 1720, leaving, with three yr s (John of Corries; James of Raray; Colin):

PATRICK CAMPBELL of Barcaldine; *b* 1677; *m* 1st Agnes Campbell, last of the family of Campbell of Kilmun, and had issue:

1 John, of Barcaldine, DL, JP Argyll, Capt Argyll Mil, one of the Earl of Breadalbane's factors, and later factor on the forfeited Perth, Strathallan, and Gask estates; *b c* 1700; *m* Margaret, dau of Campbell of Keithock, Co Forfar. Being deeply involved in debt, he sold the family estates to his half-bro Duncan, and *d* 12 April 1777, leaving issue:

(1) Alexander, Ensign Argyllshire Mil 1745, Capt in an independent company E Indies 1747 also of 1st Royals 1753, Maj Montgomery's Highrs 1757, Lt-Col 95th Buffons 1761, Dep Govr Fort George 1774, Col 1777; *b* 1729; *m* 1 Aug 1765 Helen (*d* 5 April 1787 aged 40), sis of Sir John Sinclair, Bt, of Ulbster, MP (*see* THURSO, V), and *d* 22 April 1779, having had issue:

1a Patrick, Capt Waller's Corps; *b* 9 May 1766; *d* 4 Dec 1825

2a James, RN(?)

1a Janet; *m* 15 Feb 1787 Æneas Mackay, of Scotstoun, Peeblesshire, Capt HEICS, and *d* 15 Oct 1787, leaving issue

2a Matilda; *d* unm

3a Jean; *m* 2 Jan 1784 12th Earl of Caithness (*qv*), and *d* 2nd April 1853, leaving issue

4a Mary; *d* 14 Oct 1787

5a Isobel; *b* 1773

(2) David, of Belmont, Corstorphine, WS till 1775, settled in New York 1776, Notary Public there 1777 and Attorney-at-Law 1778–83; *b* 1729/30; *m* 1st 1749/50; *m* 2nd March 1756 Jean, dau of Archibald Campbell, of the Argyll family, and had issue:

1a Archibald, Ensign 71st (Fraser's) Highrs 1775, Capt American War; *b* 1750/1; *m* Margaret (*d* by 12 Jan 1782), dau of Robert Phelp/Philip, and was *k* Battle of Videaur Bridge 3 Jan 1782, having had a dau

2a Colin, of Shelburne and Weymouth, Nova Scotia, WS; Notary Public New York 1782, went to NS with Loyalists 1783, Notary Public Shelburne, NS, 1784, admitted Nova Scotia Bar 1787, Judge of Probates, Comptroller of Customs and Crown Lands, Registrar of Deeds, Collector of Customs; *b* June 1752; *m* 1st, widow of Col Samuel Campbell, of Willington, N Carolina, Collector of Customs, to whose office he *s* 1789. She *d* 1794. He *m* 2nd 15 Nov 1796 Elizabeth, dau of Richard Hardy, a loyalist, and had issue:

1b John, MP, Queen's Co, NS; *b* 16 Aug 1797; *bapt* 28 Aug 1797; *d* 1870

2b Colin, of Weymouth, NS, Registrar for Digby Co and Notary Public; *b* 28 Oct 1798; *bapt* 30 Nov 1798; *m* Maria, dau of Col John Taylor, and *d* 1878, leaving issue:

1c Colin, MLC Nova Scotia; *b* 1822; *m* 1845 Phoebe Anne Seely and *d* 1881, having had:

1d Colin, Paymaster RNR; *b* 1846; *m* 4 Dec 1874 Christina McDonald, of N Uist, and *d* 5 Oct 1896, leaving issue:

1e Lauchlan Colin, MC, served Boer War and WW I; *b* 1880; *m* 1904 Mrs Mary Catherine Armstrong (*née* Kavanagh) and was *ka* Aug 1918, leaving issue:

1f Patrick Colin; *b* 1907

1f Dorothy; *b* 1905

2e Donald, served USN

1e Jessie; *b* 1883

2e Charlotte Eleanor; *b* 1887; *m* 1905 Alfred E Helmer, and had issue:

1f Colin Alfred; *b* 1906; *m* Agnes Jackson, and had issue:

1g Colin Dexter

2d John, MP Digby Co; *b* 1849; *d* 1888

3d Thomas, BR, MD; *b* 1851; *educ* St Andrews and Edinburgh U; *d* 1878

4d George Douglas; *b* 1852; *m* Kate Glidden Palmer and *d* 1930, having had issue:

1e George Douglas

2e Glidden, MC, Maj 85th Canadian Highrs WW I

3e Donald; *d* 1909

4e John Duncan, served with Canadian contingent WW I; *d* 1939

5e Kenneth Archibald, Lt 42nd Canadian Highrs, served WW I; *ka* at Vimy Ridge

6e Thomas, served with Canadian contingent WW I

7e Albert, served with Canadian contingent WW I

8e Colin Palmer, MC, Lt RFA, served WW I, and was *ka*

1e Florence; *d* 1928

2e Catherine; *d* 1920

1d Charlotte Elizabeth; *b* 1848; *m* F H Holyoke, and *d* 1912

2d Frances Helen; *b* 1854; *m* 1880 Rt Rev Hon John Dart, Bishop of New Westminister, and had issue

3d Agnes Jessie; *b* 1855; *m* Fenwick Williams Vroom, Archdeacon of Nova Scotia, and had issue

4d Susan Ladd; *b* 1858; *m* Rev William Hyde

5d Mary; *b* 1860; *m* Donald Kemp, and had issue

6d Marian; *b* 1863; *m* Rev Robert Holland Taylor, and had issue

2c Charles McCartney, Registrar for Digby Co; *b* 1830; *d* 1907

1c Maria; *m* 1853 James Leslie Jones, and had issue

3a Alexander; *b* 1753; Cadet 71st (Fraser's) Highrs 1776

4a Mungo; *k* Battle of New Orleans War of 1812

(3) Patrick, Capt 88th Campbell's Highrs; present Battle of Fellinghaussen 15 July 1761 against the French, Maj 44th Regt

(4) Colin, Advocate Scottish Bar; *d* unm by 1770

(5) Duncan, MD; *d* unm

(6) George, Ensign 42nd Regt and 80th Foot; *k* Martinique by 30 Sept 1762

(1) Margaret; *m* John Campbell, of Danna

(2) Ann; *m* Capt Trapaud, Dep Govr of Fort Augustus

(3) Matilda; *m* (contract 9 May 1760) Capt Neil Campbell, of Duntroon, Roy Regt N Br Fus

1 Anne; *m* (contract dated 3 Nov 1719) Charles Campbell of Ardchattan

PATRICK CAMPBELL *m* 2nd 1707 Lucia, dau of Sir Ewan Cameron of Lochiel, and by her had:

2 Colin, of Glenure, Offr Loudon's Highrs, Factor for Government on forfeited estates of Stewart of Ardsheil, Cameron of Callart, Mamore and part of that of Cameron of Lochiel; *m* 9 May 1749 Janet, dau of Col Hon Hugh Mackay of Bighouse, s of 3rd Lord Reay (*qv*), and was murdered 14 May 1752 by Allan Breck Stewart, having had three daus

3 DUNCAN, of whom presently

4 Donald, Surgeon RN; *d* unm in the W Indies

5 Alexander, Lt Earl of Loudon's Highrs; *b* 1729; *m* 1770 Elizabeth, dau of Sutherland of Uppat, and *d* 1822, having had issue:

(1) Donald, Ensign Reay Fencibles and Capt 71st Highrs, wounded Waterloo; *b* 1772; *m* 14 Feb 1804 Frances, dau of Maj Pilot, and *d* 27 Aug 1848, having had four s and a dau

(2) Hugh; *d* unm

(3) Kenneth; *d* unm

(4) Norman, Capt 71st HLI, wounded Vittoria and Waterloo; *m* 1810 Charlotte Wilson Everard and *d* 1836, having had issue:

1a William Wilson, Lt 94th Highrs; *m* 21 July 1846 Jane Elizabeth Lauretta (*d* 1910), only dau of W H C Bluett, of Holcombe Regis, Devon, and *d* 17 Jan 1878, having had issue:

1a Flora Wilde; *b* 10 Feb 1847; *m* 12 Oct 1871 John Tompson Goodridge, Surgeon, of Paignton, son of John Jackson Goodridge, and had issue

6 Robert, of Stirling, and of London; *m* Katherine (who *d* 1814), dau of Maj Cunningham of Boglas, and *d* 30 Oct 1776, having had issue:

(1) Patrick, 71st Foot, served in N America 1776–78 and with the 36th Regt of Foot at Bangalore in 1783; *d* in India 12 May 1784

(2) David, Col 98th Foot; *d* 1792

7 Archibald, Maj 43rd Regt; *d* 1755

8 Allan, Gen, Subaltern Black Watch, captured Battle of Prestonpans, Brevet-Col 36th Foot; *d* 13 Nov 1794

2 Isobel; *m* John Campbell of Achallader, and had issue

3 Mary; *m* Alexander MacDougall of Dunolly, and had issue

4 Annabel; *m* Archibald Campbell of Melfort, and had issue
5 Jane; *m* Colin Campbell of Edenchip, and had issue

PATRICK CAMPBELL of Barcaldine *d* 1738; his 2nd s by his 2nd w,

DUNCAN CAMPBELL of Barcaldine and Glenure; Sheriff Substitute for Perthshire at Killin; *b c* 1716; *m* 1744 Mary, dau of Alexander Macpherson, and *d* 14 Nov 1784, having had:

1 ALEXANDER, his heir
2 Patrick, Maj 71st (Fraser's) Highrs; *m* 1 Jan 1781 Sarah, dau of Thomas Pearsall, of New York, and *d* Sept 1782, having had issue:
(1) Duncan Pearsall; *b* 25 Dec 1781; *m* 1st 12 May 1808 Catherine, dau of William Bayard, of New York, and had issue; *m* 2nd 16 June 1817 his sis-in-law, 3rd dau of William Bayard, and by her had with other issue:
1a Thomas Pearsall; *b* 17 Dec 1820; *m* 1st 6 June 1867 Catherine Hearsey, and had issue; *m* 2nd 26 April 1893 Mary Amelia Wilde, of Newark, NJ, and *d* 26 Nov 1906
3 James, Capt 77th Atholl Highrs; *d* 1783
4 Colin, of Carrigeen, or Bernard's Hall, Co Cork, Capt 42nd Highrs, and 24th Regt; *m* 1789 Elizabeth, dau of Col Hungerford, and *d* Nov 1809, having had issue:
(1) Alexander Patrick, of Clonakilty; *d* 1818
(1) Lucy; *m* Thomas Hungerford
(2) Mary; *m* Richard Hungerford, of Clonakilty
5 William, Lt 77th Atholl Highrs
1 Louisa; *m* 2 Nov 1767 Sir Ewen Cameron, Bt, of Fassifern, and had issue

The est son,

ALEXANDER CAMPBELL of Barcaldine and Glenure, a memb of the Faculty of Advocates; *b* 30 April 1745; *m* 22 Sept 1785 Mary, dau of John Campbell, of the Citadel, Edinburgh, Dep Keeper Gt Seal Scotland, Cashier Roy Bank of Scotland, and *d* 17 March 1800, having had issue:

1 DUNCAN (Sir), **1st Bt**
2 John; *b* 3 July 1796; *dsp* 1808
3 Peter William, Lt 2nd Bn, 11th Regt, Bengal NI; *dsp* 15 Nov 1819
4 Colin Alexander, Maj 74th Foot, Adj Argyll and Bute Mil Rifles; *b* 23 Sept 1796; *dsp* 10 March 1863
1 Caroline Louisa Anne; *d* unm 19 March 1848
2 Maria Helen; *m* 8 Oct 1818 Rev Hugh Fraser, Min of Ardchattan, Co Argyll, and *d* 4 Jan 1862, having had issue

The est son,

Sir Duncan Campbell, 1st Bt (UK), so *cr* 30 Sept 1831, of Barcaldine and Glenure, JP and DL Argyll; *b* 3 July 1786; Capt 3rd Gds, served Copenhagen, Walcheren Expdn and Peninsular War, ADC to his cousin Gen Campbell (afterwards Sir Alexander Campbell, Bt, of Gartsford (*qv*)) Battle of Talavera; *m* 22 Feb 1815 Elizabeth Dreghorn, dau of James Dennistoun of Dennistoun, Dunbartonshire, heir male and rep of the Dennistouns, Lords Dennistoun, and coheir of her mother, Margaret, dau of Allan Dreghorn, of Blockhairn, and *d* 2 April 1842, having had, with other issue:

1 **Sir Alexander Campbell, 2nd Bt**, JP, Serjeant-at-Arms Roy Household, Capt Argyll and Bute Mil, cmded Lochaber Axe Men of the Roy Breadalbane Highrs on occasion of HM QUEEN VICTORIA's visit to Taymouth 1842; *b* 15 June 1819; *m* 20 Aug 1855 Harriette Augusta Royer (*d* 11 Sept 1909), dau of Adml Henry Collier, and *d* 11 Dec 1880, leaving:
(1) **Sir Duncan Alexander Dundas Campbell, 3rd Bt**, CVO, JP, and Commissioner of Supply, FSA Scot, FRGS, Capt 3rd Bn The Black Watch 1881–1887, Capt (ret as Hon Maj 1893) 3rd and 4th Bn HLI, Memb Roy Co Archers, Gentlemen Usher Green Rod 1884–95, Sec Order Thistle, Carrick Pursuivant of Arms, Queen Victoria's Diamond Jubilee Medal 1897, Coronation Silver Medals 1902 and 1911; bought 1896 the Castle and Barony of Barcaldine, the ancient seat of his family, which had been sold in 1842 on the death of Sir Duncan Campbell, 1st Bt; Keeper Barcaldine Castle and Superior of Auchachrossan, Argyllshire, of Rannaguezion, Corb and Drumturn, Galray and Wester Denhead, Hillock and Tullifergus, Perthshire; author: *The Clan Campbell* (8 vols), *Records of Clan Campbell in the Military Service of the Honourable E India Company from 1600–1858* and *Officers of the Clan Campbell in Army and Royal Marines from 1660–1924* (22 vols MSS); *b* 4 Dec 1856; *d* unm 27 May 1926
(2) Eric Reginald Duncan, Capt 2nd Bn Princess Victoria's Roy Irish Fus, Inspr Lagos Constabulary, served Lagos Expdny Force (medal), Govr Prison at Asaba, S Nigeria 1900–08; *b* 28 Nov 1857; *m* 14 Nov 1899 Rose (*d* 22 Dec 1930), dau of J E Scott, JP, of Outlands, Devonport, and *d* 21 July 1900, having had issue:
1a Erica Rose; *b* posthumously 29 Nov 1900; *d* unm Oct 1963
(1) Harriette Beatrice Mabel; *d* unm 4 March 1906
(2) Flora Mary Muriel; *d* unm 12 March 1915
2 James Robert, Lt 43rd Madras NI; *b* 24 May 1822; *d* 15 May 1843
3 John Peter William, Maj-Gen BSC; *b* 18 March 1824; *m* 1st 14 Oct 1847 Frances Charlotte (*d* 1 Jan 1874), dau of Alfred William Begbie, ICS, by Margaret Anna, only dau of James Grant, HEICS, 3rd s of Sir Ludovic Grant, 6th Bt, of Dalvey (*qv*), and had issue:
(1) **Sir Alexander William Dennistoun Campbell, 4th Bt**, Col Indian Staff Corps, formerly 16th Lancers and 15th Hus, served Afghan War 1878–80; *b* 8 Sept 1848; *d* unm 11 April 1931
(2) **Sir Duncan John Alfred Campbell, 5th Bt**, BCS, Dist Judge Centl India, Commr Burma, served Upper Burma Campaign 1886–89 (medal, two clasps); *b* 5 Aug 1854; *m* 12 July 1890 Mary Snell (*d* 25 March 1952), dau of Septimus Gibbon, MD, and *d* 13 March 1932, leaving:
1a Jean Linda Dennistoun; *b* 1893
(3) Francis James Brooke, Lt-Col IA; *b* 7 Feb 1861; *m* 7 May 1889 Ethel May, dau of Dep-Surg-Gen C E Raddock, and *d* 1918, leaving issue:
1a **Sir Eric Francis Dennistoun Campbell, 6th Bt**; *b* 17 Aug 1892; *educ* Wellington; Capt 1st Bn S Lancs Regt WW I and Afghan War 1919, Hereditary Keeper Barcaldine Castle; *d* unm 11 July 1963
1a May Lilian; *b* 4 March 1890; *m* 1 Sept 1916 Capt Henry Harman Wadeson, late IA, and had issue:
1b George Francis, served WW II 1939–41 as P/O RAF; *b* 26 Sept 1919; *ka* over Germany 5 July 1941
2b *Alexander Richard Campbell; *b* 17 May 1923; *educ* London U (LLB); *m* 25 July 1944 *Winifred Mary, dau of Richard Wilfred Thomas Dunscombe, of Topsham, and has four sons and three daus
(4) Gerald Edward Lyon, Madras CS; *b* 8 Oct 1863; *m* 12 Oct 1886 Sybil (*m* 2nd 27 March 1911 Cdr Wentworth Vernon Cole, RN and *d* 21 Jan 1958), dau of Maj-Gen Thomas Ross Church, CIE, and *d* Feb 1902, leaving issue:
1a Mary Hamilton; *b* 22 March 1888; *m* 7 June 1915 Alfred Thomas Duncan Anderson, MBE (*d* 1 Feb 1949), and had issue:
1b *Ian Duncan Hamilton; *b* 2 June 1916
2b *Alec Vernon; *b* 5 June 1921
(5) Richard Hamilton, CIE (1912), Madras CS, Priv Sec to HH Maharajah of Mysore; *b* 26 Nov 1865; *m* 29 May 1889 Ellen Emily Harington (*d* 27 April 1949), dau of Henry James Colley Gompertz, Madras Revenue Survey, and *d* 19 March 1923, having had issue:
1a Eric Lyon Hamilton; *b* 23 May 1890; *d* 20 Nov 1891
2a IAN VINCENT HAMILTON (Sir), **7th Bt**
3a Richard Henry Dennistoun, dir R G Shaw and Co, E India Merchants; *b* 8 Sept 1901; *educ* Winchester and Corpus Christi Coll Oxford; *m* 21 Nov 1936 *Kathleen Adair, yst dau of Richard Fallowes Dunn, of Wolverhampton, and *d* 1978, leaving issue:
1b *Lorne Mary Dennistoun; *b* 10 March 1939
2b *Elizabeth Gay Adair; *b* 9 Aug 1942
1a Christine May *b* 8 July 1892; *d* unm 17 March 1930
(1) Emily Frances Margaret; *m* 20 Jan 1872 Lt-Col Francis Richard Begbie, late IA, and *d* 17 March 1930, leaving issue. He *d* 17 Jan 1932
(2) Elizabeth Helen Montagu; *m* 23 Dec 1878 James R Drummond, Bengal CS, and *d* 8 June 1881, leaving issue
3 (cont.) Maj-Gen John Campbell *m* 2nd 10 Aug 1875 Louisa (*d* 25 April 1887), widow of Capt Bonar, RA, and 2nd dau of Alexander Campbell of Monzie, by Christina, only dau and heir of Sir Duncan Cameron, 2nd Bt, of Fassifern, and *d* 30 Oct 1901, having by her had issue:
(6) Ian Alastair, 2nd Lt Gordon Highrs, late RN; *b* 26 Aug 1876; *d* 23 Oct 1899 from wounds recd at Elandslaagte, S Africa
(7) Patrick Duncan; *d* an infant 29 Aug 1880
(3) Christina; *m* 14 Oct 1902 Richard Ernest Campbell, late Capt 3rd King Edward's Horse (who assumed the name of Campbell), yst son of Henry Gompertz, late Madras Survey, and *d* 1931 leaving issue

The 6th Bt's cousin,

Sir Ian Vincent Hamilton Campbell, 7th Bt, CB (1951); *educ* Cheltenham and Corpus Christi Coll Oxford; Lt King's Liverpool Regt WW I, Assist Pncpl Air Ministry 1919, Priv Sec to Ch Air Staff 1927–30, Assist Priv Sec to Sec State Air 1930–34, Pncpl 1934, Assist Sec Air Min 1939, Assist Under-Sec of State 1945, ret 1955; Hereditary Keeper Barcaldine Castle; *b* 7 May 1895; *m* 1st 14 July 1920 Madeline Lowe Reid (*d* 11 Oct 1929), est dau of H Anglin Whitelocke, MD, FRCS, of Oxford, and had issue:

1 Sir NIALL ALEXANDER HAMILTON CAMPBELL, **8th and present Bt**

Sir Ian m 2nd 2 June 1932 (*annulled* 1942) Iris Constance, only dau of Lt-Col Ronald Charles Gibb, CBE, RASC; *m* 3rd 14 Nov 1942 Agnes Louise, widow of Vsevolod Victor Watson, MBE, and est surv dau of the writer William Henry Gerhardi, and *d* 14 April 1978

CAMPBELL, Bt, of Succoth

Arms: Quarterly, 1st and 4th, gyronny of eight engrailed or and sa. (for CAMPBELL); 2nd and 3rd, az. a lion rampant arg., within a bordure counter company arg. and az. (for WALLACE of Elderslie). **Crest:** A camel's head couped ppr. **Supporters:** Dexter, a lion, rampant-guardant; sinister, a savage, wreathed about the temples and loins, all ppr. **Motto:** *Labore et perseverantia* ('with hard work and perseverance') **Creation:** Bt. (UK) 17 Sept 1808.

SIR ILAY MARK CAMPBELL, 7TH BT, of Succoth, Dunbartonshire [Sir Ilay Campbell of Succoth Bt, Crarae Lodge, by Inveraray, Argyll PA32 8YA]; *b* 29 May 1927; *s f* 1967; *educ* Eton and Ch Ch Oxford (BA 1952, MA 1970); Scottish agent Christie's 1968–73 (jtly 1973–92), chm Christie's Scotland 1978–96, Pres Assoc Protection Rural Scotland 1978–90, Convener Ch of Scotland Ctee for Artistic Matters 1987–91, Hon V-Pres Scotland's Garden Scheme 1960–, dir High Craigton Farming Co, Tstee Crarae Garden Charitable Tst 1978– and Tree Register Br Isles 1988–; memb Historic Bldgs Cncl Scotland 1989–, Gdns Ctee Nat Tst Scotland 1994–, Argyll, Lochaber and Western Isles Regnl Ctee Nat Tst Scotland 1995–, Scottish Rep Nat Art Collections Fund 1972–83; *m* 22 July 1961 *Margaret Minette Rohais, only dau of James Alasdair Anderson, formerly of Tullichewan, Dunbartonshire, by Lady Flavia Joan Lucy, only dau of 2nd Earl of Halsbury (*qv*), and has:

1 *Cecilia Margaret Lucy; *b* 3 June 1963; *m* 1988 *Maj Malcolm Gregor Charles MacGregor, Yr. of MacGregor, er s of Brig Sir Gregor MacGregor of MacGregor, 6th Bt (*qv*)

2 *Candida Harriett Rohais; *b* 7 Sept 1964; *m* 1991 *Gerard Joseph Rafferty, er s of Richard Byrne Rafferty, of Bellshill, Lanarks, and has:

(1) *Ruaraidh Ilay Byrne; *b* 1993

(2) *Fintan Campbell; *b* 1997

Lineage: Recent research indicates a descent from the CAMPBELLs of Ardkinglas via the CAMPBELLs of Reroch, Renfrewshire.

ROBERT CAMPBELL of Succoth, Dunbartonshire, which he bought 1616 from the BONTEINs; variously called *servitor* and *familius* (*i.e.*, kin) to 7th Earl of Glencairn (*see* CUNINGHAME, Bt), also 'Robert Campbell, Yr.'; maltster and Burgess of Dumbarton 1610, Cncllr 1614, Common Procurator 1617, Baillie 1621–26; *m* by 1606 Janet, dau of Duncan Glen, tailor and Burgess of Dumbarton, by Janet, dau of Duncan Glen, and *d* 1640, having had, with a yr s (James, *m* Christian, dau of Robert Paterson):

WILLIAM CAMPBELL of Succoth; Provost Dumbarton 1652, Burgess 1637, Sheriff Clerk 1641; *m* Lillias Houstoun (*d* 1704) and *d* 1658, leaving, with other issue, including another s (James, *m* 1676 Marion, dau of Patrick Williamson of Chapelton, and had a s, James, *d* 1681) and a dau (Marion, *m* John Ewing, gunner Dumbarton Castle, and had issue):

JOHN CAMPBELL of Succoth; *b c* 1645; writer (legal practitioner) Edinburgh; recorded arms 1672–77; Burgess Glasgow 1679; bought the Garscube estate, Dunbartonshire, from Sir James Colquhoun, 4th Bt, of Luss, (*qv*), 1687; MP (S Parl) Argyll 1681–82; *m* 1st 1670 Janet (*d* 1675), dau of James Hamilton, Burgess Glasgow, and had two sons (Colin, *b* 1672, *d* by 1687; Archibald, *b* 1674, Lt-Govr Dumbarton Castle, *dsp* 1701); *m* 2nd by 1677 Agnes, dau of William Stirling of Law, and by her had, with other issue, including another s (John CAMPBELL later STIRLING (1703 on inheriting Law), *d* 1753, leaving a s (James, of Law, who *m* 1757 Christian, dau of William Colquhoun of Craigton, and *dsp* 1809)) and at least two daus (Margaret, *m* 1694 John Maxwell of Dargavell; Anna, *m* 1702 Robert Campbell of Balvie, WS), the rest dying young or unm:

WILLIAM CAMPBELL of Succoth; *b c* 1679; had disposition of Garscube 1689 but resigned all his lands to the Crown 1707 for regrant as the free (territorial) Barony of Succoth; Lt-Govr Dumbarton Castle 1708-64; *m* 1701 Margaret, dau of John Walkinshaw of Barrowfield and aunt of Clementina Walkinshaw, Bonnie Prince Charlie's mistress, and *d* 1764, leaving, with other issue (*d* young or unm), a 2nd s:

ARCHIBALD CAMPBELL of Succoth; *b c* 1703; WS 1728, Commissary Pncpl Glasgow, Dep Keeper Gt Seal, a Pncpl Clerk of Session 1770; sold the Elderslie estate 1769 to Alexander Speirs; *m* 1731 Helen (*d* 1767), only child and heiress of John Wallace of Elderslie, and *d* 1790, leaving, with other issue (*d* young or unm), an est s:

1 **Sir Ilay Campbell, 1st Bt** (UK), so *cr* 17 Sept 1808; *b* 23 Aug 1734; *educ* Edinburgh High Sch; advocate 1757, Slr-Gen Scotland 1783, Ld Advocate 1784, MP Glasgow Burghs 1784–89, Ld-Pres Court of Session as Lord Succoth 1789–1808; *m* 13 Nov 1765 Susan Mary, dau of Archibald Murray of Murrayfield (*see* MURRAY, Bt, of Blackbarony), and had:

(1) ARCHIBALD (Sir), **2nd Bt**

(2) Alexander; *b* Sept 1771; WS; *d* unm in 1799

(1) Jean; *b* 1767; *m* 1797 John MacNeil of Gigha, Argyllshire, and *dsp*

(2) Margaret; *m* her cousin Sir John Connell, Judge Admlty and legal author, and had issue

(3) Anne; *b* 1773; *m* 1795 Francis Sitwell (*see* SITWELL, Bt)

(4) Susan; *b* 1775; *m* 17 June 1795 Craufurd Tait, of Harviestoun, Clackmannan, and *d* 3 Jan 1814, leaving issue. He *d* 6 May 1822

(5) Mary *b* 1777; *d* 21 Jan 1820

(6) Elizabeth Glen; *b* 1778; *m* 1801 William Dalzeil Colquhoun of Garscadden and *dsp* 1853. He *d* 27 Jan 1806

2 William; *b* 1736; Portuguese Army 1764–70 (Capt Artillery), Sub-Dir and Capt Engrs Fort George Madras 1770; *m* 1770 — (*d* in childbirth 1775), dau of Thomas Hay of Huntingdon, Ld of Session as Lord Huntingdon

3 John; *b* 1743; merchant, Provost Glasgow 1788, Receiver-Gen Customs 1790, a Dir Bank of Scotland 1815; *m* 1st 1768 Rebecca Douglas (*dsp*), allegedly dau of Robert Douglas (s of Mary Douglas of Mains by John Campbell of Woodside); *m* 2nd Elizabeth, dau of James Houston of Jordanhill and widow of Hugh Maclean of Ardgour, and by her had, with other issue (*d* young):

(1) Archibald; *b* 1770; Capt 9th Regt; *d* unm 1794

(1) Lilias; *m* 1810 James Keir of Blackshiels

4 James; HEIC contractor for army in India; *d* unm after 1827

1 Jean; *b* 1732; *m* 1750 William Wallace of Cairnhill and *d* 1781, leaving issue

The 1st Bt *d* 28 March 1823; his est s,

Sir Archibald Campbell, 2nd Bt; *b* 1 Aug 1769; advocate 1791, Ld of Session as Lord Succoth 1809–24; *m* 8 Aug 1794 Elizabeth (*d* June 1844), est dau of John Balfour, 5th of Balbirnie, Fife, and *d* 23 July 1846, having had:

1 Archibald; *b* 1795; *d* 1812

2 John; *b* 28 May 1798; advocate 1821, MP Dumbarton 1826; *m* 12 July 1824 his cousin Anna Jane (*d* 3 June 1869), dau of Francis Sitwell (*see* SITWELL, Bt), and *d* 1830, leaving:

(1) **Sir Archibald Islay Campbell, 3rd Bt**; *b* 15 May 1825; *m* 1 July 1858 Lady Agnes Grosvenor (*m* 2nd 5 Dec 1871 Philip Frank, MD, and *d* 22 Jan 1909), 7th dau of 2nd Marquess of Westminster (*see* WESTMINSTER, D), and *dsp* 11 Sept 1866

(2) **Sir George Campbell, 4th Bt**, DL Lanarks, Capt 1st Dragoons; *b* 27 April 1829; *m* 8 June 1858 Margaret Anne Maria (*d* 3 March 1904), dau of Sir Edward Borough, 2nd Bt; *dsp* 17 Feb 1874

3 George Ramsay, HEIC CS; *b* 25 March 1800; *m* 26 June 1851 Lucy (*d* 24 Nov 1886), dau of Thomas Spencer Lindsey, of Hollymount, Co Mayo, and *d* 24 Nov 1861, leaving issue:

(1) ARCHIBALD SPENCER LINDSEY (Sir), **5th Bt**

(2) James Ramsay, of Ardachy, Inverness-shire, Lt-Col Shropshire LI; *b* 23 April 1855; *m* 28 Sept 1896 Alice Mildred (*d* 13 Nov 1914), dau of Sir Victor Alexander Brooke, 3rd Bt (*see* BROOKEBOROUGH, V), and *d* 12 Jan 1924

(1) Hester Elizabeth Susan Mary; *d* unm 28 Aug 1944

4 James; *b* 10 Oct 1805; HEIC 1824–34, wine merchant, co-fndr Cockburn & Campbell, of Edinburgh; *dsp* 1850

5 Andrew Ramsay (Rev); *b* 2 Aug 1813; Rector Aston 1853–72, Preb York 1871; *m* 2 March 1848 Mary Elphinstone Charlotte (*d* 4 July 1871), dau of John Anstruther Thomson, of Charleton, Fife (*see* ANSTRUTHER, Bt), and *d* 4 Nov 1874, leaving issue:

(1) Archibald John; *b* 14 March 1849; *d* 4 Jan 1872

(2) James Wallace; *b* 9 June 1852; *d* 1891

(3) Charles Ramsay; *b* 27 April 1860; *d* 1873

(1) Clementina Elizabeth; *b* 2 April 1855; *d* unm 9 Feb 1949

(2) Mary Louisa; *b* 9 Sept 1858; *d* 1860

1 Susan; *b* 1801; *m* 1822 William Grant of Congalton, Haddington, and *d* his widow 6 Dec 1868, leaving issue

2 Elizabeth Anne; *b* 1804; *m* 21 June 1824 8th Earl of Leven and (7th Earl of) Melville (*qv*) and *d* 6 Nov 1863, leaving issue

3 Catherine Amelia; *b* 1810; *m* 22 Feb 1854 Rev Henry Peisley Herbert Stepney (*d* 1885), 2nd s of Herbert Stepney, of Durrow Abbey, King's Co, and *dsp*, and *d* 1868

The 4th Bt's cousin,

Sir Archibald Spencer Lindsey Campbell, 5th Bt, DL, JP Dunbartonshire, JP Argyll and Glasgow; advocate Scottish Bar; *b* 27 June 1852; *educ* Univ Coll Oxford (BA); *m* 18 Jan 1887 Harriett Katherine Grace (*d* 28 April 1940), 4th dau of Col Arthur John Reynell-Pack, CB, of Avisford, Sussex, and had issue:

1 GEORGE ILAY (Sir), **6th Bt**

1 Lucy Katherine Grace; *b* 24 June 1896; *m* 25 Nov 1925 Charles William Herdman (*d* 1956) and *d* 1981, leaving issue

Sir ARCHIBALD *d* 1 March 1941; his only son,

Sir George Ilay Campbell, 6th Bt, DL, JP Argyllshire; *educ* Harrow and Ch Ch Oxford, Capt Argyll and Sutherland Highrs, memb Roy Co Archers, pres Roy Scottish Forestry Soc, served WW I and WW II 1940–43 (ROC); *b* 20 Jan 1894; *m* 29 April 1926 (*divorce* in Scottish Courts 1935) Clematis Elizabeth Denys, er dau of Maj Walter Waring, JP, of Lennel, Coldstream, Berwicks, and *d* 1 April 1967, having had issue:

1 Sir ILAY MARK CAMPBELL, **7th and present Bt**

2 A son; *b* and *d* 1929

CAMPBELL OF ALLOWAY

Creation: B. (LP, UK) 1981.

THE BARON CAMPBELL OF ALLOWAY, of Ayr, in the District of Kyle and Carrick (Alan Robertson Campbell, QC 1965) [The Rt Hon The Lord Campbell of Alloway QC, 2 King's Bench Walk, Temple, London EC4Y 7DE]; *b* 24 May 1917; *educ* Aldenham, Ecole des Sciences Politiques Paris and Trinity Hall Cambridge (MA); WWII: Lt RA (SR) 1939, (POW Colditz 1940–45); barrister Inner Temple 1939, Bencher 1972, Recorder Crown Court 1976–89; Chm Legal Research Ctee Soc C Lawyers 1968–80, memb Law Advsy Ctee Br Cncl 1974–82; Memb Management Ctee UK Assoc European Law 1975–90; author: *Restrictive Trade Practices and Monopolies* (with Ld Wilberforce, 1956, 2nd ed 1966, supplements 1 and 2 1973), *Restrictive Trading Agreements in the Common Market* (1964, supplement 1965), *Common Market Law* (vols 1 and 2 1969, vol 3 1973, supplement 1975), *Industrial Relations Act* (1971), *EC Competition Law* (1980), *Trade Unions and the Individual* (1980); *m* 1957 *Vivien, dau of Comd A H de Kantzow, DSO, RN

Lineage: JOHN KENNETH CAMPBELL; had issue:

ALAN ROBERTSON, *cr* a **Baron**

CAMPBELL OF CROY

Arms: Gyronny of eight or and sable, overall on a fess ermine two pheons points upwards gules. **Crest:** Between two sprays of red roses barbed and leaved proper and tied in base with a riband or, a lyre sable. **Supporters:** Dexter, an osprey; sinister, a curlew, both proper. **Motto:** *Dulce patriæ servire* ('It is sweet to serve one's family'). **Creation:** B. (LP, UK) 1974.

THE BARON CAMPBELL OF CROY, of Croy, Co Nairn (Gordon Thomas Calthrop Campbell, MC and bar, PC 1970) [The Rt Hon The Lord Campbell of Croy MC and bar PC, Holme Rose, Cawdor, Nairn IV12 5XT]; *b* 8 June 1921; *educ* Wellington; WWII NW Europe, OC 320 Field Bty 15th (Scottish) Div 1942–45 (disabled), Maj RA; Dip Serv 1946–57: UK Mission UN New York 1949–52, Priv Sec to Sec Cabinet 1954–56, 1st Sec Vienna 1956–57; MP (C) Moray and Nairn 1959–74, Govt Whip 1961–63, Parly U-Sec Scotland 1963–64, Sec State Scotland 1970–74; consultant Chevron Cos 1975–94, chm Stoic Insur Servs 1979–93, dir Alliance Bldg Soc 1983–, Alliance and Leicester Bldg Soc 1985–92; Chm (Scotland) Internat Year Disabled People 1981; V-Lt Nairn 1988–; Pres Anglo-Austrian Soc 1991–; *m* 1949 *Nicola Elizabeth Gina, dau of Capt Geoffrey Spencer Madan (*see* NOBLE, Bt), and has issue:

1 *Colin Ian Calthrop; *b* 1950; *educ* Eton and Trin Coll Cambridge

1 *Alastair James Calthrop [Lt-Col The Hon Alastair Campbell, Holme Rose, Cawdor, Nairn]; *b* 1952; *educ* Eton and Wadham Coll Oxford (MA); comm'd Queen's Own Highlanders 1973, Lt-Col 1991, memb Roy Co Archers; FRGS; *m* 1993 *Primrose Felicia, er dau of William Henry Tugwell Palmer (*see* LONGFORD, E), of York, and has issue:

(1) *Ferdinand James Marc; *b* 1994
(2) *Edward Henry Brunel; *b* 1995
(1) *Leonora Mary Felicia; *b* 1995

2 *Christina Marjorie [The Hon Mrs Clarfelt, 8 Vicarage Gdns, London W8]; *b* 1953; *m* 1980 *Mark Michael Clarfelt, s of Jack Clarfelt, of Timsbury, Hants, and has:

(1) *Max; *b* 1986
(1) *Alice Nicola Irene; *b* 1982
(2) *Tessa; *b* 1984
(3) *Harriet; *b* 1990
(4) *Kate; *b* 1994

Lineage: Maj-Gen JAMES ALEXANDER CAMPBELL, DSO and bar; had:

GORDON THOMAS CALTHROP, *cr* a **Baron**

CAMPBELL-ORDE

Arms: Quarterly, 1st and 4th, sa., three salmon hauriant per pale arg. and or (for ORDE); 2nd and 3rd, gyronny of eight or and sa., a bordure componée erm. and vert., in the centre a crescent of the last for difference (for CAMPBELL). **Crests:** 1 An elk's head erased or, gorged with a collar invected sa. (for ORDE), 2 A dexter hand ppr., holding a spur or, strap ppr. **Mottoes:** *Mitis et fortis* ('Gentle and Strong') and 'Forget not' (over crests 1 and 2 respectively). **Creation:** Bt. (GB) 9 Aug 1790.

SIR JOHN ALEXANDER CAMPBELL-ORDE, 6TH BT, of Morpeth, Co Northumberland [Sir John Campbell-Orde Bt, PO Box 22974, Nashville TN 37202, USA]; *b* 11 May 1943; *s f* 1969; *educ* Gordonstoun; art dealer; *m* 20 March 1973 (*divorce* 1991) Lacy Ralls, only dau of T Grady Gallant, of Nashville, and has issue:

1 +JOHN SIMON ARTHUR; *b* 15 Aug 1981
1 *Alexandra Louise; *b* 8 Jan 1974
2 *Alice Theodora; *b* 3 April 1976
3 *Octavia Maie; *b* 9 May 1978

Lineage: JOHN ORDE, of Morpeth, DL (bro of 1st Baron Bolton; *qv*); had a 3rd s:

Sir John Orde, 1st Bt (GB, so *cr* 9 Aug 1790; Adml of the Red, Govr Dominica 1783–93, MP Yarmouth 1807–12; *b* 22 Dec 1751; *m* 1st 1781 Margaret Emma (*dsps* 13 Sept 1790), dau and coheir of Richard Stephens, of St Helena, S Carolina; *m* 2nd 3 Dec 1793 Jane (*d* 16 Sept 1829), er dau of John Frere, JP, FRS, FSA, of Roydon Hall, Norfolk, and Finningham, Suffolk, and *d* 19 Feb 1824, having by her had, with a dau (Anna Maria Fenn, *d* unm 17 Aug 1894 aged 88):

Sir John Powlett Orde, 2nd Bt; *educ* Ch Ch Oxford (BA); *b* 9A June 1803; *m* 1st 15 June 1826 Eliza (*d* 13 June 1829), est dau and coheir of Peter Campbell, of Kilmory, Argyll, of the Auchinbreck branch of the Campbells, and had issue, with another dau (*d* unm):

1 JOHN WILLIAM POWLETT (Sir), **3rd Bt**
1 Jane Ellen; *m* 8 Dec 1857 Rev Frederick Paget Wilkinson (*d* 29 Oct 1892, *see* SIMEON, Bt), and *d* 1 March 1893, leaving issue

Sir John *m* 2nd 14 June 1832 Beatrice (*d* 29 July 1895 aged 81), yst dau of James Edwards, of Harrow-on-the-Hill, and by her had issue, with two sons (*d* young):

2 Beatrice Catherine; *d* 23 April 1921

Sir JOHN *d* 11 Dec 1878, and was *s* by his only son,

Sir JOHN WILLIAM POWLETT ORDE later CAMPBELL-ORDE (roy licence 16 Jan 1880), **3rd Bt**, Capt 42nd Highrs; *b* 23 Feb 1827; *m* 1st 17 July 1862 Alice Louisa (*d* 7 Jan 1883), only sis of Sir Arthur Middleton, 7th Bt (*qv*), and had issue:

1 ARTHUR JOHN (Sir), **4th Bt**
2 Colin Ridley, JP Argyll, Lt Lovat Scouts IY; *b* 25 Feb 1867; *m* 18 Nov 1896 Winifred Harriet (*d* 26 Dec 1967 aged 95), dau of Capt John Campbell Stewart, of Fasnacloich, and *d* 25 Sept 1932, leaving issue, with a dau (*d* unm):

(1) Ronald Charles, Lt RFA WW I 1914–19 (wounded); *b* 24 Sept 1897; *d* 24 Feb 1926

(2) Alan Colin, CBE (1943), AFC (1919), FRAeS, served WW I (wounded, despatches) as Flt Sub Lt RNAS and F/O RAF, Instr and Advr to Chinese Govt Peking 1921–23, Instr and later Ch Test Pilot Sir W G Armstrong-Whitworth Aircraft Ltd 1924–36, Operational Mgr Br Airways 1936–39 and Imp Airways 1939–40, Operational Dir BOAC 1940–43, special duties BOAC with Tport Cmd RAF 1943–44, Assist to Chm BOAC 1944–46, Devpt Dir to 1957, aviation consultant 1958 on; *b* 4 Oct 1898; *educ* Sherborne; *m* 27 Oct 1951 Beatrice (*d* 20 Nov 1989), formerly w of Ivor Herbert McClure, DSO, OBE, of Montreal, and est dau of Rev Henry Meyrick Eliott-Drake Briscoe, MA, Rector Burnham Thorpe, Norfolk (*see* BRISCOE, Bt), and *d* 18 April 1992

(3) Bernard Arthur, pncpl Bank of England; *b* 26 Jan 1901; *m* 1st 4 Sept 1939 (*divorce* 1955) Pamela (*d* 1979), formerly w of Col Robert Hugh Arthur Lucas, of Oakash, Chaddleworth, Berks, and er dau of Brig-Gen John Cecil Wray, CB, CMG, CVO, TD, of 2 Walton St, London SW3, and had issue:

1a *Jennifer Mary [Mrs Reuben Gunn, 39 Whitworth Close, Gosport, Hants PO12 3PF]; *b* 21 May 1940; *educ* Convent Sacred Heart Woldingham, Sur-

rey; *m* 1st 25 May 1959 (*divorce* 1971) Robin Alfred Clive Salmon, MN, son of Col A W Salmon, of Channel Haven, Kingsdown Rd, Walmer, Kent, and has issue:
1b *Timothy John; *b* 24 May 1960
2b *Robert Bernard; *b* 11 Nov 1961
1b *Belinda Jane; *b* 25 March 1964
1a (cont.) Mrs Jennifer Salmon *m* 2nd 24 June 1977 *Reuben Harry Gunn and has further issue:
2b *Sarah Louise; *b* 1978
(3) (cont.) Bernard Campbell-Orde *m* 2nd 5 Oct 1955 *Nancy Mabyn Bradley [Mrs Bernard Campbell-Orde, Old Farm, Trebetherick, Wadebridge, Cornwall], dau of Maj Thomas Langdon Trethewy, DCLI, and *d* 4 Oct 1974
(4) Peter Stewart, Capt Royal Norfolk Regt, served WW II; *b* 12 June 1906; *m* 2 March 1940 *Margaret Constance (*m* 2nd 5 Jan 1946 Maj Edward Eyre Williams, 5th Fus, s of Maj Edward Eyre Williams, DSO), yr dau of Lt-Col John Clayton Atkinson, Roy Norfolk Regt, of Sheringham, Norfolk, and *d* of wounds recd in action Singapore 8 Feb 1942, having had issue:
1a Richard Stewart; *b* posthumously 29 April 1942, *d* same day
(5) Ian Ridley, AE and bar, W/Cdr RAuxAF WW II (despatches), Advsr and Dir Tactical Devpt USAF 1942–43; *b* 18 June 1907; *m* 6 Nov 1939 Myrtle Maud (*d* 1998), formerly w of — Welsh and only dau of Robert van Gruisen Adamson, of Liverpool, UK, and Boston, USA
(6) Harry Eustace, Yorks Regnl Sec Arthritis and Rheumatism Cncl for Research, W/Cdr RAF (ret 1961), Lt Roy Scots Fus (TA), served WW II Europe and Middle East; *b* 8 April 1914; *educ* Roy GS Guildford; *m* 6 July 1940 *Mary Beatrice, 2nd dau of Percy Bruce Elliott, JP, of Middleham House, Ripon, Yorks
3 Henry Campbell; *b* 14 Aug 1877; *m* 1st 1901 Marie Elizabeth (*d* 9 Dec 1913), dau of John S Barr, of Newcastle, and had issue:
(1) *Beatrice Constance; *b* 25 Feb 1903; *m* 1st 13 June 1929 Rodney Whittard Doherty, of Buenos Aires, and has issue. He *d* 15 Feb 1953. She *m* 2nd 1956 Edward Errol Heriot-Maitland, 5th son of Frederick Heriot-Maitland (*see* LAUDERDALE, E). He *d* 13 Sept 1964
3 (cont.) Henry Campbell-Orde *m* 2nd 14 Nov 1927 Ruth (*d* 1985), only dau of Robert Thomas, of Penarth, S Wales, and *d* 1 Nov 1954, having by her had issue:
(1) +Alexander Powlett [Alexander Campbell-Orde Esq, Willow Cottage, Newbridge Green, Upton-on-Severn, Worcs], Petty Offr (Radar Electrical Artificer) RN (ret); *b* 5 Sept 1928
(2) +Colin Robert [Colin Campbell-Orde Esq, Cruachan, Kingweston Rd, Charlton Mackrell, Somerton, Som TA11 6AH], CEng, MIMechE, MRAeS; *b* 19 March 1935; *m* 8 July 1959 *Audrey Isobel, dau of Raymond S Griffiths, of Brentford, Middx, and has issue:
1a +Andrew Colin [Andrew Campbell-Orde Esq, 48 Oak Terr, Board Cross, Shepton Mallet, Somerset BA4 5DY]; *b* 28 Nov 1969; *educ* Millfield; ACCA; *m* 1991 *Susan, dau of Brian Parsons and formerly w of Peter Hill, and has issue:
1b +Joseph Harry; *b* 1993
1b *Annie Grace; *b* 1995
1a *Tamzin Ruth [Mrs Dennis Elliott, 60 Grove Ave, Yeovil, Somerset BA20 2BE]; *b* 1960; *m* 1985 *Dennis David James Elliott and has issue:
1b *Adam David Stewart; *b* 1986
2b *Christopher James Robert; *b* 1988
3b *Daniel Dennis James; *b* 1991
2a *Sarah Elizabeth [Mrs David Read, Box 384, Rapid City, Manitoba ROK 1WO, Canada]; *b* 29 Nov 1965; *m* 1993 *David Montague Read and has
1b *Callum Stewart Montagu; *b* 1995
2b *Benjamin Robert; *b* 1997
(2) *Morwenna, SRN; *b* 24 Aug 1929; *m* 17 March 1951 (*divorce* 19–) George Ernest Turner, MA, son of Ernest Turner, of Cwmavon House, Cwmavon, Mon, and has issue:
1a *Ian George; *b* 13 Aug 1965
1a *Tracey Christine; *b* 6 Aug 1958
2a *Alison Meryl; *b* 1 Nov 1961; *m* 1984 *Stephen Kingdon
1 Gertrude Isabel; *m* 27 Feb 1894 Barnett Matthews, of Newcastle-on-Tyne, and *d* 1 March 1914, leaving issue
2 Louisa Beatrice; *m* 16 Dec 1891 Arthur Scott Williams, JP, FRGS, of Hill House, Yetminster, Dorset, 4th son of Montague Williams, DL, JP, of Woodland Ho, Dorset, and *d* 18 Feb 1929, leaving issue. He *d* 17 April 1953
3 Alice Constance; *m* 20 Dec 1904 (*divorce* 1939) Frederic John Poynton, MD, FRCP, and *d* 1995, leaving issue. He *d* 29 Oct 1943
Sir John *m* 2nd 20 Dec 1884 Louisa Charlotte Temple (*d* 15 Feb 1937), dau of Robert Temple Frere, MD, of Harley Street, London W, and *d* 12 Oct 1897
His est son,
Sir Arthur John Campbell-Orde, 4th Bt, DL, JP Argyllshire, JP Inverness-shire, Maj 8th Bn Cameron Highrs, Maj Lovat Scouts Yeo, formerly Lt 3rd Bn QO Cameron Highrs, Lt Lovat Scouts S Africa 1900–01 and WW I; *b* 13 April 1865; *m* 6 Jan 1892 Maie Ronald (*d* 2 Sept 1955), est dau of John Campbell Stewart, late Capt 72nd Highrs, of Fasnacloich, Argyll, and had issue:
1 John Vernon, Lt 5th Service Bn Cameron Highrs, served WW I; *b* 19 Jan 1894; *d* 14 Oct 1917
2 SIMON ARTHUR (Sir), **5th Bt**
1 Alice Maie; *b* 1897; *m* 7 Nov 1917 Rev James Humphrey Copner Macfarlane-Barrow (*d* 1943), Rector All Saints' Inveraray, Argyll, 2nd s of John Burton Barrow, of Ringwood Hall, Derby, and *d* Oct 1995, having had:
(1) Seumas Donnchadh MACFARLANE-BARROW later MACFARLANE (deed poll 1968); *b* 8 April 1922; *m* 17 Nov 1956 *Beatrice Harriet [Mrs Seumas MacFarlane, 99 Gregory St, Geraldton WA 6530, Australia], dau of Capt Christopher St Barbe Shields, of Higher Holditch, Chard, Somerset, and *d* 1981, having had issue:
1a *James Peter Raymund; *b* 31 Aug 1957
2a *Simon Ruairidh; *b* 2 Oct 1958
3a *Christopher Donnchadh Diarmad; *b* 19 Nov 1959
4a *Ian Andrew; *b* 8 April 1963
1a *Rosamund Lucy Alice; *b* 16 Sept 1961
2a *Julia Maie Louise; *b* 21 March 1967
(2) *Padruig Francis [Padruig Esq, Quaintways, Killiney Hill Rd, Killiney, Co Dublin, Ireland], DipArch Aberdeen, ARIBA; *b* 17 Sept 1929; *educ* Ampleforth; *m* 21 Jan 1967 *Ann Maria, yr dau of Thomas F Coen, of Raheen House, Raheen, Gort, Co Galway, and has issue:
1a *Sine Mary; *b* 21 Nov 1968
2a *Ailse Brighde; *b* 1970
3a *Dearbhail Anna; *b* 1971
(3) *Ian Tearlach MACFARLANE-BARROW later MACFARLANE (dropped BARROW 1977) [Ian MacFarlane Esq, Glenfinnan House, Glenfinnan, Inverness-shire]; *b* 16 Dec 1931; *m* 2 May 1966 *Isobel Nicholas, only dau of Robert Durham Alexander, of 1 Merchiston Crescent, Edinburgh 10, and has issue:
1a *Duncan James; *b* 23 Jan 1969
2a *Ian Robert; *b* 1970
1a *Jane Isabelle; *b* 7 April 1967
(4) *Calum Seumas [Calum MacFarlane-Barrow Esq, Craig Lodge, Dalmally, Argyll]; *b* 2 Dec 1932; *m* 19 May 1962 *Mary Ann, er dau of Maj Gabriel Thomas Grisewood, of Inveramie, Strathnairn, Inverness-shire, and has issue:
1a *Magnus Calum; *b* 7 Feb 1968
1a *Ruth Magdalene; *b* 14 March 1963
(4) (cont.) Mr and Mrs Calum Macfarlane-Barrow also adopted:
*Seumas Magnus; *b* 26 Sept 1965
*Fergus Paul; *b* 11 Jan 1967
*Mark Christopher Murray; *b* 1973
(1) Eilidh Marsali; *b* 31 July 1919; *d* unm 24 Aug 1968
(2) Maie Bridget; *b* 23 Nov 1926; *m* Feb 1962 Donald Joseph MacDonald (*d* 6 April 1967) and *d* 25 Sept 1996, leaving:
1a *Donald Hamish; *b* 25 Dec 1962
2a *Alastair Ninian; *b* 7 Jan 1964
1a *Eilidh Mairi; *b* 14 April 1965
2a *Catherine Margaret [Miss Catherine MacDonald, 3 Bohuntin, Roy Bridge, Inverness-shire PH31 4AH]s; *b* 1 Aug 1966
2 Winifred Beatrice; *d* unm 31 July 1952
3 *Muriel Frances
Sir ARTHUR *d* 1 Feb 1933 and was *s* by his only son,
Sir Simon Arthur Campbell-Orde, 5th Bt, TD (1954); *educ* Charterhouse, Maj Lovat Scouts Yeo (TA) WW II; *b* 15 July 1907; *m* 30 April 1938 Eleanor Hyde (*d* 18 May 1996), est dau of Col Humphrey Watts, OBE, TD, of Haslington Hall, Cheshire, and *d* 23 Aug 1969, leaving issue:
1 Sir JOHN ALEXANDER CAMPBELL-ORDE, **6th and present Bt**
2 +Peter Humphrey [Peter Campbell-Orde Esq, 53 Bell St, Shaftesbury, Dorset SP7 8AE]; *b* 18 June 1946; *educ* Gordonstoun; *m* 1st 1976 (*divorce* 1992) Mrs Perdita Bennett, dau of Alexander Peter Fordham Watt and formerly w of Richard Bennett; *m* 2nd 1992 *Penelope Jane Armstrong, dau of Mark Alexander Wynter-Blyth, MA, pncpl The Rajkumar Coll, Rajkot, India
1 *(Caroline) Jane [Mrs Christopher Davies, Westgate House, Dedham, Colchester, Essex CO7 6HJ]; *b* 21 Nov 1940; *educ* North Foreland Lodge and Sorbonne; *m* 1 April 1967 *Christopher John Davies, MA, er s of Col John A Davies, of Limes, Therfield, Herts, and has issue:
(1) *(John) Humphrey Stewart; *b* 6 May 1969
(2) *(Simon) William Gardner; *b* 6 June 1970; *educ* Colchester Roy GS and Cambridge (MA)
(1) *Caroline Celia Hyde; *b* 3 Nov 1973; *educ* Claremont Sch and Camberwell Coll of Art

CAMROSE

Arms: Arg. three bars gu., over all a pile erm. **Crest:** A griffin sejant regardant sa., collared or. **Supporters:** On either side a wolf ppr. gorged with a collar or, pendent therefrom an escutcheon sa., charged with two pens in saltire arg. **Motto:** *Vivere virtute* ('Living with courage'). **Badge:** A daffodil leaved and slipped ppr. between two roses gu., barbed, seeded, leaved and slipped also ppr., enfiled by a viscount's coronet or. **Creations:** Bt (UK) 4 July 1921; B. (UK) 19 June 1929, V. (UK) 20 Jan 1941.

THE 3RD VISCOUNT CAMROSE, of Hackwood Park, Co Southampton, **Baron Camrose**, of Long Cross, Surrey, and a **Baronet**; *see* HARTWELL, B

CARBERY

Arms: Quarterly, 1st and 4th, sa. two bars or, in chief three mullets of the last (for FREKE); 2nd and 3rd, arg. three boar's heads couped sa. (for EVANS). **Crests:** 1 A bull's head couped at the neck sa., collared and chained or (for FREKE), 2 A demi-lion rampant-regardant or, holding between the paws a boar's head as in the arms (for EVANS). **Supporters:** Two lions regardant or, ducally crowned az. **Motto:** *Libertas* ('Liberty'). **Creations:** B. (I) 9 May 1715, Bt. (I) 15 July 1768.

THE 11TH BARON CARBERY, of Carbery, Co Cork, and a **Baronet** (Sir Peter Ralfe Harrington Evans-Freke, Bt) [The Rt Hon The Lord Carbery, 2 Hayes Court, Sunnyside, London SW19 4SH]; *b* 20 March 1920; *s* unc 1970; *educ* Downside; MICE, late Capt RE in India and Burma WW II, memb London Stock Exchange, memb of IOD, dir Equine and Livestock Insur Co; *m* 27 Dec 1941 *Joyzelle Mary, only child of Herbert Binnie, of Sydney, NSW, and has issue:

1 +MICHAEL PETER; *b* 11 Oct 1942; *educ* Downside, Ch Ch Oxford (BA 1964, MA 1969) and U of Strathclyde; *m* 9 Sept 1967 *Claudia Janet Elizabeth, only dau of Capt Percy Lionel Cecil Gurney, of Little Chart, Penshurst, Kent, and has issue:

(1) +Dominic Ralfe Cecil; *b* 29 June 1969

(1) *Richenda Clare; *b* 28 Sept 1971

(2) *Isabel Lucy; *b* 3 Oct 1973

(3) *Anna-Louise; *b* 1979

2 +John Anthony [The Hon John Evans-Freke, Lynturk Home Farm, Alford, Aberdeenshire AB33 8DU]; *b* 1949; *educ* Downside and RAC Cirencester; FRICS, late land agent to Duke of Northumberland; *m* 1972 *Veronica Jane, yst dau of Maj Eric Williams, of House of Lynturk, Alford, Aberdeenshire, and has issue:

(1) +James Eric; *b* 1976

(2) +Charles William Anthony; *b* 1981

(1) *Flora Mary; *b* 1979

3 +Stephen Ralfe [The Hon Stephen Evans-Freke, The Corner House, Norfolk, Conn 06058, USA; Casa Niños, 1320 Marlborough Rd, Hillsborough, CA 94010, USA]; *b* 1952; *educ* Downside and Trin Coll Cambridge (BA); Pres Paine Webber Devpt Corp USA; *m* 1990 *Valerie Beattie Johnson, est dau of Russell Beattie, of Stonington, Conn., and has issue:

(1) +Yorick Peter; *b* 1992

(2) +Roland Charles Goodheart; *b* 1993

1 *Maura Clare [The Hon Mrs Fanshawe, Rafters, Waldron, Heathfield, E Sussex TN21 0QY]; *b* 1946; late admin assist RCM; *m* 1966 *Richard Henry William Fanshawe, and has issue (*see* LINDSEY and ABINGDON, E)

2 *Angela Mary; *b* 1954; *m* 1975 *Martin David Tomlins, and has issue:

(1) *Alexander Peter David; *b* 1978

(2) *William John Anthony; *b* 1981

Carbery, other creations: Sir William de Bermingham, of Carbery, Co Kildare, was made Baron Carbery in the Irish peerage in 1541. On the death of his son at the age of four in 1550 the title expired. Nearly 80 years later John Vaughan, of a Carmarthenshire family, and who had been MP for that county in 1601 and 1620–22, was created Earl of Carbery, Co Cork, again in the Irish peerage. His son the 2nd Earl was one of the chief royalist commanders in southwest Wales during the Civil War. With the death in January 1712/3 of the 3rd Earl, grandson of the original grantee, the earldom expired. Both the 2nd and 3rd and last Earls were patrons of men of letters, the former being the dedicatee of the devotional writer Jeremy Taylor (much of whose best work was composed at Golden Grove, Lord Carbery's Carmarthenshire seat), while the latter was a supporter of Dryden. As was often the case in the Restoration period, the 3rd Earl combined literary sensibility with what Pepys, his contemporary, called great lewdness. He also went out to Jamaica as Governor and was said to have sold many of the Welsh gentlemen who accompanied him there into slavery.

Lineage: GEORGE EVANS, PC (in or after 1688), of Bulgaden Hall, Co Limerick; barrister, MP Co Limerick and Charleville, Co Cork; *m* 1679 Mary, dau of John Eyre, PC, of Eyre Court, Co Galway, and had, with seven daus:

1 GEORGE, **1st Baron**

2 Eyre, of Portrane, Co Dublin, barrister, MP Co Limerick; *m* Sarah, 2nd dau and coheir of T Dixon, of Ballylackin, Co Cork, and had, with other issue:

(1) Hampden, Capt 54th Regt; *m* July 1769 Margaret, 2nd dau of Joshua Davis, barrister, and *d* 22 April 1820, leaving issue:

1a George, of Portrane, PC, MP Co Dublin; *m* 21 Aug 1805 Sophia (*d* 24 April 1853), only dau of Sir John Parnell, 2nd Bt (*see* CONGLETON, B), and *dsp* 2nd July 1842

2a Joshua, barrister and Commr of Bankruptcy; *m* Eleanor, only dau of R Harrison, and *dsp* 1864

3a Eyre Dixon, of Liverpool, merchant; *m* Jessie, dau of Alexander Robertson, of Edinburgh, and *d* 2 Oct 1862, leaving issue:

1b George, of Portrane; *b* 27 July 1831; *m* 28 Aug 1855 Harriet Mary (*m* 2nd 1 June 1875 John Gordon, of Milrig, Ayrshire, who *dsp* 17 Sept 1900), yst dau of Col Chidley Coote, of Huntington, Queen's Co (*see* COOTE, Bt), and *dsp* 26 May 1873

1b Margaret; *m* 1852 John Donald MacNeale, and *d* 19 May 1874, leaving three daus. He *d* 22 Oct 1883

1a Mary; *m* Gen William Lawless, and *d* 1854

2a Anne; *m* George Putland, of Baryhead, Co Wicklow, and *d* 20 Oct 1850. He *d* 18 Nov 1841

3a Sidney Elizabeth; *m* Rev Thomas Acton, of W Aston, Co Wicklow. He *d* 12 Aug 1846

3 Thomas, of Miltown Castle, Co Cork, MP Castlemartyr; *m* 18 May 1722 Mary (*d* 1762), 3rd dau of James Waller, of Castletown, Co Limerick, Govr of Kinsale, and *d* 17 Sept 1753, leaving with other issue:

(1) Eyre, of Miltown Castle; *m* 16 July 1757 Mary (*d* 29 Nov 1825), only dau and heiress of Thomas Williams, of Ballymenagh, Co Limerick, and *d* 5 April 1773, leaving, with three daus:

1a Eyre, of Ash Hill Towers, Co Limerick; *b* 23 May 1773; *m* 20 March 1805 Anna (*d* 24 June 1857), est dau of Robert Maunsell, of Rumbo Ho, E Indies, and a Memb of Cncl at Madras, and *d* 29 Jan 1856, having had issue:

1b Eyre; *b* 5 May 1806; *m* 6 Dec 1837 Hon Sophia Crofton (*d* 18 Dec 1885), sis of 2nd Baron Crofton (*qv*), and *d* 17 July 1852, leaving, with other issue (*dsp* or unm):

1c Elystan Eyre, of Ash Hill Towers; *b* 23 June 1845; *m* 21 Dec 1876 Isabella, dau of Rev Philip Smith, of Cherrymount, Co Meath, and widow of Richard Beardsley, US Consul Gen in Egypt, and *dsp* Feb 1888

2b Robert Maunsell (Ven), Archdeacon of Cloyne; *b* 4 May 1808; *m* 6 Feb 1835 Deborah, 3rd dau of William Cassubon Purdon, of Tinerana, Co Clare, and *dsp* 1 May 1890

3b George Thomas, Maj 47th Regt; *b* 17 Dec 1809; *m* 19 Jan 1841 Louisa Barbara (*d* 7 Jan 1890), 2nd dau of Trevor Corry, of Newry, and *d* 16 Oct 1898, having had issue:

1c Eyre Frederick FitzGeorge, of Clooneavin, Otago; *b* 23 Feb 1842; *m* 1st 14 April 1868 Charlotte (*d* 22 July 1882), dau of James Lees, of Oldham, Lancs, and had issue:

1d Percy; *b* 15 Sept 1871; *m* 1916 Ethel Margaret (*d* 15 Dec 1951), dau of T Dickson, of Wanganui, NZ, and *d* 26 April 1959, having had issue:

1e Maurice Lees; *b* 24 Sept 1922; *d* 14 June 1924

1e *Jean Charlotte; *b* 1917; *educ* Victoria U Coll, Wellington, NZ (MA); *m* 27 Dec 1960 Robert Gibson Bauld, 2nd son of John Bauld, of Wanganui, NZ

2e *Margaret Lees; *b* 1925; *m* 17 May 1947 (*divorce* 1991) Clifford Roy Dewe

2d Eyre; *b* 13 June 1874; *d* 26 Oct 1944

3d Lloyd; *b* 28 Sept 1875; *d* Feb 1927

4d George; *b* 15 Dec 1876; *d* 20 Jan 1877

5d Savage; *b* 5 Jan 1878; *m* 1st 26 Dec 1902 (*divorce* 1920) Jane Ann, dau of H Healey, of Naseby, NZ; *m* 2nd 11 Oct 1927 Alicia Madeline Isobel, only dau of Charles Gifford-Moore, of Omaru, NZ; *m* 3rd *Lilian Amelia, dau of Joseph Fair, of Headford, Co Galway, and *d* 1 May 1968, having by his 1st w had issue:

1e +Trevor George Corry, OBE (1946), TD, JP (W Sussex 1955), served WW II as Lt-Col Roy Sussex Regt; *b* 6 Feb 1910; *educ* abroad and RAC Cirencester; *m* 27 Nov 1937 *Sara Gwendolyn, dau of R C Drummond, of Masterton, NZ, and has issue:

1f +Michael George Corry [Michael Evans Esq, 10 Moor Lane, Clevedon, Avon BS8 4IJ]; *b* 11 June 1938; *educ* Rugby and RAC Cirencester; land agent

2f +Stephen Telford Eyre; *b* 31 Aug 1939; *educ* Rugby and RAC Cirencester; *m* 31 Jan 1970 *Susan Biron Young, dau of Michael Pallister Young, of Bishopsbourne, Kent

3f +Patrick Robert Heugh Eyre [Patrick Evans Esq, Border Farm, Closworth, Yeovil, Som BA22 9SZ]]; *b* 5 May 1944; *educ* Nautical Coll Pangbourne; *m* 26 Sept 1970 *Jennifer Robin, dau of Capt Brian Granville White, RM, of Chaldon, Surrey, and has issue:

1g +James Richard Eyre; *b* 1975

1g *Caroline Nicola Corry; *b* 1974

1e Nina Corry; *b* 30 Oct 1903; *m* 1st 16 July 1934 Walter Briggs (*d* 29 Oct 1938), of Linden Hall, Borwick, Carnforth, Lancs; *m* 2nd 1949 Robert Workman

2e *Kathleen Ann; *b* 16 July 1906; *m* 16 Dec 1943 Capt Edward Copus, late RASC, son of George Copus, of Guildford, Surrey

3e Sylvia Elizabeth; *b* 1 Nov 1907; *m* 1947 Hubert Stanley Chittick, MA, son of Charles Chittick, of Bournemouth, Hants. He *d* 1 May 1963

6d Robert; *b* 23 Feb, *d* 20 April 1879

7d James; *b* 9 Aug 1881; *ka* 1916

8d Eric (Rev), CF NZ Expdny Forces 1917–18; *b* 16 July 1882; *m* 4 Jan 1910 Dora Handforth (*d* 1980), of Onerhai, Auckland, NZ, and *d* 26 April 1970, having had issue:

1e +Philip Eyre (Rev), LTh; *b* 1910; *m* 14 Dec 1935 *Florence Anne, 2nd dau of Richard U Reeves, of Melbourne, and *d* 1980, having had issue:

1f +Rodger Eyre [Rodger Evans Esq, 13 Templemore Dve, Templestowe, Vic 3106, Australia]; *b* 19 March 1937; *m* 10 Nov 1962 *Noreen Lorraine Evans, dau of James Alexander Cook, of 94 Reynolds Pde, Pescoe Vale S, Vic, Australia, and has issue:

1g +Stephen Rodger Eyre; *b* 1970

1g *Robyn Anne; *b* 21 Aug 1963; *m* 1988 *Rodney David Johnson

2g *Melinda Joy; *b* 11 Feb 1967; *m* 1993 *Peter John McMullen

1f *Wendy Jillian [Mrs Gilbert Turnbull, 51 Harrison St, Burwood, Vic 3125, Australia]; *b* 1 Nov 1940; *m* 28 April 1962 *Dr Gilbert Wilson Turnbull, and has issue:

1g *Leeanne Jane; *b* 10 Feb 1963; *m* 1988 *Andrew Graham Edwin Cooke, and has issue

2g *Melissa Frances; *b* 1 Jan 1965; *m* 1991 *Rodney Peter Endall

3g *Penelope Jillian; *b* 2 March 1967; *m* 1989 *Timothy James Joyce, and has issue

4g *Rosemary Ferelith; *b* 1969; *m* 1993 *John Gerard Cincotta

2e +Llewellyn Handforth; *b* 1913; *m* 1st 1940 Ivy Edith (*d* Sept 1949), dau of William Elliot, of Melbourne; *m* 2nd 1951 Una Jessie (*d* 1979), dau of Charles A Drew, of Melbourne and has issue by his 1st w:

1f +Peter Handforth (Rev) [The Rev Peter Evans, 34 Cuba St, Petone, Wellington, New Zealand]; *b* 27 July 1941; LTh Stawell; Vicar of Victoria from 1968; *m* 24 June 1967 *Merlyne Leslie Chambers, and has issue:

1g *Yona Leslie; *b* 14 April 1968; *m* 1990 *Michael Heyward

2g *Megan Joan; *b* 1970

1f *Corry Margaret; *b* 1942; *m* 1964 *Peter Owen Skilbeck, and has issue

2f *Jean Rebecca; *b* 1949; *m* 1972 *Bruce David Glover, and has issue

3e +Raymond Austin [Raymond Evans Esq, 42 Jopling St, N Ryde, NSW 2113, Australia]; *b* 25 Sept 1915; *m* 11 Jan 1958 *Lucy Margaret, dau of Walter George Blomfield, of Killara, NSW, and has issue:

1f +Bruce Raymond Blomfield; *b* 16 Aug 1962

1f *Kathryn Margaret; *b* 1959; *m* 1989 *Murray Gerrard Wilson, and has issue

4e +Denison Anthony [Denison Evans Esq, 1 Gardiner Rd, Hawthorn, Vic 3122, Australia]; *b* 1925; *m* 1962 *Janette Relleen, dau of Brian William Peacocke, of Hove, Sussex, and has issue:

1f +Charles Anthony; *b* 1963; *m* 1989 *Jane Spiers

2f +John Andrew; *b* 1966

1f *Sarah Louise; *b* 1965; *m* 1988 *Mark Anderson

1e Rachel Corry; *d* May 1913

2e *Rhoda Caroline; *b* 9 Sept 1916; *m* 15 Sept 1945 *Joseph Emerson Gibson, son of Joseph Emerson Gibson, of Korumburra, Vict, Australia, and has issue:

1f *David Warwick [David Evans Esq, RMB 464, Smeaton, Vic 3364, Australia]; *b* 15 Feb 1947; *m* 1st 11 Jan 1969 (*divorce c* 1984) Miriam Felicia, dau of Rev Philip Neilson Simmons, of Box Hill, Victoria; *m* 2nd 1991 *Ivy Virginia, dau of William Gordon Lockhart, and has issue by 1st w:

1g *Janet Katherine; *b* 17 Sept 1951

1d Ethel; *m* (*divorce* 1923) Robert Milligan, JP, of Oamaru, Otago, NZ, and *d* 29 March 1948

2d Kathleen; *d unm* 22 March 1892

3d Alice; *d* an infant, 28 Jan 1873

4d Eva; *m* 1920 Clarence James, and *d* leaving issue. He *d* 1936

1c (cont.) Eyre Evans *m* 2nd 20 Dec 1888 Mary (*d* 24 July 1920), est dau of William Alderson, of Cheltenham, and *d* 1919, having by her had further issue:

9d Thomas Charles, Lt NZ Perm Staff; *b* 1890; *m* 1st 1919 Elsa Phyllis Heckler (*d* 1924), and had issue:

1e +Francis Eyre Ogilvie; *b* 1919; *m* 1942 *Marjorie Ahradsen, and has had issue:

1f +David James Ogilvie; *b* 1953; *m* 1977 *Helen Anne Cowie, and has issue:

1g +Jeremy David Ogilvie; *b* 1980

1g *Gabrielle Helen; *b* 1978

2g *Miriam Elizabeth; *b* 1982

3g *Michaela Frances; *b* 1987

2f +Christopher Paul Ogilvie; *b* 1954

1f *Jacqueline Susan; *b* 1947; *m* 1969 *Dr James Robert Crush, and has issue

2f Elizabeth Frances; *b* 1948; *d* 1952

2e +Thomas Corry Ogilvie [Thomas Evans Esq, Forest Downs, RD2, Masterton, New Zealand]; *b* 1921; *m* *Marian Jean McIndoe, and has issue:

1f +James Peter McIndoe; *b* 1958

2f +Corry Rhys Walter; *b* 1962

1f *Elsa Corrine; *b* 1952; *m* 1973 *Ian Vincent Morgan, and has issue

2f *Marilyn Brenda; *b* 1953; *m* 1979 *John Frederick David Peach, and has issue

3f *Helen Jean; *b* 1956

3e +William Phillip Ogilvie; *b* 1924; *m* 1950 *Fay St Clair Rawlins, and has had issue:

1f +Lloyd Phillip; *b* 1955

2f Stephen William; *b* 1958; *d* 1982

1f *Susan Phyllis; *b* 1952; *m* 1979 *Graeme Edmond Millow, and has issue

9d (cont.) Thomas Evans *m* 2nd 1925 Elsie Edith Smith (*d* 1964), and *d* 23 Sept 1960, having had further issue:

1e +Ashley Ogilvie; *b* 1926; *m* 1950 *Ruth Martin Napier, of Hawkes Bay, NZ, and has issue:

1f +Neil Martin; *b* 1951

2f +Robert Denis; *b* 1954

3f +Philip Leslie; *b* 1958

4f +Allan Ashley; *b* 1960

5f +Bruce Raymond; *b* 1962

2e +Lees Ogilvie; *b* 1932 (twin); *m* 18 Sept 1954 *Rae Irene Anne Croudis, of Johnsville, Wellington, NZ, and has issue:

1f +Lawrence Thomas; *b* 28 Nov 1958

1f *Suzanne Mary; *b* 29 Nov 1955

2f *Cynthia Anne; *b* 15 July 1957

3f *Kathleen Pauline; *b* 15 June 1962

4f *Helen Lucy; *b* 28 Dec 1964

5f *Patricia Frances; *b* 18 Feb 1966

1e *Olwyn Ogilvie; *b* 1927; *m* 17 May 1952 *Eion John and has issue:

1f *Garth Raynsley; *b* 15 Feb 1953

2f *Mark Thomas; *b* 15 June 1955

1f *Tracey Elizabeth; *b* 30 Aug 1958

2e *José Ogilvie; *b* 1929

3e *Fabienne Ogilvie; *b* 1932 (twin); *m* 1953 *Neale Thomas Grenfell, and has issue

2c Trevor Corry; *b* 31 Jan 1850; *m* 14 Aug 1923 Carolina (*d* 22 Aug 1928), widow of Edwart Cutten, of Temuka, S Canterbury, NZ, and *d* 26 May 1927

3e George Maurice; *b* 1 Oct 1855; *d* 28 June 1944

1c Ann Trevor Corr (Nina); *m* 24 Nov 1874 her 1st cousin 10th Earl of Seafield (*qv*), and *d* 16 Oct 1935, having had issue

4b Thomas Williams, of Crieff Lodge, Auckland, NZ, Capt 74th Highrs; *b* 6 March 1815; *m* 12 Aug 1851 Helen Elizabeth (*d* 1906), 4th dau and coheir of Rev David Stewart Moncrieffe, Rector of Loxton, Somerset, and *d* 3 Nov 1882, having had issue:

1c Stewart Eyre; *b* 24 May 1852; *m* 18 Oct 1877 Harriet (*d* 12 NOv 1882), 3rd dau of James McKenny, nephew of Sir Thomas McKenny, 1st Bt, and had issue:

1d John Stewart Moncrieffe; *b* April 1881

1d Emily Helen McKenny; *b* 11 Feb 1879

2c Hardress Eyre Graham; *b* 15 March 1857

1c Anne Moncrieffe; *m* 3 April 1878 John Gifford, of Brooklet, Oamaru, NZ, and *d* 26 April 1907, leaving issue

5b John Freke, JP, LLD, barrister; *b* 6 Feb 1817; *m* 1st 27 May 1851 Julia Bruce (*d* 10 July 1879), 3rd dau and coheir of Rev David Stewart Moncrieffe; *m* 2nd 12 Nov 1885 Charlotte Maitland (*d* 1897), dau of Rev Giles Pugh, Rector of Shapwick, and Chaplain to the Br Legation at Naples, and *d* 1892, having by his 1st w had issue:

1c Isabel Freke; *m* 25 May 1881 Rev Robert Hedges Maunsell Eyre, Vicar of Congresbury Somerset 1882–1921, and *d* 30 Sep 1916, leaving issue. He *d* 5 Feb 1928

6b Henry Frederick, Maj Cork Militia; *b* 12 April 1821; *m* 25 May 1851 Sarah Anne (*d* 1886), yst dau and coheir of Rev David Stewart Moncrieffe, and *d* 1904, having had issue:

1c Frederick Maclean; *b* 9 Oct 1856; *m* 16 Oct 1882 Ida, dau of John Greaveston

1c Caroline Susan; *m* 1st 22 Nov 1878 John Baptist Nicholas Thomas Dale, MD, of Arizona, USA, and had issue; *m* 2nd 1887 Edward James Freeman-Packer. He *d* 1909

2c Helen Frederica; *m* 18 July 1882 Charles Moore Echlin

1b Anna Maria Stone; *m* 5 Feb 1836 Rev Robert Hedges Maunsell Eyre, est son of Richard and Lady Catherine Maunsell

2b Caroline Louisa; *m* 6 April 1841 9th Earl of Seafield (*qv*) and *d* 6 Feb 1850, leaving issue

3b Elizabeth; *m* 17 Feb 1857 Peter Hay, Govr of Spike Island, and *d* 1922, leaving issue. He *d* 1899

(2) Thomas Waller (Rev), Rector of Dunmanway, Co Cork; *m* 12 April 1763 Catherine (*d* 13 April 1804), dau and heiress of James Conyers D'Arcy, and *d* 24 Feb 1797, having had issue:

1a Thomas, of Knockaderry, Co Limerick; *m* 1814 Brabazon, dau of Richard Taylour, of Holly Park, Limerick, and *dsp* 10 Dec 1833

2a James D'Arcy, of Knockaderry; *m* 1st May 1800 Arabella Massy (*d* 20 March 1833), dau of Col Samuel Leake; *m* 2nd 2 Jan 1834 Ann Maria, widow of John Fitzgerald, and *d* 7 March 1848, having by his 1st w had issue:

1b Thomas D'Arcy, of Knockaderry; *b* 20 April 1809; *m* 1st 21 May 1835 Thomasina Eliza (*d* 3 June 1874), dau of John Boles Reeves, of Belfort, Co Cork; *m* 2nd 8 Sept 1875 Elizabeth, dau of George Studdert, of Clunderlaw, Co Clare, and by his 1st w had issue:

1c Thomas; *b* 19 Feb 1836; *d* 20 July 1855

2c Eyre George Elystan; *b* 27 Feb 1837; *d* 20 Oct 1866

1c Anna Maria; *d* 1865

2c Thomasina Mary; *m* 12 April 1866 Samuel Richard Prosser, of Mount Plunkett, Lecarrow, Co Roscommon, and had issue:

3c Catherine Sophia; *m* 1 June 1863 George Pierce, MD, and *d* 12 Sept 1876, leaving issue

2b John D'Arcy; *b* 29 Sept 1817; *m* 29 July 1857 Marian (*d* 1890), dau of William Wallace, MD, of Dublin, and *d* 12 Oct 1875, having had, with other issue:

1c John D'Arcy; *b* 31 Aug 1858

2c George William Wallace, Capt Roy Irish Rifles and 20th Hus; *b* 4 Oct 1860; *m* 16 July 1889 (*divorce* 1902) Harriette George Marion Gledstanes (*d* 30 Sept 1960), dau of Capt George Gledstanes Richards, of Macmine Castle, Co Wexford, and *d* 8 Sept 1906, having had issue:

1d Elystan Eyre Cecil John George; *b* 10 July 1890; *m* —, *and d* 18 Nov 1959

2d St George Richards Waller; *b* 31 May 1891; *m* 22 July 1917 Mary Emmeline (*d* Dec 1953), only dau of Surtees Wilkinson, of Eaton Socon, Beds, and *d* 3 Nov 1927

3d Eyre Freke; *b* 21 Oct 1892; *d* 14 April 1894

4d Hardress Waller Eyre, Cdr RN; *b* 1898; *m* 1 Sept 1934 *Mary Frideswide Leslie, only child of W W Jessop Sharpe, and *d* 9 April 1962 leaving issue:

1e +John Hardress Waller; *b* 19 June 1938; *m* 1965 *Janet Barbara, dau of Francis Spencer Ware, and has issue:

1f +Andrew Hardress Eyre; *b* 1966

2f +Stephen Elystan Waller; *b* 1973

1f *Jennifer Frances; *b* 1968

1e *Wendy Nina Mary; *b* 13 May 1940; *m* 1970 *Capt M B Fowkes, and has issue

1d *Marian Sylvia Lucretia; *m* S Wilson

3c Eyre Waller; *b* 20 June 1864; *m* 18-—, and *d* 1926, leaving issue

1b Catherine; *m* 6 July 1832 Robert Dean Hay

2b Elizabeth; *m* 15 Aug 1828 John E Lucas, and *d* 28 Dec 1845, leaving issue

3b Emily; *m* 5 May 1849 Thomas Waller Evans, LLD, and *dsp* 29 Jan 1873

4b Mary Anne; *m* 11 Sept 1835 Thomas W Locke

5b Arabella; *m* 24 July 1848 William O'Hara, and had issue

3a Eyre; *m* 10 May 1821 Elizabeth (*d* 6 May 1874), est dau of Thomas Austin, and *d* 14 Nov 1847, leaving issue:

1b Thomas Waller Eyre, LLD; *b* 29 May 1826; *m* 5 May 1849 Emily (*dsp* 29 Jan 1873), dau of James D'Arcy Evans, of Knockaderry (*see* above)

1b Elizabeth

2b Catherine; *m* Richard Busteed

4a John, Capt 24 Regt, *k* at Talavera

1a Elizabeth Waller; *d* unm 1845

2a Catherine; *m* 1800 Sampson Beamish, and *d* 1849

GEORGE EVANS *d* 1720; his est son,

GEORGE EVANS, **1st Baron Carbery**, of Carbery, Co Cork (I), so *cr* 9 May 1715 *vp*, with remainder to his f's male issue, PC (I 1715), MP Co Limerick 1707–13 and Westbury Wilts 1715–22 and 1724–27; *m* 4 May 1703 Anne (*d* 30 Dec 1757), dau and eventual coheir of William Stafford, of Blatherwick, Northants, and *d* 28 Aug 1749, having had issue:

1 GEORGE EVANS, **2nd Baron Carbery**; MP (Whig) Westbury 1734–47; *m* 23 May 1732 Frances, dau of 5th Viscount FitzWilliam of Merrion, and *d* 2 Feb 1759, leaving:

(1) GEORGE EVANS, **3rd Baron Carbery**; *m* 1st 7 Feb 1760 Lady Juliana Noel (*d* 18 Dec 1760), dau of 4th Earl of Gainsborough (*qv*), and had:

1a Juliana; *m* 16 April 1782 Edward Hartopp Igley, of Dolby Ho, Leics, and *d* 20 May 1807

(1) (cont.) The **3rd Baron** *m* 2nd 13 Dec 1762 Elizabeth, 3rd dau of Christopher Horton, of Catton Hall, Derbys, and *d* 26 May 1783, having by her had:

1a GEORGE EVANS, **4th Baron Carbery**; *b* 18 Feb 1766; *educ* Eton and Trin Coll Cambridge; MP (Tory) Rutland 1802–04; *m* 13 Aug 1792 Susan (*m* 2nd 21 Jan 1806 George Freke, of Bulgaven Hall; *see* below), only dau and heiress of Col Henry Watson, and *dsp* 31 Dec 1804

(2) JOHN EVANS, **5th Baron Carbery**; *b* 1738; *m* 15 April 1759 Emma (*d* 6 Jan 1806), 4th dau of Very Rev William Crowe, Dean of Clonfort, and *d* 4 March 1807, having had:

1a John William; *b* 31 March 1763; *d* 1805

1a Emily Frances; *d* 1771

2a Frances Dorothea; *m* 1789 William Preston, Judge of Appeal, and had issue

3a Maria Juliana; *m* 1796 Col Thomas Barry, of Leighs-brook, Co Meath, and *d* June 1847, leaving two daus

(1) Frances Anne; *m* 1st Sept 1756 Edward Warter Wilson and had issue (*see* STRADBROKE, E); and 2nd Eleazer Davey, of Ubbeston Hall, Suffolk, and *d* 12 July 1802

2 John, of Bulgaden Hall; *m* June 1741 Grace, sole heiress of her bro, Sir Redmond Freke, 3rd Bt, MP (*dsp* 1764, when the btcy expired), and *d* 1758, having had issue:

(1) George; *m* —, dau of — Stamer, of Carnelly, and *dsp* 1769

(2) Sir JOHN EVANS later EVANS-FREKE, **1st Bt** (I), so *cr* 15 July 1768; *m* 15 July 1764 Lady Elizabeth Gore, dau of 1st Earl of Arran (*qv*), and *d* 20 March 1777, leaving issue:

1a **Sir John Evans-Freke, 2nd Bt**, and **6th Baron Carbery**; MP (I Parl) Donegal 1784–90 and Baltimore 1790–1800, rep I peer 1823; *b* 11 Nov 1765; *m* 25 Jan 1783 Lady Catherine Charlotte Gore (*d* 23 Feb 1852), 3rd dau of 2nd Earl of Arran (*qv*), and *dsp* 12 May 1845

2a George, MP, of Bulgaden Hall; *b* July 1772; *m* 21 Jan 1806 Susan (*d* Oct 1828), dau and heir of Col Henry Watson and widow of 4th Baron Carbery, and *dsp* 19 June 1829

3a Percy; *b* April 1774; *m* 1797 Dorothea (*d* 26 March 1835), dau of Rev Christopher Harvey, DD, of Kyle, Co Wexford, and *d* 9 Sept 1844, leaving issue (to whom rank of baron's dau/yr sons was granted by roy licence 1845):

1b GEORGE PATRICK PERCY EVANS-FREKE, **7th Baron Carbery**; *b* 17 March 1810; *m* 5 Aug 1852 Harriet Maria Catharine (*d* 19 Aug 1884) dau of Gen Edmund Shuldham, of Dunmanway, Co Cork, and *d* 25 Nov 1889, leaving:

1c Georgiana Dorothea Harriet, CBE (1920); *m* 22 June 1876 4th Earl of Bandon (*see* 1970 edn) and *d* 29 June 1942. He *d* 18 May 1924

2b Percy Augustus, Lt-Col; *d* unm 15 Jan 1847

3b Fenton John, Col 2nd Life Gds; *m* 14 Oct 1851 Lady Katherine Felicia Pakenham (*d* 26 Dec 1911), est dau of 2nd Earl of Longford (*qv*), and *d* 3 Sept 1889, leaving issue:

1c Georgiana Louisa; *b* 15 Aug 1852; *d* unm 30 Dec 1923

4b WILLIAM CHARLES, **8th Baron**

1b Catherine Charlotte; *b* 26 Dec 1811; *m* Jean Henri Pintiaux, and *d* 26 Nov 1881, leaving issue

2b Jane Grace Dorothea; *m* 25 July 1843 Rt Rev and Hon Charles Brodrick Bernard, DD, Bp Tuam, and *d* 5 June 1892, leaving issue (*see* 1970 edn BANDON, E). He *d* 31 Jan 1890

1a Jane Grace; *m* 4 June 1795 Sir Fenton Aylmer, 7th Bt (*qv*), and *d* 31 Dec 1827, leaving issue

(3) William; *b* 16 May 1747; *m* Elizabeth, dau of Richard Becher, and *d* Feb 1796, leaving issue, now extinct in the male line

(4) Ralph Evans, of Greenmount, Co Wexford, Capt 39th Regt; *b* 6 June 1748; *m* 1782 Mary (*m* 2nd C Perceval), dau of Robert Woodcock, of Killown, Wexford, and *d* 1785, leaving issue:

1a John, Offr Rifle Bde; *b* 26 Sept 1785; *m* 1 Feb 1809 Amy (*d* 1838), dau of Cadwallader Edwards, of Ballyhire, and *d* 27 March 1825, leaving issue:

1b Ralph; *b* 25 Aug 1816; *m* 8 June 1842 Caroline (*d* 6 June 1912), dau of John Wheeler, and *dsp* 17 Aug 1885

2b John; *b* 11 March 1814; *dsp* 9 March 1858

3b George William Henry; *b* 14 June 1822; *m* 8 July 1851 Sophia (*d* 1922), dau of John Wheeler, and *d* 24 Dec 1889, leaving issue:

1c George Henry; *b* 7 Oct 1852; *d* unm 27 July 1941

2c Percy Ralph, slr High Court; *b* 11 Sept 1854; *d* 5 Dec 1934

3c John Fenton, Maj IMS, late 18th Bengal LI; *b* 26 July 1858; *d* unm 13 March 1899

4c Cadwallader Edwards, MRCSE; *b* 5 July 1860; *d* unm in S Africa 29 July 1893

1c Amy Sophia; *d* unm 8 Sept 1936

2c Grace Freke; *d* unm 20 Dec 1899

1b Elizabeth; *d* unm

2b Amy Louisa; *m* George Bradney Gilpin, and had issue

1a Mary; *m* 1806 Cadwallader Edwards, of Ballyhire, Co Wexford, and *d* 26 July 1809

(5) Percy; *d* unm

(1) Grace; *m* R Baldwin

(2) Anne; *m* W Putland, and had issue

(3) Catherine; *m* G Putland

(4) Jane; *m* 1782 Richard Grace, MP, and *d* 24 March 1804, leaving issue (*see* 1967 edn GRACE, Bt)

1 Anne; *m* 1734 Maj Charles du Terme

The 7th BARON's bro,

WILLIAM CHARLES EVANS-FREKE, **8th Baron Carbery**, DL; *b* 24 May 1812; rep I peer, High Sheriff Rutland 1862; *m* 1st 23 April 1840 Sophia (*d* 23 Sept

1851), 3rd dau of 5th Earl of Harborough and widow of Sir Thomas Whichcote, 6th Bt; *m* 2nd 15 Dec 1866 Lady Victoria Cecil (*d* 22 Feb 1932), dau of 2nd Marquess of Exeter (*qv*), and by her had issue:

1 ALGERNON WILLIAM GEORGE, **9th Baron**

2 Percy Cecil, DL (Rutland), Lt-Col Leics Yeo Boer War 1900–01 and WW I; *b* 19 May 1871; *m* 24 July 1895 Eva (*d* 3 Dec 1942), yst dau of Charles Kirwan, of Dalgan Park, Co Mayo, and Mrs Maitland-Kirwan, of Gelston Castle, Kirkcudbrightshire, and was *ka* 3 May 1915, leaving issue:

(1) Maida Cecil; *b* 11 June 1897; *m* 21 Dec 1927 Capt Edmund Michael Gordon Loeventhorpe Boyle, RN, 4th son of Maj Charles John Boyle, and *d* 14 Oct 1995, leaving issue (*see* CORK and ORRERY, E)

3 Cecil Montague, Lt 16th Lancers; *b* 3 Sept 1876; *d* of wounds received at Bappisfontein, S Africa, 15 June 1900

The 6th BARON *d* 7 Nov 1894; his son,

ALGERNON WILLIAM GEORGE EVANS-FREKE, **9th Baron Carbery**, DL Co Cork, Lt 3rd Bn Northants Regt; *b* 9 Sept 1868; *m* 26 Nov 1890 Mary, author: *The Farm by Lough Gur* and *Happy World* (*m* 2nd 11 Feb 1902 Arthur Wellesley Sandford, MD, MCh (*d* 12 May 1939), son of Rev Canon Sandford, Rector of Clonmel, and *d* 6 Feb 1949), 2nd dau of Henry Toulmin, DL, JP, of Kingsbury, St Albans, and *d* 1898, leaving:

(1) JOHN EVANS-FREKE later JOHN EVANS CARBERY (deed poll 23 Nov 1921), **10th Baron Carbery**; *b* 20 May 1892; T/Flying Sub-Lt RNAS; *m* 1st 7 July 1913 (*divorce* 1920) José, dau of Evelyn James Metcalf, of 5 Chester Place, W, and had issue:

1a *Fabienne José [The Hon Mrs Claridge, Cloonagh, Monkstown, Co Cork, Ireland]; *m* 1st 6 Feb 1936 (*divorce* 1946) Cdr John Dudley Finnemore Dowse-Finnemor, RN (*d* 1971), er son of Rt Rev Charles Benjamin Dowse, DD, Bp Cork, and added with him the name FINNEMOR 1938; *m* 2nd 1947 *Philip Claridge

(1) (cont.) The **10th Baron** *m* 2nd 1922 Maia Ivy (*d* 12 March 1928), dau of Alfred Anderson, of Nairobi, and by her had issue:

2a *Juanita Virginia Sistare (does not use courtesy title); *b* 1925; served WTS (FANY) 1942–46, Br Merchant Navy 1952–58 and Norwegian MN 1958 on

(1) (cont.) The **10th Baron** *m* 3rd July 1930 June Weir Mosley (*d* 1980) and *d* 1970

(2) Ralfe, MBE (1953), Maj Rifle Bde, ADC Personal Staff 1918, Mil Sec to Govr Burma 1946–47, served WW I (wounded, despatches) and WW II, on Staff War Office 1948–55; *b* 23 July 1897; *educ* Eton and RMC Sandhurst; *m* 1st 4 March 1919 (*divorce* 1929) Vera (*d* 23 Jan 1984), dau of C Harrington-Moore, of 2 Sussex Gardens, W2, and had issue:

1a PETER RALFE HARRINGTON EVANS-FREKE, **11th and present Baron Carbery**

(2) Maj the Hon Ralfe Evans-Freke *m* 2nd 1929 (*divorce* 1940) Phyllis, dau of C W Thorpe; *m* 3rd 18 Jan 1941 Dorothy May, er dau of H G Surrey, and *d* 23 May 1969, having by his 2nd w had further issue:

1a *Anne Mary Elizabeth [Mrs Ross Young, Easters, Sandhills, Cattistock, Dorchester, Dorset DT2 0HQ]; *b* 7 July 1933; *m* 21 Aug 1957 *Ross Young, only son of A E J Young, of Bury St Edmunds, Suffolk, and has issue:

1b *Paul Ralfe; *b* 4 June 1958

1b *Clare Elizabeth; *b* 12 July 1960; *m* 1986 *Stephen Delevante, and has issue:

1c *Andrew Edward; *b* 1988

2c *Patrick Ross; *b* 1991

2b *Diane Mary [Mrs George Spence, 80 Tyneham Rd, London SW11 5XP]; *b* 26 Nov 1967; *m* 1977 *George Robert Spence

CARDEN of Molesey

Arms: Per pale sa. and gu. a staff-sling bendwise between four pheons in saltire, all arg. **Crest:** A fasces fesswise or, thereon a wolf's head erased sa., pierced in the neck by an arrow in bend sinister, point downwards gold, embrued ppr. **Motto:** *Fide et amore* ('With faith and love'). **Creation:** Bt. (UK) 14 June 1887.

Christopher Robert Carden, 5th Bt, of Molesey [Christopher Carden, Casilla 1341, Santa Cruz, Bolivia]; *b* 24 Nov 1946; *s f* 1993 but does not use title and has taken no steps to prove succession; *educ* Eton and Aberdeen U (BSc Forestry 1970); tropical rain-forest management consultant and conservationist; *m* 1st 1972 (*divorce* 1979) Sainimere Rokotuibau, of Suva, Fiji; *m* 2nd 1981 (*divorce* 1996) Clarita Peralta, of Manila, Philippines

Lineage: JAMES CARDEN, of Bedford Sq, Middx; *m* 11 Oct 1794 Mary (*d* 9 Nov 1830), dau of John Walter, of Teddington Grove, Middx, and Printing House Sq, London, and *d* 25 April 1829, having had a yst s:

Sir Robert Walter Carden, 1st Bt (UK), *so cr* 14 June 1887, JP Middx and Surrey, Alderman, Commr Ltcy for London, Sheriff London 1851, Ld Mayor 1857–58, MP Glos 1857–59 and Barnstaple 1880–85, ktd 1851; *b* 7 Oct 1801; *m* 1 Jan 1827 Pamela Elizabeth Edith (*d* 13 Nov 1874 aged 68), dau of William Smith Andrews, MD, of Richmond, Surrey, and had, with seven daus:

1 FREDERICK WALTER (Sir), **2nd Bt**

2 Robert Augustus (Rev), MA; *b* 2 Jan 1836; *m* 21 Sept 1859 Caroline Gertrude (*d* 6 Sept 1886), dau of John Arnold Mello, of Leinster Gdns, W, and *d* 25 June 1873, leaving issue:

(1) Evangeline Gertrude; *m* 1st 1887 John Effingham Lawrence (*d* 1890); *m* 2nd 1893 William Ashford Caunter (*d* 1919), of Oakfield, Exeter, and had issue

3 Alexander James; *b* 28 Aug 1839; *m* 12 April 1863 Anne Rule (*d* 6 July 1924), dau of John Thomas Clements, and *d* 23 July 1897, leaving issue:

(1) James (Rev), served WW I; *b* 13 Dec 1865; *m* 19 June 1894 Cornelia Charlotte (*d* 16 May 1941), dau of Cornelius Turner, and *d* 5 Jan 1946, leaving issue:

1a Cornelia; *b* 11 April 1895; *d* unm 1954

(2) George Frederick; *b* 2 March 1868; *m* 1895 Katherine Judith (*d* 6 Nov 1935), dau of C Mannix, and *dsp* 1952

(3) Henry; *b* 19 Oct 1872; *m* 1st 1894 Martha Vinnineda (*d* 1918), dau of Ernst Tronson, of Romsdalen, Norway; *m* 2nd 1919 Mildred Kedge (*d* 1946), and *d* New Orleans 6 Feb 1948, leaving issue by his 1st w:

1a Florence Lillian; *b* 1895; *m* 1924 Brig Francisco Rabia Muñoz, Mexican Army

(4) Robert Walter, T/Lt RE; *b* 1 July 1875; *m* 4th June 1901 Ethel May (*d* 25 Nov 1955), er dau of Lemuel Johns, of Christchurch, NZ, and *d* 23 Feb 1943, leaving issue:

1a Derick Walter; *b* 30 April 1902; *m* 27 April 1929 Lois Leila Frances, dau of Dan Weeks, of Bridport

2a Ronald Tracy; *b* 20 Sept 1903; *m* 6 July 1934 Aloysia Frances (*d* 16 Feb 1949), dau of Frank Machalak, of Plainfield, NJ, USA

(5) Alexander; *b* 12 March 1877; *d* unm 31 July 1900, while serving with the City Imperial Vols in S Africa

(1) Pamela; *b* 20 March 1871; *m* 2 June 1894 Percy William Bullock, of The Staithe, 90 Sunningfields Rd, Hendon, Middx, and *d* 30 Sept 1929

(2) Rowena; *b* 8 Feb 1880; *m* 6 March 1927 Daniel Hall, son of Maurice Hall, of Jaffa, Palestine, and *dsp* 11 May 1967. He *d* 6 April 1943

Sir ROBERT *d* 19 Jan 1888; his est son,

Sir Frederick Walter Carden, 2nd Bt, JP Hants, High Sheriff 1891, Lt-Col 5th Lancers; *b* 6 Nov 1833; *m* 23 Sept 1870 Rowena Laura (*d* 28 Aug 1910), dau of Rowand Ronald, of Manchester Sq, Middx, and widow of Capt Alexander Lester Copland, 57th Regt, and had:

1 FREDERICK HENRY WALTER (Sir), **3rd Bt**

2 Ronald James Walter, Maj 17th Lancers, T/Lt-Col 16th Roy Welch Fus; *b* 3 April 1876; *ka* 10 July 1916

1 Lilian Edith Laura; *b* 8 Aug 1871; *m* 26 July 1899 Bertram Hugh Barton, and *d* 19 Oct 1937, leaving issue. He *d* 5 Dec 1927

Sir FREDERICK *d* 4 Dec 1909; his er son,

Sir Frederick Henry Walter Carden, 3rd Bt, JP (1919) and High Sheriff Hants 1922, DL (Berks 1936); *b* 17 Oct 1873; *educ* Marlborough and Pembroke Coll Oxford; Maj 1st Life Gds, served Boer War 1899–1900 (Queen's medal with five clasps) and WW I (three medals); *m* 27 April 1901 Winifred Mary (*d* 12 Jan 1974), dau of Philip Wroughton, DL, JP, of Woolley Park, Wantage, and had issue:

1 HENRY CHRISTOPHER (Sir), **4th Bt**

1 Enid Evelyn; *b* 12 July 1902; *m* 8 Nov 1928 Alfred Henry Michell (*d* 11 July 1965), only surv son of James Alfred of Shouldham Hall, King's Lynn, Norfolk, and has issue:

(1) *John Frederick Carden; *b* 9 Feb 1933; *educ* Eton and Trin Coll Cambridge

(2) *Charles Henry Wroughton; *b* 5 May 1938; *educ* Eton

(1) *Clare Winifred Mary; *b* 27 March 1935; *m* 1st 25 April 1957 (*divorce* 1965) Geoffrey St George Schomberg, yr son of Rev Edward St George Schomberg, MA, DL, Master of Charterhouse, and has issue:

1a *Laura Carolyn; *b* 17 July 1960

2a *Julia Rachel; *b* 7 Nov 1961

(1) (cont.) Mrs Clare Schomberg *m* 2nd *Harry Dexter Lyon, son of H Lyon, of The Old Rectory, Dillington, Hently, Sussex, and has further issue:

1a *Giles Roderick; *b* 31 March 1965

Sir FREDERICK *d* 22 Sept 1966; his son,

Sir Henry Christopher Carden, 4th Bt, OBE (1945); *b* 16 Oct 1908; *educ* Eton and RMC Sandhurst; Lt-Col 17th/21st Lancers WW II, Mil Attaché Stockholm 1951–55, ret 1956, Cdr Order Sword 2nd Cl Sweden; *m* 1st 5 June 1943 (*divorce* 1961) Jane St Clare [Mrs Thomas Pilkington, Hyde Mill, Stow-on-the-Wold, Cheltenham, Glos GL54 1LA] (*m* 2nd 1962 Maj Thomas Douglas Pilkington, of Reay), yr dau of Thomas Edward St Clare Daniell, OBE, MC, and had issue:

1 (Sir) CHRISTOPHER ROBERT CARDEN, (**5th and potentially present Bt**)

1 *Melinda Jane [Mrs Andrew Wilson, Glenfall Stables, Ham, Charlton Kings, Cheltenham, Glos GL52 6NH]; *b* 17 June 1950; *m* 1975 *Andrew James Wilson, son of Capt G A J Wilson, of Ballyburn, Castledermot, Co Kildare, and has:

(1) *Fiona Jane; *b* 1981

(2) *Sarah Bobby; *b* 1984

Sir Henry *m* 2nd 8 Nov 1962 Gwyneth Sybil, FCA (*d* 19 May 1996), 2nd dau of Herbert Arthur Dyke Acland, AMICE (*see* ACLAND, Bt, of Oxford), and widow of F/Lt Roderick Stanley Emerson, RAFVR, and *d* 4 Feb 1993

CARDEN of Templemore

Arms: Arg. a mascle gu. between three pheons sa.
Crest: A pheon sa. **Motto:** *Fide et amore* ('With faith and love').
Creation: Bt. (I) 31 Aug 1787.

SIR JOHN CRAVEN CARDEN, 7TH BT, of Templemore, Co Tipperary [Sir John Carden Bt, PO Box 66, St Helier, Jersey CI JE4 8PZ]; *b* 11 March 1926; *s f* 1935; *educ* Eton; *m* 12 Nov 1947 *Isabel Georgette, yst dau of Robert de Hart, and has issue:

1 Isabel Mary; *b* 28 May 1952

Lineage: JOHN CARDEN settled at Templemore, Co Tipperary, *c* 1650; *m* Priscilla Kent and had:

1 Jonathan, ancestor of the CARDENs of Barnane
2 JOHN
3 William, of Lismore; *m* Gertrude Warburton, of Garryhinch, Queen's Co, and had issue

JOHN CARDEN *d* aged 105 in 1728; his 2nd s,

JOHN CARDEN, of Templemore; *m* 1717 Rebecca, dau of Humphrey Minchin, of Ballynakill, and had:

1 JOHN
2 Paul
3 Minchin, of Fishmoyne, Co Tipperary, ancestor of Richard George Carden, JP, of Fishmoyne

The er son,

JOHN CARDEN, of Templemore; *m* 1747 Elizabeth, dau and heir of Rev Robert Craven, by Rose, dau of Thomas Otway, of Lissenhall, Co Tipperary, and *d* 1774, having had, with a yr s and seven daus:

Sir John Craven Carden, 1st Bt (I), so *cr* 31 Aug 1787, of Templemore; *m* 1st 23 Jan 1776 Mary (*d* 28 Sept 1778), 3rd dau of 1st Viscount Harberton (*qv*), and had:

1 John; *d* unm
2 **Sir Arthur Carden, 2nd Bt**, Capt 4th Dragoon Gds; *b* 1778; *m* 10 Feb 1801 Mary (*m* 2nd Capt Joseph Smith and *d* 20 June 1857), dau of Thomas Kemmis, of Shane, Queen's Co, and *dsp* 4 March 1822

Sir John *m* 2nd 2 May 1781 Sarah, dau of John Moore, of Drumbanagher, Co Armagh, MP Ballynakill, and by her had two daus; *m* 3rd 16 Feb 1788 Mary Frances, dau of Henry Westenra and sis of 2nd Baron Rossmore (*qv*), by whom he had further issue:

3 HENRY ROBERT (Sir), **3rd Bt**
1 Frances; *m* William Blayney Wade, of Clonebraney, Co Meath
2 Harriet Amelia; *m* Henry Lloyd, of Farrinrory, and *d* his widow 13 April 1879

Sir John *m* 4th Anne (*d* 20 Dec 1823), dau of Henry Quin, MD, and widow of 1st Viscount Monck (*qv*), and *d* 21 Nov 1820

The 2nd Bt's half-bro,

Sir Henry Robert Carden, 3rd Bt; *b* 8 Feb 1789; army offr Peninsular War and Waterloo; *m* 10 March 1818 Louisa, only child of Frederick Thompson, of Woodville, Queen's Co, and had, with other issue:

1 JOHN CRAVEN (Sir), **4th Bt**
2 Frederick; *b* 26 March 1821; *d* 1844
3 Henry Daniel, DL, of Knightstown, Portarlington, Queen's Co, Hon Col 4th Bn Leinster Regt; *b* 1 May 1822; *m* 28 April 1847 Catherine Rebecca (*d* 29 Aug 19140), 3rd dau of John Parry de Winton, DL, JP, of Maesderwen, Breconshire, and *d* 4 Jan 1894, having had issue:

(1) Henry Parry, Lt-Col and Brevet Col DCLI; *b* 22 Feb 1854; *m* 26 Aug 1897 Araby (*d* 7 Jan 1942), dau of Howard Burton and widow of Edward Nugent Greer, and *d* 19 Dec 1910, leaving issue:

1a Catherine Constance; *d* unm 7 Jan 1979
2a *Sybil Parry; *m* 15 Sept 1936 Maj-Gen Francis David Rome, CB, CMG, CBE, DSO, Roy Fus, son of Francis James Rome, of W Dingle, Liverpool

(1) Frances Mary; *m* 5 Feb 1871 Maj John Aldridge, JP, late 4th Bn Leinster Regt, only son of John Aldridge, of Inholmes, Hungerford, Berks, and *d* his widow 3 March 1934
(2) Caroline Elizabeth Mary; *d* unm 18 May 1907

4 Arthur (Rev), BA; *b* 30 June 1823; *m* 13 May 1852 Rosa Emily (*d* 15 Nov 1908), dau of W Wilton Woodward, of Matson Ho, Glos, and *d* 10 Aug 1863 leaving issue:

(1) Arthur Craven; *b* 3 May 1853; *m* 23 Nov 1875 Marian, dau of John Hendy, of St Florence, Pembroke, and *d* 5 Jan 1881, leaving:

1a Edith Craven

(2) Henry Westenra; *b* 13 April 1857; Lt-Col APD, Capt 2nd Bn DCLI; *m* 1st 8 March 1886 Emily Elphinstone (*d* 17 Jan 1918), dau of Rev William Courtenay Clerk, Rector of Moreton, Devon; *m* 2nd 22 Oct 1919 Beatrice (*d* 1944), dau of Peter Sharp, of Cannock, and *d* 30 May 1928, having by his 1st w had issue:

1a Bernard Westenra; *b* 1887; Lt 8th Bn Glos Regt; *m* 1923 Gwendoline (*d* 1980), dau of Joseph Price, of Leamington, and *d* 4 July 1951, leaving issue:

1b Patrick Westenra [Patrick Carden Esq, Sandy Top, 174 Station Rd, Fordingbridge, Hants SP6 1DS]; *b* 8 Jan 1928; *educ* U of Wales (Bsc 1951); *m* 23 July 1955 *Janet Hilda, dau of William Edgar Stickland, of Myrtle Cottage, Babraham Rd, Cambridge, and has issue:

1c +David Westenra; *b* 7 Feb 1957; *m* 1984 *Jane Leslie Clough, and has issue:

1d +Benjamin Westenra; *b* 1989
2d +Timothy Peter; *b* 1992

2c +Trevor Courtenay; *b* 26 Nov 1959
1c *Angela; *b* 2 Oct 1961; *m* 1985 *Keith West, and has issue:

1d *Christopher William; *b* 1990
1d *Heather Carol; *b* 1992

2c *Carol Mary; *b* 27 March 1967

2a +Cecil Courtenay; *b* 1892
3a +Henry Elphinstone; *b* 1894
1a Violet Courtenay; *m* 1921 Lee Remeo, of Alberta, Canada
2a Beryl, MBE (1946), Nursing Matron-in-Ch Prison Serv England and Wales; *m* June 1955 S Jaggard
3a Hazel; *m* 17 Oct 1925 Langshaw Rowland, OBE, est son of Sir Leonard Bromfield Rowland
4a Sybil Rose Courtenay
5a Murel Elphinstone; *b* 1899; *m* 9 Dec 1924 Charles Pelham Thursby (*d* 1977) and had:

1b *Hugh James; *b* 24 June 1931

6a Christina Annette; *b* 1900; *m* 1924 John Elliot Weir (*d* 1976), and had:

1b *Charles Henry [Charles Weir Esq, 14003–75th Ave, Edmonton, Alberta, Canada T5R 2Y5]; *b* 1925; MSc, DLS, PEng; *m* 1949 *Kathleen McLellan, and has issue:

1c *Douglas Charles; *b* 1953
1c *Wendy Kathleen; *b* 1954
2c *Sandra Christina; *b* 1957

2b *Carden Fraser [Carden Weir Esq, 14 Atlanta Cres, Calgary, Alberta, Canada]; *b* 1927; *m* 1950 *Freda Irene McCoy, and has issue:

1c *Carlene Ann; *b* 1951; *m* 1972 *Ronald Joseph Bourassa, and has issue:

1d *Jeffery Alexander; *b* 1976
1d *Ronalee Jo-Ann; *b* 1974
2d *Danielle Lynn Patricia; *b* 1975

2c *Marion; *b* 1954; *m* 1973 *Carmon Marshall Woodworth, and has issue:

1d *Collin Matthew; *b* 1976
2d *Carl Alexander; *b* 1978

3c *Patti; *b* 1961; *m* 1984 *David Mitchell Dennis

7a Pearl Elphinstone, MCSP; *d* unm 30 May 1959

Sir HENRY *d* 23 March 1847; his est son,

Sir John Craven Carden, 4th Bt, DL, Co Tipperary; *b* 1 Dec 1819; *m* 1st 23 July 1844 Caroline Elizabeth Mary (*d* 5 Nov 1850), dau of Sir William Mordaunt Milner, 4th Bt (*qv*), and had three daus (*dsp* or unm); *m* 2nd 21 June 1852 Julia Isabella (*d* 12 Oct 1915), only dau of Adml Charles G Robinson, and by her had issue:

1 JOHN CRAVEN (Sir), **5th Bt**
2 Henry Charles, DSO, Maj Reserve Offrs Devon Regt Boer War 1899–1901 and WW I; *b* 30 Jan 1855; *m* 1881 Blanche Catherine (*d* 26 Aug 1954 aged 92), dau of R-Adml John Parry Jones-Parry, of Thelwall Hall, Cheshire, and was *ka* France 25 Sept 1915, leaving issue:

(1) Henry Craven (Rev Canon); *b* 23 Dec 1882; *educ* Durham U (MA 1908), Hon Canon of Lahore Cathedral 1934, Chaplain Roy Hants Co Hosp Winchester 1954, Vicar of Kilmeston-with-Beauworth 1934–53, RD Alresford 1946–53, Archdeacon Lahore 1929–34, Chaplain Indian Ecclesiastical Establishment 1913, CF Mesopotamia 1918 (despatches) and Afghanistan 1919; *m* Nov 1913 Olive (*d* 29 March 1966), est dau of Rev Canon Charles Vincent Gorton, and *d* 30 Oct 1964, having had issue:

1a John Rory, Lt RN (FAA) WW II; *b* 21 Aug 1917; *educ* Haileybury and RNC Dartmouth; *kas* in HMS *Audacity* Dec 1941
2a +DERRICK CHARLES, CMG (1974) [Derrick Carden Esq CMG, Flat 47, Peninsula Square, Winchester, Hants SO23 4QA]; *b* 31 Oct 1921; heir presumptive; *educ* Marlborough and Ch Ch Oxford; served in Sudan Political Serv 1942–54, Dip Serv 1954, Political Agent Doha 1955–58, 1st Sec Tripoli 1958–62, Head Chancery Cairo 1965, Consul-Gen Muscat 1965–69, dir Middle East Centre Arab Studies 1969–73, Amb Yemen Arab Repub 1973–76, Amb Sudan 1977–79 (ret); *m* 18 Oct 1952 *Elizabeth Anne, only

dau of Capt Alfred Spalding Russell, DSO, RN, of Portchester, Hants, and has issue:

1b +John Craven [John Carden Esq, 7 Cleveland Rd, Chichester]; *b* 17 Nov 1953; *m* 1983 *Celia Howitt, and has issue:

1c +Patrick John Cameron; *b* 1988

2b +Peter James Charles; *b* 8 Aug 1958

1b *Elizabeth Louise; *b* 16 June 1956

2b *Clare Margaret; *b* 17 Nov 1961

(2) John Humphry; *b* 1886; *m* 11 Oct 1923 Eileen Winifred Bourke (*d* 6 Feb 1996), yr dau of Lt-Col Thomas Patrick Shannon, RASC, and *d* 21 Sept 1957, leaving issue:

1a +Patrick Henry [Patrick Carden Esq, The Old Rectory, 91 Windmill St, Gravesend, Kent]; *b* 8 March 1928; Trinity Ho Pilotage Serv (ret); *m* 10 April 1951 *Rosalie Alice, yr dau of Rev Canon Sydney William Groom and has had:

1b +Derek Edward Trevor; *b* 15 July 1952; *educ* King's Sch Rochester and Nottingham U; *m* 1977 *Amanda Mary Smyllie and has:

1c +Toby James; *b* 1980

2c +Philip Paul; *b* 1983

3c +Oliver Mark; *b* 1987

2b +Nigel John Patrick; *b* 13 Feb 1954; *educ* King's Sch Rochester and Kings Coll London

3b +Roger Michael Colin; *b* 20 Nov 1956; *educ* King's Sch Rochester; *m* 1989 *Helena Louise Davis and has issue:

1c +Harry Grahame Patrick; *b* 1997

1c *Katy Louise; *b* 1993

4b Paul William Sydney; *b* 31 Dec 1958; *d* 19 April 1959

1b Alison Rosalie; *b* 21 Jan 1965; *d* 12 July 1976

2a Michael Humphrey; *b* 16 April 1929; Capt Worcs Regt Malaya 1952; *d* 21 Aug 1995

3 Frederick Richard; *b* 19 June 1856; *m* 1885 Miriam Beale and *d* 1935, leaving issue:

(1) Frederick Craven; *b* 1890; *ka* 1918

(2) Richard Craven; *b* 1893

(3) Selwyn; *b* 18–

(4) Rodney; *b* 18–

(5) Geoffrey; *b* 18–

(1) Helen Mary; *m* March 1912 Herbert Roger, and has issue

(2) Pattie Constance; *m* 1915 D A Morrell, of Auckland, NZ

4 Coldstream James; *b* 18 Aug 1857; Capt Connaught Rangers, served in S Africa 1881, and Sudan 1885; *m* 9 Sept 1891 Rose Margaret Ponton, yst dau of David Johnstone, of Croy, Dunbartonshire, and *d* 15 Sept 1925, leaving issue:

(1) Eileen Margaret; *b* 5 April 1893; *m* 1919 Brig Thomas Dix Perkin, DL, KSLI (*d* 1991), and *d* 1984

(2) Veronica Sybil; *b* 1896; *d* unm 20 Nov 1918

5 Derrick Alfred, Maj Seaforth Highrs, T/Lt-Col 7th Bn Argyll and Sutherland Highrs; *b* 27 March 1875; *d* 25 May 1915 of wounds recd in action

1 Julia Ellen Beatrice; *m* 8 Aug 1889 George Edward De Vere Kennedy, and *d* 6 Oct 1933, leaving issue (*see* KENNEDY, Bt)

2 Norah Ierne; *b* 28 June 1873; *m* 21 Jan 1903 Lt-Col Henry Sargeaunt (*d* 15 Jan 1950), late Cheshire Regt, yst son of John Barneby Sargeaunt, of Burton Latimer, Northants, and had a s

3 Eileen Olive; *b* 18 Aug, *d* 4 Sept 1878

Sir JOHN *d* March 1879; his est son,

Sir John Craven Carden, 5th Bt, DL, JP, Co Tipperary, High Sheriff 1882; *b* 30 Jan 1854; *m* 10 Feb 1891 Sybil Martha (*d* 1 July 1911), only surv child of Gen Valentine Baker, and had issue:

1 JOHN VALENTINE (Sir), **6th Bt**

1 Audrey; *b* 1 July 1897; *d* unm 24 Dec 1936

Sir JOHN *d* 16 Dec 1831; his son,

Sir John Valentine Carden, 6th Bt, MBE, T/Capt RASC; *b* 6 Feb 1892; *m* 1st 18 Sept 1915 (*divorce* 1925) Vera Madeleine, yr dau of William Henry Hervet-d'Egville, of Springbourne Lodge, Queen's Park, Bournemouth; *m* 2nd 13 Feb 1925 Dorothy Mary, dau of Charles Luckraft McKinnon, and was *k* in an aeroplane accident 10 Dec 1935, leaving issue:

1 Sir JOHN CRAVEN CARDEN, **7th and present Bt**

CAREW, Baron

Arms: Or, three lions passant sa. **Crest:** An heraldic antelope passant sa., crined and horned or. **Supporters:** Two heraldic antelopes gu., crined and horned or. **Motto:** *Nil admirari* ('Wondering at nothing'). **Creations:** B. (I) 13 June 1834 (Carew) and (UK) 9 July 1838 (Carew of Castle Boro).

THE 7TH BARON CAREW, of Co Wexford, and **Baron Carew of Castle Boro**, Co Wexford (Patrick Thomas Conolly-Carew) [The Rt Hon The Lord Carew, Donadea House, Naas, Co Kildare, Ireland]; *b* 6 March 1938; *s* f 1994; *educ* Harrow; late Capt RHG; *m* 1962 *Celia Mary, yr dau of Col Hon Charles Guy Cubitt, CBE, DSO, TD, DL (*see* ASHCOMBE, B), and has issue:

1 +WILLIAM PATRICK; *b* 27 March 1973

1 *Virginia Mary; *b* 13 March 1965; *m* 1985 *Neill S McGrath, 3rd son of Dr Patrick McGrath, of Brownstown Stud Farm, Curragh, Co Kildare, and has issue:

(1) *William James Thady; *b* 1987

(2) *Christopher Neil; *b* 1990

2 *Nicola Rosamond; *b* 23 Dec 1966; *m* 1991 (*divorce* 1992) Peter C G Schwerdt, est son of George Schwerdt, of Hants, and Mrs Diana Hutton, of Portbury, Bristol

3 *Camilla Sylvia; *b* 26 Nov 1969

Other titles of the same name: A Barony of Carew of Clopton in the Irish peerage was conferred on Sir George Carew in 1605. He, who was of the same family as the Carew Baronets (*qv*), that is to say of Devonian and South Walian origins, took part during the latter half of ELIZABETH I's reign in various military adventures on sea and land, on the Continent and in Ireland. His principal Irish appointment was as President of Munster. He was later promoted Earl of Totnes(s). On his death without issue in 1629 both titles expired.

Lineage: ROBERT CAREW; *m* Anne, sis of Lawrence Hyde, of Cottington, and had issue:

1 ROBERT, his successor

2 Lawrence, living in 1721

3 Peter, of Ballynamona, Co Wexford; *d* 18 April 1673, leaving by Joane, his w (who *m* 2nd David Roche, of Killineedy), a son, Robert, and three daus, Mary, Margaret, and Juliana

4 William

5 Richard

6 Henry

ROBERT CAREW *d* by June 1661. His est son,

ROBERT CAREW, of Bally Boro, Co Wexford, JP Co Wexford, High Sheriff Co Wexford 1686 and Co Waterford 1703, acquired large estates in Co Wexford by patent 9 Feb 1668 and by purchases 1669 and 1680; *m* Anne, dau of Andrew Lynn, of Ballynamona, Co Waterford, and had issue, with six daus:

1 ROBERT, his successor

2 Andrew, to whom his maternal gf left Ballynamona, and his other estates in Co Waterford, *dsp*

3 Peter; *b* 1681; had a dau, Martha, who *m* Rev Richard Burgh

4 Lynn; *m* Rebecca Palmer, who *d* 1736. He *d* 1722, and left issue:

(1) Robert, ancestor of the CAREWs of Wodenstown, Co Tipperary

(2) Peter

(3) Thomas

(1) Hannah

(2) Elizabeth

ROBERT CAREW *d* 1708; his est son,

ROBERT CAREW, of Castle Boro, JP Cos Wexford and Waterford, High Sheriff Co Waterford 1711; *m* Aug 1710 Elizabeth, dau and coheir of John Shapland, a wealthy merchant of Wexford, and *d* 1721, having had issue:

1 Robert, of Castle Boro, MP Waterford 1740; *dsp*

2 SHAPLAND, heir to his bro

3 Thomas; *b* 11 Aug 1718, ancestor of the CAREWs of Ballinamona

1 Ellen; *m* Christmas Paul, of Paulville, Co Carlow

The 2nd s,

SHAPLAND CAREW, of Castle Boro, Co Wexford, MP Waterford, barrister; *b* 1716; *m* 18 Feb 1744 Dorothy, dau and coheir of Isaac Dobson, and had, with five daus:

ROBERT SHAPLAND CAREW, of Castle Boro, MP Waterford and Co Wexford; *bapt* 23 June 1752; *m* May 1783 Anne, dau and heir of Rev Richard Pigott, DD, of Dysart, Queen's Co, by Hon Dorothea Crosbie, dau of 1st Baron Branden, and *d* 29 March 1829, having had, with three daus:

ROBERT SHAPLAND CAREW, **1st Baron Carew**, of Co Wexford (I), so *cr* 13 June 1834, also 9 July 1838 BARON CAREW OF CASTLE BORO, Co Wexford (UK), KP (1851); *b* 9 March 1787; *educ* Ch Ch Oxford; MP (Whig) Co Wexford 1812–30 and 1831–34, Ld Lt Co Wexford 1831–56; *m* 16 Nov 1816 Jane Catherine (*d* 12 Nov 1901 aged 103), dau of Maj Anthony Cliffe, of New Ross, Co Wexford, by Frances, est dau of Col Joseph Deane, of Terenure, MP Co Dublin, and *d* 2 June 1856, leaving:

1 ROBERT SHAPLAND CAREW, **2nd Baron Carew**, KP (1872); Col Wexford Militia, Ld Lt and custos rotulorum Co Wexford 1856–81; *b* 28 Jan 1818; *m* 16 July 1844 Emily Anne (*d* 24 Nov 1899), 2nd dau and coheir of Sir George Richard Philips, 2nd and last Bt, of Weston, Warwicks, and *d* 9 Sept 1881, leaving:

(1) ROBERT SHAPLAND GEORGE JULIAN CAREW, **3rd Baron Carew**, DL Co Wexford; *educ* Trin Coll Cambridge (BA); *b* 15 June 1860; *m* 27 June 1888 Julia Mary (*d* 28 Sept 1922), er dau of Albert Arthur Erim Lethbridge (*see* LETHBRIDGE, Bt), and *dsp* 29 April 1923

(2) GEORGE PATRICK JOHN CAREW, **4th Baron Carew**; *b* 1 Feb 1863; *m* 5 Oct 1888 Maud Beatrice (*d* 17 July 1955), 2nd dau of John Summons Ramsay, and *dsp* 21 April 1926

2 Shapland Francis, Lt 8th Hus, Lt-Col Wexford Mil, RM Clonmel, Co Tipperary; *b* 19 Feb 1827; *m* 7 Aug 1858 Lady Hester Georgiana Browne (*d* 10 Jan 1925), dau of 2nd Marquess of Sligo (*qv*), and *d* 6 June 1892, leaving issue:

(1) GERALD SHAPLAND, **5th Baron**

(1) Nesta Elizabeth; granted rank of baron's dau 28 Dec 1926; *b* 29 April 1861; *d* unm 22 Oct 1936

1 Anne Dorothea; *m* 7 Oct 1851 John Davies Gilbert, of Trelissick, Cornwall, and *d* 6 April 1909, leaving issue. He *d* 16 April 1854

2 Ellen Jane; *m* 29 July 1846 Charles Glynne Prideaux Brune, DL, of Prideaux Place, Cornwall, and *d* 12 Sept 1902, leaving issue. He *d* 16 Oct 1907

The 4th BARON's cousin,

GERALD SHAPLAND CAREW, **5th Baron Carew**; *b* 26 April 1860; *m* 21 April 1904 Catherine (*d* 20 March 1947), only dau of Thomas Conolly, MP, of Castletown (*see* LONGFORD, E), and had issue:

1 WILLIAM FRANCIS, **6th Baron**

2 +Gavin George, MBE (1945), TD (1956) [The Hon Gavin Carew MBE TD, The Grove, Little Bealings, Woodbridge, Suffolk IP13 6LL]; *b* 21 Sept 1906; *educ* Clifton; Maj Co of London Yeo, served WW II in W Desert, Italy, Belgium and Germany (despatches), US Legion of Merit; *m* 30 April 1932 Aileen Hilda Frances (*d* 1974), only dau of Ean Francis Cecil, of Hilltop, Sunningdale, Berks, and Fasnadarach, Dinnet, Aberdeenshire (*see* EXETER, M), and *d* 11 Oct 1997, leaving:

(1) *Anne Hilda Catherine [Mrs John Dix, Gellilyndu, Llanio, Tregaron, Cardiganshire]; *b* 3 Dec 1933; *m* 6 June 1953 *John Dix, son of Lt-Col Stephen Hamilton Dix, MC, of Chudleigh, Devon, and has issue:

1a *Stephen Gavin; *b* 11 Sept 1955

1a *Julia Anne; *b* 19 Aug 1954

2a *Anita Frances; *b* 11 March 1957

3 Peter Cuthbert; *b* 31 Dec 1908; Lt-Cdr RN (ret 1953), F/Lt RAF WW II; *m* 22 Nov 1937 *Barbara [The Hon Mrs Peter Carew, Highlands, Fitzgerald Rd, Woodbridge, Suffolk IP12 1EN], est dau of Henry Wolley Leigh-Bennett, of Knightsbridge, and *d* 1980, leaving:

(1) David Edward; *b* 2 Dec 1942; *educ* Thomas More Sch Farnham; *d* unm 3 May 1977

(2) Thomas Henry; *b* 18 May 1947; *educ* Winchester; *m* *Lucinda (*m* 2nd 1983 John Martin Harkness), yst dau of Joseph Guy Lubbock (*see* AVEBURY, B), and *d* 17 May 1978, leaving issue

(1) *Susan Catherine [Lady Madel, 120 Pickford Rd, Markyate, Herts AL3 8RL]; *b* 15 Aug 1944; *m* 16 Oct 1971 *Sir (William) David Madel, MP, er son of William R Madel, of Northwich, Cheshire, and has issue:

1a *Christopher William; *b* 1977

1a *Louise Jona; *b* 1975

The 5th BARON *d* 3 Oct 1927; his est son,

WILLIAM FRANCIS CAREW later CONNOLLY-CAREW (deed poll 25 March 1938), **6th Baron Carew**, CBE (1966); *b* 23 April 1905; *educ* Wellington; ADC to Govr Bermuda 1931–36, Capt and Brevet-Maj Duke of Cornwall's LI WW II (wounded), Nat Chm Br Legion 1963–66, Br Govt Tstee Irish Sailors' and Soldiers' Land Tst, Pres Irish Olympic Horse Soc (ret 1969), CStJ; *m* 3 June 1937 *Lady Sylvia Gwendoline Eva Maitland, CStJ, only dau of 15th Earl of Lauderdale (*qv*), and *d* 1994, having had issue:

1 PATRICK THOMAS CONNOLLY-CAREW, **7th and present Baron Carew**

2 +Gerald Edward Ian CAREW later MAITLAND-CAREW (deed poll 1971), DL (Roxburgh, Ettrick and Lauderdale 1989) [Capt The Hon Gerald Maitland-Carew DL, Thirlestane Castle, Lauder, Berwickshire TD2 6RU]; *b* 28 Dec 1941; *educ* Harrow; late Capt 15th/19th Hus; chm: Gurkha Welfare Tst Scotland 1995–, Musselburgh Racecourse 1994–, Lauderdale Hunt 1980–, Lauderdale and Galawater Branch Roy Br Legn Scotland 1976–; Pres: Border Rifle League 1975–, Scottish Horse Trials Championships 1982–; memb: Roy Co Archers 1982–, Jockey Club 1987–, cncl ILPH 1992–; *m* 1972 *Rosalind Averil, er dau of Lt-Col Neil Hanning Reed Speke, MC and bar, of Aydon White Ho, Corbridge, Northumberland, and has issue:

(1) +Edward Ian Conolly; *b* 5 Nov 1976

(2) +Peter Gerald; *b* 5 Feb 1979

(1) *Emma Rosalind; *b* 15 Dec 1974

1 *Diana Sylvia [Baroness Alexis Wrangel, Lone End, Oberstown Cross, Tara, Co Meath, Ireland]; *b* 7 April 1940; equestrian rep Ireland Olympic Games; *m* 1985 *Baron Alexis Wrangel

2 *Sarah Catherine [The Hon Mrs Macpherson, Round Ash, E Worlington, Crediton, Devon EX17 4TZ]; *b* 6 Nov 1944; *m* 5 March 1966 *Ian Arthur Cluny Macpherson, son of Maj Arthur Clarence Macpherson, of Rowana Ho, Westward Ho!, N Devon, and has issue:

(1) *John Gavin; *b* 5 April 1967

(1) *Caroline Emma Louise; *b* 7 Nov 1969

(2) *Katharine Heather Elizabeth; *b* 23 Oct 1974

CAREW, Bt

Arms: Or three lions passant in pale sa. **Crest:** A mainmast, the roundtop set off with palisadoes or, a demi-lion issuant thereout sa. **Motto:** *Nil conscire sibi* ('Conscious of no guilt'). **Creation:** Bt. (E) 2 Aug 1661.

SIR RIVERS VERAIN CAREW, 11TH BT, of Haccombe, Co Devon [Sir Rivers Carew Bt, Cherry Bounds, Hicks Lane, Girton, Cambridge CB3 0JS; Undercliffe Cottage, Clarence St, Dartmouth, Devon TQ6 9NW]; *b* 17 Oct 1935; *s f* 1976; *educ* St Columba's Coll Dublin and Dublin U (BAg (Hort), MA); jnlst, jt editor *The Dublin Magazine* 1964–69, with RTE TV 1967–87, BBC World Serv 1987–93, author: *Figures out of Mist*; *m* 1st 7 Dec 1968 (*divorce* 1991) Susan Babington, 2nd dau of Harold Babington Hill, of 30 Ovington Court, Brompton Rd, SW3; *m* 2nd 1992 *Siobhán, 2nd dau of Críostíór Seán MacCárthaigh, of Cork, and has had by his 1st w:

1 +GERALD De REDVERS; *b* 24 May 1975

2 Henry Mohunn; *b* and *d* 29 Oct 1973

1 *Marcella Tamsin; *b* 29 May 1970

2 *Marina Lys; *b* 18 July 1972

3 *Miranda Rose; *b* 29 Oct 1973

Lineage: WALTER Fitz OTHER, Castellan of Windsor (*see* LEINSTER, D); had:

GERALD Fitz WALTER; Constable Pembroke Castle *temp* HENRY I; *m* Nesta, dau of Rhys ap Griffyd ap Tudor Mawr, Prince of S Wales, and heiress of Carew Castle, and had an est s:

WILLIAM Fitz GERALD, of Carew/Carru Castle, Pembs; *d* 1173, leaving, with other issue (including William, ancestor of GERARD, B, *qv*):

OTHO; ancestor of:

JOHN CAREW, of Carew, Pembs, Moulsford, Berks, and Idrone, Ireland, where Ld Deputy; *m* Margaret, dau of John Mohun, of Dunster, and *d c* 1363, leaving:

Sir LEONARD CAREW, of Carew, Moulsford and Idrone; *b* 1342; *m* Alice, dau of Sir Edmond FitzAlan (*see* NORFOLK, D), and *d* 1370, leaving:

THOMAS CAREW, of Carew, Moulsford and Idrone; *m* Elizabeth, dau of Sir William Bonville, of Shute, and *d* 1431, leaving:

Sir NICHOLAS CAREW; feudal Ld of Carew; *m* as her 1st husb Joan (*m* 2nd Sir Robert de Vere and by him was grandmother of 15th Earl of Oxford; *see* SAINT ALBANS, D), dau of Sir Hugh Courtenay (*see* DEVON, E), and had, with five sons and three daus:

1 Thomas (Sir), of Mohun's Ottery; ancestor of the CAREWs of Mohun's Ottery, CAREWs of Bickleigh and CAREWs who held the Earldom of Totnes

2 NICHOLAS (Sir), of whom hereafter

3 Hugh, to whom his mother gave Lynham and other manors in Devon; *dsp*, when his manors passed to his bro Nicholas

4 Alexander; ancestor of the CAREWs of Antony

5 William (Sir); ancestor of the CAREWs of Carew Castle, and Crowcombe

Sir NICHOLAS *d* 1446; his 2nd son,

Sir NICHOLAS CAREW; came into possession of the manors of Haccombe, Ringmore and Milton, all Devon, through his mother; *m* Elizabeth, dau of Sir John Croker, of Lydeard St Lawrence, Somerset, and widow of John Seymour, of Berry Pomeroy (*see* SOMERSET, D), and *d* 13 Sept 1469, leaving:

JOHN CAREW, of Haccombe, who *m* Elizabeth, dau of 7th Lord (Baron) Zouche (of Haryngworth; *qv*), and had, with a yr s (Thomas) and two daus (Elizabeth, Joan):

JOHN CAREW, of Haccombe; offr in Italy in 1520s in Anglo-French forces ranged against Imperial ones; *m* Elizabeth, dau of Sir William Martin, of Dorset, and was *k* Battle of Pavia 1525, having had, with a yr s (Henry) and two daus (Mary, Christiana):

THOMAS CAREW, of Haccombe; *m* Mary (*d* 19 Nov 1558), dau of William Huddle, of Pillesdon, Dorset, and *d* 28 March 1586 aged 68, having had, with two er s (*dsp*) and six daus (Katherine, Dorothy, Barbara, Mary, Margaret, Joane):

JOHN CAREW, of Haccombe; *m* Elizabeth (*d* Ascension Day 1611), dau of Robert Hill, of Shilston, Devon, and had:

1 THOMAS
2 John; *b c* 1603
3 Robert; *b* 1605
4 Peter; *b* 1608
5 Edward; *b* 1610
1 Ursula; *b c* 1606

JOHN CAREW *d* 1620; his est son,

THOMAS CAREW, of Haccombe; *b* 1601; *m* Anne (*d* 8 Dec 1656), dau of Rev John Clifford, DD, of Ugbrook, and *d* 6 Dec 1656, having had, with a dau and four other s:

Sir Thomas Carew, 1st Bt (E), so *cr* 2 Aug 1661, of Haccombe; *bapt* 21 June 1632; MA Oxford; *m* 1st his cousin 1653 Elizabeth, est dau and coheir of Sir Henry Carew, of Bickleigh; *m* 2nd (licence 20 June 1672) Martha (*bur* 10 Jan 1673/74), dau and coheir of Arthur Duck, LLD, and *d* Sept 1673, leaving an only surv s:

Sir Henry Carew, 2nd Bt; *b* 1654; *m* 1st (licence 8 April 1673) Elizabeth (*dsp*), dau of Thomas, 1st Lord Clifford, of Chudleigh (*qv*); *m* 2nd 3 Jan 1683/4 Katharine (*dsp*), dau of John Fownes, of Whitleigh; *m* 3rd 1687 Gratiana, dau of Thomas Darell, of Trewornan, Cornwall, and *d* 1695, having by her had:

1 **Sir Henry Darell Carew, 3rd Bt**; *b* 1687; *d* unm by 7 July 1708
2 **Sir Thomas Carew, 4th Bt**, Sheriff of Devon 1731; *b* 1692; *m* 1725 Dorothy (*d* by April 1776), dau and coheir of Peter West, of Tiverton Castle, and *d* by 1746, leaving an er s:

(1) **Sir John Carew, 5th Bt**; *b* 1726; *m* 1755 Elizabeth (*d* 8 Feb 1817), dau and coheir of Rev Henry Holdsworth, of Dartmouth, and had issue:

1a THOMAS (Sir), **6th Bt**
2a John West (Rev), Rector of Bickleigh, Devon; *m* Lydson, dau of Rev Charles Smalwood, and had issue
3a Henry, Capt RN; *m* Maria, dau of Rev Henry Fownes, and had issue
1a Dorothy Christiana

Sir JOHN *d* by Feb 1773; his est son,

Sir Thomas Carew, 6th Bt; *m* 19 June 1777 Jane (*d* 4 May 1838), dau of Rev Charles Smalwood, and had, with five daus:

1 HENRY (Sir), **7th Bt**
2 Charles *dsp*
3 Thomas (Rev), of Collipriest Ho, Devon, Rector of Bickleigh; *b* 15 Feb 1788; *m* Dec 1820 Holway (*d* 3 April 1857), only dau of Robert Baker, of Collompton, Devon, and *d* 13 Nov 1848, having had issue:

(1) THOMAS, of Collipriest, Devon, JP, High Sheriff 1878; *b* 1821; *d* 1880
(2) Robert Baker (Rev), MA Oxford, Rector of Bickleigh; *b* 30 Nov 1823; *m* 13 Aug 1851 Augusta Elizabeth (*d* 1 Dec 1921), dau of Thomas Daniel, of Stoodleigh, and *d* 1899, having had issue:

1a Francis Henry, MA, 2nd Sec Dip Serv; *b* 30 June 1852; *m* 19 June 1878 Rose Matilda (*d* 2 Nov 1881), 3rd dau of Adml Hon Sir Edward Alfred John Harris, KCB, and sis of 4th Earl of Malmesbury (*qv*), and *dvp* 11 March 1888, leaving issue:

1b Dorothy Beatrice Rose; *m* 22 Oct 1908 Maj Humphrey St Leger Stucley, Gren Gds, yst son of Sir George Stucley, 1st Bt (*qv*), and *d* 29 Jan 1954, leaving issue. He was *ka* 29 Oct 1914

2a Charles Robert Sydenham, of Collipriest Ho, Devon, JP, BA Camb, MP NE Div of Devon 1915–22; *b* 7 June 1853; *m* 15 Oct 1891 Muriel Mary (*d* 4 March 1939), dau of Sir John Heathcoat-Amory, 1st Bt (*qv*), and *d* 23 March 1939, leaving issue:

1b Peter Gawen, Capt late Roy 1st Devon Yeo; *b* 1894; *educ* Winchester and Trin Coll Cambridge; *m* 15 Sept 1927 Ruth, est dau of Arthur Chamberlain, JP, of Rackenford Manor, Tiverton, and *d* 5 Sept 1967, having had issue:

1c Timothy Mohun; *b* 10 Feb 1929; *d* unm 6 Jan 1954
1c *Nichola [Nichola Lady Kennard, Gogwell, Tiverton, Devon EX16 4PP]; *b* 26 April 1930; *m* 5 Oct 1950 (*divorce* 1968) Charles Louis Breitmeyer, BA, slr (*d* 2 Sept 1969), only son of Lt-Col Gabriel Charles Alan Breitmeyer, MC, JP, of Ashlands, Billesdon, Leics; resumed her maiden name in 1968; *m* 2nd 1985 (*divorce* 1992) Lt-Col Sir George Arnold Ford Kennard, 3rd Bt (*qv*), and has issue by her 1st husb:

1d *Hugo Charles [Hugo Breitmeyer Esq, The Stables, Warnicombe, Tiverton, Devon EX16 4PP]; *b* 15 July 1951; *m* 1986 *Diana Margaret, er dau of Michael Harold Wrigley, OBE, of Ganton, Yorks, and has issue
2d *Peter Alan BREITMEYER later CAREW (1970); *b* 15 April 1953; *educ* Eton; *m* *Laura, dau of Esmond Gerahty, and has issue
3d *Henry John BREITMEYER later CAREW (1970); *b* 11 Feb 1957; *m* 1976 *Louise Star, yr dau of Maj Roger Francis Mortimer (*see* PENDER, B), and has issue
4d *Geoffrey Nicholas BREITMEYER later CAREW (1970); *b* 23 March 1962; *m* 1987 *Maxine, dau of Douglas Robson, and has issue

2b Francis Ludovic, Lt 20th Hussars; *b* 1895; *ka* 1914
1b Nesta Muriel; *b* 31 July 1892; *m* 28 June 1927 Edmund George Coryton, late Sudan Political Serv, 2nd son of William Coryton, and had issue:

1c Gillian Merowe; *b* 22 March 1928; *d* 10 Aug 1935
2c *Nancy Loveday; *b* 30 Nov 1930; *m* 12 June 1965 *Simon Charles Spencer, yr son of James Seymour Spencer, of Greenhaugh Hall, Tarset, Hexham, Northumberland, and has issue:

1d *Charles James; *b* 20 Aug 1966
2d *Andrew George; *b* 14 Aug 1968

3c *Jane; *b* 28 Feb 1933; *m* 6 July 1957 *Capt Philip Peter Davies-Cooke, 1st Roy Dragoons, er son of Col Philip Ralph Davies-Cooke, CB, TD, DL, JP, of Gwysaney, Mold, N Wales (Isee COOKE, Bt), and has issue

2b Elizabeth Dora; *b* 1897; *m* 16 May 1959 Col Colin F Tod, RA, son of Maj Alexander G W Tod, 22nd The Cheshire Regt
3c Nancy; *b* 1899

3a Walter Gawen (Rev), Rector of Bickleigh, nr Tiverton; *b* 1 Sept 1870; *m* 5 April 1899 Blanche Gwendolen (*d* 16 March 1969, aged 92), dau of W J Llewellyn, of Southwood, Tiverton, and *d* 5 June 1923, leaving issue:

1b Lorna Gwendolen; *b* 14 Aug 1902; *d* 3 Aug 1985
2b Olive Dorothea; *b* 7 March 1904; *m* 27 Oct 1928 Capt James Ian Robertson, CBE, RN (*d* 31 May 1976), son of James Peter Robertson, of Manor Ho, Bishop's Tachbrook, Leamington Spa, and *d* 18 April 1969, leaving issue:

1c *Evelyn Jean; *b* 11 April 1930; *m* 1976 Richard Noel Firth (*d* 1995)
2c *Susan Patricia [Mrs John Lake, Hollybank, West St, Hambledon, Hants]; *b* 3 Nov 1934; *m* 17 Aug 1963 *Lt-Cdr John Frederick Lake, RN, son of G F Lake, of Chichester, and has issue:

1d *Nigel John; *b* 31 Aug 1965
1d *Fiona Susan; *b* 4 July 1964; *m* 30 July 1988 *Andrew Yue and has:

1e *Alexander James; *b* 8 July 1993
1e *Hannah Louise; *b* 26 Dec 1991

1a Florence Augusta; *m* 1884 Capt Lang, and *d* 1885
2a Dora Frances; *m* 1885 Charles Fetherstonhaugh, JP, 2nd son of Timothy Fetherstonhaugh, JP, of The College, Kirkoswald, Cumberland, and *d* 31 Dec 1942, leaving issue. He *d* 20 May 1934
3a Elizabeth Beatrice; *d* unm 21 April 1911

(1) Dorothea; *m* Thomas Daniel, Jr, of Stoodleigh, and *d* March 1881, leaving issue. He *d* 14 Sept 1862

Sir THOMAS *d* April 1805; his est son,

Sir Henry Carew, 7th Bt, of Haccombe, Newton Abbot; *b* 10 Jan 1779; *m* 3 Oct 1806 Elizabeth (*d* 7 March 1862), only dau of Walter Palk, of Marley, Devon, and *d* 31 Oct 1830, leaving:

1 **Sir Walter Palk Carew, 8th Bt**; *b* 9 July 1807; *m* 25 Jan 1837 Anne Frances (*d* 8 June 1861), est dau of Maj-Gen Taylor, CB, Lt-Govr RMC Sandhurst, of Ogwell Ho, Devon, and had issue:

(1) Walter Palk, Capt RHG; *b* 13 April 1838; *m* 4 April 1872 Ellen Augusta, 2nd dau of T D Daniel, of Stuckeridge, nr Tiverton, and *dsp* 14 June 1873
(1) Elizabeth Anne; *d* 4 Nov 1921
(2) Beatrix *d* 19 Dec 1919

2 Henry; *b* 24 Oct 1808; *m* July 1858 Susan (who *m* 2nd 1 Sept 1880 Joseph Norrington), dau of John Symes, and *d* 24 Oct 1871, leaving issue:

(1) HENRY PALK (Sir), **9th Bt**
(1) Edith Elizabeth; *m* 15 Aug 1885 Richard Bazett, of Cobble Hill, Vancouver, and *d* 1914
(2) Florence Palk; *m* 1888 Gerald Gordon Bond, of Florida, USA, and *d* 13 Feb 1936, leaving issue. He *d* 2 Feb 1936
(3) Laura Susan Augusta; *m* 22 Sept 1887 Col Arthur John Breakey, OBE, late RA (*d* 20 Aug 1929), only son of Insp-Gen John Breakey, MD, RN, and *d* 31 Jan 1945, leaving, with other issue:

1a Ivy Madeline Laura; *m* 1st (*divorce* 1921) her cousin Thomas Palk Carew (afterwards 10th Bt), and had issue; *m* 2nd 27 Feb 1926 Harold Batten Coulthard Yeomans

3 Thomas, of Rattery, Devon; *b* 3 May 1810; *m* 14 Dec 1842 Charlotte (*d* 3 June 1884), dau of Sir William Curtis, 2nd Bt (*qv*), of Culland's Grove, and *d* 5 Sept 1876, leaving issue:

(1) Henry William (Rev), Vicar of Rattery, Buckfastleigh, Devon; *b* 31 May 1845; *educ* Trin Coll Dublin (BA); *m* 28 April 1885 Maude Elizabeth (*d* 22 Feb 1929), dau of Rev FitzWilliam John Taylor, Rector of Haccombe and Ogwell, and *d* 14 Dec 1901, leaving issue:

1a Peter FitzWilliam, Maj Res of Offrs, late Lt-Col and brev Col cmdg 5th Bn Devonshire Regt, formerly Maj Suffolk Regt, served during WW I 1914–19, JP Devon; *b* 3 June 1887; *m* 10 April 1919 Joyce Margaret (*d* 19 Aug 1974), only dau of Capt Hon Arthur Grenville Fortescue (*see* FORTESCUE, E), and *d* 31 March 1954, having had issue:

1b Nicolas Jasper-Grenville, Lt RA (TA), served WW II; *b* 12 April 1920; *ka* 7 Nov 1943
2b John Mohun, MC, Capt Devonshire Regt, late Lt IA, served WW II with 3rd (QAO) Gurkha Rifles, served in Burma 1943–44 (wounded), Java 1945–46, and Malaya 1948–49, ret 1952; *b* 8 July 1921; *m* 1 Dec 1950 Barbara Joan Stewart (*d* 1993), dau of Maj Arthur Neil Stewart Roberts, OBE, The Queen's Roy Regt, of Farnham, Surrey, and widow of Maj Richard Henry Baird Shakespear, The Roy Scots Fus, and *d* 1980, having had issue:

1c +Nicolas John Stewart [Nicolas Carew Esq, 20 Samian Place, Binfield, Berks RG42 4BX]; *b* 10 Aug 1952

2a Jasper, Lt PWO W Yorks Regt; *b* 29 June 1894; *ka* 14 Oct 1914
1a Margaret, VAD; *b* 11 Dec 1889; *d* unm 3 Nov 1918

(2) Alfred Curtis, Cdr RN, JP (BC); *b* 27 Jan 1847; *m* 5 July 1893 Susannah (*d* 9 Dec 1939), dau of Edmund Grantham, and *d* 11 Feb 1927, leaving issue:

1a Thomas Alfred Curtis, served in 2nd Canadian Mounted Rifles WW I 1916; *b* 7 July 1895; *m* 15 Sept 1921 Christina, dau of John Hanna, and *d* 1970, having had issue:

1b +Patrick Henry Curtis, CD [Brig-Gen Patrick Carew CD, 1070 Sunnyside Rd, Kelowna, BC V1Z ZN8, Canada]; *b* 31 March 1931; Brig-Gen, late Roy Canadian Dragoons, served in Korea 1952–53 (two medals); *m* 21 Aug 1954 *Norma Diane, dau of Claude Rupert Methune Willcox, and has issue:

1c *Janice Lynn; *b* 5 Feb 1956
2c *Diana Elizabeth; *b* 4 Feb 1958

3c *Suzanne Marie; *b* 28 March 1961
1b Verona Loraine; *b* 9 May 1922; *m* 1945 *Allan Cameron Barton, and *d* 25 June 1987, leaving:
1c *Thomas Allan; *b* July 1946
2c *Gerald Patrick; *b* 1949
3c *Donald Bruce; *b* Jan 1956
2b *Dorothy Joan [Mrs Charles de Pfyffer, 3910 Suncrest Court, Kelowna, BC, Canada]; *b* 3 Feb 1926; *m* 1948 *Charles Henry DE PFYFFER (formerly PFYFFER von ALTISHOFEN) and has issue:
1c *Charles Russell; *b* 1950
2c *Richard Louis; *b* 1956
1c *Christine Marie; *b* 1951
2c *Alice Jerryl; *b* 1955
2a Henry Walter Palk, served in 2nd Canadian Mtd Rifles WW I 1916; *b* 16 Aug 1896; *k* in RCAF flying accident at Regina, Sask, 22 April 1930
3a Nicholas John; *b* 7 Dec 1904; *m* 5 April 1930 *Violet Miken, dau of George Borge, and *d* 1970, having had issue:
1b Nicholas Darrell [Nicholas Carew Esq, 3405 27th St, Vernon, BC, Canada]; *b* 14 April 1932; *educ* U of BC, Canada
1b *Shirley Elizabeth Diane; *b* 11 April 1931; *m* 1953 —
1a Dorothy Susannah; *b* 29 March 1894; *m* 16 July 1932 Hugh Fraser Cunningham, and had issue:
1b *Dorothy Patricia; *b* 2 Aug 1934
(3) Thomas Gerald (Rev), Curate of South Brent, Devon; *b* 27 June 1848; *d* 11 Oct 1925
(4) Fitz Walter; *b* 5 Nov 1851; *d* 1860
(1) Elizabeth Constance; *d* 1863
(2) Maud Charlotte Louisa; *d* 1856
4 Robert Palk (Rev), Vicar of Rattery, Devon; *b* 20 Oct 1818; *m* 21 July 1864 Charlotte Hornsby, widow of Rev R C Clifton, Canon of Manchester and Rector of Somerton, Oxon, and *dsp* 13 April 1875

Sir WALTER *d* 27 Jan 1874; his nephew,

Sir Henry Palk Carew, 9th Bt; *b* 26 Feb 1870; *m* 1889 Frances Gertrude (*d* 16 May 1955), yst dau of Robert Lock-Roe, JP, of Lynmouth Manor, N Devon, and had issue:
1 THOMAS PALK (Sir), **10th Bt**
1 Dora Gertrude; *b* 8 Oct 1894; *m* 3 Feb 1942 Frederick John Twomey, 2nd son of Capt Patrick John Twomey, of Mumbles, Swansea

Sir HENRY *d* 21 Oct 1934; his son,

Sir Thomas Palk Carew, 10th Bt; *educ* Wellington and Pembroke Coll Oxford, late Lt IA, served WW I; *b* 1 March 1890; *m* 1st 10 Nov 1913 (*divorce* 1921), his cousin, Ivy Madeline Laura, dau of Col Arthur John Breakey, OBE, late RA (*see* above), and had issue:
1 Raymond Mohun; *b* 15 June 1916; *d* 28 March 1917
1 *Zia [Mrs David Hill, 1 Eastview Close, Wargrave, Berks RG10 8BG]; *b* 8 Sept 1914; served WW II in WAAF; *m* 1st 22 Sept 1939 Maj Hugh Richard Stirling, RA (*kas* 29 Aug 1944), only son of Hugh Walter Stirling, of Kenilworth, Ascot; *m* 2nd 1 April 1997 *David Maurice Hill, and by her 1st husb has:
(1) *Anthony Carew [Anthony Stirling Esq, 1 Eldon Farm, King's Somborne, Hants SO2 6QN]; *b* 23 July 1942; *educ* Pangbourne Nautical Coll; *m* 5 Oct 1968 *Geraldine Erica, yst dau of F/Lt Walter Frank Barber, of Wargrave, Berks
(1) *Valerie Frances; *b* 20 Sept 1943; *m* 19 April 1969 *Jeremy Hamilton Lightly, son of Capt Lightly, of Kingston-on-Thames, and has issue:
1a *Yvonne Susan; *b* 1970
2a *Nicola Jane; *b* 1973

Sir Thomas *m* 2nd 20 Aug 1927 Phyllis Evelyn (*d* 1976), only child of Neville Mayman, of Sydney, NSW, and *d* April 1976, leaving by her:
2 Sir RIVERS VERAIN CAREW, **11th and present Bt**
2 *Œnone Venetia [Mrs John O'Sullivan, 17 Brighton Ave, Rathgar, Dublin 6, Ireland]; *b* 9 June 1929; *m* 1957 *John O'Sullivan and has:
(1) *Rowan John Amadeus; *b* 19–
(1) *Kilda Mary Venetia; *b* 19–
(2) *Marney Darrell Owen; *b* 19–

CARLISLE

Arms: Quarterly of six, 1st, gules on a bend between six crosslets fitchée argent an escutcheon or charged with a demi-lion rampant, pierced through the mouth by an arrow within a double tressure flory-counterflory, all gules, and above the escutcheon a mullet sable for difference (for HOWARD); 2nd, gules, three lions passant-guardant or in pale, and in chief a label of three points argent (for THOMAS of Brotherton); 3rd, chequy or and azure (for WARREN); 4th, gules a lion rampant argent (for MOWBRAY); 5th, gules, three escallops argent (for DACRE); 6th, barry of six argent and azure, over all three chaplets gules proper (for GREYSTOCK). **Crest:** On a chapeau gules doubled ermine a lion statant guardant with tail extended or, ducally gorged argent, a mullet sable for difference. **Supporters:** Dexter, a lion argent charged with a mullet sable for difference; sinister, a bull gules, armed, unguled, ducally gorged and lined or. **Motto:** *Volo, non valeo* ('I am willing, but not worthy'). **Creations:** L. (S) 1651; E., V. and B. (E) 30 April 1661.

THE 13TH EARL OF CARLISLE, Viscount Howard of Morpeth, Northumberland, **Lord Ruthven of Freeland**, and **Baron Dacre of Gillesland** (George William Beaumont Howard) [The Rt Hon The Earl of Carlisle, 8 Mill Terrace, Easington, Co Durham]; *b* 15 Feb 1949; *s f* 1994; *educ* Eton and Balliol Coll Oxford (MA); Maj 9th/12th Roy Lancers to 1987, fought (Lib Alliance) Easington 1987 gen election and (Lib Dem) Northumbria European parly election 1989

Carlisle, previous creations: Sir Andrew de Harcla or Hartcla, *i.e.*, originally of Harcla Castle in Westmorland, was son of a Sheriff of Cumberland in EDWARD I's reign. He himself was appointed Sheriff of that county under EDWARD II and on defeating at the Battle of Boroughbridge in 1322 a rebel force led by the Earl of Lancaster, the King's cousin and formerly chief of the anti-Gaveston faction among the English nobility, was created Earl of Carlisle. He in turn now began to view EDWARD's favourites with distaste and plotted an alliance with the Scots against the (le) Despensers (*see* FALMOUTH, V). He was found out and executed, when the Earldom expired.

In the early 17th century James Hay (*see* KINNOULL, E), one of the Scots who had swarmed south on JAMES I's heels in 1603, was created Earl of Carlisle. He was a courtier to CHARLES I as well as the latter's father and undertook various diplomatic missions. His second wife, a daughter of the Earl of Northumberland (*see* NORTHUMBERLAND, D), was thought by contemporaries to have been the Parliamentarian John Pym's mistress and to have warned Pym of CHARLES I's imminent descent on the House of Commons to arrest the Five Members. One of the great beauties of the day, she appears to have been active both sides of the fence, for she was undoubtedly the lover of the Earl of Strafford, at one time CHARLES I's chief minister.

The 2nd and last Earl of Carlisle of this (the 1622) creation was nominally a royalist commander in the Civil War but sat out the conflict in the Caribbean. He inherited Barbados among other pieces of real estate (his father the 1st Earl having been at one time Governor of what were then called the Caribbee Islands). Barbados and its associated islets were accordingly known as the Carlisle Islands.

Lineage (of Howard): The 4th DUKE OF NORFOLK (*qv*) had a 3rd s:

WILLIAM ('Bald Willy' or 'Belted Will') HOWARD; restored in blood (following f's attainder) by Act of Parl 1603, Warden W Marches; *m* 28 Oct 1577 Elizabeth, sis and coheir of George, 5th Lord (Baron) Dacre (of Gilsland) (*see* DACRE, B), through whom he acquired Naworth Castle, Cumberland, and Hinderskelfe (the site of the present Castle Howard), and *d* 7 Oct 1640, having had, with other issue, including a yr s (Sir Francis, ancestor of the HOWARDs of Corby Castle, Cumberland; *see* NORFOLK, D):

PHILIP HOWARD (Sir); *b* 6 Dec 1581; *m* Margaret, dau of Sir John Carryl, of Harting, Sussex, and *dvp*, leaving, with other issue:

Sir WILLIAM HOWARD; *m* Mary, est dau of William Eure, 4th Lord (Baron) Eure, and had, with five daus:
1 William; *d* 1644
2 CHARLES, **1st Earl**
3 Philip; *d* unm

4 Thomas; *m* Mary, dau of George Villiers, 1st Duke of Buckingham (*see* JERSEY, E), and widow of Charles Stuart, Duke of Richmond and Lennox (*see* MORAY, E), and *dsp* 1678

The est surv son,

CHARLES HOWARD, **1st Earl of Carlisle**, so *cr* 30 April 1661, as also BARON DACRE OF GILLESLAND, Cumberland, and VISCOUNT HOWARD OF MORPETH, Northumberland (all E), PC (1660–79); *b* by 1629; Sheriff Cumberland 1649–50, Capt OLIVER CROMWELL's Body Gd and Col of Horse, Memb Cncl State July-Dec 1653, MP Westmorland 1653 and Cumberland 1654, 1656 and 1660; allegedly *cr* under the Protectorate 20 July 1657 Viscount Howard of Morpeth and Baron Gilsland, with remainder presumably to heirs male of the body, and was certainly called 10 Dec 1657 to CROMWELL's Ho of Lds as 'Lord Viscount Howard' but in 1660 worked to bring about the Restoration; Ld Lt Cumberland and Westmorland 1660–Feb 1684/5 and Co Durham 1672–Feb 1684/5, Amb to Czar of Muscovy 1663 and Sweden 1664, FRS 1665, Lt-Gen Forces 1667, Col Foot Regt 1673, Govr Jamaica 1677–81; *m* his cousin Anne (*d* Sept 1703), dau of 1st Baron Howard of Escrick (*see* SUFFOLK and BERKSHIRE, E), and *d* 24 Feb 1684/5, having had issue:

1 EDWARD, **2nd Earl**

2 Frederick Christian; *b* Denmark 5 Nov 1664; *ka* Siege of Lutzemburgh and *bur* Westminster Abbey 11 Oct 1684

1 Mary; *m* Sir John Fenwick, Bt (executed for high treason 27 Jan 1697), and *d* 27 Oct 1708

2 Anne; *m* 2 Aug 1670 Sir Richard Graham, 3rd Bt, 1st Viscount Preston (*d* 22 Nov 1695) (*see* GRAHAM of Esk, Bt)

3 Catherine; *d* unm and was *bur* Westminster Abbey 11 Oct 1684

The er son,

EDWARD HOWARD, **2nd Earl of Carlisle**; *b* 1646; MP (Whig) Morpeth 1666–79, Cumberland 1679–81 and Carlisle 1681, Jt Ld Lt Cumberland 1668–85; *m c* 27 April 1668 Elizabeth (*d* 30 Dec 1696), dau and coheir of Sir William Uvedale, of Wickham, Hants, and widow of Sir William Berkeley, and *d* 23 April 1692, having had, with other issue:

CHARLES HOWARD, **3rd Earl of Carlisle**; *b* 1669; MP (Whig) Morpeth 1689–92; Govr Carlisle, Ld-Lt Cumberland and Westmorland and Tower Hamlets, First Ld Treasury 1701–02 and May-Oct 1715, Constable Tower of London, Govr Windsor Castle 1723–30, Dep Earl Marshal 1701 and 1706; *m* 25 July 1683 Anne (*d* 14 Oct 1752), dau of 1st Earl of Essex (*qv*), and *d* 1 May 1738 having had, with two daus:

1 HENRY, **4th Earl**

2 Charles, KB, Col 19th Foot, comded a Bde at Dettingen and Fontenoy, Gen 1765, Govr Fort Augustus and Fort George, MP Carlisle; *d* unm 26 Aug1765

The 3rd er son,

HENRY HOWARD, **4th Earl of Carlisle**, KG (1756); *b* 1694; *educ* Eton and Trin Coll Cambridge; MP (Whig) Morpeth 1715–38; *m* 1st 27 Nov 1717 Lady Frances Spencer (*d* 27 July 1742), dau of 3rd Earl of Sunderland (see MARLBOROUGH, D), and had issue, including three s (*dsp*) and two daus (Arabella, *m* Jonathan Cope, s and heir of Sir Jonathan Cope, Bt, of Brewerne Abbey, Oxon, and *d* 1746; Diana, *m* Thomas Duncombe, of Helmesley, Yorks, and *d* 1770); *m* 2nd 8 June 1743 Isabella (*m* 2nd 10 Dec 1759 Sir William Musgrave, Bt, and *d* 22 Jan 1795), dau of 4th Baron Byron (*qv*), and *d* 3 Sept 1758, leaving, with four daus:

FREDERICK HOWARD, **5th Earl of Carlisle**, KG (1793), KT (1768–93), PC (1777); *b* 28 May 1748; *educ* Eton and King's Coll Cambridge; Treas Household 1777–79, Commr to negotiate with colonist in America 1778, 1st Ld of Trade 1779–80, Ld Lt 1780–82 Ireland and E R Yorks (also 1799–1807), Ld Steward Household 1782–83, Ld Privy Seal April–Dec 1783; *m* 22 March 1770 Margaret Caroline (*d* 27 Jan 1824), dau of 1st Marquess of Stafford, KG (*see* SUTHERLAND, D), and *d* 4 Sept 1825, leaving issue:

1 GEORGE, **6th Earl**

2 William; *b* 25 Dec 1781; *d* 25 Jan 1843

3 Frederick; *b* 6 Dec 1785; Maj 10th Hus; *m* 6 Aug 1811 Frances Susan (*m* 2nd 16 June 1819 Hon H F C Cavendish, and *d* 23 Nov 1840), only dau of William Henry Lambton, of Lambton Hall, and was *k* Waterloo 1815, leaving issue:

(1) Frederick John; MP Youghal 1837–41, DL Sussex; *b* 1 March 1814; Priv Sec to 7th Earl of Carlisle when Ld Lt Ireland; *m* 1 July 1837 Lady Fanny Cavendish (*d* 30 Dec 1885), sis of 7th Duke of Devonshire (*qv*), and *d* 28 Feb1897, leaving issue:

1a William Frederick; *b* 26 June 1838; *d* 28 May 1918

2a George Francis; *b* 28 April 1840; *d* unm 1 Aug 1913

3a Frederick Compton, JP (W R Yorks); *b* 23 Jan 1847; Lt-Col Rifle Bde, Lt-Col cmdg and Hon Col 3rd Bn Yorks Regt Afghan War 1878–79, Burmese War 1889–90; *m* 29 Feb 1876 Ann Augusta (*d* 1915), yr dau of Thomas Hitchcock, of Weeke, nr Winchester, and *d* 14 Aug 1909, having had issue:

1b Richard Fitzroy; *b* 14 May 1879; WW I as Lt 7th and 11th Bns Yorks Regt; *m* 4 June 1914 Elsie Anne (*d* 4 Dec 1938), est dau of Robert Clarkson, of Scarborough, and *d* 1962, having had issue:

1c Richard Frederick Robert; *b* 31 Jan 1916; Capt Green Howards WW II; *m* 1947 *Jean McBride, 2nd dau of Cyril Taylor, of Durban, and *d* 1978, leaving issue:

1d *Jane Anne McBride [Mrs Jane MacLennan, 8 Cleveland Rd, Westville, Durban, S Africa]; *b* 10 Nov 1951; *m* 1969 (*divorce* 1984) Andrew Hugh Ross MacLennan, and has issue:

1e *Angus; *b* 1972

1e *Morag Jean; *b* 1970

2e *Shannon Fiona; *b* 1976

2c +George William; *b* 24 April 1924; CEng, AMI FIMech E; *m* 26 July 1952 *Barbara Enid, dau of Reginald Edgar Everett, of Mill Hill, and has issue:

1d *Katherine Margaret; *b* 7 May 1954; *m* 1st 19– (*divorce* 19–) Peter Kay; *m* 2nd 1989 *Thomas Idris Bowen

2d *Lesley Jane; *b* 15 April 1957; *m* 1987 *Stephen Hutty, of Elloughton, Yorks, and has issue:

1e *William Robert; *b* 1988

1e *Katharine Jane; *b* 1990

2e *Helen Rose; *b* 1992

3d *Sarah Barbara [Mrs Sarah van der Walt, 3 Jengers Mead, Billingshurst, W Sussex RH14 9PB]; *b* 26 March 1960; MA Vet, MB, MRCVS; *m* 1987 (*divorce* 1997) Geoffrey van der Walt, of Chiltington, W Sussex

1c *Bertha Frances Grace [Mrs Bertha Haley, 73 Silkham Rd, Oxted, Surrey]; *b* 11 Sept 1914; *m* 9 Oct 1943 (*divorce* 1960) Douglas Arthur Haley, and has issue:

1d *Ian Richard [Ian Haley Esq, 30 Wellington Rd, Newark, Notts]; *b* 23 July 1944; *educ* Oxted GS; *m* 24 March 1966 *Rose Elizabeth, dau of Michael O'Reilly, of Co Cavan, and has:

1e *Damien Michael Douglas; *b* 1974

1e *Siobhan Geraldine; *b* 1972

1d *Helen Veronica; *b* 14 Nov 1946; *m* 1974 *Brian S Liddell, of Reading, and has issue:

1e *Stephen; *b* 1975

2e *David; *b* 1979

2c *Katheen Victoria; *b* 12 Nov 1918; *m* 1942 John Alan Lake (*d* 1977), and has issue:

1d *Ann Cecilia Mary; *b* 21 Sept 1942; *m* 14 Aug 1967 *Stephen John Curtis, of Upton House, Beeford, Driffield, Yorks, and has issue:

1e *Matthew John; *b* 14 Oct 1968

1e *Amelia Ann; *b* 1971

2e *Madeleine Ann; *b* 1975

2d *Susan Margaret; *b* 8 April 1949; *m* 19– *David Christopher Lavender, of 2 Lea Way, Huntington, Yorks, and has issue:

1e *Rachel; *b* 1970

3c Helen Margaret; *b* 4 Jan 1920; *d* Nov 1941

4c *Elsie Anne [Mrs William Temple, 19 Throxenby Lane, Newby, Scarborough, Yorks]; *m* 1951 *William Byass Temple, and has issue:

1d *Janet; *b* 6 July 1954; *m* 1977 *— Bjornstern

2d *Wendy; *b* 8 Sept 1956

3d *Diane; *b*18 Jan 1962

2b George Frederick; *b* 18 Oct 1894; Hon Capt KRRC, Lt 5th BnYorks Regt; *m* 19 Feb 1919 Jane Anne Scott (*d* 1961), est dau of John Young Myrtle, of Edinburgh, and *d* 18 May 1957, leaving issue:

1c *Margaret Anne Myrtle [Mrs Ralph Hardy, 13 Denleigh Gdns, Thames Ditton, Surrey]; MB; *b* 20 April 1921; ChB, DPh, Capt RAMC WW II; *m* 4 Sept 1946 Ralph Kenyon Hardy (*d* 1993), son of Geoffrey Lancelot Hardy, barrister, and has issue:

1d *Christopher Nigel [Christopher Hardy Esq, 15 St Mary's Rd, Ditton Hill, Surbiton, Surrey]; *b* 23 Aug 1947; *educ* Malvern; *m* 1977 *Carol, 2nd dau of Peter Barnes, of Surrey, and has issue:

1e *Gemma Elizabeth; *b* 1980

2e *Annabel Frances; *b* 1984

2d *Peter Ralph; *b* 20 April 1953; *educ* Surbiton Co GS

1b Margaret Louisa Mary; *b* 5 Jan, *d* 18 Feb 1877

2b Grace Mary; *m* 1901 Alder Alderson-Smith (*d* 1911), only surv son of G Alderson-Smith, of Scarborough, and *d* 1921, leaving issue

3b Evelyn Fanny Louisa; *m* 15 Jan 1908 Roger Ivan Hughes, yst son of Capt George William Bulkeley Hughes, of Carreg Bran, Anglesey, and *d* 6 Jan 1930, leaving issue

4b Helen Emma Edith; *m* 1918 Humphrey Butler (*d* 1919), and *d* 19–

5b Dorothy Ann; *m* 20 June 1916 Rev Philip Charles Walker (*d* 3 July 1933), Rector of Lockington, son of R-Adml Charles Francis Walker, JP, and *d* 4 Oct 1936, leaving issue (*see* WALKER, Bt, of Sand Hutton)

4a Alfred John; *b* 14 Oct 1848; *m* 6 May 1876 Mary Alice (*d* 14 May 1942), dau of Lord Gilbert Kennedy (*see* AILSA, M), and *d* 22 Nov 1916, leaving issue:

1b William Gilbert, CBE (1919); *b* 12 March 1877; Capt RN WW I; *m* 19 Dec 1912 Hon Agnes Caroline Sophia Parnell, JP (*d* 28 Dec 1968), only dau of 4th Baron Congleton (*qv*), and *d* 18 Jan 1960, leaving issue:

1c +Frederick Henry, DSO (1946), MC (1936) [Lt-Col Frederick Howard DSO MC, Isle of Ulva, Aros, Mull, Argyll PA73 6LZ]; *b* 25 Feb 1915; Lt-Col 3rd King's Own Hus WW II; *m* 1st 9 Nov 19– (*divorce* 1946) Estelle Georgette, yr dau of Capt John Sharpe, of Londjani, Kenya; *m* 2nd 29 Nov 1952 *Hon Jean Margaret Parnell, 2nd dau of 6th Baron Congleton (*qv*), and by her has issue:

1d +Henry James; *b* 24 Nov 1956; *educ* Eton and RMA Sandhurst; Capt Roy Scots Dragoon Gds, also Scot Yeo, memb Roy Co Archers; *m* 1983 *Philippa Charlotte, 3rd dau of Maj Lyon Balfour Paul, of Eskdale, Iverness, and has issue:

1e +William Henry; *b* 1986

1e *Kiloran Rose; *b* 1988

2d +John Dugald; *b* 20 March 1958; *educ* Gordonstoun and RMA Sandhurst; 2nd Lt Roy Scots Dragoon Gds

1d *Rose; *b* 4 Oct 1953

2c John William; *b* 18 Jan 1917; *educ* Gresham's and Magdalene Coll Cambridge (MA 1946); Colonial Admin Serv Kenya 1939–63, WW II: Capt 5th KAR Abyssinia and Madagascar (despatches twice), Home CS 1963–77; *m* 15 Oct 1949 *Elizabeth Bligh [Mrs John Howard, Appletree Cott, Staplecross, Robertsbridge, Sussex], yst dau of Capt Robert Francis Veasey, RN (ret), of Mau Summit, Kenya, and *d* 1988, leaving issue:

1d +Jonathan Arthur Francis [Lt-Col Jonathan Howard, Royal Oak, Donhead St Mary, Shaftesbury, Dorset]; *b* 16 Oct 1955; *educ* Eton and Nottingham U (BA); Lt-Col Roy Hus; *m* 1984 *Louise MariaTheodora, er dau of Richard Miles Backhouse (*see* BACKHOUSE Bt), and has:

1e +William Richard Michael; *b* 1986

2e +George Jonathan Henry; *b* 1988

3e +Henry John Arthur; *b* 1989

1d *Sarah Elizabeth Agnes; *b* 15 Feb 1951; *educ* London U (BA); *m* 1st 1973 (*divorce* 1978) Robert James Rogers; *m* 2nd 1989 *Rev Charles Patrick Sherlock, er son of Niall Patrick Sherlock, of Ewhurst, Surrey, and by him has issue:

1e *Patrick John Howard; *b* 1991

2e *Francis Alexander Howard; *b* 1994

2d *(Eva) Jane Agnes; *b* 1953; *m* 1979 *Col Hugh Charles Gregory Willing, RGJ, and has issue:

1e *Edward John David; *b* 1982

2e *Richard Hugh; *b* 1984

1e *Arabella Jane; *b* 1987

3c +Mark Alfred; *b* 13 Oct 1919 (twin); N Africa and Greece WW II with 2nd/7th AIF; *m* 1950 *Judith Ruth, dau of F Selwyn Scott, MBE, JP, of Scotsburn, Victoria, Australia, and has issue:

1d +Michael Gilbert; *b* 12 Dec 1950; *educ* Geelong GS and Australian National U (BA)

2d +William Mark; *b* 2 Nov 1959; *educ* Geelong GS and Glenormiston Ag Coll

1d *Margaret Jean; *b* 23 June 1952; *m* 1980 *Colin MacLeod Campbell, of Rockgedgiel, Quirinfdi, NSW, Australia, and has issue:

1e *Henry Mark; *b* 1982

1c *Margaret [Mrs Christopher Lloyd Browne, Dean House, West Dean, Salisbury, Wilts]; *b* 13 Oct 1919 (twin); WW II Sub ATS and FANY; *m* 30 June 1945 Brig Christopher Charles Lloyd Browne, OBE (*d* 1972), late RA, 2nd son of Lt-Col William Lloyd Browne, RA, of Newcastle-on-Tyne, and has had issue:

1d Andrew William Lloyd; *b* 27 Nov 1948; *d* in an accident 22 March 1967

1d *Elizabeth; *b* 31 Oct 1947; *educ* London U (BA); *m* 1978 *Lt-Cdr Quentin Parker, RN, and has issue:

1e *Jonathan; *b* 1980

2e *Charles Godfrey; *b* 1981

2d *Felicity; *b* 12 March 1954; *m* 1974 *Capt Charles William Granville Dobbie, KOSB, and has issue:

1e *William Arthur Charles; *b* 1980

2e *George Galahad Christopher; *b* 1986

1e *Alice Felicity; *b* 1982

3d *Carolyn; *b* 19 Oct 1958; BSc, PhD (Oxon)

2c *Agnes Nancy [Mrs John Hattersley, 20 Long View Close, Snettisham, Norfolk PE31 7RD]; *b* 30 Sept 1921; BA (OU); WW II Leading Wren WRNS; *m* 15 Dec 1945 Maj John Singleton Hattersley, RE (ret), (*d* 1992), est son of Col Sidney Martin Hattersley, MC, of Overy Staithe, Norfolk, and has issue:

1d *Charles William; *b* 22 March 1949; *educ* Marlborough and Durham U (BA), FRGS; Lt-Cdr RN (Ret); *m* 1988 *Rebecca Jane, only dau of David Smith, of Puttenham, Surrey, and has issue:

1e *Elizabeth Maryse; *b* 1989

2e *Antonia Sarah; *b* 1993

3e *Caroline; *b* 1995

1d *Margaret Sarah; *b* 16 March 1950; *educ* Lond U (BA); late Capt WRAC; *m* 1979 *John Martin Ford, son of Rev Basil Ford, and has issue:

1e *Michael John; *b* 1986

1e *Alexandra Margaret; *b* 1982

2d Anne Agnes; *b* 20 June 1952; *d* 1974

3d *Victoria Vera; *b* 21 Nov 1955; *educ* Aberystwyth U (LLB); *m* 1985 *Peter Francis Harris, and has:

1e *Sophia Anne; *b* 1997

4d *Helen Jean; *b* 25 Aug 1961; *educ* Sheffield U (BA)

2a Ronald; JP Devon; *b* 22 Aug 1878; ADC to HM 1929; V-Adml; *m* 22 Jan 1913 Ruth Evelyn (*d* 15 Nov 1968), est dau of William Coryton, DL, of Pentillie Castle, Cornwall, and *d* 24 Feb 1959, leaving issue:

1c Michael William; MC and bar ; *b* 12 March 1917; Maj Devons Regt WW II; *m* 5 May 1949 *Gillian Hester [Mrs Michael Howard, Southern Wood, Peter Tavey, Devon], yst dau of Sir John Frederick Shelley, 10th Bt (*qv*), and *d* 1994

2c +Roger Alexander, TD [Maj Roger Howard TD, 11 Knightsbridge Court, Sloane St, London SW1]; *b* 18 Aug 1919; Maj (ret) RAOC; *m* 1 Sept 1944 *Jean, dau of V-Adml Argentine Hugh Alington, of Stamford, Lincs, and has:

1d *Alexandra Nancy; *b* 14 Nov 1946; *m* 1971 *Christopher Skidmore Taylor, of Yorton Hse, Harmer Hill, Shrewsbury, and has issue:

1e *Charles Argentine Weston; *b* 1981

1e *Emily Clare; *b* 1973

2e *Alexia Lucy; *b* 1974

2d *Miranda Jane [Mrs Petar Djedovic, 12 Sedlescombe Rd, London SW6 1RD]; *b* 9 May 1948; *m* 1973 *Petar Djedovic, of Petrovac Na Moru, Montenegro, Yugoslavia, and has issue:

1e *Natasha Kate; *b* 1975

3d *Elvina Lucy [Mrs Peter Robert Siddons, 25 Addison Ave, Holland Park, London W11 4QS]; *b* 25 Dec 1949; *m* 1974 *Peter Robert Siddons, and has issue:

1e *Alastair Mark; *b* 1978

1e *Philippa Sarah; *b* 1977

2e *Melanie Sarah; *b* 1980

1c *Millicent; *b* 5 Dec 1913; *m* 5 June 1937 *Col Charles Richard Spencer, OBE, of Elfordtown, Yelverton, S Devon, DL, 12th Roy Lancers (ret), son of Capt Charles Spencer, Devonshire Regt, and has issue:

1d *Edward Charles; *b* 24 Sept 1946; *m* 1974 *Sarah Elizabeth Dewhurst, and has issue:

1e *Oliver Charles; *b* Windham 1978

1e *Caroline Tana; *b* 1976

2e *Rebecca Victoria; *b* 1983

1d *Elizabeth Janet; *b* 10 Dec 1938; *m* 1962 *Gen Sir Frank Edward Kitson, GBE, KCB, MC and bar, DL, and has issue:

1e *Catherine Alice; *b* 1963

2e *Rosemary Diana; *b* 1966

3e *Marion Ruth; *b* 1969

3b Frederick Charles; *b* 4 July 1882; Cdr RNR; *m* 3 Oct 1923 Catherine Harriet (*d* 16 Sept 1945), dau of Thomas William Bourne, of Blakeney, Norfolk, and *d* 25 Feb 1936

1b Margaret; *b* 23 March 1880; *m* 12 Dec 1906 Hon Claud William Biddulph (*d* 6 Aug 1954), yr son of 1st Baron Biddulph (*qv*), and *d* 19–, leaving issue

5a Gerald Richard; *b* 7 Nov 1853; late Lt 3rd Brig Cinque Ports Div RA; *m* 1886 Ada (*d* 7 April 1937), dau of Charles William Curtis, of Lincoln, and *d* 20 May 1945, leaving issue:

1b Alfred; *b* 5 Dec 1888; RCMP; *m* Jan 1922 Merle Ethel, dau of James McEwan, of Ontario, Canada

2b Bertram Marcus; *b* 10 Sept 1890; WW I with E R Yeo; *m* 28 April 1924 Phyllis Maude (*d* 1988), est dau of Robert James Lamb, of Surbiton, and *d* 1970, leaving issue:

1c +Michael Cavendish [Michael Howard Esq, 24 South View, Letchworth Garden City, Herts]; *b* 17 July 1926; *educ* King's Coll Taunton; REME Br W Africa 1945–47, ARIC (1955); *m* 1st 4 April 1956 Muriel (*d* 1978), widow of W T Mullings, MA BSc MD; *m* 2nd 1980 *Patricia Ellen Millicent Gwatkin, dau of William James Sandiford, of Woodford, Essex

2c +Richard Cavendish [Richard Howard Esq, Pigeonhouse Barn, Dingle Rd, Brockamin Leigh, Worcs WR6 5JX]; *b* 17 Oct 1936; *educ* King's Coll Taunton, (MBIM, MIIM); *m* 28 March 1959 (*divorce* 1979) Diana Mary, only dau of Frank B Wharton, of Lichfield, Staffs, and has issue:

1d +Dale Robin Cavendish [Dale Howard Esq, Moora-Moora Co-operative, PO Box 14, Healsville, Victoria 3777, Australia]; *b* 6 Jan 1960; *educ* Manchester U (BSc); *m* 1993 *Michelle Redman

2d +Timothy Richard Cavendish [Timothy Howard Esq, 139 Marley Fields, Leighton Buzzard, Beds LU7 8WJ]; *b* 29 Aug 1962; *m* 1986 *Anne Marcia, dau of Malcolm John McAlistair Bennett, of Harrogate, Yorks, and has issue:

1e +Daniel Timothy Cavendish; *b* 1989

1e *Ellen Francesca; *b* 1988

3d +James David Cavendish [James Howard Esq, Rose Croft, 12 Haynes Close, Thorne, Doncaster DN8 5HR]; *b* 17 March 1968; *m* 1994 *Leanda Ruston

1d *Angela Claire [Mrs Martin John Korchinsky, 14 Empress Drive, Heaton Chapel, Stockport, Cheshire SK4 2RW]; *b* 28 March 1961; *m* 1992 *Martin John Korchinsky, and has issue:

1e *Benjamin John; *b* 1990

2e *Josef James; *b* 1993

1b Mildred Rachel; *b* 3 Jan 1896; *m* 14 April 1934 Frederick George Foord, formerly of West Firle, nr Lewes, and *d* 22 Sept 1963

2b Joan Edith Barbara; Polish Grand Cross of Merit; *m* 2 Nov 1922 (*divorce* 1942) Bertram Eric Edmonds (*d* 1965), Lt Special List, and *d* 1983

3b Blanche Esther Muriel ; *b* 26 May 1904; *m* 30 April 1928 Angelo Victor John de Rin (known in Italy as The Noble Angelo de Rin de Capodistria, who *d* 27 May 1944) and *d* 21 June 1994, leaving:

1c *Diana Maria; *b* 1930; *m* 1955 *Hilary George Alfred Gosling, and has issue:

1d *Oliver Angelo de Rin; *b* 1958

1d *Jane Dorothy Blanche [Mrs Gerard Sweeting, 168 St Ann's Hill, London SW18]; *b* 1956; *m* 1983 *Gerard John Cornwallis Sweeting (*see* HAWARDEN, V), and has issue:

1e *Henry Donald Alfred Beauclerk; *b* 1984

2e *Frederick Oliver de Rin; *b* 1987

2d *Rosemary Agnes Pauline; *b* 1961

3d *Veronica Jean; *b* 1963; *m* 5 Dec 1992 *Andrew Yap, s of Robert Yap, of Sydney, NSW, and has:

1e *Noa; *b* 19 March 1994

1e *Chile; *b* 20 Aug 1996

2c *Victoria; *b* 1931; *m* 1959 *David Lynn Pratt, CBE, FIMechE, FICE, of 76 Royal Hospital Rd, Chelsea, SW3 4HN, and Fox Lodge, Guildford, Surrey, and has issue:

1d *Jonathan de Rin; *b* 1960

2d *James Lynn DE RIN (deed poll); *b* 1963; *m* 1st 19– (*divorce* 19–) —; *m* 2nd 2 Nov 1996 and has:

1e *Simon; *b* 18 June 1997

1a Louisa Blanche; *m* 22 July 1869 Cecil George Savile Foljambe (afterwards 1st Earl of Liverpool (*qv*), who *d* 23 March 1907), and *d* 7 Oct 1871, leaving issue

2a Margaret Fanny; *m* 1 Feb 1877, Hon Frederick John William Ponsonby (*d* 25 Aug 1933), 3rd son of 2nd Baron de Mauley (*qv*), and *d* 1919, leaving issue

3a Edith Susan Louisa; *d* 8 Jan 1922

(2) Villiers Frederick Francis; *b* posthumously 16 Nov 1815; *d* 30 Nov 1823

4 Henry Edward John (Very Rev), DD; *b* 14 Dec 1795; Preb York, Dean Lichfield, Rector Donington, Salop; *m* 13 July 1824 Henrietta Elizabeth (*d* 12 Nov 1892), dau of Ichabod Wright, of Mapperley, Notts, and *d* 8 Oct 1868, having had issue, with five daus:

(1) George; *b* 20 June 1826; barrister, librarian H of C; *m* 1st 18 May 1852 Marion (*d* 1896), only child of Edward Southam, MD, and widow of William Leigh Bennett; *m* 2nd 31 Jan 1903 Jean, yst dau of James Lyon Gilbert, of Aberdeen, and *dsp* 7 April 1917

(2) John Henry; *b* 30 Nov 1827; Capt RN; *m* 25 June 1874 Eliza (*d* 24 Oct 1929), dau of Rev Joseph Salt, of Standon, Staffs, and *d* 31 July 1925, having had issue:

1a Henry John; *b* 7 Aug 1875; *d* 4 Sept 1876

2a Robert John; *b* 2 Aug 1878; Cdr RN WW I, WW II in HG; *m* 22 Oct 1918 Violet Mary (*d* 12 Jan 1930), est dau of Thurstan Collins, of Newton Ferrers, Cornwall, and had issue:

1b +John Thurstan Collins, MC [Lt-Col John Howard MC, College Green Farm, East Pennard, Shepton Mallet, Somerset]; *b* 4 Dec 1919; *educ* Eton; Lt-Col SCLI, WW II; *m* 11 Oct 1949 *Margaret Mitchell, only dau of Lt-Col Courtnay Edyvean, of Cornwall

2b Henry Gerald Percival; *b* 9 June 1922; Sub-Lt RN, WW II; lost at sea 1 Nov 1942

2a (cont.) Cdr Robert Howard *d* 12 July 1965, having also adopted:

*Ruth Mary; *b* 31 Dec 1926; *m* 22 April 1948 *Maj Nicholas Robert Ogle, Northants Regt, only son of Henry William Ogle, and has had issue:

1c *Norman Robert; *b* 11 Nov 1953

1c *Bridget Rosemary; *b* 22 March 1949

2c *Elizabeth Mary; *b* 31 March 1951

3c *Frances Caroline; *b* 3 Aug 1952

4c Joanna Margaret; *b* 9 March, *d* 15 April 1955

5c *Dorothy Annandale; *b* 12 Dec 1958

3a Charles Wilbraham John; *b* 10 March 1880; Cdr RN, served WWs I and II; *m* 6 Jan 1909 Dorothy Ida Leigh (*d* 5 Dec 1968), only child of Sir Thomas Leigh Hare, 1st Bt, MVO, and *d* 27 April 1959, leaving issue:

1b +Geoffrey Charles [Maj Geoffrey Howard, Stow House, Great Somerford, Wilts SN15 5HU]; *b* 30 Jan 1910; Maj Black Watch WW II; *m* 14 Feb 1939 *Katherine, only child of Adml Sir Eric John Arthur Fullerton, KCB, DSO, of Downham Market, Norfolk

1b Susan Elizabeth; *b* 12 April 1913; *d* 2 Nov 1994

4a Edmund John; *b* 20 Feb 1891; *educ* Wellington; WW I with RA

1a Gertrude Alathea; *b* 18 Sept 1876; *d* unm 8 Feb 1939

2a Muriel Adelicia; *b* 1 Sept 1883; *d* 2 Feb 1932

3a Algitha Fanny; *b* 1 Sept 1883 (twin); *m* 22 Feb 1909 Brig-Gen Charles Graeme Higgins, CMG, DSO and bar (*d* 15 March 1961), est son of Capt CC Higgins, 13th Hus, and *d* 16 March 1940, leaving issue

4a Winifrede Alice; *b* 25 July 1886; *m* 20 Feb 1912 Francis Nevill Lloyd (*d* 27 May 1968), only son of Herbert Lloyd, of Addington, and *d* 24 May 1949, leaving issue

5a Edith Mary; *b* 3 Oct 1888; *d* unm 20 Nov 1934

(3) Edward Henry; *b* 7 June 1832; V-Adml; *m* 28 April 1873 Sophia Caroline Lucille (*d* 30 Oct 1926), est dau of Francis Robertson Lynch, of Spanish Town, Jamaica, and *d* 18 Jan 1890, leaving issue:

1a Edward John; *b* 10 Feb 1877; Midshipman RN; *d* 4 Aug 1896

2a Harold Edward; *b* 11 Sept 1879; *d* unm 5 Nov 1953

1a Eleanor Caroline Henrietta; *b* 1874; *d* unm 19 July 1967

2a Julia Margaret Lucille

(4) Charles John Henry; *b* 28 Sept 1834; Capt 71st Foot; *m* 1st 3 July 1862 Lilla (*dsp* 20 June 1876), dau of Capt Edwin L Durant, Madras Army; *m* 2nd 16 Oct 1879 Agnes Catherine (*d* 8 Feb 1919), 2nd dau of Rev Edward Randolph, Rector of Dunnington and Canon of York, and *dsp* 24 July 1907

(5) Henry Frederick (Rev); *b* 9 Nov 1844; *educ* Ch Ch Oxford (MA); *m* 3 July 1878 Eliza Minna (*d* 8 July 1938), est dau of Rev John Spearman Wasey, of Prior's Court, and *d* 6 April 1938, having had issue:

1a Bernard Henry; *b* 10 May 1879; Maj 47th Sikhs, IA; *m* 20 July 1909 Margaret Ellen Edith (*d* 1984), dau of Lt-Col Donat Edmund McMahon and was *ka* 8 March 1916, leaving issue:

1b Henry Bernhard Patrick; *b* 24 May 1912; *d* 13 May 1915

1b *Marjorie Isabella [Mrs Roger Hoyle, Swandown, Axford, Marlborough, Wilts SN8 2EX]; *b* 13 May 1910; *m* 1st 30 July 1938 Lt-Cdr Robert Lampard (*ka* 25 Feb 1941) RN, son of Percival Lampard, of S Devon; *m* 2nd 1 Sept 1945 Cdr Roger Hoyle, RN (*d* 1988), son of Rev Charles Edward Hoyle, and by him has issue:

1c *Hugo Charles John; *b* 16 May 1949; *educ* Clayesmore; *m* 22 Sept 1979 *Susan Elizabeth Haynes and has:

1d *Joshua Roger; *b* 7 Nov 1986

1d *Sarah; *b* 17 June 1984

1c *Angela Felicity; *b* 31 July 1947

2b Rosalind Alathea; *b* 1914; WW II as 3rd Offr WRNS, FO 1950; *m* 1946 (*annulled* 1949) Lt-Col James Dougal Moffatt, IA, and *d* 1970

2a Arthur Henry, OBE (1919), MC; *b* 20 March 1885; Capt Yorks Hus, WW 1 (despatches); FRGS; *d* unm 26 March 1958

3a Henry Charles Mowbray; *b* 27 Feb 1895; Lt Yorks and Lancs Regt, WW I (despatches); *ka* France 30 Sept 1915

1a Margaret Elizabeth; *b* 29 April 1880; *m* 26 Aug 1908 Richard Hicks Barneby (*d* 31 Jan 1923), of Longworth, Herefs, and *d* 26 Nov 1955, leaving issue

2a Nevill Mary; *b* 15 May 1881; *d* unm 21 Oct 1949

3a Evelyn Frances; *b* 23 March 1884; *m* 14 Feb 1912 Anthony Dod (*d* 17 Jan 1960), son of Joseph Dod, of Birkenhead, Cheshire, and had issue:

1b *Philip William; *b* 29 July 1914

2b *Michael Henry Anthony; *b* 8 Sept 1915

3b *Geoffrey Francis; *b* 31 July 1921; BSc

1b *Barbara Margaret; *b* 26 June 1913

4a Maud Agnes Minna; *b* 23 Feb 1887; WW I in Italy with Red Cross, WW II with YMCA and WVS

(5) Henrietta Dorothea; *b* 2 Nov 1892; WW I with Red Cross, WW II with CVWW Overseas

The 5th EARL's est son,

GEORGE HOWARD, **6th Earl of Carlisle**, KG (1837), pc (1806); *b* 17 Sept 1773; *educ* Eton and Ch Ch Oxford; MP (Whig) Morpeth 1795–1806 and Cumberland 1806–20, Ld Lt E R Yorks 1824–40, Ch Commr Woods and Forests May-July 1827, Ld Privy Seal 1827–28 and June-July 1834, Cabinet Min without portfolio 1830–34; *m* 21 March 1801 Georgiana (*d* 8 Aug 1858), est dau and coheir of 5th Duke of Devonshire (*qv*), and *d* 7 Oct 1848, having had:

1 GEORGE WILLIAM FREDERICK HOWARD, **7th Earl of Carlisle**, KG (1855), PC (GB and I 1835); *b* 18 April 1802; *educ* Eton and Ch Ch Oxford; MP (Whig) Morpeth 1826–30, Yorks 1830–32, W R Yorks 1832–41 and 1846–48, Ch Sec Ireland 1835–41, Ch Commr Woods and Forests 1846–50, Chllr Duchy Lancaster 1850–52, Ld Lt Ireland 1855–58 and 1859–64, author: *A Diary in Greek and Turkish Waters* (1853); *d* unm 5 Dec 1864

2 Frederick George; *b* 8 June 1805; Army Offr; accidentally *k* 18 Nov 1834

3 WILLIAM GEORGE HOWARD, **8th Earl of Carlisle**; *b* 23 Feb 1808; *educ* Eton and Ch Ch Oxford; Rector Londesborough Yorks 1832–77; *d* unm 29 March 1889

4 EDWARD GRANVILLE GEORGE HOWARD, 1st and last BARON LANERTON OF LANERTON, Co Cumberland (UK), so *cr* 8 Jan 1874; *b* 23 Dec 1809; MP (Lib) Morpeth 1833–37 and 1840–52, Adml 1870; *m* 16 Aug 1842 Diana (*d* 2 Nov 1893), only dau of Hon George Ponsonby, 4th son of 1st Baron Ponsonby of Imokilly (*see* BESSBOROUGH, E), and *dsp* 8 Oct 1880, when the Barony expired

5 Charles Wentworth George; *b* 27 March 1814; MP E Cumberland; *m* 8 Aug 1842 Mary (*d* 26 Aug 1843), 2nd dau of Rt Hon Sir James Parke, Baron Wensleydale, one of the Barons of the Exchequer, and *d* 11 April 1879, leaving issue:

(1) GEORGE JAMES, **9th Earl**

6 Henry George; *b* 22 May 1818; Sec Legation Paris; *m* 29 May 1845 Mary Wellesley (*d* 21 Feb 1850), dau of John McTavish, of Montreal, and *dsp* 10 Aug 1879

1 Caroline Georgiana; *m* 14 May 1823, Rt Hon William Saunders Sebright Lascelles (*d* 2 July 1851), 3rd son of 2nd Earl of Harewood (*qv*), and *d* 27 Nov 1881

2 Georgiana; *m* 7 March 1822 1st Baron Dover (*d* 10 July 1833; *see* 1899 edn), and *d* 17 March 1860

3 Harriet Elizabeth Georgiana; *m* 28 May 1823 2nd Duke of Sutherland (*qv*) and *d* 27 Oct 1868

4 Blanche Georgiana; *m* 6 Aug 1829 2nd Earl of Burlington, later Duke of Devonshire (*d* 21 Dec 1891; *qv*), and *d* 27 April 1840

5 Elizabeth Dorothy Anne Georgiana; *m* 12 Aug 1840 Rev Hon Francis Richard Grey (*dsp* 22 March 1890), MA, Rector Morpeth, and *d* 11 May 1891

6 Mary Matilda Georgiana; *m* 13 July 1852 Rt Hon Henry Labouchere (*d* 1869), Lord Taunton, and *d* 17 Sept 1892

The 8th EARL's nephew,

GEORGE JAMES HOWARD, **9th Earl of Carlisle**; JP Cumberland; *b* 12 Aug 1843; *educ* Eton and Trin Coll Cambridge (BA); MP (Lib) E Cumberland 1879–80 and 1881–85; *m* 4 Oct 1864 Rosalind Frances (*d* 12 Aug 1921), yst dau of 2nd Baron Stanley of Alderley (*see* STANLEY OF ALDERLEY, SHEFFIELD and, B), and *d* 16 April 1911, leaving issue:

1 CHARLES JAMES STANLEY, **10th Earl**

2 Hubert George Lyulph; *b* 3 April 1871; *ka* Battle of Omdurman Sept 1898

3 Christopher Edward;b 2 June 1873; Lt 8th Hus; *d* 1 Sept 1896

4 Oliver; *b* 14 March 1875; FSA, FRGS; Lt Bedfordshire Yeo, Resident of Bauchi, N Nigeria; *m* 17 March 1900 Muriel, MBE (*m* 2nd 27 April 1909 5th Earl of Clanwilliam(*qv*) and *d* 1 June 1952), dau of Russell Maule Stephenson, and *d* 20 Sept 1908, leaving issue:

(1) Hubert Arthur George; *b* 29 Aug 1901; *educ* Eton and Ch Ch Oxford (MA); *m* 2 June 1930 Moira (*d* 1986), 3rd dau of Rev John Arthur Victor Magee by Gwendolin Georgina Frances Mary, est dau of Sir Mathew Amcotts Wilson, 3rd Bt (*see* WILSON, Bt, of Eshton), and *d* 1986, leaving issue:

1a +David Charles Hubert [David Howard Esq, Ranvilles Farm, nr Romsey, Hants]; *b* 14 March 1940; *educ* Eton; *m* 1st 10 Oct 1962 (*divorce* 1969) Pamela Mary, only dau of Frederick Thomas Rose, of Kenilworth, Warwicks, and has issue:

1b *Susan Mary; *b* 30 Oct 1963

2b *Rosalind Emma; *b* 1966

1a (cont.) David Howard *m* 2nd *Norma Ellen, dau of Norman William Sparks, of Bridgewater, Som, and has further issue:

1b +Oliver Charles Frederick; *b* 1980

1a *Lavinia Moira; *b* 6 March 1944; *m* 21 Sept 1963 *Christopher Thomas Bernard Turville-Constable-Maxwell, yr son of Maj David Turville-Constable-Maxwell, of Bosworth, Northants (*see* NORFOLK, D), and has issue

(1) Gwendolen Georgiana; *b* 5 Oct 1902; *m* 5 Sept 1923 (*divorce* 1934) Capt Roger Bevan Crewdson, late RFA, son of Wilson Crewdson, and *d* 30 March 1936, leaving issue

5 Geoffrey William Algernon, JP; Ld Lt N R Yorks; *b* 12 Feb 1877; *educ* Trin Coll Cambridge (MA); T/Capt RND 1914, Priv Sec to: Parly Sec BOT 1909 and PM 1910, V-Chamberlain Household 1911–15, Jr Ld Treasury 1915–16, MP (Lib) Eskdale 1906–10, Westbury 1911–18 and Luton 1923–24; *m* 15 May 1915 Hon Ethel Christian Methuen (*d* 26 April 1932), dau of 3rd Baron Methuen (*qv*), and *d* 20 June 1935, leaving issue:

(1) Mark Paul Geoffrey; *b* 10 June 1918; *educ* Trin Coll Cambridge (BA), Maj Coldstream Gds, Supplementary Res of Offrs, WW II; *ka* 2 July 1944

(2) GEORGE ANTHONY GEOFFREY HOWARD, BARON HOWARD OF HENDERSKELFE (LP, UK), so *cr* 1983, JP (Yorks 1952); *b* 22 May 1920; *educ* Eton and Balliol Coll Oxford; Maj Green Howards attd IA WW II (wounded); CC 1947 N R Yorks, Pres CLA 1969–84, Countryside Commr 1969, Chm York Georgian Soc and Govrs BBC; *m* 11 May 1949 Lady Cecilia Blanche Genevieve FitzRoy (*d* 1974), yst dau of 8th Duke of Grafton (*qv*), and *d* 1984, having had issue:

1a +Henry Francis Geoffrey; *b* 17 March 1950

2a +Nicholas Paul Geoffrey [The Hon Nicholas Howard, 9 Kensington Place, London W8]; *b* 25 April 1952; *educ* Eton and Oxford; *m* 1st 1983 (*divorce* 1990) Amanda Kate Victoria, dau of Derek Nimmo, actor, of Kensington; *m* 2nd 1992 *Victoria, dau of Thomas E Barnsley OBE, of Llanelidan, N Wales, and has issue by his 1st w:

1b +George Fulco Geoffrey; *b* 1985

3a +Simon Bartholomew Geoffrey [The Hon Simon Howard, Castle Howard, Yorkshire]; *b* 26 Jan 1956; *educ* Eton; High Sheriff N Yorks 1995–96; *m* 1983 *Annette Marie, dau of Charles Anthony Russell Smallwood, of Storrington, W Sussex, and formerly w of 7th Marquess of Northampton (*qv*)

3a +(Anthony) Michael Geoffrey [The Hon Michael Howard, Leyfield Farm, Coneysthorpe, York YO6 7DF]; *b* 18 May 1958; *m* 1985 *Linda Louise, yr dau of Alexander McGrady, of Broughty Ferry, Angus, and has issue:

1b *Arabella Blanche Geneviève; *b* 1986

2b *Grania Alexandra Louise; *b* 1988

(3) Christopher John Geoffrey; *b* 31 May 1922; F/Lt RAFVR, WW II; *ka* over Germany 7 Oct 1944

(1) *Rosemary Christian, DBE (1986) [Dame Rosemary Howard DBE, Coneysthorpe, York]; *b* 5 Sept 1916; Hon MA Lambeth, memb Church Assembly

(2) *Katharine Cecelia Gabriel; *b* 12 Dec 1930; *m* 3 Oct 1953 *Stephen Nicholas Spens, yr son of Sir Will Spens, CBE, of Ely, Cambs

6 Michael Francis Stafford; *b* 23 Jan 1880; Lt 18th Hus, Res of Offrs, late 8th and 13th Hus, S African War, WW I; *m* 30 Nov 1911 Nora, JP Folkestone (*d* 23 Nov 1961), 2nd surv dau of Col William Hensman, RAMC, and was *ka* 9 Oct 1917, leaving issue:

(1) Eric Bertram; *b* 26 Feb 1917; Lt RA (80th Anti-Tank Regt) WW II; *k* 22 Feb 1943 by the Japanese after escaping from a POW camp and being recaptured

(1) *Geraldine Mary; *b* 26 Feb 1917 (twin); MB, BS, MRCS, LRCP; *m* 1st 18 Dec 1943 (*annulled* 1944) Frederick Hume Jackson, RA, only son of Maj-Gen George Hanbury Jackson, CB, CMG, DSO, of Scarborough; *m* 2nd 28 April 1944 Dr Hugh Reginald Jolly, MA, MD, BCh, MRCS, FRCP, DCH, late Capt RAMC, son of Rev Canon Reginald Bradley Jolly, of N Devon, and has issue:

1a *Christopher John Howard; *b* 13 Sept 1944; *educ* Bryanston and Bristol U (BSc)

2a *Paul Howard; *b* 9 March 1951; *educ* Bryanston

1a *Caryl Ann Howard; *b* 18 June 1947; *educ* Aberdeen U

1 Mary Henrietta; *m* 30 Nov 1889 George Gilbert Aimé Murray (*d* 20 May 1957), OM, DLitt, Hon DCL, LLD, FBA, Emeritus Prof of Greek Oxford, Tstee Br Museum, son of Sir Terence Aubrey Murray, and *d* 2 Sept 1956, leaving issue

2 Cecilia Maude; *m* 7 April 1891 Charles Henry Roberts (*d* 25 June 1959), of Boothby, Brampton, Cumberland, son of Rev Albert James Roberts, Vicar of Tidebrook, Sussex, and *d* 6 May 1947 leaving issue

3 Dorothy Georgiana; *m* 14 Oct 1913 6th Baron Henley (*d* 21 April 1962), and *d* 14 Sept 1968, leaving issue

4 Elizabeth Dacre; *d* an infant

5 Aurea Fredeswide; *m* 1st 24 May 1923 (*annulled* 1926) Denyss Chamberlaine Wace (*d* 1944), of Stanmore; *m* 2nd Aug 1928 Maj Thomas MacLeod (*d* 24 Sept 1963), OBE, Croix de Guerre avec Palme, late RFC and RAF, barrister (Queensland, Australia), son of Thomas MacLeod, of Brisbane

The 9th EARL's est son,

CHARLES JAMES STANLEY HOWARD, **10th Earl of Carlisle**; JP, DL; *b* 8 March 1867; *educ* Oxford (BA); Capt 3rd Border Regt, formerly 5th Bn Rifle Bde, S Africa 1902; CA Cumberland, MP S Birmingham 1904–11; *m* 17 April 1894 Rhoda Ankaret (*d* 9 Dec 1957), dau of Col Paget W L'Estrange, late RA, and *d* 20 Jan 1912, leaving issue:

1 GEORGE JOSSYLN L'ESTRANGE, **11th Earl**

1 Constance Ankaret; *b* 20 Jan 1897; *d* in an accident, 3 Sept 1964, unm

2 Ankaret Cecelia Caroline; *b* 23 April 1900; barrister Inner Temple 1928; *m* 7 April 1927 William Jackson, son of William Jackson, of Cheshire (*see* JACKSON, Bt, of The Manor House), and *d* in a riding accident 9 April 1945, leaving issue

3 Elizabeth Henrietta; *b* 24 Oct 1903; *m* 7 Sept 1934 Lawrence Robert Maconochie-Welwood, son of John Allan Maconochie-Welwood, of Kirknewton, Midlothian, and *d* 12 Jan 1969, leaving issue

The 10th EARL's only son,

GEORGE JOSSLYN L'ESTRANGE HOWARD, **11th Earl of Carlisle**; *b* 6 Jan 1895; Lt-Cdr RN WW I, Croix de Guerre; *m* 1st 17 Jan 1918 (*divorce* 1947) Hon Bridget Helen Hore-Ruthven (later **Lady Ruthven of Freeland** in her own right (*see* below), all of whose descendants, of both sexes, are in remainder to that title, hence the + against females and their issue), and had issue:

1 CHARLES JAMES RUTHVEN, **12th Earl**

1 +Carolyn Bridget Dacre [The Lady Carolyn Howard, 16 Brunswick Rd, Penrith, Cumbria]; *b* 18 Aug 1919; WW II in ATS and FANY (Ambulance Corps)

The **11th Earl** *m* 2nd 15 Aug 1947 Esmé (*d* 4 June 1997), yr dau of Dr Charles Edward Iredell, and by her had:

2 +Susan Ankaret [The Lady Susan de Meyer, 50 Hasker Street, London SW3]; *b* 13 Nov 1948; *m* 1st 9 Sept 1967 (*divorce* 1978) Charles James Buchanan-Jardine, yr son of Sir John William Buchanan-Jardine, 3rd Bt (*qv*), and has:

(1) +Flora Jane; *b* 1971

2 (cont.) Lady Susan *m* 2nd 1978 *Count Hubert Charles de Meyer and by him has:

(1) +Alexander Charles Benedict; *b* 1979

The 11th EARL *d* 17 Feb 1963; his only son,

CHARLES JAMES RUTHVEN HOWARD, **12th Earl of Carlisle**, MC (1945); *b* 21 Feb 1923; *educ* Eton; WW II 1942–45 with Rifle Bde (severely wounded); FLAS, memb Border RDC 1964–94, a Forestry Commr 1965–88; *m* 3 Oct 1945 Hon Ela Hilda Aline Beaumont, only dau of 2nd Viscount Allendale (*qv*), and *d* 28 Nov 1994, leaving issue:

1 GEORGE WILLIAM BEAUMONT HOWARD, **13th and present Earl of Carlisle**

2 +PHILIP CHARLES WENTWORTH; *b* 25 March 1963; heir presumptive; *educ* Eton and Reading U

1 +Jane Annabelle [The Lady Jane Ledward, Beaulieu Cottage, The Riviera, Sandgate, Folkstone, Kent CT20 3AB]; *b* 28 Feb 1947 (HRH THE PRINCESS ROYAL stood sponsor); *m* 1st 8 June 1968 (*divorce* 1977) John David Vaughan Seth-Smith, only son of Lt-Cdr David Keith Seth-Smith, RN (ret), and has issue:

(1) +Gemma Bridget Annabel; *b* 1972

1 (cont.) Lady Jane *m* 2nd 1983 *Rodney S Ledward and has further issue:

(1) +Bertie Arthur Ruthven; *b* 1985

2 +Emma Bridget [The Lady Emma Sisson, 28 Elms Road, London SW4]; *b* 20 July 1952; *m* 1st 1974 (*divorce* 1981) John Philip Charles Langton-Lockton, and has issue:

(1) +Maximilian; *b* 1980

(1) +Tabitha Jane; *b* 1978

2 (cont.) Lady Emma *m* 2nd 1983 (*divorce* 1988) Robie Patrick Maxwell Uniacke, and has further issue:

(2) +Robie Jonjo; *b* 1984

2 (cont.) Lady Emma *m* 3rd 1988 *Guy Mark Sisson, and has further issue:

(3) +Ned John Hamilton; *b* 1989

Lineage (of Ruthven of Freeland): THOR; probably identical with the nobleman Thor Sweyn's son (possibly of Northumbrian origin) who witnessed charters of DAVID I 1127–1150 and was overlord of the great mountainous district of Crawford in Clydesdale; granted the church of Tranent to the monks of Holyrood; had:

SWEYN THOR(')S SON; feudal overlord of the district of Crawford, which was held of him by his powerful vassal William de Lindsay (ancestor of the Earls of Crawford and Balcarres, *qv*); settled in Perthshire 1188–89, when he granted lands in Gowrie to the monks of Scone; had, with other issue:

ALAN SWEYN'S-SON, Laird of Ruthven (pronounced Rivven), near Perth; *m* Cecily, dau and coheir of Sir William de Maule of Foulis, and had, with other issue:

Sir WALTER OF RUTHVEN; living 1223–45; took the surname RUTHVEN soon after 1234; *m* Cecily, dau of Gilbert, Earl of Strathearn, and had, with an er s (Sir Gilbert; renounced right to Foulis 1262 and *dsp* 1266–79):

Sir WILLIAM RUTHVEN OF THAT ILK; did homage to EDWARD I 1291 and 1296; had, with other issue:

WALTER RUTHVEN OF THAT ILK; capitulated to EDWARD I 1303/4 but later joined ROBERT I (THE BRUCE) and *d* by 1330, leaving:

WILLIAM RUTHVEN OF THAT ILK; *d* by Easter 1346, leaving, with other issue:

WILLIAM RUTHVEN OF THAT ILK; *m* Joan — and *d* by 25 June 1376, leaving:

Sir WILLIAM RUTHVEN OF THAT ILK; one of the Scottish leaders Battle of Otterburn 1388, Sheriff Perth 1394; *d* in or after 1396, leaving, with other issue:

Sir WILLIAM RUTHVEN OF THAT ILK; a hostage in England for the ransom of JAMES I 1424–27; had:

Sir JOHN RUTHVEN OF THAT ILK; Sheriff Perth 1444; *d c* 1454, leaving:

Sir PATRICK RUTHVEN OF THAT ILK; Sheriff-Depute Perth 1444; *m* a dau of Sir Thomas Cranstoun of that Ilk and *d* in or after 1461, leaving:

WILLIAM RUTHVEN, 1st LORD RUTHVEN (S), so *cr* 29 Jan 1487/8, PC (S by Aug 1513); Hereditary Sheriff Perth, sat in Parl among the feudal barons as Laird of Ruthven 1471; ktd by Jan 1483/4, Conservator of the Truce with England 1484, sided with JAMES III against the rebel nobles Sauchieburn 1488, one of the four Guardians of the boy-King JAMES V from 1515; *m* 1st by March 1482/3 his mistress Isabel Levington, of Saltcoats, widow of Walter Lindsay of Beaufort (*see* CRAWFORD and BALCARRES, E), and had issue:

1 William, *Master of Ruthven*; *b* before his parents' marriage, legitimated 12 July 1480; *ka* Flodden 1513; had:

(1) WILLIAM RUTHVEN, 2nd LORD RUTHVEN, PC (S 1542); Hereditary Sheriff Perthshire, Provost Perth, Extrdy Ld of Session 1539, Ld Privy Seal 1546; *m* after 28 Nov 1514 but by 15 March 1519/20 Janet, Lady Dirletoun in her own right, dau and coheir of Patrick Halyburton, 5th Lord Dirleton, and *d* by 29 Oct 1552, having had, with other issue (including Lilian, *m* as his 2nd w 2nd LordDrummond, *see* PERTH, E):

1a PATRICK RUTHVEN, 3rd LORD RUTHVEN, PC, also (through his mother) 7th LORD DIRLETOUN, PC (S 1553); Hereditary Sheriff Perthshire, Provost Perth, Ld Warden Middle March 1558, one of the promoters of the Scottish Reformation 1560, ringleader in the assassination of Rizzio 1566 when he rose from his sick-bed clad in black armour to lead his fellow conspirators up the secret stair to MARY QUEEN OF SCOTS' apartments at Holyrood, afterwards deserted by his friend the King Consort Lord Darnley (*see* MORAY, E) and fled to England; *m* 1st Janet Douglas, allegedly illegitimate dau of Archibald, 6th Earl of Angus (*see* HAMILTON and BRANDON, D), and had, with other issue:

1b Patrick, *Master of Ruthven*; *m* Marion, dau of 5th Lord Gray (*qv*), and *dsp* & *vp* by 12 April 1561

2b WILLIAM RUTHVEN, 4th LORD RUTHVEN and 1st EARL OF GOWRIE (S), so *cr* 23 Aug 1581, PC (S 1578); Ld High Treasurer Scotland 1571, Ld Warden of the Marches 1578, an Extrdy Ld of Session 1578, Hereditary Sheriff Perthshire, Provost Perth, suspected of showing favour to MARY QUEEN OF SCOTS while she was his prisoner 1567 but fought against her at Langside 1568, kidnapped JAMES VI in the 'Raid of Ruthven' 23 Aug 1582, was pardoned after the King's escape but later arrested, convicted of high treason and beheaded Stirling 2 May 1584, having *m* 17 Aug 1561 Dorothea, dau of Henry, 1st Lord Methven (*see* MORAY, E), and had, with other issue:

1c JAMES RUTHVEN, 2nd EARL OF GOWRIE on its being restored him 1586; *bapt* 25 Sept 1575; *dsp* 1588

2c JOHN RUTHVEN, 3rd and last EARL OF GOWRIE; *b* 1577; *educ* Edinburgh and Padua Us; Hereditary Sheriff Perthshire, Provost Perth; JAMES VI was in his debt to the tune of more than £80,000 but during an unexpected visit from the King the Earl, then aged 23, was killed with his yr bro the Master of Gowrie by courtiers in his town house in Perth 5 Aug 1600; after this episode, in which the Master of Gowrie had hinted to other dinner guests that they should not accompany him and the King and then went upstairs with the King, who was soon heard and seen at a window calling for help and found by his courtiers completely unhurt but struggling with the Master of Gowrie, although the latter's sword was not drawn (JAMES VI's sexual tastes and the good looks of the Master of Gowrie suggesting at least a partly libidinous cause of the struggle), the honours and estates of the family were forfeited, and the very surname of Ruthven abolished (and their forfeited castle of Ruthven called Huntingtower) by Act of Parl 15 Nov 1600

3c Alexander, *Master of Gowrie*; *k* by JAMES VI's courtiers in the so-called Gowrie Conspiracy 1600

4c William; of scientific bent; fled abroad

5c Patrick; MD; also of scientific bent; arrested on JAMES VI's accession to the English throne and imprisoned Tower of London 19 years; petitioned CHARLES I to restore his family name and on 12 Nov 1641 was successful (ratified Act of Parl 17 Nov 1641); styled himself Lord Ruthven, believing that that specific Lordship also had been restored; *m* Elizabeth, dau of Robert Woodford, of Brightwell, and widow of Thomas, 1st Baron Gerard; *d* a prisoner King's Bench May 1652, leaving, with other issue:

1d Patrick, self-styled Lord Ruthven; opposed Parliament in Civil War; lived much in Sweden; *m* twice and *d* in or after 1667

1d Mary; Maid of Honour to QUEEN HENRIETTA MARIA; *m* Sir Anthony Van Dyck, the celebrated painter, and had issue

1c Mary; *m* 1st 5th Earl of Atholl of the 1457 *cr* and had four daus; *m* 2nd 1596 1st Earl of Atholl of the 1595/6 *cr* (*see* MORAY,E); *m* 3rd James Stewart, gs of 3rd Earl of Buchan of the 1382 *cr* (*see* MORAY, E)

2c Margaret; *m* 4th Earl of Montrose (*see* MONTROSE, D); her dau Margaret, Lady Napier of Merchiston (*qv*), was ancestor of Elizabeth Napier, Countess of Arran, great-grandmother of **Lady Ruthven of Freeland**, 11th holder of the Lordship

3c Sophia; *m* 2nd Duke of Lennox (*see* MORAY, E)

4c Jean; *m* 6th Lord Ogilvy (*see* AIRLIE, E)

5c Isabel; *m* 1st (*divorce* 1608 due his adultery) Sir Robert Gordon of Lochinvar; *m* 2nd, as his 2nd w, 1st Lord (Campbell of) Loudoun (*see* LOUDOUN, E)

3b Archibald, *Master of Ruthven* 1566–75; Gen in Swedish service; arrested 1574 after an alleged plot to assassinate JOHN III of Sweden (*see* also ERROLL, E) and *d* a prisoner Vesteras Castle Feb 1578

4b George; *k* with the Regent Lennox (see MORAY, E) nr Stirling 1571

1b Jean; *m* 1st 2nd Lord Methven (*see* MORAY, E); *m* 2nd 5th Earl of Rothes (*qv*)

1a The 3rd LORD RUTHVEN *m* 2nd Janet, dau of 2nd Earl of Atholl and widow of (a) Alexander, Master of Sutherland, (b) Sir Hew Kennedy of Girvanmains and (c) 1st Lord Methven (see MORAY, E), and *d* in exile 13 May 1566, having by her had further issue

2a Alexander, of Freeland; denounced as a rebel for his part in Rizzio's murder; *m* Elizabeth, dau of William Moncreiffe 10th of that Ilk, (*see* ERROLL, E), and *d* 9 Oct 1599, leaving, with other issue:

1b William, of Freeland; *m* Isabella Fothringham and *d* of the plague 20 Oct 1608, leaving, with other issue (including a dau Elizabeth, *m* Sir David Makgill of Rankeillour and had issue; *see* OXFUIRD, V):

1c THOMAS RUTHVEN, **1st Lord Ruthven of Freeland**

2b Harry; Tutor (guardian) of Freeland, forfeited for being present at the Gowrie House Affair 1600

3b Alexander; also forfeited for being present at the Gowrie House Affair 1600

2 John, of Cultvainy and Drumdrane, which lands he received from his f for renouncing the name of Lindsay and taking the name and arms of Ruthven; also legitimated 1480; *m* Libra Livingston and had issue

1 Margaret; *m* by 1499, as his 2nd w, 2nd Earl of Buchan (*qv*) and had issue

The 1st LORD RUTHVEN *m* 2nd Christian, dau of Sir John Forbes of Pitsligo, and *d* after 12 July 1528, having by her had:

3 William, of Ballindean; *m* Agnes, dau of Sir John Crichton of Strathord, and *d* 1528, having had, with other issue:

(1) William (Sir), of Ballindean; *m* Katharine Stewart, dau of 4th Lord Innermeath (*see* MORAY, E), and was *k* Dundee July 1603, leaving, with other issue:

1a William, of Gardyne; took the surname BALLINDEAN or BANDANE when the name RUTHVEN was proscribed; *m* Christian Barclay, of Towie (of the same family as the Russian Field-Marshal Prince Barclay de Tolly), and had, with other issue:

1b William, of Gardyne; in whose time the surname RUTHVEN was restored for services as a royalist in the Civil War; had issue

2b Francis (Sir), of Carse; in Swedish service, Govr Memel, royalist Civil War; *d* 1655

3b John (Sir), of Dunglass; Maj-Gen in Swedish service, royalist Col; *m* 1st Jean Ramsay and had issue; *m* 2nd Barbara, dau of 1st Earl of Leven (*see* LEVEN and MELVILLE, E), and by her had, with other issue:

1c William (Sir), of Dunglass; *m* Katherine, dau of 1st Marquess of Douglas (see HAMILTON and BRANDON, D), and *d* leaving female issue

2c Sir FRANCIS RUTHVEN, 1st Bt (NS), so *cr* 11 July 1666, of Redcastle; *m* Elizabeth, dau of **1st Lord Ruthven of Freeland** (*see* below), and had issue:

1d ISABEL, **Lady Ruthven of Freeland**

2a PATRICK RUTHVEN, 1st and last EARL OF FORTH (S; so *cr* 27 March 1642) and 1st and last EARL OF BRENTFORD, Co Middlesex (E; so *cr* 27 May 1644), also LORD RUTHVEN OF ETTRICK (S), so *cr* 1639, and Count of Kirchberg, in Germany, so *cr* (presumably by GUSTAVUS ADOLPHUS, King of Sweden, who then enjoyed a local ascendancy in Germany half way through the Thirty Years War (1618–48)) April 1632, PC (1645); *b c* 1573; joined Swedish army: Capt 1615, Col 1630, Maj-Gen 1632, Lt-Gen and Col of Horse 1635; ktd 1627, defeated the Imperial forces Battles of Doemitz, Lutzen, Goldberg and Koesen 1635; back in Scotland held Edinburgh Castle for CHARLES I during his war against the Scots 1639–40, Civil War in England: Marshal-Gen and C-in-C Royalist Army Edgehill 1642, defeated Parly forces Battle of Brentford 15 Nov 1642 (whence the title of his E peerage), Ld Chamberlain to CHARLES II in exile; *m* 1st —; *m* 2nd Jane, sis of Col John Henderson; *m* 3rd 1633 Clara, dau of John Berner, of Saskendorff and Ventzin, Mecklenburg, and *dspm* 2 Feb 1650/1, when all his titles expired, leaving by his 2nd w a 3rd dau:

1b Jean; *m* by July 1661, as his 2nd w, 2nd Lord Forrester of Corstorphine (*see* VERULAM, E) and *d* in or after Oct 1668

2 Elizabeth Ruthven; *m* 5th Earl of Erroll (*qv*)

The 3rd and last EARL OF GOWRIE's cousin,

THOMAS RUTHVEN, **1st Lord Ruthven of Freeland** (S), so *cr* between 31 March and 28 May 1651 (the patent of *cr* is unrecorded and its precise terms are unknown; it is said to have been destroyed 14 March 1750 when Freeland House was burned but grounds have been cited for surmising that it conferred a power of nomination in some shape and collateral proof has been advanced that heirs female were not excluded: (a) the retention of the title on the Union roll after the extinction of the issue male of the 1st Lord, (b) the votes given without protest by the 3rd and later Lords at Holyrood at a time when every dubious vote was challenged, (c) the summonses to the coronations and (d) the fact that Ruthven was not included in the careful enumeration (by the Lords of Session) of peerages as to which it was thought possible that a question could be raised; certainly the question was resolved by the creation of the Barony of Ruthven of Gowrie in 1919 which expressly recognised the grantee as holder of the 1651 title and since he held through sevral female lines it implicitly recognised the creation of 1651 as having been with remainder to heirs female; against the collateral proofs advanced above it has been observed that (a) the right to vote for rep S peers was often not challenged in the 18th century; (b) even when it was, two claimants to the same title often both voted; (c) the argument that an invitation to GEORGE I's coronation constituted proof of a peerage's existence and recognition failed 1733 in the case of the self-styled Viscount of Oxfuird), PC (S 1643); ktd 1633, MP Perths 1639–41, 1645–46 and 1649–50; Col anti-royalist regt 1644 but ennobled by CHARLES I probably to induce a change of heart; *m* Isabel, 3rd dau of Robert, Lord Balfour of Burleigh (*qv*), and *d* 6 May 1671, having had issue:

1 DAVID RUTHVEN, **2nd Lord Ruthven of Freeland**; Ld of PC 1689; entailed his estates, failing his own issue, on his sisters and their issue 26 Oct 1674, with precedence to the yst; *d* unm April 1701

1 Anne; *m* 1st Aug 1661 Sir William Cuninghame or Cunyngham of Cunninghamehead, 3rd Bt (*d* April 1671), and had:

(1) Sir William Cuninghame/Cunyngham later Ruthven (after April 1722, when he inherited the Ruthven estates from his aunt Jean (*see* below), 4th Bt; *m* Anne, dau of Sir Archibald Stewart, Bt, of Castlemilk; *dsp* Oct 1722, when the btcy became dormant

1 (cont.) Lady Anne Cunningham *m* 2nd 22 April 1673 William Cunningham, Yr of Craigends (*dsp*), and *d* by 21 March 1688/9

2 Elizabeth; *m* Sir Francis Ruthven, Bt, of Redcastle, Forfarshire, so *cr* 11 July 1666, and *d* by Oct 1674, having had issue:

(1) ISABEL Ruthven, **Lady Ruthven of Freeland** in her own right; invited as holder of a Scottish Ldship of Parl to coronation of GEORGE II 1727; *m* Col James JOHNSTONE later RUTHVEN, 3rd Regt of Foot Gds, of Graitney, Dumfriesshire, s of William Johnstone, of Graitney, and *d* 23 June 1732, having had:

1a JAMES JOHNSTONE later RUTHVEN, **5th Lord Ruthven of Freeland**; voted unchallenged at elections of rep S peers 1733–74; invited to GEORGE III's coronation 1761; *m* 1st Janet, dau of William Nisbet, of Dirleton, and had issue:

1b JAMES RUTHVEN, **6th Lord Ruthven of Freeland**; *b* 16 Dec 1733; Capt 12th Foot; voted at election of rep S peers 1784; *m* 8 or 12 Nov 1776 Mary Elizabeth (*d* 7 Oct 1820), dau of 6th Earl of Leven and (5th Earl of) Melville (*qv*), and *d* 27 Dec 1789, having had, with other issue:

1c JAMES RUTHVEN, **7th Lord Ruthven of Freeland**; *b* 17 Oct 1777; Maj 90th Foot; *m* 20 Dec 1813 Mary Hamilton (*d* 5 April 1885), dau of Walter Campbell, of Schawfield, and *dsp* 27 July 1853

1c MARY ELIZABETH THORNTON, **Lady Ruthven of Freeland**

2b William; *b* 16 Feb 1735; *d* unm

1a (cont.) The **5th Lord** *m* 2nd July 1736 Anne (*d* 28 Nov 1786), dau of 2nd Earl of Bute (*see* BUTE, M), and *d* 3 July 1783, having had by her, with other issue (*d* young or unm):

1b Anne; *b* 3 Oct 1737; *m* 1764 11th Lord Elphinstone (*qv*) and *d* 28 Oct 1801, leaving issue

2b Isabel; *b* 2 Nov 1738; *m* Capt John MacDougal, Yr. of MacDougal (*d* April 1775), and *d* 4 Sept 1775

3b Elizabeth Maria; *m* 18 July 1763 (*divorce* 2 Feb 1774) Sir Robert Laurie of Maxwellton, 5th Bt (*qv*), and had issue

4b Janet; *b* 7 Dec 1747; *m* 1 Aug 1765 Capt Wade Toby Caulfeild (*d* Aug 1800), of Raheenduff, Queen's Co (*see* CHARLEMONT, V), and *dsp* June 1785

1a Anne; *m* 1st 25 April 1724 Henry Rollo, 2nd s of 4th Lord Rollo (*qv*); *m* 2nd Frederick Bruce, of Bunzeon, and *dsp*

(2) Elizabeth; *m* James Pitcairn and had:

1a David; *m* Catherine Hamilton, of Wishaw, and had:

1b John; *m* Elizabeth Dalrymple, of Dreghorn, and was *k* Battle of Bunker Hill in War of American Independence, having had, with four s (*dsp*):

1c Anne; *m* William Campbell, Commr of the Navy, and had issue

(3) Anna; *dsp*

3 JEAN RUTHVEN, **Lady Ruthven of Freeland** in her own right; executor to bro 4 Jan 1703 and made out her title to the estates; her right to the peerage unchallenged in her lifetime; *d* unm April 1722

The 7th LORD's only surv sis,

MARY ELIZABETH THORNTON Ruthven, **Lady Ruthven of Freeland** in her own right; *b c* 1784; *m* 13 Oct 1806 Walter HORE later (with his w on her bro's death 1853) HORE-RUTHVEN (*see* below), and *d* 13 Feb 1864, having had issue (with five other daus *d* unm):

1 William; 75th Regt; *m* 16 May 1836 Dells Honoria (*d* 9 Nov 1883 aged 64), dau of Lt-Col Pierce Lowen, KH, and *dvm* 12 May 1847, leaving:

(1) WALTER JAMES, **9th Lord**

(2) Charles Edward Stewart, OBE (1920), JP (Brecon); *b* 21 April 1840; Lt 51st Regt and Capt Quebec Artillery; *m* 20 Sept 1875 Mariana (*d* 18 Nov 1941), 2nd dau of Col Edward Robert Wood, DL, late 12th Lancers, of Stouthall, Glam, and *d* 1920, leaving issue:

1a Charles; *b* 19 Aug 1878; Capt Breconshire Bn TF; *m* 21 April 1910 Elyned Rhoda (*d* 25 Jan 1965), er dau of Col Thomas Wood, DL, of Gwernfed Park, Brecon, and *d* 26 Feb 1963, leaving issue:

1b +Elcha Cecilia [Mrs Elcha Harrison, Knoll House, Aylsham, Norfolk]; *b* 3 March 1912; *m* 7 June 1934 (*divorce* 1968) William Herbert Harrison, JP, er son of Lt-Col William Edward Harrison, OBE, of Wychnor Park, Burton-on-Trent, and had issue:

1c +Rhona Moya [Mrs Edward Luddington, Wallington Hall, King's Lynn, Norfolk]; *b* 17 June 1936; *m* 8 Oct 1958 *Edward Luddington, est son of Maj James Hilton Luddington, of Wallington Hall, King's Lynn, Norfolk, and has issue:

1d +Nicholas Edward; *b* 6 Feb 1960

2d +Christopher Mark; *b* 11 Nov 1963

3d +Andrew William; *b* 15 June 1965

2c +Zara Carolyn [Mrs Alastair Campbell-Harris, Gattendon Lodge, Goring-on-Thames, Berks RG8 9LU]; *b* 29 March 1938; *m* 9 Jan 1962 *Alastair Neil Campbell-Harris, yr son of Maj Arthur Edward Campbell-Harris, MC, IA, of Belgravia, and has:

1d +James Neil; *b* 22 Jan 1966; *m* 1992 *Vanessa Hogan-Hern and has :

1e +Hugo James; *b* 8 April 1997

1e *Alexandra Charlotte; *b* 2 Aug 1995

1d +Clare Louise; *b* 4 Oct 1963

2d +Lucinda Zara; *b* 17 May 1968

3c +Susan Juliet; *b* 28 Feb 1945; *m* 20 April 1967 *Charles Bannatyne Watson, son of Ronald Kenneth Watson, of Edinburgh, and has:

1d +Adam Bannatyne; *b* 1971

1d +Sara Cecilia; *b* 19 July 1969

4c +Susannah; *b* 1946; *m* 1975 *Martin Woodnutt and has:

1d +Piers Mark; *b* 1977

1d +Emily Sophie; *b* 1979

2b +Elyned Barbara, MBE (1946) [Mrs John Barratt, Upgate House, Swannington, Norfolk]; *b* 18 April 1915; *m* 27 March 1939 *John Legh Barratt TD, yst s of Legh Barratt, of Northolt, Norfolk, and has:

1c +David John [David Barratt Esq, Manor House, Great Witchingham, Norfolk]; *b* 18 July 1947; *educ* Gresham's; *m* 1982 *Penelope Constance Isabel Loyd and has:

1d +Fergus Ralph Legh; *b* 1984

2d +Frederick David Nicholas; *b* 1987

2c +Charles William [Charles Barratt Esq, Ollands Farm, Heydon, Norfolk]; *b* 22 Oct 1949; *educ* Gresham's; *m* 1976 *Caroline, dau of Maj James Clifford Wilson, of King's Lynn, and has:

1d +William James; *b* 1979

2d +Samuel Charles Legh; *b* 1982

1c Anita Elyned; *b* 5 April 1952; *d* 1973

(1) Maria; *m* 7 June 1860 Rev Walter H Sutton, and *d* 4 Feb 1869, leaving issue

(2) Wilhelmina Dells Owena; *m* 19 June 1879 Rev Charles Bodval Griffith, Rector Bishopstone, Herefs, and *d* 29 Oct 1933, leaving issue

(3) Maria Frederica; *d* 14 Aug 1897

2 James Ruthven (Rev); *d* Jan 1839

3 Alexander Leslie Melville; Capt 2nd Berks RV; *d* 11 May 1877

4 James Stopford; *d* 1827

5 Cavendish; Lt RN; *d* 22 Oct 1854 of wounds received before Sebastopol

6 Walter; Maj HEIC's service; *d* 5 March 1856

1 Jane Stewart; *m* 1 May 1858 George O'Grady, of Plattenston, Co Wicklow (*d* 11 Nov 1872), and *dsp* 6 Oct 1917 aged 93

LADY RUTHVEN OF FREELAND's gs,

WALTER JAMES HORE later HORE-RUTHVEN, **9th Lord Ruthven of Freeland** and 1st BARON RUTHVEN OF GOWRIE, of Gowrie (UK), so *cr* by patent (in the enrollment of which the new Baron of the UK was recognised as Lord Ruthven of Freeland, although the Ld Clerk Register of Scotland had denied the Lordship's very existence before a Select Ctee 1882) 28 Oct 1919, JP and DL (Perthshire), JP (Lanarks and Herefs); *b* 14 June 1838; Lt-Col Rifle Bde Crimea, India and Abyssinia; bankrupt in the sum of £3,387 Dec 1881; in WW I joined Rifle Bde aged 76, later King's Messenger; Grand Offr Crown of Belgium 1915; *m* 21 Aug 1869 Lady Caroline Gore (*d* 17 Dec 1914), est dau of 4th Earl of Arran (*qv*), and *d* 28 Feb 1921, having had issue:

1 WALTER PATRICK; **10th Lord**

2 ALEXANDER GORE ARKWRIGHT HORE-RUTHVEN, *cr* EARL OF GOWRIE (*qv*)

3 Christian Malise, CMG (1918), DSO (1902); *b* 24 April 1880 (HRH PRINCESS CHRISTIAN stood sponsor); Col Black Watch, S Africa 1899–1902 (despatches three times, two medals with five clasps), WW I (wounded, despatches, brevet, Croix de Guerre), Cdr 15th (Durham LI) Bde 1929, ADC to HM GEORGE V 1932–33; *m* 26 May 1925 Hon Angela Margaret Manners, RRC (*d* 1 Feb 1970), dau of 3rd Baron Manners (*qv*), and *d* 3 May 1969, leaving issue:

(1) +James John Malise [James Hore-Ruthven Esq, 42 Westminster Gdns, Marsham St, London SW1 4JD]; *b* 17 Aug 1935; *educ* Eton; chm cncl management MRA; *m* 19 June 1965 *(Helen) Dron, er dau of John Sommerville Craig, of Woodridge, Milngavie, Glasgow, and has issue:

1a +Alexander Malise; *b* 21 Aug 1972

1a +Angela Dron; *b* 1976

(1) Nancy Margaret; *b* 10 March 1927; *k* in a car crash 20 Aug 1989

(2) +Sarah Constance Anne [Mrs James Baynard-Smith, 44 Sunderland Ave, Oxford]; *b* 16 Oct 1930; *m* 1 Dec 1962 *James Baynard-Smith, MA, only son of Sydney Baynard-Smith, of Wineanton, Rowlands Castle, Hants, and has:

1a +Peter James; *b* 21 March 1966; *m* 1993 *Julia Woodley, and has issue:

1b +Rebekah Clare; *b* 9 Sept 1996

2a +Christopher Ruthven; *b* 5 Oct 1972

4 Philip James Leslie; *b* 7 June 1882; Lt HLI Boer War 1901–02 (Queen's medal with three clasps); *m* 8 March 1906 Lydia Gladys (*m* 2nd 15 April 1912 Maj-Gen Hugh Wharton Myddleton Watson, CB, CMG, DSO (*d* 23 March 1938), son of Maj-Gen JC Watson, 60th Rifles, and *d c* 1950, having had issue), yst dau of Henry Adams, of Cannon Hill, Bray, Berks, and *dsp* 18 May 1908

1 Beatrix Mary Leslie; *b* 4 June 1871; *m* 1st 5th Dec 1888 (*divorce* 1894) Charles Lindsay Orr Ewing (*d* 24 Dec 1903) (*see* ORR EWING, Bt); *m* 2nd 28 Dec 1894 (*divorce* 1914) Charles Edward Malcolm (*d* 16 April 1935), of Maxstoke Castle, Coleshill. Warwicks (*see* MALCOLM, Bt); *m* 3rd 30 Dec 1914 Sir Thomas Octave Murdoch Sopwith, CBE, s of Thomas Sopwith, MICE, and *d* 24 March 1930, leaving issue by her 2nd husb

The 9th LORD's er surv son,

WALTER PATRICK HORE-RUTHVEN, **10th Lord Ruthven of Freeland**, CB (1919), CMG (1915), DSO (1900), JP and DL (Lanarks); *b* 6 June 1870; *educ* Eton; Maj-Gen late Scots Gds, Bde-Maj 4th Gds Bde 1914, cmded 1st Bn Scots Gds 1914–15, GSO(1) 47th and Gds Div 1915–16, BGS 8th Army Corps 1916–17, cmded 120th Inf Bde 1918, 1st Gds Bde 1919, Brig cmdg S Cmd India 1920, Col Cmdt cmdg a Bde India 1921, and GOC London Dist 1924–28, Lt-Gov and cmdg troops Guernsey 1929–34, S Africa 1899–1902 (Queen's medal with nine clasps, despatches three times), WW I (wounded, despatches seven times, Brevet Col), Gold Medal Montenegro; *m* 1st 23 April 1895 Jean Leslie (*d* 8 Dec 1952), only dau of Norman George Lampson, JP, DL (*see* KILLEARN, B), and had issue:

1 BRIDGET HELEN, **Lady Ruthven of Freeland**

2 Jean Elisabeth St Loe; *m* 21 June 1933 Don Francisco Larios (*d* 26 Nov 1958), only son of Don Ernesto Larios, of Monte de la Torre, Algeciras, Spain, and *dsp* 7 March 1960

3 Alison Mary; *m* 5 March 1929 Cdr Sir John Leighton Barran, 3rd Bt, RNVR (*qv*; *d* 28 Dec 1974), and *d* 2 Oct 1974, leaving issue:

(1) +John Napoleon Ruthven; *b* 14 Feb 1934; *educ* Winchester

4 Margaret Leslie (twin with her sister Alison); *m* 10 March 1932 Peter Llewelyn Davies, MC (*d* as the result of an accident 5 April 1960), son of Arthur Llewelyn Davies, barrister, by his 1st w Sylvia, dau of George du Maurier, and *d* 30 April 1970, leaving issue:

(1) +Ruthven Barrie; *b* 9 May 1933; *educ* Eton; Lt Life Gds; *m* 14 May 1960 *Mary Bridget, dau of Dr John Musser Pearce, of 156 East 79th St, New York 21, USA

(2) +George Caesar; *b* 1 June 1938; *educ* Eton

(3) +Peter Theodore; *b* 28 April 1940; *educ* Eton and Trin Coll Cambridge; *m* 1965 *Frances Jane Carson

The **10th Lord** *m* 2nd 18 Nov 1953 *Judith Gordon [Mrs Digby Peel, Tyne Hall, Bembridge, IoW] (*m* 2nd 13 Oct 1965 Maj Digby Robert Peel, MC, RA (*d* 6 Jan 1971), son of William Felton Peel), yr dau of Bertie E Bell, of Knapp, Guernsey, and *dspm* 6 April 1956, when the Barony of Ruthven of Gowrie passed to his great-nephew 2nd Earl of Gowrie (*qv*)

His est dau,

BRIDGET HELEN, **Lady Ruthven of Freeland** in her own right, CBE; *b* 27 July 1896; WW II as Sr Controller ATS and Dir WACI; *m* 1st 17 Jan 1918 (*divorce* 1947) **11th Earl of Carlisle** (*see* above) and had issue

Lineage (of Hore): MATHEW HORE; *m* Agatha, dau and heiress of Philip le Harper, of Harperstown, Taghmon, Co Wexford, and was granted the estate of Harperstown by patent 4 April 1390; ancestor of:

DAVID HORE, of Harperstown; had:

WILLIAM HORE, of Harperstown; granted Taghmon 1547; *m* Joan, dau of Sir Nicholas Cleeves, of Ballyhaly, Co Wexford, and *d* 20 Jan 1568, having had an est s:

NICHOLAS HORE; *m* by 1558 Margaret (*m* 2nd Sir Nicholas Arnold, PC, Ch Govr Ireland, and *d* 1616), dau and coheir of John Isham, of Bryanston, and was *k* by 1561, leaving:

EDMUND HORE, of Harperstown; *m* Elinor, dau of Nicholas Turnor, of Balyhaly, Co Wexford, and *d* 2 Nov 1609, leaving an est s:

WILLIAM HORE, of Harperstown; *m* 10 Dec 1607 Margaret, dau of Oliver Keating, of Kilcowan, Co Wexford, and *d* after 5 June 1662, having had an est s:

WALTER HORE; living 1618; *m* Alison, dau of Col Nicholas Devereux, and *dvp* leaving:

WILLIAM HORE; *m* —, dau and heiress of William Russell, of Newcastle, Co Wexford, and *d* between 6 May 1699 and 5 April 1700, having had an est s:

WILLIAM HORE, of Harperstown; MP Co Wexford 1711 and Taghmon 1731–41, Col; *m* 1st Anne, dau of Rev Thomas Bunbury, of Balesker, and had issue; *m* 2nd Catherine, dau and coheir of John Shapland, of Wexford, and by her had a dau; he *d* 13 April 1741, leaving, presumably by his 1st w, an est s:

WILLIAM HORE, of Harperstown; DCL; MP Taghmon 1727–31 and 1741–45, Attorney-Gen Ireland; *m* 1st Dorothy, dau of William Ponsonby, Viscount Duncannon (*see* BESSBOROUGH, E), and had issue; *m* 2nd 29 Aug 1743 Mary (*m* 3rd Charles Tottenham, of Tottenham Green, Co Wexford, ancestor of the Marquesses of Ely (*qv*)), dau of John Grogan, of Johnstown Castle, and widow of Maj Andrew Knox, of Rathmacnee Castle, and *d* Feb 1745, having by her had no issue; his only s by his 1st w:

WALTER HORE, of Harperstown; Attorney-Gen Ireland, MP Taghmon, Col Wexford Yeo, High Sheriff 1793; *m* 28 May 1758 Lady Anne Stopford (*d* March 1808), dau of 1st Earl of Courtown (*qv*), and *d* 27 Feb 1795, leaving issue:

WILLIAM HORE, of Harperstown, JP Co Wexford; High Sheriff 1788; *m* 5 Jan 1782 Eleanor Catherine (*d* 1849), dau and heiress of Sir Simon Bradstreet, Bt, and was *k* in the Uprising at the bridge of Wexford 20 June 1798, leaving an est s:

WALTER HORE, of Harperstown, JP, High Sheriff 1828; *b* 6 June 1784; *m* 13 Oct 1806 Mary Elizabeth Thornton, **Lady Ruthven of Freeland** in her own right, and *d* 16 April 1878, having had issue (*see* above)

CARLISLE OF BUCKLOW

Creation: B. (LP, UK) 1987.

THE BARON CARLISLE OF BUCKLOW, of Mobberley, Co Cheshire (Mark Carlisle, PC (1979), DL (Cheshire 1983)) [The Rt Hon The Lord Carlisle of Bucklow PC DL, 3 Holt Gdns, Mobberley, Cheshire WA16 7LH]; *b* 7 July 1929; *educ* Radley and Manchester U (LLB); barrister Gray's Inn 1953, Recorder Crown Court 1976–79 and 1981–, QC 1971, Bencher 1980, Judge Courts of Appeal Jersey and Guernsey 1990–; MP Runcorn (C) 1964–83 and Warrington S 1983–87, Jt Hon Sec C Home Affrs Ctee 1965–69 (Chm 1983–87), Memb Home Office Advsy Cncl Penal System 1966–70, C Front Bench Spokesman Home Affrs 1969–70, Parly U-Sec Home Office 1970–72, Min State Home Office 1972–74, Sec State DES 1979–81; Parole Review Ctee 1987, PM's Advsy Ctee Business Appts of Crown Servants 1988–, Criminal Injuries Compensation Bd 1989–; Treas CPA 1982–85 (dep chm UK Br 1985–87); Memb Advsy Cncl BBC 1975–79; *m* 1959 *Sandra Joyce, dau of John Hamilton Des Voeux, of St Ives, Cornwall, and has issue:

1 *(Vanessa) Lucy; *b* 19–; *m* 5 Nov 1994 *Angus W W P von Schoenberg, yr s of Baron Witold von Schoenberg

Lineage: PHILIP EDMUND CARLISLE; *m* Mary — and had:

MARK, *cr* a **Baron**

CARMICHAEL OF KELVINGROVE

Creation: B. (LP, UK) 1983.

THE BARON CARMICHAEL OF KELVINGROVE, of Camlachie, Glasgow (Neil George Carmichael) [The Rt Hon The Lord Carmichael of Kelvingrove, 53 Partick Hill Rd, Glasgow G11 5AB]; *b* Oct 1921; *educ* Eastbank Acad and Roy Coll of Science and Technology Glasgow; MP (Lab) Woodside 1962–74 and Kelvingrove 1974–83; PPS to Min Tech 1966–67, Jt Parly U-Sec Tport 1967–69, Parly U-Sec Min Tech 1969–70, DOE 1974–75 and Dept Industry 1975–76, Hon Sec Scottish Lab Gp of MPs 1979–83, Memb Select Ctee Tport 1980–83, Oppn front bench spokesman: Tport 1987–97, Scotland 1987–97; *m* 1948 (*divorce*) Catherine McIntosh, dau of John Dawson Rankin, of Glasgow, and has issue:

1 *Sheena MacIntosh; *b* 1949; *m* 1974 (*divorce* 1988, resumed maiden name) Thomas Anthony Edward Sharpe and has a s and dau

Lineage: JAMES CARMICHAEL; had issue:

NEIL GEORGE, *cr* a **Baron**

CARNARVON

Arms: Per pale az. and gu. three lions rampant arg. **Crest:** A wyvern, wings elevated vert, holding in the mouth a sinister hand, couped at the wrist gu. **Supporters:** Dexter, a panther guardant arg., semée of torteaux and hurts, flames issuant from the mouth and ears ppr.; sinister, a lion arg., each ducally gorged per pale az. and gu. and chained or, and charged on the shoulder with an erm. spot sa. **Motto:** *Ung je serviray* ('I will serve but one master'). **Creations:** B. (GB) 17 Oct 1780, E. (GB) 3 July 1793.

THE 7TH EARL OF THE TOWN AND COUNTY OF CARNARVON and **Baron Porchester of Highclere**, Co Southampton (Sir Henry George Reginald Molyneux Herbert, KCVO (1982), KBE (1976), DL (Hants 1965)) [The Rt Hon The Earl of Carnarvon KCVO KBE DL, Highclere Castle, Newbury, Berks RG20 9RN; Milford Lake House, Newbury, Berks RG20 9EL]; *b* 19 Jan 1924; *s* f 1987; *educ* Eton; late Lt RHG, Hon Col 116th (Hampshire Fortress) Engineer Regt (TA) 1963–, chm: SE Ec Planning Cncl 1971–79, Ag Research Cncl 1978–82, Game Research Assoc 1960–; Verderer New Forest 1961–65, High Steward Winchester 1977, memb Sports Cncl 1965–, Nature Conservancy 1963– and Jockey Club; racing manager to HM THE QUEEN 1969–, CA (Hants 1965–74), chm Newbury Racecourse; Hon: Fell Portsmouth Poly 1976, DSc Reading 1980; *m* 7 Jan 1956 *Jean Margaret, er dau of Hon Oliver Malcolm Wallop, of Big Horn, Wyoming, USA (*see* PORTSMOUTH, E), and has issue:

1 +GEORGE (GEORDIE) REGINALD OLIVER MOLYNEUX, *Lord Porchester* [Lord Porchester, Dairy Cottage, Highclere Pk, Newbury, Berks RG15 9RN; *b* 10 Nov 1956 (HM THE QUEEN stood sponsor); *educ* Eton and St John's Coll Oxford (BA); page of Hon to HM THE QUEEN 1969–73; *m* 1989 (*divorce* Jan 1998) Jayne M, est dau of Kenneth A Wilby, of Cheshire, by Princess Prospero Colonna di Stigliano, of Ashford, Co Wicklow, Ireland, and has issue:

(1) +George Kenneth Oliver Molyneux; *b* 13 Oct 1992

(1) *Saoirse; *b* 1991

2 +Henry Malcolm [The Hon Henry Herbert, Field House, Highclere Pk, Newbury, Berks RG15 9RN]; *b* 2 March 1959; *educ* Eton; *m* 1992 *Francesca (Chica) V, yr dau of Jonathan Stuart Vaughan Bevan, of Belgravia, and has:

(1) *Chloe Victoria; *b* 1994

(2) *Francesca Jeanie; *b* 21 Nov 1995

1*Carolyn Penelope [The Lady Carolyn Warren, The Priory, Moulton, Newmarket, Suffolk]; *b* 27 Jan 1962; *m* 1985 *John Frederick Rufus Warren, son of John Warren, of Harlow, Essex, and has issue:

(1) *Jakie James; *b* 1986

(2) *Alexander Edward; *b* 1994

(1) *Susanna; *b* 1988

Carnarvon, other creations: A grandson of the 1st Baron Dormer of Wyng was created Earl of Carnarvon in 1628 (*see* DORMER, B). His Countess's great-nephew was Henry Herbert and it was doubtless the connection with the former Earl of Carnarvon that prompted the latter to chose it as his title when promoted in the peerage in 1793. Meanwhile one of the Duke of Chandos's subsidiary titles, conferred on him five years before he was elevated to the strawberry leaves in 1719, was that of Earl of Carnarvon (*see* KINLOSS, L). It expired with the Dukedom in 1789, leaving Herbert free to press for its revival in his own favour four years later.

Lineage: The 8th EARL OF PEMBROKE AND (5th Earl of) MONTGOMERY had a 5th s:

WILLIAM HERBERT, Maj-Gen; *m* Catherine Elizabeth Tewes, of Aix-la-Chapelle (*d* 28 Aug 1770), and *d* 31 March 1757, leaving an er son:

HENRY HERBERT, **1st Earl of The Town and County of Carnarvon**, so *cr* 3 July 1793, as also earlier 17 Oct 1780 BARON PORCHESTER OF HIGH CLERE, Co Southampton, PC (1806); *b* 20 Aug 1741; *educ* Ch Ch Oxford and Magdalene Coll Cambridge; inherited the Highclere estate from his f; MP (Tory, later Whig) Wilton 1768–80, Master of the Horse 1806–07; *m* 15 July 1771 Elizabeth Alicia Maria (*d* 10 Feb 1826), dau of 1st Earl of Egremont (*see* EGREMONT, LECONFIELD and, B), and had:

1 HENRY GEORGE, **2nd Earl**

2 Charles, RN; *b* 5 July 1774; *m* 9 July 1806 Bridget Augusta (*d* 4 March 1876), dau of 5th Viscount Torrington (*qv*), and was drowned 12 Sept 1808, leaving:

(1) Augusta Elizabeth; *m* 10 May 1824 Sir Francis Vincent, 10th Bt (of 1620 *cr*, extinct 1941), and *d* 3 April 1876, leaving issue. He *d* 6 July 1880

3 William (Very Rev), LLD, Dean of Manchester; *b* 12 Jan 1778; *m* 17 May 1806 Letitia Dorothea (*d* 14 June 1878), 2nd dau of 5th Viscount Allen, and *d* 28 May 1847, leaving issue:

(1) Henry William, of The Cedars, Newark, NJ, USA; *b* 7 April 1807; *m* 31 Dec 1839 Sarah Barker (*d* March 1844), of Bangor, Maine, USA, and *d* in New York 2 Sept 1859, leaving:

1a William George, served War Office, JP Folkestone, CA Kent 1893–1910; *b* 3 Aug 1841; *m* 8 Jan 1867 Emily Eliza (*d* 30 May 1911), dau of Sir Samuel Edmund Falkiner, 5th Bt, of Annemount (*qv*), and *dsp* 17 May 1920

(2) Frederick Charles, Cdr RN; *b* 25 Feb1819; *m*12 Sept 1848 Bessie Newenham (*d* 16 Sept 1904), yst dau of Capt Henry Stuart, 69th Regt, and *d* 27 May 1868, leaving, with other issue:

1a St Leger Algernon, CMG, Priv Sec to Sir Garnet Wolseley, GCB; *b* 16 Aug 1850; *k* in the Sudan War 19 Jan 1885

1a Louisa Emily Julia; *m* 14 May 1875 Robert Hervey Monro Elwes, of Stoke College, Suffolk, and *d* July 1889. He *d* 6 Feb 1893

2a Hilda Augusta; *m* 4 Aug 1881 Rev Frederick Philip Green de Fréville, BA, vicar Oakridge, nr Stroud, and *d* 19 May 1946, leaving issue

3a Beatrice Mary; *d* unm 15 Jan 1948

(1) Louisa Catherine Georgina; *m* 6 June 1848 Maj-Gen Godfrey Charles Mundy, Lt-Govr of Jersey, and *d* 17 Feb 1904, leaving issue. He *d* 10 July 1860

(2) Cecilia Augusta Henrietta; *m* 1856 Col A T Ferguson, of Lemon Hill, Kentucky, and *d* 1860, leaving issue. He *d* 1863

4 George (Rev), Vicar Tibenham, Norfolk; *b* 21 Feb 1789; *m* 1 Sept 1806 Frances (*d* 2 Feb 1862), only child and heiress of Francis Head, of St Andrew's Hall, Norfolk, and *d* 27 March 1825, leaving a son and six daus (*d* unm)

5 Algernon, barrister; *b* 12 July 1792; *m* 2 Aug 1830 Marianne (*d* 7 Aug1870), dau of Thomas Lempriere, and *d* 11 June 1855, leaving, with a dau:

(1) Robert George Wyndham (Sir), GCB, DL, JP, DCL, LLD, of Ickleton, Cambs, barrister, Fell All Souls, Premier Queensland 1859–66, Assist Sec BOT 1867–69, Assist U-Sec Colonial Office 1869–71, U-Sec Colonies 1871–92, Chllr Order of St Michael and St George 1892–1905, Agent-Gen Tasmania 1893–96, High Sheriff Co London 1899, Order of Crown of Johore 1st Cl; *b* 12 June 1831; *d* unm 6 May 1905

(1) Elizabeth Alicia Maria; *m* 31 Dec 1857 Rev William Lempriere Lewis and had issue. He *d* 18 Jan 1872

1 Frances; *m* 6 Dec 1797 1st Earl of Ducie (*qv*), and *d* 22 Aug 1830, leaving issue

The 1st EARL *d* 3 June 1811; his est son,

HENRY GEORGE HERBERT, **2nd Earl of The Town and County of Carnarvon**; *b* 3 June 1772; MP (Whig) Cricklade 1794–1811; *m* 25 April 1796 Elizabeth (*d* 5 March 1813), dau of Col John Dyke Acland (*see* ACLAND, Bt, of Columb John), and had issue, with three daus:

1 HENRY JOHN GEORGE, **3rd Earl**

2 Edward Charles Hugh; *b* 30 March 1802; *m* June 1833 Elizabeth (*d* 10 July 1840), 2nd dau of Preb Thomas Sweet-Escott, of Hartrow Hall, Som, and *d* 30 May 1852, leaving issue:

(1) Edward Henry Charles, of Tetton Ho, Som; *b* 1 Sept 1837, murdered by brigands in Greece 1870

(2) Henry; *b* 1839; *d* 8 Feb 1847

The 2nd EARL *d* 16 April 1833; his son,

HENRY JOHN GEORGE HERBERT, **3rd Earl of The Town and County of Carnarvon**; *b* June 1800; *educ* Eton and Ch Ch Oxford; MP (Tory) Wootton Bassett 1831–32; *m* 4 Aug 1830 Henrietta Anna (*d* 26 May 1876), est dau of Lord Henry Thomas Molyneux Howard, and niece of 12th Duke of Norfolk (*qv*), and had, with other issue:

1 HENRY HOWARD MOLYNEUX, **4th Earl**

2 Auberon Edward William Molyneux, DCL Oxford, Lt 7th Hus, MP Nottingham 1870–74; *b* 18 June 1838; *m* 9 Aug 1871 Lady Florence Amabel Cowper (*d* 26 April 1886), dau of 6th Earl Cowper, and *d* 5 Nov 1906, having had, with other issue:

(1) AUBERON THOMAS; *s* uncle Earl Cowper as 8th BARON LUCAS OF CRUDWELL (*qv*) and 11th BARON DINGWALL; *ka* 4 Nov 1916

(1) NAN INO, BARONESS LUCAS OF CRUDWELL and DINGWALL in her own right

1 Eveline Alicia Juliana; *m* 15 Feb 1855 5th Earl of Portsmouth (*qv*) and *d* 1 Oct 1906, leaving issue

The 3rd EARL *d* 10 Dec 1849; his est son,

HENRY HOWARD MOLYNEUX HERBERT, **4th Earl of The Town and County of Carnarvon**, PC (1866), DL (Notts); *b* 24 June 1831; *educ* Eton and Ch Ch Oxford; High Steward Oxford U, Constable Carnarvon Castle, Sec State Colonies 1866–67 and 1874–78, Ld Lt: Ireland 1885–86 and Hants 1887–90; Hon Col 2nd Vol Bn Hampshire Regt, FSA (pres), DCL, LLD; *m* 1st 5 Sept 1861 Evelyn (*d* 25 Jan 1875), only dau of 6th Earl of Chesterfield (see 1967 edn CHESTERFIELD and STANHOPE, E), and had issue:

1 GEORGE EDWARD STANHOPE MOLYNEUX, **5th Earl**

1 Winifred Anne Henrietta Christina; *b* 2 July 1864; *m* 1st 10 Jan 1887 Capt Hon Alfred John George Byng, 7th Hus, 5th son of 2nd Earl of Strafford (*qv*). He *d* 8 Nov 1887. She *m* 2nd 4 March 1890 1st and last Baron Burghclere (*d* 6 May 1921; *see* 1921 edn), and *d* 28 Sept 1933, leaving:

(1) Juliet Mary Evelyn Stanhope; *b* 14 June 1892; *m* 1916 (*divorce* 1922 in the Scottish courts, obtained by him for desertion) Capt Alexander D Cumine Russell

(2) Alethea Margaret Guendolen Valentine; *b* 19 Aug 1893; *m* 1915 Sir Geoffrey Storrs Fry, 1st and last Bt, CB, CVO (*see* 1956 edn), and had:

1a *(Ann) Jennifer Evelyn Elizabeth [Mrs Jennifer Ross, 74 Bishops Mansions, Bishops Park Rd, London SW6]; *b* 1916; *m* 1st 1942 (*divorce* 1947), as his 1st w, Robert Vernon Heber-Percy (*see* NORTHUMBERLAND, D); *m* 2nd 1949 Alan Ross, CBE, and by him has:

1b *Jonathan Timothy de Beaurepaire [Jonathan Ross Esq, 286 Earl's Court Rd, London SW5]; *b* 16 July 1953; *m* 19– (*divorce* 1997) Diana Margaret Summers (*née* Gost)

(3) Mary Sidney Katharine Almina; *b* 27 Aug 1896; *m* 1st 1914 (*divorce* 1928) Hon Geoffrey Hope-Morley, later 2nd Baron Hollenden (*qv*), and had issue; *m* 2nd Jan 1929 Lt-Cdr Hugh Hillgarth, RN (ret) and by him had:

1a *Jocelyn Nigel Herbert Gardner Alan Aubrey [Dr Jocelyn Hillgarth, 330 Waverley St, Belmont, Mass., USA]; PhD; *b* Sept 1929; *m* 1966 *Nina, widow of Richard Foster

(4) Evelyn Florence Margaret Winifred; *b* 27 Sept 1903; *m* 1st 1928 (*divorce* 1930), as his 1st w, Evelyn Arthur St John Waugh, the novelist (*see* below), yr son of Arthur Waugh; *m* 2nd 1930 (*divorce* 1936), as his 1st w, Sir John Edward Nourse Heygate, 4th Bt (*qv*); *m* 3rd 1937 Ronald Nightingale (*d* 1977), and *d* 11 March 1994, leaving:

1a *William Benedict Herbert [William Nightingale, 40 Broomhouse Rd, London SW6]; *b* 1939; *m* 1964 *Anne, dau of Bryan C Redmon, of Bernardsville, NJ, and has:

1b *Auberon Christopher Redmon Herbert; *b* 1966

2b *John Piers Sydney; *b* 1973

1b *Elizabeth Magdalen Margaret; *b* 1969

1a *Virginia Margaret Ann [Ms Virginia Nightingale, 67 Chesil Court, Chelsea Manor St, London SW3 5QS]; *b* 1943

2 Margaret Leonora Evelyn Selina; *b* 18 Sept 1870; *m* 10 Sept 1904 Sir George Herbert Duckworth, CB, son of Herbert Duckworth, of Orchardleigh Park, Som, and half-bro of Virginia Woolf, and *d* 13 Sept 1958, leaving issue. He *d* 27 April 1934

3 Victoria Alexandrina Mary Cecil, CBE (1919), DGStJ; *b* 31 Dec 1874 (HM QUEEN VICTORIA stood sponsor); *d* unm 15 Nov 1957

The **4th Earl** *m* 2nd 26 Dec 1878 Elisabeth Catharine (*d* 1 Feb 1929), est dau of Henry Howard, of Greystoke Castle, Cumberland (*see* NORFOLK, D), and by her had further issue:

2 Aubrey Nigel Henry Molyneux, DL Carnarvonshire, MP (C) S Somerset 1911–18 and (Ind) Yeovil 1918, T/Lt-Col 1917 (SR) Irish Gds WW I (wounded), formerly Lt Roy N Devon Yeo, Hon Attaché Dip Serv, Order White Eagle Serbia 5th Cl with swords; *b* 3 April 1880; *educ* Balliol Coll Oxford (BA); *m* 20 Oct 1910 Hon Mary Gertrude Vesey (*d* 1970), only child of 4th Viscount de Vesci (*qv*), and *d* 26 Sept 1923, leaving issue:

(1) Auberon Mark Henry Yvo Molyneux; *b* 25 April 1922

(1) Gabriel Mary Hermione; *b* 29 Sept 1911; *m* 6 March 1943 Maj Alexander Dru, Intell Corps, son of Louis Gaston Dru, of Down Ho, Itchen Abbas, and had issue:

1a *Bernard Auberon Alexander; *b* 29 Dec 1951

1a *Angela Mary; *b* 5 Dec 1943

2a *Mary Sophia; *b* 6 March 1945

3a *Laura Jane Veronica; *b* 2 Sept 1946

(2) *(Anne) Bridget Domenica; *b* 22 Feb 1914; *m* 20 Nov 1935 Maj Allister Edward Grant, MC (*d* 27 Sept 1947), late 9th Lancers, son of Sir Charles Grant, KCSI (*see* MALMESBURY, E), and has issue:

1a *Robert John David [Robert Grant Esq, Nutcombe Manor, Clayhanger, Tiverton, Devon]; *b* 1942; *educ* Ampleforth and New Coll Oxford; *m* 1970 *Harriet, dau of Markway Roope Reeve, of Lower Brook Ho, Kings Somborne, Hants, and has issue:

1b *Charles Edward; *b* 1971

2b *Peter Mark Haddon; *b* 1981

1b *Katherine Bridget; *b* 1972

2b *Emma Philippa; *b* 1973

1a *Mary Christina [Mrs Michael Melotte, 102 Talfourd Rd, London SE15 6NZ]; *b* 1937; *m* 1962 *Maj Michael Edward Melotte, Irish Gds, and has:

1b Edward John; *b* 1965; Capt IG; *d* Nov 1994

1b *Victoria Mary [Mrs Jonathan Clark, 17 Crescent Grove, London SW4]; *b* 1963; *m* 1985 *Jonathan Clark

2a Evelyn Elizabeth Anne; *b* 1938; *m* 1958 *Sir Ian James Fraser, CBE, MC, and *d* 1984, leaving issue (*see* LOVAT, L)

(3) Laura Laetitia Gwendolen Evelyn; *b* 21 June 1916; *m* 17 April 1937, as his 2nd w, her 1st cousin Evelyn Gardner's former husb Evelyn Waugh (*d* 10 April 1966), and had:

1a *Auberon Alexander [Auberon Waugh Esq, 7 Phoenix Lodge Mansions, Brook Green, London W6 7BG]; *b* 17 Nov 1939; *educ* Downside and Ch Ch Oxford; served RHG 1957–58, columnist, political correspondent or book reviewer with: *Daily Telegraph* 1960–63 and 1990–, *Catholic Herald* 1963–64, Mirror gp 1964–67, *Spectator* 1967–70 and 1976–96, *Private Eye* 1970–86, *The Times* 1970–71, *New Statesman* 1973–76, *Books and Bookmen* 1973–80, *Evening Standard* 1973–80, *Daily Mail* 1981–86, *Sunday Telegraph* 1981–90 and 1996–, *Independent* 1986–89, ed *Literary Review* 1986–; author: *The Foxglove Saga* (1960), *Path of Dalliance* (1963), *Who are the Violets Now?* (1966), *Consider the Lilies* (1968), *Biafra: Britain's Shame* (with Susan Cronje, 1969), *A Bed of Flowers* (1971), *Four Crowded Years: the Diaries of Auberon Waugh* (1976), *The Last Word: an Eyewitness Account of the Thorpe Trial* (1980), *Auberon Waugh's Yearbook* (1981), *The Diaries of Auberon Waugh: a turbulent decade 1976–85* (1985), *Waugh on Wine* (1986), *Will This Do?* (autobiography, 1991), *Way of the World* (1994); fought 1979 gen election as Dog Lover's Party candidate Devon N; *m* 1961 *Lady Teresa Onslow, only dau of 6th Earl of Onslow (*qv*), and has issue

2a *James; *b* 30 June 1946

3a *Septimus; *b* 11 July 1950

1a *Maria Teresa; *b* 9 March 1938

2a Mary; *b* 1 Dec, *d* 2 Dec 1940

3a Margaret Evelyn; *b* 11 June 1942; *m* 1962, as his 1st w *Giles Eden Fitz Herbert, CMG Amb Venezuela and Dominica 1988–93, [Giles Fitz Herbert Esq CMG, Fenagh Rectory, Co Carlow, Ireland] and *d* in a road accident 28 jan 1986, leaving two sons and three daus

4a *Harriet; *b* 13 May 1944; *m* 1985 *Richard Dormant; author: *The Chaplet of Pearls (1997)*

3 Mervyn Robert Howard Molyneux, Dip Serv; *b* 2 Dec 1882; *educ* Balliol Coll Oxford (BA); *m* 1 June 1921 Mary Elizabeth (*d* 1979), dau of Joseph E Willard, US Amb Madrid, and *d* 26 May 1929, leaving issue:

(1) (Edward Alan) Mervyn Henry Molyneux, barrister Middle Temple 1952, Capt Coldstream Gds, ARIBA 1964; *b* 6 July 1926; *educ* Eton; *m* 22 March 1966 Bridget Anne (*d* 1976), er dau of Maj Hugh Washington Hibbert, of Normanton Ho, Lake, Wilts (*see* MOWBRAY, SEGRAVE and STOURTON, B), and *d* 1994, leaving:

1a +Alan Mervyn Edward Hugh; *b* 31 Oct 1971

1a *Mary Patricia; *b* 3 March 1967

2a *Elizabeth Anne [Mrs David Carter, 109 Mile End Rd, London E1]; *b* 17 Aug 1968; *m* 1996 *David Carter and has:

1b *Isadora; *b* Dec 1996

3a *Penelope Gabrielle Serena; *b* 29 Nov 1969

(1) *(Mary) Elizabeth Catherine Gwendolen [Countess Elizabeth Ledochowska, 193 Coleherne Court, Old Brompton Rd, London SW5 0DU], concert singer, composer, poetess and pianist; *b* 24 March 1922; *m* 1st 6 April 1946 (*divorce* 1957) Radu Tilea, son of Viorel Virgil Tilea, CBE, late Romanian Min UK; *m* 2nd 1970 (*divorce* 19–) Count Denys Halka Ledochowsky (*d* 1980) and by her 1st husb has:

1a *Mary Catherine Ileana Camilla [Mrs Ian Willis, Chapel Barn, Goodworth Clatford, Andover, Hants]; *b* 2 Oct 1950; *m* *Ian Henry Willis and has issue (*see* THURLOW, B)

2a *Elizabeth Helen Rodica [Mrs John Harrap, 35 Kenway Rd, London SW5]; *b* 3 Oct 1953; *m* 1973 *John Michael Darrell Harrap and has issue (*see* DARELL, Bt)

(2) Margaret Anne Antonia; *b* 13 Aug 1923; *m* 29 May 1954 Timothy Walter Horn (*d* 1989), barrister, yr son of D'Arcy Horn, of Allerly, Gattonside, Melrose, Roxburghshire, and *d* 1991, leaving:

1a *Nicholas Charles D'Arcy; *b* 22 Aug 1962

1a *Magdalen Sarah; *b* 2 May 1955; *m* 1979 (*divorce* 19–) Colin Vandeleur Stuart Studd and has:

1b *Georgina Katharine Antonia; *b* 1981

2b *Clementine Elizabeth Burden; *b* 1983

2a *Mary Virginia Louise; *b* 6 April 1957; *m* 1982 *James Richard Colville and has:

1b *Charles

2b *Edward

1b *Emma

2b *Sophia

3a *Harriet Ann Serena; *b* 23 Dec 1958

The 4th EARL *d* 28 June 1890; his est son,

GEORGE EDWARD STANHOPE MOLYNEUX HERBERT, **5th Earl of The Town and County of Carnarvon**, DL; *b* 26 June 1866; *educ* Eton and Trin Coll Cambridge; the celebrated excavator of Tutankhamen's tomb; *m* 26 June 1895 Almina Victoria Marie Alexandra (*d* 8 May 1969 aged 92, having *m* 2nd 19 Dec 1923 Lt-Col Ian Onslow Dennistoun, MVO, Gren Gds, who *d* 22 May 1938), dau of Marie, w of Frederick Charles Wombwell (*see* WOMBWELL, Bt) possibly by Alfred Rothschild (*see* ROTHSCHILD, B), and had issue:

1 HENRY GEORGE ALFRED MARCUS VICTOR FRANCIS, **6th Earl**

1 Evelyn Leonora Almina; *b* 15 Aug 1901; *m* 8 Oct 1923 Sir Brograve Campbell Beauchamp, 2nd Bt (*see* 1970 edn) and had issue

The 5th EARL *d* 5 April 1923; his only son,

HENRY GEORGE ALFRED MARIUS VICTOR FRANCIS HERBERT, **6th Earl of The Town and County of Carnarvon**; *b* 7 Nov 1898; *educ* Eton and RMC Sandhurst; Lt-Col 7th Hus, served WW I and WW II, had US Bronze Star, High Steward Newbury; *m* 1st 17 July 1922 (*divorce* 1936) Anne Catherine Tredick (*d* 1977, having *m* 2nd 1938, as his 2nd w, Lt-Cdr Geoffrey Seymour Grenfell, RN (*ka* 1940), and 3rd 1950 Don Stuart Mommand), dau of Jacob Wendell, of New York; *m* 2nd 1 Sept 1939 (*divorce* 1947) Ottilie Ethel (Tillie Losch, the dancer who *d* 1975), formerly w of Edward Frank Willis James and dau of Eugene Losch, of Vienna, and *d* 1987, having by 1st w had issue:

1 HENRY GEORGE REGINALD MOLYNEUX HERBERT, **7th and present Earl of The Town and County of Carnarvon**

1 (Anne) Penelope Marian; *b* 3 March 1925; *m* 21 April 1945 *Capt Reinier Gerrit Anton van der Woude, Gren Gds, son of Reinier Gerrit Anton van der Woude, of Heronden, Eastry, Kent, and Soton, New York, and had issue:

(1) *Michael Gerrit; *b* 25 March 1946; *educ* Aiglon Coll, Switzerland

(2) *David Anthony; *b* 7 Nov 1947; *educ* Eton

(1) *Penelope Catherine Mary; *b* 19 Aug 1952

Seat: Highclere Castle, Newbury, Berks. Despite having been described as the ultimate in high Victorian, Highclere is not strictly speaking of that era but a little before. The point is more than just pedantic. When Barry set about his designs for Highclere back in the 1830s (though it is true that the actual physical remodelling did not begin till 1841) he was working on the new Houses of Parliament, and his lightness of touch is very different from the more stolid high Victorian work of Butterfield or Scott. It is also true that Scott himself worked on Highclere, but externally at least the mansion owes more to Barry than to the architect of St Pancras and the Albert Memorial — Scott's best known secular creations. Inside there is certainly some ecclesiastical gothic, and the **4th Earl** was interested enough in church architecture to design the chapel in the park himself. (His remains were laid to rest there following his death.) But Highclere also contains rooms in oriental and neo-rococo styles, more probably reflecting the **3rd Earl**'s interests as a traveller.

CARNEGY OF LOUR

Arms: Or an eagle displayed azure, beaked and membered sable, within a bordure gules. **Crest:** A demi leopard rampant proper. **Supporters:** Dexter, a leopard proper, having a collar argent charged with three torteaux; sinister, a greyhound proper, having a collar gules charged with three escallops argent. **Motto:** Tache sans tache ('Spot without blemishes'). **Creation:** B. (LP, UK) 1982.

BARONESS CARNEGY OF LOUR, of Lour in the District of Angus (Elizabeth Patricia Carnegy of Lour, DL (Angus 1988)) [The Rt Hon The Baroness Carnegy of Lour DL, Lour, by Forfar, Angus DD8 2LR; 33 Tufton Court, Tufton St, London SW1P 3QH]; *b* 28 April 1925; *educ* Downham Sch Essex; with Girl Guides Assoc 1947–, Co Commr Angus 1956–63, Training Adviser Scotland 1958–62 and Cwlth HQ 1963–65, Pres Cncl Scotland 1979–89; memb Educn Ctee Angus CC 1967–75, Cncllr Tayside Region 1974–82, Convenor Recreation and Tourism Ctee 1974–76, Educn Ctee 1976–82; Commr Manpower Servs Commn 1979–82, Chm Working Party on Prof Training for Community Educn Scotland 1975–77, Manpower Servs Commn Ctee for Scotland 1981–83 and Scottish Community Educn Cncl 1981–88, memb Scots Ec Cncl 1981–93, Admin Cncl Roy Jubilee Tsts 1984–88, Cncl OU 1984–96, Tstee Nat Museums Scotland 1987–91, memb Court St Andrews U 1991–96; served WW II Cavendish Laboratory Cambridge; Hon Sheriff 1969–84, Hon LLD Dundee 1991, St Andrews 1997

Lineage: *see* NORTHESK, E

CARNOCK

Arms: Or three falcon's heads erased gules armed argent, in fess point an inescutcheon argent a saltire azure surmounted of an inescutcheion or charged with a lion rampant within a double tressure flory counterflory gules endigned of an Imperial Crown proper (arms of Nova Scotia as a Baronet). **Crest:** A lion issuant or armed and langued gules. **Supporters:** Two eagles or armed gules. **Mottoes:** (Over crest) *Generositate* ('with magnanimity'), *Nil sistere contra* ('Nothing to stand against'). **Creations:** Bt. (NS) 27 July 1629 and 16 Jan 1637, B. (UK) 27 June 1916.

THE 4TH BARON CARNOCK, of Carnock, Co Stirling, and **a Baronet** (Sir David Henry Arthur Nicolson of that Ilk, 16th Bt, of Lasswade, and 14th Bt, of Carnock) [The Rt Hon The Lord Carnock, 90 Whitehall Court, London SW1A 2EL; Ermewood House, Harford, Devon PL21 0JE]; *b* 10 July 1920; *s f* 1982 in barony and 1637 btcy and established right to 1629 btcy 1984, also as Chief of Clan Nicolson; *educ* Winchester and Balliol Coll Oxford; Maj Roy Devon Yeo WW II, slr 1949, ptnr Clifford Turner 1955–86

Lineage: The NICOLSONs traditionally originated on the island of Skye. According to a genealogy assembled *c* 1400 on behalf of the Lord of the Isles (*see* BOSVILLE MACDONALD, Bt):

HAROLD; had:

ASMAINNECH; had:

HAROLD; had:

TORQUIL, of Dublin; had:

OLAF; had:

TEAGUE; had:

AIRFINN; had:

ALLEN; had:

PAUL; had:

FOGHAL; had:

MURDOCH; had:

HAROLD; had:

ERBLE; had, with a yr s (ancestor of the MacKERLYs):

SDACAILL; had:

THORSTEIN; had:

TORTHA; had:

TOIRCENN; had:

GILLE *Muire* (cognate with *Mor* ['The Great']?); had:

NICHOLAS; had:

HUGH; described as kin to the MacLEODs; had:

NICHOLAS; had:

JOHN; had:

EWEN; had:

JOHN; referred to in English records of *c* 1388–1407 as 'Johan M'Nakyld' who accompanied Donald of Islay, Lord of the Isles (*see* BOSVILLE MACDONALD, Bt), on a visit to RICHARD II of England; traditionally ancestor (possibly gf) of:

ALEXANDER NICOLSON; Burgess Aberdeen 1444; had, with possibly two yr sons (John, Burgess Aberdeen 1470–74; Matthew, Chaplain 1496):

WILLIAM NICOLSON; Burgess Aberdeen 1474; *m* Marjory, dau of Gilbert Menzies, gs of the 4th Menzies of Menzies and bro of David Menzies of Pitfoddels, and *d* by 1520(?), leaving:

1 Alexander; Burgess Aberdeen, Clerk of the Cocket 1536 and 1543; *m* by 1520 Margaret Rolland and *d* by 1547, leaving:

(1) Gilbert; Burgess Aberdeen; *m* Joan — and was *ka* English victory over Scots of Pinkie 1547, leaving:

1a John; *b* (posthumously?) 1547/8; of age by 1569

(2) Thomas; Burgess Aberdeen and Clerk of the Cocket 1547; *m* 1st Barbara Low (*dsp* by 1562); *m* 2nd Agnes Menzies of Pitfoddels and *d* at sea 20 Jan 1568/9, leaving:

1a Thomas

2a George; MP, Ld Provost; had:

1b Thomas, of Pitmedden; ancestor of the NICOLSONs of Cluny, NICOLSONs of Kemnay, NICOLSONs of Trabroun and the NICOLSON Bts of Skye, whose male line is extinct but who are represented by the BADENACH-NICOLSONs of Glenbervie

3a Alexander

(3) Alexander

(4) Peter

2 David; notary public 1509, priest 1520 (Vicar Maryculter), Sheriff Clerk 1539; *d c* 1543, leaving, with another s (Robert, legitimated 1539, Sheriff Clerk Aberdeen *c* 1539–58, later apparently Bp Caithness):

(1) James; *fl* 1548–74; writer (legal practitioner) and Burgess Edinburgh 1563, Sheriff Clerk Aberdeen 1563–65; *m* 1st(?) Janet, dau of John Swinton of that Ilk; *m* 2nd by 1563 Christian, dau of John Houpe, Burgess Edinburgh, and by his 1st w had:

1a James; *dsp* young

2a JOHN, for whom *see* further below

3a Thomas

3 John; *fl* 1527–57; notary public; had:

(1) Andrew; *dsp* by 1563

The 2nd s,

JOHN NICOLSON, of Edinburgh; advocate; bought the Lasswade estate, Midlothian, 1590; *m* Elizabeth, dau of Edward Henderson/Henrison, and *d* 1605, leaving, with a 2nd s:

1 **Sir John Nicolson, 1st Bt** (NS), so *cr* 27 July 1629, with remainder to heirs male whatsoever, of Lasswade; *m* Magdalen, dau of David Preston, of Craigmillar, and *d* May 1651, having had:

(1) John, of Pilton; *dvp* 1648, leaving:

1a **Sir John Nicolson, 2nd Bt**; MP (S Parl) Co Edinburgh 1672–74; *m* Elizabeth, dau of Sir William Dick of Braid and had:

1b **Sir John Nicolson, 3rd Bt**; *dsp* May 1681

2b **Sir William Nicolson, 4th Bt**; *m* Elizabeth, dau of John Trotter of Mortonhall, and was *bur* 29 Jan 1687, leaving:

1c **Sir John Nicolson, 5th Bt**; *dspm* and was *bur* 30 Oct 1689

2c **Sir Thomas Nicolson, 6th Bt**; *dspm* and was *bur* 8 April 1693

3c **Sir James Nicolson, 7th Bt**; *m* 1st 16 Dec 1721 Isabel, dau of Henry Simpson, land agent at Eishington, Northumberland; *m* 2nd Elizabeth, dau of James Carnegie of Craigs, and *dsp* May 1743, when the btcy became dormant; it was assumed from 1826 by at least three generations of NICOLSONs of a branch descended from a younger brother of the grantee's father

2 **Sir Thomas Nicolson, 1st Bt** (NS), so *cr* 16 Jan 1637, with remainder to heirs male whatsoever, of Carnock, Stirlingshire, MP; *m* Isobel, dau of Walter Henderson, of Granton, and *d* 8 Jan 1648, leaving:

(1) **Sir Thomas Nicolson, 2nd Bt**; *b* 10 June 1628; *m* Lady Margaret Livingston (*m* 2nd 1666 Sir George Stirling of Keir (*d* 1667); *m* 3rd 6 Feb 1668 Sir John Stirling of Keir and *d* 2 Nov 1674), dau of 2nd Earl of Linlithgow (see LINLITHGOW, M, preliminary remarks), and *d* 24 July 1664, leaving:

1a **Sir Thomas Nicolson, 3rd Bt**; *b* 15 Sept 1649; *m* 1668 Jean (*d* 1680), est dau of 2nd Lord Napier of Merchistoun (*see* NAPIER, Bt, of Merchistoun) and *d* 20 Jan 1670, having had issue:

1b **Sir Thomas Nicholson, 4th Bt**, and 4th LORD NAPIER OF MERCHISTOUN (as which *s* maternal unc 1683); *b* 14 Jan 1669; *d* unm 9 June 1688, when the Lordship of Napier passed to his maternal aunt Margaret, the Carnock estate passed to his paternal aunts and the btcy to his cousin

1a Eleanor; *m* Sir John Shaw, 2nd Bt, of Greenock (*d* 1702), and had issue (*see* SHAW-STEWART, Bt)

2a Isobel; *m* 11 Feb 1679 Sir James Dunbar, 1st Bt, of Mochrum (*qv*)

3a Margaret; *m* 1st James Hamilton of Ballencrieff; *m* 2nd 1688 Sir Thomas Nicolson, 1st Bt, of Kemnay (*dspm* 31 Aug 1728)

(2) John (Sir), of Tillicoultrie; *m* Sabina, dau of Col Walter Colyear, and *d* 1683, leaving an est s:

1a **Sir Thomas Nicolson, 5th Bt**; sold Tillicoultrie 1693; *d* 2 Jan 1699, leaving an only son:

1b **Sir George Nicolson, 6th Bt**; Maj one of the Scottish regts in Dutch service to 1746; *m* Charlotte, 2nd dau of Edward Halkett, and *d* at The Hague Oct 1771, leaving:

1c **Sir Walter Philip Nicolson, 7th Bt**; *m* Helen Frances Carpenter and *d* 1788

2c **Sir David Nicolson, 8th Bt**; *d* unm at Breda 19 Oct 1808

3c Charles, who *d* at Maestricht, unm, in 1789

2a William; Lt-Col of a Scottish regt in Dutch service; *d* Ypres 1720, leaving an est s:

1b George; returned to Scotland; bought a small property, Tarviston, Lanarks; *m* Catherine Edmonstone and *d* 1769, leaving, with several daus, an only son:

1c WILLIAM (Sir), **9th Bt**

(1) Elizabeth; *m* Thomas Drummond, of Riccarton

(2) Ann; *m* Sir George Stirling, of Keir

The 9th Bt's cousin,

Sir William Nicolson, 9th Bt, Maj-Gen, entered Army 1778, served America, India, Ireland and Mauritius; *b* 1758; *m* 5 July 1804 Mary (*d* 20 Feb 1853), dau of John Russell,by Eleanor, dau of William Robertson, DD, historian, and *d* 5 Aug 1820, leaving an only child:

Sir Frederick William Erskine Nicolson, 10th Bt, CB, Adml; *b* 22 April 1815; *m* 1st 26 May 1847 Mary Clementina Marian (*d* 17 July 1851), 2nd dau of James Loch, MP, of Drylaw (*see* 1970 edn LOCH, B), and had issue:

1 Frederick, Lt RA; *b* 10 June 1848; *k* at Kambula, Zululand, 29 March 1879

2 ARTHUR, **1st Baron**

1 Clementina Ann Eleanor; *m* 26 Nov 1885 Wilhelm Beemelmans, of Strasburg, and *d* his widow 5 Dec 1931

Sir Frederick *m* 2nd 1855 Augusta Sarah (*d* 19 April 1861), only dau of Robert Cullington, of Old Lakenham, and by her had issue:

2 Frances; *d* unm 5 March 1942

3 Amy; *d* unm 1951

Sir Frederick *m* 3rd 16 Aug 1867 Anne (*d* 8 Jan 1896), only child of R Crosse, and *d* 29 Dec 1899

His only surv son,

Sir Arthur Nicolson, 11th Bt and **1st Baron Carnock**, of Carnock, Co Stirling (UK), so *cr* 27 June 1916, PC (1905), GCB (1907, KCB 1901), GCMG (1906, CMG 1886), GCVO (1905, KCVO 1903), KCIE (1888); *b* 10 Sept 1849; entered FO 1870, Assist Priv Sec to For Sec 1872–74, 3rd Sec 1874, 2nd Sec Peking 1876, Berlin 1878 and Constantinople 1879, Sec Legation Tehran 1885, Consul-Gen Hungary 1888, Sec of Embassy Constantinople 1893, Agent and Consul-Gen Bulgaria 1894, Envoy Extrdy and Min Plen Tangier and Consul-Gen Morocco 1895, Amb Madrid 1904 and St Petersburg 1906–10, Perm U-Sec FO 1910–16, Orders of St Alexander Nevsky of Russia and Charles III of Spain, Grand Cross Legion of Honour, Hon Fell BNC Oxford 1916; *m* 20 April 1882 Mary Catharine (*d* 23 March 1951), dau of Capt Archibald Rowan Hamilton, of Killyleagh Castle, Co Down (*see* DUFFERIN and CLANEBOYE, B, and *American Presidential Families*, section TAFT, 1994, Morris Genealogical Books, SA), and *d* 6 Nov 1928, leaving:

1 FREDERICK ARCHIBALD NICOLSON, **2nd Baron Carnock**, MC, barrister Inner Temple, Maj 15th Hus and GSO WW I (despatches, wounded), Legion of Honour; *b* 9 Jan 1883; *d* unm 3 May 1952

2 ERSKINE ARTHUR, **3rd Baron**

3 Harold George (Hon Sir), KCVO (1953), CMG (1920); *b* 21 Nov 1886; *educ* Wellington and Balliol Coll Oxford (MA 1930, Hon Fell 1953); Dip Serv 1909–30, fought combined Universities on behalf of Sir Oswald Mosley, Bt (*see* RAVESDALE, B)'s New Party 1931, MP (Nat Lab) Leicester W 1935–45, Parly Sec Min of Inf 1940–41, Govr BBC 1941–46, Legion of Honour, author: *Paul Verlaine* (1921), *Sweet Waters* (1921), *Tennyson* (1923), *Byron, The Last Journey* (1924), *Swinburne* (1926), *Some People* (1927), *Development of English Biography* (1928), *Lord Carnock* (1930), *People and Things* (1931), *Public Faces* (1932), *Peacemaking, 1919* (1933), *Curzon: The Last Phase* (1934), *Dwight Morrow* (1935), *Small Talk* (1937), *Helen's Tower* (1937), *Diplomacy* (1939), *Marginal Comment* (1939), *The Congress of Vienna* (1946), *Benjamin Constant* (1949), *King George V: His Life and Reign* (1952), *Sainte Beuve* (1957), *Journey to Java* (1957), *The Age of Reason* (1959), *Monarchy* (1962); *m* 1 Oct 1913 Hon Victoria Mary Sackville-West, CH (1948), JP, DLitt (*d* 2 June 1962), only child of 3rd Baron Sackville (*qv*), and *d* 1 May 1968, leaving issue:

(1) (Lionel) Benedict, MVO (1947), Capt Intell Corps WW II, Dep Surveyor King's Pictures 1939–47, ed: *Burlington Magazine*, author: *The Painters of Ferrara* (1950), *Hendrick Terbrugghen* (1958), *Wright of Derby: Painter of Light* (1968), *The Treasures of the Foundling Hospital* (1972), *Courbet: The Studio of the Painter* (1973), *Georges de la Tour* (1974); *b* 6 Aug 1914; *educ* Eton and Balliol Coll Oxford; *m* 8 Aug 1955 (*divorce* 1962) Luisa Felicita, er dau of Prof Giacomo Vertova, of via Romana 34, Florence, and *d* 1978, leaving issue:

1a *Vanessa Pepita Giovanna [Mrs Andrew Davidson, Horserace House, Sissinghurst, Cranbrook, Kent TW17 2AT]; *b* 8 Aug 1956; *m* 1991 *Andrew Cunningham Churchill Davidson, son of Harry Churchill Davidson, of Hove, Sussex, and has issue:

1b *Elena Rose; *b* 1987

2b *Rosa Ilaria; *b* 1989

(2) +NIGEL, MBE (1945) [Nigel Nicolson Esq MBE, Sissinghurst Castle, Cranbrook, Kent TN17 2AB]; *b* 19 Jan 1917; heir presumptive; *educ* Eton and Balliol Coll Oxford; MP (C) Bournemouth E and Christchurch Feb 1952–Sept 1959, Capt Gren Gds WW II (despatches), dir Weidenfeld and Nicolson 1948–92, author: *The Grenadier Guards, 1939–45* (official history 1949), *People and Parliament* (1958), *Lord of the Isles* (1960), *Great Houses of Britain* (1965), *Harold Nicolson: Diaries and Letters 1930–62* (ed, 3 vols, 1966–68), *Great Houses* (1968), *Alex (FM Alexander of Tunis)* (1973), *Portrait of a Marriage* (1973), *The Himalayas* (1975), *Mary Curzon* (1977), *Napoleon: 1812* (1985), *Two Roads to Dodge City* (with Adam Nicolson, 1986), *Kent* (1988), *The World of Jane Austen* (1991), *Vita and Harold: the letters of Vita Sackville-West and Harold Nicolson 1910–1962* (1992), *Long Life* (memoirs) (1997); FSA, FRSL; *m* 30 July 1953 (*divorce* 1970) Philippa Janet (*d* 1987), only dau of Sir Gervais Tennyson d'Eyncourt, 2nd Bt (*qv*), and has issue:

1a +Adam [Adam Nicolson Esq, Perch Hill Farm, Brightling, Robertsbridge, E Sussex TN32 5HP]; *b* 12 Sept 1957; *educ* Eton and Magdalene Coll Cambridge (MA); dir Toucan Books Ltd 1986–, jnlst *Sunday Times* 1986–92, *Sunday Telegraph* 1993–, author: *National Trust Book of Long Walks* (1981), *Long Walks in France* (1983), *Landscape in Britain* (1984), *Frontiers* (Somerset Maugham Award, 1985), *Wetland* (Br Topography Prize, 1986), *Two Roads to Dodge City* (with Nigel Nicolson, 1986), *Prospects of England* (1989), *Restoration: The Rebuilding of Windsor Castle* (1997); *m* 1st 1982 (*divorce* 1992) Olivia Mary Rokeby, est dau of Lt-Cdr Antony Charles Reynardson Fane, RN (*see* WESTMORLAND, E), and has issue:

1b +Thomas; *b* 1984

2b +William; *b* 1986

3b +Benedict; *b* 1988

1a (cont.) Adam Nicolson *m* 2nd 1993 *Sarah Clare, dau of John Earle Raven, of King's Coll, Cambridge, and has further issue:

1b *Rose Raven; *b* 1993

2b *Mollie Raven; *b* 1996

1a *Juliet [Mrs James Macmillan-Scott, 71 Chester Row, London SW1]; *b* 9 June 1954; *m* 1977 (*divorce* 1995) James Macmillan-Scott and has:

1b *Clementine; *b* 1981

2b *Flora; *b* 1985

2a *Rebecca [Mrs Rebecca Philipps, 5 Malvern Terr, London N1 1HR]; *b* 10 April 1963; *m* 1988 (*divorce* 1996) Hon Guy Wogan Philipps, est son of 3rd Baron Milford (*qv*)

1 Clementina Gwendolen Catharine, JP; *b* 3 July 1896; *m* 6 Oct 1916 3rd Baron St Levan, DL, JP (*d* 1978) (*qv*), and had issue

The 3rd BARON's bro,

ERSKINE ARTHUR NICOLSON, **3rd Baron Carnock**, DSO (1919), JP (Devon), Capt RN WW I (Legion of Honour, Offr Order Crown of Italy, Russian Order of St Anne 3rd Cl with swords); *b* 26 March 1884; *m* 9 Oct 1919 Hon Katharine Frederica Alberta Lopes (*d* 24 Aug 1968), dau of 1st Baron Roborough (*qv*), and *d* 1982, having had issue:

1 DAVID HENRY ARTHUR NICOLSON, **4th and present Baron Carnock**

2 Peter Trevylyan Erskine, DSC, Sub-Lt RNR WW II; *b* 3 Sept 1921; *ka* Aug 1942

1 Naomi Catharine Bertha; *b* 18 Jan 1925; *d* 17 June 1934

CARR OF HADLEY

Creation: B. (LP, UK) 1975.

THE BARON CARR OF HADLEY, of Monken Hadley, Greater London ((Leonard) Robert Carr, PC 1963) [The Rt Hon The Lord Carr of Hadley PC, 14 North Court, Great Peter St, London SW1P 3LL]; *b* 11 Nov 1916; *educ* Westminster and Gonville and Caius Coll Cambridge (MA); joined John Dale Ltd 1938 (dir 1948–55, chm 1958–63 and 1965–70); MP (C) Mitcham 1950–74 and Carshalton 1974–76; PPS to: For Sec 1951–55 and PM 1955, Parly Sec Min Labour 1955–58, Sec Tech Co-operation 1963–64, Sec of State Employment and Productivity 1970 and Employment 1970–72, Ld Pres Cncl and Leader H of C 1972, Home Sec 1972–74; dir: Carr Day & Martin 1947–55, Isotope Developments 1950–55, London Bd Scottish Union and Nat Insur 1958–63, Metal Closure Gp 1959–63 and 1965–70 (Dep Chm 1960–63, jt md 1960–63), Securicor Ltd and Security Servs plc 1961–63, 1965–70 and 1974–85, S Hoffnung & Co 1963 and 1965–70 and 1974–80, SGB Gp plc 1974–86, Cadbury Schweppes plc 1979–87, Prudential Assur 1976–85 (dep chm 1979–80, chm 1980–85), Prudential Corp 1978–89 (dep chm 1979–80, chm 1980–85); Govr: St Mary's Hosp 1958–63, Imp Coll 1959–63 and 1976–85, St Mary's Medical Sch Cncl 1958–63; Hon Treas Wright Fleming Inst Microbiology 1960–63; Pres Surrey CCC 1985–86; FIM 1957; Hon Fell Westminster Sch 1991, Fell Imp Coll 1985; CIPD (CIPM 1975), CIMGT (CBIM 1982); Pres Consultative Cncl of Professional Management Organisations 1976–; author: *One Nation* (jt author, 1950), *Change is Our Ally* (jt author, 1954), *The Responsible Society* (jt author, 1958), *One Europe* (1965); *m* 1943 *Joan Kathleen, dau of Dr E W Twining, and has had, with s s (*d* young):

1 *Susan Elizabeth [The Hon Mrs Bradley-Jones, Gardener's Cottage, Kingscote, Glos]; *b* 1947; *m* 1972 *(Alun) Rhodri Bradley-Jones

2 *Virginia Sarah; *b* 1957; *m* 1984 *Michael Frederick Fox

Lineage: RALPH EDWARD CARR; *m* Katie Elizabeth — and had:

(LEONARD) ROBERT, *cr* a **Baron**

CARRICK

Arms: Or a chief indented az., a crescent for difference. **Crest:** Out of a ducal coronet or a plume of five ostrich feathers arg., thereon a falcon rising of the last. **Supporters:** Dexter, a falcon, wings inverted, arg., beaked and membered or; sinister, a male griffin sans wings arg., beaked, rayed, collared and chained or. **Motto:** *Soyez ferme* ('Be steadfast'). **Creation:** V. (I) 12 May 1629, E. (I) 10 June 1748, B. (UK) 8 July 1912.

THE 10TH EARL OF CARRICK, Viscount Ikerrin, of Ikerrin, Co Tipperary, and **Baron Butler**, of Mount Juliet, Co Kilkenny (David James Theobald Somerset Butler) [The Rt Hon The Earl of Carrick, Pant yr Eos, Moelfre, Llansilin, Oswestry, Salop SY10 7QR]; *b* 9 Jan 1953; *s* f 1992; *educ* Downside; *m* 1975 *Philippa Janice Victoria, yr dau of W/Cdr Leonard Victor Craxton, RAF, of Mills Lydgate One, West Rd, Milford on Sea, Lymington, Hants, and has issue:

1 +(ARION) THOMAS PIERS HAMILTON, *Viscount Ikerrin*; *b* 1 Sept 1975

2 +Piers Edmund Theobald Lismalyn; *b* 1979

3 +Lindsay Simon Turville Somerset; *b* 1979 (twin)

Carrick, other creations: Duncan, a grandson by a junior line of Fergus, the Celtic ruler of Galloway, was recognised by KING WILLIAM (THE LION) OF SCOTS as overlord of the area of Galloway known as Carrick and made Earl thereof by 1196. His granddaughter Margaret was Countess of Carrick in her own right but when she married Robert de Bruce he became Earl of Carrick in right of his wife. It was his son, another Robert, who was the celebrated ROBERT 'THE' BRUCE and became King of Scots as ROBERT I in 1306. From this moment on the Earldom of Carrick became increasingly closely connected with the royal house, being almost invariably conferred on either a son or brother of a ruling sovereign. Indeed in 1469 an Act of the Scottish Parliament ruled that it should be evermore annexed to the eldest sons of the Kings of Scots, and it remains to this day one of the Scottish titles of the PRINCE OF WALES.

Nevertheless in the first half of the 17th century it was briefly held by John Stewart, second son of the Earl of Orkney. Even then there were objections to the designation on the grounds that it strictly appertained to an eldest son of the royal house. The 1st and last Earl of Carrick of this, the 1628 creation, died without surviving male issue fifteen years later when the problem was solved inasmuch as the title expired.

Lineage: EDMUND BUTLER le BOTILLER; granted 1 Sept 1315 a fief consisting of the castle and manors of Karryk Macgriffyn and Roscrea, whereby he has been by some sources referred to as Earl of Carrick, though the weight of evidence militates against this; *d* 13 Sept 1321, leaving, with an er s (JAMES BUTLER/le BOTILLER, 1st EARL OF ORMOND; *see* 1970 edn):

JOHN, of Clonamilchon (now Clonamicklon), in the Barony of Sleiveardagh, Co Tipperary; had:

Sir PIERCE BUTLER, **1st Viscount of Ikerrin** (I), so *cr* 12 May 1629, of Lismallin; ktd 1615; Lt-Gen forces taking part in the 1641 Uprising, being present at defence of Limerick against Gen Ireton and Battles of Liscarrol and Rosse, hence outlawed; *m* Lady Ellen Butler, dau of Walter, 11th Earl of Ormonde and (4th Earl of) Ossory (*see* 1970 edn), and apparently *d* by 20 April 1661, having had, with a yr s (Theobald, *d* 1669) and a dau (Ellen, *m* 4th Baron Dunboyne; *qv*):

JAMES BUTLER, of Fennor, Co Tipperary; *educ* Gray's Inn from 24 March 1637/8; *m* Ellen, est dau of 3rd Baron Dunboyne (*qv*), and *dvp* 1638, leaving, with two yr sons:

PIERCE BUTLER, **2nd Viscount Ikerrin**, PC (1686); *b* 3 Sept 1637; *educ* Oxford; conformed to the C of E, thus getting his lands back; *m* Eleanor, dau of John Bryan, of Bawnemore, Co Kilkenny, and had:

JAMES BUTLER, **3rd Viscount Ikerrin**; RC; Capt Grenadiers 1687; *m* in or after 1672 Eleanor, widow of Henry Warden, of Burnechurch, Co Kilkenny, and est dau and coheir of Col Daniel Redman, of Ballylinch, Co Kilkenny, and *d* 26 Oct 1688, leaving, with two intervening sons:

1 PIERCE BUTLER, **4th Viscount Ikerrin**; *b* 1679; *educ* Trin Coll Dublin; sat in JAMES II's Parl May 1689 hence outlawed after Williamite victory; outlawry annulled and he ennabled to attend I Ho Lds 1698, Col of Foot 170–05 and Dragoons 1705–11, Brig-Gen 1710l *m* 1st 14 Oct 1697 Alicia Boyle, est dau of Murrough, 1st Viscount Blesington [*sic*], and had issue; *m* 2nd 28 April 1703 Olivia (*m* 3rd 3 Oct 1719 Richard Booth (*d* 21 Nov 1726), of Epsom, Surrey, son of Sir Richard Booth, of Butlers Grove, Co Kilkenny, Govr Kinsale 1669–79, and *d* Jan 1723/4), widow of Sir Robert Colville and only dau of Sir Oliver St George, 1st Bt, but had no other issue and *d* 4 Jan 1710/1; his s by his 1st w:

(1) JAMES BUTLER, **5th Viscount Ikerrin**; *b* 6 Dec 1698; *d* unm 19 July 1712

4 THOMAS BUTLER, **6th Viscount Ikerrin**; *b* 1683; in Protestant holy orders, Chaplain-Gen to Army in Flanders during War of Spanish Succession; *m* 6 July 1713 Margaret, dau and coheir of James Hamilton, of Bangor, Co Down, and *d* 7 March 1719/20, leaving:

(1) JAMES BUTLER, **7th Viscount Ikerrin**; *b* 1714; *d* 20 Oct 1721

(2) SOMERSET HAMILTON BUTLER, **8th Viscount Ikerrin** and **1st Earl of Carrick**, Co Tipperary (I), so *cr* 10 June 1748, PC (I 1746); *b* 6 Sept 1718; *m* 18 May 1745 Lady Juliana Boyle, dau of 1st Earl of Shannon (*qv*), and had issue:

1a HENRY THOMAS, **2nd Earl**

2a Pierce BUTLER later BUTLER-COOPER, MP; *b* 15 Aug 1750; *m* 27 Dec 1774 Catherine (*d* 20 Feb 1833), est dau of Richard Rothe, of Butler's Grove, Co Kilkenny, and *dsp* 5 May 1826

1a Henrietta, twin with her bro Pierce; *m* Oct 1768 11th Viscount Mountgarret

2a Margaret; *m* 1772 1st Earl Belmore (*qv*)

The 1st EARL *d* 15 April 1774; his son,

HENRY THOMAS BUTLER, **2nd Earl of Carrick**; *b* 19 May 1746; MP Killyleagh 1768–74; *m* 7 Aug 1774 Sarah (*d* 4 April 1841), 2nd dau and coheir of Col Edward Taylor, of Askeaton, Co Limerick, and *d* 20 July 1813, having had, with other issue:

1 SOMERSET RICHARD BUTLER, **3rd Earl of Carrick**; *b* 28 Sept 1779; *m* 1st 1 Sept 1811 Anne (*d* 22 Oct 1829), est dau of Owen Wynne, of Haslewood, Co Sligo, and had issue:

(1) Sarah Juliana; *m* 8 Dec 1832 3rd Earl of Clancarty (*qv*), and *d* 28 April 1905, leaving issue

(2) Anne Margaret; *m* 7 Feb 1861 George Whitelocke Whitelocke Lloyd, of Strancally Castle, Co Waterford, and Calton, Yorks, and *dsp* 15 May 1901

1 (cont.) The **3rd Earl** *m* 2nd 12 Feb 1833 Lucy (*m* 2nd 10 Aug 1842 Hon Charles H Butler Clarke Southwell Wandesford, bro of 1st Marquess of Ormonde (*see* 1970 edn), and *d* 13 Oct 1884 aged 84), 3rd dau of Arthur French, of French Park, and *d* 4 Feb 1838, leaving:

(1) HENRY THOMAS BUTLER, **4th Earl of Carrick**; *b* Feb 1834; *d* 16 April 1846

(2) SOMERSET ARTHUR BUTLER, **5th Earl of Carrick**, Capt Gren Gds; *b* 30 Jan 1835; *d* unm 22 Dec 1901

(3) Lucy Maria; *m* 19 March 1863 6th Baron Massy (*qv*), and *d* 25 July 1896, leaving issue

2 Henry Edward, Lt-Gen, Col 94th Foot; *b* 3 Dec 1780; *m* 1st 6 Jan 1812 Jane (*d* 30 Aug 1834), dau of Clotworthy Gowan, and had, with other issue:

(1) Charles George, Capt 86th Foot; *b* 1823; *m* 29 May 1850 Jane Elizabeth (*m* 2nd 21 Nov 1861 Charles Compton Abbott, and *d* 22 March 1900), est dau of Capt Prosser, 7th Fus, and *d* 18 Dec 1854, leaving issue:

1a CHARLES HENRY SOMERSET, **6th Earl**

1a Mary Emily; granted 15 Sept 1910 rank of Earl's dau; *m* 22 Feb 1876 Rev George Platt Dew, BA, of Netherwent, Meads, Eastbourne, Rector Shire Newton, Mon, and *d* 10 Feb 1933, leaving issue. He *d* 1915

(2) Pierce (Rev), Mil Chaplain Crimea and Expdn to Kertch; rector Ulcombe, Kent; *b* 27 Feb 1826; *m* 30 July 1861 Catherine Twisden (*d* 3 Nov 1904), 2nd dau of Rev Sir William Marriott Smith-Marriott, 4th Bt (*qv*), Rector Horsmonden, and *d* 8 Feb 1868, having had, with other issue:

1a Pierce Armar (Rev), Rector Brancaster, King's Lynn; *b* 26 June 1863; *m* 1 Jan 1885 Emily (*d* 24 May 1933), dau of Capt W I Rüswurm, W India Regt, and *d* 23 March 1924, leaving, with other issue:

1b Pierce Rollo (Rev), Rector N Baddesley, Hants 1937–50, Port Chaplain Southampton 1923, Hon Chaplain RAF, Rector Melcombe Bingham Dorset 1913–23, served WW I with Italian Red Cross and RAF (despatches, Croce di Guerra); *b* 6 Nov 1885; *m* 7 Jan 1911 Ethel Florence (*d* 1943), dau of Rev Thomas Legge Symes, and *d* 1950, having had issue:

1c Theobald Rollo Pierce, BEM, Detective Sgt Metropolitan Police; *b* 18 June 1913; *m* 1st 1940 (*divorce* 1963) Christine Helen, dau of Gilbert William Harding, and had issue:

1d +Jeremy Somerset Pierce; *b* 1944

1d *Charlotte Veronica Pierce; *b* 1942

1c (cont.) Detective Sgt Theobald Butler *m* 2nd 1964 *Gwendoline May Emily [Mrs Theobald Butler, 33 Dalinghoo Rd, Wickham Market, Woodbridge, Suffolk], dau of Frederick George Jennings, and *d* 1983, having had further issue:

2d +Mark Pierce [Mark Butler Esq, 85 Beulah Rd, Walthamstow, London E17 9LD]; *b* 1960; Metropolitan Police Constable; *m* 1983 *Jane, dau of Alfred Reginald Gill, and has issue:

1e *Scarlett Frances; *b* 1986

2c James Armar Cory, F/Lt RAF; *b* 30 May 1916; *m* 1944 *Marjorie Wells [Mrs James Butler, 140 Broom Rd, Teddington, Middx], and *d* 1973, leaving issue:

1d *Sandra Leigh; *b* 1945; *m* 19– *Charles Devine, and has issue:

1e *Anthony Michael; *b* 1969

1e *Sarah Louise; *b* 1976

2d *Melanie Ann; *b* 1949; *m* 1978 *Terence Patrick Cook, and has had issue:

1e Coralie Joanna; *b* 1979; *d* 1985

2e *Natalie Jane; *b* 1982

3e *Genevere Eloise; *b* 1987

4e *Daniella; *b* 1990

3c +Kenelm Somerset Priaulx [Lt-Col Kenelm Butler, 16 Penny Lane, Durbanville, CP 7550, S Africa], Polar Medal for service in Antarctic 1945–48, Leader of Falkland Is Dependencies Survey 1947–48 (Sec 1948–50), manager Whaling Dept, Compañia Argentina de Pesca, Buenos Aires 1954–58, Lt-Col Falkland Islands Def Force and Admin Offr S Georgia, late Capt Roy Sigs (TA); *b* 24 Nov 1917; *m* 14 Aug 1954 *Janet Cooper, widow of — Horne, and dau of James Gilmour

1c Patricia Florence Pierce; *b* 13 Nov 1911; *d* 27 Nov 1931

2b Hubert Blennerhassett, Capt Dorset Regt and Maj RE WW I France and Palestine, WW II in Egypt; *b* 12 Aug 1887; *m* 4 Oct 1919 Sophie Marie (*d* 1985), dau of Jules Castravelli, of Bacos, Alexandria, Egypt, and *d* 1986, leaving issue:

1c *Marjorye Marie; *b* 4 March 1921; *m* 30 March 1944 Maj Peter Quentin Logan, S Staffs Regt (*d* 1992), yr son of Dr Roderic Walter Logan, of Ashby-de-la-Zouch, and *d* 1995, leaving:

1d *Michael Roderic Quentin; *b* 12 March 1947; *educ* Milton Abbey; *m* 1971 (*divorce* 1981) Gillian, dau of Cdr J M C C Rutherford, RNVR, of Henley-on-Thames, Oxon

2c *Noreen May [Mrs Frank Bristowe, 18 Archery Sq, Walmer, Deal, Kent]; *b* 24 May 1923; *m* 15 April 1944 Col Frank Hilary Bristowe, RM (*d* 1992), son of Arthur Hilary Bristowe, of Vayne, Budleigh Salterton, Devon, and has issue:

1d *Rosamund Gillian; *b* 3 June 1947; *m* 1969 *Charles Vivian Parryand has:

1e *Giles Hubert; *b* 1974

2e *Julian Charles; *b* 1976

2d *June Hilary [Mrs William Jamieson, 53 Loxley Rd, London SW18]; *b* 17 June 1949; *m* 1969 *William Magnus Jamieson, and has issue:

1e *Henry William Ashton; *b* 1979

2e *James Nicholas Rupert; *b* 1986

1e *Francesca Catherine Sophie; *b* 1977

2e *Leanda Georgina Hilary; *b* 1983

3d *Nicola Catherine Diana [Mrs Courtenay Inchbald, 54 Elmfield Rd, London SW17]; *b* 10 Dec 1960; *m* 1984 *Courtenay Charles Ilbert Inchbald and has:

1e *Isabella Catherine Noreen; *b* 1991

2e *Venetia Presiley Alice; *b* 1996

1b Norah Veronica Pierce; *b* 30 Aug 1904; *d* 1995

1a Harriet Frances; *b* 3 June 1862; *d* 1941

(3) James Armar; *b* 1827, army officer Crimean War; *d* 22 July 1854

2 (cont.) Lt Gen The Hon Henry Butler *m* 2nd 29 Nov 1836 Frances Mauleverer (*d* 27 June 1844), 2nd dau of John Parker Toulson and *d* 7 Dec 1856, having by her had further issue, with a dau:

(4) Edward John, Capt late 21st Fus; *b* July 1842; *m* 27 March 1879 Elizabeth Turner, dau of G E S Clark, MD, and *d* 11 Oct 1920

1 Anne; *m* 8 Sept 1798 Rev Henry Maxwell, who *s* as 6th Lord Farnham (*qv*), and *d* 29 May 1831

2 Juliana; *m* 2nd Earl Belmore (*qv*), and *d* 1861

3 Sarah; *m* 1812 Hon Charles H Butler Clarke Southwell Wandesford, bro of 1st Marquess of Ormonde (*see* MOUNTGARRET, V), and *d* 1839

The 5th EARL's cousin,

CHARLES HENRY SOMERSET BUTLER, **6th Earl of Carrick**, Maj late Welsh Regt; *b* 5 Aug 1851; *m* 1st 8 Jan 1873 Kathleen Emily Hamilton (*d* 21 June 1888), 3rd dau of Lt-Col Albert Ernest Ross, 5th Fus; *m* 2nd 1896 Emily (*d I*1915), dau of Mark Codrington Jones, and by his 1st w had, with a 2nd son:*

1 CHARLES ERNEST ALFRED FRENCH SOMERSET BUTLER, **7th Earl**

1 Kathleen, OBE (1918); *b* 20 Dec 1876; *m* 24 March 1897 Col Walter Charles Lindsay, MVO, son of Lt-Col Henry Gore Lindsay, of Glasnevin, and *d* 29 April 1953, leaving issue (*see* CRAWFORD and BALCARRES, E)

The 6th EARL *d* 6 April 1909; his son,

CHARLES ERNEST ALFRED FRENCH SOMERSET BUTLER, **7th Earl of Carrick**, OBE (1918), DL (Co Kilkenny); Comptroller Household to Ld Lt Ireland 1913–15, Lt-Col RASC, formerly Lt KOYLI, T/DAA, QMG MGC 1916, Staff Capt 1916–18 and AAG 1918; *b* 15 Nov 1873; *cr* 8 July 1912 BARON BUTLER, of Mount Juliet, Co Kilkenny (UK); *m* 16 Nov 1898 (Ellen) Rosamond Mary (*d* 15 June 1946), dau of Lt-Col Henry Gore Lindsay, of Glasnevin (*see* CRAWFORD and BALCARRES, E), and had issue:

1 THEOBALD WALTER SOMERSET HENRY BUTLER, **8th Earl**

2 (Horace) Somerset Edmond, CIE (1945), Lt IA Res of Offrs, Indian Frontier Medal 1930, memb Burma Ho of Reps 1938–41, Hon Magistrate Rangoon; *b* 23 May 1903 (twin with his bro); *m* 20 June 1928 Barbara (*d* 1977), only dau of Malcolm Sutherland Jacomb Hood, of Campton Manor, Shefford, Beds, and *d* 26 Aug 1962, leaving issue:

(1) *Georgina Carolin Eve; *b* 22 Sept 1931; the fashion designer Gina Fratini; *m* 1st 1954 (*divorce* 1961) David Goldberg; *m* 2nd 11 Oct 1961 (*divorce* 1968) Renato Candido Attilio Fratini, of Sacrofano, Rome, Italy; *m* 3rd 7 May 1969 *James Alan Short, the actor Jimmy Logan, son of Jack Short, of Glasgow

3 Guy Somerset Lionel, Lt IARO, Maj Roy Canadian Dragoons; *b* 5 Nov 1905; *educ* Tonbridge; *m* 1st 14 June 1939 (*divorce* 1961) Mrs Patricia Ann Tennant, dau of William Alexander Dunne; *m* 2nd 1961 Mrs Janet Frances Parker (*d* 1984), dau of Gordon Preston, and *d* 1983, having by 1st w had issue:

(1) +Rupert Lionel Somerset [Rupert Butler Esq, Lily Bank Farm, Lily Bottom Lane, Parslows Hillock, Princes Risborough , Bucks HP27 0RN], former F/Lt RAF; *b* 16 May 1940; *educ* Tonbridge and RAF Coll Cranwell; *m* 24 Aug 1968 *Jenifer Mary, dau of Norman James Rush, of High Wood, Henley, Haslemere, Surrey, and has issue:

1a +Piers Somerset Patrick; *b* 1970

2a +Eli Somerset James; *b* 1971

3a +Matthew Somerset Guy; *b* 1972

4a +Sebastian Somerset Lionel; *b* 1979

(2) +Dermot Somerset Launcelot [Dermot Butler Esq, Prospect House, Newcastle, Co Wicklow, Ireland]; *b* 3 April 1941; Ieduc Tonbridge and Quintin Sch; *m* 1st 1970 (*divorce* 1983) Lorna Ailsa Graham, dau of Maj Ian Graham Menzies; *m* 2nd 1986 *Mrs Victoria Marsland Nabarro, dau of John Lloyd Owen, and by 1st w has issue:

1a *Tara Siobhan Somerset; *b* 1974

4 Godfrey Claude Somerset Pierce, P/O RAFVR; *b* 22 Nov 1907; *educ* Stowe

5 Pierce Alan Somerset David, TD, Maj RA (TA); *b* 12 Nov 1909; *educ* Stowe; *m* 1st 9 June 1933 (*divorce* 1957) Leri, est dau of Dr Griffith Llewelyn-Jones, of Bryn Glas, Llangefni, Anglesey; *m* 2nd 2 July 1957 *Dorothea, yst dau of Thomas Warwick Bennett, of 40 Bishops Road, E2, and *d* 11 Jan 1964, having by 1st w had issue:

(1) +David Llewelyn Somerset [David Butler Esq, Brook Farm, Wethersfield, Braintree, Essex], dir M W Marshall and Co (Deposits) Ltd, and Marshall Dagues Bie, Geneva (subsidiaries of Cater Byder Gp); *b* 18 Dec 1937; *m* 25 June 1966 *Anne, dau of A S Haigh, of Marks Hall, White Roding, nr Dunmow, Essex, and has issue:

1a +Michael Somerset; *b* 6 May 1969

1a *Hilary Mary; *b* 1971

(1) *Helen Sarah Ann [Mrs Helen Colley, Fosters Buildings, Hartest, Bury St Edmunds, Suffolk]; *b* 4 Feb 1936; *m* 19 Oct 1957 (*divorce* 1969) Anthony Thomas Colley, 3rd son of Maj Clarence Colley, of Porridge Hall, Lindsell, Essex

1 Rosamond Kathleen Margaret, JP (1944), CC (1946), CA (1957), Herts, V-Chm Herts. CC 1961–62, Pres Herts Assoc of Parish Cncls, chm Care of Children Ctee Ware Park Hospital; *b* 31 Aug 1899; *m* 1st 12 Feb 1919 (*divorce* 1925) Lionel Gallwey Robertson (*d* 21 Jan 1926), son of Arthur Robertson, and had issue:

(1) *Patrick Somerset GIBBS (took step f's name), late Lt-Col Welsh Gds; *b* 14 Dec 1919; *m* 1949 Mairi Zoe, dau of Arthur Macmillan Evans, and *d* 27 Dec 1961, leaving issue:

1a *Andrew; *b* 8 Dec 1951; *educ* Eton

2a *David; *b* 21 April 1953; *educ* Eton

3a *Alexander; *b* 13 July 1957

1a *Teresa; *b* 12 April 1950

2a *Georgiana; *b* 22 April 1954

1 (cont.) Lady Rosamond Robertson *m* 2nd 9 June 1925 (*divorce* 1947) Maj Bryan Mortem Gibbs, MBE, Welsh Gds (*d* 23 Jan 1965), son of Arthur Gibbs, of Kingswood, Tunbridge Wells, and had further issue:

(2) *Somerset Byran; *b* l1 Jan 1926; *m* 9 Feb 1950 *Elspeth Pauline Mary Harrington, dau of Maj John Felix Russi, MC, and has issue:

1a *Brian Somerset Andrew; *b* 30 Nov 1950; *educ* Ampleforth

2a *Anthony Somerset; *b* 10 July 1952; *educ* Ampleforth

3a *Matthew Somerset; *b* 5 July 1954; *educ* Ampleforth

1a *Kathleen Oriana; *b* 19 June 1957

(1) *Brigid April; *b* 27 April 1927; *m* 7 May 1949 *Lancelot Guy Michael Hannen, MC, son of Gordon Hannen, and has issue:

1a *Peter Michael Lance; *b* 17 July 1953; *educ* Eton

1a *Caroline; *b* 7 Jan 1952

2 (Irene) June Beatrice, MBE (1943), OStJ; *b* 11 June 1901; *m* 1st 31 Oct 1923 (*divorce* 1934) John Sills Charlton, son of John Sills Charlton, of Grove Ho, Tonbridge, Kent; *m* 2nd 27 Dec 1934 Col Anthony Gordon Dobson, late IA, er son of Edward Hobson, of Butterstocks, Shipley, Sussex, and by 1st husb had issue:

(1) *Michael Tobias Peter, late Capt Skinner's Horse, IA; *b* 21 Aug 1926; *m* 1953 *Marie Margaret Celine Eda, dau of René Feuilherade, and has issue:

1a *John Sills Somerset Anthony; *b* 7 April 1957

1a *Marie Dominique Alexa; *b* 9 Move 1953

The 7th EARL *d* 2 Nov 1931; his est son,

THEOBALD WALTER SOMERSET HENRY BUTLER, **8th Earl of Carrick**; *b* 23 May 1903; *educ* Repton and Tonbridge; Cdr RNVR WW II, life V-Pres Roy Stuart Soc 1947 and Dep Govr-Gen 1948; *m* 1st 14 Aug 1930 (*divorce* 1938) Marion Caher, formerly w of Brook Edwards and dau of Daniel Charles Donoghue, of Philadelphia, and had issue:

1 BRIAN STUART THEOBALD SOMERSET CAHER BUTLER, **9th Earl of Carrick**; *b* 17 Aug 1931; *educ* Downside; memb Cncl Cotton Research Corp and Br Cotton Growing Assoc, chm Ralli Bros and Coney Ltd, dir: Reynolds and Gibson (Cotton) Ltd, Bacup Warehousing Co Ltd, James Platt (Liverpool) Ltd, Liverpool Uganda Co Ltd, Liverpool Cotton Assoc Ltd, Khartoum Cotton Co Ltd, Ralucot (Tanzania) Ltd and COTAC Le Havre; *m* 1st 20 Aug 1951 (*divorce* 1976) (Mary) Belinda (*d* 1993), est dau of David Turville-Constable-Maxwell, of Bosworth Hall, nr Rugby (*see* NORFOLK, D); *m* 2nd 1986 *Gillian Irene [The Rt Hon Gillian Countess of Carrick, 10 Netherton Grove, London SW10], dau of Leonard Grimes, and *d* 1992, having by his 1st w had issue:

(1) DAVID JAMES THEOBALD SOMERSET BUTLER, **10th and present Earl of Carrick**

(1) *Juliana Mary Philomena [The Lady Juliana Butler, 31 Greenbank Ave, Saltdean, Brighton, Sussex BN2 8QS]; *b* 20 Dec 1960

The **8th Earl** *m* 2nd 18 Oct 1938 Mrs Margaret Drum (*d* 24 July 1954), dau of Charles B Power, of Helena, Montana, USA; *m* 3rd 21 Oct 1954 Ruth, dau of Francis T M McEnery, of Chicago, USA, and *d* 31 July 1957

CARRINGTON

Arms: Or a chevron cotised between three demi-griffins, the two in chief respectant, sa. **Crest:** An elephant's head erased or, eared gu., charged on the neck with three fleurs-de-lys, two and one, az. **Supporters:** Two griffins wings elevated sa., the dexter charged with three fleurs-de-lys palewise or, the sinister with three trefoils slipped palewise of the last. **Motto:** *Tenax in fide* ('Persevering and faithful'). **Creations:** B. (I) 16 July 1796 and (GB) 20 Oct 1797.

THE 6TH BARON CARRINGTON OF UPTON, Co Nottingham, and **Baron Carrington of Bulcot Lodge** (Sir Peter Alexander Rupert Carington, KG (1985), GCMG (1988, KCMG 1958), CH (1983), MC (1945), PC (1959), JP (Bucks 1948), DL (Bucks 1951)) [Maj The Rt Hon The Lord Carrington KG GCMG CH MC PC JP DL, The Manor House, Bledlow, nr Aylesbury, Bucks HP27 9PB; 32A Ovington Sq, London SW3 1LR]; *b* 6 June 1919; *s* f 1938; *educ* Eton (Fell 1966) and RMC Sandhurst; Maj Gren Gds WW II, Parly Sec to: Min Ag and Fisheries Nov 1951–Oct 1954, MOD Oct 1954–Oct 1956, HC Australia Oct 1956–Oct 1959, First Ld Admiralty Oct 1959–63, Min without Portfolio and Leader Ho Lds Oct 1963–Oct 1964, Leader Oppn Ho Lds Oct 1964–70 and 1974–79, Defence Sec 1970–74, Sec State Energy Jan-Feb 1974, Chm C Party 1972–74, For Sec 1979–82, Sec-Gen NATO 1983–88, jt dep chm Australia and NZ Bank Ltd 1965–67 and chm 1967–69, chm: CLA 1951, Christies 1988–93 (dir 1988–), tstees V&A 1983–88 and European Community Peace Conf on Yugoslavia 1991–92, dir: Br Metal Corp 1965–68, Amalgamated Metal Corp 1969–70, Barclays Bank Ltd 1967–70 and 1974–79, Hambros 1967–70, Schweppes 1968–70 and 1974–79, RTZ 1974–79 and The Telegraph plc 1990–, pres: The Pilgrims 1983, VSO 1993, Tstee Tradescant Tst 1990–, Chllr: Reading U 1992–, Order St Michael and St George 1984–94, Order of the Garter 1994–; *m* 25 April 1942 *Iona, yr dau of Lt-Col Sir Francis Kennedy McClean, AFC, of Huntercombe Place, Henley-on-Thames, and has issue:

1 +RUPERT FRANCIS JOHN; *b* 2 Dec 1948; *educ* Eton and Bristol U; *m* 1989 *Daniela, dau of Flavio Diotallevi, of Madrid, and has issue:

(1) +Robert; *b* 7 Dec 1990

(1) *Francesca; *b* 1993

(2) *Isabella; *b* 1995

1 *Alexandra [The Hon Mrs de Bunsen, The Old Rectory, Kirby Bedon, Norwich, Norfolk]; *b* 11 April 1943; *m* 8 Sept 1965 *Capt Peter Noel de Bunsen, late Coldstream Gds, est son of Charles de Bunsen, of Eincastle, Pitlochry, Perthshire (*see* BUXTON, Bt), and has issue:

(1) *Charles Rupert; *b* 1970

(2) *Peter James; *b* 1973

(1) *Victoria; *b* 16 July, 1968; *m* 1991 *Andrew Falcon (*see* WELLINGTON, D)

2 *Virginia [The Hon Virginia Carington, 5 Rutland Gate Mews, London SW7]; *b* 23 June 1946; *m* 1973 (*divorce* 1979, resumed maiden name) 4th Baron Ashcombe (*qv*)

Lineage: JOHN SMITH, of Cropwell Boteler, Titheby, Notts, where he bought land 1623; *m* Elizabeth — and *d* 1641, leaving:

THOMAS SMITH, of Nottingham and Gaddesby, Leics; *bapt* 1 Nov 1631; draper; *m* 1st Mary Hooper and had two daus (Mary, *m* John Eggleton, *d* unm 1691); *m* 2nd Fortune, dau of Laurence Collin and sis of Abel Collin, of Nottingham, and *d* 1699, leaving:

1 Thomas, of Broxtowe, Notts; Sheriff Leics 1718; *d* 1727, leaving five daus

2 Samuel; ancestor of the DORRIEN-SMITHs of Ashlyns Hall and Tresco Abbey

3 Abel, of E Stoke and Nottingham, banker; *m* 1713 Jane, dau of George Beaumont, of Chapelthorpe, Yorks, and had issue:

(1) Sir GEORGE SMITH, 1st Bt, so *cr* 1757; had:

1a Sir GEORGE SMITH later BROMLEY, 2nd Bt (*see* BROMLEY, Bt)

(2) John, London merchant; ancestor of the HECKSTALL-SMITHs of St Mary Cray, SMITHs of Edwalton and Foelalt and BARON PAUNCEFOTE (*see* 1902 edn)

(3) Abel, of Nottingham; banker, MP Aldborough 1774, St Ives 1780 and St Germans 1785; *m* 1745 Mary, dau of Thomas Bird, of Barton, Warwicks, and *d* 12 July 1788, having had, with three daus and two other sons:

1a ROBERT, **1st Baron**

2a Samuel, of Woodhall Park, Herts; *b* 14 April 1754; *m* 2 Dec 1783 Elizabeth Frances, dau of Edmund Turnor, of Panton Ho, Lincs, and *d* 12 March 1834, leaving issue

3a George, of Selsdon

4a John, of Blendon Hall (*see* BICESTER, B)

The 3rd son,

ROBERT SMITH, **1st Baron Carrington of Bulcot Lodge** (I), so *cr* 16 July 1796, and **1st Baron Carrington of Upton**, Notts (GB), so *cr* 20 Oct 1797; *b* 22 Jan 1752; MP (Whig to 1783, Pittite thereafter) Nottingham 1779–97, Pres of Bd of Ag 1800–03, Capt Deal Castle, FRAS, DCL; *m* 1st 6 July 1780 Anne (Id 9 Feb 1827), dau of Lewyns Boldero-Barnard, of South Cave, Yorks, and had, with other issue:

1 ROBERT JOHN, **2nd Baron**

1 Harriet; *m* 28 June 1819 Col John Frederick Crewe, nephew of 1st Baron Crewe (*see* 1939 edn CREWE, M), and *d* 27 April 1856, leaving issue. He *d* 10 Nov 1840

2 Catharine Lucy; *m* 19 Nov 1803 4th Earl Stanhope (*see* 1967 edn CHESTERFIELD and STANHOPE, E), and *d* 1 Oct 1843, leaving issue. He *d* 2 March 1855

3 Charlotte Elizabeth; *m* 10 April 1809 2nd Baron Gardner (see 1970 edn) and *d* 27 March 1811, leaving issue. He *d* 22 Dec 1815

4 Hester Frances; *m* 30 Sept 1813 Hon Sir Henry Watkin Williams-Wynn, GCH, KCB (*see* WILLIAMS-WYNN, Bt), and *d* 5 March 1854, leaving issue

5 Emily; *m* 27 July 1822 Rt Hon Lord Granville Somerset, and *d* 4 Jan 1869, leaving issue (*see* BEAUFORT, D)

The **1st Baron** *m* 2nd 19 Jan 1836 Charlotte (*d* 22 April 1849), widow of Rev Walter Trevelyan (*see* TREVELYAN, Bt, of Nettlecombe), and 3rd dau of John Hudson, and *d* 18 Sept1838

His only son,

ROBERT JOHN SMITH later CARRINGTON (roy licence 26 Aug 1839), **2nd Baron Carrington of Upton**, Ld Lt Bucks and Col Roy Bucks Mil, MP (Whig) Wendover 1818–20, Bucks 1820–21 and High Wycombe 1831–88; *b* 16 Jan 1796; *m* 1st 17 June 1822 Elizabeth Katherine (*d* 23 July 1882), dau of 1st Baron Forester (*qv*), and had issue:

1 Cecil Katherine Mary; *m* 9 June 1853 1st Viscount Colville of Culross (*qv*), and *d* 2 Aug 1907, leaving issue

The **2nd Baron** *m* 2nd 10 Aug 1840 Charlotte Augusta Annabella (*d* 26 July 1879), sis and coheir of 22nd Baron Willoughby de Eresby (*qv*), jt hereditary Great Chamberlain, and descended through the Dukes of Ancaster from the WYNNs of Gwydir, and *d* 17 March 1868, having by her had issue:

1 CHARLES ROBERT CARRINGTON later CARINGTON (roy license for him and his bros 21 Aug 1880) later still WYNN-CARINGTON (roy licence 24 April 1896), **3rd Baron Carrington of Upton** and 1st and last MARQUESS OF LINCOLNSHIRE, so *cr* 26 Feb 1912, as also earlier 16 July 1895 EARL CARRINGTON and VISCOUNT WENDOVER of Cheping Wycombe, Bucks (all UK), KG (1906), PC (1881), GCMG (1885), DL, JP Bucks; MP (Lib) High Wycombe 1865–68; Capt Gentlemen-at-Arms 1881–85, Govr NSW 1885-90, Ld Chamberlain 1892–95, Pres Bd Ag and Fisheries 1905–11, Ld Privy Seal 1911–12, Lt-Col and Hon Col 3rd Bn Oxfordshire LI, Capt RHG, Jt Hereditary Ld Great Chamberlain with the Marquess of Cholmondeley (qv) and the Earl of Ancaster (see WILLOUGHBY DE ERESBY, B) and was deputed to exercise the Office during GEORGE V's reign 1911; *b* 16 May 1843; *m* 15 July 1878 Hon Cecilia Margaret Harbord, Lady of the Bedchamber to HM QUEEN ALEXANDRA 1911–25 (*d* 6 Oct 1934), est dau of 5th Baron Suffield, KCB (*qv*), and *dspms* 13 June 1928, when all his titles bar the 18th–century baronies expired, having had issue:

(1) Albert Edward Charles Robert, *Viscount Wendover*; *b* 24 April 1895 (HM EDWARD VII stood sponsor); Lt RHG; *d* 19 May 1915 of wounds recd in action

(1) Marjorie Cecilia, DGStJ; *b* 4 April 1880; *m* 1 Feb 1901 2nd Baron Nunburnholme, CB, DSO (*qv*), and *d* 17 June 1968, leaving issue

(2) Alexandra Augusta; *b* 6 March 1881 (HM QUEEN ALEXANDRA personally stood sponsor); *m* 30 June 1910 Col William Llewellen Palmer, MC, DL, JP, late 10th Hus and 4th Bn Wilts Regt (TA), of Great Somerford Manor, Chippenham, Wilts, son of Brig-Gen George Llewellen Palmer, of Lackham, Lacock, Wilts, and *d* 12 Jan 1955, leaving issue. He *d* 11 Aug 1954

(3) Ruperta; *b* 19 July 1883; *m* 7 Dec 1905 7th Earl of Dartmouth, GCVO (*qv*), and *d* 26 June 1963, leaving issue

(4) Judith Sydney Myee; *b* 27 Sept 1889; *m* 9 June 1909 Walter Egerton George Lucian, Viscount Bury, later 9th Earl of Albemarle (*qv*), and *d* 14 March 1928, leaving issue

(5) Victoria Alexandrina; *b* 7 Dec 1892 (HM QUEEN VICTORIA stood sponsor in person); Woman of the Bedchamber to HM QUEEN MARY 1930–37 and Extra Woman of the Bedchamber 1937–53; *m* 1st 3 June 1913 Nigel Walter Legge-Bourke, Coldstream Gds, of Hayes, Beau Parc, Co Heath, and had issue (*see* DARTMOUTH, E). He was *ka* 30 Oct 1914. She *m* 2nd 10 April 1916 Maj Hon Edric Alfred Cecil Weld-Forester, CVO, son of 5th Baron Forester (*qv*), and *d* 28 March 1966, leaving further issue

2 William Henry Peregrine (Sir), PC, GCVO, KCB, JP (Bucks and Berks), Lt-Col Gren Gds, MP Wycombe 1868–83, Groom-In-Waiting to HM QUEEN VICTORIA 1880–82, Actg Master Buckhounds 1883–84, Equerry to HM QUEEN VICTORIA 1881–1901, Extra Equerry to TM EDWARD VII 1902–10 and GEORGE V 1910, Comptroller and Treas to HRH THE PRINCE OF WALES 1901–10, Keeper Privy Purse 1910–14, Memb Cncl of HRH THE PRINCE OF WALES 1910–14, served in Egypt 1882; *b* 28 July 1845; *m* 23 Sept 1871 Juliet (*d* 6 Nov 1913), only dau of Francis Warden, and *dsp* 7 Oct 1914

3 RUPERT CLEMENT GEORGE CARRINGTON, **4th Baron**

2 Augusta Clementina; *m* 7 July 1864 1st Baron Blythswood (*see* 1940 edn) and *d* 23 March 1922. He *d* 8 July 1908

3 Eva Elizabeth; *m* 5 July 1869 8th Earl of Harrington (*qv*), and *d* 20 June 1919

The 3rd BARON's bro,

RUPERT CLEMENT GEORGE CARRINGTON later CARINGTON, **4th Baron Carrington of Upton**, CVO, DSO, DL (Bucks); MP 1880–85; Lt Gren Gds; served Zulu War 1879 (medal with clasp), and cmded 3rd NSW Imp Bushmen in S African War 1901–07 (medal with five clasps); *b* 18 Dec 1852; *m* 23 March 1891 Edith (*d* 26 Jan 1908), est dau of John Horsefall, of Widgiewa, NSW, and *d* 11 Nov 1929, having had issue:

RUPERT VICTOR JOHN CARINGTON, **5th Baron Carrington of Upton**, DL, JP Devon, Capt Res of Offrs Gren Gds WW I (wounded twice); *b* 20 Dec 1891; *m* 25 May 1916 Hon Sybil Marion Colville (*d* 30 Sept 1946), Lady-in-Waiting to HRH THE PRINCESS ROYAL, dau of 2nd Viscount Colville of Culross (*qv*), and *d* 19 Nov 1938, having had issue:

1 PETER ALEXANDER RUPERT CARINGTON, **6th and present Baron Carrington of Upton**

1 *Elizabeth [The Hon Mrs Dove, 6 Woolton Hill Rd, Liverpool L25 6HX]; *b* 4 June 1917; *m* 13 Nov 1943 *Capt William Lionel Dove, MB, ChB, MRCS, LRCP, RAMC, son of Edward William Dove, and has issue:

(1) *Anthony Edward [Anthony Dove Esq, Little House, Common Lane, Lower Stretton, Cheshire]; *b* 3 Sept 1946; *educ* Stowe; *m* 1st 1983 (*divorce* 1988) Jane Susan, only dau of A H Smith, of Dundrum, Queens Rd, Ilkley, Yorks; *m* 2nd 19– *Julie Maria, dau of G Williams, of Warrington, Cheshire

(2) *(John) Andrew [Andrew Dove Esq, 14 Guion Rd, London SW6]; *b* 18 April 1951; *educ* Stowe; *m* 1st 1980 (*divorce* 1984) Jane Esther, dau of Denis Horace Holland, of Park Farm, Lavenham, Sudbury, Suffolk; *m* 2nd 1994 *Clare Scott, dau of Anthony Scott, of Old Vicarage Fields, Chebsey, Staffs, and by her has:

1a *A dau; *b* 1995

Seat: The Manor House, Bledlow, Bucks. William Fitzherbert held the Manor of Bledlowe [*sic*] at the mid-17th century, when James Blanck, who is responsible for the oldest part of the present house, acquired it. Bledlow is therefore thought to date from the 1670s, when country house construction started on a serious scale again after the stagnation following the Civil War. It was remodelled during the 1720s, when it passed through the marriage of Blanck's granddaughter to Johnshall Crosse, member of a London brewing family. From the CROSSEs it passed to the WHITBREADs, also brewers, till bought by the **1st Baron Carrington** in 1801 for his eldest son. The entrance porch dates from soon afterwards.

It was probably then too that the external paint was applied, the subsequent weathering of which has contributed to the house's charm today. The **2nd Baron** carried out further alterations in the 1840s but by the end of World War II it had sunk to the status of a farm house and was occupied by one of the tenants. The **6th** and present **Baron** took up residence shortly after the War and with his wife has made substantial improvements, including the brick-paved surround to the swimming pool (itself relatively newly installed) and a section of the grounds set aside for the display of modern sculpture.

CARTER

Creation: B. (LP, UK) 1987.

THE BARON CARTER, of Devizes, Co Wilts (Denis Victor Carter) [The Rt Hon The Lord Carter, House of Lords, London SW1A 0PW]; *b* 17 Jan 1932; *educ* Xaverian Coll Brighton, E Sussex Inst Ag, Essex Inst Ag and Worcester Coll Oxford (BLitt); Nat Serv Canal Zone GHQ MELF 1950–52; farmer and ag consultant 1957–, fndr AKC Ltd 1957; Sr Research Fellowship in Ag Marketing MAFF 1970–72; ptr Drayton Farms 1975–; dir W E & D T Cave Ltd 1976–; exec producer Link TV 1988–97; opposition spokesman: Ag and Rural Affrs 1987–97, Social Security 1988–90, Health 1989–92, Dep Ch Oppn Whip Ho Lds 1990–92, Ch Govt Whip Ho Lds May 1997–; Chm: BBC Rural Affrs and Ag Advsy Ctee 1987–90, UK Co-operative Cncl 1993–; Pres: Br Inst Ag Consultants 1992–, Guild Ag Jnlsts 1994–96; Tstee: Rural Housing Tst 1992–, John Arlott Meml Tst 1993; V-Pres Shaw Tst 1991–; *m* 1957 *Teresa Mary, dau of Cecil William Greengoe, and has had:

1 Andrew Peter; *b* 1963; *d* 1982

1 *Catherine Mary; *b* 1959

Lineage: ALBERT WILLIAM CARTER; *m* Annie Julia — and had:

DENIS VICTOR, *cr* a **Baron**

CARVER

Creation: B. (LP, UK) 1977.

THE BARON CARVER, of Shackleford, Co Surrey ((Richard) Michael Power Carver, GCB 1970 (KCB 1966, CB 1957), CBE 1945, DSO 1943 and bar (1943), MC) [Field Marshal The Rt Hon The Lord Carver GCB CBE DSO and bar MC, Wood End House, Wickham, Fareham, Hants PO17 6JZ]; *b* 24 April 1915; *educ* Winchester, RMC Sandhurst; 2nd Lt Roy Tank Corps 1935; WWII: GSO(1) 7th Armoured Div 1942, OC 1st RTR 1943, Cdr 4th Army Bde 1944; Tech Staff Officer Min Supply 1947, Jt Servs Staff Coll 1950, AQMQ Allied Land Forces Centl Europe 1951, Col GS SHAPE 1952, Ch Staff E Africa 1955 (Dep 1954), IDC 1957, Dir Plans War Office 1958–59, Cdr 6th Inf Bde 1960–62, GOC 3rd Div 1962–64; Cdr Jt Truce Force Cyprus and Dep Cdr UN Force Cyprus 1964; Dir Army Staff Duties MOD 1964–66, Lt-Gen 1966, Gen 1967, C-in-C Far East 1967–69, ADC (Gen) 1969–72, Roy Tank Regt 1968–72, GOC Southern Command 1969–71, CGS 1971–73, CDS 1973–76, FM 1973, RAC 1974–77; Br Resident Commissioner Rhodesia 1977–78; Hon DLitt Southampton 1991; author: *Second to None* (1954) *El Alamein* (1962), *Tobruk* (ed, 1964) *The War Lords* (1976), *Harding of Petherton* (1978), *The Apostles of Mobility* (1979), *War since 1945* (1980), *A Policy for Peace* (1982), *The Seven Ages of the British Army* (1984), *Dilemmas of the Desert War* (1986), *Twentieth Century Warriors* (1987), *Out of Step: memoirs of Field-Marshal Lord Carver* (1989), *Tightrope Walking: British Defence Policy since 1945* (1992) and *Letters of a Victorian Army Officer: Edward Wellesley 1840–1854* (1995); *m* 1947 *Edith, dau of Lt-Col Sir Henry Lowry-Corry, MC (*see* BELMORE, E), and has issue:

1 *Andrew Richard [The Hon Andrew Carver, Bayswater Mill House, Headington, Oxford OX3 9SB]; *b* 1950; *m* 1st 1973 *Anne Rosamunde, dau of Brian Stewart, of the Broich, Crief, Perthshire; *m* 2nd 1989 *Patricia, dau of Jack Taffe, of Marco Is, Florida, USA

2 *John Antony; *b* 1961; *m* 1992 *Susan E, only dau of Alexander Graham, of Kirkcaldy, Fife

1 *Susanna Mary [The Hon Susanna Carver, 57A Broughton Rd, London SW6 2LE]; *b* 1948

2 *Alice Elizabeth [The Hon Mrs Alice Walters, 33 The Green, Brill, Aylesbury, Bucks HP18 9RU]; *b* 1954; *m* 1976 (*divorce* 1989) Capt Claude Walters, Gren Gds

Lineage: HAROLD POWER CARVER; *m* Winifred Anne Gabrielle Wellesley and had issue:

(RICHARD) MICHAEL POWER, *cr* a **Baron**

CARY

Arms: Arg. on a bend cotised sa. three roses arg., barbed and seeded ppr., in sinister chief a cinquefoil gu. **Crest:** A swan, wings elevated and addorsed ppr., between two cinquefoils gu. **Motto:** Strive.
Creation: Bt. (UK) 12 June 1955.

SIR ROGER HUGH CARY, 2ND BT, of Withington, Co Lancaster [Sir Roger Cary Bt, 23 Bath Rd, London W4 1LJ]; *b* 8 Jan 1926; *s* f 1979; *educ* Eton and New Coll Oxford (BA 1949); Lt Gren Gds (Res) WW II, Salzburg Scholar American Studies 1956, BBC: producer Overseas Servs 1951–56, talks writer European Servs 1956–58, dep ed *The Listener* 1958–61, management training organiser 1961–66, assist secretariat 1966–74, special assist Public Affairs 1974–77, special assist to md BBC TV 1977–83, ch assist to Sec BBC 1982–83, ch assist to dir programmes BBC TV 1983–86, consultant to Dir-Gen 1986–, sec Central Music Advisory Ctee BBC 1966–77 and 1983, tstee Kedleston 1988–, Assoc Roy Hist Soc; *m* 1st 30 June 1948 (*divorce* 1951) Matilda (Tilly; *d* 25 Sept 1996), dau of Maj Philip Pearson-Gregory, MC, and has issue:

1 *Marcia Susan [The Hon Mrs Robin Gibson-Watt, Gelligarn, Llandrindod Wells, Powys LD1 6EY]; *b* 12 Sept 1949; BA; landscape painter; *m* 1971 *Hon Robin Gibson-Watt, and has issue (*see* GIBSON-WATT, B)

Sir ROGER *m* 2nd 18 July 1953 *Ann Helen Katharine, er dau of Hugh Blair Brenan, OBE, of 7 Light Horse Ct, Roy Hosp, London SW1, and by her has issue:

1 +NICOLAS ROBERT HUGH [Nicholas Cary Esq, 266 Priest's Lane, Shenfield, Brentwood, Essex]; *b* 17 April 1955; *educ* St Paul's and London U (BA); *m* 1979 *Pauline Jean, dau of Dr Thomas Ian Boyd, MB, ChB, and has issue:

(1) +Alexander Robert; *b* 27 Nov 1981
(2) +Nathaniel Ian; *b* 1983
(3) +Peter; *b* 1988

2 +(Roger) Nathaniel Blair; *b* 13 Nov 1957; *m* 1978 *Tesney Vera, dau of Jasper Partington, and has issue:

(1) +Jonathan Nicolas Partington; *b* 1985

1 *Charlotte Rhoda Rosamond; *b* 10 Oct 1960; *m* 1982 *David Mayou, son of Simeon Mayou, and has issue:

(1) *George; *b* 1984
(2) *Jack; *b* 1986
(3) *Joseph Edward; *b* 1987
(4) *Joshua; *b* 1989

Lineage: Sir ROBERT CARY, of Cockington, Devon; *b c* 1380; *m* 1st Elizabeth, dau of Sir Philip Courtenay, of Powderham (*see* DEVON, E); *m* 2nd Jane (*d* 1448), widow of John Wadham, and dau of Sir William Hanksford, and had:

PHILIP CARY, of Cockington, MP Devon 1433; *b c* 1400; *m* 1422 Christian, dau of William Orchard, of Somerset, and *d* 1437, leaving:

Sir WILLIAM CARY; *b* 1437; *m* 1st Elizabeth, dau of Sir William Powlett, of Heanton St George, Somerset, and was beheaded (presumably as a Lancastrian) after the Battle of Tewkesbury 1471, leaving:

ROBERT CARY; *b* 1457; *m* 3rd *c* 1500 Margaret (*d* 1547), dau of William Fulkeram, of Dartmouth, and *d* 15 June 1540, leaving, with three er s (John, of Kegbear, *b* 1502; Thomas, *b* 1505, *d* 1567; William, *b c* 1506, *d* 1550):

ROBERT CARY, of Clovelly, MP Barnstaple 1553; *b* 1513; *m* Margaret, widow of John Gifford, of Yeo, and dau of John Milliton, and *d* 1 April 1586, leaving, with four er s (George, of Clovelly, Sheriff Devon, *b* 1543, *d* 10 July 1601; Robert, of Creedy; Gabriel; Thomas):

JAMES CARY, of Bideford; *b c* 1550; *m* 2nd Catherine (*d* 1629), dau of George Basset, of Tehidy, and *d* Sept 1632, leaving, with a yr s (Thomas, *b* 1600) and two daus (Mary, *b* 1599, *m* Robert Burgoyne; Alice, *b* 1602):

JAMES CARY, of Bideford and Alwington, merchant; *b* l597; *m* 21 Nov 1615 Elizabeth (*d* 1635), dau of Thomas Grenville, of Aldercombe, and had, with five er s (Francis, *b* 1616; Timothy, *b* 1617; James, *b* 1622, *d* 1694; Julian, *b* 1624; Francis, *b* 1628, *d* 1680;):

Rev JOHN CARY, vicar Hatherleigh; *b* 1629; *m* Mary (*d* May 1685), dau of John Yeo, of Reed, and *d* Nov 1683, leaving, with two daus (Ann, *b* 1662; Rebecka, *b* 1665, *m* 26 Nov 1684 William Williams, Vicar of Hatherleigh):

NATHANIEL CARY, of Hatherleigh, Devon; *b* 1661; *m* 14 May 1684 Margaret Rolle, of Cookbury, Devon, and had:

ROLLE CARY; *b* 1690; *m* 1720 Mary Walky (*d* Dec 1763), of Tregony, Cornwall, and had:

NATHANIEL CARY, of Grampound, Cornwall; *m* 24 Jan 1747 Sarah Pardew (*d* Dec 1811), of Creed, Cornwall, and *d* July 1779, leaving issue:

1 William; *b* 1747; *m* 20 Jan 1772 Elizabeth Pentreath (*d* April 1835), and *d* Oct 1833, leaving issue:

(1) William; *b* 1774; *m* 26 Dec 1795 Anne Trethewy, of Fowey, and had issue:

1a GEORGE ROLLE, of whom presently

2 Roulle, sailor, of Mousehole; *b* 1763; *m* 14 April 1783 Jane Harvey (*d* 11 Jan 1842), of Lanleglos, Cornwall, and *d* 3 Feb 1846, leaving issue:

(1) Charles Henry, of Paul, Cornwall; *b* 1785; *m* —, and had:

1a Nathaniel Cary; *b* 2 June 1832, only mate of the sailing ship *King Philip*, presumed drowned 1860 when the ship foundered between London and Calcutta

(2) Nathaniel; *b* 1786; *d* unm Feb 1805

(3) Roulle, of The Gurnick, Mousehole St Paul, Cornwall, Master Mariner; *b* 31 Jan 1790; *m* 25 Dec 1818 Ruth Trewavas (*d* 1 Dec 1855), and *d* 20 Oct 1876, leaving issue:

1a Rolle, Master Mariner and Captain of the barque *Spirit of the Ocean*; *b* 29 Dec 1819; *m* Elizabeth Corin, of Middx, and *d* 23 March 1866 when his ship was lost in a storm off Start Point, Devon, leaving issue:

1b Rouellena; *b* posthumously 22 Sept 1866

2a Charles Henry, Master of the *King Philip*, presumed drowned with his cousin

3a Obed; *b* 14 April 1830; *m* Martha Carolan (*d* 25 Oct 1909), of Settermore, Connemara, Ireland, and was lost at sea while on a voyage from Chile to Liverpool in 1862, leaving issue:

lb Obed Charles; *b* at sea 7 Oct 1855; *d* at Perth, W Australia, 10 June 1928, leaving issue

2b Richard Harvey. of Mousehole St Paul, Cornwall; *b* 4 April 1858; *m* his first cousin Elizabeth Carolan, of Mousehole, and *d* at Worthing 1 Nov 1922

lb Ruth; *b* at Mousehole 9 Oct 1860; *d* there 1872

4a Joseph Beardon; *b* 4 July 1833; *d* 28 Nov 1852 at sea on a voyage from Quebec to Bristol

5a Richard Harvey; *b* 18 Jan 1836; *d* 12 Dec 1923

1 Elizabeth *b* 1749; *m* 26 March 1770 Thomas Pentreath
2 Mary; *b* 1752; *d* July 1754
3 Mary; *b* 1760; *d* 1770

The ggs,

GEORGE ROLLE CARY, of Bishopsgate, and 10 Canal Place, Camberwell; *b c* 1807; *m* 1831 Elizabeth, dau of Frederick White, of Rochford, Essex, and *d* 21 Feb 1873, leaving:

1 WILLIAM
2 Frederick; *b* 26 April 1845
3 Charles; *b* 22 Jan 1849; *m* 26 Nov 1875 Alice Jane Gaffe, and had issue:

(1) George Rolle; *b* 24 May 1876; *d* 5 Aug 1886

1 Elizabeth; *b* 1833
2 Mary Ann; *b* 18 Nov 1839

The est son,

WILLIAM CARY, of Camberwell; *b* 5 Dec 1841; *m* 6 May 1866 Isabella Ann (*d* 10 Jan 1926), dau of Thomas Shilson, and *d* 29 Oct 1901, leaving issue:

1 William Richard; *b* 28 June 1869; *drowned* 16 June 1877
2 ROBERT, of whom presently
1 Isabel Ann; *b* 24 Feb 1867; *m* Henry George Shore, and *d* 18 Dec 1952
2 Alice; *b* 2 Jan 1875

The yr son,

ROBERT CARY, of Hampstead, London; *b* 2 Dec 1871; *m* 1897 Alice (*d* 18 Dec 1919), dau of Frederick Day, and *d* 4 April 1958, leaving issue:

Sir Robert Archibald Cary, 1st Bt (UK), so *cr* 12 June 1955, ktd 1915; *b* 25 May 1898; *educ* Ardingly and RMC Sandhurst; 4th Dragoon Gds WW I 1916–18, 4th/7th Roy Dragoon Gds WW II 1939, MP (C) Eccles 1935–45 and Withington 1951–55, PPS to: Civil Ld Admlty 1939–42 and Sec State India and Burma 1942–45, Assist Govt Whip 1944–45, Jr Ld Treasury May-July 1945, PPS to Ld Privy Seal and Leader H of C 1951–55, chm: Lancashire United Tport Ltd, J Compton Sons and Webb Ltd; *m* 30 April 1924 Hon Rosamond Mary (*d* 1985), yr dau of Col Hon Alfred Nathaniel Curzon (Isee SCARSDALE, V), and *d* 1979, leaving issue:

1 Sir ROGER HUGH CARY, **2nd and present Bt**

CASSEL

Arms: Per fess embattled az. and gu., in chief a pair of scales or between two swords, points upwards, pommels and hilts of the third, and in base a portcullis also of the third. **Crest:** A lion rampant gu., resting the dexter paw on a mill-rind gold. **Motto:** *Fiat justitia* ('Let justice be done'). **Creation:** Bt. (UK) 26 Jan 1920.

SIR HAROLD FELIX CASSEL, 3RD BT, TD (1975), QC (1970), JP (Herts 1959) [His Hon Sir Harold Cassel Bt TD JP, 49 Lennox Gardens, London SW1X 0DF]; *b* 8 Nov 1916; *s* bro1969; *educ* Stowe and Corpus Christi Coll Oxford; barrister Lincoln's Inn 1946, dep chm Herts QS 1959–62, Recorder Gt Yarmouth 1968–71, Hon Recorder 1972–, Circuit Judge 1976–88, Capt RA WW II; *m* 1st 27 April 1940 (*divorce* 1963) Ione Jean, est dau of Capt Evelyn Hugh Barclay, of Colney Hall Norwich; *m* 2nd 1963 *Mrs Eileen Elfrida Smedley, dau of James Herbert Rider Faulkner, of Shanghai, and has issue by 1st w:

1 +TIMOTHY FELIX HAROLD, QC (1988) [Timothy Cassel Esq QC, Studdridge Farm, Stokenchurch, Bucks HP14 3XS]; *b* 30 April 1942; *educ* Eton; barrister Lincoln's Inn 1965, Bencher 1994; *m* 1st 1971 (*divorce* 1977) Mrs Jenifer Samuel, dau of Kenneth Bridge Puckle, and has issue:

(1) +Alexander James Felix; *b* 25 May 1974

(1) *Natalia Hermione; *b* 1972

1 (cont.) TIMOTHY CASSEL *m* 2nd 1979 *Ann (Baroness Mallalieu, *qv*), only dau of Sir (Joseph Percival) William Mallalieu, and has further issue:

(2) *Bathsheba Anna; *b* 1981

(3) *Cosima Ione Harriet; *b* 1984

2 +Jeremy James; *b* 7 June 1950; *educ* Eton; *m* 1982 *Vivien Helen, dau of John David Hayter, of Kingham Farm, Hollington, Highclere, Berks, and has issue:

(1) +Hugo Timothy; *b* 1982

(2) +Felix; *b* 1988

(1) *Chloë Sieglinda; *b* 1984

3 +Evelyn Martin; *b* 5 May 1952

1 *Miranda Phyllis; *b* 18 Oct 1946; *m* 1980 *Ronald Ryer, of USA, and has:

(1) *Sarah Elizabeth Jean; *b* 1986

Lineage: M S CASSEL, of 2 Orme Sq, Bayswater; had:

Sir Felix Cassel, 1st Bt (UK), so *cr* 26 Jan 1920, PC (1937), KC (1906); *b* 16 Sept 1869; *educ* Harrow and Corpus Christi Coll Oxford (MA, Hon Fell); barrister Lincoln's Inn 1894, Bencher 1913 (Treas 1935), Judge Advocate-Gen 1916–34, memb LCC 1907–10, MP (C) St Pancras W 1910–16, Capt 1st/19th Bn London Regt WW I, pres Cassel Hosp for Functional Nervous Disorders, treas and v-chm Mount Vernon Hosp and Radium Inst, chm Cassel Educn Tst, memb cncl King Edward VII Sanatorium Midhurst, chm Ctee on Compulsory Insur 1936–37, memb ctees on Court Martial Procedure 1919 and 1938, Master Musicians' Co 1940, High Sheriff Herts 1942; *m* 18 Nov 1908 Lady Helen Grimston (*d* 7 Oct 1947), est dau of 3rd Earl of Verulam (*qv*), and *d* 22 Feb 1953, having had:

1 Ernest James, S/Lt RNVR WW II; *b* 1 Sept 1909; found shot dead 3 June 1940

2 **Sir Francis Edward Cassel, 2nd Bt**; *b* 27 May 1912; *educ* Harrow; concert pianist, chm Cassel Hosp for Functional Nervous Disorders, chm Cncl King Edward VII Br-German Fndn; *d* unm 17 April 1969

3 Sir HAROLD FELIX CASSEL, **3rd and present Bt**

1 Hermione Anna; *b* 9 Dec 1910; *d* 14 Feb 1989

2 *Josephine Helen [Mrs Griffith Pugh, Hatching Green House, Hatching Green, Harpenden, Herts]; *b* 0 Nov 1910; *m* 5 Sept 1939 Lewis Griffith Cresswell Evans Pugh, MA, BM, BCh (*d* 23 Dec 1994), son of Lewis Pugh Evans Pugh, KC, of Calcutta, and has issue:

(1) *David Sheridan Griffith [David Pugh Esq, Hatching Green House, Hatching Green, Harpenden, Herts AL5 2JY]; *b* 17 Sept 1940

(2) *Simon Francis [Dr Simon Pugh MRCP, FRCPath, 10 Coniger Rd, London SW6]; *b* 21 June 1945

(3) *Oliver Lewis Evans [Oliver Pugh Esq, 28 Redan St, London W14]; *b* 24 Aug 1955

(1) *Harriet Veronica Felicity [Mrs James Tuckey, 95 Elgin Cres, London W11 2JF]; *b* 19 Oct 1946; *m* 8 Nov 1974 *James Lane Tuckey and has:

1a *Venetia Anne; *b* 21 May 1978

2a *Elizabeth; *b* 26 Nov 1979

3a *Rose; *b* 22 June 1981

CASTLE OF BLACKBURN

Creation: B. (LP, UK) 1990.

BARONESS CASTLE OF BLACKBURN, of Ibstone, Co Buckingham (Barbara Anne Betts, PC (1964) [The Rt Hon The Baroness Castle of Blackburn, House of Lords, London SW1A 0PW]; *b* 6 Oct 1910; *educ* Bradford Girls' GS and St Hugh's Coll Oxford (Hon Fell 1966); memb St Pancras Borough Cncl 1937 and Met Water Bd 1940–43, ed *Town and County Councillor* 1936–40, housing correspondent and affrs advsr *Daily Mirror* 1944–45, MP (Lab) Blackburn 1945–50 and 1955–79 and Blackburn E 1950–55, MEP Gter Manchester N 1979–84 and Gter Manchester W 1984–89 (Ledaer Br Lab Gp 1979–85, V-Chm Socialist Gp 1979–86), Lab Pty: memb NEC 1950–85, Chm 1959, Min Overseas Devpt 1964–65, Tport Sec 1965–68, First Sec State and Sec State: Employment and Productivity 1968–70, Social Servs 1974–76; Hon DTech Bradford 1968 and Loughborough 1969, Hon Fell: Bradford and Ilkley Community Coll 1985, Umist 1991, Humberside Poly 1991, York 1992, Hon LLD: Lancaster 1991, Manchester 1993, Cross Order Merit Germany 1990, author: *The Castle Diaries 1974–76*, vol I (1980) and *1964–70* vol II (1984), *Sylvia and Christabel Pankhurst* (1987), *Fighting All the Way* (autobiography, 1993); *m* 1944 Edward Cyril Castle, *cr* Baron Castle (LP) 1974, formerly night ed *Daily Mirror* (*d* 25 Dec 1979)

Lineage: FRANK BETTS, of Yorks; tax inspr; *m* Annie Rebecca and had:

BARBARA ANNE, **BARONESS CASTLE OF BLACKBURN**

CASTLE STEWART

Arms: Quarterly, 1st, or a lion rampant gu., armed and langued or, within a double tressure flory-counterflory of the 2nd (for SCOTLAND); 2nd, or a fess chequy az. and arg., in chief a label of three points gu. (for STUART); 3rd, arg. a saltire between four roses gu., barbed and seeded ppr. (for LENNOX); 4th, or a lion rampant gu. (for MACDUFF); the whole within a bordure company arg. and az., in the dexter chief a canton of Nova Scotia. **Crest:** A unicorn's head arg., armed and maned or. **Supporters:** Two wyverns or, their tails nowed, armed ppr. and langued gu. **Motto:** Forward. **Creations:** B. (I) 7 Nov 1619, Bt. (NS) 2 Oct 1628, V. (I) 20 Dec 1793, E. (I) 29 Dec 1800.

THE 8TH EARL CASTLE STEWART, Co Tyrone, **Viscount Castle Stuart**, Co Tyrone, **Baron Castle Stuart**, of Co Tyrone, and a **Baronet** (Sir (Arthur) Patrick Avondale Stuart, 15th Bt) [The Rt Hon The Earl Castle Stewart, Manor Farm, Babcary, Somerton, Som TA11 7DT]; *b* 18 Aug 1928; *s f* 1961; *educ* Eton and Trin Coll Cambridge (BA 1950); Lt Scots Gds 1949, farmer, FIMgt 1978; *m* 20 Dec 1952 *Edna, dau of William Edward Fowler, of Harborne, Birmingham, and has issue:

1 +ANDREW RICHARD CHARLES, *Viscount Stuart* [Viscount Stuart, Combe Hayes Farm, Buckerell, nr Honiton, Devon EX14 0ET]; *b* 7 Oct 1953; *educ* Millfield and Exeter U (BSc 1996, MSc 1997); *m* 22 Dec 1973 *Annie Yvette, only dau of Robert le Poulain, of 65 Ave de Marville, St Malo, France, and has issue:

(1) Celia Elizabeth; *b* 11th May 1976

1 *Bridget Ann [The Lady Bridget Wadey, Stone House Farm, E Pennard, Shepton Mallet, Somerset]; *b* 12 Feb 1957; *educ* Wynstones Sch, Whaddon Glos; MHort (RHS) 1983, DMS 1989, lecturer in horticulture Kingston Maurward Coll, Dorset 1983–87, cider-apple grower; *m* 1990 *Robert W Wadey, only son of Thomas Wadey, of Brighton and has:

(1) *Miriam Sarah; *b* 15 May 1997

Lineage: The 2nd LORD (STEWART OF) OCHILTREE, (*see* MORAY, E) had by his 1st w with other issue:

1 Andrew, *Master of Ochiltree*; *m* by 9 March 1566/7 his cousin Margaret (*d* 1 Jan 1627), dau of 2nd Lord Methven, and *dvp* by 10 Sept 1578, having had, with seven daus (including Margaret, *m* John Stewart, Yr. of Traquair; *see* MORAY, E) and three other sons:

(1) ANDREW, 3rd LORD

2 JAMES STEWART, 1st EARL OF ARRAN (S), so *cr* 23 April 1581 (*see* ARRAN, E, preliminary remarks); a favourite of JAMES VI, Chllr Scotland; *m* 6 July 1581 his cousin Elizabeth, dau of 4th Earl of Atholl (*see* MORAY, E) and was *k* 1 Dec 1595, having been attainted 1585, and having had:

(1) JAMES STEWART (Sir), *cr* or became LORD OCHILTREE 9 June 1615 on buying the Ochiltree lands and acquiring the Ochiltree (territorial) Barony by his cousin's resignation of it to him; *m* 1st by 16 May 1622 Katherine, widow of Hew, Master of Cassillis (*see* AILSA, M), and dau of Uchtred Macdowall of Garthland, and had issue, with several daus:

1a William, *Master of Ochiltree*; *dvp* 1645 unm

(1) (cont.) LORD OCHILTREE *m* 2nd (?)by(?) 1653 Mary, sis of William Livingston, and *d c* 1659, having by her had issue:

2a WILLIAM STEWART, 2nd LORD OCHILTREE; *b c* 1659; *d* unm 12 Feb 1675, when the Lordship became dormant or expired

(2) Henry; granted Manor of Corrigan, Killyman, Ireland; had:

1a William, of Corrigan; *m* and had issue:

1b Henry, *dsp*

1a Jean; *m* 1st Hugh Halcro; *m* 2nd Patrick Smith

2a Barbara; *m* Col Stewart, and had issue:

1b James; inherited Corrigan

3a A dau; *m* 3rd and last Lord Methven (*see* MORAY, E)

3 William (Sir) of Monkton and Carstairs; *m* Helen Cunningham, widow of John Stewart, burgess of Ayr, and was *k* by Francis, Earl of Bothwell, 1588, leaving issue:

(1) William, denounced as a rebel 13 March 1610

(2) A son

(1) Margaret

4 Henry of Barskimming and Gogar; *m c* 1580 Janet, dau of Adam Reid of Barskimming, and had issue:

(1) Adam; *m* 1610 Maria Ross, dau of Margaret Wallace, Lady Haining

(1) Janet; *m* James Chalmers of Corsaith and *d* after 1605

5 Robert of Pittheustes; *m* (contract 1586) Jean, dau of John Ross, of Craigie, and had issue:

(1) William, of Easter Polquhairie

(2) Andrew (Rev), MA; *b* 1598; *m* Esther, dau of William Wallace, of Failfurd, and *d* 1634, leaving issue:

1a Andrew (Rev); *b c* 1605; *m* —, and *d* 1671, leaving issue:

1b Esther; *m* Rev Henry Hamilton

1a Janet; *b* 1627; *m* Rev Thomas Crawford, MA, of Donegore, and *d* leaving issue. He *d* 1670

2a Elizabeth; *m* Lt Paul Cunningham

(3) Archibald

(4) James

(1) Agnes

(2) Helen

1 Isabel; *m* Thomas Kennedy, of Bargary

2 Margaret; *m* 1st 1564 John Knox (*d* 1572), the Scottish Reformer and historian.; *m* 2nd Sir Andrew Ker, of Faldonside

3 Berthia; *m* Rev Thomas Cawford

LORD OCHILTREE *d* by 21 March 1601/2; his gs,

ANDREW STEWART, 3rd LORD OCHILTREE later **1st Baron Castle Stuart**, of Co Tyrone (I), so *cr* 7 Nov 1619; *b c* 1560; First Gentleman of the Bedchamber to JAMES VI and I, Gen Edinburgh Castle, Gen of Artillery, sold the territorial Barony of Ochiltree and resigned his peerage to his cousin to raise cash 1615, settled in Ulster 1611, where granted 3,000 acres in Co Tyrone, as one of the 'undertakers' (i.e., pioneers sent to colonise northern Ireland in the name of Protestantism); he was later granted further large tracts of land in northern Ireland; *m* soon after 8 Aug 1587 Margaret, dau of Sir John Kennedy of Blairquhan, and *d* Jan 1628/9, having had:

1 **Sir Andrew Stewart, 1st Bt** (NS), so *cr vp* 2 Oct 1628, and **2nd Baron Castle Stuart**; *m* 1st (contract 15 Aug 1604) Anne (*d* Oct 1635), dau of 5th Earl of Atholl (*see* MORAY, E); *m* 2nd — and *d* 30 March 1638/9, leaving an est s:

(1) ANDREW STEWART, **3rd Baron Castle Stuart**; *m* by 1635 Joyce, dau and heir of Sir Arthur Blundell, of Blundellsbury, King's Co, and *dspm c* 10 Aug 1650, leaving an only dau and heiress:

1a Mary; *m* 5th Earl of Suffolk (*see* SUFFOLK and BERKSHIRE, E) and brought him the family estate

(2) JOSIAS STEWART, **4th Baron Castle Stuart**; *m* (licence 2 April 1662) Anne (*bur* 16 Dec 1678), dau of John Madden, of Maddenstown, Co Kildare, and *dsp* 2 Dec 1662

2 JOHN STEWART, **5th Baron Castle Stuart**l; *d* unm 1685, when the barony became dormant till 1774 (*see* below against **1st Earl**)

3 Robert, of Irry, Co Tyrone, Col; *m* 2nd Jane, dau of James Richardson, of Castle Hill, Co Tyrone, and *d* 1662, having had, with other issue:

(1) ROBERT STEWART, *de jure* 6th BARON CASTLE STUART, of Irry, Co Tyrone; High Sheriff 1665, Capt Army; *m* Anne (*d* 1694), dau of William Moore, of Garvey, and *d* March 1685/6, having had:

1a ANDREW STEWART, *de jure* 7th BARON CASTLE STUART, of Irry; *b c* 1672; High Sheriff Co Tyrone 1704; *m* Eleanor, dau of Robert Dailway, of Bellahill, Co Antrim, and *d* 1715, leaving, with other issue:

1b ROBERT STEWART, *de jure* 8th BARON CASTLE STUART; *b* 3 March 1700; *m* 1 June 1722 Margaret, est dau of Thomas Edwards, of Castle Gore, Co Tyrone, and *d* 2 March 1742, leaving:

1c ANDREW THOMAS, **9th Baron** and **1st Earl**

(2) George, of Termon; *m* Margaret, dau of Col Saunderson, of Tullylogan, Co Tyrone, and had issue:

1a Alexander; *m* Jane, dau of P Wallace, and by her had issue:

1b George, Surgn-Gen Army in Ireland; *m* Frances, dau of William Stewart, of Killymoon, MP, and had issue:

1c Eleanor; *m* Robert Evans, of Gortmerron, Co Tyrone, who *dsp* 21 July 1876

2c Frances; *m* James White, of Whitehall, Co Antrim, and had issue

The *de jure* 8th BARON's s,

ANDREW THOMAS STEWART-MOORE later STEWART (dropped MOORE on taking his seat 28 Nov 1775), **9th Baron Castle Stuart** (claim allowed 24 May 1774) and **1st Earl Castle Stewart**, Co Tyrone, so *cr* 30 Dec 1800, as also previously 20 Dec 1793 VISCOUNT CASTLE STUART, Co Tyrone (both I); *b* 29 Aug 1725; High Sheriff Co Tyrone 1755; *m* 2 Aug 1782 Sarah (*d* 11 Nov 1843), dau and coheir of Godfrey Lill, Judge Court Common Pleas Ireland, and had, with other issue:

1 ROBERT, **2nd Earl**

2 Andrew Godfrey; *b* 8 Dec 1790; *m* 10 Jan 1814 Sophia Isabella (*d* 24 June 1854), dau of George Lennox Conyngham, of Spring Hill, and *d* 7 Jan 1872, having had, with other issue:

(1) Andrew Thomas; *b* 6 Nov 1814; *m* April 1840 Mary (*d* 1906), dau of John Gilmour, and *d* 1894, leaving, with other issue:

1a Andrew Godfrey; *b* 1841; *m* 1868 Rosa, dau of William Wilson, of Hobart, Tasmania, and had, with another dau:

1b Andrew William Godfrey; *b* 1869

2b George Sydney; *b* 1871

1b Rosa Mary

2a George Joseph; *b* 1842; *m* 1875 Elizabeth Sarah (*d* 1877), dau of Abraham Rheuben, and *d* 24 Sept 1916, leaving issue:

1b Arthur Burleigh; *b* 1876

3a Robert Walter; *b* 1845; *m* 1871 Annie (*d* 20 Nov 1899), dau of Charles Nichols, of Tasmania, and *d* 1918, leaving, with other issue:

1b Burleigh Walter; *b* 1875; *m* 1901 Helen Gertrude (*d* 4 June 1956) (who *m* 2nd 1913 John Martin Muir, of Sorell, Tasmania who *d* 1943), dau of Edward Mace, of Burnie, Tasmania, and *d* 1912, leaving issue

1c Burleigh Athol; *b* 8 Jan 1904; *m* 21 April 1927 Winifred May, dau of W Ernest Kerrison, and *d* 1982, having had issue:

1d +Ernest Martin, Min of Religion with Seventh Day Adventist Ch, S Australia, late technician Educn Dept Tasmania; *b* 28 Oct 1935; *educ* Hobart Tech High Sch Tasmania and Avondale Coll Cooranbong NSW; *m* 21 Dec 1965 *June Rosalyn, dau of Stanley Bastian, of Como, W Australia, and has issue:

1e +Conway Athol; *b* 29 Nov 1968

1e *Kym Robina; *b* 5 May 1967

1d *Claire Leila [Mrs Reginald Johnston, 19 Rialannah Rd, Mount Nelson, Hobart, Tasmania 7007, Australia]; *b* 26 May 1928; *m* 10 Feb 1951 *Reginald Edward Johnston, and has issue:

1e *Kent Reginald; *b* 29 March 1952; *m* 1975 *Marlene Irene Baier and has:

1f *Nathan James; *b* 26 Aug 1975

1f *Alycia Irene; *b* 23 Oct 1979

2f *Caitlin Laine; *b* 15 May 1989

1e *Vivienne Claire; *b* 9 Feb 1955; *m* 1980 *Kenneth Ross Watts and has:

1f *Samuel Neil; *b* 2 Oct 1984

1f *Emma Claire; *b* 8 July 1982

2f *Amanda Joan; *b* 8 June 1988

2e *Celia Anne; *b* 11 Feb 1963; *m* 9 May 1992 *Gregory Arnold Helbig

3e *Dianne Ruth; *b* 7 April 1965

2d *Winifred Ellen; *b* 21 Aug 1929; *m* 5 Aug 1950 *John Robert Sinclair Mackey, and has issue:

1e *Andrew John Sinclair; *b* 1 May 1956; *m* 1978 *Debbie Lee Robson, and has issue

1e *Denise Claire; *b* 16 May 1952; *m* 19– (*divorce*) Robert John Wells

3d *Alma Elaine; *b* 29 Oct 1931; *m* 2 Dec 1955 *James Maxwell Carter, and has issue:

1e *Stuart James; *b* 2 Feb 1958; *m* 1984 (*divorce*) Eleni Atzamoglou

2e *Michael Jackson; *b* 21 Dec 1960

1e *Lee Andrea; *b* 25 Sept 1956; *m* 1978 *Ian Cameron Tremayne, and has issue

1c *Sylvia Annie; *b* 27 April 1902

1b Mabel Mary; *b* 1877; *m* 1906 Archibald Charles Peacock, of Launceston, Tasmania, and *d* 14 Oct 1935, leaving issue

4a John James Ochiltree; *b* 1847; *m* Alice, dau of William Rumney, and *d* 17 May 1935, having had, with a son:

1b Mary Doris; *m* Philip Arnold

2b Isabel Vera; *m* 1922 Roy Sharrington Smith, and had issue

5a Audley Mervyn; *b* 1860; *m* 1892 Alice Anne Rogers (*d* 1897) and *d* 27 May 1942, having had issue:

1b Audley Andrew Mervyn, served in Naval Patrol (Auxiliary) 1942–45, city valuer to Hobart City Cncl 1953; *b* 1897; *m* 1934 *Beryl Elizabeth, dau of Edward Alfred Irwin, of Hobart, and had issue:

1c *Elizabeth Anne Castle; *b* 17 June 1937

2c *Helen Christine Castle; *b* 31 Dec 1939

3c *Margaret Lyndsay Castle; *b* 25 Aug 1942

1b Alice Muriel; *b* 1894; *d* 1925

1a Emily Mary; *m* 1st 1877 Hugh Hall More (*d* 1881); *m* 2nd Capt Green, and *d* 24 July 1935, leaving issue

2a Mary Henrietta; *m* 1895 Bruce Logan, and had issue

(2) George William Conyngham, Capt 75th Foot; *m* 7 Dec 1854 Marianne, only surv child of James Cruttwell and widow of Rev Aaron Foster, of Milton Lodge, Wells, and *dsp* 10 July 1871

(3) Burleigh William Henry Fitzgibbon, of Dergmony, Omagh, Co Tyrone, Maj Tyrone Fus; *b* 12 July 1823; *m* 1st 12 Oct 1863 Susan Mary (*d* 28 Feb 1870), only child of Henry Briscoe, and had, with other issue:

1a Godfrey Richard Conyngham, CB (1918), of Dergmony, Co Tyrone, DL Suffolk, Maj E Lancs Regt, Sec Suffolk and Cambs TFA; *b* 28 Jan 1866; *m* 19 Dec 1899 Alice Mabel (*d* 8 March 1936), yst dau of John Acheson Smyth, of Ardmore, Co Londonderry, and *d* 19 Jan 1955, leaving issue:

1b Godfrey Walter Burleigh; *b* 12 April 1901; Lt-Col E Lancs Regt; *m* 22 April 1933 Christine Valerie (*d* 6 May 1997), 3rd dau of Col Stephen Simpson, TD, DL, of Bowerswood, nr Garstang, Lancs, and *d* 18 March 1996, leaving:

1c *Jane Christine [Mrs Wayne Kines, RR3, Prescott, ON K0E 1T0, Canada]; *b* 15 July 1934; *educ* St Paul's Girls Sch and Brandon U (BGS); APR, DipCAM; *m* 1st 1960 (*divorce* 1972) Anthony Rossington Vickers; *m* 2nd 1974 Herbert Jackson Daniel (*d* 1974); *m* 3rd 18 Sept 1982 *Wayne Locksley Kines (pres World Media Inst Inc) and has by her 1st husb:

1d *Robin Daniel Stuart [Robin Stuart Esq, 10 Discovery Ave, CE, Morinville, AB T8R 1N5, Canada]; *b* 8 Nov 1964; *educ* Grant McEwan Coll; computer manager; *m* 27 Aug 1988 *Kathleen, dau of Erik Nielsen, of St Albert, Alberta, and has:

1e *Christopher Anthony; *b* 29 Sept 1995

1e *Samantha Ann; *b* 26 March 1992

2e *Nicole Christine; *b* 24 April 1993

3e *Michaela Marie; *b* 31 May 1997

1d *Helena Jane Stuart [Mrs Philip Ziegler, c/o Kines, RR3, Prescott, ON K0E 1T0, Canada]; *b* 8 July 1969; *educ* Roy Mil Coll Kingston (BA) and U of Geneva (MA); *m* 18 May 1992 *Rev Philip Gordon Ziegler, s of Greg Ziegler of New Hamburg, Ontario, Canada

2c *Wendy Mary [Mrs Edward Stuart-Murphy, Hillbrook House, 47 Queens Rd, Chorley, Lancs PR7 1LA]; *b* 9 Dec 1935; *educ* St Paul's Girls Sch; *m* 1st 4 June 1955 (*divorce* 1972) William Joynson; *m* 2nd 3 Sept 1983 (*divorce* 1990) John Remmett-Smith; *m* 3rd 13 May 1995 *Edward Murphy, and has by her 1st husb:

1d *Timothy William Stuart [Timothy Joynson Esq, 3 Old Post Office Cottages, Marton-cum-Gratton, N Yorks YO5 9RT]; *b* 1958; *educ* Huddersfield U (BSc), AIEE; *m* 1989 *Linda, dau of J Spencer

2d *Nicholas George Stuart [Nicholas Joynson Esq, Hubertus Straße 56, 38279 Sehnde, Salzgitter, Germany]; *b* 1960; *educ* Sunderland U (MSc), MICE, CEng, MBA; *m* 31 July 1998 *Katryn, dau of Heinrich Ahrens of Wallmoden, Germany

3d *Jeremy Duncan Stuart [Jeremy Joynson Esq, 15 Ashgrove Rd, Aberdeen AB2 5AE]; *b* 3 July 1963; *educ* Loughborough U (BSc), CEng, MIChemE; dir Performance Improvements Ltd, Aberdeen

4d *Andrew Douglas Stuart [Andrew Joynson Esq, The Garden House, West End, Stokesley, N Yorks TS9 5BN]; *b* 26 July 1965; *educ* Loughborough U (MEng)

2b John Ochiltree, Lt-Col, King's Regt attd KAR; *b* 21 Sept 1902; *m* 18 Nov 1937 Helen Winifred, of 109 Onslow Sq, SW7, yr dau of Col Charles Perceval Lynden-Bell, of Fairlawn Ho, Tadley, Basingstoke, Hants, and *dsp* 20 Nov 1968

3b Robin Charles Burleigh, Lt-Col Roy Signals, Lt Lincs Regt; *b* 1907; *educ* Ipswich Sch; *m* 19 Nov 1939 Evelyn Alice (*d* 16 Feb 1996), yr dau of Harry Freegard, of Charlton Kings, Cheltenham, and *d* 1970, leaving:

1c +(Douglas) Charles Burleigh [Charles Stuart Esq, 370 Maintongoon Rd, Bonnie Doon, Victoria 3720, Australia]; *b* 25 Oct 1940; *educ* Cheltenham and Pangbourne Nautical Coll; with Air Traffic Control Melbourne, pres Internat Fedn of Air Traffic Controllers; *m* 1st 1962 (*divorce* 1990) Pamela, dau of Gordon Sivyer, of Wembley, W Aust; *m* 2nd 1993 (*divorce* 1998) Roslyn Harriet, dau of Roy Jennings, of Brighton, Victoria, and has by his 1st w:

1d +Andrew John Burleigh [Andrew Stuart Esq, 75 Regents Park Rd, Primrose Hill, London NW1 8UY]; *b* 1967; *educ* Eltham Coll and Melbourne U (BComm); merchant banker, Goldman Sachs, NY; *m* March 1996 *Joanne Ayesha Mellor, est dau of Bill Mellor Mosman, of NSW, and has:

1e *Aisha Alexandra; *b* 6 June 1997

1d Joanne Mary; *b* 1965; *educ* Eltham Coll and Labrobe U (BA)

1c *Rosemary Anne; *b* 7 Aug 1945; *m* 9 Sept 1967 (*divorce* 1984) Capt Michael John Ridlington, Roy Corps of Signals, er son of Maj Jack Harry Ridlington by Marjorie, yst dau of Lt-Col Harold Stephen Fox Strangways (*see* ILCHESTER, E), and *dsp* 5 Oct 1995

2a Burleigh Francis Brownlow, CB (1915), CMG (1919), Hon Brig-Gen late 3rd Bn Worcs Regt, served in S African War 1900–2 (despatches, brevet, two medals with four clasps), and WW I (despatches, wounded); *b* 1 Nov 1868; *m* 26 Jan 1916 Evelyn Margaret, JP (*d* 4 May 1970), only dau of Lt-Col Sir Edward Henry St Lawrence Clarke, CMG, DSO, 4th and last Bt, of Crosses Green and Rossmore, Co Cork, and *d* 8 March 1952, leaving issue:

1b +John William Brownlow, MBE (1945), MC (1939) [Col John Stuart MBE MC, Corner Cottage, Radford, Inkberrow, Worcs WR7 4LR]; *b* 30 May 1917; *educ* Rugby and RMC Sandhurst; Col late Worcs Regt (cmded 1st Bn 1959–61), WW II (despatches twice), Kenya 1956–57; *m* 27 Feb 1954 Anthea Joan (*d* 1977), er dau of Ashley Ernest Herman, OBE, FRCS, of Shipton Hall, Hambledon, Surrey

2b +Burleigh Edward St Lawrence [Capt Burleigh Stuart, Hunter's Close, Ickford, nr Aylesbury, Bucks]; *b* 27 March 1920; *educ* Rugby and Trin Coll Oxford (BA 1950, MA 1963); Colonial Forest Serv (ret), Cwlth Forestry Bureau Oxford 1964–76, served WW II as Capt Worcs Regt; *m* 5 March 1952 *Joan Elizabeth, only dau of Col Matthew George Platts, CIE, OBE, MC, of The Down Wood, Blandford, and has issue:

1c +Edward John Burleigh [Edward Stuart Esq, 28 Sinnels Field, Shipton-Under-Wychwood, Oxon OX7 6EJ]; *b* 28 Oct 1953; *educ* Cokethorpe Sch; horologist; *m* 1976 *Alison Ann, yst dau of James Steel, of Clanfield, and has issue:

1d +Simon Francis Brownlow; *b* 20 May 1980

2d +Henry George Burleigh; *b* 10 April 1982

1c *Elizabeth Helen [The Rt Hon the Countess Howe, Penn House, Amersham, Bucks HP7 0PS]; *b* 12 Nov 1955; *m* 1983 *7th Earl Howe (*qv*) and has issue

2c *Catherine Frances; *b* 5 June 1958; *m* 1982 *Graham Ian Briggs

1a Henrietta Louisa; *b* 24 Aug 1864; *d* unm 17 Feb 1938

2a Sophia Mary; *b* 12 Aug 1867; *m* 6 March 1890 Col Charles John Lloyd Davidson, DSO, Roy Inniskilling Fus, and *dsp* 2 March 1897. He *d* 9 Oct 1916

(3) (cont.) Maj Burleigh Stuart; *m* 2nd 5 Sept 1872 Charlotte Anne (*d* 2 Sept 1931), est dau of Col Francis Ellis, of Fecarry Ho, Omagh, and *d* 9 Oct 1905, having by her had, with other issue:

3a Charles Erskine, Fell of Trin Coll Cambridge, Capt Suffolk Regt; *b* 25 May 1882; *m* 30 Dec 1916 Mary Helen (*m* 2nd 27 Oct 1921 John Woodman-Smith, son of William John Woodman-Smith, of Laithers, Aberdeenshire, and *d* 5 March 1924, leaving issue), er dau of 1st Baron Woodbridge, and *d* 15 March 1917 of wounds recd in action

3a Maud Erinvine, MBE (1965); *b* 17 Nov 1879; *d* unm 11 Jan 1969

(4) Robert Arthur Walter Charles, Lt-Col 17th Madras Native Inf; *b* 27 Dec 1828; *m* 24 May 1855 Louisa Frances (*d* 1911), dau of Edmund Singer Burton, of Churchill, Daventry, Northants, and *d* 20 Aug 1875, leaving issue:

1a Andrew Edmund Castle Stuart, CSO (1919), ICS, FGS, FLS, FRGS, Bd of Revenue Madras; *b* 24 Nov 1856; *m* 2 Oct 1879 Mary Agnes Josephine Ruth (*d* 1944), dau of Peter Kennedy, of Malahide, Dublin, and *d* 12 Sept 1936

2a Robert Charles Ochiltree (Sir), KCSI (1917), Maj-Gen formerly RA, Dir-Gen of Ordnance India 1911, served in Burmese War 1885–87; *b* 22 Aug 1861; *m* 1885 Edith Jane (*d* 6 Jan 1936), dau of Herbert Mills Birdwood, CSI, LLD (*see* BIRDWOOD, B), and *dsp* 14 Oct 1948

3a Alan Lenox Conyngham, LLD, barrister, Puisne Judge Supreme Court Cyprus, formerly DC Gold Coast, served in Ashanti War 1900; *b* 18 July 1863; *m* 1908 Marion Charlotte, dau of Herbert Robins, of Johannesburg, and widow of I A Mackay, and *d* 18 Dec 1938

1a Sophia Louisa; *m* 24 May 1882 Maj John Currey Hickson-Mahony, late Cape Inf Regt and Cape Mtd Riflemen, and *d* 3 March 1935, leaving issue. He *d* 5 Sept 1922

(1) Sophia Letitia; *m* 5 June 1862 Charles Edward Gee Barnard, of Cave Castle, Yorks, and *d* 28 Sept 1910, leaving issue. He *d* 14 Aug 1894

(2) Caroline Elizabeth Josephine; *m* 10 June 1858 Capt William Claud Cole Hamilton, and *d* 23 Jan 1930, leaving issue (*see* ENNISKILLEN, E)

(3) Charlotte; *m* Rev George Robinson, Rector of Tartaraghan, Co Armagh

1 Caroline; *m* 16 Jan 1815 Gen Sir James Bathurst, KCB, 2nd son of the Bishop of Norwich, and *d* 15 Jan 1864, leaving issue

The 1st EARL *d* 26 Aug 1809; his est son,

ROBERT STEWART, **2nd Earl Castle Stewart**; *b* 19 Aug 1784; *m* 28 April 1806 Jemima (*d* 27 April 1859), only dau of Col Robison, RA, and *d* 10 June 1854, having had, with other issue:

1 EDWARD STEWART, **3rd Earl Castle Stewart**; *b* 11 Sept 1807; *m* Feb 1830 Emmeline (*m* 2nd 27 June 1867 Alessandro Pistocchi, of Rome, and *d* 7 Jan 1893), only surv child of Benjamin Bathurst, Sec of Legation, and *d* 20 Feb 1857

2 CHARLES ANDREW KNOX STEWART, **4th Earl Castle Stewart**; *b* 23 April 1810; *m* 24 March 1835 Charlotte Raffles Drury (*d* 2 May 1807; *d* 1 Feb 1906), only dau of Acheson Quinton Thompson and niece of Sir Thomas Stamford Raffles, Govr of Java, and *d* 12 Sept 1874, having had, with other issue:

(1) HENRY JAMES STEWART later STUART-RICHARDSON (11 May 1867, also quartered arms of RICHARDSON and STUART), **5th Earl Castle Stewart**; High Sheriff Co Tyrone 1870; *b* 21 March 1837; *m* 1 Nov 1866 Augusta Le Vicomte (took by roy licence 28 Jan 1865 the name and arms of RICHARDSON in addition to those of BRADY and *d* 3 Dec 1908), yst and only surv child of Maj William Stewart Richardson-Brady, DL, of Oaklands, Co Tyrone, and widow of Maj Hugh Massy, 85th Foot (*see* MASSY, B), and *d* 5 June 1914:

1a Muriel Albany; *m* 2 June 1891 Maj Maxwell Archibald Close, DL, JP, of Drumbanagher, Poyntz Pass, Co Armagh, and Drum Manor, Cookstown, Co Tyrone, and *d* 20 March 1928, leaving issue. He *d* 31 Jan 1935

2a Mary; *m* 21 Dec 1898 Lt-Col Edward Harrison Clough-Taylor, of Firby Hall, York, son of Edward Clough-Taylor, DL, JP, of Kirkham Abbey, and Firby Hall, Yorks, and *d* 26 Aug 1967, leaving issue. He *d* 1 April 1921

(1) Mary; *m* 5 Jan 1860 Col Thomas Richard Crosse, of Shaw Hill, Lancs, and *d* 14 June 1903, leaving issue. He *d* 27 Nov 1897

(2) Ella Sophia; *m* 2 March 1875 Rev Charles Leslie Garnett, Rector of Ardtrae, Co Tyrone, and *d* 2 May 1900, leaving issue

(3) Alice Maude; *m* 16 Jan 1867 Edmund Huntly Hooper, of Shelly Hill, Christchurch, Hants, only son of Rev Edmund Westerton Hooper, and *d* 6 Aug 1921, leaving issue

(4) Margaretta Louisa; *m* 1st 28 Dec 1865 Maj-Gen Thomas Erskine Arthur Hall, son of James Traill Hall (*d* 9 Feb 1901); *m* 2nd 7 July 1903 Rev Albert Smith, Vicar of Wendover, and *d* 21 Dec 1917. He *d* 20 Aug 1914

3 Andrew Godfrey (Rev), MA, Hon Canon Peterborough, Rector Cottesmore, Rutland, RD; *b* 24 Sept 1812; *m* 1st 21 Dec 1835 Hon Catherine Anne Wingfield (*d* 25 Dec 1845), dau of 5th Viscount Powerscourt (*qv*), and had, with two other sons and two daus:

(1) ANDREW JOHN, **6th Earl**

(2) Richard Wingfield; *b* 17 Jan 1843; *m* 1st 17 Feb 1872 Jeannie Miriam (*dsp* 1889), dau of John Macdermot, of Gayfield, Sydney, Australia; *m* 2nd 1891 Isabel Clare (*d* 1953), dau of Charles Lee, of NSW, and *d* 8 Jan 1914, leaving issue:

1a John William Wingfield, CE; *b* 17 Dec 1901; *m* 15 Jan 1930 *Dorothy Eleanor, dau of T Baker Insoll, of Hamilton, NZ, and *d* 1983, having had issue:

1b *Mary Rose Dorothy Wingfield; *b* 8 April 1931; *m* 1st 1954 Rev Leonard Russell Goggs (*d* 1977), of St Peter's, S Aust; *m* 2nd *Percy Wilbur Collom, Jr, and has issue by 1st husb:

2a +Richard Godfrey; *b* 1904

3 (cont.) Canon the Hon A G Stuart *m* 2nd 24 April 1849 Mary Penelope (*d* 24 Jan 1859), 2nd dau of Rev Hon Leland Noel Noel (*see* GAINSBOROUGH, E), and *d* 19 Sept 1889, having by her had, with another s and two other daus:

(3) Horace Noel; *b* 30 Dec 1850; *m* 30 April 1881 Madeline Frances, yst dau of Walter Hemming, of Spring Grove, Bewdley; *d* 3 Aug 1900, leaving issue:

1a Robert James Noel, 2nd Lt 3rd Bn Roy Scots Fus; *b* 23 Oct 1886; *ka* 17 May 1915

(1) Janet Erskine, 6th Superior Gen of the Soc of the Sacred Heart; *d* 21 Oct 1914

The 5th EARL's cousin,

ANDREW JOHN STUART, **6th Earl Castle Stewart**; Madras CS; *b* 21 Dec 1841; *m* 23 Sept 1876 Emma Georgiana (*d* 5 Dec 1949), dau of Gen Arthur Stevens, Madras Staff Corps, by Georgiana, dau of Maj R L Dickson, 1st Life Gds, and had issue:

1 Andrew John, *Viscount Stuart*, Lt 6th Serv Bn Roy Scots Fus; *b* 27 Dec 1880; *educ* Corpus Christi Coll Oxford; *ka* France 25 Sept 1915

2 Robert Sheffield, Capt 1st Bn Roy Scots Fus; *b* 1 May 1886; *m* 9 Dec 1909 Constance Evelyn Nancye (served WW I and WW II BRCS and CD; *d* 12 Oct 1964, having *m* 2nd 1 Jan 1920 Charles Gordon Lee Elverson, Roy W Kent Regt, son of Maj Hamilton James Everson, Queen's Roy Regt, and had issue), yst dau of Capt Edward William Dunlo Croker, 93rd Highrs, of Ballynagarde, Co Limerick, and was *ka* 2 Nov 1914

3 ARTHUR, **7th Earl**

4 Charles Patrick; *b* 21 Sept 1892; *educ* Charterhouse and Pembroke Coll Cambridge; *d* unm 15 Nov 1928

1 Katherine Frances; *b* 13 Nov 1878; *d* unm 4 May 1923

The 6th EARL *d* 7 Nov 1921; his 3rd son,

ARTHUR STUART, **7th Earl Castle Stewart**, MC; *educ* Charterhouse, Trin Coll Cambridge and U of Paris; MP (U) Harborough 1929–33, Maj MGC WW I (despatches) GSO 1918–20, assist master Rugby 1920–21, barrister Inner Temple 1943; *b* 6 Aug 1889; *m* 16 Dec 1920 Eleanor May (*d* 1992), est dau of Solomon R Guggenheim, of Trillora Court, Port Washington, Long Island, USA, and *d* 5 Nov 1961, having had issue:

1 David Andrew Noel, *Viscount Stuart*, Lt 11th Hus WW II; *b* 7 Oct 1921; *educ* Eton; *ka* Middle East 10 Nov 1942

2 Robert John Ochiltree, *Viscount Stuart*, 2nd Lt 9th Lancers WW II; *b* 12 Dec 1923; *educ* Eton; *d* of wounds recd in action Italy 17 Sept 1944

3 ARTHUR PATRICK AVONDALE STUART, **8th and present Earl Castle Stewart**

4 +Simon Walter Erskine [The Hon Simon Stuart, Windyridge, Wych Cross, Forest Row, Sussex RH18 5JP]; *b* 22 Aug 1930; *educ* Eton and Trin Coll Cambridge (BA 1953, MA 1957); late 2nd Lt Scots Gds, assist master Haberdashers Aske's Sch 1961–78, formerly at King's Canterbury and Stowe, since when a writer; *m* 26 May 1973 *Deborah Jane, yr dau of Michael J Mounsey, of Backhouse, Murton, Appleby, Cumbria, and has issue:

(1) +Thomas Harry Erskine; *b* 1974

(2) +Corin Edward Leveson; *b* 1975

(3) +Tristram James Avondale; *b* 12 March 1977

CASTLEMAINE

Arms: Erm. on a chief sa. a dexter hand between two cocks arg., armed, crested and jelloped gu. **Crest:** A demi-lion rampant az., holding between the paws a fusil arg., charged with a cock gu. **Supporters:** Dexter, a lion guardant az.; sinister, a cock ppr. **Motto:** *Vigilate et orate* ('Watch and pray'). **Creation:** B. (I) 21 Dec 1812.

THE 8TH BARON CASTLEMAINE OF MOYDRUM, Co Westmeath (Lt-Col Roland Thomas John Handcock, MBE (1981)) [Lt-Col The Rt Hon The Lord Castlemaine MBE, Keepers Cottage, Winterbourne Stoke, Salisbury, Wilts]; *b* 22 April 1943; *s f* 1973; *educ* Campbell Coll Belfast and RMC Sandhurst; Lt-Col AAC (ret 1992), cmded Parachute Regt 1964, tfd Army Air Corps 1971; *m* 1st 27 Oct 1969 (*divorce* 19–) Pauline Anne, est dau of John Taylor Bainbridge, of The Moat Ho, Burston, Surrey; *m* 2nd 1989 *Lynne Christine, est dau of Maj Justin Michael Gurney, RAEC, and has issue by 2nd w:

1 +RONAN MICHAEL EDWARD; *b* 27 March 1989

Previous creations under this title: The most celebrated predecessor is Roger Palmer, the *mari complaisant* of Barbara Villiers, one of CHARLES II's mistresses, who was created Earl of Castlemaine in the Irish peerage in 1661. It is said that he felt so ashamed of the title, as being an obvious sop to a cuckold to look the other way, that he put off assuming it as long as he could. He was out of the country when the three sons of his wife by the King were born and given the slowness of travel in those days he could not possible have been their father. Accordingly although all three were called Palmer and technically born in wedlock, they were legally deemed illegitimate so that on his death in 1705 the Earldom expired.

In 1718 Richard Child, son of a nabob, was created Viscount Castlemaine and some 13 years later promoted Earl Tylney of Castlemaine. These peerages expired with the death of the 2nd Earl in 1784. It appears to be pure coincidence that the family name of the current Earls of Jersey is Child-Villiers, representing a mid-19th-century alliance between the Villierses who had produced Barbara Countess of Castlemaine two hundred years earlier and a descent from a family called Child, since the latter appears to have had no link with the Child Lords Castlemaine of the early to mid-18th century.

Lineage: WILLIAM HANDCOCK, of Twyford, Westmeath, MP Co Westmeath 1661, memb Cncl of Connaught, granted patent 12 Feb 1680 to erect his estates into the Manor of Twyford; *m* 25 July 1652 Abigail (*d* 21 Nov 1680 in her 53rd year), dau of Rev Thomas Stanley and sis of Sir Thomas Stanley, and had, with other issue:

1 Thomas, his heir

2 William (Sir), Recorder Dublin, MP Athlone 1692; *b* 10 Sept 1655; *m* 31 May 1685 Elizabeth, dau of Nicholas Coddington, and *d* Sept 1701, leaving, with other issue (including Abigail, *m* Edward Griffith and was ancestor of Sir Richard John Griffith, Bt):

(1) John, *b* 1687; inherited Ardloe and Sultonrah, Co Kilkenny, from his gs William Handcock, of Twyford; *m* — Shrigley and had:

1a Richard; *m* Mary Caulfeild and had:

1b Tobias; *m* Johanna Reily and had, with three daus:

1c Richard; Lt Col 46th Regt, *m* Jane Fraser, widow of Capt Woodham, and had issue:

1d William Fraser, in holy orders; *m* 1869 Elizabeth Jane Colville

2d Richard George, in holy orders; *m* 1855 Mary Swinhoe, dau of Gen Samuel Swinhoe, IA, and *d* 1913, leaving five s and three daus

1d Jane Eliza; *d* unm

2c Arthur

3c Tobias, and

3 Stephen (Very Rev), Dean of Kilmacduogh; *b* 3 Sept 1657, ancestor of the HANDCOCKs later TEMPLEs of Waterstown, Co Westmeath

4 Matthew (Ven), Archdeacon Kilmore, ancestor of Matthew Handcock, DQMG

1 Hannah; *m* Robert Rochford, Speaker I H of C, Ld Ch Baron Exchequer Ireland, and was with him grandparent of Robert Rochfort, *cr* Earl of Belvidere. She *d* 2 July 1733

2 Sarah; *m* Capt Chichester Philips, of Drumcondra Castle, MP Askeaton, gs of Sir Thomas Phillips, of Newtown Limavady, Co Derry, by Alicia, dau of Sir William Ussher and Isabella, dau of Adam Loftus, Archbp Dublin (*see* ELY, M), and had issue

3 Elizabeth; *m* 1696 Duke Giffard, of Castle Jordan

The est son,

THOMAS HANDCOCK, of Twyford, MP Lanesborough 1692; *b* 28 May 1654; *m* 5 July 1677 Dorothy Green and had, with other issue:

1 WILLIAM, his heir

2 Eliah, ancestor of John Handcock, Lt Govr Kinsale, and Robert, DQMG

The est son,

WILLIAM HANDOCK, of Twyford; *m* Susan Warburton and had, with three other sons and three other daus:

1 William, of Twyford, MP Fere 1739; *m* Elizabeth (*m* 2nd Agmondesham Vesey, MP, of Lucan), 2nd dau of Rt Rev Sir Thomas Vesey, 1st Bt, Bp Ossory, and sis of 1st Baron Knapton (*see* DE VESCI, V)

2 RICHARD

3 Robert; *m* Sarah, dau and coheir of Richard Blackburne, of Carrickenagh, Co Roscommon, by Jane, dau of Capt Chichester Phillips (*see* above), and had issue

1 Abigal; *m* Mark Rainsford

The 2nd son,

Very Rev RICHARD HANDCOCK, Dean Achonry; *m* Sarah (*d* 1 July 1803), only dau and heir of Richard Toler, of Ballintore, Co Kildare, and *d* 25 July 1791, having had, with other issue:

1 WILLIAM HANDCOCK, **1st Baron Castlemaine of Moydrum**, Co Westmeath (I), so *cr* 21 Dec 1812, with a special remainder failing heirs of his body to his bro, as also 12 Jan 1822 (1st and last) VISCOUNT CASTLEMAINE (also I), with ordinary remainder; *b* 28 Aug 1761; Constable and Govr Athlone 1813–39 and Govr Co Westmeath 1814–31; *m* 20 March 1782 Lady Florinda Trench (*d* 9 Feb 1851), est dau of 1st Earl of Clancarty (*qv*), and *dsp* 7 Jan 1839, when the viscountcy expired

2 RICHARD, **2nd Baron**

1 Sarah *m* 1763 Richard St George, and had issue. He *d* Feb 1820

2 Susannah; *m* 1778 Francis Whyte Edgworth, of Pallasmore, and had issue

3 Dorothy; *m* 12 Dec 1768 John Loftus Cuppage, er son of John Cuppage, of Killowing, Co Tipperary, and *d* 3 Dec 1830, leaving issue. He *d* 15 April 1797

The 1st BARON's bro,

RICHARD HANDCOCK, **2nd Baron Castlemaine**, MP (last I Parl) Athlone 1800; *b* 14 May 1767; *m* 13 Nov 1790 Anne (*d* 4 Nov 1852), dau of Arthur French, of French Park, and had, with other issue (including a dau, Sarah *m* 1817 Christopher Hamilton; *see* HOLMPATRICK, B):

1 RICHARD, **3rd Baron**

2 Arthur; *b* 5 April 1796; *m* 13 April 1817 Margaret (*m* 2nd 1 Feb 1837 Adml Hon William Le Poer Trench (see CLANCARTY, E), and *d* 4 March 1885, dau of Dawson Downing, of Rosegift, Co Londonderry, and *d* 27 July 1826, leaving issue:

(1) Anne; *m* 1 May 1845 Rev John Crampton, and *d* Aug 1855

(2) Florinda; *m* 7 April 1840 Rev Arthur Hill Griffith, Rector of Aughrim, Co Galway, yst son of Richard Griffith, of Millicent, Co Kildare, and *d* 24 Jan 1847

3 John Gustavus (Rev), Rector of Annaduff, Co Leitrim; *b* 1799; *m* 13 Nov 1827 Frances Flood (*d* 27 Nov 1848), dau of John Harward Jessop, of Doory Hall, Co Longford, and *d* 2 March 1838, leaving, with other issue:

(1) John Harward Jessop (Rev), Vicar of St Mary's, Woodlands, Sevenoaks, Kent, 1860–1907; *b* 22 Oct 1829; *m* 1st 23 July 1856 Frances (*d* 4 Feb 1864), dau of Rev Nicholas Devereux, DD, of Ballyrankin Ho, Wexford, and had issue:

1a Maria; *d* young, 20 April 1870

(1) (cont.) The Rev John Handcock *m* 2nd 16 April 1873 Lucy (*d* 25 Feb 1907), dau of Rev Edward Carr, LLD, Vicar of St Helen's, and *d* 27 Oct 1907, having by her had issue:

1a Harward Devereux; *b* 21 July 1874; *m* 1 Jan 1907 Eleanor Winifred (*d* 25 Jan 1966), only child of Henry John Potts, JP, of Glan-yr-afon, Mold, Flintshire, and *d* 8 Feb 1944, having had issue:

1b +John Harward [John Handcock Esq, Anderida, Brook Green, Cuckfield, Sussex]; *b* 12 July 1924; *m* 12 Feb 1949 *Brenda Terrill, dau of Donald Stewart Alexander Simpson, and has issue:

1c +Jeremy John; *b* 16 Oct 1953; *m* 1978 *Effie, est dau of H Hallaschek, of Stuttgart, Germany, and has issue:

1d +Alexander John; *b* 1981

2d +Thomas William Heinz; *b* 1983

2c +Timothy Charles; *b* 4 Feb 1964

1c *Fiona Elizabeth Jane; *b* 22 May 1956

1b Eleanor Lucy Vivien; *b* 29 Dec 1907; *d* 4 Feb 1919

2a Lucy Maria; *b* 18 July 1875; *d* 13 Jan 1895

(2) Richard Arthur; *b* 10 Jan 1836; *m* 21 June 1865 Harriette (*d* 7 May 1932), yst dau of Surgn-Maj Michael James MacCormack, MD, and *d* 10 June 1915, leaving issue:

2a Harriet Frances; *m* 6 July 1900 John Frederick Devenish-Meares, barrister, est son of Joseph Leycester Devenish-Meares, JP, of Meares Court, Co Westmeath. He *d* 5 March 1935

(1) Frances Flood; *m* 23 Nov 1871 John Cameron, MD, Bengal Army. He *d* Oct 1885

(2) Anne Alicia; *m* 1st 8 Dec 1858 Sir St Vincent Hawkins Whitshed, 3rd and last Bt (*d* 9 March 1871), and had issue; *m* 2nd 17 Dec 1885 James Percival Hughes, of Somerby Ho, Hove, and *d* 23 July 1908, leaving further issue

4 George; *b* 1801; *m* 16 Feb 1833 Elizabeth Alicia (*d* 1 April 1890), dau of Robert Henry French (*see* DE FREYNE, B), and *d* 20 Oct 1867, having had, with other issue:

(1) Charlotte Elizabeth; *m* 23 April 1863 Lt-Gen Hon Charles Wemyss Thesiger, 2nd son of 1st Baron Chelmsford (*qv*), and *d* 29 Oct 1880, leaving issue

(2) Henrietta; *m* 31 Dec 1862 Rt Hon Alfred Henry Thesiger, Ld Justice of Appeal, 4th son of 1st Baron Chelmsford (*qv*), and *d* 18 Feb 1921

5 Henry Robert, Lt-Col 97th Foot; *m* 15 May 1854 Ellen Georgina (*m* 2nd 31 Aug 1859 Col Richard Wellesley Bernard (*d* 29 Sept 1877) and *d* 28 Jan 1907), est dau of Lt-Col Henry Williams, RA, and was *ka* Sebastopol 8 Sept 1855

6 Charles, of Creaghduff, Athlone, barrister; *b* 31 Jan 1808; *m* 25 April 1845 Elizabeth (*d* 26 June 1878), dau of Daniel Kelly, of Cargins, Co Roscommon, by Mary French, sis of 3rd Baron De Freyne (*qv*), and *d* 13 Feb 1879, having had, with other issue:

(1) Richard, JP (Cos Westmeath and Roscommon), land agent, of Victoria Sq, Christchurch, NZ; *b* 2 Sept 1859; *educ* Trin Coll Dublin; *m* April 1908 Louisa Isabella, yst dau of John C Ogilvie Urquhart, of Huntly, Aberdeenshire, and *d* 21 March 1921

(1) Mary Harriett; *m* 8 July 1879 William James Mackie later Mackay, MD, of Holmwood, Nelson, NZ, and had issue

(2) Elizabeth; *m* 23 July 1891 Edward Green, of Nelson, NZ, and *d* 19 Nov 1918, leaving issue

(3) Louisa; *m* 1896 Samuel L Hadden, of Compass Hill, Kinsale, Co Cork, and *d* 23 Dec 1922, leaving issue

7 Robert French, Capt Army, Lt-Col Dublin City Art; *m* 11 April 1848 Isabella Louisa (*d* 19 April 1898), only dau of James Gordon, and *d* 3 Dec 1871, having had with other issue:

(1) Robert Gordon, Maj late BSC; *b* 25 April 1849; *m* 30 March 1882 Hon Audrey Mary Florence Abbott (*d* 24 Nov 1945, having *m* 2nd 8 July 1915 William Harry Nash, barrister (*d* 25 Feb 1929), 2nd son of John Nash, of Langley Marish, Bucks), dau of 3rd Baron Tenterden (*see* 1939 edn), and *dsp* 13 Dec 1906

(2) Stannus Henry; *b* 11 April 1852; *m* 11 Sept 1883 Theodosia Violet (*d* 18 Aug 1931), dau of Murray McGregor Blackor, DL Co Mayo, of Goldingham Hall, Sudbury, Suffolk, and *d* 31 Jan 1938

(3) Edward Stanley; *b* 6 Aug 1953; *m* 1st 3 July 1880 Lucy Eleanor (*d* 1882), dau of Capt Clement Archer, 4th Dragoon Gds, of Hill Ho, Hampton, and widow of Capt Hugh Campbell, RN, and had issue:

1a Robert Harris Temple, of Karura, Br E Africa; *b* 5 May 1881; *m* 30 Dec 1907 Norah Isabel (*d* 29 Dec 1932, having *m* 2nd 18 Aug 1917 Capt Henry Edmund Harvey Spencer- Cooper, MVO, RN), yr dau of Lt-Col John Sherston, DSO, Rifle Bde and *d* 11 Dec 1913, having had issue:

1b William Stanley, Cdr RN WW II, *b* 26 Oct 1908; *m* 5 Dec 1933 *Joan Mary, of Sparshott House, Hambledon, Hants, 2nd dau of Sir Ralph Molyneux Combe, of Bunce's Shaw, Farley Hill, Berks, and *d* 25 Jan 1954, leaving issue:

1c +Timothy Stannus [Timothy Handcock Esq, Holmwood Cottage, Stroud, Petersfield, Hants GU32 3PJ]; *b* 20 May 1938; *educ* Sherborne;

1c *Deidre Elizabeth; *b* 16 June 1935; *m* 17 Sept 1960 *Capt Colin Prinsep James, MC, late Rifle Bde, only son of Col Cecil Paulglase James, DSO and bar, Argyll and Sutherland Highrs, of Meadowfield, Cranleigh, Surrey, and has issue:

1d *Emma Louise; *b* 20 June 1962

2d *Belinda Anne Nonie; *b* 26 Aug 1964

2c *Luleen Annette; *b* 17 July 1946; *m* 1st 1977 Michael Poynder; *m* 2nd 1981 *Frederick Moseley Wanklyn

2b John Richard; *b* 18 Nov 1912; *d* 30 July 1913

(3) (cont.) Edward Handcock *m* 2nd 13 April 1889 Rose Marion (*d* 14 Feb 1945), yst dau of Col W A Middleton, CB, RA, and *d* 22 April 1928, having by her had issue:

1a Marion Dorothy; *b* 9 Oct 1890; *m* 1st 19 March 1910 (*divorce* 1920) Maj Bryan Ricco Cooper, DL (*d* 5 July 1930), of Markree Castle, Co Sligo, and had issue; *m* 2nd 4 July 1920 Basil Lascelles Rose (*d* 5 Nov 1953), son of Edward George Rose, of 18 Burnleigh Place, SW7, and *d* 7 April 1967, leaving further issue

2a Muriel Gordon; *b* 2 Feb 1892; *m* 2 July 1931 (*divorce* 1956) Brian Henry Stock, only surv son of James Henry Stock, MP, of Glenapp Castle, Ballantrae, Ayrshire, and The White Hall, Tarporley, Cheshire. He *d* 18 March 1967

(1) Mary Louisa Helen; *m* 4 April 1877 Thomas Mercer Cliffe Vigors, of Burgage, Co Carlow, and *d* 13 Feb 1933, leaving issue. He *d* 30 Jan 1908

(2) Florence; *m* 29 Dec 1877 Henry Charles Jackson Warren, of Derrintovey, Carrickmines, Dublin, only son of Rt Hon Robert Richard Warren, and *d* 14 Dec 1944, leaving issue (*see* WARREN, Bt)

(3) Minna Gordon; *m* 2 Aug 1881 Harry Ashworth Taylor, MVO, late 47th Regt, only son of Sir Henry Taylor, KCMG, and *d* 30 Jan 1947, leaving issue. He *d* 5 March 1907

(4) Amy Georgina; *m* 11 April 1889 Anthony Ashley Hanbury, of The White Ho, nr Slough, yst son of Robert Culling Hanbury, MP, of Bedwell Park, Herts, and *d* 8 April 1921, leaving issue. He *d* 3 Jan 1914

The 2nd BARON *d* 18 April 1840; his est son,

RICHARD HANDCOCK, **3rd Baron Castlemaine**; rep I peer; *b* 17 Nov 1791; *m* 17 April 1822 Margaret (*d* 27 Jan 1867), 2nd dau of Michael Harris, of Dublin, and *d* 4 July 1869, having had issue:

1 RICHARD HANDCOCK, **4th Baron Castlemaine**; rep I peer, Ld Lt and Custos Rotulorum Co Westmeath 1888–92; *b* 25 July 1826; *m* 10 Feb 1857 Louisa Matilda (*d* 31 Jan 1892), day of 2nd Baron Harris (*qv*), and *d* 26 April 1892, having had, with other issue:

(1) ALBERT EDWARD HANDCOCK, **5th Baron Castlemaine**; *b* 26 March 1863; *educ* Eton and Ch Ch Oxford; Lt 4th Bn Roy Inniskilling Fus, Ld Lt, Custos Rotulorum 1899 and CC Co Westmeath, rep I peer 1898; *m* 25 Sept 1895 Annie Evelyn (*d* 14 Nov 1955), only dau of Col Joseph Thoms Barrington, of Charlton, Kent (*see* BARRINGTON, Bt), and *dspm* 6 July 1937, leaving:

1a Evelyn Constance; *b* 3 Dec 1897; *m* 19 May 1925 Lt-Gen Sir Charles Henry Gairdner, KCMG, CB, CBE, 10th Hus, Govr W Australia 1951–63, est s of Charles Arthur Gairdner, of Lisbeg Ho, Co Galway

(2) ROBERT ARTHUR HANDCOCK, **6th Baron Castlemaine**, DL, JP Co Westmeath, T/Lt RASC WW I; *b* 19 April 1864; *m* 16 Jan 1894 Ethel Violet (*d* 13 July 1934), only dau of Col Sir Edmond Bainbridge, KCB, RA, and had issue:

1a Richard Edmond Guy; *b* 21 July 1896; *d* 11 Nov 1909

1a Violet Louisa; *b* 26 May 1895; *m* 12 Feb 1919 Maj Charles R Moorhouse Duncan, MC, RFA, only son of Col T A Duncan, of Cullen, Banff, and had issue. He *d* 22 Jan 1939

(1) Agnes Isabella; *m* 5 Feb 1885 Capt Conway Richard Dobbs Higginson, RA, son of Sir James Higginson, KCB, and *d* 4 Jan 1908, leaving issue

(2) Florence Margaret; *m* 14 Jan 1886 Hubert John Broughton Adderley, of Barlaston Hall, Staffs, and Coton Hall, Sudbury, Derbys, and *d* 1 April 1934, leaving issue. He *d* 9 April 1931

(3) Edith Louisa; *m* 10 Oct 1891 2nd and last Baron Rosmead (*see* 1933 edn) and *d* Jan 1936, leaving issue. He *d* 26 May 1933

(4) Meta; *m* 30 June 1891 David Knox Ruttledge, of Barbersfort, Co Galway, and *d* 1 March 1937

(5) Alice; *m* 12 Oct 1892 Col Meade James Crosbie Dennis, CB, RA, of Fort Granite, Co Wicklow, and *d* 26 Feb 1937, leaving issue. He *d* 27 Oct 1945

2 Robert John, BA Dublin, Lt 48th Regt; *b* 19 Sept 1830; *m* 10 Jan 1856 Caroline Emily Louisa (*d* 1922), dau of Gen Henry Pester, RHA, and *d* 10 April 1902, leaving, with other issue:

(1) Richard Henry, Lt 104th Regt (Roy Munster Fus); *b* 9 July 1858; *m* 9 Feb 1886 Katherine Eleonora (*d* 1936), dau of Ven Arthur Palmer, Archdeacon of Toronto, and *d* 1 Nov 1891, leaving, with other issue:

1a Kathleen Margaret Victoria; *m* 4 Jan 1912 Edward Otto Reis, Commr Chinese Maritime Customs Service, est son of Adolph Reis, of Shanghai, and *d* 1914

2a Dorothy Madeline

3a Florence Guy; *b* posthumously; *m* 4 Oct 1924 (*divorce* 1941) Reginald John Foort, est son of R C Foort, of Rugby, and had issue

(2) Robert John; *b* 19 Sept 1860; *educ* Trin Hall Cambridge (BA 1889); *m* 1903 Eleanor Annie Ether (*d* 29 Oct 1963), er dau of Jones Hodder Staveley, barrister, of Glanduff Castle, Charleville, Co Cork, and *d* 26 Sept 1951, leaving issue:

1a JOHN MICHAEL SCHOMBERG STAVELEY, **7th Baron**

1a Leonie Caroline Esther; *b* 30 Nov 1905; *m* as his 2nd w 9 March 1931 Thomas MacGregor Greer, DL, JP, of Tullylagan Manor, Co Tyrone, son of Thomas Greer, MP, FRGS, of Sea Park, Co Antrim, and Grove Ho, Regent's Park, NW. He *d* 9 June 1941

(3) Henry; *b* 26 June 1869; *m* 26 Sept 1892 Charlotte (*d* 22 June 1922), dau of Richard Cole, and *d* 17 June 1917, having had, with other issue:

1a Richard Henry Algernon (Dick); *b* 23 July 1895; *m* 1943 Catherine (*d* 1971), dau of Emmanuel Breham, of Pont de l'Arche, France, and widow of Lt John Morgan Keeley Knight, RFC, and *d* 27 April 1974, having had issue:

1b +Clifford Marcel [Clifford Handcock Esq, Rancher, Beaconsfield, Farnham Royal, Bucks]; *b* 1925; CQMS KOSB, WW II with 1st Airborne Div; *m* 1944 *Joyce Morton, and has issue:

1c *Linda; *b* 1945

2b +Claude Desmond Richard; *b* 1928; *m* 1948 *Enid Perry, and has issue:

1c +Andrew Patrick James; *b* 1950

2c +Peter Michael Roland; *b* 1951

1c *Teresa Catherine Rose; *b* 1954

1b *Sheila Annette Kathleen; *b* 1927; *m* 19– *Brinley Aurelius, and has issue

2b *Heather; *b* 1939; *m* 1961 *Robert Henry Harvey, and has issue

2a Clifford Frederick; *b* 3 Oct 1896; *educ* Westham, Weymouth; *m* 14 Nov 1928 Margaret (*d* 25 July 1954), dau of Capt Philip Nicholls, RFC, of Penzance, Cornwall, and *dsp* 13 Jan 1983

3a +Terence Robin, surveyor and valuer, principal of Handcock and Co, served WW II 1940–44 in Metropolitan Police Res; *b* 3 Dec 1902; *m* 1933 *Eva Mary, dau of Charles Taylor, and has issue:

1b +Michael Robin [Michael Handcock Esq, The Annexe, 6 Pond Rd, Blackheath, London SE3]; *b* 1934; *m* 21 March 1961 *Jean Anne, only dau of J T Smoker, and has issue:

1c *Jenny Samantha; *b* 1969

4a Desmond Fitzgerald; *b* 10 Dec 1903

5a +Patrick Francis Denys [Patrick Handcock Esq, 6 Westrope Way, Bedford MK41 7YU]; *b* 3 Jan 1913; *m* 1st 1933 Kathleen Joan (*d* 6 March 1972), dau of Frederick Lyle; *m* 2nd 11 May 1972 *Hilary Maybelle, widow of S/Ldr D W Willis, RAF and has issue by 1st w:

1b +Patrick Michael; *b* 1934

1a Evelyn Violet Muriel; *b* 22 Jan 1894; *m* 16 June 1914 Lt-Cdr Henry Guy Stanton, RN, er son of Henry Stanton, of Snelston Hall, Derbys, and *d* Jan 1960, leaving issue (*see* POWER). He *d* 19 Dec 1960

2a Monica Ciceley Joyce; *b* 21 March 1898

(1) Emily Anette; *m* 5 Oct 1896 Percy Wright, and had issue

(2) Alexandra Louisa; *m* 13 Dec 1892 John Minchin Carden, son of Col William Joseph Carden, APD, and has issue. He *d* Jan 1912

(3) Edith Anne Ernestine; *m* 6 Feb 1900 Lt-Col Herbert Stoney Smith, DSO, Leics Regt, son of Arthur Smith, of Hempstead, and *d* 12 May 1909, leaving issue. He was *ka* 22 Oct 1915

(4) Sydney

1 Florinda; *m* 25 July 1854 Samuel Stephen Bateson, 2nd son of Sir Robert Bateson, 1st Bt, and *d* 26 April 1906. He *dsp* 9 March 1879

2 Annetta; *m* 2 Feb 1858 5th Viscount Charlemont (*qv*) and *d* 10 Nov 1888, leaving issue

The 6th BARON *d* 31 May 1954; his kinsman,

JOHN MICHAEL SCHOMBERG STAVELEY HANDCOCK, **7th Baron Castlemaine**; WW II with Irish Def Forces (Adj), joined Prov Bank of Ireland 1923, ret 1957, chm Mancunian Bldg Soc, dir Irish Int Bank; *b* 10 March 1904; *m* 8 Oct 1930 Rebecca Ellen (*d* 25 Jan 1978), only dau of William Thomas Soady, RN, and *d* 31 July 1973, having had issue:

1 RONALD THOMAS JOHN HANDCOCK, **8th and present Baron Castlemaine**

1 *Eileen Esther; *b* 14 Nov 1931; *m* 12 Oct 1959 *F/Lt Terence Frank Adams, RAF (ret), son of Joseph Adams, of Wolverhampton, and has issue:

(1) *Patrick Joseph John; *b* 29 Oct 1960

(2) *Niall Michael; *b* 2 April 1968

(1) *Siobhan Mary; *b* 13 Aug 1962

2 *Edith Deidre; *b* 20 Aug 1936; *m* 1st 21 Dec 1957 (*divorce* 1974) Keith Moss, BEM, est son of Eric G Moss, AMIEE, of Ludgershall, Hants; *m* 2nd 1976 *Terence Hook, and has issue by 1st husb:

1a *Julian Duncan; *b* 1962

CATHCART

Arms: Azure, three cross crosslets fitchée, issuing from as many crescents argent. **Crest:** A dexter hand couped above the wrist and erect proper, grasping a crescent argent as in the arms. **Supporters:** Two parrots, wings inverted proper. **Motto:** I hope to speed.

Creations: L. (S) *c* 1452, V. and B. (UK) 9 Nov 1807, E. (UK) 16 July 1814.

THE 6TH EARL CATHCART, Viscount Cathcart of Cathcart, Co Renfrew, **Lord Cathcart** and **Baron Greenock** of Greenock, Co Renfrew (Alan Cathcart, CB (1973), DSO (1945), MC (1944)) [Maj-Gen The Rt Hon The Earl Cathcart CB DSO MC, Moor Hatches, W Amesbury, Salisbury, Wilts SP4 7BH]; *b* 22 Aug 1919; *s* f 1927; *educ* Eton and Magdalene Coll Cambridge; Maj-Gen Scots Gds WW II (despatches), Adj RMA Sandhurst 1946–47, Regtl Adj Scots Gds 1951–53, Bde Maj 4th Gds Bde 1954–56, cmded 1st Bn Scots Gds 1957–59, Lt-Col cmdg Scots Gds 1960, Col AQ Scottish Cmd 1962–63, IDC 1964, cmded 152nd Highland Bde (TA) 1965–66, Brig SHAPEX and Exercise Branch SHAPE 1967–68, Maj-Gen cmdg Yorks Dist 1969–70, GOC and Br Cmdt Berlin 1970–73, ret 1973; Ensign Roy Co Archers; Dep Speaker and Dep Chm Ctees Ho Lds 1975, Pres ACFA 1975–82, Dep Grand Pres Br Cwlth Ex-Servs League 1976–86, Pres Roy Soc Prevention Accidents 1982–86, Cdre Roy Yacht Sqdn 1974–80, GStJ 1986 (KStJ 1985, Ld Prior 1986–88, V-Chllr 1984–86); *m* 10 July 1946 Rosemary Clare Marie Gabrielle (*d* 6 July 1980), yr dau of A/Cdre Sir (Henry) Percy Smyth-Osbourne, CMG, CBE, of Holmedown, Exbourne, N Devon, and has issue:

1 +CHARLES ALAN ANDREW, *Lord Greenock* [Lord Greenock, Gateley Hall, Dereham, Norfolk; 18 Smith Terrace, London SW3]; *b* 30 Nov 1952; *educ* Eton; 2nd Lt Scots Gds 1973–75; *m* 12 Sept 1981 *Vivien Clare, only dau of Francis Desmond McInnes Skinner, of North Farm, Snetterton, Norfolk, and has issue:

(1) +Alan George; *b* 16 March 1986

(1) *Laura Rosemary; *b* 1984

1 *Louisa [The Lady Louisa Cosgrave, Totterdown Lodge, Inkpen, nr Hungerford, Berks]; *b* 27 April 1948; *educ* Convent of Sacred Heart, Woldingham; *m* 7 Oct 1975 Norman Kirkpatrick Cosgrave (*d* 1991), yst son of Dr Alexander Kirkpatrick Cosgrave, of Hove, Sussex

2 *Charlotte Mary [The Lady Charlotte McCallum, Week Green Farm, Froxfield, Petersfield, Hants]; *b* 29 Oct 1951; *educ* Convent of Sacred Heart, Woldingham; *m* 16 June 1972 *Capt Anthony Colin McCallum, 1st Queen's Dragoon Gds, er son of Colin McCallum, of Mead End, Sway, Lymington, Hants, and has issue:

(1) *Charles Colin; *b* 1973

(2) *Anthony James; *b* 1977

(1) *Sophie Charlotte; *b* 1975

The 6th EARL *m* 2nd 1984 *Marie Isobel, dau of Hon William French, 3rd son of 4th Baron de Freyne (*qv*) and widow of Sir Thomas Brian Weldon, 8th Bt (*qv*)

Lineage: RAINALDUS de KETHCART; living 1178; alleged ancestor of:

Sir ALAN CATHCART; fought Battle of Loudoun Hill 1307; *m* a sis of Sir Duncan Wallace of Sundrum, and had:

ALAN de KATHKERT; ggf of:

Sir ALAN CATHCART, **1st Lord Cathcart** (S), so *cr* *c* 1452; granted lands and territorial Barony of Cathcart by charter 31 July 1452, Warden West March and Master of Artillery 1484; *m* Janet Maxwell and *d* by 3 Oct 1497, having had issue:

ALAN, *Master of Cathcart*; *m* and *dvp*, leaving issue:

JOHN CATHCART, **2nd Lord Cathcart**; *m* 1st Margaret, dau of John Kennedy, of Blairquhan, and had issue; *m* 2nd by Aug 1499 Margaret, dau of William Douglas of Drumlanrig (*see* QUEENSBERRY, M, and BUCCLEUCH and QUEENSBERRY, D), by her was ancestor of the CATHCART Bts (now extinct), and *d* Dec 1535; his s by his 1st w:

ALAN, *Master of Cathcart*; *m* by Aug 1507 Agnes, dau of Robert, 2nd Lord Lyle, and was *k vp* Battle of Flodden 9 Sept 1513, leaving:

ALAN CATHCART, **3rd Lord Cathcart**; *m* Helen, est dau of 2nd Lord Sempill (*qv*), and was *ka* Battle of Pinkie 10 Sept 1547, leaving an only son:

ALAN CATHCART, **4th Lord Cathcart**; *b c* 1537; *m* 1st Margaret, dau of John Wallace of Craigy; *m* 2nd Florence McDougall, widow of John Kennedy of Baltersane, and *d* Dec 1618, having had:

ALAN, *Master of Cathcart*; *b* 1562; *m* by 24 June 1594 Isabel, dau of Thomas Kennedy of Bargeny, and *dvp* 1603, leaving:

ALAN CATHCART, **5th Lord Cathcart**; *b c* 1600; *m* 1st *c* Aug 1621 Lady Margaret Stewart (*dsp*), dau of 1st Earl of Bothwell (*see* MORAY, E); *m* 2nd *c* 29 Oct 1626 Jean, dau of Sir Alexander Colquhoun of Luss (*see* COLQUHOUN, Bt), and *d* 18 Aug 1628, leaving:

ALAN CATHCART, **6th Lord Cathcart**; *b* 1628; *m* by July 1643 Marion, est dau of David Boswell, 5th of Auchinleck, and *d* 13 June 1709, leaving issue:

ALAN CATHCART, **7th Lord Cathcart**; *b c* 1648; *m c* 12 Oct 1672 Elizabeth Dalrymple, dau of 1st Viscount Stair (*see* STAIR, E), and *d* 19 Oct 1732, leaving a 2nd s:

CHARLES CATHCART, **8th Lord Cathcart**; *b* 1686; Capt 1702, Maj Scots Greys 1709, later Lt-Col, played leading role in defeating Jacobite left wing Battle of Sheriffmuir 1715, Lt-Col 9th Foot 1717, Col: 31st Foot 1728–31, 8th Dragoons 1731–33 and 7th Horse of King's Carabiniers 1733–40, rep S peer 1734–40, Brig Gen 1735, Maj Gen 1739, apptd C-in-C Br Forces America *d* at sea en route to his post 20 Dec 1740; *m* 1st 29 March 1718 Marion (*d* 21 March 1733), only child of Sir John Shaw (or Schaw), Bt, of Greenock, and had, with twin est bros (*d* young):

1 CHARLES SCHAW, **9th Lord**

2 Schaw; Offr in the Gds; *ka* Battle of Fontenoy 1745

1 Eleanor; *m* Sir John Houston

2 Marie Anne; *m* 7th Lord Napier of Merchistoun (*see* NAPIER and ETTRICK, L)

The **8th Lord** *m* 2nd 1739 Elizabeth (*m* 4th 18 May 1745 Lt-Col Hugh Macguire and *d* 3 Aug 1789), dau of Thomas Malyn and widow of (a) James Fleet, of Tewin, Herts, and (b) Joseph Sabine, of Tring, but by her had no issue

The 8th LORD's er surv son,

CHARLES SCHAW CATHCART, **9th Lord Cathcart**, KT (1763), PC (1768); *b* 21 March 1721; rep S peer 1752–76, ADC to Duke of Cumberland, dangerously wounded at Battle of Fontenoy 30 April 1745, Lt-Gen, Amb St Petersburg 1768–71; *m* 24 July 1753 Jane (*d* 13 Nov 1771), dau of Lord Archibald Hamilton and gdau of 4th Duke of Hamilton (*qv*), and *d* 14 Aug 1776, having had issue:

1 WILLIAM SCHAW, **1st Earl**

2 Charles Allan; *b* 8 Dec 1759; Col, MP Clackmannanshire; *dsp* 10 June 1788

3 Archibald Hamilton (Rev); *b* 25 July 1764; Preb York; *m* 3 June 1790 Frances Henrietta (*d* 26 April 1821), dau of John Fremantle, and *d* 10 Oct 1841, leaving, with other issue:

(1) Catherine Selina; *m* 21 Nov 1839 Robert Smith, of Capenhurst House, Chester

(2) Isabella Sophia; *m* 3 Nov 1829 Sir Samuel Crompton, Bt (*d* 27 Dec 1848), and *d* 1896

(3) Elizabeth Sarah; *m* 2 June 1842 Maj Robert Stuart, UK Min Haiti (*d* 17 June 1901)

1 Jane; *m* 26 Dec 1774 4th Duke of Atholl (*qv*), and *d* 4 Dec 1790, leaving issue

2 Mary; *m* 26 Dec 1774 Sir Thomas Graham, 1st and last Baron Lynedoch (*dsp* 18 Dec 1843), and *dsp* 26 June 1792

3 LOUISA Cathcart, COUNTESS OF MANSFIELD in her own right; *m* 1st 5 May 1766 David MURRAY, 2nd Earl of Mansfield (*d* 1 Sept 1796; *see* MANSFIELD and MANSFIELD, E), and had issue; *m* 2nd 19 Oct 1797 Hon Robert Fulke Greville (*d* 27 April 1824), bro of 2nd Earl Brooke and Warwick (*qv*), and *d* 11 July 1843, leaving further issue

The 9th LORD's er son,

WILLIAM SCHAW CATHCART, **1st Earl Cathcart**, so *cr* 16 July 1814, as also earlier 9 Nov 1807 VISCOUNT CATHCART of Cathcart, Co Renfrew, and BARON GREENOCK of Greenock, Co Renfrew (all UK), KT (1805), PC (GB 1798, I 1803); *b* Aug 1755; *educ* Eton and Lincoln's Inn; advocate 1776, joined 7th Dragoons 1777, Maj 98th Regt 1779, QMG Forces America to 1779–80, Lt-Col Coldstream Gds 1781, Col 29th Foot 1792–97, rep S peer (Tory) 1788–1812, Maj-Gen 1794, Lt-Gen 1801, C-in-C Copenhagen Expdn 1807, Amb St Petersburg 1805–06 and 1812–20, Col 2nd Life Gds, Gen 1812, Jt Min Plen Congress Vienna 1814–15, Memb Bd Gen Offrs, Commr RMC and Roy Mil Asylum, V-Adml Scotland; *m* 10 April 1779 Elizabeth (*d* 14 Dec 1847), dau of Andrew Elliot, of Greenwells, Roxburghshire, Govr New York and unc of 1st Earl of Minto (*qv*), and *d* 16 June 1843, having had, with other issue:

1 William, Master of Cathcart; *b* 13 June 1782; *educ* Eton; Capt RN March 1804; *dvp* unm 5 June 1804 of yellow fever at Jamaica when cmdg HMS *Clarinda*

2 CHARLES MURRAY, **2nd Earl**

3 Frederick CATHCART later McADAM, of Craigengillan; *b* 28 Oct 1789; Col, Kt Russian Order of St Anne; *m* 18 Oct 1827 Jane (*d* 25 April 1878), dau and heir of Quentin McAdam, and *d* 5 March 1865

4 George (Sir), GCB; *b* 12 May 1794; Gen, ADC to Duke of Wellington Battle of Waterloo 1815, Govr and Cdr Forces Cape of Good Hope, Dep-Lt Tower of London, cmd 4th Div Crimea; *m* 12 May 1824 his cousin Lady Georgiana Greville (*d* 12 Dec 1871), dau of Louisa, Countess of Mansfield and her 2nd husb Hon Robert Fulke Greville (*see* above), and was *ka* Battle of Inkerman 5 Nov 1854, having had, with a son and six other daus:

(1) Emily Sarah, VA; Maid of Honour 1855–79 and Woman of the Bedchamber 1888–1901 to HM QUEEN VICTORIA; *d* unm 16 Feb 1917

5 Adolphus Frederick, of Caldra, Berwicks; *b* 28 June 1803; Lt-Col; *m* 2 July 1832 Margaret (*d* 29 April 1861), 2nd dau of William Forman Home of Wedderburn and Paxton, Berwicks, and *dsp* 6 April 1884

The 1st EARL's 2nd but est surv son,

CHARLES MURRAY CATHCART, **2nd Earl Cathcart**, GCB (1859, KCB 1838); *b* 21 Dec 1783; *educ* Eton; Lt-Col 1810, served Peninsula and Waterloo, Gen, Col 1st Dragoon Gds, Govr Edinburgh Castle, Cdr Forces Scotland, Govr-Gen and C-in-C England; *m* 12 Feb 1819 Henrietta (*d* 24 June 1872), 2nd dau of Thomas Mather, and *d* 16 July 1859, having had, with other issue:

1 ALAN FREDERICK, **3rd Earl**

2 Augustus Murray; *b* 18 Aug 1830; JP (Yorks), Col Gren Gds Crimean War; *m* 28 Nov 1866 Hon Jean Mary Orde-Powlett (*d* 27 Jan 1931), only dau of 3rd Baron Bolton (*qv*), and *d* 14 July 1914, having had, with other issue:

(1) Frederick Adrian, of Drumgrange, Ardendee, Kirkcudbright; *b* 26 June 1873; Maj 3rd Bn York and Lancaster Regt, S African War and WW I; V-Convener Kirkcudbrightshire; *m* 15 Nov 1904 Margaret Cecil Anne (*d* 2 March 1956), yr dau of Lt-Col Hon William Fitzwilliam Elliot (*see* MINTO, E), and *d* 2 May 1943, leaving issue:

1a Alan Reginald, of Drumgrange; *b* 6 June 1908; *educ* Edinburgh Acad; WW II as Maj IA; *m* 5 April 1934 Daphne Victoria Catherine (*d* 1993), yr dau of Maj-Gen John Archibald Henry Pollock, CB, of Ardendee, Kirkcudbright (*see* MONTAGU-POLLOCK, Bt), and *d* 26 April 1967, leaving issue:

1b +Charles Alan [Charles Cathcart Esq, Culraven, Borgue, Kirkcudbright DG6 4SG]; *b* 1 April 1940; *educ* Oundle; *m* 1973 *Carol Ann, yr dau of A E Jenner, and has issue:

1c +Daniel Edward; *b* 24 Sept 1974

1c *Emma Katherine; *b* 22 June 1976

1b *Julia Mary [Mrs Angus Millar, 24 Buckingham Terrace, Edinburgh EH4 3AE]; *b* 14 June 1936; *m* 25 April 1959 *Angus George Millar, WS, son of George William Russell Millar, of Port Dickson, Malaya, and has issue:

1c *James George; *b* 16 Jan 1961; *m* 1992 *Katherine Ann, yr dau of John Danielson, and has issue:

1d *Hector George; *b* 1994

2d *Ludovic Angus Danielson; *b* 1996

2c *Charles Angus; *b* 15 June 1963

3c *Roderick Alan; *b* 23 May 1967

2a Charles Frederick, of Pitcairlie, Newburgh, Fife, DSO (1942), and bar (1945), DL (Fife 1953); *b* 26 March 1912; *educ* Sedbergh; Lt-Col The Black Watch, WW II (despatches); *m* 1st 25 Aug 1939 (*divorce* 1954) Pamela Violet, er dau of Lt-Col Patrick Douglas Stirling, OBE, MC, JP, of Kippenross, Dunblane, Perthshire, and *d* 1971, leaving issue:

1b *Clovannis Jane (twin) [Mrs Colin Innes, Easter Dunbeg, Newburgh, Fife KY14 6JF]; *b* 18 April 1942; *m* 30 Sept 1961 *Colin Berowald Innes, Black Watch (RHR), (*see* INNES, Bt, of Balvenie), and has:

1c *Andrew Berowald; *b* 28 Dec 1963

1c *Katherine Candida [Mrs Giles Peppiatt, Aston Mullins Farm, Ford, Bucks]; *b* 30 May 1967; *m* May 1994 *Giles Ernest Peppiatt and has:

1d *Dominic Andrew Slingsby; *b* 19 March 1997

2c *Emily Jane; *b* 14 Jan 1969; *m* June 1997 *Edward John Timothy Taylor, of Gondhurst, Kent

2b *Miranda Jane (twin); *b* 18 April 1942; *m* 1984 *Anthony C Henderson, of Sydney, NSW, and *dsp* 1987

3b *(Sarah) Camilla; *b* 25 June 1946; *m* 1977, as his 3rd w, *Baron Jauncey of Tullichettle (*qv*) and has issue

2a (cont.) Lt-Col Charles Cathcart *m* 2nd 15 Feb 1955 *Pamela Vera, twin dau of Maj Harry Sebastian Garrard, of Welston Place, Daventry, Northants, and widow of Maj Sir Arthur Ralph Wilmot, 7th Bt (*qv*), and *d* 15 March 1971

1a Mary Leta; *b* 11 Oct 1905; *m* 2 Feb 1935 Philip James Lee Hobson, of 8 New Street, Deal, Kent, son of C J Hobson, RI, RMS, and *d* 24 Dec 1965, leaving:

1b *Andrew James Alan; *b* 1936

(2) Augustus Ernest; *b* 4 March 1875; Capt KRRC, S Africa 1900–02 and WW I 1914; *m* 10 June 1913 Hilda Renée (*d* 29 May 1958), est dau of William Frederick Lee, of Grove Hall, Knottingley, Yorks, and was *ka* Sept 1914, leaving issue:

1a Eva Renée, OBE (1971), JP (NR Yorks) [Miss Eva Cathcart OBE JP, Warwick House, Aiskew, Bedale, Yorks]; *b* 10 March 1914; Jr Cdr ATS WW II, raised Mauritius Women's Vol Corps 1945

(3) William Harold; *b* 3 May 1880; Lt 3rd Bn Worcester Regt, S Africa; *d* 7 Jan 1902

(1) Mary Mildred; *b* 10 May 1876; *m* 1st 6 Aug 1925 Lt-Col Ferdinand Cospatrick Logan-Home (*d* 28 June 1931), son of Col George Logan-Home, of Broom House and Edrom, Berwickshire; *m* 2nd 4 Dec 1943 Rev Sir Frederick Sullivan, 7th Bt (*qv*), and *dsp* 25 Dec 1952

(2) Constance; *b* 17 Aug 1877; *m* 1 June 1897 William Harris Ferrand (*d* 25 Aug 1954), of Bilton Dene, Harrogate, and *d* 28 Dec 1943, leaving issue

(3) Leta Adine; *b* 10 April 1882

(4) Vera; *b* 10 June 1883; *m* 10 Aug 1914 Alan Peter Slingsby (*d* 2 July 1938), 3rd son of Rev Charles Slingsby Slingsby, of Scriven Pk, Yorks, and *dsp* 13 Oct 1967

1 Elizabeth; *m* 1 June 1843 Gen Sir John Douglas, GCB (*d* 8 Sept 1887), of Glenfinart, Col 79th Foot, and sometime Cdr Forces in Scotland, est son of Lt-Gen Sir Neil Douglas, KCB, and *d* 27 Feb 1896, leaving issue

2 Adelaide; *m* 13 July 1850 John Randolphus de Trafford, of Croston Hall, Lancs (*d* 3 Feb 1879), 2nd son of Sir Thomas Joseph de Trafford, 1st Bt (*qv*), and *d* 15 Feb 1871, leaving issue

The 2nd EARL's er son,

ALAN FREDERICK CAHCART, **3rd Earl Cathcart**, DL (N R Yorks); *b* 14 Nov 1828; Hon Col 1st Vol Bn Yorks Regt, VD, LLD Honoris Causa Glasgow; *m* 2 April 1850 Elizabeth Mary (*d* 13 April 1902), est dau and heiress of Sir Samuel Crompton, 1st Bt, and *d* 30 Oct 1905, having had issue:

1 ALAN CATHCART, **4th Earl Cathcart**, JP, DL (NR Yorks); *b* 18 March 1856; Lt 6th Dragoon Gds and Scots Gds; *d* unm 2 Sept 1911

2 Charles; *b* 23 Dec 1858; Lt 79th Regt; *d* 21 May 1880

3 GEORGE, **5th Earl**

4 Reginald; *b* 9 Nov 1870; Capt 3rd Bn KRRC; *ka* Relief of Ladysmith, S Africa 22 Feb 1900

5 Archibald Hamilton; *b* 30 Jan 1873; *d* unm 3 Feb 1955

1 Isabel; *d* young 29 Nov 1856

2 Cecilia; *b* 5 Dec 1857; *m* 26 July 1883 Capt Edward Temple Rose (*d* 1920), late 10th Hus, son of Sir John Rose, 1st Bt, of Montreal, PC, GCB, and *d* 2 Oct 1932

3 Ida; *b* 26 April 1866; *m* 24 July 1886 Sir Thomas Leigh Hare, 1st Bt, MVO (*d* 22 Feb 1941), and *d* 25 Jan 1929, leaving issue
4 Marion; *b* 14 June 1867; *d* unm 5 Oct 1955
5 Emily; *b* 27 Dec 1868; *d* unm 9 Oct 1960
6 Eva; *b* 12 May 1874; *d* unm 3 June 1960

The 4th EARL's next surv bro,

GEORGE CATHCART, **5th Earl Cathcart**; *b* 26 June 1862; Lt 4th Bn Princess of Wales's Own Yorkshire Regt; *m* 6 Jan 1919 (Idivorce 1922) Vera, dau of John Fraser, of Cape Town, S Africa, and widow of Capt Henry de Grey Warter, 4th Dragoon Gds, of Cruck Meole, Salop, and *d* 19 Nov 1927, leaving issue:
1 ALAN CATHCART, **6th and present Earl Cathcart**

CATTO

Arms: Or on a chevron between three lymphads sa. as many boar's heads couped of the field. **Crest:** A wild cat sejant ppr., resting the dexter paw on a garb or. **Supporters:** On either side a tiger ppr., charged on the shoulder with an ivy leaf or. **Motto:** Touch not gloveless. **Creations:** Bt. (UK) 5 July 1921, B. (UK) 24 Feb 1936.

THE 2ND BARON CATTO, of Cairncatto, Co Aberdeen, and a **Baronet** (Sir Stephen Gordon Catto, Bt) [The Rt Hon The Lord Catto, 41 William Mews, Lowndes Sq, London SW1X 9HQ]; *b* 14 Jan 1923; *s* f 1959; *educ* Eton and Trin Coll Cambridge; served RAFVR 1943–47, dir Morgan Grenfell 1957–79 (ch exec 1973–74 and chm 1973–79), chm Morgan Grenfell Gp plc (now Deutsche Morgan Grenfell Gp plc) 1980–87 (pres 1987–), memb Advsy Cncl Export Credits Guarantee Dept 1959–65, part-time memb London Tport Bd 1962–68, chm Yule Catto 1971–, dir: News Internat plc 1969–96, Times Newspapers Hldgs 1981–, chm RAF Benevolent Fund 1978–91; *m* 1st 28 July 1948 (*divorce* 1965) Josephine Innes, er dau of George Herbert Packer, of Alexandria, Egypt, and has issue:
1 +INNES GORDON CATTO [The Hon Innes Catto, House of Schivas, Ythanbank, Ellon, Aberdeen AB41 0TN]; *b* 7 Aug 1950; *educ* Grenville Coll and Shuttleworth Coll
2 +Alexander Gordon [The Hon Alexander Catto, Holmdale, Holmbury St Mary, Surrey RH5 6NR]; *b* 22 June 1952; *educ* Westminster and Trin Coll Cambridge (BA 1983); *m* 6 June 1981 *Elizabeth Scott, twin dau of Maj T P Boyes, of Brookvale Cottage, Whitford, Devon, and has issue:
(1) +Thomas Innes Gordon; *b* 18 Oct 1983
(2) +Alastair Gordon; *b* 6 March 1986
(1) *Charlotte Gordon; *b* 19 May 1988
1 *Christian Victoria Gordon [The Hon Mrs Menzies-Wilson, Newport House, Newport Lane, Braishfield, nr Romsey, Hants SO51 0PL]; *b* 24 Feb 1955; *educ* The Manor Ho, Westwood Ho Peterborough and Hatfield Poly; *m* 16 April 1983 *Charles N Menzies-Wilson, er son of W N Menzies-Wilson, of Holland Park, W11, and has issue:
(1) *Richard Napier; *b* 25 April 1988
(2) *James Benedict; *b* 7 Oct 1991
(1) *Cathryn Lucy; *b* 16 Jan 1986
2 *Ariane Madeleine Gordon; *b* 22 Aug 1960; *educ* Francis Holland Sch, Westwood Ho Peterborough and Aiglon Coll Switzerland

The 2nd BARON *m* 2nd 27 Jan 1966 Margaret (*d* 5 June 1998), dau of James Stuart Forrest, of Dilston, Tasmania, and by her has:
3 +James Stuart Gordon [The Hon James Catto, Lower Lutheredge Farm, Shortwood, Nailsworth, Glos GL6 0SJ]; *b* 20 Dec 1966; *educ* Gordonstoun; *m* 17 May 1997 *Kathryn Mary Lawton, er dau of Robert Lawton of Aldbourne, Wilts
(3) *Georgina Lucinda Gordon [The Hon Mrs Newman, Sandford House, Avening, Tetbury, Glos GL8 8NF]; *b* 21 May 1969; *educ* Riddlesworth Hall Norfolk; *m* 1993 *Robert Alistair Newman, er son of Alistair Newman, of Sutton Green, Guildford, and has:
1a *Charles Guy Gordon; *b* 6 Nov 1994
2a *Tobias James Gordon; *b* 25 March 1997

Lineage: WILLIAM CATTO, of Peterhead, Scotland; *m* Isabella, dau of William Yule, and had issue:
1 William; *b* 1864; *d* 1917
2 John; *b* 1867; *m* Harriet (*d* 5 Feb 1963, aged 85), and *d* 1942
3 Andrew Yule, CBE, Lt-Cdr RN; *b* 1869; *m* 18 Nov 1922 Ella Grosvenor, widow of Lt-Cdr Arthur Bruce Nesling, RN, and *d* 20 Jan 1939
4 Adam Yule, Lt RNR; *b* 1871; *d* 1933
5 THOMAS SIVEWRIGHT, **1st Baron**
1 Mary *b* 1876; *d* 1942

The yst son,

Sir Thomas Sivewright Catto, 1st Bt, and **1st Baron Catto**, of Cairncatto, Co Aberdeen, so *cr* 5 July 1921 and 24 Feb 1936 respectively (both UK), PC (1947), CBE (1918), LLD; *b* 15 March 1879; Govr Bank of England 1944–49, Fin Advsr to Chllr Exchequer 1940–44, Dir Gen Equipment and Stores and memb Supply Cncl 1940, dir Morgan Grenfell, Andrew Yule and Co Calcutta, Yule Catto and Co London, Mercantile Bank of India and Roy Exchange Assur; Br Admlty Rep on Russian Commn to USA 1915–17, memb Br Food Mission USA 1917, Chm Allied Provisions Commn and Head Br Min Food in USA and Canada 1918–19; Order Leopold Belgium 1919, memb Indian Govt Retrenchment Ctee (Inchcape Ctee) 1922–23, Br Govt Ctee on Coal Selling 1926; OStJ; *m* 20 Oct 1910 Gladys Forbes (*b* 5 June 1885, *d* 8 Oct 1980), of Holmdale, Holmbury St Mary, Dorking, Surrey, dau of Stephen Gordon, of Elgin, and *d* 23 Aug 1959, having had issue:
1 STEPHEN GORDON CATTO, **2nd and present Baron Catto**
1 Isabel Ida Gordon, OBE (1952); *b* 1912; Govr PNEU Schs, World Pres YWCA 1955–63, Pres YWCA GB 1966–72; *d* unm 13 Oct 1997
2 Gladys Gordon; *b* 1917; *m* 25 Nov 1939 W/Cdr Euan Owens Richmond-Watson, RAFVR (*d* 15 April 1954) , 3rd son of Richmond Watson, of Chalfont Grove, Chalfont St Giles, Bucks, and *d* as the result of a motor accident, 17 Feb 1967, leaving issue:
(1) *Anthony Euan; *b* 8 April 1941; *educ* Westminster
(1) *Marilyn Olivia; *b* 25 Sept 1945
(2) *Zoë Isabel; *b* 4 Feb 1950
3 *Ruth Gordon; *b* 1919; *m* 14 Feb 1947 *Francis Ernest Herman Bennett, CBE, est son of Sir Ernest Nathanial Bennett, MP, and has issue:
(1) *David Francis; *b* 13 April 1948; *educ* Westminster; *m* 1980 *Lynn D, dau of Lt-Col Allan Burton, DSO, TD, of Limestone Hall, Milton, Ontario, Canada, and has issue:
1a *Nicholas Gordon; *b* 1982
1a *Audrey Claire; *b* 1984
(2) *Adam Gordon Greverus; *b* 31 Aug 1954; *educ* Westminster; *m* 1986 *Zoë Diana, er dau of Prof Terence John Bew Spencer, of Birmingham U, and has issue:
1a *Oscar Francis; *b* 1986
1a *Isabel Diana; *b* 1989
(1) *Olivia Gay; *b* 8 Oct 1950

CAVAN

Arms: Gu. three narcissi pierced arg. **Crest:** On a mount vert a centaur ppr., drawing his bow gu. stringed or, arrow of the last, pheon arg. **Supporters:** On either side a knight in complete armour, visor open all ppr., garnished and spurred or, out of the helm a plume of four feathers alternately arg. and gu., pendant from a belt of the last a sword also ppr., pommel and hilt gold.
Motto: *Ut quocunque paratus* ('Prepared on every side').
Creations: B. (I) 17 Feb 1617/8, V. and E. (I) 15 April 1647.

THE 13TH EARL OF THE COUNTY OF CAVAN, **Viscount Kilcoursie**, King's County, and **Lord Lambart, Baron of Cavan**, Co Cavan (Roger Cavan Lambart) [The Rt Hon The Earl of Cavan, 34 Woodleigh Gdns, London SW16]; *b* 1 Sept 1944; *s* fourth cousin of the halfblood 1988; *educ* Wilson's Sch, Wallington, Surrey

Lineage: JOHN LAMBERT, of Preston; living *c* 1474; had:

RICHARD LAMBERT, of Long Preston; *m* — Burton, of Carshalton, and had:

WALTER LAMBERT, of Stone Court, Carshalton, Surrey, London citizen and goldsmith, Warden Goldsmiths' Co 1541; *m* by 1 Dec 1516 Margaret, dau of Robert Gaynsford, of Allington Castle, Kent, and *d* between 11 Sept and 17 Sept 1545, leaving a 3rd s:

WALTER LAMBERT, of Southampton; *m* 1st Rose, dau of Sir Oliver Wallop (*see* PORTSMOUTH, E) and had issue (including a dau, Anne, *m* Henry Calthorp); *m* 2nd Elizabeth, dau of Sir George Paulet, bro of 1st Marquess of Winchester (*qv*), and widow of — Reniger, and by her had two other daus (Barbara and Elizabeth); his only s (who was by his 1st w):

Sir OLIVER LAMBART, **1st Lord Lambart, Baron of Cavan** Co Cavan (I), so *cr* 17 Feb 1617/8, PC (I 1603); ktd 1596, offr under Earl of Essex in Ireland, Master of the Camp 1599, cmded 200 Foot at Enniscorthy, Co Wexford; Govr Connaught 1601, Sgt-Major of the Army, MP Cavan 1613–15; *m* by 3 Jan 1598/9 Hester (*d* 12 March 1639), est dau of Sir William Fleetwood, of Cranford, Middx, and Cardington Manor, Beds, and was *bur* 10 June 1618, having had, with, a yr s (Cary (Sir), ktd 1622, *d* unm 1627) and three daus:

CHARLES LAMBART, **1st Earl of the County of Cavan**, so *cr* 1 April 1647, as also VISCOUNT KILCOURSIE, in King's County (both I), PC (I); *b c* 1600; MP Bossiney 1626 and 1628–29, Seneschal Co Cavan and Kells, cdr Dublin 1642, helped suppress 1641 Uprising with a 1,000–strong inf regt; *m* by 30 June 1625 Jane Robartes, yr dau of 1st Baron Robartes of Truro, and *d* 25 June 1660, leaving, with a yr s (Oliver, of Painstown, ancestor of LAMBART, Bt; *see* 1970 edn):

RICHARD LAMBART, **2nd Earl of the County of Cavan**; MP Kilbeggan 1647–49; *m* 1st 12 Nov 1648 Rose (*d* 29 Dec 1649), 2nd dau of Sir James Ware, of Macestown, Co Dublin, and had an only son; *m* 2nd Elizabeth, widow of Francis Derenzi *alias* Keane, of Tinecross, King's Co, who was appointed the person responsible for him after he became insane 1670, and *d* just before May 1691, leaving by his 1st w:

CHARLES LAMBART, **3rd Earl of the County of Cavan**; *b* 7 Sept 1649; *m* Castilina, sis of St Leger Gilbert, of Kilminchy, Queen's Co, and *d* 5 Dec 1702, leaving:

1 RICHARD LAMBART, **4th Earl of the County of Cavan**, PC (I 1729); *m* Margaret (*d* 5 Aug 1737), dau of Richard Trant, Govr Barbados, and niece of the essayist Sir Richard Steele, and *d* 10 March 1741, leaving a 2nd but surv s:

(1) FORD LAMBART, **5th Earl of the County of Cavan**; *b* 1718; *m* 24 March 1741/2 Elizabeth (*d* 4 Oct 1766), dau of James Wall, of Dublin, and *d* 29 Sept 1772, leaving an only dau:

1a Gertrude; *m* Sir Michael Cromie, Bt

2 Henry; *m* Dorothea, dau of Thomas Higgison, of Portumna, Co Galway, and had:

(1) RICHARD LAMBART, **6th Earl of the County of Cavan**; Lt-Gen 1777, Col 55th Foot; *m* 1st Sophia (*d* May 1749), dau and heir of his unc, Hon Oliver Lambart, but by her had no issue; *m* 2nd 13 Nov 1762 Elizabeth (*d* 27 Feb 1811), est dau and coheir of William Davies, Commr RN, and by her had issue:

1a RICHARD, **7th Earl**

1a Elizabeth Jane; *m* 1st 9 Nov 1793 Captain William Henry Ricketts Jervis, RN; *m* 2nd March 1800 Rev Richard Brickenden and *d* 17 Jan 1830, leaving issue

3 Oliver; *m* Frances Stewart, (previously?) mother illegitimately by 1st Duke of the County of Buckingham and of Normanby of Sir Charles Sheffield, 1st Bt (*qv*)

The 6th EARL *d* 2 Nov 1774; his son,

RICHARD LAMBART, **7th Earl of the County of Cavan**; *b* 10 Sept 1763; Gen, Col 45th Foot 1823–37, cmded a Div in Egypt 1800 under Abercrombie; *m* 1st 11 July 1782 Honora Margaretta (*d* 1 Oct 1813), yst dau and coheir of Sir Henry Gould, Judge Court of Common Pleas, and had, with other issue:

1 GEORGE FREDERICK AUGUSTUS, *Viscount Kilcoursie*; *b* 9 March 1789; *m* 14 May 1811 Sarah (*d* 30 Dec 1823), only dau of J P Coppin, of Cowley, Oxon, and *dvp* 28 Dec 1828, leaving issue (the yr son and daus granted rank of earl's daus/yr s 1838):

(1) FREDERICK JOHN WILLIAM, **8th Earl**

(2) Oliver George, Capt late 12th Foot, late Hon Lt-Col 3rd Bn Hants Regt; *b* 29 June 1822; *m* 13 July 1847 Elizabeth (*d* 24 June 1904), 3rd dau of William Spear, of Monkton, Dorset, and *dsp* 16 June 1898

(1) Henrietta Augusta; *m* 11 Aug 1845 Sir Robert John Harvey Harvey, 1st Bt, and *d* 3 July 1874, leaving issue. He *d* 19 July 1870

(2) Alicia; *m* 13 April 1849 Rev James Stevenson Blackwood, DD, LLD, and *dsp* 30 July 1913. He *d* 27 March 1882

(3) Julia; *m* 3 Aug 1841 Rev Theodore Bouwens, MA, Preb of Lincoln and Rector of St Mary's, Bedford, and *d* 13 Feb 1897, leaving issue. He *d* 18 Feb 1869

1 Alicia Margaretta Hockmore; *m* 5 Jan 1813 Philip Duncombe Pauncefort-Duncombe, of Brick Hill, Bucks, and *d* 3 April 1818, leaving issue (*see* PAUNCEFORT-DUNCOMBE, Bt)

The **7th Earl** *m* 2nd 11 Aug 1814 Lydia (*d* 7 Feb 1862), 2nd dau of William Arnold, of Slatwoods, IoW, by his w Martha, dau of John Delafield, and by her had, with other issue:

2 Oliver William Matthew, Cdr RN; *b* 26 Aug 1822; *m* 26 Nov 1844 Anne Elizabeth (*d* 24 Nov 1881), 2nd dau of Capt George W Willes, RN, and *d* 28 April 1863, having had, with other issue:

(1) Ford Edward Willes, Cdr RN, served in Egypt 1882 (medal with three clasps and bronze star); *b* 16 April 1849; *m* 17 May 1894 Geraldine Elizabeth (*d* 19 Feb 1922), dau of William Westropp Brereton, Prof at Queen's Coll Galway, and *d* 21 Jan 1906, leaving issue:

1a Oliver Ford Westrop, late Lt RFA; *b* 17 Feb 1895; *m* 1921 Hilda, dau of I Digby, and *dsp* 1 Jan 1960

(2) Frederick Richard Henry, Maj late Roy Scots Fus, served in Zulu and Boer Wars; *b* 10 June 1850; *m* 10 June 1873 Catherine Adeline Maxwell (*d* 1897), only child of Walter H Gill, late Cape Mounted Riflemen, and *d* 19 Aug 1888, leaving issue:

1a Ernest Oliver Cavan, MC, Lt late Roy Berks Regt, served WW I 1914–16 (despatches); *b* 1 Jan 1874; *m* Josephine Drake (*d* 1929), and *d* in NY, 27 June 1945

2a Richard Frederick Lacon, DSO (1915), Capt Intell Corps, served WW I (despatches); *b* 26 June 1875; *m* 1st 1899 (*divorce* 1909) Enid (*d* 21 Feb 1963, aged 89), dau of Spencer Brunton; *m* 2nd 2 May 1913 (*divorce*) Faith Bevan; *m* 3rd 1922 Kitty Gibbens (who *m* 2nd 1924 (*divorce*) Herbert Alfred Rich, *m* 3rd 1941 Capt Horace Lacy Bullimore), and *d* 6 Jan 1924, having by her had issue:

1b *(Kathleen) Joy Lydia Lacon; *b* 1923

3a Henry Godfrey Randolph, late Capt Kimberley Light Horse, formerly 4th Hus, served in S African War, and WW I, Intell Dept, USA; *b* 9 July 1876; *m* 1st 1901 Ruby, dau of M J Kerchoff, of Cape Town; *m* 2nd (*divorce*) Winifred Harris; *m* 3rd Minnie Jago (*d* 11 Nov 1959), and *d* 11 June 1949, having by her had issue:

1b *Angele Patricia Victoria; *b* 1 March 1925; *m* 1956 — Ström, of Stockholm, Sweden

2b *Eileen Ann Cavan; *b* 16 Oct 1927

4a Charles Edward Kilcoursie, Maj 21st Roy Scots Fus; *b* 3 Nov 1877; *m* 1st (*divorce*) Isobel Dora (*d* 16 Nov 1936), dau of Edward Jeffery, of Boar's Hill Ho, Berks; *m* 2nd 14 Sept 1901 Florence Marion (*d* 1961), dau of Frederick Manasseh Brandon, and was *ka* 5 June 1916, leaving issue:

1b Frederick Cavan; *b* 16 July 1902; *m* 1st 19 April 1924 (*divorce* 1942) Adelaide Constance, dau of Ottywell Babler, and had issue:

1c *Olivia Marianne (abandoned the Christian name of Olive); *b* 22 Oct 1925; *m* 27 Dec 1950 (*divorce* 1970) Ernest Ephraim Corrett, and has issue:

1d *Paul [Paul Corrett Esq, 2 Erskine Mews, Regent's Park, London NW3]; *b* 7 Sept 1952; *educ* Stowe; *m* 1984 *Anne Margaret, dau of Ernest Joseph Ferridge, of 35 Dunbar Rd, N22, and has issue:

1e *Catherine Marianne; *b* 1986

2d *Graham; *b* 4 April 1954; *educ* Corona Stage Sch; *m* 1982 (*divorce* 1988) Kelly Elaine, dau of Seymour Arnold Hoppen, of 7 Egerton Place, London SW3, and formerly of S Africa, and has issue:

1e *Natasha; *b* 1983

1b (cont.) Frederick Cavan *m* 2nd 1942 (*divorce* 1948) *Audrey May [Mrs Audrey Lambart, 34 Woodleigh Gdns, London SW16], only dau of Albert Charles Dunham, and by her had issue:

1c ROGER CAVAN LAMBART, **13th and present Earl of the County of Cavan**

1b (cont.) Frederick Cavan *m* 3rd 1958 *Kathleen Elizabeth [Mrs John Wiggin, The Anchor Hotel, Shepperton, Middx] (she *m* 2nd 1965 Frederick Rufus Lawrence (*d* 1969); *m* 3rd 1970 John Armstrong Wiggin), er dau of Edward James Henry Darvill, of Port Vale Ho, Hertford, and *d* 13 May 1963, having by her had issue:

2c *Elizabeth; *b* 1959

(3) Percy Francis, Lt-Col, formerly 5th Fus, JP and CC for E Sussex, served in Afghan War 1879–80 (medal), and WW I 1915–18 as a King's Messenger and GSO; *b* 2 Oct 1851; *m* 1st 28 March 1881 Helen Ann (*d* 8 April 1918), dau of Capt Alexander Ellice, RN; *m* 2nd 8 Aug 1918 Mary Louisa (*d* 12 Jan 1936), dau of Capt Henry Stone, 13th Som LI, and *dsp* 10 July 1933

(4) Arthur Oliver, of E London, S Africa; *b* 21 July 1854; *m* 27 Nov 1879 Annie Louisa (*d* 25 Oct 1918), dau of Augustus Hillier, and *d* 4 April 1903, leaving issue:

1a Ford Augustus Oliver, late temp Lt Roy Berks Regt, served in Bechuanaland 1897, in S African War 1899–1902, and WW I 1917–19; *b* 30 June 1880; *m* 1908 Daisy Elizabeth Margaret (*d* 21 July 1959), er dau of A Reid Nicholson, of Edinburgh, and *d* 10 June 1940, leaving issue:

1b Arthur Oliver Reid; *b* 1909

1a Honoria Kathleen; *b* 5 May 1884; *d* unm 5 April 1962

2a Alice Mary Helen Barclay; *b* 27 Aug 1888

3a Blanche Mary; *b* 9 Sept 1893; *m* 9 Jan 1919 Samuel Alexander Vintcent Melvill (*d* 25 Jan 1963), and had issue:

1b *Jack Vintcent; *b* 1 April 1921; *m* 1959 *Shirley, yr dau of L A Wyndham, of Fresnaye, Sea Point, Cape Town, S Africa, and has issue:

1c *David Leonard Vintcent; *b* 1960

2c *Eric Wyndham; *b* 1961

3c *Robert John; *b* 1964

1b Maureen May Vintcent; *b* 24 Dec 1919; *m* 1945 John James Austen, of Apdale Farm, Que Que, Rhodesia, and *d* 28 Jan 1959, leaving issue, four daus

4a May Hensleigh; *b* 24 Aug 1889; *m* 17 March 1927 Stephen Peter Meintjes, and had issue:

1b *John Lambart; *b* 4 April 1928; *m* 4 June 1955 (*divorce* 1963) Jean Paton, dau of J W Davidson, and has issue:

1c *Peter James; *b* 18 March 1958

1b *Muriel Edgar; *b* 16 Nov 1931; *m* 29 April 1955 *Sidney Charles Housdon, and has issue:

1c *Michael Charles; *b* 29 July 1963

1c *Jennifer May *b* 27 July 1961

2c *Carolyn Janet; *b* 4 April 1969

2b *Elizabeth Ann; *b* 25 April 1938; *m* 27 June 1960 *Edward James Wyndham Quin, and has issue:

1c *Michael John Wyndham; *b* 17 June 1965

1c *Ann Sharon Wyndham; *b* 13 Jan 1961

2c *Margaret Lynn Wyndham; *b* 10 Feb 1962

(5) Edgar Alan, CB (1917), Col in the Army, Hon Brig-Gen 1919, served in Afghan War 1879–80 (medal with clasp), in S African War 1901–2 (medal with four clasps), and WW I 1914–17 (despatches); *b* 2 Jan 1857; *m* 1st 29 Dec 1884 Hannah Geraldine (*d* 29 Jan 1887), dau of Capt James Stirling Crawford Stirling-Stuart, of Castle Milk, Lanarkshire, and had issue:

1a Gerald Edgar Oliver Fortescue, Capt 1st Bn Roy Scots Fus, formerly 19th Hus; *b* 30 Nov 1885; *d* 28 March 1916, of wounds received in action

1a Lily Georgiana Harriet Gordon; *b* 16 Jan 1887; *d* unm 29 March 1974

(5) (cont.) Brig Edgar Lambart *m* 2nd 14 April 1891 Mary Louisa (*d* 31 Jan 1948), est dau of Sir James Robert Walker, 2nd Bt (*see* WALKER, Bt, of Sand Hutton), and *d* 30 June 1930, having by her had issue:

2a Julian Harold Legge, V-Provost of Eton Coll 1959–67, assist master Eton Coll 1919, Lower Master 1945–49, late Capt RFA, served WW I, had Croix de Guerre; *b* 7 May 1893; *educ* Eton and King's Coll Cambridge; *m* 28 July 1948 *Margaret, only child of Rev Canon William Evans, Rector of

Narberth, Pembrokes, and widow of Sir (Henry) Walford Davies, KCVO, OBE, MusD, Organist of St George's Chapel, Windsor

(6) Alfred Charlemagne; *b* 19 Jan 1861; *m* 1st 16 June 1897 (*divorce* 1914) Constance (*d* 12 Dec 1948), est dau of Capt Edmund Lyons Green, RN, and had issue:

1a Lydia Abigail Mary; *b* 20 June 1901; *m* 25 April 1925 Ivan Estridge, son of S Estridge, and had issue:

1b *Christopher Robert Ivan; *b* 10 July 1926; *m* 7 June 1952 *Patricia, er dau of John Archibald, and has an adopted son and dau:

*Christopher Ivan; *b* Feb 1960

*Lydia Margaret; *b* April 1962

2a Helen Sybil Mary; *b* 19 Sept 1912; *m* 7 April 1938 Hon Richard Frederick Hope, OBE, 3rd son of 1st Baron Rankeillour, PC (*qv*), and *d* 1971, having had issue

(6) (cont.) Alfred Lambart *m* 2nd 1 June 1920 (*divorce* 1926) Anne (*d* 11 Feb 1943), dau of Rev Andrew Belcher, of Fasque, Kincardineshire, and widow of 5th Earl of Mexborough (*qv*), and *d* 15 Feb 1943

(1) Lydia Annie Georgiana; *b* 14 Sept 1846; *m* 9 Oct 1888 Rev Alfred Arthur Kaye Legge, MA (*see* DARTMOUTH, E), and *d* 25 Nov 1931

(2) Alicia Gundreda Henrietta Caroline; *b* 24 July 1859; *d* unm 6 Jan 1938

The 7th EARL *d* 21 Nov 1837; his gs,

FREDERICK JOHN WILLIAM LAMBART, **8th Earl of the County of Cavan**; *b* 30 Dec 1815; *m* 24 July 1838 Hon Caroline Augusta Littleton (*d* 18 Jan 1892), 3rd dau of 1st Baron Hatherton (*qv*), and had issue, six sons and two daus, of whom:

1 FREDERICK EDWARD GOULD, **9th Earl**

2 Octavus Henry, late Lt 2nd Som Militia; *b* 10 Jan 1855; *m* 15 Oct 1878 Hannah Sarah (*d* 10 March 1911), dau of Hiram Edward Howard, of Buffalo, USA, and *d* 24 Jan 1919, having had, with other issue:

(1) Howard Frederick John, FRGS 1926; *b* 30 Dec 1880; *educ* McGill U Canada (BSc 1904); *m* 1st 10 March 1908 Helen Marianne (*d* 17 Sept 1932), only dau of Samuel Shelley Wallbridge, LLB, of Belleville, Canada; *m* 2nd 1938 May, dau of Hon Robert Bickerdike, of Montreal, and *d* 12 Jan 1946, leaving issue by 1st w:

1a Frederick Arthur Henry, F/O RAF served WW II; *b* 28 Nov 1910; *kas* 13 Aug 1940

2a Edward Howard Wallbridge, Capt RCHA, served WW II; *b* 19 Aug 1917; *ka* in Italy, 17 Dec 1943

1a Helen Hyacinthe; *b* 9 Oct 1908; *educ* McGill U Canada (BA 1930)

2a *Evelyn Mary [Miss Evelyn Lambart, Mudgett Rd, RR 4, Sutton, Quebec, Canada]; *b* 23 July 1914

(1) Caroline Augusta; *b* 14 May 1883; *d* unm 13 July 1949

3 Arthur, Maj RA; *b* 11 Aug 1858; *m* 1883 Winifred Edith (*d* 22 Nov 1926), widow of George Broughton, and *d* 3 April 1937

1 Mary Hyacinthe; *m* 6 May 1875 Baron Hans Von Essen, of Tidaholm, Stockholm, Sweden, and *d* 22 Aug 1933, leaving issue. He *d* 2 July 1894

2 Sarah Sophia; *m* 14 July 1875 Lt-Col Joseph Sladen, late RA, of Ripple Court, Kent, and *d* 8 July 1914, leaving issue. He *d* 17 April 1930

The 8th EARL *d* 16 Dec 1887; his est son,

FREDERICK EDWARD GOULD LAMBART, **9th Earl of the County of Cavan**, KP (1894), PC, DL Somerset; MP (Lib) Somerset S 1885–92, Lt RN, V-Chamberlain Household Feb-July 1886; *b* 21 Oct 1839; *m* 22 July 1863 Mary Sneade (*d* 2 Aug 1905), only child of Rev John Olive, MA, Rector of Ayot St Lawrence, and had issue:

1 FREDERICK RUDOLPH, **10th Earl**

2 Lionel John Olive, DSO (1916), JP Dorset; *b* 16 July 1873; Capt RN, served WW I (despatches); *m* 8 May 1906 Adelaide Douglas (*d* 1972), yr dau of Capt Arthur Randolph Randolph, of Eastcourt, Wilts, and was *ka* June 1940, leaving issue:

(1) Edith Sybil; *b* 11 June 1918; granted rank of earl's dau 1947; *m* 28 Feb 1940 (*divorce* 1974) Ivan Cottam Foxwell, late Maj Roy Norfolk Regt, est son of Lt-Col Herbert Somerton Foxwell, and *d* 31 March 1996, leaving:

1a *Zia [Mrs Zia Kruger, Mill House, W Kington, Chippenham, Wilts SN14 7JQ]; *b* 3 Dec 1940; novelist: *Nothing Lasts Forever* and *Borrowed Time*; *m* 1st 1 Oct 1968 (*divorce* 1991) David Joseph Kruger, est son of Bernard John Kruger, of 1455 Sherbrooke St, W Montreal, Canada, and has issue:

1b *Patrick Gene; *b* 9 Aug 1972

1a (cont.) Mrs Zia Kruger *m* 10th June 1995 (*divorce* 1996, has resumed former married name) Pierre Vacher

2a *Atalanta Edith; *b* 17 Feb 1956; *m* 1973 *Don Stefano, Prince Massimo of Roccasecca dei Volsci, of Rome, and 44 Fernshaw Rd, SW10, s of the actress Dawn Addams, and has issue:

1b *Valerio Francesco; *b* 1973

2b *Cesare Camillo Alessandro; *b* 1977

1b *Tancredi Rara; *b* 1986

3 HORACE EDWARD SAMUEL SNEADE, **11th Earl**

1 Ellen Olive; *b* 12 Aug 1867; *d* unm 17 March 1945

2 Maud Edith Gundreda; *b* 17 April 1869; *m* 1st 25 June 1892 Henry J Barrett, of Swakeleys, Uxbridge (*d* 5 June 1901); *m* 2nd 15 Oct 1930 Geoffrey Birkbeck, JP of Stoke Holy Cross, Norwich, and *d* 2 Nov 1940. He *d* 25 April 1954

The 9th EARL *d* 14 July 1900; his est son,

FREDERICK RUDOLPH LAMBART, **10th Earl of the County of Cavan**, KP (1916), GCB (1926, KCB 1918, CB 1915), GCMG (1919), GCVO (1922, MVO 4th Cl 1910), GBE (1927), DL and JP (Herts); rep I peer 1915, Hon LLD Cambridge 1920, Hon DCL Oxford 1926, chm Nat Playing Fields Assoc 1936, Col Irish Gds 1925 and Beds and Herts Regt 1928–35, cmded 1st Bn Gren Gds 1908–12, T/Brig-Gen cmdg 4th Gds Bde BEF 1914–15, Maj-Gen cmdg Gds Div 1915, Lt-Gen cmdg XIVth Army Corps 1916–17, T/Gen C-in-C BEF Italy 1918–19, Lt Tower London 1920, ADC Gen to HM GEORGE V and GOC-in-C Aldershot 1920, Mil Advsr Br Delegn Washington 1921, CIGS and memb Army Cncl 1922–26, when ret, Ch Staff to HRH THE DUKE OF YORK Australian and NZ Tour 1927, Capt Gentlemen-at-Arms 1929–31, Maj-Gen 1915, Lt-Gen 1917, Gen 1921, FM 1932, served Boer War 1899–1902 (despatches, two medals, five clasps), and WW I (despatches nine times), cmded troops Coronation 1937, Grand Offr Legion of Honour, Crown of Belgium and Savoy, Grand Cross St Maurice and St Lazarus of Italy, Croix de Guerre, Order of Wen-Hu of China 1st Cl, US DSM; *b* 16 Oct 1865; *m* 1st 1 Aug 1893 Caroline Inez (*d* 15 June 1920), est dau of George Baden Crawley (*see* CRAWLEY-BOEVEY, Bt); *m* 2nd 27 Nov 1922 Lady (Hester) Joan Mulholland, DBE (1927) (*d* 31 Aug 1976), yst dau of 5th Earl of Strafford (*qv*) and widow of Capt Hon Andrew Edward Somerset Mulholland, est son of 2nd Baron Dunleath (*qv*), and had issue:

1 *Elizabeth Mary [The Lady Elizabeth Longman, The Old Rectory, Todenham, Moreton-in-Marsh, Glos GL56 9PA]; *b* 16 Oct 1924 (HM QUEEN MARY and HRH THE PRINCESS ROYAL stood sponsors); a bridesmaid to HRH THE PRINCESS ELIZABETH 20 Nov 1947; *m* 20 July 1949 Mark Frederic Kerr Longman, publisher (*d* 6 Sept 1972), 5th son of Henry Kerr Longman, of Wildwood, Pyrford, Surrey, and has issue:

(1) *Caroline Elizabeth; *b* 24 Dec 1951 (HM THE QUEEN stood sponsor); *m* 25 Sept 1982 *Peter Zevenbergen, son of Jan Zevenbergen, of Elcet, Nigeria, and has issue:

1a *Frederick Christian Edmund; *b* 1985

2a *Raphael James; *b* 1991

(2) *Jane; *b* 11 July 1955

(3) *Emma; *b* 14 Jan 1959; *m* 1980 *Timothy James Hanbury, son of James Robert Hanbury, of Burley-on-the-Hill, Oakham, Rutland, and has issue:

1a *David Mark James; *b* 1986

1a *Marina Jane; *b* 1982

2a *Rose Sarah; *b* 1984

2 *Joanna; *b* 8 Dec 1929 (HM QUEEN ELIZABETH THE QUEEN MOTHER stood sponsor); *m* 3 Nov 1955 *Maj Michael Godwin Plantagenet Stourton, Gren Gds, er son of Maj Hon John Joseph Stourton, TD, of Miniature Hall, Wadhurst, Sussex, and has issue (*see* MOWBRAY, SEGRAVE and STOURTON, B)

The 10th EARL *d* 28 Aug 1946; his bro,

Ven HORACE EDWARD SAMUEL SNEADE LAMBART, **11th Earl of the County of Cavan**, Archdeacon Emeritus of Salop and Preb Emeritus of Lichfield Cathedral; *educ* Magdalen Coll Oxford (MA), Vicar of Holy Trinity, Leaton, Shrewsbury 1908–13, Market Drayton 1913–18, and St Mary's Shrewsbury 1918–25, Archdeacon of Salop 1916, Provost of Denstone 1928, late Lt 1st Vol Bn Oxon LI (TD), served in S Africa 1900, and WW I 1914–18; *b* 25 Aug 1878; *m* 9 July 1907 Audrey Kathleen (*d* 8 April 1942), only dau of Alfred Basil Loder, JP, of Aldwickbury, Herts (*see* LODER, Bt), and had issue:

1 MICHAEL EDWARD OLIVER, **12th Earl**

1 Mary Veronica; *b* 12 April 1908; *m* 4 April 1934 Col Edward Henry Cadogan, CBE, late RWF, only child of Lt-Col Henry Osbert Samuel Cadogan, RWF, and had issue:

(1) *Henry Michael Edward, Maj RWF; *b* 18 Jan 1935; *educ* Winchester and RMA Sandhurst; *m* 17 Dec 1966 *Daphne Jane Richards, dau of Harold Ashley Mason, and has issue:

1a *A son; *b* 3 March 1970

1a *Camilla Mary; *b* 4 Nov 1968

(2) *Alexander John; *b* 5 June 1937; *educ* Radley; commnd Kent and Co of London Yeo (Sharpshooters) 1965

(3) *Oliver Roger; *b* 29 Jan 1946; *educ* Radley

2 *Daphne Olive [The Lady Daphne Grierson, 24F Four Limes, Wheathampstead, Herts AL4 8PW]; *b* 22 Dec 1909; *m* 22 Dec 1944 Maj Kenneth Gordon Grierson, E Surrey Regt (*d* 1976), son of Douglas Grierson, barrister, of Shirley, Warwicks, and has issue:

(1) *William; *b* 17 Oct 1947; *educ* Lancing; with BBC since 1967; *m* 1972 *Barbara Edwina, dau of Edwin Locke, of Haywards Heath, Sussex, and has issue:

1a *James Nicholas; *b* 1981

2a *Victoria Caroline; *b* 1977

The 11th EARL *d* 9 Dec 1950; his only son ,

MICHAEL EDWARD OLIVER LAMBART, **12th Earl of the County of Cavan**, TD (1950), DL (Salop 1959) V-Ld Lt (Salop 1975), served WW II (despatches), cmded Shropshire Yeo1955-58, Hon Col from 1974 QO Mercian Yeo TAVR; *b* 29 Oct 1911; *educ* Radley; *m* 10 April 1947 *Essex Lucy [The Rt Hon Essex Countess of Cavan, The Glebe House, Stockton, Shifnal, Salop T11 9EF], only dau of Henry Cholmondeley, of Shotton Hall, Shrewsbury (*see* DELAMERE, B), and *d* 1988, having had:

1 Sarah Audrey; *b* 12 June 1948; *m* 12 Sept 1968 *Capt Alistair Charles Sinclair, late 17th/21st Lancers [Alistair Sinclair Esq, Piccadilly Cottage, Kingston Lisle, Wantage, Oxon OX12 8QU], son of Col David Charles Stranach Sinclair, OBE, JP, of Court Close, Southmoor, Abingdon, Berks, and *d* 26 July 1981 leaving issue:

(1) *Harry Charles Lambart; *b* 28 Jan 1972; *educ* Radley

(2) *Rupert Alistair Grenville; *b* 15 Dec 1973; *educ* Radley

2 Jane Mary; *b* 25 Oct 1949; *d* 17 Dec 1954

3 *Katherine Lucy [The Lady Katherine Lambart, 174 Broomwood Rd, London SW11]; *b* 2 March 1955; has resumed her maiden name; *m* 25 Oct 1978 (*divorce* 1986) Lorenzo Ruiz Bannero, yr son of Lorenzo Ruiz Jimenez and Guadalupe Barrero Alonso, of Jorge Juan 55, Madrid, and has issue:

(1) *Lorenzo Cavan; *b* 28 Aug 1980

(1) *Natasha Pepa; *b* 1982

Cave

Arms: Az. fretty arg., on a fess or a greyhound courant sa., collared of the 2nd, a bordure of the 3rd pelletée. **Crest:** A daisy flower slipped ppr., issuant therefrom a greyhound's head, per pale arg. and sa. guttée counterchanged. **Motto:** *Cave* ('Beware'). **Creation:** Bt. (UK) 21 July 1896.

SIR JOHN CHARLES CAVE, 5TH BT, of Sidbury Manor, Devon [Sir John Cave Bt, Buckley Farm, Sidbury, Sidmouth, Devon EX10 0PS]; *b* 8 Sept 1958; *s f* 1997; *educ* Eton and RAC Cirencester; *m* 24 June 1984 *Carey Diana, er dau of John Lloyd, of Tiverton, Devon, and has:

1 +GEORGE CHARLES; *b* 8 Sept 1987

2 +William Alexander; *b* 7 May 1992

1 *Alice Elizabeth; *b* 28 June 1989

Lineage: THOMAS CAVE/KAVE, of Leigh, Worcs; paid subsidies to the Abbot of Pershore 1453, 1459–60 and 1472; *m* Margaret, widow of (a) Richard Bolles and (b) Richard Rock, of Leigh Sinton, Worcs, and dau of Thomas Hall, and had:

JOHN CAVE/KAVE, of Leigh Sinton; *m* Margaret, widow of — Rufford and dau of Thomas Acton, and had issue:

1 THOMAS

2 Richard; *d* between 30 Nov 1576 and 8 Jan 1576/7; ancestor of the CAVEs of Larport

The er son,

THOMAS CAVE, of Leigh Sinton; *m* Elizabeth Tovy and *d* between 19 Dec 1548 and 30 March 1549, leaving a 2nd son:

RICHARD CAVE, of Leigh Sinton; living 1576 and 1591; *m* Margaret de la Hay and had, with other issue:

1 WILLIAM

2 Thomas, of St Helen's, Worcs; living 1591; *m* Katherine, dau of Walter Jones, of Whitney, Oxon, and had, with other issue:

(1) Richard (Sir); royalist Govr Hereford Castle Civil War; *m* Elizabeth (*m* 2nd Rev Thomas Yates, DD, Pncpl BNC Oxford (ld 22 April 1681), and *d* 11 Jan 1688), dau of Sir Thomas Bartlett, of Senbury, Glos, and was *k* Battle of Naseby 1645, leaving:

1a Henry

1 Catherine; *m* Richard Robinson, of Worcester, and *d* 20 Jan 1587 aged 23, leaving issue

The est son,

WILLIAM CAVE, of Leigh Sinton, living 1576 and 1590/1; fined for not taking knighthood at the coronation of CHARLES I; *m* 1st Eleanor Beale, of Eldersfield, Glos, and had a son; *m* 2nd — and *d* 1654 aged 80, having by her had a dau (*m* — Luddington and had issue); his only son:

WILLIAM CAVE; *m* Anne (*d* 1665), dau of John Browning, of Martley, Worcs, and *dvp* 16 Jan 1617/8, leaving, with daus:

THOMAS CAVE, of Leigh Sinton and Martley; *b* 1612; *m* Elizabeth (*d* 19 April 1693), dau of Richard Arden, of Martley, and *d* 11 June 1692, leaving, with other issue:

1 Richard, Chamberlain of Evesham, Under-Sheriff Worcs; *bapt* 7 Feb 1636; *m* 1656 Anne (*d* 13 oct 1685), dau of John Hunt, of Parkhall, Worcs, by Anne, dau of Thomas Burlton, of Ombersley, Worcs, and *d* 12 July 1690

2 Walter (Rev), Chaplain Ch Ch Oxford, Sizar St John's Coll Cambridge 31 March 1655; MA 1662; incorporated at Oxford 18 Feb 1662/3; *bapt* 21 Dec 1637; *d* 6 Dec 1704

3 William, of Martley; *b* 1654; *m* Oct 1678 Elizabeth (*bur* 23 April 1699), dau of John Ingram, of Rodge Hill, Martley, and *d* Aug 1727, leaving a 3rd son:

(1) Walter, of Avenbury, Herefs; *b* 18 March 1686; *m* Hannah — (*d* 27 April 1741) and *d* 10 July 1731, leaving a 2nd son:

1a Edward, of Pool Hall, Bromyard, which he bought 1742; *bapt* 29 April 1712; *m* Nov 1732 Mary Hallward and was *bur* 9 Jan 1752, leaving, with other issue:

1b Edward, of Buckland, Docklow, Herefs; *bapt* 1733; *d* 1787; ancestor of the CAVEs of Pool Hall, Bromyard

2b John, of Arno's Vale, Bedminster, Somerset, and Bristol; *bapt* 6 April 1736; *m* 1 May 1762 Susanna (*d* 1806), dau and heiress of Stephen Cox, of Sturminster Newton, Dorset, and Bristol, and *d* 1800, leaving, with two other sons:

1c STEPHEN

2c John, of Brentry, Henbury, Glos, and Powick; *b* 1765; *m* Penelope, dau of Thomas Oliver (the last pre-Independence Lt-Govr of Massachusetts; *d* Bristol, UK, 1815), and *d* 1842; ancestor of the CAVEs of Brentry

1c Susanna; *b* 1767; *m* Thomas Daniel, of Bristol

The est son,

STEPHEN CAVE, of Cleve Hill, Glos, DL, JP Glos, Quartermaster Bristol Vols 1803; *b* 8 March 1763; *m* 1 May 1787 Anne (*d* 1851), dau of Thomas Daniel, of Bristol and Barbados, and *d* 18 Feb 1838, leaving:

1 DANIEL

2 Charles, of 23 Lowndes St, London; *b* 1796; *m* Sarah, dau of Edward Carlton Cumberbatch, of Bristol and Barbados, and *d* 1887, leaving issue

3 George, of Burfield, nr Bristol, DL, JP Glos; *b* 21 Feb 1798; *m* Anne (*d* 1888), dau of Capt Halliday, RN, and *d* 15 April 1877, leaving issue

Harriet; *b* 1801; *m* John New, of Cradoch, Devon, and *d* 1883, leaving issue

The est son,

DANIEL CAVE, of Cleve Hill, Glos, and Sidbury Manor, Devon, JP, MA Oxford, High Sheriff Bristol 1836; *b* 22 April 1789; *m* 15 April 1820, Frances (*d* 1 May 1854), dau of Henry Locock, MD, of Northampton, and *d* 9 March 1872 having had, with other issue:

1 Stephen Cave (Rt Hon Sir), of Cleve Hill and Sudbury Manor, PC, GCB, DL, JP Glos, FSA; *b* 28 Sept 1820; MA, barrister; MP New Shoreham and Rape of Bramber 1859; Paymaster-Gen and V-Pres BOT July 1866–Dec 1868; JAG Jan 1874–Nov 1875; Paymaster-Gen from Jan 1874; special envoy to Egypt 1875–76; Commr in Paris for negotiating fishery convention 1886–87; *m* 1852 Emma Jan (*d* 13 Nov 1905), est dau of Rev William Smyth, of Elkington Hall, Lincoln, Preb Lincoln, and *dsp* 7 June 1880

2 CHARLES DANIEL (Sir), **1st Bt**

1 Frances; *m* 1855 George Lyall, of Headley, Surrey, MP Whitehaven, and *d* 1893, having had issue. He *d* 1881

2 Susannah; *m* 1851 John J L Bayley, of Alderley, Glos, and had issue. He *d* 1860

3 Eleanor; *m* 1873 Rev Charles A Alington, of Swinhope, and *d* 5 May 1874. He *d* 30 May 1899

The 3rd son,

Sir Charles Daniel Cave, 1st Bt (UK), so *cr* 21 July 1896, JP (Glos and Devon), DL (Glos); *b* 17 Sept 1832; *educ* Exeter Coll Oxford (MA), High Sheriff Bristol 1863, and Devon 1898, dir Union of London and Smith's Bank Ltd; *m* 1 Sept 1859 Edith Harriet (*d* 5 Aug 1912), dau of John Addington Symonds, MD, of Clifton, and had issue:

1 Daniel Charles Addington, FSA, JP Glos and Devon; *b* 17 May 1860; *d* unm 23 July 1901

2 CHARLES HENRY (Sir), **2nd Bt**

3 Walter Frederick; *b* 17 Sept 1863; *m* 21 June 1892 Jessica Maria (medal of Queen Elisabeth of Belgium) (*d* 11 Oct 1934), dau of Hugh Cochrane, of Montreal, Canada, and *d* 7 Jan 1939, leaving issue:

(1) Richard Walter Dundonald; *b* 15 Sept 1901; *educ* Eton; *m* 22 March 1934 Joan Elizabeth, yst dau of Charles Lyon Liddell, JP (*see* RAVENSWORTH, B)

4 Arthur Stephen, Maj late Princess Charlotte of Wales's Roy Berks Regt; *b* 24 June 1865; *m* 10 Jan 1905 Emily Ina Graham, (*d* 20 March 1972 aged 89), est dau of Roland Lyons Nosworthy Mitchell, CMG, of 22 Lansdowne Crescent, W11 and *d* 13 July 1945, leaving issue:

(1) Ronald Arthur, ACSM, AMIMM; *b* 20 June 1910; *educ* Cambridge U (BA); *m* 2 Jan 1937 *Audrey Oenone [Mrs Ronald Cave, Ramblers, Holford, Somerset], yst dau of Dr Francis Joseph Child, of Penlee, Weybridge, and *d* 18 Sept 1964, leaving issue:

1a *Diana Ann; *b* 11 April 1938; *m* 21 July 1957 *Charles Thoburn Maxwell II, son of Charles Thoburn Maxwell, of Indianapolis, Indiana, USA, and has issue:

1b *Bruce Maxwell; *b* 1959

2b *Steven Maxwell; *b* 1961

3b *Brandon Maxwell; *b* 1964

2a *Sylvia Margaret; *b* 26 April 1944; *m* 1992 *Richard Antony Hackney

1 Edith Frances; *d* unm 17 Nov 1949

Sir CHARLES *d* 29 Oct 1922; his son,

Sir Charles Henry Cave, 2nd Bt, JP (Glos and Devon); *b* 17 Mar 1861; *educ* New Coll Oxford (BA), High Sheriff Devon 1926; *m* 12 Jan 1892 Beatrice Julia, OBE (1918) (*d* 7 Nov 1951), 3rd dau of Sir Frederick Martin Williams, 2nd Bt, of Tregullow, Cornwall (*qv*), and had issue:

1 EDWARD CHARLES (Sir), **3rd Bt**

2 Walter Henry Charles, Lt Dorset Regt; *b* 15 March 1895; *ka* 15 March 1915

3 Victor Charles; *b* 20 June 1897; *d* unm 5 Nov 1960

Sir CHARLES *d* 26 July 1932; his est son,

Sir Edward Charles Cave, 3rd Bt, JP; *b* 2 Jan 1893; *educ* Eton and Magdalene Coll Cambridge; served with Somerset LI WWI 1915–19; *m* 19 July 1922 (*divorce* 1942) Betty Christabel Gertrude (*d* 1979), only dau of Maj Rennell Coleridge (*see* COLERIDGE, B), and *d* 4 Oct 1946, leaving:

1 **Sir Charles Edward Coleridge Cave, 4th Bt**, JP (Devon 1972), DL (Devon 1977); *b* 28 Feb 1927; *educ* Eton; FRICS, High Sheriff Devon 1969; Lt Devonshire Regt 1946–48, CC Devon 1955–64; *m* 15 June 1957 *Mary Elizabeth [Mary Lady Cave, Sidbury Manor, Sidmouth, Devon EX10 0QE], yr dau of John Francis Gore, CVO, TD, of Littlehay, Burley, Hants (*see* ARRAN, E), and *d* 1 Nov 1997, having had:

(1) Sir JOHN CHARLES CAVE, **5th and present Bt**

(2) +Nicholas Stephen [Nicholas Cave Esq, Bishops Court, Fluxton, Ottery St Mary, Devon EX11 1RJ]; *b* 22 April 1961; *m* 1991 *A Frances, er dau of Simon Hicks, of Battersea, and Mrs Patty Gordon, and has:

1a +Frederick Stephen; *b* 9 Sept 1995
1a *Harriet Patricia; *b* 9 Sept 1995
2a *Louisa Elizabeth; *b* 10 Sept 1996
(3) Thomas; *b* 26, *d* 27 July 1962
(4) +Thomas Henry; *b* 23 Sept 1964
(5) +Richard Hugh; *b* 4 May 1967; *m* 27 April 1996 *Emily Heber-Percy (*see* NORTHUMBERLAND, D) and has:
1a *Olivia Jane; *b* 23 April 1997
1 Rosemary Betty; *b* 14 Oct 1924; *d* 1 Sept 1964
2 *Daphne Frances [Miss Daphne Cave, Greenhead, Sidbury, Sidmouth, Devon]; *b* 3 March 1930

CAVE-BROWNE-CAVE

Arms: Quarterly, 1st and 4th, az. fretty arg. (for CAVE); 2nd and 3rd, az. a chevron between three escallops or, a bordure engrailed gu. (for BROWNE). **Crests:** 1, A greyhound courant sa., collared arg., 2, A stork ppr., winged and gorged with a ducal crown or, beaked and membered gu. (for BROWNE). **Motto:** *Gardez* ('Beware'). **Creation:** Bt. (E) 30 June 1641.

SIR ROBERT CAVE-BROWNE-CAVE, 16TH BT, of Stanford, Co Northampton [Sir Robert Cave-Browne-Cave Bt, 20901–83 Ave, RR11, Langley, BC V3A 6Y3, Canada]; *b* 8 June 1929; *s f* 1945; *educ* St George's Sch Vancouver, U Sch Victoria, U of BC (BA 1951); pres Seaboard Chemicals Ltd, KStJ 1986; *m* 1st 12 June 1954 (*divorce* 1975) Lois Shirley, dau of John Chalmers Huggard, of Winnipeg, Manitoba, Canada; *m* 2nd 1977 *Joan Shirley, dau of Dr Kenneth Ashe Peacock, of W Vancouver, BC, and has issue by 1st w:

1 +JOHN ROBERT CHARLES; *b* 22 June 1957
1 *Lisé Irene; *b* 19 May 1955

Lineage: WYAMARUS de CAVE; granted 1080 land in N Cave and S Cave, Yorks, but *dsp*, having made it over to his bro:

JORDAN de CAVE; had:

BRIAN de CAVE; had:

ROBERT de CAVE; *m* —, dau of Thomas de Metham, and had:

THOMAS de CAVE; *m* Joyce, dau of William St Quintin, feudal Ld of Byrans Burton, and had, with other issue:

GEOFFREY de CAVE; *m* Mabel, dau of Robert de Talso, and had, with another s (Alexander de Cave, Dean of Durham, *dsp*):

PETER de CAVE; *m* —, dau and heir of Sir Thomas Bromflete, and had, with three daus:

1 ALEXANDER
2 Thomas, ancestor of the CAVEs of Flinton

The er son,

Sir ALEXANDER CAVE; living 1275; *m* —, dau of Peter de Malodaen, feudal Ld of Mulgrave, and had, with four daus (Jane, *m* Thomas Skelton, of Skelton; Ursula, *m* Sir John Ella, of Kirk Ella; Joyce, *m* Sir Thomas Pollington; Margaret, *m* Ralph Andleby):

PETER CAVE; *m* Anne, dau of Sir Simon Ward, Kt, and had, with two daus:

Sir ALEXANDER CAVE; *m* Amphelicia, dau of Sir Jeoffrey Hotham, and had, with four daus (Margaret, *m* Ansel St Quintin, of Brayns Burton; Jane, *m* Sir Roger Kelke; Mary, *m* Sir John Risbye; Elizabeth, *m* William Ellerker):

Sir JOHN CAVE; *m* —, dau and heir of Peter Genille, of S Cliffe, and had an est s:

Sir ALEXANDER CAVE; *m* Katharine, dau of Roger Somerville, of Grindall, Yorks, and had, with a yr s (Alexander (Sir)) and three daus (Grace; Katharine, *m* Sir John Markenfield; Anne, *m* Gilbert Stapleton, of Boyton, Yorks):

PETER CAVE; *m* Anne, dau of Ralph Ingleby, and had, with two yr s:

PETER CAVE; *m* Mary, dau of — Burdett, of Rothwell, Northants, and had:

THOMAS CAVE; *m* Thomasine, dau of Passamer, of Essex, and had, with three other s:

1 RICHARD, his heir
2 John, ggf of Francis Cave, of Sinecross, Leics

The est son,

RICHARD CAVE, of Stanford, Northants; *m* 1st Elizabeth, dau of John Marvyn, of Church Lawford, Warwicks, and had, with a dau:

1 Edward, of Wenwick, Northants; had two daus and coheirs (Catharine, *m* Sir Thomas Andrews; Margaret, *m* Thomas Boughton)

RICHARD CAVE *m* 2nd Margaret, dau of Sir Thomas Saxby, of Northants, by whom he had, with other daus:

2 THOMAS (Sir)
3 Anthony, of Chicheley, Bucks; had four daus and coheirs (the est, Judith, *m* Wm Chester)
4 Ambrose (Sir), PC *temp* ELIZABETH I; Chllr Duchy Lancaster; *m* Margery, dau and coheir of William Willington, of Barcheston, Warwicks, and *d* 2 April 1568, leaving an only dau:
(1) Margaret; *m* Henry Knollys
5 Francis; ancestor of the CAVEs of Bargrave
6 Richard, of Pickwell, Leics; *m* Barbara, dau of Sir William Feilding, of Newnham (*see* DENBIGH and DESMOND, E), and was ancestor of the CAVEs of Yateley, Hants
7 Brian, of Ingarsby, Leics; *m* 1st Margaret, dau of Sir George Throckmorton; *m* 2nd Bridget, dau of Sir William Skipwith

The est son of the 2nd marriage,

Sir THOMAS CAVE, of Stanford, Northants; *m* Elizabeth, dau and coheir of Sir John Danvers, of Waterstock, Oxon, and had, with other issue:

1 ROGER, his heir
1 Margaret, w of Sir William Meringe, of Meringe
2 Elizabeth, w of Sir Humphrey Stafford, of Blatherwick, Northants

The son and heir,

ROGER CAVE, of Stanford; *m* Margaret, sis of 1st Baron Burghley (*see* EXETER, M), and *d* 26 July 1586, having had, with three s (including Sir William Cave) and three daus (including Margaret, *m* Sir William Skipwith, of Coates; and Frances, *m* Sir Edmund Bussey):

Sir THOMAS CAVE; *m* Eleanor, dau of Nicholas St John, of Lydiard Tregoze, Wilts, and had, with at least two daus (Eleanor, *m* 1st Sir Thomas Rowe, Chllr of the Garter, *m* 2nd Sir George Beeston; Alice (7th dau), *m* John Skeffington; *see* MASSEREEN, E and FERRARD, V):

Sir THOMAS CAVE; *m* Elizabeth, dau of Sir Herbert Croft, of Croft Castle, Herefs (*see* CROFT, Bt, of Croft), and left, with a dau (Dorothy, *m* Sir Rowland Berkeley, of Cotheridge), an only s:

Sir Thomas Cave, 1st Bt (E), so *cr* 30 June 1641; ktd, royalist Civil War; *m* 1st Katharine, dau of Sir Anthony Haslewood, of Maydwell, Northants, but by her had no issue; *m* 2nd Penelope, 2nd dau and coheir of 2nd Viscount Wenman, and by her had, with other issue:

1 ROGER (Sir), **2nd Bt**
2 Ambrose, Brig Life Gds; *k* 1690 by one Biron, an offr who bore a long-standing grudge against him and ran a sword through Ambrose's back as he sat in the banqueting hall at Greenwich; Biron was never caught
1 Mary; *m* by licence 28 Sept 1670 Sir Oriando Bridgeman, 2nd Bt, of the second *cr* (*see* BRADFORD, E)

The 1st Bt *d* by Feb 1671; his est son,

Sir Roger Cave, 2nd Bt, MP Coventry; *m* 1st 24 Feb 1675/6 Martha, dau and heir of John Browne, of Eydon, Northants, Clerk of Parl, and had, with other issue:

1 **Sir Thomas Cave, 3rd Bt**, MP Leics; *m* 20 Feb 1703 Margaret (*d* 17 May 1774), dau of 1st Viscount Fermanagh (*see* VERNEY, Bt, of Claydon), and *d* 21 April 1719, having had an er s:
(1) **Sir Verney Cave, 4th Bt**; *b* 4 Jan 1704/5; *d* unm 13 Sept 1734
(2) **Sir Thomas Cave, 5th Bt**, barrister Inner Temple; *b* 27 May 1712; *m* 1736 Elizabeth (*d* 15 May 1760), only dau and heir of Griffith Davies, MD, by Elizabeth, dau of Sir John Burgoyne, Bt, and *d* 7 Aug 1778, leaving:
1a **Sir Thomas Cave, 6th Bt**; *b* 22 Aug 1737; *m* Sarah (*d* July 1819), dau of John Edwards, London merchant, and *d* 30 May 1780, leaving:
1b **Sir Thomas Cave, 7th Bt**, MP Leics; *b* 6 Oct 1766; *m* 3 June 1791 Lucy (*m* 2nd 20 Aug 1798 Hon Philip Bouverie-Pusey, son of 1st Viscount Folkestone (*see* RADNOR, E), and *d* 27 March 1858), only dau of 4th Earl of Harborough, and *dsp* 15 Jan 1792, when his estates passed to his sis
1b Sarah, heiress to her bro; *m* 25 Feb 1790 Henry Otway (*d* 13 Sept 1815), er bro of Adml Sir Robert Otway, Bt, and had issue (*see* BRAYE, B)
2a **Rev Sir Charles Cave, 8th Bt**, MA Oxford, FSA, Rector of Finedon, Northants; *b* 1747; *d* unm 21 March 1810
(1) Elizabeth; *m* Sir John Cheshire, Serjeant-at-Law, and *d* 16 Aug 1705

Sir Roger *m* 2nd Mary (*d* 22 Nov 1721, dau of Sir William Bromley, KB, and *d* 11 Oct 1703, having by her had:

2 Roger, of Eydon, Northants, and Raunston, Leics; *m* 1721 Catherine (*d* 6 May 1772), dau and coheir of William Browne, of Stretton, Derbys (*see* below, **Lineage (of Browne):**), and *d* March 1741, leaving, with other issue:
(1) John CAVE later CAVE-BROWNE (added by Act of Parl 1752 on inheriting the Stretton estate from his gf William Browne); *m* 1st 6 Dec 1757 Frances (*dsp*, *bur* 25 Oct 1758), dau of Theodore William Inge, of Thorpe Constantine; *m* 2nd 3 Jan 1764 Catherine (*d* 8 Sept 1811), dau and heir of Thomas Asteley, of Wood Eaton, Staffs, and Asteley, Salop, and *d* 2 Oct 1798, leaving, with other issue:
1a WILLIAM (Sir), **9th Bt**
2a John (Rev), Rector of Stretton; *b* 20 Sept 1767; *m* 1 May 1798 Margaret (*d* 21 Nov 1851), dau of Robert Haymes, and *d* 23 March 1843, leaving issue
3a Edward, Lt-Col HEICS; *b* 15 Nov 1779; *m* 8 Oct 1815 Ann (*d* 11 July 1876), dau of Thomas Raban, of Calcutta, and *d* 26 July 1841, leaving, with other issue:
1b John (Rev), MA Oxford, Vicar of Detling, Maidstone; *b* 17 Jan 1818; *m* 1st 7 May 1851 Selina Mary (*d* 7 Sept 1881), dau of Lt-Col William Turner, Bengal Army, and had issue:

1c Edward; *b* 14 Sept 1856; *m* 20 July 1886 Norah (*d* 19 March 1955), dau of Lt-Col William Joseph Gorman, and *d* 21 June 1895, leaving issue:

1d Edward Raban, planter; *b* 5 Jan 1889; unm 9 Dec 1958

1d Dorothy Sela; *m* 7 Sept 1922 Robert Flemyng Prideaux, Town Clerk of Shrewsbury, 2nd son of Rev Canon Walter Cross Prideaux, of Bristol, and Halberton, Devon, and had issue. He *d* 26 April 1952

2c John Asteley, Assist Commr Chittagong Hill Tracts, India; *b* 15 Nov 1860; *m* 13 Jan 1894 Amy Burvill (*d* 29 Oct 1904), dau of Lt-Col W B Holmes, RE, and *dsp* 30 Aug 1904

3c William Charles, Assist Auditor S Indian Railway; *b* 25 Aug 1867; *m* 12 Dec 1895 Maude Alice (*d* 7 July 1949), dau of Maj-Gen W J Jones, MSC, and *d* 4 Nov 1916, leaving issue:

1d Selina Verney Cleveland; *m* 18 June 1923 Alan Kingsford Watts (*d* 18 March 1957), son of W H Watts, of Folkstone, and had issue:

1e *Patricia Sela; *b* 15 Sept 1927; *m* 1 Nov 1947 Harold Keith Gerow, son of Archibald Cameron Gerow, and has issue:

1f *Rodney Dale; *b* 8 Dec 1948

2f *Donald Keith; *b* 26 April 1952; *m* 1978 *Carol Newnes, and has issue

3f *Terry Francis; *b* 24 March 1954

4f *Randal Kingsford; *b* 15 May 1958; *m* 1980 *Debbie Scott, and has issue

5f *Cameron Lee; *b* 2 March 1962; *m* 1984 *Dianne Kinnear, and has issue

2e *Joan Genille; *b* 14 Jan 1931; *m* 1st 8 Nov 1949 Iain Blair MacAlister (*d* 1970); *m* 2nd 1973 *George Wilfred Yates, and by 1st husb has issue:

1f *Laurence Blair; *b* 19 June 1950; *m* 1974 *Janice Hodges, and has issue

2f *Robert Kingsford; *b* 22 Nov 1951

1f *Vicki Joan; *b* 20 Nov 1952; *m* 1972 *Sheldon Winston Hotte, and has issue

2d Joyce Marian Asteley; *m* 4 Dec 1934 Rev Canon Florian Morgan Sanger-Davies, 5th son of Rev Joseph Sanger-Davies. He *d* 4 Jan 1963

1c Annette Forbes; *m* 9 Sept 1880 Arthur George Burney, barrister, of The Weir, Hereford, and *d* 30 Aug 1937 leaving issue. He *d* 20 Jan 1924

2c Selina Margaret; *m* 9 May 1901 Rev George Thomas Palmer, MA, Hon Canon of Rochester and Rector of St Mary's, Newington, SE, and *d* 26 April 1934. He *d* 7 Dec 1908

3c Edith Mary; *d* unm 4 Nov 1916

4c Mabel Catherine; *m* 4 July 1893 James Murray Dale, of Aldeburgh, son of James Murray Dale, of Aldeburgh, Suffolk, and *d* 16 Aug 1960, leaving issue. He *d* 4 Dec 1921

1b (cont.)The Rev John Cave-Browne *m* 2nd 19 Aug 1884, Marian (*d* 6 June 1926), dau of William Tiffin Iliff, MD, of Newington, Surrey, and widow of Samuel Bastock, of Walton Heath, Surrey, and *d* 13 June 1898

2b William Henry (Rev), MA Oxford, late Rector of Wickham St Paul, Essex; *b* 26 Nov 1827; *m* 1st 29 July 1852 Henrietta (*d* 16 May 1856), dau of Philip Selfe, of Marten, Wilts, and had, with other issue:

1c Henry; *b* 30 April 1856; *m* 22 Nov 1900 Nina Christiana (*d* 11 Jan 1950), yst dau of Rev Newton J Spicer, Rector of E Woodhay, and *dsp* 17 Dec 1947

2b (cont.) The Rev William Cave-Browne *m* 2nd 22 Aug 1865 Louisa (*d* 17 Oct 1885), dau of George Munday, of Kennington, and *d* 2 May 1908, having by her had issue

3b Edward Raban, CSI, late Accountant-Gen India Office 1893–1901; *b* 29 May 1835; *m* 17 July 1879 Caroline Anne (*d* 26 Sept 1931), dau of William Abbott Green, Inspr-Gen of Hospitals, Bengal, and *d* 16 June 1907, leaving issue:

1c William, CBE (1937), DSO (1919), MC, Maj-Gen, late RE, Ch Engr Malaya 1935–38, Ch Engr Eastern Cmd 1938–40, and Dir of Fortifications and Works, War Office 1940–41, served in Abor operations 1911–12 (despatches), and WW I (despatches three times), and WW II 1939–41 (despatches twice), Order of Nile 4th Cl; *b* 18 Sept 1884; *educ* Shrewsbury; *m* 14 Feb 1916 Muriel (*d* 19 July 1971), er dau of J W Wainwright, AMICE, and *d* 1 Nov 1967, having had issue

1d John Raban, MC, Brig late RE, served WW II (despatches); *b* 6 Jan 1917; *educ* King's Sch, Bruton, and Pembroke Coll Cambridge (BA 1939); *m* 3 Dec 1940 *Ulrica Ellen, dau of Maj Frank Paget-Hoblyn, IA, and *d* 1989, having had issue:

1e *Susan Margaret; *b* 24 July 1942; *m* 12 Dec 1969 *Richard Laybourne Perry, er son of Lt-Col H St M Perry, of Warren Ho, Merrion, nr Pembroke, and has issue

2e *Ulrica Sarah; *b* 18 June 1946; *m* 7 June 1969 Patrick Lawrence Covernton, yr son of Maj John Lawrence Covernton, of Burywood Cottage, Bovington, Herts, and has issue

2d William Geoffrey; *b* 3 Oct 1920; *d* unm March 1941

3d Edward Henry, F/O RAFVR, served WW II; *b* 8 March 1923; *k* on air operations, Feb 1943

1d *Caroline Jane [Mrs Derek Brightman, Keepers, Dunsfold, Surrey]; *b* 11 Aug 1926; *m* 20 March 1948 *Derek Marten Brightman, DSC, only son of Cecil Frederick Brightman, of 13 Frognal Lane, NW3, and has issue:

1e *Christopher Marten; *b* 20 Jan 1949; *educ* Fettes

2e *Jeremy Richard; *b* 22 May 1951; *educ* Harrow

1e *Elizabeth Jane; *b* 11 Oct 1953

2e *Nicola Anne; *b* 10 Feb 1959

2c Horace, Maj late 23rd Cav FF and PAVO, Cavalry FF, IA, served WW I in Mesopotamia; *b* 1 Jan 1886; *educ* Charterhouse; *m* 7 July 1920 Alice Rose (*d* 18 Jan 1972, aged 83), dau of Col Patrick Alexander, Weir, IMS, of Farnham Common, Bucks, and *d* 15 March 1960, leaving issue:

1d +Patrick Norman Rose [Maj Patrick Cave-Browne, 150 Greenbank Rd, Edinburgh EH10 5RN], Maj 1st N Rhodesia Regt (ret 1961), formerly Capt Seaforth Highrs, and Rhodesia and Nyasaland Staff Corps; *b* 5 Jan 1926; *educ* Charterhouse; *m* 3 Nov 1956 *Mary Davy, yr dau of Lt-Col Montagu Francis Davy Cobbold, 4th Gurkhas, and has issue:

1e *Margaret Alison; *b* 26 Sept 1959; *m* 1981 *Alan MacLellan Millar and has:

1f *Robert Ewan MacLellan; *b* 19 Nov 1987

2f *Stuart Alexander Cave; *b* 2 June 1989

2e *Ann Mary; *b* 17 June 1961; *m* 3 Sept 1994 *Gerald Reginald Clark and has:

1f *Keith Charles Cave; *b* 31 May 1995

1f *Kenna Mary Rose; *b* 5 March 1997

1d *Alison Barbara Rose; *b* 3 Oct 1932; served WRNS; *m* 2 March 1954 Maj Robin John Ronald Campbell, Seaforth Highrs, er son of Col Robert Campbell, DSO, Cameron Highrs (*see* CAWDOR, E), and has issue

3c Frederick; *b* 10 April 1889; *d* unm 19 Nov 1956

1c Ann; *b* 2 Feb 1881; *d* unm 15 Feb 1947

2c Mary; *m* 20 Sept 1906 Spencer Domett Secretan, MP, yr son of Holford Secretan, of Reigate, Surrey, and *d* 19 June 1934, leaving issue. He *d* 27 March 1965

3 Mary; *m* Sir William Dixwell, Bt, who *dsp* Feb 1712/3

4 Eleanor; *m* 1st Sir Holland Egerton, Bt (*see* GREY EGERTON, Bt); *m* 2nd John Brooke, and *d* Sept 1734, leaving issue

The 8th Bt's cousin,

Sir WILLIAM CAVE-BROWNE later CAVE-BROWNE-CAVE (added soon after his inheriting the btcy, and confirmed to his male issue by roy lience 18 Jan 1839), **9th Bt**, of Stanford; *b* 19 Feb 1765; *m* 1st 13 Oct 1788 Sarah (*dsp* 21 June 1790), dau of Thomas Prinsep; *m* 2nd 4 Jan 1793 Louisa (*d* 23 April 1824), 4th dau of Sir Robert Meade Wilmot, Bt (*qv*), and by her had, with other issue:

1 JOHN ROBERT (Sir), **10th Bt**

2 William Astley (Rev), MA Oxford, Rector of Stretton-en-le Field 1843–62; *b* 3 Aug 1799; *m* 1st 2 May 1828 Elizabeth Martha (*dsp* 6 Nov 1828), yr dau of Samuel Wathen, of New House, Glos; *m* 2nd 25 March 1830 Julia (*d* 6 Sept 1866), dau of Thomas Minton, of Stoke, Staffs, and *d* 13 June 1862, leaving, with other issue:

(1) William Cecil (Rev), MA Oxford, Vicar of St Thomas, Sydney, NSW; *b* 8 Oct 1835; *m* 1st Feb 1864 Rachel Perrins (*d* 1904), dau of Rev Hugh Smith Cumming; *m* 2nd Edith Evans, and *d* July 1913

(2) Fitzherbert Astley (Rev), Vicar of Longridge, Lancs, MA Oxford; *b* 26 Oct 1839; *m* 1st 5 Jan 1869 Harriet Ellen (*d* 20 May 1873), dau of William Beckwith, of Seacox Heath, and had issue:

1a Cecil Beckwith; *b* 22 Nov 1871; *educ* Eton and BNC Oxford (BA); *m* 1st 4 Feb 1896 Sarah Eleanor (*d* 16 March 1928), dau of J W Nicholson, and had issue:

1b Cecil Fitzherbert *b* 29 Aug 1901; *d* an infant

1a (cont.) Cecil Cave-Browne-Cave *m* 2nd 1 June 1929 Edith Beatrice (*d* 20 Aug 1948), dau of Alfred Evans, of Chesham Bois, Bucks, and *d* 5 Jan 1953 having by her had issue:

1b *Penelope Margaret Cecil [Mrs Timothy ffrench-Mullen, c/o Barclays Bank, 31 Ave de la Costa, Monaco 98000]; *b* 5 Dec 1931; *m* 4 Sept 1965 Timothy Fitzgerald ffrench-Mullen (*d* 1987), of 4 Smith St, SW3, s of Lt-Col Douglas ffrench-Mullen, and has had:

1c Candetta Lydia Cecil; *b* 18 Sept 1966; *d* 1982

2c *Tara Eve Siobhan; *b* 6 May 1970; *m* 4 Dec 1993 *Mark Burnyeat

2b *Catherine Priscilla Astley; *b* 27 Feb 1937; *m* 14 Oct 1958 *David Edward Stuart Bates, 39, Camino de la Luz, La Orotava, Tenerife, Canary Islands, only son of Capt S A Bates, of Palstre Court, Wittersham, Kent, and has issue

1c Joanna; *b* 23 July 1959

(2) (cont.) The Rev F A Cave-Browne-Cave *m* 2nd 23 June 1875 Frances Esther Anne (*d* 8 Oct 1916), yst dau of Courtney Kenny Clarke, of Larch Hill, Co Dublin, and *d* 14 Jan 1894, having by her had issue:

2a William Astley; *b* 15 Nov 1884; *d* unm 1 July 1908

3a Courtney Priestley Edwards; *b* 4 Dec 1890; *m* 6 Jan 1915 Helen Freda (*d* 26 July 1955), only dau of A J Cable, of Epping, and *d* 31 Aug 1961, leaving issue:

1b +Paul Astley, JP (Southampton) [Paul Cave-Browne-Cave Esq, 32 Crofton Close, Highfield, Hants SO2 1XB]; *b* 27 Feb 1917; printer and publisher, served WW II as Capt Gen List in Germany; *m* 7 Dec 1940 *Joan Myfanwy, dau of Thomas Norman Jones, JP, of Rhyl, and has issue:

1c +Paul; *b* 1 May 1954; *educ* Manchester U (BA); *m* 1979 *Jane, dau of Maj J Reeves, of St Austell, Cornwall

1c *Jane; *b* 31 Aug 1943; *m* Birmingham U (BSc); *m* 1980 *Eugene Versluysen

2c *Adrienne; *b* 23 Jan 1947; *educ* New Hall, Cambridge; *m* 1968 *Clifford Burrows, BA, son of Frederick Burrows, of Haresflinch, Lancs

3c *Sarah; *b* 1959; *m* 1983 *James Chiriankandath and has issue

2b +Lyndon Fraser, [Lyndon Cave-Browne-Cave Esq, 24 Portland St, Leamington Spa, Warwicks CV32 5EY]; *b* 4 July 1923; *educ* Liverpool U (Dip Arch), MPhil (Warwick U), FSA; *m* 1952 *Betty, only dau of Walter Rush, of Dinnington, Yorks, and has issue:

1c +Anthony John; *b* 1952; LLB London; *m* 1980 *Susan Margaret, dau of K G L Chalk, of Leamington Spa, and has issue:

1d +Edmund Jonathan; *b* 1981

1d *Melissa Betty; *b* 1983

2c +Bernard James William (Rev) [Rev Bernard Cave-Browne-Cave, 97 Barton Rd, Lancaster, Lancs]; *b* 1954; *educ* Cambridge U (MA); Chaplain Lancaster U; *m* 1977 *Rosalind, GRNCM, LRAM, only dau of Col Oliver Robert Corbett, ERD, and has issue:

1d +James William; *b* 1979
1d *Lucy Marie; *b* 1983
3b +Anthony, DSO (1945) [Anthony Cave-Browne-Cave Esq DSO, Cheney Longville, Craven Arms, Salop SY7 8DR]; *b* 4 March 1925; Capt 6th Bn S Wales Borderers, served WW II Burma, and in Indonesia as Bde Intell Offr, 4th Indian Inf Bde; ARIBA (1954); *m* 10 Dec 1957 *Dinah Ann, dau of John William Mitchell, of E Wall, Longville, Much Wenlock, Salop, and has had issue:
1c Genille Anthony; *b* 1 Jan 1959; *d* 1977
2c +Courtney Peter; *b* 23 April 1961; *m* 1988 *Rachel Sarah, dau of Brian Fish, of Ettington, Warwicks, and has issue:
1d +Jack Priestley; *b* 1994
1d *Amy Ann; *b* 1995
3c +Jonathan Lyndon; *b* 14 July 1962
4c +William Astley; *b* 4 Jan 1967; *m* 1988 *Lorraine Katharine, dau of Philip Wood, of Leamington Spa, and has issue:
1d *Alexandra Grace
2d *Isabella Poppy; *b* 1995
3d *Verity Jade; *b* 1997
4b +Bernard Adrian [Bernard Cave-Browne-Cave Esq, 49 Sunvale Crescent SE, Calgary, Alberta T2X 2S7, Canada]; *b* 8 May 1926; Lt 2nd Bn Middx Regt, served WW II in Germany and Palestine; *m* 7 Oct 1961 (*divorce* 1975) Ann, dau of Richard George William Pritchard, JP, of Roddis Ho, Wellesbourne, Warwicks, and has issue:
1c +Richard Ambrose; *b* 1962
2c +Rowland Fraser; *b* 1966
1c Helen Ann; *b* 1963; *m* 1991 *Rui Manuel Martins, and has issue
1a Frances Catharine Delia; *d* unm 9 Feb 1926
2a Mary Julia Minton; *d* unm 5 Dec 1953
3a Violet Gertrude; *d* unm June 1928
4a Florence Mabel Fitzherbert; *d* unm
5a Lucy Wilmot; *d* unm 23 April 1929
6a Elsie Lilian; *d* an infant, 21 May 1888
(1) Louisa Wilmot; *m* 3 Aug 1854 Colin Minton Campbell, MP, DL, of Hartshill, Stafford, and *d* 9 Aug 1909, leaving issue. He *d* 8 Feb 1885
3 Thomas, of Cliff Hall, Warwicks, and Repton Lodge, Derbys; *b* 16 June 1801; *m* 10 April 1827 Anne (*d* 27 March 1875), dau of John Walker, of Levenshulme, Lancs, and *d* 17 April 1854, leaving, with other issue:
(1) John Walker (Rev), of Lifford Hall, King's Norton, Worcs, and Clarence Ho, Southport; *b* 5 Sept 1828; *m* 3 Feb 1850 Hannah (*d* 23 Jan 1896), dau of Edward Johnson, of Full-Sutton, Yorks, and *d* 21 Oct 1902, leaving, with other issue:
1a Edward Johnson; *b* 14 Dec 1851; *m* 1 July 1880 Phoebe Hannah (*d* 9 Oct 1923), dau of Stephen Andrews, and *d* 16 Oct 1930, leaving issue:
1b Edward Jordayne; *b* 9 Aug 1885; *m* 16 Aug 1910 Ella (*d* 1968), dau of Joseph Hilton Cant, of Appleby, and *d* 1970, having had issue:
1c +Genille Hilton Jordayne; *b* 28 June 1912; *educ* BC U (MA 1940), and MIT (PhD 1951); Prof of Chemistry, McGill U; *m* 19 May 1944 *Mary Margaret Elizabeth, dau of Lt-Col Robert Henry Palmer, DSO (*see* PALMER, Bt, of Carlton)
2c +Wilmot Wyamarus; *b* 28 July 1915; *m* 1969 *Janet Kyle, dau of Thomas Peddie, MA
1b Mabel Phoebe; *b* 21 June 1881; *d* unm 21 April 1958
2b Florence Beatrice; *b* 6 May 1883
2a Henry Wilmot, MRCS, LRCP; *b* 6 April 1863; *d* 5 Aug 1915
1a Mary Ann Sophia; *d* 11 May 1920
2a Hannah Louisa; *m* 25 June 1889 Rev James Leigh, MA, Vicar of Tinsley Yorks 1906–38, and *d* 13 Aug 1922
3a Emily Wilmot; *m* 30 June 1877 George David Welding, of Freshfield, King's Norton, and *d* 14 July 1912. He *d* 5 July 1912
(2) William, of Wellington Lodge, Harborne, Birmingham; *b* 26 Oct 1831; *m* 1st 1853 and had issue:
1a Lizzie; *d* unm
(2) (cont.) William Cave-Browne-Cave *m* 2nd 1 Aug 1877 Maria (*d* 28 Jan 1921), dau of John Thornicroft, of The Ravenhurst, Harborne, and *d* 20 April 1907, having by her had issue:
1a Stretton; *b* 8 Sept 1878; *educ* Malvern; *m* 2 Oct 1907 Ethel Milbro (*d* 6 May 1943), er dau of William Higgin-Birket, of Birket Houses, Lancs, and *d* 17 Sept 1961, leaving issue:
1b +Glen Myles LEVERING [Glen Levering Esq, Topham's Farm, Conistone-with-Kilnsey, nr Skipton, Yorks], an aeronautical engr, assumed the names of Glen Myles Levering, in lieu of Myles Verney Cave-Browne-Cave 1944; *b* 18 July 1918; *m* 18 April 1936 (*divorce* 1943) Christine Elizabeth, only dau of Wilfred Bentley, of Inglewood, Huddersfield
2b +Stretton Patrick, late Warwicks Yeo; *b* 24 Nov 1911; *educ* Sedbergh; *m* 1 Nov 1954 *Pamela, dau of Col H S Cole, of Stonebank, Ilkley, Yorks
3b Bryan William, OBE (1946); *b* 12 Dec 1915; *educ* Shrewsbury and St Edmund Hall, Oxford (BA 1938); late Lt-Col Roy Northumberland Fus, served WW II, Head Programmes BBC N Region 1953, Dir Br Forces Broadcasting Serv 1963; *m* 9 Aug 1947 Margaret Royston, MBE (*d* 5 April 1978), only dau of Alfred Cooke, of Gorse Hill, Linton, nr Wetherby, Yorks, and *d* 1980, having had issue:
1c +Myles Alfred; *b* 26 Aug 1949; *educ* Rugby and St Edmund's Hall Oxford (MA); slr 1974; *m* 1986 *Sally Jayne, dau of Geoffrey Lilley, and has issue:
1d *Sam; *b* 1990
1c *Claire Birket; *b* 17 July 1948; *m* 25 April 1970 *Stuart William Brown, yst son of E Brown, of 50 The Drive, Rickmansworth, Herts, and has issue:
1d *Matthew Myles Anthony; *b* 1980
1d *Laura Zoë; *b* 1977
2c *Elise Margaret; *b* 10 Nov 1952; *m* 1972 *Franz Nadernau, er son of F E Nadernau, of Aachen, W Germany, and has issue:
1d *Stefan; *b* 1974
2a Mary; *m* 29 April 1903 Herbert Vaughan Craster, LRCP, LRCS, (Edin), LRPS (Glas), of Keston Ho, Keston, Kent, and *d* 23 Feb 1933, leaving issue. He *d* 27 Feb 1929
3a Margaret Wilmot; *m* 3 Jan 1906 Rev Hubert Bernard Drew, MA, Vicar of Sutton-on-the-Forest, Yorks, and Rural Dean of Easingwold, son of George Bernard Drew, barrister, of London, and *d* 16 April 1959. He *d* 27 Jan 1928
(3) Thomas (Sir), ktd 1911, CB (1907), a Commr of the Roy Hosp, Chelsea 1899–1923, late Dep Acc-Gen of the Army 1897–1900; *b* 11 April 1835; *m* 30 April 1870 Blanche Matilda Mary Ann (*d* 20 Oct 1928), dau of Sir John Milton, CB, of High Elms, Streatham Common, and *d* 9 Dec 1924, leaving issue:
1a Thomas Reginald, CBE (1919), FRSA, MIMechE, W/Cdr RAF, RN, Prof Engrg U Coll Southampton 1931–50, Prof Emeritus U of Southampton, Dep Dir Airship Research Air Min 1920–21, Dir Camouflage Min Home Security 1941–45, FRAeS; *b* 11 Jan 1885; *educ* Dulwich; *m* 1st 8 June 1918 Marjorie Gwynne (*d* 8 Nov 1969), only dau of Albert Wright, of Idle, Yorks; *m* 2nd 19 Nov 1969 Elsie May (*d* 1991), of Southampton, dau of James Ricks, and *d* 26 Nov 1969, having by his 1st w had:
1b John Evelyn; *b* 4 July 1921; *d* unm 9 Nov 1949
2b +Thomas Milton [Thomas Cave-Browne-Cave Esq, The Old Rectory, Clatworthy, Wiveliscombe, Taunton TA4 2EQ]; *b* 29 July 1926; *educ* Reading U; *m* 30 March 1964 *Anne, only dau of Ralph P Symons, of Truro, Cornwall, and has issue:
1c Thomas Edward; *b* 3 Feb 1968
1c Janet Mary; *b* 4 July 1965; BSc Manchester and London
1b *Gillian Mary; *b* 3 Aug 1923; BSc London
2a Henry Meyrick, CB (1936), DSO (1918), DFC, A/V/M RAF, Dep Dir of Tech Development at Air Min 1922–27, cmdg Far E Flight RAF 1927, Dir of Tech Develop Air Min 1931–34, Air Offr cmdg RAF Cranwell and Cmdt RAF Coll 1934–7, Air Offr cmdg No 16 (Reconnaissance) Gp RAF 1937–38 and Air Offr cmdg No 25 (Armament) Gp RAF 1938; *b* 1 Feb 1887; *educ* Dulwich; *d* unm 5 Aug 1965
1a Blanche Isabel; *b* 12 July 1871; *d* 10 Aug 1871
2a Jeanette Gertrude, MBE (1945); *d* unm 9 March 1950
3a Beatrice Mabel, MBE (1920), AFRAeS; *d* unm 9 July 1947
4a Frances Evelyn, MA, Fell and Govr of Girton Coll Cambridge; *d* unm 30 March 1965
(4) Wilmot; *b* 3 June 1838; *m* 24 Dec 1860 Marie Anne (*d* 1879), dau of William Skinner, of Calcutta, and *d* 13 Feb 1898, leaving issue:
1a Annie Rebecca; *d* unm 1951
(5) Henry (Rev), Vicar of Edington, nr Westbury, Wilts 1880–90; *b* 27 Jan 1840; *m* 11 Oct 1865 Maria Louisa (*d* 3 March 1908), yst dau of George Chance, of Edgbaston, and *d* 4 Feb 1890, leaving issue:
1a Eustace Henry; *b* 3 Feb 1879; *m* 7 Dec 1904 Helen Mildred, yst dau of Hon George Irvine, of Quebec, and *d* 21 May 1924, leaving issue:
1b Harold; *b* 17 Sept 1905; *d* 11 Nov 1933
1a Cornelia Maria; *m* 28 Aug 1919 Thomas Collett
2a Maude Evelyn (Sister Mary Evelyn); *d* 22 Jan 1959
3a Irene de Peyster, ARRC, QARNNS (R)
(6) Frank Wyamarus; *b* 1 Oct 1844; *m* 4 Dec 1883 Annie Mabel (*d* 18 Aug 1923), dau of Joseph Barrows, The Limes, Himley, Staffs, and *d* 4 Feb 1925, leaving issue:
1a Nigel Frederick, late Capt RE, MIEE, Dep Regnl Dir Post Off, Home Counties Region 1939–43, served WW I 1915–19 (despatches); *b* 10 May 1885; *educ* Birmingham U (BSc Eng); *m* 7 Feb 1911 May (*d* 18 May 1968, aged 83), dau of George Titterton, JP, of Moseley, nr Birmingham, and *d* 24 May 1943, having had issue:
1b Roger, F/Lt RAF; *b* 10 Feb 1913; *d* 23 July 1938
1b Margaret; *b* 23 July 1917; *m* 25 July 1942 Capt Joseph Lees Bickerton, RA, son of William Peter Jardine Bickerton, and *d* 27 Jan 1956, leaving issue, two daus
2a Frank Wyamarus, late Lt 1st Vol Bn S Staffs Regt, served WW I 1915–19, with Canadian Expdny Force, and RAF; *b* 18 April 1886; *m* 16 March 1926 Kathleen (*d* 1983), dau of John M Douglas de Fenzi, and *d* 24 Aug 1942, leaving issue:
1b +Norman John [Norman Cave-Browne-Cave Esq, Trefeddian Hotel, Aberdovey, Gwynedd LL35 0SB]; *b* 5 Jan 1927; *m* 1st 19 Jan 1952 (*divorce* 1957) Eveline Fay (*d* 1989), yr dau of John Stanley Hill, of W Didsbury, and of Mrs J Stanley Hill, MP for Wythenshawe, Manchester; *m* 2nd 1957 *Margaret Dobbs, dau of John Stanley Maw, and by 1st w has issue:
1c +Peter Stanley; *b* 1955; *m* 1987 *Caroline Anne, est dau of Gerald Smith, and has issue:
1d +Thomas Edward; *b* 1991
1d *Lucy Fay; *b* 1989
1b (cont.) Norman Cave-Browne-Cave adopted:
*Helen; *b* 1966; *m* 1997 *Marc Joseph Hatch, s of Joseph Hatch, of Marlow, Bucks, and has:
*Rosie Ellen; *b* 1994
*Joanna; *b* 1967; *m* 1992 (*divorce* 1996) Andrew J Pearce and has:
*Molly Harriet; *b* 1997
1b *Anne Molly; *b* 11 Jan 1920; *m* 25 Oct 1952 *Selwyn Wootton Hill, son of Ernest Hill, of Aberdovey, Merioneth, and has issue:
1c *Anthony Wootton; *b* 8 June 1966
1c *Frances Anne; *b* 31 March 1954
2c *Judith Wootton; *b* 6 Aug 1955
3c *Stacey Wootton; *b* 6 Feb 1961
3a Norman, AIMM, FGS, Mining Engr in Mexico, late Capt 7th RWF (TA); *b* 1893; *m* 1st 1915 Ida (*d* 1923), dau of E J Bennett, of Camborne; *m* 2nd 27 Nov 1929 Ursula Jane, dau of D O Jones, of Towyn, Merioneth, and *dsp* 16 May 1946

1a Mabel Jane; *b* 1 April 1936

2a Isabelle Verney; *m* 12 Aug 1922 George FitzEdward Summers, of 70 Goodwin's Rd, Kings Lynn, Norfolk, son of Henry Summers of Chorley Wood, Herts, and *d* 24 July 1954

4 Edward Sacheverell (Rev), MA Oxford, Vicar of Stow and Gayton, Staffs; *b* 3 Oct 1804; *m* 7 July 1830 Mary (*d* 14 Sept 1874), only surv dau of John Farsyde Watson, DL, of Bilton Park, Yorks, and *d* 7 Aug 1842, having had issue:

(1) Edward Farsyde (Rev), of Holbrook, Hampton Park, Hereford, Rector of Bretherton, Lancs 1871–74; *b* 10 Oct 1833; *educ* Jesus Coll Cambridge (MA); *m* 14 Oct 1873 Sarah Maria (*d* 23 Dec 1899), yst dau of William Marshall, DL, of Penwortham Hall, Lancs, and *dsp* 9 March 1915

Sir WILLIAM *d* 24 Aug 1838; his est son,

Sir John Robert Cave-Browne-Cave, 10t Bt, High Sheriff Derbys; *b* 4 March 1798; *m* 22 Nov 1821 Catherine Penelope (*d* 13 March 1871), dau and coheir of William Mills, of Barlaston Hall, Staffs, and *d* 11 Nov 1855, having had, with two other s and three daus:

1 **Sir Mylles Cave-Browne-Cave, 11th Bt**, DL, JP Derbys, Leics, and Warwicks, Maj Derbys Yeo Cav, formerly Lt 11th Hus; *b* 1 Aug 1822; *m* 15 May 1855 Isabelle (*d* 13 Aug 1922), dau and coheir of John Taylor, of The Newarke, Leics, and *d* 22 Jan 1907, having had:

(1) Geoffry Lisle; *b* 5 Nov 1857; *d* 17 Sept 1880

(2) **Rev Sir Genille Cave-Browne-Cave, 12th Bt**, Rector of Londesborough, Yorks, RGA, formerly Capt Legion of Frontiersmen, served in Boxer Expdn in China and in American-Spanish War 1898–99, and WW I 1918–19; *b* 3 Sept 1869; *m* 1 June 1926 Mary Elizabeth (*d* 23 March 1960), dau of John Wreghitt, of E Thorpe, E Yorks, and *dsp* 29 Oct 1929

(1) Millicent Rosamund; *m* 3 Feb 1885 William Wentworth Clapham, of Crumpshall Ho, Lancs and *d* 15 Oct 1907, leaving issue. He *d* 8 June 1920

(2) Mabel; *d* unm 21 Jan 1941

(3) Muriel; *d* unm 29 Feb 1956

2 Ambrose Syned, BA Oxford, sometime Rector of Stretton-en-le-Field, Derbys; *b* 31 Aug 1834; *m* 9 Sept 1858 Caroline Mary Anne Elizabeth (*d* 16 April 1903), est dau of Ven James Saurin, MA, Archdeacon of Dromore, and *d* 22 July 1895, having had issue:

(1) James Saurin, Capt 2nd Bn Yorks LI; *b* 21 July 1859; *d* unm 14 Feb 1892

(2) **Sir Reginald Ambrose Cave-Browne-Cave, 13th Bt**, Capt RN; *b* 21 Oct 1860; *m* 1 Oct 1890 Evelyn (*d* 4 Jan 1939), yst dau of Rev Charles and Lady Georgina Oakley (*see* DUCIE, E), and *dsp* 4 July 1930

(3) Wilmot; *b* 11 April 1862; *d* 26 Dec 1923

(4) **Sir Rowland Henry Cave-Browne-Cave, 14th Bt**, T/Capt RFA; *b* 14 April 1865; *m* 1 June 1895 Honora Phoebe Gertrude (*d* 17 March 1924), dau of Benjamin Bright, of Colwall, and widow of Edward Seymour Fowler, and *dspm* 21 Dec 1943, leavinge:

1a Phoebe Hyacinth, MBE (1956), a missionary in Uganda

(5) Bernard, Capt Res of Offrs, Inspr Sierra Leone Police, Lt 2nd Bn Wilts Regt; *b* 23 Feb 1868; *m* 21 Jan 1903 Katherine Elizabeth Frere *d* 7 Nov 1953), yst dau of Gen Sir John William Cox, KCB, and widow of Francis Haden Cope, and *d* 5 April 1917

(6) Edward Lambert; *b* 5 Jan 1870; *m* 6 June 1895 Rachel Marion (*d* 7 Feb 1942), dau of Rev A L Fortin, and *d* 4 July 1932, leaving issue:

1a CLEMENT CHARLES (Sir), **15th Bt**

(7) Clement Andrew, late Lt KRRC; *b* 7 Aug 1871; *m* —, and *d* 27 Oct 1920

(8) Alfred William; *b* 1 June 1873; *d* 8 Jan 1874

(9) Anthony Stanhope; *b* 4 Jan 1879

(1) Mary Geneviève; *m* 17 July 1894 George Arthur Chenery

(2) Catherine Penelope; *m* 1st 15 Sept 1887 (*divorce* 1905) William Crewdson Howard, and had issue; *m* 2nd 24 July 1905 Sir John William Salusbury-Trelawny, 11th Bt (*qv*), and *d* 23 Jan 1930, leaving further issue

(3) Rosamund Harriet; *m* 29 April 1899 Edward Mason Munby, son of Edward Charles Munby, of Oswaldkirk, Yorks, and *d* 25 June 1937

(4) Caroline Emma; *d* young 29 Jan 1878

The 14th Bt's nephew,

Sir Clement Charles Cave-Browne-Cave, 15th Bt; *b* 28 Nov 1896; *m* 24 Nov 1923 *Dorothea Plewman, yst dau of Robert Greene Dwen, of Chicago, Illinois, USA, and *d* 21 April 1945, having had issue:

1 Sir ROBERT CAVE-BROWNE-CAVE, **16th and present Bt**

2 David; *b* 19, *d* 22 May 1932

Lineage (of Browne): Sir JOHN BROWNE; Ld Mayor London; *m* Alice, dau of Sir William Swinsted, and had:

Sir WILLIAM BROWNE; Ld Mayor London 1513; *m* Alice, dau of Sir H Kevell, and had, with a dau (Anne; *m* Sir William Petre, PC, of Fogalestone, Essex, Chllr Order Garter):

JOHN BROWNE, of London, Horton Kirby, Kent, and Stretton-en-le-Field, Derbys; Ld Almoner and Master Mint *temp* HENRY VIII, EDWARD VI, MARY and ELIZABETH I; *m* Christiana, dau of William Crokell, of London, and had:

CHARLES BROWNE, of Stretton-en-le-Field; had:

JOHN BROWNE, of Stretton-en-le-Field; *m* 1st Magdalen, dau of Anthony Grey, Earl of Kent; *m* 2nd Winifred, dau of Sir John Harper, of Harperstone, Derbys, and *d* 17 May 1669, leaving:

JOHN BROWNE, of Stretton-en-le-Field; *m* Dorothy, dau of Thomas Brudenell, of Stanton-in-the-Stones, Leics, and had:

THOMAS BROWNE, of Stretton-en-le-Field; *m* Thomazine, dau of John Fitzherbert, of Somershall, Derbys, and had:

WILLIAM BROWNE, of Stretton-en-le-Field; *m* Catherine, dau of Zouche Tate (*see* ZOUCHE, B), and had:

CATHERINE *m* Roger CAVE, of Eydon (*see* above)

Cavendish of Furness

Arms: Sable three buck's heads cabossed argent. **Crest:** A serpent nowed proper. **Motto:** *Cavendo tutus* ('Safe by keeping watch') **Creation:** B. (LP, UK) 1990.

THE BARON CAVENDISH OF FURNESS, of Cartmel, Co Cumbria ((Richard) Hugh Cavendish, DL 1988)) [The Rt Hon The Lord Cavendish of Furness DL, Holker Hall, Cark-in-Cartmel, Cumbria LA11 7PL]; *b* 2 Nov 1941; *educ* Eton; Titular Abbot of Furness; internat banker 1961–71, chm Holker Estate Gp 1971–, Morecambe and Lonsdale C Assoc 1975–78; High Sheriff Cumbria 1978, Memb: Cumbria CC 1985–90, Commn on Historic Buildings and Monuments (English Heritage) 1992–; Chm: Govrs St Anne's Sch Windermere 1983–89, Lancs and Cumbria Fndn for Med Research 1994–; Ld in Waiting 1990–92; dir UK Nirex Ltd 1993–; FRSA 1988; *m* 1970 *Grania Mary, dau of Brig Toby St George Caulfeild, CBE (*see* CHARLEMONT, V), and has issue:

1 *Frederick Richard Toby; *b* 1972

1 *Lucy Georgiana; *b* 1973

2 *Emily Moyra; *b* 1980

Lineage: *See* DEVONSHIRE, D

Seat: Holker Hall, Cark-in-Cartmel, Cumbria. The estate of which Holker is the hub comprises monastic lands which originally belonged to Cartmel Priory and Furness Abbey. After the suppression of these two religious houses in the 1530s (along with all the rest in England) their lands were granted to the PRESTONs of Lancashire, from an earlier branch of which the Viscounts Gormanston (*qv*) may descend. Catherine, daughter and heiress of Thomas Preston, married in the late 17th century Sir William Lowther, 1st Bt, of Marske in Yorkshire, and their grandson Sir William, the 3rd and last Baronet, left what was by now the Holker estate on his death in 1753 to his cousin Lord George Augustus Cavendish, younger brother of the 4th Duke of Devonshire (*qv*), Sir William's mother having been a daughter of the 2nd Duke.

The house had been built in the early 17th century but was almost completely reconstructed in the mid-19th by the 7th Duke of Devonshire, to whom it had passed since Lord George died without issue. One wing dates from the early years of Queen Victoria's reign, the other, which is set at a right-angle, from a third of a century later following a fire in 1871. The result is externally unattractive, or at any rate unfashionable, albeit formidable. Internally some of the 18th-century elements survive, notably staircases. There is also some good panelling dating from the time the original house was built, though it comes not from Holker itself but a farm house nearby.

CAWDOR

Arms: Quarterly, 1st, or a hart's head cabossed sa., attired gu. (for CALDER); 2nd, gyronny of eight or and sa. (for CAMPBELL); 3rd, arg. a galley with her oars in action sa. (for LORNE); 4th, parted per fess az. and gu., a cross or (for LORT). **Crest:** A swan ppr., crowned or. **Supporters:** Dexter, a lion rampant guardant gu., armed or; sinister, a hart ppr. **Mottoes:** (over Crest) *Candidus cantabit moriens* ('The pure of heart shall sing when dying'); (under Arms) Be mindfull. **Creations:** B. (GB) 21 June 1796, E. and V. (UK) 5 Oct 1827.

THE 7TH EARL CAWDOR OF CASTLEMARTIN, Co Pembroke, **Viscount Emlyn**, of Emlyn, Co Carmarthen, and **Baron Cawdor of Castlemartin**, Co Pembroke (Colin Robert Vaughan Campbell) [The Rt Hon The Earl Cawdor, Cawdor Castle, Nairn IV12 5RD]; *b* 30 June 1962; *s* f 1993; *educ* Eton and St Peter's Coll Oxford; architect; *m* 21 Oct 1994 *Lady Isabella Stanhope, yr dau of 11th Earl of Harrington (*qv*)

Lineage: The 2nd EARL OF ARGYLL (*see* ARGYLL, D) had a 3rd s:

Sir JOHN CAMPBELL; *m c* 1510 Muriel (*d c* 1575), dau and heir of John Calder, of Calder/Cawdor, Nairnshire, rep of the old Thanes of Cawdor, and *d* 1 May 1546, having had, with a dau (Janet, *m* 4th Lord (Fraser of) Lovat, *qv*) an est s:

ARCHIBALD CAMPBELL of Cawdor; *m* Isabel, dau of James Grant, 3rd of Freuchie (*see* STRATHSPEY, B), and *d* Dec 1551, having had issue:

JOHN CAMPBELL of Cawdor; *m* 1st 1575 Lady Mary Keith, dau of 4th Earl Marischal; *m* 2nd Jean, dau of Lauder of Hatton, and was *k* by Campbell of Ardkinglas Feb 1591, leaving by his 1st w an est s:

Sir JOHN CAMPBELL of Cawdor; *m* 1st 1601 Jean, dau of Sir Duncan Campbell of Glenorchy; *m* 2nd Elizabeth, sis of 1st Marquess of Douglas (*see* HAMILTON and BRANDON, D), and *d* 1642, having by his 1st w had:

1 John, MP Nairnshire, to whom his f made over the estate of Cawdor 1622; *m* 1622 Elizabeth, dau of Sir Thomas Urquhart of Cromarty, and *d* 1654, having had, with a s (Colin, *dvp*):

(1) Jean; *m* 1648, as his 1st w, 12th Lord Forbes (*qv*) and had issue

(2) Christian; *m* 1653 Nicholas Dunbar, a burgess of Edinburgh of the family of Bogs, and had an only child:

1a Lilias; *m* 1679 Alexander Campbell of Torrich

2 Colin, of Ardersier; *m* Elizabeth, dau of David Brodie of Brodie, and *d* 12 Sept 1642, having had: HUGH (Sir), who *s* to Cawdor, and other issue

Sir JOHN's gs,

Sir HUGH CAMPBELL of Cawdor; ktd 1660; *m* 1662 Henrietta, dau of 3rd Earl of Moray (*qv*), and *d* 11 March 1716, having had an est s:

Sir ALEXANDER CAMPBELL; *m* 1689 Elizabeth (*d* 28 Sept 1714), sis and heir of Sir Gilbert Lort, Bt, of Stackpole Court, Pembs, and *dvp* 1697, leaving:

JOHN CAMPBELL of Cawdor; a Ld of the Admlty and later Treasury; *b* 1695; *m* 30 April 1726 Mary, dau and coheir of Lewis Pryse, of Gogirthen, and *d* 6 Sept 1777, having had, with other issue:

1 Pryse, of Stackpole Court, MP Nairnshire; *m* 20 Sept 1752 Sarah (*d* 20 May 1767), dau and coheir of Sir Edmund Bacon, Bt (*qv*), and *dvp* 14 Dec 1768, leaving with other issue (including a dau Sarah, *m* Thomas Wodehouse; *see* KIMBERLEY, E):

(1) JOHN, **1st Baron**

(2) George (Sir), GCB, Adml of the White; *m* his cousin Eustacia, dau of John Campbell Hooke, Lyon King-of-Arms, and *dsp* 28 Jan 1821

2 John Hooke CAMPBELL later CAMPBELL-HOOKE, of Bangeston, Pembs; Lyon King-of-Arms 1754 to his death; *m* Eustacia, dau of Francis Basset, of Heanton Court, Devon, and had, with a s and two other daus:

(1) Eustacia; *m* Adml Sir George Campbell, and *dsp*

(2) Charlotte; *m* Sir Thomas Gage, Bt, and *d* 1849

3 Alexander, Lt-Col; *m* Frances (*d* 1770), dau of Philip Meadows, and *d* Nov 1785, leaving:

(1) Henry Frederick (Sir), KCB, GCH, Gen; *b* 10 July 1769; *m* 10 April 1808 Emma (*d* 20 March 1847), dau of Thomas Williams and widow of Col Thomas Knox, and *d* 2 Sept 1856, leaving, with other issue:

1a George Herbert Frederick, Col, DL, JP Northants; *b* 19 June 1811; *m* 1838 Louisa, dau of R H Cox, and had, with other issue:

1b George Augustus, of Market Ho, Brackley; *b* 1847; *m* 23 July 1868 Hon Alice Barrington (*d* 31 July 1928), dau of 8th Viscount Barrington (*see* 1970 edn), and *d* 12 Sept 1930, leaving issue

2b Henry Algernon; *m* Jan 1872 Edith (*d* 7 May 1930), dau of Prideaux Selby, of Pawston, Northumberland, and *d* 20 June 1904, leaving issue

3b Francis Alexander (Sir), KCMG, CB, Assist Under-Sec For Affrs 1902–11; *b* 1852; *m* 1880 Dora Edith, dau of Hugh Hammersley, and *d* 1911

1b Fanny Georgina; *m* 29 June 1859 Col Hon Henry Walter Campbell, and *d* 9 Jan 1934, leaving issue (*see* below)

1a Frances Augusta; *m* 10 Dec 1836 Col Hon Charles J Fox Stanley, 3rd son of 13th Earl of Derby (*qv*)

1 Anne; *m* 8 July 1752 2nd Baron Fortescue (*see* FORTESCUE, E)

JOHN CAMPBELL's gs,

JOHN CAMPBELL, **1st Baron Cawdor of Castlemartin**, Co Pembroke (GB), so *cr* 21 June 1796, DCL, FRS, FSA, MP (Tory) Nairnshire 1777–80 and Cardigan 1780–96; *b c* 1753; *m* 28 July 1789 Lady Caroline Howard (*d* 8 March 1848), est dau of 5th Earl of Carlisle (*qv*), and had issue:

1 JOHN FREDERICK, **2nd Baron** and **1st Earl**

2 George Pryse, R-Adml; *b* 1793; *m* 13 Oct 1821 Charlotte, 2nd dau of Gen Isaac Gascoyne, and *d* 12 Jan 1858

The 1st BARON *d* 1 June 1821; his er son,

JOHN FREDERICK CAMPBELL, **1st Earl Cawdor of Castlemartin**, Co Pembroke, so *cr* 5 Oct 1827, as also VISCOUNT EMLYN of Emlyn, Co Carmarthen (both UK); *b* 8 Nov 1790; *educ* Ch Ch Oxford; MP (Whig) Carmarthen 1813–21, Ld Lt Carmarthenshire 1852–60; *m* 5 Sept 1816 Lady Elizabeth Thynne (*d* 16 Feb 1866), dau of 2nd Marquess of Bath (*qv*), and had, with other issue:

1 JOHN FREDERICK VAUGHAN, **2nd Earl**

2 Archibald George (Rev), MA Oxford, Rector of Knipton, Leics; *b* 11 Jan 1827; *m* 29 Sept 1853 Charlotte Henrietta (*d* 3 Oct 1896), 2nd dau of Very Rev Hon Henry Edward Howard, Dean of Lichfield (*see* CARLISLE, E), and *d* 2 May 1902, leaving with other issue:

(1) Donald; *b* 10 Feb 1860; *m* 26 July 1888 Edith Mary (*d* 15 May 1931), dau of Henry Smith Wright, MP, and *d* 31 March 1923, leaving issue:

1a Mary Charlotte; *m* 22 June 1931 Patrick Herbert Humphris Dawes, son of Alfred Dawes, formerly of Bryn Marion, Blaenau Festiniog, N Wales, and *d* 6 Nov 1956

2a Evelyn Hope; *b* 10 April 1894; *m* 7 Feb 1935 Arthur William Glenton Lennard, only son of Arthur Lennard, barrister. He *d* 4 Sept 1943

3 Henry Walter, Lt-Col late Coldstream Gds, Kt of the Legion of Honour and of the Medjidie, JP Carmarthenshire; *b* 23 March 1835; *m* 29 June 1859 Fanny Georgina (*d* 9 Jan 1934), est dau of Col George Herbert Frederick Campbell (*see* above), and *d* 17 Dec 1910, having had, with other issue:

(1) Alice Mary; *m* 28 April 1880 Seymour Pleydell-Bouverie, 2nd son of Philip Pleydell-Bouverie, of Brymore, Somerset, and *d* 11 Sept 1948, leaving issue (*see* RADNOR, E)

1 Emily Caroline; *m* 31 March 1842 Hon Octavius Duncombe, MP, yst son of 1st Baron Feversham (*qv*), and *d* 22 May 1911, leaving issue

2 Georgiana Isabel; *m* 25 June 1840 Col John Balfour, 7th of Balbirnie, DL, JP, and *d* 3 Dec 1884, having had issue. He *d* 25 July 1895

3 Elizabeth Lucy; *m* 28 June 1842 3rd Earl of Desart, and *d* 26 April 1898, leaving issue (*see* 1934 edn). He *d* 1 April 1865

4 Mary Louisa; *m* 29 April 1846 2nd Earl of Ellesmere (*see* SUTHERLAND, D), and *d* 24 Nov 1916, aged 91, leaving issue

The 1st EARL *d* 7 Nov 1860; his est son,

JOHN FREDERICK VAUGHAN CAMPBELL, **2nd Earl Cawdor of Castlemartin**, DL (Inverness); *b* 11 June 1817; *educ* Eton and Ch Ch Oxford; MP (C) Pembs 1841–60, Ld Lt and Custos Rotulorum Carmarthenshire 1861–98; *m* 28 June 1842 Sarah Mary (*d* 21 April 1881), 2nd dau of Hon Henry Frederick Compton-Cavendish (*see* DEVONSHIRE, D), and had, with other issue:

1 FREDERICK ARCHIBALD VAUGHAN, **3rd Earl**

2 Ronald George Elidor, Capt Coldstream Gds; *b* 30 Dec 1848; *m* 17 Dec 1872 Katharine Susanna (*d* 12 Feb 1934), dau of Rev Thomas Legh Claughton, DD, Bishop of St Albans, and was *k* in the Zulu War, 28 March 1879, having had issue:

(1) Guy Ronald (Rev), Rector of Wilton, Salisbury 1912–43; *b* 2 Dec 1874; *educ* New Coll Oxford (MA); *m* 23 July 1901 Hon Vere Annesley (*d* 18 May 1975), est dau of 11th Viscount Valentia (*qv*), and *d* 10 Feb 1950, leaving issue:

1a Colin Arthur Ronald, Capt 5th Bn Wilts Regt; *b* 2 June 1910; *educ* Eton; *d* unm 10 March 1976

1a Hester Maud Vere, CBE (1963); *b* 3 Jan 1904; *m* 8 June 1929 (*divorce* 1938) Eric Rupert Walter Barrington, only son of Hon Rupert Edward Selborne Barrington, DSO (*see* 1970 edn BARRINGTON, V), and *d* 6 April 1982

2a Margaret Helen; *b* 5 Oct 1907; *m* 29 Dec 1937 Bruce Delacour Hylton Stewart, yst son of Canon Hylton Stewart, and *d* Sept 1975, leaving:

1b *Richard Anthony; *b* 22 April 1945

(2) John Vaughan, VC (1916), CMG (1918), DSO (1900), Col Coldstream Gds, Hon Brig-Gen 1933, Bde Cdr and Brig-Gen 1916–23, and cmdg Coldstream Gds and the Regimental Dist 1923–27, ADC to HM 1919–33, memb Gentlemen-at-Arms 1934, served in S African War 1899–1902, and WW I (despatches brevet), Croix de Guerre with Palm and Star, and Legion of Honour; *b* 31 Oct 1876; *m* 1st 18 July 1904 Amy Dorothy (*d* 9 March 1927), er dau of John Penn, MP, and had issue:

1a John Ronald, Maj Coldstream Gds WW II; *b* 18 Sept 1905; *m* 12 June 1935 Ethel Mildred (*d* 17 May 1967), yst dau of Thomas Reginald Hague

Cook, JP, of 46 Portman Sq, W1, and widow of Capt Frank Brian Frederic Bibby (*see* BIBBY, Bt), and was *ka* France 30 May 1940

1a Diana Marion; *b* 11 Oct 1909; *m* (*divorce*) John Carney and *d* Nov 1975, leaving issue

(2) (cont.) Brig John Campbell *m* 2nd 6 Feb 1937 *Margaret Emily Robina, yr dau of Alfred Tennyson Smith, OBE, MD, CM, of Rodborough Grange, Bournemouth, and *d* 22 May 1944

(3) Robert, DSO and bar (1917); Lt-Col late Cameron Highrs, served WW I (despatches); *b* 23 June 1878; *m* 15 Nov 1926 Mary Emelda (*d* 1979), dau of William Robert Wood, and *d* 16 March 1945, leaving issue:

1a +Robin John Ronald, Maj Queen's Own Highrs (Seaforth and Camerons) (despatches Malaya, 1951) [Maj Robin Campbell, Kinrara, Aviemore, Inverness-shire PH22 1QA]; *b* 30 Sept 1927; *educ* Eton; *m* 2 March 1954 *Alison Barbara Rose, only dau of Maj Horace Cave-Browne, IA (*see* CAVE-BROWNE-CAVE, Bt), and has issue:

1b +Ian Robert; *b* 27 Sept 1956; *educ* abroad

2b +James Farquhar Robin [James Campbell Esq, Old Cowpastures Farm House, Hook Norton, Oxon]; *b* 26 Nov 1958; *educ* Gordonstoun; late Capt Queen's Own Highrs; *m* 1985 *Marina Caroline Vere, er dau of Maj Charles Pepler Norton (*see* OGILVY, Bt), and has issue:

1c +Guy James Farquhar; *b* 17 March 1991

2c +Hugh Robin Farquhar; *b* 16 Sept 1997

1c *Ishbel Elizabeth Rose; *b* 30 Nov 1988

2c *Isla Sophia Rose; *b* 16 Sept 1997

2a +Alan (Seaforth and Camerons), served Malaya 1952 (despatches) [Lt-Col Alan Campbell, Crossways House, Bartlow, Cambridge CB1 6PN]; *b* 25 May 1929; *educ* Eton, Lt-Col Queen's Own Highrs; *m* 2 Nov 1963 Sylvia Ann (*d* 1994), est dau of Richard Hermon, of Langar Ho, Langar, Notts, and has:

1b +Alexander; *b* 22 Sept 1964; *educ* Eton

2b +James; *b* 14 May 1967; *educ* Eton; Maj Highrs (Seaforth Gordons and Camerons)

3b +Andrew; *b* 8 May 1969; *educ* Eton; *m* 6 Sept 1997 *Louise Ann, only dau of John Richardson, of Constitution Hill, Norwich

4b +Nicholas; *b* 25 March 1971; *educ* King's Sch Ely; *m* 4 Oct 1997 *Anita Karen, yst dau of Ian Packman, of School Close, Fittleworth, W Sussex

1b *Theresa Ann; *b* 18 Nov 1965; *educ* St Swithun's Winchester; *m* 1 Oct 1994 *Robert George Seton Adams, est s of His Hon Judge John Roderick Seton Adams, of Frizley Old Hall, Frizing Hall Rd, Bradford, W Yorks, and has:

1c *James Alexander Seton; *b* 21 Sept 1997

1c *Lucy Sylvia Seton; *b* 18 July 1995

(1) Maud; *b* 27 Sept 1873; *d* unm 21 Jan 1900

3 Alexander Francis Henry, JP Carmarthenshire, formerly Lt 12th Lancers and Scots Gds, and late Capt 3rd Bn Roy Scots; *b* 3 Sept 1855; *m* 1st 3 Sept 1879 Constance (*d* 24 Jan 1887), 4th dau of Philip Pleydell-Bouverie, of Brymore (*see* RADNOR, E), and had, with other issue:

(1) Duncan Elidor, DSO (1918), TD, Maj late Northumberland Yeo; *b* 10 Oct 1880; *m* 6 June 1914 Hon Florence Evelyne Willey (*d* 1978), only dau of 1st Baron Barnby (*see* 1967 edn), of Blyth Hall, Notts, and *d* 2 Sept 1930, leaving:

1a Alister Henry, DSO, MC and bar, Maj Probyn's Horse, att 7th Light Cav Bde, SEAC, served WW II (severely wounded); *b* 5 April 1918; *educ* Stowe; *d* of wounds recd in action in Burma 30 Aug 1945

2a +Ian Robert, CB (1976), CBE (1965), AFC (1948), A/V/M RAF [Air Vice-Marshal Ian Campbell CB CBE AFC, Pike Farm, Fossebridge, Cheltenham, Glos GL54 3JR]; *b* 5 Oct 1920; *educ* Eton and RAF Coll Cranwell; served WW II (POW), Air Attaché, Br Embassy Bonn 1968, Dir Management and Support Intell, MoD 1970–73, Ch of Staff, 18 Gp Strike Cmnd 1973–75 (ret); *m* 1st 26 June 1953 Beryl Evelyn (*d* 1982), yr dau of Brig Thomas Kennedy Newbigging, MC, of Bardfield End Green, Thaxted, Essex; *m* 2nd 1984 *Elisabeth, yr dau of Maj Richard Kennedy Lingard-Guthrie, and by 1st w has issue:

1b +Alister Neil [Alister Campbell Esq, 41 Rusholme Rd, London SW15 3LF]; *b* 11 April 1955; *educ* Eton; *m* 1982 *Ceril Diana, only dau of A Barnato-Kahan, and has issue:

1c +Rory Dominic Alexander; *b* 1987

1c *Arabella Louise Evelyn; *b* 1984

(2) Neil Alister Henry, Lt-Col 2nd Bn Som LI WW I (wounded); *b* 29 Oct 1881; *m* 7 Oct 1919 Enid Muriel Money, Moyles Cottage, Quenington, nr Cirencester, Glos, 2nd dau of Col Charles Henry Dudley Ryder, CB, CIE, DSO (*see* HARROWBY, E), and *d* 1 March 1950

3 (cont.) Capt The Hon Alexander Campbell *m* 2nd 1888 Rosa Rebecca (*d* 28 Feb 1929), dau of E M Blyton, of Woodhall, Lincs, and *d* 5 March 1929

1 Victoria Alexandrina Elizabeth; *m* 24 Jan 1866 Lt-Col Francis William Lambton, late Scots Gds, 3rd son of William Henry Lambton, of Biddick Hall, Durham, bro of 1st Earl of Durham (*qv*), and *d* 30 March 1909, leaving issue. He *d* 6 Oct 1921

2 Muriel Sarah; *m* 20 April 1876 Sir Courtenay Edmund Boyle, KCB (*see* CORK and ORRERY, E), and *d* 30 Sept 1934

3 Rachel Anne Georgina; *m* 21 Sept 1876 Sir Edward Stafford Howard, KCB, of Thornbury Castle, Glos, and *d* 6 Oct 1906, leaving issue (*see* NORFOLK, D)

The 2nd EARL *d* 29 March 1898; his est son,

FREDERICK ARCHIBALD VAUGHAN CAMPBELL, **3rd Earl Cawdor of Castlemartin**, PC, JP Cos Carmarthen and Pembroke, DL and JP for Inverness, Nairn, and Carmarthen, Ld Lt and Custos Rotulorum of Pembs and Pres of Pembs TFA, a Memb of the Cncl of HRH PRINCE OF WALES 1908–11, one of the Ecclesiastical Commrs for England, MP Carmarthens 1874–85, chm GWR 1895–1905, First Ld of the Admlty 1905, ADC to HM, Col Carmarthen Art, W Div RA; *b* 13 Feb 1847; *m* 16 Sept 1868 Edith Georgiana (*d* 2 Sept 1926), est dau of Christopher Turnor, of Stoke Rochford, Lincs, and had issue:

1 HUGH FREDERICK VAUGHAN, **4th Earl**

2 Nigel (Rev), Rector of Milton Keynes, Bucks 1910–14, Rector of Stifford, Grays, Essex, 1914–16, and Curate of St Martin's-in-the-Fields, London 1918–20; *b* 18 Nov 1873; *educ* Ch Ch Oxford (MA); *m* 30 April 1902 Violet (*d* 15 March 1940), dau of Charles Wyndham Rodolph Kerr, son of Lord Charles Lennox Kerr (*see* LOTHIAN, M), and *d* 20 July 1951, having had issue:

(1) Frederick Charles; *b* 26 April 1905; *d* 10 July 1927

(1) Olivia; *b* 10 Jan 1905; *m* 1st 1 Dec 1934 (*divorce* 1940) Arthur Edmund Leveson, only son of Adml Sir Arthur Cavanagh Leveson, GCB; *m* 2nd 21 Jan 1943 Maj Samuel John Rennie Bucknill, Irish Gds (*ka* in Tunisa, 30 March 1943), only son of Samuel Pratt Berens Bucknill, of Melbury Lodge, Wimborne, Dorset; *m* 3rd 16 April 1947 Hon Roger Nathaniel Frankland (*see* ZOUCHE, B), and *d* 19–

(2) Jean Edith; *b* 20 Jan 1911; *d* 19–

3 Ralph Alexander, CBE (1919), Lt-Col late Cameron Highrs, served in Soudan 1898, and S Africa 1899–1902 (despatches twice); *b* 18 Feb 1877; *educ* Eton; *m* 1st 1 Dec 1906 Marjorie Theophila (*d* 30 Nov 1911), dau of Sir John Arthur Fowler, 2nd Bt, and had issue:

(1) Myrtle Alice; *b* 27 Aug 1911; *m* 16 Sept 1944 Maj Colin Lachlan Kennedy, late Canadian Forestry Corps, son of Colin Robert Campbell Kennedy, of 2834 Spruce St, Vancouver, BC, and *dsp* 10 April 1965

3 (cont.) Lt-Col The Hon Ralph Campbell *m* 2nd 14 Jan 1914 Marjorie Edith (*d* 1984), er dau of Horace George Devas, and *d* 1 Aug 1945, leaving issue:

(1) +David Archibald, CBE (Civil 1988, OBE (Mil) 1954), TD [Col David Campbell CBE TD, Paxton House, Bucklebury, Reading, Berks]; *b* 13 Feb 1915; *educ* Eton and Trin Hall Cambridge (BA); FRICS, Lt-Col and Brevet Col late Berks Yeo, served WW II

(2) +Angus Mervyn, TD, [Maj Angus Campbell Esq TD, Wasing Lodge, Aldermaston, Reading, Berks RG7 4LZ]; late Maj Surrey Yeo, served WW II (despatches); *b* 29 March 1918; *educ* Eton; *m* 20 June 1950 *Rosemary Madeline Hamilton, only dau of Hugh Alastair Hamilton Fraser, of Mill Place, Stanton Drew, Somerset, and has issue:

1a +Ian Angus Ralph; *b* 26 June 1951; *educ* Bradfield; *m* 1984 *Jacqueline, dau of John Jowett, and has issue:

1b +Edward Alastair Ian; *b* 1988

2b +Frederick Hugh; *b* 1990

1b *Laura Beatrice; *b* 1995

2a +James Malcolm (Rev) [The Rev James Campbell, Holly Cross Vicarage, Binstead, Hants GU34 4NX]; *b* 8 April 1955; *educ* Eton, RAC Cirencester and Wycliffe Hall, Oxford; ordained 1991; *m* 1984 *Mary, est dau of John Rolston, and has issue:

1b +John (Jack) Alexander; *b* 1988

2b +Harry David; *b* 1990

1b *Chloe Elizabeth; *b* 1992

2b *Alice Violet; *b* 1994

1a *Catherine Rosemary [Miss Catherine Campbell, Wasing Lodge, Aldermaston, Berks RG7 4LZ]; *b* 29 Nov 1964

(2) *Rosemary Edith [Miss Rosemary Campbell, Pond Cottage, Padworth Common, Reading, Berks]; *b* 23 June 1921

4 Elidor Ronald, barrister Inner Temple, attd Embassy Washington 1918; *b* 7 May 1881; *educ* Magdalen Coll Oxford (BA); *m* 29 Jan 1913 Violet Antoniette (*d* 28 June 1975), dau of Octavius Edward Bulwer-Marsh, of Bryngwyn Manor, Raglan, Mon, and *d* 15 Dec 1957, leaving issue:

(1) Elidor Diarmid Calder, Maj RA WW II; *b* 14 Feb 1916; *m* 15 Dec 1947 *Liliana, dau of Maj Anthony Zarich, of Kifissia

(1) *Fiona Mary [Mrs Iain MacDonald, Blaen-y-Myarth, Llangynidr, nr Crickhowell, Powys]; *b* 1 Nov 1925; *m* 1973 *Iain Alastair MacDonald

5 Ian Malcolm, DSO (1918), TD, Ld Lt Nairnshire 1949–58, Col late TAR, formerly Lovat Scouts Yeo, Fell and Bursar Trin Hall Cambridge 1919–28, served WW I in Gallipoli, Egypt and France (despatches), Dist Commr CD, N Dist (Scot) 1939–45; *b* 17 Nov 1883; *educ* Eton and Trin Coll Cambridge (BA 1905, MA 1919); *m* 16 July 1928 Marion Louisa (*d* 20 Feb 1971, aged 80), dau of William Stirling of Fairburn, and widow of Ewen James Brodie of Lethen, Capt Cameron Highrs, and *dsp* 11 March 1962

6 Eric Octavius, DSO (1915) and bar (1918), T/Lt-Col Seaforth Highrs WW I (wounded, despatches three times, brevet); *b* 3 Dec 1885; *d* 4 June 1918, from illness contracted on active serv

1 Edith Aline Caroline; *b* 11 July 1869; *m* 21 Nov 1908 Charles Alexander Ferguson, yst son of Lt-Col George Alexander Ferguson, DL, of Pitfour, Aberdeenshire, and *d* 20 May 1944, leaving issue. He *d* 13 March 1945

2 Mabel Marjorie; *b* 24 Feb 1876; *m* 7 July 1904 Maj Sir Henry Bernard De la Poer Beresford-Peirse, 4th Bt (*qv*), and *d* 13 Jan 1966, leaving issue

3 Lilian Katharine; *b* 13 July 1879; *m* 21 July 1910 Rev Richard Windham De la Poer Beresford-Peirse, Vicar of Christ Church, Lancaster Gate, 2nd son of Sir Henry Morson De la Poer Beresford-Peirse, 3rd Bt (*qv*), and *d* 2 Jan 1918, leaving issue

4 Muriel Dorothy; *b* 25 July 1887; *d* unm 23 Oct 1934

The 3rd EARL *d* 8 Feb 1811; his est son,

HUGH FREDERICK VAUGHAN CAMPBELL, **4th Earl Cawdor of Castlemartin**, DL (Nairn), JP (Carmarthenshire and Pembs), BA Oxford, late Capt and Hon Maj Carmarthen Art; *b* 21 June 1870; *m* 11 June 1898 Joan Emily Mary (*d* 26 July 1945), dau of John Charles Thynne (*see* BATH, M), and had issue:

1 JOHN DUNCAN VAUGHAN, **5th Earl**

2 Andrew Charles, Maj RARO, QO Cameron Highrs; *b* 26 Oct 1907; *educ* Eton and Ch Ch Oxford (BA 1929, MA 1933); *m* 15 Aug 1935 *Helen Christina, only dau of Hon Douglas Halyburton Cairns, of Carnach, Nairn (*see* CAIRNS, E), and *dsp* 11 April 1976

1 Janet Helena; *b* 2 March 1899; *m* 14 April 1926 John Francis Gore, CVO, barrister, 3rd son of Sir Francis Charles Gore, KCB, and *d* 2 Nov 1982, leaving issue (*see* ARRAN, E)

2 Mary Agatha; *b* 6 Jan 1905; *m* 5 Feb 1931 Brig Henry Claude Warrington Eastman, DSO, MVO, late RA (*d* 1975), only surv son of Thomas Eastman, MA, of Northwood Park, Winchester, and *d* 1997, leaving:

(1) *David William [David Eastman Esq, Pandy Newydd, Halfway Bridge, Bangor, Gwynedd]; *b* 7 Aug 1937; *educ* Eton; *m* 17 July 1969 *Antonia Catherine, dau of Anthony Dorman, of Mill Ho, Netherbury, Bridport, Dorset

(1) *Sylvia; *b* 23 Feb 1935; *m* 1967 Peter Leth (*d* 1987)

The 4th EARL *d* 7 Jan 1914; his est son,

JOHN DUNCAN VAUGHAN CAMPBELL, **5th Earl Cawdor of Castlemartin**, TD, JP (Pembs 1928), served WW I in RN, Lt-Col 4th Bn QO Cameron Highrs, served WW II (despatches), FSA, FSA Scot, FRGS, Convenor Nairn CC 1953–64, Chm Jt CC of Moray and Nairn 1957–64, Chm Historic Bldgs, Cncl for Scotland, Tstee Nat Museum of Antiquities of Scotland; *b* 17 May 1900; *m* 1st 15 May 1929 (*divorce* 1961) Wilma Mairi, (*d* 27 Aug 1982), est dau of Vincent Cartwright Vickers, of Edge Grove, Aldenham, Herts; *m* 2nd 29 June 1961 *Elizabeth Topham, dau of John Topham Richardson, JP, of Harps Oak, Merstham, Surrey, and widow of Maj Sir Alexander Penrose Gordon Cumming, 5th Bt (*qv*), and by 1st w had issue:

1 HUGH JOHN VAUGHAN, **6th Earl**

2 +James Alexander; *b* 21 July 1942; *educ* Eton and RCA; ARCA; *m* 1st 14 Nov 1964 (*divorce* 1973) Brigid Carol Dolben, dau of Capt Patrick Owen Lyons, RA (*see* MACKWORTH, Bt), and has issue:

(1) *Slaine Catherine; *b* 18 July 1966

(2) *Cara Jenny; *b* 19 June 1968

2 (cont.) The Hon James Campbell *m* 2nd 1973 (*divorce* 1986) Ann Elizabeth, dau of Col Argyle Henry Gillmore, OBE, and has further issue:

(3) *Lucy Georgia Elizabeth; *b* 1973

(4) *Sarah Ann; *b* 1977

1 Caroline Mairi; *b* 10 May 1930; *m* 4 Feb 1953 Baron Bernard Henry Hubert Friesen, only son of Baron Eduard Friesen, of Virnberg, Bavaria, and Majorca, and had issue:

(1) *Alexander Christian Edward; *b* 22 Sept 1961

(1) *Hero Arabella Mairi Elizabeth; *b* 18 Nov 1963

The 5th EARL *d* 9 Jan 1970; his er son,

HUGH JOHN VAUGHAN CAMPBELL, **6th Earl Cawdor of Castlemartin**; *b* 6 Sept 1932; *educ* Eton, Magdalen Coll Oxford and RAC Cirencester; High Sheriff of Carmarthenshire 1964, FLAS, underwriting memb of Lloyd's; *m* 1st 19 Jan 1956 (*divorce* 1979) Cathryn, 2nd dau of Maj-Gen Sir (William) Robert Norris Hinde, CBE, DSO, ADC, of Shrewton Ho, Salisbury, Wilts, by Evelyn Muriel, 3rd dau of Henry Fitzherbert Wright, JP, of Yeldersley Hall, Derbys, and had issue:

1 COLIN ROBERT VAUGHAN CAMPBELL, **7th and present Earl Cawdor of Castlemartin**

2 +FRED(ERICK) WILLIAM; *b* 29 July 1965; heir presumptive; *educ* Eton, UEA, Heriot Watt U and Inst of Holy Land Studies Jerusalem; *m* 7 Dec 1996 *Katherine (Katie) J M, 3rd dau of Richard Barrett, of Dallas, Texas, and Mrs Jennifer Barrett, of Fulham

1 *Emma Clare [The Lady Emma Marrian, PO Box 45465, Nairobi, Kenya]; *b* 15 March 1958; *m* 29 Jan 1983 (in Kenya) *David Marrian, son of Peter Marrian, of Nairobi, and has issue:

(1) *Jack Alexander Wolf; *b* 1985

(2) *Hunter James; *b* 1988

(3) *Finlay David; *b* 1991

2 *Elizabeth [The Lady Elizabeth Athill, 14 Almeric Rd, London SW11]; *b* 24 Sept 1959; *m* 1990 *William Robert Charles Athill, 3rd son of Maj Andrew Athill, Roy Norfolk Regt, of The Cottage, Morston, Norfolk, and has issue:

(1) *Atticus Ocean; *b* 1992

(1) *Storm; *b* 1990

3 *Laura Jane; *b* 26 Dec 1966

The **6th Earl** *m* 2nd 28 Dec 1979 Countess Angelika Lazansky [The Rt Hon The Dowager Countess Cawdor, Cawdor Castle, Nairn IV12 5RD], yr dau of Count Prokop Lazansky von Bulowa, of Chieska, Bohemia, and Salisbury, Rhodesia, and *d* 1993

Seat: Cawdor Castle, Cawdor, Nairn. The central block is a Scottish tower house of *c* 1370, constructed about a century after the Calders had first acquired land there. Accordingly any connection between the Castle and the historic figure of Macbeth is sheer romance since Macbeth lived in the mid-11th century. The tower was fortified in the 15th century and greatly added to with an ordinary dwelling house in the 17th. This replaced the 'curtain' wall that had surrounded the tower. In the ground floor room of the tower are the remains of a hawthorn tree. This commemorates legendary instructions in a dream to the first of the Calders that wherever a certain donkey carrying gold lay down to rest was where he should site his castle. The hawthorn remains genuinely date from the period when the tower was built.

CAWLEY

Arms: Sa. three swan's heads erased arg. guttée de poix, a chief arched or, thereon a rose gu. barbed and seeded ppr. between two garbs az. **Supporters:** On either side a swan, wings surgeant tergiant arg. guttée de poix, each standing upon a garb fesswise or.
Crest: Upon a mount vert a swan's head erased arg. between six bullrushes stalked and leaved, three on either side or.
Motto: *Cupio, credo, habeo* ('I desire, I believe, I have').
Creation: Bt. (UK) 1 Dec 1906, B. (UK) 16 Jan 1918.

THE 3RD BARON CAWLEY, of Prestwich, Co Lancs, and a **Baronet** (Sir Frederick Lee Cawley, Bt) [The Rt Hon The Lord Cawley, Bircher Hall, Leominster, Herefs HR6 0AX]; *b* 27 July 1913; *s f* 1954; *educ* Eton and New Coll Oxford (BA 1935, MA 1942); barrister Lincoln's Inn 1938 (Patent Bar 1946–73), Capt RA Leics Yeo WW II (wounded), memb Woking UDC 1949–57, Dep Chm Ctees Ho Lds 1958–67, Memb Jt Parly Ctees 1956–95; *m* 12 Dec 1944 *Rosemary Joan, yst dau of Reginald Edward Marsden, of Bishopsgate Place, Englefield Green, former Bursar of Eton Coll, by Hon Vere Mary, sis of 19th Viscount Dillon (*qv*), and has issue:

1 +JOHN FRANCIS [The Hon John Cawley, Castle Grounds, Ashton, Herefs HR60 DN]; *b* 28 Sept 1946; *educ* Eton; *m* 4 May 1979 *Regina Sarabia, est dau of Marqués De Hazas, of Madrid, and has issue:

(1) +William Robert Harold; *b* 2 July 1981

(2) +Thomas Frederick José-Luis; *b* 1982

(3) +Andrew David; *b* 1988

(1) *Susan Mary; *b* 20 Jan 1980

2 +William (Bill) Frederick [The Hon William Cawley, Stable House, Bircher Hall, nr Leominster, Herefs]; *b* 7 Dec 1947; *educ* Eton and New Coll Oxford (BA 1970, MA 1974); *m* 9 June 1979 (*divorce* 1988) Philippa Jane, er dau of Philip Hoare, DFC, of The Playne, Weycombe Rd, Haselmere, Surrey, and has issue:

(1) +Edward Frederick; *b* 1980

(1) *Elizabeth Lena; *b* 1982

3 +Richard Kenneth; *b* 14 April 1949; *educ* Eton, Durham U (BA 1973), and City U Business Sch (MBA); MBIM; *m* 8 Sept 1976 *Tsugumi, 2nd dau of S Ota, of Takarazuka, Japan

4 +Justin Robert [The Hon Justin Cawley, 41 Moreton Eye, Leominster, Herefs]; *b* 15 June 1953; *educ* Milton Abbey; *m* 1986 (*divorce* 1994) Margaret Lee Greatorex-Davies

5 +Charles Michael; *b* 9 Feb 1955; *educ* Milton Abbey and Manchester U (BA 1977); *m* 11 Oct 1980 (*divorce* 1987) Justine Jane, dau of John Frederick Barwise Parry, of Hockley, Essex

6 +Mark Andrew; *b* 3 Nov 1957; *educ* Eton, New Coll Oxford (MA 1979) and INSEAD (MBA)

1 *Vanessa Mary [The Hon Mrs Marston, Gorwell House, Barnstaple, N Devon]; *b* 30 Dec 1951; BA OU; *m* Sept 1971 *Dr John Anthony Marston, only son of Donald A Marston, OBE, and has issue:

(1) *Cicely Alice; *b* 10 June 1973

(2) *Emma Elizabeth; *b* 6 Jan 1975

(3) *Camilla Vere; *b* 9 May 1977

(4) *Annabel Sarah; *b* 11 July 1979

Lineage: THOMAS CALYE, of Chester; living 26 Oct 1469; had:

RICHARD CALLYE; living 1539; had:

RICHARD CALLIE or CAWLEY, of Chester; *d* April 1570, leaving, with a yr s (Richard, of Chester; *d* 1614, leaving issue):

ROBERT CAWLEY, of Hallowes Gate, Kelsall, Cheshire; *m* Alice Vernon and *d* Nov 1601, leaving, with other issue, including an er s (Robert, of Willington, Cheshire, left issue):

JOHN CAWLEY, of Kelsall; *d* by 1607, leaving a 2nd s:

WILLIAM CAWLEY, of Kelsall; *m* 10 June 1628 Anne Ithell (*d* 1644) and had:

WILLIAM CAWLEY, of Burton, Tarvin, Cheshire; *b* Feb 1633; *d* Jan 1669, leaving:

ROBERT CAWLEY, of Burton; *m* 1st 18 Oct 1680 Margarey Ince (*d* 1683) and had issue; *m* 2nd Elizabeth (*d* July 1689) and had further issue; *m* 3rd Elizabeth and had a 4th s:

STEPHEN CAWLEY, of Moat Ho, Alpraham, Cheshire; *b* Dec 1695; *m* Anne (*d* 28 Sept 1771), dau of John Catterall, and *d* 20 July 1773, leaving:

ROBERT CAWLEY, of Burland, Cheshire; *b* 1725; *m* Elizabeth Holbrook (*d* 15 Feb 1805) and *d* 20 March 1803, leaving:

JOHN CAWLEY, of Ridley Hall, Cheshire; *b* 1774; *m* Mary Woodfield (*d* 28 Dec 1860) and *d* 30 Nov 1860, leaving:

THOMAS CAWLEY, of Priestlands, Bunbury, Cheshire; *b* 13 Feb 1806; *m* 14 Oct 1829 Harriet (*d* 11 Oct 1886), dau of Samuel Bird, of Beeston Hall, Cheshire, and *d* 5 Oct 1875, leaving, with other issue:

Sir Frederick Cawley, 1st Bt, and **1st Baron Cawley**, of Prestwich, Co Lancs (both UK), so *cr* 1 Dec 1906 and 16 Jan 1918 respectively, PC (1916), JP (Lancs and Herefs), MP (Lib) Prestwich 1895–1918, Chllr Duchy Lancaster 1916–18; *b* 9 Oct 1850; *m* 24 Aug 1876 Elizabeth (*d* 21 March 1930), dau of John Smith, of Kynsal Lodge, Audlem, Cheshire, and had:

1 ROBERT HUGH, **2nd Baron**

2 Harold Thomas, barrister Inner Temple 1902, MP (Lib) Heywood 1910–15, PPS to Rt Hon R McKenna 1911–15, served WW I Capt 6th Bn Manchester Regt; *b* 12 June 1878; *educ* New Coll Oxford (MA), *ka* Dardanelles 23 Sept 1915

3 John Stephen, Maj 20th Hus Boer War 1902 (Queen's medal with four clasps), WW I 1914 as Bde Maj 1st Cav Bde (despatches); *b* 27 Oct 1879; *ka* 1 Sept 1914

4 Oswald, Capt Shropshire Yeo, MP Prestwich 1918; *b* 7 Oct 1882; *educ* New Coll Oxford (BA); *ka* 22 Aug 1918

1 Hilda Mary; *b* 20 May 1881; *m* 27 July 1904 Capt Charles Edwin Percival Long, late 3rd Bn KOYLI, son of C E B Long, of Down End, Fareham, Hants, and *d* 14 March 1956, leaving issue. He *d* 14 April 1930

The 1st BARON *d* 30 March 1937; his est and only surv son,

ROBERT HUGH CAWLEY, **2nd Baron Cawley**, JP Lancs; Lt 77th Co Imp Yeo Boer War (Queen's Medal with four clasps); *b* 16 May 1877; *m* 26 Sept 1912 Vivienne (*d* 4 Jan 1978 aged 100), dau of Harold Lee, of Fairfield, Broughton Park, Manchester (*see* 1967 edn, LEE, Bt), and *d* 24 Sept 1954, having had issue:

1 FREDERICK LEE CAWLEY, **3rd and present Baron Cawley**

2 Stephen Robert, JP Herefs and Worcs Supplemental 1970–78, Kidderminster (Active) 1978–83, Surrey Supplemental since 1983; *b* 22 Oct 1915; *educ* Eton and New Coll Oxford (BA 1937, BSc 1938, MA 1946); served WW II with Roy Signals, Prime Warden Dyers' Co 1970–71; *m* 28 June 1952 his bro's w's sister *Iris Edrica [The Hon Mrs Stephen Cawley, Marlow, Beaconhill Rd, Hindhead, Surrey GU26 6QD], 2nd dau of Reginald Edward Marsden, and *d* 29 Dec 1995, having had issue:

(1) Peter Edward; *b* 14, *d* 17 April 1953

(2) +Robin Alexander; *b* 20 July 1954; *educ* Eton; *m* 1982 *Roslyn, only dau of George Latham, of Newport, Gwent, and has:

1a +Hugh Edward; *b* 3 Nov 1984

2a +Timothy James; *b* 19 June 1987

(3) +James Edward; *b* 19 April 1956; *educ* Eton; *m* 1984 *Mary Fiona, only dau of Lt-Cdr E J Wright, of Elm Ho, Ampleforth, Yorks, and has issue:

1a +Joseph Edward John; *b* 1989

(4) +Martin Harold; *b* 17 July 1959

(1) *Yoland Diana; *b* 29 Dec 1957; *m* 1988 *Mark Jonathan Dodgson, Prof Australian National U, and has:

1a *Jack Andrew; *b* 7 Dec 1986

1a *Kate Suzanne; *b* 1989

2a *Rosie Jane; *b* 1 Feb 1991

3 Harold Kenneth John, Capt KSLI, served WW II; *b* 22 May 1919; *ka* in Tunisia, May 1943

Seat: Bircher Hall, Leominster, Herefs. The origins of this house lie in the third quarter of the 18th century, its earliest constructor, Adam Ward, having died in 1772. It was then enlarged, chiefly in depth away from the front elevation, and to considerable extent, in the 19th century. Despite this eye-catching stretch effect the front is capable of holding its own, having a porch supported by doric columns. The **3rd Baron** bought it some 30 years ago, by which time it had passed through the hands of the DUNNEs, a prominent county family, and those of the sister of the present Viscount Hereford (*qv*).

CAYLEY

Arms: Quarterly, arg. and sa., a bend gu. charged with three mullets of the first. **Crest:** A demi-lion rampant or, charged with a bend gu., thereon three mullets arg., in the paws a battle-axe arg., handle also gu, with an ornamental tuft on it gold. **Motto:** *Nul q'un* ('Nothing but one') **Creation:** Bt. (E) 26 April 1661.

SIR DIGBY WILLIAM DAVID CAYLEY, 11TH BT, of Brompton, Co York [Sir Digby Cayley Bt, Morris House, Marlborough College, Marlborough, Wilts SN8 1PA]; *b* 3 June 1944; *s* kinsman 1967; *educ* Malvern and Downing Coll Cambridge (BA 1967, Dip Ed 1968, MA); Assist Classics Master and Master i/c Shooting Marlborough 1994–, Assist Classics Master: Portsmouth GS 1968–73, Stonyhurst 1973–81, Marlborough 1989–90, Abingdon Sch 1990–94; antique dealer 1981–89; *m* 1st 19 July 1969 (*divorce* 1987) Christine Mary, only dau of Derek Francis Gaunt, of Ilkley, Yorks, and has issue:

1 *Emma Jane; *b* 1974

2 *Catherine Mary; *b* 1975

Sir DIGBY *m* 2nd 1993 *Cathryn (Kate) Mary Russell and by her has:

1 +THOMAS THEODORE WILLIAM; *b* 17 Feb 1997

Lineage: WILLIAM de CAYLEY, of Heacham, Norfolk; lived *temp* HENRY I.

The CAYLEYs held Heacham by *c* 1190.

In the second half of the 13th century four bros existed (Elias and Ralph de Cailly, who gave to the monks of Lewes all their f's land in Massingham, Norfolk; also Roger); the 4th:

HUGH de CALY, of Heacham and Yorks; *m* Agnes de Hemstede and *d* 1286, leaving:

JOHN CAYLY, of Owby; had:

Sir WILLIAM CAYLEY, of Owby; sold *c* 1316 the manor of Heacham to Simon Kenyng, of Kenyngham; had:

1 William (Sir), of Owby; *m* Alice, dau of Sir John Braose, and had:

(1) Agnes; *m* John Harsike, of Norfolk

(2) Eva; *m* Edmund Clipsby, of Clipsby, Norfolk, who assumed the arms of CAYLEY

2 JOHN

The yr son,

JOHN CAYLEY; moved to Yorks and settled at Normanton; had:

1 Hugh, *dsp*

2 William, of Normanton; had an only dau and heiress:

(1) Jennet; *m* John Lake and was ancestor of the LAKEs of Normanton

3 JOHN

The yst son,

JOHN CAYLEY; had:

WILLIAM CAYLEY; had, with another s (John, *dsp*):

EDMUND CAYLEY, of Thormanby; had, with a yr s (John, priest, incumbent of Thormanby):

WILLIAM CAYLEY, of Thormanby; had:

JOHN CAYLEY, of Thormanby, had, with two yr s (William, incumbent Thormanby; Lawrence):

EDWARD CAYLEY, of Thormanby; had:

WILLIAM CAYLEY, of Thormanby; *m* Joan, dau of Richard Gouldthorp, and *d* 1586, having had, with a yr s (James, *m* Mary, dau of Ralph Bell, of Sowerby, Yorks, and had Matthew, a royalist in the Civil War):

EDWARD CAYLEY; bought the estate of Brompton, Pickering, Yorks; *m* 1604 Anne, dau of William Walters, of Cundall, Yorks, and *d* 7 Dec 1642, having had, with a yr s (Arthur (Sir), of Newland, Coventry):

Sir William Cayley, 1st Bt (E), so *cr* 26 April 1661, of Brompton; *bapt* 5 May 1610; ktd March 1640/1, royalist Civil War; *m* 1633 Dorothy (*bur* 24 Nov 1684), est dau of Sir William St Quintin, 1st Bt, of Harpham, and had four s and two daus, of whom:

1 WILLIAM (Sir), **2nd Bt**

2 Arthur, of The Low Hall, Brompton; *m* 14 April 1662 Elizabeth, dau of Thomas Shipton, of Lyth and Mulgrave, and had issue; ggggf of:

(1) Edward Stillingfleet Cayley, of Wydale, MP; *b* 13 Aug 1802; *m* 30 Aug 1823, his cousin Emma (*d* 2 Aug 1848), dau of **Sir George Cayley, 6th Bt**, and *d* 25 Feb 1862, leaving, with other issue:

1a George John; *b* 26 Jan 1826; *m* 11 Sept 1860 Mary Anne Frances (*m* 2nd 4 Dec 1888 Baron Emile de Royer, and *d* 5 Jan 1908), dau of Montagu Wilmot, and *d* 11 Oct 1878, having had, with other issue:

1b Hugh, of Wydale; *b* 6 Sept 1861; *m* 9 July 1903 Rosa, dau of Johann Seelig, of Hanover, and *d* 5 Nov 1924

2a Charles Digby, RN; *b* 22 March 1827; *d* 17 May 1844

3 Cornelius, of York; *b* 10 Aug 1644; *m* 11 Aug 1681 Ann, dau of Cecil Tyrwhitt, and *d* before 15 March 1734, leaving issue. His 5th son:

(1) Cornelius, barrister, Recorder of Hull; *b* 16 April 1692; *m* 18 Nov 1723 Elizabeth (*d* Feb 1750), dau of Leonard Smelt, of Kirkby Fleetham, and *d* 17 Nov 1779, leaving issue:

1a William (Rev), Preb of Southwell, and Rector of Burton Agnes and Rudstone, Yorks; *b* 1724; *dsp*

2a John, Consul-Gen at St Petersburg; *b* 7 Oct 1730; *m* 19 Dec 1756 Sarah (*d* 12 Nov 1803), dau of Richard Cozens, and *d* 9 July 1795, leaving, with other issue:

1b John, of Wallington, Surrey; *b* 11 April 1761; *m* 1st 8 Feb 1792 Anna (*dsp* 8 Sept 1793), dau of Matthew Halliday, MD; *m* 2nd 20 Oct 1799 Harriett (*d* 23 Feb 1870), dau of Timothy Raikes, and *d* 30 March 1831, leaving with other issue:

1c William, of Toronto, MP, Inspr-Gen Canada; *b* 26 May 1807; *m* 12 April 1836 Emma Robinson (*b* 15 March 1890), dau of D'Arcy Boulton, and *d* 23 Feb 1890, leaving, with five other s and another dau:

1d John D'Arcy (Rev), DD, Canon and Precentor St Alban, Rector St George's, Toronto; *b* 15 March 1837; *m* 18 June 1861 Mary Magdalene (*d* 10 Oct 1900), dau of J S Cartwright, and *d* 20 Aug 1911, leaving issue:

1e Edward Cartwright (Rev), MA, DD, Rector of St Simon's Church, Toronto, Prof of Theology in Trinity Coll, Toronto; *b* 13 Feb 1864; *m* 25 Sept 1895 Alice (*d* 1951), dau of Rev A J Broughall, Rector of St Stephen's, Toronto, and *d* 11 April 1921, leaving issue:

1f Arthur Bowen, Lt RGA, served WW I (wounded, POW); *b* 28 Nov 1898; *m* 3 Sept 1921 Katharine Vanderwerken (*d* 1973), dau of Peleg Howland, of Toronto, and *d* 1973, having had issue:

1g +Edward Cartwright [Edward Cayley Esq, 44 Jackes Av Apt 1713, Toronto, Ont M4T 1E5, Canada]; *b* 11 May 1922; *educ* Trin Coll Sch, Port Hope, Toronto, and U of Toronto (BA), MA 1957 Columbia U; Lt-Cdr RCNVR WW II, Headmaster of Stanstead Coll Quebec, Assist Headmaster Holderness Sch; *m* 1st 1944 (*divorce* 1956) Margaret Noble, of Mansfield, Notts, and has issue:

1h +David Cartwright [David Cayley Esq, 242 Havelock St, Toronto, Ont M6H 3B9, Canada]; *b* 26 March 1946; *educ* Holderness Sch Plymouth and Harvard; author and broadcaster; *m* 1st 1968 (*divorce* 1976) Mary Josephine Breen and has:

1i *Rachael Catherine; *b* 1968

1h (cont.) David Cayley *m* 2nd 19– *Jutta Bechmann and by her has:

1i +Jesse Luke Edward; *b* 1980

2i +Richard Daniel; *b* 1983

2i *Katharine Emmanuel Cartwright; *b* 1978

1h *Susan Margaret; *b* 1948

2h *Catherine Jane; *b* 1952

1g (cont.) Edward Cayley *m* 2nd 1956 *Catherine Norma, dau of Alexander Stuart, of Eganville, Ontario

2g +Peleg Howland [Capt Peleg Cayley RCN, Glenlea, High Pitfold, Hindhead, Surrey]; *b* 5 Feb 1924; *educ* Trin Coll Sch, Port Hope, and RNC Dartmouth; Capt RCN; *m* 1st 1945 (*divorce* 1953) Freda Rosemary, dau of Alfred Cotter, of 8 Cherryhill, Beechlands, Belfast, and has issue

1h *Jennifer Margaret; *b* 1947

2g (cont.) Capt Peleg Cayley *m* 2nd 1955 *Patricia Challinor, dau of Dr John C Poole, of Cranbourne, Horley, Surrey, and by her has further issue:

1h +John Howland; *b* 1956

2h +Richard Arthur; *b* 1960

3h +Christopher Peter; *b* 1966

3g David; *b* 15 Dec 1927; *d* 1934

2f Hugh Cartwright, Capt 48th Highrs of Canada, served WW II; *b* 1901; *educ* Trin Coll Toronto (BA 1925); *m* 1st Sept 1928 Ethel Ann Farquharson (*d* 1934), dau of Wilmot L Matthews, of Toronto, Canada; *m* 2nd 1940 *Gladys, dau of J T Large, and *d* 1967, leaving by his 1st w:

1g Hugh Cartwright; *b* 30 Aug 1932; *d* 1987

1f Alice Margaret; *m* 12 Sept 1925 Arthur Arundell Harcourt Vernon and had issue (*see* VERNON, B)

2f Cicely; *d* 1906

3f Sylvia; *b* 1909; *m* Oct 1937 Ven Terence Patrick Crosthwait (*d* 1995), Archdeacon York, Rector St Clement's N Toronto, and *d* 1990, leaving issue

4f *Ray D'Arcy; *b* 1912; *m* 1947 William Ramsay Osler (*d* 1988), RCAF

2e Arthur Macaulay, Maj RA; *b* 15 Jan 1867; *d* unm Nov 1910

1e Mary Augusta; *d* 3 Aug 1926

2e Cecil Maud; *d* unm 17 Sept 1916

3e Emma Madeline; *m* 27 Feb 1902 Noël Burn Rosher, OBE, MIME, and *d* 3 March 1940, leaving issue. He *d* 4 Sept 1936

2d Francis; *b* 7 Feb 1845; *m* 15 Oct 1874 Jane Isabel (*d* 1920), dau of Henry Easton, of Ontario, and *d* 1909, leaving issue:

1e +William Henry; *b* 30 Dec 1881

1e *Emma Robinson

2e *Adelaide Mary; *m* R G Strickland, of Salt Lake City, Utah, USA

3e *Muriel Isabel; *m* Jay Scholefield, of Santa Monica, California, USA

3d Hugh St Quintin, Sr Co Court Judge, Vancouver, BC; *b* 19 Nov 1857; *m* 6 Sept 1897 Nora Adelaide, dau of William Maurice Cochrane, of Vernon, BC, and *d* May 1934, leaving issue:

1e Beverley Cochrane; *b* 25 Oct 1898

1d Mary; *m* 23 Aug 1866 Capt W Glascott, and *d* 1890, leaving issue

2d Sophia Emma

2c John, of Holmdene, Bickley, Kent; *b* 11 Feb 1816; *m* 1st 4 Aug 1841 Catherine Mary (*dsp* Sept 1845), dau of Capt Maine; *m* 2nd 5 Oct 1847 Clara Louisa (*d* 1898), dau of Hon Henry John Boulton, Ch Justice of Newfoundland, and *d* 1900, leaving issue:

1d Claud Thornton; *b* 9 June 1854; *m* 1st 1 June 1881 Esther Mary (*d* Dec 1926), dau of William Bayley; *m* 2nd May 1927 Blanche Graham (*d* 23 Aug 1942), dau of John Ford, late of Tancred, York, and widow of Arthur H Clemow, MD, FRCP, and *d* 31 July 1928, having by 1st w had issue:

1e Claud D'Arcy, Lt 5th Bn Middx Regt; *b* July 1882; *m* 1917 Lilian Gertrude (*d* 13 May 1942), dau of R Hall, of Retford, Notts, and *d* 30 Nov 1948, leaving issue:

1f +Robert Edward Digby; *b* 10 Aug 1918; *m* 19 Aug 1942 *Mary Florence Louvain Robins

2e Edward St Quentin, Lt RFA (TF); *b* 7 June 1887; *m* 4 May 1916 Sybil Frances (*d* 14 July 1975), dau of Canon Joseph Alfred Halloran, Rector of Eastwell, Kent, and *d* 14 July 1941, leaving issue:

1f *Patricia St Quentin; *b* 23 Oct 1922; *m* 3 April 1948 Anthony Bruce Askew (*d* 1980), 2nd son of Sidney Bruce Askew, of Buxshalls, Lindfield, Sussex, and has issue:

1g *Rory Anthony Rank; *b* 15 April 1949; *educ* Bradfield; *m* 1978 *Susan Mary Mawson, and has issue

1g *Cleone St Quentin; *b* 10 Aug 1952; *m* 1977 *Maxim Hastings Pengelly, and has issue

3e Charles Knightley, Lt Kent Fortress, RE; *b* 3 Aug 1888; *m* 15 Sept 1915 Isabella Alice (*d* 1956), dau of Benjamin Edward Leach, of PO Coalbrook, OFS, and *d* 22 June 1916, leaving issue:

1f *Alice Knightley; *b* 1916; *m* 11 May 1940 *Christian John Rosslee, son of Hendry Rosslee, of Cape Town, and has issue

1e Adela Mary; *b* July 1883; *m* 9 June 1915 Brig William Albany Fetherstonhaugh, CB, CBE, DSO, 8th Cav IA, son of Col William Albany Fetherstonhaugh, and *d* 13 Oct 1954, leaving issue. He *d* 25 Oct 1947

2e Mabel Boulton; *b* Sept 1884; *m* 11 July 1907 Rev Henry Lynden Potter, Vicar of Collier St, Marden, son of Dean Potter, of Raphoe, Ireland, and had issue. He *d* 19 Oct 1943

3e Dorothy Gladys; *b* Feb 1886; *m* 20 April 1911 (*divorce* 1927) Edward George Tewson, son of Edward Arthur Tewson, of Tunbridge Wells, and *d* 4 July 1936, leaving issue

2d Francis Osmond, of Toronto; *b* 30 Sept 1856; *m* 7 July 1882 Marion Louisa (*d* 1943), dau of Sir James Lukin Robinson, 2nd Bt of Toronto (*qv*), and *d* 1921, leaving issue:

1e Clara Gwendoline; *b* 1884

2e Julia Isabel; *b* 1885; *m* 12 Feb 1913 Robert Alexander Laidlaw, of 35 Jackes Ave, Toronto, and *d* 20 April 1961, leaving issue

3e Hilda Marion; *b* 1887; *m* 21 April 1910 Charles Delamere Magee, son of Charles Magee, of Ottawa, and *d* 10 Dec 1915, leaving issue

4e Marjorie Gordon; *b* 5 April 1897; *m* 27 June 1925 John William Gamble Boyd, son of J W G of Toronto, and has issue:

1f *John William Gamble, RCAF; *b* 26 Sept 1929

2f *Philip Cayley, BA, RCAF; *b* 6 March 1932

3f *Peter Beverley; *b* 12 June 1935

1d Adela Sidney; *b* 9 Dec 1850; *m* 8 May 1873 Christopher Wolston, MD, and *d* 26 Jan 1931, leaving issue. He *d* 1923

2d Clara Louisa; *b* 13 Feb 1852; *m* 6 Jan 1894 William Fitzwilliam Burton, JP, of Burton Hall, Co Carlow, and *d* 11 Dec 1914, leaving issue. He *d* 29 April 1909

1c Lucy; *m* Rev C E Hutchinson, Canon of Chichester, and had issue. He *d* 1870

2c Maria; *m* 24 Sept 1840 Charles Chevall Tooke, of Hurston Clays, and *d* 10 Nov 1885, leaving issue

2b Henry, of St Petersburg and Blackheath; *b* 21 Dec 1768; *m* 18 Feb 1814 Mary Antonia, dau of William Doughty, and *d* 11 July 1850, leaving, with other issue:

1c Arthur, of Trin Coll Cambridge, Sadlerian Prof of Pure Mathematics; *b* 16 Aug 1821; *m* 8 Sept 1863 Susan (*d* 27 May 1923), dau of Robert Moline, and *d* 26 Jan 1895, leaving issue:

1d Henry, JP, ARIBA; *b* 12 Feb 1870; *educ* Trin Coll Cambridge (MA); *m* 26 June 1907 Kate (*d* 18 Feb 1967, aged 91), dau of Walter Dixon, late of St Albans, and *dsp* 22 Aug 1949

1d Mary; *d* unm 14 June 1950

3a Edward, of Whitby, Yorks; *b* 6 Sept 1733; *m* 1st 8 Nov 1760 Anne, dau of William Simpson, and had issue; *m* 2nd Mary, dau of Jonas Brown, JP, of Whitby, and *d* 12 Jan 1805, having by her had issue:

1b Edward, of Stamford, Lincs; *b* 12 Aug 1782; *m* 24 Sept 1828 Frances (*d* 1 June 1851), dau of Rev Richard Twopeny, MA, Rector of Little Casterton, Rutland, and *d* 10 April 1868, leaving issue:

1c Edward (Rev), MA (Camb), Vicar of S Leverton, Notts; *b* 15 June 1829; *m* 20 May 1862 Catherine Isabella (*d* 29 Dec 1919), dau of Henry Blenkarne, and *d* 5 Dec 1908, leaving issue:

1d Agnes Mary, had Order of Mercy, and bar; *m* 1887 Richard Lake Harrison, of 1 New Court, Lincoln's Inn, and *d* 1956, leaving issue. He *d* 1916

2d Margaret Isabella, had Order of Mercy, and bar; *d* unm 10 Jan 1945

3d Henrietta; *m* 7 April 1891 Maj Frank H M Savile, Tank Corps, of Castle Ashby, Northants, and *d* 18 Feb 1926

2c George, of Ketton Priory, Stamford; *b* 12 July 1831; *m* 17 Nov 1859 Margaret (*d* 1899), dau of Ven Robert Bateman Paul, and *d* 1891, leaving issue:

1d Nowell Paul; *b* 18 Nov 1865; *m* 16 Nov 1893 Gertrude Stephanie (*d* 4 Sept 1948), dau of Sir Richard Cayley, of Ryhall (*see* below), and *d* 15 Jan 1928, leaving issue:

1e John Oliver; *b* 6 April 1906; *d* 24 Feb 1938

2d Arthur George, Lt PWO Regt; *b* 6 Jan 1867; *d* 1892

3d Frank Peirson; *b* 1 Nov 1868; *educ* Trin Coll Cambridge (MB, BA); *dsp* Dec 1914

1d Frances Bateman; *d* unm 20 Dec 1902

2d Rosa Elizabeth; *d* unm 27 Sept 1940

3d Edith Margaret; *m* 19 Dec 1891 Julian Edward Bellamy; barrister, of 3 New Inns Sq, WC, and *d* 22 June 1935, leaving issue

4d Ida Mary; *d* unm 4 Jan 1951

5d Helen Maria; *d* unm 7 May 1943

3c Richard (Sir), JP Rutland and Northants, MA Cambridge, barrister, Ch Justice of Ceylon; *b* 22 April 1833; *m* 17 April 1866 Sophia Margaret (*d* 25 June 1921), dau of David Wilson, of Ceylon, MLC, and *d* 5 April 1908, leaving issue:

1d Hugh Charles, T/Lt E Lancs Regt WW I; *b* 6 Aug 1869; *educ* Trin Coll Cambridge (BA); *m* 25 Nov 1899 Annie Beatrice (*d* 1951), dau of Alfred Wilkins, and *d* 10 April 1945, leaving issue:

1e Kymer Frank Hugh; *b* 12 Dec 1900; *d* 5 Feb 1917

2e Richard Wilkins, BSc Lond, ACGI, AMIMechE, Capt RAOC and REME, served WW II; *b* 5 April 1902; *educ* Aldenham; *m* 29 June 1935 Joan Harvey (*d* 1990), dau of Dr E Harvey Sutcliff, of Torrington, N Devon, and *d* 1991, having had issue:

1f Hugh James; *b* 4 Sept; *d* 12 Oct 1936

2f +William Richard [William Cayley Esq, 2 Meadow Rd, Corn Meadow Lane, Claines, Worcs]; *b* 28 May 1944; *educ* Taunton Sch; *m* 1972 *Mary Elizabeth, dau of George Arthur Baillie, of Selkirk, and has issue:

1g +Alexander Richard; *b* 1973

2g +Arthur Edward (twin); *b* 1973

1g *Lucy Claire Christina; *b* 1984

1f *Mary Catherine [Mrs Richard Wood, Ashlar, Church Row, Hilton, Dorset DT11 0DD]; *b* 21 June 1938; *m* 3 Aug 1963 *Richard John Wood, MA, er son of Joseph Gordon Wood, of 25 Monkhams Ave, Woodford Green, Essex, and has issue:

1g *James Julian; *b* 4 Aug 1965; *m* 1992 *Samantha Schofield

2g *Jonathan Mark; *b* 20 April 1968

2f *Janet Rose [Mrs Barry Palmer, 20 Queen's Dve, Great Malvern, Worcs]; *b* 11 Sept 1940; *m* 10 July 1965 *Barry Keith Palmer, yr s of Eric Palmer, and has issue:

1g *Daniel Barry; *b* 1970

1g *Louise Janet; *b* 13 April 1967

2g *Eleanor Mary; *b* 20 May 1969

1d Frances Sophia Henrietta; *m* 23 May 1898 Sir Francis Du Pré Oldfield, ICS, Judge of Madras High Court, and *d* 27 March 1932, leaving issue. He *d* 14 Feb 1928

2d Gertrude Stephanie; *m* 16 Nov 1893 her cousin Nowell Paul Cayley and *d* 4 Sept 1948, having had issue (*see* above)

3d Adeline Matilda; *m* 30 Aug 1902 William Sidney Hargreaves, est son of William Hargreaves, of Shipley Hall, Yorks, and *d* 4 Oct 1965, leaving issue. He *d* July 1943

4d Dorothy Mary, mycologist; *d* unm 5 Dec 1954

5d Gwladys Eva; *d* unm 17 Jan 1954

4c Henry, CMG, Hon Surg to the King, Dep Surg-Gen late Bengal Army, FRGS; *b* 20 Dec 1834; *m* 10 July 1862 Letitia Mary (*d* 29 April 1920), dau of Rev Nicholas Walters, and *d* 19 March 1904, leaving issue:

1d Walter de Sausmarez (Sir), KCMG, CB, DL, Maj-Gen late W Yorks Regt, Hon Col 5th Bn W Yorks Regt 1927–33, served in Ashanti 1895–96, in S African War 1901–02, on N W Frontier of India 1908 and WW I 1914–18 (despatches), had Order of Karageorge of Serbia 3rd Cl with swords; *b* 8 Aug 1863; *m* 8 Dec 1896 Constance (*d* 23 May 1966), dau of Rev Canon Richard Paul Blakeney, LLD, DD, and *d* 21 July 1952

2d Cyril Henry, JP, MD, FRCS, MA Cambridge; *b* 1865; *m* 1893 Maria Charlotte (*d* 27 May 1960, aged 91), dau of William Black, and *d* 31 July 1905, having had issue:

1e Henry Douglas, OBE (1946), late Ch Gen Manager Nat and Grindlays Bank Ltd, London (ret as Dir 1972); *b* 20 Jan 1904; *educ* Epsom Coll; *m* 14 Aug 1940 *Nora Innes, est dau of Maj Nigel Paton, of Covehithe, Wrentham, Suffolk, and *d* 1991, leaving issue

1f +Neil Henry [Neil Cayley Esq, 7 Coolena Rd, Elanora Heights, Sydney, NSW, Australia]; *b* 7 Aug 1943; *educ* Marlborough; ARICS, FVLE, dir Cayleys Pty, property consultants; *m* 31 Jan 1970 *Julie, dau of A L Bowen, and has issue:

1g +Henry James; *b* 1972

1g *Victoria Anne; *b* 1971; *m* *Patrick Andrew Dare

1f *Innes Margaret; *b* 6 Oct 1941; *m* 1971 *Terence John Benson, and has issue:

1g *Andrew Douglas; *b* 1973

2g *Mark David; *b* 1975

2f *Lindsay Mary; *b* 6 June 1948; *m* 7 Nov 1970 Ian James, and has issue:

1g *Alison Mary; *b* 1980

2g *Kirsty Innes; *b* 1982

2e Cyril, MC (1942), Maj IA WW II (wounded); *b* 4 Dec 1905

1e Dorothy St Quintin

3d Douglas Edward, CB (1919), CMG (1915), Col late 4th Bn Worcs Regt, Hon Maj-Gen ret 1920, served Boer War 1900–02 (two medals, five clasps), WW I (wounded, despatches) and WW II (CD), had Order of White Eagle of Serbia, 3rd Cl with swords, Croix de Guerre of France and Belgium, and Order of Crown of Belgium; *b* 15 July 1870; *m* 7 Nov 1906 Jessie Eyre Duff (*d* 23 Nov 1955), yst dau of Sir William Duff Gibbon, of Bournemouth, late of Kandy, Ceylon, and *d* 19 Dec 1951, leaving issue:

1e Richard Douglas, DSO (with 2 bars), Cdr RN, served WW II; *b* 6 Oct 1907; *m* 22 April 1933 *Nancy (*m* 2nd H S Gild, FRCS), yr dau of Edward Coutts, of Sweffling, Fleet, Hants, and was *ka* Jan 1943, whilst in cmd of HM Submarine *P 311*, leaving issue:

1f *Jennifer Jane; *b* 14 April 1934; *m* 18 Aug 1956 *S/Ldr Arthur Christopher Doggett, RAF, est son of Arthur Francis Doggett, of The Hill, Strumpshaw, Norwich, by Hon Elizabeth Mary, yr dau of 1st Baron Horder (*qv*), and has issue:

1g *Antonia Clare; *b* 9 April 1958

2g *Jessica; *b* 19 May 1963

4d Bernard; *b* 22 Aug 1871; *m* 1904 Gertrude Mary (*d* 1942), dau of J C Large, and *d* 8 July 1914, having had issue:

1e John Norman; *b* 8 Aug 1905; *d* 14 Dec 1906

2e William Bernard, Capt IA WW II (POW); *b* 17 Sept 1907; *educ* Clifton and Wye Ag Coll; *m* 1935 Bronwen, dau of R C Young, of Yanco, NSW, and *d* 28 Oct 1963, leaving:

1f +John William Douglas [John Cayley Esq, 56 Rippon Rd, Hamilton, Vict 3300, Australia]; *b* 1938; *educ* Geelong GS and Melbourne U (BSc Ag); *m* 1 Dec 1964 *Glenys Robertson, dau of William Ross Wilson, of Edinburgh, and has issue:

1g +Ross Andrew; *b* 18 Sept 1965; *educ* Hamilton Coll, Victoria and Melbourne U (BSc)

1g *Fiona Bronwen; *b* 18 July 1968; *educ* Hamilton Coll, Victoria, Melbourne U (BA), New Hall Cambridge (MPhil) and Jesus Coll Cambridge (PhD)

3e Hugh Edward, Capt RE WW II; *b* 1910; *educ* Clifton and Wye Agric Coll

1e *Agnes Mary; *b* 7 Aug 1906; *m* 16 Feb 1926 Maj Charles Fraser Raper, 3rd Madras Regt, Rajputana Rifles, IA (*d* 22 June 1965), yr son of John Charles Dogson Raper, of Eastbourne, and has issue:

1f *John James; *b* 4 Oct 1927

2f *Charles Richard; *b* 30 May 1929

5d Norman, T/Lt RGA WW I; *b* 1874; *educ* Pembroke Coll Cambridge (BA); *d* unm 8 Dec 1952

6d Henry Priaulx, R-Adml RAN WW I; *b* 1877; *m* 14 July 1906 Ethel Mary (*d* 1940), only dau of Thomas Hewitt, of Sandcroft, Baynards, Horsham, and *d* 31 Dec 1942, leaving:

1e Henry Francis; *b* 23 Feb 1910; *educ* Geelong GS; *m* 18 April 1940 *Marea, dau of Colin Borthwick, of Sydney, Australia, and *d* 1981, leaving issue:

1f +Charles Francis; *b* 18 Aug 1943

1f *Susan Aneva Mary; *b* 6 July 1947

2f *Mary Lorraine; *b* 25 Feb 1950

1d Mary Louisa, had Order of Mercy; *m* 9 June 1892 Sir Charles Campbell McLeod, 1st Bt (*qv*), and *d* 19 Feb 1951, leaving issue

2d Evelyn Wynne; *m* 13 Feb 1893 Maj-Gen Sir Hayward Reader Whitehead, KCB, son of Rev T C Whitehead, MA, and *dsp* 9 Feb 1958. He *d* 28 Sept 1925

5c William, MD, FRCP London, consulting physician to Middx Hosp; *b* 14 Dec 1836; *d* unm 17 Dec 1916

6c Arthur; *b* 16 April 1840; *m* 12 May 1868 Caroline Ada (*d* 13 April 1927), dau of Rev F Forde, MA, Rector of St Peter's, Chester, and *d* 10 April 1905, leaving issue:

1d Osbert Arthur, slr; *b* 15 June 1869; *m* 19 March 1910 Dorothy (*d* 25 July 1942), dau of Rev George Herbert Lewis, Chaplain (ret) Indian Govt, and *d* 18 Aug 1947, leaving issue:

1e +Forde Everard de Wend, MBE (1946) [Dr Forde Cayley MBE, 67 Wish Rd, Hove, Sussex BN3 4LN]; *b* 1 Nov 1915; MD, MRCS, FRCP, Consultant Physician Brighton and Lewes Gp of Hosps in Diseases of Chest, Capt RAMC, WW II (POW); *m* 16 Sept 1941 Eileen Lilian (*d* 12 Oct 1997), dau of Arthur Claud Dalton, and had:

1f +(Arthur) Charles Digby [Dr Charles Cayley, 17 Conolly Rd, Hanwell, London W7 3JW]; *b* 8 Nov 1946; *educ* Brighton Coll and Middx Hosp Med Sch; MB, BS, MRCP; *m* 1969 *Jeanette Ann, MSc, MB, BS, MFFP, dau of G Avery, of Plymouth, and has:

1g +George Cornelius Forde; *b* 23 Nov 1971

2g +Adam Charles Francis; *b* 27 Dec 1975

3g +Seth Marcus Hugo; *b* 7 June 1980

2f +Michael Forde [Michael Cayley Esq, 13 Grove Rd, East Molesey, Surrey KT8 9JS]; *b* 26 Feb 1950; *educ* Brighton Coll and St John's Coll Oxford (MA); *m* 1987 *Jennifer, MA, MB, BS, dau of Patrick Lytle, of Southsea

1e *Frances Dorothy [Mrs Sidney Yates, 33 Kenilworth Rd, Ealing, London W5 5PA]; *b* 23 Dec 1912; *m* 23 Aug 1941 Sidney Alfred Yates (*d* 1977), s of Frederick John Yates, of London

1d Marjorie; *d* unm 12 Jan 1915

1 Anne; *m* Francis Wyvill, 2nd son of Sir Christopher Wyvill, 3rd Bt, of Constable Burton, and had issue. He *d* 22 Oct 1717

2 Dorothy; *m* 1695 Sir John Legard, 2nd Bt (*qv*), of Ganton, and *d* 11 July 1739, having had issue

Sir WILLIAM *d* 2 May 1681; his est surv son,

Sir William Cayley, 2nd Bt; *bapt* 23 June 1635; *m* 1653 Mary (*bur* 25 April 1709), dau and heir of Barnaby Holbech, of Birchley Hall, Warwicks, and *d* between 13 Sept 1706 and 16 March 1708, leaving, with other issue (including Hester, *m* Reginald Heber, of Marton, Yorks, and Dorothy, *m* Sir John Legard, 2nd Bt, *qv*):

Sir Arthur Cayley, 3rd Bt; *m* 28 May 1699 Everilda (*d* 12 Sept 1733), dau of George Thornhill, of Fixby, Yorks, and *d* 19 May 1727, leaving an only surv s:

Sir George Cayley, 4th Bt; *m* 31 May 1730 Philadelphia (*d* 14 Jan 1765), dau of John Digby, of Mansfield Woodhouse, Notts and had, with other issue:

1 THOMAS (Sir), **5th Bt**

1 Frances; *m* Rev John Cayley, of Low Hall, Brompton (descended from the 2nd son of the 1st Bt), and had:

(1) John; had:

1a Edward Stillingfleet, MP, of Wydale Ho (*see below*)

Sir GEORGE *d* Sept 1791 aged 84; his est son,

Sir Thomas Cayley, 5th Bt; *b* Aug 1732; *m* 1763 Isabella (*d* 30 July 1828), dau of John Seton, of Parbroath, and *d* 15 March 1792, having had, with four daus:

Sir George Cayley, 6th Bt; *b* 27 Dec 1733; aeronautical pioneer; *m* 9 July 1795 Sarah (*d* 8 Dec 1854), only dau of Rev George Walker, of Nottingham, FRS, Pres Manchester Literary and Philosophical Soc, and had, with other issue:

1 DIGBY (Sir), **7th Bt**

1 Isabella; *m* 28 Oct 1822 Sir Thomas Charles Style, 8th Bt (*qv*), of Wateringbury, and *dsps* 27 Dec 1881

2 Emma; *m* 30 Aug 1823 her cousin Edward Stillingfleet Cayley, of Wydale Ho, Yorks (*see above*), MP, and *d* 2 Aug 1848, having had issue. He *d* 25 Feb 1862

3 Sarah Philadephia; *m* 18 Jan 1827 Sir William Worsley, 1st Bt (*qv*), of Hovingham, Yorks, and *d* 23 April 1885, aged 82, leaving issue

4 Katherine; *m* 1st 19 May 1831 Henry Ralph Beaumont, of Newby Park, Ripon, and had issue (*see* ALLENDALE, V); *m* 2nd 6 May 1845 Capt James Legard, RN, and *d* 12 March 1887, aged 75, leaving issue (*see* LEGARD, Bt)

Sir GEORGE *d* 15 Dec 1857; his est son,

Sir Digby Cayley, 7th Bt; *b* 13 March 1807; *m* 8 July 1830 Dorothy (*d* 4 April 1881), 2nd dau and eventually sole heiress of Rev George Allanson, of Middleton, Quernhow, Yorks, Prebendary of Ripon and Rector of Hodnet, and *d* 21 Dec 1883, leaving issue:

1 **Sir George Allanson Cayley, 8th Bt**, DL, High Sheriff of Denbighshire 1883; *b* 31 Dec 1831; *m* 5 July 1859 Catherine Louisa (*d* 19 Jan 1907), est dau of Sir William Worsley, 1st Bt (*qv*), and *d* 10 Oct 1895, leaving:

(1) **Sir George Everard Arthur Cayley, 9th Bt**, JP (Flints, N R Yorks, and Denbighs), DL Flints, High Sheriff of Denbighshire 1898, Capt Roy Defence Corps, and Capt 3rd Bn RWF; *b* 8 July 1861; *m* 17 Sept 1884 Lady Mary Susan (*d* 11 Dec 1941), dau of Hon Francis Dudley Montagu Stuart Wortley (*see* WHARNCLIFFE, E), and *d* 15 Nov 1917, having had:

1a Francis Digby Edward, Lt 1st Bn KRRC; *b* 4 Feb 1894; *dvp, ka* 29 Sep 1915

2a **Sir Kenelm Henry Ernest Cayley, 10th Bt**, JP; *b* 24 Sept 1896; *educ* Trin Coll Cambridge; Lt 3rd Bn Suffolk Regt served WW I (wounded, prisoner), and WW II 1939–41 with rank of Maj, CA (NR Yorks), chm: Muston and Yedingham Drainage Bd, Scarborough and Dist Disablement Advisory Ctee; *m* 17 Sept 1929 (Frances) Elizabeth Edwyna (*d* 21 Jan 1974), est dau of Lt-Col Francis Bertie Brewis of Norton Grove, Malton, and *d* 27 Dec 1967, having had issue:

1b *Angela Elizabeth [Angela Lady Frank, Brompton, Scarborough, Yorks]; *b* 22 Aug 1930; *m* 10 May 1950 (*divorce* 1959), as his 1st w, Sir Robert John Frank, 3rd Bt (*qv*), and has issue

2b *Susan Dorothy Marie Gabrielle; *b* 19 March 1934; *m* 1st 17 Sept 1955 (*divorce* 1977) Maldwin Andrew Cyril Drummond (*see* PERTH, E), and has issue; *m* 2nd 8 Sept 1978 *Sir Henry Lawson-Tancred, Bt (*qv*)

3b *Virginia Anne [The Hon Lady Storey, Settrington House, Malton, Yorks; 7 Douro Pl, London W8]; *b* 1 July 1936; *m* 30 Sept 1961 *Hon Sir Richard Storey, 2nd Bt (*qv*), and has issue

4b *Belinda Jane [Mrs Mark Evans, Manor House, Brompton-by-Sawdon, Scarborough, Yorks]; *b* 6 Aug 1940; *m* 15 Dec 1962 *Mark Singleton Evans, only son of Arthur Singleton Evans, of Hormead Bury, Torquay, Devon, and has issue:

1c *Arthur Nicolas Singleton Cayley; *b* 15 Dec 1963

2c *Alexander Kenelm Singleton Cayley; *b* 10 March 1970

1c *Amanda Elizabeth Singleton Cayley; *b* 9 Jan 1966; *m* 1990 *Damien Peter Adam Doyle McCrystal, son of Cal C McCrystal, of Totteridge Lane, N20

5b *April Mary [Mrs Thomas Partridge, 40 Princedale Rd, London W11]; *b* 3 April 1945; *m* 28 June 1969 *Thomas Vernon Partridge, son of T D Partridge, of Booton Manor, Reepham, Norfolk, and has issue:

1c *William Kenelm Thomas; *b* 27 Jan 1972

1c *Annabel Elizabeth Diana; *b* 1 Feb 1974

6b Alison Rose (twin) [Mrs Patrick Maloney, The Green, Brompton-by-Sawdon, Scarborough, Yorks]; *b* 3 April 1945; *m* 14 Oct 1972 *Patrick Dermot Maloney, er son of Dermont Maloney, of Guildford, and has:

1c *Elizabeth Mary; *b* 6 Feb 1974

2c *Katharine Olivia; *b* 1976

3c *Caroline Rose; *b* 1979

7b *Joanna Storm [The Rt Hon The Lady Grey, High Legh House, Knutsford, Cheshire WA16 0QR]; *b* 19 Feb 1947; *m* 28 Sept 1974 *6th Lord (Baron) Grey (*qv*) (of Codnor), and has issue

1a Dorothy Frances; *b* 14 May 1888; *m* 10 Sept 1918 (*divorce* 1930) Capt Hon John de Bathe Crossley, 2nd son of 1st Baron Somerleyton (*qv*), and *d* 28 Feb 1955, leaving issue

2a Margaret Renée; *b* 7 Dec 1892; *m* 1st 4 June 1915 Cdr Ernest Henry Rideout, RN (d 8 Jan 1923), son of Maj-Gen Rideout, RHA, and had issue:

1b Mary Renée; *b* 14 Feb 1917; *m* 22 June 1945 Maj Desmond Hewitt, son of Col Alfred Hewitt, of Boars Hill, Oxford, and *d* 21 March 1951, leaving a s and dau

2b *Monica Winifred Mary; nun; *b* 15 Aug 1918

2a (cont.) Mrs Ernest Rideout *m* 2nd 17 Dec 1929 William Philip Jeffcock (*d* 18 Nov 1963), only son of Capt James William Gully Philip Jeffcock, JP, and *d* 3 April 1975, leaving further issue:

1b *David Philip; *b* 8 July 1933; *educ* Ampleforth and Trin Coll Camb; *m* 14 Dec 1963 *Josephine Anne, SRN, only dau of Maj Harold George Warde-Norbury, DL, JP, of Hooton Pagnell Hall, Doncaster, Yorks, and has issue:

1c *John Philip Harold Patience; *b* 8 May 1968

1c *Venetia Mary; *b* 11 Sept 1964

2c *Cordelia Caroline; *b* 5 Sept 1965

3c Anne Lætitia Mary, BEM (1944); *b* 17 March 1899; *m* 5 Feb 1925 Lt-Col Henry John Cator, MC, son of John Cator, of Woodbastwick Hall, Norfolk (*see* STRADBROKE, E), and *d* 15 Jan 1960, leaving issue. He *d* 27 March 1965

(2) Digby William; *b* 16 Sept 1862; *d* 25 March 1928

(1) Ethel Barbara; *b* 9 Sept 1865; *d* unm 1956

2 Digby, of Norton Grove, Malton, Yorks, JP and CC E Riding; *b* 7 June 1834; *m* 15 Nov 1859 Charlotte Philadelphia (*d* 1901), dau of Robert Bower, of Welham, Yorks, and *d* 26 June 1912, having had, with other issue:

(1) Digby Leonard Arthur, Lt Yorks Hus Yeo Cav, JP Lancs, and DL Herefs; *b* 25 Sept 1864; *m* 18 April 1864 Beatrice (*d* 23 Aug 1945), only child of Sir William Coddington, 1st Bt, of Wycollar, Blackburn, and *d* 19 July 1948, leaving:

1a Digby Coddington, JP Lancs, Maj KOSB and MGC WW I Gallipoli and France; *b* 15 July 1895; *educ* Eton; *m* 6 Feb 1924 Beatrice Elizabeth Eleanora, 2nd dau of Robert Charles Campbell-Renton, of Lamberton and Mordington, and Id 2 Feb 1965, leaving issue:

1b Pauline Grace; *b* 26 Nov 1924

2b *Katherine Sonia; *b* 2 Dec 1926; *m* 5 Aug 1954 7th Baron ffrench (*qv*) and has issue

3b *Amanda Beatrice *b* 23 July 1938

2a William Arthur Seton, Lt-Cdr RN (ret), served WW I and WW II; *b* 11 Sept 1896; *m* 9 June 1937 *Natalie Maud, BA, yr dau of Ernest Grey, of N Beacons, Conway, and *d* 15 Aug 1964, leaving issue:

1b Sir DIGBY WILLIAM DAVID CAYLEY, **11th and present Bt**

1b *Josephine Beatrice Seton [Contessa Giacomo Bertolini, Via Bergognone 27, Milan, Italy]; *b* 3 June 1944 (twin with her bro); *m* 18 May 1968 *Giacomo Bertolini, son of Count Francesco Bertolini, of Rovetta, nr Bergamo, Italy

3a Cuthbert John, FRGS, F/O RAFVR WW II; *b* 9 June 1907; *educ* Eton and Pembroke Coll Cambridge; *m* 21 July 1938 *Cecil Lilla Iris, dau of Adml George Cuthbert Cayley, CB (*see below*)

(2) George Cuthbert, CB (1916), Adml, T/Maj-Gen RAF and GOC NW Area 1918, Offr Legion of Honour; *b* 30 Aug 1866; *m* 1897 Cecil Mildred May (*d* 5 Aug 1937), dau of Col Price Jones, and *d* 21 Dec 1944, having had issue:

1a Paul Charles Cuthbert, T/Capt RE WW II; *b* 18 Dec 1906; *m* 26 July 1939 *Cassandra Rosamond Elaine (*m* 2nd 24 Aug 1946 John Sarginson, of Bermuda Lodge, Eye, Suffolk, er son of James Sarginson, of Great Barton, Suffolk), only dau of Sir Digby Algernon Hall Legard, 13th Bt (*qv*), and *d* as the result of an accident, 25 May 1945, leaving issue:

1b +George Paul [George Cayley Esq, Applegarth, Brewers Green, Roydon, Diss, Norfolk IP22 3SD]; *b* 23 May 1940; *educ* Felsted; *m* 1967 *Shirley Southwell, dau of Frank Woodward Petford, and has issue:

1c +Paul Alistair; *b* 1971

2c +Kevin George; *b* 1974

1b *Sarah Philadelphia; *b* 22 Feb 1943

1a *Cecil Lilla Iris; *b* 26 July 1901; *m* 21 July 1938 her cousin Cuthbert John Cayley (*see above*)

2a Ivy Violet; *b* 25 March 1903; *d* unm 5 Aug 1936

(3) Valentine Charles Hugh; *b* 11 Jan 1868; *d* 1949

(4) Harry Francis, DSO (1917) and bar (1919), Capt RN; *b* 4 July 1873; *m* 19 April 1900 Margery (*d* 4 March 1901), dau of Sir Thomas George Freake, 2nd Bt, and *d* 31 March 1954, leaving issue:

1a *Alexandra Margery Eileen; *b* 21 Feb 1901; *m* 18 Dec 1928 Cdr Arthur Frank Armitage, RN, only surv son of Alfred Armitage, JP, of Northfield Cottage, Henley-on-Thames, and has issue:

1b *Mark Cecil Christopher; *b* 24 June 1937; *educ* Eton; memb London Stock Exchange 1964

1b *Diana Eileen; *b* 13 July 1932; *m* 30 Oct 1956 John Trevor Lewis and has:

1c *Beryn Charles Martin; *b* 19 April 1958

(5) Lewis Richard; *b* 19 Aug 1877; *m* 2 Sept 1926 Etheldrida Mary (*d* 1 March 1954), dau of Capt Charles Hall, Roy Dragoons, and *d* 12 Aug 1932

(1) Helen Dora; *m* 1 March 1892 Christopher John Leyland, of Haggerston Castle, Northumberland, and *d* 23 Dec 1940, leaving issue. He *d* 21 Oct 1926

(2) Julia Philadelphia, MBE; *m* 1st 3 Feb 1891 Ernest Richard Bradley Hall Watt, DL (*d* 4 July 1908), of Bishop Burton, Yorks, and had issue; *m* 2nd 25 Sept 1913 Gervas Malcom Eyre, OBE, er son of Col Henry Eyre, CB, of Rampton, Notts and *d* 29 April 1923. He *d* 19 May 1926

(3) Beatrice Mary Eugenia; *m* 26 Oct 1898 John William Coulthurst, JP, of Gargrave Ho, Yorks, and *d* 4 April 1938. He *dsp* as result of an accident, 14 June 1949

(4) Alice Erica; *d* unm 22 Jan 1937

(5) Catherine Eleanor Millicent; *m* 13 Feb 1901 Adml Sir Walter Henry Cowan, 1st Bt, KCB, DSO, MVO, and *d* 21 April 1934, leaving issue. He *d* 14 Feb 1956

(6) Mary Caroline Charlotte; *d* unm

(7) Lucy Violet; *m* 31 Oct 1916 Philip Francis Bouverie-Pusey (*see* RADNOR, E) and *d* 20 Feb 1959

(8) Octavia; *m* 16 June 1921 Cdr (S) George Thomson, OBE, RN, S/Ldr RAF, son of Maj J Thomson, and *dsp* 4 Jan 1957

3 Reginald Arthur (Rev), Rector of Stowell, Somerset 1897–1916; *b* 15 Aug 1837; *educ* Merton Coll Oxford (MA); *m* 3 May 1864 Mary Louisa (*d* 18 Jan 1924), 5th dau of Rev Edmund Hiley Bucknall-Estcourt, of Estcourt, Glos, and *d* 9 Oct 1918, leaving issue:

(1) Cecil Reginald; *b* 5 Feb 1865; *m* 7 Sept 1893 Ida Rutherford (*d* 25 Nov 1931), dau of George Rutherford Gibbs, and *d* 21 May 1935, leaving issue:

1a Philip Estcourt, MBE (1943), Capt IA and T/Lt Col KRRC, Res of Offrs, served WW I on NW Frontier of India, in Mesopotamia 1917, in Waziristan 1919–20 (despatches) and WW II 1939–43, Chevalier Order of Star of Romania; *b* 17 Dec 1894; *m* 22 July 1931 *Louise, yst dau of Richard Bobbett, of 20 Princes Gate, SW, and Cooldrinagh, Leixlip, Co Kildare, and *dsp* 22 May 1947

(2) Lionel Richard; *b* 15 March 1867; *d* 24 Oct 1950

(3) Edmund Henry George, Capt late RF Reserve; *b* 4 Aug 1870; *m* 1st 3 Aug 1898 Marie Olga (*d* 3 May 1910), dau of Otto Martin, Consul at Valparaiso; *m* 2nd 27 Dec 1913 Laura Eugénie Beatrice (*d* 1949), only dau of George Fox, of Hampstead, NW, and *d* 2 March 1945, having by 1st w had issue:

1a Digby Edgar Martin, master mariner, late Colombo Pilot Service, Lt-Cdr RNVR (Ceylon), and Examination Offr 1939–46; *b* 7 Aug 1904; *m* 14 Jan 1931 *Dorothy, only surv dau of Thomas Allen Harper of Edgbaston, Birmingham, and Sandgate, Queensland

2a Reginald Estcourt; *b* 2 May 1907; *d* 15 Aug 1908

3a Damyon Edmund Martin, S/Ldr RAF; *b* 6 May 1909; *m* 17 June 1944 *Mary Ann, QAIMNSR, dau of Stephen Taylor, of Sheffield, and *d* 14 Jan 1957, leaving issue:

1b *Barbara Ann; *b* 14 June 1945; *m* 1 Jan 1962 *Victor Mason and has:

1c *Michael Shaun; *b* 4 Feb 1965

1c *Deborah Ann; *b* 4 April 1963

1b *Patricia Janis; *b* 11 March 1948

1a Evelyn Olga Vivienne; *b* 6 May 1899; *m* 30 May 1923 William Christian Alwin Wilkendorf, of Quilpue, Chile, son of Ferdinand Wilkendorf, of Danzigerstrasse, 54, Hamburg, Germany, and had issue:

1b *Heinz Ferdinand Otto; *b* 30 Jan 1927; *m* 1958 *Ursula Wilckens, of Valparaiso, and has issue:

1c *Richard; *b* 1959

1c *Astrid; *b* 1960

2b *Harold Christian; *b* 22 June 1934; *m* 1966 *Senta Schwarzenberg, of Santiago, and has issue:

1c *Robert Christian; *b* 1970

2c *Stephen Alfred (twin); *b* 1970

1c *Helga Veronica; *b* 1968

(1) Edith Margaret; *d* young

(2) Dora, MBE (1918); *b* 21 Dec 1871; *d* unm 22 Nov 1941

(3) Isabel Mary; *b* 25 July 1873; *d* unm 6 July 1957

(4) Hester Charlotte; *b* 10 March 1876; *d* unm 30 Aug 1952

1 Sarah; *d* young

2 Dora; *m* 22 Sept 1870 George Arthur Thompson, 12th Lancers, only son of Col Thompson, of Kirk Hammerton, Yorks, and *d* his widow 11 April 1931, leaving issue

CAYZER, Baron

Arms: 1st and 4th, per chevron az. and arg. two estoiles or and an ancient ship with three masts, sails furled sa., colours flying gu., on a chief of the third three fleur-de-lys of the first (for CAYZER); 2nd and 3rd, er. on a pale gu., three passion nails (for TRICKEY). **Crest:** A sea-lion erect ppr., gorged with a naval crown and holding in his dexter paw a fleur-de-lys gold. **Motto:** *Caute sed impavide* ('Cautiously, but without fear'). **Creation:** Bt. (UK) 17 Jan 1921; B (LP, UK) 1981.

THE BARON CAYZER, of St Mary Axe in the City of London, so *cr* 1981, and a **Baronet**, of Roffey Park, Horsham, Co Sussex (Sir (William) Nicholas Cayzer, Bt) [The Rt Hon The Lord Cayzer, 95 Eaton Sq, London SW1W 9AQ; The Grove, Walsham-le-Willows, Suffolk IP31 3AD]; *b* 21 Jan 1910; *s f* 1943; heir presumptive to Btcy of Cayzer of Gartmore (*qv*); *educ* Eton and Corpus Christi Coll Cambridge; memb Nat Dock Labour Bd 1947–52, chm: Liverpool Steamship Owners Assoc 1944–45, Gen Cncl Br Shipping 1959, Br and Cwlth Shipping Co Ltd 1958–87, Cayzer, Irvine & Co Ltd, Clan Line Steamers Ltd, Union-Castle Steamship Co Ltd, Caledonia Investments plc 1958–94, Cayzer Steel Bowater Holdings 1974–, chm English and Scottish Investors; dir: Sun Alliance & Lond Insur Gp; pres: Inst Marine Engrs 1963–64, and Gen Cncl of Br Shipping 1959; Prime Warden Shipwrights' Co 1969–70; *m* 29 July 1935 Elizabeth (Betty) Catherine (*d* 12 Oct 1995), est dau of Owain Williams and gdau of Morgan Stuart Williams, of Aberpergwn, and St Donats Castle, Glam, and has issue:

1 *Nichola [The Hon Mrs Colvin, Tangley House, nr Andover, Hants SP11 0SH]; *b* 27 May 1937; *m* 15 Sept 1956 *Michael Keith Beale Colvin, MP, late Lt Gren Gds, er son of Capt Ivan Beale Colvin, RN, of Kilmeston, Hants, and has issue:

(1) *James Michael Beale CAYZER-COLVIN; *b* 1 April 1965; *m* 1992 *Esther Anne Mary, adopted dau of Michael Tree, of Shute Ho, Donhead St Mary, Dorset (*see* DEVONSHIRE, D)

(1) *Amanda, MBE (Civil 1990); *b* 12 June 1957; *m* 1985 *Rupert Spencer Ponsonby, 2nd son of Sir Ashley Charles Gibbs Ponsonby, 2nd Bt (*qv*)

(2) *Arabella Nichola [Mrs James Gaggero, calle Doñana 8, 11310 Sotogrande, (Cadiz), Spain]; *b* 11 April 1960 ; *m* 1983 *James Gaggero, only son of Joseph Gaggero, CBE, of King's Yard Lane, Gibraltar, and has issue:

1a *Nicholas James; *b* 1985

2a *Alexander Charles; *b* 1987

2 *Elizabeth; *b* 16 Jan 1946; *m* 1992 *Nigel Christopher Gilmour, MD

Lineage: Sir CHARLES WILLIAM CAYZER, 1st Bt, of Gartmore (*qv*); had a 3rd s:

Sir August Bernard Tellefsen Cayzer, 1st Bt (UK), so *cr* 17 Jan 1921, JP Glasgow, Lt-Cdr (Emergency List) RN, chm: Cayzer, Irvine and Co, Ltd, the Clan Line, Houston Line and Scottish Shire Line of Steamers, dir Suez Canal; *b* 21 Jan 1876; *m* 28 April 1904 Ina Frances (*d* 25 Sept 1935), 2nd dau of William Stancomb, of Blount's Court, Potterne, Wilts, and *d* 28 Feb 1943, leaving:

1 Sir WILLIAM NICHOLAS CAYZER, **2nd and present Bt and Baron Cayzer**

2 Bernard Gilbert Stancomb, Maj Queen's Westminster, KRRC (TA), served WW II; *b* 14 March 1914; *educ* Eton and Magdalene Coll Cambridge

1 Ina Heather; *b* 28 Nov 1907; *m* 1st 26 June 1934 (*divorce* 1939) Frederick Herbert Marsden Kaye (*d* 30 March 1952), only son of Sydney Herbert Kaye, OBE, of Lodsworth Ho, Petworth, Sussex, and had issue:

(1) *Pamela Heather; *b* 7 March 1936; *m* 5 April 1956 *Lt-Col Thomas Nigel Bromage, OBE, Gren Gds, son of James Vincent Bennet Parkes Bromage, of Dunfield, Ruyton, Herefs, and has issue:

1a *Charles Nigel; *b* 27 Nov 1960; *m* 1987 *Hon Jaqumine Thellusson, dau of 8th Baron Rendlesham (*qv*), and has issue

1a *Nichola; *b* 18 May 1963

1 (cont.) Mrs Ina Kaye *m* 2nd 11 April 1940 *Maj Edward Richard Buckley, JP, The HLI (*d* 25 July 1971), only son of Lt-Col Percy Neville Buckley, CBE, of Strood Park, Horsham, and had further issue:

(1) *Peter Neville; *b* 23 Sept 1942; *educ* Eton; *m* 2 Feb 1967 *Mary Barabel, yr dau of A G Stewart, of Corsliehill, Houston, Renfrewshire

(2) *Hermione Mary; *b* 29 Dec 1944

CAYZER, Bt

Arms: Party chevron az. and arg. in chief two fleurs-de-lys or and in base an ancient ship with three masts, sails furled sa. colours flying gu.; a chief invected of the third, thereon three estoiles of the first. **Crest:** A sea-lion erect ppr., holding in his dexter paw a fleur-de-lys and supporting with the sinister an estoile, both or. **Motto:** *Caute sed impavide* ('Cautiously but fearlessly'). **Creation:** Bt. (UK) 12 Dec 1904.

SIR JAMES ARTHUR CAYZER, 5TH BT, of Gartmore, Perthshire [Sir James Cayzer, Bt, Kinpurnie Castle, Newtyle, Angus PH12 8TW]; *b* 15 Nov 1931; *s* bro 1943; *educ* Eton

Lineage: EDWARD CAISER; had:

JOHN CAISER, of St Newlyn in Pydar, Cornwall; *bur* 1570, leaving:

INIGO CAISER/KEASER; *bur* 1612, leaving:

GILBERT CAYSER; *m* Genever — and was *bur* 1630, leaving:

EDWARD CAISER/KEASER; *m* 1612 Honor Kevall and had:

GILBERT CAYSER; *b* 1613; *m* Grace — and was *bur* 1694, leaving:

GILBERT CAYSER; *m* 1684 Elizabeth Crips and was *bur* 1692, leaving:

BENET CAYZER, of St Columb, Cornwall; *b* 1689; *m* 1st 1720 Mary Angel (*d* 1741) and had an only surv child (Martha); *m* 2nd 1744 Christian Northcott and by her had an only s:

JOHN CAYZER, of Hatherleigh; *b* 1745; *m* 1774 Sarah Metheril and left an only s:

JOHN CAYZER; *b* 1775; *m* Jane Hooper and left, with an er s (John Tyack, *b* 1802):

CHARLES WILLIAM CAYZER, of Plymouth; *b* 1808; *m* Mary Elizabeth, only dau of William Nicklin, of Hackney, and *d* 27 March 1900, leaving an only s:

Sir Charles William Cayzer, 1st Bt (UK), so *cr* 12 Dec 1904, of Gartmore, Perthshire, JP (Dunbartonshire, Stirlingshire and Renfrewshire); *b* 15 July 1843; MP (C) Barrow-in-Furness 1892–96, Hon Col 3rd Lowland Bde RFA, head Cayzer, Irvine and Co, steamship owners, ktd 1897; *m* 16 May 1868 Agnes Elizabeth (*d* 15 Nov 1919), only dau of William Trickey, of Clifton, Bristol, and had issue:

1 CHARLES WILLIAM (Sir), **2nd Bt**

2 John Sanders, Maj late 7th Dragoon Gds, served in S African War 1899–1900 (brevet, Queen's medal with six clasps); *b* 24 Oct 1871; *m* 2 June 1894 Sibyll (who *m* 2nd 14 July 1908 Capt J C Hartley, late Roy Fus), dau of Herbert Hall, CE, late of Bombay, and *d* 14 Jan 1908

3 AUGUST BERNARD TELLEFSEN (Sir), *cr* a Bt (*see* CAYZER, B (LP), also for the heir presumptive to the above btcy, *cr* 1904)

4 Arthur Edward Bryant; *b* 1 Oct 1878; *m* 3 Aug 1905 Louise Margaret (*d* 14 April 1966 aged 87), 4th dau of John Birkett, of Kendal, and *d* 22 June 1909, leaving issue:

(1) Nancy Avis Louise; *b* 22 April 1909; *m* 7 March 1936 Alister Curtis Leeson (*d* 1991), son of Capt Leeson, and *d* 11 Oct 1996, leaving:

1a *Ian Arthur [Ian Leeson Esq, Eaton House, 7 Eaton Park, Cobham, Surrey KT11 2JF]; *b* 13 March 1937; *educ* Rugby and U Coll Oxford (MA); *m* 7 Aug 1965 *Eileen Margaret, only dau of Lt-Col Anderson K Tennent, of W Kilbride, and has issue:

1b *Sally Louise; *b* 20 June 1968

2b *Patricia Anne; *b* 17 March 1971

5 HERBERT ROBIN CAYZER, *cr* BARON ROTHERWICK (*qv*)

6 Harold Stanley; *b* 8 Aug 1882; Maj 11th Hus (SR) DAAG BEF 1915–19, Adj Oxfordshire Yeo WW I (wounded), High Sheriff Warwicks 1935; *m* 5 Dec 1908 Mary Kate (*d* 25 Feb 1946), est dau of Joseph Hume Dudgeon, of Merville, Co Dublin, and *d* 27 Feb 1948, leaving issue:

(1) +Harold Stanley; *b* 1 Feb 1910; *educ* Eton; Maj Reserve of Offrs 11th Hus WW II (wounded); *m* 1st 8 Aug 1943 (*divorce* 1956) Doussa, est dau of Fahmy Bey Wissa, Egyptian Min CD; *m* 2nd 2 Oct 1959 (*divorce* 1968) Pamela Estelle, er dau of Geoffrey Myers, FRCS, of Christchurch, NZ; *m* 3rd 14 March 1971 *Mrs Beatrice Fairbanks Murray, writer and jlnst, yst dau of former US Amb at Large

(1) Mary; *b* 30 April 1914; *m* 1st 25 June 1935 (*divorce* 1959) Brig Wilfred Penfold Wyatt (*d* 9 March 1966), late 17th/21st Lancers, son of Gerald Wyatt, of White Ho, Rustington, Sussex, and had a s; *m* 2nd 10 Oct 1959 James Kenneth Cattenach Munro, of Chippenham Lodge, Ely, Cambs, son of Donald Munro, of Balnaglaie, Inverness-shire, and *d* 26 June 1969

1 Mary Agnes; *m* 1st 15 Nov 1892 (*divorce* 1914) Maj John Medlicott Vereker and had issue (*see* GORT, V); *m* 2nd 30 Sept 1915 (*annulled* 1916) Robert Lachlan McGlashan; *m* 3rd 15 Oct 1917 Capt Ernest Douglas Black, Canadian Engrs, and *d* 15 May 1930

2 Florence Gwendoline; *m* 1 July 1902 1st Earl Jellicoe (*qv*) and *d* 12 May 1964, leaving issue

3 Constance Winifred; *m* 28 June 1905 Sir Charles Edward Madden, 1st Bt (*qv*), and *d* 18 Nov 1964, leaving issue

The 1st Bt *d* 28 Sept 1916; his est son,

Sir Charles William Cayzer, 2nd Bt; *educ* Ch Ch Oxford (MA); *b* at Colaba, Bombay, 19 July 1869; *m* 1 June 1893 Annie Mabel (*d* 19 Jan 1954), dau of Thomas Jennings White, QC, of Frogmore Lodge, St Albans, and had issue:

1 CHARLES WILLIAM (Sir), **3rd Bt**

2 Arnold Tellefsen; *b* 7 May 1897; *d* unm 8 Aug 1914

1 Winifred Mary; *m* 13 April 1917 R-Adml Neil O'Neill, son of Major Edward Armstrong O'Neill, 45th Regt, of Craythorne, Teignouth, Devon, and had a s and three daus

2 Estelle Agnes; *m* 15 Sept 1923 Capt Philip George Marr, RFC and RAF, yr son of Alexander Marr, of Englefield Green, Surrey, and had two daus. He *d* 13 Feb 1966

3 *Iris Cecilie [Mrs Iris McKellar, 14 Victoria Court, Grand Ave, Hove]; *b* 1905; *m* 26 Sept 1938 (*divorce* 1968) Duncan Alistair McKellar (*d* 26 Sept 1969), son of Alexander McKellar, and has issue:

(1) *Heather Joy [Mrs Kenneth Hyman, Flat 1, Little Silver, Marsham Way, Gerrard's Cross, Bucks]; *b* 7 Nov 1943; *m* 17 July 1965 *Kenneth Leonard Hyman, and has issue:

1a *Jeanne Cecile; *b* 5 Nov 1966

2a *Tara Penelope; *b* 15 Nov 1968

4 *Berenice Amice

Sir CHARLES *d* 20 July 1917; his only surv son,

Sir Charles William Cayzer, 3rd Bt; Lt 19th Hus WW I, MP Chester 1922–40, memb Roy Co Archers, Staff Capt 22nd Heavy Armoured Bde WW II; *b* 6 Jan 1896; *m* 1 Oct 1919 Beatrice Eileen, OBE (1963) (*d* 1981), Co Pres Angus BRCS 1945–81, er dau of James Meakin, of Westwood Manor, Staffs, and Countess Sondes (*see* 1970 edn), and *d* 18 Feb 1940, leaving:

1 **Sir Nigel John Cayzer, 4th Bt**, Lt, Scots Gds, served WW II; *b* 16 Nov 1920; *ka* Salerno 11 Sept 1943

2 Sir JAMES ARTHUR CAYZER, **5th and present Bt**

1 *Deva [Mrs John Brownrigg, 2 The Court, Ridgeway Lane, Lymington, Hants SO41 9NR]; *b* 22 Jan 1923; served WW II as 3rd Offr WRNS; *m* 20 July 1946 Lt-Cdr John Studholme Brownrigg, DSC, RN (*d* 1971), only son of Adml Sir (Henry John) Studholme Brownrigg, KBE, CB, DSO, and has issue:

(1) *Henry John Studholme; *b* 22 May 1961; *m* 1985 *Sally Anne, dau of Barry Jepson, and has issue:

1a *Jonathan Studholme; *b* 1990

1a *A dau; *b* 1988

2 *Angela [Mrs Anthony Galliers-Pratt, Mawley Hall, Cleobury Mortimer, Worcs DY14 8PN]; *b* 6 March 1926; *m* 19 April 1950 *Anthony Malcolm Galliers-Pratt, CBE, only son of George Kenneth Galliers-Pratt, of Alderbury Ho, Salisbury, Wilts, and Gelston Castle, Kirkcudbrightshire, and has issue:

(1) *Rupert Anthony [Rupert Galliers-Pratt Esq, Mawley Hall, Cleobury Mortimer, Salop SY14 8PN; *b* 9 April 1951; *educ* Eton; *m* 11 June 1973 *Alexandra Mary, est dau of Maj Hugh Rose, of Buriton Ho, Buriton, nr Petersfield, and has issue:

1a *George Anthony; *b* 1979

2a *Frederick Hugh; *b* 1981

1a *Isabella Eileen; *b* 1985

2a *Alexandra Georgina Angela; *b* 1988

(2) *Nigel Kenneth [Nigel Cayzer Esq, Thriepley House, Lundie, Dundee DD2 5PA]; *b* 30 April 1954; assumed surname of Cayzer by deed poll 1982; *educ* Eton; *m* 1986 *Henrietta Caroline Rose, yr dau of Sir Richard Tatton-Sykes, 7th Bt (*see* SYKES, Bt, of Sledmere), and has issue:

1a *Arthur James Richard; *b* 1988

2a *John Nigel; *b* 30 Oct 1996

1a *Virginia Angela; *b* 1990

2a *Angelica Eileen Rose; *b* 1992

(3) *Anthony Charles [Anthony Galliers-Pratt Esq, 61 Rutland Gate, London SW7 1PT]; *b* 15 Dec 1958

CECIL OF ESSENDON

Creation: B. (E) 13 May 1603 (current holder called up to Ho Lds *vp* 1992 in one of his f's subsidiary titles by the process known as a writ of acceleration).

THE 13TH BARON CECIL OF ESSENDON, Co Rutland (Robert Michael James (Gascoyne-)Cecil, PC (1994), DL (Dorset 1987)) [Viscount Cranborne PC DL, Manor House, Cranborne, Dorset BH21 5PP]; *b* 30 Sept 1946; *educ* Eton; MP Dorset S 1979–87, Parly U-Sec MOD 1992–94, Ld Privy Seal and Leader Ho Lds 1994–97, Shadow Leader Ho Lds 1997–, Patron Politeia (think tank) 1995–; *m* 7 Jan 1970 *Hannah Ann, er dau of Lt-Col William Joseph Stirling of Keir (*see* 1970 (HERON-MAXWELL, Bt) and has issue:

1 +ROBERT EDWARD WILLIAM; *b* 18 Dec 1970; Page of Honour to HM THE QUEEN 1983–86

2 +James Richard; *b* 1973

1 *Elizabeth Ann; *b* 30 May 1972

2 *Georgiana; *b* 1977

3 *Katherine (twin); *b* 1977

Lineage: *See* SALISBURY, M

CHADLINGTON

Creation: B. (LP, UK) 1996

THE BARON CHADLINGTON (Peter Selwyn Gummer) [The Rt Hon The Lord Chadlington, 61 Grosvenor St, London W1X 9DA]; *b* 24 Aug 1942; *educ* King's Sch Rochester and Selwyn Coll Cambridge; dir CIA Gp 1990–94, Halifax Bldg Soc 1994–, memb NHS Policy Bd 1991–95, Arts Cncl 1991–96, chm Shandwick plc 1974– and ROH 1996–97; *m* 1982 *Lucy Rachel, er dau of A Ponsonby Dudley-Hill and has a s and three daus

Lineage: Rev Canon SELWYN GUMMER; *m* Sybille Mason and has:

1 John Selwyn [The Rt Hon John Gummer MP, House of Commons, London SW1A 0AA], PC (1985); *b* 26 Nov 1939; *educ* Kings Sch Rochester and Selwyn Coll Cambridge (Pres Union 1962); chm Fedn C Students 1962, ed Business Publicns 1962–64, ed-in-ch Max Parrish & Oldbourne Press 1964–66, special assist to chm BBC Publishing 1967, memb ILEA Educn Ctee 1967–70, dir: Shandwick Publishing 1966–81, md EP Gp 1975–81, chm Selwyn Shandwick Internat 1976–81 and Siemssen Hunter 1979–80; MP (C) Lewisham W 1970–Feb 1974 (fought Greenwich 1964 and 1966), Eye 1979–83 and Suffolk Coastal 1983–, PPS to Min Ag 1972, addnl V-Chm C Party 1972–74 (Chm 1983–85), Assist Govt Whip 1981, a Ld Commr Treasury 1981–83, Parly U-Sec Employment Jan-Oct 1983, Min State Employment 1983–84, Paymaster-Gen 1984–85, Min State MAFF 1985–86 and DOE 1988–89, Min Ag Fisha dn Food 1989–93; author: *When the Coloured People Come* (1966) and *Christianity and Conservatism* (1990); *m* 1977 *Penelope Jane, yr dau of John Gardner, and has two sons and two daus

2 PETER SELWYN, *cr* a Baron

CHADWYCK-HEALEY

Arms: 1st and 4th, gules four fusils engrailed and conjoined in bend ermine between two lilies leaved and slipped proper (for HEALEY); 2nd and 3rd, gules an anchor cabled within an orle argent, charged with eight martlets of the field (for CHADWYCK). **Crests:** 1 In front of four fusils engrailed and conjoined fesswise ermine a lily, as in the arms (for HEALEY), 2 A talbot's head couped gules, charged on the neck with an escutcheon argent, thereon a martlet as in the arms (for CHADWYCK). **Motto:** *Crede mihi* ('Believe in me'). **Creation:** Bt. (UK) 6 May 1919.

SIR CHARLES EDWARD CHADWYCK-HEALEY, 5TH BT, of Wyphurst, Cranleigh, Surrey, and New Place, Luccombe, Somerset [Sir Charles Chadwyck-Healey Bt, Manor Farm, Bassingbourn, Cambs SG8 5NX]; *b* 13 May 1940; *s f* 1986; *educ* Eton and Trin Coll Oxford (BA, MA 1968); chm: Chadwyck-Healey Ltd 1973– and Chadwyck-Healey Inc 1981–; commr Marshall Aid commn, co-commr Library and Info commn; Liveryman Fishmongers', Stationers' and Newspaper Makers Co; *m* 1967 *Angela Mary, est dau of John Metson, of Brook End, Little Dunmow, Essex, and has issue:

1 +EDWARD ALEXANDER; *b* 2 June 1972

1 *Catherine; *b* 1 Sept 1970

1 *Faith; *b* 10 Aug 1977

Lineage: EDWARD CHARLES HEALEY, JP, of Wyphurst, Surrey, *d* 22 July 1906, leaving issue:

Sir CHARLES EDWARD HELEY CHADWYCK HEALEY later CHADWYCK-HEALEY, **1st Bt** (UK), so *cr* 6 May 1919, KCB, KC, JP (Surrey), DL, FSA; *b* 26 Aug 1845; Hon Capt RNR, Bencher Lincoln's Inn, CA Somerset, chm QS Somerset, High Sheriff 1911, Chllr Diocese of Salisbury, Bath and Wells, and Exeter; *m* 1st 6 Feb 1872 Rosa (*d* 20 July 1880), only dau of John Close, of York, and had issue:

1 Sir GERALD EDWARD, **2nd Bt**

Sir CHARLES *m* 2nd 17 May 1884 Frances Katharine (*d* 5 May 1909), est dau of William Killigrew Wait, MP, and *d* 5 Oct 1919, leaving issue:

2 Oliver Nowell; *b* 19 Dec 1886; barrister Lincoln's Inn 1911, dir Morgan Bros (Publishers) Ltd, chm Vol Hospitals Ctee for London 1934–41, Cncl King Edward's Hosp Fund London 1935–60, management ctee 1938–41 and 1949–60, T/Maj Roy Berks Regt (despatches) and Staff WW I; *educ* Eton and Trin Coll Oxford (BA 1908, MA 1917); *m* 2 Sept 1916 Gwendoline Mary (*d* 13 July 1979), dau of Maj Hugh Charrington, of Hill Cottage, Taplow, Bucks, and *d* 4 Feb 1960, leaving issue:

(1) +John Hugh [John Chadwyck-Healey Esq, 9d Thistle Grove, London SW10 9RR]; *b* 23 July 1922; *educ* Eton; Capt Rifle Brigade 1941–45 (wounded) WW II

(1) *Patience Mary [Mrs Peter Maxwell, Pettistree Grange, Woodbridge, Suffolk IP13 0HP]; *b* 1917; Jr Cdr ATS WW II; *m* 30 Nov 1946 Lt-Col Peter St George Hereward Maxwell, MC, Highland LI (*d* 25 May 1997), er s of Capt Hugh St George Maxwell, of Pettistree Grange, and has issue:

1a *Philip Hugh; *b* 1947; *m* 1976 *Briar Royle-Bantoft, and has:

1b *Rory Nairne; *b* 1977

2b *Andrew Philip; *b* 1979

2a *Ian Peter; *b* 1949; *m* 1971 *Elisabeth Weddell and has:

1b *Peter Ross; *b* 1982

1b *Catherine Elisabeth; *b* 1980

1a *Gillian Mary; *b* 1954; *m* 1980 *Hamish Clifton and has:

1b *Thomas Wykeham; *b* 1983

2b *Alastair Maxwell; *b* 1985

1b *Louise Venetia; *b* 1988

2a *Penelope Frances; *b* 1956; *m* 1993 *David Smart and has:

1b *James Alexander; *b* 1994

1b *Sophie Victoria; *b* 1996

3 Hilary Philip; *b* 11 Jan 1888; Capt 5th Bn E Surrey Regt (TA); *educ* Eton; *d* unm 30 March 1976

1 Elizabeth Frances; *m* 14 April 1925 Brig Edward Stephen Bruce Williams, CBE, Rifle Bde, only s of Maj-Gen Sir Hugh Bruce-Williams, KCB, DSO, RE, and *d* 24 Feb 1934

Sir CHARLES CHADWYCK-HEALEY, 1st Bt's est s,

Sir Gerald Edward Chadwyck-Healey, 2nd Bt, CBE (1919), DL (Ayrshire); *b* 16 May 1873; *educ* Eton and Trin Coll Oxford (BA 1896, MA 1900), Lt RNVR, Assist to Controller Admlty 1917–18, Dir Materials and Priority Admlty 1918–19, Cdr Crown of Italy; *m* 2 March 1897 Mary Verena (*d* 24 Mar 1957), dau of George Arthur Watson, of East Court, Finchampstead, Berks, and *d* 2 Feb 1955, leaving issue:

1 **Sir Edward Randal Chadwyck-Healey, 3rd Bt**, MC (1917) and bar (1943); *b* 23 Jan 1898; *educ* Eton; Maj RA, served WWs I and II (wounded), Croix de Guerre, tstee City Parochial Fndn 1942, Prime Warden Fishmongers' Co 1954, pres: London Chamber Commerce 1955–57, Freshwater Biological Assoc 1960–79, v-pres Marine Biological Assoc 1969–79; *m* 24 June 1924 Rachel, TD (*d* 26 Aug 1978), Ch Cmmdt ATS, dau of Lionel Charles Whitehead Phillips, JP, of Unsted Park, Godalming, Surrey, by Lilian Marion Estelle, OBE, yst dau of Edward Bourchier Savile, of Okehampton, and *d* 1979

2 **Sir Charles Arthur Chadwyck-Healey, 4th Bt**, OBE (1945); *b* 27 May 1910; *educ* Eton and Trin Coll Oxford (BA 1932) (MA 1936); Lt-Col RA (TA), served WW II (despatches twice); *m* 2 May 1939 Viola (*d* 14 March 1995), yst dau of Cecil Lubbock, of 8a Chelsea Park Gardens, SW3 (*see* AVEBURY, B), and *d* 1986, leaving issue:

(1) Sir CHARLES EDWARD CHADWYCK-HEALEY, **5th and present Bt**

(2) +Nicholas Gerald [Nicholas Chadwyck-Healey Esq, Yew Tree House, 4 Finborough Rd, Stowmarket, Suffolk IP14 1PW]; *b* 8 July 1946; *educ* Eton; *m* 1978 *Alison Jill, only dau of Dr N Stevens, of Morris House, Fishmarket St, Thaxted, Essex, and has issue:

1a +Gerald Norton; *b* 1979

1a *Cherry Kathleen; *b* 1980

(3) +Peregrine James [Peregrine Chadwyck Healey Esq, Vern Leaze, Calne, Wilts]; *b* 5 May 1950; *educ* Eton; *m* 12 May 1973 *Julia Mary, est dau of Sir Richard Boughey, 10th Bt, and has issue:

1a +Oliver Peregrine; *b* 11 May 1982

1a *Alice Rachel; *b* 11 Oct 1977

2a *Rose Henrietta; *b* 1980

(1) *Philippa Harriet [Mrs Philippa Lubbock, 24 Delancey St, London NW11 7NH]; *b* 13 May 1943; *m* 1974 (*divorce* 1987) Jeremy Michael Lubbock (*see* AVEBURY, B) and has issue

(2) *Serena Margaret [Mrs Jeremy Nickson, Mount Pleasant House, Gt Shefford, Berks]; *b* 18 May 1948; *m* 16 Oct 1971 *Jeremy David Nickson, yr s of John Nickson, of The Elms, High Easter, Sussex, and has issue:

1a *George Howard; *b* 12 Jan 1977

1a *Francesca Verena; *b* 1975

2a *Theresa Viola; *b* 1980

1 Rosa Mary Philippa; *b* 1907; *m* 21 July 1933 Cyril George Holland-Martin, JP (*d* 1983), s of Robert Martin Holland-Martin, CB, of Overbury Court, Tewkesbury, and *d* 1997, leaving:

(1) *Timothy David; *b* 1936; *educ* Eton; 2nd Lt 12th Roy Lancers; *m* 1977 (*divorce* 1988) Caroline Mary, only dau of Thomas Francis Blackwell, of Langham Hall, Bury St Edmunds

(2) *Robert George [Robert Holland-Martin Esq, 18 Tite St, London SW3]; *b* 1939; *educ* Eton; *m* 1976 *Dominique, dau of Maurice Pierre Gabriel Fromaget, of Paris, and has issue:

1a *Emily Marie Charlotte; *b* 1978

2a *Tamara Sophie; *b* 1980

(1) *Faith Mary [Mrs Anthony Hallett, 26 Nassau Rd, London SW13 9QE]; *b* 1949; *m* 1972 *Capt Anthony Hallett, RN, and has issue:

1a *James Anthony; *b* 1976

2a *Edward George; *b* 1978

3a *Thomas Alexander Pitfield; *b* 1981

CHALFONT

Arms: Gules a sword point downwards proper, pommel and hilt or, within an orle of two branches of olive fructed gold. **Crest:** A dragon sejant gules supporting a column sable charged with nine bars argent, the capital also argent. **Supporters:** Dexter, a private of the Grenadier Company, 24th Foot (South Wales Borderers), in uniform of *c* 1751, supporting with the exterior hand a bamboo cane leaved proper; sinister, a herald vested in a tabard of the arms proper and holding in the exterior hand a sprig of olive fructed or.

Motto: *Cedant arma togæ* ('Let weapons of war give way to the magistrate's robe') **Creation:** B. (LP, UK) 1964.

THE BARON CHALFONT, of Llantarnam, Co Monmouth (Alun Arthur Gwynne Jones, OBE (1961), MC (1957), PC (1964)) [The Rt Hon The Lord Chalfont OBE MC PC, 65 Ashley Gdns, London SW1P 1QG]; *b* 5 Dec 1919; *educ* W Monmouth Sch; commissioned S Wales Borderers 1940; served: Burma 1941–44, Malaya 1955–57, Cyprus 1958–59; Brevet Lt-Col 1961; def correspondent *The Times* 1961–64; Min State FCO 1964–70, UK Perm Rep WEU 1969–70, for ed *New Statesman* 1970–71; Chm: VSEL plc 1987–, Industrial Cleaning Papers 1979–86, All Party Defence Gp Ho Lds 1980–, UK Ctee for Free World 1981–89, European Atlantic Gp 1983–, Peter Hamilton Security Consultants Ltd 1984–86, Radio Authority 1991–94, Marlborough Stirling Gp 1994–; Dep Chm IBA 1989–90; dir: W S Atkins Internat 1979–83, IBM UK 1973–90 (memb IBM Europe Advsy Cncl 1973–90), Lazard Bros 1983–90, Shandwick plc 1985–, Triangle Holdings 1986–90; Pres: Hispanic and Luso Brazilian Cncl 1975–80, Llangollen Internat Music Festival 1979–90, RNID 1980–87, Abington Corp (Consultants) Ltd 1981–, Freedom in Sport 1982–88, Nottingham Building Soc 1983–90; memb Nat Defence Industries Cncl 1992–, IISS, Bd of Govrs Sandle Manor Sch; MRI, MinstD, FRSA, Hon Fell U of Aberystwyth 1974; Hon Col Wales U OTC 1991–94; Liveryman Paviors' Co; Freeman City of London; author: *The Sword and the Spirit* (1963), *The Great Commanders* (1973), *Montgomery of Alamein* (1976), *Waterloo — Battle of Three Armies* (ed, 1979), *Star Wars — Suicide or Survival* (1985), *Defence of the Realm* (1987), *By God's Will: A Portrait of the Sultan of Brunei* (1989); *m* 1948 *Mona, MB, ChB, dau of Harry Douglas Mitchell, of Grimsby, and has had a s

Lineage: ARTHUR GWYNNE JONES; *m* Eliza Alice Hardman and had issue:

ALUN ARTHUR GWYNNE, *cr* a **Baron**

CHALKER OF WALLASEY

Creation: B. (LP, UK) 1992.

THE BARONESS CHALKER OF WALLASEY, of Leigh-on-Sea, Co Essex (Lynda Bates, PC (1987)) [The Rt Hon The Baroness Chalker of Wallasey PC, House of Lords, London SW1A 0PW]; *b* 29 April 1942; *educ* Roedean, Heidelberg U, Westfield Coll London and Centl London Poly; statistician Research Bureau Ltd (Unilever subsidiary) 1963–69, mkt research Shell Mex and BP 1969–72, ch exec Internat Div Louis Harris Internat 1972–74, Chm Gtr London YCs 1969–70, Nat V-Chm 1970–71, memb BBC Gen Advsy Ctee 1975–79, RIIA 1977; MP (C) Wallasey 1974–92, Jt Sec C Health and Social Servs Ctee 1975–76, Parly Under Sec DHSS 1979–82 and Tport 1982–83, Min State Tport 1983–86 and FCO (Min Overseas Devpt) 1986–97, Dep For Sec 1987–89; dir Capital Shopping Centres 1997–, memb bd BRC 1998–, Hon Fell Queen Mary and Westfield Coll London 1998–; *m* 1st 1967 (*divorce* 1973) Eric Robert Chalker; *m* 2nd 1981 *Clive Landa

Lineage: SIDNEY HENRY JAMES BATES; *m* Marjorie Kathleen Randell and had issue:

LYNDA, *cr* a **Baroness**

CHANCE

Arms: Gu. a saltire vair between two fleurs-de-lys in pale and as many towers in fess arg. **Crest:** A demi-lion rampant gu. semé of annulets or, holding between the paws a sword erect, entwined by a wreath of oak all ppr. **Motto:** *Deo non fortuna* ('Through God, not by chance'). **Creation:** Bt. (UK) 19 June 1900.

SIR (GEORGE) JEREMY FFOLLIOTT CHANCE, 4TH BT, of Grand Avenue, Hove, Co Sussex [Sir Jeremy Chance Bt, Rhosgyll Fawr, Chwilog, Pwllheli, Gwynedd LL53 6TQ]; *b* 24 Feb 1926; *s* f 1987; *educ* Gordonstoun and Ch Ch Oxford (MA); Lt RNVR 1944–47, dir Massey-Ferguson (UK) 1973–78; *m* 4 March 1950 his cousin *Cecilia Mary Elizabeth, 2nd dau of Sir (William) Hugh Stobart Chance, CBE (*see* below), and has issue:

1 +(JOHN) SEBASTIAN; *b* 2 Oct 1954; *educ* Dartington Hall and Stourbridge Coll of Art (BA); *m* 3 Sept 1977 *Victoria Mary, dau of Dennis McClean, of Newcastle-upon-Tyne, and has issue:

(1) +Thomas Hugh Jeremy; *b* 14 May 1983

(2) +Michael John Ferguson; *b* 1987

(1) *Madeleine Katharine Eustacia; *b* 1981

2 +Roger William Tobias (Toby); *b* 8 May 1960; *educ* Eton and Fitzwilliam Coll Cambridge (BA)

1 *Victoria Katherine Elizabeth; *b* 9 Nov 1952

2 *Helena Mary ffolliott; *b* 7 July 1957; *m* 1979 *John Christopher (Toby) Beaufoy, er son of Harold Beaufoy, of 76 High St, Kenilworth, Warwicks, and has issue:

(1) *William Tobias Roland; *b* 1986

(1) *Joanna Mary Constance; *b* 1988

Lineage: RICHARD CHAUNCE, of Bromsgrove, Worcs; *d* between 1 Sept and 28 Nov 1558, leaving, with two yr s (Richard, William):

THOMAS CHAUNCE, of Bromsgrove; tenant of the Manor of Dyers; *m* Eleanor — (*d* between 28 Oct 1585 and 29 Aug 1586) and *d* by 28 Oct 1585, having had, with a dau (Isabel, *m* — Stoure):

JOHN CHAUNCE, of Shepley, Bromsgrove; tenant of the Manor of Dyers; *m* Bennet (*bur* 18 March 1633/4) and *d* between 12 and 27 Feb 1617/8, leaving:

WILLIAM CHAUNCE, of Shepley; tenant of the Manor of Dyers; *m* 18 July 1599 Anne, dau of John Butler, of Timberhanger, Bromsgrove, and had, with an er s and three daus:

JOHN CHAUNCE, of Shepley; *m* 2nd Anne Christopher (*bur* 17 Jan 1669/70) and was *bur* 3 Jan 1669/70, leaving, with four yr s and two daus:

WILLIAM CHAUNCE, of Shepley; *m* 18 April 1656 Elizabeth, widow of Wheeler Perkes, of Fairfield, Belbroughton, and had:

WILLIAM CHANCE, of Shepley; *bapt* 4 Oct 1660; *m* Frances (*bur* 16 Sept 1742 aged 85) and *d* 26 Dec 1739, having had, with an er s and two daus:

JOHN CHANCE, of Bromsgrove; *m* Sarah (*d* 19 Aug 1762 aged 81) and *d* 29 Oct 1771 aged 84, having had, with four yr s and a dau:

JOHN CHANCE, of Bromsgrove; *b* 6 Oct 1711; *m* 1st 24 Oct 1743 Hannah (*d* 3 Feb 1746 aged 34), dau of Thomas Hunt, of Bromsgrove, and had two daus; *m* 2nd 15 Oct 1746 Mary (*m* 2nd George Bell, of Bromsgrove, and *d* 12 May 1812 aged 91), dau of Joshua Tilt, of Bromsgrove, and *d* 13 Feb 1749/50, having by her had further issue:

1 WILLIAM

1 Sarah; *b* 12 Oct 1747; *m* 3 March 1773 Edward Homer, of Birmingham, afterwards of West Town, Somerset, son of Edward Homer, slr, of Sutton Coldfield, Warwicks, and *d* 14 Sept 1776, having had issue. He *d* 19 March 1825

The only son,

WILLIAM CHANCE, settled in Birmingham in 1771; *b* 16 May 1749; *m* 30 June 1778 Sarah (*d* 7 Sept 1809 aged 53), 7th dau of Robert Lucas, of Bristol (8th son of Clement Lucas, of Feckenham Park, Hanbury, Worcs), by Elizabeth, dau of John Butler, of Hanbury, Worcs, and *d* 21 March 1828, having had, with other issue:

1 Robert Lucas, of Summerfield, Birmingham; *b* 8 Oct 1782; *m* 7 May 1811 his cousin Louisa (*d* 24 Dec 1873), 3rd dau of Edward Homer, of West Town,

Somerset, by his 2nd w Mary, 5th dau of Robert Lucas, of Bristol, and *d* 7 March 1865, having had issue

2 WILLIAM

3 George, of Birmingham and NY, USA; *b* 26 July 1790; *m* 19 May 1825 Cornelia Maria (*d* 30 Dec 1881), dau of Arent Schuyler de Peyster, of NY, and *d* 16 Sept 1861, having had issue

The 4th son,

WILLIAM CHANCE, of Spring Grove, Birmingham; High Bailiff of Birmingham 1829–30, JP (Birmingham, Warwicks and Worcs); *b* 29 Aug 1788; *m* 6 Aug 1811 Phoebe (*d* 13 April 1865), 4th dau of James Timmins, of Birmingham, and *d* 8 Feb 1856, having had an est s:

Sir James Timmins Chance, 1st Bt (UK), so *cr* 19 June 1900, of Grand Ave, Hove, Sussex, DL, JP (Worcs and Staffs), High Sheriff of Staffs 1868; *b* 22 March 1814; *educ* Trin Coll Cambridge (BA 1838, MA 1841), MA *ad eundem* Oxford 1848, student of Lincoln's Inn, and Fell UCL; *m* 26 June 1845 Elizabeth (*d* 27 Aug 1887), 4th dau of George Ferguson, of Houghton Hall, Carlisle, and *d* 6 Jan 1902, leaving:

1 **Sir William Chance, 2nd Bt**; *educ* Trin Coll Cambridge (MA), barrister Inner Temple, High Sheriff of Surrey 1911; *b* 2 July 1853; *m* 15 Oct 1884 Julia Charlotte (*d* 30 Aug 1949), only child of Lt-Col Henry Strachey, Bengal Army (*see* 1970 edn STRACHIE, B), and *dsp* 9 April 1935

2 George Ferguson, High Sheriff of Worcs 1910; *b* 25 Sept 1854; *educ* Trin Coll Cambridge (MA); *m* 21 April 1891 Mary Kathleen (*d* 7 July 1953), 2nd dau of Rev Henry Stobart, of Wykeham Rise, Totteridge, formerly Rector of Warkton, Northants, and *d* 4 Feb 1933, having had issue:

(1) ROGER JAMES FERGUSON (Sir), **3rd Bt**

(2) (William) Hugh (Stobart) (Sir), ktd 1945, CBE (1958), DL (Worcs 1952); *b* 31 Dec 1896; *educ* Eton and Trin Coll Cambridge (BA 1920, MA 1924); dir Chance Bros Ltd 1924–64, CC Worcs 1946–74 (v-chm 1949–53), High Sheriff 1942, chm Worcs Educn Ctee 1958–64, Hon BSc Aston U, Hon Col The Parachute Regt (TA), memb: Roy Commn on Scottish Affairs 1952, Percy Ctee on Higher Technological Edcn and Ld Chllr's Ctee on Intestacy, Willis Jackson Ctee on Technical Teachers 1957, pres W Midlands Union of Cons Assocs 1957–67, late Lt Worcs Regt (TF) and RFC, served WW I 1914–18; *m* 1st 20 April 1926 (*divorce* 1961) Cynthia May, er dau of Maj Addison Francis Baker-Cresswell, of Cresswell and Harehope; *m* 2nd 3 Feb 1961 *Rachel, dau of Lt Cyril Henry Cameron, RHA, of Tasmania, and of Mrs Patrick Stormonth Darling, of 7 Swan Walk, SW3, and formerly w of James W Carr, and *d* 1981, having by his 1st w had issue:

1a +William John Ferguson [William Chance Esq, 15 Monteith Place, Durban N 4051, Natal, S Africa]; *b* 19 Dec 1929; *educ* Eton and RAC Cirencester; *m* 1st 26 May 1951 Elizabeth Kathleen, er dau of Victor J S Crookes, of Chartwell, Umzinto, Natal; *m* 2nd 1989 (*divorce* 1992) Mrs Ingrid Bonnet, née von Christierson, and has issue by 1st w:

1b +Christopher John Hugh; *b* 3 June 1952; *m* 1976 *Merilyn Koller, and has issue:

1c +Justin William Timmins; *b* 1988

1c *Lara; *b* 1978

2c *Sarah; *b* 1982

2b +James William Frederick; *b* 29 Aug 1953; *m* 1978 *Tessa Stretton-Barry, and has issue:

1c +David; *b* 1981

1c *Philippa; *b* 1979

2c *Camilla; *b* 1985

3b +Richard George Ferguson; *b* 10 Nov 1956; *m* 1987 *Nicola Anne Butcher, and has issue:

1c +Michael John William; *b* 1989

1c *Natasha Anne; *b* 1991

1b *Sarah Elizabeth; *b* 26 March 1960

2a +Hugh Nicholas [Hugh Chance Esq, Harcourt Farm, Chorley, nr Bridgnorth, Salop]; *b* 6 March 1940; *educ* Gordonstoun, McGill U (BEng (Mech) 1964), and RAC Cirencester; *m* 1st 4 Dec 1963 (*divorce* 1977) his cousin Caroline Susan, est dau of Patrick Edward Michael Holmes, MBE, MA, AMICE, of Stourton Ho, Stourbridge, Worcs, by Eleanor, 2nd dau of Geoffrey Robert Lucas Chance, of Stourton Court, Stourbridge, Worcs; *m* 2nd 1990 *Mrs Rose E Baldwin, er dau of — Heft, of Wisconsin, USA, and has issue by 1st w:

1b +Timothy William Holmes; *b* 19 Sept 1966

2b +Henry Charles Hugh; *b* 28 Jan 1969

1b *Lucy Emma; *b* 14 May 1971

1a *(Kathleen) Idonea Cresswell; *b* 27 March 1927; *m* 1st 8 July 1948 (*divorce* 1956) William Henry Dunamace Heaton-Armstrong, only son of Capt Sir John Dunamace Heaton-Armstrong, MVO, Clarenceux King of Arms, of 46 Carlisle Mansions, SW1, and has issue:

1b *Anthony Eustace John; *b* 27 Sept 1950; *educ* Ampleforth and Bristol U; barrister, Gray's Inn 1973; *m* 1st 1973 Susan Margaret, dau of Ian Peter Allnut, of Karen Cottage, Boulters Lane, Maidenhead, Berks; *m* 2nd 1982 *Anne Frances, dau of Mrs E E M Robigo, and formerly w of Marcus Hugh Lecky, and has issue by 2nd w:

1c *John William; *b* 1983

1c *Eleanor Katharine; *b* 1985

2c *Celestine Anne; *b* 1988

1b *Mary Suzanne Bertha; *b* 19 April 1949; *m* 1977 *John Beresford-Iles, of Melbourne, Australia

2b *Bridget Cynthia; *b* 29 May 1952; has issue:

1c *Morgan Lei (a dau); *b* 1973

2b (cont.) Bridget Heaton-Armstrong *m* 1982 (*divorce* 1991) Michael Roger David Dansey, of Auckland, NZ, and has further issue:

2c *Katherine Marie Bridget; *b* 1984

3c *Georgina Michaela Celestine; *b* 1986

3b *Rachel Catherine; *b* 28 Aug 1954

1a (cont.) Mrs Idonea Heaton-Armstrong *m* 2nd 31 March 1956 (*divorce* 1965) Lt-Cdr John Timothy Fetherston-Dilke, CBE, RN (ret), yr son of Beaumont Albany Fetherston-Dilke, MBE, JP, of Maxstoke Castle, Coleshill, Warwicks; *m* 3rd 4 Dec 1965 (*divorce* 1975) Colin Frederick Rogers, LDS, son of Frederick Arthur Rogers, of Gorleston-on-Sea, Norfolk; *m* 4th 1992 *Martin Joseph Crossley, and by her 2nd husb has further issue:

2b *Timothy Hugh; *b* 9 June 1958

4b *Miranda Catherine; *b* 6 May 1956; *m* 1985 *William Murray Lindsay (*see* MANSFIELD and MANSFIELD, E), and has issue:

1c *Alicia Flora; *b* 1987

2c *Harriet Idonea; *b* 1987 (twin)

2a *Cecilia Mary Elizabeth; *b* 17 Nov 1928; *m* 4 March 1950 her cousin **+Sir (George) Jeremy ffolliott Chance, 4th Bt**, and has issue

3a *Bridget Nicola [Mrs John Eastaugh, Willow Cottage, Kingsland, Leominster, Herefs HR6 9RU]; *b* 14 April 1931; *m* 22 Oct 1963 Rt Rev John Richard Gordon Eastaugh, sometime Bishop of Hereford (*d* 1990), er son of Gordon Eastaugh, of 36 Greenways Crescent, Shoreham-by-Sea, Sussex, and has issue:

1b *James Gordon Mark; *b* 11 Oct 1964; *m* 1 Oct 1994 *Philippa Jane Skeats, and has:

1c *Samuel John Timothy; *b* 19–

2b *Edward John Hugh; *b* 16 Feb 1970

1b *Katharine Elizabeth Sophia; *b* 23 July 1967

(3) Eustace George St Clair, 2nd Lt Coldstream Gds; *b* 11 March 1899; *ka* 27 Sept 1918

(1) Katharine Dorothea, JP Hants

3 James Frederick; *b* 9 April 1856; *educ* Trin Coll Cambridge (MA); *d* 18 Oct 1938

1 Frances Elizabeth; *d* unm 23 Jan 1940

2 Edith Mary; *m* 4 May 1875 Archibald Edward Dobbs, MA, barrister, of Castle Dobbs, Co Antrim, and *d* 18 Dec 1922, leaving issue. He *d* 9 Aug 1916

3 Margaret Anne; *d* unm 13 Oct 1932

4 Eleanor Phoebe; *m* 5 Dec 1877 Rev William Campbell Riland-Bedford, MA Cambridge, late Rector of Sutton Coldfield, Hon Canon of Birmingham, est son of Rev William Kirkpatrick Riland-Bedford, and *d* 15 Sept 1928, leaving issue. He *d* 15 Aug 1922

5 Bertha Louisa; *d* young, 14 March 1867

6 Katharine; *d* unm 8 June 1893

7 Marian Georgiana; *d* unm 23 Jan 1950

The 2nd Bt's nephew,

Sir Roger James Ferguson Chance, 3rd Bt, MC; *educ* Eton, Trin Coll Cambridge (BA 1918, MA 1921), London U (PhD 1927), Capt The Rifle Bde, formerly Capt and Adj 4th Roy Irish Dragoon Gds, Press Attaché, Br Embassy, Berlin 1938, served WW I 1914–18 (wounded twice, despatches twice), and WW II 1940–41, as S/Ldr, RAFVR, author: *Until Philosophers are Kings* (1928) and *The End of Man* (1974); *b* 26 Jan 1893; *m* 12 April 1921 Mary Georgina, 2nd dau of Col William Rowney, RAMC, and *d* 1987, having had issue:

1 Anthony Ferguson, late Lt The Rifle Bde; *b* 20 July 1923; *educ* Eton; *d* unm 17 Jan 1970

2 Sir (GEORGE) JEREMY FFOLLIOTT CHANCE, **4th and present Bt**

1 Serena Mary Benedicta; *b* 19 Aug 1928; *m* 25 July 1953 (*divorce* 1985) Baron Armstrong of Ilminster (LP; *qv*), and *d* 19–, leaving issue

3 *Teresa Margaret; *b* 22 March 1930; *m* 6 Aug 1955 *George Gilbert Kennedy, DFC, 4th son of George Lawrence Kennedy, of Cashelnagor, Co Donegal, and has issue:

(1) *Seamus Michael ffolliott; *b* 17 Jan 1963

(2) *Miles Thomas Pitt; *b* 29 Oct 1965

CHANDOS

Arms: Arg. a chevron between three escallops sa., a cross moline gu. for difference. **Crest:** A Moor's head couped at the shoulders ppr., wreathed round the temples arg. and sa., a cross moline gu. for difference. **Supporters:** On either side a merman ppr. holding in the outer hand a trident, pendant from a rope around the inner shoulder an escutcheon or charged with a pile gu. **Motto:** *Fais ceque dois advienne que poussa* ('Do what you must, come what may'). **Creation:** V. (UK) 9 Sept 1954.

THE 3RD VISCOUNT CHANDOS, of Aldershot, Co Southampton (Thomas Orlando Lyttelton) [The Rt Hon The Viscount Chandos, 149 Gloucester Ave, London NW1 8LA]; *b* 12 Feb 1953; *s* f 1980; *educ* Eton and Worcester Coll Oxford (BA 1974); dir: Kleinwort Benson 1985–93, Capital and Regnl Properties, Chrylasis Gp to 1996, Botts 1993–97 and Lopex (chm 1997–); Oppn Spokesman Treasury matters 1995–97; chm Media-Key 1998–, dir Video Networks 1998–; *m* 1985 *Arabella Sarah Lucy, dau of John Adrian Bailey (*see* HADDINGTON, E), and has:

1 +OLIVER ANTONY; *b* 21 Feb 1986
2 +Benedict; *b* 1988
1 *Rosanna Mary; *b* 1990

Previous creations: In 1337 Sir Roger de Chaundos, of a family from the Herefordshire-Shropshire borders, was called to Parliament by writ, thus being created Lord (Baron) Chaundos according to later doctrine, although none of his successors were ever called to Parliament under this title. Candos, of which both Chaundos and Chandos appear to be corruptions, is in Normandy, some ten miles northwest of Rouen. (The famous Garter Knight Sir John Chaundos was of a different family, settled in Derbyshire.) On the death in 1428 of Roger's grandson Sir John, any peerage created by the writ of 1337 would have fallen into abeyance, though within 30 years this abeyance would have been terminated by the death of the only other coheir and the notional Barony would have become vested in Sir John's great-nephew Giles Brugge.

In 1554 the problematical nature of any barony of 1337 was resolved when Giles Brugge's great-grandson Sir John Bruges, Brugge or Brydges was created Baron Chandos of Sudeley. The peerage was a reward for having suppressed Wyatt's rising against QUEEN MARY. Four days after his ennoblement the new Lord Chandos of Sudeley escorted LADY JANE GREY to the headsman's block in his capacity as Lieutenant of the Tower of London, a post to which he had been appointed the previous year.

The 9th Lord Chandos of Sudeley was created Duke of Chandos in 1719. He was a patron of Handel, whose Chandos anthems commemorate the fact and who acted as a kind of composer in residence at the Duke's magnificent seat of Canons, at Little Stanmore, Middlesex. With the death of the 3rd Duke in 1789 all his titles expired bar the Scottish Lordship of Kinloss (*qv*), of which he was *de jure* rather than *de facto* holder, though the Chandos of Sudeley Barony was later claimed by the genealogical writer Sir Egerton Brydges.

Meanwhile the 3rd and last Duke of Chandos's sole surviving daughter and heiress had married in 1796 the 2nd Marquess of Buckingham. The latter, on being promoted a Duke in 1822, chose the title Buckingham and Chandos to commemorate the alliance. This Dukedom too became extinct with the death of its third holder (in 1889), but his Viscountcy of Cobham passed to a cousin, Lord Lyttelton of Frankley, an ancestor of the present holder of the Viscountcy of Chandos (*see* COBHAM, V).

Lineage: ALFRED LYTTELTON, PC, KC, MA (*see* COBHAM, V); had:

Sir OLIVER LYTTELTON, **1st Viscount Chandos**, of Aldershot, Co Southampton (UK), so *cr* 9 Sept 1954, KG (1970), PC (1940), DSO (1916), MC (1918); *b* 15 March 1893; *educ* Eton and Trin Coll Cambridge; Capt Gren Gds, Bde Maj 1918 WW I, Controller non-ferrous metals Min Supply 1939–40, MP (C) Aldershot 1940–54, Pres BOT 1940 and 1945, Min State Middle East (War Cabinet) 1941, Min Production (War Cabinet) 1942–45, Sec State Colonies 1951–54, chm AEI 1954–63, dir: ICI, Alliance Assur, chm Nat Theatre Bd 1962, memb South Bank and Opera Ho Bd, pres: Roy Marsden Hosp, IoD 1954–63, Queen Elizabeth Ho Oxford 1955, tstee: Nat Gallery 1958–65, Churchill Coll 1958, author: *From Peace to War*; *A Study in Contrast (1857–1918)*, and a volume of memories; *m* 30 Jan 1920 Lady Moira Godolphin Osborne (*d* 20 May 1976) (took name Lady Moira Lyttelton 1972), 4th dau of 10th Duke of Leeds (*see* 1963 edn), and had issue:

1 ANTHONY ALFRED, **2nd Viscount**
2 Julian, Capt Gren Gds WW II; *b* 30 Aug 1923; *educ* Eton; *ka* Italy Oct 1944
3 +(Nicholas) Adrian Oliver [The Hon Adrian Lyttelton, 30 Paulton's Sq, London SW3]; *b* 26 March 1937; *educ* Eton and Magdalen Coll Oxford; Fell All Souls; *m* 3 April 1960 Margaret (*d* 1993), only dau of Sir Harold Hobson, the drama critic, of Grenville Ho, Dolphin Square, SW1, and has issue:
(1) +Francis Sebastian Jasper; *b* 28 May 1967
(1) *Celia Melissa Francesca; *b* 28 Oct 1960; art critic and painter; *m* 1985 *Dr Andrew Rae, actor as Andrew Heath, est son of John Rae, of Brook Ho, Johannesburg
1 *Rosemary [The Rt Hon The Viscountess Chaplin, 61 Ladbroke Rd, London W11 3PN]; *b* 30 May 1922; *m* 16 March 1951, as his 2nd w, 3rd Viscount Chaplin (*d* 1981) (*see* 1970 edn)

The 1st VISCOUNT *d* 21 Jan 1972; his er son,

ANTHONY ALFRED LYTTELTON, **2nd Viscount Chandos**; *b* 23 Oct 1920; *educ* Eton and Trin Coll Cambridge (MA 1962); served WW II on Gen Staff, Mediterranean 1942–45 (despatches), memb London Stock Exchange 1950, ptnr Panmure Gordon and Co 1950–75; *m* 20 May 1949 *Caroline Mary (*m* 2nd 1985, as his 2nd w, Hon David Hervey Erskine, bro of 13th Earl of Mar and Kellie (*qv*)) [The Hon Mrs David Erskine, Felsham House, Felsham, Bury St Edmunds, Suffolk], yr dau of Sir Alan Frederick Lascelles, PC, GCB, GCVO, CMG, MC, formerly Priv Sec to HM THE QUEEN (*see* HAREWOOD, E), and *d* 1980, having had issue:

1 THOMAS ORLANDO LYTTELTON, **3rd and present Viscount Chandos**
2 +Matthew Peregrine Antony; *b* 21 April 1956; *educ* Eton and Trin Coll Cambridge (BA 1977)
1 *Laura Katherine; *b* 18 May 1950; *educ* Cranborne Chase, St Anne's Coll Oxford (BA) and London U (BSc)
2 *Deborah Claire; *b* 18 Sept 1963

CHAPMAN

Arms: Per chevron arg. and gu. a crescent counterchanged, in dexter chief a portcullis chained sa., over all in pale a sword, point downwards, ppr., pommel and hilt or. **Crest:** Issuant from a wreath of oak ppr. a dexter arm embowed, vested gu., cuffed arg., grasping in the hand a harpoon, also ppr. **Motto:** *Suaviter sed fortiter* ('Mildly but firmly'). **Creation:** Bt. (UK) 30 Jan 1958.

SIR DAVID ROBERT MacGOWAN CHAPMAN, 3RD BT, of Undercliff, Cleadon, nr Sunderland, Co Durham, DL (Tyne and Wear 1997) [Sir David Chapman Bt DL, Westmount, 14 West Park Rd, Cleadon, Sunderland, Tyne and Wear SR6 7RR]; *b* 16 Dec 1941; *s* f 1987; *educ* Marlborough, Grenoble U, McGill U Montreal (BCom); High Sheriff Tyne and Wear 1993, dir: Wise Speke (stockbrokers), Newcastle-upon-Tyne 1987– (ptnr 1971–87), N of E Bldg Soc, Northern Rock Bldg Soc 1994–, chm Northern Unit of Stock Exchange 1988–91; govr St Aidan's Coll Durham 1987–; *m* 19 June 1965 *Maria Elizabeth de Gosztonyi-Zsolnay, dau of Dr Nicholas de Mattyasovszky-Zsolnay, of Pecs, Hungary, and Montreal, Canada, and has:

1 +MICHAEL NICHOLAS; *b* 21 May 1969
1 *Christina Elizabeth; *b* 14 Dec 1970

Lineage: ROBERT CHAPMAN, of S Shields, Co Durham; *b* 6 Oct 1811; *m* 14 Jan 1841 Elizabeth Robson, of S Shields and *d* 31 Dec 1892, leaving issue:

HENRY CHAPMAN, of Seacroft, Westoe, S Shields, FCA, 3rd Durham Vol Art; *b* 18 March 1850; *educ* Roy GS Newcastle-upon-Tyne; *m* 8 Aug 1876 Dora (*d* 17 May 1938), dau of George Gibson, of Harton, Co Durham, and *d* 5 Feb 1936, having had issue:

1 Henry; *b* 21 Aug 1878; *d* 29 Jan 1926
2 ROBERT (Sir), **1st Bt**
3 George Gibson; *b* 3 May 1882; *educ* Peterhouse Cambridge (BA); *m* Isabella Wilson and *d* 31 Dec 1954, leaving issue:
4 Alan Edward; *b* 4 July 1883; *d* 20 Dec 1898
5 Lawrence Alfred; *b* 18 March 1886; *d* 3 Feb 1943
6 Frederick Ernest; *b* 4 July 1887; *d* 8 May 1938
7 Charles Lancelot, MC (1916), Capt RA, served WW I; *b* 1 Aug 1892; *ka* 22 Aug 1917
1 Ethel; *b* 2 May 1877; *d* 16 Dec 1938
2 Hilda; *b* 3 March 1881; *m* Sidney Howard Smith, son of James Smith, of Stroud, Glos, and *d* 6 July 1929, leaving issue
3 Dora Elizabeth; *b* 20 Dec 1884; *m* 10 Jan 1914 Lt-Cdr Wallace Moir Annand, RND, son of Robert Cummings Annand, of Harton, Co Durham, and *d* 26 July 1935, having had issue. He was *ka* at Gallipoli, 4 June 1915
4 Marion Dorothy, VAD Nurse; *b* 10 Sept 1890; *d* at Alexandria, 10 Aug 1918

The 2nd son,

Sir Robert Chapman, 1st Bt (UK), so cr 30 Jan 1958, ktd 1950, CB (1944), CMG (1918), CBE (1945), DSO (1916), TD (1918), DL (1921), JP (Co Durham 1930), High Sheriff 1940, V-Lt 1946 and 1949, JP (S Shields 1920), MP (C) Houghton-le-Spring 1931–35, Mayor of S Shields 1931–32, Cncllr 1921–51, Alderman 1936–51, a Church Commr 1950–57, sr ptnr Henry Chapman Son & Co, ACA 1902, FCA 1919, WW I: (wounded, despatches 4 times), Lt-Col RFA (TF) 1916, Brevet Col 1924, Col 1925, ret 1937, Hon Col 74th Field Regt RA 1935–50, chm Co Durham TA 1941–48, chm Ingham Inf S Shields 1930–45 and Tstee 1933–45, Co Durham Orthopaedic Assoc 1938, Finchale Abbey Training Centre for Disabled 1943–60, Chev Legion Honour 1917, OStJ; *b* 3 March 1880; *educ* S Shields High Sch and London U (BA 1899); *m* 10 Nov 1909 Hélène Paris, er dau of James George MacGowan, of Paris and London, and had issue:

1 ROBERT MacGOWAN (Sir), **2nd Bt**
2 +(Henry James) Nicholas; *b* 3 Feb 1914; *educ* Marlborough and Corpus Christi Coll Cambridge (Scholar, BA 1936, MA 1967); CC Dorset (1962), Colonial Serv, Gold Coast 1937–57 (ret) Perm Sec Mins of Communicns and Labour 1952–57, Underwriting memb Lloyd's 1959, memb Dorset Area Health Auth 1974–82, Govr Sherborne Sch 1967–80, memb cncl Sherborne Sch for Girls 1965–84; *m* 11 Feb 1950 *Anne Barbara, only dau of Sir William Dawson Croft,

KCB, KBE, CIE, CVO, of 2 Kingsbury Sq, Wilton, nr Salisbury, and *d* 1991 leaving issue:

(1) *Caroline Anne; *b* 9 Oct 1955; *m* 1985 *Christopher John Steane, and has issue:

1a *Sebastian James David; *b* 1986

1a *Isobel Sarah; *b* 1988

Sir ROBERT *d* 31 July 1963; his er son,

Sir Robert (Robin) MacGowan Chapman, 2nd Bt, CBE (1961), TD and bar (1948), DL (1952), JP (1946) Co Durham, High Sheriff 1960, V-Ld Lt Tyne and Wear from 1974; *b* 12 Feb 1911; *educ* Marlborough and Corpus Christi Coll Cambridge (BA 1933, MA 1936), 2nd Lt RA (TA) 1934, served WW II as Capt GSO (3), AA Cmd 1940, Maj GSO (2), 1st AA Corps 1940, cmdg Batt 124th HAA Regt RA 1942, Maj (TA) 1947, Lt-Col cmdg 325th Regt Light AA Regt RA (TA) 1948, Hon Col 463 Light AD Regt RA (TA) 1963, memb Durham Co TA from 1948; chartered accountant and co dir, ACA (1938), FCA (1945), pres N Soc of Chartered Accountants 1958–59, tstee Ingham Inf S Shields 1946–49, Hon Treas Co Durham Boy Scouts Assoc 1947–68, chm: Co Durham Scout Cncl from 1972; N Area Cons Party 1954–57, Jarrow Cons Assoc 1957–60, Durham Diocesan Bd of Finance 1966–70, Govr Utd Newcastle Hosps 1957–64; *m* 18 Jan 1941 *Barbara May [Barbara Lady Chapman, Pinfold House, Cleadon, Sunderland, Tyne and Wear SR6 7RR], dau of Hubert Tonks, of Delmar, Halgranoya, Ceylon, and Harvington, nr Evesham, Worcs, and *d* 1987, having had issue:

1 Sir DAVID ROBERT MacGOWAN CHAPMAN, **3rd and present Bt**

2 +Peter Stuart; *b* 24 Aug 1944; *educ* Marlborough, Sorbonne, Trin Coll Cambridge (MA) and LSE (MSc); dir Chapman Hendy Assocs; *m* 1972 *Joan, dau of R S V Hewitt, of Middle Barton, Oxon, and has issue:

(1) +Christopher Edward; *b* 1974

(1) *Victoria Rose; *b* 1977

(2) *Katherine Rebecca; *b* 1980

(3) *Rachel Emily; *b* 1981

1 *Elizabeth Mary [Mrs Mark Levy, 126 Corte Madera Ave, Mill Valley, Cal 94941, USA]; *b* 11 May 1946; *educ* Benenden, St Aidan's Coll Durham, and Columbia U NY (Phi Beta Kappa); *m* 11 March 1967 *Dr Mark Ivan Levy, er son of Lee Levy, of W Hempstead, NY, USA, and has issue:

(1) *Noah; *b* 1970

(1) *Gabriel; *b* 1972

CHAPPLE

Creation: B. (LP, UK) 1985.

THE BARON CHAPPLE, of Hoxton, Greater London (Francis (Frank) Joseph Chapple) [The Rt Hon The Lord Chapple, House of Lords, London SW1A 0PW]; *b* Aug 1921; *educ* elementary sch; Memb ETUC 1937–83 (Shop Steward and Branch Official, memb Exec Cncl 1958, Assist Gen Sec 1963–66), Gen Sec EETPU 1966–83; memb: Ctee of Inquiry into Shipping 1967, Roy Commn Environmental Pollution 1973–77, Horserace Totalisator Bd 1976–90, Energy Commn 1977–79, NEDC 1979–83, Nat Nuclear Corp 1980–86, Southern Water Authority 1983–89; dir: Inner City Enterprises 1983–88, N G Bailey Orgn 1989–; Memb: Gen Cncl TUC 1971–83 (Chm 1982–83), NEC Lab Party; Gold Badge of Congress 1983; author: *Sparks Fly* (1984); *m* 1944 Joan Jeanette (*d* 1994), dau of James Nicholls, and has:

1 *Roger Francis; *b* 1947; *educ* Brooke House Comprehensive Sch; *m* 1969 *Susan Audrey, dau of Charles F W Brown

2 *Barry Joseph; *b* 1951; *educ* Hawes Down Comprehensive Sch; *m* 1980 *—

Lineage: FRANK CHAPPLE; *m* Emily — and had:

FRANCIS (FRANK) JOSEPH, *cr* a **Baron**

CHARLEMONT

Arms: Quarterly, 1st and 4th, barry of ten arg. and gu., on a canton of the second a lion passant-guardant or (for CAULFEILD); 2nd and 3rd, or a chevron chequy arg. and az. between three martlets sa. (for HOUSTON). **Crest:** A dragon's head erased gu., gorged with a bar gemel arg. **Supporters:** Two dragons gu., wings addorsed sa., each gorged with a bar gemel arg. **Motto:** *Deo duce ferro comitante* ('God my leader, the sword my companion').

Creations: B. (I) 22 Dec 1620, V. (I) 8 Oct 1665.

THE 14TH VISCOUNT CHARLEMONT, Co Armagh, and **Lord Caulfeild, Baron of Charlemont**, Co Armagh (John Day Caulfeild) [The Rt Hon The Viscount Charlemont, 39 Rossburn Dve, Etobicoke, Ontario M9C 2P9, Canada]; *b* 19 March 1934; *s* unc 1985; *m* 1st 15 Aug 1964 Judith Ann (*d* 29 April 1971), dau of James E Dodd, of Islington, Ontario; *m* 2nd 19 Aug 1972 *Janet Evelyn, dau of Orville Ross Nancekivell, of Salford, Ontario, and has issue:

1 +JOHN DODD; *b* 15 May 1966

1 *Janis Ann; *b* 26 Aug 1968

Lineage: ALEXANDER CALFEHILL/CAULFEILD, of Gt Milton, Oxon; had:

1 George CAULFEILD; Recorder of Oxford; *m* Martha, dau of Richard Taverner, of Wood Eaton, Oxon, and had:

(1) WILLIAM, **2nd Baron**

2 Sir TOBY CAULFEILD, **1st Lord Caulfeild, Baron of Charlemont**, Co Armagh (I), so *cr* 22 Dec 1620 (with special remainder to his nephew Sir William Caulfeild), PC (I 1613); *bapt* 2 Dec 1565; served at sea under Frobisher and Howard, notably in the taking of Cadiz 1596, subsequently served as cavalry cdr under Earl of Essex (*see* HEREFORD, V) in Ireland, notably the taking of Kinsale 1601, made cdr of Fort Charlemont on the River Blackwater 1601; ktd 1603; acquired 1,000 acres of the O'Neill Earls of Tyrone's estates 1610 (he being official Receiver superintending their confiscation 1607–10), Govr Cos Armagh and Tyrone 1608, MP Co Armagh 1613–15; *dsp* unm 17 Aug 1627

The 1st BARON's nephew,

Sir WILLIAM CAULFEILD, **2nd Lord Caulfeild, Baron of Charlemont**; *bapt* 8 Oct 1587; ktd 1618, Govr Fort Charlemont 1621, Master-Gen Ordnance 1627–34; *m* Mary (*d* between 16 July and 15 Aug 1633), dau of Sir John King (ancestor of the Earls of Kingston (*qv*)), and *d* 1640, having had, with other issue:

1 TOBY CAULFEILD, **3rd Lord Caulfeild, Baron of Charlemont**; *b c* Oct 1621; *educ* Lincoln's Inn and Exeter Coll Oxford; MP Co Tyrone 1639–40, Govr Fort Charlemont 1640; murdered 6 Jan 1641/2 by followers of Sir Phelim O'Neill, who had taken him prisoner during the 1641 Uprising after being his guest (Sir Phelim, however, is thought not to have known of the murder beforehand)

2 ROBERT CAULFEILD, **4th Lord Caulfeild, Baron of Charlemont**; *b c* 1622, Capt in army; *d* unm 1 Jan 1643/4 from an overdose of opium

3 WILLIAM, **1st Viscount**

4 Thomas, of Donamon, Co Roscommon, Master in Chancery 1655, MP for Charlemont 1661; *m* 1657 Anne (*bur* 3 Dec 1672), dau of 2nd Viscount Moore of Drogheda (*see* DROGHEDA, E), and *d c* 1691, leaving, with other issue:

(1) William, of Donamon, MP Tulske 1662, Justice of the King's Bench 1715–34; *m* Lettice, dau of Sir Arthur Gore, 1st Bt (*see* ARRAN, E), and *d* 24 Aug 1737, leaving, with other issue:

1a William; *m* Frances Gunter, and *d* 1745, leaving a son, Gore

2a Robert (Rev), MA, Rector Monasterevan, Kildare; *m* Mary Browne, of Castlehill, Co Down, and had three daus

(2) Toby (Rev); Archdeacon of Killaloe; *m* Anne, dau of Adam O'Hara, of Nymphsfield, and had three daus

1 Anne; *m* 1st 1640 Sir Ralph Gore, 2nd Bt (*qv*); *m* 2nd Sir Paul Harris; *m* 3rd Sir John Moore

2 Mary; *m* William Basill, of Donnacarney, and *d* 24 Sept 1668, leaving issue. He *d* 1693

3 Margaret; *m* 3 Nov 1659 Sir George Acheson, 3rd Bt (*see* GOSFORD, E)

The 4th BARON's bro,

WILLIAM CAULFEILD, **1st Viscount Charlemont**, Co Armagh (I), so *cr* 8 Oct 1665, PC (I 1660); captured Sir Phelim O'Neil and had him executed for rebellion; life Govr Fort Charlemont but parted with the office to the Crown for £3,500 (over £140,000 in late 1990s terms); *m* 1653 Sarah (*bur* 3 Dec 1712), 2nd dau of Charles, Viscount Moore (*see* DROGHEDA, E), and had, with other issue:

1 WILLIAM, **2nd Viscount**

2 Toby, Capt of Foot, served in Spain; *m* Rebecca, dau of Oliver Walsh, of Ballykilcavan, Queen's Co, and had issue:

(1) Toby, of Clone, Co Kilkenny, High Sheriff 1721; *m* by 16 March 1720 Lucy (*d c* 18 Feb 1758), dau of Frederick Trench (*see* CLANCARTY, E), and *d* 26 Feb 1758, leaving three daus

(2) William, Col, Lt-Govr Fort George, Inverness; *m* Catherine, dau and heir of Rev Francis Moore, of Raheenduff, Queen's Co, son of Rev John Moore, Archdeacon of Cloyne, and had, with other issue:

1a Wade Toby, of Raheenduff and Catcombe, Wilts, Capt 3rd Dragoon Gds; *b* 1732; *m* 1st 1 Aug 1765 Jessie (*dsps* June 1785), dau of 3rd Lord Ruthven (*see* CARLISLE, E); *m* 2nd 1786 Anne (*m* 3rd François le Chartier de Bolleville), widow of John Cowper, dau of Jonathan Cope and sis of Sir Jonatham Cope, 4th and last Bt, of Brewerne, and *d* Aug 1800, having by her had, with two daus:

1b Edwin Toby, Cdr RN, of Raheenduff and Beckford Ho, Bath; *b* 14 Jan 1793; *m* 1st Jan 1818 Frances Sally (*d* 13 Nov 1841), dau of Eyles Irwin, of Slieve Russell, Co Fermanagh, and had issue:

1c Henry Cope, of Raheenduff, MA, barrister; *b* 29 Dec 1819; *m* 1st 20 April 1847 Anne Louisa (*d* 7 May 1882), yst dau of J R Francklin; *m* 2nd 3 Oct 1883 Eleanor (*d* 1 April 1910), dau of Charles Richard Harford, and *dsp* 11 March 1905

1b (cont.) Cdr Edwin Caulfeild *m* 2nd 9 May 1846 Alicia Almeria (*d* 27 Dec 1882), widow of Capt Henry Pooley, RE, and yst dau of Lt-Gen Sir David Latimer Tinling Widdrington, and *d* 24 Feb 1881, having by her had issue:

2c Edwin James Stuart Widdrington, of Raheenduff; *b* 14 Jan 1848; *m* 20 June 1872 Florence Elizabeth Middleton (*d* 9 April 1925), yst dau of Col John Frederick Sales Clarke, late Scots Greys, and *d* 23 Oct 1914, leaving issue:

1d Edwin Vivian Stuart, of Raheenduff; *b* 7 March 1874; *m* 5 May 1903 Edith Helen (*d* 4 Feb 1966 aged 89), 2nd dau of Claude Ferneley, of Loughborough, and *d* 11 Oct 1958, having had, with other issue:

1e +Stewart Frederick Barry; *b* 20 Jan 1907

1e *Leonore Alicia; *b* 31 Jan 1906

1d *Florence Madeline Lenore; *m* 11 March 1915 Leslie Sloane Palmer

2b Edward Warren (Rev), MA, Rector of Beechingstoke, Wilts; *b* 5 July 1796; *m* 1st 17 Nov 1825 Anne (*d* 26 May 1841), dau of John Pybus, of Cheam, Surrey, and had a s and four daus; *m* 2nd 20 Oct 1842 Millicent (*d* 18 April 1878), yst dau of Joseph Hellicar, and *d* 30 June 1871, having by her had issue:

1c Francis William, MA; *b* 29 Aug 1843; *m* 11 June 1868 Anne Charlotte Eliza (*d* 15 Feb 1934), only day of Cdr George Bunbury, RN, and *d* 6 March 1934, leaving, with other issue:

1d Francis Wade, CBE (1936), V-Adml, Order Crown of Italy, Fndr/Pres Assoc of Retired Naval Offrs 1925; *b* 25 Jan 1872; *m* 18 June 1898 Katherine Ann (*d* 24 Oct 1940), dau of John Clarke Hawkshaw, MA, JP, MInstCE, of Holycombe, Liphook, Hants, and *d* 7 Nov 1947, leaving issue:

1e Wade Toby, dir Antofagasta Railway Co; *b* 24 June 1902; *educ* Eton and New Coll Oxford; *m* 29 June 1935 Philippa Mary (*d* 1996), yst dau of Capt Henry Cyril Royds Brocklebank, CBE, RN, of Charlton Ho, Shaftesbury, Dorset, and *d* 1991, leaving issue:

1f +James Alexander Toby [James Caulfeild Esq, Hookland, Redford, W Sussex GU29 0QF], 2nd Lt KRRC 1956–57; *b* 30 March 1937; *educ* Eton and New Coll Oxford; *m* 1976 *Diana Penelope, dau of Col Martin Pound, RM, and has issue:

1g *Harriet Katharine; *b* 1980

2g *Victoria Louise; *b* 1982

3g *Charlotte Frances; *b* 1984

4g *Sophie Elizabeth; *b* 1987

1f *Charlotte Antonia [Mrs David Evans, 59 Walcot Sq, Kennington, London SW11 4UB]; *b* 17 April 1939; *m* 27 Sept 1975 *Rev David Burton Evans, er son of Thomas Evans, of Shrewsbury

1e Cicely; *b* 14 March 1899; *m* 21 July 1921 Henry Vernon Flower Barran, only son of Henry Barran (*see* BARRAN, Bt), and had issue

2e Ann Katharine, ARCM; *b* 19 Feb 1907; *d* 1992

1d Dorothy; *m* 19 Dec 1905 Professor (Arthur Frederic) Basil Williams, OBE, FBA, only son of F G A Williams, barrister, and *d* 19 March 1948, leaving issue. He *d* 5 Jan 1950

1c Grace Henrietta; *m* 6 May 1873 Col Henry Thomas Thompson Sandes, late RA, and *d* 3 May 1934, leaving issue. He *d* 2 Dec 1906

2a John (Ven), of Benown, Westmeath, Archdeacon of Kilmore; *m* Euphemia Gordon, of Kenmuir, Dumfries, and had issue:

1b William, of Benown, Col Roscommon Militia; *m* 1st Lucy, dau of Sanderson of Clover Hill; *m* 2nd Anna, dau of White Baker, of Castle Bamford, and *d* 1831, having by his 1st w had three sons and four daus, of whom:

1c John, of Bloomfield, Westmeath, High Sheriff Co Roscommon 1826, Lt-Col; *b* 2 Jan 1792; *m* 17 May 1824 Anne Lovell (*d* 22 July 1888), dau of James Bury, of Nazeing, and *d* 3 Feb 1865, having had, with other issue:

1d Robert, of Camolin Ho, Co Wexford, Col 7th Madras Cav, JP (Co Longford); *b* 16 March 1829; *m* 2 Dec 1857 Caroline Henriette (*d* 23 Aug 1918), dau of William Magill, of Lyttelton, Co Westmeath, and *d* 6 Sept 1905, having had, with other issue:

1e Francis William John, CBE (1919), of Camolin, Brig-Gen 65th Inf Bde, 3rd New Army, Col IA; *b* 7 July 1859; *m* 9 March 1897 Alice (*d* 19 Dec 1950), dau of James Hornidge Finnemor, and *d* 12 Oct 1938, leaving, with other issue:

1f Robert, OBE (1952), Col KOSB WW II, ADC to Govr United Provinces 1935; *b* 15 May 1907; *educ* Bromsgrove; *d* 26 July 1990

1f Joan; *b* 10 Aug 1903; *m* 27 Oct 1926 Capt Ludovic Ernest Porter, RN (*d* 28 Feb 1976), only child of Reginald Hugh Porter, and *d* 22 Dec 1995, having had:

1g *Simon Hugh Ludovic [Simon Porter Esq, Stanley House, Stanley Hill, Ledbury, Herefs HR8 1HB]; *b* 7 March 1934; *educ* Eton; *m* 5 Oct 1963 *Patricia Anne, dau of Maj Ynyr Alfred Burges, DL, JP, of Catsfield Manor, Battle, Sussex, and has issue:

1h *Alison Joan; *b* 21 June 1966

2h *Rosemary Anne; *b* 15 Dec 1967

2g Jeremy Michael, Capt RN; *b* 2 Jan 1937; *educ* Eton; *m* 12 June 1965 *(Elizabeth) Caroline (*m* 2nd 6 March 1991 *Kennett Anderson, of Gifford Hall, Broughton Gifford, Wilts), yr dau of Maj Hugh Washington Hibbert (*see* MOWBRAY, SEGRAVE and STOURTON, B), and *d* 4 May 1985, leaving:

1h *James Robert; *b* 11 Oct 1967; *m* 22 April 1995 *Elizabeth Lyne, dau of Michael Lyne, of Ufford, Suffolk

2h *Toby Hugh Washington; *b* 4 May 1969

2e Gordon Napier, DSO (1893), Col DLI; *b* 27 Jan 1862; cmded 17th Serv Bn DLI; *m* 21 May 1902 Mildred (*d* 8 Dec 1963), yst dau of Philip O'Reilly, DL, of Coolamber, Co Westmeath, and *d* 17 March 1922, leaving issue:

1f *Judith Mary; *m* 3 Jan 1938 Robert D FitzRichard Barry, yst son of Richard Fitzwilliam Barry, of Elmgrove, Birr, Co Offaly, and has issue:

1g *Gordon Robert; *b* 20 Nov 1938; *educ* Glenstal and Nat U of Ireland (BA 1959)

2g *Robert James; *b* 16 May 1943; *educ* Glenstal and Nat U of Ireland (BE 1965)

1g *Jennifer Frances; *b* 3 April 1941; *m* 18 Sept 1965 Gerard Clarke, est son of Maurice Clarke, of Lansdowne Park, Ennis Rd, Limerick, and has issue:

1h *Stephen; *b* 8 April 1968

1h *Catherine Anne; *b* 22 Sept 1966

2f *Irene Mildred; *b* 1909; a nun

3e Charles Trevor, CMG (1916), Col RA, Brig-Gen 1914, cmdg RA Home Counties Div 1913–14, W Riding Div 1915–16, 71st Div 1917, 2nd Rawalpindi Div 1918–19 and 1920 (ret 1920); served WW I (despatches) and Afghan War 1919 (despatches); *b* 30 June 1863; *m* 15 July 1903 Kathleen Mary (*d* 11 Aug 1946), dau of Sir John Edge, PC, KC, and *d* 25 Sept 1947, leaving issue:

1f John Trevor, Capt USAF; *b* 2 Aug 1908; *educ* Lancing and Trin Coll Oxford (MA); *m* 10 July 1948 Elizabeth Allie Madeleine de Mestral (*d* 20 Oct 1968), est dau of Gérard de Mestral-de Bülow, of Steinerstrasse 22A, Berne, Switzerland, and *d* 20 Oct 1968, leaving issue:

1g *Catherine Norah [Mrs Nicholas Hall, 28 New Close, Knebworth, Herts SG3 6NU]; *b* 18 June 1949; *m* *Nicholas William Hall, yr son of Francis George Hall, of Sharmans How, Digswell, Herts, and has issue:

1h *Andrew Nicholas Francis William; *b* 1988

1h *Clare Elisabeth Alexandra; *b* 1987

1f Norah Frances; *b* 3 July 1904; *d* 19 Feb 1993

4e St George Robert Sanderson, Lt-Col RE; *b* 5 March 1868; *m* 27 Nov 1902 Winifred Mary (*d* 20 May 1963), 2nd dau of Reginald Butterworth, JP, of Rockwell, Henbury, and Bath, and *d* 1916, leaving issue:

1f Francis St George; *b* 7 Oct 1903; *educ* Cheltenham and Queen's Coll Oxford (BA 1927, MA 1939); *d* unm 10 July 1963

2f +Arthur James, Lt-Col RA WW II; *educ* Cheltenham; *m* 20 Dec 1945 *Marie Antoinette, yr dau of M H G Tholen, of Sittard, Holland

1e Alice Marion Caroline; *m* 5 Aug 1885 Henry Ernest William Fetherstonhaugh-Whitney, of New Pass, Co Westmeath, and *d* 30 Dec 1920. He *d* 3 Sept 1921

2e Violet; *m* 7 March 1900 Richard Francis Caulfeild Orpen, of Coologe, Carrickmines, Co Dublin. He *d* 27 March 1938

3e Hilda Louisa Hamilton; *m* 23 Aug 1920 Lt-Col Ambrose Boxwell, CIE, late IA, son of John Boxwell, ICS, of Butlerstown, Co Wexford. He *d* Jan 1959

2d John, late Capt 90th Foot, JP; *b* 10 Oct 1830; *m* 4 March 1870 Theresa Eliza Stafford (*d* 3 May 1911), yr dau of Maj John Palmer Caulfeild, Bengal Cav (*see below*), and *d* 12 Dec 1892, leaving issue:

1e Walter Stafford, late Lt 3rd Bn Roy Irish Regt; *b* 31 Dec 1874; *d* unm 1942

2e Gordon, Lt Somerset LI; *b* 25 Feb 1885; *ka* at Cambrai, 30 Nov 1917, unm

1e Gwendoline Theresa; *m* 7 Dec 1891 George Caulfeild Prideaux Brune (*see* KILMAINE, B) and *d* 6 Jan 1937

2e Edith Adela Roberta; *d* unm 15 Oct 1968

3e Geraldine Muriel; *m* 4 March 1903 Frederick James Bird, only son of Frederick Bird, of Midsomer Norton, and *d* 22 Feb 1949, leaving issue

1d Anna Julia; *m* 18 April 1850 Maj Francis Winter, late Bengal Army, yst son of John Pratt Winter, of Agher, Co Meath, and *d* his widow, 29 Jan 1909

2d Fanny Elizabeth; *m* 24 Nov 1846 Col Henry Law Maydwell, and *d* 4 Dec 1907, leaving issue. He *d* 15 April 1879

3d Lucy; *m* 2 Aug 1854 Maj Charles Yelverton Balguy, and *d* 3 Sept 1865, leaving issue:

2c James, of The Moorings, Athlone, Cdr RN; *m* 1st 8 May 1823 Hon Augusta Crofton (*d* 29 Sept 1832), dau of Sir Edward Crofton, 2nd Bt (*see* CROFTON, B); *m* 2nd Emily, dau of Col John French, of Clonyquin, Co Roscommon, and *d* 22 Oct 1851, having by his w had:

1d William Montgomerie Stewart, Lt-Col late Roy Dublin Fus, of Weston Park, Dublin; *b* 15 June 1824; *m* 8 June 1847 Dora Jane (*d* 23 March 1916), dau of William French, of Clonyquin, and *d* 4 March 1894, leaving with other issue:

1e Montgomerie Crofton, late Lt 19th Regt; *b* 24 Aug 1851; *d* 18 July 1940

2e James Montgomerie, CBE (1919), Capt RN, sometime Harbour Master at Mauritius, served Egyptian War 1882 (medal, Khedive's Bronze Star), Sudan Campaign 1883–84, Brass River Punitive Expdn 1895, in command of Niger Coast Protectorate Yacht *Evangeline*, WW I as Div Coast-Watching Offr, on Boundary Survey between Cameroons (German Colony) and Niger Coast Protectorate 1894, cmded HMS *Agincourt* at Jubilee Review 1897 (medal); *b* 22 Feb 1855; *m* 6 Feb 1889 Kathleen Ruth (*d* 30 Aug 1951), dau of Lt-Col Hugh Augustus Crofton (*see* CROFTON, Bt, of Mohill), and *dsp* 26 Oct 1946

3e Algernon Montgomerie, DSO, of the Moorings, Farnham, Surrey, Maj late 1st Bn Border Regt, served Afghanistan 1878–80, Burma 1886–90, Chin Lushai Expdn, Egypt 1892–93 and WW I; *b* 9 July 1858; *m* 4 Feb 1897 Edith Mabel (*d* 24 March 1956), dau of Henry Bainbridge Browning, of 9 Cadogan Square, SW, and was *ka* Gallipoli 9 Aug 1915, leaving issue:

1f Kathleen Montgomerie; *b* 25 June 1901; *m* 16 Jan 1929 Rev Thomas Western Page-Phillips, MA, Vicar of Puddletown, Dorchester, Preb of Chisenbury and Chute, and Hon Canon of Salisbury Cathedral, son of Henry Western Page-Phillips, of Marden Ho, Milford-on-Sea, Hants, and *d* 9 Jan 1964, leaving a son. He *d* 8 July 1961

1e Emily Augusta; *m* 7 Feb 1878 Hon Francis George Crofton, and *d* 2 Jan 1924, leaving issue (*see* CROFTON, B)

2e Maud Laura; *d* unm 12 July 1953, in her 90th year

2b Thomas Gordon, Cdre RN, of Curraghmore, Co Roscommon; *b* 1768; *m* 1802 Theodosia, dau of W Talbot, of Mount Talbot, and *d* 23 June 1821, leaving, with four daus (all left issue):

1c William (Rev), Rector Mullahiffe; *b* 2 Dec 1813; *m* 9 July 1840 Ellen (*d* 1890), est dau of J Wilmot Smyth, of Silver Hills, King's Co, and *d* 28 Oct 1867, leaving, with other issue:

1d James Edward Wilmot Smyth, CMG (1917), Hon Brig-Gen, late Col 2nd W India Regt and Brig-Gen Cmdg troops in Jamaica 1902–06, 96th Inf Bde 1914 and 8th Res Inf Bde 1915–16; *b* 4 Sept 1850; *educ* Trin Coll Dublin (BA); *m* 22 May 1876 Sophia Morley (*d* 20 Dec 1932), dau of William Alexander Parker, Ch Justice of British Honduras, and *d* 19 Sept 1925, leaving issue:

1e William Talbot McClintock, Lt RE; *b* 7 Aug 1879; *d* unm 28 May 1907, accidentally *k* in a military balloon

2e St George Frederick Gordon, Col RM, JP W Sussex, chm W Sussex Magistrates Courts Ctee 1952–55, WW I (despatches) and WW II with Naval Staff Admiralty, Order of Rising Sun of Japan; *b* 25 Jan 1881; *educ* Bradfield; *m* 28 July 1917 Eila Rosslyn (*d* 12 Jan 1973), er dau of Reginald John, of Colombo, Ceylon, and *d* 26 Nov 1973, leaving issue:

1f +Toby St George, CBE (1974, MBE 1952) [Brig Toby Caulfeild CBE, PO Box 11, Girne, Mersin 10, Turkey], Brig RA WW II and Korea 1952–54, Instr Staff Coll 1955–57, served Malaya 1958–59, OC 7th Parachute Regt RHA 1960–62, GSO(1) Brixmis 1962–64, Col GS RAF Staff College 1964, UK Nat Mil Rep SHAPE 1971–74; *b* 22 April 1919; *educ* Wellington; *m* 1st 16 Feb 1942 (*divorce* 1951), Mary, er dau of Sir William Lindsay Murphy, KCMG, of Milford, Tuam, Co Galway; *m* 2nd 16 May 1959 *Agnes Sheila (Robin), QARNNS, dau of Edward Buckmaster Robinson, of Cranmore, Queen's Rd, Tankerton, Kent, and by 1st w has issue:

1g +Toby John St George [Toby Caulfeild Esq, Newlands Grange, Shotley Bridge, Consett, Co Durham]; *b* 3 Nov 1943; *educ* Wellington; *m* 1st 26 Aug 1967 Gillian, only dau of C M Rhead, of 6 Ashleigh Rd, Horsham, Sussex; *m* 2nd 1980 *Joanna, dau of Arthur R Yates Hunter, of Saskatoon, Canada, and by 1st w has issue:

1h +Patrick William St George; *b* 6 June 1968

1g *Grania Mary [The Rt Hon The Lady Cavendish of Furness, Holker Hall, Cark-in-Cartmel, Cumbria]; *b* 19 April 1947; *m* 3 Oct 1970 *Baron Cavendish of Furness (LP; *qv*), and has issue

3e Wilmot Smyth, MC, Lt-Col RA, Maj E Surrey Regt, Capt Leinster Regt, served WW I (despatches twice, Croix de Guerre), WW II in RA; CD Long Serv Medal 1967; *b* 7 April 1887; *educ* Bradfield; *m* 1st 9 Jan 1923 Meredith de Lisle (*d* 27 Oct 1924), yr dau of Reginald John, of Merryworth Lawn, Wrotham, and 31 Kensington Court, W8, and had issue:

1f *Pamela Ann de Lisle, JP (Westmorland 1961) [Mrs Walter Godsal JP, Little Edbrooke, Winsford, Som TA24 7AE]; *b* 1924, served WW II in WRNS; *m* 1st 19 Dec 1944 (*divorce* 1970) Maj Philip Hugh Godsal, FLAS (*d* 1982), er son of Lt-Col Philip Godsal, MC, JP, of Iscoyd Park, Salop; *m* 2nd 7 Nov 1970 *Capt Walter Edward Browning Godsal, RN, yr son of Lt-Col Philip Godsal, MC, JP, and by her 1st husb has:

1g *Philip Caulfeild [Philip Godsal Esq, Iscoyd Park, Whitchurch, Salop SY13 3AT]; *b* 1945; *educ* Eton; High Sheriff Clwyd 1993; FRICS; land agent; *m* 1st 1969 (*divorce* 1985) Lucinda Mary, dau of Lt-Cdr Percival Royston Dancey, RNVR, of Old Shalesbrook, Forest Row, Sussex; *m* 2nd 1986 *Mrs Selina Baber, dau of Thomas William Brooke-Smith, of Canford Cliffs, Dorset, and by his 1st w has:

1h *Philip Langley; *b* 1971

2h *Benjamin Rupert Wilmot; *b* 1976

3h *Thomas Henry; *b* 1977

1h *Laura Sophie; *b* 1973

2g *David Hugh, MBE (1983); *b* 1947; *educ* Eton and Exeter U (BA), Col late RGJ; *m* 1971 *Tamsin Annette, dau of Capt Thomas Keppel Edge-Partington, RN, of Arnoldsfield, Fairfield Rd, Quenington, Cirencester, Glos GL7 5RT, and has issue:

1h *James Keppel; *b* 1977

2h *Jonathan Hugh; *b* 1981

1h *Nicola Jane; *b* 1974

3g *Rupert Charles [Rupert Godsal Esq, Horris Hill Prep School, Newtown, Newbury, Berks]; *b* 1952; *educ* Eton; Dep Headmaster Horris Hill Prep Sch

1g *Caroline Mary [Mrs Robert Miller, Stowbridge House, Moreton-in-Marsh, Glos]; *b* 1950; *m* 1974 *Robert Thornewill Miller, and has issue:

1h *David Robert; *b* 1982

1h *Clare Serena; *b* 1983

2g *Meredith Jane; *b* 1956; *m* 1981 *Maj Adam H C MacMillan-Scott, KOSB, son of W T R MacMillan-Scott, of 2 Grove Meadow, Sticklepath, Okehampton, Devon, and has issue:

1h *Katherine Rachel Sarah; *b* 1982

2h *Charlotte Meredith Lucy; *b* 1984

3h *Isobel Sophie de Lisle; *b* 1986

3e (cont.) Lt-Col Wilmot Caulfeild *m* 2nd 21 Sept 1928 Sheilah (*d* 1992), Civil Def Long Serv Medal (1968), served WW II, yr dau of John J Beven, of Dublin, and *d* 1980, having by her had issue:

1f Toby Bevan St George; *b* and *d* 15 Aug 1942

2f *Eileen Ruth Morley; *b* 1929; *m* 20 Sept 1952 Henry Edward Percy (*d* 1985), er son of Lord William Percy, and has issue (*see* NORTHUMBERLAND, D)

3f *Barbara Joan Sheilah [Mrs Preston Prichard, The Croft, Says Lane, Upper Langford, Bristol]; *b* 1932; *m* 17 May 1969 *Preston Caradoc Hardinge Mostyn Prichard (*see* HARDINGE, V), er son of Rev George Mostyn Prichard, of 24 Palace Ct, W2, and has issue:

1g *Julian Caulfeild Mostyn; *b* 3 June 1970; *educ* Milton Abbey

1g *Diana Mostyn; *b* 20 Sept 1973

4e James Crosbie, Lt 2nd Bn Manchester Regt; *b* 21 Feb 1892; *ka* 18 Nov 1914

1e Grace Hardyman, OBE (1948), RRC, Matron QAIMNS 1932, served WW I in France 1914–19 (despatches); *d* unm 27 Dec 1956

2e Ellen Mary; *d* unm 11 Aug 1963

3e Charlotte Morley; *d* Dec 1885

4e Ruth; *m* 1 Aug 1912 Rev Benjamin Hayward Fisher (*d* 10 June 1962), and has issue:

1f *Stella Margaret; *b* 3 June 1915

2f *Ruth Mary; *b* 26 May 1918; *m* 23 April 1963 John Walter Rocke Swayne, MC, son of Lt-Col O R Swayne, of Tillington Ho, Hereford

5e Stella Evelyn, ARRC, served WW I in France with VAD, Br Expdny Forces

3d St George Henry Wandesford (Rev), late HM Prison Serv, formerly Rector of Melrose, S Australia; *b* 9 Aug 1859; *m* 1890 Annie Lovel Caulfeild, dau of Col Henry Law Maydwell, and *d* 19 July 1934

3b James, CB, Lt-Gen, MP Abingdon; *b* 30 Jan 1782; *m* 1st 14 Dec 1814 Letitia (*d* Aug 1826), dau of Lt-Gen Hugh Stafford, and had a son; *m* 2nd Annie Rachel (*d* 17 May 1890), dau of Maj Blake, and *d* 4 Nov 1852, having by her had, with two other s:

1c George, JP (Co Limerick), of Copeswood, Pallaskenry, Co Limerick; Rifle Bde, High Sheriff Co Limerick; *b* 3 Jan 1841; *m* 6 Dec 1871 Thomasina (*d* 1910), dau of Thomas Royce, and *d* 15 June 1922, leaving, with other issue:

1d George Blake; *b* 10 May 1875; *m* 10 Jan 1899 Lilian (*d* March 1944), 2nd dau of Capt Edward Bacon, DL, late 18th Hus, and *d* 28 June 1939, leaving issue:

1e Leslie Alexander; *b* 1900; *m* 5 Nov 1930 (*divorce* 1936) Jennie Ida, dau of Charles Deering Manson, and was believed *k* in an air raid 1940, leaving issue:

1f +A son; *b* 193–

2e Jack Harley; *b* 13 Nov 1903; *m* 3 July 1929 Gweneth (*m* 2nd 20 June 1933 Col Alexaner Frederick Sholto Douglas, KOYLI, son of Alexander Forbes Douglas, of Hutton Buscel, Yorks), dau of Alexander Henry Morris, of Orchard Ho, Aston Tirrold, Berks, and *d* 30 July 1929, as result of a flying accident

3e William Henry, Maj RASC WW II; *b* 7 Oct 1911; *m* 9 April 1935 *Lorna [Mrs William Caulfeild, Flat 9, 26 Sussex Sq, Brighton, Sussex BN2 5AB], dau of Cuthbert Wilkinson, of The Clock Ho, Nether Stowey, Somerset, and was *ka* in India 2 Dec 1943, leaving issue:

1f *Anne Marie [Mrs Rupert Travis, 97 Balham Park Rd, London SW12 8EB]; *b* 25 Feb 1941; *educ* Bristol U (BA Econ); *m* 23 Jan 1965 *Rupert Alan Travis, est son of Norman John Travis, of Howe Green Hall, nr Hertford, and has issue:

1g *Benjamin William Norman; *b* 27 Oct 1973

2g *Toby Rupert Dale; *b* 1979

1g *Amanda Tiffany; *b* 15 May 1972

1e Phyllis Daphne; *b* 1905; *m* 9 Sept 1954 Paul Albeck, son of Vilhelm Theodor Albeck, of 14 Kronprinsensvej, Fredriksberg, Copenhagen, Denmark, and *d* 7 May 1964

1d Ada; *m* 14 July 1904 Maj George Henry Wyndham Bayley, late RA, and *d* 16 Oct 1960 aged 85, leaving issue. He *d* 16 Aug 1941

1c Annie Rachel; *m* 5 Sept 1867 George Frederick Robert Purdon, of Tinerana, Co Clare, and *d* 23 June 1882, leaving issue

(1) Edith; *m* by 1717 William Flower, 1st Baron Castle Durrow, and had issue (*see* ASHBROOK, V)

3 John, of Tullydowy, Co Tyrone; Lt-Col; *m* Sydney (*d* 4 July 1725), dau of James Somerville, of Tully Kilter, Co Fermanagh, and was *bur* 22 Nov 1752, leaving issue

1 Mary; *m* 1st Arthur Dillon, of Lismullen, Co Meath (*d* Dec 1684); *m* 2nd 1686 6th Baron Blayney (*d* 3 Jan 1705/6) and *d* 8 Aug 1724

2 Alice; *m* 1st John Margetson; *m* 2nd 20 Jan 1693/4 1st Baron Carpenter of Killaghy and *d* 7 Oct 1731, leaving issue. He *d* 10 Feb 1731/2

3 Elizabeth; *m* 1st John Chichester (*see* DONEGALL, M) and had issue (*see* O'NEILL, B); *m* 2nd Edward Walkington, Bp Down and Connor, and *d* 1694. He *d* Jan 1698

The 1st VISCOUNT was *bur* 25 May 1671; his 2nd, but est surv son,

WILLIAM CAULFEILD, **2nd Viscount Charlemont**, PC (I 1726); Williamite in post-Glorous Revolution Ireland, accordingly attainted by JAMES II's I Parl May 1689; restored by WILLIAM III, Govr Fort Charlemont, Col 36th Foot 1701–06, Maj Gen 1708; *m* 11 July 1678 Anne (*d* 1729), only dau of Dr James Margetson, Archbp Armagh, and *d* 21 July 1726, having had, with other issue:

1 JAMES CAULFEILD, **3rd Viscount Charlemont**; MP Charlemont 1703–04 and 1713–26; *bapt* 29 July 1682; *m* Elizabeth (*m* 2nd 9 Oct 1740 Thomas Adderley and *d* 30 May 1743), only dau of Francis Bernard, of Castle Mahon, Co Cork, Judge Court Common Pleas Ireland (*see* 1970 edn BANDON, E), and *d* 21 April 1734, having had:

(1) JAMES CAULFEILD, **4th Viscount Charlemont** and 1st EARL OF CHARLEMONT, Co Armagh (I), so *cr* 23 Dec 1763, KP (1783), PC (I 1783); *b* 18 Aug 1728; C-in-C Irish Volunteers 1780; *m* 2 July 1768 Mary (*d* April 1807), dau of Thomas Hickman, of Brickhill, Co Clare, yr bro of Luke Hickman, of Fenloe, Co Clare, and *d* 4 Aug 1799, having had, with other issue:

1a FRANCIS WILLIAM CAULFEILD, **5th Viscount Charlemont** and 2nd EARL OF CHARLEMONT, KP (1831), PC (I 1832); *b* 3 Jan 1775; MP Co Armagh 1797–99, rep I peer 1806–63; *cr* 13 Feb 1837 BARON CHARLEMONT, of Charlemont, Co Armagh (UK), with remainder to his bro and the latter's male issue; *m* 9 Feb 1802 Anne (*d* 23 Nov 1876), yst dau and coheir of William Bermingham, of Ross Hill, Co Galway, and *dsps* 26 Dec 1863, having had:

1b James William, *Viscount Caulfeild*; *b* Aug 1803; *d* 13 Jan 1823

2b William Francis; *b* 1805; *d* 1807

1b Maria Melosina; *b* Jan 1807; *d* unm 4 March 1827

2b Emily Charlotte; *b* 1808; *d* unm Oct 1829

2a Henry, of Hockley, Co Armagh; MP Armagh; *b* 29 July 1779; *m* 30 Aug 1819 Elizabeth Margaret (*d* 20 Oct 1878), 2nd dau of Dodwell Browne, of Rahins, Co Mayo, and *d* 4 March 1862, leaving (yr son and dau granted in, the precedence of children of an Earl):

1b JAMES MOLYNEUX CAULFEILD, **6th Viscount Charlemont** and 3rd and last EARL OF CHARLEMONT, KP (1865); *b* 6 Oct 1820; Ld Lt Co Armagh 1849–64 and Co Tyrone 1864–92, MP (Lib) Co Armagh 1847–57; *m* 1st 18 Dec 1856 Hon Elizabeth Jane Somerville (*d* 31 May 1882), only dau of 1st Baron Athlumney (*see* 1929 edn); *m* 2nd 10 May 1883 Anna Lucy (*d* 7 March 1925), dau of Rev Charles James Lambart, Rector of Navan, Co Meath (*see* CAVAN, E), and *dsp* 12 Jan 1892, when the Earldom and UK Barony expired

2b Henry William; *b* 1822; granted Feb 1864 with sis rank of earl's dau/yr s; *d* 28 Feb 1867

1b Margaret Zoe; *m* Sept 1848 Sir John Calvert Stronge, 4th Bt (*qv*), and *d* 14 Sept 1903, leaving issue

(2) Francis, MP Charlemont; *m* Oct 1760 Mary, only dau of John, Lord Eyre, and was lost with his w, infant child and servant in a storm on his passage to Ireland from London Nov 1775, leaving:

1a James Eyre, Col; *b* 14 July 1765, *dsp*

1a Eleanor; *m* 31 March 1787 3rd Earl of Wicklow (*see* 1970 edn) and *d* 1807

(1) Alicia; *m* 23 April 1763 1st Baron Kilmaine (*qv*)

2 Charles (Rev), Rector of Donaghenry, Co Armagh; *bapt* 27 Dec 1686; *m* Alice (*d* April 1760), dau of John Houston, of Castlestewart, Co Tyrone, and *d* Jan 1768, leaving, with other issue:

(1) James, of Drumcairn, Co Tyrone; *m* 1765 Catherine, dau of Thomas Burgh, of Oldtown, and *d* 1825, leaving:

1a James, of Drumcairn; *m* 22 May 1806 Hon Harriet Crofton (*d* 6 July 1837), dau of Sir Edward Crofton, 2nd Bt, MP, of Mote Park (*qv*), by Baroness Crofton (*see* CROFTON, B), and had issue:

1b Edward Houston, of Drumcairn, DL, JP; *b* 28 Feb 1807; *m* 26 April 1828 Charlotte (*d* 11 Nov 1840), dau of Piers Geale, and *d* 7 March 1883, leaving:

1c JAMES ALFRED CAULFEILD, **7th Viscount Charlemont**, CB (1892), DL, JP, V-Lt Co Tyrone, High Sheriff 1868, Hon Col 3rd Bn Roy Inniskilling Fus, Capt Coldstream Gds (served Crimea), Comptroller Household of Ld Lt Ireland 1868–95, Usher Black Rod Order St Patrick to 1913; *b* 20 March 1830; *m* 2 Feb 1858 Hon Annetta Handcock (*d* 10 Nov 1888), yr dau of 3rd Baron Castlemaine (*qv*), and *d* 4 July 1913, leaving:

1d Constance Elizabeth; *m* 10 Feb 1880 5th Earl of Ranfurly (*qv*), and *d* 25 July 1932, leaving issue

2c Marcus Piers Francis, CB; granted with siblings by roy warrant 26 May 1894 rank of viscount's dau/yr s; with Admlty, Maj Mid-Ulster Art Militia; *b* 3 Nov 1840; *m* 15 Aug 1878 Louisa Gwyn (*d* 14 Nov 1916), 4th dau of Robert Griffith Williams and niece of Sir Richard Williams-Bulkeley, 10th Bt (*qv*), and *d* 15 April 1895, leaving:

1d JAMES EDWARD GEALE CAULFEILD, **8th Viscount Charlemont**, PC (NI 1926); *b* 12 May 1880; *educ* Winchester; Hon ARIBA, Hon LLD Queen's U Belfast; rep I peer 1918–49, V-Lt Co Tyrone 1922–39, Min Educn NI and Leader Senate 1926–37, chm Advsy Ctee Ancient Monuments NI; *m* 1st 26 Nov 1914 (*divorce* April 1940) Evelyn Fanny Charlotte (*k* by enemy action 14 Oct 1940), dau of Edmund Charles Pendleton Hull, of Park Gate Ho, Ham Common, Surrey; *m* 2nd 25 July 1940 Hildegarde, Chev Order of Leopold of Belgium and Order of St Sava of Yugoslavia (*d* 22 Jan 1969), dau of Rodolphe Slock-Cotell, of Malstapel, Ruiselede, Belgium, and *dsp* 30 Aug 1949

1d Dorothy; granted with sisters by roy warrant 4 June 1914 rank of viscount's daus; *m* 2 Jan 1906 Adml Philip Nelson-Ward, CVO, of Crocker Hill, nr Chichester, Sussex, Extra Gentleman Usher to HM, son of Rev Horatio Nelson Nelson-Ward, Rector of Radstock, and was *k* by enemy action 27 April 1942. He *d* 27 June 1937

2d Rachel; *k* by enemy action 27 April 1942

1c Harriet Charlotte; *d* unm 24 Dec 1909

1b Harriet Anna; *m* 1837 William John French, and *d* 27 Feb 1890, leaving issue (*see* DE FREYNE, B)

(2) Charles (Rev), Rector of Killyman; *m* Margaret, dau of Hans Widman Wood, of Rosmead, Co Westmeath, by Frances, dau of Sir Henry King, 3rd Bt (*see* KINGSTON, E) and had issue:

1a Hans (Rev), Rector of Kilmanagh, Co Kilkenny; *m* 13 March 1803 Anne (*d* 13 April 1852), dau of John Rothe, of Bloomhill, Co Kilkenny, and *d* June 1854, having had, with other issue:

1b Charles (Rt Rev), DD, Bishop of Nassau, Bahamas; *b* 1804; *m* 6 Feb 1832 Grace Anne (*d* 1 Dec 1896), dau of Sir Richard Bligh St George, 2nd Bt (*qv*), and *d* 4 Sept 1862, leaving, with other issue:

1c Hans St George; *b* 5 Aug 1837; *m* 1 March 1878 Emily Bertha (*d* 21 Aug 1932), dau of Edward James, JP, MD, of Edgbaston, and *d* 14 Feb 1899, leaving issue:

1d CHARLES EDWARD ST GEORGE CAULFEILD, **9th Viscount Charlemont**, FSS, Lt RFC (Mil Wing), served Admin Staff E Cmd 1916–17; Min Nat Serv 1917–18; served WW II; Hon V-Pres Nat Union of Mfrs, dir of Membership 1919–50; pres Sutton and Cheam branch RFA Assoc; *b* 12 July 1887; *m* 2 Sept 1911 Mabel (*d* 15 Feb 1965), est dau of James Frederick William Hawthorn, and *d* 18 Jan 1964, leaving:

1e Shelah St George; *b* 24 Dec 1914; *m* 18 May 1946 John Arnold Hawkes, BCom, ACA, son of Arnold Hawkes, of Birmingham, and *d* 5 March 1982, leaving issue:

1f *Richard John; *b* 25 Sept 1947; *educ* St John's Leatherhead

2e *Patricia St George [The Hon Patricia Caulfeild, 55 New Rd, Lewes, E Sussex], WW II as 3rd Offr WRNS; *b* 17 Sept 1920

1d Lilian Mary St George; *b* 5 July 1888; *m* 3 June 1911 William Henry Garside, 2nd son of Alfred Garside, and had issue. He *d* 1965

2d Dorothy Gladys St George; *b* 21 March 1890; *m* 20 March 1915 Austen Gordon Hutchins, late Lt RA, only son of George D'Oyly Hutchins, CBE, of Clive Ho, Oxshott, Surrey, and *d* 28 Jan 1954. He *d* 1949

2c Theophilus William St George; *b* 30 March 1844; *m* 21 Dec 1876 Annie Florence (*d* 1944), dau of Frederick W Marsden, and *d* 1911, leaving issue:

1d Grace St George; *b* 25 Sept 1877; *m* 18 June 1903 William McDonald (*d* 7 Feb 1918), of Melbourne, Victoria, Australia, and had issue:

1e Ian; *b* 17 Nov 1908; *m* 16 April 1938 *Verna, only dau of Theodore Harrison, of Aloha, Highfield Grove, Kew, Melbourne, and had issue:

1f *Graham William Andrew; *b* 26 Feb 1941

2f *Ian Ross; *b* 13 July 1944

1e Catherine St George; *b* 14 May 1904; *m* 22 April 1954 Frederick William Faulkner, son of William George Faulkner, of Melbourne

2d Linda St George; *b* 14 Dec 1881; *m* 21 Dec 1909 Alfred George Henry Couchman, of St Kilda, Melbourne, and *d* 13 March 1937, leaving issue. He *d* 23 March 1953

3c Francis John Rothe Toby St George, ISO (1904), MICE, Dir of Public Works, FMS 1901–07; *b* 20 Feb 1852; *m* 11 Nov 1880 Helen Isabel (*d* 27 April 1958), dau of Henry John Simonds, JP, of Caversham, and *d* 17 Oct 1933, leaving, with other issue:

1d Harry Frowd St George, Maj RA WW I (wounded); *b* 14 Aug 1881; *m* 7 Dec 1914 Geraldine Marguerite (*d* 17 Jan 1922), dau Lt-Col Charles Boyd, RE, and *d* Oct 1961, leaving issue:

1e *Geraldine St George [Mrs Hugh Mason, Orchard Leigh, Prinsted, Emsworth, Hants]; *b* 3 Oct 1918; SRN; *m* 1st 27 Sept 1947 Maj Peter Lawry Matthews, TD, RASC (*d* 1970), only surv son of H Matthews, FSMC, FIO, of St Margaret's, Hayle, Cornwall; *m* 2nd 1975 Hugh Alan Mason (*d* 1992), and by 1st husb has issue:

1f *Toby St George; *b* 1 April 1950

1f *Helen Brontë; *b* 18 Nov 1953; *m* 1st 1980 (*divorce* 1988) Charles Kroller, of California; *m* 2nd 1989 *Phillip Warren Kunz, and has issue:

1g *Sarah Kaitlyn; *b* 1990

1c Theodosia Mary; *m* 26 Sept 1866 Rev Thomas Cosgrave

2c Grace Ellen Sophia; *d* unm 25 June 1943

2b James, Treasurer of Ceylon; *b* 1805; *m* Eliza Thomas, widow of Maj Rehé, of Ceylon, and dau of Basil Gray, and *d* 4 May 1861, leaving, with other issue:

1c James Campbell; *b* 18 June 1843

2c Henry St George, Queensland CS; *b* 1 Sept 1851; *m* 14 May 1877 Jane (*d* 22 Oct 1924), dau of William Goldsmith, and *d* 22 May 1943, leaving issue:

1d James Charles Russell St George (Rev), Missionary Br Solomon Is 1904–09; *b* 26 April 1878; *m* 3 Feb 1934 May Jane (*d* 26 April 1959), dau of Thomas Mitchell, of Moredur Station, Ben Lomond, NSW, and *dsp* 1 Jan 1956

2d ROBERT TOBY ST GEORGE CAULFEILD, **10th Viscount Charlemont**, JP (Queensland 1907); *b* 30 Sept 1881; *educ* Von Schultz GS, Bundaberg, Australia; Capt Australian Res of Offrs WW I (wounded); *d* unm 26 Nov 1967

3d CHARLES ST GEORGE CAULFEILD, **11th Viscount Charlemont**; *b* 1884; *educ* Von Schultz GS, Bundaberg; manager Bank of NSW, Camboya, Queensland; *m* 24 Nov 1915 Lydia Clare (*d* 1973), dau of Charles James Kingston, of Aramac, Qld, and *d* 1971, leaving:

1e *Constance Ada [The Hon Mrs Pearce, 254 Mooroondu Rd, Thorneside, Qld 4158, Australia]; *b* 16 Feb 1918; *m* 27 Feb 1943 *Henry Edward Pearce, and has issue:

1f *Edward Charles [Edward Pearce Esq, 44 Dawson, Rd, Ormiston Heights, Qld 4163, Australia]; *b* 25 Nov 1943; AAIA; *m* 1967 *Beverly Ellen, dau of Cyril Edward Cooper, of 15 Wyeth St, Wynrthum North, Qld, Australia, and has issue:

1g *Rodney Edward; *b* 1975

1g *Sandra Ellen; *b* 1970

2f *Donald John; *b* 27 June 1947; BEng; *m* 1971 *Rasa Janina Zvirblis, and has issue:

1g *Scott Ramon; *b* 1975

1g *Kristie Louise; *b* 1977

1f *Pamela Ann [Mrs Hendrik Veenstra, 18 Gallang St, Rochedale, Qld 4123, Australia]; *b* 18 Feb 1946; *m* 30 April 1966 *Hendrik Wouter Veenstra, son of Martin Hubert Heinrich Veenstra, and adopted:

*Wade Hendrik; *b* 1971

*Annelies Pamela; *b* 1973

2f *Janet May *b* 17 April 1950; BEd

3f *Wendy Roslyn; *b* 12 Oct 1958; DipT

2e *Janie St George [The Hon Mrs Moore, 30 Maxwell St, Turramurra, Sydney, NSW 2074, Australia]; *b* 9 April 1921; *m* 27 June 1942 *David Dominic Moore, BSc, AMIE (Aust), and has issue:

1f *Colleen Janie; *b* 22 Oct 1944; *m* 9 Sept 1967 *Alan Charles Watts, MB, ChB, LRCP, MRCS, son of Thomas Watts, and has issue:

1g *Tracey Colleen; *b* 21 June 1968

2g *Kellie Mary Jane; *b* 1972

3g *Christine Judith; *b* 1975

4g *Sarra Alaine; *b* 1979

2f *Margaret Louise; *b* 24 Dec 1947; *m* 1972 *Keith Douglas Brodie, LLB, CA, of Sydney, NSW, and has issue:

1g *Barry; *b* 1977

1g *Paula Louise; *b* 1975

2g *Claire Elizabeth; *b* 1980

4d RICHARD WILLIAM ST GEORGE CAULFEILD, **12th Viscount Charlemont**; with Directorate of Works, Air Ministry, also Colonial Civ Serv, FMS; *b* 13 March 1887; *m* 7 Oct 1914 Dorothy Laura (*d* 18 May 1961), only dau of Frank Giles, ICS, of 24 The Grange, Wimbledon, and *d* 18 June 1979, leaving:

1e *Dorothy Frances Lucy St George [The Hon Mrs Trowbridge, Drumcairn, Lane End, Elmstead Market, Essex CO7 7BB]; *b* 1915; *m* 1945 F/Lt Robert Hender Trowbridge, RAAF (*d* 1993), and has issue:

1f *Mark Robert; *b* 27 April 1947

2f *(Richard) Keith Giles; *b* 23 Aug 1950; *m* 1980 *Pamela Mary, dau of Philip N Bradshaw, of Gt Driffield, N Yorks, and has issue:

1g *Laura Frances; *b* 1986

2g *Emma Kathryn; *b* 1988

2e *Alicia St George [The Hon Mrs Stuart, 3 Lovel Hill, Windsor Forest, Berks]; *b* 1918; *m* 1939 *G/Capt Gordon Hackworth Stuart, MD, DPH, BS, MRCS, LRCP, RAF, and has issue:

1f *Colin Gordon Cameron; *b* 17 Oct 1940; *educ* Badingham Coll; *m* 1st 5 June 1965 (*divorce* 1971) Jane Susan, dau of Maj A E Dennis Michell, KAR; *m* 2nd 1981 *Eve Lin-Yau, dau of Yau Shan Shan, of Peking, and has issue:

1g *Alicia Frances Sarah; *b* 1983

1c Anne Ellen; *d* unm 17 Jan 1937

2c Sophia, Isabella; *m* 3 Oct 1872 George Francis Green, and *d* 11 Oct 1940, leaving issue. He *d* 9 Oct 1918

3b Wilberforce (Rev), Rector of St Mary, Kilkenny; *b* 1806; *m* 1832 Catherine (*d* 2 June 1858), dau of E Butler, and *d* 27 April 1872, leaving, with other issue:

1c Hans (Rev); *b* 2 Dec 1833; *m* 4 Feb 1861 Rachel (*d* 1912), dau of Thomas Reade, of Callan, Co Kilkenny, and *d* 10 Dec 1874, leaving issue:

1d Charles Hans; *b* 8 June 1869; *m* 21 March 1898 Ethel Jessie, dau of D G R Mann, of Ottawa, and *d* 2 Nov 1950, leaving issue:

1e CHARLES WILBERFORCE CAULFEILD, **13th Viscount Charlemont**; Canadian Civ Serv; *b* 10 March 1899; *m* 24 Sept 1930 *Dorothy Jessie, dau of Albert Allan Johnston, of Ottawa, Canada, and *d* 1985

2e Eric St George; *b* 19 April 1900; *m* 3 June 1933 *Edith Evelyn [Mrs Eric Caulfeild, 43 Smithwood Dve, Islington, Ont M9B 48I, Canada], dau of F W Day, of Ottawa, and *d* 1975, leaving issue:

1f JOHN DAY CAULFEILD, **14th and present Viscount Charlemont**

1f *Edith Jane [Mrs Edward Cobean, 106 Brown's Ave, Walkerton, Ont N0G 2VO, Canada]; *b* 19 Sept 1941; *m* 1963 *Edward Cobean, and has issue:

1g *Robert Edward; *b* 1967

2g *Stephen John; *b* 1971

1g *Susan Jane; *b* 1966

3e +Arthur Edward Lampay (Ven); *b* 21 Sept 1906; *educ* Bishop's U (BA), DD King's Coll; LST, Rector Trinity Ch, and Archdeacon St John, New Brunswick, Chaplain RCAF (Res) 1940–51; *m* 5 June 1940 *Emilie Kathleen Irene, dau of Rev E Frank Salmon, DD, of Philadelphia, and has:

1f +David Arthur; *b* 9 May 1942; BArch, MASc, MRAIC, PEng; architect; *m* 4 Sept 1965 *Diane, dau of F W Du Vernet, of Ottawa, Canada, and has issue:

1g +Sean David; *b* 14 June 1966

2g +Derek Arthur; *b* 1969

2f +Charles Patrick [Charles Caulfeild Esq, 883 Safari Rd, Kingston, Ontario K7M 6W2, Canada], BEng; *b* 2 June 1946; *m* 18 Aug 1968 *Marjorie Agnes, dau of Robert Reid, of St John, NB, Canada

1d Catherine; *b* 1 May 1863; *d* unm 1947

2d Mary Rachel; *b* 6 Feb 1865; *m* 11 July 1898 William Ayres McCarthy, of Cleveland, Ohio, USA, and *d* 1967, leaving issue. He *d* 1923

4b Hans, MD; *b* 1814; *m* 1847 Mary Anne, dau of Henry Ellis, and *d* 1863, leaving, with other issue:

1c Hans James; *b* 9 Aug 1849; *m* 1st 1872 Jenny (*d* 1901), dau of Samuel Brasher, and had issue:

1d Alfred Hans Waring, MB Toronto U, sometime Capt Canadian AMC, Consultant Dept of Nat Health and Pensions, Res Memb Connaught Laboratories, U of Toronto, Canada; *b* 1879; *m* 1st 19 Dec 1917 (*divorce* 1934) Mary Harris (*d* 27 Dec 1968), widow of Maj George Malcolm Nixon Harman, DSO, Rifle Bde, and er dau of Sir Evan Davies Jones, 1st Bt; *m* 2nd 30 Aug 1934 Adele Edith (*d* June 1940), dau of Melfort Boulton, of Toronto, and *d* 2 May 1940, having by 1st w had issue:

1e Evan Michael St George, CA, WW II 1939–40 in Br Army and 1940–46 with Canadian Forces; *b* 9 Dec 1918; *educ* Toronto U (BA 1948); *m* 25 June 1948 *Shirley Joyce [Mrs Evan Caulfeild, 2 Clearside Place, Etobicoke, Ont M9C 2G6, Canada], dau of Harry Scutt Burt, of Richmond Hill, Ontario, Canada, and *d* 1993, having had issue:

1f +Toby Michael Hans; *b* 24 June 1949; *educ* Toronto U (BA, BEd)

1d Lilian May; *m* 1894 Henry Nevill Sanders, Professor at Pennsylvania U, and had issue

2d Mabel Violet; *m* 1st 1901 Hubert Valentine Hamilton (*d* 1905); *m* 2nd 1907 Ernest Gutmann and had issue. He *d* 1946

3d Kathleen Crofton; *d* unm 23 Oct 1949

1c (cont.) Hans Caulfeild *m* 2nd 1904 Ida Mary (*d* 4 Sept 1908), dau of George Rowntree; *m* 3rd 1909 Mary Louise Burkart (*d* 25 Nov 1963), and *d* 7 Feb 1928, having by her had issue:

2d (James) Gordon; *b* 1917; *m* 1943 *Olive (Irene), dau of Thomas Henry Bradley, of Goderich, Ontario, and *d* 1975, leaving issue:

1e +Roddy Terence [Dr Roddy Caulfeild, Tavistock, Ontario N0B 2RO, Canada]; *b* 5 April 1946; MD; *m* 1969 *Patricia Ann Rogers, and has issue:

1f +Stephen Michael; *b* 1972; *m* 17 May 1997 *Victoria Jayne Wright

2f +Jonathan David; *b* 1975

1e *Caroline Diane [Mrs Peter Wardell, 74 Derby Court, Newmarket, Ontario L3Y 5Z9, Canada]; *b* 13 May 1948; *m* 1969 *Peter Stanley Wardell, and has issue:

1f *Peter Alexander; *b* 1975

1f *Stephanie Suzanne; *b* 1978

2c Henry Ellis; *b* 1 Aug 1852; *m* Annie (*d* 1944), dau of Thomas Jenkins, and *d* 31 Oct 1919, leaving issue:

1d *Hester

2d *Alice

3c Alexander Theophilus; *b* 12 Jan 1854; *m* 1874 Rosetta, dau of Samuel Knowlton, and had issue:

1d Olive Marion; *m* 1892 C W Godwin, late of Allience, Ohio, USA, and had issue

2d Ida May; *m* 1896 Royle Seymour, of Los Angeles, and has issue

4c James Bellairs, Master of St Luke's Church School, Toronto, Ontario; *b* 21 April 1861

1c Annie Isabella; *d* unm Jan 1936

2c Helen Ruth; *m* 1 Sept 1881 Kingston Reed Waring, of Hamilton, Ontario, and *d* 8 Oct 1943, leaving issue. He *d* 10 Feb 1918

3c Margaret

5b Abraham St George (Rev), DD, Rector of Windsor; *b* 17 Sept 1823; *m* 9 Dec 1846 Mary Anne, dau of William Waring, and *d* 17 Sept 1882, leaving issue:

1c Charles; *b* 4 Dec 1848; *m* 28 Oct 1873 Eliza Caroline, dau of Daniel Hanvey, and had issue:

1d Charles St George Stewart Hanvey; *b* 24 Aug 1874

1d Kathleen Elizabeth

(3) John, Col, of Donomon, Co Roscommon; *m* Mary, dau of Henry Irvine, yr bro of William Irvine, of Castle Irving, MP Fermanagh, and had issue:

1a St George, of Donamon; *b* 19 Aug 1780; *m* 2 April 1802 Hon Frances Crofton, dau of Sir Edward Crofton, 2nd Bt, of Mote (*qv*), by Baroness Crofton (*see* CROFTON, B), and had issue:

1b Francis St George, of Donamon Castle, Co Roscommon, JP, late 1st Life Gds; *b* 8 March 1806; *m* 17 Aug 1830 Hon Susannah Anne Crofton (*d* 10 Jan 1894), sis of 3rd Baron Crofton (*qv*), and *d* 28 Oct 1896, having had, with other issue:

1c Alfred Henry, of Cottesmore Hall, Oakham, Rutland; *b* 29 Dec 1834; *m* 1st 14 Nov 1872 Augusta (*dsp* 1 April 1873), widow of 7th Earl of Kingston (*qv*) and dau of 1st Baron Templemore (*see* DONEGALL, M); *m* 2nd 4 Aug 1874 Rosamond (*d* 10 Dec 1888), widow of Lord Alan Spencer Churchill (*see* MARLBOROUGH, D) and dau of Thomas Dowker, and *d* 14 July 1904

1c Emily Susan; *m* 31 July 1852 3rd Earl of Lonsdale (*qv*), and *d* 15 July 1917, leaving issue

2c Fanny Florence; *m* 18 Aug 1862 Maj-Gen Owen Lewis Cope Williams, of Craig-y-Don, Anglesey, and Temple Ho, Gt Marlow, and *dsp* 28 July 1876. He *d* 2 Oct 1904

1b Frances Henrietta; *m* 10 July 1827 Frederick Hamilton Cornwall, of Delbury Hall, Salop, est son of the Bishop of Worcester

2b Harriet; *m* Feb 1830 Count Achille de la Marre

1a Harriet; *m* 12 Aug 1796 James Cuffe, of Deel Castle, Co Mayo, MP Tralee 1819–28

1 Mary; *m* July 1724 John Moore, of Drumbanagher, and *d* 26 Jan 1769, leaving issue (*see* DROGHEDA, E)

CHARTERIS OF AMISFIELD

Arms: Quarterly; 1st and 4th, argent a fess azure within a double tressure flory counterflory gules (for CHARTERIS); 2nd and 3rd, or a lion rampant gules, armed and langued azure (for WEMYSS); over all at the fess point a crescent sable for difference. **Crest:** A dexter hand issuant paleways, holding between the thumb and forefinger in bend sinister a pair of sulptor's callipers, all proper. **Supporters:** Dexter, a scribe soberly attired holding in his exterior hand a quill pen proper; sinister, an officer of the King's Royal Rifle Corps in the uniform worn *c* 1904, proper. **Motto:** *Ecce charta mea* ('Lo, here is my charter'). **Creation:** B. (LP, UK) 1978.

THE BARON CHARTERIS OF AMISFIELD, of Amisfield, E Lothian (Sir Martin Michael Charles Charteris, GCB (1977, KCB 1972, CB 1958), GCVO (1976, KCVO 1962, MVO 1953), OBE (1946), QSO (1978), PC (1972)) [The Rt Hon The Lord Charteris of Amisfield GCB GCVO QSO OBE PC, 11 Kylestrome House, Cundy St, London SW1W 9JT; Wood Stanway House, Wood Stanway, Cheltenham, Glos GL54 5PG]; *b* 7 Sept 1913; *educ* Eton and RMC Sandhurst; Lt KRRC 1933, WWII: Middle East, Lt-Col 1944; Private Sec to HRH PRINCESS ELIZABETH 1950–52, Assist Priv Sec to HM THE QUEEN 1952–72, Extra Equerry 1956, Priv Sec and Keeper Archives 1972–77, Perm Ld in Waiting 1978–; Provost Eton 1978–91; dir: Claridge's 1978–96, Connaught 1978–97, De La Rue 1978–85, RTZ 1978–84; Chm Tstees Nat Heritage Memorial Fund 1980–92; Tstee: British Museum 1979–89, Police Convalescence and Rehabilitation Tst 1987–96; Pres Prayer Book Soc 1987–; Grand Offr Legion Honour, Roy Victorian Chain 1992; Hon DCL Oxon 1978, Hon LLD London 1981, Hon RA 1981; *m* 1944 *Hon (Mary) Gay Hobart Margesson, dau of 1st Viscount Margesson (*qv*), and has issue:

1 *Andrew Martin [The Hon Andrew Charteris, 11 Grove Rd, Hitchin, Herts]; *b* 1947; *educ* Milton Abbey

2 *Harold Francis [The Hon Harold Charteris, 94 Talfourd Rd, London SE15 5NZ]; *b* 1950; *educ* Eton and Pembroke Coll Oxford; *m* 1984 *Blandine Marie, er dau of Roger Desmons, of 14 rue Wilhelm, Paris 16me, and has issue:

(1) *Zoe France; *b* 1984

(2) *Julia Marie; *b* 1985

1 *(Francesca) Mary [The Hon Mrs Mary Pearson, 3 Shepherd's Close, London W1Y 3RT]; *b* 1945; *m* 1977 (*divorce* 1996), as his 2nd w, Baron Pearson of Rannoch (LP, *qv*) and has issue

Lineage: *See* WEMYSS and MARCH, E

CHATFIELD

Arms: Or, a griffin segreant sa., on a chief purpure an anchor between two escallops of the first. **Crest:** A heraldic antelope's head erased arg., gorged with a naval crown or. **Supporters:** Dexter, an Admiralty messenger holding in the exterior hand his staff; sinister, a gunner of the Royal Navy resting the exterior hand on a shell, all ppr. **Motto:** *Pro aris et focis* ('For our altars and our hearths'). **Creation:** B. (UK) 4 June 1937.

THE 2ND BARON CHATFIELD, of Ditchling, Co Sussex (Ernle David Lewis Chatfield) [The Rt Hon The Lord Chatfield, 535 Island Rd, Victoria, BC V8S 2T7, Canada]; *b* 2 Jan 1917; *s f* 1967; *educ* RNC Dartmouth and Trin Coll Cambridge; late Hon Lt RNVR; ADC to Govr Gen of Canada 1940–45; *m* 16 May 1969 *(Felicia Mary) Elizabeth, dau of Dr John Roderick Bulman, of Hereford

Lineage: ROBERT CHATFIELD, of Chiltington, Sussex; *d* 1610, leaving:

ROBERT CHATFIELD, of Newick and Beards, Ditchling, Sussex; *m* 1st 1596 Margery, dau and heir of Thomas Haslegrove, of Bedells, Ditchling, and widow of John Cowper; *m* 2nd 1600 Mary, sis of John Godley, of Chailey, Sussex, and *d* 1629, leaving an est s:

ROBERT CHATFIELD, of Bedells; *b* 1597; *d* 1660, leaving an est s:

ROBERT CHATFIELD, of Cuckfield, Sussex; *b* 1622; *m* 2 Dec 1658 Mary (*d* 1692), dau of Robert Abbot, of Cuckfield, and *d* 1680, leaving an est s:

ROBERT CHATFIELD, of Hanly, Cuckfield; *b* 23 Oct 1659; *m* 1st 24 Nov 1684 Susanna (*dsp* 1692), dau of John Warden, of Cuckfield; *m* 2nd 23 Nov 1693 Katherine (*d* 25 May 1745), yst dau of Allen Savage, of Westhouse, Cuckfield, and *d* 21 May 1726, having had, with three daus:

1 Robert, of Hanly; *dspm* 14 March 1780

2 Charles, of Cuckfield; surgn, whose issue male became *extinct* in 1851

3 ALLEN, of whom below

The 3rd son,

ALLEN CHATFIELD, of Croydon, Surrey; *b* 18 March 1712; *m* 1st Sarah (*d* 19 Feb 1741) and had four children (*d* young); *m* 2nd 14 July 1747 Mary (*d* 18 Sept 1761), er dau of Robert Osborn, of Croydon, and *d* 30 April 1772, leaving an est surv s:

ROBERT CHATFIELD, HEICS, of Croydon, and Cooper's Row, Hart St, JP Surrey, High Sheriff 1805; jr clerk Pay Office HEIC 1764; 2nd Assist to Paymaster and Clerk to Ctee of Shipping 1793; 1st Assist to Paymaster of Seamen's Wages 1798, Paymaster 1802, ret 1809; *b* 23 July 1748; *m* Ann Storrow (*d* 28 Sept 1830) and *d* 21 May 1811, having had, with a s (John, *dvp*):

1 ROBERT (Rev), of whom presently

2 Samuel, of Battersea Rise, Surrey, and Cooper's Row, Crutched Friars; *m* Letitia (*m* 2nd Capt Charles Close, RA, of Haslemere, Surrey, son of Rev Henry Jackson Close, of St Clement's, Ipswich, Rector of Bentworth, Hants, and *d* 31 May 1866), dau of William Lewis, HEICS, of Leatherhead, Surrey, and York Place, St Marylebone, memb Cncl Bombay, and *d* by 29 July 1822, having had issue:

(1) Lewis; *b* 5 Feb 1811, apparently *dvp*

(2) Samuel; *b* 11 Aug 1813, apparently *dvp*

3 William, of Goulburn, NSW; *b* 22 May 1815; *m* and had issue

1 Mary Anne; *b* 28 March 1810

2 Letitia; *b* 11 March 1812; *m* 10 Dec 1836 George Richard Griffiths, of Castle Hill, Englefield Green, and Sydney, NSW, and *d* 28 Dec 1891, having had issue. He *d* 7 Aug 1859

The est son,

Rev ROBERT CHATFIELD, LLD, Vicar of Chatteris, Cambs, JP Cambs and Isle of Ely; *b* 2 Oct 1775; *m* 17 July 1800 Susannah (*d* 15 April 1857), 4th dau of William Money, of Homme Ho, Herefs, and Whetham, Wilts, and *d* 10 Sept 1853, leaving with other issue:

1 ROBERT (Rev), of whom presently

1 Mary; *m* 17 Nov 1829, as his 2nd w, David Barclay Chapman, of Roehampton, and *d* 7 Feb 1881, leaving issue. He *d* 1891

The est son,

Rev ROBERT MONEY CHATFIELD, MA Cambridge, Vicar of Wilsford with Woodford, Wilts; *b* 19 Aug 1804; *m* 18 June 1829 Anna Maria (*d* 4 April 1880),

3rd dau of Thomas Jesson, of Hill Park, Kent, and *d* 21 Sept 1882, leaving an est surv s:

ALFRED JOHN CHATFIELD, CB (1887), KStJ, Adml, served Baltic Expdn 1854, Black Sea Crimean War and Ashanti Campaign 1874; *b* 27 Aug 1831; *m* 27 Aug 1868 Louisa (*d* 29 Sept 1916), er dau of Thomas Faulconer, of Hampstead, and *d* 25 Aug 1910, leaving issue, with six other children, including a dau (Gwendolen Percy Elizabeth, *d* unm 24 Dec 1968 aged 89), an est s:

ALFRED ERNLE MONTACUTE, **1st Baron Chatfield**, of Ditchling, Co Sussex, so *cr* 4 June 1937, PC (1939), GCB (1934, KCB 1922, CB 1916), OM (1939), KCMG (1919, CMG 1916), CVO (1912); Hon DCL Oxford (1934), Hon LLD Cambridge (1939); *b* 27 Sept 1873; entered RN 1886, Capt 1909, R-Adml 1920, V-Adml 1926, Adml 1930, Adml of the Fleet 1935; Flag-Capt in HMS *Lion* (Heligoland Bight 1914, Dogger Bank 1915, Jutland 1916), and HMS *Queen Elizabeth* as Flag-Capt and Fleet Gunnery Offr to C-in-C Grand Fleet, Cdr HMS *Excellent* 1906–09, Capt HMS *Medina* during tour in India of TM GEORGE V and QUEEN MARY 1911–12; 4th Sea Ld Admlty 1919, Assist Ch Naval Staff 1920–22, Br Naval Rep Washington Naval Conf 1921–22, cmdg 3rd Light Cruiser Sqdn 1922–24, 3rd Sea Ld and Controller Navy 1925–28, C-in-C Atlantic Fleet 1929–30 and Mediterranean Fleet 1930–32, 1st Sea Ld Admlty and Ch Naval Staff 1933–38, pres Inst Naval Architects 1941–48; tstee Imp War Mus 1943–50; chm: Roy Empire Soc 1948–51, CD Gallantry Ctee 1940–45; Min Co-ordination of Defence 1939–40 with Seat in War Cabinet; Gold Medal Roy Soc of Arts 1947; Grand Cross Order Phoenix Greece, Order Aviz Portugal; *m* 29 July 1909 Lillian Emma, CStJ (*d* 30 Sept 1977 aged 88), dau of Maj George L Matthews, TF, and *d* 15 Nov 1967, having had issue:

1 ERNLE DAVID LEWIS CHATFIELD, **2nd and present Baron Chatfield**

1 Angela; *m* 25 April 1938 Sir Patrick William Donner, MP, only son of Ossian Donner, of 22 Prince's Gdns, SW7, and *dsp* 18 Aug 1943

2 *(Mary) Katharine Medina, OBE (1946) [The Hon Mrs Duckworth OBE, Dalingridge Place, Sharpthorne, Sussex RH19 4JB]; *b* 1911; WVS 1939–46; *m* 22 Sept 1947 Henry George Austen de l'Etaing Herbert Duckworth (*d* 1992), est son of Sir George Herbert Duckworth, CB, FSA (*see* CARNARVON, E), and has issue:

(1) *Sarah Margaret Katharine; *b* 2 May 1951; *m* 1974 *Hector William Munro of Foulis (*see* MUNRO, Bt) and has issue

(2) *Harriet Angela Victoria (twin) [Countess von Einsiedel, 63 Wood Vale, London SE23]; *b* 2 May 1951; *m* 1979 *Count Andreas Jean-Paul von Einsiedel, s of Count Wittigo von Einsiedel, of Frankfurt, W Germany, and has issue:

1a *Orlando Ernie Benedict; *b* 1980

2a *Evelyn; *b* 1982

3a *Robin; *b* 1988

1a *Gwendolen; *b* 1985

CHAYTOR

Arms: Per bend dancettée arg. and az. four quatrefoils counterchanged. **Crest:** A buck's head couped lozengy arg. and sa., attired or, in the mouth a trefoil slipped vert. **Motto:** *Fortune le veut* ('Fortune wills it'). **Creation:** Bt. (UK) 30 Sept 1831.

SIR GEORGE REGINALD CHAYTOR, 8TH BT, of Croft, Yorks [Sir George Chaytor Bt, 103–9372 Fletcher Ave, Chilliwack, BC V2P 4Z2, Canada]; *b* 28 Oct 1912; *s* kinsman 1976; patron (alternatively) of Witton-le-Wear V; *m* 1970 *Mrs Elsie Magdeline Rogers

Lineage: CHRISTOPHER CHAYTOR, of Butterby; *b* 1494; Surveyor-Gen for ELIZABETH I; *m* Elizabeth, sole heiress of the Clervaux family which had owned estates at Croft since 1246, and was ggf of:

Sir WILLIAM CHAYTOR, 1st Bt, so *cr* 1671, but the title became *extinct* 1720 and the Croft estate passed to his n:

HENRY; *b* 1689; *m* Jane, dau of Mattew Smales, of Gilling, and *d* 1774, leaving an est s:

WILLIAM CHAYTOR; MP Hedon, Recorder of Richmond; *b* 1732; *m* Jane Lee and *d* 1819, leaving an est s:

Sir William Chaytor, 1st Bt (UK), *cr* 30 Sept 1831, of Croft, Yorks; MP Sunderland; *b* 29 April 1771; *m* 18 Aug 1803 Isabella (*d* 23 Dec 1855), yr dau and coheir of John Carter, of Tunstall and Richmond, Yorks, and had, with other issue:

1 WILLIAM RICHARD CARTER (Sir), **2nd Bt**

2 John Clervaux, of Croft; *b* 8 Sept 1806; *m* 30 Jan 1834 Lydia Frances (*d* 2 Oct 1889), est dau of Thomas Brown, of New Grove, and *d* 8 May 1894, having had, with other issue:

(1) John Clervaux; *b* 28 Jan 1836; *m* 30 Jan 1867 Emma (*d* 8 May 1913), dau of Edward Fearon, of Nelson, New Zealand, and *d* 2 April 1920, having had, with other issue:

1a Edward Walter Clervaux (Sir), KCMG, KCVO, CB, Maj-Gen, GOC NZ Forces 1919–24, ADC to HM GEORGE V 1917–21, Hon Col 8th NZ Mtd Rifles 1923, served in S Africa 1900–02 (severely wounded, despatches, two medals with five clasps) and WW I (twice wounded, despatches seven times), Order of White Eagle of Serbia 3rd Cl with swords, Order Nile 2nd Cl; *b* 21 June 1868; *m* 17 Oct 1898 Louisa Jane (*d* 26 May 1948), dau of Charles Sweeney Collins, of Wharton Street, W, and *d* 13 June 1939, having had issue:

1b Edward John Clervaux, Brig RA WW II (despatches twice); *b* 16 Nov 1903; *educ* Wanganui Collegiate Sch NZ and RMA Woolwich; *m* 1st 12 Nov 1938 Margaret Frances Morgan (*d* 19 March 1969), only child of Charles Archibald Vlieland, of Alton, Hants; *m* 2nd 28 Oct 1970 *Mrs (Carina Mary) Marcelle Anderson, and *dsp* 27 Nov 1976

1b Katharine Clervaux; *b* 9 June 1900; *m* 10 Nov 1926 Col Sir Robert Eric Sherlock Gooch, 11th Bt (*qv*), KCVO, DSO, Life Gds, and *d* 1 March 1974, leaving issue

2b Dorothy Clervaux; *b* 24 May 1902; *m* 25 Oct 1933 Ian Douglas McNeill (*d* 12 Jan 1950), son of Neil McNeill, of Ardnacross, Argyllshire, and had issue:

1c *Nigel Edward Ian; *b* 3 Feb 1938

2a Alfred Henry, KC, of Clervaux Castle, Croft, Yorks and Iridge Place, Sussex, late Capt 8th City of London Regt; *b* 28 Oct 1869; *educ* Clare Coll Cambridge (MA); *m* 1 Aug 1899 Dorothy Elizabeth (*d* 14 May 1960), dau of Harry Percy Burrell, of Brooklands, Alton, Hants, and *d* 12 July 1931, leaving issue:

1b (Alfred) Drewett, barrister Inner Temple 1925; *b* 16 Feb 1901; *educ* Eton and Trin Coll Cambridge (BA 1922); *m* 6 Nov 1929 *Rachel Elizabeth, yst dau of Canon William Hartley Carnegie, Sub-Dean of Westminster Abbey, and *d* 1977, leaving issue:

1c +William Drewett [William Chaytor Est, The Hall, Croft, nr Darlington]; *b* 13 Sept 1937; *educ* Eton; *m* 20 June 1964 *Susan Philippa, est dau of James Lawrence Bunting Ansell, BA, MRCS, LRCP, of Wood Farm, Wolferton, King's Lynn, Norfolk, and has issue:

1d +Clervaux James; *b* 6 Nov 1967

2d +Nicholas John Drewett; *b* 16 Feb 1976

1d *Katharine Elizabeth; *b* 1970

1c *Elizabeth [Mrs David Ashwin, Hill Farm, Dedham, Colchester, Essex]; *b* 5 May 1934; *m* 9 May 1959 *Lt David Henry Ashwin, RN, est son of Philip C Ashwin, of Holway Farm, Sherborne, Dorset, and has issue:

1d *Philip David; *b* 1 June 1960

2d *Henry William; *b* 26 July 1962

1d *Rachel Elizabeth; *b* 19 Oct 1964

2c *Jane [Mrs John Watherston, 39 Sutherland St, London SW1]; *b* 16 Dec 1935; *m* 1st 22 Oct 1966 John Richard Evelyn Atkinson (*d* 1973), only son of John Atkinson, of Temple Sowerby Ho, Penrith, Cumberland, and has issue:

1d *Richard Matthew Clervaux; *b* 30 June 1968

1d *Harriet Rachel; *b* 1972

2c (cont.) Mrs John Atkinson *m* 2nd 27 March 1976 *John Anthony Charles Watherston, yr son of Sir David Charles Watherston, KBE, CMG, and has further issue:

2d *Charles Crispin; *b* 1977

3c *Susannah Albinia [Mrs John Ewart, Astrop Park, Northants]; *b* 13 Nov 1939; *m* 1st 1971 Hon Edward Lawies Jackson (*d* 1982), son of 3rd Baron Allerton (*see* 1970 edn), and has issue:

1d *Olivia Susannah; *b* 1975

2d *Katharine Elizabeth; *b* 1978

3c (cont.) The Hon Mrs Edward Jackson *m* 2nd 2 April 1997 *John W D Ewart

2b Christopher William Drewett, MBE (1945); *b* 19 Oct 1902; *educ* Eton and Trin Coll Cambridge (BA and LLB 1924); *m* 26 July 1949 *Rachel, only dau of John Henry Pease, of Broadwindsor, Beaminster, Dorset and *dsp* 20 Feb 1969

3b +Edward Drewett, MC [Lt-Col Edward Chaytor MC, 6 Bridle Path, Cherry Cross, Totnes, Devon], Lt-Col W Yorks Regt WW II; *b* 5 Aug 1913; *educ* Eton and Clare Coll Cambridge (BA); *m* 17 Sept 1938 *Mary Monica, only dau of Rev Canon Thomas John Woodall, of The Close, Salisbury, and has issue:

1c +Richard Clervaux; *b* 22 Dec 1939; *educ* King's Sch Bruton; *m* 1983 *Janet, dau of Irving D Miller, of Malboro, USA

2c +Michael Clervaux; *b* 10 Jan 1944; *educ* King's Sch Bruton

1b Catherine Beatrice; *b* 9 Sept 1907; *d* unm 23 Oct 1983

2b *Dorothy Anne; *b* 24 May 1912; *m* 19 June 1937 *George Egerton Lambert Manley, yr son of Maj William Edward Manley, OBE, of Mayfield, Horley, Surrey, and has issue:

1c *Robert John Lambert; *b* 1938

2c *Christopher Michael; *b* 1948

3c *Peter George; *b* 1949; *m* 1975 *Elaine Mary, only dau of John Bernard Dancer, MRCS, LRCP

1c *Jessica Helen [Mrs Charles Mansfield, 23 Hawthorn St, Roma, Qld, Australia]; *b* 1940; *m* 1968 *Charles James Mansfield, son of Hon Sir Alan James Mansfield, KCMG, KCVO, and has issue:

1d *Anthony Roderick; *b* 1969

2d *David William; *b* 1970
1d *Ruth Sarah; *b* 1978
3b *(Margaret) Clare; *b* 27 Dec 1918; *m* 14 Feb 1939 Lt Anthony William Kellie-Smith, RA (*d* 9 June 1942), son of William Kellie-Smith, of Kellas Ho, Perak, FMS, and has issue:
1c *David Anthony; *b* 4 June 1940; *m* 1963 *Griselda, dau of George Williams, of Toronto, Canada, and has issue:
1d *Samuel Anthony; *b* 12 May 1966
2d *Owen William; *b* 20 July 1968
3a D'Arcy, CMG (1918), CBE (1919), VD, JP, Col NZ Mil Forces, Lt-Col RM, served S Africa 1899–1901 (medal with four clasps) and WW I (despatches three times), Order of the Nile 3rd Cl; *b* 1873; *educ* Clare Coll Cambridge; *m* 1908 Avis Anne (*d* 3 Feb 1954), dau of Cdr Robert Atherton Edwin, RN, and *dsp* 9 Oct 1960
4a Lawrence Clervaux, MC, TD, Col (Res) WW I with Canterbury Mtd Rifle Regt and NZ, MGC (wounded twice, 1914 star, two medals); *b* 1892; *m* 4 Feb 1920 Dorothy Mary Bullen, dau of John Robert Bullen Tripe, of Palmerston North, NZ, and *d* 8 July 1954, leaving issue:
1b John Lawrence Clervaux; *b* 28 Feb 1926; *m* 3 Dec 1954 *Susan Ruth [Mrs John Chaytor, Marshlands, Spring Creek, Marlborough, New Zealand], dau of George M Turrell, of Canterbury, NZ, and *d* 1976, leaving issue:
1c *Sarah Frances Clervaux; *b* 25 Aug 1956
2c *Miranda Jane Clervaux; *b* 23 May 1958
3c *Frances Alexandra Clervaux; *b* 1961
2b +Anthony David Clervaux; *b* 8 June 1934
1b *Jocelyn Dorothy Clervaux [Mrs Michael Hall, Pendeen, Hororata, Canterbury, New Zealand]; *b* 11 Feb 1921; *m* 23 Aug 1947 *Michael Fearon Hall, son of Godfrey Hall, of Canterbury, NZ, and has issue:
1c *Micahel Timothy Chaytor; *b* 11 May 1949
1c *Annabel Rose; *b* 30 Nov 1954
2c *Georgina Miranda Mary; *b* 28 Sept 1959
2b *Frances Anne; *b* 17 March 1922; *m* 20 April 1956 *Michael Kenneth Macdonald, son of G K Macdonald, of Canterbury, NZ, and has issue:
1c *Fiona Anne; *b* 25 June 1958
2c *Caroline; *b* 1959
5a John Clervaux, Col RA, served WW I (wounded) and WW II; *b* 3 Feb 1896; *m* 7 Aug 1930 Olive Mary (*d* 8 Nov 1957), only dau of Col Reginald Brittan, DSO, OBE, late Sherwood Foresters, of Failand Hill, Failand, Somerset, and *d* 8 Nov 1957, leaving issue:
1b *Pamela June [Mrs Henry Fooks, Reves Hall Farm, Eyke, Woodbridge, Suffolk]; *b* 1 June 1934; *m* 5 Dec 1959 *Capt Henry Raymond Harvey Fooks, King's Dragoon Gds, only son of Sir Raymond Hatherell Fooks, CBE, DL, of Broomhill Copse, Boars Hill, Oxford, and has issue:
1c *Caroline Mary; *b* 6 June 1961
2c *Serena Alice; *b* 9 April 1963; *m* 26 June 1993 *Graeme Weston Elliot Murray, s of Alexander Elliot Murray, and has:
1d *James Alexander Elliot; *b* 19 Oct 1994
1d *Isobel Alice Elliot; *b* 13 May 1996
3c *Sarah Clervaux; *b* 25 June 1965; *m* 11 Sept 1993 *Jonathan de Hoghton Dumergue Veale, er s of Dr Michael H Dumergue Veale, and has:
1d *Edward Henry Charles; *b* 13 March 1996
2b *Jennifer Margaret [Mrs Martin Dean, Oak Farm, Gwehelog, Usk, Mon]; *b* 22 Nov 1936; *m* 1st 24 Sept 1959 (*divorce* 1985) Thomas Barrington Cubitt, of Forbury Ho, Kintbury, Berks, 4th son of Maj Charles Cyril Cubitt, MC, of Edge of the Hill, Crowthorne, Berks; *m* 2nd 1985 (Edward) Martin Dean (*d* 1985), son of Col Frank Longueville Dean, and by 1st husb has issue:
1c *Annabelle Jane; *b* 7 Feb 1964; *m* 1995 *John Newell, of Christchurch, NZ
2c *Alicia Mary; *b* 14 June 1965; *m* 1992 *Christopher Edward Howard Guinness, er son of Lt-Cdr Sir Howard Christian Sheldon Guinness, VRD, RNR (*see* GUINNESS, Bt)
3c *Miranda Louise; *b* 13 March 1967; m 1967 *Alexander Shaw
4c *Sophia Henrietta; *b* 19 Aug 1968
5c *Natasha Isabelle; *b* 1976
1a Beatrice Emma; *d* unm 24 Nov 1950
2a Elinor Mary; *m* 1906 Percy Watt Stuart, of Spring Creek, NZ, and *d* 1917, leaving issue. He *d* 1948
3a Jane; *m* Oct 1910 Henry Joseph Stace, of Spring Creek, Picton, Marlborough, NZ, and had issue
4a Constance Clervaux; *m* 17 June 1914 Maj Godfrey Percy Burrell, MC, of Ackender Ho, Alton, Hants, 4th Hampshire Regt, er son of Harry Percy Burrell, of Brooklands, Alton, Hants, and *d* 17 Aug 1945, leaving issue. He *d* 2 July 1931
5a Frances Emily; *m* 23 Jan 1912 Harry Aldwyn Burrell, of Alton, Hants, and *d* 30 Nov 1919, leaving issue
6a Isabel Clervaux
(2) Arthur; *b* 27 July 1843; *m* 1st 9 April 1872 Mary Ellen Gibbard (*d* 13 Jan 1898), dau of Thomas Gibbard Burrell, of Nelson, NZ; *m* 2nd Evelyn, dau of John Allen, of Picton, New Zealand, and *d* 1 Sept 1937, having by 1st w had issue:
1a Arthur Cuthbert; *b* 21 Jan 1873; *m* 13 May 1908 Linda (*d* 1971), yst dau of Charles Martin, of Stoke, Nelson, NZ, and *d* 29 June 1948, leaving issue:
1b +Jose Melva [Jose Chaytor Esq, 22B Evelyn Rd, Howick, Auckland, New Zealand]; *b* 5 May 1909
2b +Jack Martin [Jack Chaytor Esq, 298 Didsbury Dve, Waiti Beach, New Zealand 3060]; *b* 7 Feb 1913; *m* 1937 *Ida Kathleen, dau of E A Russell, of Dannevirke, NZ, and has issue:
1c +Warren John [Warren Chaytor Esq, 40 Beach Rd, Waiti Beach, New Zealand 3060]; *b* 19–; *m* 19– *Susan Mary Rohl, and has issue:
1d *Melanie Elizabeth; *b* 19–
2d *Kathryn Alanna; *b* 19–
1c *Lynne Marie; *b* 19–; *m* Clifton Hallam, and has issue:
1d *Richard Wayne; *b* 19–
1d *Donna Adele; *b* 19–
2d *Kathryn Marie; *b* 19–
2a Walter Henry; *b* 1875; *m* 1909 Frederica Mary, dau of William Howard Stafford, of Upper Montere, Nelson, NZ
3a Frank Clervaux, Capt NZ Inf, Wellington Regt, WW I (despatches twice); *b* 1884; *m* 31 Oct 1922 Alice (*d* 1983), dau of John Hill, of Winslow, and *d* 2 April 1962, leaving issue:
1b *Joan Clervaux; *b* 11 March 1925; *m* 21 June 1952 *Ian McKelvie Bull, er son of Allan Russell Bull, of Paraparaumu, NZ, and has issue:
1c *Mary Clare; *b* 2 July 1953
2c *Susan Alice; *b* 6 April 1958
1a Frances Mary; *d* unm 24 June 1962
2a Kathleen; *m* 1905 Hubert Francis Vaughan Miller, and *d* 5 Jan 1955, leaving issue
3 Matthew Hutton; *b* 31 Dec 1807; *m* 1838 Elizabeth, dau of Nathan Horn, of Bishopwearmouth, and *d* 1882, leaving, with other issue:
(1) D'Arcy; *b* 28 Aug 1840; *m* 25 July 1893 Lily, dau of T J Watkins, and *dsp* 23 July 1903
1 Isabella; *b* 11 April 1810; *m* 3 March 1836 Thomas Drewett-Drewett, of Jarrow Hall, Co Durham, who *d* 15 July 1870, leaving issue
Sir WILLIAM *d* 28 Jan 1847; his est son,
Sir William Richard Carter Chaytor, 2nd Bt, MP Durham City 1831–34; *b* 7 Feb 1805; *m* 1st 27 Sept 1936 Annie (*d* 11 Sept 1837), dau of — Lacy, of Easingwold, and had issue:
1 **Sir William Chaytor, 3rd Bt**; *b* 10 Sept 1837; *m* 25 Aug 1866 Mary (*d* 11 Oct 1917), yst dau of Lt-Col Henry van Straubenzee, of Spennithorne, Yorks, and *d* 8 Aug 1896, having had issue:
(1) **Sir William Henry Edward Chaytor, 4th Bt**, DL and JP Co Durham (High Sheriff 1902) and N R Yorks; *b* 14 June 1867; *d* unm 25 April 1908
(2) **Sir Walter Clervaux Chaytor, 5th Bt**, JP Co Durham and N R Yorks, Cdr RN; *b* 27 Feb 1874; *m* 7 Jan 1909 Alexandra Leila (*m* 2nd 5 Sept 1914 George Pym Gore (*d* 25 June 1959) and *d* 9 Dec 1970), only child of Rev Canon Frederick Alfred John Hervey, CVO (*see* BRISTOL, M), and *d* 9 July 1913
(3) **Sir Edmund Hugh Chaytor, 6th Bt**, 2nd Lt Scots Gds and RASC; *b* 11 Nov 1876; *m* 19 Feb 1912 Isobel (*m* 2nd 27 June 1935 Edwin Burton Fiske (*d* 1940), of Denewood, Broadlands Rd, Highgate, N6, son of Charles E Fiske, of Greenfield, Mass, USA; resumed name CHAYTOR 1944 and *d* 20 Nov 1968), dau of Thomas Scott, of Darlington, and *d* 6 Feb 1935, leaving issue:
1a **Sir William Henry Clervaux Chaytor, 7th Bt**; *b* 4 May 1914; *m* 28 July 1947 *Patricia Nora, formerly w of George Walkley Alderman and dau of Loftus Joseph McCaffry, and *d* 5 Sept 1976, leaving:
1b *Carol Miranda [Miss Carol Chaytor, 24 Cruden St, London N1]; *b* 9 April 1948
1a Lilian Mary; *m* 26 Oct 1935 Sir Ralph Henry Lawson, 4th Bt (*see* HOWARD-LAWSON, Bt), and *d* 13 June 1968, leaving issue
2a *Isobel Clare; *m* 1st 12 Sept 1936 Maj Hugh Manford Vaux, Durham LI (*d* 25 Jan 1949), yst son of Maj C Vaux, of Low Startforth Hall, Barnard Castle, Co Durham, and has issue:
1b *Richard High Chaytor, Capt Durham LI; *b* 7 Aug 1937; *m* *Rosita Morton-Fisher, and has issue:
1c *Robina; *b* 6 July 1966
1b *Francesca Margaret; *b* 23 Oct 1946; *m* 22 Jan 1965 *Peter Harold Kenchington, and has issue:
1c *Andrew Edward; *b* 29 July 1965
2c *Heath Peter; *b* 20 Aug 1966
3c *Robert John; *b* 6 Feb 1968
2b *Amanda Clare; *b* 19 Jan 1949
2a (cont.) Mrs Hugh Vaux *m* 2nd 1950 Gordon William Ham, The Manchester Regt (*d* 16 Oct 1964), and has further issue:
2b *William Gordon; *b* 1952
3a *Anne; *m* 6 July 1946 Peter Dickinson, 4th son of Robert Dickinson, of Styford Hall, Stocksfield, Northumberland, and has issue:
1b *Simon Clervaux; *b* 26 Oct 1948
2b *Mark Chaytor; *b* 17 May 1951; *m* 1978 (*divorce* 1992) Amanda Evelyn Fraser (*see* FEILDEN, Bt) and has:
1c *Maximillian Chaytor; *b* 1981
1c *Olivia Esme; *b* 1983
2c *Georgia Eve; *b* 1987
3b *John Joicey; *b* 20 Aug 1953
(4) Clervaux Arthur, late Lt 3rd Bn Yorks and Lancs Regt
(1) Lillian Emma; *d* unm 12 March 1953
(2) Marion Henrietta
(3) Annie Julia; *m* 26 May 1897 (*divorce* 1913) Allan Havelock-Allan, yr son of Lt-Gen Sir Henry Marshman Havelock-Allan, 1st Bt, VC (*qv*), and *d* 10 Nov 1953, leaving issue
Sir William *m* 2nd 16 March 1852 (*d* May 1904), 4th dau of John Whitney Smith, of Northallerton, and *d* 9 Feb 1871, having by her had, with other issue:
2 Reginald Clervaux; *b* 6 Oct 1857; *m* 1878 Margaret Ann (*d* 1953), dau of Archibald McCurdie, of Dalhousie, New Brunswick, Canada, and *d* 1952, leaving issue:
(1) William Richard Carter; *b* 10 Jan 1881; *m* 1st 1909 Anna Laura (*d* 1947), dau of George Fawcett; *m* 2nd 1949 Clara Ethel (*d* 3 Feb 1966), dau of John E Parker, and *d* 1973, having by 1st w had issue:
1a Sir GEORGE REGINALD CHAYTOR, **8th and present Bt**
1a Ruth Willena; *b* 1911; *m* 1st 1931 James Leroy Watson (*d* 1938); *m* 2nd 1947 Nelson Reid Anderson
2a Florence Bernice; *b* 4 March 1915; *m* 1942 Thorbjorn and had issue:

1b *George William; *b* 1943
2b *Larry Elof; *b* 1944
3b *Ronald Edward; *b* 1948
3a *Florine May; *b* 1 May 1920; *m* 1951 *Edwin John Dauncey, and has:
1b *Darwin Ross; *b* 1953
2b *Dale Allan; *b* 1956
3b *Douglas Edwin; *b* 1960
4a *Doreen Isabelle; *b* 1 May 1920 (twin); *m* 1941 *Herbert William Scott, and has issue:
1b *Edward William [Edward Scott Esq, 6896 Winnifred Place, Saanichton, BC VO5 1MO, Canada]; *b* 2 May 1946
1b *Beverley Ann [Miss Beverley Scott, B6520 Bella Vista Dve, Victoria BC V8Z 6Y4, Canada]; *b* 22 Sept 1949
(2) Herbert Archibald; *b* 1884; *m* 1911 Effie Bell, dau of William Smith, and *d* 1979, leaving issue:
1a +(HERBERT) GORDON [Gordon Chaytor Esq, 1899 Deborah Dve, Duncan, BC V9L 5A5, Canada]; *b* 15 June 1922; heir presumptive; *m* 1947 *Mary Alice, dau of Thomas Craven, and has issue:
1b +Bruce Gordon [Bruce Chaytor Esq, 2785 Sooke Rd, Victoria, BC V9C 2P7, Canada]; *b* 31 July 1949; *m* 1969 *Rosemary Lea, dau of Reid Stephen, of Lake Cowichan, and has issue:
1c +John Gordon; *b* 17 Jan 1973
1c *Sharon Kathleen; *b* 1969
2b +Kenneth Reginald; *b* 1952; *m* 1973 *Susan Shroetter, of Toronto, and has issue:
1c *Wisteria Willow; *b* 1974
2c *Naomi Sage; *b* 1976
3b +Robert David; *b* 1958
1a *Dorothy May [Mrs George Blewett, 406–1010 MacKenzie Ave, Victoria BC V8X 4B2, Canada]; *b* 30 May 1912; *m* 25 April 1936 George Walker Blewett (*d* 19–), son of Edward Blewett, and has issue
1b *Gordon Edward; *b* 30 March 1937
1b *Maybelle Alice; *b* 12 June 1940
(3) Perley Edgar; *b* 1886; *m* 1907 Dora May Lodge, and *d* 1939, having had issue:
1a *Jean Pearl; *b* 1908; *m* 19– *John H Sutherland
2a *Rita Alberta [Mrs Donald Cowan, 1368 Duncan Dve, Delta, BC V4L 1R4, Canada]; *b* 1909; *m* 1936 *Donald S Cowan, and has issue:
1b *Donald R; *b* 1943; *m* 1966 *Louise, dau of Robert Coltart, and has issue:
1c *Steven M; *b* 1971
2c *Michael; *b* 1975
1c *Andrea E; *b* 1973
1b *Barbara L; *b* 1941; *m* 1963 *Ken Matsuzaki, son of I Matsuzaki, of Delta, BC, and has issue:
1c *Dean Scott; *b* 1972
1c *Dana Jane; *b* 1970
2a *Audrey [Mrs George Laing, 1657 East 62nd Ave, Vancouver BC V5P 2K8, Canada]; *b* 1913; *m* 19– *George S Laing
(1) Elizabeth Alberta; *b* 1879; *m* 1951 Thomas N Dickie

CHELMSFORD

Arms: Gu., a gryphon segreant or, within an orle of roses arg., barbed and seeded ppr. **Crest:** A cornucopia fesswise, the horn or, the fruit ppr., thereon a dove holding in the beak a sprig of laurel, also ppr. **Supporters:** On either side a gryphon or, winged vairé.
Motto: *Spes et fortuna* ('Hope and fortune')
Creation: B. (UK) 1 March 1858, V. (UK) 3 June 1921.

THE 3RD VISCOUNT CHELMSFORD and **Baron Chelmsford of Chelmsford**, Co Essex ((Frederic) Jan Thesiger) [The Rt Hon The Viscount Chelmsford, 26 Ormonde Gate, London SW3 4EX]; *b* 7 March 1931; *s f* 1970; late Lt Inns of Court Regt, Lloyd's insur broker (ret), dir Willis Faber plc 1979–91; *m* 16 Aug 1958 *Clare Rendle, dau of Dr George Rendle Rolston, of Bambers, Haslemere, Surrey, and has issue:
1 +FREDERIC CORIN PIERS; *b* 6 March 1962; *educ* Sherborne
1 *Tiffany Gay; *b* 23 April 1968

Lineage: JOHN ANDREW THESIGER; *b* 1722, of a family originating in Dresden, Saxony; *m* Sarah Gibson (*bur* 29 March 1814), of Chester, and was *bur* 1 June 1783, having had, with other issue:
1 Frederic (Sir), Capt RN, Kt Order St George of Russia, ADC to Nelson Copenhagen 1801; *d* unm 26 Aug 1805
2 CHARLES, of whom presently
3 Augustus, of Weybridge, Surrey, Dep Surveyor-Gen of Customs; *b* 2 Jan 1767; *d* unm 8 June 1837
4 George, Maj, Barrack-Master-Gen Canada; *d* unm Quebec Aug 1812
The 2nd son,
CHARLES THESIGER, Collector of Customs on the island of St Vincent; the destruction of his estate there in a volcanic eruption 1812 decided his 2nd son to exchange the navy for the bar as a career, as less dangerous and more lucrative; *m* Mary Anne (*d* 13 Feb 1796), dau of Theophilus Williams, of London, and *d* 18 Feb 1831, having had, with other issue:
1 Charles Theophilus; *b* 9 June 1786; *d* Sept 1787
2 FREDERIC, **1st Baron**
1 Augusta; *m* Dec 1840 Ralph Hewett, of Lincoln
The 3rd son,
FREDERIC THESIGER, **1st Baron Chelmsford of Chelmsford**, Essex (UK), so *cr* 1 March 1858, PC (1858), KC (1834), DCL, FRS; *b* 15 July 1794; Midshipman RN 1807; barrister Gray's Inn 1818 (Inner Temple 1824), MP (C) Woodstock 1840–44, Abingdon 1844–52 and Stamford 1852–58, Slr-Gen and ktd 1844, Attorney-Gen 1845–46 and Feb-Dec 1852, Ld Chllr 1858–59 and 1866–68; *m* 9 March 1822 Anna Maria (*d* 9 April 1875), yst dau and coheir of William Tinling, of Southampton, and n of Maj Pierson, defender of Jersey against the French 1781, and had with other issue:
1 FREDERIC AUGUSTUS, **2nd Baron**
2 Charles Wemyss, Lt-Gen, Col 14th Hus, ADC to Ld Lt Ireland 1858, served China War 1860 (medal with two clasps), Inspr Yeo Cav 1878–83, cmded Curragh Bde, Inspr-Gen Cav in Ireland 1885–90 (ret 1895); *b* 12 Oct 1831; *m* 23 April 1863 Charlotte Elizabeth (*d* 29 Oct 1880), est dau of Hon George Handcock (*see* CASTLEMAINE, B), and *d* 29 July 1903, leaving issue:
(1) George Handcock, CB, CMG, ADC, Lt-Col and Brevet Col cmdg 4th Bn Rifle Bde, Inspr-Gen KAR 1909–13, T/Maj-Gen 1915, served Nile Expdn 1898 (despatches, brevet, two medals), S Africa 1899–1900 (severely wounded, despatches, medal), WW I 1914–15 (despatches); *b* 6 Oct 1868; *m* 9 Jan 1902 Frances (*d* 25 Sept 1950), dau of Maj-Gen Fitzroy William Fremantle, CB (*see* COTTESLOE, B), and was *ka* 27 Sept 1915, leaving issue:
1a Gerald Alfred (Sir), ktd 1958, MBE (1946), KC (1948); *b* 25 Dec 1902; *educ* Gresham's and Magdalen Coll Oxford (BA 1925, MA 1929); barrister Inner Temple 1926, Bencher 1956, memb Gen Cncl Bar 1936–41 and 1958, memb Fulham Cncl 1934037 and Chelsea Cncl 1937 (Alderman 1946, Mayor 1944–46), Recorder Rye 1937, Hastings 1942, Southend-on-Sea 1957, High Court Judge Queen's Bench 1958–78, Dep Chm Boundary Commn England 1962, Maj Office of Judge Advocate-Gen WW II, chm: W Kent QS 1947–58, govrs United Westminster Sch 1948–58, ctee on Licensing Rd Passenger Servs 1952–53; *m* 28 July 1932 Marjorie Ellen (*d* 25 March 1972), dau of Raymond Guille, of Long Island, NY, and *d* 1981 leaving issue:
1b *Oonah Caroline [Mrs Vincent Vine, 16 Painted Cup Court, The Woodlands, Texas 77380, USA]; *b* 13 Feb 1936; *m* 21 Sept 1957 Vincent Vine, MA, yr son of Laban Edwin Vine, OBE, MB, BS, MRCS, LRCP, of Highett St, Mansfield, Victoria, Australia, and has issue:
1c *Peter Gerald; *b* 10 Dec 1958
1c *Juliet Mary; *b* 20 June 1960
2c *Anita Oonah; *b* 18 April 1962
2b *Virginia Mary; *b* 25 Feb 1941; *m* 15 Aug 1968 *John Carlton Pinckney, and has:
1c *Gerald; *b* 3 March 1970
2c *Philip; *b* 10 July 1971
3b *Juliet Elizabeth; *b* 23 Aug 1943; *m* 1st 16 April 1966 (*divorce* 1977) Roderick Car Warwick Neville, only son of Roderick Charles Neville, of 40 Dean Court Rd, Rottingdean, Sussex; *m* 2nd 1977 *David Halliwell Sutcliffe, and has issue by 1st husb:
1c *Roderick Thomas Gerald; *b* 20 April 1968; *m* 1993 *Frances Johnson
1c *Nicola Ingalisa; *b* 28 March 1967
1a Oonah Pamela; *m* 5 Oct 1928 John McLean Buckley, MA Oxford, slr, er son of St John Buckley, of Redcastle, Oamaru, NZ, and had issue:
1b *Thomas George McLean [Thomas Buckley Esq, 34 Petersham Ho, Harrington Rd, London SW7 3HD]; *b* 14 Jan 1932; *educ* Eton and Magdalen Coll Oxford (MA); slr; *m* 4 May 1963 *Valerie Frances, 2nd dau of Lt-Col (Edgar) Donald Reid Shearer, of The Pheasantry, Finniebrogue, Co Down, and has issue:
1c *William Donald McLean; *b* 31 March 1965
2c *Edward John McLean; *b* 20 June 1967
3c *Thomas Fitzpatrick; *b* 18 June 1971
2b *(Guy) James McLean [James Buckley Esq, 75 Lansdowne Rd, London W11 2LG]; *b* 25 May 1936; *educ* Eton and Magdalen Coll Oxford (BA); slr; *m* 24 Feb 1968 *Elena Rose, er dau of Hamish Holdsworth Deans, of Auchenflower, Darfield, Canterbury, NZ, and has:
1c *Virginia Rose; *b* 11 Nov 1969
2c *Elizabeth Oonah; *b* 9 April 1972
(2) Gerald Edward Peirson, Maj late Surrey Yeo, formerly Asst Resident in N Nigeria, served in S Africa 1900 and WW I; *b* 24 May 1872; *m* 9 April 1908 Ruby Le Nora Marguerite (*d* 16 Jan 1947), 2nd dau of John McCulloch, and *dsp* 9 Oct 1947

(1) Ethel Mary; *d* 24 Oct 1920

3 Alfred Henry, Ld Justice of Appeal, PC, QC, Attorney-Gen to HRH THE PRINCE OF WALES; *b* 15 July 1838; *m* 31 Dec 1862 Henrietta (*d* 18 Feb 1921), 2nd dau of Hon George Handcock (*see* CASTLEMAINE, B), and *dsp* 20 Oct 1880

4 Edward Peirson (Sir), KCB, Clerk Parl Office 1862, Sec of Presentations to successive Lds Chllr 1866–90, Clerk-Assist Parls 1890–1917; *b* 19 Dec 1842; *m* 13 May 1869 Georgina Mary (*d* 22 Dec 1906), 3rd dau of William Bruce Stopford (*see* COURTOWN, E), and *d* 11 Nov 1928, leaving issue:

(1) Arthur Lionel Bruce ; *b* 19 Oct 1872; *educ* Winchester; barrister Inner Temple, CC Judge, Circuit No 1 (Northumberland) 1931–37, and Circuit No 57 (Exeter, etc) 1938 (ret Oct 1947); *m* 26 April 1902 Florita Maria Engracia, OBE (1920) (*b* 9 Dec 1966), dau of Edward J Knight, of Tregroes, Pencoed, Glam, and *d* 20 Feb 1968, leaving issue:

1a Richard Edward Knight, OBE (1953); *b* 28 March 1912; *educ* Winchester and Magdalen Coll Oxford; barrister Inner Temple 1936, served WW II as Lt-Col Devonshire Regt, Assist Slr Ld Chllr's Office; *m* 1st 12 Jan 1934 (*divorce* 1947) Carolin Sophie (*d* 3 March 1948), yr dau of Norman M Grant, of NY, USA, and had issue:

1b +David Arthur Grant [David Thesiger Esq, 74 Herne Rd, Surbiton, Surrey KT6 5BP]; *b* 7 Dec 1934; *educ* Winchester and Trin Hall, Cambridge; slr 1965; *m* 23 Feb 1963 *Margaret Evelyn, only dau of Albert Edward Thomas, of 29 Maelog Place, Cardiff, and has issue:

1c *Amanda Carolin Thomas [Mrs Timothy Meachan, 29 Balcorn St, London E8 7AY]; *b* 28 June 1964; *educ* Roy Acad Art (MA) and Br Sch Rome; *m* 19 Oct 1996 *Timothy Meachan, s of Rev John Meachan, of Salisbury, and has:

1d *Milo Douglas; *b* 1997

2c *Clare Margaret Thomas [Clare Thesiger, 32 rue de Chevalier de la Barne, 58175 Tremplemous,, France]; *b* 4 May 1966; *educ* Kent U (BA); *m* Sept 1991*François Germain Tison, s of Jean René Tison, and has:

1d *Madeleine Patience TISON-THESIGER; *b* 1992

2d *Leah Emilienne TISON-THESIGER; *b* 1995

1a (cont.) Lt-Col Richard Thesiger *m* 2nd 15 Nov 1947 Eileen Alice (*d* 1991), only dau of John Still, of Ceylon, and *d* 1984, having by her had further issue:

2b +John Still [John Thesiger Esq, 7 Herne Rd, Surbiton, Surrey KT6 5BX]; *b* 11 Sept 1948; *educ* Winchester and Magdalen Coll Oxford; social work manager (CQSW 1975); *m* Sept 1979 *Nefise Serpil, dau of Mehmet Bayböru, of Küçükyali, Istanbul, and has issue:

1c +Osman Richard Bayböru; *b* 1987

1c *Hatice Emma; *b* 1989

1b *Anne Alice Florita [Mrs Paul Towner, The Rectory, Hanwood, nr Shrewsbury, Shropshire SY5 8LJ]; *b* 24 Sept 1951; *educ* Bristol U (BA); *m* Aug 1973 *Preb Paul Towner, only son of Reginald Towner, of Fleet, Hants, and has issue:

1c *Andrew Paul John; *b* 1976

1c *Katherine Anne; *b* 1975; *educ* Newcastle U (BA 1997)

2c *Elizabeth Marjorie; *b* 1979

2b *Frances Georgina [Miss Frances Thesiger, 107 Upper Brook St, Winchester, Hants]; *b* 7 Oct 1956

1a *Patience Elizabeth Florita, MBE (1994), TD [Miss Patience Thesiger MBE TD, Eleven Plus, Hungershall Park, Tunbridge Wells, Kent]; *b* 20 March 1908; served in ATS WW II 1939–45, Borough Cncllr 1959, Mayor Tunbridge Wells 1969–70, v-chm Kent CC 1982–84

2 Bertram Sackville (Sir), KBE (1942), CB (1916), CMG (1911), DL (Co Southampton) Adml, ADC to HM GEORGE V 1921–22, Adml Sup of Portsmouth Dockyard 1925–27, and C-in-C E Indies Station 1927–29, WW I (despatches), WW II as Cdre RNR in command of Convoys and FOIC, Falmouth; Russian Orders of St Anne 2nd Cl with swords and St Vladmir with swords, US Legion of Merit; *b* 14 Jan 1875; *m* 3 March 1921 Violet (*d* 21 May 1973), only dau of Joseph Arthur Henley, of Waterperry, Oxon, and widow of William Brodrick Cloete, of Hare Park, and *dsp* 12 May 1966

(3) Ernest Frederic Graham, CBE (1960), FRSA, Fell UCL, actor, served QV Rifles 1914–15; *b* 15 Jan 1879; *educ* Marlborough; *m* 29 May 1917 Janette Mary Fernie (*d* 21 May 1970 aged 92), dau of Robert Burt Ranken, of Edinburgh, and *dsp* 14 Jan 1961

(1) Sibyl Adeline, MBE (1954), memb Church Assembly; *b* 16 Feb 1883; *d* unm 19 Feb 1954

1 Augusta; *m* 1 July 1843 William Frederic Higgins, Master of the Court of Bankruptcy, est son of Col Sir Samuel Gordon Higgins, KCH, and *d* 14 Jan 1912, leaving issue. He *d* 1891

2 Julia Selina; *m* 19 July 1851 Maj-Gen Sir John Eardley Wilmot Inglis, KCB, Col of the 32nd Foot, and *d* 3 Feb 1904, leaving issue. He *d* at Homburg, 27 Sept 1862

The 1st BARON *d* 5 Oct 1878; his est son,

FREDERIC AUGUSTUS THESIGER **2nd Baron Chelmsford of Chelmsford**, GCB (1979, KCB 1878, CB 1868), GCVO (1902); Gen 1888, ADC to HM QUEEN VICTORIA 1868–77, Lt Tower London 1884–89, Col 2nd Life Gds, formerly Col Sherwood Foresters, served Crimea, Indian Mutiny and Abyssinia, commanded UK Forces Kaffir and Zulu Wars; *b* 31 May 1827; *m* 1 Jan 1867 Adria Fanny (*d* 25 March 1926), est dau of Maj-Gen Heath, Bombay Army, and had, with other issue:

1 FREDERIC JOHN NAPIER, **1st Viscount**

2 Percy Mansfield, MBE (1918), Capt Roy E Kent Yeo WW I (despatches); *b* 7 Nov 1869; *m* 6 Nov 1900 Katharine Frances (*d* 16 Aug 1958), dau of Alexander Falconer Wallace, of Candacraig, Strathdon, Aberdeenshire, and *d* 3 Aug 1959, leaving issue:

(1) Donald Adrian Wallace; *b* 28 Oct 1901; *educ* Winchester and Peterhouse, Cambridge; *m* 29 July 1927 Frances Nina (*d* 29 March 1968), only dau of Brig-Gen Sylvester Bertram Grimston, CMG, of The White Ho, Willingdon, Sussex, and *d* 1978 leaving issue:

1a *Nina Frances [Miss Nina Thesiger, Flat 59, Roebuck Ho, Palace St, London SW1E 5BB]; *b* 22 Aug 1928

2a Rua Susan; *b* 27 Oct 1930; *m* 8 July 1961 Lt-Col Michael Alistair Lowry, MC, son of G L B Lowry, MC, of Les Bougainvillées, Rue Général Ferrié, Cannes, France, and had issue:

1b *Robert; *b* 8 April 1967

1b *Susan Jane; *b* 28 June 1964

2b *Patricia Gillian; *b* 30 Nov 1965

3a *Zara Jane; *b* 4 April 1933; *m* 31 Oct 1969 *(Arthur) Mark Farrer, slr, er son of Hugh Frederick Francis Farrer, of Finchingfield, Essex, and has:

1b *Lucy Frances; *b* 1971

(2) Alec Pierson; *b* 26 Oct 1904; *d* unm 16 March 1971

(3) Anthony Frederic Lewis; *b* 30 June 1906; *educ* Winchester and Magdalen Coll Oxford; *m* 9 March 1939 *Virginia Margaret, dau of Capt Harry Jocelyn Clive Graham, and *dsp* 10 Aug 1969

3 Wilfred Gilbert, DSO (1900); *b* 25 March 1871; Hon Capt Army, V-Consul Taranto 1897–1900, V-Consul Belgrade and 2nd Sec Dip Corps 1901–06, Consul St Petersburg 1905–08 and Boma, Congo, 1908–09, Consul-Gen and Min Plen Addis Ababa 1909–19, 1st Cl Star Ethiopia, served Boer War 1900–01 (despatches) and WW I (despatches); *m* 21 Aug 1909 Kathleen Mary, CBE (1920) (*d* 1973 having *m* 2nd 8 Oct 1931 Reginald Basil Astley (*d* 6 Oct 1942), 5th son of Lt-Col Francis L'Estrange Astley (*see* HASTINGS, B)), er dau of Thomas Mercer Cliffe Vigors, of Burgage, Co Carlow, and *d* 31 Jan 1920, leaving issue:

(1) +Wilfrid Patrick (Sir), KBE (1995, CBE 1968), DSO (1941) [Sir Wilfred Thesiger KBE DSO, 15 Shelley Court, Tite St, London SW3 4JB]; *b* 3 June 1910; *educ* Eton and Magdalen Coll Oxford (MA); Sudan Civ Serv 1935–44, attd to HRH THE DUKE OF GLOUCESTER's Mission to Abyssinia 1930 (Star of Ethiopia 3rd Cl), served WW II as Maj Sudan Defence Force and Spec Airborne Serv (despatches), Hon DLitt Leicester 1968 and Bath 1992, Fndr's Gold Medal of Roy Geog Soc 1948, Lawrence of Arabia Medal, Roy Central Asian Soc 1955, Roy Scottish Geog Soc 1961, David Livingstone Medal, Roy Soc of Literature Award 1964, Heinemann Award, Roy Soc of Literature 1965, and Burton Memorial Medal, Roy Asiatic Soc 1966, author: *Arabian Sands* (1959), *The Marsh Arabs* (1964), *Desert, Marsh and Mountain* (1979), *The Life of My Choice* (autobiog, 1987), *Visions of a Nomad* (1987), *My Kenya Days* (1994), *The Danakil Diary* (1996)

(2) Brian Peirson THESIGER later DOUGHTY-WYLIE (deed poll 26 Sept 1933), MC; *b* 4 Oct 1911; *educ* Eton and New Coll Oxford; Hon Col formerly Maj RWF (ret 1957), served WW II, Col (Intell) in HQ 2 Br Corps in Suez Operation 1956; *m* 6 July 1937 Diana (*d* 1976), only dau of Capt Vere de Hoghton (*see* DE HOGHTON, Bt), and *d* 1982 leaving issue:

1a *Daphne Susan [Mrs Jeremy Case, New Marton Hall, New Marton, Oswestry, Shropshire]; *b* 19 April 1940; *m* 1st 29 July 1961 Capt Jonathan Harvey William Reeves, RWF, son of Col William Robert Reeves, DSO, of Pennant Hall, Eglwysbach, Denbighs; *m* 2nd 1983 *Jeremy David Michael Case, and has issue by 1st husb:

1b *Thomas Somerville Thesiger; *b* 11 Jan 1969

1b *Emma de Hoghton; *b* 18 Oct 1963; *m* 1988 *Richard Charles Farquhar (*see* FARQUHAR, Bt), and has issue

2b *Katharine Rebecca; *b* 11 April 1966

2a *Philippa Vere Thesiger [Mrs John Harvey, Halston, Whittington, Oswestry, Shropshire SY11 4NS]; *b* 18 May 1942; *m* 2 May 1964 *Maj John Lewarne Harvey, SCLI, est son of H G L Harvey, MRCVS, of Penmellyn, St Columb, Cornwall, and has issue:

1b *Rupert Lewarne; *b* 30 Oct 1965

2b *James Thesiger; *b* 1969

1b *Pippa Vere Karenza; *b* 1971

2b *Joanna Demelza; *b* 1975

(3) Dermot Vigors, P/O RAFVR WW II; *b* 24 March 1914; *educ* Eton and Magdalen Coll Oxford (BA); *ka* 28 April 1942

(4) +Roderic Miles Doughty [Roderic Thesiger Esq, The Paddocks, Lucton, Leominster, Herefs HR6 9PG]; *b* 8 Nov 1915; *educ* Eton, Ch Ch Oxford (BA 1938) and Courtauld Inst; served WW II in Welsh Gds and 1st Para Bde (wounded twice, PoW); dir P and D Colnaghi 1955–71; *m* 1st 21 Sept 1940 (*divorce* 1946) Mary Rose (*d* 21 Dec 1962), yst dau of Hon Guy Charteris (*see* WEMYSS and MARCH, E); *m* 2nd 10 Jan 1946 *Ursula Joan, yst dau of Aymer William Whitworth, of Woollas Hall, Pershore, by his w Alice Lucy Patience, dau of Col Constantine Rodney William Hervey, RA (*see* BRISTOL, M), and has issue by his 2nd w:

1a +Simon Dermot [Simon Thesiger Esq, Old Manor Cottage, Stapley, Taunton, Som]; *b* 25 May 1950; *m* 27 July 1973 *Concepción, dau of Pérez Chavez, of Coyuca de Catalan, Mexico, and has issue:

1b *A dau; *b* 1980

1a *Sarah Elizabeth [Mrs Christoher Wintle, 49 Stradella Rd, London SE24]; *b* 12 April 1947; *m* 26 June 1974 *Christopher Simon Wintle, er son of Julian Wintle, and has issue:

1b *Alice Marina; *b* 1977

2b *Emily Miranda; *b* 1981

4 Eric Richard, DSO (1919), TD, Hon Capt and Lt Col, late TA Res, Page-of-Honour to HM QUEEN VICTORIA, served Boer War 1900–2 and WW I (despatches twice, wounded twice), Croix de Guerre and Order of Crown of Belgium; *b* 17 Feb 1874; *educ* Winchester; *m* 1st 29 Oct 1904 Pearl Marie (*d* 14 Feb 1922), only dau of John Coupland, and had issue:

(1) Osric Wilfred; *b* 5 Oct 1905; *educ* Beaumont; A/Capt IA and GSO, E Cmd, India; *m* 27 Sept 1934 Cecily Mary (*d* 1988), dau of F Vandertaelen, and *d* 29 March 1977, leaving:

1a +Michael Eric [Michael Thesiger Esq, Ridgecrest, Church Rd, St John's, Redhill, Surrey]; *b* 13 Jan 1936; *educ* Downside; FCA; Kt of Grace and Devotion SMO Malta; *m* 3 Oct 1964 *Patricia Low, only dau of George Waddington, of Highfield Ho, Blackwell, Worcs, and has issue:

1b +Edward Osric; *b* 3 Oct 1967; *educ* Downside, RMA Sandhurst and Nottingham U (BA); Capt RGJ; *m* 20 Sept 1997 *Joanna, dau of Peter Wooley-Stafford, of Harwin, Little Kingshill, Bucks

2b +Antony Martin; *b* 21 Sept 1968; *educ* Downside and Oxford Polytechnic (BSc); ARICS

3b +Justin Michael; *b* 3 May 1970; *educ* Downside and Oxford Polytechnic (BSc)
4b +Robert Cedric; *b* 3 May 1970; *educ* Downside and Exeter U (BA)
1b *Georgina Mary; *b* 12 Oct 1965; *m* 1993 *David Charles Dowden, s of Lt-Col Ronnie Dowden, of Axminster, Devon, and has:
1c *Charles Edward; *b* 20 March 1995
2c *William George; *b* 13 Oct 1997
(2) Cedric Paul; *b* 21 March 1915; *educ* Eton; BA (Architecture) 1938; *m* 9 May 1942 *Barbara Cecilia [Mrs Cedric Thesiger, 1/31 Dominion St, Takapuna, Auckland, New Zealand], yr dau of Maj Hubert Cecil Delacour Jarrett, IA, and *d* 1987, having had issue:
1a +Peter Hubert [Peter Thesiger Esq, 4934–2A Ave, Delta, BC, Canada]; *b* 2 Dec 1943; *educ* The Oratory Sch and Simon Fraser U (MBA 1977); *m* 4 Oct 1969 *Jill Patricia, dau of Lt-Cdr E J Worthy, RCN (ret), and has issue:
1b +James Edward; *b* 1980
1b *Julia Mary; *b* 29 April 1983
2a +Richard Paul [Richard Thesiger Esq, Box 14–530, Panmure, Auckland, New Zealand]; *b* 25 Feb 1945; *educ* The Oratory Sch; *m* 1st 1971 (*divorce* 1981) Susan, dau of J Sydes, of 602 E Coats Rd, Bowns Bay, Auckland, NZ; *m* 2nd 1981 *Jennifer Diane, dau of Jonathan David Sharp, RNZAMC, of 12 Stewart Ave, Panmure, Auckland, and has issue by 1st w:
1b *Robin Bruce; *b* 2 Feb 1973
1b *Clare Louise; *b* 31 Oct 1975
3a +John Bede [John Thesiger Esq, 9 Castleton St, Birkenhead, Auckland, New Zealand]; *b* 5 June 1947; *educ* Blackfriars Sch, Laxton; *m* 1981 *Christine Joyce, dau of G A Edmond, BEM, and has issue:
1b +David George; *b* 1986
2b +Kevin Ryan; *b* 1988
(1) *Désirée (Mother Mary Peter), a nun; *b* 29 April 1908
4 (cont.) Lt-Col Eric Thesiger *m* 2nd 3 Oct 1929 Sydney Hilda (*d* 16 July 1930), dau of George Arthur Hutton-Croft, of Aldborough Hall, Yorks, and widow of Maj George Du Plat Taylor, OBE, Gren Gds; *m* 3rd 27 March 1953 Mrs Mary Anderson (*d* 16 Nov 1954), dau of Rev F W Pudsey, of Stainton-in-Cleveland, Yorks, and *d* 2 Oct 1961

The 2nd BARON *d* 9 April 1905; his est son,

FREDERIC JOHN NAPIER THESIGER, **1st Viscount Chelmsford**, of Chelmsford, Co Essex, so *cr* 3 June 1921, PC (1916), GCSI (1916), GCMG (1912, KCMG 1906), GCIE (1916), GBE (1917); *b* 12 Aug 1868; *educ* Magdalen Coll Oxford (MA, Hon Fell 1917), Fell All Souls 1892–99 and 1929, Warden 1932, barrister, Capt late 4th Bn Dorset Regt, memb London Sch Bd 1900–04 and LCC 1904–05, Alderman LCC 1913, Govr Queensland 1905–09 and NSW 1909–13, Viceroy India 1916–21, First Ld Admlty Jan-Nov 1924; Agent-Gen London for NSW 1926–28, v-pres Roy Empire Soc, KJStJ, Chllr Order St Michael and St George 1914–16, ex-officio Grand Master Orders Star India and Indian Empire 1916–21; Hon DCL Oxford 1929, Hon LLD Birmingham 1927, Edin and Sheffield 1932, Fell of Winchester Coll 1921, Warden 1930–32; *m* 27 July 1894 Hon Frances Charlotte Guest, GBE (1917), CI (*d* 24 Sept 1957), est dau of 1st Baron Wimborne (*see* WIMBORNE, V), and had issue:

1 Frederic Ivor, Lt RFA; *b* 17 Oct 1896; *d* May 1917 from wounds recd in action in Mesopotamia
2 ANDREW CHARLES GERALD, **2nd Viscount**
1 Joan Frances Vere; *b* 1 Aug 1895; *m* 16 March 1920 Capt Sir Alan Frederick Lascelles, PC, GCB, GCVO, CMG, MC, son of Cdr Hon Frederick Canning Lascelles, and *d* 15 May 1971, leaving issue (*see* HAREWOOD, E)
2 Anne Molyneux; *b* 17 Dec 1898; *m* 13 Dec 1921 16th Baron Inchiquin (*qv*), and *d* 10 Aug 1973, leaving issue
3 Bridget Mary; *b* 7 Aug 1900; *m* 1st 24 June 1919 (*divorce* 1937) Maj Richard Hasell Sheepshanks, DSO, MVO, IA, and had issue (*see* NOBLE Bt, of Ardmore and Ardardan Noble); *m* 2nd 8 Jan 1938 Nello Beccari, est son of Dr Odoardo Beccari, botanist, of Florence, Italy. He *d* 20 March 1957
4 Margaret St Clair Sidney; *b* 7 May 1911; *m* 10 July 1934 John Monck (formerly Monk Goldman), est son of Maj Charles Sydney Goldman, of Sydney Lodge, Hamble, and had issue:
(1) *Robert Frederic; *b* 1 Nov 1938; *educ* Millfield; *m* 1962 *Barbara, dau of A Lloyd, of Liverpool, and has issue:
1a *Amanda Elizabeth; *b* 28 Jan 1963
2a *Margaret Frances; *b* 22 May 1964
(1) (cont.) Mr and Mrs R F Monk adopted 11 March 1965:
*James; *b* 3 Aug 1961
(2) *Charles Sydney Penryn; *b* 7 April 1945; *educ* Marlborough and Magdalene Coll Cambridge

The 1st VISCOUNT *d* 1 April 1933; his est surv son,

ANDREW CHARLES GERALD THESIGER, **2nd Viscount Chelmsford**; *b* 25 July 1903; *educ* Winchester and Christ's Coll Cambridge; Lt RNVR; with Willis Faber, insur brokers, dir J E A Marshall 1970, assoc from 1976; *m* 14 July 1927 Gillian (*d* 22 April 1978, aged 71), only dau of Arthur Nevile Lubbock, of Bassets, Farnborough, Kent (*see* AVEBURY, B), and *d* 27 Sept 1970, having had issue:

1 +(FREDERIC) JAN THESIGER, **3rd and present Viscount Chelmsford**
1 *Dawn Loraine [The Hon Dawn Thesiger, Hazelbridge Court, Chiddingford, Surrey]; *b* 23 Nov 1934
2 *Philippa Merryn [The Hon Philippa Thesiger, Hazelbridge Court, Chiddingford, Surrey]; *b* 27 July 1939

CHESHAM

Arms: Sa. three stag's heads cabossed arg. **Crest:** A snake nowed, ppr. **Supporters:** Dexter, a buck ppr., gorged with a chaplet of roses arg. and az.; sinister, a greyhound arg., gorged with a plain collar gu., thereon three buckles or. **Motto:** *Cavendo tutus* ('Secure by caution'). **Creations:** B. (UK) 15 Jan 1858.

THE 6TH BARON CHESHAM, of Chesham, Co Buckingham (Nicholas Charles Cavendish) [The Rt Hon The Lord Chesham, The Old Post House, Church St, Ropley, Hants SO24 0DR]; *b* 7 Nov 1941; *s f* 1989; *educ* Eton; ACA, Capt Yeomen Gd (Dep Govt Ch Whip) 1995–97; *m* 1st 4 Nov 1965 (*divorce* 1969) Susan Donne, est dau of Frederick Guy Beauchamp, MD, MRCS, of 119 Harley St, W1, by Hon Susan Silence, yr sis of 13th Baron North (*see* 1970 edn); *m* 2nd 1973 *Suzanne Adrienne, er dau of Alan Gray Byrne, of Rose Bay, Sydney, Australia, and has issue:

1 +CHARLES GRAY COMPTON; *b* 11 Nov 1974; *educ* King's Sch, Parramatta, and Durham U
2 +William George Gray; *b* 13 April 1980

Lineage: The 1st EARL OF BURLINGTON (*see* DEVONSHIRE, D) had a 4th s:

CHARLES COMPTON CAVENDISH, **1st Baron Chesham**, of Chesham, Co Buckingham (UK), so *cr* 15 Jan 1858; *b* 28 Aug 1793, MP (Whig, later Lib) Aylesbury 1814–18, Newtown (IoW) 1821–30, Yarmouth (IoW) 1831–32, E Sussex 1832–41, Youghal, Co Cork, 1841–47 and Bucks 1847–57; *m* 16 June 1814 Catherine Susan (*d* 14 Dec 1866), est dau of 9th Marquess of Huntly (*qv*), and had issue:

1 WILLIAM GEORGE, **2nd Baron**
1 Susan Sophia; *m* 12 Jan 1937 22nd Lord Dacre (*see* HAMPDEN, V), and *d* 13 Aug 1896
2 Harriet Elizabeth; *m* 16 March 1848 2nd Earl of Strafford (*qv*), and *d* 26 June 1892, leaving issue

The 1st BARON *d* 10 Nov 1863; his son,

WILLIAM GEORGE CAVENDISH, **2nd Baron Chesham**; *b* 29 Oct 1815; *educ* Eton; offr 10th Light Dragoons, MP (Lib) Peterborough 1847–52 and Bucks 1857–63; *m* 24 July 1840 Henrietta Frances (*d* 21 May 1884), dau of William Saunders Sebright Lascelles (*see* HAREWOOD, E), and had, with other issue:

1 CHARLES COMPTON WILLIAM, **3rd Baron**
2 William Edwin, MVO (1908), Lt-Col and Brev Col late Gren Gds, Bde Cdr and T/Brig-Gen 1916, served Br Centl Africa 1895, Nile Expdn 1898, S African War 1899–1902, and WW I; *b* 18 May 1862; *m* 25 March 1885 Elizabeth Janet, OBE (1918) (*d* 2 May 1935), dau of Thomas Baillie, and sis of Sir George Baillie, 3rd Bt (*qv*), and *d* 28 Aug 1931, leaving:
(1) Evan George Charles, OBE (1935); *b* 23 Feb 1891; Cdr RN (ret); Capt RNVR, ADC to HM 1936–37, had Orders of the Nile, El Nahda, and Rising Sun of Japan, Silver Jubilee medal 1935 and Coronation medal 1937; *m* 25 Jan 1923 Esmé Frances Sylvia Irby (*d* 6 Oct 1959), dau of Hon Gilbert Neville Smyth, of Ashton Court, Bristol (*see* BOSTON, B), and *d* 4 Sept 1955, leaving issue:
1a +Greville Adrian; *b* 22 Dec 1925; *m* 1st 9 Aug 1952 (*divorce* 1974) Hazel Colleen Elizabeth, only dau of John Henry Many, of Amani Cliffe Ave, Mombasa, Kenya; *m* 2nd 1974 *Gillian, dau of Leslie George Webb, of W Hagley, Yorks, and has issue by 1st w:
1b +Rupert Edward Greville; *b* 4 Sept 1955
2b +Piers Antony Charles [Piers Cavendish Esq, 58 St John's Hill Grove, London SW11 2RG]; *b* 29 Dec 1956; *m* 1986 *(Rose Vivien) Louise, est dau of Gerard Dacres (Dickie) Oliver, and of Mrs Hester St John Ives, of Chain Ho, Modbury, S Devon, and has issue:
1c +Patrick Alexander; *b* 1990
1c *Georgia Claire; *b* 1989
1b *Kiloran Arabella; *b* 8 May 1959
1a *Susan [Mrs Leslie Graham, Mount Farm, Highwood, nr Ringwood, Hants]; *b* 10 May 1924; PO WRNS; *m* 1st 17 July 1951 (*divorce* 1955) David Murray Martin, son of Reginald Martin, of Rose and Ivy Cottage, King's Somborne, Hants, and has issue:

1b *Trudy Carol; *b* 4 June 1952
2b *Amanda Jane; *b* 19 Feb 1954
1a (cont.) Mrs Susan Martin *m* 2nd 1 Dec 1955 *Leslie Gordon Graham, son of Sidney Graham, of 84 Tylecroft Rd, Norbury, SW16, and has further issue:
3b *Sarah Frances; *b* 28 Sept 1956
(1) Elizabeth Compton *m* 25 April 1917, R-Adml Sir Wellwood George Courtenay Maxwell, KBE, CMG, DCL, son of George Maxwell of Glenlee, Stewartry of Kirkcudbright, and *d* Oct 1974, leaving issue. He *d* 9 July 1965
1 Georgiana Caroline; *m* 26 Aug 1875 2nd Earl of Leicester, KG (*qv*), and *d* 26 Feb 1937, leaving issue
2 Mary Susan Caroline; *m* 19 Oct 1878 8th Viscount Cobham (*qv*), and *d* 28 Jan 1937, leaving issue
3 Katherine Caroline, CBE (1920); *m* 19 July 1882 1st Duke of Westminster, KG (*qv*), and *d* 19 Dec 1941, leaving issue

The 1st BARON *d* 26 June 1882; his est son,

CHARLES COMPTON WILLIAM CAVENDISH, **3rd Baron Chesham**, PC, KCB, DL (Warwicks); *b* 13 Dec 1850; Master of the Buckhounds 1900, Ld Bedchamber to HRH PRINCE OF WALES, Hon Col Roy Bucks Hus, Inspr-Gen Imp Yeo, Lt Coldstream Gds, Capt 10th Hus and 16th Lancers, Maj-Gen Imp Yeo Boer War; *m* 13 Nov 1877 Lady Beatrice Constance Grosvenor, RRC (*m* 2nd 4 Oct 1910 Maj John Alexander Moncreiffe, MC (*d* 21 June 1933), son of Sir Thomas Moncreiffe, 7th Bt (*see* ERROLL, E), and *d* 12 Jan 1911), 2nd dau of 1st Duke of Westminster (*qv*), and *d* 9 Nov 1907, having had issue:
1 Charles William Hugh, 2nd Lt 17th Lancers; *b* 13 Sept 1878; *ka* at Diamond Hill, nr Pretoria, S Africa, 11 June 1900
2 JOHN COMPTON, **4th Baron**
1 Lilah Constance, OBE (1920); *b* 20 March 1884; *m* 8 July 1903 Sir Mervyn Edward Manningham-Buller, 3rd, Bt, MP, and *d* 27 April 1944, leaving issue (*see* DILHORNE, V)
2 Marjorie Beatrice; *b* 18 Sept 1888; *d* 2 July 1897

The 3rd BARON *d* 1907; his only surv son,

JOHN COMPTON CAVENDISH, **4th Baron Chesham**, MC, DL, JP, Capt late 10th Hus WW I (wounded), and WW II as S/Ldr RAFVR; *b* 13 June 1894; *m* 1st 17 Aug 1915 (*divorce* 1937) Magot, dau of John Layton Mills, of Tansor Court, Oundle, Northants, and had issue:
1 JOHN CHARLES COMPTON, **5th Baron**

The **4th Baron** *m* 2nd 20 Oct 1938 Marion Caher, memb for Iringa Constituency in Nat Assembly of Tanganyika 1958, served WW II in ATS, and with American Red Cross (*d* 6 Sept 1973), dau of Daniel Charles Donoghue, of Philadelphia, USA, and formerly w of 8th Earl of Carrick (*qv*), and *d* 26 April 1952

His only son,

JOHN CHARLES COMPTON CAVENDISH, **5th Baron Chesham**, PC (1964), JP (Bucks 1946); *b* 18 June 1916; *educ* Eton and Trinity Coll Cambridge; Capt RA (TA), served WW II; Ld-in-Waiting to HM THE QUEEN Jan 1955–Oct 1959, Jt Parly Sec Min of Tport Oct 1959–64, exec v-chm RAC 1966–70, chm: Br Rd Fedn 1966–72 (v-pres 1972), Inernat Rd Fdn 1973–76; Chllr Primrose League 1957–59; *m* 28 Sept 1937 *Mary Edmunds [The Rt Hon The Dowager Lady Chesham, Meadow House, Preston Candover, Basingstoke, Hants], 4th dau of David Gregory Marshall, MBE, of White Hill, Fen Ditton, Cambs, and *d* 1989, having had issue:
1 NICHOLAS CHARLES CAVENDISH, **6th and present Baron Chesham**
2 +John Charles Gregory [The Hon John Cavendish, Hall Farm, Farringdon, nr Alton, Hants]; *b* 23 Nov 1952; *educ* Eton and Jesus Coll Cambridge (BA 1974); *m* 3 July 1976 *Lucinda Mary, dau of Richard Hugh Corbett, of Manor Farm, Beauworth, Hants
1 *Joanna Mary [The Hon Mrs Price, Pin Hill Farm, Sidbury, Devon EX10 0QT]; *b* 20 July 1938; *m* 23 July 1960 *Peter Henry Mabille Price, son of Cdr Maurice Price, RN, of Sutton, Surrey, and has issue:
(1) *Nicholas Henry Maurice; *b* 12 Aug 1971; *m* 5 Oct 1996 *Celina, dau of Charles Llewellyn, of Leigh, Reigate, Surrey
(1) *Caroline Mary; *b* 8 June 1967; *m* 1st 1988 (*divorce* 1996) Christopher G Marler, son of Geoffrey Marler; *m* 2nd 1997 *Henry St John Symes Bullen, son of Michael Bullen, of Borough Court, Hants
2 *Georgina Mary [The Hon Mrs Tufnell, High Dell Farmhouse, Bighton, Alresford, Hants]; *b* 8 Sept 1944; *m* 11 Nov 1967 *(Michael) Wynne Tufnell, only son of Capt Michael Neville Tufnell, DSC, RN, of Curdridge Grange, Botley, Hants, and has issue:
(1) *Christopher Wynne; *b* 13 April 1969
(2) *Michael Greville; *b* 3 Sept 1971; *m* 1 Nov 1997 *Katharine, yr dau of David Adam, of Halland, E Sussex
(3) *Simon Charles *b* 3 Sept 1977

CHETWODE

Arms: Quarterly, arg. and gu., four crosses pattée counter-changed. **Crest:** Out of a ducal coronet or a demi-lion rampant issuant gu. **Supporters:** Dexter, a crusader in chain armour and surcoat, resting the exterior hand proper on a shield of the arms of Chetwode; sinister, an officer of the 19th Royal Hussars, resting his exterior hand on the hilt of his sword proper. **Motto:** *Corona mea Christus* ('Christ is my crown'). **Creation:** Bt. (E) 6 April 1700, B. (UK) 10 July 1945.

THE 2ND BARON CHETWODE, of Chetwode, Co Buckingham, and a **Baronet** (Sir Philip Chetwode, Bt) [The Rt Hon The Lord Chetwode, The Mill House, Chilton Foliat, Hungerford, Berks RG17 0TG]; *b* 26 March 1937; *s* gf 1950; *educ* Eton; commnd RHG 1956 (ret as Capt 1966); *m* 1st 10 Aug 1967 (*divorce* 1979) Susan Janet, er dau of Capt Voltelin James Howard van der Byl, DSC, RN, of North Lodge, The Avenue, Alverstoke, Hants, and formerly w of Alwyn Richard Dudley Smith; *m* 2nd 1990 *Mrs Fiona Holt, dau of Christos Tsintsaris, of 15 Alexandrou Mihailidi, Thessaloniki, Greece, and has issue by 1st w:
1 +ROGER; *b* 29 May 1968; *educ* Harrow
2 +Alexander; *b* 19 Nov 1969; *educ* Harrow
1 *Miranda; *b* 24 Jan 1974

Lineage: Sir JOHN CHETWODE, of Chetwode, Bucks; lived *c* 1100; alleged ancestor of:

PHILIP CHETWODE, of Oakley; *m* Hester, dau and heir of William Touchet, of Nether Whitley, Cheshire, and had:

Sir John Chetwode, 1st Bt (E), so *cr* 6 April 1700, of Oakley; *m* 1st 1695 Mary, dau of Alderman Sir Jonathan Raymond, of the City of London, and had a s and three daus; *m* 2nd Catherine, dau of John Tayleur, of Rodington, Shropshire, and *d* 22 April 1733, leaving:

Sir Philip Touchet Chetwode, 2nd Bt; *m* 1727 Elizabeth, only dau and heir of George Venables, of Agdon, Cheshire, and *d* 15 Nov 1764, leaving, with five other surv children, an est s:

Sir John Chetwode, 3rd Bt; *m* Dorothy, 3rd dau and coheir of Tobias Bretland, of Thorncliffe, Cheshire, and *d* 25 May 1779, having had, with seven other children (all *dvp*):

Sir John Chetwode, 4th Bt; *b* 11 May 1764; *m* 1st 26 Oct 1785 Lady Henrietta Grey (*d* 12 July 1826), est dau of 5th Earl of Stamford (*see* 1970 edn), and had, with other issue:
1 Sir JOHN CHETWODE later NEWDIGATE-LUDFORD-CHETWODE (sign manual 1826), **5th Bt**; *b* 12 Nov 1788; *m* 1st 16 Oct 1821 Elizabeth Juliana (*d* 17 June 1859), est dau and coheir of John Newdigate Ludford, of Ansley Hall, Warwicks; *m* 2nd 17 Jan 1861 Arabella Phillis (*d* 26 June 1873), widow of James Reade, of Lower Berkeley St, Portman Sq, and *dsp* 8 Sept 1873
2 George (Rev), of Chilton Ho, Bucks, MA, Rector of Ashton-under-Lyne, Lancs, and perpetual Curate of Chilton; *b* 1 Nov 1791; *m* 1st 26 Aug 1818 Charlotte Anne (*d* 19 Jan 1837), dau of Morton Walhouse, and sis of 1st Lord Hatherton (*qv*), and by her had, with other issue:
(1) GEORGE (Sir), **6th Bt**
(1) Emily Hyacinth Anne; *m* 24 July 1845 Joseph Baily, of Shenley Ho, Bucks, and *d* 18 Aug 1899, leaving issue
(2) Hyacinthe Laura; *m* 7 July 1868 Rev William Mondeford Bramston, MA, 3rd son of T W Bramston, MP, of Skreens, Essex, and had issue. He *d* Jan 1892
2 (cont.) The Rev George Chetwode *m* 2nd 1 Sept 1840 Anna Maria, dau of Very Rev Dr Shipley, Dean of St Asaph, and widow of Leslie Jones; *m* 3rd 27 Feb 1849 Elizabeth Anne (*d* 13 June 1861), widow of Fiennes Trotman; *m* 4th 30 April 1868 Elizabeth Sophia Ricketts, of Dorton and Boarstall, Bucks, widow of Charles Spencer Ricketts, RN, and *d* 4 Aug 1870
3 Philip, Lt RN; *b* 16 May 1805; *m* 10 Aug 1836 Joanna (*d* 7 July 1868), dau of J G Alleyn, and *d* 15 Sept 1843, leaving an only child:
(1) Henrietta Dorothy Boughey; *m* 16 Aug 1864 Rev John T Vaudrey, MA, of Wyke Regis, Dorset

4 Frederic, in the Army; *b* 24 June 1818; *m* 26 March 1835 Elizabeth, dau of James Finlay, and *d* 3 March 1863, leaving issue:

(1) Elizabeth Louisa; *m* 16 April 1856 Richard King, and *d* 1879, leaving issue

1 Henrietta Dorothy; *m* 9 Feb 1808 Sir John Fenton Fletcher Boughey, 2nd Bt (*qv*), and *d* 22 Jan 1849, leaving issue

Sir John *m* 2nd 1827 Elizabeth (who *m* 2nd 22 May 1848 Andrew Kennedy Hutchinson, of Chester Sq), dau of John Bristow, and *d* 17 Dec 1845

The 5th Bt's nephew,

Sir George Chetwode, 6th Bt, Lt-Col 8th Hus; *b* 20 July 1823; *m* 21 Oct 1868 Alice Jane (*d* 26 Nov 1919), 2nd dau of Michael Thomas Bass, of Rangemore, MP, and sis of 1st Baron Burton (*qv*), and had issue:

1 PHILIP WALHOUSE, **1st Baron**

2 George Knightley (Sir), KCB, CBE; *b* 10 Dec 1877; ADC to HM GEORGE V 1928, Naval Sec to First Ld of the Admlty 1929–31, cmdg 1st Cruiser Sqdn Mediterranean Fleet 1932–33, and Adml Cmdg Reserves 1933–36, R-Adml 1928, V-Adml 1933, Adml 1936, served in China 1900 (medal), WW I (despatches), Russian Order of St Stansias 2nd Cl with Swords, Legion of Honour, Hellenes Medal of Military Merit; *m* 1st 4 Feb 1908 Alice Clara (*d* 19 June 1937), yst dau of Maj Vaughan Hanning Vaughan Lee, DL, of Dillington Park, Somerset; *m* 2nd 13 Jan 1939 Elizabeth Jane (*d* 1979), dau of Frederick Taylor, of Jericho, Queensland, Australia, and formerly w of Capt Lionel Dawson, RN (ret), and *d* 11 March 1957, having by his 1st w had issue:

(1) John, Paymaster Lt RNR, served WW II; *b* 28 May 1909; *m* 2nd 28 July 1934 Joan Muriel (*k* in a motor accident, 7 Sept 1951) (who *m* 2nd 8 Aug 1947 Capt Joseph Anthony (Tony) Collings, MBE, late N Somerset Yeo (*k* in an air accident, 8 April 1954), only son of Joseph Chamberlayne Collings, of Porlockford Ho, Porlock, Som, and had further issue), er dau of Lt-Col Frederick George Glyn Bailey, late RA, by Lady Janet, 2nd dau of 1st Earl of Inchcape (*qv*), and was *ka* in HMS *Gloucester*, off Crete, 22 May 1941, leaving issue:

1a John Simon Knightley; *b* 21 Aug 1935; *educ* Eton and Ch Ch Oxford; student Inner Temple from 1960, Lt Roy Wilts Yeo (TA), formerly 2nd Lt 12th Roy Lancers 1954–56, and 2nd Lt Derbys Yeo (TA) 1956–57; *d* unm 4 Aug 1977

1a *Janet Amanda Alice [Miss Janet Chetwode, c/o The Lansdowne Club, 9 Fitzmaurice Place, London W1]; *b* 22 May 1937; *educ* Westonbirt and St Clare's Coll Oxford

(2) +(George) David, MBE (1944) [Major David Chetwode MBE, Swiss Farm House, Upper Slaughter, Cheltenham, Glos GL54 2JP]; *b* 24 Aug 1914; *educ* RNC Dartmouth and RMC Sandhurst; Maj Coldstream Gds, served WW II (wounded), ADC to Govr of Bombay 1937; *m* 9 Oct 1946 *Lady Willa Elliot, yr dau of 5th Earl of Minto (*qv*), and has issue:

1a +Joshua Lariston Knightley; *b* 20 July 1967; *educ* Eton and LSE

1a *Davina Marion [Mrs Joshua Miller, 33 Summer St, Northampton, Mass 01060, USA]; *b* 23 July 1947; *m* 1st 22 June 1968 (*divorce* 1975) William John N Moore, son of W Moore, of Thornhill Ho, Stalbridge, Dorset, and has issue:

1b *Lucy; *b* 1970

1a (cont.) Mrs Davina Moore *m* 2nd 1977 *Joshua Miller, son of Prof Irving Miller, of NY, and has further issue:

2c *Corina Emily; *b* 1979

3c *Sophie Claire; *b* 1983

2a *Sarah Alice [Mrs Sarah Cox, 94 Cambridge Gdns, London W10 6HS]; *b* 14 Nov 1948; *m* 26 July 1969 (*divorce* 1983) Andrew Donald Cox, son of Donald Nugent Cox, of Gourdie, Fife, and has issue:

1b *Damian; *b* 1975

1c *Indiajane; *b* 1970

2c *Alice Dawn; *b* 1972

3c *Flora Eileen Gian; *b* 1976

3a *Emma Bridget [Mrs Simon Keswick, Rockcliffe, Upper Slaughter, Cheltenham, Glos GL54 2JW]; *b* 17 Oct 1950; *m* 12 June 1971 *Simon Lindley Keswick, yst son of Sir William Keswick, of Glenkiln, Shawhead, Dumfries, and has issue:

1b *Benjamin William; *b* 1972

2b *Archibald David; *b* 1980

1b *Poppy Teresa; *b* 1978

2b *Willa Mary China; *b* 1984

4a *Willa Mary Gabrielle; *b* 25 May 1954; *m* 22 April 1978 18th Lord Elphinstone (*qv*), and has issue

5a *Georgina Caroline; *b* 27 Dec 1955; *m* 1983 *Edward Charles Markes, 2nd son of John Edward Markes, of Recess, Co Galway, and has issue:

1b *Dominic John; *b* 1989

2b *Gerard David; *b* 1991

1b *Araminta Victoria; *b* 1987

1 Evelyn Hamar, MBE (1918); *b* 18 Nov 1870; *m* 19 March 1892 Percy Alfred Leyland Laming, of Alresford Place, Alresford, Hants, and *d* 16 June 1931

2 Laura Grey; *b* 1 July 1872; *m* 3 July 1897 Hon Christian Edward Cornwallis Eliot, OBE, of Sunhill, Alresford, Hants, son of Col Hon Charles Eliot, and *d* 22 Jan 1938, leaving issue (*see* ST GERMANS, E)

3 Florence Hyacinthe; *b* 11 Dec 1876; *m* 21 Oct 1903 Gen Sir James Frederick Noel Birch, GBE, KCB, KCMG, RHA (*d* 3 Feb 1939), of 11 Kensington Gore, SW7, son of Maj R E Birch, of St Asaph, and *d* 4 Oct 1938, leaving issue (*see* WOLSELEY, also 1970 edn RHYL OF HOLYWELL, B)

Sir GEORGE *d* 28 June 1905; his son,

PHILIP WALHOUSE (Sir), **7th Bt**, and **1st Baron Chetwode**, of Chetwode, Co Buckingham (UK), so *cr* 10 July 1945, GCB (1929, KCB 1918), OM (1936), GCSI (1934), KCMG (1917), DSO (1900); *b* 21 Sept 1869; *educ* Eton; cmded 19th KAO Hus 1909, Col Roy Scots Greys 15th/19th Dragoons, cmded 5th Cav Bde and 2nd Cav Div France, Desert Corps and 20th Army Corps Palestine and Syria, Mil Sec to Sec State War 1919–20, Dep CIGS 1920–22, memb Army Cncl 1920–23, Adj-Gen Forces 1922–23, GOC-in-C Aldershot 1923–27, ADC Gen to HM GEORGE V 1927–31, CGS India 1928–30, C-in-C Army in India and memb Exec Cncl Govr-Gen 1930–35, Gen 1926, FM 1933, Constable Tower London 1943–48, GCStJ; served Chinwir Hills Expdn Burma 1892–93 (medal and clasp), Boer War 1899–1902 (despatches two medals, six clasps), WW I (wounded, despatches), Croix de Guerre, Order Nile 2nd Cl, Order Sacred Treasure Japan 1st Cl, Cdr Legion of Honour, Hon DCL Oxford 1936; *m* 1 June 1899 Alice Hester Camilla (*d* 29 June 1946), est dau of Col Hon Richard Cotton (*see* COMBERMERE, V), and *d* 6 July 1950, having had issue:

1 Roger Charles George, Capt 11th (City of London Yeo), Light AA, Bde, RA (TA); *b* 18 April 1906; *m* 19 May 1936 Hon (Molly) Patricia Berry (*d* 1995, having *m* 2nd 23 March 1942 (*divorce* 1948) 1st and last Baron Sherwood (*d* 1 April 1970), *m* 3rd 21 July 1958 Lt-Col Sir Richard Charles Geers Cotterell, 5th Bt (*qv*)), 3rd dau of 1st Viscount Camrose (*qv*), and *dvp* 14 Aug 1940, leaving issue:

(1) PHILIP CHETWODE, **2nd and present Baron Chetwode**

(2) +Christopher Roger [The Hon Christopher Chetwode, Hill House, Cheriton, Hants SO24 0PT]; *b* 24 March 1940; *educ* Eton; granted rank of baron's yr s March 1951; *m* 25 July 1961 *Hon Philippa Mary Imogen Brand, yr dau of Lt-Col 5th Viscount Hampden (*qv*), and has issue:

1a +Michael Walhouse David; *b* 31 Aug 1962; *m* 1986 *Louise Ann, dau of R W Wood, of Maldon, Essex, and has issue:

1b +George; *b* 1992

1b *Emma Louisa Patricia; *b* 1987

2b *Holly; *b* 1989

3b *Daisy; *b* 1992 (twin)

2a +Richard Christopher; *b* 6 May 1964; *educ* Eton and Edinburgh; *m* 1993 *Sheelagh Maria, dau of Desmond Francis Boylan, of Marion, Mass., USA (*see* O'BRIEN, Bt), and has:

1b +Harry Thomas Christopher; *b* 2 Nov 1996

1b *Lucy Imogen Brigid, *b* 14 April 1998

3a +Charles Philip; *b* 17 Aug 1967

4a +William Robin; *b* 12 Sept 1973

5a +James Nicholas; *b* 8 Aug 1975

1 *Penelope Valentine Hester; *b* 14 Feb 1910; *m* 29 July 1933 Sir John Betjeman, CBE, Hon DLitt (*d* 1984), Poet Laureate, only son of Ernest Edward Betjeman by Mabel Bessie, dau of James Dawson, and has issue

CHETWYND, Viscount

Arms: Quarterly, 1st and 4th az. a chevron between three mullets or (for CHETWYND), 2nd and 3rd arg, three chevronels gu. each charged with a mullet of the field, a canton gu. (for CASSON). **Crest:** A goat's head erased arg., attired or. **Supporters:** Two unicorns arg., each gorged with a chaplet of roses gu., thereto affixed, reflexed over the back, a line of roses of the last. **Motto:** *Probitas verus honos* ('Probity is true honour'). **Creation:** V. (I) and B. (I) 29 June 1717.

THE 10TH VISCOUNT CHETWYND OF BEARHAVEN, Co Kerry, and **Baron of Rathdowne**, Co **Dublin** (Adam Richard John Casson Chetwynd) [The Rt Hon The Viscount Chetwynd, c/o J G Ouvry Esq, Lee Bolton & Lee, 1 The Sanctuary, Westminster, London SW1P 3JT]; *b* 2 Feb 1935; *s* f 1965; *educ* Eton; Lt QO Cameron Highrs 1954–56, Freeman Guild of Air Pilots and Air Navigators, with Colonial Mutual Life Assur, Salisbury, Rhodesia, 1968–78, unlt manager 1972, agency manager Johannesburg 1975, exec consultant Liberty Life Assoc of Africa 1984–; Fell Inst of Life and Pension Advisers 1982, Liveryman Guild Air Pilots and Air Navigators 1996–; *m* 1st 19 Feb 1966 (*divorce* 1974) Celia Grace, er dau of Cdr Alexander Robert Ramsay, DSC, RNVR (*see* RAMSAY, Bt); *m* 2nd 15 Aug 1975 *Angela May, only dau of Jack Payne McCarthy, of Aspley, Notts, and by his 1st w has:

1 +ADAM DOUGLAS; *b* 26 Feb 1969

2 +Robert Duncan; *b* 26 Feb 1969

1 *Emma Grace; *b* 5 May 1967

Lineage: ADAM de CHETWYND, feudal Ld of Chetwynd, Salop; living 1180; had:

Sir JOHN CHETWYND; *d c* 1240, having had issue:

1 John (Sir); *d* 1280, leaving:

(1) A son; made over Chetwynd to his cousin

2 PHILIP

3 Adam; had:

(1) John; became feudal Ld of Chetwynd on his cousin's resignation; *d* 1354, leaving:

1a Reginald; had a dau and heiress:

1b Joan de Chetwynd; *m* Richard de Peshall, Sheriff Salop 1374–76, and had:

1c Joyce; *m* — Pigott and brought him Chetwynd

2c Isabella; *m* Thomas Grosvenor, of Bellaport

The 2nd son,

Sir PHILIP de CHETWYND; *m* Isabella (*m* 2nd Roger Thornton), dau of Sir Adam de Mutton, through her acquired Ingestre, Staffs, and *d* 1294, leaving:

PHILIP de CHETWYND; *m* Isabella de Pulesdon and *d* 1306, leaving:

Sir PHILIP de CHETWYND; *m* Alice, dau and (with her sis Johanna, w of Sir Roger Chetwynd, bro of Sir Philip) coheir of Sir Ralph Grendon, of Grendon, and *d* 1346, having had four s, of whom the 3rd:

Sir WILLIAM CHETWYND, of Ingestre; *m* Matilda, dau of Elyas de Verdien, and *d* 1373, leaving:

Sir WILLIAM CHETWYND, of Ingestre; *m* Aline St Paul and *d* 1396, leaving issue:

1 Roger, of Ingestre; *m* twice and *dsp* 1397 aged 22

2 Richard, of Ingestre; *m* Thomasina Frodsham and *d* 1417 aged 36, leaving:

(1) Philip (Sir); *m* 1st 1438 Elene, dau of Thomas de la Roche and widow of Lord Ferrers (of Chartley; *see* HEREFORD, V); *m* 2nd 1442 Johanna, dau and coheir of Sir William Burley, of Bromsgrove, and *dsp* 1444

3 John, of Alspath; *s* his nephew; *d* 1445, leaving:

(1) Thomas, of Alspath; *d* 1451, leaving:

1a William, of Alspath and Ingestre; Gentleman-Usher of the Chamber to HENRY VII; *m* Alice, dau of Hugh Egerton, of Wrienhill, Staffs, and was *k* in an affray at Tixall Heath by followers of Sir Humphrey Stafford, of Pipe, Staffs, with whom he was on bad terms at Court, having been inveigled there early in the morning by a forged letter, leaving, with two other sons and two daus:

1b William (Sir), of Alspath and Ingestre; *m* Elizabeth, dau of Sir John Ferrers, of Tamworth, and *d* 1547, having had, with a dau:

1c Thomas, of Ingestre; sold Alspath; *m* Joanna (*m* 2nd Sir William Sneyde, of Bradwell, Sneyde and Tunstall, Staffs), dau of heir of Sir John Salter, of Salters Hall, Newport, Salop, Ch Justice N Wales, and *d* 1555, leaving, with other issue:

1d John, of Ingestre; *m* 1st Mary, only dau of Louis Meverill, of Bold, Staffs, and had:

1e William (Sir), of Ingestre; *m* 1st 1574 (*divorce*) Atlanta (*d* 1618), dau of Robert Huick (Physician to ELIZABETH I); *m* 2nd 1604 Catherine, widow of Stephen Slaney (s of a Ld Mayor of London) and dau of Sir Walter Aston, of Tixall, but *dsp* 1612

1d (cont.) John Chetwynd *m* 2nd Marjory (*d* 20 Dec 1602), 2nd dau of Robert Middlemore, of Edgbaston, Warwicks, and *d* 15 April 1592, having had by her, with other issue:

2e Walter (Sir), of Ingestre; MP Newcastle-under-Lyme 1584 and 1603, High Sheriff Salop 1607; *m* 1st Mary (*d* 1588), only dau of John Mullins, Archdeacon of London; *m* 2nd 1605 Lady Catherine Hastings, dau of 4th Earl of Huntingdon (*qv*) and widow of Sir Edward Unton, and *d* 1638, having had by his 1st w, with other issue:

1f Walter, of Ingestre; *m* 1632 Frances (*m* 2nd 1 Sept 1670, as his 2nd w, Sir Wolstan Dixie, Bt (*see* 1970 edn), and *d* 1686), dau and heir of Edward Haslerig, of Arthingworth, and *d* 1670 leaving:

1g Walter, of Ingestre; *m* 14 Sept 1656 Anna, dau of Edward Bagot, of Blithfield, but *dsp* 21 March 1693, leaving his estates devolved to his cousin the **1st Viscount**

3e Thomas, of Rugeley, Staffs; *m* Dorothy, dau of Walter Colman, of Cannock, Staffs, and was ancestor of the CHETWYNDs of Grendon (*see* CHETWYND, Bt)

2d Robert; *m* Elizabeth Hamersley and had issue

1d Dorothy; *m* Sir Walter Smyth, of Therford, Warwicks

2c Anthony, of Ridge; *m* Katherine, dau of Ralph Thickness, and had:

1d John; *m* Mary, dau of Richard Welles, of Horecross, and had:

1e John, of Ridge; *m* Susannah, dau of John Broughton, of Whittington, and *d* 1674, leaving:

1f John, of Ridge and Meare, later Ingestre; MP Stafford; *m* Lucy, dau of Thomas Roane, of Chaldon, Surrey, and *d* 9 Dec 1702, leaving:

1g WALTER CHETWYND, **1st Viscount Chetwynd of Bearhaven**, Co Kerry, and BARON OF RATHDOWNE, Co Dublin (both I), so *cr* 29 June 1717, with special remainder to the heirs male of the body of his f, of Rudge and Ingestre; *b c* 1678; *educ* Ch Ch Oxford; MP (Tory to 1708, Whig from 1708 till he got his peerage then Tory again) Stafford 1702–11, 1712–22 and 1725–34, Master Buckhounds 1705–11, Ranger St James's Pk and Keeper the Mall 1714–27, High Steward Stafford 1717; *m* 27 May 1703 Mary (*d* 28 Feb 1736/7), dau and coheir of John Berkeley, 4th Viscount Fitzhardinge and Baron Berkeley of Rathdowne (*see* BERKELEY, B), and *dsp* 21 Feb 1735/6

2g JOHN CHETWYND, **2nd Viscount Chetwynd of Bearhaven**, Envoy Savoy 1706–10, a Ld of Trade 1714–28, MP (Whig) St Mawes 1715–22, Stockbridge (Whig to 1727, Tory thereafter) 1722–34 and Stafford 1738–47, Envoy Madrid in 1717–18, a Ld Admlty 1717–27; *m* by 1720 — (*d* 21 Feb 1738/9) and *dspms* 21 June 1767, having had, with other issue:

1h William Richard, MP Stafford; *m* 1753 Elizabeth (*m* 2nd Dr Jeffrey Thompson, MD), dau of William Wollaston, and *dvp* Feb 1765, leaving:

1i Isabella; *m* John Parsons

1h Catherine; *m* 1748 John, son of 1st Baron Talnbot of Hensol, and had; by this marriage the Earls of Shrewsbury and Waterford (*qv*) acquired the Ingestre estate

3g WILLIAM RICHARD, **3rd Viscount**

1g Lucy; *m* Edward Yonge, Bath King-of-Arms, and had:

1h Lucy; *m* 1740 William, Earl of Rochfort, KG, but *dsp* 1773

The 2nd VISCOUNT's bro,

WILLIAM RICHARD CHETWYND, **3rd Viscount Chetwynd of Bearhaven**; *b c* 1684; *educ* Westminster and Ch Ch Oxford; Envoy Genoa 1708–12, MP (Whig to 1727, thereafter Tory) Stafford 1715–22 and 1734–70 and Plymouth 1722–27, a Ld Admlty 1717–27, Under-Sec of State North 1744–46, Master of the Mint 1744–69; *m* (settlement 3 June 1715) Honora (*d* 1 Sept 1726), dau of William Baker, Consul at Algiers, and had, with other issue:

1 WILLIAM, **4th Viscount**

2 John (Rev); *m* Judith Pigott and had, with two daus:

(1) William; *m* Penelope, dau of John Carleton, of Woodside, Co Cork, and was *k* Battle of Saintfield during the 1798 Uprising, leaving, with other issue:

1a Lucy Esther; *m* Adml Charles Philip Boteler Bateman (*d* 23 Nov 1857)

1 Mary; *m* 20 May 1755 Rev Hon Richard Henry Roper (*see* TEYNHAM, B), and *dsp* Jan 1758

The 3rd VISCOUNT *d* 3 April 1770; his er son,

WILLIAM CHETWYND, **4th Viscount Chetwynd of Bearhaven**; *b* 25 Nov 1721; MP (Whig) Stockbridge 1747–54; *m* 28 Oct 1751 Susannah (*d* 3 March 1790), yst dau of Sir Jonathan Cope, 1st Bt (*see* 1967 edn COPE, Bt, of Hanwell), and had issue:

1 RICHARD, **5th Viscount**

2 Granville Anson CHETWYND later CHETWYND-STAPYLTON, Maj-Gen; *b* 1758; *m* 29 July 1783 Martha (*d* 20 Nov 1822), only dau of Henry Stapylton, of Wighill, Yorks, and *d* 2 Dec 1834, leaving, with other issue:

(1) Henry Richard, Maj 10th Hus; *b* Jan 1789; *m* 13 Dec 1820 Margaret (*d* 24 July 1882), dau of George Hammond, of Portland Place, W, and *d* 4 April 1859, leaving issue:

1a Henry Edward, of Shenley Lodge, Herts, JP (Herts, Middx and London); *b* 12 March 1822; *educ* Univ Coll Oxford (BA); *m* 1st 29 April 1851 Esther Charlotte (*d* 3 July 1853), only surv dau of Edward Goulburn, Serjeant-at-law, by his 2nd w Hon Esther Chetwynd (*see* below), and had issue:

1b Henry Goulburn, of Hilliers, Petworth, Sussex, JP, barrister; *b* 20 May 1852; *educ* Univ Coll Oxford (MA); *m* 1 June 1886 Mary (*d* 9 Jan 1951), dau of Charles Watkin Williams Wynn (*see* WILLIAMS-WYNN, Bt), and *d* 8 July 1926, having had issue:

1c Henry Miles, Capt RFA; *b* 21 Aug 1887; *m* 25 Oct 1915 Muriel Kathleen (who *m* 2nd 24 Nov 1921 Lt-Col Ronald Henry Antrobus, MC, DL, RA, and had issue (*see* ANTROBUS, Bt)), er dau of Richard Henry Gosling, of Hawthorn Hill, Bracknell, Berks, and *d* of wounds received in action 14 Nov 1916

1c Annora Esther; *b* 16 Sept 1889; *m* 30 March 1921 Arthur Edward Osmaston, JP, late Imp Forest Serv, India, son of John Osmaston, of Osmaston Manor, Derby, and Hawkhurst Court, Sussex, and *d* 1 Aug 1977, leaving issue. He ld 30 June 1972

1a (cont.) Henry Chetwynd-Stapylton *m* 2nd 23 Oct 1856 Ellen (*d* 27 Feb 1870), widow of Rev James Lewis Venables, of Shenley Lodge, and dau of Henry Hoyle Oddie, of Colney Ho, Herts, and had issue:

2b Miles, late Capt 7th Bn KRRC; *b* 22 June 1860; *m* 7 Feb 1888 Helen (*d* 25 Dec 1940), dau of Arthur Preston, of Norwich, and *d* 24 Sept 1933, leaving issue:

1c Philip Miles; *b* 11 Feb 1889; *educ* Radley and Pembroke Coll Cambridge (BA 1910); *m* 7 April 1920 Esmé Louise (*d* 1990), dau of William George Eveleigh, and *d* 13 Jan 1965, having had issue:

1d +Henry Philip [Henry Chetwynd-Stapylton Esq, 8 Jubilee Terrace, Chichester, W Sussex PO19 1XL]; *b* 10 Jan 1921; *educ* Radley; BArch 1952, ARIBA, FRSA, Capt IA WW II; *m* 6 Oct 1962 Elizabeth Bentinck (*d* 1992), yst dau of Ernest Edward Chambers, of Holly Hill, Ringwood, Hants, and has issue:

1e +(Henry) Edward; *b* 17 March 1966; *educ* Radley; BSc, DipTP, FRGS

1e *Diana Rachel; *b* 5 July 1970

2d Edward Miles, P/O (N) RAF WW II; *b* 17 April 1924; *k* on operations over Germany 9 Feb 1945

1d *Esmé Elizabeth [Mrs Robert Waight, Charcroft, Maddington St, Shrewton, Wilts SP3 4JL]; *b* 14 Feb 1927; *m* 16 Jan 1954 *Col Robert Edward Waight, OBE, late LI, only son of Col Dennis Edward Francis Waight, MC, 5th Fus, of Fareham, and has issue:

1e *Richard Edward Charles; *b* 18 Dec 1960; Maj LI

1e *Deborah Anne; *b* 20 Aug 1957

2c Geoffrey, Capt 4th Bn Yorks LI and Hon Capt RAF WW I (despatches); *b* 27 Dec 1892; *m* 24 Oct 1964 *Alice Mary, dau of Herbert Shaw, of Purston, Yorks

1b Beatrice; *d* unm 29 June 1954

2b Evelyn Mary; *b* 1864; *d* unm 24 May 1963

1a (cont.) Henry Chetwynd-Stapylton *m* 3rd 15 Aug 1871 Hon Sophia Catherine Chetwynd (*see* below), dau of 6th Viscount Chetwynd, and *d* 21 Jan 1900

2a Granville George, Lt-Gen and Col DCLI; *b* 22 March 1823; *m* 8 Dec 1864 Lady Barbara Emily Maria Leeson (*d* 27 April 1915), dau of 4th Earl of Milltown, KP (*see* 1967 edn), and *d* 27 April 1915, having had, with other issue:

1b Granville Joseph, Maj RAF, served in S Africa 1900–02 (two medals, seven clasps), and WW I; *b* 11 Sept 1871; *m* 17 Feb 1906 Elizabeth Grace (*d* 14 April 1930), dau of Christopher Lethbridge, of Chester Sq, SW, and was *ka* 25 Aug 1914, leaving issue:

1c +Granville Richard [Lt-Col Granville 1a Shelton Fields, Shrewsbury, Salop], Lt-Col Somerset LI; *b* 30 Aug 1909; *educ*

Charterhouse; *m* 8 Sept 1934 *Emma, yst dau of Col William Arthur Young, of Lockerley Manor, Romsey, Hants, and has issue:

1d +Richard Granville Hugh [Lt-Col Richard Chetwynd-Stayplton, Beckets House, Lapford, Crediton, Devon EX17 6PZ] Lt-Col The LI; *b* 13 Feb 1939; *educ* Charterhouse and RMA Sandhurst; *m* 10 Aug 1968 *Janet Mary Agnes, dau of Cdr Alastair Shand Cumming, RN, of Arlington Ho, Barrow-in-Furness, and has issue:

1e *Margot Emma; *b* 27 Aug 1969; *m* 6 May 1995 *Matthew Alan Walton, s of Michael Walton, of Romsey, Hants and has issue:

1f *Poppy Olivia; *b* 13 March 1997

2e *Polly Rose; *b* 16 Oct 1971

1d *Sarah Elizabeth; *b* 5 Feb 1936; *m* 17 Nov 1962 *Lt-Col Ian Guy Mathews, late 1st Bn, Somerset and Cornwall LI, yr son of Lt-Col Stanley Mathews, MC, of Cheltenham, Glos, and has issue:

1e *Nicola; *b* 15 Oct 1963

2e *Amanda; *b* 26 Sept 1965

2c (Christopher) George, Lt-Col RA WW II; *b* 31 Jan 1913; chm Northern Radio Associates 1973; *m* 28 June 1952 *Bridget, formerly w of Ian Urquhart Wilson, and dau of Harry Selwyn Dixon-Spain, of Little Massingham Manor, King's Lynn, and *d* 1988, leaving issue:

1d *Elizabeth Alice; *b* 24 Feb 1954; *m* 1979 *Lt-Col Michael Anthony Hart, MBE, QGM, The Cheshire Regt, er son of Maj R F S Hart, of Gt Clacton, Essex, and has issue:

1e *Christopher James Seymour; *b* 1984

1e *Rebecca Louise; *b* 1981

1c *Barbara Mary Elizabeth; *b* 25 Jan 1907; *m* 30 June 1934 Ronald Anthony Edward Birch, er son of Lt-Col Julius Guthlac Birch, DSO, OBE, of Bude, Cornwall, and has issue:

1d *George Anthony; *b* 1935

2d *William; *b* 1938

3d *John Montagu; *b* 1941

2b Bryan Henry, CBE (1922), Col, Staff Capt and DAAG War Office 1910–14, AAG 1919–20, cmded 1st Bn Cheshire Regt 1919–23 (ret 1930), served in S Africa 1899–1902 (despatches, two medals, seven clasps) and WW I; *b* 10 June 1873; *educ* Charterhouse and RMC Sandhurst; *m* 5 Dec 1905 Dorothy Constance (*d* 23 Aug 1942), dau of Chambré Brabazon Ponsonby, of Kilcooley Abbey (*see* BESSBOROUGH, E), and *d* 29 May 1958, leaving issue:

1c Edward Henry, Maj Cheshire Regt WW II; *b* 29 April 1912; *educ* Eton and RMC Sandhurst; *m* 18 July 1957 *Priscilla [Mrs Edward Chetwynd-Stapylton, Ewelands House, Felixkirk, Thirsk, N Yorks], dau of Maj Robert Gerald Wright, of Tunstall Grange, Richmond, Yorks, and *d* 1992, having had issue:

1d +Miles Edward [Miles Chetwynd-Staplyton Esq, 51 Marston St, Oxford]; *b* 30 June 1958; *educ* Bradfield; *m* 1987 *Caroline, dau of Jan Siwy, of Bedford Park, London, and has issue:

1e *Rachel Caroline; *b* 1992

1c *Mary Blanche [Mrs Ralph Turton, Forge Cottage, Kildale, Whitby, Yorks]; *b* 15 Sept 1910; *m* 22 Feb 1936 Ralph Meredyth Turton, TD (*d* 1988), slr, 3rd son of Maj Robert Bell Turton, of Kildale Hall, Whitby, and has:

1d *Cecilia Mary; *b* 1936; *m* 1959 *John Harold Vick Sutcliffe, CBE, of Gt Broughton Middlesborough, and has issue:

1e *Andrew Harold Wentworth of Kildale Hall; *b* 1960; *m* 1988 *Emma Elisabeth, er dau of Sir Angus Duncan Æneas Stirling (*see* DUNMORE, E), and has had issue:

1f Ralph Andrew Æneas; *b* 1991; *d* 1992

1f *Rose Cecilia; *b* 1990

2f *Helena Tertia Morar; *b* 1993

3f *Laura Mary; *b* 1995

2e *John Ralph Beaumont; *b* 1964; *m* 1991 *Marcella, yr dau of Giovanni Pellegrino, of Milan, and has issue:

1f *Edward John Ralph; *b* 1995

1f *Francesca Renata; *b* 1993

3e *Mark David Chetwynd; *b* 1967

1e *Henrietta Cecilia; *b* 1961; *m* 1987 *Matthew Williams, er son of Sir John Williams, of Hanging Langford, Wilts, and has issue:

1f *Joshua John Ralph; *b* 1989

2f *Jonathan Frederick Matthew; *b* 1991

1f *Katherine Mary Elizabeth; *b* 1994

2d *Lavinia Rose [Lady Horsbrugh-Porter, Bowers Croft, Coleshill, Amersham, Bucks HP7 0LS]; *b* 1939; *m* 1964 *Sir John Simon Horsbrugh-Porter, 4th Bt (*qv*), and has issue

3d *Victoria Harriet Lucy [The Rt Hon The Viscountess Bridgeman, Watley House, Sparsholt, Hants; 19 Chepstow Rd, London W2]; *b* 1942; *educ* Trin Coll Dublin (MA); *m* 1966 *3rd Viscount Bridgeman (*qv*), and has issue

4d *Sylvia Dorothy [Mrs Martin Oakley, 24 Warnborough Rd, Oxford]; *b* 1947; *m* 1st 1977 David Laurence (Jeremy) Booth; *m* 2nd 1983 *Martin Oakley, and has issue:

1e *Oliver Ronald; *b* 1984

2e *Edmund Ralph; *b* 1986

1e *Esther Amelia Blanche; *b* 1990

1b Barbara Margaret; *d* unm 4 Jan 1955

3a William (Rev), MA Oxford, Hon Canon of Rochester, and Rector of Hallaton, Leics, 1893–1907; *b* 15 May 1825; *m* 1st 26 Oct 1852 Elizabeth Biscoe (*d* 18 Sept 1893), dau of Rev Robert Tritton (*see* TRITTON, Bt); *m* 2nd 21 April 1898 Mary Elizabeth (*d* 1 May 1921), only dau of Fred Johnson, and *d* 4 March 1919, having by his 1st w had:

1b Edward; *b* 10 July 1855; *m* 1st 27 Sept 1879 Beatrice Mary (*d* 13 Nov 1923), dau of Henry Cowie, of Calcutta; *m* 2nd 12 Aug 1924 Elizabeth Gordon (*d* 31 March 1940), widow of Maj Cavaliere Scipione Giordano, of Turin, Italy, and dau of Capt Robert W Ker, RNR, and *d* 25 April 1938, having by his 1st w had issue:

1c Richard; *b* 28 June 1880; *m* 21 Jan 1915 Vera Helen (*d* 28 April 1959), dau of Andrew Maitland-Makgill-Crichton (*see* LAUDERDALE, E), and *d* 26 April 1945, leaving issue:

1d Miles Richard John, DFC, F/Lt RAFVR WW II; *b* 10 May 1918; *educ* Winchester and Magdalene Coll Cambridge; *d* unm 9 Feb 1970

2d Edward Mark, Maj KRRC WW II (despatches); *b* 23 Nov 1919; *educ* Winchester and Magdalene Coll Cambridge; *m* 20 Feb 1946 *Anne Phillida, late WRNS [Mrs Edward Chetwynd-Stapylton, 110 Western Rd, Lewes, E Sussex BN7 1RR] dau of Sir Edward Pease, 2nd Bt (*see* PEASE, Bt, of Hutton Lowcross), and *d* 1 July 1995 leaving:

1e *Judy Anne [Mrs John Lambert, 5 Bridgefield Rd, Cheam, Surrey SM1 2DG]; *b* 22 April 1948; *m* 1977 *John Trevor Lambert, and has issue:

1f *Sophie Alice Doanda; *b* 1977

2f *Hannah Madeleine Harriet; *b* 1983

2e *Phillida Helen [Ms Phillida Chetwynd-Stapylton, Brackmound House, Castle Precincts, E Sussex BN7 1YT]; *b* 20 Dec 1949

3e *Joanna Elizabeth [Mrs Joanna Fuller, 30 Lansdowne Place, Lewes, E Sussex BN7 2JU]; *b* 19 July 1951; *m* 1978 (*divorce* 1983) Kim Stephen Fuller and has:

1f *Jessie Alison; *b* 1980

1d Helen; *b* 16 Jan 1916; *m* 10 Jan 1939 Lt-Col Baron Adeane, GCB, GCVO, PC, (LP, *d* 1984), and *d* Aug 1994, having had:

1e *(George) Edward, CVO (1985) [The Hon Edward Adeane CVO, B4 Albany, Piccadilly, London W1V 9RE]; *b* 4 Oct 1939; *educ* Eton and Magdalene Coll Cambridge (BA); Page of Honour to HM THE QUEEN 1954–56, barrister Middle Temple 1962; Priv Sec to HRH THE PRINCE OF WALES 1979–85 and HRH THE PRINCESS OF WALES 1984–85, dir Hambros Bank

1e Rosemary Jane; *b* 22 Dec 1942; *d* 10 May 1952

2d Vera Rosemary; *b* 23 March 1924; *m* 30 March 1946 (*divorce* 1970) Maj Derek Leslie Lloyd, MC, 5th Fus (*d* 1990), est son of Leslie S Lloyd, of Manatons, St George's Hill, Weybridge, and *d* 13 Oct 1996, leaving:

1e *Julian Richard Leslie [Julian Lloyd Esq, The Glebe, Leixlip, Co Kildare, Ireland]; *b* 7 March 1947; *educ* Eton; *m* 1972 *Hon Victoria Mary Ormsby-Gore, dau of 5th Baron Harlech (*qv*), and has issue:

1f *Lester Guy Julian; *b* 1982

1f *Poppy Zita Aline; *b* 1972

2f *Zita Crystal Rosemary; *b* 1974

1e *Carolyn Rosemary [Mrs John Hall, The Old Vicarage, Sprey-ton, Crediton, Devon EX17 5AL]; *b* 28 May 1948; *m* 1978 *John Derek Hall, son of Sidney Hall, and has issue:

1f *Jack Julian Bunker; *b* 1980

1f *Rosie Niamh; *b* 1977

2e *Althea Victoria; *b* 11 Feb 1950; *m* 1977 *Roderick David Alasdair Boyle and has issue (*see* GLASGOW, E)

2c William Eric, Capt 8th Serv Bn London Regt; *b* 10 Nov 1895; *m* 1st 2 Feb 1924 Vivienne (*d* 18 Oct 1961), est dau of Harry Baker Spurling, of Upton Park, Slough; *m* 2nd 12 Nov 1962 Audrey Margaret Read (*d* 17 July 1983), widow of Ian Theodore Bright Cash and dau of Percival Hardy, of 12 Curzon St, W1, and *d* 30 Dec 1978, having by 1st w had issue:

1d *Mary Violet, late WRNS; *b* 18 Sept 1926; *m* 24 Sept 1955 *Richard Nevill Vaughan Fairbank, TD, of Coopers Green, Windlesham, Surrey, est son of Lt-Col Henry Nevill Fairbank, DSO, MC, DL, of The Grove, Clifton, Bristol, and has issue:

1e *David Richard Stapylton [David Fairbank Esq, Perry Leigh, Grove Rd, Selling, Faversham, Kent ME13 9RN]; *b* 14 Nov 1956; *m* 1981 *Clare Arabella, er dau of Peter Leonard Eckersley (*see* HARDY, Bt), and has:

1f *Thomas David Peter; *b* 25 Oct 1984

1f *Arabella Clare Mary; *b* 11 Jan 1987

2e *Anthony William Vaughan; *b* 2 Aug 1963; *m* 1989 *Harriet Caroline, er dau of Cdr Oliver Lascelles, MBE, DSC, RN (*see* HAREWOOD, E), and has issue:

1f *Emily Rose; *b* 1991

2f *Olivia Alice; *b* 1992

1e *(Victoria) Mary Nevill [Mrs James Thompson, Milton Bank Farm, Sandfield Lane, Acton Bridge, Northwich, Cheshire]; *b* 26 March 1959; *m* 1983 *James Harman Thompson, late Maj Queen's Roy Irish Hussars, and has issue:

1f *William James Richard; *b* 1986

2f *Jack Peter; *b* 1992

1f *Rosanna Patricia Mary; *b* 1988

1c Lilian Beatrice; *b* 14 Aug 1881; *m* 28 Sept 1901 Harold Hallocombe Gordon, son of John Gordon, and *d* 23 Jan 1965, leaving issue. He *d* 24 July 1945

2c Dorothy; *b* 23 Dec 1883; *m* 1st 13 Oct 1909 Lt-Cdr Walter John Fletcher, RN, 3rd son of Lionel John William Fletcher, DL, and had issue. He *d* 12 May 1916. She *m* 2nd 18 Sept 1919 William Miskin, est son of Arthur Miskin, of Chart Sutton, Kent

3c Grace Mary; *b* 24 Aug 1887; *m* 14 Oct 1911 Edgar Reginald Godson (*d* 8 April 1963), son of Clement Godson, MD, and had issue:

1d *Clement Patrick Chetwynd; *b* 17 Feb 1913; *educ* Charterhouse; *m* 27 March 1941 *Dorothy Frances, dau of Lt-Col George Frederick Graham, MD, FRCSI, IMS, and has issue:

1e *Mark Chetwynd, Lt RTR; *b* 8 Feb 1943; *educ* Charterhouse

2e *Antony Graham; *b* 9 March 1946; *educ* Bradfield

3e *Richard Hugh; *b* 26 March 1947; *educ* Bradfield

2d Michael Stapylton, DSC, Lt-Cdr (A) RN WW II (despatches); *b* 24 Aug 1916; *ka* 12 May 1945

4c Vera; *b* 22 Jan 1890; *m* 1st 7 July 1909 Edgar William Hutton, of Hainford Lodge, Norfolk, only son of Col Edmund Bacon Hutton, Roy Dragoons, and had a s and one dau. He *d* 13 Feb 1923. She *m* 2nd 27 Sept 1924 Arthur Henry Habgood, DSO, MB, BCh, late Lt-Col RAMC (SR), er son of Dr Henry Habgood, of Stafford Ho, Eastbourne, and *d* 9 Dec 1968, leaving further issue:

1d *JOHN STAPYLTON HABGOOD, *cr* a BARON (LP, *qv*)

1d *Pamela; *b* 24 Oct 1925; *m* 1948 *Joseph Cyril Talbot Garman, yr son of Edmund Garman, of Hythe, Kent, and has issue

2b Frederick; *b* 15 Oct 1857; *m* 27 June 1891 Maud (*d* 30 Aug 1948), dau of William H Morrison, of Newport, RI, USA, and *d* 21 April 1942, having had issue:

1c Alan; *b* 14 June 1892; *d* 27 Sept 1897

1c Helen Maud; *b* 13 March 1895; *m* 15 Feb 1915 12th Lord Rollo (*qv*) and *d* 15 Aug 1928, leaving issue

3b Granville; *b* 11 Dec 1858; *m* 15 Dec 1885 Elizabeth (*d* 29 June 1943), dau of James Routledge, and *d* 29 Oct 1902, leaving issue:

1c Granville Brian, CB (1949), OBE (1946), TD, DL (Surrey 1931), JP (Surrey 1941), High Sheriff 1952–53, Col (ret), 5th Bn E Surrey Regt (TA), Hon Col 381 Light Regt RA (TA) 1947–57, served WW I (Bde Maj 1916, GSO 1917), and WW II (SE Cmd Welfare Offr 1943–44), chm TA&AFA Surrey 1931; *b* 19 Sept 1887; *educ* Charterhouse; *m* 14 June 1922 Catherine (*d* 1981), dau of Herbert Lyne, of Newport, Mon, and *d* 20 Jan 1964, leaving issue:

1d *Lucy [Mrs Lucy Robinson, Jesus Fellowship Community, Festal Grange, Church Rd, Pattishall, nr Towcester, Northants]; *b* 17 May 1923; *m* 12 May 1945 (*divorce* 1980) F/O Paul Anthony Robinson, RAFVR, yst son of Rufus Robinson, of Kettering, and has issue:

1e *Nigel Anthony; *b* 18 March 1946; *m* 31 July 1971 (*divorce* 1986) Sandra Anne Coggs, and has issue:

1f *Howard Charles; *b* 1978

1f *Suzanne Louise; *b* 1974

1e *Jennifer Chetwynd; *b* 16 July 1949; *m* 1974 *Malcolm Colin Bowden, and has issue:

1f *David; *b* 1981

1f *Josephine; *b* 1980

2d *Bridget [Mrs John Sewter, Harlequin Cottage, High St, Broughton, Stockbridge, Hants]; *b* 27 Oct 1924; served WW II 1942–46 in WAAF; *m* 1st 12 June 1948 Dennis Worsley Wilks, MB, BS Lond (*d* 4 May 1969), son of William Harrison Worsley Wilks, of Thames Ditton; *m* 2nd 1978 *John Baron Sewter, and by 1st husb has issue:

1e *David Michael Worsley; *b* 26 May 1949; *educ* St John's Leatherhead; MB, BS; *m* 1972 (*divorce* 1992) Patricia Dorothea Joyce, dau of Charles Anthony Philip Hackforth, DSO, and has issue:

1f *Anthony Peter Worsley; *b* 1983

1f *Philippa Carla; *b* 1977

2f *Nicola Catherine; *b* 1980

2e Peter Brian Chetwynd; *b* 24 Jan 1951; *educ* Cranleigh and Exeter Coll Oxford; *d* 1972

3e *John Richard Stapylton; *b* 16 July 1955; *educ* Cranleigh and Balliol Coll Oxford (MA, ARCM); *m* 1983 *Suzan Jane Scothern, and has issue:

1f *Naren Richard; *b* 1985

4e *Nicholas Paul; *b* 28 Feb 1960; *educ* Ch Ch Oxford (BA)

3d *Mary Elizabeth [Mrs Grahame Nicholls, 12A Lillington Ave, Royal Leamington Spa, Warwicks CV32 5UJ]; *b* 8 Aug 1926; *m* 28 May 1949 Grahame Archer Nicholls, BSc (Ag) (*d* 22 Aug 1997), son of Stanley Harold Nicholls, of Estcourt, Hadley Wood, and has issue:

1e *Granville Richard; *b* 27 July 1952; *educ* The Cathedral Sch, Salisbury, and Dauntsey's Sch

2e *David Chetwynd; *b* 7 April 1957; *m* 1988 *Karen Jane Hodgkinson

1e *Janet Archer; *b* 22 June 1950

1c Ella Mabel, JP; *b* 22 Nov 1889; *m* 14 June 1911 Col Sir (William) Alan Gillett, TD, DL, est son of William Edward Gillett, of Streatham, Surrey, and *d* June 1974, leaving issue (*see* TOLLEMACHE, Bt). He *d* 18 Feb 1959

1b Ella; *m* 5 June 1886 Henry Cockburn, est son of Archibald William Cockburn, and *d* 27 Jan 1938, leaving issue. He *d* 14 Jan 1936

1a Margaret Diana; *m* 25 Sept 1856 George Carnac Barnes, CB, Commr of the Cis-Sutlej States, East Indies, and *d* 1 July 1927, leaving issue. He *d* 13 May 1961

1 Susannah; *m* 6 June 1782 Munbee Goulburn, of Jamaica, and *d* 1818. He *d* 1790

2 Anderlechtia Clarissa; *m* 2 May 1806, as his 2nd w, Lord Robert Seymour, 3rd son of 1st Marquess of Hertford, KG (*qv*), and *dsp* 3 June 1855 aged 90

The 4th VISCOUNT *d* 12 Nov 1791; his est son,

RICHARD CHETWYND, **5th Viscount Chetwynd of Bearhaven**; *b* 29 Sept 1757; *m* 30 July 1791 Charlotte (*d* 7 April 1845), dau of Thomas Cartwright, of Aynho, Northants, and had, with other issue:

1 RICHARD WALTER, **6th Viscount**

1 Esther; *m* 13 Aug 1825 Edward Goulburn, DCL, Serjeant-at-law, and *d* 26 March 1829, leaving issue, He *d* 24 Aug 1868

The 5th VISCOUNT *d* 27 Feb 1821; his son,

RICHARD WALTER CHETWYND, **6th Viscount Chetwynd of Bearhaven**; *b* 13 Dec 1800; *m* 1st 30 Aug 1822 Mary (*d* 5 Dec 1857), dau of Robert Moss and niece of Rt Rev Charles Moss, Bishop of Oxford; *m* 2nd 24 Sept 1861 Mary (*dsp* 7 June 1901), only surv dau of John Hussey, DL, JP, Recorder of Lyme Regis, and *d* 6 Dec 1879, having by his 1st w had, with other issue:

1 RICHARD WALTER CHETWYND, **7th Viscount Chetwynd of Bearhaven**, DL Staffs; 14th Dragoons; *b* 26 July 1823; *m* 16 March 1858 Harriet Johanna (*d* 12 Jan 1898), est dau of Walter Campbell, of Sunderland, and *d* 23 Jan 1911, having had issue:

(1) Richard Walter, Maj 3rd Bn S Staffs Regt; *b* 27 Nov 1859; *m* 8 Jan 1889 (*divorce* 1900) Florence Mary (*d* 28 April 1955), only dau of Col Tom Naylor Leyland, of Nantclwyd, and *dvp* 6 March 1908, leaving issue:

1a Mary Eleanora; *b* 7 March 1890; *m* 6 Oct 1917, as his 2nd w, Maj Robert Charles Otter, VD, DL, JP, of Royston Manor, Clayworth, Retford, Notts, 2nd son of Henry Otter, of Swinton Ho, Yorks, and *d* 30 Oct 1936, leaving issue. He *d* 25 Oct 1939

2a Amélie Mary; *b* 2 Feb 1892; *m* 17 Sept 1912 Claude Edward Reynard, late Capt 12th Lancers and Maj E Riding Yeo, est son of Frederick Reynard, DL, JP, of Sunderlandwick and Hob Green, Yorks, and had issue

(1) Eleonora, MBE (1920); *m* 29 June 1907 James Lloyd-Anstruther, of Knapp Ho, Gillingham, Dorset, 3rd son of Capt James Hamilton Lloyd-Anstruther, of Hintlesham Hall, Ipswich (*see* ANSTRUTHER, Bt), and *dsp* 20 Feb 1949

(2) Katherine Frances; *m* 6 June 1889 George Blezard, only son of Robert Blezard, JP, of Pool Park, Ruthin, and *d* 29 June 1949, leaving issue. He *d* 26 Jan 1928

2 Henry Weyland, Capt RN; *b* 8 Oct 1829; *m* 8 Feb 1858 Julia Bosville (*d* 17 Oct 1901), dau of Duncan Davidson, of Tulloch, by his 1st w, est dau of 3rd Lord Macdonald of the Isles (*qv*), and *d* 27 Nov 1893, leaving issue:

(1) Henry Goulburn Willoughby, AMICE; *b* 12 Dec 1858; *m* 7 Nov 1893 Eva Constance Elizabeth Fanny (*d* 16 Aug 1936), er dau of Augustus Berney, of Bracon Hall, Norwich, and *d* 1 July 1909, leaving issue:

1a Dorothy Constance; *b* 13 Nov 1895; *m* 20 Oct 1921 Hon Harry Robert Chichester Balfour, son of 1st Baron Kinross (*qv*), and *d* 8 Nov 1963, leaving issue

2a *Sylvia Evelyn; *b* 4 Sept 1902; *educ* Newnham Coll Cambridge (MA); *m* 22 Dec 1931 Anthony Makower (*d* 1984), MA, AIMM, son of Stanley Victor Makower, of Steep, Petersfield, and has issue:

1b *Peter [Peter Makower Esq, 2 Lillian Rd, Barnes, London SW13]; *b* 12 Sept 1932; *educ* Trin Coll Cambridge (BA 1955, MA 1959); ARIBA 1961, FRIBA, MRTPI; *m* 20 Aug 1960 *Katharine, MA Oxford, er dau of James Howarthe Paul Chadburn, MBE, BLitt, of Church Ho, Bisley, Glos, and has had issue:

1c *Andrew; *b* 5 Oct 1961

2c *Timothy; *b* 14 June 1965

1c Mary; *b* 5 Jan 1963; *d* 1979

2b *Michael Stanley [Michael Makower Esq, Gogar House, Blairlogie, by Stirling FK9 5QB]; *b* 12 Sept 1936; *educ* Trin Coll Cambridge (BA 1959, MA 1963), and LSE (Dip OR 1962); *m* 1 Oct 1960 *Selina Elizabeth, 5th dau of Henry Vernon Flower Barran (*see* BARRAN, Bt), and has:

1c *Sophia Galiena; *b* 26 March 1962

2c *Janet Elizabeth Agnes; *b* 10 Jan 1964; *m* 30 March 1991 *Darby Edwards, s of Brian Darby Edwards, and has issue:

1d *Florence Isabel; *b* 2 Sept 1993

2d *Phoebe Mary; *b* 9 May 1996

3c *Margaret Eleanor; *b* 7 June 1966

3b *Malory (Rev) [The Rev Canon Dr Malory Makower, 9 Dunverlin Close, Norwich NR4 6HS], Deacon 1966, Priest 1967, Assist Curate St Paul's Onslow Sq, Tutor Ridley Hall 1969– pncpl E Anglian ministerial trg course; team Vicar Gt Yarmouth, pncpl Norwich Diocese local non-stipendiary ministry course, ret 1997; *b* 6 June 1938; *educ* Dublin U (BA 1961, MA) and St John's Coll Oxford (MA, DPhil 1964); *m* 2 Sept 1967 (*divorce* 1987) Mary Noel, dau of Ralph Edward Stokes, of Malvern, Worcs, and has:

1c *Philip; *b* 27 Sept 1969

2c *William; *b* 1976

1c *Caroline; *b* 16 July 1968

2c *Sandra; *b* 1972

1b *Anne [Mrs Christopher Fitz-Simon, 8 Richmond Hill, Monkstown, Dublin, Ireland]; *b* 9 June 1934; *educ* Dublin U (BA 1956); *m* 15 May 1964 *Christopher Lennox Killen O'Connell Fitz-Simon, MA, er son of Lt-Col Christopher Richard Daniel Manners O'Connell Fitz-Simon, MC, of Glencullen Ho, Co Dublin, and has issue:

1c *Adrian Christopher; *b* 1967

1c *Vanessa Una; *b* 1965

3a Enid Elizabeth; *b* 29 July 1907; *m* 19 Sept 1933 Rev Eric Campbell Douglas, 5th son of Dr Justyn G D Douglas, and has issue. He *d* 12 July 1971, aged 86

(2) GODFREY JOHN BOYLE, **8th Viscount**

(3) Walter James Bosville (Rev), OBE; *b* 30 April 1865; granted with surv siblings 4 May 1911 rank of viscount's daus/yr s; Vicar Penistone with Midhope 1913–15, Rector Clifton with Glapton, Nottingham 1915, Lt Berks Yeo Cav; *m* 5 March 1890 Ashton Yate (*d* 2 April 1947), dau of Ashton Benyon, of Stetchworth Park, Cambs, and *d* 11 Feb 1920

(4) Louis Wentworth Pakington, Capt RN; *b* 15 Dec 1866; *m* 17 Jan 1903 Augusta Frances Beverley (*d* 23 July 1955), yr dau of E R Robinson, of New York, and *d* 18 April 1914, leaving issue:

1a Wentworth Randolph, MBE (1954), Maj Gren Gds WW II, War Office 1945–56; *b* 16 Dec 1903; *educ* Eton and New Coll Oxford; *m* 1st 26 Sept 1931 (*divorce* 1964) Bridget (*d* 28 Nov 1970), dau of Col Theobald Alfred Walsh, DSO, and had issue:

1b +Rupert Milo Talbot [Rupert Chetwynd Esq, The New Stables, Ingestre, nr Stafford], Lt Gren Gds; *b* 7 Jan 1934; *educ* Stowe; *m* 1st 22 Aug 1956 (*divorce* 1970) Antonia, only child of Denis Clark, DFC, of 32 Tite St, SW3, and has issue:

1c +Rupert Jonathan Richard; *b* 11 April 1957

2c +Dominic Jeremy; *b* 19 April 1959

3c +Crispin; *b* 19 Jan 1961

4c +Alexander Anthony; *b* 9 May 1964

1c *Persephone Catherine; *b* 30 Aug 1965
1b (cont.) Rupert Chetwynd *m* 2nd 1970 *Luciana Maria, er dau of Count Ernest Arrighi, and has further issue:
5c +Aaron St George Francesco Arrighi; *b* 1971
2c *Alalia; *b* 19–
2b +Tom Wentworth Guy [Tom Chetwynd Esq, 12 Mornington Terr, London NW1 7RR], late 2nd Lt 14th/20th King's Hus; *b* 7 April 1938; *m* 9 Oct 1959 *Hélène, dau of Baron Pierre de Bosmelet, of Château de Bosmelet, Auffay, SM, France, and has issue:
1c *Yolanda; *b* 16 Aug 1960; *m* 29 Dec 1987 *Suresh Advani and has:
1d *Madhu; *b* 12 Aug 1989
1d *Diana; *b* 24 Sept 1995
2c *Natasha; *b* 2 Nov 1961; *m* 10 Sept 1983 *Mark Latimer and has:
1d *Jack; *b* 12 Oct 1985
2d *Joseph; *b* 23 Dec 1992
3c *Bridget; *b* 9 June 1966; *m* 6 July 1985 *Daniel Cairns and has:
1d *Oliver; *b* 29 Jan 1997
1d *Isobel; *b* 7 April 1992
1a (cont.) Maj Wentworth Chetwynd *m* 2nd 18 July 1964 *Mary, dau of Francis Rosser, and *d* 1987
2a Philip Henry; *b* 28 Jan 1906; *d* 1 Nov 1933
1a Elizabeth Julia; *b* 25 Nov 1907; *d* unm 9 Nov 1961
2a *Victoria Edith Joan; *b* 24 May 1912; *m* 9 March 1933 (*divorce* 1945) Archibald William Laurence Patrick Kirwan, CMG, TD, BLitt, son of Patrick Kirwan, and has issue:
1b *Anne Jennifer; *b* 4 Dec 1933; *m* 14 Aug 1965 *Antony Martin Preston
(1) Ida Helen Lizzie; *m* 14 Nov 1899 Archibald William Merry, RHG, of Belladrum, Beauly, and 18 Hill St, W1, son of James Merry, DL, JP, MP, of Belladrum, Inverness-shire, and *d* 3 Jan 1950, leaving issue. He *d* 16 Aug 1933
(2) Katharine Adelaide, JP (1931); *m* 8 Nov 1893 Douglas Vickers, of Tulloch Castle, Dingwall, and Chapel Ho, Charles St, Berkeley Sq, est son of Col Thomas Edward Vickers, CB, of Bolsover Hill, Sheffield, and *d* 24 Aug 1944, leaving issue. He *d* 23 Nov 1937
(3) Margaret Diana Hopetoun; *m* 2 June 1894 Sir Thomas Stanley Birkin, 2nd Bt (*qv*), of Ruddington Grange, Nottingham, and *d* 24 July 1927, leaving issue
3 Charles Cornwallis, Maj 10th Regt; *b* 17 Sept 1834; *m* 30 Oct 1860 Emily Hannah (*d* 24 Sept 1919), only dau of W H Blaauw, of Beechland, Sussex, and *d* 31 March 1884, leaving with other issue:
(1) Emily Mary Frances; *d* unm 29 Nov 1947
(2) Margaret Adelaide; *m* 5 June 1890 Frank Bousfield Hudson, of Oakwood, Roundhay, Leeds, son of Henry Hudson, of Roundhay, Yorks, and *d* 21 Jan 1951, leaving issue. He *d* May 1912
(3) Louisa Charlotte; *d* unm 1 March 1967, aged 98
(4) Julia Alice, Sister of Bethany; *d* unm 19 Jan 1959, aged 88
(5) Katharine Philippa; *m* 1 Sept 1908 Rev Knowlton Harold Hampshire, 3rd son of Rev William Knowlton Hampshire, and *d* 27 April 1956, leaving issue. He *d* 1914
1 Sophia Catherine; *m* 15 Aug 1871 Henry Chetwynd-Stapylton, of Shenley Lodge, Herts (*see* above), and *dsp* 3 May 1899
2 Charlotte Adelaide; *m* 5 July 1855 Rev James Augustus Atkinson, MA, DCL, Vicar of St Michael's, Coventry, and Hon Canon of Manchester, and *d* 16 Sept 1912 leaving issue. He *d* 18 Nov 1911
The 8th VISCOUNT's n,
GODFREY JOHN BOYLE CHETWYND, **8th Viscount Chetwynd of Bearhaven**, CH, JP (W R Yorks); md National Shell Filling Factory, Chilwell, Notts 1915–19; *b* 3 Oct 1863; *m* 1st 12 April 1893 (*divorce*) Hilda, dau of Baron George von Alvensleben Rusteberg and gdau of Gen Sir Beauchamp Walker, KCB; *m* 2nd 10 Feb 1904 Hon Mary Eden (*d* 22 Jan 1925), 3rd dau of 4th Baron Auckland (*qv*), and by her had issue:
1 ADAM DUNCAN, **9th Viscount**
2 John Julian; *b* 10 Aug 1906; *educ* Eton and King's Coll Cambridge; T/Sec Br Embassy Washington; *m* 6 April 1937 Margaret Agnes (*d* 1993), est dau of Maj-Gen Hugh Clement Sutton, CB, CMG (*see* SUTTON, Bt), and *d* 22 April 1966, leaving issue:
(1) Richard Walter; *b* 23 Feb 1938; *educ* Eton; *m* 7 April 1964 Judith Mary (*d* 21 March 1998), only dau of Capt Selwyn Victor Jephson, RN, of The Red Ho, Hambledon, Hants, and *d* 1990, leaving issue:
1a +Mark Richard; *b* 1972
1a *Katharine Margaret [Mrs Michael Toogood, 102 Ritherdon Rd, London SW17 8QQ]; *b* 24 June 1965; *m* 1990 *Michael William Toogood, est son of James Anthony Gordon Toogood, and has:
1b *William Richard Stanley; *b* 1 June 1996
1b *Emma
2b *Alexandra
2a *Sarah Alexandra; *b* 6 Oct 1967
(2) +John Hugh [John Chetwynd Esq, South Hay Cottage, Kingsley, Borden, Hants]; *b* 29 May 1942; *educ* Stowe; *m* 1st 23 April 1966 (*divorce* 1971) Denyse Jacqueline, only dau of Col H de Frisching, of Berne, Switzerland, and has issue:
1a +Hugh Nigel; *b* 1967
2a +Philip Mark; *b* 27 March 1969
(2) (cont.) John Chetwynd *m* 2nd 8 May 1973 (*divorce* 1977) Caroline L, er dau of John Fitzwilliams, of Greatford, Stamford, Lincs; *m* 3rd 1983 *Mrs Lorna Butler (née Menzies), and has further issue:
1a *Fleur Alicia Camilla; *b* 1983
1 (Mary Diana) Eve; *b* 19 July 1908; SRN, SCM, MTD, HV; Hon Life Memb Roy Coll of Nursing, 1st pres E Herts br of RCN; *d* 6 Feb 1997
The 8th VISCOUNT *d* 22 March 1936; his son,
ADAM DUNCAN CHETWYND, **9th Viscount Chetwynd of Bearhaven**, FSA; *educ* Eton and New Coll Oxford; Hon Lt-Col RA WW II (2nd Lt RA (TA) May 1939, Capt Sept 1939, Maj 1941, Lt-Col 1946), staff Control Cmmn Germany 1947–53; *b* 14 Nov 1904; *m* 1st 28 April 1928 (*divorce* 1951) Joan Gilbert (*d* 1979) (formerly S/O WAAF), formerly w of Victor Alexander Charles Findlay and only child of Herbert Alexander Casson, CSI, of Tyn-y-Coed, Arthog, Merionethshire, and had issue:
1 ADAM RICHARD JOHN CASSON CHETWYND, **10th and present Viscount Chetwynd of Bearhaven**
1 *Philippa Mary Agnes Joan [The Hon Mrs Luard, Maidenford, Goodleigh, nr Barnstaple, Devon EX32 7NG]; *b* 17 Nov 1930; *m* 4 July 1959 *Maj John Anthony Hawtrey Luard, Coldstream Gds, only son of Richard Lestocq Erskine Luard, of The Red Lion, Hellidon, Daventry, Northants, and has issue:
(1) *David Andrew John; *b* 6 Oct 1961
(1) *Sophia Mary [Mrs Gianfranco Goddi, 57 Oxford Gdns, London W10]; *b* 6 June 1960; *m* 1982 *Gianfranco Goddi, only son of Sra Mele-Goddi, of Rome, and has issue:
1a *Lucrezia Ruth Jessica; *b* 1983
2 Julian Isabella; *b* 9 Dec 1932; *m* 6 Feb 1960 *Philip David Miles, yr son of Maj Walter Harold Miles, MBE, of North Park Farm, Godstone, Surrey, by his w Joyce Marjorie, est dau of Sir Bernard Eyre Greenwell, 2nd Bt, MBE (*qv*), and had issue:
(1) *Charles Philip Chetwynd; *b* 15 Oct 1962
(1) *Sara Isabella; *b* 6 Jan 1961
The **9th Viscount** *m* 2nd 17 Jan 1952 Dorothea Marianne, MBE, OStJ (*d* 1990), dau of Lt-Col Angus Colin Duncan-Johnstone, MBE, ED, of Oakwood, Hermitage, Berks, and *d* 12 June 1965, having by her had issue:
3 *Catherine Sophia Marianne; *b* 5 Oct 1956
4 *Frances Diana Dorothea; *b* 19 Jan 1959

CHETWYND, Bt

Arms: Quarterly, 1st and 4th, az. a chevron between three mullets or; 2nd and 3rd, arg. two chevrons gu. **Motto:** *Quod Deus vult fiet* ('What God wills, let it be done'). **Creation:** Bt. (GB) 1 May 1795.

SIR ARTHUR RALPH TALBOT CHETWYND, 8TH BT, of Brocton Hall, Staffs [Sir Arthur Chetwynd Bt, 117 King St East, Apt 3, Coburg, Ontario K9A 1L2, Canada]; *b* 28 Oct 1913; *s* unc 1972; *educ* Vernon Prep Sch Vernon BC and U of BC; dir Remedial Gymnastics BC Workmen's Compensation Bd 1942, ch instructor medical reconditioning RCAF 1943–45, Associate Physical and Health Educn U of Toronto, publicity offr U of Toronto Athletic Assoc 1946–52, chm Chetwynd Films Ltd Toronto 1977– (fndr-pres and gen manager 1950–76), pres: Brocton Hall Communications Toronto 1978–88, Post Productions Inc; KCLJ; *m* 26 Aug 1940 *Marjory May MacDonald, est dau of Robert Bruce Lang, of Vancouver, BC, and has issue:
1 +ROBIN JOHN TALBOT; *b* 21 Aug 1941; film producer Chetwynd Films Ltd; *m* 23 Sept 1967 *Heather Helen, dau of George Bayliss Lothian, of Baie d'Urfe, Quebec, and has:
(1) +Peter James Talbot; *b* 1973
(1) *Kimberly Anne; *b* 1971
2 +(William) Richard Talbot [Richard Chetwynd Esq, 1090 Sycamore Cres, Oshawa, Ontario L1G 6S7, Canada]; *b* 18 June 1946; *m* 1971 *Patricia Anne, dau of Geoffrey Senior, of Manchester, and has issue:
(1) +Hugh Geoffrey Talbot; *b* 1973
(2) +Brian William Talbot, *b* 1977

Lineage: JOHN CHETWYND, of Ingestre (*see* CHETWYND, V); had a 4th s:
THOMAS CHETWYND, of Rugeley, Staffs; *m* Dorothy, dau of Walter Colman, of Cannock, Staffs, and *d* 1633, leaving, with other issue:
1 William, merchant at Bristol; *m* Elizabeth Long and *d* 1651, leaving:
(1) William, of Rugeley, MP Stafford; *d* unm 9 April 1691
(2) Edward
(1) Mary
(2) Elizabeth; *m* John Hill, merchant of Bristol
2 RALPH, of whom presently
3 Thomas, of Heywood; *m* 1st Mary, dau of Francis Congreve, of Stretton, and had a dau (Anne, *m* Thomas Melward); *m* 2nd Dorothy, dau of Robert Harcourt, and *d* Sept 1641, leaving William, of Heywood, and Mary

The 2nd s,

RALPH CHETWYND; *m* Dorothy, dau and coheir of Sir William Twysden, and *d* 1653, leaving issue:

1 Charles, of Salters Hall and St James's St; *m* Sarah, dau of Gamaliel Purefoy, of Wolverhill, Staffs, and *d* 1719, leaving issue

2 RICHARD, of whom presently

3 John; *d* 1692, leaving a s, Ralph, and dau, Sarah

The 2nd son,

RICHARD CHETWYND, of Rugeley; *m* Ann, dau of William Launder, of Rugeley, and widow of William Sprott, and *d* 1693, leaving, with a yr s (Francis, of the Middle Temple, *m* 1730 Elizabeth Gordon):

WALTER CHETWYND, of Brocton, Staffs; *m* Mary (*d* 1761), dau of William Sneyd, of Keele, Staffs, and *d* 7 Nov 1750, leaving:

WILLIAM CHETWYND, of Brocton; *m* 1738 Martha, only dau of James St Amand, of St Paul's, Covent Garden, and widow of Thomas Hesketh, of Rufford, and had, with another s (James, *d* unm 1 March 1774):

Sir George Chetwynd, 1st Bt (GB), so *cr* 1 May 1795, of Brocton; *b* 26 July 1739; ktd 1787, Clerk to PC; *m* 1782 Jane (*d* 1841 aged 83), dau of Richard Bantin, of Little Faringdon, Berks, and had, with other issue:

1 GEORGE (Sir) **2nd Bt**

2 William Fawkener, of Brockton Hall, Maj; *b* 15 Oct 1788; *m* 25 April 1843 Mary Anne (*d* 20 Dec 1890), 4th dau of Sir Oswald Mosley, 2nd Bt (*see* RAVENSDALE, B), and *d* 25 April 1873, having had with other issue:

(1) Charles, of Brocton Hall, DL; *b* 1 July 1851; *m* 2 Feb 1888 Mary (*d* 1948), est dau of George Meakin, of Creswell Hall, Staffs, and *d* 17 Sept 1895, leaving issue:

1a Charles William George; *b* 29 Oct 1894; *educ* Haileybury; 2nd Lt Wilts Yeo; *m* 1st 26 Nov 1914 (*divorce* 1932) Olive Mary, yr dau of J Hall, of Huntingdon, and had issue:

1b Basil Charles Fawkener; *b* 20 Aug 1915; marine engr with Shell Co; *m* 11 Jan 1944 Margaret Joan (*d* 1992), yr dau of George Ernest Welch, of Charlton Ho Farm, Creech St Michael, nr Taunton, Somerset, and *d* 1980, leaving issue:

1c +Paul Ernest Fawkener [Paul Chetwynd Esq, Greenacres, Charlton Rd, Creech Heathfield, Taunton, Somerset]; *b* 16 Jan 1945; *m* 1972 *Shirley Evelyn, est dau of Raymond Godfrey Manuel, of Creech Heathfield, and has issue:

1d *Karen Lynne; *b* 1975

2d *Wendy Caroline; *b* 1977

2c +Raymond Charles Fawkener [Raymond Chetwynd Esq, Westlake, Cockpit Rd, Gt Kings Hill, nr High Wycombe, Bucks]; *b* 4 Aug 1950; *m* 1974 *Susan Jane, er dau of John Kershaw, of Taunton, Som, and has issue:

1d *Joanne Louise; *b* 1978

2d *Rebecca Claire; *b* 1978 (twin)

3d *Sarah Jane; *b* 1982

2b Ronald John Trevor; *m* 1st 1940 (*divorce* 1956) Alice Sybil, dau of Frank Baker, of Stoke St Mary, Somerset; *m* 2nd 1963 *Mrs Gwendoline Blodwyn Cullen, yr dau of William Richard Williams, of Chester

1b *Rhona Mary; *b* 23 Dec 1916; *m* 30 Dec 1940 *Philip Graham Stacey Brinson, and has issue:

1c *John; *b* 1948

1a (cont.) Charles Chetwynd *m* 2nd 19––; *m* 3rd 19–*Mary Elizabeth, dau of Arthur Griffiths, of Worcs, and *d* 1975, having by her had issue:

1b *Valerie Elizabeth; *b* 20 June 1940; *m* 1st 27 May 1961 Rupert Paul Carrington, er son of H M F Carrington, of Heskin Hall, nr Chorley, Lancs; *m* 2nd 1978 *Lt-Col Mark F Murray, RM

1a Beatrice Ada

2a Mildred Florence Mary

(1) Sophia Ann; *m* 10 Jan 1870 Francis Peter Conolan, only son of Peter Conolan, MD, RN, of Sligo, and had issue

(2) Caroline

3 Henry, of Brocton Lodge, Staffs; *b* 15 Aug 1791; *m* 6 Sept 1827 Mary Anne (*d* 5 Jan 1888), 2nd dau of Rev John Hayes Petit, of Hilton, Staffs, and *d* 9 Aug 1870, leaving issue, with two daus:

(1) John; *b* 13 July 1840; *m* 21 Feb 1867 Mary Ellen, est dau of Henry Hull, of Warminster, Wilts, and *d* 1885, leaving issue:

1a Henry Walter Petit; *b* 1869

2a William Jelf Petit; *b* 1872

1a *Emma Louise Petit

2a *Mary Anne Petit

Sir GEORGE *d* 24 March 1824; his son,

Sir George Chetwynd, 2nd Bt, MP Stafford; *b* 23 July 1783; *m* 30 Aug 1804 Hannah Maria (*d* 7 June 1860), est dau and coheir of John Sparrow, of Bishton Hall, Staffs, by Elizabeth, dau and coheir of Ralph Moreton, and *d* 1850, having had, with other issue:

1 **Sir George Chetwynd, 3rd Bt**; *b* 6 Sept 1809; *m* 2 Aug 1843 Lady Charlotte Augusta Hill (*d* in a fall from her horse 24 Nov 1861), est dau of 3rd Marquess of Downshire (*qv*), and *d* 24 March 1869, having had, with other issue:

(1) **Sir George Chetwynd, 4th Bt**, JP; *b* 31 May 1849; High Sheriff Warwicks 1875; *m* 6 June 1870 Lady Florence Cecilia (*d* 3 Feb 1907), dau of 2nd Marquess of Anglesey (*qv*), and widow of 4th Marquess of Hastings, and *d* 10 March 1917, having had, with other issue:

1a **Sir George Guy Chetwynd, 5th Bt**; *b* 6 Dec 1874; *m* 1st 2 Jan 1902 (*divorce* 1909) Rosalind (*d* 8 Oct 1922), dau of William Holt Secor, of NY; *m* 2nd 11 Oct 1917 Constance Winifred, only dau of Albert Amor, of 11 Park Village W, Regent's Park, and *d* 27 Aug 1935, having had issue by his 1st w:

1b **Sir Victor James Guy Chetwynd, 6th Bt**; *b* 14 Nov 1902; *m* 1st 8 July 1926 Annie Dorothy Christian (*d* 10 Jan 1927), dau of Francis Wigley Greswolde Greswolde-Williams, DL, JP, of Bredenham Court, and widow of Alfred Noel Granville Summers, 9th Lancers; *m* 2nd 16 Jan 1929 Valian Betty Masson, of Paris (*k* in air crash at Le Bourget, France, 4 Sept 1946), and *dsp* 25 Nov 1938

1a Lilian Florence Maud; *b* 10 March 1876; *m* 1st 20 Jan 1898 her cousin 5th Marquess of Anglesey (*dsp* 14 March 1905); *m* 2nd 11 Dec 1909 John Francis Grey Gilliat, son of Howard Gilliat, of Honington Hall, and *d* 20 Feb 1962, leaving issue. He *d* 22 Sept 1948

2a Olive Nina Mary; *b* 24 Feb 1877; *d* unm 15 Oct 1946

(2) Walter Hill, Capt 16th Lancers; *b* 13 Jan 1856; *m* 14 June 1890 Hon Edomé Eliza Theodosia Monson (*d* 30 May 1950), dau of 8th Baron Monson (*qv*), and *d* 23 Feb 1916, leaving issue:

1a Phyllis Marion; *b* 5 April 1893

(1) Isabel Marian; *m* 1st 24 May 1870 Cudworth Halsted Poole, of Marbury Hall, Salop, and had issue; *m* 2nd 22 June 1880 3rd Viscount Combermere (*qv*), and *d* 17 Sept 1930, leaving further issue

(2) Georgiana; *m* 4 May 1874 7th Earl of Guilford (*qv*), and *d* 13 May 1931, leaving issue

2 William Henry, of Longdon Ho, Staffs, DL, JP; *b* 17 Sept 1811; *m* 1st 15 Aug 1854 (*divorce* 1865) Blanche (*d* 1898), est dau of Rev Hon Arthur Chetwynd-Talbot (*see* SHREWSBURY and WATERFORD, E); *m* 2nd 7 Dec 1875 Mary, dau of James Parkin, and *d* 5 July 1890, having by his 1st w had issue:

(1) Arthur, of Longdon Hall, Rugeley, JP, Capt 3rd and 4th Bns S Staffs Regt; *b* 22 July 1857; *m* 23 June 1886 Kinbarra Swene (*d* 23 July 1930), dau of Samuel Lipscombe Seckham, DL, of Beacon Place, and *d* 15 Aug 1926, leaving issue:

1a **Sir (Arthur Henry) Talbot Chetwynd, 7th Bt**, OBE (1919), MC, of Brocton Hall; *educ* Wellington; Capt 16th and 9th Lancers, Col Frontiers Camel Corps Egyptian Army 1924–31, served WW I (despatches twice) and WW II (Cmdt War Res Spec Constab, Co Monmouth), Acting Ch Constable Mon 1939–44, 4th Cl Order of the Nile; *b* 13 April 1887; *m* 1st 25 Oct 1914 (*divorce* 1940) Evelyn Margaret (*d* 23 Aug 1972, aged 82), yr dau of Leonard Wodehouse Andrews, of Southborough, Kent; *m* 2nd 29 July 1940 Violet Mary (*d* 13 Oct 1955), est dau of William Charles Cripps, of The Lawn, Camden Park, Tunbridge Wells; *m* 3rd 4 April 1956 (Frances) Audrey, only dau of Dr Thomas Flawith-Smith, of Timbers, Boldre, Hants, and formerly w of John Taylour Boumphrey, and *dsp* 24 July 1972

2a William Ralph Talbot, MC (1918), Lt RFA (SR) WW I, memb Provincial Govt BC 1952 for Cariboo; Min Trade and Industry, Rlwys and Fisheries 1952, Min Ag; *b* 1890; *m* 8 Oct 1912 Frances Mary (*d* 1986), 2nd dau of James Jupe, of Mere, and *d* 3 April 1957, leaving issue:

1b Sir ARTHUR RALPH TALBOT CHETWYND, **8th and present Bt**

(1) Florence; *m* 5 June 1877 Lord Berkeley Charles Sydney Paget and *d* 26 May 1936, leaving issue (*see* ANGLESEY, M)

1 Georgiana; *m* Sept 1833 John Baron Hanmer, and *d* 21 March 1880

CHEYNE

Arms: Az. on a bend between six crosses patée fitchée arg. an oak tree eradicated ppr., fructed or. **Crest:** A cross patée fitchée arg.
Motto: *Patientia vincit* ('He conquers by patience').
Creation: Bt. (UK) 20 July 1908.

SIR JOSEPH LISTER WATSON CHEYNE, 3RD BT, of Leagarth, Fetlar, Zetland, OBE (1976) [Maj Sir Joseph Cheyne Bt OBE, Leagarth, Fetlar, Shetland; The Haa, Gloup, Cullivoe, Yell, Shetland ZE2 9DD]; *b* 10 Oct 1914; *s f* 1957; *educ* Stowe and Corpus Christi Coll Cambridge; Maj The Queen's Westminsters KRRC WW II; 2nd Sec (Info) Br Embassy Rome 1968–70, 1st Sec 1970–73, 1st Sec (Info) 1973–76; curator Keats-Shelley Memorial Ho Rome 1976–90; *m* 1st 14 Jan 1938 (*divorce* 1955) Mary Mort (*d* 29 Oct 1959), er dau of V-Adml John Derwent Allen, CB, and has issue:

1 +PATRICK JOHN LISTER [Patrick Cheyne Esq, 37 Chapel Lane, Hale Barns, Altrincham, Cheshire WA15 0AG]; *b* 2 July 1941; *educ* Lancing; late Lt RN; *m* 8 June 1968 *(Helen) Louise Trevor, yr dau of Louis Smith, of Marine Lodge, 25 Driftwood Gdns, Southsea, Hants PO4 9ND, and has issue:

(1) +Louis Richard Patrick Lister; *b* 25 March 1971

(1) *Elizabeth Hennrietta Louise; *b* 9 Nov 1969

(2) *Mary Catherine Fleur; *b* 1974

(3) *Caroline Victoria Alice; *b* 12 July 1979

1 *Ann Caroline Lister [Mrs Ronald Adam, Coombe House, Sharnden, Mayfield, E Sussex TN20 6QA]; *b* 3 March 1939; *m* 22 July 1961 *Lt-Col Ronald Eric Croll Adam, QO Highrs, er son of Lt-Col John Croll Adam, TD, MB, ChB, of Duncryne, Forres, Morayshire

Sir JOSEPH *m* 2nd 6 Aug 1955 *Cicely, dau of Thomas Metcalfe, of Padiham, Lancs, and by her has issue:

2 +John Joseph Peter [Mr John Cheyne, La Vignaccia, Via Del Bandino 6, Pergine Val D'Arno, Arizzo, Italy]; *b* 17 March 1956; *m* 1980 (*annulled* 19–) Emma, 2nd dau of Luciano Sestini, of Arezzo, Italy, and has:

(1) +Edward William Watson; *b* 1980

3 +James Andrew Watson [James Cheyne Esq, 140 Viale Regina Margerita, Roma 00198, Italy]; *b* 20 Aug 1957; *educ* Stowe; *m* 1984 *Frederica Elda Cristina, yr dau of Paolo Napolitani, of Rome, and has issue:

(1) +William Giovanni Joseph Watson; *b* 1986

(1) *Victoria Emma Watson; *b* 1991

2 *Helen Margaret Watson [Sra Rinaldo Rinaldi, 44 Via Tolmino, Roma 00198, Italy]; *b* 14 June 1959; *educ* Downe Ho Newbury; *m* 1989 *Rinaldo G M Rinaldi, er son of Francesco Rinaldi, of Naples, and has:

(1) *Cecilia Pauline; *b* 1 Feb 1992

Lineage: ANDREW CHEYNE; had:

Sir William Watson Cheyne, 1st Bt (UK), so *cr* 20 July 1908, KCMG, CB, MP Edinburgh and St Andrews Us 1917–18 and Scottish Us 1918–23; MB and CM Edin, FRCS England, FRS Hon FRCS, and Hon FRRCP Edin, Hon LLD Edin and Birmingham, Hon DSc Oxford, Pres of Cncl of Roy Coll of Surgeons 1914–17, Prof Clinical Surgery King's Coll London, Hon Surgn-in-Ordinary to HM GEORGE V 1910; Consulting Surgn King's Coll Hosp and Examiner in Surgery at London U, Ld Lt Orkney and Shetland Islands 1919–30, Hunterian Prof Roy Coll Surgeons 1888–90, Consulting Surgn Forces S Africa 1900–01 (despatches, medal) and Naval Medical Dept, Surgn R-Adml WW I; Lister Memorial Medal and prize for distinguished surgical work; *b* 14 Dec 1852; *m* 1st 29 Jan 1887 Mary Emma (*d* 6 Feb 1894), dau of Rev William Servanté, of Plumstead, Kent, and had issue:

1 (JOSEPH) LISTER (Sir), **2nd Bt**

2 William Hunter Watson, MB, MRCS, LRCP, late Surg RN; *b* 26 June 1889; *m* 15 Dec 1923 Grizel (*d* 4 Sept 1975 aged 83), er dau of Isaac Fenton Bayley, of Halls, Dunbar, and *d* 19 April 1957, leaving issue:

(1) George Watson, barrister Gray's Inn 1955; *b* 16 May 1929; *educ* Sherborne and Corpus Christi Coll Cambridge (MA, LLM); *m* 1 Feb 1964 *(Alison) Diane [Mrs George Cheyne, The Priory, Monk Sherborne, Basingstoke, Hants RG26 5HY], barrister Middle Temple 1960, dau of Cyril Muir Jones, of Hawarden, Chester, and *d* 23 Dec 1996, leaving:

1a +Piers William Watson; *b* 10 May 1965; *educ* Radley and Bristol U (BA); *m* 1994 *Anne, est dau of Jean-Louis Richard, of St Germain-en-Laye, France, and has:

1b +Hugo Edouard Watson; *b* 30 March 1997

1a *Phyllida Alison; *b* 14 Sept 1968; MA, MPhil Cambridge; barrister Inner Temple 1992

2a *Catriona Helen; *b* 1971

(1) *(Janet) Mary Watson [The Rt Hon The Lady Cochrane of Cults, Cults, Cupar, Fife]; *b* 13 April 1931; *m* 18 Dec 1956 *4th Baron Cochrane of Cults (*qv*), and has issue

1 Mary Frances; *b* 10 July 1891; *d* 4 May 1892

Sir William *m* 2nd 12 Dec 1894 Margaret (*d* 9 April 1922), dau of George Smith, of Lerwick, and *d* 19 April 1932, having by her had issue:

3 George Basil Watson; *b* 12 Oct 1898; *d* 2 July 1922

2 Grace Ella Margaret Watson; *b* 30 Oct 1895; *m* 21 Sept 1926 H T Browne, son of H S Browne, of 91, Cambridge St, Eccleston Sq, SW, and *d* 28 Jan 1931

3 Julia Millicent Watson; *b* 25 April 1900; *d* 22 Feb 1901

The est son,

Sir (Joseph) Lister Cheyne, 2nd Bt, MC and bar, Col 16th/5th Lancers, AAG Southern Cmd 1933–37, cmded 16th/5th Lancers 1929–33, served WW I (despatches twice) and WW II, AQMG 46th Div 1939–40; *b* 12 Jan 1888; *m* 19 June 1912 Nelita Manfield (*d* 16 May 1977), er dau of Andrew Pringle, of Borgue, Kirkcudbright, and *d* 20 Sept 1957, having had issue:

1 Sir JOSEPH LISTER WATSON CHEYNE, **3rd and present Bt**

2 William Watson, DSO (1966), OBE (1963, MBE 1946), Brig QO Highrs; *b* 2 Feb 1920; *educ* Stowe; served WW II (POW 1940–45), cmded 1st Bn Seaforth Highrs 1959–61, cmdg 4th Bn KAR 1961–62, 1st Bn Uganda Rifles 1962–63 and 99th Gurkha Bde on active service 1964–66, IDC 1967; *m* 1 Oct 1946 *Laurel Audrey (Polly) [Mrs William Cheyne, 12 Crondace Rd, London SW6], er dau of Lt-Gen Sir Balfour Hutchison, KBE, CB, of Rendham Court, Rendham, Saxmundham, Suffolk, and *d* 16 May 1970, leaving issue:

(1) +Julian Lister Hutchison; *b* 20 Aug 1947; *educ* Stowe and Oriel Coll Oxford (BA)

(2) +David Watson [David Cheyne Esq, 19 Ladbroke Gdns, London W11 2PY]; *b* 30 Dec 1948; *educ* Stowe and Trin Coll Cambridge (BA); *m* 1978 *(Judith) Gay McAuslane, er dau of David Anstruther Passey, of The Hall, Kirkby Fleetham, Northallerton, Yorks, and has issue:

1a +Alexander William David; *b* 1980

2a +Rory Alistair Watson; *b* 1984

3a +Rupert Valentine Hutchinson; *b* 1989

(3) +(William) Gerald [Gerald Cheyne Esq, 32 Ringmer Ave, London SW6 5LW]; *b* 13 April 1950; *educ* Stowe and Trin Coll Cambridge (BA); served QO Highrs; *m* 1978 (*divorce* 1984) Clare Rosdew, dau of Stamford Robert Francis Vanderstegen-Drake, of The Old Tannery, Ecchinswell, Newbury, Berks (*see* MOWBRAY, Bt), and has issue:

1a *Katherine Clare; *b* 1980

(1) *Bridget Nelita [Mrs Richard Lanyon, 16 Dryburgh Rd, London SW15 1BL]; *b* 5 Dec 1955; *m* 1984 *Richard Patrick Lanyon, est son of Maj Patrick Lanyon, of Popesfield House, Timberscombe, Somerset, and has:

1a *William Patrick; *b* 1988

2a *Oliver James; *b* 8 May 1996

1a *Frances Alice; *b* 1986

2a *Alexandra Polly; *b* 1990

3 +Andrew Watson [Andrew Cheyne Esq, 49 Hurlingham Court, Ranelagh Gdns, London SW6], AMInstCE, FICE, Capt RE WW II (despatches); *b* 15 Oct 1921; *educ* Stowe and Loughborough Coll; *m* 21 Dec 1946 *Joyce Mary, only dau of Conway Stanton, of Kensington

CHICHESTER, Earl of

Arms: Quarterly, 1st and 4th, az. three pelicans arg., vulning themselves ppr.; 2nd and 3rd, gu. two broken belts palewise, the buckles upwards arg. **Crest:** A peacock in pride arg. **Supporters:** Dexter, a horse of a mouse colour; sinister, a bear ppr., each collared with a belt arg., buckle and pendant or. **Motto:** *Vincit amor patriæ* ('The love of my country prevails'). **Creation:** Bt. (E) 22 May 1611, B. (GB) 4 May 1762, E. (UK) 23 June 1801.

THE 9TH EARL OF CHICHESTER, Baron Pelham of Stanmer, Co Sussex, and a **Baronet** (Sir John Nicholas Pelham, Bt) [The Rt Hon The Earl of Chichester, Little Durnford Manor, Salisbury, Wilts SP4 6AH]; *b* posthumously 14 April 1944; *s* f 1944; *educ* Stanbridge Earls Sch, Romsey, Hants; *m* 10 Dec 1975 *Mrs June Marijke Hall, dau of G/Capt E D Wells, DSO, DFC, RAF (ret), of Marbella, Spain, and has issue:

1 *Eliza Catherine; *b* 12 May 1983

Chichester, earldom of: The medieval Aubigny Earls of Arundel were occasionally referred to in contemporary documents as Earls of Chichester, as also was Roger de Montgomery Earl of Shrewsbury (*see* SHREWSBURY and WATERFORD, E, preliminary remarks) since among his other fiefs was the Earldom of Arundel. These first few post-Conquest Earls of Arundel held the town and castle of Chichester, whence their being credited with an earldom under that denomination. But the administrative nature of an earldom at that remote period was such that its holder might be referred to by the name of the place where he officiated rather than a more personal entity such as his chief manor.

It was not till the 17th century that a specific Earldom of Chichester was conferred. In 1644 Sir Francis Leigh, 1st Bt, who had been ennobled as Baron Dunsmore sixteen years earlier, was promoted to this title. The creation was with remainder to Leigh's son-in-law Thomas Wriothesley, who in addition held the Earldom of Southampton (*see* SOUTHAMPTON, B, preliminary remarks). On Thomas's death without surviving male issue in 1667 the title expired.

It was revived for a bastard of CHARLES II's by Barbara Villiers, Duchess of Cleveland. This took place on 10 Sept 1675 and was one of three titles conferred that day on the 13-year old Charles FitzRoy, being subsumed in the much grander Dukedom of Southampton, the previous concurrence of the Earldom of Chichester and Southampton held by Thomas Wriothesley doubtless suggesting the names of the new titles. This Earldom expired on the death without issue of the 2nd Duke of Southampton (who was also 3rd Duke of Cleveland) in 1774.

Lineage: WALTER de PELHAM; held Pelham, Herts, *c* 1293; presumably ancestor of:

Sir JOHN de PELHAM; did mil service *temp* EDWARD III; *m* Joan (dau of Vincent Herbert *alias* Finch), who brought him property in Winchelsea, Sussex, and had:

Sir JOHN PELHAM, KB; MP Sussex *temp* HENRY IV, Constable of Pevensey Castle; ancestor of:

Sir WILLIAM PELHAM, of Laughton, E Sussex; *b* 1468?; *m* 1st Mary, dau of Sir Richard Carew, of Beddington, Surrey, and had, with a yr s and dau:

1 NICHOLAS (Sir)

2 Anthony, of Buxstepe in Warbleton, ancestor of the PELHAMs of Swineshead

Sir WILLIAM *m* 2nd, as her 1st husb, Mary (*m* 2nd John Palmer), dau of 1st Baron Sandys, of The Vyne, Hants, Ld Chamberlain to HENRY VIII, and *d* 1538, leaving further issue (with possibly another s, er than Sir Edmund):

3 William (Sir), ancestor of the PELHAMs of Brocklesby (*see* YARBOROUGH, E)

4 Edmund/Edward (Sir), PC (1602); memb Gray's Inn 1563, MP Hastings 1597, Serjeant-at-Law 1601, Ch Baron Exchequer Ireland 1602–06, ktd 1604; *m* and *d* 4 June 1606, leaving issue:

(1) Herbert; *b c* 1587; ancestor of the PELHAMs of Catsfield, Sussex

The est son,

Sir NICHOLAS PELHAM, of Halland-in-Laughton, Sussex; *b* 1517; defended Seaford, E Sussex, against an attempted French invasion 1545, MP Arundel 1547–52 and Sussex Jan 1557/8–60, Sheriff Surrey and Sussex 1549, ktd 1549; *m* Anne, dau of John Sackville, and *d* 15 Dec 1559, having had, with eight other children:

1 John (Sir), of Laughton; MP Sussex 1571; *m* Judith, dau of Oliver, 1st(?) Baron St John of Bletso (*qv*), and *d* 13 Oct 1580, leaving an only child:

(1) Oliver, of Laughton; *dsp* 19 Jan 1584

2 **Sir Thomas Pelham, 1st Bt** (E), so *cr* 22 May 1611, of Laughton, Sussex; MP Lewes 1584–85 and Sussex 1586–90, Sheriff Sussex and Surrey 1589; *b c* 1540; *m* by 1590 Mary (*bur* 7 March 1634), dau of Sir Thomas Walsingham, of Scadbury, Kent, and niece to Secretary Sir Francis Walsingham, and *d* 2 Dec 1624, having had, with a dau (Judith, *m* Henry Carey, 1st Earl of Dover; *see* ALDENHAM and HUNSDON OF HUNSDON, B, preliminary remarks), an only son:

(1) **Sir Thomas Pelham, 2nd Bt**, MP E Grinstead 1621–22 and Sussex 1624–25, 1640–48 and 1654; *bapt* 22 Sept 1597; *m* 1st Mary (*bur* 7 March 1634), 3rd dau and coheir of Sir Roger Wilbraham, and had, with other issue:

1a JOHN (Sir), **3rd Bt**

1a Judith; *m* Sir John Monson and had issue (*see* MONSON, B)

(1) **Sir Thomas** *m* 2nd Judith (*bur* 21 Nov 1638), dau of Sir Robert Honeywood and widow of John Shirley, but by her had no surv issue; *m* 3rd Margaret, dau of Sir Henry Vane, of Fairlawn, Kent, by whom he had surv issue:

2a Nicholas (Sir), of Catsfield Place, Sussex, MA Oxford, MP Sussex; *m* Jane, dau and coheir of James Huxley, of Dornford, Oxon, and had at least one dau (Margaret, *m* Sir William Ashburnham, 2nd Bt; *qv*); was ancestor of the CRESSETT-PELHAMs of Crowhurst, Sussex

2a Philadelphia; *m* 8 July 1673 6th Baron Howard of Effingham (*see* EFFINGHAM, E) and *d* 13 Aug 1685, having had issue

3a Elizabeth; *m* as his 2nd w her distant cousin Charles Pelham, of Broclesby (*see* YARBOROUGH, E), and *dsp*

Sir THOMAS was *bur* 28 Aug 1654; his est son,

Sir John Pelham, 3rd Bt, MP Hastings 1645–46 and Sussex 1654–58 and 1660–98; *m* 20 Jan 1647 Lady Lucy Sydney (*bur* 19 Oct 1685), 2nd dau of 2nd Earl of Leicester (*see* DE L'ISLE, V, and LEICESTER, E, preliminary remarks), and was *bur* 20 Jan 1702/3, having had, with other issue:

1 **Sir Thomas Pelham, 4th Bt**, and 1st BARON PELHAM OF LAUGHTON, Co Sussex ((GB), so *cr* 16 Dec 1706; *b c* 1653; MP (Whig) E Grinstead 1678–79, Lewes 1679–1702 and Sussex 1702–05; Commr Customs 1689–91 and a Ld Treasury March 1689/90–March 1690/1, 1698–99 and 1701–02; *m* 1st 26 Nov 1679 Elizabeth (*bur* 13 Oct 1681), dau of Sir William Jones, Attorney-Gen to CHARLES II, and had, with another dau:

(1) Elizabeth; *m* 3 July 1698 2nd Viscount Townshend and *d* 11 May 1711, leaving issue (*see* TOWNSHEND, M)

1 (cont.) **Sir Thomas** *m* 2nd 21 May 1686 Lady Grace Holles (*d* 13 Sept 1700), dau of 3rd Earl of Clare and sis of 1st and last Duke of Newcastle-upon-Tyne of the 1694 *cr*, and *d* 23 Feb 1711/2, having had, with other further issue:

(1) Sir THOMAS PELHAM later PELHAM-HOLLES (added on death of his maternal uncle John Holles Duke of Newcastle, whose estates he inherited, 15 July 1711), **5th Bt**, 2nd BARON PELHAM OF LAUGHTON, also 1st and last DUKE OF NEWCASTLE-UPON-TYNE and MARQUESS OF CLARE, both *cr* 11 Aug 1715, and 1st and last VISCOUNT HAUGHTON, Co Nottingham, and EARL OF CLARE, Co Suffolk, both *cr* 19 Oct 1714, with special remainder in the case of all four (which were GB creations) to his bro; in addition *cr* 17 Nov 1756 (1st) DUKE OF NEWCASTLE-UNDER-LINE (GB), with special remainder to his niece Catherine's husb the 9th Earl of Lincoln (*qv*; *see* also below) and the heirs male of the latter's body by her, and lastly *cr* 4 May 1762 BARON PELHAM OF STANMER, Co Sussex (GB), with remainder to his cousin and heir male Thomas Pelham, of Stanmer, later **1st Earl of Chichester** (*see* below), KG (1718), PC (1717); *b* 1 July 1693; *educ* Westminster and Clare Hall Cambridge; Ld Lt Middx and Westminster 1714–62, Notts 1714–62 and 1756–58 and Sussex 1761–62, Ld Chamberlain 1717–24, Sec State for the South 1724–48 and the North 1748–54, First Ld of the Treasury and PM 1754–56 and 1757–62 (unusually, for an 18th-century statesman, ending poorer after his term of office than before it — to the tune of £400,000), Ld Privy Seal 1765–66; *m* 2 April 1717 Henrietta (*d* 17 July 1776), est dau and coheir of 2nd Earl of Godolphin by Henrietta, Duchess of Marlborough (*qv*) in her own right, but *dsp* 17 Nov 1768, when all his titles expired bar the Dukedom of 1756, the Barony of 1762 and the btcy

(2) Henry, PC (1725); *b* 1696; *educ* Westminster and Hart Hall Oxford; Capt Brig Dormer's Regt 22 July 1715 and helped defeat the Jacobites at the Battle of Preston Nov 1715; MP (Whig) Seaford 1717–22 and Sussex 1722054, a Ld Treasury 1721, Sec at War 1724, Paymaster Forces 1730, 1st Ld Treasury and PM 25 Aug and Chllr Exchequer 12 Dec 1743 (though his er bro (*see* above) had equal power in the Cabinet), resigned 11 Feb 1746 but reappointed 14 Feb 1746; *m* 29 Oct 1726 Lady Catherine Manners (*d* 18 Feb 1780), est dau of 2nd Duke of Rutland (*qv*), and *d* in office 6 March 1754, leaving, with two other daus (*d* unm):

1a Catherine; *b* 24 July 1727; *m* 3 Oct 1744 9th Earl of Lincoln (*qv*)

2a Grace; *b* 18 Aug 1728; *m* 12 Oct 1752 1st Baron Sondes of Lees Court and *d* 31 July 1777, leaving issue (*see* MONSON, B)

(2) Frances; *m* 31 May 1715 2nd Viscount Castlecomer and *dsp* 1756. He *d* 23 June 1719

(3) Lucy; *m* 16 May 1717 7th Earl of Lincoln (*qv*) and had issue

(4) Margaret; *m* 16 March 1726/7 Sir John Shelley, 4th Bt (*qv*), and *d* 23 Nov 1758, leaving issue

2 Henry, of Stanmer, Sussex, Clerk of the Pells; *m* Frances, dau and coheir of John Bine, of Rowdell, Sussex, and *d* 1 April 1721, leaving with other issue:

(1) Thomas, of Stanmer; MP Lewes 1727–37, merchant at Constantinople; *m* Annetta (*d* 9 Oct 1733), dau of Thomas Bridges, merchant at Constantinople, and *d* 1737, leaving by her:

1a THOMAS, **1st Earl**

1a Harriet; *m* 1st 18 May 1748 Hon Richard Temple, MP (*see* TEMPLE OF STOWE, E) and had issue; *m* 2nd 5 Feb 1753 1st Earl of Abergavenny (*see* ABERGAVENNY, M) and *d* 31 Aug 1768, leaving issue

(1) Grace; *m* William Poole, nephew of Sir James Poole, 1st Bt, of Poole, but *dsp*

(2) Frances; *m* Sir Francis Poole, 2nd Bt, of Poole, and *d* 30 April 1760, leaving issue

(3) Lucy; *m* 1726 Talbot Yelverton, Earl of Sussex, and *d* 25 May 1730, leaving issue (*see* GREY, B)

1 Elizabeth; *m* 1st 30 May 1678 Edward Montagu, bro of 1st Earl of Halifax (see HALIFAX, E, preli inary remarks), and had issue; *m* 2nd Thomas Woodcock (*dsp* 3 July 1732) and *d* 13 July 1723

2 Lucy; *m c* 10 March 1679/80 1st and last Baron Pierrepont of Hanslape and *dsp* 8 July 1721

The 5th Bt's cousin,

Sir Thomas Pelham, 6th Bt, **2nd Baron Pelham of Stanmer** and **1st Earl of Chichester** (UK), so *cr* 23 June 1801, PC (1765); *b* 28 Feb 1728; MP (Whig) Rye 1749–54 and Sussex 1754–68, Commr Trade 1754–61, a Ld Admlty 1761–62, Comptroller Household 1765–74; *m* 15 June 1754 Anne (*d* 5 March 1813), only dau and heiress of Frederick Meinhart Frankland, and had, with other issue:

1 THOMAS, **2nd Earl**

2 Henry; *b* 1759; *m* 1788 Catherine, est dau of Col Thomas Cobbe, MP (*see* WATERFORD, M), and *d* 1797, leaving two daus

3 George, DD, Bp Bristol, Exeter and Lincoln; *b* 13 Oct 1766; *m* 1792 Mary, 3rd dau of Sir Richard Rycroft, 1st Bt (*qv*), and *dsp* 1827

1 Henrietta Anne; *m* 24 May 1789 13th Earl of Rothes (*qv*) and *d* 1797

2 Frances; *m* 5 Dec 1778 4th Viscount Midleton (*qv*), and *d* 1783

3 Lucy; *m* 26 Dec 1794 1st Earl of Sheffield and *dsp* 18 Jan 1797. He *d* 30 May 1821

The 1st EARL *d* 8 Jan 1805; his est son,

THOMAS PELHAM, **2nd Earl of Chichester**, PC (I 1783, GB 1795); *b* 28 April 1756; *educ* Westminster and Clare Hall Cambridge; MP (Whig to 1794, Pittite thereafter) Sussex 1780–1801 and (I Parl) Carrick-on-Shannon 1783–90 and Clogher 1795–97, Ch Sec to Ld Lt Ireland 1783–84 and 1795–98, Sec State Ireland 1796–97, called up to Ho Lds vp in f'a barony of Pelham of Stanmer June 1801, Home Sec 1801–03, Chllr Duchy Lancaster 1803–04, Capt Yeomen Gd a few weeks June 1804, Jt PMG 1807–23, PMG; *m* 16 July 1801 Lady Mary Henrietta Juliana Osborne (*d* 21 Oct 1862), dau of 5th Duke of Leeds (*see* 1963 edn), and had, with other issue:

1 HENRY THOMAS, **3rd Earl**

2 Frederick Thomas, CB, R-Adml, a Kt of San Fernando, a Ld Admlty 1859; *b* 2 Aug 1808; *m* 26 July 1841 Ellen Kate (*d* 8 Jan 1900), dau of Rowland Mitchell, of Upper Harley St, and *d* 21 June 1861, having had, with other issue:

(1) Frederick Sidney, CBE (1919), Adml; *b* 25 Oct 1854; Adml-Supt at Gibraltar 1909–12, Naval ADC to HM; *m* 23 Nov 1886 Louise Elizabeth (*d* 26 Dec 1949), dau of Maj-Gen William John Chads, CB, and *d* 19 Oct 1931

(1) Constance Mary Kate; *d* unm 5 Jan 1926

(2) Beatrice Emily Julia; *d* unm 27 Feb 1939

3 John Thomas (Right Rev), DD, Bishop of Norwich 1857–93; *b* 21 June 1811; *m* 6 Nov 1845 Henrietta (*d* 31 Dec 1893), 2nd dau of Thomas William Tatton, of Wythenshawe Hall, Cheshire, and *d* 1 May 1894, leaving with other issue:

(1) Henry Francis, MA Oxford, FSA, Hon LLD, FBA, Pres Trin Coll Oxford, Camden Prof of Ancient History and Fell BNC Oxford, Hon Fell Exeter Coll Oxford; *b* 19 Sept 1846; *m* 30 July 1873 Laura Priscilla (*d* 2 Nov 1918), 3rd dau of Sir Edward North Buxton, 2nd Bt (*qv*), and *d* 12 Feb 1907, having had issue:

1a Edward Henry (Sir), KCB, Perm Sec Bd of Educn 1931–37, chm Grants Ctee for England and Wales, apptd under Physical Training and Recreation Act 1936; *b* 20 Dec 1876; *educ* Harrow and Balliol Coll Oxford; *m* 5 Dec 1905 Hon Irene Lubbock (*d* 14 Feb 1961), yst dau of 1st Baron Avebury (*qv*), and *d* as result of an accident, 18 Dec 1949, having had issue:

1b Henry John; *b* 28 July 1907; *educ* Harrow; *m* 17 Sept 1932 *Althea Muriel, only dau of J R Beavan, of Northwing, Kempsey, Worcs, and *d* 28 May 1939

2b Eric Thomas, Maj Welsh Gds WW II; *b* 19 Aug 1915; *educ* Harrow and Balliol Coll Oxford; *m* 27 July 1940 Barbara Hilda (*d* 28 May 1969), yst dau of Henry John Fordham, JP, of Therfield, Royston, Herts, and *d* 8 Jan 1984, leaving issue:

1c +Henry Thomas; *b* 10 June 1943; *educ* Harrow; *m* 24 Feb 1978 *Sarah, yr dau of John Charlton, of Culworth Fields, Banbury, Oxon, and has issue:

1d +Charles Thomas; *b* 1987

1d *Sophie; *b* 1980

2d *Clare; *b* 1981

2c +Richard John, of Montreal, Canada; *b* 7 Jan 1945; *educ* Harrow and Oxford U

3c +Charles Herbert; *b* 17 April 1947; *educ* Harrow; *m* 1st 1972 (*divorce* 1979) Thérèse Annabella, er dau of Maj James Richard Edwards Harden, DSO, MC (*see* RAYLEIGH, B); *m* 2nd 19– *Sarah —, and has issue:

1d +Henry; *b* 1986

1d *Katharine; *b* 1984

4c +William Robert; *b* 14 Jan 1950; *educ* Harrow

1b *(Alice) Catherine; *b* 20 May 1911; *m* 9 Oct 1933 Patrick Robert Sandars, OBE (*d* 3 June 1977), 4th son of Rev Canon George Russell Sandars, Rector of Davenham, Cheshire, and has issue:

1c *Patrick George Henry; *b* 29 March 1935; *educ* Wellington and Balliol Coll Oxford (MA, DPhil, Fell); *m* 3 Oct 1959 *Patricia Barbara, dau of E J Hall, of 116 London Rd, Headington, Oxford

2c *Anthony Thomas; *b* 28 May 1937; *educ* Wellington; *m* 27 Sept 1969 *Beatrice Valerie Kirk

2b *Irene Joan [Mrs Maurice Hayne, 11 Heathfield Court, Crookham Rd, Fleet, Hants GU13 8DX]; *b* 10 Dec 1912; *m* 20 Feb 1961 Brig Maurice Leslie Hayne, CBE (*d* 1971), 4th son of Frederick Underwood Stokes Hayne, of Reading, Berks

3b *Susan [Mrs Cresswell Clementi, Navigator's Cottage, 44 Strand-on-the-Green, Chiswick, London W4]; *b* 30 July 1918; *m* 28 Nov 1940 A/V/M Cresswell Montagu Clementi, CB, CBE, MA (*d* 1981), Senior RAF Instructor, IDC, only son of Sir Cecil Clementi, GCMG, of Holmer Court, Holmer Green, Bucks, and has issue:

1c *Christopher Pelham [Christopher Clementi Esq, Uplands, 13 Edgehill Rd, Purley, Surrey CR8 2ND]; *b* 8 July 1943; *educ* Bradfield; *m* 1976 Pamela Juliette Nollan (*d* 1992) and has:

1d *Richard Adam; *b* 1978; *m* 1994 *Frances Kathleen Chivers

2c *David Cecil; *b* 25 Feb 1949; *educ* Winchester, Lincoln Coll Oxford and Harvard Business Sch; *m* 1972 *Sarah Louise, dau of Dr A B Cowley, of E Molesey, Surrey, and has issue:

1d *Thomas Cowley; *b* 1979

1d *Anna Lucy; *b* 1976

1c *Nancy; *b* 2 Feb 1946; *m* 1972 *Peter Lambert Tribe and has:

1d *Mark Lambert; *b* 1978

2d *Howard Clementi; *b* 1981

1d *Natalie Clare; *b* 1975

2a Arthur John; *b* 4 Dec 1878; *d* 11 Aug 1883

3a Herbert Sidney (Rt Rev), Bishop Suffragan of Barrow-in-Furness 1926–44; *b* 25 June 1881; *educ* Harrow and Univ Coll Oxford (MA); *d* unm 11 March 1944

1a Catherine Harriet; *b* 8 Sept 1885; *d* 20 Nov 1894

2a Laura Grace; *b* 20 Sept 1888; *m* 2 Sept 1915 David Francis Bickmore, DSO, Norfolk Regt, acting Lt-Col Cmdg 4th Bn Gordon Highrs, son of Rev F A Bickmore, and had issue. He was *ka*, 20 July 1918

(2) John Barrington (Rev), Vicar of Higham, Suffolk 1889–1908, Hon Canon of Norwich 1906–08, and Vicar of Thundridge, Ware, Herts 1908–14; *b* 7 Jan 1848; *educ* Trin Coll Cambridge (MA); *m* 19 July 1884 Caroline (*d* 4 Aug 1917), dau of Rev William Buller, of Lanreath, Cornwall, and *d* 10 Jan 1941

(3) Sidney (Rev), Hon Canon of Norwich 1896–1901, and from 1916, Archdeacon of Norfolk 1901–16; *b* 16 May 1849; *educ* Magdalen Coll Oxford (MA); *m* 3 June 1897 Caroline Elizabeth, dau of Canon John Patteson, Rector of Thorpe St Andrew, Norfolk, and *d* 14 July 1926

1 Amelia Rose; *b* 17 June 1806; *m* 5 Sept 1854 Maj-Gen Sir Joshua Jebb, KCB, RE, Surveyor-Gen Convict Prisons, Inspr Mil Prisons, and *d* 2 Jan 1884. He *d* 26 June 1863

2 Catherine Georgiana; *b* 21 July 1814; *m* 26 Oct 1837 Rev Hon Lowther John Barrington, MA, Rector of Watton, Herts (*see* 1970 edn BARRINGTON, V), and *d* 18 Jan 1885. He *d* 17 March 1897

3 Lucy Anne; *b* 3 Nov 1815; *m* 24 Aug 1858 Sir David Dundas, 2nd Bt, of Beechwood (*see* 1970 edn), and *dsp* 16 Jan 1901. He *d* 23 March 1877

The 2nd EARL *d* 4 July 1826; his est surv son,

HENRY THOMAS PELHAM, **3rd Earl of Chichester**, Ld Lt and Custos Rotulorum of Sussex; *b* 25 Aug 1804; *m* 18 Aug 1828 Mary (*d* 22 May 1867), 5th dau of 6th Earl of Cardigan (*see* AILESBURY, M), and *d* 15 March 1886, having had, with other issue:

1 WALTER JOHN PELHAM, **4th Earl of Chichester**, DL Sussex, MA Cambridge, MP Lewes 1865–74; *b* 22 Sept 1838; *m* 18 June 1861 Elizabeth Mary (*d* 7 Dec 1911), only dau of Hon Sir John Bligh, KCB (*see* DARNLEY, E), and *dsp* 28 May 1902

2 FRANCIS GODOLPHIN, **5th Earl**

3 Thomas Henry William, CB, barrister Inner Temple 1871, Assist Sec BOT 1895–1913; *b* 21 Dec 1847; *educ* Trin Coll Cambridge (MA); *m* 26 July 1883 Louisa Keith, OBE (*d* 3 April 1940), dau of William Bruce, yr of Kennet (*see* BALFOUR OF BURLEIGH, L), and *d* 23 Dec 1916, leaving issue:

(1) Walter Henry (Rev), JP Wilts, Hon CF, Rector of Chilton Foliat, nr Hungerford 1925–45; *b* 22 July 1886; *educ* Trin Coll Cambridge (MA); *m* 26 Aug 1914 Ruth Mary (*d* 20 May 1950), dau of Claude Leatham, DL, of The Red Ho, Wentbridge, Yorks, and *d* 3 Oct 1949, leaving issue:

1a Thomas Bertram (Rev), Capt RIASC WW II, Presbyter in Ch of S India 1949, Rector of Great and Little Somerford and Seagry 1966; *b* 28 Sept 1915; *educ* Charterhouse; *m* 13 Dec 1948 *Gudrun Elisabeth [Mrs Thomas Pelham, 2 Upper Grange, Lovedays Mead, Stroud, Glos GL5 1XB], dau of Rev Uno Axel Valdemar Almgren, of Halmstad, Sweden, and *d* 1984, leaving issue:

1b +Philip Henry [Philip Pelham Esq, 15 Ethelbert Rd, Canterbury, Kent]; *b* 1 Oct 1949; *educ* Lushington Hall, Ootacamund and Malmesbury GS and Sch of Herbal Medicine, Tunbridge Wells; *m* 1983 *Mrs Jennifer B Wellington, dau of Col J D Power, of Tetherings, Mystole, nr Canterbury, Kent, and has issue:

1c +Andrew Timothy; *b* 1984

1c *Annabel Claire; *b* 1985

2c *Elizabeth Rose; *b* 1990

2b +David Almgren [David Pelham Esq, 28 York Rd, Colwyn Bay, Clwyd]; *b* 9 Sept 1950; *educ* Lushington Hall, Ootacamund, Malmesbury GS, Derby U and Rhodes U, Grahamstown, S Africa (MSc); *m* 1980 *Julie Ann, dau of D G Killingley, of Wolverhampton, and has issue:

1c +Thomas James; *b* 1982

1c *Lucy Jane; *b* 1985

3b +Peter Thomas [Peter Pelham Esq, 48 Leighton Hill Flats, 16 Link Rd, Happy Valley, Hong Kong]; *b* 29 Feb 1952; *educ* Lushington Hall, Ootacamund, Malmesbury GS and Manchester U; *m* 1974 (*divorce* 1994) Linda Margaret, dau of Capt P H Phillips, of Benallack, Grampound Rd, Truro, Cornwall, and has issue:

1c +Henry William; *b* 1983

3b (cont.) Mr and Mrs Peter Pelham also adopted:

*Suyin; *b* 1985

4b +Erik John; *b* 8 July 1954; *educ* Lushington Hall, Ootacmund, Malmesbury GS and Lancaster U; *m* 1988 *Jane, dau of John Souter Henley, and has issue:

1c +Alexander; *b* 1990

2c +Joseph; *b* 1992

1c *Laura; *b* 1988

5b +(James) Richard [Richard Pelham Esq, 27 Hill Head, Glastonbury, Somerset]; *b* 25 Aug 1955 (twin); *educ* Lushington Hall, Ootacamund, and Bremilham Sch, Malmesbury; has issue (by Mary Chipper):

1c *Isaac Roy; *b* 1994

1b *Astrid Louisa [Mrs Richard Flaye, Kettlehouse, Chapel Lane, Belchford, Lincs]; *b* 25 Aug 1955 (twin); *m* 1978 (*divorce* 199–) Richard Michael FLAYE (formerly FLEAY), s of Martin Fleay, of Rydon Acres, Stoke Gabriel, Devon, and has:

1c *Thomas Charles; *b* 1983

2c *Tobias Pelham; *b* 1985

1c *Ella; *b* 1988

2b *Susan Margaret [Miss Susan Pelham, 1 Wraxhill Rd, Street, Somerset]; *b* 15 March 1959; has issue:

1c *Robin David Pelham; *b* 1985

2b (cont.) Susan Pelham has further issue by Jonny Green:

1c *Maia; *b* 1992

2a Robert Henry, Capt RA WW II; *b* 28 Feb 1919; *educ* Canford; *m* 3 March 1951 Anne Farebrother Dalziel (*d* 19–), only dau of Capt Geoffrey Dalziel Mayer, and *d* 1980, leaving:

1b +Michael Henry; *b* 16 Sept 1953

1b *Sarah Mary; *b* 20 March 1955

1a Patricia Mary; *b* 17 March 1917; *m* 1st 26 June 1937 (*divorce* 1949) Lt-Col Charles Reginald Clayton Albrecht, OBE, RA, son of Frank Albrecht, of W Kensington, and had issue; *m* 2nd 12 July 1949 Harold Holtby, MB, BS (*d* 26 April 1961), son of Rev Tom Rookledge Holtby, MA, DD, of Rudston Manor, Holtby, Yorks, and *d* 19–

(1) Mary Louisa, OBE (1918); *b* 16 May 1885; *m* 14 April 1915 1st Baron Piercy, CBE (*qv*), and *d* 8 Jan 1953, leaving issue

(2) Maud Katherine, OBE (1918), JP Co London; *b* 20 Sept 1887; *d* unm 28 Feb 1963

4 Arthur Lowther; *b* 28 Dec 1850; *educ* Trin Coll Cambridge (MA); *m* 30 April 1879 Evelyn Georgiana (*d* 21 Jan 1937), est dau of Sir Reginald John Cust (*see* BROWNLOW, B), and *d* 12 Feb 1929

1 Harriet Mary; *m* 31 Aug 1850 6th Earl of Darnley (*qv*), and *d* 4 Sept 1905, leaving issue

2 Susan Emma; *m* 7 April 1853 Abel Smith, MP, of Woodhall Park, Hants, and *d* 1875

3 Isabella Charlotte; *m* 9 July 1855 Samuel Whitbread, of Southill, Biggleswade, late MP for Bedford, and *d* 11 Dec 1916, leaving issue. He *d* 25 Dec 1915

The 4th EARL's bro,

Rev FRANCIS GODOLPHIN PELHAM, **5th Earl of Chichester**, MA Cambridge, Rector of Lambeth; *b* 18 Oct 1844; *m* 4 Aug 1870 Alice Carr (*d* 1 Feb 1934), dau of 1st Baron Wolverton (*qv*), and had issue:

1 JOCELYN BRUDENELL, **6th Earl**

2 Henry George Godolphin, late Sudan CS, had Order of the Osmanieh 4th Cl, and Order of the Nile 4th Cl, served WW I (despatches); *b* 5 March 1875; *m* 1st 19 April 1906 Agnes Lee (*d* 22 Oct 1930), dau of Thomas James Ollerhead, of Minehead, Som; *m* 2nd 3 Aug 1938 Dorothy Mary (*d* 15 April 1972), est dau of George Bridger Shiffner, JP, of West Riding of Yorks (*see* SHIFFNER, Bt), and *d* 28 June 1949, having by 1st w had issue:

(1) Anthony George, WW II as Maj RA (despatches), Sudan Political Serv; *b* 4 Sept 1911; *educ* Eton and King's Coll Cambridge (BA 1933, MA 1938); *m* 19 Sept 1938 Ann Margaret (*d* 1990), dau of Direktor Axel Bergengren, of Borås, Sweden, and *d* 10 March 1969, leaving issue:

1a +RICHARD ANTHONY HENRY [Richard Pelham Esq, Hisomley Farm House, Westbury, Wilts BA13 4DD]; *b* 1 Aug 1952; heir presumptive; *educ* Eton; *m* 1987 *Georgina Levinge, dau of David Gilmour, of Ringshall Grange, Suffolk, and has issue:

1b +Duncan James Bergengren; *b* 24 Nov 1987

2b +Christopher (Kit) Douglas Gilmour; *b* 28 July 1990

1a *Ella Christine [Mrs John Perring, 21 Somerset Rd, Wimbledon, London SW19 5JZ]; *b* 20 July 1940; *m* 21 July 1961 *John Raymond Perring, est son of Alderman Sir Ralph Edgar Perring, 1st Bt (*qv*), and has issue

2a *Judith Henrietta [Mrs Christopher Chetwood, The Bell House, Ellisfield, Hants RG25 2QD]; *b* 13 March 1943; *m* 26 Oct 1968 Christopher John Chetwood, MA, ACA (*d* July 1990), only son of Leonard William Chetwood, of Sheffield, and has issue:

1b *Thomas William; *b* 13 March 1970

2b *Henry Jonathan; *b* 1972

3b *Matthew James; *b* 1981

1b *Henrietta Rose; *b* 1983

(1) Joan Ursula, JP (Surrey 1951); *b* 24 Feb 1907; *m* 9 April 1929 John Edward Sealy, MA (*d* 30 March 1968), only son of George Elliot Sealy, of Ringmer Park, nr Lewes, Sussex, and *d* 1989, leaving:

1a *Nicholas John Elliot [Nicholas Sealy Esq, Timber Hill, Chobham, Surrey]; *b* 1938; *educ* Eton; late Capt Rifle Bde; *m* 1971 *Hon Lavinia Caroline Piercy, twin dau of 2nd Baron Piercy (*qv*), and has issue

1a *Agnes Coral Pelham [Mrs James Curwen, Deep Ford Cottage, Chobham, Surrey]; *b* 1932; *m* 1954 *James Gilbert Curwen and has:

1b *Henry James Gospatric; *b* 1957

2b *Simon Charles Edward; *b* 1959; *m* 1984 *Jane Kathrine, dau of Robert Snell, of Dinas Powis, S Glam, and has:

1c *Carolyn Sara; *b* 1986

2c *Nicola Helen; *b* 1988

3c *Georgina; *b* 1994

3b *Philip Mark Ivo; *b* 1963
1b *Rachel Helen Vanessa; *b* 1962
2a *Ann Pelham [Mrs Fereydoun Ala, Hall Farm, Weatheroak Hill, Alvechurch, Birmingham B48 7EG]; *b* 1934; *m* 1957 *Fereydoun Ala, MB, ChB, MRCPE, FRCP, and has issue:
1b *Arjan; *b* 1957
2b *Souren; *b* 1960; *m* 1990 *Natalyn and has issue:
1c *Mary; *b* 1994
3b *Tour; *b* 1967
(2) Beryl Northup; *b* 5 Nov 1908; *m* 14 Dec 1940 Lawrence Swan (*d* 1994), late S/Ldr RAFVR, son of Lt-Col Norman Edward Swan, Green Howards, of Oxford, and *d* 1992
3 Anthony Ashley Ivo, Capt RE, Sudan CS, Order Medjidie (4th Cl), WW I France and Palestine (despatches); *b* 23 Oct 1879; *m* 1st 5 Aug 1908 Muriel Spear (*d* 5 July 1927), dau of Capt George Spear Lindeman, RN, of Sydney, NSW; *m* 2nd 11 Sept 1928 Barbara Clare (*d* 1992) dau of Col James Edward Doidge Taunton, DQMG Australian Mil Forces, and *d* 15 Oct 1951
4 Herbert Lyttelton, Lt and Adjt Roy Sussex Regt, had Cross of Legion of Honour; *b* 3 April 1884; *ka* at battle of the Aisne, 14 Sept 1914
1 Ruth Mary, Sister of the Community of the Holy Trinity, Ascot; *b* 30 May 1873; *d* unm 5 March 1943

The 5th EARL *d* 21 April 1905; his est son,

JOCELYN BRUDENELL PELHAM, **6th Earl of Chichester**, OBE (1918), DL and JP Sussex, Capt and Brevet Lt-Col late 5th Bn Roy Sussex Regt; *b* 21 May 1871; *educ* Trin Coll Cambridge (BA); *m* 17 May 1898 Ruth (*d* 8 Feb 1965), est dau of Francis William Buxton (*see* BUXTON, Bt), and *d* 14 Nov 1926, leaving:

1 FRANCIS GODOLPHIN HENRY PELHAM, **7th Earl of Chichester**; *b* 23 March 1905; *d* unm 22 Nov 1926
2 JOHN BUXTON, **8th Earl**
1 Elizabeth Jocelyn; *b* 27 March 1899; *m* 27 Oct 1948 Capt Charles Murray Beazley, son of Arthur George Beazley, of Orwell, Walton-on-the-Hill, and *dsp* Aug 1975. He *d* 27 April 1965
2 Prudence Mary BUHLER; *b* 6 April 1910; *m* 25 March 1939 F/O Guy Rawstron Branch, EGM, AAF, yst son of Charles Churchill Branch, OBE, and *d* 13 Oct 1952. He was *ka* in the Battle of Britain, 11 Aug 1940

The 7th EARL's bro:

JOHN BUXTON PELHAM, **8th Earl of Chichester**, Hon Attaché Warsaw 1931 and Washington 1933, Hon Priv Sec to Br HC Canada 1934, 3rd Sec and Press Attaché The Hague 1939, Capt Scots Gds WW II; *b* 12 June 1912; *m* 27 March 1940 Ursula (*m* 2nd 8 May 1957 (*divorce* 1971) Ralph Gunning Henderson, only son of E W Henderson, of Argentina, and *d* 1989), dau of Walter de Pannwitz, of Hartekamp, Beenebroek, Holland, and was *kas* 21 Feb 1944, leaving issue:

1 JOHN NICHOLAS PELHAM, **9th and present Earl of Chichester**
1 *Georgiana Joceleyn [The Lady Georgiana Caranci, La Catalina, Diego de Alvear, Santa Fe, Argentina]; *b* 7 June 1942; *m* 1974 *Helios Alberto Caranci, son of Helios Jorge Caranci, of Arredondo 2015, Castelar, Buenos Aires, Argentina, and has issue:
(1) *Helios Nicolas; *b* 1983
(1) *Cecilia Catalina; *b* 1976
(2) *Ursula Claudia; *b* 1978

Seat: Little Durnford Manor, Wilts. Although dating chiefly from the 1740s, the Manor in which Little Durnford is situated is known to have been owned between 1548 and 1795 by a family called Young or Yonge, one of whom, Edward, Bath King-of-Arms, married a sister of the 1st Viscount Chetwynd (*qv*). (It was in his time that the dining room was plastered in an elaborate baroque design.) Moreover the tower on the north side may well date from before the Civil War. And the three-storey northeast wing could have been added as early as 1710, well before the major remodelling of the mid-18th century, since some of its features clearly go back to that period.

The most noticeable aspect of Little Durnford is the enchanting stippling effect given by the alternating flint and stone material of the elevations. This is seen to best advantage on the western side, where the ground floor windows have alternating triangular and D-shaped pediments and globular finials at either end of the parapet above the second and top storey which effectively break up the otherwise over rectinlinear outline. But the same chequer-board effect is to be found on the stable block too, for the whole property is remarkably harmonious.

A certain Edward Hinxman bought the house in the late 18th century and was almost certainly responsible for the pretty wrought-iron balustrades set against the first-floor windows of the south front, where the main entrance of triangular-pedimented portico over twin columns is situated. A century later Little Durnford was acquired by the general manager of a Wessex bank, whose granddaughter wrote an admirable book about it entitled *A Wiltshire House*. The **9th** and present **Earl of Chichester** bought it in 1966, his old family seat having been sold in 1947.

CHICHESTER, Bt

Arms: Chequy or and gu., a chief vair. **Crest:** A heron rising with an eel in his beak, ppr. **Motto:** *Ferme en foi* ('Firm in faith')
Creation: Bt. (E) 4 Aug 1641.

SIR (EDWARD) JOHN CHICHESTER, 11TH BT, of Raleigh, Devon [Sir John Chichester Bt, Battramsley Lodge, Boldre, Lymington, Hants SO41 8PT]; *b* 14 April 1916; *s* f 1940; *educ* Radley and RMC Sandhurst; Capt Roy Scots Fus and RNVR WW II, King's Messenger 1947–50, with ICI 1950–60; *m* 23 Sept 1950 *Hon Anne Rachel Pearl, 3rd dau of 2nd Baron Montagu of Beaulieu (*qv*) and widow of Maj Howel Joseph Moore-Gwyn, Welsh Gds, and has had issue:

1 +JAMES HENRY EDWARD; *b* 15 Oct 1951; *educ* Eton; *m* 1990 *(Margaret) Anne, only dau of Maj John Walkelyne Chandos-Pole, JP, DL, of Radbourne Hall, Derbys, and has issue:
(1) +Edward John Chandos-Pole; *b* 27 July 1991
(2) +Charles James; *b* 1992
2 +Julian John Raleigh; *b* 29 Sept 1963; *educ* Eton; *m* 12 Nov 1994 *Holly J B, yr dau of Capt J H B Hartley and Mrs Keith Martin, and has:
(1) +Linus; *b* 5 Feb 1997
(1) *Sylvi [*sic*]; *b* 28 Feb 1998
1 *Coral Anne [Mrs Christopher McEwen, Aldhams, Bromley Rd, Lawford, Manningtree, Essex CO11 2NE]; *b* 7 Jan 1954; *m* 18 June 1977 *Christopher Angus McEwen, MICE, yr son of Capt Donald McEwen, DSC, RN, of Boskey Dell, Bunch Lane, Haslemere, Surrey, and has issue:
(1) *Rosanna Clare; *b* 1981
(2) *Alexia Catherine; *b* 1982
(3) *Sabrina Caroline; *b* 1988
2 *Georgina Caroline [Mrs Christopher Leyland, Greymare Farm, Belford, Northumberland NE70 7PG]; *b* 19 Nov 1955; *m* 1985 *Christopher J Leyland, son of John Christopher Michael Leyland (*see* COTTERELL, Bt), and has issue:
(1) *Benjamin John; *b* 1994
(1) *Emma Rose; *b* 1989
3 Mary Rose; *b* 3 March 1957; *m* 1978, as his 2nd w, *Greville Patrick Charles Howard (*see* SUFFOLK and BERKSHIRE, E) and *d* 1980

Lineage: Sir JOHN CHICHESTER, yr bro of 1st Viscount Chichester of Carrickfergus (*see* DONEGALL, M); had an est s:

Sir JOHN CHICHESTER, of Raleigh, Devon; *m* Anne, dau of Sir Robert Dennis, of Holcombe, Devon, and *d* from disease caught from the prisoners in Exeter Castle spring 1585, leaving:

Sir ROBERT CHICHESTER, KB, of Raleigh; *m* 1st Frances Harington, yst dau of 1st Baron Harygnton of Exton, and had an only dau (Anne, *m* 1st Earl of Elgin (*see* ELGIN and KINCARDINE, E, also AILESBURY, M)); *m* 2nd Ursula (*m* 2nd Sir Ralph Sydenham), dau of Robert Hill, of Shilston, Devon, and *d* 24 April 1624, having by her had, with a dau:

Sir John Chichester, 1st Bt (E), so *cr* 4 Aug 1641, of Raleigh; MP Barnstaple 1661–67; *b* 23 April 1623; *m* 1st Elizabeth (*dsp* 1654), dau of Sir John Rayney, Bt; *m* 2nd 18 July 1655 Mary (*m* 3rd 1668 Edward Buller), widow of George Warcup and dau of Theodore Colley, and *d* 1667, having by her had, with other issue:

1 **Sir John Chichester, 2nd Bt**; *b* 1658; *m* 4 Nov 1679 Elizabeth, dau of Sir Charles Bickerstaffe, of The Wilderness, Seal, Kent, and was *bur* with her 16 Sept 1680
2 ARTHUR (Sir), **3rd Bt**
3 Henry; *m* Dorothy, widow of John Chichester, of Hall, and dau and coheir of Sir Henry Carew, of Bickleigh, Devon

The 2nd Bt's bro,

Sir Arthur Chichester, 3rd Bt, of Youlston; MP Barnstaple 1685–90 and 1713–18; *m* Elizabeth, dau of Thomas Drewe, of The Grange, Devon, and *d* 3 Feb 1717/8, leaving, with seven daus:

Sir John Chichester, 4th Bt, of Youlston; MP Barnstaple 1734–40; *bapt* 2 Jan 1688/9; *m* 1st Anne (*bur* 16 July 1723), dau of John Leigh, of Newport, IoW; *m* 2nd 1733 Frances (who survived him), widow of Francis Hall, of Sandford, Crediton, Devon, and dau of Andrew Quicke, of Newton St Cyres, and *d* 2 Sept 1740, having had by his 1st w, with five daus (also by his 1st w?):

1 **Sir John Chichester, 5th Bt**, of Youlston; High Sheriff Devon 1753; *bapt* 26 March 1721; *m* Frances, 2nd dau and coheir of Sir George Chudleigh, of Haldon, and *d* 18 Dec 1784, leaving:

(1) **Sir John Chichester, 6th Bt**, of Youlston; High Sheriff Devon 1788–89; *d* unm 30 Sept 1808

2 William (Rev), Rector Sherwell and Georgeham, Devon; *b c* 1722; *m* 29 Dec 1748 Mary, dau of John Bellamine, of Hart, Devon, and *d* Sept 1770, leaving, with four daus:

(1) John, of Hart; *b c* 1752; *m* 26 June 1787 Elizabeth Cory (*d* June 1837), of Newton, Devon, and *d* 1 Aug 1800, leaving, with other issue:

1a **Sir Arthur Chichester, 7th Bt**, of Youlston; High Sheriff Devon 1816–17; *b* 25 April 1790; *m* 8 Sept 1819 Charlotte (*d* 18 Aug 1834), yst dau of Sir James Hamlyn Williams, 2nd Bt, of Clovelly Court, and *d* 30 May 1842, having had, with three other s and another dau:

1b ARTHUR (Sir), **8th Bt**

1b Blanche, *m* 30 Aug 1855 John Toller Nicholetts, of S Petherton, Som (*d* 1910), and *d* 7 Feb 1918, leaving issue

The 7th Bt's est s,

Sir Arthur Chichester, 8th Bt, DL and JP; Capt 7th Hus, Hon Col N Devon Yeo Cav; *b* 4 Oct 1822; *m* 1st 20 Nov 1847 Mary (*d* 28 June 1879), est dau of John Nicholetts, of S Petherton; *m* 2nd 23 Jan 1883 Rosalie Amelia (*d* 22 Aug 1908), widow of Sir Alexander Palmer Bruce Chichester, 2nd and last Bt of Arlington, and dau of Thomas Chamberlayne, of Cranbury Park Hants, and by his 1st w had, with other issue:

1 EDWARD (Sir), **9th Bt**

2 Henry; *b* 26 Nov 1851; *m* 13 May 1876 Adah Georgiana (*d* 25 Jan 1944), yst dau of Horatio Francis Kingsford Holloway (formerly Martelli), DL, JP, of Marchwood Park, Hants, and *d* 4 July 1929, leaving issue:

(1) Arthur Raleigh, Lt Roy N Devon Yeo; *b* 30 May 1879; *m* 16 Dec 1903 Isabel Edith Thomasine (*d* 26 March 1967), er dau of Sir George Sidney Meade Thomas, 6th Bt (*see* 1970 edn THOMAS, Bt, of Yapton), and *dsp* 18 June 1949

(2) John, Lt 4th Bn N Staffs Regt; *b* 1890; *d* 17 Sept 1914

(1) Thomasine; *m* 29 Nov 1905 Walter Grenfell White, son of S Francis White, of 13 Bolton Gardens, SW and *dsp* 15 April 1956. He *d* 30 May 1943

(2) Vera; *m* 1st 17 Dec 1910 Lt-Cdr George Harley Pownall, RN, son of Frank Pownall, barrister. He was *ka* 25 April 1915. She *m* 2nd 20 June 1921 Lt-Col Herbert Hallilay, only son of Richard Hallilay, barrister Middle Temple, and *dsp* 20 Aug 1967. He *d* 14 Feb 1940

3 Gerard, Capt 98th Prince of Wales's Regt, Maj and Hon Lt-Col 4th Bn N Staffs Regt; *b* 31 Oct 1859; *m* 15 Oct 1891 Alice (*d* 3 Feb 1932), dau of George Pinckney, of Feniton Court, Devon, and *d* 15 Dec 1906, leaving issue:

(1) Ronald Gerard, Cdr RN; *b* 28 May 1896; *m* 16 May 1946 *Anna Maria, dau of Gottfried Mauracher, of Maurach, Tyrol, Austria, and *dsp* 11 Aug 1956

(1) Alice Mary; *m* 31 July 1923 Capt (Andrew) Stuart Hibberd, MBE, late IA, formerly Ch Announcer BBC, son of W H Hibberd, of Broadstone, Dorset

(2) Geraldine Maud; *d* unm 2 March 1977

(3) Christine Margaret; *d* unm 11 Oct 1947

4 George; *b* 7 Aug 1865; *m* 1st 17 Jan 1900 Frances Caroline (*d* 9 Feb 1904), yst dau of Col Hugh Robert Hibbert, Roy Fus, of Birtles Hall, Cheshire, and had issue:

(1) Patrick George, OBE (1965), G/Capt RAF WW II 1939–43 (Greek AFC); *b* 18 March 1901; *educ* Sherborne; *m* 22 April 1931 Gladys Evelyn Vesta Clemency (*d* 1977), er dau of William Carnegie Barnes, of Hayne Manor, Lewdown, Devon, and *d* 1983, leaving issue:

1a +Jeremy Patrick [Jeremy Chichester Esq, Hawthorn Cottage, Congresbury, nr Bristol, Somerset BS19 5BE]; *b* 11 Sept 1932; *educ* Kelly Coll; *m* 3 Nov 1956 *Kathleen Anne, only dau of William George Lloyd, of Nashley Ho, Weston-super-Mare, Som, and has issue:

1b +Mark Arlington Raleigh [Cdr Mark Chichester RN, The Lodge, Hayne Manor, Lewdown, nr Okehampton, Devon]; *b* 9 Nov 1957; *educ* Malvern BSc (Hons); RN in submarines; *m* 1984 (*divorce* 19-) Adrienne Valmai, yr dau of Douglas Henry Cook, of Sutherland Dve, Hutton, Avon, and has issue:

1c *Amelia Henryetta Frances; *b* 1989

2c *Alicia Vesta Anne; *b* 1991

2b +Matthew Patrick Lloyd [Matthew Chichester Esq, Apt 6, Nevsky Prospect, 3 St Petersburg, Russia]; *b* 25 Feb 1966; *m* 1997 *Jill Katherine, 2nd dau of David Allen, of Burcottla, Brierton, Bucks

1a (cont.) Mr and Mrs J P Chichester also adopted:

*Miranda Frances Louise; *b* 19 Feb 1962; *m* 1987 *Trevor D Jones, son of K H Jones, of Tenterden, Kent and has:

1c *Hugo George Hearn; *b* 1993

2c *Oscar Joseph Lloyd; *b* 1996

1a *Patricia Gladys Clemency; *b* 8 Sept 1930; *m* 7 Dec 1963 *F/Lt Anthony Arthur Greves Quinton, MD, RAF, only son of A G Quinton, of 16 Waverley Way, Carshalton, Surrey, and has issue:

1b *Lucinda Clemency; *b* 16 Nov 1965

2a *(Caroline Sandra Pietre) Katrina; *b* 31 Dec 1943; *m* 1970 *R-Adml Michael George Temple Harris (*see* HARRIS, B) and has issue

3a *Clarissa Evelyn Georgette; *b* 23 April 1948; *m* 1972 *Keith James Keating, of Cloncurry, W Qld, Australia, and has issue:

1b *Simon Keith; *b* 1979

1b *Melissa Evelyn; *b* 1973

2b *Georgina Naomi; *b* 1974

(2) Adrian Francis; *b* 3 June 1903

4 (cont.) George Chichester *m* 2nd 15 Feb 1908 Essex Mary, 2nd dau of Col Hugh Robert Hibbert, of Birtles Hall, and *d* 24 July 1933

5 Charles (Rev), Rector of Shirwell, Barnstaple, Devon 1894–1936; *b* 19 Aug 1868; *educ* BNC Oxford (MA); *m* 24 June 1896 Emily Annie (*d* 23 April 1962), dau of Samuel Page, and *d* 7 Jan 1938, leaving issue:

(1) James John, late Lt Duke of Edinburgh's Wilts Regt, served WW I 1916–18; *b* 19 Nov 1897; *m* 3 Sept 1932 Beatrice Walton Milward (*d* 28 April 1963), widow of Robert Webster, of Uvakellie, Madulsima, Ceylon, and Parkwood, Harrietsham, Kent, and 2nd dau of William Milward Jones, JP, of Rosebank, Rathfarnham, Co Dublin, and *dsp* 7 Jan 1968

(2) Francis Charles (Sir), KBE (received accolade from HM with Drake's sword at Greenwich 1967, CBE 1964), FIN, chm Francis Chichester Ltd, Map and Guide Publishers, aviator, navigator, ocean racer, second person to fly solo England to Australia 1929, first person to make long distance flight solo in a seaplane 1931, Johnston Memorial Trophy for Air Navigation 1931, winner of first solo Trans-Atlantic Yacht Race 1960, solo one-stop global circumnavigation at record speed in *Gypsy Moth IV* 27 Aug 1966–28 May 1967 (this epic voyage via Cape Horn achieved numerous records and various awards), Yachtsman of the Year Trophy 1960, Gold Medal Inst of Navigation 1961, Blue Water Medal of Cruising Club of America 1962 and 1967, Silver Globe Award, Br Inst of Navigation 1967, Achievement Medal, American Inst of Navigation 1967, Marconi Memorial Medal of Honour New York 1967, Italian Polhena da Bravura San Remo 1967, memb d'honneur of Yacht Club de France 1967, Gold Medal RGS 1967, Yr Bro Trin House 1968, Freeman Barnstaple, author: *The Lonely Sea and the Sky* (autobiography) and other books on solo flights, sailing and navigation; *b* 17 Sept 1901; *educ* Marlborough; *m* 1st 1923 Muriel Eileen (*d* 21 Dec 1929), dau of M F Blackiston, and had issue:

1a George Beresford; *b* 30 May 1926; *m* 10 July 1965 *Elizabeth Gay, yr dau of Beresford Button, of Telarah Station, Coonamble, NSW, and *dsp* 18 Oct 1967

(2) (cont.) Francis Chichester *m* 2nd 25 Feb 1937 Sheila Mary (*d* 1989), chm Francis Chichester map publishers from 1972, yr dau of Gerald Craven, of Belle Eau Park, Notts, and Coln St Aldwyn, Glos, and by her had issue:

2a +Giles Bryan [Giles Chichester Esq MEP, 9 St James's Place, London SW1A 1PE]; *b* 29 July 1946; *educ* Westminster and Ch Ch Oxford; MEP (C) Devon and E Plymouth 1994–; dir Francis Chichester, map publishers, 1971– (co sec 1970–89, md 1983–, chm 1989–); FRGS 1972; *m* 8 Sept 1979 *Virginia, dau of Edwin Ansell, and has issue:

1b +George Arthur Francis; *b* 1981

2b +Charles Edward Orlando; *b* 1990

1b *Jessica Mary; *b* 1984

(1) Barbara, JP; *b* 20 Jan 1907; *m* 25 Sept 1951 John Charles Fanshawe Royle, JP, MA (*d* 1973), son of Arthur Fanshawe Waterloo Royle, of Lympsham Manor, Somerset, and *d* 23 Dec 1995

(2) Cicely; *b* 16 Aug 1913; *d* unm 11 July 1997

6 Orlando, Capt late 6th Bn Devon Regt; *b* 6 Nov 1873; *m* 8 April 1899 Isabel Clare (*d* 28 Feb 1952), dau of Egerton Parks-Smith, late RA, of Clifton, Bristol, and *d* 3 March 1933, leaving issue:

(1) Angela Clare Rosalind; *b* 16 Jan 1909; *m* 7 May 1928 Michael Nial Slade (later Sir Michael Slade, 6th Bt), 2nd son of Sir Cuthbert Slade, 4th Bt (*qv*), and *d* 4 Sept 1959, leaving issue

1 Beatrice; *m* 2 Aug 1870 Charles Chichester, DL, JP, of Hall, Barnstaple, and *d* 14 May 1931, leaving issue. He *d* 5 Nov 1912

2 Norah; *m* 1899 Francis Bernard Parr Manning, LRCP, and *d* 30 May 1933. He *d* 25 March 1937

3 Evelyn; *m* 3 April 1877 Edward Fairfax Studd, late Capt RFA, of Exleigh, Starcross, S Devon, and *d* 11 Feb 1947, leaving issue. He *d* 20 Sept 1942

4 Geraldine; *m* 20 Sept 1888 Percy William Barons Northcote, 2nd son of Rev G Barons Northcote, MA, of Somerset Court, Somerset, and *d* 11 Oct 1930. He *dsp* Dec 1899

Sir ARTHUR *d* 13 July 1898; his est surv son,

Sir Edward Chichester, 9th Bt, CB, CMG, Adml Supt Naval Establishment Gibraltar 1904–06, ADC to TM QUEEN VICTORIA and EDWARD VII 1899–1902, served in S Africa 1881, Egypt 1882 and 1884–85 and S Africa 1900–01; *b* 20 Nov 1849; *m* 12 Oct 1880 Catharina Emma (*d* 24 July 1937), est dau of Cdr R C Whyte, RN, of Instow, N Devon, and had issue:

1 EDWARD GEORGE (Sir), **10th Bt**

2 Arthur Whyte, Col RASC WW I; *b* 17 Jan 1885; *m* 8 June 1921 Marthe Lucie Madeleine, dau of Col Richet, of Belgium, and *d* 6 Sept 1951, leaving issue:

(1) +Gilbert; *b* 16 Sept 1924

(1) *Marie-José (twin); *b* 16 Sept 1924

3 Robert Charles, Lt RN WW I; *b* 29 Oct 1889; *ka* Battle of Jutland 31 May 1916

4 Marcus Beresford, Capt Roy N Devon Yeo WW I; *b* 10 April 1896; *m* 11 June 1925 Myra Brownrigg (*d* 1985), yst dau of Maj Harvey Brownrigg Jay, and *d* 1985, leaving issue:

(1) *Imogen Ann [Mrs Arthur Hamilton, Crawley Lodge, Yarcombe, Honiton, Devon]; *b* 1926; *m* 10 Feb 1948 Maj Arthur John Digby Hamilton, Scots Gds (*d* 1980) (*see* FAIRLIE-CUNNINGHAME, Bt), only son of Col Arthur Cochrane Hamilton, 6th Dragoon Gds, and has issue:

1a *Philip Arthur Marcus; *b* 3 Jan 1949

2a *Edward Digby Hamilton; *b* 28 Sept 1953

3a *James John; *b* 24 Oct 1959

4a *Thomas Patrick (twin); *b* 24 Oct 1959

1a *Kate Antonia [Mrs Simon Dewhurst, Sicily Oak, Cholmondeley, Malpas, Cheshire]; *b* 9 June 1950; *m* 1st 1972 (*divorce* 1979) Robin Salt, and has issue:

1b *Thomas Bertram; *b* 1972

1b *Antonia Jane; *b* 1974

1a (cont.) Mrs Kate Salt *m* 2nd 1981 *Simon Peter Dewhurst, and has further issue:

2b *Patrick Digby; *b* 1983

3b *Frederick Oliver; *b* 1989

(2) *Jane Catherine [Mrs Roger Longrigg, Orchard House, Crookham, Hants]; *b* 1929; *m* 20 July 1957 *Roger Erskine Longrigg, 2nd son of Brig Stephen Hemsley Longrigg, OBE, DLitt, of Chancellor Ho, Tunbridge Wells, and has issue:

1a *Laura Jane; *b* 21 June 1958

2a *Frances Angelica; *b* 26 March 1961

3a *Clare Selina; *b* 23 Aug 1963

1 Catherina Edina; *m* 27 June 1905 Maj Charles Venables Beresford, Worcs Regt, 2nd son of His Honour Judge Cecil Hugh Wriothesley Beresford, and *d* 18 April 1968, having had issue. He *d* 1963

2 Janet; *m* 3 Feb 1904 Edward Hornby Beckwith, of Cranfield, East Grinstead, 2nd son of Rev G L Beckwith, Vicar of Collingham, and *d* 18 Nov 1966, aged 82, leaving issue. He *d* 22 Jan 1921

3 Victoria May, OBE (1951); *m* 2 Dec 1914 1st Baron Dulverton (*qv*), and *d* 5 April 1968, leaving issue

4 Edith Mary; *m* 26 Jan 1911 (*divorce* 1939) Sir Charles Stephen Bine Renshaw, 2nd Bt (*qv*), and had issue

5 Fanny; *m* 2 June 1930 (*divorce* 1943) Capt Patrick Maitland Campbell, MC (*d* 29 Aug 1961), son of P W Campbell, of Edinburgh, and had issue:

(1) *Fiona Patricia; *b* 6 Oct 1932; *m* 10 Dec 1955 *Derek Gilbert, son of Charles Vincent Gilbert, Sudan CS, and has issue:

1a *Patrick Charles; *b* 12 May 1966

1a *Joanna Catherine; *b* 22 April 1957

2a *Daphne Mary; *b* 3 Feb 1959

3a *Erica Claire; *b* 21 Dec 1962

6 Joanna

Sir EDWARD *d* 17 Sept 1906; his est son,

Sir Edward George Chichester, 10th Bt, Cdr RN, served in the Naval Bde in S African War; *b* 22 Jan 1883; *m* 1st 5 Jan 1915 (*divorce* 1933) Phyllis Dorothy, dau of Henry Francis Compton, DL, of Minstead Manor Ho, Lyndhurst and Mapperton Ho, Dorset, and had issue:

1 Sir EDWARD JOHN CHICHESTER, **11th and present Bt**

1 *Mary; *b* 29 Sept 1917; *m* 29 March 1941 *Cdr John Blakeley Russell, DSC, RN, son of Maj George Blakeley Russell, of Instow, N Devon, and has issue:

(1) *Christopher John; *b* 1954

(1) *Hermione Anne; *b* 1942; *m* 1962 *Robin Labron Johnson, and has issue:

1a *Nicolas Patrick Amyas Labron; *b* 1963

2a *Tristan Alexander Labron; *b* 1965

(2) *Cherry Rose; *b* 1952; *m* 1977 *F/Lt Andrew Renshaw and has issue (*see* RENSHAW, Bt)

Sir Edward *m* 2nd 5 June 1924 (*divorce* 1935) Hon Moira Faith Lilian, formerly w of Capt John Robert Rankin Fullerton, 15th/19th Hus, and only dau of 3rd Baron Deramore (*qv*), and by her had issue:

2 Patrick D'Arcy Robert; *b* 13 Oct 1925; *d* 12 April 1945

Sir Edward *m* 3rd 21 Dec 1935 Gladys Ethel (*m* 3rd 22 April 1961 Cdr Robert S Heffner, USN (ret)), formerly w of Maj Francis Herbert Cairnes, 5th Inniskilling Dragoon Gds, and dau of John Fordham, and *d* 26 Sept 1940

CHILD

Arms: Per chevron az. and gu., on a chevron engrailed erm. between three eagles close arg. a fylfot sa. **Crest:** An eagle, wings expanded arg., charged on the breast with a fylfot sa., holding in the beak by its neck a serpent entwined round the body vert. **Motto:** *Imitare quam invidere* ('To imitate rather than to envy'). **Creation:** Bt. (UK) 16 Sept 1919.

SIR (COLES JOHN) JEREMY CHILD, 3RD BT, of Bromley Palace, Bromley, Kent [Sir Jeremy Child Bt, c/o Representation, Joyce Edwards, 275 Kennington Rd, London SE11 6BY]; *b* 20 Sept 1944; *s* f 1971; *educ* Eton and Poitiers U; actor; *m* 1st 19 March 1971 (*divorce* 1976) Deborah Jane, dau of Henry Percival Snelling, of 20 Grange Rd, London W5, and has issue:

1 *(Honor) Melissa; *b* 1973

Sir JEREMY *m* 2nd 21 July 1978 (*divorce* 1987) Jan Todd, yst dau of Bernard Todd, of Kingston-upon-Thames, and has further issue:

1 +(COLES JOHN) ALEXANDER; *b* 10 May 1982

2 *Leonora; *b* 1980

Sir JEREMY *m* 3rd 1987 *Elizabeth (Libby), yst dau of Rev Grenville Morgan, of Canterbury, Kent, and has further issue:

2 +Patrick Grenville; *b* 1991

3 *Eliza Caroline; *b* 1989

Lineage: ROBERT CHILDE, of Woodside, Amersham, Bucks; *m* Katherine — (*bur* 7 May 1563) and was *bur* 3 April 1578, having had, with another s (also John):

JOHN CHILD, of Woodside; *b c* 1530; *m* Mary — (*bur* 9 Dec 1592) and was *bur* 13 Aug 1599, having had, with other issue:

ROBERT CHILD, of Woodside; *b* 1569; *m* 10 Feb 1592 Margaret Batchelor (*d* 20 April 1617) and *d* 1649, leaving a 2nd son:

WILLIAM CHILD, of Woodside; *b* 1601; *m* 1st Martha —; *m* 2nd 15 Nov 1632 Prudence Carter and *d* 1649, leaving by his 1st w:

JOHN CHILD, of Yaxley, Hunts; *b* 1625; *m* Frances (*d* 3 March 1717 aged 80), dau of Uriah Harris, and *d* 11 Dec 1705, leaving, with other issue:

JOHN CHILD, of Yaxley; *b* 1677; *m* Isabella (*d* 18 Jan 1747), dau of William Coles, of London, and *d* 19 Jan 1743, leaving issue:

WILLIAM CHILD, of Yaxley; *b* 1700; *m* Elizabeth, dau of William Nicholls, of Yaxley, and *d* 30 June 1770, leaving with other issue:

COLES CHILD, of Yaxley; *b* 1738; *m* 1762 his first cousin Isabella, dau and heir of Col Coles Child, and *d* 3 May 1798; his 2nd son:

COLES CHILD, Clerk Cheque Yeomen Gd *temp* GEORGEs III and IV; *b* 1775; *m* 16 May 1811 Ann Martha (*d* 21 March 1862), dau of George Frederick Casimar Stahischmidt, and *d* 25 July 1831, having had issue:

COLES WILLIAM JOHN CHILD, of Bromley Palace, Kent, DL, JP; *b* 23 March 1813; *m* 3 Oct 1850 Elizabeth Letitia, dau of Robert Jones, of Peckham, Surrey, and *d* 16 Jan 1873, having had an only son:

Sir Coles Child, 1st Bt (UK), so *cr* 16 Sept 1919, DL, JP, Hon Col 3rd Vol Bn Roy W Kent Regt, CA Kent, chm W Kent QS 1911, Ld Manors of Bromley, E Farleigh and E Peckham; *b* 6 April 1862; *m* 5 Aug 1885 Eliza Caroline (*d* 28 July 1932), only dau of Richard Bolton Barton, LLD, JP, of Stour Lodge, Bradfield, Essex, and had issue:

1 COLES JOHN (Sir), **2nd Bt**

1 Marjorie Isabel Knox; *b* 28 April 1886; *m* 17 April 1909 Maj Arthur Dunbar Whatman, son of George Dunbar Whatman, JP, and *d* 19 Dec 1969, leaving issue. He *d* 28 May 1965

2 Dorothy; *b* 28 April, *d* 2 May 1886

3 Audrey Eleanor Mary; *b* 17 May 1887

4 Norah Phyllis Amy; *b* 17 May 1889; *m* 17 March 1917 Rev Charles Hallam Edwards, Maj RWF, son of Maj Henry Herbert Edwards, RWF, and had issue

5 Kathleen Ida Rachael; *b* 4 Jan 1893; *d* unm 8 March 1934

Sir COLES *d* 29 Jan 1929; his son,

Sir (Coles) John Child, 2nd Bt, DL (Surrey 1960); *educ* Eton; Maj Coldstream Gds, Ld of the Manor of Bromley, ADC to Govr and C-in-C Canada 1931–33; *b* 11 Feb 1906; *m* 2 Feb 1933 Sheila (*d* 1 May 1964), est dau of Hugh Mathewson, of Pine Ave, Montreal; *d* 26 May 1971, having had issue:

1 Sir (COLES JOHN) JEREMY CHILD, **3rd and present Bt**

1 *Deirdre Kathleen [Mrs Antony Woodall, Mill House, Gt Hormead, Herts SG9 0NY]; *b* 13 Sept 1934; *m* 23 May 1959 *Antony Edward Woodall, yr son of Edward Corbet Woodall, OBE, of The Red Ho, Clifton Hampden, Oxon (*see* CRAWLEY-BOEVEY, Bt), and has issue:

(1) *James Henry; *b* 25 Oct 1960

(2) *Andrew Hugh; *b* 1 June 1963; *m* 1990 *Jane Mary Ashton, and has issue:

1a *Gabriel Sanderson; *b* 1992

2a *Leo Vincent; *b* 1996

1a *Constance Rose; *b* 1991

(3) *Edward Antony John; *b* 6 Sept 1967; *m* *Amanda Pritchett

2 *Honor Diana; *b* 31 May 1936; *m* 1st 27 June 1959 Capt Noel Hardwick Matterson (*d* 1982), late 1st The Roy Dragoons, only son of George Hardwick Matterson, of Stable Hills, Keswick, Cumberland; *m* 2nd 1985 *Robin Patrick Fremantle (*see* COTTESLOE, B), and by her 1st husb has issue:

(1) *Charles John Hardwick; *b* 26 Dec 1960; *m* 1987 *Elizabeth Caroline McGregor Moffat

(2) *Justin George Hardwick; *b* 26 July 1962

(3) *Nicholas Noel Hardwick; *b* 18 Dec 1963; *m* 1992 *Georgia Cadwaladr

(4) *Dominic Graham Hardwick; *b* 16 Feb 1965; *m* 1992 *Camilla Mary Roche

CHILSTON

Arms: Quarterly, 1st and 4th, arg. a man's heart gu. ensigned with an imperial crown ppr. and pierced by an arrow fesswise, the pheon towards the dexter also ppr., a chief az., thereon three mullets of the field (for DOUGLAS); 2nd and 3rd, gu. three escallops or, within a bordure arg. charged with eight acorns ppr. (for AKERS).
Crests: 1 An arm embowed in armour holding in the hand a sword all ppr. (for DOUGLAS), 2 An arm embowed in armour ppr., garnished or, holding in the hand a flagstaff also ppr., therefrom flowing a pennon barry of four az. and arg. (for AKERS).
Supporters: On either side a horse arg., that on the dexter supporting a flagstaff erect ppr., therefrom flowing a banner az. charged with three mullets arg., that on the sinister supporting a like flagstaff also ppr., therefrom flowing a banner erm. charged with a heart gu. crowned and pierced by an arrow, as in the arms.
Motto: *Sapientia et veritas* ('Wisdom and truth').
Creation: B. and V. (UK) 6 July 1911.

THE 4TH VISCOUNT CHILSTON, of Boughton Malherbe, Co Kent, and **Baron Douglas of Baads**, Co Midlothian (Alistair George Akers-Douglas) [The Rt Hon The Viscount Chilston, The Old Rectory, Twyford, Hants SO21 1NS]; *b* 5 Sept 1946; *s* cousin 1982; *educ* Eton and Madrid U; film producer; *m* 5 June 1971 *Juliet Anne, dau of Lt-Col Nigel Lovett, of The Old Rectory, Inwardleigh, Devon, and has:

1 +OLIVER IAN; *b* 13 Oct 1973
2 +Alexander Hugh; *b* 30 July 1975
3 +Dominic Lovett; *b* 31 July 1979

Lineage (of Douglas): Sir JAMES DOUGLAS; ancestor of:

LEONARD DOUGLAS, of Baads or Baddis in Midlothian, an estate he acquired 16 April 1551; had:

WILLIAM DOUGLAS, of Baads; *m* Jean, dau of Bruce of Clackmannan, and had:

JOSEPH DOUGLAS, of Baads; *m* 1st Jean Denham, of W Shields; *m* 2nd Beatrix Brown and by her had, with two daus:

JAMES DOUGLAS, of Baads; *m* Jean, dau of James Sandilands, of Muirhouse Dykes, by Margaret Somervell, and had, with two daus and a yr s (James, *s* to Muirhouse Dykes and had issue):

WILLIAM DOUGLAS, of Baads; *m* 3 March 1664 Joan, dau of Mason of Park of Blantyre, and had, with other issue:

1 Walter, Col, Govr-Gen Leeward Islands; *b* 1670; *s* to Baads on the renunciation of his bro William but sold it 1720, though in 1787 it was bought by his nephew Alexander (*see* below); *d* 1739, leaving:
(1) John
(2) James George; merchant in London
2 William; *b* 1679; Gen; *s* his f at Baads but renounced it to his er bro; *m* his cousin Jean, dau of James Douglas of Muirhouse Dykes
3 John; *b* 1682; Memb Assembly St Kitts, WI; Col; *d* 1783, leaving:
(1) John; MP Hindon, Wilts; had:
1a John
2a William
1a A dau; *m* her cousin Adml John Leigh Douglas
(2) James; Col 3rd Foot Gds
4 Rev Alexander; Min Skirling 1718 and E Calder, Midlothian, 1725; *m* 22 April 1726 Isabel, dau of Andrew Houstoun, of Calder Hall, and had, with other issue:
(1) Alexander, of Baads, which he bought 1787; *b* 1731; *m* 26 Sept 1765 Elizabeth Taylor and *d* 1787, leaving:
1a Isobel; had, with a s:
1b Elizabeth; *s* to Baads on the death of her bro 1852 and took the name DOUGLAS; *d* unm 1873
and was *s* by her cousin, James Douglas Stoddart Douglas (*see* below)
(2) John Leigh, Adml of the White; *b* 1741; *m* his cousin Charlotte, dau of John Douglas, MP (*see* above), but *dsp* Nov 1810
(1) Jean; *m* 4 Dec 1752 Aretas Akers (*see* below)
(2) Isobel; *m* 1st her cousin Sir James Douglas, Br Min Naples; *m* 2nd John Walcot and *d* 1817
(3) Mary Euphan; *m* Rev James Stoddart, Min Kirkintulloch, and had, with other issue:
1a George Alexander; *b* 1765; *m* — Bridges and *d* 1796, leaving, with another s:
1b James Douglas STODDART later DOUGLAS, of Baads, which he inherited 1873 from his cousin Elizabeth (*see* above); *b* 1793; *m* 1st 1830 Margaret Braziere (*dsp* 1858), adopted dau of George Douglas, of Chilston; *m* 2nd Jane Sarah, dau of James Jenkin, RE, but *dsp* 1875, when Baads passed to his cousin, **1st Viscount Chilston**

Lineage (of Akers): CHRISTOPHER AKERS descended from the AKERSes of Akers Hall, Lancs, settled in the W Indies *c* 1620; had:

CHRISTOPHER AKERS; living Barbados 1650–78; had, with a yr s (Christopher, *b* 1658):

JONAS AKERS; *b* 1654; *m* Rebecca, — (*d* 1726) and *d* 1727, having had:

JONAS AKERS; *m* 1703 Anne James (*d* 1763) and had, with other issue, including a yr s (James, *m* 1760 Jane Abbot (*d* 1789) and *d* 1791, having had three s):

EDMUND AKERS; *b* 1710; *m* 1st Sarah (*d* 1746), dau of Aretas Seton, Govr Leeward Isles, and had, with other issue:

1 ARETAS
1 Rebecca; *b* 1739; *m* 23 June 1763 Rev James Ramsay, Min Ch Ch, Nicola Town, and Rector Teston and Nettlestead, Kent, and had issue

EDMUND AKERS *m* 2nd Rachel Vance and *d* 1780, having by her had further issue

His est son,

ARETAS AKERS; *b* 1734; *m* 4 Dec 1752 Jean (*d* 11 Jan 1769), dau of Rev Alexander Douglas, Min E Calder, and *d* 1785, having had, with other issue:

1 Edmund, of Berrymead Priory, Acton, Middx; *b* 15 Jan 1757; *m* 1st 9 Sept 1784 Frances, dau of Joseph Rawlings, of St Kitts, and had:
(1) Elizabeth Rosa; *m* Maj — Hartmann and had an only dau
1 (cont.) Edmund Akers *m* 2nd Catherine Deerhurst and *d* 1821, having had:
(1) Aretas; *d* young
2 Aretas; *b* 1759; *m* 19 March 1795 his cousin Jean, dau of Rev James Ramsay, Rector Teston and Nettlestead, Kent, by Rebecca, dau of Edmund Akers (*see* above), and had, with other issue:
(1) ARETAS
(2) James Ramsay; *b* 1813; *educ* Caius Coll Cambridge (MA); *m* 1840 Mary Louisa Goodrich and *d* 1877, leaving, with two s:
1a Louisa; *m* John Beale, of Maidstone, and *d* 1865, leaving issue
2a Ellen; *m* Maj-Gen Arthur Saunders, RA, and had issue
(1) Caroline; *m* 1st J Allot Osborne; *m* 2nd John Borton, MA Cambridge, and *d* 1867, leaving issue

ARETAS AKERS *d* 15 Dec 1816; his est son,

ARETAS AKERS, of Malling Abbey, Kent, DL, JP; *b* 1799; *m* 9 May 1821 Isabella, dau of John Larking, of Clare Ho, Kent, and *d* 21 April 1855, having had, with other issue:

1 ARETAS (Rev)
2 Charles Style, Maj-Gen RE; *b* 21 Sept 1828; *m* 16 Oct 1851 Henrietta Margaret (*d* 2 May 1903), dau of Gen Despard, CB, and *d* 1887, having had, with seven other children:
(1) Charles Edmund; *b* 1861; *m* Charlotte Mabel Dwight, of Stockbridge, Mass., USA, and had issue:
1a James Dwight, Capt Gren Gds; *b* 1904; *educ* Eton; *m* 1st 17 July 1928 Dorothy Helen Fellows; *m* 2nd 12 Sept 1946 Pamela Corrie Bowmann, of Sydney, NSW; *m* 3rd 7 Nov 1960 *Lilian Alice Bentley
1a Henrietta Frances Ruth; *m* Lewis Gordon Campbell, of Craignish, and *d* 27 April 1977, leaving issue. He *d* 1944
2a *Teresa; *m* Capt Haynes Hubbard, RN, and has issue. He *d* 1963
(1) Mary Sophia; *m* Maj Henry Lyall, late RA, and *d* 1909, leaving issue
1 Jane Mary; *m* 25 March 1857 John P Green, of Hucking Ho, Kent, and *d* 1863, leaving issue
2 Caroline Ramsay; *m* 1849 Rev William Lewis Wigan, of Clare Ho, Kent, Vicar of East Malling, and *d* 6 April 1910, leaving issue. He *d* 8 Jan 1876
3 Mary Elizabeth; *m* 10 Oct 1860 Bertie Peter Cator, of Beckenham, Kent, and *d* 1 Jan 1918, leaving issue. He *d* 30 March 1875

The est son,

Rev ARETAS AKERS, of Malling Abbey; *b* 18 Nov 1824; *educ* Worcester Coll Oxford (MA); *m* 7 Aug 1849 Frances Maria (*m* 2nd 11 July 1866 William Whitmore and *d* 18 May 1900), 2nd dau of Francis Holles Brandram, DL, of Underriver Ho, Kent, and had issue:

1 ARETAS, **1st Viscount Chilston**
1 Isabel Frances; *d* unm 23 April 1903, aged 50
2 Eleanor Mary; *m* 10 Aug 1875 Edward Norman, of Chelsfield Ho, Kent, and *d* 28 Dec 1911, leaving issue

The Rev ARETAS AKERS *d* 19 Aug 1856; his son,

ARETAS AKERS later AKERS-DOUGLAS (roy licence 20 May 1875 under terms of will of his cousin Alexander Douglas of Baads), **1st Viscount Chilston**, of Boughton Malherbe, Co Kent, so *cr* 6 July 1911, as also BARON DOUGLAS OF BAADS, Co Midlothian (both UK), PC (1891), GBE (1920), DL, JP, *b* 21 Oct 1851; *educ* Eton and Univ Coll Oxford; barrister Inner Temple 1874, MP (C) E Kent 1880–85 and St Augustine's Kent 1885–1911, Ecclesiastical Commr, memb Ctee Cncl Educn Scotland, Patronage Sec Treasury 1885–86, 1886–92 and 1895, First Commr of Works 1895–1902, Home Sec 1902–05, KGStJ; *m* 10 June 1875 Adeline Mary (*d* 25 Feb 1929), dau of Horatio Austen-Smith, of Hayes, Kent, and *d* 15 Jan 1926, leaving issue:

1 ARETAS AKERS-DOUGLAS, **2nd Viscount Chilston**, PC (1939), GCMG (1935, KCMG 1927, CMG 1918); *b* 17 Feb 1876; Capt 3rd Bn Roy Scots; Dip Serv: Attaché 1898, served Cairo, 3rd Sec 1900, served Madrid, Constantinople and Athens, 2nd Sec 1905, Actg Agent and Consul-Gen Sofia 1907, served Rome 1907 and Vienna 1909, 1st Sec 1912, Chargé d'Affaires Montenegro 1911, 1913 and 1914, Romania 1914, FO 1915, Envoy Extrdy and Min Plen Vienna 1921–28 and Budapest 1928–33, Amb Extrdy and Min Plen Moscow 1933–38; *m* 6 Aug 1903 Amy (*d* 11 Aug 1962), dau of John Robert Jennings Bramly, late RHA, and *d* 25 July 1947, having had issue:

(1) Aretas; *b* 7 Nov 1905; *m* 1stly 25 May 1932 (*divorce* 1938) Irene, dau of George Richard Goss; *m* 2nd 1939 Marcia Victoria (*d* 3 Nov 1945), dau of John Myddleton Brace, of Mapitigama, Ceylon, and *d* following a motor accident 28 Feb 1940

(2) ERIC ALEXANDER AKERS-DOUGLAS, **3rd Viscount Chilston**; *b* 17 Dec 1910; *educ* Eton and Trin Coll Oxford; F/Lt RAFVR; *m* 15 Feb 1955 Marion (*d* 9 Jan 1970), dau of Capt Charles William Howard, RE, and *dsp* 10 April 1982

2 George Alexander, Maj and Brevet Lt-Col Roy Fus, formerly Capt Argyll and Sutherland Highrs, ADC to Viceroy of India 1904, served in S African War 1900 and WW I 1914; *b* 7 June 1878; *m* 5 Jan 1909 Doris (*d* 24 Sept 1971), dau of Stanley Christopherson, of Bramley, Surrey, and *d* 11 July 1955, having had issue:

(1) Ian Stanley, Capt WW II in Kent Yeo and Berks Yeo; *b* 16 Nov 1909; *m* 1st 5 Oct 1933 (*divorce* 1943) Joan Holroyd, only child of Maj Charles Bowring Toms, of 109 Oakwood Court, Kensington, W14, and had issue:

1a *Jennifer [Mrs Charles Smith-Bingham, Stag Cottage, Bagnor, Newbury, Berks]; *b* 30 Oct 1938; *m* 1st 24 June 1958 George David Henry Wiggin (*d* 1990), er son of Lt-Col Peter Milner Wiggin, JP, late 11th Hus, of Ashe Ho, Overton, Basingstoke, Hants, and has issue (*see* WIGGIN, Bt); *m* 2nd 1993 *Charles Arthur Smith-Bingham

(1) (cont.) Ian Akers-Douglas *m* 2nd 12 July 1945 *Phyllis Rosemary [Mrs John Shaw, 1 Garden Cottages, Amesbury Abbey, Amesbury, Wilts] (*m* 2nd 9 Oct 1965 Maj John Anthony Cobham Shaw, MC), dau of Arthur David Clere Parsons (*see* ROSSE, E), and *d* following an accident 16 Dec 1952, leaving by her:

1a ALASTAIR GEORGE AKERS-DOUGLAS, **4th and present Viscount Chilston**

2a *Diana [Mrs Simon Harrap, Perryland, Bentley, Farnham, Hants]; *b* 17 Sept 1948; *m* 24 May 1969 *Simon Richard Harrap, est son of Michael Harrap, of Marsh Ho, Bentley, Hants, and has issue (*see* DARRELL, Bt)

(2) Anthony George, Maj late 13th/18th Roy Hus, served WW II; *b* 21 Dec 1914; *educ* Eton; *m* 9 Aug 1941 *Dorothy Louise [Mrs Anthony Akers-Douglas, 23 Mytten Close, Cuckfield, W Sussex RH17 5LN], only dau of Brig-Gen Moreton Foley Gage, DSO (*see* GAGE, V), and *d* 1991, leaving:

1a +Adrian Anthony [Adrian Akers-Douglas Esq, PO Box 257, Limassol, Cyprus], late F/Lt RAF; *b* 17 Sept 1943; *educ* Eton; *m* 1st 2 April 1974 (*divorce* 1995) Janet Penelope (Penny), only dau of Sir Frederick Cecil, Mason, KCVO, CMG, of The Old Forge, Ropley, Alresford, Hants; *m* 2nd 11 May 1996 *Artemis Edith Coudounari, er dau of Louis Aristide Coudounaris, of Limassol, Cyprus, and by his 1st w has:

1b *Lara Victoria; *b* 13 May 1983

2b *Nicola Antonia; *b* 1991

2a +Francis Alexander Moreton [Francis Akers-Douglas Esq, Warrie Wood House, Windmill Hill, St Mary Platt, Kent TN15 8QR]; *b* 23 Sept 1948; *educ* Eton; *m* 1st 4 Oct 1974 (*divorce* 1997) Hon Julian Mary, er dau of 2nd Baron Bruntisfield (*qv*), and has:

1b +Joseph Michael Aretas; *b* 1979

2b +James George; *b* 1989

2a (cont.) Francis Akers-Douglas *m* 2nd 18 Feb 1998 *Mrs Lorna Stables, yr dau of John Farquharson

1a *Laura Dorothy; *b* 3 Sept 1957; *m* 1985 *Nicholas James Bell, er son of Dr Anthony Bell, of Woodruffs Farm, Fittleworth, Sussex, and has issue:

1b *Joshua Anthony Fernie; *b* 1988

2b *Benedict William James; *b* 1991

1b *Eliza Dorthy Thalia; *b* 1994

(1) Sonia *b* 9 Nov 1917; *d* 10 March 1918

(2) Angela Evelyn; *b* 6 March 1919; *m* 15 March 1940 Lt Douglas Shankland, RNVR, son of Andrew Shankland, of 3, Bristol Court, Brighton, and *d* 30 Nov 1959 leaving issue

1 Adeline Frances; *m* 30 Sept 1899 Fedor Andrew Satow, Judge of the Court of Appeal, Egypt, and *d* 19 Aug 1959, leaving issue. He *d* 23 Oct 1909

2 Ethel Margaret; *m* 27 April 1925 (*m annulled* 1928) Capt John William Haughton, son of W J Haughton, of Morley Hall, Wymondham, Norfolk, and *d* 25 Jan 1951. He *d* 1930

3 Bertha Marion; *m* 2 June 1905 Maj-Gen Sir Arthur Lynden Lynden-Bell, KCB, KCMG, DL, JP, late Col of the Buffs, 3rd son of Maj-Gen T L Lynden-Bell, of Brookhill, Co Wexford, and *d* 27 Jan 1960, leaving issue. He *d* 14 Feb 1943

4 Evelyn Amy; *m* 29 Oct 1910 Bernard Godfrey Samuelson, er son of Godfrey Blunden Samuelson, of Kenfield Hall, Canterbury, and *d* 13 July 1914, leaving issue (*see* SAMUELSON, Bt)

5 Cara Mary; *m* 3 May 1916 Maj John Esmond Longuet-Higgins, OBE, MC, late 13th London Regt, 2nd son of Henry Longuet Longuet-Higgins, of Turvey Abbey, Beds, and *d* 10 Oct 1969, leaving issue. He *d* 27 Jan 1968

CHILVER

Creation: B. (LP, UK) 1987.

THE BARON CHILVER, of Cranfield, Co Beds (Sir (Amos) Henry Chilver) [The Rt Hon The Lord Chilver, Lanlawren House, Trenewan, Looe, Cornwall PL13 2PZ]; *b* 30 Oct 1926; *educ* Southend High Sch and Bristol U; structural engrg assist BR 1947; lecturer: Bristol U 1952–54, Cambridge 1958–61; Fell Corpus Christi Coll Cambridge 1958–61; Prof Civil Engrg UCL 1961–69, Dir Centre for Environmental Studies 1967–69, V-Chllr Cranfield Inst Tech 1970–89; Assessor Inquiry on Lorries, People and the Environment 1979–80; dir: SKF (UK) 1972–80, De La Rue 1973–81, SE Regn Nat West Bank 1975–83, Delta Gp 1977–84, Powell Duffryn 1979–89, TR Technology Investment Tst 1982–88, Hill Samuel Gp 1983–87, Britoil 1986–88, ICI 1990–93, Zeneca Gp 1993–95; Chm: ICE Ctee on Educn and Trg 1973, PO 1980–81, Higher Educn Review Body NI 1978–81, U's Computer Bd 1975–78, RAF Trg and Educn Advsy Ctee 1976–80, RMCS Advsy Cncl Shrivenham 1978–83, Working Gp Advanced Ground Transport 1978–81, Electronics EDC 1980–85, ACARD 1982–85, Milton Keynes Devpt Corp 1983–93, Interim Advsy Ctee Teachers' Pay 1987–91, UFC 1988–91, BASE Int 1983–88, Innovation Advsy Bd DTI 1989–93, English China Clays 1989–95 (dir 1973–95), RJB Mining 1993–97; memb: Ferrybridge Enquiry Ctee 1965, Management Ctee Inst of Child Health 1965–69, ARC 1967–70 and 1972–75, SRC 1970–74, Beds Educn Ctee 1970–74, Planning and Tport Research Advsy Cncl 1972–79, Ctee for Industl Technologies 1972–76, CNAA 1973–76, Roy Commn Environmental Pollution 1976–81, Standing Commn Energy and Environment 1978–81, Cncl Birkbeck Coll 1980–82, Cncl Cheltenham Coll 1980–88, Advsy Bd for Research Cncls 1982–85, Bd Nat Advsy Body for Local Authority Higher Educn 1983–85; ktd 1978; Hon Fell Corpus Christi Coll Cambridge 1981, FEng 1977, FRS 1982, CIM; Hon DSc: Leeds 1982, Bristol 1983, Salford 1983, Bath 1986, Strathclyde 1986, Cranfield 1989, Buckingham 1990, Compiègne 1990; author: *Problems in Engineering Structures* (with R J Ashby, 1958), *Strength of Materials* (with J Case, 1959), *Thin-Walled Structures* (ed, 1967), *Strength of Materials and Structures* (with J Case and C T Ross, 3rd edn of *Strength of Materials*, 1993); *m* 1959 *Claudia Mary Beverley, only dau of Sir Wilfrid Grigson, CSI, of Pelynt, Cornwall, and has issue:

1 *John; *b* 1964; *educ* Bedford Sch

2 *Mark; *b* 1965; *educ* Bedford Sch

3 *Paul; *b* 1967; *educ* Bedford Sch

1 *Helen; *b* 1960; *m* 1979 *Geoffrey Prentice

2 *Sarah; *b* 1962

Lineage: AMOS HENRY CHILVER; *m* A E Mack and had:

(AMOS) HENRY, *cr* a **Baron**

CHITNIS

Creation: B. (LP, UK) 1977.

THE BARON CHITNIS, of Ryedale, Co N Yorks (Pratap Chidamber Chitnis) [The Rt Hon The Lord Chitnis, Beverley House, Shipton Rd, York; Quartier des Trois Fontaines, 84490 Vaucluse, France]; *b* 1 May 1936; *educ* Stonyhurst, Birmingham U (BA) and Kansas U (MA); admin asst NCB 1958–59; Lib Party: Local Govt 1960–62, Training Offr 1962–64, Press Offr 1964–66, Organisation Head 1966–69, Sec 1969–75, ch exec and dir 1975–88; ch exec Rowntree Social Serv Tst 1969–88; memb: Community Relations Commn 1970–77, BBC Immigrants Programme Advsy Ctee 1972–77 (chm 1979–83); Chm: Refugee Action 1981–86, Br Refugee Cncl 1986–89; *m* 1964 *Anne, dau of Frank Mansell Brand, and has had a s (*d* young)

Lineage: CHIDAMBER N CHITNIS; *m* Lucia Mallik and had:

PRATAP CHIDAMBER, *cr* a **Baron**

CHITTY

Creation: Bt. (UK) 25 Jan 1924.

SIR THOMAS WILLES CHITTY, 3RD BT, of the Temple [Sir Thomas Chitty Bt, Bow Cottage, W Hoathly, Sussex RH19 4QF]; *b* 2 March 1926; *s f* 1955; *educ* Winchester and Univ Coll Oxford; served in RN 1944–47, Shell Petroleum Co 1953–60, Granada Arts Fell U of York 1964–65, visiting lecturer U of Illinois, USA 1965–67, Visiting Prof Boston U 1969–70; author (as Thomas Hinde) (fiction): *Mr Nicholas* (1952), IHappy as Larry (1957), *For the Good of the Company* (1961), *A Place Like Home* (1962), *The Cage* (1962), *Ninety Double Martinis* (1963), *The Day the Call Came* (1964), *Games of Chance* (1965), *The Village* (1966), *High* (1968), *Bird* (1970), *Generally A Virgin* (1972), *Agent* (1974), *Our Father* (1975), *Daymare* (1980); non-fiction: *On Next to Nothing* (with w as Susan Hinde, 1976), *The Great Donkey Walk* (with w as Susan Chitty, 1977), *The Cottage Book* (1979), *Sir Henry and Sons* (autobiography, 1980), *A Field Guide to the English Country Parson* (1983), *Stately Gardens of Britain* (1983), *Forests of Britain* (1985), *Capability Brown* (1986), *Courtiers* (1986), *Tales from the Pumproom* (1988), *Imps of Promise* (1990), *Looking Glass Letters* (1991), *Paths of Progress* (1993), *A History of Highgate School* (1993), *A History of King's College School* (1994), *Carpenter's Children* (1995), *The University of Greenwich* (1996); *m* 23 Aug 1951 *Susan Elspeth Russel, writer, biographer of Charles Kingsley, dau of Rudolph Glossop, and has issue:

1 +ANDREW EDWARD WILLES; *b* 20 Nov 1953
1 *Cordelia Anne; *b* 21 July 1955
2 *Miranda Jane; *b* 15 July 1967
3 *Jessica Susan; *b* 6 June 1971

Lineage: JOSEPH CHITTY; *b* 1658; *m* Sarah Huse, and had, with other issue:

JACOB CHITTY; *b* 1693; had:

JOSEPH CHITTY; *b* 1729; *m* Sarah Cartwright (*d* 4 May 1820) and had:

JOSEPH CHITTY, barrister Middle Temple; *b* 1776; *d* 1841, leaving:

THOMAS CHITTY, of 47 Lancaster Gate, W; *b* 1802; *m* Eliza Cawston and *d* 13 Feb 1878, leaving:

THOMAS EDWARD CHITTY, of 44 Blandford Sq, NW; *b* 1827; *m* 1854 Mary Ann (*d* 1875), dau of Dr James Willes, of Cork, and sis of Rt Hon Sir James Shaw Willes, Judge Court Common Pleas, and *d* 4 May 1868, having had, with other issue:

1 THOMAS WILLES (Sir), **1st Bt**

2 James Charles Martin (Rev); *b* 28 March 1865; *educ* Pembroke Coll Oxford (MA); Rector Hanwood 1899–1920 and Yockleton, Salop, 1920–38, RD Pontesbury 1916–23; *m* 1890 Gwen Ethlin Georgiana Jones (*d* 2 Nov 1933), and *d* 7 Jan 1938, leaving issue:

(1) John Heighway (Rev), MRCS, LRCP (1926), MB, BCh (1930), Deacon 1959, Priest 1960, Assist Curate St Dogfan's, Llanrhaiadr, 1960–63, medical missionary S Africa 1963–77; *b* 19 Sept 1898; *educ* Winchester and New Coll Oxford (MA); *m* 14 Feb 1927 Phyllis Margaret (*d* 2 Jan 1953), dau of H G Stevens, and *d* 18 Aug 1977, having had issue:

1a James Redmond Harrison; *b* 13 June 1928; *educ* Winchester and Univ Coll Oxford (BA); lost at sea from SS *Monowai* on his way to New Zealand, 28 April 1955

1a *Margaret Ethlin, MB, BS (Durham) 1953 [Mrs John Yelland, 10 Henry St, Wooloowin, Brisbane, Qld, Australia]; *b* 5 Jan 1930; *m* 26 Nov 1955 *John Douglas Newman Yelland, MB, FRCS (Eng), FRACS, and has issue:

1b *Michael John; *b* 26 June 1960
2b *David Ernest; *b* 11 April 1962
3b *Stephen Douglas; *b* 13 Oct 1964
1b *Philippa Margaret; *b* 28 Sept 1956
2b *Catherine Elizabeth; *b* 31 July 1958

2a *Rachel Mary; *b* 1 Dec 1932; *m* 15 Sept 1965 *Alfred Ernest Collins

3a *Elisabeth Georgina; *b* 14 Feb 1936; *m* 20 June 1959 *Derek Anthony Simpson, BSc (Eng), MIMechE, and has issue:

1b *Ian David; *b* 11 Nov 1960
2b *Peter Charles; *b* 5 April 1963
3b *Nigel Christopher *b* 25 Feb 1966

(2) Derwas James (Rev); *b* 2 June 1901; *educ* Winchester and New Coll Oxford (MA); Rector of Upton, Didcot, Berks 1931–68, T/Chaplain RNVR 1940–46, author of *The Desert a City* (1966); *m* 5 July 1943 *Anna Mary Hawthorn, MA, FSA, dau of Lt-Col Edwin Kitson Clark, TD, MA, FSA, of Meanwoodside, Leeds, and *d* as the result of an accident, 19 Feb 1971, leaving issue:

1a *Anna Georgina; *b* 12 July 1947; *m* 27 Sept 1969 *Christopher J Sanson, er son of J G Sanson, of Borehamwood

(1) *Lily Frances, OBE (1956), FSA, Hon MA, U of Wales (1957), Ch Correspondent for Shropshire of Ancient Monuments br of Min of Works

1 Elizabeth Isabella Helen; *m* 1887 Lt-Col Francis Du Vernet, and *d* 6 Nov 1937.

He *dsp* 5 Dec 1911

The est son,

Sir Thomas Willes Chitty, 1st Bt (UK), so *cr* 25 Jan 1924, KC (1927); *b* 24 June 1855; barrister Inner Temple 1877, Bencher 1925; joined NE Circuit; Master Supreme Court 1901–20, Srn Master Supreme Court and King's Remembrancer 1920–26, ed *Archbold's Practice, Chitty's Forms, Smith's Leading Cases*; managing ed *Lord Halsbury's Laws of England*, ed-in-ch *English and Empire Digest*; ktd 1919; *m* 1st 21 Dec 1888 Emily Eliza (*d* 17 Aug 1903), dau of Rev H F Newbolt, of Bilston; *m* 2nd 1 Sept 1904 Beatrice Maud (*d* 19 March 1937), dau of Rev Edward Hale, of Eton College, and by his 1st w had issue:

1 (THOMAS) HENRY WILLES (Sir), **2nd Bt**

2 Robert Michael Willes, QC Canadian Bar; *b* 13 Oct 1893; *educ* Marlborough; *m* 26 April 1922 Norah, dau of W Cooke of Toronto, Canada, and *d* 5 Feb 1970, leaving issue:

(1) +Thomas Michael Willes; *b* 2 June 1930; *m* 19 July 1952 *Edith Jeremy Weir, of Toronto, and has issue:

1a +Robert Arthur; *b* 6 Oct 1953
1a *Diana; *b* 24 Dec 1956
2a *Susan Elizabeth; *b* 1957

(1) *Norah Elizabeth; *b* 20 Nov 1926; *m* 1958 *Ross Alexander Wilson, and has issue:

1a *Lesley; *b* 7 July 1959

1 Diana Willes; *m* 18 Dec 1915 John Erskine Read KC, BA, Hon DCL, Hon LLD, Hon Fell Univ Coll Oxford, Hon Bencher, Gray's Inn, son of Dr H H Read, and has issue

2 Elizabeth Willes; *m* 31 Aug 1918 Henry Matthew Philipson Philipson-Stow, 3rd son of Sir Frederic Samuel Philipson Philipson-Stow, 1st Bt (*qv*), and has issue

The 1st Bt *d* 15 Feb 1930; his er son,

Sir (Thomas) Henry Willes Chitty, 2nd Bt, MA, barrister Inner Temple; *b* 30 July 1891; *m* 4 Jan 1922 Ethel Constance (*d* 1 Jan 1971), dau of Samuel Henry Gladstone, of Darley Ash, Bovingdon, Herts, and *d* 26 Feb 1955, having had issue:

1 Sir THOMAS WILLES CHITTY, **3rd and present Bt**

2 +Michael Willes [Michael Chitty Esq, Leonora Cottage, Mithian, St Agnes, Cornwall]; *b* 10 June 1929; *m* 18 Dec 1954 *Janet Leonora, 2nd dau of William A Messenger, of Forest Down, Pyford, Surrey, and has issue:

(1) +Sebastian William; *b* 28 Oct 1958
(1) *Anne-Marie; *b* 13 Jan 1966

3 +John Henry Willes [John Chitty Esq, 31 Church Way, Sanderstead, Surrey], late Lt RA; *b* 1 Feb 1932; *educ* Winchester; *m* 17 May 1968 *Diana Mary, dau of Geoffrey D B Dear, of Coulsdon, Surrey, and has issue:

(1) *Antonia Mary Willes; *b* 1970
(2) *Louise Elizabeth Willes; *b* 1973

CHOLMELEY

Arms: Gu. two esquire's helmets in chief ppr. and a garb in base or.
Crest: A demi-griffin segreant sa., beaked, winged and membered or, holding between the claws an esquire's helmet or.
Creation: Bt. (UK) 4 March 1806.

SIR MONTAGUE JOHN CHOLMELEY, 6TH BT, of Easton Hall, Co Lincoln [Sir Montague Cholmeley Bt, Church Farm, Burton le Coggles, Grantham, Lincs]; *b* 27 March 1935; *s* f 1964; *educ* Eton; late Capt Gren Gds (ret 1964); *m* 18 Oct 1960 *Juliet Auriol Sally, yr dau of Maj-Gen Sir (Eustace) John Blois Nelson, KCVO, CB, DSO, OBE, MC, of Burpham Lodge, Arundel, Sussex, by Jane, er sis of 9th Duke of Grafton (*qv*), and has issue:

1 +(HUGH JOHN) FREDERICK SEBASTIAN; *b* 3 Jan 1968; *educ* Eton; *m* 1993 *Ursula Ann, est dau of Hugh Peter Derwyn Bennett, QC, of Highbrook, Ardingly, Sussex, and has:

(1) +Montague (Monty) Hugh Peter; *b* 19 May 1997

1 *Camilla; *b* 23 April 1962; *m* 1982 *William Murdoch, est son of Andrew Murdoch, of Parsonage Farm, Hurstbourne Tarrant, Hants, and has:

(1) *Andrew William; *b* 1991
(2) *John Oliver; *b* 1994

2 *Davina; *b* 30 Jan 1964; *m* 1985 *Nicholas Morgan, and has issue:

(1) *Peter; *b* 1987
(2) *James; *b* 1990

Lineage: WILLIAM de CHOLMONDELY (*see* CHOLMONDELEY, M); *d* 1422, leaving a yr s:

JOHN CHOLMELEY, of Copenhall, Staffs; *m* —, dau of — Pickstock, and had two sons of the same name:

1 John, of Copenhall; *m* — Allynn and had issue:

(1) Thomas, of Copenhall; *m* Margery, dau of Morrys Aynion, and had issue (extinct in the male line after two generations)

(2) William, of Penkeridge; *d* on or after 1 April 1551

2 John; settled at Bletchingley, Surrey, by 1493; *m* Mary, dau and heir of John Turner, of Bletchingley, and *d* 1534, having had, with other issue:

(1) Richard, of Bletchingley; *m* 1st Elizabeth Mitchell and had, with other issue:

1a Humphrey, of Bletchingley; *m* Elizabeth, dau of Roger Slade, and *d* between 1 March 1558 and 1559, leaving:

1b John, of Ashby-de-la-Zouch
1b Betterich

2a John, of Bletchingley; *m* — Eaton and *d* 1589, leaving, with three yr s:

1b Richard, of Bletchingley; living 1623; had three sons

(1) Richard Cholmeley *m* 2nd Dionisia, dau of — Phillips and widow of — Homden, and *d* between 20 Feb 1556/7 and 1558, having by her had, with other further issue, a yst son:

1a John, of Old Windsor, Berks, and Bletchingley; *m* Isabel, dau of John Hare, of London and Homersfield, Suffolk, and widow of John Brook, and *d* soon after 12 Jan 1572, having had, with three yr s and four daus:

1b Henry (Sir), of Easton, Lincs; *b* 1562; inherited property from an uncle called Robert 1590; *m* Elizabeth (*bur* 18 June 1619), dau of William Lacy, of Stamford, and was *bur* 20 Nov 1620, leaving, with six yr s and three daus:

1c Henry, of Easton; *bapt* 29 May 1589; *m* 1614 Elizabeth (*d* 30 Sept 1631), sis of 1st Earl of Feversham of the 1676 *cr* and dau of Sir Richard Sondes by Susan, sis of 1st Earl of Manchester (*see* MANCHESTER, D), and *d* 5 Dec 1632, having had:

1d Montague, of Easton; had a warrant 16 July 1642 for a btcy but the patent never made out; *bapt* 7 March 1615; *m* 12 Sept 1637 Elizabeth (*m* 2nd Henry Hall, of Burton Coggles, and was *bur* 29 Jan 1676), dau of Sir Edward Hartopp, Bt, of Buckminster (*see* CRADOCK-HARTOPP, Bt), and *d* 3 Feb 1652, having had:

1e Montague, of Easton; *m* 1st Alice (*d* 2 Sept 1678), dau of Sir Edward Brownlow, Bt, of Great Humby, Lincs (*see* BROWNLOW, B), and had two daus; *m* 2nd Elizabeth, dau of Richard Booth, London Alderman, of a cadet branch of the Booth Earls of Warrington, and *d* 5 March 1700, leaving:

1f James, of Easton; *m* Catherine (*d* 1 Dec 1770), dau of John Woodfine, of Ragley, Bucks, and had, with other issue:

1g JOHN

1g Elizabeth; *m* 12 Aug 1727 Sir Robert Cocks, 4th and last Bt, and *d* 30 Jan 1749. He *dsps* 4 April 1765

2g Catherine; *m* William Welby, of Denton, Lincs (*d* 29 June 1792), and had issue (*see* WELBY, Bt)

JAMES CHOLMELEY *d* 2 Oct 1735; his est son,

JOHN CHOLMELEY, of Easton; *m* Penelope (*d* 10 Dec 1760), dau of Sir Joseph Herne, of Tywford, by Penelope, dau of Sir John Mordaunt, Bt, of Massingham (*qv*), and *d* 7 Jan 1768, leaving an only surv son:

MONTAGUE CHOLMELEY, of Easton; *bapt* 8 July 1743; *m* 31 Dec 1768 Sarah, dau of Humphrey Sibthorp, of Canwick, Lincs, and had, with other issue:

1 MONTAGUE (Sir), **1st Bt**

1 Mary Elizabeth; *m* 22 June 1799 James Raymond Johnstone, of Alva, Clackmannanshire, and *d* 9 Sept 1843, leaving issue (*see* JOHNSTONE, Bt)

MONTAGUE CHOLMELEY *d* 15 April 1803; his est son,

Sir Montague Cholmeley, 1st Bt (UK), so *cr* 4 March 1806, of Easton; MP, V-Pres London Soc for Promoting Christianity among the Jews 1821; *b* 20 March 1772; *m* 1st 14 Sept 1801 Elizabeth (*d* 22 Nov 1822), dau and heir of John Harrison, of Norton Place; *m* 2nd 26 March 1826 Catherine (*dsp* 2 Feb 1864), 4th dau of Benjamin Way, of Denham Place, and by his 1st w had, with other issue:

1 MONTAGUE JOHN (Sir), **2nd Bt**

2 Henry Daniel, of The Priory, Woodchester, Glos, Capt 27th Regt; *b* 1810; *m* 1st 19 Feb 1852 Georgiana Millicent (*d* 5 May 1855), yst dau of Rev Lewis Way, of Stanstead Park, Sussex; *m* 2nd 25 March 1862 Penelope (*dsp* 3 Jan 1912), only surv dau of John Goodford, of Chilton Cantelo, Somerset, and *d* 1 June 1865, having by 1st w had issue:

(1) Catherine Maude; *m* 4 Nov 1889 Edward Metcalfe, yst son of Francis Metcalfe, of Metcalfe Park, Co Kildare, and *d* 3 March 1933. He *d* 6 Dec 1891

(2) Olivia Millicent; *m* 15 Dec 1891 Rev Francis Collins Norton, Vicar of Ditchling, Sussex, and *d* 25 Aug 1934, leaving two daus. He *d* 8 Oct 1921

1 Elizabeth; *m* 5 Aug 1825 Sir John Jacob Buxton, 2nd Bt, of Shadwell, and *d* 28 Aug 1884

2 Frances; *m* 6 March 1828 Sir Glynne Earle Welby-Gregory, 3rd Bt, and *d* 9 Oct 1881

The 1st Bt *d* 10 March 1831; his est son,

Sir Montague John Cholmeley, 2nd Bt, MP N Lincs; *b* 5 Aug 1802; *m* 10 Feb 1829 Lady Georgiana Beauclerk (*d* 8 Jan 1880), 5th dau of 8th Duke of St Albans (*qv*), and had, with other issue:

1 HUGH ARTHUR HENRY (Sir), **3rd Bt**

1 Flora Caroline Elizabeth; *m* 14 July 1853 Sir Henry Hussey Vivian, Bt, of Singleton (afterwards 1st Baron Swansea (*qv*)), and *d* 25 Jan 1868, having had issue

Sir MONTAGUE *d* 18 Jan 1874; his 2nd son,

Sir Hugh Arthur Henry Cholmeley, 3rd Bt, DL, JP, and CA, Lincs, High Sheriff 1885, MP Grantham 1868–80, Capt Gren Gds; *b* 18 Oct 1839; *m* 12 Aug 1874 Edith Sophia (*d* 26 Dec 1910), dau of Sir Charles Robert Rowley, 4th Bt (*see* ROWLEY, Bt, of Tendring Hall), and had issue:

1 MONTAGUE AUBREY ROWLEY (Sir), **4th Bt**

1 Margaret Georgina Louisa; *b* 20 July 1875; *m* 5 Oct 1898 John Robarts, est son of Abraham John Robarts, and *dsp* 1 July 1967. He *d* 22 Jan 1954

2 Mary Selina; *b* 17 July 1877; *d* unm 15 Dec 1952

3 Winifred Susan; *b* 4 Nov 1879; *m* 18 July 1906 Lt-Col Charles Archibald Calvert, DSO, DL, (*d* 21 Nov 1956) yr s of Col Archibald Motteux Calvert, RA, of Ockley Court, Dorking, *d* 18 Nov 1957, leaving issue (*see* BUXTON, Bt)

4 Aline Marie Janette; *b* 16 April 1884; *d* unm 12 Sept 1960

Sir HUGH *d* 14 Feb 1904; his only son,

Sir Montague Aubrey Rowley Cholmeley, 4th Bt, Capt Gren Gds, served in S African War 1899–1902 (Queen's and King's medals) and WW I 1914; *b* 12 June 1876; *m* 18 April 1903 Mabel Janetta (*m* 2nd 28 June 1921 Brig-Gen Walter John Lambert, DSO (*d* 28 July 1944), son of Sir John Lambert, KCIE, and *d* 9 May 1964), est dau of Montagu Richard Waldo-Sibthorp, of Canwick Hall, Lincs, and had issue:

1 HUGH JOHN FRANCIS SIBTHORP (Sir), **5th Bt**

1 Rosamond Mary Edith; *m* 13 July 1927 Lt-Col Hon (Charles) Guy Cubitt, DSO, TD, RA (TA), yst son of 2nd Baron Ashcombe, CB (*qv*), and had issue

The 4th Bt was *ka* 24 Dec 1914; his only son,

Sir Hugh John Francis Sibthorp Cholmeley, 5th Bt, CB (1963), DSO (1944), DL (1939), V-Lt (1963), JP (1939) Lincs, High Sheriff 1961; *b* 7 Feb 1906; *educ* Eton and RMC Sandhurst; Maj Gren Gds WW II, Hon Col 4th/6th Bn Roy Lincs Regt (TA) 1947; *m* 23 July 1931 Cecilia, er dau of William Henry Ellice, of Ewhurst Manor, Shermanbury, Horsham, and *d* 1 Feb 1964, having had issue:

1 Sir MONTAGUE JOHN CHOLMELEY, **6th and present Bt**

CHOLMONDELEY

Arms: Gu., in chief two helmets in profile arg., and in base a garb or. **Crest:** A demi-griffin segreant sa., beaked, winged and membered or, holding between the claws a helmet, as in the arms. **Supporters:** Dexter, a griffin sa., beaked, winged and membered or, langued gu.; sinister, a wolf or, gorged with a collar vair, armed and langued gu. **Motto:** *Cassis tutissima virtus* ('Virtue is the safest helmet'). **Creation:** V. (I) 29 March 1661 (Cholmondeley of Kells) and (E) 29 Dec 1706 (Malpas); B. (E) 10 April 1689 (Cholmondeley of Namptwich), (I) 12 April 1715 (Newborough of Newborough) and (GB) 10 July 1716 (Newburgh); E. (E) 29 Dec 1706 (Cholmondeley) and (UK) 22 Nov 1815 (Rocksavage); M. (UK) 22 Nov 1815.

THE 7TH MARQUESS OF CHOLMONDELEY, Earl of Rocksavage, Earl Cholmondeley, Viscount Cholmondeley of Kells, Co Meath, **Viscount Malpas**, Co Chester, **Baron Cholmondeley of Namptwich**, Co Chester, **Baron Newborough of Newborough**, Co Wexford, and **Baron Newburgh** in the Isle of Anglesey, and (David George Philip Cholmondeley, DL (Cheshire 1992)) [The Most Hon The Marquess of Cholmondeley DL, Cholmondeley Castle, Malpas, Cheshire; Houghton Hall, King's Lynn, Norfolk]; *b* 27 June 1960; *s* f 1990; *educ* Eton and Sorbonne; Page of Hon to HM THE QUEEN 1974–76, Jt Hereditary Ld Great Chamberlain of England (acting for reign of ELIZABETH II 1990–), film dir as David Rocksavage: *Other Voices, Other Rooms* (1995)

Lineage: WILLIAM le BELWARD; feudal Ld of half the Barony of Malpas including Calmundelai in right of his w; *m* an illegitimate dau of Hugh Kevelioc, Earl of Chester, and had:

1 David; inherited the territorial Barony of Malpas; ancestor of the EGERTONs

2 ROBERT

3 Richard

The second son,

ROBERT de CHOLMONDLEY; feudal Ld of Cholmondely; *m* Mabel, dau of Sir Robert FitzNigel, feudal Baron of Halton, and had:

Sir HUGH de CHOLMONDELY; feudal Ld of Cholmondely; living *temp* HENRY III; had, with two yr s:

ROBERT de CHOLMONDELY; feudal Ld of Cholmondely; had:

RICHARD de CHOLMONDELY; feudal Ld of Cholmondely; living *temp* EDWARD I; *m* Margery, dau and heir of Richard de Kingsleigh, and had a 2nd s:

HUGH de CHOLMONDLEY; feudal Ld of Cholmondely; living temp EDWARD II; *m* Katherine, dau of William de Spurstow, and had issue:

1 Richard; feudal Ld of Cholmondely; living 1340; had by his 2nd w:

(1) Richard; feudal Ld of Cholmondely; *dsp* 1361

2 Hugh; living 1337; *m* the dau and coheir of Robert de Harcourt, of Chorley, and *d* by 1362, leaving:

(1) WILLIAM

3 Robert; ancestor of the CHOLMELEYs of Chorley and Withby

The eventual heir,

WILLIAM de CHOLMONDELY; feudal Ld of Cholmondely; *m* Elizabeth, dau of Sir William Brereton, of Brereton, and *d* 1375, leaving an only son:

RICHARD de CHOLMONDELY; feudal Ld of Cholmondely; not yet of age 1376; *m* Ann, dau of Sir John Bromley, of Badington, and had an only son:

WILLIAM de CHOLMONDELY; *m* Maud (*m* 2nd William Lee, of Aston), dau and heir of Sir John Cheney, of Willaston, and *dvp* 1422, having had, with a yr s (John, ancestor of the Cholmeley Bts; *qv*):

RICHARD de CHOLMONDELY; feudal Ld of Cholmondely; *m* Ellen, dau of John Davenport, of Davenport, and *d c* 1489, having had, with three yr sons:

RICHARD de CHOLMONDELY; *m* Alinora, dau of Sir Thomas Dutton, of Dutton, and *dvp* by 1488, leaving an only son:

RICHARD CHOLMONDELY; *b c* 1474; *m* Elizabeth — and *d* 1518, having had three sons and four daus; his 2nd s:

Sir HUGH CHOLMONDELEY; five times Sheriff Cheshire, Sheriff Flintshire, DL Cheshire; *m* twice but had issue only by his 1st w Anne, dau and coheir of George Dorman, of Malpas, and *d* 1577/8, leaving:

Sir HUGH CHOLMONDELEY, of Cholmondeley; *m* Mary (*d* 1625), only dau and heir of Christopher Holford, of Holford, and *d* 23 July 1601, having had, with four other sons and two other daus:

1 Sir ROBERT CHOLMONDELEY, 1st and last Bt (E), so *cr* 29 June 1611, and 1st and last EARL OF LEINSTER, so *cr* 5 March 1645/6, as also VISCOUNT CHOLMONDELEY OF KELLS, Co Meath (both I), and 1 Sept 1645 BARON CHOLMONDELEY OF WICHEMALBANK, Co Chester (E); *b* 26 June 1584; *educ* Queen's Coll Oxford; High Sheriff Cheshire 1621, MP Cheshire 1625–26, raised royalist troops for Civil War 1642; later fined £7,742 following Parly victory; *m* Catherine Stanhope (*d* 15 June 1657), dau of 1st Baron Stanhope of Harrington (see HARRINGTON, E), and *dspl* 2 Oct 1659, when all his titles expired, leaving an illegitimate s:

(1) Thomas CHOLMONDELEY; inherited the Holford estate from his f; *d* 6 Jan 1667 leaving issue

2 Hugh; *m* Mary, dau of Sir John Bodville, of Bodville Castle, Caernarvs, and *d* 11 Sept 1655, leaving an est s:

(1) ROBERT, **1st Viscount**

3 Thomas, of Vale Royal, ancestor of the Barons Delamere (*qv*)

1 Lettice; *m* as his 1st w Sir Richard Grosvenor, 1st Bt (*see* WESTMINSTER, D)

The EARL's nephew,

ROBERT CHOLMONDELEY, **1st Viscount Cholmondeley of Kells**, Co Meath (I), so *cr* 29 March 1661; *m* Elizabeth, dau and coheir of George Cradock, of Caverswall Castle, Staffs, and *d* 22 May 1681, having had, with other issue:

1 HUGH CHOLMONDELEY, **1st Earl of Cholmondeley**, so *cr* 29 Dec 1706, as also VISCOUNT MALPAS, Co Chester, and previously 10 April 1689 BARON CHOLMONDELEY OF WITCH MALBANK otherwise NAMPTWICH, Co Chester (all E, with remainder to his yr bro), PC (1705); *b c* 1662; *educ* Ch Ch Oxford; Ld Lt N Wales 1702–13 and 1714–25 and Cheshire 1704013 and 1714–25, Comptroller (Whig) Household May-Oct 1708, Treasurer Household 1708–13 and 1714–25; *d* unm 18 Jan 1724

2 GEORGE CHOLMONDELEY, **2nd Earl of Cholmondeley**, PC (1706); *b c* 1666; *educ* Westminster and Ch Ch Oxford; Capt Queen Consort (MARY OF MODENA)'s Regt of Horse 1686 but deserted to WILLIAM III 1688 and became Lt-Col 1st Horse Gds 1689, cmdg them Battle of the Boyne 1690, also fought Battle of Steinkirk 1692, Col 1st Horse Gren Gds 1693–1715, Brig-Gen 1697, Maj Gen 1702, Lt Gen 1704, Col 3d Horse Gds 1715–33, Gen of Horse 1727; Groom Bedchamber 1691–1702, MP (Tory) Newton 1690–95, *cr* 12 April 1715 BARON NEWBOROUGH OF NEWBOROUGH, Co Wexford (I), and 10 July 1716 BARON OF NEWBURGH in the Isle of Anglesey (GB); Ld Lt and V-Adml Cheshire and Ld Lt N Wa;les 1725–33, Govr Hull 1725–32 and Guernsey 1732–33; *m c* 1701 Elizabeth van Ruytenburg, whose mother Anne Elizabeth was sis of Henry d'Auverquerque, Earl of Grantham, and had, with three daus and another s:

(1) GEORGE, **3rd Earl**

(2) James; *b* 18 April 1708; Col 34th Foot 1742; fought Battle of Fontenoy 11 May 1745, and later that year in Scotland against the Jacobites, also the next year 17 Jan 1746 Battle of Falkirk; Gen; *m* (*divorce* 1736) Lady Penelope Barry, dau of 4th Earl of Barrymore by his 2nd w Elizabeth, dau and heir of Richard Savage, 4th Earl Rivers, whereby the Rock Savage property came to the Cholmondeleys (Rock Savage being originally the name of a splendid house erected by Sir John Savage in the late 16th century but which had fallen into considerable disrepair by the late 18th) and *dspl* 13 Oct 1775

The 2nd EARL *d* 7 May 1733; his est surv son,

GEORGE CHOLMONDELEY, **3rd Earl of Cholmondeley**, KB (1725), PC (1736); *b* 2 Jan 1702/3; MP (Whig) E Looe 1724–27 and Windsor 1727–33, a Ld of Admlty 1727–29, a Ld of Treasury 1735–36, Chllr Duchy Lancaster 1736–43, Ld Privy Seal 1743–44, Lt-Gen 1759; *m* 14 Sept 1723 Lady Mary Walpole (*d* 1731), only dau of Robert Walpole, 1st Earl of Orford, the first PM, and had, with another s:

1 George, *Viscount Malpas*, MP (Whig) Bramber 1754–61 and Corfe Castle 1761–64; *b* 17 Oct 1724; *m* 19 Jan 1747 Hester (*d* 10 April 1805), dau and heiress of Sir Francis Edwardes, 14th Bt, of Shrewsbury, and Idvp 15 March 1764, leaving issue:

(1) GEORGE JAMES, **1st Marquess**

(1) Hester; *m* 6 Sept 1773 William Clapcott Lisle, of Upway, Dorset, and had:

1a Marcia Mary Anne; *m* 23 Feb 1799 Charles Arbuthnot, PC, and had:

1b Marcia; *m* her cousin **3rd Marquess of Cholmondeley**

2 Robert (Rev), Rector St Andrews, Hertford; *b* 1 Nov 1727; served Army; *m* 30 Nov 1746 Mary (*d* 4 April 1811), dau of Arthur Woffington and sis of the actress Peg Woffington; *d* 5 June 1804, leaving with other issue:

(1) George James, Receiver-Gen of Excise; *b* 22 Feb 1752; *m* 1st 17 Aug 1790 Marcia (*d* May 1808), dau of John Pitt, of Encombe, Dorset, and had issue; *m* 2nd 10 May 1814 Catherine (*d* 11 Sept 1823), dau of Sir Philip Francis, KB, by whom he had no issue; *m* 3rd 4 Oct 1825 Hon Mary Elizabeth (*m* 2nd 8 Feb 1832 2nd Earl of Romney (*qv*)), dau of John Thomas, 2nd Viscount Sydney, and *d* 5 Nov 1830, having by her had issue:

1a Frances Sophia; *m* 16 April 1846 Rev J C B Riddell, 2nd son of Sir John B Riddell, 9th Bt, of Riddell (*qv*)

(1) Hester Frances; *m* 3 Dec 1783 Sir William Bellingham, 1st Bt, of Castle Bellingham (*qv*), and *dsp* 10 Jan 1844

The 3rd EARL *d* 1770; his gs,

GEORGE JAMES CHOLMONDELEY, **1st Marquess of Cholmondeley**, so *cr* 22 Nov 1815, as also EARL OF ROCKSAVAGE, Co Chester (both UK), KG (1822), GCH (1819), PC (1783); *b* 11 May 1749; Ld Steward Household 1812–21, Chamberlain Cheshire 1770–1827; *m* 25 April 1791 Lady Georgiana Charlotte Bertie (*d* 23 June 1838), 2nd dau of 3rd Duke of Ancaster (*see* WILLOUGHBY DE ERESBY, B), whereby the jt right to act as Ld Gt Chambrlain came to the Cholmondeleys, and *d* 10 April 1827, having had:

1 GEORGE HORATIO CHOLMONDELEY, **2nd Marquess of Cholmondeley**, PC (1830); *b* 16 Jan 1792; called up 5 Jan 1822 *vp* to Ho Lds in f's Barony of Newburgh; *m* 1st 20 Oct 1812 Caroline (*d* 12 Oct 1815), 2nd dau of Lt Gen Sir Colin Campbell; *m* 2nd 11 May 1830 Lady Susan Somerset (*d* 4 Feb 1886 aged 81), 4th dau of 6th Duke of Beaufort (*qv*), and *dsp* 8 May 1870

2 WILLIAM HENRY HUGH, **3rd Marquess**

1 Charlotte Georgiana; *m* 18 May 1818 Lt-Col Hugh Seymour, and *d* 24 June 1828, leaving issue (*see* HERTFORD, M)

The 2nd MARQUESS's bro,

WILLIAM HENRY HUGH CHOLMONDELEY, **3rd Marquess of Cholmondeley**; *b* 31 Aug 1800; *educ* Eton and Ch Ch Oxford; MP (Tory) Castle Rising 1822–32 and S Hants 1852–57; *m* 28 Feb 1825 his cousin Marcia Emma Georgiana (*d* 3 Nov 1878), dau of Rt Hon Charles Arbuthnot, and had, with other issue:

1 Charles George; *b* 9 July 1829; *m* 31 Oct 1854 Susan Caroline (*d* 1891), dau of Sir George Dashwood, 4th Bt (*see* DASHWOOD, Bt, of Kirtlington Park), and *dvp* 7 Dec 1869, having had, with other issue (his daus being granted by roy warrant 1885 rank of marquess's daus):

(1) GEORGE HENRY HUGH, **4th Marquess**

(1) Marcia Charlotte Maria; *m* 21 May 1891 Percy John de Paravicini, CVO, of Riverside, Datchet, son of Baron James Prior de Paravicini, and *d* 14 May 1939, having had issue. He *d* 11 Oct 1921

(2) Mabel Frances Georgiana; *d* unm 24 May 1944

(3) Eva Harriet, MBE (1943); *m* 27 Nov 1913 Harry Farquhar de Paravicini, son of Baron de Paravicini, and *d* 12 Nov 1954. He *d* 28 Oct 1942

2 Henry Vere; *b* 4 Oct 1834; *m* 17 July 1860 Frances Isabella Catherine (*d* 13 Feb 1900), 2nd dau of Lt-Col Hon George Augustus Spencer (*see* CHURCHILL, V), and *d* 25 Feb 1882, leaving issue:

(1) George Vere Hugh, of Hatten, Cheshire, JP Devon; *b* 13 Sept 1871; *m* 19 Jan 1899 Ida Sophia (*d* 1 Aug 1938), 5th dau of John Saunders Gilliat, MP, of Cedars, Chorleywood, Herts, and *d* 28 March 1925, leaving issue:

1a Hugh Henry Vere; *b* 4 Dec 1899; *d* 31 July 1914

1a Irene Marcia; *b* 13 April 1902; *d* unm 27 March 1965

2a Joan Cicely; *b* 24 June 1906; *m* 1st 11 April 1927 Cdr Eric Alonzo Stocker, DSC, RN, and had issue; *m* 2nd — Marshall, of Newton Abbot, Devon

(2) Charles Almeric John, Capt Border Regt; *b* 5 March 1880; *ka* 28 Oct 1914

(1) Edith Charlotte Frances; *m* 1st 2 June 1892 Robert Edward Heaven, est son of Joseph Robert Heaven, of the Forest of Birse, Aberdeenshire. He *dvp* 27 April 1910. She *m* 2nd 9 Dec 1913 Col Matthew Burrow Ray, DSO, OBE, MD, late AMS (TA), son of Richard Ray, of Harrogate, and *d* 28 Sept 1954. He *d* 5 July 1950

(2) Caroline Marcia Cicely; *b* 13 Nov 1873; *m* 20 March 1906 George Charles Ker Mahon, of Ballydonellan and Killereeny, and *d* 24 Dec 1952. He *d* 8 June 1936

1 Charlotte Georgiana; *m* 27 April 1852 Rev Edward Gladwin Arnold, MA, Rector of Gt Massingham, Norfolk and *d* 17 Aug 1912, leaving issue. He *d* 12 June 1887

2 Marcia Susan Harriet; *d* unm 10 June 1927

The 3rd MARQUESS *d* 16 Dec 1884; his gs,

GEORGE HENRY HUGH CHOLMONDELEY, **4th Marquess of Cholmondeley**, PC (1901), DL Norfolk; Lt Cheshire Yeo Cav; *b* 3 July 1858; *m* 16 July 1879 Winifred Ida, OBE (1920) (*d* 14 Oct 1938), dau of Col Sir Robert Nigel Fitzhardinge Kingscote, GCVO, KCB, DL, JP, of Kingscote, Glos, and had issue:

1 GEORGE HORATIO CHARLES, **5th Marquess**

2 George Hugo, OBE (1919), MC, Maj Notts RHA WW I (despatches), WW II as Lt-Col Northern Cmd and in Egypt; *b* 17 Oct 1887; *educ* Eton; *m* 1st 7 March 1911 (Idivorce 1921) Clare Elizabeth (*d* 27 June 1925), formerly w of Maj John Alexander Stirling, DSO, MC, and dau of Charles Henry Taylor, of Washington, USA, and had issue:

(1) *Irene; *b* 3 May 1913; *m* 3 May 1947 Stephen Falkland (formerly Stanislaw Falkowski), MD, late Maj RAMC (*d* 1986), Sr Offr WHO, son of Richard Falkowski, of Warsaw, and has issue:

1a *Priscilla Susan [Mrs Robert Dicketts, Rosemary Cottage, Wards Lane, Wallcrouch, Wadhurst, Susssex TN5 6HN]; *b* 4 June 1948; *m* 1974 *Robert A I Dicketts, and has issue:

1b *Oliver Simon; *b* 1979

2 (cont.) Lt-Col Lord George Cholmondeley *m* 2nd 7 Dec 1921 (*divorce* 1948) Ina Marjorie Gwendoline, OBE (1934) (*d* 9 July 1969), formerly w of Maj Hon Christopher Hugh Lowther (*see* ULLSWATER, V) and dau of Canon Raymond Percy Pelly (*see* PELLY, Bt); *m* 3rd 21 Dec 1948 Diana (*d* 10 Feb 1965), widow of Capt Albany Kennett Charlesworth, MC, and 3rd dau of Hon Rupert Evelyn Beckett (*see* GRIMTHORPE, B), and *d* 26 Aug 1958

1 Lettice Joan, ARRC; *b* 23 May 1882; *m* 1st 20 April 1911 (*divorce* 1923) Maj Cecil Pryce Harrison, DSO, RHA, yr son of Lt-Col Robert John Harrison, DL, JP, of Caerhowel, Montgomeryshire, and had issue; *m* 2nd 24 March 1923 Cecil William Shepard, son of William Peter Shepard, of Wimbledon, and *d* 2 Nov 1946. He *d* 29 May 1963

The 4th MARQUESS *d* 16 March 1923; his er son,

GEORGE HORATIO CHARLES CHOLMONDELEY, **5th Marquess of Cholmondeley**, GCVO (1953), Capt late 9th Lancers (SR), ADC to Viceroy of India, served Boer War 1901 and WW I; *b* 19 May 1883; *m* 6 Aug 1913 Sybil Rachel Betty Cecile, CBE (1946), Supt WRNS 1939–46, only dau of Sir Albert Edward Sassoon, 2nd Bt, of Kensington Gore (*see* 1939 edn), and had issue:

1 GEORGE HUGH, **6th Marquess**

2 John George, Lt (A) RNVR WW II; *b* 15 Nov 1920; *educ* Eton and Magdalene Coll Cambridge; *m* 6 June 1957 *Maria-Cristina [The Lady John Cholmondeley, 22 Hyde Park Gdns, London W2], only dau of Giorgio Solari, of Genoa, and *d* 1986, leaving issue:

(1) +CHARLES GEORGE; *b* 18 March 1959; heir presumptive

(1) *Joanna Antonia; *b* 7 Feb 1958

1 *Aline Caroline [The Lady Aline Cholmondeley, 39 Eaton Sq, London SW1W 9DH]; *b* 5 Oct 1916

The 5th MARQUESS *d* 16 Sept 1968; his er son,

GEORGE HUGH CHOLMONDELEY, **6th Marquess of Cholmondeley**, GCVO (1977), MC (1943), DL (Cheshire 1955); *b* 24 April 1919; *educ* Eton and Magdalene Coll Cambridge; Maj Gren Gds WW II, and with 1st Roy Dragoons Middle

East, Italy, France and Germany; *m* 14 June 1947 *Lavinia Margaret, DL (Cheshire 1992) [The Most Hon Lavinia Marchioness of Cholmondeley DL, Cholmondeley Castle, Malpas, Cheshire], only dau of Col John Leslie, DSO, MC, DL, of Appletree Cottage, Brancaster, Norfolk (*see* SKIPWITH, Bt), and *d* 1990, leaving issue:

1 DAVID GEORGE PHILIP CHOLMONDELEY, **7th and present Marquess of Cholmondeley**

1 *Rose Aline [The Lady Rose Cholmondeley, 44 Bassett Rd, London W10 6JL]; *b* 20 March 1948; ARCM

2 *Margot Lavinia [The Lady Margot Huston, Village Farm, Houghton, King's Lynn, Norfolk]; *b* 27 Jan 1950; *m* 18 Nov 1978 *(Walter) Anthony Huston, only son of John Huston, the film dir, of Las Caletas, Puerto Vallarta, Mexico, and has issue:

(1) *Mathew; *b* 6 Sept 1979

(2) *Jack Alexander; *b* 1982

(1) *Laura Sybil; *b* 1981

3 *Caroline Mary [The Lady Caroline d'Erlanger, Grey Court, Kings Sutton, Banbury, Oxon]; *b* 10 April 1952; *m* 7 June 1982 *Rodolphe d'Erlanger, son of Leo d'Erlanger, and has issue:

(1) *Leo Frederick Hugh; *b* 31 Aug 1983

(2) *David Joshua Robert; *b* 1987

Seats: Houghton Hall, King's Lynn, Norfolk; Cholmondeley Castle, Malpas, Cheshire.

Sir Robert Walpole, father-in-law of the **3rd Earl of Cholmondeley**, built Houghton to Colen Campbell's designs amended by Thomas Ripley's. It was finished in 1735, seven years before its owner's fall from power, though the original plans dated from his accession to the premiership. The magnificent Palladian Houghton we see today replaced an early 17th-century structure, but for once even the most hardened devotee of the Jacobethan need not repine, for Houghton's proportions are near perfection. The four cupolas which rescue it from being just another dull Norfolk squire's monument to Whig Ascendancy triumphalism were, oddly enough, Ripley's idea rather than the better known Campbell's. It was Ripley also who selected the stone, which came from Aislaby in Yorkshire hundreds of miles away and was transported by sea.

Walpole was of course very far from being a dull country squire (though he could affect a bucolic oafishness when it suited him during carousals with his East Anglian cronies). His magnificent art collection would testify to that even if Houghton had never existed. Inside he hired William Kent to superintend every detail of the decorations and they accordingly have a harmony that is almost unique among English country mansions. The Stone Hall is probably the masterpiece of the entire layout. It is cuboid, measuring 40' x 40' x 40', and sports a carved ceiling frieze by Atari, augmented by Rysbrack reliefs over the chimney piece and door lintels.

Although called a castle Cholmondeley is a 'Gothick' mansion dating from the Napoleonic Wars. The threat then of invasion might conceivably have justified its crenellations, though in 1805, the year the first phase was finished, Nelson destroyed the possibility of French cannon bombarding English gentlemen's seats by his victory at Trafalgar and even the real thing would have been at risk against Napoleonic-era artillery. A second phase of improvements was carried out between 1815 and 1819, the executant in both cases being William Turner of Whitchurch, originally a mere carrier-out of his employer's ideas but occasionally an originator, as for instance with the arcade setting for the portico and the north-side clock tower.

But Cholmondeley is a castle by courtesy, fantasy rather than fortification. The original family home seems not to have been much of a castle either, for it is referred to as a 'house' and was timber-framed. On the other hand it was undeniably moated, which the present castle is not, though there is an abundance of water in the form of two lakes in the grounds. The family chapel is all that survives from the original building, though reroofed in 1300, restored in the early 18th century and enlarged just over a hundred years after that. The restoration of the early 18th century was part of an overall refurbishment programme by the **1st Earl** encompassing the entire house, and using brick to make a standard Queen Anne mansion. William Smith of Warwick (*see* also BRAYE, B, section **Seat**) was the architect. Some of the work of this period also survives.

The architect of the present structure was chiefly the **1st Marquess** himself. He pulled down the Queen Anne building because of its rickety state, though fashion undoubtedly had something to do with the decision to build anew, and took the opportunity to move the site of the house up onto a slight rise in the parkland. His successor the **2nd Marquess** called in Robert Smirke, the architect of the British Museum, to advise on further embellishments at the end of the 1820s. The round tower at the southwest corner and the three-side bow window swelling out from the central west-front tower are the chief result. Nelson's old service, the Royal Navy, occupied the place during World War II and after it was repossessed by the family the task of restoring the grounds was embarked upon following years of neglect. The Temple Garden, with its waterfall, is now considered Cholmondeley's chief jewel externally. The Gothick style has been maintained in a Pavilion by the swimming pool dating from the early 1970s. The gardens, but not the house, are open to the public on mid-week afternoons throughout the summer.

CHORLEY

Arms: Per chevron arg. and vert, in chief two blue-bottles ppr. and in base a fountain. **Crest:** In front of two torches in saltire or and in flames a teazle, stalked and leaved ppr. **Supporters:** On either side a buzzard ppr. **Motto:** *Propositi tenax* ('Tenacious of purpose').
Creation: B. (UK) 16 Nov 1945.

THE 2ND BARON CHORLEY, of Kendal, Co Westmorland (Roger Richard Edward Chorley) [The Rt Hon The Lord Chorley, House of Lords, London SW1A 0PW]; *b* 14 Aug 1930; *s* f 1978; *educ* Stowe and Gonville and Caius Coll Cambridge (BA 1952); FCA, joined Cooper Bros (later Coopers and Lybrand) 1955 (ptnr 1967–89); visiting Prof Dept of Management Science Imperial Coll 1979–82; memb cncl: RGS 1984– (pres 1987–90), RSA 1987–89; chm Nat Tst 1991–, dep chm Br Cncl 1990–; Hon Fell Central Lancs U 1993, Hon DSc: Reading 1990 and Kingston 1992, Hon LLD Lancaster 1995; *m* 31 Oct 1964 *Ann Elizabeth, yr dau of Archibald Scott Debenham, of Ingatestone, Essex, and has issue:

1 +NICHOLAS RUPERT DEBENHAM; *b* 15 July 1966; *educ* privately

2 +Christopher Robert Hopkinson; *b* 28 June 1968

Lineage: CLEASBY CHORLEY, of Fern Lea, Kendal, Westmorland; had:

RICHARD FISHER CHORLEY, of Chapel Close, Kendal; *b* 21 June 1860; *educ* Kendal Sch; slr; *m* Annie Elizabeth (*d* 20 Aug 1933), dau of Samuel Frost, of Hardingstone, Northampton, and *d* March 1922, leaving:

ROBERT SAMUEL THEODORE CHORLEY, **1st Baron Chorley**, of Kendal, Co Westmorland (UK), so *cr* 16 Nov 1945, JP (Westmorland), QC (1961); *b* 29 May 1895; *educ* Kendal Sch and Queen's Coll Oxford (BA 1916, MA 1921); Jr Clerk FO 1916–17, Min Labour 1917–19, barrister Inner Temple 1920, Pncpl Home Office 1940–41, Assist Sec Min Home Security 1941–42, Dep Regnl Commr CD NW Regn 1942–44; memb Ctee on Nat Pks 1945 and Roy Commn on JPs 1946; Prof Commercial and Industl Law London U 1930–47, chm Ctee Salaries of Higher Civ Servs 1949; chm Westmorland QS 1944–68, Hon Sec CPRE 1936–67 (v-pres 1969); pres: Assoc U Teachers 1947–48, Inst for Study and Treatment Delinquency 1956, Commons Preservation Soc 1961, Friends of Lake District 1961; a v-chm Nat Tst 1960, a Ld-in-Waiting 1946–50;; *m* 15 April 1925 Katharine Campbell (*d* 1986), only dau of Edward Hopkinson, MP, DSc, of Alderley Edge, Cheshire, and *d* 27 Jan 1978, leaving:

1 ROGER RICHARD EDWARD CHORLEY, **2nd and present Baron Chorley**

2 +(Geoffrey) Patrick Hopkinson [The Hon Patrick Chorley, 7 Chalcot Crescent, London NW1]; *b* 15 Aug 1933; *educ* Stowe and New Coll Oxford; *m* 1st 9 July 1955 (*divorce* 1972) Daria Antonia Maria, dau of Raoul, Marquis de Merindol, of Kensington; *m* 2nd 1975 *May Amaryllis, dau of Prof A Ashmore, of Didsbury, Manchester, and by his 1st w has:

(1) *Alexandra (Asya) Maria; *b* 13 Nov 1956; *m* 1981 *Hugh Bett, son of Cdr R T Bett, of Paxtons, E Lavant, Sussex

(2) *Elizabeth Henrietta Marianne; *b* 11 Sept 1961

1 *Gillian Theodora Marianne [The Hon Mrs Goodwin, 29 Chalcot Sq, London NW1]; *b* 5 April 1929; *educ* Liverpool Coll for Girls, Huyton Coll, and St Anne's Coll Oxford; *m* 19 Jan 1965 *F Godfrey Goodwin, yr son of Robert Goodwin, and has issue:

(1) *Robert Theodore Chorley; *b* 1969

CHURCHILL

Arms: Quarterly, 1st and 4th, quarterly, arg. and gu., in the 2nd and 3rd quarters a fret or; over all on a bend sa. three escallops of the first (for SPENCER); 2nd and 3rd, sa. a lion rampant arg., on a canton of the last a cross gu. (for CHURCHILL). **Crest:** Out of a ducal coronet or a griffin's head between two wings, expanded arg., gorged with a bar gemelle gu. armed gold. **Supporters:** Dexter, a griffin, wings erect, per fess arg. and or, gorged with a collar of the last, thereon three escallops sa., a line reflexed over the back also or; sinister, a wyvern, the wings erect gu., collared as the dexter.
Motto: *Dieu defend le droit* ('God defend the right').
Creation: B. (UK) 11 Aug 1815, V. (UK) 14 July 1902.

THE 3RD VISCOUNT CHURCHILL, of Rolleston, Co Leicester, and **Baron Churchill of Whichwood or Wychwood**, Co Oxford (Victor George Spencer) [The Rt Hon The Viscount Churchill, 6 Cumberland Mansions, George St, London W1H 5TE]; *b* posthumously 31 July 1934 (HM GEORGE V stood sponsor); *s* half bro 1973; *educ* Eton and New Coll Oxford (BA 1958, MA 1966); Lt Scots Gds 1953–55, with Morgan Grenfell 1958–74, Investment Manager Centl Bd Finance C of E 1974– and Charities Official Investment Fund 1974–95; dir CCLA Investment Management Ltd 1987–, Kleinwort Charter Investment Tst 1992–, Schroder Split Fund 1993–, For & Colonial Income Growth Investment Tst 1994 Allchurches Tst 1994–;

Lineage: The 4th DUKE OF MARLBOROUGH (*qv*) had a 2nd s:

FRANCIS ALMERIC SPENCER, **1st Baron Churchill of Wychwood**, Co Oxford (UK), so *cr* 11 Aug 1815, DCL; *b* 26 Dec 1779; MP (Tory) Oxon 1801–15, FRS 1818; *m* 25 Nov 1800 Frances (*d* 7 Jan 1866), dau of 3rd Duke of Grafton (*qv*), and had, with other issue:

1 FRANCIS GEORGE, **2nd Baron**

2 George Augustus, Lt-Col; *b* 6 Feb 1804; *m* 17 Jan 1834 Charlotte (*d* 18 June 1875), only dau of Maj-Gen John Munro, of Teaninich, Alness, Ross-shire, and *d* 18 Jan 1877, leaving with other issue:

(1) John Winston Thomas SPENCER later MUNRO-SPENCER (1911), of Teaninich; Lt-Col and Brevet Col RA; *b* 27 Sept 1849; *m* 1st 17 Jan 1884 Synolda Ellen Le Petit (*d* 4 Nov 1890), dau of James William Fitzgerald Butler and gdau of Hon James Butler, of Lamberton Park (*see* DUNBOYNE, B); *m* 2nd 31 Oct 1899 Helen (*d* 27 March 1919) dau of Alexander Crum Ewing, of Strathleven, and *d* 27 Nov 1916, having by 1st w had issue:

1a Almeric Stuart John, of Teaninich; Capt 4th Bn Seaforth Highrs; *b* 26 Aug 1885; *m* 17 July 1912 (*divorce* 1928) Phyllis Margaret Rivers (*d* 1971), only child of Charles Richard Rivers Rivers, of Orrell Mount, Wigan, Lancs, and Brighton, and *d* 16 March 1960, leaving:

1b *Synolda Joan Margaret [Mrs Cecil Hardy, Church View, West St, Hinton St George, Somerset TA17 8SA]; *b* 19 Jan 1914; *m* 27 Sept 1949 Capt Cecil Campbell Hardy, DSO, RN (*d* 8 Dec 1963), son of Col Charles Richard Hugh Hardy, and has issue:

1c *Charles Rupert Almeric; *b* 28 April 1951; *educ* Wellington and Magdalene Coll Cambridge (BA); MBA (INSEAD); *m* 1982 *Helen, dau of Lt-Col R C Orgill, OBE, and has issue:

1d *Robin Campbell Richard; *b* 1984

2d *Jack Spencer; *b* 1986

3d *Christopher Munro; *b* 1992

1c *Theodora Margaret; *b* 18 Feb 1953; DO, MRO, *m* 1989 *Jeremy Gilson Lowe and has:

1d *Nicholas Jaspar; *b* 4 April 1994

1d *Jessamy Synolda; *b* 1991

(1) Charlotte Frances Bona; *m* 8 Jan 1873 Lt-Col George FitzRoy (*see* GRAFTON, D) and *d* 18 June 1919

(2) Fanny Isabella Catherine; *m* 17 July 1860 Lord Henry Vere Cholmondeley, 2nd son of 3rd Marquess of Cholmondeley (*qv*), and *d* 13 March 1900, leaving issue

(3) Caroline Louisa Elizabeth; *m* 7 July 1860 Hon Charles Murray Hay Forbes, 3rd son of 18th Lord Forbes (*qv*), and *d* 30 March 1901

3 Augustus Almeric (Sir), GCB, Gen, Offr Legion of Honour, Order Medjidie, Col 96th Foot and 1st Bn Oxon LI, cmded 44th Regt at the Alma and Inkerman and Siege of Sebastopol; *b* 25 March 1807; *m* 6 Feb 1836 Helen Maria (*d* 17 July 1899), 2nd dau of Lt-Gen Sir Archibald Campbell, 1st Bt, GCB, and *d* 28 Aug 1893, leaving, with other issue:

(1) Augustus Campbell, Lt-Col 5th Lancers and 1st Dragoon Gds; *b* 19 April 1851; *m* 12 Oct 1886 Hilda (*d* 10 July 1952), est dau of Alexander William Thorold Grant-Thorold, of Weelsby Ho, Lincs, and *d* 27 Feb 1912, leaving issue:

1a Richard Augustus, DSO (1917), OBE (1945), Col late RA, served WW I (despatches twice), and WW II; *b* 14 Dec 1888; *educ* Wellington; *m* 12 Sept 1925 Maud Evelyn (*d* 1989), er dau of Lt-Col Henry Lushington Ramsay, late IA (*see* DALHOUSIE, E), and *d* 20 Feb 1956, leaving issue:

1b +RICHARD HARRY RAMSAY [Richard Esq, The Old Vicarage, Vernham Dean, Hants]; *b* 11 Oct 1926; heir presumptive (to Barony only); *educ* Wellington; ARIBA, AA Dipl, Principal Harry Spencer and Associates, architects, late Lt Coldstream Gds; *m* 19 April 1958 *Antoinette Rose-Marie, dau of Godefroy de Charrière, of Les Pignets, Prévérenges, Lausanne, Switzerland, and has issue:

1c +Michael Richard de Charrière; *b* 9 Nov 1960; *educ* Bedstone School

2c +David Anthony; *b* 11 March 1970

2b +Charles Geoffrey Campbell [Charles Spencer Esq, Stokke Common, Savernake Forest, Marlborough, Wilts], late Lt Coldstream Gds, served in Malaya 1949–50 (wounded), and in Kenya 1954–56; *b* 25 May 1928; *educ* Wellington and RMA Sandhurst; *m* 26 Sept 1964 *Cherry Elizabeth, er dau of William Carlyle Clarke

2a Edward Almeric, OBE (1945), Lt-Col RA, WW I (wounded), WW II (despatches); *b* 26 Dec 1892; *educ* Wellington; *m* 9 July 1918 Elsie Winifred (*d* 1969), yst dau of Arthur Macan, DL, of Drumcashel, Co Louth, and *d* 1984, leaving issue:

1b *Augusta Elsie [Mrs Guinevere Williamson, Lower House, Ashley, Box, Corsham, Wilts]; *b* 6 Nov 1920; *m* 6 Oct 1945 (*divorce* 1975) Maj Charles Arthur Wellesley Williamson, MC, MD, MA, Sherwood Foresters (*d* 1997), yr son of Rev Charles Arthur Williamson, and has:

1c *Richard Almeric Spencer; *b* 20 March 1949; *educ* Winchester; *m* 1st 11 April 1970 (*divorce* 1982) June, dau of Wilfrid Mansfield; *m* 2nd 1982 *Aura Figueroa, and by 1st w has issue:

1d *Sasha; *b* 1971

2d *Damian; *b* 1974

3d *Mischa; *b* 1977

2c *Michael Anthony Wellesley; *b* 13 Feb 1952; *educ* Winchester and Durham U (BA); ARCM; *m* 1981 *Pascale Eyre

3c *Francis Charles FitzRoy; *b* 11 July 1959; *educ* Wellington; MSc, CEng, MIMechE; *m* 1995 *Ana Bhageloe

4c *Patrick Alexander Campbell; *b* 11 Oct 1960; *educ* Wellington and UEA (BA); *m* 1995 *Lydia Girot

1c *Sarah Lavinia [Mrs Michael Danny, The Manor House, Wellow, Bath]; *b* 25 Nov 1946; BA; *m* 1976 *Michael Danny and has:

1d *William; *b* 1979

2d *Christopher; *b* 1981

1d *Melissa; *b* 1976; *educ* Exeter U (BA Hons)

(1) Helen Frances; *m* 10 Oct 1870 Col Robert Spencer Liddell, late 10th Hus, and *d* 29 Aug 1932, leaving issue. He *d* 16 June 1903

(2) Augusta Melita; *m* 1st 10 Oct 1870 Lt-Col Sussex Vane Stephenson, Scots Fus Gds, and had issue. He *d* 28 June 1872. She *m* 2nd 15 Aug 1882 Rev Edward Mallet Young, son of Capt Sir George Young, 2nd Bt, RN, of Formosa Place (*qv*), and *d* 29 Aug 1920

4 William Henry (Rev), Rector of Gt Houghton, Northampton; *b* 12 April 1810; *educ* Ch Ch Oxford (MA); *m* 1st 23 Jan 1838 Elizabeth Rose (*d* 25 March 1851), 2nd dau of Thomas Thornhill, of Woodleys, and had issue:

(1) William Francis, JP Worcs, late Capt 46th Foot; *b* 10 Oct 1838; *m* 17 Jan 1874 Margaret Georgiana (*d* 21 Jan 1935), est dau of Walter Hemming, of Spring Grove, Worcs, and *d* 3 July 1923, leaving issue:

1a John Almeric Walter, CMG (1919), DSO (1918), Col late Rifle Bde, cmdg 163rd Inf Bde (TA) 1931–35, Hon Brig-Gen 1935, served WW I 1914–18 (despatches), Legion of Honour; *b* 21 July 1881; *m* 7 Aug 1913 Eleanor Georgiana (*d* 11 June 1967), 2nd dau of William Peel, of Knowlmere Manor, Clitheroe, Lancs, and *d* 12 Feb 1952, leaving issue:

1b John Lawrence, DSO, MC, Capt late RHA, served WW II; *b* 9 Jan 1917; *educ* Winchester and Magdalene Coll Cambridge; *m* 1 May 1943 *Jane Lilian [Mrs John Spencer, Ghyllas, Sedbergh, Cumbria LA10 5LT] dau of Col Granville Duff, MC, of Heydon, Norfolk, and was *k* in an accident 28 Jan 1967, leaving issue:

1c +John William James [John Spencer Esq, Ghyllas, Sedbergh, Cumbria LA10 5LT]; *b* 26 Dec 1957; *educ* Sedbergh, Magdalene Coll Cambridge (MA) and Open Business Sch (MBA); *m* 1st 1982 (*divorce* 1987) Leonie Margaret, dau of Ralph Jameson; *m* 2nd 1987 *Jane Elizabeth, dau of Andrew Young, and has issue:

1d +Charles William Alexander; *b* 1990

1d *Rosanagh Jane Katharine; *b* 1991

2d *Caitlin Anne Sophia; *b* 1996

1c *Caroline Mary [Mrs Robin Sandys-Clarke, Raff Yard House, Staindrop, Darlington, Co Durham DL2 3AH]; *b* 30 Oct 1948; *m* *Robin Peter Sandys-Clarke, and has issue

1d *Peter Edward David; *b* 1981

1d *Jessica Jane; *b* 1975

2d *Lucinda Mary; *b* 1977

1a Sibyl Frances; *b* 25 Feb 1875; *m* 20 Jan 1903 William Moat, OBE, DL, JP, MA, of Johnson Hall, Eccleshall, Stafford, late Maj Staffs Yeo, and *d* 4 June 1948, leaving issue. He *d* 17 Sept 1941

(2) Almeric George, Col, late cmdg 33rd Regimental Dist and Essex Regt; *b* 16 Oct 1841; *m* 1st 11 Aug 1869 Alice Isabel (*d* 23 May 1913), dau of Col T G Fraser; *m* 2nd 1914 Ada (*d* 8 Dec 1929), dau of Henry Downing, of Stratford-on-Avon, and *d* 5 Sept 1929, having by 1st w had issue:

1a Almeric Arthur William, Lt-Col late W Yorks Regt, served WW I 1914–18 (despatches thrice, Brev of Lt-Col, Legion of Honour); *b* 21 Nov

1874; *m* 1st 16 Oct 1907 (*divorce* 1927) Sybil, 2nd dau of Frederick William Lawson, of Adel, Leeds. He *m* 2nd 22 July 1930 *Charlotte [Mrs Cecil Whiteside, 34 Ashgarth Court, Harrogate, N Yorks] (who *m* 2nd 8 Aug 1941 Capt Cecil Trevor Hamilton Whiteside, MC, MRCS, RAMC (*d* 14 April 1965), son of Hon Mrs Borras Whiteside (*see* BELHAVEN AND STENTON, L)), dau of Rev John Lesley Parker, Vicar of Lanteglos-by-Fowey, Cornwall, and *d* 21 Oct 1934, leaving issue:

1b *Ann Frances; *b* 10 May 1931; *m* 1st 29 Jan 1957 (*m annulled* 1963) Rev Leslie Vandernoll Wright, MA, son of Ernest Wright, CBE, of 1 Emberton Ho, 22, Shakespeare Rd, Bedford; *m* 2nd 1979 *Patrick Joseph Healy

1a Rose Frances; *m* 1st 10 Sept 1890 Capt Charles Greenway, Dorsetshire Regt, and had issue. He *d* 1892. She *m* 2nd 9 June 1894 Maj-Gen Raymond Northland Revell Reade, CB, CMG, of Stutton Manor, Ipswich, Col KSLI, son of John Page Reade, of Crowe Hall, Suffolk, by his w Lady Mary, dau of 2nd Earl of Ranfurly (*qv*), and *d* 28 April 1947, leaving further issue. He *d* 18 Oct 1943

2a Alice Katharine; *m* 3 Nov 1894 Lt Col Francis Hugh Neish, late Gordon Highrs, son of W Neish, of Tannadyce and Clepington, Angus, and *d* 1944, leaving issue. He *d* 1945

3a Dorothy Julia; *m* 17 July 1902 George Willoughby Fraser, FSA, Egyptian Govt Serv, son of Maj-Gen Sir Thomas Fraser, KCB, and *d* 30 Sept 1925. He *d* 24 Nov 1923

(1) Frances Rose; *m* 23 Oct 1879 Rev Sir Henry John Gunning, 4th Bt (*qv*), and *d* 24 Dec 1927. He *d* 30 June 1885

(2) Isabella Elizabeth *m* 25 Jan 1865 Marten Harcourt Griffin, of Lang Field, Bude, Cornwall, and *d* 6 Jan 1934, leaving issue. He *d* 3 June 1924

4 (cont.) The Rev William Spencer *m* 2ndly 15 June 1852 Louisa Mercer (*dsp* 31 Aug 1892), 3rd dau of Sir William Call, 2nd Bt, of Whiteford; *m* 3rd 1893 Anna Maria Cowley (*d* 25 Jan 1924), widow of Robert Francis Allan, and dau of John Horton Sheppard, of Towcester, and *d* 21 Aug 1900

5 Robert Charles Henry, Col late RHA; *b* 10 June 1817; *m* 14 July 1845, his cousin, Lady Louisa Spencer-Churchill (*d* 23 March 1882), dau of 6th Duke of Marborough (*qv*), and *d* 17 June 1881, having had, with other issue:

(1) Gerald Robert, Maj, Roy Def Corps, late Capt RA; *b* 21 Feb 1853; *m* 20 Aug 1878 Emma Douglas (*d* 29 May 1934), est dau of Sir George Tapps-Gervis-Meyrick, 3rd Bt (*qv*), of Hinton Admiral, Hants, and *dsp* 13 May 1918

(1) Blance Louisa; *m* 5 July 1876 Henry George Fane, late Capt 52nd Regt, 2nd son of Col John William Fane, DL, JP, MP, of Wormsley, Oxon (*see* WESTMORLAND, E), and *d* 24 Feb 1919, leaving issue

6 Charles Frederic Octavius (Rev), Vicar of Sutton, Isle of Ely; *b* 9 Sept 1824; *educ* Clare Coll Cambridge (MA); *m* 17 June 1847 Hester Eliza (*d* 5 March 1905), est dau of Rev Henry Fardell, Vicar of Wisbech and Canon of Ely Cathedral, and *d* 12 Aug 1895, having had, with other issue:

(1) Charles Francis Henry, Lt-Col late Roy Inniskilling Fus; *b* 11 June 1848; *m* 17 March 1879 Emily Lydia (*d* 14 Dec 1941), yr dau of William Walker Ball, of Carlow, and *d* 30 July 1922, leaving issue:

1a Francis Elmhirst, DSO (1918), MC (1916), Col late RA, Brig i/c Admin W Command 1934–38, Hon Brig 1938, served in China 1900, in Tibet Expdn and occupation of Lhasa, 1904, and WW I 1914–18 (despatches five times), and WW II 1939–45 (RARO; Regl Offr London CD, Admiralty); *b* 25 July 1881; *educ* Dover Coll; *m* 26 Feb 1916 Augusta (Vera) (*d* 18 Dec 1956), yr dau of Col Arthur Tracey, late RA, and *d* 1972, leaving issue:

1b Francis Tracey, Capt, York and Lancs Regt; *b* 27 Jan 1917; *educ* Blundell's; *m* 12 May 1962 *Rev Diana Margaret Colton [The Rev Diana Spencer, 3013 Jasette Place, Victoria, BC V8T 4Z9, Canada], er dau of Dennis Haines, of Wattisfield, Suffolk, and *d* 1989, leaving issue:

1c +Philip Henry [Philip Spencer Esq, c/o Math Dept, Toronto University, Toronto, Ont, Canada]; *b* 28 Jan 1966; *educ* Glenlyon Sch, Victoria, Victoria U (BSc) and Harvard (PhD)

1b *Joan Elizabeth [Mrs Geoffrey Shell, Gomorin, Court Wood, Newton Ferrers, Plymouth, Devon], late QARNNS; *b* 22 May 1921; *m* 23 April 1949 *Surgn-Cdr Geoffrey Norman Shell, RN, son of Rev Alfred Shell, Chaplain RN, and has issue:

1c *Peter Geoffrey [Peter Shell Esq, Southways, 5 Kingsdale Rd, Berkhamsted, Herts]; *b* 10 Aug 1951; *educ* Haileybury; *m* 1984 *Marianne Jane, er dau of Paul Pierre Tissier, FRSS, Abingdon and has:

1d *Timothy Geoffrey; *b* 3 Aug 1987

2d *Jonathan Paul; *b* 22 Sept 1992

2c *David Spencer [David Shell Esq, 11 Lumsdale Terrace, Lumsdale, Matlock, Derbys]; *b* 21 Nov 1954; *educ* Milton Abbey

(2) Henry Montagu, VD, JP Worcs, late Capt and Hon Maj 5th Bn Glos Regt; *b* 13 Nov 1851; *m* 7 Sept 1880 Ethel Louisa (*d* 5 Nov 1925), yr dau of Gen Marcus Beresford (*see* DECIES, B), and *d* 26 Oct 1924, leaving issue:

1a Henry Beresford, Lt W Som Yeo, attd Tank Corps, late Lt 2nd Vol Bn Glos Regt, served in S Africa, and WW I; *b* 5 July 1881; *educ* BNC Oxford (BA); *m* 14 Jan 1908 Dorothy Acton (*d* 17 Nov 1950), yst dau of Rev Frederick Farrer, of Brayfield, Bucks, and was *ka* 3 Sept 1918, leaving issue:

1b Denis Henry, F/O RAF; *b* 29 Aug 1913; *k* 18 July 1936, as result of a flying accident

1b *Audrey Joan; *b* 3 Sept 1911; *m* 19 Dec 1939 Maj John Alexander Sneyd Hawkins, RA, son of John Sneyd Hawkins, MD, of Fernihurst, Cheltenham, and has issue:

1c *John David; *b* 11 Sept 1940; *educ* Bradfield and Univ Coll Oxford

2c *Timothy Spencer; *b* 15 June 1945; *educ* Bradfield

1c *Denzil Audrey; *b* 11 Jan 1946; *educ* St Mary's Wantage

1a Hilda Agnes; *b* 25 June 1882

2a Eleanor Cicely; *b* 5 Sept 1883

1 Caroline Elizabeth; *m* 22 June 1830 3rd Baron Clonbrock, and *d* 17 Dec 1864, leaving issue. He *d* 4 Dec 1893

The 1st BARON *d* 10 March 1845; his er son,

FRANCIS GEORGE SPENCER, **2nd Baron Churchill of Wychwood**; *b* 6 Oct 1802; *m* 19 May 1849 Lady Jane Conyngham, VA (*d* 25 Dec 1900), a Lady of the Bedchamber to QUEEN VICTORIA, est dau of 2nd Marquess Conyngham, KP (*qv*), and *d* 24 Nov 1886, having had issue:

VICTOR ALBERT FRANCIS CHARLES SPENCER, **1st Viscount Churchill**, of Rolleston, Co Leicester (UK), so *cr* 14 July 1902, GCVO (1902, KCVO 1900), JP (Oxon and Leics); a Prince of the Holy Roman Empire, a Page of Honour 1876–81 to HM QUEEN VICTORIA, who stood his sponsor, Lt-Col late TAR, formerly Maj Oxon Yeo and Lt Coldstream Gds, T/Col WW I, Ld-in-Waiting 1889–92, 1895–1901 and 1901–05; Master of the Buckhounds 1900–01, Ld Chamberlain 1902; chm: GWR and Br Overseas Bank, dir: P&O and Br India Steamship Co and Grand Union Canal; *b* 23 Oct 1864; *m* 1st 1 Jan 1887 (*divorce* in Scottish Courts 1927) Lady Verena Maud Lowther, VA (*d* 25 Dec 1938), dau of 3rd Earl of Lonsdale (*qv*), and *d* 3 Jan 1934, having had issue:

1 Victor Almeric Lancelot; *b* and *d* 18 Jan 1888

2 VICTOR ALEXANDER SPENCER, **2nd Viscount Churchill**; *b* 1 Aug 1890 (QUEEN VICTORIA stood sponsor); *educ* Eton; Maj Res of Offrs, late KOSB, GSO(3) War Office 1917–19, a Prince of the Holy Roman Empire, Page of Honour to HM EDWARD VII 1901–07, served WW I (despatches), WW II in USAF; FRAS; *m* 1st 15 July 1916 Katherine Emily (*d* 1 Dec 1943), widow of Capt Stanley Venn Ellis, RN, and dau of Hon Robert Beaven, formerly Premier of Victoria, BC; *m* 2nd 19 Oct 1949 Joan (*d* 12 May 1957), est dau of Joseph Baron Black, of Belfast, and *dsp* 21 Dec 1973

1 Victoria Ivy Louise; *b* 15 Oct 1897 (QUEEN VICTORIA and PRINCESS LOUISE, DUCHESS of ARGYLL stood sponsor); *m* 10 Nov 1920 Capt Hon Cecil Henry Brassey, late 1st Life Gds, est son of 1st Baron Brassey of Apethorpe (*qv*)

2 Ursula; *b* 21 June 1901; *m* 16 July 1928 Lt-Col Alick Frederick Tod, DSO, RHA, son of Col George Russell Tod, JP, of the Red Ho, Dorchester, and *d* 1 June 1934

The **1st Viscount** *m* 2nd 29 Aug 1927 Christine McRae (*b* 24 Sept 1895; *d* 22 May 1972) (had Order of Leopold of Belgium) (who *m* 2nd 12 June 1937 (*divorce* Reno USA 1938) Lt-Col Ralph Heyward Isham, CBE (*d* 13 June 1955), son of Henry Heyward Isham, of New York; *m* 3rd 6 Nov 1939 Sir Lancelot Oliphant, KCMG, CB (*d* 2 Oct 1965)), est dau of William Sinclair, and by her had issue:

3 VICTOR GEORGE SPENCER, **3rd and present Viscount Churchill**

3 *Sarah Faith Georgina (MBE) [The Hon Mrs Palmer MBE, Queen Anne's Mead, Swallowfield, Berks RG7 1ST]; *b* 5 June 1931 (HM GEORGE V stood sponsor); *m* 17 Dec 1951 *Richard John Palmer, JP, DL (*see* PALMER, B), and has:

(1) *David Charles; *b* 3 May 1955; *educ* Eton; *m* 1989 *Lucy Belinda, er dau of Capt Patrick John Boteler Drury-Lowe (*see* EARLE, Bt), and has:

1a *George Richard Charles; *b* 1992

2a *Shamus Patrick John; *b* 1993

3a *Edward; *b* 1996

(2) *James Nicholas [James Palmer Esq, 10 rue de la Source, 75016 Paris, France]; *b* 21 May 1963; *m* 1988 *Cybele I, dau of Francis Bullock, of Egypt Farm, Hamptons, Kent, and has issue:

1a *Oliver Victor George; *b* 1990

1a *Sophie Rose; *b* 1995

(3) *Christopher Richard; *b* 24 July 1967

(1) *Caroline Mary [Mrs Mark Dickinson, Newbrough Lodge, Newbrough, Hexham, Northumberland]; *b* 16 Dec 1952; *m* 1st 11 Dec 1975 (*divorce* 1991) Maj Hon Richard Nicholas Bethell, MBE, er son of 5th Baron Westbury (*qv*); *m* 2nd 1992, as his 2nd w, *Mark Chaytor Dickinson (*see* CHAYTOR, Bt)

CHURSTON

Arms: Quarterly, 1st and 4th, sa. on a cross arg. quarterly pierced four eagles displayed of the field (for BULLER); 2nd and 3rd, arg. a chevron gu. between three water-bougets sa.(for YARDE).
Crest: A Saracen's head couped ppr. **Supporters:** Dexter, an ostrich ppr., in the beak a horseshoe or; sinister, an eagle sa.
Motto: *Aquila non capit muscas* ('The eagle does not catch flies').
Creations: Bt. (GB) 13 Jan 1790, B. (UK) 2 Aug 1858.

THE 5TH BARON CHURSTON OF CHURSTON FERRERS AND LUPTON, Co Devon, and a **Baronet** (Sir John Francis Yarde-Buller, Bt) [The Rt Hon The Lord Churston, Yowlestone House, Puddington, Tiverton, Devon EX16 8LN]; *b* 29 Dec 1934; Is f 1991; *educ* Eton; 2nd Lt RHG 1954; *m* 25 Oct 1973 *Alexandra Joanna

Philippa, only dau of Anthony Contomichalos, of 23 Eaton Pl, London SW1, and has issue:
1 +BENJAMIN FRANCIS ANTHONY; *b* 13 Sept 1974; *educ* Eton
1 *Katherine Marina; *b* 23 Dec 1975
2 *Francesca Elisabeth; *b* 17 Dec 1980

Lineage: JAMES BULLER, of Morval, Cornwall; had a 4th s:

Sir Francis Buller, 1st Bt (GB), so *cr* 13 Jan 1790, KC (1777); *b* 17 March 1745/6; barrister 1772; Second Judge Chester Circuit 1777, Judge: King's Bench 1778, Common Pleas 1794; *m c* 1771 Susannah, only dau and heir of Francis Yarde, of Churston Ferrers and Ottery St Mary, Devon, and *d* 4 June 1800, leaving an only son:

Sir FRANCIS BULLER later BULLER-YARDE (under terms of maternal uncle's will) later still BULLER-YARDE-BULLER (sign-manual), **2nd Bt**; *b* 28 Sept 1767; *m* 27 May 1793 Elizabeth Lydia (*d* 8 Nov 1851), only dau and heir of John Holliday, of Lincoln's Inn, and Dilhorne Hall, Staffs, and had, with other issue:
1 JOHN, **1st Baron**
2 Sir EDWARD BULLER-YARDE-BULLER later MANNINGHAM-BULLER, 1st Bt (*see* DILHORNE, V)
1 Susan Elizabeth; *m* 1st 13 Aug 1814 16th Earl of Morton (*qv*); *m* 2nd 17 Sept 1831 Edward Godfrey, of Old Hall, Suffolk, and *d* 23 July 1849. He *d* 1842

Sir FRANCIS *d* 17 April 1833; his er surv son,

Sir JOHN BULLER-YARDE-BULLER later YARDE-BULLER (roy licence 13 Feb 1860), **3rd Bt**, and **1st Baron Churston of Churston Ferrers and Lupton**, Co Devon (UK), so *cr* 2 Aug 1858; *b* 12 April 1799; MP (C) S Devon 1835–58; *m* 1st 24 Jan 1823 Elizabeth (*d* 20 Feb 1857), dau of Thomas Wilson-Patten, of Bank Hall, Lancs, and had issue:
1 John, Col; *b* 23 Dec 1823; *m* 1 Jan 1845 Charlotte (*d* 15 March 1895, 3rd dau of Edward Sacheverell Chandos-Pole, of Radborne Hall, Derbys, and *dvp* 6 May 1867, having had issue (his children were granted rank of baron's daus/yr s 14 June 1873):
(1) JOHN, **2nd Baron**
(2) Walter, Lt 2nd Bn Devon Regt; *b* 21 Jan 1859; *m* 1st 1886 Leilah (*d* 1904), widow of D Boyle Blair and dau of Gen R W Kirkham, of California; *m* 2nd 19 Aug 1913 Alianore (*d* 24 Feb 1952), yst dau of Edward Sacheverell Chandos-Pole, of Radborne Hall, and *d* 28 April 1935
(3) Geoffrey; *b* 24 Oct 1861; *m* 19 May 1892 Olegaria Venancia, dau of Florencio Alvarez, of Argentina, and *d* 1952, leaving issue:
1a John; *b* 21 March 1893
2a Geoffrey; *b* 14 Aug 1894; *m* 1st 13 March 1919 Hortensia (*d* 25 Sept 1957), 2nd dau of Leon Naboulet, of Paraná, Argentina, and had issue:
1b +Norberto [Sr Norberto Yarde-Buller, La Tribuna 1705, Castelar, Buenos Aires, Argentina]; *b* Dec 1922; *m* 20 June 1946 *Yolanda Adela, 3rd dau of Carlos Devillier, of Florida, Argentina, and has issue:
1c +Daniel Carlos; *b* 1954; *m* 1976 *Elda Beatriz Martinez, and has issue:
1d *Soledad Jorgelina; *b* 1980
2c +Norberto Luis; *b* 1959; *m* 1987 *Viviana Sandra Masseo, and has issue:
1d +Alexis; *b* 1988
1d *Jimena; *b* 1989
1c *Rita Adela; *b* 1947; *m* 1979 *Ingeniero Jorge Daniel Balan, and has issue:
1d *Gonzolo Daniel; *b* 1992
2c *Susana Hortensia; *b* 1952; *m* 1985 *Marcelo Esteban Gilberto
2b +Eduardo [Sr Eduardo Yarde-Buller, Luis Maria Campos 4029, Villa Insuperable, La Matanza, Buenos Aires, Argentina]; *b* Dec 1926; *m* 13 Aug 1953 *Isabel Ester, 2nd dau of Francisco Hinojosa, of Buenos Aires, Argentina, and has issue:
1c +Eduardo Guillermo; *b* 1972
1c *Liliana Beatriz; *b* 1955; *m* 1976 *Luciano Dal Cin, and has issue:
1d *Mariano; *b* 1983
2d *Ignacio; *b* 1985
3d *Dario; *b* 1988
1d *Luciana; *b* 1991
2c *Jaquelina Ines; *b* 1968; *m* 1985 *Marcelo Romero, and has issue:
1d *Frederico Alizeri; *b* 1991
1d *Maria Azul; *b* 1987
1b *Lilian [Sra de Victor Olivera, Arias 1955–5° Piso, Dto C, Buenos Aires, Argentina]; *b* 24 Dec 1920; *m* 1st 1944 Oswaldo Alizeri (*d* 1962); *m* 2nd 1968 *Victor Antonio Olivera, Capt de Corbeta de la Armada Argentina, and by 1st husb has issue:
1c Stella Maria; *b* 1945; *d* 1967
2c Diana; *b* 1947; *m* 1973 *Juan Jose Molero, and *d* 1980, leaving issue:
1d *Frederico Jose; *b* 1977
2d *Enrique Marcelo; *b* 1979
2b *Delia [Sra de Rafael Parravicini Piaggio, Av Maipu 1864–2° Piso, Vicente Lopez, Buenos Aires, Argentina]; *b* 22 Feb 1932; *m* 27 Oct 1949 Don Rafael M Parravicini Piaggio (*d* 1967), author, and has issue:
1c *Octavio Horacio; *b* 1950; *m* 1972 *Raquel O Melgarejo Dutra, and has issue:
1d *Octavio Ovidio; *b* 1976
1d *Mercedes; *b* 1980
2d *Florencia Soila; *b* 1985
3d *Delmira Soita; *b* 1985 (twin)
2c *Rafael Guido; *b* 1952; *m* 1980 *Ana Maria Liria Laurant, and has issue:
1d *Alejo Andres; *b* 1989
1d *Lucia Florencia; *b* 1981
1c *Denise Oriental; *b* 1959
3b *Doris [Sra de Jorge Gattino Av Maipu 1468–2° Piso, Vicente Lopez, Buenos Aires, Argentina]; *b* 1934; *m* 1962 *Jorge Gattino Cuesta, and has issue:
1c *Gabriela Amalia; *b* 1965; *m* 1988 *Ingeniero Leonardo Omar Lanzilotta
4b *Estella [Sra de Ismael Sabino Salvatierra, Feliciano Chiclana 61, 1708 Morón, Buenos Aires, Argentina]; *b* 1939; *m* 1961 *Prof Ismael Sabino Salvatierra, and has issue:
1c *Alejandro Ismael; *b* 1962; engineer
2c *Eduardo Pablo; *b* 1964; teacher; *m* 1993 *Adrioma Marcela Viggiano
3c *Gustavo Fabian; *b* 1968
1c *Adriana Hortensia; *b* 1970
2a (cont.) Geoffrey Yarde-Buller *m* 2nd 19– (*divorce* 1972) Elsa Cejas, and *d* 1993, having by her had further issue:
5b *Silvia Veronica; *b* 1966; *m* 1984 *Luis Cosenza, and has issue:
1c *Alexis; *b* 1985
3a Edmond; *b* 1897; *m* *Adela Jmelnisky, and *d* 19–, leaving issue:
1b +Reinaldo Alberto [Sr Reinaldo Yarde-Buller, Avenida 9 de Julio 3260, Chajari (Entre Rios), Argentina]; *b* 19–; *m* *Martha Elena Melgar, and has issue:
1c +Cristian; *b* 17 Dec 1964
2c +Adrian; *b* 9 Jan 1966
3c +Alann; *b* 21 Feb 1970
2b +Jorge; *b* 19–
1b *Anita Sofia; *b* 19–; *m* *Rodolfo Juan Carlos Nux
2b *Cecilia Olegaria; *b* 19–; *m* *Eduardo Tirado
4a +Henry; *b* 1899
5a +Manuel; *b* 1901
6a +Albert; *b* 6 March 1908; *m* 23 Oct 1942 *Ella Cristina, dau of Dugaldo Farquharson
7a +Reginald; *b* 15 Feb 1911
1a *Olga
2a *Agnes
3a *
(4) Henry (Sir), KBE (1919), CB (1917), DSO (1900), MVO (1908), Hon Brig-Gen formerly Rifle Bde, served with Waziristan Expdn 1894–95, Nile Expdn 1898, in Crete 1898, S African War 1899–1902, and WW I 1914–16; was Mil Attaché in Belgium, The Hague and at Northern Courts 1906–10, and Paris, Madrid and Lisbon 1912–15, Head of Mil Mission, French HQ 1914–17, and Mission to Scandinavia 1917–19, had Orders of Leopold of Belgium, St Olav of Norway, Dannebrog of Denmark, and Epée of Sweden, and the Cross of Cdr of the Legion of Honour; *b* 2 Nov 1862; *m* 11 Dec 1902 Adelaide Maud Sophia (*d* 23 April 1950), dau of Lt-Col Charles Meeking, of Riching's Park, Colnbrook, and *d* 15 March 1928
(5) Reginald John (Rev Canon), Vicar of Dean Prior, Devon 1931–39, Canon Emertius of Truro Cathedral 1931; *b* 12 July 1864; *educ* Ch Ch Oxford (MA); *m* 29 Jan 1919 Hon Mary Vere Agar-Robartes (*d* 9 April 1946), est dau of 6th Viscount Clifden (*see* 1970 edn), and *dsp* 13 June 1950
(1) Charlotte Mildred; *m* 1st 11 July 1872 (*divorce* 1892) Lt-Col John Richard Malone, of Baronston, Co Westmeath, and had issue. She *m* 2nd 23 Nov 1892 Count Charles de Beaumont d'Autichamp
(2) Louisa Maud; *m* 1st 24 Oct 1871 Hon Reginald Greville-Nugent, 4th son of 1st Baron Greville. He *d* 28 Feb 1878. She *m* 2nd 17 July 1879 James Charles Hope-Vere (*see* LINLITHGOW, M), and *dsp* 20 April 1882
(3) Eleanor Isabel; *m* 1 Sept 1890 Capt Herbert Frederick Northey Hopkins, late Seaforth Highrs, of Marchington Hall, Staffs, and *d* 6 July 1913. He *dsp* 27 Nov 1910
(4) Bertha; *m* 4 Dec 1883 Capt Robert Henry Dewhurst, late 4th Hus, of Clonsilla, Co Dublin, and *d* 13 Sept 1931. He *d* 11 Dec 1936
1 Bertha; *m* 11 May 1854 Sir (Lopes) Massey Lopes, 3rd Bt, PC, MP, and *d* 13 Jan 1872, leaving issue (*see* ROBOROUGH, B)

The **1st Baron** *m* 2nd 16 Aug 1861 Caroline (*d* 27 Nov 1866), 3rd dau of Sir Robert William Newman, 1st Bt, of Mamhead (*qv*), and *d* 4 Sept 1871

His gs,

JOHN YARDE-BULLER, **2nd Baron Churston of Churston Ferrers and Lupton**, JP Devon, Capt Scots Fus Gds and afterwards Maj Devon Art; *b* 26 Oct 1846; *m* 23 Sept 1872 Hon Barbara Yelverton (*d* 1 Oct 1924), only child of Adml Sir Hastings Reginald Yelverton, GCB, by his w Barbara, Baroness Grey (of Ruthin) (*see* GREY, B), Marchioness of Hastings (*see* SAINT DAVIDS, V), and had:
1 JOHN REGINALD LOPES, **3rd Baron**
2 Giles Yelverton; *b* 10 Dec 1875; *d* unm 9 Sept 1900
1 Barbara Lois; *b* 5 Jan 1875; *d* unm 31 Oct 1945

The 2nd BARON *d* 30 Nov 1910; his only surv son,

JOHN REGINALD LOPES YARDE-BULLER, **3rd Baron Churston of Churston Ferrers and Lupton**, MVO, OBE, Lt-Col late 3rd Res Bn Scots Gds, and formerly Lt-Col and Insp of Quartermaster-Gen's Services, ADC to the Viceroy of India 1902003, and to HRH DUKE OF CONNAUGHT 1904–06, served in S African War 1900–01 (medal with four clasps); *b* 9 Nov 1873; *m* 24 April 1907 (*divorce* 1928) Jessie (*d* 20 Oct 1960), only dau of Alfred John Smither, and had issue:
1 RICHARD FRANCIS ROGER, **4th Baron**
2 John Reginald Henry, served WW II; *b* 13 June 1915; *m* 25 Nov 1939 *Guendolen Margaret Osborn [The Hon Mrs John Yarde-Buller, Le Vallon, Mont Félard, Jersey, CI], only dau of Rev Charles Roots, of Heathfield, Sussex, and *d* 10 Oct 1962, leaving issue:
(1) +Roger Charles John; *b* 30 June 1942
(2) +Anthony Reginald Lawrence; *b* 24 Aug 1946
1 Joan Barbara; *b* 22 April 1908; *m* 1st 4 July 1927 (*divorce* 1936) G/Capt (Thomas) Loel Evelyn Bulkeley Guinness, OBE, AAF (Res) (*d* 1988), and had issue (*see* GUINNESS, Bt); *m* 2nd 18 May 1936 (*divorce* 1949) Prince Aly Khan

(*d* following a motor accident, 12 May 1960), son of the Aga Khan, GCSI, GCIE, GCVO, PC, and had by him:

(2) *Karim [HH The Aga Khan, Aiglemont, 60270 Gouvieux, France]; *b* 1936; *educ* Le Rosey and Harvard (BA Hons); *s* gf as 4th Aga Khan 1957; spiritual leader and Imam of Ismaili Muslims all over the world; received personal title of Highness 1957 from HM THE QUEEN; a leading racehorse owner and breeder in France and Ireland; pres Aga Khan Fndn Geneva 1967, Fndr and Chllr Aga Khan U Pakistan 1983; *m* 1969 (divorce 1995) Sarah (Sally) Frances, only dau of Lt-Col A E Croker Poole, of 95 Eaton Sq, London SW1, and formerly w of Lord James Charles Crichton-Stuart (*see* BUTE, M), and has issue:

1a *Rahim; *b* 1971

2a *Hussain; *b* 1974

1a *Zahra; *b* 1970; *educ* Harvard; *m* 21 June 1997 *Mark Boyden

(3) *Amyn Mohamed [Prince Amyn Aga Khan, 276 Route de Lausanne, 1292 Chambesy, Geneva, Switzerland; 69 rue de Lille, 75007 Paris, France]; *b* 1937; *educ* Le Rosey and Harvard

1 (cont.) The Hon Princess Aly Khan *m* 3rd 1986 2nd Viscount Camrose (*qv*) and *d* 25 April 1997

2 *Denise Margaret [Denise Lady Ebury, Bartons Lodge, Eversholt, Bletchley, Bucks]; *b* 24 Oct 1916; *m* 21 Nov 1941 (*divorce* 1954) 5th Baron Ebury, (*qv*), and has issue

3 *Lydia [Lydia Duchess of Bedford, Little Ribsden, Windlesham, Bagshot, Surrey]; *b* 17 Oct 1917; *m* 1st 26 Jan 1938 Capt Ian Archibald de Hoghton Lyle, Black Watch, est son of Sir Archibald Moir Park Lyle, 2nd Bt, MC (*qv*), of Glendelvine, Perthshire, and has issue. He was *ka* in the Middle East Oct 1942. She *m* 2nd 12 Feb 1947 (*divorce* 1960) 13th Duke of Bedford (*qv*) and has further issue

4 Primrose Lillian; *b* 24 Dec 1918; *m* 11 June 1936 (*divorce* 1960) 7th Earl Cadogan (*qv*) and *d* 6 Dec 1970, leaving issue

The 3rd BARON *d* 19 April 1930; his er son,

RICHARD FRANCIS ROGER YARDE-BULLER, **4th Baron Churston of Churston Ferrers and Lupton**, VRD (1949); *b* 12 Feb 1910; *educ* Eton; Lt-Cdr RNVR WW II; *m* 1st 5 Jan 1933 (*divorce* 1943) Elizabeth Mary (*d* 23 Sept 1951, having *m* 2nd 1943 Maj Peter Laycock (*d* 1978)), 2nd dau of Lt-Col William Baring Du Pre, of Wilton Park, and had issue:

1 JOHN FRANCIS YARDE-BULLER, **5th and present Baron Churston of Churston Ferrers and Lupton**

1 *Nicole [The Hon Mrs Russell, Wilby Hall, Wilby, Norwich, Norfolk]; *b* 11 March 1936; *m* 1st 10 April 1958 (*divorce* 1962) Richard Wilfred Beavoir Berens, est son of Herbert Cecil Berens, MC, of Bentworth Hall, Hants, and has issue:

(1) *Thomas Richard; *b* 2 June 1960; *educ* Bishop Wordsworth Sch, Salisbury

(1) *Jessica Primrose; *b* 19 April 1959; *educ* Cranbourne Chase; journalist

1 (cont.) The Hon Mrs Nicole Berens *m* 2nd 6 Feb 1963 *Michael Russell, son of Edward Dennis Russell, of The Well Ho, Wick, Bournemouth, Hants, and has further issue:

(2) *Francis; *b* 15 March 1966; *educ* Harrow; *m* 1993 *Penelope G, yr dau of Maj J I L Syddall, of Puddletown, Dorset

(3) *Alexander; *b* 28 Dec 1969; *educ* Eton and Edinburgh U; *m* 27 Sept 1997 *Rose M, dau of John Fairbairn

(2) *Lorna; *b* 21 Dec 1963; *educ* St Mary's, Calne

The 4th Baron *m* 2nd 31 March 1949 Sandra (*d* 1 Dec 1979) formerly w of (a) Claud Harold Bertram (Arthur) Griffiths and (b) Jack Dunfee and dau of Percy Needham; *m* 3rd 1981 Mrs Olga Alice Muriel Blair (*d* 1992), illegitimate dau of 2nd Baron Rothschild by Marie Barbara, dau of Maximilian Fredenson, of Newton Sq, Bayswater, London W2, and formerly w of Bryce Evans Blair, and *d* 1991

CITRINE

Arms: Argent on waves of the sea in base an ancient three-masted ship in full sail proper, on a chief gules a Saxon crown between two seaxes points downwards or, the dexter in bend and the sinister in bend sinister. **Crest:** A cubit arm habited azure cuffed argent, the hand grasping a citrine proper. **Supporters:** Dexter, an Alsatian wolfhound proper, on the shoulder a terrestrial globe or charged with a human heart gules; sinister, a lion proper, on the shoulder a torteau charged with a spade and a pick-axe in saltire and a pen-nib in pale or. **Motto:** *Pro recto labora* ('Strive for what is right'). **Creation:** B. (UK) 16 July 1946.

Ronald Eric Citrine [Dr Ron Citrine, 1 Rosella Place, Maunu, Whangarei, New Zealand]; *b* 19 May 1919; *s* bro 1997 but does not use title; *educ* U Coll Sch and London U (MD, MRCS, LRCP); late house physician Westminster Hosp; *m* 27 July 1945 *Mary, dau of Reginald Williams, of Wembley.

Lineage: FRANCIS THOMAS CITRINE, of Liverpool; *b* 1816; *m* 28 Aug 1848 Mary Cope, of Liverpool, and *d* 29 Dec 1899, leaving issue:

ALFRED CITRINE, of Wallasey, Liverpool; *b* 9 March 1852; *educ* elementary sch; *m* 19 Dec 1881 Isabella (*b* 23 April 1847; *d* 6 Nov 1913), dau of George McLennan, of Arbroath, Angus, and *d* 8 July 1937, leaving issue:

WALTER McLENNAN CITRINE, **1st Baron Citrine**, of Wembley, Co Middx (UK), so *cr* 16 July 1946, GBE (1958, KBE 1935), PC (1940): *b* 22 Aug 1887; *educ* elementary sch; Assist Gen Sec ETU 1920–23, Assist Sec TUC 1924–26 and Gen Sec 1926–46, Pres IFTU 1928–45, dir and v-chm Daily Herald Ltd 1929–46, Tstee Imp Relations Tst 1937–49, memb Cinematograph Films Cncl 1938–48, V-Pres Nat Safety First Assoc, memb: Ec Advsy Cncl 1930–33, Roy Commn on W Indies 1938–39, Exec Ctee Red Cross and St John War Organisation 1939–46, Consultative Cncl Treasury 1940–46, NCB, (part-time) Electricity Cncl 1958–62 and UKAEA 1958–62; Tstee Nuffield Trust Forces of the Crown 1939–46, Chm: Ctee Regnl Bds (Munitions Production) 1942, Miners' Welfare Commn 1946–47 and Br Electicity Authority 1947–57; Pres WFTU 1945–46, Visiting Fell Nuffield Coll 1939–47, author: *The Trade Union Movement of Great Britain, Labour and the Community, I Search for Truth in Russia, ABC of Chairmanship, Men and Work, Two Careers*; Hon LLD Manchester; *m* 28 March 1913 Doris Helen (*d* 13 July 1973), dau of Edgar Slade, of Pendleton, Manchester, and *d* 22 Jan 1983, having had issue:

1 NORMAN ARTHUR CITRINE, **2nd Baron Citrine**; *b* 27 Sept 1914; *educ* U Coll Sch Hampstead and London U (LLB 1938); WW II as Lt RNVR; slr 1937–84, legal advsr TUC 1946–51, Pres Devon and Exeter Law Soc 1971–72, FIDE 1990, author: *War Pensions Appeal Cases* (1946), *Guide to Industrial Injuries Acts* (1948), *Citrine's Trade Union Law* (1950, 3rd edn 1967); *m* 4 Jan 1939 Kathleen Alice (*d* 1993), dau of George Chilvers, of Saxmundham, Suffolk, and *d* 18 March 1997, leaving:

(1) *Patricia Deirdre; *b* 1 Dec 1939

2 RONALD ERIC CITRINE, **3rd and present Baron**

CLANCARTY

Arms: Quarterly, 1st and 4th, argent a lion passant gules between three fleurs-de-lys azure, on a chief of the third the sun in splendour (for TRENCH); 2nd and 3rd, argent a chief indented sable (for LE POER); over all an escutcheon or, ensigned with a coronet of a Marquess of the Netherlands and charged with a wheel of six spokes gules. **Crests:** 1 An arm in armour embowed holding a scimitar, all proper, 2 A lion rampant or, imperially crowned, holding in his dexter paw a sword argent, pommel and hilt gold, in the sinister paw a sheaf of arrows of the last, 3 A stag's head cabossed argent, attired or, between the attires a crucifix. **Supporters:** Dexter, a lion gules semée of fleurs-de-lys or; sinister, a stag guardant proper, attired or, between the attires a crucifix, and supporting with the sinister forepaw a lance resting bendwise over the shoulder proper, thereon a banner of the arms of LE POER. **Mottoes:** *Consilio et prudentia* ('By counsel and prudence') and *Dieu pour la Tranche, qui contre?* ('If God is for Trench, who can be against?'). **Creations:** B. (I) 25 Nov Nov 1797 (Kilconnel of Grabally), V. (I) 3 Jan 1801 (Dunlo of Dunlo and Ballinasloe), E. (I) 11 Feb 1803, B. (UK) 4 Aug 1815 (Trench of Garbally), V. (UK) 8 Dec 1823 (Clancarty), M. (Netherlands) 18 July 1818.

THE 9TH EARL OF CLANCARTY, Co Cork, **Viscount Dunlo of Dunlo and Ballinasloe**, Cos Galway and Roscommon, **Viscount Clancarty**, of Co Cork, **Baron Kilconnel of Garbally**, Co Galway, **Baron Trench of Garbally**, Co Galway, and **Marquess of Heusden** (The Netherlands) (Nicholas Power Richard Le Poer Trench) [The Rt Hon The Earl of Clancarty, House of Lords, London SW1A 0PW]; *b* 1 May 1952; *s* unc 1995; *educ* Ashford GS, Plymouth Poly and U of Colorado

Clancarty, earlier creation: Donough Maccarty, who succeed his father as 2nd Viscount Muskerry of the 1628 creation in 1640, commanded royalist forces in southwest Ireland against CROMWELL during the Civil War and was rewarded with promotion to the Earldom of Clancarty in 1658 by the exiled CHARLES II. Donough had fought with the Confederate Irish against the English in 1641–42 and was a Catholic. His younger son, the 3rd Earl (the 2nd one having died a child), had taken his religion seriously enough in youth to profess vows as a monk but accession to a title seems to have induced a more worldly attitude and he conformed to the established church, though by the time of his death his membership of it had lapsed. The 4th and last Earl presumably reverted to Catholicism; he was certainly a devoted Jacobite, commanding an infantry regiment in JAMES II's army in Ireland in 1689 and later following his master into exile in France.

His wife meanwhile had stayed behind in England but Lord Clancarty could not bear the separation and visited her clandestinely in 1698, only to be given away by his brother-in-law, Charles Spencer, 2nd Earl of Sunderland (*see* MARLBOROUGH, D). This apparently despicable action can perhaps be explained by the fact that Sunderland was an ultra-Whig and doubly anxious to save his sister from the Jacobite taint inasmuch as his elder brother had turned Catholic before his death. Clancarty had been stripped of his titles and had his estates confiscated some years earlier, precisely for such Jacobite sympathies. He was now imprisoned in the Tower of London but released provided he settled abroad. He ended his days as a kind of superior ticket-of-leave-man on an island in the Elbe, near Hamburg.

His son Robert Maccarty tried in vain to get the his father's attainder reversed and lived some years as a remittance man in Boulogne, till his meagre pension of £1,000 p.a. was stopped after he had got involved in the '45 Uprising (meagre at any rate in comparison with the rental he could have expected had his estates been restored him). He too may have died near Hamburg.

The 1st Earl's youngest sister married John Power, whose great-grandson David Power was father-in-law of the 1st Earl of the 1803 creation covered below.

Lineage: FREDERIC, allegedly SEIGNEUR de La TRENCHE, Poitou; migrated *c* 1575 to Northumberland, presumably because he was a Huguenot; *m* 1576 Margaret Sutton and had, with a dau:

1 THOMAS
2 James (Rev); Rector Clongell, Co Meath; bought land in Co Cavan; *m* 1605 Margaret Montgomery and *d* 13 March 1631, leaving an only dau:
(1) Anna; *m* her cousin Frederick Trench, of Garbally, Co Galway (*see* below)
3 Adam; settled in Scotland and left descendants, among whom was Thomas Trench, London merchant (*bur* 1699)

The est son,

THOMAS TRENCH; MA 1599; *m* 1610 Catherine, dau of Richard Brooke, of Pontefract, Yorks, and had, with two daus:

FREDERICK TRENCH; moved to Ireland 1631, buying the lands and castle of Garbally, Co Galway; *m* 1632 his cousin Anna (*see* above) and *d* 1699, having had issue:

1 FREDERICK
2 John (Very Rev); Dean Raphoe; ancestor of the Barons Ashtown (*qv*)
3 William; *b* 1642; *m* Ruth — and left issue:
(1) Robert; *dsp*
(1) Anne; *m* Rev Sutton Morgan

The est son,

FREDERICK TRENCH, of Garbally; *b* 1633; bought more land from the Commrs for the Sale of Forfeited Estates 1690; *m* Elizabeth, dau of Richard Warburton, of Garryhinch, and *d* 1704, having had, with other issue, including a yr s (John (Rev), *m* Mary, dau of Sir Samuel Cooke, Alderman of Dublin, and had two daus):

FREDERICK TRENCH, of Garbally; *b* 1681; MP Co Galway, Col Galway Militia; *m* 1703 Elizabeth, dau of John Eyre, of Eyrecourt, Co Galway, and *d* 1752, having had, with other issue:

1 RICHARD
2 Eyre, of Ashford, Co Roscommon; ancestor of the TRENCHes of Clonfert, Co Galway
3 William (Ven); Archdeacon Kilfenora; *m* 1771 Anne Colpoys, of Co Tipperary, and left issue
1 Elizabeth; *m* Rt Rev Nicholas Synge (*see* SYNGE, Bt) and had issue

The est surv s,

RICHARD TRENCH; *b* 1710; MP (Whig) Co Galway 1761; *m* 13 March 1732 Frances, only dau and heir of David Power (*see* above, **Clancarty, earlier creation**), of Coorheen, Co Galway, by Elizabeth Keating, and *d* 1768, having had:

1 Frederick; *d* an infant
2 David; *d* an infant
3 WILLIAM POWER KEATING, **1st Earl**
4 John Power; Maj
5 Eyre Power; Lt-Gen; *m* 1797 Charlotte, dau of Gen Johnstone, of Overstone, and widow of Sir John Burgoyne, Bt, and *d* 14 April 1820
6 Nicholas Power; *m* Jane, dau of Sir Richard Butler, 5th Bt, of Cloughgrenan (*qv*), and *d* 31 Aug 1824, leaving issue
1 Elizabeth Power; *m* 1 Oct 1753 John Nugent, of Clonlost, and had issue (now extinct in the male line)
2 Hester Power; *m* Walter Taylor, of Castle Taylor, and had issue, including a dau (Anne, *m* her cousin Most Rev Power Trench)
3 Rose Power; *m* James Galbraith
4 Jane Power
5 Anne Power; *m* 1756 Charles Cobber, of Newbridge, MP (*d* 1798), and *d* 1835, leaving issue

The est surv s,

WILLIAM POWER KEATING TRENCH, **1st Earl of Clancarty**, Co Cork, so *cr* 11 Feb 1803, as also earlier 25 Nov 1797 BARON KILCONNEL OF GARBALLY, Co Galway, and 3 Jan 1801 VISCOUNT DUNLO OF DUNLO AND BALLINASLOE in the Counties of Galway and Roscommon (all I); *b* 1741; MP (Whig to 1791, Pittite thereafter) Co Galway 1768–97, Sheriff Co Kilkenny 1777; *m* 30 Oct 1762 Anne (*d* 8 July 1829), est dau of Rt Hon Charles Gardiner and sis of 1st Viscount Mountjoy of Mountjoy, and *d* 27 April 1805, having had, with other issue:

1 Francis; *d* an infant
2 RICHARD, **2nd Earl**
3 Charles; *d* an infant
4 Power (Most Rev), DD; *b* 10 June 1770; Archbp Tuam; *m* 29 Jan 1795 his cousin Anne (*d* 15 Aug 1844), yst dau of Walter Taylor, of Castle Taylor, and *d* 26 March 1839, having had, with other issue:
(1) William (Rev); Rector Cloone; *m* 25 Dec 1830 his cousin Lady Louisa Trench (*d* 7 Feb 1881), est dau of **2nd Earl of Clancarty** (*see* below), and *d* 11 May 1854, leaving issue:
1a Harriet Anne; *m* 12 April 1862 Henry William Meredyth (*d* 6 Nov 1878), only s of Sir Henry Meredyth, 4th Bt, and *d* 2 March 1895 leaving issue:
1b Frances Anne; *m* 1st 18 March 1840 her cousin Charles Trench (*d* 1854); *m* 2nd Rev William Newton Guinness (*see* GUINNESS, Bt), Rector Christchurch, Victoria, formerly Rector Collonoy, Co Sligo, and had issue
5 William Le Poer; *b* 4 July 1771; R-Adml; *m* 1st 1880 Sarah, dau of John Loftus Cuppaidge, and had, with other issue:
(1) William (Rev), DD; *b* 2 Feb 1801; Preb Tuam, Rector Moylough, Co Galway; *m* 26 March 1827 Mary Anne (*d* 25 Aug 1874), est dau of Edward Hardman, and *d* 10 July 1868, leaving issue:
1a Sarah Rebecca; *m* 7 Sept 1859 William John Digby, of Moat Lodge, Moylough (*d* 1886), and *d* 26 Feb 1922, leaving issue
(2) John Le Poer (Rev); *b* 11 March 1802; *m* Jan 1834 Ellen (*d* 22 Nov 1870), yst dau of Charles Rice Davis, and *d* 29 Sept 1866 leaving issue:
1a Charles Edward Le Poer, of Westcliff-on-Sea; *b* 6 Aug 1838; *m* 28 June 1870 Harriet Laura (*d* 23 Jan 1915), dau of Charles A Johnston and widow of Capt Robert Taylor, and *d* 25 May 1905 leaving issue:
1b Charles Edward Le Poer; *b* 18 April 1877; *educ* Hertford Coll Oxford (MA); Educnl Dept Egypt, Order Nile 4th Cl; *m* 31 July 1919 Evelyn

Agnes (*d* 1967), yr dau of H J Salmon, of St Ives, Cornwall, and *d* 20 Oct 1935, leaving issue:

1c Laura Joan; *b* 25 Jan 1912; *m* 18 Jan 1932 Maj Charles Smith, Roy Tank Regt, and had issue

3 (cont.) Adml William Trench *m* 2nd 1 Feb 1837 Margaret (*d* 4 March 1885), dau of Dawson Downing, of Rosegift, Co Londonderry, and widow of Arthur Handcock (*see* CASTLEMAINE, B), and *d* 14 Aug 1846, having by her had further issue:

(1) Frederick Netterville, QC, JP; *b* 12 July 1845; barrister; *m* 30 July 1878 Sarah Frances (*d* 1913) dau of Very Rev John Fiennes Twistleton Crampton, Rector Aughrim, Co Galway, and *d* 24 Nov 1893, leaving issue:

1a William Netterville; *b* 1882; *m* 21 Feb 1916 Mary Agnes (*d* 1953), 4th surv dau of Patrick John Mullarney, of Dublin, and *dsp* 9 April 1961

1a Margaretta Louise (Pearl); *b* 10 June 1879; *m* 24 Jan 1911 Robert Thompson, s of Samuel Thompson, of Muckamore Abbey, Co Antrim (*d* Feb 1952), and *d* 26 Nov 1966, leaving issue

2a Emily Frances; *m* 19 Jan 1916 Lt-Col William Trench Digby, RE (ret) (*d* 9 Nov 1952), only surv s of William John Digby, of Moat Lodge, and *d* 23 March 1965, leaving issue

3a Eileen May; memb United Soc Artists; *m* 21 April 1910 Rev Gairdner Wyon, FRBS (*d* 26 Feb 1962), est s of Allan Wyon, FSA, and *d* April 1969, leaving issue

(1) Harriette Mary; *m* 8 June 1864 Charles Dennis O' Rorke, JP (*d* 1915), of Clonbern, Co Galway, and *d* 10 April 1916, leaving issue

6 Charles Le Poer (Ven); *b* Dec 1772; DD; Archdeacon Ardagh; *m* 1806 Frances, 2nd dau of Thomas Elwood, of Ashford Park, Co Mayo, and *d* 1839, leaving issue:

(1) Frederick William (Rev); *b* 8 Jan 1808; MA; Rector Moore and Drum, Diocese of Tuam; *m* 14 April 1846 Matilda Sophia (*d* 1914), dau of Capt John Ireland, RN, of Prospect, St Heliers, and *d* 26 Jan 1860, having had, with other issue:

1a Frederick Emilius, CB (1900), CBE (1919); *b* 6 July 1857; Lt-Col and Brevet Col ASC, served S Africa; *m* 1st 29 March 1883 Mary Phoebe Gertrude (*d* 19 June 1928), dau of C W Roberts, MRCS, of Radstock, Somerset; *m* 2nd 21 Oct 1929 Frances Lee (*d* 18 May 1937), dau of T J Bryant, of Brighton, and *dsp* 4 Jan 1942

1a Gertrude Frances; *m* 15 March 1871 James Robert Stewart (*d* 1891) and had issue

(2) Henry Luke; *b* 16 Jan 1820; Maj-Gen Bengal Staff Corps; *m* 1st 23 June 1852 Clara (*d* 2 Feb 1878), yst dau of Christopher Nugent, of Snape House, Beaminster, and cousin of Rt Hon Edmund Burke, and had issue:

1a Charles Henry; *b* 1860

2a Frederick Augustus; *b* 1862

3a Arthur Osborne; *b* 1864

4a Robert Morgan

1a Emily Louisa; *m* 17 Oct 1876 Thomas Walter Penrice Gape (*d* 28 Feb 1890), and *d* 22 Nov 1905, leaving issue

2a Helen Randal; *m* 4 Jan 1877 Brig-Gen O'Donnel Colley Grattan, CBE, DSO, Liverpool Regt (*d* 5 March 1929), and *d* 2 July 1952, leaving issue

3a Ada Blanch; *m* 14 May 1885 Cdr Edward Arthur Richmond, RN, and *d* 2 June 1930, leaving issue

(2) (cont.) Maj-Gen Henry Trench *m* 2nd 21 Dec 1881 Amy (*d* 17 Oct 1916), dau of Rev William Mackanley Oliver, and *d* 8 March 1907

(1) Anne Letitia; *m* 25 July 1842 Maj Thomas Osborne, Madras Army, 2nd s of Sir Daniel Toler Osborne, 12th Bt (*qv*); both *d* the same day of cholera 18 Feb 1846, leaving a s (*d* unm 16 Oct 1862)

7 Thomas; *b* 1774; *d* 1795

8 Luke Henry; *b* 1775; *d* 1799

9 Frederick; *b* 1778; *d* 1800

10 Robert Le Poer (Sir), KCB, KTS; *b* 1782; Col; *m* 21 Nov 1805 Hon Letitia Susanna Dillon (*d* Nice 25 March 1865), yst dau of 1st Baron Clonbrock (*see* 1926 edn), and *d* 14 March 1823, leaving issue:

(1) Fanny Catherine; *m* 3 Aug 1840 Col R E Burrowes, KH (*d* 17 Sept 1877), and *d* 28 Dec 1888, leaving issue

(2) Elizabeth; *m* 1 Sept 1840 Samuel Walker, of The Grange, Leicester, and *d* 9 Dec 1867, leaving issue

(3) Emily; *m* 18 Jan 1842 Rev Joseph Mansfield (*d* 1 Dec 1895), and *d* 13 Sept 1899, leaving issue

(4) Augusta; *m* 1st 3 Feb 1858 Rev William Henry Priestly (*d* 28 Sept 1861) and had issue; *m* 2nd 10 June 1869 Rev Charles Childers, Canon Gibraltar (*d* Feb 1896), and *d* 10 Dec 1914, leaving issue

1 Florinda; *m* 20 March 1782 1st and last Viscount Castlemaine (*see* CASTLEMAINE, B), and *dsp* 9 Feb 1851

2 Anne; *b* 1766; *m* 1789 William Gregory

3 Kouisa; *d* 1785

4Elizabeth; *b* 1784; *m* 1805 John McClintock

5 Harriet; *m* Jan 1805 Sir Daniel Toler Osborne, Bt (*qv*), and *d* 17 Nov 1855, leaving issue

3 Frances; *m* 28 July 1806 1st Earl of Rathdowne and *d* 22 Nov 1843, leaving issue (*see* MONCK, V)

The 1st EARL'S est s,

RICHARD TRENCH later LE POER TRENCH, **2nd Earl of Clancarty**, GCB (1815), PC (I 1809, GB 1807); *b* 18 May 1767; MP Newtown Limavady 1796–97, Co Galway 1797–1800 and 1801–05 and (Tory) Rye April-July 1807, Commr Indian Affrs 1804–06, Govr Co Galway 1805, Jt PMG (I) April-Nov 1807, PMG (I) 1807–09, rep I peer 1808–37, Master Mint 1812û14, Pres BOT 1812–18, Amb The Hague 1813–15 and 1816–23, Jt PMG (GB) 1814–16, a Plen Congress Vienna 1814; *cr* 4 Aug 1815 BARON TRENCH OF GARBALLY, Co Galway, and 8 Dec 1823 VISCOUNT CLANCARTY, of Co Cork (both UK) and by the King of the Netherlands 18 July 1818 Marquess of Heusden; *m* 9 Feb 1796 Henrietta Margaret (*d* 30 Dec 1847) 2nd dau of Rt Hon John Staples, and had issue, with four daus:

1 WILLIAM THOMAS, **3rd Earl**

2 Richard John; *b* 1805

3 Frederick Robert; *b* 23 July 1808; Cdr RN; *m* 14 April 1847 Catherine Maria (*d* 7 Sept 1874), dau of John Thompson, of Clonfin, Co Longford, and *d* April 1867 leaving a s

1 Louisa Augusta Anne; *b* 1796; *m* her cousin Rev William Le Poer Trench, s of Most Rev Power Le Poer Trench

2 Harriete Margaret; *m* 28 Feb 1825, as his 2nd w, Thomas Kavanagh, MP (*d* 20 Jan 1837), and had issue

The 2nd EARL *d* 24 Nov 1837; his er s,

WILLIAM THOMAS LE POER TRENCH, **3rd Earl of Clancarty**; *b* 21 Sept 1803; *m* 8 Sept 1832 Lady Sarah Juliana Butler (*d* 28 April 1905), dau of 3rd Earl of Carrick (*qv*), and had:

1 RICHARD SOMERSET, **4th Earl**

2 Frederick; *b* 10 Feb 1835; Maj 40th Foot, Indian Mutiny 1857, 52nd Oxfordshire LI (medal and clasp) and 40th Regt NZ War 1864–66 (despatches, brevet, medal); *m* 1st 6 Feb 1883 Hon Harriet Mary Trench (*dsp* 16 July 1884), dau of 2nd Baron Ashtown (*qv*); *m* 2nd 1891 Catherine (*d* 18 Feb 1925), dau of George Simpson, and *d* 17 Dec 1913, leaving issue:

(1) Frederick Power; *b* 1891; Lt 3nd Bn Leinster Regt; *d* of wounds received in action 9 April 1916

(1) Dorothy Marian; *b* 1895; *m* 25 June 1918 Hugh Lloyd Williams, CBE, DSO, MC, barrister (*d* 2 Dec 1968), and *dsp* 18 Jan 1967

3 William, CVO (1912), JP (Bucks, Middx and London and Westminster); *b* 17 June 1837; Col RE China 1857–58, cmdg ladder party capture Canton and Nankow (medal with clasp, despatches); MP Galway 1872–74; *m* 21 April 1864 Harriet Maria Georgina (*d* 24 Feb 1909), only dau and heir of Sir William Martins, and *d* 16 Sept 1920, leaving issue:

(1) William Martins, of Coorheen, Vancouver; *b* 26 Sept 1866; *m* 17 April 1891 Elinor Mary (*m* 2nd 6 Nov 1905 Hon Sydney Trench (*see* ASHTOWN, B) and 3rd 7 Jan 1908 Brig-Gen Ronald Campbell Maclachlan, DSO, Rifle Bde, who was *ka* 11 Aug 1917), dau of Dr J C Cox, of Sydney, and *dsp* 13 Sept 1904

(2) Power; *b* 19 July 1869; *educ* Trin Hall Cambridge (BA); barrister Inner Temple; *m* 3 Dec 1896 Gladys, dau of George Carew Carew-Gibson, of Sandgate Park, Sussex, and *d* 14 June 1926, leaving issue:

1a Gladys Marjorie; *b* 22 Dec 1899; *m* 1st 8 April 1920 (*divorce* 1937) Henry Saxe Wyndham (*d* 14 Nov 1940), er s of Henry Wyndham, and had issue; *m* 2nd 18 March 1839 Eric Charles Edwards (*d* 30 July 1960), est s of Osman Adams Edwards, of Cleator, Brooklyn, Hawkesbury River, NSW, and *d* 19 May 1960

4 Power Henry; *b* 11 May 1841; Sec Embassy Berlin 1888–93, Envoy Extrdy and Min Plen Mexico 1893–94 and Japan 1894–95; *d* unm 30 April 1899

1 Anne; *m* 30 April 1867 Hon Frederick Sidney Charles Trench (*d* 2 March 1879), er s of 2nd Baron Ashtown (*qv*), and *d* 12 March 1924, leaving issue

The 3rd EARL *d* 26 April 1872; his est s,

RICHARD SOMERSET LE POER TRENCH, **4th Earl of Clancarty**; *b* 13 Jan 1834; *educ* Cheltenham and Trin Coll Cambridge; Hon Col 5th Connaught Rangers; *m* 29 Nov 1866 Lady Adeliza Georgiana Hervey (*d* 7 Nov 1911) dau of 2nd Marquess of Bristol (*qv*), and *d* 29 May 1891, having had, with a yr s (Richard John, *b* 25 Dec 1877, *d* unm 10 Aug 1960) and a dau (Katherine Anne, *b* 12 Aug 1871, *d* unm 25 Feb 1953):

WILLIAM FREDERICK LE POER TRENCH, **5th Earl of Clancarty**, JP and DL (Co Galway); *b* 29 Dec 1868; *educ* Eton; bankrupt Ireland 1907 and England 1910; *m* 1st 10 July 1889 'Isabel' Maude Penrice, actress at the Empire Theatre (*d* 31 Dec 1906), dau of John George Bilton, Sgt RE and operative Woolwich Dockyard, and had issue:

1 RICHARD FREDERICK JOHN DONOUGH LE POER TRENCH, **6th Earl of Clancarty**; *b* 27 Dec 1891; *educ* Repton; sometime RNAS; *m* 1st 28 Oct 1915 (*divorce* 1918) Edith Constance (*d* 7 July 1950), dau of Maj Albermarle Alexander Rawlinson, 8th Hus, of 4 Aldford St, London W1; *m* 2nd 1919 Cora Maria Edith, er dau of H H Spooner, of Thornton Hall, Surrey, and *d* 5 June 1971, having by her had issue:

(1) William John Hervey; *b* 6 March, *d* 5 May 1926

(1) *Maureen Isabel [The Lady Maureen Cooper, Old Tannery, Donnington Village, Newbury, Berks RG13 2JT]; *b* 20 Dec 1923; *m* 16 March 1949 *Christopher Colin Cooper, only s of Maj Colin Cooper, of Barnwell Castle, Northants, and has issue:

1a *Simon Richard Colin; *b* 14 Feb 1956; *educ* Eton; wood sculptor; *m* 1979 *Julia C, yst dau of E B Teesdale, of The Hogge House, Buxted, Sussex

1a *Claudia [Miss Claudia Cooper, Old Tannery, Donnington Village, Newbury, Berks RG13 2JT]; *b* 3 Feb 1952; lecturer Sana'a U, S Yemen

(2) Patricia Ann; *b* 20 Jan 1928; *m* 1st 24 Aug 1946 Eugene Nicodemus de Szpiganowicz, late purser Polish MN (*d* 30 Dec 1965), only s of Baron Klemens de Szpiganowicz, of Dobrynie, Poland; *m* 2nd 1977 *Alan Sidney Andrews

(3) *Caragh Seymour [The Lady Caragh Le Poer Trench, PO Box 47788, San Antonio, Texas 78265, USA]; *b* 20 Feb 1933; *m* 1st 6 June 1953 (*divorce* 1961) Lt-Cdr John Anthony Lake, RN, only s of V-Adml Walter John Challoner Lake, CBE, of 40 Roehampton Gate, London SW15, and has issue:

1a *Henry John Challoner; *b* 18 Aug 1955

1a *Catherine Challoner; *b* 12 Dec 1957

2a *Jean Challoner; *b* 24 Aug 1959

(3) (cont.) The Lady Caragh Lake *m* 2nd 25 Nov 1961 (*divorce* 1966) Lt Arthur Jay Oken, USAF, twin s of Dr H M Oken, of New York; *m* 3rd Capt Donald Van Horn Lee, USAF; *m* 4th 19–; *m* 5th 19– *— Jefferson

2 Power Francis William; *b* 27 Dec 1891; *d* 9 June 1894

3 Roderic Charles Berkeley, MC; *b* 19 Oct 1895; Lt Lincs Yeo and MGC; *d* 23 Jan 1937

4 GREVILLE SYDNEY ROCHFORT LE POER TRENCH, **7th Earl of Clancarty**; *b* 10 Dec 1902; *educ* RNCs Osborne and Dartmouth; *m* 26 July 1926 Beatrice Georgiana (*d* 8 July 1979), yst dau of Capt James Gordon Miller, of Thurlow Pk, Little Thurlow, Suffolk, and *dsp* 15 Sept 1975

1 Beryl Franziska Kathleen Bianca; *b* 8 Oct 1893; *m* 1st 18 May 1914 Capt Hon Richard Philip Stanhope, Gren Gds (*ka* 15 Sept 1916, *see* 1967 edn CHESTERFIELD and STANHOPE, E); *m* 2nd 5 July 1917 (*divorce* 1927) Lt-Cdr Walter Raleigh Gilbert, RN (*d* 26 Jan 1977), er s of Rev Walter Raleigh Gilbert, MA, of The Priory, Bodmin, Cornwall, and had issue; *m* 3rd 2 Dec 1931 Francis Edward Selby Groves, of Westfield, Leasingham, Sleaford, Lincs, s of Herbert John Groves, VD, JP, of Weymouth, and *d* 17 May 1957

The **5th Earl** *m* 2nd 7 Oct 1908 Mary Gwatkin (*d* 31 Oct 1974), dau of W F Ross-Lewin Ellis, barrister, and *d* 16 Feb 1929, having by her had further issue:

5 (WILLIAM FRANCIS) BRINSLEY LE POER TRENCH, **8th Earl of Clancarty**; *b* 18 Sept 1911; *educ* Nautical Coll Pangbourne; ed *Flying Saucer Review*, author: *The Sky People* (1960), *Men among Mankind* (1962), *Forgotten Heritage* (1964), *The Flying Saucer Story* (1966), *Operation Earth* (1969), *The Eternal Subject* (1973) and *Secret of the Ages* (1974); *m* 1st 6 June 1940 (*divorce* 1947) Diana Joan, yr dau of Sir William Younger, 2nd Bt (*qv*); *m* 2nd 16 June 1961 (*divorce*) Wilma Dorothy Millen, dau of S R Vermilyea, of USA, and formerly w of William Burke Belknap, Jr; *m* 3rd 1974 Mrs Mildred Allewyn Spong (*d* 1975), dau of R Bensusan; *m* 4th 1976 *Mary Agnes (May) [The Rt Hon The Countess of Clancarty, 51 Eaton Place, London SW1], only dau of E Radonicich and widow of Cdr Frank M Beasley, RN, and *d* 18 May 1995

6 Power Edward Ford; *b* 22 Jan 1917; *educ* Cheltenham; *m* Jocelyn Louise Courtney (*d* 1962) and *d* 29 Jan 1975, leaving issue:

(1) NICHOLAS POWER RICHARD LE POER TRENCH, **9th and present Earl of Clancarty**

(1) *Caroline Jessica Mary; *b* 3 Dec 1954; *educ* St Paul's Girls' Sch and Wadham Coll Oxford; *m* 1st 1981 (*divorce* 1984) Alan Rodger; *m* 2nd 1991 *Robert Richard Hill and has issue:

1a *Theodore Alexander; *b* 23 Feb 1994

2 (Sibell) Alma Kathleen; *b* 21 May 1918; *m* 28 June 1938 Stewart Croft Jolly, s of Henry Stewart Jolly, Ch Registrar Supreme Court, and had issue:

(1) *Venetia Alma Mary; *b* 19 Jan 1940; *m* 15 July 1961 Laurence John Champniss, yr s of George Champniss, of South Acre, Mount Park, Harrow-on-the-Hill, Middx, and has had issue:

1a *Jeremy Stewart John; *b* 11 Sept 1963

2a *Robert Henry James; *b* 3 June 1966

3a *James Alexander; *b* 1974

1a *Suzy Joanne; *b* 21 Jan 1968

(2) *Maureen Pamela Stewart; *b* 10 Oct 1943; *m* 24 June 1967 *Brian Nicholas Danby Smith, s of Wilfred S Smith, of 19 Kingsway, Petts Wood, Kent, and has issue:

1a *Anthony John Nicholas; *b* 18 April 1969

2a *Philip James Edward; *b* 1970

CLANMORRIS

Arms: Az. a bend cotised between six crosses patée or. **Crest:** A rock, thereon an eagle rising, all ppr. **Supporters:** Two lions az. **Motto:** *Spes mea Christus* ('Christ is my hope'). **Creation:** B. (I) 31 July 1800.

THE 8TH BARON CLANMORRIS OF NEWBROOK, Co Mayo (Simon John Ward Bingham) [The Rt Hon The Lord Clanmorris, c/o Child & Co, 1 Fleet St, London EC4Y 1BD]; *b* 25 Oct 1937; *s f* 1988; *educ* Downside and Queens' Coll Cambridge (BA 1961, MA 1965); 2nd Lt 13th/18th Roy Hus 1957–58; ACA 1965, FCA 1975; *m* 28 Aug 1971 *Gizella Maria, dau of Zandor Zverkó, of Budapest, Hungary

1 *Lucy Katherine Gizella; *b* 15 Jan 1974

Lineage: GEORGE BINGHAM (*see* LUCAN, E); had a yr s:

JOHN BINGHAM, of Foxford, Co Mayo; had:

CHARLES BINGHAM, of Newbrook and Foxford; Maj; *m* Mary, 2nd dau of Henry Blennerhassett, and had:

HENRY BINGHAM, of Newbrook; a Ld Justice Ireland; *m* Anne, dau of John Vesey, Archbp Tuam, and had:

JOHN BINGHAM, of Newbrook; *m* 1 June 1738 Frances, est dau and coheir of Sir Arthur Shaen, 2nd Bt, of Kilmore, and had:

HENRY BINGHAM, of Newbrook; *m* 1760 Letitia, dau of Denis Daly, of Raford, Co Galway, by Lady Anne de Burgh, sis of 11th Earl of Clanricarde (*see* SLIGO, M), and had, with six daus:

1 JOHN, **1st Baron**

2 Henry; gf of Denis Bingham, of Bingham Castle, Co Mayo

3 Denis, of Bingham Castle

HENRY BINGHAM *d* 1790; his est son,

JOHN BINGHAM, **1st Baron Clanmorris of Newbrook**, Co Mayo (I), so *cr* 31 July 1800; *b* 1762; MP Tuam 1797–1800, exchanging his two seats in that rotten borough with the Govt for £8,000 and an Irish peerage; *m* 21 May 1791 Hon Anne Maria Yelverton (ld 27 April 1865 aged 88), only dau of 1st Viscount Avonmore, and *d* 18 May 1821, having had, with other issue:

1 CHARLES BARRY BINGHAM, **2nd Baron Clanmorris of Newbrook**; *b* 1796; said to be the handsomest man in Ireland; *m* 1816 Sarah (*m* 2nd 29 May 1830 Edward S Hickman), dau of Walter Lambert, of Castle Lambert, Co Galway, and *dsp* 3 June 1829

2 DENIS ARTHUR, **3rd Baron**

1 Louisa Catherine; *m* in 1838 Rev Benjamin Chapman Frederick Yelverton, and *d* his widow, 14 May 1891, leaving issue

The 2nd BARON's bro,

DENIS ARTHUR BINGHAM, **3rd Baron Clanmorris of Newbrook**; *b* 22 Jan 1808; *m* 1 May 1825 Maria Helena (*d* 27 Aug 1899 aged 96), 2nd dau of Robert Persse, of Roxborough, Co Galway, and *d* 24 Feb 1847, having had, with other issue:

1 JOHN CHARLES ROBERT BINGHAM, **4th Baron Clanmorris of Newbrook**; *b* 28 Nov 1826; *m* 24 May 1849 Sarah Selina (*d* 28 Nov 1907), 4th dau of Burton Persse, of Moyode Castle, Co Galway, and *d* 5 April 1876, having had, with other issue:

(1) JOHN GEORGE BARRY, **5th Baron**

(2) Burton Percy; *b* 11 Sept 1853; *m* 3 Jan 1895 Frances Matilda (*d* 29 July 1935), 3rd dau of Burton Robert Parsons Persse, DL, of Moyode Castle, Co Galway, and *dsp* 10 Dec 1898

(1) Matilda Maria Helena, OBE (1919); *m* 12 Jan 1871 Albert Brassey, of Heythrop, Oxon, 14th Hus, formerly MP for Banbury, and *d* 16 July 1943, leaving issue (*see* BRASSEY OF APETHORPE, B)

(2) Florence Madeline; *m* 1st 17 April 1873 John Pollok, of Lismany, Co Galway, and had issue. He *d* Aug 1891. She *m* 2nd 6 June 1895 Maj James David Barry, late RHA, er son of Rt Hon C R Barry, and *d* 20 Dec 1941

(3) Rose Elizabeth (Médaille de la Reconnaisance Française); *m* 29 Sept 1885 Maj-Gen Sir Hugh McCalmont, KCB, CVO, and *d* 28 April 1935, leaving issue. He *d* 2 May 1924

2 Denis Arthur; *b* 6 Nov 1829; *m* 6 Nov 1864 Eugenie Colette Gabriele de Lacretelle (*d* 1893), of Burgundy, and *d* 8 July 1897, leaving issue:

(1) Jeanne Aimée

3 Albert Yelverton, DL Mayo; *b* 11 Feb 1840; *m* 1st 24 June 1858 Caroline (*d* 1879), dau of James Begbie, MD, and had issue:

(1) Bentinck Yelverton Warburton; *b* 18 Jan 1862; *m* 11 April 1907 Letitia Charlotte May, dau of William Henry Madill, of Paki Kohi, New Zealand, and *d* 28 Sept 1911

(1) Elizabeth Caroline; *m* 1st 1 March 1883 (*divorce* by Act of Parl 1906) Henry Aubrey Beaumont Wallis, of Drishane Castle, Co Cork, and had issue; *m* 2nd 27 July 1906 William John Wallace, son of Capt Henry Ritchie Wallace, 92nd Gordon Highrs. He *d* 1 April 1908. She *m* 3rd 8 Aug 1914 Maj Alan Rowley Sale-Hill, Somerset LI, only son of Gen Sir Rowley Sale-Hill, KCB (*see* HILL, Bt), and *d* 1 July 1924

(2) Helen Augusta Mary, OBE (1919), Order of Mercy; *m* 20 Nov 1884 Capt William Augustus Turpin, and *d* Feb 1944, leaving issue

3 (cont.) Albert Bingham *m* 2nd 20 March 1883 Jean Crawford (*d* 13 July 1924), only child and heir of Thomas Service, of Cranley, Lanarkshire, and *d* 31 March 1907, having by her had a son (*d* young)

1 Anna Maria; *m* 2 Oct 1856 Rev Ferdinand Cotter Spiller, est son of W A Spiller, of Uplands, Bandon, Co Cork, by Anne, dau of Rev George Sackville Cotter, Prebendary of Cloyne (*see* COTTER, Bt), and *dsp* 1 May 1923

2 Elizabeth Caroline; *m* 23 July 1856 St John Legh Clowes, of Cheltenham, and *d* 21 Sept 1919, leaving issue. He *d* 18 April 1915

The 4th BARON's est surv son,

JOHN GEORGE BARRY BINGHAM, **5th Baron Clanmorris of Newbrook**, DL (Co Mayo), JP (Cos Down and Galway); *b* 27 Aug 1852; *educ* Eton; Lt Rifle Bde, ADC to Ld Lt Ireland; *m* 27 June 1878 Matilda Catherine Maude (*d* 14 Feb 1941), only child and heiress of Robert Edward Ward, of Bangor Castle, Co Down (*see* BANGOR, V), and had issue:

1 ARTHUR MAURICE ROBERT, **6th Baron**

2 (John) Denis Yelverton, DSO (1918), Lt-Col 15th/19th Hus WW I (despatches twice, Legion of Honour, Brev Lt-Col); *b* 11 Aug 1880; *m* 29 July 1926 Vera Mary (*d* 19 Aug 1972 aged 81), est dau of Maj Norman Darbyshire, of Sefton Park, nr Liverpool, and *d* 28 Dec 1940, leaving issue:

(1) *Elizabeth Rosemary [Mrs Maxwell Denham, Lock Farm, Tixall, nr Stafford ST18 0XR]; *b* 19 May 1927; *m* 23 April 1949 *Maxwell William John Denham, MBE, only son of William John Denham, of Wembley Park, Middx, and has issue:

1a *(John) Alistair Campbell [Alistair Denham Esq, 19 Vanderbilt Rd, London SW18 3BG]; *b* 7 Feb 1955

2a *Iain Maxwell [Iain Denham Esq, 5 Gloucester Rd, Kew Green, Richmond, Surrey]; *b* 17 Oct 1957; *m* 1988 *Wendy Ann, dau of Albert Edward Johnson, of Hastings, Sussex, and has issue:

1b *Jonathan Maxwell; *b* 1991

1b *Jessica Sarah; *b* 1989

(2) *(Mary) Mavourneen Denise [Mrs Albert Schiff, Ambrose Farm House, Ramsbury, Wilts SN8 2PW]; *b* 30 Nov 1931; *m* 22 Sept 1951 *Albert Werner Schiff, son of Harry Edmund Schiff, of Sopron, and Budapest, Hungary, and has had issue:

1a Robert John Denis; *b* 5 May 1958; *educ* Eton; *m* 1983 *Lucinda Mary [Mrs Andrew Bengough, Church Farm House, Longparish, Hants] (who *m* 2nd 1992 Andrew Nigel Crosbie Bengough, er son of Col Sir Piers Henry George Bengough, KCVO, OBE, DL (*see* ALBU, Bt), of Great Ho, Canon Pyon, Herefs), er dau of Capt John Geoffrey Sherston, of Terry Ho, Warehorne, Ashford, Kent, and drowned 1990, leaving issue:

1b *Frederick John Albert; *b* 1984

2b *Maximilian Robert Denis; *b* 1986

3b *Robert Edmund Bingham; *b* (posthumously) 1990

1a *Miranda Caroline [Mrs Derek Hearn, Muntins, The Gardens, Adstock, Bucks]; *b* 27 July 1952; *m* 1980 *Derek Hearn

3 (Edward) Barry Stewart, VC (1916), OBE (1919), R-Adml, Naval ADC to HM GEORGE V 1931, served WW I (despatches), Russian Order of St Stanislas 2nd Cl with swords; *b* 26 July 1881; *m* 18 May 1915 (*divorce* 1937) Vera Maud Temple (*d* 30 Dec 1972), only child of Edward Temple Patterson, and *d* 24 Sept 1939, leaving:

(1) John Temple; *b* 22 Feb 1923; *m* 28 April 1949 Joan Muriel Bown (*d* 1955) and *d* 25 July 1997

(1) *Lavinia Mary [Mrs Simon Campbell, Inchivore, Old Connaught Ave, Bray, Co Wicklow, Ireland]; *b* 7 July 1921; *m* 31 Oct 1946 *Simon Campbell (*see* HAWARDEN, V) and has issue

4 (Hugh) Terence de Burgh, AMICE, Ch Engr in the Indian Service of Engineers, served in Indian Defence Force 1914–18; *b* 31 Dec 1885; *m* 2 Nov 1912 Dorothea Minnie (*d* 8 Dec 1976) 3rd dau of John Alexander Sinclair, ICS, barrister, of Lahore, India and *d* 27 Feb 1957, having had issue:

(1) (John) Peter Derrick; *b* 14 Sept 1913; *educ* Cheltenham and RMC Sandhurst; *m* 1st Jan 1939 (*divorce* 1954) Mary Machen, er dau of Robert Morehead Rose, of Sydney, NSW; *m* 2nd 10 Oct 1954 *Jean, est dau of Robert Harold Hogarth, of Waverley, Tasmania, and *d* 1978, having by 1st w had issue:

1a (Robert) Michael Terence; *b* 8 Feb 1941; *d* unm 198–

1a *Angela Rose; *b* 3 June 1944; *m* 22 Aug 1969 *Anthony William Martin Steyn, MB, BS, of Sydney, NSW, Australia

(2) (Hugh) Denis Sinclair, Capt Roy Inniskilling Fus WW II; *b* 6 Sept 1914; *m* 29 Sept 1939 Margaret Douglas (*m* 2nd 17 March 1948 (*divorce* 1953; resumed ex-husb's name by deed poll 1951) George Lennox Barrow, yst son of Maj Ronald Edmund Barrow, and *d* 1980), dau of Maj Robert Stevenson, DL, of Aloha, Dungannon, Co Tyrone, and *d* 18 July 1946, leaving issue:

1a +(ROBERT) DEREK DE BURGH [Derek Bingham Esq, Cooks Barn, Chillesford Lodge, Sudbourne, Suffolk IP12 2AN]; *b* 29 Oct 1942; heir presumptive; *educ* Stowe; publisher; *m* 12 July 1969 *Victoria Mary, yr dau of P A Pennant-Rea, of Broadlands Court, Bourton-on-the-Water, Glos, and has:

1b *Alexandra Louise Clare; *b* 25 April 1974

2b *Georgina Mary Margaret; *b* 30 Sept 1976

3b *Rosamunde Jessica Elizabeth; *b* 1979

1a *(Jane) Victoria (Clare); *b* 6 March 1941; *m* 22 Jan 1966 (*divorce* 1985 resumed maiden name) Béla Peter Daranyi, yr son of Bela de Daranyi and Countess Margit Haller von Hallerstein, of Budapest, and has issue:

1b *Imre Patrick Béla; *b* 1973

1b *Katherine Emma Margaret; *b* 17 Feb 1967; *m* 1991 *Angus W Macgregor Jurkschat, 2nd son of Rudolf Jurkschat

2b *Sophie Jane Clare; *b* 5 April 1968

(1) *Elizabeth Maude [Mrs Jelle Veenbaas, Erwarton Hall Farm, nr Ipswich, Suffolk]; *b* 21 Jan 1922; *m* 27 July 1944 *Jelle Roel Hogeveen Veenbaas, son of Dr Anne Veennbaas, of Leeuwarden, Holland, and had issue:

1a *Peter Hans; *b* 27 Oct 1946; *educ* Oundle; *m* 1978 *Veronica Anne, dau of Carl Christian Moore, of Warminghurst, W Sussex

5 Henry Derrick Thomas; *b* 17 Oct 1887; *d* 22 Feb 1902

6 George Roderick Bentinck, Capt RWF WW I, Waziristan 1921, WW II as S/Ldr RAFVR; *b* 10 May 1894; *m* 4 April 1921 Barbara Melvill, yst dau of Col Charles Henry Joubert de la Ferté, MB, IMS, and *dsp* 10 Dec 1972

7 Richard Gerald Ava, 2nd Lt RAF; *b* 8 March 1896; *ka* 10 Oct 1918

1 Harriette Ierne Maude; *b* 18 July 1882; *m* 22 Dec 1908 Sir Herbert Lightfoot Eason, CB, CMG, MD, son of Edward Henry Physick Eason, of Forest Hill, and *d* 11 Jan 1917, leaving issue. He *d* 2 Nov 1949

2 Emily Ina Florence; *b* 3 March 1884; *m* 25 Nov 1905 1st Baron Glentoran, PC, OBE (*qv*), and *d* 25 April 1957, leaving issue

3 Eleanor Clare Alice; *b* 18 Jan 1892; *m* 15 Sept 1915 Maj Harold Murray Fleming, 1st Dragoon Gds, only son of Col Fleming, RA, of Belville, Co Cavan, and *d* 25 Nov 1972, having had issue. He *d* 8 Nov 1953

The 5th BARON *d* 4 Nov 1916; his est son,

ARTHUR MAURICE ROBERT BINGHAM, **6th Baron Clanmorris of Newbrook**; *b* 22 June 1879; *educ* Eton; Capt 5th Lancers, ADC to Govr-Gen NZ 1904–07, served Boer War 1899–1902 (Queen's medal with five clasps, King's medal with two clasps) and WW I; *m* 5 June 1907 Leila (*d* 3 June 1969 aged 88), 4th dau of Gordon Cloete, JP, of Rosebank, Cape Town, and *d* 24 June 1960, having had issue:

JOHN MICHAEL WARD BINGHAM, **7th Baron Clanmorris**; *b* 3 Nov 1908; *educ* Cheltenham; WW II with RE and attd Gen Staff; author (as John Bingham) of detective novels; *m* 28 July 1934 Madeleine Mary (*d* 16 Feb 1988), authoress and playwright, est dau of Clement Ebel, of Copyhold Place, Cuckfield, Sussex, and *d* 6 Aug 1988, having had issue:

1 SIMON JOHN WARD BINGHAM, **8th and present Baron**

1 *Charlotte Mary Thérèse [The Hon Mrs Brady, Hardway House, Hardway, Bruton, Somerset]; *b* 29 June 1942; *educ* The Priory, Haywards Heath and Sorbonne; playwright and novelist, author: *Coronet Among the Weeds* (1963), *Lucinda* (1965); *m* 15 Jan 1964 *Terence Joseph Brady, actor and writer, son of Noel Brady, of Macroon, Co Cork, and has issue:

(1) *Matthew Joseph Mulligan; *b* 11 March 1972

(1) *Candida Marie Thérèse; *b* 19 April 1965; *m* 1994 *Titus M Ogilvy

CLANWILLIAM

Arms: Gu. a chevron erm. between three trefoils, slipped arg. **Crest:** An eagle displayed with two heads sa., armed or. **Supporters:** Dexter, an eagle close sa.; sinister, a falcon close ppr., beaked and legged or, each collared and chained of the last. **Motto:** *Toujours prest* ('Always ready'). **Creations:** Bt. (I) 29 May 1703; V. and B. (I) 17 Nov 1766; E. (I) 20 July 1776; B. (UK) 28 Jan 1828.

THE 7TH EARL OF CLANWILLIAM, Viscount Clanwilliam, Co Tipperary, **Baron Gillford**, of the Manor of Gillford, Co Down, in Ireland; **Baron Clanwilliam**, of Co Tipperary, and a **Baronet** (Sir John Herbert Meade, Bt) [The Rt Hon The Earl of Clanwilliam, Blundells House, Tisbury, Wilts]; *b* 27 Sept 1919; *s* cousin 1989; *educ* RNC Dartmouth; *m* 1956 *Maxine, only dau of James Adrian Hayden-Scott, of Isère, France, and formerly w of Michael John Willson Levien, and has issue:

1 +PATRICK JAMES, *Lord Gillford*; *b* 28 Dec 1960; *educ* Eton and RMA Sandhurst; 2nd Lt Coldstream Gds 1979–83, exec Hanson plc 1983–90, special advsr Home Sec 1986–88, with Ian Greer & Assocs 1990–93, memb (C) Kensington and Chelsea Cncl 1990–, md Westminster Policy Ptnrship 1993–; *m* 1st 1989 (*divorce* 1994) Serena Emily, adopted dau of Lt-Col Brian Joseph Lockhart, Glos (*see* GRAY, L), and has:

(1) *Tamara Louise; *b* 1990

1 (cont.) Lord Gillford *m* 2nd 1995 *Cara de la Peña and by her has:

(1) +John Maximillian; *b* 28 Jan 1998

1 *Rowena Katharine [The Lady Rowena Crichton-Stuart, 1 Sloane Gdns, London SW1]; *b* 2 April 1957; *m* 1991, as his 2nd w, *(Patrick) James Crichton-Stuart (Isee BUTE, M)

2 *Tania Frances [The Lady Tania Compton, Coombe Cottage, Hanging Langford, Salisbury, Wilts SP3 4NW]; *b* 6 Oct 1963; *m* 1989, as his 2nd w, *James Alwyn Compton (*see* NORTHAMPTON, M)

Lineage: JOHN MIAGH (the family was also called 'Meagh' and 'Myagh'); held the fishery weir of Lochmacen in the Haven of Cork *c* early 15th century; had:

JOHN MIAGH 'the younger'; had:

WILLIAM MIAGH; *d* by 1488, leaving:

JOHN MIAGH, had:

WILLIAM MEAGH; *d* in or after 1558, leaving:

JOHN MEAGH/MEADE/MIAGH; MP for City of Cork 1559 and 1585; Recorder of Cork, Queen's Attorney for Munster, Second Justice of Munster 1570; *d* by 1589, leaving:

JOHN MEADE, of Ballintubber and Cork; *d* after 22 Feb 1611, leaving:

Sir JOHN MEADE, of Ballintubber; ktd 1623; *m* (settlements 22 Feb 1611) Catherine, dau of Sir Dominick Sarsfield, Bt, Viscount Kilmallock, and *d* 28 Sept 1629, having had, with a yr s (John):

WILLIAM MEADE, of Ballintubber; *b c* 1612; Lt-Col, raised a troop of horse for CHARLES II in 1666; *m* Elizabeth, dau of Sir Robert Travers, and had issue:

1 JOHN (Sir), **1st Bt**

2 Robert, of Kinsale; *m* Francis, dau of Sir Peter Courthope, of the Little Island, and had issue

3 Patrick, Brig-Gen; *dsp* between 9 April 1726 and 30 June 1732

4 Dominick (Ven), Archdeacon of Cloyne; *b* 1661; *m* Mary, dau of Francis Smyth, of Rathcourcy, and had issue

1 Elizabeth; *m* John Galway, of Lota

2 Eleanor; *m* Godwin Swift, Attorney-Gen to the Duke of Ormonde and uncle of Jonathan Swift

3 Katherine; *m* William Dunscombe, of Cork

Col MEADE's est son,

Sir John Meade, 1st Bt (I), so *cr* 29 May 1703, of Ballintubber, Co Cork; Attorney-Gen Ireland, Judge Palatinate of Tipperary, MP Dublin U 1689 and Co Tipperary 1692–93, 1695–99 and 1703–07; ktd 1678; *m* 1st 1671 Mary (*dsp*), dau and heir of James Coppinger; *m* 2nd 14 June 1680 Elizabeth, dau and coheir of Maj Daniel Redman, of Ballyinch Castle, by whom he had a dau; *m* 3rd 14 June 1688 Hon Elizabeth Butler (*d* Dec 1757), dau of 2nd Viscount Ikerrin, and *d* 12 Jan 1706/7, having by her had, with two other s and four other daus:

1 **Sir Pierce Meade, 2nd Bt**; *educ* Trin Coll Dublin (BA); *bur* 18 July 1711

2 RICHARD (Sir), **3rd Bt**

1 Elizabeth; *m* 1st Sir Ralph Freke, Bt, of Rathbarry; *m* 2nd 4th Baron Kingston (*see* KINGSTON, E)

Sir PIERCE's bro,

Sir Richard Meade, 3rd Bt; *b* 1697; *educ* Trin Coll Dublin (BA); MP Kinsale 1725–44; *m* 1736 Catherine (*m* 2nd 6 Oct 1748 Sir Henry Cavendish, 1st Bt, and *d* 21 March 1779), 2nd dau of Henry Prittie, of Dunalley, Co Tipperary, and had issue:

1 JOHN, **1st Earl**

1 Elizabeth; *m* 1760 3rd Earl of Mayo (*qv*), and *d* 1807

Sir RICHARD *d* 26 May 1744; his son,

JOHN MEADE, **1st Earl of Clanwilliam**, so cr 20 July 1776, as also earlier 17 Nov 1766 BARON GILLFORD of the Manor of Gillford, Co Down, and VISCOUNT CLANWILLIAM of Co Tipperary (all I); *b* 21 April 1744; *educ* Trin Coll Dublin (BA); MP Banagher 1764–66; *m* 29 Aug 1765 Theodosia (*d* 2 March 1817), only dau and heir of Robert Hawkins Magill, of Gill Hall, Co Down, and had, with other issue:

1 RICHARD, **2nd Earl**

2 Robert, of Burrenwood, Co Down, Gen, Col 12th Regt; *b* 29 Feb 1772; *m* 20 June 1808 Anne Louise (*d* 18 March 1853), dau and heir of Gen Sir John Dalling, Bt, and *d* 11 July 1852, having had, with other issue:

(1) John, of Earsham Hall, Norfolk, and Burrenwood, Co Down; *b* 23 March 1812; *m* 18 June 1846 Elvira (*d* 31 Dec 1905), 2nd dau of Robert Ibbetson, and *d* 5 May 1886, leaving, with other issue:

1a John Percy, of Earsham Hall, and Burrenwood, JP Norfolk and Suffolk, and DL Co Down, Capt 52nd Oxf LI; *b* 17 May 1847; *m* 2 Jan 1894 Helena Frances, JP Norfolk (*d* 23 July 1946), est dau of Sir Allen Johnson Walsh, 4th Bt, and *d* 23 June 1919, leaving with other issue:

1b John Windham, JP (Co Down 1956), Ld of the Manor of Doubles-Earsham, Norfolk, Maj Oxon and Bucks LI WW I (wounded twice), in N Russian (Archangel) Campaign 1919, and WW II, formerly Perm Pres Field Gen Courts Martial to 30th and 12th Corps of Hanover Dist and to Br Troops in Berlin; *b* 28 Nov 1894; *educ* Eton and RMC Sandhurst; *m* 6 Feb 1932 Grace Dorothea (*d* 26 Feb 1977) 3rd dau of Sir Cecil Fane De Salis, KCB, and *d* 1984, leaving issue:

1c +John Michael [John Meade Esq, Manor Farm House, Hedenham, Suffolk NR35 2DG], late Lt Oxon and Bucks LI; *b* 5 Sept 1935; *educ* Stowe and RMA Sandhurst; *m* 23 Jan 1967 *Princess Valentine Galitzine, 2nd dau of Prince Nicholas Galitzine, of 39 Abinger Rd, Bedford Park, W4, and has issue:

1d +Nicholas; *b* 20 Nov 1969

1d *Tatiana; *b* 3 Feb 1968; *m* 1994 *Prince Andrei Mikhailovitch Galitzine, son of Prince Mikhail V Galitzine, of Moscow, and has issue:

1e *Alexei; *b* 25 Feb 1997

1e *Helena; *b* 6 Nov 1994

2d *Catherine; *b* 3 Feb 1968; *m* 1994 *Gary Meyer and has:

1e *Anastasia; *b* 1995

2e *Kira; *b* 11 Dec 1996

3d *Elizabeth; *b* 1971

2c +Francis Windham; *b* 24 March 1941; *educ* Stowe and London U (BSc 1962)

1c *Theodosia Frances; *b* 3 Dec 1932

1a Rose Harriette Theodosia; *m* 28 Sept 1880 Lt-Col James Edward Harris, Suffolk Regt, son of T J Clarke Harris, JP, of The Shade, Hinckley, Leics, and *d* 27 Aug 1944, leaving issue. He *d* 30 Nov 1925

2a Elvira Adela; *m* 4 Feb 1891 Capt Roger Hall, DL, 2nd Bn Roy Fus, of Narrow Water, Co Down, and *d* 14 Sept 1923, leaving issue. He *d* 16 April 1915

(1) Theodosia; *m* 11 June 1836 Sir Robert Alexander Shafto Adair, 2nd Bt (afterwards Baron Waveney) (*see* 1970 edn ADAIR, Bt), and *dsp* 10 May 1871. He *d* 5 Feb 1886

(2) Louisa; *m* 23 May 1842 Hon George Liddell, 4th son of 1st Baron Ravensworth (*qv*), and *d* 19 May 1873

(3) Anne; *m* 15 July 1833 Sir David Thurlow Cunynghame, 6th Bt (*qv*), and *d* 10 June 1864, leaving issue

(4) Adelaide; *m* 25 Oct 1855 Col Rt Hon William Brownlow Forde, of Seaforde, Co Down, and *dsp* 5 Sept 1901. He *d* 8 Feb 1902

(5) Caroline; *m* 12 July 1854 Sir William Compton Domvile, 3rd Bt (*see* 1970 edn), and *d* 8 July 1890, leaving issue. He *d* 29 Sept 1884

3 John, CB, Lt-Gen; *m* 2 Oct 1816 Urania Caroline (*d* Nov 1851), dau of Hon E Ward, and *d* 6 Aug 1849, having had, with other issue:

(1) Richard Raphael, Maj 8th Foot; *b* 24 Oct 1826; *m* 14 Dec 1869 Rica Nunes (*d* 14 April 1908), dau of David Nunes Carvalho, and *d* 26 March 1873, leaving issue:

1a Richard John Edward, OBE (1920), FLAS, Land Agent to Duke of Norfolk and Earl of Albemarle to 1946; *b* 20 Aug 1870; *educ* Clare Coll Cambridge (BA); *m* 15 Aug 1894 Helen Venetia Digby (*d* 19 Dec 1944), dau of Rev George Digby Newbolt, Rector of Knotting-with-Souldrop, and *d* 24 Oct 1957, having had issue:

1b Richard Gilbert Trevor, Lt 14th Hus; *b* 31 May 1895; *d* 10 Oct 1917 of wounds recd in action

1b Patricia Helen Isabel; *b* 17 March 1899

2b Ulrica Nina Elizabeth; *b* 29 June 1902; *m* 21 July 1937 Kenneth Richard Bennett, son of Richard Simpson Bennett, of Market Drayton, Salop, and *d* 28 Feb 1964, leaving issue. He *d* 24 Feb 1938

1a Urania Frances Jane; *m* 1st 17 June 1897 Robert Salusbury Trevor, MA Cambridge, est son of Col S T Trevor, RE; *m* 2nd 4 April 1918 Thomas Rowland Charles Whipham, MD, son of T T Whipham, MD, of Fishleigh Ho, Hatherleigh, and *d* 27 Feb 1941

4 Pierce (Ven), Archdeacon of Dromore; *b* 21 Nov 1776; *m* 6 April 1801 Elizabeth (*d* 26 Sept 1823), dau of Rt Rev Thomas Percy, Bishop of Dromore, and *d* 22 Nov 1834, having had, with other issue:

(1) Edward Richard; *b* 30 Nov 1805; *m* 9 April 1850 Eleanor Eliza (*d* 4 April 1880), est dau of William George Ives Bosanquet, HEICS, and *d* 19 Jan 1890, leaving issue:

1a Mary Frances; *m* 15 May 1873 Brig-Gen Arthur Broadwood, CVO, late Scots Gds, son of Henry Broadwood, and *d* 30 Oct 1925, leaving issue. He *d* 2 Jan 1928

2a Constance Isabel; *d* unm 26 Dec 1941

3a Helen Adelaide; *m* 19 Sept 1888 Gen Sir Montagu Gilbert Gerard, KCB, KCSI, and *d* 3 Jan 1925, leaving issue. He *d* 26 July 1905

(1) Theodosia Barbara; *m* 11 April 1833 Rev John Whalley, of Ecton, Northants, and had issue

1 Catherine; *m* 4th Viscount Powerscourt (*qv*), and *d* 1793

2 Theodosia Sarah Frances; *m* Baron Howden, GCB

3 Melosina Adelaide; *m* 10th Earl of Meath (*qv*), and *d* 26 March 1866

The 1st EARL *d* 19 Oct 1800; his est son,

RICHARD MEADE, **2nd Earl of Clanwilliam**; *b* 10 May 1766; *m* 1st at Schuschitz, Bohemia, 6 Oct 1793 Caroline (*d* 1800), dau of Count von Thun; *m* 2nd 6 July 1803 or 1805 Margaret Irene, widow of (a) John Harcourt, of Ankerwycke, Bucks, and (b) Molyneux, Baron Shuldham, and dau of John Sarney, and by his 1st w had, with another s and dau:

1 RICHARD, **3rd Earl**

1 Caroline; *m* 1811 Count Paul Szechenyi, Chamberlain to the EMPEROR OF AUSTRIA, and *d* 29 Aug 1820

2 Selina; *m* 1821 Gen Count Clam-Martinitz, ADC-Gen to the EMPEROR OF AUSTRIA, and *d* 29 Aug 1872

The 2nd EARL *d* 3 Sept 1805; his only son,

RICHARD CHARLES FRANCIS CHRISTIAN MEADE, **3rd Earl of Clanwilliam**, GCH (1826); *b* 15 Aug 1795; *educ* Eton; Dip Serv: attd Lord Castlereagh's (*see* LONDONDERRY, M) suite Congress Vienna 1814, Priv Sec to Lord Castlereagh at FO 1817–19, U-Sec For Affairs 1822–23, Envoy Berlin 1823–27; *cr* 28 Jan 1828 BARON CLANWILLIAM of Co Tipperary (UK); *m* 5 July 1830 Lady Elizabeth Herbert (*d* 20 Sept 1858), dau of 11th Earl of Pembroke and (8th Earl of) Montgomery, KG (*qv*), and had, with other issue:

1 RICHARD JAMES, **4th Earl**

2 Robert Henry (Sir), GCB, PUS Colonies, Extra Groom Bedchamber to HRH THE PRINCE OF WALES; *b* 16 Dec 1835; *m* 1st 19 April 1865 Lady Mary Elizabeth Lascelles (*d* 7 Feb 1866), dau of 3rd Earl of Harewood (*qv*), and had issue:

(1) Mary Elizabeth Blanche; *d* 13 June 1897

2 (cont.) Sir Robert Meade *m* 2nd 13 April 1880 Caroline Georgiana (*d* 5 March 1881) est dau of Charles William Grenfell, MP (*see* GRENFELL, B), and *d* 8 Jan 1898, having by her had issue:

(1) Charles Francis, Lt Surrey Yeo WW I, cmded 5th Montgomeryshire Bn HG WW II, author: *Approach to the Hills* and *High Mountains*; *b* 25 Feb 1881; *m* 26 Sept 1913 Lady Aileen Hilda Brodrick (*d* 30 Sept 1970), dau of 1st Earl of Midleton (*see* MIDLETON, V), and *d* 11 Jan 1975, leaving issue:

1a +Simon Robert Jasper [Simon Meade Esq, Pen-y-lan, Meifod, Montgomeryshire], Gen Sec of Cncl for Protection of Rural Wales; *b* 13 Feb 1928; *educ* Shrewsbury and RAC; *m* 13 July 1957 *Lady Catherine Sophia Gathorne-Hardy, 2nd dau of 4th Earl of Cranbrook, CBE (*qv*), and has issue:

1b +Jasper Gathorne; *b* 12 July 1962

2b +Benjamin; *b* 17 Dec 1963

1b *Camilla; *b* 31 July 1958

2b *Rachel; *b* 28 May 1965

1a Antonia Mary Hilda, JP (Parts of Kesteven, Lincs 1957, and Co of London 1964); *b* 12 Sept 1914; *m* 21 Dec 1933 Col Ralph George Edward Jarvis, DL (*d* March 1973), of Doddington Hall, Lincoln, only son of Lt-Col Charles Francis Cracroft Jarvis, OBE, DL, JP, of Doddington Hall, and *d* 26 July 1970, leaving issue:

1b *Anthony George; *b* 2 Feb 1938; *m* 25 July 1962 *Victoria Ena Mary, dau of Anthony Mathias, of Weston Turville, Bucks, and has issue:

1c *Claire Victoria; *b* 22 May 1963

2c *Sophia Camilla; *b* 10 Dec 1964

3c *Katherine Antonia; *b* 5 April 1968

1b *Caroline; *b* 18 Dec 1935; *m* 9 May 1968 *5th Earl of Cranbrook (*qv*), and has issue

2a *Evelyn Clodagh [Mrs Colin Mackenzie, Kyle House, Kyleakin, Isle of Skye]; *b* 10 Sept 1916; *m* 20 Jan 1940 Colin Hercules Mackenzie, CMG (*d* 1986), only son of Maj-Gen Sir Colin John Mackenzie, KCB, and has issue:

1b *Christian Fiona [Mrs Nicholas Phipps, 9 Queen's Mansions, Douglas, Isle of Man IM2 4ND]; *b* 1941; *m* 3 June 1966 *(Charles) Nicholas Phipps, only son of Charles Bathurst Hele Phipps, JP, of Chalcot, Wilts (*see* BUCCLEUCH and QUEENSBERRY, D), and has issue:

1c *Charles Mackenzie; *b* 22 March 1967

1c *Alice Christian; *b* 25 March 1969

3a *Flavia Mary [The Rt Hon The Lady Ebbisham, St Ann's, Church St, Mere, Wilts BA12 6DS]; *b* 20 Nov 1920; *m* 26 Oct 1949 2nd and last Baron Ebbisham, TD (*d* 1991), and has issue:

1b *Susan Mary [The Hon Mrs Stevenson, The White House, Whitehouse Loan, Edinburgh EH9 2EY]; *b* 1951; *m* 1980 *Peter D Stevenson, son of Alexander Stevenson, of Westfield Ho, W Calder, Midlothian, and has issue:

1c *George Dennistoun; *b* 1987

1c *Mary Flavia; *b* 1984

2b *Emma Caroline [The Hon Mrs Brooke-Hitching, Osmington House, Kintbury, Newbury, Berks]; *b* 1954; *m* 1977 *Franklin Brooke-Hitching, son of Desmond Brooke-Hitching, of 12 Porchester Terr, London W2, and has issue:

1c *Edward Robert; *b* 5 Dec 1982
2c *Matthew Thomas; *b* 24 Feb 1985
3c *William Franklin; *b* 6 Feb 1987
1c *Georgia Emma; *b* 22 March 1992
3b *Catherine Anne [The Hon Mrs Spencer, Search Farm, Stourton, Warminster, Wilts]; *b* 1955; *m* 1981 *Charles J Spencer, son of Kenneth Spencer, of St Martin's Farm, Zeals, Wilts, and has issue:
1c *Thomas James; *b* 1985
2c *Henry Charles Blades; *b* 1990
1c *Flora Antonia Blades; *b* 1987
3 Sidney (Rev), JP Wilts, Canon of Salisbury, Rector of Wylye, Wilts 1869–82; *b* 29 Oct 1839; *m* 9 Dec 1868 Lucy Emma (*d* 21 July 1918), 2nd dau of J H Jacob, of The Close, Salisbury, and *d* 11 Feb 1917, having had issue:
(1) Francis Henry, CBE (1920), barrister; *b* 6 Dec 1870 *m* 1st 19 April 1900 (*divorce* 1923) Beatrice Mary (*d* 6 March 1959), dau of Lord Esmé Stuart Gordon (*see* HUNTLY, M), and had issue:
1a Robert Sidney Stuart, JP Glos, served WW II 1939–45 as Lt-Col RA (TA) (despatches); *b* 16 Feb 1901; *educ* Eton and Magdalene Coll Cambridge; *m* 1st 31 May 1930 Veronica Augusta (*d* 10 Feb 1968), dau of Lt-Col Herbert Vere Wilbraham, and had issue:
1b *Daphne Theresa; *b* 10 July 1936
2b *Jane Cecilia [Mrs David Corsellis, c/o Nat Westminster Bank, Bishops Stortford, Herts]; *b* 27 Jan 1940; *m* 15 July 1967 *Col David Henry George Corsellis, RE, only son of Henry Alexander Corsellis, of Tudor Ho, Stansted, Essex, and has issue:
1c *Nicholas Robert Alexander; *b* 12 Dec 1968; barrister, Lincoln's Inn 1993
2c *James Henry Merrick; *b* 1970
1a (cont.) Lt-Col Robert Meade *m* 2nd 1970 *Baroness Maria Elisabeth Johanna Rosalia Ottilia [Mrs Robert Meade, The Hangingshaw, Yarrorford, Selkirk], widow of Count Ferdinand Zdenko Karl Emmerich Maria von Thun und Hohenstein, and dau of Baron (Freihem von) August Hermann George Victor Ranberg, Korvetten Kapitaen Imperial Navy, of Gimmden, Austria, and *d* 1971
(1) (cont.) Francis Meade *m* 2nd 13 Oct 1923 Dorothy Elizabeth (*d* 10 June 1962), widow of Lt-Col Joseph Scott Plummer, and dau of Humphrey Pocklington-Senhouse, of Netherhall, Maryport, and *d* 10 July 1953
(1) Elizabeth Cecilia; *m* 9 Aug 1904 Capt John Somerled Thorpe, MC, Scots Gds, of Coddington Hall, Notts, and Ardbrecknish, Argyll, and *d* 13 Nov 1950, leaving issue. He was *ka* 15 Sept 1916
(2) Constance Selina; *m* 19 Aug 1902 Brig-Gen William Henry Sitwell, CB, DSO, of Barmoor Castle, Northumberland, and *dsp* 21 July 1908. He *d* 7 Sept 1932
1 Selina Catherine; *m* 1st 23 Nov 1854 Granville Edward Vernon, MP, est son of Granville Harcourt Vernon, of Grove Hall, Notts (*see* VERNON, B). He *d* 1 Feb 1861. She *m* 2nd 8 July 1862 John Bidwell, of the FO (*d* 22 Aug 1873); *m* 3rd 14 Aug 1880 Henry Arthur William Hervey, CB, and *d* 20 Nov 1911. He *d* 11 May 1908

The 3rd EARL *d* 7 Oct 1879; his est son,

RICHARD JAMES MEADE, **4th Earl of Clanwilliam** GCB (1895, KCB 1887, CB 1877), KCMG (1882); *b* 3 Oct 1832; entered RN 1845, Lt 1852, Capt 1859, R-Adml 1876, V-Adml 1881, Adml 1886, Adml of the Fleet 1895; served Baltic 1854–55, severely wounded assault on Canton 1857; Jr Ld Admlty 1874–78, cmded detached sqdn 1880–81, C-in-C: N American Station 1885–86 and Portsmouth 1891–94; *m* 17 June 1867 Elizabeth Henrietta (*d* 31 March 1925), dau of Sir Arthur Edward Kennedy, GCMG, CB, Govr Queensland, and *d* 4 Aug 1907, having had issue:
1 Richard Charles, *Lord Gillford*, Capt 3rd Vol Bn (Cumberland) the Border Regt, Lt RN; *b* 10 June 1868; *m* 5 Sept 1895 Lady Mary Douglas Home (*d* 21 April 1951), est dau of 12th Earl of Home (*qv*), and *dvp* 14 Oct 1905, leaving issue:
(1) Theodosia Beatrix Catherine Mary; *b* 1 Feb 1898; *m* 11 Nov 1961 Angus Julian Drummond, yr son of Charles Drummond (*see* PERTH, E)
2 ARTHUR VESEY MEADE, **5th Earl of Clanwilliam**, MC, DL (Co Down); Capt RHG, Extra ADC to Viceroy of India, APM and Staff Capt, served Boer War 1900–02 (severely wounded) and WW I, Order of Crown of Italy; *b* 14 Jan 1873; *m* 27 April 1909 Muriel, MBE (1920) (*d* 2 June 1952), widow of Hon Oliver Howard (*see* CARLISLE, E) and dau of Russell Maule Stephenson, and *d* 23 Jan 1953, leaving:
(1) JOHN CHARLES EDMUND CARSON MEADE, **6th Earl of Clanwilliam**; *b* 6 June 1914; *educ* Eton; Maj Coldstream Gds (ret 1948) WW II Middle East and France (despatches twice); Ld Lt Co Down 1975–79 (HM Lt 1962–75, DL 1957–62), CStJ 1975; *m* 1 Dec 1948 *Catherine [The Rt Hon The Dowager Countess of Clanwilliam, Maizley Cottage, Oare, Marlborough, Wilts SN8 4HZ], yst dau of Arthur Thomas Loyd, OBE, of Lockinge, Wantage, Berks, and *d* 1989, leaving:
1a *Selina Catherine [The Lady Selina Timpson, Ardington Croft, Wantage, Oxon]; *b* 14 March 1950; *m* 28 Oct 1972 *Nicholas George Lawrence Timpson, late Scots Gds, est son of Maj (John) Alastair Livingston Timpson, MC, late Scots Gds, of 51 Rostrevor Rd, SW6, by his 1st w (Elizabeth) Phoebe, only surv child of Sir George Reginald Houston-Boswall, 4th Bt (*qv*), and has issue:
1b *Lawrence Rupert John; *b* 5 July 1974
1b *Catherine Selina Alexandra; *b* 13 Jan 1979
2a *Mary Jane [The Rt Hon The Countess Belmore, Castle Coole, Enniskillen, Co Fermanagh, Ireland]; *b* 12 July 1952; *m* 1984 *8th Earl Belmore (*qv*), and has issue
3a *Julia Elizabeth [The Lady Julia Hiscox, Rainscombe Park, Oare, Marlborough, Wilts SN8 4HZ]; *b* 31 Dec 1953; *m* 1985, as his 2nd w, *Robert Ralph Scrymgeour Hiscox, son of Ralph Hiscox, CBE, and has issue:
1b *Milo Edmund; *b* 1987
2b *Henry Charles; *b* 1989
3b *Sidney John; *b* 1993
4a *Laura Louise; *b* 11 March 1957; *m* 25 April 1981 *W Scott B Reid, son of Howard Reid, of Bronxville, USA, and has issue:
1b *Nicholas John Howard; *b* 30 Dec 1982
1b *Amelia Louise Catherine; *b* 1984
2b *Clementine Julia; *b* 1988
5a *Katharine Anne [The Lady Katharine Wills, Litchfield Down, Whitchurch, Hants]; *b* 10 Aug 1959; *m* 1987 *Christopher Aubrey Hamilton Wills, er son of Hon Victor Patrick Hamilton Wills, and has issue (*see* DULVERTON, B)
6a *Sophia Hester; *b* 14 Oct 1963; *m* 1990 *Jonathan G Heywood, son of Brig Anthony Heywood, of Monkton Ho, Monkton Deverill, Wilts, and has issue:
1b *A son; *b* 1993
(1) Mary Katharine Selina; *b* 16 Feb 1910; *m* 1st 29 Aug 1934 (*divorce* 1946) Col Robert Arthur Hermon, DSO, OBE, The Royals, of Breda, Alford, Aberdeenshire, est son of Lt-Col Edward William Hermon, of Brook Hill Ho, Cowfold, Sussex, and had issue. He *d* 7 Oct 1963. She *m* 2nd 1946 Lt-Col A Frank Stanley-Clarke. He *d* 16 Jan 1947. She *m* 3rd Oct 1954 S/Ldr David Beckwith Rodd, DFC, son of Thomas Rodd, of Pittsburgh, USA, and *d* 26 July 1965
(2) Elizabeth Louise Margaret; *b* 18 April 1911; *m* 7 Oct 1933 Lt-Col Charles Rankin Scott, KRRC (*d* 4 Dec 1965), yst son of James Henry Scott, of Eredine, Argyll, and had issue:
1a *Edward John Rankin; *b* 3 Jan 1939; *educ* Eton
2a *(William) Nigel Charles; *b* 19 March 1941; *educ* Eton
3 Herbert MEADE later MEADE-FETHERSTONHAUGH (roy licence 15 Dec 1931) (Hon Sir), GCVO (1934), CB, DSO; *b* 3 Nov 1875; Adml, Naval ADC to HM GEORGE V 1924, Hon Naval ADC, and cmdg HM's Yachts 1931–34; Extra Equerry to: TM GEORGE V 1934–36, EDWARD VIII 1936 and GEORGE VI 1937–52; served WW I (despatches) and WW II 1939–44 as Cdre Convoys and Lt-Col HG, Serjeant-at-Arms Ho Lds 1939–46; *m* 6 July 1911 Margaret Isabel Frances (*d* 15 June 1977), er dau of Rt Rev Hon Edward Carr Glyn, DD, Bishop of Peterborough (*see* WOLVERTON, B), and *d* 27 Oct 1964, having had issue:
(1) Richard James, Lt Army WW II 1939–42 (POW); *b* 14 Dec 1913; *educ* Eton; *m* 26 Aug 1948 *Jean Phyllis [Mrs Richard Meade-Fetherstonhaugh, 14 Limerston St, London SW10; Uppark, Petersfield, Hants], est dau of Maj Basil Falkner, of Matt's Ho, Thornby, Northants, and *d* 7 July 1958, leaving issue:
1a *Harriet Sarah [Mrs Harriet Cossart, Uppark, Petersfield, Hants GU31 5QR]; *b* 31 July 1949; *m* 21 June 1969 (*divorce* 1997) John de Bianchi Cossart, only son of Peter de Bianchi Cossart, of Madeira, and has had:
1b Charles Richard; *b* 27 May 1972; *d* 4 Feb 1997
2b *Edward James; *b* 12 March 1984
1b *Henrietta-Maria; *b* 14 May 1974
2a *Emma Mary [Mrs Geoffrey Goad, Deerkeepers, Uppark, Petersfield, Hants]; *b* 2 July 1951; *m* 3 Jan 1976 *Geoffrey Wanklyn Goad, and has issue:
1b *Oliver Edward; *b* 1977
2b *Harry Frederick; *b* 1978
1b *Matilda Rose; *b* 1989
3a *Sophia Teresa; *b* 22 March 1954; *m* 1985 *Angus Warre [Mrs Angus Warre, Dalcross Castle, Croy, Inverness], est son of Maj John Antony Warre, MC, of Barrowden Oakham, Rutland (*see* DEVONSHIRE, D), and has issue:
1b *Theodora; *b* 1986
(2) JOHN HERBERT MEADE, **7th and present Earl of Clanwilliam**
(1) *Anne Margaret; *b* 15 June 1912; *m* 9 May 1933 2nd Baron Rockley (*qv*), and has issue
(2) *Jean Mary; *b* 31 May 1917; granted rank of earl's dau 1990; *m* 28 Sept 1943 Brig Michael James Babington Smith, CBE, TD (*d* 1984), est son of Sir Henry Babington Smith, GBE, CH, KCB, CSI, by Lady Elizabeth, dau of 9th Earl of Elgin and Kincardine (*qv*), and has issue:
1a *Alan; *b* 1946; *educ* Eton and Trin Coll Cambridge
1a *Louisa [Mrs James Macfarlane, Riverwood, Wickham, Hants PO1Y 5AY]; *b* 1944; *m* 1967 *Lt-Col James Richard Macfarlane, Coldstream Gds, and has issue:
1b *Edward Michael Richard; *b* 1969; Capt Coldstream Gds
2b *David Peter; *b* 1970
2a *Susan Mary [Mrs John Hemming, 10 Edwardes Sq, London W8]; *b* 1950; *m* 1979 *John Henry Hemming, CMG, and has issue:
1b *Henry Sebastian; *b* 1979
1b *Beatrice Margaret Louisa; *b* 1981
4 Edward Brabazon, Capt 10th Hus (SR) Boer War 1900 (medal) and WW I as ADC on personal Staff (despatches); *b* 10 Sept 1878; *educ* Eton; *m* 1st Dec 1907 Hon Elizabeth Kate Shelley Gully (*d* 26 Feb 1908), yr dau of 1st Viscount Selby (*qv*); *m* 2nd 28 June 1910 (*divorce* 1924) Angela Anna Rosing Theresa Maximilian, dau of Thury von Thurybrugg; *m* 3rd 23 Dec 1925 Beatrice (*d* 16 March 1975), widow of Arthur Godfrey, and dau of Rt Rev Douglas Herbert Brunner, of Boston, Mass, USA, and *dsp* 13 April 1963
1 Elizabeth Selina Georgiana, Woman of the Bedchamber to HM QUEEN MARY; *m* 27 April 1898 Capt Hon Edward Stanley Dawson RN, 2nd son of 1st Earl of Dartrey, and *d* 13 Oct 1924, leaving issue. He *d* 13 Oct 1919
2 Katharine, Lady-in-waiting to TRH THE DUCHESS OF ALBANY 1910–22 and THE DUCHESS OF YORK 1923–26; *d* unm 19 Oct 1954
3 Beatrice; *d* unm 19 June 1952
4 Adealaide Jane; *m* 6 Dec 1902 Adml Hon Sir Stanley Cecil James Colville, GCB, GCMG, GCVO, 2nd son of 1st Viscount Colville of Culross (*qv*), and *d* 31 March 1960, leaving issue

CLARENDON

Arms: Arg. on a cross gu. five escallop shells or. **Crest:** A lion rampant arg., ducally crowned or. **Supporters:** Two eagles, wings endorsed sa., ducally crowned or, charged on the breast with a plain cross arg. **Motto:** *Fidei coticula crux* ('The cross, the test of faith').

Creations: B. (GB) 3 June 1756, E. (GB) 14 June 1776.

THE 7TH EARL OF CLARENDON, and **Baron Hyde of Hindon**, Wilts (George Frederick Laurence Hyde Villiers) [The Rt Hon The Earl of Clarendon, Holywell House, Swanmore, Hants SO32 2QE]; *b* 2 Feb 1933 (HM GEORGE V stood sponsor); *s* gf 1955; *educ* Eton and Madrid U; Page of Hon to HM GEORGE VI 1948–49, Lt RHG (AER) 1951–53, md Seccombe, Marshall and Campion plc 1962–93 (chm 1985–93); *m* 17 July 1974 *Jane Diana, twin dau of Edward Wilham Dawson, of The Old Rectory, Idmiston, Salisbury, Wilts, and has issue:

1 +GEORGE EDWARD LAURENCE, *Lord Hyde*; *b* 12 Feb 1976; Page of Hon to HM THE QUEEN 1988–90

1 *Sarah Katherine Jane; *b* 20 Oct 1977

Clarendon, previous creation: Edward Hyde, the father-in-law of JAMES II, chief minister to CHARLES II for the first years of his reign and the historian of the Civil War, was created Earl of Clarendon in 1661. His grandson, the 4th and last Earl of this creation, was grandfather-in-law of the 1st Earl of the present creation (*see* below).

Lineage: The 2nd EARL OF JERSEY (*qv*) had a 2nd s:

THOMAS VILLIERS, **1st Earl of Clarendon**, so *cr* 14 June 1776, as also earlier 3 June 1756 BARON HYDE OF HINDON, Wilts, with remainder in the latter case to the heirs male of his body by his then w and in default thereof to her and the heirs male of her body, PC (1763); *b* 1709; *educ* St John's Coll Cambridge; Envoy to Poland and Saxony 1740–47, Vienna 1742–43 and Berlin 1746–48 (*cr* a Baron of the Kingdom of Prussia and allowed to use title in GB by sign-manual), MP (Whig) Tamworth 1747–56, a Ld Admlty 1748–56, Jt PMG 1763–65 and Sept-Dec 1786, Chllr Duchy Lancaster 1771–82 and 1783–86; *m* 30 March 1752 Charlotte (*d* 3 Dec 1790), est surv dau of 3rd Earl of Essex (*qv*) by Jane, est surv dau of Henry Hyde, 4th and last Earl of Clarendon of the 1661 *cr*, and *d* 11 Dec 1786, leaving:

1 THOMAS VILLIERS, **2nd Earl of Clarendon**, MP (Tory) Christchurch 1774–80 and Helston 1780–86; *b* 26 Dec 1753; *d* unm 7 March 1824

2 JOHN CHARLES VILLIERS, **3rd Earl of Clarendon**, PC (1787), MP (Tory) Old Sarum 1784–90, Dartmouth 1790–1802, Wick Burghs 1802–05 and Queenborough 1807–12 and 1820–24, Comptroller Household 1789–90, Envoy Portugal 1807–10; *b* 14 Nov 1757; *m* 5 Jan 1791 Maria Eleanor (*d* 18 March 1844), 2nd dau and coheir of Adml Hon John Forbes (*see* GRANARD, E), and *d* 22 Dec 1838, leaving:

(1) Mary Harriet; *d* unm 20 Jan 1835

3 George; *b* 23 Nov 1795; *m* 17 April 1798 Theresa (*bur* 10 Jan 1856), only dau of 1st Baron Boringdon of Boringdon (*see* MORLEY, E), and *d* 21 March 1827, leaving issue (his living yr children being granted Feb 1839 rank of earl's daus/yr s):

(1) GEORGE WILLIAM, **4th Earl**

(2) Thomas Hyde; *b* 24 Jan 1801; MA Cantab 1825; Colonial Office 1822–25, Agent for Berbice and Newfoundland, Sec Bd Control, MP Hedon 1826–30, Wotton Bassett 1830, Bletchingly 1831; *d* 3 Dec 1832, having by Charlotte, dau of Surgn-Maj Harte had either illegitimately or through a secret marriage:

1a Charles LAWRENCE later VILLIERS (roy licence Aug 1876) (Rev); *b* 1830; Chaplain to Bps Carlisle and Durham 1857–61, Rector Croft, Yorks; *m* 19 Oct 1860 Florence Mary Tyssen Amherst (*d* 7 Oct 1927), sis of 1st Baron Amherst of Hackney (*qv*), and *d* 15 Oct 1893, leaving:

1b Charles Hyde, CVO, TD, Lt-Col RHG, Boer War (medal and three clasps) and WWI (despatches), memb Gentlemen-at-Arms; *m* 1901 Victoria Alexandrina (*d* 22 May 1970), 2nd dau of 7th Duke of Roxburghe (*qv*), and *d* 23 May 1947, leaving:

1c Alastair Edward Hyde, Lt-Col Gren Gds, Legion of Honour, Croix de Guerre; *b* 1905; *m* 1938 Gaudencia Isabel (*d* 1962), dau of E G Fraser-Luckie, of Anduhnasi, Peru, by Guadencia, dau of general Miguel Iglesias, Pres Peru, and *d* 24 March 1968, leaving issue:

1d *Alastair Michael Hyde; *b* 1939; *m* 1st 27 June 1962 (*divorce* 1976) Hon Elizabeth Mairi Keppel, er dau of Viscount Bury (*see* ALBEMARLE, E) and has:

1e *Charles Alastair Hyde [Charles Villiers Esq, Milton House, Milton, Dunbartonshire GS2 2TU; *b* 4 April 1963; *educ* Eton and Edinburgh U; stationer, newspapermaker, Freeman City London; *m* 30 April 1994 *Emma Mary Jane Goodall and has:

1f *Clarissa Elizabeth Mairi; *b* 4 Aug 1995

1e *Charlotte Mairi; *b* 27 Oct 1965; *m* 1995 *Rupert Edinmore Gather and has:

1f *Felix Edinmore; *b* 1997

1d (cont.) Lt-Col Alastair Hyde Villiers *m* 2nd 12 March 1976 *Mrs Lamorne Jessica Elliot (*see* SAINT LEVAN, B) and has further issue

2c Algernon Richard John, Brig RA WW II France and Iceland, on Staff 47th Inf Div 1943, SHAEF 1944 (France and Holland) and with SHAPE 1951–53, Mil Attaché Brussels 1957–61, ret 1961; *b* 16 April 1907; *educ* Wellington and RMA Woolwich; *m* 1953 Alice (*d* 13 Dec 1973), dau of Captain Baron Alexander von Gröller, and *d* 25 April 1977

1c (Victoria) Angela Mary; *b* 1903; *m* 1933 Col Charles Naunton Turner, and *d* 22 Nov 1966. He *d* 8 June 1968

2c Isabel Alexandrina; *b* 1907; *m* 19 Sept 1951 Rupert Leigh, son of Rev R E Leigh, of Sherfield-on-Loddon, Hants, and had issue

3c Violet Rosamund; *b* 1911; *m* 1934 Archibald Adam Gordon Black, publisher, son of Adam Black, and had issue

4c Cecily Irene; *b* 1914; *m* 1934 Cdr Denis Courage, RN, son of Capt A Courage, RN, of Offham Ho, Lewes, Sussex, and had issue

2b Ernest Amherst, MP (Lib) Brighton 1906–10; *b* 14 Nov 1863; *m* 30 April 1898 Hon Elaine Augusta Guest (*m* 2nd 28 July 1933 Robert Lewin Hunter), 3rd dau of 1st Baron Wimborne (*see* WIMBORNE, V), and *d* 26 Sept 1923, leaving issue:

1c Charles Amherst; *b* 9 Dec 1900; motor car engr, inventor; *m* 1st (*divorce*) Maya de Lisle Adam, widow of George Strokosch; *m* 2nd (Ju)Anita Lorraine (*d* 17 Sept 1968), dau of Charles Brown, of Minneapolis, and *d* 1993, leaving:

1d *Charles Churchill

1d *Jane [Miss Jane Villiers, 46a Holland St, London W8

2c George; *d* unm

1c Barbara; *b* 1899; *m* 11 Dec 1925 Brig-Gen Sir Smith Hill Child, 2nd and last Bt, GCVO, CB, CMG, DSO, of Newfield, and *d* 23 Dec 1971, leaving issue (*see* 1959 edn). He *d* 11 Nov 1958

2c *Veronica [Mrs Ray Milner, Long Distance, Qualium Beach, Victoria Is, BC, Canada]; *b* 1909; *m* 9 Jan 1929 Desmond Wyndham Otho FitzGerald, 28th Knight of Glin, and has issue. He *d* 2 April 1949. She *m* 2nd 2 Feb 1954 (Horatio) Ray Milner, CC (Canada), QC, DCL, BA, LLB (*d* 1975), of Edmonton, Alberta, son of William Cochrane Milner, LLD, BSc of Sackville, New Brunswick

3b William Noel; *b* 1864; *m* 7 Dec 1903 Susan Dorothea FitzPatrick Watson-Armstrong (*d* 1961), sis of 1st Baron Armstrong (*see* 1970 edn), and *dsp*

4b Bertram; *b* 1865; *d* unm

5b Edward Cecil, CMG, R-Adml; *b* 16 Feb 1866; *m* 1900 Anne Gordon (*d* 1963), dau of Sir William Frederick Haynes-Smith, KCMG, Govr and C-in-C Cyprus, and *d* 16 April 1939, leaving issue:

1c Louis Alexander, Lt-Col Roy Norfolk Regt, Queen's Messenger 1955–67; *b* 1902; *m* 8 Sept 1939 (*divorce* 1963) Muriel Sinclair, dau of Col J S Liddell and Baroness Porcelli, and *d* 22 May 1970 aged 92, having had issue:

1d *Louisa; *b* 4 Sept 1943; *m* 1st 1967 Michael Leonard Grogan, yst s of John Reginald Grogan; *m* 2nd 19– *Tim Maskell, London estate agent

2c William Amherst, BSc, ACGI, WW II in RAF; *b* 1903 *m* 1942 *Joan, dau of Basil Griffin, of S Africa, and had issue:

1d *Susan; *b* 1944; *m* 1965 *Lt Frederick Mead

3c (John) Michael (Sir), KCB (1962, CB 1960), OBE (1943), V-Adml, served WW II (despatches), cmded HMS *Ursa* 1945, HMS *Snipe* 1946–47, on directing staff of Jt Services Staff Coll 1948–49, Assist Dir of Plans, Admiralty 1950–51, Capt Dockyard, Malta 1952–54, cmded HMS *Bulwark* 1954–57, Ch of Naval Staff NZ 1958–60, Fourth Sea Ld 1960–63, Lt-Govr and C-in-C Jersey 1964–69, KStJ 1964; *b* 22 June 1907; *educ* Oundle and RNC; *m* 3 Nov 1936 *Rosemary, CStJ, 2nd dau of Lt-Col Bernard Salwey Grissell, DSO, and had issue:

1d *Valerie Anne; *b* 28 March 1940; *m* 15 Dec 1962 *V-Adml Sir John Morrison Webster, KCB, son of Frank Morrison Webster, of Lea Ho, Lymington, Hants, and has issue:

1e *Lucilla Jane; *b* 6 March 1964

2e *Anna Rozelle; *b* 24 Dec 1966

2d *Camilla Rosemary; *b* 26 Jan 1943; *m* 12 July 1969 *Richard Weston Warner, er son of John Weston Warner, of The Old Rectory, Stanton, nr Broadway, Worcs, and has issue:

1e *Michael Weston; *b* 18 July 1971

1e *Miranda Jane; *b* 13 June 1973

4c Edward Gordon; *b* 18 Oct 1909; *d* unm 1933

1c *Ellen Margaret

6b Evelyn Fountaine, CMG, DSO; *b* 4 May 1875; Lt-Col; *m* 1st 1901 Muriel, 3rd dau of Col Wisden; *m* 2nd Edith Ellen, dau of Richard Scroffin, of Grantham, and *d* 3 Jan 1955, having by 1st w had issue:

1c Patrick; *b* 1908; W/Cdr RAF, King's Flight pre-WW II and Malta WWII; *m* 1939 Margot, dau of Charles Robinson, of Alexandria, Egypt, and *d* 1993, leaving:

1d *Carol Anne; *b* 1940; *m* 1959 *Kenneth Fawcett, of Nairobi, and has:

1e *Mark Ashley Villiers; *b* 1960

2e *Alan Gregory Villiers; *b* 1962

1c Winifred; *b* 1902; *m* 1st 1922 Brig Henry Ayerst Young, DSO (*d* 19–; *m* 2nd Brig Claude Vallentin (*d* 19–); *m* 3rd Brig Reginald Hudson, DSO (*d* 1995), and *dsp* 1990

2c Audrey; *b* 1905; *m* 1st 1930 (*divorce* 194–) Derrick Clayton (*d* 1973) and had:

1d Michael Denzil Grierson; *b* 1931; *m* 1966 *Georgina, dau of Sir Charles Buchanan, Bt (*qv*) and *d* 1991, leaving issue

2c (cont.) Mrs Audrey Clayton *m* 2nd 1945 William (Ben) Hutchinson, of Mollington, Cheshire, and *d* 1981, leaving by him:

2d *John Villiers; *b* 1946; *m* 1997 *Sylvie —, of Toronto

3d *Anthony Broadbent; *b* 1951

3c Esme; *b* 1906; *m* 19– Tom Wisden, RN and *dsp* 196–

1b Gertrude Mary Amelia; *m* 20 Aug 1896 Canon Hon Robert Grimston, 3rd son of 2nd Earl of Verulam (*qv*), and *d* 8 July 1928, leaving issue

2b Florence Margaret Rose; *m* 7 July 1896 Henry Minshull Stockdale, of Mears Ashby Hall, Northants (*see* STOCKDALE, Bt), and *d* 20 Jan 1952, leaving issue

3b Gwendoline; *d* unm 1961

1a Gertrude; *bapt* 1 Aug 1834; *m* 4 Aug 1853 Rev William Frederick Bickmore, Vicar Kenilworth 1856–75, Rector Stone, both Worcs, 1875–96, and *d* 2 July 1896, having had ten children, one of whom was gf of Peter Bickmore, who *m* 22 July 1975 Margaret Fitzalan Howard (*see* NORFOLK, L)

(3) Charles Pelham, PC; *b* Jan 1802; (granted Feb 1839 with yr siblings rank of earl's dau/yr s), MA, barrister, MP Wolverhampton 1835–98, JAG, Pres Poor Law Bd; *d* unm 16 Jan 1898

(4) Edward Ernest; *b* 23 March 1806; *m* 1 Aug 1835 Hon Elizabeth Charlotte Liddell (*d* 15 April 1890), 5th dau of 1st Baron Ravensworth (*qv*), and *d* 30 Oct 1843, leaving issue:

1a Ernest, Hon Col 21st Bn Co of London Regt, VD, ADC to HM, formerly Capt 43rd LI; *b* 18 July 1838; *m* 1st 10 April 1866 Elizabeth (*d* 16 Feb 1867), est dau of Sir Charles Alexander Wood, and had issue:

1b Edward Ernest; *b* 7 Feb 1867; *m* 27 June 1891 Florence (*d* 21 May 1956), est dau of Francis Ricardo, of The Friary, Old Windsor, and *d* 22 Sept 1942, leaving issue:

1c Algernon Edward, MIEE, Capt KRRC (SR) WW I; *b* 16 Aug 1892; *educ* Eton and Univ Coll Oxford (MA 1918); *m* 29 July 1924 Annie Augusta Mereweather (*d* 1978), dau of George Latham Massy, of Berridge, Sunningdale, and ld 1991, leaving issue:

1d +George Edward, TD (1965) [Maj George Villiers TD, 98 Ravenscourt Rd, London W6 0UG], Maj Berks and Westminster Dragoons (TA), 2nd Lt 4th Regt RHA 1950–51, pres Oxford U Athletic Club 1953–54; *b* 3 Aug 1931; *educ* Wellington and BNC Oxford (BA 1956, MA 1959); *m* 25 Aug 1962 *Anne Virginia, er dau of Cuthbert Raymond Forster Threlfall, of Warstone Ho, Bewdley, Worcs, and has issue:

1e +Edward Richard; *b* 6 July 1963; *m* 29 March 1995 *Lisa Alexandra Bryer, est dau of Lionel Bryer, of Chelsea and has:

1f +James Lionel Edward; *b* 15 Oct 1997

2f +Frederick George Edward; *b* 15 Oct 1997

2e +Henry Raymond; *b* 1 Nov 1965

1e *Theresa Anne; *b* 5 March 1968

1d Elizabeth Anne; *b* 7 Sept 1925

2d *Barbara Jane [Miss Barbara Villiers, Flat 17, 55 Shepherds's Hill, London N6 5QP]; *b* 4 Jan 1927

1c Constance Irene, of Pine Acre, Sunningdale, Berks; *b* 27 April 1900; *d* unm 17 Oct 1973

2c Victoria Florence Louisa; *b* 28 May 1905; *m* 18 Jan 1947 James Wilson, MA, MB, MRCS, LRCP, yr son of Dr James Wilson, of Redhurst, Irvine, Ayrshire, and *dsp* 2 Jan 1970

1a (cont.) Col Ernest Villiers *m* 2nd 21 July 1869 Adela Sarah (*d* 19 Dec 1936), only dau of Col Charles Parke Ibbetson, and *d* 22 April 1921, having by her had issue:

1b Clementina Elizabeth Charlotte; *b* 3 July 1870; *m* 1st 16 July 1892 Montague Whittingham Price, DL, of 67 Eaton Place, SW, and had issue. He *d* 5 Jan 1928. She *m* 2nd 16 Feb 1931 Edward Henry Loyd, of Langleybury, Herts and 43 Cadogan Sq, SW, and *d* 6 Feb 1933. He *d* 6 Nov 1938

2b Adela Constance; *b* 19 March 1872; *m* 27 July 1901 Sir Francis Edward James Smith, of Ashdown Ho, Dane Hill, East Grinstead, son of John Smith, of Britwell Ho, Oxon, and *d* 24 Oct 1956, leaving issue. He *d* 27 Feb 1950

3b Sara Georgina; *b* 1 Aug 1880; *m* 31 Aug 1914 Capt John Elphinston Hugh Orr, late RA, and *d* 20 Feb 1969

1a Maria Theresa; *m* 14 April 1864 Capt Charles William Earle, Rifle Bde, and *d* 27 Feb 1925, leaving issue. He *d* 7 June 1897

2a Edith, CI, VA, Lady of the Bedchamber to TM QUEEN VICTORIA and QUEEN ALEXANDRA, twin with Elizabeth; *m* 4 Oct 1864 1st Earl of Lytton (*qv*), and *d* 17 Sept 1936, leaving issue

3a Elizabeth, LG StJ; *m* 7 May 1862 1st Baron Loch, PC, GCB, GCMG (*see* 1970 edn), and *d* 12 March 1938, leaving issue. He *d* 20 June 1900

(5) Henry Montagu (Rt Rev), DD, Bishop of Durham; *b* 4 Jan 1813; *m* 30 Jan 1837 Amelia Maria (*d* 5 Feb 1871) est dau of William Hulton, of Hulton Park, Lancs (*see* 1970 edn HULTON, Bt), and *d* 9 Aug 1861, leaving issue:

1a Henry Montagu (Rev), MA Vicar St Paul's Knightsbridge, Preb St Paul's Cathedral; *b* 13 Nov 1837; *m* 1st 16 April 1861 Victoria (*d* 9 May 1880), 2nd dau of 1st Earl Russell, KG (*qv*), and had, with other issue:

1b Henry Montagu, MVO (1908), V-Consul Bogota 1894–1900, Consul Faroe Islands 1900–06, Stockholm 1906–13 and Malaga 1913–19, Commercial Sec Madrid and Lisbon 1919, retired 1 Nov 1919; *b* 30 March 1863; *m* 7 April 1896 Carmen (*d* 2 Sept 1953), dau of Dr Luhrsen, German Envoy Extrdy and Min Plen Colombia, and *d* 23 Sept 1948, having had issue:

1c Cecil Montagu John; *b* 24 Jan 1897; *d* 21 Jan 1912

2c George Dumba, Cdr RN, served WWs I and II; with BBC; *b* 6 March 1900; *m* 10 May 1926 Anne Hilda Whellens (*d* 1990), dau of James Barton Hall, of Longframlington, Northumberland, and *d* 18 May 1977, leaving issue of:

1d +Simon William George [Maj Simon Villiers, 16B Harmony St, Rusthall, Kent TN4 8NS], late Maj RA, seconded to Fedn of Malaya Armed Forces, served Malaya from 1955 (despatches, Order of Ali Manghu Negara); *b* 1927; *m* 1956 *Patricia de Lacey, and has issue:

1e +Clive Matthew George; *b* 1957

1e *Virgina Anne [Mrs Nigel Batchelor, Parkfield, Wallaford Rd, Buckfastleigh, Devon]; *b* 1959; *m* 1979 *Nigel Mark Batchelor, and has issue:

1f *Matthew Joseph; *b* 1979

2f *Christopher Luke; *b* 1981

2e *Moira Lillian [Mrs Michael Rudd, 31 Bramley Hill, Mere, Wilts BA12 6JX]; *b* 1963; *m* 1st 1983 Terence Michael Rodden, and has issue:

1f *Sally Anne; *b* 1985

2e (cont.) Mrs Moira Rodden *m* 2nd 1994 *Michael Rudd and by him has issue:

1f *Sean Thomas; *b* 1996

1d *Janet Mary [Miss Janet Villiers, Tormead, Daddyhole Plain, Torquay, Devon TQ1 3EQ], formerly headmistress Middle Sch, Tormead Sch for Girls, Guildford; *b* 1929

3c Edmund Rollo Stanley, CA, Fin and Ec Advsr Nat Bank Nigeria, WW II in RAFVR, Colonial Serv 1952–56; *b* 13 May 1909; *educ* Cheltenham; *m* 1st 12 Oct 1934 (*divorce* 1957) Margit Cleland, dau of Robert Rogerson, of Marchmount, Dumfries, and had issue:

1d +Charles Russell [Charles Villiers Esq, Wargrave Lodge, Wargrave-on-Thames, Berks]; *b* 14 Nov 1938; *educ* Cheltenham and Corpus Christi Coll Cambridge (BA 1960); MB, BCir, DMRD, FFR; *m* 22 May 1971 *Barbara Clare, dau of Fredwin McMaster, of Nottinghill, Belfast

3c (cont.) Edmund Villiers *m* 2nd 31 July 1957 *Christine Joan, yr dau of Cdr Walter Odwin Hutton Lambert, RN, of The Toll, Buxted, Sussex, and *d* 30 April 1960

1c Victoria Mary; *b* 1 Aug 1903; *m* 11 June 1928 Hon Nigel Amyas Orde-Powlett, afterwards 6th Baron Bolton (*qv*), and *d* 1 Nov 1933, leaving issue

2c *Margaret Adelaide Rhoda; *b* 15 Feb 1913; *m* 9 Nov 1936 *Rupert Huber, and has issue:

1d *Anita Margaret; *b* 17 April 1939; *m* 7 Jan 1958 *Eduard Bacher, and has issue:

1e *Hannes; *b* 27 June 1959

2e *Ewald; *b* 16 Dec 1960

3e *Tristan; *b* 7 June 1964

4e *Christoph; *b* 10 Dec 1966

2d *Renate Krexentia; *b* 27 Nov 1941

3c *Margaret Anne Theresa, twin; *b* 15 Feb 1913; *m* 1944 *Ronald Basil Strickland, of Bow River, W Australia, and has issue

2b John Russell; *b* 15 Jan 1866; *m* 19 April 1893 Grace Elizabeth (*d* 31 May 1962, aged 93), yr dau of Maj-Gen William Earle, CB, CSI (*see* EARLE, Bt), and *d* 6 Feb 1958, leaving issue:

1c Arthur Henry, MC, late 2nd Lt 6th Bn KRRC; *b* 27 March 1894; *educ* Radley; *m* 6 Oct 1919 Vera Adeline (*d* 1976), only dau of Charles Howe, of Durban, S Africa, and *d* 6 Sept 1975, leaving issue:

1d +Peter William, late Lt KRRC, electrical engineer, film producer; *b* 26 Jan 1922; *educ* Lancing; *m* 1st 17 Nov 1945 (*divorce* 1958) Juneica, only child of William Friedhoff; *m* 2nd 1959 *Alice, dau of A J Startup, and by 1st w has had issue:

1e +Roger Peter; *b* 1946; *m* 1975 *Julia Helen, dau of A S Rymer, and has issue:

1f +Mark Roger; *b* 1980

1f *Helen Fiona; *b* 1977

1e Jennifer Ann; *b* 31 Oct 1948; *d* 21 Aug 1970

2d +Geoffrey Richard [Geoffrey Villiers, 1301 Jefferson St, Napa, Calif, USA], WW II as Sub-Lt RNVR; *b* 9 Dec 1924; *educ* Lancing; *m* 23 Oct 1948 *Janet Myra, twin dau of Dr Leonard W Trott, of Carawatha, Edwin Terr, Gilberton, Adelaide, S Australia, and has issue:

1e *(Mary) Jane; *b* 8 Sept 1954

2e *Lesa Kathleen [Mrs George Smith, 1815 Silverado Trail, Napa, Calif 94558, USA]; *b* 20 Aug 1959; *m* 1988 *George Emerson Smith

3d +Christopher Nigel; *b* 22 Jan 1929; *educ* Lancing; *m* 2 May 1953 (*divorce* 1964) Brenada Margaret, yr dau of Duncan Richard Penny, of Ferring, Sussex, and has issue:

1e +Nigel Richard; *b* 5 March 1956; *m* 1980 *Valerie Reeling, and has issue:

1f *Kirstie June; *b* 1982

1e *Gillian Grace; *b* 5 May 1958; *m* 1977 (*divorce* 1984) Alan Lawrence Sussex, and has issue:

1f *Charlene Louise; *b* 1978

2c William Earle, Capt 5th Bn KRRC; *b* 6 Jan 1897; *ka* 10 Nov 1917

3c John Michael; *b* 22 Oct 1899; *m* 9 April 1947 May (*d* 3 Jan 1966), dau of John Horwood, of Headington, Oxon

4c Richard Montagu, DSO (1944) and bar (1945), Brig Cameronians (Scottish Rifles) WW II (despatches, wounded); *b* 10 Sept 1905; *educ* Winchester and RMC Sandhurst; *m* 9 June 1932 *Nancy [Mrs Richard Villiers, 4 Orford Mews, Puddletown, Dorchester, Dorset DT2 8TL, er dau of Lt-Gen Sir Charles Alexander Campbell Godwin, KCB, CMG, DSO, and *d* 8 Aug 1973, leaving issue:

1d +Timothy Charles, Lt-Col 15th/19th The King's Roy Hus; *b* 16 March 1943; *educ* Eton and RMA Sandhurst, *m* 1971 *Maureen McCahearty, and has issue:

1e +Nicholas Charles; *b* 20 Feb 1976

2e +Richard Henry; *b* 1980

1e *Louise Elizabeth; *b* 29 Jan 1973

1d *(Judith) Annette [Mrs Rupert McCarthy, Rew Cottage, Buckland Newton, Dorchester DT2 7DN]; *b* 11 April 1935; *m* 30 April 1960 *Brig Rupert Henry George McCarthy, 15th/19th The King's Roy Hus, 2nd son of George McCarthy, of The Old Rectory, Ash-by-Wrotham, Kent, and has issue:

1e *William Rupert; *b* 28 Feb 1963; *m* 19 April 1997 *Louise Stickland

1e *Sarah Victoria; *b* 28 Feb 1961; *m* 20 Dec 1997 *Simon Robert James Thornton, of Trevone, Cornwall

2e *Meriel Anne; *b* 8 April 1966; *m* 9 Sept 1995 *Andrew David Lane, of Balaklava, Adelaide, Australia and has:

1f *Henry George Harold; *b* 6 April 1997

2d *Victoria Belinda [Mrs Robert Yeatman, 9 Clarendon Rd, Cambridge CB2 2BH]; *b* 24 March 1938; *m* 1 June 1963 *Robert Quentin Yeatman, yr son of Harry Morgan Yeatman, of 6 Morpeth Mansions, SW1, and has issue:

1e *Catherine Victoria; *b* 25 Aug 1964

2e *Lucy Belinda; *b* 22 Nov 1966

3e *Rosanna Charlotte; *b* 1973

3d *Carol Elspeth [Mrs Charles Hammick, Higher Waterston Farm, Dorchester, Dorset DT2 7SW]; *b* 27 Dec 1944; *m* 1st 18 Sept 1965 (*divorce* 1981) Maj Gerald Charles Mordaunt, yr son of Eustace John Mordaunt, of Oathall Cottage, Haywards Heath, Sussex (*see* MORDAUNT, Bt), and has issue; *m* 2nd 1984, as his 3rd w, Maj Charles Cyril Willmott Hammick (*see* HAMMICK, Bt)

3b Thomas Lister (Sir), MLC Ceylon 1924–31; *b* 31 Oct 1869; *m* 1st 4 Nov 1896 Evelyn (*d* 19 Dec 1938), dau of William Higgin Walker, of Bellwood, Ceylon; *m* 2nd 23 Sept 1953 Marjorie Glencora (*d* 9 Dec 1964), dau of Edwin Keyt, of Colombo, Ceylon, and *d* 21 Dec 1959, having by 1st w had issue:

1c Henry Lister, Lt 6th Dragoons, and RFC; *b* 21 July 1896; *ka* 4 Feb 1917

2c Thomas Hyde, Cdr RN WW II; *b* 15 Jan 1902; *m* 19 June 1925 Eleanor (*d* 12 May 1958), yst dau of Francis Edgar Croft (*see* CROFT, Bt, of Cowling Hall), and *d* 31 Oct 1955, leaving issue:

1d Nicholas Lister; *b* 19 May 1926; *educ* Eton; Lt RN; *m* 3 April 1954 *Betty Midelton [Mrs Nicholas Villiers, Heatherlands, Orford Rd, Bromeswell, nr Woodbridge, Suffolk IP12 2PP], 2nd dau of Capt Sidney Ralph Midelton Barlow, of Wayside, Chalfont St Giles, Bucks (*see* BARLOW, Bt, of Bradwall Hall), and *d* 1984, leaving issue:

1e +Derek Midelton Lister [Derek Villiers Esq, Willows End, Orford Rd, Bromeswell, nr Woodbridge, Suffolk IP12 2PP]; *b* 2 May 1958; *m* 1984 *Deborah, dau of Christopher John Randall, of 22 Glos Glanlliw, Pontlliw, Swansea, Glam, and has issue:

1f +Nicholas Christopher Lister; *b* 1985

2f +George Alexander; *b* 1991

1f *Catriona Sarah; *b* 1987

1e *Caroline Patricia [Miss Caroline Villiers, 8 Ravenswood, New Town Rd, Colchester, Essex CO1 2EG]; *b* 22 April 1960

2d +Stephen Hyde; *b* 15 May 1931; *educ* Eton; *m* 14 June 1958 *Elizabeth Jill, only dau of John Stewart Jeffrey Chapple, of Clayton, Hadham Rd, Bishops Stortford, Herts, and has issue:

1e +Harry Hyde; *b* 28 April 1959

2e +Timothy Stewart; *b* 3 July 1960

3e +Hugo James; *b* 1962

1e *Lucinda Victoria; *b* 24 July 1961

4b Godfrey Robert Randell; *b* 22 Aug 1877; *m* 10 July 1907 Sylvia (*d* 7 Dec 1926), dau of James Moore Bennett, MD, and *d* 23 Oct 1925, leaving issue:

1c *Sylvia Betty; *b* 18 June 1915; *m* 28 Dec 1934 *Stavros Sirakos, son of Nicholas Sirakos, of Smyrna, and has issue:

1d *Denise Catherine; *b* 25 Nov 1935; *m* 5 July 1961 *Lt Philippe Moulierac, son of Cdr Jean Moulierac, of Chateau Bresson, St Jeannet, AM, France, and has issue:

1e *Christophe Jean Philippe; *b* 12 May 1964

1e *Pascale Mireille Monique; *b* 29 Nov 1967

1b Frances Adelaide; *m* 1st 6 June 1893 Arthur Francis Walrond, son of Theodore Walrond, CB. He *dsp* 17 Jan 1906. She *m* 2nd 26 July 1910 Col Charles William Ernest Duncombe, only son of Hon Cecil Duncombe (*see* FEVERSHAM, B), and *d* 3 July 1934

2b Gwendolen Mary; *d* unm 2 May 1941

3b Margaret Evelyn, Sister of Mercy at St Peter's Home, Grahamstown, S Africa; *d* unm 15 Feb 1961

4b Dorothy; *m* 27 July 1898 Rev Preb William Frederick Herbert Randolph, Sub-Dean of Wells, son of Rev Canon Randolph, Chllr of York, and *d* 10 Feb 1961. He *d* 19 March 1946

5b Mabel Agatha; *d* unm 6 Nov 1966

6b Katharine Helen, Sister of Mercy at St Peter's Home, Grahamstown, S Africa; *d* unm Nov 1951

1a (cont.) The Rev Henry Villiers *m* 2nd 9 Jan 1883 Charlotte Louisa Emily (*d* 3 June 1947), dau of Hon Frederick William Cadogan (*see* CADOGAN, E), and *d* 9 Sept 1908, having by her had issue:

5b Paul Frederick, DSO (1917), Maj late 14th Hus Canadian Local Forces, and GSO(2) 1917, Fell Roy Cwlth Soc, Order of Danilo of Montenegro 4th Cl; *b* 8 July 1884; *educ* Harrow and RMC Sandhurst; *m* 24 Oct 1912 Evelyn (*d* 1*1973), *dau of Edward S Webb, of Park Crescent, Brighton, and d* 24 May 1968, leaving issue:

1c *Pauline Mary Lethbridge [Mrs Dennis Dunnill, 8 St Lucia, West Parade, Bexhill-on-Sea, E Sussex TN39 3DT]; *b* 31 Jan 1914; *m* 29 Sept 1936 Dennis Estyn Dunnill, MB, BS, MRCS, LRCP, DA, Maj RAMC (*d* 1986), yr son of Arthur Harry Dunnill, and has issue:

1d *Richard Paul Hyde [Richard Dunnill Esq, Dairy Farm House, Avon, nr Ringwood, Hants BH23 7BG]; *b* 10 Oct 1945; *educ* Charterhouse and Guys Hosp; MB, BS, LRCP, MRCS, FFARCS; *m* 1st 1971 (*divorce* 1977) Rosamund Strange, and has issue:

1e *Robert James Hyde; *b* 1975

1d (cont.) Richard Dunnill *m* 2nd 1978 *Charlotte Gorter, and has further issue:

2e *Charles William Hyde; *b* 1981

1e *Elizabeth Anna; *b* 1979

2e *Sarah Denise; *b* 1986

1d *Veronica Mary [Mrs Andrew Gottlieb, 34 Boston Close, Sovereign Harbour, Eastbourne BN23 6RA]; *b* 7 Sept 1937; *m* 1st 14 Sept 1963 (*divorce* 1973) Timothy Mawdsley Welch, 2nd son of Ronald Gordon Welch, of Old Barn Ho, Gt Canfield, Dunmow, Essex; *m* 2nd 1982 *Andrew Charles Gottlieb, and by 1st husb has issue:

1e *Andrew Ronald Mawdsley; *b* 20 July 1968

1e *Nicola Mary; *b* 16 June 1966

2d *Angela Evelyn, JP (W Yorks) [Mrs Raymond Barker JP, 109 Tadcaster Rd, Dringhouses, York YO2 2XA]; *b* 15 April 1939; *m* 23 July 1966 *(William) Raymond Barker, son of Frederick Barker, of Bradford, Yorks, and has issue:

1e *Christopher Paul Howard; *b* 24 Sept 1967

1e *Caroline Susan; *b* 15 Sept 1969

6b Gerald Berkeley, OBE (1919), Capt RN, served WWs I and II and with CCG 1945–47, Order of Crown of Italy, Chev Legion of Honour; *b* 14 June 1885; *m* 10 Oct 1918 Rachel Joan, dau of Rev Henry Vernon Heber-Percy (*see* NORTHUMBERLAND, D), and *d* 21 Feb 1959, leaving issue:

1c +Anthony Henry Herbert [Anthony Villiers Esq, The Old Priory, N Woodchester, Stroud, Glos], MFH, Capt Grenadier Gds WW II; *b* 19 March 1921 *educ* Nautical Coll Pangbourne; *m* 9 April 1948 *Rosemary Elizabeth, yr dau of Maj (William) Bertram Bell, JP, 12th Lancers, of Fota Island, Queenstown, Co Cork, and has issue:

1d +(Anthony James) Valentine [Valentine Villiers Esq, The Kennels, Petworth Park, Petworth, W Sussex GU28 9LR]; *b* 8 Sept 1949; *educ* Aiglon Coll; *m* 1st 1974 Sally Wilson, and has issue:

1e +Henry Anthony Edward; *b* 1978

1d (cont.) Valentine Villiers *m* 2nd 1984 *Sara A, dau of Basil Gotto, of Willowhill Ho, Carrigaline, Co Cork, and has further issue:

1e *Delia Dorothy; *b* 1989

2e *Geraldine Olive; *b* 1990

2d Charles Henry; *b* 10 May 1954; *educ* Milton Abbey; *d* 1980

1d *(Rosemary) Henrietta Dorothy; *b* 8 Sept 1950; *m* 1st 17 Nov 1973 (*divorce* 1978) Peregrine Banbury, son of Ralph Banbury; *m* 2nd 1978 *William Murray Lucas (*d* 1982) and adopted:

*Elizabeth Jacquetta; *b* 1981

2d *Emma Helen; *b* 16 Oct 1963; *m* 1988 *Richard Henry Ronald Benyon, and has issue (*see* SHELLEY, Bt)

7b Oliver George Graham, DSO (1918), Maj RAF, Sr Assist Staff of Directorate Civil Aviation Air Min 1919–39, Dir Special Intell Branch Min of Home Security 1939–48, MOD 1948–51, served WW I (despatches), Croix de Guerre and Legion of Honour of France; *b* 28 June 1886; *educ* Harrow; *m* 6 July 1918 Aleen Judith (*d* 1976), 2nd dau of Rev Henry Vernon Heber-Percy (*see* NORTHUMBERLAND, D), and *d* 1981, having had issue:

1c David Hugh, DFC, W/Cdr RAFVR WW II (despatches twice), freelance film director and writer; *b* 30 Sept 1921; *educ* Stowe; *m* 1st 4 March 1942 (*divorce* 1946) Freida Patricia, only child of Richard Payne, and had issue:

1d +Robin Julian; *b* 20 Oct 1945; *m* 1974 *Birgitte, dau of Peter Stafford

1c (cont.) W/Cdr David Villiers *m* 2nd 21 May 1954 *Elizabeth Barbara [Mrs John Rumble, White Horse Cottage, School St, Stoke-by-Nayland, Suffolk CO6 4QY] (*m* 2nd 1992 Capt John B Rumble (*d* 2 July 1996)), dau of Leonard Hobbins, and *d* 12 Sept 1962, leaving by her:

2d +Christopher Francis [Christopher Villiers Esq, 100 Elsenham St, London SW18 5NT]; *b* 7 Sept 1958; actor; *m* 1985 *Katherine, only dau of William Threlfall, of London SW6, and has issue:

1e +Charles Sebastian; *b* 1987

2e +Frederick James; *b* 1988

3d +Jonathan Paul [Jonathan Villiers Esq, Flat 4, 74 Casenove Rd, London N16 6AA]; *b* 23 Aug 1961; actor

1d *Catherine Judith [Ms Catherine Villiers, 18 Lenthall House, Claverton St, London SW1]; *b* 20 Dec 1955; film producer

1c *(Judith) Rosemary [Mrs Peter Locke-Wheaton, 3 West End, Spilsby, Lincs PE23 5ED]; *b* 17 Dec 1919; *m* 16 Sept 1949 Peter George Locke-Wheaton (*d* 1981), est son of George Locke Wheaton, of Fernheath Rd, Ensbury Park, Bournemouth, and has issue:

1d *Henry George [Henry Locke-Wheaton Esq, 36 Medgbury Rd, Swindon SN1 2AS]; *b* 14 March 1950; *educ* Lindsey Coll Lincoln; *m* 1st 1973 (*divorce* 1986) Cynthia Jane, dau of Eric Bagley; *m* 2nd 14 Feb 1995 *Mrs Christine Pokovel, *née* Mulcocke, and by his 1st w has:

1e *David George; *b* 1983

1e *Sarah Jane; *b* 1977

2e *Annabelle; *b* 1980

2d *John Antony Charles [John Locke-Wheaton Esq, 18 Evergreen Dve, Calcot, Reading, Berks]; *b* 14 Sept 1952; *educ* King Edward Sch, Louth, and Cambridge (MA); *m* 1977 *Margaret Patricia, dau of Rev George Clifford Hunt, and has issue:

1e *Stephen Antony; *b* 1983
1e *Jennifer Anne; *b* 1981
3d *Philip James [Philip Locke-Wheaton Esq, 64 Baldwin Rd, Kidderminster, Worcs]; *b* 24 July 1955; *m* 1980 *Janet Rosemary, dau of George Danks, and has issue:
1e *Daniel Philip; *b* 1981
2e *Luke Peter; *b* 1983
3e *Simon George; *b* 1990
1e *Naomi Janet; *b* 1985
2e *Miriam Rachel; *b* 1988
4d *Richard Oliver [Richard Locke-Wheaton Esq, Mill Cottage, Toynton-all-Saints, Lincs]; *b* 25 Feb 1957; *m* 1979 *Janice Sheila, dau of Peter Rothery, and has issue:
1e *Christopher James; *b* 1985
1e *Nicola Claire; *b* 1983
1d *(Henrietta) Mary-Anne [Mrs Graham Elliker, Roburs, The Common, W Chiltington, W Sussex]; *b* 4 June 1951; *m* 1st 1970 (*divorce* 1975) Richard Peter Noble, and has issue:
1e *Sarah Louise; *b* 1974
1d (cont.) Mrs Mary-Anne Noble *m* 2nd 1982 *Graham Roy Elliker, and has further issue:
1e *Hallam Piers Oliver; *b* 1983
2e *Camilla Aleen; *b* 1987
2d *Caroline Elizabeth [Mrs Caroline Hendy, 76 Newmarket Rd, Bulwell, Nottingham]; *b* 17 Sept 1953; *m* 1979 (*divorce* 1989) Capt Paul Hendy, Salvation Army, and has issue:
1e *Stuart James; *b* 1982
1e *Corrine Louise; *b* 1981
8b (Francis) Edward Earle (Sir), Lt RAF WW I and Afghan War 1919, MLC Bengal 1924–26, pres European Assoc of India 1931 and 1932; *b* 1 Jan 1889; *educ* Harrow and Ch Ch Oxford; *m* 20 Dec 1933 Katherine Mary Wakefield (*d* 21 Nov 1965), only dau of Hugh White, of Edinburgh, and *dsp* 20 March 1967
7b Edith Mary; *b* 24 Sept 1887; *m* 10 Oct 1916 (*divorce* 1927) Capt Montague W Hocker, MC, Scots Gds (SR), and *d* 1959
2a Frederick Ernest, Maj Herts Yeo Cav, JP Dumfriesshire and Ayrshire, memb Roy Co Archers; *b* 16 Nov 1840; *m* 20 July 1869 Jane Isabella (*d* 27 April 1943), dau and coheir of Douglas Baird, of Closeburn, and *d* 14 Oct 1922, having had issue:
1b George Frederick Montagu, Capt and Hon Maj 3rd Bn Roy Scots Fus; *b* 13 Sept 1870; *m* 2 Sept 1908 Mary Seton (*d* 17 Nov 1949), er dau of Thomas Jackson, son of Thomas Jackson, of Coats, by his w Jane, 2nd dau of Alexander Baird, of Lockwood (*see* KINTORE, E), and *d* 13 July 1934, having had issue:
1c *Jean Baird; *b* 21 July 1909
2c Barbara Mary; *b* 28 June 1911; *d* unm 11 May 1933
3c Constance Adelaide, WW II as Subaltern ATS; *b* 24 Aug 1913; *d* unm as a result of war service 8 May 1946
2b Charles Walter, CBE (1919), DSO (1916), Lt-Col Coldstream Gds (SR), memb Roy Co Archers, Lt 3rd Bn Roy Scots Fus WW I (despatches four times), Order of White Eagle of Serbia 5th Cl, Order Redeemer 3rd Cl Greece, Croix de Guerre, CStJ; *b* Sept 1873; *m* 1 Aug Lady Kathleen Mary Cole (*d* 17 June 1956), 2nd dau of 4th Earl of Enniskillen, KP (*qv*), and *d* Sept 1938, leaving issue:
1c (Francis) Berkeley Hyde, OBE (1945), Lt-Col RAOC WW II; *b* 8 Nov 1906; *educ* Eton; *m* 21 June 1938 *Rose Marie [Mrs Berkeley Villiers, Stone House, nr Kidderminster, Worcs], dau of Consul-Gen von Passavant, of Vienna (and niece of Sir George Franckenstein), and *d* 1991, leaving issue:
1d +Nicholas Hyde [Nicholas Villiers Esq, Stone House, nr Kidderminster, Worcs]; *b* 3 Dec 1939; *educ* Eton
1d Florence Angela; *b* 1 Nov 1934; *m* 31 July 1930 1st Baron Teviot, DSO, MC (*qv*), and *d* 1979, leaving issue
1c Helen Mary; *b* 17 April 1915; *m* 1st 25 April 1939 (*divorce* 1947) Capt Lord Eliot, DCLI, later 9th Earl of St Germans (*qv*), and had issue. She *m* 2nd 19 Nov 1947 Capt Ralph Benson, Coldstream Gds, son of Maj George Reginald Benson, of Lutwyche Hall, Salop, and *d* 6 Dec 1951, leaving further issue
3b Reginald Hyde, DSO (1900), Lt 12th Lancers SAfrica 1899–1902 (despatches); *b* 4 Aug 1876; *m* 31 Oct 1906 Florence Marianne (*d* 4 July 1937), dau of George Stockwell, of Dunedin, NZ, and *d* 20 July 1953, leaving issue:
1c +Frederick Montagu Hyde [Maj Frederick Villiers, Braemar, 13 Dixon Rd, Buderim, Qld 4556, Australia], Maj Ceylon L Inf; *b* 15 July 1907; *m* 1st 18 March 1936 (*divorce* 1947) Maisie Marguerite Hunt, and has issue:
1d *Judith Marianne [Mrs Geoffrey Hill, Ferndale RMB 4055, Limestone Rd, Yea, Vic 3717, Australia]; *b* 9 June 1937; *m* 1st 1958 (*divorce* 1973) David Price; *m* 2nd 1991 *Geoffrey Alan Hill, and by 1st husb has issue:
1e *Brett Alexander Hyde; *b* 1960; *m* 1986 *Lindy Sue Ferry, and has issue:
1f *Maddison Hyde; *b* 1988
2e *James Stuart; *b* 1961; *m* 1987 *Roslyn Anne Dimech, and has issue:
1f *Brock David; *b* 1987
1f *Tamsin Jean; *b* 1992
1c (cont.) Maj Frederick Villiers *m* 2nd 26 Jan 1948 (*divorce* 1959) Ann Sybella Chetwode, formerly w of Count Carl Otto Werner Schimmelmann, of Ahrensburg, Holstein, and dau of Rev Nixon Chetwode Ram, MA, of Petersfield, Hants; *m* 3rd 16 July 1959 *Sheila Joyce, 3rd dau of Charles Alexander Squair, of Reigate, Surrey, and widow of Douglas Montagu Baird, of Durris

2c George Pelham; *b* 23 March 1909; *m* 1st 7 July 1937 (*divorce* 1945) Gladys Mildred Moehr (*d* 1977); *m* 2nd 1945 Ursula Alison Paterson (*d* 26 June 1957), dau of John Hodgson, of Kotapala, Ceylon, and *d* 1989, having by 1st w had issue:
1d *Ursula Georgette Victoria Maria [Mrs Jonathan Burch, 10 Pitman Court, Gloucester Rd, Lower Swainswick, Bath, Avon]; *b* 1943; *m* 1st 1965 Lt John Philip Bear, RN (*d* 1967); *m* 2nd 1976 *Capt Jonathan Alexander Burch, CBE, RN, and by 1st husb has issue:
1e *Alexander George Philip Villiers; *b* 1966
1c Lyspeth Desirée; *b* 5 July 1911; *m* 1st 28 Nov 1931 (*divorce* 1944) F/Lt James Bryan Robertson, only son of James Robert Robertson, JP, CC, of Fairkytes, Hornchurch, Essex, and had issue; *m* 2nd 20 Oct 1944 Cdr Leonard Evelyn Romaine Govett, RNVR, yst son of F A Govett, of Sunningdale. He was *k* in an aeroplane accident, in Sydney, 19 July 1945. She *m* 3rd 19 Jan 1949 Maj Richard Vernon Lea, and *d* 19–
4b Evelyn Charles Arthur, Memb State Cncl Ceylon 1939; *b* 16 July 1884; *m* 17 July 1907 Dorothy Katherine (*d* 11 Sept 1976 aged 92), dau of Col George Howard Moore Lane, CMG, and *d* 27 Oct 1968, leaving issue:
1c (Robert) Alexander, CBE (1952), Capt RN, served WW II 1939–45 (despatches). and in Korea 1950–52; *b* 3 April 1908; *m* 1st 7 Jan 1933 Leila Alexandra (*d* 23 Aug 1938), est dau of Lt-Col William Alexander Victor Findlater, Roy Irish Fus, of The Croft, Tenterden, Kent, and has issue:
1d *(Diana) Susan [Mrs Ian Watt, Kingswood House, 8 Lower Green Rd, Esher, Surrey]; *b* 1 March 1935; *m* 1963 Ian Buchanan Watt, CMG (*d* 1988), son of John Watt, of Woodend, Barnhill, Perth, and has issue:
1e *James Alexander Macdonald; *b* 30 June 1965
2e *Robin John Macdonald; *b* 1969
1e *Harriet Leila Elizabeth; *b* 30 Dec 1970
1c (cont.) Capt Alexander Villiers *m* 2nd 21 Dec 1939 (*divorce* 1958) Elizabeth Mary (*d* 1985), dau of Maj-Gen Arthur Leslie Irvine Friend, CB, CBE, MC, DL, of Dynes Farm, Bethersden, Kent, and by her had issue:
1d Michael Alexander, Capt 11th Hus (PAO), Maj 1975; *b* 25 Jan 1941; *educ* Eton and RMA Sandhurst; *m* 1st 12 Oct 1968 (*divorce* 1982) Annabell Vanessa, dau of F R G N Sherrard, of South Lodge, Dorchester; *m* 2nd 1989 *Jean Annette Mary [Mrs Michael Villiers, Woodhouse Farm, Kingsworthy, Hants SO23 7LB], dau of Brig Robert Angus Graham Binny, CBE, of Pitt Farm Ho, Skilgate, Taunton, Somerset (*see* COVENTRY, E), and formerly w of Lt-Col William Robert Wilson FitzGerald, Roy Dragoons (*see* HARRINGTON, E), and *d* 1996, having had:
1e Patrick Alexander; *b* 1971; *d* 1972
1e *Annabel Jane; *b* 1975
2d +Charles Nigel [Charles Villiers Esq, 8 Sutherland St, London SW1], ACA; *b* 25 Jan 1941 (twin); *educ* Winchester and New Coll Oxford (BA), dir Nat Westminster Bank 1985–88 and Abbey National 1989–; *m* 1970 *Sally Priscilla, dau of Capt D H Magnay, RN, and has issue:
1e +Christopher Frederick Pelham; *b* 1976; *educ* Winchester and Edinburgh U
1e *Caroline Harriet; *b* 1974; *educ* St Mary's Calne, Charterhouse and Edinburgh U
1d *Sarah Jane Amanda; *b* 5 Jan 1956
1c (cont.) Capt Alexander Villiers *m* 3rd 8 July 1960 *(Irene) Mary [Mrs Alexander Villiers 33 Ennismore Gdns, London SW7], formerly w of Peter L Foulsham, and dau of William Ellis-Jones, of Isfryn, Eddisbury Rd, West Kirby, Cheshire, and *d* 1990
2c Kenneth Charles Howard; *b* 27 June 1912; Lt-Cdr RN WW II Burma and Far East (wounded), owner of Charles Howard Decoration Ltd and South River Furnishing Contracts, memb Exec Ctee Interior Designer and Decorators Assoc; *d* 1992
1c *Marjorie Francis [Mrs Henry Hoare, Sanctuary, 54 Copers Cope Rd, Beckenham, Kent]; *b* 28 March 1909; *m* 8 Feb 1932 *Henry Samuel Malortie Hoare, 3rd son of Lt-Col Arthur Fanshawe Hoare, CB, and has issue:
1d *Charles Antony Richard; *b* Jan 1934; *educ* King's Sch Canterbury and Merton Coll Oxford (MA); Prof Queen's Coll Belfast
2d *Arthur Malortie; *b* Dec 1934; *educ* King's Sch Canterbury and Trin Coll Oxford (MA, PhD)
3d *Henry Ronald John; *b* 1936; *educ* King's Sch Canterbury and St John's Coll, Cambridge (BA, MSc)
1d *Dorothy Ann Katherine; *b* 1945; *educ* St Hugh's Coll, Oxford (MA)
2d *Janet Frances Mary; *b* 1948; *educ* St Aidan's Coll Durham (BA)
1b Florence Katherine; *b* 6 March 1872; *m* 31 Aug 1893 Henry Robert Baird, of Durris, Drumoak, Aberdeenshire, and *d* 1955, leaving issue. He *d* 12 Feb 1929
2b Blanche Evelyn; *b* and *d* 1875
3b Freda Ernestine; *b* 8 May 1879; *d* unm 24 Dec 1940
1a Amy Maria; *m* 11 April 1860 Rev Edward Cheese, MA, Rector of Haughton-le-Skerne, Durham, and *d* 20 Oct 1934 leaving issue. He *d* 1886
2a Gertrude Fanny; *m* 22 Aug 1865 Berkeley Paget, DL, and *d* 31 Dec 1906, leaving issue (*see* ANGLESEY, M)
3a Mary Agneta; *m* 4 April 1872 Rev James Hughes Cooper, Vicar of Cuckfield, Sussex, and Hon Canon of Chester, and 22 May 1935, leaving issue. He *d* 21 July 1909
4a Evelyn Theresa; *d* unm 29 Dec 1943
(6) Augustus Algernon, Lt RN; *b* 14 April 1817; *d* 1843
(1) Maria Theresa; *m* 1st 6 Nov 1830 Thomas Henry Lister, of Armytage Park, Staffs, and had issue. He *d* 5 June 1842. She *m* 2nd 25 Oct 1844 Rt Hon Sir George Cornewall Lewis, 2nd Bt, MP, and *d* 9 Nov 1865. He *dsp* 13 April 1863

1 Charlotte Barbara; *b* 27 March 1761; *d* 9 April 1810

The 3rd EARL's nephew,

GEORGE WILLIAM FREDERICK VILLIERS, **4th Earl of Clarendon**, KG (1849), GCB (1837), PC (1840); *b* 26 Jan 1800; *educ* St John's Coll Cambridge; Attaché St Petersburg 1820–23, Commr Customs 1824–33, Envoy Madrid 1833–39, Ld Privy Seal (Lib) 1840–41, Chllr Duchy of Lancaster 1840–41 and 1864–65, Pres BOT 1846–47, Ld Lt Ireland 1847–52, For Sec 1853–58, 1865–66 and 1868–70, DCL Oxon 1856; *m* 4 June 1839 Lady Katharine (*d* 4 July 1874), widow of John Foster Barham, of Stockbridge, Hants, and dau of 1st Earl of Verulam (*qv*), and had issue:

1 Edward Hyde, *Lord Hyde*; *b* 30 Jan 1845; *d* 26 Feb 1846

2 EDWARD HYDE, **5th Earl**

3 George Patrick Hyde, CB, CMG, Col Gren Gds, Mil Sec to Govr-Gen India, Mil Attaché St Petersburg, Berlin and Paris; *b* 27 Sept 1847; *m* 9 Oct 1884 Louisa Maria (*m* 2nd 28 June 1894 Maj Hon Gilbert Legh, Gren Gds, 2nd son of 1st Baron Newton (*qv*), and *d* 22 Nov 1932), dau of George Disney Maquay, of Florence, and *d* 10 Jan 1892, having had issue:

(1) George John Theodore Hyde, Lt Gren Gds (SR) WW I (wounded), served in Press Censorship 1939–40; *b* 1 Oct 1891; *m* 16 Sept 1931 Marjorie (*d* 3 Aug 1982), dau of Maj-Gen Sir Francis Howard, KCB, KCMG (*see* NORFOLK, D), and *d* 12 March 1942, having had issue:

1a Michael George; *b* 10, *d* 25 Dec 1937

(1) Katharine Alice (Hon), Maid of Honour to HM QUEEN MARY 1911, Actg Lady-in-Waiting to HRH PRINCESS PATRICIA OF CONNAUGHT 1913–19; *b* 16 Aug 1885; *d* unm 5 May 1944

(2) Constance Barbara; *b* 2 Aug 1886; *d* 24 Jan 1922

(3) Beryl Emily Edith; *b* 18 Dec 1888; *d* 31 March 1889

4 Francis Hyde (Sir), PC, GCMG, GCVO, CB, FO: joined 1870, Priv Sec to PUS 1875–92, Actg Sec Dip Serv 1885, Priv Sec to For Sec 1886 and 1892–94, Assist U-Sec 1896–1905, Envoy Extrdy and Min Plen Lisbon 1906–11 and Brussels 1911–19, Amb 1919–20, Grand Cross Christ Portugal and Leopold Belgium; *b* 13 Aug 1852; *m* 28 June 1876 Virginia Katharine (*d* 12 Dec 1937), 2nd dau of Eric Carrington Smith, DL, of Ashfold, Handcross, Sussex, and *d* 18 Nov 1925, having had issue:

(1) Eric Hyde, DSO (1919), Capt 1st Bn HLI WW I (despatches); *b* 2 Feb 1881; *educ* Wellington; *m* 11 Dec 1928 Joan Ankaret (*d* 1986), yr dau of John Edward Talbot (*see* SHREWSBURY and WATERFORD, E), and *d* 16 May 1964, having had issue:

1a +Henry Hyde, JP (Kent) [Henry Villiers Esq JP, Icknor House, South Green, Sittingbourne, Kent]; *b* 8 March 1931; *educ* Wellington; High Sheriff Kent 1992; *m* 1 Oct 1959 *Mary Elizabeth Cavan, dau of Robert Hugh Swan Corbett, of Yalding, Kent, and has had issue:

1b Alexander Robert Hyde; *b* 24 Aug, *d* 13 Dec 1966

2b +Charles James Hyde; *b* 4 Nov 1967

3b +Robert Henry Hyde; *b* 17 June 1969

1b *Charlotte Amelia; *b* 11 Feb 1961; *m* 1988 *Christopher H C Figg, est son of Sir Leonard Clifford William Figg, KCMG, of Gt Missenden, Bucks, and has issue:

1c *Orlando; *b* 1992

2b *Henrietta Barbara; *b* 21 Jan 1962; *m* 1986 *Alastair Henderson Scott, son of Paul Henderson Scott, CMG, of Dolphin Sq, London SW1

2a James Michael Hyde; *b* 29 Sept 1933; *educ* Wellington; actor; *m* 1st 20 Aug 1966 (*divorce* 1984) Patricia, est dau of William Victor Donovan, of Fern Ho, Pembroke, and adopted Sept 1967:

*Alan Michael Hyde (formerly Alan Donovan)

2a (cont.) James Villiers *m* 2nd 30 July 1994 *Lucinda Claire, dau of Nita Jex, of Washington, W Sussex, and *d* 18 Jan 1998

3a +John Francis Hyde [John Villiers Esq, 21 Overstrand Mansions, Prince of Wales Dve, London SW11 4EZ]; *b* 24 Jan 1936; *educ* Winchester and King's Coll Cambridge (BA 1957, MA 1960, PhD 1962) Br Cncl Offr from 1960–79, dir Br Inst SE Asia 1978–86, Fell Roy Asiatic Soc, FRSA; *m* 19 July 1958 *Myee Miranda, est dau of Lt-Col David McKenna, CBE, late RE, of 21 Kylestrom House, Cundy St, London, and Rosteague House, Portscatho, Truro, Cornwall, by Lady Cecilia Elizabeth, er dau of 9th Earl of Albemarle (*qv*), and has:

1b +Daniel James Hyde; *b* 20 Oct 1960; *educ* Ampleforth and Harrow Coll of Art

1b *Cecilia Ankaret [Mrs David Holdsworth, Vigeau, St Mézard, Lectoure 32700, France]; *b* 20 Feb 1962; *m* 1983 *David Michael Holdsworth, yr son of G M Holdsworth, of Seal, Kent

2b *Antonia Aniela [Miss Antonia Villiers, Meadows Born, Blakeney Rd, Letheringsett, Norfolk NR25 7YD]; *b* 21 Sept 1965

3b *Susanna Sophia [Miss Susanna Villiers, 68A Prince of Wales Mansions, Prince of Wales Dve, London SW11 4BJ] (twin); *b* 21 Sept 1965

1a Penelope Barbara; *b* 10 Jan, *d* 15 May 1930

(2) Gerald Hyde, CMG (1923), Assist Sec Dept Ec Warfare FO, Counsellor 1903–29, Min Ec Warfare WW II, Cdr Order Orange-Nassau; *b* 31 Aug 1882; *d* unm 10 Feb 1953

(3) Algernon Hyde, Lt Lothians and Border Horse, attached MGC; *b* 1 Feb 1886; *m* 4 Oct 1911 Beatrix Elinor (*m* 2nd 6 Nov 1919 4th Baron Aldenham and (2nd Baron) Hunsdon of Hunsdon (*qv*)), only dau of Herbert Woodfield Paul, late MP, and was *ka* 23 Nov 1917, leaving issue:

1a Charles English Hyde (Sir), ktd 1975, MC (1945), Lt-Col Gren Gds SR WW II; OStJ, chm: BSC 1976–80, Guinness Mahon 1971–76, dir: Bass Charrington, Courtaulds, Sun Life Assur; memb Chelsea Borough Cncl 1950–53, tstee ROH 1974–79; Order of the People Yugoslavia 1970, Grand Offr Leopold Belgium 1974; *b* 14 Aug 1912; *educ* Eton and New Coll Oxford; *m* 1st 9 June 1938 Pamela Constance (*d* 17 Oct 1943), dau of Maj John Flower, 60th Rifles, and had issue:

1b +Nicholas Hyde [Nicholas Villiers Esq, St Leonard's Grange, Beaulieu, Hants], Lt Gren Gds (AER); *b* 10 April 1939; *educ* Eton; *m* 1983 *Hon Mrs Catherine Mary Wilbraham, 2nd dau of 1st Viscount De L'Isle, VC, KG, GCMG, GCVO, PC (*qv*)

2b Robert Hyde; *b* and *d* 17 Oct 1943

1a (cont.) Sir Charles *m* 2nd 26 Oct 1946 *Countess Marie José de la Barre [Lady Villiers, Blacknest House, Sunninghill, Berks], dau of Count Henri de la Barre d'Erquelinnes, of Jurbise, Belgium, and *d* 1992, having by her had issue:

1b *Diana Mary, Chevalier Leopold Belgium 1974; *b* 14 Aug 1947; *m* 14 Dec 1976 *Hon John Dimitri Negroponte, US Foreign Serv Offr, son of Dimitri Negroponte

2b *Anne Hyde; *b* 25 Jan 1950; *m* 1st 1 Sept 1973 Paul Nuttall Kesterton, son of Robin N Kesterton, of Robin Hill, Poole, Dorset; *m* 2nd 1993 *Thomas Martin, and by 1st husb has issue:

1c *Toby; *b* 1977

1c *Lara Beatrice; *b* 1979

1a *Mary Theresa, served WW II in WRNS; *b* 16 Sept 1917; *m* 14 March 1945 Lt-Col Sir Peter Allix Wilkinson, CMG, DSO, OBE, Dep U-Sec of State and Ch Clerk FCO 1968, late The Roy Fusiliers, only child of Capt Osborn Cecil Wilkinson, 15th Foot (E Yorks), and has issue:

1b *Virginia Caroline; *b* 3 May 1947; *m* 1971 *Daniel Worsley

2b *Alexandra Mary; *b* 21 Sept 1953

(1) Dorothy; *b* 20 Feb 1879; *m* 1st 9 July 1904 Capt Hugh Craufurd Keith-Fraser, and had issue (*see* 1970 edn FRASER, Bt, of Ledeclune). He *d* 19 May 1906. She *m* 2nd 8 Feb 1910 Capt Jocelyn Henry Clive Graham, Coldstream Gds, son of Sir Henry Graham, KCB, and *d* 11 Jan 1942, leaving issue. He *d* 30 Oct 1936

(2) Marjory Mildred; *b* 9 May 1890; *m* 1 Sept 1919 Capt Ivan Snell, MC, barrister (*d* 29 Aug 1958), only son of Edward Snell, of 5 Rutland Gate, SW, and had issue:

1a Christopher Villiers Ivan, Lt Gren Gds, served WW II; *b* 29 Nov 1921; *educ* Eton and Trin Coll Oxford; *ka* 27 June 1944

2a *Francis Ivan, served WW II 1942–46; *b* 9 May 1923; *educ* Canford; *m* 3 Aug 1968 *Francesca Braithwaite Bell, and has issue:

1b *Ivan Francis; *b* 5 June 1969

1a Julianna Mary Ivan; *b* 23 June 1920; WRNS WW II; *m* 8 Dec 1945 Sir Ralph Walford Selby, CMG (*d* 21 Feb 1997), Consul-Gen at Boston from 1966, er son of Sir Walford Harmood Selby, KCMG, CB, CVO, and *d* 19 March 1994, leaving:

1b *(Mary) Virginia; *b* 13 May 1947

2b *Pamela Marjory Dorothy; *b* 26 July 1953

3b *Cynthia Elizabeth Mildred; *b* 19 July 1953

1 Constance; *m* 31 May 1864 16th Earl of Derby, KG (*qv*), and *d* 17 April 1922, leaving issue

2 Alice; *m* 16 Aug 1860 1st Earl of Lathom, GCB (*see* 1930 edn), and *d* 23 Nov 1897, leaving issue. He *d* 19 Nov 1898

3 Emily Theresa, VA; *m* 5 May 1868 1st Baron Ampthill, GCB, GCMG (*qv*), and *d* 22 Feb 1927, leaving issue

4 Florence Margaret; *d* an infant, 25 Aug 1851

The 4th EARL *d* 27 June 1870; his est surv son,

EDWARD HYDE VILLIERS, **5th Earl of Clarendon**, PC (1900), GCB (1902), GCVO (1905), DL, JP Warwicks; *b* 11 Fen 1846; *educ* Harrow and Trin Coll Cambridge; Ld Lt and Custos Rotulorum Herts, Pres and Chm Herts TA, MA Cambridge, Ld-in-Waiting 1895–1900, Ld Chamberlain 1900–05, Hon Col cmdg Herts Yeo (TD), ADC to TM QUEEN VICTORIA, EDWARD VII and GEORGE V, MP (Lib) Brecon 1869–70; *m* 1st 6 Sept 1876 Lady Caroline Elizabeth Agar (*d* 9 May 1894), est dau of 3rd Earl of Normanton (*qv*); *m* 2nd 5 Aug 1908 Emma Mary Augusta (*d* 9 March 1935), widow of Maj Hon Edward Roden Bourke (*see* MAYO, E) and er dau of Lt-Gen George Cliffe Hatch, CSI, and by his 1st w had issue:

1 GEORGE HERBERT HYDE, **6th Earl**

1 Edith; *b* 8 Nov 1878; *m* 15 May 1911 5th Earl of Mount Edgcumbe (*qv*), and *d* 1 Aug 1935

The 5th EARL *d* 2 Oct 1914; his only son,

GEORGE HERBERT HYDE VILLIERS, **6th Earl of Clarendon**, KG (1937), PC (1931), GCMG (1930), GCVO (1939), DL, JP Herts, Hon LLD U of Witwatersrand 1937, dir GEC, Extra ADC to Ld-Lt Ireland 1902–05, Chllr Primrose League 1919–21, Hon Lt-Col, Ld-in-Waiting to HM GEORGE V 1921–22, Ch Conservative Whip Ho Lds and Capt Gentlemen-at-Arms 1922–25, ParlyU-Sec Dominion Affs and chm Overseas Settlement Ctee 1925–27, chm BBC 1920–30, Govr-Gen and C-in-C Union of South Africa 1931–37, Ld Chamberlain and Chllr Roy Victorian Order 1938–52, Roy Victorian Chain 1952, Chllr St Michael and St George 1942, Grand Cross Legion of Honour, Orange-Nassau, St Olav of Norway and Dannebrog Denmark; *b* 7 June 1877; *m* 5 Aug 1905 Hon Adeline Verena Ishbel, JP, DGStJ, Hon LLD U of Witwatersrand (*d* 6 Feb 1963), only surv dau of Herbert Haldane Somers Cocks and sis of 6th Baron Somers (*qv*), and *d* 13 Dec 1955, having had:

1 George Herbert Arthur Edward Hyde, *Lord Hyde*; *b* 6 May 1906 (HM GEORGE V stood sponsor); *educ* Eton and Trin Coll Oxford (BA); 2nd Lt RHG; *m* 18 April 1932 Hon Marion Feodorovna Louise Glyn, DCVO (1961, CVO 1945), Woman of the Bedchamber to HM THE QUEEN (later QUEEN ELIZABETH THE QUEEN MOTHER) 1937–61, Extra Woman of the Bedchamber 1961–70 (*d* 13 Dec 1970), er dau of 4th Baron Wolverton (*qv*), and *d* 27 April 1935, leaving issue:

(1) GEORGE FREDERICK LAURENCE HYDE VILLIERS, **7th and present Earl of Clarendon**

(1) *Rosemary Verena Edith [The Lady Rosemary Steel, Glebe House, Notgrove, Cheltenham, Glos]; *b* posthumously 29 June 1935; granted rank of earl's dau 20 July 1956; *m* 15 Jan 1959 *Richard Hugh Jordan Steel, er son of Sir Christopher Eden Steel, GCMG, MVO (*see* BUXTON, Bt), and has issue:

1a *James Thomas Jordan [James Steel Esq, 66 Manville Rd, London SW17 8JL]; *b* 16 April 1960; *m* 1989 *Lindsay J, er dau of Michael Farrell, of Much Hadham, Herts, and has issue:

1b *Frederick James Edward; *b* 1993

1b *Sophie Mary Verena; *b* 1991

2a *Oliver George Nigel; *b* 5 April 1962; *m* 1992 *Jacqueline E, yr dau of Colin Quaife, of Lea, Wilts

1a *Arabella Rosemary Louise; *b* 14 March 1966
2 +(William) Nicholas Somers Laurence Hyde, JP (Hants 1957), Maj Gren Gds, Supp Res of Offrs served WW II 1939–45, OStJ [Major The Hon Nicholas Villiers JP, Firs Farm, Milbourne, Malmesbury, Wilts]; *b* 17 July 1916 (HRH the DUKE OF CONNAUGHT stood sponsor); *educ* Eton and New Coll Oxford; *m* 4 May 1939 *Mary Cecilia Georgina, er dau of Maj Hon Edric Alfred Cecil Weld-Forester, CVO (*see* FORESTER, B), and has issue:
(1) *Caroline Jane [Mrs Caroline Havard, 21 Glycena Rd, London SW11 5TP]; *b* 14 June 1940; *m* 2 May 1964 (*divorce* 1974) John Kenneth Holmes Havard, yr son of Rt Rev William Thomas Havard, Bishop of St Davids
(2) *Nerena Anne Hyde [Mrs Nerena Stephenson, Old Posting House, Didmarton, nr Badminton, Glos]; *b* 18 July 1941; *m* 14 April 1966 (*divorce* 1980) Timothy Congreve Stephenson, est son of Augustus William Stephenson, of Saxbys Mead, Cowden, nr Edenbridge, Kent (*see* HAWARDEN,V), and has issue:
1a *Guy Congreve; *b* 23 Nov 1969
2a *Henry Frederick; *b* 1978
1a *Lucinda Mary Pamela; *b* 19 April 1967
2a *Henrietta Cecilia; *b* 1975
(3) *(Elizabeth) Georgina Gail [Mrs Edward Jewson, Wacton House, Norwich, Norfolk NR15 2UF]; *b* 19 Oct 1952 (HM THE QUEEN stood sponsor); *m* 1980 *Edward R R Jewson, only son of Col John Jewson, MC, of Mergate Hall, Norwich, and has issue:
1a *Sophie Emily Josceline; *b* 1987
2a *Isobel Mary Elizabeth; *b* 1988
1 (Nina) Joan Edith Virgina, DStJ; *b* 10 Dec 1908; *m* 27 June 1933 George Christopher Newman, MA, FRICS, only son of Frank Newman, of The Lodge, 6 Egerton Terrace, SW, and *d* 28 Oct 1971, leaving issue:
(1) *Robin George, Lt Coldstream Gds; *b* 15 July 1936; *educ* Eton and Ch Ch Oxford
(1) *Jillian Ann, MCSP, MNZSP; *b* 24 April 1934; *educ* Downham, Sorbonne, and St Mary's Hosp, Paddington

CLARK of Dunlambert

Arms: Barry wavy of four arg. and az., a galley with sail set and flags flying, all or, on a chief of the second a thistle slipped with two leaves between two roses of the third. **Crest:** A demi-huntsman ppr., habited az., blowing a horn or. **Motto:** Free for a blast.
Creation: Bt. (UK) 6 July 1917.

SIR JONATHAN GEORGE CLARK, 5TH BT, of Dunlambert, Belfast [Sir Jonathan Clark Bt, Somerset House, Threapwood, Malpas, Cheshire SY14 7AW]; *b* 9 Oct 1947; *s f* 1995; *educ* Eton; Capt RGJ 1966–78; md Paragon Homes Ltd 1992–; *m* 1971 *Susan Joy, dau of Brig Thomas Ian Gordon Gray, and has issue:
1 +SIMON GEORGE GRAY; *b* 3 Oct 1975; *educ* Shrewsbury
1 *Polly Caroline; *b* 1973
2 *Tessa Louise; *b* 1978

Lineage: ALLEN CLARK, of Dykebar; *m* 20 Aug 1673 Janet Stuart and *d* in or after 1710, leaving an est s:
ALLAN CLARK, of Dykebar; *b* 19 Dec 1677; *m* 7 June 1700 Agnes, dau of James Snodgrass, of Carriagehill, and had a 2nd s:
WILLIAM CLARK, of Dykebar; *b* 4 Dec 1710; *m* 6 May 1736 Agnes Bryson, of Yoker, Renfrew, and had a 5th s:
JAMES CLARK, of Paisley; *b* 12 Sept 1747; *m* 8 Oct 1768 Margaret (*d* 9 Nov 1825), est child of Andrew Campbell, and *d* 6 Oct 1829, leaving, with an est s, another s and seven daus:
1 JAMES
2 John, of Gateside; *see* STEWART-CLARK, Bt
The 2nd son,
JAMES CLARK, of Chapel Ho, Paisley; *b* 1782; *m* 20 April 1830 Agnes (*d* 10 Sept 1836), dau and coheir of James McFarlane, and *d* 19 Oct 1865, having had, with a dau (*d* an infant):
1 JAMES
2 Robert, of The Hollies, Kirn, Argyll; *b* 8 March 1833; *m* 22 July 1857 Ellen Elizabeth, dau of Robert Corry, of Belfast, and *d* 6 May 1928, leaving. with other issue:
(1) Alexander King; *b* 8 Sept 1872; *m* 9 April 1907 Katherine Margaret Elizabeth Mainwaring (*d* 18 Oct 1927), dau of Col Cuthbert George Knocker, and *d* 28 Oct 1918, leaving issue:
1a Robert KING-CLARK, MBE, MC, Lt-Col Manchester Regt and The Glider Pilot Regt, matriculated arms at Court of Ld Lyon 13 June 1967; *b* 27 Nov 1913; *m* 16 Jan 1950 *Jean May Evelyn, only dau of Roland Campbell, and has issue:
1b *Robert Campbell; *b* 28 Oct 1950; *educ* Loretto
1b *Catherine Mainwaring; *b* 30 Oct 1952
2a Cuthbert King, WW II in RAF; *b* 29 Aug 1916; *ka* 19 June 1940
1a Elspeth King; *m* 29 April 1929 Sir John William Spencer Maclure, 3rd Bt (*qv*), and *d* 1991, having had issue
2a *Jean King
The er son,
JAMES CLARK, of Chapel Ho, Paisley, Provost of Paisley 1882–85; *b* 27 Feb 1831; *m* 1st 3 March 1858 Jane (*d* 28 Nov 1868), dau of George Smith, of Glasgow, and had issue:
1 James, CB (1911), KC, MA Glasgow, LLB Edin, Lt-Col cmdg 9th Bn Argyll and Sutherland Highrs, Memb of the Roy Company of Archers; *b* 2 Jan 1859; *m* 25 April 1889 Norah Kathleen (14 July 1959), dau of Stewart Clark, of Dundas, Linlithgow (*see* STEWART-CLARK, Bt), and was *ka* 10 May 1915
2 GEORGE SMITH (Sir), **1st Bt**
3 Robert, shipowner; *b* 22 Aug 1886; *m* 9 Feb 1886 Alice (*d* 27 Feb 1907), dau of Henry Matler, of Dunlambert, Belfast, and *d* 22 Nov 1942, having had issue:
(1) James Henry Maurice, VD, Capt RNVR; *b* 18 Feb 1892; *d* 4 Sept 1941
JAMES CLARK *m* 2nd 1 June 1871 Katherine (*d* 14 April 1915), dau of Maj-Gen George King (*see* KINGSTON, E), and by her had issue:
4 Gerald FitzGerald KING-CLARK; *b* 23 June 1874; *m* 4 June 1902 Maida Eekhout (*d* 24 April 1950) and *d* 11 Dec 1915, having had issue:
(1) Douglas Gerald FitzGerald; *b* 8 April 1910; *d* 22 March 1919
(1) *Maida Katherine King; *m* 6 June 1944 John Cunningham Watt (*d* 27 May 1954), yr son of Thomas Watt, of High St, Paisley, Renfrewshire, and has issue:
1a *Maida Cunningham; *b* 18 Nov 1945; *m* 6 Sept 1967 James Ingram Watson, MB, ChB, and has issue:
1b *Margaret Maida King-Clark; *b* 16 May 1969
2b *Helen Caroline; *b* 17 Aug 1972
(2) *Mabel Hope Geraldine
5 Rudolph John Campbell; *b* 17 Feb 1878; *m* 20 Nov 1907 Mary Rebecca Graham Abercrombie (*d* 196–), and *d* 24 Oct 1936, leaving issue:
(1) *Katherine May Abercrombie
1 Agnes MacFarlane; *b* 15 May 1872; *m* 13 Oct 1897 Byng Montgomery Wright, VD, JP, Hon Maj 8th Bn Argyll and Sutherland Highrs, and *d* 13 April 1929, leaving issue. He *d* 17 Nov 1940
2 Katherine King; *b* 19 March 1876; *d* unm 4 Jan 1918
3 Jane Smith; *b* 24 Aug 1880; *m* 7 June 1905 John Henning Wilson, and *d* 22 Oct 1926, leaving issue
4 Williamina King, of Chapel Ho, Paisley; *b* 8 Feb 1882; *d* 1 March 1938
JAMES CLARK *d* 6 March 1910; his 2nd son,
Sir George Smith Clark, 1st Bt (UK), so *cr* 6 July 1917, DL; MP N Belfast 1907–10, Senator NI 1925, dir Bank of Ireland and Henry Matier and Co, linen mfrs, of Belfast, chm Gt Northern Rlwy Co (Ireland); *b* 8 Nov 1860; *m* 28 Sept 1881 Frances Elizabeth (*d* 3 May 1929), dau of Henry Matier, of Dunlambert, Belfast, and had issue:
1 GEORGE ERNEST (Sir), **2nd Bt**
2 Henry Douglas, MA Cambridge, barrister Inner Temple 1919, late Capt 9th Bn Argyll and Sutherland Highrs; *b* 9 Feb 1889; *d* unm 30 Sept 1952
Sir GEORGE *d* 23 March 1935; his est son,
Sir George Ernest Clark, 2nd Bt, DL, MA Cambridge, MINA, dep chm Gt Northern Rlw Co (Ireland), Commr of Irish Lights; Hon Col 3rd Searchlight Regt RA (TA) 1939–46, High Sheriff Cos Antrim 1940 and Down 1941; *b* 25 July 1882; *m* 20 July 1910 Norah Ann, JP (Belfast 1938), OStJ (*d* 12 March 1966), dau of W G Wilson, of Glasgow, and *d* 10 Nov 1950, leaving:
1 **Sir George Anthony Clark, 3rd Bt,** DL (Co of City of Belfast 1961), Capt Black Watch WW II, Senator NI 1951–69, MP Belfast Dock 1938–45, High Sheriff Co Antrim 1954, Grand Master Grand Orange Lodge Ireland 1957, Imperial Grand Master of Imperial Grand Orange Cncl of the World 1961, Imp Grand Pres of Imp Grand Orange Cncl 1958–61; *b* 24 Jan 1914; *educ* Canford; *m* 15 Feb 1949 *Nancy Catherine [Dowager Lady Clark, Tullygirvan House, Ballygowan, Co Down], 2nd dau of George Wallis Newport Clark, of Carnabane, Upperlands, Co Londonderry, and *d* 1991, leaving:
(1) *Elizabeth Frances Catherine [Mrs Nicholas Reid, Overbury Hall, Layham, Suffolk IP7 5RP]; *b* 22 March 1960; *m* 1981 *Nicholas James Reid, late RGJ, and has issue:
1a *Henry George Donald; *b* 1984
1a *Georgina Charlotte Elizabeth; *b* 1987
2 COLIN DOUGLAS (Sir), **4th Bt**
3 +Peter Aubrey [Peter Clark Esq, Cillenamara, Ringhaddy, Killinchy, Co Down BT23 6TU]; *b* 19 June 1927; *educ* Campbell Coll; *m* 3 April 1951 *Rosemary Frazer, only dau of Thomas Frazer Mackie, of Guincho, Helen's Bay, Co Down, and has:
(1) +Richard Henry Frazer [Richard Clark Esq, 4 Beechfield Dve, Conlig Newtownards, Co Down BT23 7ZW]; *b* 28 Oct 1952; *educ* Trin Coll Glenalmond; *m* 1977 *Hazel Yvonne Elizabeth, dau of Edmund Irvine Smith, of Ellenvine, Craigavad, Co Down, and has issue:
1a *Linda Helen; *b* 1978
2a *Fiona Elizabeth; *b* 1980
(2) +Michael Peter George [Michael Clark Esq, 4 Chaple Acres, E Abercromby St, Helensburgh, Dunbartonshire]; *b* 14 March 1955; *educ* Trin

Coll Glenalmond; *m* 1976 *Sandra Muriel Jane Foster, dau of Martin Reid-Foster, of Flagpoint, Campbell St, Helensburgh, and has issue:

1a +Paul Michael Frazer; *b* 1978

2a +Jamie Stewart; *b* 1979

3a +Garry Martin; *b* 1982

1a *Katie Jane; *b* 1984

1 Beatrice Norah; *b* 24 Nov 1911; *m* 1st 1 July 1931 (*divorce* 1946) Maj Theodore Bertram Doxford, JP, RASC, only son of Albert Ernest Doxford, of Newby Wiske, Northallerton, Yorks, and had issue:

(1) *Angela Beatrice [Mrs Ernest Beeson, Hawthorns, Coin Colin, St Martins, Guernsey, CI GY4 6AH]; *b* 13 Aug 1935; *m* 1st 20 March 1958 (*divorce* 1968) Dr Martin William Robert Heinzl, son of Martin Johann Josef Heinzl, of Vienna, and has issue:

1a *Philip Carlos Martin [Philip Heinzl Esq, Fairfield, Mill Lane, S Chailey, E Sussex]; *b* 1 Sept 1960; *m* 1986 *Yvonne Clemence

2a *Robert Peter Douglas [Robert Heinzl Esq, 14 Cranedown, Lewes, E Sussex]; *b* 17 Jan 1962; *m* 22 March 1997 *Susan Cumming

1a *Martina Georgina Angela [Mrs David White, 26 Lloyde Rd, Hove, Sussex BN7 3NA]; *b* 13 March 1959; *m* 1981 *David Angus Stewart White, and has issue:

1b *Alexander Martin Stewart; *b* 1982

2b *George Robert David; *b* 1984

3b *Jolyon Ronald; *b* 1989

4b *Dominic Antony; *b* 1991

(1) (cont.) Mrs Angela Heinzl *m* 2nd 6 Sept 1968, as his 2nd w, *Ernest Edward Giles Beeson, s of Ernest Herbert Beeson, and by him has:

2a *Julia Mary [Mrs Robert Alder, Lea Crest, Le Foulon, St Peter Port, Guernsey, CI]; *b* 1969; *m* 1991 *Robert Alder and has issue:

1b *Luke Robert; *b* 17 June 1998

1b *Sophie Julia; *b* 1992

2b *Chloe Beatrice; *b* 7 July 1994

3a *Sarah Elizabeth [Mrs John Wise, Hollies, School Hill, Barcombe, Sussex BN8 5DU]; *b* 1970; *m* 6 May 1995 *John Lewis Wise

1 (cont.) Mrs Beatrice Doxford *m* 2nd 12 June 1953 Col William Buckley Nicholl Roderick, OBE, late Coldstream Gds (*d* 18 March 1957), s of William Buckley Roderick, of Llanelly, S Wales; *m* 3rd 7 July 1961 John Wrench (*d* 1981), son of Maj Alfred John Chamberlain Wrench, and *d* 3 July 1994

The 3rd Bt's bro,

Sir Colin Douglas Clark, 4th Bt, MC; *b* 20 July 1918; *educ* Eton and Trin Coll Cambridge (BA 1939, MA 1944); Maj RE WW II (despatches), md G Heyn and Sons Ltd Belfast, dir: Cladox Ltd, The Ulster Steamship Co Ltd, The North Continental Shipping Co Ltd, Mountain Steamship Co Ltd, Northern Irish and Scottish Investment Tst Ltd, Ulster Unit Tst Management Ltd; Belfast Harbour Commr; *m* 19 Dec 1946 *Margaret Coleman, yst dau of Maj-Gen Sir Charlton Watson Spinks, KBE, DSO, and widow of Maj Guy William Going Threlfall, MC, 8th Hus, and *d* 27 April 1995, having had issue:

1 Sir JONATHAN GEORGE CLARK, **5th and present Bt**

1 *Sarah Louise [Mrs Michael Kohler, 16a Marlborough Rd, Richmond, Surrey TW10 6JR]; *b* 18 March 1949; *m* 1975 *Michael Alan de Cheveley Kohler, and has issue:

(1) *Rosalie de Cheveley; *b* 1979

(2) *Mirabel Margaret Macadam; *b* 1982

(3) *Katharine Isobel Lisoipa; *b* 1985

2 *Gillian Margaret Anne [Mrs Roger Dixon-Spain, The Old Hall, Whitecross Lane, Tilney All Saints, Norfolk PE34 4SR]; *b* 15 Nov 1957; *m* 1987 *Roger Dixon-Spain

CLARK of Melville Crescent

Arms: Az. a fess or, between a castle triple towered arg. masoned sa. in chief, and a crescent of the 2nd in base. **Crest:** A demi-lion rampant az. holding in his dexter paw a battle-axe ppr.
Motto: *In Deo speravi* ('In God I have trusted').
Creation: Bt. (UK) 28 Sept 1886.

SIR FRANCIS DRAKE CLARK, 5TH BT, of Melville Crescent, Edinburgh [Sir Francis Clark Bt, Woodend Cottage, Wood Lane, Burgh-next-Aylsham, Norfolk NR11 6TS]; *b* 16 July 1924; *s* bro 1991; *educ* Edin Acad; WW II 1943–46 in RN, dir Clark Travel Service Ltd, London, 1948–80; *m* 14 Aug 1958 Mary (*d* 1994), dau of John Alban Andrews, MC, FRCS, and has issue:

1 +EDWARD DRAKE; *b* 27 April 1966; *educ* Westminster and St Andrews U

Lineage: JOHN CLARK, of Edinburgh; magistrate; *m* Margaret, dau of Maurice Lothian, of Edinburgh, and *d* 29 Aug 1860, leaving:

Sir Thomas Clark, 1st Bt (UK), so *cr* 28 Sept 1886, JP (Edin), DL (City and Co of Edinburgh), of Melville Crescent, Edinburgh; *b* 5 Sept 1823; Ld Provost 1885–88; FRSE; *m* 13 June 1851 Eliza Maule (*d* 15 Dec 1906), dau of Rev George Ramsay Davidson, DD, and had issue:

1 JOHN MAURICE (Sir), **2nd Bt**

2 Thomas George Ramsay Davidson, TD, Lt-Col 9th Bn the Roy Scots; *b* 10 Nov 1867; *m* 1st 13 June 1894 Eliza (*d* 24 Feb 1943), dau of James Raeburn; *m* 2nd 29 June 1944 Evelyn Agnes Nelson-Smith (*d* 26 March 1954), and *d* 29 Feb 1948, having by 1st w had issue:

(1) Thomas George, Capt 7th Bn Roy Scots WW I, sr ptnr T and T Clark, publishers, Edinburgh; *b* 15 June 1895; *m* 17 Dec 1921 Mary Hall (*d* 1987), dau of Thomas Aldcorn, of Johannesburg, S Africa, and *d* 1986, leaving issue:

1a +Thomas George Ramsay Davidson [Thomas Clark Esq, Tyneford House, Ford, Midlothian]; *b* 21 Oct 1922; WW II in RAF; CA, ptnr T and T Clark; *m* 10 Nov 1956 *Sheila Campbell, dau of Herbert Campbell Brown, of Littleacre, Strathkinnes Rd, St Andrews, Fife, and has issue:

1b +Thomas George Nigel; *b* 10 Aug 1965

1b *Sheena Campbell; *b* 18 Feb 1959

2b *Karen Ramsay (twin); *b* 18 Feb 1959; *m* 1985 *Christopher John Heaton-Armstrong, est son of Capt Thomas Michael Robert Heaton-Armstrong, of Couligarton, Aberfoyle, Perth, and has issue:

1c *Gabrielle Louise; *b* 1991

3b *Gillian Davidson; *b* 15 Feb 1962

1a *Wendy Margaret [Mrs George Brown, Kingshot, Edward Rd, St Cross, Winchester, Hants]; *b* 13 Jan 1935; *m* 16 Aug 1968 *Maj George Gordon Brown, late 9th/12th Roy Lancers, barrister, son of Arthur Frederick Brown, of Dagnal, St Nicholas Hill, Leatherhead, Surrey, and has issue:

1b *Richard Gordon; *b* 1973

1b *Melanie Ann; *b* 1969

(2) Cecil Edward, Maj RM; *b* 11 Nov 1899; *m* 24 June 1937 *Mary, dau of Patrick Murray, of Clegg, Carrick-on-Suir, Co Tipperary, and *dsp* 27 Oct 1954

(1) Eliza Lilian

(2) Kathleen Muriel; *m* 12 Dec 1936 *Hugh MacIntyre, est son of Hugh MacIntyre, of Henley-on-Thames, and had issue:

1a *Alison Dora; *b* 3 Feb 1942

2a *Jessica Margaret; *m* 9 July 1966 *William Sinclair Hays, est son of Henry Sinclair Hays

1 Jessie Stuart; *b* 3 Sept 1852; *m* 27 July 1878 James Ritchie, of Edinburgh, MD, FRCSE, and *d* Nov 1900. He *d* Nov 1925

2 Margaret Helen Lothian; *b* 14 July 1855; *d* 6 July 1940

3 Eliza Lilian; *b* 12 Oct 1875; *m* 13 July 1909 Rev William Ross, BD, and *d* 21 Aug 1941. He *d* 23 Nov 1942

Sir THOMAS *d* 24 Dec 1900; his er son,

Sir John Maurice Clark, 2nd Bt, MBE, Lt-Col and Hon Col cmdg 7th Bn Roy Scots 1905–10, VD, JP Edinburgh, and DL Midlothian, v-chm Midlothian TFA; *b* 7 March 1859; *m* 3 June 1885 Helen Marder (*d* 4 May 1942), dau of Rev Henry M Douglas, Min of the Free Ch, Kirkcaldy, and had issue:

1 THOMAS (Sir), **3rd Bt**

2 Henry James Douglas, MC, DL (Stirlingshire 1952), Brig late cmdg 1st Bn Argyll and Sutherland Highrs 1935–37, Assist Cmdt and Ch Instructor, SA Sch Netheravon 1937, cmded an Inf Bde (TA) 1938, served WW I 1914–19 (despatches, severely wounded), and WW II 1939–45; *b* 7 June 1888; *educ* Edinburgh Acad; *m* 30 Nov 1915 Isobel Wentworth (*d* 1969), yr dau of Lt-Col George Wentworth Forbes, KDG, of Brackley, Northants, and *d* 1978, having had issue:

(1) +Wentworth Douglas [Lt-Col Wentworth Clark, Jesus Hospital, High St, Bray, Berks SL6 2AN]; *b* 11 Sept 1916, Lt-Col Argyll and Sutherland Highrs, WW II (wounded); *m* 1st 5 June 1948 Florence Mary (*d* 1987), formerly w of Alexander Addis Leslie, and dau of Duncan Richard Ricketts; *m* 2nd 15 Dec 1989 *Margaret Doris Baker, and by his 1st w has:

1a *(Wentworth Mary) Carolyn; *b* 4 Oct 1949; *m* 1st 1972 (*divorce*) G/Capt Peter Butt, RAF; *m* 2nd 1992 *Richard Northcote and by her 1st husb has:

1b *Susannah Jane; *b* 1974

2b *Annabel Laura Mary; *b* 1988

(2) Ian Ronald Wentworth, Sgt RAF, served WW II; *b* 10 Dec 1921; *k* on air operations, 4 Feb 1941

3 +John Maurice, MBE (1944) [Maj John Clark MBE, Little Thornbank, Long St, Sherborne, Dorset DT9 3BS]; *b* 7 Nov 1903; *educ* Edin Acad, and Leys Sch Cambridge; Hon Major RE (ret) (Movement Control), served WW II 1940–45, on staff of UN Secretariat 1946–63; *m* 14 Oct 1933 *Winnie Stratton, dau of Dr Campbell Highet, of Reading, Berks, and has had issue:

(1) Ian Campbell, Lt RM, served in Cyprus, Aden, Borneo and Sarawak; *b* 9 March 1937; *educ* Nautical Coll Pangbourne, and Millfield; *m* 14 April 1962 *Melita (who *m* 2nd 1971 (*divorce* 1979) Anthony Hurst), only dau of Ivor Gerald Powell, of Woking, Surrey, and was *ka* in Sarawak, 16 March 1966 (despatches posthumously), leaving issue:

1a +Timothy Ian Hugh; *b* posthumously, 6 April 1966

(2) +Hugh Lothian [Lt-Col Hugh Clark, Belstone Cottage, Blackford, Queen Camel, nr Yeovil, Somerset]; *b* 5 March 1939; *educ* King's Sch Canterbury, and RMA Sandhurst; Lt-Col Argyll and Sutherland Highrs, served in Borneo, Sarawak and Aden; *m* 1 April 1967 *Deborah Mary Ann, 2nd dau of Col William Innes Moberly, CBE, of Belstone Cottage, Blackford, Yeovil, Somerset, and has issue:

1a +Hugo Ian Moberly; *b* 1970; Capt Argyll and Sutherland Highrs

2a +Harry James Lothian; *b* 1972

3a +Benedict John Innes; *b* 1975
4a +Luke Edward Campbell; *b* 1979
(3) +Hamish Douglas, Maj Argyll and Sutherland Highrs, served in Sarawak 1965–66, and Aden 1967 (despatches); *b* 7 Jan 1945; *educ* St Edward's Sch, Oxford and RMA Sandhurst; *m* 21 March 1969 *Wendy Ann Macdonald, only dau of Ian MacDonald Harper, of Redlairdston, Buchlyvie, Stirlingshire, and has issue:
1a +Ian Nicholas Harper; *b* 1971
2a +Mark James Macdonald; *b* 1974
1 Isabella Douglas, ARRC, Hon Life Memb BRCS; *b* 22 March 1891; *m* 10 June 1920 (Arthur) Cedric Mears Coxon, TD, MA Cantab, MB, BCh, MRCS, LRCP, LDS, Capt late 5th Bn Norfolk Regt (*d* 9 June 1968), yr son of Maj S A T Coxon, of King's Lynn, Norfolk, and had issue:
(1) *Arthur John Douglas, Lt-Cdr RN; *b* 22 March 1927; *m* 7 April 1951 *Pamela Ann, yr dau of Frank A Longman, and has issue:
1a *Douglas Charles; *b* 13 Nov 1952; *educ* Portsmouth GS
2a *Mark Peter; *b* 13 Aug 1954; *educ* Allhallows Sch
(1) *Helen Florence Howard; *b* 9 March 1923; *m* 27 March 1948 *Capt Kenneth Roderick McKilliam, BA, HM Colonial Serv (ret), Gordon Highrs (ret), son of Capt Robert Basil Vincent McKilliam, Master Mariner, of Aberdeen, and has issue:
1a *Robert Douglas; *b* 8 March 1950; *educ* King's Sch Canterbury, and Imp Coll London
1a *Isobel Jean; *b* 2 Oct 1952; *educ* Lillesden Sch, Hawkhurst, Kent
Sir JOHN *d* 27 May 1924; his est son,
Sir Thomas C1ark, 3rd Bt, DL (Co and City of Edinburgh 1955); *b* 30 March 1886; *educ* Edin Acad and Univ Coll Oxford; Maj late 7th Bn Roy Scots, apptd Hon Col Forth Heavy Regt RA (TA), later 414 Coast Regt RA (Forth) (TA) 1938–49; chm City of Edinburgh T and AFA Assoc 1947–50, FRSE; *m* 18 June 1914 Ellen Mercy, only dau of Francis Drake, by his w Laura, dau of Cdr William Hobson Moubray, RN, DL, of Otterston and Cockairnie, Fife, and *d* 1977, leaving:
1 **Sir John Douglas Clark, 4th Bt**; *b* 9 Jan 1923; *educ* Gordonstoun; *m* 1969 *Anne [Dowager Lady Clark, 52 Ormidale Terrace, Edinburgh 12], dau of Angus Gordon, of Beauly, Inverness-shire, and widow of William Swan, of Edinburth, and *dsp* 1991
2 Sir FRANCIS DRAKE CLARK, **5th and present Bt**
1 *Laura Moubray [Mrs Hugh Renwick, Greenacres, 49 Gogar Bank, Edinburgh 12]; *b* 1916; *m* 1 June 1940 Maj Hugh Mackinlay Renwick, RAC (*d* 1991), er son of William Barr Renwick, of Millburn Tower, Midlothian, and has issue:
(1) *William Norman Hugh; *b* 18 April 1950; *educ* Melville Coll Edinburgh; *m* 1970 (*divorce* 1982) Patricia Jamieson, and has issue:
1a *George Martin; *b* 1970
2a *Paul William; *b* 1974
(1) *Diana Elizabeth [Mrs David Richardson, Carlesgill, Langholm, Dumfriesshire]; *b* 4 Aug 1942; *m* 1st 1967 (*divorce* 1972) Allan Miller Duthie; *m* 2nd 1972 *David Richardson, and has issue:
1a *Susan Carolyn; *b* 1975
(2) *Cynthia Caroline; *b* 4 Dec 1947
2 Cynthia Adeline (twin); *b* 16 July 1924; served WW II 1943–46 in WRNS

CLARK OF KEMPSTON

Arms: Erminois on a pile azure between two quills pilewise, points in base argent, penned or, a portcullis chained in centre in chief or and five roundels in pile of the last. **Crest:** A demi-unicorn azure, winged, armed, crined and unguled or, collared chequy argent and azure and supporting with the forelegs a thistle plant flowered proper. **Supporters:** Dexter, a lion gules gorged with a collar chequy argent and azure, pendent therefrom by a cord or an escallop argent and resting the interior hind paw on a portcullis gold; sinister, a unicorn azure, winged, horned, unguled and crined or, gorged with a collar chequy argent and azure, pendent therefrom by a cord gold an escallop argent and resting the interior hoof on a bezant. **Motto:** *Perseverantia cum perceptione* ('Perseverance allied with insight'). **Creation:** B. (LP, UK) 1992.

THE BARON CLARK OF KEMPSTON, of Kempston, Co Beds (Sir William Gibson Clark, PC (1990)) [The Rt Hon The Lord Clark of Kempston PC, The Clock House, Box End, Bedford MK43 8RT; 3 Barton St, London SW1P 3NG]; *b* 18 Oct 1917; *educ* in London; served Army UK and India 1941–46 (Maj); memb: CACA 1941, Wandsworth Borough Cncl 1949–53 (V-Chm Finance Ctee); Chm: Clapham C Assoc 1949–52, Mid-Beds C Assoc 1949–52, MP (C) Nottingham S 1959–66, E Surrey 1970–74 and S Croydon 1974–92, Oppn Spokesman EC 1964–66, Chm Select Ctee Tax Credits 1973, Jt Dep-Chm C Party 1975–77 (Jt Treasurer 1974–75), Chm C Finance Ctee 1979–92; Hon Nat Dir Carrington C Appeal 1967–68; Chm Anglo-Austrian Soc 1983–; Pres: City Gp Smaller Companies (CISCO) 1993–, ktd 1980, ACA 1941, Freeman City London 1987, Fell Industry and Parly Tst, Austrian Grand Gold Cross 1989, Austrian Grand Decoration of Honour in Gold with Star 1994; *m* 1944 *Irene Dorothy Dawson, dau of Edward Francis Rands, of Grimsby, Lincs, and has issue:
1 *Richard Anthony [The Hon Richard Clark, Manor Farm House, Potterne, nr Devizes, Wilts]; *b* 1947; *educ* Charterhouse and Sorbonne; slr; *m* 1st 1973 Susan Kirstie Macgregor, dau of Hamish Edgar Donaldson Adamson, and has issue:
(1) *Oliver Hamish William; *b* 1978
(1) *Lucy Caroline; *b* 1976
(2) *Polly Catherine Isabel; *b* 1981
1 (cont.) The Hon Richard Clark *m* 2nd 25 Jan 1996 *Sue, yr dau of Michael Haslam and widow of Oliver Gregory
2 *David William Francis [The Hon David Clark, 3 Godmersham Park, Godmersham, Kent]; *b* 1948; *educ* Charterhouse and Sorbonne; FCA; *m* 1972 (*divorce* 1997) Elizabeth Grace, dau of Cdr Thomas Woodrooffe, and has issue:
(1) *Serena Elizabeth; *b* 1974
(2) *Camilla Georgina Grace; *b* 1977
3 Charles Edward Hugh; *b* 1959; *educ* Haileybury; *m* 1991 *Nicoletta Luisa Caroline, dau of Dr Mario Lentati, of Nice, and *d* 29 Jan 1997
1 *Angela Margaret Grayson [The Hon Mrs 5 Chelsea Embankment, London SW5]; *b* 1950; *m* 1st 1971 Hugh Duncan Sinclair (*d* 1987); *m* 2nd 1992 *Peter Thomas Labey and has by her 1st husb:
(1) *Hugh; *b* 1973
(1) *Harriet Emily Margaret; *b* 1975
Lineage: HUGH CLARK, of Cautley Av, London SW4; had:
WILLIAM GIBSON, *cr* a **Baron**

CLARKE of Dunham

Arms: Erm. on a bend cotised gu. three swans arg., between three annulets sa., two and one. **Crest:** A mount vert, thereon a lark, wings elevated or, in the beak an ear of wheat ppr, the dexter claw resting on an annulet, as in the arms. **Motto:** *Sapientia melior fortitudine* ('Wisdom is the better part of valour'). **Creation:** Bt. (UK) 30 Sept 1831.

SIR (CHARLES MANSFIELD) TOBIAS (TOBY) CLARKE, 6TH BT, of Dunham Lodge, Norfolk [Sir Toby Clarke Bt, 80 Campden Hill Rd, London W8 7AA; The Church House, Bibury, Glos GL7 5NR]; *b* 8 Sept 1939 (added forename Tobias 1962); *s f* 1973; *educ* Eton, Ch Ch Oxford (MA), Sorbonne and New York U Graduate Business Sch; v-pres London br Bankers Trust Co of NY 1974–80, assoc dir Swiss Bank Corp London 1992–94, MSI 1993, chm Standing Cncl Btge 1993–96, tstee Bts Tst 1989–95 (chm 1996–), ed and originator *The Baronets' Journal* 1987–; *m* 1st 28 Jan 1971 (*divorce* 1979) Charlotte, er dau of Roderick Walter, of Stanford Ct, Cornwall Gdns, London SW; *m* 2nd 1984 *Teresa Lorraine Aphrodite, dau of Somerset Struben de Chair (*see* 1970 edn FITZWILLIAM, E), of St Osyth's Priory, St Osyth, Essex, and has issue:
1 +(CHARLES SOMERSET) LAWRENCE; *b* 12 March 1990
1 *Theodora Roosevelt; *b* 1985
2 *Augusta Elfrida; *b* 1987

Lineage: Sir Charles Mansfield Clarke, 1st Bt (UK), so *cr* 30 Sept 1831, MD, LLD, FRS, Physician to QUEEN ADELAIDE (and son of John Clarke, London surgn, by Biddy, dau of William Mansfield, of Thrapston, Northants); *b* 28 May 1782; *m* 17 Jan 1806 Mary Anna (*d* 3 July 1856), dau of Wright Thomas Squire, of Peterborough, and *d* 1857, having had, with other issue:

1 CHARLES (Sir), **2nd Bt**
2 John, MD, FRCP; *b* 16 Aug 1823; *m* 30 Jan 1855 Helen (*d* 1899), 2nd dau of Henry Alexande, of Cork St, London, and *d* 8 May 1906, having had issue:
(1) John; *b* 1857
1 Mary Anna; *m* Jan 1832 Rev George Coldham, MA, rector Glemsford, Suffolk, and *d* 13 Sept 1841, leaving issue:
2 Catherine; *m* 16 Aug 1842 Rev Charles Roe, rector Welnetham, Suffolk. He *d* 1878
3 Maria Agnes; *m* 16 Aug 1842 Rev Walter Partridge, rector Caston, Norfolk, and *d* 26 Feb 1847, leaving issue. He *d* 28 Dec 1891
The est son,
Rev Sir Charles Clarke, 2nd Bt, MA, of Dunham Lodge, Norfolk, JP Essex, rector Hanwell, Middx; *b* 15 June 1812; *m* 24 April 1838 Rosa Mary (*d* 26 Aug 1885), dau of Henry Alexander, and *d* 25 April 1899, having had, with other issue:
1 **Sir Charles Mansfield Clarke, 3rd Bt**, GCB, GCVO, Gen, 57th Regt, Cmdt-Gen Colonial Forces Cape of Good Hope 1880–82, AAQMG Aldershot 1883–84, AAG HQ 1884–86, DAG Ireland 1886–88, Brig-Gen Aldershot 1889–91, DAG HQ 1892–93, C-in-C Madras Army and Memb Cncl Govr Madras 1893–95, Lt-Gen Cmdg Madras 1895–98, QMG 1899–1903, Govr and C-in-C Malta 1903–07; *b* 13 Dec 1839; *m* 1st 19 Dec 1867 Gemma Cecilia (*d* 23 Dec 1922), only child of William Pitt Adams; *m* 2nd 26 April 1929 Constance Marion (*d* 12 Dec 1964), est dau of Herbert Warner, and *d* 22 April 1932, having by his 1st w had:
(1) Charles Henry Geoffrey Mansfield, MVO (1907), Maj Rifle Bde; *b* 26 March 1873; *m* 27 March 1915 Hon Linda Blanche Douglas-Pennant (*d* 8 July 1965), est dau of 3rd Baron Penrhyn (*qv*), and *d* 27 July 1919, leaving issue:
1a Sara Louise Mansfield; *b* 14 March 1917; *d* unm 13 Jan 1962
(1) Æthel Rosa; *m* 1st Oct 1894 Capt Ernest George Campbell, Rifle Bde. He *dsp* of wounds recd in action in S Africa 29 Aug 1900. She *m* 2nd 29 Dec 1906 Brig-Gen Hon Charles Granville Fortescue, CB, CMG, DSO, 6th son of 3rd Earl Fortescue (*qv*), and *d* 2 April 1967 aged 98, leaving issue
(2) Kathleen; *m* 10 June 1896 Maj-Gen Hon Sir Francis Richard Bingham, KCB, KCMG, 3rd son of 4th Earl of Lucan (*qv*), and *d* 18 Sept 1963, leaving issue
2 Frederick, barrister, Assist Sec Legislative Cncl of Bengal, officiating Admin-Gen of Bengal, Sec of Siamese Legation, Paris; *b* 17 March 1846; *educ* Exeter Coll Oxford (MA); *m* 22 Nov 1877 Adelaide Catherine (*d* 22 March 1920), est dau of Roger Allday Kerrison, of Queensborough Terr, W, and *d* 8 June 1921, leaving issue:
(1) ORME BIGLAND (Sir), **4th Bt**
(1) Mary Theodora; *m* 18 Dec 1909 Robert Pringle Davidson, and *d* 28 Feb 1937
3 William Alexander, slr; *b* 19 Nov 1848; *educ* Magdalen Coll Oxford (BA); *m* 10 Aug 1886 Helen (*d* 28 Nov 1911), dau of G R Woodward, of Kingswear, Devon, and *d* 12 Oct 1920, leaving issue:
(1) William Peter Dunham, OBE (1927), local dir Barclay's Bank Ltd, formerly in Sudan CS, had Order of Nile (3rd Cl); *b* 8 Nov 1888; *m* 27 Sept 1915 Ethel, dau of Edmund Ethelston, of Hinton, Salop, and *d* 28 Jan 1967, having had issue
1a Peter Ethelston, served WW II 1939–45 as Capt Intell Corps (despatches), Co Sec The Times Publishing Co Ltd 1955–67, in charge of *Times* Foreign News Service from 1967; *b* 11 July 1916; *educ* Eton and King's Coll Cambridge (BA 1938, MA 1946); *m* 5 Sept 1940 *Isabel Helen, est dau of Philip Elton Longmore, CBE, TD, of Whyke Grange, Chichester, Sussex, and was *k* in a motor accident 30 Jan 1975, leaving issue:
1b +Peter Alexander; *b* 25 Sept 1941; *educ* Eton and Trin Coll Cambridge; *m* 29 July 1967 *Lilah Victoria Mary, only dau of John Forrester, of Ardnacross, Isle of Mull, and has issue:
1c +Paul Sebastian; *b* 1971
2c +Timothy Forrester; *b* 1975
3c +Robert Theodore; *b* 1983
2b +John Elton; *b* 16 Dec 1948; *educ* Eton and Kent U; *m* 1979 *Caroline Anne Bannatyne, dau of Edward Michael Courage, and has issue:
1c +Edward Peter; *b* 1985
1c *Helena Margaret; *b* 1981
2a Charles Ivor; *b* and *d* 20 Aug 1921
(2) Paul Humphrey, MC, Lt late RGA (SR); *b* 17 June 1891; *m* 25 Sept 1927 Joyce Chicheley (*d* 6 Aug 1934) 2nd dau of Richard Chicheley Plowden, and *d* 17 July 1946, leaving issue:
1a +Humphrey [Humphrey Clarke Esq, 124 Off Lane, Gladstone, Qld, Australia]; *b* Dec 1929
2a Paul Ivor; *b* 4 June 1931; *educ* Prince of Wales Sch Nairobi and Cape Town U (BSc); *m* 13 April 1963 *Angela Mary [Mrs Paul Clarke, Elgon, Tilsmore Rd, Heathfield, E Sussex], dau of Thomas George Cleaver, and *d* 1977, leaving issue:
1b *Fiona Mary; *b* 29 April 1964
2b *Rosemary Ann; *b* 7 Sept 1965
1a *Barbara [Mrs Barbara Arlaud, 46 Hargreaves Ave, Chelmer, Brisbane, Qld 4068, Australia]; *b* Aug 1928; *m* 14 April 1951 (*divorce* 1973) Anthony Lucien Noon Arlaud, and has issue:
1b *Anthony Stephen; *b* 25 April 1953
2b *David Paul; *b* 20 Nov 1955; *m* 1981 *Hilary Dawn, dau of John Goldsworthy Palmer, and has issue:
1c *Kimberly Rose; *b* 1992
3b *Christopher John; *b* 18 July 1961; *educ* Qld Inst of Technology (BB Comn); *m* 1984 (*divorce* 1990) Mette Slej, dau of Villy Bertlesen
(1) Rhoda Margaret
1 Rosa Helen; *m* 16 June 1863 Col William Garrow Waterfield, CSI, Indian Staff Corps, and *d* 7 Sept 1905, leaving issue. He *d* 3 Feb 1897
2 Mary Anna; *m* 8 Nov 1865 Lawrence Harrison, and *d* 1893, having had issue
3 Florence Lucy; *m* 19 Feb 1867 Roger Kerrison, JP, and *d* 26 April 1903, leaving issue. He *d* 6 March 1924

The 3rd Bt's n,
Sir Orme Bigland Clarke, 4th Bt, CBE; *b* 8 Oct 1880; *educ* Magdalen Coll Oxford (BA), barrister Inner Temple; *m* 19 June 1905 Elfrida (*d* 16 Jan 1963), er dau of Alfred Roosevelt, of New York, and had issue:
1 HUMPHREY ORME (Sir), **5th Bt**
2 Alfred Roosevelt Orme; *b* 29 Aug 1909 (twin); *d* 22 Jan 1911
3 +Charles Frederick Orme [Charles Clarke Esq, Weltpoststrasse 18/032, 3015 Berne, Switzerland]; *b* 29 Aug 1909 (twin); *educ* Eton and Ch Ch Oxford; *m* 11 April 1942 *Sylvia Vera, only child of Leo Kaelin, of Rorschach, Switzerland, and has had issue:
(1) +William Oliver; *b* 17 Aug 1943; *educ* Gordonstoun and Trin Coll Dublin; *m* 1981 *Elizabeth, dau of John Ivimy, and has issue:
1a +Frederick William Michael; *b* 1982
2a +Percival John Theodore; *b* 1983
3a +Maximillian Tobias Ivimy; *b* 1986
(2) Michael Nicholas; *b* 23 March 1945; *educ* Eton and Ch Ch Oxford; *d* unm 11 Oct 1968
(1) *Katherine Sybil; *b* 26 July 1950; *educ* St Mary's Convent Ascot and Bristol U; *m* 1981 (*divorce* 1991, resumed maiden name) Michael Pearl
The 4th Bt *d* 31 March 1949; his er surv son,
Sir Humphrey Orme Clarke, 5th Bt; *b* 6 July 1906; *educ* Eton and Ch Ch Oxford; Br Embassy Washington 1941–44, FO 1944–46; *m* 1st 12 June 1931 (*divorce* 1936) Frances Mary Powys, only dau of Maj Frederick Powys Sketchley, DSO; *m* 2nd 1 Sept 1938 (*divorce* 1947) Elisabeth (*d* 7 Nov 1967), formerly w of Colin Leiter Campbell and dau of Dr William Alexander Cook, of Santa Barbara, Calif, and had issue:
1 Sir (CHARLES MANSFIELD) TOBIAS CLARKE, **6th and present Bt**
Sir Humphrey *m* 3rd 11 Feb 1947 (*divorce* 1953) Constance Elizabeth, formerly w of John Stephen Langton and dau of Herbert Gray Gibbs, of Charnwood, Blackwater, Hants, and *d* 22 Jan 1973, having by her had issue:
2 Orme Roosevelt; *b* 30 Nov 1947; *educ* Eton; *m* 1st 31 July 1971 (*divorce* 1989) Joanna Valentine, only dau of Maj John Schuster, TD, DL, of the Manor Farm, Nether Worton, Oxon (*see* WYFOLD, B), and had issue
(1) +Nicholas Orme; *b* 1976
2 (cont.) Orme Clarke *m* 2nd 1991 *Christine V [Mrs Orme Clarke, 41 Kensington Place, London W8], dau of J G O'Flaherty, of Melbourne, Australia, and *d* 1992, leaving further issue:
(2) +Alexander; *b* 1992

CLARKE of Rupertswood

Arms: Or two bars az. between four escallops, three in chief and one in base gu., between two flaunches of the second. **Crest:** In front of a dexter arm embowed in armour, the hand in a gauntlet ppr. grasping an arrow in bend sinister or, flighted arg., three escallops also or. **Motto:** *Signum quærens in vellere* ('Seeking the sign in the wool'). **Creation:** Bt. (UK) 29 Dec 1882.

SIR RUPERT WILLIAM JOHN CLARKE, 3RD BT, MBE (1943) [Maj Sir Rupert Clarke Bt MBE, 500 Bourke St, Melbourne 3000, Australia]; *b* 5 Nov 1919; *s* f 1926; *educ* Eton and Magdalen Coll Oxford (MA 1945); FAIM; Capt (Hon Maj) Irish Gds (Res of Offrs) WW II (despatches), ADC to C-in-C Middle East 1942–43; chm: United Distillers Co 1960–88, Nat Australia Bank 1986–92 (dir from 1955), P & O Australia Ltd 1983–96 (Hon pres 1996), Cadbury Schweppes (Australia) Ltd 1955–89, Cadbury Schweppes 1977–85, Bank of S Pacific 1986–92, and First National Ltd 1986–92; pres Roy Humane Soc of Australasia Inc, memb Bd and v-pres Howard Florey Inst (Melbourne), Hon Consul-Gen Monaco in Melbourne 1975–, Hon Fell Trinity Coll Melbourne, Chev Legion of Honour, Offr Order Leopold Belgium, Order Grimaldi Monaco; *m* 21 Jan 1947 *Kathleen, dau of Peter Grant Hay, of Egoline, Toorak, Victoria, Australia, and has had issue:
1 +RUPERT GRANT ALEXANDER; *b* 12 Dec 1947; *educ* Melbourne U (LLB); *m* 1978 *Susannah, dau of Sir (Richard) Robert Law-Smith, and has issue:
(1) +Rupert Robert William; *b* 24 June 1981
(1) *Samantha Kathleen; *b* 1980
(2) *Joanna; *b* 1983
2 Ernest William Grant; *b* 4 Nov 1949; *d* as result of an accident 5 Sept 1961

3 +Peter Robert Justin John; *b* 15 March 1955; *m* 1983 *Andrea Wilkes, dau of Joshua Pitt, and has issue:
(1) +William Peter Norman Grant; *b* 1986
(1) *Alexandra Kathleen; *b* 1984
1 *Vanessa Margaret; *b* 7 Jan 1952; *m* 1975 *Roden David Cutler, son of Sir Arthur Roden Cutler, VC, AK, KCMG, KCVO, CBE, and has issue:
(1) *Jonathan Roden Rupert David; *b* 1981
(2) *Richard William Grant Clarke; *b* 1983
(3) *James Robert Oliver David; *b* 1986
(1) *Christina Annabelle Kate; *b* 1988

Lineage: — CLARKE, of Greinton, Somerset; living *temp* ELIZABETH I; *m* Joane — (*d* between 30 Jan 1628 and 9 Aug 1633) and predeceased her, leaving, with a dau (*m* Robert Cooke):
WILLIAM CLARKE, of Greinton; *m* Joane — (*d* between 8 Dec 1671 and 30 Nov 1672) and had:
1 WILLIAM
2 John; *m* Joane — and *d* 1686, leaving a dau (*m* her cousin William, son of Gabriel Clarke, of Greinton)
1 Joane
WILLIAM CLARKE *d* 1671; his er son,
WILLIAM CLARKE, of Greinton; owned the lands called Comers and part of Catcott Heath, Moorlinch, adjoining Weston Zoyland; *m* Elizabeth — and *d* between 6 Dec 1685 and 6 Nov 1686, leaving, with a yr s (Thomas, inherited from his f lands at Aller Moore, Somerset):
WILLIAM CLARKE, of Greinton; *m* Mary — and *d* between 8 Jan and 18 May 1709, leaving, with three daus (Hannah, *m* — Hurman; Elizabeth; Jane, *m* John Hart):
PHILIP CLARKE, of Willake, Middlezoy; in possession after 1700 of his father's holding of Catcott Heath; settled at Weston Zoyland 1714 (Churchwarden 1737); *m* 1st Jane (*d* 12 May 1702), dau of Mrs Joan Daunton, widow, and had:
1 Hester; *m* — Harris, of Mark, Somerset
PHILIP CLARKE *m* 2nd Alice — (*bur* 26 Aug 1710) and had:
2 Joan; *bapt* 2 April 1704; *bur* 26 April 1712
3 Mary; *bapt* 15 Jan 1708
PHILIP CLARKE *m* 3rd Hester — (*d* by 24 March 1766) and *d* 11 Dec 1742 aged 69, having had, with five more daus:
1 William, of Willake; *bapt* 27 Dec 1726; *m* 1st Elizabeth — (*bur* 23 April 1762) and had, with anoth er s and three daus:
(1) WILLIAM
1 (cont.) William Clarke *m* 2nd *c* 26 July 1762 Mrs Mary Keene (*bur* 30 Sept 1789) and was *bur* 29 March 1771, having had no issue by her
His est son,
WILLIAM CLARKE; Churchwarden Weston Zoyland 1784; *m c* 2 May 1771 Amy Sparke, of Chedzoy, near Bridgwater, and had, with other issue:
1 WILLIAM
2 Joseph, of Wiveliscombe; *bapt* 2 Dec 1779; had two sons
3 Richard Perry, of Barnstaple, Devon; *m* Mary Snow, of Marley, and had issue
His est son,
WILLIAM CLARKE, of St Botolph, Aldgate, London; *bapt* 11 July 1772; *m* 18 Feb 1796 Sarah Turner, of Weston Zoyland, and had issue:
1 Charles, of Chelsea; *m* Elizabeth, dau of John Howe, of Merridge, nr Bridgwater, and *d* March 1878, leaving two surv sons and four daus
2 WILLIAM JOHN TURNER
3 Lewis, settled in Australia; left two sons and seven daus
WILLIAM CLARKE *d* 1819; his 2nd son,
WILLIAM JOHN TURNER CLARKE; went to Australia 1840; MLC Victoria; *m* Elizabeth, dau of Rev George Pyke Dowling, curate Puckington, Somerset, and had issue:
1 WILLIAM JOHN (Sir), **1st Bt**
2 Thomas Biggs; *b* 1833; settled in Australia; *m* Hannah, dau of Henric Nicholas, of Tasmania
3 Joseph, of Toorak, near Melbourne; *m* his cousin Caroline, dau of his uncle Lewis Clarke
The est son,
Sir William John Clarke, 1st Bt (UK), so *cr* 29 Dec 1882, of Rupertswood, Bourke Co, Victoria, Australia, LLD, MLC; *b* 1831; *m* 1st 23 Nov 1860 Mary (*d* 1871), dau of Hon John Walker, MLC and Exec Cncl Tasmania, and had issue:
1 RUPERT TURNER HAVELOCK (Sir), **2nd Bt**
2 Ernest Edward Dowling, Lt RN; *b* 19 May 1869; *d* unm 13 Jan 1941
1 Alice Blanche; *b* 4 Aug 1862; *m* 8 Dec 1887 Chesborough Falconer John Macdonald, of Wantabadgery, Wagga Wagga, NSW, and Falcon Manor, Towcester, Northants, est son of C C Macdonald, late 22nd Regt, and *d* April 1940, leaving issue. He *d* 1919
2 Ethel Maude; *b* 12 July 1867; *m* 1stly 1895 Hon George Alexander Cruikshank, of Bryon Inverell, NSW, MP Australia. He *d* 11 April 1904. She *m* 2nd 12 Feb 1907 Prof Horatio Scott Carslaw, ScD, DSc, LLD, FRS, of Sydney U, 4th son of Rev Dr William Henderson Carslaw, of Helensburgh, Scotland, and *d* 3 June 1907. He *d* Nov 1954
Sir William *m* 2nd 21 Jan 1873 Janet Marian (*d* 4 April 1909), dau of Hon Peter Snodgrass, of Victoria, MLC, son of Col Snodgrass, and by her had, with other issue:
3 William Lionel Russell (Hon); *b* 31 March 1876; late MLC S Province, Victoria, JP, served WW I 1915–19 as Lt Aust FA; *m* 23 Sept 1908 Florence Douglas (*d* 23 Jan 1961), dau of Col Henry Douglas Mackenzie, Aust Mil Force, late RN (*see* MACKENZIE, Bt, of Coul), and *d* 14 May 1954, leaving issue:
(1) John Russell, served WW II with AIF; *b* 15 Dec 1909; *m* 12 April 1934 (*divorce* 1940) Alison Mary, est dau of Clive Milne, of Adelaide, Australia, and *d* 1963, having had issue:
1a Timothy Ian Russell; *b* 5 May 1935; *d* 1939
(2) +Michael Alastair [Hon Michael Clarke, 82 Mathoura Rd, Toorak, Victoria, Australia], late Lt Australian Imp Forces, served WW II, MLC Victoria; *b* 28 Sept 1915; *educ* Harrow and New Coll Oxford (BCL 1938, MA 1941); *m* 1948 *Helen Rosalind, dau of Essington Lewis, CH, and has issue:
1a *Andrea Rosalind; *b* 30 Oct 1950
2a *Louise Merilyn; *b* 6 Feb 1953
3a *Rosemary Janet; *b* 28 Jan 1956
(1) *Janet Marjorie Nina; *b* 3 Nov 1911; *m* 1941 Capt Henry Armstrong Hammond, 5th Light Horse, AIF, and has issue:
1a *Rupert Russell; *b* 7 July 1945; *m* 1973 *Cheryl Gay, dau of W R Harvey
4 Francis Grenville (Hon Sir), KBE, Pres Legislative Cncl of Victoria 1923–43; V-Chm Nat Bank of Australasia, and a dir of Goldsborough Mort and Co, memb Felton Art Bequest Ctee; *b* 14 March 1879; *m* 24 July 1901 Nina Ellis (*d* 27 June 1948), dau of Thomas Cotton, banker, of Melbourne, Victoria, and *d* 13 Feb 1955, having had issue:
(1) John Hollywell; *b* 1902; *d* 1917
(2) William Anthony Francis, WW II as Capt AIF; *b* 1908; *m* 1939 *Jessie Deakin, dau of Herbert Brookes, of Melbourne, Victoria, and *d* 22 Oct 1953, leaving issue:
1a +Francis Brookes; *b* Sept 1940; *educ* Massey U Coll NZ; *m* 1st 1969 (*divorce* 1976) Jacqueline, dau of Graham Crossley; *m* 2nd Vivica Spens, and has issue:
1b +Antony Graham; *b* 1970
2a +William Severn; *b* Dec 1945; BA, BSc, MBA
1a *Janet Deakin [Mrs Robert Hogarth-Scott, 6 Selbourne Rd, Toorak, Vict, Australia]; *b* July 1942; *educ* Melbourne U (Dip OT); *m* 1970 *Robert Stirling Hogarth-Scott, and has issue
2a *Barbary Cotton; *b* March 1950 ; *educ* Melbourne U (BA)
(3) Colin Grenville, WW II as Sgt AIF and F/O RAAF; *b* 1914; *educ* Geelong GS and Reading U; *m* 6 Nov 1943 *Elizabeth Lennox, dau of Dr Lennox Spiers, CBE, ED, FRACS, of Melbourne, and *d* 10 June 1962, leaving issue:
1a +Jason William; *b* 5 Dec 1952
1a *Sally Miranda; *b* 5 Nov 1949
(1) *Margaret Mary; *m* 19– (*divorce* 1952) John Egerton LLB, Australian External Affairs Dept, Australian HC Pakistan, son of Arthur Egerton Oldham, of St Kilda, Victoria, and has issue:
1a *John Christopher Clarke; *b* 10 Feb 1934
1a *Patricia Anne; *b* 14 June 1950
(2) *Patricia Kathleen; *b* 1906; *m* 21 Dec 1939 S/Ldr Raymond Vincent O'Burne, JP, RAAF (*d* 1973), son of Patrick Augustus O'Bryne, of Launceston, Tasmania
(3) *Valerie Janet Cotton; *m* 1946 *Capt Robert Southey, late Coldstream Gds, and has issue:
1a *Robert Clarke Allen; *b* 4 Feb 1948
2a *Guy Frances; *b* 7 Sept 1950
3a *Jonathan Edward; *b* 20 Dec 1951
4a *William Blaise; *b* 23 Feb 1957
5a *Patrick Richard Christian; *b* 30 Dec 1963
5 Reginald Hastings, Lt-Col Cwlth Forces of Australia, late Lt 15th Hus; *b* 26 Oct 1880; *m* 1904 Ernestine Maud (*d* 24 Dec 1926), dau of Edmund Govett, and *d* 17 March 1914, leaving issue:
(1) Reginald Clive Nevil, served WW II in RAAF; *b* 29 Sept 1910; *m* 1935 Elizabeth Blanche Macpherson (*d* 15 Sept 1965), and *d* 26 Feb 1964, leaving issue:
1a +Robin; *b* 1935; *m* 21 Aug 1958 *Prunella, dau of Wilfred Weigall, of Cobden, Victoria, and has issue:
1b +Anthony Clive; *b* 5 May 1963
1b *Sara Elizabeth; *b* 7 May 1965
1a *(Ernestine) Lucilla; *b* 1937
(1) *Joan Rosemary; *b* 29 Sept 1908; *m* 1st 30 Nov 1931 John Francis St Barbe Barclay, only son of John Barclay. He was *ka* 1940. She *m* 2nd 1941 Frederick Norman Hill, and has issue:
1a *Elizabeth Jane; *b* 25 Aug 1942; *m* 27 Nov 1963 *Gordon Macquarie Douglass, son of Herbert Douglass, of Darling Point, Sydney, NSW, and has issue:
1b *Hamish Macquarie; *b* 21 Aug 1968
1b *Sybella Jane; *b* 10 June 1966
2a *Susan Diana; *b* 21 Oct 1944; *m* 1967 *Simon Creswick, son of Alec Creswick, of Avenel, Victoria, Australia
(2) *Ernestine Elizabeth Hastings; *b* 1914; *m* 15 May 1937 Tim Harry Collins, and has issue:
1a *David Timothy Henry; *b* 19 March 1939
1a *Penelope Anna; *b* 20 Dec 1943
3 Mary Janet; *b* 25 Dec 1874; *m* 23 April 1903 Maj Hon Robert Hamilton Lindsay, Scots Greys, 3rd son of 26th Earl of Crawford and Balcarres (*qv*), and *d* 30 April 1960, leaving issue
4 Lily Vera Montague Douglas; *b* 21 Sept 1883; *m* 9 Nov 1911 Maj George Landale, late 3rd Hus, and *d* 1949, leaving issue. He *d* 1949
5 Ivy Victoria; *b* 2 Oct 1887; *m* 11 Nov 1914 Sir Robert Wilson Knox, of Greenknowe, Toorak, Melbourne, and had issue
The 1st Bt *d* 15 May 1897; his son,
Sir Rupert Turner Havelock Clarke, 2nd Bt, late Lt RASC, sometime MLC, Victoria, Australia; *b* 16 March 1865; *m* 1st 22 Dec 1886 (*divorce* 1909) Aimée Mary, dau of Hon Thomas Forrest Cumming, MLC, of Victoria, and had issue:
1 Phyllis Mary; *m* 1 June 1909 Reginald Power, son of Herbert Power, of Melbourne, Australia. He *d* 1951
2 Aimée Gwendolyn; *m* 1st 19 Oct 1915 (*divorce* 1930) Col Charles Robert Tolver Michael Gerard, DSO, OBE, late Gren Gds, son of Hon Robert Joseph Gerard-Dicconson, and had issue (*see* GERARD, B). He *d* 14 Jan 1971. She *m* 2nd 24 Jan 1940 Cdr Humphrey Ranulph Brand, RN, son of R-Adml Hon Thomas Seymour Brand (*see* HAMPDEN, V)

Sir Rupert *m* 2nd 6 Nov 1918 Elsie Florence (*m* 2nd 18 Sept 1928 5th Marquess of Headfort (*qv*) and *d* 16 May 1972), dau of James Partridge Tucker, of Sydney, Australia, and *d* 25 Dec 1926, having by her had issue:

1 Sir RUPERT WILLIAM JOHN CLARKE, **3rd and present Bt**

2 Ernest Edward Dowling, served WW II in RAF; *b* 17 Dec 1920; *kas* 14 Dec 1950

3 *Elizabeth Elsie Faith [Mrs Willoughby Lake, Ashleigh, Much Hadham, Herts]; *b* 12 July 1924; *m* 13 Sept 1952 Willoughby Alfred Lake (*d* 1986), 2nd son of Capt Sir Atwell Henry Lake, 9th Bt, CB, OBE, RN (*qv*), and has issue

CLAY

Arms: Arg. a chevron engrailed paly sa. and or, between three trefoils of the second. **Crest:** Two wings arg., each charged with a chevron engrailed between three trefoils slipped sa. **Motto:** *Per orbem* ('Throughout the world'). **Creation:** Bt. (UK) 20 Sept 1841.

SIR RICHARD HENRY CLAY, 7TH BT, of Fulwell Lodge, Middlesex [Sir Richard Clay Bt, The Copse, Shiplate Rd, Bleadon, Avon BS24 0NX]; *b* 2 June 1940; *s* f 1985; *educ* Eton; FCA 1966; *m* 14 Sept 1963 *Alison Mary, only dau of Dr James Gordon Fife, of Summer Hill, Alde House Dve, Aldeburgh, Suffolk, and has issue:

1 +CHARLES RICHARD; *b* 18 Dec 1965; *educ* Manor Sch Cambridge and UEA (BA)

2 +Thomas Henry; *b* 28 July 1967; *educ* Manor Sch Cambridge

3 +James Felix; *b* 13 April 1969; *educ* Manor Sch Cambridge and York U (BA)

1 *Virginia Rachel [Mrs Robin Taylor, Elton Farm, Elton, Salop SY8 2HP]; *b* 9 July 1964; *m* 1988 *Robin P Taylor, yst son of Richard Taylor, of Grange Farm, Bourn, Cambs, and has issue:

(1) *Richard James; *b* 1993

(1) *Megan Catherine; *b* 1992

2 *Catherine Victoria; *b* 1971; *educ* Bath U (BA)

Lineage: GEORGE CLAY, of a yr branch of the CLAYs of Chapel and Crick, Derbys, settled for two generations at Cambridge (the er branch male line died out between 1680 and 1690); *m* 1670 Elizabeth, 2nd dau of Felix Calbert, of Albury Park, Herts, and had:

FELIX CLAY, of Enfield; had:

WILLIAM CLAY, of City of London; had:

GEORGE CLAY; *b* 1757; merchant and shipowner; *m* 1784 Mary, dau of Richard Moorsom, of Whitby and Scarborough, Yorks, by Elizabeth Fairfax, and *d* 1836, leaving an only surv son:

Sir William Clay, 1st Bt (UK), so *cr* 20 Sept 1841; *b* 15 Aug 1791; MP Tower Hamlets 1832–1857, Sec Bd of Control India 1839–41; *m* 26 Sept 1822 Harriet (*d* 10 Dec 1867), dau and coheir of Thomas Dickason, of Fulwell Lodge, Middx, and *d* 13 March 1869, having by her had, with other issue:

1 **Sir William Dickason Clay, 2nd Bt**; *b* 21 Dec 1828; *m* 19 April 1855 Mariana Emily (*m* 2nd 3 Nov 1877 Baron Haliburton (*d* 21 April 1907) and *d* 19 March 1919), est dau of Leo Schuster, of Upper Belgrave St, London, and *dsp* 14 Oct 1876

2 **Sir George Clay, 3rd Bt**; *b* 14 Aug 1831; Lt-Col Crimean War, present Battles of Alma and Inkerman and Siege of Sebastopol (Crimean Medal with three clasps, Order of the Medjidie 5th Cl, Turkish Medal); *m* 1st 8 March 1862 Caroline Elizabeth (*d* 6 April 1873), only dau of Sir John Palmer Bruce Chichester, 1st Bt, of Arlington, and had issue:

(1) Lilian Caroline Georgiana; *d* unm 16 Feb 1918

(2) Rosalie Violet Marion; *d* unm

2 (cont.) **Sir George** *m* 2nd 5 Oct 1876 Mary Caroline (*m* 2nd 28 Feb 1881 Lt-Col Walter Henry Holbech, KRRC, who *d* 6 March 1901, and *d* 8 April 1933), dau of Sir John Walrond, 1st Bt, and *d* 30 June 1878, having by her had issue:

(3) Sybil Mary; *b* 18 Jan 1878; *m* 18 July 1905 Samuel Horace Law, MD, FRCSI, est son of Thomas Pakenham Law, KC, and *d* 2 June 1952, leaving issue. He *d* 27 Feb 1940

3 ARTHUR TEMPLE FELIX (Sir), **4th Bt**

1 Harriet; *m* 28 June 1853 John Morgan Edwardes Jones, of Loub Croy, Wimbledon Hill, son of H R Jones, of Garthmyl, and *d* 2 Feb 1917 aged 93, leaving issue. He *d* 8 March 1903 aged 83

2 Mary; *m* 16 Dec 1851 Capt John Walrond Clarke, 10th Hus, 2nd son of T E Clarke, of Tremlett Ho, Wellington, and *d* 17 Dec 1907, leaving issue. He *d* 26 March 1903

3 Elizabeth; *m* 1st 26 June 1847 her cousin James Temple-Bowdoin, 4th Dragoon Gds, who *d* 9 April 1871. She *m* 2nd 11 Jan 1872 Rt Hon Sir William Henry Gregory, KCMG, MP, Govr Ceylon 1872–76, and *dsp* 28 June 1873. He *d* 6 March 1892

4 Emma Georgiana Christina; *m* 1st 15 July 1850 Lt-Col Henry Wedderburn Cumming, late Coldstream Gds, est son of Gen Sir Henry Cumming, Col 12th Lancers, and had issue. He *d* 1870. She *m* 2nd 4 July 1871 Horatio Mansfield, barrister (*see* SANDHURST, B), and *d* 25 Nov 1908

5 Laura Felicia Susan; *m* 22 Feb 1859 Walter Montiford Westropp-Dawson, of Charlesfort, Co Wexford, DL, Capt 19th Regt, and *d* 19 Feb 1901, leaving issue. He *d* 17 April 1896

The 3rd Bt's bro,

Sir Arthur Temple Felix Clay, 4th Bt, barrister Inner Temple; *b* 9 Dec 1842; *educ* Trin Coll Cambridge (BA); landscape and portrait painter; *m* 1 June 1869 Margaret (*d* 25 Dec 1915), 5th dau of Arthur Kett Barclay, FRS, DL, JP, of Bury Hill, Dorking, Surrey, and *d* 18 March 1928, having had, with an er s (William Temple, *b* 26 June 1870, *d* unm 6 April 1893):

Sir (George) Felix Neville Clay, 5th Bt; *b* 24 Nov 1871; *educ* Trin Coll Cambridge (BA); FRIBA, Architect to Bd of Educn 1904–27; *m* 9 March 1904 Rachel, est dau of Rt Hon Henry Hobhouse, PC, of Hadspen Ho, Castle Cary, and had issue:

1 HENRY FELIX (Sir), **6th Bt**

2 +Anthony George Hobhouse [Dr Anthony Clay, 8 Springfield Crescent, Sherborne, Dorset], MA, MB, BCh (Cambridge 1939), Maj RAMC TARO WW II, SBStJ; *b* 9 July 1914; *m* 1st 20 Oct 1938 (*divorce* 1959) Elizabeth Alice, dau yst dau of Sir Gilbert Charles Upcott, KCB, of Highgate, and has:

(1) +Christopher George Anthony [Prof Christopher Clay, 48 Clarendon Rd, Redland, Bristol], PhD (1967), lecturer Ec History Bristol U; *b* 27 Jan 1940; *educ* Sherborne and Trin Coll Cambridge (BA 1961, MA); *m* 1st 1973 (*divorce*) Diana, dau of Edward Hippolyte Joseph Burbidge; *m* 2nd 19– *Rachel Redford and by his 1st w has:

1a +Felix Temple; *b* 1974

2a +Francis Benjamin; *b* 1976

1a *Caroline Emily; *b* 1978

2 (cont.) Dr Anthony Clay *m* 2nd 31 Oct 1960 Patricia Barbara (*d* 18 Dec 1967), yst dau of Archibald Foulcher, of W Wickham, Kent, and by her has:

(2) +Timothy Paul; *b* 27 Aug 1961; *educ* Southampton U (BA 1983); *m* 29 July 1989 *Alison Fiona, dau of Douglas Cuthbert Short, of Woking, Surrey and has had:

1a *Katherine Lucy; *b* 10 July 1992

2a Jessica Holly; *b* 17 March, *d* 28 Sept 1996

2 (cont.) Dr Anthony Clay also adopted:

*Ann Yvonne; *b* 3 Sept 1951

*Elaine Clare; *b* 22 July 1954

2 (cont.) Dr Anthony Clay *m* 3rd 1971 *Pamela Joan, dau of Edward Farley Oaten, of Walton-on-Thames

1 Margaret Imogen; *b* 5 Dec 1904; *m* 17 Aug 1938 Joseph Cleverly Lister (*d* 1984), s of Sir William Lister, KCMG, KCVO, MD, FRCS, and *d* 1984 leaving issue

2 Janet; *b* 9 March 1907; *m* 4 Dec 1948 Humphrey Seymour Outterson Wood, est son of Ernest Seymour Wood (*d* 29 March 1971), of Cornwall Ho, Murton, Co Durham, and *d* 1997

3 Theresa Rachel, DSc Edin (1955), Pncpl Scientific Offr Br Museum Nat Hist; *b* 7 Feb 1911; *m* 1974 Rodney G Searight (*d* 1991), and *d* 1995

Sir FELIX *d* 11 Nov 1941; his er son,

Sir Henry Felix Clay, 6th Bt, MIEE; *educ* Gresham's and Trin Coll Cambridge (BA 1930, MA 1935); ptnr McLellan and Ptnrs, consulting engrs, Past Chm Assoc of Consulting Engrs, Chm Br Overseas Engineering Services Bureau; *b* 8 Feb 1909; *m* 4 Nov 1933 Phyllis Mary (*d* 4 Oct 1997), yr dau of Richard Horace Paramore, MD, FRCS, of 4 Bilton Rd, Rugby, and *d* 1985, leaving issue:

1 Sir RICHARD HENRY CLAY, **7th and present Bt**

1 *Jenny Elizabeth [Mrs Jenny Murray, 31 The Terrace, Aldeburgh, Suffolk]; *b* 28 March 1936; *educ* Bristol U (BA); *m* 11 July 1959 (*divorce* 1975) Oswyn Murray, MA, only surv son of (Malcolm) Patrick Murray, CB, of Scotsland, Bramley, Surrey, and has issue:

(1) *James Augustus Henry; *b* 8 Sept 1961

(1) *Octavia; *b* 10 Feb 1965

2 *Sarah Richenda [Mrs Frederic Wise, 9 Market Cross Place, Aldeburgh, Suffolk]; *b* 12 Aug 1938; *m* 1979 *Frederic Henry Wise

CLAYTON

Arms: Arg. a cross sa. between four pellets. **Crest:** A leopard's gamb erased and erect arg., holding a pellet. **Mottoes:** 1 *Virtus in actione consistit* ('Virtue consists in action') 2 *Quid leone fortius* ('What is braver than the lion?'). **Creation:** Bt. (GB) 13 Jan 1732.

SIR DAVID ROBERT CLAYTON, 12TH BT, of Marden, Surrey [Capt Sir David Clayton Bt, Rock House, Kingswear, Dartmouth, Devon TQ6 0BX]; *b* 12 Dec 1936; *s* f 1985; *educ* HMS *Conway* and John Cass Coll, London; Capt Merchant Navy 1970, dir Oceanic Liners (UK) Ltd 1989–; *m* 1971 *Julia Louise, dau of Charles Henry Redfearn, and has issue:

1 +ROBERT PHILIP; *b* 8 July 1975

2 +John Richard; *b* 1978

Lineage (of Clayton): Sir ROBERT CLAYTON, descended from the CLAYTONs of Bulwick, Northants, Ld Mayor London 1679, MP City of London, Commr Customs, benefactor to Christ's Hospital; *b* 29 Sept 1629; *m* Martha (*d* 25 Dec 1705), dau of Perient Trott, London merchant, and *dsp* 16 July 1707

His n,

Sir William Clayton, 1st Bt (GB), so *cr* 13 Jan 1732, MP Bletchingley 1715–44; inherited large estates from his f William as well as those which he derived from his uncle; bought 1716 the Manor of Marlow; *m* Martha (*d* 14 Dec 1739), est dau of John Kenrick, of Flore, Surrey, by his w, a sis of Sir Robert Clayton's w, and *d* 28 Dec 1744, having had surviving issue, with two daus (including Mary, *m* Jonathan Rashleigh and had issue; *see* RASHLEIGH, Bt):

1 **Sir Kenrick Clayton, 2nd Bt**, MP Bletchingley 1754–69; *m* 1740 Henrietta Maria (*d* 25 July 1774, est dau and coheir of Henry Herring, and *d* 10 March 1769, leaving issue

(1) **Sir Robert Clayton, 3rd Bt**, MP Bletchingley 1768–83; *m* 1 June 1767 Elizabeth (*d* 27 Feb 1803), est dau of Frederick Standish, and *dsp* 10 May 1799

(1) Henrietta Mary; *m* 2 June 1765 Sir John Gresham, 6th Bt, and *d* 26 Jan 1804, leaving an only dau. He *d* 20 Sept 1801

(2) Martha; *d* unm 1802

2 William, of Harleyford, Bucks, MP; *m* 1st Mary (*d* 2 Jan 1760), dau of John Warde, of Squerryes, Kent, and had issue:

(1) Catherine; *m* 11 June 1765 4th Baron Howard de Walden (*qv*), who *dsp* 25 May 1797. She *d* 15 Aug 1807

2 (cont.) William Clayton *m* 2nd 3 May 1761 Maria Eliza Catherine (*d* Dec 1763), er dau and coheir of Rice Lloyd, of Alltycadno and Gwaleod-y-maes, Carmarthenshire, and had issue:

(1) WILLIAM (Sir), **4th Bt**

(2) Marianne; *m* 14 Feb 1786 Gen Hon Edward Fox (*see* ILCHESTER, E), and *d* 15 Oct 1808, leaving issue

2 (cont.) William Clayton *m* 3rd 24 Sept 1767 Louisa (*d* 30 June 1809), dau of Thomas, Earl of Pomfret (see HESKETH, B), and *d* 3 July 1783, having by her had issue:

(2) George, of Stonehall Surrey, Lt-Col 3rd Fus Gds, served in campaign in the Low Countries 1793; *b* 29 June 1768; *m* 22 Sept 1798 Frances (*d* 16 Aug 1849), dau of Rt Rev John Hinchcliffe, DD, Bishop of Peterborough, and *d* 17 Oct 1828, leaving, with other issue:

1a Emilius, Capt Scots Fus Gds; *b* 15 Jan 1803; *m* 25 Sept 1838 Eliza (*d* 3 Dec 1886), dau of William Hazlewood, of Slaugham Park, Sussex, and *d* 20 March 1887, leaving issue:

1b Emilius, JP Somerset, Col late RA, V-Consul at Van, Turkey, 1879–82, Prof of Staff Coll 1883–90, ret 1898; *b* 17 Oct 1841; *m* 14 June 1883 Ellen (*d* 2 Feb 1947), dau of Richard Laurence Pemberton, of Hawthorn Tower, Co Durham, and *d* 25 June 1921, leaving issue:

1c Emilius, OBE (1919), CA (1961) Devon, Lt-Col RA WW I (wounded), Mil Mission to Poland 1920–27, T/Brig on special duty 1939, memb Devon CC 1948 and Exmouth UDC 1939–45 (Chm 1947); *b* 19 June 1884; *m* 26 June 1915 Irene Dorothy Constance (*d* 12 Nov 1971), dau of Col T E Strong, IA, and *d* 10 June 1967, leaving issue:

1d Michael Thomas Emilius, CB (1976), OBE (1958); War Office 1939–76; *b* 15 Sept 1917; *m* 5 Feb 1942 Mary Margery (*d* 29 June 1994), er dau of Dr J Roberts Pate, of Oxford, and *d* 27 May 1995, leaving:

1e *Amanda Rosemary [Dr Amanda Hobson, 2 Tregonning Parc, St Keverne, Cornwall TR12 6QF]; *b* 12 April 1949; *educ* Reading (BA, PhD) and Exeter Us (Dip Law); *m* 1976 (*divorce* 1997) Peter Hobson, MA

2d +Anthony Hugh Le Quesne, TD (1965) [Lt-Col Anthony Clayton TD, April Cottage, 43 Ford Lane, Lower Bourne, Farnham, Surrey GU10 4SF], Lt-Col Intell Corps (TAVR), Kenya Civil Service 1952–65, Sr Lecturer RMA Sandhurst 1965; *b* 3 Sept 1928; *educ* St Andrews U (MA 1950, PhD); FSA Scot; *m* 1973 *Judith Mary, dau of P L Blackstone, of Rhu, Dunbartonshire, and has:

1e +Robert Anthony Emilius; *b* 1975; *educ* Edinburgh U (BSc)

1e *Penelope Fleur; *b* 1977

2c Ralph Arthur, Lt RA; *b* 16 Oct 1885; *d* unm 12 Nov 1910

3c George Edward, MC, Straits Settlements Civil Service, Capt RFA (TF) WW I; *b* 17 Dec 1896; *d* 30 March 1932

1c Janet Betha; *b* 2 June 1887; *d* unm 31 Oct 1975

2c Bridget Eleanor; *b* 28 Aug 1889; *m* 1 Dec 1914 Capt Winstanley Robert Coverdale Moorsom, OBE, RN (*d* 27 Dec 1966), and *d* 9 July 1981

3c Lucy Emilia; *m* 29 Sept 1920 John Vassle Buchanan, MD, and *d* 10 Sept 1921, leaving issue

2b Arthur Granville, Lt-Col RE; *b* 13 Aug 1843; *m* 12 Nov 1870 Elizabeth (*d* 12 July 1932), dau of John Kierman, and *d* 2 June 1892, leaving issue:

1c Arthur John Granville, served WW I, and WW II with RNVR; *b* 14 March 1872; *m* 1st 4 Aug 1894 Emily (*d* 21 Feb 1933), dau of William Freeman, of Gosport, Hants. He *m* 2nd 15 Nov 1946 Elizabeth (*d* 2 Feb 1965), dau of Frederick Mason, of Apsley End, Herts, and *dsp* 23 Feb 1956

2c Harold Robert, Capt Lancs Fus Boer War (medal, four clasps) and WW I (despatches); *b* 4 Nov 1874; *ka* 4 June 1915

3c Frank Guy (Rev), Vicar Spreyton Bow Devon 1935–53, vicar St Paul's Camden Sq, NW1, 1930–35; *b* 31 Dec 1875; *d* unm 14 Dec 1960

1c Kathleen Mary, WW II CD; *b* 1880; *d* unm Jan 1963

1b Betha Frances; *d* unm 17 June 1929

2b Horatia Louisa; *d* unm 4 Aug 1912

3b Florence Augusta; *m* 8 March 1883 Col Alexander William Croker Bell, IA , and *d* 9 April 1925

2a Henry, Maj-Gen, served at Bhurtpoor 1826, DQMG Cavalry Maharajpoor 1843; *b* 8 Sept 1804; *m* 9 Aug 1826 Jean Henrietta (*d* 1 Feb 1880), dau of Gen Sir Robert Blair, KCB, and *d* 17 May 1869, leaving, with other issue:

1b Edward Gilbert (Sir), CB, Maj RE, JP Surrey, Inspector of Prisons, Sec to Prison Commrs 1895–1908; *b* 16 July 1841; *m* 4 Nov 1864 Georgina Elizabeth Sykes (*d* 8 Aug 1931), dau and heir of Sykes Clayton, of The Manor Ho, Rufforth, Yorks, and *d* 5 March 1917, leaving issue:

1c Henry Edward Gilbert, Lt-Col RE S African War 1900–2 (despatches) and WW I (despatches); *b* 24 Aug 1867; *m* 7 Jan 1900 Huberta, 2nd dau of Capt Hubert H Grenfell, RN, and *d* 9 Feb 1948, leaving issue:

1d Henry Hubert, Head of Theoretical Physics Br Nat Research Laboratories, Chalk River, Ontario, WW II as Maj RCA; *b* 9 Feb 1906; *educ* U of Br Columbia (MA); *m* 17 June 1944 Isobel Mary (*d* 1 Jan 1990), dau of W G Winter, of Pembroke, Ontario, and *d* 10 Sept 1989, leaving issue:

1e +William Edward [William Clayton Esq, 14007-23A Ave, Surrey, BC V4A 9V3, Canada]; *b* 24 March 1945; *m* 19 Aug 1967 *Sharon Joan, dau of Kenneth Campbell, of Edmonton, Alberta, and has issue:

1f *Stacey Anna; *b* 17 Feb 1972

2f *Susan Amanda; *b* 28 March 1975

1e *Florence Nancy Thackeray; *b* 12 June 1947; *m* 2 Oct 1971 (*divorce* 1997) Erik van Veenen and has:

1f *Hendrick Hubert Clayton; *b* 3 Oct 1982

1f *Vanessa; *b* 17 June 1977

2f *Erica Maegan; *b* 30 July 1979

2d George Edward; BASc, MCIME, MAIME; *b* 5 Aug 1907; *m* 7 Jan 1940 *Olive, dau of H M Selfe, of Vancouver, BC, and *d* 1 Dec 1987

1d Petronilla; *b* 1 Dec 1903; *m* 1940 Richard Baden Whaley, ARICS (*d* 19–), and *d* 1984, leaving

1e *Richard H Grenfell [Richard Whaley Esq, 2 Rotherwick Court, Alexandra Rd, Farnborough, Hants GU14 6BD]; *b* 1940

2d Blanche Petite; *b* 9 Jan 1905; *educ* McGill U (MA); *d* 1960

3d *Grace Cynthia Maude [Mrs Philip Amsden, Headquarters Rd, RR4, Courtenay, BC V9N 7J3, Canada]; *b* 22 Feb 1908; *m* 27 Oct 1934 Philip Hennell Amsden (*d* 19–), son of Stanley Amsden, of 3 Arden Ho, Sydenham, and has issue:

1e *Michael Phillip; *b* 5 Aug 1935; *m* 29 Aug 1959 *Lorna Ryder and has:

1f *Brian; *b* 1964; *m* 12 July 1993 *Sharon Audrey Johnston and has:

1g *Natasha Elizabeth; *b* 10 Nov 1994

2g *Rachel; *b* 12 April 1997

1f *Lisa; *b* 25 July 1959; *m* 24 June 1989 *Robert Mallony, and has issue:

1g *Connor Michael; *b* 30 Dec 1992

2g *Stephen Padraich; *b* 28 July 1995

1g *Erin Maria; *b* 10 Oct 1990

2f *Sherri; *b* 14 Dec 1961; *m* 13 July 1985 *John McCall and has:

1g *Kyle Alexander; *b* 15 April 1988

2g *Thomas Michael; *b* 18 Jan 1990

3f *Susan Maureen; *b* 20 Sept 1962

4f *Julia Jane; *b* 2 Feb 1968; *m* 6 May 1992 *Gino Celebre and has:

1g *Jordan Robert; *b* 19 May 1993

2e *Harry Linton; *b* 4 June 1938; *m* 28 Dec 1965 *Josephine Venebles and has:

1f *Sarah; *b* 10 Aug 1974

3e *Stephen Oliver; *b* 7 Feb 1944; *m* 17 Aug 1968 *Janet Ives and has:

1f *Jessica Ann; *b* 1 June 1975

2f *Jacqueline Cynthia; *b* 1 Oct 1978

3e *Robin Petite; *b* 1941; *m* 1966 (*divorce* 1972) Allen Cripps and has:

1f *Cynthia; *b* 11 Feb 1968

2c Gerald Facourt, Capt Queen's Roy Regt WW I (wounded), joined Prison Serv, ret 1940; *b* June 1886; *m* 29 Aug 1916 Anabel Mary Margaret, only dau of Col Henry Maxwell Robertson, RA, of Hartfield Court, Eastbourne, and *d* 13 Sept 1963

1c Blanche Georgine; *m* 14 Dec 1893 Rev William Francis Sorsbie, MA Oriel Coll Oxford, rector Swainswick, Bath, 1927–34, CF, and *d* 2 Jan 1952, leaving issue. He *d* 1943

2c Grace Louisa; *m* 28 Jan 1897 Maj-Gen Sir Ernest Dunlop Swinton, KBE, CB, DSO, MA, late RE, and *d* 1 July 1952, leaving issue. He *d* 15 Jan 1951

3c Frances Jean; *d* unm 16 Sept 1961 aged 89

4c Eva; *m* 20 Nov 1904 Samuel Booth Brereton, and *d* 18 June 1949, leaving issue. He *d* 24 April 1930

2b Ernest William; *b* 28 April 1853; *m* 24 June 1880 Ellen Maude (*d* 16 July 1930), 3rd dau of Edward Tayloe, MRCS, and *d* 25 Aug 1917, having had:

1c Kenrick Edward, Capt 7th Bn Somerset LI S Africa 1901–02; *b* 26 May 1881; *m* 2 July 1918 Elizabeth May, 2nd dau of James Phillips, of Arley, Worcs

2c Harry Swinton, Indian Police; *b* 27 Oct 1883; *d* unm 26 Dec 1904

3c Reginald Ernest Thornbury, Lt Roy Guernsey Artillery WW I (severely wounded twice); *b* 20 Aug 1888; *m* 10 Dec 1925 Mabel, dau of Joseph Preston Ward, of Jersey, and *d* 3 April 1948

The 3rd Bt's cousin,

Sir William Clayton, 4th Bt; *b* 16 April 1762; *m* 16 July 1785 Mary (*d* 9 Aug 1833), only dau of Sir William East, Bt, of Hall Place, Berks, and *d* 26 Jan 1834, having had issue:

1 **Sir William Robert Clayton, 5th Bt**, Gen, present Battles of Vittoria, the six-days action in the Pyrenees, Genappe, Quatre-Bras (wounded) and Waterloo, MP Marlow 1832–42; *b* 28 Aug 1786; *m* 10 May 1817 Alice Hugh Massey, only child and heir of Col Hugh O'Donel, est son of Sir Neil O'Donel, Bt, and *d* 19 Sept 1866, having had issue, with an er dau:

(1) William Capel, Capt Coldstream Gds; *b* 14 April 1818; *m* Georgiana (who *m* 2nd J C de Wynter and *d* 12 Jan 1882), dau of Charles Wood, and *d* 9 June 1848, leaving issue:

1a **Sir William Robert Clayton, 6th Bt**, of Marden Park, Surrey, MA Cambridge, JP Carmarthenshire, Norfolk, Surrey and Bucks, DL, High Sheriff Bucks 1876, and Norfolk 1878, sometime Capt Roy Bucks Mil; *b* 3 Aug 1842; *m* 29 Oct 1872 Aimée Gertrude (*d* 3 Feb 1930), 5th dau of Edward Mackenzie, DL, JP, of Fawley Court, Bucks, and Auchenskeoch, Kirkcudbrightshire, and *dsp* 7 Oct 1714

(2) Henry Hugh O'Donel, 2nd Life Gds; *b* 2 April 1823; *m* 19 March 1846 Augusta (*m* 2nd 20 Oct 1863 Maj Robert George Manley, 6th Dragoon Gds, and *d* 15 Nov 1879), dau of Sir Charles Oakeley, 2nd Bt (*qv*), and niece of the Marquis Latour-Maubourg, and *d* 17 March 1857, leaving issue:

1a Charles Edward Ferdinand, Capt Grenadier Gds; *b* 17 Aug 1847; *m* 22 March 1880 Isabella Julia, dau of Edward George Lloyd, and *dsp* 11 Jan 1886

(1) Caroline Margaret; *m* 28 May 1840 at Gretna Green and 2 June 1840 8th Marquess of Queensberry (*qv*) and *d* 14 Feb 1904, having had issue

2 Sir EAST GEORGE CLAYTON later CLAYTON EAST (roy licence 6 April 1829), 1st Bt (UK), of Hall Place; *b* 9 April 1894; *m* 20 June 1815 Marianne Frances (*d* 5 Jan 1876), est dau of Charles Bishop, of Sunbury, Middx, late Procurator-Gen, and *d* 6 March 1851, having had, with five daus:

(1) Sir GILBERT EAST CLAYTON EAST later GILBERT EAST (roy licence 4 April 1839), 2nd Bt, of Hall Place; *b* 13 Nov 1823; *m* 29 Jan 1845 Emma Jane Lucretia (*d* 28 July 1872), est dau of Sebastian Smith, of Connaught Place West, and *d* 12 Aug 1866, leaving:

1a Sir GILBERT AUGUSTUS GILBERT EAST later CLAYTON EAST (1870), **7th Bt**, of Marden, and 3rd Bt, of Hall Place, JP; *b* 25 April 1846; *m* 3 Sept 1867 Eleanor Theresa (*d* 11 July 1924), dau of Maj-Gen Alexander Robert Fraser, and *d* 26 Sept 1925, having had issue:

1b Gilbert William; *b* 7 May 1869; *dsp* 23 Nov 1924

2b **Sir George Frederick Lancelot Clayton East, 8th Bt**, of Marden, and 4th Bt, of Hall Place, OBE; Maj RA WW I (despatches); *b* 3 Sept 1872; *m* 13 Oct 1906 Frances Louise Helen, JP Berks (*d* 29 Jan 1950), yr dau of Lt-Col James Colquhoun, DL, JP (*see* COLQUHOUN, Bt), and *d* 27 April 1926 had issue:

1c Sir ROBERT ALAN CLAYTON EAST later CLAYTON-EAST-CLAYTON (deed poll 22 Jan 1932), **9th Bt**, of Marden, and 5th and last Bt, of Hall Place; Lt RN; *b* 7 April 1908; *m* 29 Feb 1932 Dorothy Mary (*d* 15 Sept 1933 following an aeroplane accident), dau of Rev Arthur Durrant, Vicar Leverstock Green, Herts, and *dsp* 1 Sept 1932, when the btcy *cr* 1838 expired

1c *Cynthia Anne [Mrs Walter Graham, Knabbs Farmhouse, Fletching, Sussex TN22 3SX]; *b* 2 March 1914; Section Offr WAAF WWII; *m* 21 Oct 1949 *Walter Gerald Cloete Graham, CBE, HM Amb Libya 1955–59, son of Lance Graham Cloete Graham, and adopted:

*Alan Richard; *b* 1956

*Harriet Jane; *b* 1954; *m* 1986 *Fulvio Richetto

2c Erica Martia; *b* 4 Aug 1915; *m* 23 April 1938 (*divorce* 1958) Col John Kenneth Maitland Gordon, The Welch Regt (*d* 17 June 1967), 2nd son of Alexander Stillingfleet Gordon, of Lessland, Nettlestone, IoW, and has issue:

1d *Alan Julyan Maitland; *b* 20 Dec 1941; *educ* Eton; *m* 8 June 1968 *Diana Margaret Elonwy, dau of George William Harns James, of North Ave, Salisbury, Rhodesia

2d *Cosmo Gerald Maitland, barrister Middle Temple 1966; *b* 26 March 1945; *educ* Eton

1b Eleanor Alexandra; *d* young, 31 Dec 1878

2b Agnes Emma; *d* unm 13 Oct 1941

1a Emma Frances Louisa; *m* 9 Sept 1872 Reginald Gough Paynter, and *d* 16 May 1894, leaving issue. He *d* 1900

2a Frederica Julia; *m* 1 July 1874 Walter Grey Bellairs, of 6 Eaton Mansions, Cliveden Place, SW, and had issue. He *d* 4 July 1929

3a Ella Theresa; *d* 17 Feb 1870

(2) Augustus Henry, RN; *b* 1824; *d* off the coast of Borneo 23 Aug 1845

(3) Charles William, Lt 15th Regt; *b* 1826; *m* 1st 15 May 1847 Lillie Campbell (*d* 8 Aug 1747), dau of Campbell MacLachlan; *m* 2nd 14 Sept 1854 Eliza Spooner, est dau of Thomas Spooner Palmer, of Bayview, Co Sligo, and *dsp* 21 Aug 1866. She *d* 25 Sept 1906

(4) Frederick Richard, Capt 8th Madras Cav; *b* 19 Feb 1828; *m* 24 Aug 1854 Caroline Louisa (*d* 28 March 1912), yst dau of Thomas Spooner Palmer, of Bayview, Co Sligo, and *d* 15 Sept 1860, leaving issue:

1a George Frederick, late Lt 2nd Bn Roy Inniskilling Fus; *b* 18 Oct 1857; *d* unm 29 Jan 1898

1a Augusta Marianne; *d* unm 9 Nov 1944

3 John Lloyd, Lt RN; *b* 19 Aug 1796; *m* 10 April 1832 Louisa Sophia (*d* 2 March 1841), only dau of Charles Littledale, of Portland Place, and *d* 6 Oct 1855, leaving issue:

(1) John William, FRGS, Capt 13th Light Dragoons; *b* 23 Feb 1833; *m* 1st 4 Sept 1862 Mary Harietta Charlotte (*d* 8 Sept 1880), dau of Lt-Col Henry Charles Capel Somerset, of Elm Lodge, Hempstead, Glos (*see* BEAUFORT, D), and had issue:

1a Harold Hugh Kenrick John; *b* 13 Aug 1867; *d* unm 6 Aug 1890

1a Isabel Emily Florence; *m* 18 Jan 1893 Ernest Brooke Cozens-Brooke and *d* 1946, leaving issue

(1) (cont.) Capt John Clayton *m* 2nd 7 April 1892 Catherine Mary (*d* 11 Jan 1943), dau of James Gibson, MLC, of Tasmania, and *d* 18 April 1913, having by her had issue:

2a Kenrick; *b* 3 March 1896; *d* 13 Feb 1909

2a Violet; *b* 13 Feb 1893; *m* 1st 11 June 1914 (*divorce* 1921) Maj Edgar Henry Stocker, late 13th Hus, yst son of Alonzo Henry Stocker, MD, MRCS, LRCP, of Craigwell Ho, Aldwick, Sussex; *m* 2nd 23 June 1923 (*divorce* 1926) Maj Richard William Rice Jeudwine, late Roy Irish Fus, son of William Wynne Jeudwine, of Walton Lodge, Chesterfield, Derbys. He *d* 31 Dec 1956. She *m* 3rd 12 Jan 1932 Lt-Col Frederick Charles Goddard, IA, 2nd son of A C Goddard, of Pershore, Worcs. He *d* 28 Oct 1962

3a Winifred Ianthe; *b* 23 Jan 1895; *m* 1st May 1919 (*divorce* 1936) Capt Martin George Byard Copeman (*d* Feb 1942), late Leics Regt, son of Thomas Copeman, of Aylsham Old Hall, Norfolk, and has issue:

1b *Michael George Auchel, WW II as Maj RA, with Libyan Arab Force 1942–45, and Cyrenica Def Force 1945–50; *b* 7 April 1920; *educ* Aldenham

3a (cont.) Mrs Winifred Copeman *m* 2nd 21 Oct 1943 Col Philip Herbert Catt, KJStJ, FRGS, late Scots Gds, er son of George Herbert Catt, of The Depot Ho, Chichester, Sussex

4 Rice Richard, of Hedgerley Park, Bucks, MP Aylesbury 1841–47, MA, JP, and DL, High Sheriff 1838; *b* 15 Nov 1797; *m* 3 July 1832 Maria Amelia (*d* 30 Dec 1880), 2nd dau of FM Sir George Nugent, 1st Bt, GCB (*see* NUGENT, Bt, of Waddesdon), and *d* 4 May 1879, having had surv issue:

(1) Richard Nugent, Capt late 13th Regt; *b* 3 Sept 1833; *d* 8 Feb 1914

(2) George Augustus; *b* 1840; *m* Elizabeth, dau of Henry Godbere, late of Dawlish, and *d* 3 March 1918

(3) Francis Edmund; *b* Dec 1844; *m* 15 Sept 1881 Eliza (*d* 1882), dau of Henry Liggins, of Antigua, and *d* 11 April 1905, leaving issue:

1a Leila Cecilia; *m* 1903 her cousin **Sir Harold Dudley Clayton, 10th Bt** (*see* below), and *d* 8 Aug 1976, leaving issue

(4) Arthur John; *b* 5 Dec 1846; *m* 1893 Alice Rose (*d* 10 April 1922), dau of William Jones, of Hereford, and *d* 22 Dec 1922, leaving issue:

1a Marjorie Ida May Rose; *m* 16 Nov 1915 Capt R G Thompson, 8th Bn Roy W Surrey Regt, son of R H Thompson, of Reigate, Surrey. He *d* 13 May 1963

2a Mildred; *m* 5 July 1928 Constantine Hotham Crichton, son of Alexander William Crichton. He *d* 6 June 1946

3a Muriel Edith Lily; *b* 17 April 1900; *m* 1927 Arthur Harold Clayton, later 11th Bt (*see* below), and *d* 8 April 1929

(1) Louisa Maude; *m* 1 June 1876 Francis Arthur Hervey, and *d* 8 July 1923, leaving issue (*see* BRISTOL, M)

(2) Emily Rosa; *m* 1881 James Melvill Davidson, of Old Windsor, Berks, and *d* 27 Dec 1936. He *d* 4 July 1928

5 Augustus Philip (Rev), of Combe Bank, Kent; *b* 11 Oct 1799; *m* 4 Sept 1828 Georgiana Elizabeth (*d* 23 June 1885), dau of Very Rev Charles Talbot, DD, Dean of Salisbury, by Lady Elizabeth, dau of 5th Duke of Beaufort (*qv*), and *d* 2 Feb 1871, leaving issue:

(1) FitzRoy Augustus Talbot (Sir), KCVO, of Fyfield Ho, Maidenhead, Berks, JP, Chm of RNLI, sometime Lt-Col Gren Gds; *b* 28 March 1834; *m* 4 April 1872 Lady Isabel Frances Taylour (*d* 17 Nov 1909), dau of 3rd Marquess of Headfort (*qv*), and *d* 1 Aug 1913, leaving issue:

1a HAROLD DUDLEY (Sir), **10th Bt**

2a Lionel Arthur, Lt RAF and SA Constabulary; *b* 29 Jan 1878; *m* 30 Oct 1913 Rita Eleanor, only child of James W Ayrs, of Sunningdale, Berks and *d* 14 April 1954, leaving issue:

1b *Margaret Isabel; *b* 1914; *m* 1940 Edward John Wigan (*d* 1949), and has issue:

1c *Nicholas John; *b* 1941

3a Cecil Fraser Talbot, Capt Warwicks Yeo, formerly Capt 5th Bn KRRC, Lt 1st Bn Gren Gds; *b* 12 Aug 1880; *m* 1st 14 April 1909 (*divorce* 1918) Kathleen Agnes (*d* 27 Sept 1969), only dau of Lt-Col William Edward Bradish-Ellames, of Manor Ho, Little Marlow . He *m* 2nd 1918 Alice (*d* 1957), dau of John T Hatton, JP, and *d* 10 March 1940, leaving issue:

1b +Gilbert Talbot Hatton [Gilbert Clayton Esq, Cobbles, Broadstone, Dorset]; WW II 1942–45 in RAFVR; *b* 1920

(1) Elizabeth Georgiana

1 Catherine Emilia; *m* 16 July 1821 John Shawe Manley, of Manley Hall, Staffs, and *d* 7 Feb 1864, having had issue. He *d* 19 May 1857

The 9th Bt's cousin,

Sir Harold Dudley Clayton, 10th Bt, Lt RNVR WW I, AINA; *b* 28 Jan 1877; *m* 1903 Leila Cecilia (*d* 8 Aug 1976), only child of Francis Edmund Clayton (*see* above), and had issue:

1 ARTHUR HAROLD (Sir), **11th Bt**

2 FitzRoy Richard Henry, Lt RASC; *b* 1907; *m* 1st 1930 Morwen (*d* 11 June 1941), dau of Judge Fedor Andrew Satow (*see* CHILSTON, V), and had issue:

(1) +Barry Drew Satow, MRIBA; *b* 20 Jan 1935; *educ* Sherborne

(1) *Ailsa; *b* 24 Feb 1932; *m* 1 Jan 1952 *William Findlay Key, er son of William Key, of Mowbray, Cape Town, S Africa, and has issue:

1a *Richard William; *b* 1960

1a *Philippa Margaret; *b* 1954; *m* 1974 *Anthony Victor Lithgow

2a *Gail Morwen; *b* 1956

2 (cont.) FitzRoy Clayton *m* 2nd 1 July 1944 Moira Consuelo (*d* 17 June 1971), dau of Philip Fidelis Ryan, of Ceylon, and by her had issue:

(2) Roderick John; *b* 21 May 1945; *educ* Beaumont; *m* 25 July 1968 *Diana Melissa [Mrs Diana Corbett, 24 Duke's Ave, London W4 2AE] (*m* 2nd 1985 (*divorce* 1995) — Corbett), yr dau of Sir H Alan Walker, of Belgravia, and *d* 1980, leaving:

1a +Patrick Justin FitzRoy; *b* 1970; *educ* Downside

1a *Louisa Jane; *b* 1972; *educ* St Mary's Shaftesbury

2 (cont.) FitzRoy Clayton *m* 3rd 1973 *(Phyllis) Margaret [Mrs FitzRoy Clayton, 108A Alderney St, London SW1V 4EZ], dau of Reginald Tindal, of Wirral, Cheshire, and widow of Sydney James Pullan, of Lillington Manor, Leamington Spa, and *d* 1989

1 Elfreda Isabell Stella; *b* 1904; *d* unm 1956

Sir HAROLD *d* 19 Oct 1951; his er son,

Sir Arthur Harold Clayton, 11th Bt, DSC, Lt-Cdr RNVR WW II (despatches); *b* 14 Oct 1903; *educ* Haileybury; *m* 1st 1927 Muriel Edith (*d* 8 April 1929), yst dau of Arthur John Clayton (*see* above); *m* 2nd 19 Dec 1931 (*divorce* 1954) Alexandra, only child of Sergei Andreevsky, and had issue:

1 Sir DAVID ROBERT CLAYTON, **12th and present Bt**

1 *Ann; *b* 19 Sept 1933; *m* 1st 4 Oct 1951 (*divorce* 1977) Alfred Plew, slr, son of Edwin Plew, of Pendennis, Paignton, Devon; *m* 2nd 1978 John Hawksely Martin

Sir Arthur *m* 3rd 29 May 1954 Dorothy (Jill) (*d* 8 April 1964), formerly w of S Hamer and 2nd dau of Arthur John Greenhalgh, of Llanrhos, Llandudno; *m* 4th 1965 *Diana Katherine Mary [Diana Lady Clayton, Colonsay, Kingswear, Devon], only child of Capt Charles Alverey Grazebrook, 60th Rifles, and formerly w of (a) Peter Neve and (b) — Bircham, and *d* 1985

Lineage (of East): WILLIAM EAST (son of William East, of the Middle Temple, who *d* 1726), of Hall Place, Hurley, Berks, the site of which he bought 1728 and finished the house *c* 1735, barrister; *m* Anne, dau of Sir George Cooke, of Harefield, Ch Prothonotary of the Common Pleas, and *d* 1737, leaving:

Sir WILLIAM EAST, 1st Bt, of Hall Place, Berks, so *cr* 5 June 1766, High Sheriff 1766–67; *b* 27 Feb 1737/8; *m* 1st 29 June 1763 Hannah, 2nd dau of Henry Casamajor; *m* 2nd 28 July 1768 — Jackson and *d* 12 Oct 1819, having by his 1st w had issue:

1 Sir GILBERT EAST, 2nd and last Bt, High Sheriff Berks 1822–23; *b* 17 April 1764; *m* 10 May 1788 Eleanor Mary (*m* 2nd 31 March 1834 Hon John Craven Westenra (*see* ROSSMORE, B) and *dsp* 17 Dec 1838), est dau of William Joliffe, of Petersfield, and *dsp* 11 Dec 1828, when the btcy expired

2 Augustus Henry; *m* 22 Dec 1792 Caroline Anne, est dau of George Vansittart, of Bisham Abbey, and *dsp* 1828

1 Mary; *m* 16 July 1785 **Sir William Clayton, 4th Bt**, of Marden (*see* above), and *d* 9 Aug 1833, having had issue

CLEDWYN OF PENRHOS

Creation: B. (LP, UK) 1979.

THE BARON CLEDWYN OF PENRHOS, of Holyhead in the Isle of Anglesey (Cledwyn Hughes, CH (1977), PC (1966)) [The Rt Hon The Lord Cledwyn of Penrhos CH PC, Penmorfa, Trearddur, Holyhead, Gwynedd]; *b* 14 Sept 1916; *educ* Holyhead GS and U Coll of Wales Aberystwyth (LLB); slr 1940; F/Lt RAFVR 1940–46; memb Angelsey CC 1946–52; MP (Lab) Anglesey 1951–79, memb Ctee Public Affrs 1957–64, Chm: Welsh Parly Party 1953–54, Welsh Lab Gp 1955–56; Oppn Spokesman Housing and Local Govt 1959–64, Min State Cwlth Affrs 1964–66, Sec State Wales 1966–68, Min MAFF 1968–70, memb Ctee Privileges 1974–79, Jt Chm TUC-Lab Party Liaison Ctee 1974–79, V-Pres Britain in Europe 1975, PM's Emissary Southern Africa 1978, Chm: PLP 1974–79, Welsh Ctee Ec and Industl Affrs 1982–84, Oppn Leader Ho Lds 1982–92, memb Political Honours Ctee 1992–; dir: Shell UK 1980–84, Anglesey Aluminium 1980–, Holyhead Towing 1980–; Regnl Advsr Wales Midland Bank 1979–94, Memb CC Assoc 1980–, Chm Welsh Theatre Co 1981–85; Pres: Housing and Town Planning Cncl 1980–92, Age Concern Wales 1980–85, Soc of Welsh People Overseas 1979–91, UCW Aberystwyth 1974–84, Assembly of Welsh Counties 1990–, U Wales Bangor 1995–; Pro-Chllr U of Wales 1984–94; Fell UCW Aberystwyth 1988, Trinity Coll Carmarthen 1993; Hon Freedom Beaumaris 1972, Freeman Borough Anglesey 1976; Hon LLD: Wales 1970, Sheffield 1992, Glamorgan 1996; Alderman Anglesey CC 1973; author: *Report on Conditions in St Helena* (1958); *m* 1949 *Jean Beatrice, JP, dau of Capt Jesse Hughes, and has:

1 *Harri Cledwyn; *b* 1955; *m* 1986 *Jennifer Meryl, dau of R P Hughes, of Coedlys Valley, Anglesey, and has issue

1 *Emily Ann; *b* 1950; *m* 1976 *Peter Wright and has issue

Lineage: Rev HENRY DAVID HUGHES, descendant of Morus ap William, who lived in Fachwen in 1702 after leaving Clynnog, home of his family; *m* Emily Hughes and had:

CLEDWYN, *cr* a **Baron**

CLERK

Arms: Or a fess chequy azure and argent between two crescents in chief gules, and a boar's head couped in base sable. **Crest:** A demi-huntsman winding a horn proper. **Supporters:** Dexter, a savage wreathed about the middle with oak, in the dexter hand a bow, a quiver of arrows over his shoulder, and the skin of a wild beast hanging behind his back, all proper; sinister, a druid priest with flowing beard proper, vested and hooded argent, holding in the sinister hand an oak branch acorned vert. **Mottoes:** (above crest) Free for a blast; (below arms) *Amat victoria curam* ('Victory desires care'). **Creation:** Bt. (NS) 24 March 1679.

SIR JOHN DUTTON CLERK, 10TH BT, of Penicuik, Edinburgh, CBE (1966), VRD, JP (Midlothian 1955) [Sir John Clerk Bt CBE VRD JP DL, Penicuik House, Penicuik, Midlothian EH26 9LA]; *b* 30 Jan 1917; *s f* 1943; *educ* Stowe; Cdre RNR (ret 1967), WW II; Midlothian: Ld-Lt 1972–92 (V-Lt 1965–72, DL 1956–72), Lt Roy Co Archers 1973; *m* 10 June 1944 *Evelyn Elizabeth, er dau of William Robertson, and has issue:

1 +ROBERT MAXWELL OBE (1995), DL [Robert Clerk Yr of Penicuik OBE DL, Penicuik House, Penicuik, Midlothian EH26 9LA]; *b* 3 April 1945; *educ* Winchester and Wye Coll London (BSc Ag); FRICS; memb Roy Co of Archers; *m* 5 Sept 1970 *(Felicity) Faye, yr dau of George Collins, of Grayshott House, Bampton, Oxon, and has:

(1) +George Napier; *b* 27 May 1975

(2) +Edward James 1986

(1) *Julia Elizabeth; *b* 28 Oct 1973

2 +Piers Edward John [Piers Clerk Esq, Newport House, Weston-under-Lizard, Shifnal, Shropshire TF11 8JT]; *b* 22 June 1955; *educ* Winchester and Aberdeen U (BLE); ARICS; *m* 23 July 1983 *Lucy Ann, only dau of Michael Hewens, of Crookham Manor, Thatcham, Berks, and has issue:

(1) +William James; *b* 1987

(1) *Iona Mary; *b* 1985

1 *Aymée Lavinia [Mrs George Ferguson, 5 Windsor Terr, Clifton, Bristol]; *b* 4 June 1947; *m* 24 May 1969 *George Robin Paget Ferguson, er son of Maj Robert Ferguson, of Pewsey, Wilts, and has issue:

(1) *John Spencer Guy; *b* 1974

(1) *Alice Rose; *b* 1971

(2) *Corinna May; *b* 1979

2 *Honor Elizabeth; *b* 24 April 1957

Lineage: JOHN CLERK; held the lands of Kilhuntley, in Badenoch; supported MARY QUEEN OF SCOTS in opposition to his superior, the Earl of Huntly (*see* HUNTLY, M), and consequently moved to Fettercairn, Kincardineshire; his s:

WILLIAM CLERK; merchant-burgess Montrose; *d* 1620, leaving:

JOHN CLERK, of Penicuik, Edinburgh; *b* 22 Dec 1611; settled Paris 1634, acquiring a fortune; returned to Scotland; in 1646 bought the lands and Barony of Penicuik, Edinburgh; *m* Mary, dau of Sir William Gray of Pittendrum, and *d* 1674, leaving, with four yr sons and five daus:

Sir John Clerk, 1st Bt (NS), so *cr* 24 March 1678/9, of Penicuik; MP Co Edinburgh 1690–1702, bought the lands and Barony of Lasswade 1700; *m* 1st 1674 Elizabeth, dau of Henry Henderson, of Elrington, and had three sons and three daus; *m* 2nd Christian, dau of the Rev James Kirkpatrick, and had four other sons and four daus; *d* 1722; his est s:

Sir John Clerk, 2nd Bt; FRS, FSA, MP Whithorn 1702–08; *b* 8 Nov 1676; Baron Exchequer in Scotland 1707–55, Commr for the Union; *m* 1st 23 Feb 1701 Lady Margaret Stewart (*d* 15 Nov 1709), dau of 3rd Earl of Galloway (qv), and had a son John (*dvp* unm 1722); *m* 2nd 15 Nov 1709 Janet (*d* 29 Jan 1760), dau of Sir James Inglis, Bt, of Cramond, and *d* 4 Oct 1755, having by her had, with five other sons and six daus, an est surv s:

1 **Sir James Clerk, 3rd Bt**; *m* Elizabeth, dau of Rev John Cleghorn, and *dsp* 6 Feb 1782

2 **Sir George Clerk, 4th Bt**; Commr Customs, Ld Treasurer's Remembrancer Exchequer, tstee for the improvement of fisheries and manufactures of Scotland; *m* Dorothea (*d* 28 Dec 1793), dau and heir of his uncle William Clerk-Maxwell by Agnes Maxwell, and *d* 29 Jan 1784, having had, with four daus:

(1) **Sir John Clerk, 5th Bt**; *m* Rosemary, dau of Joseph Dacre Appleby, of Kirklington, Cumberland, and *dsp* 1798

(2) George; *d* unm

(3) James; HEICS; *m* 18 Oct 1786 Janet, dau of George Irving of Newton, and *d* 1793, leaving issue:

1a GEORGE (Sir), **6th Bt**

2a John CLERK-MAXWELL, of Middlebie, Co Dumfries; *b* 1790; *m* 1826 Frances (*d* 6 Dec 1839), dau of Robert Cay, of Charlton, and *d* 3 April 1856, leaving:

1b James, of Middlebie; *b* 13 June 1831; FRS, Prof Experimental Physics Cambridge; *m* 2 June 1858 Katherine Mary, dau of the Very Rev Daniel Dewar, DD, and *dsp* 5 Nov 1879

1a Isabella; *m* 28 Oct 1813 Rt Hon James Wedderburn (*see* OGILVY-WEDDERBURN, Bt) and *d* 2 Nov 1865, having had issue

(4) William

(5) Robert

The 5th Bt's nephew,

Sir George Clerk, 6th Bt, PC (1845); *b* 1787; FRS, DCL, MP Midlothian 1811–20, Stamford 1838–47 and Dover 1847–52, Master of the Mint, V-Pres BOT 1845; *m* 13 Aug 1810 Maria (*d* 7 Sept 1866), 2nd dau of Ewan Law, of Sussex, and 1st cousin of Earl of Ellenborough (*qv*), and *d* 23 Dec 1867, having had issue:

1 JAMES (Sir), **7th Bt**

2 George Edward, of Montreal; *b* 18 March 1815; *m* 27 Nov 1849 Marie Louise Elizabeth, dau of Casimir Dupuis, of Montreal, and *d* 30 Sept 1875, leaving issue, with three daus:

(1) George Edward; *b* 4 Sept 1850; *m* 1st 12 Jan 1875 Henrietta Davignon (*d* 1889), and had issue:

1a George Edward, MD, CM; *b* 1877; Capt RAMC; *m* 1903 Annie, dau of Eugene Manny, and *d* 15 Nov 1938, leaving issue:

1b Douglas Leo; *b* 1904; *m* 29 May 1937 Madeline St Jean

2b George Henry; *b* 1907; *d* 1910

3b +Sydney Percy; *b* 1912; *m* 8 Oct 1938 *Thérèse, only dau of Louis St Laurent, and had issue:

1c *Michelle Marie Madeleine; *b* 1940

2c *Helene; *b* 1943

4b +Joseph Harry; *b* 1914; *m* 1950 *Alberta Therese, dau of Armand Drouin, and had issue:

1c *Irene Gail; *b* 1952

(1) (cont) George Edward *m* 2nd 1889 Regina (*d* 1950), dau of F X Renois, and *d* 29 Sept 1906, having by her had:

2a Abel; *b* 1897; *m* 1927 Cecile, dau of R Poisson, and *d* 1964, leaving issue:

1b +André Arthur [André Clerk Esq, 10430 Meunier St, Ahuntsic, Montreal, Canada]; *b* 4 Feb 1929; *m* 1955 *Claire, dau of Armand Charbonneau, and has issue:

1c +Georges Edward; *b* 1 Aug 1958

2c +Benoit; *b* 1962

3c +Bruno; *b* 1964

1c *Micheline; *b* 25 Oct 1956

1a *Lucette; *m* 1908 Edmond Chasse who *d* 1951

2a *May; *b* 25 Feb 1894

(2) Charles François; *b* 15 Oct 1851; *m* 1st 30 June 1873 Néomi Bertrand; *m* 2nd Delphine Barsalon, and *d* 1927, having had issue by his 1st w:

1a Charles (Rev); *d* 1932

2a Henry; went to USA

1a Néomi; *m* Paul Quimet (*d* 1918), and had issue

2a Marie; *m* O Gelinas, and had issue

(3) Henry Joseph; *b* 22 Aug 1856; *m* Nellie Coogan (*d* 1930), and *d* 28 Oct 1929, leaving issue:

1a *Louise; *m* 1930, Ben Pitt, of Canada

2a Eva; *d* unm 20 Aug 1960

3a Mabel; *d* Dec 1955

(4) Edmund Antoine; *b* 27 Feb 1858; *m* 1886 Malvina Tourville (*d* 1900), and *d* 6 Jan 1921, leaving issue:

1a Walter Charles; *b* 1891; *m* 1st 1915 Jeanne Beauchamp (*d* 1920), and had issue:

1b *Francoise; *b* 1917; *m* 1943 Lt-Cdr Pierre R Gendron, DSC, RCNVR (*d* 1983)

2b *Marguerite; *b* 1919; *m* 1943 Jacques de Tounancour, artist

1a (cont) Walter Charles *m* 2nd1922 *Gabrielle Beauchamp, and *d* 23 Dec 1937, having by her had issue:

1b +George; *b* 1925; *m* 1950 *Lucette C Barbeau, and has issue:

1c +Philippe; *b* 1959

2c +Patrice; *b* 1964

1c *Josée; *b* 1951

2c *Michelle; *b* 1953

3c *Danie; *b* 1957

2b +Robert; *b* 1926

3b *Suzanne; *b* 1924

2a Guy; *b* 1893; Customs Officer; *m* 1916 Jeanne Mongeau

3a Henry; *b* 1896; *m* 1918 Liliane Payette, and had issue:

1b +Gérard; *b* 1919; Capt Canadian Army; *m* 1949 *Lucille McCaughan and has:

1c *Joanne; *b* 1955

2b +Jacques; *b* 1922; P/O RCAF; *m* *Rejane Gauvain

1b *Raymonde; *b* 1918; *m* 1940 Paul Fortin, and has issue:

1c *Micheline; *b* 1941

2c *Monique; *b* 1943

1a Aline; *b* 1894; *m* 1916 C Henri Rouleau

(5) Alexander Marie Joseph; *b* 30 Aug 1861; *m* 1888 Blanche Gelinas (*d* 1942), and *d* 27 July 1932, leaving issue:

1a Edouard; *b* 19 Feb 1889; architect; *m* 1917 Fernande (*d* 1969), dau of Dr Ernest Choquette, MLC, of Quebec, and *d* 1982, leaving issue:

1b +Michel; *b* 29 Jan 1920; *m* 1952 *Monique Martineau and has:

1c +Philippe; *b* 1953

2c +Cyril; *b* 1954

3c +Emmanuel; *b* 1960

1c Catherine; *b* 1957; *d* 1987

2c Sophie; *b* 1964; *d* 1987

2b +Marc; *b* 19 June 1923; *m* 1949 *Gabrielle Brunet, PhD, and has issue:

+David; *b* 1952

*Nathalie; *b* 1950

3b Stephan, BA, BCL, QC; *b* 6 Feb 1926; *m* 1954 *Thérèse, dau of Maurice Saint-Jacques, of St Hyacinthe, Quebec, and *d* 1989, having had issue:

1c +Eric Fraser; *b* 1955; *m* 1982 *Elleana Balladares Diez, and has issue:

1d *Christina; *b* 1993

2c Nicolas; *b* 1957; *d* 1976

3c +Jean (twin); *b* 1957

4b +Pierre; *b* 26 April 1928; painter; *m* 1953 *Adriana Bertolini, and has issue:

1c *Jessica; *b* 1954

2a Paul; *b* 15 Sept 1891; *m* 1927 Alice Gascon (*d* 3 March 1947), and *d* 1960, and having had issue:

1b Paul; *b* 9 Aug 1930; *m* 1975 *Vivian Winsor and *d* 1997

2b +Andrée; *b* 31 July 1933; *m* 1959 Réne Beaucage (*d* 1991), and has issue:

1c +Michel; *b* 1956

2c +Dominique; *b* 1959

1c +Edith; *b* 1962

1b *Françoise; *b* 14 July 1928; *m* 1953 Léon Des Lauriers, and has issue:

1c *François; *b* 1959

1c *Nathalie; *b* 1962; *m* 1989 *Alain Barrette, and has issue:

1d *Nicolas; *b* 1990

1d *Amélie; *b* 1993

3a Maurice; *b* 1 Jan 1893; *m* 1926 Marguerite Lajoie, and *d* 1926, leaving issue:

1b *Louise; *b* 1926; *m* 1948 Léopold Brégent

4a Bernard; *b* 11 May 1902

1a Marie; *b* 21 May 1894; *d* 28 Jan 1987

2a Pauline; *b* 3 July 1896; *d* 10 Aug 1997

3a Marcelle; *b* 20 Aug 1898; *m* Fabien Geoffrion, and *d* 31 Dec 1934, leaving issue

4a *Yvette; *b* 1912; *m* 1937 Jacques Trépanier, LLD, jnlst, and has issue:

1b *François; *b* 1938

2b *Maurice; *b* 1942

1b *Hélène; *b* 1943

2b *Josette; *b* 1946

3b *Micheline; *b* 1947

(6) Jean Pio Robert; *b* 9 June 1870; *m* 1898 Marie Alma David (*d* 7 Jan 1947), dau of Senator L O David, and *d* 1932, leaving issue:

1a David Douglas; *b* 1901; *m* 29 Oct 1931 Jeanne, dau of Hon C A Caron

2a Jacques Donald; *b* 1904; Administrator, L'Union Medicale du Canada; *m* Elizabeth Labreque, and had issue:

1b +Robert; *b* 13 Aug 1929

2b +Gilles; *b* 14 Feb 1931

3b +Jacques; *b* 7 March 1936

1b *Lise; *b* 30 May 1928

2b *Jeannine; *b* 4 July 1933

3b Denise; *b* 24 Oct 1938

4b Andrée; *b* 29 Jan 1940

3a +Louis Philippe Duncan; *b* 1907; *m* 1936 *Gabrielle, dau of Hon George A Simard, and had issue:

+Henri; *b* 1941

*Michelle; *b* 25 July 1937

4a +Jean Elton; *b* 1910; *m* 1942 *Monique, dau of Albert Olivier, and has issue:

1b +Jean Elton; *b* 18 Jan 1944

1b *Suzanne; *b* 5 March 1948

2b *Hélène; *b* 5 Oct 1954

1a Jeanne Isabella; *b* 1899; *m* Theodore Fauteux, and had issue:

1b +Pierre; *b* 1928

1b *Louise; 1927

2a Camille Gertrude; *b* 1902

3a Simone Corinne; *b* 1909; *d* 26 July 1936

3 John, QC, JP Leics; *b* 16 April 1816; *m* 9 Dec 1845 Rose Alice Clothilde (*d* 6 Nov 1899), 2nd dau of Thomas Greene, of Slyne, and Whittington Hall, MP, and *d* 10 April 1900, leaving issue:
(1) George Thomas; *b* Dec 1846; *d* 4 Feb 1897
(2) John Frederick; *b* May 1848; BA Oxford; barrister; *m* 16 Dec 1884 Eleanor (*d* 29 May 1937), dau and coheir of Gustavus Smith, of Goldicote, and *d* 4 April 1931, leaving issue:
1a Aylmer Gustavus, DSO (1917), MC, TD; *b* 1888; *educ* Winchester; Maj 1st Bn Herts Regt TA WW I (despatches three times); *m* 25 June 1938 (*divorce* 1952) Blanche, dau of Emile Marchal, and *dsp* 5 April 1968
1a Violet; *m* 13 Feb 1909 Francis Maurice Gustavus Du Plat Taylor, CB (*d* 22 May 1954), and had issue
2a Sybil Alice; *b* 29 June 1892; *d* unm 27 Dec 1970
3a Nancy Eleanor; *m* 1934 Philip Giles Tennant
(3) Malcolm Henry; *b* May 1853; *dsp* 1887
(4) Duncan Edward; *b* Jan 1863; *m* 1890 Madge (*d* 25 June 1942), dau of Rev David Bruce, DD, and *d* 5 Nov 1941, having had issue:
1a Eric; *b* 1891; *ka* 1917
1a Mabel Thorold Bruce; *b* 1895
(1) Alice Henrietta; *d* April 1874
(2) Helen Georgina; *d* unm 15 June 1925
(3) Mabel Gertrude; *m* Addison Bright, and *d* 1924, leaving issue
4 Edward; *b* 24 June 1824; Maj late 4th Madras Cav; *m* 28 April 1864 Alice (*d* 30 May 1925), yst dau of T W Bramston, MP, of Skreens, Essex, and *d* 1 May 1917, leaving issue:
(1) William Henry; *b* 19 Sept 1867; *m* 1906 Sarah Cecilia Reeves (*d* 1964), and *d* 1915, leaving issue:
1a +William Robert; *b* 1907
2a +Edward (twin); *b* 1907; *m* 1940 *Dora Appleby, and had issue
1b +Edward Peter; *b* 1941
(2) Herbert Edward; *b* 15 April 1871; *m* 15 Aug 1908 Helen (*d* 21 May 1946), dau of Julius A Heuer, and *d* 6 July 1931, leaving issue:
1a Margery Alice, CBE (1959), JP (1966); *b* 18 May 1913; *educ* St Paul's and St Hugh's Coll Oxford (MA 1948); Chelsea Borough Cncllr 1945–56, Cncllr LCC 1946–58, Dep Chm LCC 1957–58, a Govr Hammersmith Hosp 1959–65; *m* 30 Nov 1937 Maj Richard Thornton, RT Regt, er s of Richard Thornton, of East Ashling House, nr Chichester, and had issue:
1b *Richard George Clerk; *b* 21 April 1944; *educ* Marlborough
2b *Anthony Christopher Lawrence; *b* 18 Aug 1947; *educ* Eton and Keble Coll Oxford
1b *Anna Sara Constance; *b* 1 May 195
2a Mary Helen; *b* 13 Feb 1915; *m* 22 Dec 1939 Michael George Russell Adams, MA (*d* 27 April 1995), 2nd son of Capt Henry George Homer Adams, CBE, RN, of Hereford, and *d* 15 Feb 1989, leaving:
1b *Nicholas Henry Harvey [Lt-Col Nicholas Adams, Hollies Farm, Postland, Crowland, Peterborough PE6 0LS]; *b* 5 Oct 1943; *educ* Eton, RMA Sandhurst and Corpus Christi Coll Cambridge (MPhil 1983); Lt-Col Light Div (Roy Grn Jackets) (ret); *m* 8 Dec 1964 *Leila, only dau of Maj Gilbert Mahon King, of Mullingar, Co Westmeath, and has issue:
1c *Mark Henry Leo; *b* 8 May 1966; *educ* Eton, RMA Sandhurst and Corpus Christi Coll Cambridge (MA); *m* 3 Sept 1994 *Frances, dau of William Montgomery, of Grey Affey, Co Down
1c *Clare Laura Catherine; *b* 1971; *educ* St John's Coll Durham (BA)
2b *George Miles Bramston [George Adams Esq, 131 Percy Rd, London W12]; *b* 18 Aug 1956; *m* 1987 *Christine Martin and has:
1c *Abigail; *b* 1988
1b *Daffodil Jane Florence [Mrs Charles Marriage, Netherhill Cottage, Botley, Southampton]; *b* 3 April 1946; *m* 1971 *Charles Brian Marriage and has:
1c *Thomas Charles; *b* 1976
1c *Louise Caroline; *b* 1974
2c *Ellen Elizabeth; *b* 1980
(1) Florence Eliza; *d* unm 6 May 1952
(2) Maud Alice; *d* unm 17 Aug 1918
5 Alexander; *b* 22 Dec 1828; Col ASC; *m* 1 Dec 1857 Edith Mary (*d* 7 March 1904), dau of Andrew Buchanan, MD, and *d* 11 Nov 1912, leaving issue:
(1) Hugh Edward, CIE (1914); *b* 11 June 1859; India PW Dept, Ch Engr and Jt Sec Madras 1911–14; *m* 1885 Edith Elizabeth (*d* 4 March 1933), est dau of Willoughby James Beauchamp (*see* PROCTOR-BEAUCHAMP, Bt,), and Id 17 Feb 1942, having had issue:
1a Beauchamp; *b* 22 Aug 1886; Capt IA; *ka* 11 March 1915
(2) Arthur Stanley; *b* 26 Nov 1864; *m* 1897 Edith Maud (*d* 19 Dec 1955), dau of C E Sheffield, of Nova Scotia, and *d* 1948, leaving issue:
1a Alexander Stanley; *b* 1901; *m* 1927 Jennie Waters, and *dsp* 3 Dec 1953
2a Charles Beverley; *b* 1904; *m* 1925 Angela Herbin (*d* 1969), and *d* 1983, leaving issue:
1b +Alexander Simpson; *b* 12 Jan 1930; *m* 19 Sept 1953 *Shirley Evangeline, dau of Robert S Cook, of Kentville, Nova Scotia, and has issue:
1c +Charles Alexander; *b* 20 Aug 1954; *m* 1987 *Friedel Moser
2c +Thomas Richard; *b* 29 March 1956; *m* 1980 *Kimberley Denhartog, and has issue:
1d *Courtney Ruth; *b* 1980
2d *Kendra Ann; *b* 1983
1c *Katherine Lois; *b* 9 Feb 1958; *m* 1980 *Peter Charles Cooper, of Kentville, Nova Scotia, and has issue:
1d *Christopher Allan; *b* 1984
2d *Jason Alexander; *b* 1986
1d *Elizabeth Katherine; *b* 1988
2c *Susan Bernice; *b* 2 March 1961; *m* 1986 *Mark Stuart Hersey, and has issue:
1d *Justin Robert; *b* 1986
2d *Benjamin Stuart; *b* 1988
1d *Angela Faye; *b* 1985
3c *Faye Marie; *b* 22 Jan 1965
1b *Mary Beverley; *b* 1 Jan 1929; *m* 5 Jan 1954 William H Stevens (*d* 1979), and has issue:
1c *William Charles; *b* 29 Oct 1954
1c *Marylynne Margaret; *b* 5 June 1958; *m* 1980 *Michael Karl Middelkoop, of Halifax, NS, and has issue:
1d *Adam Jason; *b* 1985
2d *Stephanie Anne; *b* 1983
1a Mary Adela; *b* 1899; *m* 1st 1926 Thornton Pineo who *d* 1928; *m* 2nd 1935 Maj G K Peake, DSO, son of Col G Peake, of Charlottetown, Prince Edward Island, and *d* 1942
2a *Dorothy Evangeline [Mrs Arthur Merlin, 82 Broadway Ave, Apt 1, Toronto M4P 1T7, Ontario, Canada]; *b* 1902; *m* 1926 Arthur F Merlin (*d* 1983), and had issue:
1b *Marilyn; *b* 1928; *m* 1st (*divorce* 1967) Kenneth Arthur Wynne; *m* 2nd 1967 *Richard Arthur and has issue by 1st husb:
1c *Kenneth Arthur; *b* 1955; *m* 1983 *Barbara Anne Jame, and has issue
2c *Derrick Andrew; *b* 1957; *m* 1988 *Brenda Lee Crack
(1) Agnes Isabella; *m* 1883 Andrew Williamson, of Dover, and had issue
(2) Cecilia Mary
(3) Isabella Edith; *m* 20 July 1893 Rev William Russell Fox (*d* 30 March 1938), Rector of North Bovey, Newton Abbot, Devon, and *d* 5 May 1949, leaving issue
(4) Charlotte Elizabeth; *d* unm
(5) Dorothea Emma; *m* 8 Jan 1903 Frederick Alexander Bowlby, of Ingatestone who *d* 1911; she joined the Sisters of Vincent of Paul 1913

The 6th Bt's est son,

Sir James Clerk, 7th Bt, JP and DL (Midlothian); *b* 17 July 1812; Capt Cmdt 3rd Midlothian Vols, formerly 9th Lancers; *m* 26 June 1851 Jane Calvert (*d* 29 Sept 1895), est dau of Maj-Gen Mercer Henderson, CB, and *d* 17 Nov 1870, having had issue:
1 GEORGE DOUGLAS (Sir), **8th Bt**
2 Robert James; *b* 1857; *d* April 1860
1 Susan Edith; *m* 5 June 1883 Sir Alan Henry Seton-Steuart, 4th Bt, of Allanton (*d* 3 April 1913; *see* 1930 edn), and *dsp* 21 April 1907
2 Jane Isabella Maria; *d* unm 25 Jan 1936
3 Mary Elizabeth; *d* unm 9 Dec 1940

The 7th Bt's only surv son,

Sir George Douglas Clerk, 8th Bt, JP and DL (Midlothian); *b* 17 May 1852; Lt-Col and Hon Col cmdg 3rd Bn E Surrey Regt 1899–1904, Lt 2nd Life Gds Boer War; *m* 4 Jan 1876 Aymée Elizabeth Georgiana Milliken (*d* 8 May 1947), 2nd dau of Sir Robert John Milliken Napier, 9th Bt (*see* NAPIER, Bt, of Merchiston), and *d* 30 Nov 1911, leaving an only s:

Sir George James Robert Clerk, 9th Bt, JP, DL (Midlothian); *b* 4 Oct 1876; Capt 3rd Bn Roy Scots; *m* 19 Aug 1903 Hon (Mabel) Honor (*d* 23 June 1974), yst dau of Col Hon Charles Dutton (*see* 1970 edn SHERBORNE, B), and *d* 21 Nov 1943, leaving:
1 Sir JOHN DUTTON CLERK, **10th and present Bt**
1 *Susan Rosemary Dacre [Mrs Francis Law, Barony House, Lasswade, Midlothian]; *b* 29 Nov 1905; *m* 4 Oct 1928 Col Hugh Francis d'Assisi Stuart Law, DSO, OBE, MC, TD, DL, late Irish Gds (*d* 1984), only son of Hugh Law, of Marble Hill, Co Donegal, and had issue:
(1) *Hugh Francis Stephen John; *b* 4 Nov 1931; *educ* Eton and RMA Sandhurst; Capt late 9th Lancers
(2) *Francis Robin Luke Alexander; *b* 29 June 1946; *educ* Eton and Edinburgh U
(1) *Rosemary Bridget Honor Stuart; *b* 13 Feb 1930
2 *(Aymée) Lavender [Mrs Alan Dower, Swinbrook Cottage, Swinbrook, Oxon OX18 4DY]; *b* 18 June 1907; radionic therapist, Chm Inst for Complementary Medicine; *m* 11 Feb 1928 Col Alan Vincent Gandar Dower, TD, DL, FRGS, Res of Offrs, 2nd Dragoon Gds (*d* 1980), 2nd son of Joseph William Gandar Dower, and has issue:
(1) *Natalie Gay Stuart, of Estoril; *b* 4 Nov 1931

Clerke

Arms: Arg. on a bend gu. between three pellets as many swans of the field; on a sinister canton az. a demi-ram salient of the first, and in chief two fleurs-de-lys or, the whole debruised by a baton. **Crest:** A ram's head couped ppr. **Creation:** Bt. (E) 13 July 1660.

SIR JOHN EDWARD LONGUEVILLE CLERKE, 12TH BT, of Hitcham, Co Buckingham [Sir John Clerke Bt, Longueville, 48 Savernake Ave, Melksham, Wilts SN12 7HD]; *b* 29 Oct 1913; *s* gf 1930; *educ* Eton and Magdalene Coll Cambridge (BA 1934); FCA 1948, Capt Roy Wilts Yeo (TA) WW II; *m* 6 July 1948 (*divorce* 1986) Mary Beviss, of Cape Town, dau of Lt-Col Ivor Reginald Beviss Bond, OBE, MC, of Prosperity, Natal, S Africa, and has issue:

1 +FRANCIS LUDLOW LONGUEVILLE; *b* 25 Jan 1953; *educ* Diocesan Coll Cape Town, Stellenbosch U (BA) and Witwatersrand U (LLB); *m* 1982 *Vanessa Anne, only dau of Charles Cosman Citron, of Cape Town, and has issue:

(1) +William Francis Talbot; *b* 1987

(1) *Camilla Frances; *b* 1984

1 *Albinia Jennifer; *b* 6 Sept 1949

2 *Teresa Mary [Mrs Michael Waller-Bridge, 62 Creffield Rd, London W3 9PS]; *b* 6 July 1951; *m* 1982 *Michael Cyprian Waller-Bridge (*see* GRAYSON, Bt) and has:

(1) *Jasper Cyprian; *b* 1987

(1) *Isobel Noeline; *b* 1984

(2) *Phoebe Mary; *b* 1985

Lineage: WILLIAM CLERKE, of Willoughby, Warwicks (son of Richard Hamund, *alias* Clerke, by Collett -); *m* Alice — and had:

WILLIAM CLERKE, of Willoughby; *m* Elizabeth — and had:

WILLIAM CLERKE; *m* Agnes — and had:

1 Richard; had:

(1) Collett; *m* Richard Beaumont, of Cole Orton

2 Robert; *m* Elizabeth Clerke and had:

(1) Henry; ancestor of the CLERKEs of Kingsthope, Northants, and Uscombe, Kent

(2) William

(3) Clement; had:

1a George (Sir), of Watford, Northants; Alderman and Sheriff London 1641–42; *m* Barbara, dau of Robert Palmer, of Hill, Beds, and *d* 30 Jan 1648/9, having had issue:

1b George, of Watford, MP

2b Robert, of Long Buckley

3b Sir CLEMENT CLERKE, 1st Bt (E), so *cr* 18 June 1661, of Laund Abbey, Leics; Gentleman Privy Chamber 1661; *m* Catherine or Sarah, dau of George Talbot, of Ridge, Salop, and was *bur* 10 Dec 1693, leaving, with a 2nd s:

1c Sir TALBOT CLERKE, 2nd Bt; *m* 17 March 1688/9 Hannah Tilecote and *d* in or just before 1708, leaving:

1d Sir CLEMENT CLARKE, 3rd Bt; *d* unm by 1715

2d Sir TALBOT CLERKE, 4th Bt; *m* by 1719 Barbara, dau and coheir of Thomas Gladin, of Durrant Hall, Chesterfield, Derbys, and *d* 16 Feb 1723/4, leaving:

1e Sir TALBOT CLERKE, 5th Bt; *b c* 1719; *educ* Westminster; *d* unm 21 Nov 1732

3c George; *m* Dorothy Pearse, of Oakfield, Berks, and had:

1d Sir TALBOT CLERKE, 6th and last Bt; *m* Lucy, dau of Rev — Rogers, of Painswick, Glos, and *dsp* 10 July 1759, when the btcy expired

1d Dorothy; *m* Philip Jennings, of Duddleston, Salop, and with him was ancestor of:

1e Sir PHILIP JENNINGS CLERKE, 1st Bt (GB), so *cr* 26 Oct 1774, of Duddleston (extinct 22 April 1788)

3 John (Sir), of Weston; campaigned in France 1513 were on 14 Aug he captured Louis d'Orleans, Duke of Longueville, at Borny, near Thérouanne, and was accordingly granted by HENRY VIII an honourable augmentation to his coat of arms; *m* — Ashby and *d* 1539, leaving:

(1) Nicholas, of North Weston; *m* Elizabeth (*m* 2nd Roger Alford), dau of Thomas Ramsay, of Hitcham, and had:

1a William (Sir); *m* Mary, dau of Sir John Brown, of Holt Castle, Warwicks, Sec of State, and *d* 1624, having had, with four other s (*d* young) and three daus:

1b Francis (Sir), of Hitcham; *m* Grisel, dau of Sir David Woodruffe, of Poyle, Surrey, and *d* 18 March 1631, leaving an est surv son:

1c **Sir John Clerke, 1st Bt** (E), so *cr* 13 July 1660, of Hitcham; *m* Philadelphia (*d* 9 Aug 1668), est dau and coheir of Sir Edward Carr, of Hillingdon, and *d* 7 Oct 1667, having had, with four other sons and three daus:

1d **Sir William Clerke, 2nd Bt**, of Shabbington, Bucks; *b* 9 July 1643; *m* Elizabeth, dau of William Muschamp, of Row-Barnes, and *d* 6 Sept 1678 , having had, with other issue:

1e **Sir William Clerke, 3rd Bt**; *m* 11 July 1683 Catherine (*d* 14 March 1741), 2nd dau of Sir Arthur Onslow, 2nd Bt, and sis of 1st Baron Onslow (*see* ONSLOW, E), and *d* between 14 July and 1 Dec 1699, having had, with a yr s and four daus:

1f **Sir John Clerke, 4th Bt**; *dsp* 27 Feb 1726/7

2f **Sir William Clerke, 5th Bt**; *m* — Brunsrow, of London, but *dsp* by Nov 1738

2e John; *m* Catherine, dau of Henry Jennings, of Devonshire, and *d* 1708, leaving:

1f **Sir Francis Clerke, 6th Bt**; *b* 12 July 1682; *d* unm 12 Feb 1769

2d Richard (yst son); *b* 4 March 1659; *m* 13 March 1675 — Day and had:

1e Francis Carr; *m* Catherine — and had an only son:

1f Francis, of North Weston; *b* 23 Sept 1724; *m* 3 March 1746 Susannah Elizabeth, 3rd dau of Thomas Henry Ashurst, of Waterstock, Oxon, and *d* 30 April 1760, having had issue:

1g **Sir Francis Carr Clerke, 7th Bt**; *b* 24 Oct 1748; army offr; *ka* Saratoga 15 Oct 1778

2g WILLIAM HENRY (Sir), **8th Bt**

1g Diana Susanna; *m* Rev Edward Willes, of Newbold Comyn, Warwicks, and had issue. He *d* 10 Dec 1820

2g Susannah; *m* 18 Oct 1805 Sir Robert Peel, 1st Bt (*see* PEEL, E), of Drayton, Staffs, but *dsp* 10 Sept 1824

The 7th Bt's bro,

Rev Sir William Henry Clerke, 8th Bt, Fell All Souls, DCL, rector Bury, Lancs; *b* 25 Nov 1751; *m* 5 May 1792 Byzantia (*d* 30 April 1815), est dau of Thomas Cartwright, of Aynhoe, Northants, and had, with other issue:

1 WILLIAM (Sir), **9th Bt**

2 Charles Carr (Ven), DD, Archdeacon Oxford, Canon Christ Church, rector Milton, nr Abingdon; *b* 23 Dec 1798; *m* 15 April 1847 Caroline (*d* 25 Dec 1904), dau of William Henry Ashurst, of Waterstock, Oxon, and *dsp* 24 Dec 1877

The 8th Bt *d* 10 April 1818; his est son

Sir William Henry Clerke, 9th Bt; *b* 13 Sept 1793; served 52nd Regt Peninsular War, Lt-Col at Waterloo; *m* 2 May 1820 Mary Elizabeth (*d* 12 June 1873), only dau of George Watkin Kenrick, of Mertyn, Flint, and had, with other issue:

1 WILLIAM HENRY (Sir), **10th Bt**

1 Mary Dora; *m* 26 May 1863 Rev Theodore Beale, rector Hopton Castle, Salop, and *d* 31 March 1918, leaving issue. He *d* 1887

The 9th Bt *d* 16 Feb 1861; his est son,

Sir William Henry Clerke, 10th Bt; *b* 17 Nov 1882; *m* 28 Nov 1849 Georgina (*d* 12 April 1909), est dau of Robert Gosling, of Botley's Park, Surrey, and had issue:

1 WILLIAM FRANCES (Sir), **11th Bt**

2 Charles John; *b* 8 Sept 1857; *m* 26 July 1892 Augusta Laura, dau of Rev Henry Arthur Daniel, of Stockland Manor, Bridgewater, and *d* 7 Nov 1944, leaving issue:

(1) Nicholas John, 2nd Lt 62nd (Northumbrian) AA Bde RA (TA) WW II; *b* 9 March 1912; *educ* Corpus Christi Coll Cambridge (MA); *ka* at Dunkirk, June 1940

3 Henry Carr; *d* an inf, 28 Aug 1861

1 Mary Georgina; *m* 19 April 1890 Basil Thomas Fanshawe, of The Park, Lunugala, Ceylon, and The Manor Ho, Bratton Fleming, N Devon, and *d* 24 May 1945, leaving issue. He *d* 4 April 1944

The 10th Bt *d* 8 Feb 1882; his er son,

Sir William Francis Clerke, 11th Bt, barrister, chm Roy Hosp for Incurables, Putney, 1923–30; *b* 16 Jan 1856; *educ* Ch Ch Oxford (BA); *m* 21 June 1884 Beatrice (*d* 6 Nov 1954), er dau of Graham Menzies, of Hallyburton, Coupar Angus, and *d* 27 June 1930, having had, with other issue:

1 Francis William Talbot, Lt Coldstream Gds; *b* 6 March 1886; *m* 4 Oct 1911 Albinia Mary (who *m* 2nd 6 March 1920 Capt Anthony Henry Evelyn Ashley, Coldstream Gds (*d* 14 Jan 1921) (*see* SHAFTESBURY, E) and 3rd 3 Feb 1923 A/C/M Sir Edgar Rainey Ludlow-Hewitt, GCB, GBE, CMG, DSO, MC, RAF (*d* 15 Aug 1973), and *d* 16 April 1972), er dau of Edward Henry Evans-Lombe, DL, of Marlingford Hall, Norwich, and was *ka* 26 Sept 1916, leaving issue:

(1) Sir JOHN EDWARD LONGUEVILLE CLERKE, **12th and present Bt**

(2) Rupert Francis Henry, DFC, G/Capt RAF WW II; *b* 13 April 1916; *educ* Eton and Magdalene Coll Cambridge; *m* 1st 15 June 1945 (*divorce* 1972) Ann Jocelyn, dau of Maurice Julian Tosswill, of The Top Ho, Paignton, Devon; *m* 2nd 1975 *Pamela Emily [Mrs Rupert Clerke, 3 Havelock Court, Warsash, Hants], dau of F H Bayliss, and *d* 1988, leaving by 1st w issue:

1a +Robert William; *b* 19 April 1952; *educ* Eton

1a *Nicola Frances; *b* 30 May 1950

2 David Herbert Hamund, Lt Res of Offrs, 15th/19th Hus, served WW I 1917–18; *b* 14 March 1897; *educ* Eton; *d* unm 16 May 1965

1 Beatrice Janet Elsie; *b* 16 Nov 1891; *m* 19 Sept 1916 Robert Evelyn Henderson, late Lt Household Cav, of Sedgwick Park, Horsham, and had issue. He *d* 6 Nov 1925

CLIFFORD, Bt

Arms: Chequy or and az. a fess gu. **Crest:** Out of a ducal coronet or a wyvern rising gu. **Motto:** *Semper paratus* ('Always ready'). **Creation:** Bt. (UK) 16 July 1887.

SIR ROGER JOSEPH GERRARD CLIFFORD, 7TH BT, of Flaxbourne, in the province of Marlborough, in the colony of New Zealand [Sir Roger Clifford Bt, 135 Totara St, Christchurch 4, New Zealand]; *b* 5 June 1936; *s* f 1982; *educ* Beaumont; *m* 12 April 1968 *Joanna Theresa, dau of Cyril James Ward, of Christchurch, NZ, and has issue:

1 *Angela Mary Jane; *b* 24 March 1971
2 *Annabel Mary Louise; *b* 16 June 1973

Lineage: The 3rd BARON CLIFFORD OF CHUDLEIGH (*qv*); had a yr s:

THOMAS CLIFFORD; had a 5th s:

GEORGE LAMBERT CLIFFORD; *b* 9 Jan 1779; *m* 6 April 1812 Mary (*d* 22 July 1854), dau of Walter Hill Coyney, of Weston Coyney, and *d* 31 Jan 1854, leaving, with six yr sons and three daus:

Sir Charles Clifford, 1st Bt (UK), so *cr* 16 July 1887; ktd 1858, Speaker NZ Ho Reps 1853–60; *b* 1 Jan 1813; *m* 13 Jan 1847 Mary Anne (*d* 6 Oct 1899), dau of John Hercy, DL, of Cruchfield Ho, Berks, and *d* 27 Feb 1893, having had issue:

1 **Sir George Hugh Charles Clifford, 2nd Bt**; *b* 10 Oct 1847; *m* 1st 7 April 1880 Mary (*d* 29 Dec 1880), dau of Sir John Lawson, 2nd Bt, of Brough Hall (*qv*); *m* 2nd 24 Aug 1884 Janet (*d* 3 Aug 1885), dau of James Burnett, of Nelson, NZ, and by her had issue:

(1) **Sir Charles Lewis Clifford, 3rd Bt**, Lt Lancs Hus Yeo; *b* 17 July 1885; *d* unm 13 Sept 1938

1 (cont.) **Sir George** *m* 3rd 27 Dec 1891 Helen Frances Stonyhurst, dau of Rev James Dennis, and *d* 17 April 1930, having by her had issue:

(1) Beatrice Mary; *b* 13 Nov 1892; *m* 14 Feb 1922 George Ranald Macdonald, son of Ranald Macintosh Macdonald

(2) Mary Edith; *b* 30 March 1894; *m* 14 Dec 1920 Henry Bruce Douglas, son of James Douglas, and *d* 9 Aug 1948, leaving issue. He *d* 26 Jan 1961

(3) Helen Mary; *b* 1897; *m* 1926 Joseph A Sapio de Belmonte, DSc, and had issue

2 **Sir Walter Lovelace Clifford, 4th Bt**; *b* 20 May 1853; *m* 14 Nov 1883 Catherine (*d* 24 May 1928), dau of Edward Bath, of Bryn-y-Mor, Glam, and *dspm* 26 May 1944, having had issue:

(1) Catherine Mary; *b* 24 May 1885; *m* 1st 21 May 1907 Roland Richards (*ka* 7 Dec 1915), and had issue; *m* 2nd 16 Feb 1924 William Herbert Wallis, and *d* *c* 1956. He *d* 1965

(2) Bertha Mary; *b* 6 Aug 1887; *m* 14 Nov 1912 Lt-Cdr Ian C Shiriff Hilton, RN, er son of C H Shiriff Hilton, and had issue. He *d* 27 June 1927

(3) Mary Lucy; *b* Aug 1908; *m* 23 Sept 1931 Alf Christoffer Brustad, son of Aska Brustad, of Norway, and *d* Dec 1933

3 Charles William, JP Salop; *b* 31 Aug 1854; *m* 1st 19 Jan 1881 Mary Eliza (*d* 7 Dec 1881), dau of Col Raleigh Chichester, of Runnamoat, Co Roscommon, and had issue:

(1) Charles Aston; *b* 16 Nov 1881; *d* 23 March 1898

3 (cont.) Charles Clifford *m* 2nd 2 June 1892 Sicele Agnes (*d* 5 Feb 1948), dau of Sir Humphrey de Trafford, 2nd Bt (*qv*), and *d* 21 Sept 1939, having by her had issue:

(2) George Gilbert Joseph, Capt 8th Hus, served WW I and WW II 1939–40; *b* 13 April 1893; *m* 12 May 1925 *Alice Mary [Alice Lady Clifford, 52 Onslow Square, London SW7 3NX] (granted rank of bt's widow Aug 1958), 2nd dau of John Joseph Calder, JP, of Ardargie, Perthshire. and was *kas* in France 21 May 1940, leaving issue:

1a *Anne Caroline [Miss Anne Clifford, 52 Onslow Sq, London SW7 3NX]; *b* 21 March 1926

(3) Walter Francis Joseph, Lt Irish Gds; *b* 6 Sept 1894; *ka* at Loos 27 Sept 1915(4) **Rev Sir Lewis Arthur Joseph Clifford, 5th Bt**; *b* 9 April 1896; *educ* Beaumont; RC priest, Rector Beaumont 1950–56, BA London, WW II as CF; *d* unm 8 Dec 1970

(5) ROGER CHARLES JOSEPH GERRARD, **6th Bt**

(1) Agnes Mary Annette; *b* 23 March 1899; *m* 18 Nov 1924 Hon Francis Joseph Southwell, RWF, 2nd son of 5th Viscount Southwell (*qv*), and had issue

(2) Rosamond Mary Clare, WW II as Jr Cdr ATS; *b* 10 Aug 1904

4 Francis Charles; *b* 15 Dec 1856; *m* 1st 14 Nov 1894 Fanny Dora (*dsp* 6 June 1906), dau of Thomas Broughton Charlton, of Chilwell Hill, Notts; *m* 2nd 29 July 1911 Mrs Geraldine McKean (*d* 9 April 1925), er dau of William George Coventry (*see* COVENTRY, E), and *d* 15 Sept 1931

1 Mary Lucy; *m* 7 Feb 1877 Arthur John Moore, DL, JP, MP, of Mooresfoot, Co Tipperary, and *d* 21 Jan 1936, leaving issue. He *d* 5 Jan 1904

The 5th Bt's bro,

Sir Roger Charles Joseph Gerrard Clifford, 6th Bt; *b* 28 May 1910; *m* 1st 1934 Elizabeth (*d* 1971), dau of Charles Kiver, of Christchurch, NZ; *m* 2nd 1973 Grechen Patrice Pollock, and *d* 1982, having by his 1st w had issue:

1 Sir ROGER JOSEPH CLIFFORD, **7th and present Bt**
2 +CHARLES JOSEPH [Charles Clifford Esq, 2/44 Wairarapa Terrace, Fendalton, Christchurch, New Zealand]; *b* 5 June 1936 (twin); heir presumptive; *m* 1983 *Sally Madeline, dau of William Hartgill Pennefather Green
1 *Elizabeth Mary Jane [Mrs Godfrey Goodson, 4 Golf Rd, Heretaunga, Wellington, New Zealand]; *b* 24 April 1938; *m* 1972 *Godfrey Matthew Goodson, of Wellington, NZ, and has issue:

(1) *Charles Godfrey; *b* 1974
(1) *Catherine Cecilia Mary; *b* 1973

CLIFFORD OF CHUDLEIGH

Arms: Chequy or and azure a fess gules. **Crest:** Out of a ducal coronet or a demi-wyvern rising gules. **Supporters:** Two wyverns purpure. **Motto:** *Semper paratus* ('Always ready'). **Creation:** B. (E) 22 April 1672.

THE 14TH BARON CLIFFORD OF CHUDLEIGH, Devon (Thomas Hugh Clifford) [The Rt Hon The Lord Clifford of Chudleigh, Ugbrooke Park, Chudleigh, S Devon TQ13 0AD]; *b* 17 March 1948; *s* f 1988; *educ* Downside and RAC Cirencester; Capt 1st Bn Coldstream Gds, ADC to CDS 1972–73, Adj Gds Depot 1973–75 (ret); *m* 1980 (*divorce* 1993) (Muriel) Suzanne, dau of Maj Campbell Austin; *m* 2nd 21 Nov 1994 *Clarissa, interior decorator, er dau of His Honour Anthony C Goodall, MC, DL, and by his 1st w has:

1 +ALEXANDER THOMAS HUGH; *b* 24 Sept 1985
2 +Edward George Hugh; *b* 1988
1 *Georgina Apollonia; *b* 20 June 1983

Lineage: The alleged descent of the Barons Clifford of Chudleigh from the medieval Lords (Barons) Clifford is as follows:

Sir LEWIS de CLIFFORD, KG, Amb to France 1392, 5th son (or perhaps bro) of Roger, 5th Lord (Baron) Clifford (*see* DE CLIFFORD, B); *m* Eleanor, dau of John, Lord (Baron) Delawarr (*see* DE LA WARR, E), and *d* between 17 Sept and 5 Dec 1404, leaving, with a dau:

WILLIAM CLIFFORD; *m* Eleanor, dau of Sir Arnold Savage, of Bobbing Court, Kent, and heir of her bro Arnold Savage, and had, with an er s (Lewis, of Bobbing Court, whose issue later died out):

JOHN CLIFFORD; had:

THOMAS CLIFFORD, of Borscombe, nr Salisbury, Wilts; had:

WILLIAM CLIFFORD, of Borscombe; had:

HENRY CLIFFORD, of Borscombe; *m* — Hungerford, of Downe Omney, Wilts, had:

ANTHONY CLIFFORD, of Borscombe; *m* Anne, dau and coheir of Sir Peter Courtenay, of Ugbrooke, Chudleigh, Devon, and had, with an est s (Henry, ancestor of the CLIFFORDs of Borscombe and King's Teignton, whose heiress Mary *m* Col Hugh Bampfylde) a 2nd s:

THOMAS CLIFFORD; inherited Ugbrooke; *m* Amy, dau and heir of Hugh Steplehill, of Bremble, Devon, and *d* 1634, having had, with a yr s (Thomas) and four daus:

HUGH CLIFFORD, of Ugbrooke; *b c* 1603; Col; *m* Mary, dau of sir George Chudleigh, Bt, of Ashton, Devon, and *d* 1639, having had, with a yr s (George):

(Sir THOMAS CLIFFORD, **1st Baron Clifford of Chudleigh**, Devon (E), so *cr* 22 April 1672, PC (1666); *b* 1 Aug 1630; MP Totnes 1660–72, fought in several naval battles during Dutch Wars and was ktd, Comptroller Household 1666–68, a Commr Treasury 1667–72, Treasurer Household 1668–72, one of CHARLES II's five-man clique of acronymic advsrs known as the CABAL (his forming the 'C') and architect of the Treaty of Dover 1670, including its secret clause by which CHARLES was to declare himself RC, Ld High Treasurer 1672–73 but forced to resign by Test Act, which made public office impossible for RCs (of which he, unlike his master, had at least openly declared himself to be one); *m* Elizabeth (*d* 21 Sept 1709), dau and coheir of William Martin, of Lindridge, Devon, and *d* (seemingly by suicide, hanging himself from the bed tester by his scarf) 17 Oct 1673, having had seven sons (four *d* unm and *vp*) and eight daus; his 5th and est surv son:

HUGH CLIFFORD, **2nd Baron Clifford of Chudleigh**; *bapt* 21 Dec 1663; *m* by 1685 Anne (*d* 5 July 1734), dau and coheir of Sir Thomas Preston, of Furness, Lancs, and had, with several other sons who *d* young and three daus (nuns):

1 Thomas; *b* 1687; *m* 22 Dec 1713 Charlotte Maria, Countess of Newburgh (*qv*) in her own right (*m* 2nd 24 June 1724 Charles Radcliffe, titular Earl of Derwentwater, and *d* 4 Aug 1755), and *dvp* 21 Feb 1718/9, having had issue

2 HUGH, **3rd Baron**

1 Elizabeth; *b* 6 April 1689; *m* 1st William Constable, 4th and latest Viscount Dunbar (*dspl* 15 Aug 1718, when his title became dormant); *m* 2nd 17 Nov 1720 Charles Gregory Fairfax, later 9th and last Viscount Fairfax of Emley, and *dsp* 23 April 1721

2 Anne; *m* George Cary, of Tor Abbey, Devon

3 Amy; *m* Cuthbert Tunstall, who on the death of Viscount Dunbar *s* to Burton Constable and took the name Constable

The 2nd BARON *d* 12 Oct 1730; his est surv son,

HUGH CLIFFORD, **3rd Baron Clifford of Chudleigh**; *b* 14 April 1700; *m c* 14 Oct 1725 Elizabeth (*d* Nov 1778), dau of Edward Blount, of Blagden, Devon, sis of Mary, w of Edward, 9th Duke of Norfolk (*qv*), and had, with other issue:

1 HUGH, **4th Baron**

2 Thomas; *b* posthumously 22 Aug 1732; *m* 2 Feb 1762 Barbara (*d* 2 Aug 1786), yr dau and coheir of James, 5th and latest Lord Aston of Forfar (*dspm* 24 Aug 1751, when the title became dormant), and *d* 16 July 1787, having had, with other issue (*see* CLIFFORD, Bt):

(1) Sir THOMAS HUGH CLIFFORD later CONSTABLE (sign manual 1821), 1st Bt (UK), so *cr* 22 May 1815 at the request of LOUIS XVIII OF FRANCE, of Tixall, Staffs; *b* 4 Dec 1762; *m* 17 June 1791 Mary McDonald (*d* 16 Sept 1825), 2nd dau of John Chichester, of Arlington, Devon, and *d* 25 Feb 1829, leaving issue:

1a Sir THOMAS ASTON CONSTABLE, 2nd Bt; *b* 3 May 1806; *m* 1st 27 Sept 1827 Marianne (*d* 13 Dec 1862), yst dau of Charles Joseph Chichester, of Calverleigh Court, Devon; *m* 2nd 15 May 1865 Rosina (*m* 2nd 23 March 1872 Edgar Trelawny (*d* 1872) and 3rd 23 Aug 1876 Francis John Hartley (*d* 27 March 1880) and *d* 28 June 1908), yst dau of Charles Brandon, and *d* 23 Dec 1870, having by his 1st w had issue:

1b Sir FREDERICK AUGUSTUS TALBOT CONSTABLE, 3rd and last Bt, DL, Maj York Militia; *b* 30 June 1828; *m* Mary Ann (*d* 24 Feb 1902), est dau of William Herring, of St Mary's, Scilly Is, and *dsp* 24 Oct 1894, when the btcy expired

1b Mary Barbara; *m* 13 April 1826 Col Sir Charles Chichester, yst son of Charles Joseph Chichester, of Calverleigh, and *d* 14 Dec 1876, leaving issue. He *d* 4 April 1847

2b Mary Isabella; *m* 27 Sept 1827 Henry Raymond Arundell, of Kenilworth, Warwicks, and *d* 2 Oct 1828, leaving issue (*see* 1940 edn ARUNDELL OF WARDOUR, B)

(1) Lucy Bridget; *m* 7 June 1796 Thomas Weld and *d* 1 June 1815, leaving issue. After her death he took RC orders, became Bp of Amycla 1825 and Cardinal 15 March 1830. He *d* 10 April 1837

(2) Mary; *m* 13 Dec 1792, as his 1st w, Sir Charles Wolseley, 7th Bt, of Wolseley (*qv*)

1 Mary; *m* 14 April 1766 Sir Edward Smythe, 4th Bt, of Eshe and Acton Burnell, who *d* 2 Nov 1784, and had issue

The 3rd BARON *d* 26 March 1732; his est son,

HUGH CLIFFORD, 4th Baron Clifford of Chudleigh; *b* 29 Sept 1726; *m* 17 Dec 1749 Lady Anne Lee (*d* 9 Dec 1802), 5th dau of 2nd Earl of Lichfield (*see* LICHFIELD, E), and *d* 1 Sept 1783, having had, with other issue:

1 HUGH EDWARD HENRY CLIFFORD, **5th Baron Clifford of Chudleigh**; *b* 2 July 1756; *m* 2 May 1780 Apollonia, yst dau and coheir of Marmaduke, 5th and last Baron Langdale of Holme, but *dsp* 15 Jan 1793

2 CHARLES, **6th Baron**

3 Robert Edward; *b* 16 Oct 1767; *d* unm 18 Feb 1817

4 Thomas Edward; *d* 5 Dec 1774; *m* 17 Nov 1807 Henrietta Philippina, Baroness de Lutzow (*d* 20 Nov 1822), and *d* 2 April 1817, leaving issue:

(1) Laura Maria; *m* 25 July 1833 Ambrose Lisle March Philipps de Lisle, of Garendon Park and Grace Dieu, and *d* 15 Aug 1896, leaving issue. He *d* 5 March 1878

(2) Mary; *d* unm

(3) Henrietta Maria; *m* 3 June 1841 Henry B G Whitgreave, of Mosely Court, Staffs, and *d* 19 Feb 1852, leaving issue. He *d* 13 Aug 1881

The 5th BARON's bro,

CHARLES CLIFFORD, **6th Baron Clifford of Chudleigh**, FSA; *b* 28 Nov 1759; *m* 28 Nov 1786 Eleanor Mary (*d* 24 Nov 1835), yst dau of 8th Baron Arundell of Wardour (*see* 1940 edn) and had, with other issue:

1 HUGH CHARLES, **7th Baron**

2 Charles Thomas, of Irnham Hall, Lincs; *b* 27 May 1797; *m* 14 Jan 1822 Theresa (*d* 24 April 1885), yr dau of Marmaduke William Constable-Maxwell, of Everingham Yorks (*see* HERRIES OF TERREGLES, L), and *d* 11 Sept 1870, having had issue:

(1) Christina Maria; *m* 12 Feb 1811 Humphrey Weld, of Chideock, Dorset, and *d c* 19 March 1857. He *d* 9 Jan 1852

The 6th BARON *d* 29 April 1831; his son,

HUGH CHARLES CLIFFORD, **7th Baron Clifford of Chudleigh**; *b* 22 May 1790; *educ* Stonyhurst; *m* 1 Sept 1818 Mary Lucy (*d* 15 May 1831), only dau of Thomas Weld, of Lulworth Castle, Dorset (later Cardinal Weld; *see* above), and had issue:

1 CHARLES HUGH, **8th Baron**

2 William Joseph Hugh (Rt Rev), DD, RC Bp Clifton; *b* 24 Dec 1823; *d* 14 Aug 1893

3 Henry Hugh (Sir), VC, KCMG, CB, Chev Legion of Honour, Maj-Gen; *b* 12 Sept 1826; *m* 21 March 1857 Josephine Elizabeth (Id 15 Jan 1913), only child of Joseph Anstice, of Madeley Wood, Salop, and *d* 12 April 1883, having had issue:

(1) Hugh Charles (Sir), GCMG, GBE, entered Malay CS 1883; Resident Pahang 1896 and 1901, Govr Labuan and Br N Borneo 1899–1901, Colonial Sec Trinidad and Tobago 1903–07 and Ceylon 1907–12, Govr and C-in-C Gold Coast 1912–19, Nigeria 1919–25, Ceylon 1925–27 and Straits Settlements 1927–29; *b* 5 March 1866; *m* 1st 15 April 1896 Minna (*d* 14 Jan 1907), dau of Gilbert à Beckett; *m* 2nd 24 Sept 1910 Elizabeth Lydia Rosabelle, CBE (1918) (*d* 30 Oct 1945), widow of Henry Philip Ducarel de la Pasture and dau of Edward Bonham, of Bramling, Kent, and *d* 18 Dec 1941, having had by his 1st w issue:

1a Hugh Gilbert Francis, Lt Lincs Regt; *b* 20 Jan 1897; *ka* 1 July 1916

1a Mary Agnes Philippa; *b* 2 April 1898; *m* 19 June 1920 Maj-Gen Sir Noel Galway Holmes, KBE, CB, MC, Roy Irish and E Yorks Regts, son of Capt Harry W Holmes, of Rockwood, Co Galway, and had issue:

1b *Hugh Clifford, WW II in RA 1942–46, Political Administrator Gold Coast 1947–51, memb Sheffield City Cncl 1959–61, Head of Executive Selection Peat Marwick Mitchell; *b* 7 Jan 1924; *educ* Beaumont and Trin Coll Cambridge; *m* 27 June 1953 *Gloria Joan Mary, only dau of Sir Harold Ernest Georges West, JP, of Muswell Lodge, Brincliffe Cres, Sheffield, and has issue:

1c *Robert Hugh; *b* 29 June 1955

2c *Mark David; *b* 16 June 1958

1c *Loretta Anne; *b* 3 Aug 1954

2c *Michèle Therese; *b* 2 Oct 1956

1b *Bettine Mary; *b* 22 April 1921; *m* 27 May 1949 Maj Peter George Frederick Sutton, MC, RWF (*ka* in Malaya, 29 Aug 1958), son of Lt-Col George Frederick S Sutton, of Western Green Rd, Esher, Surrey, and has issue:

1c *Paul Anthony; *b* 7 April 1950; *educ* Beaumont

2c *Piers Hugh; *b* 17 April 1953

1c *Térèse Mary; *b* 27 Oct 1951

2a Monica Elizabeth Mary; *b* 4 May 1903; *m* 1st 9 June 1925 Maj Cecil Edward Trafford, MC (*d* 15 Dec 1948), 2nd son of Edward Southwell Trafford (*see* PETRE, B), and had issue; *m* 2nd 10 Oct 1952 Maj Richard Désiré Girouard, only son of Maj-Gen Sir Edward Percy Cranwill Girouard, KCMG, DSO, and *d* 11 Jan 1965

(2) Henry Frederick Hugh, DSO, Lt-Col and brevet Col Suffolk Regt, and Brig-Gen cmdg bde BEF, served in S Africa 1899–1902 (Queen's medal with three clasps, King's medal with two clasps), and WW I 1914 (wounded, despatches, Brevet Col), 3rd Cl Order of St Stanislas of Russia; *b* 13 Aug 1867; *ka* 11 Sept 1916

(3) Everard Louis Hugh (Rev), a Benedictine monk, served in S Africa, 1900; *b* 2 June 1871; *d* 16 Dec 1935

(1) May; *b* 29 July 1859; *d* 6 Oct 1861

(2) Emily Josephine; *b* 23 July 1860; *m* 22 April 1885 Maj Hubert George Howard Galton, RFA, of Hadzor Ho, Droitwich, and *d* 28 Dec 1923, leaving issue. He *d* 21 Sept 1928

(3) Blanche Winifred Mary; *b* 3 Nov 1861; *m* 1 July 1885 William Fitzherbert Brockholes, CBE, DL, of Claughton Hall, Lancs, and *d* 1 Oct 1918, leaving issue. He *d* 21 Jan 1924

(4) Alice Mary; *b* 26 Nov 1862; *m* 7 Nov 1882 Sir Walter Hamilton-Dalrymple, 8th Bt (*qv*), and *d* 8 April 1927, leaving issue

(5) Sibyl Mary; *b* 12 Oct 1864; *d* unm 1 Aug 1948

4 Walter Charles Hugh (Rev), DD, RC priest; *b* 5 Dec 1830; *d* 20 Feb 1902

1 Eleanora Mary, a nun of the Sacré-Coeur; *d* 1871

2 Mary Constantia; *m* 1st 12 Jan 1846 William Vavasour, 3rd son of Hon Sir Edward Vavasour, 1st Bt (*qv*), and had issue. He *d* 11 Jan 1860. She *m* 2nd 7 Feb 1865 Maurice Denis Kavanagh, LLD, barrister, and *d* 18 March 1898, having had further issue

The 7th BARON *d* 28 Feb 1858; his son,

CHARLES HUGH CLIFFORD, **8th Baron Clifford of Chudleigh**; *b* 27 July 1819; *m* 30 Sept 1845 Hon Agnes Catherine Louisa (*d* 25 May 1891), yst dau of 11th Baron Petre (*qv*), and *d* 5 Aug 1880, having had, with seven daus:

1 LEWIS HENRY HUGH CLIFFORD, **9th Baron Clifford of Chudleigh**, VD, DL, JP Devon, v-chm Devon TFA, barrister; *educ* London U (BA); Hon Col Wessex Div T and S Column ASC, Col cmdg bde Terr Force 1908–10, late Hon Col 5th Vol Bn Devon Regt, ADC to HM; *b* 24 Aug 1851; *m* 23 Jan 1890 Mabel (*d* 24 Jan 1921), yst dau of John Towneley, of Towneley, Lancs (*see* O'HAGAN, B), and *dsp* 19 July 1916

2 Bede William Hugh; *b* 3 Oct 1852; *d* 6 March 1853

3 Edmund Charles Hugh; *b* 11 May 1857; *d* 2 May 1867

4 WILLIAM HUGH, **10th Baron**

5 Walter Charles Ignatius; *b* 14 Oct 1862; *d* unm July 1956

The 9th BARON's bro,

WILLIAM HUGH CLIFFORD, **10th Baron Clifford of Chudleigh**, FGS, FZS; *b* 17 Dec 1858; *m* 1st 1886 Catherine Mary (*d* March 1943), dau of R Bassett; *m* 2nd 26 May 1943 Grace Muriel (*d* 18 Feb 1963), dau of W St Clair-Munro, of Glasgow and London, and *d* 5 July 1943, having by his 1st w had issue:

1 CHARLES OSWALD HUGH CLIFFORD, **11th Baron Clifford of Chudleigh**; *b* 24 April 1887; *educ* Downside; Capt late 5th Bn Devon Regt TA, Sub-Lt RNVR,

served WW I from 1914; *m* 1st 6 Nov 1917 Dorothy (*d* 3 Dec 1918), only dau of Alfred Joseph Hornyold, of 97 Eaton Place, SW; *m* 2nd 3 Jan 1940 Clare Mary (*d* 26 April 1975), widow of Charles Struthers White Ogilvie, dau of Capt Jasper Greham Mayne, CBE, of Gidleigh Park, Chagford, and gdau of Sir Frederick Weld, GCMG, of Chideock, and *d* 1 Feb 1962, having by his 1st w had issue:

(1) Agnes Mary; *b* 26 Nov 1918; *m* 22 April 1944 *Lt Robert Weatherhead Stallybrass, RNVR [Robert Stallybrass Esq, The Old Laundry, Oakhill, nr Bath, Somerset BA3 5BG], 2nd son of Greville Stallybrass, and *d* 10 March 1995, having had:

1a Hugh Greville; *b* 29 Jan 1948; *educ* Downside; *m* 1969 *Carey, dau of L R Pullen, of Worthing, and *d* 1992, leaving:

1b *Alexander Hugh; *b* 1978

1b *Kate Helen; *b* 1974

1a *Helen Hope; *b* 12 March 1945

2a *Emma Catherine; *b* 28 Nov 1951; *m* 1980 *John Bowles and has:

1b *George David; *b* 1981

2b *Patrick William; *b* 1987

1b *Caroline Louise; *b* 1984

2 LEWIS JOSEPH HUGH, **12th Baron**

3 Bede Edmund Hugh (Sir), GCMG (1931), CB (1945), MVO (4th Cl 1920), FRGS, Capt Res of Offrs, late Roy Fus, served WW I 1914–18, Priv Sec to Govr-Gen Australia 1918–20, Sec to HRH PRINCE ARTHUR OF CONNAUGHT when Govr-Gen of S Africa 1921–24, Sec to Govr-Gen and C-in-C Union of S Africa, Imperial Sec to High Commr 1924–31, Rep in Union of S Africa of UK Govt 1927–31, Govr and C-in-C: Bahamas 1931–37, Mauritius 1937–42 and Trinidad and Tobago 1942–46, KStJ; *b* 1890; *m* 21 Oct 1925 Alice Devin, CStJ (*d* 1980), dau of John Murton Gundry, of Cleveland, Ohio, and *d* 6 Oct 1969, leaving issue:

(1) *Anne Frances May; *b* 5 Jan 1929; *m* 5 Aug 1952 (*divorce* 1985) 2nd Viscount Norwich (*qv*), and has issue

(2) (Patricia David) Pandora ; *b* 29 Jan 1930 (HRH THE DUKE OF WINDSOR stood sponsor); *m* 1st 23 Jan 1948 (*divorce* 1960) Timothy Angus Jones, est son of Sir Roderick Jones, KBE, of Rottingdean, Sussex; *m* 2nd 12 July 1961 (*divorce* 1968) Hon Michael Langhorne Astor (*d* 1980), 3rd son of 2nd Viscount Astor (*qv*), and *d* 1988, having by her 1st husb had issue:

1a *Alexander Roderick; *b* 1955

1a *Annabel Lucy Veronica; *b* 1948; *m* 1st 11 Nov 1969 (*divorce*) Sir Reginald Adrian Berkeley Sheffield 8th Bt (*qv*), and has issue; *m* 2nd 14 Jan 1976 *4th Viscount Astor (*qv*)

(3) *(Alice Devin) Atalanta; *b* 10 May 1932 (HRH PRINCESS ALICE, COUNTESS OF ATHLONE stood sponsor); *m* 1st 10 Sept 1955 Richard Fairey (*d* 27 July 1960), er son of Sir (Charles) Richard Fairey, MBE, of Bossington Ho, Houghton, Hants, and has issue:

1a *Leanda Alice Devin Joan; *b* 8 Sept 1957 (HRH PRINCESS ALEXANDER OF YUGOSLAVIA stood sponsor)

(3) (cont.) Mrs Richard Fairey *m* 2nd 31 Oct 1963 (*divorce*) W/Cdr Timothy Ashmead Vigors, DFC, RAF, 2nd son of Capt Ludlow Ashmead Cliffe Vigors, of Coolmore, Fethard, Co Tipperary, and has further issue:

1a *Thomas Ashmead Merton; *b* 8 April 1969

(3) (cont.) Mrs Atalanta Vigors; *m* 3rd 1972 *Michael Henry Dennis Madden, and has further issue:

2a *Henry George Bede; *b* 1973

The 11th BARON's bro,

LEWIS JOSEPH HUGH CLIFFORD, **12th Baron Clifford of Chudleigh**; *b* 7 Feb 1889; *m* 1st 1914 Amy (*d* 15 Jan 1926), dau of John Arthur Webster, MD; *m* 2nd 14 Dec 1934 Mary Elizabeth (*d* 198–), dau of Rt Hon Sir Adrian Knox, PC, KCMG, KC, Ch Justice Cwlth of Australia, and by his 1st w had issue:

1 (LEWIS) HUGH, **13th Baron**

1 *Mary; *b* 1919; *m* 17 Aug 1943 *Maj Jack Philip Albert Galvin Clifford Wolff, MBE, late Intell Corps, yst son of Philip Wolff, of Bushey, Herts, and has issue:

(1) *Rosamund Elizabeth [Mrs John Wallinger, The Major House, Upton Grey, Basingstoke, Hants RG25 2RD]; *b* 16 May 1944; *m* 22 Feb 1966 *John David Arnold Wallinger, son of Sir Geoffrey Arnold Wallinger, GBE, KCMG

(2) *Antoinette Mary; *b* 16 Dec 1946; *m* 20 Jan 1970 *David B Parkes, son of S E Parkes

2 *Rosamund Ann [The Rt Hon The Lady Fisher, Marklye, Rushlake Green, nr Heathfield, Sussex]; *m* 1st 21 July 1945 (*divorce* 1965) Geoffrey Forrester Fairbairn, only son of James Valentine Fairbairn, of Mount Elephant, Derrinallum, Victoria, Australia; *m* 2nd 1970 *3rd Baron Fisher (*qv*), and by her 1st husb has issue:

(1) *James Clifford; *b* 16 June 1950; *educ* Downside; *m* 1979 *Catherine Elizabeth, dau of Prof E K Cruickshank, of Ore, Wilts, and has issue:

1a *Paul; *b* 1982

1a *Julia; *b* 1984

(2) *Charles Marcus Clifford; *b* 26 Oct 1956; *m* 1984 *Sarah Jane, dau of P A Coveney, of Burgess Hill, Sussex, and has issue:

1a *Rory Tobias; *b* 1987

1a *Chloe Rebecca; *b* 1985

(1) *Katrina Elizabeth Clifford; *b* 3 March 1947; *m* 1st 1968 (*divorce* 1982) Robert Moss, and has issue:

1a *Pandora; *b* 1971

2a *Candida Rebecca; *b* 1978

(1) (cont.) Katrina Moss [Mrs Peter Wise, 6 St Stephen's Ave, London W12 8JH]; *m* 2nd 1986 *Peter Laurence Wise, and has issue:

3a *Serena Alice; *b* 1988

The 12th BARON *d* 27 Aug 1964; his only son,

(LEWIS) HUGH CLIFFORD, **13th Baron Clifford of Chudleigh**, OBE (1962), DL (Devon 1964); *b* 13 April 1916; *educ* Beaumont and Hertford Coll Oxford (BA); Col Devon Regt, ADC (TA) 1963, Hon Col Devon Territorials TAVR III 1968, served WW II (POW, escaped 1943), Dep Hon Col Wessex Yeo (March 1972), Hon Col (April 1972), Pres Devonshire Assoc 1978, Pres Devon Assoc of Parish Cncls 197715088; *m* 29 Jan 1945 *Hon Katharine Vavasseur Fisher [The Rt Hon Katharine Lady Clifford of Chudleigh, Flat 3 The Care House, Les Blancs Bois, Rue Cohu, Guernsey, CI], 2nd dau of 2nd Baron Fisher (*qv*), and *d* 1988, having had issue:

1 THOMAS HUGH CLIFFORD, **14th and present Baron Clifford of Chudleigh**

2 +Rollo Hugh [The Hon Rollo Clifford, Worthy Manor, Porlock Weir, Minehead, Somerset TA24 8PG]; *b* 15 March 1954; *educ* Downside; *m* 1st 2 Sept 1977 Fiona Margaret, only dau of Richard Andrew Palethorpe Todd, OBE, actor, of Little Ponton Ho, Grantham, Lincs, and has issue:

(1) +Christopher Rollo; *b* 28 Nov 1982

(2) +Alasdair Rollo; *b* 1986

(1) *Elizabeth Alice; *b* 4 Feb 1981

2 (cont.) Hon Rollo Clifford *m* 2nd 1989 *Mrs Caroline Peta Versen, only dau of Peter Marshall Roberts, of Sydney, Australia, and has issue:

(2) *Sophie Katharine Rose; *b* 1991

1 *Cecilia Alice [The Hon Mrs Cecilia Kirby, 43 Wilson Rd, Blairgowrie, Victoria 3942, Australia]; *b* 15 Nov 1945; *m* 15 April 1968 (*divorce* 1997) Capt Nicholas Breakspear Kirby, BSc, RN, of Melbury Bubb, nr Dorchester, son of Ronald Kirby, of Ruscombe Ho, West Milton, Bridport, Dorset, and has had issue:

(1) *Julian Breakspear Bede; *b* 1975

(1) *Samantha Mary; *b* 17 July 1969

(2) *Christina Mary Anna; *b* 4 June 1971

(3) Patricia Katherine Mary; *b* 9 March 1973; *d* 28 Nov 1974

(4) *Caroline Mary Julia; *b* 22 May 1977

2 *Sarah Amy [The Hon Mrs Richardson, Greatcombe, Holne, Devon TQ13 7SP]; *b* 22 June 1956; *m* 25 April 1981 *Robert Carwithen Richardson, 2nd son of Christopher Richardson, of Ash, Dartmouth, Devon, and has issue:

(1) *Amy Natasha; *b* 1984

(2) *Jessie Katharine; *b* 1987

Seat: Ugbrooke Park, Chudleigh, S Devon. An older house on the site, including a family chapel of around 1670, was almost entirely replaced by Robert Adam in the 1760s. This was not entirely due to changes in fashion, certainly not where the chapel was concerned. The penal laws forbade Catholics such as the CLIFFORDs to erect free-standing places of worship and the chapel had to be incorporated into the southwest wing of the main house. In the mid-1830s, following the Act of Catholic Emancipation of 1829, the **7th Baron** was able to redress this furtive treatment of a major spatial feature, beautifying the apse with marble and installing an organ loft.

Some features had been retained at the time of the mid-18th century transformation, the curving wings on the northwest side, for instance. But they only dated from *c* 1740. And then there were budgetary considerations. So Ugbrooke emerged from the Adam treatment as a toy fortification, crenellated, somewhat box-like as to shape, being of two storeys with eleven bays by ten, and enlivened by towers at each corner. A curious feature, which has come in for some criticism, are the rounded tubular mouldings to the windows in composition stone, and a larger version surrounding the main entrance, all added in the 1850s. In the mid-1870s the appearance of the battlements was rendered a bit more formidable by enlargement. But the arts of peace were by no means neglected: the conservatory dates from 1863.

During the War Ugbrooke was occupied by a school. Just after it a Polish Military Hospital moved in. The CLIFFORDs took up residence again in the late 1950s.

CLINTON, Bt

Arms: Argent semy of cross crosslets fitchy sable, in a chief azure two mullets or pierced gules (for CLINTON), charged with an inescutcheon quarterly, 1st, argent, on a fess azure three dexter gauntlets appaumy or (for FANE), 2nd, argent, a chevron between three spindles sable (for TREFUSIS), 3rd, azure, three boar's heads couped argent, muzzled gules, a cross crosslet argent for distinction (for FORBES OF PITSLIGO), 4th, or, a bend gules surmounted by a fess checky azure and argent, in chief crescent azure, a canton ermine for difference (for STUART). **Crest:** A bull's head erased sable armed, and about the neck an ancient crown attached thereto a line or, in the mouth a rose gules, barbed, seeded, slipped and leafed proper. **Supporters:** On either side a greyhound argent collared, with line reflexed over the back gules, in the mouth a gauntlet as in the arms (for CLINTON). **Motto:** *Tout vient de Dieu* ('Everything comes from God'). **Creation:** B. (E) 6 Feb 1298/9.

THE 22ND LORD (Baron) **CLINTON** (Gerard Nevile Mark FANE later FANE TREFUSIS (deed poll 1959), JP (Bideford 1963), DL (Devon 1977)) [The Rt Hon The Lord Clinton JP DL, Heanton Satchville, Okehampton, Devon EX20 3QE]; *b* 7 Oct 1934; *educ* Gordonstoun; *s* on termination of abeyance 18 March 1965; memb cncl of HRH THE PRINCE OF WALES 1968–79, SBStJ 1972; *m* 18 July 1958 *Nicola Harriette, High Sheriff Devon 1998–99, est dau of Maj Charles Robert Purdon Coote, of Ballyclough Castle, and Bearforest, Co Cork (*see* COOTE, Bt), and has issue:

1 +CHARLES PATRICK ROLLE [The Hon Charles Fane Trefusis, Kitts Hayes, Colaton Raleigh, Devon EX10 OHY]; *b* 21 March 1962; *educ* Millfield; *m* 1992 *Rosanna (Rosy), yr dau of (Alexander) John Rennie Izat, of High Cocklaw, Berwick upon Tweed, and has issue:

(1) +Edward Charles Rolle; *b* 26 Feb 1994

(2) +James Henry Rolle; *b* 16 July 1996

1 +Caroline Harriet; *b* 23 May 1960; *m* 19– *Charles Fowle and has:

(1) +Thomas Trefusis; *b* 15 Oct 1997

2 +Henrietta Jane; *b* 31 Jan 1964

Lineage: GEOFFREY de CLINTON; Treasurer and Ld Chamberlain to HENRY I, unc of:

OSBERT; ancestor of:

THOMAS de CLINTON; *m* Mazera, dau and heir of James de Bisey, of Baddesley, and *d* by 12 Jan 1277/8, leaving issue:

1 THOMAS

2 John, of Coleshill, Warwicks; *d* 1315/6, and had issue:

(1) John; *m* Alice, dau of Robert de Grendon, and had a s who *dspm c* 1347

THOMAS de CLINTON's er s,

THOMAS de CLINTON, of Amington, Warwicks; *m* Maud, dau of Sir Ralph Bracebridge, of Kinsbury, Warwicks, and *dvp* by 1264, having had issue, with an er s (*d* young):

JOHN de CLINTON, **1st Lord** (Baron) **Clinton** (E), so cr according to later doctrine by writ of summons to Parl 6 Feb 1298/9 (though never again thereafter); the peerage is heritable by heirs general, which can include females, hence the + against each living female and her issue; *b c* 1258; Ld Manor of Maxstoke, Warwicks, through his w; served Scottish and French Wars of EDWARD I, MP Warwicks 1300–01, Constable Wallingford Castle 1308; *m c* 1290 Ida, 1st dau of William de Odingsells, Ld of Maxtoke Castle, Warwicks, and sis and coheir of Edmund de Odingsells, and *d* 1310, leaving issue:

1 JOHN, **2nd Lord**

2 WILLIAM de CLINTON, 1st and last EARL OF HUNTINGDON (E), so *cr* 13 March 1336/7, earlier (6 Sept 1330) called to Parl by writ made out to 'William de Clynton', thus according to later doctrine being *cr* LORD (Baron) CLINTON even though his er bro was at one point sitting in Parl under an identical 'title'; ktd by 1324; Custodian Halton Castle, Cheshire, Sept 1327–48, Justice Chester 1330–33 and Kent 1332, Constable Dover Castle and Warden Cinque Ports 1330–43, Adml of the W 1333–35, served Scottish Wars and Hundred Years War, fighting at Sluys 24 June 1340, took part in Crécy expedition 1346 but only as Adml in command of the ships; *m* by 17 Oct 1328 Juliane (*d* between 31 Oct and 2 Nov 1367), dau and heir of Sir Thomas de Leyburne, and widow of (a) Sir Thomas Le Blount and (b) 3rd Lord (Baron) Hastings of the putative 1264 *cr*; *dsp* 25 Aug 1354, when his titlesexpired

The 1st LORD (Baron) CLINTON'S est s,

JOHN de CLINTON, **2nd Lord** (Baron) **Clinton**; *b c* 1300; fought with the roy army which defeated EDWARD II's cousin Thomas, Earl of Lancaster, at Battle of Boroughbridge 16 March 1321/2, ktd by 1324; *m* by 24 Feb 1328/9 Margery, dau of Sir William Corbet, of Chaddesley Corbet, Worcs, and *d* by 1 April 1335, having had issue:

1 JOHN de CLINTON, **3rd Lord** (Baron) **Clinton**; *b c* March 1325/6; fought Battle of Poitiers 1356, Constable Warwick Castle 1390–97; *m* 1st Idonea de Saye, dau of the 2nd Lord (Baron) Say of the 1313 *cr*, and had issue:

(1) William (Sir); *m* Elizabeth, dau of 2nd Lord (Baron) Deincourt of the 1299 *cr*, and *dvp* 25 Oct 1383, leaving issue:

1a WILLIAM, **4th Lord**

(2) Thomas (Sir), of Amington; had:

1a Anne; *m* Sir Robert Frauncys, of Foremark, Derbys

1 (cont.) The **3rd Lord** (Baron) **Clinton** allegedly *m* 2nd — and had further issue:

(3) Thomas; *b c* 1368; living 1398

1 (cont.) The **3rd Lord** (Baron) **Clinton** *m* 3rd after 6 July 1367 Joan (*d* 21 Feb 1387/8), widow of Sir Philip Limbury, and had further issue:

(4) Edward; *b c* 1374; living 1398

1 (cont.) The **3rd Lord** (Baron) **Clinton** *m* 4th by 24 Oct 1388, as her 3rd husb, Elizabeth (*m* 4th licence 24 Dec 1398 Sir John Russell and *dsp* after 1 Sept 1423), dau and heir of William de la Plaunche, of Haversham, Bucks, and widow of (a) 5th Lord (Baron) Grey, of Rotherfield, and (b) Sir John de Bermingham, and *d* 8 Sept 1398

The 3rd LORD's gs,

WILLIAM de CLINTON, **4th Lord** (Baron) **Clinton**; *b c* 1378; on the death 1399 of his cousin *s* to part of the Say lands in right of his grandmother and styled himself LORD (Baron) SAY; *m* 1st Anne, dau of Sir Thomas Trivett by his w Elizabeth, his f's half sis through their mother; *m* 2nd between 13 Aug and Nov 1409 Alice/Anne (*d* 17 Oct 1420), dau of 2nd Lord (Baron) Botreaux of the 1368 *cr* and widow of 6th Lord (Baron) Fitzwarine of the 1295 *cr*; *m* 3rd, as her 2nd husb, Mary (*m* 3rd Sir John Heron, of Northumberland, and *d* 2 Feb 1458/9), widow of Sir Henry Retford, of Carlton Paynel and Castlethorpe, Lincs, and *d* 30 July or 20 Aug 1431, leaving issue by his 2nd w:

JOHN de CLINTON, **5th Lord** (Baron) **Clinton**; *b* 1410; taken prisoner 1441 when serving in France and held more than six yrs till ransomed for 6,000 marks, exchanged the Ldship (Manor) of Maxstoke *c* 1438 with Humphrey, Earl of Stafford, for the Ldships (Manors) of Whiston and Woodford, Northants; coheir to the Barony of Say but relinquished all claim to it 1 Nov 1448 in favour of Sir James Fiennes (*see* SAYE AND SELE, B); attainted 1459 for his Yorkist sympathies but restored 1461; *m* 1st — ; *m* 2nd Margaret (*m* 2nd Walter Hungerford, 3rd s of Sir Edmund Hungerford (*see* SAINT DAVIDS, V); *m* 3rd Sir John Heveningham and *d* 1 Feb 1495/6), dau of John St Leger, of Ulcombe, Kent, and *d* 24 Sept 1464, leaving by his 1st w:

JOHN CLINTON (or FIENNES?), **6th Lord** (Baron) **Clinton**; *b c* 1429/34; apparently recognised 1471 as Lord Clinton and Say but never called to Parl under either title; *m* 1st Elizabeth, dau of Sir Richard Fiennes by Joan Baroness Dacre in her own right (*see* DACRE, B); *m* 2nd Anne (*m* 2nd Richard Willoughby; *m* 3rd Thomas Willicote), allegedly dau of Sir Humphrey Stafford, and *d* 29 Feb 1487/8, leaving issue (but by which w is unknown):

JOHN CLINTON alias FIENNES, **7th Lord** (Baron) **Clinton**, KB (1501); *b c* 1470/1; *m* 1st by 1490 Elizabeth (*d* by 1501), dau of Sir John Morgan, of Tredegar, Mon; *m* 2nd by 1501 Anne — and *d* 4 June 1514, leaving issue:

THOMAS CLINTON alias FIENNES, **8th Lord** (Baron) **Clinton**; *b c* 1490; ktd 1513; *m* (settlement 4 May 1510) Joan (*m* 2nd after 4 July 1519 Sir Robert Wingfield; *see* POWERSCOURT, V), illegitimate dau of Sir Edward Poynings, KG, and *d* 7 Aug 1517, leaving issue:

EDWARD CLINTON alias FIENNES, **9th Lord** (Baron) **Clinton** (and Say) (so addressed in writ of summons to Parl 1536) and 1st EARL OF LINCOLN (*qv*) (E), so *cr* 4 May 1572, KG (1551), PC (1550, 1557, 1558); *b* 1512; ktd 1544, Ch Capt of Boulogne 1548–50, Ld High Adml May 1550–Oct 1553 and Feb 1557/8–85, Ld Lt Lincs 1552–85, Constable Tower of London 7–19 July 1553, cmmded 1569 the army that crushed the rebellion of the northern earls (*see* NORTHUMBERLAND, D, ABERGAVENNY, M, and WESTMORLAND, E, preliminary remarks) and was promoted Earl in reward, Lt Order of the Garter 1570 and 1573, Ld Steward 1572–84; *m* lst between 15 April 1530 and 12 Feb 1534/5 Elizabeth (previously mistress of HENRY VIII by whom she was mother of Henry FitzRoy, Duke of Richmond and Somerset of the 1525 *cr*), dau of Sir John Blount and widow of 1st and last Lord (Baron) Tailboys of the 1529 *cr*, and had three daus; *m* 2nd by 15 June 1541 Ursula (*d* 4 Sept 1551), dau of 7th Baron Stourton (*see* MOWBRAY, SEGRAVE and STOURTON, B); *m* 3rd (settlement 1 Oct 1552) Elizabeth FitzGerald (*dsp* March 1589/90) 'the fair Geraldine', dau of 9th Earl of Kildare (*see* LEINSTER, D), and widow of Sir Anthony Browne, and *d* 16 Jan 1584/5, leaving, with other issue:

1 HENRY, **10th Lord**

1 Frances Clinton alias Fiennes; *m* by Sept 1573 3rd Baron Chandos of Sudeley of the 1554 *cr* (*see* CHANDOS, V, preliminary remarks) and *d* 12 Sept 1623, leaving issue

The 9th LORD's s,

HENRY CLINTON alias FIENNES, **10th Lord** (Baron) **Clinton** and 2nd EARL OF LINCOLN, KB (1553); *b* 1540; MP Lincs 1571; *m* 1st between 10 Dec 1555 and 30 April 1557 Catherine Hastings (*d* by 20 Oct 1586), dau of 2nd Earl of Huntingdon (*qv*), and had issue:

1 THOMAS, **11th Lord**

2 Edward (Sir); *m* Mary, dau of Thomas Dighton, of Stourton, Lincs, and had, with two er s (*dsp*):

(1) Francis, of Stourton Parva, Lincs; *m* Priscilla, dau of John Hill, and had issue:

1a FRANCIS CLINTON, 6th EARL OF LINCOLN (*qv*)

The **10th Lord** *m* 2nd after 20 Oct 1586 Elizabeth (*d c* 4 July 1611), dau of Sir Richard Morrison, of Cassiobury, Herts, and widow of William Norreys, s of 1st Lord (Baron) Norreys (of Rycote) (*see* LINDSEY and ABINGDON, E), and *d* 29 Sept 1616, leaving further issue:

3 Henry (Sir), of Kirkstead, Lincs; *b* 1587; *m* 1st Eleanor, dau of Sir James Harrington; *m* 2nd 1624 Elizabeth, dau of Dr Henry Hickman, and *d* 1641, leaving issue (*see* WILLOUGHBY DE ERESBY, B)

4 Kendal

The 10th LORD's er s,

THOMAS CLINTON alias FIENNES, **11th Lord** (Baron) **Clinton** and 3rd EARL OF LINCOLN; *b c* 1568; *educ* Ch Ch Oxford (MA 1588); MP Gt Grimsby 1601 and Lincs 1604–10, called up to Ho Lds *vp* 8 Feb 1609/10 in his f's supposed barony of CLINTON DE SAY; *m c* 21 Sept 1584 Elizabeth, dau and coheir of Sir Henry Knyvett, of Charlton, Wilts (*see* SUFFOLK and BERKSHIRE, E), and *d* 15 Jan 1618/9, having had, with eight other children:

1 THEOPHILUS, **12th Lord**

2 Charles; living 25 Nov 1615

3 Knevet, Knevitt or Knyvett; living 25 Nov 1615

4 John; living 25 Nov 1615

1 Frances

2 Arabella; *m* Isaac Johnson, of Clipsham, Rutland, who emigrated to New England 1629 with John Winthrop and *d* Aug 1630 at Salem, Mass

3 Susan; *m* as his 2nd w John Humphrey, of Chaldon, Dorset, who emigrated to New England 1635 and had two daus

4 Dorcas

5 Sara

6 Elizabeth

The 11th LORD's est s,

THEOPHILUS CLINTON alias FIENNES, **12th Lord** (Baron) **Clinton** and 4th EARL OF LINCOLN, KB (1616); *b c* 1600; *educ* Queens' Coll Cambridge; raised 300 volunteers Nov 1624 to assist the dispossessed Elector Palatine, bro-in-law of CHARLES I, during the Thirty Years War, imprisoned 1626 Tower of London for opposing CHARLES I's forced loan, supported Parl Civil War, Col Regt of Foot 1642, Resident Commr for Parl with Scottish Army 16 Dec 1645, Speaker Ho of Lds 1 Aug 1647, Commr Colonies Dec 1660; *m* 1st *c* 1622 Bridget Fiennes, dau of 1st Viscount Saye and Sele (*see* SAYE AND SELE, B); *m* 2nd his cousin Elizabeth (*bur* 5 May 1675), dau of Sir Arthur Gorges, of Chelsea, by his w Elizabeth, dau of 2nd Earl of Lincoln and widow of Sir Robert Stanley, and *d* 21 May 1667, leaving issue by his 1st w:

1 Edward, *Lord Clinton*; *bapt* 30 Dec 1624; MP Callington Cornwall 1646–48; *m* (settlement 30 March 1652) Anne Holles (*m* 2nd Charles Bates and *d* Oct 1707), dau of 2nd Earl of Clare of the 1624 *cr*, and *dvp* by 21 April 1657, leaving issue:

(1) EDWARD CLINTON alias FIENNES, **13th Lord** (Baron) **Clinton** and 5th EARL OF LINCOLN, KB (1661); *m* 1674 Jeanne (*dsp* 25 Aug 1688), dau of Pierre de Gulière, Ld of Verune, France, and *dsps* 25 Nov 1692, when the barony of Clinton fell into abeyance between his aunts or their issue, while the Earldom of Lincoln passed to his cousin and heir male

1 Catherine; *m* Sir George Booth, 2nd Bt, subsequently *cr* 1661 1st Baron Delamere, and *d* 5 Aug 1643, leaving a dau (*d* unm)

2 Arabella; *m* Robert ROLLE (*d* 1663), of Hainton Satchville, Devon, and had issue:

(1) Samuel ROLLE, of Hainton; *bapt* 20 Nov 1646; *m* Margaret (*m* 2nd John Harris, and *d* 1754), sis and heir of Roger Tuckfield, and *d* Oct 1719, leaving issue an only dau:

1a MARGARET Rolle, **Baroness Clinton** in her own right (15th holder of the title); *b* 17 Jan 1709; *m* 1st 26 March 1724 2nd Earl of Orford (*see* WALPOLE, B); *m* 2nd 25 May 1751 Hon Sewallis Shirley (*d* 25 Oct 1765), 4th s of 1st Earl Ferrers (*qv*), and *d* 13 Jan 1781, leaving issue by her 1st husb:

2a GEORGE WALPOLE, **16th Lord** (Baron) **Clinton** and 3rd EARL of ORFORD; *b* 2 April 1730; *educ* Eton; High Steward King's Lynn and Yarmouth 1751–91, Ld-Lt Norfolk 1757–91, Col Norfolk Militia 1759–91; *d* unm 5 Dec 1791

(2) BRIDGET Rolle; *b* 1648; *m* 23 July 1672 Francis TREFUSIS (*d* Nov 1680), of Trefusis, Cornwall, and *d* 28 Aug 1721, having had issue:

1a Francis; *b c* 1673; *d* unm Sept 1692

2a Samuel, of Trefusis; *b c* 1677; *m* Elizabeth Affleck and *d* 4 April 1724, leaving issue:

1b Robert, of Trefusis; *b* 1708; *m* and *d* Aug 1742, leaving issue:

1c Robert Cotton; *b* 1759; *m* Hon Anne St John, dau of 10th Lord St John of Bletso (*qv*), and *d* Aug 1778, leaving issue:

1d ROBERT GEORGE WILLIAM, **17th Lord**

3 MARGARET Trefusis; *m* Hugh BOSCAWEN (*bur* 10 June 1701), of Tregothnan, Cornwall, s of Hugh Roscawen, Recorder Truro, and Margaret his w, dau of Robert Rolle (*see* FALMOUTH, V), and was *bur* 1 Nov 1688, leaving an only dau and heiress:

(1) BRIDGET Boscawen; *m* Hugh FORTESCUE, of Filleigh, Devon (*m* 2nd Lucy, dau of 1st Baron Aylmer (*qv*), and by her was ancestor of the Earls Fortescue (*qv*)), and *d* 1708, leaving, with other issue:

1a HUGH FORTESCUE, **14th Lord** (Baron) **Clinton**, KB (1725); *b* 1696; called to Parl 15 March 1720/1 as LORD CLINTON; Ld Lt Devon 1721–23, LLD Cambridge 1728; *cr* 5 July 1749 BARON FORTESCUE OF CASTLE HILL, Co Devon (with special remainder to his half-bro), and EARL CLINTON (both GB); *d* unm 2 May 1751, when the Earldom expired, the Barony of Fortescue passed to his half bro and the Barony of Clinton fell once more into abeyance

1a Margaret; *d* unm 14 March 1760

The **16th Lord** (Baron) **Clinton**'s cousin,

ROBERT GEORGE WILLIAM TREFUSIS, **17th Lord** (Baron) **Clinton**; *b* 5 Oct 1764; *m* 28 April 1786 Albertina Marianna (*d* 7 Feb 1798), dau of John Abraham Rodolph Gaulis, of Lausanne, Switzerland, magistrate, and *d* 28 Aug 1797, leaving, with other issue:

1 ROBERT COTTON ST JOHN TREFUSIS, **18th Lord** (Baron) **Clinton**; *b* 28 April 1787; *educ* Harrow; Col 1825, ADC to Duke of Wellington Peninsular War, Capt 16th Light Dragoons; *m* 4 Aug 1814 Frances Selina Isabella (*m* 2nd July 1835 Sir Horace Beauchamp Seymour, KCH (*see* HERTFORD, M), and *dsp* 29 Aug 1875), dau of William Stephen Poyntz, of Cowdray, Sussex, by Elizabeth Mary, dau of 7th Viscount Montagu of the 1554 *cr*, and *dsp* Oct 1832

2 CHARLES RODOLPH, **19th Lord**

3 George Rolle Walpole; *b* 8 April 1793; Capt RN; *m* 8 Jan 1839 Margaret Frances (*d* 6 March 1848), 2nd dau of John James, of Houghton Lodge, Hants, and *d* May 1849, leaving, with a dau:

(1) George Rodolph; *b* 22 Oct 1840; Lt RN; *d* 10 May 1867

(2) Robert Edward (Rt Rev), DD; *b* 24 Jan 1843; Bp Crediton 1897–1930; *m* 7 May 1874 Emma Mary (*d* 11 April 1927), dau of Owen Wethered, JP, of Remnantz, Marlow, Bucks, and *d* 9 July 1930, having had issue:

1a George Rodolph; *b* 24 Feb 1875; Maj Loyal N Lancs Regt, Boer War 1902 and WW I 1914; *m* 1 June 1911 Elsie Jane (*d* 16 April 1946), er dau of James S Harrison, of Sydney, Australia, and *d* 23 May 1927, leaving:

1b (Robert) John (Jack) Rodolph; *b* 17 Oct 1914; *educ* Brighton Coll; CEng, MICE, FIMechE, Maj Scots Gds WW II, For Serv 1946–54, Dir Gen Hydraulic Assoc, Chm Prayer Book Soc 1973–89, Offr Order Crown of Belgium; *m* 2 Sept 1955 *Shirley Adeline Scott, only dau of Charles Scott Barton, of Fordye, Sullington, Warren, Sussex, and *d* 13 May 1997, leaving:

1c +Charles Rodolph (Rev) [The Rev Charles Trefusis, Christ Church Vicarage, 38 Woodcote Valley Rd, Purley, Surrey CR8 3AJ]; *b* 1 Sept 1961; *m* 1989 *Catherine (Kate), dau of Brian Dudgeon, of Guildford, Surrey, and has issue:

1d +William Henry Rodolph; *b* 15 Oct 1997

1d +Harriet Sarah Patricia; *b* 1991

2d +Charlotte Rosanna; *b* 1993

3d +Eleanor Rachel; *b* 26 Sept 1995

1c +Rosemary Jane; *b* 14 Sept 1959; *m* 1988 Lt-Cdr David Richard RN, est s of Capt R G Fry, of Whitchurch Canonicorum, Bridport, Dorset, and has issue:

1d +Edward James; *b* 1993

1d +Emma Katherine; *b* 1991

2d +Georgina Sarah; *b* 16 April 1996

2a Robert Peel; *b* 16 June 1880; *d* 17 April 1947

3a Haworth Walter; *b* 20 July 1882; Capt 3rd (attached 2nd) Bn Northampton Regt, served S Africa 1902 and WW I 1914–16; *ka* 7 Nov 1916

4a Arthur Owen; *b* 2 June 1884; Capt 9th Bn Loyal N Lancs Regt; *m* 19 Jan 1916 Alice Marjorie (*m* 2nd 10 Aug 1918 (*annulled* 1928) Adml Sir George Francis Hyde, KCB, CVO, CBE, RAN (*d* 28 July 1937), and *d* 23 Feb 1956), 2nd dau of Rev Angel Spicer, rector East Anstey, and was *ka* 7 July 1916

5a Francis Mackworth (Rev); *b* 22 July 1886; *educ* Exeter Coll Oxford (MA, BM, BCh); Hon CF, Pncpl St Paul's Coll Liuli, Tanganyika Territory, 1937, served WW I 1915–17 as CF, fndr St Francis Hosp, Katete, Zambia 1947, rector Cheriton Bishop, Exeter, 1958–60; *m* 18 July 1961 Margaret Ermyntrude (*d* 1 July 1979), 3rd dau of Arthur Edward Drake Lovell, of Wells, Somerset, and widow of Lt-Col Everard Graham Stanley Trotter, IA, and *d* 6 Nov 1962

1a Mary Hyeritha; *b* 24 July 1876; *d* unm 5 Jan 1941

2a Hilda; *b* 2 Jan 1891; *d* -

1 Anne Matilda; *m* 1827 Rev Hon Edward Moore, (*d* 8 Feb 1876), canon Windsor, 3rd s of 2nd Earl Mountcashell (*see* 1915 edn), and *d* 24 Feb 1876

2 Louisa; *m* 1822 1st and last Baron Rolle of the 1796 *cr* and *d* 20 Nov 1885 aged 91

The 18th LORD's yr bro,

CHARLES RODOLPH TREFUSIS, **19th Lord** (Baron) **Clinton**; *b* 9 Nov 1791; *educ* Eton and Oriel Coll Oxford (BA 1814, MA 1817); MP (Tory) Callington 1813–18, Commr Excise 1819–33; *m* 25 Oct 1831 Lady Elizabeth Georgiana Kerr (*d* 19 March 1871), dau of 6th Marquess of Lothian (*qv*), and *d* 10 April 1866, leaving, with other issue:

1 CHARLES HENRY ROLLE, **20th Lord**

2 Mark George Kerr TREFUSIS later ROLLE (roy licence 30 Jan 1852), of Stevenstone, Devon, DL; *b* 13 Nov 1835; High Steward Barnstaple, High Sheriff Devon 1864; *m* 6 Oct 1860 Lady Gertrude Jane Douglas (*d* 21 March 1924), 5th dau of 17th Earl of Morton (*qv*), and *d* 27 April 1907, leaving issue:

(1) Gertrude Emily; *m* 15 May 1889 Brig-Gen Sir Hugh Henry John Drummond, 1st and last Bt, CMG (*d* 1 Aug 1924), and *d* 14 April 1954

(2) Mary Frances; *m* 7 June 1894 Maj Arthur Scott Browne (*d* 14 Feb 1946), of Buckland Filleigh, N Devon, 4th s of William James Browne, and *dsp* 23 Nov 1945

3 Walter Rodolph, CB, Col cmdg 2nd Bn Scots Gds; *b* 5 Jan 1838; *m* 24 July 1877 his cousin Lady Mary Charlotte Montagu Douglas-Scott (*d* 13 Dec 1908), yst dau of 5th Duke of Buccleuch (*qv*), and *d* 3 Dec 1885, leaving issue:

(1) Adela Mary Charlotte: *b* 3 Feb 1879; *m* 1st 9 July 1902 Capt William Lenox Naper, MC, DL, JP (*d* 24 Oct 1942), RHG, of Loughcrew, Co Meath; *m* 2nd 1946 Rodney Richard Matthews later Matthews-Naper (deed poll; disappeared presumed *k* in an air crash 1 April 1953), of Qld, Australia, and *d* 11 Oct 1952

(2) Eva Mary Louise; *b* 12 May 1880; *d* unm Sept 1942

(3) Katherine Helen Elizabeth; *b* 25 June 1881; *m* 13 June 1906 Hon Arthur Owen Crichton (*d* 11 July 1970), 3rd s of 4th Earl of Erne (*qv*), and *d* 12 April 1964, leaving issue

(4) Marion Gertrude; *b* 3 Aug 1882; *m* 2 Dec 1905 4th Earl of Leicester (*qv*) and *d* 23 Nov 1955, leaving issue

(5) Margaret Harriet; *b* 18 Oct 1885; *m* 26 Jan 1911 Lt-Col Edgar Hugh Brassey, MVO, (ld 11 April 1946), 1st Life Gds, 3rd s of Henry Arthur Brassey, DL (*see* BRASSEY OF APETHORPE, B), and *d* 2 Nov 1966, leaving issue

4 John Schomberg, CMG (1902), JP (Somerset), DL and JP (Devon); *b* 24 June 1852; Col cmdg 4th Bn Devonshire Regt; *m* 19 July 1883 Eva Louisa, RRC, dep pres Branch BRCS (*d* 20 Aug 1949), only dau of James Bontein, Gentleman Usher to HM QUEEN VICTORIA, by Katherine Cecilia, gdau of Sir John Shelley, 6th Bt (*qv*), and *d* 29 Dec 1932, having had issue:

(1) Schomberg Kerr; *b* 2 Oct 1888; *m* 29 April 1919 Alberta Mary (*d* 26 Dec 1942), dau of Gen Hon Sir Arthur Edward Hardinge, KCB, CIE (*see* HARDINGE, V), and widow of Hon Evelyn Henry Ellis, and *dsp* 21 June 1963

(2) Denys Robert, MC (1919); *b* 30 March 1890; Maj RHG (SR); *m* 16 June 1919 Violet, Chevalier Legion of Honour (*d* 1 March 1972), er dau of Hon George Keppel, MVO (*see* ALBEMARLE, E), and *d* 2 Sept 1929

(3) Edward Hervey; *b* 31 May 1894; *d* 20 May 1901

(1) Beatrice Morwenna; *b* 8 Sept 1884 (HRH PRINCESS BEATRICE stood sponsor); *m* 11 Sept 1916 her cousin Hon Schomberg Charles Hepburn-Stuart-Forbes-Trefusis, 5th s of **20th Lord** (Baron) **Clinton** (*see* below), and *d* 18 Nov 1962

(2) Elizabeth Katharine Mary; *b* 4 May 1887; *m* 10 Oct 1907 Capt Garth Neville Walford, VC, RHA (*ka* 26 April 1915), only s of Col Neville Walford, LKI, and *d* 9 Oct 1976, leaving issue:

1a +Phyllida [Mrs Kenneth Ellis, Grapperies, W Porlock, Somerset TA24 8NV]; *b* 1915; *m* 1944 Kenneth Ellis (*d* 1972)

1 Evelyn Anne; *m* 27 Sept 1881 Hon Edward William Douglas (*d* 7 May 1918), 4th s of 17th Earl of Morton (*qv*), and *d* 28 Feb 1911, leaving a dau (*d* unm)

2 Helen Georgina; *d* 7 March 1923

3 Gertrude Albertina; *m* 17 Oct 1876 Lt-Col Hon George Herbert Windsor-Clive, MP (*d* 26 April 1918), and *d* 11 April 1878, leaving issue (*see* PLYMOUTH, E)

4 Alice Morwenna; *d* unm 16 Nov 1930

The 19th LORD's est s,

CHARLES HENRY ROLLE TREFUSIS later HEPBURN-STUART-FORBES-TREFUSIS (roy licence 4 Sept 1867, quartered the arms of Stuart and Forbes with those of Trefusis), **20th Lord** (Baron) **Clinton**, DL (Kincardine); *b* 2 March 1834; *educ* Eton and Ch Ch Oxford (BA 1856, MA 1859); MP (C) N Devon 1857–66, Parly Under-Sec India 1867–68, Ld Lt Devon 1887–1904, chm Devonshire CC 1888 and QS 1863–99, Lt-Col Roy N Devon Hus, Capt 25th Aberdeenshire RVC; *m* 1st 29 July 1858 his 1st cousin Harriet Williamina (*d* 4 July 1869), only dau of Sir John Stuart Hepburn-Forbes, 8th Bt (*see* STUART-FORBES, Bt), and had issue:

1 CHARLES JOHN ROBERT, **21st Lord**

2 Henry Walter, DL, JP (Cornwall); *b* 8 Dec 1864; Sheriff Cornwall 1923, Dep Warden Stannaries, Lt-Col Res of Offrs Scots Gds, cmded 4th Bn Duke of Cornwall's LI 1909–14 and 9th Bn 1914–16, employed London Dist 1917–19, ADC to Gen cmdg Troops Hong Kong 1898–1903; *m* 6 May 1905 Lady Mary Lygon (*d* 12 Sept 1927), Lady of the Bedchamber to HM QUEEN MARY, est dau of 6th Earl Beauchamp (*see* 1970 edn), and *d* 2 June 1948, leaving issue:

(1) Henry HEPBURN-STUART-FORBES-TREFUSIS later TREFUSIS (statutory declaration 1939); *b* 4 June 1908 (HM QUEEN MARY stood sponsor); *educ* Winchester and New Coll Oxford (BA 1930); High Sheriff Cornwall 1967, Lt-Cdr RNVR WW II; *m* 11 May 1940 *Sheila Margaret [Mrs Henry Trefusis, 20 Tregew, Flushing, Falmouth, Cornwall], 2nd dau of Herman Bryan, and *d* 27 April 1975, leaving issue:

1a +Nicholas John, JP (Cornwall) [Nicholas Trefusis Esq JP, Trefusis, Falmouth, Cornwall]; *b* 21 Oct 1943; *educ* Sherborne; *m* 23 Oct 1973 *Servane M J F, yst dau of L Mélénec, of Brest and Landévennec, Brittany, France, and has issue:

1b +Jan Henry Nicholas; *b* 27 April 1977

1b +Tamara Jane; *b* 19 Dec 1974

1a +Thomasine Mary [Mrs Philip Heycock, 62 Hamilton Park West, London N5 1AB]; *b* 23 June 1942; *m* 1970 *Philip Henry Faudel Heycock, only s of Raworth Henry Faudel Heycock, of Broadley House, and has issue:

1b +Thomas Henry Trefusis; *b* 5 Dec 1971

1b +Eleanor Rachel; *b* 24 May 1974

2b +Sarah Kerensa Faudel; *b* 30 April 1977

2a +Morwenna Jane [Mrs Robert Orton, 11 Radlett Av, London SE26 4BZ]; *b* 17 July 1945 (twin with a stillborn son); *m* 1973 *Robert Michael Orton and has:

1b +Magdalen Jane Dorothy; *b* 15 Feb 1975

2b +Ann Emily; *b* 2 June 1977

3a +(Ann) Kerensa [Mrs Andrew Pearson, 7 Gussiford Lane, Exmouth, Devon EX8 2SD]; *b* 30 March 1949; *m* 1973 *Andrew Michael Pearson, er s of H C R Pearson, of Pennant End, Start Lane, Whalley Bridge, and has issue:

1b +Timothy Mark; *b* 14 May 1977

2b +William Hugh; *b* 7 June 1979

1 Ada Harriet; *d* unm 14 Oct 1945

2 Mary Elizabeth; *d* unm 7 June 1954 aged 92

3 Margaret Adela; *m* 18 Jan 1897 Rt Rev Leonard Jauncey White-Thomson (*d* 31 Dec 1933), Bp Ely, and *d* 20 March 1939, leaving issue

The **20th Lord** *m* 2nd 30 March 1875 Margaret (*d* 19 Jan 1930), 2nd dau of Sir John Walrond Walrond, 1st Bt (*see* 1963 edn WALERAN, B), and *d* 29 March 1904, leaving further issue:

3 John Frederick, DSO; *b* 14 Jan 1878; Brig-Gen, Maj and T/Lt-Col Irish Gds; *d* unm of wounds recd in action 24 Oct 1915

4 Walter Alexander; *b* 1 July 1879; temp Lt-Col Roy Marines, RND, Capt Scots Gds, served S African War 1899–1900 (medal with two clasps) and WW I 1914; *m* 27 June 1911 (*divorce* 1919) Marjorie Winifred (*d* June 1937), yr dau of Sir Henry John Lowndes Graham, KCB, and *d* 11 July 1926

5 Schomberg Charles; *b* 22 March 1882; *educ* Eton; *m* 11 Sept 1916 his 1st cousin Beatrice Morwenna (*d* 18 Nov 1962), er dau of Col Hon John Schomberg Trefusis, CMG (*see* above), and *dsp* 11 Oct 1974

6 Robert Henry; *b* 1 July 1888; *m* 5 Aug 1914 Lady Dorothy Marguerite Elizabeth Herbert, OBE (1919) (*d* 25 Dec 1956), dau of Col Edward William Herbert, of Orleton, Salop, and sis of 5th Earl of Powis (*qv*), and *d* 1 July 1958, leaving issue:

(1) +Helen Beatrice Margaret [Mrs Simon Whitbread, 31 Egerton Gardens, London SW3]; *b* 6 May 1917; *m* 26 May 1936 Maj Simon Whitbread, DL, JP (*d* 1985), KRRC (60th Rifles), er s of Samuel Howard Whitbread, CB, of Southill, Biggleswade, Beds, and 9 Montagu Square, London W1 (*see* MAYO, E), and has issue:

1a +Samuel Charles, JP (1969–83), DL (Beds) [Samuel Whitbread Esq JP DL, Southill Park, Biggleswade, Beds]; *b* 22 Feb 1937; *educ* Eton and Trin Coll Cambridge; Beds: High Sheriff 1973–74, Ld-Lt 1991–, chm Whitbread & Co 1984–92; *m* 31 Aug 1961 *Jane Mary, dau of Charles Hugh Hayter, of Pudlicote House, Chilson, Oxon, and has issue:

1b +Charles Edward Samuel; *b* 3 Jan 1963; *m* 1991 *Jane Elizabeth, dau of David Evans, of Warsash, Hants, and has issue:

1c +Emily Victoria; *b* 1992

2c +Catherine Helen; *b* 1994

2b +Henry George Simon; *b* 2 Feb 1965; *m* 1994 *Serena Caroline, dau of Anthony J Barclay, of Nineveh Farm, Nuneham Courtenay, Oxon

3b +William John Howard; *b* 29 July 1966

1b +Victoria Clare Helen; *b* 1969; *m* 1993 *Sebastian Finch Morley (*see* BEAVERBROOK, B)

1a +Elizabeth Anne [Mrs James Bennett, 65 Eccleston Sq Mews, London SW1]; *b* 21 April 1939; *m* 3 Oct 1962 James Carthew Cavendish Bennett (*d* 1969), Dip Serv, s of James Cavendish Bennett, and has issue:

1b +Nicholas James; *b* 4 Sept 1964

2b +Simon Patrick; *b* 17 Nov 1965

3b +Charles David; *b* 1969

4 Edith; *b* 12 Feb 1876; *d* unm 13 April 1934

5 Evelyn Mary; *b* 3 July 1883; *m* 22 Feb 1911 Col Harry Stuart Ravenhill, CMG (*d* 17 April 1930), s of Maj-Gen Frederick George Ravenhill, RA, and *d* 5 Jan 1963, leaving issue

6 Harriet Margaret; *b* 20 March 1891; *m* 4 Aug 1914 Lt-Col Eustace Widdrington Morrison-Bell (*d* 13 Dec 1947), 4th s of Sir Charles William Morrison-Bell, 1st Bt (*qv*), and *d* 2 Feb 1975, leaving issue

The 20th LORD's est s,

CHARLES JOHN ROBERT TREFUSIS later HEPBURN-STUART-FORBES-TREFUSIS, **21st Lord** (Baron) **Clinton**, PC (1926), GCVO (1933), JP, DL (Kincardine); *b* 18 Jan 1863; Convener Kincardineshire 1898–1904, High Steward Barnstaple 1908, Memb Cncl Duchy of Cornwall 1911–33, Keeper Privy Seal to HRH THE PRINCE OF WALES 1913–33, Lt-Col Roy N Devon Yeo Cav (cmdg 1914–18), Jt Parly Sec Bd of Ag and Fisheries 1918–19, Forestry Commr 1919–29 (chm 1927–29), Ld Warden Stannaries Cornwall and Devon 1921–23; *m* 1 June 1886 his 3rd cousin Lady Jane Grey McDonnell, CStJ (*d* 27 Aug 1953), dau of 5th Earl of Antrim (*qv*), and *d* 5 July 1957, when the barony fell into abeyance between his two daus, leaving issue:

1 HARRIET; *b* 14 Nov 1887; *m* 28 April 1910 (*divorce* 1935) Maj Henry Nevile FANE (*d* 2 Aug 1947), Coldstream Gds, only s of Sir Edmund Douglas Veitch Fane, KCMG, of Boyton Manor, Wilts, and *d* 15 March 1958, having had issue:

(1) Charles Nevile; *b* 7 Feb 1911; Capt Coldstream Gds, served WW II, ADC; *m* 20 Dec 1933 Gladys Mabel (*m* 2nd 14 Feb 1942 Lt-Col James Hayton Greenhill Black (*d* 23 Dec 1966), Argyll and Sutherland Highlanders, only s of Robert Greenhill Black, of Ardmay, Dunbartonshire, and has further issue), dau of Sir Gerald Lowther, 1st and last Bt, PC, GCMG, CB (*see* LONSDALE E), and was *ka* Belgium 21 May 1940, leaving issue:

1a GERALD NEVILE MARK FANE later FANE TREFUSIS, **22nd and present Lord** (Baron) **Clinton**

1a +Carol [Mrs Hugo Bevan, The Old House, Lt Everdon, Daventry, Northants]; *b* 12 Aug 1937; *m* 1 July 1959 *Hugo Peter Charles Bevan, er s of Morier Geoffrey Bosanquet Bevan, of Warmington, nr Peterborough, and has issue:

1b +Rupert Charles; *b* 4 Feb 1965; *m* 1992 *Sophie Louise, only dau of Clement Michael Charles Royds, of Armthwaite, Cumbria, and has issue:

1c +Orlando; *b* 1994

1b +Georgina Lucy; *b* 8 Jan 1963; *m* 1991 *Rupert Patrick Fordham, est s of John Rupert Fordham, of 94 Portland Rd, London W11, and has issue:

1c +Patrick Hugo John; *b* 1993

2b +Charlotte Adèle; *b* 13 Oct 1966

3b +Sophia Alexandra; *b* 20 Nov 1968

2a +Fiona [Mrs Sylvanus Connolly, The Long Barn, Monkton Deverill, Wilts]; *b* 9 March 1939; *m* 22 Feb 1963 *Sylvanus John Connolly, er s of Lt-Cdr Patrick Joseph Connolly, RN, of Durban, S Africa, and has issue:

1b +Daniel Charles; *b* 1970

1b +Nichola Jane; *b* 5 Feb 1964; *m* 1991 *Michael Leslie John Beck, only s of Roger Beck, of Dinton, Wilts

2b +Alice Louise; *b* 5 May 1965

3b +Claudia Gay; *b* 17 April 1969

(2) Edmund John; *b* 16 April 1914; *d* 13 March 1915

(3) John Henry Mark, MBE (1944); *b* 28 July 1917; Capt Green Howards, served WW II (POW, escaped); *m* 1st 23 June 1939 (*divorce* 1954) Catherine Adelaide Anne, only dau of Gerald Noel Dyer (*see* LEGARD, Bt); *m* 2nd 1954 (*divorce* 1964) (Eleanor) Sybil Ruth, er dau of Albert Henry Archdeacon, of 22 Station Rd, Hastings; *m* 3rd 1964 *Elizabeth [Mrs John Fane, 6 Ollivier St, Alderney, CI], only dau of Kenneth W Cowell, of Les Butes, Alderney, and *d* 31 July 1995, having had by his 2nd w:

1a Charles Mark Anthony; *d* an infant

2a +Simon John Nevile; *b* 1954 (twin with his bro)

3a +Robert Trefusis; *b* 1958

1a +Harriet Jane; *b* 4 April 1956

2a +Briony Anne; *b* 1957

(1) +Idonea Elizabeth; *b* 27 Feb 1912

(2) +Rosemary Jean; *b* 16 April 1914 (twin with her bro)

(3) (Anne) Charmian Fane (resumed maiden surname); *b* 13 March 1916; *m* 1st 1 June 1937 (*divorce* 1949) Robert Rivers-Bulkeley, CMG, MVO, Scots Gds (*see* WEMYSS and MARCH, E); *m* 2nd 12 Feb 1949 *Peter Richard Hampton, MC, only s of Robert W Hampton, of Moffat Cottage, Ashtead, Surrey, and *d* 15 Feb 1990, leaving by her 1st husb:

1a +Miranda Jane [Mrs John Goglis, 4 Psaron St, Glyfada, Athens, Greece]; *b* 1938; *m* 1963 *John Goglis (actor as John Voglis) and has issue:

1b +Dimitri; *b* 1965

2b +Robertos Nicholas; *b* 1969

(4) +Ethelreda Flavia; *b* 30 Dec 1922

2 Fenella; *b* 19 Aug 1889; *m* 29 Sept 1914 Hon John Herbert Bowes-Lyon (*d* 7 Feb 1930), 2nd s of 14th Earl of Strathmore (*qv*), and *d* 19 July 1966, leaving issue

CLINTON-DAVIS

Creation: B. (LP, UK) 1990.

THE BARON CLINTON-DAVIS, of Hackney, in the London Borough of Hackney (Stanley Clinton Clinton-Davis) [The Rt Hon The Lord Clinton-Davis, c/o S J Berwin & Co, 222 Gray's Inn Rd, London WC1X 8HB]; *b* 6 Dec 1928; *educ* Hackney Downs Sch, Mercers' Sch and King's Coll London (LLB 1950); slr 1953–; memb Exec Cncl Nat Assoc Lab Students' Orgnsns 1949–50, memb Hackney Cncl 1959–71, Mayor Hackney 1968–69, MP (Lab) Hackney Centl 1970–83, Parly U-Sec Trade 1974–79, Oppn Spokesman: Trade 1979–81, For and Cwlth Affrs 1981–83, Tport 1990–97, Min State DTI 1997–; Chm: Advsy Ctee Protection Sea 1984–85, Refugee Cncl 1989–, Packaging Standards Cncl 1992–; memb: Commn ECs 1985–89, UN Selection Ctee Sasakawa Environment Project 1989–; V-Pres Soc Lab Lawyers 1987– (Jt-Pres 1991–); dir *Jewish Chronicle* 1989–; consultant European Affrs: S J Berwin & Co 1989–, Hill & Knowlton Int 1989–; V-Pres Chartered Inst Environmental Health Officers; Dep-Chair Lab Finance and Indust Gp 1993–; memb: APEX, RIIA, Bd Deputies Br Jews, Br Maritime League 1989–, Law Soc Members Cncl Parly Relations Sub-Ctee; Pres: AMA 1992, Hackney Branch Br Multiple Sclerosis Soc, UK Pilots Assoc (Marine) 199150, BALPA 1994–; Tstee: NUMAST, Bernt Carlsson Tst; Hon Memb Exec Cncl of Justice; Grand Cross Order Leopold II Belgium 1990, FRSA 1992, Hon Fell QMW 1993, Hon Dr Polytechnical Inst Bucharest 1993; *m* 1954 *Frances Jane, dau of Marcus Gershon Lucas, and has issue:

1 *Henry; *b* 1960

1 *Joanna; *b* 1955; *m* 19– *— Lavell

2 *Susanna; *b* 1962; *m* 19– *— Fox

3 *Melissa; *b* 1964

Lineage: SIDNEY DAVIS, had

STANLEY CLINTON later CLINTON-DAVIS (deed poll 1990), *cr* a **Baron**

CLITHEROE

Arms: Arg. a mullet sa. pierced of the field. **Crest:** On a cap of maintenance a mower, vested and capped quarterly arg. and sa., sleeves and stockings counter-changed, holding a scythe az., handled or, the point of the blade towards the dexter.
Supporters: Dexter, a labrador dog sa.; sinister, a bull arg., armed or.
Motto: *Nec arrogo, nec dubito* ('I am neither proud nor afraid').
Creation: Bt. (UK) 4 Sept 1945, B. (UK) 20 June 1955.

THE 2ND BARON CLITHEROE, of Downham, Co Lancaster, and **a Baronet** (Sir Ralph John Assheton, Bt, DL (Lancs 1986)) [The Rt Hon The Lord Clitheroe, Downham Hall, Clitheroe, Lancs BB7 4DN]; *b* 3 Nov 1929; *s f* 1984; *educ* Eton and Ch Ch Oxford (BA 1954, MA 1956); V-Lt Lancs 1995–, 2nd Lt The Life Gds 1948–49, chm Yorkshire Bank plc 1990–, formerly dep ch exec RTZ, Borax Hldgs, dir: First Interstate Bank of California, Touche Remnant Natural Resources, American Mining Congress, Chemical Industries Assoc, Halliburton Co Texas 1987–; Liveryman Skinners' Co, pres Assoc of Lancastrians in London 1990; FCIB, FRSA; *m* 2 May 1961 *Juliet, only dau of Col Christopher Lionel Hanbury, MBE, TD, JP, DL, of Juniper Hill, Burnham, Bucks, and has issue:

1 +RALPH CHRISTOPHER; *b* 19 March 1962; *educ* Eton and RMA Sandhurst; commnd Life Gds, Ld Manors of Downham and Cuerdale; *m* 19 Oct 1996 *Olivia Sarah, only dau of Anthony Warrington (*see* HASTINGS, B)

2 +John Hotham; *b* 12 July 1964; *educ* Harrow; *m* 1989 *Amanda, dau of Geoffrey Freeman, of Red Lion Ho, Nettlebed, Oxon, and has issue:

(1) +William Hotham; *b* 1992

(1) *Charlotte; *b* 12 Sept 1994

1 *Elizabeth Jane; *b* 6 Oct 1968; *m* 6 May 1995 *Capt Robin A E Tarling, Life Gds, s of Timothy Tarling, of Dulverton, Somerset

Lineage: AILWARD; had:

ORM; fndr market town of Ashton-under-Lyne, Salford Hundred, Lancs; *m c* 1115 Emma, dau of Albert de Grelley, jt feudal Ld of the Hundred of Blackburn and later feudal Ld of Manchester, and had:

ROGER de KIRKBY, of Kirkby Ireleth; held Ashton of the feudal Ld of Manchester; had with another s (William, ancestor of the KIRKBYs of Kirkby Ireleth):

ORM Fitz ROGER or de ASSHETON; living between 1195 and 1201; had:

THOMAS de ASSHETON; granted lands to Richard de Byron; had, with another s (William):

ROBERT de ASSHETON; living 1254; had:

THOMAS de ASSHETON; won 1284 a 10-year lawsuit with John de Kirkby over right to the Manor of Ashton; *d* by 1320, leaving:

Sir JOHN de ASSHETON; called to the Gt Cncl at Westminster 1324, ktd 1342; *m* Margaret (*m* 2nd William de Radclyffe, of Todmorden), dau of Robert Legh, of Adlington, and sis of Sir Perkyn de Legh, of Lyme, and *d c* 1360, leaving:

Sir JOHN de ASSHETON; allegedly present Siege of Noyon during Hundred Years War 1370, memb retinue of JOHN OF GAUNT (s of EDWARD III) Spain 1386, commissioned by HENRY IV to muster forces against the PERCYs in their rebellion 1403; drowned in a well at Norham, leaving, with other issue:

Sir JOHN de ASSHETON, KB (1399); Seneschal of Bayeux 1412, Govr Hadupais and Bailiff Coutances 1419, MP Lancs 1411 and 1413, cmded troops Battle of Agincourt 1415; *m* 1st Jane, dau of Sir John Savile, of Tankersleigh, and had issue (including Sir Thomas Assheton, alchemist, ancestor of the extinct ASSHETONs of Ashton-under-Lyne, ASSHETONs of Chadderton and ASHTONs of Shepley); *m* 2nd Margaret, dau of Sir John Byron, of Clayton, and *d* 3 Sept 1428, leaving by her:

Sir RALPH ASSHETON, called 'The Black Knight of Ashton', Page of Honour to HENRY VI 1428, Kt Marshal of England, Lt Tower of London, Sheriff Yorks 1473–74, V-Constable of England 1483 and supported RICHARD III but pardoned by HENRY VII 6 June 1486; *m* 1st *c* 1439 Margaret (*d* in or after 1480), dau and heiress of John Barton, of Middleton, through whom he came into the Middleton estate, and had issue, including an er son (Sir Richard, of Middleton, ancestor of the extinct Assheton Bts); *m* 2nd Elizabeth (*m* 3rd Sir John Bourchier, nephew of Richard, Duke of York, and *d* 1499), widow of John Kerielle, of Stockling, Kent, and dau of John Chichele, of Wimpole, and *d* by 1490; his 2nd son by his 1st w:

Sir RALPH ASSHETON; *m* Margaret, dau and sole heir of Adam Leaver, of Great Leaver, and had, with other issue:

RALPH ASSHETON, of Great Leaver; *b* by 1483; *m* Eleanor, dau of Adam Hulton, of the Park, and had issue:

1 RALPH

2 Richard, protegé of 1st Baron Burleigh (*see* EXETER, M); bought Whalley Abbey and the Downham and Malham estates; *m* Jane, dau and heiress of Ralph Harbottle, of Northumberland, but *dsp* 29 Jan 1578, leaving Whalley and Malham to his nephew Ralph (*see* below) and Downham to his great-nephew Richard (*see* also below)

The er son,

RALPH ASSHETON, of Great Leaver; Receiver Duchy of Lancaster, MP Liverpool 1553; *m* Margaret, dau of William Orrell, of Turton Tower, Lancs, and left, with other issue:

RALPH ASSHETON, of Great Leaver, Whalley and Malham, Receiver Duchy of Lancaster, DL, High Sheriff Lancs 1579; *m* Alice, dau of William Hulton, of Farnworth, and *d* 1587, leaving, with other issue (including at least one dau, Jane, *m* Richard Towneley; *see* O'HAGAN, B):

1 RALPH

2 Richard, of Downham; had:

(1) Nicholas, diarist; *d* 1625, leaving Downham to Sir RALPH ASSHETON, 1st Bt, of Leaver (*see* below)

The est son,

RALPH ASSHETON, of Great Leaver, Whalley and Malham; Receiver Duchy of Lancaster, High Sheriff Lancs 1594; *m* 1st Joanna, dau of Edward Radclyff, of Todmorden, and coheiress through her mother of her kinsman, William Radclyffe, of Wymersley; *m* 2nd Anne, widow of James Assheton, of Chadderton, and dau of Thomas Talbot, of Gatehouse, and *d* 1616, leaving, with other issue by his 1st w:

1 Sir RALPH ASSHETON, 1st Bt (E), so *cr* 28 June 1620, of Great Leaver, Whalley, Malham and Downham, High Sheriff Lancs 1624; *b* 1579; *m* 1st 1604 Dorothy, dau of Sir James Bellingham, of Levens, Westmorland, and had:

(1) Sir RALPH ASSHETON, 2nd Bt, of Whalley and Downham; *b c* 1605; MP Clitheroe in several Parls, including the Long Parl of 1640; *m* 1st Lady Dorothy Tufton (*d* 1635), dau of 1st Earl of Thanet (*see* DE CLIFFORD, B); *m* 2nd Elizabeth, dau of Sir Sapcote Harrington, and *dsps* 30 Jan 1679/80

1 (cont.) The 1st Bt *m* 2nd 1610 Eleanor, dau of Thomas Shuttleworth, of Smethells, Lancs, and was *bur* 18 Oct 1644, having by her had:

(2) Sir EDMUND ASSHETON, 3rd Bt; *b* 1620; *dsp* 31 Oct 1695

(3) Sir JOHN ASSHETON, 4th Bt; *b* 1621; *dsp* 19 June 1697

(1) Anne; *m* Sir Ralph Assheton, Bt, of Middleton (extinct), and had issue

2 Radclyffe, Clerk Common Pleas Lancs 1608, bought with his f in 1614 the Hall and Manor of Cuerdale; *b* 1582; *m* Elizabeth, dau and coheir of John Hyde, citizen and grocer of London, and *d* 19 Jan 1644, leaving an est son:

(1) John, of Cuerdale, royalist Capt of Foot Civil War; *m* Anne, est dau of Richard Shuttleworth, of Gawthorpe, and *dvp* of wounds recd at Edgehill Oct 1642, leaving an only child:

1a Richard, of Cuerdale and Downham, which had been settled on him by his cousin the 2nd Bt of the 1620 *cr* (*see* above); *b c* 1642; *m* 1665 Mary, dau and heiress of George Pigott, of Preston, and *d* 1709, leaving an est s:

1b Ralph; *b* 1666; *m* 1695 Sarah (*d* 1700 aged 20), dau of Tilston Bruen, of Bruen Stapleford, Cheshire, and *dvp* 1705, leaving:

1c RALPH

2c Richard; *dsp*

The er s,

RALPH ASSHETON, of Downham and Cuerdale; *b* 1696; *m* 1716 Mary, dau of Thomas Lister, of Gisburne, and *d* 1729, leaving, with other issue:

RALPH ASSHETON, of Downham and Cuerdale; *b* 1719; *m* Rebecca (*d* 1812 aged 79), er dau and coheir of William Hulls, of Freelands, Kent, and Popes, Herts, and *d* 1758, having had, with other issue:

WILLIAM ASSHETON, of Downham and Cuerdale, High Sheriff Lancs 1792; *b* 19 June 1758; *m* 20 Nov 1786 Lettice (*d* 30 Dec 1834), dau of Sir Richard Brooke, 4th Bt (*qv*), of Norton, Cheshire, and *d* 29 Jan 1833, having had, with other issue:

WILLIAM ASSHETON, of Downham and Cuerdale, DL, JP Lancs; *b* 16 March 1788; *m* 9 Aug 1816 Frances Annabella (*d* 25 July 1835 aged 40), dau of Hon William Cokayne and coheiress of 6th Viscount Cullen (*see* CULLEN OF ASHBOURNE, B), and *d* 8 Aug 1858, having had, with other issue:

RALPH ASSHETON, of Downham and Cuerdale DL, JP Lancs and JP W R Yorks, MP Clitheroe 1868–1880; *b* 20 Dec 1830; *educ* Trin Coll Cambridge (MA); *m* 3 Aug 1854 Emily Augusta (*d* 19 Sept 1916 aged 82), 4th dau of Joseph Feilden, MP, of Witton Park, Lancs; *d* 22 June 1907, having had issue:

1 RALPH COCKAYNE (Sir), **1st Bt**

2 Richard, ScD, FRS; *b* 23 Dec 1863; *educ* Eton and Trin Coll Cambridge (MA); *m* 5 Jan 1892 Frances Annette Ellen, JP Cambs (*d* 19 June 1945), 3rd dau of Sir Thomas Sebastian Bazley, 2nd Bt (*qv*), of Hatherop Castle, Glos, and *d* 23 Oct 1915, leaving issue:

(1) Richard Thomas, Housemaster Eton, Capt Cambs Regt, T/Maj MGC WW I; *b* 4 July 1894; *educ* Eton and Trin Coll Cambridge; *m* 11 Dec 1918 Beryl Elizabeth (*d* 15 May 1967), only dau of Ernest William Slater, of Peterborough, and *d* 1 March 1946, having had:

1a *John Richard; *b* 15 Nov 1919; *educ* Eton; *m* 21 Oct 1957 (*divorce*) Betty, formerly w of Stanley Wilson Mase and dau of Fred P Murphy, of Stamford and Bronxville, NY

2a Edmund; *b* 21 Aug 1922; *d* 28 March 1923

(1) Dulcia; *b* 3 Dec 1902; *m* 10 Jan 1934 Wilfrid James Hemp (*d* 14 April 1962), s of James Kennerley Hemp, of High Wycombe, Bucks and *d* 26 Oct 1994

(2) Sylvia Lois; *b* 5 April 1905; *m* 2 April 1932 Cecil Henry Coben Haslam (*d* 1 June 1972), son of Henry Cobden Haslam, ScD, MP, of 30 Eaton Sq, SW1, and Delamere, Skegness, and had issue:

1a *Henry William; *b* 21 Oct 1940; *educ* Eton and Trin Coll Cambridge (BA 1962, MA 1966, PhD 1965); *m* 2 Nov 1968 *Wendy Sheila, dau of Dudley Arthur Robinson, of Salisbury, Rhodesia, and has issue:

1b *Michael Henry; *b* 9 April 1972

1b *Mary Jean; *b* 20 Aug 1969

2a *Richard Michael; *b* 27 Sept 1944; *educ* Eton, New Coll Oxford (BA, MA) and Inst of Art London (MA); *m* Charlotte Sophia (*d* 1 Jan 1997), dau of Lt-Cdr Thomas Mervyn Smith-Dorrien-Smith, of Tresco Alley, Scilly Isles, and has:

1b *Nicholas; *b* 19–

2b *Felix; *b* 19–

1a *Sylvia Mary, Lecturer in Biology, Roy U of Malta; *b* 28 June 1934; *educ* Newnham Coll Cambridge (MA , PhD 1961)

3 William Orme (Rev), Rector Bilton, Warwicks 1895–1935, Canon Coventry Cathedral 1937, Canon Emeritus 1939; *b* 16 Feb 1866; *m* 14 June 1898 Winifred Maude (*d* 14 Nov 1958), 3rd dau and coheiress of John Henry Master, JP, of Montrose Ho, Petersham, and *d* 20 Nov 1953, leaving issue:

(1) Nicholas Master, Colonial Serv 1928–50, CC (1966–74) Warwicks, Rugby Borough Cncl (1962–74), Mayor Rugby 1965, Ald 1970; *b* 2 June 1905; *educ* Sherborne and Jesus Coll Cambridge (BA 1927); *m* 15 May 1947 *Mary Nest, BA Westfield Coll London (1934), dau of Very Rev David John Jones, of The Deanery, Llandaff, and *d* 20 Feb 1994, leaving:

1a *William Francis; *b* 17 March 1957; *educ* Rugby; *m* 2 June 1990 *Harriet Emilie, dau of Peter Fromanteel Cobbold (*see* COBBOLD, B), and has:

1b *Richard; *b* 6 Feb 1994

1b *Emilie; *b* 6 Feb 1992

1a *Cecilia Mary; *b* 13 June 1948; *educ* Reading U (BSc 1969); *m* 2 June 1973 *Philip Hawkins and has:

1b *William; *b* 13 May 1975

2b *Benjamin N; *b* 17 Sept 1977

3b *A son; *b* 18 June 1980

(1) (cont.) Nicholas Assheton also adopted:

*David Nicholas; *b* 13 Dec 1953; *educ* Malvern and Kesteven Ag Coll; *m* 29 June 1974 *Christine Anne Rodwell, of Rugby, Warwicks, and has issue:

1b *Richard J; *b* 13 July 1977

1b *Naomi Clare; *b* 9 Jan 1975

(1) Margaret; *b* 27 May 1902; ATS WW II; *d* unm 2 Jan 1967

4 Nicholas Radclyffe; *b* 5 July 1870; *educ* Eton; *m* 15 April 1915 Mary Nina (*d* 10 March 1933), er dau of William Peel, of Knowlmere Manor, and *d* 14 April 1960, leaving issue:

(1) *William Radclyffe, DFC, S/Ldr RAF WW II (fighter pilot Battle of Britain); *b* 12 Dec 1917; *educ* Sherborne and Jesus Coll Cambridge; *m* 20 July 1940 *(Lilian) Dorothy Andrews and has issue:

1a *Juliette Mary; *b* 13 June 1942; *m* 26 April 1965 *Capt Peter Woolley, Prince of Wales's Own Regt of Yorks, son of S/Ldr F E Woolley, RAF, of Frampton Cotterell, Bristol, and has had issue:

1b Simon; *b* 31 Oct, *d* 12 Nov 1968

2a *Penelope Jane; *b* 18 Feb 1950; *m* *Paul Thomas Grimwood and has:

1b *Kate; *b* 19–

(1) *(Nina) Joanna, BA (Phil) London 1949; *b* 28 Feb 1919

1 Frances Annabella; *m* 20 Oct 1886 Sir Mervyn Lloyd Peel, KBE, DL, JP, of Danyrallt, Carmarthenshire, and *d* 5 March 1939, leaving issue. He *d* 4 Jan 1929

2 Dorothy; *m* 1 July 1886 Edward Henry Burrows, est son of Capt Montagu Burrows, RN, of Norham Ho, Oxford, and *dsp* 2 Feb 1908. He *d* 29 March 1910

3 Joan; *d* unm 21 Jan 1962

The est son,

Sir Ralph Cockayne Assheton, 1st Bt (UK), so *cr* 4 Sept 1945, JP (Lancs and W R Yorks), DL (Lancs); *b* 13 Sept 1860; *educ* Eton and Jesus Coll Cambridge; High Sheriff Lancs 1919, memb Lancs CC from 1892 (Alderman 1902–49); Ld of the Manor of Downham; *m* 27 Sept 1898 Mildred Estelle Sybella, CBE (1934), JP Lancs (*d* 18 Aug 1949), 2nd dau and coheiress of John Henry Master, JP, of Montrose Ho, Petersham, Surrey, and had issue:

1 RALPH, **1st Baron**

1 Dorothy Winifred, Girl Guide Co Commr Beds, 1938–41; *b* 7 Aug 1899; *m* 18 June 1924 Capt Robin Coventry Barrett, MA, FRICS, FLAS, 6th Duke of Wellington's Regt, er son of Robert Bell Barrett, JP, of Skipton Castle, Yorks, and had:

(1) Robert Assheton, late KOYLI, slr 1954; *b* 10 Dec 1927; *educ* Winchester and Trin Coll Cambridge (BA 1951, MA 1958); *m* 22 June 1957 *April Joy, yst dau of Percy Marsden, CIE, of Sutton Waldron Ho, Blandford, Dorset, and has issue:

1a *Robert James Michael; *b* 27 Nov 1958

2a *Anthony Charles; *b* 22 Jan 1963; *m* 16 Nov 1991 *Sarah Margaret Torrie and has:

1b *George Robin; *b* 3 Dec 1992

2b *Edward Ronald; *b* 30 Sept 1995

1a *Juliet Susannah; *b* 17 July 1960; *m* 25 April 1990 *Simon Francis Cavendish Egerton and has issue (*see* SUTHERLAND, D)

(1) Hazel Monica; *b* 22 March 1926; *m* 21 June 1949 *Raymond Michael Martin, BSc, late Lt RNZNVR, and *d* 5 Jan 1997, leaving:

1a *Christopher Edward; *b* 22 May 1951

2a *Robert John; *b* 8 April 1958; *m* 19– *Margaret Pasak and has issue

3a *David Michael; *b* 23 June 1961; *m* 19– *Mary —

1a *Catharine Ruth; *b* 18 June 1954; *m* 19– *Peter Pinkham and has issue

2a *Sarah Anne; *b* 1 March 1956; *m* 19– *Graham Bulford and has issue

3a *Elizabeth Jane; *b* 3 May 1959

2 Mary Monica, JP Lancs; *b* 6 May 1903; *m* 20 July 1940 Capt (Charles) Peter Fleetwood Fleetwood-Hesketh, TD, DL, Duke of Lancaster's Own Yeo, 2nd son of Charles Hesketh Fleetwood-Hesketh, of Stoken Hall, Rutland, North Meols, Lancs, and Holcombe Court Devon (*see* BIBBY, Bt), and *d* 14 June 1982, having had issue

(1) *Everilda Dorothea; *b* 2 June 1941; has:

1a *Esther Mary Hollingshead; *b* 16 Jan 1979

3 *Eleanor, CBE (1956) [Mrs John Yorke CBE, Halton Place, Hellifield, Skipton, Yorks]; *b* 2 May 1907; v-chm Yorks Privincial Area of Nat Union of C and U Assocs 1952–55; *m* 30 Sept 1926 Maj John Edward Evelyn Yorke, JP (*d* 4 Jan 1997), of Halton Place, Hellifield, Skipton, Yorks, and has issue:

(1) *David John, JP, DL (Lancs), FRICS, FLAS, ptnr Ingham and Yorke, surveyors and land agents, Clitheroe, late Life Gds; *b* 26 Oct 1927; *educ* Eton and Trin Coll Cambridge (BA 1950, MA 1956); *m* 29 July 1957 *Susan Alexandra, 2nd dau of Lt-Col Scrope Arthur Francis Sutherland Egerton (*see* SUTHERLAND, D) and has:

1a *John Alexander; *b* 21 Jan 1959; *educ* Eton

2a *Charles Scrope Edward; *b* 3 Feb 1965; *educ* Eton

1a *Sophia Caroline Annabel; *b* 7 Jan 1961; *m* 1984 *Nicholas Anthony Bevil Acland (*see* ACLAND, Bt, of St Mary Magdalen)

(1) *Felicity Anne [Mrs James Cooper, Hexton Manor, Hitchin, Herts]; *b* 19 Jan 1931; *m* 16 April 1955 *James Patrick Ashley Cooper, only son of Sir Patrick Ashley Cooper, of Hexton Manor, and has:

1a *Patrick John Ashley; *b* 19 Oct 1957; *educ* Eton and Trin Hall Cambridge; *m* 1989 *Belinda Jane, dau of Christopher Firth, of Brantingham Hall, Brough, E Yorks, and has issue:

1b *Christopher Patrick Ashley; *b* 20 Dec 1990

2b *Thomas James Ashley; *b* 28 April 1992

1b *Amelia Clare; *b* 7 Dec 1994

2a *Edward James Ashley; *b* 8 Jan 1966

1a *Katharine Mary; *b* 10 June 1956; *m* 1991 *Dr Peter Foot and has:

1b *Sarah Elizabeth; *b* 1993

2a *Felicity; *b* 17 Feb 1961; *m* 1997 *Ian Gorton

The 1st Bt *d* 21 Sept 1955; his only son

Sir Ralph Assheton, 2nd Bt, and **1st Baron Clitheroe**, of Downham, Co Lancaster (UK), so *cr* 20 June 1955, PC (1944), KCVO (1977), JP (Lancs 1934), DL (1955), V-Lt 1956–70, Ld Lt 1970–76, High Steward of Westminster from 1962, memb Cncl of Duchy of Lancaster, FSA, barrister Inner Temple 1925, memb London Stock Exchange 1927–39, chm Mercantile Investment Tst Ltd, Borax Holdings Ltd, dep chm Nat Westminster Bank, dir: RTZ, Coutts and Co, John Brown and Co, Tube Investments Ltd, memb Ho of Laity of Nat Assembly for Blackburn 1930–50, MP (C) Rushcliffe 1934–45, City of London 1945–50 and Blackburn W 1950–55, PPS to First Commr of Works and Sec of State Colonies 1936–38, Parly Sec to: Min of Labour 1939–42, Min of Supply Feb-Dec 1942; Fin Sec to Treasury 1942–45, chm: C and Ut Party Orgn 1944–46, Public Accts Ctee 1948–50, Select Ctee of Nationalised Industries 1951–53, memb Roy Commn to W Indies 1938–39, Ld of the Manors of Downham, Slaidburn and Cuerdale, KStJ 1972; *b* 24 Feb 1901; *educ* Eton and Ch Ch Oxford (MA 1923); *m* 24 Jan 1924 Hon Sylvia Benita Frances Hotham (*d* 1991), FRICS, govr Westminster Hosp, memb Cncl Lancaster U, er dau of 6th Baron Hotham (*qv*), and *d* 1984, having had issue:

1 RALPH JOHN ASSHETON, **2nd and present Baron Clitheroe**

2 +Nicholas [The Hon Nicholas Assheton, 15 Hammersmith Terr, London W6 9TS]; Ld of the Manor and Liberty of Slaidburn, Grindleton and Bradford, late 2nd Lt The Life Gds and Lt Inns of Court Regt, Liveryman Vintners' Co, memb London Stock Exchange (memb Cncl 1968–88), ptnr Montagu, Loebl, Stanley and Co 1960–87 London, bd Nat Mutual Life Assoc of Australia 1972, dep chm Coutts & Co; *b* 23 May 1934; *educ* Eton and Ch Ch Oxford (BA 1957, MA 1960); FSA; *m* 29 Feb 1960 *Jacqueline Jill, yst dau of Marshal of the RAF Sir Arthur Travers Harris, 1st Bt, GCB, OBE, AFC (*see* 1970 edn HARRIS, Bt, of Chepping Wycombe), and has issue:

(1) +Thomas [Thomas Assheton Esq, Manor Farm, Longborough, Glos GL56 0QR]; Capt Life Gds (ret); *b* 8 July 1963; *educ* Eton, Reading U (BSc) and RMA Sandhurst; *m* 1989 *Katherine Sophie, dau of David Alphy Edward Raymond Peake (*see* INGLEBY, V), and has issue:

1a +Noah Frederick; *b* 26 Jan 1991

1a *Molly; *b* 9 Aug 1992

(1) *Caroline; *b* 2 May 1961

(2) *Mary Thérèse; *b* 26 Sept 1967; has:

1a *Arthur Travers GORDON; *b* 22 April 1994

1a *Alice GORDON; *b* 20 July 1988

1 Anne; *b* and *d* 22 Dec 1924

2 *Bridget [The Hon Lady Worsley, Hovingham Hall, York]; served WW II in WRNS; *b* 20 Aug 1926; *m* 10 Dec 1955 *Sir (William) Marcus John Worsley, 5th Bt (*qv*), and has issue

Seat: Downham Hall, Clitheroe, Lancs. Richard Assheton, uncle of the 1st Baronet of the 1620 creation, bought the Manor of Downham in 1558, having five years earlier acquired part of the lands formerly belonging to the dissolved Whalley Abbey, which had lain close by. Downham may well date from about that time, for despite its predominantly 19th-century appearance there is evidence of an older building underneath in the rubblestone material of the south-facing walls (which also display the remains of mullion windows), the E-shape, typical of later Tudor buildings, of the north facade and most cogently a date stone marked 1589. In the late 18th century a survey was carried out which suggested the main house had been completed by the time of CHARLES I's accession. On the other hand it has been suggested that Downham could have been erected on the site of a medieval tower.

Whatever the truth, William Assheton, who attained his majority in 1779, knocked down much of his ancestral dwelling, only to settle in foreign parts a few years later. Fairly major changes were effected by 1809, however, namely the reconstruction of the west wing and the central block. His son, another William, inherited in 1833 and employed George Webster of Kendal to carry out further improvements. The only major change since the mid-1830s is the section containing the school-room, which was added to the east wing, though Mildred, mother of the **1st Baron**, carried out a good deal of internal redecoration.

The result is a handsome but not spectacular mansion, its somewhat grim-coloured building materials being more than compensated for by the magnificent vista out towards Pendle Hill. The asymmetrical north facade, its central branch of the E pedimented, focuses at ground-floor level on a portico with a flat roof on four unfluted doric columns. The chimney stacks and a dormer window on the left hand side of the roof are particularly prominent against the skyline.

CLWYD

Arms: Per fess az. and arg. a lion rampant between three ostrich feathers, all countercharged. **Crest:** A lion rampant per fess arg. and az., holding in the paws an ostrich feather or. **Supporters:** Dexter, a dragon ppr.; sinister, a bear sa., each gorged with a collar or. **Motto:** *Tra anadl gobaith* ('While there's breath there's hope'). **Creation:** Bt. (UK) 25 July 1908, B. (UK) 19 May 1919.

THE 3RD BARON CLWYD, of Abergele, Co Denbigh, and **a Baronet** (Sir (John) Anthony Roberts, Bt) [The Rt Hon The Lord Clwyd, 24 Salisbury Ave, Cheam, Surrey SM1 2DJ]; *b* 2 Jan 1935; *s* f 1987; *educ* Harrow and Trin Coll Cambridge; barrister Gray's Inn 1970; *m* 20 Dec 1969 *(Linda) Geraldine, yr dau of Charles Engene Cannons, of Sanderstead, Surrey, and has issue:

1 +JOHN MURRAY; *b* 27 Aug 1971

2 +Jeremy Trevor; *b* 26 Oct 1973

3 +Hugh Gerald Arthur; *b* 21 Jan 1977

Lineage: DAVID ROBERTS, of Tanyrallt, Abergele, Denbighs; *b* 9 March 1806; *m* 5 Oct 1832 Jane (*d* 17 Jan 1864), dau of Richard Roberts, of Liverpool, and *d* 3 Oct 1886, having had, with other issue:

JOHN ROBERTS, of Bryngwenallt, Abergele, JP, MP Flintshire Boroughs 1878–92; *b* 14 July 1835; *m* 23 May 1861 Catherine Tudor (*d* 13 Sep 1880), dau of Rev John Hughes, of Liverpool, and *d* 24 Feb 1894, having had an est son:

Sir John Herbert Roberts, 1st Bt, so *cr* 25 July 1908, as also 19 May 1919 **1st Baron Clwyd**, of Abergele, Co Denbigh (both UK), JP (Denbighs); MP W Denbighs 1892–1918, a Commr for Temporalities under the Welsh Church Act from 1914, chm Welsh Lib Parly Party 1912–18 (sometime Sec); *b* 8 Aug 1963; *educ* Trin Coll Cambridge (BA 1884, MA 1888); *m* 1 Aug 1893 Hannah Rushton (*d* 1 Jan 1951), er dau of William Sproston Caine, MP Camborne, and had issue:

1 (JOHN) TREVOR ROBERTS, **2nd Baron**

2 David Stowell (twin), Sr History Master Christ's Hospital, Horsham; *b* 28 Nov 1900; *educ* Trin Coll Cambridge (BA 1922, MA 1927); *m* 11 Aug 1936 *Aileen Mary Box [Mrs David Roberts, 24 Long Ashton Rd, Bristol BS18 9LB], only dau of Charles Edward Burrow, of Sale, Cheshire, and *d* 28 April 1956, leaving issue:

(1) +(Hugh) Martin [Martin Roberts Esq, 29 Chalfont Rd, Oxford OX2 6TL]; *b* 9 Oct 1941; *educ* Christ's Hosp and Merton Coll Oxford; Headmaster Cherwell Comprehensive Sch; *m* 13 Aug 1966 *Diana, dau of Denis C Cochran, of Cape Town, S Africa, and has issue:

1a +Thomas Owen; *b* 1973

1a *Sarah Megan; *b* 1971

(2) +Peter Gareth [Peter Roberts Esq, 11 Sandford Rd, Hotwells, Bristol]; *b* 5 Jan 1947; *educ* Christ's Hosp, UEA and Columbia U (NY); *m* 1982 *Susan Browne, and has issue:

1a +Matthew Lewis; *b* 1984

(1) *Fenella [Mrs Peter Rosenwald, 39 Drayton Gardens, London SW10 9RY]; *b* 19 Jan 1940; *m* 27 Dec 1968 *Peter Rosenwald, son of Joseph Sanger Rosenwald, of New Rochelle, NY, USA, and has issue:

1a *David Joseph; *b* 1972

1a *Celia Janet; *b* 1974

3 (William Herbert) Mervyn, JP (Denbighs 1954), ARCM, ALCM, *b* 23 Nov 1906; *educ* Gresham's and Trin Coll Cambridge (BA 1928); composer and teacher; *m* 15 April 1947 *Eileen Margaret [Mrs Mervyn Roberts, 17 Wimblehurst Rd, Horsham, W Sussex RH12 2EA], only dau of Alfred Thomas Easom, of Hillside, Abergele, and *d* 1990, leaving issue:

(1) *Catherine Angela [Mrs David Arnold, 17 Wimblehurst Rd, Horsham, W Sussex RH12 2EA]; *b* 14 Dec 1950; *m* 1984 *David James Arnold

The 1st BARON *d* 19 Dec 1955; his est son,

(JOHN) TREVOR ROBERTS, **2nd Baron Clwyd**, JP (Co London 1950), barrister Gray's Inn 1930, Assist Sec of Commns Ld Chllr's Office 1949–61; *b* 28 Nov 1900; *educ* Gresham's and Trin Coll Cambridge (BA 1922); *m* 4 Jan 1932 Joan de Bois (*d* 1985), er dau of Charles Robert Murray, of Woodbank, Partickhill, Glasgow, and *d* 1987, having had issue:

1 JOHN ANTHONY ROBERTS, **4th and present Baron**

1 *Alison de Bois [The Hon Mrs Brown, 9 Royal Terrace, Glasgow G3 7NT]; *b* 24 Feb 1939; *m* 1st 19 Feb 1965 (*divorce* 1972) George Stricevic, son of Milorad Stricevic, of Banjaluke, Yugoslavia, and has issue:

(1) *Milorad; *b* 8 Feb 1967; *educ* Rugby

1 (cont.) The Hon Mrs Alison Stricevic *m* 2nd 23 Sept 1972 *Anthony Harold Brown, er son of Peter Beale Harold Brown, of Woodlands, Balmaha, Drymen, Glasgow, and has further issue:

(2) *Barnaby Joseph; *b* 8 Aug 1973

(3) *Benedict Samuel; *b* 9 Sept 1975

(4) *Lionel Trevor; *b* 1978

CLYDE

Arms: Per fess argent and azure a fess wavy per fess wavy azure and argent,two bushes upon mounds vert in chief and a tower or window and port gules in base. **Crest:** Issuant from a mount vert a tree with a branch of mountain ash, of beech and of cherry proper. **Supporters:** Dexter, the figure of Justice, without blindfold, and holding in her exterior hand a pair of scales; sinister, the figure of Apollo holding in his exterior hand a lyre proper. **Motto:** (over the crest) *Diligens integer lætus* ('Hard-working, fulfilled, happy') **Creation:** B. (LP, UK) 1996.

THE BARON CLYDE, of Briglands, Perthshire and Kinross (James John Clyde, PC (1996)) [The Rt Hon The Lord Clyde PC, House of Lords, London SW1A 0PW]; *b* 29 Jan 1932; *educ* Edinburgh Acad, Corpus Christi Coll Oxford and Edinburgh U; advocate 1959, QC Scotland 1971, Advocate-Depute 1973–74, Chllr to Bp Argyll and the Isles 1972–85, Judge Jersey and Guernsey Cts Appeal 1979–85, Ld of Session 1985–96, Chm Med Appeal Tbnl 1974–85, V-Pres Roy Blind Asylum and Sch 1987–, a Ld Appeal in Ordinary 1996–; DUniv Heriot-Watt 1991, Hon DLitt Napier 1995; ed *Armour on Valuation* (3rd edn 1961, 5th edn 1985); *m* 1963 *Anne Clunie Hoblyn and has two sons

Lineage: BARON CLYDE; had:

JAMES JOHN, *cr* a **Baron**

CLYDESMUIR

Arms: Argent a cross moline sable, on a chief of the last a thistle slipped proper between two bull's heads, also argent. **Crest:** A hind's head erased proper. **Supporters:** A roebuck and a doe, both proper. **Motto:** (above the crest) *Oublier ne puis* ('I cannot forget'). **Creation:** B. (UK) 5 March 1948.

THE 3RD BARON CLYDESMUIR, of Braidwood, Co Lanark (David Ronald Colville) [The Rt Hon The Lord Clydesmuir, Langlees House, Biggar, Lanarkshire ML12 6NP]; *b* 8 April 1949; *s* f 1996; *educ* Charterhouse; ACA; *m* 9 Sept 1978 *Aline Frances, er dau of Peter Merriam, of Holton Lodge, Holton St Mary, Suffolk, gs of 3rd Marquess of Ailsa (*qv*), and has issue:

1 +RICHARD DAVID RONALD; *b* 21 Oct 1980

2 +Hamish; *b* 1989

1 *Rachel; *b* 23 Feb 1983

2 *Harriet; *b* 1985

Lineage: JAMES COLVILLE of Barnweill; living between *c* 1526 and 1548 (a cousin of the COLVILLEs of Hiltoun and Ochiltree (*see* COLVILLE OF CULROSS, V); had:

WILLIAM COLVILLE of Barnweill; *m* Elizabeth Dunlop (*d* Nov 1580) and *d* between 10 Nov 1580 and Aug 1584, having had, with a yr s (James, had three sons (William, merchant; James; Philip) and a dau (Isobel, *d* Feb 1622)) and three daus (Janet; Isobel; Christian):

MUNGO COLVILLE of Barnweill; *m* Janet Wallace and *d* between 17 June 1601 and 5 Jan 1602, leaving, with two yr sons (Philip; William, Ayr merchant, *d* 6 Oct 1610) and a dau (Agnes, *m* 1st James Blair and had a s, *m* 2nd Robert Rankin):

WILLIAM COLVILLE, of Underwood, Barnweill, by 1622 (later in Raith); had, with four yr sons (Robert, Ayr merchant and burgess, *m* Janet Rankin (*d* Aug 1671) and had a s James; Philip; James, of Ladykirk; Hugh) and two daus (Sarah, *m c* 13 Dec 1640 John Millar, Yr., in Kirkindeall; Elizabeth):

WILLIAM COLVILLE, of Lesnessock, which he acquired between 23 July 1631 and 17 Feb 1644; *m c* 22 July 1631 Jean, dau of Robert Stewart of Robertoun by Katharine Kennedy, and *d* Dec 1677, leaving issue, with a yst s (John, *bapt* 28 Oct 1645) and four other daus:

1 ROBERT

2 William, in Craignock; *m* Marion Cunyngham

3 Matthew, of Edinburgh; writer (lawyer), one of the Gentlemen of the Guard of Horse; *m* 20 Nov 1660 Helen (*bur* 16 Sept 1699), dau of John Bineing, of Dalvenan, and *d* on or after 30 July 1687, having had, with four other children (*d* young), a s (William, *bapt* 25 Dec 1664) and two daus (Helen, *bapt* 7 July 1663; Eupheme, *bapt* 14 Jan 1666)

1 Anna; *bapt* 29 Nov 1643; *m* 31 Jan 1671 William Wallace

2 Jean; *bapt* 27 Oct 1950; *m* James Muir, in Crookmilne

The est son,

ROBERT COLVILLE, of Lesnessock and Kintyre, Argyllshire, which acquired between 13 April 1670 and 20 March 1687; *m* 20 Sept 1660 Elizabeth Wallace and *d* by 1698, leaving, with a yr s (Robert) and dau (Margaret, *bapt* 10 July 1672):

WILLIAM COLVILLE, of Lesnessock and later Tradigal, Argyllshire; *bapt* 27 April 1662; *m* 14 March 1695 Janet, dau of James Armour, of Campbelltown, and *d* after 1707, leaving, with three yr sons (Alexander, *bapt* 19 March 1699; William, *bapt* 14 Feb 1703; James, *bapt* 18 Feb 1711) and a dau (Janet, *bapt* 4 May 1701):

ROBERT COLVILLE, of Tradigal; *bapt* 7 July 1696; *m* 8 Dec 1724 Margaret Cuthbertson, and *d* after 1755, leaving, with an est s (William, *bapt* 8 Aug 1725), four yr sons (James, *bapt* 9 June 1728; John, *bapt* 6 Nov 1731; Robert, *bapt* 27 Aug 1733; Robert, *b* 18 Oct 1748) and two daus (Isobel, *bapt* 14 April 1730; Mary, *bapt* Nov 1743):

ARCHIBALD COLVILLE, of Peninver 1755 and Drumgarve 1772; *bapt* 30 Nov 1726; *m* Jan 1752 Elizabeth Templeton and *d* between 1772 and 1780, leaving, with four yr sons (Thomas, *bapt* 15 Aug 1756; John, *bapt* 29 April 1759; Archibald, *b* 28 Feb 1761; Charles, *b* 1770, *m* 12 Aug 1798 Janet Dunlop, of Killean, and *d* 15 April 1828, leaving three sons (two of whom *d* young) and five daus) and two daus (Anne, *b* 27 July 1765; Jean, *b* 20 May 1768):

ROBERT COLVILLE, of Drumgarve; *bapt* 8 May 1753; *m* Janet (*d* 15 Sept 1832), dau of Archibald Mitchell by Mary Ferguson, and *d* 29 May 1835, leaving, with another s and two daus (all *d* young):

1 Archibald; *b* 29 March 1792; *m* 19 June 1827 Catherine Harvey (*d* 5 March 1838), and *d* 10 Nov 1838, leaving issue:

(1) Janet; *b* 11 Sept 1830; *m* 17 July 1856 Robert Greenlees, of Burnbank Ho, nr Campbeltown, Argyllshire, and *d* 2 Dec 1893, leaving, with two yr daus:

1a Catherine Harvey; *m* her cousin David Colville (*see* below)

2 John, of Muasdale; *b* 11 Dec 1795; *m* his cousin Margaret Colville, sis of David Colville of Eastcliffe, and had issue:

(1) Robert, of Muasdale; *m* Elizabeth Colville

(2) John, of Burnside, Campbeltown; *b* 10 Aug 1827; *educ* Glasgow U (MA); *m* Mary Agnes (*d* 19 May 1933), dau of Thomas Bodington, of Harborne Pk, Warwicks, and *d* 27 July 1886, leaving issue:

1a Mary Theodora; *b* 4 Feb 1886; *m* 3 Sept 1909 Rev David Colville Lusk, MA, 2nd son of John Lusk, of Dunavon, Strathaven, Lanarks, by Janet Colville (*see* below), and *d* 7 May 1938, leaving three sons and two daus

3 Robert; *b* 1 July 1804; *m* his sis-in-law Janet Colville

4 James; *b* 5 May 1807; *d* unm

5 DAVID

1 Mary; *b* 17 Feb 1790; *m* Alexander Greenlees, of Seafield, Campbeltown

2 Jean; *b* 24 Dec 1799; *m* Hugh Greenlees, of Burnbank Ho, nr Campbeltown

3 Elizabeth; *b* 13 May 1802; *m* Andrew Smith, of Bleachfield, Argyllshire

ROBERT COLVILLE's yst son,

DAVID COLVILLE, of Cliftonhill Ho, Lanarks, and Claremont Terr, Glasgow, JP (Lanarks); *b* 15 Feb 1813; Commr of Supply; *m* 18 June 1845 Janet Amelia (*d* 19 Nov 1897), dau of Rev John Barr, DD, of Dovehill, Glasgow, by Elizabeth Houston, and *d* 29 Oct 1898, leaving, with an est s (*d* an infant):

1 JOHN

2 Archibald; *b* 27 Sept 1853; *m* 3 March 1886 Jane (*d* 1936), dau of John Millar, of Fernhill, and Lambhill, Lanarks, and *d* 11 Dec 1916, leaving issue:

(1) David; *b* 21 April 1890; *educ* Fettes and Pembroke Coll Cambridge (MA); Capt Fife and Forfar Yeo WW I (despatches); *m* 9 Aug 1916 Elizabeth, 3rd dau of Sir Henry Beyer Robertson, of Palé, Llandderfel, N Wales, and *d* 12 April 1964, having had issue:

1a Archibald; *b* 12 Feb 1918; *educ* Shrewsbury; Capt KOSB WW II; *m* 27 July 1949 *Margaret Mary, dau of Dennis Wheeler-Carmichael by Violet Penelope Gibson-Carmichael (*see* GIBSON-CRAIG-CARMICHAEL, Bt), and *d* 30 Jan 1970, leaving issue:

1b *Thomas David; *b* 21 July 1952; *educ* Radley

2b *William Henry Archibald; *b* 30 April 1955; *educ* Radley

1b *Rosemary Elizabeth; *b* 27 June 1950; *m* 10 Aug 1974 *Neil Robert Colquhoun, yst son of W R Colquhoun, and has issue:

1c *A son; *b* 16 Sept 1976

2a David; *b* 26 April 1919; *educ* Eton; Capt KOSB WW II; *d* of wounds 18 Feb 1945

3a *Wynn Robert [Wynn Colville Esq, Islabank, Coupar Angus, Perthshire]; *b* 7 May 1927; *educ* Eton; *m* 25 July 1951 *Deirdre Joan, yr dau of Alastair Montague Dixon, of Broadleys, Gleneagles, Auchterarder, Perthshire, and has:

1b *Philip John; *b* 16 July 1952; *educ* Eton

2b *David Alastair; *b* 15 Feb 1955; *educ* Millfield

1a *Hazel Jean Elizabeth [Mrs Alexander Leslie, Wester Gavin, Howwood, Renfrewshire]; *m* 7 June 1949 Alexander Leslie, TD, MA, CEng, FICE, MIWE, FASCE, son of James Leslie, of Edinburgh, and has issue:

1b *James; *b* 23 Aug 1950; *educ* Fettes

2b *Robert Colville; *b* 4 Nov 1954; *educ* Fettes

1b *Susan Elizabeth; *b* 1 Nov 1953

2b *Mary Helen; *b* 3 Nov 1957

(2) *John Millar; *b* 15 May 1902; *educ* Eton and Pembroke Coll Cambridge (MA); *m* 28 Dec 1934 *Helen, dau of Walter Thomas Markillie, of San Francisco, and has issue:

1a *Virginia; *b* 15 Feb 1936; *m* 10 Sept 1966 Sir Peter Craft Hutchinson, 2nd Bt, of Rossie (*qv*), and has issue

2a Marilyn Jean [Mrs William Crawford, Kitty Frist House, Hexham, Northumberland]; *b* 7 June 1938; *m* 31 July 1965 William Hamilton Raymund Crawford, er son of Col Mervyn Crawford, DSO, of Dalgonar, Dunscore, Dumfriesshire, and has issue:

1b *Alexander Mervyn Colville; *b* 14 May 1966

1b *Catharine Clare; *b* 26 Feb 1968

2b *A dau; *b* 25 July 1971

(1) Nora Jane Craig Millar; *m* 9 June 1915 Capt James Russell Pelham-Burn (*d* 4 July 1963), Seaforth Highrs, yst son of Charles Maitland Pelham-Burn, Seaforth Highrs, of Grange Pk, Edinburgh, and *d* 9 Sept 1964, leaving issue

(2) Maud; *m* 4 Sept 1915 Capt John Wyndham, JP (*d* 24 Nov 1966), 3rd son of William Wyndham, JP, DL, of Dinton Ho, Wilts, and *d* 6 Oct 1972, leaving issue:

1a *George Colville, JP (1952), of Orchard Wyndham, Williton, Somerset; *b* 19 June 1916; *educ* Stowe and Corpus Christi Coll Cambridge (BA); ICS (ret 1947), CC Somerset 1949, chm CC 1959–62 and 1964–69, memb Somerset Ag Exec Ctee 1949–59, memb SW Regnl Ec Cncl 1965–, V-Chm CLA 1967–69; *m* 26 Aug 1939 *Anne Dorothy Hodder, est dau of Ralph Hodder-Williams, MC, of Duddings, Dunster, Somerset, and has issue:

1b *William Wadham; *b* 4 Aug 1940; *educ* Eton and Wadham Coll Oxford

2b *Edmund Sydenham; *b* 25 July 1954

1b *Sylvana Margery Glazebrook; *b* 9 Sept 1944; *m* 15 May 1965 *Richard David Chandler, son of Lt-Col C Roger T Chandler, and has issue:

1c *Christopher James Elphinstone; *b* 24 Feb 1967

2c *Edward Nicholas Colville; *b* 27 Nov 1968

1c *Katherine Stafford Heathcote; *b* 27 Nov 1947

1a *Barbara [Mrs John Forster-Cooper, 10 rue des Heraults, Brunoy, Seine-et-Oise, France; *b* 14 June 1917; *m* 23 Aug 1943 John Forster-Cooper, son of Sir Clive Forster-Cooper, FRS, FZS, and has a s and dau

2a *Lorna Marion; *b* 28 May 1919

3a *Stella Margaret; *b* 28 May 1919

(3) Margaret Wallace; *m* 26 March 1924 Maj Thomas Vernon Booth-Jones, JP, DL (*d* 13 March 1966), only son of Thomas Booth-Jones, of Park Ho, Whitefield, Lancs, and had issue

(4) Edith; *m* 11 Nov 1920 Lt-Col Ralph George Snead Cox, MC, Roy Inniskilling Fus (*ka* Burma 9 April 1942), son of Col Richard Charles Clement Snead Cox, 27th Regt, and had issue:

1a *(Geoffrey) Richard, of Slaney Cottage, Hartley Wintney, Hants; *b* 29 April 1927; *educ* Ampleforth; Maj Roy Inniskilling Fus (ret 1964), Malaya, Cyprus, Kenya, and Arabian Peninsula, UN Peace Force Cyprus 1964, GSO(3) NI Dist 1955–56, 2nd Para Regt 1957–59; *m* 15 Feb 1962 *Ann Nina Marion, er dau of Lt-Col Thomas Leslie Ovens, IA, of Stillorgan Grove, Blackrock, Co Dublin, by Christina Mary, dau of John Cahill, of Ballyconra Ho, Ballyragget, Co Kilkenny

2a *Michael Guy, of Inverclune, Killiecrankie, Perthshire; *b* 29 Sept 1928; *educ* Ampleforth; late Seaforth Highrs

1a *Mary Johanna Jean; *m* 11 April 1950 (Edward Henry) Vernon Harington, er son of Judge Edward Harington, JP, and has issue (*see* HARINGTON, Bt)

(5) Elizabeth Georgina; *b* 6 Oct 1903; *d* unm 23 Sept 1936

3 David, of Jerviston House, Lanarks, JP (Lanarkshire); *b* 10 March 1860; *educ* Glasgow U; *m* 18 Aug 1887 his 3rd cousin Catherine Harvey (*d* 10 Sept 1932), dau of Robert Greenlees by Janet Colville (*see* above), and *d* 16 Oct 1916, leaving issue:

(1) David; *b* 5 July 1888; *d* 7 March 1889

(2) Norman Robert, MC; *b* 11 Sept 1893; *educ* Fettes and Clare Coll Cambridge; WW I Capt Argyll and Sutherland Highrs (despatches twice) ret 1919, WW II as Gp Cdr HG 1940–41; High Sheriff Cornwall 1940–41; *m* 1st 10 Nov 1915 Marjorie Southworthe (*d* 26 Oct 1937), 2nd dau of Philip Edelston, of Penworthan Ho, Lancs, and had issue:

1a Gavin David; *b* 20 June 1922; *educ* Eton; RAF WW II; *ka* over Tripoli 2/3 Nov 1941

1a *Anne Lindsay; *b* 1 Aug 1916

(2) (cont.) Norman Colville *m* 2nd 14 July 1938 André Manuela Alexandre Joaquina (*d* 8 May 1940), dau of Germain Bapst, of Paris, by Queta Narischkine (*née* de Laski); *m* 3rd 1 June 1951 *Diana Evelyn [Mrs Norman Colville, Penheale Barton, Launceston, Cornwall PL1 8RX; 11 Kensington Sq, London W8], High Sheriff Cornwall 1988–89, only child of Lt-Col Hon Sir Piers Walter Legh, GCVO, CMG, CIE, OBE (*see* NEWTON, B, also Section Polk AMERICAN PRESIDENTIAL FAMILIES, 1994, Morris Genealogical Books SA), and formerly w of 4th Earl of Kimberley (*qv*), and *d* 26 Aug 1974, leaving by her:

2a *James Charles David; *b* 16 April 1952; *educ* Eton; Page of Honour to HM THE QUEEN 1966–68; *m* 2 April 1983 *Fiona Gaylor and has:

1b *Robert John James; *b* 14 June 1984

1b *Saraha Elizabeth Rose; *b* 27 June 1986

2b *Lucy Isabel Amy; *b* 14 Aug 1988

(1) Amy Janet; *m* 16 Feb 1922 1st Baron Bilsland (*d* 10 Dec 1970; *see* 1970 edn), *d* 19–

4 Robert; *b* 25 March 1863; *d* unm 1931

1 Elizabeth; *b* 30 Dec 1847; *m* 14 June 1877 John Boyle Lindsay (*d* 16 Jan 1885), and *d* 7 May 1884, leaving a dau

2 Janet; *b* 14 Aug 1849; *m* 10 Aug 1876 John Lusk (*d* 6 April 1913), and *d* 29 Oct 1929, leaving two sons and a dau

3 Mary Amelia; *b* 4 Dec 1850; *m* 19 Aug 1875 Rev William Young Turner, BD, MD (*d* 23 Dec 1927), of Glasgow, and *d* 21 Nov 1876, leaving a s

4 Jane; *b* 28 May 1855; *m* 5 June 1884 Alexander Bilsland (*d* 8 Feb 1919), of Glasgow, 3rd son of James Bilsland (*see* 1970 edn BILSLAND, B), in Ballat, Stirlingshire, and *d* 4 April 1940, leaving a s and dau

5 Margaret Anne; *b* 28 May 1855; *m* 13 Sept 1883 George Bishop Douglas (*d* 26 Jan 1933), of New York, and *d* 3 Oct 1929, leaving three daus

6 Jemima; *b* 14 Feb 1857; *d* unm 12 April 1932

7 Georgina; *b* 26 May 1861; *m* 17 Jan 1889 Zachary Taylor Emery, MD (*d* 7 Oct 1924), of New York, and *dsp* 15 June 1941

DAVID COLVILLE's est surv son,

JOHN COLVILLE, of Cleland, Lanarks; *b* 3 July 1852; MP NE Lanarks; *m* 1st 1878 Janet (*dsp* 23 July 1883), dau of Rev Joseph Brown, DD, of Glasgow; *m* 2nd 31 Aug 1885 Christian (*d* 7 Jan 1936), dau of James Downie, JP, of Kirkintilloch, and *d* 22 Aug 1901, leaving issue:

1 (DAVID) JOHN, **1st Baron**

1 Christian Hendrie, MBE (1944); *b* Dec 1888; *m* 3 Dec 1915 Sir Alexander Galloway Erskine-Hill, 1st Bt (*qv*), and *d* 13 Sept 1947, leaving issue

JOHN COLVILLE's only son,

(DAVID) JOHN COLVILLE, **1st Baron Clydesmuir**, of Braidwood, Co Lanark (UK), so *cr* 5 March 1948, GCIE (1943), TD, PC (1936), JP (1925), DL (1933); *b* 13 Feb 1894; *educ* Charterhouse and Trin Coll Cambridge (BA 1914, MA 1920); Ld Lt Lanarks 1952 (V-Lt 1949), Brig Roy Co Archers, MP (U) N Midlothian and Peebleshire May 1929–Jan 1943, PPS to Parl U-Sec Scotland 1931, Parly Sec Dept Overseas Trade 1931–35, Parly U-Sec Scotland 1935–36, Fin Sec Treasury 1936–38, Sec State Scotland 1938–40, 6th Bn Cameronians (TA) WW I 1914–19 (wounded twice), T/Col Staff 1940–42, Hon Col 6th Cameronians 1941–46, Govr Bombay March 1943–Jan 1948 (Actg Viceroy India 1945, 1946 and 1947), dir Colville's Ltd, Steelmakers 1948–54, Govr BBC 1950–54, KGStJ; *m* 6 Oct 1915 Agnes Anne, CI (1947), CStJ, Kaisar-i-Hind Gold Medal (*d* 29 Dec 1970), er dau of Sir William Bilsland, 1st Bt, LLD (*see* 1970 edn), and *d* Oct 1954, having had issue:

1 RONALD JOHN BILSLAND, **2nd Baron**

1 Mary Helen; *b* 24 Oct 1922; *m* 23 July 1949 *Capt North Edward Frederick Dalrymple-Hamilton of Bargany, CVO, MBE, DSC, JP, DL, RN, only son of Adml Sir Frederick Hew George Dalrymple-Hamilton, KCB, and *d* 1981, leaving issue (*see* STAIR, E)

2 *Rosemary Anne Heather [The Hon Mrs Whitcombe, Green Cross Farm, Churt, Farnham, Surrey]; *b* 27 Sept 1927; *m* 14 July 1954 *Philip Arthur Whitcombe, late Capt RA, yr son of Maj-Gen Philip Sidney Whitcombe, CB, OBE, JP, of the Grange, Lake, Amesbury, Wilts, and has:

(1) *Robert John; *b* 28 Nov 1955; *m* 1988 *Sophie E, dau of T O Roberts, of Petersfield, Hants

(1) *Susan Anne Clare [Mrs Robin Marriott, Park View Farm, Headley, Hants]; *b* June 1957; *m* 1985 *Robin R Marriott, yr son of Anthony Marriott

The 1st BARON *d* 31 Oct 1954; his est son,

RONALD JOHN BILSLAND COLVILLE, **2nd Baron Clydesmuir**, KT (1972), CB (1965), MBE (1949), TD, DL (Lanarks 1955); *b* 21 May 1917; *educ* Charterhouse and Trin Coll Cambridge (BA); Brevet-Col Cameronians WW II (despatches), commissioned 6th/7th Cameronians (TA) 1953056 (Hon Col 1967–71), chm Lanarks T&AFA 1957, v-chm Cncl T&AFA 1961; dir Br Steel Corp Strip Mills Div 1970–73, govr Bank of Scotland 1972–81, dir Barclays Bank 1972–82, dir Colvilles Ltd 1958–70, dep govr Br Linen Bank 1966–71 and dir Scottish Provident Inst 1954–88, chm Scottish br Nat Playing Fields Assoc, tstee King George's Fields Fndn, King George's Jubilee Tst, Pres Scottish Cncl Physical Recreation, chm Scottish Cncl (Development and Industry) 1966–78 (Pres 1978–86), Captain Gen 1988–96 Roy Co of Archers (memb 1953–96), Ld HC Gen Assembly Ch Scotland 1971 and 1972, Hon Memb Merchants' Co Edinburgh, Ld Lt Lanarks 1963–92 (V-Lt 1959–63), Hon LLD Strathclyde 1968, Hon DSc Heriot-Watt 1971; *m* 10 April 1946 *Joan Marguerita, er dau of Lt-Col Ernest Brabazon Booth, DCO, MD, of Darver Castle, Co Louth, and *d* 2 Oct 1996, having had issue:

1 DAVID RONALD COLVILLE, **3rd and present Baron Clydesmuir**

2 +Andrew John [The Hon Andrew Colville, 40 Pembroke Rd, London W8]; *b* 30 May 1953; *educ* Harrow and Magdalene Coll Cambridge (BA 1975); slr 1976–80, merchant banker 1980–; *m* 30 Sept 1978 *Elaine Genevieve, dau of E G Davy, of Corner Farm, Holton St Peter, Halesworth, Suffolk, and has issue:

(1) +Patrick Edwin Ronald; *b* 1988

(1) *Emily Christine Rose; *b* 1986

1 *Diana Mary [The Hon Mrs Munro, 26 Pembroke Sq, London W8]; *b* 21 Jan 1947; Ldy in Waiting to HRH THE DUCHESS OF GLOUCESTER 1980–; *m* 22 Sept 1973 *Christopher Ian Craddock Munro, only son of William Hutton Munro, of Warrix, Troon, Ayreshire, and has:

(1) *Andrew James William; *b* 26 Feb 1979

(1) *Fiona Mary; *b* 1976

2 *(Elizabeth) Anne; *b* 26 June 1955; *m* 1983 *Christopher J V R Baker, son of Maj Valentine Baker, and has issue:

(1) *Lucy Florence; *b* 1986

COATES

Arms: Gules a chevron cotised argent, on a chief ermine two bells or; on an escutcheon of pretence, quarterly, 1st and 4th, argent, a fir tree growing out of a mount in base vert surmounted by a sword in bend supporting a crown in the dexter canton proper, and in chief and base a lion's head erased, armed and langued gules; 2nd and 3rd, gules three bear's heads couped argent, muzzled sable. **Crest:** A cock statant, wings closed, gules. **Motto:** Watchful and bold. **Creation:** Bt. (UK) 15 July 1921.

SIR DAVID FREDERICK CHARLTON COATES, 3RD BT, of Haypark, in the City of Belfast [Sir David Coates Bt, 30 Hauxton Rd, Little Shelford, Cambs CB2 5HJ]; *b* 16 Feb 1948; *s* f 1994; *educ* Millfield; *m* 1973 *Christine Helen, dau of Lewis F Marshall, of Ely, Cambs, and has issue:

1 +JAMES GREGORY DAVID; *b* 12 March 1977

2 +Robert Lewis Edward; *b* 1980

Lineage: ISRAEL COATS, of The Falls, Belfast; *m* Grace, dau and coheir of Edward Harris, of Belfast, and *d* 1764, leaving, with other issue:

VICTOR COATS, of Snugville, Belfast; *b* 1760; *d* 22 Oct 1822, leaving:

WILLIAM COATES, of Glentoran, Belfast, JP; *b* 1798; *m* Mary, dau of Maurice Lindsay, of Ashfield, and *d* 31 March 1878, leaving, with other issue:

DAVID LINDSAY COATES, of Clonallon, Strandtown, Belfast, JP; *b* 16 Sept 1840; *m* 10 Nov 1864 Sara (*d* 18 Nov 1915), only dau of George Mulligan, of Banbridge, Co Down, and *d* 26 May 1894, leaving issue:

1 WILLIAM FREDERICK (Sir), **1st Bt**

2 Harold Vivian Edmund; *b* 23 Oct 1874; *d* 3 Oct 1936

1 Anna Maria; *d* 7 Oct 1939

The er son,

Sir William Frederick Coates, 1st Bt (UK), so *cr* 15 July 1921, JP Co Antrim, DL, JP Belfast; *b* 1 March 1866; High Sheriff Belfast 1906, High Sheriff Co Antrim 1931, Ld Mayor Belfast 1920, 1921, 1922, 1929 and 1930; First Senator NI 1921, Freeman Belfast 1931, sr ptnr William F Coates and Co; *m* 27 Nov 1907 Elsie Millicent, Hon Burgess of Belfast (*d* 26 June 1958), yr dau of Col Frederick William Gregory, Essex Regt, and had:

1 FREDERICK GREGORY LINDSAY (Sir), **2nd Bt**

1 *Jean Ann Dorothy [Mrs Thomas Sinclair, 610 Bridlespur Lane, Earlysville, VA 22936, USA]; *m* 7 Dec 1938 Thomas Roland Lecky Sinclair (*d* 1991), only son of Capt Sir Kenneth Duncan Lecky Sinclair, DL, RNR, of Beech Leigh, Windsor Park, Belfast, and has issue:

(1) *Francis David Nicholas [Francis Sinclair, RTI, Box 196, Earlysville, VA 22936, USA]; *b* 26 Aug 1940; *m* 1st 1963 (*divorce* 1966) Peggy Elizabeth Biller; *m* 2nd 1984 *Mary Virginia Otto, and by her has issue:

1a *Thomas William Patrick; *b* 1985

2a *Frederick Duncan Andrew; *b* 1990

(2) *Kenneth Richard Coates [Kenneth Sinclair, 1204 Colonial Way, Charleston, W Va, USA]; *b* 29 Jan 1946; *m* 1972 *Marion Evans Jefferds, of W Va, and has issue:

1a *Joseph Jefferds; *b* 1975

1a *Elizabeth Young; *b* 1973

2a *Catherine Coates; *b* 1978

(1) Eleanor Margaret; *b* 29 Sept 1943; *m* 1st 1962 (*divorce* 1981) Walter Roger Shope, Lt-Col US Army; *m* 2nd 1986 *James Edwin Lewis and *d* 1996 leaving by her 1st husb:

1a *Thomas Roger; *b* 1968; *m* 1992 *Lisa Ann Crandall and has:

1b *Zachary Sinclair; *b* 1995

1a *Jean Marie; *b* 1964; *m* 1996 *Delbert Scott Cottrill

Sir WILLIAM *d* 19 Jan 1932; his only son,

Sir Frederick Gregory Lindsay Coates, 2nd Bt; *b* 19 May 1916; *educ* Eton and RMC Sandhurst; served WW II in N Africa and NW Europe (twice wounded), Brig late RTR, Assist Mil Attaché Stockholm 1953–56, memb Br Jt Services Mission Washington 1956–58, Cmdt RAC Sch of Tank Technology 1958–61, Assist Dir Fighting Vehicles and Col GS War Office and MOD (Army Dept) 1961–66, Dir Munitions R and D Staff and Assist Mil Attaché, Br Embassy Washington 1966–69, Dir Overseas Sales (Army) 1969–71 (ret); *m* 20 Sept 1940 *Joan Nugent [Joan Lady Coates, Launchfield House, Briantspuddle, Dorset DT2 7HN], 2nd dau of Maj-Gen Sir Charlton Watson Spinks, KBE, DSO, and *d* 1994, leaving:

1 Sir DAVID FREDERICK CHARLTON COATES, **3rd and present Bt**

1 *Elizabeth Sara Ann [Mrs Carol Gurney, Higham Lodge, Higham, Stratford St Mary, Suffolk CO7 6ND]; *b* 12 Jan 1941; *m* 6 March 1964 *Maj Carol James Hay Gurney, late 60th Rifles, High Sheriff Suffolk 1993, only son of Brig Cecil Hay Gurney, CBE, of Higham Lodge, Stratford St Mary, Suffolk, and has issue:

(1) *Christopher Hay; *b* 22 April 1968

(1) *Sara Catherine; *b* 30 Aug 1965; *m* 1990 *Rupert Lyle Charles Eley, son of Oliver John Maxwell Eley, and has:

1a *Cuthbert Oliver; *b* 28 July 1997

2 *Moira Louise [Mrs Anthony Hunt, 74 Lynn St, Swaffham, Norfolk]; *b* 23 Jan 1945; *m* 12 Aug 1967 *Anthony Hunt and has issue:

(1) *Nigel David Antony Howard; *b* 10 Jan 1968

(2) *Michael William Richard; *b* 1971

(3) *Jonathan Andrew Frederick; *b* 1974

COATS

Arms: Or three mascles sable, a chief engrailed azure, semée of fleur-de-lys of the field. **Crest:** A stag's head erased proper charged on the neck with an escarbuncle or. **Motto:** *Cœur fidèle* ('Faithful heart'). **Creation:** Bt. (UK) 7 Dec 1905.

SIR ALASTAIR FRANCIS STUART COATS, 4TH BT, of Auchendrane, Ayrshire [Sir Alastair Coats Bt, Birchwood House, Durford Wood, Petersfield, Hants GU31 5AW]; *b* 18 Nov 1921; *s* f 1966; *educ* Eton; Capt Res of Offrs Coldstream Gds WW II; *m* 6 Feb 1947 *Lukyn, dau of Capt Charles Gordon, of Birchwood, Durford Wood, Hants, and has issue:

1 +ALEXANDER JAMES [Alexander Coats Esq, 5 Bina Gdns, London SW5 0LD]; *b* 6 July 1951; *educ* Eton

1 *Sarah Mary [Mrs Archibald Lloyd, 122 Pelham Rd, London SW19 1PA]; *b* 18 Aug 1948; *m* 1st 3 July 1972 (*divorce* 1976) Viscount Ednam, only son of 4th Earl of Dudley (*qv*); *m* 2nd 29 May 1976 *Archibald David Sampson Lloyd, son of David Lloyd, of Pipewell Hall, Kettering, Notthants, and has issue:

(1) *Katherine Mary; *b* 11 Jan 1978

(2) *Amy Constance; *b* 6 Jan 1981

Lineage: DAVID COATES/COITTIS, of Barnhill, Blantyre; *b c* 1545; *m* Katherine Clerk (*d* Nov 1617) and *d* on or after 12 Oct 1607, having had, with two yr s:

JOHN COITTIS, of Barnhill; bought lands in the Barony of Blantyre 1623; *m* Isabel Pollock and had, with a dau:

JOHN COATES; received a charter of the lands of Barnhill, Blantyre, 22 Feb 1673 and of Birdsfield, Belfield and Syd, Blantyre, 30 Jan 1692; *m* Isobell Mason (*d* 1664) and *d* by 3 March 1696, having had:

JOHN COATES, of Barnhill; *m* Margaret Miller and *d* by 1696, having had, with other issue:

1 John, of Barnhill; *m* 4 Sept 1674 Christian, dau of John Murray, of Flemington, and had issue

2 JAMES

3 William, of Old Place, Blantyre; *m c* 1 Feb 1677 Katherine, dau of John Clark, of Auchinraith, and had issue

4 Thomas, of Barnhill, living 1692; *m* Jane Zuil, and had issue

The 2nd son,

JAMES COATES, of Easter Kitochsyde, E Kilbride, Lanarks; had sasine of the lands of Dykehead 9 Feb 1699; *m* Jane, dau of James McGie, of Braehead, and had, with two yr s:

JAMES COATS, of Dykehead, portioner of Easter Kitochsyde, had sasine of Dykehead 12 June 1711; *m* 20 Dec 1706 Jean, second dau of Patrick Graham, of Lymekilns, East Kilbride, and had an est son:

JAMES COATS, of Dykehead; *bapt* 7 Dec 1707; *m* 13 Feb 1736 Agnes, dau of George Tod, of Haghill, Glasgow, and had four s and a dau; the 3rd s:

GEORGE COATS, of Paisley; *b* 14 March 1743; *m* Katherine Haywood and had:

JAMES COATS, of Paisley; *b* 1 Oct 1774; *m* 22 Nov 1802 Catherine (*d* 11 Feb 1857), dau of Peter Mitchell, and *d* 19 Aug 1857, having had, with other issue:

1 James, fndr with his bro Sir Peter of J and P Coats Ltd; *b* 20 Aug 1803; *dsp*

2 George; *b* 4 Dec 1805; had two s (*dsp*)

3 PETER (Sir)

4 Thomas, of Ferguslie (*see* 1970 edn GLENTANAR, B)

5 William; *b* 9 Aug 1812; had a dau (Marianne)

6 Andrew, of Pitcullen Ho, Perth, JP; *b* 22 June 1814; *m* 1 June 1854 Agnes Hamilton (*d* 1906), dau of James Stirling of Dalquhurn and Cordale, and *d* 10 Feb 1900, leaving issue

The 3rd son,

Sir PETER COATS, of Auchendrane, Ayrshire, and Campagne du Sahel, Mustapha Superieur, Algeria, DL, JP; Commr of Supply Ayrshire, JP Renfrewshire, FRSE; *b* 18 July 1808; *educ* Paisley GS and Glasgow U; co-fndr J and P Coats, ktd 1869; *m* 5 Nov 1832 Gloranna (*d* 21 April 1877), dau of Daniel McKenzie, of Sandbanke, Holy Loch, Argyllshire, Lt 74th Regt, and *d* 9 March 1890, having had, with other issue:

1 JAMES (Sir), **1st Bt**

2 Archibald, of Battleby, Perthshire, and Woodside, Renfrewshire; *b* 23 March 1840; *m* April 1864 Elizabeth, dau of William Hodge, of Paisley, and *d* 11 May 1912, leaving issue

3 George, of Staneley, Renfrewshire; *b* 25 June 1846; *m* 18 Aug 1868 Mary Thompson, dau of John McAlister Symington, of Oakshaw Ho, Paisley, and *d* 9 Oct 1901, leaving issue:

(1) Ernest Symington, JP; *b* 5 Nov 1873; *educ* Marlborough and Geneva; *m* 20 April 1898 Nora (*d* 30 Nov 1948), dau of Dr W Pountney, of Bristol, and *d* 4 Aug 1938, leaving issue:

1a Ian Pountney, DL (Renfrewshire 1945); *b* 12 Jan 1901; Lt RN (ret), Hon Col 2nd Bn Renfrewshire Army Cadet Force 1945–; *m* 11 Jan 1927 Hilda May, MBE (1960), dau of James Gilmour Latta, of Auchenfail, Ayrshire, and has issue:

1b James Alexander Pountney; *b* 31 Dec 1927; Lt-Cdr RN; *m* 26 Aug 1961 *Sarah Margaret [Mrs James Coats, Gorten Lodge, Carse, Tarbert, Argyll], yr dau of Adml Sir Mark Pizey, GBE, CB, DSO, of Abbots Barton, Seavington, nr Ilminster, Somerset, and had issue:

1c *Amanda May *b* 16 March 1964

2c *Fiona Mary; *b* 23 April 1966

3c *Anne; *b* 22 Sept 1969

1b *Fiona Mary Mackenzie [Lady Byatt, Leargnahension, Tarbert, Argyll PA29 6YB]; *b* 25 Feb 1929; *m* 19 June 1954 *Sir Hugh Campbell Byatt, KCVO, CMG, Amb Portugal 1981–86, est son of Sir Horace Archer Byatt, GCMG, JP, of Meesden Hall, nr Buntingford, Herts, and has issue:

1c *Andrew Lorne Campbell; *b* 27 Sept 1955

2c *Duncan Ian Arthur Campbell; *b* 24 Jan 1962

1c *Lucinda Margaret Campbell; *b* 27 Aug 1957

2b *Ann Gillian Douglas; *b* 18 April 1932; *m* 16 Dec 1954 Capt Peter Lorne Mackie-Campbell, JP, The Rifle Bde, only son of Col Geordie Osmond Lorne Mackie-Campbell, MC, of Stonefield, Tarbert, Argyllshire, and has issue

2a *Archibald James, Maj late Scots Gds; *m* 18 April 1952 *Prudence Elizabeth, only dau of Col Eric Francis Dashwood Shettell, OBE

1 Margaret; *b* 1 Feb 1836; *m* 1859 Anthony Hutton, of Liverpool, and left issue

2 Jessie Mackenzie; *b* 6 March 1850; *m* 20 Aug 1874 Sir Alexander Cross, 1st Bt (*d* 13 Feb 1914), of Marchbankwood, Dumfriesshire, and *d* 1901, leaving issue

3 Eliza; *b* 17 Nov 1854; *m* 24 April 1884 James Louis Alexander Hope (*d* 15 Oct 1904), of Whitney Court, Herefs, and *d* 7 May 1906, leaving issue (*see* LINLITHGOW, M)

The est son,

Sir James Coats, 1st Bt (UK), so *cr* 7 Dec 1905, of Auchendrane, Ayrshire, JP (Ayr and Renfrew); *b* 12 April 1834; Capt 2nd Bn Renfrewshire Rifles (Vols), sr dir J and P Coats; *m* 1st 15th Oct 1857 Sarah Ann (*d* 8 June 1887), dau of John Auchincloss, of New York, and had issue:

1 STUART AUCHINCLOSS (Sir), **2nd Bt**

2 Alfred Mainwaring; *b* 12 April 1869; *m* 5 Sept 1895 Elizabeth (*d* 1940), dau of Morris Barnewall, of Flushing, Long Island, USA, and *d* 1942, having had issue:

(1) Archibald, Lt US Army; *b* 20 Aug 1896; *das* 1918

(1) Mabel; *m* B William MacColl, and had issue

(2) Elizabeth Barnewall; *b* 1902; *m* (*divorce* 1938) Kenneth MacColl, of Providence, RI, USA, and had issue

3 James Monro; *b* 6 Jan 1875; *m* 27 April 1899 Anne Baldwin, dau of Edward Thompson Caswell, of Providence, RI, and *dsp* 1 Feb 1946

1 Elizabeth Winthrop; *m* 26 Sept 1888 Thomas Glen Arthur (*d* 2 Feb 1907), of Barshaw, Renfrewshire, and *d* 28 Jan 1923, leaving issue (*see* GLENARTHUR, B)

2 Annie McKenzie; *m* 16 June 1891 George Gordon King (*d* 30 March 1922), of Newport, RI, and had issue

3 Alice Dudley; *m* 25 Aug 1885 Theodore Frelinghuysen, of Newark, NJ, son of Hon Frederick Frelinghuysen, US Sec of State, and *d* 2 March 1889, having had issue

Sir James *m* 2nd 19 Sept 1889 Marie Jeanne Augustine, OBE (1920), DGStJ (*d* 22 Jan 1940), dau of Charles Henri Adam, of Marmoutiers, Alsace, memb of Conseil General de Basse Alsace, and *d* 20 Jan 1913

His est son,

Sir Stuart Auchincloss Coats, 2nd Bt; *b* 20 March 1868; MP Wimbledon 1916–18 and E Surrey 1918–22, Private Chamberlain of Sword and Cape to TH PIUS X, XI and XII and BENEDICT XV, Kt Cdr (with star) Order of Pius; Kt Cdr Order of St Gregory the Great; Cdr Crown of Italy; *m* 8 Sept 1891 Jane Muir (*d* 23 Jan 1958), dau of Thomas Greenlees, of Paisley, and had issue:

1 JAMES STUART (Sir), **3rd Bt**

2 Muir Dudley, MC (1918); *b* 15 Sept 1897; Capt Res of Offrs. late Scots Gds (SR); *m* 25 March 1922 Audrey Evelyn (*m* 2nd 18 Aug 1930 (*divorce* Reno, USA, 1934) Marshall Field, of Chicago; *m* 3rd 25 Nov 1938 (*divorce* 1946) Hon Peter Pleydell-Bouverie, 5th son of 6th Earl of Radnor (*qv*), and *d* 14 Feb 1968), yst dau of William Dodge James, CVO, of West Dean Park, and *d* 7 Aug 1927, having had issue:

(1) Peter; *b* 16, *d* 20 Feb 1923

1 Margaret Mary Josephine; *m* 11 Oct 1928 2nd Viscount Knollys (*qv*) and *d* 1987, having had issue

Sir STUART *d* 15 July 1959; his only surv son,

Sir James Stuart Coats, 3rd Bt, MC (1918); *b* 13 April 1894; *educ* Downside and Magdalen Coll Oxford; Lt-Col Res of Offrs Coldstream Gds, served WW I (wounded, despatches) and WW II; *m* 11 Dec 1917 Lady Amy Gwendoline Gordon-Lennox, er dau of 8th Duke of Richmond and Gordon (*qv*), and *d* 26 Oct 1966, having had:

1 Ian Charles James; *b* 18 Nov 1919; *educ* Eton; Capt Res of Offrs Irish Gds WW II; *m* *Irka Brennan and *dsp* Los Angeles 27 Jan 1959

2 Sir ALISTAIR FRANCIS STUART COATS, **4th and present Bt**

3 +Ivor Paul [Ivor Coats Esq, 110c Victoria Rise, London SW4 0NW]; *b* 25 Jan 1923; *educ* Eton; Lt 12th Lancers WW II (wounded, POW); *m* 21 Jan 1959 *Caroline Gay, dau of Charles Percy Pinckney, MA, MB, BChir, MRCS, FRCP, of 76 Albert Hall Mansions, London SW7, and has issue:

(1) +Dominic Peter; *b* 7 May 1962

(2) +James Charles; *b* 19 Oct 1964

(1) *Emma Lucinda; *b* 25 July 1960

(2) *Sophia Louise; *b* 9 May 1966

4 James Raymond; *b* 31 Aug 1928; *educ* Eton; *d* 15 Sept 1996

COBBOLD

Arms: Sable a chevron or between in chief two bezants and in base a lion passant guardant gold, on a chief dancetty of the last two ducal coronets azure. **Crest:** A lion statant guardant argent crowned with a ducal coronet azure, supporting with the dexter paw an escutcheon vert, thereon three escutcheons also argent, each having a bordure engrailed or. **Supporters:** On either side a yellow labrador dog proper, each resting the interior hind foot on a battering ram fesswise, the head inward also proper, headed and garnished azure. **Motto:** *Rebus angustis fortis* ('Brave in adversity'). **Creation:** B. (UK) 23 Nov 1960.

THE 2ND BARON COBBOLD, of Knebworth, Co Herts (David Antony Fromanteel COBBOLD later LYTTON COBBOLD (deed poll 4 Dec 1960), DL (Herts 1993)) [The Rt Hon The Lord Cobbold DL, Knebworth House, Knebworth, Herts SG3 6PY]; *b* 14 July 1937; *s* f 1987; *educ* Eton and Trin Coll Cambridge (BA 1960); P/Offr RAF 1955–57, Fell Assoc of Corporate Treasurers, BP Finance Int 1979–87, Gen Manager Treasury, TSB England & Wales plc 1987–88, md Gaincorp UK Ltd 1989–, dir: Hill Samuel 1988–89, Close Bros Gp plc 1993–; chm and md Lytton Enterprises Ltd 1971–, Hon Treasurer HHA 1988–97, pres U of Hertfordshire Devpt Ctee 1992– (memb Bd of Govrs 1993–), tstee The Pilgrim Tst 1993150, chm Stevenage Community Tst 1990–; *m* 7 Jan 1961 *Christine (Chryssie) Elizabeth, 3rd dau of Maj Sir Dennis Frederic Bankes Stucley, 5th Bt (*qv*), and has issue:

1 +HENRY FROMANTEEL; *b* 12 May 1962; *educ* Eton and Kent U (BA 1983); *m* 1987 *Martha Frances, dau of James Buford Boone, Jr, of Tuscaloosa, Alabama, USA, and has issue:

(1) +Edward; *b* 23 April 1992

(1) *Morwenna Gray; *b* 1989

2 +Peter Guy Fromanteel; *b* 25 Nov 1964; *educ* Eton and Durham U (BA 1986); *m* 1988 *Ginette Elizabeth, dau of Bernard Keigher, of Holland Park, London W11, and has issue:

(1) +Frederick Alexander; *b* 1992

(1) *Natasha Elizabeth; *b* 1995

3 +Richard Stucley Fromanteel; *b* 31 July 1968; *educ* Eton and Bristol U; Page of Honour to HM THE QUEEN 1980–82; *m* 24 Sept 1994 *Frankie, dau of Jeremy Lancaster, of Broadwell, Glos

1 *Rosina Kim; *b* 14 Dec 1971; proprietor Rosina Cobbold Ltd (furniture mfrs)

Lineage: ROBERT COBBOLD, of Tostock; *d* 1603, leaving:

REYNOLD COBBOLD, of Rattlesden, Suffolk; *b c* 1564; *d* 1666, having had:

THOMAS COBBOLD; *dvp*, leaving:

JOHN COBBOLD, of Rattlesden; had:

THOMAS COBBOLD, of Rattlesden; *b* 1680; *d* 1753, leaving:

THOMAS COBBOLD, of Bury St Edmunds; *b* 1708; *m* Sarah Cobbold, of Trimley, Suffolk, and *d* 1767, leaving, with other issue:

JOHN COBBOLD, of Holywells, Ipswich; *b* Jan 1745/6; *m* 1st 1773 Elizabeth, dau of James Wilkinson, and had seven s and eight daus; *m* 2nd 1791 Elizabeth, dau of Robert Knipe, and had six more sons and another dau; his est s by his 1st w:

JOHN COBBOLD, of Holywells; *b* 1774; *m* 1796 Harriet (*d* 1851), 3rd dau of Rev Temple Chevallier, of Aspall Hall, Suffolk, and *d* Feb 1860, leaving issue:

1 JOHN CHEVALLIER

2 Henry; *b* 1799; *m* Mary Bampton, and *dsp*

3 Walter Temple; *b* 1801; *dsp*

4 Francis (Rev), Rector of Hemby, Suffolk; *b* 1803; *m* Mary Anne Cobbold and had a dau

5 Alfred; *b* 1814; *m* Fanny Worship

6 Arthur Thomas, of Brightlingsea Park, Essex; *b* 1815; *m* 1838 Sarah, dau of Robert and Elizabeth Elliston, and *d* 11 Oct 1898, having had eight sons and two daus

1 Mary Caroline; *m* Alexander Henry Bartlet, and *d* 1876

2 Louisa Emily; *m* David Hanbury

3 Georgiana Kate; *m* 3 Jan 1832 William Charles Fonnereau (*d* 31 July 1855)

4 Agnes; *m* Capt Frederick Chevallier Syer RN

5 Emily; *m* 1st George Dixon; *m* 2nd Henry Cobbold

6 Harriet Ann; *m* 1st Edward Hanbury; *m* 2nd Thomas Rose; *m* 3rd Borlase Adams

7 Charlotte; *m* Rev John Bampton, and *d* 1915

8 Jane Octavia; *m* Rev Thomas Preston

The est son,

JOHN CHEVALLIER COBBOLD, of Holywells, DL, JP, MP Ipswich 1847–68, High Steward Ipswich; *b* 24 Aug 1797; *m* 14 May 1827 Lucy (*d* 1879), 3rd dau of Rev Henry Patterson, Rector Drinkstone and Wortham, Suffolk, and *d* 6 Oct 1882, having had issue:

1 John Patterson, JP, MP Ipswich; *b* 12 July 1831; *m* 20 April 1858 Adela Harriette (*d* 1917), dau of Rev John George Dupuis, V-Provost Eton, and *dvp* 9 Dec 1875, leaving issue

2 Henry Chevallier; *b* 1 Sept 1832; *m* 1st 24 May 1860 Louisa Ann (*d* 15 April 1861), dau of Charles Montagu Pocock, 2nd Light Dragoons, King's German Legion, and had a son; *m* 2nd 1865 Charlotte Key (*d* 26 Oct 1920), and *d* Sept 1902, having by her had another son

3 Thomas Clement, CB, MP Ipswich, Chargé d'Affaires: Baden-Baden 1867, Rio de Janeiro 1870 and Lisbon 1873–75; *b* 22 July 1833; *educ* Charterhouse; *d* 21 Nov 1883

4 Herbert Wilkinson; *b* 8 Aug 1835; *d* in the E Indies 1852

5 Temple Francis; *b* Oct 1836; *d* an infant

6 NATHANIEL FROMANTEEL

7 Ernest St George, of Ufford, Suffolk, JP, formerly Lt RA, Hon Maj 1st Suffolk RV; *b* April 1840; *m* 1864 Helen Emma (*d* 19 Nov 1917), dau of Philp Cazenove, of Clapham, and *d* 23 Feb 1895, leaving issue

8 Felix Thornley, JP Suffolk, MP Stowmarket 1885–86 and Ipswich 1906–09, MA and Fell King's Coll Cambridge, barrister; *b* 8 Sept 1841; *d* 6 Dec 1909

1 Lucy; *m* 14 June 1855 Col Henry Jervis-White-Jervis, RA (*see* 1939 edn), and *d* 22 Feb 1916, leaving issue. He *d* 22 Sept 1881

2 Anna Frances; *m* Very Rev Dean Spooner, of Hadleigh, and *d* 28 Dec 1906

3 Harriet Sophia; *d* an infant

4 Sophia Mariana Edwyna; *d* an infant

5 Constance Sophia; *m* 1876 Richard Green, of The Whittern, Lyonshall, Herefs

The 6th son,

NATHANIEL FROMANTEEL COBBOLD; *b* Jan 1839; *m* 1st 1860 Caroline (*d* 1876), dau of Rev Charles Drage, Rector of Resterfield, Suffolk; *m* 2nd Oct 1881 his cousin Caroline Ellen Alice (*d* 1882), dau of Rev Charles Boutell, heraldic writer, by Mary, dau of Rev John Chevallier, of Aspall Hall, Suffolk, and had issue:

1 CLEMENT JOHN FROMANTEEL

NATHANIEL COBBOLD *m* 3rd 1884 his cousin Caroline (*d* 2 Nov 1922), dau of Thomas Kinder, of St Albans, Herts, by his w Frances, dau of Rev John Chevallier, above mentioned, and *d* Feb 1886, having by her had issue:

2 Guy Fromanteel, MC (1916); *b* 10 April 1885; *educ* Eton and Trin Coll Cambridge (MA); Maj York and Lancaster Regt WW I, Capt HG WW II; *d* unm 14 June 1969

The er son,

CLEMENT JOHN FROMANTEEL COBBOLD, Lt-Col Suffolk Regt WW I (despatches), barrister Inner Temple, Sec Roy Cancer Hosp London SW 1933–34; *b* 27 Aug 1882; *educ* Eton and Trin Coll Cambridge; *m* 1st 1 Oct 1903 Stella Willoughby Savile (*d* 2 Dec 1918), dau of Charles Cameron, and had issue:

1 CAMERON FROMANTEEL, **1st Baron**

Lt-Col COBBOLD *m* 2nd 26 Sept 1919 Mabel Ethel (*d* 20 Sept 1967), dau of Richard Morris, and *d* 24 Jan 1961, having by her had issue:

2 *Peter Fromanteel, MC [Peter Cobbold Esq MC, Elkington Lodge, Welford, nr Rugby, Warwicks]; *b* 24 June 1922; *educ* Dover Coll; Capt KRRC WW II; *m* 26 Jan 1949 *Liselotte Emilie, dau of Albert Meyers, and has issue:

(1) *John Guy Fromanteel; *b* 26 May 1952; *educ* Eton

(1) *Corinna; *b* 16 Dec 1949

(2) *Harriet Emilie; *b* 14 April 1957; *m* 2 June 1990 *William Francis Assheton (*see* CLITHEROE, B) and has issue

(3) *Sara Frances; *b* 9 Oct 1958

1 *Naomi Moira; *b* 9 March 1920; *m* 15 Jan 1943 *John Howard Jacobs, MA Cambridge, FRPS, Fell Socs of Motion Picture and Television Engrs and Photographic Scientists and Engrs, Pncpl Research Physicist Bell and Howell, late RAFVR, son of Maj Cecil Jacobs, of Little Glade, West Hill, Ottery St Mary, Devon, and has issue:

(1) *Peter Howard; *b* 15 June 1944; *educ* U of California (BA)

(2) *Roger Howard; *b* 24 May 1959

(1) *Anne Imogen; *b* 21 Aug 1946

2 Muriel Alice; *d* 27 June 1921

The est son,

CAMERON FROMANTEEL COBBOLD, **1st Baron Cobbold**, of Knebworth, Co Hertford (UK), *so cr* 23 Nov 1960, KG (1970), PC (1959), GCVO, DL (Herts 1972); *b* 14 Sept 1904; *educ* Eton (Fell, Steward of the Courts 1973–87) and King's Coll Cambridge, Hon LLD McGill 1961, Hon DSc Econ London 1963, High Sheriff Co of London 1946, Lt City of London, joined Bank of England 1933, Dir 1938, Dep Govr 1945, Govr 1949–61, Lt London Rifle Bde 1925–29, dir Royal Exchange Assur, BP and Hudson's Bay Co, Ld Chamberlain 1963–71, chm Middx Hosp and Medical Sch Cncl 1963–74, pres Br Heart Fndn 1969–76, Ld-in-Waiting 1971–87, chm Italian Internat Bank to 1974, chm Stevenage Youth Tst and Herts County Playing Fields Assoc; *m* 3 April 1930 *Lady (Margaret) Hermione Millicent Bulwer-Lytton [The Rt Hon Hermione Lady Cobbold, Lake House, Knebworth, Herts], er dau of 2nd Earl of Lytton (*qv*), and *d* 1987, having had issue:

1 DAVID ANTONY FROMANTEEL LYTTON COBBOLD, **2nd and present Baron Cobbold**

2 +Rowland John Fromanteel [The Hon Rowland Cobbold, Hallam House, Ogbourne St George, Wilts SN8 1SG]; *b* 20 June 1944; *educ* Eton and Trin Coll Cambridge (MA 1970); dir: Cathay Pacific Airways Ltd 1987–94, Air London Internat plc 1996–, Ecco Tours Ltd 1995–; *m* 3 June 1969 *(Sophia) Augusta, dau of Benjamin White-Spunner, of Lansdowne, Nenagh, Co Tipperary, and has:

(1) Patrick Alexander Fromanteel; *b* 11 March 1974

(1) Lorna Bridget; *b* 19 April 1971

1 Jane; *b* 10 May 1931; *d* 16 Feb 1937

2 *Susan Victoria [The Hon Mrs Blount, Manor Farm, Barkway, Herts]; *b* 24 May 1933; High Sheriff Herts 1989; *m* 12 Nov 1957 *S/Ldr Christopher Charles Blount, MVO, late RAF, yr son of AVM Charles Hubert Boulby Blount, CB, OBE, MC and has issue:

(1) *James Hubert Rowland; *b* 31 Aug 1958; *educ* Harrow and Ch Ch Oxford

(2) *Oliver Charles; *b* 11 Oct 1959; *educ* St John's Coll Cambridge and RMA Sandhurst; *m* 17 Sept 1994 *Vivien, yr dau of Cdr Peter Barton, RN (ret), of Monks Eleigh, Suffolk

(1) *Catherine Victoria Jane; *b* 15 Dec 1962; *m* 1988 *Richard M Glaister, 5th son of Thomas Glaister, of Crofthead, Kentmere, Kendal, Cumbria, and has issue:

1a *Cosima Susan Ruth; *b* 1990

2a *Davina Millicent Jane; *b* 1991

(2) *Pamela Jane; *b* 24 March 1965; *m* 1991 *Rupert A W Goodman, er son of Nigel Goodman, of Eton Coll, Berks, and has issue:

1a *Felix Christopher Woodward; *b* 1993

Seat: Knebworth House, Knebworth, Herts. An apparently late medieval house was acquired in HENRY VII's reign by Sir Robert Lytton, who refashioned it around a courtyard. Virtually nothing of that date is now left apart from the hall and its immediately ancillary chambers. A little over one hundred years later the hall was remodelled, the most important additions being a screen of oak wood after Inigo Jones which dates from early in the 17th century, and panelling and a pediment in pine wood which date from near its end.

The Lytton male line became extinct early in the 18th century and the house was inherited by William Robinson [?] and from his male-line descendants by Elizabeth Bulwer-Lytton, mother of Edward the novelist (*see* LYTTON, E). Elizabeth had already knocked down most of the old house when her son came to inherit and what she hadn't destroyed she ornamented in the fashionable Gothic style and smothered in rendering, thus hiding the brickwork. Her son went still further, rebuiding Knebworth in the 1840s as the belvedered, crenellated, pinnacled and machicolated pile that, with its proximity to London hence attractiveness as location to film and television directors, is familiar to an unusually wide public today.

Even in Edward's day it was the haunt of celebrities, such as his brother scribbler Dickens or the priapic portraitist Daniel Maclise. A generation later Lutyens, who had married into the family, refurbished parts of the interior, John Dibblee Crace having already contributed some fanciful neo Gothic, particularly in the State Drawing Room. Knebworth is also home to pop concerts. It passed to the COBBOLDs by the marriage of Lady Hermione Lytton with the **1st Baron**.

COBHAM

Arms: Argent a chevron between three escallops sable. **Crest:** A Moor's head in profile, couped at the shoulders proper, wreathed about the temples argent and sable. **Supporters:** On either side a merman proper, in his exterior hand a trident or. **Motto:** *Ung Dieu, ung roy* ('One God, one king'). **Creations:** Bt. (E) 25 July 1618; B. (GB) 23 May 1718 (Cobham), (I) 29 April 1776 (Westcote of Ballymore) and (GB) 13 Aug 1794 (Lyttelton); V. (GB) 23 May 1718.

THE 11TH VISCOUNT COBHAM, Baron Cobham, Baron Westcote of Ballymore, Co Longford, **Lord Lyttelton, Baron of Frankley,** Co Worcester, and a **Baronet** (Sir John William Leonard Lyttelton, Bt) [The Rt Hon The Viscount Cobham, Hagley Hall, nr Stourbridge, W Midlands DY9 9LG; 20 Kylestrome House, Cundy St, London SW1Y 9JT]; *b* 5 June 1943; *s f* 1977; *educ* Eton, Christ's Coll Canterbury NZ and RAC Cirencester; Hagley Hall Farm 1976–; *m* 1st 2 Feb 1974 (*divorce* 1995) Penelope Ann, er dau of Roy Cooper, of Moss Farm, Knutsford, Cheshire; *m* 2nd 1 Aug 1997, as her 2nd husb, *Lisa Romaine, round-the-world yachtswoman, er dau of Dan and Gwen Clayton, of Edgbaston

Cobham, other creations: In January 1312/3 one Henry de Cobham, of a Kentish family and son of a Baron of the Exchequer, was called to Parliament, his writ of summons according to later doctrine making him Lord Cobham. He was Constable of Dover Castle and Rochester and a Warden of the Cinque Ports. This Barony, which had been forfeited by attainder in 1603 and even if restored would have fallen into abeyance forty years later, was both restored to and called out of abeyance in favour of Gervase Disney Alexander in 1916 but fell again into abeyance in 1933 on his death. It fell once more into abeyance, having been called out of abeyance in favour of Gervase's brother Robert, on the latter's death in 1951. (*See* 1970 edn.)

Another barony of Cobham by writ of summons is deemed to have been created for Sir Ralph de Cobham in late 1324. No connection with Henry de Cobham is known of. After his death his son was never called to Parliament.

In late 1326 Stephen de Cobham, of Rundale, also in Kent, is deemed to have been created Lord Cobham by writ of summons to Parliament. He was first cousin of the Henry created Lord Cobham in 1312/3. None of his descendants were called to Parliament either. Yet a third cousin, Reynold de Cobham, of Sterborough, Lingfield, Surrey, was called to Parliament by writ in 1347 and thus deemed by later doctrine to have been created Lord Cobham too. He is the most distnguished of the medieval Lords Cobham, of whatever creation, being a Knight of the Garter, an Admiral, commissioned to look after the Black Prince at the Battle of Crécy (1346) and Marshal of the Prince's Army at Poitiers ten years later. His son at any rate was summoned to Parliament but after the latter's death no more writs were issued to this branch of the de Cobhams.

A cousin of the Lord Cobham attainted in 1603, one John Brooke, of Heckington, Lincolnshire, was created Baron Cobham by letters patent in January 1644/5. On his death without issue in 1660 this peerage too expired.

Lineage: THOMAS de LUTTELTON; held substantial amount of land in the Vale of Evesham, Worcs, particularly at South Lyttelton *c* 1235; *m* 1st Emma, only dau and heir of Sir Simon de Frankley, and had an only dau (Emma, *m* Augerus de Tatlynton); *m* 2nd Anselm, dau and heir of William Fitzwarren, of Upton, Worcs, Judge Common Pleas 1228 and Sheriff Worcs 1229, by whom he had, with an est s (Edmund, lived at Coulesdon, held land at Naunton, Worcs) and 2nd s, a yst one:

THOMAS de LUTTELTON; MP Worcs 1316–61; had an est son:

THOMAS de LUTTELTON; inherited the manor of Frankley from his de Tatlynton cousins; Esq of the Body to RICHARD II, HENRY IV and HENRY V; *d* 1422, leaving an only dau:

ELIZABETH; *m* Thomas Westcote, of Devon, Escheator Worcs 1450, and had, with three yr sons and four daus:

Sir THOMAS LUTTELTON/LYTTELTON (took mother's name), KB (1475); Serjeant-at-Law 1454, King's Serjeant 1455, Judge Common Pleas 1475–81; author: *Treatise on Tenures*; *m* Joan, widow of Sir Philip Chetwynd, of Ingestre (*see* CHETWYND, V), and dau and coheir of Sir William Burley, of Bromscroft Castle, Salop, and had (with two daus, *d* unm):

1 WILLIAM

2 Richard, ancestor of the Barons Hatherton (*qv*)

3 Thomas, of Spetchley, Worcs, ancestor of 1st and lst Baron Lyttelton of Mounslow, so *cr* 18 Feb 1640/1 (*b* 1589; royalist Ld Chllr Civil War; *dspm* 9 Aug 1645) and Sir William Lyttelton, Speaker H of C *temp* WILLIAM III

Sir THOMAS *d* 23 Aug 1481; his est son,

Sir WILLIAM LYTTELTON, of Frankley; *m* 1st Ellyn, widow of Thomas Fielding and dau and heir of William Walsh, of Wanlip, Leics, and had, with an only dau (Joan, *m* Sir John Aston, of Heywood, Staffs; *m* 2nd Mary, dau of William Whittington, of Pauntley, Glos, and *d* 1507):

JOHN LYTTELTON; *m* Elizabeth, dau and coheir of Sir Gilbert Talbot, of Grafton, Worcs (*see* SHREWSBURY and WATERFORD, E), and *d* 17 May 1532, having had, with six other sons and two daus:

Sir JOHN LYTTELTON; Constable Dudley Castle, Staffs, 1553; memb Cncl of Wales and JP and DL Worcs and Staffs *temp* ELIZABETH I; ktd 1566; *d* 15 Feb 1589/90; his est son:

GILBERT LYTTELTON; MP Worcs 1571–72, High Sheriff Worcs 1583; *m* Elizabeth, dau of Humphrey Coningsby, of Nyend-Solers, Salop, and Hampton Court, Herefs, and *d* 1 June 1599, leaving an est son:

JOHN LYTTELTON, MP Worcs *temp* ELIZABETH I; *m c* 12 Dec 1590 Meriel, dau of Sir Thomas Bromley, Ld Chllr, and after being convicted of high treason 20 Feb 1600/1 for participation in the Earl of Essex's Conspiracy (*see* HEREFORD, V) *d* in prison July 1601 (his attainder was reversed in the following reign), leaving, with two yr sons and five daus (including Jane, *m* 13 Oct 1627 Sheringham Talbot (*see* SHREWSBURY and WATERFORD, E); Bridget, *m* by 1617, as his 1st w, 2nd Baron and Viscount Tracy of Rathcoole; *see* SUDELEY, B):

Sir Thomas Lyttelton, 1st Bt (E), so *cr* 25 July 1618; ktd, Worcs: High Sheriff 1613, MP 1621–2 and 1640, royalist Civil Wars (hence imprisoned Tower of London); *m* Catherine (*d* 24 June 1666), dau and sole heir of Sir Thomas Crompton, of Driffield, Yorks, and *d* 22 Feb 1649/50, leaving, with other issue:

1 **Sir Henry Lyttelton, 2nd Bt**, MP Lichfield 1678–79; imprisoned as a royalist 17 months in Tower of London after CHARLES I's defeat Civil War; *m* 1st Philadephia (*d* 2 Aug 1663), dau and coheir of Thomas Carey, 2nd son of Robert, Earl of Monmouth; *m* 2nd Elizabeth (*m* 2nd Edward Harvey), dau of Francis, Viscount Newport (*see* BRADFORD, E), and *dsp* 24 June 1693

2 **Sir Charles Lyttelton, 3rd Bt**, Brig-Gen, Govr: Jamacia 1663, Harwich 1667 and Sheerness 1680; MP Bewdley 1685–87; *m* 1st Catherine (*dsp* 26 Jan 1662), widow of Martin Lister and dau of Sir William Fairfax, of Steeton, Yorks; *m* 2nd 23 May 1666 Anne (*d* 22 Aug 1718), dau of Thomas Temple, of Frankton, and had issue:

(1) Charles *m* Anne (*d* 25 Dec 1718), dau and heir of Thomas Saunders, of Beechwood, and widow of Sir Edward Sebright, 3rd Bt (*qv*), and *dvp* 16 Aug 1712

(2) THOMAS (Sir), **4th Bt**

(1) Cary; *m* Sir Theophilus Biddulph, 3rd Bt (*qv*)

(2) Mary; *m* as his 3rd w William Plowden (*see* PLOWDEN, B)

(3) Anne; *m* Joseph Amphlett, of Clent, Staffs

Sir CHARLES *d* 2 May 1716; his only surv son,

Sir Thomas Lyttelton, 4th Bt, MP Worcs, a Ld Admlty 1727; *m* 8 May 1708 Christian, sis of Sir Richard Temple, 4th Bt (*cr* 23 May 1718 **Viscount Cobham**, as also BARON COBHAM of Cobham, Kent (both GB), with special remainder, failing heirs male of his body and of his 2nd sister Hester, to those of his 3rd sister Christian, Lady Lyttelton (*see* above), a contingency which took place on the death *spm* 26 March 1889 of Richard, 3rd Duke of Buckingham and Chandos and 7th Viscount and Baron Cobham, Hester's last heir male (*see* TEMPLE OF STOWE, E), and *d* 14 Sept 1751, having had, with other issue:

1 **Sir George Lyttelton, 5th Bt**, and 1st BARON LYTTELTON OF FRANKLEY, Co Worcester (GB), so *cr* 18 Nov 1756, PC (1754); *b* 17 Jan 1708/9; *educ* Eton and Ch Ch Oxford; MP (Whig) Okehampton 1735–56, Pncpl Sec to PRINCE OF WALES 1737–44; a Ld of the Treasury 1744–54; Cofferer to the Household 1754–55, Chllr Exchequer 1755–56; *m* 1st June 1742 Lucy (*d* 19 Jan 1747), dau of Hugh Fortescue, of Filleigh, Devon, and sis of 2nd Baron Fortescue of Castle Hill; *m* 2nd 10 Aug 1749 Elizabeth, dau of Sir Robert Rich, 4th Bt (*see* 1970 edn), and *d* 22 Aug 1773, having by his 1st w had issue:

(1) **Sir Thomas Lyttelton, 6th Bt**, and 2nd and last BARON LYTTELTON OF FRANKLEY, PC (1775); *b* 30 Jan 1743/4; *educ* Eton and Ch Ch Oxford; MP (Whig) Bewdley 1768–69 (unseated), Ch Justice in Eyre 1775; *m* 22 June 1772 Apphia (*d* 11 April 1840), 2nd dau of Broome Witts, of Chilling Norton, and widow of Joseph Peach, Govr of Calcutta, and *dsp* 27 Nov 1779, when the peerage expired

(1) Lucy; *b* 13 March 1742/3; *m* 10 May 1767 8th Viscount Valentia (*qv*) and *d* 20 May 1783, leaving issue

2 Richard (Sir), KB; *m* 14 Dec 1745 Rachel, est dau of 2nd Duke of Bedford (*qv*) and widow of 1st Duke of Bridgwater (*see* GREY EGERTON, Bt), but *dsp* 1 Oct 1770

3 **Sir William Henry Lyttelton, 7th Bt**, and **1st Lord Lyttelton, Baron of Frankley**, Co Worcester (GB), so *cr* 13 Aug 1794, as also peviously 29 April 1776 BARON WESTCOTE OF BALLYMORE, Co Longford (I); *b* 24 Dec 1724; *educ* Eton and St Mary Hall Oxford; barrister Middle Temple 1748, MP (Whig) Bewdley 1748–55 and (Tory 1774–83, Pittite thereafter) 1774–90, Govr South Carolina 1755–60 and Jamaica 1760–66, Envoy Extrdy and Min Plen Lisbon 1766–71, a Ld Treasury 1777–82; *m* 1st 2 June 1761 Mary (*d* 28 May 1765), est dau and coheir of James Macartney, of Longford, Co Longford, nephew and coheir of Ambrose Aungier, Earl of Longford (*see* LONGFORD, E, preliminary remarks), and had issue:

(1) GEORGE FULKE LYTTELTON, **2nd Lord Lyttelton, Baron of Frankley**; *b* 27 Oct 1763; MP (Tory) Bewdley 1790–96 and Granard 1797–1800; *d* unm and insane 12 Nov 1828

(2) Charles Adam, RN Offr; *ka* 1781

(1) Hester; *m* 1783 Sir Richard Colt Hoare, 2nd Bt (*see* HOARE, Bt, of Barn Elms), and *d* 1785

3 (cont.) The **7th Bt/1st Lord** *m* 2nd 19 Feb 1774 Caroline (*d* 19 Sept 1809), dau of John Bristow, of Quiddenham, in Norfolk, and *d* 14 Sept 1808, having by her had issue:

(3) WILLIAM HENRY, **3rd Baron**

(2) Caroline Anne; *m* 4 May 1808 Rt Hon Reginald Pole-Carew, of Anthony Ho, Cornwall, and had issue (*see* CAREW-POLE, Bt)

The 2nd LORD's half-bro,

WILLIAM HENRY LYTTELTON, **3rd Lord Lyttelton, Baron of Frankley**; *b* 3 April 1782; *educ* Rugby and Ch Ch Oxford; MP (Whig) Worcs 1806–20, Ld Lt Worcs 1833–37; *m* 4 March 1813 Lady Sarah Spencer (*d* 13 April 1870), est dau of 2nd Earl Spencer (*qv*), and had issue:

1 GEORGE WILLIAM, **4th Baron**

2 Spencer; *b* 19 June 1818; Marshal Ceremonies Roy Household; *m* 10 Aug 1848 Henrietta (*d* 20 May 1917), est dau and coheir of Frederick Hamilton Cornewall, of Delbury, Salop, and *d* 4 Feb 1889, having had:

(1) William Henry Cornewall; *b* 9 June 1849; *d* 22 May 1882

3 William Henry (Rev), MA, Canon Gloucester, Rector Hagley; *b* 3 April 1820; *m* 1st 28 Sept 1854 Emily (*d* 12 Sept 1877), yst dau of Rev Henry Pepys, DD, Bp Worcester; *m* 2nd 5 Feb 1880 Constance Ellen (*d* 24 Dec 1920), dau of Very Rev Hon Grantham Yorke, Dean Worcester (*see* HARDWICKE, E), and *dsp* 24 July 1884

1 Caroline Lavinia; *b* 1 Feb 1816; *d* unm 8 April 1902

2 Lavinia; *m* 14 Oct 1843 Rev Henry Glynne (*d* 29 July 1872), MA, Rector Hawarden, bro of Sir Stephen Glynne, 9th Bt (*qv*), and *d* 3 Oct 1850, leaving issue

The 3rd BARON *d* 30 April 1837; his son,

GEORGE WILLIAM LYTTELTON, **4th Lord Lyttelton, Baron of Frankley**, PC (1869), KCMG (1869); *b* 31 March 1817; *educ* Eton and Trin Coll Cambridge; Ld Lt and custos rotulorum Worcs 1839–76, High Steward Bewdley, Parly U-Sec Colonies Feb-July 1846, Ch Commr of Endowed Schools 1869–74 , DCL, LLD, FRS; *m* 1st 25 July 1839 Mary (*d* 17 Aug 1857), sis of Mrs W E Gladstone (*see* GLADSTONE, Bt) and dau of Sir Stephen Glynne, 8th Bt, by Mary, dau of 1st Baron Braybrooke (*qv*), and had issue:

1 CHARLES GEORGE LYTTELTON, **5th Lord Lyttelton, Baron of Frankley** and **8th Viscount Cobham**

2 Albert Victor (Rev); *b* 29 June 1844; *educ* Trin Coll Cambridge (MA); public preacher London diocese, priest-in-charge St John, Hawarden, Mold, Flints 1903–18; *d* unm 4 April 1928

3 Neville Gerald (Rt Hon Sir), PC (1908), GCB (1907), GCVO (1911), of Bell Hall, Belbroughton, Worcs; *b* 28 Oct 1845; Gen, Col Cmdt Rifle Bde, AAG War Office 1894–97, Assist Mil Sec 1897–99, Maj-Gen Inf Bde Aldershot 1899 and S Africa 1899–1900, Lt-Gen S Africa 1900–03, cmded forces S Africa 1903–04, CGS and first mil memb Army Cncl 1904–08, C-in-C Ireland 1908–12, Govr Roy Hosp Chelsea 1912–31, a Commr Duke of York's Roy Mil Sch 1919–31, served Canada 1866, Jowaki Expdn 1877, Egypt 1882, Nile Expdn 1898 and S Africa 1899–1902; *m* 1 Oct 1883 Katherine Sarah (*d* 27 March 1943), dau of Rt Hon James Archibald Stuart Wortley, MP (*see* WHARNCLIFFE, E), and *d* 6 July 1931, leaving issue:

(1) Lucy Blanche *b* 19 July 1884; *m* 2 June 1908 Rt Hon Charles Frederick Gurney Masterman, PC (*d* 17 Nov 1927), late MP, son of Thomas William Masterman, of Rotherfield Hall, Sussex; *d* 22 April 1977, leaving issue

(2) Hilda Margaret, OBE (1944), V-Pres of World's YWCA; *b* 13 Jan 1886; *m* 23 Feb 1909 Lt-Col Arthur Morton Grenfell, DSO (*d* 24 Nov 1958), 6th son of Pascoe du Pré Grenfell, and *d* 10 June 1972, leaving issue (*see* GRENFELL, B)

(3) Mary Hermione, CBE (1950), ARRC, JP, and CA Co Oxford (chm Educn Ctee); *b* 15 Oct 1894; served QAIMNS WW I (despatches), memb Roy Commn on distribution of Industrial Population 1937; *m* 1 March 1919 William Lionel Hichens (*d* as a result of enemy action 14 Oct 1940), son of John Hichens, of St Ives, Cornwall, and had issue

4 George William Spencer, CB, FRGS, JP (Worcs), Priv Sec to PM 1873–74, 1882–85 and 1892–94; *b* 12 June 1847; *educ* Trin Coll Cambridge (MA); *d* unm 5 Dec 1913

5 Arthur Temple (Rt Rev), DD; *b* 7 Jan 1852; *educ* Trin Coll Cambridge (MA); Bishop of Southampton, Provost of St Nicholas College, Lancing, Archdeacon Winchester; *m* 3 Aug 1880 Kathleen Mary (*d* 12 Jan 1907), dau of George Clive, of Perrystone, Herefs, and *d* 19 Feb 1903, leaving issue:

(1) Archer Geoffrey, DSO (1919); *b* 7 May 1884; *educ* Haileybury and Trin Coll Cambridge (BA 1906); Lt Col The Welch Regt, Lt-Col RA (TA), served WW I (despatches, brevet) and WW II (cmdg Cardiff Garrison); *m* 1st 2 April 1921 Mwyndeg Dorothea Winchester, MBE (1945) (*d* 17 Nov 1951), dau of Winchester Clowes, of Hitchin, Herts, and had issue:

1a *Judith Hazel [Mrs Henry Johnson, 13 Sloane Ave, London SW3]; *b* 8 Aug 1925; *m* 23 June 1950 *Henry James Johnson, OBE, TD, only son of Paul Johnson, of 8 Cordova Court, Sandgate Rd, Folkestone, Kent, and has:

1b *Rupert Charles Gavin; *b* 16 Oct 1954; *educ* Eton

1b *Charlotte Mary; *b* 19 Jan 1959

(1) (cont.) Archer Lyttelton *m* 2nd 5 Aug 1953 *Cynthia Violet, dau of Edgar Anderson, of Greenth, Bramley, Surrey, and *d* 11 Dec 1959

(2) Stephen Clive, OBE (1919), DSC (1917), Sheriff Calcutta 1937–38, Cdr RN, Croix de Guerre; *b* 17 June 1887; *educ* Haileybury; *m* 1st 11 March 1919 (*divorce* 1933) Maureen Nina, only child of Harold Anthony Smith, of 6 Dean's Yard, Westminster, and had issue:

1a *Barbara Meriel [Mrs Charles Fawcus, High Drive House, Woldingham, Surrey]; *b* 13 Nov 1921; *m* 1 Nov 1947 Charles Russell Fawcus (*d* 1985), yr son of Russell Evans Fawcus, of Hindcap Farm, Forest Row, Sussex, and has issue:

1b *Mark Russell [Mark Fawcus Esq, 22 Hill View Rd, Hildenborough, Kent]; *b* 9 March 1951; *educ* Clifton; *m* 1975 *Cynthia, dau of Ronald Stephen Blair, and has issue:

1c *Philip Russell; *b* 1981

2c *James Russell; *b* 1989

1b *Meriel Clare [Mrs Benjamin Carver, The Old Vicarage, Uppington, Telford, Shropshire]; *b* 12 May 1949; *m* 1974 *Benjamin J Carver, and has issue:

1c *Annabel Jane; *b* 1976

2c *Victoria Meriel; *b* 1978

(2) (cont.) Stephen Lyttelton *m* 2nd 11 Feb 1938 Mary Cicely (*d* 12 March 1945), only dau of Brig-Gen Sir Frederick Gascoigne, KCVO, CMG, DSO, of Ashtead Lodge, Surrey, and by her had issue:

1a +Edward Gascoigne [Edward Lyttelton Esq, 306 Delaware Ave, Toronto, Ontario, Canada M6H 2T6]]; *b* 7 May 1944; *educ* Eton, King's Coll Cambridge and Ripon Hall Theological Coll

2a *Mary Kathleen [Mrs Malcolm Fraser, Reelig House, Kirkhill, Inverness-shire]; *b* 27 Dec 1939; *educ* St Mary's Wantage and St Andrews U (BA); *m* 25 July 1970 *Malcolm Robert Fraser, er son of Maj Charles Ian Fraser of Reelig, CBE, TD, DL, JP

(2) (cont.) Stephen Lyttelton *m* 3rd 16 Oct 1947 *Phoebe Hermione [Mrs Stephen Lyttelton, Reeling House, Kirkhill, Inverness-shire], est dau of Archibald Knightley Graham, of 9 Sloane Terrace Mansions, London SW1, and *d* 19 Feb 1959, having by her had issue:

3a *Cicely Phoebe Lavinia [Mrs Peter Northrop, Moor of Clunes, Kirkhill, Inverness]; *b* 11 Oct 1950; *m* 1979 *Peter John Northrop, son of D F Northrop, of Teynham, Kent

(1) Margaret Lucy; *b* 15 July 1882; *m* 30 July 1914 Lt-Col Lancelot Edward Becher, DSO, late RE (*d* 28 Feb 1960), 2nd son of John Henry Becher, of Southwell, and had issue

6 Robert Henry; *b* 18 Jan 1854; *educ* Trin Coll Cambridge (MA); *m* 1st 14 July 1884 Edith (*d* 14 Feb 1926), dau of Sir Charles Santley; *m* 2nd 19 July 1926 Olive Agneta (*d* 25 Nov 1941), dau of Rev James Langton Clarke, DD, of 25 Clarendon Sq, Leamington, and *dsp* 7 Nov 1939

7 Edward (Rev), DD; *b* 23 July 1855; *educ* Trin Coll Cambridge (MA); Headmaster: Haileybury 1890–1905 and Eton 1905–16, Hon Canon St Albans 1895–1905, Rector Sidestrand Norfolk 1918–20, Dean of Whitelands Coll London 1920–29, Hon Canon Norwich 1931, Order Leopold Belgium; *m* 21 Dec 1888 Caroline Amy (*d* 6 July 1919), yr dau of Very Rev John West, DD, Dean St Patrick's, and *d* 26 Jan 1942, leaving issue:

(1) Norah Joan, Assist Co Dir Red Cross Norfolk 1942–50; *b* 15 June 1890; *d* unm 4 Oct 1965

(2) Delia, Dip Theo (Lambeth) 1927; *b* 19 Nov 1892; *d* unm 25 March 1964

8 Alfred (Rt Hon), PC, QC (1899); *b* 7 Feb 1857; MA Cambridge, Hon MA Oxford; High Steward Cambridge U, barrister Inner Temple 1881, Recorder Hereford 1893–94 and Oxford 1894–1903, MP Warwick and Leamington 1895–1906 and St George's, Hanover Sq, 1906–13, Chllr Rochester Diocese 1903, Sec State Colonies 1903–05; *m* 1st 21 May 1885 Octavia Laura (*d* 24 April 1886), sis of 1st Baron Glenconner (*qv*), and had issue:

(1) Alfred Christopher; *b* 1886; *d* 1888

8 (cont.) The Rt Hon Alfred Lyttelton *m* 2nd 18 April 1892 Edith Sophy, GBE, JP London (*d* 2 Sept 1948), Dep Dir Women's Br Min Ag 1917–19, Chm: ESU, Nat Theatre Co; Br Substitute Delegate to League of Nations Assembly 1923, 1926, 1927, 1928 and 1931, dau of Archibald Balfour, and *d* 5 July 1913, having by her had issue:

(2) OLIVER LYTTELTON, *cr* VISCOUNT CHANDOS (*qv*)

(3) Anthony George; *b* 3 June 1900; *d* 17 Dec 1901

(1) Mary Frances; *m* 18 Dec 1928 Sir George Lillie Craik, 2nd Bt, MC (*d* 9 July 1929), and *d* 24 Oct 1982

1 Meriel Sarah; *m* 19 July 1860 Rt Hon John Gilbert Talbot, PC, MP (*d* 1 Feb 1910), and *d* 22 April 1925, leaving issue (*see* SHREWSBURY and WATERFORD, E)

2 Lucy Caroline, Hon LLD Leeds, Maid-of-Honour to HM QUEEN VICTORIA; *m* 7 June 1864 Lord Frederick Charles Cavendish, MP (murdered Phoenix Park, Dublin, 6 May 1882), 2nd son of 7th Duke of Devonshire, KG (*qv*), and *d* 22 April 1925

3 Lavinia; *m* 29 June 1870 Rt Rev Edward Stuart Talbot, DD (*d* 30 Jan 1934), Bp Winchester, son of Hon John Chetwynd Talbot, KC, and *d* 9 Oct 1939, leaving issue (*see* SHEWSBURY and WATERFORD, E)

4 Mary Catherine; *b* 21 March 1875

The **4th Lord** *m* 2nd 10 June 1869 Sybella Harriet (*d* 9 Dec 1900), widow of Humphrey Francis St John Mildmay, MP (*see* St JOHN-MILDWAY, Bt), and dau of George Clive, MP, and by her had issue:

5 Sarah Kathleen; *b* 12 May 1870; *m* 26 April 1900 John Cann Bailey (*d* 29 June 1931), MA Oxford, barrister, author, 3rd son of Edward Cann Bailey, Clerk of the Peace for Norwich, and *d* 1 Oct 1942, leaving issue

6 Sybil; *b* 17 Feb 1873; *m* 16 July 1895 Sir Lionel Henry Cust, KCVO (*d* 12 Oct 1929), and *d* 2 Oct 1934, leaving issue (*see* BROWNLOW, B)

7 Hester Margaret, CBE (1949); *b* 26 Dec 1874; *m* 5 April 1904 Rev Cyril Argentine Alington, DD, DCL (*d* 16 May 1955), Dean of Durham 1933–51, Chaplain to HM 1921–33, Headmaster Eton 1908–33, 2nd son of Rev Henry Giles Alington, of Candlesby, Lincs, and *d* 26 March 1958, leaving issue (*see* HOME, E)

The 4th BARON *d* by his own hand (jumping down the stairs) 19 April 1876; his son,

CHARLES GEORGE LYTTELTON, **5th Lord Lyttelton, Baron of Frankley** and **8th Viscount Cobham** (as which, with Barony of Cobham, he *s* his kinsman the 3rd Duke of Buckingham and Chandos (*see* TEMPLE OF STOWE, E) 1889), JP, DL; *b* I*27 *Oct 1842*; *educ* Eton (Fell) and Trin Coll Cambridge (MA); MP (Lib) E Worcs 1868–74, High Steward Bewdley, Land Commr England and Wales 1881–89, Commr under Railway and Canal Traffic Act 1891–1905, CC Worcs; Hon Col 7th Bn Worcs Regt, and Worcs Yeo, Tstee Nat Portrait Gallery; *m* 19 Oct 1878 Hon Mary Susan Caroline Cavendish (*d* 28 Jan 1937), 2nd dau of 2nd Baron Chesham (*qv*), and had:

1 JOHN CAVENDISH, **9th Viscount**

2 George William; *b* 6 Jan 1883; *educ* Eton and Trin Coll Cambridge (BA 1905, MA 1930); Assist Master at Eton; *m* 3 April 1919 Pamela Marie (*d* 17 Oct 1975 aged 86), est dau of Charles Robert Whorwood Adeane, CB, of Babraham, Cambs, and *d* 1 May 1962, leaving issue:

(1) +Humphrey Richard Adeane [Humphrey Lyttelton Esq, Alyn Close, Barnet Rd, Arkley, Herts]; *b* 23 May 1921; *educ* Eton and Camberwell Sch of Art; jazz musician, composer, jnlst, WW II in Gren Gds, leader Humphrey Lyttelton's Band 1953–, author: *Take It From The Top* (1975), Pres Soc for Italic Handwriting 1990–; Hon Prof Music Keele U 1993–, Hon DLitt: Warwick 1987, Loughborough 1988, Hon DMus: Durham 1989, Keele 1992; *m* 1st 19 Aug 1948 (*divorce* 1952) Patricia Mary Braithwaite, only dau of J Wellesley Gaskell, and has issue:

1a *Henrietta Maria; *b* 23 Oct 1949

(1) (cont.) Humphrey Lyttelton *m* 2nd 1 Nov 1952 *Elizabeth Hill, 2nd dau of Albert E Richardson, of 5 Exbury Dve, Bournemouth, and by her has issue:

1a +(Anthony) Stephen; *b* 12 Oct 1955; *m* 1989 *Emma, dau of J de Vere Hunt, of Kensington Sq, London W8, and has issue:

1b +Charles; *b* 1991

2b +Oliver Stephen; *b* 1993

1b *Lucy Elizabeth Joanie; *b* 1989

2a +David George; *b* 16 July 1958

2a *Georgina Pamela; *b* 20 March 1963

(1) *Diana Maud, CVO (1957, MVO 1952), Assist Press Sec to TM GEORGE VI 1947–52 and THE QUEEN 1952–57; *m* 30 April 1957 7th Viscount Hood (*qv*), and has issue

(2) *Helena Frances [Mrs Peter Lawrence, Simeons, Little Milton, Oxford]; *m* 10 Aug 1940 *Peter Stafford Hayden Lawrence, sometime Eton house master, yr son of Aubrey Trevor Lawrence, MBE, KC (*see* LAWRENCE, Bt, of Ealing Park), and has issue

(3) *Margaret Rose [Mrs Robert Bourne, 25 Nine Mile Ride, Finchampstead, Wokingham, Berks]; *m* 4 Aug 1949 *Robert Morice Anthony Bourne, Assist Master Eton 1947–84, er son of Capt Rt Hon Robert Croft Bourne, PC, MP, of Fyfield Manor, Abingdon, Berks, and has issue:

1a *Robert Humphrey; *b* 28 May 1954; *educ* Eton

2a *George Julian; *b* 23 April 1960

1a *Harriet Madeline; *b* 6 June 1950

2a *Charlotte Elizabeth; *b* 6 April 1952

3a *Lucy Jane; *b* 20 March 1956

4a *Emily Hester; *b* 11 Nov 1963

(4) *Mary Pamela [Mrs Arthur Cox, Long Mead, Brixton Deverill, Warminster, Wilts]; *b* 29 Nov 1929; *m* 3 Oct 1953 *Lt-Col Arthur George Ernest Stewart Cox, DFC, RA, yst son of Lt-Col Arthur Stewart Cox, of Balcote Manor, nr Oxford, and has issue:

1a *Rupert Lyttelton; *b* 4 Sept 1956; *m* 1984 *Mary Catherine, yst dau of J M Mitchell, of Tullymurdoch, Alyth, Perthshire, and has issue:

1b *Georgina Helen; *b* 1987

2b *Phoebe; *b* 1991

2a *Jonathan May *b* 8 Oct 1957

3a *Charles Arthur; *b* 10 Oct 1960

1a *Belinda Jane; *b* 18 Sept 1954

3 Charles Frederick (Rev), MC (1919); *b* 26 Jan 1887; *educ* Trin Coll Cambridge (MA); Rector Cranleigh, Surrey, CF 4th Cl 1917–19; *m* 11 May 1920 Sibell Eleanor Maud (*m* 3rd 27 Sept 1937 Roger Fulford, son of Canon F J Fulford), widow of Hon Edward Kay-Shuttleworth (*see* SHUTTLEWORTH, B), and dau of Charles Robert Whorwood Adeane, CB, of Babraham, Cambs, and *d* 3 Oct 1931, having had issue:

(1) John Anthony, Lt Gren Gds WW II; *b* 21 July 1921; *das* of wounds at Anzio 24 Feb 1944

(2) Martin William; *b* 11 March and *d* 16 March 1923

4 Richard Glynne; *b* 16 Oct 1893; *educ* Eton and Trin Coll Cambridge; Hon Col 73rd AA Bde RA (TA) WW I (wounded, Croix de Guerre), with GKN 1919–64; *m* 23 July 1931 Judith (*d* 1993), est dau of Lt-Col Percy Archer Clive, MP, late Gren Gds, of Whitfield, Herefs, and *d* 3 Oct 1977, leaving issue:

(1) Spencer Clive; *b* 26 March 1939; *educ* Highgate Sch; with GKN; *d* 27 Aug 1996

(2) +Thomas Glynne [Thomas Lyttelton Esq, 7 The Grove, Highgate Village, London N6 6JU]; *b* 29 April 1940; *educ* Eton and Trin Coll Cambridge; Assist Master Eton 1968–94

1 Maud Mary; *b* 22 July 1880; *m* 25 Feb 1908 4th Baron Leconfield (*see* EGREMONT, LECONFIELD and, B), and *dsp* 22 July 1953

2 Frances Henrietta; *b* 11 June 1885; *m* 12 July 1911 Hon (Christian) Henry Charles Guest, MP (*d* 9 Oct 1957), 2nd son of 1st Baron Wimborne, and *d* 20 Jan 1918, leaving issue (*see* WIMBORNE, V)

3 Rachel Beatrice; *b* 21 Jan 1892; *m* 28 Aug 1919 Capt Sir Walter Buchanan Riddell, 12th Bt (*qv*), and *d* 26 Aug 1965, leaving issue

The 8th VISCOUNT *d* 9 June 1922; his est son

JOHN CAVENDISH LYTTELTON, **9th Viscount Cobham**, KCB (1942, CB 1937), TD; *b* 23 Oct 1881; Ld Lt City and Co of Worcester, JP and CA Worcs, High Steward Bewdley, Lt-Col and Brevet Col RA (TA), Lt Rifle Bde, DAA and QMG 1916, ADC and Assist Priv Sec to HC S Africa 1905, MP (Lib U) Droitwich 1910–16, Pres MCC 1935 and Treasurer 1938–49, chm Cncl T&AFA 1942–49, served Boer War 1901–02 (medal with three clasps) and WW I 1915–17 (despatches), Order Sacred Treasure Japan 4th Cl, KJStJ, Parly U-Sec War 1939–40, Hon Col 53rd AT Regt RA 1939; *m* 30 June 1908 Violet Yolande (*d* 28 Feb 1966), yst dau of Charles Leonard, of Kensington Palace Gdns, W8, and Gloria, Cape Colony, and had issue:

1 CHARLES JOHN, **10th Viscount**

1 Meriel Catharine; *b* 1 May 1911; *d* unm 11 Nov 1930

2 Viola Maud, F/O WAAF WW II (despatches); *b* 10 June 1912; *m* 3 Dec 1946 5th Duke of Westminster, TD (*qv*), and had issue

3 *Audrey Lavinia [The Hon Mrs Lindsay, Poplar Cottage, Fore St Hill, Budleigh Salterton, Devon]; *b* 3 Aug 1918; *m* 21 June 1950, as his 3rd w, David Edzell Thomas Lindsay (*d* 14 July 1968), yst son of Col Henry Edzell Morgan Lindsay, CB, DL, JP, of Ystrad Mynach, Glam (*see* CRAWFORD and BALCARRES, E), and has issue

4 *Lavinia Mary Yolande [The Hon Mrs Dennys, Fore St, Budleigh Salterton, Devon]; *b* 21 Aug 1921; served WW II in ATS; *m* 1st 15 Feb 1945 Capt Cecil Francis Burney (Nick) Rolt, 23rd Hus (*ka* 6 April 1945), yst son of Very Rev Cecil Henry Rolt, Dean of Cape Town; *m* 2nd 12 Dec 1949 Maj John Edward Dennys, MC, ARIBA (*d* Aug 1973), only son of Maj-Gen Lance Ernest Dennys, MC, IA, and has issue:

(1) Nicholas Charles Jonathan, QC (1991) [Nicholas Dennys Esq QC, The Old Rectory, Arborfield, Berks RG2 9HZ]; *b* 14 July 1951; *educ* Eton and BNC Oxford (BA); barrister Middle Temple 1975; *m* 1977 *Frances Winifred, dau of Rev Canon Gervase William Markham, of Morland Ho, Penrith, and has issue:

1a *Harriet; *b* 1979

2a *Sophie; *b* 1981

3a *Romilly Mary; *b* 1984

4a *Katharine; *b* 1986

The 9th VISCOUNT *d* 31 July 1949; his only son,

CHARLES JOHN LYTTELTON, **10th Viscount Cobham**, KG (1964), GCMG (1957), GCVO (1972), TD, PC (1967), JP (Worcs 1938) and DL (1952–57 and 1963); *b* 8 Aug 1909; *educ* Eton and Trin Coll Cambridge (BA 1932); Ld Lt 1963–74, Govr-Gen NZ 1957–62, Ld Steward Household 1967–72, Chllr Order of the Garter 1972–77, Lt-Col RA (TA) WW II, Hon Col Warwicks Yeo (March 1972), Dep Hon Col (April 1972), Maj (Hon Col) A Sqdn The Queen's Own Mercian Yeo RAC TAVVR (ret 1975), dir: Lloyds Bank Ltd, AEI and Cerebos Ltd, J Brockhouse & Co 1973–77, played Cricket for Worcs XI 1932–48 (Capt 1936–39), V-Capt MCC in NZ and Australia 1935–36, pres Worcester City C Assoc 1947, Pres: MCC 1954 (Treas 1963–64), Roy Inst for the Blind 1964; Tstee Nat Portrait Gallery 1972–77, KStJ; *m* 30 April 1942 Elizabeth Alison, CStJ (*d* 1986), yr dau of John Reeder Makeig-Jones, CBE, ICS, of Southerton Ho, nr Ottery St Mary, Devon, and *d* 20 March 1977, having had:

1 JOHN WILLIAM LEONARD LYTTELTON, **11th and present Viscount Cobham**

2 +CHRISTOPHER CHARLES [The Hon Christopher Lyttelton, 28 Abbey Gdns, London NW8]; *b* 23 Oct 1947; *educ* Eton; chm NCL Investments (stockbrokers); *m* 1973 *(Teresa) Tessa Mary, dau of Col Alexander George Jeremy Readman, DSO, of The Old Rectory, Fairstead, Essex, by Mary Kay, yr dau of Maj Timothy Herbert William Curtis, cousin of Sir Francis Egerton Curtis, 5th Bt (*see* CURTIS, Bt), and has issue:

(1) +Oliver Christopher; *b* 24 Feb 1976

(1) *Sophie Emma; *b* 1978

3 +Richard Cavendish [The Hon Richard Lyttelton, 5 Queen's Gate Place Mews, London SW7 5BG]; *b* 24 July 1949; *educ* Eton; pres EMI Classics; *m* 24 April 1971 *Romilly, dau of H Michael Barker, and has issue:

(1) +Thomas Charles Henry; *b* 1986

(1) *Mary Viola; *b* 26 Dec 1976

4 +Nicholas Makeig; *b* 3 Jan 1951; *educ* Shiplake Coll; *m* 1980 June Carrington (*d* 1993), and has issue:

(1) +David Charles; *b* 1981

1 *Juliet Meriel [The Hon Mrs Dugdale, Birch Farm, Kinlet, Bewdley, Worcs DL12 3DS]; *b* 28 July 1944; *m* 8 July 1967 *John Michael Dugdale, only son of Maj John Eldon Marshall Dugdale, DL, RWF, of Lower Cefn Perfa, Kerry, Newtown, Powys, and has issue:

(1) *Mark Rupert Marshall; *b* 30 Sept 1968

(1) *Helen Riba; *b* 5 Jan 1970

(2) *Clare Lucinda; *b* 1973

(3) *Rowena Sarah; *b* 1976

2 *(Elizabeth) Catherine; *b* 7 Feb 1946; *m* 14 Jan 1967 *8th Baron Forester (*qv*), and has issue

3 *Lucy [The Hon Mrs Beech Tree Cottage, Preston Candover, Basingstoke, Hants RG25 2EJ]; *b* 10 June 1954; *m* 1980 *Mark Kemp-Gee, yr son of Bernard Kemp-Gee, of 16 Airlie Gdns, London and has issue:

(1) *Henry Alfred; *b* 1981

(2) *Robert Arthur; *b* 1984

(3) *John Andrew; *b* 1987

4 *Sarah (twin) [The Hon MrsArmsworth Hill Cottage, Old Alresford, Hants]; *b* 10 June 1954; *m* 1976 *Nicholas Bedford and has issue:

(1) *Minna Lucy; *b* 1978

(2) *Olivia Alison; *b* 1982

Seat: Hagley Hall, Stourbridge, W Midlands. A house on the site of the present one had been in existence long before and been acquired by the LYTTELTONS in the mid-16th century. Two hundred years later **Sir George**, the **5th Baronet**, who was soon to be created Lord Lyttelton of Frankley, commissioned Sanderson Miller to build him a plain structure, his wife adding that there must be no touch of the Gothick. Miller complied and the result, at any rate compared with the other buildings on the estate (*see* below), would surely have been almost perversely austere — externally. Inside it is a very different matter and although a fire on Christmas Eve 1925 did considerable damage the flames did at least spare the drawing-room with its Soho tapestries of 1720, by common consent the gem of the entire place. Miller was sufficiently disobedient to his patroness to throw up a charming little Gothick Castle in the grounds, pillaging stones from Halesowen Abbey to do so. What with a Rotunda and James 'Athenian' Stuart's Greek Temple of Theseus (the first Greek revival building in all Britain) the landscape surrounding the house must have looked quite exceptionally eclectic.

COCHRANE OF CULTS

Arms: Quarterly, 1st, arg. a chevron gu. between three boar's heads erased az., armed and langued of the second, within a bordure contre-erm. (for COCHRANE); 2nd, gu. a fess erm., in chief a stag's antler fessways or (for CRAWFORD of Kilbirnie); 3rd, gu. a fess chequy arg. and az., in chief three mullets of the second (for LINDSAY of The Byres); 4th, arg. on a saltire sa. nine lozenges of the field, in centre chief a mullet gu. (for BLAIR). **Crest:** A horse passant arg. between two stag's attires gu. **Supporters:** Two ermines erm. **Motto:** *Virtute et labore* ('By virtue and labour'). **Creation:** B. (UK) 16 May 1919.

THE 4TH BARON COCHRANE OF CULTS, of Crawford Priory, Co Fife ((Ralph Henry) Vere Cochrane, DL (Fife))[The Rt Hon The Baron Cochrane of Cults DL, Cults, Cupar, Fife KY15 5RD]; *b* 20 Sept 1926; *s* bro 1990; *educ* Eton and King's Coll Cambridge (BA 1951, MA 1967); Lt RE 1945–48, memb Roy Co Archers 1965–96, chm Craigtoun Meadows Ltd, underwriting memb Lloyd's, Gen Commr Income Tax; *m* 18 Dec 1956 *(Janet) Mary Watson, only dau of William Hunter Watson Cheyne (*see* CHEYNE, Bt), and has :

1 +THOMAS HUNTER VERE; *b* 7 Sept 1957; *educ* Eton and Exeter U (LLB); barrister Inner Temple 1980; ACII

2 +Michael Charles Nicholas; *b* 4 March 1959; *educ* Glenalmond and RNC Dartmouth; Cdr RN

Lineage: The 11th EARL OF DUNDONALD (*qv*) had a 3rd son:

THOMAS HORATIO ARTHUR ERNEST COCHRANE, **1st Baron Cochrane of Cults**, of Crawford Priory, Co Fife (UK), so *cr* 16 May 1919, JP and DL (Fifes); *b* 2 April 1857; MP (Lib U) N Ayrshire 1892–1910, PPS to Sec State Colonies 1895–1901 and U-Sec Home Dept 1902–05, Hon Maj 1901, Maj and Hon Lt-Col 4th Bn Argyll and Sutherland Highrs 1900–07, served Boer War 1900–01 (medal, three clasps); Lt-Col cmdg 2nd/7th Black Watch 1914–17 and Hon Lt-Col TFR 1917, Capt Res of Offrs late Scots Gds, Hon LLD St Andrews 1934; *m* 2 Dec 1880 Lady Gertrude Julia Georgina Boyle (*d* 12 Dec 1950), est dau of 5th Earl of Glasgow (*qv*), and had issue:

1 THOMAS GEORGE FREDERICK, **2nd Baron**

2 Archibald Douglas (Hon Sir), GCMG, KCSI, DSO and bar; *b* 8 Jan 1885; served WW I (despatches thrice), MP E Fife 1924–29 and Dunbartonshire 1932–36, Govr Burma 1936–41, Capt RN WW II 1941–45, KStJ; *m* 6 Jan 1926 Hon Julia Dorothy Cornwallis, CBE (1952), CStJ (*d* 15 June 1971), est dau of 1st Baron Cornwallis (*qv*), and *d* 16 April 1958, leaving issue:

(1) +Douglas Fiennes [Douglas Cochrane Esq, 20 Minerva Mews, London SW1W 9JD]; *b* 28 July 1928; *educ* Eton and Trin Coll Cambridge; *m* 1969 (*divorce* 1987) Patricia Ann, dau of Frank Renshaw, of Puddletown, Dorset, and has issue:

1a +Alexander Douglas; *b* 1972

2a +James Archibald; *b* 1976

(1) *Mabel Dorothy [Mrs Douglas Gill, Camino Son Toels 5, San Augustin, 07015 Palma de Mallorca, Spain]; *b* 15 April 1932; *m* 27 May 1958 Col (Geoffrey) Douglas Gill, MBE, King's Regt (*d* 1990), yr son of Geoffrey Murton Gill and adopted:

*Peter Geoffrey Fiennes; *b* 9 Oct 1966

3 Ralph Alexander (Hon Sir), GBE (1950, KBE 1945, CBE 1939), KCB (1948, CB 1943), AFC; *b* 24 Feb 1895; ACM RAF, CAS to RNZAF 1937–39, Air ADC to HM GEORGE VI 1939–40, AOC-in-C Tport Cmd 1945–47 and Flying Training Cmd 1947–50, V-Ch Air Staff 1950–52, served WW I and WW II (despatches twice); *m* 22 Dec 1930 Hilda Frances Holme (*d* 1982), 3rd dau of Francis Holme Wiggin, and *d* 1977, leaving issue:

(1) +John Alexander [John Cochrane Esq, Fairspear House, Leafield, Oxford, OX8 5NY]; *b* 6 Jan 1935; *educ* Eton and Balliol Coll Oxford (BA 1959); *m* 26 Nov 1966 *Margaret, dau of Sir Charles Henry Rose, 3rd Bt (*see* ROSE, Bt, of Hardwick), and has issue:

1a +Thomas Hugh; *b* 31 Aug 1973

1a *Phoebe Clare; *b* 26 Nov 1967

2a *Alexandra; *b* 12 Jan 1969

3a *Katherine Grizel Rose; *b* 1975

(2) +Malcolm Ralph [Malcolm Cochrane Esq, Grove Farmhouse, Shipton-under-Wychwood, Oxon]; *b* 8 Aug 1938; *educ* Eton; *m* 5 Aug 1972 *Mary Anne, 4th dau of Ralph Henry Scrope, JP, of South Thorpe, Barnard Castle, Co Durham, and has issue:

1a +William Ralph; *b* 1974

1a *Alice Anne; *b* 1976

2a *Harriet Mary; *b* 1979

(1) *Ann Grizel [Mrs Robert Stewart, Arndean, Dollar, Clackmannanshire]; *b* 26 June 1932; *m* 21 May 1953 *Robert Christie Stewart, CBE, TD, Argyll and Sutherland Highlanders, Ld Lt Kinross-shire 1966–74 and Clackmannanshire 1974–, only son of Maj Alexander Caldwell Stewart, MC, of Arndean, and has:

1a *Alexander Christie [Alexander Stewart Esq, Clarehaven, Newmarket, Suffolk]; *b* 21 June 1955; *m* 1986 *Katherine Lake, er dau of Denys Barry Herbert Domvile (*see* BELLEW, B), and has issue:

1b *Archie Christie; *b* 1989

1b *Georgina Elizabeth; *b* 1987

2a *John Cochrane; *b* 21 Aug 1957

3a *David Coldwells; *b* 10 Feb 1960; *m* 1989 *Lucy, dau of Maj Michael Paxton

1a *Catriona Ann; *b* 10 March 1954; *m* 1975 *Julian Charles Marsham (*see* ROMNEY, E)

2a *Sara Jane; *b* 6 Oct 1966

4 Roger; *b* 2 June 1898; *d* 1908

1 Louisa Gertrude Montagu; *d* 24 Oct 1916

2 Marjorie Julia; *d* an infant, 29 May 1886

3 Katherine Elizabeth, DBE (1938); *m* 5 Jan 1921 10th Earl of Elgin and Kincardine, KT (*qv*), and had issue

4 Dorothy Agnes; *m* 21 July 1923 Sir Thomas Fowell Buxton, 5th Bt (*qv*), and *d* 17 Sept 1927, leaving issue

The 1st BARON *d* 17 Jan 1951; his est son,

THOMAS GEORGE FREDERICK COCHRANE, **2nd Baron Cochrane of Cults**, DSO; *b* 19 March 1883; *educ* Eton and Ch Ch Oxford (BA 1908); barrister Inner Temple 1908, Maj Black Watch WW I (wounded thrice, despatches thrice); *m* 1st 14 Oct 1920 Hon Elin Douglas-Pennant (*d* 19 Feb 1934), yst dau of 2nd Baron Penrhyn (*qv*); *m* 2nd 22 Oct 1948 Millicent Agnes Mary (*d* 1981), est dau of Alexander Duckham, PhD, and formerly w of Wilfred Neill Foster, and *d* 8 Dec 1968, having by his 1st w had issue:

1 THOMAS CHARLES ANTHONY COCHRANE, **3rd Baron Cochrane of Cults**; *b* 31 Oct 1922; *educ* privately; fndr and tstee Gardners' Memorial Trust; *d* unm 1990

2 (RALPH HENRY) VERE COCHRANE, **4th and present Baron Cochrane of Cults**

3 (John Douglas) Julian [The Hon Julian Cochrane, Townend House, Hopton, Derbys]; *b* 12 June 1929; *educ* Eton; *m* 27 Nov 1965 *Vaila Rose, yr dau of Cdr Robert Dalby, RN, of Castle Donnington, Leics, and has issue:

(1) +John Colin; *b* 30 June 1969

(1) *Julietta Anne; *b* 26 Sept 1966

(2) *Alice Georgina; *b* 29 Oct 1974

COCHRANE

Arms: Azure on a chevron engrailed argent, between in chief two boar's heads erased or, and in base a sun in splendour of the last, a thistle proper between two trefoils slipped vert. **Crest:** In front of two tilting spears in saltire a bay horse passant all proper. **Motto:** *Virtute et labore* ('By strength and hard work'). **Creation:** Bt. (UK) 8 Oct 1903.

SIR (HENRY) MARC SURSOCK COCHRANE, 4TH BT, of Woodbrook, Old Connaught, Bray, Co Wicklow, Lisgar Castle, Ballieborough, Co Cavan, and Kildare Street, Dublin [Sir Marc Cochrane Bt, Woodbrook, Bray, Co Wicklow, Ireland; Palais Sursock, PO Box 154, Beirut, Lebanon]; *b* 23 Oct 1946; *s* f 1979; *educ* Eton and Trin Coll Dublin (BBS, MA); Hon Irish Consul Gen in Lebanon

1979–84, dir: Hambros Bank Ltd 1979–85 and GT Management plc 1986–, tstee Chester Beatty Library and Gallery of Oriental Art, Dublin; *m* 28 June 1969 *Hala, 2nd dau of Fouad Mahmoud Bey es-Said, of Beirut, Lebanon, and has issue:

1 +ALEXANDER DESMOND; *b* 7 May 1973
2 +Patrick Talal; *b* 1976
1 *Faiza Maria Rosebud; *b* 1971

Lineage: THOMAS COCHRANE, of Graughlough Ho, Co Cavan; *m* 1789 Jane, dau of J McKibben, and *d* 1833, leaving:

WILLIAM COCHRANE, of Graughlough Ho; *m* Sarah (*d* 29 Jan 1877), dau of Henry McQuade, and *d* 31 Dec 1873, leaving:

Sir Henry Cochrane, 1st Bt (UK), so *cr* 8 Oct 1903, of Woodbrook, Old Connaught, Bray, Co Wicklow, Lisgar Castle, Bailieborough, Co Cavan, and Kildare Street, Dublin, JP Cos Dublin, Wicklow and Cavan, DL City of Dublin; *b* 21 Dec 1836; High Sheriff Co Wicklow 1897 and Co Cavan 1899, Alderman Dublin Corp (Mansion Ho Ward) for over 25 years, Gov Dir Cantrell and Cochrane Ltd, mineral and aerated water mfrs, chm Bray Township Commrs, ktd 1887; *m* 10 May 1865 Margaret (*d* 7 Dec 1901), only dau of Richard Gilchrist, and had:

1 Richard Gilchrist; *b* 26 May 1868; *d* 4 July 1871
2 Henry John Nassau; *b* 13 Aug 1871; *d* unm 15 April 1892
3 ERNEST CECIL (Sir), **2nd Bt**
4 Sir STANLEY HERBERT COCHRANE, 1st and last Bt (UK), so *cr* 10 Feb 1915, of Woodbrook, Bray, Co Wicklow, JP, DL Co Dublin, JP Co Wicklow, High Sheriff 1911; *b* 19 Sept 1877; *educ* Trin Coll Dublin (MA); Capt 7th Serv Bn Roy Dublin Fus, High Sheriff Co Wicklow 1912; *d* unm 23 Oct 1949, when the btcy expired
1 Sarah Elizabeth Graham; *m* 27 Dec 1883 Joseph M Day, LLD, barrister, and *dsp* 30 April 1953
2 Eleanor Maude; *b* 29 March 1870; *d* 14 April 1883
3 Margaret Louise Creighton; *m* 7 April 1902 Lt-Col James Dunne Day, RAMC, and *d* 18 Feb 1911

The 1st Bt *d* 11 Sept 1904; his er surv s,

Sir Ernest Cecil Cochrane, 2nd Bt, JP Co Cavan; *b* 12 Sept 1873; barrister Inner Temple 1904; Capt 3rd Bn Connaught Rangers and Gentleman-in-Waiting to Ld Lt Ireland 1908–09; dramatist as Ernest Cecil: *A Matter of Fact* (Comedy Theatre 1921) and *Monica* (Everyman Theatre 1924); *m* 1st 8 June 1898 (*divorce* 1910) Ethel Amy (*d* 9 April 1953), dau of John Henry Davis, of Cressingham Ho, Carshalton, Surrey, and had:

1 Beatrice Dorothea; *b* 2 Dec 1900; *m* 16 Feb 1924 Capt Richard Esmond Curwen Escombe, RFA, s of Edmund Escombe, of 39 Gloucester Sq, London, and adopted:
*Delia Susan; *b* 11 Feb 1945

Sir Ernest *m* 2nd 12 Sept 1911 (*divorce* 1933) Elsa Dorothea Marie (*d* 7 June 1966), yst dau of Erwin Albert Schumacher, of S Kensington, and by her had:

1 Ernest Henry, MC; *b* 3 Feb 1913; Maj Inniskilling Fus WW II; *d* following an accident in Austria 21 July 1945
2 DESMOND ORIEL ALASTAIR GEORGE WESTON (Sir), **3rd Bt**
2 *Elizabeth Margaret [Mrs Robert Steen, Elstow, Foxrock, Co Dublin, Ireland]; *b* 20 June 1915; *m* 9 Sept 1939 Robert Elsworth Steen, MD, FRCPI (*d* 1981), s of David Steen, barrister, of Mountsandel, Carrickmines, Co Dublin, and has:
(1) *(David) Michael Cochrane Elsworth [David Steen Esq, Neville's Mattingley, Hants RG27 8JU]; *b* 5 March 1945; *educ* Eton and Oriel Coll Oxford (MA); FCA; *m* 1971 *Rosemary Florence, er dau of Maj William Bellingham Denis Dobbs (*see* VESTEY, B), and has:
1a *Peter Robert Denis Elsworth; *b* 1977
1a *Jane Elizabeth Norah; *b* 1973
2a *Lucy Alannah Rosemary; *b* 1975
3a *Rosalie Frances Elsworth (twin); *b* 1977
(1) *Sarah Fiola Elsworth; *b* 13 March 1942; *m* 1975 *Capt Lewis Dixon-Brown, RM (ret), only s of Brig Cecil Thomas Dixon-Brown, OBE, RM (*ka* 1942), and has:
1a *Elizabeth-Olga Cochrane; *b* 1977
2a *Cecily Anne Cochrane; *b* 1979
3a *Nicola Frances Cochrane; *b* 1982

Sir Ernest *m* 3rd 23 Feb 1933 (*divorce* 1948) Flora (author of *Thelma Svane, Still She Smiles, Under the Pepper Trees, The Milk White Unicorn* and other novels), dau of Fritz Arnold Sandstrom, of Finland, and by her had:

3 *Jan Asa Helen Grahame; *b* 31 Oct 1939

Sir Ernest *m* 4th 26 Aug 1948 Margaret Eileen (Peggy) Cooper (*d* 16 Jan 1959), yst dau of John Wilfred Fowler, of Harrogate, and *d* 6 March 1952

The 2nd Bt's only surv son,

Sir Desmond Oriel Alastair George Weston Cochrane, 3rd Bt; *b* 22 Oct 1918; *educ* Eton; Maj Lancs Fus WW II (Lt 1940, Staff Offr 59 Div 1940, N Cmd 1941, War Office 1942, GHQ ME Forces 1943, Mil Sec to GOC 9th Army 1944), Hon Consul-Gen in Ireland for Syria and the Lebanon; dir: Tst Corp of Bahama, Roy Bank of Canada Tst Corp, Banque des Activités Economiques; *m* 12 Jan 1946 *Yvonne [Yvonne Lady Cochrane, Palais Sursock, Rue Sursock, Beirut, Lebanon], only child of Alfred Bey Sursock by Maria and gdau of 8th Duke of Cassano, and *d* 1979, having had:

1 Sir (HENRY) MARC SURSOCK COCHRANE, **4th and present Bt**
2 +Alfred Stanislas Marie Sursock [Dr Alfred Cochran, Cork Lodge, Woodbrook, Bray, Co Wicklow, Ireland]; *b* 8 May 1948; *educ* Eton and Rome U (DrArch, MIDI)
3 +Roderick Marie Inigo Sursock; *b* 16 Sept 1952; *educ* Le Rosey and American U of Beirut
1 *Isabelle Marie Elsa Sursock; *b* 26 April 1962; *m* 1987 *Count Gregorio Riccardi, s of Count Roberto Riccardi and Giulia Pascucci-Righi

COCKBURN

Arms: Quarterly, 1st and 4th, argent three cocks gules (for COCKBURN); 2nd and 3rd, gules six mascles or, three, two and one (for WEAPONT); all within a bordure vert. **Crest:** A cock crowing proper. **Mottoes:** (above crest) *Accendit cantu* ('He arises with a song'), (below arms) *Vigilans et audax* ('Watchful and bold').
Creation: Bt. (NS) 24 May 1671.

SIR JOHN ELLIOT COCKBURN OF THAT ILK, 12TH BT [Sir John Cockburn of that Ilk, Bt, 48 Frewin Rd, London SW18 3LP]; *b* 7 Dec 1925; *s* f 1949; *educ* RNC Dartmouth and RAC Cirencester; RAF WW II 1944–48 (invalided); md Cellar Management Ltd; *m* 7 Sept 1949 *Glory Patricia, er dau of Nigel Tudway Mullings, of Sea Spray, The Lizard, Cornwall, and has issue:

1 +CHARLES CHRISTOPHER [Charles Cockburn Esq, West Dene House, 84 Medstead Rd, Beech, Hants GU34 4AE]; *b* 19 Nov 1950; *educ* Emanuel Sch, London Poly (BA) and Garnett Coll; *m* 1st 1978 Beverley, dau of B Stangroom, of Richmond, Surrey; *m* 2nd 1985 *Margaret Ruth, dau of Samuel Esmond Bell, of Cheshunt, Herts, and has issue:
(1) +Christopher Samuel Alexander; *b* 24 March 1986
(2) +William James John; *b* 26 Feb 1996
(1) *Charlotte Elspeth Catherine (twin); *b* 24 March 1986
2 +James Chandos; *b* 1 April 1952
3 +Jonathan McQueen (twin); *b* 4 July 1956
1 *Julia Georgina; *b* 10 May 1954
2 *Catherine Isabel (twin); *b* 4 July 1956; *m* 1982 *Stephen Edward Keal

Lineage: ALEXANDER de COCKBURN; *m* Mary de Vipont or Weapont and had:

ALEXANDER DE COCKBURN; *cr* Heritable Usher of the White Rod 10 Feb 1473, Keeper Gt Seal of Scotland *temp* ROBERT II and ROBERT III; ggf of:

Sir WILLIAM COCKBURN, feudal Baron of Langton, Berwicks; *m* Anna Home and was *k* with other members of his family at the English victory over the Scots of Flodden 9 Sept 1513, leaving:

1 Alexander, *ka* Flodden; ancestor of:
(1) Sir WILLIAM COCKBURN, 1st Bt (NS), so *cr* 22 Nov 1627, of Langton, whose line failed, the btcy becoming dormant, when Sir ALEXANDER JAMES EDMUND COCKBURN, 12th Bt, of Langton, Ld Ch Justice Queen's Bench, *d* unm 20 Nov 1880
2 WILLIAM, for whom *see* below
3 Christopher, of Chouslie (possibly bro, not son, of Sir William Cockburn); ancestor of JAMES COCKBURN, of Ryslaw, Co Berwick, allegedly *cr* a Bt (NS) 1628; his line failed *c* 1782

Sir WILLIAM's 2nd son,

WILLIAM COCKBURN of that Ilk; granted charter by David, Earl of Crawford (see CRAWFORD and BALCARRES, E), of the lands and Barony of Inverarity, Forfar, confirmed 5 April 1527; *m* Isobel Home; his est s:

ALEXANDER COCKBURN of that Ilk; *m* Helena, dau of Sir Patrick Hepburn of Bolton, and *d c* 9 July 1583; his est s:

WILLIAM COCKBURN of that Ilk; *m* Helen, dau of John Renton of Billie; his est s:

WILLIAM COCKBURN of that Ilk; *m* 3 May 1596 Elizabeth, dau of John Kincade of Warriston; his est s:

JOHN COCKBURN of that Ilk; *b* 1598; *m* Oct 1652 and had, with an est s (William, *dsp* March 1663, having sold Cockburn 1657 to his next bro):

Sir James Cockburn of that Ilk, 1st Bt (NS), so *cr* 24 May 1671, presumably with remainder to heirs male of the body; *b* 7 Nov 1628; Burgess Edinburgh 1658; bought 6 May 1690 from his cousin Sir Archibald Cockburn, 4th Bt, of Langton, the estate of Langton and office of Usher; *m* 8 Jan 1658 Grissel, dau of Hay of Barra, and was *bur* 3 Jan 1704, having had, with other issue:

1 **Sir William Cockburn of that Ilk, 2nd Bt**; *b* 11 Sept 1662; advocate 1686; *m* Helen (*d* 28 Nov 1764), dau of Mark Lermonth, advocate, and was *bur* 10 Jan 1751, having had, with five daus, an only s:
(1) **Sir James Cockburn of that Ilk, 3rd Bt**; sold Langton and the office of Usher 15 Dec 1757; Lt-Col 48th Foot at Quebec 1760; *m* 8 April 1764 Mary (*d* 5 Sept 1766), dau of Robert Rochead, of Masterton, and had an only s:

1a **Sir Williams James Cockburn of that Ilk, 4th Bt**; Lt-Col 1st Foot; *d* unm 9 Jan 1800

(1) (cont.) **Sir James** allegedly *m* 2nd Phoebe Sharman and *d* 13 March 1780, having by her had three s (*dsp*)

2 John, of Kilkenny; *b* 22 April 1675; surgeon; *m* 1720 Martha Rich, of Kilkenny (*d* 14 Jan 1756), and *d* 12 Dec 1758, having had issue, with a dau:

(1) William (Ven), LLD; *b* 1721; Archdeacon of Ossory 1762; *m* 10 Dec 1763 Susanna Savage and *d* 7 June 1776, having had a son and four daus

(2) JAMES (Sir), **5th Bt**

1 Barbara; *b* 22 July 1660; *m* 30 Dec 1680 10th Lord Sinclair (*qv*), and had issue

The 4th Bt's cousin,

Sir James Cockburn of that Ilk, 5th Bt; *b* 1723; Lt-Col 35th Regt Brig-Gen and QMG N America; *m* Laetitia (*d* 11 Nov 1804), dau and coheir of Luke Little, of Carlow, and *d* 9 June 1809, having had, with other issue:

1 WILLIAM (Sir), **6th Bt**

1 Lucy; *d* young

2 Mary; *m* Col John Cockburn, RA, and had issue

3 Margaret; *m* Maj Cole, of Kilkenny

The 5th Bt's only son,

Sir William Cockburn of that Ilk, 6th Bt; *b* 1769; Lt-Gen 73rd Foot, DCL Oxford; *m* 1st 1 June 1791 Eliza Anne (*d* 30 June 1829), dau of Col Henry Frederick Creutzer, of Mannheim, Germany, and widow of (a) Maj Charles Clifton, RA, and (b) Thomas Davis, MD, and had issue:

WILLIAM SARSFIELD ROSSITER (Sir), **7th Bt**

Katherine; *m* 6 May 1828 Edward Cludde, of Orleton, Salop, and had issue

Sir William *m* 2nd 2 July 1834 Martha Honora Georgina (*d* 26 Feb 1865), dau and coheir of Capt William Henry Ricketts-Jervis, RN, of Longwood, Hants (*see* ST VINCENT, V), and widow of Osborne Markham, and *d* 19 March 1835

His only son,

Sir William Sarsfield Rossiter Cockburn of that Ilk, 7th Bt; *b* 11 June 1796; *educ* Exeter Coll Oxford (MA); *m* 15 Oct 1823 Ann (*d* 12 April 1879), er dau of Rev Francis Coke, of Lemore, Eardisley, Herefs, Preb Hereford, and *d* 12 April 1858, having had issue, with five daus:

1 EDWARD CLUDDE (Sir), **8th Bt**

2 George William; *b* 14 Jan 1838; Capt 42nd Highrs (Black Watch) Indian Mutiny, Col cmdg Native Forces Hyderabad; *m* 5 June 1761 Emily Sarah (*d* 18 Dec 1923), only dau of Ven John Cleugh, Archdeacon of Malta, and *d* 17 March 1924, leaving, with other issue (*d* in infancy or unnamed):

(1) William Alexander Crawford; *b* 7 May 1863; DCS Nigeria, Maj Queen's Bays, in Benin Expdn 1897 (despatches, medal with clasp), W Africa 1898 and 1902 (clasp), Boer War (Queen's medal with clasp); *d* 30 Aug 1924

(2) Charles Edward Stuart; JP and CA Derbyshire; *b* 27 Oct 1867; *m* 8 Aug 1894 Lilian (*d* 23 Nov 1943), dau of Sir Morton Edward Maningham-Buller, 2nd Bt (*see* DILHORNE, V), and *d* 12 Dec 1917, leaving issue:

1a Sylvia; *m* 10 Nov 1919 Col Reginald William Welfare Hills, OBE, MC, IA (*d* 5 Feb 1962), only son of Jacob William Hills, of Riverhead, Kent, and *dsp* 27 Jan 1967

2a Rosalind, MBE (1962); *m* 7 April 1921 Cdr Guy Darracott Millar, RN (*d* 24 Aug 1940), s of Charles Christian Hoyer Millar, of Feldon, Boxmoor, Herts, and had a s (*see* INCHYRA, B)

(3) Ronald Abercromby, OBE; *b* 1 April 1872; Lt-Col and Brevet Col 4th Bn Suffolk Regt (TA), Lt-Col RAF, Maj Suffolk Regt; Sierra Leone Frontier Police and W African Field Force 1900–05, WW I (wounded, despatches); *m* 17 Dec 1910 Gladys Huxtable, er dau of William Pearce, of Standen Elms, Newport, IoW, and *d* 26 July 1951, leaving:

1a Rona Abercromby; *b* 27 Oct 1911; *m* 22 Sept 1933 Capt Harry George Cowdell, 4th QOH, yr s of H S Cowdell, and *d* 2 Feb 1943

(4) Donald Graham (twin); *b* 1 April 1872; *m* 1st 15 Sept 1915 Dorothy Agnes (*d* 15 Nov 1916), dau of Lewis Evans, of Gwelo, Rhodesia; *m* 2nd 6 March 1922 Nova (*d* 1947), er dau of C Walton and widow of H D Douglas, and *d* 25 March 1938, having had issue by his 1st w:

1a *Edith Penelope; *b* 20 June 1916

(1) Constance Anne Cleugh; *d* unm 8 Dec 1940

(2) Ethel Marie Louise; *m* 24 Oct 1894 Reginald Nevill Boustead, and *d* 25 Jan 1905, leaving issue

(3) Violet Selina Margaret; *m* 20 Sept 1911 Adml Edward Montgomery Phillpotts, CB (*d* 9 April 1952), 3rd son of Rev H J Phillpotts, of Shadwell, Speldhurst, and *d* Oct 1949, leaving issue

(4) Muriel Evelyn Kathleen MBE (1918); *m* 29 April 1902 John Houston Sinclair, CMG, CBE (*d* 17 Aug 1961), son of William Houston Sinclair, of Morton Manor, Brading, IoW, and *d* 5 June 1952, leaving issue

(5) Kathleen Beatrice Melita; *m* 2 Aug 1913 Robert Raymond Smith Barry, AFC (*d* 23 April 1949), son of James Hugh Smith Barry, of Stowell Park, Pewsey, Wilts, and *d* 18 May 1941

The 7th Bt's est son,

Sir Edward Cludde Cockburn of that Ilk, 8th Bt, JP and DL (Herefs); *b* 10 June 1834; High Sheriff 1866, Capt 11th Hus Crimea; *m* 13 Oct 1859 Mary Anne Frances (*d* 30 Oct 1917), dau of Robert Kerr Elliot, of Harwood and Roxburghshire, and *d* 24 Dec 1903, having had, with other issue:

1 **Sir Robert Cockburn of that Ilk, 9th Bt**, JP (Herefs); *b* 7 Dec 1861; Maj Shropshire LI WW I, AMICE; *m* 10 Nov 1925 Katharine May Meetkerke (*d* 7 July 1937), dau of Rev Alexander Ewing, and *dsp* 26 Aug 1938

2 **Sir James Stanhope Cockburn of that Ilk, 10th Bt**; *b* 11 Nov 1867; Capt Gen List Boer War (Queen's medal with clasp) and WW I; *m* 28 Nov 1828 Ethel Frances Sophia (*d* 20 May 1953), er dau of Lord Francis Horace Pierrepont Cecil (*see* EXETER, M) and widow of Maj Edward Crichton Parry-Hawkshaw, JP, and *dsp* 1 April 1947

3 JOHN BRYDGES (Sir), **11th Bt**

1 Florence; *d* unm 1 Oct 1943

2 Annie; *m* 30 June 1893 Francis George Sherlock, of Irton Hall, Cumberland, and *d* 23 June 1938, leaving issue

3 Eleanor; *m* 28 Aug 1902 James Tuder Hereford (*d* 1952), of Sufton, Herefs, and *d* 22 May 1928, leaving issue

4 Mary; *d c* 1950

The 10th Bt's bro,

Sir John Brydges Cockburn of that Ilk, 11th Bt; DSO (1919); *b* 23 Dec 1870; *educ* Cheltenham; Lt-Col 1st Bn Roy Welch Fus W Africa 1897–98 (medal with clasp), 1901–02 (Queen's medal with five clasps) and 1906 (medal with clasp), N Nigeria 1900 (despatches, clasp), WW I in Cameroons and France (despatches three times, brevet of Lt-Col, twice severely wounded, 1914 Star, British War Medal, Victory medal); Roy Humane Soc silver medal, Legion of Honour, memb Ross-on-Wye UDC 1928–31; *m* 9 April 1919 Isabel Hunter (*d* 10 March 1978), yst dau of James McQueen, of Crofts, Stewartry of Kirkcudbrigth, and *d* 2 May 1949, leaving:

1 Sir JOHN ELLIOT COCKBURN OF THAT ILK, **12th and present Bt**

1 *Frances Isabel; *b* 12 May 1921

COCKBURN-CAMPBELL

Arms: Grand quarterly 1st and 4th, quarterly, 1st and 4th, gyronny of eight or and sa.; 2nd, arg. a galley, sails furled, oars in action, sa.; 3rd, or a fess chequy az. and arg., over all a chief arg., charged with a rock ppr. subscribed 'GIBRALTAR' between two medals for Seringapatam and Talavera (for CAMPBELL); 2nd and 3rd, quarterly, 1st and 4th arg., an ostrich feather ensigned with an imperial crown ppr. between three cocks, two and one, gu.; 2nd and 3rd, gu. six mascles, three, two and one or (for COCKBURN). **Crest:** A dexter hand holding a scimitar ppr. **Motto:** 'Without fear' **Creation:** Bt. (UK) 3 July 1821.

SIR THOMAS COCKBURN-CAMPBELL, 6TH BT, of Gartsford, Co Ross [Sir Thomas Cockburn-Campbell Bt, 21 Cardwell, York, WA 6302, Australia]; *b* 8 Dec 1918; *s* f 1935; *educ* C of E GS Melbourne, Australia; author: *Land of Lots of Time*, served WW II in Australian Forces; *m* 1st 24 June 1944 (*divorce* 1981) Josephine Zoi, est dau of Harold Douglas Forward, of Cunjardine, W Australia; *m* 2nd 1982 (*divorce* 1990) Janice Laraine, yst dau of William John Pascoe, of Bundoora, Victoria, and has issue by 1st w:

1 +ALEXANDER THOMAS [Alexander Cockburn-Campbell Esq, 11 Templetonia Retreat, Livingston Estate, Canning Vale, WA 6155, Australia]; *b* 16 March 1945; *m* 1969 *Kerry Ann, er dau of Sgt K Johnson, of Mt Hawthorne, W Australia, and has issue:

(1) +Thomas Justin; *b* 10 Feb 1974

(1) *Felicity Ann; *b* 1981

Lineage: JOHN CAMPBELL, JP, 2nd of Achalader, Perthshire, had a yst s:

Sir Alexander Campbell, 1st Bt (UK), so *cr* 6 May 1815 with a new patent 3 July 1821 extending the limitation to his gs Alexander and after him to the issue male of his 2nd dau, Isabella, Lady Malcolm; *b* 20 Aug 1760; served at Siege of Gibraltar, Col 80th Regt, Lt-Col cmdg 4th Div Battle of Talavera (severely wounded), ktd; *m* 1st 1783 Olympia Elizabeth (*d* 24 Dec 1794), est dau of William Morshead, of Cartuther, Cornwall, and had issue:

1 John Morshead, Lt Inf; *k* Battle of Assaye

2 Allan William, Lt-Col; *k* Battle of the Pyrenees 28 July 1813

1 Olympia; *m* Alexander Cockburn, of Madras, banker, 3rd s of Thomas Cockburn, of Bowchester, Berwickshire, Dep Keeper Gt Seal of Scotland, by Agnes, dau of John Scott, of Belford, Roxburghshire, gs of Sir John Scott, Bt, of Ancrum, and had:

(1) ALEXANDER THOMAS COCKBURN (Sir), **2nd Bt**

2 Isabella Charlotte; *m* 4 June 1807 Gen Sir John Malcolm, GCB (*d* 31 May 1833), son of George Malcolm, of Burnfoot, and *d* 26 June 1867 having had issue:

(1) George Alexander, CB, Gen; *b* 21 Jan 1810; *m* 4 Dec 1845 Georgiana (*d* 29 Oct 1886), dau of Most Rev Edward Harcourt, Archbp York, s of 1st Baron Vernon (*qv*), and *dsp* 2 June 1888

(1) Margaret; *m* 20 June 1827 her cousin **Sir Alexander Thomas Cockburn-Campbell, 2nd Bt**, and *d* 1841, leaving issue (*see* below)

(2) Olympia; *m* Count Usedom, of Rügen, and had issue

(3) Catherine Wellesley

3 Amelia Harriet; *m* Lt-Col Sir John Kinnier Macdonald, CB, of Sanda, Argyll, Br Envoy Persia, and *dsp* 16 Oct 1860. He *d* 11 June 1830

Sir Alexander *m* 2nd Elizabeth Anne (*d* 20 Jan 1870), dau of Rev Thomas Pemberton, and by her had issue:

4 Flora Elizabeth; *m* 19 Nov 1833 Rev Hon Henry Reginald Yorke, and *d* 12 Jan 1852, leaving issue (*see* HARDWICKE, E)

Sir ALEXANDER *d* 11 Dec 1824; his gs,

Sir ALEXANDER THOMAS COCKBURN later COCKBURN-CAMPBELL (roy licence 1825), **2nd Bt**, RM Albany, W Australia; *m* 1st 20 June 1827 his cousin Margaret (*d* 1841), est dau of Sir John Malcolm, GCB (*see* above), and had issue:

1 Charlotte Isabella

2 Olympia; *m* 1st 4 Nov 1857 Charles Uhde (*d* 1859), of Hanschucheim, Baden; *m* 2nd 1863 Friedrich von Pällnitz, of Ippesheim, Bavaria

Sir ALEXANDER *m* 2nd 1842 Grace (*d* 31 July 1870), dau of Joseph Spence, of Birstwith, Yorks, and by her had issue:

1 **Sir Alexander Cockburn-Campbell, 3rd Bt**; *b* 1843; *d* unm 6 Sept 1871

2 THOMAS (Sir), **4th Bt**

3 Cecilia

Sir ALEXANDER *m* 3rd 4 April 1871 Sophie Jane Trimmer (*d* Sept 1890) and *d* 23 April 1871

The 3rd Bt's bro,

Sir Thomas Cockburn-Campbell, 4th Bt, MLC and Chm Ctees W Australia; *b* 1845; *m* 1870 Lucy Ann (*d* 9 July 1924), dau of Arthur Trimmer by Mary Anne, dau of Capt Sir Richard Spencer, CB, KH, RN, of Pootenes, W Australia, and had issue:

1 ALEXANDER THOMAS (Sir), **5th Bt**

2 John Stothart; *b* 31 Oct 1878; *d* unm in S Australia

1 Grace Lucy; *b* 12 July 1871; *d* unm 16 June 1918

2 Olympia Sophia Cecilia; *b* Jan 1874; *m* 30 April 1895 Theophilus Rodda Lowe, of Perth, W Australia, and *d* 16 June 1901. He *d* 7 Feb 1912

3 Rachel Mary Anne; *b* 8 July 1878; *m* 29 April 1903 Cecil Hedley Salmon, of Keane St, Cottesloe, W Australia, and *d* 17 Aug 1956, leaving issue. He *d* 20 April 1948

4 Lalla; *b* 2 Aug 1882; *d* unm 19 May 1964

Sir THOMAS *d* 27 Sept 1892; his est son,

Sir Alexander Thomas Cockburn-Campbell, 5th Bt; *b* 8 Aug 1872; *m* 1918 Maude Frances Lorenzo (*d* 12 Feb 1923), only dau of Alfred Giles, of Bowrook Stn, N Territory, and *d* 1 July 1935, having had issue:

1 Sir THOMAS COCKBURN-CAMPBELL, **6th and present Bt**

2 Urban Alfred, Cpl AIF WW II; *b* 31 May 1921; *m* 24 Feb 1954 *Betty McGuinness

3 +Alexander Bruce [Alexander Cockburn-Campbell Esq, 90 Evans St, Shenton Park, W Australia]; *b* 25 May 1923; LAC RAAF WW II; *m* 5 May 1951 *Beryl, dau of William Elder, of 275 Onslow Rd, Shenton Park, W Australia, and has issue:

(1) *Susan Peta; *b* 7 Feb 1954

(2) *Nola Gay; *b* 10 July 1957

(3) *Judith Ann; *b* 20 Aug 1961

(4) *Alison Lee; *b* 29 Jan 1964

COCKFIELD

Creation: B. (LP, UK) 1978.

THE BARON COCKFIELD, of Dover, Co Kent (Sir (Francis) Arthur Cockfield, PC (1983)) [The Rt Hon The Lord Cockfield PC, House of Lords, London SW1A 0PW]; *b* 28 Sept 1916; *educ* Dover GS and LSE (LLB, BSc (Ec)); barrister Inner Temple 1942; joined Home Civil Service Inland Revenue 1938, Bd Inland Revenue: Assist Sec 1945, Dir Statistics and Intelligence 1945–52, memb 1951–52, Commr Inland Revenue 1951–52; Boots Pure Drug Co: Finance Dir 1953–61, md and chm Exec Managing Ctee 1961–67; memb NEDC 1962–64 and 1982–83, Pres Roy Statistical Soc 1968–69, Advsr Taxation Policy to Chllr Exchequer 1970–73, Chm Price Commn 1973–77; Min State Treasury 1979–82, Sec State Trade 1982–83, Chllr Duchy Lancaster 1983–84; V-Pres European Commn 1985–88, memb Court Govrs Nottingham U 1963–67, ktd 1973, Hon Fell LSE 1972; Hon LLD: Fordham NY 1989, Sheffield 1990; Hon DU Surrey 1989; Grand Cross Order Leopold Belgium 1990; author: *The European Union: creating the single market* (1994); *m* 19– Aileen Monica Mudie, choreographer (*d* 1992)

Lineage: Lt C F COCKFIELD (*ka* Somme 1916); *m* Louisa James and had:

(FRANCIS) ARTHUR, *cr* a **Baron**

COCKS OF HARTCLIFFE

Creation: B. (LP, UK) 1987.

THE BARON COCKS OF HARTCLIFFE, of Chinnor, Co Oxfordshire (Michael Francis Lovell Cocks, PC (1976)) [The Rt Hon The Lord Cocks of Hartcliffe PC, House of Lords, London SW1A 0PW]; *b* 19 Aug 1929; *educ* Bristol U; Lecturer Bristol Poly 1968; MP (Lab) Bristol S 1970–87, Assist Govt Whip 1974–76, Parly Sec Treasury and Govt Ch Whip 1976–79, Oppn Ch Whip 1979–85; V-Chm Govrs BBC 1993–; *m* 1st 1954 Janet Macfarlane and has two sons and two daus; *m* 2nd 1979 *Valerie Davis

Lineage: Dr HARRY F LOVELL COCKS, of Amersham, Bucks, had:

MICHAEL FRANCIS, *cr* a **Baron**

CODRINGTON
of Dodington (1721)

Arms: Argent a fess embattled counter-embattled sable fretty gules between three lions passant of the third. **Motto:** *Vultus in hostem* ('Face to the enemy'). **Creation:** Bt. (GB) 21 April 1721.

SIR WILLIAM ALEXANDER CODRINGTON, 8TH BT, of Dodington, Co Gloucester [Sir William Codrington Bt, 73 Backchurch Lane, London E1 1LQ]; *b* 5 July 1934; *s* f 1961; *educ* St Andrew's Grahamstown and S African Naval Coll; joined Merchant Navy 1952, Master Mariner's Certificate of Competency 1962, Cadet Training Offr Br and Commonwealth Training Scheme, Port Capt Hong Kong for World-Wide Shipping Agency Ltd 1979– (dir 1994–), dir Worldwide Shipping Agency 1994–98; FNI 1976, memb Hon Co of Master Mariners

Lineage: ROBERT CODRINGTON (son or nephew of Robert Codrington, living 1399); had:

JOHN CODRINGTON; *m* Mary — and had:

EDWARD CODRINGTON; had:

THOMAS CODRINGTON; *m* Mary Kelway, of Tregorthen, Cornwall, and had, with a dau (Ann, *m* 27 Oct 1593 Robert Isaac):

SIMON; *m* Agnes, dau and heir of Richard Seacole, of Didmarton, Glos, and had:

ROBERT CODRINGTON, of Didmarton; *m* Anne Stubbs and had, with an er s (John, High Sheriff Glos 1683, *m* Frances, dau of William Guise, of Elmore, and was ancestor of the CODRINGTONs of Wroughton, Wilts):

CHRISTOPHER CODRINGTON; settled *temp* CHARLES I in Barbados and had:

1 Christopher; Lt-Govr Barbados, Capt-Gen Leeward Islands; had, with a yr s:

(1) Christopher; Govr Leeward Islands; *d* 7 April 1710, leaving to All Souls, Oxford, £10,000 for a library plus his own collection of books, also £2,000 p.a. to the SPG to found a Coll at Barbados

2 John; Treasurer Barbados, Col Life Gds there; *m* —, dau of Col Bates, and had with a yr s:

(1) **Sir William Codrington 1st Bt** (GB), so *cr* 21 April 1721, of Dodington, Co Gloucester; *m* 12 March 1717/8 Elizabeth (*d* 5 Feb 1761), dau of William Bethell, of Swindon, Yorks, and had issue:

1a WILLIAM (Sir), **2nd Bt**

2a John Archibald, of Chingford Hatch, Essex; *b* 26 Nov 1721; *m* Sarah, dau of Henry Capper, of Wincanton, Som, and *dsp* 18 March 1759

3a Christopher CODRINGTON later BETHELL, of Dyrham Park, Middx; *b* 10 Aug 1728; *m* 21 July 1768 Hon Anne Sandys, dau of 1st Baron Sandys (*qv*), and *dsp* Sept 1797

4a Edward, ancestor of the CODRINGTON Bts, *cr* 1876 (*qv*)

1a Bridget; *m* 15 Nov 1747 William Dowdeswell (*d* 1775), PC, of Pall Court, Worcs, MP Tewkesbury, and had issue

2a Caroline; *m* Richard Cox (*d* 1818), Army Agent and fndr Cox's Bank 1747

The 1st Bt *d* 17 Dec 1738; his est son,

Sir William Codrington, 2nd Bt, PC, MP Tewkesbury; *b* 26 Oct 1719; *m* 22 Feb 1735/6 Anne Acton, of Fulham, and *d* 11 March 1792, having had, with a dau (Mary, *m* George Bernard (*d* 1818)):

Sir William Codrington, 3rd Bt; *b* 1739; disinherited by his f, who bequeathed his extensive estates to his great-nephew Christopher William (*see* CODRINGTON, Bt, *cr* 1876; possibly because of a confused idea that the btcy went with the estates the title *cr* in 1721 was disputed for over 60 years and was assumed by Christopher William, f of the Gerald *cr* a Bt in 1876, though it was also assumed by Christopher William's f Christopher, who was not heir to the estates); lived in France; *m* 1st Mary (*dsp* 20 April 1789), sis of Godfrey Kirke, of London; *m* 2nd his w's niece Eleanor (*d* 13 Feb 1816), dau of Godfrey Kirke, of London, and *d* 5 Sept 1816, having by her had:

1 WILLIAM RAYMOND (Sir), **4th Bt**

1 Mary Anne Eleanor; *m* 1826 Charles Magon, Offr in 60th Regt of French Hus, and *d* 1834

The only son,

Sir William Raymond Codrington, 4th Bt; *b* 25 Jan 1806; *m* 20 May 1828 Anne Mary (*d* 27 Oct 1876), dau of Joseph Raphael Agrippin Lefer de Bonabon, and *d* 17 Dec 1873, having had, with other issue, including dau (Nancy Mary, *m* 29 Jan 1856 Marquis de la Moussaye):

Sir William Mary Joseph Codrington, 5th Bt; *b* 12 March 1829; *m* 12 April 1866 Mary (*d* 1 Sept 1915), dau of Robert Roskell, of Park Ho, Fulham, and had issue:

1 WILLIAM ROBERT (Sir), **6th Bt**

2 George Raymond; *b* 14 Aug 1868; *d* unm 15 Jan 1939

3 Alexander Joseph; *b* 9 Aug 1870; *m* 24 July 1905 Mary (*d* 25 Oct 1928), est dau of Nicholas R Roskell, of Warwick Gdns, London, and *dsp* 19 July 1941

4 Charles Arthur; *b* 7 Aug 1878; *d* 10 Dec 1902, drowned at Rennes, France

The 5th Bt *d* 1 March 1904; his est son,

Sir William Robert Codrington, 6th Bt; *b* 18 April 1867; Lt-Col, Capt and Brevet Maj 11th Hus, served NW Frontier India 1897–98 (medal and clasp) and Boer War 1899–1902 (despatches, wounded, brevet, two medals with six clasps); *m* 25 April 1903 Joan (*d* 18 Aug 1963), est dau of Harry Adams Rogers, of Johannesburg, and had:

1 WILLIAM RICHARD (Sir), **7th Bt**

2 Frank Christopher; *b* 8 May 1908; *educ* Victoria Coll Jersey and Pembroke Coll Oxford; *m* 12 Dec 1933 Monica Bawn (*d* 1983), est dau of Sir James Philip Reynolds, 1st Bt, DSO, MP (*qv*), and *d* 1992, leaving issue:

(1) +Christopher Michael; *b* 29 April 1937; *educ* St Andrew's Coll Grahamstown; *m* 1972 *Christine Beatrice, est dau of Lt-Col Max Emil Bürki, of Château Surpierre, Switzerland, and has issue:

1a *Rosalind Bawn; *b* 1974

2a *Emily Jane; *b* 1977

The 6th Bt *d* 7 Nov 1932; his er son,

Sir William Richard Codrington, 7th Bt; *educ* Shrewsbury and Victoria Coll Jersey; Lt-Cdr RNVR WW II; *b* 22 April 1904; *m* 3 May 1933 (*divorce* 1952) Joan Kathleen Birelli, est dau of Percy E Nicholas, and *d* 23 March 1961, having had issue:

1 Sir WILLIAM ALEXANDER CODRINGTON, **8th and present Bt**

2 +GILES PETER [Giles Codrington Esq, Villa Félipe, Ave Fernand Martin, Villefranche-sur-Mer, France]; *b* 28 Oct 1943; heir presumptive; *m* 1989 *Shirley Linda Duke, and has issue:

(1) +Christopher Harry; *b* 1988

(2) +Daniel Peter; *b* 1993

(1) *Michele Anne; *b* 1990

3 +Andrew Richard [Capt Andrew Codrington, 5 Cambridge Mews, Kingsley, Perth, WA 6026, Australia]; *b* 23 April 1947; Capt; *m* 1975 *Claire Marie Agnes Frichot, of Mahé, Seychelles, and has issue:

(1) +Adrian Christopher; *b* 1981

(1) *Estelle Louise; *b* 1985

1 *Sally Ann [Mrs Philip Collingwood, 51 Longcroft Lane, Welwyn Garden City, Herts]; *b* 12 Nov 1939; *m* 8 Sept 1962 *Philip John Francis Collingwood, son of Wilfrid Arthur Denis Collingwood, of 28 Selsey Ave, Bognor Regis, Sussex, and has issue:

(1) *Richard Francis; *b* 18 Aug 1964

(1) *Sophia Catherine Mary; *b* 8 July 1963; *m* 1989 *Julian Thomas Rowe

(2) *Charlotte Mary; *b* 13 June 1966

CODRINGTON of Dodington (1876)

Arms: Argent a fess embattled counter-embattled sable fretty gules between three lions passant of the third. **Crest:** Issuant from a coronet composed of four roses set upon a rim or, a dragon's head gules between two dragon's wings per fess or and azure.
Motto: *Immersabilis est vera virtus* ('True virtue is imperishable').
Creation: Bt. (UK) 25 Feb 1876.

SIR SIMON FRANCIS BETHELL CODRINGTON, 3RD BT, of Dodington Park, Co Gloucester [Major Sir Francis Codrington Bt, Bean Cottage, Dodington, Chipping Sodbury, Bristol BS17 6SF]; *b* 14 Aug 1923; *s* f 1979; *educ* Eton; Hon Maj Coldstream Gds WW II 1942–45 in Italy; *m* 1st 3 May 1947 (*divorce* 1959) Joanne, dau of John William Molineaux, of Rock Castle, Kilmacsimon, Co Cork, and widow of William Humphrey Austin Thompson; *m* 2nd 1959 (*divorce* 1979) Pamela Joy Halliday, only dau of Maj George Walter Bentley Wise, MBE, and has issue:

1 +CHRISTOPHER GEORGE WAYNE [Christopher Codrington Esq, The Old Hundred, Tormarton, Badminton, Avon]; *b* 20 Feb 1960; *educ* Millfield and RAC Cirencester; *m* 1991 *Noelle Lynn, dau of Dale Wilford Leverson, of Texas, USA, and Mrs Genell Benner, of Ohio, and has issue:

(1) +Alexander Edward Kristoffer; *b* 9 Nov 1993

(1) *A dau; *b* 12 Aug 1996

2 +Bethell; *b* 22 May 1961; *educ* Eton

3 +Hugo John; *b* 5 June 1964; *m* 1992 *Antonia Hannah Beaufort, est dau of Andrew McCullough, of Windsor, Berks, and has:

(1) +Charles; *b* 8 June 1996

Sir SIMON *m* 3rd 1980 (*divorce* 1987) Sarah Gwynne Gaze (*née* Pennell); *m* 4th 1989 *Shirley Ann, dau of Percival Lionel Davis

Lineage: Sir WILLIAM CODRINGTON, 1st Bt, of Dodington, so *cr* 1721 (*qv*); had a 4th s (all of whose male-line descendants are therefore in remainder to the older btcy as well as the 1876 one):

EDWARD CODRINGTON; *b* 22 June 1732; *m* 4 May 1759 Rebecca le Sturgeon (*d* 1770), and *d* Feb 1775, leaving, with a dau:

1 CHRISTOPHER

2 William John CODRINGTON later BETHELL (roy licence 12 March 1798); *b* Nov 1768; *m* Anna Maria (*d* 7 Dec 1861), dau of William Chaloner, of Guisborough, Yorks, and had a dau (Emma, *d* unm 1874)

3 Edward (Sir), GCB, Adml of the Blue; *b* 27 April 1770; cmded HMS *Orion* at Trafalgar 1805 and the allied fleets at Navarino 1827, MP Devonport 1832–39, Kt St Lazarus, Kt St George Greece; *m* 27 Dec 1802 Jane (*d* 21 Jan 1837), dau of Jasper Hall, of Otterburn, Hexham, and Old Windsor, Berks, and *d* 28 April 1851, having had, with another s and three daus (including Jane Barbara, *m* Capt Sir Thomas Bourchier, KCB, RN, and *d* 3 April 1884):

(1) William John (Sir), GCB; *b* 26 Nov 1804; Gen, Col Coldstream Gds, C-in-C Br forces Crimea 1855, MP Greenwich 1857–59, Govr Gibraltar 1859–1865; *m* 7 May 1836 Mary, VA (*d* 28 June 1898), Woman of the Bedchamber to HM QUEEN VICTORIA, dau of Levi Ames, of The Hyde, Herts, and *d* 6 Aug 1884, having had, with other issue:

1a Alfred Edward (Sir), GCVO, KCB, JP, DL Rutland; *b* 4 May 1854; Lt-Gen, Col Coldstream Gds from 1918, formerly cmdg London District 1909–13, Mil Sec to Sec of State for War 1914, cmdg 3rd Army, Home Defences 1914–16, Gd Offr Legion of Honour, Kt Grand Cross Redeemer Greece, served Egypt and S Africa; *m* 20 May 1885 Adela Harriet, CBE, DGStJ (*d* 14 Feb 1935), dau of Melville Portal, of Laverstoke, Hants (*see* PORTAL, Bt) and *d* 12 Sept 1945, leaving issue:

1b Geoffrey Ronald (Sir), KCVO (1953, CVO 1948), CB (1932), CMG (1951), DSO (1918), OBE (1916), TD, High Sheriff Wilts 1955; *b* 13 May 1888; *educ* Harrow and Ch Ch Oxford (BA 1910, MA 1934); Col TA, late Leics Yeo, served WW I (despatches four times, wounded) and WW II 1939–46 at HQ London District, Gentleman Usher to TM GEORGE VI and THE QUEEN, Order of St Maurice and St Lazarus of Italy, and American Bronze Medal; *m* 24 May 1923 Cecilia Mary (*d* 1979), yst dau of Ernest James Wythes, CBE, DL, JP, of Copped Hall and The Wood Ho, Essex, and Birkley Hall, Kent and *d* 18 June 1973 leaving issue:

1c +Michael Christopher Alfred [Major Michael Codrington, Beech Cottage, Farm Lane, Gt Bedwyn, Wilts]; *b* 19 April 1926; *educ* Eton; late Maj 16th/5th Lancers; *m* 1st 12 Dec 1953 (*divorce* 1986) Irene Margaret (*d* 1994), only dau of Col Mark Edward Makgill Crichton Maitland, CVO, DSO, of The Island Ho, Wilton, Salisbury (*see* LAUDERDALE, E), and has issue:

1d *Camilla Ann; *b* 10 Feb 1957

2d *Bridget Margaret [Mrs Ross Witherow, 116 Portland Rd, London W11 4LX]; *b* 7 Nov 1958; *m* 1st 1979 George Daniel Rossiter (*d* 1984) and has:

1e *Peter Goodman; *b* 1983

2d (cont.) Mrs Rossiter *m* 2nd 1990 *Ross O'N Witherow, and has further issue:

2e *Thomas Edward; *b* 1991

3d *Katherine Alice; *b* 22 Oct 1965

1c (cont.) Michael Codrington *m* 2nd 1986 Alma Patricia (*d* 20 May 1997), dau of Patrick Sheridan and widow of Norman G Batcheller

2c +James Geoffrey [James Codrington Esq, Lyde Barn, Lower Lyde, Herefs HR1 3AC]; *b* 1 Sept 1935; *educ* Harrow; chm Appledore Investments Ltd; *m* 2 Sept 1961 *(Clare) Lorraine, er dau of Richard Guy Arthur Wells, of Stable Cottage, Winchelsea, and has issue:

1d +Richard Melville; *b* 16 Oct 1962

2d +Charles Sebastian; *b* 21 Sept 1964; *m* 1995 *Sarah Juliette, yr dau of Michael Style, and has:

1e +Benjamin Michael; *b* 30 May 1997

1d *Annabelle Cecilia; *b* 21 April 1967; *m* 1991 *Graham P Sylvester, only son of Dr Derek Sylvester, of Almondsbury Field, Lower Almondsbury, Bristol, and has:

1e *Thomas James Hogarth; *b* 20 Oct 1994

2e *Nicholas Alexander Hogarth; *b* 11 April 1996

1c *Mary Alice, JP (Co London 1961); *b* 1924; *m* 19 Nov 1949 *Robert Thomas Boscawen, PC, MC, MP, yst son of 8th Viscount Falmouth (*qv*), and has issue

2c *Emma Cecilia [Miss Emma Codrington, West Lodge, Wilton, Salisbury, Wilts]; *b* 18 Sept 1930

2b William Melville, CMG (1946), MC (1919), High Sheriff Rutland 1947, Ld Lt from 1951; *b* 16 Dec 1892; *educ* Harrow and New Coll Oxford (MA); Capt Res of Offrs late 16th Lancers, attd Army Signal Serv, served WW I (despatches), Assist U-Sec FO (unpaid) 1940–45, Ch Security Offr War

Cabinet 1942–45; chm Nyasaland Railways Ltd; dir: Sun Alliance Insur Co, Powell Duffryn Ltd; *m* 26 Feb 1935 *Katherine Theodosia [Mrs Edward Kirkpatrick, The Cottage, Hambleton, Oakham, Rutland] (*m* 2nd 24 Oct 1968 Lt-Col Edward Kirkpatrick (*d* 1972), yr son of Sir Cyril Reginald Sutton Kirkpatrick, TD, of Loudham, Amersham, Bucks), er dau of John Houston Sinclair, CMG, CBE, of Tangier, Morocco, by Muriel Evelyn Kathleen, MBE, 4th dau of George William Cockburn (*see* COCKBURN, Bt), and *d* 29 April 1963, having had issue:

1c *Jane Evelyn [Mrs Richard Micklethwait, Preston Hall, Oakham, Rutland LE15 9NJ]; *b* 1 June 1937; *m* 26 Jan 1961 *Richard Miles Micklethwait, (*see* NORFOLK, D) and has issue

2c Sarah Elizabeth; *b* 4th Nov 1939; *d* as result of a point-to-point accident 15 April 1961

3c *Teresa Anne [Mrs John Wheeler, 73 The Chase, London SW4 0NP]; *b* 26 Sept 1944; *m* 1979 *John Stuart Wheeler (*see* GIBBONS, Bt), and has issue:

1d *Sarah Rose; *b* 1980

2d *Jacquetta Lydia; *b* 1981

3d *Charlotte Mary; *b* 1985

3b John Alfred; *b* 28 Oct 1898; *educ* Harrow and Ch Ch Oxford (MA 1930); Lt-Col Coldstream Gds WW I 1917–18, attd Mil Mission Smyrna 1920, Br Liaison Offr French Forces Syria 1926–29, ADC to C-in-C India 1934–36, attd FO 1939–42, Assist Ch Staff Gibraltar 1942–43, Special Liaison Offr Algiers 1943–44, Greek MC, Cdr Order Phoenix Greece, OStJ; *m* 21 Dec 1936 (*divorce* 1942) Primrose, yr dau of Dr. Vaughan Harley, of Walton Hall, Bletchley, Bucks

1b Mary Adela, OBE (1942), Pres Rutland BRCS; *m* 12 Aug 1931, as his 2nd w, Maj Robert Wentworth Doyne (*d* 25 Sept 1942), of Lois Weedon Ho, Towcester, Northants, and *dsp* 11 July 1961

1a Jane Emily; *m* 13 Sept 1867 Sir Robert Uniacke-Penrose-Fitzgerald, 1st Bt (*dsp* 10 July 1919), of Corkbeg and Lisquinlan, Co Cork, and *d* 27 Oct 1924

2a Mary; *m* 21 July 1864 Maj-Gen William Earle, CB, CSI, and *d* 27 Jan 1928, leaving issue (*see* EARLE, Bt)

(2) Henry John (Sir), KCB, Adml of the Fleet; *b* 17 Oct 1808; *m* 1st 9 April 1849 Helen Jane, dau of C Webb Smith, and had issue:

1a Anne Jane; *m* 12 Jan 1882 13th Earl of Winchilsea and Nottingham (*qv*), and *d* 20 June 1924, leaving issue

2a Ellen; *m* 27 July 1878 Sir John Roche Dasent, CB (*d* 21 Nov 1914), est son of Sir George Webbe Dasent, and *d* 29 March 1924, leaving issue

(2) (cont.) Sir Henry *m* 2nd 9 Oct 1869 Catherine (*d* 4 April 1880), widow of Adml A'Aitchinson, and dau of Henry Combe Compton, of The Manor Ho, Minstead, Hants, and *d* 4 Aug 1877

The est son,

CHRISTOPHER CODRINGTON later BETHELL-CODRINGTON (roy licence 17 Nov 1797), of Dodington; *b* Oct 1764; *m* 16 Aug 1796 Harriet (*d* 1 Jan 1843), dau of 2nd Baron Foley (*qv*), and *d* 4 Feb 1843, leaving, with other issue:

1 CHRISTOPHER WILLIAM

2 Edward, Capt 7th Dragoon Gds; *b* 6 Aug 1813; *m* 15 July 1863 Jane Brown (*d* 13 Feb 1904), dau of William White, and *dsp* 4 Dec 1870

1 Caroline Anna Maria; *m* 3 Jan 1826 Hon Arthur Thellusson (*d* 15 July 1858) and *d* 19 June 1877 aged 79, leaving issue (*see* RENDLESHAM, B)

2 Georgina Elizabeth; *m* 18 April 1828 Sir Henry Peyton, 3rd Bt (*d* 18 Feb 1866; *see* 1959 edn), and *d* 7 Nov 1866 aged 67

3 Charlotte Octavia; *m* 10 Dec 1833 Henry Lannoy Hunter (*d* 23 March 1876), of Beechill, Berks, and *d* 16 Oct 1895, leaving issue

4 Emma; *m* 1 Aug 1843 John Harvey Lovell, and *d* 28 May 1884, leaving issue

The est son,

CHRISTOPHER WILLIAM BETHELL-CODRINGTON, of Dodington, MP E Gloucester; *b* 12 March 1805; *m* 29 Dec 1836 Lady Georgiana Charlotte Anne Somerset, VA (*d* 2 Dec 1884), dau of 7th Duke of Beaufort, KG (*qv*), and *d* 24 June 1864, having had, with other issue:

1 GERALD WILLIAM HENRY, **1st Bt**

2 George John Granville Christopher, Capt and Hon Maj Glos Yeo Cav, with Glam Imp Yeo Boer War 1900 (medal with three clasps), Coronation Medal 1911; *b* 24 Dec 1855; *d* 4 Sept 1932

1 Alice Emily Georgiana Olivia; *m* 27 Aug 1891 Sir Henry Mervyn Vavasour, 3rd Bt (*qv*), and *d* 28 Feb 1920

The est son,

Sir Gerald William Henry Codrington, 1st Bt (UK), so *cr* 25 Feb 1876, JP, High Sheriff 1880, Hon Maj Glos Yeo Cav; *m* 3 Feb 1887 Lady Edith Henrietta Sybil Denison (*d* 6 May 1945), dau of 2nd Baron Londesborough (*qv*), and had:

1 CHRISTOPHER WILLIAM GERALD HENRY (Sir), **2nd Bt**

1 Edith Georgiana Veronica; *b* 15 July 1888; *m* 10 July 1916 Maj Frank Leslie Gilliat (*d* 5 March 1955), Northants Yeo, *s* of Howard Gilliat, JP, of Abbots Ripton Hall, Hants, and had issue

2 Cecilia Grace Adelaide Sybil; *b* 28 Jan 1904; *d* unm 7 May 1923

Sir GERALD *d* 3 Nov 1929; his son,

Sir Christopher William Gerald Henry Codrington, 2nd Bt; *b* 6 Oct 1894; *educ* Uppingham; Capt 19th Hus WW I (wounded), High Sheriff Glos 1938; *m* 1st 3 Dec 1921 Joan Mary (*d* 29 Aug 1961), 2nd dau of Thomas Reginald Hague-Cook, of 46 Portman Sq, London, and had issue:

1 Sir SIMON FRANCIS BETHELL CODRINGTON, **3rd and present Bt**

Sir Christopher *m* 2nd 19 Oct 1963 Henrietta Desirée Moutray (*d* 15 May 1979), dau of Maj Beresford Moutray Read, of Bampton, Tiverton, Devon, and *d* 10 November 1979

COGGAN

Creation: B. (LP, UK) 1980.

THE BARON COGGAN, of Canterbury and Sissinghurst, Co Kent ((Frederick) Donald Coggan, PC (1961)) [The Rt Rev and Rt Hon The Lord Coggan PC, 28 Lions Hall, St Swithun St, Winchester, Hants SO23 9HW]; *b* 9 Oct 1909; *educ* Merchant Taylors', St John's Coll Cambridge (MA 1935), Wycliffe Hall Oxford and Wycliffe Coll Toronto (BD 1941); Assist Lecturer Semitic Lang and Lit Manchester U 1931–34, Curate St Mary's Islington 1934–37, Prof New Testament Wycliffe Coll Toronto 1937–44, Pncpl London Coll Divinity 1944–56, Examining Chaplain to: Bps of Lincoln 1946–56, Manchester 1951–56, Southwark 1954–56, Chester 1955–56; Bp Bradford 1956, Chm Liturgical Commn 1960–64; Preacher Oxford U 1961, Archbp York 1961, Pro-Chllr: York U 1962–74, Hull U 1968–74; Pres Soc Old Testament Studies 1967–68, Prelate OStJ 1967–90 (Sub-Prelate 1960), Archbp Canterbury 1974–80, Chm Coll Preachers and exec ctee Cncl Christians and Jews 1983–87; DD Lambeth 1957, Hon DD: Wycliffe Coll Toronto 1944, Leeds 1958, Cambridge, Hull 1963, Aberdeen 1963, Toyko 1963, Saskatoon 1963, Huron 1963, Manchester 1972, Moravian Theological Seminary 1976, Virginia Theological Seminary 1979; HHD: Westminster Choir Coll and Princeton 1966; Hon DLitt Lancaster 1967, Hon STD General Theological Seminary NY 1967; Hon LLD Liverpool 1972; Hon DCL Kent 1975; D U York 1975; Hon Freeman Canterbury 1976; FKC 1975; Royal Victorian Chain 1980; author: *A People's Heritage* (1944), *The Ministry of the Word* (1945), *The Glory of God* (1950), *Stewards of Grace* (1958), *Five Makers of the New Testament* (1962), *Sinews of Faith* (1969), *Word and World* (1971), *Convictions* (1975), *Paul: Portrait of a Revolutionary* (1984), *The Sacrament of the Word* (1987), *Cuthbert Bardsley: Bishop, Evangelist, Pastor* (1989), *The Voice from the Cross* (1993), *The Servant-Son* (1995), *A New Way for Preaching* (1996), *Meet Paul!* (1997); *m* 1935 *Jean Braithwaite, dau of Dr William Loudon Strain, and has:

1 *Dorothy Ann [The Hon Dorothy Coggan, 1 King Alfred Place, Hyde, Winchester, Hants]; *b* 1938

2 *Ruth Evelyn [The Hon Ruth Coggan, 15 Plough Way, Badger Farm, Winchester, Hants]; *b* 1940

Lineage: CORNISH ARTHUR COGGAN; *m* Fannie Sarah — and had:

(FREDERICK) DONALD, *cr* a **Baron**

COGHILL

Arms: Quarterly, 1st and 4th, ermine a chevron argent, three cocks gules (for COGHILL); 2nd and 3rd, gules on a chevron argent three pellets, a chief indented of the second (for CRAMER). **Crest:** On a mount vert a cock gules, charged on the breast with a bezant. **Motto:** *Non dormit qui custodit* ('He who keeps guard does not sleep'). **Creation:** Bt. (GB) 31 Aug 1778.

SIR EGERTON JAMES BEVILL TOBIAS (TOBY) COGHILL, 8TH BT, of Coghill, Co York, [Sir Toby Coghill Bt, Sourden, Rothes, Moray AB38 7AE]; *b* 26 March 1930; *s* f 1983; *educ* Gordonstoun and Pembroke Coll Cambridge; former headmaster; *m* 12 April 1958 *Gabriel Nancy, est dau of Maj Dudley Claud Douglas Ryder (*see* HARROWBY, E), and has:

1 +PATRICK KENDAL FARLEY [Patrick Coghill Esq, 26 Gowrie Rd, London SW11]; *b* 3 Nov 1960

1 *Elizabeth Louisa Gay; *b* 11 June 1962

Lineage (of Coghill): JOHN COCKHILL of Cockhill, living at Knaresborough, Yorks, *temp* RICHARD II and HENRY IV; ancestor in the 7th generation of:

Sir JOHN COGHILL, of Coghill Hall, W R Yorks, and Drumcondra, Co Dublin, LLD, Master in Chancery Ireland; *m* Hester, dau of Tobias Cramer, of Ballyfoile, Co Kilkenny, and *d* 1699, leaving issue:

1 Marmaduke, PC, LLD, Judge Prerogative Court, Chllr Exchequer, MP U of Dublin; *d* unm 9 March 1738

2 James, LLD; Registrar Prerogative Court; *m* Mary, sis of Thomas Pearson, of Rathmore, Co Meath, and *d* 4 Sept 1734, having had an only dau and heir:

(1) Hester; *m* 1st 13 Oct 1737 Charles Moore, 1st and last Earl of Charleville of the 1758 *cr* (*dsp* 17 Feb 1764); *m* 2nd Maj Sir John MAYNE later COGHILL, 1st and last Bt (*dsp* 14 Nov 1785), so *cr* 24 March 1781, and *dsp* 28 July 1789, leaving her property to her cousin Sir JOHN CRAMER later COGHILL, **1st Bt**

1 Hester Coghill; *m* 15 Nov 1700 Oliver CRAMER, of Ballyfoile (*see* below **Lineage (of Cramer)**), and left, with other issue:

(1) Balthazar John; *m* 23 April 1724/5 Judith (*d* 13 May 1749), dau of 1st Viscount Lanesborough (*see* LANESBOROUGH, E), and *d* 18 June 1741, leaving, with other issue:

1a JOHN (Sir), **1st Bt**

2a Marmaduke (Rev), ancestor of the CRAMER-ROBERTSes of Sallymount, Co Kildare

BALTHAZAR CRAMER's son,

Sir JOHN CRAMER later COGHILL (by 1778), **1st Bt** (GB), so *cr* 31 Aug 1778, of Coghill, Co York; *b* 14 July 1732; MP Belturbet 1754–60, 1761–68 and 1776; *m* 17 Oct 1754 Mary (*d* 14 Dec 1815), dau of Most Rev Josiah Hort, DD, Archbp Tuam, and sis of Sir John Hort, 1st Bt, and *d* 8 March 1790, having had, with other issue:

1 Sir JOHN CRAMER later COGHILL (roy licence 7 June 1807), **2nd Bt**; *b* 2 Feb 1766; *d* unm 21 May 1817

2 JOSIAH COGHILL (Sir), **3rd Bt**

1 Sophia; *m* 1801 Lt-Gen Sir Charles W Doyle, GCH, and had issue (*see* 1970 edn DOYLE, Bt)

The 2nd Bt's bro,

Sir JOSIAH CRAMER later COGHILL (roy licence 7 June 1817), **3rd Bt**, V-Adml; *b* 1773; *m* 1st 31 Aug 1803 Sophia (*d* 1817), dau of John Dodson, and had, with another dau:

1 Emmeline Katherine Egerton; *m* 27 Aug 1839 Rev Charles Bushe (*d* 25 Aug 1866) and *d* 26 Aug 1879, leaving issue

2 Josephine; *m* 1844 George De Morgan (*d* 13 March 1890), and *d* 8 Aug 1905, leaving issue

Sir JOSIAH *m* 2nd 27 Jan 1819 Anna Maria (*d* 8 March 1848), est dau of Rt Hon Charles Kendal Bushe, Ld Ch Justice King's Bench Ireland, and by her had, with other issue:

1 JOHN JOSCELYN (Sir), **4th Bt**

2 Kendal Josiah William, CB (1882), JP Co Cork, Lt-Col 19th Hus; *b* 21 Aug 1832; *d* 16 July 1919

3 Rosanna Louisa; *m* 7 Feb 1849 John Harrison Aylmer, of Walworth Castle, and was *k* with her husb and est son in a railway accident nr Abergele 20 Aug 1868

4 Sydney Katherine; *m* 18 Oct 1854 Rev Samuel Allen Windle (*d* 1880), Vicar Market Rasen, Lincs, and *d* 12 Feb 1910, leaving issue

5 Alicia Elizabeth Judith; *m* 11 Feb 1850 Rev George Henry Ray (*d* 1893), of Heanor Hall, Derbys, and *d* 8 March 1910, leaving issue

6 Anne Georgina; *m* 19 Sept 1860 Rev William Izon Chavasse (*d* 15 Sept 1864), only son of Pye Henry Chavasse, of Priory Ho, Birmingham, and *d* 3 Jan 1899, leaving issue

7 Adelaide Eliza; *m* 29 June 1857 Lt-Col Thomas Henry Somerville (*d* 15 March 1898), DL, of Drishane, Co Cork, and *d* 3 Dec 1895, leaving issue

8 Sylvia Maria; *m* 15 May 1856 Thomas Greene, son of Rt Hon Richard Greene, Baron Exchequer Ireland, and *d* 4 Jan 1907, leaving issue

Sir JOSIAH *d* 20 June 1850; his est son,

Sir John Joscelyn Coghill, 4th Bt, DL, JP, Co Dublin, High Sheriff 1859; *b* 11 Feb 1826; *educ* Rugby; served 59th Regt; *m* 1 Feb 1851 Katherine Frances (*d* 25 Aug 1881), 2nd dau of 3rd Baron Plunket (*qv*), and had, with other issue:

1 Nevill Josiah Aylmer, VC, Lt 24th Foot; *b* 25 Jan 1852; *ka* Zulu War at Isandhlwana (while saving the Colours of his Regt), 22 Jan 1879, *dsp*

2 EGERTON BUSHE (Sir), **5th Bt**

3 Claude Plunkett, JP Meath; *b* 13 Nov 1859; *m* 25 June 1885 Maude Mary (*d* 14 March 1948), dau of Ferdinand McVeagh, of Drewstown, Meath, and *d* 27 Sept 1922, leaving issue:

(1) Joscelyn Kendal Bushe, late Lt 3rd Bn S Wales Borderers; *b* 7 Dec 1893; *m* 21 Nov 1925 Maud Evelyn, 2nd dau of Leslie Phillips Filder, of Crawley, Sussex, and *d* 3 Feb 1959, leaving issue:

1a +John Kendal Plunket, OBE (Civil 1990) [Lt-Col John Coghill OBE, 8 East Meads, Onslow Village, Guildford, Surrey GU2 5SP]; *b* 17 July 1929; *educ* Sherborne and RMA Sandhurst; late Lt-Col RAOC (ret 1976), late Lt S Wales Borderers; *m* 6 Oct 1951 *Diana Mary, yr dau of Frederick Charles Callen, of Mombasa, Kenya, and has issue:

1b *Michèle Mary [Mrs Julian Lyon, 4 East Meads, Onslow Village, Guildford, Surrey GU2 5SP]; *b* 11 June 1957; *m* 1988 *Julian David Sinclair Lyon, 2nd son of Stewart Lyon, of Guildford, and has issue:

1c *Georgina Mary Coghill; *b* 1991

2b *Amanda Patricia [Mrs Stephen Downing, 22 Bowood Rd, London SW11]; *b* 23 May 1960; *m* 1985 *Stephen John Lowcock Downing, and has issue:

1c *Thomas Peter; *b* 1989

1c *Katherine Louise; *b* 1991

3b *Samantha Jane; *b* 7 Feb 1967; *m* 1990 *Peter James Wilken

1a *Sheila Mary [Mrs David Cooper, Pine Trees, 3 Ferguson Ave, Greendale, Harare, Zimbabwe]; *b* 6 Aug 1926; *m* 22 Feb 1952 *David Polwhele Cooper, er son of Dr Daniel Stirling Cooper, of Minehead, Som, and has:

1b *Shaun David Coghill; *b* 10 Aug 1956

1b *Sally Muara Coghill; *b* 9 May 1954

2b *Julie Rosalind Coghill; *b* 7 Aug 1965

3b *Lucinda Jane Coghill; *b* 20 Dec 1966

2a *Muara Ann; *b* 10 May 1928; *m* 23 May 1953 (*divorce* 1964) James Alan Bannerman Kellagher (*d* 21 Aug 1974), 2nd son of George Bannerman Kellagher, of Bude, Cornwall, and has issue:

1b *Richard Brian Bannerman; *b* 10 March 1954

1b *Belinda Jane; *b* 4 June 1955

(1) Elfrida Hester Brooke, LRCS, LRCP, Dr to 1967, Assist MOH Eastbourne, Assist Schools MO Cornwall CC 1940–45

(2) Ethel Maude Wynch; *d* unm 27 Feb 1956

1 Ethel Charlotte; *m* 30 Dec 1880 James Edward Penrose, MVO, JP (*d* 27 Sept 1936), of Alton Lodge, Hartley Wintney, Basingstoke, formerly of Wood Hill, Co Cork, and *d* 1 June 1938, leaving issue

2 Violet Alice Penrose, MB, ChB Edin; *d* unm 14 Feb 1951

The 4th Bt *d* 29 Nov 1905; his est son,

Sir Egerton Bushe Coghill, 5th Bt, DL, JP, Co Cork; *b* 7 Feb 1853; landscape painter (studied Barbizon Sch, Paris); *m* 11 July 1893 his cousin Elizabeth Hildegarde Augusta (*d* 6 March 1954), yr dau of Lt-Col Thomas Henry Somerville, DL, of Drishane, Co Cork, and *d* 9 Oct 1921, leaving issue:

1 **Sir (Marmaduke Nevill) Patrick Somerville Coghill, 6th Bt**, TD, DL (Herts 1942); *b* 18 March 1896; *educ* Hailbury; Lt-Col RA (TA) WW I 1916–18 Flanders (two medals), WW II (despatches twice); Spec Serv Offr Turkey and Iraq 1919–25; cmded Herts Yeo 1939–41; Col Arab Legion Jordan 1952–56; OStJ 1957, Order of Istiqlal Jordon 2nd Cl 1956; *d* unm 6 June 1983

2 Nevill Henry Kendal Aylmer; *b* 19 April 1899; *educ* Haileybury and Exeter Coll Oxford (BA 1922, MA 1925, Fell 1925–67), late Lt RFA, served WW I 1917–19, Merton Prof of English Lit, Oxford 1957–66, Chaucerian scholar, edited various Chaucer editions, co-adaptor of *The Canterbury Tales* for the stage; *m* 24 March 1927 (*divorce* 1933) Elspeth Nora, dau of Richard James Harley, of Ochterlony, Guthrie, Forfar, and had issue:

(1) *Rosemary Caroline; *b* 25 July 1928

3 JOCELYN AMBROSE CRAMER, **7th Bt**

1 Katherine Adelaide Hildegarde; *b* 5 May 1906; WW II in WAAF; *m* 19 Jan 1944 Maj Terence Greer Johnston (*d* 18 Oct 1972), son of Frederick William Johnston, of Raheen Ho, Spa, Ballynahinch; *d* 19–

The 6th Bt's bro,

Sir Joscelyn Ambrose Cramer Coghill, 7th Bt; *b* 30 Sept 1902; *educ* Haileybury; E African CS, 2nd Lt S Wales Borderers, WW II as Lt-Cdr RNVR, Admin Offr UN (London Office) 1945–46, Ch Sec Allied Secretariat CCG Berlin 1947–50; *m* 1st 7 Aug 1926 (*divorce*1949) Elizabeth Gwendoline (*d* 1980), er dau of John Black Atkins, of 3 Burford Lodge, Elstead, and had:

1 Sir (EGERTON JAMES BEVILL) TOBIAS COGHILL, **8th and present Bt**

1 *Faith Patricia Elizabeth [Mrs James Garson, Hill Farm, Elsfield, Oxford OX3 9SW]; *b* 13 July 1928; *m* 21 April 1955 *James Leslie Garson, son of Herbert Leslie Garson, of Blakeway, Allport Rd, Bromborough, Wirral, Cheshire, and has issue:

(1) *Jeremy James; *b* 6 June 1961

(1) *Elizabeth Lucy; *b* 28 April 1956

(2) *Rachel Margaret; *b* 10 Jan 1958; *m* 4 Sept 1982 *Michael Dickinson and has:

1a *Samuel Caradoc; *b* 17 March 1985

1a *Hannah Beatrice; *b* 4 June 1987

2a *Phoebe Rose; *b* 1990

3a *Eleanor Grace (twin); *b* 1990

(3) *(Isobel) Laura; *b* 23 Aug 1968; *m* 1992 *Tobias Andrew Baxter and has:

1a *Joshua James; *b* 1994

2a *Izaac Jeremy; *b* 1996

Sir Joscelyn *m* 2nd 4 July 1949 *Louise Fernande, dau of Col Gaston Berdonneau, of Paris, and *d* 6 June 1983, having by her had:

2 Christopher Michael Jerome; *b* 4 Sept 1950; *d* 6 Jan 1951

2 *Bridget Olivia Françoise; *b* 15 June 1949; by *Derek Holt has:

(1) *Lewis COGHILL; *b* 1 Nov 1986

(1) *Gwen COGHILL; *b* 23 June 1989

3 Jocelyn Edith Louise; *b* 24 March 1952; *m* 8 Jan 1972 *Stephen George Thomas [Stephen Thomas Esq, 135 Sommerville Rd, Ashley Down, Bristol] and *d* 9 Oct 1983, leaving:

(1) *Daniel; *b* 24 Oct 1975

(2) *Luke; *b* 26 Feb 1977

(3) *Oliver; *b* 27 April 1980

4 *Deborah Katherine Hildegrade [Mrs Alan Nye, 35 Nevil Rd, Bishopston, Bristol]; *b* 14 Oct 1954; *m* 1987 *Alan Nye and has:

(1) *Alistair William James; *b* 1989

(1) *Lucy Elizabeth Katherine; *b* 1991

Sir Joscelyn also adopted:

*Isabelle Edith; *b* 4 Jan 1945; *m* 27 June 1964 *Nicholas Rodney Carpenter and has issue

Lineage (of Cramer): Col TOBIAS KRAMER, of Lower Germany; made a free denizen of Ireland 28 May 1639; had issue:

BALTHAZER CRAMER; *d* on or after 9 Dec 1650, having had:

TOBIAS CRAMER; served under OLIVER CROMWELL; granted lands of Ballyfoile, Co Kilkenny; Sheriff Dublin 1653, *d* 1655, leaving:

BALTHAZER CRAMER, of Ballyfoile; High Sheriff Co Kilkenny 1683; *b* 1644; *m* 1st Elizabeth (*dsp*), widow of Hugh Drysdale; *m* 2nd Sarah, dau of Cl Oliver Jones, and had:

OLIVER CRAMER, of Ballyfolle; *m* Hester Coghill (*see* above)

COLERAINE

Arms: Argent a saltire azure between four cocks proper. **Crest:** Issuant from a chaplet of maple leaves vert a demi-salmon proper. **Supporters:** Dexter, a Basenji dog; sinister, a kid, both proper. **Motto:** *Lex tua meditatio mea* ('Thy law my thought'). **Creation:** B. (UK) 16 Feb 1954.

THE 2ND BARON COLERAINE, of Haltemprice, E Riding, Co Yorks (James Martin Bonar Law) [The Rt Hon The Lord Coleraine, 5 Kensington Park Gdns, London W11 3HB]; *b* 8 Aug 1931; *s f* 1980; *educ* Eton and Trin Coll Oxford; slr 1958; *m* 1st 30 April 1958 (*divorce* 1966) Emma Elizabeth, only dau of Nigel Richards and Mrs Herbert Copeland Cary Batten, of Aldon, Yeovil, Somerset, and has issue:

1 *Elizabeth Mary; *b* 4 Feb 1961; *m* 1985 *Hon Charles Edmund Grenville Ironside, only son of 2nd Baron Ironside (*qv*)

2 *Sophia Anne; *b* 12 July 1964

The 2nd BARON *m* 2nd 31 Aug 1966 (Anne) Patricia (accidently drowned in Portugal 1993), yr dau of Maj-Gen Ralph Henry Farrant, CB, of King's Acre, Wareham, Dorset, and by her has:

1 +JAMES PETER BONAR; *b* 23 Feb 1975; *educ* Eton

3 Henrietta Margaret; *b* 17 Nov 1968; accidently drowned in Portugal 1993

4 *Juliana Caroline Matilda; *b* 19 June 1971

Lineage: Rev JAMES LAW, MA, of New Brunswick; *m* Eliza, dau of William Kidston, of Glasgow, and had issue:

ANDREW BONAR LAW, PC, LLD; *b* 16 Sept 1858; *educ* High Sch Glasgow; MP (U) Glasgow Blackfriars 1900–06, Dulwich 1906–10, Bootle 1911–18 and Glasgow Centl 1918–23, Ldr Opposition 1911–15, Colonial Sec 1915–16, Chllr Exchequer 1916–18, Ld Privy Seal 1919–21, Plen Peace Conference, Ldr H of C 1916–21, Memb War Cabinet 1916–19, Ldr Unionist Party 1911–21, PM and First Ld Treasury 1922–23; *m* 1891 Annie Pitcairn (*d* 1909), dau of Harrington Robley, of Glasgow, and *d* 30 Oct 1923, leaving issue:

1 RICHARD KIDSTON, **1st Baron**

2 Harrington; Cdr RN; *d* 31 May 1958

1 Isabel Harrington; Kalsar-i-Hind Medal; *m* 3 June 1920 Maj-Gen Sir Frederick Hugh Sykes, PC, GCSI, GCIE, GBE, KCB, CMG (*d* 30 Sept 1954), son of Henry Sykes, of Addiscombe, and *d* 30 Nov 1969, leaving issue

2 Catherine; *m* 1st 1926 (*divorce* 1941) Kent Colwell, and had issue; *m* 2nd 15 Nov 1961 1st Baron Archibald, CBE (*see* 1970 edn)

The Rt Hon ANDREW BONAR LAW's est son,

RICHARD KIDSTON LAW, **1st Baron Coleraine**, of Haltemprice, E Riding, Co York (UK), so *cr* 16 Feb 1954, PC (1943); *b* 27 Feb 1901; *educ* Shrewsbury and St John's Coll Oxford (BA 1923, MA 1945); MP (C) Hull SW Oct 1931–June 1945, S Kensington Nov 1945–Feb 1950, Hull Haltemprice Feb 1950–Jan 1954, Fin Sec War Office 1940–41, Parly U-Sec FO 1941–43, Min State FO 1943–45, Min Educn 1945, Ldr UK Delegn Hot Springs Conference on Food and Ag 1943; memb MRC 1936–40 and Industl Health Research Bd 1936–40; chm Cncl of Br Socs for Relief Abroad 1945, Hon LLD New Bunswick 1951; *m* 26 Jan 1929 Mary Virginia (*d* 3 April 1978), dau of Abram Fox Nellis, of Rochester, NY, and *d* 1980, having had issue:

1 (JAMES) MARTIN BONAR LAW, **2nd and present Baron Coleraine**

2 +Andrew [The Hon Andrew Law, Shankhill Castle, Shankhill, Co Dublin, Ireland]; *b* 27 July 1933; *educ* Rugby and Trin Coll Dublin; *m* 11 March 1961 *Joanna Margarette, er dau of Raymond Neill, of Fairview, Delgany, Co Wicklow, and has issue:

(1) +Richard Pitcairn Bonar; *b* 19 Feb 1963; *educ* Clifton

(1) *Charlotte Mary de Montmorency; *b* 2 April 1964

COLERIDGE

Arms: Argent on a mount vert, in base an otter proper; a chief gules charged with a dove of the first between two crosses patée fitchée or. **Crest:** On a mount vert, therefrom issuing ears of wheat proper, in front of a cross gules, an otter also proper. **Supporters:** Dexter, an otter proper; sinister, a lion sable, each gorged with a garland of roses gules, leaved vert. **Motto:** *Qualis vita finis ita* ('As life so the end'). **Creation:** B. (UK) 10 Jan 1874.

THE 5TH BARON COLERIDGE OF OTTERY ST MARY, Devon (William Duke Coleridge) [The Rt Hon The Lord Coleridge, The Chanter's House, Ottery St Mary, Devon EX11 1DQ]; *b* 18 June 1937; *s f* 1984; *educ* Eton and RMA Sandhurst; Maj Coldstream Gds (ret 1977), served King's African Rifles and Kenya Army 1961–63, cmded Guards Independent Parachute Co 1970–72; *m* 1st 17 Feb 1962 (*divorce* 1977) Everild Tania (Judy), only dau of Lt-Col Beauchamp Hambrough, OBE, of Wispers Farm, Box 1543, Nairobi, and has issue:

1 +JAMES DUKE; *b* 5 June 1967

1 *Tania Rosamund; *b* 22 Jan 1966

2 *Sophia Tamsin *b* 9 Nov 1970

The 5th BARON *m* 2nd 1977 *Pamela, dau of George William Baker, CBE, VRD, and has further issue:

3 *Vanessa Leyla; *b* 1978

4 *Katharine Suzannah; *b* 1981

Lineage: Rev JOHN COLERIDGE, Vicar of Ottery St Mary (son of John Coleridge, of Crediton); *b* 21 Jan 1719; *m* 1st 24 May 1743 Mary Lendon (*d* 1753) and had three daus; *m* 2nd Anne (*d* 1809), dau of Roger Bowden, and *d* 1781, having by her had, with other issue:

1 JAMES

2 Edward (Rev), of Ottery St Mary; *m* 1st Elizabeth Wagg (*dsp*); *m* 2nd 18 Aug 1802 Anne, dau of Robert Bowden, and had a son (*dsp*) and dau (*d* unm)

3 George (Rev), Master GS at Ottery; *m* Jenny, dau of Richard Hart, of Exeter, and *d* 12 Jan 1828, leaving a son (*d* unm)

4 Luke Herman, of Thorverton, Devon, surgeon; *b* 18 Oct 1765; *m* Sarah, dau of Richard Hart, of Exeter, and *d* 1790, leaving an only son:

(1) William Hart (Rt Rev), DD, Bp Barbados; *b* 27 June 1789; *m* 11 Oct 1825 Sara Eliza (*d* 29 Aug 1869), dau of Very Rev Thomas Rennell, Dean Winchester, and *d* 20 Dec 1849, leaving an only son:

1a William Rennell, of Salston Ho, Devon, DL, JP, Maj Devon Mil; *b* 1833; *m* 9 Aug 1855 Katherine Frances (*d* 15 Oct 1903), only surv dau of Capt Robert Cutts Barton, RN, and *d* 19 Jan 1904, leaving, with other issue:

1b Rennell, of Salston, Ottery St Mary; *b* 29 Jan 1858; High Sheriff 1925, BA Oxford, barrister Inner Temple, Maj 4th Bn Devonshire Regt (TD), Roy 1st Devon Yeo; *m* 17 June 1891 Ellen Gertrude OBE (*d* 22 July 1944), only child of Frederick Swabey, of 69 Pont St, London, and *d* 15 Oct 1934, having had issue:

1c Luke Frederick Rennell, 2nd Lt Coldstream Gds (SR); *b* 20 Nov 1892; *ka* 22 Dec 1914

(2) Derek William Rennell; *b* 14 Feb 1894; *d* unm 29 June 1972

1c Betty Christabel Gertrude; *b* 11 Nov 1895; *m* 19 July 1922 (*divorce* 1942) Sir Edward Charles Cave, 3rd Bt (*qv*), and had issue

1b Mary Rennell, OBE (1920); *m* 24 April 1878 Col Sir Edward Thomas D'Avenant Cotton Jodrell, KCB (*d* 13 Oct 1917), and *d* 18 April 1932, leaving issue (*see* COMBERMERE, V)

2b Marion; *m* 27 Dec 1888 Arthur Melville Hood Walrond (*d* 21 June 1946), and *d* 25 May 1922, leaving issue

5 Samuel Taylor, the poet; *b* 20 Oct 1772; *m* Aug 1795 Sarah (*d* 24 Sept 1845), dau of Stephen Fricker, a sis of Mrs Southey, and *d* 25 July 1834, leaving issue:

(1) Hartley, author; *d* 6 Jan 1849

(2) Derwent (Rev), MA, Preb St Paul's; *b* 14 Sept 1800; *m* 6 Dec 1827 Mary Simpson (*d* 11 Sept 1887), est dau of John Drake Pridham, of Plymouth, and *d* 28 March 1883, having had, with other issue:

1a Ernest Hartley; *b* 8 Dec 1846; *m* 20 April 1876 Sarah Mary (*d* 3 Feb 1917), dau of William Bradford, and *d* 19 Feb 1920, leaving issue

(1) Sara; *b* 1803; *m* 3 Sept 1829 her cousin Henry Nelson Coleridge (*see* below), and *d* 3 May 1852, leaving issue

The est surv son,

JAMES COLERIDGE, of The Chanter's Ho, Ottery St Mary, JP; *b* 3 Dec 1759; Capt 6th Foot, Lt-Col E Devon local militia in 1809; *m* 28 Feb 1788 Frances (*d* 5 Aug 1838), dau of Bernard Frederick Taylor and coheir of Robert Duke, of Otterton, and *d* 10 Jan 1836, leaving issue:

1 James Duke (Rev), DCL, Preb Exeter; *b* 13 June 1789; *m* 9 June 1814 Sophia, dau of Col Stanhope Badcock, and *d* 26 Dec 1857, leaving two daus

2 JOHN TAYLOR (Sir)

3 Francis George; *b* 25 Dec 1794; *m* Harriet, dau of Thomas Norris, and *d* 26 Aug 1854, leaving issue

4 Henry Nelson; *b* 25 Oct 1798; *m* 3 Sept 1829 his cousin Sara (*d* 3 May 1852), dau of S T Coleridge, and *d* 26 Jan 1843, having had two sons and three daus

5 Edward (Rev), Vicar Mapledurham, Oxon, Fell Eton; *b* 11 May 1800; *m* 1st 3 Aug 1826 Mary (*d* 10 Dec 1859), dau of Rev John Keate, DD, and had four sons and a dau; *m* 2nd 4 Sept 1862 Mary Caroline (*d* 5 March 1907), dau of Rev George Jones Bevan, and *d* 18 May 1883 aged 83

1 Frances Duke; *m* Rt Hon Sir John Patteson (*d* 28 June 1861) and had three sons and two daus

Capt COLERIDGE's 2nd son,

Sir JOHN TAYLOR COLERIDGE, of The Chanter's Ho, Ottery St Mary, PC, MA, DCL; *b* 9 July 1790; Recorder Exeter, Judge Queen's Bench, Serjeant-at-law; *m* 7 Aug 1818 Mary, 2nd dau of Rev Gilbert Buchanan, DD, and *d* 11 Feb 1876, having had, with other issue:

1 JOHN DUKE, **1st Baron**

2 Henry James (Rev), RC priest, SJ, DD; *b* 20 Sept 1822; *d* 13 April 1893

1 Alethea Buchanan; *m* 7 Aug 1849 Rt Rev John Fielder Mackarness, DD, Bp Oxford (*d* Sept 1889), and *d* 30 March 1909, leaving issue

The est son,

JOHN DUKE COLERIDGE, **1st Baron Coleridge of Ottery St Mary**, Devon (UK), so *cr* 10 Jan 1874, PC (1873), QC (1861); *b* 3 Dec 1820; *educ* Eton and Balliol Coll Oxford; Fell Exeter Coll Oxford 1843–46, barrister Middle Temple 1846 (Bencher 1861), Recorder of Portsmouth 1855–66, MP (Lib) Exeter 1865–73, Slr-Gen 1868–71, Attorney-Gen 1871–73, Ld Ch Justice Common Pleas 1873–80 and Ld Ch Justice 1880–94, DCL Oxon 1877, FRS 1877; *m* 1st 11 Aug 1846 Jane Fortescue (*d* 6 Feb 1878), dau of Rev George Turner Seymour, of Farringford, IoW; *m* 2nd 13 Aug 1885 Amy Augusta Jackson (*d* 27 May 1933), dau of Henry Baring Lawford, Bengal CS, and by 1st *w* had issue:

1 BERNARD JOHN SEYMOUR, **2nd Baron**

2 Stephen William Buchanan, barrister, Clerk of Assize S Wales Circuit; *b* 1854; *educ* Trin Coll Cambridge (MA); *m* 1st 5 April 1879 Geraldine Beatrice (*d* 10 May 1910), dau and coheir of Charles Manners Lushington, of Norton Court, Kent, and niece of 1st Earl of Iddesleigh (*qv*); *m* 2nd 8 July 1911 Susan (*d* 18 April 1960), 2nd dau of Allan Duncan Stewart, of Inverhadden and Bun Rannoch, Perthshire, and *d* 10 April 1936, having by his 1st *w* had issue:

(1) John Duke, FRIBA, Lt RNVR WW I; *b* 10 Nov 1879; *m* 11 June 1904 Hon Katharine Euphemia Godley (*d* 25 Sept 1941), yst dau of 1st Baron Kilbracken (*qv*), and *d* 9 Sept 1934, leaving issue:

1a Peter Duke, V-Consul Göteborg, Sweden; *b* 27 April 1905; *educ* Rugby and Trin Coll Oxford (MA); *m* 8 Aug 1936 (*divorce* 1953) Sigrid, dau of Paulus Stahl-Christensen, of Göteborg, and *d* 11 Sept 1958, leaving issue:

1b +John Duke [John Coleridge, 11644 N 52nd St, Scottsdale, Arizona 85254, USA]; *b* 9 Jan 1940; *educ* Sigtuna and U of Göteborg Medical Sch; *m* 16 Nov 1963 *Carin Eva Christina, dau of Karl Olof Lennart Cassmark, of Löten, Varnhem, and has issue:

1c +Peter John; *b* 8 Aug 1966; attorney; *m* 1994 *Rosemary Kathleen, dau of Harvey Widroe, MD, of Orinda, Calif. and has:

1d +Samuel John; *b* 4 March 1997

1c *Christina; *b* 15 Aug 1964

2c *Malin Charlotta; *b* 19 Jan 1970

2a Arthur Nicholas, barrister Middle Temple 1939, Capt Irish Gds WW II; *b* 19 Nov 1915; *educ* Rugby and New Coll Oxford (BA 1937, MA); *m* 20 Sept 1941 *Lady (Marguerite) Georgina Hay [The Lady Georgina Coleridge, 33 Peel St, London W8 7PA], writer, 2nd dau of 11th Marquess of Tweeddale (*qv*), and *d* 1988, leaving issue:

1b *Frances Marguerite Katharine [Mrs Neil Smith, Park Hill, Appledore, Kent]; *b* 11 May 1943; *m* 7 April 1964 *Neil Lindsay Vaughan Smith, er son of Donald Neil Vaughan Smith, of Little Court, Buntingford, Herts, and has issue:

1c *Julian Arthur Vaughan; *b* 7 Feb 1969; *m* 1994 *Suzanne Hearne

1c *Candida Louise Vaughan; *b* 8 Oct 1967; *m* 1992 *Robert Lindsay Machin and has:

1d *Miles Robert Arthur; *b* 13 April 1996

1d *Tabitha Eleanor Frances; *b* 6 May 1994

1a Nancy Katharine; *b* 22 Jan 1907; *m* 27 Oct 1928 Maj-Gen (Reginald) Llewellyn Brown, CB, CBE, MA, FRGS, FRICS (*d* 1983), son of Col Francis David Millett Brown, VC, 101st Roy (Munster) Fus, and *d* 1989, leaving:

1b *David Arthur Llewellyn [David Brown Esq, Guston, Chelwood Gate, Sussex RH17 7LP]; *b* 19 Nov 1929; *educ* Wellington, New Coll Oxford (MA), King's Coll Cambridge and Imp Coll of Tropical Ag (DTA); FRGS; *m* 10 July 1954 *Priscilla Mary, dau of Rev George Day, of Headington, Oxford, and has issue:

1c *Alexander Edmund Llewellyn; *b* 13 March 1956

2c *Richard Arthur Llewellyn; *b* 23 April 1957

3c *William David Llewellyn; *b* 22 April 1959

(2) Guy Lushington, FRGS, Capt RN WW I, barrister Middle Temple 1919, Order of St Anne of Russia; *b* 15 April 1884; *m* 22 Jan 1910 (Hester Christabel) Margaret (*d* 30 Sept 1969), only dau of Rev Richard Henry Dickson, Rector of Eastchurch, Sheerness, and *das* 28 Oct 1941, leaving issue:

1a Geraldine Margaret Joan; *b* 24 April 1911; *m* 1st 24 April 1929 (*divorce* 1946) Capt Cyril Aubrey Hamilton Brooking, CBE, RN (*d* 29 Nov 1961), son of Arthur Holdsworth Brooking, and had issue:

1b *Patrick Guy [Patrick Brooking Esq, Little Langley, Chobham, Surrey], Maj 5th Roy Inniskilling Dragoon Gds; *b* 4 April 1937; *educ* Charterhouse; *m* 11 April 1964 *Pamela Mary, yr dau of Lt-Col John Erskine Scott Walford, MBE, of Earls Court, and has:

1c *Jonathan Guy; *b* 13 Dec 1967

1c *Samantha Sara; *b* 11 March 1965

1b Sara Ann; *b* 14 Oct 1934; *d* 7 June 1953

1a (cont.) Mrs Geraldine Brooking *m* 2nd 26 Aug 1947 Maj-Gen (Percival) Napier White, CB, CBE, son of Alfred John White, of Norton, Worcs, and by him has:

2b *John Napier; *b* 7 June 1949; *educ* Winchester

3b *Robert James; *b* 29 Sept 1952; *educ* Charterhouse

(3) Paul Humphrey, MC, FRIBA, Capt 16th Bn Sherwood Foresters, served WW I (wounded) and WW II; *b* 17 Feb 1888; *m* 27 June 1914 Margaret Frances (*d* 6 Sept 1964), 2nd dau of George Campbell Giffard, JP, of Bulkeley Ho, Englefield Green, Berks, and *d* 23 May 1955, having had issue:

1a +Antony Duke [Antony Coleridge Esq, Ottery, Harwood Rd, Marlow, Bucks SL7 2AR]; *b* 18 June 1915; *educ* Stowe; Capt Queen's Bays WW II (despatches); *m* 1st 4 July 1942 (*annulled* 1946) Kathleen Crozier, yst dau of Herbert Taylor; *m* 2nd 26 April 1947 *June Marian, 2nd dau of George Frederick Charles Caswell, of Barnes, Surrey, and has had:

1b Jeremy Charles Duke; *b* 5 Nov 1949; *d* 8 Feb 1955

2b +Nicholas Antony; *b* 11 Nov 1955; *educ* Bedford Coll; *m* 1983 *Gayl June, yr dau of Clive O J Grove-Palmer, of Oxford, and has issue:

1c +Matthew Oliver Duke; *b* 1984

1c *Laura Claire May; *b* 1986

3b +David George; *b* 22 June 1957; *m* 1981 *Naomi Jean, 2nd dau of Dr Harry Vere White, of Gosforth, Northumberland, and has:

1c *Katherine Natasha; *b* 1989

2c *Hannah Lucy; *b* 1991

3c *Emily Claire; *b* 2 July 1994

1b *Geraldine Margaret [Mrs David Leeming, 113 Calabria Rd, London N5 1HS]; *b* 25 May 1948; ptnr Rogers Coleridge and White, Literary Agency 1988–; pres Assoc of Authors' Agents 1988–91; *m* 1974 *David Roger Leeming and has:

1c *Robert Antony Dundas; *b* 1978

2c *Toby Alexander David; *b* 1981

2a James Bernard; *b* 9 May 1919; *educ* Charterhouse and King's Coll Cambridge; Maj Roy Signals WW II; *m* 30 March 1946 *Jane Eveline [Mrs James Coleridge, 85 Erpingham Rd, London SW15], dau of Campbell Walter Giffard, of St John's Wood, by his 1st *w* Ethel Miriam, dau of Felix Albu (*see* ALBU, Bt), and *d* 1991, leaving:

1b +Paul James Duke, QC (1993); *b* 30 May 1949; *educ* Cranleigh and Coll of Law London; barrister Middle Temple 1970; *m* 1973 *Judith Elizabeth (Lisa), dau of H T Rossiter, of Ringwood, Hants, and has:

1c +William Paul Hugh Duke; *b* 5 July 1976

2c +Edward James; *b* 1980

1c *Alice Evelina; *b* 19 Sept 1974

1b *Susan Margaret Ethel [Mrs Peter Cunard, Ivy Lodge, London Rd, Woburn, Beds]; *b* 24 May 1947; *m* 1970 *Peter John Cunard and has:

1c *Nicholas Peter; *b* 1971

2c *Sebastian James; *b* 1972

1c *Catherine Jane; *b* 1976

2b *Lucy Veronica; *b* 1 July 1954; *m* 1977 *Stuart John Selleck, and has issue:

1c *Samuel George; *b* 1978

2c *Leo James; *b* 1986

1c *Georgina Jane; *b* 1980

3a Francis Stephen, DSC; *b* 30 Dec 1920; *educ* Charterhouse; Lt RNVR WW II; *m* 1st 24 July 1948 (*divorce* 1973) Jane Dealtry, 3rd dau of Maj George Arthur Howson, MC, of The Hyde, Hambleden, Bucks; *m* 2nd 1980 *$IColeridge, Jean Roberts Jean Roberts McFadyean Mrs [Mrs Francis Coleridge, Sontut, Camino de San Vicente, Pollensa, Mallorca, Spain], and *d* 1992, having by his 1st *w* had issue:

1b +Stephen John [Stephen Coleridge Esq, Cherry Tree Pottery, Common Rd, Headley, Newbury, Berks]; *b* 30 Aug 1953

1b *Harriet Sibell; *b* 25 Sept 1959; *m* 1st 1988 (*divorce* 1994) Martin F Wright; *m* 2nd 1994 *Alexander Victor Akoulitchev

4a Paul Michael; *b* 30 June, *d* 19 Dec 1923

1a Helen Bridget; *b* 19 March, *d* 29 April 1928

3 Gilbert James Duke, JP (Surrey); *b* 15 Feb 1859; *educ* Eton and Trin Coll Oxford (MA); barrister Middle Temple 1886, Assist Master in Crown Office Dept of the Supreme Court 1892–1921, author: *An Instinctive Criminal*, *Eton in the 'Seventies*, etc; poet and sculptor, exhibited RA; v-pres: RBA Arts Club and Modern Churchmen's Union; *m* 1st 24 Oct 1888 Annie Marion (*d* 1 Dec 1917), dau of Duncan Darroch, of Gourock, and Torridon; *m* 2nd 30 April 1921 Marguerite Winifred Pierpoint (*d* 14 July 1964), only dau of Pierpoint Mitchell, of Gateways, Beaconsfield, and *d* 6 Nov 1953, having by 1st *w* had issue:

(1) Wilfred Duke, barrister Middle Temple 1914, Ch Clerk of Arraigns Centl Criminal Court 1949–56, Capt 7th Bn London Regt WW I; *b* 6 Oct 1889; *m* 22 Sept 1923 Frances Mary Farie (*d* 17 Feb 1964), dau of Thomas Walker, of Saltburn, Yorks, and *dsp* 31 May 1956

1 Mildred Mary; *m* 24 June 1885 Charles Warren Adams, and *d* 14 Jan 1929. He *d* 31 July 1903

The 1st BARON *d* 14 June 1894; his est son,

BERNARD JOHN SEYMOUR COLERIDGE, **2nd Baron Coleridge**, JP (Devon), QC (1892); *b* 19 Aug 1851; *educ* Eton and Trin Coll Oxford (MA 1877, Hon Fell 1910); barrister 1877 Middle Temple (Bencher 1894, Treas 1918), High Court Judge 1907–23, MP (Lib) Sheffield Attercliffe 1885–94, chm: Devon QS and Conciliation Bd for Coal Trade of the Federated Districts 1912–18; *m* 3 Aug 1876 Mary Alethea (*d* 2 April 1940), est dau of Rt Rev John Fielder Mackarness, DD, Bp Oxford, and had issue:

1 GEOFFREY DUKE, **3rd Baron**

1 Audrey Jane; *b* 4 Oct 1878; *d* 22 Aug 1922

2 Phyllis Mary; *b* 11 May 1883; *d* unm 26 Dec 1950

The 2nd BARON *d* 24 Sept 1927; his son,

GEOFFREY DUKE COLERIDGE, **3rd Baron Coleridge**, JP (Devon 1929); *b* 23 July 1877; *educ* Eton and Trin Coll Oxford (BA 1900); Capt Devonshire Regt; *m* 14 Sept 1904 Jessie Alethea (*d* 25 April 1957), yst dau of George Evelyn Mackarness, of Lahard, Co Cavan, and had issue:

1 RICHARD DUKE, **4th Baron**

2 John Seymour Duke; *b* 1 Oct 1908; *m* 8 Sept 1934 *Dora Lovelace, dau of George Coplestone Carter

3 (Ronald) James Duke; *b* 12 June 1911; *m* 9 Jan 1937 Ursula Mary (*d* 1987), only child of Rev William Turner Long, of Cheltenham, and *d* 1972, leaving issue:

(1) +Syndercombe James Duke; *b* 21 May 1941; *educ* King's Sch Worcester and RNC Dartmouth; Lt RN (ret), Flag-Lt to Cdre-in-Charge Hong Kong 1965; *m* 1st 12 Dec 1964 (*divorce* 1969) Barbara Jane, only dau of Frank Lionel Dawson, of Rio de Janeiro, and has:

1a *Christina Joanne; *b* 1965

(1) (cont.) Syndercombe Coleridge *m* 2nd 1969 (*divorce* 1972) Deborah Coburn, dau of Rev Marcus Brown Hall, of Vermont, USA; *m* 3rd 1977 *Susan Elizabeth, only dau of Derrick Vernon Littlejohn, of St Alban's Mansions, London W8, and by her has issue:

1a +Robert James Duke; *b* 1979

2a +Nicholas John; *b* 1981

(1) *Sara Louise Sydney; *b* 15 Feb 1945; *m* 1st 11 July 1964 Alexander Arthur Luttrell Reid, PhD, only son of Capt Philip Reid, OBE, RN, of Greenhill, Thorncombe, Chard, Som; *m* 2nd 1988 *Alexander Milne, and by 1st husb has issue:

1a *Anna Louise; *b* 1965

2a *Katharine Louise; *b* 13 April 1967

The 3rd BARON *d* 27 March 1955; his est son

RICHARD DUKE COLERIDGE, **4th Baron Coleridge**, KBE (1971, CBE 1951 (OBE 1944), DL (Devon 1973), Capt RN; *b* 24 Sept 1905; *educ* RNCs Osborne and Dartmouth; served WW II, War Cabinet Office 1940–41, Jt Staff Mission Washington 1941, Dep Sec to Br Jt Staff and Combined Chiefs of Staff 1942–45, UK Sec Mil Staff Ctee of UN 1946–48, Sec to Br Jt Services Mission Washington 1948, Ch Staff Offr to Marshal of RAF Lord Tedder, Chm of Br Chiefs of Staff Ctee and Br Rep on Standing Gp NATO 1950–51, Exec Sec NATO and Sec N Atlantic Cncl; US Legion of Merit 1945, chm: Devon and Exeter Savings Bank 1971–75, TSB 1975–84; *m* 28 Aug 1936 (Cecilia) Rosamund (*d* 1991), er dau of Adml Sir William Wordsworth Fisher, GCB, GCVO, and *d* 1984, having had issue:

1 WILLIAM DUKE COLERIDGE, **5th and present Baron Coleridge**

2 +Samuel John Taylor [The Hon Samuel Coleridge, 43 Vogesenstrasse, 7570 Baden-Baden, Germany]; *b* 5 Feb 1942; *educ* Winchester and Trin Coll Oxford; Brig Gren Gds, attd Army Air Corps 1964–68, Mil Attaché Algiers and Tunis 1985–88; *m* 25 April 1973 *Patricia Susan, yr dau of J B Edwards, CBE, of Cradley, nr Malvern, Worcs, and has issue

(1) *Jessica Alice Seymour; *b* 24 March 1974

(1) *Clara Emily Taylor *b* 21 Jan 1976

COLFOX

Arms: Sable, three spinning-cogs erect and in fess or, on a chief argent as many fox-heads couped at the neck gules. **Crest:** A fox proper, charged on the body with two fleur-de-lys in fess sable and resting the sinister paw on a fleur-de-lys in fess sable. **Motto:** *Lux, lex, libertas* ('Light, law, liberty'). **Creation:** Bt. (UK) 4 July 1939.

SIR (WILLIAM) JOHN COLFOX, 2ND BT, of Symondsbury, Co Dorset, JP (Dorset 1962), DL (Dorset 1977) [Sir John Colfox Bt JP DL, Symondsbury House, Bridport, Dorset DT6 6HB]; *b* 25 April 1924; *s f* 1966; *educ* Eton; Lt RNVR WW II, Qualified Land Agent 1950, High Sheriff Dorset 1969; chm Land Settlement Assoc 1980–81; *m* 13 Jan 1962 *Frederica Loveday, only dau of Adml Sir Victor Alexander Charles Crutchley, VC, KCB, DSC, DL, of Mappercombe Manor, Powerstock, Bridport, Dorset, and has issue:

1 +PHILIP JOHN [Philip Colfox Esq, 117 Eccleston Mews, London SW1X 8AQ]; *b* 27 Dec 1962; *educ* Eton; *m* 19– *Julia R, yr dau of Geoffrey St George Schomberg, of Durfort, France, and Mrs H D Lyon, of Dallington, Sussex, and has:

(1) *Alice; *b* 1993

(2) *Lily (twin); *b* 1993

(3) *Mary Rose (Mamie); *b* 5 April 1997

2 +Edward Timothy; *b* 14 Jan 1969

1 *Victoria Mary; *b* 17 Jan 1964; *m* 12 Oct 1996 *Fergus Byrne, s of James J Byrne, of Co Kildare

2 *Charlotte Ismay Joan; *b* 28 Jan 1966; *m* 1987 *Capt James William Harwood Daniel, Welsh Gds, est s of Col John Daniel, and has issue:

(1) *Olivia Mary Frederica; *b* 1988

3 *Constance Ruth; *b* 20 July 1971

Lineage: RICHARD or JOHN COLFOX; *d* 1593, leaving, with four sons and six daus:

WILLIAM COLFOX; *d* 1647, leaving issue:

WILLIAM COLFOX; *b* 1607; *m* Mary James and *d* 1682, leaving issue:

JOSHUA COLFOX; *b* 1635; *m* Elizabeth Way (*d* 1721), and *d* 1690, leaving issue:

JOSHUA COLFOX; *b* 1681; *m* 1712 Susannah Warne and *d* 1744, leaving, with a dau (Hannah, *m* John Carter (*d* 1786) and *d* 1784, leaving issue):

JOHN COLFOX; *b* 1714; *m* Mary (*d* 1798), dau of Rev Collins, of Horton, and had issue:

THOMAS COLLINS COLFOX; *b* 1755; *m* Elizabeth (*d* 1793), dau of Joseph Stone, of Bridport, and *d* 1835, having had issue, with six daus (all *d* young) and two er sons (one *d* young; the other, Thomas, *b* 1788, *d* 1806):

WILLIAM COLFOX; *b* 1784; *m* 1821 his second cousin Hannah (*d* 1873), dau of Andrew Abbott, of Bradford Abbas, by Betty, dau of John Carter (*see* above), and had issue:

1 Thomas; *b* 1823; *m* Louisa, 13th child of Henry Wansey, and *d* 1886, leavinga dau (Harriet, *b* 1856, *m* Edgar Crookshank and *d* 1930, leaving issue)

2 William, of Westmead, Dorset, JP, DL, High Sheriff 1899; *b* 1826; *m* 1855 Anna Elizabeth (*d* 1907), 14th child of Henry Wansey, of Sambourne, Warminster, Wilts, and *d* 1906, leaving issue:

(1) THOMAS ALFRED

(1) Alice Lee, of Westmead, Dorset; *b* 1856; *d* unm 9 Oct 1936

(2) Margaret Wansey; *b* 14 July 1864; *m* Oliver Lupton, and *d* 1949, leaving issue

The only son,

THOMAS ALFRED COLFOX, of Coneygar, Bridport, Dorset, DL, JP, High Sheriff 1920; *b* 29 Sept 1858; Lt-Col QO Dorset Yeo (TD), Hon Col 94th (Dorset Yeo) Field Regt RA (TA) 1928–37; *m* 14 April 1886 Constance (*d* 21 June 1950), 2nd dau of Edward John Nettlefold, of Edgbaston, Birmingham, and *d* 18 April 1945, leaving issue:

1 WILLIAM PHILIP (Sir), **1st Bt**

2 Thomas David; *b* Oct 1898; *educ* Eton and RMA Woolwich; *ka* June 1918

1 Constance Alice; *b* 12 Jan 1887; *m* 1917 Cdr Francis Theodore Hare, RN, 2nd son of Evan Hering Hare, MA, FRCS, of London

2 Agatha Frances; *b* 13 Oct 1890; *m* 30 Aug 1911 Alan Spencer Gaskell Kennard (*d* 17 Aug 1951), Capt TA Res, yst son of Adam Steinmetz Kennard, JP, of Belmore, Bishop's Waltham, Hants (*see* KENNARD, Bt), and had issue

The er son,

Sir (William) Philip Colfox, 1st Bt (UK), so *cr* 4 July 1939, MC (1918), JP, DL (both Dorset); *b* 25 Feb 1888; *educ* Eton and RMA Woolwich; CC Dorset 1919–22 and 1941–54, CA 1954–66, also memb RDC, High Sheriff Dorset 1946–47; MP N Dorset 1908–22 and W Dorset 1922–41, commnd RFA 1908; Capt 1914, Maj 1917 (ret 1923) WW I (twice wounded, 1914 star, two medals), Lt-Col HG WW II, PPS to Min Pensons 1920–21 and Parly U-Sec Colonies 1921–22, Assist Govt Whip 1922–23; Govr Sherborne Sch; *m* 27 Jan 1920 Mary Frances, JP (Dorset 1931) (*d* 21 Nov 1973 aged 81), only dau of Col John Bullen Symes-Bullen, JP, DL, of Catherston-Leweston, Charmouth, Dorset, and *d* 8 Nov 1966, having had issue:

1 Thomas Andrew; *b* 2 Dec 1921; *d* 27 Dec 1935

2 Sir WILLIAM JOHN COLFOX, **2nd and present Bt**

1 *Susan Helen Frances [Mrs William Batten, Church Farm, Ryme Intrinsica, Dorset]; *b* 16 June 1929; *m* 2 Sept 1950 *William Henry Batten, only son of Col Herbert Copeland Cary Batten, DSO, of Aldon, Yeovil, and has:

(1) *David Henry Cary; *b* 3 March 1952; *educ* Eton; *m* 1981 *Sarah Bagnell

(2) *Michael John; *b* 29 Jan 1960; *m* 1984 *Joanna Winslade, and has two sons and a dau

(1) *Tessa Mary; *b* 22 Oct 1953; *m* 1976 *John Mackenzie-Green and has two sons and a dau

(2) *Caroline Bridget; *b* 13 July 1955; *m* 1978 *Angus Handasyde Dick and has two sons and a dau

2 *Bridget Alice [Mrs Alexander Mure, Pevington Farm, Pluckley, Kent TN27 0PF]; *b* 30 Nov 1931; *m* 1st 15 March 1958 Lt-Col Peter Amyand Brenton Wickham, RHA (*d* 30 June 1967), only child of Brig John Charles Wickham, DSO, RE, of Shoddesden Manor, Andover, by Augusta Phyllis Amyand, only dau of Maj Edward Arthur Haggard, and has had issue:

(1) *Anthony John Macarthur; *b* 2 July 1960; *m* 1994 *Georgina Dimity Cumberland-Brown and has:

1a *Adelaide; *b* 13 Oct 1996

(2) *Mark Andrew; *b* 31 Oct 1962; *m* 1992 *Corinne Lynne Barker and has:

1a *William Peter Mure; *b* 23 May 1993

1a *Charlotte Alice; *b* 26 Nov 1994

(1) *Tania Catherine; *b* 23 April 1959

(2) Anna Frances; *b* 20 Feb 1965; *d* 29 June 1966

2 (cont.) Mrs Wickham *m* 2nd 8 May 1968 *

COLGRAIN

Arms: Gyronny of eight or and sable, on a chief azure a bezant between two crescents of the first. **Crest:** A boar's head erect and erased azure issuing from a wreath of myrtle leaved and flowered proper. **Supporters:** Dexter, a horse argent; sinister, a boar azure. **Motto:** *Fac et spera* ('Act and hope'). **Creation:** B. (UK) 28 Jan 1946.

THE 3RD BARON COLGRAIN, of Everlands, Co Kent (David Colin Campbell) [The Rt Hon The Lord Colgrain, Bushes Farm, Weald, Sevenoaks, Kent TN14 6ND]; *b* 24 April 1920; *s* f 1973; *educ* Eton and Trin Coll Cambridge (BA 1941); WW II in 9th Lancers (wounded 1942), manager National & Grindlays Bank Ltd, India and Pakistan 1945–49; dir Anthony Gibbs Holdings Ltd 1954–83, chm Alexander and Berendt Ltd 1967–, Hon Treas Roy Assoc for Disability and Rehabilitation; *m* 1st 30 June 1945 (*divorce* 1964) Veronica Margaret, yr dau of Lt-Col William Leckie Webster, RAMC, and has issue:

1 +ALASTAIR COLIN LECKIE; *b* 16 Sept 1951; *educ* Eton and Trin Coll Cambridge (BA 1973); *m* 14 July 1979 *Annabel Rose, yr dau of Hon Robin Hugh Warrender of Widcombe Manor, Bath, and gdau of 1st Baron Bruntisfield, MC (*qv*), and has issue:

(1) +Thomas Colin Donald; *b* 9 Feb 1984

(2) +Nicholas Robin; *b* 12 Dec 1986

1 *Virginia Charlotte Angela [The Hon Mrs Gattertop, Leominster HR6 0JY]; *b* 19 Oct 1948; *m* 8 June 1973 *Maj Jonathan Charles Mackay-Lewis, yr son of Maj-Gen Kenneth Frank Mackay-Lewis, CB, DSO, MC, of Stamps and Crows, Layer Breton, Essex, and has issue:

(1) *James Edward; *b* 5 Dec 1978

(2) *George Mungo Pyne; *b* 1985

(1) *Gemma Elizabeth; *b* 2 Nov 1977

The 3rd BARON *m* 2nd 10 Jan 1973 *Sheila McLeod, dau of Robert McLeod Mitchell and formerly w of Martin Morgan Hudson

Lineage: This family descends from a yr bro of Alexander Campbell, 1st of Possil, and is therefore a cadet of the Campbells of Kinloch, a yr branch of the Campbells, Earls of Breadalbane (*qv*).

COLIN CAMPBELL (3rd son of John Campbell of Morriston); acquired the former Dennistoun property of Colgrain, Dunbartonshire, 1836; *b* 8 Jan 1782; *m* 24 Oct 1814 Janet Miller, est dau of John Hamilton, of North, and *d* 1863, having had:

1 John; *b* 9 Aug 1815; Capt Roy Scots Greys; *d* May 1846

2 Colin, 2nd of Colgrain

3 Alexander Henry; JP (Herts), DL (Cornwall); *b* 31 July 1822; MP Launceston 1865–68; *m* 20 Oct 1858 Agnes, est dau of John Campbell Douglas of Mains, and had issue:

(1) Douglas, of Mains

(1) Caroline Agnes; *m* 2 Nov 1895 Brig-Gen Ernest William Stewart King Maconchy, CB, CMG, CIE, DSO (*d* 1 Sept 1945), of Edenmore, Hook, Hants, and *d* 15 July 1953, having had issue

(2) Evelyn Mary; *b* 26 Nov 1873; *d* unm 19 Aug 1965

4 Archibald Hamilton; *b* 17 Dec 1823; Lt-Col IA; *m* 25 June 1868 Mary Agnes, est dau of Charles Lionel Maitland-Kirwan, of Dalgin Park, Co Mayo, and Gelston Castle, Kirkcudbrightshire, and *d* March 1897, leaving issue

5 Thomas; *b* 2 March 1825; *m* 1st Sept 1851 Mary (*d* Aug 1852), dau of Col Campbell of Possil; *m* 2nd 14 Jan 1869 Katherine Caroline, est dau of Lt-Col Robert Vansittart (*see* 1956 edn VANSITTART, B), of The Chuffs, nr Maidenhead, and by her had, with other issue:

(1) Arthur Vansittart; *m* 4 July 1905 Marjorie Jane, yr dau of Frederick Chatfield Smith, of Bramcote Hall, Notts, and *d* 3 Aug 1958, leaving issue:

1a Nigel Arthur; *b* 25 Dec 1906; *m* 30 April 1938 *Philippa Janet, dau of Leonard Ferdinand de Smidt, of Tiverton Castle, Devon, and had issue:

1b +Neil Vanisittart [Neil Campbell Esq, Ballyenvis, 39 Salterton Rd, Exmouth, Devon]; *b* 2 Dec 1947; *educ* Sherborne

1b *Jane Susannah [Mrs Anthony Bennett, c/o Barclays Bank, Tiverton, Devon]; *b* 19 March 1940; *m* 10 Sept 1960 *Anthony Cecil Harley Bennett, SCLI, yst son of Maj R H E Bennett, of Uphays, Otterton, Devon, and has issue:

1c *Richard Neil Harley; *b* 25 June 1963

2c *Henry Robert Campbell; *b* 16 May 1966

1c *Caroline Sarah; *b* 5 Aug 1961

2c *Joanna Elizabeth (twin); *b* 25 June 1963

2a Tom Vansittart; *b* 18 April 1910; *educ* Shrewsbury

3a +Guy; *b* 16 April 1915

6 George William; *b* 3 June 1826; *educ* Edinburgh Acad; *m* 8 May 1865 Florence (*d* Feb 1916), dau of Rt Hon Sir James Weir Hogg, 1st Bt (*qv*), and *d* 2 Dec 1896, leaving issue:

(1) COLIN FREDERICK, **1st Baron**

(2) Charles Alexander; *b* 1868; *educ* Eton and Trin Coll Cambridge; *d* 1906

(3) George Augustus (Rev); *b* 1874; *educ* Eton and Trin Coll Cambridge (MA 1902); Rector St Mary-at-the Walls, Colchester, 1933–46, RD Colchester 1933–46, Hon Canon Chelmsford 1934, Canon Emeritus 1947, Vicar Witham Essex 1921–33; *d* unm Dec 1955

(1) Mabel Mary; *m* 11 June 1895 Rev Canon Arthur Blackburn Goulburn Lillingston (*d* 19 April 1943), Canon Res Durham Cathedral, and *d* 4 May 1922, leaving issue

(2) Florence Ishbel, OBE (1917); *d* unm 23 Dec 1968

(3) Constance Harriet; *d* unm 17 Sept 1960

7 James; *b* 14 Oct 1828; *d* 1905

8 Robert; *b* 13 March 1830; Maj 12th Lancers; *d* 4 July 1866

9 Mungo Septimus; *b* 31 March 1831; *d* 26 Aug 1859

10 William; *b* 18 June 1832; Col 100th Regt; *d* 1887

1 Helen Bogle; *m* 15 Jan 1851 John Campbell, 2nd of Possil, and *d* 8 July 1851

2 Marion; *m* 3 June 1840 Alexander S Finlay, of Castle Toward, MP Argyll, and *d* 27 Jan 1865, leaving issue

3 Mary; *d* 17 April 1872

4 Elizabeth Anne; *b* 6 Aug 1882

5 Janet Hamilton; *m* 1st 10 June 1857 Maj William Middleton (*d* 18 April 1859), 7th Dragoon Gds, and had issue; *m* 2nd 7 July 1867 George Maconchy (*d* 30 Oct 1889), of Rathmore, Co Longford, and *d* May 1910, leaving issue

COLIN CAMPBELL's gs,

COLIN FREDERICK CAMPBELL, **1st Baron Colgrain**, of Everlands, Co Kent (UK), so *cr* 28 Jan 1946, JP (Kent 1905); *b* 13 June 1866; *educ* Eton; dir: Nat Prov Bank 1903 (chm 1933–46), London Assur 1897 (govr 1914–33), Alexanders Discount Co 1912 (chm 1916–50), Telegraph Construction and Maint Co 1897 (chm 1932–); pres Br Bankers Assoc and chm of Ctee of London Clearing Banks 1938–46, memb Bp of London's Commn on City Churches; *m* 9 May 1890 Lady Angela Mary Alice Ryder, MBE (*d* 10 Nov 1939), 2nd dau of 4th Earl of Harrowby (*qv*), and had issue:

1 DONALD SWINTON, **2nd Baron**

2 Angus Dudley, CBE (1939), JP 1943; *b* 8 Oct 1895; *educ* Eton; 2nd/1st Surrey Yeo and 9th Lancers WW I, dir: Haighton and Dewhurst Ltd, Manchester Ship Canal, Martins Bank, memb Lancs Mission to India 1933 (chm 1936, 1938 and 1955), memb Industl Mission Pakistan 1950, Pres Manchester Chamber Commerce 1940–41, chm UK Cotton Industry Export Mission Br E Africa 1953; *m* 30 June 1926 *Joan Esther Sybella, JP (Cheshire 1949) [The Hon Mrs Angus Campbell JP, Beech Cottage, 24 Cheerbrook Rd, Willaston, Nantwich, Cheshire], est dau of Col Hercules Arthur Pakenham CMG (*see* LONGFORD, E), and *d* 5 Dec 1967, leaving issue:

(1) *Judith Averil; *b* 12 Nov 1927; *m* 16 Dec 1954 Lt-Cdr Gerard St John Roden Buxton, RN, yr son of Capt Roden Henry Victor Buxton, CBE, RN, of Smallburgh Hall, Norwich (*see* BUXTON, Bt), and has issue

(2) Fiona Mary; *b* 7 Jan 1930; *m* 3 Oct 1953 *Donald Dundas Scott [Donald Scott Esq, Harsfold Manor Farm House, Wisborough Green, Sussex RH14 0BD], only surv son of James Douglas Scott, of Harsfold Manor Farm, by Bridget Violet, 2nd dau of John Arthur Penfold Wyatt, of Harsfold Manor, and *d* 20 Oct 1996, having had:

1a *Roderick (Rory) Arthur [Roderick Scott Esq, Harsfold Manor, Wisborough Green, W Sussex RH14 0BD]; *b* 16 Feb 1958; *m* 1990 *(Petrina) Jane, yr dau of John Frederick Edward Trehearne (*see* HARVINGTON, B), and has:

1b *Sebastian Angus Edward; *b* 1993

1b *Hannah Augusta; *b* 1991

2b *Angela Fiona; *b* 19–

2a *Angus Malcolm; *b* 15 Feb 1964

1a Arabella Joan; *b* 5 Nov and *d* 17 Nov 1955

2a *Henrietta Sara [Mrs William Drake, Twinstead Manor, Sudbury, Suffolk]; *b* 18 Jan 1957; *m* 1982 *William Eric Drake, yr son of Sir Eric Drake, CBE, and has issue:

1b *Hector Donald Arthur; *b* 1986

2b *Milo Edmund Courtney; *b* 1991

1b *Edwina Margaret Fiona; *b* 1987

3a *Rosanna Harriet [Mrs Rupert Dickinson, 3 Beechmore Rd, London SW11 4ET]; *b* 23 Feb 1962; *m* 1990 *Rupert Jerome Dickinson, 2nd son of Ian Dickinson, MC, of The Manor Ho, Riding Mill, Northumberland, and has issue:

1b *Caspar; *b* Nov 1994

2b *Joshua; *b* Nov 1994

1b *Atalanta Bella; *b* 1992

(3) *Linda Ishbel [Lady Cubitt, Chapel House, Westhumble, Dorking, Surrey RH5 6AY]; *b* 4 May 1934; *m* 26 June 1958 Sir Hugh Guy Cubitt (*see* ASHCOMBE, B) and has issue

1 Marjorie Angela; *b* 19 Jan 1893

2 Rachel Audrey; *b* 27 July 1894; *m* 31 Jan 1917 Sir Godfrey Middleton Bosville Macdonald, 15th Bt (*qv*), and has issue

The 1st BARON *d* 3 Nov 1954; his er son,

DONALD SWINTON CAMPBELL, **2nd Baron Colgrain**, MC (1917), JP (Kent 1942); *b* 6 Nov 1891; *educ* Eton and Trin Coll Cambridge; 10th Bn The Buffs and Capt W Kent Yeo (TF) WW I, WW II as Maj Roy W Kent Regt and HG, dir: Nat

Overseas and Grindlays Bank Ltd; dir Forbes, Forbes and Campbell, India, and London Produce Clearing House; chm Grindlays Bank; memb TocH and Roy Br Legion; *m* 1 Aug 1917 Margaret Emily (*d* 1989), est dau of Percy William Carver, of Courtlands, W Hoathly, Sussex, and *d* 20 Oct 1973, leaving:

1 DAVID COLIN CAMPBELL, **3rd and present Baron Colgrain**

2 +Robert Dudley [The Hon Robert Campbell, Sharp's Place, Bough Beech, Edenbridge, Kent]; *b* 6 July 1921; *educ* Eton and Trin Coll Cambridge; Capt Scots Gds WW II (wounded), dir Balfour Williamson and Co; *m* 1st 23 July 1954 (*divorce* 1978) Cecilia Barbara, er dau of Cdr George Alexander Rankin Johnston Leslie, RN, of Old Manor Cottage, Lympne Hill, Kent, and has:

(1) *Lenore Robina Cecilia; *b* 10 Jan 1957; *m* 1985 *Michael C Maynard, son of Ronald Maynard, of Epping, Essex, and has issue:

1a *Chantal Robina; *b* 1987

2a *Alexandra Samantha; *b* 1992

(2) *Zephyrine Alexandra; *b* 27 Aug 1967; *m* 6 June 1996 *Christopher Bennett, s of Peter Bennett, of Hanslope, Bucks

2 (cont.) The Hon Robert Campbell *m* 2nd 1983 *Mrs Muriel Anne Kandal, dau of George Tuson, RN, of Loughborough, Leics

3 +Neil Donald, DSC (1945) [The Hon Neil Campbell DSC, York's Hill Farm, Ide Hill, Sevenoaks, Kent TN14 6HY]; *b* 24 Aug 1922; *educ* RNC Dartmouth; late Lt RN, ptnr James Capel and Co; *m* 11 July 1951 *Angela Louise Vereker, est dau of Rt Hon Sir Ronald Hibbert Cross, 1st and last Bt, KCMG, KCVO, PC (*see* 1967 edn), and has had issue:

(1) Andrew Donald; *b* 23 Oct 1954; *educ* Harrow; *m* 1 June 1974 *K Dominique, er dau of Peter Juul, Copenhagen, Denmark, and *d* 1980, leaving:

1a Claire; *b* 1974; *d* 1978

(2) +Roderick Hugo; *b* 4 March 1960; *educ* Eton; *m* 1988 *Sophie Louise, dau of Richard Hicks, and has issue:

1a +Arthur Frederick; *b* 1988

1a *Edie Blanche; *b* 1990

(3) +Martin Emmott [Martin Campbell Esq, Fernhill, Ide Hill, Kent TN14 6LG]; *b* 12 Nov 1963; *educ* Marlborough; has by *Penelope Jane Wilson, est dau of Alan Wilson, of Napier, NZ:

1a *Kiloran Diana Claire; *b* 13 July 1990

(1) *Joanna Louise; *b* 9 July 1953; *m* 1st 1980 (*divorce* 1987) Michael L Wennink, yr son of Cornelis Wennink, and has issue:

1a *Oliver Neil; *b* 1981

2a *(Jonathan Roelof) Donald; *b* 1982

(1) (cont.) Mrs Joanna Wennink *m* 2nd 1992 *Robert M Tennant, son of Cecil Tennant, and by him has:

3a *A child; *b* 1992

1 *Gillian Margaret [The Hon Mrs Young, Orchard House, Langton Green, Tunbridge Wells, Kent TN3 0RA]; *b* 21 Aug 1925; *m* 28 April 1951 Peter Scott Young (*d* 1988), only son of James John Bertram Young, of Calcutta, and has issue:

(1) *Robert James Campbell; *b* 1 June 1954; *educ* Marlborough; *m* 1986 *Josynane Noelle, dau of Jean Pierard, of Le Figueret, Flayosc, Haut-Var, France, and has issue:

1a *Sam Peter Antoine; *b* 1987

2a *Yannick Robert Pierard; *b* 1989

(2) *Mark Peter; *b* 14 Jan 1961; *m* 1990 *Andrea C S, dau of Maj Geoffrey Browne, MBE, of Jasmine Cottage, Harwell, Didcot, Oxon, and has issue:

1a *Fergus Scott Antony; *b* 1993

2a *Luke Peter James; *b* 1997

1a *Pollyanna Gillian; *b* 1995

(1) *Bridget Margaret [Mrs Patrick Macdougall, 40 Stevenage Rd, London SW6 6EJ]; *b* 11 July 1952; *m* 1983 *Patrick L Macdougall, son of J A Macdougall, of Midhurst, and has issue:

1a *Laura Margaret Valerie; *b* 1984

2a *Nicola Elizabeth Bridget; *b* 1987

3a *Vanessa Emily Hope; *b* 1990

(2) *Deborah Mary; *b* 8 Aug 1957; *m* 1983 *Steven H Hewlett, son of Maurice Hewlett, of 9 The Old Nurseries, Grange-over-Sands, Cumbria, and has issue:

1a *Jacob (Jake) Robert; *b* 1986

2a *Adam James; *b* 1988

1a *Megan Ruth; *b* 1991

COLLETT

Arms: Azure on a chevron couped or between three hinds trippant proper, collared of the second, an arch sable between two open books, also proper. **Crest:** A demi-hind proper, collared or, resting the sinister foot on an escutcheon gold, charged with a maul sable. **Motto:** Keep straight on. **Creation:** Bt. (UK) 1 Nov 1934.

SIR IAN SEYMOUR COLLETT, 3RD BT, of Bridge Ward in the City of London [Sir Ian Collett Bt, The Red House, Ufford, Woodbridge, Suffolk IP13 6EL]; *b* 5 Oct 1953; *s* gf 1971; *educ* Lancing; memb Law Soc 1979, Notary Public 1985, Freeman City of London; *m* 18 Sept 1982 *Philippa, only dau of James R I Hawkins, of Preston St Mary, Suffolk, and has issue:

1 +ANTHONY SEYMOUR; *b* 1984

1 *Georgina; *b* 1986

Lineage: HENRY COLLETT; *m* 14 June 1808 Ann, dau of Joseph Fletcher, of Somerford, and *d* 1852, leaving:

HENRY JOHN COLLETT; *b* 17 May 1809; *m* 14 Aug 1834 Amelia Sophia Mawby, and had:

HENRY JOHN RICHARD COLLETT, of The Hall, Peasenhall, Suffolk, JP; *b* 17 Nov 1838; *m* 23 Dec 1862 Jane Johnson Thomas, of Bungay, and *d* 1923, leaving:

Sir Charles Henry Collett, 1st Bt (UK), so *cr* 1 Nov 1934; ktd 1933; *b* 8 July 1864; Lt City London, Common Councilman Bridge Ward 1912–27, Alderman 1927–38, Sheriff London 1932–33, Ld Mayor 1933–34; *m* 1st 20 April 1892 Lilian Louisa (*d* 2 Sept 1935), dau of Seymour Ionn, of Dulwich; *m* 2nd 30 Dec 1936 Grace Audrey (*d* 13 Sept 1978), est dau of Thomas Livingstone Ashford, of Gillingham, Beccles, Suffolk, and by his 1st w had issue:

1 HENRY SEYMOUR (Sir), **2nd Bt**

2 Stanley Beresford; *b* 1896; S/Ldr AAF, cmdg City of London Sqdn 1931, Assist Slr then Assist Sec GWR, RFC WW I; *m* 12 April 1923 Olga Kathleen, OBE (1955), yst dau of Col Frank Griffith, and was *k* in a flying accident at RAF Display, Hendon, 30 June 1934

3 Norman Charles, RNAS; *b* 8 Nov 1899; *k* in a flying accident, Jan 1918

4 Richard Ionn; *b* 19 May 1901; *m* 1926 Helen Alice (*d* 1992), dau of Harry Hayns, and *d* 1993 leaving issue:

(1) +Norman Ionn [Norman Collett Esq, 561 Hallsor Dve, Victoria, BC V9C 1K9, Canada]; *b* 4 Sept 1927; *educ* Ipswich Sch, Perse Sch Cambridge and HMS *Conway*; *m* 1st 22 Sept 1954 (*divorce* 19–) Ethne Maureen, dau of Samuel Chadwick; *m* 2nd 19– *Patricia Jean Williams and by his 1st w has:

1a +Kevin Samuel Richard; *b* 1955

2a +Norman Michael; *b* 1959

1a *Helen Margaret; *b* 1962

(2) +James Masterman [James Collett Esq, Owl's Hoot, 23 Bramley Ave, Coulsdon, Surrey CR3 2DS]; *b* 5 Aug 1930; *educ* Ipswich Sch, Perse Sch Cambridge and Bishops Stortford Coll; *m* 2 June 1962 *Rosalind Mary, dau of John Humphrey Lane, of Wallington, Surrey, and has:

1a *Lucinda Mary; *b* 1963

(3) Richard Patrick, Capt RE (TA); *b* 2 Oct 1932; *educ* Ipswich Sch, Perse Sch Cambridge and Bishops Stortford Coll; *m* 23 Aug 1958 *Gillian Anne, dau of Alfred James Remes, of Thatches, Witnesham, and *d* 1982, leaving issue:

1a *Jane Louise; *b* 22 Oct 1960

2a *Johanna Mary; *b* 31 Dec 1962

(4) +Henry Alexander; *b* 15 April 1944; *educ* Bishops Stortford Coll; ACA (1969); *m* 23 Aug 1969 *Joy Eileen, dau of Rev Ross McPherson Heard, of The Rectory, Hatch Beauchamp, Taunton, Somerset, and has issue:

1a +Christian Tom; *b* 1972

2a +Ross Tobias; *b* 1973

5 John Collison; *b* 6 June 1903; *m* 5 Sept 1928 *Ethel Ruth [Mrs John Collett, Stable End, Windhill, Bishops Stortford, Herts], dau of Benjamin A Glanvill, and *d* 26 Oct 1956, leaving issue:

(1) +John Brian Glanvill [John Collett Esq, Countess Wells Farm, Framlingham, Suffolk]; *b* 18 July 1929; *educ* Bishops Stortford Coll; *m* 17 May 1959 *Phyllis Ivy Sybil, 2nd dau of Hastings Kiddy, of Hunt's Park Farm, Gt Thurlow, Norfolk, and has issue:

1a +Robert Glanvill; *b* 29 Oct 1961

2a +John Charles; *b* 1969

1a *Helen Mary; *b* 17 Feb 1960

(2) +Peter Glanvill, JP Herts [Peter Collett Esq JP, Stable End, Windhill, Bishops Stortford, Herts CM23 2ND]; *b* 5 Nov 1933; *educ* Bishops Stortford Coll; *m* 1st 7 Feb 1959 Cecilia Judith (Sally) (*d* 1966), er dau of Gerald Eliot Maysey Bromley-Martin, of Hardley Hall, London, Norfolk, and has issue:

1a +Gerard Henry Glanvill [Gerard Collett Esq, 11 Clarence Rd, Stansted, Essex]; *b* 7 Feb 1961; *m* 1989 *Nicola May Marie, dau of William Robson, and has:

1b +Charles Henry; *b* 1992

1b *Sally Elizabeth; *b* 1990

2a +Thomas John Elliot; *b* 17 July 1962

3a +Alexander Peter Glanvill; *b* 1965

1a *Nicola Mary; *b* 29 Nov 1959

(2) (cont.) Peter Collett *m* 2nd 1973 *Mary Jean, dau of Leonard George Truelove, and has further issue:

2a *Rebecca Mary; *b* 1974

3a *Anna Catherine; *b* 1976

(1) *Sheila Mary [Mrs John Sewell, Brettenham Park, Ipswich, Suffolk]; *b* 26 Nov 1931; *m* 20 Aug 1955 *John Donald Sewell, yr son of T J E Sewell, of Old Buckenham Hall, Norfolk, and has:

1a *David John Elliott; *b* 9 June 1956

2a *Andrew William *b* 20 March 1961

3a *Michael James; *b* 12 May 1968

1a *Jean Mary; *b* 3 April 1958

(2) *Diana [Mrs Robert MacDonald, Box 204, N Gower, Ontario, Canada]; *b* 24 Aug 1940; *m* 1st 2 Sept 1959 (*divorce* 1969) Thomas Joseph Henighan, only son of Thomas A Henighan, of Mount Vernon, NY, USA, and has:

1a *Stephen Patrick Glanvill; *b* 1960

1a *Phoebe Clare; *b* 1964

(2) (cont.) Mrs Diana Henighan *m* 2nd 1971 *Robert Hugh MacDonald

6 (Thomas) Kingsley (Sir), ktd 1968, CBE (1956); *b* 7 March 1905; *educ* Bishops Stortford Coll; dir Adams Bros and Shardlow Ltd (Creative Printers) London and Leicester, memb Court Common Cncl City London (Ward of Bridge) 1945, Ch Commoner and Chm City Lands Ctee 1955, Chm Special Ctee 1956–66, HM Lt City London 1958, Chm Govrs Bishops Stortford Coll 1964, memb Bd PLA 1959–67, Freeman City London 1930, Liveryman Distillers' Co (Upper Warden 1959, Master 1960–61), commnd RA (TA) 1923–28, served 54th Kent Bn HG 1940–44, cmded 51st Kent HG Bn 1952–57, memb TAVRA Gtr London, Chev Order Christ Portugal 1956; *m* 10 July 1930 Beatrice Olive, er dau of Thomas H Brown, of Englefield, Bickley, Kent

7 +David Brooke [David Collett Esq, 3 Buckenham Court, Southwold, Suffolk]; *b* 6 Nov 1907; *educ* Bishops Stortford Coll; DTech (Hons), Freeman City London, Fell The Plastics and Rubber Inst, dir Dunlop Co 1952067, Hon Memb and Past Pres Rubber and Plastics Research Assoc GB, former Memb LEB and Sr Pro-Chllr Loughborough U of Tech 1966–80; *m* 29 April 1933 *Mary Cecily Beatrice, dau of Hugh C Aston, and has issue:

(1) +Anthony Hugh [Anthony Collett Esq, 7 Drayton Close, Fetcham Park, Surrey KT22 9EZ]; *b* 12 Dec 1936; *educ* Liverpool Coll, Upper Canada Coll Toronto, Bishops Stortford Coll and Emmanuel Coll Cambridge (BA 1959, MA 1964); CEng and FICE 1987, Freeman City London; *m* 5 May 1962 *Christine Ann, er dau of James Hiddleston Little, of Sheffield, and has:

1a *Gail Christine; *b* 25 Jan 1964; *m* 1993 *Robert Dean, s of Brian Dean of Feteham, Surrey, and has:

1b *Jonathan James; *b* 1996

1b *Eloise Christine; *b* 1994

2a *Clare Elizabeth; *b* 4 Jan 1967; *m* 1993 *Guy Wordley Williams, s of Col David Williams, of Rye, Sussex, and has:

1b *Thomas Wordley; *b* 1994

2b *Oliver Brooks; *b* 1996

3a *June Alison; *b* 3 June 1969

(1) *Elizabeth Anne [Mrs David Boult, Southwold, Suffolk], Freeman City London; *b* 22 Jan 1934; *m* 15 July 1957 *David Luard Boult, yst s of Peter Swinton Boult, MC, of New Bunnee, Hoylake, Cheshire, and has:

1a *David Mark; *b* 28 Feb 1960; Freeman City London; *m* 1996 *Sally Anne White, yr dau of Trevor White, of Maldon, Essex

2a *Edward William; *b* 3 Nov 1963; Freeman City London

1a *Nicola Anne Louise; *b* 10 July 1958; Freeman City London; *m* 1989 *Clive William Huish, s of George Huish, of Devon, and has:

1b *George Brooke; *b* 1993

(2) *Bridget Mary [Mrs James Blackburn, Railroad Mills Rd, Pittsford, NY, USA]; *b* 12 Feb 1945; *m* 1981 *James David Blackburn and has:

1a *David Peter; *b* 1986

(2) (cont.) Mr and Mrs James Blackburn also adopted:

*Barbara Ann; *b* 1972; *m* 1997 *Thomas Vincent Sadowski, s of Frank Sadowski Jr, of Pittsford, NY

8 Roger; *b* 14 July 1909; *m* 21 July 1934 (*divorce*) Doreen Frances Alvie, est dau of Sydney Platt, of The Spinney, Bickley, Kent, and *d* 15 Jan 1972, leaving:

(1) +Roger James [Roger Collett Esq, 8 Vanbrugh Fields, London SE3 7TZ]; *b* 14 March 1942; *educ* Ellesmere Coll; *m* 1966 *Valerie Doreen, dau of Prof Cyril George Beasley, and has issue:

1a +Christopher James; *b* 1973

1a *Nicola Valerie; *b* 1971

(1) *Susan Marjory [Mrs James Coombe, Glenmore, Church Lane, Chipstead, Surrey]; *b* 7 Feb 1939; *m* 16 July 1960 *James Stafford Coombe, er son of William Stafford Coombe, of Bearsted, Kent, and has issue:

1a *Andrew James Grant; *b* 4 Sept 1964

2a *John Edward; *b* 1979

1a *Caroline Jane; *b* 10 June 1961

2a *Edwina Gay; *b* 27 Jan 1963

3a *Georgina Susan; *b* 1974

4a *Genevieve Frances; *b* 1983

1 Elsa Mary; *b* 6 Sept 1894; *m* 16 Feb 1922 Sir Frank Samuel Alexander, 1st Bt (*see* ALEXANDER, Bt, of Sundridge Park), and *d* 20 Jan 1959, leaving issue

2 Margaret Edith; *b* 27 April 1898; *d* Aug 1913

Sir CHARLES *d* 23 Nov 1938; his est son,

Sir Henry Seymour Collett, 2nd Bt; *b* 14 Feb 1893; *educ* Bishops Stortford Coll; Lt Suffolk Regt and RFC WW I (twice wounded, POW), Freeman City London 1918, Pres City London Retail Traders' Assoc 1951–68, Common Councilman Bridge Ward City London 1958–71, Liveryman Glovers' Co, Cdr Nat Order Ivory Coast 1962, Cdr Roy Order Phoenix Greece 1963; *m* 22 Nov 1920 Ruth Mildred (*d* 1994), er dau of William Thomas Hatch, MICE, of Bromley, Kent, and *d* 6 Jan 1971, having had issue:

1 David Seymour; *b* 14 June 1924; *educ* Bishops Stortford Coll and Emmanuel Coll Cambridge; For Serv, Lt Middx Regt; *m* 20 Oct 1951 *Sheila Joan (*m* 2nd as his 2nd w Sir James Miskin, QC (*d* 1993)) [Lady Miskin, 15 North View, London SW19 4UJ], only dau of Harold R Scott, of 24 Inverleith Gdns, Edinburgh 4, and *dvp* 14 Nov 1962, leaving:

(1) Sir IAN SEYMOUR COLLETT, **3rd and present Bt**

(1) *Joanna Ruth; *b* 9 May 1956; Freeman City London; *m* 1984 *Nigel E Wicks, est son of Malcolm E Wicks, of Peterborough, and has issue:

1a *Jennifer Ruth; *b* 1989

2 +Christopher (Sir), GBE (1988), JP (City of London 1979) [Sir Christopher Collett GBE JP, 13 Somerset Ho, Somerset Rd, London SW19 5JA]; *b* 10 June 1931; *educ* Harrow and Emmanuel Coll Cambridge (BA 1954, MA 1960); FCA (1969, ACA 1957), ptnr Ernst and Young (ret 1993), Freeman City London, Capt RA (TARO), Liveryman: Glovers' Co (Master 1981–82), Chartered Accountants' Co and Haberdashers' Co, Common Councilman 1973–79, Alderman 1979, Sheriff 1985, Ld Mayor London 1988–89, Hon DSc City U, KStJ 1988, Cdr Order Merit Fed Republic Germany; *m* 12 Sept 1959 *Christine Anne, only dau of Oswald Hardy Griffiths, of Nunthorpe, Yorks, and has issue:

(1) +Alastair John Calvert [Alastair Collett Esq, 77 Faraday Rd, London SW19]; *b* 1 Dec 1961; *m* 1992 *Tiana J, only dau of Anthony Peck, of Kingston upon Thames, Surrey

(2) +Angus Christopher Calvert; *b* 23 Nov 1964

(1) *Alexandra Louise; *b* 9 June 1972

1 *Margaret Ruth, MBE, JP [Mrs George Chadd MBE JP, Mardle House, Wangford, nr Beccles, Suffolk NR34 8AU]; *b* 7 June 1922; AMIA, Freeman City of London; *m* 10 June 1950 Col George Victor Nudd Chadd, OBE, TD, JP, DL (*d* 12 June 1997), yr son of George B Chadd, of Four Stones, Corton, Suffolk, and has:

(1) Christopher George Andrew; *b* 20 June 1951; *educ* Harrow; drowned in *Morning Cloud* tragedy 1974

(2) *Richard Jonathan [Richard Chadd Esq, Ditchingham Cottage, Ditchingham, nr Bungay, Suffolk]; *b* 14 Aug 1953; *educ* Harrow and Oxford U (MA); notary public; *m* 1977 *Jane, dau of Dr William Ayles, of Edinburgh, and has:

1a *Hugo George William; *b* 1987

1a *Emma Louise Mary; *b* 1981

(3) Timothy Charles; *b* 4 Dec 1955; *educ* Harrow; *d* 1976

(4) *Nicholas Martyn Philip [Nicholas Chadd Esq, Thatched Cottage, Rushmere, nr Lowestoft, Suffolk]; *b* 30 March 1958; *educ* Harrow; Freeman City London, Liveryman Farriers' Co; *m* 1987 *Amelia Catherine, dau of Timothy Sallitt, of France, and has issue:

1a *Edward George Alexander; *b* 1991

2a *Rollo Nicholas William; *b* 29 Oct 1995

1a *Eleanor Alice; *b* 1993

COLMAN

Arms: Erm. on a pale rayonnée or between two crosses flory sa., a lion rampant gu. **Crest:** On a wreath or and az. in front of two wings arg., each charged with an estoile az., a rock proper, thereon a caltrap or. **Badge:** Issuant through an antique crown or a grey hound's head ppr. **Motto:** *Sat cito, si sat bene* ('Quick enough if it be well enough'). **Creation:** Bt. (UK) 26 Nov 1907.

SIR MICHAEL JEREMIAH COLMAN, 3RD BT, of Gatton Park, Gatton, Surrey [Sir Michael Colman Bt, Malshanger, Basingstoke, Hants RG23 7EY; 40 Chester Sq, London SW1W 9HT]; *b* 7 July 1928, *s f* 1961; *educ* Eton; Capt Queen's Own Yorks Yeo (RARO), chm Reckitt & Colman plc 1986–95; 1st Church Estates

Commr 1993–, dir Reckitt & Colman plc 1970–95 and Foreign & Colonial Ventures Advisors Ltd 1988–, memb Cncl of Roy Warrant Holders 1977– (pres 1984–85), Associate of Trin House and Memb of Lighthouse Bd 1985–94, Yr Brother 1994, Memb Court Skinners' Co 1985– (Master 1991–92), memb Gen Cncl and Fin Ctee King Edward's Hosp Fund for London, Special Tstee St Mary's Hosp Paddington, FRSA, Hon LLD; *m* 29 Oct 1955 *Judith Jean Wallop, yst dau of V-Adml Sir Peveril William Powlett, KCB, CBE, DSO (*see* PORTSMOUTH, E), and has issue:

1 +JEREMIAH MICHAEL POWLETT; *b* 23 Jan 1958; *educ* Eton and Leicester U (LLB); *m* 1981 *Susan Elizabeth, yr dau of John Henry Britland, of 15 Straylands Grove, York, and has issue:

(1) +Joseph Jeremiah; *b* 31 Oct 1988

(2) +Nathaniel James; *b* 1990

(1) *Eleanor Mary; *b* 1985

2 +John Powlett; *b* 5 June 1962

1 *Olivia Helena Judith; *b* 7 Aug 1956; *m* 1979 *Rev Patrick J Whitworth, yr son of Maj-Gen Reginald Henry Whitworth, CB, CBE, of Abbey Ho Farm, Goosey, Wantage, Oxon, and has issue:

(1) *David John William; *b* 1990

(1) *Emma Rachel; *b* 1982

(2) *Louisa Judith; *b* 1984

(3) *Sophia Rose; *b* 1987

2 *Victoria Rose [Mrs Matthew Persson, 41 Marloes Rd, London W8 6LA]; *b* 11 Nov 1960; *m* 1988 *Rev Matthew S Persson, er son of Rt Rev William Michael Dermot Persson, Bp Doncaster, and has issue:

(1) *Augustus William; *b* 1990

(2) *Bartholomew Jo; *b* 1993

3 *Alice Mary; *b* 8 Jan 1965; *m* 1994 *Timothy A C Page, est son of Col (John Patrick) Anthony Page, of Croft Ho, Brackley, and has issue

Lineage: WILLIAM COLMAN, of Wymondham, Norfolk; *d* 1354, leaving:

ROGER COLMAN, of Wymondham; *d* 1399, leaving:

JOHN COLMAN, of Wymondham; *d* 1438, leaving:

ROBERT COLMAN, of Wymondham; *m* Agnes — and *d* 1481, leaving:

JOHN COLMAN, of Wymondham; *m* Katherine — and *d* 1550, leaving:

RICHARD COLMAN, of Wymondham; made a settlement of his lands 1527; *d* 1594, leaving:

ROBERT COLMAN, of Wymondham; *m* Mary — and had, with other issue:

EDWARD COLMAN, of Wymondham; *m* Elizabeth — and *d* 1609, leaving:

JEREMIAH COLMAN, of Wymondham; *m* Rebecca — (*d* 1663) and *d* 1656, having had, with other issue:

EDWARD COLMAN, of Wymondham; *b* 1627; *m* Sarah — and *d* 1681, leaving, with other issue:

JEREMIAH COLMAN, of Wymondham; *b* 1657; *m* 10 April 1683 Rebecca Bubbin (*d* 1747) and had, with seven other children:

JEREMIAH COLMAN, of Wymondham, *bapt* 14 May 1690; *m* 1st 6 Feb 1716 Deborah Weavers and had seven children; *m* 2nd 7 Jan 1748 Esther Barnard and had three children; his son by his 1st w:

JEREMIAH COLMAN, of Wreningham; *bapt* 21 April 1717; *m* 24 Sept 1745 Mary Juby and had:

ROBERT COLMAN, of Ashwellthorpe, Norfolk; *b* 1749; *m* 21 July 1774 Mary (*b* 7 Jan 1750; *d* 6 May 1826), dau of Thomas Harmer, of Denton, Norfolk, and *d* 9 Jan 1807, having had:

ROBERT COLMAN, of Rockland, Norfolk; *b* 4 May 1775; *m* 22 Oct 1799 Anne Mills (*d* 5 June 1856) and had, with other issue:

1 James, of Stoke Holy Cross, Norwich; *b* 18 Nov 1801; *m* 1 Aug 1826 Mary (*d* 15 Sept 1898), dau of John Burlingham, of Old Burlingham, Norfolk, and *d* 19 Oct 1854, leaving issue

2 Joseph; *b* 29 Dec 1803; *m* Maria Elizabeth Mills and *d* 3 July 1858, leaving issue

3 John, of Longnor Ho, Kilburn; *b* 3 April 1806; *m* 1st Charlotte Farey (*dsp* 22 April 1841); *m* 2nd 1 Sept 1842 Hannah (*d* 1 July 1908), dau of John Gardner, and *d* 17 April 1884, leaving issue

4 JEREMIAH

5 Edward; *b* 12 May 1808; *m* 7 July 1840 Eliza (*d* 19 Dec 1899), dau of Benjamin Farey, and *d* 27 Sept 1874, leaving issue

6 William; *b* 24 Sept 1812; *m* 1st Aug 1839 Philippa Wilson; *m* 2nd Clarissa Ann Carter and *d* 19 Jan 1882, leaving issue

7 Henry, of Rockland St Peter, Norfolk; *b* 10 Feb 1814; *m* 1st 28 Nov 1848 Sarah (*d* 15 July 1852), dau of John Palmer, of Welborne, and had issue; *m* 2nd 24 Aug 1853 Harriett, dau of John Palmer, of Welborne, and *d* 15 March 1895, having by her had issue

8 Thomas; *b* 4 June 1815; *m* 14 April 1840 Mary (*d* 12 July 1881), dau of James Page, and *d* 28 Oct 1849, having had issue

9 Samuel; *b* 14 Sept 1816; *m* 26 Sept 1854 Mary (*d* 12 May 1893), dau of William Bowles, of Little Ellingham, Norfolk, and *d* 20 Oct 1894, leaving issue

1 Mary Anne; *b* 31 Aug 1809; *m* 5 July 1836 William Fielding (*d* 4 April 1881), and *d* 2 March 1881, leaving issue

ROBERT COLMAN *d* 26 Jan 1867; his 4th son,

JEREMIAH COLMAN, of Carshalton Park, Surrey, HM's Lt City London; *b* 4 April 1807; *m* 25 July 1855 Isabella Cocksedge (*d* 17 March 1897), dau of James Button, of Hopton, nr Ixworth, Suffolk, and *d* 21 May 1885, having had issue:

1 JEREMIAH (Sir), **1st Bt**

2 Frank; *b* 1 Feb 1862; *d* 19 Jan 1867

1 Isabella Mary; *b* 19 Nov 1856; *m* 30 July 1881 Sir Charles Tyrrell Giles, KC, DL (*d* 16 Jan 1940), of Copse Hill Ho, Wimbledon, MP Wisbech, 3rd son of Alfred Giles, of Cosford Ho, Godalming, MP Southampton, and Id 4 March 1949, leaving issue

The only surv son,

Sir Jeremiah Colman, 1st Bt (UK), so *cr* 26 Nov 1907, JP, DL, High Sheriff 1893–94; *b* 24 April 1859; *educ* St John's Coll Cambridge (MA); Lt City London, chm Reigate Petty Sessions Court 1902–28; pres Surrey CCC 1916–23, v-pres: Boy Scouts' Assoc and YMCA; Freeman Borough of Reigate; Master Skinners' Co 1899–1900; Order of Leopold; KStJ, chm J & J Colman Ltd, of Norwich and London; *m* 25 Feb 1885 Mary, Order of Mercy (*d* 9 Nov 1954), 3rd dau of James Short McMaster, of Mitcham, Surrey, and *d* 16 Jan 1942, leaving:

Sir Jeremiah Colman, 2nd Bt, JP Surrey 1909–38, JP Southampton; *b* 1 Jan 1886; *educ* Winchester and Trin Coll Cambridge (BA 1908); dir Reckitt & Colman Hldgs, Master Skinners' Co 1924–25; *m* 23 Oct 1924 Edith Gwendolen, est dau of Sir Alfred Ernest Tritton, 2nd Bt (*qv*), and *d* 8 Jan 1961, having had issue:

1 Sir MICHAEL JEREMIAH COLMAN, **3rd and present Bt**

2 +Oliver James [Oliver Colman Esq, 7 Tor Gdns, London W8 7AB]; *b* 8 Feb 1933; *educ* Winchester; *m* 4 March 1967 *Hon Cynthia Makins, twin dau of 1st Baron Sherfield (*qv*), and has issue:

(1) +Thomas James; *b* 12 Aug 1969

(1) *Camilla Mary; *b* 11 Dec 1972

1 *Gillian Veronica [Miss Gillian Colman, Bartlett's Farm, Mattingley, nr Basingstoke, Hants]; *b* 9 Dec 1926

COLQUHOUN

Arms: Argent a saltire engrailed sable. **Crest:** A hart's head couped gules, attired argent. **Supporters:** Two ratchhounds argent, collared sable. **Mottoes:** 1. *Cnoc ealachan* ('Hill of the willow tree'); 2. *Si je puis* ('If I can'). **Creation:** Bt. (GB) 27 June 1786.

SIR IVAR IAIN COLQUHOUN OF LUSS 8TH BT, of Luss, Argyllshire, JP (1951), DL Dunbartonshire (1952), [Captain Sir Ivar Colquhoun of Luss Bt JP DL, Camstraddan, Luss, Argyll G83 8NX]; *b* 4 Jan 1916; *s f* 1948, also as Chief of Clan Colquhoun; *educ* Eton; Gren Gds WW II, Capt 1945, Hon Sheriff Substitute 1956; *m* 17 April 1943 *Kathleen, 2nd dau of Walter Atholl Duncan, of Chelsea, and has had:

1 Torquil Ian; *b* 7 April 1944; *educ* Eton; *d* unm 22 July 1963

2 +MALCOLM RORY, Yr. of Luss [Malcolm Colquhoun Yr of Luss, 74 Nightingale Lane, London SW12 8NR]; *b* 20 Dec 1947; *educ* Eton and London U; *m* 1st 1978 (*divorce* 1983) Susan, er dau of Stewart W Timmerman, of Harrisburg, Pa., and has:

(1) +Patrick John; *b* 17 Dec 1980

2 (cont.) MALCOLM COLQUHOUN, Yr. of Luss, *m* 2nd 1989 *Katharine A H, est dau of A C Mears, of Canberra, Australia, and by him has:

(2) +Fergus Alexander Mears; *b* 1991

(1) *Georgina Iona Helena; *b* 1993

1 *Iona Mary; *b* 22 June 1945; *m* 4 July 1964 *12th Duke of Argyll (*qv*) and has issue

Lineage: UMFRIDUS de KILPATRIK; acquired *temp* ALEXANDER II (1214–49) from Maldwin, Earl of Lennox, the lands of Culchone or Colquhoun which lay within the territory of that Earldom and which his descendants took as their surname.

HUMPHREY of Colquhoun; had charters of Colquhoun and Sauchy from ROBERT I (THE BRUCE) (1306–29)

Sir ROBERT OF COLQUHOUN; living *temp* DAVID II (1329–71); acquired the lands of Luss, supposedly by marriage with the heiress of Luss of that Ilk, and had, with other issue:

1 HUMPHREY (Sir)

2 Robert; in 1395 acquired from his bro Camstradden, Dunbartonshire, and was ancestor of the chief cadet branch; ancestor in the 17th degree of:

(1) Robert Gilmour (Sir), of Camstradden, KCB, Consul-Gen Danubian Principalities, Dip Agent Egypt; bought Fincastle, Perthshire, 1833; *m* 1st 1837 Margaret Charlotte (*dsp*), dau of Thomas Hog, of Newliston; *m* 2nd 1886 Anna (*m* 2nd W A Atkinson), only child of William Cathrow, of Stoke Lodge, Bucks, and *d* 1870, having by her he had a dau. The COLQUHOUNs of Garscadden, Killermont and Craigallan descend from a yr son of John, 7th Laird of Camstradden

Sir ROBERT's est son,

Sir HUMPHREY COLQUHOUN of Luss; witnessed charters 1390–95; had, with an est s (Robert, *dsp c* 1408) and a yst s (Patrick, ancestor of the COLQUHOUNs of Kenmure):

Sir JOHN COLQUHOUN of Luss; Govr Dumbarton Castle during minority of JAMES II; murdered 24 Sept 1439 by marauding Highlanders, having had, with a dau (Isabel, *m* David Douglas, of Mains):

MALCOLM; *dvp*, leaving:

Sir JOHN COLQUHOUN of Luss; granted 1457 a charter incorporating his lands into the (territorial) Barony of Luss, another of forestry of Rossdhu and Glenmuckerne 1458 and one of Kilmardinny 1465; Sheriff Dumbarton, Comptroller Roy Household 1464–66, Keeper Dumbarton Castle 1477; envoy 1474 to negotiate a marriage between the Scottish heir apparent and CECILIA, dau of EDWARD IV; *m* 1st — Boyd and had:

1 HUMPHREY

2 Robert, Bp Argyll 1473–95

1 Margaret; *m* 1430 Sir David Murray of Tullibardine (*see* ATHOLL, D)

Sir JOHN *m* 2nd *c* 1462, as her 3rd husb, Elizabeth, 2nd dau and coheir of 4th Earl of Moray of the March 1371/2 *cr*, (*see* DUNBAR, Bt, of Mochrum) and widow of Archibald Douglas, Earl of Moray (*see* QUEENSBERRY, M), and was *k* 1479 by a cannon ball at the Siege of Dunbar Castle

His est s by his 1st w,

HUMPHREY COLQUHOUN of Luss; *m* 1st Helen, dau of 2nd Lord Erskine and *de jure* 13th Earl of Mar (*qv*), and had:

1 JOHN (Sir)

2 Walter, of Lettyr

3 Patrick

4 Humphrey, of Lettyr

5 Archibald

1 Agnes; *m* 1st James Galbraith, 13th Chief of Galbraith (*see* STRATHCLYDE, B); *m* 2nd Lord Somerville (*see* 1868 edn)

2 Elizabeth; *m* James Cunningham of Polmaise

HUMPHREY COLQUHOUN of Luss *m* 2nd Mariota, dau of William Baillie of Lamington and widow of 2nd Lord Somerville (*see* 1870 edn), and *d* Aug 1493

His son and heir,

Sir JOHN COLQUHOUN of Luss; conspired 1514 with his f-in-law to seize Dumbarton Castle; *m* 1st Margaret, dau of 10th Earl of Lennox and (1st Earl of) Darnley (*see* MORAY, E), and had:

1 HUMPHREY

2 James

3 Walter; ancestor of the COLQUHOUNs of Kilmardinny and of Craigton

4 John, Rector of Stobo

1 Marion; *m* 1st 4th Lord Boyd (*see* KILMARNOCK, B); *m* 2nd Thomas Crawford of Jordanhill

2 Marjory; *m* Sir Duncan Campbell of Glenorchy (*see* 1970 edn BREADALBANE AND HOLLAND, E)

3 Katherine; *m* Duncan Macfarlane of that Ilk

Sir JOHN COLQUHOUN of Luss *m* 2nd Margaret, dau of William Cunningham of Craigends, and by her had, with two daus (including Giles *m* William Chirnside, Rector of Luss):

5 Thomas

6 Archibald

Sir JOHN *d* 1536; his est son,

HUMPHREY COLQUHOUN of Luss; *m* Katherine, dau of 1st Earl of Montrose (*see* MONTROSE, D), and *d* Jan 1537/8, having had, with other issue:

1 JOHN (Sir)

2 James, of Garscube

1 Helen; *m* James Cunningham of Aiket

2 Marion; *m* Colin Campbell of Ardkinglas

His est son,

Sir JOHN COLQUHOUN of Luss; *m* 1st Christian (*d* 1564), dau of *de jure* 15th Earl of Mar (*qv*); *m* 2nd 15 Nov 1564 Agnes, dau of 5th Lord Boyd (*see* KILMARNOCK, B), and *d* Jan 1574/5, having by her had:

1 Humphrey (Sir), of Luss; *b* 1565; feuded with the McFARLANs and McGREGORs and was *k* 1592 in his castle of Bannachra; *m* 1st 1583 Jean (*d* 1584), dau of 5th Earl of Glencairn (*see* CUNINGHAME, Bt) and widow of 5th Earl of Argyll (*see* ARGYLL, D); *m* 2nd 1585/6 Jean, dau of 1st Marquess of Hamilton (*see* HAMILTON AND BRANDON, D), by whom he had three daus (including Anna, *m* 1610 Colin Campbell, Yr. of Carrick), who resigned any right in Luss to their uncle Alexander

2 John, passed over in the succession, possibly because he was, as alleged by some sources, accessory to his bro's death

3 ALEXANDER

1 Jean; *m* Sir Matthew Stewart of Minto

2 Margaret; *m* Sir James Edmonstone of Duntreath (*see* EDMONSTONE, Bt)

Sir HUMPHREY's bro,

ALEXANDER COLQUHOUN of Luss; continued the feud with the McGREGORs, reaching a climax in an encounter at Glenfruin 1603; *m* Helen, dau of Sir George Buchanan of that Ilk, and *d* 23 May 1617, leaving, with other issue:

1 JOHN (Sir), 1st Bt

2 Humphrey, of Balvie, MP Dunbartonshire 1643–49, by whose interposition in his bro's time the estates were saved; *m* Margaret, dau of 8th Lord Somerville, and *dsp*

1 Jean; *m* 1st 1626 5th Lord Cathcart (*see* CATHCART, E); *m* 2nd Sir Duncan Campbell, 2nd Bt, of Auchinbreck (*qv*); *m* 3rd Sir William Hamilton, 3rd s of 1st Earl of Abercorn (*see* ABERCORN, D)

2 Nancy

3 Katherine; *m* Sir John Mure of Auchindraine

The est son,

Sir JOHN COLQUHOUN of Luss, 1st Bt NS, so *cr* 30 Aug 1625, with remainder to heirs male whatsoever; warrant issued for his arrest 1632 on charge of abducting his sis-in-law, Katherine, the life-rents of his estates made over to Sir Robert Douglas of Spott, 1st and last Viscount Belhaven, but Sir JOHN's bro Humphrey recovered the estates and conveyed them 1646 to Sir JOHN's est son; *m* 6 July 1620 Lilias, dau of 4th Earl of Montrose (*see* MONTROSE, D), and *d c* 1650, having had issue:

1 Sir JOHN COLQUHOUN of Luss, 2nd Bt, acquired Balloch from the Duke of Lennox 1652 and Lochend (which he sold in 1676) by marriage; *m* 17 Feb 1636 Margaret (*m* 2nd April 1677 Archibald Stirling, 3rd of Garden, and *d* 20 July 1679, leaving further issue), dau and heir of Sir Gideon Baillie, 1st and last Bt, of Lochend, and *d* 11 April 1676, having had, with other issue:

(1) Sir JAMES COLQUHOUN of Luss, 3rd Bt, *d* unm 1680

(1) Lilias; *m* 1st 1675, as his 2nd w, Sir John Stirling, 8th of Keir and 5th of Cawder, and had issue; *m* 2nd Charles, s of 3rd Earl of Lauderdale (*qv*)

(2) Christian; *m* William Cunningham of Craigends

(3) Helen; *m* Robert Dickson of Sornbeg

2 Sir JAMES COLQUHOUN of Luss, 4th Bt; *m* by 1669 Penuel, dau of James Cunningham, of Ballyachen, Co Donegal, and *d* 1688, having had issue:

(1) HUMPHREY (Sir), 5th Bt

(2) James; *m* Deborah (*d* 1699), dau and coheiress of Henry Blennerhassett, of Castle Hassett, and had, with a yr dau:

1a Lillias *m* Alexander Squire and had issue

(1) Elizabeth; *m* Alexander Falconer of Kipps

3 Alexander, of Tilliquhoun; *m* Annabella, dau of Archibald Stewart of Scotstoun, and *d* 1718, having had:

(1) John, of Tilliquhoun; as heir male of the 1st Bt from 1718 assumed the btcy, though his right had been barred by the regrant 1704 (*see* below); *m* Elizabeth, dau of Andrew Anderson, King's Printer Scotland, and had:

1a Humphrey, of Tilliquhoun; also assumed the btcy; *d* unm 19 Aug 1722

(2) James; Capt 3rd Foot Gds; *m* Elizabeth of Tilliquhoun, dau of John Colquhoun of Auchintarlie, and had:

1a George, of Tilliquhoun; Col in serv of States General; assumed btcy on death of his cousin Humphrey 1722; *m* 1st 7 Jan 1751 Rebecca (*dspm*), only dau of William Jones, Collector Stamp Duties; *m* 2nd 1777 Charlotte (*d* 1 Feb 1816), dau of David Barclay, and *d* 1785, leaving by her:

1b James, of Tilliquhoun; Lt 19th Foot; assumed the btcy 1785; *d* unm 1799

2b George, of Tilliquhoun; Capt 2nd Royals; assumed btcy 1799; *d* unm Salamanca 22 July 1812

3b Robert David, of Tilliquhoun; *b* posthumously 1786; Brevet Maj Bengal Army; assumed btcy 1812; *m* Feb 1822 Anna Maria, 2nd dau of James Colvin, of Calcutta, and *dsp* 2 June 1838, when the issue male of the 1st Bt expired

1b Rebecca; *m* Gen James Alexander Farquharson, of Oakley, and had issue

(1) Jean; *m* 1647 Walter Stewart

(2) Lilias; *m* 1649 John Napier, Yr. of Kilmahew

(3) Katherine; *m* 1659 John Drummond of Pitkellonie

The 4th Bt's er son,

Sir HUMPHREY COLQUHOUN of Luss, 5th Bt; MP (S Parl) Dunbartonshire 1703; having no sons he resigned his btcy to the Crown 30 March 1704 and obtained 29 April 1704 a new patent with the former precedency and limitation, failing heirs male of his body, to James Grant of Pluscardine and the heirs male of the latter's marriage with his (Sir HUMPHREY's) dau; in 1706 he entailed his lands on Humphrey Grant, his dau's est son, and the heirs male of the latter's body, whom failing on the other sons of the marriage, and the heirs male of their body, with the proviso that the Grant and Colquhoun estates were never to be united; *m* 4 April 1684 Margaret, dau of Sir Patrick Houstoun of that Ilk, 1st Bt, and *d* 1718, having had:

ANNE Colquhoun; *b* 1685; *m* 29 Jan 1702 Sir JAMES GRANT later COLQUHOUN (on inheriting his f-in-law's btcy 1718) later still GRANT again (on inheriting the Grant estates of his er bro 1719) of Pluscardine (*d* 16 Jan 1747), 2nd son of Ludovic Grant of Grant, and *d* 25 June 1724, having had, with other issue (*see* STRATHSPEY, B):

1 Sir LUDOVIC COLQUHOUN, 7th Bt; *b* 13 Jan 1707; advocate 1728, MP Moray 1741–61; became heir apparent to the Grant estates 1732 so that he was obliged to make over the Colquhoun estates, which he had till then held, to his bro James; *s f* in Grant estates 1747 and was ancestor of the Earls of Seafield (*qv*) and Barons Strathspey (*qv*), to the latter of whom the btcy *cr* in 1625 eventually passed, though male heirs of the junior line dealt with below are in remainder to it

2 JAMES (Sir), **1st Bt**

The 4th son,

Sir James Colquhoun of Luss, 1st Bt (GB), so *cr* 27 June 1786; *b* 22 Feb 1714; *s* to the Colquhoun estates as heir under the entail of 1706 after considerable litigation with his bro, Sir Ludovic; built the modern mansion of Rossdhu; *m* 12 April 1740 Helen (*d* 7 Jan 1791), sis of 17th Earl of Sutherland (*qv*), and had, with other issue:

1 JAMES (Sir), **2nd Bt**

1 Ludovic; *b* 25 July 1757; Lt-Col; *m* 19 Dec 1801 Barbara Camilla, dau of Rev Dr Joseph McIntyre, and *d* 5 Jan 1835, leaving five sons and a dau

The 1st Bt's son,

Sir James Colquhoun of Luss, 2nd Bt; *b* 28 July 1741; Sheriff Dunbartonshire 1775, Pncpl Clerk of Session 1779; *m* 22 July 1773 Mary, dau and coheir of James Falconer, of Monktown, Co Edinburgh, and had, with other issue:

1 JAMES (Sir), **3rd Bt**

1 Jane Falconer; *m* 28 Sept 1803 David Kemp of Balsusney

2 Wilhelmina; *m* 15 July 1808 John Campbell of Stonefield and *d* 22 Dec 1833

3 Catherine Falconer; *m* 21 July 1815 Alexander Miller of Earnock and *d* 22 Nov 1862

Sir JAMES *d* 20 April 1805; his est son,

Sir James Colquhoun of Luss, 3rd Bt; *b* 28 Sept 1774; *m* June 1799 Janet (*d* 21 Oct 1846), dau of Sir John Sinclair of Ulbster, 1st Bt (*see* THURSO, V), and *d* 3 Feb 1836, having had, with another s and daus:

1 **Sir James Colquhoun of Luss, 4th Bt**; *b* 1804; Dunbartonshire: MP 1837–41, Ld Lt; *m* 14 June 1843 Jane (*d* 3 May 1844), 2nd dau of Sir Robert Abercromby, 5th Bt (*qv*), and was drowned in Loch Lomond 18 Dec 1873, leaving an only child:

(1) **Sir James Colquhoun of Luss, 5th Bt**; *b* 20 March 1844; Ld Lt Dunbartonshire; MA Cambridge; *m* 1st 8 Dec 1875 Charlotte Mary Douglas (*d* 9 Jan 1902), dau of Maj William Monro, 79th Highrs, by Elizabeth, dau of Sir Robert Abercromby, 5th Bt (*qv*), and had issue:

1a Constance Janet Sinclair Flora Abercromby; *b* 1 Sept 1884; *m* 7 Nov 1908 Frederick Charles Lockhart Robertson, er son of Charles Alexander Lockhart Robertson, MD, of Guns Green, and *d* March 1948, leaving issue

2a Dorothea Helen Mary Elizabeth Sutherland; *b* 28 Sept 1885; *m* 29 Feb 1908 Evelyn George Massey Carmichael of Carmichael, OBE, JP, FSA, MA Oxford (*d* 14 July 1959), barrister, only son of Lt-Col George Lynedoch Carmichael, and *d* 2 Sept 1963, leaving issue

(1) (cont.) **Sir James** *m* 2nd 9 Nov 1904 Ivie Muriel Helen (*m* 2nd 7 Sept 1909 Col Henry Harington, W Yorks Regt (*d* 18 Jan 1941), son of Rev James Douglas Harington, of Crewe Green, Cheshire), only dau of Maj Ives McLean Urquhart, Roy Inniskilling Fus, of The Avenue, Kew, and *dspm* 13 March 1907

2 John, DL and JP; *b* 6 March 1805; author: *The Moor and the Loch*, 4th Roy Irish Dragoon Gds; *m* 29 Jan 1834 Frances Sarah (*d* 28 May 1877), 4th dau of E Fuller Maitland, of Park Place, Stansted Hall, Essex, and Garth House, Breconshire, and *d* 1885, having had, with other issue:

(1) James, DL Dunbartonshire; *b* 3 March 1835; Lt-Col Highland Borderers and 4th Dragoon Gds; *m* 26 Jan 1876 Anna Maria (*d* 18 Dec 1913), yst dau of Robert Kerr Elliot, DL, of Harwood, and Clifton Park, Roxburghshire, and *dvp* 1883, having had:

1a Violet Annie Douglas; *m* 1913 Brig James Melville Hamilton, DSO, Gordon Highrs, and 24 April 1950

2a Frances Louisa Helen; *m* 13 Oct 1906 Maj Sir George Frederick Lancelot Clayton-East, 8th Bt, OBE (*see* CLAYTON, Bt), and *d* 29 Jan 1950, leaving issue

(2) ALAN JOHN (Sir), **6th Bt**

(3) Roderick William; *b* 29 Aug 1847; Maj and Hon Lt-Col 3rd Bn Argyll and Sutherland Highrs, DL, JP Dunbartonshire; *m* 28 June 1882 his cousin Alice (*d* 7 Oct 1930), dau of William Fuller Maitland, of Stansted Hall and Garth House, and *dsp* 15 Nov 1918

(1) Helen Augusta; *m* 8 Sept 1863 Very Rev Norman Macleod (*d* 11 Dec 1911), DD, Pncpl Clerk Gen Assembly Ch of Scotland

(2) Flora Maitland; *m* 22 June 1877 Sir Colin George Macrae (*d* 9 Dec 1925), of Glenflora, Colinton, Edinburgh, and *d* 24 Nov 1921, leaving issue

(3) Janet Sinclair; *m* 17 Oct 1872 Rev Arthur Hastings Berger, Vicar Cobham, Kent, and had issue

(4) Lucy Bethia, novelist; *m* 23 June 1869 Alfred Saunders Walford (*d* 31 July 1907), of 17 Warwick Sq, London, and *d* 11 May 1915, leaving issue

1 Helen; *m* 9 April 1829 John Page Reade, of Stutton Ho, Suffolk, and *d* 17 Oct 1852, leaving a son

The 5th Bt's cousin,

Sir Alan John Colquhoun of Luss, 6th Bt, KCB, JP, DL Co Dumbarton; *b* 19 Sept 1838; Hon Col Duke of Edinburgh's Own RF Res Art, Lt-Col and Hon Col cmdg 3rd Bde Scottish Div RA, formerly 42nd Roy Highrs (Black Watch) and 16th Lancers; *m* 1st 17 April 1884 Justine Henrietta (*d* 24 June 1905), dau of John Kennedy, of Underwood; *m* 2nd 3 July 1906 Anna Helena (*d* 26 March 1947), dau of Duncan MacRae of Conchra, DL, JP, and by his 1st w had issue:

1 IAIN (Sir), **7th Bt**

2 Alan Roderick, Capt 3rd Bn Argyll and Sutherland Highrs; *b* 21 Jan 1891; *d* unm 19 April 1954

1 Mary; *m* 23 June 1922 Cdr John Wyndham Cookson, RN (*d* 29 Sept 1958), son of William Reginald Cookson, of Binfield Park, Berks, and *d* 30 March 1963, leaving issue

2 Helen Margaret; *m* 16 Aug 1926 Capt Michael Conder Harewell Smith-Carington (*d* 19 Nov 1973), er son of Richard Smith-Carington, of Southbury Ho, Great Malvern, and *dsp* 12 Oct 1955

3 Justina Rose; *d* unm 10 Nov 1958

The 6th Bt *d* 14 March 1910; his er son,

Sir Iain Colquhoun of Luss, 7th Bt, KT (1937), DSO (1916) amd bar (1918), LLD; *b* 20 June 1887; Hon Col 9th Bn Argyll and Sutherland Highrs, Lt-Col Scots Gds, Hon Col Glasgow U OTC 1934, Pres Dumbarton TAA, Hon Col RA (TA) 1939, Ld Lt and Convener Dunbartonshire, Scottish Ecclesiastical Commr 1930, Ld HC Gen Assembly Ch Scotland 1932, 1940 and 1941, memb Roy Commn Ancient and Historical Monuments and Constructions Scotland 1934, chm Nat Tst Scotland, Ld Rector Glasgow U 1934–37, Grand Master Mason Scotland 1936, served WW I (wounded, despatches); enthusiastic proponent of the manly aspects of Highland stalking, going out in the deer forests himself barefoot; *m* 10 Feb 1915 Geraldine Bryde (Dinah) (*d* 20 July 1974), 2nd dau of Francis John Tennant, of Innes, Morayshire (*see* GLENCONNER, B), and *d* 12 Nov 1948, having had:

1 Sir IVAR IAIN COLQUHOUN of Luss, **8th and present Bt**

2 Donald Alen, Capt Scots Gds WW II 1939–46; *b* 19 Jan 1920; *educ* Eton; *m* 19 Nov 1946 *Josephine Griselda, only dau of Charles Wilfrid Janson, of 16 Wilton Crescent, London SW1, and *d* 1992, leaving issue:

(1) +James; *b* 22 Sept 1947; *educ* Gordonstoun

(2) +Iain; *b* 1 Jan 1949; *educ* Gordonstoun

(1) *Catherine; *b* 8 Oct 1959

1 *Fiona Bryde [The Rt Hon Fiona Countess of Arran, Pimlico House, Hemel Hempstead, Herts]; *m* 11 June 1937 8th Earl of Arran (*d* 1983; *qv*), and has issue

2 *Robina; WRNS; *m* 26 Oct 1950 *Alan Lewis Wigan, KRRC (Res), yr son of Sir Rod Wigan, 3rd Bt (*qv*), and has issue

3 *(Frances) Mary [Miss Mary Colquhoun, 15 Shawfield St, London SW3]; *b* 27 Sept 1925; served in WRNS

COLT

Arms: Argent a fess between three colts in full speed sable. **Crest:** A colt passant or. **Motto:** *Vincit qui patitur* ('He conquers who endures'). **Creation:** Bt. (E) 2 March 1693/4.

SIR EDWARD WILLIAM DUTTON COLT, 10TH BT, of St James's, Westminster, Middlesex [Sir Edward Colt Bt, 12 E 88th St, New York, NY 10128, USA]; *b* 22 Sept 1936; *s* unc 1951; *educ* Douai and U Coll Hosp (MB, MRCP, BS); Assoc Clinical Prof of Medicine, Columbia U, Assoc Attending Physician St Luke's Hosp, New York, formerly Medical Registrar UCH, House Physician Brompton Hosp; FRCP, FACP; *m* 1st 20 Aug 1966 (*divorce*1972) Jane Caroline, dau of James Histed Lewis, of Pont Céard, Versoix, Geneva, and Washington, DC; *m* 2nd 1979 *Suzanne Nelson (*née* Knickerbocker) and by her has had:

1 Tristan Charles Edward; *b* 27 June 1983; *d* 19 May 1992

1 *Angela Cecily; *b* 1979

Lineage: THOMAS COLT, of Carlisle, Cumberland; *m* —, dau of Nicholas Girlington, of Hackforth, Yorks, and had:

THOMAS COLT, PC *temp* EDWARD IV, of Netherhall, Roydon, Essex; administrator of the estates of RICHARD, DUKE OF YORK, f of EDWARD IV, Keeper of the Hanaper of Chancery, Keeper of the Rolls of Chancery in Ireland; *m* Johanna (*m* 2nd Sir William Parr and *d* 1473), dau and heir of John Trusbut, of Runcton Holme, Norfolk, and *d* 22 Aug 1471, having had:

JOHN COLT, of Netherhall (Newhall), Essex, and Grays Colt's Hall, Cavendish, Suffolk; had livery of his lands 5 Nov 1485; *m* 1st Elizabeth, dau of his guardian in minority Sir John Elrington, Treasurer of the Household to EDWARD IV, and had, with several daus (includingJoan or Jane *m* Sir Thomas More; *see* TEYNHAM, B):

1 GEORGE (Sir)

JOHN COLT *m* 2nd Mary (*m* 2nd — Higham, of Essex), dau of Sir John de Lisle, and by her had:

2 Thomas; *m* Magdalen Middleton and had issue

JOHN COLT *d* by 25 Nov 1521; his er son,

Sir GEORGE COLT, of Colt's Hall; ktd 1578; *m* Elizabeth (*d* 15 Sept 1569), dau of Henry Mackwilliam, of Stambourne, Essex, and *d* 23 March 1578/9, having had, with a yr son (John):

HENRY COLT, of Netherhall, Essex; *m* 1st Elizabeth, dau of John Coningsby, of N Mimms, Herts; *m* 2nd Margaret (*bur* 6 May 1603), dau of John Heath, and *dvp* 1577, leaving by his 1st w an est son:

GEORGE COLT, of Colt's Hall, Suffolk, and Netherhall, Clay Hall and Little Paringdon, Essex; High Sheriff Suffolk 1587; *m* Mary, dau of William Poley, of Boxted, Suffolk, and was *bur* 5 Jan 1615/6, leaving:

Sir HENRY COLT, of Colt's Hall and Netherhall; ktd Feb 1604/5; *m* Bridget (*bur* 24 Jan 1633/4), dau of Sir William Kingsmill, of Sydmonton, Hants, and *d* abroad *c* 1635, having had an est son:

GEORGE COLT, of Colt's Hall; *bapt* 17 Aug 1614; *m* Elizabeth (*d* by 22 Dec 1674), est dau and coheir of John Dutton, MP, of Sherborne, Glos (*see* 1970 edn SHERBORNE, B), by Elizabeth, dau of Sir Henry Baynton, of Bromham, Wilts, and *d* in exile with CHARLES II 20 Jan 1658/9 drowned at sea, having had, with other issue:

1 John Dutton, MP Leominster; *bapt* 16 March 1642/3; *m* 1st 31 Aug 1671 Mary (*d* 15 Feb 1702/3), dau and heir of John Booth, of Letton Court, Herefs, and had issue; *m* 2nd Margaret (*bur* 30 Oct 1730), widow of John Arnold, MP, and dau of Edward Cooke, of Highnam Court, Glos, and was *bur* 4 May 1722, having had by his 1st w, with other issue:

(1) John Dutton, High Sheriff Herefs 1719; *bapt* 19 May 1673; *m* Mary (*d* 6 Aug 1761), yst dau of John Arnold, MP, of Llanvihangel Court, Mon, and was *bur* 4 Feb 1730/1, having had issue:

1a JOHN DUTTON (Sir), **2nd Bt**

1a Sophia Maria; *m* 1 Aug 1751 Rev John Lacy (*d* March 1768), of Weobley, Herefs, and *d* by 22 June 1803

2 William Dutton (Sir); *bapt* 2 March 1645/6; Master of the Horse to PRINCE RUPERT, ktd 1684, Hon MD Oxford 1680; Envoy to Hanover, Celle, Brunswick and Dresden 1689–93; *m* 1st Lucy, dau of Thomas Webb; *m* 2nd Dorothy, dau

of Henry Sanderson; m 3rd 20 Nov 1684 Mary, dau and coheir of John Garneys and widow of William Shipman, and *d* at Heilbronn Aug 1693, leaving issue by his first and last marriages (*see* 1963 edn BURRARD, Bt)

3 **Sir Henry Dutton Colt, 1st Bt** (E), so *cr* 2 March 1693/4, with remainder, in default of direct male issue, to his bro John; Adj to PRINCE RUPERT, Ensign Yeomen Gd, MP Westminster *temp* WILLIAM III and ANNE; *m* Cecilia, dau of Francis Brewster, of Wrentham, Suffolk, and widow of Sir Thomas Hatton, and *dsp* 25 April 1731

4 Edward Dutton, Col of a Regt of Foot which was formed into Marines 1698, *k* in a duel Hyde Park 7 Dec 1700

The 1st Bt's gn,

Rev Sir John Dutton Colt, 2nd Bt, JP Herefs; Rector Letton and Willersley, Herefs, and Cold Weston, Salop; *m* 24 June 1747 Mary Powell, of London, and was *bur* 4 May 1809, having had issue:

1 JOHN (Sir), **3rd Bt**

2 James (Rev), BA Cambridge; *m* Mallet (*d* 13 Jan 1827), dau of James Bowman Clarke, of Leominster, and *dsp* 31 Aug 1832

1 Anne; *m* 4 May 1784 Rev John Lodge (*d* 23 July 1830), BA Oxford, Vicar Bosbury, Herefs, and *d* 21 Feb 1785

The 2nd Bt's er son,

Sir John Colt, 3rd Bt; *bapt* 12 Nov 1750; *m* 24 July 1774 Mallet (*d* 5 Jan 1824), est dau of Capt George Langley, RM, of Golding, Cound, Salop, by Hon Mallet Vaughan, only dau of 2nd Viscount Lisburne (*see* LISBURNE, E), and was *bur* 29 June 1810, having had, with other issue:

1 **Sir John Dutton Colt, 4th Bt**, High Sheriff Radnorshire 1838; *bapt* 6 Nov 1774; *d* unm 10 Jan 1845

2 EDWARD VAUGHAN (Sir), **5th Bt**

1 Anne Sophia; *m* 4 Feb 1828 Rev George Woodhouse (*d* 21 Oct 1846), Vicar Leominster, and *d* 25 Nov 1876

The 4th Bt's bro,

Sir Edward Vaughan Colt, 5th Bt; *bapt* 17 Feb 1782; *m* 6 Sept 1804 Frances Martha (*d* 16 July 1865), dau of Harry Gough, yst son of Walter Gough, of Oldfallings and Perry Hall, Staffs, and first cousin of Richard Gough, antiquary, and *d* 9 June 1849, having had issue:

1 **Rev Sir Edward Harry Vaughan Colt, 6th Bt**, Vicar Hill, Glos; *bapt* 13 Jan 1807; *educ* Queen's Coll Oxford (BA); *m* 6 March 1844 Ellen Cotton (*d* 30 April 1870), yst dau of Dr Francis Hickin Northen, MD, of Lea Ho, Staffs, and *d* 15 Oct 1882, leaving:

(1) Frances Sophia Vaughan; *m* 1st 1 Dec 1863 (*divorce* 1881) Frederick Henry Cator and had issue; *m* 2nd 22 Feb 1882 Maj Walter Illingworth Haynes, late Roy Sussex Regt (*d* 19 Nov 1898), and *d* 27 Nov 1904

2 THOMAS ARCHER (Sir), **7th Bt**

1 Martha Elizabeth Flora; *m* 16 July 1845 Rev David Williams (*d* 24 Feb 1882), MA Oxford, Hon Canon St Asaph, Rector Nannerch, Flints, and Castle Caereinion, Montgomeryshire, and *d* 25 Sept 1888, leaving issue

2 Sophia Leonora; *m* 2 July 1851 Rev G H Kirwood, MA (*d* 30 Nov 1898), Vicar St Martin's, Hereford, and *dsp* 23 Feb 1854

The 6th Bt's bro,

Sir Thomas Archer Colt, 7th Bt, MD; *bapt* 14 Nov 1815; *m* 13 Sept 1849 Frances (*d* 31 March 1892), yst dau of Elias Chadwick, of Swinton Hall, Lancs, and *d* 26 Feb 1893, leaving:

1 **Rev Sir Edward Harry Dutton Colt, 8th Bt**; *b* 3 Oct 1850; *educ* Merton Coll Oxford (MA), Rector Monk Okehampton Devon 1889–97; *m* 4 Sept 1889 Alice (*d* 8 Dec 1952), dau of William Jefferys Strange, of Mile Ho, Sulhampstead, Berks, and *d* 23 June 1931, leaving:

(1) Flora Margaret Frances Sophia Dutton Vaughan; *m* 26 Jan 1921 Maj John Maunder Webb Gill (*d* 21 July 1935), 3rd Devon Regt, son of John Maunder Gill, of Moombye, NSW, and had issue

(2) *Stella Theodora Dutton Vaughan; *m* 15 Nov 1932 Rev Claude Alfred Wigglesworth Russell (*d* 9 Jan 1955), Preb Exeter

2 Thomas Archer, OBE (1920), LRCP (Edin), MRCS (Eng); *b* 29 Dec 1851; *m* 1st 27 June 1881 (*divorce* 1895) Mabel Marion Aileen, 2nd dau of Rev H L Nicholson, DD, and had issue:

(1) **Sir Henry Archer Colt, 9th Bt**, DSO, MC; *b* 16 Sept 1882; Lt-Cdr RN, WW I as Lt-Col 12th Bn Glos Regt (severely wounded, despatches twice), S/Ldr RAFVR WW II, Area Cdr Ulster Special Constab Co Tyrone 1922–26; *m* 1927 Louisa May (*d* March 1952), dau of Joseph Edward Whitaker, of Paignton, Devon, and widow of John Cuthbert Whittam, of Branksome Park, Bournemouth, and *dsp* 10 Feb 1951

(1) Mabel Emily; *b* 26 July 1884; *m* 7 June 1915 Henry Trevor Meredith (*d* 1966), and had a son (*ka* WW II)

(2) Helen Enid; *b* 5 April 1887; *d* unm 30 Nov 1968

2 (cont.) Thomas Colt *m* 2nd 1897 Annie Mercy (*d* 28 June 1937), dau of William Kennett, of Chidham, Sussex, and *d* 23 April 1930, having by her had issue:

(2) John Rochfort, Maj N Staffs Regt WW II; *b* 6 June 1900; *m* 15 Dec 1928 Angela Miriam Kyan (*m* 2nd 29 Nov 1946 Capt Robert Leslie Cock, N Staffs Regt), and *das* 21 Nov 1944, having had issue:

1a John Archer; *b* 6 Dec 1929; *d* an infant

2a Sir EDWARD WILLIAM DUTTON COLT, **10th and present Bt**

1a *Joan Margaret Roper, MA (Aberdeen) 1953, MB, ChB 1959; *b* 16 Feb 1932; *m* 3 Oct 1964 *John Malcolm Campbell, son of Arthur James Campbell, of The Old Barn, Uplyme, Lyme Regis, Dorset, and has issue:

1b *Gay Lindsey Helen; *b* 30 Dec 1965

1 Francis Alice; *d* unm 1928

2 Maud; *d* 28 Nov 1923

3 Lucy Sophia; *d* 17 July 1924

COLTHURST

Arms: Argent on a fess azure between three colts courant sable as many trefoils slipped or. **Crest:** A colt statant sable. **Motto:** *Justum ac tenacem* ('Just and persevering'). **Creation:** Bt. (I) 3 Aug 1744.

SIR RICHARD LA TOUCHE COLTHURST, 9TH BT, of Ardrum, Co Cork [Sir Richard Colthurst Bt, Blarney Castle, Co Cork, Ireland]; *b* 14 Aug 1928; *s f* 1955; *educ* Harrow and Peterhouse Cambridge (MA); memb Internat Dendrology Soc, host and organiser Blarney Castle Internat Three Day Event 1992–, Liveryman Grocers' Co; *m* 24 Oct 1953 *Janet Georgina, only dau of Leonard Almroth Wilson-Wright, of Coolcarrigan, Co Kildare, by Florence Janet Margaret, er dau of James Ivory, of Brewlands, Glenisla, Angus, and has issue:

1 +CHARLES ST JOHN [Charles Colthurst Esq, Turret Farm, Blarney, Co Cork, Ireland]; *b* 21 May 1955; *educ* Eton, Magdalene Coll Cambridge (MA) and U Coll Dublin; slr Cork, memb Irish Timber Growers; *m* 1987 *Nora Mary, dau of Mortimer Kelleher, of Dooniskey, Lissarda, Co Cork, and has issue:

(1) +John Conway La Touche; *b* 13 Oct 1988

(1) *Charlotte Louisa Margaret; *b* 1990

(2) *Isabel Janet Denys; *b* 1991

(3) *Olivia; *b* 199–

2 +James Richard [James Colthurst Esq FRCS, Balsdon Farm House, Folly Rd, Inkpen, Berks RG17 9DH]; *b* 7 March 1957; *educ* Eton (rowed for England Youth Internat 1973–74) and St Thomas's Med Sch, London U (BSc, MB, BS) 1982, FRCS (Edin) 1985; MBA (Brunel) 1992, inventor, medical business consultant; *m* 1990 *Dominique G, er dau of Gale Coles, of Little Streele, Framfield, E Sussex, and has:

(1) *Leah Alexandra; *b* 23 Oct 1994

(2) *Cecily Rachel; *b* June 1997

3 +Henry Nicholas Almroth [Henry Colthurst Esq, Asserton House, Berwick St James, Wilts SP3 4TZ]; *b* 10 Jan 1959; *educ* Eton and Christ's Coll Cambridge (MA); Liveryman Grocers' Co; *m* 5 June 1983 *Sophia Selina Irene, dau of Sir John Hervey-Bathurst, 7th Bt (*qv*), and has issue:

(1) +Edward Henry John; *b* 1986

(1) *Harriet Sophia; *b* 1984

(2) *Caroline Georgina; *b* 1991

1 *Georgina Margaret; *b* 16 Feb 1961; organiser Blarney Castle Internat Three Day Event 1992–, author: *Fighting Back* (1990)

Lineage (of Colthurst): HENRY COLTHURST, of Standen in Great Mitton, Yorks; *b c* 1460; *m* —, dau of Christopher Parker, of Radholme in Bolland, and *d* by 1516, leaving issue:

1 Giles, of Standen; *m* and *d* 1552, leaving issue:

(1) Henry; *b* 1526

2 Thomas, of Edisford in Gt Mitton; *m* 1517 Isabel, dau of Ralph Catterall, of Catterall, by Elizabeth, dau of James Butler, of Rawcliffe, and had issue:

(1) Henry, of Edisford Hall; *m* 1st —, dau of Roger Knolles, of Over Browsholme, Yorks, and had issue:

1a Thomas, of Edisford; *m c* Nov 1552 Anne, dau of Oliver Breres, of Preston, Lancs, and *d* 1586, leaving:

1b Isabel; *m* Walter Hawkesworth (*d* 11April 1620), of Hawkesworth, who obtained Edisford

2b Grace; *m* Nicholas Curwen, of Stubbs

3b Ann; *m* Henry Dyneley, of Bramhope, Yorks, and had issue

2a William, *dsp* by 18 Sept 1566

3a Richard, living 1586, when he claimed the Edisford estates as heir male

4a Henry, ancestor of the COLTHURSTs of Upleatham, Yorks

1a Isabel; *m* 1st 1558 Giles Parker (*d* 1572), of Horrocksford; *m* 2nd 1573 Robert Walbank (living 1592)

2a Jane; *m* after 1558 Thomas Heber (*d* by 1601), of Marton, and had issue

(1) (cont.) Henry Colthurst *m* 2nd Anne (*m* 2nd Reginald Heber, of Marton), dau of John Malham, of Elslack, by Lucy, dau of William Clapham, of Beamley, and *d* between 6 May 1554 and 5 Oct 1558, having by her had:

5a Christopher, captained the London ship *Passport* (80 tons) against the Spanish Armada 1588

3 HENRY, of whom presently

The yst son,

HENRY COLTHURST; living 1573; *m* —, dau of Giles Parker, of Horrocksford and Brownsholme, Yorks, and had issue:

1 Matthew, of Wardour Castle, Wilts, Treasurer of the Ordnance 1554, acquired much monastic property in Somerset; *m* 1st Anne, dau of Thomas Grimston, of Suffolk, and had issue:

(1) Edmund, of Hinton Priory, Somerset, which he sold together with most of his other estates; *b* 1527; *m* Elinor (*bur* 27 April 1586), dau of Thomas de la Rivere, of Bransbye, Yorks, and *d* after 1611, having had issue:

1a Henry, of Treley, Cornwall; *b c* 1565; *m* Dorothy (*bur* 13 March 1640), dau of John Trengove, of Nance, Cornwall, and *d* after 1620, leaving issue:

1b Margery; *m c* 23 Sept 1620 Hugh Pollard, of Horwood, Devon

2a Edward; *bapt* 29 July 1570; *bur* 2 Jan 1579

3a Walter; *bapt* 28 May 1576

4a Delariver; *bapt* 7 March 1579

1a Jane; *bur* 11 March 1581

2a Elizabeth; *bapt* 20 Oct 1566

3a Dorothy

4a Mary; *bapt* 13 June 1574

(2) Matthew, living 1559

(3) Andrew, went to Ireland with Sir Walter Raleigh, who granted him lands there, later of Stoney Littleton in Wellow, Som; *bur* 20 Oct 1603

(4) Richard (Rev), Rector Claverton, Somerset 1556; *d* 1581

(5) Thomas, went to Ireland and was granted the castle and manor of Shane and other lands there 8 Sept 1589; had issue:

1a Thomas; *bapt* 2 Jan 1573/4

(1) Mary

1 (cont.) Matthew Colthurst *m* 2nd Anne (*m* 2nd Lawrence Hyde, of West Hatch, 3rd son of Robert Hyde, of Norbury, Cheshire, and was great-grandmother of QUEENs MARY II and ANNE), dau of Nicholas Sybill, of Chamblains, Eynsford, Kent, and *d* 8 July 1559, having by her had issue:

(2) Elizabeth; *m* John Dackcombe, of Iwerne Stapleton, Dorset, and had issue

(3) Anne; *m* — Crane

2 Henry, of Clitheroe, Lancs; *m* and had issue:

(1) Matthew

(2) Henry

(3) Roger

(4) Thomas; *m* Katherine Audley, of York, and *d* on or after 18 June 1588

3 JOHN

4 James, living 1559

The 3rd son,

JOHN COLTHURST; living 1559, allegedly settled in Ireland, Col; *m* and was allegedly *k* by native Irish 1607, having had issue:

1 John, of Aunsby, Lincs; owned land in S Petherton, Somerset; *m* Mary (*m* 2nd John Lake, of Normanton, Yorks), dau of William Beane, and *d* between 21 May and 12 June 1572, leaving three sons (John; Edmond; Thomas) and six daus (Bridget; Mary; Gertrude; Elizabeth; Alice; Anne)

2 EDWARD

The yr son,

Rev EDWARD COLTHURST, Vicar Tilshead, Wilts; *m* Margery — and *d* between 24 Nov 1598 and 27 Feb 1598/9, leaving issue, with four daus (Anne; Constance; Margery; Thomasine):

1 CHRISTOPHER

2 Edward, ancestor of the COLTHURSTs of North Petherton

3 William, of Lyncombe and Widcombe, Somerset; living 1630; *m* Elizabeth — and had issue:

(1) William; *bapt* 24 Feb 1631

(2) Edward; *bapt* 2 May 1633

(3) Thomas, of Lyncombe and Widcombe; *m* 1st Sarah —, and had issue:

1a Thomas, of Hornscombe; *bapt* 24 Sept 1672; *m* Martha, dau of Benjamin James, attorney, and was *bur* 4 April 1724, leaving his property to his cousin Thomas Colthurst, of North Petherton

2a William; *bapt* 27 Oct 1681; *m* —, *and had issue:*

1b William; *bapt* 29 March 1717

3a Edward; *bapt* 12 Feb 1683

1a Elizabeth; *bapt* 28 Nov 1678; *m* William Barber

2a Eleanor

(3) (cont.) Thomas Colthurst *m* 2nd 15 March 1676 Mary Covery

(4) Adam; *bapt* 6 July 1640

(1) Ann; *bapt* 28 Feb 1630; *bur* 17 Feb 1673/4

(2) Elizabeth; *bapt* 22 March 1634

The est son,

CHRISTOPHER COLTHURST, of City of Cork; *k* nr Macroon, Co Cork, in the 1641 Uprising, leaving issue:

JOHN COLTHURST, of Coolevissanally, Co Cork; *m* Elizabeth Beaghan and *d* by 1658, leaving issue:

JOHN COLTHURST, of Coolevissanally; *m* Ann Weeks and *d* by 1682, leaving issue:

JOHN COLTHURST, of Ballyally, Co Cork, granted extensive land in Co Cork 1684; *m* Eliza, dau of Sir Nicholas Purdon, of Ballyclough, Co Cork, and had issue:

1 Nicholas, of Ballyally; Col, High Sheriff Co Cork 1736; *m* Penelope, 3rd dau of Sir John Topham, of Dublin, Master in Chancery, and *d* 1754, leaving issue:

(1) Elizabeth; *m* Rowland Bateman, JP, of Oak Park, Co Kerry, and had issue

(2) Penelope; *m* George Dunscombe, of Mount Desert, Co Cork

2 John, of Ardrum, Co Cork, MP Tallagh 1734–57, High Sheriff Co Cork 1738; *m* 1st Alice, dau and heir of James Conway, of Clohane, Co Kerry, by Katherine, dau of Patrick FitzGerald, son of the Knight of Kerry (*see* FitzGERALD, Bt, of Valentia), and had issue:

(1) JOHN CONWAY (Sir), **1st Bt**

(2) James, of Dripsey Castle, Co Cork, High Sheriff Co Cork 1747; *m* Elizabeth (*m* 2nd 7 Aug 1763 Joseph Oates, of Kilmahouse, Co Cork, and *d* 1775), dau of Col Christopher Russell, of Pemsey, Govr of Minorca, and *d* 1757 leaving issue

(1) Honora; *m* Hawes Cross, of Cronody More, Co Cork

(2) Elizabeth

2 (cont.) John Colthurst *m* 2nd Mahetabel, dau of William Wallis, of Drishane Castle, Co Cork, and *d* 12 July 1756, having by her had issue:

(3) Wallis, of Carrigrohane Castle, Co Cork, High Sheriff Co Cork 1761; *m* Helena, sis and coheir of Barraehia Wallis, of Carrigrohane Castle, and had issue

The est son,

Sir John Conway Colthurst, 1st Bt (I), so *cr* 3 Aug 1744; MP Doneraile 1751–60, Youghal 1761–8 and Castle Martyr 1769–75; *m* 1741 Lady Charlotte FitzMaurice (*d* 9 Oct 1774), 3rd dau of 1st Earl of Kerry (*see* LANSDOWNE, M), and *d* 19 Sept 1775, having had, with three other sons:

1 **Sir John Conway Colthurst, 2nd Bt**; *d* unm 15 Feb 1787, *k* in a duel by Dominick Trant

2 **Sir Nicholas Colthurst, 3rd Bt**, High Sheriff Co Cork 1788, MP Johnstown, Co Longford, 1783–90 and Castle Martyr 1791–95; *m* 8 May 1788 Harriet (*m* 2nd 1798 Lt-Gen Gray and *d* 1841), dau of Rt Hon David La Touche, and had issue:

(1) NICHOLAS CONWAY (Sir), **4th Bt**

(1) Elizabeth; *m* Ven Edward St Lawrence (*dsp* 21 June 1842), Archdeacon of Ross, gs of 1st Earl of Howth (*see* 1909 edn)

(2) Charlotte; *m* Col William Henry Moor Hodder, of Hoddersfield, Co Cork, and *dsp* 7 March 1832

The 3rd Bt *d* July 1795; his son,

Sir Nicholas Conway Colthurst, 4th Bt; *b* Jan 1789; *educ* Eton; Col Cork Militia, Capt 68th Foot, MP City of Cork 1812–29; *m* 11 Nov 1819 Elizabeth, only dau and heir of Col George Vesey, of Lucan Ho, Co Dublin, and had, with two other sons and a dau:

1 GEORGE CONWAY (Sir), **5th Bt**

2 Charles Vesey COLTHURST later COLTHURST-VESEY (roy licence 1860), of Lucan Ho, Co Dublin, DL, High Sheriff 1858, Lt-Col 5th Bn Roy Dublin Fus; *b* 13 June 1826; *m* 20 July 1858 Annie (*d* 19 March 1911), dau of Col David Fraser, and *d* 11 May 1885, having had three sons

The 4th Bt *d* 22 June 1829; his son,

Sir George Conway Colthurst, 5th Bt, DL (Londonderry and Co Cork), JP (Co Cork); *b* 1824; *educ* Harrow and Ch Ch Oxford; High Sheriff Co Cork 1850; MP Kinsale 1863–74; *m* 16 Jan 1846 Louisa Jane (*d* 30 March 1915), only dau and heir of St John Jefferyes, of Blarney Castle, Co Cork (*see* below), and had, with other issue:

1 GEORGE ST JOHN (Sir), **6th Bt**

1 Louisa Julia; *m* 17 June 1878 Samuel Bruce, DL (*d* 1 Sept 1922), of Comber, Co Down, and *d* 19 Oct 1953 aged 96, leaving issue

3 Alice Conway; *m* 16 July 1891 Francis Pym (*see* PYM, B), and *dsp* 24 Dec 1948

The 5th Bt *d* 24 Sept 1878; his son,

Sir George St John Colthurst, 6th Bt, DL, JP; *b* 29 June 1850; *educ* Harrow; served 43rd Foot, ADC to Ld Lt Ireland; *m* 27 Aug 1881 Edith Jane Thomasina (*d* 2 Oct 1930), dau of Capt Jonas Morris, 1st Roy Dragoons, of Dunkathal, Co Cork, and *d* 25 Dec 1925, having had issue:

1 **Sir George Oliver Colthurst, 7th Bt**; *b* 24 Aug 1882; *educ* Harrow and Trin Coll Cambridge; Capt S Irish Horse WW I, Croix de Guerre, MFH Muskerry 1930–44; *d* unm 28 Feb 1951

2 RICHARD ST JOHN JEFFERYES (Sir), **8th Bt**

1 Edith Dorothy; *b* 28 April 1884; *d* 13 Nov 1892

The 7th Bt's bro,

Sir Richard St John Jefferyes Colthurst, 8th Bt; *b* 19 July 1887; *educ* Harrow and Trin Coll Cambridge (MA); High Sheriff Co Dublin 1920–21; Capt London Regt WW I; *m* 1st 2 Aug 1911 (*divorce* 1927) Cecily Charlotte (*d* 1 Jan 1958), only child of Brig-Gen Hugh Cecil Cholmondeley, CB, CBE, of Edstaston Ho, Wem, Salop (*see* DELAMERE, B), and had issue:

1 Mary Penelope, of Blarney Castle, Co Cork; *b* 16 Oct 1912; *m* 1st 27 April 1937 (*divorce* 1952) Brig Godfrey John Hamilton, CB, CBE, DSO, QVO Corps of Guides IA, er son of Lt-Col Frederick Arthur Hamilton, OBE, FRGS, of Great Osbaston, Mon, by Phyllis Addams, 2nd dau of Maj-Gen Sir Godfrey Williams, KCIE, CB, JP, and had issue:

(1) *Adriana Louise; *m* 18 March 1968 *Lt-Col Charles John Dawnay (*see* DOWNE, V)

1 (cont.) Mrs Mary Hamilton *m* 2nd 10 Sept 1952 Maj Jack Montagu Hillyard (*d* 16 Feb 1983 aged 92), late of Blarney Castle, Co Cork, son of Cdr G W Hillyard, and *d* Sept 1975

2 *Shournagh Dorothy [Mrs Robert Combe, Hundry Lodge, Hambridge, nr Langport, Somerset]; *b* 24 July 1914; *m* 20 July 1937 Lt Robert Tristram Combe, Coldstream Gds (*d* of wounds recd in action at Dunkirk 2 June 1940), only surv son of Maj Robert Thomas Combe, DL, JP, of Earnshill, Somerset, and has issue:

(1) *Richard Tristram, JP [Richard Combe Esq JP, Earnshill, Hambridge, nr Langport, Somerset]; *b* 1938; *educ* Eton; Capt Coldstream Gds, underwriting memb Lloyd's; *m* 1985 *Mrs Bridgett Anne Glide, dau of Charles Fleetwood Crombie, of S Hillside, Strete, Dartmouth, Devon

(2) *Henry Cecil; *b* 1940; *m* 1st 1968 Gillian Margaret (*d* 1973), dau of Ralph Hancock, of Port Elizabeth, S Africa, and has issue:

1a *Nicholas Hamilton; *b* 1969; Dip Eng; with Leighton Engineering Ltd, Tsing Yi Is, Hong Kong

(2) (cont.) Henry Combe *m* 2nd 1975 (*divorce* 1992) Ingerise Andersen, and has further issue:

1a *Kirstina Louise; *b* 1977

2a *Andrea Shournagh Margrethe; *b* 1979

Sir Richard *m* 2nd 3 Feb 1927 Denys Maida Hanmer (*d* 25 July 1966), er dau of Augustus William West, of Leixlip Ho, Co Kildare, by Fanny Madeline Jane, dau of Thomas Hanmer, of Talgai, Australia (*see* HANMER, Bt), and *d* 18 Feb 1955, having by her had issue:

1 Sir RICHARD LA TOUCHE COLTHURST, **9th and present Bt**

2 +(George Silver) Oliver Annesley [Oliver Colthurst Esq, Le Bourg 16450, Beaulieu-sur-Sonnette, Charente, France]; *b* 1 March 1931; *educ* Harrow and Trin Coll Cambridge (MA); late 2nd Lt The Life Gds, memb London Stock Exchange, ptnr de Zoete and Bevan 1961–81, Liveryman Goldsmiths' Co, memb Court Common Cncl (Broad St Ward) 1976–80; *m* 1st 10 Oct 1959 (*divorce* 1966) Hon Elizabeth Sophia Sidney, est dau of 1st Viscount De L'Isle (*qv*), and has:

(1) *Shaunagh Anne Henrietta; *b* 30 April 1961; *m* 1st 1980 (*divorce* 1990) Thomas Peter William Heneage and has issue (*see* MORTON, E); *m* 2nd 2 Aug 1995 *Hon Crispin Money-Coutts, est s of 8th Lord (Baron) Latymer (*qv*)

2 (cont.) Oliver Colthurst *m* 2nd 22 May 1968 *Caroline Romaine, 2nd dau of Cdr Anthony Boyce Combe, RN (*see* FARQUHAR, Bt), of Little Ferry Ho, Golspie, Sutherland, and by her has issue:

(2) *Romaine Louisa; *b* 9 April 1969

(3) *Rowena Barbara; *b* 15 Sept 1971

Lineage (of Jefferyes): Sir JAMES JEFFERYES, of Blarney Castle, Co Cork; *b* Perthshire 1685; Brig-Gen, Govr Duncannon and later Cork, Br Resident Danzig, ret to Ireland, MP Lismore 1703–13 and 1713–14; *m* 1st — Vandensinden, of Sweden (*d* there 1685), and had issue:

1 JAMES

2 Gustavus, Ensign Gds of CHARLES XII OF SWEDEN; *k* aged 16 in battle against the Danes

3 Laurence, Lt RM; *k* Siege of Gibraltar aged 19

1 Eleanor; *b* by 1682; *m* 1st *c* 1723 — Cox, est son of Sir Richard Cox, Ld Chllr Ireland (1725); *m* 2nd — Parker, son of Robert Parker, of Cork, and *dsp c* 1742

2 Elizabeth; *m* 1715 Loftus Cliffe, of Co Wexford, and had issue

3 Jane; *m* Capt William Taylor, of Perthshire, and *dsp*

Sir JAMES *m* 2nd Catherine Dranchintutin, of Sweden, and by her had issue:

4 George, *dsp*

5 Charles, *dsp*

4 Wilhelmina Maria; *m* — Hamit, and *dsp*

5 Catherina; *m* Peter Smith

The est son,

JAMES JEFFERYES, of Blarney Castle, Co Cork, Capt, Govr of Cork, Min Plen Sweden; *b* at Halmstad 1677; *m* 1st Louisa, dau of — Colman, of Danzig, and had issue:

1 Elizabeth

2 Louisa

JAMES JEFFERYES *m* 2nd Anne (*d* May 1762), est dau and coheir of Rt Hon St John Brodrick, PC, MP (*see* MIDLETON, V), and *d* 1739, having by her had issue:

1 JAMES ST JOHN

2 Allen, *dsp* 16 Feb 1759 aged *c* 21

3 Arthur, *dsp* 1 March 1760 aged *c* 18

The est son,

JAMES ST JOHN JEFFERYES, of Blarney, Co Cork, Maj 22nd Regt of Foot, Govr of Cork; *b* 1734; *m* Arabella, est dau of John Fitzgibbon, MA, barrister, of Mount Shannon, Co Limerick, and sis of John, 1st Earl of Clare, Ld Chllr Ireland, and *d* 1796, having had issue:

1 GEORGE CHARLES

1 Mary Anne; *m* 1st 27 April 1784 (*divorce* 1796) 7th Earl of Westmeath (*qv*), and had issue; *m* 2nd Hon Augustus Cavendish Bradshaw

2 Albinia Jane; *m* 1st Col Stephen Francis William Fremantle (*d* on passage from Gibraltar 1794; *see* COTTESLOE, B), and had issue; *m* 2nd 24 April 1798 Lt-Gen Sir John Taylor, KCB (*d* Dec 1843), of Castle Taylor, Co Galway, and had further issue

3 Anne; *d* unm aged *c* 17

4 Emilia; *m* 13 Aug 1793 1st Earl of Glengall (*d* 30 Jan 1819) and *d* 1836, leaving issue

The only son,

GEORGE CHARLES JEFFERYES, of Blarney, Co Cork; *m* Anne (*d* 1798), dau of Rt Hon David La Touche, PC, MP, of Dublin, and *d* 1841, leaving:

ST JOHN GEORGE JEFFERYES, of Blarney; *b* 1798; *m* Harriet (*d* 1857), dau of Col Taylor, and *d* 1862, leaving:

1 St John George, of Paris; *educ* Eton; *d* 1896

1 Louisa Jane; *m* 16 Jan 1846 **Sir George Conway Colthurst, 5th Bt** (*see* above), and had issue

Seat: Blarney Castle, Co Cork, Ireland. Originally built in the mid-15th century, when it belonged to the Maccartys or McCarthys of Muskerry, Blarney was confiscated in the late 17th century after the 4th Earl of Clancarty of the 1658 creation had sided with JAMES II against WILLIAM III. (Clancarty was the title under which Donough Maccarty was ennobled after he had laid down his arms following the defeat of the Confederation of Kilkenny in 1641–42 and fought for CHARLES I's forces against Cromwell; *see* CLANCARTY, E, preliminary remarks). The Jefferyes family bought it and added a Gothick house onto the massive keep around 1745. The house burnt down in 1828, though the keep proved (and continues to prove, despite the osculatory attrition of the eponymous stone by thousands of tourists every year) practically indestructible. An uncompromisingly Scottish baronial building was erected in the mid-1870s some way away from the original castle.

COLVILLE OF CULROSS

Arms: Quarterly, 1st and 4th, argent a cross moline sable (for COLVILLE); 2nd and 3rd, gules a fess chequy argent and azure (for LINDSAY). **Crest:** A hind's head, couped argent. **Supporters:** Dexter, a rhinoceros proper; sinister, a Hercules covered with a lion's skin, holding on his exterior shoulder a club, all proper. **Motto:** *Oublier ne puis* ('I cannot forget'). **Creations:** L. (S) 24 April 1604, B. (UK) 31 Dec 1885, V. (UK) 12 July 1902.

THE 4TH VISCOUNT COLVILLE OF CULROSS, Co Perth, **Lord Colville of Culross, Baron Colville of Culross**, Co Perth (John Mark Alexander Colville, QC (1978)) [The Rt Hon The Viscount Colville of Culross QC, c/o House of Lords, London SW1A 0PW]; *b* 19 July 1933; *s* f 1945; *educ* Rugby and New Coll Oxford (BA 1957, MA 1963); Lt Gren Gds (RARO); barrister Lincoln's Inn 1960, Bencher 1986, Min State Home Off 1972–74, memb Roy Co of Archers, Chm Parole Bd 1988–92, Recorder 1990, Circuit Judge 1993, Memb Cncl UEA 1968–72, Hon memb Rating and Valuation Assoc, dir BET 1974–; *m* 1st 4 Oct 1958 (*divorce* 1973) Mary Elizabeth, only dau of Col Mostyn Hird Wheeler Webb-Bowen, RM, of Beccles, Suffolk, and has issue:

1 +CHARLES MARK TOWNSHEND, *Master of Colville* [The Master of Colville, Rookyards, Spexhall, nr Halesworth, Suffolk]; *b* 5 Sept 1959; *educ* Rugby and Durham U (BA)

2 +(Richmond) James Innys; *b* 9 June 1961; *educ* Rugby and Bristol U (BSc) and London U (MSc); MB, BS; *m* 1993 *(Aurea) Katherine, dau of Sir Philip Manning Dowson, CBE, PRA (*see* BACON, Bt), and has:

(1) +Oliver; *b* 18 April 1996

3 +Alexander Fergus Gale; *b* 9 July 1964; *educ* Wellington and Nottingham Poly (BSc); *m* 1993 *Elizabeth, yst dau of John Desmond O'Hare, of Liverpool

4 +Rupert George Streatfeild; *b* 17 May 1966; *educ* Milton Abbey

The 4th VISCOUNT *m* 2nd Aug 1974 *Margaret Birgitta, JP (Inner London), memb Parole Bd England and Wales 1976–80, dau of Maj-Gen Cyril Henry Norton, CB, CBE, DSO, of Dunn House, Long Melford, Suffolk, and former w of 2nd Viscount Davidson (*qv*), and by her has further issue:

5 +Edmund Carleton; *b* 14 July 1978

Lineage: PHILIP de COLVILLE held Heiton and Oxnam, Roxburghshire, in the 12th century, and his s and gs added Kinnaird, Stirling, and Ochiltree, Ayrshire, to the family possessions; ancestor of:

ROBERT COLVILLE of Hiltoun, of which he had a charter 10 Oct 1483; King's Chamberlain and Steward to MARGARET OF DENMARK, Consort of JAMES III; *m* Margaret Logan and *d c* Jan 1495/6, leaving:

ROBERT COLVILLE of Hiltoun; Dir of Chancery, acquired Ochiltree and Oxnam 1509 from Elizabeth, dau of Sir William Colville of Ochiltree, but sold Oxnam soon after; *m* Elizabeth (*d* 1527), dau of Walter Arnot, of Balbarton, and was *ka* Flodden 1513, having had, with other issue (including Janet, *m* Alexander Boyd (*see* KILMARNOCK,B); Margaret, *m* as his 1st w 1st Lord Semphill; *qv*):

Sir JAMES COLVILLE of Ochiltree; Comptroller Household 1526, a Judge Court of Session on its institution 1532, obtained Easter Wemyss from Sir James Hamilton of Finnart in exchange for Ochiltree 1530; attainted for treason 1540/1; *m* 1st Alison, dau of Sir David Bruce of Clackmannan; *m* 2nd 21 May 1536 Margaret, sis of David Forrester of Garden, and *d c* 4 Dec 1540, having had, with other issue:

1 James (Sir), of Easter Wemyss; *b* 1532; had f's attainder reversed 1543; *m* Janet, dau of Sir Robert Douglas of Lochleven (*see* MORTON, E), and *d c* 16 May 1561, having had:

(1) Sir JAMES COLVILLE, **1st Lord Colville of Culross** (S), so *cr* in Parl 24 April 1604 (though a slightly earlier document starts to refer to him halfway through as a Ld of Parl; he also had another charter with remainder to heirs whomsoever 20 Jan 1609), of Easter Wemyss; *b c* 1551; served in Huguenot forces France during Wars of Religion; granted Culross as temporal Barony 20 June 1589; returned to France where ktd by HENRY IV, granted lands in Ireland 1614; *m* 1st (charter 22 Aug 1570) Isabel, 2nd dau of Patrick, Lord Ruthven, and sis of 1st Earl of Gowrie (*see* CARLISLE, E), and had two s and three daus; *m* 2nd *c* May 1599 Helen Shaw, widow of Robert Moubray of Barnbougie, and *d* Sept 1629; his s by his 1st w:

1a Robert, *Master of Colville*; *m c* 24 Sept 1603 Christian, dau of George Bruce of Carnock, and *dvp* by 14 Dec 1614, having had an er s:

1b JAMES COLVILLE, **2nd Lord Colville of Culross**; *b* 1604; *m* 1st 1622 Magdalen (*dsp, bur* 28 Oct 1638), dau of Sir Peter Young of Seton; *m* 2nd — and by her had issue:

1c WILLIAM COLVILLE, **3rd Lord Colville of Culross**; *d* unm 12 April 1656

2c JOHN COLVILLE, **4th Lord Colville of Culross**; *dsp* after 1678

1c Marjorie; *m* April 1662 Isaac Dobson

1b (cont.) The **2nd Lord** *m* 3rd Margaret Clynton (*m* 2nd John Arthur; *m* 3rd Nicholas Hooper and *d c* 11 Aug 1686) and *d* 1654

1a Jean; *m* 23 June 1595 Sir James Campbell of Lawers (*see* CAMPBELL, Bt, of Aberuchill) and had issue

2 Alexander; Commendator of Culross Abbey, of which he had a charter 4 Feb 1566/7, a Ld of Session 1572 on; *m* Nicolas, dau of Alexander Dundas of Fingask, and *d* 1597, having had, with other issue:

(1) John, Laird of Comrie; *b* 1573; *m* Elizabeth, dau of Sir James Melvill of Halhill, and *d* 1645–50, having had, with other issue:

1a Alexander (Rev); *b* 1610; DD; Pncpl St Mary's Coll St Andrews; *m* Anne le Blanc, and *d* 1676, leaving:

1b John (Rev); *b* 1640; DD; Regent Old Coll of St Andrews; *m* 1665 Mary, dau of Sir John Preston of Valleyfield, and *d c* 1677/8, having had, with other issue:

1c ALEXANDER COLVILLE of Kincardine, *de jure* 5th LORD COLVILLE OF CULROSS; *b c* 1666; did not assume the title; *m* 1687 Mary, dau of Sir Charles Erskine of Cambo, 1st Bt, Lord Lyon King of Arms (*see* MAR and KELLIE, E), and *d* 9 Aug 1717, having had, with other issue, including a dau (Margaret, *m* Alexander Blair and *d* 1794, leaving issue):

1d JOHN COLVILLE, **6th Lord Colville of Culross**; *b* 1690; claim to peerage allowed 27 May 1723; cmded a regt Siege of Cartagena 1741; *m* 1716 Elizabeth Johnston (*d* 3 March 1748) and *d* Cartagena 20 April 1741, having had, with two other s:

1e ALEXANDER COLVILLE, **7th Lord Colville of Culross**; *b* 28 Feb 1717; V-Adml of the White, cmded the *Northumberland* Siege of Quebec 1759; C-in-C N America 1760; *m* 1 Oct 1768 Lady Elizabeth Erskine (*d* 1794), dau of 5th Earl of Kellie (*see* MAR and KELLIE, E) and widow of Walter Macfarlane of Macfarlane, antiquary, and *dsp* 21 May 1770

2e JOHN, **8th Lord**

3e James; Capt RN; *d* unm with all the crew of the *Sunderland* Pondicherry 21 Jan 1761

1e Margaret; *m* Paul Castleman, of Horsley, Glos, and had issue

2e Elizabeth; *m* Robert Petrie, and had issue

The 7th LORD's bro,

JOHN COLVILLE, **8th Lord Colville of Culross**; *b* 24 Jan 1724/5; Inspr-Gen Outposts Scotland, served 21st Fus Battles of Fontenoy 1745 and Culloden 1746; *m* 18 July 1758 Amelia Webber (*d* 5 Aug 1788) and *d* 8 March 1811, having had, with other issue:

1 James John, *Master of Colville*; *b* 10 Aug 1763; RN; *d* unm 18 Feb 1786

2 JOHN COLVILLE, **9th Lord Colville of Culross**; *b* 15 March 1768; Adml of the White, rep S peer 1818–49; *m* 1st 14 Oct 1790 Elizabeth (*dsp* 19 Aug 1839), dau of Francis Ford (*see* ST CLAIR-FORD, Bt); *m* 2nd 15 Oct 1841 Hon Anne Law (*dsp* 30 May 1852), sis of 1st Earl of Ellenborough (*qv*), and *d* 22 Oct 1849

3 Charles (Sir), GCB, GCH; *b* 7 Aug 1770; Gen, Col 5th Foot, Peninsular War and Waterloo campaign with distinction; *m* 16 Feb 1818 Jane (*d* 27 May 1843), est dau of William Mure, of Caldwell, Ayrshire, and *d* 27 March 1843, leaving issue:

(1) CHARLES JOHN, **1st Viscount**

(2) William James (Sir), KCVO, CB; *b* 9 March 1827; Crimean War, Rifle Bde and staff of Gen Sir J Simpson, ret as Col 1872; Lt Yeomen Gd, Comptroller Household of HRH DUKE OF SAXE-COBURG and GOTHA 1871–94, Master Ceremonies to TM QUEEN VICTORIA and EDWARD VII 1894–1903; *m* 20 Jan 1857 Georgiana Mary Montague (*d* 29 March 1918), dau of Evan Baillie of Dochfour by Lady Georgiana Montagu, dau of 5th Duke of Manchester (*qv*), and *d* 16 Oct 1903, leaving issue:

1a Arthur Edward William, CB (1902); *b* 20 Nov 1857; Col and Hon Brig-Gen Rifle Bde Afghan War 1878–9, Waziri Expdn 1881, NW Frontier India 1897, S African War 1899–1903 (despatches), Brig-Gen cmdg 60th Inf Bde 1914; *m* 6 Nov 1883 Olivia (*d* 28 May 1943), dau of Lord Alfred Spencer-Churchill (*see* MARLBOROUGH, D), and *d* 26 Feb 1942, leaving issue:

1b Robert Alfred, MC; *b* 15 Feb 1888; Maj Cameron Highrs, late Capt Worcs Yeo, formerly Coldstream Gds, WW I 1915–19 (despatches); *m* 1 Dec 1951 Honora Violet, dau of John Stapleton Martin, barrister, of Norton, Worcester, and *dsp* 25 Dec 1959

1a Mary Catherine; *m* 19 April 1899 Rt Hon Sir John Winfield-Bonser, PC, Ch Justice Ceylon (*d* 9 Dec 1914), only s of Rev John Bonser, of Hastings, Sussex, and *d* 6 Feb 1945, leaving issue

(1) Anne Amelia; *m* 29 July 1839 Francis Jack Needham, Viscount Newry and Morne (*dvp* 1851), s of 2nd Earl of Kilmorey (*qv*), and *d* 6 Jan 1900, leaving issue

(2) Catherine Dorothea; *m* 2 Oct 1861 Sir John Simeon, 3rd Bt (*d* 21 May 1870), and *d* 26 Feb 1904, leaving issue

(3) Georgiana Clementian; *m* 13 July 1865 Joseph Ridgway, of Fairlawn, Sevenoaks, Kent, and *d* 18 March 1871

1 Catherine; *m* 14 June 1792 Rev Roger Frankland, Canon of Wells (*d* 25 March 1826), and *d* 19 Sept 1843, leaving issue

The 9th LORD's n,

CHARLES JOHN COLVILLE, **1st Viscount Colville of Culross**, Co Perth, so *cr* 12 July 1902, as also earlier 31 Dec 1885 BARON COLVILLE of Culross, Co Perth (both UK), KT (1874), GCVO (1896), PC (1866), JP (Hants and Middx); *b* 23 Nov 1818; Ch Equerry and Clerk Marshal to HM QUEEN VICTORIA 1852–58, Master Buckhounds 1866–68, Ld Chamberlain to HM QUEEN ALEXANDRA 1873–1903, Capt 11th Hus, rep S peer 1850–85; *m* 6 June 1853 Hon Cecil Katherine Mary (*d* 2 Aug 1907), dau of 2nd Baron Carrington (*qv*), and *d* 1 July 1903, having had issue:

1 CHARLES ROBERT WILLIAM, **2nd Viscount**

2 Stanley Cecil James (Sir), GCB (1921, KCB 1912, CB 1896), GCMG (1919), GCVO (1915); *b* 21 Feb 1861; Adml, ADC to HM EDWARD VII 1905–06; cmdg Nore Div 1908–09, 1st Cruiser Sqdn 1909–11, 1st Battle Sqdn 1912–14, C-in-C Orkney and Shetlands 1914–16, C-in-C Portsmouth 1916–19, First and Pncpl ADC to HM GEORGE V 1919–22, R-Adml 1927–29, served Zulu War 1879, Egyptian Campaign 1882, Nile Expdn 1884–85, Dongola Expdn 1896, WW I, Grand Offr Legn of Honour, 1st Cl Russian Order St Stanislas, V-Adml 1929–39; *m* 6 Dec 1902 Lady Adelaide Jane Meade (*d* 31 March 1960), yst dau of 4th Earl of Clanwilliam (*qv*), and *d* 9 April 1939, having had issue:

(1) George Cecil, CBE (1953, OBE 1942); *b* 9 Sept 1903 (HM GEORGE V stood sponsor); Capt RN, ADC to HM THE QUEEN 1953, ADC to Govr-Gen S Africa; *m* 19 Sept 1935 Gabrielle, dau of Gen Sir Arthur Power Palmer, GCB, GCIE, and widow of Col Frances Leger Christian Livingstone Learmonth, CMG, RA, of Southover House, Tolpuddle, Dorset, and *d* 18 Aug 1983, leaving issue:

1a *Rona Alice Gabrielle [Mrs Rona Dixon, Gazebo, The Plantation, Curdridge, nr Southampton]; *b* 28 Dec 1936; *m* 12 Jan 1959 (*divorce* 1975) Capt Hon (Thomas) Robin (Valerian) Dixon, MBE, Gren Gds, er s of 2nd Baron Glentoran (*qv*), and has issue

(2) Edward Charles, CB (1955), DSO (1944) and bar (1945), JP (W Sussex 1960), DL (Sussex 1962) of Old Bartons, Stoughton, nr Chichester, Sussex; *b* 1 Sept 1905; *educ* Marlborough and RMC Sandhurst; Maj-Gen Gordon Highrs, ADC to Govr-Gen Canada 1932–34, WW II (despatches), Brig Gen Staff HQ Northern Army Gp 1952–54, Ch Staff Far East Land Forces 1954–58, cmdg 51 Highland Div 1956–59; *m* 29 Sept 1934 Barbara Joan (*d* 1983), yr dau of Edward Henry Marland Denny, of Stapleford Place, Stapleford, Sussex, and *d* 10 Jan 1982, leaving issue:

1a *Jane [Mrs Bingham Hartley, 19 Cliveden Place, London SW1]; *b* 16 March 1936; *m* 1st 17 Jan 1957 (*divorce* 1968) Sir Archibald Bruce Charles Edmonstone, 7th Bt (*qv*), and has issue; *m* 2nd 28 July 1967 HSH Prince Martin Lubomirski (*d* 1977), of El Mundo, Marbella, Spain, only s of HSH Prince Adam Lubomirski, of Poland, and has issue; *m* 3rd 1983 *Capt (John Holliday) Bingham Hartley, late Coldstream Gds

2a *Antonia [HRH Princess Carol of Romania, 36 Doria Rd, London SW6]; *b* 29 May 1939; *m* 1st 20 March 1962 (*divorce* 1973) Garry Lacon Jock Ropner, yr s of Sir Robert Desmond Ropner, of Camp Hill, Bedale, Yorks (*see* ROPNER, Bt), and has issue; *m* 2nd 1984 HRH PRINCE CAROL OF ROMANIA

(3) Richard (Sir), KCVO (1965, CVO 1953, MVO 1950), CB (1960), DSC (1943); *b* 26 Sept 1907; *educ* Harrow; Cdr (S) RN, joined RN 1925, WW II, Press Sec to TM GEORGE VI 1947–52 and THE QUEEN 1952–68, Extra Equerry to HM THE QUEEN 1968–75; *m* 2 Jan 1933 Dorothy (*d* 3 April 1972), dau of Brig-Gen Halhed Brodrick Birdwood, of Deaks Farm Ho, Cuckfield, Sussex (*see* BIRDWOOD, B), and *d* 14 June 1975, leaving issue:

1a +Peter Alan [Peter Colville Esq, Golden Hill House, Stourton Caundle, Dorset DT10 2JW]; *b* 6 Aug 1935; *educ* Wellington; late Lt RM; *m* 25 April 1964 *Jane Helen, er dau of Capt Thomas Harland RN, of Walton House, Kineton, Warwicks, and has issue:

1b +James Richard; *b* 9 Oct 1976

1b *Julia Mary; *b* 10 Nov 1965; *m* 1995 *Jeremy Minchin, yr s of Peter Minchin, of Wadhurst, E Sussex

2b *Annabel Clare; *b* 18 June 1967

3b *Joanna Elizabeth [Mrs Nicholas Waite, of Oak Cottage, Wambrook, Somerset]; *b* 9 Oct 1969; *m* 22 Aug 1992 *Nicholas Alexander Waite, er s of Michael Waite, of E Coker, Somerset, and has:

1c *Rosalind Emma Corlyon; *b* 22 June 1996

4b *Sarah Dorothy Louise; *b* 19 May 1972

1a *Anne Bridget [Mrs Hugh Spankie, The Manse, Iden Green, nr Cranbrook, Kent]; *b* 22 March 1939; *m* 15 June 1963 (*divorce* 19–) Hugh Oliver Spankie, RM, s of Lt-Col Hugh Spankie, of Tonbridge, Kent, and has:

1b *Hugh Nicholas; *b* 11 May 1967

1b *Rosemary Bridget; *b* 5 Sept 1964

2a *June Claire; *b* 15 June 1948; *m* 1977 *Anthony Barrington Prowse, of Rose Cottage, Coombe, Shute, Stoke Gabriel, S Devon, and has issue:

1b *Sebastian Irwin Barrington; *b* 1978

2b *Nicholas Richard Barrington; *b* 1982

1b *Alexandra Rose Barrington; *b* 1979

(4) Frederick James; *b* 30 May 1913; Capt Gordon Highrs WW II; *m* 28 Sept 1938 Dorothy Louisa (*m* 2nd 27 Dec 1941 (*divorce* 1962) Lt Clifford John Maddocks, RNVR, only s of John Maddocks, of Rhymney House, Mon, and has issue; *m* 3rd 8 Sept 1962 Lt-Col John Anthony Russell Freeland, late The Queen's Roy Regt, Douglas Lake House, Fittleworth, Sussex, only s of Col John Cavendish Freeland, CB, CBE), only dau of Hubert William Fane, of 24 Dawson Place, London W2 (*see* WESTMORLAND, E), and was *ka* Dunkirk June 1940

3 George Charles, MBE (1918); *b* 22 Feb 1867; *educ* Trin Coll Cambridge (BA); barrister, High Sheriff Co London 1930; *m* 21 Jan 1908 Lady (Helen) Cynthia Crewe-Milnes, DCVO (1937), DBE (1953), FRCM, LLD (Hon) Leeds U, OStJ, JP Co London, a Woman of the Bedchamber to HM QUEEN MARY 1923–53 (*d* 15 June 1968), 3rd dau of 1st and last Marquess of Crewe, KG (*see* 1939 edn), and *d* 19 Sept 1943, leaving issue:

(1) David Richard; *b* 11 May 1909; *educ* Harrow and Trin Coll Cambridge (BA 1930); Lt RNVR WW II; *m* 21 Jan 1933 *Lady Joan Child-Villiers, er dau of 8th Earl of Jersey (*qv*), and *d* 1986, leaving issue:

1a +Robert (Robin) John [Robert Colville Esq, Duxhams, Dulverton, Somerset TA22 9EJ]; *b* 20 May 1941; *educ* Harrow; *m* 25 April 1997 *Elizabeth Mary, only dau of Leonard White, of Duxhams

2a +James Richard Charles [James Colville Esq, Windflower House, Halfway Pitch, Pitchcombe, Glos GL6 6LJ]; *b* 26 Jan 1952; *educ* Harrow; *m* 25

Sept 1982 Mary Virginia Louise, yr dau of Timothy Horn (*see* CARNARVON, E), and has issue:

1b +Charles David James; (twin) *b* 12 Nov 1987

2b +Edward Timothy George; *b* 30 Dec 1988

1b *Emma Virginia Anne; (twin) *b* 12 Nov 1987

2b *Sophia Antonia Louise; *b* 20 Oct 1994

1a *Sarah Anne [Sarah Lady Pigot, Gardle House, St Luke's Drive, Bembridge, IoW PO35 5XA]; *b* 25 Nov 1933; *m* 28 Sept 1968 Maj-Gen Sir (Robert) Anthony Pigot, 7th Bt (*qv*), and has issue

2a *Catherine [Mrs Warren Gilchrist, Rookhill, Monk Sherborne, nr Basingstoke, Hants]; *b* 25 April 1935; *m* 1 March 1958 *Cdr Warren Llewellyn Russell Euan Gilchrist, RN (ret), s of Maj Euan James Leslie Warren Gilchrist, MC, DFC, BA, of Monk Sherborne House, and has issue:

1b *Charles Warren; *b* 8 Jan 1962

2b *David Warren; *b* 4 Oct 1967

1b *Catherine Anne; *b* 29 June 1960

2b *Julia Mary; *b* 25 April 1969

3a *Mary Julia [Mrs Aubrey Bowden, The Old Vicarage, Winkfield, Windsor, Berks]; *b* 1 Dec 1947; *m* 4 Oct 1969 *Aubrey Bowden (*see* BOWDEN, Bt)

(2) Philip Robert, MBE; *b* 1910; *educ* Harrow and Trin Coll Cambridge (BA 1932), (MA 1935); Maj Gren Gds NW Europe 1944–45 (despatches); *d* unm 11 April 1997

(3) John Rupert (Jock) (Sir), CB (1955), CVO (1949); *b* 28 Jan 1915; *educ* Harrow and Trin Coll Cambridge (BA 1936, MA 1941); Page of Honour HM GEORGE V 1927–31; F/Lt RAF WW II; Dip Serv 1937–55, Assist Priv Sec to PM 1939–45, Priv Sec HRH THE PRINCESS ELIZABETH 1947–49, Pncpl Priv Sec to PM 1951–55, dir Hill Samuel, Coutts, Nat & Grindlay's Bank, Dep Chm Lond Ctee Ottoman Bank, Provident Life Assoc, author: *Gort, Man of Honour*, ktd 1974; *m* 20 Oct 1948 Lady Margaret Egerton [The Lady Margaret Colville, The Close, Broughton, Stockbridge, Hants] (Ldy-in-Waiting to HRH PRINCESS ELIZABETH 1946–49), 5th dau of 4th Earl of Ellesmere (*see* SUTHERLAND, D), and *d* 1987, leaving issue:

1a +Alexander George; *b* 21 May 1955 (HRH THE PRINCESS ROYAL stood sponsor); *educ* Harrow; Page of Honour to HM THE QUEEN 1968–71

2a +Rupert Charles; *b* 18 Jan 1960; *educ* Harrow and Trinity Coll Oxford (MA); *m* 1991 *Sarah Catherine, dau of Richard Russell, of Kidlington, Oxford

1a *(Elizabeth) Harriet; *b* 3 Dec 1952 (HM THE QUEEN, Sir Winston Churchill and the Earl of Home stood sponsors); a Ldy-in-Waiting to HRH THE PRINCESS ROYAL 1990–; *m* 17 Nov 1976 *David James Bowes-Lyon, yr s of Maj-Gen Sir (Francis) James Cecil Bowes-Lyon (*see* STRATHMORE and KINGHORNE, E)

1 Blanche Cecile; *m* 26 July 1890 R-Adml Richard Frederick Britten, DL, of Kenswick, Worcester, and *d* 3 April 1940, leaving issue

The 1st VISCOUNT's est s,

CHARLES ROBERT WILLIAM COLVILLE, **2nd Viscount Colville of Culross**; *b* 26 April 1854; Maj Gren Gds and Lt-Col TFR 1915, Zulu War 1879 (despatches), ADC to C-in-C Bombay, Mil Sec to Govr-Gen Canada; *m* 7 Oct 1885 Ruby (*d* 14 Dec 1943), dau of Lt-Col Henry Dorrien Streatfeild, JP, DL, of Chiddingstone, Kent, and *d* 25 March 1928, having had issue:

1 CHARLES ALEXANDER, **3rd Viscount**

2 John Gilbert; *b* 24 Dec 1892; Lt RNVR, served WWs I and II; *d* unm 19 Jan 1952

1 Margaret; JP (Kent 1941, Devon 1944), WVS Centre Organiser 1938–40; *d* 30 April 1975

2 Sybil Marion; Ldy-in-Waiting to HRH THE PRINCESS ROYAL; *m* 25 May 1916 5th Baron Carrington (*d* 19 Nov 1938), and *d* 30 Sept 1946, leaving issue

The 2nd VISCOUNT's er s,

CHARLES ALEXANDER COLVILLE, **3rd Viscount Colville of Culross**, DL (Co Kincardine); *b* 26 May 1888; Cdr RN Battle of Jutland 1916 (despatches), served WW II; *m* 21 May 1931 Kathleen Myrtle, OBE (1961) (*d* 1986), est dau of Brig-Gen Henry Richmond Gale, CMG, RE, of Bardsea Hall, and *das* in a flying accident Azores 14 March 1945, having had issue:

1 JOHN MARK ALEXANDER COLVILLE, **4th and present Viscount Colville of Culross**

2 +(Charles) Anthony [The Hon Anthony Colville, Rydes Nevill Court, Tunbridge Wells, Kent TN4 8NL]; *b* 5 Aug 1935; *educ* Rugby and Magdalen Coll Oxford (BA 1958); late Sub-Lt RNVR; slr 1969; Overseas Civ Serv Kenya 1958064; *m* 2 Oct 1965 *Katherine, dau of Humphrey John Sankey, of Kinangop, Kenya, and Mrs Elizabeth Cowling, of Lime House, Herstmonceux, Sussex, and has issue:

(1) +Robert Quintin Oxnam; *b* 2 June 1971

(2) +Charles Alexander; *b* 11 July 1974

3 Angus Richmond; *b* 29 April 1939; *educ* Rugby; 2nd Lt Gren Gds (AER) 1957–59; ARICS, FRICS, QALAS; *d* unm (murdered by thieves in Guatemala City)

COLWYN

Arms: Per chevron gules and argent, in chief two cocks of the second and in base a whale spouting proper. **Crest:** Upon a whale a cock, both as in the arms. **Supporters:** Dexter, a miner holding in his exterior hand and resting on his shoulder a pick-axe suspended from his belt a miner's lamp all proper; sinister, a female weaver holding in her exterior hand a shuttle all proper. **Motto:** *Gratias ago* ('I give thanks'). **Creations:** Bt. (UK) 9 July 1912, B. (UK) 22 June 1917.

THE 3RD BARON COLWYN, of Colwyn Bay, Co Denbigh, and **a Baronet** (Sir (Ian) Anthony Hamilton Smith, Bt, CBE (1989)) [The Rt Hon The Lord Colwyn CBE, 2 Painswick Rd, Cheltenham, Glos]; *b* 1 Jan 1942; *s* f 1966; *educ* Cheltenham and Roy Dental Hosp, London U (BDS), LDS, RCS (Eng); dental surgeon 1966–, musician; dir: Three B Consultants Ltd 1978–94, Dental Protection Ltd 1990–, Med Protection Soc, Big City Radio Ltd 1992–; pres: Natural Medicines Soc 1989–, Huntington's Disease Assoc 1991–; *m* 1st 30 May 1964 (*divorce* 1977) Sonia Jane, er dau of Peter Henry Geoffrey Morgan, of Malvern, Worcs, and has issue:

1 +CRAIG PETER; *b* 13 Oct 1968

1 *Jacqueline Jane; *b* 5 March 1967

The 3rd BARON *m* 2nd 24 March 1977 *Nicola Jeanne, dau of Arthur Tyers, of Sunbury on Thames, Middx, and has further issue:

2 *Kirsten Antonia; *b* 17 Jan 1981

3 *Tanya Nicole; *b* 14 Jan 1983

Lineage: JOHN SMITH, of Colne, Lancs, had a son:

JOSHUA SMITH, of Eccles, Lancs, JP; *b* 1837; *m* 7 June 1852 Elizabeth (*d* 28 Dec 1860), dau of John Henry Whalley, of Trawden, Lancs, and *d* 16 April 1906, having had issue:

Sir Frederick Henry Smith, 1st Bt, and **1st Baron Colwyn**, of Colwyn Bay, Co Denbigh (both UK), so *cr* 9 July 1912 and 22 June 1917 respectively, PC (1924), JP (Cheshire, Denbighs, Caernarvonshire and Salford), DL (Denbighs); *b* 24 Jan 1859; Mayor Colwyn Bay 1934, High Sheriff Carnarvonshire 1917–18, India Rubber and Cotton mfr, dir of Collieries and Rlys, dir Martins Bank, chm: Roy Commn on Income Tax, Bank Amalgamation Ctee, Govt Contracts Ctee; v-chm PO Advisory Cncl 1921, Hon LLD Manchester, Hon Lt-Col late 2nd Vol RWF; *m* 3 April 1882 Elizabeth Ann (*d* 26 Jan 1945), dau of Hamilton Savage, of Eccles, Manchester, and had issue:

1 Frederick Henry Hamilton, MA, LLB Cambridge, Lt Lancashire RGSC, MT; *b* 5 June 1887; *m* 14 Oct 1913 Hilda (*m* 2nd 20 Dec 1932 Maj J F Hardy-Smith (*d* Sept 1945) and *d* 4 Sept 1964), est dau of John Ross, of Alexandria, and *d* 7 Jan 1931, leaving issue:

(1) FREDERICK JOHN VIVIAN SMITH, **2nd Baron**

(1) *Elisabeth Joan Babette Hamilton [Mrs John Ferguson, Ashcraig, The Croft, Bures, Essex]; *b* 8 July 1919; *m* 1 Sept 1939 *Lt-Col John Baddeley Bagot Ferguson, RTR, er son of Victor Bruce Ferguson, of Abbotsdene, Charlton Kings, Cheltenham, and has issue:

1a *Nicholas John [Nicholas Ferguson Esq, Ashcraig, The Croft, Bures, Essex]; *b* 17 March 1941; *educ* Michaelhouse, Balgowan, Natal; *m* 8 May 1965 *Karen Elisabeth, dau of Niels Ladefoged Christensen Svansø, of Whitegates, Mere, Cheshire, and has issue:

1b *James Fergus; *b* 1966

1b *Kate Venetia Elisabeth; *b* 1967

2 Hubert Constantine; *b* 11 Oct 1890; Capt late RAF; *m* 6 Oct 1917 Marjorie Methwold, OBE (1957) (*d* 1984), dau of Arthur Birkett, of Langford Lodge, Southwold, Suffolk, and *d* 15 Feb 1956, leaving issue:

(1) +Michael Constantine, TD [Michael Smith Esq TD, Maes Nant, Pant Glas, Garndolbenmaen, Gwynedd], Capt RA (HAA) WW II; *b* 30 Aug 1919; *educ* Radley; *m* 1st 13 June 1945 (*divorce* 1970) Veronica, only dau of Thomas Flanagan, of Tralee, Co Kerry, and has issue:

1a +Christopher Michael Constantine; *b* 4 Sept 1953; *educ* Radley

1a *Sally Constantine; *b* 12 July 1947

2a *Judy Jennifer Constantine; *b* 4 March 1951

(1) (cont.) Michael Smith *m* 2nd 18 April 1970 *Marie Therese, yr dau of Patrick Stuart Martin, of Hillside Rd, Glasgow

(2) +Anthony Methwold Constantine; *b* 13 Jan 1923; *m* 16 April 1955 *Susan Muriel, only child of Frederick B Staveacre, of Braeside, Colwyn Bay, N Wales, and has issue:

1a +David Anthony Constantine; *b* 8 Feb 1962

1a *Caroline Constantine; *b* 28 Feb 1957

2a *Nicola Constantine; *b* 16 June 1959

(1) *Elizabeth Pamela Constantine [Mrs Michael Malim, Little Court, High St, Stock, Ingatestone, Essex CM4 9BA]; *b* 31 July 1918; *m* 15 Aug 1945 Lt Michael William Malim, RINVR (*d* 1 Feb 1974), 4th son of Frederick Blagden Malim, formerly Master of Wellington Coll, of Myddylton Ho, Saffron Walden, Essex, and has issue:

1a *Flavia Constantine Eve; *b* 29 Dec 1949

2a *Lydia Elisabeth Constantine [Mrs Nicholas Umney, 62 London Rd, Riverhead, Sevenoaks, Kent TN13 2DJ]; *b* 31 March 1952; *m* 1985 *Nicholas David Umney, and has issue:

1b *Michael David; *b* 1987

3a *Julia Pamelia Constantine; *b* 11 Dec 1956

4a *Delia Constantine; *b* 15 Dec 1959

1 Winifred; *m* 24 Oct 1917 Maj Thomas Roy Irons, late RAF (*d* 1950), son of Thomas Irons, of Sydney, NSW, and *d* 1951, leaving issue:

2 Dorothy Elizabeth; *b* 20 July 1910 Alan George Boumphrey (*d* 21 April 1946), son of Arthur Burrows Boumphrey, of Baycliffe, Lymm, Cheshire, and *d* 7 May 1958, leaving issue

3 Kathleen Whalley, MBE (1946); *m* 22 Sept 1945 Robert Cullen Howie, er son of Robert Hood Howie, of 2 Milnthorpe Court, Meads Rd, Eastbourne

The 1st BARON *d* 26 Jan 1946; his gs,

FREDERICK JOHN VIVIAN SMITH, **2nd Baron Colwyn**; *b* 26 Nov 1914; *educ* Malvern; stockbroker, Capt 2nd Bn Gordon Highrs WW II (wounded); *m* 1st 21 Dec 1940 (*divorce* 1951) Miriam Gwendoline (*d* 8 Jan 1996), only dau of Victor Bruce Ferguson, of Abbotsdene, Charlton Kings, Cheltenham, and had:

1 (IAN) ANTHONY HAMILTON SMITH, **3rd and present Baron Colwyn**

2 +Timothy Hamilton [The Hon Timothy Smith, Diocesan Coll, Rondebosch 7700, Cape, S Africa]; *b* 28 June 1944; *educ* Cheltenham and Oxford U (BA, DipEd, MA); *m* 29 July 1967 *Carolyn, dau of Bernulf Llewelyn Hodge, MRCS, LRCP, of The Old Cottage, Jac-na-Pare, Polperro, S Cornwall, and has issue:

(1) *Annabel; *b* 1972

(2) *Fiona; *b* 1974

The **2nd Baron** *m* 2nd 18 July 1952 (*divorce* 1954) Hermione Sophia O'Bryen, only dau of Cyril Bertie Edward O'Bryen Hoare, of d'Avigdor House, Hove, Sussex (*see* HOARE, Bt, of Annabella); *m* 3rd 8 Jan 1955 Beryl (*m* 4th 1969 Sir George Taylor, FRS (*d* 1993), and *d* 1987), dau of Harvey Walker, JP, of Heathgates Ho, Heathgates, Salop, widow of Mortimer Philip Reddington, FRCS, and previously w of Edward Chorley Cookson, MBE, BS, and *d* 29 May 1966

COLYER-FERGUSSON

Arms: Arg. a lion rampant az., armed and langued gu., on a chief engrailed of the last a mullet between two cinquefoils of the first. **Crest:** A dexter hand grasping a broken spear in bend sinister, all ppr. **Motto:** (over the crest) *Vi et arte* ('By strength and skill'). **Creation:** Bt. (UK) 23 Jan 1866.

SIR JAMES HERBERT HAMILTON COLYER-FERGUSSON, 4TH BT, of Spitalhaugh, Peebleshire [Sir James Colyer-Fergusson Bt, Flat 8, 61 Onslow Square, London SW7 3LS]; *b* 10 Jan 1917; *s* gf 1951; *educ* Harrow and Balliol Coll Oxford (BA 1939, MA 1945); Capt The Buffs WW II (POW 1943–45)

Lineage: EDWARD FERGUSSON, of Lochmaben, Dumfriesshire; *m* Janet Kerr and *d c* 1690, leaving issue:

JAMES FERGUSSON, Burgess of Lochmaben 1672; had:

JOHN FERGUSSON, of Lochmaben; *b* 1729; *m* 18 Dec 1762 Janet Bell and *d* 1819, leaving:

JAMES FERGUSSON, of Prestonpans; *b* 7 Jan 1766; *m* 1793 Elizabeth (*d* Jan 1818 aged 51), dau of Andrew Hodge, of Anstruther, Fifeshire, and *d* 17 June 1834, having had, with other issue, including a dau (Jean Bell, *b* 16 June 1805, *m* 1826 Thomas Melvill and *d* March 1834, leaving issue):

Sir William Fergusson, 1st Bt (UK), so *cr* 23 Jan 1866; *b* 20 March 1808; LLD, FRS, Prof Surgery King's Coll and Surgn to its Hosp, PRCS, Surgn to HRH PRINCE CONSORT, Serjeant Surgn to HM QUEEN VICTORIA, author: *System of Practical Surgery*; *m* 10 Oct 1833 Helen Hamilton (*d* 19 June 1861), dau of William Ranken, of Spitalhaugh, and had, with other issue:

1 JAMES RANKEN (Sir), **2nd Bt**

2 Charles Hamilton, Maj Seaforth Highrs; *b* 27 May 1849; *d* 23 May 1913

1 Katherine Hamilton; *d* unm 23 Dec 1932 aged 92

2 Helen Seymour; *d* unm 17 Aug 1938 aged 94

Sir WILLIAM *d* 10 Feb 1877; his son,

Sir James Ranken Fergusson, 2nd Bt; JP and V-Lt Peebleshire, barrister, FSA, memb Roy Co Archers; *b* 10 Aug 1835; *m* 1st 13 Dec 1862 Mary Ann Somes (*d* 14 April 1868), er dau of Thomas Colyer, of Wombwell Hall, Kent, and had issue:

1 William Hamilton Colyer; *b* 25 Feb 1864; *d* 2 April 1873

2 THOMAS (Sir), **3rd Bt**

Sir James *m* 2nd 17 Oct 1877 Louisa (*d* 12 Sept 1878), 2nd dau of William Forbes, of Medwyn, Peeblesshire, and by her had issue:

3 Louis Forbes (Sir), KCVO (1945), Clerk Cncl and Keeper Records Duchy Lancaster 1927–45; *b* 5 Sept 1878; *educ* Harrow and Univ Coll Oxford (BA); *m* 1922 Elizabeth Frances Ethel (*d* 1986), dau of Seth Lewis, of Old Woking, Surrey, and *d* 10 Jan 1962, leaving issue:

(1) *Christine Forbes [Mrs Charles Evans, 6 Fabye House, Cumberland Rd, Kew, Surrey TW9 3HH]; *b* 24 Feb 1934; *m* 1966 *Charles Raymond Evans, MA

Sir James *m* 3rd 1 June 1886 Alice Fanny (*d* 6 April 1926), dau of John Price Simpson, and by her had issue:

4 James Adam Hamilton, Lt HLI; *b* 22 March 1892; *ka* Battle of the Aisne Sept 1914

5 Charles Hamilton, Lt Northants Regt; *b* 9 Aug 1894; murdered by natives on his farm in Kenya 1 Jan 1953

1 Margaret Alice Hamilton; *b* 18 Feb 1889; *m* 21 Oct 1913 Cuthbert Archibald Lambton, er surv son of Col Francis William Lambton, of Brownslade, Pembroke, by Lady Victoria, dau of 2nd Earl Cawdor (*qv*), and *d* 1 Feb 1969, leaving issue. He *d* July 1946

2 Helen Hamilton; *b* 28 Aug 1890; *m* 1st 2 June 1919 Arthur Julian de Spiganovicz, MD (*d* 7 April 1925), and had issue; *m* 2nd 16 April 1933 Allan Rigden Finn, MD, FRCS, of Westwood Speen, Newbury, Berks, and had further issue. He *d* 13 May 1971

Sir JAMES *d* 28 Oct 1924; his est son,

Sir THOMAS COLYER FERGUSSON later COLYER-FERGUSSON (added 1890), **3rd Bt**, JP Kent, High Sheriff 1906; *b* 11 July 1865; *educ* Ch Ch Oxford (MA); *m* 1st 30 Jan 1890 Beatrice Stanley (*d* 17 June 1902), only surv dau of Prof Friedrich Max Muller, PC, and had:

1 Max Christian Hamilton; *b* 30 Dec 1890 (HRH PRINCESS CHRISTIAN stood sponsor); Lt and T/Capt RASC WW II; *m* 23 July 1913 Edith Jane (*d* 18 June 1936), only child of William White Miller, of Portage la Prairie, Manitoba, Canada, and was *kas* 13 Aug 1940, leaving:

(1) Sir JAMES HERBERT HAMILTON COLYER-FERGUSSON, **4th and present Bt**

2 William Porteous; Lt Northants Regt WW I (wounded); *b* 18 Oct 1893; *educ* Harrow and Univ Coll Oxford; *m* 1st 4 June 1919 (*divorce* 1938) Doris Dunstan, dau of William Dunstan Ford-Smith; *m* 2nd Jan 1964 *Isobel Mary, dau of Rev Robert Trotter Fairbairn, of Inverkip Renfrewshire, and *dsp* 2 March 1974

3 Thomas Riversdale, VC, A/Capt Northants Regt; *b* 18 Feb 1896; *d* 31 July 1917 of wounds recd in action that day

1 Mary Adelaide Somes; *b* 6 Feb 1892; *m* 18 July 1914 (*divorce* 1947) 1st Viscount Monckton of Brenchley (*qv*) and *d* 30 April 1964, leaving issue

2 Phillis Katherine St Ledger; *b* 18 April 1900; *m* 1st 29 June 1922 (*divorce* 1934) Capt John Naylor Hodgson-Wilson (*d* 31 March 1960), 3rd son of William Hodgson-Wilson, of Hexgreave Park, Southwell, Notts, and had issue; *m* 2nd 14 May 1938 (*divorce* 1947) Theobald Henry Hinkson

3 Beatrice Helen Valentine; *b* 14 Feb 1902; *m* 9 Dec 1930 Leonard Riddle and *d* 2 Nov 1963, leaving issue. He *d* 29 Nov 1963

Sir THOMAS *m* 2nd 28 July 1914 Mary Freda (*d* 11 Nov 1964 aged 92), 3rd dau of Arthur Cohen, PC, KC (*see* 1970 edn COHEN, B), and *d* 7 April 1951

COLYTON

Arms: Azure on a chevron argent between three mullets of six points or as many mascles gules, a bordure engrailed or. **Crest:** A demi-lion sable between two mullets of six points or. **Supporters:** On either side an angel proper habited azure, winged or, the dexter holding in the exterior hand a Saxon Crown and the sinister likewise holding a trumpet gold. **Badge:** In front of a portcullis chained or a grasshopper proper. **Motto:** Look forward. **Creation:** B. (UK) 19 Jan 1956.

THE 2ND BARON COLYTON, of Farway, Co Devon, and Taunton, Somerset (Alisdair John Munro Hopkinson) [The Rt Hon The Lord Colyton, Lindertis, by Kirriemuir, Angus DD8 5NT]; *b* 7 May 1958; *s* gf 1996; *m* 1980 *Philippa J, yr dau of Peter J Bell, of Harefield, Itchen Abbas, Hants, and has issue:

1 +JAMES PATRICK MUNRO; *b* 1983
2 +Thomas Charles Robert; *b* 1985
1 *Kate Alice; *b* 1988

Lineage: JAMES HOPKINSON; *b c* 1600; Wagon Master Gen for the Northern Association of the Parliamentary forces; *m* Anne — and *d* by 1658, leaving, with an er s (John, *b* by 1667):

THOMAS HOPKINSON, of the parish of St Olave, Old Jewry; *b c* 1630; apothecary; *m* Alice — and *d* 1679, leaving issue:

MATTHEW HOPKINSON, of Gt Marlborough St, St James's; *b* 1650; scrivener, memb of Middle Temple; *d* 1710, leaving issue:

1 Matthew; *b c* 1676; *m* Hannah — and *d* 1723, having had four children (*d* as infants)
2 Isaac
3 Thomas, of St James's; *b c* 1678; scrivener; *m* Mary Nicholls, of St James's, and had:
(1) Thomas, Judge of Admlty for Pennsylvania; *b* 1709; *m* 1736 Mary (*d c* 1804), dau of Baldwin Johnson, of Antigua and Philadelphia, and *d* 5 Nov 1751, leaving issue:
1a Francis, signed American Declaration of Independence; *b* 1737; *d* 1791
(2) Francis, of Thorne, Yorks; *b* 1710; *m* Dorothy Harrison, widow of Newark-on-Trent, and probably *dsp*
(3) JOHN
(1) Catherine; *m* Joseph Maleham, of Portland St, London

The yst son,

JOHN HOPKINSON; *b* 1712; *d* leaving issue:
1 Charles *b* 1740; had a son and dau
2 Joseph; *b* 1774; had:
(1) John; *b* 1789
(2) Charles; *b* 1790
(1) Mary; *b* 1795
(2) Elizabeth; *b* 1798
3 BENJAMIN
1 Mary; *b* 1746
2 Rachel; *b* 1748

The yst son,

BENJAMIN HOPKINSON, of Highbury Park, Islington, Middx; *b* 1751; *m* 1779 Mary Gresley (*d* 1828), and *d* 22 Sept 1821, leaving issue:
1 John; *b* 23 Aug, *d* 30 Sept 1780
2 Luke; *b* 18 Oct 1781; *m* 1807 Elizabeth (*d* 24 Dec 1859), dau of Robert Wrightson, and *d* 14 Feb 1852, having had, with two other sons (*d* infants):
(1) Luke; *b* 1811; *d* unm 7 May 1842
(2) Alfred; *b* 1813; *d* unm
(1) Amelia; *m* 27 Jan 1841 John Henry Briggs, of the Admlty, and *d* 1888, having had two sons and three daus
(2) Emma; *d* unm 1842
(3) Ellen; *m* 17 Aug 1848 Sir George Edmund Hodgkinson, JP, DL (*d* 1886), Sheriff of London, of 44 Wimpole St, London W, son of George Hodgkinson, merchant, of London, and *d* 1864, leaving two sons
(4) Elizabeth; *b* 15 Sept 1825; *m* 15 Aug 1855 Alexander Pulling (*d* 15 Jan 1895), Serjeant-at-law, and *d* 6 July 1896, having had two sons
3 Charles (Sir), ktd 1837, CB (1826); *b* 14 Sept 1783; Gen Cmdg Artillery in India; *d* unm 17 Dec 1864
4 William; *b* Dec 1785; *m* 5 Feb 1814 Elizabeth (*d* 1862), dau of Christopher Ibberson, and *d* 9 Feb 1866, having had issue:
(1) William; *b* 1 Dec 1821; *m* Eliza Hamilton, and *d* 26 Aug 1878, having had issue:
1a William; *b* 1861; *d* unm 15 June 1884
2a James Sewell; *b* 1865; *m* Sarah Callaway Hewett, and *d* 1888
3a John Hamilton
1a Elizabeth; *m* Hildebrand Oglemoore, and *dsp*
(2) Christopher; *b* 26 Sept 1832; *m* 1863 Annie Orleana Joyce, and had issue:
1a Charles; *b* 11 Nov 1867; *m* Daisy Maude Schneider
2a Francis; *b* 10 July 1869; *d* 29 Jan 1875
3a Ernest Francis; *b* 9 Jan 1876; *m* Constance Ellen Davis, and had issue:
1b *Gwladys Dora; *b* 26 March 1905
1a Emily; *b* 12 July 1871; *d* 1 Feb 1875
2a Annie Elizabeth; *b* 3 Oct 1873
(1) Mary; *b* 18 Sept 1818; *m* Richard Cattarns, and *d* 22 April 1885, having had a son and two daus
(2) Isabella; *b* 14 June 1823; *m* Dr Robert Druitt and had four sons and four daus
(3) Emily; *b* 2 Nov 1829; *m* Benjamin Ferrey, and *dsp*
5 BENJAMIN
6 George; *b* 25 Feb 1795; *m* Isabella Bowles, and *d* 24 Oct 1861 or 1871, leaving:
(1) William, Col; *m* his cousin Louisa, dau of Richard Cattarns, by Mary Hopkinson (*see* above), and had issue:
1a Montague; *m* Aimée Brand, of Saskatchewan, Canada
2a Charles, slr; *b* 1878
1a Ethel; *b* 1868; *m* Rev Thomas Landulph Smith
2a Bertha; *b* 1870
3a Louisa; *b* 1876
(2) George; *d* of yellow fever at Charleston
(3) Samuel
(4) David; *d* at sea
(1) Isabella; *m* — Thornton
(2) Mary *m* — Goss
(3) Sarah; *m*
(4) Kezia; *m*
7 James; *b* 30 Sept, *d* 27 Nov 1798
8 Robert; *b* 4 Aug 1800; *d* unm 24 Aug 1831
1 Mary; *b* 21 Oct 1788; *m* William Benson Stones, and *d* 25 Aug 1863, having had three sons and four daus
2 Isabella; *b* 8 July 1791; *m* William Sotheby, and *d* 26 Oct 1859, having had a son
3 Sarah; *b* 23 Oct 1796; *m* William Grove, and *d* 16 Jan 1818, leaving a son

The 5th son,

BENJAMIN HOPKINSON; *b* 20 April 1793; *m* 10 July 1817 Louisa Ann Stedman (*d* 8 Jan 1869), and *d* 18 April 1844, having had issue:
1 Francis; *d* an infant
2 HENRY
3 Arthur; *d* an infant
4 Edward; *m* Eliza Jones, of New Zealand
5 Robert; *d* an infant
1 Fanny; *m* Charles Law, and had a son and five daus
2 Margaret; *m* Alfred B Langmore (*d* 16 March 1894), and *d* Feb 1895, having had six daus
3 Louisa; *d* unm 23 June 1891
4 Eleanor; *m* Rev Horatio J Ward (*d* 16 May 1894), and *dsp* 1903

The est surv son,

HENRY HOPKINSON, CSI (1874); *b* 7 Aug 1820; *educ* Coll de Menars, France; Indian SC, joined 15th Regt Bengal NI 1838, Commr of Arakan 1852, Commr Tenasserim Provs 1858, Commr for Assam and Agent to Govr-Gen of India on NE Frontier 1860, served in Punjab 1848–49, Burma 1852, Bhutan 1865, ret as Gen; *m* 10 Sept 1849 Jean (*d* 16 Nov 1891), est dau of Dr William Montgomerie, HEICS, and *d* 22 Dec 1899, having had issue:
1 Archibald Montgomerie, 47th Regt; *b* 18 Jan 1850; *d* 22 July 1874, in Jamaica
2 HENRY LENNOX (Sir)
1 Norah Montgomerie Margaret Maynard; *m* 28 April 1886 Thomas Arthur Hill, of Normanton-on-the-Wolds, Plumtree, Notts, and had a son

The yr son,

Sir HENRY LENNOX HOPKINSON, KCVO (1936), JP, of Duntesbourne Manor Ho, Cirencester, Glos; *b* 23 Oct 1855; *educ* Cheltenham and Trin Coll Cambridge; FSA, memb Cncl of Roy Albert Hall 1900–36 and Hon Treas 1927–34, Almoner St Bartholomew's Hosp 1916, Master Merchant Taylors' Co 1910; *m* 6 Dec 1900 Marie Ruan (*d* 11 July 1949), dau of Francis Blake du Bois, of St Croix, Virgin Is, and New York, and *d* 9 Dec 1936, leaving issue:
1 HENRY LENNOX D'AUBIGNÉ, **1st Baron**
2 John Montgomerie, TD; *b* 28 Nov 1902; *educ* Eton and Trin Coll Cambridge (MA); FICA, WW II as Lt-Col RA, Master Merchant Taylors' Co 1953; *m* 26 Sept 1933 Alexandra Martha Ingeborg Pauline, dau of Baron Erik Stjernstedt, of Stockholm, and had issue:
(1) +Anthony Erik [Anthony Hopkinson Esq, 12 Queensdale Place, London W11], late Capt Scots Gds; *b* 18 March 1935; *educ* Eton; *m* 7 Sept 1966 *Syl-

via Christina, only dau of Sir Alfred Stanley Fordham, of Melbourn Bury, Cambs, and has issue:

1a +Francis John Fordham; *b* 21 Oct 1967

2a +Edward; *b* 1 Nov 1972

1a *Christina Alexandra Isabel; *b* 20 Aug 1969

(1) Marika; *b* 9 Sept 1938; journalist; *m* 14 Jan 1959 *(Airling) Robin Hanbury Tenison, OBE, author and explorer, yst son of Capt Gerald Evan Farqhar Tenison, of Lough Bawn, Castleblayney, Co Monaghan, and Overbury Hall, Suffolk, and *d* 24 Oct 1982, leaving issue:

1a *A son; *b* 19–

1a *Lucy Antonia; *b* 20 Jan 1960

3 Francis Archibald; *b* 30 Sept 1904; *educ* Eton and Trin Coll Cambridge; CC Kent (1961), barrister Inner Temple 1927, Maj Scots Gds WW II; *m* 14 Sept 1935 *Ursula Joan Tyldesley, yr dau of William Everard Tyldesley Jones, KC, of Roche Court, Winterslow, nr Salisbury, Wilts, and had issue:

(1) *Elizabeth Anne; *b* 7 July 1936; *m* 1st 27 July 1955 (*divorce* 1968) David Charles Watney, yr son of Col Charles Watney, CIE, TD, of Ivy Hatch, nr Sevenoaks, and Bishops Caundle, Sherborne, Dorset, and has issue:

1a *(Anne) Louise; *b* 10 March 1956

2a *Caroline Teresa; *b* 22 July 1958

(1) (cont.) Mrs Elizabeth Watney *m* 2nd 3 July 1968 *Michael Raymond Minoprio, yst son of Frank Charles Minoprio, of Broadlands, Ascot, Berks, and Haulfryn, Caernarvonshire

(2) *Theresa Mary; *b* 1 Dec 1938; *m* 1 Oct 1960 *Maj John Norman Stewart Arthur, The Roy Scots Greys, er son of Lt-Col Evelyn Stewart Arthur, DL, of Longnor Hall, nr Shrewsbury, Salop (*see* GLENARTHUR, B), and has had issue

Sir HENRY's est son,

HENRY LENNOX D'AUBIGNÉ HOPKINSON, **1st Baron Colyton**, of Farway in the Co of Devon, and Taunton in the Co of Somerset (UK), so *cr* 19 Jan 1956, PC (1952), CMG (1944); *b* 3 Jan 1902; *educ* Eton and Trin Coll Cambridge (BA Hons 1923); Dip Serv 1924–46: 3rd Sec Washington 1924–29, 2nd Sec FO 1929–31, Stockholm 1931–32, Assist Priv Sec to For Sec 1932–34, 2nd Sec Cairo 1934–38, 1st Sec 1936: Athens 1938–39, War Cabinet Secretariat 1939–40, Priv Sec to PUS FO 1940–41, Counsellor 1941 and Dip Advsr to Min State Middle East 1941–43, Min Plen Lisbon 1943–44, Dep HC Rome and Political Advsr to Allied Commn Italy 1944–46, Head C Parly Secretariat and jt dir CRD 1946–50, MP (C) Taunton 1950–56, Sec Overseas Trade 1951–52, Min State Colonial Affairs 1952–55, chm: Anglo-Egyptian Resettlement Bd 1957–60, Jt E and Centl African Bd 1960–65, Tanganyika Concessions Ltd 1966–72, dir: London Tin Corp, Union Minière, Roy Humane Soc's Award for Saving Life from drowning 1919; OStJ, Grand Cross Order of Prince Henry the Navigator of Portugal, Grand Star Order Paduka Stia Negara of Brunei, Cdr Order of Zaire; *m* 1st 10 Nov 1927 Alice Labouisse (*d* 30 April 1953), dau of Henry Lane Eno, of Bar Harbor, Maine, and Princeton, NJ, USA, and had issue:

1 Nicholas Henry Eno; *b* 18 Jan 1932; *educ* Eton and Trin Coll Cambridge (BA 1957); Lt 11th Hus; *m* 10 Aug 1957 Fiona Margaret (*d* 15 May 1996), only dau of Sir Thomas Torquil Munro, 5th Bt, of Lindertis (*qv*), and *d* 1991, leaving issue:

(1) ALISDAIR JOHN MUNRO HOPKINSON, **2nd and present Baron Colyton**

(2) +Charles Henry Kenneth; *b* 2 May 1960; *m* 1988 *Karen Anne, est dau of E Snowdon, of Melbourne, Australia, and has issue:

1a +Frederick Nicholas Hugo; *b* 1990

2a +Henry Jonathan Arthur; *b* 1992

1 Olivia (twin with Nicholas); *b* 18 Jan, *d* 22 Jan 1932

The **1st Baron** *m* 2nd 11 Dec 1956 *Barbara Estella [The Rt Hon Barbara Lady Colyton, Le Formentor, Av Princess Grace, Monte Carlo, Monaco], formerly w of the cartoonist Charles Samuel Addams and dau of Stephen Barb, of New York, and *d* 6 Jan 1996

COMBERMERE

Arms: Quarterly, 1st and 4th, az. a chevron between three hanks of cotton arg.; in chief, pendant from a ribbon gu., a representation of the medal presented to the 1st Viscount after the battle of Salamanca (for COTTON); 2nd and 3rd, arg. a lion rampant sa. (for STAPLETON). **Crests:** 1 A falcon ppr., wings expanded, belled or, holding in the dexter claw a belt az. buckled of the second, 2 (of augmentation) Upon a mount vert a soldier of the 3rd Regt. of Light Dragoons mounted all ppr. in the attitude of charging the enemy, over him in an escrol az. the word SALAMANCA in letters of gold, 3 Out of a ducal coronet or a saracen's head couped at the shoulders affrontée wreathed round the temples arg. and sa. **Supporters:** Two falcons, wings expanded and addorsed ppr., belled or, the dexter supporting a spear also ppr., therefrom flowing a standard swallow-tailed vert semé of estoiles or, streamers and tassels of the last, the sinister supporting a like spear therefrom flowing a yellow standard swallow-tailed, streamers and tassels of the last.

Motto: *In utraque fortuna paratus* ('Prepared against all outcomes').

Creations: Bt. (E) 29 March 1677, B. (UK) 17 May 1814, V. (UK) 8 Feb 1827.

THE 5TH VISCOUNT COMBERMERE OF BHURTPORE, Baron Combermere, of Combermere, Co Chester, and a **Baronet** (Sir Michael Wellington Stapleton-Cotton, Bt) [The Rt Hon The Viscount Combermere, Vanners, Bucklebury Common, Berks RG7 6RU]; *b* 8 Aug 1929; *s* f 1969; *educ* Eton and King's Coll London (BD 1965, MTh 1967); F/Lt RAF Res, Palestine Police 1947–48, RCMP 1948–49, short serv commn gen duties pilot RAF 1950–58, sales rep Teleflex Products Ltd 1959–62, staff lecturer biblical and religious studies London U Dept Extra-Mural Studies 1972–94, sr lecturer religious studies Birkbeck Coll Centre Extra-Mural Studies 1988–94, chm World Congress of Faiths 1983–88; *m* 4 Feb 1961 *Pamela Elizabeth (Jill), er dau of Rev Robert Gustavus Coulson, of Stansted, Kent, and has issue:

1 +THOMAS ROBERT WELLINGTON; *b* 30 Aug 1969

1 *Tara Christabel; *b* 26 Nov 1961; *educ* N Foreland Lodge; *m* 1992 *Laurent Saglio

2 *Sophia Mary; *b* 20 July 1963; *m* 1995 *Greville Worthington

Lineage: Sir GEORGE COTTON, PC; Esq of the Body to HENRY VIII, acquired the lands of Combermere, formerly a Benedictine Abbey, at the Dissolution of the Monasteries; V-Chamberlain Household to EDWARD VI when Prince of Wales; *m* Mary, dau of John Onley, of Catesby, Northants, and had an only son:

RICHARD COTTON, of Combermere; *m* 1st Mary, dau of Sir Arthur Mainwaring, of Ightfield, Salop, and had two s and a dau; *m* 2nd —; *m* 3rd —; his est s by his 1st w:

GEORGE COTTON, of Combermere; *m* Mary, dau of Sir George Bromley, Ch Justice Chester, and had:

THOMAS COTTON; *m* 1st Frances, dau of 3rd Viscount Kilmorey (*see* KILMOREY, E) and had a s (George, *dsps* 1647); *m* 2nd Elizabeth, dau and coheir of Sir George Calveley, of Lea, Cheshire, and *d* by 1649, having by her had an est surv son:

Sir Robert Cotton, 1st Bt (E), so *cr* 29 March 1677, of Combermere; *b c* 1635; MP Cheshire 1679–1702; ktd 1660; *m* Hester (*d* 1710), sis and heir of John Salusbury, 3rd Bt, of Llewenny, Denbighs, and *d* 17 Dec 1712, having had, with other issue, including an er s (Hugh Calveley, *m* Mary, only dau and heiress of Sir William Russell, Bt, and *dvp* leaving an only dau) an only surv one:

Sir Thomas Cotton, 2nd Bt; *b c* 1672; Sheriff Cheshire 1712–13; *m c* 18 Nov 1689 Philadephia (*m* 2nd Thomas King and *d* 30 Dec 1758), dau and heir of Sir Thomas Lynch, of ; Esher, Surrey, Govr Jamaica, and *d* 12 June 1715, having had:

1 **Sir Robert Salusbury Cotton, 3rd Bt** *bapt* 2 Jan 1694/5; *educ* BNC Oxford; MP Cheshire 1727–34 and Lostwithiel 1741–47; *m* Elizabeth (*d* 16 Aug 1745), est dau of 3rd Earl of Dysart (*qv*), and *dsp* 27 Aug 1748

2 LYNCH SALUSBURY (Sir), **4th Bt**

The yr s,

Sir Lynch Salusbury Cotton, 4th Bt; *b c* 1705; MP Denbighs 1749–74; *m* by 1738 Elizabeth (*d* 4 Jan 1777), dau of Rowland Cotton, of Etwall, Derbys, and had, with other issue (living membs of whom are in remainder, where at all, to the btcy only):

1 ROBERT SALUSBURY (Sir), **5th Bt**

2 Rowland, Adml RN; *m* 29 June 1792 Elizabeth, dau of Sir Willoughby Aston, Bt, and *d* 3 Nov 1794, having had, with a dau (Sydney Arabella, *m* Richard Moore):

(1) Willoughby (Sir), GCB, KCH, Gen, Col 32nd Foot; *b* 1783; *m* 16 May 1806 Augusta Maria (*d* 1 Nov 1865), est dau of 7th Earl of Coventry (*qv*), and *d* 4 May 1860, having had:

1a Willoughby; Capt 44th Regt; *b* 3 Sept 1807; *d* 21 April 1846

2a Corbet; Maj-Gen formerly 49th Regt; *b* 10 Aug 1808; *m* 11 May 1847 Christina Augusta (*d* 23 Jan 1892), dau of Sir Charles Des Voeux, 2nd Bt, (*see* 1940 edn), and *d* 1885, leaving issue:

1b Willoughby; *dsp* 14 March 1903

2b Corbet Stapleton; 60th Rifles; *dsp*

1b Augusta Charlotte; *m* 1887 Lt-Col Wyatt William Turnor, 4th Bn Yorks Regt, of Pinkney Pk, Malmesbury, and *d* 23 Dec 1927, leaving issue. He *d* 3 March 1931

2b Chinty Mary Chatherine; *m* 1 June 1876 William Robert Percival LOCKWOOD formerly WOOD and *d* 18 July 1938, leaving issue. He *d* 28 Feb 1929

3b Florence Champagne; *m* 27 Jan 1880 Augustus William Craven, est son of W G Craven, of Horseleath Lodge, Cambs, and *dsp* Aug 1899. He *d* 23 Feb 1929

1a Augusta Mary; *m* Col Henry Vaughan Brooke, CB, and had issue

3 George (Rev) LLD, Dean Chester; *b* 1742; *m* 1771 Katherine Maria (*d* Dec 1818), er dau of James Tomkinson, and *d* 10 Dec 1805, leaving, with other issue:

(1) James Henry (Very Rev), Dean Bangor; *b* 8 Feb 1781; *m* 1st 14 April 1810 Mary Anne, dau of Rt Rev W H Majendie, Bp Bangor; *m* 2nd 1826 Mary, dau of Samuel Fisher, MD, and *d* May 1862, having by his 1st *w* had issue:

1a Henry James (Rev), Rector Dalbury; *b* 1 May 1811; *m* 15 April 1847 Elisabeth Emma (*d* 1902), dau of John Sparrow Stovin, and *d* 1884, leaving issue:

1b Frederick Henry; *b* 1 March 1848; *m* 8 Dec 1870 Florence Hester Lavinia (*d* 1915), dau of Charles Richard Banastre Legh, DL, JP, of Adlington, Cheshire, and *d* 1 June 1921, leaving issue:

1c Caroline Mary Florence; *m* 28 June 1892 Arthur Masterton Robertson RENNY later LEGH (1897), of Adlington, Cheshire, and *d* 6 July 1940, leaving issue. He *d* 25 Dec 1933

2c Gwendoline Mabel Lucy; *m* 19 Jan 1898 Frank Thomas Wisden, of Henfield, Sussex, and *d* 25 July 1960, leaving issue. He *d* 20 Jan 1922

2b James Stapleton (Rev), Vicar Audlem, Cheshire 1896–1924, Hon Canon Chester 1917; *b* 25 June 1849; *m* 5 Feb 1880 Louisa Jessie (*d* 11 April 1922), er dau of Colin Minton Campbell, of Woodseat, Staffs, and *d* June 1932, leaving issue:

1c Frederick Arthur Stapleton, Capt Res of Offrs Roy Scots Fus WW I (severely wounded); *b* 1884; *educ* Selwyn Coll Cambridge (MA); *m* 3 July 1912 Evelyn Mary (*d* 20 Aug 1968), dau of Col Samuel Ormsby Rogers, Army Ordnance Corps, of Congleton, Cheshire, and *d* 1 Aug 1927, leaving issue:

1d Hugh Philip Stapleton, WW II as Capt RA; *b* 1 May 1913; *educ* Felsted; *m* 28 May 1938 *Mary Josephine, dau of Frederick Thomas Wheeler, of Three Ways, Edenbridge, Kent, and *d* 1979, leaving issue:

1e +Stephen Hugh Stapleton; *b* 31 Aug 1949; *educ* Tonbridge and Reading U (BSc Estate Management); FRICS; *m* 1970 *Josephine Katharina, dau of Owen Eric Goddard, Consul Oporto, and has issue:

1f +Rufus Tom Stapleton; *b* 1976

1f *Gabriele Pippa; *b* 1974

2f *Hannah Stephanie; *b* 1977

3f *Olivia Jo; *b* 19–

1e *Jennifer Mary [Mrs Jennifer Chettle, Whistle Cottage, Cowden, Edenbridge, Kent]; *b* 24 Feb 1943; *m* 5 Sept 1964 (*divorce* 1983) Peter Ivan Chettle, son of William Clarence Chettle, and has issue:

1f *Dominic Mark; *b* 12 Dec 1967

1f *Deborah Jane Emma; *b* 1970

2e *Marilyn Elizabeth [Mrs Steven Linehan, 30 Stanford Ave, Hassocks, W Sussex]; *b* 5 June 1946; *educ* Sussex U (BEd), Dip RSA; *m* 1st 1977 (*divorce* 1988) Christopher David Jones; *m* 2nd 1989 *Steven John Linehan, and by 1st husb has issue:

1f *Benjamin Kester; *b* 1973

2f *Daniel Ian; *b* 1975

1d Sheila Evelyn Ormsby; *b* 18 Jan 1915; *m* 7 May 1940 Maj Arthur Richard Burch, DSC, RM (*d* 11 Feb 1964), s of Arthur Rodney Burch, of Heathfield, Sussex, and *d* 14 Feb 1996, leaving:

1e *Peter Ronald [Lt-Cdr Peter Burch RN, 760 San Mario Dve, Solana Beach, Calif, USA]; *b* 11 April 1946; *educ* Tonbridge; *m* 1980 *Mary Lou, dau of Gordon Galligan, of San Diego, and has:

1f *Andrew Richard; *b* 18 Feb 1986

2f *Matthew David; *b* 18 Feb 1986

1f *Sarah Louise; *b* 15 Oct 1983

2e *David John [Dr David Burch, Monastery House, Priory St, Newport Pagnell, Bucks MK16 9AH]; *b* 19 Nov 1949; *educ* Durham Sch and Leeds (BSc), Sussex (DPhil) and Brunel Us (MSc); *m* 1 Sept 1984 *Pauline Heather, dau of George Twitchen, and has issue:

1f *Henry Arthur; *b* 24 June 1987

1f *Lucy Hester; *b* 29 Sept 1985

2f *Hazel Joan; *b* 7 Aug 1989

1e *Sally Louise; *b* 28 Jan 1943; *educ* Southampton (BA) and London Us (PhD); *m* 1972 (*divorce* 1980) David John North

2c Hugh Stapleton, T/Lt RE WW I (wounded); *b* 1885; *d* unm 7 Oct 1957

3c George Edward Stapleton; despatch rider 1st Canadian Contingent WW I 1914–17; *b* 1888; *m* 1918 Lillie (*d* 28 Jan 1963), dau of William Henry Price, of Shrewsbury, and *dsp*

4c Henry Wilmot Stapleton (Rev Canon), Chaplain Indian Ecclesiastical Establishment 1925–46, Archdeacon Lucknow 1937–47, Rector Bredfield with Boulge Suffolk 1947–52, Debach 1949–52 and Lavenham 1952–64, Hon Canon Bury St Edmunds, RD Lavenham 1955, on staff Bury St Edmunds Cathedral 1964–66, Canon Emeritus 1964, T/Capt Cheshire Regt WW I (despatches, wounded); *b* 1894; *educ* Radley and Queens' Coll Cambridge (BA 1920, MA 1923); *m* 9 April 1923 Elaine Christine Isobel, dau of Joseph Henry Iredale, of Rock Ferry, Cheshire, and The Towers, Capel Curig, Caernarvs

1c Beatrice Jessie; *b* 1880; *m* 16 April 1912 Rev Percy Edward Mainwaring, MA, Rector Whitmore, Staffs, 5th s of Rev Charles Mainwaring, JP, and *dsp* 29 Sept 1945. He *d* 22 June 1927

2c Constance Muriel; *b* 1883; *m* 20 April 1915 Maj Geoffrey Pearson Rogers, King's Liverpool Regt (TA), son of Fletcher Rogers, of Aigburth, Lancs, and *d* 27 Dec 1930, leaving issue

3c Mildred Lucy; *b* 1890; *d* 1891

4c Hester Evelyn; *b* 11 Feb 1897

3b George Stovin Egerton; *d* unm

4b Charles Harington; *b* 28 Jan 1857; *m* 14 April 1898 Julia Katherine, widow of Rev Gerard Duke Wyatt and dau of Rev Howard Gough, of Colwall Ct, Malvern

1b Caroline Lucy; *d* unm

2b Constance Mary Anne; *m* 1881 Charles G H Shorting, and *d* 1926, leaving issue. He *d* 1897

3b Florence Isabel; *m* 1887 Frank Marven Southwell, of Bridgnorth, Salop, and *d* 3 May 1930, leaving issue

2a James; *b* 1815; *dsp*

1a Mary; *b* 1827; *d* 1894

2a Anne; *m* 11 Oct 1859 Rev Evan Lewis, and *d* 22 Dec 1860

(2) Thomas Davenant; Capt Roy Fus; *m* 25 June 1810 Mary Burnley, and was *k* 13 Nov 1813, leaving:

1a George Edward Lynch (Rt Rev), Bp Calcutta; *b* 29 Oct 1813; *m* 26 June 1845 Sophia Ann (*d* 24 Feb 1907), dau of Rev Henry Tomkinson, of Reaseheath, Cheshire, and *d* 6 Oct 1866, leaving issue:

1b Edward Thomas Davenant COTTON later COTTON-JODRELL (roy licence 1890) (Sir), KCB, of Yeardsley and Reaseheath, Nantwich, Cheshire, and Shallcross, Derbys, DL, JP Cheshire; Capt RA, Col TF, Lt-Col and Hon Col cmdg Cheshire RE (Rlwy Bn), DADG Staff HQ 1906–12, MP Wirral 1885–1900; *b* 29 June 1847; *m* 24 April 1878 Mary Rennell, OBE (1920) (*d* 18 April 1932), dau of William Rennell Coleridge, of Salston, Devon (*see* COLERIDGE, B), and *d* 13 Oct 1917, having had issue:

1c George Henry Coleridge; *d* an infant 1882

1c Dorothy Lynch, CBE (1920), JP Derbys; *m* 3 June 1902 Lt-Col Henry RAMSDEN later RAMSDEN-JODRELL, CMG, RA, son of John Charles Francis Ramsden, DL, of Willinghurst, Surrey, and *d* 24 April 1958, leaving issue (*see* RAMSDEN, Bt)

2c Olive Harriet, OBE (1920); *m* 9 Aug 1910 Adml Richard Greville Arthur Wellington Stapleton-Cotton, CB, CBE, MVO (*see below*), and *dsp* 31 July 1978 aged 94. He *d* 5 Jan 1953

1b Ursula Mary; *m* 1st 29 Jan 1879 Rev Walter Hillyard, Vicar Worleston, Cheshire, and had issue. He *d* 21 July 1881. She *m* 2nd 25 June 1884 Rev Arthur Atkinson, MA, Vicar Audlem, Cheshire, Hon Canon of Chester, and *d* 31 Jan 1928, having had further issue. He *d* 24 Oct 1915

4 Henry Calveley, of Woodcote, Oxon; *b* 25 July 1755; *m* 14 April 1788 Matilda (*d* 3 Feb 1848), dau and heiress of John Lockwood, of Dews Hall, Essex, and *d* 15 May 1837, leaving, with other issue:

(1) Henry Calveley (Rev), Vicar Greatness; *b* 25 March 1789; *m* 24 May 1815 Eloisa (*d* 17 Aug 1872), dau of William Mostyn Owen, of Woodhouse, Salop, and *d* 4 Oct 1850, leaving issue:

1a Henry Calveley, Capt 21st Roy Scots Fus; *b* 16 April 1823; *m* 4 March 1856 Georgiana (*d* 24 July 1914), dau of Edward Bolton King, DL, MP, of Chadshunt, Warwicks, and *d* 16 Dec 1909, leaving issue:

1b Henry Robert Stapleton, Capt 1st Bn Oxon LI, Maj and Ch Recruiting Offr 1914–18, served Red Cross Ambulance French Army 1918–19; *b* 8 June 1859; *m* 12 Sept 1900 Isabella Scott (*d* 18 April 1953), widow of Arthur Lyon and yst dau of John Johnstone, of Halleaths, Dumfries, and *dsp* 25 Jan 1946

2b Willoughby Lynch; Capt 3rd Bn Salop LI; *b* 22 Aug 1863; *m* 1st 1888 Rosina Mary Adelaide (*d* 29 Jan 1914), est dau of Andrew Jones, of Shelton, Salop; *m* 2nd April 1916 Eleanor Mary, widow of Walter Sutton Salt and est dau of James Henry Sprott, and *dvs* 6 Jan 1918, having by his 1st *w* had issue:

1c Vyvian Stapleton; *b* 1889; matron Polack's House, Clifton Coll; *d* unm 23 April 1973

1b Frances Georgina; *d* 11 Nov 1936

2b Eloisa Alice; *m* 3 April 1888 Lt-Col Henry Vane Russell, 3rd Bn Salop LI, and *d* 2 Nov 1906. He *d* Aug 1914

1a Matilda Eloisa; *m* 15 Aug 1844 Rev Charles Orlando Kenyon, son of Hon Thomas Kenyon, and *d* 1892, leaving issue (*see* KENYON, B)

(2) Sydney John (Sir), GCB, Gen, Col 10th Foot; *b* Dec 1792; *m* 1820 Marianne (*d* 1854), dau of Capt Hackett, 22nd Light Dragoons, and *d* while Govr Roy Hosp Chelsea 20 Feb 1874, having had, with another s and two daus:

1a Lynch Stapleton, Maj-Gen, AA & QMG, Cmdt Roy Hibernian Mil Sch; *b* 21 Dec 1828; *m* 20 March 1855 Jane Gordon (*d* 8 Jan 1923), dau of James Inglis, of Fairley, Aberdeenshire, and *d* 7 March 1899, leaving surv issue:

1b Stapleton Lynch, Maj King's Liverpool Regt Afghan, Burmese, Boer Wars (severely wounded) and WW I; *b* 15 Jan 1860; *d* 3 May 1928

1b Charlotte Gordon; *d* 11 April 1916

2b Matilda; *d* unm 4 Dec 1945

(3) Richard Lynch (Rev), DD; Provost Worcester Coll Oxford; *b* 14 Aug 1794; *m* 25 June 1839 Charlotte Bouverie (*d* 2 July 1883), dau of Hon Philip Pusey (*see* RADNOR, E), and *d* 8 Dec 1880, leaving a dau

(4) Charles Robert, of Knolton Hall, Flints, JP; *b* 22 Nov 1796; *m* 26 May 1841 Mary Anne Elizabeth (*d* 5 July 1902), dau of Sir Philip Grey Egerton, 9th Bt (*qv*), and *d* 18 May 1873, leaving issue:

1a Charles Calveley; *b* 18 Aug 1847; *m* 9 Oct 1873 Kate (*d* 7 Sept 1936), dau of William Frederick de la Rue, and *d* 25 April 1892, leaving issue:

1b Charles William Egerton, CSI (1931), CIE (1920); ICS, Ch Sec Govt Madras; *b* 14 Aug 1874; *educ* Eton and Univ Coll Oxford (BA); *m* 12 Dec 1925 Violet (*d* 17 May 1971), yr dau of Sir Philip Mainwaring, 4th Bt (*see* 1934 edn), and *d* 6 Sept 1931

2b Ronald Egerton, DSO (1919), Lt-Col Serv Bn Yorks Regt, served Boer War 1900–01 (medal with three clasps) and WW I (wounded, despatches thrice); *b* 8 March 1876; *m* 8 Feb 1917 Hilda (*d* 15 March 1967), yr dau of Capt Charles Dickson Inglis, RN, of Grianach, Nairn, and *d* 3 Sept 1932, leaving issue:

1c Patricia Daphne; *b* 20 Feb 1920; *d* 8 April 1991

3b Arthur Egerton, DSO (1917), cmded 11th Serv Bn Rifle Bde; *b* 8 March 1876 (twin); *m* 1 July 1909 Beryl Marie (*m* 2nd 1923 John Lee Booker JP (*d* 1942), of Swarthdale, Carnforth, Lancs, and *d* 26 Jan 1966), dau of Henry Jack Cumming, and *d* 10 June 1922, leaving issue:

1c *Elizabeth Egerton; *b* 9 Nov 1910; *m* 1st 21 Feb 1934 (*divorce* 1949) Francis Mortimer Montgomery, son of Robert Mortimer Montgomery, KC, and has issue:

1d *John Ayrton, manager City Magazines Ltd, dir Impress Internat Merchandising; *b* 22 Feb 1935

1c (cont.) Mrs Elizabeth Montgomery *m* 2nd 1 May 1951 *Stafford William Somerfield, son of Albert George Somerfield, of Barnstaple, Devon

2c *Anne Rebecca; *b* 6 July 1912; *m* 1943 (*divorce* 1951) Auriol Earsdon Thornton Magor, only son of George Furniss Auriol Magor, of The Lelant, Cornwall. He *d* 5 Nov 1956

3c *Diana Sara [Mrs Brooke Crutchley, 39 High St, Great Shelford, Cambs]; *b* 9 Nov 1914; *m* 20 March 1936 *Brooke Crutchley, CBE, er son of Lt-Col Ernest Tristram Crutchley, CB, CMG, CBE, and has issue:

1d *Edward Brooke; *b* 18 Feb 1950; *m* 1982 *Eugenie Tsirmoula, and has issue:

1e *James Edward Brooke; *b* 1986

2d *Christopher Miles; *b* 18 June 1951

1d *Anna Maria; *b* 28 June 1954

4b Sydney Egerton; *b* 23 May 1884; *educ* Haileybury; *m* 2 July 1923 Mabel (*d* 31 July 1954), widow of Francis Neville Carter, and *d* 18 March 1938

5b Vere Egerton, CBE (1937), TD (1927), Hon LLD Liverpool U 1953, High Sheriff Lancs 1956, Ld Mayor Liverpool 1951–52, Hon Alderman City Liverpool (Chm Libraries, Museums and Arts Ctee), Pro Chllr Liverpool U, memb Arts Cncl, Lt-Col and Brevet Col TA, Hon Col 470 Heavy AA Regt RA (TA) WW I (despatches three times, Croix de Guerre France and Italy); *b* 5 May 1888; *educ* Repton and Magdalene Coll Cambridge (MA); *m* 2 Feb 1922 Elfreda Helen, JP (*d* 1992 aged 100), dau of William Francis Moore, of Greenbank Cottage, Liverpool, and *d* 19 Nov 1970, leaving issue:

1c +Simon Arthur, JP [Simon Cotton Esq JP, 28 Sauncey Ave, Harpenden, Herts]; barrister Gray's Inn 1951, served WW II; *b* 17 Aug 1924; *educ* Repton and Magdalene Coll Cambridge (BA 1949); *m* 18 June 1960 *Barbara Helen Ralston, yr dau of Albert James Sutcliffe, of The Church Cottage, Dodleston, Cheshire, and has issue:

1d +William Andrew Calveley; *b* 27 Nov 1962; *educ* Radley and Bristol U

1d *Emma Jane; *b* 27 May 1961; *educ* Sidney Sussex Coll Cambridge (BA)

2d *Helen Clare; *b* 10 Oct 1965; *educ* Durham U

2c +Robert Charles [Robert Cotton Esq, Cherry Orchard, Badgemore, Henley-on-Thames, Oxon RG6 4NR], late Lt RA (TA); *b* 31 Dec 1925; *educ* Repton and Magdalene Coll Cambridge (MA 1984); *m* 30 Oct 1954 *Nicolette Anne, 2nd dau of Capt Robert Lionel Brooke Cunliffe, CBE, RN, of The Garden Ho, Pakenham, Bury St Edmunds, Suffolk (*see* CUNLIFFE, Bt), and has issue:

1d +Richard Robert [Richard Cotton Esq, The Malt House, Bromdean, Alresford, Hants]; *b* 10 Jan 1956; *educ* Bradfield and UEA (BA); *m* 1984 *Corin, dau of Carel Wevers, of The Hague, and has issue:

1e +Oliver Charles; *b* 1987

2e +Anthony Vere; *b* 1988

1e *Pavania Sarah; *b* 1991

2d +Philip Egerton [Philip Cotton Esq, 42 Buckmaster Rd, London SW11]; *b* 22 March 1960; *educ* Shiplake Coll; *m* 1st 1987 (*divorce* 1996) Rosie Louise, dau of Capt James Pack, OBE, RN, of Wickham, Hants; *m* 2nd 1998 *Juliet, dau of Barry Edwards, of Macclesfield, and by his 1st w has:

1e +Charles Egerton; *b* 1989

1d *Penelope Clare [Mrs John Arnold, 1 Deepdene, Park Rd, Dorking, Surrey RH5 4AL]; *b* 7 Nov 1957; *educ* Queen Anne's Caversham and Roy Free Med Sch (MB, BS); *m* 1983 *John Christopher Arnold, son of Rev Eric Joseph Arnold, of Tiverton, and has issue:

1e *William Henry; *b* 1991

2e *Hugh James; *b* 1993

1e *Frances Helen; *b* 1996

2d *Caroline Harriet [Mrs Thomas Emlyn Jones, 40 Lady Somerset Rd, London NW5]; *b* 16 March 1963; *educ* St Mary's Calne and Manchester U (BA); *m* 1992 *Thomas Emlyn Jones, son of J H Emlyn Jones, of Ivinghoe, Bucks, and has issue:

1e *Jack; *b* 1995

1e *Kate; *b* 1993

3c Henry Egerton, JP, Lt RA (TA), Ld Lt Merseyside 1989–93; *b* 21 July 1929; *educ* Rugby and Magdalene Coll Cambridge (BA 1952); *m* 18 June 1955 *Elizabeth Margaret Susan, JP, DL [Mrs Henry Cotton JP DL, Norwood, Grassendale Pk, Liverpool L19 0LP], yr dau of Clifford James Peard, DSO, JP, of N Curry, Taunton, and *d* 1993, leaving issue:

1d +Timothy James Egerton; *b* 30 March 1958

1d *Catherine Susan [Mrs Yianni Psillou, Roussa Limni, Aghios Nikolaos 72100, Crete, Greece]; *b* 3 Sept 1956; *educ* Benenden and Cambs Sch of Art & Tech (RSA); *m* 1996 *Yianni Psillos, of Kritsa, Crete

2a Francis Egerton, Maj Denbighs Imp Yeo; *b* 7 Aug 1849; *m* 8 May 1879 Helen Louisa Muriel (*d* 18 July 1910), yr dau of Capt Francis Mostyn-Owen, of Althrey Hall, Wrexham, and *d* 27 Oct 1923, leaving issue:

1b Gilbert Francis Egerton, Maj Denbighs Imp Yeo; *b* 14 March 1880; *m* 22 Dec 1913 Nora (*d* 11 Nov 1956), dau of Matthew Williams, of Whiston Hall, Albrighton, and *d* 1971, leaving issue:

1c +Francis Brian Egerton; Maj RWF WW II; *b* 14 July 1916; *educ* Eton; *m* 28 April 1955 *Ruth Margery, MBE, er dau of Richard Stratton, CBE, of Kingston Deverill, Wilts, and has issue:

1d +Charles Egerton; *b* 26 Aug 1958

1c *Helen Viola Egerton; *b* 3 Oct 1917; *m* 1st 6 April 1940 Capt Sir John Hargreaves Pigott-Brown, 2nd Bt, Coldstream Gds, and has issue (*see* PIGGOTT-BROWN, Bt). He was *ka* 25 Dec 1942. She *m* 2nd 20 April 1948 *Capt Charles Raymond Radclyffe, late Scots Greys, only son of Raymond Augustus Edward Radclyffe, of Lew, and has further issue:

1d *Sarah [Miss Sarah Radclyffe, 15 Shirlock Rd, London NW3 2RH]; *b* 1950; film producer

1b Violet Mary Egerton; *b* 11 May 1883; *d* unm 2 Aug 1967

(5) Hugh Calveley, Col HEICS; *b* 13 Feb 1798; *m* 25 April 1825 Louisa (*d* 1 July 1862), dau of W Brodie of Brodie, and *d* 13 Oct 1881, having had issue:

1a Henry Calveley Lynch, CE; *b* 6 Nov 1829; *m* 18 Sept 1862 Clara (*d* 1905), dau of John Loch, of Australia, and *d* 1897, leaving issue:

1b Calveley William Gordon; *b* 28 April 1865; *m* 3 June 1889 *Marian Annie, est dau of Henry George Baylis, of Calcutta, and *d* 28 Dec 1933

1b Clara Louisa

2b Marion; *m* 9 Oct 1894 John Stewart Hamilton, of Devizes. He *d* 1919

3b Ethel

2a William Gordon Lynch, MICE, PWD India; *b* 9 Aug 1838; *m* 1st 27 Jan 1866 Emma (*d* 1885), 2nd dau of John Clough, of Newbold Hall, Market Weighton, Yorks, and had issue:

1b Hugh Gordon; *b* 23 July 1869; *m* 5 Jan 1903 Gertrude Mary, dau of Charles Parsons, and *d* 1942, leaving issue:

1c *Vivienne Mary; *b* 1903

2b Thomas Calveley; *b* 8 Sept 1873; *d* 1895

3b John Delves Lynch; *b* 25 Nov 1881; *d* 1887

1b Ella Blanche; *m* 1st 1889 Herbert Charles Crosley, of Darjeeling, Bengal, and had issue. He *d* 1905. She *m* 2nd 1918 A S Wrigley, and *d* Jan 1950

2a (cont.) William Cotton *m* 2nd 1889 Maggie Miller (*dsp* 2 June 1902), dau of Robert Hay, of Dalmuir, Dunbartonshire; *m* 3rd 3 April 1905 Adelaide Cicely (*d* 21 Sept 1906), widow of John Martin Dwyer, PWD, and dau of Charles Vavasour, of Sandford, Ireland, and *d* 23 Jan 1911

1a Frances Matilda; *m* 18 Feb 1865 Capt Sir William Burgess Goldsmith, RN, Serjeant-at-Arms in Ordinary to HM QUEEN VICTORIA, and *d* 8 Oct 1911, leaving issue. He *d* 23 Dec 1912

2a Isabella Hester; *d* unm 29 March 1924

(6) Arthur Thomas (Sir), KCSI, Gen; *b* 15 May 1803; *m* 1841 Elizabeth (*d* 5 Dec 1907), est dau of Thomas Livingstone Learmonth, of Parkhall, and *d* 24 July 1899, leaving issue:

1a Alfred Fox, Maj Indian Staff Corps; *b* 11 Jan 1850; *m* 1881 Marion Emma (*m* 2nd Maj Richard Crofton, RHA (*dsp* 24 Jan 1899), and *d* 14 May 1949), est dau of V-Adml Sir Leopold George Heath, KCB, of Ainstie Grange, Holmwood, Surrey, and *dsp*

1a Elizabeth Reid; *m* 1st 2 Dec 1877 Adml of the Fleet Sir James Hope, GCB. He *d* 9 June 1881. She *m* 2nd 27 Sept 1893 Thomas Anthony Denny, 3rd son of Henry Denny, of Newtown Ho, Co Waterford, and *d* 8 March 1922. He *d* 25 Dec 1909

(7) Frederic Conyers, CSI, Maj-Gen HEIC; *b* 30 July 1807; *m* 9 April 1849 Mary (*d* 1896), dau of Brooke Cunliffe (*see* CUNLIFFE, Bt), and *dsp* 12 Oct 1901

(1) Maria Frances; *m* Rev Joseph Hordern, Rector Burton Agnes, Yorks, and had issue

1 Hester Salusbury; *m* Sir Corbet Corbet, (*see* 1970 edn CORBET, Bt)

Sir LYNCH *d* 14 Aug 1775; his est son,

Sir Robert Salusbury Cotton, 5th Bt; *b c* 1739; MP Cheshire 1780–96; *m* 1767 Frances (*d* 20 April 1825), dau and coheir of Col James Russell Stapleton (*see* LANGFORD, B), and had, with other issue:

1 STAPLETON, **1st Viscount**

2 Lynch; Col; *m* Louisa Margaret — (*m* 2nd 1807 Lt-Gen Sir William Lumley, KCB (*d* 15 Dec 1850), and *d* 11 Sept 1859) and *d* 1799

1 Frances; *b* 1 Dec 1769; *m* 10 Jan 1792 11th Viscount Kilmorey (*see* KILMOREY, E) and *d* 26 Nov 1818

2 Sophia; *m* Sir Harry Mainwaring Mainwaring, 1st Bt, of Over Peover, Cheshire (*see* 1934 edn), and *d* 24 May 1838

Sir ROBERT; *d* 24 Aug 1809; his est surv son,

Sir STAPLETON COTTON later STAPLETON-COTTON (roy licence 21 Nov 1827), **6th Bt**, and **1st Viscount Combermere of Bhurtpore**, so *cr* 8 Feb 1827, as also earlier 17 May 1814 BARON COMBERMERE, of Combermere, Co Chester (both UK), with on the latter occasion (but former in point of time) a grant of £2,000 p.a. to be continued to his two successors in the title, GCB (1815, KB 1812), GCH (1817), KSI (1861), PC (GB 1834, I 1822); *b* 14 Nov 1773; *educ* Westminster; 2nd Lt 23rd Regt (Welsh Fus) 1790, Lt 1791, Capt 6th Dragoon Gds 1793, Lt-Col 25th Light Dragoons 1794 (served Siege Seringapatam), Col and Lt-Col 16th Light Dragoons 1800, Maj-Gen 1805 (cmded a bde Peninsular War, recd thanks of Parl for servs Talavera 1809, cmded 1st Div Cav retreat to Torres Vedras 1810 and Allied Cav 1811–14 as 2ic to Wellington, leading the decisive charge at Salamanca 1812), Lt Gen 1812, Col 20th Light Dragoons 1813–18, cmded Allied Cav occupation France 1815–16, Govr and C-in-C Barbados 1817–20, Col 3rd Light Dragoons 1821–29, Govr Sheerness 1821–52, C-in-C Ireland 1822–25, Gen 1825, C-in-C E Indies (as which took Bhurtpore 1825), Col 1st Life Gds and Gold Stick 1829–65, FM 1855; MP (Tory) Newark 1806–14, Constable Tower London and Ld Lt Tower Hamlets 1852–65; Kt Grand Cross: Tower and Sword Portugal 1813 and St Ferdinand and Charles III Spain; *m* 1st 1 Jan 1801 Lady Anna Maria Pelham-Clinton (*dsp* 31 May 1807), est dau of 3rd Duke of Newcastle (*see* LINCOLN, E); *m* 2nd 18 June 1814 Caroline (*d* 25 Jan 1837), 2nd dau of William Fulke Greville (*see* WARWICK, BROOKE and, E), and by her had issue:

1 WELLINGTON HENRY, **2nd Viscount**

1 Caroline Frances; *m* 23 Aug 1837 4th Marquess of Downshire, KP (*qv*), and *d* 10 May 1893, leaving issue

2 Meliora Emily Anna Maria; *m* 18 June 1853 John Charles Frederick Hunter, of Straidarran, Co Londonderry, and *d* 18 Sept 1897

The **1st Viscount** *m* 3rd 2 Oct 1838 Mary Woolley (*d* 31 Aug 1889 aged 90), only child of Robert Gibbings, of Gibbings Grove, Co Cork, and *d* 21 Feb 1865

His only son,

WELLINGTON HENRY STAPLETON-COTTON, **2nd Viscount Combermere of Bhurtpore**, DL, Col 1st Life Gds, MP Carrickfergus 1847–1857; *b* 24 Nov 1818; *m* 29 July 1844 Susan Alice (*d* 12 Aug 1869), est dau of Sir George Sitwell, 2nd Bt (*qv*), and had issue:

1 ROBERT WELLINGTON, **3rd Viscount**

2 Richard Southwell George, JP (Cheshire and Salop), DL (Anglesey), Col Scots Gds and 3rd Bn Wilts Regt, Inspr-Gen Police Br Guiana 1889–91; *b* 9 Oct 1849; *m* 18 Oct 1870 Hon Jane Charlotte Methuen (*d* 10 Aug 1924), dau of 2nd Baron Methuen (*qv*), and *d* 24 Nov 1925, leaving issue:

(1) Wellington Robert Paul; Lt 19th Hus; *b* 29 Aug 1872; *d* Ladysmith, S Africa, 29 Jan 1900

(2) Richard Greville Arthur Wellington, CB (1926), CBE (1919), MVO (1905), Adml, Naval ADC to HM GEORGE V 1922–23, Adml Supt Gibraltar Dockyard 1925–27, Gentleman Usher Scarlet Rod Order Bath 1928–32, Registrar and Sec Order Bath 1932–53, served WW I, Order Crown Italy, OStJ; *b* 7 Nov 1873; *m* 9 Aug 1910 Olive Harriet, OBE (1920) (*d* 31 July 1978 aged 94), yr dau of Lt-Col Sir Edward Thomas Davenant Cotton-Jodrell, KCB (*see* above), and *dsp* 5 Jan 1953

(3) Robert Francis, Lt-Col RAF, served Matabele campaign 1896–97, Boer War 1899–1900 and WWs I and II (HG); *b* 15 Feb 1876; *m* 22 July 1905 Violet Maude (*d* Aug 1959), 3rd dau of Sir Frederick Hervey-Bathurst, 4th Bt (*qv*), and *dsp* 26 Feb 1958

(1) Alice Hester Camilla; *b* 19 July 1871; *m* 1 June 1899 1st Baron Chetwode (*qv*) and *d* 29 June 1946, leaving issue

(2) Pauline Edith, Dep Administrator WRAF; *b* 4 Sept 1877; *d* unm 20 Feb 1964

(3) Jane Primrose; *b* 19 April 1882; *m* 28 Feb 1911 5th Viscount Hood (*qv*), and *d* 5 March 1919

1 Susan Caroline Mary; *m* 3 Jan 1867 Lt-Col Cecil Lennox Peel, yst son of Lawrence Peel, and *d* 28 May 1916, leaving issue (*see* PEEL, Bt)

2 Hester Alice; *m* 26 Aug 1880 Lord Alexander Victor Paget, 3rd son of 2nd Marquess of Anglesey (*qv*), and *d* 17 March 1930, leaving issue

The 2nd VISCOUNT *d* 1 Dec 1891; his son,

ROBERT WELLINGTON STAPLETON-COTTON, **3rd Viscount Combermere of Bhurtpore**, JP; *b* 18 June 1845; *educ* Eton; Lt Salop Yeo Cav; *m* 1st 2 June 1866 (*divorce* 1879) Charlotte Ann, only dau of Jacob Fletcher, of Peel Hall, Lancs; *m* 2nd 22 June 1880 Marian (*d* 17 Sept 1930), yst dau of Sir George Chetwynd, 3rd Bt (*qv*), and *d* 20 Feb 1898, having by her had issue:

FRANCIS LYNCH WELLINGTON STAPLETON-COTTON, **4th Viscount Combermere of Bhurtpore**, DL (Herefs 1953–60); *b* 29 June 1887; *educ* Harrow; Lt RGA (SR) WW I 1916–19 (wounded); *m* 1st 30 Oct 1913 (*divorce* 1926) Hazel Louisa (*d* 15 April 1943), yr dau of Henry de Courcy Agnew, 2nd son of Sir Andrew Agnew, 8th Bt, of Lochnaw (*qv*); *m* 2nd 1 Jan 1927 Constance Marie Katherine (*d* 29 June 1968), yst dau of Lt-Col Sir Francis Dudley Drummond, KBE, of Hafodneddyn, Llandilo, Carmarths (*see* 1970 edn WILLIAMS-DRUMMOND, Bt), and *d* 8 Feb 1969, leaving by her:

1 MICHAEL WELLINGTON STAPLETON-COTTON, **5th and present Viscount Combermere of Bhurtpore**

2 +David Peter Dudley [The Hon David Stapleton-Cotton, The Old Buffers, 9 Station Rd, Darling 7345, Cape, S Africa]; late Capt Life Gds; *b* 6 March 1932; *educ* Eton; *m* 9 Feb 1955 *Susan Nomakepu, 2nd dau of Sir George Werner Albu, 2nd Bt (*qv*), and has issue:

(1) +Simon; *b* 29 March 1959; *m* 1993 *Tessa, dau of Dr John Cummings, of Cape Town, and has:

1a +Oliver Dudley; *b* 14 June 1994

2a +James Peter George; *b* 15 March 1996

(2) +Toby James; *b* 13 Jan 1966

(1) *Nicola Caroline Louisa; *b* 20 July 1957; *m* 1994 *Martin Street, son of Brian Street, of Evesham, Worcs, and has:

1a *Rhiannon Madeleine; *b* 20 Nov 1995

(2) *Polly; *b* 19 Feb 1961; *m* 1990 *Bernard John Harton, son of Mrs D Barker, of Worcester

CONANT

Arms: Quarterly, 1st and 4th, per saltire gules and azure billetée or (for CONANT); 2nd and 3rd, ermine on a bend vert between three lion's heads erased azure, two and one, as many roses or (for WHISTON). **Crest:** On a mount vert a stag proper, the dexter foreleg resting on a shield gules billetée or. **Motto:** *Conanti dabitur* ('It shall be given to him who tries'). **Creation:** Bt. (UK) 30 June 1954.

SIR JOHN ERNEST MICHAEL CONANT, 2ND BT, of Lyndon, Co Leicester [Sir John Conant Bt, Periwinkle Cottage, Lyndon, Oakham, Rutland LE15 8TU]; *b* 24 April 1923; *s f* 1973; *educ* Eton and Corpus Christi Coll Cambridge (BA 1949); Lt Gren Gds WW II 1942–45, farmer and landowner, High Sheriff Rutland 1960; *m* 1st 16 Sept 1950 Periwinkle Elizabeth (*d* 1985), er dau of Dudley Thorp, of Brothers Ho, Kimbolton, Hunts; *m* 2nd *Mrs Clare Attwater, yr dau of W E Madden, and by 1st w has had issue:

1 Christopher John Roger; *b* 19 March 1952; *d* as result of an accident 28 April 1958

2 +SIMON EDWARD CHRISTOPHER; *b* 13 Oct 1958; *educ* Eton and RAC Cirencester

3 +William John Nathaniel; *b* 1970

1 *Fiona Elizabeth; *b* 27 Jan 1955; *m* 1987 *Jonathan P N Driver, er son of R M Driver, of Warren Bay, Watchet, Som, and has issue:

(1) *Alexander Edward; *b* 1990

2 *Melanie Lucinda; *b* 17 Nov 1961; *m* 1986 *Richard Alastair Firmston-Williams, son of Gordon Firmston-Williams, and has issue:

(1) *Hamish Alastair; *b* 1991

(1) *Jessica Alice; *b* 1989

(2) *Emily Periwinkle; *b* 1994

Lineage: RICHARD CONANT, of E Budleigh, Devon (s of John Conant, of E Budleigh (1520–96)); *b c* 1548; *m* Agnes, dau of John Clarke, of Colyton, and *d* 1630, leaving, with other issue:

1 Richard; *b* 1581; *d* 1625

2 ROBERT, of whom presently

3 John, Rector Lymington, Somerset, St Botolph, London, and St Thomas à Becket, Salisbury, preached before H of C 1643; *b* 1586; *educ* Exeter Coll Oxford (BD, MA); *d* 1653

4 Christopher; *b* 1588; emigrated to Plymouth, Mass., 1623

5 Roger; *b* 1592; emigrated to Plymouth, Mass., 1623; *m* 1618 Sarah Horton and *d* 1679; ancestor of the CONANTs in N America

The 2nd son,

ROBERT CONANT, of Bicton, Devon; *m* Elizabeth Morris and *d* 1638, leaving, with other issue:

JOHN CONANT, DD; *b* 18 Oct 1608; Rector Exeter Coll Oxford 1549–62 (expelled for non-conformity), Regius Prof Divinity 1654–60, V-Chllr Oxford U 1657–60; a Commr to review Prayerbook 1661, Minister of St Mary Aldmanbury 1670, Vicar All Saints Northampton 1671, Archdeacon Norwich 1676, Preb Worcester 1681; *m* Elizabeth, dau of Dr Edward Reynolds, Bp Norwich, and *d* 12 March 1694, leaving, with other issue:

ROBERT CONANT, London merchant; *b* 1670; *m* Mary Medlicot and *d* 1756, leaving, with other issue:

Rev JOHN CONANT; *b* 1706; *educ* Pembroke Coll Oxford (MA); Rector Hastingleigh, Vicar Elmstead, Kent, Preb Llanfair 1735; *m* 1733 Mary, dau and coheir of Rev William Wake, MA, Rector Hannington and Waldegrave, Northants, and *d* 1779, leaving, with other issue:

1 John, Rector St Peter's, Sandwich; *b* 1734; *educ* Lincoln Coll Oxford (MA); *d* 1811

2 NATHANIEL, of whom presently

3 Culpepper; *b* 1748; *educ* Trin Coll Cambridge (MA); *d* 1815

4 Elias; *b* 1750; *d* Bengal *c* 1765

The 2nd son,

Sir NATHANIEL CONANT ; *b* 10 April 1745; ktd 1813, Police Magistrate Marlborough St, Ch Magistrate Bow St; *m* 1776 Sarah, dau and coheir of John Whiston, and *d* 12 April 1822, leaving, with other issue, including a yr s (William CONANT later STAINSBY-CONANT on inheriting property from Mrs Stainsby, of Southampton Row, WC2, *b* 1783, *educ* Trin Coll Cambridge (BA 1806), *d* 1835):

JOHN EDWARD CONANT; *b* 18 Oct 1777; Cdr RN, Police Magistrate Marlborough St 1817; *m* 1817 Catherine, dau of Edward Brown, of Barn Hill, Stamford, and Horbling, Lincs, and *d* 13 Oct 1848, leaving issue:

1 EDWARD NATHANIEL, of whom presently

2 John William, of Surfleet and Gosberton, Lincs; *b* 21 Feb 1824; *educ* Eton and St John's Coll Oxford (BA); *m* Frances Catherine, dau of Col P Groves, of Boughton, Kent, and *d* 20 Feb 1884, leaving issue:

(1) Henry John, of Grafton Regis, Northants, JP; *b* 1852; Capt W Kent Regt; *m* 1st 23 Nov 1878 Emily (*d* 18 June 1881), yst dau of Col Charles Edward Gostling Murray, DL, JP, of Whitton Park, Middx (*see* ATHOLL, D), and had issue:

1a Eric Edward Wake; *b* 1879

2a Charles Henry, Lt E Lancs Regt; *b* 1880; *k* S Africa 21 Sept 1903

(1) (cont.) Henry Conant *m* 2nd 1883 Geraldine Effie (*d* 8 May 1945), only dau of Charles Livius Grimshawe, DL, JP, of Goldington Grange, Beds, and *d* 17 May 1914, having by her had issue:

3a Malcolm Vaughan; *b* 28 Oct 1883; *d* unm 8 March 1955

4a Nigel Cecil Peter; *b* 9 July 1891; *educ* Harrow; Capt Durham LI WW I, ADC to Govr Victoria 1915–19, HG WW II; *m* 20 June 1941 Morfydd, dau of W Williams, of Treaddwr Bay, Anglesey, and had issue:

1b *Fane Charles (Rev) [The Rev Fane Conant, St Philip's Vicarage, Chester Rd, Kelsall, Tarporley, Cheshire CW6 0SA]; *b* 13 Jan 1944; trained Oakhill Theological Coll, priest 1986, Vicar Kelsall 1989–; *m* 1970 *Susan Eileen, dau of Robert Shield Goodale, of Guildford, and has issue:

1c *Tobias Charles; *b* 14 May 1971

2c *Matthew Fane, *b* 6 April 1973

3c *Benjamin Paul; *b* 11 Sept 1975

1c *Hannah Florence; *b* 11 Jan 1988

1 Catherine; *b* 25 Oct 1818; *m* 1840 Charles Ellis, of Waltham Place, Maidenhead

The er son,

EDWARD NATHANIEL CONANT, of Lyndon Hall, Oakham, Rutland, which he inherited 1862 from his maternal uncle Rev Edward Brown, DL, JP; *b* 15 May 1820; *educ* Rugby and St John's Coll Oxford (BA 1842, MA 1845); barrister; *m* 27 Aug 1844 Gertrude Mary (*d* 27 March 1860), 2nd dau of Rev Charles Proby, Vicar Twickenham, Canon Windsor, and *d* 17 Sept 1901, leaving issue:

1 Edward Henry; *b* 20 Oct 1847; *educ* Eton; Lt 5th Dragoon Gds; *d* unm 26 Sept 1897

2 ERNEST WILLIAM PROBY, of whom presently

1 Gertrude Catherine; *b* 30 Sept 1845; *d* unm 28 Aug 1930

2 Frances Ann; *b* 7 Nov 1846; *m* 24 Sept 1874 Byam Alartin Davies (*d* 13 Oct 1924), son of Gen Francis John Davies, of Danehurst, and *d* 11 July 1910, leaving issue

3 Emily Agnes; *b* 5 April 1849; *m* July 1876 Frank Edward Vandeleur (*d* 1900), est son of Capt Thomas Pakenham Vandeleur, and *d* 12 Sept 1931, leaving issue

4 Amy Louise Emily; *b* 20 Dec 1850; *d* unm 9 June 1937

5 Eleanor Mary; *b* 14 Oct 1854; *d* unm 10 Aug 1944

6 Cecilia Eva; *b* 13 Aug 1356; *m* 7 Sept 1878 Maj Frederick Gustavus Fowke (*d* 16 Feb 1893), Leics Regt, JP, est son of Sir Frederick Fowke, 2nd Bt (*qv*), and *d* 28 March 1933, leaving issue

7 Catherine Agnes; *b* 6 July 1859; *m* 17 Dec 1884 Sir Arthur Denman, son of Rt Hon George Denman, and *d* 10 Feb 1917, leaving issue (*see* DENMAN, B)

8 Beatrice Alice; *b* 8 Nov 1860; *m* 17 Nov 1886 Malcolm Wolryche-Whitmore (*d* 8 Dec 1940), 2nd son of Rev Francis Henry Wolryche-Whitmore, of Dudmaston Hall, Salop, and *d* 12 Jan 1944, leaving issue

9 Grace Mary; *b* 17 June 1862; *m* 25 March 1885 Edmond Henry Stuart Nugent, JP, DL (*d* 13 June 1935), yr but only surv son of Thomas Vesey Nugent, of Portaferry Ho, Co Down, and *d* 7 May 1925, leaving issue

The 2nd son,

ERNEST WILLIAM PROBY CONANT, of Lyndon Hall, JP; *educ* Eton and Oxford U; High Sheriff Rutland 1907; *b* 7 March 1852; *m* 12 July 1898 Eva Mildred (*d* 6 Sept 1957), est dau of Lt-Col Thomas Tryon, of Bulwick Park, Northants (*see* TRYON, B), and *d* 14 Aug 1920, leaving issue:

1 ROGER JOHN EDWARD (Sir), **1st Bt**

2 Rupert Thomas; *b* 3 Dec 1901; *educ* Eton and RMC Sandhurst; Maj Oxon and Bucks LI; *m* 10 Sept 1938 Rachel Faith (*m* 2nd 4 Nov 1955 Merrik de Sampajo Cecil Ward, yr son of Cecil Ward), 2nd dau of Maj Harry Grant-Thorold, JP, of Cranford Hall, Northants (*see* THOROLD, Bt), and was *ka* Dunkirk May 1940, leaving issue:

(1) *Joanna Faith; *b* posthumously, 10 Nov 1940; *m* 8 May 1969 *Simon Stewart Forster, son of Brig Stewart Forster

The er son,

Sir Roger John Edward Conant, 1st Bt (UK), so *cr* 30 June 1954, CVO (1953), JP (1932), DL (Rutland 1946), of Lyndon Hall; High Sheriff Rutland 1927; *b* 28 May 1899; *educ* Eton and RMC Sandhurst; Maj Gren Gds, MP (C) Chesterfield 1931–35, Bewdley 1937–50 and Rutland and Stamford 1950–59, Oppn Whip 1946–51, Comptroller Household (Sr Whip) 1951–54; *m* 9 Nov 1920 Daphne Lorraine, yst dau of Alfred Ernest Learoyd, of Huddersfield, and *d* 1973, leaving:

1 Sir JOHN ERNEST MICHAEL CONANT, **2nd and present Bt**

2 +(Guy) Timothy Geoffrey, JP (1960) and DL Northants, High Sheriff 1969 [Tim Conant Esq JP DL, Bulwick Park, nr Corby, Northants NN17 3DZ]; *b* 7 Oct 1924; *educ* Stowe; late F/Lt RAF; *m* 1st 27 June 1953 (*divorce* 19–) Elizabeth, dau of Alfred Trevor Handley, of IoW, and has had:

(1) +Rupert Edward Geoffrey; *b* 28 April 1964; *m* 1993 *Kathryn Jean, 4th dau of Harold Miller, of Bridgend, Glam

(1) *Sheena Lorraine; *b* 13 July 1954

(2) *Elizabeth Jane; *b* 15 Nov 1955

(3) Sally Gillian; *b* 21 Nov 1957; *d* 6 May 1958

(4) *Diana Juliet; *b* 26 July 1960; *m* 1985 *Peter S McMahon, 2nd son of R F McMahon, of NZ

2 (cont.) Timothy Conant *m* 2nd 1981 *Davina Huntley, er dau of Sir Guy Hope Holland, 3rd Bt (*see* ZOUCHE, B), and by her has:

(5) *Melissa Eva; *b* 11 May 1984

3 +Charles Richard [Charles Conant Esq, Rose House, Gaddesby, Leics LE7 4WD]; *b* 8 Nov 1929; *educ* Eton; BSc (Eng), CEng, MIEE; *m* 26 July 1958 *Katherine Anne Ross, yr dau of Hubert George Anthony Ross-Wilson, of Gaddesby, Leics, and has issue:

(l) *Caroline Rose [Mrs Timothy Hawkins, 35 Nansen Rd, London SW11]; *b* 20 April 1959; *m* 1988 *Timothy John Hawkins, yr son of Lt-Col Tony Hawkins, OBE, of Chelsea, and has issue:

1a *William Anthony Charles Horatio; *b* 1992

2a *Charlotte Lucy; *b* 1990

(2) *Francesca Louise [Mrs Philip Kendall, 7 Cheltenham Terr, London SW3]; *b* 30 May 1962; *m* 1986 *Philip Henry Kendall, and has issue:

1a *Josephine Louise; *b* 1988

2a *Claudia Daphne; *b* 1991

CONGLETON

Arms: Gules two chevronels, in chief three escallops argent. **Crest:** A boar's head erased or between two wings gules, each charged with two chevronels argent. **Supporters:** Dexter, an angel vested argent, wings gold and radiated of the same; sinister, a hermit vested proper, a staff in his exterior hand and an escallop or in his hat. **Motto:** *Te digna sequere* ('Honours have followed thee'). **Creations:** Bt. (GB) 3 Nov 1766, B. (UK) 18 Aug 1841.

THE 8TH BARON CONGLETON, of Congleton, Co Chester, and a **Baronet** (Sir Christopher Patrick Parnell, Bt) [The Rt Hon The Lord Congleton, West End Lodge, Ebbesbourne Wake, Wilts SP5 5JR]; *b* 11 March 1930; *s* bro 1967; *educ* Eton and New Coll Oxford (BA 1954, MA 1987); memb Salisbury and Wilton RDC 1964–74, v-pres: RDCA 1973–74, Assoc of Dist Cncls 1974–79; pres: Nat Ski Fedn of GB 1976–81, Ski Club of GB 1991–; tstee: Wessex Medical Tst 1984–90 (chm 1997–), Southampton U Develt Tst 1986–95 (chm 1986–94); Hon LLD Southampton 1990; *m* 19 Nov 1955 *Anna Hedvig, er dau of Gustav Adolf Sommerfelt, of Oslo, and has:

1 +JOHN PATRICK CHRISTIAN; *b* 17 March 1959; *m* 1985 *Marjorie-Anne (Annie), only dau of John Hobdell, of Cobham, Surrey, and has:

(1) +Christopher John Edward; *b* 1987

(2) +Harry Gustav Willem; *b* 1990

(1) *Anna Hedvig; *b* 1992

2 +Thomas David Howard; *b* 6 June 1963

1 *Anne Cathrine; *b* 3 Oct 1956; *m* 1980 *(Michael) Robin Long and has:

(1) *Richard Per; *b* 1981

(2) *Willum Jan; *b* 1984

2 *Elizabeth Dagny; *b* 13 June 1960

3 *Mary Clare; *b* 18 March 1965

Lineage: THOMAS PERNELL, of Rode, nr Congleton, Cheshire; living 1427; had:

JAMES PERNELL; Yorkist in Wars of Roses; pardoned by HENRY VI 1460; had:

HENRY PERNELL, of Rode; had:

RICHARD PERNELL; bought property in Congleton; had a 2nd son:

THOMAS PARNELL; Mayor Congleton 1625; had:

TOBIAS PARNELL; Alderman; had:

THOMAS PARNELL; *b* 1625; bought an estate in Ireland *temp* CHARLES II; *d* 1686, having had issue:

1 Thomas (Rev), DD, Archdeacon of Clogher 1705, Preb Dublin 1713, Vicar Finglas 1716; minor poet and friend of Pope, who in 1721 published a posthumous collection of his verse; *m* Anne, dau of Thomas Minchin, and *d* July 1717, leaving surv issue:

(1) Theobald Tobias, of Dublin; *b* 1711; *educ* Trin Coll Dublin (BA); *d* 1736

(1) Jane; *m* 23 Oct 1734 Charles Broughton, of Dublin, Usher of Court of Chancery

2 John, of Rathleague, Queen's Co; MP, Judge Court of King's Bench Ireland 1722–27; *m* Mary, sis of Ld Ch Justice William Whitshed, and *d* 7 July 1727, leaving an only surv son:

(1) **Sir John Parnell, 1st Bt** (I), so *cr* 3 Nov 1766, of Rathleague; High Sheriff Queen's Co 1753, MP Maryborough (modern Portlaoise) 1761–82; *m* 1744/5 Anne (*d* April 1795), 2nd dau of Michael Ward, of Castle Ward, Co Down, Judge Court of King's Bench, and sis of 1st Viscount Bangor (*qv*), and *d* 14 April 1782, leaving an only son:

1a **Sir John Parnell, 2nd Bt**, PC (1787), MP Queen's Co 1783–1801, Commr Revenue Ireland 1780, Chllr Exchequer, a Ld Treasury 1793; *m* 19 July 1774 Letitia Charlotte (*d* 11 Nov 1783), dau and coheir of Rt Hon Sir Arthur Brooke, 1st and last Bt, of Colebrooke (*see* BROOKEBOROUGH, V), and *d* 5 Dec 1801, having had, with other issue:

1b **Sir John Augustus Parnell, 3rd Bt**; *b* May 1775 a mute cripple; *d* 30 July 1812

2b HENRY, **1st Baron**

3b William PARNELL later PARNELL-HAYES, of Avondale, Co Wicklow; *b* Aug 1780; *m* 1 Oct 1810 Frances (*d* 11 Aug 1814), est dau of Hon Hugh Howard (*see* 1970 edn WICKLOW, E), and *d* 2 April 1821, leaving issue:

1c John Henry PARNELL, of Avondale, Co Wicklow: DL, JP, High Sheriff 1836; *b* 14 Aug 1811; *m* 31 May 1834 Delia Tudor (*d* 1898), only dau of Cdre Charles Stewart, USN, and *d* 3 July 1859, leaving, with other issue:

1d John Howard, of Avondale; Dublin City Marshal, MP S Meath 1895–1900; *b* 1843; *m* 13 June 1907 Olivia Isabella, widow of Archibald Mateer, JP Co Louth, and er surv dau of Col James Smythe, 69th Regt, and *d* 3 May 1923

2d Charles Stewart, of Avondale, JP; the celebrated Irish Nationalist; High Sheriff Co Wicklow 1874, MP Co Meath 1875–80 and Cork 1880–91, leader of Irish Parly Party 1874, Pres Land League 1879; *b* June 1846; *m* 2 July 1891 Katherine (Kitty) (*d* 5 Feb 1921), formerly w of Capt William Henry O'Shea and yst dau of Rev Sir John Page Wood, 2nd Bt (*qv*), and *dsp* 6 Oct 1891

3d Henry Tudor, barrister; *b* Dec 1850; *educ* Trin Coll Cambridge (BA); *m* 21 Oct 1882 Penelope Jane, dau of Rev Thomas Luby, DD, and *d* 24 Nov 1915, leaving issue:

1e Henry Maurice Stewart; *b* 1884; *d* 19 Nov 1934

2e Harold de Mowbray; *b* 1889

le Maude Yolan Howard

1d Emily Letitia Georgina; *m* 1st 30 April 1867 Capt Robert Munro Dickinson, 10th Foot (*d* 1883), and had issue; *m* 2nd Cuthbert S Bengough Ricketts and *d* 18 May 1918 aged 80

2d Sophia; *m* 13 Sept 1862 Alfred McDermott, and had issue

3d Theodosia; *m* 21 July 1880 Cdr Claude Paget, RN (*see* ANGLESEY, M), and *d* 17 March 1920, leaving issue

1c Catherine; *m* 18 Aug 1835 George Vicesimus Wigram (*see* WIGRAM, Bt)

1b Sophia; *m* 21 Aug 1805 Rt Hon George Hampden Evans, PC (*dsp* 2 July 1842), of Portrane, MP Co Dublin (*see* CARBERY, B), and *d* 24 July 1853

The 3rd Bt's bro,

Sir Henry Brooke Parnell, 4th Bt, and **1st Baron Congleton**, of Congleton, Co Chester (UK), so *cr* 18 Aug 1841, PC (1831); *b* 3 July 1776; *educ* Eton, Winchester and Trin Coll Cambridge; inherited family estates (bypassing his bro, whose aflictions made him incapable of administering them) direct from his f by special Act of Parl 1789; MP (I Parl) Maryborough 1797–1800, Queen's Co (Whig, UK Parl) April-June 1802 and 1806–32, Portarlington July-Dec 1802 and Dundee 1833–41, a Ld Treasury (I) 1806–07, Sec at War 1831–32, Treasurer Navy 1835–36 and Paymaster-Gen 1835–41, author of financial treatises; *m* 17 Feb 1801 Lady Caroline Elizabeth Dawson (*d* Paris 16 Feb 1861), est dau of 1st Earl of Portarlington (*qv*), and hanged himself 8 June 1842, leaving:

1 JOHN VESEY PARNELL, **2nd Baron Congleton**; *b* 16 June 1805; *educ* in France and at Edinburgh U; Plymouth Brethren missionary in Baghdad from 1831; *m* 1st 1828 or 1831 Nancy (*d* 1832), dau of Edward Cronin, of Cork; *m* 2nd 1833 one of his converts, Khatun (*d* 30 May 1865), dau of Ovauness Moscow, of Shiraz, Persia, and widow of Yusuf Constantine, of Bushire, Persia, Armenian merchant; *m* 3rd 21 Feb 1867 Margaret Catherine (*d* 1 Nov 1910), only dau of Charles Ormerod, of the India Bd, and *d* 23 Oct 1883, having by her had issue:

(1) Sarah Cecelia; *b* 5 Aug 1868; *m* 21 Nov 1895 Henry Ambrose Mandeville (*d* 23 May 1917), of Anner Castle, Clonmel, Co Tipperary, and *d* 26 April 1912, leaving issue

2 HENRY WILLIAM, **3rd Baron**

3 George Damer (Rev), *b* Nov 1810; *m* Aug 1833 Catherine (*d* 17 March 1899), dau of Sir John St Aubyn, 4th Bt, and *d* 17 Dec 1882

1 Caroline Sophia; *m* 15 Dec 1831 Most Rev Charles T Longley, DD, Archbp Canterbury, and *d* 9 March 1858

2 Mary Letitia; *m* 1st 27 Sept 1824 Lord Henry Seymour Moore (*d* Aug 1825), bro of Charles, Marquess of Drogheda (*see* DROGHEDA, E), and had issue; *m* 2nd 30 Dec 1830 Edward H Cole, of Twickenham, Middx, and Lyne, Oxon, and *d* his widow 6 May 1881

3 Emma Jane; *m* 26 July 1825 6th Earl of Darnley (*qv*), and *d* 15 March 1884, leaving issue

The 2nd BARON's bro,

HENRY WILLIAM PARNELL, **3rd Baron Congleton**; *b* 23 March 1809; served RN, present Battle of Navarino 1827; *m* 1st 28 May 1835 Sophia (*d* 5 April 1846), only dau of Col Hon William Bligh (*see* DARNLEY, E), and had, with other issue:

1 William Henry, Lt-Col Gren Gds; *b* 7 Oct 1837; *d* 4 May 1879

2 HENRY, **4th Baron**

3 Arthur; *b* 4 Jan 1841; Col RE; *m* 15 Oct 1868 Mary Anne (*d* 11 Sept 1920), dau of Alfred Rouse Dunn, of Hillgrove Ho, Glos, and *d* 28 July 1914, leaving issue:

(1) Arthur Reginald Bligh; *b* 27 Nov 1871; *d* unm 24 Sept 1956

(2) Bertram Damer; *b* 29 March 1876; playwright; Lt RNVR; *m* 1st 1899 Madeleine (*d* 14 July 1929), dau of James Byrne; *m* 2nd 1930 Lucy Margaret, dau of John Hersohn, of S Africa, and *d* 1960, having by his 1st w had issue:

1a Desmond Damer; *b* Jan 1900; gen manager Books Div, George Newnes Ltd; *m* 11 Jan 1930 Ivy Maude (*d* 1972), dau of Mark Hunt Harding, and *d* 1972, leaving issue:

1b +John Desmond [John Parnell Esq, 6 Gayton Court, Gayton Rd, Harrow, Middx]; *b* Nov 1930; *m* 26 Aug 1961 *Barbara Jean, formerly w of Coleson John King and dau of Laurence Chappell, of Leeds, and has issue:

1c *Sally Dee; *b* 1 May 1966

1b *Jean Pamela [Mrs Ronald Johnson, 59 Sutton Lane, Langley, Berks]; *b* 11 Nov 1943; *m* 1976 *Ronald James Johnson, and has issue:

1c *Philip Andrew; *b* 1981

1c *Joanna; *b* 1976

2a Myles Bligh Damer PARNELL later FARMILOE (deed poll 3 May 1929); *b* 25 May 1903; *educ* Winchester and New Coll Oxford (MA); *m* 1 Aug 1929 Cynthia Joyce (*d* 1990), dau of Maj Henry Percy Holt, and *d* 11 Oct 1983, leaving issue:

lb Michael John; *b* 31 Dec 1931; *educ* Winchester; *m* 14 Oct 1953 Mary Elizabeth (*d* 1980), only dau of Vivian Ewart Berry, of 118 Berkeley Court, NW1 (*see* CAMROSE, V), and *d* 27 Feb 1983 leaving issue:

1c +Simon Charles; *b* 7 March 1961

1c *Sarah Elizabeth [Mrs John Kiddell, Sandy Bottom, 8 Beech Close Court, Cobham, Surrey]; *b* 26 May 1959; *m* 1986 *John Kiddell, son of Percy Edgar Kiddell, and has issue:

1d *Jamie Michael; *b* 1992

2d *Lewis; *b* 1994

2b +Timothy Miles [Timothy Farmiloe Esq, Little Brookwood, 30 Woodfield Lane, Ashtead, Surrey KT21 2BE]; *b* 22 Feb 1935; *educ* Winchester and New Coll Oxford (MA)

1a Nancy Stewart; *educ* Liverpool U (BA 1922)

2a Mary Margaret

(3) Harold Stewart; *b* 7 April 1880; Lt RNVR, Commr Chinese Postal Service; *m* 25 Oct 1919 Marjorie Eva, dau of Herbert Dixon Summers, of Peking and Exmouth, Devon, and *d* 16 Aug 1945, leaving issue:

1a Joan Letitia Brooke; *b* 7 Nov 1920; *m* 24 Oct 1945 Richard Bencraft Joly (*d* 7 Feb 1956), 2nd son of Cecil Henry Bencraft Joly, of Wainscote Cottage, Kivernell Rd, Milford-on-Sea, Hants, and had issue:

1b *Antony Stewart Bencraft; *b* 12 June 1949; *educ* Christ's Hosp

2b *Simon Michael Bencraft; *b* 14 Oct 1952; *educ* Christ's Hosp

(4) Geoffrey Brooke; *b* 9 Sept 1882; Maj Queen's Roy W Surrey Regt; *ka* 15 July 1916

(1) Winifred Mary; *d* unm 22 Jan 1942

(2) Edith Caroline; *m* 7 April 1891 Ven Wllliam Thomas Farmiloe, MA, Archdeacon of Sudbury, and *d* 26 March 1921

(3) Gwendolen Muriel; *d* unm 2 Dec 1957

(4) Muriel Alice; *d* 1902

(5) Yseulte Geraldine; *b* 26 July 1886; *d* unm 9 June 1969

(6) Marjorie; *b* 4, *d* 5 Dec 1887

1 Emma Sophia; *m* 17 May 1866 Rev George B Perry Ayscough (*d* 31 Aug 1885), Vicar Brabourne, and *d* 26 Nov 1910, leaving issue (*see* TURING, Bt)

The **3rd Baron** *m* 2nd 10 March 1851 Hon Caroline Margaret Dawson (*d* 17 Jan 1912), Maid of Honour to HM QUEEN VICTORIA, dau of Hon Lionel Charles Dawson (*see* PORTARLINGTON, E), and by her had issue:

4 Victor Alexander Lionel Dawson, barrister; *b* 25 Aug 1852; *d* unm 6 Jan 1936

5 Lionel Charles Nugent; *b* 17 Aug 1864; *m* 1899 Marjorie Gore, dau of William Millar, and *d* 1940, leaving issue:

(1) Harold Charles Stewart; *b* 1900; *m* 1938 Marjorie J Carvell (*d* 1990), and *d* 1973 leaving issue:

1a +Christopher Charles Stewart [Christopher Parnell Esq, 213a Northfield Ave, London W13 9QU]; *b* 1946; *m* 1982 *Joy E Johnson

(2) Hugh Francis; *b* 1903

(1) Evelyn Molly; *b* 1906

(2) Louisa Catharine; *b* 1910

2 Madeline Catherine; *m* 10 Jan 1895 Charles Augustus Este Wells (*d* 21 April 1923), of Heathfield, Albury, son of Rev John Wells, and *d* 18 Oct 1925, leaving issue

3 Louisa Anna Maria; *m* 30 July 1884 Lt-Col Francis Henry Launcelot Errington, CB (*d* 8 July 1942), barrister, of The Red Ho, Berkhamsted, son of Gen Arnold Charles Errington, and *d* 21 Feb 1933, leaving issue

4 Elizabeth Mary Emily; *m* 30 Nov 1881 Col Willoughby Cole Verner (*d* Jan 1922), of Hartford Bridge, Winchfield, Hants, formerly Rifle Bde, and *d* 10 July 1936, leaving issue

5 Mabel Frances Laetitia; *m* 13 Dec 1898 Col Henry Charles Barwick Hopkinson, CMG, CBE (*d* 19 April 1946), Capt Seaforth Highrs, son of George Henry Hopkinson by Blanche Isabella, dau of Col Henry Charles Capel Somerset (*see* BEAUFORT, D), and *d* 15 March 1947, leaving issue

The 3rd BARON *d* 10 Oct 1890; his est surv son,

HENRY PARNELL, **4th Baron Congleton**, CB (1879); *b* 10 July 1839; Maj-Gen, served Crimea after fall of Sebastopol, ADC to GOC Windward and Leeward Islands 1864–66, cmded 2nd Bn The Buffs Zulu War (present Battle of Inyezane and occupation of Ekowe), Cmdt Straits Settlements 1880–82 and Inf Bde Malta 1895–1902; *m* 17 June 1885 Elizabeth Peter (*d* 22 Jan 1931), dau of Dugald Dove, of Nutshill, Renfrewshire, and *d* 12 Nov 1906, leaving issue:

1 HENRY BLIGH FORTESCUE PARNELL, **5th Baron Congleton**; *b* 6 Sept 1890; *educ* Eton and New Coll Oxford (BA 1912); Lt Gren Gds WW I (despatches); *ka* 10 Nov 1914

2 JOHN BROOKE MOLESWORTH, **6th Baron**

3 William Alastair Damer, MC, Lt Gren Gds SR; *b* 30 Aug 1894; *ka* at Somme 25 Sept 1916

1 Agnes Caroline Sophia, JP Sussex; *b* 23 Feb 1889; *m* 19 Dec 1912 Capt William Gilbert Howard, CBE, RN (*d* 18 Jan 1960), est son of Alfred John Howard, and *d* 28 Dec 1968, leaving issue (*see* CARLISLE, E)

The 5th BARON's bro,

JOHN BROOKE MOLESWORTH PARNELL, **6th Baron Congleton**; *b* 16 May 1892; *educ* McGill U (BSc 1921), MIME; Lt-Cdr RN (Emerg List); *m* 6 April 1918 Hon Edith Mary Palmer Howard, MBE (1941), JP (1948–56) (Im 2nd 5 July 1946 F/Lt Alfred Eric Rowland Aldridge (*d* 11 June 1950), took by deed poll 1951 name CONGLETON and *d* 1979), formerly CC Hants and chm New Forest RDC, v-pres BRCS New Forest N Div 1937–43, Assist City Organiser WVS 1939–44, Order of Mercy with bar, 2nd dau of Robert Jared Bliss Howard, MD, by Margaret Charlotte, Baroness Strathcona and Mount Royal (*qv*) in her wn right, and *d* 21 Dec 1932, having had issue:

1 Harry Douglas; *b* 14 Dec 1920; *d* 7 Jan 1928

2 WILLIAM JARED PARNELL, **7th Baron Congleton**; *b* 8 Aug 1925; *educ* Eton; Lt RN (Emerg List); *d* as result of a motor accident 12 Oct 1967

3 CHRISTOPHER PATRICK PARNELL, **8th and present Baron Congleton**

4 Timothy John; *b* 6 May 1931; *d* 14 Feb 1936

1 *Mary Elizabeth [The Hon Mrs Turnbull, 74 St Ann St, Salisbury, Wilts SP1 2DX]; *b* 21 Feb 1919; *m* 20 July 1956 Percy Purvis Turnbull (*d* 1976), son of James Turnbull, of Newcastle-upon-Tyne

2 *Jean Margaret [The Hon Mrs Howard, Isle of Ulva, Aros, Mull, Argyll PA73 6LZ]; *b* 4 June 1922; *m* 29 Nov 1952 *Lt-Col Frederick Henry Howard, DSO, MC and bar, 3rd The King's Own Hus, est son of Capt William Gilbert Howard, CBE, RN, of The Oast Ho, Stonegate, Sussex (*see* above and CARLISLE, E), and has issue

3 *Sheila Helen [The Hon Mrs Sheila Duvollet, River House, Golant, Par, Cornwall]; *b* 25 Nov 1923; *m* 21 March 1959 (*divorce* 1979) Roger Henry Duvollet, son of Henri Ulysse Duvollet, and has issue:

(1) Annette Frances; *b* 16 June 1961; *d* 1982

4 *Ann Bridget [The Hon Mrs Russell, Lyscombe, Piddletrenthide; Dorset]; *b* 27 April 1927; *m* 15 Nov 1947 Maj Derek Campbell Russell, RE, son of Edgar Campbell Russell, of Lynchburg, Virginia, USA

5 *Heather Doreen [The Hon Mrs Bell, Sarsen House, 5 Mead Rd, St Cross, Winchester, Hants]; *b* 11 Jan 1929; *m* 23 April 1960 *(Robert) Peter Mangin Bell, 2nd son of Rev Robert William Bell, MA, Vicar Stamfordham, Newcastle-on-Tyne, and has issue:

(1) *(Robert) Simon Parnell; *b* 1 Nov 1961; *m* 1986 *Fiona J, MD, er dau of David Sanders, of Winchester, and has issue:

1a *(Robert) Edward Sanders; *b* 1989

2a *Jack Digby; *b* 1993

1a *Alice Seymour; *b* 1990

(2) *Aidan William George; *b* 1 Feb 1967; *m* 17 May 1997 *Judith, dau of Richard Harrison, of Cheltenham

(l) *Penelope Edith; *b* 2 Sept 1963; *m* 1991 *Peter M Melville, er son of Rev P K Melville, of Albury, NSW, Australia

CONSTANTINE OF STANMORE

Creation: B. (LP, UK) 1981.

THE BARON CONSTANTINE OF STANMORE, in Greater London (Sir Theodore Constantine, CBE (1956), DL (Greater London 1967)) [The Rt Hon The Lord Constantine of Stanmore CBE DL, House of Lords, London SW1A 0PW]; *b* 15 March 1910; *educ* Acton Coll; WWII: RAAF (AE 1945); Chm Nat Union of C and U Assocs 1968– (Pres 1980), ktd 1964, Freeman City London 1949, Master Coachmakers' Co 1975, Tstee Sir John Wolstenholme Charity; *m* 1935 Sylvia Mary (*d* 1990), dau of Wallace Henry Legge-Pointing, of London, and has issue:

1 *Roy [The Hon Roy Constantine, 11 Grove Park Terr, London W4]; *b* 1936; *m* 1972 *Stella Helena (*née* Rogers) and has:

(1) *Claire; *b* 1976

1 *Jill Diane [The Hon Mrs Murray, 46 Linkway, Northwood, Middx]; *b* 1938; *m* 1965 *Geoffrey Murray, and has issue:

(1) *Guy John; *b* 1968

(1) *Tracy Diane; *b* 1966

Lineage: LEONARD CONSTANTINE; *m* Fanny Louise —, and had:

(Sir) THEODORE, *cr* a **Baron**

CONYNGHAM

Arms: Arg. a shake-fork between three mullets sa. **Crest:** A unicorn's head erased arg., armed or, crined and tufted sa. and maned or. **Supporters:** Dexter, a horse arg., maned, hoofed and charged on the breast with an eagle, displayed or; sinister, a buck ppr., attired, unguled and charged on the breast with a griffin's head erased or. **Motto:** Over fork over. **Creations:** B. (I) 4 Jan 1781 (Conyngham of Mount Charles), V. (I) 6 Dec 1789 (Conyngham of Mount Charles), V. (Mount Charles) and E. (I) 27 Dec 1797 (Conyngham), V. (Slane), E. (Mount Charles) and M. (I) 15 Jan 1816, B. (UK) 17 July 1821 (Minster of Minster Abbey).

THE 7TH MARQUESS CONYNGHAM, Earl Conyngham, Earl of Mount Charles, Viscount Conyngham of Mount Charles, Co Donegal, **Viscount Slane, Viscount Mount Charles, Baron Conyngham of Mount Charles**, Co Donegal, and **Baron Minster of Minster Abbey**, Co Kent (Frederick William Henry Francis Conyngham) [The Most Hon The Marquess Conyngham, Myrtle Hill, Andreas Rd, Ramsey, Isle of Man]; *b* 13 March 1924; *s f* 1974; *educ* Eton; late Capt Irish Gds; *m* 1st 29 April 1950 (*divorce* 1970) Eileen Wren, only dau of Capt Clement Wren Newsam, of Ashfield, Beauparc, Co Meath; *m* 2nd 1971 Elizabeth Ann, yr dau of Frederick Molyneux Hughes, of Fareham, Hants, and formerly w of David Sutherland Rudd; *m* 3rd 1980 Daphne Georgina Adelaide (Id 1986), est dau of R C Armour, formerly of Kenya, and formerly w of C P V Walker, of Nairobi; *m* 4th 1987 *(Emma Christianne) Annabelle, only dau of (Denys) Martin Agnew, of Grosvenor Ct, 22 Grove Rd, East Cliffe, Bournemouth (*see* AGNEW, Bt), and by 1st w has issue:

1 +HENRY VIVIAN PIERPOINT, *Earl of Mount Charles* [Earl of Mount Charles, Slane Castle, Co Meath, Ireland; Beau Parc, Navan, Co Meath, Ireland]; *b* 23 May 1951; *educ* Harrow; stood for Irish Senate 1997; *m* 1st 1971 (*divorce* 1985) Juliet Ann, yr dau of Robert R B Kitson, of Churchtown, Morval, Cornwall, and has issue:

(1) +Alexander Burton, *Viscount Slane*; *b* 30 Jan 1975

(1) *Henrietta Tamara Juliet; *b* 1976

1 (cont.) *Earl of Mount Charles m* 2nd 1985 *Lady Iona Charlotte Grimston, yst dau of 6th Earl of Verulam (*qv*), and has further issue:

(2) *Tamara Jane; *b* 1991

2 +Simon Charles Eveleigh Wren; *b* 20 Nov 1953; *educ* Harrow; *m* 1st 1978 (*divorce* 19–) Emma S, dau of W/Cdr F W Breeze, and has issue:

(1) *Chloe Wren; *b* 1980

2 (cont.) Lord Simon Conyngham *m* 2nd 1990 *Mrs Carole Crossman Yorke, yst dau of Eldon F le Poer Power, of Ashfield, Beauparc, Co Meath, and formerly w of Nicholas Roger Yorke (*see* HARDWICKE, E), and has further issue:

(2) *Frances; *b* 1991

3 +(Frederick William) Patrick [The Lord Patrick Conyngham, North Wing, Severn End, Hanley Castle, Worcs]; *b* 23 March 1959; *m* 1st 1990 (*divorce* June 1995) Charlotte Mary Temple Gordon (unsuccessfully fought (C) Kirkcaldy 1997 gen election), er dau of (Michael) Donald Gordon Black, MC, of Edenwood, Cupar, Fife; *m* 2nd 29 Nov 1995 *Mrs Siobháin Ramos

Lineage: ALEXANDER CONYNGHAM, of Scotland; moved to Ireland; first Protestant minister of Enver and Killymard, Co Donegal, 1611; Dean of Raphoe 1630; settled at Mount Charles, Co Donegal; *m* Marian, dau of John Murray, of Broughton, and *d* 3 Sept 1660, having had, with 26 other children (including Katherine, *m* Bp John Leslie; *see* LESLIE, Bt), an est surv s:

Sir ALBERT CONYNGHAM; Lt Gen Ordnance Ireland 1660; fought for WILLIAM III Battle of the Boyne 1690, present Siege Limerick 1691; *m* Margaret, dau of Rt Rev Henry Leslie, Bp Meath, and was *k* by rapparees near Colooney, Co Sligo, leaving an only surv s:

HENRY CONYNGHAM, of Slane, Co Meath (an estate forfeited after the 1641 Uprising by Lord Slane); MP Co Donegal, Capt Ld Mountjoy's Regt, Maj-Gen; *m* 9 Dec 1696 Mary (*m* 3rd Col Robert Dalway and *d* Dec 1710), dau and heir of Sir John Williams, 2nd Bt, of Minster Court, Kent, and widow of Charles Petty, Baron Shelburne (*see* LANSDOWNE, M), and was *ka* 1705/6 at St Estevans during the War of the Spanish Succession, leaving:

1 William; *d* 26 Oct 1738

2 HENRY CONYNGHAM, **1st Baron Conyngham of Mount Charles**, Co Donegal, so *cr* 4 Jan 1781, with remainder (in the case of this peerage only) to his nephew Francis Pierpoint Burton, as also 4 Jan 1781 EARL CONYNGHAM OF MOUNT CHARLES, Co Donegal, and previously 3 Oct 1753 BARON CONYNGHAM OF MOUNT CHARLES, Co Donegal, also 20 July 1756 VISCOUNT CONYNGHAM in Ireland (all I), PC (I 1748); *b* 1705; MP (I Parl) Killybegs 1727–53, Tiverton (Whig, GB Parl) 1747–54 and Sandwich 1756–74, Govr Co Donegal 1746 and Co Londonderry 1754, V-Adml Ulster 1748–79, Capt of Horse; *m* Dec 1744 Ellen (*d* 15 June 1816 aged 97), only dau and heir of Solomon Merrett, London merchant, by Rebecca, dau of Charles Savage, packer, of London, and *dsp* 3 April 1781, when all his titles expired bar the Barony of 1781

1 Mary; *m* Rt Hon Francis Burton, of Buncraggy, Co Clare, MP Coleraine 1721–7, and Co Clare 1727–43 (*d* 20 March 1743), son of Francis Burton, MP Ennis 1692–1714, of Buncraggy, and *d* 1737, having had, with two daus:

(1) FRANCIS PIERPOINT, **2nd Baron**

(2) William BURTON later CONYNGHAM (on inheriting the Co Donegal and Slane estates of his uncle the 1st and last EARL OF CONYNGHAM of the 1781 *cr*), PC (I), MP, Teller Exchequer; *m* — Studdert and *d* unm 31 May 1796, leaving the Donegal and Slane estates to his n the **1st Marquess**

The 1st BARON CONYNGHAM OF MOUNT CHARLES's n,

FRANCIS PIERPOINT BURTON later CONYNGHAM (roy licence 3 May 1781 on inheriting his unc the 1st and last EARL's Co Limerick estates), **2nd Baron Conyngham of Mount Charles**; MP Killybegs 1753–60; *m* 19 March 1750 Elizabeth (*d* 31 Oct 1814), est dau of Rt Hon Nathaniel Clements and sis of 1st Earl of Leitrim (*see* 1953 edn), and had, with three daus:

1 HENRY, **1st Marquess**

2 Francis Nathaniel Pierpoint BURTON CONYNGHAM (Sir), GCH, MP Co Clare 1790–1827, Col Clare Mil, Govr Lower Canada 1808–25; *b* 26 Dec 1766 (twin with his bro); *m* 4 June 1801 Hon Valentina Letitia Lawless (*d* 4 Feb 1844), 2nd dau of 1st Baron Cloncurry (*see* 1929 edn), and *d* 27 Jan 1832, leaving issue:

(1) Henry Stuart, of Carrigaholt Castle, Co Clare, DL, JP; *b* 14 Sept 1808; *m* 24 July 1836 Alicia Mary (*d* 17 March 1887), only dau of Very Rev Valentine Simpson, DD, and *d* 10 Feb 1867, having had issue:

1a Francis Nathaniel Valentine, of Carrigaholt Castle, DL, JP, High Sheriff 1870, late 10th Regt; *b* 13 Sept 1842; *m* 8 Nov 1866 Marie, dau and heiress of Savory, Duke de Rovigo, and *dsp* 1883

2a William Conyngham Vandeleur, of Carrigaholt Castle, DL, JP Co Clare, High Sheriff 1868, 68th Durham LI; *b* 19 Sept 1846; *m* 16 Jan 1896 Lilias (*d* 27 July 1935), dau of Thomas Green, of Wilby and Athellington, Suffolk, and *dsp* 5 Feb 1919

3a Henry Stuart; *b* 12 June 1849; *d* unm

1a Lucy Anne; *m* 1st 17 Oct 1863 Capt Ormsby Rose. He *d* Sept 1870. She *m* 2nd 2 Oct 1872 Col Ambrose Edward Saunders, and *d* 6 Dec 1874, leaving issue

2a Valentina Henrietta; *m* 23 Oct 1860 Francis Wise Low, of Kilshaw, and *d* 1 July 1861, leaving issue

3a Elizabeth Cecilia; *d* unm 6 Nov 1870

4a Alice Katherine Lawless; *m* 6 Nov 1879 (*divorce* 1893) Gustav Leon Albert, Count de Hamel de Manin, and had issue. He *d* 1906

(2) William Conyngham, Capt Scots Fus; *b* 31 Dec 1809; *dsp*

The 2nd BARON *d* 22 May 1787; his er son,

HENRY CONYNGHAM, **1st Marquess Conyngham**, so *cr* 15 Jan 1816, as also VISCOUNT SLANE and EARL OF MOUNT CHARLES, and previously 6 Dec 1789 VISCOUNT CONYNGHAM OF MOUNT CHARLES, Co Donegal, then 27 Dec 1797 VISCOUNT MOUNT CHARLES and EARL CONYNGHAM (all I), and finally 17 July 1821 BARON MINSTER OF MINSTER ABBEY, Co Kent (UK), KP (1801), GCH (1821), PC (1821); *b* 26 Dec 1766; FSA 1789, Maj-Gen 1808, Lt-Gen 1812, Gen 1830, rep I peer 1801–32, Govr Co Donegal 1803–31, Custos Rotulorum Co Clare 1808–32, Ld Steward Household 1821–30, Constable Windsor Castle 1829032; *m* 5 July 1794 Elizabeth (*b c* 1769; GEORGE IV's mistress, replacing Lady Hertford (*see* HERTFORD, M); *d* 11 Oct 1861), dau of Joseph Denison, London banker, and sis and eventually sole heir of William Joseph Denison, of Seamer, E R Yorks, and had issue:

1 Henry Joseph, *Earl of Mount Charles*; *b* 6 April 1795; *educ* Trin Coll Cambridge; MP (Tory) Co Donegal 1818–24; *d* unm 26 Dec 1824

2 FRANCIS NATHANIEL, **2nd Marquess**

3 ALBERT DENISON, *cr* BARON LONDESBOROUGH (*qv*)

1 Elizabeth Henrietta; *m* 2 March 1826 10th Marquess of Huntly (*qv*) and *dsp* 24 Aug 1839

2 Harriet Maria; *m* 22 Dec 1832 Sir William Meredyth Somerville, Bt (*see* 1970 edn), afterwards Baron Athlumney (*see* 1929 edn), and *d* 3 Dec 1843, leaving an only child:

(1) Elizabeth Jane; *b* 21 June 1834; *m* 18 Dec 1856, as his 1st w, 3rd Earl of Charlemont (*see* CHARLEMONT, V) and *dsp* 31 May 1882

The 1st MARQUESS *d* 28 Dec 1832; his er surv son,

FRANCIS NATHANIEL CONYNGHAM, **2nd Marquess Conyngham**, KP (1833), GCH (1823), PC (1835); *b* 11 June 1797; Gen 1874, V-Adml Ulster, Lt Co Meath, MP (Tory) Westbury 1818–20 and Co Donegal (Tory to 1830, then Whig) 1825–31, Under-Sec For Affrs 1823–26, a Ld Treasury 1827–33, PMG 1834–35, Ld Chamberlain 1835–39; *m* 23 April 1824 Lady Jane Paget (*d* 28 Jan 1876), dau of 1st Marquess of Anglesey (*qv*), and had, with four daus:

1 GEORGE HENRY, **3rd Marquess**

2 Francis Nathaniel, Lt RN, MP Co Clare 1857–1859 and 1874–1880; *b* 24 Sept 1832; *m* 28 Sept 1857 Georgina Charlotte (*m* 2nd 27 April 1882 Lt-Col Alan Chichester, OBE (*see* DONEGALL, M), and *d* 22 April 1886), 5th dau of 1st Baron Tredegar (*see* 1959 edn), and *dsp* 14 Sept 1880

The 2nd MARQUESS *d* 17 July 1876; his er son,

GEORGE HENRY CONYNGHAM, **3rd Marquess Conyngham**, Lt-Gen 1st Life Gds, Equerry to HM QUEEN VICTORIA 1870–73, Extra Equerry 1873–82, Lt-Col cmdg Roy E Kent Yeo Mtd Rifles; *b* 3 Feb 1825; *m* 17 June 1854 Lady Jane St Maur Blanche Stanhope (*d* 28 Nov 1907), only surv child of 4th Earl of Harrington (*qv*), and had issue:

1 HENRY FRANCIS, **4th Marquess**

2 Charles Arthur; Capt Roy Def Force and TFR, Lt Rifle Brigade; *b* 1 Feb 1871; *m* 1st 1899 Lena Barbara (*dsp* 24 Feb 1902), dau of Lewis Richard Morgan, of Mordon, Rhyl; *m* 2nd 6 Aug 1910 Annie Brewer (*d* 14 April 1955), widow of Andrew Wilson Hunter and dau of Daniel Morgan, and *d* 7 March 1929

1 Blanche; *d* unm 13 April 1946

2 Constance Augusta; *m* 20 Oct 1881 Richard Combe, 2nd son of Richard Henry Combe, of Pierrepont, Surrey, and *d* 14 June 1941, leaving issue. He *d* 14 April 1939

3 Jane Seymour; *m* 26 July 1883 Capt Christian Combe, RHG, est s of Richard Henry Combe, of Pierrepont, Surrey, and *d* 30 Oct 1941, leaving issue (*see* SCARSDALE, V)

4 Elizabeth Maud; *m* 30 July 1887 Capt Frederick William Ramsden, Coldstream Gds, and *d* 27 May 1949, leaving issue (*see* RAMSDEN, Bt)

5 Florence; *m* 1st 30 April 1887 Bertram Frankland Frankland-Russell-Astley, of Chequers Court, Bucks, and had issue (*see* HASTINGS, B). He *d* 11 Feb 1904. She *m* 2nd 17 June 1905 Lt-Col Hon Claud Heathcote-Drummond-Willoughby, 3rd son of 1st Earl of Ancaster (*see* WILLOUGHBY DE ERESBY, B), and *d* 28 Jan 1946. He *d* 24 Feb 1950

The 3rd MARQUESS *d* 2 June 1882; his er son,

HENRY FRANCIS CONYNGHAM, **4th Marquess Conyngham**, V-Adml Ulster, DL, Lt Scots Gds; *b* 1 Oct 1857; *m* 21 March 1882 Hon Frances Elizabeth Sarah Eveleigh De Moleyns (*m* 2nd 27 April 1899 Maj John Russell Bedford Cameron and *d* 8 July 1939), dau of 4th Baron Ventry (*qv*), and *d* 28 Aug 1897, having had issue:

1 VICTOR GEORGE HENRY FRANCIS CONYNGHAM, **5th Marquess Conyngham**, Lt S Irish Horse, formerly 3rd Bn Wilts Regt; *b* 30 Jan 1883; *d* unm 9 Nov 1918

2 FREDERICK WILLIAM BURTON **6th Marquess**

1 Blanche Frances; *b* 10 March 1884; *m* 29 July 1905 Maj Sir Edward Seymour, KCVO, DSO, OBE, late Gren Gds, 3rd son of Lt-Col Leopold Richard Seymour, Gren Gds, and *d* 11 Feb 1956, leaving issue (*see* HERTFORD, M)

2 Mildred Martha; *b* 2 June 1886; *d* unm 16 Feb 1955

3 Hersey Constance Evelyn; *b* 24 Sept 1887; *m* 28 Jan 1908 William Arthur Baird, yr son of Sir David Baird, 3rd Bt (*see* BAIRD, Bt, of Newbyth), and *d* 6 Aug 1962, leaving issue

4 Edina Dorothy Hope; *b* 18 Oct 1888; *m* 1st 9 Feb 1911 (*divorce* 1925) Sir Thomas Ainsworth, 2nd Bt (*qv*), and had issue; *m* 2nd 27 Oct 1925 2nd Baron Holm Patrick (*qv*), and *d* 13 April 1964, leaving further issue

5 (Barbara) Helen; *b* 13 Nov 1893; *m* 3 June 1918 Maj Dermot Hugh Bingham McCalmont, MC, 7th Hus, of Mount Juliet, Thomastown, Co Kilkenny, only son of Gen Sir Hugh McCalmont, KCB, CVO, and *d* 24 Dec 1938, leaving issue. He *d* 24 Feb 1968

The 5th MARQUESS's bro,

FREDERICK WILLIAM BURTON CONYNGHAM, **6th Marquess Conyngham**; *b* 24 June 1890; *educ* Winchester; Lt 3rd Bn Roy Innisikilling Fus, Capt HG; *m* 1st 28 Nov 1914 (*divorce* 1921) Bessie Alice (*d* 1933), dau of William Andrew Tobin, of Australia; *m* 2nd 8 Nov 1922 Antoinette Winifred (*d* 29 May 1966), formerly w of Maj Studley Neville Custance, RFA, and er dau of John William Howard Thompson, of Bratton Ho, Wincanton, Som, and 25A N Audley St, W; *m* 3rd 4 Nov 1966 Stella (*d* 1985), widow of Robert Newton Tory, of Dorset, and er dau of Francis Barrallier Thompson, and *d* 1974, having by his 2nd w had issue:

1 FREDRICK WILLIAM HENRY FRANCIS CONYNGHAM, **7th and present Marquess Conyngham**

2 John Victor Albert Blosse, Lt RN; *b* 4 April 1926; *educ* RNC Dartmouth; *m* 25 March 1950 *Olivia Phoebe [The Lady John Conyngham, Windmill Cottage, Yapton Rd, Barnham, Bognor Regis, W Sussex] (*m* 2nd 4 Aug 1963, as his 4th w, Hon Francis Alexander Innys Eveleigh-Ross-de-Moleyns (*d* 29 April 1964), yr son of 6th Baron Ventry (*qv*), and who has reverted to her former style), only dau of Capt Percy Neave Leathers, of Fayre Cottage, Robertsbridge, Sussex, and *dsp* 31 May 1963

1 Antoinette Fredericka Hersey Cecilia; 3rd Offr WRNS WW II; *m* 30 Oct 1948 2nd Baron Croft (*qv*) and *d* 15 June 1959, leaving issue

Seats: Slane Castle, Co Meath, Ireland; Beau Parc, Navan, Co Meath, Ireland. Slane was one of the first Gothic Revival structures built in Ireland, being started in the mid-1780s by the **2nd Baron Conyngham of Mount Charles**. At that point James Wyatt was the architect but by the time the project was completed the **1st Marquess** had inherited and he employed Francis Johnston, though chiefly to take charge of the internal decoration. There had indeed been a genuine castle there once, but it was built over around 1700, well before Wyatt got to work. Indeed his brief was to turn a William III house (it seems, appropriately, to have had a decidedly Dutch appearance) into a castle that looked both backwards to a fantasy Middle Ages and yet was up to date.

As well as the two main architects already mentioned, Slane benefited from advice by several others, including Capability Brown, who was responsible for the stables despite never setting foot in Ireland, James Gandon and Thomas Hopper (*see* also PARKER, Bt of Melford Hall). The result is remarkably homogeneous, being effectively a massive slab of Classicism with some rather vestigial fortifications such as the crenellations, square towerlets at the corners and a machicolated gallery over the main entrance. The house of *c* 1700 had had various towers surrounding it and as far as these were concerned Wyatt did no more than join them properly to the house, though given the apparently variegated nature of the originals it was something of a triumph to draw them into a coherent whole. Inside there was no attempt at medievalising other than the exquisite library-cum-ballroom with its plasterwork ceiling that simulates filigree. Slane has been the site of several pop concerts in recent years and was badly damaged by fire in the autumn of 1991.

From the external point of view Beau Parc is arguably more successful, despite being the work of amateurs. The first, in the mid-18th century, is generally agreed to have been Nathaniel Clements, father-in-law of the **2nd Baron Conyngham of Mount Charles**. The other two, about a quarter of a century later, were Charles Lambart and the Rev Daniel Beaufort. The Lambarts, a cadet branch of the Earl of Cavan's family (*qv*), had owned Beau Parc for at least two generations beforehand. (Charles's grandson, the 1st Baronet, married a daughter of the **2nd Marquess Conyngham**; *see* **Lineage** above.)

Beau Parc, like Slane, enjoys a vista out over the Boyne. Such a feature is apt, for it was the Battle of the Boyne, at which Sir Albert Conyngham fought, that established the Conynghams among the first families in Ireland.

COOK

Arms: Gules a rose argent barbed and seeded proper between three crescents of the second, a chief vair. **Crest:** Issuant from a chaplet of roses gules a dexter arm embowed proper holding in the hand a mullet of six points or, between two branches of oak vert. **Motto:** *Esse quam videri* ('Being rather than seeming'). **Creation:** Bt. (UK) 10 March 1886.

SIR CHRISTOPHER WYMONDHAM RAYNOR HERBERT COOK, 5TH BT, of Richmond, Surrey, and **4th Visconde de Monserrate** in Portugal [Sir Christopher Cook Bt, La Fosse Equievre, Bouillon Rd, St Andrews, Guernsey, CI GY6 8YN]; *b* 24 March 1938; *s* f 1978; *educ* King's Canterbury; late RAF, dir Diamond Guarantees Ltd 1980–91; *m* 1st 1958 (*divorce* 1975) Malina, dau of Aster Gunasekera, of Ceylon, and formerly w of Cyril Wettasinghe, of Ceylon, and has issue:

1 +RICHARD HERBERT ASTER MAURICE; *b* 30 June 1959

1 *Priscilla Melina; *b* Oct 1969

Sir CHRISTOPHER *m* 2nd 1975 *Margaret, dau of John Murray and formerly w of Ronald Miller, and has further issue:

2 +Alexander James Frederick; *b* 1980

2 *Caroline Emma; *b* 1978

Lineage: WILLIAM COOK, of Wymondham, Norfolk, and Roydon Hall, Kent; *m* Mary Anne, sis of Alderman Lainson, of London, and had, with three daus:

1 William; *b* 1814; *dspm* 1852

2 FRANCIS (Sir), **1st Bt**

3 Edwin Adolphus, of Roydon Hall, DL, JP Kent; *b* 1831; Maj 11th Hus; *m* 1867 Minnie Augusta (*m* 2nd 3 Aug 1875 Lord George Charles Gordon Lennox, MP, son of 5th Duke of Richmond and Gordon (*qv*), and *d* 21 Sept 1913), dau of W H Palmer, of Portland Place, and *d* 1872, leaving issue

The 2nd son,

Sir Francis Cook, 1st Bt (UK), so *cr* 10 March 1886, of Doughty House, Richmond, Surrey; Visconde de Monserrate, Cintra, in the Kingdom of Portugal, FSA; *b* 23 Jan 1817; *m* 1st 10 Aug 1841 Emily Martha (*d* 12 Aug 1884), dau of Robert Lucas, of Lisbon; *m* 2nd 1 Oct 1885 Tennessee Celeste (*d* 18 Jan 1923), dau of Reuben-Buckman Claflin, of New York, and by his 1st w had issue:

1 FREDERICK LUCAS (Sir), **2nd Bt**

2 Wyndham Francis; *b* 21 Aug 1860; *m* 22 Nov 1887 Frederica Evelyn Stillwell (*d* 9 Jan 1925), 3rd dau of F J Freeland, of Chichester, and *d* 17 May 1905, leaving issue:

(1) Humphrey Wyndham; *b* March 1893; *educ* Harrow and Ch Ch Oxford; *m* 1st 18 Aug 1926 (*divorce* 1932) Gillian, er dau of Frederick William Hedderly, of Tilbury, Oxford; *m* 2nd 4 Feb 1941 Mrs Anne Blakeley (*d* 197–), dau of John Moffet, of Ballynhinch, Co Down, and d 1978, having by his 1st w had issue:

1a +William Wyndham Humphrey; *b* 1928

(1) Cecil Emily Freda Wyndham; *b* 1 July 1896; *m* 1 March 1920 Sir Terence James O'Connor, KC, MP (*d* 8 May 1940), Slr-Gen, Capt 4th HLI, est son of James O'Connor, of Bridgnorth, and had issue

(2) Ursula Maud Wyndham; *b* 20 Nov 1900; *m* 1st 31 Jan 1921 (*divorce* 1924) Lt-Cdr Cecil Highat Harcourt Smith, RN (*d* 18 March 1956), er son of Sir Cecil Harcourt Smith, CVO; *m* 2nd 18 Dec 1924 Cecil Walter Lazenby, est son of Frank Lazenby, of Wood Hall, Sunningdale

1 Emily Jane; *b* 8 Jan 1849; *m* 22 Dec 1874 Maj-Gen Euston Henry Sartorius, VC, CB (*d* 19 Feb 1925), son of Adml Sir George Rose Sartorius, GCB, of Old Swan Ho, Chelsea, and *d* 6 Jan 1915, leaving issue

Sir FRANCIS *d* 17 Feb 1901; his son,

Sir Frederick Lucas Cook, 2nd Bt, Visconde de Monserrate in Portugal; *b* 21 Nov 1844; *educ* Harrow; MP Kennington 1895–1906, Lt City London, Head of Cook, Son and Co, warehousemen, of St Paul's Churchyard; *m* 7 Jan 1868 Mary Anne Elizabeth (*d* 9 Aug 1913), dau of Richard Payne Cotton, MD, of Cavendish Sq, and had issue:

1 HERBERT FREDERICK (Sir), **3rd Bt**

1 Edith Laura; *b* 13 Nov 1870; *m* 1893 Rev Alfred Percivall Pott (*d* Dec 1943), Rector Thursley, Godalming, and *d* 2 April 1954, leaving issue

2 Mabel Emily; *b* 30 July 1875; *m* 6 July 1897 Sir William Symington McCormick, GBE, LLD (*d* 22 March 1930), of Frognal Priory, Hampstead, NW, est son of William McCormick, and had issue

Sir FREDERICK *d* 21 May 1920; his son,

Sir Herbert Frederick Cook, 3rd Bt; *b* 18 Nov 1868; *educ* Harrow and Balliol Coll Oxford (MA); barrister, tstee Nat Gallery 1923–30 and Nat Portrait Gallery 1916–30; Hon Memb Roy Academy, Milan; Visconde de Monserrate in Portugal, author: *Giorgione, Reviews and Appreciations*, and other works on art criticism, chm Cook, Son & Co (St Paul's) Ltd, ret 1931; *m* 21 April 1898 Hon Mary Hood (*d* 28 Nov 1943), dau of 2nd Viscount Bridport (*qv*), and had issue:

1 FRANCIS FERDINAND MAURICE (Sir), **4th Bt**

1 Vera Mary; *b* 15 Feb 1899; *m* 1st 12 April 1921 (*divorce* 1938) George Mervyn Anstey Hamilton-Fletcher, JP (*d* 2 April 1958), of Shermanbury Place, nr Henfield, Sussex, and had issue; *m* 2nd 14 Oct 1938 Dudley Claud Douglas Ryder, of Rempstone, Corfe Castle, Dorset (*see* HARROWBY, E), and by him had a son

2 Rachel Margaret; *b* 7 April 1903; *m* 1st 24 May 1922 (*divorce* 1937) Sir John Serocold Paget Mellor, 2nd Bt, MP, and had issue; *m* 2nd 1939 Capt William Eric Lloyd, Roy Berks Regt (*ka* 1943)

Sir HERBERT *d* 4 May 1939; his son,

Sir Francis Ferdinand Maurice Cook, 4th Bt; *b* 21 Dec 1907; *educ* Bradfield; artist and musician, FRSA (1940), ARBA 1938–48, memb: Jersey Soc Artists 1949, Chelsea Art Soc and St Ives Soc of Artists Cornwall 1938, Roy Instn of Cornwall (Truro), exhibited RA, RBA, etc, paintings in permanent Collections of Walker Art Gallery, Liverpool, Manchester, Northampton and Bournemouth, as well as private collections, specialist in research into mediums of the Old Masters, Patron Br Picture Restorers Assoc; *m* 1st 15 Feb 1928 (*divorce* 1930) Molly Violet, dau of Thomas Wilson Mappin (*see* 1967 edn MAPPIN, Bt); *m* 2nd 25 Feb 1933 (*divorce* 1935) Dorothea Alice, only dau of Col William Bennett, DSO, OBE, of Belbins, Romsey, Hants; *m* 3rd 8 June 1937 (*divorce* 1942) Joan Loraine (*d* 21 July 1995), dau of John Aloysius Ashton Case, of Durban, S Africa, and by her had issue:

1 Sir CHRISTOPHER WYMONDHAM RAYNOR HERBERT COOK, **5th and present Bt**

Sir Francis *m* 4th Oct 1942 (*divorce*1947) Barbara Frances, est dau of Mrs Cora Lang, of Seaford, Sussex; *m* 5th 5 Sept 1947 (*divorce* 1951) Juliet Berry, yr dau of Christopher Edward Perkins, of The Stone, Sudbury, Suffolk, and late of Chiswick Mall, W4; *m* 6th 10 Aug 1951 (*divorce* 1956) Jane Audrey, er dau of Christopher Nott, and by her had issue:

1 *(Cleone) Willa Johanne Vera Rosemary [Mrs Willa Wilson, 25 Ampthill St, Norwich, Norfolk]; *b* 6 June 1952; *m* 6 June 1970 (*divorce* 1983) Peter Wilson, and has issue:

(1) *Stuart Francis James; *b* 1971

(1) *Catherine Jane Brenda Rachael; *b* 26 Nov 1972

Sir Francis *m* 7th 3 Dec 1956 *Bridget Brenda [Dowager Lady Cook, Le Coin, La Haule, St Aubin, Jersey CI], dau of Thomas David Lynch, of Galway, and formerly w of Capt John Barclay Polland, and *d* 12 Sept 1978

COOKE

Arms: Or a chevron gules between two lions passant-guardant sable. **Crest:** Out of a mural crown argent a demi-lion guardant issuant sable, gorged with a ducal coronet or. **Creation:** Bt. (E) 10 May 1661.

SIR DAVID WILLIAM PERCEVAL COOKE, 12TH BT, of Wheatley Hall, Co York [Lt-Col Sir David Cooke Bt, c/o Midland Bank, Knutsford, Cheshire WA16 6BZ]; *b* 28 April 1935; *s* f 1978; *educ* Wellington, RMA Sandhurst and OU (BA 1983); commnd 4th/7th RDG 1955, tfd to RASC (later RCT) 1958, Silver Jubilee medal 1977, Col 1984, ret 1990; consultant and researcher, FCIT, FBIM, AMInstTA, AssocRAeS; *m* 30 April 1959 *Margaret Frances, only dau of Herbert Skinner, of Knutsford, Cheshire, and has issue:

1 *Sara Elizabeth Mary; *b* 11 Feb 1960; *m* 1984 *Darren P Grosvenor, and has issue

2 *Louise Diana Margaret; *b* 27 Jan 1962; *m* 1986 (*divorce* 1988) Michael Moriarty

3 *Catherine Faith Maria; *b* 24 July 1968

Lineage: EDWARD COOKE, of Arksey, Mayor Doncaster 1504, 1505, 1506, 1507 and 1508, had, with an er s (Lawrence, Prior Doncaster 1536–38, participant Pilgrimage of Grace 1536, executed 1540):

WILLIAM COOKE, of Doncaster, had:

BRYAN COOKE, of Sandall Yorks; had:

BRYAN COOKE, of Sandall; Mayor Doncaster 1630; royalist Civil War; *m* Sarah (*d* 3 Dec 1647), dau and heir of Henry Ryley, of Doncaster, and *d* 26 Dec 1653 aged 83, having had issue:

1 Bryan, of Wheatley, Yorks, barrister; *d* unm 5 Jan 1660/61

2 **Sir George Cooke, 1st Bt** (E), so *cr* 10 May 1661, with remainder, in default of male issue, to his next bro; *d* unm 16 Oct 1683

3 HENRY (Sir), **2nd Bt**

1 Susan; *m* Charles Butler, of Coates, Lincs

2 Sarah; *m* 1st John Copley, of Batley, Yorks; *m* 2nd Thomas Nevile, of Thorney, Notts; *m* 3rd Christopher Ayscough, of Kelsey, Lincs

3 Margaret; *m* Acton Burnell, of Winkburne, Notts

The 1st Bt's bro,

Sir Henry Cooke, 2nd Bt; *b* 29 Oct 1633; *m* 1st 29 Aug 1659 Diana (*d* 5 Jan 1668), only dau of Anthony Butler, of Coates, Lincs, and sis and coheir of Charles Butler, of Coates; *m* 2nd Anne (*bur* 16 Jan 1686), dau of William Stanhope, and by his 1st w had, with other issue:

1 GEORGE (Sir), **3rd Bt**

2 Henry, of Owston, Yorks; *b* 26 May 1665; *m* Anne, dau and coheir of Rev Ralph Eaton, Rector Darfield, and *d* 2 May 1717, leaving issue:

(1) Bryan, of Owston, Recorder of Doncaster; *d* unm 1754 aged 52

(2) Anthony, of Owston; *b* 1710; *m* 26 Oct 1752 Mary, dau of Anthony Eyre, of Rampton, and *d* 1761 leaving, with a dau (Anne, *m* Sir Andrew Warde, of Hooton Pagnell):

1a Bryan, of Owston, Col 3rd W York Mil, High Sheriff Denbighs 1794, MP Malton 1811; *b* 8 June 1756; *m* 1st 18 Dec 1786 Frances (*d* 1 Jan 1818), dau and heir of Philip Puleston, of Hefod-y-wern, Denbighs, by Mary, sis and coheir of John Davies, of Llanerch and Gwysaney; *m* 2nd 17 April 1821 his cousin Charlotte Bulstrode (*d* 16 Oct 1850), dau of **Sir George Cooke, 7th Bt**, of Wheatley (*see* below), and *d* 8 Nov 1821, having by his 1st w had:

1b Philip COOKE later DAVIES-COOKE, of Owston, Hafod-y-wern and Gwysaney, DL, JP Yorks, Denbighs and Flints, High Sheriff Flints 1824, FLS, FHS, FGS, and FZS; *b* 11 Aug 1793; *m* 8 Dec 1829 Lady Helena Caroline King (*d* 9 May 1871), est dau of 3rd Earl of Kingston (*qv*), and *d* 20 Nov 1853, having had issue:

1c Philip Bryan, of Owston, Gwysaney and Hafod-y-wern, DL, JP, High Sheriff Flints 1858 and W R Yorks, FSA; *b* 2 March 1832; *m* 17 July 1862 Emma Julia (*d* 7 Oct 1907), 6th dau of Sir Tatton Sykes, 4th Bt, of Sledmere (*qv*), and *d* 29 Sept 1903, leaving issue:

1d Philip Tatton, OBE (1920), of Owston and Gwysaney and Maes Alyn, Mold, JP and V-Lt Flints, High Sheriff 1915, V-Chm Flints TAA, Lt 1st W Yorks Yeo Cav, Maj Denbighs Hus Yeo; *b* 15 May 1863; *m* 14 Aug 1894 Doris (*d* 20 March 1935), 2nd dau of Charles Donaldson-Hudson, MP Cheswardine, Salop, and *d* 10 June 1946, leaving issue:

1e Philip Ralph, CB (1958), TD, JP (W R Yorks 1933) and DL (1947), JP (Flints 1923), High Sheriff Flints 1949, V-Lt 1957–74; *b* 27 Nov 1896; *educ* Eton; Col Yorks Dragoons Yeo, Capt 5th Bn RWF, TA, formerly Roy Dragoons; served WWs I and II on Staff HQ N Command, Hon Col 4th Bn RWF (TA) 1953–61, chm Denbigh and Flints T&AFA, Rep Chm for Wales Cncl T&AFA 1956–61, chm Mold Petty Sessional Div and N Wales Regnl Advsy Forestry Cncl; *m* 12 June 1924 his cousin Kathleen Mabel, OBE (1964) (*d* 1994), 2nd dau of William Hugh Davies-Cooke, of Maes Alyn, Mold (*see* below), and *d* 15 Nov 1974, leaving:

1f +(Philip) Peter [Peter Davies-Cooke Esq, Gwysaney Hall, Mold, Clwyd CH7 6PA]; *b* 4 July 1925; *educ* Eton; late Capt 1st Roy Dragoons; *m* 1st 6 July 1957 Jane (*d* 1981), yr dau of Edmund George Coryton (*see* CAREW, Bt), of Linkincorn Ho, Yelverton, S Devon; *m* 2nd 1985 *Mrs Zinnia Mary Arfwedson (Charlton), er dau of Col Reggie Hodgkinson, of Shennington Ho, Stratford upon Avon, and by his 1st w has issue:

1g +Richard Piers; *b* 1 July 1960; *m* 1986 *Sarah Jane, est dau of John Latham, of Caldecott Hall, Farndon, nr Chester, and has issue:

1h +James Portland; *b* 1988

1h *Sophie Jane; *b* 1989

2g +Paul Bryan; *b* 30 March 1962

3g +Michael Antony; *b* 2 Nov 1965; *m* 1993 *Helen Marie, dau of Eric Roberts, of Nercwys, Clwyd

2f +David Ralph [David Davies-Cooke Esq, 25 Barkston Gdns, London SW5 0ER]; *b* 15 May 1930; *educ* Eton and Magdalene Coll Cambridge (MA); late Capt 384 Light Regt RA (RWF), TA, formerly 2nd Lt 1st Bn RWF; *m* 23 April 1955 *Henrietta Sarah Angénis, only dau of Edward Jan Hoos, of Thistleton Grange, Oakham, Rutland, by Hon Sarah Mary Adelaide, yr dau of 5th Baron Brownlow (*qv*), and has issue:

1g +(Philip) Rupert Hugh [Rupert Davies-Cooke Esq, 56A Queenstown Rd, London SW8]; *b* 11 May 1960; *m* 10 June 1995 *Chiena, only dau of Dr Yoshiharu Hiruta, of 17-10-716 Nishiyamacho, Japan

2g *Nichola Sarah Angénis [Mrs Ian Reed, Colpa, Gilgandra, NSW 2827, Australia]; *b* 13 Feb 1958; *m* 23 April 1988 *Ian William Reed, yr son of D C Reed, of Molong, NSW, and has:

1h *Hugh William Bryan; *b* 6 Dec 1994

1h *Emma Sarah Annabel; *b* 24 July 1989

2h *Alice Bronwyn Diana; *b* 31 July 1991

1f *Philippa Marjorie [Mrs William Warde-Norbury, Hooton Pagnell Hall, Doncaster, Yorks]; *b* 17 Oct 1938; *m* 15 April 1961 *William George Antony Warde-Norbury, late Capt Coldstream Gds, only son of Maj Harold George Warde-Norbury, of Hooton Pagnell Hall, Doncaster, by his w Mary Betty, only dau of Col William St Andrew Warde-Aldam, DSO, of Hooton Pagnell Hall, and has issue:

1g *Mark William Antony; *b* 29 July 1962

2g *Alastair George; *b* 8 April 1966

2e Richard Anthony, Capt late RWF; *b* 9 Oct 1909; *educ* Eton and Trin Coll Cambridge; *m* 2 June 1934 Berys (*d* 9 Aug 1966), dau of Maj Thomas Fanning-Evans, DL, JP, of Plas Cadnant, Anglesey, and *d* 28 Dec 1962, leaving issue:

1f *Doris Caroline [Mrs Arthur Grant, Tal-y-Bont, Dwyran, Anglesey, N Wales]; *b* 31 Aug 1935; *m* 1971 *Arthur Henry Grant, and has issue:

1g *Arthur Paul; *b* 1972

3e Paul John, F/O RAF WW II; *b* 14 Nov 1916; *ka* 27 Sept 1940

2d Henry George; *b* 3 May 1867; *d* 27 Feb 1872

1d Mary Helena; *d* unm 15 Dec 1933

2d Emma Katharine; *d* unm 5 Jan 1941

3d Mildred Emily; *d* unm 17 Sept 1910

4d Helena Frances Anna; *d* 14 March 1919

2c Bryan George, of Colomendy, Denbighs, DL, JP Flints, High Sheriff 1865, ADC, Col and Lt-Col Flint Vol, Capt 73rd Regt; *b* 3 Jan 1835; *m* 24 Jan 1860 Judith Caroline Halsted (*d* 25 Feb 1922), 3rd dau of Capt William Halsted Poole, RHA, of Terwick Hall, Salop, and *d* 20 Sept 1913, having had issue:

1d Bryan Davies COOKE later POOLE (roy licence 26 Sept 1907), JP Salop, DL, JP Cheshire, Capt Denbighs and Merioneths Militia; *b* 9 Sept 1861; *m* 1890 Georgiana Mary (*d* 1944), 2nd dau of Charles R Fenwick, of Harpenden, Herts, and *d* 1 Dec 1930, leaving issue:

1e Bryan Cudworth Halsted, Capt RWF; *b* 9 Nov 1892; *educ* Wellington and RMC Sandhurst; *m* 11 Nov 1925 Margaret (*d* 1948), dau of Sir Adrian Knox, PC, KCMG, KC, of Osterley, Sydney, NSW, and *d* 1971, leaving issue:

1f +Adrian Bryan [Adrian Poole Esq, Dellawong, Box 279, Wellington 2820, NSW, Australia]; *b* 4 Dec 1927; *m* 1957 *Philippa, dau of Judge Adrian Herbert Curlewis, CVO, CBE, and has issue:

1g +Adrian Peter; *b* 1958

2g *Bryan David Edward; *b* 1964

1g *Belinda Margaret; *b* 1960

2g *Susan Philippa; *b* 1962

1f *Bronwen Margaret Knox; *b* March 1932; *m* 30 June 1955 *Maj Basil Hugh Philips Heaton, MBE, RA, er son of Cdr Hugh Edward Heaton, RN, DL, JP, of Rhual, Mold, and has issue:

1g *Sara Margaret; *b* 28 April 1956

2g *Julia Mary; *b* 1959

2e Richard Domville, Lt-Col Rifle Bde; *b* 26 Jan 1900; *educ* Charterhouse and RMC Sandhurst

1e Judith Mimi; *m* 1st 19th July 1914 Capt Alfred Spencer Mason Summers, 19th Hus (*ka* 1916); *m* 2nd 21 Aug 1918 Maj Sir Bache McEvers Athole Hay, 11th Bt, of Smithfield (*see* 1970 edn), and *dsp* 9 Jan 1978

2d William Hugh, JP Flints; *b* 13 Oct 1862; *m* 27 June 1900 Mabel Louisa (*d* 21 Dec 1956), dau of Capt Edwin William Philips, late 36th Regt of Rhûal, Flints, and *d* 28 Nov 1941, having had issue:

1e *Sybil Gwyndd; *b* 20 July 1901

2e *Kathleen Mabel, OBE (1964), Chm Exec Ctee Girl Guides Assoc of GB 1948–51; *b* 5 Jan 1903; *m* 12 June 1924 her cousin Col Philip Ralph Davies-Cooke, CB, TD, JP (*d* 1974), and has issue (*see* above)

3e Mary Frances Helena; *b* 13 April 1904; *m* 1 July 1933 Cdr Gordon Gratwicke Peters, RN, yr son of Sir Byron Peters, and *d* 8 Jan 1961, leaving two daus

4e Marjorie Judith; *b* 15 March 1905; *d* 12 Oct 1915

5e *Doris Sara; *b* 22 Dec 1907; *m* 7 Feb 1940 Lt-Col Anthony Lawrence Allpress, JP, and has issue:

1f *William Anthony Toulmin [William Allpress Esq, 931 Briarwoods Rd, Franklin Lakes, NJ 07417, USA]; *b* 7 Aug 1942

1f *Alyn Diana [Mrs Roger Newmarch, PO Box 206, Norton, Zimbabwe]; *b* 5 April 1941; *m* 25 Feb 1967 *Roger William Newmarch, son of George Herbert Newmarch, of Carrick Creagh Estates, Rhodesia, and has issue:

1g *Steven William; *b* 13 Oct 1968; *m* 15 Sept 1990 *Debbie Anne, dau of Richard Homann, of Mutepatepa, Zimbabwe, and has:

1h *Ian Steven; *b* 8 Aug 1991

1h *Keri Lee; *b* 28 Sept 1993

2g *Christopher George; *b* 11 Nov 1969; *m* 4 July 1993 *Samantha Leigh, dau of W Harlacz, and has:

1h *Jake Chris; *b* 4 Dec 1993

2h *Ben David; *b* 7 April 1994

3d Frederick Anthony; *d* March 1869

1d Helena Adelaide Sara, MBE (1920), JP Flints; *m* 12 Feb 1896 Lt-Col Basil Edwin Philips (*ka* 10 Aug 1915), 5th Bn RWF, of Rhûal, Mold, Flintshire, and *d* 19 April 1943, leaving issue

2d Gwendoline Mary, OBE (1950), JP Denbighs 1925; *d* unm 9 Aug 1956

3c George Robert (Rev), Vicar Hythe, Hants; *b* 29 May 1836; *educ* Ch Ch Oxford (BA); *m* 10 Feb 1863 Diana (*d* 2 May 1908), est dau of Henry Yarborough Parker, of Streethorpe, Yorks, and *dsp* 1910

4c James Robert, Maj RA, 4 July 1837; *m* 2 July 1868 Clara Louisa (*d* 11 Feb 1929), only child of John Webb, and *d* 1 Sept 1883, leaving issue:

1d Aubrey George King, Capt 10th Roy Hus; *b* 18 June 1873; *d* unm 25 March 1908

1d Kathleen Mary; *d* 2 April 1899

2d Beatrice Helena Mary; *d* unm 7 Oct 1962 aged 92

1c Helena Frances Adelaide; *d* 30 Nov 1833

2c Adelaide Flora Frances Isabella; *d* unm 10 Jan 1902

2b Robert Bryan (Rev), Rector Wheldrake, Preb York Minster; *b* 26 Aug 1800; *m* 15 Jan 1824 Emily Carteret (*d* 16 Aug 1880 aged 80), yst dau of Philip Smith Webb, of Milford Ho, Surrey, and *d* 17 Oct 1887, having had:

1c Anthony Charles, CB, Lt-Gen, Col Cmdt RE Siege Sebastopol, 5th Cl Medjidie; *b* 15 Feb 1826; *d* unm 6 April 1905

1c Emily Charlotte Hannah; *m* 9 Aug 1848 Oliver William Farrer (*d* 6 Nov 1876), of Binnegar Hall, Wareham, Dorset, 3rd son of James William Farrer, of Ingleborough, and had issue

Sir HENRY was *bur* 16 July 1689; his er son,

Sir George Cooke, 3rd Bt, MP Aldborough 1698; *b* 16 May 1662; *m* 19 June 1683 Catherine (*bur* 9 April 1703), dau of Sir Godfrey Copley, Bt, and had issue:

1 BRYAN (Sir), **4th Bt**

2 George; *b* 28 Dec 1687; *m* 28 Oct 1736 Mary (*d* 5 Nov 1742), dau and coheir of Tobias Harvey, and *d* 12 Sept 1763, leaving an only son:

(1) George COOKE later COOKE-YARBOROUGH (added 7 July 1802 after death 23 Nov 1801 of his first cousin Elizabeth Yarborough, last descendant of Thomas Yarborough, of Campsall), of Streethorpe, Doncaster; *b* 23 Nov 1737; *m* 26 Jan 1764 Mary (*d* 3 Dec 1778), dau and heir of Richard Sare Newsome, and *d* 19 Jan 1818, leaving, with other issue:

1a John, of Campsmount, Yorks; Lt-Col 3rd W York Militia; *b* 1765; *m* his second cousin Mary (*d* 4 Nov 1824), dau of Rev George Cooke, Rector Darfield, and *d* 30 March 1836, having had, with other issue:

1b George, of Campsmount; *b* 19 July 1794; *m* 1st 16 May 1837 his first cousin Emily Sarah (*dsp* 31 Dec 1840), 2nd dau of George Cooke, of Carr Ho, nr Doncaster; *m* 2nd 9 June 1842 Mary Louisa (*d* 23 Nov 1906), yst dau of Richard Heathfield, of Green Lanes, Middx, and *d* 2 Feb 1870, having had issue:

1c George Bryan, of Campsmount; BA Oxon, DL, JP W R Yorks, chm W R QS, Lt 14th Hus; *b* 1 Dec 1843; *m* 14 Feb 1871 Mary Elizabeth (*d* 6 May 1931), yr dau of Henry Yarborough Parker, of Streethorpe, Yorks, and *d* 4 April 1915, having had issue:

1d George Eustace, JP, of Campsmount; barrister Inner Temple, chm W R Sessions Doncaster; *b* 12 Jan 1876; *m* 5 Aug 1914 Daphne Isabel (*m* 2nd 6 July 1950 Capt Tadeusz Adam Gabriel Mincer (*d* 3 April 1969) and *d* 1984), yr dau of Henry Cordy Wrinch, and *d* 12 May 1938, leaving issue:

1e +Edmund Harry [Edmund Cooke-Yarborough Esq, Lincoln Lodge, Longworth, nr Abingdon, Oxon OX13 5DU]; *b* 25 Dec 1918; *educ* Canford Sch and Ch Ch Oxford (BA 1940, MA 1944); Dep Ch Scientist UKAEA, FEng, FIEE, FInstP; *m* 7 June 1952 *Anthea Katharine, er dau of John Alexander Dixon, of Whirlow, Hook Heath, Woking, by his w Beryl Roza Luis, yst dau of George Walker Luis Fernandes, of Haddon Lodge, Dorset, and has:

1f +Anthony Edmund [Anthony Cooke-Yarborough Esq, Barton House, Middle Barton, Oxon OX7 7DH]; *b* 6 Aug 1956; *educ* Eton and Gonville and Caius Coll Cambridge (MA); *m* 1990 *Joanna S, dau of Anthony Northrop, of Felgate Farm, Ashfield-cum-Thorpe, Stowmarket, Suffolk, and has issue:

1g +George Edmund; *b* 1991

1g *Eliza Flora; *b* 1993

1f *Jane Anthea [Mrs Giles Vicat, Woodbine Cottage, Bucknell, Bicester, Oxon OX6 9RS]; *b* 27 July 1958; *m* 1986 *Giles Vicat, er son of Alan Vicat, of Shoreham-by-Sea, Sussex, and has issue:

1g *Felix; *b* 1989

2g *Theodore; *b* 1993

2d Henry Alfred, AEI; *b* 27 March 1877; *m* 1916 Agnes Dagg (*d* 1949), and *d* 1947

3d Orfeur Frederic, ASI, Capt RAF; *b* 28 Nov 1878; *m* 9 Aug 1906 Anne Henrietta Lucy (*d* 4 May 1965), est dau of Rev William Wyatt, Rector Broughton, Lincs, and *d* 14 May 1965, leaving issue:

1e Bryan Orfeur Eustace; *b* 13 Sept 1907; *m* 1938 Ellen Martha (Nellie) (*d* 1974), er dau of John Myers, of Mount Silinda, Rhodesia, and *d* 1987 leaving issue:

1f +Edmund Orfeur [Edmund Cooke-Yarborough Esq, 160 Marimba Rd, Matsheumhlope, Bulawayo, Zimbabwe]; *b* 12 Feb 1940; *m* 1966 *Jennifer Anne, dau of Lt-Col John Winterton Scott, and has issue:

1g +David Jon Orfeur; *b* 1970

1g *Nichola Joan; *b* 1966; *m* 1987 *Roderick Young

1f *Rosemary Anne [Mrs Rodney Buckley, 60A Padfield Rd, Pinetown 3600, Natal, S Africa]; *b* 16 May 1945; *m* 1966 *Rodney Franklin Buckley, and has issue:

1g *Craige Franklin; *b* 1970

1g *Samantha Anne; *b* 1974

2f *Susan Mary; *b* 5 Aug 1951; *m* 1973 *Jacobus Petrus van Lelyveld, and has issue:

1g *Darren Richard; *b* 1974

1g *Tracy Lee; *b* 1977

2g *Sherryl Lyn; *b* 1979

2e Thomas Nicholas, RAF; *b* 18 Dec 1910; *m* 1940 *Elizabeth Thomson [Mrs Thomas Cooke-Yarborough, 6 Westbury Court, Hedge End, Southampton], dau of William Gilmore, of Edinburgh, and *d* 1991, leaving:

1f +Nicholas Michael; *b* 1941; *m* 1967 *Sheila, dau of R Symonds, of Southampton, and has issue:

1g *Sarah Louise; *b* 1969; *m* 19– *Stephen Searle and has:

1h *Harrison Thomas; *b* 7 Feb 1998

1h *Chloë; *b* 19–

2h *Elizabeth; *b* 19–

2g *Claire Elizabeth; *b* 1972

1e *Nancy Penelope Mary [Mrs George Wingate, Spicers, Newtown, Heytesbury, nr Warminster, Wilts BA12 0HN]; *b* 14 Nov 1912; *m* 5 Sept 1939 Lt-Col George Michael Donaldson Wingate, RA (*d* 1977), son of Lt-Col G F R Wingate, of Chesham, Bucks, and has issue:

1f *Elizabeth Anne; *b* 1940

2f *Sarah Penelope; *b* 1944; *m* 1964 Lt Michael R R Peever, RN (*d* 1982), and has issue:

1g *Richard Charles; *b* 1971

2e *Henrietta Rosemary Orfeur [Mrs William Smith, March Wall, King's Drive North, Caldy, Wirral, Cheshire L48 1LL]; *b* 13 Sept 1918; served in FANY; *m* 14 March 1944 Maj William Victor Smith, Lancs Yeo (RHA) (*d* 1994), slr, Liverpool, er son of R P Smith, of Lingdale Cottage, West Kirby, Cheshire, and has issue:

1f *Richard Orfeur Bateson [Richard Smith Esq, 12 Thurstaston Rd, Irby, Wirral]; *b* 1949; *m* 1984 *Vivien Dovey

1f *Rosemary Julia [Mrs John Cheshire, 14 Maes-y-Llan, Llanfairtalhaiarn, Clwyd]; *b* 1945; *m* 1972 *John Brian Cheshire, and has issue:

1g *Melissa Rosemary Jean; *b* 1972

2g *Alkana Susan; *b* 1978

4d Humfrey Charles, slr; *b* 24 Dec 1880; *m* 4 Oct 1911 Honor Lake (*d* 1977), 2nd dau of Col Henry Lake Wells, CIE, RE, and *d* 19 May 1955, having had issue:

1e Henry George Peter; *b* 13 July 1913; *d* 21 Feb 1914

2e Michael Humfrey; *b* 20 Sept 1915; architect; *m* 11 Dec 1942 Pamela (*d* 10 Aug 1996), yr dau of Sir John Baldwin, KCMG, CB, of Dumfries Aldeburgh, Suffolk, and *d* 29 May 1995, leaving:

1f *Ann [Mrs Ann Cooke-Yarborough, 36 Rue de Chabrol, 75010 Paris, France]; *b* 29 Sept 1944; *m* 9 Dec 1967 (*divorce* 1997, resumed maiden name) Alain Paul René Nérot, son of Georges Joseph Edme Nerot, of Paris, by Yvonne Monique Roger, and has issue:

1g *Alex; *b* 1975

1g *Lucie; *b* 1974

2f *Penelope [Mrs George Wallbridge, The Chapel, Roe Green, Sandon, Buntingford, Herts SG9 0QJ]; *b* 4 April 1946; *m* 1974 *George Roger Frank Wallbridge

3e +Steven Sandford [Steven Cooke-Yarborough Esq, 3555 Crystal Court, Miami, FL 33133, USA]; lb 26 June 1919; civil engr, late Capt RE; *m* 13 Oct 1941 *Evelyn, dau of Charles Buccleuch Scott, of Port-of-Spain, Trinidad, and has issue:

1f +Christopher [Christopher Cooke-Yarborough Esq, 6802 SW 64th Ave S, Miami, FL 33143, USA]; *b* 24 Dec 1949

2f +Nicholas [Nicholas Cooke-Yarborough Esq, 701 SE 51st Ave, Ocala, FL, USA]; *b* 1 April 1952; *m* 1983 *Tina, dau of Marco Sierra, of Miami, Florida, and has issue:

1g +Michael Charles; *b* 1988

1g *Stephanie Marie; *b* 1986

4e +Eustace [Eustace Cooke-Yarborough Esq, Spring House, Priors Way, Aldeburgh, Suffolk], industrial designer; *b* 22 Nov 1921; *m* 1981 *Patricia Marion Gardiner

5d Edmund Selwyn, WW I in 3rd Dragoon Gds; *b* 4 Feb 1882; *ka* 17 Nov 1914

6d Geoffrey Arthur; *b* 10 June 1883; *m* 1913 Grace, dau of William Knapp Cargill, and *d* 31 May 1946

1d Mary Alice; *d* unm 19 May 1969

2d Mary Violet; *d* unm 11 Nov 1965

2c Alfred; *b* 12 Aug 1847; *m* 1874 Mary (*d* 1919), dau of J Ferguson, and *d* 28 May 1925, having had issue:

1d Bryan Alfred; *b* 1877; *dsp* Nov 1921

2d Alfred Graeme, MBE (1955); *b* 1879; *m* 1911 Charlotte Elsie, dau of Robert Jarvie

3d Archibald George; *b* 1881; *dsp* July 1922

4d Randall Francis; *b* 1883; *m* 1917 Norma (*d* 1970), dau of George Downes, of Kohu Kohu, Hokianga, NZ, and *d* 1980, leaving issue:

1e *Pauline; *b* 17 Feb 1923; *m* 1947 *Raymond Leslie Gerrard Rogers, son of Leslie Alexander Gerrard Rogers, of Nilgris, S India, and has issue:

1f *Sandra Frances; *b* 31 July 1956

2f *Diana Leslie; *b* 4 April 1958

1d Gertrude Mary

2d Mabel Christina Margaret; *m* 1912 George Andrewes (*d* 1948), and has issue

3d Mildred May; *m* 1917 Roland Octavius Philips (*d* 1944), and has issue

4d Ethel Winifred; *m* 1923 James Joseph Molloy, and has issue

3c Arthur, slr, Mayor Boston, Lincs, 1917–19; *b* 8 May 1852; *m* 20 June 1877 Ethel Constance (*d* 23 Sept 1935), dau of Rev William Rawlins Capel, vicar Bickenhill, Warwicks, and *d* 1 May 1933, having had issue:

1d Arthur Capel; *b* 22 Nov 1880; *d* 15 Oct 1924

2d Ethel Dorothy Marion; *d* unm 17 June 1965

2d Norah Gladys; *d* unm 30 Aug 1910

3d (Edith) Muriel

1c Julia Elizabeth; *m* 8 Feb 1872 William James Brown (*d* 17 Dec 1927), of Hermeston Hall, Old Cotes, Rotherham, and *d* 12 Nov 1917

2c Gertrude Flora; *m* 1884 Lyster Andrew Nolan, LRCSI, and *d* his widow, 23 April 1934, having had issue

2b Richard; *b* 19 Aug 1805; *m* 2 June 1842 Mary Utten (*d* 1891), dau of James Utten Easson, of Jamaica, and *d* 1889, leaving issue:

1c John Disney; *b* 19 Dec 1848; *m* 1st Mary (*d* 1896), dau of Ellis Hills; *m* 2nd 7 May 1898 Sarah Mary (*d* 10 March 1924), dau of N Keating, of Ballinastraw, Co Wexford, and *d* 11 April 1916

2c Richard; *b* 22 Aug 1851; *m* 4 Aug 1898 Cornelia Clara (*d* 24 Nov 1935), 2nd dau of John Dixon, CE, of Surbiton, and *d* 2 Jan 1907, leaving issue:

1d John Richard, Lt RGA; *b* 12 July 1899; *d* following a rail accident N Rhodesia 21 March 1948

2d Francis Michael; *b* 14 Aug 1904; *educ* King's Sch Canterbury; *m* 12 Sept 1933 Mary (*d* 9 June 1965), dau of Everett L Hudson, of Tyneholme, Beechgrove Rd, Newcastle-upon-Tyne, and *d* 27 Sept 1970, leaving issue:

1e +Richard Everett [Richard Cooke Esq, 2 Ramsay Ave, West Pymble, NSW, Australia]; *b* 14 May 1935; BSc (Hons), FAIAS (1983), Ag Offr to Bank of NSW; *m* 1960 *Sheila Margaret, dau of John Hugill, of Cumberland, and has issue:

1f *Helena Margaret [Mrs John Croker, 17 Constitution Hill, Dulwich Hill, NSW, Australia]; *b* 12 Sept 1960; BSc (Hons); *m* 1983 *John Robert Croker

2f *Claire Mary; *b* 9 April 1963

3f *Ruth Meryl; *b* 13 Dec 1967

1e *Jean Christine [Mrs Alan Martin, Dalmore, Greenhead, Mauchline, Ayrshire], AISTD; *b* 25 April 1937; *m* 22 Oct 1960 *Alan Keith Martin, BSc, PhD, ARIC, son of Leslie M Martin, of Bourton-on-the Water, Glos, and has issue:

1f *Colin Seath; *b* 7 Oct 1962

1f *Patricia Anne; *b* 27 Jan 1964

2f *Christine Fiona; *b* 7 Feb 1966

3f *Mary Kay; *b* 29 July 1967

2e *Mary Elizabeth [Mrs Robert Porteous, 65 Lyncroft Gdns, Hounslow, Middx], NNEB, ARSH; *b* 21 July 1942; *m* 27 March 1965 *Robert Alexander Porteous, yr son of Alexander Porteous, of Dawes Rd, London, and has:

1f *Alexander Michael; *b* 26 Aug 1967

2f *Robert James; *b* 19 Dec 1968

3c William Henry; *b* 31 Aug 1853; *m* 1883 Charlotte Georgina (*d* 22 Dec 1943), dau of Morgan Charles Chase, MCS, and *d* 23 Nov 1916, leaving issue:

1d Wilfred Ernest, Lt RE (SR) WW I; *b* 1887; *d* unm 12 Dec 1947

2d Geoffrey Michael, BA, Lt RE WW I, Croce di Guerra Italy; *b* 1888; *d* unm 14 Feb 1958

1d Constance Mary; *b* 18 April 1884; *d* unm Dec 1965

2d Dorothy Maud; *m* 12 May 1917 W/Cdr Harold Edward Mostyn Watkins, AFC, RD, RAF, and *dsp* 22 Jan 1954

4c John James (Rev), Hon Canon Winchester 1909–41, Rector Puttenham, Guildford, 1918–25; *b* 7 Oct 1855; *educ* Keble Coll Oxford (MA); *m* 19 June 1890 Emily (*d* 2 March 1947), dau of Richard Foster, of Homewood, Chislehurst, and *d* 1941, leaving issue:

1d Richard James; *b* 10 Sept 1901; *d* 18 April 1904

1d Margaret Hope; *b* 4 July 1891; *m* 19 Oct 1915 Herbert Prior Ingram (*d* 1943), er son of Henry Ingram, of Newcastle, and had issue:

1e *Margaret Jane [Mrs Peter Fraser, 51 Hertford Ave, East Sheen, London SW14]; *b* 13 Nov 1916; *m* 1945 *Peter Hallett Fraser, and has issue:

1f *Richard Thomas Yarborough; *b* 1951

2f *Robert Peter; *b* 1954

1f *Judy Rosemary; *b* 1947

2e *Rosamund Marion; *b* 11 May 1918; *m* 1944 *Alan Robson, and has issue:

1f *Anthony Prior; *b* 1946

1f *Alicia Ann; *b* 1950

2d *Mary Honor; *b* 18 Sept 1893; *m* 1st 29 Dec 1920 Laurence Hodgson Archer-Hind (*d* 20 March 1923), of Ovington Lodge, Northumberland; *m* 2nd 30 Jan 1928 Charles Ernest Augustine Jeffery, MBE (*d* 18 July 1964), son of Rev C Jeffery, of St John's, Newfoundland

3d Dorothea Alice; *b* 15 July 1897; *m* 25 April 1935 Richard Keith van Sickle (*d* 9 July 1961), of Schloss Marbach, Austria, and had issue

4d Jean Lily, memb Soc Scottish Women Artists, author: *The Palm Sunday Case*; *b* 2 Feb 1900; *m* 12 Feb 1925 3rd Earl of Balfour (*qv*), and had issue

5d *Elizabeth Serena [Mrs Elizabeth Jackson-Taylor, 9 Belgravia Ho, Halkin Place, London SW1]; *b* 9 April 1904; *m* 21 April 1927 (*divorce* 1941) S/Ldr Philip Stuart Jackson-Taylor, RAF (*ka* 1945)

1c Mary Emily; *d* unm 29 May 1905

2c Avis Frederica; *m* 11 June 1873 John Hooke, of Croydon, and *d* 25 Oct 1917, leaving issue

3c Julia Louisa Elizabeth; *m* 1886 Louis Michael Simon (*d* 13 May 1901), of Croydon, and *d* 22 April 1937, having had issue

3b Charles, CB, of Woodlands, Camden Park, Col 91st Regt; *b* 25 June 1807; *m* 1st 28 Nov 1853 Flora Emily Sophia (*d* 5 Jan 1855), dau of David Grant, of Forres, and had issue:

1c Sophia Flora, OBE (1918); *m* Sept 1887 Col Grey Townsend Skipwith, RE Bengal Presidency (*d* 12 Aug 1900), and *d* 19 Dec 1940, leaving issue (*see* SKIPWITH, Bt)

3b (cont.) Charles Cooke *m* 2nd 5 June 1859 Esther Anne (*dsp* 14 July 1894), dau of Rev Alexander Cooke, of Loversall Hall, Doncaster (*see* below), and *d* 1891

2a Alexander Cooke (Rev), of Lovershall Hall, Rector Warmsworth, Vicar Arksey, Yorks; *b* 12 Jan 1767; *m* 10 Sept 1811 Catherine Esther (*d* 21 Sept 1870), dau and coheir of Samuel Buck, of New Grange, Recorder Leeds, and *d* 14 June 1849, leaving issue:

1b Samuel Alexander; *b* 1 Feb 1814; *m* Mary, dau of John Robinson, of Loversall, and *d* 15 June 1853, leaving issue:

1c Frederick; *b* 23 June 1850; *d* 1890

1b Esther Anne; *m* 5 July 1859 her cousin Col Charles Cooke-Yarborough, CB (*see* above), and *dsp* 14 July 1894

3a George, of Carr Ho, Doncaster; *m* 26 May 1803 Mary (*d* 17 May 1840), dau of William Hamilton, of London, and *d* 14 Oct 1842, leaving surv issue three daus

3 Henry

4 Godfrey

5 William

6 Alexander

7 John, of Doncaster; *m* Margaret (*bur* 24 June 1771), dau of Rev Francis Mosley, and was *bur* 20 Jan 1767, leaving:

(1) George (Rev), Rector Darfield; *m* Mary, dau of Henry Hollings, of Horton Hall, Yorks, and had:

1a Henry (Rev), Rector Darfield; *m* 1st Mary, dau of John Bowen, of Woodbridge Hall, Suffolk, and had issue:

1b Henry Bowen (Rev), LLD, Rector Darfield; *b* 29 March 1797; *m* 1st 27 June 1822 Juliana Mary (*d* 1 Sept 1859), dau of William R L Serjeantson, and had issue; *m* 2nd 29 Sept 1864 Georgina Helena Elizabeth (*dsp* 24 March 1915), dau of George Whigham, of Allanton and Halliday Hill, and *d* 27 Feb 1879

1a (cont.) The Rev Henry Cooke *m* 2nd Elizabeth, dau of — Cope, and *d* 1842, having by her had issue:

1b Emily Elizabeth; *m* Rev Thomas R Langhorne (*d* 1891), and *d* 1905

(2) Brian, of Doncaster; *m* Elizabeth, dau of W M Darwin, MD, and *d* 29 March 1786, leaving:

1a William Brian Darwin, of Alverley Grange, Yorks; *b* July 1764; *m* Oct 1794 Catherine, dau of John Griffith, and *d* 26 April 1823, leaving issue:

1b John Francis, of Alverley Grange, HEICS; *b* 8 Sept 1800; *d* 1885

2b Brian William Darwin, Capt Bengal Army; *b* July 1806; *m* 21 July 1835 Harriette, dau of Charles Scott, of Helstone, and *d* 1850, leaving issue:

1c Brian William Darwin; *b* 1837

2c Charles Edward, AMICE; *b* 1846; *m* 1874 Marian Elizabeth (*d* 1936), dau of Rev Arthur Guyon Purchas, and *d* 1929, having had issue:

1d Arthur Charles Darwin, Capt NZ Forces WW I; *b* 1876; *m* 1913 Muriel (*d* 16 Sept 1958), er dau of Leonard Brownlow Horrocks, and *d* 23 Aug 1963, leaving issue:

1e +David Charles Darwin; *b* 1917; Lt NZ Forces WW II; *m* 1944 *Phyllis Edith, dau of Capt Arthur Henry Prosser, OBE, and has issue:

1f +Richard Charles Darwin; *b* 1947; *m* 1972 *Dorothy Jane, dau of Eric George Woollams

1f *Elizabeth Angela Darwin; *b* 1948; *m* 1970 *Martin John Beattie, LLB, and has issue:

1g *James Brian David; *b* 1976

1g *Rosemary Ann; *b* 1971

2g *Amanda Jane; *b* 1973

1d John Alfred Selwyn; *b* 1881; *d* unm 1903

2d Philip Bryan, Transport Offr HMS *Tahiti* WW I; *b* 1886; *m* 1st 1909 Florence Alma (*d* 5 June 1950), dau of James Leamy, of Vancouver, BC, and had issue:

1e +Bryan Edward; *b* 1910; Maj (res) Australian Forces WW II 1939–42 (POW); *m* 1st 1933 (*divorce* 1945) Margaret Ida (*d* 1965), dau of Walter Hiskens, of Melbourne, Australia, and has:

1f *Robin May [Mrs Robin Rickard, Ganamead, Rocks Crossing, via Mt George, 2424 NSW, Australia]; *b* 1936; *m* 1st 1956 (*divorce*1960) Michael Threlfall, son of M M Threlfall, of Sydney, NSW, and has issue:

1g *Philip; *b* 26 June 1957

1f (cont.) Mrs Robin Threlfall *m* 2nd 1961 (*divorce*1983) Bruce Arthur Rickard, and has further issue:

2g *Samuel Bruce; *b* 1962

3g *James Arthur; *b* 1963

4g *Nicholas Lancelot; *b* 1965

1e (cont.) Maj Bryan Cooke *m* 2nd 29 May 1946 *June Mary, dau of Arthur Tregea, of Strathfield, Sydney, NSW, and by her has issue:

2f *Elizabeth Alice [Mrs Robert Drury, 5 Crampton Court, West Lakes, Adelaide 5021, S Australia]; *b* 19 Jan 1948; *m* 1st 1966 (*divorce* 1979) John Curley, and has issue:

1g *Louise Alice; *b* 1967

2g *Amanda June; *b* 1970

3g *Penelope Anne; *b* 1971

2f (cont.) Mrs Elizabeth Curley *m* 2nd 1980 *Robert Michael Drury, and has further issue:

4g *Kathleen Bethal; *b* 1981

2d (cont.) Philip Cooke *m* 2nd Dec 1951 Katharine (*d* 1963), dau of Walter Price, of Westerly, RI, USA, and *d* 1968

1d Marion Hariette Olivia; *m* 1896 Hubert Pullen Burry, and had issue
1d Agnes Gertrude, MBE; *m* 7 Sept 1905 James Thomas Maling, OBE (*d* 15 Aug 1952), of Christchurch, NZ, and *d* 2 July 1967, leaving four sons and two daus
3d Amy Francis; *d* unm 1962
4d Ethelwynne Beatrice Victoria; *b* 1883; *m* 1911 William Martin Simcox (*d* 4 May 1957), est son of William Henry Simcox, of Forest Lakes, Otaki, NZ, and had three sons and two daus
5d Elsie Mary Emily, RRC; *m* 1920 Maj Lewis Clayton Timperley (*d* 27 Dec 1947), and had issue
6d Elaine Mildred
7d Vera Durelle; *m* 1926 Capt John Stuart Robertson, BEM, IA, and had a son and dau
1c Harriett; *m* 1857 Gen Philip Henry Farrell Harris, CB, IA (*d* 23 April 1913), son of Maj-Gen P Harris, Bengal Army, and *d* 20 March 1910, leaving issue
2c Maria Jane Durrell; *m* 1861 Maj-Gen Robert Nixon Tronson, Bengal SC (*d* 9 Nov 1882)
3b William Augustus, Lt-Col Bengal Army; *b* 14 May 1808; *d* unm 1 June 1864
4b Charles (Rev), Rector Withycomb, Somerset; *b* 8 March 1810; *m* 17 March 1859 Charlotte (*d* 1916), dau of Rev Samuel Medlicott, and *d* 1887, leaving issue:
1c Charles Herbert (Rev), Vicar Stourpaine, Dorset, RD Blandford 1923–27; *b* 4 Oct 1862; *m* 1890 Ida Beatrice (*d* 11 Dec 1941), dau of Rev G F Armstrong, and *d* Aug 1946, leaving issue:
1d Lancelot Darwin, MA Oxford 1921, Capt 5th Bn Dorset Regt (T); *b* 17 Aug 1891 (twin); *m* 29 July 1922 Edith Euphemia Catherine (Halimah), dau of Maj Allan Ewen Grant, IMS, and *d* 1975 leaving issue:
1e Charles Bryan; *b* 31 July 1925; MA Oxford; *m* 3 July 1952 *Vajira Wijesinghe Kannangara, of Ceylon, and *d* 1975 leaving:
1f +Arjuna Bryan [Arjuna Cooke, 21/9 Polhengoda Gdns, Colombo 5, Sri Lanka]; *b* 27 Sept 1953; BSc (Eng) (Sri Lanka), AMIEE (London); *m* 1990 *Ramyamala Dhana Lakshmie Gunawardane
1e *Sheila Beatrice [Mrs John Nelson, 6630 Linda Vista Rd, Apt 3, San Diego, CA 92111, USA]; *b* 7 June 1923; *m* 1943 Capt J A Nelson, Medical Corps US Army (*d* 1963), and has issue:
1f *James Darwin; *b* 26 June 1946
2f *Lance Edward; *b* 8 Sept 1947
3f *Richard Crosby; *b* 22 Dec 1949; *m* 1973 *Nancy Mack and has:
1g *Colin Douglas; *b* 1981
1g *Dael Byrony; *b* 1978
1d Grace Dorothy; *m* 25 Aug 1931 Samuel Nevill Neild, only son of H W Neild
2d Ida Muriel; *d* unm 19 Feb 1953
3d *Marjorie Sheila; *m* Thomas Murray MacDougall, OBE, MC
4d Barbara Helen; *b* 19 April 1902; *educ* St Anne's Coll Oxford (MA 1936)
5d *Betty Mary; *m* 14 Sept 1929 Louis Dennis Martin, MA, son of S A Martin, of Teddington, Middx, and has had issue:
1e *Patrick Graeme [Patrick Martin Esq, Midleton Park, Cobh, Co Cork, Ireland]; *b* 26 June 1930; *m* 24 Sept 1964 *Margaret Mary Hester, dau of Samuel John Whitaker, of Coolbeg, Glanmire, Co Cork, and has issue:
1f *Richard Louis; *b* 1 Sept 1966
1f *Sarah Jean; *b* 28 June 1965
1e Bridget Jean (twin); *b* 26 June 1930; *d* 3 June 1951
6d *Elinor Beatrice
2c Henry D'Arcy Medlicott, Capt Res of Offrs The Queen's Roy Regt; *b* 1875; *m* 1914 Helen Elizabeth (*d* 8 Oct 1961), dau of Stephen Hall, of Jesmond, Newcastle-upon-Tyne, and *d* 1960, leaving issue:
1d *Vivienne Madge; *b* 1915; *m* 1943 Maj-Gen Sir (Wilfrid) John Potter, KBE, CB, Col Cmdt RCT, son of Maj Benjamin Henry Potter, OBE, MC, and has issue:
1e *Simon Michael John; *b* 9 Aug 1950
1e *Jacqueline Vivienne; *b* 19 March 1944
1c Ada Jeanette
2c Helen Isabella
3c Agnes Mary; *m* 1889 Robert Sanderson, MB Oxford, MRIS, Capt RAMC (TF), of Little Houghton, N Lancing, Sussex, and had issue
4c Julia May; *m* 1898 Rev William Maynard Raymond, MA, son of Rev Charles Raymond, of Bray, and had issue
1 Diana
2 Elizabeth

Sir GEORGE *d* 5 Oct 1732; his est son,

Sir Bryan Cooke, 4th Bt, MP Retford 1711–18; *bapt* 17 Dec 1684; *m* Priscilla (*bur* 22 June 1731), dau and coheir of Robert Squire, MP, and *d* 25 Oct 1734, leaving:
1 **Sir George Cooke, 5th Bt**, High Sheriff 1739; *m* Catherine, dau and coheir of John Sunderland, of Doncaster, and *d* 16 Aug 1756 leaving two daus
2 **Sir Bryan Cooke, 6th Bt**; *m* Mary, dau of Col Foley, and *d* 1769, leaving an only son:
(1) **Sir George Cooke, 7th Bt**, of Wheatley, Col 3rd Bn W York Militia; *m* 1st 1770 Frances Jory (*d* 1796), dau of Sir John Lambert Middleton, 4th Bt (*qv*), of Belsay Castle, Northumberland; *m* 2nd —, widow of Thomas Hewett, of Bilham, and dau of James Farrer, and *d* 2 June 1823, having by his 1st w had (with a dau, Frances, *m* Rev John Ramsden, *see* RAMSDEN, Bt) a 2nd son:
1a **Sir William Bryan Cooke, 8th Bt**, offr Foot Gds; *b* 3 March 1782; *m* 8 April 1823 Isabella Cecilia Viviana (*d* 25 Nov 1869), yst dau of Sir William Middleton, 5th Bt (*qv*), of Belsay Castle, Northumberland, and had issue:
1b WILLIAM RIDLEY CHARLES (Sir), **9th Bt**
2b Charles Edward Stephen, JP, Lt-Col Yorks Yeo Cav; *b* 1 Aug 1829; *m* 13 Aug 1874 Lady Mary Louisa Stewart (*d* 23 Feb 1929), 2nd dau of 9th Earl of Galloway (*qv*), and *dsp* 21 Oct 1895
1b Louisa Janetta; *d* 12 July 1838
2b Isabella Cecilia; *d* unm 28 Dec 1904

The 8th Bt *d* 24 Dec 1851; his er son,

Sir William Ridley Charles Cooke, 9th Bt, DL, Capt 7th Hus; *b* 5 Oct 1827; *m* 1st 17 April 1855 (*annulled* 1863) his cousin Harriet Eloise, dau of Rev Jonathan Trebeck, vicar Melbourne, Cambs; *m* 2nd 27 April 1871 Blanche Harriet Juanita Georgina (*d* 24 Feb 1930), yst dau of Sir William Henry Feilden, 2nd Bt (*qv*), and had issue:
1 WILLIAM HENRY CHARLES WEMYSS (Sir), **10th Bt**
2 Arthur Gordon Wyatt; *b* 1876; *educ* Radley; *m* 5 Oct 1905 Blanche Elia Catherine (*d* 14 Feb 1949), dau of Charles Eldon Clarke, of Newtown Ho, Thurles, Co Tipperary, and *d* 29 April 1969, leaving issue:
(1) William Bryan, Capt IA, tea planter; *b* 15 July 1909; *m* 13 May 1959 *Marion June, yr dau of Maj Mervyn H Corsellis, and *d* 1974 leaving issue:
1a *Marion Nathalie COOKE; *b* 27 Dec 1960; MA 1983, MA 1987, PhD 1990; Assist Prof English Dept McGill U; retained maiden name after marriage; *m* 1984 *Samuel Altman, LLB, MBA, of Toronto, Canada, and has issue:
1b *Jordan Saul Cooke; *b* 1988
2b *Bryan Jeremy; *b* 1990
3b *Simon Zev; *b* 1993
(1) *Blanche Elia Ruby; *b* 4 Feb 1908; *m* 18 Jan 1933 Rev John Bernard White, CF, Chaplain to Compañia Petrolera Lobitos, Lobitos, Talara, Peru, and has issue:
1a *Anthony John [Anthony White Esq, 730 Wharncliffe Rd, Duncan, Vancouver Is, BC, Canada]; *b* 28 Sept 1938
2a *Jeremy Nicholas [Jeremy White Esq, 1461 Harwood St, 501 Vancouver, BC, Canada]; *b* 23 Sept 1940; *m*
1 Ruby Blanche Juanita; *b* 3 June 1879; *d* unm 21 July 1950

The 9th Bt *d* 27 Sept 1894; his er son,

Sir William Henry Charles Wemyss Cooke, 10th Bt, High Sheriff 1903, DL (W R Yorks); Lt Yorks Dragoons, T/Lt E Kent Regt; *b* 21 June 1872; *m* 1st 15 July 1902 (*divorce* 1925) Lady Mildred Denison (ld 25 Jan 1953), yst dau of 1st Earl of Londesborough (*qv*), and had issue:
1 William Francis Henry; *b* 29 Sept 1903; *m* 5 June 1946 *Irene Mary (*m* 3rd — Herbert), widow of Capt O Bellingham-Smith, and *d* 12 March 1950, leaving issue:
(1) *Patricia Irene Mildred; *b* 24 June 1949
2 CHARLES ARTHUR JOHN (Sir), **11th Bt**

Sir William *m* 2nd 6 Aug 1927 Margaret (*d* 11 March 1964), dau of Richard Ross, and by her had issue:
1 *Elizabeth Hera; *b* 2 Oct 1928; *m* 7 May 1968 G/Capt Cecil Edgar Arthur Garton, RAF, son of Leopold Frederick Garton, of Worcester, and has issue:
(1) *Patrick William; *b* 1969
(1) *Dorothy Margaret; *b* 1970

The 10th Bt *d* 11 June 1964; his only surv son,

Sir Charles Arthur John Cooke, 11th Bt; *b* 12 Nov 1905; *educ* Wellington and RMC Sandhurst, Maj 4th/7th Dragoon Gds WW II 1939–40 (POW); *m* 12 July 1932 Diana (*d* 1989), only dau of Maj-Gen Sir Edward Maxwell Perceval, KCB, DSO, JP, of The Grange, Farnham, Surrey, and *d* 5 July 1978, having had issue:
1 Sir DAVID WILLIAM PERCEVAL COOKE, **12th and present Bt**
1 *Amanda Norah Mildred [Mrs Robert Watson, 15 Bilton Grove Ave, Harrogate, N Yorks]; *b* 14 June 1939; *m* 1st 10 Oct 1964 (*divorce* 1970) David Hervey Old, son of Frederick Hervey Old, of The Croft, Trevone, Cornwall; *m* 2nd 1975 *Robert W Watson (*d* 1982), FAIA, FCIS, FFAA, FBAA, FCommA, FRES, and by her 1st husb has issue:
(1) *Amanda Mary Perceval; *b* 21 June 1966

COOKE OF ISLANDREAGH

Creation: B. (LP, UK) 1992.

THE BARON COOKE OF ISLANDREAGH, of Islandreagh, Co Antrim (Victor Alexander Cooke, OBE 1981, DL (Co Antrim 1970)) [The Rt Hon The Lord Cooke of Islandreagh OBE DL, House of Lords, London SW1A 0PW]; *b* 18 Oct 1920; *educ* Marlborough and Trin Coll Cambridge (MA); Lt (E) RN 1940–46; Henry R Ayton Ltd Belfast 1946–89 (Chm 1970–89), chm: Springvale EPS 1964–, Belfast Savings Bank 1963, Harland & Wolff Ltd 1980081 (dir 1970–87); dir NI Airports 1970–85; Memb Senate NI Parl 1960–68, NI Ec Cncl 1974–78; Commr: Belfast Harbour 1968–79, Irish Lights 1983– (Chm Commrs 1990–92); CEng, FIMechE; *m* 1951 *Alison Sheila, only dau of Maj-Gen Francis Casement, DSO, of Craigtara, Ballycastle, Co Antrim, and has issue:
1 *Michael John Alexander; *b* 1955; *educ* Marlborough and Van Mildert Coll Durham (BSc); *m* 1983 *Anne Helen Madeleine, est dau of Maj Michael Henry Armstrong, MBE, DL, of Dean's Hill, Co Armagh, and has issue:
(1) *Robert Michael James; *b* 1990
(1) *Helen Frances Alice; *b* 1985
(2) *Katharine Mary Elizabeth; *b* 1987
(3) *Susannah Madeleine Jane; *b* 1993
2 *James Victor Francis; *b* 1960; *educ* Marlborough, Trin Coll Cambridge (MA) and Cranfield Business Sch (MBA)

1 *Victoria Sally; *b* 1956; *educ* Cobham Hall, Marlborough and Edinburgh U (MA); *m* 1982 *Nicholas Patrick yst s of Cdr Philip Evelyn Yonge, OBE, DSC, RN (ret), and has issue:

(1) *Cyprian Alexander; *b* 1990

(2) *Charlotte Emma Rosaleen; *b* 1988

Lineage: (NORMAN) VICTOR COOKE; *m* Alice Harman Peavey and had:

VICTOR ALEXANDER, *cr* a **Baron**

COOKE OF THORNDON

Creation: B. (LP, UK) 1996.

THE BARON COOKE OF THORNDON, of Wellington in New Zealand and of Cambridge in the County of Cambridgeshire (Sir Robin Brunskill Cooke, KBE (1986), PC (1977)) [The Rt Hon The Lord Cooke of Thorndon KBE PC, House of Lords, London SW1A 0PW]; *b* 9 May 1926; *educ* Wanganui Collegiate Sch, Victoria U Coll Wellington, Clare Coll Cambridge and Gonville and Caius Coll Cambridge (Resident Fell 1952–56, Hon Fell 1982); barrister Inner Temple 1954, Hon Bencher 1985, practised NZ Bar 1955–72, QC 1964, Judge Supreme Court 1972–76, Pres W Samoa Court Appeal 1982 and 1994– and Cook Islands 1981 and 1982, Judge Fiji Supreme Court 1995–, memb Internat Commn Jurists 1993–, special status memb American Law Inst 1993–; ktd 1977; Hon LLD Victoria U Wellington 1989 and Cambridge 1990; Hon DCL Oxford 1991; *m* 1952 *Phyllis Annette Miller and has three sons

Lineage: PHILIP BRUNSKILL COOKE, MC, Judge Supreme Court; *m* Valmai Digby Gore and had:

ROBIN BRUNSKILL (Sir), *cr* a **Baron**

COOPER of Gadebridge

Arms: Vert a fess embattled or between two pheons in chief, points downwards, and in base two human thigh-bones in saltire arg.
Crest: Out of a mural crown arg. a demi-spear erect ppr., fringed or, pointed arg., surmounted of two palm branches in saltire vert.
Motto: *Nil magnum nisi bonum* ('Nothing is great that is not good').
Creation: Bt. (UK) 31 Aug 1821.

SIR PATRICK GRAHAM ASTLEY COOPER, 6TH BT, of Gadebridge, Herts [Sir Patrick Cooper Bt, The White Cottage, 3 Townside, Haddenham, Aylesbury, Bucks HP7 8BG]; *b* 4 Aug 1918; *s* kinsman 1959; *educ* Marlborough; WW II 1939–40 with RA 52 AA Bde (TA) (invalided); QALAS 1949, Sr Assist Land Commr Min Ag and Fisheries 1950–59, joined Crendon Concrete Co Ltd 1959 (dir 1973–83); *m* 7 April 1942 *Audrey Anne Jervoise, yr dau of Maj Douglas Philip Jervoise Collas, Mil Kt Windsor, and has issue:

1 +ALEXANDER PASTON ASTLEY [Alexander Cooper Esq, 8 Berkshire Close, Leigh-on-Sea, Essex SS9 4RJ]; *b* 1 Feb 1943; *educ* Kelly Coll; *m* 1974 *Minnie Margaret, dau of Charles Harrison

1 *Patricia Ann Astley [Mrs Michael Snodin, 28 Leybourne Park, Kew, Surrey]; *b* 13 March 1950; *educ* Malvern Girls' Coll and UEA; *m* 1979 *Michael Robert Snodin and has issue:

(1) *Oliver Karl Astley; *b* 1985

2 *Helena Rosalind Collette Astley [Mrs Jonathan Holford, 76 King St, Maryport, Cumbria]; *b* 15 Sept 1958; *m* 1982 *Jonathan David Holford, and has issue:

(1) *Graham Richard Desmond; *b* 1984

(1) *Diana Sophia; *b* 1986

Lineage: SAMUEL COOPER, of Norwich; *m* Henrietta Maria, gdau of Thomas Newton (by Mary (*m* 2nd Sir Thomas Jermyn, of Rushbrook, and *d* 19 Sept 1679), dau of Edward Barber, of Bury), and Lady of the Manor of Edgefield Ellingham; gf of:

Rev SAMUEL COOPER, DD; Rector Great Yarmouth, Yelverton and Morley; *m* 1761 Maria (*d* July 1807), dau and heir of James Bransby, of Shottisham, Norfolk, by Anna Maria, dau and eventually heir of James Paston, of Harleston, and *d* 8 Jan 1800, leaving, with another son:

1 Robert Bransby, MP Gloucester 1818–29; *b* 21 Feb 1762; *m* 6 May 1784 Anne (*d* 20 Sept 1804), dau and heiress of William Purnell, of Dursley, and *d* 10 May 1845, leaving, with other issue:

(1) Purnell Bransby COOPER later PURNELL (roy licence 22 Feb 1805), of Stancombe Park, Glos

(2) Robert Jermyn (Rev), Rector W Chiltington; *b* 2 Nov 1795; *m* 8 Sept 1817 Arabella, dau of Edward Wallington, and *d* 19 May 1873, leaving, with two daus:

1a Robert Jermyn (Rev), Vicar Fylingdales, Yorks, MA Oxford; *b* 12 July 1830; *m* 27 Sept 1857 Fanny, dau of Robert Hicks, and had issue

(1) Henrietta Maria; *m* Maj Henry Heathcote, 88th Regt, 2nd son of Sir Henry Heathcote (*see* HEATHCOTE, Bt)

2 Samuel Lovick (Rev), Rector Ingoldesthorpe and Barton, Norfolk; *b* 4 Feb 1763; *m* 29 Nov 1787 Sarah Leman (*d* 13 March 1823), dau of Thomas Rede, of Letheringham Abbey, Suffolk, by Theophila, heiress of William Leman, and *d* 2 June 1817, leaving with other issue:

(1) Bransby Blake, FRS; *b* 2 Sept 1792; *m* 21 May 1816 Mary Anne, only dau of John Keeling. She *d* 21 Jan 1868. He *d* 18 Aug 1853, leaving with other issue:

1a Bransby Henry, HEICS; *b* 13 July 1820; *m* 7 Aug 1840 Marianne, dau of Thomas Bruce Swinhoe. She *d* 26 Aug 1865. He *d* 9 Nov 1857, leaving issue:

1b Bransby Beauchamp; *b* 15 March 1844; *m* 9 Sept 1875 Helen Ormsby, dau of Rev G Wilkinson

1b Mary Edith; *m* 17 Dec 1872 Freeman H Jackson, and had issue

2a Astley Paston; *b* 15 Dec 1827; *m* 17 Jan 1856 Elizabeth (*d* 3 April 1907), dau of Thomas Crofts, and *d* 11 Aug 1901, leaving:

1b Mary Florence Astley

1a Henrietta; *m* 15 Nov 1859 Gen George Staunton, CB (*d* 4 April 1880), and had issue

(2) Robert COOPER later REDE (roy licence 17 Sept 1822) (Rev), of Ashmans, Suffolk; *b* 10 April 1794; *m* 17 Nov 1821 Louisa (*d* 16 Oct 1870), dau and coheir of B Henshaw, of Moor Park, Essex, and *d* 13 April 1852, leaving issue:

1a Louisa Charlotte; *m* 22 March 1845 Capt Frank Fowke, and *d* 30 Nov 1874, leaving issue. He *d* 4 Dec 1865

2a Anne Cooper; *m* 5 Aug 1846 R O Buckley, and 5 Oct 1891, leaving issue

3a Marian Sarah; *m* 10 Jan 1850 Charles Henry Tottenham, and *d* 13 Feb 1893, leaving issue. He *d* 10 April 1871

4a Madeline Nainton; *m* 26 Jan 1859 Adml T P Thompson (*d* 5 March 1892)

(3) ASTLEY PASTON (Sir), **2nd Bt**

(4) Thomas Lovick (Rev), Rector and Patron Mablethorpe, Lincs, Rector Empingham, Rutland; *b* 3 Sept 1802; *m* 1st 18 June 1821 Emily Mary Swinfen (*d* 1 Aug 1838), only dau of Sir T Durrant, Bt, of Scottow, Norfolk (*qv*), and by her had a son:

1a Lovick Emilus, offr Rifle Bde; *b* 29 Nov 1837; *ka* Lucknow 19 March 1858

(4) (cont.) The Rev Thomas Cooper *m* 2nd 15 July 1841 Harriette, est dau of Jacob Ricardo, and had by her a son and two daus

(1) Anne; *m* Charles Aston Key, MD, and had issue

(2) Frances Susanna; *m* 1st Frederick Tyrrell; *m* 2nd 2 Aug 1854 Sir Charles G Young, DCL, Garter King of Arms (*d* 31 Aug 1869), and *d* 21 Nov 1876

3 Beauchamp Newton; *b* 16 July 1764; *m* 31 July 1798 Frances (*m* 2nd 31 March 1807 Edward Morgan and *d* 8 Dec 1839), heiress of Rev James Adams, of Jenkins, Essex, and *d* 9 Nov 1802, leaving issue, with a dau:

(1) Charles Beauchamp (Rev), Rector Morley, Norfolk, MA; *b* 31 Jan 1803; *m* 31 July 1829 Harriet (*d* 6 Jan 1866), dau of G D Harvey, and *d* 21 Jan 1878, leaving issue:

1a Charlotte Elizabeth; *m* 23 April 1863 Rev Frederick Blackett de Chair, JP, est son of Rev Frederick de Chair, Rector E Langdon, Kent, and Manton, Lincs, and *d* 1922, leaving issue. He *d* 23 Oct 1932

4 **Sir Astley Paston Cooper, 1st Bt** (UK), so *cr* 31 Aug 1821, with remainder, in default of male issue, to his n, Astley Paston; of Gadebridge, Herts; *b* 23 Aug 1768; surgn; *m* 1st 12 Dec 1791 Anne (*d* 10 June 1827), dau of T Cocks; *m* 2nd 5 July 1828 Catherine (*d* 8 Jan 1870), dau of J Jones, of Derry Ormond Park, Cards, and *dsp* 12 Feb 1841

1 Susanna Maria; *m* Henry Loftus Reade, of Rathbeg, Co Tipperary, only son of Capt Henry Reade, of Rathbeg, and *d* 3 Aug 1851

The 1st Bt's n,

Sir Astley Paston Cooper, 2nd Bt, High Sheriff Herts 1864; *b* 13 Jan 1798; *m* 29 Nov 1821 Elizabeth Harriet (*d* 6 Sept 1878), only child and heiress of William Rickford, MP Aylesbury, and *d* 6 Jan 1866, having had, with other issue:

1 Sir ASTLEY PASTON COOPER later PASTON-COOPER (roy licence 1884), **3rd Bt**, DL, JP Herts, High Sheriff 1885, JP Suffolk, Mayor Hemel Hempstead 1898–99, Capt Rifle Bde 1848, served Crimea (medal and clasp); *b* 23 Feb 1824; *m* 1st 7 Nov 1855 Etheldreda Julia (*d* 17 July 1888), dau of George Newton, of Croxton Park, Hunts, and had issue:

(1) George Frederick Paston, Capt 4th Bn Beds Regt; *b* 25 Jan 1861; *d* unm 11 Jan 1895

(2) Edmund Courtenay Astley Paston, Lt RN; *b* 10 Aug 1863; *m* 29 Dec 1887 Constance Mary (*m* 2nd 3 March 1898 Lt-Col Bertie St John Clarkson, CMG, DSO, Dorset Regt (*d* 24 Jan 1954), son of Thomas Hollingsworth Clarkson, Lancs Fus), est dau of Rt Hon Sir John Eldon Gorst, MP, and *dsp* 1 April 1892

(3) **Sir Charles Naunton Paston Paston-Cooper, 4th Bt**; *b* 27 Sept 1867; *m* 25 Jan 1899 Tatiana, only child of Prince Dmitri Dolgorouki, of Russia, and *dsp* 4 Dec 1941

(1) Margaret Paston; *d* unm 18 March 1923

(2) Mary Ethel Paston; *m* 29 Jan 1885 Lt-Col Lionel HERVEY-BATHURST later PASTON-COOPER (roy licence 7 Oct 1905), Rifle Bde, 2nd son of Sir Frederick Hervey-Bathurst, 3rd Bt (*qv*), and *d* 16 Aug 1931, leaving issue

1 (cont.) Sir ASTLEY *m* 2nd 12 Aug 1890 Sophia (*d* 4 Feb 1928), widow of Col John Stephenson Ferguson, 2nd Life Gds, and yst dau of John Holford, of Rusholme Hall, Lancs, and *d* 19 Oct 1904

2 William Rickford Astley (Rev), Vicar Froyle, Hants, 1864–76; *b* 21 Feb 1826; *educ* Univ Coll Oxford (MA); *m* 1st 3 Oct 1861 Elizabeth (Id 27 March 1864), 2nd dau of R-Adml Evan Nepean, and had issue; *m* 2nd 4 Nov 1869 Lucy Elizabeth (*d* 22 Oct 1923), dau of Rev J R Burgess, Vicar Streatley, and *d* 26 June 1876, having by her had issue:

(1) William Astley; *bapt* 3 May 1874; *dec*

(2) **Sir Henry Lovick Cooper, 5th Bt**; *b* 2 April 1875; *m* May Adams (*d* 1911) and *d* 25 Aug 1959, leaving:

1a *Lucy Elizabeth; *b* 1905

(1) Mary Elizabeth; *b* 11 Oct 1872; *d* unm 24 Aug 1950

3 Samuel Lovick Astley (Rev), MA, Rector Croxton and Vicar Eltisley, Cambs; *b* 16 Oct 1827; *m* 5 Dec 1855 Margaretta Sarah (*d* 21 July 1909), dau of Frederick Corbin Lukis, FRS, of The Grange, Guernsey, and *d* 1895, leaving issue:

(1) Ernest Henry Astley; *b* 22 Aug 1858; *m* 17 Feb 1903 Mary, widow of Percy William Charrington and only dau of Maj Beverley Randolph, of Millwood, Virginia, and *dsp* 1 Jan 1942

(2) Francis William Astley; *b* 16 Nov 1859; *m* 4 May 1897 Lyonesse Mathilda Dora (*d* 1944), dau of Rev Ralph William Lyonel Tollemache-Tollemache (*see* TOLLEMACHE, Bt), and *d* 1945, leaving issue:

1a Theodora Mary Astley

(3) Arthur Rickford Astley; *b* 8 May 1861; *m* 1890 Charlotte Emma (*d* 16 Aug 1945), dau of Richard Richards, and *d* 1950, having had issue:

1a Dorothy Lukis Astley; *m* 25 March 1916 Capt Anthony Laurence Carr, BA, only son of Canon Laurence Carter Carr, of Holbrooke Hall, Derbys, and Boscobel, Salop, and *d* 29 Nov 1949, leaving issue. He *d* 30 May 1963

(1) Edith Mary Astley; *m* 10 Oct 1899 Sydney Hawker Williams, of Hemingford Park, Hunts, and *dsp* 10 Oct 1947

4 Loftus Lewis Astley, Maj 98th Foot; *b* 29 Jan 1838; *m* 20 Aug 1874 Florence Louisa (*d* 4 July 1931), dau of Augustus Briggs, Speaker of Ho Assembly, Barbados, and *d* 24 Aug 1925, having had issue:

(1) Percy Beauchamp Astley, Lt-Cdr RN; *b* 17 Jan 1876; *ka* 4 May 1916 serving in the ranks E Kent Regt

(2) Lewis Vernon Astley, late Lt 3rd Bn DCLI; *b* 1878; *d* unm 18 April 1941

(3) Clifton Graham Astley, DSO (1917), Col RA; *b* 13 July 1881; *m* 21 Dec 1915 Ida Margaret Mary (*d* 2 Nov 1968 aged 81), dau of Henry Lumsden Forbes, of Invery, Guildford, and *d* 30 July 1951, having had issue:

1a Sir PATRICK GRAHAM ASTLEY COOPER, **6th and present Bt**

2a Donald Lewis Astley, Capt KRI Hus WW II; *b* 26 Dec 1920; *ka* nr Seoul Jan 1951

(1) Florence Winifred Astley; *m* 6 Sept 1905 Col William Arthur Travell Bowly, CVO, CBE, MC, Roy Warwicks Regt, son of Cdr J E Bowly, RN, and *d* 2 Feb 1962, leaving issue. He *d* 24 Oct 1957

(2) Gladys Astley; *m* 10 April 1907 Brig Colin Burton, CBE, DSO, late RASC, 2nd son of Edward P Burton, of East Molesey, Surrey, and *d* 18 Nov 1937, leaving issue. He *d* 4 May 1945

5 Albert Beauchamp Astley, Capt RA, JP Devon; *b* 14 Aug 1841; *m* 16 April 1879 Eva Cornelia (*d* 14 Dec 1917), yst dau of Anthony O'Reilly, of Baltrasna, Co Meath, and *d* 9 June 1921, leaving issue:

(1) Geoffrey Beauchamp Astley, OBE, Lt-Col IA; *b* 5 Feb 1884; *m* 1st 22 Dec 1911 Gladys Mary (*d* 26 Aug 1912), 3rd dau of Lt-Col Orbell Henry Oakes, of Nowton Court, Suffolk; *m* 2nd 17 Aug 1914 Louisa Maude (*d* 1972), 4th dau of Isaac William Hewitt White, of West Lea, Meanwood, Leeds, and *d* 5 March 1948, having by her had issue:

1a +Gerald Nigel Astley [Maj Gerald Cooper, Five Bells Cottage, Hessett, nr Bury St Edmunds, Suffolk], Maj 1st RGJ WW II; *b* 8 June 1916; *educ* Wellington; *m* 1st 19 July 1941 (*divorce* 1945) Mary Constance, dau of Capt Basil Hamilton Piercy, RN, and has issue:

1b *Juliet Jane [Mrs Peter Bellfield, The Old Rectory, Clopton, Woodbridge, Suffolk IP13 6QB]; *b* 20 April 1942; *m* 21 Nov 1964 *Peter Robert Bellfield, son of Ernest Robert Bellfield, of Creek Cottage, Budock Vean, Falmouth, Cornwall, and has issue:

1c *Robert James Astley; *b* 28 July 1965; *educ* Framlingham Coll; Lt-Cdr RN; *m* 1994 *Zoë, dau of Capt Thomas Le Marchand, RN, of Hasketon, Woodbridge, Suffolk, and has:

1d *Eleanor Charlotte; *b* 27 April 1997

2c *Charles Peter; *b* 12 Nov 1969; *educ* Uppingham

3c *Edward Jonathan; *b* 26 Jan 1972; *educ* Uppingham

1a (cont.) Maj Gerald Cooper *m* 2nd 26 July 1951 *Joan Ryland, est dau of Dr Bernard Wall, of Coleshill, Warwicks, and by her had issue:

1b +Desmond Beauchamp; *b* 19 April 1955; *educ* Wellington and St Peter's Coll Oxford; with Algo Saibi of Bahrain; *m* 1984 *Randa, dau of Dr Joseph Yammine, and has issue:

1c +Kimball; *b* 1986

2c +Joseph; *b* 1986

2b *Felicity Ann; *b* 20 Jan 1954; *educ* Roy Sch Bath and Durham U; *m* 1981 *Maj-Gen Anthony David Pigott, CBE, of Hessett, Bury St Edmunds, Suffolk, twin son of Lt-Col P J Pigott, of Bexhill-on-Sea, and has issue:

1c *James Anthony Alexander; *b* 1991

2c *Matthew Thomas Michael; *b* 1992

1c *Anna Louisa; *b* 1984

2a Geoffrey Desmond, Sub-Lt RN; *b* 29 Dec 1918; *ka* July 1940

1a *Rosemary Anne [Mrs Peter Lewis, Thedwastre, Thurston, Bury St Edmunds, Suffolk]; *b* 21 Aug 1920; *m* 21 Sept 1946 Lt-Col Peter Jarret Lewis, late The Buffs (*d* 1983), son of Maj Ernest Hastings Lewis, of Corstorphine, Ryde, IoW, and has issue:

1b *Virginia Rosemary; *b* 23 Oct 1949; *m* 1974 *Maj-Gen Roderick Alexander Cordy-Simpson, CB, OBE, Light Dragoons, and has issue:

1c *Angus John; *b* 1978

1c *Zoë Finovola; *b* 1976

(1) Olive Sylvia Beauchamp; *d* unm 29 April 1959

(2) Rosalind Beauchamp; *d* unm 27 March 1959

6 Clement Paston Astley, JP Herts, Capt 29th Foot; *b* 30 May 1845; *m* 10 July 1877 Evangeline Julia (*d* 19 Nov 1944), yst dau of George Marshall, of Portland Place, and sis of Walter Marshall, of Hambleton, and *d* 12 Feb 1927, leaving, with other issue:

(1) Stephen Clement Paston, Lt 3rd Bn London Regt; *b* 12 June 1885; *m* 1915 Florence Gertrude Taylor (*d* 1966), and *d* 30 Dec 1935, leaving issue:

1a Elizabeth Margaret; *m* 1st 7 Nov 1935 (*divorce* 1950, resumed maiden surname by deed doll 19 Dec 1967) Maj Roderick Walter Sholto Douglas, RAC (TA), son of Hon Archibald Roderick Sholto Douglas, of Loddington, Leicester (*see* MORTON, E), and had issue; *m* 2nd 1949 Sir Basil Antony Trevor Mostyn, 13th Bt (*qv*); *m* 3rd 1959 (*divorce* 1966) David George Longman

2a *Diana Susan [Mrs Clive Windsor-Richards, Golf Lodge, Steepways, Hindhead, Surrey GU26 6PQ]; *b* 1919; *m* 1st 8 Sept 1939 (*divorce* 1967) Cdr Cecil John Grenfell, RN, 2nd son of Lt-Col John Pascoe Grenfell, of The Rookery, Wymondham, Oakham (*see* GRENFELL, B); *m* 2nd 24 May 1969 *Clive Walter Edwin Windsor-Richards, and by her 1st husb has issue:

1b *John Stephen [Captain John Grenfell RN, 58 Heath Rd, Petersfield, Hants GU32 4EJ]; *b* 1940; Capt RN; *m* 1967 *Stephanie Ann, dau of Capt James Marigold, RN, and has issue:

1c *James Christopher; *b* 1969

2c *Nicholas Ian; *b* 1969

3c *Alaistar Mark; *b* 1974

2b *Richard Francis [Richard Grenfell Esq, 12 Grindlestone Court, Whittinghame Lane, Goosnargh, Lancs PR3 2AU]; *b* 1944; *m* 19– *Jennifer, dau of -

3b *Michael Gerrard; *b* 1947

1b *Sally Angela; *b* 1947; *m* 1980 *Francis Robert Gugen, and has issue:

1c *Lucy Francesca; *b* 1981

3a Monica Mary

4a *Pamela Jane [Mrs Pamela Anderton, Cheyne Lodge, Brook Rd, Wormley, Godalming, Surrey]; *b* 1921; *m* 29 Jan 1966 (*divorce* 1974) Lt-Cdr John Woolven Anderton, VRD, RNVR (ret), son of Edward Cooke Anderton, of Ainsdale, Lancs

(1) Phyllis Mary; *m* 28 Nov 1899 Lt-Col Leonard Temple Ashworth, RFA, of Hambleton, Oakham, son of Charles Frederick Ashworth, and *d* 28 Oct 1925. He *d* 22 March 1918

(2) Elizabeth Monica Astley, twin with her bro; *m* 23 July 1906 Humphrey Charles Walrond, son of Rev Main Swete Alexander Walrond, and *d* 18 March 1956, leaving issue. He *d* 29 Aug 1928

1a Elizabeth Harriette Astley; *m* 2 May 1854 Rev James Charles Wharton, Vicar Gilling, Yorks, and *d* 19 July 1913, leaving issue. He *d* 13 Sept 1900

2 Augusta Fanny Astley; *m* 25 April 1865 Rev Frederick Edward Horne, BD, Rector Drinkstone, Suffolk, son of Rev William Horne, MA, of Epping Ho, Herts, Vicar Baroning, Kent, and *d* 18 Aug 1919. leaving issue. He *d* 1913

3 Alice Louisa Astley; *m* 3 July 1876 Gilfrid George Baker Cresswell, JP, of Preston Tower, Chathill, 2nd son of Oswin Addison Baker Cresswell, of Harehope, Northumberland, and *d* 15 June 1936, leaving issue. He *d* 24 Jan 1943

COOPER of Shenstone

Arms: Erm. on a pile arg. three martlets, two and one sa., and on a chief gu. two boar's heads couped or. **Crest:** Between two sprigs of holly erect a lion's gamb, grasping in the paw a like sprig in bend sinister, all ppr. **Motto:** *Conata perficio* ('I complete things I have attempted'). **Creation:** Bt. (UK) 20 Dec 1905.

SIR RICHARD POWELL COOPER, 5TH BT, of Shenstone Court, Shenstone, Staffs [Sir Richard Cooper Bt, Lower Farm, Chedington, Beaminster, Dorset DT8 3JA]; *b* 13 April 1934; *s f* 1987; *educ* Marlborough; chm Rare Breeds Survival Tst 1978–80 and 1990–92; *m* 2 Oct 1957 *Angela Marjorie, er dau of Eric Wilson, of Norton-on-Tees, Durham, and has issue:

1 +RICHARD ADRIAN; *b* 21 Aug 1960; *educ* Millfield

1 *Jane Alice; *b* 25 July 1958

2 *Belinda Gay; *b* 29 Aug 1963

Lineage: HENRY COOPER, of Clunbury, Aston-on-Clun, Salop (son of William Cooper, of Clunbury, by Sarah -); *bapt* 7 Oct 1821; *m* 13 April 1844 Ann Mason and *d* 19 March 1876, leaving:

Sir Richard Powell Cooper, 1st Bt (UK), so *cr* 20 Dec 1905, of Shenstone Court, Shenstone, Staffs, DL, JP, High Sheriff 1901, memb Staffs CC 1892–1913, V-Pres Cncl Roy Ag Soc, MRCVS London 1868; *b* 21 Sept 1847; *m* 30 April 1872 Elizabeth Anne (*d* 30 Jan 1915), er dau of Elias Ashmole Ashmall, of Hammerwich, Lichfield, Staffs, and had issue:

1 RICHARD ASHMOLE (Sir), **2nd Bt**

2 William Francis, MB, BCh Cambridge, MRCS, LRCP; *b* 9 Jan 1878; *m* 1st 29 April 1914 Christine Maud (*d* 27 Feb 1919), yr dau of M Jones, of Earls Court, SW, and had issue:

(1) *Christine Elisabeth, OBE (1967), MB, BCh, FRCP, DCH, paediatrician Dept of Child Health, U of Newcastle-upon-Tyne, Consultant Paediatrician Govt of Sierra Leone; *b* 21 July 1918; *educ* Girton Coll Cambridge (MA)

2 (cont.) William Cooper *m* 2nd 27 March 1920 Eileen Beryl, dau of Percy J Hall, of Cambridge, and *d* 21 Dec 1950, having by her had issue:

(2) *Eileen Frances, Assoc Inst of Linguists; *b* 18 Aug 1921; *m* 1st 22 June 1944 (*divorce* 1948) her cousin, Maj Richard Philip Cooper, The Glider Pilot Regt, 2nd son of Sir Richard Ashmole Cooper, 2nd Bt (*see* below); *m* 2nd 1948 *G/Capt Gordon Slade, OBE, FRAES, 2nd son of William of Worthing, Sussex, and has had:

1a A son; *b* 25 July 1949; *d* an inf

2a *Patrick Charles Gordon; *b* 24 Nov 1955

3a *Jonathan Francis William; *b* 7 July 1958

1a *Elisabeth Mary Frances; *b* 28 Feb 1951

2a *Patricia Mary Ann; *b* 6 Oct 1952

(3) *Rosemary Anne, MA, MB, BCh Cambridge, MRCP; *b* 6 April 1925; *m* 14 Jan 1956 *Walter van t'Hoff, MA, MB, BCh, MRCP, son of Robert van t'Hoff, and has issue:

1a *William Gordon; *b* 21 Feb 1958

2a *Hugh Colin; *b* 4 April 1960

3a *Graham Robert; *b* 20 Dec 1961

1 Lucy Anne; *m* 30 March 1902 Brig-Gen Richard Mildmay Foot, CB, CMG, DSO, DL, Roy Inniskilling Fus, 3rd son of Rev Cunningham Noel Foot, BA Cantab, Rector Dogmersfield, and *d* 20 Sept 1946. He *d* 16 Oct 1933

2 Mary Mabel; *m* 19 May 1903 Kenward Stuart Barker, of Watchbury, Barford, Warwicks, er son of Christopher Dove Barker, of Radnor Ho, Gt Malvern, and *d* 5 March 1953, leaving issue. He *d* 8 Oct 1946

3 Edith Maud; *m* 20 July 1910 Lt-Col Robert Essington Negus, DL, JP, N Staffs Regt, er son of Thomas Addison Negus, of Shenstone Lodge, Lichfield, and *d* 2 Feb 1923, leaving issue. He *d* 5 May 1970

The 1st Bt *d* 30 July 1913; his er son,

Sir Richard Ashmole Cooper, 2nd Bt, MP Walsall 1910–22, JP Berkhamsted, Staffs Imp Yeo; *b* 11 Aug 1874; *m* 18 April 1900 Alice Elizabeth (*d* 12 Jan 1963), dau of Rev Edward Priestland, of Spondon, Derbys, by Lucy Mary, dau of Rev Thomas Gascoigne, and *d* 5 March 1946, leaving:

1 **Sir William Herbert Cooper, 3rd Bt**, JP (Herts 1957), High Sheriff 1956; *b* 7 March 1901; *educ* Wellington and Trin Coll Cambridge, Hon Pres (former Chm) Cooper McDougall and Robertson Ltd, Berkhamsted, Chm Ashmole Investment Tst, V-Pres Cncl Roy Smithfield Club (Pres 1964), MFH Herts 1927–38, WW II in Roy Observer Corps 1939–41 and RAF 1941–45; *m* 1 March 1948 Eileen Dolores Patricia, formerly w of W P George, of USA, and er dau of G P Hayes, of Dunloe Castle, Co Kerry, and *d* 8 June 1970

2 (Richard) Philip, TD (1949), barrister Inner Temple 1929, Maj Glider Pilot Regt WW II; *b* 26 July 1902; *educ* Malvern and King's Coll Cambridge (MA 1942); *m* 1st 22 June 1944 (*divorce* 1948) Eileen Frances, 2nd dau of Dr William Francis Cooper, of Hertcombe, Kingston (*see* above); *m* 2nd 21 July 1951 *Kathleen Duncan, widow of Edward Andreas Priestland and 3rd dau of W E D Knight, of Limuru, Kenya, and *dsp* 22 Aug 1966

3 **Sir Francis Ashmole Cooper, 4th Bt**, PhD London 1936, MIChemE; *b* 9 Aug 1905; *educ* Lancing and King's Coll Cambridge (MA 1942); *m* 8 July 1933 *Dorothy Frances Hendricka [Dowager Lady Cooper, Mas Folie, 320 Route de la Madeleine, 06140 Tourrettes S/Loup, France], dau of Emile Deen, of Berkhamsted Hill, Herts, and *d* 1987, having had issue:

(1) Sir RICHARD POWELL COOPER, **5th and present Bt**

(1) Elizabeth Sally Ann, BVSc, MRCVS; *b* 18 Sept 1936; *m* 30 June 1962 *Peter James Glendinning, 2nd son of Harold Whittingham Glendinning, of Little Hay, Berkhamsted, Herts

(2) *Jacqueline Margaret [Mrs Peter Flaherty, Glen Cottage, Butlers Dene Road, Woldingham, Surrey]; *b* 23 Aug 1939; *m* 28 Sept 1962 *Peter Desmond Flaherty, son of James Flaherty, of Dublin, and has issue:

1a *Andrew Niall; *b* 1970

1a *Sally Clodagh; *b* 27 June 1963

2a *Sheena Mary; *b* 8 Dec 1964

3a *Julia Siobhan; *b* 18 Oct 1966

(3) *Dione Frances; *b* 15 Aug 1944; *m* 1970 *Christopher Bruce Jones, of Ashmole, RD Manurewa, Auckland, NZ

COOPER of Woollahra

Arms: Az. a chevron engrailed between two lions passant in chief and a star of eight points in base or. **Crest:** A lion sejant or, collared az., supporting with the dexter paw a lance erect ppr., suspended therefrom by a chain gold an escutcheon also az, charged with a star, as in the arms. **Supporters:** Dexter, Faith, holding in the sinister hand a mullet of six points or; sinister, Hope, holding in the dexter hand a like mullet. **Motto:** *Perseverantia omnia vincit* ('Perseverance conquers all things'). **Creation:** Bt. (UK) 26 Jan 1863.

SIR WILLIAM DANIEL CHARLES COOPER, 6TH BT, of Woollahra, NSW [Sir William Cooper Bt, 1 Victoria Cottages, Andover Rd, Micheldever Station, Hants SO21 3AX]; *b* 5 March 1955; *s* f 1984; *educ* Northease Manor; dir The Garden Maintenance Service and GMS Vehicles; *m* 1988 *Julia Nicholson

Lineage: THOMAS COOPER, of Bolton-le-Moors, Lancs (son of Thomas Cooper); *b* 1759; *m* 1st Hannah Holt and had a son (Daniel, of Sydney, *dsp* 3 Nov 1853); *m* 2nd Ellen (*d* 21 Jan 1814), dau of Richard Haslam, and *d* 18 Feb 1824, having by her had issue:

THOMAS COOPER, of Sydney, merchant; *b* 13 Sept 1795; *m* 1814 Jane (*d* 29 Sept 1871), dau of Nathaniel Ramsden, and had, with other issue:

1 DANIEL (Sir), **1st Bt**

2 John; *b* 23 June 1829; *m* and had issue

3 James; *b* 13 Jan 1832; *m* 8 June 1853 Adelaide, dau of William Macdonald, and had issue

4 Charles; *b* 2 March 1835; *m* 17 July 1856 Anne, dau of Thomas Baker, and had a dau

1 Hannah; *m* 8 June 1838 John Robert Cropper, and had issue. He *d* 1871

2 Sarah; *m* 30 July 1844 James Booth, surgeon, of Montrose, Scotland, and had issue

THOMAS COOPER *d* 4 June 1866; his est son,

Sir Daniel Cooper 1st Bt (UK), so *cr* 26 Jan 1863, GCMG, first Speaker Legislative Assembly NSW 1856–60; *b* 1 July 1821; ktd 1857; *m* 3 Sept 1846 Elizabeth (*d* 1 April 1906), 3rd dau of William Hill, and *d* 5 June 1902, leaving:

1 **Sir Daniel Cooper 2nd Bt**, DL, JP Cambs, JP Suffolk; *b* 15 Nov 1848; *m* 12 July 1886 Harriet (*d* 25 April 1941), dau of Sir James Grant Suttie, 6th Bt, of Balgone (*qv*), and *d* 13 June 1909, leaving:

(1) Dorothy; *m* 22 July 1908 Col Henry Sidney John Streatfeild, DSO, TD, Gren Gds, only son of Col Sir Henry Streatfeild, GCVO, CB, DL, of Chiddingstone, Kent, and *d* 13 March 1961, leaving issue. He *d* 22 May 1949

(2) Hilda Susan Ellen; *m* 1st 12 June 1912 Viscount Northland, only s of 5th Earl of Ranfurly (*qv*), and had issue; *m* 2nd 26 Feb 1917 Hon Geoffrey Edward Mills, s of 1st Baron Hillingdon (*d* 14 Aug 1917; *see* 1970 edn); *m* 3rd 30 April 1918 (*divorce* 1929) Capt John Stewart Michael Wardell, 10th Hus, only son of Harold Wardell, of Nannau, Dolgelly, N Wales, and had further issue; *m* 4th 24 April 1929 Julien Joseph Lezard, est s of Louis Flavien Lezard, of 49 Hallam St, W1, formerly of Kimberley, S Africa, and had further issue. He *d* 31 Aug 1958

2 WILLIAM CHARLES (Sir), **3rd Bt**

1 Ellen Sophia; *d* 6 June 1922

2 Alice Jane; *m* 9 July 1868 Sir Frederick Green, KBE, JP, of Oaklawn, Wimbledon Park, and *d* 24 June 1927, leaving issue. He *d* 18 Feb 1927

3 Mary Elizabeth; *m* 29 April 1886 William Palfrey Burrell, barrister, Consul Port Said, and *d* 2 Nov 1931, leaving issue. He *d* 1919

4 Florence Eva; *m* 10 June 1882 Hugh Arundell Trevanion, only son of Hugh Charles Trevanion by Lady Frances, sis of 13th Earl of Strathmore and Kinghorne (*qv*), and *d* 3 March 1916, leaving issue. He *d* 25 Feb 1918

5 Elizabeth Edith; *m* 25 April 1883 Henry Valentine Macnamara, DL, JP, of Doolin and Ennistymon Ho, Co Clare, and *d* 20 Oct 1944, leaving issue. He *d* 30 Oct 1925

The 2nd Bt's bro,

Sir William Charles Cooper 3rd Bt, JP Northants; *b* 22 Oct 1851; *m* 18 Nov 1876 Alice Helen (*d* 2 Aug 1937), 3rd dau of George Hill, of Surrey Hills, Sydney, NSW, and had issue:

1 WILLIAM GEORGE DANIEL (Sir), **4th Bt**

2 Arthur Hamilton, DL Middx, OStJ, Maj 4th Bn Essex Regt Boer War 1901–02 and WW I, Freeman City of London; *b* 18 Jan 1881; *educ* Eton; *m* 25 Jan 1910 Mabel Alice (*d* 20 June 1973), yst dau of Sir William Henry Smith-Marriott, 5th Bt (*qv*), and *d* 25 May 1973, leaving issue:

(1) Arthur William Douglas, Fell All Souls Oxford 1958, RAF, Croix de Guerre with Palm; *b* 20 Feb 1911; *educ* Repton and Trin Coll Cambridge

(2) Geoffrey Mervyn, 13th/18th Roy Hus (QMO), WW II as Capt Roy Sussex Regt; *b* 19 Jan 1916; *educ* Eton; *m* 1st 11 March 1941 (*divorce* 1955) Elise Marie, dau of George McGregor Richmond, of Balmacraig, Perthshire; *m* 2nd 10 Jan 1957 (*divorce* 1967) Jean Margaret, yst dau of William Ross-Brown, of Durban, S Africa; *m* 3rd 9 May 1967 *Jean Mellor, dau of Cdr J W W M Standring, RN, and *d* 1984, leaving by his 1st w issue:

1a *Marie Frances Richmond, JP Cornwall; *b* 8 April 1942; *m* 1st 1979 A R Lusk, of Comrie, Perthshire (*d* 1981); *m* 2nd 1983 Hon (Montagu) Robert Vere Eliot (*d* 1994; *see* SAINT GERMANS, E)

(3) Robert Henry, JP (Dorset 1967); *b* 12 Jan 1922; *educ* RNC Dartmouth; Lt RN WW II (wounded); *m* 19 Sept 1946 *Teri, er dau of Emin Agolli Doshishti by HH PRINCESS ADILE ZOG, sis of HM KING ZOG OF ALBANIA, and *d* 1 Oct 1994, leaving:

1a +William Jeremy Daniel [William Cooper Esq, The Down House, Blandford Forum, Dorset DT11 9AD]; *b* 4 March 1951; *educ* Eton; *m* 1975 *Teresa Margaret, dau of Ralph Ernest Bamford, of Winterbourne Whitchurch, Dorset, and has:

1b +Daniel Alexander Westrow; *b* 1982

2b +Richard Gregory Christopher; *b* 1984

3b +Samuel Robert Paul; *b* 1988

2a +Westrow Gerald Alan; *b* 20 May 1956; *m* 1986 *Helen Margaret, dau of George William Stokes, of Croydon, and has issue:

1b *Katherine Teri Helen; *b* 1988

3 Gerald Melbourne, MC, Lt Scots Gds (SR); *b* 13 Sept 1892; *d* unm 17 Nov 1947

1 Alice Nellie; *m* 18 April 1905 5th Baron Penrhyn (*qv*), and *d* 17 Dec 1965, leaving issue

Sir WILLIAM *d* 2 Sept 1925; his est son,

Sir (William George) Daniel Cooper 4th Bt, T/Capt RASC, Lt 7th Hus; *b* 14 Dec 1877; *educ* Eton and Trin Coll Cambridge; *m* 18 April 1904 Hon Lettice Margaret Long (*d* 1 Sept 1950), yr dau of 1st Viscount Long, PC (*qv*), and had issue:

1 CHARLES ERIC DANIEL (Sir), **5th Bt**

2 +Sydney Michael; *b* 29 Aug 1909; *educ* Harrow

1 *Joyce Mabel (twin with Sydney Michael); *m* 1st 12 July 1932 Lt-Col Henry Balfour Scott (*d* 24 Jan 1955), Roy Dragoons, 3rd son of James Henry Scott, of Eredine, Argyllshire, and has issue; *m* 2nd 7 July 1955 *George Beeby

Sir DANIEL *d* 27 Dec 1954; his er son,

Sir Charles Eric Daniel Cooper, 5th Bt, Maj Roy Dragoons; *b* 5 Oct 1906; *educ* Harrow and RMC Sandhurst; *m* 1st 8 Oct 1931 Alice Estelle (*d* 8 Oct 1952), dau of William T Manifold, of Purrumbete, Weerite, Victoria, Australia; *m* 2nd 17 Dec 1953 *(Mary) Elisabeth [Elisabeth Lady Cooper, Pudley Cottage, Castle St, Aldbourne, Wilts SN8 2DA], formerly w of Robert Erland Nicholai d'Abo and er dau of Capt John Eagles Henry Graham-Clarke, JP of Frocester Manor, Stonehouse, Glos, and *d* 1984, having had issue:

1 Sir WILLIAM DANIEL CHARLES COOPER, **6th and present Bt**

2 +GEORGE JOHN [George Cooper Esq, Hinton Ho, Ablington, Bibury, Cirencester, Glos GL7 5NY]; *b* 28 June 1956; *educ* Harrow

COOTE

Arms: Arg. a chevron sa. between three coots close ppr. **Crest:** A coot close ppr. **Mottoes:** *Coûte que coûte* ('Cost what it may'), *Vincit veritas* ('Truth conquers'). **Creation:** Bt. (I) 2 April 1621.

SIR CHRISTOPHER JOHN COOTE, 15TH BT [Sir Christopher Coote Bt, Monkton House, Broughton Gifford, Melksham, Wilts SN12 8PA]; *b* 22 Sept 1928; *s f* 1978; *educ* Winchester and Ch Ch Oxford (MA 1957); late Lt 17th/21st Lancers, coffee and tea merchant; *m* 23 Aug 1952 *Anne Georgiana, yr dau of Lt-Col Donald James Handford RA, of Guyers, Corsham, Wilts, and has:

1 +NICHOLAS PATRICK; *b* 28 July 1953; *educ* Winchester; *m* 1980 *Mona Rebecca, dau of Moushegh Bedelian, and has issue:

(1) +Rory Alasdair; *b* 3 April 1987

(1) *Eleanor Marianne; *b* 20 May 1984

1 *Vanessa Jean; *b* 10 Aug 1955; *educ* Southampton U (BSc), Camborne Sch of Mines (MSc) and UCL (PhD); FGS

Lineage: Sir NICHOLAS COOTE, of Norfolk; had:

Sir Charles Coote, 1st Bt (I), so *cr* 2 April 1621, of Castle Cuffe, Queen's Co; *b* 1581; Capt of 100 Foot in wars against O'Neill, Earl of Tyrone (at Siege of Kinsale); Provost Marshal Connaught *temp* JAMES I; V-Pres Connaught 1620; helped relieve Birr, King's Co, 1642 during Uprising by Confedn of Kilkenny; *m c* 1604 Dorothea, yst dau and coheir of Hugh Cuffe, of Cuffes Wood, Co Cork, and was *k* 7 May 1642 in a sally to protect the town of Trim, Co Meath, during the Uprising, having had, with other issue:

1 **Sir Charles Coote, 2nd Bt**, and 1st EARL OF MOUNTRATH in Queen's County, so *cr* 6 Sept 1660, as also BARON COOTE OF CASTLE CUFFE in Queen's County and VISCOUNT COOTE OF CASTLE COOTE, Co Roscommon (all I); *b c* 1605; ktd 1626, MP Co Leitrim 1634–35, Parly Ld Pres Connaught 1645, MP (E Parl) Cos Galway and Mayo 1654–55, 1656–58 and 1659 but conspired to bring about the Restoration as early as 1659; Pres Connaught 1660; *m* 1st Mary, 2nd dau and coheir of Sir Francis Ruish, PC, MP, of Castle Jordan, Co Meath, and had with other issue:

(1) **Sir Charles Coote, 3rd Bt**, and 2nd EARL OF MOUNTRATH; *b c* 1622; ktd 1660, MP Co Roscommon April-Dec 1661; *m* 1653 Alice, dau of Sir Robert Meredyth, of Greenhills, Co Kildare, and *d* 30 Aug 1672, leaving, with two other sons and two other daus:

1a **Sir Charles Coote, 4th Bt**, and 3rd EARL OF MOUNTRATH, PC (I 1695 and 1702); *b* 1656; *m c* 4 Aug 1679 Lady Isabella Dormer, dau of 2nd Earl of Carnarvon (*see* DORMER, B), and *d* May 1709, leaving issue:

1b **Sir Charles Coote, 5th Bt**, and 4th EARL OF MOUNTRATH, PC (I *c* 1711); *b c* 1680; *d* unm 14 Sept 1715

2b **Sir Harry Coote, 6th Bt**, and 5th EARL OF MOUNTRATH, PC (I 1718); *b* 4 Jan 1683/4; MP (Whig) Knaresborough 1715–20; *d* unm 27 March 1720

3b **Sir Algernon Coote, 7th Bt**, and 6th EARL OF MOUNTRATH; *bapt* 6 June 1689; *educ* St Paul's and Trin Coll Cambridge; *m* 28 Nov 1721 Lady Diana Newport (*d* 14 July 1766), dau of 2nd Earl of Bradford of the 1694 *cr* (*see* BRADFORD, E), and *d* 27 Aug 1744, leaving an only son:

1c **Sir Charles Henry Coote, 8th Bt**, and 7th and last EARL OF MOUNTRATH, PC (I 1761); *b c* 1725; *cr* 31 July 1800 BARON CASTLE COOTE (I), with special remainder to his kinsman Rt Hon Charles Henry Coote (*see* below); *dspl* unm 1 March 1802, when all his titles expired bar the btcy and the Barony of 1800, leaving by Mary Preston:

1d Charles; *b* 30 July 1761

1a Anne; *m* Nov 1672, as his 2nd w, 1st Viscount Blesington (*see* CORK and ORRERY, E) and *d* 6 April 1725

1 (cont.) **Sir Charles, 2nd Bt**, *m* 2nd by May 1645 Jane (*m* 2nd Sir Robert Reading, 1st Bt), dau of Sir Robert Hannay, 1st Bt, and *d* 18 Dec 1661, having by her had, with other issue:

(2) Richard, of Tullaghmain, Co Kilkenny; *m* July 1666 Penelope, dau of Arthur Hill, of Hillsborough (*see* DOWNSHIRE, M), and had issue:

1a Jane; *m* 1st Sir William Evans, Bt; *m* 2nd, as his 2nd w, Capt Henry Gorges, Inniskilling Dragoons (*d* 1696), yst son of John Gorges, of Summerseat, Co Londonderry, and had issue; *m* 3rd Jervais Price; *m* 4th Maj William Billingsly and *d* 25 June 1729

2a Rose; *m* as his 1st w 2nd and last Viscount Blesington (*see* CORK and ORRERY, E) and *dsp*

2 Chidley, of Killester, Co Dublin, and Mount Coote, Co Limerick; *m* 1st —, dau (*dsp*) of Sir Francis Willoughby; *m* 2nd Alice/Anne (*bur* 25 Sept 1680), only dau of Sir Thomas Philips, and *d* 19 Nov 1668, leaving issue:

(1) Chidley, of Kilmallock, Co Limerick; Lt-Col; *m* 26 June 1675 Catherine, dau of Col Robert Sandys, and had issue:

1a Chidley (Rev), DD, of Ash Hill, Co Limerick; *m* 31 June 1702 Jane (*d* Feb 1763), dau of George Evans and sis of 1st Baron Carbery (*qv*), and *d* 1 Aug 1730, leaving, with other issue:

1b Robert, of Ash Hill, Co Limerick; *m* Feb 1730 Anne (*m* 2nd William Cole), dau and coheir of Bartholomew Purdon, of Ballyclough, Co Cork, and *d* Dec 1745, having had issue:

1c CHIDLEY, for whom see further below

2c Bartholomew COOTE later PURDON-COOTE, of Ballyclough; *m* April 1762 Mary, dau of Henry Wrixon, and *d* Oct 1780, leaving a son and four daus

3c Charles (Rev), Rector Ballyclough; *m* Mary, dau of Mary Evatt, and had issue

1c Jane; *m* William Purdon

2c Catherine; *m* Rev William Dobbin, DD

2b Charles (Very Rev), DD, Dean of Kilfenora; *m* 1st 31 July 1753 Grace (*d* 20 Dec 1766), widow of Thomas Cuffe and dau of Thomas Tilson; *m* 2nd 1 July 1771 Catherine (*dsp* 1801), dau of Benjamin Bathurst, of Lydney, Glos, and *d* 12 Feb 1796, having by his first w had issue:

1c CHARLES HENRY COOTE, 2nd BARON CASTLECOOTE; *b* 25 Aug 1754; *m* 23 May 1779 Elizabeth Ann, dau and coheir of Rev Henry Tilson, DD, of Eagle Hill, Co Kildare, and *d* 22 Jan 1823, leaving:

1d EYRE COOTE, 3rd BARON CASTLECOOTE; *b* 21 Sept 1793; *m* July 1822 Barbara (*m* 2nd July 1828 4th Earl of Milltown, KP (*d* 31 Jan 1866; *see* 1970 edn), and *d* 14 Feb 1874, leaving issue), dau and coheir of Sir Joshua Colles Meredyth, 8th Bt, of Greenhills, and *dsp* 1827, when the Barony expired

2c Eyre (Sir), GCB, of West Park, Hants; MP, Gen; *m* 1st 9 Nov 1786 Sarah (*d* 30 Oct 1795), dau and coheir of John Rodbard, and had three daus; *m* 2nd 25 Oct 1805 Jane, dau of John Bagwell, of Marlfield, Co Tipperary, and *d* 1824, leaving:

1d Eyre, of West Park, MP; *b* 7 Sept 1806; *m* 13 April 1828 Elizabeth Rosetta (*m* 2nd 2 Nov 1842 R-Adml Armar Lowry Corry, was granted rank of a KCB's widow 1856 and *d* 7 Jan 1858), dau of James Hewitt

Massy-Dawson, of Ballynacourte, Co Tipperary (*see* MASSY, B), and *d* 30 May 1834, having had, with a dau (Katherine, *m* 20 Feb 1850 V-Adml Sir William Houston-Stewart, GCB):

1e Eyre, of West Park; *b* 4 Oct 1830; *m* 17 Feb 1857 Jessie Mary (*m* 2nd 21 May 1867 William Selby-Lowndes, JP, of Whaddon Hall, and Winslow, Bucks (*d* 3 Nov 1920), and *d* 9 Jan 1938, leaving further issue), dau of Lt-Gen Henry Lechmere Worrall, ISC, of The Cottage, Clifton, Bristol, and *d* 23 Aug 1864, having had, with another dau:

1f Eyre (Sir), of West Park, JP Wilts and Hants, DL Queen's Co, High Sheriff 1886, High Sheriff Co Dublin 1903; *b* 31 Dec 1857; *m* 24 Nov 1892 Evelyn Mary (*d* 23 April 1944), dau of Rev Edward Cadogan, Rector Wicken, Northants, and *d* 6 May 1925

2f Charles Henry Eyre, of Highgate Ho, Creaton, Northants, JP, DL, Maj 11th Hus, Lt-Col and Hon Col Northants Yeo; *b* 5 Aug 1859; *m* 10 Dec 1895 Evelyn Alice (*d* 1 Sept 1968 aged 99), yst dau of J H Gartside, of Overstone Park, Northants, and *d* 23 Nov 1938, leaving issue:

1g Charles Gartside Eyre, 2nd Lt 11th Hus; *b* 2 Dec 1896; *ka* 22 March 1918

1g Evelyn Gertrude Eyre; *b* 17 Feb 1900; *m* 18 Nov 1924 Maj Ronald Leslie Downing Kaye, TD, est son of Robert W Kaye, of Great Glenn Manor, Leics, and *d* 21 Feb 1960, leaving issue

2g Nina Violet Eyre; *b* 9 May 1904; *m* 16 Sept 1931 Peter Thomas Wellesley Sykes, the Queen's Bays, er son of Lt-Col Harold Platt Sykes, of Longford Hall, Newport, Shropshire, and *d* 12 Sept 1935, leaving issue

1f Florence Anita Eyre, CBE (1920); *m* 1st 26 June 1888 Sir Robert John Abercromby, 7th Bt, of Birkenbog (*qv*), and had issue; *m* 2nd 10 June 1899 2nd Earl of Northbrook (*qv*) and *d* 4 Dec 1946

1e Catherine Elizabeth; *m* 20 Feb 1850 as his 1st w, Sir William Houston Shaw-Stewart, GCB (*see* SHAW-STEWART, Bt), and *d* 23 Nov 1867, leaving issue

1c Grace; *m* 16 Sept 1780 Right Rev Henry Bathurst, DD, Bp Norwich, and *d* 16 April 1823, leaving issue

3b Thomas, of Charleville, Co Cork; *m* Eleanor, dau of Dr Grove White, of Charleville, and had, with four other sons:

1c Thomas, Capt RA; had:

1d Charles Eyre, of Farway Ho, Clifton; *dsp*

2c Eyre, Maj 27th Regt; *m* Theodosia (*d* 8 Feb 1833), dau of Michael Creagh, and *d* 1 Oct 1802, leaving, with other issue:

1d Richard Gethin Creagh, of Bridge View, Mallow, Co Cork; Capt 54th Regt Burmese War 1824–25, present taking of Ava; *b* 13 June 1797; *m* 1834 Hester (*d* 1874), dau of James Tarrant, and *d* 19 Dec 1872, leaving, with other issue:

1e Edmund Eyre, Lt-Col and Staff Paymaster APD, Capt 58th Regt, served Afghan War 1879–80 (medals); *b* 3 Jan 1842; *m* 17 Jan 1865 Eliza Olivia, dau of Nicholas Gray, of Jamestown, Co Wexford, and *d* 10 May 1907, having had issue:

1f Chidley Eyre; *b* 1871; *d* 22 Nov 1874

1e Theodosia Isabella; *m* 1 Feb 1859 Edward Bullen and *d* 1872, leaving issue. He *d* 1873

1d Jane; *m* 6 July 1821 Rev James Grant (*d* 3 Aug 1874) and had issue

4b Eyre (Sir), of West Park, KB, C-in-C India; *b* 1726; *m* 8 July 1763 Susannah, dau of Charles Hutchinson, and *dsp* 26 April 1783

1a Anne; *m* Bartholomew Purdon, of Ballyclough

2a Catherine; *m* 1715, as his 1st w, 1st Henry Boyle, Earl of Shannon (*qv*)

(2) Philips (Sir), of Mount Coote; *bapt* 10 March 1658; *m* 1st Jane, dau of Henry Jones, Bp Meath, and had an only child (Anne, *d* young); *m* 2nd Elizabeth, dau and coheir of 3rd Earl of Meath (*qv*), and had, with two daus:

1a Charles; *m* Katherine, dau of Sir Robert Newcomen, Bt, and *d* 1761, leaving:

1b Chidley, of Mount Coote, Co Limerick; *m* Jane, dau of Sir Ralph Gore, 4th Bt (*qv*), and *d* 24 Feb 1764, leaving, with a dau (Elizabeth, *m* James King, of Gola):

1c Charles; *m* 1775 Elizabeth dau and coheir of Philip Oliver, of Altamira, MP, and *d* 17 Sept 1792, having had issue:

1d Chidley, of Mount Coote; *b* 14 Feb 1776; *m* 24 July 1797 Anne (*d* 11 Dec 1842), dau and coheir of Hon William Williams Hewitt (*see* LIFFORD, B), and *d* 11 July 1843, leaving with other issue:

1e Charles Eyre; *b* 5 June 1801; *m* 8 Jan 1828 Caroline Dillon (*d* 4 March 1878), dau of Maj Crofton Croker, and *d* 12 March 1858, leaving, with other issue:

1f Mary Ann Harriet; *m* 5 Feb 1856 William Uniacke Townsend, and *d* 15 Feb 1915, leaving issue. He *d* 1888

2f Caroline Alicia; *m* 26 June 1866 Walter James Cummins and *d* 8 Dec 1911, leaving issue

2e Charles James; *b* 1814; Lt-Col 18th Roy Irish Regt; *m* Anne (*d* 24 May 1853), dau of Thomas Stewart, of Limerick, and had, with other issue:

1f Charles James, of Mount Coote; Capt 18th Roy Irish Regt; *b* 19 Aug 1837; *m* 6 June 1867 Emily (*dsp* 23 May 1896), dau of Very Rev Hon Henry Pakenham, DD (*see* LONGFORD, E), and *d* 11 March 1925

1f Ann Hewitt; *m* 20 Dec 1866 Henry John Norman, of Gadsden, Hayes, Kent, er son of Henry Norman, of Oakley, Bromley, Kent, and *d* 14 Nov 1926, leaving issue. He *d* 4 June 1905

2f Ada; *m* 17 Nov 1868 Hon Henry Leslie Pepys, and *d* 21 April 1936, leaving issue (*see* COTTENHAM, E)

1e Alicia; *m* 14 June 1831 John Wingfield King, and *d* 14 Sept 1855. He *d* 19 Sept 1868

2d Charles Phillips (Rev), Rector Doon, Co Limerick; *m* Anne, dau of Charles Atkinson, of Rehins, Co Mayo, and *d* 1838, having had seven sons and six daus

3 RICHARD COOTE, 1st LORD COOTE, BARON OF COLOONY, Co Sligo (I), so *cr* 6 Sept 1660, PC (I 1660); *b c* 1620; *m* Mary, sis of Sir Oliver St George, 1st Bt (*qv*), and *d* 10 July 1683, leaving, with an est s (*d* young):

(1) RICHARD COOTE, 2nd LORD COOTE, BARON OF COLOONY, and 1st EARL OF BELLOMONT (I), so *cr* 2 Nov 1689; MP (Whig) Droitwich 1689–95, apptd by WILLIAM III Govr Leitrim 1689 with grant of 77,000 acres of confiscated lands (having been attainted by JAMES II's Irish Parl May 1689), Govr Massachusetts and New York 1695–March 1700/1 and 1697–March 1700/1 respectively ; before leaving England he prepared a privateer to help him suppress freebooters in the American Colonies — this being one of the chief reasons for his gubernatorial appointments — but made the mistake of putting in charge of her one William Kidd, better known as Captain Kidd, thereby launching the career of a pirate more infamous than any he was supposed to suppress; *m* 19 Aug 1680 Catharine, dau of Sir Bridges Nanfan, and *d* 5 March 1700/1, leaving:

1a NANFAN COOTE, 2nd EARL OF BELLOMONT; *b c* 1681; *m* 17 Feb 1705/6 Lucia Anna, sis of Henry de Nassau, 1st Earl of Grantham, and yst dau of Henry, Count de Nassau and feudal Ld of Auverquerque, Holland, and *dspm* 14 June 1708

2a RICHARD COOTE, 3rd and last EARL OF BELLOMONT; *m* 1st Judith, dau of Francis Wilkinson, of Southwark, a purveyor of rabbit's fur; *m* 2nd 4 May 1721 Anne, dau of John Holloway, of Oxford, and widow of Sir Henry Oxenden, 4th Bt, and *dspms* 10 Feb 1766, when the Earldom expired but the Barony passed to his cousin Charles

(2) Thomas, of Coote Hill, Co Cavan; Justice King's Bench Ireland; had:

1a Charles, of Coote Hill; MP Co Cavan 1727–50; *m* Prudence, dau of Richard Geering, and *d* 19 Dec 1750, having had, with six other daus:

1b Sir CHARLES COOTE, 1st Bt (GB), so *cr* 12 or 18 May 1774 (with special remainder to his illegitimate s), 5th LORD COOTE, BARON OF COLOONY (as which he s his cousin 1766), and 1st and last EARL OF BELLAMONT [*sic*] (I), so *cr* 4 Sept 1767, KB (1764), PC (1774); *bapt* 12 April 1738; MP Co Cavan 1761–66, DQMG Forces 1766–73; *m* 20 Aug 1774 Lady Emily Mary Margaretta FitzGerald, dau of 1st Duke of Leinster (*qv*), and *dspmsl* (apart from the 2nd Bt he had eleven other children by five different women) 20 Oct 1800, when the Earldom and Barony expired, but the btcy passed to his s by Rebecca Palmer *alias* Sheldon:

1c Sir CHARLES COOTE, 2nd Bt, of Donnybrook, Co Dublin, and Bagot St, Dublin; *b* 1765; *m* by 1798 — Richardson and *d* 25 May 1857, leaving:

1d Sir CHARLES COOTE, 3rd Bt, of Rathmines, Dublin; *b* 1798; *m* 1846 Helena Melefont, dau of Anthony O'Ryan, MD, and widow of — Smith, and *d* 5 Nov 1861, leaving:

1e Sir CHARLES ALGERNON COOTE, 4th Bt, of Dublin; *b* 1847; Lt Kilkenny Militia, LRCS (I) 1883; *dsp* 1 Feb 1920, when the btcy expired

1b Elizabeth; *b* 1735; *m* 26 Oct 1756, as his 1st w, her cousin Chidley Coote (see below) and had issue

(1) Mary; *m* Sir William Stewart, 3rd Bt, of Ramelton (*qv*), who was also 1st Viscount Mountjoy of the March 1682/3 *cr*, and had issue

1 Letitia; *m* Sir Francis Hamilton, Bt, of Killeshandra

The 8th Bt's cousin,

CHIDLEY COOTE, of Ash Hill, Co Limerick; *m* 1st 26 Oct 1756 his cousin Elizabeth (*d* 1781), sis of 1st and last EARL OF BELLAMONT, and had issue:

1 Anne; *m* 26 Oct 1784 John Grogan, of Johnstown

CHIDLEY COOTE *m* 2nd 31 Aug 1790 Elizabeth Anne (*d* 31 March 1831), dau of Rev Ralph Carr, of Bath, and *d* 6 June 1799, having had by her had issue:

1 CHARLES HENRY (Sir), **9th Bt**

2 Robert Carr, Capt 18th Light Dragoons; *b* 1796; *m* Margaret Grier (*d* 1854), and *d* 5 Nov 1834, leaving, with other issue:

(1) Charles Purdon, Offr 3rd Dragoon Gds; *m* 1846 Lydia Lucy (*m* 2nd 8 Dec 1851 4th Viscount Lifford (*qv*) and *d* 28 April 1919), est dau of Rev John Digby Wingfield-Digby, Vicar Coleshill, Warwicks, and *d* 3 Sept 1848, leaving issue:

1a Charles Purdon, of Ballyclough Castle, and Bearforest, Co Cork, DL, JP, Gentleman Usher to Ld-Lt Ireland; *b* 8 Aug 1847; *m* 22 June 1871 Harriette Louisa (*d* 29 Dec 1935), 4th dau of Robert Perceval Maxwell, DL, of Finnebrogue, and Groomsport, Co Down, and Moore Hill, Co Waterford, and *d* 20 Sept 1893, leaving issue:

1b Charles Robert Purdon, of Ballyclough Castle, and Bearforest; T/Maj RASC WW I, Belgian Croix de Guerre; *b* 23 Jan 1875; *m* 30 Sept 1933 *Noel Margaret Jephson [Mrs Charles Coote, Durham House, Balsham, Cambs CB1 6EZ], est dau of Lt-Col Ernest Henry Denne Stracey, of Cross Lane, Ticehurst, Sussex (*see* STRACEY, Bt), and *d* 28 March 1954, leaving issue:

1c *Nicola Harriette; *b* 6 Jan 1937; *m* 18 July 1959 *22nd Baron Clinton (*qv*), and has issue

2c *Margaret Lydia Faith; *b* 28 Feb 1939; *m* 9 July 1966 *Colin Patrick Annesley Martin Hill, only son of William Martin Hill, MA, of Princeton, NJ, by Diana Patricia, twin dau of Richard Arthur Grove Annesley, of Annesgrove, Co Cork (*see* ANNESLEY, E), and has issue

3c *Caroline Anne; *b* 7 Dec 1940; *m* 16 April 1963 *Baron Lambert Frederick Casijn Royal Netherlands Navy, er son of Capt Baron G N H van Till, ADC, Royal Netherlands Navy, of Boomgaard, Bussum, Holland, and has issue:

1d *Rupert Maurice Casijn; *b* 28 May 1967

2d *Edward Nicholaas Frederick; *b* 1970

1d *Lydia Julie; *b* 20 Oct 1964

2d *Vanessa Caroline; *b* 1975

4c *Rosamond Aileen [Mrs Timothy Bulwer-Long, Balsham House, Balsham, Cambs]; *b* 5 July 1943; *m* 22 April 1965 *Timothy Hetherington Earle Bulwer-Long, 15th/19th King's Roy Hus, yr son of Brig Hetherington Bulwer-Long, OBE, MC, of Heydon, Norfolk, and has issue:

1d *Lucy Wiggett; *b* 28 Aug 1966

2d *Charlotte Louise; *b* 6 June 1968

3d *Harriet Elizabeth; *b* 6 July 1977
4d *Laura Rose; *b* 31 Jan 1979
5c *Mary Patricia; *b* 20 Sept 1945
1b Lydia Purdon; *b* 5 July 1872; *d* unm 4 Sept 1960
2b Aileen Selina; *b* 16 Oct 1878; *m* 8 Oct 1903 11th Baron Farnham (*qv*), and *d* 1 Feb 1964, leaving issue
3b Harrie Helena; *b* 13 Nov 1884; *d* 26 Feb 1886
1a Maria; *m* 3 Dec 1855 Henry M Smythe, of New Park, Co Roscommon, and was murdered at Barbavilla, Co Westmeath, 2 April 1882, leaving issue
3 Chidley, of Huntington, Queen's Co, JP, Col Scots Gds; *b* 10 Jan 1798; *m* 1st 8 May 1827 Jane Deborah (*d* 2 Dec 1857), 2nd dau of Rev Samuel Close, of Elm Park, and had, with other issue:
(1) Maxwell Henry (Rev), of Ross, Tullamore, King's Co, Rector Killoughy; *b* 4 May 1832; *m* 21 June 1865 Charlotte (*d* 9 March 1905), 2nd dau of Maj Barry Fox, of Annaghmore, King's Co, and *dsp* 21 June 1905
(1) Jane Elizabeth Anna; *m* 2 Jan 1855 Rev Charles Lyndhurst Vaughan, son of Sir John Vaughan (*see* SAINT JOHN OF BLETSO, B), and *d* 26 Dec 1873
(2) Harriet Mary; *m* 1st 28 Aug 1855 George Evans, of Portrane. He *d* 26 May 1873; *m* 2nd 1 June 1875 John Gordon, of Milrig, Ayrshire, and *d* 3 Oct 1927 aged 96. He *dsp* 17 Sept 1900
3 (cont.) Col Chidley Coote *m* 2nd 3 May 1859 Catherine Maria (*d* 1910), dau of William Philip Brabazon (*see* MEATH, E) and *d* 21 July 1876, having by her had issue:
(2) Ralph Brabazon; *b* 7 Feb 1860; *d* unm
4 Ralph (Rev), incumbent of Fercall, Tullamore; *m* 1825 Harriet, yst dau of Rev Samuel Close, and *dsp*
1 Mary; *m* 15 Jan 1815 Charles Lancelot Sandes, of Indiaville, Queen's Co, and *d* 6 Feb 1852, leaving issue. He *d* May 1855
The est son,
Sir Charles Henry Coote, 9th Bt; *b* 2 Jan 1792; *m* 1814 Caroline (*d* 11 March 1871), dau of John Whaley, of Whaley Abbey, Co Wicklow, and *d* 8 Oct 1864, having had, with other issue:
1 **Sir Charles Henry Coote, 10th Bt**, DL; *b* Sept 1815; *d* unm 15 Nov 1895
2 John Chidley, Capt 43rd LI; *b* 6 Sept 1816; *m* 6 Dec 1855 Margaret Mary Pole (*m* 2nd 14 July 1880 Sir Charles Robert Pigott, 3rd Bt (*qv*), and *d* 9 Dec 1924), dau of Sydney Cosby, of Stradbally Hall, Queen's Co, and *dsp* 26 April 1879
3 ALGERNON (Sir), **11th Bt**
4 Robert, CB, Adml; *b* 1 June 1820; *m* 14 Feb 1854 Lucy (*d* 7 Feb 1906), dau of Adml Sir William E Parry, and *d* 17 March 1898, having had issue:
(1) Stanley Victor, JP Roscommon, High Sheriff 1900; *b* 30 May 1862; *educ* Oriel Coll Oxford (MA); *m* 26 Oct 1889 Louisa (*d* 20 Oct 1939), dau of Ven Frederick Bathurst, Archdeacon of Bedford, and *d* 3 May 1925, having had issue:
1a Margaret Stanley; *b* 24 Oct 1893; *d* 21 June 1894
2a Honor Dorothea; *b* 18 Nov 1896; *m* 12 May 1920 Col Anthony Charles Barnes, DSO, OBE, son of Sir George Stapylton Barnes, KCB, KCSI, and *d* 3 Oct 1984, leaving:
1b *George Stanley Coote; *b* 23 April 1925; *educ* Eton and Trin Coll Cambridge; *m* 6 Aug 1961 *Priscilla Ann, yr dau of Hon Walter Judd Post, of Spofford, NH, USA, memb Gen Court of New Hampshire
1b *Margaret Honor; *b* 3 June 1921; *m* 6 Sept 1976 *Peter James Sisam
2b *Catherine Lucy; *b* 4 June 1923; *m* 10 June 1957 Hugh David Phillimore, est son of Capt William Raigersfeld Phillimore, CBE, RN, of Folkestone, Kent, and has issue (*see* PHILLIMORE, B)
(1) Caroline Maud; *b* 22 Feb 1864; *m* 6 Aug 1884 Maj-Gen Cecil William Park, CB, Devonshire Regt, son of Rev J Allen Park, Vicar Methwold, Norfolk, and *d* 4 Sept 1947, leaving issue. He *d* 29 March 1913
5 Chidley Downs, 52nd Foot; *b* 1829; *m* 1868 Thérèse (*d* 25 Nov 1918), dau of Capt John Anthony Reinbod, of Nice, and *dsp* 10 March 1872
1 Caroline; *m* 1842 Marquis de Massingy de la Pierre (*d* 1889) and *d* 1848, leaving a dau
The 10th Bt's bro,
Rev Sir Algernon Coote, 11th Bt, of Ballyfin, Queen's Co; *b* 29 Sept 1817; *educ* BNC Oxford (MA), Vicar Nonington, Kent; *m* 1st 12 Feb 1847 Cecilia Matilda (*d* 24 May 1878), dau of John P Plumptre, MP, of Fredville, and had, with other issue:
1 ALGERNON CHARLES PLUMPTRE (Sir), **12th Bt**
2 John Pemberton Plumptre; *b* 15 Sept 1850; Cdr RN; *m* 26 Dec 1880 Eleanor Agnes (*d* 17 March 1925), dau of John Osmaston, of Hawkhurst Court, and *d* 10 June 1938, leaving issue:
(1) Mervyn Chidley, Lt-Col 4th Hazara Pioneers, IA; *b* 5 June 1885; *m* 10 July 1915 Cecil Maud Vera (*d* 1989), dau of Maj-Gen Cecil William Park, CB, and *d* 18 Aug 1950, leaving issue:
1a +Chidley; *b* 6 March 1918; *m* 1954 *Mavis Ellen Thompson
1a *Eleanor Patricia [Mrs James Hayter, Rocklands, Golden Bay, Nelson, New Zealand]; *b* 1916; *m* 1940 *James Chilton Francis Hayter and has had:
1b Stephen James; *b* 1945; *d* 1987
2a *Maureen Joyce [Mrs Samuel Nicholson, 93 Coronation Rd, Morrisville, Waikato, New Zealand]; *b* 1923; *m* 1963 *Samuel Nicholson and has:
1b *Ian Andrew; *b* 1964
3a *Rosemary Cecilia [Mrs Joseph Clark, 21 Kakenga Rd, Stoke, Nelson, New Zealand]; *b* 1929; *m* 8 Sept 1951 *Joseph Trevor Clark, and has issue:
1b *Anthony Joseph; *b* 1952; *m* 1979 *Cushla Kerr, and has issue:
1c *Benjamin Joseph; *b* 1981
1c *Anna Louise; *b* 1984
2b *Peter Andrew; *b* 1954
3b *Geoffrey Robert; *b* 1956
4b *Jeremy John; *b* 1961; *m* 1992 *Elizabeth Annandale Dodd, and has issue:
1c *Ashton Thomas; *b* 1995
1c *Olivia Jessie; *b* 1993
(1) Emily Cecilia; *m* 18 Nov 1909 Albert Leslie Wright, JP, of Butterley Hall, Derbys, and *d* 28 April 1955, leaving issue. He *d* 4 Sept 1938
(2) Joyce Margaretta; *m* 31 Dec 1924 Frederick Arthur Leaf, son of Arthur H Leaf, of Oxted, and had issue. He *d* 1959
3 Orlando Robert, JP, Co Roscommon; *b* 14 March 1855; *m* 24 Aug 1882 Edith Mary (*d* 17 Jan 1920), dau of Adophus William Hume, of Ferndale, Tunbridge Wells, Kent, and *d* 22 March 1927, leaving issue:
(1) Nina Edith; *b* 23 Sept 1883; *d* unm 6 Jan 1945
4 Cecil Henry; *b* 2 Oct 1856; *m* 1888 Blanche Mabel (*d* 14 May 1947), dau of John Oldham, of New Zealand, and *d* 16 Nov 1926, leaving issue:
(1) John Cecil, MM, Lt NZ MGC WW I; *b* 1889; *m* 1915 Edith Blechynden (*d* 1976), and *d* 26 Oct 1937, leaving issue:
1a +John Robin [Maj John Coote, 88 Valley, Wakefield, New Zealand]; Maj 20th NZ Armoured Regt WW II; *b* 1916; *m* 1947 *Anna May McDonald, and has had issue:
1b +John McDonald [John Coote Esq, Damian Grove, Lower Hutt, New Zealand]; *b* 1949; Lt RNZAC; *m* 1976 *Stephanie Buchanan, and has issue:
1c +Jack Buchanan; *b* 1980
2c +Evan Blechynden; *b* 1985
1c *Anna Dolougħan; *b* 1982
1b *Isobel Anne; *b* 1950; *m* 1978 *Mark Rodger Taylor, of Havelock N, NZ
2b Alison May; *b* 27 May 1954; *d* 1975
3b *Ann Cecile; *b* 1956; *m* 1979 *Dr Duncan Bull, of Erin, Ontario, Canada, and has issue:
1c *Alexandra Alison; *b* 1981
2c *Ainsley Frances; *b* 1984
2a Peter Chidley, F/O, RNZAF; *b* 1921; *m* 1942 *Nancy Bower-Playter, and *d* 1991, leaving issue:
1b +Robin Maxwell; *b* 5 Sept 1943; *m* 1st 10 Feb 1969 (*divorce* 1987) Philippa Jacqueline, only dau of Howard Harvey McLaren Elliott, of Christchurch, NZ; *m* 2nd 1991 *Glennis Susan Hinch
3a +Richard Eyre [Richard Coote Esq, Ballyfin, Enner Glynn Rd, Nelson, New Zealand], Lt NZ Artillery Korea 1950–52; *b* 1929; *m* 3 Jan 1953 *Janet Patricia Armatage Holmes and has issue:
1b +Stephen Richard; *b* 1955; *m* 1978 *Judith Goff, and has issue:
1c +Logan Eyre; *b* 1981
1c *Tyler Lesley; *b* 1982
2b +David Eyre; *b* 1959; Warrant Offr US Army; *m* 1979 *Jody Susan Bishop
3b +Jonathan Robert; *b* 1966
1b *Sarah Patricia; *b* 1965
1a *Edith Jane [Mrs Ralph Holmes, Armatage, Wakapuaka Rd, RD1, Nelson, New Zealand]; *b* 1919; *m* 20 June 1953 *Ralph Armatage Holmes, and has issue:
1b *Marion Jane; *b* 1954
(2) Frederick Stanley, OBE (1956), KGStJ (1955), Gen Manager Far East, Cable and Wireless Ltd 1952–56; *b* 1896; *m* 1920 Edith Farquharson Crowe (*d* 1985), and *d* 1967, leaving issue:
1a John Oldham; *b* 1921; Capt RN WW II, dep chm Beaverbrook Newspapers; *m* 18 Sept 1944 *Sylvia, er dau of R-Adml (S) John Luxmoore Syson, OBE, of Enderby, Marnhull, Dorset, and *d* 11 June 1993, leaving:
1b *Judith Sylvia; *b* 13 Sept 1945; *m* 19–
2b *Angela Mary; *b* 1 April 1947
3b *Belinda Jane; *b* 10 Nov 1953
(3) Eric Royds Methuen, Lt NZ Defence Forces 1940–44; *b* 1902; *m* 1932 Vivienne Patricia Vercoe (*d* 1993), and *d* 1974, leaving issue:
1a +Philip Arthur Cecil [Philip Coote Esq, Mountrath, 26 Mount Street, Nelson, New Zealand], BDS (NZ); *b* 30 March 1935; *m* 5 Sept 1957 *Gabrielle Alice, dau of Russell Stanley Goodman, of Timaru, NZ, and has:
1b +John Anthony Royds; *b* 8 Nov 1959; *m* 1992 *Kris Vollebright, and has issue:
1c +Jack Eric; *b* 27 Aug 1992
2c +Wilbur; *b* 9 June 1994
2b +Richard Philip; *b* 21 March 1964
3b +Timothy Philip; *b* 21 March 1964
4b +Thomas Stanley Eyre; *b* 7 Nov 1967
1b *Catherine Alice; *b* 14 March 1958
2b *Bridget Ann; *b* 16 Sept 1961; *m* 1990 *Lloyd James Harwood, and has issue:
1c *George Sebastian; *b* 1994
1c *Amelia Alice; *b* 1993
2c *Lucy Helen; *b* 1996
2a +Robert Malcolm [Robert Coote Esq, Mountrath, 23 Browallia Cres, Loftus 2232, Sydney, NSW, Australia]; *b* 11 July 1947; *m* 1971 *Rhondda Beverly Kenny, of Sydney, NSW, and has issue:
1b *Justin Russell Royds; *b* 1977
1b *Deborah Michelle; *b* 1974
1a *Jennifer Margaret [Mrs Arthur Maskill, 213 Main Rd, Annesbrook, Nelson, New Zealand]; *b* 21 Oct 1933; *m* 18 June 1959 *Arthur Edward Maskill, and has issue:
1b *Patricia Anne; *b* 23 Jan 1960
2b *Margaret Kaye; *b* 19 April 1961
3b *Virginia Robyn; *b* 12 Jan 1964
4b *Dianna Mary; *b* 28 Feb 1965
(1) Ivy Mabel; *m* 1916 Charles William Thorp (*d* 4 April 1961), of Motueka, NZ, son of Rev Robert John Thorp, Rector Armthorpe, Doncaster, and *d* 1991, leaving issue
(2) Myrtle Cecilia; *d* 1997

5 Herbert Chidley (Rev), Rector St Peter's, RD Dorchester; *b* 8 July 1861; *educ* Corpus Christi Coll Cambridge (MA) *m* 1 June 1886 Elizabeth Margaret (*d* 28 April 1936), dau of Brenton Haliburton Collins, of Dunorlan, Kent, and *d* 14 May 1919

1 Catherine Cecilia; *m* 1896 Rev A de Vlieger, DLitt, and had issue. He *d* 1 Dec 1908

Sir Algernon *m* 2nd 25 Sept 1879 Constance (*d* 16 Aug 1936), dau of T H Headlam, of Wavertree, and *d* 20 Nov 1899, having by her had, with a son (*d* an infant):

2 Cecilia Constance, JP; *m* 6 June 1900 Henry Western Plumptre, of Fredville, Kent, and *d* 7 Jan 1966, leaving issue. He *d* 16 July 1939

3 Dora Maud; *d* unm Jan 1953

The 11th Bt's son,

Sir Algernon Charles Plumptre Coote, 12th Bt, JP ; *b* 14 Dec 1847; *educ* Eton, St John's Coll Cambridge (MA 1875) and Trin Coll Dublin (MA 1903); Lt and Custos Rotulorum Queen's Co; *m* 1st 28 Aug 1873 Jean (*d* 15 April 1880), dau of Capt John Trotter, of Dyrham Park, Herts, and had issue:

1 RALPH ALGERNON (Sir), **13th Bt**

2 John Methuen, OBE (1918), DC E African Protectorate, Hon Maj Special List, Hon Attaché Teheran 1902; *b* 13 March 1878; *m* 24 Sept 1912 Leonora Wray (*d* 7 June 1969 aged 83), yr dau of John Townsend Trench (*see* ASHTOWN, B), and *d* 4 Oct 1967, leaving issue:

(1) *Joanna Frances [Miss Joanna Coote, Gins, Beaulieu, Hants]; 1st Offr WRNS WW II; Dip Serv 1948–73; *b* 6 Aug 1913

(2) *Diana Jean, MBE (1946) [Mrs Edmund Luxmoore MBE, Staindrop Hall, Staindrop, Darlington, Co Durham DL2 3NH]; WW II as Sr Cdr ATS; *b* 14 Nov 1914; *m* 1 June 1946 Edmund Luxmoore (*d* 17 Dec 1997), son of Allan Aylmer Luxmoore, of The Herds Ho, Croxdale, Co Durham, and has:

1a *Michael John; *b* 5 April 1948; *educ* Harrow and Trin Coll Cambridge; *m* 1st 1973 (*divorce* 19–) Margaret Rosemary, dau of Surgn-Cdr John Graham More-Nisbett, RN, of The Drum, Gilmerton, Edinburgh; *m* 2nd Ann Dalrymple-Smith, and by his 1st w has issue:

1b *Andrew Aylmer; *b* 1976

2b *James; *b* 1979

2a *Richard Aylmer; *b* 11 July 1955; *m* 3 Sept 1994 *Samantha Emmerich and has:

1b *Alasdair William; *b* 2 March 1997

1a *Elizabeth Jean [Mrs Alexander Macdonald, Ardslignish, Glenborrodale, Ardnamurchan, Argyll PH36 4JG]; *b* 23 April 1950; *m* 1st 1976 Geoffrey Wells Abbot, of Harare, Zimbabwe; *m* 2nd 1987 *Alexander Lindsay Macdonald and by her 1st husb has:

1b *Jessica; *b* 1980

2b *Lucy; *b* 1983

3 Bernard Trotter, OBE (1919), Cdr RN; *b* 9 April 1880; *m* 3 April 1907 Grace Harriet (*d* 23 Aug 1958), er dau of Very Rev John Joseph Robinson, DD, Warden of St John's Coll, Winnipeg, and *d* 3 Sept 1955, having had issue:

(1) Denis Ivor (Rev), CBE (1951), G/Capt RAF WW II (despatches), ordained 1963, Rector East Stoke with East Holme 1965–67 and St James's Shaftesbury 1967; *b* 19 Feb 1908; *educ* Woking GS; *m* 1st 22 April 1933 Olive Sheelagh (*d* 1978), F/O WAAF, only dau of Hugh Crompton Bischoff (*d* 24 Jan 1978), of Woodhayes, Woodlands, Southampton; *m* 2nd 1979 Mary (*d* 1996), dau of William McDonough, of Newcastle, and *d* 1985, having had by his 1st w:

1a Timothy Chidley; *b* 8 April, *d* 18 Oct 1940

1a *Caragh Mary [Mrs Caragh Harford, 42 Orchardstown Drive, Rathfarnham, Dublin, Ireland]; *b* 21 Nov 1949; *m* 1st 1973 (*divorce* 1983) Patrick O'Fáoláin; *m* 2nd 1984 (*separated* 19–) Gerald Harford and by her 1st husb has:

1b *Tamsin Emilie; *b* 1973

(2) Patric Bernard, W/Cdr RAF WW II; *b* 7 Jan 1910; *m* 1 June 1935 Muriel (*d* 1995), er dau of Maj-Gen Alexander Montagu Spears Elsmie, CB, CMG, of Ealing, and was *ka* 13 April 1941, leaving issue:

1a Ann Patricia; *b* 14 Oct 1937; *d* unm 19 Sept 1994

2a *Susan Brigid [Mrs Geoffrey Young, 78 Harpenden Rd, St Albans, Herts AL3 6DA]; *b* 28 Sept 1939; *m* 15 Aug 1970 *Geoffrey Maurice Young, and has issue:

1b *Michael Patrick; *b* 1971

1b *Catherine Ann; *b* 1974

(3) +Michael Henry, FMInstI [Michael Coote Esq, 13 Laurelton, Bushy Park Rd, Rathgar, Dublin 6, Ireland]; *b* 31 May 1913; *educ* Woking GS; chm and md Coote Gp; *m* 1st 14 Oct 1939 Barbara Netterville (*d* 1987), yr dau of Richard Netterville Eaton, of Roslyn-Churchtown, Dundrum, Co Dublin; *m* 1987 *Joan May, dau of W W G Stevenson, of Cowper Drive, Dublin 6, and by his 1st w has issue:

1a +David Brian [David Coote Esq, Slieve Thoul, Brittas, Co Dublin, Ireland]; *b* 11 Aug 1942; *educ* St Columba's Coll ; dir M H Coote Co Ltd 1969; *m* 18 May 1968 *Elizabeth Joy, dau of Anthony Purdon Brooks, of Dublin, and has issue:

1b *Susan Barbara; *b* 1972

2b *Linda Elizabeth; *b* 1975

1a *Deirdre Joan; *b* 16 Sept 1940; *m* 1973 *Sean Rowsome, of Ballintober, Hollywood, Co Wicklow

2a *Sheila Ann, SRN [Mrs Patrick Robeson, 2 Wellhead Lane, Westbury, Wilts]; *b* 16 April 1946; *m* 24 Feb 1968 *Maj Patrick Brian Hemming Robeson, 6th Queen Elizabeth's Own Gurkha Rifles, only son of Mrs J D W Craig, of Killodiernan Rectory, nr Nenagh, Co Tipperary, and has issue:

1b *Simon Michael Hemming; *b* 1970

2n *Nicholas Andrew Hemming; *b* 1973

1b *Philippa Charlotte; *b* 22 Jan 1969

3a *Jennifer Hazel; *b* 4 April 1949; *m* 1969 *Peter Stuart Todd, of Monastery, Enniskerry, Co Wicklow, and has issue:

1b *Sam Stuart; *b* 1981

1b *Sarah Stuart; *b* 1972

2b *Jane Stuart; *b* 1974

3a (cont.) Mr and Mrs Peter Todd also adopted:

*Cathy; *b* 1976

(4) +Roderic Norman (Rt Rev) [The Rt Rev Roderic Coote, Friday Woods, Stoke Rd, Cobham, Surrey KT11 3AS], DD, Bp Gambia and Rio Pongas 1951–57, Fulham 1957–66 and Colchester 1966–87 (Archdeacon of Colchester 1969–72); *b* 13 April 1915; *educ* Woking GS and Trin Coll Dublin (BA 1937, MA 1941, DD 1945); *m* 2 May 1964 *Erica Lynette, dau of Rev Eric Gordon Shrubbs, MBE, of The Rectory, Lawshall, Suffolk, and has issue:

1a +Patrick Shrubbs; *b* 1972

1a *Antoinette Alexandra; *b* 24 Oct 1965; *m* 29 July 1995 *Dean Buckley, s of Ian Buckley, of Colchester, and has:

1b *Carl Roderick; *b* 12 June 1997

2a *Bernadette Sophia; *b* 7 Oct 1966

(5) Brian Philip, MC, W/Cdr RAF Regt; Capt Reconnaissance Corps WWII; Pncpl Queen Elizabeth's Training Coll Leatherhead 1972–79; Dep Dir Queen Elizabeth's Foundation for the Disabled 1979–84; *b* 11 Jan 1919; *educ* Woking GS and St Columba's Coll Dublin; *m* 28 May 1949 *Elizabeth Helen [Mrs Brian Coote, The Hollies, Church St, Rudgwick, W Sussex], dau of William James Rutt, of Trimley St Mary, Suffolk, and *d* 5 Nov 1997, leaving:

1a *Grace Elizabeth; *b* 31 Dec 1956; *m* 1984 *Ian Arthur Bagster, of Furneaux Pelham, Herts

1 Ethel Jean, OBE (1919); *b* 29 April 1876; *m* 14 July 1896 (*divorce* 1921) Ivor Bevan, 6th son of Francis Augustus Bevan, of Trent Park, Middx, and *d* 27 July 1941. He *d* Dec 1941

Sir Algernon *m* 2nd 21 April 1882 Ellen Melesina (*d* 21 April 1923), dau of Philip Charles Chenevix Trench, of Botleyhill, Hants (*see* ASHTOWN, B), and by her had issue:

4 Charles Chenevix, OBE (1939), Lt 4th Bn Leinster Regt; *b* 11 Sept 1884; *m* 16 June 1908 Alice Maud (*d* 16 Jan 1948), only dau of Most Rev John Baptist Crozier, DD, Archbp Armagh and Primate of All Ireland, and *d* 26 July 1944, leaving issue:

(1) Mervyn Charles, BSc, MIMechE, Maj RE; *b* 12 Sept 1913; *m* 1949 *Inger Dahl, dau of Dahl Sorensen, of Bellahojvei, Copenhagen, and *d* 1985, leaving:

1a +Peter Mervyn Dahl; *b* 6 Feb 1950; *m* 1976 *Ann Patricia Taylor and has issue

(2) +Dermot Chenevix, OBE; [Cdr Dermot Coote OBE RN, 21 Carlton Court, Wells, Somerset BA5 1SF]; *b* 30 April 1915; Cdr RN WW II (despatches); *m* 3 March 1945 *Dorothy, 2nd Offr WRNS, dau of Richard Oliver, of Plymouth, and has:

1a +Christopher Chenevix [Lt-Cdr Christopher Coote RN, 11 Warsash Rd, Warsash, Hants]; *b* 17 May 1946; *educ* St Edward's Sch Oxford, RNC Dartmouth and RNEC Manadon (BSc Eng); Lt-Cdr RN; *m* 1971 *Cheryl, late QARRNS, dau of William Bridge, and has issue:

1b +James Chenevix; *b* 1971; *educ* Canford, Reading U (BEng) and RMA Sandhurst; Capt POW Roy Regt

2b +Timothy Charles; *b* 1973; *educ* Canford, TCD (BA) and RMA Sandhurst; 2nd Lt Irish Gds

2a +Richard Anthony [Richard Coote Esq, 9 Fordham Close, Ashwell, Herts SG7 5LJ]; *b* 14 July 1950; *educ* St Edward's Sch Oxford and U of Kent (BSc); *m* 1974 *Lynne BA, dau of Sydney Matthews, and has issue:

1b +Christopher Neil; *b* 1977

2b +William Richard; *b* 1987

1b *Emma Louise; *b* 1980

(1) *Cecilia Maud [Mrs John Gordon, 4 Chapel Lane, Alnwick, Northumberland NE66 1XT]; *b* 29 June 1911; *m* 1st 21 Dec 1935 (*divorce* 1945) Benjamin Thomas Bowman; *m* 2nd 25 March 1950 (*divorce* 1952) Mortimer Wilmot Bennitt, U-Sec Min of Works, son of Frederick Wilmot Bennitt, of Bletchley, Bucks; *m* 3rd 19 Jan 1962 *John Ainsworth Gordon, son of George Sutton Gordon, of 26 Violet Bank Rd, Sheffield, and by her 1st husb has issue:

1a *Charles Christopher Benjamin [Charles Bowman Esq, Mariners, Anglesea Rd, Wivenhoe, Colchester, Essex CO7 9JR]; *b* 26 July 1939; *educ* Royal GS Newcastle-upon-Tyne and HMS *Worcester*; *m* 1961 *June Vivian, dau of William Murray, of Arcadia, Mount Healey, Rothbury, Northumberland, and has issue:

1b *Timothy Charles; *b* 9 March 1968

1b *Susan Louise; *b* 20 Oct 1962

2b *Emma Lucy; *b* 23 April 1966

2a *James Thomas CBE (1997) [James Bowman Esq CBE, 4 Brownlow Rd, Reigate, Surrey RH1 6AW]; *b* 6 Nov 1941; *educ* Newcastle Cathedral Choir Sch, King's Sch Ely and New Coll Oxford (BA, Dip Ed)

(2) *Patricia Aileen [Mrs Nelles Timmerman, 55 Waterford Drive, House No 407, Weston, ON M9R 2N7, Canada], Section Offr WAAF, attd RAF Delegation, Washington, USA; *b* 20 Dec 1919; *m* 28 June 1943 *A/Cdre Nelles Woods Timmerman, DSO, DFC, CD, RCAF, and has issue:

1a *Mark; *b* 4 Sept 1945

2a *Peter; *b* 4 Dec 1950

1a *Nicola Mary; *b* 15 May 1952; *m* 1979 *Eric Jean Pierre Maillé and has:

1b *Victor Alfred; *b* 1993

1b *Dominique Patricia; *b* 1986

5 Arthur Philip, Dep Govr Red Sea Province, Inspr Sudan Civ Serv, Order Nile 4th Cl; *b* 24 Jan 1887; *m* 5 Sept 1918 Margaretta (*d* 17 Sept 1977), 2nd dau of Albert Leslie Wright, of Butterley Hall, Derbyshire (*see* FITZWALTER, B), and *d* 5 Oct 1954, leaving issue:

(1) Richard Leslie St George (Rev), Lt RE, curate Yardley, Birmingham 1950–54, vicar St Peter's, Tile Cross, Birmingham 1954–57, Vicar All Saints, Gravelly Hill, Birmingham 1957; *b* 23 April 1922; *educ* Repton, Trin Coll Cambridge (MA 1949) and Westcott Ho Theol Coll Cambridge; *d* unm 13 Aug 1967

(2) +Stephen Arthur [Stephen Coote Esq, Pippins, Adforton, Leintwardine, Salop SY7 0NF]; *b* 12 Sept 1925; *educ* Repton, Selwyn Coll Cambridge and

RAC Cirencester; late Lt Rifle Bde; *m* 17 Feb 1951 *Sheila Mary, dau of Basil Archibald Collett Healey, of Brockworth, Glos and has:

1a +Michael Philip John [Michael Coote Esq, 55 Mid Lavant, Lavant, W Sussex]; *b* 26 March 1952; *educ* Repton and Merristwood Ag Coll; *m* 23 Sept 1978 *Barbara Jean, dau of Darrell Cecil Phipps of Branscombe, Devon, and has:

1b +Samuel Jack [Samuel Coote Esq, 4 Abbey Passage, Winchester, Hants]; *b* 7 June 1980; *educ* Westgate Sch and Peter Symonds Coll Winchester

2b +Thomas Michael; *b* 22 Dec 1982; *educ* Westgate Sch Winchester

1b *Ellen Jean; *b* 29 Aug 1984; *educ* Westgate Sch Winchester

2a Timothy Stephen; *b* 3 April 1954; *educ* Repton and Merristwood Ag Coll; *k* in a motor accident 23 Oct 1976

3a +Nicholas Anthony [Nicholas Coote Esq, 20a New Quebec St, London]; *b* 26 Nov 1955; *educ* Repton and Bingley Coll W Yorks

4a +Peter Richard [Peter Coote Esq, 41 Potters Close, Ludlow, Salop]; *b* 26 March 1965; *educ* Ludlow Sch and Hereford Tech; *m* 27 April 1996 *Sharon Ann, dau of Jean Margaret Mytton, of Ludlow, and has:

1b *Amber Danielle; *b* 12 Nov 1993

1a Bryony Mary; *b* 10 March 1958; *k* in a motor accident 23 Oct 1976

(1) (Margaretta) Anne, SRN, RAFNS; *b* 7 June 1919; *m* 8 March 1946 *Geoffrey Cecil Morris, son of Cecil Morris, and had issue:

1a *William Philip; *b* 28 Jan 1947; *educ* Uppingham

1a *Sally Margaretta; *b* 24 June 1948

(2) *Bridget [Mrs Reginald Whinney, Brickfield Cottage, Brickfield Lane, Walhampton, Lymington, Hants SO41 5RD]; *b* 4 Feb 1924; *m* 30 July 1959 Capt Reginald Fife Whinney, DSC, RN (*d* 1992), er son of Lt-Col Harold Fife Whinney, DSO, OBE, Oxon and Bucks LI, and has issue:

1a *Alison Bridget; *b* 18 March 1963; *m* 1991 *Jonathan West, of Petersfield, Hants, and has issue:

1b *Bede Robert Fife; *b* 1992

1b *Fritha Anne; *b* 1995

6 Maxwell Henry, Capt RFA, W/Cdr RAF, WW I with RFA, RFC and RAF, regular service with RAF to 1929 (ret), WW II with RAF (despatches); *b* 1 June 1895; *m* 22 Jan 1935 Muriel Evelyn (*d* 15 March 1970), widow of Walter Jagger, MB, CM, dau of Evelyn Arthur Rich (*see* 1970 edn RICH, Bt)

2 Ella Cecilia; *b* 12 April 1883; *d* 7 Feb 1901

3 Mary Melesina; *b* 14 Sept 1888; *m* 9 May 1917 John Henry Goldsmith, late Sudan Pol Serv, er son of Rev Henry Goldsmith, CMS, and *d* 24 Nov 1964, leaving issue. He *d* 27 Jan 1935

Sir ALGERNON *d* 22 Oct 1920; his est son,

Sir Ralph Algernon Coote, 13th Bt, Capt 17th Lancers; *b* 22 Sept 1874; *m* 12 April 1904 Alice Matilda Mary (*d* 12 Aug 1975), yr dau of Thomas Wingfield Webber, DL, JP, of Kellyville, Queen's Co, and had issue:

1 JOHN RALPH (Sir), **14th Bt**

2 Thomas Charles, MBE (1946); Pncpl Planner Min Housing and Local Govt; *b* 24 Aug 1907; *educ* Tonbridge and UCL (BSc Eng 1928); *m* 14 June 1932 Zulimah Paton Sherriff (*d* 1996), dau of William Paton Sherriff, of Delgany, Co Wicklow, and *d* 1981

Sir RALPH *d* 2 July 1941; his est son,

Sir John Ralph Coote, 14th Bt, CB (1957), CBE (1946), DSC, R-Adml (ret 1958); *b* 10 Jan 1905; *educ* RNCs Osborne and Dartmouth; served WW II; *m* 14 Dec 1927 Noreen Una, JP (Wilts 1950) (*d* 4 March 1996), only dau of Wilfred Tighe, of Rossanagh, Ashford, Co Wicklow, and *d* 23 Jan 1978, having had issue:

1 Sir CHRISTOPHER JOHN COOTE, **15th and present Bt**

2 +Terence Eyre [Terence Coote Esq, Rushmoor, The Warren, Radlett, Herts WD7 7DU]; *b* 22 May 1933; *educ* Winchester; *m* 22 May 1976 *Jennifer W, only dau of H B Cumming, of Bulawayo, Rhodesia, and has issue:

(1) +Jonathan Eyre; *b* 1977

(1) *Sarah Jane; *b* 1980

COPE OF BERKELEY

Creation: B. (LP, UK) 1997.

THE BARON COPE OF BERKELEY, of Berkeley, Co Gloucester (Sir John Ambrose Cope, PC (1988)) [The Rt Hon the Lord Cope of Berkeley PC, House of Lords, London SW1A 0PW]; *b* 13 May 1937; *educ* Oakham Sch Rutland; chartered accountant; Offr RA and RE Nat Serv and TA; Staff C Party 1965–70; Special Assist to Sec State DTI 1972–74, MP (C) S Glos 1974–83, Northavon 1983–97, Govt Whip 1979–87, Ld Commr Treasury 1981–83, Dep Ch Whip 1983–87, Min State Employment and Min for Small Business 1987–89, Dep Chm C Party and Jt Treas 1990–92, ktd 1991, Paymaster Gen 1992–94, Sec: C Parly Fin Ctee, Parly Gp for Concorde, C Parly Smaller Business Ctee 1975–77 (V-Chm 1977–79); Sr Comr Roy Hosp Chelsea 1992–94, Pres Inst Business Counsellors 1988–90, Hon V-Pres Nat Chamber Trade; Patron Avon Riding for Disabled; author: *Acorns to Oaks (Policy for Small Business)* (with Bernard Weatherill, 1967), *A Funny Thing Happened* (ed, 1991), *I'm Sorry You Were In When I Called* (1992); *m* 1969 *Djemila Lovell, dau of Col P V L Payne, of Dorset, and Mrs Tanetta Blackden, and has two daus

Lineage: GEORGE COPE, MC, of Leicester; FRIBA; had:

JOHN AMBROSE (Sir), *cr* a **Baron**

CORK and ORRERY

Arms: Per bend embattled arg. and gu. **Crest:** Out of a ducal coronet or a lion's head per pale embattled arg. and gu. **Supporters:** Two lions per pale embattled, the dexter gu. and arg., the sinister arg. and gu. **Motto:** God's providence is mine inheritance. **Creations:** B. (I) 6 May 1616 (Lord Boyle, Baron of Youghal); V. (I) (Dungarvan) and E. (I) (Cork) both 26 Oct 1620; B. (I) 28 Feb 1627/8 (Lord Boyle Baron of Broghill and Baron of Bandon Bridge), V. (I) (Boyle of Kinalmeaky) all 28 Feb 1627; E. (I) (Orrery) 5 Sept 1660; B. (GB) 5 Sept 1711 (Boyle of Marston).

THE 14TH EARL OF THE COUNTY OF CORK and 14TH EARL OF ORRERY, Viscount of Dungarvan, Viscount Boyle, of Kinalmeaky, **Lord Boyle, Baron of Youghal**, Co Cork, Baron of Bandon Bridge, **Lord Boyle, Baron of Broghill** and **Baron Boyle of Marston**, Co Somerset (Lt-Cdr John William Boyle, DSC, VRD) [Lt-Cdr The Rt Hon The Earl of Cork and Orrery DSC, VRD, Nether Craigantaggart, Dunkeld, Perthshire PH8 0HQ]; *b* 12 May 1916; *s* bro 1995; *educ* Harrow and King's Coll London (BSc 1937); Lt-Cdr RNVR WW II (despatches twice), FICE; *m* 16 Oct 1943 *Mary Leslie, only dau of Gen Sir Robert Gordon-Finlayson, KCB, CMG, DSO, of Wickerstreet Ho, Kersey, Suffolk, and has:

1 +JOHN RICHARD, *Viscount Dungarvan* [Lt-Cdr Viscount Dungarvan RN, Lickfold House, Petworth, W Sussex GU28 9EY]; *b* 3 Nov 1945; *educ* Harrow and RNC Dartmouth; dir E D & F Man Sugar Ltd, memb Baltic Exchange 1979; *m* 2 June 1973 *Hon Rebecca Juliet Noble, yst dau of Baron Glenkinglas, PC (LP, *d* 1984), and has:

(1) +Rory Jonathan Courtenay; *b* 10 Dec 1978

(1) *Cara Mary Cecilia; *b* 16 June 1976

(2) *Davina Claire Theresa; *b* 10 Dec 1978

2 +Robert William [The Hon Robert Boyle, 30 Durand Gardens, London SW9 0PP]; *b* 5 March 1948; *educ* Harrow and Ch Ch Coll Oxford (MA); FCA, ptnr Coopers and Lybrand; *m* 1987 *Fiona Mary, dau of Hon (Oliver) Piers St Aubyn, MC (*see* SAINT LEVAN, B), and has issue:

(1) +Richard Piers; *b* 1988

3 +(Charles) Reginald [The Hon Reginald Boyle, 6840 West 83rd St Terrace, Bloomington, MN 55438, USA]; *b* 3 Jan 1957; *educ* Harrow and RMA; late Capt Coldstream Gds, now stockbroker with Morgan Stanley Dean Witter; *m* 1987 *Susan Shields, dau of Philip Hoene, of Duluth, Min., and has:

(1) +(John) Arthur Hoene; *b* 30 Nov 1994

(1) *Georgina Margaret; *b* 1989

Cork, previous creations: EDWARD III's grandson Edward, 2nd Duke of York, was before succeeding his father in that title created Earl of Cork (Feb 1389/90). He had earlier been made Earl of Rutland (*see* also RUTLAND, D, preliminary remarks).

Lineage: LUDOVIC BOYLE; living *temp* HENRY III; ancestor of:

LEWIS BOYLE, of Bidney; living *temp* HENRY VI; founded a friary in Hereford; *m* Elizabeth, dau of William Russell, of Hereford, and had, with an er s:

ROGER BOYLE, of Canterbury; *m* Jane, dau of Thomas Patishall, of Hereford, and had, with other issue:

1 John, of Hereford; *m* Alice, dau of Alexander Haworth, of Burop Hall, Herefs, and had issue

2 ROGER

3 Michael; had:

(1) Michael Boyle, Archbp Armagh; *b c* 1609; *m* 1st Margaret, dau of Rt Rev George Synge (*see* SYNGE, Bt); *m* 2nd Mary, dau of 5th Baron Inchiquin (*qv*), and *d* 10 Dec 1702, leaving by her:

1a MURROUGH BOYLE, 1st VISCOUNT BLESINGTON [*sic*], Co Wicklow, so *cr* 23 Aug 1673, as also BARON BOYLE (both I), with special remainder to the heirs male of the body of his f, PC (I 1675); *b* 1648; MP Kilmallock 1665–66, Govr 1679–92, Ld Justice Ireland 1696; *m* 1st Mary, dau of John Parker, Archbp Dublin; *m* 2nd Nov 1672 Lady Anne Coote, dau of 2nd Earl of Mountrath (*see* COOTE, Bt), and *d* 26 April 1718, leaving by her:

1b CHARLES BOYLE, 2nd and last VISCOUNT BLESINGTON; MP Blessington 1711–18; *m* 1st Rose, dau of Hon Charles Coote by Penelope, dau of Arthur Hill (*see* COOTE, Bt); *m* 2nd 11 July 1709 Martha, dau of Samuel Matthews, of Bennetstown, Co Kilkenny, and *dsps* 2 June 1732, when his titles expired

1b Anne; *m* 1st Sir William Stewart, 4th Bt, of Ramelton (*qv*), who was also 2nd Viscount Mountjoy; *m* 2nd John Farquharson and *d* 27 Oct 1741

1a Honora; *m* 1st 3rd Earl of Ardglass (*see* CROMWELL, B, preliminary remarks); *m* 2nd by 1687 Francis Cuffe, MP (1 Parl) Co Mayo (*d* 26 Dec 1694); *m* 3rd Sir Thomas Burdett, 1st Bt, of Garahill, Co Carlow (*see* WELDON, Bt)

The 2nd son,

ROGER BOYLE, of Canterbury and Preston, by Faversham, Kent; *m* 16 Oct 1564 Joan (*d* 20 March 1586), dau of John Naylor, of Renvile, Kent, and *d* 24 March 1576, having had, with another s and dau:

1 John (Rt Rev), DD Oxon, Bp Cork and Cloyne 1617; *m* Elizabeth (*m* 2nd Sir William Hull, of Lemcon, Co Cork), est dau and coheir of Matthew Lacy, of Melton, Leics, and *d* 10 July 1620, having had, with other issue:

(1) Edward; *m* Mary, dau of Sir William Hull, of Lemcon, Co Cork

(2) John, of Borris, Co Cork; admitted Gray's Inn 3 Aug 1626; *m* Anne, widow of Martin Dodsworth and dau of Jasper Scoales, of Waterford, and left, with other issue:

1a Barbara; *m* Sir John Browne, of the Hospital, Co Limerick

2 RICHARD, **1st Earl (of Corke)**

1 Mary; *m* Sir Richard Smyth, of Ballynatray, Co Waterford

The 2nd son,

RICHARD BOYLE, **1st Earl of the County of Corke** [*sic*], so *cr* 26 Oct 1620, as also VISCOUNT OF DUNGARVAN, Co Waterford, and earlier 6 May 1616 LORD BOYLE, BARON OF YOUGHAL, Co Cork (all I), PC (I Feb 1612/3, E 1640); *b* 13 Oct 1566; *educ* King's Canterbury, Corpus Christi Coll Cambridge and Middle Temple; settled Ireland, where in 1602 he bought up all Sir Walter Raleigh's former estates (*c* 12,000 acres in Cos Cork, Tipperary and Waterford) for £1,500 (just over £103,000 in late 1990s terms); ktd 1603, MP Lismore 1613–15, Ld Justice Ireland 1629, Ld High Treasurer Ireland 1631, author: *The True Remembrancer* (autobiography); *m* 1st 6 Nov 1595 Joan (*dsp* 14 Dec 1599), dau and coheir of William Apsley, of Limerick, with whom he acquired an estate of £500 a year; *m* 2nd 25 July 1603 Catherine (*d* 16 Feb 1629/30), dau of Sir Geoffrey Fenton, Pncpl Sec State for Ireland, and *d* 15 Sept 1643, having had:

1 RICHARD BOYLE, **2nd Earl of the County of Corke** (as which *s f* 1643), **2nd Viscount Boyle** (as which *s* yr bro 1642) and 1st EARL OF BURLINGTON, Co York, so *cr* 20 March 1663/4, as also earlier 4 Nov 1644 BARON CLIFFORD OF LANESBOROUGH, Co York (both E), PC (I March 1684/5 and 1690); *b* 20 Oct 1612; ktd 1624, MP Appleby 1640–43, Govr Youghal 1641, Ld Treasurer Ireland 1660–95, Ld Lt W R Yorks March-Nov 1667 and 1679–87, attainted by JAMES II's Irish Parl May 1689 but restored 1690; *m* 3 July 1634 Elizabeth (*d* 6 Jan 1698), *de jure* Baroness Clifford of the 1628 *cr* in her own right, dau and heiress of 5th Earl of Cumberland (*see* DE CLIFFORD, B), and *d* 15 Jan 1697/8, having had, with other issue:

(1) CHARLES BOYLE, 2nd BARON CLIFFORD OF LANESBOROUGH, as which called up to E Ho Lds *vp* 16 July 1689, having been earlier called up to I Ho Lds *vp* 20 Feb 1662/3 in f's Viscountcy of Dungarvan; *bapt* 12 Dec 1639; MP (Tory) Tamworth 1670–79 and Yorks 1679–81; *m* 1st 7 May 1661 Lady Jane Seymour (*d* 23 Nov 1679), 3rd dau of 2nd Duke of Somerset (*qv*), and had issue:

1a CHARLES BOYLE, **3rd Earl of the County of Corke** and 2nd EARL OF BURLINGTON, PC (I 1695, E Jan 1701/2); *b* by 1674; MP (Tory) Appleby 1690–94, Govr Co Cork 1691, Ld Treasurer Ireland 1695–Feb 1703/4; *m* 26 Jan 1687/8 Juliana (*d* 17 Oct 1750), dau and heiress of Hon Henry Noel, of Luffenham, Rutland (*see* GAINSBOROUGH, E), and *d* 9 Feb 1703/4, having had issue:

1b RICHARD BOYLE, **4th Earl of the County of Corke** and 3rd and last EARL OF BURLINGTON, KG (1730), PC (I 1714, E 1729); *b* 25 April 1695; his claim admitted 25 May 1737 to the 1628 Barony of Clifford; architect of Chiswick House, connoisseur of paintings, patron of Gay and Pope in literature and Kent in architecture and interior decoration; *m* 21 March 1720/1 Lady Dorothy Savile (*d* 21 Sept 1758), er dau and coheir of William, Marquess of Halifax (*see* HALIFAX, E, preliminary remarks), and *d* 3 Dec 1753, when all his titles expired bar the Earldom of Corke) and Barony of Clifford, having had, with two other daus (*d young*):

1c Charlotte; *m* 4th Duke of Devonshire (*qv*) and had, with other issue:

1d AUGUSTUS HENRY CAVENDISH, BARON CLIFFORD (as which *s* maternal gf) and 1st EARL OF BURLINGTON of the 1831 and present *cr* (*see* DEVONSHIRE, D)

1b Elizabeth; *m* 28 Aug 1719 Sir Henry Arundell Bedingfeld, 3rd Bt (*see* PASTON-BEDINGFELD, Bt), and *d* 25 Nov 1751

2b Juliana; *m* 16 Jan 1719, as his 2nd w, Charles, Lord Bruce, afterwards 4th Earl of Elgin and 3rd Earl of Ailesbury (*see* ELGIN AND KINCARDINE, E, also AILESBURY, M), and *dsp* 26 March 1739

3b Henrietta; *m* Sept 1726 1st Earl of Shannon (*qv*) and *d* 13 Dec 1746, leaving issue

2a HENRY BOYLE, 1st and last BARON CARLTON, of Carleton, Co York (GB), so *cr* 19 Oct 1714, PC (1701); MP (Whig) Tamworth 1689–90, Aldborough Feb-May 1690, Cambridge U 1692–1705 and Westminster 1705–10, a Ld Treasury 1699–1701, Chllr Exchequer 1701–08, Ld Treasurer Ireland 1704–10, Pncpl Sec State for North 1708–10, Ld Pres Cncl 1721–25; *d* unm 14 March 1725, when the Barony expired

1a Elizabeth; *m* 1st 4th Earl of Barrymore (*d* 5 June 1747)

2a Mary; *m* 1 Dec 1685 2nd Marquess of Queensberry (*qv*) and *d* 2 Oct 1709

3a Arabella; *m* 1699 Henry, Earl of Shelburne (*see* LANSDOWNE, M), and *dsp* Oct 1740

(1) (cont.) The 2nd BARON CLIFFORD OF LANESBOROUGH *m* 2nd Lady Arethusa Berkely (*d* 11 Feb 1742/3), 6th dau of 1st Earl of Berkeley (*see* BERKELEY, B), and *dvp* 12 Oct 1694, having by her had issue:

4a Arethusa; *m* James Vernon

(1) Frances; *m* 1st Col Francis Courtenay; *m* 2nd April 1662 Wentworth, Earl of Roscommon

(2) Elizabeth; *m* 11 April 1664 Nicholas, Earl of Thanet (*see* DE CLIFFORD, B), and *d* 1725

(3) Anne; *m* Jan 1668 2nd Earl of Sandwich (*qv*)

(4) Henrietta; *m* 1665 Laurence, Earl of Rochester, and *d* 12 April 1687

2 LEWIS BOYLE, **1st Viscount Boyle of Kinalmeaky**, Co Cork, so *cr* 28 Feb 1627/8, as also BARON OF BANDON BRIDGE (both I), with special remainder to the heirs male of his f's body, failing whom, to the heirs male of his f forever; *b* 23 May 1619; ktd 1628; *m* 26 Dec 1639 Lady Elizabeth Feilding (*d* Sept 1667, when her own title expired), Countess of Guildford in her own right (so *cr* 14 July 1660), dau of 1st Earl of Denbigh (*see* DENBIGH AND DESMOND, E), and *dsp*, *ka* Battle of Liscarroll 2 Sept 1642, when his titles passed to his er bro

3 ROGER BOYLE, **1st Earl of Orrery**, so *cr* 5 Sept 1660, as also earlier 28 Feb 1627/8 LORD BOYLE, BARON OF BROGHILL (both I), PC (1665–79); *b* 25 April 1621; memb of CROMWELL's Other House (one of only nine peers summoned and three who actually took their seats); Pres Munster 1660; *m* 27 Jan 1640/1 Lady Margaret Howard, 3rd dau of 2nd Earl of Suffolk (*see* SUFFOLK and BERKSHIRE, E), and *d* 16 Oct 1679, leaving, with five daus (including Elizabeth, *m* 1660 1st Viscount Powerscourt (*qv*) of the Feb 1664/5 *cr*):

(1) ROGER BOYLE, **2nd Earl of Orrery**; *bapt* 24 Aug 1646; *m* 6 Feb 1664/5 Lady Mary Sackville (*d* 4 Nov 1710), dau of 5th Earl of Dorset (*see* SACKVILLE, B), and *d* 29 March 1681/2, leaving issue:

1a LIONEL BOYLE, **3rd Earl of Orrery**; *b* 1670; *m* Feb 1692/3 his cousin Mary, illegitimate dau of 6th Earl of Dorset (*see* SACKVILLE, B), and *dsp* 24 Aug 1703

2a CHARLES BOYLE, **4th Earl of Orrery**, KT (1705), PC (Feb 1710/1); *b* 28 July 1674; *educ* St Paul's and Ch Ch Oxford; Maj-Gen 1710–16 when sacked for suspected Jacobitism (imprisoned Tower of London 1722–March 1722/3), Envoy Extrdy and Plen to negotiate Treaty of Utrecht 1713, *cr* 5 Sept 1711 BARON BOYLE OF MARSTON, Co Somerset (GB); his name given to a new astronomical instrument by its inventor, George Graham; he also was a controversialist, disputing with the scholar Dr Bentley as to the authenticity of the Epistles of Phalaris (the debate inspiring Swift to the *Battle of the Books*); *b* 28 July 1674; *m* 30 March 1706 Lady Elizabeth Cecil (*d* 12 June 1708), only dau of 5th Earl of Exeter (*see* EXETER, M), and *d* 28 Aug 1731, leaving an only son:

1b JOHN BOYLE, **5th Earl of Orrery** and **5th Earl of the County of Corke**

(2) HENRY, f of 1st EARL OF SHANNON (*qv*)

4 FRANCIS BOYLE, 1st VISCOUNT SHANNON, Co Limerick (I), so *cr* 6 Sept 1660, PC (I); *b* 25 June 1623; *educ* Eton; Govr City and Co of Cork 1672; *m* 24 Oct 1638 Elizabeth, dau of Sir Robert Killigrew, and was *bur* 19 April 1699, having had:

(1) Richard; *m* Elizabeth, est dau of Sir John Ponsonby, of Bessborough (*see* BESSBOROUGH, E), and *dvp* in or after Sept 1679, leaving:

1a RICHARD BOYLE, 2nd and last VISCOUNT SHANNON; *b c* 1675Col 25th Foot Jan 1714/5–21, Lt-Gen Staff Ireland 1715, C-in-C Ireland 1720 and 1727–40, Col 7th Horse Gds 1721–27, Col 4th Troop of Horse Gds March 1726/7–40, Gen 1735, FM 1739; MP (Whig) Arundel 1708–10, Hythe 1710–11 and E Grinstead 1715–22 and 1722–34; *m* 1st after Aug 1703 Mary, widow of his cousin **3rd Earl of Orrery**; *m* 2nd Jan 1720/1 Grace, dau of John Senhouse, of Netherhall, Cumberland, and *dspm* 20 Dec 1740, when the Viscountcy expired, leaving by his 2nd w:

1b Grace; *m* 30 Oct 1744 2nd Duke of Dorset (*see* SACKVILLE, B) and *dsp* 10 May 1763

5 Robert, of Stalbridge, Dorset; fndr memb and Govr New England Co 1662–91; *b* 25 Jan 1626/7; *educ* Eton; chemist (proponent of Boyle's Law, which states the relationship between pressure and volume of gas at a given temperature), fndr memb Roy Soc 1660, philosopher, author: *The Sceptical Chymist* (1661), *Occasional Reflections on Several Subjects* (1665), *The Origin of Forms and Qualities* (1666) and a romance *The Martyrdom of Theodora and Didymus* (1687); *d* 30 Dec 1691

1 Alice; *m* 1st 21 July 1631 David, 1st Earl of Barrymore; *m* 2nd John Barry, of Liscarrol, and *d* 1667

2 Sarah; *m* 1st Sir Thomas Moore, yr son of Garrett, Viscount Moore of Drogheda (*see* DROGHEDA, E); *m* 2nd 1st Baron Digby (*qv*) and *d* 14 July 1633

3 Lettice; *m* 25 July 1629 George, Lord Goring (son and heir of George Goring, Earl of Norwich; *see* GORING, Bt), who survived her, and *dvp* July 1657

4 Joan; *m* 15 Aug 1630 16th Earl of Kildare (*see* LEINSTER, D)

5 Catherine; *m* 2nd Viscount Ranelagh and *d* 23 Dec 1691, leaving issue (*see* ROSSE, E)

6 Dorothy; *b* 31 Dec 1617; *m* 1st 1627 Sir Arthur Loftus, son of Sir Adam Loftus, of Rathfarnham; *m* 2nd Col Gilbert Talbot (*see* TALBOT OF MALAHIDE, B), and *d* 26 March 1668, leaving by her 1st husb:

(1) ADAM LOFTUS, 1st and last VISCOUNT LISBURNE, so *cr* 29 Jan 1685/6, as also BARON OF RATHFARNHAM (both I), PC (I March 1684/5); MP Lismore 1661–66; *m* Lucy, dau of 6th Baron Chandos of Sudeley, and *dspm* 15 Sept 1691, *ka* cmdg a Williamite regt Siege of Limerick, when his titles expired, leaving:

1a Lucy; *m* Thomas, 1st Marquess of Wharton (*see* WHARTON, B) and had issue

7 Mary; *m* 21 July 1641 4th Earl of Warwick (*see* WARWICK, BROOKE and, E)

8 Margaret, *d* unm

The 4th EARL OF CORK's cousin (and 4th EARL OF ORRERY's s),

JOHN BOYLE, **5th Earl of the County of Corke** and **5th Earl of Orrery**; *b* 13 Jan 1706/7; author: *Remarks* (commentary on Swift, a friend of his); *m* 1st 9 May 1728 Lady Henrietta Hamilton (*d* 22 Aug 1732), yst dau of George, 1st Earl of Orkney (*qv*), and had issue:

1 Charles, *Viscount Dungarvan*; *b* 20 Feb 1728/9; *m* 18 May 1753 Susannah (*m* 2nd 17 Feb 1761 1st Earl of Ailesbury (*see* AILESBURY, M) and *d* 4th Feb 1783), dau of Henry Hoare, of Stourhead, Wilts, and *dvp* 16 Sept 1759, leaving an only child:

(1) Henrietta; *m* 18 Oct 1777 1st Viscount O'Neill (*see* O'NEILL, B)

2 HAMILTON BOYLE, **6th Earl of the County of Corke** and **6th Earl of Orrery**; *b* 3 Feb 1729/30; *educ* Westminster and Ch Ch Oxford; MP (I Parl) Charleville

1759–60 and (Whig, GB Parl) Warwick 1761–62, DCL Oxford; *b* 3 Feb 1729; *d* unm 17 Jan 1764

1 Elizabeth; *m* 1749 Sir Thomas Worsley, Bt (*d* 16 Jan 1800), and had issue

The **5th Earl** *m* 2nd 30 June 1738 Margaret (*d* 24 May 1758), dau and sole heir of John Hamilton, of Caledon, Co Tyrone, and *d* 23 Nov 1762, having by her had issue:

3 EDMUND, **7th Earl**

2 Lucy; *m* 20 July 1765 4th Viscount Torrington (*qv*) and *d* 18 March 1792, leaving issue

3 Catherine Agnes, *d* unm

The 6th EARL's half-bro,

EDMUND BOYLE, **7th Earl of the County of Corke** and **7th Earl of Orrery**; *b* 21 Nov 1742; *educ* Westminster and Ch Ch Oxford; *m* 1st 31 Aug 1764 (*divorce* 1782) Anne, dau and eventual coheir of Kelland Courtenay, of Painsford, Devon; *m* 2nd 17 June 1786 Mary (*d* 30 May 1840), yst dau of 1st Viscount Galway (*qv*), and by his 1st w had, with another son:

1 John Richard, *Viscount Dungarvan*; *b* 27 May 1765; *dvp* 8 March 1768

2 EDMUND, **8th Earl**

3 Courtenay (Sir), V-Adml, KCH; *b* 3 Sept 1770; *m* 16 April 1799 Carolina Amelia (*d* 7 Oct 1851), dau of William Poyntz, of Midgham, Berks, and *d* 21 May 1844, leaving, with other issue:

(1) Courtenay Edmund William, R-Adml; *b* 3 Aug 1800; *m* 12 Nov 1836 Mary (*m* 2nd at Paris 11 July 1860 Paul de Mocombe, Judge Tbnl de Première Instance Rouen), dau of W Wallace Ogle, of Causey Park, Northumberland, and *d* 11 Feb 1859, having had a dau (*d* young 1851)

(2) Charles John; *b* 10 May 1806; *m* 3 July 1849 Zacyntha (*d* 5 March 1907), dau of Gen Sir Lorenzo Moore, and *d* 20 Aug 1885, leaving, with other issue:

1a Mordaunt Charles, Maj KRRC; *b* 21 June 1850; *m* 12 July 1877 Charlotte Jane (*d* 21 April 1917), yst dau of Col Hon Robert Boyle, Coldstream Gds (*see* below), and *d* Kurol, Upper Egypt, 5 May 1885, leaving issue:

1b Robert; *b* 31 Aug 1880; *d* 16 April 1921

2a Lionel Richard Cavendish, CMG (1918), MVO (1903), TD (1919), Lt-Col and Hon Col cmdg 2nd Bn HAC WW I, formerly RN; *b* 24 Nov 1851; *m* 4 Sept 1883 Alice (*d* 11 March 1946), dau of Rev Richard Thomas Pulteney Pulteney, of Ashley, Northants, and *d* 2 Jan 1920, leaving issue:

1b Richard Courtenay, DSC, DL (Herts 1976), Capt RN; *b* 20 May 1902; served WW II, Dir Boom Defence Admlty 1949, ADC to HM THE QUEEN 1953; *m* 17 Dec 1936 *Guendolen Mabel Maclean, DL (Herts) [Mrs Richard Boyle DL, 14 Mandeville Close, Broxbourne, Herts EN10 7PN], yst dau of Lt-Col Edward Hugh Griffith, CBE, of 16 Craven Hill, W2, and *d* 1986, leaving issue:

1c +John Richard [John Boyle Esq, 40 Drayton Gardens, London SW10], late Midshipman RNVR, dir Wm Dawson & Sons Ltd (Antique Books); *b* 28 Feb 1938; *educ* Eton and Trin Coll Cambridge; *m* 1st 8 Feb 1964 (*divorce* 1978) Jeannine Mary (*m* 2nd 1978, as his 2nd w, Sir David Barber, 3rd Bt; *qv*), er dau of Capt Timothy John Gurney, of The White House, Hare Street, nr Buntingford, Herts (*see* 1935 edn DE BATHE, Bt), and has issue:

1d +Richard Burlington; *b* 27 June 1966

2d +Charles Robert; *b* 10 March 1969; *m* 30 Aug 1997 *Laura J, dau of John Shaw by his w Jean

3d +Patrick William; *b* 3 March 1971

1c (cont.) John Boyle *m* 2nd 1978 *Lena Jupp, yst dau of Maj G B Rahr, and has issue:

4d +Harry Courtenay; *b* 1979

1d *Olivia Mary; *b* 1982

2c +William Robert Cavendish [William Boyle Esq, The Mallard, Easton, nr Newbury, Berks]; *b* 21 May 1944; *educ* Eton; *m* 1994 *Jane Anne, dau of John Bainbridge

1c *Belinda [Mrs Thomas McMicking, Miltonise, New Luce, Wigtownshire DG8 0LY; 32 Peel St, London W8 7PD]; *b* 10 Nov 1940; *m* 21 Sept 1963 *Brig Thomas Neil McMicking, late Black Watch, er son of Maj-Gen Neil McMicking, CB, CBE, DSO, MC, of Eastferry, Dunkeld, Perthshire, and has:

1d *Charles Neil; *b* 1965; *m* 1993 *Diana Hall, dau of John Hall, of Newham Buildings, Chathill, Northumberland and has:

1e *Hector Neil Hall; *b* 1996

1e *Isobella Jane Sophia; *b* 1994

2d *James Richard; *b* 1968

1d *Henrietta Sophia; *b* 1972

1b Mary Agneta Francis; *b* 9 Aug 1884; *m* 24 Sept 1912 Capt William Raymond Croft Murray, Gren Gds, only child of Col Denman Murray, of Horsendon, Ryde, IoW, and *d* 17 Oct 1973, leaving issue. He *d* from wounds received in action 25 Feb 1917

2b Alice Leonora Zacyntha; *b* 23 Feb 1886; *m* 29 April 1912 John Francis Eastwood, OBE, KC, barrister, Maj Res of Offrs Gren Gds, est son of John Edmund Eastwood, of Gosden Ho, Surrey, and *d* 23 July 1933, leaving issue. He *d* 30 Jan 1952

3b Audrey Janet; *b* 22 Jan 1888; *m* 1st 18 Sept 1916 Maj Hedworth George Ailwyn Fellowes, MC, son of 1st Baron Ailwyn, PC, KCVO, KBE (*see* 1970 edn). He was *ka* 12 May 1917. She *m* 2nd 24 Jan 1922 Wilfred Valentine Denison, son of Brig-Gen Henry Denison, CB, CBE, and has issue. He *d* 28 Aug 1964

3a Cecil William, Capt Oxon Hus; *b* 16 March 1853; *m* 7 Feb 1877 Eleanor Margaret (*d* 28 May 1922), dau of Charles Buxton, of Fox Warren, MP (*see* BUXTON, Bt), and was *ka* nr Boshof, S Africa, 5 April 1900, leaving issue:

1b Hugo Lionel Charles; *d* young

1b Dorothea Cecil; *m* 22 Sept 1909 Rupert Beresford Butler, son of Dr Alfred James Butler, of BNC Oxford, and *d* 23 April 1965, leaving issue

2b Elisabeth Adeline Cecil; *m* 12 Feb 1919 Col Geoffrey Ernald William Lane, OBE, JP, late Rifle Bde, only son of Very Rev Ernald Lane, Dean of Rochester, and *d* 3 Sept 1969, leaving issue:

4a Henry Charles; *b* 11 June 1857; *d* unm

5a William Lewis, MP Mid Norfolk 1910–18; *b* 27 May 1859; *m* 11 Oct 1887 Charlotte Mary (*d* 23 Oct 1946), est dau of Charles Loyd Norman, and *d* 2 Oct 1918, leaving issue:

1b Charles Norman Cavendish, MC, Capt 5th Bn Rifle Bde, served WWs I (despatches) and II (despatches, US Legion of Merit); *b* 1890; *m* 15 May 1919 Margaret Constance Neville (*d* 28 Jan 1969 aged 86), widow of Bertram Hambro (*see* HAMBRO, B) and dau of Sir Nevile Lubbock (*see* AVEBURY, B), and *dsp* 10 June 1961

1b Evelyn Vere; *m* 3 Feb 1925 Rev Henry Alexander Macnaghten (*see* MACNAGHTEN, Bt) and *d* 7 Nov 1939

6a Ernest Charles Patrick, DSO, Capt Res of Offrs, T/Lt-Col HAC, Capt 1st Co London Imp Yeo, served Boer War 1900–02 (medal with four clasps) and WW I (despatches); *b* 21 Nov 1860; *ka* 7 Feb 1917

1a Audrey Georgiana Florence; *m* 25 June 1884 2nd Baron Tennyson (*qv*) and *d* 7 Dec 1916, leaving issue

(3) Cavendish Spencer, Capt 72nd Regt; *b* 12 May 1814; *m* 19 Dec 1844 Rose Susan (*d* 5 Dec 1902), dau of Lt-Col C C Alexander, RE, and *d* 21 Nov 1868, leaving issue:

1a Courtenay Edmund (Sir), KCB; *b* 21 Oct 1845; MA Oxford; Perm Sec BOT, Priv Sec to Lds Lt Ireland 1868–73 and 1882–85; *m* 20 April 1876 Lady Muriel Sarah Campbell (*d* 30 Sept 1934), dau of 2nd Earl Cawdor (*qv*), and *dsp* 19 May 1901

2a (Charles) Cavendish (Sir), KCMG; *b* 29 May 1849; AMInstCE, Colonial Sec Bermuda 1882–88 and Gibraltar 1888–94, Lt-Govr and Govt Sec Br Guiana 1894–1900, Govr Newfoundland 1901–04 and Mauritius 1904–11; *m* 9 July 1914 Louise Judith, MBE (*d* 10 Feb 1964 aged 90), yst dau of Reuben David Sassoon, MVO, and *dsp* 17 Sept 1916

1a Caroline Louise; *m* 13 July 1871 Rev Charlton George Lane, Rector Little Gaddesden, est son of Rev Charlton Lane, Vicar Hampstead, and *d* Jan 1883, leaving issue. He *d* 2 Nov 1892

(1) Carolina, Maid of Honour to QUEEN ADELAIDE; *d* unm 23 Jan 1883

1 Lucy Isabella; *m* 28 July 1792 Rev Hon George Bridgeman and *d* 7 Sept 1801, leaving issue (*see* BRADFORD, E)

The 7th EARL *d* 6 Oct 1798; his est surv son,

EDMUND BOYLE, **8th Earl of the County of Cork** (first holder of the title to adopt the modern spelling) and **8th Earl of Orrery**, KP (1835); Gen 1825, ADC to GEORGE III; *b* 21 Oct 1767; *m* 9 Oct 1795 Isabella Henrietta (*d* 29 Nov 1843), 3rd dau of William Poyntz, of Midgham, Berks, and *d* 9 June 1856, having had, with other issue:

1 Edmund William, *Viscount Dungarvan*; *b* 2 April 1798; *dvp* 1 Jan 1826

2 Charles, *Viscount Dungarvan*; *b* 5 Dec 1800; *m* 10 March 1828 Catherine (*d* 4 April 1879), yst dau of 2nd Earl of Howth (*see* 1909 edn), and *d* 25 Aug 1834, leaving issue:

(1) RICHARD EDMUND ST LAWRENCE BOYLE, **9th Earl of the County of Cork** and **9th Earl of Orrery**, KP (1860), PC (1866); *b* 19 April 1829; *educ* Eton and Ch Ch Oxford; Ld Lt Somerset 1864–1904, Hon Col N Somerset Yeo, MP Frome 1854–56, Master Buckhounds 1866, 1868–74 and 1880–85, Master Horse 1886 and 1894–95, Speaker Ho Lds 1882, ADC to HM QUEEN VICTORIA 1889–99; *m* 20 July 1853 Emily Charlotte (*d* 10 Oct 1912), 2nd dau of 1st Marquess of Clanricarde, KP (*see* SLIGO, M), and *d* 22 June 1904, having had, with other issue:

1a CHARLES SPENCER CANNING BOYLE, **10th Earl of the County of Cork** and **10th Earl of Orrery**, DL Somerset; *b* 24 Nov 1861; Lt-Col and Hon Col N Somerset Imp Yeo Boer War 1900–02; *m* 21 Nov 1918 Mrs Rosalie Gray (*d* 15 March 1930), dau of William Waterman de Villiers, of Romsey, Hants, and *dsp* 25 March 1925

2a ROBERT JOHN LASCELLES BOYLE, **11th Earl of the County of Cork** and **11th Earl of Orrery**; *b* 8 Nov 1864; Orders of Crown of Belgium and St Maurice and St Lazarus of Italy; *m* 30 April 1890 Josephine Catherine (*d* 2 April 1953), only child of Joseph P Hale, of San Francisco, and *dsp* 13 Oct 1934

1a Emily Harriet Catherine; *m* 27 Jan 1885 James Dalison Alexander, DL, of Oakbank, Sevenoaks, and *d* 28 July 1931, leaving issue. He *d* 21 Oct 1914

2a Grace Elizabeth; *m* 13 Feb 1878 Hon Francis Henry Baring, bro of 2nd Earl of Northbrook (*see* NORTHBROOK, B), and *d* 23 May 1935, leaving issue

3a Honora Janet; *m* 3 July 1875 Robert Kirkman Hodgson, DL, only son of Kirkman Daniel Hodgson, MP, of Ashgrove, Kent and *d* 11 March 1953, leaving issue. He *d* *d* 26 May 1924

4a Dorothy Blanche; *m* 1 Aug 1878 1st Viscount Long (*qv*) and *d* 7 June 1938, leaving issue

5a Isabella Lettice Theodosia; *m* 29 June 1889 James Walker Larnach, of Adderbury, Banbury, Oxon, and *d* 6 April 1904, leaving issue. He *d* 24 Jan 1919

(2) William George, JP Somerset; granted with surv siblings rank of earl's daus/yr sons; Lt-Col Coldstream Gds, MP Frome 1856–57; *b* 12 Aug 1830; *d* unm 24 March 1908

(3) Edmund John, DL Somerset, Maj 85th Foot, Gentleman Usher to Ld Lt Ireland; *b* 25 Nov 1831; *m* 24 April 1866 Ida Waldegrave (*d* 8 Feb 1930), dau of Gen Archibald Money, CB, by Lady Laura Annette, dau of 6th Earl Waldegrave (*qv*), and *d* 21 April 1901, leaving issue:

1a Ida Frances; *d* unm 29 Jan 1924

(1) Louisa Caroline Elizabeth; *m* 3 June 1863 6th Earl of Essex (*qv*), and *d* 5 May 1876, leaving issue

(2) Mary Emily; *m* 1st 24 July 1857 William Edward Hope-Vere (*see* LINLITHGOW, M); *m* 2nd 24 Feb 1873 Lord David Kennedy, bro of 2nd Marquess of Ailsa (*qv*), and *d* 25 Nov 1916, leaving issue

3 John; *b* 13 March 1803; *m* 10 Dec 1835 Hon Cecilia de Ros (*d* 6 Oct 1869), dau of Lord Henry FitzGerald (*see* LEINSTER, D) and Charlotte, Baroness de Ros (*qv*) in her own right, and *d* 6 Dec 1874, leaving issue:

(1) Gerald Edmund, Col Rifle Bde; *b* 20 June 1840; *m* 1st 23 July 1864 Lady Elizabeth Theresa Pepys (*d* 24 Jan 1897), dau of 1st Earl of Cottenham (*qv*), and had issue:

1a Arthur Gerald, Maj and Hon Lt-Col W Som Yeo, Capt Prince Albert's Somersetshire LI; *b* 26 July 1865; *m* 7 June 1890 Elizabeth Evelyn (*d* 15 April 1926), dau of Rev R J Pulteney, Rector Ashley, and *d* 30 June 1912

2a WILLIAM HENRY DUDLEY BOYLE, **12th Earl of the County of Cork** and **12th Earl of Orrery**, GCB (1936, KCB 1931), GCVO (1935); *b* 30 Nov 1873; Naval Attaché Rome 1913–15, Sr Offr Red Sea Patrol and cmded HMS *Repulse* WW I (despatches three times), ADC to HM GEORGE V 1922, R-Adml 2nd Battle Sqdn Atlantic Fleet 1924, R-Adml cmdg 1st Cruiser Sqdn 1926–28, V-Adml cmdg Reserve Fleet 1928, Adml 1932, Pres RNC Greenwich 1929–32, C-in-C Home Fleet 1933–35, C-in-C Portsmouth 1937–39, Adml of the Fleet; First and Pncpl Naval ADC to TM EDWARD VIII and GEORGE VI 1936–38; WW II 1939–40 at Admlty and cmdg combined expdn Narvik 1940; tstee Nat Maritime Museum Greenwich 1939–47, Pres: RN Fund 1942, Shaftesbury Homes and *Arethusa* Training Ship 1943–53 Seamen's Hosp Soc 1946; Grand Cross Legion of Honour, Croix de Guerre avec Palme, Cdr Order of St Maurice and St Lazarus of Italy, Grand Cross Order of St Olav of Norway, 3rd Cl Order of the Nile and 2nd Cl Order of El Nahda of the Hedjaz; *m* 24 July 1902 Lady Florence Cecilia Keppel (*d* 30 June 1963), dau of 7th Earl of Albemarle (*qv*), and *dsp* 19 April 1967

3a Frederick John; *b* 4 July 1875; Capt 3rd Bn Oxon LI, WW I as Capt RASC; granted 7 March 1935 with siblings rank of earl's daus/yr sons; *m* 27 March 1920 Frances Marion Grace, dau of Francis Barndon, and *dsp* 18 Oct 1955

4a Reginald Courtenay, MBE, MC (1919), JP Somerset, Maj W SomYeo WW I; *b* 22 Nov 1877; *educ* Magdalen Coll Oxford (MA); *m* 29 Oct 1908 Violet (*d* 23 Jan 1974), dau of Arthur Flower, of 36 Prince's Gate, SW, by Isabel Margaretta Cockayne, dau of Sir Philip Pauncefort-Duncombe, 1st Bt (*qv*), and *d* 16 Feb 1946, leaving issue:

1b PATRICK REGINALD BOYLE, **13th Earl of the County of Cork** and **13th Earl of Orrery**; *b* 7 Feb 1910; *educ* Harrow and RMC Sandhurst; WW II as Capt Roy Ulster Rifles, Burma Rifles, Cameronians in Special Force (Chindits) and Parachute Regt (severely wounded), Maj 1943; Hereditary Life Govr and Chm Exec Ctee Christian Faith Soc, pres and chm Exec Ctee Br Cancer Cncl 1973–77, cncl memb Cancer Research Campaign 1973–77; Dep Speaker and Dep Chm Ctees Ho Lds 1973–78; Dir St Christopher's Hospice, Sydenham, and American Cncl for Cultural Exchange Inc 1973–78, FRSA, author *Sailing in a Nutshell* (1935), co-author *Jungle, Jungle, Little Chindit* (1946); *m* 1st 28 Jan 1952 (*divorce*) Dorothy Kate (*d* 26 Feb 1978), formerly w of (a) Marquis Demetrio Imperial di Francavilla and (b) G F Scelsi and only dau of Robert Ramsden, of Meltham, Yorks; *m* 2nd 24 Jan 1978 *Mary Gabrielle, widow of Kenneth McFarlane Walker and only dau of Louis Ginnett, and *d* 8 Aug 1995

2b JOHN WILLIAM BOYLE, **14th and present Earl of the County of Cork and 14th and present Earl of Orrery**

1b Elizabeth Theresa; *b* 19 July 1920; *m* 4 July 1947 *Adrian Noble Dodd-Noble, only son of Capt Cecil Kingsley Dodd by Hon Mrs Dodd-Noble (*see* 1935 edn KIRKLEY, B), of The Old Anchor, Sandon, Buntingford, Herts, and had issue:

1c *Adrian Michael; *b* 20 April 1948; *educ* Eton

2c *Patrick Robin; *b* 10 Nov 1951; *educ* Eton

3c *Simon Thomas Antony; *b* 17 Feb 1955; *educ* Radley

4c *Antony William; *b* 10 Dec 1961

1c *Joanna Susan [Mrs Barry Fife Hunt Kennels, Ceres, Fife]; *b* 8 Jan 1950; *m* *Barry A Godfrey, son of W E Godfrey, of Hoddesdon, Herts, and has issue:

1d *Elizabeth; *b* 10 May 1979

1a Caroline Elizabeth; *m* 7 Sept 1892 Charles Drummond, est son of Robert Drummond, and *d* 4 Dec 1958, leaving issue (*see* PERTH, E)

2a Cecilia Georgiana; *m* 20 Sept 1915 Matthew Joseph Patrich Corbally, 2nd son of Matthew Corbally, of Rathbeale Hall, Swords, Co Dublin, and *d* 16 April 1952. He *d* 18 Feb 1930

3a Theresa Selina; *m* 14 Dec 1899 Arthur Stewart Herbert, DL, JP, of Cahirnane, Co Kerry, and *d* 29 June 1956, having had issue. He *d* 28 Oct 1954

4a Evelyn Blanchet; *d* unm 29 June 1898

(1) (cont.) Col Gerald Boyle *m* 2nd 8 June 1898 Hermione (*d* 5 March 1944), er dau of John Campbell Arthur Houghton, of Sparnon, Torquay, and *d* 28 Dec 1927, having by her had issue:

5a Geraldine Lilian

(2) Robert Frederick; *b* 13 June 1841; *m* 17 April 1873 Minna Antoinetta Beatrice (*d* 21 June 1876), est dau of Edmund William Elton (*see* ELTON, Bt), and *d* 15 May 1883, having had a dau

(3) Edmund Montague; *b* 17 July 1845; *d* 11 Aug 1885

(1) Georgiana Olivia; *b* 27 Jan 1843; *m* 16 June 1868 R-Adml Richard Robert Quin (*see* HEADFORT, M), and *d* 15 Jan 1931

4 Robert Edward, MP, Lt-Col Coldstream Gds; *b* March 1809; *m* 23 Oct 1844 Georgiana (*d* 28 Aug 1911), yst dau of Abraham Wildey Robarts, and *d* 3 Sept 1854, having had, with other issue:

(1) Edmund Robarts, Capt Coldstream Gds; Page of Honour to HM QUEEN VICTORIA; *b* 10 Feb 1846; *d* unm 4 Sept 1908

(1) Emily Cecilia; *m* 20 Jan 1870 Cecil Chaplin, of Whissendine, Oakham, Rutland, and *d* 31 March 1924, leaving issue (*see* 1970 edn CHAPLIN, V). He *d* 28 Dec 1909

(2) Charlotte Jane; *m* 12 July 1877 Maj Mordaunt Charles Boyle, 60th Rifles, est son of Charles John Boyle (*see* above), and *d* 21 April 1917, leaving issue. He *d* 5 May 1885

5 Richard Cavendish (Rev), MA Oxford, Rector Marston Bigott, Som, and Chaplain in Ordinary to HM QUEEN VICTORIA; *b* 28 Feb 1812; *m* 23 Sept 1845 Eleanor Vere (*d* 30 July 1916), yst dau of Alexander Gordon, of Ellon Castle, Aberdeenshire, and *d* 30 March 1886, having had, with other issue:

(1) Hamilton Richard, Lt 23rd RWF; *b* 3 Feb 1848; *m* 17 June 1890 Harriet Marcia Jane (*d* 8 Jan 1933), est dau of Hon James Terence FitzMaurice (*see* ORKNEY, E), and *dsp* 12 Nov 1909

(2) Charles John, JP Oxon, Capt and Hon Maj 4th Bn Oxon LI, Capt 52nd LI, served Zulu War 1879 and WW I in Roy Defence Corps; *b* 17 March 1849; *m* 4 June 1885 Lilian Kennedy (*d* 15 Feb 1953), only dau of Charles Norman Pochin, HEICCS, of Barkby Hall, Leics, and *d* 1 Nov 1922, leaving issue:

1a Charles Roger Cavendish, DSO (1918) and bar (1918), Lt-Col Oxon and Bucks LI WW I (wounded, despatches twice); *b* 16 Aug 1886; *educ* Winchester; *d* unm 5 Feb 1971

2a Richard Frederick Robert Pochin, Capt Oxon and Bucks LI WW I (wounded); *b* 11 Oct 1888; *m* 12 Feb 1918 Marion Elisa Hill (*d* 12 April 1969), dau of Maj-Gen Hill Wallace, CB, RA, and *d* 6 Feb 1953, leaving:

1b Richard Michael Charles; *b* 12 Nov 1918; *d* 1994

3a John Parke, FZS; *b* 30 July 1893; *educ* Bradfield; *d* unm 24 Feb 1969

4a Edmund Michael Gordon Loeventhorpe; *b* 12 Nov 1895; Capt RN, WWs I and II; *m* 21 Dec 1927 Maida Cecil (*d* 14 Oct 1995), only dau of Lt-Col Hon Percy Cecil Evans-Freke (*see* CARBERY, B), and *d* 1982, leaving:

1b +George Hamilton, DL (Rutland 1997) [George Boyle Esq DL, Nozieres, 07270 Lamastre, France]; *b* 15 Sept 1928; *educ* Canford and Imperial Coll Lond (BSc 1953); ARSM, High Sheriff Rutland 1964 and Leics and Rutland 1976; *m* 25 July 1953 *Alathea Henriette Mary, er dau of John Adrian Frederick March Phillipps de Lisle, of Stockerston Hall, Leics, and has:

1c +Robert Edmund John [Robert Boyle Esq, Bisbrooke Hall, Uppingham, Rutland, Leics]; *b* 28 Sept 1954; *educ* Eton, RMA Sandhurst RAC Cirencester; Capt Irish Gds; *m* 1985 *Gabrielle Georgiana, only dau of Patrick Tobias Telfer Smollet, MC, DL, of Bonhill, Cameron, Alexandria, Dunbartonshire (*see* 1959 edn FOX, Bt), and has issue:

1d +Patrick Gordon Tobias; *b* 1991

1d *Albinia Mary; *b* 1988

2c +Richard William [Richard Boyle Esq, The Priory, Great Milton, Oxon OX44 7PB]; *b* 8 Jan 1959; *educ* Gordonstoun and Wanganui Coll; *m* 1990 *Suzanna Jean, est dau of Charles Bingham, of West Down, Tavistock, Devon, and has:

1d *Clementine Pamela; *b* 1997

3c +Rupert Lancelot Cavendish [Rupert Boyle Esq, The Park House, Laxton, Northants]; *b* 19 Sept 1960; *educ* Gordonstoun; *m* 1986 *Sarah Daphne, est dau of Simon Anthony Berry, of Cloggs Hall, Great Conrad, Suffolk, and has issue:

1d +Angus Hugo Edmund; *b* 1989

2d +Christopher Simon Hamilton; *b* 1992

2b Edmund Charles Percy, Sub-Lt RN; *b* 20 May 1932; *d* unm 7 July 1975 (accident)

3b +(Patrick Stephen) Crispin [Crispin Boyle Esq, 5 Weech Rd, London NW6]; *b* 24 Dec 1935; *m* 1975 *Heather Ann Williamson and has:

1c +Edmund Charles Thomas; *b* 1976

1c *Katharine Anna Cecil; *b* 1978

1a Lillian Joanna Vere; *m* 9 June 1909 7th Earl of Macclesfield (*qv*), and *d* 9 April 1974, leaving issue

(3) Algernon Edward Richard, JP Aberdeenshire; *b* 17 Sept 1854; *m* 28 May 1890 Edith Caroline (*d* 20 Jan 1926), widow of W S Mercer, of Oranmore, Co Down, and dau of William Crossley, of Belfast, and *dsp* 26 June 1914

(1) Isabella Albinia; *m* 9 Sept 1873 Sir George Gough Arbuthnot and *d* 25 Aug 1929, leaving issue (*see* ARBUTHNOT, Bt, of Edinburgh)

CORNWALLIS

Arms: Quarterly, 1st and 4th, sa. guttée d'eau on a fess arg. three Cornish choughs ppr. (for CORNWALLIS); 2nd and 3rd, sa. on a fesse embattled counter-embattled between three goats passant arg. as many pellets (for MANN). **Crest:** On a mount vert a stag lodged regardant arg., attired or, gorged with a chaplet of laurel ppr. and vulned on the shoulder gu. **Supporters:** On either side a stag arg., attired or and gorged with a chaplet of oak vert, fructed gold. **Motto:** *Virtus vincit invidiam* ('Virtue overcomes envy'). **Creation:** B. (UK) 31 Jan 1927.

THE 3RD BARON CORNWALLIS, of Linton, Co Kent (Fiennes Neil Wykeham Cornwallis, OBE (1963), DL (Kent 1976)) [The Rt Hon The Lord Cornwallis OBE DL, Ruck Farm, Horsmonden, Tonbridge, Kent TN12 8DT; 25B Queen's Gate Mews, London SW7 5QL]; *b* 29 June 1921; *s f* 1982; *educ* Eton; Lt Coldstream Gds

WW II 1940–44 (invalided); chm English Apples and Pears Ltd 1990–94, pres Nat Assoc Ag Contractors 1958–63 and 1986–; memb: Ag Export Cncl, Bd Tstees Chevening Estate 1979–; chm Smaller Firms Cncl CBI 1978–81; *m* 1st 17 Oct 1942 (*divorce* 1948) Judith, only dau of Lt-Col Geoffrey Lacy Scott, TD, of Ashcroft, Wadhurst, Sussex, and has had issue:

1 +(FIENNES WYKEHAM) JEREMY [The Hon Jeremy Cornwallis, 15 Mabelthorpe Rd, London SW6]; *b* 25 May 1946; *educ* Eton and RAC Cirencester; *m* 29 March 1969 *Sara Gray de Neufville, da of Lt-Col Nigel Stockwell, of Mill Street Ho, Iden Green, Benenden, Kent, and has issue:

(1) +(Fiennes) Alexander Wykeham Martin; *b* 25 Nov 1987

(1) *Anna Julia Gray; *b* 15 Jan 1971

(2) *Charlotte Louise; *b* 3 Sept 1972

1 Anne Judy; *b* 13 Nov 1943; *d* unm 26 June 1966

The 3rd BARON *m* 2nd 1 June 1951 *Agnes Jean Russell, yr dau of Capt Henderson Russell Landale, of Ewell Manor, W Farleigh, Maidstone, Kent, and by her has issue:

2 +(Patrick Wykeham) David [The Hon David Cornwallis, Hamnish Court, Hamnish, Leominster, Herefs]; *b* 28 May 1952; *educ* Lancing and Aiglon, Switzerland; *m* 1977 *Susannah, dau of William Edward Guest, of The Old Vineyard, Rufford Abbey, Notts, and widow of Stephen Thursfield, and has issue:

(1) +(Patrick Wykeham) James; *b* 1977

(2) +Thomas Wykeham Charles; *b* 1980

(3) +William Wykeham George; *b* 1982

2 *Cecily Mary Clare; *b* 23 Oct 1954; *m* 1980 *Ian McCulloch, yr son of Mrs E McCulloch, and has issue:

(1) *Ruari Alexander Fiennes; *b* 27 March 1982

(2) *Rohan Grey; *b* 1984

(3) *Fiennes; *b* 1989

(1) *Skye; *b* 1987

3 *Vanessa Rachel [The Hon Mrs Middleton, 104 Prince Albert Rd, Mosman, Sydney, NSW, Australia]; *b* 27 July 1958; *m* 1986 *H Jeremy Middleton

4 *(Susan Patricia) Rose; *b* 30 March 1963; *m* 1986 *Scott Simon Crolla, designer, son of Romano Crolla, of Queen's Gate, London

Lineage (of Cornwallis): THOMAS CORNWALLEYS; Sheriff London 1378, merchant; *d* 1384, leaving:

JOHN CORNWALLIS; MP Suffolk *temp* RICHARD II; *m* Philippa, dau and coheir of Robert Bucton, through whom he acquired the manorial ldships of Bro(o)me and Oakley, Suffolk, and *d* 1446, leaving:

THOMAS CORNWALLIS; *m* Philippa, dau and heir of Edward Tyrrel, of Downham, Essex, and *d* 1447, leaving:

THOMAS CORNWALLIS; MP Suffolk *c* 1450; had, with three er s (*dsp*):

Sir WILLIAM CORNWALLIS, KB, of Bro(o)me; *m* Elizabeth, dau and coheir of John Stanford, and *d* Nov 1519, leaving an est s:

Sir JOHN CORNWALLIS; Steward Household to EDWARD VI when PRINCE OF WALES; *d* 1544, leaving an est s:

Sir THOMAS CORNWALLIS, PC (1554–58); helped suppress Ket's Rebellion 1549 and Wyatt's Rebellion 1554; Sheriff Norfolk and Suffolk; Treasurer Calais 1554, MP Suffolk 1557–58, Comptroller Household to 1558; built Brome Hall, Norfolk, which was substantially remodelled on behalf of the 2nd Marquess Cornwallis in the early 19th century by George Wyatt and pulled down 1963; *m* Anne, dau of Sir John Jerningham, and *d* 24 Dec 1604, having had, with three daus:

1 WILLIAM (Sir)

2 Charles (Sir), Envoy Spain *c* 1603–04; *m* 1st Elizabeth, dau of Thomas Farnham, of Fincham, and had an est s:

(1) William (Sir); essayist; had issue

2 (cont.) Sir Charles *m* 2nd Elizabeth/Anne, dau of Thomas Barrow and widow of Ralph Skelton; *m* 3rd Dorothy, dau of Richard Vaughan, Bp London, and widow of John Jegon, Bp Norwich, and *d* 21 Dec 1629, having had by one of his ws (probably his 3rd) a dau Dorothy, who *m* Sir John Fytche

The er son,

Sir WILLIAM CORNWALLIS; *m* 1st Lucy (*d* 30 April 1608), 3rd dau and coheir of John Nevill(e), 4th Lord (Baron) Latymer (*qv*), by whom he acquired the Scampston and Earls Court (Kensington) properties, and by whom he had, with four daus:

1 Thomas; MP Suffolk *temp* CHARLES I; *d* unm 1626

Sir WILLIAM *m* 2nd Jane, dau of Hercules Mewtas, and had, with an er s (*d* young):

2 Sir FREDERICK CORNWALLIS, 1st Bt (E), so *cr* 4 May 1627, and 1st BARON CORNWALLIS OF EYE, Suffolk (E), so *cr* 20 April 1661; *b* 14 March 1610; ktd 1630, MP Eye April-May 1640 and Nov 1640–Sept 1642 (when ejected as royalist) and Ipswich Oct-Dec 1660, fought in Civil War at Battle of Cropredy Bridge 30 June 1644, accordingly fined £800 by Parl 1648, Treasurer Household 1660–Jan 1661/2; *m* 1st *c* 1630 Elizabeth, dau of Sir John Ashburnham by Lady Cramond (S Ldship of Parl) in her own right (dau of Sir Thomas Beaumont, himself gf of Sir Thomas Beaumont, 1st Bt; *qv*); *m* 2nd by 1641 Elizabeth, half sis of William, Baron Crofts of Saxham, and dau of Sir Henry Crofts, of Saxham, Suffolk, and *d* 7 or 31 Jan 1661/2, leaving by his 1st w:

(1) CHARLES CORNWALLIS, 2nd BARON CORNWALLIS OF EYE, KB (1661); *bapt* 19 April 1632; MP Eye 1660–62, Gent Privy Chamber 1660; *m* Margaret, dau of Sir Thomas Playsted, of Arlington, Sussex, and *d* 13 April 1673, having had, with two er s (*d* young):

1a CHARLES CORNWALLIS, 3rd BARON CORNWALLIS OF EYE, PC (March 1691/2); *bapt* 28 Dec 1655; acquitted of manslaughter 1676 after having been a drinking companion of a Mr Gerard who had killed a lad called Robert Clerk for supposed disrespect, Ld Lt Suffolk 1689–98; *m* 1st 27 Dec 1673 Elizabeth, half-sis of 1st Earl of Ilchester (*qv*); *m* 2nd 6 May 1688 Anne, Duchess of Buccleuch in her own right (*see* BUCCLEUCH and QUEENSBERRY, D), widow of James, Duke of Monmouth, and *d* 29 April 1698, leaving by his 1st w:

1b CHARLES CORNWALLIS, 4th BARON CORNWALLIS OF EYE; *b* 1675; MP (Whig) Eye 1695–98, Ld Lt Suffolk 1698–1703, Jt PMG 1715–21, Paymaster Gen 1721–Jan 1721/2; *m* 6 June 1699 Lady Charlotte Butler, dau of Richard, Earl of Arran (*see* ARRAN, E, preliminary remarks), and *d* 20 Jan 1721/2, leaving, with four other sons (two of whom *d* unm) and three daus (*d* unm):

1c CHARLES CORNWALLIS, 5th BARON CORNWALLIS OF EYE and 1st EARL CORNWALLIS, so *cr* 30 June 1753, as also VISCOUNT BROME of Co Suffolk (both GB), PC (1740); *b* 29 March 1700; Constable Tower of London and Ld Lt Tower Hamlets 1740–62; *m* 28 Nov 1722 Elizabeth, est dau of 2nd Viscount Townshend of Raynham (*see* TOWNSHEND, M), and *d* 23 June 1762, leaving:

1d CHARLES CORNWALLIS, 2nd EARL CORNWALLIS and 1st MARQUESS CORNWALLIS (GB), so *cr* 8 Oct 1792, KG (1786), PC (1770); *b* 31 Dec 1738; *educ* Eton and Mil Acad Turin, Italy; Ensign Gren Gds 1756, ADC to Marquess of Granby (*see* RUTLAND, D) Germany 1758–59, Lt-Col 12th Foot 1761 (fought Battles of Minden 1759 and Kirck Donkern 1762), MP (Whig) Eye 1760–62, Ld Bedchamber 1765, ADC to GEORGE III 1765–66, Col 33rd Foot 1766–1805, Maj-Gen 1775, Lt Gen 1777, Gen 1793, V-Treasurer Ireland 1769–70, Constable Tower of London 1770–84 and Nov 1784–1805, served War American Independence: victor Battle of Brandywine 13 Sept 1777, took Philadelphia 14 Sept 1777, victor Battle of Camden, NJ, 16 Aug 1780 and Guildford 15 March 1781; his strategy of invading Virginia was frustrated by his incompetent superior the C-in-C Sir Henry Clinton and he was forced by this intransigence to stay at his untenable post of Yorktown; accordingly he had no choice but to surrender with his 4,000 troops to overwhelmingly superior numbers of French and American forces, which he did 19 Oct 1781; this was effectively the end of British attempts to subdue the American Colonies although hostiltities dragged on for two more years; Envoy Extrdy Prussia Aug-Sept 1785; Govr-Gen Bengal and C-in-C E Indies 1786–93 (and 1797 but did not take up the appointment, also 1805 but died shortly after arriving at his post), conducting the Siege of Seringapatam and a successful war against the rulers of Mysore; Master Gen Ordnance 1795–1801; Ld Lt Ireland 1798–1801, in which capacity put down the 1798 Uprising and forwarded the Union of Irish and British Parls 1800; Envoy Plen to sign Treaty of Amiens 1802; *m* 14 July 1768 Jemima Tulikens, sis of Arnoldus Jones later Skelton, of Branthwaite, Cumberland, and *d* 5 Oct 1805 at Ghazipur, Benares, India, leaving, with a dau:

1e CHARLES CORNWALLIS, 2nd and last MARQUESS CORNWALLIS; *b* 19 Oct 1774; *educ* Eton and St John's Coll Cambridge; MP (Tory) Eye 1795–96 and Suffolk 1796–1805; *m* 17 April 1797 Lady Louisa Gordon, dau of 4th Duke of Gordon (*see* RICHMOND and GORDON, D), and *dspm* 9 Aug 1823, when the Marquessate expired, leaving, with two other daus (*d* unm):

1f Jane; *m* 13 May 1819 3rd Baron Braybrooke (*qv*) and *d* 23 Sept 1856, leaving issue

2f Jemima; *m* 2 Sept 1824 3rd Earl of St Germans (*qv*) and *d* 1 July 1856, leaving issue

2d JAMES CORNWALLIS, 4th EARL CORNWALLIS; *b* 25 Feb 1742/3; *educ* Eton and Ch Ch Oxford; Rector: Ickham, Kent, 1769–73, Adisham-with-Staple, Kent, 1770–81, Newington, Oxon, 1770, and Boughton Malherbe, Kent, 1773–85, Preb Westminster 1770–75, Vicar Wrotham, Kent, 1771–85, Dean Canterbury 1775–81, Bp Lichfied and Coventry 1781–1824, Dean: Windsor 1791–94 and Durham 1794–1824; *m* 30 April 1771 Catherine, dau of Galfridus Mann, (*see* LILFORD, B), and *d* 20 Jan 1824, leaving:

1e JAMES CORNWALLIS later MANN (roy licence 9 April 1814 following death of his maternal uncle Sir Horace Mann, Bt, whose estate of Linton, Kent, he inherited)), 5th and last EARL CORNWALLIS; *b* 20 Sept 1778; *educ* Eton and St John's Coll Cambridge; MP (Tory) Eye 1799–1806 and Jan-April 1807; *m* 1st 18 Dec 1804 Maria Isabella, est dau of Francis Dickens, of Woollaston House, Northants, and by her had, with a s (*d* young unm):

1f Jemima Isabella; *m* 12 April 1828 Charles Wykeham-Martin (*see below*) and had issue

1e The 5th and last EARL *m* 2nd 22 Jan 1829 Laura, dau of William Hayes; *m* 3rd 4 Aug 1842 Julia, dau of Thomas Bacon, of Redlands, Berks, and *dspms* 21 May 1852, when all his titles expired, leaving by her an only child:

1f Julia Mann later Cornwallis (roy licence 22 Oct 1844); *b* 2 July 1844; inherited the Linton estate; *m* 27 Aug 1862 William, Viscount Holmesdale, later Earl Amherst (*see* AMHERST OF HACKNEY, B), and *dsp* 1 Sept 1883

1d Elizabeth; *m* 1753 Bowen Southwell (*see* SOUTHWELL, V)

2c Stephen; Maj-Gen; *b* 1703; *m* Mrs Pearson and *dsp* May 1743

3c Edward; *b* Feb 1713; Lt-Gen, Govr Gibraltar; *m* 1763 Mary, dau of 2nd Viscount Townmshend of Raynham (*see* TOWNSHEND, M), and *dsp* 14 Jan 1776

Lineage (of Wykeham and Wykeham-Martin): RICHARD WYKEHAM, of Swalcliffe; *m* Vere Alicia, sis and coheir of Richard Fiennes, last Viscount Saye and Sele (*see* SAYE AND SELE, B), and had, with another s (William Humphrey, of Swalcliffe, gf of Baroness Wenman), a 3rd son:

Rev RICHARD WYKEHAM, Vicar Sulgrave and Chacombe, Northants, Rector Newton Purcell, Oxon; *m* Mary, only surv dau of Charles Fox, of Chacombe Priory, son of Charles Fox by Mary (dau of John Martin, of Rye, and aunt of Denny Martin, f by Hon Frances Fairfax of Rev Denny MARTIN later FAIRFAX (assumed on inheriting Leeds Castle, Kent, and an IoW estate from his maternal uncle, 7th Lord Fairfax of Cameron (*qv*; *see* also the Introduction to AMERICAN PRESIDENTIAL FAMILIES, 1994, Morris Genealogical Books SA))), and *d* 1805, having had, with another s and two daus:

FIENNES WYKEHAM later WYKEHAM-MARTIN (roy licence 18 Oct 1821), of Leeds Castle (which he inherited from his kinsman Gen Martin) and Chacombe

Priory, Banbury; *b* 12 Jan 1769; High Sheriff Kent 1824; *m* Eliza, dau of Richard Bignell, of Doddington, Oxon, and *d* 14 Sept 1840, having had, with six yr sons and six daus (including Eliza; *m* 1st Philip Thomas Wykeham and 2nd Edward Simeon; *see* SIMEON, Bt):

CHARLES WYKEHAM-MARTIN, of Leeds Castle, DL, JP, MP W Kent; *b* 11 Sept 1801; *m* 1st 12 April 1828 Lady Jemima Isabella Mann (*d* 17 Deb 1836; *see* above); *m* 2nd 18 June 1838 Matilda, dau of Sir John Trollope, 6th Bt (*qv*), and *d* 30 Oct 1870, leaving by his 1st w, with an est and yst s and a dau:

FIENNES WYKEHAM-MARTIN later CORNWALLIS (roy licence 15 Oct 1859); Maj 4th Light Dragoons; *b* 1 Nov 1831; *m* 29 July 1863 Harriet Elizabeth (*m* 2nd Rev Arthur Edward Robinson, MA, Rector Wootton, who *d* 1884), dau of John Thomas Mott, of Barningham Hall, Norfolk, and *d* 24 April 1867, leaving issue:

1 FIENNES STANLEY WYKEHAM, **1st Baron**

2 Arthur Wykeham; *b* 24 April 1865; *m* 1890 Marcia Blanche Florence (*d* 28 July 1939), dau of Robert Bower, of Welham, Yorks, by Marcia, dau of Sir John Lister-Kaye, 2nd Bt (*qv*), and *d* 9 Feb 1952, leaving issue:

(1) Iris Beryl *m* 18 July 1916 Capt Edward Henry Lee-Warner, OBE, late RA, only son of Edward Lee Warner, of Denton Ho, Harleston, Norfolk, and *d* 4 June 1975, leaving issue. He *d* 7 Sept 1963

1 Helen Florence; *d* unm 5 Sept 1957

2 Caroline Vere; *d* unm 13 Nov 1909

The est son,

FIENNES STANLEY WYKEHAM CORNWALLIS, **1st Baron Cornwallis**, of Linton, Co Kent (UK), so *cr* 31 Jan 1927, CBE, TD, DL, JP; chm Kent CC, Lt-Col and Hon Col cmdg W Kent Imp Yeo, Hon Col Thames and Medway Heavy Bde RA (TA) 1933, MP Maidstone 1888–95 and 1898–1900; *b* 27 May 1864; *m* 10 Feb 1886 Mabel (*d* 6 March 1957 aged 91), est dau of Oswald Peter Leigh, of Belmont, Cheshire, and had issue:

1 Fiennes Wykeham Mann, MC, Lt 17th Lancers WW I (Croix de Guerre); *b* 21 Aug 1890; *k* in Ireland 15 May 1921

2 WYKEHAM STANLEY, **2nd Baron**

3 Oswald Wykeham, OBE (1919), Capt RN; *b* 16 March 1894; *educ* RNCs Osborne and Dartmouth; *m* 5 Dec 1923 Hon Venetia Jane Digby (*d* 16 March 1956), 3rd dau of 10th Baron Digby (*qv*), and *d* 28 Jan 1974, leaving issue:

(1) +Michael Wykeham [Lt-Cdr Michael Cornwallis RN (ret), 10 Ravelston House Rd, Edinburgh EH4 3LW]; *b* 29 Nov 1924; *educ* Eton; *m* 18 Aug 1953 *Margaret Dorothy, dau of John Wilson Cannon, MB, ChB, of Wester Ross, Upper St Ann's Rd, Faversham, Kent, and has issue:

1a +Richard Wykeham; *b* 16 Nov 1959

1a *Diana Margaret [Mrs David Casey, 22 St Vincent Crescent, Alloway, Ayr KA7 4QW]; *b* 27 Aug 1957; *m* 1991 *David Casey, son of A Casey, of Dunblane, and has issue:

1b *Colin Wykeham; *b* 11 April 1994

(2) Charles Wykeham; *b* 22 Sept 1937; *d* unm 15 Dec 1978

(1) *Venetia Mabel; *b* 8 Nov 1928; *m* 25 Oct 1956 *Lt-Cdr Geoffrey Arthur George Brooke, DSC, RN, only son of Capt John Brooke, DSC, RN, of Hart's Gorse, Beddingham, nr Lewes, Sussex (*see* BROOKE, Bt), and has issue

1 Julia Dorothy, CBE (1952), CStJ; *m* 6 Jan 1926 Capt Hon Sir Archibald Douglas Cochrane, GCMG, KCSI, DSO, RN, 2nd son of 1st Baron Cochrane of Cults (*qv*), and *d* 15 June 1971, leaving issue

2 Vere Mabel; *m* 3 Aug 1910 Sir Samuel Strang Steel, 1st Bt (*qv*), and *d* 8 Oct 1964, leaving issue

3 Yvonne; *m* 27 Jan 1923 Cdr Hon Henry Mitford Amherst Cecil, OBE, RN, and had issue (*see* AMHERST OF HACKNEY, B)

4 Bridget Frances Kate; *m* 4 July 1921 Lt-Col John Cecil Petherick, OBE, MC, Res of Offrs, 3rd Hus, son of George Petherick, of Porthpaean, St Austell, Cornwall, and had issue

The 1st BARON *d* 26 Sept 1935; his est surv son,

WYKEHAM STANLEY CORNWALLIS, **2nd Baron Cornwallis**, KCVO (1968), KBE (1945), MC, DL (1972), JP (1926) and CA (1936) Kent; *b* 14 March 1892; *educ* Eton and RMC Sandhurst; Capt RSG WW I (wounded, despatches), Hon Col 5th Bn The Buffs (TA) 1957–67, Hon Col 415 Coast Regt (Thames and Medway) RA (TA) 1937–57, Hon Col 8th Bn The Queen's Regt TAVR 1967–68, chm Kent CC 1935–36, Ld Lt and custos rotulorum Kent 1944–72, Lt City London, chm Kent War Ag exec Ctee 1939–46, KStJ, pres MCC 1947–48, Prov GM Kent (Freemasons), v-pres SE Area TA&AFA, v-patron Kent Co Soc and Assoc of Men of Kent and Kentishmen, chm Fremlins Ltd, Isherwood, Foster & Stacey and Warden Insur Co, local dir Barclays Bank Ltd, pres Kent Assoc Boy Scouts, pres OStJ Kent, Tstee RASE and MCC, Kt Cdr Order of Dannebrog Denmark, Pro-Chllr U of Kent at Canterbury (Hon DCL), Edward Hardy Gold Medal for Services to Kent; *m* 1st 30 Jan 1917 Cecily Etha Mary (*d* 10 Oct 1943), dau of Sir James Heron Walker, 3rd Bt, of Sand Hutton (*qv*); *m* 2nd 26 Feb 1948 Esmé Ethel Alice (*d* 5 June 1969), widow of Sir Robert James Milo Walker, 4th Bt, of Sand Hutton, and dau of Capt Montmorency d'Beaumont, 5th Roy Irish Lancers, and *d* 4 Jan 1982, having by his 1st w had issue:

1 FIENNES NEIL WYKEHAM CORNWALLIS, **3rd and present Baron Cornwallis**

1 (Rosamond) Patricia (Susan Anne); *b* 15 May 1918; *d* unm 3 Sept 1960

CORRY

Arms: Gu. a saltire engrailed arg. between in chief a rose of the last, barbed and seeded ppr., in fess two thistles slipped also ppr., and in base a trefoil, slipped or. **Crest:** A cock combed and wattled ppr., charged with a trefoil as in the arms. **Motto:** *Vigilans et audax* ('Watchful and bold'). **Creation:** Bt. (UK) 15 Sept 1885.

SIR WILLIAM JAMES CORRY, 4TH BT, of Dunraven, Co Antrim [Lt-Cdr Sir William Corry Bt RN (ret), East Hilleton House, Spreyton, Crediton, Devon EX17 5AB]; *b* 1 Aug 1924; *s f* 1987; *educ* RNC Dartmouth; RN 1938–77, served WW II; *m* 8 Dec 1945 *Diana Pamela Mary (WRNS), only dau of Lt-Col James Burne Lapsley, MC, IMS, and has issue:

1 +JAMES MICHAEL [James Corry Esq, Beetslaan 4, 2252 TT Voorschoten, The Netherlands]; *b* 3 Oct 1946; *educ* Downside; *m* 1973 *Sheridan Lorraine, dau of Arthur Peter Ashbourne, of Crowland, Peterborough, and has:

(1) +William James Alexander; *b* 7 Dec 1981

(2) +Robert Philip John; *b* 1984

(3) +Christopher Myles Anthony; *b* 1987

2 +Timothy William; *b* 14 June 1948; *educ* Downside; Lt-Col RGJ; *m* 1971 *Bridget Isabella, dau of Sydney Litherland, of Tenerife, and has:

(1) +Edward Charles; *b* 1976

(1) *Georgina Katharine; *b* 1974

(2) *Charlotte Louise; *b* 1981

3 +Nicholas John; *b* 21 July 1958; *educ* Downside

4 +Simon Myles; *b* 9 Oct 1961; Lt-Cdr RN

1 *Jane Susanna [Mrs John Redman, 32 Glenmore Rd, Minehead, Somerset]; *b* 26 Aug 1949; *m* 1976 *John Anthony Redman, only son of Henry Gordon Redman, OBE, of Brockenhurst, Hants, and has issue:

(1) *Angus Richard William; *b* 1986

2 *Patricia Diana [Mrs Mark Hassell, 2 Esher Rd, E Molesey, Surrey KT8 0AA]; *b* 25 Sept 1956; *m* 1987 *Mark Hassell, only son of M Hassell, of Woodbank Ho, Teddesley Rd, Penkridge, Staffs, and has issue:

(1) *Oliver James Bowen; *b* 1990

(2) *George Frederick; *b* 28 May 1997

(1) *Rebecca Holly; *b* 1990

Lineage: JOHN CORRY; *b* 1638 (allegedly of a Dumfriesshire family who had settled at Turnagardy, nr Newtownards, Co Down, *temp* JAMES I); Provost Newtownards; *d* 1708, leaving:

ROBERT CORRY, of Turnagardy; *m* Mary Porter (*d* 1828 aged 84) and had:

JOHN CORRY, of Turnagardy; *b* 1771; *m* Susan White (*d* 1838) and *d* 1851, leaving:

ROBERT CORRY, of Turnagardy; *b* 1800; *m* 1825 Jane (*d* 1880), dau of James Porter, of Ballyrussell, Co Down, and *d* 1869, having had, with two yr sons and three daus:

Sir James Porter Corry, 1st Bt (UK), so *cr* 15 Sept 1885, of Dunraven, Co Antrim; MP Belfast 1874–85 and Mid-Armagh 1886–91; *b* 8 Sept 1826; *m* 10 July 1849 Margaret (*d* 25 Jan 1869), dau of William Service, of Glasgow, and had, with other issue:

1 WILLIAM (Sir), **2nd Bt**

1 Margaret; *b* 15 Jan 1853; *m* 30 Dec 1874 Arthur Charles Gotto, CE, of Rushmere, Belfast, and *d* 26 Nov 1925, leaving issue

Sir JAMES *d* 28 Nov 1891; his son,

Sir William Corry, 2nd Bt, dir Cunard Steamship Co; *b* 20 March 1859; *m* 31 Oct 1889 Charlotte Georgina Frances Catherine (*d* 23 Oct 1896), only dau of J Collins, and had issue:

1 JAMES PEROWNE IVO MYLES (Sir), **3rd Bt**

2 William Myles Fenton, MC; Capt RFA (TF); *b* 3 Oct 1893; *educ* Trin Coll Cambridge (BA); *m* 1st 4 Sept 1929 (*divorce* 1938) Jessica Walker, dau of William Waller; *m* 2nd 7 July 1938 Vera Elizabeth Kathleen, formerly w of F A Forde and dau of John Hemingway, MD, and *dsp* 20 May 1958

1 Myleta Fenton; *m* 30 July 1912 John Benjamin LINDENBAUM later LINDON (roy licence 1914), OBE, QC, MA, LLM, barrister (*d* 13 July 1960), and *d* 9 Nov 1966, leaving a s and dau

Sir WILLIAM *d* 9 June 1926; his est son,

Sir James Perowne Ivo Myles Corry, 3rd Bt; *b* 10 June 1892; *educ* Eton and Trin Coll Cambridge (BA 1914, MA 1918); Sub-Lt RNVR; *m* 1st 7 July 1921 (*divorce* 1937) Molly Irene (*m* 2nd 1938 Capt John Forster Cochrane, DSC, RN (*d* 1970), yst dau of Maj Otto Joseph Bell, and had issue:

1 Sir WILLIAM JAMES CORRY, **4th and present Bt**

1 Anne; *b* 12 Nov 1922; 3rd Offr WRNS; *m* 2 Oct 1945 *Lt Norman Wilkins Trembath, late Roy Warwicks Regt, est son of David Trembath, of Frinton-on-Sea, Essex, and *d* 17 June 1992, leaving:

(1) *Anthony David; *b* 31 Aug 1946; *educ* Wellington

(2) *Timothy Mark; *b* 24 April 1948; *educ* Wellington

(1) *Sandra Rosalind; *b* 14 Nov 1949

2 Susan; *b* 1926; *d* 14 March 1995

Sir James *m* 2nd 29 Jan 1946 *Cynthia Marjorie Patricia [Dowager Lady Corry, Dunraven, Fauvic, Jersey, CI], widow of Capt David Alexander Polson, Seaforth Highrs, and dau of Capt Frederick Henry Mahony, The Cheshire Regt, and *d* 1987, having by her had issue:

3 *Amanda Jane [Mrs Hamlyn Jones, 1 Hazel Drive, Dundee DD2 1QQ]; *b* 22 Nov 1947; *educ* Newnham Coll Cambridge; *m* 28 Oct 1972 *Hamlyn (Lyn) Gordon Jones, MA, PhD, FIHort, yr son of D Gordon Jones, of Little Ash, Smarden, Kent, and has issue:

(1) *Katherine Myleta Gordon; *b* 16 June1974

(2) *Julia Patricia Gordon; *b* 30 Nov 1976

CORY

Arms: Argent a saltire between two quatrefoils in pale sable, on a chief azure a griffin's head erased between two quatrefoils or. **Crest:** In front of a griffin's head erased or, between two wings per pale of the last and gules, three quatrefoils sable. **Motto:** *Cor unum via una* ('One heart, one way'). **Creation:** Bt. (UK) 13 May 1919.

SIR (CLINTON CHARLES) DONALD CORY, 5TH BT, of Coryton, Whitchurch, Co Glamorgan [Sir Donald Cory Bt, 18 Cloisters Rd, Letchworth, Herts SG6 3JS]; *b* 13 Sept 1937; *s* f 1991; *educ* Brighton Coll and abroad; FRGS 1961

Lineage: Sir (James) Herbert Cory, 1st Bt (UK), so *cr* 13 May 1919, of Coryton, Whitchurch, Glamorgan (son of John Cory, shipowner), DL, JP Glamorgan, High Sheriff 1913, JP Cardiff, MP (C) Cardiff 1915–18 and S Cardiff 1918–23, dir John Cory and Sons Ltd, shipowners; *b* 7 Feb 1857; *m* 1st 1879 Elizabeth Hoskin (*d* 1 Feb 1908), dau of George Hoskin Wills, and had issue:

1 HERBERT GEORGE DONALD (Sir), **2nd Bt**

2 Frederick Harold; *b* 1883; *d* 1951

3 Edward Douglas, JP; *b* 1885; *d* 13 Sept 1935

4 Francis Oswald; *b* 1888; *d* 9 March 1934

1 Edith Winifred; *b* 1881; *m* 1901 H T Thornley, and had issue

Sir Herbert 2nd 1910 Elizabeth Cansh, CBE, JP (*d* 23 Nov 1956), dau of Alexander Walker, JP, and by her had issue:

2 *Jessie Rosalie; *b* 1911; *m* 2 Feb 1933 Lt-Col William Handley Ferguson, late RHA (*d* 4 Aug 1972), son of Rev William Hambro Ferguson, of Trynanny Ho, Glasslough, Co Monaghan, and has issue:

(1) *Shane Steuart Cory; *b* 23 Feb 1934; *educ* Eton; *m* 1962 *Jill Huber, of Durban, S Africa, and has two daus

(1) *Fiona Dawn Cory; *b* 16 Feb 1947; *m* 17 July 1969 *Greville Edward Vernon, er son of Maj Mervyn Sydney Bobus Vernon, MVO, of Bowldown, Tetbury, Glos (*see* LYVEDEN, B)

3 Carmen; *b* 1914 ; *m* 22 April 1937 2nd Baron McGowan (*qv*) and *d* 1966, leaving issue

The 1st Bt *d* 7 Feb 1933; his est son,

Sir (Herbert George) Donald Cory, 2nd Bt; *b* 31 Dec 1879; *m* 7 June 1904 Gertrude, dau of Henry Thomas Box, and *d* 7 May 1935, leaving:

1 **Sir Vyvyan Donald Cory, 3rd Bt**; *b* 2 Nov 1906; *educ* Harrow and Clare Coll Cambridge (BA); *d* 17 March 1941 as a result of enemy action

2 **Sir Clinton James Donald Cory, 4th Bt**; *b* 1 March 1909; *educ* Brighton Coll; S/Ldr RAFVR; *m* 14 Sept 1935 *Mabel Mary [Lady Cory, 18 Cloisters Rd, Letchworth, Herts SG6 3JS], only dau of Arthur Douglas Hunt, MD, ChB, of Park Grange, Derby, and *d* 1991, having had issue:

(1) Sir (CLINTON CHARLES) DONALD CORY, **5th and present Bt**

3 Philip Cecil Donald; *b* 20 Feb 1913; *d* 13 Jan 1996

1 *Valerie Donald [Lady Gane, Sandaig, Knoydart, Inverness-shire]; *b* 23 June 1905; *m* 1st 10 Jan 1928 (*divorce* 1948) William Walter Pidcock Woolland (*d* 18 June 1949), only son of M Woolland, of 69 Evelyn Gardens, SW7 and Baydon Manor, Ramsbury, Wilts; *m* 2nd 7 Oct 1954 Sir Irving Blanchard Gane, KCVO (*d* 1972), of Newmans, Pirbright, Surrey, son of Douglas Montagu Gane, MBE, of Richmond, Surrey, and by her 1st husb has issue:

(1) *David Anthony Walter [David Woolland Esq, Baydon Manor Cottage, Marlborough, Wilts SN8 2HG]; *b* 1929

(2) *Peter Donald Cory [Peter Woolland Esq, Sandaig, Knoydart, Inverness-shire, Scotland]; *b* 1931

2 *Diana Ethel Muriel Donald [Mrs Andrew Lyell, Wester Auchleuchrie, Forfar, Angus DD8 3TU], served WW II in WRNS; *b* 14 Jan 1918; *m* 6 Feb 1943 *Maj Andrew Lyell, DFC, RA, barrister, late Maj Dorset Yeo, yr son of Col David Lyell, of Angus, and has issue:

(1) *Vivien Diana; *b* 6 June 1944

(2) *Clementina Lindsay; *b* 26 March 1949

CORY-WRIGHT

Arms: Or a fess company countercompany azure and argent, between in chief two eagle's heads erased, and in base a unicorn passant regardant of the second. **Crest:** Upon a mount proper, between two caltraps or, a unicorn passant regardant argent, armed, crined and unguled gold. **Motto:** *Dum vivimus vivamus* ('Let us live while we are alive'). **Creation:** Bt. (UK) 28 Aug 1903.

SIR RICHARD MICHAEL CORY-WRIGHT, 4TH BT, of Caen Wood Towers, Highgate St Pancras, Co London, and Hornsey, Co Middx [Sir Richard Cory-Wright Bt, 21 Trenchard Close, Wallingford, Oxon OX10 9BB]; *b* 17 Jan 1944; *s* gf 1969; *educ* Eton and Birmingham U (BSc 1965); late Lt Leics and Derbys Yeo, patron one living; *m* 1976 (*divorce* 1994) Veronica Mary, dau of James Harold Lucas Bolton, of Church Farm, Morningthorpe, Norwich, and has issue:

1 +ROLAND ANTHONY; *b* 11 March 1979

2 +Jonathan James; *b* 1981

3 +Felix Michael; *b* 1986

Lineage: Rev WILLIAM WRIGHT, of Ringwood, Hants, and St Ives, Hunts, later Bath, incumbent Oundle, Northants; inherited the Manors of Wrangle and Leake, Lincs, from Jane Woodcock (*d* between 30 April 1767 and 15 June 1768); *m* Rebecca — and had, witha yr s and nine daus:

Rev WILLIAM WRIGHT; *b* 16 Nov 1754; Rector Cotterstock, Northants; *m* Mary Charlotte — and *d* Jan 1823, having had, with three yr s and two daus:

WILLIAM WRIGHT, of Charlton, Kent; *b* 20 April 1795; Lt 95th Regt 1813, served Holland 1813–14, present at Waterloo (severely wounded); *m* 30 Aug 1825 Elizabeth (*d* 30 June 1888), dau of Rev Thomas Hooper, MA, Rector Yatton Keynell, Wilts, by Elizabeth, dau of Rev Race Godfrey, DD, of Queen's Coll Oxford, and *d* 24 Feb 1877, leaving, with other issue:

Sir CORY FRANCIS WRIGHT later CORY-WRIGHT (roy licence 1903), **1st Bt** (UK), so *cr* 28 Aug 1903, of Caen Wood Towers, Highgate, and Hornsey, Middx, JP and DL (Middx), JP (London); *b* 11 Aug 1838; CA Middx, High Sheriff 1902, chm William Cory and Sons; *m* 25 Sept 1867 Mima (*d* 31 March 1927), yst dau of Sir Hugh Owen, Welsh educnl reformer, fndr Univ Coll Aberystwyth, by Ann, dau of Richard Wade and sis of Sir Hugh Owen, GCB, and had issue:

1 ARTHUR CORY (Sir), **2nd Bt**

2 Dudley, of Red House, Westcott, Surrey, JP (Middx); *b* 2 Dec 1872; *educ* Harrow and Merton Coll Oxford (MA); barrister Inner Temple; *m* 1905 Alice Cross (*d* 11 Feb 1965) and *d* 28 Feb 1931, leaving:

(1) Reginald Dudley; *b* 7 Sept 1906; *educ* Harrow; *m* 1st (*divorce*) Patricia Elliott; *m* 2nd 28 Sept 1949 Margit Elisabeth (*d* 22 July 1962), dau of Stephen Heger, PM Hungary, and formerly wife of Gyulane Szarvas Szechenyi, and *dsp* 15 Feb 1959; his wife's s by her 1st marriage, Julian Gabriel (*b* 28 April 1942; *d* 28 Oct 1962), changed his name by deed poll from Szechenyi to CORY-WRIGHT

(2) Esmond Godrey; *b* 28 Oct 1908; *educ* Eton and Merton Coll Oxford (MA 1935); *m* 1st 22 May 1931 (*divorce* 1942) Amanda, dau of Edward Peter Menhinick, of 31 Gresham Gdns, London NW11, and had issue:

1a +Edward James Dudley [Edward Cory-Wright Esq, 26 Broadmark Lane, Rustington, W Sussex BN16 2HL]; *b* 13 April 1932; *educ* King Edward VI GS Bury St Edmunds and Merton Coll Oxford; *m* 20 July 1955 *Jean Olive, dau of George Young, of St Albans, Herts, and has:

1b +James Edward [James Cory-Wright Esq, 6 Westbourne Street, Hove, East Sussex BN3 5PG]; *b* 6 Dec 1956; *educ* UEA (BA); *m* 1st 1978 (*divorce* 1991) Susan Laura, dau of Sydney Bricknell, of Sutton Grove, Shrewsbury; *m* 2nd 26 July 1996 *Jill Wendy Ann, dau of Gwynfryn John Williams, of Rayleigh, and has:

1c +Max James; *b* 4 March 1996

2b +Nicholas John [Nicholas Cory-Wright Esq, 64 Summerlee Ave, London N2 9QH]; *b* 28 March 1964; *m* 1991 *Ana, dau of Rodolfo Sanchez-Martin, of Madrid, and has:

1c *Alexandra Delia; *b* 2 April 1995

1b *Juliet Amanda; *b* 11 Aug 1959; *m* 1984 *Philip Fielder, of Church House, Timsbury, Hants, and has issue:

1c *Mark Edward; *b* 26 May 1988

2c *Charles John; *b* 4 July 1995

1c *Victoria Frances; *b* 24 June 1986

1a *Amanda Menhinick; *b* 18 Sept 1933

(2) (cont.) Esmond Cory-Wright *m* 2nd 9 July 1949 Pepita Jane Grey (*d* 25 June 1995), dau of Harry William Grey Bell, and *d* 1989

(1) Althea Frances; *b* 19 Jan 1917

1 Elsie Maud; *m* 18 Jan 1899 Rev Gilbert Montague Hall, MA Oxford (*d* 5 April 1937), Rector of Bushey, Herts, and *d* 13 Oct 1961

2 Mabel Owen; *m* 18 April 1901 Sir Herbert Nield, PC, KC, DL and CA (Middx) (*d* 11 Oct 1932), 2nd son of William Robert Nield, of Midge Hall, Saddleworth, Yorks, and *d* 23 Nov 1948

3 Hilda Jessie; *d* unm 31 May 1960, aged 84

Sir FRANCIS *d* 30 May 1909; his er son,

Sir Arthur Cory Cory-Wright, 2nd Bt, JP (Herts and Middx); *b* 18 Nov 1869; *educ* Harrow and Merton Coll Oxford (BA 1891, MA 1896); High Sheriff Herts 1921, memb PLA 1919; *m* 18 Nov 1891 Elizabeth Olive (*d* 1 Sept 1928), est dau of Henry Clothier, MD, of Highgate, and had issue:

1 GEOFFREY (Sir), **3rd Bt**

2 Ronald, MC; *b* 19 Dec 1893; *educ* Eton; Lt 3rd Bn Royal Warwicks Regt WW I (despatches, wounded); *m* 16 June 1917 Geraldyn Mary (*d* 1976), dau of Maj Henry Charles Windsor Villiers-Stuart (*see* BUTE, M), and *d* 27 Dec 1932, leaving issue:

(1) +Francis Newman [Francis Cory-Wright Esq, Oakridge, Little Gaddesden, Herts HP4 1PH]; *b* 21 July 1925; *educ* Eton and Merton Coll Oxford (BA 1949, MA 1954); Lt 15th/19th King's Roy Hus WW II (wounded)

(1) Elisabeth Grace; *b* 23 Feb 1919; *d* unm 2 June 1966

(2) *Rosemund Ina [Countess Stanislaw Saryusz-Bielski, 27 Brunswick Rd, Hove, Sussex]; *b* 29 Aug 1923; *m* 30 April 1946 Count Stanislaw Andrzej Saryusz-Bielski (*d* 25 Oct 1958), son of Count Jan Andrzej Saryusz-Bielski, of Warsaw, and has issue

3 Alan, DSC (1918), of Hatfield Park, Takeley, Essex; *b* 6 March 1896; Lt-Cdr RN (Emergency List) WW I (severely wounded, despatches); *m* 5 July 1923 Leila Yda Cyrilla (*d* 1982), only child of Arthur Lobb, of Hatters Croft, Sawbridgeworth, Herts, and *d* 3 Feb 1964, leaving issue:

(1) +Godfrey William [Godfrey Cory-Wright Esq, Hatfield Park, Takeley, Essex]; *b* 9 April 1928; *educ* Harrow; *m* 27 Dec 1958 *Nicole Emma, only dau of E Vermeiren, of Brussels, and has issue:

1a +Alan William [Alan Cory-Wright Esq, Auchessan, Crianlarich, Perthshire FK20 8QS]; *b* 31 March 1965; *m* 1989 *Nicki, 2nd dau of Rt Rev John Richardson, Bp of Bedford, and has issue:

1b +Hamish Bean William; *b* 1991

2b +Jack; *b* 1993

1a *Elizabeth Yda [Mrs Christopher Mannion, Ploughdens, Bush End, Bishops Stortford, Herts CM22 6NG]; *b* 29 Sept 1961; *m* 1989 *Christopher Edward Mannion and has issue:

1b *Zacharia Ernest Gustave (Pingu); *b* 1993

1b *Sassi Edward Paris (dau); *b* 1990

2b *Araminta Tanzy Ophelia; *b* 1992

4 Douglas, CBE (1969); *b* 29 Dec 1901; Midshipman RN WW I, chm Chamber of Coal Traders, High Sheriff Herts 1963; *m* 29 April 1924 Margaret Vivien Sarina (Peggy) (*d* 1987), dau of Rudolph Levy, of Birkdale, Lancs, and *d* 1987, leaving issue:

(1) *June; *b* 12 Feb 1926; *m* 2 Oct 1948 Sir John James MacDonald Horlick, 5th Bt (*qv*), and has issue

(2) (Olive) Marigold [Mrs David Curling, The Rosary, Coleshill, nr Amersham, Bucks]; *b* 16 June 1929; MB, BS, MRCS, LRCP; *m* 9 Oct 1954 David Richard Michael Curling (*d* 1993), only son of Lt-Col Richard Robinson Curling, DSO, RA, of The Old Rectory, Bursledon, Hants, and has issue:

1a *Richard Michael; *b* 24 Oct 1958

1a Rosanna Virginia; *b* 29 Sept 1960; *m* 1990 Nicholas Guy Charles della Casa and is presumed murdered (with her husb) N Iraq 1991

2a *Davina Cordelia; *b* 21 Feb 1964

(3) *Cleone Anne [Mrs John Thellusson Wood, Lois Weedon House, Weedon Lois, nr Towcester, Northants]; *b* 25 Aug 1935; *m* 1956 *John Wedgwood Thellusson Wood, er son of Rt Rev Bp Claud Thomas Thellusson Wood, MC, of Redcote, Harpenden, Herts, and has issue:

1a *Nicholas John Wedgwood; *b* 28 Nov 1961

1a *Amelia Jane; *b* 28 Jan 1959

2a *Rebecca Anne Wedgwood; *b* 5 Feb 1964

3a Anna; *b* 7 Oct 1969

1 Beatrice Gwenda; *b* 29 Aug 1897; *d* unm 2 Dec 1947

Sir ARTHUR *d* 21 April 1951; his est son,

Sir Geoffrey Cory-Wright, 3rd Bt; *b* 26 Aug 1892; *educ* Harrow and Univ Coll Oxford; Capt 3rd Bn E Kent Regt and F/Cdr RFC WW I (wounded); *m* 10 Nov 1915 Felicity (*d* 1978), 2nd dau of Sir Herbert Beerbohm Tree, the actor-manager, and *d* 23 March 1969, having had:

1 (Anthony John) Julian; *b* 29 Aug 1916; *educ* Eton; Capt RA WW II; *m* 1 June 1940 Susan Esterel (*m* 2nd 26 May 1949 Lt-Col Jocelyn Eustace Gurney, DSO, MC, Welsh Gds (*d* 1973), 2nd son of Sir Eustace Gurney, JP, of Walsingham Abbey, and Sprowston Hall, Norfolk, and *d* 1993, having had further issue), est dau of Capt Robert Hamond Arthur Elwes, JP, of Congham House, King's Lynn, and was *ka* St Mauvais, Normandy, 26 June 1944, leaving issue:

(1) Sir RICHARD MICHAEL CORY-WRIGHT, **4th and present Bt**

(1) Virginia Caroline; *b* 8 May 1941; *m* 26 May 1966 David de Ferrière Faurot, only son of George F Faurot, of Sugar Hollow Farm, North Carolina, USA; both were *drowned* in a boating accident in America 24 Dec 1966

(2) *Juliet Susan [Mrs John Webster, Beech Grove Farm House, Hethersett, Norwich]; *b* 22 Oct 1942; *m* 1977 *John Frederick Webster, and has issue:

1a *Robert John Julian; *b* 1983

1a *Charlotte Josephine; *b* 1981

2 Michael; *b* 5 March 1920; *educ* Eton; Lt RA (TA) WW II (POW); *m* 2 July 1954 Elizabeth (*d* 16 Dec 1995), yr dau of Lt-Col James Archibald Morrison, DSO, of Basildon Park, Berks (*see* MARGADALE, B), widow of Eric Martin-Smith, MP, and previously wife of Nigel Eric Murray Gunnis, and *d* 3 Jan 1997

3 +David Arthur [Capt David Cory-Wright, Quoin Cottage, Biddestone, Chippenham, Wilts SN14 7DQ]; *b* 19 March 1925; *educ* Eton; Capt Scots Gds; *m* 25 Aug 1949 (*divorce* 1985) Lady Jane Katherine Douglas, yr dau of 11th Marquess of Queensberry (*qv*), and has issue:

(1) +Antony Jonathan; *b* 22 July 1950; *educ* Millfield; *m* 1988 *Susanna M, only dau of Alfonso Torrents Prats, of Geneva and London SW5, and has:

1a +James Alfonso; *b* 1994

1a *Emma Mercedes; *b* 1992

(2) +Simon; *b* 20 Feb 1952; *educ* Millfield

(3) +Christopher James; *b* 16 Dec 1965

3 (cont.) David Cory-Wright *m* 2nd 1985 Joy Elizabeth Jefferson (*d* 10 March 1996), only dau of Albert Edward Dursley, of Hanham, Bristol

4 Jonathan Francis; *b* 19 March 1925 (twin); *educ* Eton; Lt Scots Gds WW II; *ka* Germany 9 April 1945

5 +Mark Richard Geoffrey [Mark Cory-Wright Esq, Tilhill House, Tilford, Surrey]; *b* 21 March 1930; *educ* Eton; late 2nd Lt 10th Royal Hus; *m* 10 April 1956 *Tania Beatrice, only dau of John Culcheth Holcroft (*see* HOLCROFT, Bt), and has issue:

(1) +Charles Alexander; *b* 6 Sept 1958; *m* 1988 *Dorothy McNaughton, dau of Samuel Watson, of Penwortham, Lancs, and has issue:

1a *Ella Doone; *b* 1991

2a *Poppy Maud; *b* 1993

(2) +Harry William Mark; *b* 9 July 1963

COTTENHAM

Arms: Sable on a bend or between two nag's heads erased argent three fleurs-de-lys of the field. **Crest:** A camel's head erased or, bridled and gorged with a ducal coronet sable. **Supporters:** On either side a horse argent, bridled and gorged with a ducal coronet sable, pendent therefrom an escutcheon or, charged with a fleur-de-lys of the second. **Motto:** *Mens cujusque is est quisque* ('Mind makes the man'). **Creations:** Bt. (GB) 22 Jan 1784 and (UK) 23 June 1801, B. (UK) 20 Jan 1836, V. and E. (UK) 11 June 1850.

THE 8TH EARL OF COTTENHAM, Viscount Crowhurst, of Crowhurst, in Surrey, **Baron Cottenham**, of Cottenham, Co Cambridge, and a **Baronet** (Sir (Kenelm) Charles Everard Digby Pepys, Bt) [The Rt Hon The Earl of Cottenham, House of Lords, London SW1A 0PW]; *b* 27 Nov 1948; *s f* 1968; *educ* Eton; *m* 15 March 1975 *Sarah, dau of Capt S Lombard-Hobson, CVO, OBE, RN, and has issue:

1 +MARK JOHN HENRY, *Viscount Crowhurst*; *b* 11 Oct 1983

2 +Sam Richard; *b* 26 April 1986

1 *Georgina Marye; *b* 9 Oct 1981

Lineage: PEPYSes lived at Cottenham, Cambs, at least as early as 1290 and continued there till the early 16th century, though no connected pedigree can be traced either between them or with subsequent persons of that name.

ROBERT PEPYS; had an only s:

WILLIAM PEPYS, of Cottenham; *m* Margaret (*d* on or after 4 Jan 1529), dau of Robert Whiston, and *d* between 20 March 1518/9 and 20 May 1519, leaving, with two er sons and three daus:

WILLIAM PEPYS, of Cottenham; *m* Alice, dau of John Smith, of Wighton, Norfolk, and had six sons and two daus; the 2nd son:

JOHN PEPYS, of Cottenham, and Impington Manor, Cambs; *m* 1st Edith (*bur* 25 Sept 1583), dau and heir of Edmund Talbot, and had, with four other sons and four daus:

1 John, of Cottenham; *m* Elizabeth, dau of John Bendish, of Bower Hall, Essex, and was *bur* 21 March 1606, having had six sons; the 2nd son:

(1) Richard, Serjeant-at-Law, MP Sudbury 1640, Baron Exchequer May 1654, Ch Justice Ireland Sept 1654; *m* 1st 14 Aug 1620 Judith (*bur* 14 April 1634), dau of Sir William Cutte, of Arkesden, Essex, and had four sons and three daus; *m* 2nd Mary (*d* 10 Oct 1659), sis of Peter Gosnold, and *d* 2 Jan 1659; the est son:

1a Richard, of Stoke by Clare, Suffolk; *m* Mary (*d* 1664), dau of John Scott, of Belchamp Walter, Essex, migrated to New England April 1634, lived at Boston till 1650, returned to England, settled at Ashen Clare, Suffolk, and had three sons; the 2nd son:

1b John, of St Dunstan's W, Middx; Master Clock-Makers' Co; *m* 17 April 1683 Mary Gibson and *d* Nov 1737, leaving, with two er sons and a dau:

1c William, of London; *bapt* 3 Oct 1698; banker, bought in 1705 Ridley Hall (burnt down 1706) from Orlando Bridgeman (*see* BRADFORD, E); *m* 1st 15 Jan 1735 Susanna, widow of — Austin, and had a son; *m* 2nd 8 June 1738 Hannah (*d* between 29 July 1760 and 8 Nov 1761), widow of Alexander Weller and dau of Nathaniel Russell, surgn, of Lewes and Ranscomb Manor, Sussex, and *d* Sept 1743, having by her had:

1d **Sir William Weller Pepys, 1st Bt** (UK), so *cr* 23 June 1801; *b* 1 Jan 1740/1; one of the Masters in Chancery; *m* 24 June 1777 Elizabeth (*d* 21 Oct 1830), est dau of Rt Hon W Dowdeswell, Chllr Exchequer, and *d* 2 June 1825, having had, with other issue (of whom those with a + immediately below are in remainder, of the two btcies, to the 1801 one only):

1e **Sir William Weller Pepys, 2nd Bt**; *b* 4 May 1778; *d* unm 5 Oct 1845

2e CHARLES CHRISTOPHER, **1st Earl**

3e Henry (Rt Rev), DD, Bp Sodor and Man 1840–41 and Worcester 1841–60; *b* 18 April 1783; *m* 27 Jan 1824 Maria (*d* 17 June 1885 aged 89), dau of Rt Hon John and Lady Harriet Sullivan, and *d* 13 Nov 1860, having had issue:

1f Philip Henry, barrister; *b* 14 Nov 1824; *m* 14 Dec 1848 Louisa Eleanor Anne (*d* 22 Dec 1885), only dau of Lt-Col Disbrowe, and *dsp* 6 Feb 1886

2f Herbert George (Rev), Hon Canon of Worcester, vicar Hallow, Worcs; *b* 31 Oct 1830; *educ* Trin Coll Cambridge (MA); *m* 6 May 1863 Louisa Harriet (*d* 25 Oct 1917), est dau of John Whitmore Isaac, of Broughton Ho, Worcs, and *d* 21 Feb 1918, leaving issue:

1g Herbert Frederick; *b* 24 May 1865; *m* 24 Sept 1901 Alice Neame (*d* 8 June 1947), dau of John L Oliver, and *d* 1 Sept 1944, leaving issue:

1h Frederick Courtenay; *b* 20 Oct 1904; *m* 24 March 1935 *Mary Caroline Bradley, of Los Angeles, and *d* 1983, having had:

1i +Eric Courtenay [Eric Pepys, 526 S Bayfront, Newport Beach, California 92662–1039, USA]; *b* 10 Jan 1936; *m* 16 May 1964 *Shirley Ann Dietrich, of Corona del Mar, California, and has issue:

1j +Noel Dietrich; *b* 1970

2j +Maximillian Paul; *b* 1972

1j *Renée Catherine; *b* 24 Dec 1964

2j *Tiffany Ann; *b* 20 March 1968

2i +Mark Bradley [Mark Pepys, 6065 Via Sonoma, Rancho Palos Verdes, CA 90274, USA]; *b* 5 Aug 1937; *m* 1970 *Anne Claire Bowden, and has issue:

1j +Craig Brian; *b* 1974

1j *Kirsten Anne; *b* 1976

3i Noel Oliver; *b* 17 April 1944; *d* 19 March 1945

4i +Keith Alan [Keith Pepys, 8223 Woodland Drive, Buena Bark, CA 90620, USA]; *b* 20 Jan 1948

1i *Christine [Mrs Ronald Heusser, 1816 Lark Ellen Fullerton, CA 92635, USA]; *b* 10 Nov 1939; *m* 20 Aug 1960 *Ronald Vincent Heusser, and has issue:

1j *Melinda Christine; *b* 17 Nov 1965

2j *Noelle Pepys; *b* 1 April 1968

3j *Hilary Dawn; *b* 1971

2i *Mary Noel; *b* 8 Feb 1946

2g Charles Henry; *b* 10 Oct 1871; *m* 17 Oct 1901 Daisy Louise (*d* 8 Dec 1902), only dau of Rev N W Motheral, of California, and *dsp* 9 March 1940

3g Reginald Whitmore, Capt Worcs Regt; *b* 3 Jan 1883; *m* 27 July 1914 Maud Mabel (*m* 2nd 16 Sept 1919 Eric Ayton Dickson, son of Sir Frederick Dickson, KCMG), dau of William Foster, of Beechwood, Iffley, and *d* 21 Sept 1914 of wounds recd in action

1g Evelyn; *b* 24 June 1864; *d* unm 13 Aug 1940

2g Marion Emily; *b* 1 Aug 1866; *d* unm 19 Jan 1956

3g Florence, deaconess; *b* 15 Jan 1868; *d* unm 28 May 1958

4g Helen Beatrice; *b* 13 March 1870; *d* unm 9 Aug 1946

5g Gertrude Amy; *b* 1 July 1875; *d* unm 18 April 1908

6g Constance Charlotte; Benedictine nun; *b* 4 Aug 1877; *d* 17 June 1948

7g Bertha Geraldine; *b* 28 Sept 1870; *d* unm 21 Oct 1908

1f Maria Louisa; *m* 16 Dec 1847 Rev Edward Winnington-Ingram (*d* 30 April 1892), rector Stanford-on-Teme, Worcs, and *d* 11 Jan 1924, leaving issue (*see* WINNINGTON, Bt)

2f Emily; *m* 28 Sept 1854 Rev Hon William Henry Lyttelton, yst son of 3rd Baron Lyttelton (*see* COBHAM, V), and *dsp* 12 Sept 1877

1e Isabella Sophia; *m* 19 Jan 1813 Rev Thomas Whately (*d* 10 May 1864), rector Chetwynd, Salop, and *d* 21 April 1870, leaving issue

2d **Sir Lucas Pepys, 1st Bt** (GB), so *cr* 22 Jan 1784, with remainder in default of male issue to his bro; MD, FRS, FAS; *b* 24 May 1741; *m* 1st 31 Oct 1772 Jane Elizabeth, Countess of Rothes (*see* ROTHES, E); *m* 2nd 29 June 1813 Deborah (*dsp* 21 June 1848), dau of Anthony Askew, and *d* 17 June 1830, leaving by his 1st w:

1e Sir CHARLES PEPYS later LESLIE (Sir), **2nd Bt**; *b* 28 Sept 1774; *d* unm 4 Feb 1833

2e **Sir Henry Leslie, 3rd Bt**, Rector Sheephall, Herts, Preb Exeter; *b* July 1781; *m* 15 Feb 1816 Elizabeth Jane (*d* 12 Dec 1816), dau of Rev James Oakes, and *dsp* 9 Dec 1849, when the btcy passed to the **1st Earl of Cottenham** (*see* below)

1e Henrietta; *m* 25 Nov 1804 10th Earl of Devon (*qv*) and *d* 16 Dec 1839, leaving issue

2 Thomas (5th son); *m* by licence 8 July 1596 Maria Day, of Wisbech, and had, with two other sons and two daus:

(1) John, of Brampton, Hunts; tailor; *bapt* 14 Jan 1600/1; *m* Margaret — (*d* 25 March 1667) and *d* by 19 Oct 1680, having had:

1a Samuel, of Brampton; *b* 23 Feb 1632; *educ* St Paul's and Magdalene Coll Cambridge (MA); author: *Pepys's Diary*, Sec to Admlty 1684, MP Castle Rising 1673 and Harwich 1685; *m* 10 Oct 1655 Elizabeth (*d* 10 Nov 1669), dau of Alexander Merchant de St Michel, and *dsp* 26 May 1703

2a Thomas, *s* his f in his tailor's shop; *d* aged 30

3a John; *b* 1641; *educ* St Paul's and Christ's Coll Cambridge; Clerk to Trinity House 1670; *d* unm 1677

1a Paulina; *m* John Jackson and had:

1b John; heir to his uncle; had:

1c Frances; *m* John Cockerell

2c Anne; *m* Brabazon Hallowes

3c Paulina; *m* Adml Collins

JOHN PEPYS *m* 2nd 15 Oct 1587 Anne Jenison, of Saltfleete, and was *bur* 15 July 1589

The 2nd Bt (of the 1801 *cr*)'s bro,

Sir Charles Christopher Pepys, 3rd Bt (as which *s* bro 1845), and **4th Bt** (as which *s* cousin 1849), and **1st Earl of Cottenham**, so *cr* 11 June 1850, as also earlier 20 Jan 1836 BARON COTTENHAM, of Cottenham, Co Cambridge, and VISCOUNT CROWHURST, of Crowhurst, Surrey (all UK), DCL; *b* 29 April 1781; Queen's Slr-Gen to QUEEN ADELAIDE 1830–32, Slr-Gen 1833, Master of the Rolls 1834, Ld High Commr Gt Seal 1835, Ld Chllr 1836–41 and 1846–50; *m* 30 June 1821 Caroline Elizabeth (*d* 6 April 1868), dau of William Wingfield Baker by Lady Charlotte Maria Digby, sis of 2nd Earl Digby (*see* DIGBY, B), and *d* 29 April 1851, having had, with other issue:

1 CHARLES EDWARD PEPYS, **2nd Earl of Cottenham**; *b* 30 April 1824; *d* unm 18 Feb 1863

2 WILLIAM JOHN, **3rd Earl**

3 Henry Leslie; *b* 28 Nov 1830; *m* 17 Nov 1868 Ada (*d* 21 April 1936), yr dau of Lt-Col Charles James Coote, 18th Regt (*see* COOTE, Bt), and *d* 18 March 1891, leaving issue:

(1) Charles John Leslie; *b* 11 May 1874; *d* unm 5 Jan 1905

(2) Arthur Guy Leslie, MC; *b* 24 Aug 1875; Lt-Col Essex Regt, served Matabeleland and Mashonaland 1896–97 (medal and clasp), Boer War 1900–02 (two medals, five clasps) and WW I 1914–16 (wounded, despatches twice); *m* 6 March 1915 Olive Grace (*d* 1 Aug 1961), yst dau of John Frederick Starkey, DL, JP, of Bodicote Ho, Banbury, Oxfordshire, and *d* 9 April 1953, leaving issue:

1a Samuel Guy Leslie, Lt-Col Essex Regt WW II 1939–40 (despatches); *b* 13 Dec 1915; *educ* Wellington; *m* 8 Dec 1945 *Lettice Gayford, yst dau of Thomas Leonard Partridge, of Stowmarket, Suffolk, and *dsp* 16 June 1970

1a *Iris Leslie [Mrs Norman Boffee, 1B Little Green Lane, Chertsey, Surrey]; *b* 28 Nov 1918; F/O WRAF 1940–53; *m* 6 June 1953 W/Cdr Norman Maxwell Boffee, DFC, RAF, only son of Charles Boffee, of Wimbledon, and has issue:

1b *Mark Guy; *b* 4 April 1956; *m* 1982 *Jean, dau of Noshir Rumwalla, of Hounslow, Middx

(3) Gerald Leslie, CB (1933), DSO (1916), Col IA, GSO at India Office 1931–33, Personal Asst to Mil Sec India Office 1933–36, served Mohmand Expdn 1908 (medal with clasp) and WW I (despatches); *b* 30 Jan 1879; *m* 20 June 1907 Charlotte Helen (*d* 21 Feb 1965), yst dau of Charles William Lambe Forbes, of Auchrannie, Forfarshire, and *d* 23 Feb 1936, leaving issue:

1a +Charles Donald Leslie (Tom) [Lt-Col Charles Pepys, 30/31 Lyfield Court, Kidmore End Rd, Emmer Green, Reading, Berks RG4 8AP]; *b* 25 Sept 1909; *educ* Radley; Lt-Col KOYLI; *m* 3 Feb 1941 *Hon (Pamela Sophia) Nadine Stonor, er dau of 5th Baron Camoys (*qv*)

2a John Evelyn Leslie; WW II as Capt Recce Corps; *b* 15 Aug 1911; *educ* Sherborne and Corpus Christi Coll Oxford (BA 1934, MA 1946); *m* 19 Jan 1943 *Zita Mary, yst dau of Robert Emilius Noble, Puisne Judge Leeward Is, and *d* 6 Sept 1981

3a Peter Andrew Leslie, Maj IA, librarian Warwick Castle; *b* 25 June 1914; *educ* Sherborne; *d* unm 30 Dec 1978

1a Geraldine Mary Leslie; *b* 16 Aug 1908; *m* 2 July 1935 Lt-Col William Louis Barnard, Oxon and Bucks LI (*d* 26 Nov 1953), son of Rev Gilbert William Barnard, and *d* 18 April 1994, leaving:

1b *Simon William Leslie [Simon Barnard Esq, 92b Underhill Rd, London SE22]; *b* 11 June 1938; *educ* Winchester and Magdalene Coll Cambridge; *m* 22 Dec 1962 *Joy, dau of Thomas Frank Prior Pavely, of Cambridge, and has issue:

1c *Jonathan James; *b* 17 May 1969; *educ* Edinburgh U (MA) and Sussex U (MA); barrister Middle Temple 1997

1c *Emma Louise; *b* 18 Dec 1966; *educ* Keele U (BA)

(1) Evelyn; *b* 22 July 1872; *m* 3 June 1902 Col John Monteith, CB (*d* 2 June 1928), late IA, son of Robert Thomas Monteith, V-Consul St Malo, and *dsp* 29 Aug 1949

4 George, MA Cambridge, barrister; *b* 21 July 1832; *m* 21 July 1864 Anna Eliza (*d* 26 March 1916), dau of John Foster, of Malverleys, Hants, and *d* 6 Sept 1890, leaving issue:

(1) George Digby, CBE (1931), barrister Inner Temple 1897, Sr Official Receiver in Companies Liquidation; *b* 7 June 1868; *educ* Winchester and Oriel Coll Oxford (BA 1890, MA 1894); *m* 30 Dec 1902 Margaret Mary Humphrey (May) (*d* 7 July 1954 aged 82), est dau of George Walter Davidson, of Queen's Gate, SW, and Mauritius, and *d* 2 May 1957, leaving issue:

1a Mary Joyce; *b* 28 Dec 1903; *d* 1980

2a *Anna Margaret; *b* 24 March 1906; *m* 14 April 1931 Peter Pryor (*d* 1980), son of Roderick Pryor, of Weston Lodge, Hitchin, Herts, and has issue:

1b *Roderick [Roderick Pryor Esq, Weston Lodge, Hitchin, Herts]; *b* 10 Dec 1932; *educ* Eton, Trin Coll Cambridge and Ch Ch Oxford; *m* 25 April 1959 *Carolyn Vaughan, er dau of Donald Smith, of Old Mill Ho, Sandwich, Kent, and has issue:

1c *Peter David [Peter Pryor Esq, 29 Chesson Rd, London W14]; *b* 1 June 1965; *m* 1993 *Melanie Ruth, dau of Malcolm Palmer, of Woodsford Sq, London W14, and has:

1d *Rose Elizabeth; *b* 1995

1c *Louise Margaret [Dr Louise Pryor, 115 Hanover St, Edinburgh]; *b* 20 April 1960

2c *Victoria Jane; *b* 1 March 1962; *m* 1987 *Denis Henry Clough, son of Peter Clough, of Hampsthwaite, Yorks, and has issue:

1d *Hugh Peter; *b* 1993

1d *Alice Eleanor; *b* 1991

2d *Clare Helen; *b* 1996

2b *George [George Pryor Esq, Otavi Klein Farm, Namibia]; *b* 27 Dec 1936; *m* 3 Sept 1960 *Virginia Anne, yst dau of Rev Charles M Jones, of Chapel Hill, NC, and has:

1c *Richard; *b* 29 Oct 1965; *m* 1993 *Philippa, dau of Colin Brannigan, OBE

2c *Mark; *b* 8 May 1967

1c Nicola; *b* 28 Dec 1963; *d* 18 Oct 1965

2c *Catherine Eleanor; *b* 1970; *m* 1994 *Alan Roy Jones and has:

1d *Charles Alan; *b* 1995

1b *Clova Margaret [Mrs David Morris, 42 Frenchay Rd, Oxford OX2 6TG]; *b* 9 Feb 1935; *m* 1st 31 Dec 1960 (*divorce* 1983) Glyn Tudor, son of Leonard Willoughby Tudor; *m* 2nd 1990 *David Elwyn Morris, son of Rev S M Morris, and by her 1st husb has issue:

1c *Adam; *b* 11 May 1966

1c *Anna Morwena; *b* 31 Oct 1962; *m* 1992 *Marcel Goudsblom, of Amsterdam, and has:

1d *Isadora; *b* 1994

2c *Gay Elizabeth; *b* 6 Oct 1964

2b *Mary [Mrs Roy Hodges, Newnham Grounds, Daventry, Northants NN11 6EP]; *b* 29 Nov 1944; *m* 15 March 1969 *Roy Hodges, est son of Francis H Hodges, of Tangley, Shenfield, Essex, and has issue:

1c *Jeremy George; *b* 1972

2c *Jonathan Francis; *b* 1976

(2) Charles Sidney (Rev), Vicar Aylesbury, Hon Canon St John's Cathedral, Buenos Aires 1914–17, CF WW I (despatches); *b* 1 April 1875; *educ* Winchester and Oriel Coll Oxford (BD, MA); *m* 14 Aug 1913 Adelaide Mary Elizabeth (*d* 16 Aug 1968), only dau of Charles Duncan Cutts, of Buenos Aires, and *d* 21 Sept 1927, leaving issue:

1a (George) Christopher Cutts (Rt Rev), Rector Hartfield Sussex 1946–51, Vicar St Mark's North End Portsmouth 1951–58, Rector Liverpool 1958–64, Hon Canon Liverpool 1959, Suffragan Bp Buckingham 1964–74, WW II as Chaplain RNVR; *b* 29 June 1914; Ieduc Winchester and Oriel Coll Oxford (BA 1937, MA 1944); *m* 12 April 1947 *Elizabeth Margaret (*m* 2nd 1991 Rt Rev Michael A Mann, Dean of Windsor) [Mrs Elizabeth Mann, Lower End Farm Cottage, Eastington, Northleach, Glos], er dau of Maj-Gen Roger Gillies Ekin, CIE, late IA, of Hereford, and *d* 4 April 1974, leaving issue:

1b +(Charles) Richard Ekin [Richard Pepys Esq, Thoke House, Hall Lane, Farringdon, Alton, Hants]; *b* 1 Dec 1951; *educ* Winchester; BA; *m* 1979 *Jane Elizabeth Cracroft, dau of Lt-Cdr Gervis Frere-Cook, RN, of Exton, Hants (*see* BROWN, Bt), and has issue:

1c +(George) Oliver Frere; *b* 1982

1c *Suzannah Mary Elizabeth; *b* 1985

2c *Clemency Rosemary Eleanor; *b* 1987

1b *Caroline Elizabeth [Miss Caroline Pepys, 53 Hayfield Rd, Oxford]; *b* 27 Feb 1948

2b *Sarah Priscilla [Mrs William Davies, Norcott, 68 Foreland Rd, Bembridge, IoW]; *b* 5 April 1950; *m* 1980 *William Howard Davies, and has issue:

1c *William Christopher Pepys; *b* 1985

1c *Holly Pepys; *b* 1983

3b *Frances Mary [Miss Frances Pepys, 12A Clifford Gdns, London NW10]; *b* 13 Jan 1954

4b *Anna Margaret [Mrs Robert Agnew, 1 Hogg End, Chipping Warden, Banbury, Oxon OX17 1LY]; *b* 25 July 1956; *m* 1982 *Robert Peter Agnew, son of Dr Sydney Alexander Agnew, of South Molton, Devon, and has issue:

1c *Alexander Christian Pepys; *b* 1984

2c *Thomas Robert Pepys; *b* 1987

1c *Eleanor Josephine; *b* 1990

2a Charles Richard; *b* 13 Sept 1920; *d* 4 Jan 1921

1a *Elizabeth Sidney [Mrs Guy Daniel, 2 Gervis Court, Penwerris Ave, Osterley, Middx TW7 4QU]; *m* 1 June 1939 Rev (Arthur) Guy St John Daniel, est s of Rev Arthur Owen Daniel, of St Benedict's, Newbury, and has:

1b (Arthur) Jeremy Pepys; *b* 30 Aug 1940; *educ* St Paul's; *d* following a car crash 27 April 1964

2b *Nicholas Guy [Nicholas Daniel Esq, 24 Third Ave, Ottawa, Ontario K15 2JG, Canada]; *b* 27 May 1942; *educ* St Paul's; *m* 1st 1974 (*divorce* 1983) Menna Matthews; *m* 2nd 1984 *Susan Cartwright

3b *Timothy Peter Charles [Timothy Daniel Esq, 37 St Gabriel's Rd, London NW2 4DT]; *b* 3 May 1941; *educ* St Paul's and Bristol U; *m* 1974 *Rosalie Horner

2a Ursula Mary Evelyn; *b* 2 March 1917; *m* 14 May 1941 Leighton Erle Gray (*d* 1980), son of Frank Gray, of Ripley, Surrey, and *d* 16 Jan 1993, having had:

1b John Leighton; *b* 24 Sept 1945; *d* in a road accident 29 Feb 1952

2b *Paul Leighton [Paul Gray Esq, 26 Gloucester St, Faringdon, Oxon SN7 7HY]; *b* 11 Jan 1958; *educ* George Abbot Sch Guildford and Westfield Coll London (BA); *m* 30 May 1992 *Sarah Elizabeth Sinclair, er dau of Spencer Kendal, of The Old Barn, Malmesbury, Wilts, and has:

1c *Christopher Spencer Pepys; *b* 14 March 1995

1c *Jennifer Ursula Sinclair; *b* 22 Nov 1997

1b *Mary Ann [Mrs Bryan Harris, The Old Post Office, Hatherop, Glos]; *b* 4 May 1943; *m* 1972 *Bryan Harris and has:

1c *Mark; *b* 29 April 1966

2c *Charles; *b* 5 Oct 1967

1c *Jane; *b* 22 Sept 1970

3a *(Phyllis) Ann Jennifer [Mrs Alexander Paton, Knollbury, Chadlington, Oxon OX7 3NJ]; *b* 1924; *m* 12 July 1947 *Alexander Paton, MD, FRPC Consultant Physician, er son of Col Alexander Paton, DSO, MC, RA, of Willow Cottage, Hillhead, Fareham, Hants, and has had issue:

1b *Alexander; *b* 8 June 1948; *educ* Sebright Sch, Wolverley; *m* 19– *Alison Kirkland McGilp, and has issue:

1c *Rose; *b* 1984

2c *Eleanor; *b* 1986

3c *Anna; *b* 1990

2b Charles Pepys, RN; *b* 22 Feb 1950; *educ* Solihull Sch; RN; *d* 1973

3b *Antony Grimwood; *b* 24 Sept 1954; *educ* Solihull Sch; *m* 1983 *Pauline Marion Gibbins and has issue:

1c *Benjamin Charles; *b* 1985

1c *Nicola Marion; *b* 1990

1b *Clare Jennifer; *b* 11 March 1952; *m* 1st 1972 (*divorce* 1983) Terence Patrick Mead, and has issue:

1c *Samuel James; *b* 1979

1c *Jessica Ann; *b* 1976

1b (cont.) Mrs Clare Mead *m* 2nd 1988 *George Albert Kitcher, and has further issue:

2c *Nathan John; *b* 1991

2c *Naomi Mary; *b* 1993

2b *Rachel Mary; *b* 30 May 1953; has:

1c *Christopher James; *b* 1994

4a *Alison Margaret [Mrs Peter Courtenay, 9190 Canora Rd, Sidney, BC V8L 1N9, Canada]; *b* 19 Jan 1927; *m* 10 Dec 1955 *Peter Harold Edwin Courtenay, MB, BS, FRCS, only son of Harold Edwin Courtenay, of Sandhill, Dorking, Surrey, and has issue:

1b *Stephen Harold Pepys; *b* 27 Dec 1956; *m* 1989 *Mara Anna Gottler

2b *Simon Charles; *b* 22 Nov 1958; *m* 1991 *Hélène Marie Claire Dupuis and has issue:

1c *Maia Alison; *b* 1992

2c *Kesia Claire; *b* 17 May 1994

3b *Michael Peter; *b* 15 June 1962; *m* 1996 *Susan Cunningham

1b *Ann Elizabeth; *b* 20 Oct 1963

(1) Alice Evelyn; *b* 10 June 1871; *d* unm 12 July 1942

5 Walter Courtenay, barrister, Lt 60th Rifles; *b* 27 Nov 1840; *m* 4 Aug 1874 Amy Harriet (*d* 7 July 1908), only dau of Lt-Col Charles William Thompson, of Ballyherin, Co Donegal, and *d* 4 Nov 1914, having had issue:

(1) Charles Courtenay; *b* 17 Feb 1883; *d* 12 April 1884

(2) Walter Evelyn, CMG (1938), Malayan CS 1908–40, U-Sec FMS 1930, Commr Trade and Customs FMS, and SS 1932, Gen Adviser Johore 1935, ret 1940, Liaison Offr Sarawak and N Borneo 1940–42, POW at Singapore; *b* 12 April 1885; *educ* Malvern and BNC Oxford (BA 1907, MA 1910); *m* 24 Sept 1932 Violet Maude (*d* 26 Aug 1960), dau of Thomas Carr Ramsey, of Dunvegan Ho, Swatow, China, and *dsp* 15 Nov 1966

(1) Helen Emily; *b* 18 April 1876; *m* 5 Jan 1903 Col William McCombie Duguid-McCombie, DSO, JP, RSG (*d* 24 May 1970 aged 96), son of Peter Duguid-McCombie, of East Shee, and Lynturk, Aberdeenshire, and *dsp* 9 Dec 1903

(2) Amy Theresa; *b* 26 April 1878; *m* 29 July 1901 Gerard Tarver Whiteley, MA, son of George Crispe Whiteley, barrister, and *d* 1 Feb 1963, leaving, with a dau:

1a Derek Pepys-Whiteley, Keeper Pepys Library and archivist Magdelene Coll Cambridge 1959–70; *d* 10 Oct 1944

(3) Dorothy Caroline *b* 18 June 1879; *m* 17 June 1909 Lt-Col Herbert Hastings Harington, IA (*ka* 1916), son of Herbert Baring Harrington, ICS, and *d* 16 Dec 1969, leaving issue:

1a Charles Henry Pepys (Sir), GCB (1969, KCB 1964, CB 1961), CBE (1957, OBE 1953), DSO (1944), MC (1940); *b* 5 May 1910; *educ* Malvern and RMC Sandhurst; Gen late Cheshire Regt, served WW II (despatches), Cmdt Sch of Inf 1958, GOC 3rd Div 1959–61, Cmdt Staff Coll Camberley 1961–63,

C-in-C Middle East Cmd 1963–65, Dep CGS 1965–68, Ch of Personnel and Logistics MOD 1968–71 (ret), Col Cheshire Regt 1962–68, Col-Cmdt Prince of Wales's Div 1968–71, Col-Cmdt Small Arms Sch Corps 1964–70, ADC (Gen) to HM 1969–71; pres CCF Assoc 1971–80, commr: Roy Hosp Chelsea 1970–79, Duke of York's Roy Mil Sch 1971–89; Kt Offr (with swords) Order of Orange-Nassau (Holland) 1945; *m* 21 March 1942 *Victoire Marion, dau of Lt-Col Arthur Peere Williams-Freeman, DSO, OBE, and had issue:

1b *Guy Charles; *b* 12 Dec 1946; *educ* Malvern and Univ Coll Oxford

1b *Louise Frances Amy; *b* 23 Sept 1949

2b *Clare Marion; *b* 7 Oct 1956

1a Amy Melicent Pauline Pepys; *b* 25 Jan 1912; *m* July 1935 Dr Charles Watson, MD, MA, and *d* 23 May 1945, leaving issue

2a *Dorothy Joy Nora Pepys (Joy Harington), BBC TV producer; *b* 22 Feb 1914; *m* Aug 1942 James Grant Smith, Canadian Army (*ka* 1943), and has issue:

1b *Teresa Caroline Harington; *b* 23 May 1943

1 Caroline; *m* 25 May 1852 Lister Lister-Kaye, est son of Sir John Lister Lister-Kaye, 2nd Bt (*qv*), and *d* 21 Jan 1902, leaving issue

2 Elizabeth Theresa; *m* 23 July 1864 Col Gerald Edmund Boyle, late Rifle Bde, and *d* 24 Jan 1897, leaving issue (*see* CORK and ORRERY, E)

3 Evelyn; *m* 12 June 1762 Lord Courtenay (*dvp* 27 May 1898), est son of 14th Earl of Devon (*qv*), and *d* 7 Oct 1910, leaving issue

The 2nd EARL's bro,

WILLIAM JOHN PEPYS, **3rd Earl of Cottenham**, DL Surrey; *b* 15 Aug 1825; *m* 11 Oct 1870 Theodosia Selina (*d* 27 Feb 1919), only dau of Sir Robert Charles Dallas, 2nd Bt (*see* 1902 edn), and had issue:

1 KENELM CHARLES EDWARD, **4th Earl**

2 Everard Digby; *b* 21 June 1876; *m* 20 May 1897 Katharine Louise (*d* 13 Dec 1959), dau of Charles Diehl, of Metz, Germany, and *d* 14 Dec 1943, leaving issue:

(1) Everard Charles; *b* 8 April, *d* 15 May 1901

(1) Honor Mary Evelyn, OStJ; *b* 4 Nov 1899; *m* 19 July 1923 Brig (Thomas) Denis Daly, CBE, MC, KStJ, late RWF (*d* 21 Nov 1956), est son of James Thomas Daly, of Raford, Leamington

(2) Yolande Katharine Rosabelle; *b* 25 July 1902; *m* 20 Feb 1928 Christopher Reginald Turnor, only son of Maj Reginald Charles Turnor, 1st Life Gds, and had issue:

1a *Clive Christopher; *b* 8 Feb 1929; *educ* Bryanston

1a *Gillian Yolande; *b* 1 June 1931

(3) Audrey Marion Caroline; *b* 27 April 1906; *m* 19 April 1928 Humphrey Charles Vaughan Jones, est son of Sir Francis Adolphus Jones, KBE, CB, and had issue:

1a *Philip Charles; *b* 1 April 1933; *educ* Malvern and Slade Sch of Fine Art

1a *Janet Katherine Vaughan; *b* 21 Jan 1930; *m* 8 Dec 1951 *Cdr Julian Richards, RN, son of Rev Herbert John Kingsley Richards, MA, and has issue:

1b *Charles Oliver; *b* 21 March 1955; *educ* Winchester

1b *Lucinda Mary; *b* 18 April 1953

2b *Frances Julia; *b* 31 March 1958

3b *Katharine Anne; *b* 6 Jan 1963

2a *Barbara Caroline; *b* 13 June 1935

1 Mary; *b* 7 Aug 1878; *m* 26 Nov 1910 Elias Mary Benedict Corbally, DL (*d* 18 July 1933), and *d* 4 May 1957, leaving issue

The 3rd EARL *d* 20 Jan 1881; his est son,

KENELM CHARLES EDWARD PEPYS, **4th Earl of Cottenham**; *b* 18 May 1874; *m* 1st 29 Nov 1899 Lady Rose (*d* 2 May 1913), formerly w of John Blundell Leigh and dau of 1st Marquess of Abergavenny (*qv*); *m* 2nd 16 Aug 1916 Patricia (*d* 26 March 1962), dau of John Humphrey Burke, of Galway and California, and *d* 22 April 1919, having by his 1st w had issue:

1 KENELM CHARLES FRANCIS PEPYS, **5th Earl of Cottenham**; *b* 13 May 1901; *d* unm 29 Dec 1922

2 MARK EVERARD PEPYS, **6th Earl of Cottenham**; *b* 29 May 1903; Lt Leics Yeo TA; *m* 19 Jan 1927 (*divorce* 1939) Sybil Venetia, only dau of Capt John Vickris Taylor, of North Aston Manor, Oxford, and *d* 19 July 1943, leaving issue:

(1) *Rose Edith Idina [The Lady Rose Pepys, Flat B, 101 Earls Court Rd, London W8 6QS]; *b* 5 Nov 1927; SRN St Mary's Hosp; *m* 24 Sept 1994 *Col Oliver Berger

(2) *Paulina Mary Louise [The Lady Paulina Hadley, White Hill House, Upham, Hants SO32 1JL]; *b* 14 June 1930; *educ* Oxford (MA 1956); *m* 1973 *Denis Bernard Hadley

3 JOHN DIGBY THOMAS PEPYS, **7th Earl of Cottenham**; *b* 14 June 1907; *educ* Eton and RMC Sandhurst; Lt 10th Roy Hus, pres: Arundel and Shoreham C Assoc 1961–65 (chm Thakenham branch 1947–62), Br Show Pony Soc 1963, Ponies of Britain Club, Tunbridge Wells and SE Counties Ag Soc, West Grinstead and Dist Ag Soc, Queen's Park Rangers Football Club and Metropolitan and S Counties AAA; memb National Hunt Ctee 1954, National Hunt Fin Ctee 1957–62, Tattersalls Ctee 1957–62, Steward National Hunt Ctee 1962, Sr Steward 1964, dir: Peter Merchant Ltd 1933–52 (chm 1943–52, md 1933–52), Lockhart Gp Ltd (chm 1946–60, md 1946–52), Trust Houses Ltd 1962–68, Lingfield Park Racecourse Ltd; *m* 3 Oct 1933 Lady Angela Isabel Nellie Nevill, only dau of 4th Marquess of Abergavenny (*qv*), and *d* 12 May 1968, having had issue:

1 (KENELM) CHARLES EVERARD DIGBY PEPYS, **8th and present Earl of Cottenham**

1 Marye Isabel; *b* 18 Oct 1934; *m* 23 July 1953 (*divorce* 1956) Hon Luke Robert White, only son of 4th Baron Annaly, MC (*qv*), and *d* 4 June 1958, leaving issue

2 Davina Rose; *b* 9 Feb 1940; *m* 28 Oct 1959 Kenneth Drake Kleinwort, only son of Ernest Greverus Kleinwort, of Heaselands, Haywards Heath, Sussex, and 50 South Audley St, London (*see* KLEINWORT, Bt), and *d* 5 March 1973, leaving issue

3 *Gillian Angela; *b* 7 July 1941; *m* 16 May 1962 *3rd Baron McGowan (*qv*), and has issue

COTTER

Arms: Quarterly, 1st and 4th, argent a chevron gules between three serpents proper (for COTTER); 2nd and 3rd, azure a fess between a fleur-de-lys in chief and a mullet in base or (for ROGERSON).
Crest: A dexter arm embowed, armed and grasping a dart, all proper. **Motto:** *Dum spiro spero* ('While I breathe I hope').
Creation: Bt. (I) 11 Aug 1763.

SIR DELAVAL JAMES ALFRED COTTER, 6TH BT, of Rockforest, Co Cork, DSO (1944), JP (Wilts 1962) [Lt-Col Sir Delaval Cotter Bt DSO JP, Green Lines, Iwerne Courtney, Blandford Forum, Dorset DT11 8QR]; *b* 29 April 1911; *s f* 1924; *educ* Malvern and RMC Sandhurst; Lt-Col 13th/18th Roy Hus WW II NW Europe 1944–45, cmded 13th/18th Roy Hus 1953–56, ret 1959; *m* 1st 29 Sept 1943 (*divorce* 1949) Roma, only dau of Adrian Rome, of Dalswinton Lodge, Salisbury, S Rhodesia, and widow of S/Ldr Kenneth A Kerr MacEwen, RAF, of Debdale, Spratton, Northants; *m* 2nd 9 Dec 1952 Eveline Mary (ld 1991), widow of Lt-Col John Frederick Paterson, OBE, RHA, and est dau of Evelyn John Mardon, ICS, of Halsway Manor, Crowcombe, nr Taunton, Somerset, and by 1st w has issue:

1 *Sarah Gay Lisette; *b* 18 Dec 1944; *m* 1976 *Michael Vigneron

2 *Charnisay Ann; *b* 13 Dec 1946; *m* 1971 *Capt Charles A H Gwyn, Scots Gds, and has issue:

(1) *Simon; *b* 1979

(1) *Victoria; *b* 1972

(2) *Rebecca; *b* 1975

(3) *Jessica; *b* 1977

Lineage: WILLIAM COTTYR; living Co Cork *temp* EDWARD IV, of an allegedly Danish-origin family; had:

WILLIAM COTTYR, of Innismore, Co Cork; *b c* 1498; *m* a dau of Thomas Hodnett, of Belvelly Castle, Co Cork, and had:

GARRETT COTTIR, of Innismore; *b c* 1546; *m* Elizabeth, dau of Garret Barry, of the family of the Viscounts Buttevant, and had:

EDMOND COTTER, of Innismore and Anngrove, Co Cork; *m* 1st Elizabeth, dau of John Connell, of Barry's Court, and sis of the Hon Mrs Sarsfield, and had issue:

1 Garrett; *d* unm

2 JAMES (Sir), his heir

3 John; *m* and had issue:

(1) Edward, of Aylsham, Norfolk, who left his estate to his nephew, Capt F Cotter

(2) Martin, Capt in Sardinian Army, who left a son, Francis, Capt in Sardinian Army, heir to his uncle

(1) Anne; *m* D O'Brien

1 Ellen; *m* John Evans

2 Mary; *m* William Barry

3 Catherine; *m* John Gwinn, and had:

(1) John (Sir); *d* unm

EDMOND COTTER *m* 2nd Ellen Sarsfield, of Lord Kilmallock's family, and by her had issue:

4 Edmond

5 William

6 Patrick

4 Anne

5 Eleanor

6 Alice

EDMOND COTTER *d* 1660; his 2nd son,

Sir JAMES COTTER; MP, of Anngrove, Col Dragoons, Marshal and Sec certain W Indies Islands 1676, C-in-C JAMES II's forces Cos Cork, Limerick and Kerry, Govr Cork, MP Cork, Ranger of the Royal Park of Shannon; *m* 1st Mary (*dsp*), dau of Sir William Stapleton, 1st Bt (*qv*), Govr-Gen Leeward Is; *m* 2nd 30 July 1688 Hon Eleanora Plunkett, est dau of 7th Baron Louth (*qv*), and had issue:

1 JAMES, his heir

2 Laurence; *b* 17 Sept 1697; *d* unm in his 88th year
1 Mary; *b* 15 April 1695; *m* William Mahony, barrister
2 Alice Monica; *b* 4 May 1696; *d* young

Sir JAMES *d* 1705; his est son,

JAMES COTTER, of Anngrove; *b* 4 Aug 1689; executed as a Jacobite 7 May 1720; *m* 1706 Margaret, est dau of Maj George Mathew, of Thurles (*d* 1725, of the family of the Earls of Llandaff) by Mary, dau of Sir Richard Aldworth, and had:
1 JAMES (Sir), **1st Bt**
2 Edmond; *m* Miss O'Brien, of Co Clare, and had issue:
(1) George, Capt; *dvp*
(2) Edmond, Maj
1 Ellen; *m* Michael Galwey, of Rockspring, Co Cork
2 Elizabeth; *m* Kean Mahony, MD

The er son,

Sir James Cotter, 1st Bt (I), so *cr* 11 Aug 1763, of Rockforest; MP Askeaton, Co Limerick; *b* 1714; *m* 1746 Arabella, widow of Col Casaubon, MP Carrig, Co Cork, and dau and coheir (with her sisters, Elizabeth *m* 1st Baron Erne (*see* ERNE, E), and Hannah, wife of A Jephson, MP) of Rt Hon John Rogerson, Ld Ch Justice King's Bench, by Elizabeth, dau of Stephen Ludlow, ancestor of the Earls of Ludlow, and nephew of the famous republican, General Ludlow, and had issue:
1 JAMES LAURENCE (Sir), **2nd Bt**
2 Edmund; *b* 1749; *educ* Ch Ch Oxford (BA); *d* unm Sept 1770
3 Rogerson, MA, Wrangler and Fell Trin Coll Cambridge, barrister and MP Charleville; *m* Jane, widow of William Grady and dau of R Harrold, and had an only child:
(1) Jane; *m* 1822 Gen Viscomte de la Hitte, Peer of France, ADC to the DAUPHIN, son of CHARLES X, and Min For Affairs, and had issue
4 George Sackville (Rev); *educ* Trin Coll Cambridge (MA), Preb of Cloyne, Vicar Kilmacdonough, Rector Kilcredan, Garryvoe, and Ightermorragh, diocese of Cloyne; *m* Margaret, dau of Basil Rogers, by Martha, sis of Hon Mrs J Chetwynd, and dau of E Pigott, MP, ancestor of the Pigotts, Bts, of Knapton (*qv*), and *d* 1831, leaving issue:
(1) James Laurence (Rev), LLD Cambridge, Vicar Buttevant; *b* 1783; *educ* Trin Coll Dublin (BA); *m* 1st Sept 1807 Matilda, dau of A Sampayo, and had, with other issue:
1a George Sackville, CB, Col RA; *b* 17 June 1808; *m* 1st Margaret, dau of Rev William Butler; *m* 2nd 1 Aug 1836 Agnes (*d* July 1846), dau of Martin Kilgour, and had issue:
1b George Sackville; *b* 1837; *d* 1859
2b James Lawrence, Ch Factor Hudson's Bay Co; *b* 24 Dec 1838; *m* 1868 Frances, dau of Capt Ironside, and *d* 6 Aug 1889, leaving issue:
1c George Sackville; *b* 1870
2c Wemyss M'Kenzie Osborne; *b* 1872
3c Henry Martin Stuart; *b* 1873
4c Arthur Douglas; *b* 1878; *m* 1904 Marion Church Solmes, and *d* 1918, leaving issue:
1d +George Clinton Solmes; *b* 1905; *m* 19–, and has issue
2d +James Guthrie Sackville; *b* 1906; *m* 19–, and has issue
1d *Frances Marion Louise; *b* 1908; *m* 1926 Alexander Nicholson Salisbury (*d* 19–), and has issue:
1e *Virginia Puella; *b* 1927; *m* 19– *Lloyd Fieley, and has issue
1f *A son; *b* 19–
1f *A dau; *b* 19–
2f *A dau; *b* 19–
5c Oliver Wendell Holmes; *b* 1879
1c Agnes Mary
2c Evadne Kilgour
3c Ada Margaret
4c Katherine
5c Anne Winifred Ruth
1b Agnes Mary
1a (cont.) Col Cotter *m* 3rd 14 Jan 1850 Katharine (*d* 7 Oct 1851), dau of Abraham Mann, and *d* 25 June 1878, having by her had issue:
2b Katharine
1a Georgiana Isabella; *m* 1st 21 Jan 1845 Richard Kenah Exham (*d* 19 May 1871), of Co Cork, and had issue; *m* 2nd 13 Oct 1874 Capt Sheffield P F Betham (*d* 1890), Dublin Herald, and *d* 8 Aug 1905
2a Matilda; *m* 30 Oct 1845 Rev Frederick Kent (*d* 1885), of Blickling, Aylsham, Norfolk
(1) (cont.) The Rev James Cotter *m* 2nd 1827 Harriet Louisa (*d* Aug 1845), dau of Rev E Carleton, and *d* Sept 1850, having by her had issue:
2a Edward Carleton; *d* unm Sept 1866
3a William Henry (Rev), Rector Buttevant, Co Cork, LLD, MA Dublin; *b* 1844; *m* 1st 1878 Catherine Letitia (*d* 1894), dau of George Stawell, of Crobeg, Co Cork, and had issue:
1b James Laurence Stawell, Lt E Lancs Regt; *b* 23 July 1879; *d* unm 17 Sept 1903
2b George Edmund Sackville, Capt RGA; *b* 24 Feb 1882; *m* 24 Nov 1914 Beatrice Mary Grove (*m* 2nd 27 July 1921 Brig John Keily Gordon, DSO, RFA, and *d* 1981 leaving further issue), dau of Cdr Hans Thomas Fell White, RN, of Springfort Hall, Mallow, Co Cork, and *d* 19 April 1917, leaving issue:
1c *Benita May [Mrs Derek Savile, Crossways, Middle Gordon Rd, Camberley, Surrey]; *b* 13 Sept 1915; *m* 1st 2 Dec 1936 Maj Arthur William Granville Dobbie, RE (*d* of wounds in Italy, 19 June 1944), er son of Lt-Gen Sir William George Shedden Dobbie, GCMG, KCB, DSO, and has issue:
1d *William Ian Cotter, Brig RE; *b* 21 April 1939; *educ* Wellington, London U (BSc), and RMA Sandhurst
1c (cont.) Mrs Arthur Dobbie *m* 2nd 22 July 1950 Maj Derek Wrey Savile, RA (*d* 1992), est son of Lt-Col Lawrence Wrey Savile, DSO, RA, of Lych Gates, Liphook, Hants, and has further issue:
2d *George Keith Wrey; *b* 2 Sept 1951; *m* 1987 *Philippa Mary, er dau of Brian Dudgeon, of Broadfield, Guildford, and has issue:
1e *Joshua Andrew Keith; *b* 1990
2e *Samuel Christopher; *b* 1992
1e *Hannah Elizabeth; *b* 1989
1b *Catherine Anna Harriet; *m* 1904 Ven Edwin Sikes, BD (*d* 1950), Archdeacon of Ross and rector Skibbereen, Co Cork, and has issue
3a (cont.) The Rev William Cotter *m* 2nd 1896 Eva (*d* 1903), dau of J T Sikes, and *d* Feb 1931, having by her had issue:
3b William Henry Edwin, Maj Roy Inniskilling Fus; *b* 19 March 1900; *m* 19 March 1937 *Eugénie Isabelle Cory, and *d* 8 Jan 1942
2b *Eva Maud; *b* 1901; *m* 28 Dec 1921 Lt-Col Alexander Patrick Cathcart Hannay, OBE, MC, QO Cameron Highrs and S/Ldr RAF (*d* 1977), and has issue:
1c *Patrick Victor Cathcart, MA [Patrick Hannay Esq, 16 via Privata Cieli, La Spezia, Italy]; *b* 27 June 1923; *m* 1st 1943 Maria Benita Rosalia Greco (*d* 1944); *m* 2nd 28 Aug 1948 Elvira Leonora (*d* 29 Sept 1964), dau of — Fachetti; *m* 3rd 4 Oct 1965 Iride Antonietta Giuseppina (*d* 1986), dau of Cav Pietro Ercolini, of La Spezia, Italy
2c *Timothy John [Timothy Hannay Esq, Hope Cottage, Dalry, Castle Douglas, Kirkcudbrightshire DG7 3UT]; *b* 2 Sept 1929; F/Lt RAF; *m* 1st 25 Aug 1956 (*divorce* 1974) Judith, dau of Colin Harpham Butler, of Tickhill, Yorks, and has issue:
1d *Patrick George; *b* 15 Nov 1958; *m* 1988 *Urasa, dau of Aim Sanasen, of Bangkok, Thailand, and has issue:
1e *Pimon; *b* 1991
2e *Tim; *b* 1993
3e *Guy; *b* 1996
2d *William Victor Bladsworth; *b* 22 March 1963
2c (cont.) Timothy Hannay *m* 2nd 1974 *Linda Jess Elizabeth Callan, of Edinburgh, and has further issue:
3d *Neil Lennox Cotter; *b* 1976
4d *Timothy Alexander; *b* 1977
3a Elizabeth; *m* 11 March 1862 George T Galbraith, and had issue
4a Jane Harriett; *m* 18 April 1860 C G Vinall (*d* 20 June 1903) and had issue
(2) George Sackville, Col 69th Regt, served in the Peninsular and Waterloo; *b* 1 July 1783; *m* 10 March 1819 Jane, 3rd dau and coheiress of William Crofts, of Danesfort, Mallow, Co Cork, and *d* 9 April 1869, having had issue:
1a George Sackville; *b* 24 Nov 1829; *m* 4 March 1858 Frances (*d* 1901), dau of J Stewart, and *d* 1907, having had, with other issue:
1b George Sackville; *b* 16 Dec 1858; *m* June 1889 Margaret, dau of John McAvella, and *d* 1904, having had issue:
1c Marguerite Stewart; *b* 1892; *m* July 1920 Maj Frank Warren Burnham, MC, of Hamilton, Ontario, Canada
2b James Laurence; *b* 16 Nov 1864; *m* 1897 Mary, dau of Henry Morrison Dee, and had issue:
1c James Laurence; *b* 1900; *m* July 1924 Anna, dau of R Harris, of Pennsylvania, USA, and *d* 1960 leaving issue:
1d +James Laurence; *b* 12 July 1925; Lt-Cdr US Navy (ret); *m* 1st 1950 (*divorce* 1972) G Cerra, and has issue:
1e +Thomas J; *b* 1954; *m* 1977 *Karen Jones, and has issue:
1f +Thomas J; *b* 1979
2f +Matthew R; *b* 1981
1e *Gwendolyn A; *b* 1957
1d (cont.) Lt-Cdr James Cotter *m* 2nd 1972 *Mariruth Reed
1d +Joyce Marie; *b* 2 May 1929
3b Henry Crofts; *b* 18 May 1875; *m* 1907 Alice, dau of Richard Chambers
1b Frances Eleanor; *m* 1891 Thomas Hobson, KC (*d* 9 April 1936), of 66 Herkumer St, Hamilton, Ontario
2b Kate Alfrida; *m* 1895 Edward Rand Niblett, of Hamilton, and had issue
3b Mary Susannah
2a William Crofts; *b* 4 April 1831; *m* 4 Feb 1858 Georgina D'Aguilar, dau of Fred Hyde, and had issue:
1b George Sackville; *b* 14 Feb 1859; *m*
2b Francis
3b James Laurence; *m* 1916 Jane, dau of William Blyth, of Edinburgh, and *d* 1943, leaving issue:
1c +Laurence Meldrum; *b* 1917
2c +James Lawrence [James Cotter Esq, Box 473, Claresholm, Alberta, Canada]; *b* 1919; WW II with Roy Canadian Army Serv Corps; *m* 1948 *Phyllis, dau of Frank Peters, and has issue:
1d +Garry Laurence; *b* 1953
1d *Marianne Phyllis; *b* 1957
2d *Karen Jean; *b* 1959
3c +Blyth Sackville; *b* 1921
1b Caroline Alexandria; *m* 1886 George Alfred Blake, of Wimbledon, and had issue
2b Louisa
3b Georgina; *m* Alexander Bethune, and *dsp* 1954
4b Jane
5b Wilhelmina; *m* Frank Whitmore, and *dsp* 1945
3a James Laurence Rogerson, Clerk of the Peace in Simcoe, Ontario; *b* 26 Jan 1836; *m* 24 June 1857 Hannah, dau of George Lount, and *d* 3 Oct 1928, leaving, with other issue:
1b Margaret Lount; *b* 20 June 1861; *m* 20 June 1888 R L Barwick, of Toronto, and had issue

2b Wilhelmina Eliza; *b* 15 July 1870; *m* 19 Oct 1898 S C Macdonald, of Hamilton, Ontario, and had issue
1a Kate; *m* 18 Jan 1870 Thomas Bower Docker
2a Wilhelmina Margaret; *m* 10 July 1853 J Yorris, and had issue
3a Mathilda; *m* 24 July 1857 H T Johnson, and had issue
(3) Rogers, MD; *d* 1847, leaving issue, with four daus:
1a George
2a James
3a John
(4) Joseph Rogerson (Rev), Rector Donoughmore, Sr Preb of Cloyne, Rural Dean; *b* 2 Sept 1790; *m* 1st 25 Sept 1814 Annie Charlotte, dau of Capt J B Butler, and niece of Dr Bennet, Bp Cloyne, and had, with other issue:
1a George Sackville, MD; *b* June 1816; *m* 15 Jan 1844 Henrietta (*dsp* 7 July 1878), dau of Rev Thomas Hoare, and gdau of Sir Edward Hoare, 2nd Bt, MP (*see* HOARE, Bt, of Annabella)
(3) (cont.) Preb J R Cotter *m* 2nd 5 Aug 1819 Mary (*d* 15 April 1851), est dau of George Purcell, JP, and by her had issue:
2a Joseph Rogerson (Rev), BA, Rector St Mary Magdalene, Colchester; *b* 9 June 1822; *m* 1st 29 Jan 1850 Philadelphia Louisa (*d* 1897), dau of Thomas Hall, of Harpsden Court, Oxon, and had issue:
1b Mary Elizabeth; *m* 4 Nov 1884 Marcus Seton Blackden (*d* 16 June 1916), son of John Chalfont Blackden, and *d* May 1904, leaving issue
2b Katherine Louisa; *d* unm 3 Oct 1913
3b Grace; *d* unm 31 July 1934
2a (cont.) Joseph Cotter *m* 2nd 8 Dec 1899 Frances (*d* 8 March 1919), dau of Hugh Green, of Newton Hall, Suffolk, and *d* 7 Jan 1900
3a James Laurence (Rev), MD, BA, TCD, MRCS, Vicar Cheadle Hulme, Cheshire; *b* 14 Aug 1824; *m* 1st 19 Oct 1854 Mary (*dsp* 12 June 1855), dau of Rev Richard Gaggin, Rector Clonmult; *m* 2nd 3 Sept 1856 Mary Beatrice (*d* 1919), dau of William Bromilow, of Haresfinch Ho, Lancs, and *d* 1892, leaving issue:
1b James Laurence; *b* 17 Dec 1869; *m* 1st 1904 Barbara (*d* 1910), dau of Thomas Jones; *m* 2nd 1920 Grace, yst dau of Edward Irvine Herbert, of Irby, Cumberland, and *d* 1939, leaving issue:
1c Dudley Laurence; *b* 6 Sept 1922; *d* 1942
1b Mary Blanche Monica; *m* 1883 T C Mather (*d* 1908), of Oak Hill, Lydiate, Ormskirk, and *d* 10 March 1950, leaving issue
2b Miriam Laurence
3b Jessie Grace Ernestine; *m* 1901 George Gerard Baker, and *d* 24 Feb 1940, leaving issue
4b Muriel Beatrice Kathleen; *m* 1905 Henry Johnstone McGee (*d* 7 Feb 1925), and had issue
4a Charles Purcell (Rev), MA, Vicar Stantonbury with New Bradwell, Bucks; *b* 17 Feb 1826; *m* 13 July 1852 Mary Anne Caroline (*d* 1889), only child and heiress of John Frederick Gaitskell, BCS (son of Capt Henry Gaitskell), and *d* 16 May 1892, leaving, with other issue:
1b Charles Plunkett Rogerson, Lt 2nd Roy Tower Hamlets Mil; *b* 16 Aug 1855; *m* 24 June 1885 Eleanor Grace, dau of Maj John Francis Garstin, and *d* 18 Oct 1887
1b Alice Harriet; *m* 23 April 1892 Charles Henry Miles, LRCP, LSA, son of Martin Miles, LRCP, and *d* 27 Nov 1927
5a Richard Henry (Rev), BA, Incumbent of Ardcanny, Co Limerick; *b* 5 Feb 1831; *m* 18 May 1861 Sarah Pearce, dau of W J Lawrenson, and *d* 1898, leaving, with other issue:
1b Joseph Henry, JP Manitoba; *b* 1 Jan 1867; *m* 1896 Ethel Mary (*d* 31 July 1960), dau of Surgn-Col Samuel Kyle Cotter (*see* below), and *d* 1937, leaving issue:
1c Charles Henry, CA, late Lt RFA (SR); *b* 1898; *m* 1924 Louise, dau of John Wesley Ray, of Miami, Manitoba, Canada, and *d* 1976 leaving issue:
1d +Charles Roy Henry [Charles Cotter Esq, 584 Victoria Ave, Belleville, Ontario, Canada]; *b* 1927; *m* 1953 *Gertrude Elizabeth, dau of Hugh V McCann, of Ottawa, Canada, and has issue:
1e +Joseph Henry; *b* 27 Jan 1957
1e *Patricia Ann; *b* 1954
2e *Mary Elizabeth; *b* 21 Oct 1960
3e *Barbara Jane; *b* 4 April 1963
4e *Catherine Louise; *b* 28 May 1965
2d +John Raymond [John Cotter Esq, 338 Hartviksen St, Port Arthur, Ontario, Canada]; *b* 1929; *m* 21 Dec 1957 *Vivienne Margaret, dau of Henry A Patton, of 4 Cotesbach Rd, Clapton, E5, and has issue:
1e +Stephen Henry; *b* 13 Nov 1960
1e *Karen Louise; *b* 25 Aug 1959
2e *Susan Margaret; *b* 20 Dec 1961
1d *Marjorie Ethel; *b* 1930; *m* 1954 *John Durward Johnson, and has issue:
1e *David Robert; *b* 8 July 1955
2e *Eric Charles; *b* 22 Jan 1957
3e *Bruce Allan; *b* 24 June 1958
4e *John Andrew; *b* 7 May 1965
1e *Susan Elizabeth; *b* 23 Jan 1961
2c Walter Richard; *b* 1902; *m* 15 Sept 1923 Lois, dau of George Benton King, of Prescott, Arizona, USA, and *d* 1971, leaving issue:
1d +Eugene Richard [Eugene Cotter, 210E 8th South, Springville, Utah, USA]; *b* 1924; *m* 1947 *Mary Agnes, dau of Robert Ramsay, and has issue:
1e +Charles Eugene; *b* 1952
2e +Neil Edward; *b* 5 July 1957
1e *Jennifer Marie; *b* 1954
2d +George Henry; *b* 1926; *m* 1st 1949 (*divorce* 19–) Barbara Gene, dau of Glenn Maxwell, and has issue:
1e +Walter Richard; *b* 14 Jan 1953
2e +Kevin George; *b* 22 Nov 1966
2d (cont.) George Cotter *m* 2nd 1971 *Judith Kay, dau of Rex Clark, of Indianapolis, Indiana, USA
3c Laurence Cecil; *b* 1906
1c Adelaide Beatrice Ethel; *b* 1903; *m* 1931 Wilfred Joseph Gagnon (*d* 1977) and *d* 1996, leaving:
1d *Wilfred Joseph; *b* 1934; *m* 1st 1954 (*divorce* 19–) Glenda Mae Johnston and has:
1e *Garry John; *b* 1962
2e *Robert Allan; *b* 1966
1d (cont.) Wilfred Gagnon *m* 2nd 19– *Diane Dean
2d *Paul Martin [Paul Gagnon Esq, 59 Coleridge Crescent NW, Calgary, Alberta T2K 1X8, Canada]; *b* 1937; BE Geology; MP Calgary North; *m* 1961 *Maureen, and has:
1e *Paul James; *b* 1965; *m* 1988 *Nancy Fryk and has:
1f *Christopher Michael; *b* 1994
2f *Benjamin James; *b* 1997
1e *Deanna Louise; *b* 1962; *educ* U of Saskatchewan (BEGeol) and U of Calgary (MBA); *m* 1993 *Allan Lau and has:
1f *David James; *b* 1995
2e *Yvonne Michele; *b* 1963; *educ* U of Calgary (BA) and U of Ottawa (LLB); *m* 1988 *Kelvin Choy
3e *Jennifer Ann (uses maiden name); *b* 1967; *m* 1993 *Todd Bolianatz
4e *Lisa Marie; *b* 1970; *educ* U of Calgary (BSc) and U of Victoria (MSc)
1d *Winnifred Alice [Mrs George Istace, Box 190, Whitewood, Saskatchewan SOG 5CO, Canada]; *b* 1932; *m* 1st 1953 *Stephen Ivan Berkes (*d* 1990), and has issue:
1e *Stephen Michael; *b* 1958
1e *Linda Ann; *b* 1954; *m* 1974 *Edward Istace, and has issue:
1f *Craig Stephen; *b* 1978
2f *Drew; *b* 1983
1f *Dana (twin); *b* 1983
2e *Nancy Lynn; *b* 1956; *m* 1979 *Garth Simms, and has issue:
1f *Kelly James; *b* 1979
2f *Kirk Michael; *b* 1982
1f *Michele Leslie; *b* 1983
1d (cont.) Mrs Berkes *m* 2nd George Frank Istace
2c *Lillian Muriel Edith [Miss Lillian Cotter, Suite 22, 1830 Portage Ave, Winnipeg 12, Monitoba, Canada]; *b* 1910
2b Joseph Rogerson, MA, ScD (Hon), Trin Coll Dublin; *b* 10 Dec 1869; *m* 1913 his cousin Ellen Harriet (*d* 15 Sept 1948), dau of Surgn-Col Samuel Kyle Cotter (*see* above), and *d* 31 March 1957, leaving issue:
1c *Joan Jamieson [Mrs Henry Ferrell, 511 Cathedral Dve, Alexandria, VA 22314, USA]; *b* 7 Aug 1916; *educ* Trin Coll Dublin (BA 1938); late Subaltern ATS; *m* 20 May 1944 Henry Haskins Ferrell Jr, MD, Fell American Coll of Surgs, late Capt US Med Corps, son of Henry Haskins Ferrell, of Goochland, Virginia, USA, and has issue:
1d *Henry Haskins III; *b* 12 Jan 1951; MD; *m* 1984 (*divorce* 1987) Anne Elizabeth Edmunds
1d *Leslie Cotter; *b* 20 Jan 1949; *m* 1974 *José Manuel Kauffmann, and has issue:
1e *Alejandro José; *b* 1980
2d *Ana Elena; *b* 1982
2d *Joan Pinson; *b* 1 June 1954
3b Alexander McCaul; *b* 25 Nov 1871; *m* 1896 Mildred Bertha Eveline (*d* 1925), dau of George Edwards, and *d* 1929, leaving issue:
1c Charles Rogerson; *b* 1897; *m* 1934 Isabella Millie (*d* 1963), dau of Nelson Young
2c +Felix Alexander; *b* 1900; *m* 1929 *Ella Elenor Christopherson, of Brock, Sask, and has issue:
1d +William Leroy; *b* 1935
1d *Bernice Evelyn; *b* 1930
3c +Louis Stephen [Louis Cotter Esq, RR2, Mannville, Alberta, T0B 2WO, Canada]; *b* 1913; WW II with Canadian Army; *m* 1941 *Elizabeth Ellen, dau of Harry Thomas, of Mannville, Alberta, and has issue:
1d +Gavin Bryson [Gavin Cotter Esq, 98 Larose Dr, St Albert, Alberta, Canada T8N 2TZ]; *b* 1947; *m* 1972 (*divorce* 1988) Rita Maureen, dau of Allan McDonell, of St Albert, Alberta, Canada, and has issue:
1e +Tyler Bryce; *b* 1975
2e +Kelly Shannon; *b* 1978
1d *Arlene Berna [Mrs Richard Danziger, 3211 Erie St, San Diego, CA 92117, USA]; *b* 1942; *m* 1968 *Dr Richard Ellis Danziger, PhD, Capt USN, of Longmeadow, Mass, USA, and has issue:
1e *Derek Scott; *b* 1972
1e *Kathryn Erin; *b* 1975
4c David Grenfell, P/O RCAF, served WW II; *b* 1916 (twin); *d* of wounds received in action in Burma, 1945
5c Lloyd George, late RCAF; *b* 1916, twin; *m* 1945 *Iris Webb (*m* 2nd 1970 Charles Rogerson Cotter (*d* 1983), and *d* 8 Nov 1968, leaving issue:
1d +Burney Thomas; *b* 1946; *m* 1969 *Rosemarie, dau of Michael Koroluk, Geraldton, Ont, Canada, and has issue:
1e +Kevin Michael; *b* 1980
1e *Christine Michelle; *b* 1975
2e *Shari Diane; *b* 1977

1d *Bonnie Mildred (twin); *b* 1946; *m* 1972 *Paul Halagaza, and has issue:
1e *Mark Leonard; *b* 1975
1c Lilian Kate; *m* 1927 (*divorce* 1954) Harry Bowers and had three sons and a dau
2c *Florence Mildred; *b* 1906; *m* 1929 William James Shury, and has issue:
1d *David William; *b* 1930; *educ* Sask U (LLB); *m* 1956 *Jane Miller, and has issue:
1e *William Brent Cotter; *b* 1963
1e *Debra Elizabeth; *b* 1956
2d *Garry Clair; *b* 1938; *m* 1960 *Claudia Fradette, and has issue:
1e *Brian Keith; *b* 1963
2e *Todd Kevin; *b* 1964
3d *Harold Lloyd; *b* 1942; *m* 1961 *Alice Hartman, and has issue:
1e *Dale Lloyd; *b* 1962
2e *Kyle Damon; *b* 1971
4d *Terrance James; *b* 1944; *m* 1965 *Mary, dau of Doyle Edwards, of Saskatoon, and has issue:
1e *Gregory Doyle; *b* 1970
1e *Sandra Lynn; *b* 1966
2e *Laurie Ann; *b* 1971
1d *Donaline Elizabeth; *b* 1932; *m* 1955 *Harold Jones, and has issue:
1e *Glenn Harold; *b* 1960
2d *Evelyn Mildred; *b* 1933; sch teacher; *m* 1955 *Donald MacKenzie, and has issue:
1e *Janice; *b* 1957
2e *Valerie; *b* 1958
3e *Wendy; *b* 1963
4b Gerald de Purcell, FGS, FRASB, Geological Survey of India; *b* 1881; *educ* Trin Coll Dublin (BA, ScD); *m* 1917 Rosalind (*d* 12 Sept 1962), dau of James Billington Coughtrie, and *d* as a result of enemy action, 19 June 1941, leaving issue:
1c Hilary James Coughtrie; *b* 20 March 1918; *educ* Westminster, Pembroke Coll Oxford (BA 1948, MA 1954), and Manitoba U (BEd); Lt (S) RN (ret), served WW II (invalided), ADC to Govr Somaliland Protectorate 1949–50, Dept of Nat Def Canadian Armed Forces Base, Cold Lake; *m* 1957 *Patricia Kathleen Angela Mary Esther, dau of James Doyne, of Castlerickard, Moyvalley, Co Meath, and *d* 16 May 1997, leaving:
1d +Godwin Arthur Mary; *b* 1 Jan 1959; *educ* Toronto U (BSc)
2d +Hilary Patrick; *b* 22 Dec 1959; *educ* Toronto U (BSc)
3d +Marcian Gerald; *b* 17 June 1962
1d *Rosalind Catherine; *b* 19 Jan 1958; *educ* Magdalen Coll, New Hampshire, USA (BA); *m* 1983 *Brian David Pouliot, and has issue:
1e *Dominic John Pio; *b* 1984
2e *Thomas Aquinas; *b* 1986
3e *Benedict Joseph-Marie; *b* 1988
4e *Francis Joseph-Marie; *b* 1990
5e *Jerome Joseph-Marie; *b* 1994
6e *Monique Marie; *b* 1992
2d *Rebecca Angela Claire; *b* 14 March 1961; *educ* U of Toronto, and Toronto York U (BA, BSc); SRN
3d *Mary Jane Frances; *b* 18 Aug 1963; SRN; *m* 1993 *Ogden Michael Forbes
4d *Rowena Josephine; *b* 29 Dec 1964; SRN
5d *Rachel Anne Monica; *b* 16 Sept 1967; SRN
2c +Arthur Gerald Purcell; *b* 16 Dec 1924; *educ* Westminster, Oxford U and Trin Coll Dublin (BA, MB, ChB); Capt RE WW II; *m* 1959 *Isabel Sadie, dau of William Adams, of Lislap, Omagh, Co Tyrone, and has issue:
1d +Colin Arthur; *b* 9 May 1961
1d *Lynda Marie; *b* 10 April 1962
1c *Angela Mary Purcell [Mrs Edward Eborall, Tally Ho House, Castletownshend, Co Cork, Ireland]; *b* 29 March 1921; *m* 1st 28 March 1951 Ulick O'Connor Milborne-Swinnerton-Pilkington (*d* 14 June 1979) and has issue (*see* MILBORNE-SWINNERTON-PILKINGTON, Bt); *m* 2nd 1981*Cdr Edward Alfred Eborall, RNVR, FIEE
1b Mary Susannah, BA; *d* unm 1940
6a John Quarry; *b* 30 May 1832; *m* 20 March 1857 Katherine, dau of J Wentz, and *d* 1904, leaving issue:
1b George Sackville; *b* 20 Nov 1865
2b John Quarry; *b* 2 March 1871
1b Mary Susannah
2b Anna Maria
3b Catharine
4b Louisa Purcell
5b Mabel
6b Ellen Purcell
7a Arundel Hill, LRCP, late 8th Foot; *b* 15 April 1837; *m* 1st 12 May 1863 Williamina Grant, dau of J Maclean of Advie Ho, Lancs, and had issue:
1b Joseph Rogerson John; *b* 21 Feb 1864
7a (cont.) Arundel Cotter *m* 2nd Alice Amelia, dau of W M Anderson, of Jamaica, and *d* 1883
8a Duncan Donald Darroch, Offr 6th Foot; *b* 12 Sept 1838; *m* 1st 7 July 1864 Helen, dau of Thomas Musson, of Stockton, Barbados, and had issue:
1b Joseph Dudley Musson; *b* 22 June 1866; *educ* Trin Coll Cambridge (BA); *d* 14 Jan 1890
2b George Edmond Wentworth, MRCS, LRCP (London); *b* 1868; *educ* Trin Coll Cambridge (MA, MB); *m* 1906 Muriel Isobel, yst dau of Samuel James Musson, of Kinnaird Ho, Upper Norwood, and *d* 1 April 1916
8a (cont.) Duncan Cotter *m* 2nd 2 June 1874 Ella Margaret (*d* 9 April 1907), dau of William Paterson, of Morant Bay, Jamaica, and *d* 1890, having by her had issue:
3b Gerard William Ludlow; *b* 15 June 1877; *d* June 1879
4b Duncan Paterson; *b* 17 July 1879; *d* 24 Feb 1940
5b Arundel John Plunkett, Maj US Army, served WW II; *b* 1 June 1883; *m* 26 April 1911 Emma Stothard, dau of William Carter, and *d* 27 Oct 1952, leaving issue:
1c +Arundel, Lt-Col US Army (Res) served WW II; *b* 24 July 1912; *m* 1st 2 Jan 1942 (*divorce* 1952) Madelyn, dau of Forest Mitchell, and has issue:
1d +Arundel; *b* 20 Jan 1944
1c (cont.) Lt-Col Arundel Cotter *m* 2nd *Gabrielle Pauline, dau of Harry Tarter, of Washington DC, and by her has issue:
2d +Harry Bruce; *b* 28 Jan 1955
3d +Robert Darrock; *b* 22 Sept 1956
1c *Joyce; *b* 5 Oct 1914; *educ* Connecticut Coll for Women (BS); *m* 3 Nov 1948 *Lt-Col George Kern, US Army
6b Harry Norman, DMD Tufts, DDS Coll Dental and Oral Surgery; *b* 26 Jan 1885; *m* 9 July 1912 Rose Isabel (*d* 1975), dau of Henri Malabre, of Kingston, Jamaica, and *d* 4 Nov 1960, leaving issue:
1c +Harry Norman Rogerson [Harry Cotter Esq, 533 Driftwood Rd, North Palm Beach, FL 33403, USA]; *b* 11 June 1922; *educ* Cornell (BSME 1948); 1st Lt USMCR, WW II; *m* 29 July 1950 *Beverley Jane, dau of Alfred Edmund Hayes, of Winchester, NH, and has:
1d +Thomas Joseph; *b* 3 Oct 1952; *educ* U of Florida (BS); *m* 1st 19– (*divorce*) Victoria Shaw; *m* 2nd 19– *Jayne Anderson and by his 1st w has:
1e +Nicholas Anthony; *b* 3 Dec 1982
2d +Anthony John; *b* 14 Sept 1962; *educ* U of Florida (BS 1984, Juris Dr 1990); *m* 19– *Cheryl Mae Smith and has:
1e *Abigail Grace; *b* 26 Nov 1994
3d +Patrick Hayes; *b* 16 Aug 1963; *educ* U of Florida (BS); *m* 19– *Jacqueline, dau of Howard Veraby, and has:
1e *Joanna Danielle; *b* 18 Nov 1991
2e *Kacey Michelle; *b* 3 May 1997
1d *Lark Ellen; *b* 12 May 1951; *m* 19– *Michael Robert Frantz and has:
1e *Bryan Michael; *b* 21 April 1977
2d *Noreen Ann; *b* 15 Jan 1954; *educ* Dakota State Sch of Science and U of N Dakota (BS Hons); MD Army Nat G; *m* 19– (*divorce*) Robert Schwartz; *m* 2nd 19– *Stephen Vincent Waller and by her 1st husb has:
1e *Nicholas Robert; *b* 5 Dec 1977
1e *Nicole Andrea; *b* 14 May 1979
3d *Andrea Jane; *b* 20 April 1955; *educ* Atlantic U (BS) and Barry U (MS); advanced practice registered nurse; *m* 19– *Michael Evan Perry and has:
1e *Matthew Michael; *b* 2 Dec 1981
2e *Jonathan Adam; *b* 12 June 1987
3e *Andrew Steven; *b* 14 Aug 1994
1e *Beverly Lynn; *b* 12 Sept 1984
2c Richard Duncan Rogerson; *b* 11 June 1922; *educ* Yale U (AB); 1st Lt USMCR, WW II, FBI Special Agent 1948; *m* 18 June 1949 *Mary Theresa [Mrs Richard Cotter, 5337 Ravensworth Rd, N Springfield, VA, USA], dau of James Joseph Kelleher, of White Plains, NY, and *d* 1976, leaving issue:
1d +Richard Duncan; *b* 19 June 1950
2d +Michael Patrick; *b* 5 March 1952
3d +Peter James; *b* 12 Oct 1953
4d +David Henry; *b* 18 Feb 1955
5d +Matthew Joseph; *b* 18 Feb 1961
1d *Eileen Mary; *b* 21 Dec 1956
2d *Elizabeth Ann; *b* 14 Feb 1960
1c *Margaret Charlotte [Mrs Cæsar Pitassy, 11 Hidden Green Lane, Larchmont, NY, USA]; *b* 22 Oct 1917; *m* 30 June 1942 *Cæsar Leopold Pitassy, AB New York U, LLB Fordham U, son of Julian Pitassy, of New York, and has issue:
1d *Richard Norman; *b* 21 July 1943
9a Samuel Kyle, MD, BA, Surgn-Col; *b* 10 Nov 1841; *m* 1st 8 June 1868 Alice, dau of Capt Thomas Jamieson, and had issue:
1b Ethel Mary; *m* 1896 her cousin Joseph Henry Cotter, and *d* 31 July 1960, leaving issue (*see* above)
2b Ellen Harriett; *m* 1913 her cousin Joseph Rogerson Cotter, MA, and *d* 15 Sept 1948, leaving issue (*see* above)
9a (cont.) Surgn-Col Samuel Cotter *m* 2nd Mary Elizabeth (*d* 12 Jan 1937), dau of Robert Anderson, and *d* 1890, having by her had issue:
1b Vere Rogerson, Lt-Col late IA, Surv of India Dept; *b* 18 Feb 1882; *m* Nancy —, and *d* 26 Aug 1948
2b Raymond Kyle, MC, Maj IA; *b* 12 Aug 1889; *m* 6 May 1914 Beryl Jessica Macdonald (*d* 1972), dau of Charles Macdonald Wintle, and *d* 8 June 1948, leaving issue
1c +Derek Raymond Kyle [Derek Cotter Esq, 18 Castleton Close, Mannamead, Plymouth, Devon PLE 5AE]; *b* 10 Oct 1916; *m* 1st 1938 Daphne Cushion (*d* 19–), and has issue:
1d +Anthony Derek Kyle; *b* 28 March 1941; *m* 6 Oct 1962 *Maureen Louvain Swindell, and has issue:
1e +Andrew Anthony Kyle; *b* 30 Jan 1966

1d *Merril Victoria; *b* 1942; *m* 19– *Brig K J Davey, MC, of Abergavenny, Gwent
2d Carolyn; *b* 1948; *m* 19– *Capt K R McKee, of Madison, Conn.
1c (cont.) Derek Cotter *m* 2nd 1968 *Amelia Helena, dau of Maurice Walsh, of Clonmel, and by her has:
2d +Nicholas Paul Kyle; *b* 196 March 1970; BSc, PhD
1c *Kathleen Beryl Kyle [Mrs Stanley Chapman, 87 Dartford Rd, Sevenoaks, Kent]; *b* 14 March 1915; *m* 1st 19 Dec 1933 (*divorce* 1942) Reginald Barnes Elwin, ICS (*d* 4 May 1961), ICS, and has issue:
1d *Verity Ann; *b* 1934; *m* 1959 *Terry Nicholas Blows, and has issue
1c (cont.) Mrs Elwin *m* 2nd 20 April 1942 Maj Denis Erskine Ward (*see* BANGOR,V.) (*ka* 27 Oct 1942); remarried Reginald Elwin 5 July 1946, and had further issue:
1d *David Michael Harrison; *b* 1948
2d *Peter John Ashton; *b* 1950
1c (cont.) Mrs Elwin *m* 4th 1978 Stanley Chapman
3b Alice Mary; *m* 1904 Allan Campbell (*d* 9 Nov 1946), of Natal, only son of Henry Cooke Campbell, ISO, sometime Judge Pres of Native High Court of Natal, and *d* 26 Aug 1948, leaving issue
2a Margaret Anne; *m* 17 July 1845 Rev Edward Pringle Hodgins, DD, Incumbent of St Stephen's, Liverpool, and had issue
3a Isabella; *m* 11 April 1850 Rev William Ridley, BA (*d* 26 Sept 1878), and had issue
4a Catherine Louisa; *m* 14 Oct 1854 Rev John William Stubbs, DD, Fell Trin Coll Dublin (*d* 10 Jan 1897), of Stubton and Rowlestown, Co Dublin, and had issue
5a Jane Emily Perceval; *m* Rogerson Cotter Butler (*d* 1892)
6a Sarah Phillips *m* 23 May 1865 Maj-Gen Edward Langford Dillon, and *d* 1903, leaving issue
7a Georgina Purcell; *m* 24 May 1864 Surg-Maj Hunter A Coghlan, 18th Foot, MRCSE, and *d* 14 April 1865, leaving issue
8a Mary Grace Jessie; *m* 1st 10 Aug 1868, as his 2nd w, George Washington Brasier-Creagh, JP (*d* 3 June 1876), of Creagh Castle, Co Cork, and had issue; *m* 2nd 1877 Rev Ernest Arthur Firth (*d* 1890)
(4) (cont.) Preb Joseph Rogerson Cotter *m* 3rd 1 May 1852 Mary Anne (*d* 13 Aug 1864), widow of Rev E B Vardon, and dau of Capt Henry Gaitskell, LLB, and *d* 4 Feb 1868

The 1st Bt *d* 9 June 1770; his est son,

Sir James Laurence Cotter, 2nd Bt, MP, of Rockforest, Col Mallow Regt Mil; *b* 1748; *m* 1st Anne (*d* 1773), only dau of Francis Kearney, of Garretstown, nr Kinsale; *m* 2nd Isabella (*d* April 1832), widow of George Brereton, of Carrigslaney, Co Carlow, and dau of Rev James Hingston, of Aglish, Co Cork, Preb of Donoughmore, by his w Catherine, only child of Rev Benezer Murdock, Rector Kilshanick, and *d* 9 Feb 1829, leaving, with other issue:
1 JAMES LAURENCE (Sir), **3rd Bt**
2 John Rogerson (Rev), Rector Innishannon; *m* 1st Ellen, dau of Rev Robert Scott, of the city of Dublin; *m* 2nd 30 April 1840 Ellen (*d* 10 May 1841), dau of Rev T Hoare, of Castletown Roche; *m* 3rd May 1845 Caroline (Id 9 Nov 1864), dau of Sir Robert Shaw, 1st Bt (*qv*), and *dsp* 31 March 1847
3 George Edmond (Rev), Rector Monanimy; *b* 2 June 1795; *m* 13 May 1828 Grace, dau of William Digges La Touche, of Sans Souci, and Stephen's Green, Dublin, and *d* 6 Aug 1880, having had a son and two daus
4 Nelson Kearney, MD; *b* 1806; *m* 1842 Mary, dau of R Nason, of Bettyville, Co Cork, and *d* 18 July 1869, having had issue, with two other daus:
(1) Isabella Mary; *m* 12 June 1869 Bertram William Seton (*d* 19 March 1907), 4th son of Miles Charles Seton, late 85th Regt, and gs of 1st Viscount Sidmouth (*qv*), and *d* 30 June 1925, leaving issue
1 Isabella; *m* James Digges La Touche, of Sans Souci, near Dublin, and had issue:
2 Henrietta *m* John Wise, of Cork, and had issue
3 Thomasine; *m* Arundel Hill, of Graig, Co Cork, and had issue

The est son,

Sir James Laurence Cotter, 3rd Bt, of Rockforest, MP Mallow; *m* 1 Jan 1820 Helena Trydell (*d* 1 June 1870), 3rd dau and coheiress of James Lombard, of Lombardstown, Co Cork, by Ann, dau of John Townsend Becher, of Creagh, and aunt of Sir William Wrixon Becher, 1st Bt (*qv*), of Ballygiblin and Creagh, Co Cork, and *d* 31 Dec 1834, leaving:

Sir James Laurence Cotter, 4th Bt, JP Co Cork, High Sheriff 1882, DL Tower Hamlets, Lt 27th Regt; *b* 4 April 1828; *m* 1st 14 June 1851 Julia Emily (*d* 5 Feb 1863), dau of Frederick Albert Loinsworth, MD, Inspr-Gen of Hosps, Calcutta, and had, with other issue:
1 Ludlow (Sir), 3rd Bn Roy Munster Fus; *b* 11 June 1853; *dvp* unm 23 Nov 1882
2 James Lombard, Lt 1st Bn Glos Regt; *b* 1 Sept 1859; *m* 8 May 1884 Claire Mary (*m* 2nd 1897 John Francis O'Connor), dau of Capt Thomas Segrave, RM, late 14th Regt, and *dvp* 12 April 1893, leaving, with other issue:
(1) JAMES LAURENCE (Sir), **5th Bt**
(2) Thomas Lombard; *b* 7 Nov 1888; *m* 1912 Victoria Jean Robertson (*d* 1923), and *d* 1923, leaving issue:
1a Ian Peter; *b* 1916
1a *Bettine [Mrs Alan Douglas, 37 Eagle Court, Wanstead, London E11]; *b* 1920; *m* 1st 1943 J Harrison Owen (*ka* 1943), of Melbourne, Australia; *m* 2nd 1946 (*divorce* 1956) W/Cdr Richard Cresswell, RAAF; *m* 3rd 1956 *G/Capt Alan Graham Douglas, CBE, MC, ADC, RAF Regt, son of Fred Douglas, of 65 Snakes Lane, Woodford Green, Essex

Sir James *m* 2nd 30 April 1864 Jane Veargitt (*d* 21 March 1902), dau of W K Maughan, of Sedgwick Ho, Middx, and by her had issue:
3 Guy *b* 1865; *d* an infant

The 4th Bt *d* 10 Oct 1902; his gs,

Sir James Laurence Cotter, 5th Bt, T/Capt RFA, Lt S of Ireland Imp Yeo, Sub-Lt RNVR; *b* 11 July 1887; *m* 1st 6 Aug 1908 (*divorce* 1924) Ethel Lucy (*d* 12 April 1956), dau of Alfred Wheeler, late 9th Lancers; *m* 2nd 11 Aug 1924 Griselda Winifred (*m* 2nd 13 Sept 1934 Ernest Schargel), dau of Edwin James Wenyon, MB, MRCS, of Skailbrae, Dundee, and *d* 22 Aug 1924, having by his 1st w had issue:
1 Sir DELAVAL JAMES ALFRED COTTER, **6th and present Bt**
2 Laurence Stopford Llewellyn; *b* 22 Aug 1912; *m* 13 March 1935 *Grace Mary (*m* 2nd 6 Sept 1945 Lt-Col Geoffrey Rittson Thomas (*d* 1975), late Manchester Regt), dau of Ivor Vincent Downing, of Llanishen, Cardiff, and was *ka* Sicily July 1943, leaving issue:
(1) +PATRICK LAURENCE DELAVAL; *b* 21 Nov 1941; heir presumptive; *educ* Blundell's and RAC Cirencester; *m* 1967 *Janet, dau of George Potter, of Barnstaple, and has issue:
1a +Julius Laurence George; *b* 5 Jan 1968
1a *Jemima Grace Mary; *b* 1970
2a *Jessica Lucy Kathleen; *b* 1972
(1) *Peta Natalie; *b* 6 Nov 1935; *m* 8 July 1963 (*divorce* 1972) George Derek Wilson, only son of G R Wilson, of Park Rd, W Hartlepool, and has issue:
1a *Paul Sean; *b* 20 Aug 1964
2a *William Robin; *b* 16 July 1966
3a *Adam; *b* 11 May 1969
1a *Charlotte Emma; *b* 1971
(2) *Primrose Anne [Mrs Charles Burnett-Hitchcock, 2 Southdean Gdns, London SW19]; *b* 26 May 1939; *m* 1st 14 April 1960 (*divorce* 1967) (Robert Hugh) Nicholas Creswell, and has issue:
1a *Belinda Jane; *b* 26 Nov 1960; *m* 1986 *James Roger Glinn Eaton
2a *Amanda Robin; *b* 27 July 1961
(2) (cont.) Mrs Primrose Cresswell *m* 2nd 1 Jan 1968 (*divorce* 1969) 5th Earl Sondes (*see* MONSON, B); *m* 3rd 1976 *Charles Denys Burnett-Hitchcock and by him has:
1a *Jacob Nicholas; *b* 1978
1 Violet Rosa Sonia; *b* 10 Oct 1909; *m* 1st 19 July 1930 (*divorce* 1938) Arthur Alec (Peter) Banes-Walker, only surv son of H Banes-Walker, of Verriers, N Petherton, Somerset; *m* 2nd 9 Aug 1941 (*divorce* 1955) Basil Kennedy, and *d* 24 July 1983, having had issue

Seat: Garnons, Mansell Gamage, Herefs. A late Tudor-early Stuart house was supplemented rather than entirely replaced about the end of the Napoleonic Wars by a castellated mansion to its east which consisted of a chunky tower keep (liberally fenestrated, however) under a towerlet belvedere and a slightly lower wing to one side. Each section had three bays, the tower on three storeys, the wing on two, though the latter's tall chimnney pots made it reach to the battlements of its higher neighbour. The architect was William Atkinson. The elaborately Gothic internal decor and windows were swept away by Sir Reginald Blomfield a few years before World War I, to be replaced by a more conventional neo-Georgian look and sash ones respectively. The fireplaces inserted about now were mostly genuine 18th-century, however.

Meanwhile the Jacobethan house had been turned into a lower but similar-looking castellated annexe, though much longer than its easterly fellow and culminating in an almost vestigial tower one-bay wide rather than the three-bay wide keep of Atkinson's design. The man responsible for this epigone of a castle was Thomas Blashill. The vista, enhanced by terraces around both sets of buildings, is breathtaking.

The estate belonged to the GEERSes till an heiress married the father of the **1st Bt**.

COTTERELL

Arms: Quarterly or and argent, a cross engrailed per pale sable and gules, in the 2nd quarter two escallops, in the 3rd one, all of the third; over all a bend, also sable. **Crest:** An arm in armour embowed, the hand in a gauntlet proper, resting on an escutcheon argent, charged with a talbot's head sable, collared and lined or. **Motto:** *Non rapui sed recepi* ('I did not seize it, I recovered it'). **Creation:** Bt. (UK) 2 Nov 1805.

SIR JOHN HENRY GEERS COTTERELL, 6TH BT, of Garnons, Herefordshire [Sir John Cotterell Bt, Downshill House, Bishopstone, Herefs HR4 7JT]; *b* 8 May 1935; *s* f 1978; *educ* Eton and RMA Sandhurst; commnd RHG 1955 (ret as Capt 1961), chm: Radio Wyvern 1981, Herefs Community Health NHS Tst 1991–, Herefs and Worcs CC 1977–81 (v-chm 1973–77); pres Nat Fedn of Farmers Clubs 1986–91 (dep pres 1979–86), chm Hereford Mappa Mundi Tst 1990–; V-Ld Lt Herefs 1998; *m* 7 Oct 1959 *(Vanda) Alexandra (Clare), High Sheriff Hereford and Worcester 1992, only dau of Maj Philip Alexander Clement Bridgewater, 5th Roy Inniskilling Dragoon Gds, and has issue:

1 +HENRY RICHARD GEERS; *b* 22 Aug 1961; *m* 1986 *Carolyn Suzanne, Extra Lady in Waiting to SARAH DUCHESS OF YORK 1989–, er dau of John Moore Beckwith-Smith, of Maybanks Manor, Rudgwick, Sussex, and has:

(1) +Richard John Geers; *b* 1 May 1990

(2) +George Dominic Geers; *b* 1994

(1) *Poppy; *b* 1988

2 +James Alexander Geers; *b* 10 Aug 1964; *m* 1991 *Maria C B, dau of W F McManus, of Bryngwyn Close, Hereford, and has issue:

(1) +William John Geers; *b* 1992

3 +David George Geers; *b* 2 Dec 1968

1 *Camilla Jane; *b* 20 May 1963; *m* 1993 *Mark James Kenneth Houldsworth (*see* MORTON, E)

Lineage: JOHN BROOKES, of Broadway, Worcs; *m* Anne, only dau of Edward Cotterell, of Saintbury, Glos, and left an only son:

JOHN BROOKES later COTTERELL (under terms of will of his maternal uncle Thomas Cotterell), of Broadway; *m* Mary, dau of Thomas Jackson, of Welsbourn, Warwicks, and *d* 1763, leaving:

Sir JOHN BROOKES-COTTERELL, High Sheriff Herefs 1761, ktd 1761; *m* Anne, only dau and heir of John Geers, of Garnons, Herefs, and *d* 1790 leaving:

Sir John Geers Cotterell, 1st Bt (UK), so *cr* 2 Nov 1805, of Garnons; *b* 21 Sept 1757; Col Herefs Militia 1796–1803, MP Herefs 1804–31; *m* 4 Jan 1791 Frances Isabella (*d* 3 July 1813), only dau and heir Henry Michael Evans, and *d* 26 Jan 1845, having had, with other issue:

1 John Henry; *b* 15 April 1800; *m* Aug 1828 Pyne Jesse Brand (*m* 2nd 22 Nov 1845 Granville Harcourt Vernon, son of the Archbishop of York (*see* VERNON, B), and *d* 3 March 1872), est dau of 21st Baron Dacre (*qv*), and *d* 3 Jan 1834, leaving issue:

(1) **Sir John Henry Cotterell, 2nd Bt**; *b* 20 Aug 1830; *d* unm at Eton 17 Feb 1847

(2) GEERS HENRY (Sir), **3rd Bt**

1 Mary; *m* 27 March 1820 Thomas Taylor, of Valetta Lodge, Clifton, and *d* 26 Aug 1868, leaving issue

2 Sarah Frances; *m* 27 April 1848 Newton Byron Hanson, of Gilstead Ho, Essex, and *d* 25 July 1868

3 Caroline *m* April 1828 William Leigh, of Roby Hall, Lancs, and *d* 15 Oct 1878, leaving issue

4 Harriet; *m* 13 Sept 1838 Rev Edwin Hotham (*d* 1875), and *d* 30 Dec 1891 aged 91

The 2nd Bt's bro,

Sir Geers Henry Cotterell, 3rd Bt, DL, JP Herefs, High Sheriff 1863, MP Hereford 1857–59; *b* 22 Aug 1834; *m* 14 Sept 1865 Hon Katherine Margaret (*d* 22 May 1896), dau of Gen 1st Baron Airey, GCB, and had issue:

1 JOHN RICHARD GEERS (Sir), **4th Bt**

1 Alice; *d* unm 10 March 1924

2 Louisa

The 3rd Bt *d* 17 March 1900; his son,

Sir John Richard Geers Cotterell, 4th Bt; *b* 13 July 1866; Capt 1st Life Gds; Herefs: Ld Lt and Custos Rotulorum, Pres TAA 1904–33, High Sheriff 1879, CA; memb Roy Commn Historical Monuments England 1930; *m* 4 Jan 1806 Lady Evelyn Gordon-Lennox (*d* 17 Feb 1922), est dau of 7th Duke of Richmond and Gordon (*qv*), and had issue:

1 RICHARD CHARLES GEERS (Sir), **5th Bt**

1 Sylvia Evelyn; *b* 14 Nov 1896; *m* 1st 16 Nov 1916 (*divorce* 1929) Capt Christopher Digby Leyland, JP, Res of Offrs 1st Life Gds (*d* 1 Dec 1971), of Haggerston Castle, Northumberland (*see* RICHMOND and GORDON, D), and had issue; *m* 2nd 2 Nov 1929 Roland Norris Fawcett (*d* 1 Dec 1933), and *d* 4 Feb 1944, leaving further issue

2 Cicely Violet; *b* 16 Aug 1898; *m* 1st 29 Jan 1921 Capt William Adrian Vincent Bethell, 2nd Life Gds (*d* 16 July 1941), of Rise Park, Hull, and had issue (*see* RADNOR, E); *m* 2nd 28 Nov 1946 Roden Powlett Graves Orde, est son of Roden Horace Powlett Orde, OBE, and *d* 30 Nov 1974

3 Mildred Katherine; *b* 24 Nov 1902; *m* 29 Sept 1925 Lt-Col Sir Terence Edmond Patrick Falkiner, 8th Bt, Coldstream Gds (*qv*), and *d* 1989, having had issue

The 4th Bt *d* 13 Nov 1937; his only son,

Sir Richard Charles Geers Cotterell, 5th Bt, CBE (1965), TD, JP (Herefs 1938); *b* 1 June 1907; *educ* Eton and RMC Sandhurst; Lt-Col RA Shropshire Yeo (TA), RHG, WW II cmdg 76th Shropshire Yeo Medium Regt RA Middle East and Italy 1943–45 (despatches), Ld Lt and Custos Rotulorum Herefs 1945–57, Forestry Commr 1945–64, chm Wye River Authority 1968, KStJ; *m* 1st 16 June 1930 (*divorce* 1958) Lady Lettice Lygon (*d* 18 July 1973), pres BRCS Herefs 1940, chm WLA Herefs 1941–49, est dau of 7th Earl Beauchamp, KG (*see* 1970 edn), and had issue:

1 Sir (JOHN) HENRY GEERS COTTERELL, **6th and present Bt**

2 +Thomas Richard Geers [Thomas Cotterell Esq, 30 Belsize Rd, London NW6], late RHG, dir Curtis Distillery Co Ltd 1966–; *b* 17 Sept 1939; *educ* Eton; *m* 31 March 1966 Caroline Wan-Cheng (*d* 1991), er dau of Foong Chong, of Ipoh, Malaysia

1 *Rose Evelyn [Mrs Rose Hambro, Barton House, Guiting Power, nr Cheltenham, Glos]; *b* 4 Oct 1932; *m* 1 July 1954 (*divorce* 1976) Baron Hambro (*qv*), and has issue

2 *Anne Lettice [The Rt Hon The Lady Sinclair, Knocknalling, Dalry, Kircudbrightshire]; *b* 16 Oct 1933; *m* 6 Jan 1968 *17th Lord Sinclair (*qv*), and has issue

Sir Richard *m* 2nd 21 July 1958 Hon Molly Patricia (*d* 31 Aug 1995), formerly w of 1st Baron Sherwood, previously widow of Capt Roger Charles George Chetwode (*see* CHETWODE, B) and 3rd dau of 1st Viscount Camrose (*qv*), and *d* 5 Dec 1978

COTTESLOE

Arms: Vert three bars ermine, surmounted by a lion rampant gules, murally crowned or, in chief two plates. **Crest:** A demi-lion gules issuing out of a mural crown or, holding a banner quarterly argent, and vert, the staff gold, and charged on the shoulder with a plate. **Supporters:** On either side an eagle, wings expanded and inverted sable. **Motto:** *Nec prece nec pretio* ('Neither by entreaty nor bribery'). **Creations:** Bt. (UK) 14 Aug 1821, B. (UK) 2 March 1874.

THE 5TH BARON COTTESLOE, of Swanbourne and Hardwick, Co Buckingham, and a **Baronet**, JP (Bucks 1984) (Cdr Sir John Tapling Fremantle, 5th Bt, RN, JP) [Cdr The Rt Hon The Lord Cottesloe JP RN (ret), The Old House, Swanbourne, Milton Keynes, Bucks MK17 0SH]; *b* 22 Jan 1927; *s* f 1994; *educ* Eton; joined RN 1944, cmded HMS *Palliser* 1959–61, ret 1966 as Cdr, High Sheriff Bucks 1969–70, Ld Lt 1984–97, a Baron of the Austrian Empire, v-pres: RASE 1991–, Br Assoc for Shooting and Conservation 1975–, The Hosp Saving Assoc 1979–, Bucks Co Ag Assoc 1988–, pres Bucks CLA 1983–97 (chm 1976–79); govr Stowe 1983–89, a Radcliffe Tstee 1983–, Hon DUniv Buckingham 1993, KStJ 1984; *m* 1958 *Elizabeth Ann, er dau of Lt-Col Henry Shelley Barker, DSO, of Walcote Ho, nr Rugby, and has issue:

1 +THOMAS FRANCIS HENRY; *b* 17 March 1966; *educ* St Edmund's Oxford and RAC Cirencester

1 *Elizabeth Wynne; *b* 15 Feb 1959; *m* 1982 *George Iain Duncan Smith, MP, and has issue:

(1) *Edward St Alban; *b* 1987

(2) *Henry St John; *b* 1990

(1) *Alicia Cecilia; *b* 1989

(2) *Rosanna Tatiana; *b* 1993

2 *Frances Ann (Fanny); *b* 7 June 1961; *m* 1984 *Shaun Richard Stanley and has:

(1) *Joshua John; *b* 1988

(2) *Theo Peter; *b* 1996

(1) *Isabella; *b* 1990

Lineage: JOHN FREMANTLE, of a Hants family; Lisbon merchant; had:

JOHN FREMANTLE; Sec Customs Bd; *d* 30 Dec 1766, leaving issue:

JOHN FREMANTLE, of Aston Abbots, Bucks; *m* Frances, dau and coheir of John Edwards, of Bristol, and *d* 1784, leaving, with two other daus:

1 John Edwards, Lt-Col Coldstream Gds; *m* 27 March 1790 Hon Catherine Henley-Ongley (*d* 18 March 1821), dau of 1st Baron Ongley of Old Warden, and *dsp* 21 March 1798

2 Stephen Francis William, Col; *m* Albinia Francis (*m* 2nd 24 April 1798 Lt-Gen Sir John Taylor, KCB, of Castle Taylor, Co Galway, and had further issue), 2nd dau of James St John Jefferyes, of Blarney Castle, Co Cork (*see* COLTHURST, Bt), and *d* 1794, leaving:

(1) John, CB, Maj-Gen, Lt-Col Coldstream Gds, ADC to Duke of Wellington Peninsular War and Waterloo and to HM QUEEN VICTORIA; *b* 17 Jan 1790; *m* 17 Jan 1829 Agnes (*d* his widow 20 Feb 1864), 3rd dau of David Lyon, and had issue:

1a Arthur James Lyon (Sir), GCMG, CB, KGStJ, Gen Coldstream Gds, Govr Malta, DAG Aux Forces, Sardinian War Medal; *b* 11 Nov 1835; *m* 14 Sept 1864 Mary (*d* 16 Aug 1898), dau of Richard Hall, and *dsp* 25 Sept 1901

2a Fitzroy William, CB, Maj-Gen Coldstream Gds, served Crimea (wounded at the Redan); *b* 15 Dec 1836; *m* 25 Sept 1862 Julia E H (*d* 27 June 1910), yst dau of Sir Guy Campbell, 1st Bt (*qv*), and *d* 12 Feb 1894, leaving issue:

1b Guy, Maj Coldstream Gds; *b* 26 May 1867; *m* 7 June 1899 Alice Florence (*dsp* 24 March 1908), widow of Col Dickson, of Chatto, and dau of J W Seaburne May

1b Agnes; *m* 9 Jan 1890 Capt Charles Henry Sheffield Pretyman, JP, RN (*d* 23 July 1918), er son of Rev Henry George Middleton Pretyman, Vicar Lowick, and *d* 25 Nov 1942

2b Pamela; *d* unm 13 Jan 1937

3b Frances; *m* 9 Jan 1902 Maj-Gen George Handcock Thesiger, CB, CMG, ADC, Rifle Bde (*ka* 27 Sept 1915), son of Lt-Gen Hon Charles W Thesiger, and *d* 25 Sept 1950, leaving issue (*see* CHELMSFORD, V)

3a John Charles Stephen, Lt 2nd Life Gds; *b* 2 Sept 1841; *d* 17 Feb 1874

4a Delvin David, Lt RN; *b* 7 Oct 1842; *m* 3 Jan 1868 Emma (*m* 2nd 30 Oct 1879 Maj Francis Matthew Robinson, late RA), dau of Hon Robert Mackintosh Isaacs, of Sydney, NSW, and *d* 6 Nov 1873, having had:

1b Albinia Grace; *m* 7 July 1894 Charles Yate Lee, and *d* 1 Feb 1956

2b Leila Hope; *m* 1 Dec 1896 Adml Sir Sydney Robert Fremantle, GCB, MVO, and *d* 8 Oct 1930, leaving issue (*see* below)

1a Augusta Wilhelmina Louisa; *m* 6 July 1864 Lt-Gen Julian Hamilton Hall, late Coldstream Gds (*d* 15 Aug 1911), yst son of Sir John Hall, 5th Bt (*see* HALL, Bt, of Dunglass), and *d* 1 March 1906, leaving issue

(1) Albinia; *m* 27 June 1827 her first cousin Henry Wells, 3rd son of Adml Thomas Wells, of Holmewood, Hunts, and *dsp* 1877

(2) Francis Arabella; *m* 29 Aug 1815 5th Earl of Lanesborough (*qv*), and *dsp* 5 Oct 1850

3 THOMAS FRANCIS (Sir), of whom presently

4 William Henry (Rt Hon Sir), GCH, PC, of 6 Stanhope St, Mayfair, and Englefield Green, Surrey, Treas of the Household, Dep Ranger of Windsor Great Park, MP Burlington 1821; *b* 28 Dec 1766; *m* 21 Sept 1797 Selina Mary (*dsp* 22 Nov 1841), widow of Felton Lionel Hervey (f of Col Sir Felton Hervey-Bathurst, 1st Bt, CB (*qv*)) and only dau of Sir John Elwell, Bt, and *d* 19 Oct 1850

1 Sarah Bridget; *m* 19 Dec 1784 Thomas Wells (*d* 31 Oct 1811), of Holmewood, Hunts, Adml of the White, and *d* 1848, leaving issue

The 3rd son,

Sir THOMAS FRANCIS FREMANTLE, GCB; *b* 20 Nov 1765; V-Adml of the Blue, fought Battles of Copenhagen and Trafalgar, *cr* 29 Nov 1816 Kt Cdr Order of Maria Theresa and a Baron of the Austrian Empire; *m* 12 Jan 1797 Elizabeth (*d* 2 Nov 1857), dau and coheir of Richard Wynne, of Falkingham, Lincs, and *d* 19 Dec 1819 leaving, with other issue:

1 THOMAS FRANCIS, **1st Baron**

2 Charles Howe (Sir), GCB, Adml, served Crimean War; *b* 1 June 1800; *m* 8 Oct 1836 Isabella (*d* 26 Dec 1876), widow of James Webberburn and 2nd dau of David Lyon, of Portland Place, W, and Jamaica, and *dsp* 25 May 1869

3 William Robert (Very Rev), DD, Dean of Ripon 1876–95; *b* 30 Aug 1807 *m* 1st 4 Nov 1835 Emily Caroline (*d* 14 July 1877), 2nd dau of Gen Sir Harry Calvert, 1st Bt, GCB; *m* 2nd 9 Oct 1879 Caroline (*d* 10 Feb 1926), 3rd dau of Hon Alexander Leslie Melville, of Branston Hall, Lincs, bro of 7th Earl of Leven and Melville (*qv*), and *dsp* 8 March 1895

1 Augusta Harriet; *m* 27 Sept 1826 Sir James FitzGerald, Bt (*d* 25 Sept 1839), and *d* 11 June 1863

2 Cecilia Mary; *m* 7 Sept 1844 Lord William Hervey (*d* 6 May 1850), son of 1st Marquess of Bristol (*qv*), and *d* 24 Nov 1871, leaving issue

The est son,

Sir Thomas Francis Fremantle, 1st Bt (UK), so *cr* 14 Aug 1821, with remainder to the heirs male of his father, and 2 March 1874 **1st Baron Cottesloe**, of Swanbourne and of Hardwick, Co Buckingham, PC (UK 1844, I 1845); *b* 11 March 1798; *educ* Oriel Coll Oxford (BA); MP (Tory) Buckingham 1827–46, Sec Treasury 1834–35 and 1841–45, Sec War 1844–45, Ch Sec Ireland 1845–46, Dep Chm 1846 and Chm Customs Bd 1847–73; roy licence for himself and his sons to use his father's Austrian title; *m* 24 Nov 1824 Louisa Elizabeth (*d* 17 Aug 1875 from accidental poisoning,) est dau of FM Sir George Nugent, 1st Bt, GCB (*see* NUGENT, Bt, of Waddesdon), and had issue:

1 THOMAS FRANCIS, **2nd Baron**

2 William Henry (Very Rev), Dean of Ripon 1895–1915, Canon Canterbury, DD; *b* 12 Dec 1831; *educ* Balliol Coll Oxford (MA); *m* 1st 6 Aug 1863 Isabella Maria (*d* 13 July 1901), 2nd dau of Sir Culling Eardley Eardley, 3rd Bt, of Bedwell Park, Herts; *m* 2nd 16 April 1903 Sophia Frances (*d* 30 Aug 1943), er dau of Maj G F Stuart, 3rd Dragoon Gds, and *d* 24 Dec 1916, having by his 1st w had, with other issue:

(1) William Archibald Culling (Rev), MA Oxford, with CMS in NWP India; *b* 20 July 1865; *m* 21 June 1892 Grace Eleanor (*d* 30 May 1934), only surv dau of Maj-Gen Arthur George Burrows, RA, and *d* 2 Nov 1894, leaving issue:

1a Mary Isabel; *b* 15 June 1893; *d* unm 18 May 1917

2a Winifred Grace Culling; *b* postumously 10 June 1895; *m* 1st 27 Nov 1916 (*divorce* 1923) Capt Frederick William Guy Hamilton, 8th Bn King's Own Roy Lancaster Regt; *m* 2nd 10 Nov 1923 Sir Francis Henry Dent, CVO (*d* 4 June 1955), 2nd son of Adml C B Calmady Dent, and *dsp* 17 May 1970

(2) Francis Edward (Sir), ktd 1932, OBE (1919), TD, DL, JP Herts, FRCS, FRCP, DPH, MP St Albans 1919, Lt-Col RAMC (TA), memb LCC 1919–22, Consulting MOH Herts (MO 1902–16), Plague MO Punjab, S Africa 1899–1900, special correspondent for *The Lancet* Russo-Japanese War 1904, WW I in Gallipoli, Egypt and Mesopotamia (despatches); *b* 29 May 1872; *educ* Balliol Coll Oxford (MA, MD, MCh) *m* 22 July 1905 Dorothy Marion Travers (*d* 31 Dec 1960), only dau of Henry Joseph Chinnery, JP, of Fringford Manor, Bicester, and *d* 26 Aug 1943, leaving issue:

1a (Francis) David (Eardley), TD, of Bayford Ho, Herts, DL (1959), JP (1951) Herts, FCA, Lt-Col RA (TA) WW II, manager Hops Mktg Bd 1946; *b* 27 May 1906; *educ* Eton and Balliol Coll Oxford (BA 1927, MA 1935); *m* 21 April 1936 *Emmeline Amy (*m* 2nd 1973 Lt-Col Edward Peter Fletcher Boughey, OBE (*d* 1986)) (*see* BOUGHEY, Bt) [Mrs Edward Boughey, 1 Regency Terrace, Elm Place, London SW7], 2nd dau of Brig-Gen Vigant William de Falbe, CMG, DSO, DL, JP, formerly of Whittington Ho, Lichfield, Staffs, and *d* 1 July 1968, leaving issue:

1b +Edward Vigant Eardley [Edward Fremantle Esq, 4 Sutherland St, London SW1V 4LB]; *b* 10 June 1942; *educ* Eton and Balliol Coll Oxford (BA 1963, MA); FCA; *m* 19 May 1973 *Sarah Maud, yst dau of Col William Henry Whitbread, TD, of Hazelhurst, Bunch Lane, Haslemere, Surrey, and has issue:

1c *Anna Elizabeth; *b* 1981

2c *Katherine Fiona; *b* 1984

2b +Thomas David [Thomas Fremantle Esq, Wayside Cottage, E Markham, Newark, Notts]; *b* 18 Aug 1944; *educ* Eton and RNC Dartmouth; late Lt RN; *m* 26 June 1971 *Alice Marian, yst dau of Cyril Reginald Egerton (*see* SUTHERLAND, D), and has:

1c +Mark Thomas; *b* 22 Oct 1975; *educ* Eton and Edinburgh U

2c +Christopher Richard; *b* 7 March 1978; *educ* Eton and Trin Coll Oxford

1c *Emily Teresa Alice; *b* 22 June 1981; *educ* Wycombe Abbey

3b Richard Francis; *b* 15 July 1946; *educ* Eton and Keble Coll Oxford; *d* unm 9 Aug 1976

1b *Marion Jane [Mrs David Hanbury, The Old Rectory, Ruckinge, Kent TN26 2PE]; *m* 1972 *David Christopher Hanbury, yr son of Lt-Col Christopher Lionel Hanbury, MBE, TD, DL, JP, of Juniper Hill, Burnham, Bucks, and has issue:

1c *Jonathan Christopher; *b* 1975

1c *Susannah Mary; *b* 1977

2c *Caroline Jane; *b* 1981

(3) Henry Eardley Stephen; Prof English and Philosophy S African Coll Cape Town 1899–1904, ed *S African News* 1903–08 and 1910–11, MLA Uitenhage Cape Colony 1906–10 and Union of S Africa 1910–15, Chm Educn Commn Cape Colony 1910–11, fndr and first Chm Nat Party Cape Province 1915, fndr Economic Soc of S Africa 1924, memb Bd of Trade and Industries of S Africa 1921–25; *b* 6 Aug 1874; *educ* Oriel Coll Oxford (MA); *m* 1st 20 April 1899 Margaret Elizabeth (*d* 17 June 1909), 2nd dau of Alexander Macdonald, Keeper of University Galleries Oxford; *m* 2nd 20 Sept 1910 Helen (*d* 8 May 1948), 3rd dau of Jacobus Johannes Eksteen, of Deze Hoek, nr Piquetberg, S Africa, and *d* 6 Sept 1931, having by his 1st w had issue:

1a Isabella Margaret Eleanor, MA and BEd U of Cape Town, teacher of Latin High Sch Cambridge, East London, Lecturer Greek Huguenot Coll Wellington; *b* 30 Aug 1901; *d* unm 14 Jan 1935

(4) John Morton, CMG (1927), MBE (1918), Maj 3rd Co London Yeo, served S Africa 1900–02 (DCM), Priv Sec to Sec State for War 1903, Resident N Nigeria 1904–10 and 1911–29, Comptroller Household of Govr-Gen Canada, Actg Lt-Govr Nigeria 1925, Sec N Provinces 1928, retired 1929; *b* 31 March 1876; *educ* Eton and Hertford Coll Oxford (MA); *m* 4 Dec 1915 Violet (*d* 21 Aug 1944), dau of Adml Charles Lister Oxley, of The Hall, Ripon, Yorks, and *d* 21 Dec 1936, leaving issue:

1a +John Godfrey, JP (1967); *b* 28 Dec 1916; *educ* Eton and Balliol Coll Oxford (BA 1938, MA 1944), CC 1963 Kincardineshire, late Lt KOYLI; *m* 8 Sept 1955 *Gillian Daphine, only dau of Harry Easton Stedham, of 23 Addison Ave, London W11, and *d* 22 Jan 1974

1a Elisabeth Benue; *b* 23 April 1918; *d* unm 13 Jan 1942

(5) Stephen Frederick, Lt 2nd King Edward's Own Gurkhas, IA; *b* 14 Jan 1881; *educ* Univ Coll Oxford (scholar, MA) *d* unm 15 April 1910

(1) Isabella Louisa; *b* 29 June 1864; *m* 20 Oct 1894 Cyril Hamilton Aitken, of Vernon Grange, Canterbury, son of Canon James Aitken, Chaplain Roy Memorial Church, Cannes, and *d* 4 Aug 1936, leaving issue

(2) Anna Mary; *b* 7 July 1867; *m* 1 Oct 1891 Sir (Frederick) Sydney Parry, KBE, CB (*d* 22 May 1941), Dep Chm Customs and Excise, son of Rt Rev Edward Parry, DD, Bp Dover, and *d* 13 Feb 1962, leaving issue

3 Charles William (Sir), KCB, JP Middx, London and Westminster; *b* 12 Aug 1834; memb Conseil d'Administration Suez Canal Co 1868–94; *m* 20 April 1865 Sophia (*d* 22 Dec 1944), yst dau of Abel Smith, of Woodhall, and *d* 8 Oct 1914, having had, with other issue:

(1) Maurice Abel, Lt Coldstream Gds, ADC to Govr Hong Kong; *b* 26 Nov 1866; *d* 16 Jan 1892

(2) Ronald Aubrey; *b* 23 Oct 1872; *m* 23 Jan 1899 Eleanor Susan (*d* 14 July 1946), est dau of Charles John Fletcher, of Dale Park, Sussex, and *d* 5 June 1947, having had issue:

1a (Maurice Alan) Patrick, Maj 11th Hus, ADC to Govr Madras 1927; *b* 31 July 1900; *educ* Eton and RMC Sandhurst; *m* 2 Dec 1928 (Ida) Thelma Gordon Wells (*d* 6 Feb 1976), dau of Edward Reginald Stirling Bloxsome, of The Rangers, Copthorne, Sussex, and *d* 26 June 1972, leaving issue:

1b +Robin Patrick; *b* 3 Aug 1930; *educ* Wellington and RMA Sandhurst; late Capt 4th Queen's Own Hus, Capt Ayrshire (ECO) Yeo (TA), assist md Springbank Pre-Cast Concrete Ltd, Airdrie, chm The Economic League 1989–93, principal Fremantle & Co 1980–; *m* 1st 4 April 1962 (*divorce* 1980) June Helen, yr dau of Brig Ereld Wingfield Boteler Cardiff, CB, CBE, of Easton Court, Ludlow, Salop; *m* 2nd 1985 *(Honor) Diana, yr dau of Sir (Coles) John Child, 2nd Bt (*qv*), and widow of Noel H Matterson, and by 1st w has issue:

1c +Charles Ereld Patrick; *b* 21 Oct 1964

1c *Serena Katherine; *b* 29 Dec 1967

2a John Michael Charles; *b* 26 June 1911; *d* 12 Jan 1913

1a Bridget; *b* and *d* 12 Sept 1903

2a *Helen Antonia Theresa Susan; *b* 1914; *m* 1 March 1940 John Miller (*d* 1988), only son of John Miller, of Lethen Grange, Sydenham

(3) Charles Albert, DSO (1918), Capt RN, memb Lloyd's 1922, served WW I (despatches), Chev Legion of Honour and Russian Order of St Stanislas 2nd Cl with swords; *b* 15 March 1878; *m* 19 April 1906 Margaret Griselda (*d* 21 March 1918), yr dau of Sir William Wedderburn, 4th Bt (*see* OGILVY-WEDDERBURN, Bt), and *d* July 1952, leaving issue:

1a *Priscilla Jane; *b* 2 Nov 1911; *m* 1 July 1938 Henry Bourdillon Imlach Bett, only son of Stafford Henry Imlach Bett, of Thornham Manor, Norfolk

4 Edmund Robert (Sir), GCB, GCVO, CMG, JP Bucks, Adml, ADC, C-in-C: E Indian station 1888–91, China station 1892–95, Plymouth 1896–99, R-Adml United Kingdom and of Admlty 1901–26, served Burmese War 1852, New Zealand War 1864–66, Ashanti Campaign 1873–74 (severely wounded), Expdn to Vitu 1890, Crown of Prussia 1st Cl and Brilliant Star of Zanzibar 1st Cl; gold, silver and copper medals of Roy Humane Soc, gold medal of Shipwrecked Mariners Soc, FRGS; *b* 15 June 1836; *m* 31 Aug 1866 Barberina Rogers, CBE (1920)

(*d* 5 May 1923), est dau of Hon Robert McIntosh Isaacs, MLA, LLD, of Sydney, NSW, and *d* 10 Feb 1929, having had issue:

(1) Sydney Robert (Sir), GCB, MVO, Adml; *b* 16 Nov 1867; served WW I (despatches), Dep Ch Naval Staff Admlty 1918–19, cmdg 1st Battle Sqdn Atlantic Fleet 1919021, C-in-C Portsmouth 1923–26, Cdr: Legion of Honour, Order of S Maurice and S Lazarus of Italy, Order of Redeemer of Greece and Rising Sun of Japan 2nd Cl, American DSM; *m* 1st 1 Dec 1896 Lelia Hope (*d* 8 Oct 1930), dau of Lt Delvin David Fremantle, RN (*see above*); *m* 2nd 1 Aug 1931 (Geraldine) Margaret (*d* 28 Nov 1974), widow of Lt-Col James Stephens Fitzgerald, The Roy Irish Regt, and dau of Col William Cooke-Collis, CMG, of Castle Cooke, Co Cork, and *d* 29 April 1958, having by his 1st w had issue:

1a Edmund Seymour Denis, DSC (1944), Cdr RN, served WW II (despatches twice); *b* 2 June 1904; *m* 1st 26 June 1928 (*divorce* 1943) Dorothy Clare Haldane (*d* 1980), er dau of Maj W M Sinclair, OBE, RM, and had issue:

1b Robert Edmund Sinclair; *b* 27 June 1929; *d* 18 March 1930

2b +Charles Alan [Cdr Charles Fremantle RN (ret), Langley Corner, Langley Burrell, Chippenham, Wilts SN15 4LL]; *b* 20 Feb 1935; *educ* Sutton Valence Sch and RNC Dartmouth; memb: Nautical Inst, N Wilts Dist Cncl 1987–91; *m* 30 July 1960 *Caroline Mary, er dau of Cdr Sydney Andrew Boyd Morant, OBE, DSC, RN, of Roughover, Worplesdon Hill, Woking, Surrey, and has issue:

1c +Timothy Charles; *b* 13 June 1967; *educ* Plymouth Poly (BSc)

2c +James Justin; *b* 26 July 1971; *educ* Portsmouth U (BA)

1c *Naomi Juliet [Mrs Stuart Hill, Hammonds Cottage, Waltham Chase, Hants SO3 2LQ]; *b* 19 Aug 1961; *educ* Keele U (BA); *m* 1990 *Stuart John Hill, son of Michael John Hill, Eastleigh, Hants, and has issue:

1d *Matthew Augustus Fremantle; *b* 1992

1d *Georgina; *b* 1994

2d *Hannah; *b* 1996

3b +Sydney Walter [Sydney Fremantle Esq, 4 Strafford Rd, Twickenham, Middx]; *b* 5 Nov 1936; *educ* Sherborne and Oriel Coll Oxford (BA); *m* 2 Sept 1961 *Susan Delia Aiton, only child of Brig John Aiton Bell, CBE, of Long Valley, Echo Barn Lane, Farnham, Surrey, and has had issue:

1c +Samuel Patrick; *b* 17 March 1967

1c Joanna Mary Aiton; *b* 23 May 1964; *d* 1986

1b *Ann Penelope [Mrs Sirio Morgia, Summerfields, Via Tito Poggi 21, Via Ardeatina, Rome 00134, Italy]; *b* 22 June 1931; *m* 14 April 1966 Sirio Morgia, son of L Morgia, of Rome, Italy

1a (cont.) Cdr Edmund Fremantle *m* 2nd 3 April 1946 *Edna Maud [Mrs Edward Fremantle, Redlands, Hookhills Rd, Churston Ferrers, Paignton, Devon], formerly w of James Richard Lyddon and dau of Albert John Tweed Cusselle, of Dartford Kent, and *d* 1980 leaving further issue:

4b +Richard William [Richard Fremantle Esq, 40 Denmark Rd, London W13]; *b* 14 Oct 1948; *educ* Kelly Coll; *m* 1975 *Alison, dau of Arnold Cruse, and has issue:

1c +Edmund Richard; *b* 1979

2c +Peter Thomas; *b* 1985

1c *Mary Grace; *b* 1980

5b +Stephen Antony [Stephen Fremantle Esq, 9 Stavordale Way, Weymouth, Dorset]; *b* 18 July 1950; *m* 1st 1972 (*divorce* 1976) Hanna Elizabeth Fiona, dau of K Sierakowski, of Bickley, Kent, and has issue:

1c Melanie Leila; *b* 1973

5b (cont.) Stephen Fremantle *m* 2nd 1976 *Patricia Mary, adopted dau of Miss Margaret Lewin, and has further issue:

2c *Holly; *b* 1978

2a David Robert, Lt-Cdr RNVR WW II; *b* 12 June 1906; m 1st 17 March 1939 (*divorce* 1951) Patience Anne, yr dau of Lt-Cdr Evelyn Culme-Seymour, RN (*see* CULME-SEYMOUR, Bt); *m* 2nd 5 Feb 1954 (*divorce* 1976) Rosabel, formerly w of Maj Arthur Ivor Stewart-Liberty, MC, Roy Bucks Yeo, and dau of Arthur Henry Fynn, of Helston, Cornwall, and *d* 1989, having by 1st w had issue:

1b *Francesca Mary [Dr Francesca Fremantle, 13 Child's St, London SW5 9RZ]; *b* 3 Jan 1941; *educ* London U (PhD)

1a Barbara Sybil; *b* 15 Feb 1898; *m* 15 Feb 1923 Capt Douglas John Claris, RN (*d* 19 March 1959), son of Sydney Claris, formerly of Rowley Bank, Arkley, and had issue

2a Margery Hilda; *b* 27 May 1900; *m* 1st 6 June 1921 (*divorce* 1929), as his 1st w, Raymond Massey, the actor, son of Chester D Massey, of Toronto, and had issue; *m* 2nd 1929 Lt-Col Sir Giles Edward Sebright, 13th Bt (*qv*), and had further issue

(2) Selwyn Howe (Sir), CSI (1920), CIE (1915), entered ICS 1890 (ret and ktd 1925), CC Bucks 1934; *b* 11 Aug 1869; *educ* Eton and Magdalen Coll Oxford; *m* 3 Jan 1906 Vera Evelyn Selina, MBE (1918) (*d* 24 Dec 1965), er dau of Henry Marsh, CIE, India PWD, and *dsp* 16 March 1942

(3) Arthur William, Indian Ag Service; *b* 20 Aug 1870; *d* unm 23 Oct 1932

(4) Algernon Francis; *b* 19 Nov 1871; *d* 9 Nov 1875

(5) Alan Frederick, ICS, was T/Lt IA 1915–18; *b* 7 June 1877; *educ* Eton and Magdalen Coll Oxford (BA); *m* 24 April 1909 Ethel May (*d* 20 Aug 1962), dau of Rev Albert Augustus Harland, MA, FSA, Vicar Harefield, and *dsp* 20 March 1953

(6) Alfred Ernest Albert, Midshipman RN, Sr Master Modern Languages Stowe 1923–27, Lt RNVR WW I, Order of Redeemer of Greece; *b* 26 Sept 1884 (HRH the late DUKE OF EDINBURGH stood sponsor); *educ* Eton (KS) and Univ Coll Oxford (BA); *m* 19 Feb 1908 Gladys Hamilton (*d* 15 April 1945), and *d* 15 March 1955, having had issue:

1a Paris Oscar René Francesco, Maj King's Regt WW II; *b* 28 Aug 1908; *m* 21 July 1934 Rosamond Carnegie (*m* 2nd 19 April 1947 Brig Gordon de Bruyne, OBE, late 60th Rifles (*d* 1972), of Eastbourne, Sussex, 3rd son of Peter Adrian de Bruyne, of Magallanes, Chile) [Mrs Gordon de Bruyne, 4 Ravens Court, St John's Rd, Eastbourne], dau of Arthur Knox, of Fairfield, Wargrave, Berks, and *d* of wounds March 1944, leaving issue:

1b *(Valerie Rosamond) Christina [Miss Christina Fremantle, 39 Kensington Mansions, Trebovir Rd, London SW5 9TQ]; *b* 29 Jan 1942

5 Stephen James (Rev), BA, Sr Student of Ch Ch Oxford; *b* 2 April 1845; *d* unm 16 Sept 1874

1 Mary; *m* 19 Sept 1848 Richard Aubrey Cartwright, DL, JP (*d* 3 Feb 1891), of Edgcote, Banbury, and *d* Nov 1885, aged 59, leaving issue

2 Eliza Maria; *m* 29 June 1854 Henry Richard Farrer (*d* 9 Nov 1906), of Green Hammerton Hall, York, and *d* 19 May 1891 aged 64, leaving issue

3 Augusta Mary; *m* 25 Oct 1853 8th Viscount Midleton (*qv*), and *d* 1 June 1903, leaving issue

4 Emily Caroline; *m* 26 Jan 1882 Rev Charles Leslie Alexander (*d* 13 May 1888), rector Stanton-by-Bridge, Derby, and *dsp* 10 Feb 1929

5 Cecilia Elizabeth; *m* 3 Sept 1867 Rev Edmund Hugh McNeile (*d* Jan 1893), Hon Canon of Liverpool, and *dsp* 15 Feb 1929

6 Louisa Frances; *d* unm 20 March 1909

The 1st BARON *d* 3 Dec 1890; his est son,

THOMAS FRANCIS FREMANTLE, **2nd Baron Cottesloe**, DL, JP Bucks; *educ* Eton and Balliol Coll Oxford (Scholar, MA 1844) barrister Lincoln's Inn 1855, MP Bucks 1876–85, chm: Quarter Sessions 1899–1910, Bucks CC 1897–1904; *b* 30 Jan 1830; *m* 9 Sept 1859. Lady Augusta Henrietta (*d* 4 Nov 1906), 2nd dau of 2nd Earl of Eldon (*qv*), and had issue:

1 THOMAS FRANCIS, **3rd Baron**

2 Reginald Scott; *b* 11 Feb 1863; *educ* Eton and Balliol Coll Oxford (BA); *m* 26 July 1900 Hilda Lucy (*d* 2 Sept 1953), dau of Edward Middleton Barry, RA, and *d* 30 Sept 1956, leaving issue:

(1) Gerald Barry; *b* 8 Jan 1906; *d* unm 24 Feb 1967

(1) *Rosamund Beatrice; *b* 17 March 1902; *m* 7 May 1931 Thomas Gilbert Standing (*d* 6 June 1942), of Prince Edward Sch, Salisbury, S Rhodesia, Capt Nigeria Regt, son of Thomas Henry Standing, of 116 Hare St, Rochdale, Lancs, and has issue:

1a *Roderick Fremantle; *b* 1932

2a *Caspar Vernon; *b* 1933

3a *Lionel Gilbert; *b* 1940

(2) *Joan Lucy [Mrs Caleb Trevor, 72 Talbot Rd, Highgate, London N6]; *b* 16 June 1904; *m* 29 April 1930 Caleb Henry Trevor, son of Rev Henry John Trevor, and has issue:

1a *Malcolm Henry; *b* 1932

3 Cecil, JP Bucks; *b* 12 Dec 1865; *d* unm 17 July 1927

4 Walter, Capt late Oxf and Bucks LI (TF); *b* 13 March 1869; *educ* Trin Coll Cambridge (MA); *d* unm 3 Jan 1936

1 Mary Louisa; *d* unm 19 Sept 1926

2 Gertrude Charlotte; *b* 28 July 1864; *d* 23 Sept 1873

The 2nd BARON *d* 13 April 1918, and was *s* by his est son,

THOMAS FRANCIS FREMANTLE, **3rd Baron Cottesloe**, CB (1926), JP and CA Co Buckingham and JP Leics, Ld Lt Bucks 1923–54, v-chm Bucks CC and Pres CC Assoc; chm Bucks QS 1925–37, Pres Bucks TAA, Assoc Memb Ordnance Bd, chm Small Arms Ctee; chm NRA, Assist Sec to Sec of State for War 1900–03, Hon Col, Lt-Col cmdg Bucks Bn Oxf and Bucks LI (VD, TD), KJStJ; *b* 5 Feb 1862; *educ* Eton and Balliol Coll Oxford (BA 1885, MA 1889); *m* 16 April 1896 Florence (*d* 4 April 1956), only surv child of Thomas Tapling, and had:

1 Thomas Francis Halford, 2nd Lt 5th Serv Bn Oxf and Bucks LI; *b* 2 Jan 1897; *educ* Eton; *d* unm 17 Oct 1915, of wounds received in action in Flanders

2 JOHN WALGRAVE HALFORD, **4th Baron**

3 Edward St John; *b* 23 Aug 1901; *d* 24 Feb 1913

4 Christopher Evelyn; *b* 1906; *educ* Eton and Balliol Coll Oxford (BA 1930); with Min of Information 1941–45, Br Cncl 1945–46, ed: *Studio Publications* (1947), *Reporter Publications* 1950–57, *World Encyclopedia of Textiles* 1959–60; *m* 12 Nov 1930 *Anne Marie Huth, 2nd dau of Rt Hon Frederick Huth Jackson, PC (*see* JACKSON, Bt, of The Manor House), and *d* 1979, leaving issue:

(1) +Adam; *b* 18 March 1934; *educ* Eton and Balliol Coll Oxford (MA) and Fordham U NYC (JD); barrister Inner Temple 1957, New York Bar Assoc 1967; *m* 18 May 1963 (*divorce* 1978) Princess Christine Sapieha, only dau of Prince Paul Sapieha, of 1 Lycabettus St, Athens, Greece and Mrs Charles Gouverneur Paulding, of 163 East 81st St, NYC, USA, and has issue:

1a +Christopher Nicholas; *b* 31 Aug 1965; *educ* Worth and Aberdeen U (MA, MLitt); Govr Dr Johnson's House Tst, memb Children's Panel; *m* 1989 *Gillian, yst dau of Peter Hainey, of Bitterne, Southampton

2a +Paul Zachary [Paul Fremantle Esq, 84 Addison Rd, Reading, Berks RG1 8EG]; *b* 5 Dec 1968; *educ* Worth and Balliol Coll Oxford; *m* 1991 *Jane Pamela, dau of Rev John William Hunwicke, Chaplain Lancing Coll

(2) +Richard Christian Wynne [Richard Fremantle Esq, Via Matteo Palmieri 9, Florence 50122, Italy); *b* 1 May 1936; *educ* Portsmouth Priory, RI, and Columbia U (BA 1959, MA 1968); *m* 4 Sept 1971 (*divorce* 19–) Chloë Sarabella, yr dau of Sir Geoffrey Cecil Ryvers Eley, CBE, of The Change Ho, Great Yeldham, Essex (*see* WALKER, Bt, of Oakley House), and by *Camilla Baines has:

1a *Oskar Frederick Cornelius Baines-Freemantle; *b* 25 May 1990

(3) +Hugh Dominic Christopher, with Peace Corps 1966–68; *b* 6 Aug 1944; *educ* Georgetown U, Washington, DC (BA 1966); *m* 19– *Susan —

1 Florence Mary; *b* 11 March 1898; Missionary under CMS, Palestine 1928–32, and Egypt 1932–35, Linguist FO 1941–42, Sub-Editor BBC Arabic News Service 1942–46; *d* unm 3 March 1969

2 Margaret Augusta; *b* 2 Dec 1904; *educ* Oxford U (MA, DM), Lecturer Pathology Oxford 1945–72, Fell of LMH Oxford 1952–72; *m* 1st 9 April 1930 (*divorce* 1946) Denys Arthur Jennings, MA, BM, BCh Oxford, only son of A E Jennings; *m* 2nd 6 June 1967 Baron Florey , OM, FRS (Life Peer) (*d* 21 Feb 1968), and *d* 14 Nov 1994

3 *Bride Faith Louisa [The Hon Mrs Berry, The Garden House, Tayfield, Newport-on-Tay, Fife DD6 8HA]; *b* 1 July 1910; *educ* Girton Coll Cambridge (BA 1935, MA 1938); *m* 20 Aug 1936 John Berry, CBE, DL, LLD, PhD, DSc, FRSE, only son of William Berry, of Tayfield, Newport, Fife, and has issue:

(1) *William [William Berry Esq, 31 Stafford St, Edinburgh; Tayfield House, Newport-on-Tay, Fife]; *b* 26 Sept 1939; *educ* Eton, St Andrews U (MA 1961), and Edinburgh U (LLB 1963), WS, slr, notary public; *m* 15 Dec 1973 *Elizabeth, only dau of Sir Edward Redston Warner, KCMG, OBE, of Old Royal Oak, Blockley, Glos, and has issue:

1a *John; *b* 1976

2a *Robert Edward Alexander; *b* 1978

(2) *Peter Fremantle [Peter Berry Esq, 58 Pyrland Rd, London N5 2JD]; *b* 17 May 1944; *educ* Eton and Lincoln Coll Oxford (BA 1966, MA); Crown Agent 1988; *m* Feb 1972 *Paola Padovani, and has:

1a *Richard John; *b* 1979

1a *Sara; *b* 1974

2a *Anna; *b* 1977

(1) *Margaret Wilhelmina [Mrs Ronald Alexander, 81 Balfour Rd, London N5]; *b* 23 Aug 1937; *m* 4 April 1962 *Ronald Lindsay Alexander, ARIBA, 2nd son of George Alexander, of Edinburgh, and has:

1a *Adam George; *b* 1971; BA

1a *Jane Louise (Rev); *b* 16 Jan 1969; MA Oxon; *m* 1992 *Rev Duncan Arthur Spencer MacLaren and has:

1b *Duncan Alexander John; *b* 1997

4 *Katharine Dorothy Honor [The Hon Dr Katharine Fremantle, Dennenlaan 48, Hollandsche Rading, Netherlands]; *b* 23 May 1919; BA Cambridge 1941, PhD London 1956

The 3rd BARON *d* 19 July 1956; his er surv son,

JOHN WALGRAVE HALFORD FREMANTLE, **4th Baron Cottesloe**, GBE (1960), TD, DL (Co London 1951–76); *b* 2 March 1900; *educ* Eton and Trin Coll Cambridge (BA 1921, MA 1925), Lt-Col RA (TA), served WW II 1939–45 as GSO(1), Sr Mil Liaison Offr and as Lt-Col cmdg 21st LAA Regt, chm: DL's Ctees in Bermondsey 1952–58 and Deptford 1955–58, Arts Cncl of GB 1960–65, Postgraduate Medical Sch of London 1949–58 (Fell 1975) Br Postgraduate Medical Fedn 1958–94; Northwick Park Hosp Adv Ctee 1973–94, Heritage in Danger, Govr National Theatre and Sadler's Wells 1957–60, NRA 1960–94; memb: Bucks T&AFA 1939–94, Hampstead Borough Cncl 1945–53 and LCC 1945–55, PLA 1947–67 (v-chm 1956–67), Govr King Edward VIII's Hosp Fund for London 1973–94; Pres Hosp Saving Assoc 1975–94, Hammersmith and St Mark's Hosp 1966–94, Teaching Hosps Assoc Postgraduate Ctee 1968–94, NW Metropolitan Regional Hosp Bd 1953–60 and Advsy Cncl and Reviewing Ctee Export of Works of Art 1953–72, Tstee Tate Gall 1953–60 (Chm 1959–60), Dep Pres Royal Russell Sch, Tstee City Parochial Fndn 1953–94, Pres: London Smallbore Rifle Assoc 1953–94, Bucks County Rifle Assoc 1956–94 and Leander Club 1957–62, Steward Henley Regatta 1947–94, Hon Sec Amateur Rowing Assoc 1932–46, rowed for Cambridge in Universities' Boat Race 1921–22, won Match Rifle Championship six times and shot in English Eight thirty-seven times, coached at Bisley; *m* 1st 16 Feb 1926 (*divorce* 1944) Lady Elizabeth Harris, only dau of 5th Earl of Malmesbury (*qv*), and had issue:

1 JOHN TAPLING FREMANTLE, **5th and present Baron Cottesloe**

1a *Ann [The Hon Mrs Brooks, Wistow, Leicester LE8 0QF]; *b* 21 Oct 1930; *m* 29 Nov 1951 *Timothy Gerald Martin Brooks (*see* CRAWSHAW, B) and has issue

The **4th Baron** *m* 2nd 26 March 1959 *Gloria Jean Irene Dunn [The Rt Hon The Dowager Lady Cottesloe, 78 Orbel St, London SW11 3NY], adopted dau of W E Hill, of Barnstaple, Devon, and *d* 1994, leaving by her:

2 +Edward Walgrave [The Hon Edward Freemantle, 4 Merivale Rd, Putney, London SW15 2NW]; *b* 18 June 1961; *m* 1991 *Sara E, dau of Lt-Cdr Harry Chillingworth, of Bembridge, IoW, and has:

(1) +Henry John; *b* 1996

(1) *Louisa Clare; *b* 1994

2 *Elizabeth Cecilia Jane; *b* 28 Aug 1962; assumed additional forename Elizabeth 1977, jnlst; *m* 1991 *Olivier Philippe Haguenauer, est son of Dr Pierre Haguenauer, of Neuilly-sur-Seine, France

3 *Flora Catherine *b* 12 Sept 1967; *m* 1993 *Dan Miyonga, of Kisumu, Kenya

COTTS

Arms: Azure on a chevron between in chief two lions rampant and in base a representation of the Southern Cross or, three lymphads sable. **Crest:** A quadriga or. **Motto:** *Deo fidens proficio* ('Forward trusting in God'). **Creation:** Bt. (UK) 15 June 1921.

SIR RICHARD CRICHTON MITCHELL COTTS, 4th BT, of Coldharbour Wood, Rogate, Sussex [Sir Richard Mitchell Cotts Bt, c/o Mrs Tristram Barran, The Oldall, Brent Eleigh, Sudbury, Suffolk CO10 9NP]; *b* 26 July 1946; *s f* 1995; *educ* The Oratory Sch

Lineage: JOHN COUTTS, of Glencairn, Dumfriesshire; *m* 25 April 1704 Mary Grierson, and had issue:

1 JOHN

2 James; *b* 2 July 1708

1 Agnes

The er son,

JOHN COUTTS, of Dalry; living 1773; had:

JOHN COUTTS, of Dalry and later Kells; *m* 30 Dec 1773 Agnes McCreery, of Dalry, and had, with a yr s (Gilbert, *b* 1781):

JOHN COUTTS, of Snade, Glencairn; *b* 1779; *m* Agnes, dau of John Kennon, and had, with other issue:

WILLIAM COUTTS later COTTS, of Sanquhar; *b* 2 March 1812; *m* 1st 23 Dec 1831 Mary Wright, of Kirkconnel, Dumfries, and had issue:

1 Elizabeth; *b* 1833

WILLIAM COTTS *m* 2nd 1838 Marion Russell and *d* 5 April 1878, having by her had issue:

1 WILLIAM

2 James; *b* 1847

3 Robert; *b* 1852

2 Elizabeth Russell; *d* unm 19 Jan 1871

3 Agnes; *b* 1842

The est son,

WILLIAM COTTS, of Sanquhar; *b* 6 Nov 1843; *m* 1st Sarah Muir and had issue; *m* 2nd Lilias Hastings and *d* 12 Sept 1908; his est s by his 1st w:

Sir William Dingwall Mitchell Cotts, 1st Bt (UK), so *cr* 15 June 1921, KBE, MP (Nat Lib) Western Isles 1922–23, JP Sussex and London and Borough of Hampstead, colonial merchant, shipowner and colliery proprietor, helped in recruiting in S Africa WW I, OStJ; *b* 15 July 1871; *m* 18 March 1901 Agnes Nivison (*d* 27 Feb 1966 aged 91), dau of Robert Sloane, of Sanquhar, and *d* 20 Jan 1932, leaving:

1 Sir (WILLIAM) CAMPBELL COTTS later MITCHELL-COTTS (deed poll 9 Feb 1932), **2nd Bt**; *b* 12 April 1902; *educ* Trin Hall Cambridge (MA); barrister Inner Temple 1928, 1st Lt Black Watch (Roy Highland Regt) WW II, OStJ, Palmes d'Officier d'Academie; *m* 20 Dec 1934 (*divorce* 1939) Princess Hélène Marie de la Trémoïlle, 3rd dau of Louis Charles Marie, 11th Duke de la Trémoïlle, and *dsp* 20 Feb 1964

2 ROBERT CRICHTON MITCHELL (Sir), **3rd Bt**

3 Cameron

1 Agnes Nivison (twin); *b* 12 April 1902; *m* 1st 1 Dec 1926 (*divorce* 1930) Brig Claude Frederick Forestier-Walker, OBE, MC, 3rd Hus (*see* FORESTIER-WALKER, Bt); *m* 2nd 2 Jan 1941 (*divorce* 1952) S/Ldr Claude Alastair Blyth Rome, RAFVR, son of Brig Claude Rome, CMG, DSO, by his w Hon Grace Loudenne, dau of 1st Baron Blyth (*qv*)

The 2nd Bt's bro,

Sir (Robert) Crichton Mitchell Cotts, 3rd Bt; *b* 20 Oct 1903; *educ* Harrow and Balliol Coll Oxford (MA); Maj Irish Gds WW II; *b* 20 Oct 1903; *m* 14 Oct 1942 Barbara (*d* 16 Sept 1982), only dau of Capt Herbert John Anthony Throckmorton, RN (*see* 1970 edn THROCKMORTON, Bt), and *d* 17 Jan 1995, leaving:

1 Sir RICHARD CRICHTON MITCHELL COTTS, **4th and present Bt**

2 +HAMISH WILLIAM ANTHONY MITCHELL; *b* 15 Sept 1951; heir presumptive; *educ* Ampleforth

1 Lucinda Nancy Mitchell; *b* 3 March 1944; *m* 19– *Christopher Kerrison, and *d* 1987

2 *Susan Marie-Josephe Mitchell; *b* 15 March 1945; *m* 1971 *John Davies, of Cheshire, and has issue:

(1) *Justin; *b* 1981

3 *Miranda Clare Frances Mitchell [Mrs Tristram Barran, The 'Oldall, Brent Eleigh, Sudbury, Suffolk CO10 9NP]; *b* 18 Feb 1948; *m* 5 Nov 1973 Tristram Cosmo Barran (*d* 1992 in a motor accident), est son of Sir David Barran, of Brent Eleigh Hall, Sudbury, Suffolk, and 36 Kensington Sq, London W8 (*see* BARRAN, Bt)

COUPER

Arms: Or a chevron gules, charged with another ermine, between three laurel-leaves slipped vert. **Crest:** Out of a mural crown argent, a hand holding a garland proper. **Motto:** *Virtute* ('By valour'). **Creation:** Bt. (UK) 23 June 1841.

SIR (ROBERT) NICHOLAS OLIVER COUPER, 6TH BT [Sir Nicholas Couper Bt, 79 Devonshire Rd, London W4 2HU]; *b* 9 Oct 1945; *s* f 1975; *educ* Eton and RMA Sandhurst; property consultant; late Maj Blues and Royals (ret 1975), formerly 2nd Lt 1st Roy Dragoons; *m* 1st 6 Dec 1972 (*divorce* 1986) Kirsten Henrietta, dau of Maj George Burrell MacKean, JP, DL, of Loughanmore, Dunadry, Co Antrim, and has issue:

1 +JAMES GEORGE; *b* 27 Oct 1977

1 *Caroline Doune; *b* 8 May 1979

Sir NICHOLAS *m* 2nd 1991 *Katrina Frances, dau of Sir (Charles) Michael Walker, GCMG, of W Chiltington, W Sussex

Lineage: GEORGE COUPER, of Bafer, near Sorby; **had:**

ROBERT COUPER, MD, FAS, of Fochabers, Moray of; *m* 1786 Grace, dau of Rev Ebenezer Stott, of Minigaff, and had, with a yr s and three daus:

Sir George Couper, 1st Bt (UK), so *cr* 23 June 1841, CB, KH; *b* 1788; Col, Comptroller Household to DUCHESS OF KENT (mother of QUEEN VICTORIA), Capt 92nd Foot Battle of Copenhagen, ADC to Lt-Gen Earl of Dalhousie (*qv*) Peninsular War (medal with five clasps), Mil Sec in Canada to Gen Sir James Kempt and 1st Earl of Durham (*qv*); *m* 20 June 1820 Elizabeth (*d* 14 March 1880), dau of Hon Justice Sir John Wilson, of The Howe, Westmorland, and had issue:

1 GEORGE EBENEZER WILSON (Sir), **2nd Bt**

2 James Kempt; *b* 2 Nov 1827; Gen Indian Staff Corps; *m* 1854 Emily Jane (*d* 9 April 1922), dau of Col J L Earle, Bengal Army, and *d* 14 May 1901, leaving issue:

(1) Arthur Edward; *b* 6 Aug 1857; Maj E Surrey Regt, served Afghan War 1878–80 and Egypt 1884, and *d* 4 April 1927

(2) George; *b* 5 April 1861; Capt RN, served Egypt 1882, and *d* 27 Nov 1916

(3) Charles James; *b* 6 Oct 1866; *d* unm Dec 1940

(4) William Lemprière; *b* 17 Feb 1874; *m* 10 Oct 1919 Isabel (*m* 2nd 1952 Arthur Alfred Hitch (*d* 1965), and *d* 10 Dec 1968), dau of Thomas John Hodgson, of Hatzic, BC, Canada, and *d* 12 Nov 1925, leaving issue:

1a *Cara Jocelyn Mary [Mrs Verne Dickey, 45540 Spruce Drive, Chilliwack, BC V2R 1E6, Canada]; *b* 14 Feb 1921; *m* 27 Dec 1952 Verne Barrett Dickey (*d* 1984), son of Miles McInnes Dickey, of Charles St, Chilliwack, BC, and has issue:

1b *William Miles; *b* 1 Nov 1955; *m* 1992 *Tulia Carranza and has:

1c *Matthew Verne; *b* 1993

2c *Christopher Miles; *b* 30 July 1996

2b *Roy Couper; *b* 10 Nov 1957

3b *Alan Verne; *b* 2 Feb 1960

1b *Mary Isabel; *b* 2 Nov 1953; *m* 1974 (*divorce* 1989) M Borden and has:

1c *Jeffrey Wayne; *b* 1975

1c *Lisa Marie; *b* 1977; *m* June 1997 *Robert Slack

(1) Cara Georgie; *d* unm 13 Feb 1932

(2) Emily Margaret; *d* unm 10 Jan 1939

(3) Harriet Clara; *m* 19 Dec 1891 Col Manners Charles Wood, 10th Hus (*d* 12 Sept 1941), and *d* 29 June 1962, aged 99, leaving issue

(4) Elizabeth; *d* 5 Dec 1937

(5) Mary Emmeline Bertha; *m* 7 Feb 1895 Lt-Col Roger Marriott Dodington, OBE (*d* 22 Dec 1925), of Horsington, Templecombe, and *d* 10 Aug 1940, leaving issue

3 Ramsay Hamilton; *b* 11 Oct 1829; *d* 1875

4 Arthur Charles; *b* 22 Nov 1831; *d* on board HMS *Dauntless*, 16 Nov 1852

5 Henry Edward; *b* 18 May 1835; Capt 70th Foot; *d* unm 6 June 1876

1 Georgina Christian Mary Anne; *d* 10 Sept 1894, aged 69

The 1st Bt *d* 28 Feb 1861; his est son,

Sir George Ebenezer Wilson Couper, 2nd Bt, KCSI, CB, CIE, HEICS; *b* 29 April 1824; Govr NW Provinces 1877–82, ADC to Sir Henry Lawrence Siege of Lucknow and later to Sir James Outram at the Alumbagh (medal with two clasps); *m* 29 April 1852 Caroline Penelope (*d* 28 Nov 1910), sis of Sir Henry Flower Every, 10th Bt, of Egginton (*qv*), and *d* 5 March 1908, leaving:

1 **Sir Ramsay George Henry Couper, 3rd Bt**, Lt 60th Foot Afghan War 1878–80 (medal with two clasps and bronze star); *b* 1 Nov 1855; *m* 22 Jan 1884 Nora Emma (*d* 1 Jan 1925), dau of Horatio Willson Scott, formerly of Buccleuch Ho, Adelaide Rd, Hampstead, and *d* 20 March 1949, having had issue:

(1) **Sir Guy Couper, 4th Bt**, WW I 1916–18 with AIF; *b* 12 March 1889; *d* 1975

(1) Sybil

(2) Evelyn; *m* 1915 George Edward Jamieson (*d* 4 July 1923), and *d* 16 Nov 1939, leaving issue

2 Victor Arthur (Sir), KCB (1918); *b* 4 April 1859; Maj-Gen Rifle Bde, served Burma 1888–89, NWF India 1897–98 and WW I 1915–18, cmded a Div 1914–18, ret 1919, Col cmdg 1st Bn The Rifle Bde 1927–29, Order of Danilo of Montenegro (2nd Cl); *d* unm 16 May 1938

3 Edward Edmonstone; *b* 15 Dec 1860; Lt-Col 4th Gurka Rifles, served Waziristan 1894–95 and China; *m* 28 June 1899 Daisy Ethel Aylmer, dau of Henry E Rose, of Bourton-on-the-Water, and *d* 3 Nov 1954, leaving issue:

(1) John Victor Hay; *b* 1902; *d* unm

4 James Robert; *b* 24 June 1863; *m* 1897 Jessie (*d* 17 Jan 1922), 2nd dau of John Kissock, of Drummore, Lochrutton, Kirkcudbrightshire, and *d* 7 June 1917, leaving issue:

(1) GEORGE ROBERT CECIL, **5th Bt**

(2) John Every, MBE (1957), Maj REME; *b* 15 Nov 1900; *educ* RNCs Osborne and Dartmouth; *m* 19 April 1928 Katherine Audrey Mary (*d* 1987), dau of William Renfrew Alexander, formerly of Cupar, Fife, and *d* 8 June 1966, leaving issue:

1a +Jonathan Every [Jonathan Couper Esq, 18 Montague Rd, Ealing, London W13]; *b* 26 Feb 1931; *educ* Douai Sch

(3) Jem Ramsay; *b* 14 Nov 1904; *educ* Marlborough; T/Capt 27th Lancers WW II 1941–45; *m* 14 June 1940 *Aileen Jessie [Mrs Jem Couper, Estancia Los Amigos, Santa Eleadora, FCNG, General San Martin, Argentina], dau of Thomas Robert Lamb Abbott, and *d* 1979 leaving issue:

1a +Francis Jem; *b* 14 April 1946; *educ* Marlborough

1a *Caroline Mary [Sra de Enrique Avendano, 6405 30 de Agosto, FCNDFS, Prov de Buenos Aires, Argentina]; *b* 13 Oct 1941; *m* 17 April 1968 *Enrique Avendano, son of Miguel Avendano, of 30 de Agosto, Argentina, and has issue:

1b *Diego; *b* 1970

2b *Enrique Maria; *b* 1977

1b *Cecilia Maria; *b* 16 April 1969

(1) *Doris Helen [Mrs Thomas Jefferies, Hollyville House, Wexford, Ireland]; *m* 8 Aug 1941 *Capt Thomas Charles Jefferies, son of Thomas William Jefferies, of Carrigbyrne, Adamstown, Co Wexford

5 Charles James; *b* 17 Nov 1873; *d* 15 Feb 1881

1 Caroline Georgina Jane Elizabeth; *b* 1 Feb 1854; *m* 6 Sept 1881 Maj-Gen Sir Frederick William Benson, KCB, 17th Lancers (*d* 19 Aug 1916), and *d* 8 Feb 1924

2 Ada Lucy; *b* 2 Nov 1866; *d* unm 14 Nov 1951

3 Maude Madeleine; *b* 1 April 1871; *d* unm 28 Jan 1963

The 4th Bt's cousin,

Sir George Robert Cecil Couper, 5th Bt; *b* 15 Oct 1898; *educ* Uppingham; Lt MGC WW I, Hon Maj 1st Roy Dragoons WW II (despatches); *m* 15 March 1941 Margaret Grace (*d* 1984), dau of Robert George Dashwood Thomas, of Southwick, Kirkcudbrightshire, and *d* 26 May 1975, leaving issue:

1 Sir (ROBERT) NICHOLAS OLIVER COUPER, **6th and present Bt**

1 *Jennifer Susan Amanda (twin); *b* 9 Oct 1945

COURTOWN

Arms: Az. semée of crosses crosslet, three lozenges or. **Crest:** A wyvern, wings displayed vert. **Supporters:** Two stags ppr., collared and chained or, each charged on the shoulder with a lozenge of the last. **Motto:** *Patriae infelici fidelis* ('Faithful to an unhappy country'). **Creations:** B. (I) 19 Sept 1758 (Courtown); E. and V. (I) 12 April 1762, B. (GB) 7 June 1796 (Saltersford).

THE 9TH EARL OF COURTOWN, Viscount Stopford, Baron Courtown, Co Wexford, **Baron Saltersford,** of Saltersford, Co Palatine of Chester (James Patrick Montagu Burgoyne Winthrop Stopford) [The Rt Hon The Earl of Courtown, House of Lords, London SW1A 0PW]; *b* 19 March 1954; *s f* 1975; *educ* Eton, Berkshire Coll of Ag and RAC Cirencester; ARICS, a Ld in Waiting (Govt Whip) 1995–97, Oppn Whip 1997–; *m* 1985 *Elizabeth Dorothy, yr dau of Ian Rodger Dunnett, of Broad Campden, Glos, and has issue:

1 +JAMES RICHARD IAN MONTAGU, *Viscount Stopford*; *b* 30 March 1988

1 *Rosanna Elisabeth Alice; *b* 1986

Lineage: WILLIAM STOPFORD, of Ulneswalton, Lancs; *m* Mary, dau and eventual coheir of Henry ffarington, 2nd s of William ffarington, of Worden, by Margaret, dau and heiress of Edward Broster, of Saltersford, Cheshire, and *d* 1647, having had, with a yr s (William):

JAMES STOPFORD, of Saltersford, Cheshire, later New Hall, Co Meath; Capt Parly Army Ireland, where he bought or was granted large estates at the Restoration; *m* 1st Ellinor (*d* 27 Feb 1660), 4th dau of John Morewood, of the Oaks, Yorks, and had, with a dau:

1 William; *m* Mary, dau of Col Francis Willoughby, and *dvp* 22 May 1683, leaving with other issue:

(1) JAMES, successor to his gf

2 James; *b* 1650; *educ* Trin Coll Dublin; left issue

3 Joseph, Lt-Col in Col Richard Gorges' Regt of Foot; *m* Elizabeth, dau of Godfrey Boate and widow of Richard Brooking, of Totnes, Devon, and *d* by 25 Oct 1707, leaving issue

JAMES STOPFORD *m* 2nd Mary, dau of Rt Hon Sir Robert Forth, by whom he had, with further issue:

1 Emily; *m* 24 March 1701 1st Baron of Newtown-Butler (*see* LANESBOROUGH, E)

2 Dorothy, the 'Countess Doll' of Dean Swift, whose epitaph on her and her husband was entitled 'Doll and Dickey'; *m* 1st 22 Sept 1704 4th Earl of Meath (*qv*; *dsp* 22 Feb 1707); *m* 2nd Dec 1716, as his 2nd w, Lt-Gen Richard Gorges, and *d* 10 April 1729. He *d* 12 April 1728

JAMES STOPFORD *d* 18 March 1685; his gs,

JAMES STOPFORD, of Courtown; MP Co Wexford 1713–21; *m* Frances (*d* 22 May 1721), only dau of Roger Jones and gdau and heiress of Thomas Jones, of Courtown, Co Wexford, and had, with other issue:

1 JAMES, **1st Earl**

2 William, Capt Army; *d* Dec 1760, leaving issue

3 Thomas, a Master in Chancery; *bapt* 12 June 1704; *d* 15 March 1771, leaving a dau Mary

4 Joseph, Capt 2nd Regt of Horse; *m* July 1743 Anne, dau of Knightley Chetwode, and had issue

1 Anne; *m* James Stopford, DD, Bishop of Cloyne

JAMES STOPFORD *d* 9 July 1721; his est surv son,

JAMES STOPFORD, **1st Earl of Courtown,** Co Wexford, so *cr* 12 April 1762, as also VISCOUNT STOPFORD and earlier 19 Sept 1758 BARON COURTOWN, Co Wexford (all I); *b c* 1700; barrister Middle Temple 1719, MP Co Wexford 1721–1727 and Fethard 1727–58; *m* 24 Feb 1726/7 Elizabeth, only dau of Rt Rev Edward Smyth, DD, Bishop of Down and Connor, and had, with other issue:

1 JAMES, **2nd Earl**

2 Edward, Lt-Gen, *b* 1732; *m* Oct 1783 Letitia (*d* 15 Feb 1841), dau of William Blacker, of Carrick Blacker, Co Armagh, and *d* 22 Oct 1794, having had, with four other s:

(1) William Henry STOPFORD later STOPFORD-BLAIR (roy licence 6 May 1842), of Penninghame Ho, Wigton, Col RA; *b* 13 Jan 1788; *m* 3 March 1825 Mira Sophia (*d* 9 July 1830), dau of Lt-Col Robert Bull, CB, and *d* 20 Sept 1868, having had issue:

1a Edward James, of Penninghame Ho, DL; *b* 3 Feb 1826; *m* 22 June 1853 Elizabeth Letitia Morgan (*d* 25 Feb 1906), er dau of Very Rev Hugh Usher Tighe, Dean of Derry, and *dsp* 17 Sept 1875

1a Elizabeth Ellen, of Penninghame; *m* 20 Oct 1847 Edward Heron-Maxwell, DL, of Teviot Bank, Roxburgh. They assumed the additional name of BLAIR. She *d* 28 June 1901, leaving issue (*see* HERON-MAXWELL, Bt)

(1) Jane Letitia; *m* 1809 Lambert Blair, of Courtland, Devon, and *d* 5 April 1871

(2) Elizabeth Catherine; *m* 27 Dec 1815 James Blair, of Penninghame, Co Wigton, and *d* 1886. He *d* 9 Sept 1841

The 1st EARL *d* 12 Jan 1770; his est son,

JAMES STOPFORD, **2nd Earl of Courtown,** KP (1783), PC (I 1775, GB 1784), MP (I Parl) Taghmon 1761–1768, (GB Parl) Gt Bedwyn 1774 and Marlborough 1780–93, Ld of the Bedchamber to the PRINCE OF WALES 1780–84, Treasurer Household 1784–93, *cr* 7 June 1796 BARON SALTERSFORD, of Saltersford, Co Chester (GB); *m* 19 April 1762 Mary (*d* 3 Jan 1810), dau and coheir of Richard Powys, of Hintlesham Hall, Suffolk, and had, with other issue:

1 JAMES GEORGE, **3rd Earl**

2 Edward (Sir), GCB, Lt-Gen; *b* 28 Sept 1766; *d* unm 14 Sept 1837

3 Robert (Sir), Adml of the Red, GCB, GCMG, Govr Greenwich Hosp; *b* 5 Feb 1768; *m* 29 June 1809 Mary (*d* 4 June 1866), dau of Robert Fanshawe, and *d* 25 June 1847, having had, with other issue:

(1) Robert Fanshawe, Adml; *b* 19 Dec 1811; *m* 1st 31 Aug 1843 Emily Anna (*d* 6 Oct 1862), dau of Capt William Wilbraham, RN, and had, with other issue:

1a Robert Wilbraham, V-Adml; *b* 24 June 1844; *m* 23 Sept 1885 Etheldreda (*d* 20 June 1938), dau of Ralph Neville Grenville, of Butleigh Court (*see* BRAYBROOKE, B), and *d* 9 June 1911, leaving issue:

1b Robert Neville, Cdr RN, Order of the Brilliant Jade of China; *b* 4 July 1888; *m* 4 June 1919 (*divorce* 1948) Ursula, dau of Ernest Arthur Ebblewhite, FSA, barrister, of The White Cottage, West Hill Ave, Epsom, and *dsp* 3 Nov 1949

1b Audrey; *b* 14 June 1887; *m* 10 Sept 1913 Rev Canon Charles Hawkins Syndercombe Bower, MA, Rector of Childe Okeford, Dorset, 2nd son of Henry Syndercombe Bower, of Fontwell Parva, Dorset, and *d* 28 Nov 1928, leaving issue. He *d* 18 March 1961

2a Arthur Bouverie, Col RA, AA-Gen RA India 1895; *b* 21 Oct 1845; *m* 7 Sept 1881 Evelyn Fanny, dau of Lt-Gen George Samuel Montgomery, CSI, and *dsp* 10 June 1902

3a Frederick George, V-Adml; *b* 10 May 1852; *m* 28 Dec 1889 Maria Mary (*d* 1 Feb 1915), est dau of Rev Thomas Frederick Bigg, Rector St Andrew, Deal, and *d* 18 Jan 1928, having had, with two other s and a dau:

1b Robert Edward Wilbraham; *b* 24 May 1897; *m* 3 Aug 1925 Alicia Ellen Saunders (*d* 27 Nov 1967), and *d* 1982, having had issue:

1c *Mona Alicia [Mrs Mona Stopford, RR3, Tottenham, Ontario L0G 1W0, Canada]; *b* 2 July 1926; resumed maiden name; *m* 19– (*divorce* 19–) — Anderson, and has issue:

1d *Robert Edward; *b* 1952

2d *Alec; *b* 1954

1d *Susan Jean; *b* 1956 (took name STOPFORD by court order)

2d *Ellen Pegeen; *b* 1960 (took name STOPFORD by court order)

2c Emily Wilbraham; *b* 9 March 1894; *m* 1st 6 July 1915 Lt-Cdr J W Pugh, RN, son of Cdr H J M Pugh, RN; *m* 2nd James William Livingston

4a Francis James, barrister, late Lt 52nd Regt; *b* 6 July 1857; *m* 6 June 1894 Catherine Mary Howard, 2nd dau of Charles George Tripp, of Orari Gorge, Canterbury, NZ, and *d* 25 Aug 1928

1a Mary Louisa; *m* 12 Sept 1882 Rev William Ulyat, late Vicar of Freeland. He *d* 17 Jan 1929

2a Eleanor Anna; *m* 1897 Leonard de Carteret Malet, and *d* 3 Sept 1943. He *d* 10 June 1938

(1) (cont.) Adml Robert Stopford *m* 2nd 1 June 1865 Lucy Hester (*d* 10 Dec 1891), 4th dau of Adml Sir Phipps Hornby, GCB, and *d* 4 Jan 1891

(2) James John, V-Adml; *b* 17 April 1817; *m* 21 Aug 1862 Fanny (*m* 2nd 23 April 1873 Rev T G Luzard), 3rd dau of Lt-Col Gubbins, CB, and *d* 12 May 1868

(1) Christiana Fanshawe; *m* 30 April 1846 Rev William Frederick Douglas, 3rd son of Lt-Col Sir Howard Douglas, Bt, and *d* 3 Oct 1855

(2) Henrietta Maria; *m* 1st 21 Sept 1841 Lord Henry Russell, RN (*see* BEDFORD, D); *m* 2nd 7 Dec 1853 Col Cecil William Forester, and *d* 4 Feb 1869

(3) Charlotte Anne; *m* 16 July 1861 Very Rev Robert Gregory, Dean St Paul's, and *d* 19 March 1904, leaving issue. He *d* 2 Aug 1911

4 Richard Bruce (Rev), Chaplain to HM QUEEN VICTORIA, Canon Windsor, Preb Hereford; *b* 2 March 1774; *m* 10 Nov 1800 Hon Eleanor Powys (*d* 10 Dec 1854), est dau of 1st Baron Lilford (see 1970 edn), and *d* 12 Dec 1844, having had, with other issue:

(1) Charles (Rev), Rector Barton-Seagrave; *b* 19 Jan 1805; *m* 2 Sept 1845 Maria Charlotte (*d* 1894), dau of Rev J Johnson, and *d* 10 March 1864, having had, with a dau (Alice Mary, *d* unm 3 April 1903):

1a Arthur Charles; *b* 2 July 1846; *m* 19 Dec 1872 Catharine Ann (*d* 2 Sept 1925), widow of C Hendy and dau of Charles Godfrey, and *d* 11 May 1895, leaving issue:

1b Hilda Frances Marguerite; *b* 20 Aug 1874; *m* 2 Aug 1900 Arthur Alison Barnard, barrister, son of Samuel Barnard, JP, MLC, St Lucia, W Indies, and *d* 21 Aug 1937, leaving issue

(2) William Bruce STOPFORD SACKVILLE, of Drayton Ho, Thrapston, Northants, JP and DL, High Sheriff 1850; *b* 1 April 1806; *m* 20 June 1837 Caroline Harriet Sackville (*d* 16 Jan 1908), dau of Hon George Germain, and niece and heir of 5th and last Duke of Dorset (*see* SACKVILLE, B). They

added by roy licence 26 March 1870 name and arms of SACKVILLE. He *d* 29 May 1872, leaving, with other issue:

1a Sackville George, of Drayton Ho, DL, JP, CA, chm: CC Northants and QS, MP N Northants 1867–80 and 1900–06, Hon Col 3rd Bn Northants Regt; *b* 19 March 1840; *educ* Ch Ch Oxford (MA); *m* 4 Feb 1875 Edith Frances (*d* 15 Dec 1905), only child of William Rashleigh, of Menabilly, Cornwall, by Caroline, dau of 11th Lord Blantyre (*see* 1900 edn), and *dsp* 6 Oct 1926

2a Lionel Richard, Brevet Col, cmdg 4th Bn Rifle Bde; *b* 4 Jan 1845; *m* 6 Jan 1887 Constance Evelyn (*d* 20 Dec 1945), dau of Maj George Gosling and *d* 30 July 1906, leaving:

1b Lionel Charles, DSO (1915), Capt and Brevet Maj 4th Bn Rifle Bde WW I (despatches, brevet, Croix de Guerre avec Palmes); *b* 30 April 1891; *d* 31 Dec 1920

2b Geoffrey William, Sub-Lt RN; *b* 22 May 1893; *das* 21 May 1915 of wounds recd Gallipoli

3b Nigel Victor, CBE (1963, OBE 1945), TD (1944), DL (1965), JP, CA Northants, Lt 14th/20th Hus, Lt-Col Northants Yeo, Hon Col 1953, served WW II (despatches) as Col RAC; *b* 27 Jan 1901; *educ* Repton; *m* 1st 17 July 1929 (*divorce* 1943) Beatrix Helen Constance (*d* 1990), dau of Col Hercules Arthur Pakenham, CMG, late Gren Gds, of Langford Lodge, Co Antrim (*see* LONGFORD, E), and had issue:

1c +Lionel Geoffrey [Lionel Stopford Sackville Esq, Drayton House, Lowick, Kettering, Northants N14 3BB]; *b* 4 Nov 1932; *educ* Eton; CA (1959); late Lt Northants Yeo (TA), formerly Lt 14th/20th Hus, served in Libya, chm Beralt Tin & Wolfram 1973, dir Charter Consolidated Ltd, chm Cape Asbestos Co, Union Jack Oil plc, Lowick Manor Farms Ltd, J Goedhuis & Co Ltd; dir Mercury World Mining Trust plc, Dartmoor Investment Tst plc, Pantheon Int Participations plc; *m* 1st 27 April 1960 Susan Jenkin, only dau of Jenkin Coles, of The Abbey, Knaresborough, Yorks, and has had:

1d +Charles Lionel; *b* 14 Feb 1961; *m* 1992 *Shona, yst dau of Donald McKinney, CBE, of Nassau, Bahamas, and has issue:

1e +Luke Mordaunt; *b* 3 June 1993

1e *Ela Lucinda; *b* 8 April 1995

2d +Thomas Nigel; *b* 14 Aug 1968

1d Lucinda Mary; *b* 15 Oct 1963; *k* in a motor accident 1992

1c (cont.) Lionel Stopford Sackville *m* 2nd 1980 Hon (Mary) Teresa Pearson, er dau of 3rd Viscount Cowdray, TD (*qv*), and by her has:

2d *Camilla Anne; *b* 1981

1c (cont.) Lionel Stopford Sackville *m* 3rd 12 May 1997 *Mary Stoddart

1c *Venetia Mary [Mrs Venetia Chetwynd Talbot, 50 Vera Rd, London SW6]; *b* 10 May 1930; *m* 19 April 1952 (*divorce* 1968) Maj Benjamin Robert Chetwynd Talbot, TD and bar, only son of Maj Benjamin Chetwynd Talbot, TD, of Carlbury Hall, Piercebridge, Co Durham, and has issue:

1d *Benjamin Simon Robert; *b* 28 Oct 1956

1d *Victoria Mary; *b* 30 Aug 1958

3b (cont.) Col Nigel Stopford-Sackville *m* 2nd 14 Nov 1946 *Lilah Mary [Mrs Nigel Stopford-Sackville, The Weirs, Chilton Foliat, Hungerford, Berks], formerly w of George Seton Wills (*see* WILLS, Bt, of Hazlewood) and yst dau of Capt Percy Richard Hare (*see* LISTOWEL, E)

1b Elinor Beryl; *b* 7 Feb 1888

2b Diana Mary; *b* 21 March 1889; *d* unm 20 Dec 1971

3a Alexander William; *b* 31 Aug 1846; *m* 24 Jan 1903 Effie Redesdale (*m* 2nd 15 Jan 1927 Frederick Anthony White, of Trevor Ho, Belgrave Place, SW1, and *d* 1932), dau of John Collinson James, and *d* 25 Feb 1925, leaving issue:

1b Vere Elizabeth; *b* 18 Feb 1906; *d* 1968

4a Sydney Robert; *b* 22 Jan 1850; *m* 23 Aug 1883 Janet (*d* 12 Feb 1929), dau of John Shields, of Perth, and *d* in California, 6 Jan 1888, leaving, with other issue:

1b Edward Rupert Sydney; *b* 30 April 1887; *d* unm 9 Dec 1943

1a Fanny Louisa; *m* 3 Jan 1877 Rt Rev Hon Augustus Legge, Bp Lichfield, son of 4th Earl of Dartmouth (*qv*), and *d* 23 Dec 1911, leaving issue

2a Georgina Mary; *m* 13 May 1869 Hon Sir Edward Peirson Thesiger, KCB, yst son of 1st Baron Chelmsford (*see* CHELMSFORD, V), and *d* 22 Dec 1906, leaving issue

3a Margaret Elizabeth; *m* 12 Jan 1882 William Edmund Wood Collins, late of Langley Place, Slough, and had issue

4a Eleanor Mary Agnes; *m* 23 Sept 1879 Lionel John William Fletcher, DL, of Elmscroft, Maidstone, 4th son of Maj-Gen Edward C Fletcher, DL, of Kenward, Kent, and *d* 10 Dec 1943, leaving issue. He *d* 4 Feb 1911

5a Beatrice Evelyn; *m* 3 Aug 1874 Sir Harry Samuel Cumming Clarke Jervoise, 5th Bt, and *d* 4 July 1943, leaving issue. He *d* 28 May 1911

6a Grace; *m* 30 Aug 1881 5th Baron Norton (*qv*), and *d* 16 Feb 1944, leaving issue

(3) James Sydney; *b* 11 April 1808; *m* 1st 16 Sept 1847 Frances (*dsp* 20 Sept 1856), yst dau of Edward Loyd, banker, of Coombe Ho, Surrey; *m* 2nd 10 March 1868 Katherine Mary (*d* 1 May 1884), est dau of Sir Thomas Wathen Waller, 2nd Bt (*qv*), and *d* 8 July 1885, having by her had, with other issue:

1a George Waller, Capt 4th Bn Beds Regt WW I, JP, Mayor Daventry 1928 and 1929; *b* 26 May 1870; *m* 7 Dec 1911 his cousin Alice Emily (*d* 21 March 1939), dau of Adml Sir William Robert Kennedy, GCB (*see* AILSA, M), and *dsp* 14 March 1959

2a Philip James, Capt RN; *b* 14 Jan 1872; *m* 18 Nov 1902 Margaret Louise (*d* 1958), yst dau of Maj Frederick Napleton Dew, DL, JP, late 88th Regt, Connaught Rangers, and *dsp* 22 April 1952

3a Heneage Frank, Maj RFA; *b* 14 July 1877; *m* 31 Oct 1908 Margaret Amelia (*d* 22 Aug 1960), dau of Edward Briggs Kennedy, of Deanyers, Alton, Hants (*see* AILSA, M), and was *ka* 15 Sept 1916, leaving, with other issue:

1b James Coverley, OBE (1940), Capt RN WW II; *b* 27 Sept 1909; *m* 24 July 1936 Katherine Sheila (*d* 1986), dau of Capt G C S MacLeod, Black Watch, and *d* 1985, leaving:

1c +Robert Heneage [Robert Stopford Esq, Cool Bank Cottage, Winstone, Cirencester, Glos]; *b* 11 March 1945; *educ* Wellington

2c +Christopher George; *b* 29 Aug 1947

1c *Serena Margaret [Mrs Christopher Holmes, Allergarth, Burswell Villas, Hexham, Northumberland]; *b* 5 April 1939; *m* 24 Oct 1964 *F/Lt Christopher H M Holmes, RAF, est son of W/Cdr K E M Holmes, RAF, of Rochesters, Great Leighs, Essex, and has issue:

1d *Andrew David; *b* 11 Sept 1965

2d *Richard Mark; *b* 20 July 1967

1d *Bridget Constantia; *b* 20 July 1967

2b Edward Kennedy, CB (1955), Under-Sec War Office 1954–64 and MOD 1964–71; Ib 10 Oct 1911; *educ* Winchester and New Coll Oxford (BA 1933); *m* 6 Sept 1952 Patricia Iona Mary (*d* 1989), widow of Duncan George Stewart, CMG, and dau of W Howard Carrick, and *d* 6 Nov 1983, leaving issue:

1c +Michael John; *b* 22 June 1953; *educ* Radley

4a Wyndham Horace, Capt RMLI; *b* 1 June 1878; *m* 4 June 1903 Dorothy Eleanor (*m* 2nd 18 June 1906 Col Frank Truscott Phillips, RMLI (*d* 20 Jan 1936), son of Col George Hutchinson Phillips, and *d* June 1967), est dau of Rev Wilfrid Nevill Lesson, of Hove, and *d* 26 Dec 1903, leaving issue:

1b Wyndham Horace; *b* postumously 15 Aug 1904; *m* 1st 7 July 1928 May (*d* Aug 1967), dau of Col John White Craig, of Manila; *m* 2nd 22 Feb 1968 *Charlotte, dau of Rev James Graham Clark, of Barrhead, Scotland, and *d* 1984, having by 1st w had issue:

1c +Neville Craig; *b* 2 July 1932; *m* 9 Feb 1963 *(Helen) Alison, 2nd dau of William Leslie Baty, of Cheviot View, Ponteland, Northumberland, and has issue:

1d +Wyndham Leslie; *b* 17 Sept 1965

2d +Angus Craig; *b* 26 May 1967

2c +Craig Leeson [Mr Craig Stopford, Marbridge Foundation, Manchaca, Texas, USA]; *b* 17 April 1939

1c *Ann; *b* 4 July 1935; *m* 20 Feb 1959 *Michael William Frewen Jenkin, Guardian Insur Co of Canada, Toronto, 3rd son of Charles Oswald Frewen Jenkin, and has issue:

1d *Andrew Wyndham; *b* 12 Dec 1960

2d *Richard Frewen; *b* 26 Oct 1962

1a Mabel Catherine; *m* 17 Oct 1912 Rev Wathen Henry Waller, Vicar of St George, Tombland, Norwich 1921–27, only son of Rev Adolphus Waller (*see* WALLER, Bt), and *dsp* 23 Sept 1952

(4) Edward, Capt RN; *b* 20 Aug 1809; *m* 6 Aug 1840 Julia Maria (*d* 8 Aug 1924, aged 105), est dau of Capt William Wilbraham, RN, and *d* 14 Oct 1895, leaving issue:

1a Henry Edward, Lt-Col late 36th Regt; *b* 13 Nov 1841; *m* 25 Oct 1882 Constance Maria (*d* Jan 1930), dau of Montolieu Hammersley, and *dsp* 26 Dec 1895

2a Grosvenor, Cdr RN; *b* 15 Nov 1845; *m* 9 June 1874 Sara (*d* 12 Aug 1903), only child of John Palmer Palmer, of Physgill Ho, and *dsp* 14 Nov 1875

1a Edith Louisa; *m* 11 June 1868 Adml Sir William Robert Kennedy, GCB, and *d* 28 Nov 1936, leaving issue (*see* AILSA, M)

(5) Robert; *b* 16 April 1813; *m* 11 Aug 1853 Matilda Caroline (*d* 25 Dec 1907), 2nd dau of Gen Birch Reynardson, of Holywell Hall, Lincs, and *d* 25 May 1878, having had issue:

1a Horace Robert, Lt-Col Coldstream Gds; *b* 29 Oct 1855; *m* 19 May 1886 Marguerite Louisa Greathed (*d* 18 June 1944), 3rd dau of Benjamin George MacDowell, MD, of Merrion Sq, Dublin, and was *ka* at Modder River, S Africa, 28 Nov 1899, leaving issue:

1b Robert Maurice, DSC (1918), Cdr RN, served WW I (despatches) and WW II; *b* 16 July 1890; *m* 11 Feb 1920 Elsie Helen (*d* 30 Nov 1967), dau of Capt Francis William Lawson, Connaught Rangers, and *d* 22 Nov 1978, leaving issue:

1c +Michael Robert Horace [Major Michael Stopford, The Lodge, Tarrant Monkton, Blandford Forum, Dorset DT11 8RU], Maj (ret) The Queen's Roy Surrey Regt, served WW II in Rifle Bde; *b* 27 April 1921; *educ* The Oratory Sch; *m* 3 Sept 1945 *Megan, dau of Arthur Reyner Williams, and has had issue:

1d +Robert Michael Hastings; *b* 2 Oct 1949; *educ* Downside; *m* 7 Aug 1st 1976 Jennifer, dau of Maj J H Walmesley-Cotham; *m* 2nd 1984 *Alexandra E, dau of Douglas G Hartley, and has issue:

1e +Joshua Gordon; *b* 1984

2e +Benjamin Charles; *b* 1986

1e *Zoë Megan Patience; *b* 1989

2d Charles Michael Reyner, Capt 9th/12th Roy Lancers; *b* 14 Oct 1950; *educ* Downside, and RMA Sandhurst; *m* 1979 *J Clare [Mrs J Harris, 50 Barclay Rd, London SW6] (who *m* 2nd 1986 Jonathan J Harris), yst dau of M H J Villeneuve, of Byway Ho, Fordwich, Kent, and *d* 1980 as the result of a flying accident

1d *Laura Cecilia Mary; *b* 17 Nov 1947; *m* 22 Aug 1969 *Capt Kenneth Andres Courtenay, RN, of Henstridge, Somerset, est son of H A Courtenay, of Butlers Manor, Northall, Beds, and has issue:

1e *Edward Michael Andres; *b* 23 Aug 1970

1e *Tamsin Mary Andres; *b* 22 July 1972

2d *Teresa Megan Marguerite [Mrs Anton Simon, 8 Chepstow Villas, London W11 2RB]; *b* 28 July 1955; *m* 1st 25 Jan 1975 Nigel A S Healey, son of Cdr A J T Healey, of Southampton; *m* 2nd 1984 *Anton D Simon, 2nd son of Arthur G Simon, of Portsmouth, and has had issue:

1e *Charles Stephen; *b* 1987

2e Harry Eugene; *b* and *d* 1991

3e *Eugene Michael; *b* 1992

2c +Stephen Robert Anthony, CB (1988), MBE (1971) [Maj-Gen Stephen Stopford CB MBE, c/o Child & Co, 1 Fleet St, London EC4] Maj-Gen late The Roy Scots Greys; *b* 1 April 1934; *educ* Downside, Millfield, and RMA Sandhurst; *m* 8 Feb 1963 *Vanessa Marianna, dau of Theodore Baron, of 18, Rex Place, South St, W1

1c *Rosemary (Rosa) Dolores; *b* 9 Sept 1926; *m* 19 April 1963 *John Walter Mills, TD, High Sheriff Warwicks 1959–60, son of George Tom Mills, of Park House, Park Hill, Kenilworth, Warwicks, and Mrs G M Mills, OBE, JP

1b Norah Grace; *b* 14 July 1889; *m* 18 July 1911 Maj Edward Spencer Dickin, late 2nd Dragoon Gds, 3rd son of Capt Thomas Acherley Massy Dickin, of Loppington Ho, Salop, and *d* 27 Oct 1966, leaving issue. He *d* 28 Oct 1960

1a Evelyn Emma; *b* 16 July 1858; *m* 12 Nov 1889 Walter Copland Perry (*d* Dec 1911), barrister, and had issue:

1b Evelyn Walter Copland, RFC; *b* 4 Dec 1890; *d* 16 Aug 1914, the first British officer *k* in France in WW I

(1) Eleanor Elizabeth; *m* 26 July 1832 Ambrose Isted, of Ecton, and *dsp* 12 Oct 1851. He *d* 13 May 1881

(2) Harriet Jane; *m* 15 Oct 1850 Bartholomew Tunnard, Capt 27th Regt, and *d* 13 Dec 1902, leaving issue. He *d* 30 June 1875

The 2nd EARL *d* 30 March 1810; his est son,

JAMES GEORGE STOPFORD, **3rd Earl of Courtown**, KP (1821), PC (1793); *b* 15 Aug 1765; MP (Tory) Gt Bedwyn 1790–96 and 1806–07, Linlithgow Burghs 1796–1802, Dumfries Burghs 1803–06 and Marlborough 1807–10, Treas Household 1793–1806 and 1807–12; *m* 29 Jan 1791 Lady Mary Scott (*d* 21 April 1823), est dau of 3rd Duke of Buccleuch (*see* BUCCLEUCH and QUEENSBERRY, D), and had, with other issue:

1 JAMES THOMAS, **4th Earl**

2 Edward, Lt-Col Scots Fus Gds; *b* 11 June 1795; *m* 5 July 1830 Horatia Charlotte (*d* 9 Feb 1838), widow of Richard Tibbits, of Barton-Seagrave, and only dau of Thomas Lockwood, and *d* 5 July 1840, leaving issue:

(1) Frederick Manners (Rev), MA Oxford, Hon Chaplain to TM EDWARD VII 1901–10 and GEORGE V 1910–12, Chaplain-in-ordinary to HM QUEEN VICTORIA, Rector of Tichmarsh Northants 1861–1912; *b* 1 Nov 1831; *m* 1st 8 June 1857 Florence Augusta (*d* 18 Aug 1876), yr dau of Charles Alexander Saunders, of Westbourne Lodge, and had, with other issue:

1a Algernon Edward; *b* 27 June 1858; *m* 23 Aug 1887 Emma Lucy (*d* 1941), dau of Arthur Francis William Saunders, and *d* 14 Sept 1911, having had, with other issue:

1b Grosvenor Francis (Rev), DACG 1940–44, Rector of Fretherne, Glos 1945–49, served WW I 1915–20 (wounded); *b* 15 Dec 1889; *m* 8 Oct 1917 Rachel Norman, dau of Rev Anthony Reginald Martin, of Coolong Ave, Vaucluse, NSW, and *dsp* 1 March 1949

1b Eveleen Emma; *b* 8 Aug 1891

2a Albert Henry; *b* 16 May 1860

3a Francis Powys; *b* 6 Dec 1861; *m* 11 Dec 1894 Kathleen Edith (*d* 8 Dec 1956), dau of Henry James Colley Gompertz, of Madras, and *d* 21 Jan 1935, leaving issue:

1b Mary Horatia, BA (Hist Hons); *b* 28 Jan 1896; *m* 1 Feb 1933 Reginald Cuthbert Stockdale Ellison, MA, FRSA, barrister, yr son of J C Ellison, and had issue

2b Eveleen Emily, Headmistress of St Elphin's Sch 1941–58; *b* 23 Feb 1897; *educ* St Hugh's Coll Oxford (MA); *d* unm 11 Sept 1971

3b Kathleen Stewart; *b* 27 April 1900

4b Eleanor Montagu; *b* 27 April 1900

4a Gerald Frederick; *b* 2 March 1870

5a Walter Montague; *b* 1874; *m* 1919 Mary Josephine, dau of Patrick O'Neill, of Enniscorthy, Co Wexford, and *d* 1933, leaving issue:

1b +Lionel Frederick John [Lionel Stopford Esq, 153 Fraser St, Kenilworth, Johannesburg 2190, S Africa], served WW II 1944–45 in Welsh Gds; *b* 1921; *m* 1950 (*divorce* 1960) Violet Eira, dau of Harold Dart, of Cefn, Murch Rd, Dinas Powis, Glam, and has issue:

1c +John Martin; *b* 25 June 1958

1c *Linda Mary; *b* 1951

2c *Wendy Margaret; *b* 1953

1a Mary Kathleen; *m* 7 Oct 1890 Rev William Percy Powys (*see* 1970 edn LILFORD, B), and *d* 5 July 1941. He *d* 19 Jan 1918

2a Eveleen Frances; *m* 23 April 1903 Rev Wentworth Watson (*see* MONSON, B), and *dsp* 11 March 1953. He *d* 5 July 1925

(1) (cont.) The Rev Frederick Stopford *m* 2nd 7 Nov 1878 Caroline Louisa (*d* 19 March 1924), dau of Very Rev Augustus Page Saunders, DD, Dean of Peterborough, and *d* 24 Feb 1912

(2) Walter James, CB, Capt 52nd LI, a Gentleman Usher of the Privy Chamber to TM QUEEN VICTORIA and EDWARD VII, Inspr-Gen Mil Prison Dept, Commr of Prisons; *b* 4 July 1833; *m* 7 Oct 1863 his cousin Annette Jane (*d* 17 Dec 1921), 3rd dau of Adml Hon Sir Montagu Stopford, KCB (*see* below), and *d* 14 June 1908, leaving, with other issue:

1a Edward Montagu; *b* 29 Jan 1872; *m* 3 June 1903 Lydia, widow of Lt-Col Wilbraham Evelyn Morley, late RMLI, and *dsp* 27 March 1911

2a Cyril Montagu, Capt late Queen's Westminster Rifles, late Page of Honour to HM QUEEN VICTORIA; *b* 4 June 1874; *d* 18 June 1936

1a Horatia Winifred; *m* 12 Jan 1898 Edward Constable Curtis, son of Capt Constable Curtis, 12th Lancers, by his w Henrietta Mary Anne, dau of Charles Berwick Curtis (*see* CURTIS, Bt), and *d* 10 March 1914, leaving issue. He *d* 13 Feb 1947

2a Louise (for whom HRH PRINCESS LOUISE, DUCHESS OF ARGYLL, stood sponsor); *d* unm 15 Oct 1935

3a Nina; *d* unm 10 Oct 1952

(1) Horatia Charlotte Frances, VA, Maid of Honour 1857–77, and one of the Bedchamber Women-in-Ordinary to QUEEN VICTORIA 1877–1901; *d* 6 Feb 1920

3 Montagu (Sir), KCB, Adml; *b* 11 Nov 1798; *m* 1st 25 Aug 1827 Cordelia Winifreda (*d* 4 Sept 1851), dau of Maj-Gen Sir George Whitmore, and had, with other issue:

(1) George Montagu, Maj RE, Kt of the Order of Medjidie; *b* 23 June 1828; *m* 1 June 1854 Caroline Mary (*d* 18 May 1915), dau of FM Sir John Fox Burgoyne, 1st Bt, GCB, and *d* 7 Aug 1860, having had, with other issue:

1a Charlotte Mary Leycester; *m* 1st 23 Feb 1881 John Arden Birch, son of John William Birch, FRGS, of Rickmansworth Park, Herts, and had issue. He *d* 1896. She *m* 2nd 19 Jan 1905 9th Viscount Barrington (*see* 1970 edn) and *d* 22 Oct 1935. He *d* 12 Sept 1933

2a Caroline Anne Kate; *m* 25 Oct 1882 William Morton Philips, of Heybridge, Staffs, and *d* 14 July 1955, leaving issue. He *d* 2 June 1940

(1) Mary Cordelia; *m* 7 Oct 1856 Gen Sir John Miller Adye, GCB, and *d* 14 Feb 1912, leaving issue. He *d* 28 Aug 1900

(2) Emily Winifreda; *m* 6 Jan 1857 Lt-Col A J Nixon, Rifle Bde, and *d* 1891, leaving issue. He *d* 31 March 1875

(3) Annette Jane; *m* 7 Oct 1863 her cousin Capt Walter James Stopford, CB, and *d* 17 Dec 1921, leaving issue (*see* above)

3 (cont.) The Hon Sir Montagu Stopford *m* 2nd 29 Sept 1853 Lucy (*d* 3 Dec 1883), yst dau of John Cay, of N Charlton, and *d* 10 Nov 1864, having by her had, with other issue:

(2) Lionel Arthur Montagu (Sir), KCVO (1919), CB (1916), DL (Kent), Col and Hon Maj-Gen late Derby Regt and Irish Gds, Cmdt RMC Sandhurst 1911–14, and again 1916–19, Bde Cdr 1914–16, DA and QMG 1916, served Egypt 1882 (medal, bronze star), Sikkim Expdn 1888 (medal with clasp), and WW I 1915–19 (despatches); *b* 10 May 1860; *m* 21 July 1891 Mabel Georgina Emily (*d* 28 Sept 1951), only child of George Alexander Mackenzie, of Applecross, Ross-shire, and *d* 13 Sept 1942, leaving, with other issue:

1a Montagu George North (Sir), GCB (1948, KCB 1947, CB 1942), KBE (1944), DSO (1940), MC (1917), DL (Oxon 1962), Gen late The Rifle Bde, served WW I (despatches), and WW II, cmdg 17 Inf Bde BEF 1939–40 (despatches), cmdg 56 (London) Div 1940–41, Cmdt Staff Coll 1941–42, cmdg 12 Corps 1942–43, cmdg 33 Indian Corps Burma 1943–45 (despatches), cmdg 12th Army and Burma Cmd 1945–46, C-in-C Allied Forces Netherlands E Indies 1946, C-in-C Allied Land Forces S E Asia 1946–47, GOC-in-C N Cmd 1947049, ADC Gen to HM GEORGE VI 1947–49, ret 1949, v-pres Army Cadet Force Assoc, Cdr US Legion of Merit 1945; *b* 16 Nov 1892; *educ* Wellington and RMC; *m* 12 April 1921 Dorothy (*d* 4 Oct 1982 aged 90), dau of Lt-Col Henry Foulkes Deare, late 8th Hus, and *dsp* 10 March 1971

2a Lionel Montagu Phipps, Capt Seaforth Highrs WW I, Sec Kent TAA; *b* 24 Sept 1897; *educ* Wellington; *m* 20 Feb 1934 Sheila Frances, MBE (*d* 1978), dau of Gen Sir Cecil Francis Romer, GCB, KBE, CMG, of The Knoll, Ightham, Kent (*see* 1939 edn ROMER, B) and *d* 1985, leaving issue:

1b +Robert Cecil Montagu [Robert Stopford Esq, Kintail, Hobhole Bank, Old Leake, Boston, Lincs PE22 9RX]; *b* 16 Nov 1935; *educ* Radley; *m* 15 March 1958 *Elizabeth Ann, dau of Alexander Krott, of Terskaya, Russia, and has issue:

1c +Andrew Alexander Montagu [Andrew Stopford Esq, Zakres, Situ da Ribeira, S João da Boa Vista, 3420 Tabua, Portugal]; *b* 20 Nov 1959

1c *Sara Elizabeth Fiona [Miss Sara Stopford, 2A Radbourne Ave, off Little Ealing Lane, London W5 4XD]; *b* 2 June 1967

(4) Emily Evelyn Lucy; *m* 8 Feb 1877 Lt-Gen Sir Edwin Markham, KCB, RA, and *d* 16 Feb 1919, leaving issue. He *d* 1 April 1918

(5) Dora; *m* 6 Oct 1885 Lt-Col Richard Henry Atkinson, Border Regt, and *d* 31 May 1922, leaving issue. He *d* 24 Jan 1905

1 Jane; *m* 11 April 1833 Rev Abel John Ram, of Clonattin, Co Wexford, Rector Rolleston, Staffs, Hon Canon Rochester, and *d* 28 Dec 1873, leaving issue. He *d* 18 Aug 1883

The 3rd EARL *d* 15 June 1835; his est son,

JAMES THOMAS STOPFORD, **4th Earl of Courtown**; *b* 27 March 1794; MP (Tory) Co Wexford 1820–30; *m* 1st 4 July 1822 his cousin Lady Charlotte Albinia Montagu Scott (*d* 29 Feb 1828), dau of 4th Duke of Buccleuch (*see* BUCCLEUCH and QUEENSBERRY, D), and had, with other issue:

1 JAMES GEORGE HENRY, **5th Earl**

The **4th Earl** *m* 2nd 29 Oct 1850 Dora (*d* 10 Dec 1859), dau of Rt Hon Edward Pennefather, Ch Justice Queen's Bench Ireland, and by her had issue:

2 John Montagu, Lt Gren Gds, late 52nd Foot; *b* 15 April 1853; *m* 5 May 1881 Winifred Ellen (Lady-in-Waiting to PRINCESS CHRISTIAN 1886–89) (who *m* 2nd 29 July 1889 5th Earl of Arran, KP (*qv*), and *d* 12 Nov 1921), dau of John Reilly, of St Bridgid's, Co Dublin, by his w Hon Augusta Sugden, dau of 1st Baron St Leonards (*see* 1970 edn), and *d* 22 Oct 1885, leaving issue:

(1) Dora Claire; *b* 4 Sept 1883; *m* 20 June 1910 Sir Dougal Orme Malcolm, KCMG, formerly of the Colonial Office, yr son of William Rolle Malcolm, of Walton Manor, Surrey, and *d* 11 Nov 1920. He *d* 30 Aug 1955

3 Frederick William (Sir), KCB, KCMG, KCVO, Lt-Gen, Maj Gren Gds, Lt Tower London 1912–14 and 1915–17 (ret 1920), 5th Cl Medjidie, served Egypt, Sudan, Ashanti, S Africa and WW I, Page of Honour to QUEEN VICTORIA 1866–70; *b* 22 Feb 1854; d unm 4 May 1929

4 Walter George, R-Adml, ADC to HM EDWARD VII 1906–07; *b* 18 Sept 1855; *m* 11 Jan 1893 Florence Mary (*d* 12 Oct 1950), dau of Hon Loran E Baker, of Beacon Ho, Yarmouth, Nova Scotia, MLC, and *d* 18 Dec 1918, leaving issue:

(1) Walter John, MC, Lt-Col RA WW I (despatches, Cdr Order Nile) and WW II 1939–42 (despatches) as GSO attd Bomber Cmd RAF; *b* 25 July 1897; *educ* Winchester; *m* 10 Oct 1931 *Baroness Renira, dau of Adml Sir Rudolf Walter Bentinck, KCB, KCMG (*see* PORTLAND, E), and *d* 198–

(2) Frederick Victor, CBE (1952), R-Adml (E) (ret 1952), served WW I and WW II, ADC to HM GEORGE VI 1949–50; *b* 6 July 1900; *m* 10 April 1924 *Mary Guise [Mrs Frederick Stopford, Varndean House, St Leonards, Ringwood, Hants], only dau of Capt Frederick Charles Ulick Vernon Wentworth, CB, RN (*see* GUISE, Bt), of Black Heath, Saxmundham, Suffolk, and *d* 19 Jan 1982, leaving issue:

1a +John Walter [John Stopford Esq, 10 Douglas Rd, Amberley, N Canterbury, S Island, New Zealand]; *b* 7 March 1926; Capt (ret) Roy Canadian

Armoured Corps; *m* 1st 18 June 1960 Barbara Jean (*d* 19–), only dau of Maj W J McHaffie, of Donshuan, Aberlour-on-Spey, Banffshire; *m* 2nd 19– *— and by his 1st w has:

1b +Michael John; *b* 12 March 1966

1b *Susan Caroline; *b* 1961

2b *Jennifer Claire; *b* 1965

2a +Robin Frederick [Robin Stopford Esq, 4 Park Homer Rd, Colehill, Wimborne, Dorset BH21 2SP]; *b* 9 Nov 1929; *m* 1960 Patricia Ann (*d* 18 Dec 1997), er dau of Lt-Col Leo Dominic Gleeson, DSO, and has issue:

1b +Jonathan Paul Michael; *b* 1964

1b *Sarah Frances Ann; *b* 1969

3a +Timothy Patrick [Timothy Stopford Esq, 17 Allington Dve, Strood, Rochester, Kent]; *b* 4 Dec 1935; *educ* Sherborne; Lt-Cdr (SCC) RNR, RMR 1953–54; author *Admiralty Ship's Badges 1919–94*

1a *Catherine Jill [Mrs Garry Oman, 1 Appledale Rd, Islington, Ontario, Canada]; *b* 25 Sept 1939; *m* 11 March 1961 *Capt Garry Joseph Oman, CD, RCNR, and has issue:

1b *Christopher David; *b* 1966

1b *Catherine Mary; *b* 5 Aug 1964

2b *Elizabeth Frances Anne; *b* 1972

(1) Dora Mary Loraine; *m* 1 July 1922 Maj-Gen Francis Lothian Nicholson, CB, DSO, MC, son of Gen Sir Lothian Nicholson, KCB, and *d* 8 Oct 1923. He *d* 18 July 1953

The 4th EARL *d* 20 Nov 1858; his est son,

JAMES GEORGE HENRY STOPFORD, **5th Earl of Courtown**, DL, JP, Co Wexford 1848, sometime Capt Gren Gds; *b* 24 April 1823; *educ* Eton; *m* 3 Sept 1846 Hon Elizabeth Frances Milles (*d* 12 March 1894), 2nd dau of 4th Baron Sondes (*see* MONSON, B), and had:

1 JAMES WALTER MILLES, **6th Earl**

2 Edward Barrington Lewis Henry, Capt S of Ireland Imp Yeo, Maj 3rd Bn Roy Irish Regt and Capt Roy Irish Fus; *b* 20 Nov 1858; *m* 1st 21 Nov 1888 Isabel Alice (*d* 6 March 1890), only child of Capt Barrington Dashwood, RN, and had issue:

(1) Barrington George Dashwood, Lt-Cdr RN; *b* 13 Sept 1889; *m* 27 Nov 1918 Muriel Florence Mary (*d* 1980), est dau of Rev Nathaniel Nicholas Lewarne, Vicar of Yealmpton, Devon, and *d* 19 July 1930, leaving issue:

1a +Brian Barrington Dashwood, LVO (1971) [Brian Stopford Esq LVO, 122 High St, Lewes, Sussex], Assist Slr Duchy of Cornwall 1950, slr 1954–72; *b* 13 July 1923; *educ* Stowe and Trin Coll Cambridge (BA 1943); *m* 1st 3 April 1948 Alison Honor (*d* 1986), est dau of Maurice Sylvester Gibb, CBE, of Longdown Cottage, Guildford; *m* 2nd 19– *Heather Mary Sally, dau of John Basil Collingwood, and by 1st w has issue:

1b +Justin Montagu Dashwood [Justin Stopford Esq, 27 Warwick Rd, Hale, Altrincham, Cheshire WA15 9NP]; *b* 21 Feb 1949; *educ* St John's, Leatherhead and Salford U; *m* 1972 *Gillian, dau of Eric Heatherington, and has issue:

1c +Jeremy Lewis Dashwood; *b* 1982

1c *Nicola Louise; *b* 1979

1b *Yolande Honor [Mrs Owen Reynolds, Lower Ellenden Farm, Water Lane, Hawkhurst, Kent]; *b* 1 Oct 1951; *educ* Dartford Coll of Educn; *m* 1982 *Owen Arthur Reynolds, and has issue:

1c *Thomas; *b* 1984

2c *Oliver; *b* 1986

2 (cont.) Maj Edward Stopford *m* 2nd 18 Sept 1895 Alice Maud Pashley (*d* 22 Dec 1942), widow of Rev F E Haviland, and dau of James Pashley Burbeary, of Stainton, Yorks, and *d* 9 June 1909, having by her had issue:

(1) Patricia Eileen; *b* 12 June 1896; *m* 25 Nov 1916 Alec Ernest Saxton, T/Lt DCLI, and had issue:

1a Sheila Stopford; *b* 19 Nov 1917; *m* 1938 Herbert Milton Irwin, Jr, USN, and had issue. He *d* at sea 1942. She *m* 2nd David G Black, and *d* 1960, leaving further issue

2a *Natalie Moyra, dir Louisville Unit of Recording for the Blind, Inc, formerly journalist on *Courier Journal and Louisville Times*; *b* Sept 1922; *m* 1940 George Weaver Shroeder, and has issue:

3a *Doreen Patricia; *b* Sept 1926; *m* 1948 Paul Walton Jones, and has issue

(2) Violet Elizabeth; *b* 25 June 1902; *m* 20 Nov 1931 Capt John Cameron, CIE, RIN, son of Maj John Cameron, Q O Cameron Highrs

(3) Yolande Valerie; *b* 12 March 1904; *m* 12 May 1938 Stephen Thomas Colvin Turner (*d* 15 Jan 1969), and had issue:

1a *Michael James Stopford; *b* 1945; *m* 20 April 1968 *Elizabeth, dau of J Combes, of The Old Manor, Bishop's Canning, Wilts

1a *Angela Yolande; *b* 1939; *m* 8 Aug 1959 James Barry Colquhoun, son of J Clifton Colquhoun, of 61c, Eaton Sq, SW1, and has issue:

1b *James Timothy; *b* 1961

2b *Charles Stopford; *b* 1965

3b *Philip; *b* 1965

2a *Elizabeth Alice; *b* 7 Oct 1940; *m* 10 Aug 1963 *Hamish John Mackenzie, son of Dr Donald Couper Mackenzie, of Fort Rd, Alverstoke, Hants; and has issue

1b *Alasdair Hamish; *b* 25 Oct 1966

1b *Arabella Jane; *b* 20 Aug 1968

(4) Dorothy Jaqueline; *b* 12 Jan 1906; *m* 30 April 1936 Rev Thomas Gerald German Strangeways, MA, son of T S P Strangeways, and *d* 1944, leaving issue, two daus

3 George Frederick William; *b* 1 Dec 1859; *m* 31 Jan 1889 Marie Clare (*d* 25 June 1952), 2nd dau of Capt Henry Segrave, of Kiltimon, Co Wicklow, and Cabra, Co Dublin, and *d* 28 Sept 1933, having had issue:

(1) George Christian Noel, Capt Australian Forces, late 3rd Bn Roy Irish Regt (SR), served WW I 1914–15 (wounded); *b* 25 Dec 1891; *educ* Radley; *m* 19 Oct 1915 Mary Georgina (*d* 1967), dau of Rev Canon Edward Newland, of Buncrana, Co Donegal, and *d* 1969, leaving issue:

1a Edward Montagu, RAN; *b* 11 Feb 1917; *m* 1914 Dora, dau of T W Flood, of Warwick, Queensland, and *d* 1988, leaving issue:

1b +Peter [Peter Stopford, PO Box 59, Innisfail, Qld 4860, Australia], Authorised Surveyor (1966); *b* 23 July 1942; *m* 2 Jan 1965 *Lorraine Dawn, dau of Percy Denman Day, of Atherton, Qld, and has issue:

1c +Mark Peter; *b* 3 April 1968

1c *Tracey Dawn; *b* 29 Jan 1966

1b *Wendy; *b* 11 May 1944; *m* 1965 *Allan David Stephens, of Toowoomba, Qld, Australia and has issue:

1c *David Allan; *b* 1966

2c *Peter Brian; *b* 1974

1c *Christine Louise; *b* 1968

2b *Robin; *b* 31 Jan 1946

1a *$IMcIlwraith, ClaireClaire [Mrs James McIlwraith, Unit 10, Cascade Walk, 56 Burnett St, Buderim, Qld 4556, Australia]; *b* 1922; Dip of Physiotherapy, Queensland U 1944, served as Lt Aust Army Med Corps (AIF) 1944–46; *m* 17 Sept 1948 James Gordon McIlwraith (*d* 1984), son of James Samuel McIlwraith, of Maryborough, and has issue:

1b *James Edward; *b* 28 Feb 1955; *m* 1990 *Claire Elizabeth Davis, and has issue:

1c *Jesse; *b* 1989

2b *Duncan George; *b* 3 Oct 1956; *m* 1986 *Yoshiko Hiramatsu, and has issue:

1c *Ria Asuka; *b* 1987

2c *Ellie; *b* 1989

1b *Margaret Anne (Annie Stopford); *b* 23 Sept 1951; *m* 1st 1975 Dennis Morrison (*d* 19–); *m* 2nd 1989 *Ayi Mensah, of Ghana, and has issue:

1c *Nii-ayitey (a son); *b* 1990

2b *Janet Claire; *b* 24 Nov 1953; *m* 1973 *Roger O'Shaunessy, and has issue:

1c *Nye (a son); *b* 1974

2c *Tristan; *b* 1978

1c *Keely (a dau); *b* 1976

3b *Judith Pamela; *b* 10 July 1958; *m* 1977 *Stuart Tutchen, and has issue:

1c *Bradley; *b* 1978

2c *Duane (a son); *b* 1982

1c *Shari (a dau); *b* 1980

(2) Montagu Henry Aubrey, Capt late S Irish Horse (SR), formerly Lt 3rd Bn Roy Irish Regt, served WW I 1914–15; *b* 25 Nov 1894; *m* Oct 1926 Nancy Pauline Hunt, dau of Paul Hunt, of Kilfera, Kilkenny

(3) Sydney Vivian James; *b* 19 Oct 1901; *d* 3 Dec 1931

(1) Cynthia Mareli Mabel; *b* 3 Aug 1899

1 Charlotte Elizabeth; *b* 23 July 1847; *d* unm 13 July 1934

2 Eleanor Margaret; *b* 30 July 1849; *d* unm 2 Feb 1929

3 Mary Jane Jemima; *b* 25 March 1851; *m* 3 Aug 1869 Sir Charles Shelley, 5th Bt (*qv*), and *d* 17 Nov 1937, leaving issue

4 Grace Harriet; *b* 3 Dec 1854; *m* 19 Sept 1878 Capt John Strachan Bridges, of Woodcote, Fleet, Hants, and *d* 23 Nov 1916, leaving issue (*see* LIMERICK, E)

5 Lily Frances; *b* 11 Jan 1862; *m* 2 Oct 1884 Sir William Conygham Greene, PC, GCMG, KCB, and *d* 25 Jan 1950, leaving issue. He *d* 30 June 1934

The 5th EARL *d* 28 Nov 1914; his est son,

JAMES WALTER MILLES STOPFORD, **6th Earl of Courtown**, HM Lt Co Wexford, High Sheriff 1877 and Co Carlow 1878, Lt-Col and Hon Col cmdg 3rd Bn Roy Irish Regt; *b* 3 March 1853; *m* 1st 27 April 1876 Catherine Elizabeth (*d* 12 Aug 1884), est dau of 4th Baron Braybrooke (*qv*), and had issue:

1 JAMES RICHARD NEVILLE, **7th Earl**

2 Arthur, CMG, (1919), V-Adml, Naval Attaché Washington 1925–28, ADC to HM GEORGE V 1929, served Boer War 1900–01 (medal and clasp) and WW I, Legion of Honour and Russian Order St Stanislas 2nd Cl with swords; *b* 29 April 1879; *m* 1st 25 Nov 1908 (*divorce* 1924) Mary Augusta Grace, dau of Godfrey Cornewall Chester-Master, of Rangeworthy Court, Glos, and had issue:

(1) (Godfrey) Vyvyan, Capt RA (TA), ptnr Quilter Hilton Goodison & Co; *b* 22 Oct 1909; *educ* Radley and New Coll Oxford; *m* 21 July 1934 *Marjorie Alice, yr dau of Alan Cecil Lupton, of Rooksbury Mill, Andover

(1) Anne Frances Joan; *b* 16 Nov 1919; *m* 24 Feb 1940 Lt-Gen Sir Peter Mervyn Hunt, GCB, DSO, OBE, QO Cameron Highrs, est son of H V Hunt, of Fearnan, by Aberfeldy, Perthshire, and *d* 19 July 1966, leaving issue

2 (cont.) V-Adml Arthur Stopford *m* 2nd 29 Sept 1932 Elsa, widow of Carl von Wendt, of Abo, Finland, and dau of William Edward Hinke, of Gothenburg, Sweden, and *d* 25 May 1955

3 Guy, Capt RN, DL (Co Durham 1948); *b* 3 Aug 1884; served WW I; *m* 20 Dec 1923 Rosalinde Cecil, MBE, Sr Cdr ATS 1940–41 (*d* 9 July 1978), 2nd dau of Rev Charles Francis Townley, CBE, DL, of Fulbourn Manor, Cambridge and *d* 10 June 1954

1 Sybil; *b* 25 April 1882; *m* 27 July 1920 (*divorce* 1930) Capt Colin Laurence, DSC, late RAF, yst son of F Laurence, of Half Yoke, Maidstone, and *d* 31 March 1946, leaving issue

The **6th Earl** *m* 2nd 25 Sept 1886 Gertrude (*d* 15 March 1934), dau of Gen Charles James Conway Mills, of Cardington, and by her had further issue:

4 Charles William, Lt RGA WW I (wounded, despatches), Capt Gen List WW II 1940–43; *b* 1 Aug 1892

2 Eileen; *b* 11 Oct 1887; *m* 3 March 1924 Maj Montagu Richard William Duberly, OBE, 3rd Sikh Pioneers, son of Lt-Col Arthur Grey Duberly, of The Barns, Fenlake, Bedford, and *d* 11 Aug 1978, having had issue. He *d* 4 April 1976

3 Alma; *b* 24 Jan 1889; *m* 10 Oct 1922 Lt-Col Geoffrey Lennard Hoare, CBE, est son of William Hoare, of Staplehurst, Kent, and had issue. He *d* 28 Feb 1960

4 Edith Mary, formerly Co Cdr ATS; *b* 31 Oct 1890; *m* 23 Oct 1923 Brig Walter Headfort Brooke, CBE, MC, son of John Monck Brooke, and had issue

5 Marjorie Gertrude; *b* 14 Aug 1904; *d* 27 Oct 1996

The 6th EARL *d* 18 July 1933; his est son,

JAMES RICHARD NEVILLE STOPFORD, **7th Earl of Courtown**, OBE, DL Co Wexford, Maj Gen List, served Boer War 1900–01 (medal) and WW I (despatches), Mayor Aylesbury 1927–28, Staff Capt War Office 1939–41, DAAG 1941–47; *b* 16 Sept 1877; *m* 26 April 1905 Cicely Mary, OBE (1942), JP (Bucks 1936), OStJ (*d* 6 Feb 1973), yr dau of John Arden Birch by Charlotte Mary Leycester, er dau of Maj G M Stopford (*see* above), and had:

1 JAMES MONTAGU BURGOYNE, **8th Earl**

2 Edward Richard Barrington, Capt Roy Norfolk Regt; *b* 5 Feb 1914; *educ* Stowe; *m* 1st 10 May 1946 Ann Marie Elizabeth Douglas (*d* 1976), only dau of Brig Harold Gordon Henderson, CBE, of Hyde Ho, Chalford, Glos; *m* 2nd 1978 *Mrs Millicent Davies [Mrs Millicent Davies, 8 Turner's Lane, N Ferriby, N Humberside HU14 3JP], er dau of Geoffrey Watt, and formerly w of Trevor Waterson, and *d* 1990, having by his 1st w had issue:

(1) +Michael James Patrick [Michael Stopford Esq, Pilgrim Cottage, Morchard Bishop, Devon]; *b* 7 March 1950; *m* 1985 *Mrs Prudence Jane Louise Fayers, est dau of Noel Scott Unsworth, of Morchard Bishop, Devon

(2) +Christopher Gordon Edward; *b* 18 Dec 1953

(1) *Penelope Ann [Mrs Philip Leigh, 28 Great Cob, Chelmsford, Essex]; *b* 15 March 1948; *m* 1977 *Philip Henry Leigh, and has isssue:

1a *Rosemary Ann; *b* 1980

2a *Alice Margaret; *b* 1983

3 Terence Victor, Capt RN (ret 1969), served WW II, Assist Naval Adviser to UK High Commr Canada 1959–60, Assist Dir Underwater Weapons Admlty 1961–63, Capt Inshore Flotilla Fast East Fleet and CO HMS *Manxman* 1963–64, Ch Staff to C-in-C Naval Home Cmd 1965, Ch Staff Offr to Flag Offr Gibraltar 1967–69, ADC to HM THE QUEEN 1969; *b* 3 Oct 1918; *educ* Eton; *m* 1 Sept 1951 Sheila Adèle (*d* 1994), only dau of Philip H Page, and *d* 8 Feb 1998, leaving:

(1) +(Henry) Philip Terence [Philip Stopford Esq, 2 Ralston Rd, London SW3 4DS]; *b* 10 Sept 1953; *educ* Eton, Brunel (LLB) and Virginia U (LLM); Harkness Fellowship; *m* 1981 *Michele Susan, dau of Orlando Hyndman Lobo, of Bethesda, Md. and has:

1a +Philip Christian Andrew; *b* 1983

1a *Susannah Louise Adele; *b* 1985

2a *Alexandra Frances Ileara; *b* 1991

(2) +Robert Edward James; *b* 11 March 1958; *educ* Pangbourne; *m* 1987 *Anne Louise, dau of Lt-Cdr P J Patrick, RN, of Bedford Lodge, Bourne End, and has:

1a +James Charles Frederick; *b* 31 Oct 1996

1a *Louise Frances Catherine; *b* 14 Dec 1994

(3) +James Richard Hugh; *b* 8 Aug 1961; *educ* Pangbourne; Maj Irish Gds; *m* 1989 *Michelle, yr dau of Michael N Reeves, of St Catherines, Iver, and has:

1a +Milo Victor Michael; *b* 17 July 1995

1a *Isabella Frances; *b* 1992

(1) *Catherine Mary Adèle; *b* 20 March 1965

1 *Patricia Mary [The Lady Patricia Hayward, White Hart House, Haddenham, Aylesbury, Bucks]; *b* 1 Feb 1906; *m* 26 May 1934 *Maurice John Hayward, Malayan Civil Serv, only son of Sir Maurice Hayward, KCSI, of Wade Hill Ho, Totton, Hants, and has issue:

(1) *Maurice Richard [Maurice Hayward Esq, 28 Weymouth Dve, Four Oaks, Sutton Coldfield, Warwicks]; *b* 16 Aug 1939; *m* 27 April 1968 *Christina, dau of Matthew Hyland, of The Glebe, Coolrain, Co Laois, and has issue:

1a *David Maurice; *b* 1970

2a *Philip Matthew; *b* 1973

1a *Jane Margaret; *b* 1969

(1) *Bridget Mary [Mrs John Kitchin, 18 Gloucester Rd, Hampton, Middx TW12 2UH]; *b* 4 April 1935; *m* 22 Aug 1964 *John Everard Kitchin, er son of A E Kitchin, of Fort End, Haddenham, Bucks, and has issue:

1a *Hugh Everard; *b* 28 July 1965

2a *Simon John; *b* 2 Aug 1967

(2) *Caroline Patricia [Mrs Myles Saker, Rose Cottage, Cuddington, Aylesbury, Bucks]; *b* 17 Sept 1936; *m* 23 July 1960 *Myles Anthony Clive Saker, son of G/Capt H J Saker, MVO, of Jersey Cottage, Cowfold, Sussex, and has issue

1a *John Anthony; *b* 1962

1a *Deborah Ann; *b* 7 Dec 1967

(3) *Sarah Elizabeth [Miss Sarah Hayward, Church Square Cottage, Islip, Oxon]; *b* 25 Aug 1946

2 Rosemary Katharine, formerly 2nd Offr WRNS; *b* 23 Oct 1911

3 *Moyra Charlotte, BEM [The Lady Moyra Streatfeild BEM, Redberry House, Bierton, Aylesbury, Bucks]; *b* 7 Sept 1917; *m* 10 April 1943 *Lt-Cdr David Henry Champion Streatfeild, RN, yst son of Rev Claude Arthur Cecil Streatfeild, of Symondsbury Rectory, Dorset, and has issue:

(1) *David Anthony [David Streatfeild Esq, 63 Roehampton Lane, London SW15]; *b* 6 Aug 1945; *educ* Eton; *m* 1971 *Jill Katherine, dau of William Macfarlane, of The Old Cottage, Potters Lane, Send, Surrey, and has issue:

1a *James Anthony; *b* 1973

2a *Charles David; *b* 1979

1a *Katherine Moyra; *b* 1975

(2) *Timothy James [Timothy Streatfeild Esq, The Former Vicarage, North Stoke, Wallingford, Oxon]; *b* 3 April 1947; *educ* Eton; *m* 1976 *Jane, dau of Denis McVicar Merritt, MRCS, LRCP, of Grove Ho, Birchington, Kent, and has issue:

1a *Rupert Champion; *b* 1980

1a *Anna Eleanor; *b* 1978

(3) *Peter Stopford [Peter Streatfeild Esq, Royal Cottage, Kew Green, Kingston-on-Thames, Surrey]; *b* 27 May 1954; *m* 1981 *Caroline J, dau of D S M (Roy) Webster, of Farnham, Surrey, and has issue:

1a *Alexander David Stopford; *b* 1988

2a *Henry Peter Champion; *b* 1990

1a *Emma; *b* 15 Jan 1998

(1) *Cicely Mary [Mrs Michael Smith, Redlands, Clifton Rd, Chesham Bois, Bucks]; *b* 24 Dec 1950; *m* 1975 *Dr Michael R Smith, son of Bryan Crossley Smith, CBE, of Wendover, Bucks, and has issue:

1a *Harriet May Crossley; *b* 1982

2a *Lucy Patricia Streatfield; *b* 1985

4 *Cecilia Norah [The Lady Cecilia Page, Toller House, Toller Porcorum, Dorchester, Dorset DT2 0DE], formerly Jr Cdr ATS; *b* 7 Sept 1917; *m* 3 May 1947 Cdr Thomas Frederick Philip Urquhart Page, RN (*d* 24 Oct 1994), er son of Sir Leo Francis Page, of Newton Ho, Faringdon, Berks, and has:

(1) *Nicholas Leo Thomas [Nicholas Page Esq, Shoelands, Grayswood, Haslemere, Surrey]; *b* 24 Nov 1948; *educ* Eton; *m* 4 Sept 1971 *Sarah June, er dau of Leslie Bramhall, of Wheatsheaf Corner, Liphook, Hants, and has:

1a *Thomas Leslie; *b* 1973

1a *Alexia Frances; *b* 1976

(1) *Victoria Cecilia; *b* 9 Feb 1951; *m* 1979 *Robin E Furber, son of Dr Stanhope Furber, of Somerton Cottage, Winkfield, Berks, and has issue:

1a *George Frederick Edward; *b* 1986

1a *Eleanor Primrose; *b* 1988

(2) *Juliet Mary [Mrs Bruce Richardson, 117 Grandison Rd, London SW11]; *b* 13 Sept 1955; *m* 19– *Bruce Richardson and has:

1a *Daniel Hardy; *b* 1996

1a *Sophie Olivia; *b* 1992

2a *Angelica Molly; *b* 1993

The 7th EARL *d* 25 Jan 1957; his est son

JAMES MONTAGU BURGOYNE STOPFORD, **8th Earl of Courtown**, OBE (1950, MBE 1945), TD, DL (London 1951), served WW II 1939–44, 1st Bn London Irish Rifles 1941–45, cmded No 2 Army Film and Photo Section (MBE), Lt-Col cmdg 1st Bn London Irish Rifles (TA) 1947–51, Brevet Col 1951; *b* 24 Nov 1908; *educ* Eton; *m* 1st 1 Aug 1934 (*divorce* 1946) Christina Margaret, 3rd dau of Adml John Ewen Cameron, CB, MVO, of Brunton Ho, Christon Bank, Alnwick, and had issue:

1 *Mary Christina, JP, DStJ [The Lady Mary Holborow JP, Ladock House, Ladock, nr Truro, Cornwall TR2 4PL]; *b* 19 Sept 1936; Ld Lt Cornwall; *m* 8 Aug 1959 *Geoffrey Jermyn Holborow, OBE, High Sheriff Cornwall 1977, FRICS, FLAS, yst son of George Holborow, of Red Ho, Alderholt, Dorset, and has issue:

(1) *Crispin David Jermyn [Crispin Holborow Esq, 40 Canford Rd, London SW11 6PD]; *b* 7 March 1963; *educ* Eton *m* 1994 *Louise Cecilia Midleton, dau of Maj J Powell (*see* KENNARD, Bt) and has:

1a *George Jermyn Maunsel; *b* 1997

(1) *Katharine Mary [Mrs Robert Wild, 22 Brackenbury Rd, London W6 0BH]; *b* 25 March 1961; *m* 1990 *Robert Anstey Preston Wild, son of Anstey Wild, of The White Cottage, Brailsford, Derbys, and has issue:

1a *James Anstey Preston; *b* 1991

1a *Madeleine Christina Audrey; *b* 1993

2a *Isobel Anstey Jermyn; *b* 8 Oct 1997

2 *Elizabeth Cameron DStJ [The Lady Elizabeth Godsal DStJ, Haines Hill, Twyford, Berks]; *b* 10 April 1939; High Sheriff Berks 1990, Ch Pres St John Ambulance 1990–96, High Steward Wokingham 1992–; *m* 24 April 1962 *Alan Anthony Colleton Godsal, only son of Hugh Godsal, of Haines Hill, Twyford, and has:

(1) *Hugh Colleton; *b* 14 Oct 1965; *m* 1994 *Samantha Jane, er dau of Ian Angus, of El Campillo, Madrid

(1) *Lucy Violet; *b* 15 March 1964; *m* 1992 *Christopher J Zeal, 2nd son of Michael Zeal, of Westcott, Surrey

(2) *Laura Christina; *b* 28 Feb 1968

The **8th Earl** *m* 2nd 23 Feb 1951 *Patricia [The Rt Hon Patricia Countess of Courtown, Threeways, Jordans, Bucks], 3rd dau of Harry Stephen Winthrop, of Auckland, NZ, and *d* 23 July 1975, having by her had issue:

1 JAMES PATRICK MONTAGU BURGOYNE WINTHROP STOPFORD, **9th and present Earl of Courtown**

2 +Jeremy Neville, LVO; *b* 22 June 1958; *educ* Eton and RMA Sandhurst; Capt Irish Gds, T/Equerry to HM QUEEN ELIZABETH THE QUEEN MOTHER 1982–84; *m* 1984 *Bronwen, dau of Lt-Col David MacDonald Milner, of Asford Hill, Newbury, Berks, and has:

(1) *Clementine Lucy Patricia; *b* 1986

(2) *Matilda Rose Philippa; *b* 1988

(3) *Violet Mary Renée; *b* 1992

3 *Felicity Aileen Ann [The Lady Felicity Rosenquist, 9 Franche Court Rd, London SW17]; *b* 17 Dec 1951; *m* 1st 11 June 1977 (*divorce* 1981) Leslie Edward Archer-Davis, son of Thomas Archer-Davis; *m* 2nd 11 March 1982 (*divorce*) (John) Andrew McIndoe, chartered surveyor, and has issue:

(1) *Harry James; *b* 1985; *educ* Ludgrove

3 (cont.) Lady Felicity McIndoe *m* 3rd 20 March 1997 *Terry Rosenquist, advertising exec

COVENTRY

Arms: Sa. a fess erm. between three crescents or. **Crest:** A garb or lying fessways, thereon a cock gu., comb, wattles, and legs of the first. **Supporters:** Two eagles, wings expanded and inverted arg., beaked and legged or. **Motto:** *Candide et constanter* ('Candidly and constantly'). **Creation:** V.and E. (E) 26 April 1697.

THE 11TH EARL OF COVENTRY, Co Warwick, and **Viscount Deerhurst**, of the hundred of Deerhurst, Co Gloucester (George William Coventry) [The Rt Hon The Earl of Coventry, Earls Croome Court, Earls Croome, Worcs WR8 9DE]; *b* 25 Jan 1934; *s f* 1940; *educ* Eton and RMA Sandhurst; late 2nd Lt Gren Gds; *m* 1st 22 March 1955 (*divorce* 1963) Marie (Mimi) Farquhar-Medart, dau of William S Medart, of St Louis, Mo.; *m* 2nd 5 Dec 1969 (*divorce* 1975) Ann, dau of Frederick William James Cripps, of Bickley, Kent; *m* 3rd 1980 (*divorce* 1988) Valerie Anne Birch; *m* 4th 1992 *Rachel Wynne, dau of Jack Mason, and by his 1st w has issue:

1 Edward (Ted) George William Omar, *Viscount Deerhurst*; *b* 24 Sept 1957; *educ* Santa Monica High Sch Calif.; *d* unm 4 Oct 1997

Lineage: VINCENT COVENTRY, of Cassington, Oxon; had:

RICHARD COVENTRY, of Cassington; had a 2nd s:

Sir THOMAS COVENTRY; lawyer; *b* 1547; BA Oxon 1565 (Fell Balliol Coll 1566); barrister 1568, Bencher Inner Temple 1591, Serjeant-at-law 1603, King's Serjeant 1605, Judge Common Pleas 1606, when ktd; *m* Margaret, dau of William Jefferies, of Croome D'Abitot, Worcs, and *d* 12 Dec 1606, having had, with other issue:

1 THOMAS, 1st BARON

2 William; ancestor of the COVENTRYs of Ridmarley, Worcs

3 Walter; had:

(1) Walter, of London; *m* Anne, dau of Humphrey Holcombe, London merchant, and had, with three other sons:

1a WILLIAM, **5th Earl**

1 Catharine; *m* William Childe, of Northwick

The est son,

THOMAS COVENTRY, 1st BARON COVENTRY OF AYLESBOROUGH, Co Worcester (E), so *cr* 10 April 1628; *b* 1578; *educ* Balliol Coll Oxford; barrister Inner Temple 1603, Bencher 1614, Recorder London 1616, Slr-Gen 1617, when ktd, Attorney-Gen 1621, MP Droitwich 1621–22, Ld Keeper Gt Seal 1625–Jan 1639/40; *m* 1st by 1606 Sarah, sis of Sir Edward Sebright, 1st Bt (*qv*), of Besford, Worcs, and had issue:

1 THOMAS, 2nd BARON

1 Elizabeth; *m* Sir John Hare, of Stow Bardolph, Norfolk

The 1st BARON *m* 2nd by 1610 Elizabeth (*bur* 25 May 1653), widow of William Pitchford and dau of John Aldersey, of Spurstow, Cheshire, and by her had issue:

2 John; *m* Elizabeth, widow of Herbert Doddington, and dau of John Coles, of Barton, Somerset, and had:

(1) Sir John, of Pitminster, Somerset, KB; MP Weymouth; made remarks in Parl supposedly critical of CHARLES II, attacked by a party of courtiers 21 Dec 1670 and badly hurt, resulting in The Coventry Act, which banished the assailants if identified and preventing CHARLES II from pardoning them; *d* unm

3 Francis; barrister; *b* 1612; *m* thrice and *d* 1680, leaving by his 1st w Elizabeth, dau of John Manning, of Warbelton, Essex, and widow of Robert Caesar, together with an only s:

(1) Elizabeth; *m* Sir William Keyt, Bt

(2) Ultra Trajectina; *m* Sir Lacon William Childe, of Kinlet

4 Henry; MA, BCL Oxon, MP Droitwich 1661–81, Amb Sweden 1671, Sec of State 1672–80; *b* 1618; *d* unm 7 Dec 1686

5 William (Sir), DCL Oxon, MP Gt Yarmouth 1661–79, Sec to Admlty, Commr Treasury; *d* 23 June 1686

2 Anne; *m* 1st Sir William Saville, 3rd Bt, and had issue:

(1) George, Marquess of Halifax (*see* HALIFAX, E, preliminary remarks)

2 (cont.) Lady Saville *m* 2nd Thomas Chichele, of Wimpole, Cambs

3 Mary; *m* Sir Henry Frederick Thynne, 1st Bt (*see* BATH, M)

4 Margaret; *m* 25 Feb 1639 1st Earl of Shaftesbury (*qv*) and *dsp* 11 July 1649

5 Dorothy; *m* Sir John Packington, 2nd Bt, and was *bur* 13 May 1679

The 1st BARON *d* 14 Jan 1639/40; his est son,

THOMAS COVENTRY, 2nd BARON COVENTRY OF AYLESBOROUGH; *b* 1606; MP Droitwich 1625–26, royalist Civil War; *m* 2 April 1627 Mary (*d* 18 Oct 1634), sis of 1st and last Earl of Craven (*qv*) of the March 1664/5 *cr*, and *d* 27 Oct 1661, leaving:

1 GEORGE COVENTRY, 3rd BARON COVENTRY OF AYLESBOROUGH; *b* 1628; *m* 18 July 1653 Lady Margaret Tufton, dau of 2nd Earl of Thanet, and *d* 15 Dec 1680, having had:

(1) JOHN COVENTRY, 4th BARON COVENTRY OF AYLESBOROUGH; *b* 2 Sept 1654; *d* unm 25 July 1687

(1) Margaret; *m* 10 July 1679 2nd Duke of Bolton (*see* WINCHESTER, M)

2 THOMAS COVENTRY, 5TH BARON COVENTRY OF AYLESBOROUGH and **1st Earl of Coventry**, so cr 26 April 1697, as also VISCOUNT DEERHURST, of the hundred of Deerhurst, Co Gloucester (both E), with remainder to the sons of Walter Coventry, n of the 1st BARON; *b c* 1629; MP Droitwich 1660, Camelford 1661–79 and Warwick 1681 and 1685–87; *m* 1st Winifred (*d* 11 June 1694), dau of Pierce Edgcumbe, of Mount Edgcumbe, Devon (*see* MOUNT EDGCUMBE, E), and had surv issue:

(1) THOMAS COVENTRY, **2nd Earl of Coventry**; *b c* 1662; *m* 4 May 1691 Lady Anne Somerset (*d* 17 Feb 1763), dau of 1st Duke of Beaufort (*qv*), and *d* Aug 1710, having by her had an only surv s:

1a THOMAS COVENTRY, **3rd Earl of Coventry**; *b* 7 April 1702; *d* at Eton 28 Jan 1711/2

(2) GILBERT COVENTRY, **4th Earl of Coventry**; *b c* 1668; *m* 1st (licence 30 Nov 1694) Dorothy (*d* 1705), dau of Sir William Keyt, 2nd Bt, of Ebrington, Glos, and had:

1a Anne; *m* 5 Jan 1713/4 Sir William Carew, Bt, of Anthony, Cornwall

(2) (cont.) The **4th Earl** *m* 2nd 25 June 1715 Anne (*m* 2nd 1752 Edmund Pytts, MP, of Kyre, Worcs, and *d* 21 March 1788), dau of Sir Streynsham Master, of Codnor Castle, Derbys, and *d* 27 Oct 1719 without further issue, when the Barony expired, while the other titles and most of the estates passed to the descendant of Walter Coventry, bro of the 1st BARON

2 The **1st Earl** *m* 2nd 16 July 1695 his housemaid Elizabeth (*m* 2nd May 1700 Thomas Savage, of Elmley Castle, Worcs, and was *bur* 10 April 1724), dau of Richard Graham/Grimes and n of his housekeeper, and *d* 15 July 1699 withouth further issue

The 4th EARL's cousin,

WILLIAM COVENTRY, **5th Earl of Coventry**, PC (March 1719/20); *b* by 1688; DCL, Clerk of the Green Cloth, MP (Whig) Bridport 1708–19, Ld Lt and Custos Rotulorum Worcs; *m* Elizabeth (*d* 23 Nov 1738), dau of John Allen, of Westminster, and had issue:

1 Thomas Henry, *Viscount Deerhurst*; MA Oxon, MP Bridport 1742–44; *b* 27 March 1721; *d* unm 20 May 1744

2 GEORGE WILLIAM, **6th Earl**

3 John Bulkeley COVENTRY later COVENTRY-BULKELEY; *d* 1801

The 5th EARL *d* 18 March 1750/1; his est surv son,

GEORGE WILLIAM COVENTRY, **6th Earl of Coventry**; MP (Tory) Bridport 1744–47 and Worcs 1747–51, Ld Lt and Custos Rotulorum Worcs 1751–1808, Recorder of Coventry; *b* 26 April 1722; *m* 1st March 1752 Maria (*d* 30 Sept 1760), sis of the Duchesses of Hamilton and Argyll (*qv*) and est dau of John Gunning, of Castle Coote, Co Roscommon, by Hon Bridget Bourke, dau of 6th Viscount Bourke of Mayo (*see* GUNNING, Bt), and had:

1 GEORGE WILLIAM, **7th Earl**

1 Mary Alicia; *m* 29 June 1777 Sir Andrew Bayntun-Rolt, 2nd and last Bt, and *d* 8 Jan 1784. He *dsp* 12 Aug 1816

2 Anne Margaret; *m* 1st 20 Oct 1778 Hon Edward Foley, MP (*see* FOLEY, B); *m* 2nd Captain Samuel Wright

The **6th Earl** *m* 2nd 27 Sept 1764 Barbara (*d* 25 Nov 1804), dau of 10th Baron St John of Bletso (*qv*), and by her had issue:

2 John; *b* 20 June 1765; *m* 1st 1788 Anne Clayton (*d* Aug 1809) and had, with other issue:

(1) Frederick; *b* 4 Feb 1791; *m* 18 Oct 1819 Louisa (*d* 30 Sept 1865), only dau of Sir Henry Halford, 1st Bt, and *d* 10 Aug 1859, having had, with other issue:

1a St John, Cdr RN; *b* 5 Jan 1828; *m* 27 Sept 1860 Mary Elizabeth (*m* 2nd 12 Jan 1875 George William Culme Soltau-Symons (*d* 1916), of Chaddlewood, and *d* 8 July 1919), only dau of Lt-Col Frederick William Todd, Madras Army, and *d* 9 Feb 1871, leaving issue:

1b St John Halford, of The Knoll and Henbury Manor, Dorset; Capt Gren Gds; *b* 29 May 1866; *m* 5 Nov 1895 Lillian Emmeline (*m* 2nd 30 May 1922 Charles E Allen, and *d* 27 Oct 1948), dau of George Russell (*see* BEDFORD, D), and *d* 9 June 1920, leaving issue:

1c George St John, MC, late Lt S Wales Borderers, served WW I 1915–16 (despatches); *b* 21 Sept 1896; *m* 1924 Mrs Ward Dymond, and *d* 21 July 1932

1c Laura; *b* 31 Aug 1899; *m* 1st 22 July 1919 (*divorce* 1928) Hon William Arthur de la Poer Horsley Beresford, yst son of 3rd Baron Decies (*qv*), and had issue; *m* 2nd 8 Oct 1932 (*divorce* 1946) Reginald Robert Nicholls. They assumed by roy licence, 8 June 1933, the surname and arms of COVENTRY in lieu of NICHOLLS; *m* 3rd 2 Dec 1950 John Hamilton Hamilton

2b Beauchamp St John; *b* 19 Nov 1869; *d* 30 June 1870

1b Mary Louisa; *m* 30 April 1884 Charles Ethelston Parke, of Henbury Ho, Wimborne, and *dsp* 22 Feb 1953. He *d* 12 April 1919

2a Henry Halford, CE; *b* 24 Feb 1834; *m* 1st 14 May 1857 Mary Susanna (*d* 6 June 1863), yst dau of Henry Vincent, of Stanstead, Essex, and had, with other issue:

1b Harry; *b* 9 March 1858; *m* 1896 Evangeline, JP (1940) (*d* 29 April 1963, aged 86), dau of Gustave August Hermann Hohenzollern Rockel, of Carnarvon, NZ, and *d* 29 Sept 1943, leaving issue:

1c St John; *b* 30 March 1901; *m* 13 Sept 1930 *Caroline Gertrude, dau of John David Hocking, of Vancouver, Canada, and *d* 4 Dec 1963, leaving issue:

1d +Henry John, S/Ldr RNZAF, Queen's Commendation (1964); *b* 28 Jan 1932; *m* 12 April 1958 *Frances Winifred Clarke, and has issue:

1e +Simon St John; *b* 26 July 1963

2e +David Henry Halford; *b* 2 Oct 1969

1e *Rosalyn Barbara; *b* 25 Jan 1959; BA Victoria; *m* 1989 *Rev Dr Uili Feleterika Nokise

2e *Adrienne Clare; *b* 17 Sept 1960; *m* 1988 *Niel Douglas Brown

3e *Anna Louise; *b* 23 March 1967; BA Canterbury

2d +Roger Michael [Roger Coventry Esq, Merrivale, Battersea Line, Greytown, New Zealand]; *b* 10 Nov 1934; *m* 21 Jan 1961 *Margaret Ann Cooke, and has issue:

1e +Geoffrey Alan; *b* 17 May 1969

1e *Jennifer Beryl; *b* 19 June 1965; *m* 1988 *Bill Biber

2e *Sylvia Ann; *b* 18 Feb 1967

3e *Marilyn Gay; *b* 8 June 1968

3d +Alan Francis [Alan Coventry Esq, 22 Lynmore Ave, Rotorua, New Zealand], electronic technician NZ Dept of Civil Aviation (ret); *b* 5 Jan 1940; *m* 20 May 1st 1961 (*divorce* 1972) Patrina Rathbride, est dau of Patrick Francis Dwan, of 17, Stratford St, Fendalton, Christchurch, NZ, and has issue:

1e +Charles Raymond St John; *b* 26 April 1963; *m* 19– *Pauline Wendy Dyer and has:

1f +Sean James St John; *b* 1985

2f +Benjamin St John; *b* 1987

1f *Alyson Patrina; *b* 1983

2e +Andrew Francis Patrick; *b* 22 Oct 1964; *m* 1988 *Irene Florence, dau of David Alan Parr

1e *Charmaine Louise; *b* 12 Dec 1961; *m* 19– *Andrew Bryan Duxfield, and has issue:

1f *Michael Thomas; *b* 1984

2f *Timothy Edward; *b* 1986

1f *Amy Georgiana; *b* 1988

3d (cont.) Alan Coventry *m* 2nd 1972 *Alison Leslie, dau of Dallas Evans, and has further issue:

3e +Richard Alan Penrose; *b* 1971

2e *Katherine Margaret; *b* 1973

1d *Bernadine Helen Mary [Mrs Endo McBride, 27 Tennyson St, Trentham, Upper Hutt, New Zealand]; *b* 6 Feb 1945; *m* 8 Feb 1964 *Endo Francis McBride, and has issue:

1e *Lenore Frances; *d* 12 Sept 1965; *m* 1989 *Michael Cunningham

2e *Joanna Claire; *b* 29 July 1967; *m* 1988 *Robert Stuart Nicol

2c Frederick Halford, mural and stained glass painter; *b* 19 Jan 1905; *m* 27 March 1940 Dolores Rosamund Christine (Lola) (*d* 24 June 1994), yr dau of Leon Dominic Ashton, of Cairo, Egypt, and *d* 10 Feb 1997, leaving:

1d +Edward Bernard Halford St John [Edward Coventry Esq, 103 Castelnau, London SW13 9EL]; *b* 30 May 1943; *educ* London U (BSc)

1d *Elizabeth Mary Hephzibah; *b* 15 April 1947; *educ* St Martin's Sch of Art (Dipl in Art and Design (Dress) 1968); *m* 1st 30 Nov 1968 (*divorce* 1980) Terence M R Carville, only son of M T Carville, of Osterley, Middx; *m* 2nd Jan 1981 *John Henry Brierley, and has issue:

1e *Alexandra Frances Mary; *b* Dec 1981

1c *Barbara Vincent; *b* 15 Jan 1907; *m* 29 Oct 1938 *Geoffrey Ralston Anderson

2b Thomas; *b* 31 May 1863; *m* 18 Oct 1902 Eleanor Mona (*d* 14 Jan 1925), 2nd dau of Rev Hugh Stowell, and *d* 25 June 1928, leaving issue:

1c Mona Barbara; *b* 17 Aug 1903; *d* 7 June 1937

1b Gertrude; *m* 1906 John Joline Ross, of Newark, New Jersey, and *d* 24 Feb 1934

2a (cont.) Henry Coventry *m* 2nd 16 Feb 1864 Malvina Antonina (*d* 9 March 1902), dau of Marshal Hlasko, of Russia, and *d* 20 July 1914, having by her had issue:

3b John Vladislav; *b* 17 Aug 1868; *d* 30 Jan 1918

2b Mary Stanislava; *m* 1887 K Siwicki, of Kurland, Russia, and had issue

1a Barbara Louisa; *m* 10 Dec 1845 Rev John Paul

2a Matilda Barbara; *m* 8 Nov 1843 Rev Thomas Grey Clarke, and *d* 22 May 1862, leaving issue

(2) John, of Burgate Ho, Hants; *b* 14 April 1793; *m* 1st 1818 Elizabeth (*d* 1856), dau of Rev George Wilson, Vicar of Corbridge, Northumberland, and had, with other issue:

1a John (Rev), of Burgate Ho, formerly Rector of Twyardreath, Cornwall; *b* 22 April 1819; *m* 21 June 1842 Catherine (*d* 19 Feb 1901), yst dau of Col Seton, of Brookheath, Hants, and *d* 19 Nov 1897, leaving issue:

1b John, JP Hants; *b* 19 Feb 1845; *m* 25 Oct 1876 Emily Mary (*d* 22 Sept 1937), 2nd dau of Joseph Weld, JP, of Lymington, Hants, and *d* 10 Dec 1933, having had issue:

1c John Joseph, late T/Capt RASC, served WW I 1914–18 (despatches); *b* 9 Feb 1882; *m* 9 June 1910 Margaret Camilla (who *m* 2nd 24 Sept 1955 Adrian Leonard Moreton, MS, FRCS, yr son of Thomas Moreton, of 12 Serjeants' Inn, EC4, and *d* 26 April 1958), 2nd dau of Carlyle Henry Hayes Macartney, of Foxhold, Newbury, and *d* 20 Dec 1950, leaving issue:

1d Angela Mary Camilla; *b* 7 May 1911; *m* 6 Dec 1936 Herman George Richard March (*d* 2 Oct 1955), only son of Herman Molvo March, of Palais du Printemps, Blvd de Belgique, Monaco, and had issue:

1e Richard Alexander; *b* 4 Jan 1941; *educ* Bryanston; *d* unm 12 May 1968

2e *Maxwell James; *b* 26 Nov 1947; *educ* Charterhouse

1e *Clare Elisabeth; *b* 10 June 1939; *m* 9 April 1960 *Nigel Warrack, son of Guy Warrack, BA, Hon ARCM, of 72 Courtfield Gardens, SW5, and has issue:

1f *Richard Sebastian; *b* 7 Dec 1963

1f *Camilla Valentine; *b* 4 June 1961

2f *Tamsin Julia; *b* 21 June 1967

2d *Barbara Mary St John, MBE (Mil 1945) [Dr Barbara Coventry MBE, 68 Prebend Gdns, London W6 0XU], MB, BS Lond, LRCP, MRCS (1952), D(Obst) RCOG (1953), T/Jr Cdr ATS WW II; *b* 6 June 1912

3d *Catherine Margaret Mary [Mrs Herbert Jones, 4 Earl's Court Gdns, London SW5]; *b* 27 Jan 1915; *m* 24 Oct 1936 *Herbert Alan Jones, son of Maj-Gen Lewis Jones, of Stoke Lodge, Stoke Poges, and has issue:

1e *Charles Alan [Charles Jones Esq, 10 Rodway Rd, Roehampton, London SW15]; *b* 29 Aug 1937; *educ* Marlborough; *m* 1961 *Margaret Elizabeth Cowper, and has issue:

1f *Timothy Charles; *b* 1963

2f *Nicholas Alan; *b* 1967

1f *Patricia Margaret; *b* 1965

1e *Celia Margaret; *b* 27 Aug 1948

4d *Dorothea Olivia; *b* 10 April 1918; *m* 6 March 1937 (*divorce* 1952) Adrian Charles Enthoven (*d* 17 Jan 1994), son of F V Enthoven, of St John's Wood, and has:

1e *Stephen Andrew [Stephen Enthoven Esq, 15 Ladbroke Sq, London W11 3NA]; *b* 1939; *m* 1965 *Fiona Valerie Maclean, and has issue:

1f *Thomas Samuel Donald; *b* 1974

2f *John Henry William; *b* 1978

2e *John Christopher; *b* 1945; *m* 1st 1968 (*divorce* 1991) Valerie Kathleen Roberts; *m* 2nd 1995 *Sally Abdool, and by his 1st w has:

1f *Andrew James; *b* 1975

1f *Alexandra Louise; *b* 1973

5d Elizabeth Jacqueline; *b* 1 Oct 1919; *d* 29 Dec 1927

2c (Bernard) Seton; *b* 30 March 1887; *m* 31 March 1910 Annie (*d* 18 June 1960), dau of James Cunningham, MICE, of Cyprus, and *d* 7 Sept 1965, leaving issue:

1d Anthony James Seton; Maj REME; *b* 18 Oct 1913; *m* 15 Aug 1942 *Mollie Rosina [Mrs Harold Hayles, 20 St Anne's Gdns, Lymington, Hants SO4 9HT] (who *m* 2nd 16 Sept 1961 Harold J Hayles (*d* 1972)), dau of J Grummett, of St Abb's Head, Coldingham, Berwickshire, and *d* 15 Aug 1955, leaving issue:

1e +John James Seton [John Coventry Esq, Chapel House, Tregawne, Bodmin PL30 5NR]; *b* 3 Feb 1955; *educ* Downside; FRICS; *m* 1 July 1993 *Naomi Elizabeth Margaret, dau of John Selwyn Jones, of Dawlish, Devon, and has:

1f *Isobelle Florence Elisabeth; *b* 15 May 1997

1d (cont.) Mr and Mrs A J S Coventry adopted:

*Margaret Elizabeth [Mrs Nigel Brooks, Shilton House, Pitmore Lane, Lymington, Hants]; *b* 29 April 1946; *m* 1978 *Nigel James Brooks, son of Lt-Cdr F L Brooks, MBE, RD, RN, of Lymington, Hants, and has issue:

1f *Richard John; *b* 1981

2f *Anthony James; *b* 1982

1f *Nicola Kate; *b* 1985

2d +John Joseph Seton (Rev) [The Rev John Coventry SJ, 114 Mount St, London W1Y 6AH]; *b* 21 Jan 1915; *educ* Stonyhurst and Campion Hall Oxford (MA); Priest Sept 1947 (SJ), Rector Beaumont College 1956–58, Provincial Eng Prov Soc of Jesus 1958–64, Master St Edmund's Ho Cambridge 1976–85

3c William St John; Lt Beds Regt WW I (despatches); *b* 7 Feb 1893; *ka* 22 Oct 1914

1c Mary Flora; *b* 2 Nov 1877; *d* unm 14 May 1970

2c Constance Catherine Mary, a Nun; *b* 7 Feb 1879; *d* March 1961

3c Philomena Barbara Mary; nun; *b* 12 Sept 1880; *d* 27 Oct 1966

4c Annette Emily Mary; *b* 6 July 1884; *m* 27 Nov 1907 Maj-Gen Sir Philip Gordon-Grant, KCB, CMG, RE, yst son of Col J M Grant, RE, and *d* 13 May 1963, leaving issue (*see* TALBOT OF MALAHIDE, B). He *d* 14 July 1943

5c Dorothy Mary; *b* 28 April 1889; *m* 30 June 1909 Lt-Col George Leslie Hall, OBE, late RE, son of E T Hall, of Dulwich, and *d* 17 Jan 1971, leaving issue. He *d* 1947

2b James Seton; *b* 26 Feb 1849; *d* 12 April 1917

3b Walter Bulkeley, MICE; *b* 26 Feb 1950; *d* unm 8 June 1939

4b Alexander Moray (Rev); RC priest; *b* 7 July 1853; *d* 7 Nov 1925

5b Bernard, CIE (1912); Dir Ag Research Inst, Pncpl Ag Coll Pusa Bengal 1904–16, Ag Advsr Govt of India 1912–16 and Native States Centl India 1916–18; *b* 10 Dec 1859; *m* 7 Jan 1892 Ella Gordon (*d* 9 Feb 1951), est dau of Edward Dagleish, and *d* 26 Jan 1929, leaving:

1c Muriel Mary; *b* 26 Nov 1895

2c Catherine Mary Aline; *b* 15 March 1898; *m* 4 Sept 1919 Lt-Col Frederick Legh Richmond Munn, DSO, MC, late IA, only son of Maj F H Munn, DSO, and had issue

3c Bernardine Mary Joan; *b* 24 Aug 1903; *d* unm 15 July 1968

4c *Isabelle Mary; *b* 5 Oct 1905

6b Francis Martin; *b* 20 July 1863; *m* 10 Oct 1896 Amy Maud (*d* 13 Dec 1949), est dau of Henry W J Hill, of 17 Cleveland Sq, Hyde Park, and *d* 7 July 1917, leaving issue:

1c Henry Francis; indigo planter West Indies; *b* 13 May 1898

2c Gerald Leslie; lay brother Redemptorist Order; *b* 11 March 1900

1c Catharine Nora; *m* May 1925 Hubert de Burgh Williams (*d* 24 Sept 1949) and had:
1d *Evan John; *b* 2 March 1926; *m* Sept 1952 *Janet, dau of Boyd Hill, of Dean End, Lea, Ross-on-Wye, and has issue:
1e *Alan Christopher; *b* 30 Oct 1956
1e *Sheila Anne; *b* 11 June 1954
2d Hubert Michael; *b* 7 March 1927; *d* 19–
2c *Cicily Maud; *m* 21 June 1937 Maj William Geoffrey Harker, The W Yorks Regt, son of Capt H E Harker
1b Margaret Elizabeth; *d* unm 30 Oct 1894
2b Florence Catharine; *d* unm 8 Feb 1936
3b Marion; nun; *d* 2 March 1934
4b Isabella Anne; nun; *d* 2 Mar 1936
5b Barbara; nun; *d* 31 May 1946
6b Gertrude Mary Philomena; *m* 15 Jan 1896 Capt Henry Joseph Francis Radcliffe, Cameron Highers, 2nd son of Sir Joseph Percival Pickford Radcliffe, 3rd Bt (*qv*), of Rudding Park, Yorks, and *d* 15 March 1955, leaving issue
2a Charles Farmar; Lt RN, HMS *Rapid*; *b* 25 Aug 1824; *d* 12 March 1855
1a Charlotte; *m* 20 April 1852 John Pybus, and *d* 1913, leaving issue. He *d* 1895
(2) (cont.) John Coventry *m* 2nd 1857 Louisa Maria (*dsp* 6 Sept 1857), widow of — Berens and 2nd dau of Lancelot Rolleston, of Watnall, Notts; *m* 3rd 30 Sept 1858 Ellen Wyndham (*dsp* 11 Aug 1905), 4th dau of Capt Thomas Penruddocke, 3rd Foot Gds, and *d* 13 Oct 1871
(1) Anne; *m* 1823 Thomas William Coventry (*see* below), and *d* 31 Jan 1869
2 (cont.) The Hon John Coventry *m* 2nd Aug 1809 Anna Maria (*d* 28 March 1837), widow of Ebenezer Pope, and dau of Francis Eves, and *d* 12 Nov 1829
3 Thomas William; *b* 24 Dec 1778; *m* — Clarke (*d* Dec 1806), and *d* April 1816, leaving, with other issue:
(1) Thomas William; *b* 23 July 1800; *m* 20 July 1823 Anne (*d* 31 Jan 1869), 2nd dau of Hon John Coventry, and *d* 16 Feb 1882, having had, with other issue:
1a Gilbert Walter; 79th Highrs, of Christchurch, NZ; *b* 4 April 1837; *m* 29 May 1880 Margaret (*d* 28 Aug 1894), dau of Hugh Milligan, of Ballymacrelue, Co Donegal, and *d* 28 Feb 1909, leaving issue:
1b Gilbert Francis; *b* 1892; *m* 1929 Clara Dorothy (*d* 1970), dau of Robert Charles Brown, and *d* 1960, leaving issue:
1c +Noel [Noel Coventry Esq, 72 Station Rd, Paeroa, New Zealand]; *b* 1933; *m* 1960 *Nola Elsie May, dau of Robert Archibald Lindsay
2c +Francis Henry; *b* 1934; *m* 1961 *Shirley Ann, dau of Thomas Henry Lionel Turner
2b Arthur Roger; *b* 1894; *m* 19– Alma Rale (*d* 1980), and *d* 1975
1b Olivia Beryl
2b Bathilda Adéle
2a Corbet John; Lt 7th Roy Fus, Capt E Kent Mil; *b* 4 June 1838; *m* 21 April 1870 Honora Maria (*d* 1 May 1906), yst dau of J W Sutherland, of Coombe, nr Croydon, and *d* 29 Jan 1916, leaving issue:
1b Leslie Corbet, Maj Notts Yeo, Boer War 1900–01 and WW I; *b* 15 July 1872; drowned at sea through enemy action 26 May 1918
1b Kathleen; *b* 18 April 1871; *m* 28 Sept 1895 Maj Francis de Berckem Hancock, IA, and had issue. He *d* 1916
2b Gladys Anne Violet; *b* 21 Aug 1883; *d* unm 13 March 1957
1a Sophia Mary; *m* 17 Sept 1862 Joseph Noble Beasley, and had issue. He *d* 1904
2a Olivia Emile; *m* 11 Aug 1863 Stanley Sutherland Sutherland, 2nd son of J W Sutherland, of Coombe, Croydon, and *d* 30 June 1865
1 Augusta Elinor; *m* 1 March 1830 Sir George Edward Pocock, 2nd Bt, and *d* 30 April 1868, leaving issue. He *d* 3 Sept 1866
2 Julia Catherine; *m* 25 Aug 1825 Augustus Pocock, 2nd son of Sir George Pocock, 1st Bt, and *d* 9 Oct 1826, leaving issue

The 6th EARL *d* 3 Sept 1809; his est son,

GEORGE WILLIAM COVENTRY, **7th Earl of Coventry**; Recorder Worcester, High Steward Tewkesbury; *b* 28 April 1758; *m* 1st 18 March 1777 Lady Catherine Henley (*dsp* 19 Jan 1779), 4th dau of 1st Earl of Northington; *m* 2nd 10 Jan 1783 Peggy (*d* 15 Jan 1840), 2nd dau and coheir of Sir Abraham Pitches, of Streatham, Surrey, and by her had, with other issue:
1 GEORGE WILLIAM, **8th Earl**
2 William James; *b* 1 Jan 1797; *m* 26 July 1821 Mary (*d* 29 Dec 1892), dau of James Laing, and *d* 11 March 1877, having had issue:
(1) William George; *b* 5 Sept 1826; *m* 27 April 1865 Frances Cecilia (*d* 9 Feb 1906), 2nd dau of Thomas Norbury, of Sherridge Ho, and *d* 16 Feb 1874, leaving issue:
1a Gilbert William; *b* 17 April 1868; *m* 1st 3 June 1902 Georgina Blanche (*d* 1922), dau of Maj William H P G Bluett, of Fenton, Paignton, 10th Regt, and had issue:
1b William George; Lt IA; *b* 12 June 1903; *m* 1st 2 Aug 1928 Charlotte Dorothy, only dau of Verner George Lyman, of Shanghai; *m* 2nd 6 March 1968 *Ethel Wilmot
2b Cecil Dick Bluett, DSC, RD; Lt-Cdr RNR WW II (despatches); *b* 14 July 1905; *m* 1939 Anne Josephine Hale (*d* 1974), dau of Maj H J Sherwood, RE, and *d* 6 Jan 1952, leaving:
1c +George William [George Coventry Esq, 21 Malvern Rd, Hampton, Middx]; *b* 5 Oct 1939; *educ* Prince of Wales Sch, Nairobi; *m* 11 Sept 1965 *Gillian Frances, dau of W R Randall, of Wyke Regis, Weymouth, Dorset, and has issue:
1d *Diana Elizabeth Sherwood; *b* 1980
2c Peter Harold Sherwood; *b* 10 Jan 1941; *educ* Prince of Wales Sch Nairobi, and School of Navigation, Southampton; *m* 16 Aug 1969 *Kay Sandra [Mrs Peter Coventry, Hillsborough, Bere Ferrers, Yelverton, Devon], dau of Lt-Cdr Roy S Baker-Falkner, and *d* 20 Oct 1985, leaving:
1d +David Duncan Sherwood; *b* 5 March 1973
1d *Lynn Karen Sherwood; *b* 20 July 1970
3b Charles Henry Gerald; *b* 27 July 1906; MLC Kenya 1953, Capt EA Sig Corps
4b Arthur John Clifford; *b* 2 April 1909; *m* 1st 1937 (*divorce* 1947) Dulcie Alice Saxton, and had issue:
1c +Gilbert John Henry [Mr Gilbert Coventry, 15 Queen St, Guildford, NSW 2161, Australia]; *b* 1939; *m* 1961 *Patricia Anne, dau of Reginald Charles Deeley, of Balgowaie, NSW, and has issue:
1d +Wesley John; *b* 1965
1d *Anne Maree; *b* 1962; *m* 1993 *Xavier Hogan
2d *Robyne Michelle; *b* 1971; has issue:
1e *Justin Alan COVENTRY; *b* 1992
2c Geoffrey Robert; *b* 1941; *m* 1964 *Lynette, dau of Patrick Salmon, of Corrimal, NSW, and *d* 1964
1c *Margaret Elaine [Mrs Barrie Stanford, 10 Jennifer Crescent, Thirroul, NSW 2515, Australia]; *b* 1943; *m* 1964 *Barrie Robert Stanford, and has issue:
1d *Cheryn Lee; *b* 1968; *m* 1st 1992 (*divorce* 1994) Charles Goudman; *m* 2nd 1996 *David Craig Porter
2d *Karlyn Leslie; *b* 1970; *m* 1992 *Sean Johns and has:
1e *Alexandra Lee; *b* 1995
4b (cont.) Arthur Coventry *m* 2nd 1952 Margaret Nancy (*d* 1986), only dau of W E Gell, of Gosford, NSW, and *d* 8 Sept 1965, having by her had issue:
2c +Richard William [Mr Richard Coventry, 11 Fergus Rd, Queanbeyan, NSW 2620, Australia]; *b* 9 Aug 1953; *m* 1st 19— — and has:
1d +Richard John; *b* 1972
2c (cont.) Richard Coventry *m* 2nd 1984 *Carolyn, dau of William John Dray, of 11–13 Frederick St, Marburg, Qld, and by her has:
1d *Sarah Margaret; *b* 1986
2c *Elizabeth Nancy [Mrs Colin Hickey, 9 Marston Close, Macarthur, ACT 2905, Australia]; *b* 29 March 1955; *m* 1986 *Colin Hickey and has:
1d *Penelope Lee COVENTRY; *b* 1973
5b +(Gilbert) Hugo Gordon [Hugo Coventry Esq, Fermoy Cottage, Vermont Dve, E Preston, Sussex]; Lt-Cdr RINVR, manager Kuala Muda Rubber Estate, Kedah, Malaysia (ret 1960); *b* 31 March 1911; *m* 1st 1948 (*divorce* 1953) Alice, widow of Frank Tabran; *m* 2nd at Port Moresby, New Guinea, 19 Nov 1959 Mary (*d* 1991), widow of Gordon Graham, of Mile End Ho, Aberdeen
1a (cont.) Gilbert Coventry *m* 2nd 1 Dec 1923 Margaret Charlotte (*d* 1981), widow of Maj G D'Arcy Elliott-Cooper, and *d* 11 Nov 1947, having by her had issue:
1b *Anne [Mrs Stanley Keevil, The Barn, W Ogwell, nr Newton Abbot, Devon]; *b* 31 Jan 1925; *m* 21 June 1951 *Stanley Arnold Peter Keevil, son of Stanley Peter Keevil, of Watcombe Hill Ho, Torquay, and has issue:
1c *Sarah Anne [Mrs Paul Kane, Three Oaks, 65 Worthing Rd, Horsham, Sussex]; *b* 1952; *m* 1975 *Paul Kane
2c *Charlotte Fiona [Mrs Anthony Ferens, Château de Beysserat, Monségur, 33580 Gironde, France]; *b* 1956; *m* 1990 *Anthony Ferens
2a Richard George Temple; *b* 22 Oct 1869; *d* unm 19 Jan 1939
1a Geraldine; *m* 1st 13 July 1886 Andrew Edward McKean, of The Manor Ho, Walsall, s of Andrew McKean of Walsall Manor, Staffs, and had issue; *m* 2nd 29 July 1911 Francis Charles Clifford, of Stanshaw Court, Yale, Glos, yst son of Sir Charles Clifford, 1st Bt (*qv*), and *d* 9 April 1925
2a Mary Cecilia; *m* 2 Aug 1893 Hugh Hamilton Martin, JP, of Oakwood, West Malvern, Worcs, and *d* 31 Dec 1946, leaving issue. He *d* 30 Dec 1936
(2) Henry William (Rev), JP, Rector of Seven Stoke, Worcester, RD and Hon Canon of Worcester; *b* 24 Dec 1829; *m* 21 April 1868 Leila Louisa (*d* 1899), 2nd dau of Goodwin Charles Colquitt-Craven, of Brockhampton Park, Glos, and *d* 10 April 1920, leaving:
1a Fulwar Cecil Ashton, OBE (1918), Supt of Road Tport GWR; *b* 14 June 1874; *m* 7 Feb 1917 Lorna Mary (*d* 18 March 1965), dau of Capt Peregrine Henry Thomas Fellowes, Ch Constable of Hampshire, and *d* 24 July 1944, leaving issue:
1b Geoffrey Fulwar; *b* 30 Nov 1917; *d* 31 March 1928
2b +Digby Colquitt, served WW II (despatches, Chev Order of Leopold with Palm, Belgian Croix de Guerre with Palm); *b* 19 Jan 1919; *m* 1946 *Marina, formerly w of Willie Gosse, and only dau of Wilhelm George Viktor von Wahl, and had issue:
1c +Sebastian; *b* 1946; *m* 5 Dec 1965 *Helen Koslow, and has issue:
1d +Adrian; *b* 1967
1d *Alexandra; *b* 1966
2d *Christine; *b* 1971
3d *Catherine; *b* 1976
2c +Mark; *b* 1952
1c *Elizabeth; *b* 1947; *m* 1967 *Henry J C Pauwels
2c *Xenia; *b* 1949
1b *Lorna Peggy Maria; *b* 16 Oct 1922
1a Blanche Katherine Adine; *m* 6 Jan 1904 Rev George Le Strange Amphlett, and *d* 28 Dec 1968, aged 99, leaving issue. He *d* 12 Sept 1944
2a Sybil Augusta; *m* 3 Feb 1904 12th Baron Dudley (*qv*) and *d* 5 Nov 1958, leaving issue
3a Winifred Leila; *m* 14 Nov 1906 Rev Francis Herbert Horne, late Rector of Drinkstone, Woolpit, Suffolk, and *d* 22 Dec 1952, leaving issue. He *d* Nov 1943
(3) John Willoughby, late 48th and 15th Regts; *b* 28 April 1837; *m* 1st 28 March 1867 Frances Elizabeth (*d* 26 April 1870), est dau of Le Baron Drury, of St John's, New Brunswick, and had a s; *m* 2nd 30 Aug 1873 Edith Alice (*m* 2nd John Maitland, MP Kirkcudbright, and *d* May 1919), est dau of Rev E A Litton, Rector of Naunton, Andoversford, Cheltenham, and *d* 3 March 1905

(4) Gilbert George (Rev), Rector of Woolstone, and Vicar of Oxenton; *b* 18 July 1842; *m* 11 Jan 1870 Mary (*d* 25 Sept 1890), dau of Thomas Jackson, and *dsp* 16 April 1906

(5) George Walter Thomas; slr 1871; *b* 19 Dec 1843; *m* 1st 2 June 1877 Constance Jane (*d* 3 May 1907), est dau of Rev Edward Winnington-Ingram, of Ribbesford, Rector of Stanford-on-Teme, Worcs (*see* WINNINGTON, Bt), and had issue:

1a Harold Theodore; *b* 10 May 1880; *d* unm 21 Oct 1905

2a Frederick William; 2nd Lt Roy Fus; *b* 21 May 1882; *d* unm 28 Aug 1952

1a Sylvia Kathleen; *b* 16 April 1878; *m* 15 Dec 1900 Arthur Edward Morgan, of Spring Valley, Marengo, NSW, and *d* 1943, leaving issue

2a Constance Mary Adeline; *b* 25 June 1886; *m* 26 July 1911 Lt-Col Claud Broughton Grice-Hutchinson, DSO, RA, son of Capt Grice-Hutchinson, Scottish Rifles, and *d* 20 April 1962, leaving issue. He *d* 22 June 1955

(5) (cont.) George Coventry *m* 2nd 15 Sept 1910 Charlotte Matilda Grace (*d* 1955), dau of George W Chapman, of The Pound, Oxenhall, Newent, Glos, and Gamage Hall, Much Marcle, Herefs, and *d* 23 Jan 1927

(1) Eleanora Julia; *m* 4 July 1843 Rev Hon William Whitworth Chetwynd Talbot, bro of 18th Earl of Shrewsbury (*see* SHREWSBURY and WATERFORD, E), and *d* 15 Dec 1897, leaving issue

(2) Frederica Mary; *m* 2 Sept 1854 Maj J T Kearney, 15th Hus, and *d* 10 March 1898, leaving issue. He was *k* in China, 1 June 1857

(3) Barbara Frederica Beaujolois; *m* 4 Oct 1853 John Gaspard Fanshawe, of Parsloes, Essex, and *d* 31 Jan 1903, leaving issue. He *d* 27 Dec 1903

(4) Mary Theresa Burdett; *m* 1st 12 Feb 1873 George Seaham Tucker de Windt, est son of Capt Clayton de Windt, 15th Hus. He *dsp* 26 Oct 1876. She *m* 2nd 22 July 1879 John Henry Empson, of Yokefleet Hall, Yorks. He *d* 29 Aug 1881. She *m* 3rd 1881 Hon Frederick Standish O'Grady, afterwards 6th Viscount Guillamore (*see* 1953 edn), and *dsp* 12 Jan 1910. He *d* 11 Oct 1927

1 Augusta Maria; *m* 16 May 1806 Lt-Col Sir Willoughby Cotton, GCB, and *d* 1 Nov 1865, leaving issue (*see* COMBERMERE, V)

2 Barbara; *m* 23 July 1818 Lt-Col Alexander Charles Crauford, son of Sir James Gregan-Crauford, 2nd Bt, of Kilbirney, and *d* 4 Sept 1838. He *dsp* 12 March 1838

3 Sophia Catherine; *m* 1st 2 June 1821 Sir Roger Gresley, 3rd Bt (*d* 12 Oct 1837); *m* 2nd 16 July 1839 Sir William Des Vœux, 3rd Bt (*see* 1940 edn), and *dsp* 29 March 1875. He *d* 4 Jan 1868

The 7th EARL *d* 1831; his est son,

GEORGE WILLIAM COVENTRY, **8th Earl of Coventry**; *b* 16 Oct 1784; MP (Tory) Worcester 1818–26, Ld Lt and Custos Rotulorum of Worcs; *m* 1st 16 Jan 1808 Lady Emma Susanna Lygon (*d* 8 Aug 1810), 2nd dau of 1st Earl Beauchamp (*see* 1970 edn), and had:

1 George William, *Viscount Deerhurst*; *b* 25 Oct 1808; *m* 15 March 1836 Harriet Anne (*d* 7 Jan 1842), dau of Sir Charles Cockerell, Bt, and *dvp* 5 Nov 1838, having had issue:

(1) GEORGE WILLIAM, **9th Earl**

(1) Maria Emma Catherine; granted rank of earl's dau; *m* 7 Feb 1858 Hon Gerald Henry Brabazon Ponsonby and *d* 7 Feb 1912, leaving issue (*see* BESSBOROUGH, E)

The **8th Earl** *m* 2nd 6 Nov 1811 Lady Mary Beauclerk (*d* 11 Sept 1845), dau of 6th Duke of St Albans (*qv*), and by her had further issue:

2 Henry Amelius; army offr; *b* 15 Oct 1815; *m* 2 Aug 1837 Caroline Stirling (*d* 1 Jan 1862), 2nd dau of James Dundas, 28th of Dundas, and *d* 3 April 1873, having had, with other issue:

(1) Henry Amelius Beauclerk, Capt Gren Gds; *b* 15 May 1842; *m* 4 Dec 1869 Evelyn Mary (*d* 7 Nov 1924), widow of George John Brudenell-Bruce (*see* AILESBURY, M), and dau of 2nd Earl of Craven (*qv*), and *d* 29 June 1885, leaving issue:

1a Henry Robert Beauclerk; *b* 20 Sept 1871; *m* 18 July 1893 Lady Mary Muriel Sophie Howard, JP (*d* 19 Feb 1938), est dau of 18th Earl of Suffolk and (11th Earl of) Berkshire (*qv*), and *d* 25 June 1953, having had:

1b Henry Dan Beauclerk; *b* 28 Nov 1899; *d* unm 8 Sept 1946

2b Arthur Beauclerk, DSC, OBE (1950), MIMech E, Capt RN; *b* 7 Dec 1900; *m* 30 April 1928 Muriel Ethel Francis (*d* 1986), only dau of Hugh B Craven, of Wheathills Ho, Kirk Langley, Derbys, and *d* 8 June 1971, leaving:

1c Sara Mary; *b* 25 May 1929; *d* unm 5 Feb 1987

2c *Auriol Susan [Mrs Wallace Reid, 36 St Peter's Sq, London W6 9NW]; *b* 21 Oct 1932; *m* 18 Feb 1966 *Wallace McMillan Reid, yr son of James Henderson Reid, of Broadlea, Galloway, and has had:

1d *Caspar James Beauclerk; *b* 18 May 1971

1d *Frances Elizabeth; *b* 3 Jan 1967

2d Polly Venetia; *b* 12 June, *d* 13 June 1968

1b Muriel Joan Vi Vi Eleanor; *b* 6 Nov 1897; *d* unm 6 Dec 1943

(2) Henry Adam Frederick Fergusson; Lt 60th Rifles; *b* 2 Oct 1843; *m* 7 May 1889 Margaret Blencowe, 3rd dau of Rev John Henry Noyes, Vicar of Ketton, and *dsp* 10 Jan 1900

(3) Henry Aubrey; RHG; *b* 10 Oct 1845; *m* 1st 2 July 1870 Lady Alexina Duff (*dsp* 30 April 1882), sis of 1st Duke of Fife (*qv*); *m* 2nd 15 Aug 1892 Mary (*d* 15 July 1937) (*m* 2nd 10 July 1912 Nigel Richard Fitzhardinge Kingscote, DL, of Kingscote, Glos (*d* 24 Nov 1921), dau of Col Charles William Miles, of Burtonhill, Malmesbury, and *d* 13 May 1909, having by her had issue:

1a Nesta Helen Mary; *b* 18 July 1894; *m* 18 Feb 1941 Edward Trefaulx Harper, yr son of William Harper, of Sunderland, and *d* 27 Dec 1970. He *d* 21 Sept 1943

(1) Mary Frederick Dundas; *b* 25 May 1838; *m* 30 May 1860 John Alexander Burn Callender, of Preston Hall, Midlothian, and *d* 6 Nov 1876, leaving issue. He *d* 25 Sept 1865

(2) Mary Eleanor Lauderdale; *b* 25 Sept 1847; *m* 2 Dec 1868 18th Earl of Suffolk and Berkshire (*qv*) and *d* 31 Oct 1928, leaving issue

(3) Mary Caroline; *b* 11 Sept 1848; *m* 28 Nov 1874 George Dixon Atkinson-Clark, of Belford Hall, Northumberland, and *d* 9 April 1912, leaving issue. He *d* 2 April 1921

1 Mary Augusta; *m* 9 May 1833 4th and last Baron Holland (*see* ILCHESTER, E), and *d* 23 Sept 1889. He *dsp* 18 Dec 1889

The 8th EARL *d* 15 May 1843; his gs,

GEORGE WILLIAM COVENTRY, **9th Earl of Coventry**; CC Croome, Ld Lt and Custos Rotulorum Worcs 1891–1923, High Steward Tewkesbury, Hon Col 5th and 6th Bns Worcs Regt, Col Worcs Vol Regt, Capt Gentlemen-at-Arms 1877–80 and 1885–86, Master of the Buckhounds 1886–92 and 1895–1900, Pres Worcs TAA 1905; *b* 9 May 1838; *m* 25 Jan 1865 Blanche (*d* 16 March 1930), 3rd dau of 2nd Earl of Craven (*qv*), and had issue:

1 George William, *Viscount Deerhurst*, DL, JP; CC Worcs, Lt-Col TFR, Comdt Worcs Nat Reserve 1912, Lt-Col 2nd Vol Bn Worcs Regt and Lt Worcs Regt WW I (despatches), v-chm Worcs TAA; *b* 15 Nov 1865; *m* 10 March 1894 Virginia Lee, DGStJ (*d* 8 Nov 1948), only dau of William Daniel and step-dau of Charles William Bonynge, of 42 Princes Gate, SW, and *d* 8 Aug 1928, leaving issue (the yr s and daus were granted rank of earl's daus/yr s 1930):

(1) GEORGE WILLIAM REGINALD VICTOR, **10th Earl**

(2) John Bonynge; Capt Gren Gds, Mayor Worcester 1929, Alderman and JP City of Worcester 1930, CC Worcs; *b* 9 Jan 1903; *educ* Eton and Magdalen Coll Oxford; *m* 29 Dec 1942 Mrs Sybil Duse (*d* 18 Dec 1972), 2nd dau of Alan Tattam, JP, of Sydney, Australia, and *dsp* 4 July 1969

(1) Helena Blanche; *b* 19 Jan 1895; *m* 31 Jan 1922 6th Earl of Harrowby (*qv*), and *d* 1974, having had issue

(2) Peggy Virginia; *b* 24 Oct 1897; *m* 11 Dec 1925 Eustace Benyon Hoare, est son of Alfred Ernest Hoare, OBE, DL, JP, of Chelsworth, and *d* 18 May 1955, leaving issue. He *d* 9 July 1961

2 Charles John, CB (1923), JP and DL, Lt-Col and Brevet-Col late RA (TA), Hon Col 1927, formerly Capt 3rd Bn Worcs Regt, served in Bechuanaland Border Police 1888–96, in Jameson's Raid 1896, in W Africa Frontier Force 1898–99, in Matabele War (medal, despatches), and WW I (despatches); *b* 26 Feb 1867; *m* 16 Jan 1900 Lily (*d* 1 March 1970), yst dau of William Fitzhugh Whitehouse, of Eastbourne Lodge, Newport, USA, and *d* 2 June 1929, leaving issue:

(1) Charles William Gerald, Lt-Cdr RN, served WW I and II; *b* 2 Nov 1900; *educ* RNCs Osborne and Dartmouth; *das* Norfolk, Virginia, USA, 10 Oct 1941

(2) +FRANCIS HENRY [Francis Coventry Esq, Contrada S Rocco 10, 6987 Caslano, Switzerland], Lt-Cdr RNVR, served WW II, late Lt RA (TA); *b* 27 Sept 1912; heir presumptive; *educ* Eton and New Coll Oxford (BA 1934); *m* 14 May 1945 *Yolande Lucienne, yr dau of Lucien P di Benedetto, of Alexandria, and viale del Vignola, Rome, and has:

1a *Patricia Caroline Mary; *b* 8 Dec 1950; *m* 1st 22 Feb 1969 (*divorce* 1984) Antonio Morisani, only son of Col Rodolf P Morisani, of Rome; *m* 2nd 1986 *Raymond P Bianchi, of Castel S Pietro, and by her 1st husb has:

1b *Gian-Marco; *b* 1970

(1) Pamela Elizabeth; *b* 16 Oct 1901; *m* 1st 24 April 1928 (*divorce* 1940) Lt-Cdr James George Greville Dugdale, RN (*d* 15 Nov 1964), of Wroxall Abbey, Warwick, and had issue; *m* 2nd 18 April 1940 9th Earl of Aylesford (*qv*), and *d* 4 May 1990

(2) Diana Bruen; *b* 22 Aug 1910; *m* 28 Feb 1933 (*divorce* 1969) John Sidney Mason, late Lt Gren Gds, er son of Maj James Sidney Mason, of 20 Wigmore Street, W1, and *d* 27 April 1990

3 Henry Thomas; *b* 3 May 1868; *m* 3 Dec 1907 Mrs Edith McCreery (*d* 8 March 1949), dau of Col Lawrence Kip, of New York, USA, and *d* 2 Aug 1934, having had issue:

(1) Victor Henry; *b* 4 Dec 1909; *m* 6 Aug 1943 *Winifred Louise, dau of Arthur E Cooper

(2) Cecil George; *b* 21 March 1911; *d* 16 May 1912

4 Reginald William (Sir), ktd 1923, DL, JP Worcs, KC (1921); memb Bar Cncl, barrister Inner Temple 1896, Bencher 1928, Recorder of Stoke-on-Trent 1921, Chm Worcester QS 1927, Dep Chm Middx QS 1936; *b* 29 Aug 1869; *educ* New Coll Oxford (BA); *m* 1st 27 July 1911 Gwenllian Pascoe (*d* 3 Nov 1925), formerly w of St John Browne Killery and 2nd dau of Edward Vaughan Morgan, of S Kensington (*see* 1970 edn VAUGHAN-MORGAN, Bt), and had:

(1) Peter; *b* 20, *d* 29 July 1913

(2) Arthur Reginald; *b* 9 April 1919; 2nd Lt Coldstream Gds; *d* 19–

(1) *Mary Gwenllian [Mrs George Finnegan, 274 Cooden Dve, Bexhill, Sussex]; *b* April 1912; *m* 1 June 1935 George Albert Finegan, LRCP(I), LRCS(I) (*d* 1965), and has issue:

1a *Barbara Jane; *b* 1936

2a *Sonia Mary; *b* 1939

(2) Joan Bettine Gwenllian; *b* 24 June 1916; *m* 2 Aug 1945 Simon Birch, Capt Coldstream Gds, only son of Col Wyndham Birch, DSO, MBE, DL, of Beaumont Hall, Thorpe-le-Stoken, Essex, and *d* 19–, leaving:

1a *Julian Wyndham; *b* 6 March 1950; *educ* Eton

2a *James Lovel; *b* 24 July 1956

1a *Jacqueline Anne; *b* 1 Sept 1946; *m* 15 Jan 1968 A Lincoln Taber, son of A Lincoln Taber, of Pacific Palisades, California, USA

4 (cont.) Sir Reginald Coventry *m* 2nd 17 Dec 1926 Frances Constance (*d* 13 March 1943), widow of Walter P Jeffreys, of Cynghordy, and *d* 3 Dec 1940

5 William Francis; *b* 6 Aug 1875; *d* 11 Dec 1937

6 Thomas George; Lt Wilts Regt, WW I with Canadian Expdny Force, MIC, Br Columbia 1924–28, Market Commr in London for BC Govt 1929; *b* 25 Aug 1885; *educ* Eton and RMC Sandhurst; *m* 25 July 1910 Alice (*d* 1961), dau of Thomas Ward, of Hasketon, Woodbridge, Suffolk, and *d* 9 Dec 1972, having had issue:

(1) +William Thomas; Lt-Cdr RCNVR (ret); *b* 1 July 1911; *educ* BC U; *m* 1st 1940 Gwendolyn V Burton; *m* 2nd 13 Oct 1950 *Irene Muriel Shay, of Nova Scotia, and *d* 1993

(2) Robert George; F/Lt RAF; *b* 9 April 1913; *m* 1936 Olga (*d* 1985), only dau of John Henry Warhurst, and was *ka* 21 Sept 1940, leaving issue:

1a *Monica Anne; *b* 1939; *m* 4 Jan 1967 James Stuart Underhill, son of H S Underhill, of New York, USA

(3) Henry Reginald, DFC, W/Cdr RAF; *b* 10 Feb 1915; *ka* 12 Oct 1943

(4) +Gerald Victor, CD [Gerald Coventry Esq CD, 1739–148 A St, Surrey, BC V4A 6G5, Canada], Lt (QM) Canadian Militia 1961, served WW II 1940–45,

in Canadian Army, Appraiser Customs-Excise, Victoria, BC, Canada (Fed Govt); *b* 4 Oct 1917; *m* 12 June 1943 *Constance Hilda, dau of Henry Edward Green, of 19 Gladesmore Road, N15 and has had:

1a John Stephen; *b* 20 Feb 1949; *d* unm 31 May 1972

1a *Angela Barbara; *b* 7 June 1944; *m* 1974 *Robert Arthur Chapman, and has issue:

1b *Lloyd Steven; *b* 1979

1b *Susan Teresa; *b* 1977

1 Barbara Elizabeth, JP; *b* 27 Oct 1870; *m* 26 July 1894 Gerald Dudley Smith, DL, JP, of Levant Lodge, Earls Croome, Worcester and *d* 29 Nov 1946, leaving issue. He *d* 29 Dec 1936

2 Dorothy; *b* 6 Feb 1872; *m* 30 Aug 1910 Sir Keith Alexander Fraser, 5th Bt (*see* 1970 edn FRASER, Bt, of Ledeclune), and *d* 2 Dec 1965, leaving issue. He *d* 21 Sept 1935

3 Anne Blanche Alice, Médaille de la Reconnaissance Français, Médaille de la France Liberée; *b* 27 Jan 1874; *m* 4 Jan 1898 Prince Victor Albert Jay Duleep Singh, of Lahore, late Capt Roy Dragoons, and *d* 2 July 1956. He *dsp* 7 June 1918

The 9th EARL *d* 13 March 1930; his gs,

GEORGE WILLIAM REGINALD VICTOR COVENTRY, **10th Earl of Coventry**, JP Pembs, DL Worcs; Lt Worcs Regt, Lt Worcs Yeo (TA); *b* 10 Sept 1900; *m* 17 Sept 1921 Hon Nesta Donne Philipps, TD, DL (Carmarthenshire 1965), Ch Commr ATS WW II (*m* 2nd 17 Jan 1953 Maj Terrance Vincent Fisher-Hoch, RA (*d* 1978), son of John Henry Fisher-Hoch, of Basle, Switzerland), est dau of 1st and last Baron Kylsant (*see* ST DAVIDS, V), and was *ka* Givenchy May 1940, having had:

1 GEORGE WILLIAM COVENTRY, **11th and present Earl of Coventry**

1 *Anne Donne; *b* 17 June 1922

2 Joan Blanche; *b* 10 Nov 1924; *d* unm 6 May 1948

3 *Maria Alice [The Lady Maria Coventry, Levant Lodge, Earls Croome, Worcester]; *b* 2 Oct 1931; *m* 6 May 1954 (*divorce* 1968, resumed maiden name) John Richard Lewes, er son of Capt John Hugh Lewes CBE, DSC, RN, of White Willows, Yelverton, Devon

Seat: Earls Croome Court, Earls Croome, Worcs. This is a large black-and-white timber mansion dating from the 16th and 17th centuries. It is not to be confused with the much grander Croome Court at Croome d'Abitot, which was also a Coventry property from 1751, when its largely Palladian structure was embarked upon (mostly by Capability Brown, it would seem) to 1948, when it was sold, the actual estate having been in the hands of the family since 1597 (*see* above).

COWDRAY

Arms: Per fess indented gu. and or two suns in splendour in chief and a demi-gryphon couped, wings elevated and addorsed, in base, all counterchanged. **Crest:** In front of a demi-gryphon as in the arms, holding between the claws a mill stone ppr., thereon a mill rind sa., a sun in splendour. **Supporters:** Dexter, a diver holding with the exterior hand his helmet; sinister, a Mexican peon, both ppr. **Motto:** Do it with thy might. **Creations:** Bt. (UK) 26 June 1894, B. (UK) 16 July 1910, V. (UK) 2 Jan 1917.

THE 4TH VISCOUNT COWDRAY, of Cowdray, in the Co of Sussex, **Baron Cowdray**, of Midhurst, in the Co of Sussex, and a **Baronet** (Sir Michael Orlando Weetman Pearson, Bt) [The Rt Hon The Viscount Cowdray, Cowdray Park, Midhurst, W Sussex GU29 0AY]; *b* 17 June 1944; *s f* 1995; *educ* Gordonstoun; *m* 1st 1977 (*divorce* 1984) Ellen (Fritzi), dau of Hermann Erhardt, of Munich; *m* 2nd 1987 *Marina Rose, 2nd dau of John Howard Cordle (*see* POWERSCOURT, V), and by her has:

1 +PEREGRINE JOHN DICKINSON; *b* 27 Oct 1994

2 +Montague Orlando William; *b* 17 May 1997

1 *Eliza Anne Venetia; *b* 1988

2 *Emily Jane Marina; *b* 1989

3 *Catrina Sophie Lavinia; *b* 1991

Lineage: GEORGE PEARSON, of Brickendonbury, Herts; *m* Sarah (*d* 10 Feb 1911), dau of Weetman Dickinson, of High Hoyland, Yorks, and *d* 3 March 1899, leaving, with other issue:

Sir Weetman Dickinson Cowdray, 1st Bt, and **1st Viscount Cowdray**, of Cowdray, Co Sussex, so *cr* 26 June 1894 and 2 Jan 1917 respectively, as also earlier 16 July 1910 BARON COWDRAY, of Midhurst, Co Sussex, PC (1917), GCVO (1925), DL (Aberdeenshire); High Steward Colchester, MP (Lib) Colchester 1895–1910, Rector Aberdeen U 1917–21, Head of S Pearson and Son, Lt-Col Eng and Rly Staff Corps, Pres Air Bd 1916–17; *b* 15 July 1856; *m* 22 June 1881 Annie, GBE (*d* 15 April 1932), LGStJ, High Steward Colchester 1927, dau of Sir John Cass, of Bradford, Yorks, and had issue:

1 WEETMAN HAROLD MILLER, **2nd Viscount**

2 (Bernard) Clive; Maj TAR, formerly Sussex Yeo, High Sheriff Sussex 1940, chm BOAC 1940–43; *b* 12 Aug 1887; *educ* Rugby and Trin Coll Cambridge (BA 1908); *m* 14 Oct 1915 Hon Alicia Mary Dorothea Knatchbull-Hugessen (*d* 15 Jan 1974), dau of 1st Baron Brabourne (*qv*), and *d* 22 July 1965, leaving issue:

(1) Veronica Mary; *b* 15 Aug 1916; *m* 1st 17 May 1940 Lt Albert Marcus Rueff, Tower Hamlets Rifles, 9th Bn Rifle Bde, only son of Leon Rueff, of West Lodge Park, Hadley Wood, Herts. He *d* of wounds received in action at Derna, Libya, 8 April 1941. She *m* 2nd 18 Sept 1950 Patrick Arthur Tritton, est son of Arthur Francis Tritton, of Denford Mill, Hungerford, Berks (*see* TRITTON, Bt)

(2) Lavinia; *b* 7 Feb 1919; *m* 15 Sept 1939 Maj (Charles) Michael Smiley, late Rifle Bde, only son of Capt Hubert Stewart Smiley, and had issue (*see* SMILEY, Bt)

(3) *(Elisabeth) Dione [The Rt Hon The Lady Gibson, Penn's Rocks, Groombridge, Sussex]; *b* 16 July 1920; *m* 14 July 1945 *Baron Gibson (LP), Maj late Middlesex Yeo, only son of Thornely Gibson, of 2 Kensington Gate, W, and has issue:

1a *Hugh Marcus Thornely, DL (Derbys) [The Hon Hugh Gibson DL, The Fold, Parwich, Ashbourne, Derbys DE6 1QL]; *b* 23 June 1946; *educ* Eton and Magdalen Col Oxford (BA); *m* 31 March 1967 *Hon Frances Towneley Strachey, sis of 4th Baron O'Hagan (*qv*), and has:

1b *Jasper Tallentyre; *b* 1975

1b *Effie Dione; *b* 13 Sept 1970

2b *Amelia Mary; *b* 1973

2a *Clive Patrick [The Hon Clive Gibson, 29A Hyde Park Gate, London SW7 5DJ]; *b* 24 Jan 1948; *educ* Eton and Magdalen Coll Oxford (BA); *m* 1974 *Anne Marie Jeanne, dau of Count Jacques de Chauvigny de Blot, and has:

1b *Patrick Clive; *b* 1975

1b *Beatrice Dione Elizabeth; *b* 1978

3a *William Knatchbull [The Hon William Gibson, 46 Victoria Rd, London W8 5RO]; *b* 26 Aug 1951; *educ* Eton and Magdalen Coll Oxford (BA); *m* 1988 *Lori Frances, only dau of Herbert Mintz, of Miami, and has:

1b *Matthew Charles; *b* 1990

1b *Sarah Claire; *b* 1992

4a *Piers Nathaniel [The Hon Piers Gibson, Grove Farm House, Paddockhurst, W Sussex RH10 4SF]; *b* 15 March 1956; *educ* Eton and Magdalen Coll Oxford (BA); *m* 1981 *Melanie Jane Stella, er dau of Jack Walters, OBE, of Monaco, and has:

1b *Harry Maximilian; *b* 1988

2b *Theodore Charles; *b* 1991

1b *Lucy Lavinia; *b* 1986

2b *Martha Camilla; *b* 1996

3 Francis Geoffrey; attd Motor Tport Section BEF WW I; *b* 23 Aug 1891; *m* 6 Aug 1909 Ethel Elizabeth (*d* 10 Jan 1982, having *m* 2nd 11 April 1918 (*divorce* 1926) A/Cdre Henry John Francis Hunter, CBE, MC, RAF, late Rifle Bde, son of Henry Charles Vicars Hunter, and resumed her former name of Pearson 1928), dau of John J Lewis, of Hove, and was *ka* 6 Sept 1914, leaving issue:

(1) *Joan Cinnetta [Mrs William Acton, Post Box 31, Post Restante, Corfu, Greece]; *b* 19 Jan 1912; *m* 29 June 1932 William Anthony Acton (*d* 1993), only son of William Walter Acton, of Wolverton Hall, Worcs, and has issue:

1a *Caroline Jane [Lady Dawson, 11 Burton Court, Franklin's Row, London SW3]; *b* 12 May 1933; *m* 7 July 1955 Maj Sir (Hugh Halliday) Trevor Dawson, Scots Gds, 3rd Bt (*qv*), and has issue

1 Gertrude Mary, GBE (1950, DBE 1933), JP Sussex; Hon Dir WLA 1939–45; *m* 26 Nov 1903 3rd Baron Denman (*qv*) and *d* 2 June 1954, leaving issue

The 1st VISCOUNT *d* 1 May 1927; his est son,

WEETMAN HAROLD MILLER PEARSON, **2nd Viscount Cowdray**, DL Sussex; Maj late Sussex Yeo, MP Eye 1906–18; *b* 18 April 1882; *m* 14 Nov 1905 Agnes Beryl (*d* 19 Feb 1948), yr dau of Lord Edward Spencer Churchill (*see* MARLBOROUGH, D), and had issue:

1 WEETMAN JOHN CHURCHILL, **3rd Viscount**

1 Daisy Yoskyl Consuelo; *b* 5 Aug 1906; *m* 1st 20 Jan 1932 Lt Hon Robert Brampton Gurdon, Coldstream Gds, only son of 2nd Baron Cranworth (*qv*), and had issue. He was *ka* in the Middle East July 1942. She *m* 2nd 11 Nov 1944 Lt-Col Alistair Monteith Gibb, late Roy Wilts Yeo (*k* in a polo accident 29 July 1955), est son of Brig-Gen Sir Alexander Gibb, GBE, and had further issue:

(1) Jane Elizabeth Angela; *b* 21 Aug 1946; *m* 1972 (*divorce* 1990) 13th Marquess of Huntly (*qv*)

1 (cont.) The Hon Mrs Gibb *m* 3rd 26 Jan 1962 1st and last Baron McCorquodale of Newton (*d* 25 Sept 1971; *see* 1970 edn) and *d* 1979

2 *(Beryl) Nancy; *b* 25 Feb 1908; *m* 31 Jan 1934 1st Viscount Blakenham (*qv*) and has issue

3 Angela; chm Westminster Press Prov Newspaper; *b* 27 Feb 1910 (twin with her bro); *m* 1st 25 Aug 1930 Lt-Col George Anthony (Tony) Murray, OBE, Scottish Horse, only son of Sir George Evelyn Pemberton Murray, KCB, of 19 Manchester Square, W1 (*see* ATHOLL, D), and had issue. He was *ka* in Italy, April 1945. She *m* 2nd 5 June 1950 Lt-Col Robert Mordan Thorne Campbell-Preston, OBE, MC, TD, DL (*d* 14 June 1996), est son of Lt-Col Robert William Pigott Clarke Campbell-Preston, DL, JP, of Ardchattan Priory, Argyllshire (*see* also MALMESBURY, E), and *d* 1981, having had further issue

4 Brenda Ruby; *b* 15 Nov 1912; *m* 1st 11 June 1934 (*divorce* 1948) G/Capt Paul Willert, RAF, only son of Sir Arthur Willert, KBE, of 12 Sloane Terr Mansions, SW1, and had issue; *m* 2nd 16 Dec 1948 Hugh Carter and had further issue

5 *(Helena) Daphne [The Hon Mrs Lakin, Hammerwood House, Iping, Midhurst, Sussex]; *b* 13 Sept 1918; *m* 10 Aug 1939 Lt-Col John Lakin, TD, JP (*d* 1989), late Warwicks Yeo, only surv son of Henry Gilbert Lakin, of Temple Cottage, Harbury, Warwicks, and has issue (*see* LAKIN, Bt)

The 2nd VISCOUNT *d* 5 Oct 1933; his son

WEETMAN JOHN CHURCHILL PEARSON, **3rd Viscount Cowdray**, TD, DL (Sussex 1945); *educ* Eton and Ch Ch Oxford; Capt RA (TA) WW II (severely wounded), Lt-Col HG 1940–41, PPS to Parly U-Sec Air Sept 1941–Dec 1942; *b* 27 Feb 1910; *m* 1st 19 July 1939 (*divorce* 1950) Lady Anne Pamela Bridgeman, dau of 5th Earl of Bradford (*qv*), and had:

1 MICHAEL ORLANDO WEETMAN PEARSON, **4th and present Viscount Cowdray**

1 *Mary Teresa [The Hon Mrs Stopford Sackville, Idbury House, Idbury, Kingham, Oxon OX7 6RU]; *b* 3 June 1940 (HRH THE PRINCESS ROYAL, COUNTESS OF HAREWOOD, stood sponsor); *m* as his 2nd w *Lionel Geoffrey Stopford Sackville and has issue (*see* COURTOWN, E)

2 *Liza Jane [The Hon Mrs MacNaughton, Old Law House, 395 Miramontes Rd, Woodside, Calif 94062, USA]; *b* 30 March 1942; *m* 19 Dec 1967 *Malcolm MacNaughton, Jr, est son of Malcolm MacNaughton, of Honolulu, and has:

(1) *Justin John; *b* 1972

(1) *Natasha Anne; *b* 17 July 1969

The **3rd Viscount** *m* 2nd 4 March 1953 *Elizabeth Georgiana Mather, 2nd dau of Anthony Henry Mather Jackson (*see* JACKSON, Bt), and *d* 19 Jan 1995, leaving by her:

2 +Charles Anthony of The Manor House, Birkenhead [The Hon Charles Pearson, Pitshill, Midhurst, W Sussex]; *b* 5 March 1956; *m* 1992 *Baroness Benedicte Blixen-Finecke, dau of Ifver Iuul, of Fyn, Denmark, and Mrs Gerald Barry, of Cookham, Berks, and has :

(1) +George; *b* Nov 1995

(1) *Carinthia Alexandra; *b* 1993

3 *Lucy [The Hon Mrs Fraser, Blackdown Park, Lurgashall, W Sussex]; *b* 11 April 1954; *m* 1st 17 May 1972 (*divorce* 1978) Luis Hector Juan Sosa Basualdo, of Argentina, and has issue:

(1) *Rupert Peregrine PEARSON; *b* 9 March 1976

(1) *Charlotte PEARSON; *b* 1974

3 (cont.) The Hon Mrs Lucy Basualdo *m* 2nd 1988 *Charles Torquil de Montalt Fraser, late Life Gds, er s of Maj Michael Quintin Fraser, 7th Hus (*see* MOLESWORTH, B), and by him has:

(2) *Emerald Chloe; *b* 1989

(3) *Iona Violet; *b* 1991

(4) *Iolanthe Maude; *b* 1993

(5) *Nairne Constance; *b* 1995

4 *Rosanna; *b* 1 July 1959; *m* 1988 *Palma Taylor, of Jamaica, and has:

(1) *Annie Glennah; *b* 1990

COWDREY OF TONBRIDGE

Creation: B. (LP, UK) June 1997.

THE BARON COWDREY OF TONBRIDGE, of Tonbridge, Co Kent (Sir (Michael) Colin Cowdrey, CBE (1972)) [The Rt Hon The Lord Cowdrey of Tonbridge CBE, Angmering Park, Littlehampton, W Sussex BN16 4EX]; *b* 24 Dec 1932; *educ* Tonbridge (Capt Cricket XI 1949–50, Capt Public Schs XI 1950) and BNC Oxford (Capt Oxford U XI 1954); cricketer: capped for Kent 1951 and Capt 1957–71, played for England 114 times 1954–75, Capt 23 times; Chm Internat Cricket Cncl 1986–87 and Internat Cricket Cncl 1989–93; dir Bilton plc, consultant Barclays Bank; ktd 1992; Master Skinners' Co 1985, Freeman City London 1962; Dep Chm Br Sportsman's Club; author: *Cricket Today* (1961), *Time for Reflection* (1962), *Tackle Cricket This Way* (1969), *The Incomparable Game* (1970), *MCC: The Autobiography of a Cricketer* (1976); *m* 1st 1956 (*divorce* 1985) Penelope Susan Chiesman and has three sons and a dau; *m* 2nd 1985 *Lady Herries of Terregles (*qv*)

Lineage: ERNEST ARTHUR COWDREY; *m* Kathleen Mary Taylor, BEM, and had:

(MICHAEL) COLIN (Sir), *cr* a **Baron**

COWLEY

Arms: Quarterly, 1st and 4th, gu. a cross arg, in each quarter five plates in saltire (for WELLESLEY); 2nd and 3rd, or a lion rampant gu. (for COWLEY); over all an annulet. **Crest:** Out of a ducal coronet or a demi-lion rampant gu, holding a forked pennon of the last flowing to the sinister, one third per pale from the staff arg, charged with the cross of St George. **Supporters:** Two lions gu, ducally gorged and chain reflexed over the back, or and charged on the shoulder with an annulet for difference. **Motto:** *Porro unum est necessarium* ('Moreover, one thing is needful'). **Creations:** B. (UK) 21 Jan 1828, E. and V. (UK) 11 April 1857.

THE 7TH EARL COWLEY, Viscount Dangan, Co Meath, and **Baron Cowley of Wellesley**, Co Somerset (Garret Graham Wellesley) [The Rt Hon The Earl Cowley, House of Lords, London SW1A 0PW]; *b* 30 July 1934; *s* n 1975; *educ* S California U (BS 1957) and Harvard MBA 1962); US Army Counter-Intell Corps France 1957–60, investment analyst Wells Fargo Bank San Francisco 1962–64 (research dir 1966–67), investment counsel Dodge and Cox 1964–66, v-pres and investment counsel Thorndike, Doran, Paine & Lewis Los Angeles 1967–69, sr v-pres Shareholders Capital Corp Los Angeles 1969–74, Bank of America: sr v-pres San Francisco 1974–78, gp v-pres (md) Int Investment Management Serv London 1978–85, ch investment offr London 1978–85, dir 1978–83, ind fin advsr and Co dir 1985–90, investment ptnr Thos R Miller & Son (Bermuda) 1990–, memb Assoc C Peers 1981–; *m* 1st 1960 (*divorce* 1967) Elizabeth Suzanne, dau of Haynes Lennon, of SC; *m* 2nd 1968 (*divorce* 1981) Isabelle O'Bready, of Quebec; *m* 3rd 1981 *Paige Deming, of Reno, and has issue by 1st w:

1 +(GARRET) GRAHAM, *Viscount Dangan*; *b* 30 March 1965; *m* 1990 *Claire L, only dau of Peter W Brighton, of Stow Bridge, Norfolk, and has issue:

(1) +Henry Arthur Peter; *b* 3 Dec 1991

(1) *Natasha; *b* 19s–

1 *Tara Lennon; *b* 26 Aug 1962

By either his 2nd or 3rd w the 7th EARL also has:

2 *Sarah Paige; *m* 10 Aug 1996 *Frank Mosier, er s of Frank Mosier, of Saratoga, NY

Lineage: The 1st Earl of Mornington (*see* WELLINGTON, D) had a yst s:

HENRY WELLESLEY, **1st Baron Cowley of Wellesley**, Co Somerset (UK), so *cr* 21 Jan 1828, GCB (1815, KB 1812), PC (1809); *b* 20 Jan 1773; offr 1st Foot Gds 1791–94, Sec Legn Stockholm 1792, MP (I Parl) Trim 1795 and (UK Parl, Tory) Eye 1807–09, Sec to Lord Malmesbury's Embassy Lille 1797, Priv Sec to er bro 1st Earl of Mornington as Govr Gen India 1798–1805, Envoy Lucknow 1801, Lt-Gen Nawab of Oude's ceded territories 1801–02, a Ld Treasury May-Aug 1804, a Sec Treasury 1807–09, Envoy Spain 1810 and Amb there 1811–22, Austria 1823–31 and France March-May 1835 and 1841–46; *m* 1st 20 Sept 1803 (*divorce* for adultery 1810) Charlotte (*m* 2nd 1810, as his 2nd w, 1st Marquess of Anglesey (*qv*); *d* 8 July 1853), 2nd dau of 1st Earl Cadogan (*qv*), and had issue:

1 HENRY RICHARD, **1st Earl**

2 William Henry George, Capt RN; *b* 2 Feb 1806; *m* 12 July 1842 Amelia St John (*d* 3 Oct 1889), dau of Rev Joseph White Niblock, DD, and *d* 21 Dec 1875, having had, with other issue:

(1) Gerald Edward; *b* 7 Jan 1846; *m* 7 Oct 1880 Ada Hamilton (*d* 18 Dec 1933), 3rd dau of John Martin, of The Upper Hall, Ledbury, and *d* 13 Jan 1915, having had, with other issue:

1a Gerald Valerian, MC; *b* 31 July 1885; *educ* Eton; Capt Oxfordshire Yeo (TA) WW I (wounded, despatches), Medaille de Sauvetage France; *m* 15 Oct 1931 Elizabeth Thornton (*m* 3rd 22 Oct 1965 Basil Harvey; *d* 1981), dau of Otho Ball, of Chicago, and formerly w of Quintin Holland Gilbey (*see* GILBEY, Bt), and *d* 3 April 1961, leaving issue:

1b Julian Valerian; *b* 9 Aug 1933; *educ* RNC Dartmouth; Lt RN 1951–61, chm Charles Barker Gp 1978–83; *m* 26 Aug 1965 *Elizabeth Joan [Mrs Julian Wellesley, Northgate House, Ticehurst, E Sussex TN5 7AE], dau of Cyril Alfred Stocken and formerly w of David Hall, and *d* 13 Sept 1996, leaving issue:

1c +William Valerian [William Wellesley Esq, 403 Fulham Rd, London SW10 9TU]; *b* 2 Oct 1966; *educ* Eton and Trin Coll Oxford; ch operating offr St James's Place Capital plc 1995–97; *m* Sept 1994 *Emma, dau of Sir Brian Jenks, 3rd Bt (*qv*)

1c *Kate Elizabeth; *b* 2 Feb 1970

1a Georgina Victoria; *b* 12 Aug 1881; *m* 24 April 1906 (*divorce* 1919) 5th Visount de Vesci (*qv*) and *d* 22 April 1930

(1) Mary Amelia; *m* 16 Sept 1890 Farnham Chidley Close and *d* 10 Nov 1925. He *dsp* 13 Jan 1901

(2) Charlotte Anne; *d* 19 Aug 1930

(3) Emily Grace; *m* 1880 Edward Calthrop and *d* 19 Aug 1916, leaving issue. He *d* 1912

(4) Georgina Spencer; *m* 12 April 1877 William Fitzwilliam Burton, of Burton Hall, Co Carlow, and *d* 27 May 1943, leaving issue. He *d* 16 Sept 1927

(5) Louisa Christiana; *d* unm 27 Oct 1933

3 Gerald (Very Rev), Dean Windsor, Chaplain and Ld High Almoner to HM QUEEN VICTORIA; *b* 1809; *m* 16 Sept 1856 Magdalen Montagu, VA (*d* 30 Sept 1919), dau of 6th and last Baron Rokeby of Armagh, and *d* 17 Sept 1882, having had a s

1 Charlotte Arbuthnot; *m* 17 May 1831 1st Baron Ebury (*qv*) and *d* 21 Nov 1891, leaving issue

The **1st Baron** *m* 2nd 27 Feb 1816 Georgiana Charlotte Augusta (*d* 18 Jan 1860), est dau of 1st Marquess of Salisbury (*qv*), and *d* 27 April 1847, having by her had further issue:

2 Georgiana Charlotte Mary; *b* 11 June 1817; *m* 9 Dec 1848 1st and last Baron Dalling and Bulwer of Dalling (*see* LYTTON, E) and *d* 2 Aug 1878

The 1st BARON's est s,

HENRY RICHARD WELLESLEY, **1st Earl Cowley**, so *cr* 11 April 1857, as also VISCOUNT DANGAN, Co Meath (both UK), KG (1866), GCB (1853, KCB 1851, CB 1848), PC (1852; *b* 17 June 1804; *educ* Eton and BNC Oxford; Attaché Vienna 1824, The Hague 1829, Sec Legn Stuttgart 1832–43, Sec Embassy 1843–48 and Min ad interim 1846–48 Constantinople, Envoy: Switzerland Feb 1848, Frankfurt July 1848, Germanic Confedn 1851, Amb France 1852–67; *m* 23 Oct 1833 Olivia Cecilia (*d* 21 April 1885 aged 78), dau of Lord Henry FitzGerald (*see* LEINSTER, D) by Charlotte, Baroness de Ros in her own right (*qv*), and had issue:

1 WILLIAM HENRY, **2nd Earl**

2 Cecil Charles Foley, RN; *b* 1842; *d* 28 March 1916

3 Frederick Arthur, Col Coldstream Gds, 1st Sec Vienna, Mil Attaché St Petersburg; *b* 24 May 1844; *m* 1st 15 Dec 1873 (*divorce* 1882) Emma Anne Caroline Bloomfield, dau of Lord Augustus Loftus (*see* ELY, M), and had issue:

(1) Victor Alexander Augustus Henry (Sir), KCMG, CB, FO 1899–1936 (Controller Commercial and Consular Serv 1916–24, Assist Under-Sec 1924–25, Dep Under-Sec 1925–36), Page Honour to HM QUEEN VICTORIA 1887–92; *b* 1 March 1876; *m* 20 July 1909 Alice Muriel (*d* 22 Jan 1949), est dau of Oscar Leslie Stephen, of 7 Eaton Terrace, London SW, and *d* 20 Feb 1954, having had issue:

(1) Anne Muriel; *b* 22 May 1913; *d* 20 Feb 1919

3 (cont.) Col The Hon Frederick Wellesley *m* 2nd 3 June 1884 (*divorce* 1897) Catherine Candelin (Kate Vaughan) (*d* 21 Feb 1903); *m* 3rd his nephew's sis-in-law Evelyn Katrine Gwenfra (*d* 11 March 1939), widow of 3rd Duke of Wellington (*qv*) and dau of Col Thomas Peers Williams, MP, of Temple House, Berks, and *d* 9 Feb 1931

1 Feodorovna Cecilia; *m* 11 April 1874 1st Viscount Bertie of Thame (*see* LINDSEY and ABINGDON, E) and *d* 30 March 1920, leaving issue

2 Sophia Georgiana Robertina; *m* 16 Feb 1863 5th Earl of Hardwicke (*qv*) and *d* 3 June 1923, leaving issue

The 1st EARL *d* 15 July 1884; his est s,

WILLIAM HENRY WELLESLEY, **2nd Earl Cowley**, Lt-Col Coldstream Gds, Kt Medjidie 5th Cl; *b* 25 Aug 1834; *educ* Eton; *m* 8 Aug 1863 Emily Gwendolen (*d* 9 Nov 1932), 2nd dau of Col Thomas Peers Williams, and *d* 28 Feb 1895, leaving (with a dau Eva Cecilia Margaret, *m* 23 Nov 1898 Randolph Gordon Erskine-Wemyss of Wemyss (*see* WEMYSS and MARCH, E); *d* 4 March 1948):

HENRY ARTHUR MORNINGTON WELLESLEY, **3rd Earl Cowley**, JP (Wilts), Lt Roy Glos Hus 1893; Ib 14 Jan 1866; *educ* Eton; *m* 1st 17 Dec 1889 (*divorce* 1897) Lady Violet Nevill (*d* 28 March 1910), yst dau of 1st Marquess of Abergavenny (*qv*), and had issue:

1 CHRISTIAN ARTHUR, **4th Earl**

The **3rd Earl** *m* 2nd 14 Dec 1905 (*divorce* 1913) Hon Millicent Florence Eleanor (*d* 29 Nov 1952), formerly w of Sir Charles Edward Cradock-Hartopp, 5th Bt (*qv*), and est dau of 1st Baron Nunburnholme (*qv*), and had issue:

2 (Henry) Gerald Valerian Francis; *b* 8 Aug 1907; *m* 1st 17 June 1929 (*divorce* 1953) Doris Caroline Sabia, est dau of Edward Robert Kennedy, of Bishops Court, Straffan, Co Kildare (*see* KENNEDY, Bt); *m* 2nd 11 Jan 1954 (*annulment* 1955) Nancy Joan, only dau of Bentley Collingwood Hilliam; *m* 3rd 30 Jan 1957 (*divorce* 1969) Marina Isobel Sherlock, only dau of Capt Rowland Francis Eustace, formerly w of (a) Capt George James Wellwood Moncreiffe and (b) Cdr John Bremer Richards Horne, DSC, RN, and widow of Lt Robert Charles Henry Dundas, RN (*see* DUNDAS, Bt); *m* 4th 1969 *Valerie Rose [The Hon Mrs Gerald Wellesley, Priestown House, Mulhuddart, Co Dublin, Ireland], 2nd dau of Christian Ernest Pitman, CBE, and *d* 25 Dec 1981, leaving by her:

(1) +Henry Arthur Winston Butler; *b* 1970

(2) +Richard Valerian; *b* 1972

The **3rd Earl** *m* 3rd 19 Jan 1914 Clare Florence Mary (*d* 8 May 1949), formerly w of Maj Geoffrey Charles Buxton (*see* BUXTON, Bt) and only child of Sir Francis George Stapleton, 8th Bt (*qv*), and by her had issue:

1 Diana Mary; *m* 20 July 1933 Col 2nd Baron Glentoran (*qv*) and *d* 1984, having had issue

2 Cecilia Katherine; *m* 1st 4 Dec 1936 (*divorce* 1942) John Claude Smiley, 2nd s of Sir John Smiley, 2nd Bt (*qv*), and had issue; *m* 2nd 1942 (*divorce* 1950) Lt-Col Norman David Melville Johnstone, MBE, Gren Gds, s of Maj Charles Melville Johnstone, of Croy, Dunbartonshire, and had further issue; *m* 3rd 18 March 1950 Norman Hyman Wachman, s of Woolf Wachman, and *d* following an accident 30 Sept 1952

The 3rd EARL *d* 15 Jan 1919; his er s,

CHRISTIAN ARTHUR WELLESLEY, **4th Earl Cowley**, Lt 5th Lancers, RMA; *b* 25 Dec 1890; *m* 1st 23 Feb 1914 (*divorce* 1933) Mae Pickard, actress (*d* 3 June 1946), of Memphis, Tenn., and had issue:

1 Michael, *Viscount Dangan*; *b* 24 May 1915; *d* 13 Feb 1922

2 DENIS ARTHUR WELLESLEY, **5th Earl Cowley**, BEM (1942), RAF WW II; *b* 25 Dec 1921; *m* 1st 16 Nov 1944 (*divorce* 1950), as her 2nd husb, Elizabeth Anne (*m* 3rd 1953 Freeman Winslow Hill), yr dau of Lt-Col Pelham Rawstorn Papillon, DSO, of Crowhurst Park, Sussex, and widow of F/Lt Stephen Alers Hankey, RAF, and had issue:

(2) RICHARD FRANCIS WELLESLEY, **6th Earl Cowley**; *b* 12 June 1946; *educ* Eton; Govt Whip 1974; *m* 1971 *Maria Delia (*m* 2nd 1980, as his 2nd w, Maj Robin James Stirling Bullock-Webster, OBE, Irish Gds), dau of Henri Buenaño, of Buenos Aires, and *d* playing squash Dec 1975, leaving:

1a *Alexia Anne Elizabeth; *b* 30 Oct 1973

2a *Caroline Maria Frances; *b* (posthumously) 11 May 1976

2 (cont.) The **5th Earl** *m* 2nd 11 July 1950 Annette Nancy Doughty (*d* following a car crash 29 Oct 1959), formerly w of Lt Arthur Simmonds, previously a widow and dau of Maj J J O'Hara, of Northumberland; *m* 3rd 15 Feb 1961 (*divorce* 1968) Janet ('Tiger') Elizabeth Mary (*m* 2nd 1976 (*divorce* 1981), as his 2nd w, Piers (Pierson John Shirley) Dixon (*see also* MARLBOROUGH, D), s of Sir Pierson Dixon, GCMG, CB), dau of Ramiah Doraswamy Aiyar, FRCS, LRCP, of Ystrad, Denbigh, N Wales, and *d* 23 March 1968

1 Patricia Mary Anne; *b* 19 Feb 1918; WRNS WW II; *das* unm 28 Aug 1944

2 *Colleen [The Lady Colleen Hanlon, 543 Westmoreland Ave, Kingston, PA, USA]; *b* 21 March 1925; WRNS WW II; *m* 9 Aug 1945 *Dr Paul A Hanlon, MD, late Capt US Army, s of Edward F Hanlon, MD, of Hazelton, PA, and has issue:

(1) *Paul Christian; *b* 18 Nov 1946

(2) *Gavin Edward; *b* 18 July 1948

(3) *Christopher Peter; *b* 23 April 1951

(4) *Timothy Patrick; *b* 25 Sept 1955

(5) *Richard Francis; *b* 30 March 1957

(1) *Colleen Patricia; *b* 18 Dec 1958

(2) *Jennifer Mary; *b* 14 Oct 1960

The **4th Earl** *m* 2nd 1933 *Mrs (Mary) Elsie Himes, and *d* 29 Aug 1962, leaving by her:

3 GARRET GRAHAM WELLESLEY, **7th and present Earl Cowley**

4 +Brian Timothy; *b* 28 Feb 1938; *educ* Arizona State Coll, Denver U Colorado, Nevada U (BS 1965) and US Treasury Law Enforcement Acad Washington; Instr US Missile Systems USAF 1958–62, Dir IRS US Treasury 1965; *m* 1st June 1961 (*divorce* 1964) Patricia P Tribbey, of Temple, Mesa, Ariz.; *m* 2nd 9 April 1966 (*divorce* 1980) Karen Elizabeth Bradbury, of Reno, Nev.; *m* 3rd 1988 *Katherine Samaniego, of New Mexico, and has issue:

(1) *Johnna (dau)

Cox

Arms: Azure a sword in fess, the blade couped at the point argent, the hilt, pommel and quillons to the sinister or, between two ancient lamps also or, enflamed proper. **Supporters:** Dexter, a horse argent, crined and hoofed or; sinister, a unicorn argent, its horn or, crined and unguled gold. **Motto:** Think and thank.
Creation: B. (LP, UK) 1982.

THE BARONESS COX, of Queensbury, Greater London (Caroline Anne Love) [The Rt Hon The Baroness Cox, The White House, Wyke Hall, Dorset SP8 5NS; 1 Arnellan House, 144–146 Slough Lane, London NW9 8XJ]; *b* 6 July 1937; *educ* Channing Sch Highgate and London U (BSc Sociology, MSc Econ 1969), FRCN 1985, SRN London Hosp 1958, staff nurse Edgware Gen Hosp 1960, research assoc U of Newcastle-Upon-Tyne 1967–68, head Sociology Dept N London Poly 1974–77, Visiting Prof Faculty of Health and Social Work Anglia Poly Essex U 1990–, Dir CPS 1983–85, Nursing Educn Research Unit Chelsea Coll London 1977–84, Baroness in Waiting April-Aug 1985, Dep Speaker Ho Lds 1986–; ,

Chllr Bournemouth U 1992–, Jagiellonian Tst 1984–93, Parental Alliance for Choice in Educn 1985–, Health Studies Ctee CNAA 1987093; V-Pres RCN 1990–, IAPS 1991–; co-dir Educn Research Tst 1980–; Tstee Medical and Emergency Relief Internat; Patron: Medical Aid for Poland Fund; co-ed Internat Jnl Nursing Studies; Hon PhD Polish U London, Commander's Cross Order of Merit Poland 1990; Hon FRCS 1996, Hon DSS Queen's U Belfast 1996; William Wilberforce Award 1995; author: *A Sociology of Medical Practice* (1975), *Rape of Reason: The Corruption of the Polytechnic of North London* (jt au 1975), *The Right to Learn* (jt au 1982), *Sociology: A Guide for Nurses, Midwives and Health Visitors* (jt au 1983); *The Insolence of Office* (jt au 1989); *Choosing a State School: how to find the best education for your child* (jt au 1989); *Trajectories of Despair; misdiagnosis and maltreatment of Soviet orphans* (with John Eibner 1991), *Ethnic Cleansing in Progress: war in Nagorno Karabakh* (1993), *Made to Care: the case for residential and village communities for people with a mental handicap* (with M Pearson, 1995); *m* 10 Jan 1959 Dr Murray Newell Cox, FRCPsych (*d* 28 June 1997), and has issue:

1 *Robin Michael COX later COX MCNEILL LOVE; *b* 18 Nov 1959; *educ* Kingsbury High Sch and Roy Free Hosp Sch of Medicine (MB BS); Surgn Cdr RN, Pncpl MO HMY *Britannia* and HMS *Illustrious*; *m* 1985 *Penelope Jane, dau of Dr Richard Michael Griffin, of 64 Warwick Rd, Bishops Stortford, Herts

2 *Jonathan Murray; *b* 30 Nov 1962; *educ* Kingsbury High Sch

1 *Philippa Ruth Dorothy; *b* 31 Aug 1965; *educ* Channing Sch Highgate

Lineage: ROBERT JOHN McNEILL LOVE, MS, FRCS; *m* Dorothy Ida Borland and has issue:

CAROLINE ANNE, *cr* a **Baroness**

CRADOCK-HARTOPP

Arms: Quarterly, 1st and 4th, sa. a chevron between three otters arg. (for HARTOPP); 2nd and 3rd, per saltire gu. and arg. crusilly three boar's heads, two and one, couped, counterchanged (for CRADOCK). **Crest:** Out of a ducal coronet or a pelican arg., vulning herself ppr. (for HARTOPP).Motto: *De tout mon coeur* ('With all my heart'). **Creation:** Bt. (GB) 12 May 1796.

SIR KENNETH ALSTON CRADOCK-HARTOPP, 10TH BT, of Freathby, Co Leicester, MBE (1946), DSC (1952) [Lt-Cdr Sir Kenneth Cradock-Hartopp Bt MBE DSC RN (ret), Keepers, Yeovilton, Yeovil, Somerset BA22 8EX]; *b* 26 Feb 1918; *s* cousin 1996; served RN WW II and in Korea (cmded HMNZ frigate *Taupo* 1951–52), Legn Merit USA 1953, AMIM, FRGS 1949; *m* 18 June 1942 *Gwendolyn Amy Lillian, only dau of Capt Victor Crowther Upton, Malay States Guides, of Taiping, Malaya, and has issue:

1 *Christina [Mrs Thomas Hickman, 60 Acre Lane, London SW2]; *b* 2 April 1948; *m* 1977 *Thomas Montagu Hickman, and has issue (*see* HICKMAN, Bt)

Lineage: WILLIAM HARTOPP, of Burton Lazers, Leics; *m* Eleanor Adcock and *d* 2 Sept 1586, leaving, with a yr s (George, ancestor of the HARTOPPs of Dalby House, Leics):

Sir EDWARD HARTOPP, 1st Bt (E), so *cr* 24 Oct 1619, of Freathby, Leics; Sheriff Leics 1617–18, MP Leicester 1628–29; *m* Mary, 2nd dau of Sir Erasmus Dryden, 1st Bt (*qv*), and *d* 1652, leaving, with at least one dau (Anne, *m* Thomas White; *see* WHITE, Bt, of Wallingwells), an est s:

Sir EDWARD HARTOPP, 2nd Bt, of Freathby and Buckminster, Leics; *b* 1608; ktd 1634; raised a Parly regt Civil War; *m* Mary, dau of Sir John Coke, of Melbourne, Derbys, and *d* 1657, leaving an est s:

Sir JOHN HARTOPP, 3rd Bt, of Freathby; *bapt* 21 Oct 1637; *educ* St John's Coll Oxford and Lincoln's Inn; MP Leics 1679–81; *m* 8 Nov 1666 Elizabeth, dau of Gen Charles Fleetwood, the Parly Cdr and s-in-law of OLIVER CROMWELL, by the Gen's 1st w Frances, dau of Thomas Smith, of Winston, Norfolk, and *d* 1 April 1722, leaving:

Sir JOHN HARTOPP, 4th and last Bt, of Freathby; *b* 1680; *m* 1st 1716 Sarah, dau of Alderman Sir Joseph Wolfe, of Hackney; *m* 2nd Sarah Marsh and *dspm* 13 Jan 1762, leaving by his 1st w (with a yr dau Elizabeth, *m* Timothy Dallowe, MD, and *dsp*):

SARAH Hartopp; *m* Jan 1755 Joseph HURLOCK, of Fort Marlborough, Govr Bencoolen, Dir HEIC (*bur* 15 Aug 1793 aged 78), and was *bur* 4 April 1766, leaving an only child:

ANNE Hurlock; inherited her gf's property, also the Fleetwood estate, Norfolk, of her cousin Jane Fleetwood; *m* 7 Aug 1777 Sir EDMUND BUNNEY later (from Michaelmas 1777) CRADOCK-HARTOPP, **1st Bt** (GB), so *cr* 12 May 1796 (*d* 10 June 1883), s of Joseph Bunney, merchant, of Newark, Notts, by Mary, dau of Edmund Cradock, of Kyntiton, Leics, and *d* Sept 1837, having had surv issue:

1 George Harry William CRADOCK-HARTOPP later CRADOCK-HARTOPP-FLEETWOOD (added to commemorate his descent from the Gen); *b* 20 Aug 1785, MP Dundalk; *dvp* unm 31 March 1824

2 **Sir Edmund Cradock-Hartopp, 2nd Bt**; *b* May 1789; *m* 23 Sept 1824 Hon Mary Jane Eden (*d* 12 Sept 1843), dau of 1st Baron Henley (*qv*), and *dsp* 3 April 1849

3 WILLIAM EDMUND (Sir), **3rd Bt**

1 Anna Maria; *m* 6 June 1811 Charles Clement Adderley, of Hams Hall, Warwicks, and *d* a widow 20 April 1827, leaving issue

2 Emilia; *m* 15 May 1809 Edward Grove, of Shenstone Park, Staffs, and had issue

Sir EDMUND's bro,

Sir William Edmund Cradock-Hartopp, 3rd Bt; *b* 11 Dec 1797; *m* 1825 Jane Mary (*d* 1 Nov 1881), est dau of Henry Bloomfield Keane, and *d* 16 Oct 1864, leaving:

1 **Sir John William Cradock-Hartopp, 4th Bt**; *b* 1829; Capt 17th Lancers; *m* 14 Aug 1855 Charlotte Frances (*d* 17 Nov 1889), est dau of Edward Gyles Howard, nephew of 12th Duke of Norfolk (*qv*), and *d* 25 May 1888, leaving:

(1) **Sir Charles Edward Cradock-Hartopp, 5th Bt**, JP Warwicks; *b* 1858; Lt Scots Gds Egypt 1882; *m* 10 June 1895 (*divorce* 1905) Hon Millicent Florence Eleanor (*d* 29 Nov 1952), est dau of 1st Baron Nunburnholme (*qv*), and *dsp* 20 Feb 1929

(2) Alick William; *b* 7 Nov 1860; *m* 10 Oct 1888, Janet Susan Webbe (*d* 26 Oct 1942), yst dau of John William Gooch Spicer, of Spye Park, Wilts, and *d* 5 Aug 1912, leaving issue:

1a **Sir Charles William Everard Cradock-Hartopp, 6th Bt**; *b* 4 Sept 1893; 1st Sec Dip Serv, served in France WW I (despatches, Maj 1918); *d* unm 14 March 1930

1a Susan Cynthia Frances; *b* 16 March 1898; *m* 23 July 1924 Lindsay Drummond and has issue (*see* PERTH, E)

(3) **Sir Frederick Cradock-Hartopp, 7th Bt**; *b* 11 July 1869; *dsp* 26 Feb 1937

(4) **Sir George Francis Fleetwood Cradock-Hartopp, 8th Bt**; *b* 20 July 1870; *m* 28 July 1909 Ethel Caroline Jane (*d* 8 May 1953), widow of Maj Bernard Hamilton Gunston (*see* GUNSTON, Bt) and 6th dau of Col William Henry Charles Wellesley (*see* WELLINGTON, D), and *dsp* 5 Sept 1949

(1) Eveline Frances; *m* 17 June 1884, Audley Charles Miles, 2nd son of Col Charles William Miles, MP, of Burton Hill, Wilts, and *d* 23 Jan 1946, leaving issue. He *d* 6 Sept 1919

(2) Ada Mary; *m* 24 April 1884, James FitzRoy Wilberforce Farquhar, 13th Hus, 5th son of Sir Walter Rockcliffe Farquhar, 3rd Bt (*qv*), and *d* 24 June 1944, leaving issue

(3) Catherine Louisa, OBE (1919); *m* 14 June 1883 Alfred Edward Miller-Mundy, of Shipley, Derbyshire, and *d* 29 Jan 1935, leaving issue. He *d* 15 April 1920

(4) Beatrice Anne; *m* 12 Oct 1903 Newton Charles Ogle, JP, DL, of Kirkley Hall, Northumberland, and *d* 21 May 1951, leaving issue. He *d* 23 July 1912

(5) Mary Eleanor; *d* unm 5 April 1954

2 Edmund Charles, Hon Col 7th Bn KRRC; *b* 29 Sept 1846; *m* 29 Dec 1870 Frances Emily (*d* 1 Nov 1923), 2nd dau of William Charles Alston, of Elmdon Hall, Warwicks, and *d* 24 Dec 1904, having had, with two sons (*d* in infancy):

(1) William Edmund Cecil, Lt RGA; *b* 18 March 1872; *d* 14 Dec 1932

(2) Francis Gerald; *b* 6 June 1877; *m* 20 Oct 1908 Elizabeth Mary (*d* 23 April 1955), only dau of John Windsor Stuart, of Foley House, Rothesay (*see* BUTE, M), and *d* 27 Aug 1946, leaving issue:

1a **Sir John Edmund Cradock-Hartopp, 9th Bt**; *b* 8 April 1912; *educ* Uppingham; Maj RE WW II (despatches twice), dir Firth Brown Tools 1961–96; *m* 29 April 1953 *Prudence [Prudence Lady Cradock-Hartopp, The Cottage, 27 Wool Rd, London SW20 0HN], 2nd dau of Sir Frederick William Leith-Ross, GCMG, KCB, and *d* 7 Aug 1996, leaving:

1b *Melinda Anne; *b* 17 Feb 1954; *m* 1984 *Murray Lewis, only son of Rev Raymond Lewis, of E Dean, E Sussex, and has issue:

1c *Jonathan Murray; *b* 1988

1c *Katherine; *b* 1990

2b *Nicola Jane; *b* 20 Jan 1957

3b *Joanna Elizabeth; *b* 20 Jan 1960; *m* 1985 *Michael Victor Charter, 2nd son of Victor Noël Charter, of Chelmsford, Essex, and has:

1c *Thomas Michael; *b* 25 July 1994

1c *Nicola Bryony; *b* 17 May 1996

1a *Gwendoline Mary [Mrs John Morrison, The Lea, Dogmersfield, Basingstoke, Hants]; *b* 29 Dec 1909; *m* 10 Nov 1938 G/Capt John Stanton Fleming Morrison, DFC and bar, RAFVR (*d* 28 Jan 1961), er son of John Fleming Morrison, and has issue:

1b *Elizabeth Mary; *b* 15 April 1942

(3) Ronald Arthur Charles; WW I as Lt RAF; *b* 27 Oct 1881; *m* 27 Nov 1912 Ellen Dora, only child of Henry Cox, of Radipole Manor, Dorset, and *dsp* 23 June 1957

(4) Louis Montague, Maj W Yorks Regt (PWO) and Roy Tank Corps WW I (despatches) *b* 8 Feb 1884; *m* 6 Nov 1916 Marjorie Somerville (*d* 19 June 1971), only dau of James Falshaw Watson, MICE, MIME, of Park House, Codsall Wood, Staffs, and *d* 29 Jan 1957, leaving issue:

1a Sir KENNETH ALSTON CRADOCK-HARTOPP, **10th and present Bt**

1a *Virginia Anne [Mrs Michael Carter, Dormer Cottage, Long Sutton, Lincs PE12 9AG]; *b* 9 April 1922; *m* 5 July 1952 Michael Henry Tindall Carter (*d* 7 March 1995), yr son of Arthur Herbert Carter, JP, CA, and has issue:

1b *Christopher Henry James; *b* 10 April 1953; *educ* Uppingham; *m* 1980 *Jane Anne Hardie and has issue:

1c *Sophie Louise; *b* 1987

1b *Geraldine Anne Louise [Mrs William Fletcher, Pulvertoft Hall, Gedney Broadgate, Lincs]; *b* 20 May 1956; *m* 1st (*divorce*) 1985 Bruce Gordon Scott Coles and has:
1c *Alexander Henry Rufus Scott; *b* 1987
2c *James Edward Rupert Scott; *b* 1989
1b (cont.) Mrs Geraldine Coles *m* 2nd *William Sam Fletcher and by him has:
3c *Charles William Louis; *b* 18 Nov 1996
2b *Paula Margaret; *b* 30 March 1962
(1) Mildred Eveline Norah; *b* 16 July 1889; *m* 25 Nov 1913 Capt Reginald Montagu Alston-Roberts-West, RN (ret), 3rd son of James Alston-Roberts-West, DL, JP, of Alscot Park, Glos, and *d* 6 Oct 1975, leaving issue. He *d* 14 Dec 1944
1 Mildred Anne; *m* 1st 5 Jan 1854 Sir Francis Edward Scott, 3rd Bt, and had issue (*see* 1970 edn SCOTT, Bt, of Gt Barr and ST AUDRIES, B). He *d* 21 Nov 1863. She *m* 2nd 12 Sept 1868 Edward Pakenham Alderson, est son of Sir Edward Hall Anderson, Baron of the Exchequer, and *d* 3 Dec 1909. He *dsp* 3 Dec 1876
2 Gertrude Emily; *m* 2 July 1851 Edward Basil Farnham, DL, JP, of Quorndon House, Leics and *d* 9 Oct 1911, leaving issue. He *d* 13 May 1878
3 Matilda Jane; *m* 22 Aug 1865 Lord Edward Pelham Clinton, 2nd son of 5th Duke of Newcastle, KG (*see* LINCOLN, E), and *dsp* 23 Oct 1892
4 Anna Maria; *m* 7 Oct 1858 Lord Walter Charles Montagu Douglas Scott, 3rd son of 5th Duke of Buccleuch (*see* BUCCLEUCH and QUEENSBERRY, D), and *d* 29 May 1886, leaving issue
5 Louisa Margaret Emily; *m* 11 May 1867 Capt Thomas Charles Douglas Whitmore, RHG, of Orsett Hall, Essex, and *d* 29 Nov 1892, leaving issue (*see* WHITMORE, Bt)
6 Julia Charlotte; *m* 14 Jan 1868 5th Earl of Shannon (*qv*), and *d* 27 Dec 1921, leaving issue

CRAIG OF RADLEY

Arms: Ermine an arrow in bend gules feathered or, the point upwards proper, transfixing a mullet vert, over all on a chevron sable three delta figures argent. **Crest:** Rising from an astral crown or a knight on horseback in full armour, his dexter hand holding a broken tilting spear, all proper, his helm surmounted by three ostrich plumes gules, argent and sable. **Supporters:** On either side a double-headed eagle, wings displayed per pale gules and azure, beaked and legged or, the dexter charged on the breast with two keys in saltire, wards upwards also gold, and the sinister charged on the breast with a rose argent, barbed and seeded proper; a compartment comprising a grassy mount traversed palewise by a runway both proper bordered by four crosses formy gules.
Motto: *Nec degenero* ('And I do not deteriorate')
Creation: B. (LP, UK) 1991.

THE BARON CRAIG OF RADLEY, of Helhoughton, Co Norfolk (Sir David Brownrigg Craig, GCB (1984, KCB 1980, CB 1978), OBE (1967)) [The Rt Hon The Lord Craig of Radley GCB OBE, Park House, Helhoughton, Norfolk]; *b* 17 Sept 1929; *educ* Radley and Lincoln Coll Oxford; commissioned RAF 1951: ADC to the Queen 1967–71, OC RAF Cranwell 1968–70, Dir Plans and Ops HQ Far East Cmd 1970–71, OC RAF Akrotiri 1972–73, ACAS (Ops) MOD 1975–78, AOC No 1 Gp RAF Strike Command 1978–80, V-Ch Air Staff 1980–82, AOC-in-C Strike Command and C-in-C UKAF 1982–85, Ch Air Staff and Air ADC to the Queen 1985–88, Marshal RAF 1988, CDS 1988–91; dir M L Hldgs 1991–92; Hon Fell Lincoln Coll Oxford 1984; FRAeS 1986, Hon DSc Cranfield 1988; *m* 1955 *Elisabeth June, dau of Charles James Derenburg, of W Byfleet, Surrey, and has issue:
1 *Christopher Charles Brownrigg [The Hon Christopher Craig, Royal Bank of Scotland, 9 Pall Mall, London SWIY 5LX]; *b* 1957; *educ* Radley and Jesus Coll Cambridge; *m* 1981 *Marilyn Ashmead
1 *Susan Elisabeth; *b* 1960; *m* 1997 *Michael Tomlin, s of C S N Tomlin, of Binham, Norfolk

Lineage: Maj FRANCIS BROWNRIGG CRAIG, of Dublin; *m* Olive — and had:
DAVID BROWNRIGG, *cr* a **Baron**

CRAIGAVON

Arms: Gu. a fess erm. between three bridges of as many arches ppr. **Crest:** A demi-lion rampant per fess gu. and sa., holding in the dexter paw a mullet or. **Supporters:** Dexter, a constable of the Ulster Special Constabulary, his hand resting on a rifle; sinister, a private of the Royal Ulster Rifles, armed and accoutred, both ppr.
Motto: Charity provokes charity. **Creations:** Bt. (UK) 5 Feb 1918, V. (UK) 20 Jan 1927.

THE 3RD VISCOUNT CRAIGAVON, of Stormont, Co Down, and a **Baronet** (Sir Janric Fraser Craig, Bt) [The Rt Hon The Viscount Craigavon, House of Lords, London SW1A 0PW]; *b* 9 June 1944; *s* f 1974; *educ* Eton and London U (BA, BSc); FCA

Lineage: JAMES CRAIG, JP, of Craigavon and Tyrella, Co Down; *m* Eleanor Gilmour, dau of Robert Brown, and *d* 20 April 1900 aged 72, leaving a 6th s:

Sir James Craig, 1st Bt, and **1st Viscount Craigavon**, of Stormont, Co Down, so *cr* 5 Feb 1918 and 20 Jan 1927 respectively (both UK), PC (I 1921, NI 1922), DL (Co Down), JP (Belfast); MP E Devon 1906–18, Mid-Down 1918–21 and Co Down (Parl of NI 1921–40), 1st PM of NI 1921–40, Hon LLD Queen's U Belfast 1922, Hon DCL Oxford 1926, Associate of Inst of Naval Architects, Pres Ulster Unionist Cncl, Freeman Londonderry, Hon Lt-Col, formerly Capt, 3rd Bn Roy Irish Rifles, Hon Capt RNVR, AAG and QMG Ulster Div WW I, Treas Household 1916–19, Parly Sec Min Pensions 1919–20, Fin Sec Admlty 1920–21, KStJ, served in S African War 1900–02; *b* 8 Jan 1871; *m* 22 March 1905 Cecil Mary Nowell Dering, DBE (1941), CStJ, pres Ulster Women's Unionist Cncl 1923–43 (*d* 17 March 1960), only child of Sir Daniel Alfred Anley Tupper, MVO, Assist Comptroller Ld Chamberlain's Dept and Serjeant-at-Arms to HM GEORGE V, and had issue:
1 JAMES, **2nd Viscount**
2 (Patrick William) Dennis, MBE (1942); served WW II 1939–45 (despatches twice) as Maj and DAM Sec to C-in-C, MEF; author: *Horse Racing, The Breeding of Thoroughbreds* and *A Short History of the English Turf*; *b* 2 March 1906 (twin); *educ* Eton and Magdalen Coll Oxford; *m* 1st 1931 (*divorce* 1933) Aline Margaret Mary McClaren, dau of J Cumming; *m* 2nd 21 March 1947 Marjorie Joy (*d* 22 Aug 1974), formerly w of Igor Vinogradov, of 10 Gower St, WC1, and dau of Algernon Cecil Newton, RA, and *d* 15 Aug 1972, leaving by his 1st w:
(1) *Deirdre [Mrs Peter Levi, Austin's Farm, Stonesfield, Oxford]; *b* 4 Dec 1931; *m* 1st 9 July 1951 (*divorce* 1959) Jonathan Craven, only s of Maj Alfred Eric Lawrence Craven, JP, of Ringwell Ho, Ditcheat, Somerset, and has:
1a *Simon James [Simon Craven Esq, 50 Stevenage Rd, London SW6 6HA]; *b* 7 April 1954; *educ* Eton
1a *Sarah; *b* 20 April 1952; *m* 1973 (*divorce* 1983) Martin J Bradbury and has:
1b *Arthur John; *b* 1976
2b *Jack Daniel; *b* 1978
(1) (cont.) Mrs Deirdre Craven *m* 2nd 27 April 1959 Cyril Vernon Connolly, CBE (*d* 26 Nov 1974), critic, son of Maj Matthew William Kemble Connolly, KOYLI, of The Lock Ho, Deepcut, Surrey, by Muriel Maud, dau of Col Edward Vernon, DL, JP, of Clontarf Castle, Dublin; *m* 3rd 1977 *Peter Chad Tigar Levi, Prof Poetry Oxford 1984–89, and by her 2nd husb has:
1a *Matthew Vernon; *b* 14 April 1970
2a *Cressida Louisa Vernon [Mrs Charles Hudson, Wick Manor, Wick, Pershore, Worcs]; *b* 14 Jan 1960; jnlst; *m* 1st 1982 (*divorce* 1983) Adrian A Gill; *m* 2nd 1985 *Charles Alexander Burnell Hudson and by him has:
1b *Gabriel Charles More; *b* 1994
1b *Violet Isobel Connolly; *b* 1988
2b *Ellen Rose; *b* 1990
1 Ellinor Aileen Cecil; *b* 20 Aug 1907; *m* 19– (*divorce* 1946) Cdre Robert Gordon Hood Linzee, CB, CBE, RN, only son of Alexander Grosvenor Linzee, and *d* 1929, leaving:
(1) *Robin Alexander Craig LINZEE later LINZEE-GORDON (decree of Lyon Court 1967) [Robin Linzee-Gordon Esq, Corrennie Schoolhouse, Sauchen, Aberdeenshire]; *b* 25 Oct 1930; *m* 7 June 1958 Frances Sheena (*d* 1995), yr dau of Colin MacLennan, of Rhinduie, Lentran, Inverness, and has issue:

1a *Robert James Nicholas; *b* 23 June 1959
2a *Philip Alexander Hood; *b* 17 April 1962
3a *Andrew Damian; *b* 26 Nov 1966
1a *Frances Susannah; *b* 26 Nov 1966

The 1st VISCOUNT *d* 24 Nov 1940; his er son

JAMES CRAIG, **2nd Viscount Craigavon**; *b* 2 March 1906; *educ* Eton; Lt-Cdr (S) RNVR WW II; *m* 22 Nov 1939 *(Angela) Fiona, yr dau of Percy Tatchell, MRCS, LRCP, of S Kensington, and *d* 18 May 1974, leaving:

1 JANRIC FRASER CRAIG, **3rd and present Viscount Craigavon**

1 *Janitha Stormont; *b* 31 Aug 1940; *m* 1965 *Gordon Robert MacInnes, est s of Robert Wood MacInnes, of Ruislip, Middx, and has:

(1) *Avila; *b* 19 Oct 1967
(2) *Córdova; *b* 1972
(3) *Jimena; *b* 20 March 1975

2 *Jacaranda Fiona [The Hon Mrs Jacaranda Macdonald, 23 Kelso Place, London W8 5QG]; *b* 8 Jan 1949; *m* 1972 (*divorce* 1983) Dudley Francis Macdonald, of 26 Paroman Towers, George St, W1, and has issue:

(1) *Toby James Francis; *b* 1975
(1) *Rose Carole; *b* 1978

CRAIGMYLE

Arms: Erm., a fir tree growing out of a mount in base ppr. between two piles az. issuant from a chief or, charged with a scroll arg., its seal pendant ppr., between two lymphads or. **Crest:** A demi-savage holding in his dexter hand a club resting on his shoulder ppr.
Supporters: Dexter, a lion rampant gu.; sinister, a kangaroo ppr.
Motto: *Misericordia fidelitas jus* ('Mercy, Fidelity, Right').
Creations: B. (UK) 7 May 1929.

THE 4TH BARON CRAIGMYLE, of Craigmyle, Co Aberdeen (Thomas Columba Shaw) [The Rt Hon The Lord Craigmyle, Court Farm, St Catherine, Bath BA1 8HA]; *b* 19 Oct 1960; *s* f 1998; *m* 1987 *(Katharine) Alice, 2nd dau of David Floyd, OBE, of Priory Close, Combe Down, Bath, and has:

1 +ALEXANDER FRANCIS; *b* 1 July 1988
2 +Finnian Donald; *b* 1990
3 +Calum Edward; *b* 1993
4 +Joseph Thomas; *b* 1996

Lineage: ALEXANDER SHAW, of Dunfermline, Fifeshire; had:

THOMAS SHAW, **1st Baron Craigmyle**, of Craigmyle, Co Aberdeen, so *cr* 7 May 1929, as also earlier 22 Feb 1909 BARON SHAW, of Dunfermline, Co Fife (LP; both UK), PC (1906), QC (1894); *b* 23 May 1850; MA and LLB Edin, Hon LLD St Andrews, Aberdeen, Edinburgh and Philadelphia, called to Scottish Bar 1875, Hon Bencher of Middle Temple 1910, Slr-Gen Scotland 1894–95, Ld Advocate 1905–09, a Ld of Appeal in Ordinary 1909–29, MP (Lib) Hawick Burghs 1892–1909; *m* 1879 Elsie Stephen (*d* 31 May 1939), dau of George Forrest, of Ludquharn, Aberdeenshire, and had issue:

1 ALEXANDER, **2nd Baron**

1 Elsie; *m* 5 Jan 1909 Surgn R-Adml Sir William Ireland de Courcy Wheeler, MD, BCh, BAO, FRCSI, and *d* 3 Oct 1951, leaving issue. He *d* 11 Sept 1943

2 Mary Emma Louise; *m* 16 Nov 1910 Alexander Forrester-Paton, JP, son of late A P Forrester-Paton, of Inglewood, Alloa, and *d* 8 Sept 1974, leaving issue. He *d* 8 April 1954

3 Isabel; *m* 6 Feb 1915 Capt Richard Henry Vaughan Thompson, 11th Bn Roy Fus, only son of E Vaughan Thompson, of East Sheen. He was *ka* 26 Sept 1916

The 1st BARON *d* 28 June 1937; his son,

ALEXANDER SHAW, **2nd Baron Craigmyle**, DL Selkirk; *educ* Trin Coll Oxford (MA, Pres Union Soc 1905); a Lt for City of London, High Sheriff 1931, barrister Inner Temple 1908, MP (Lib) Kilmarnock Burghs 1915–18 and Kilmarnock 1918–23, chm Special Arbitration Tbnls under Munitions Acts 1917–18, dir: Bank of England 1923, Atlas Assur, P&O and Br India Steam Navigation Co (chm 1932–38), Hain Steamship Co Ltd and Anderson, Green and Co; v-pres Canadian-Australasian Line, pres UK Chamber of Shipping 1927; memb: BOT Advsy Cncl 1927, Imp Shipping Ctee 1931; Lt RMA 1915, Hon Capt RNR 1935, Hon Col RAMC 1940; served WW I 1915–16; *b* 28 Feb 1883; *m* 24 July 1913 Lady Margaret Cargill Mackay (*d* 31 May 1958), est dau of 1st Earl of Inchcape (*qv*), and *d* 29 Sept 1944, leaving:

1 THOMAS DONALD MACKAY SHAW, **3rd Baron Craigmyle**; *b* 17 Nov 1923; *educ* Eton and Trin Coll Oxford (MA); FRSA, served WW II as Sub-Lt (A) RNVR 1943–46, Bailiff Grand Cross SMO Malta, Pres Br Assoc (Pres 1989–93), Pres Catholic Union of GB, Kt Cdr with Star Order of Pius IX 1993, KStJ 1989; *m* 22 Sept 1955 *Anthea Esther Christine Theresa [The Rt Hon Anthea Lady Craigmyle, 18 The Boltons, London SW10 9SY], yst dau of Edward Charles Rich, of 31 Yeomans Row, London SW3, and *d* 30 April 1998, having had:

(1) Alexander; *b* 10, *d* 11 June 1957
(2) +THOMAS COLUMBA SHAW, **4th and present Baron Craigmyle**
(3) +Justin Edward Magnus [The Hon Justin Shaw, 32 Thurloe Sq, London SW7 2SD]; *b* 1 April 1965; *educ* Eton, and Gonville and Caius Coll Cambridge
(4) +(Alexander) Joseph (Ranald); *b* 1971; *educ* Ampleforth and St Benet's Hall Oxford
(1) *Alison Margaret [The Hon Mrs Heggs, 6/6 Collingham Gdns, London SW5 0HW]; *b* 8 Aug 1956; *educ* Harvard (BA 1979) and Antioch U (MA 1991); *m* 16 Dec 1995 *Oliver Heggs, yr s of Geoffrey Heggs
(2) *Catriona (Kate) Mary [The Hon Mrs MacGreevy, 1 Fernshaw Rd, London SW10 0TB]; *b* 30 Oct 1958; *educ* Byam Shaw Sch of Art; *m* 1986 *Dr Brian Irial Patrick MacGreevy, er son of Dr Brian MacGreevy, of S Kensington, and has:

1a *Ivo Alexander Patrick; *b* 1987
2a *Hubert Donald Brian; *b* 1989
1a *Christabel Elizabeth Anthea; *b* 1991
2a *Flora Catherine Mary; *b* 1993
3a *Madeleine Sarah Isabel; *b* 1996

(3) *Madeleine Claire; *b* 23 Oct 1963

1 *(Margaret) Jean [The Hon Mrs Mussell, 3 Birkenhead Rd, Sheffield S6 3NL]; *b* 20 Feb 1915; *m* 10 Dec 1949 Laurence Shirl Mussell (*d* 27 Dec 1956), only surv son of Shirl Mussell, and has:

(1) *Anabel Margaret; *b* 26 June 1954; *m* 1978 (*divorce* 19–) Francisco Parra
(2) *Lisabel Jean; *b* 28 Aug 1956

2 *Thalia Mary [The Hon Mrs Dean, Hambledon Hurst, Godalming, Surrey GU8 4HF]; *b* 7 Aug 1918; *m* 4 Sept 1939 *Winton Basil Dean, author and musical scholar, est son of Basil Dean, CBE, and has had:

(1) *Stephen Nicholas Winton [Stephen Dean Esq, Fairnilee, Galashiels, Selkirkshire TD1 3PR]; *b* 18 Nov 1946; *educ* Seaford Coll and U of Kent
(1) Brigid Miriam; *b* 14 March 1943; *d* 10 Oct 1945
(2) Diana Margaret; *b* 22, *d* 28 March 1948

2 (cont.) Mr and the Hon Mrs Dean adopted:

*Diana Rosamund Thalia [Mrs Michael Bracewell, 49 Windsor Rd, Kew, Surrey TW9 2EJ]; *b* 1955; *m* 1978 *Michael William Bracewell

3 *Elspeth Ruth [The Hon Mrs Macdonald, 22 Heath Dve, London NW3 7SB]; *b* 17 Feb 1921; *m* 12 Sept 1945 Archibald James Florence Macdonald, JP (*d* 1983), er s of Dr G B D Macdonald, of Hampstead, and has:

(1) *Michael Christopher Archibald; *b* 25 May 1947; *educ* U Coll Sch and Merton Coll Oxford; *m* 7 July 1979 (*divorce* 1989) C Ann, yr dau of R G Searight, of 129 Oakwood Court, W14
(2) *Ian Alexander James [Ian Macdonald Esq, Coldred Court Cottage, Coldred, nr Dover, Kent CT15 5AQ]; *b* 2 Dec 1950; *educ* U Coll Sch and Atlantic Coll

CRANBROOK

Arms: Quarterly, 1st and 4th, arg., on a bend invected plain cotised gu. three catherine wheels or, on a chief of the second as many leopard's faces of the the third for HARDY); 2nd and 3rd, per pale arg. and or, a bend company az. and gu. between two pellets, each within an annulet sa. (for GATHORNE). **Crest:** 1 A dexter arm embowed in armour ppr., garnished or, entwined by a branch of oak vert, charged with two catherine wheels gu., the one above and the other below the elbow, the hand grasping a dragon's head erased ppr. (for HARDY), 2 In front of a wolf's head erased arg. a staff raguly fesswise or (for GATHORNE). **Supporters:** Two leopards guardant ppr. each gorged with a collar gu., therefrom pendant an escutcheon of the last charged with a catherine wheel or. **Motto:** *Armé de foi hardi* ('Armed with hardy faith'). **Creations:** V. (UK) 4 May 1878, E. and B. (UK) 22 Aug 1892.

THE 5TH EARL OF CRANBROOK, Viscount Cranbrook of Hemsted, Kent, and **Baron Medway of Hemsted Park**, Co Kent (Gathorne Gathorne-Hardy, DL (Suffolk)) [The Rt Hon The Earl of Cranbrook DL, House of Lords, London SW1A 0PW]; *b* 20 June 1933; *s f* 1978; *educ* Eton and Corpus Christi Coll Cambridge (MA 1960), PhD (Birmingham 1960); chm English Nature 1991–, late RA (TA), assist Sarawak Museum 1956–58, Fell Jajasan Siswa Lokantara (Indonesia) 1960–61, sr lecturer Zoology U of Malaya Kuala Lumpur 1961–70, ed *Ibis* 1973–80, memb Suffolk Coastal DC 1976–83, chm Panel of Enquiry into Shooting and Angling 1976–79, pres Suffolk Wildlife Tst 1979–, tstee Nat History Museum 1981–86, memb: Roy Commn Environmental Pollution 1981–92, Natural Environment Research Cncl 1982– 88, Bd Anglian Water Authority 1987–89, Broads Authority 1988– and Harwich Haven Authority 1989–, ch exec RSPB to 1998, author: *Mammals of Borneo, Wild Mammals of SE Asia*, ed *Key Environments: Malaysia*, co-author: *Birds of the Malay Peninsula*, vol 5, and *Belalong: a tropical rainforest*; Skinner and Freeman City of London, FLS, FZS, FRGS, MBOU, FIBiol, Hon DSc Aberdeen 1989, OStJ; *m* 9 May 1967 *Caroline, only dau of Col Ralph George Edward Jarvis, DL, of Doddington Hall, Lincs, and has issue:

1 +JOHN JASON, *Lord Medway* [Lord Medway, 7 Woodfall St, London SW3 4DJ]; *b* 26 Oct 1968; *educ* Woodbridge Sch and Pembroke Coll Oxford (BA)

1 +Angus Edward; *b* 28 March 1973; *educ* Woodbridge Sch, Gresham's, King's Coll London and Trin Coll Dublin

1 *Flora; *b* 10 Oct 1971; *educ* Woodbridge Sch, Bryanston and Emmanuel Coll Cambridge (BA)

Lineage: Sir JOHN HARDY, 1st Bt (*qv*); had a yr bro:

Sir GATHORNE HARDY later GATHORNE-HARDY (also quartering arms of GATHORNE, roy licence 11 May 1878), **1st Earl of Cranbrook**, so *cr* 22 Aug 1892, as also BARON MEDWAY OF HEMSTED PARK, Co Kent, and earlier 4 May 1878 VISCOUNT CRANBROOK OF HEMSTED, Kent (all UK), PC (1866), GSCI (1880), JP (Kent and W R Yorks), DL, DCL, LLD; *b* 1 Oct 1814; *educ* Shrewsbury and Oriel Coll Oxford (BA 1836, DCL 1866, Hon Fell 1894); barrister 1840, Bencher Inner Temple 1868, MP (C) Leominster 1856–65 and Oxford U 1865–78, U-Sec Home Dept 1858–59, Pres Poor Law Bd 1866–67, Home Sec 1867–68, Sec State: War 1874–78 and India 1878–80, Ld Pres Cncl 1885–86 and 1886–92; Hon LLD Cambridge 1892; *m* 29 March 1838 Jane, CI (*d* 13 Nov 1897), 3rd dau of James Orr, of Ballygowan and later Hollywood Ho, Co Down, and had, with other issue:

1 JOHN STEWART, **2nd Earl**

2 Charles Gathorne; Col Gren Gds, formerly 60th Rifles; *b* 11 May 1841; *educ* Eton; *m* 16 April 1872 Lady Cicely Louisa Nevill (*d* 1 May 1932), est dau of Marquess of Abergavenny (*qv*), and *d* 17 Feb 1919, leaving issue:

(1) Violet Caroline; *m* 23 Jan 1902 Henry Ernest Crawley, son of George Baden Crawley, and *d* 19 Nov 1952, leaving issue. He *d* 18 June 1931

(2) Cicely Muriel, DGStJ; *m* 7 July 1904 Charles Comyn Scott Scott-Gatty, Maj Herts Regt, 2nd son of Sir Alfred Scott-Gatty, KCVO, Garter King-at-Arms, and *d* 29 Sept 1956, leaving a dau. He *d* 24 July 1916

3 Alfred Erskine, JP (Berks), DL (Co London and Kent); *b* 27 Feb 1845; *educ* Eton and Balliol Coll Oxford (MA); barrister Inner Temple, MP Canterbury 1878–80 and East Grinstead 1886–95, Commr of Railways and Canals 1905; *m* 3 Aug 1875 Isabella Louisa (*d* 17 Aug 1924), only dau of John Malcolm of Poltalloch, Argyll, and *d* 11 Nov 1918, leaving:

(1) Geoffrey Malcolm, MC; Capt late 4th Bn Roy Berks Regt, PhD Oslo (1946), barrister Inner Temple 1903, served in S African War and WW I (despatches), Croix de Guerre (Belgium), Assist Librarian Ho Lds 1923–28, Hon Sec Roy Inst Internat Affrs 1920–35, author: *The Norse Discoverers, A Short History of International Affairs, A Royal Impostor*; *b* 28 Jan 1878; *educ* Eton and New Coll Oxford (MA, Pres Union 1899); *m* 12 March 1914 Kathleen Eleanor, yst dau of Henry Goschen, of Heathfield, Addington (*see* GOSCHEN, V), and *dsp* 7 Jan 1972

(2) Alfred Cecil; barrister, T/Capt 9th Serv Bn Cameronian Scottish Rifles; *b* 26 March 1881; *educ* Balliol Coll Oxford (BA); *ka* 25–26 Sept 1915

(1) Isabel Edith; *b* 7 Aug 1876; *m* 24 Oct 1905 Lionel Portman, yr son of Rev Hon Walter Berkeley Portman (*see* PORTMAN, V), and *dsp* 4 Feb 1959. He *d* 12 Oct 1940

1 Edith Elizabeth; *m* 15 June 1869 Sir Henry John Lowndes Graham, KCB, and *d* 8 Jan 1875, leaving issue. He *d* 5 Dec 1930

2 Margaret Evelyn, CI, DGStJ, Kaisar-i-Hind Gold Medal; *m* 26 Jan 1893 2nd Viscount Goschen (*qv*), and *d* 11 July 1943, leaving issue

The 1st EARL *d* 30 Oct 1906; his est son,

JOHN STEWART GATHORNE-HARDY, **2nd Earl of Cranbrook**, VD, DL, JP, CA Kent; chm Kent TAA, Hon Col 5th Weald of Kent Bn The Buffs, Lt Rifle Bde, MP Rye 1868–80 and Mid Kent 1884–92; *b* 22 March 1839; *m* 12 June 1867 Cicely Marguerite Wilhelmina (*d* 20 Feb 1931), dau and heir of Joseph Ridgway, of Fairlawn, Kent, and Wallsuches, Lancs, and had issue:

1 GATHORNE, **3rd Earl**

2 (John) Francis (Sir), GCB, GCVO, CMG, DSO, Gren Gds, DL Wilts, Brig-Gen Gen Staff 1916–18, Maj-Gen 1919, Lt-Gen 1928, Gen 1932, Dir Mil Training 1922–25, cmdg Deccan Dist 1926–28, GOC-in-C N Cmd 1931–33, GOC-in-C Aldershot Cmd 1933–37; ADC Gen to TM GEORGE V 1934–36, EDWARD VIII 1936 and GEORGE VI 1936–1937; served in S Africa 1900–02 (despatches twice) and WW I (despatches ten times), Gold Medal of Montenegro, Offr Legion of Honour, Croix de Guerre, Mil Order of Savoy; *b* 14 Jan 1874; *m* 10 Dec 1898 Lady Isobel Constance Mary Stanley, DCVO (*d* 30 Dec 1963), dau of 16th Earl of Derby (*qv*), formerly Woman of the Bedchamber to HM QUEEN MARY, and *d* 21 Aug 1949, leaving issue:

(1) Elizabeth Constance Mary; *b* 23 Aug 1904; *m* 21 Jan 1933 (*divorce* 1949) Brig Godfrey Pennington Hobbs, CBE, Northumberland Fus, son of Maj Frederick Manoli Baltazzi Hobbs, RMLI, of Barnaboy, Ireland, and *d* as the result of a motor accident 3 March 1953, leaving issue

3 Ralph Cecil North, Cdr RN; *b* 19 March 1876; *d* unm 30 Dec 1911

4 Nigel Charles, DSO (1918), JP Oxon, Lt-Col late Rifle Bde, formerly Capt Northumberland Fus, ADC to Govr-Gen of New Zealand 1907–10, served in S Africa 1902 as Lt 37th Bn Imp Yeo and WW I (despatches four times); *b* 31 March 1880; *m* 11 June 1910 Doris Cecilia Featherstone (*d* 17 Dec 1973), dau of Hon Sir Charles John Johnston, Speaker of Leg Cncl, of Karori, NZ, and *d* 17 Dec 1958, leaving issue:

(1) Patrick Guy, TD, Maj Roy Sigs, formerly Maj RA (TA), served WW II, local dir (Pall Mall) Barclays Bank; *b* 21 March 1911; *educ* Wellington; *m* 19 July 1947 *Julia (*m* 2nd 29 May 1974 *Lt-Col Edward C Croft), 3rd dau of Henry Wolley Leigh-Bennett, of Wickham Ho, nr Newbury, Berks, and *dsp* 21 Jan 1966

(1) *Margaret Doris [Lady Cameron of Lochiel, Achnacarry, Spean Bridge, Inverness-shire PH34 4EJ]; *b* 29 Jan 1913; *m* 21 July 1939 *Col Sir Donald Hamish Cameron of Lochiel, KT, CVO, TD, DL, JP, FCA, 26th Chief of Clan Cameron, late Lovat Scouts (*see* MONTROSE, D), and has issue:

1a *Donald Angus, yr of Lochiel, DL (Lochaber, Inverness and Badenoch and Strathspey 1986); *b* 1946; *educ* Harrow and Ch Ch Oxford; *m* 1974 *Lady Cecil Nennella Therese Kerr, er dau of 12th Marquess of Lothian (*qv*), and has issue:

1b *Donald Andrew John; *b* 1976

1b *Catherine Mary; *b* 1975

2b *Lucy Margot Therese; *b* 1980

3b *Emily Frances; *b* 1986

2a *John Alastair Nigel; *b* 1954; *m* 1982 *Julia R, dau of R C Wurtzburg, of Kensington Court Place, London W8, and has issue:

1b *Hamish; *b* 1985

2b *Robert Andrew; *b* 1991

1b *Kirsty Anne; *b* 1987

1a *Margaret Anne [Mrs Timothy Nott-Bower, Buckwood, Chisbury Lane, nr Marlborough, Wilts]; *b* 1942; *m* 1968 *Timothy E Nott-Bower, son of Sir John Reginald Hornby Nott-Bower, KCVO, and has issue:

1b *John William; *b* 1972

1b *Katherine Margot; *b* 1970

2a *Caroline Marion [Mrs Blaise Hardman, Farley House, Farley Chamberlayne, Romsey, Hants]; *b* 1943; *m* 1967 *Blaise Noel Anthony Hardman, son of Air Chief Marshal Sir (James) Donald Innes Hardman, GBE, KCB, DFC, and has issue:

1b *Thomas; *b* 1977

1b *Jane; *b* 1969

2b *Annabel; *b* 1971

3b *Elizabeth; *b* 1974

4b *Rosanna; *b* 1979

1 Selina Marguerite; *m* 2 Dec 1897 Capt Reginald Hughes-D'Aeth, of Woodlands View, Ashurst, Lyndhurst, Hants, late The Buffs, and *d* 29 May 1934, leaving issue. He *d* 29 July 1947

2 Jane Ethel; *d* unm 26 Jan 1943

3 Dorothy Milner; *m* 1st 6 June 1907 (*divorce* 1942) Rupert D'Oyly Carte, yr son of Richard D'Oyly Carte, and had issue; *m* 2nd 2 July 1942 St Yves de Verteuil, and *d* in Tobago 21 Feb 1977. He *d* 2 Sept 1963, aged 88

The 2nd EARL *d* 13 July 1911; his est son,

GATHORNE GATHORNE-HARDY, **3rd Earl of Cranbrook**, DL, JP, late Capt 2nd Vol Bn The Buffs; *b* 18 Dec 1870; *m* 25 April 1899 Lady Dorothy Montagu Boyle, JP (1923), and CC (1940–49) East Suffolk (*d* 17 March 1968, aged 89), yst dau of 7th Earl of Glasgow (*qv*), and had issue:

1 JOHN DAVID, **4th Earl**

2 (Ralph) Edward; *b* 4 June 1901; *educ* Eton and Ch Ch Oxford; *d* 18 June 1978

3 Robert; *b* 31 July 1902; *educ* Eton, and Ch Ch Oxford; poet, novelist, botanist and bibliographer, part-time sec to Logan Pearsall Smith; author: *Lacebury Manor, the biographies, Recollections of Logan Pearsall Smith* (1949), *Ottoline* (1963) and *Wildflowers in Britain* (1978), ed *Ottoline at Garsington 1915–18*, Fellow of Linnaean Soc 1960, Chm Bradfield RDC 1953–61; *d* unm 11 Feb 1973

4 Antony Gathorne, OStJ, Surgn Cdr RN (ret 1962); *b* 13 July 1907; *educ* Eton and Edinburgh U (MB, BCh 1935); *m* 1st 8 July 1931 Ruth Elizabeth (*d* 8 July 1973), est dau of Cdr Arthur Penton Napier Thorowgood, DSO, RN (*see* HUNTER-BLAIR, Bt), of The Green Cottage, Trull, Somerset; *m* 2nd 1974 *Mary Catherine [The Hon Mrs Antony Gathorne-Hardy, 21 Cranebrook Manor Rd, Twickenham, Middx TW2 5DJ], and *d* 1976, leaving by his 1st w:

(1) +Jonathan Gathorne [Jonathan Gathorne-Hardy Esq, 31 Blacksmith's Yard, Binham, Norfolk NR21 0AL]; late Lt RSF, author: *One Foot in the Clouds* (1961), *The Office* (1970), *The Rise and Fall of the British Nanny* (1972), *The Public School Phenomenon* (1977), *Love, Sex, Marriage and Divorce* (1981), *Doctors* (1983), *A Life of Gerald Brenan—The Interior Castle* (1993), *The Centre of the Universe is 18 Baedekerstrasse* (1985), *The City Beneath the Skies* (1986), *Particle Theory—a novel* (1996); *b* 17 May 1933; *educ* Bryanston and Trin Coll Cambridge (BA); *m* 1st 4 Oct 1963 (*divorce* 1977) Sabrina Viola, yst dau of Hon David Francis Tennant (*see* GLENCONNER, B); *m* 2nd 1985 *Nicolette, dau of Dr Kenneth William Cripps Sinclair-Loutit, MBE, and by his 1st w has:

1a +Benjamin; *b* 22 Feb 1967; *m* 1992 *Philippa, yr dau of David Heimann, and has:

1b *Nell; *b* 25 Oct 1994

1a *Jenny; *b* 16 Aug 1965; *m* 1996 *Joseph Mellen and has:

1b *Rudi; *b* 7 Jan 1996

(2) +Samuel Gathorne [Samuel Gathorne-Hardy Esq, Old Bullock Sheds, Great Glemham, Saxmundham]; late 2nd Lt RSF, Lt Parachute Regt TA; *b* 31 Aug 1936; *educ* Gordonstoun; *m* 30 April 1965 *Grace D'Cruz and has:

1a +Robert Dee; *b* 1973

1a *Lydia; *b* 1964

2a *Penelope Rose; *b* 1965

(1) *(Elizabeth) Rose; *b* 18 April 1949; *m* 30 June 1974 *Ian Richmond Battye, only son of Maj Richmond Keith Molesworth Battye, 1A, and has issue:

1a *Thomas Gathorne; *b* 1975

1a *Nell Aurore; *b* 1977

1 *Anne Catherine Dorothy [The Lady Anne Hill, Snape Priory, Saxmundham, Suffolk]; *b* 12 Oct 1911; *m* 9 Feb 1938 (George) Heywood Hill (*d* 1986), only son of George Hill, OBE, of Great Orchard, Bignor, Sussex (*see* JOHNSTONE, Bt), and has issue:

(1) *Harriet; *b* 1943; *m* 1st 1963 (*divorce* 1981) Timothy John Behrens; *m* 2nd 1985 *Simon Frazer, and by her 1st husb has:

1a *Algernon Kenneth; *b* 1966

2a *Charlie Corrado Heywood; *b* 1979

1a *Frances Anne; *b* 1963

(2) *Rabea (Lucy) [Mrs Abdul Redpath, The Tithe Barn, Stoke Holy Cross, Norwich, Norfolk]; *b* 1946; *m* 1970 *Abdul Azis (George James) Redpath, and has issue:

1a *Justin Abd'Allah; *b* 1971

2a *Abdul Razzaq; *b* 1977

1a *Hafidha; *b* 1975

2a *Aisha Iman; *b* 1983

3a *Khyria; *b* 1985

The 3rd EARL *d* 23 Dec 1915; his est son,

JOHN DAVID GATHORNE-HARDY, **4th Earl of Cranbrook**, CBE (1955), DL, JP for Suffolk, Alderman E Suffolk CC (chm 1950–57); *educ* Eton and RMA Woolwich; Hon MA Camb, Lt late RA, Alderman LCC 1928–30, chm E Anglian Regnl Hosp Bd 1946–50, PPS to First Cmmr of Works 1927–28, Dep Regnl Commnr East CD Region 1940–45, KStJ, Hon A/Cdre No 3169 (Suffolk) Fighter Control Unit RAuxAF 1950–61, treas and v-pres Linnean Soc 1958, treas UEA 1964, tstee Br Museum (Natural History) 1964–1973, memb: Br Commn Museums and Galleries 1965, Nature Conservancy 1967; *b* 15 April 1900; *m* 1st 7 Oct 1926 (*divorce* 1931) Bridget Cicely, dau of Robert D'Oyly Carte by Lady Dorothy, 3rd dau of 2nd Earl of Cranbrook (*see* above); *m* 2nd 26 July 1932 *Fidelity, OBE (1972), JP (Suffolk 1943) [The Rt Hon The Dowager Countess of Cranbrook OBE JP, Red House Farm, Great Glemham, Saxmundham, Suffolk], chm Aldeburgh Festival, dau of Hugh Exton Seebohm, JP, of Poynder's End, Hitchin, Herts, and *d* 21 Nov 1978, leaving:

1 GATHORNE GATHORNE-HARDY, **5th and present Earl of Cranbrook**

2 +Hugh [The Hon Hugh Gathorne-Hardy, The Hall Farm, Great Glemham, Saxmundham, Suffolk]; *b* 30 Dec 1941; *educ* Eton and Corpus Christi Coll Cambridge (BA 1963, MA); *m* 4 July 1971 *Caroline Elizabeth, only dau of William Nigel Ritchie (*see* RITCHIE OF DUNDEE, B), and has issue:

(1) +Frederick Jasper; *b* 1972

(2) +Alfred; *b* 1978

(1) *Alice; *b* 1974

(2) *Daisy; *b* 1977

1 *Juliet [The Lady Juliet Simpson, The White House, Rooks Hill, Underriver, Sevenoaks, Kent]; *b* 12 Dec 1934; *m* 30 Aug 1958 (*divorce* 1970) (Charles) Colin Simpson TD, only son of Charles Walter Simpson, MC, DM, of Seeley's Orchard, Beaconsfield, Bucks, and has issue:

(1) *Charles Duncan; *b* 8 Jan 1962

(2) *Edward Colin; *b* 8 Oct 1965

(1) *Fidelity Anne; *b* 29 March 1960

(2) *Amanda Juliet; *b* 7 March 1964

2 *(Catherine) Sophia [The Lady Sophia Meade, Bron Fedw, Meifod, Powys SY22 6DN]; *b* 11 March 1936; *m* 13 July 1957 *Simon Robert Jasper Meade and has issue (*see* CLANWILLIAM, E)

3 *Christina [The Lady Christina Letanka, Pepsall End, Pepperstock, Luton LU1 4LH]; *b* 1 May 1940; *educ* Homerton Teachers Training Coll Cambridge; *m* 11 June 1967 *Stanley Edward Letanka, MRCS, LRCP, son of Simon John Letanka, of Krom Kuil, S Africa, and has issue:

(1) *Peter Edward; *b* 1974

(1) *Stella Dorothy; *b* 21 March 1968; *m* 1996 *Richard Daniel Jeffs

(2) *Florence Ruth; *b* 1969

CRANWORTH

Arms: Sa. three leopard's faces jessant-de-lys or. **Crest:** A goat climbing up a rock with sprigs issuant therefrom, all ppr. **Supporters:** On either side a goat ppr., gorged with a collar gemel or and standing on a rock, also ppr. **Motto:** *In arduis viget virtus* ('Virtue flourishes in danger'). **Creation:** B. (UK) 28 Jan 1899.

THE 3RD BARON CRANWORTH OF LETTON AND CRANWORTH, Co Norfolk (Philip Bertram Gurdon) [The Rt Hon The Lord Cranworth, Grundisburgh Hall, Woodbridge, Suffolk IP13 6TW]; *b* 24 May 1940; *s* gf 1964; *educ* Eton and Magdalene Coll Cambridge; late Lt Roy Wilts Yeo; *m* 18 Jan 1968 *Frances Henrietta, twin dau of Lord William Walter Montagu Douglas Scott, MC, of Beechwood Ho, Melrose (*see* BUCCLEUCH, D), and has:

1 +(SACHA WILLIAM) ROBIN; *b* 12 Aug 1970

2 +(Brampton) Charles; *b* 28 May 1975

1 *Louisa-Jane; *b* 14 May 1969

Cranworth, previous creation: *see* NELSON, E.

Lineage: ADAM de GURDON; held a rent in Tystede from KING JOHN; *d* 1214, leaving:

Sir ADAM de GURDON; held lands in Tystede and Selborne, Hants; *d* 1231, leaving by Ameria, his w, two sons, of whom the er:

Sir ADAM de GURDON; bailiff Alton *temp* HENRY III; outlawed for treason and rebellion as one of Simon de Montfort's followers in the Barons' War; after the Battle of Evesham 1265 he fled with a band of followers to the New Forest, where he was defeated in single combat by PRINCE EDWARD later EDWARD I, who pardoned him, made him Keeper of the Forest of Wolmer and employed him in high military commands; *m* by special papal licence Constantia de Venuz and lived at The Temple, Selborne, Hants (later Gurdon Manor); his n (s of his yr bro):

ROBERT GURDON, of London; Sheriff 1314; *d* 1343, leaving:

JOHN GURDON; London merchant; *d* 1385, leaving:

THOMAS GURDON, of Clyne, Kent; *d* 1439, leaving:

JOHN GURDON, of Clyne; *d* 1465, leaving:

JOHN GURDON, of Dedham, Essex; *d* 1487, leaving:

JOHN GURDON, of Dedham; *d* 1505, leaving:

JOHN GURDON, of Dedham; *m* 1st Mary, dau of John Butter, of Dedham, but had no issue; *m* 2nd Anne, dau of John Coleman, of Lynes Hall, Suffolk, and *d* 1536, leaving, with eight daus:

ROBERT GURDON; bought Assington Hall from Sir Miles Corbet; *m* Rose, dau and heiress of Robert Sexton, of Lavenham, Suffolk, and *d* 1577, leaving:

JOHN GURDON, of Assington; High Sheriff Suffolk 1585; *m* Amy, dau and heir of William Brampton, of Letton, Norfolk, and *d* 1623, leaving:

BRAMPTON GURDON, of Assington Hall and Letton; High Sheriff Suffolk 1629, MP Sudbury; *m* 1st Elizabeth, dau of Edward Barrett, of Belhouse, Essex; *m* 2nd Muriel, dau of Martyn Sedley, of Morley, Norfolk, by a dau of Sir Thomas Knyvett, of Ashwellthorp, and had issue by both. By his 1st w he was ancestor of the GURDONs of Assington. By his 2nd w he had an est s:

BRAMPTON GURDON; barrister, MP Sudbury 1640–54, Col Regt of Horse Civil War, fought Battle of Naseby, at Siege of Colchester, one of the court-martial on Sir Charles Lucas and Sir George Lisle; *m* Mary, dau of Henry Polsted, of London, and *d* 1669, leaving:

BRAMPTON GURDON, of Letton; *m* Elizabeth, dau of Col Thornhagh, MP, of Fenton, Notts, s of Sir Francis Thornhagh, and *d* 1691, leaving:

THORNHAGH GURDON, of Letton; Receiver-Gen Norfolk *temp* QUEEN ANNE, author: *Origin and Rights of Parliament*; *m* Elizabeth, dau and coheir of Sir William Cooke, Bt, of Brome Hall, Norfolk, MP Norfolk, and *d* 1733, leaving, with three daus (two *d* unm; the other, Letitia, *m* Rev Nathaniel Saltier, of Ashdon, Essex):

THORNHAGH GURDON, of Letton; *m* Sarah, dau and heir of Theophilus Dillingham, of Shelton, Beds, and *d* 1783, leaving:

BRAMPTON GURDON later DILLINGHAM, of Letton, Norfolk, and Grundisburgh, Suffolk; High Sheriff Norfolk 1789; *m* 1st Mary, dau of Philip Bedingfeld, of Ditchingham, and had three s; *m* 2nd Mary, dau and coheir of Samuel Howard, and *d* 1820, having by her had a dau (Mary, *m* 4 May 1810 William Frere, DCL, Serjeant-at-Law and Master Downing Coll Cambridge (*d* 25 May 1836), 5th son of John Frere, JP, FRS, FSA, of Roydon Hall, Norfolk, and *d* 4 May 1864, leaving issue); his s by his 1st w:

THEOPHILUS THORNHAGH GURDON, of Letton, Norfolk, and Grundisburgh, Suffolk, DL, JP; Lt-Col W Norfolk Mil, High Sheriff 1824; *b* 24 Aug 1764; *m* 25 July 1796 Anne (*d* 23 Dec 1850), dau of William Mellish, MP, of Blyth, Notts, and had issue:

1 BRAMPTON

2 John, ancestor of the GURDON-REBOWs of Wyvenhoe Park

3 Philip (Rev), MA, JP, Rector Cranworth-cum-Letton, Southburgh and Reymerston, Norfolk; *b* 20 June 1800; *m* 3 July 1832 Henrietta Laura (*d* 17 Aug 1898), dau of John Pulteney, of Northerwood Ho, Hants, and *d* 1 Aug 1874, leaving issue

4 William, of Brantham, Suffolk, JP, MA; Recorder Bury, Judge Essex Co Court; *b* 1804; *d* Nov 1884

5 Edward (Rev), JP, MA; Rector Barnham Broom and Kimberley, later Hingham; *b* 26 Feb 1812; *m* 1st 20 Oct 1846 his cousin Mary Wilhelmina Frederica (*dsp* 3 Nov 1850), 3rd dau of William Frere, DLC, Serjeant-at-Law and Master Downing Coll Cambridge (*see* above); *m* 2nd 23 Sept 1853 Catherine Mary Jane Temple (*d* 9 March 1892), est dau of Rev Temple Frere, DL, JP, Rector of Roydon and Canon of Westminster, son of John Frere, JP, FRS, FSA, of Roydon Hall, Norfolk, and *d* 31 July 1873, having by her had issue

1 Anne; *m* 7 April 1825 Henry Wodehouse, DL, JP, and *d* 14 Jan 1880, leaving, with other issue, 1st Earl of Kimberley (*qv*)

Col GURDON *d* March 1849; his est son,

BRAMPTON GURDON, of Letton and Grundisburgh, DL, JP, MP W Norfolk, High Sheriff Norfolk 1855; *b* 25 Sept 1797; *m* 12 Aug 1828 Henrietta Susannah (*d* 28 May 1880), est dau of 1st and last Baron Colborne of West Harling, and *d* 28 April 1881, leaving issue:

1 ROBERT THORNAGH, **1st Baron**

2 William Brampton (Rt Hon Sir), PC, KCMG, CB, of Assington Hall, Suffolk; Ld Lt Suffolk 1907–10, MP N Norfolk 1899–1910; *b* 5 Sept 1840; *m* 20 Sept 1887 Lady Eveline Camilla (*d* 13 Sept 1894), 2nd dau of 5th Earl of Portsmouth (*qv*), and *dsp* 31 May 1910

1 Charlotte; *m* 8 May 1860 Horace Broke, only child of Lt-Gen Broke and cousin of Sir George Broke Myddleton, Bt (*see* 1887 edn), and *d* 11 Jan 1868, leaving issue

2 Amy Louisa, *d* unm 6 Feb 1864

The er son,

ROBERT THORNHAGH GURDON, **1st Baron Cranworth of Letton and Cranworth**, Co Norfolk (UK), so *cr* 28 Jan 1899, DL, JP, MA Camb, MP (Lib) S Norfolk 1880–85 and (Lib U) Mid-Norfolk 1885–92 and 1895, chm QS 1868–1901 and Norfolk CC 1889–1901, Col 4th Vol Bn Norfolk Regt; *b* 18 June 1829; *m* 1st 4 Sept 1862 Harriot Ellin (*d* 7 April 1864), dau of Sir William Miles, 1st Bt (*qv*), of Leigh Court, and had issue:

1 Amy Harriott, JP (W Suffolk); *b* 23 March 1864; *m* 1st 19 Aug 1884 Lionel Charles Drummond (*see* PERTH, E; *dsp* 5 March 1891); *m* 2nd 17 April 1895 Capt Alfred Bayley Ridley, late King's Own Roy Lancaster Regt (*see* RIDLEY, V). He *dsp* 26 March 1894. She *m* 3rd 22 Aug 1905 Maj Charles Stirling, RHA, er son of Gen Sir William Stirling, KCB, and *d* 13 May 1944, leaving issue. He *d* 19 Nov 1914

The **1st Baron** *m* 2nd 27 July 1874 Emily Frances (*d* 3 April 1934), dau of Rev Robert Boothby Heathcote, JP, MA, of Friday Hill, Essex (*see* WILLOUGHBY DE ERESBY, B), and by her had issue:

1 Bertram Robert; *b* 20 May, *d* 27 June 1875

2 BERTRAM FRANCIS, **2nd Baron**

2 Muriel Charlotte; *b* 18 April 1876

The 1st BARON *d* 13 Oct 1902; his only surv son,

BERTRAM FRANCIS GURDON, **2nd Baron Cranworth of Letton and Cranworth**, KG (1948), MC (1918), DL and JP Suffolk, V-Lt 1947–64, Hon Col 58th Suffolk Med Bde RA (TA), 1937–47, Capt Res of Offrs, late RA, formerly Lt PWO Norfolk RFA, served in S African War 1901–02, and WW I 1914–18, had Croix de Guerre; *b* 13 June 1877; *educ* Trin Coll Cambridge (BA); *m* 18 July 1903 Vera Emily, CBE (1945) (*d* 15 Nov 1966), er dau of Arthur William Ridley (*see* RIDLEY, V), and *d* 4 Jan 1964, having had:

1 Robert Brampton, Lt Coldstream Gds WW II; *b* 21 June 1904; *m* 20 Jan 1932, as her 1st husb, Hon Daisy Pearson (*d* 1979), est dau of 2nd Viscount Cowdray (*qv*), and was *ka* Libya July 1942, leaving issue:

(1) Charles Harold; *b* 15 Jan 1936; *d* as the result of an accident 23 Jan 1945

(2) PHILIP BERTRAM GURDON, **3rd and present Baron Cranworth of Letton and Cranworth**

(1) *Jeryl Marcia Sarah, DL (Warwicks 1990) [The Hon Lady Smith-Ryland DL, Old Hall, Medbourne, Leics LE16 8DZ]; granted rank of baron's dau 5 Aug 1964, DStJ (1990, CStJ 1981); *b* 3 Nov 1932; *m* 30 Oct 1952 Sir Charles Mortimer Tollemache Smith-Ryland, KCVO, JP, Ld Lt Warwicks (*d* 1989), only son of Capt Charles Ivor Phipson Smith-Ryland, JP, of Barford Hill, Warwicks, and has issue:

1a *Robin Charles; *b* 19 Oct 1953; *educ* Eton

2a *David James; *b* 23 Feb 1961

1a *Sarah Yoskyl; *b* 30 Aug 1955

2a *Joanna; *b* 22 June 1959

3a *Petra; *b* 24 Aug 1970

1 Camilla Elizabeth; *b* 9 Aug 1909; *m* 30 July 1932 George Marcus Tomline Pretyman, of Orwell Park, Suffolk, and *d* 1985, leaving:

(1) *Gillian Enid [Mrs Mark Bence-Jones, Glenville Park, Glenville, Co Cork, Ireland; Orwell Park House, Nacton, Suffolk IP10 0JG]; *b* 16 March 1934; *m* 2 Feb 1965 *Mark Adayre Bence-Jones, author, only child of Col Philip Reginald Bence-Jones, MC, of Glenville Park, and has:

1a *Nicholas George Winthrop; *b* 30 Sept 1966; *educ* Ampleforth

1a *Miranda Beatrice May; *b* 15 Dec 1971; *educ* Cobham Hall and St Paul's

2a *Silvia Camilla Coromandel; *b* 31 Oct 1980; *educ* Amberfield and Riddlesworth

2 Judith Florence; *b* 8 May 1914; *m* 20 March 1943 Maj Thomas Henry Bull, TD, MA, RA, yst son of William Perkins Bull, KC, of Toronto, Canada, and *d* 1992

CRATHORNE

Arms: Erm. a cross moline gu. between four hurts. **Crest:** A gryphon's head erm., wings addorsed erminois, gorged with a collar az., therefrom pendant a cross as in the arms. **Supporters:** Dexter, a crow sa., beaked and membered or, in the beak a sprig of blackthorn flowered ppr.; sinister, a stag sa., attired, unguled and gorged with a mural crown gold, charged on the shoulder with a thistle slipped and leaved ppr **Motto:** *Perseverando* ('By persevering'). **Creations:** Bt. (UK) 31 Jan 1945, B. (UK) 15 July 1959.

THE 2ND BARON CRATHORNE, of Crathorne, N R Co York, and a **Baronet** (Sir (Charles) James Dugdale, Bt, DL (Cleveland 1983, N Yorks 1996)) [The Rt Hon The Lord Crathorne DL, Crathorne House, Yarm, N Yorks TS15 0AT]; *b* 12 Sept 1939; *s* f 1977; *educ* Eton and Trin Coll Cambridge (MA); FRSA; consultant and lecturer in fine art, assist to Pres Parke-Bennet New York 1965–69, James Dugdale & Associates London, Independent Fine Art Consultancy Serv 1969–77, James Crathorne & Associates 1980–, memb: Yorks Regnl Ctee Nat Tst 1978–84 and 1988–94, Court Leeds U 1985–97, Conservative Advisory Gp Arts and Heritage 1988–; chm Georgian Gp 1990–, tstee: Georgian Theatre Royal Richmond 1970–, Capt Cook Tst 1978– (chm 1993–), Christian Inheritance 1989– and Nat Heritage Memorial Fund 1992–95, dir: Woodhouse Securities Ltd 1989– and Cliveden plc 1997–; author: *Edouard Vuillard* (1967), co-author: *Tennant's Stalk* (1973), *History of Crathorne* (1988) and *Cliveden The Place and The People* (1995); *m* 8 Jan 1970 *Sylvia Mary, yr dau of Brig Arthur Montgomery, OBE, TD (*see* MONTGOMERY, Bt), and has issue:

1 +THOMAS ARTHUR JOHN; *b* 30 Sept 1977

1 *Charlotte Patricia; *b* 11 Dec 1972

2 *Katharine Feodora Nicola; *b* 1980

Lineage: EDMUND DUGDALE, of Gt Harwood, Clitheroe, Lancs; *bapt* 11 March 1693; *m* 26 Dec 1721 Ann Dagon, of Gt Harwood, and was *bur* 2 July 1737 leaving, with other issue:

JOHN DUGDALE, of Gt Harwood; *bapt* 23 Sept 1722; *m* 24 Sept 1749 Ann (*bur* 23 May 1795), dau of Nathaniel Aspden, of Gt Harwood, and was *bur* 6 July 1791, having had issue:

1 Edmund, of Gt Harwood; *b* 12 April 1757; *m* 16 Sept 1793 Peggy, dau of Thomas Hindle, and was *bur* 5 July 1809, leaving issue:

(1) Ann; *m* 11 Oct 1810 her cousin William Dugdale, of Ivy Bank, and had issue (*see* below)

2 NATHANIEL, of whom presently

3 Thomas; *bapt* 18 May 1766; *m* 7 Sept 1793 Grace, dau of Edward Pickles, and had issue

4 John; *bapt* 28 May 1769; *d* unm 10 July 1826

5 Adam, of Dovecot Ho, Lancs; *b* 6 Jan 1771; *m* 25 Dec 1800 Mary, dau of John Hargraves, of Burnley, Lancs, and *dsp*

1 Anne; *m* 3 Sept 1775 James Haworth, and *d* Feb 1823, leaving issue

2 Charlotte; *m* 24 May 1791 James Sykes, of Accrington, Lancs, and *d* 5 Aug 1821, leaving issue

The 2nd son,

NATHANIEL DUGDALE, of Gt Harwood; *bapt* 30 May 1762; *m* 27 March 1785 Ellen (*bur* 4 Aug 1828), dau of John Smalley, and *d* 23 Sept 1816, having had issue:

1 John, of Dovecot, nr Liverpool and Llwyn, Llanfillin, Montgomeryshire
2 JAMES, of whom presently
3 William, of Ivy Bank, Lancs; *b* 21 Sept 1793; *m* 1st 11 Oct 1810 his cousin Ann (*d* 12 Jan 1823), dau of Edmund Dugdale (*see* above); *m* 2nd 24 Aug 1826 Sarah (*d* 9 Aug 1841) est dau of Henry Roberts, and *d* 11 Nov 1839, leaving issue by both ws
4 Thomas, DL, JP, of Griffin Lodge, Lancs; *b* 14 May 1797; *m* 13 March 1824 Elizabeth (*d* 9 April 1866), dau of Thomas Walmsley, and *d* 17 March 1875, leaving issue
1 Mary

The second son,

JAMES DUGDALE, of Lower House, Lancs; *bapt* 12 Feb 1792; *m* Ellen, dau of John Martland, of Padiham, Lancs, and had an est s:

JOHN DUGDALE, of Irwell Bank, Eccles, Lancs, and Crathorne, Yorks; *b* 12 Aug 1823; *m* 16 May 1860 Charlotte Mary (*d* 18 March 1891), dau of Robert Artindale, of Burnley, Lancs, and *d* 29 Dec 1881, leaving, with three daus:

JAMES LIONEL DUGDALE, DL, JP, of Crathorne Hall, Yorks, High Sheriff 1921; *educ* Eton and Ch Ch Oxford; Capt Princess of Wales's Own Yorks Hus Yeo Cav; *b* 19 Sept 1862; *m* 11 Dec 1894 Maud Violet (*d* 23 Feb 1940), yr dau of George William Plukenett Woodroffe, and *d* 17 Oct 1941, leaving issue:

1 **Sir Thomas Lionel Dugdale, 1st Bt**, and **1st Baron Crathorne**, of Crathorne, N Riding of Yorkshire (both UK), so *cr* 31 Jan 1945 and 15 July 1959 respectively, PC (1951), TD, JP (N R Yorks 1928), V-Lt (1957); *educ* Eton and RMC Sandhurst; Maj Princess of Wales's Own Yorks Hus Yeo Cav (TA), formerly Capt Roy Scots Greys, served WW I 1917–18 (two medals) and WW II 1940–41 in Middle East, MP (C) Richmond (Yorks) 1929–59, PPS to: Pres BOT 1931, Sec State Colonies 1931–35 and Sec State Air 1935 and PM 1935–37, Jr Ld Treasury 1937–40, Dep Ch Govt Whip and V-Chm C Party Org 1941–42, Chm C Party 1942–44, Pres Nat Union Conservative and Unionist Assocs 1952, Min Ag and Fisheries 1951–54, memb Standing Ctee NATO Parly Conf 1958–65 (pres 1963), UK memb Gen Assembly Cncl Europe 1958–59 and 1961–65, v-pres Cncl of Europe 1962–65, memb Advsy Commn Centl Africa 1960, chm Political Honours Scrutiny 1961, Steward Jockey Club 1960–62, Sr Steward 1962, chm NE England Advsy Ctee Civil Aviation 1964, Ld of the Manor and Patron living Crathorne; *b* 20 July 1897; *m* 22 Sept 1936 Nancy, OBE (1961) (*d* 17 May 1969), formerly w of Sylvester Govett Gates, CBE, and yst dau of Sir Charles Tennant, 1st Bt (*see* GLENCONNER, B), and *d* 26 March 1977, leaving issue:

1 (CHARLES) JAMES DUGDALE, **2nd and present Baron Crathorne**
2 +David John [The Hon David Dugdale, Park House, Crathorne, Yarm, N Yorks TS15 0BD], GradMIMech E; *b* 4 May 1942 ; *educ* Eton and Trin Coll Cambridge (MA); High Sheriff Cleveland 1995–96; *m* 1972 *Susan Louise, yr dau of Lewis A Powell, and has issue:
(1) +Jonathan William Shaun; *b* 1980
(1) *Clare Nancy Louise; *b* 1978
1 Beryl Violet; *m* 17 July 1926 20th Earl of Rothes (*qv*), and *d* 1994, having had issue

CRAUFURD

Arms: Arg. two tilting spears in saltire ppr. between four erm. spots sa., a bordure chequy gu. and of the field. **Crest:** An ermine ppr. **Motto:** *Sine labe note* ('Distinction without a stain'). **Creation:** Bt. (GB) 8 June 1781.

SIR ROBERT JAMES CRAUFURD, 9TH BT, of Kilbirney, North Britain [Sir Robert Craufurd Bt, East Grove, Grove Rd, Lymington, Hants SO41 3RF]; *b* 18 March 1937; *s f* 1970; *educ* Harrow and Univ Coll Oxford (MA 1965); memb London Stock Exchange 1969; *m* 1st 1 Feb 1964 (*divorce* 1987) Catherine Penelope, yr dau of Capt Horatio Westmacott, RN, of Torquay; *m* 2nd 1987 *Georgina Anne, dau of John Dennis Russell, of Lymington (*see* 1970 edn CORBET, Bt), and by his 1st w has issue:

1 *Caroline Anne; *b* 10 Jan 1965
2 *Penelope Jane; *b* 14 July 1967
3 *Veronica Mary; *b* 10 April 1969

Lineage: JOHN, stepson of Baldwin de Biggar (ancestor of the Earls of Wigton), possessed *c* 1153 the northern part of the territorial Barony of Crawford, later called Crawfordjohn, and took the surname CRAUFURD; had:

Sir REGINALD de CRAUFURD; 1st Sheriff Ayr; *b c* 1165; *m* Margaret, dau and heir of James de Loudoun, and had five s, of whom four were witnesses between 1229 and 1232. His son John inherited the estate but his line ended in coheirs shortly before 1259.

Another son, probably the 2nd:

HUGH CRAUFURD; inherited his mother's property of Loudoun, granted 1226 and 1228 by Alan, Lord of Galloway, Constable of Scotland, the lands of Crosbie and Monnoch; had an est s:

HUGH CRAUFURD; *m* Alicia —, had with her a charter of the lands of Draffen 1271, and had, with a dau (Margaret, mother of Sir William Wallace, Guardian of Scotland):

Sir REGINALD CRAUFURD; Sheriff Ayr; murdered by the English garrison at the Black Parl of Ayr *c* 1297; *m* Cecilia — and had, with a yr s:

Sir REGINALD CRAUFURD; Sheriff Ayr; executed by the English at Carlisle 13 Feb 1307, leaving:

SUSAN; *m* Sir Duncan Campbell, of Reidcastle (see LOUDOUN, E), to whom she conveyed the Loudoun estates, but the Castle of Crosbie and the adjacent estate of Monnoch appear to have held from her and her descendants by the CRAUFURDs of Auchenames, the first of whom appears to have been her uncle:

HUGH CRAUFURD of Auchenames; living 1335; had:

REGINALD CRAUFURD of Auchenames; living 1401; had:

REGINALD CRAUFURD of Auchenames; had:

THOMAS CRAUFURD of Auchenames; endowed a chapel at Kilbarchan 1401; had, with an er s (Robert, ancestor of the CRAUFURDs of Auchenames):

ARCHIBALD CRAUFURD of Previck and Thirdpart; had:

THOMAS CRAUFURD of Previck and Thirdpart; had:

ARCHIBALD CRAUFURD of Previck and Thirdpart; *m* Agnes Galbraith and had an est s:

JOHN CRAUFURD of Previck and Thirdpart, which he sold to Lord Sempill (*qv*) *c* 1520; murdered 1524, leaving:

JOHN CRAUFURD of Drummure; *b* 1516; had:

WILLIAM CRAUFURD; tenant of the lands of Drings; had:

ANDRO CRAUFURD; bought the lands of Drings; *m* Marion Cathcart and had, with another s (William, whose male line died out four generations later):

Rev GEORGE CRAUFURD; Min W Kilbride; *m* Agnes, dau of John Montgomery of Bridgend and had an est s:

ROBERT CRAUFURD; *m* Agnes Kennedy of Balsarroch and *d* 1682, leaving an est s:

JAMES CRAUFURD; bought 1687 the lands of Newark; *m* 28 May 1687 Ann, dau of Quentin Kennedy of Drummellane and had:

QUENTIN CRAUFURD of Newark; justiciary baillie for West Seas of Scotland; *m* 18 Sept 1729 Ann, dau of James Robinson, merchant of Irvine, and *d* 1749, having had, with other issue:

1 ALEXANDER (Sir), **1st Bt**
2 Quentin; *b* 22 Sept 1743; nabob, settled in Paris, where friend of MARIE ANTOINETTE, whom he helped to escape in the Flight to Varennes; author; *d* 23 Nov 1819

The er son,

Sir Alexander Craufurd, 1st Bt (GB), so *cr* 8 June 1781; *m* 30 May 1760 Jane (*d* 6 May 1794), dau of James Crokatt, of Luxborough, Essex, and *d* 15 Dec 1797, leaving (with other issue who *dsp*):

1 Sir JAMES CRAUFURD later GREGAN-CRAUFURD (added by sign manual 1812 in the mistaken belief that he descended from Sir Gregan Craufurd *temp* DAVID I KING OF SCOTS), **2nd Bt**; *b* 11 Oct 1761; *m* 2 March 1792 Maria Theresa (*d* 21 April 1832), sis of 3rd Viscount Gage (*qv*), and *d* 9 July 1839, having had:

(1) Thomas Gage, Gds Offr; *b* 1792; *ka* Hougoumont 18 June 1815
(2) Alexander Charles, Lt-Col; *b* 30 June 1794; *m* 23 July 1818 Barbara (*d* 4 Sept 1838), dau of 7th Earl of Coventry (*qv*), and *dsp* 12 March 1838
(3) **Rev Sir George William Craufurd, 3rd Bt**, MA and Fell of King's Coll Cambridge; *b* 10 April 1797; *m* 1st 15 Feb 1843 Hon Hester King (*d* 18 March 1848), sis of 1st Earl of Lovelace (*qv*), and had:

1a **Sir Charles William Frederick Craufurd, 4th Bt**, Lt-Cdr RN; *b* 28 March 1847; *m* 23 Nov 1870 Hon Isolda Caroline Vereker (*d* 10 Sept 1927), est dau of 4th Viscount Gort (*qv*), and *d* 24 Sept 1939, leaving:

1b **Sir Standish George Gage Craufurd, 5th Bt**, CB (1919), CMG (1916), CIE (1913), DSO (1900), DL, JP, Ayr, late Gordon Highrs, Hon Brig-Gen 1928, ADC to HM GEORGE V 1918–28, served in Chitral 1895, in Tirah 1897–98 (wounded), in Dargai in S African War 1899–1902 (wounded), W African Frontier Force 1905–08, in Persian Gulf 1909–13 and WW I (wounded three times); FRGS; *b* 10 Nov 1872; *m* 19 Dec 1923 (*annulled* 1927) Ellen Alexandra (*d* 2 Jan 1976), only dau of Capt Alexander Price Haig, of Blairhill, and *dsp* 6 Jan 1956

2b **Sir Quentin Charles Alexander Craufurd, 6th Bt**, Capt RN, FRSA, AMIEE, FInst P; *b* 11 Feb 1875; *m* 1 Oct 1899 Anne (*d* 1957), est dau of Thomas Blackwell, of Rodeen, Borrisokane, Co Tipperary, and *dsp* 8 May 1957

3b **Sir Alexander John Fortescue Craufurd, 7th Bt**; *b* 22 March 1876; *educ* Wellington and Camborne Sch of Mines; *m* 25 Sept 1911 Alexa Campbell (*d* 8 July 1955), dau of Robert Little, MD, of Singapore, and had issue:

1c *Isolda Vereker [Mrs James Clement, 21 Glendale Dve, London SW19]; *b* 28 June 1912; *m* 5 July 1945 *Maj James Robertson Clement, Transvaal Scottish, son of Robert Clement, of Dunlop, Ayrshire, and has issue:

1d *James Robert Alexander; *b* 16 Oct 1949
1d *Helen Alexa Caroline; *b* 11 Nov 1950

2c *Cynthia; *b* 17 Aug 1917; *m* 1st 1 July 1944 Jacques Pinkasfeld (*d* 30 Jan 1963), son of Henry Pinkasfeld, of Vienna and Cairo; *m* 2nd 1972 Lt-Col Albert Francis Lamb (*d* 1981), and by 1st husb has:

1d *Peter Charles; *b* 10 Sept 1950

1d *Rosemary; *b* 30 Oct 1952

4b Charles Edward Vereker, Cdr RN; *b* 17 July 1884; *m* 24 Nov 1923 (*annulled* 1934) Sonia, 3rd dau of S Russell, of Stirling Ho, Clapton Common, and *d* 11 April 1947

5b Robert Henry Dukinfield (twin with Charles Edward Vereker); *d* 25 Jan 1885

1b Hester Jane Laline; *d* unm 21 Nov 1946

2b Laline Isolda; *m* 1st 9 Nov 1909 Hugh Walton-Wilson (*d* 1 March 1921), only son of John Walton-Wilson, JP, of Shotley Hall, Northumberland, and had issue; *m* 2nd 2 June 1923 Frederick Thomas Clifton Crump, son of Thomas Crump, of The Manor Ho, Cleobury Mortimer, Shropshire, and *d* 5 June 1965. He *d* 24 April 1944

3b Isolda Mabel Cecil; *m* 15 Oct 1912 Geoffrey Parker, 3rd son of Hon Cecil Thomas Parker, and *d* 11 June 1955, leaving issue (*see* MACCLESFIELD, E)

4b Eleanor Mary Dorothea; *m* 22 Sept 1911 Charles Thackeray Wilbraham, son of Henry Wilbraham, and *dsp* 10 Oct 1953. He *d* 26 Feb 1954

5b Margaret Elizabeth Maria; *m* 15 June 1918 Professor Owen Lambert Vaughan Simkinson de Wesselow, MD, FRCP, son of Rev C H de Wesselow, and *d* 22 Nov 1948, leaving issue. He *d* 6 July 1959

2a Henry Thomas Gage; *b* 26 Feb 1848; *bur* 5 July 1848

(3) (cont.) The **Rev Sir George** *m* 2nd 3 May 1849 Martha (*d* 5 July 1865), widow of William Cooke and dau of John Holland, of Carrington Ho, and *d* 24 Feb 1881

(1) Jane; *m* 1st 12 Oct 1823 Gen Christopher Chowne (formerly Tilson). He *d* 15 July 1834. She *m* 2nd 29 Aug 1836 Rev Sir Henry R Dukinfield, 7th and last Bt, and *d* 25 May 1884. He *d* 24 Jan 1858

2 Charles Gregan (Sir), GCB, MP, Lt-Gen; *b* 12 Feb 1763; *m* 7 Feb 1800 Anna Maria (*d* 18 Oct 1834), widow of 3rd Duke of Newcastle (*see* LINCOLN, E) and dau of 2nd Earl of Harrington (*qv*), and *dsp* 26 March 1821

3 Robert, Maj-Gen cmdg Light Div Peninsular War; *b* 5 May 1764; *m* 7 Feb 1800 Mary Frances (*d* 1842), dau of Henry Holland, of Hans Place, Chelsea, and *d* 24 Jan 1812 (*k* leading his troops Ciudad Rodrigo), having had, with a dau (Louisa Mary Frances, *m* Rev Robert Farquharson, Rector of Langton, Dorset, and *d* 14 Oct 1839, leaving issue):

(1) Charles Henry Gregan (Rev), MA; *b* 14 Dec 1802; Rector of Old Swinford, Worcs; *m* 2 March 1836 Eliza (*d* 25 Nov 1864), dau of Richard Hickman, of Old Swinford Ho, and *d* 24 Feb 1876, leaving issue:

1a Charles Richard; *b* 4 July 1839; *d* unm 26 May 1866

2a Robert; *b* 19 Jan 1841; *d* 16 Feb 1880

3a Alexander Henry (Rev); *b* 16 Feb 1843; *educ* Oriel Coll Oxford (MA); *d* unm 9 Sept 1917

4a William Devereux; *b* 11 Nov 1855; *m* 15 Sept 1880 Ada Mary (*d* 24 Aug 1942), dau of John Bagshaw, and *d* 8 Dec 1938, leaving issue:

1b Cecil Alfred; *b* 16 April 1885; *educ* Brighton Coll; *m* 26 Dec 1914 Edith Mary Dutton, 2nd dau of Rev J R Dutton Tompson, Chaplain at Dinan, France, and *dsp* 6 Dec 1958

1b Mabel Florence; *d* unm April 1963

2b Elfreda Marion; *d* as a result of enemy action, 24 Sept 1942

1a Caroline Julia; *m* 31 March 1870 Alexander Asher, KC, MP, late Solicitor-Gen for Scotland, and *dsp* 31 Aug 1922. He *d* 5 Aug 1905

2a Mary Frances; *m* 5 Sept 1876 Rev Robert Henry Streeten, MA Oxford, late Vicar of St Mary, Kingswinford, and *d* 12 Nov 1943, leaving issue .He *d* 1921

3a Emily; *m* 17 April 1879 Rev C S Wordsworth, MA, Rector of Old Swinford, and *d* March 1930, leaving issue. He *d* 1909

4a Charlotte; *m* 25 April 1873 Bond Douglas Atkinson, of Claygate, Surrey, and *d* 11 Feb 1927, having had issue. He *d* 30 July 1909

(2) Robert Gregan; *b* 25 Dec 1804 in Lisbon; *m* 9 Sept 1844 Fanny Louisa (*d* 14 July 1874), dau of Adml Thomas Wolley, and *d* 16 July 1868, leaving issue:

1a Henry Robert, JP (Herts), formerly Lt RA; *b* 13 Aug 1845; *m* 1st 18 July 1872 Fanny (*dsp* 16 Dec 1876), dau of Rev James Williams, of Tring Park; *m* 2nd 30 July 1878 Alice Jane (*d* 15 June 1930), dau of Rev R M Wood, Rector of Aldbury, and *d* 28 Nov 1920, leaving issue:

1b Robert Quentin, DSO (1918), CC Herts, Col, late Roy Scots Fus, served in S African War 1899–1902 (two medals, seven clasps), and WW I 1914–18 (despatches, Croix de Guerre of France); *b* 9 March 1880; *m* 1st 5 Oct 1909 Mildred Mary (*d* 2 Nov 1929), yst dau of Rt Hon William Kenny, PC, of Cabinteely, Co Dublin, Judge of High Court of Justice in Ireland, and had issue:

1c *Dorothy Mary, a Nun, memb of Order SHCJ; *b* 20 Oct 1910

2c Mary Elizabeth; *b* 19 Jan 1912; *m* 28 Sept 1940 Michael de Lancey Wilson, TD, BA, son of William Henry Wilson, of Blandford Forum, Dorset, and *d* 3 Dec 1972, leaving:

1d *Peter Michael [Peter Wilson Esq, 23 Beechwood Ave, Kew Gardens, Richmond, Surrey]; *b* 9 June 1941; *educ* Downside and Oriel Coll Oxford (MA); *m* 5 Sept 1964 *Lissa, dau of Olaf Trab, of Copenhagen, Denmark

1d *Gillian Mary; *b* 26 Sept 1944; *m* Jan 1974 *Roger Hoffen and *d* 9 June 1984, leaving:

1e *Rupert Peter Rogers; *b* 23 Oct 1974

2e *Harry Michael Rogers; *b* 15 Sept 1976

1e *Lucy Gillian Mary; *b* 12 Dec 1977

3c Alice Gwendoline; *b* 22 Nov 1913; *m* 4 Sept 1959 Maj William Henry Murray, Irish Gds (*d* 16 Jan 1983), son of Maj William Murray, TD, of Reedley, Woodsgate, Bexhill, Sussex, and *d* 12 Aug 1990

4c *(Mildred) Heather Mary [Miss Heather Craufurd, 61 Finborough Rd, London SW10 9DL]; *b* 23 June 1916

1b (cont.) Col Robert Craufurd *m* 2nd 31 Jan 1931 Muriel Frances (*d* 16 Feb 1969), dau of George Edward Darroch, of 40 Stanhope Gardens, SW, and Braidley, Canford Cliffs, Bournemouth, and *d* 10 Jan 1943

2b Archibald, Lt-Col Res of Offrs, late Gordon Highrs, attd Egyptian Army, served WW I; *b* 2 Aug 1881; *d* 11 July 1932

3b JAMES GREGAN (Sir), **8th Bt**

1b Emma Katherine; *b* 23 Oct 1891; *d* unm after a motor accident 3 April 1967

2a Charles Quentin Gregan, Master Attendant at Singapore, Cdr RN; *b* 2 Dec 1847; *m* 1 June 1878 Esmeralda Calligary (*d* 3 May 1927), dau of Countess Valsamachi, of Corfu, and *d* 10 March 1917, having had issue:

1b Quentin; *b* 24 April 1879; *d* 23 Jan 1934

2b Robert; *b* 29 July 1880; *d* 1 Jan 1881

1b Maud Katherine; *b* 29 Sept 1882; *m* 19 April 1906 Edward Hayes Dashwood, and *d* 13 Feb 1966, leaving issue. He *d* May 1951

1a Emma Katherine; *m* 26 Sept 1874 Edward Broughton Pillans, of Milan, and *d* 7 Aug 1933, having had issue. He *d* 1889

(3) Alexander Quentin (Rev); *b* Sept 1808; *d* unm 19 March 1876

4 Daniel; *b* 11 Sept 1768; *m* 26 April 1798 Bridget (*m* 2nd 26 May 1817 Sir Robert Wilmot, 3rd Bt (*qv*), and *d* 18 July 1842), dau of Henry Holland, and was lost at sea 1810, leaving issue:

(1) Charlotte Anne; *m* 1st Sir James John Fraser, 3rd Bt (*see* 1967 edn FRASER, Bt, of Ledeclune), and had issue. He *d* 5 June 1834. She *m* 2nd July 1837 Sir Ralph Howard, 1st and last Bt, and *d* 7 May 1867. He *d* 15 Aug 1873

Sir ALEXANDER *dspm* 10 July 1966; his kinsman,

Sir James Gregan Craufurd, 8th Bt, JP (Herts 1930); *educ* Harrow and Univ Coll Oxford (MA); barrister Lincoln's Inn 1914; *b* 23 Feb 1886; *m* 11 April 1931 Ruth Marjorie (*d* 13 Feb 1998), dau of Frederic Corder, of Ipswich, and *d* 7 April 1970, leaving:

1 Sir ROBERT JAMES CRAUFURD, **9th and present Bt**

1 *Jane Elizabeth [Mrs John Hoyle, 12 Linkfield, E Molesey, Surrey]; *b* 22 July 1932; *m* 1st 29 Oct 1960 (*divorce* 1979) Maj Michael Cumby Spurrier, DLI, son of Rev William Horatio Sandys Cumby Spurrier, OBE, TD, MA, of Trafalgar (formerly Heighinton) Ho, Heighinton, Co Durham; *m* 2nd 1979 *John Robson Hoyle

2 *Margaret Ruth; *b* 28 Nov 1934; *educ* St Andrews (MA); *m* 3 May 1962 (*divorce* 1989) John Peter Hudson, son of Col Christopher John Peter Hudson, of Butlers' Cross, Wendover, Bucks, and has issue:

(1) *Alexander Matthew HUDSON later HUDSON CRAUFURD (deed poll); *b* 18 Feb 1965; *educ* Edinburgh U (BA)

(1) *Emma Caroline; *b* 4 May 1963

(2) *Erica; *b* 27 Oct 1968

CRAVEN

Arms: Arg. a fess between six cross crosslets fitchée gu. **Crest:** On a chapeau gu. doubled erm. a griffin statant, wings elevated erm., beaked and foremembered or. **Supporters:** Two griffins, wings elevated erm., beaked and foremembered or. **Motto:** *Virtus in actione consistit* ('Virtue consists in action'). **Creations:** B. (E) 11 Dec 1666, E. and V. (UK) 18 June 1801.

THE 9TH EARL OF CRAVEN, Co York, **Viscount Uffington**, Co Berks, and **Baron Craven of Hampsted Marshall**, Berks (Benjamin Robert Joseph Craven) [The Rt Hon The Earl of Craven, Hawkwood House, Hawkhurst Lane, Waldron, E Sussex]; *b* 13 June 1989; *s f* 1990

Lineage: JOHN CRAVEN, of Appletreewick, Craven, Yorks; *m* 1539 Beatrix (*d* 1597), dau of John Hunter, and had:

1 Henry, of Appletreewick; *b* 1543; *m* Margaret Brockden (*d* 1613) and *d* 1604, having had, with other issue:

(1) Robert, of Appletreewick; *b* 1574; *m* by 1603 Mary Shearwood (*d* 1670) and *d* 1661, having had, with other issue:

1a William (Sir), of Lenchwick, Worcs; *b* 1610; *m* Elizabeth, dau of 2nd Lord Fairfax of Cameron (*qv*), and *d* 12 Oct 1655, having had issue:

1b William; included in the 1st extension of the remainder (*see* below) made in March 1664/5; *d* unm 1665 aged 16

2a Thomas, of Burnsall; *b* 1611; *m* 1634 Anne (*d* 1681), dau of Francis Proctor, of Beckwith, and *d* 15 April 1682, leaving, with three daus:

1b Sir WILLIAM CRAVEN, of Benham Valence, Berks, and Coombe Abbey, Warwicks; *b* 26 Aug 1638; included (with his male issue) in the 2nd extension of the remainder (*see below*) made in Dec 1666; *m* Margaret (*d* 1711), dau of Sir Christopher Clapham, of Beamsley, and *d* 28 Oct 1695, leaving, with five other sons and six daus:

1c WILLIAM CRAVEN, **2nd Baron Craven of Hampsted Marshall**; *b* 24 Oct 1668; Ld Lt Berks 1702–11, Ld Proprietor 1705/6 and Ld Palatine of Carolina (*i.e.*, holding the territory in North America know as Carolina of the King as a county palatine); *m* 12 Oct 1697 Elizabeth (*d* 16 May 1704), sis of Sir Fulwar Skipwith, 2nd Bt, of Newbold Hall, Warwicks, and *d* 9 Oct 1711, leaving:

1d WILLIAM CRAVEN, **3rd Baron Craven of Hampsted Marshall**; *b* 1700; *educ* Rugby and St John's Coll Cambridge; *m* 1 June 1721 Anne (*d* 5 Feb 1729/30), dau of Frederick Tylney, of Tylney Hall, Hants, and *dsp* 10 Aug 1739

2d FULWAR CRAVEN, **4th Baron Craven of Hampsted Marshall**; *educ* Rugby and Magdalen Coll Oxford; *d* unm 10 Nov 1764

2c John, of Whitley, Warwicks; *b* 23 Nov 1673; *m* Maria Rebecca, dau of Henry Green, of Wykin, Leics, and *d* 6 Dec 1726, leaving, with two other sons and another dau:

1d WILLIAM CRAVEN, **5th Baron Craven of Hampsted Marshall**; *b* 19 Sept 1705; MP (Tory) Warwicks 1746–64, High Steward of Newbury; *m* 27 April 1749 Jane, dau of Rev Rowland Berkeley, formerly Green, of Cotheridge, Worcs, and *dsp* 17 March 1769

2d John (Rev), Vicar of Stanton Lacy, MA, LLB; *b* 7 Feb 1708; *m* Mary, dau of Rev Baptist Hickes, and *d* 21 Aug 1752, leaving an only son:

1e WILLIAM, **6th Baron**

1d Maria; *m* 4th Baron Leigh of Stoneleigh of the 1643 *cr* (*see* LEIGH, B)

3c Charles; Govr of Carolina *temp* QUEEN ANNE; *b* 1682; *m* Elizabeth Staples and *d* 27 Dec 1754, leaving an only son:

1d John (Rev), of Chilton Ho, Wilts; *m* 1st Elizabeth, dau of Sir Jemmett Raymond; *m* 2nd 6 July 1779 Catherine (*d* 31 March 1839), dau of James Hughes, of Letcombe, Berks, and *d* 19 June 1804, leaving issue:

1e Fulwar, of Brockhampton Park, Glos; *b* 25 June 1782; *m* 26 Nov 1809 Laura (*d* 8 Feb 1844), dau of George Vansittart, of Bisham Abbey, Berks, and *d* 14 April 1860, leaving, with other issue:

1f Fulwar William; *b* 12 Sept 1810; *m* 11 Nov 1831 Louisa (*d* 19 April 1856), dau of Rev John Orde, and *d* 7 March 1844, leaving, with other issue:

1g Edmund Filmer, late Police Magistrate and JP for Queensland, formerly RN; *b* 21 Nov 1836; *m* 10 March 1866 Caroline (*d* 1932), dau of William Smith, of Bedford, and *d* 4 Aug 1910, leaving issue:

1h Fulwar; *b* 26 May 1873; *m* 1916 Elizabeth A Wheatley, and had issue:

1i +Edmund Filmer [Edmund Craven, 11 Buckley Ave, Mount Isa 4825, Cloncurry, Qld, Australia], late RAAF; *b* 1917; *m* 1944*Ada Clemence Adelaide, dau of C Richardson, of Cloncurry, Queensland, and has issue:

1j +John Edmund; *b* 1946; *m* 1980 (*divorce* 1987) Julie Ann Airie, and has issue:

1k *Jillian Lee; *b* 1980

1i *Evelyn Caroline [Mrs Donald Whitehouse, 58 Alma Rd, Clayfield, Brisbane 4011, Qld, Australia]; *b* 1929; *m* 1952 Donald Leslie Whitehouse (*d* 1981), and has issue:

1j *Gregory Thomas; *b* 1954; *m* 1990 *Kerryn Wilson, and has issue:

1k *Edward Anthony; *b* 1991

1j *Jennifer Lynette; *b* 1953; *m* 1976 *Clive Baylis, of London, and *dsp* 1979

2i +Fulwar Guy; *b* 1920

3i George Edward James, RAF; *b* 1921; *ka* 1942

2h +Edmund Cecil Codrington, served in S Africa 1901–02; *b* 2 April 1875

3h Arthur Leonard; *b* 12 June 1876; *d* 23 Jan 1879

4h Rupert Dudley Orde Berkeley; *b* 1886; *d* 1888

1h Ethel Laura; *m* 1889 John Cowper Linedale, Police Magistrate, Cloncurry, Queensland, and *d* 1919, leaving issue

2h Georgiana Louisa

3h Evelyn Caroline Jocelyn; *d* 1920

4h Constance Lilian

5h Florence Lucy; *m* 2 Nov 1899 Edward Goddard Blume, JP, and had issue

6h Beatrice Violet; *m* 1908 E Pringle, of Fermoy, and *d* 1910, leaving issue

7h Mabel Carleton; *m* 1909 Rev Ernest Clarence Landeman, sometime Rector of Geraldton, N Queensland, and had issue

8h Blanche Gwendoline; *m* 1913 Hubert Macnish, and had issue

1g Laura Louisa; *m* 7 Jan 1862 Maj Edmund Garland Horne, late 25th Regt, and *d* 7 Nov 1925, leaving issue. He *d* 15 Oct 1905

2g Georgina; *m* 28 July 1863 Rev Thomas Grey Clarke, MA Oxford, Vicar of Odiham, Hants, and left issue

1f Georgina Maria; *m* 17 June 1841 Goodwin Charles Colquitt Craven, of Brockhampton Park, and *d* 10 April 1878, leaving issue. He *d* 29 June 1899

2e Charles John; *b* 14 March 1784; *m* 23 Oct 1817 Penelope (*d* 21 Sept 1857), dau of Edward Wheler, and *d* 24 Oct 1864, leaving, with other issue:

1f Charles, late Capt Scots Greys; *b* 2 Aug 1818; *m* 1st 13 Nov 1847 (*divorce* 1873) Harrietta (*d* 29 May 1917), dau of Capt Robert Streatfeild, RN; *m* 2nd 1874 Eliza, dau of Francis Smith, and *d* 21 Sept 1892, having by 1st w had issue:

1g Alfred Eugene; *b* 21 Sept 1848; *m* 1st 20 July 1881 (*divorce* 1897), Edith dau of Frederick Urban Sartoris, of Rushden Hall, Northants; *m* 2nd 5 March 1898 Sarah Annie (*d* 14 Jan 1931), dau of Walter Carey, and *d* 6 Jan 1937, having by 1st w had issue:

1h Harold Evelyn Andrew, late Lt RASC, served WW I 1914–19; *b* 6 July 1885; *m* 22 Aug 1914 (*divorce* 1932) Florence Mary Jackson, dau of Capt J Moore, of Conoor, India

1h Thyra

2g Godfrey Leopold; *b* 25 Aug 1856; *d* 3 Nov 1857

1f Cecilia Catherine; *m* 1st 23 Feb 1847 W Ricardo (*d* 14 April 1859); *m* 2nd 10 Sept 1867 F J Owen, and had issue

1e Charlotte Elizabeth; *m* 9 Sept 1819 Sir John Walter Pollen, 2nd Bt (*qv*), and *dsp* 7 Oct 1877

3a Anthony (Sir); *dsp* 1670

1a Margaret; *b* 1603; *m* 1624 Thomas Craven, and had, with other issue, Sir Anthony Craven, Bt

2 Anthony, of Darley, left issue, William, Ellen, and three other daus

3 William (Sir); Ld Mayor London 1610 and 1618; *m* Elizabeth, dau of William Whitmore (*see* WHITMORE, Bt), and *d* 18 July 1618, having had issue:

(1) WILLIAM, **1st Baron Craven of Hampsted Marshall**, Berks (E), so *cr* 12 March 1626/7, with remainder, failing heirs male of his body, to his yr bro John and Thomas and heirs male of their bodies; this remainder was extended 16 March 1664/5 to include his paternal gf's senior male line descendant (a gggs) William Craven (the grantee's 1st cousin twice-removed) and William's paternal uncle Sir Anthony Craven (the grantee's 1st cousin once-removed), and further extended 11 Dec 1666 to Sir William Craven, of Coombe Abbey, another gggs of the grante's paternal gf, being another 1st cousin twice-removed; also *cr* 16 March 1664/5 (1st and last) VISCOUNT CRAVEN OF UFFINGTON, Berks, and (1st and last) EARL OF CRAVEN, Co York (both E, with standard remainders), PC (1666–79 and March 1680/1–Feb 1688/9); *bapt* 26 June 1608; *educ* Trin Coll Oxford; ktd March 1626/7, cdr English force fighting on behalf of the Elector Palatine in Thirty Years War in Germany 1632, fought there again 1637, subsidised the ex-Queen of Bohemia (w of the Elector Palatine and dau of JAMES I) and CHARLES II during their repective years of exile, Col Regt Foot 1662, a Ld Proprietor Carolina 1663, Col Coldstream Gds 1670–89, Ld Lt Middx and Southwark 1670–89, commr for got Tangier 1673, Lt-Gen 1678–8; *d* 9 April 1697, when the earldom and viscountcy expired, but the Barony of Craven of Hampsted Marshall passed to his cousin

(2) JOHN CRAVEN, 1st and last BARON CRAVEN OF RYTON, Co Salop (E), so *cr* 21 March 1642/3; *bapt* 10 June 1610; MP Tewkewsbury 1640–41 (when election declared void); *m* 4 Dec 1634 Elizabeth (*m* 2nd 7 July 1648 Hon Henry Howard, 3rd s of 1st Earl of Berkshire (*see* SUFFOLK and BERKSHIRE, E); *m* 3rd 1st and last Baron Crofts of Saxham (*d* 11 Sept 1677) and *d* 11 Aug 1672), dau of 2nd Baron Spencer of Wormleighton (*see* MARLBOROUGH, D), and *dsp* by 26 Feb 1647/8, when the barony expired

(3) Thomas; *d* unm before 13 Feb 1636/7

(1) Mary; *m* 2 April 1627 2nd Baron Coventry (*qv*)

(2) Elizabeth; *m* 19 Nov 1622 2nd Baron Powis, (*see* POWIS, E), and had issue

The 5th BARON's nephew,

WILLIAM CRAVEN, **6th Baron Craven**; *b* 11 Sept 1738; *m* 30 May 1767 Lady Elizabeth Berkeley (*m* 2nd 13 Oct 1791 Christian Frederick, Margrave of Brandenburg Anspach and Bayreuth and *d* 13 Jan 1828), dau of 4th Earl of Berkeley (*see* BERKELEY, B), and had, with other issue:

1 WILLIAM, **1st Earl**

2 Henry Augustus Berkeley; Maj-Gen; *b* 21 Dec 1776; *m* 1829 Marie Clarisse Trebhault (*d* 4 April 1865), and *d* 1836

1 Maria Margaret; *m* 1 Jan 1792 2nd Earl of Sefton (*see* 1970 edn) and *d* 9 March 1851, leaving issue. He *d* 20 Nov 1838

2 Arabella; *m* 6 April 1793 Gen Hon Frederick St John, and *d* 9 June 1819, leaving issue (*see* BOLINGBROKE and ST JOHN, V)

The 6th BARON *d* 26 Sept 1791; his est son,

WILLIAM CRAVEN, **7th Baron** and **1st Earl of Craven**, Co York, so *cr* 18 Jun 1801, as also VISCOUNT UFFINGTON, Co Berks (both UK); *b* 1 Sept 1770; Gen 1825, Recorder of Coventry, and Ld Lt of Berks; *m* 12 Dec 1807 Louisa (*d* 27 Aug 1860 aged 78), a celebrated actress, dau of John Brunton, of Norwich, originally a Drury Lane grocer but later an actor-manager, and had issue:

1 WILLIAM, **2nd Earl**

2 George Augustus; army offr; *b* 15 Dec 1810; *m* 23 Dec 1833 Georgina (*m* 2nd 19 Oct 1844 Edmond, Duc de la Force, and *d* 11 Dec 1867), dau of Walter Smythe, of Bembridge Ho, Hants, and *d* 26 July 1836, leaving issue:

(1) William George; 1st Life Gds; *b* 12 May 1835; *m* 20 July 1857 Lady Mary Catherine Yorke (*d* 14 Dec 1890), 2nd dau of 4th Earl of Hardwicke (*qv*), and *d* 2 Jan 1906, leaving:

1a Augustus William; Lt Roy Berks Militia; *b* 3 May 1858; *m* 1st 27 Jan 1880 Florence Champagne (*dsp* Aug 1899), dau of Gen Corbet Cotton (*see* COMBERMERE, V); *m* 2nd 1900 Lilian, dau of John Hearn, and *d* 23 Feb 1929, leaving issue:

1b *Violet Lilian Mary [Mrs Ronald Wimbush, Lullington Manor, Alfriston, Sussex]; *b* 1906; *m* 1935 Ronald Crosley Wimbush (*d* 1964), and has issue:

1c *Jennifer; *b* 1940; *m* 1965 *James Charles Tempest Bouskell, and has issue:

1d *James Henry Tempest; *b* 1968

1d *Louisa Jane; *b* 1967; *m* 1994 *James Richard Symington

2a Caryl Walter; *b* 7 Oct 1860; *d* unm 27 Feb 1942

3a Francis; *b* 9 April 1869; *d* unm

1a Constance Georgina; *m* 10 May 1886 Capt Francis Marmaduke Henry Sandford, late Gren Gds, and *d* 1946, leaving issue. He *d* 30 May 1904

2a Isabel Sophie; *m* 3 July 1882 7th Duke of Richmond and Lennox (*see* RICHMOND and GORDON, D), and *d* 20 Nov 1887, leaving issue

(2) Walter Arthur Keppel; Lt RN, served Burma 1852 and China 1860 (despatches); *b* 16 March 1836; *m* 22 Sept 1864 Countess Elisabetta Maria Luigia Tadea (*d* 12 Nov 1881), dau of Count Ercole Oldofredi Tadini, and *d* 21 Dec 1894, leaving issue:

1a Arthur Julius, DSO (1918); Col RE, Hon Brig-Gen 1924, served in S African War 1899–1902, and WW I 1915–18 (despatches, brevet); *b* 11 Dec 1867; *m* 23 Oct 1909 Edith Maude (*d* 20 July 1935), dau of Albert Smallwood, and *d* 30 April 1933

2a Louis Bertrand; Lt RNVR WW I; *b* 16 Aug 1869; *d* 15 June 1945

1a Maria Julia; *b* 8 Aug 1865; *d* unm at Varese, Italy, 22 Feb 1956

2a Julia Elizabeth; *b* 4 Aug 1877; *d* unm at Varese, Italy, 24 Nov 1952

3 Frederick Keppel; *b* 11 April 1812; *d* unm 21 June 1864

1 Louisa Elizabeth Frederica; *m* 24 Oct 1840 Sir G F Johnstone, 7th Bt (*qv*). He *d* 7 May 1841. She *m* 2nd 15 Aug 1844 Alexander Oswald, of Auchencruive, Ayrshire, and *d* 20 Oct 1858

The 1st EARL *d* 30 July 1825; his est son,

WILLIAM CRAVEN, **2nd Earl of Craven**; Ld Lt Warwicks, Recorder of Coventry, and High Steward of Newbury; *b* 18 July 1809; *m* 5 Sept 1835 Lady Emily Mary Grimston (*d* 21 May 1901), 2nd dau of 1st Earl of Verulam (*qv*), and had issue:

1 William Augustus Frederick, *Viscount Uffington*, Capt Gren Gds; *b* 24 Aug 1838; *d* 18 April 1865

2 GEORGE GRIMSTON, **2rd Earl**

3 Osbert William; Lt-Col and Hon Col Berks Imp Yeo, JP, CC Berks; *b* 6 Feb 1848; *d* 5 March 1923

4 Robert Walter, RN; *b* 4 Jan 1850; *d* 5 March 1866 on board HMS *Spiteful* at Montevideo

1 Elizabeth Charlotte Louisa; *m* 1st 11 Aug 1858 3rd Earl of Wilton (*qv*); *m* 2nd 14 Sept 1886 Arthur Vickris Pryor, of Hylands, Essex, and *d* 8 March 1919. He *d* 18 June 1927

2 Evelyn Mary; *m* 1st 7 Aug 1862 George John Brudenell-Bruce, est s of 3rd Marquess of Ailesbury (*qv*), and had issue; *m* 2nd 4 Dec 1869 (*divorce* 1877) Capt Henry Amelius Beauclerk Coventry (*see* COVENTRY, E) and had issue; *m* 3rd 30 Aug 1877 George William Hutton Riddell, of Muselee, Roxburghshire, Capt 16th Lancers, and *d* 7 Nov 1924, leaving further issue. He *d* 9 Feb 1915

3 Blanche; *m* 25 Jan 1865 9th Earl of Coventry (*qv*), and *d* 16 March 1930, leaving issue

4 Beatrix Jane, VA; *m* 16 May 1865 5th Earl Cadogan (*qv*) and *d* 9 Feb 1907, leaving issue

5 Emily Georgiana; *m* 6 Aug 1868 Victor William Bates Van de Weyer, of New Lodge, Windsor, JP, CA Berks, Lt-Col Roy Berks Militia, eit son of Jean Sylvain Van de Weyer, Belgian Min to UK, and *d* 6 Jan 1932, leaving issue. He *d* 31 Oct 1915

The 2nd EARL *d* 25 Aug 1866; his est surv son,

GEORGE GRIMSTON CRAVEN, **3rd Earl of Craven**, DL (Warwicks), Ld Lt of Berks, Capt Scots Fus Gds; *b* 16 March 1841; *m* 17 Jan 1867 Hon Evelyn Laura Barrington (*d* 9 Nov 1924), 2nd dau of 7th Viscount Barrington (*see* 1970 edn), and had issue:

1 WILLIAM GEORGE ROBERT, **4th Earl**

2 Rupert Cecil, OBE (1919), Maj late 3rd Bn Roy Scots Fus, formerly Capt 3rd Bn Roy Berks Regt, and Midshipman RN, served in S African War 1900–02, and WW I 1914–18 (despatches, wounded three times); *b* 19 April 1870; *m* 1st 9 April 1899 (*divorce* 1908) Inez Morton, dau of George Broom; *m* 2nd 18 June 1925 Josephine Marguerite (*d* 13 April 1971), widow of Capt Charles William Banbury (*see* BANBURY OF SOUTHAM, B), and dau of Don José Reixach y Gisbert, and *d* 9 July 1959, leaving issue:

(1) +RUPERT JOSÉ EVELYN, JP Hants [Lt-Cdr Rupert Craven JP RN, Swordly, Bettyhill by Thurso, Caithness KW14 7TA]; *b* 22 March 1926; heir presumptive; *educ* RNC Dartmouth; Lt-Cdr RN; *m* 22 Oct 1955 Margaret Campbell (*d* 1985), dau of Alexander Smith, MBE, of Glasgow and Alness

3 Charles Frederick; *b* 10 April, *d* 7 June 1873

4 Charles Eric, formerly Lt Scots Gds; *b* 6 Feb 1879; *m* 3 Oct 1901 Amalia Kolowratek (*d* 10 Aug 1950), and *d* 19 July 1909, leaving issue:

(1) William Anthony Hubert; *b* 25 Jan 1904; *d* 15 Dec 1929

1 Mary Beatrix; *b* 26 Nov 1867; *d* 26 April 1881

2 Helen Emily; *b* 13 Dec 1874; *m* 23 April 1901 Lt-Col Ian Rose Innes Forbes, DSO, DL, JP, of Rothiemay Castle, Banffshire, and *d* 13 Oct 1926, leaving issue. He *d* 18 Sept 1957

The 3rd EARL *d* 7 Dec 1883; his est son,

WILLIAM GEORGE ROBERT CRAVEN, **4th Earl of Craven**, OBE (1919), Ld Lt and Pres TA Warwicks; Capt Yeomen of the Gd 1911–15, Capt Berks Yeo Cav, ADC to Ld Lt Ireland, Legion of Honour and Order of the Crown of Belgium; *b* 16 Dec 1868; *m* 18 April 1893 Cornelia (*d* 19 May 1961), only dau of Bradley Martin, of New York, and was accidently drowned 10 July 1921, having had issue:

WILLIAM GEORGE BRADLEY CRAVEN, **5th Earl of Craven**; Lt 3rd Bn Hampshire Regt WW I (wounded); *b* 31 July 1897; *m* 4 Oct 1916 Mary Williamina (*d* 14 Sept 1974), dau of William George, ODE, JP, of Invergordon, Scotland, and *d* 15 Sept 1932, having had issue:

WILLIAM ROBERT BRADLEY CRAVEN, **6th Earl of Craven**; memb E Sussex CC 1957; *b* 8 Sept 1917; *educ* Downside and Northants Inst of Ag; 2nd Lt Coldstream Gds SR Offrs, WW II as Lt (E) RNVR, Kt SMO Malta 1959; *m* 1st 3 May 1939 (*divorce* 1954) Irene (*m* 2nd, as his 2nd w, Sir Andrew MacTaggart (*d* 20 June 1978)), yst dau of Ferdinand Richard Holmes Meyrick, MD, of 59 Kensington Court, W8, and had issue:

1 *Sarah Jane [The Lady Sarah Thomson Glover, La Gratitude, 6 De Villiers St, Somerset West 7130, S Africa]; *b* 9 Jan 1940; *m* 4 March 1961 *David John Traill Thomson Glover, son of Lt-Col John William Thomson Glover, CBE, IA, and has had :

(1) Katherine; *b* 10, *d* 13 Feb 1963

(2) *Suzanna Gwendoline; *b* 10 Aug 1964

(3) Priscilla Traill; *b* 28 July 1967; *d* 28 Feb 1971

(4) *Vanessa Kate; *b* 31 Jan 1972

The **6th Earl** *m* 2nd 25 Sept 1954 *Elizabeth Gwendolen Teresa [Mrs Kenneth Banner, Peelings Manor, Pevensey, Sussex BN24 5AP] (*m* 2nd 27 July 1966 Kenneth Harmood Banner), only dau of Robert Sholto Johnstone-Douglas (*see* QUEENSBERRY, M), and *d* 27 Jan 1965, leaving by her:

1 THOMAS ROBERT DOUGLAS CRAVEN, **7th Earl of Craven**; *b* 24 Aug 1957; *d* unm 22 Oct 1983

2 SIMON GEORGE CRAVEN, **8th Earl of Craven**; *b* 16 Sept 1961; student nurse; *m* 1988 *Teresa Maria Bernadette [The Rt Hon The Countess of Craven, Hawkwood House, Hawkhurst Lane, Waldron, E Sussex], dau of Arthur John Downes, of Black Hall, Clane, Co Kildare, and *d* 1990 in a car crash, leaving:

(1) BENJAMIN ROBERT JOSEPH CRAVEN, **9th and present Earl of Craven**

2 *Ann Mary Elizabeth [The Lady Ann Tarassenko, 68 Old Rd, Headington, Oxford OX3 7LP]; *b* 9 April 1959; BA; *m* 1978 *Dr Lionel Tarassenko, MA DPhil, CEng, MIEE, er son of Sergei Tarassenko, of Swanage, Dorset, and has issue:

(1) *Luke Ivan Thomas; *b* 1988

(2) *Simon Robert Serge; *b* 1991

(1) *Naomi Rachel Elizabeth; *b* 1989

CRAWFORD and BALCARRES

Arms: Quarterly, 1st and 4th, gules a fess checky argent and azure (for LINDSAY); 2nd and 3rd, or a lion rampant gules, debruised of a ribbon in bend sable (for ABERNETHY). **Crest:** A swan's head, neck and wings proper, issuing from an antique ducal coronet or. **Supporters:** Two lions, rampant guardant gules. **Motto:** *Endure fort* ('Suffer bravely'). **Creations:** E.(S) 21 April–2 May 1398 (of Crawford), L.(S) first so styled 1443 (Lindsay) and recognised as a creation 11 Aug 1848, L. (S) 27 June 1633 (Lindsay of Balcarres), E. (Balcarres) and L. (Lindsay and Balniel) (S) 9 Jan 1650/1, B. (UK) 5 July 1826 and (LP) 1974. Although the Earldoms of Mar and Sutherland are of earlier origin, mere antiquity was not the predominant factor in deciding precedence in Scotland before the Act of Union of Scottish and English Parliaments of 1707 and in that year the primacy of the Earldom of Crawford over all other Scottish titles of like rank was reaffirmed.

THE 29TH EARL OF CRAWFORD AND 12TH EARL OF BALCARRES, Lord Lindsay, Lord Lindsay of Balcarres, Lord Lindsay and Balniel, Baron Wigan of Haigh Hall and **Baron Balniel** (LP) (Robert Alexander Lindsay, KT (1996), PC (1972), DL (Fife 1953)) [The Rt Hon The Earl of Crawford and Balcarres KT PC DL, Balcarres, Colinsburgh, Fife KY9 1HL]; *b* 5 March 1927; *s f* 1975; *educ* Eton and Trin Coll Cambridge; Lt Gren Gds 1945–49; MP (C) Hertford May 1955–74 and Welwyn and Hatfield Feb-Sept 1974, PPS: to Fin Sec Treasury 1955–57 and Min Housing and Local Govt 1957–60; Opposition front-bench spokesman Health and Social Security 1967–70; Min of State: MOD 1970–72 and FCO 1972–74, Pres RDCs Assoc 1959–65, chm: Nat Assoc Mental Health 1963–70, Lombard North Central Ltd and Historic Blds Cncl for Scotland 1976–83, dir Nat West Bank 1975–88, First Crown Estate Cmmr 1980–85, chm Roy Commn Ancient Historical Monuments Scotland 1985–95, Crown Tstee and Chm Tstees Nat Library of Scotland 1990–, Ld Chamberlain to HM QUEEN ELIZABETH THE QUEEN MOTHER 1992–; *m* 27 Dec 1949 *Ruth Beatrice, dau of Leo Meyer-Bechtler, of 49 Keltenstrasse, Zürich, and has issue:

1 +ANTHONY ROBERT, *Lord Balniel* [Lord Balniel, 6 Pembridge Place, London W2 4XB]; *b* 24 Nov 1958; *educ* Eton and Edinburgh U; dir J O Hambro Investment Management 1987–; *m* 1989 *Nicola A, yst dau of Antony Bicket, of N Wales, and has issue:

(1) +Alexander Thomas, *Master of Lindsay*; *b* 5 Aug 1991

(2) +James Antony; *b* 10 Nov 1992

(1) *Katherine Ruth Vere; *b* 4 Sept 1996

2 +Alexander Walter [The Hon Alexander Lindsay, Studio 5, Neckinger Mills, 162 Abbey St, London SE1]; *b* 18 March 1961; *educ* Eton; Endure Pursuivant to his f

1 *Bettina Mary [The Lady Bettina Drummond-Hay, 86 Rowayton Ave, Rowayton, Conn 06853, USA]; *b* 26 June 1950; *m* 1975 *Peter Charles Drummond-Hay (*see* KINNOULL, E) and has issue

2 *Iona Sina [The Lady Iona Mackworth-Young, 18 The Chase, London SW4 0NH]; *b* 10 Aug 1957; *m* 1983 *Charles Gerard Mackworth-Young (*see* YOUNG, Bt, of Formosa Place) and has issue:

(1) *Robin Gerard Lindsay; *b* 6 Oct 1994

(1) *Rose; *b* 23 Oct 1987

(2) *Constance; *b* 5 April 1990

Lineage: Sir WALTER de LINDISSI or LIND(E)SAY (almost certainly 3rd *s* of Gilbert de Ghent) probably accompanied David, Earl of Huntingdon, subsequently KING DAVID I, in his anglicising of the Lowlands in the early 12th century; he was witness 1116 to an inquisition concerning the see of Glasgow; had:

WILLIAM de LIND(E)SAY; had:

WALTER de LIND(E)SAY, sat in Scots Parl 1145, a justiciar of Scotland, witness to charters of KING MALCOLM; had:

Sir WILLIAM de LIND(E)SAY; sat in Scots Parl 1164, hostage for KING WILLIAM 1174, afterwards Justiciary, first appears as feudal Ld of Crawford but styled Baron of Luffness in Parl; *m c* 1174 Aleanora, dau of Gerard, Lord of Limesay or Limesis (and coheir of her bro), by Amicia de Bidun (Gerard was gs of Randolph de Limesay or Limesis, fndr Hertford Priory and a tenant-in-chief of large estates 1086; the name de Limesay/Limesis derives from a fief near Caux in Normandy and those who bore it were allegedly cadets of the house of de To(s)ny, legitimate heirs male of the Dukes of Normandy). Sir WILLIAM was heir of Randolph de Lindesay, a great feudal lord of Northumbria in right of his w Ethelreda, gdau of Earl Gospatric (*see* ABERGAVENNY, M). He *d c* 1200, having had issue:

1 David (Sir); Justiciary 1208; *m* Marjory, a memb of the Scottish royal house, and *d* 1214, having had issue:

(1) David, High Justiciary Lothian 1238, 3rd feudal Ld of Crawford, also *s* maternal great-uncle as feudal Ld of Limesay/Limesis and Wolverley in England

(2) Gerard; 4th feudal Ld of Crawford; *dsp*

(3) William; Chllr Scotland, Dean Glasgow; *dsp*

(1) Alice; *m* Sir Henry Pinckney; *s* to her bro's English estates, though the Ldship of Crawford reverted to the heir male

2 Walter (Sir); High Justiciary Lothian, Constable Berwick, Scottish Amb to KING JOHN of England 1215; became by marriage feudal Ld of Lamberton and *d* 1221, having had issue:

(1) William (Sir), feudal Ld of Lamberton; *m* Alice, dau and coheir of William de Lancaster, feudal Ld of Kendal, thus acquiring the territories of Windermere, Grasmere etc, and had issue:

1a Walter, feudal Ld of Lamberton; had issue:

1b William; held estates in Cumberland, Lancs and 25 Scottish counties; *m* Ada, sis and eventual coheir of KING JOHN BALLIOL, and had issue an only dau:

1c Christiana; *m* Ingelram de Coucy, 2nd *s* of Count Arnold III of Guignes, and was ancestor of the Dukes of Parma

2a John; Bp Glasgow

3 William; had issue (with a yr *s*, ancestor of the LINDSAYs of Craigie):

(1) William; had:

1a David (Sir); feudal Ld of Brenevil, had charter of the Byres 1233 from Gilbert, Earl of Pembroke, and of Chirden in Tyndale 1244 from Margaret, Countess of Pembroke, dau of ALEXANDER II; Justiciary 1243–49; had issue:

1b DAVID (Sir)

2b John (Sir); Ld Chamberlain; *m* Dyonysia, dau and heir of Alexander Beneyt, and had issue:

1c Philip (Sir), of Lincs

2c Simon (Sir), also of Lincs, ancestor of the LINDSAYs of Wauchopdale

Sir DAVID's er *s*,

Sir DAVID de LINDSAY; one of the Regents 1255, High Chamberlain 1256; *d* in the crusade of St Louis 1268, leaving by his w Margaret:

1 ALEXANDER (Sir)

2 William (Sir), feudal Ld of Symontoun, Ayrshire; *m* 1st Alicia Lockhart; *m* 2nd by 1310 Margaret, Countess of Buchan, yr dau of Alexander Comyn, Sheriff Aberdeen in 1305 and niece of John Comyn, 7th Earl of Buchan (*see* BUCHAN, E, preliminary remarks)

Sir DAVID's er *s*,

Sir ALEXANDER de LINDSAY; *s* 1244 to lands in Northumberland granted to his f by Margaret Countess of Pembroke, also to Breneville and the Byres and afterwards to Crawford. He was a conspicuous supporter of Sir William Wallace and ROBERT I (THE BRUCE) and sat in Parl 1308; had issue:

1 DAVID (Sir)

2 Alexander (Sir)

3 Reginald; all three bros were prisoners of EDWARD I

1 Beatrix; *m* 1st Sir Archibald Douglas and had issue (*see* (QUEENSBERRY, M); *m* 2nd Sir Robert Erskine, and had issue (*see* MAR, E)

Sir ALEXANDER's est *s*,

Sir DAVID de LINDSAY, feudal Ld of Crawford; Amb to England 1349 and 1351, Custodian Edinburgh and Berwick Castles; *m* (dispensation 1325) Mary, dau of Alexander Abernethy of that Ilk (*see* SALTOUN, L) and widow of Andrew de Leslie of Leslie (*see* ROTHES, E), and *d* 1355, having had, with another *s* (David, *dsp*):

1 James (Sir), feudal Ld of Crawford; hostage for KING DAVID 1351, Amb to England 1357; *m* by dispensation 1346 Egidia, dau of Walter, High Steward Scotland, and half-sis to ROBERT II; *d* 1357, leaving issue:

(1) James (Sir), feudal Ld of Crawford; Amb to England 1395; *m* Margaret, dau of Sir William Keith, Marshal of Scotland, and *dspm* 1397, leaving:

1a Margaret; *m* Sir Thomas Colville, of Oxenham

2a Eufemia; *m* Sir John Herries of Terregles (*see* HERRIES OF TERREGLES, L)

(1) Elizabeth; *m* 1st Sir John Maxwell (*see* HERON-MAXWELL, Bt); *m* 2nd Sir Henry de Prestoun

2 Alexander (Sir), of Glenesk, Angus; *s* his mother in her share of the Abernethy lands, Esq to the Earl of Angus, ktd 1368, Justiciary 1378; *m* 1st 1358 Catherine, dau of Sir John Stirling of Edzell and heiress of Glenesk, and *d* 1381, having had issue:

(1) DAVID, **1st Earl of Crawford**

(2) Alexander (Sir), of Baltrody

2 (cont.) Sir Alexander *m* 2nd Marjory, niece of ROBERT III, and *d* 1381 at Candia, Cyprus, on his way to the Holy Land, having had by her, with other issue:

(3) William (Sir), of Rossie

3 William (Sir), feudal Ld of Abercorn and Byres; ancestor of the Earls of Lindsay (*qv*)

A dau; mother of Sir Alexander de Ramsay

Sir DAVID's gs,

DAVID de LINDSAY, **1st Earl of Crawford** (S), so *cr* between 21 April and 2 May 1398; *b c* 1360; Justiciary 1389, Sheriff Banff; *s* cousin as 9th feudal Ld of Crawford 1397; represented the chivalry of Scotland in what contemporary chroniclers refer to as a 'passage of arms' (*i.e*, a friendly joust) with Lord Welles on 23 April (St George's Day) 1390 on London Bridge before RICHARD II and his Queen ANNE OF BOHEMIA, when he unhorsed his opponent; Adml Scotland 1403, Amb to England 1404 and 1406; *m c* 22 Feb 1374/5 Elizabeth, dau of ROBERT II by his 2nd w Eupheme, dau of Hugh Earl of Ross, and by her acquired the feudal Ldship of Strathnairn; *d* Feb 1406/7, having had, with two other sons (*dsp*):

1 ALEXANDER, **2nd Earl**

1 Marjory; *m* Sir William Douglas of Lochleven and had issue (*see* MORTON, E)

2 Elizabeth; *m de jure* 12th Earl of Mar (*qv*)

The 1st EARL's *s*,

ALEXANDER de LINDSAY, **2nd Earl of Crawford**, ktd 1424, a hostage for JAMES I and imprisoned Tower of London 1424, obtained a new entail of his comitatus (county, here in the sense of domains appertaining to an earl of a county) 1421 (an early example of a royal charter containing a name and arms clause); *d* after 31 March 1438/9, leaving by his w Marjory:

1 DAVID, **3rd Earl**

1 Janet; *m* 6th Earl of Douglas (*see* QUEENSBERRY, M)

2 Elizabeth; *m* Sir Simon Glendonwyne, Yr. of Glendonwyne

The 2nd EARL's only *s*,

DAVID de LINDSAY, **3rd Earl of Crawford**, hereditary Sheriff Aberdeenshire (a post which remained in the Lindsay family till the first half of the 16th century and which helped them maintain a quasi-independent status as princes); *m c* March 1422/3 Marjory, dau of Alexander Ogilvie of Auchterhouse; *k* 17 Jan 1445/6 four days after being injured in an affray at Arbroath between the Lindsays (led to victory by his son and heir) and his wife's relatives the Ogilvies, despite his efforts to prevent it, leaving issue:

1 ALEXANDER de LINDSAY, **4th Earl of Crawford**, 'Earl Beardie' or 'The Tiger', hereditary Sheriff Forfar as well as Aberdeenshire, Amb to England 1451, rebelled against JAMES II 1452 but defeated at Battle of Brechin, following which he was stripped of his title (pardoned 1453); *m* Margaret (later w of William Wallace of Cragie), dau and heir of Sir David Dunbar of Cockburn (bro of the Earl of Dunbar or March), and *d* Sept 1453, having had issue:

(1) DAVID de LINDSAY, **5th Earl of Crawford**, PC (S Feb 1489/90); *b* 1440; granted 1472 the Ldships of Brechin and Forfar for life, Keeper Berwick 1473–76, High Adml Scotland 1476, Master Household 1480, Ld Great Chamberlain lc 1483, Jt High Justiciary of the North 1487, entailed 1474 the family estates on his heirs male forever, *cr* by JAMES III 18 May 1488 DUKE OF MONTROSE (S) but this annulled following JAMES III's death at Battle of Sauchieburn 9 June 1488, granted a new patent of the Dukedom 19 Sept 1489, though the title was not assumed by his immediate successors in the possibly mistaken belief that it was a life peerage; an unsuccessful claim to it was put forward by the 24th Earl in 1853 (*see* below); *m* 1st 1459 (*divorce c* 1484) Elizabeth, dau of James, 2nd Lord Hamilton; *m* 2nd by 27 Sept 1484 Margaret Carmichael (*d* 1534) and *d* 1495, leaving by his 1st w, with two daus (including Elizabeth *m c* Sept 1505 David Lyon of Baky and cossins and Haltoune of Erse; *see* STRATHMORE AND KINGHORNE, E):

1a Alexander, *Master of Crawford*; *m* Janet (*m* 2nd 3rd Lord Gray (*qv*)), 2nd dau of 2nd Earl of Huntly (*see* HUNTLY, M), and *dsp* & *vp* 16 Sept 1489, being murdered in his bed by suffocation, allegedly with the connivance of his w and bro, with whom he had often quarrelled (as also with his f)

2a JOHN de LINDSAY, **6th Earl of Crawford**, accused with his sis-in-law of murdering his brother, but was *k* Battle of Flodden before any action taken in the matter; *m* by Aug 1493 Mariot, dau of Alexander, 2nd Lord Home (*see* HOME, E), and *dspl* 9 Sept 1513

(2) Sir ALEXANDER de LINDSAY of Auchtermonzie, **7th Earl of Crawford**; *b c* 1443; Sheriff Depute Forfar 1483, High Justiciary N of Forth 1515; *m* by 18 March 1470 Isobel, dau of — Campbell of Ardkinglass, and *d* May 1517, leaving (with a dau Margaret, *m* James, 3rd Lord Ogilvy of Airlie (*see* AIRLIE, E)) an er s:

1a Sir DAVID de LINDSAY, **8th Earl of Crawford**; ktd 1512; as a result of the violent behaviour shown by his son he resigned the Earldom and had a new confirmation of it 1541 by which it was to pass, subject to his own life interest and in default of his having further male issue of his own, to his cousin and next heir male David Lindsay of Edzell with further remainder to the latter's heirs male; *m* 1st by 6 Nov 1500 Elizabeth, dau of 3rd Earl of Erroll (*qv*), and had issue:

1b Alexander, *Master of Crawford*, 'the Wicked Master'; seized and imprisoned his f, found guilty of constructive parricide, which carried the death penalty and by the law as it then stood prevented him succeeding to the Earldom; *m* Jean, dau of 1st Lord Sinclair (*qv*), and was *k* in a brawl shortly before 5 July 1542, having had, with another s:

1c DAVID de LINDSAY, **10th Earl of Crawford**, PC (S, 1565); *b c* 1527; fought for MARY QUEEN OF SCOTS Battle of Langside 1568; *m c* 10 April 1546 Margaret, illegitimate dau of Cardinal Beaton, Archbp St Andrews, by Marion, dau of 1st Lord Ogilvy of Airlie (*see* AIRLIE, E), and *d* just before 1 Nov 1574, leaving issue:

1d DAVID de LINDSAY, **11th Earl of Crawford**, PC (S, 1575); *b c* 1552; *m* 1st 12 Feb 1572/3 Lilias, dau of 2nd Lord Drummond (*see* PERTH, E); *m* 2nd *c* 1582 Lady Grizel Stewart, dau of 4th Earl of Atholl (*see* MORAY, E), and *d* 22 Nov 1607, leaving by her:

1e DAVID de LINDSAY, **12th Earl of Crawford**, PC (S, 1608), 'the Prodigal'; *bapt* 8 March 1575/6; squandered most of the family wealth (though his f had been known as a spendthrift too); *m c* 1608 Jean, dau of 1st Earl of Lothian (*see* LOTHIAN, M) and widow of Robert, Master of Boyd (*see* KILMARNOCK, B), and *d* June 1620, leaving an only dau:

1f Jean; lived at one point by begging but eventually granted a pension of £100 p.a. by CHARLES II

1e Mary; mistress to 1st Lord Reay (*qv*) by whom she had issue

2d HENRY LINDSAY later CHARTERIS, **13th Earl of Crawford**; adopted 1584 by Sir John Charteris of Kinfauns and his w Janet Chisholm; *m* 1st 1586 Helen Chisholm, heiress of Kinfauns and thought to have been either sis or niece of his adoptive mother, and had issue:

1e John (Sir), KB; *m* 1608 Jean, dau of Lord Saltoun (*qv*), and *dvp*, leaving two daus

2e GEORGE LINDSAY, **14th Earl**; *m c* 1621 Lady Elizabeth Sinclair, dau of 5th Earl of Caithness (*qv*), and *dspm* 1633 (his only child Margaret *d* unm 1655)

2d (cont.) The **13th Earl** *m* 2nd 1599 Margaret, dau of Sir James Shaw, of Sauchie, and *d* 1623, having had issue, with two daus:

3e ALEXANDER LINDSAY, **15th Earl**; *dsp* and insane 1639

4e LUDOVIC LINDSAY, **16th Earl** 'The Loyal Earl'; took part in a plot to capture the leading Covenanters (Presbyterians opposed to CHARLES I's anglicising tendencies in Scottish ecclesiastical matters) but was found out and imprisoned, was later set free allegedly through the good offices of his cousin the Earl of Lindsay (*qv*), who apparently made it a condition that he should obtain from the King a regrant of the Earldom of Crawford (which Earl Ludovic did 15 Jan 1641/2) with limitation to the heirs male of his (Earl Ludovic)'s body, then to the Earl of Lindsay and the heirs male of the latter's body and only after that to Earl Ludovic's collateral heirs male; this had the effect of supplanting the LINDSAYs of Spynie, Edzell and Balcarres; the 'Loyal Earl' fought as a royalist in the Civil War at the Battles of Edgehill 1642, Newbury 1643 and Marston Moor 1644, being captured by the Parliamentarians at Newcastle 1644 and excluded from the list of royalists pardoned by Parl 1646; *m c* 1643 Lady Margaret Graham, widow of Alexander Stewart, Lord Garlies, and dau of William, Earl of Menteith, and *dsp* in exile abroad *c* 7 Nov 1652, when the Earldom of Crawford, together with the undifferenced arms and chiefship of the Name of Lindsay, passed to John, Earl of Lindsay (for whom and his successors in the title of Crawford, until they died out 1808, *see* LINDSAY, E), while first Lord Spynie and then the head of the branches of Edzell and Balcarres became the heir male

3d John (Sir), KB, of Ballinscho; *d* 6 Jan 1609, having by his 2nd w Catherine, dau of John Lindsay of Balcarres, Lord Menmuir, had three sons (*dsp*)

4d Sir ALEXANDER LINDSAY, 1st LORD SPYNIE (S); *cr* 4 Nov 1590, PC (S, 1590); *b c* 1564 ; *m* Jean Lyon, dau of 8th Lord Glamis (*see* STRATHMORE AND KINGHORNE, E) and widow of (a) 8th Earl of Angus (*see* HAMILTON and BRANDON, D) and (b) Robert Douglas, Master of Morton (*see* MORTON, E), and *d c* 16 June 1607, having had, with other issue:

1e ALEXANDER LINDSAY, 2nd LORD SPYNIE, fought in Germany in Thirty Years War under KING GUSTAVUS ADOLPHUS OF SWEDEN; *m* Lady Margaret Hay, dau of 1st Earl of Kinnoull (*qv*), and had issue, with another dau:

1f Alexander; *m* Jean (*m* 2nd John Lindsay of Edzell), dau of John Carnegie, 1st Earl of Northesk (*qv*), but *dsp* & *vp* after 29 June 1643

2f GEORGE LINDSAY, 3rd LORD SPYNIE, ruined himself raising forces for CHARLES I. On the death of the 16th Earl of Crawford he became heir male of the Lindsays but not chief of the house and Earl of Crawford because of the regrant of 15 Jan 1641/2 with its changed terms of limitation; *dsp* and seemingly unm (*bur* 21 Jan 1670/1)

1f Margaret, whose descendant, Lt-Col William Fullarton of Glenquich, unsuccessfully claimed the Lordship of Spynie 1785

1a The **8th Earl** *m* 2nd Katherine Stirling, by whom he had a son; *m* 3rd by 1526 Isobel (*m* 2nd 4th Earl of Rothes, *qv*), dau of — Lundy of that Ilk, and *d* 27 Nov 1542, having by her had, with a son (*dsp*):

1b Isobel; *m* 1st 5th Lord Borthwick (*qv*); *m* 2nd George Preston of Cameron

(1) Elizabeth; *m* 1st Lord Drummond (*see* PERTH, E)

2 Walter, Lord of Beaufort and Edzell; tutor (guardian) to his nephew David; *m* 1470 Isabel Livingstone (afterwards w of William, Lord Ruthven) and *d* 1476, leaving issue:

(1) David (Sir); *m* 1st Katherine, dau of Thomas Fotheringham of Pourie, and by her had issue:

1a Walter, *k* Battle of Flodden 1513, leaving, with other issue, by his w, who was of the family of Erskine of Dun:

1b DAVID LINDSAY, **9th Earl of Crawford**; with the consent of the Crown reconveyed the Earldom to his kinsman, s of the 'Wicked Master', whom he brought up and educated; *m* 1st Janet (*dsp*), dau of 2nd Lord Gray (*qv*) and widow of 2nd Lord Lovat (*qv*); *m* 2nd 1549 Katherine (*d* 1 Oct 1578), widow of James, Master of Oglivy, and dau of Sir John Campbell of Calder, and *d* 1558, having by her had, with other issue:

1c David (Sir), heir to Ldship of Edzell, Ld of Session as Lord Edzell; completed Castle of Edzell; *m* 1st his cousin Lady Helen Lindsay, dau of **10th Earl of Crawford**, and *d* Dec 1610, having had:

1d David Lindsay of Edzell; *m* Margaret, dau of John Wishart of Pitarrow, and had issue:

1e Alexander; *m* Anne, dau of 1st Earl of Wemyss (*see* WEMYSS and MARCH, E), and had issue:

1f Jean; *m* 6th Lord Torphichen (*qv*)

2d Alexander; f of:

2e John; f of:

1f David, of Edzell; became heir male of the Lindsays (but not chief of the house because of the entail) on the death of the 3rd Lord Spynie (*see* above); f of:

1g David, last of Edzell, *dsp* 1744, having sold his estates to Lord Panmure

1g Margaret; *m* David Watson of Aitherny

2g Janet; *m* Ensign Edward Whitmore

1d Margaret; *m c* 8 Oct 1595 1st Earl of Southesk (*see* FIFE, D)

1c (cont.) Sir David Lindsay of Edzell *m* 2nd 1 Dec 1585, as her 2nd husb, Isobel, dau of Arthur Forbes of Logie and Balfour and widow of Alexander Innes, 18th of that Ilk (*see* ROXBURGHE, D) and by her had:

2d Margaret; *m* Sir James Keith of Benholme 2nd s of 5th Earl Marischal (*see* KINTORE, E), and had issue (*see* ROSEBERY, E)

2c John; Sec of State, granted ecclesiastical revenues of Menmuir, Lethnot and Lochlee; Ld of Session as Lord Menmuir; one of the Octavians or eight persons in charge of the royal finances; *m* 1st 29 Nov 1581 Marion, widow of David Borthwick of Lockhill and dau of Alexander Guthrie; bought Balcarres, Fifeshire, from his stepson and established his family there; *m* 2nd 7 Feb 1590 Jane Lauder, widow of (a) Sir James Forrester of Costorphine and (b) John Campbell of Calder, but had no issue by her, and *d* 3 Sept 1590, having had, with other issue:

1d DAVID, **1st Lord Lindsay of Balcarres**, for whom see further below

1d Katherine; *m* 1st her cousin Sir John Lindsay of Ballinscho, s of **10th Earl of Crawford**; *m* 2nd Thomas Brown of Fordel

3c Walter (Sir), of Balgawies

1c Elizabeth; *m* by 21 Oct 1572, as his 1st w, Patrick, 3rd Lord Drummond (*see* PERTH, E), and *d* May 1585, having had issue

2c Margaret; *m* 1580 1st Earl of Atholl of the 1595/6 *cr* (*see* MORAY, E)

2b Alexander, of Haltoun; f of:

1c David, Bp of Ross; f of:

1d Jerome (Sir), Ld Lyon King of Arms, from whom the LINDSAYs of Virginia claim descent

(1) (cont.) Sir David *m* 2nd Elizabeth Spens (afterwards w of John Anstruther of Anstruther) and by her had a s and dau

3 William, of Lekoquhy; ancestor of the extinct LINDSAY Bts of Evelick

4 John (Sir), of Brechin; ancestor of the LINDSAYs of Pitcairlie

5 James; went to Germany with PRINCESS ELEANOR STUART and founded a line of LINDSAYs at Augsburg

The 9th EARL'S gs by his 2nd s Lord Menmuir,

DAVID LINDSAY, **1st Lord Lindsay of Balcarres** (S), so *cr* 27 June 1633, with limitation to his heirs male bearing the name of Lindsay; *bapt* 17 March 1587; *s* his est bro John 1601; ktd; *m* 16 Feb 1611/2 Lady Sophia Seton, dau of Alexander, 1st Earl of Dunfermline, and *d* March 1640/1, leaving an er s:

ALEXANDER LINDSAY, **2nd Lord Lindsay of Balcarres** and **1st Earl of Balcarres**, so *cr* 9 Jan 1650/1, as also LORD LINDSAY AND BALNIEL (both S) by CHARLES II when in exile at The Hague; *b* 6 July 1618; hereditary Govr Edinburgh Castle, Sec of State, Ld HC Gen Assembly Ch Scotland; Im April 1640 Lady Anna Mackenzie (*m* 2nd Jan 1670 9th Earl of Argyll; *d* 2 May 1707), dau and coheir of 1st Earl of Seaforth (*see* CROMARTIE, E), and *d* in exile at Breda, The Netherlands, 30 Aug 1659, having had issue:

1 CHARLES LINDSAY, **2nd Earl of Balcarres**; *d* unm 15 Oct 1662

2 COLIN, **3rd Earl**

1 Henrietta; *m* Sir Duncan Campbell, 4th Bt, of Auchinbreck (*qv*), and had issue

2 Anne; a nun

3 Sophia; *m* Col Hon Charles Campbell

The 2nd EARL's yr bro,

COLIN LINDSAY, **3rd Earl of Balcarres**; *bapt* 23 Aug 1652; as a Jacobite at the time of the Glorious Revolution in 1688 went into exile on the Continent for ten years, later received permission to return, but supported the Stuarts again in the 1715 uprising, though once again pardoned owing to friendship with the 1st Duke of Marlborough (*qv*); *m* 1st *c* 1670 Mauritia de Nassau, dau of Louis, Baron of Lecke and Beverwaert (illegitimate son of Maurice Prince of Orange), by whom he had no surv issue; *m* 2nd Lady Jean Carnegie, est dau of 2nd Earl of Northesk (*qv*), and had issue:

1 Anne; *m* 1st 4th Earl of Kellie (*see* MAR and KELLIE, E); *m* 2nd 3rd Viscount of Kingston (*see* EGLINTON and WINTON, E) and *d* 3 Feb 1743

The **3rd Earl of Balcarres** *m* 3rd Jean, dau of 2nd Earl of Roxburghe (*see* ROXBURGHE, D), and by her had issue:

1 Colin, ADC to 1st Duke of Marlborough; *d* unm

2 Margaret; *m* 6th Earl of Wigtoun and had issue (*see* ROSEBERY, E)

The **3rd Earl of Balcarres** *m* 4th by 4 July 1689 Lady Margaret Campbell, dau of 2nd Earl of Loudoun (*qv*), and *d* 1722, having by her had, with other issue:

2 ALEXANDER LINDSAY, **4th Earl of Balcarres**; rep S peer 1734–36, became on the death of David Lindsay of Edzell 1744 heir male of the Lindsays, thus reuniting the arms and chiefship; *m* 1718 Elizabeth (*d* 4 Sept 1768), dau of David Scott of Scotstarvet, but *dsp* 25 July 1736

3 JAMES, **5th Earl**

3 Eleanor; *m* 1726 James Fraser, s of 12th Lord Saltoun (*qv*) of Abernethy

The 3rd EARL OF BALCARRES's yst s,

JAMES LINDSAY, **5th Earl of Balcarres**; *b* 14 Nov 1691; *m* 24 Oct 1749 Anne, dau of Sir Robert Dalrymple of Castleton, and *d* 20 Feb 1768, having had, with other issue:

1 ALEXANDER, **6th Earl**

2 Robert, of Balcarres, Fife; with HEICS; *b* 25 Jan 1754; *m* 25 Nov 1788 Elizabeth (*d* 4 July 1835), dau of Sir Alexander Dick, 3rd Bt, of Prestonfield (*see* DICK-CUNYNGHAM, Bt), and *d* 18 May 1936, leaving, with other issue:

(1) James; MP Wigan 1825–31 and Fifeshire 1831–32, Lt-Gen; *b* 17 April 1793; *m* 1st 5 Feb 1819 Mary Ann (*dsp* 14 July 1820), dau of Francis Grant, of Kilgraston; *m* 2nd 2 April 1823 Anne (*d* 10 Aug 1894), est dau and coheir of Sir Coutts Trotter, 1st Bt (*d* 1 Sept 1837), of Westville, Lincs (*cr* a Baronet 4 Sept 1821 (UK) with special remainder to the male issue of his dau Anne), and *d* 5 Dec 1855, having by her had issue:

1a Sir COUTTS LINDSAY, 2nd and last Bt, of Westville; *b* 2 Feb 1824; *s* to his maternal gf's btcy; DL, JP Fifeshire, Capt Gren Gds, cmded 1st Regt Italian Legion Crimea, Lt-Col Fife Vols 1864–84; *m* 1st 30 June 1864 Caroline Blanche Elizabeth (*d* 4 Aug 1912), only surv child of Rt Hon Henry FitzRoy (*see* SOUTHAMPTON, B), and had issue:

1b Harriet Euphemia Susan; *b* 15 May 1865; *m* 3 Aug 1897 Rev Thomas Selby Henrey (*d* Jan 1941), Vicar St George, Old Brentford, Middx, and *d* 9 Aug 1946

2b Anne Helen; *b* 18 Oct 1868; *m* 10 March 1917 George Hegarty Ramsay, Pastor Hillcrest Chapel, Thorpe-next-Norwich, and *d* 11 Aug 1955

1a (cont.) Sir COUTTS *m* 2nd 10 Aug 1912 Katie Harriet (*d* 4 April 1937), widow of — Madley and dau of William Burfield, and *d* 7 May 1912, when the btcy expired

2a ROBERT JAMES LINDSAY later LINDSAY-LOYD (roy licence), 1st and last BARON WANTAGE OF LOCKINGE, Co Berks (UK), so *cr* 23 July 1885, VC, KCB, Ld Lt Berks, MP (Lib) 1865–85, Lt-Col Scots Fus, Col-Cmdt Berks Roy Vols, Lt-Col cmdg HAC, Brig-Gen cmdg Home Counties Inf Vol Bde, Fin Sec War Office 1877–80; *b* 16 April 1832; *m* 17 Nov 1858 Hon Harriet Sarah Loyd (*d* 9 Aug 1920), only surv dau and heir of 1st and last Baron Overstone of Overstone and of Fotheringhay, and *dsp* 10 June 1901, when the Barony expired

1a Margaret; *m* 23 July 1846 her cousin **25th Earl of Crawford** and *d* 28 Dec 1909, leaving issue (*see* below)

2a Mary Anne; *m* 5 Aug 1854 Robert Stayner Holford, of Westonbirt, Glos, and *d* 13 Feb 1901, leaving issue. He *d* 22 Feb 1892

(2) Robert, of Stralton, Fife; *b* 13 July 1795; *m* 2 Aug 1824 Frances (*d* 13 May 1865), dau of Sir Robert Henderson, Bt, and *d* 5 Sept 1869, having had, with other issue:

1a Alexander William, Hon Col; *b* 1833; *m* 4 Sept 1880 Mary Louisa, widow of Maj H Wellesley and dau of Rev Nathaniel Cotton, and *dsp* 1891

1a Elizabeth Frances; *m* 20 Jan 1864 Capt Thomas Nourse Underwood, RN

2a Marianne; *m* 15 April 1857 Maj-Gen Hickman Thomas Molesworth and *d* 25 March 1920, leaving issue (*see* MOLESWORTH, V)

(3) Colin, Bengal CS, Judge Delhi; *b* 6 March 1800; *m* 1st 19 March 1824 Augusta (*d* 19 Feb 1831), dau of Charles Blair, and had issue:

1a Charles Robert, Bengal CS; *b* 18 Jan 1826; *m* 24 March 1848 Rhoda Charlotte (*d* 7 Dec 1921), dau of Maj-Gen Edward Gwatkin, and *d* 23 Feb 1895, leaving issue:

1b Mary Augusta, CI; *m* 28 Jan 1871 Sir Richard Temple, 1st Bt (*qv*), and *d* 9 March 1924, leaving issue. He *d* 15 March 1902

2b Laura Anne; *m* 6 Dec 1873 Charles Edward Buckland, CIE, of Cornwall Gdns, London, and *d* 1918, leaving issue

3b Rhoda Gordon; *m* 28 Sept 1882 Gen Carl von Schubert, of Russia, and *d* 19 Jan 1931, leaving issue. He *d* 29 July 1889

1a Charlotte Augusta; *m* Sept 1846 Maj-Gen John Christie, CB, and *d* 1 March 1909, leaving issue. He *d* 7 May 1869

(3) (cont.) Colin Lindsay *m* 2nd 1832 Margaret Browne (*d* Oct 1833) and by her had issue:

2a Margaret; *m* 1851 Maj-Gen Henry Dimsdale Manning and had issue. He *d* 1892

(3) (cont.) Colin Lindsay *m* 3rd 1834 Emma (*d* 12 Aug 1903), dau of H Watson, and *d* 18 Aug 1864, having by her had, with other issue:

3a Emma Anne Elizabeth; *m* 30 Aug 1860 Lt-Col W D Macdonald, 93rd Highrs, est s of Capt Hon and Mrs Panmure Macdonald, of Caithnesshire, and *dsp* 29 March 1864. He *d* 1862

(4) Charles Bazil; *b* 31 July 1804; Madras Cav; *m* 19 July 1842 Anna (*m* 2nd 17 Feb 1852 Hugh Hamilton Lindsay (*see* below)), dau of Eneas Ronald McDonnell, Chief of Glengarry, and *dsp* 31 Aug 1848

(1) Mary Butler; *m* 18 Nov 1815 Charles Maitland Christie of Durie and *d* 27 March 1829, leaving issue. He *d* 1872

(2) Cecilia Martha Harvey; *m* 25 July 1821 Capt James Head, HEICS, and *d* 31 July 1847, leaving issue (*see* HEAD, Bt)

3 Charles Dalrymple, DD, Bp Kildare; *b* 15 Dec 1760; *m* 1 Jan 1790 Elizabeth (*d* 7 Feb 1797), only dau of Thomas Fudell, of Boston, and had, with other issue:

(1) Charles, Archdeacon Kildare; *b* 12 Oct 1790; *m* 28 Sept 1819 Anne (*d* 18 Sept 1876), est dau of Owsley Rowley, of Priory Hill, Hunts, and *d* 23 April 1855, leaving issue:

1a Caroline Frances; *m* 30 Oct 1849 George Dawson Rowley and *d* 3 Jan 1900, leaving issue. He *d* 21 Nov 1878

(2) Philip Yorke; *b* 7 Feb 1795; *m* 4 April 1816 Helena Elizabeth (*d* 14 Dec 1879), dau of Charles Blane, and *d* 16 Dec 1832, leaving a s and two daus

(1) Elizabeth Frances; *m* 21 Oct 1811 Sir Compton Pocklington Domville, Bt (*see* 1970 edn), and *d* 10 Aug 1812, leaving issue. He *d* 23 Feb 1857

3 (cont.) The Rt Rev Charles Lindsay *m* 2nd 2 June 1798 Catherine Eliza, dau of Evert George Coussmaker, of Dane Court, Kent, and *d* 8 Aug 1846, having by her had issue:

(3) George Hayward; DL, JP; *b* 10 June 1799; *m* 3 Sept 1828 Lady Mary Catherine Gore (*d* 28 April 1885), sis of 4th Earl of Arran (*qv*), and *d* 5 Jan 1886, leaving, with other issue:

1a Henry Gore; *b* 26 Aug 1830; Lt-Col Rifle Bde, Ch Constable Glam, DL, JP Co Dublin and Breconshire, served S Africa 1852–53, Crimea 1855 and Indian Mutiny 1857 (despatches); *m* 14 May 1856 Hon Ellen Sarah (*d* 19 May 1912), dau of 1st Baron Tredegar (*see* 1959 edn TREDEGAR, V), and *d* 15 Dec 1914, leaving, with other issue:

1b Henry Edzell Morgan, CB (1911); *b* 13 Feb 1857; Capt RE, Hon Col Roy Mon RE 1924, JP Glam and Co Dublin, DL Glam, served Transvaal 1880–81, Suakin 1885, S Africa 1899–1901 (despatches) and WW I, KJStJ; *m* 24 July 1889 Ellen Katherine (*d* 3 Aug 1937), est dau and coheir of George William Griffith Thomas, of Ystrad Mynach, and *d* 1 Nov 1935, having had issue:

1c George Walter Thomas; *b* 29 Jan 1891; Capt RFA and RFC; accidentally *k* while flying 26 June 1917

2c Claud Frederic Thomas ; *b* 20 Jan 1892; *educ* Wellington and RMA Woolwich; Capt and Actg Maj RFA WW I (despatches); *m* 10 June 1915 Dorothy Lindsay (*m* 2nd 24 April 1923 Lt-Col Eric Denis Corkery, MC, Devonshire Regt (*ka* 4 Dec 1942), er s of Col Thomas Herbert Corkery, and *d* 30 May 1969), er dau of Sir Henry James Forde, JP, of Waterford, and was *ka* 31 March 1918, leaving issue:

1d George Morgan Thomas, psc 1950; *b* posthumously 16 Nov 1918; *educ* Wellington and RMA Woolwich; Maj RA WW II (despatches); *m* 8 May 1954 *Jennifer Mary [Mrs George Lindsay, Glanmor, Southern Down, Bridgend, Glam], only dau of Col John Geoffrey Ferry, RA, of Wymering Lodge, Farnborough, Hants, and *d* 1990, leaving issue:

1e +David Charles Thomas; *b* 9 April 1955; *educ* Wellington; *m* 1987 (*divorce* 1991) Alexandra Wendy, dau of Robert Emmas

2e +William George Thomas; *b* 6 Feb 1958*educ* Wellington

3c Archibald Thurstan Thomas; *b* 17 June 1897; Lt RE; *ka* 26 March 1918

4c David Edzell Thomas; *b* 28 Feb 1910; *educ* Wellington and Clare Coll Cambridge (BA 1931); OStJ; *m* 1st 2 Dec 1933 (*divorce* 1939) Katherine Mary, yr dau of Austin Green, of Penarth, and had issue:

1d +David Claud; *b* 26 Sept 1934; *educ* Eton; *m* 18 Nov 1964 *Sheela Mary, est dau of Michael Edward FitzGerald, of Co Galway

4c (cont.) David Lindsay *m* 2nd 18 May 1940 (*divorce* 1946) Eleanor Margaret, dau of Kenneth Campbell; *m* 3rd 21 June 1950 *Hon Audrey Lavinia Lyttelton [The Hon Mrs Lindsay, Poplar Cottage, Fore St Hill, Budleigh Salterton, Devon], 2nd dau of 9th Viscount Cobham (*qv*), and *d* 14 July 1968, having by her had issue:

2d Hugh Charles Lyttelton; *b* 30 May 1953; *educ* Millfield; Maj 9th/12th Lancers (Prince of Wales's), Equerry to HM THE QUEEN; *m* 1987 *Sarah Patricia, MVO (*m* 2nd 20 Dec 1996, as his 2nd w, Paul Horsley), dau of Brian J Brennan, of Surrey, and *d* in an avalanche in the Alps 1988 while skiing with HRH THE PRINCE OF WALES and his party, leaving issue:

1e *Alice Rose; *b* postumously 1988

3d +Andrew Edzell Thomas [Andrew Lindsay Esq, Durdham Park, Bristol BS6 6XB]; *b* 12 Sept 1956; *m* 1991 *Patricia May, dau of David Thesen, of Bude, Cornwall

1d *Emma Katrina; *b* 3 July 1955; *m* 1986 *Lt-Col Ian M Daniell, RE, er s of Dr B L Daniell, and has issue:

1e *Tobias Hugh; *b* 1989

1e *Amy Meriel; *b* 1987

1c Ellen Blanche, BEM (1955); *b* 22 Dec 1893; *m* 16 Aug 1921 Maj Richard Cope Wilson, MBE, er s of H Wilson. He *d* 1949

2c Nesta Jessie, MBE (1943), OStJ; *b* 23 May 1898; *m* 22 July 1927 S/Ldr Gerald Towell Stoneham, of Kitale, Kenya, s of Frederic Stoneham, of Echo Hurst, Guildford, and *dsp* 11 June 1957

2b Lionel Arthur, MVO (1912), OBE (1920); *b* 27 March 1861; Ch Constable Glam 1891–1937, OStJ, Adj, Maj and Inspr Egyptian Police; *d* unm 15 April 1945

3b David Balcarres; *b* 15 Feb 1863; Maj Glos Imp Yeo; *m* 11 Jan 1898 Grace Maud (*d* 11 July 1945), dau of George Miller, and was *k* while hunting 9 March 1943, leaving issue:

1c Madeline; *b* 2 Jan 1899; *m* 15 Jan 1936 Thomas Morgan, of Wantage, Berks, and *d* 18 Dec 1996, leaving:

1d *John Patrick [John Morgan Esq, 12 Maiden Erlegh Drive, Earley, Reading RG6 7HP]; *b* 20 May 1937; *m* 6 July 1968 Raine (*d* 7 Jan 1996), er dau of G F Tredwell, and has issue:

1e *James Christopher; *b* 1984

2e *Edward Patrick; *b* 1987

2d *Bernard Lawrence [Bernard Morgan Esq, Ivy Lodge, Letcombe Bassett, Berks]; *b* 3 Aug 1938; *m* 1st 12 Nov 1960 (*divorce* 1976) Chong Siew Yong and has issue:

1e *Michael Gary; *b* 1963

2e *David; *b* 1965

1e *Susan Jane; *b* 1961

2d (cont.) Bernard Morgan *m* 2nd 1977 *Monique Huart, of Zaire, and has further issue:

3e *Michael David; *b* 1978

4e *Philip; *b* 1979

2c Juliet Mary; *b* 27 Jan 1904; *m* 1st 14 Oct 1939 7th Marquess of Waterford (*qv*); *m* 2nd 17 Dec 1946 Lt-Col John Eric Durnford Silcock, s of Charles Silcock, of Co Tipperary, and *d* 1987, having had issue by her 1st husb

3c *Winifred Laura; *b* 24 May 1907

4b Walter Charles, MVO (1904); *b* 11 March 1866; High Sheriff Co Kilkenny 1911, CC Kilkenny 1911–20, Gent-in-Waiting to Ld Lt Ireland 1898–1904, V-Chamberlain 1904–06, Lt-Col and Brevet Col Roy Dublin Fus WW I (despatches, brevet); *m* 24 March 1897 Lady Kathleen Butler, OBE (1918) (*d* 29 April 1953), only dau of 6th Earl of Carrick (*qv*), and *d* 4 June 1929, leaving issue:

1c Doreen, MVO (1954); *b* 29 June 1899; *m* 12 Oct 1929 Maj Richard Archer Houblon, DSO, RA (ret), 6th s of Col George Bramston Archer Houblon, of Hallingbury Place. He *d* 11 June 1957

2c Kathleen; *b* 7 Aug 1902; *m* 10 Sept 1924 Cdr Denys Brocklebank, RN (*d* 22 Feb 1947), est surv s of Ralph Eric Royds Brocklebank, and had issue:

1d *Ralph Wilfrid; *b* 18 July 1927; *educ* Lakefield Ontario and Trin Coll Cambridge (BA 1950); *m* 8 Feb 1954 *Beryl, est dau of Harold Francis Raymond Seabury, of Wollaston, Stourbridge, Worcs, and has issue:

1e *Guy Philip; *b* 24 Aug 1954

1d (cont.) Ralph Brocklebank also adopted:

*Mark Eric; *b* 7 Sept 1959

*Leo; *b* 14 Aug 1965

*Susan; *b* 8 July 1956

*Karen; *b* 27 Dec 1960

1d *Ann; *b* 12 April 1926; *m* 1st 16 Feb 1952 (*divorce* 1960) John Ronald Lindsay Antrobus, only s of Lt-Col Ronald Henry Antrobus, MC, late RA (*see* ANTROBUS, Bt), and has issue; *m* 2nd 1 April 1967 *Maurice Stanley Gooding, s of Harold Charles Gooding by Dorothy Eliza Taylor-Wyman

2d *Eve; *b* 7 March 1929; *m* 30 Dec 1952 *Anthony Victor Kaye, of Dunsdale, Forest Row, Sussex, only s of Victor Kaye, of Pre-Sec, St Brelade, Jersey, and has issue:

1e *Tobias John; *b* 5 April 1956

2e *Denys Michael; *b* 9 Oct 1957

1e *Gabriel Fiona; *b* 3 Dec 1954

2e *Sandra Juliet; *b* 6 July 1959

3e *Emma Lucy; *b* 15 Nov 1962

4e *Charlotte Mary; *b* 27 Sept 1964

3d *Una; *b* 9 Dec 1930; MCSP; *m* 27 Aug 1960 *Christopher John Lewers, yr s of Alfred Joseph Lewers, and has:

1e *Angela Jane Lindsay; *b* 28 July 1962

2e *Katherine Elizabeth Lindsay; *b* 8 April 1964

5b George Mackintosh, CB (1936), CMG (1919), CBE (1946), DSO (1917); *b* 3 July 1880; KStJ, Maj-Gen (1934) Roy Tank Corps, dir Brit Nat Cadet Assoc, formerly Col Rifle Bde, ADC to HM GEORGE V 1928, Brig Gen Staff Egypt 1929–32, Brig 7th Inf Bde 1932–34, cmded Presidency and Assam Dist India 1935–39, Col Cmdt Royal Tank Corps 1938–47; served S Africa 1900–02 and WW I 1914–19 (despatches, brevet), Order Leopold Belgium and Croix de Guerre, Kaisar-i-Hind Medal, WW II in CD, BRC; OStJ; *m* 9 July 1907 Constance, dau of George Stewart Hamilton, and *d* 28 Nov 1956, having had issue:

1c Constance; *b* and *d* 16 May 1910

2c *Joan Mary; *b* 8 Sept 1911; *m* 23 Feb 1938 Lt-Col Charles Holwell Thomas, OBE, er s of Robert George Dashwood Thomas, and has issue:

1d *Robert Heriot Lindsay; *b* 2 Jan 1941; *educ* Eton and Ch Ch Oxford (BA)

2d David Charles Morgan; *b* 12 May 1942; *educ* Eton; *m* 11 April 1970 *Ann Tresina, dau of R H B Benger, of Johannesburg, and *d* 1987, leaving issue:

1e Rupert James Morgan ; *b* 1972; *k* in motor accident 1992

3d *George Francis Maitland; *b* 8 July 1944; *educ* Nautical Coll Pangbourne; *m* 1976 *Geraldine, dau of Adrian van der Kwast, of Curaçao, Netherlands Antilles, and has issue:

1e *Morgan Adrian Maitland; *b* 1979

1e *Georgiana Elaine Lindsay; *b* 1980

1d *Sarah Elizabeth Lindsay; *b* 13 Nov 1946; *m* 1971 *Henry Charles Alfred Rowe, of Dorset, and has issue:

1e *Charles Edward Kingsley; *b* 1973

1e *Louise Arabella; *b* 1975

2e *Serena Elizabeth Henrietta; *b* 1977

1b Ellen Rosamond Mary; *m* 16 Nov 1898 7th Earl of Carrick (*qv*) and *d* 15 June 1946, leaving issue

2a William John Coussmaker (Rev), MA Dublin, Rector Llanvair, Abergavenny, RD Raglan; *b* 7 Dec 1832; *m* 18 May 1859 Rosamond Emily (*d* 1 March 1885), est dau of Frederic Clinton Mundy, and *dsp* 23 June 1912

1a Georgiana Kathleen; *m* 16 March 1858 William O'Connor Morris, of Gartnamona, King's Co, County Judge, and *d* 24 June 1910, leaving issue. He *d* 3 Aug 1904

2a Mary Catherine Caroline; *m* 6 April 1864 Thomas Spencer Lindsay, of Co Mayo, and *d* 8 Feb 1881, leaving issue. He *d* 14 July 1874

4 John; *b* 15 March 1762; Col 71st Highrs; *m* 2 April 1800 Lady Charlotte North (*d* 25 Oct 1849), 3rd dau of 2nd Earl of Guilford (*qv*), and *dsp* 6 March 1826

5 Hugh; *b* 30 Oct1765; Dir HIEC, Marshal Court of Admlty; *m* 14 Jan 1799 Jane (*d* 26 May 1865), 2nd dau of Hon Alexander Gordon, a Ld of Session as Lord Rockville (*see* ABERDEEN AND TEMAIR, M), and *d* 23 April 1844, leaving issue:

(1) Hugh Hamilton; *b* 12 Aug 1802; *m* 17 Feb 1852 Anna (*d* 17 Oct 1900), widow of Charles Basil Lindsay (*see* above) and dau of Eneas R McDonnell, and *dsp* 29 May 1881

(1) Anne; *m* 16 Oct 1817 Sir Edmund Antrobus, 2nd Bt (*qv*), and *d* 1 Dec 1885 aged 85, leaving issue

1 Anne, author: *Auld Robin Gray*; *m* 31 Oct 1793 Andrew Barnard and *dsp* 6 May 1825

2 Margaret Janet; *m* 1st Alexander Fordyce; *m* 2nd 8 Sept 1812 Sir J B Burges (later Lamb), Bt, and *dsp* 1 Dec 1814

3 Elizabeth Scot; *m* 24 July 1782 3rd Earl of Hardwicke (*qv*) and *d* 26 May 1858, leaving issue

The 5th EARL OF BALCARRES's est s,

ALEXANDER LINDSAY, **6th Earl of Balcarres** and *de jure* 23rd EARL OF CRAWFORD following death of his cousin George, Earl of Crawford and Lindsay (*see* LINDSAY, E); *b* 18 Jan 1752; rep S peer 1784–96 and 1802–25, joined army 1767 (wounded Ticonderoga 1777, Lt-Col 24th Foot 1777, Col 63rd Foot 1789–1825, Maj-Gen 1793, Cdr Forces Jersey 1793, Lt-Gen 1798, Gen 1803), Lt-Govr Jamaica 1794–1801 where he put down a slave rebellion; *m* 1 June 1780 his first cousin Elizabeth (*d* 10 Aug 1816), only child of Charles Dalrymple (*see* HAMILTON-DALRYMPLE, Bt) and heiress of the Haigh estates on failure of male issue in her maternal family, that of Sir Roger Bradshaigh, Bt, of Haigh (her ggf), and *d* 27 March 1825, having had, with other issue (including an allegedly mad son Richard, who his f put away on the Orkney island of Shapinsay under the care of the local minister, and another s, Edwin, who his f arranged to have certified as insane although he may not have been; it is said that Edwin returned to Europe after service with the HEICS but displeased his f by refusing to fight a duel; he was then inveigled into going up to Shapinsay to look for his bro and left in those parts by his f without money for 25 years; he became known as the 'prisoner of Papa Stour' (in the Shetland Islands); Edwin eventually escaped and successfully sued for restitution):

1 JAMES, **24th/7th Earl**

2 Charles Robert; *b* 20 Aug 1784; Collector Customs Agra, India; *m* 12 Feb 1814 Elizabeth (*d* 8 Nov 1852), dau of Thomas William Thompson, and *d* 4 July 1835, leaving, with other issue:

(1) Hugh Barlow; *b* 21 March 1832; Bombay CS; *m* 3 Oct 1863 Jane (*d* 13 July 1921), widow of 4th Baron Muncaster and dau of 2nd Marquess of Westminster (*see* WESTMINSTER, D), and *d* 13 April 1913, leaving, with other issue:

1a Nigel Crawford; *b* 15 Oct 1870; *m* 27 June 1893 Nelda, dau of Dr Carl Schlund, and *d* 10 July 1922

1a Evelyn Agnes; *b* 14 Feb 1869; *m* 3 Aug 1892 Henry William Grant Gordon-Cumming and *d* 30 Oct 1948, leaving issue (*see* GORDON-CUMMING, Bt)

2a Rose Margaret Sandford; *b* 25 Jan 1876

1 Elizabeth Keith; *m* 13 Dec 1815 R E Heathcote, of Stafford, and *d* 1825, leaving issue

2 Anne; *m* 16 April 1811 Robert Wardlaw Ramsay, of Balgarvie, Fife, and *d* 14 Jan 1846, leaving issue. He *d* 1837

The 23rd/6th EARL's est s,

JAMES LINDSAY, **24th Earl of Crawford** (as which confirmed 1848 but failed in his attempt to claim the Dukedom of Montrose 1853) and **7th Earl of Balcarres**; *b* 24 April 1783; MP (Tory) Wigan 1820–25, *cr* 5 July 1826 BARON WIGAN OF HAIGH HALL, Co Lancaster (UK); *m* 21 Nov 1811 Hon Maria Margaret Francis Pennington (*d* 16 Nov 1850), only surv child of 1st Baron Muncaster, and *d* 15 Dec 1869, leaving:

1 ALEXANDER WILLIAM CRAWFORD, **25th/8th Earl**

2 James (Sir), KCMG; *b* 25 Aug 1815; Lt-Gen, MP Wigan for 19 years, Gren Gds, Col 3rd Buffs, Mil Sec HQ to FM HRH THE DUKE OF CAMBRIDGE, C-in-C; *m* 6 Nov 1845 Lady Sarah Elizabeth Savile (*d* 16 Dec 1890), VA, Woman Bedchamber to HM QUEEN VICTORIA, only dau of 3rd Earl of Mexborough (*qv*), and *d* 13 Aug 1874, leaving, with two s and another dau:

(1) Mabel; *m* 13 Feb 1877 Lt-Col William John Frescheville Ramsden, Coldstream Gds (*see* RAMSDEN, Bt), and *d* 12 June 1928. He *d* 8 Jan 1927

(2) Mary Egidia; *m* 9 Feb 1875 John Coutts Antrobus, of Eaton Hall, Cheshire, and *d* 1 July 1911, leaving issue (*see* ANTROBUS, Bt)

3 Charles Hugh, CB; *b* 11 Nov 1816; MP Abingdon 1865–74, Groom-in-Waiting to HM QUEEN VICTORIA, Lt-Col Gren Gds, Col cmdg St George's Rifles; *m* 24 April 1851 Emilia Anne (*d* 15 Feb 1873), dau of Very Rev Hon Henry Montague Browne (*see* KILMAINE, B), and *d* 25 March 1889, having had, with three other s and two other daus:

(1) Henry Edith Arthur, OBE (1918), JP Berks; *b* 9 April 1866; Commr Br Red Cross France 1914, Staff Capt RFC 1915–17, Lt-Col RAF 1917–19 and Capt Gordon Highrs WW I (despatches twice); *m* 27 April 1895 Norah Mary Madeline (*d* 20 June 1948), dau of Hon Edward Roden Bourke (*see* MAYO, E), and *d* 6 May 1939, having had issue:

1a (David Ludovic) Peter, DSO; *b* 30 April 1900; T/Lt-Col Irish Gds WW II; *m* 1st 12 Oct 1940 (*divorce* 1946) Ursula Jane, yr dau of Capt Robert Orlando Randolph Kenyon-Slaney, Gren Gds (*see* KENYON, B); *m* 2nd 14 Jan 1950 *Barbara Joan Dunn, dau of Edward Oliver Dunn, of London, and Mrs Margarita Byers, and had issue:

1b +David Michael; *b* 10 Sept 1956; *m* 1991 *Sarah Jane, est dau ofAnthony Poat

1b *Jane Caroline; *b* 7 Feb 1951

2b *Sarah Jacqueline; *b* 3 July 1952; *m* 1988, as his 2nd w *Hon James Malise Dundas Jauncey, er s of Baron Jauncey of Tullichettle (*qv*)

1a Nancy Winifred Robina

(1) Marion Margaret Violet; *m* 25 Nov 1882 8th Duke of Rutland (*qv*) and *d* 22 Dec 1937, leaving issue

4 Colin; *b* 6 Dec 1819; *m* 29 July 1845 Lady Frances Howard (*d* 20 Aug 1897), dau and er coheir of 4th Earl of Wicklow (*see* 1970 edn), and *d* 28 Jan 1892, leaving with other issue:

(1) William Alexander, CVO (1924), QC (1897), DL, JP Devon; *b* 8 June 1846; *educ* Eton and Trin Coll Cambridge (MA); barrister 1873, bencher Middle Temple 1906, Portcullis Pursuivant of Arms 1882–94, Windsor Herald 1894–1919, Norroy King of Arms 1919–22 and Clarenceux King of Arms 1922–26, memb Lloyd's from 1868; *m* 7 May 1870 Lady Harriet Gordon (*d* 15 Feb 1942), 2nd dau of 5th Earl of Aberdeen (*see* ABERDEEN AND TEMAIR, M), and *d* 13 Sept 1926, having had, with other issue:

1a James Howard, DSO (1917); *b* 29 April 1871; *educ* Trin Coll Cambridge (MA LLB); barrister; Lt-Col 14th Bn (Lond Scottish) Co Lond Regt WW I 1914–17 (despatches, wounded); *m* 15 Aug 1906 Joanna Lucy (*d* 25 Dec

1965), est dau of Thomas Duff Gordon Duff, CBE, of Drummuir, Banffshire, and *d* 22 April 1940, leaving issue:

1b Michael; *b* 1 April 1908; Lt-Cdr RN WW II; *m* 21 Dec 1939 *Isabel (*m* 2nd 6 March 1946 Maj John Poë, RA, s of Col John Poë, CMG, DSO), dau of Brig Mainwaring Ravell Walsh, CB, CMG, and was *ka* July 1940

2b Harry Lachlan; *b* 25 Oct 1912; Maj RHA WW II; *ka* Italy Sept 1944

2a Michael William Howard; *b* 7 Aug 1872; Capt 2nd Bn Seaforth Highrs and Scottish Horse Boer War (despatches); *k* Brakenlaagte, S Africa, 30 Oct 1901

3a Francis Howard; *b* 9 March 1876; *educ* Clare Coll Cambridge (BA); Capt and T/Maj 14th Bn (Lond Scottish) Co Lond Regt; *m* 14 April 1910 Helen Margaret (*d* 1 Feb 1941), est dau and coheir of Lt-Col Stewart MacDougall, of Lunga, Argyll, and was *ka* 1 July 1916, leaving issue:

1b John Stewart LINDSAY later LINDSAY-MacDOUGALL (April 1932), DSO, MC; *b* 28 Feb 1911; Maj Argyll and Sutherland Highrs WW II 1939–43; *m* 4 Sept 1934 *Sheila Marion Roma (*m* 2nd 7 Oct 1949 Lt-Col Aubrey Wynter Gibbon, OBE, Arygll and Sutherland Highrs, s of Rev Henry Hensham Gibbon, OBE, TD, MA), only dau of Capt James William Lennox Sprot, The Black Watch, and *d* of wounds in Italy while in enemy hands 5 Aug 1943, leaving issue:

1c +Colin John Francis [Colin Lindsay-MacDougall Esq, Lunga, Ardfern, Lochgilphead, Argyllshire]; *b* 21 July 1939; *educ* Radley; late 2nd Lt The Queen's Own Hus; *m* 11 Feb 1961 (*divorce* 1978) Hon Frances Phoebe Phillimore, only dau of Capt Hon Anthony Francis Phillimore, 9th Lancers (*see* PHILLIMORE, B), and has issue:

1d +James Alexander; *b* 4 Dec 1964

2d +Lucien Coll; *b* 3 Oct 1966

3d +Aidan John; *b* 23 Oct 1968

1d *Antonia Frances; *b* 4 Oct 1961

2d *Joanna Theresa; *b* 28 Oct 1962

1c Cecilia Anne; *b* 2 Aug 1941; *educ* Girton Coll Cambridge

2b David William; *b* 24 March, *d* 16 June 1914

1b *Katherine Frances LINDSAY later LINDSAY-MacDOUGALL (1949) [Miss Katherine Lindsay-MacDougall, Innisaig, Ardfern, Argyll]; *b* 26 Dec 1915; MA, BLitt Oxon, late 1st Offr WRNS, Curator Mss. Nat Maritime Museum, Greenwich, 1945–59

4a John Colin Howard, DL, JP Clackmannanshire; *b* 27 Dec 1877; Capt RN WW I 1914–19, Legion of Honour; *m* 8 Aug 1918 Katherine Claudia Bruce (*d* 25 April 1952), yst dau of Claud Hamilton Hamilton, of Dunbartonshire, and *dsp* 17 Jan 1954

5a David Howard, JP; *b* 4 June 1882; Capt RGA (Res), served WWs I and II (despatches), Croix de Guerre with Palms; chm Lambeth Juvenile Ct; *d* unm 28 July 1961

1a Mary Haddo, LRAM; *b* 2 Oct 1873; *d* unm 14 Jan 1961

2a Margaret Louisa; *b* 22 Aug 1880; *d* unm 14 Nov 1949

(2) Walter James; *b* 28 Sept 1847; Lt-Col late Rifle Bde; *m* 23 April 1883 Henrietta Julia (*d* 30 July 1933), dau of FitzMaurice Gustavus Bloomfield, of Co Waterford, and *d* 12 May 1922, leaving issue:

1a Frances Ruby Vera; *m* 21 July 1909 (*divorce* 1923, resumed maiden name 1926) Ralph Harding Peto (*d* 3 Sept 1945), est s of William Herbert Peto, and *d* 27 July 1951, leaving issue (*see* PETO, Bt)

(3) Alfred; *b* 7 April 1853; *m* 7 Nov 1882 Isabel Katherine (*d* 3 Dec 1935), dau of Rev George Barons Northcote, Rector Feniton, Devon, and *d* 2 April 1901, leaving issue:

1a Humphrey George Maurice LINDSAY later BROUN-LINDSAY (added on marriage) (Sir), ktd 1947, DSO (1919); DL, JP E Lothian (V-Lt 1949–64); *b* 23 Oct 1888; *educ* Cheltenham; Maj KOSB, Bde Maj France and Italy WW I 1918–19, DAA and QMG Italy 1919–20, DAAG Egypt 1920–21, Memb Roy Co Archers, Pres CCs Assoc Scotland 1946–47; MP Partick 1924–49; *m* 26 July 1921 Edith Christian Broun, OBE (1965), dau of John George Alexander Baird, of Wellwood, Muirkirk, and *d* 23 June 1964, leaving issue:

1b Colin George; *b* 4 Nov 1926; *educ* Eton; Capt Lothians and Border Horse (TA) and Gren Gds; *m* 4 Aug 1952 *Countess Beatrice d'Ursel, dau of Count Conrad d'Ursel, of Château de Moulbaix, Belgium, and *d* 1989, leaving issue:

1c +Ludovic David; *b* 12 Jan 1954; *educ* Ampleforth

1c *Christian Georgiana; *b* 30 Dec 1956

1a Margaret Frances Catherine; *d* unm 30 July 1954

2a *Violet Isabella Harriet; *b* 1886; *m* 12 Aug 1915 Arnold Churchill, 3rd s of Rev William Henry Churchill, MA. He *d* 28 March 1964

(4) Leonard Cecil Colin, JP; *b* 23 June 1857; FSA; Chamberlain to TH POPEs LEO XIII, PIUS X, BENEDICT XV and PIUS XI; Priv Sec to Earl Marshal for Coronation 1902, memb Lloyd's 1887–1941; *m* 23 Jan 1902 Clare Mary Elizabeth (*d* 26 April 1950), est dau of Col Francis Baynham Vaughan, DL, of Courtfield, Herefs, and *dsp* 15 Oct 1941

(5) Claud Reginald (Very Rev); *b* 9 Nov 1861; Domestic Chamberlain to TH POPEs LEO XIII, PIUS X and BENEDICT XV; *d* 23 July 1918

(1) Isabella; *b* 1 April 1849; *m* 22 Oct 1878 Frederick Butler Molineux Montgomerie, barrister, and *d* 4 July 1930, leaving issue. He *d* 11 Nov 1913

(2) Alexina Frances; *m* 2 July 1878 Col E J T Ross, of Bladensburg, RE, and *d* 26 Sept 1897, leaving issue. He *d* 25 April 1923

The 24th/7th EARL's est son,

ALEXANDER WILLIAM CRAWFORD LINDSAY, **25th Earl of Crawford** and **8th Earl of Balcarres**; *b* 16 Oct 1812; *educ* Eton and Trin Coll Cambridgeridge; author: *The Lives of the Lindsays* and *The History of Christian Art*; *m* 23 July 1846 Margaret (*d* 28 Dec 1909), er dau of Lt-Gen James Lindsay of Balcarres (*see* above), and *d* 13 Dec 1880, leaving issue:

1 JAMES LUDOVIC, **26th/9th Earl**

1 Alice Frances; *m* 17 April 1873 Col George Bramston Archer-Houblon, of Hallingbury Place, Essex, and Welford Park, Berks, and *d* 28 Sept 1915, leaving issue. He *d* 9 Nov 1913

2 Margaret Elizabeth; *m* 8 Jan 1870 Lewis Ashurst Majendie, of Hedingham Castle, Essex, and *d* 4 Jan 1912, leaving issue. He *d* 22 Oct 1885

3 Mary Susan Félicie; *m* 9 May 1878 Hon Frederick George Lindley WOOD later MEYNELL, yst s of Viscount Halifax (*see* HALIFAX, E), and *d* 27 Nov 1937, leaving issue

4 Anne Catharine Sybil; *m* 22 Nov 1883 Hon Francis Bowes-Lyon, of Ridley Hall, Bardon Mill, Northumberland, s of 13th Earl of Strathmore and Kinghorne (*qv*), and *d* 15 Dec 1936, leaving issue

5 Jane Evelyn; *b* 14 May 1862; *d* unm 2 Jan 1948

6 Mabel; *d* unm

The 25th/8th EARL's only son,

JAMES LUDOVIC LINDSAY, **26th Earl of Crawford** and **9th Earl of Balcarres**, KT (1891), VD, JP Lancs and Aberdeenshire; *b* 28 July 1847; *educ* Eton and Trin Coll Cambridge; Lt Gren Gds, MP (C) Wigan 1874–80, Hon LLD Edin 1882, FRS 1878, FSA 1885, Tstee Br Museum, Pres Roy Astronomical Soc 1878–80, Hon Col 5th Bn Manchester Regt, KGStJ, Cdr Legion of Honour, Dep for Gt Steward of Scotland Coronations 1902 and 1911; *m* 22 July 1869 Emily Florence (*d* 15 Jan 1934), 2nd dau of Col Hon Edward Bootle-Wilbraham (*see* SKELMERSDALE, B), and *d* 31 Jan 1913, having had issue:

1 DAVID ALEXANDER EDWARD, **27th/10th Earl**

2 Walter Patrick; *b* 13 Feb 1873; T/Capt 12th Service Bn Middx Regt WW I (wounded); civil engr; *m* 26 Nov 1902 (*divorce* 1927) Ruth (*d* 11 Sept 1933), dau of Isaac A Henderson, and *d* 2 July 1936, leaving issue:

(1) Kenneth Andrew; *b* 3 Nov 1903; served WW II 1940–45 S African Forces; *m* 15 Feb 1928 Kathleen Mary (*d* 1975), dau of H E Lovemore, of Queenstown, Cape Province, and *d* Feb 1970, leaving issue:

1a *Patricia Jane; *b* 6 March 1932; *m* 28 Nov 1956 Noël Gwynne Harpur and has issue:

1b *Patrick Leslie Gwynne; *b* 2 Sept 1957

2b *Colin Andrew Lindsay; *b* 26 Sept 1959

(1) Margaret Elspeth; *b* 24 Aug 1905; *educ* LMH Oxford (BA 1928); *m* 8 April 1938 George Shirley Rawlings, Malayan CS (*k* motor accident Afghanistan 8 June 1963), er s of Rev George William Rawlings, MA, and had issue:

1a *Rodney Lindsay; *b* 25 Jan 1939

2a *Walter Parker; *b* 20 June 1940

3a Hugh Lionel; *b* 5 Dec 1944; *k* with his f Afghanistan 8 June 1963

4a *Guy Evelyn (twin); *b* 5 Dec 1944

3 Robert Hamilton; *b* 30 March 1874; Maj 2nd Dragoons, RSG S African War 1899–1900, ADC to Viceroy India; *m* 23 April 1903 Mary Janet (*d* 30 April 1960), 3rd dau of Sir William John Clarke, 1st Bt, and *d* 8 Dec 1911, leaving:

(1) +Robert William Ludovic, OBE (1971); *b* 18 Aug 1905; *educ* Eton and RMC Sandhurst; Maj Gren Gds WW II, Capt Trans-Jordan FF 1931–34; Memb Australian Ho of Reps for Flinders 1954–66; *m* 17 Dec 1946 *Rosemary Catherine Marion, only dau of Sir Robert Knox, of Toorak, Melbourne, and has had issue:

1a Robin David; *b* 5 Oct 1947; *d* 6 June 1965

2a +Andrew William Michael; *b* 9 March 1949

3a +Ian Alexander; *b* 26 April 1957

4a +James Malcolm; *b* 16 June 1961

1a Victoria Mary Jacobena; *b* 9, *d* 10 April 1953

(1) *Joyce Emily [Joyce Lady Lindsay, 40 Ladbroke Rd, W11 3PH]; *b* 5 May 1904; *m* 15 Dec 1932 (*divorce* 1967) Sir Martin Alexander Lindsay, 1st Bt, CBE, DSO (*qv*), and has issue

(2) Rosemary Jean Aline; *b* 8 Oct 1908; *m* 17 July 1928 (*divorce* 1951) William Charles Sanford and had issue. He *d* in a motor accident 6 April 1974

4 Edward Reginald (Rev), MM; *b* 15 March 1876; *educ* Magdalen Coll Oxford (MA); served WW I, RC priest parish of Stone; *d* 17 June 1951

5 Ronald Charles (Sir), PC, GCB, GCMG, CVO; *b* 3 May 1877; Hon LLD Harvard 1933; Dip Serv, Under Sec Finance Egypt 1913–19, Min Plen Paris 1920, Assist Under Sec FO 1921–24, HM Rep then Amb Constantinople 1924–25 and 1925–26 respectively, Amb Berlin 1926–28, PUS FO 1928–30, Amb Washington 1930–39, Grand Offr Order Nile; *m* 1st 18 March 1909 Martha (*d* 28 April 1918), dau of Senator James Donald Cameron, of Pennsylvania; *m* 2nd 14 July 1924 Elizabeth Sherman (*d* 3 Sept 1945), dau of Colgate Hoyt, of New York, and *dsp* 21 Aug 1945

6 Lionel, MC; *b* 20 July 1879; *educ* Charterhouse and Trin Coll Cambridge; Capt 16th Serv Bn KRRC WW I (despatches), Legn Honour; *m* 25 Oct 1921 Kathleen Yone (*d* 16 May 1970), er dau of Sir John Gordon Kennedy, KCMG (*see* AILSA, M), and *d* 18 Aug 1965, leaving issue:

(1) +Colin Paul [Colin Lindsay Esq, Hambrook House, Chichester, W Sussex PO18 8UD], FCA; *b* 6 Nov 1922; *educ* Eton and New Coll Oxford; *m* 10 Sept 1965 *Jennifer Ann, only dau of Capt Thomas Marcus Brownrigg, CBE, DSO, RN, of Vann House, Finchampstead, Berks, and has issue:

1a +Christopher Ronald; *b* 16 Sept 1957; *m* 1986 *Anna Giulia, dau of Andrea Orsini Baroni, of Florence, and has issue:

1b +Alexander Cosmo; *b* 7 Aug 1995

1b *Giulia Joyce; *b* 16 Aug 1988

2b *Francesca Sophia Katherine; *b* 18 Jan 1993

2a +Andrew Mark; *b* 26 Nov 1962; *m* 21 Jan 1995 *Katharine Annabel, est dau of David Weaver, of Guildford

1 Evelyn Margaret, OBE (1920); *b* 8 May 1870; LGStJ, Silver Jubilee Medal 1935 and Coronation Medal 1937; *m* 9 Feb 1895 James Francis Mason, JP, of Eynsham Hall, Oxon, only s of James Mason, JP, of Eynsham Hall, and *d* 3 April 1944, leaving issue (*see* KINTORE, E). He *d* 2 April 1929

The 26th/9th EARL's son,

DAVID ALEXANDER EDWARD LINDSAY, **27th Earl of Crawford** and **10th Earl of Balcarres**, KT, PC (1916), DL Lancs; *b* 10 Oct 1871; *educ* Eton and Magdalen Coll Oxford (MA, Hon Fell 1923), Hon LLD St Andrews 1911, Hon LLD Manchester 1923, Hon Col 5th Bn Manchester Regt, Capt 1st Vol Bn Manchester Regt, Offr Order Leopold of Belgium, served RAMC WW I 1915, Chllr Manchester U 1923–40, Hon DCL Cambridge 1924, Hon LLD Edin 1926, Hon DLitt Liverpool 1928, FRS 1924, FSA Lond, FSA Scot, FRIBA, Tstee Nat Portrait Gallery and Br Museum, memb Cncl Br Sch Rome, Chm Roy Fine Arts Commn, Jr Ld Treasury 1903–05, MP (C) Chorley 1895–1913, Pres Bd of Ag and Fisheries 1916, Ld

Privy Seal 1916–19, Chllr Duchy of Lancaster 1919–21, First Commr Works and Public Bldgs 1921, Min Tport with Cabinet seat 1922; *m* 25 Jan 1900 Constance Lillian (*d* 8 Jan 1947), yr dau and coheir of Sir Henry Carstairs Pelly, 3rd Bt (*qv*), and *d* 8 March 1940, having had issue:

1 DAVID ALEXANDER ROBERT, **28th/11th Earl**

2 James Louis; *b* 16 Dec 1906; *educ* Eton and Magdalen Coll Oxford; Maj KRRC WW II, MP N Devon 1955–59; *m* 26 April 1933 *Hon Bronwen Mary Scott-Ellis, est dau of 8th Baron Howard de Walden (*qv*), and *d* 27 Aug 1997, leaving:

(1) +Hugh John Alexander [Hugh Lindsay Esq, The Old Rectory, Litton Cheney, Dorset DT2 9AH]; *b* 30 July 1934; *educ* Eton and Magdalen Coll Oxford; ACA, late 2nd Lt Black Watch; *m* 7 Oct 1961 *(Constance) Carolyn, yr dau of Maj Sir Charles James Buchanan, 4th Bt (*qv*), and has issue:

1a +David Charles [David Lindsay Esq, 26 Avondale Pk Gdns, London W11]; *b* 3 Sept 1962; *educ* Eton and Southampton U; chartered accountant

2a +Alastair James [Alastair Lindsay Esq, Alexander Wood House, Sotterley, Suffolk NR34 8EZ]; *b* 24 Aug 1964; *educ* Eton and Southampton U; chartered accountant; *m* 1992 *Heather J, dau of Denis Adair, of Newtownabbey, Co Antrim, and has:

1b +James Oliver; *b* 23 Oct 1995

1b *Polly Alexandra; *b* 7 Sept 1997

3a +Robert Hugh; *b* 12 March 1967; *educ* Eton and Reading U; Maj Scots Gds; *m* 8 April 1995 *Joanna, dau of Stuart Shoesmith, and has:

1b *Eliza Sophie Paget; *b* 19 Oct 1996

1a *Serena Clare [Mrs Matthew Jones, 59 Oakworth Rd, London W10 6DF]; *b* 18 March 1970; *educ* St Andrews U and Homerton Coll Cambridge; *m* 13 April 1996 *Dr Matthew Jones, BSc, MPhil, PhD, s of Prof Glyn Jones

(2) +Alexander Thomas [Col Alexander Lindsay, The Manor, Yatesbury, Calne, Wilts SN11 8YE]; *b* 18 Dec 1936; *educ* Eton and Magdalen Coll Oxford (MA); Col 17th/21st Lancers; *m* 31 Dec 1966 *(Jessie) Miranda Cecilia, dau of Col John Anthony Tristram Barstow, DSO, TD, DL, and has issue:

1a +James Alexander Tristram; *b* 29 Oct 1968; *educ* Eton

2a +Roderick Charles; *b* 27 Sept 1970; *educ* Eton and London U

3a +Felix Thomas; *b* 18 July 1973; *educ* Eton and Bristol U

(3) +Stephen James [Lt-Col Stephen Lindsay, Invermoidart, Acharacle, Argyll PH36 4LR]; *b* 2 March 1940; *educ* Eton and RMA Sandhurst; Lt-Col Black Watch; *m* 8 Jan 1966 *Margaret Ann, yr dau of Maj John Henry Courthope Powell and Mrs John William Gardner Hume (*see* SPENCER-NAIRN, Bt), and has issue:

1a +Richard Stephen; *b* 18 Feb 1969; *educ* Eton and St Catherine's Coll Oxford; *m* 8 Feb 1997 *Xanthe Lorraine Critchett

2a +Charles Ludovic; *b* 24 April 1974; *educ* Eton and St Andrews

3a +Andrew James Ronald; *b* 1977; *educ* Eton and BNC Oxford

1a *Jane Margaret [Mrs Charles Graham, 56 Chepstow Rd, London W2 5BE]; *b* 1966; *educ* Edinburgh U; *m* 1991 *Charles R Graham, s of Maj Stephen Graham, of Flint House, Goodworth, Hants, and has:

1b *Cosmo Stephen Buckle; *b* 5 Sept 1995

2b *Ludovic James Buckle; *b* 18 Aug 1997

(1) *Julia Margaret [Mrs Peter Barton, 3 Aubrey Rd, London W8 7JJ]; *b* 24 Sept 1941; *m* 7 Sept 1963 *(Malcolm) Peter Speight Barton, yr s of Maj Michael Barton, 1st Green Jackets, and has issue:

1a *Henry James; *b* 5 July 1967; *educ* Eton and Durham U

2a *Christopher Charles; *b* 10 Nov 1970; *educ* Eton and Durham U

1a *Fenella Jane; *b* 10 March 1965; *educ* Benenden and Exeter U; *m* 1996 *Nicholas Clements, s of Arthur Clements

1 Margaret Cynthia, ARRC; *b* 27 June 1902; *m* 18 Dec 1928 Lt-Col Henry Cyril Harker Illingworth, MC, JP, KRRC (*d* 17 July 1979), s of Harry Holden Illingworth, JP, of Wyndale

2 (Cynthia) Anne; *b* 21 June 1904; *m* 1st 12 Nov 1931 Per Erik Folke Arnander, First Sec Swedish Legation Rome (*d* as the result of a motor accident 26 Feb 1933), and has issue:

(1) *Christopher James Folke; *b* 22 Dec 1932; *educ* Harrow and Oriel Coll Oxford (BA 1956); *m* 7 April 1961 *Pamela Primrose, 2nd dau of Lt-Col David McKenna, OBE, by Lady Cecilia Elizabeth, est dau of 9th Earl of Albemarle (*qv*), and has two s and a dau

2 (cont.) Lady Anne Arnander *m* 2nd 2 April 1934 Giovannia Fummi (*d* 29 June 1970), s of Pietro Fummi, and *d* 5 Jan 1997, having had further issue:

(1) *Francesca Giovanna Maria; *b* 27 Jan 1935; *educ* St Andrews U (MA 1956); *m* 28 June 1961 *Christopher Robin St Quintin Wall (*see* PEEL, E) and has:

1a *Dominic John St Quintin; *b* 21 June 1964

1a *Camilla Mary; *b* 10 May 1962; *m* 1990 *Charles Ranfurly Plunkett-Ernle-Drax (*see* DUNSANY, B), and has issue

3 Elizabeth Patricia; *b* 15 Sept 1908; *d* unm 4 Feb 1937

4 *Mary Lilian; *b* 27 Sept 1910; *m* 18 Dec 1930 1st Viscount Dilhorne (*qv*) and has issue

5 Katharine Constance; *b* 26 Aug 1912; *m* 30 June 1936 Sir Godfrey Nicholson, 1st and last Bt (*see* NICHOLSON OF WINTERBOURNE, B), and *d* 19–, leaving issue

6 *Barbara [The Lady Barbara Hurst, Porters Farm, Rusper, Horsham, W Sussex]; *b* 31 Dec 1915; *m* 23 May 1939 Col Richard Lumley Hurst (*d* 26 Feb 1962), Roy Sussex Regt (TA), barrister, s of Sir Cecil James Barrington Hurst, GCMG, KCB, and has issue:

(1) *Robert Andrew; *b* 1945; *m* 1977 *Cristina, er dau of J J Couper Edwards, of Rusper Nunnery, Horsham, W Sussex, and has issue:

1a *Andrew; *b* 1981

1a *Sarah; *b* 1978

2a *Mary; *b* 1982

(1) *Elizabeth; *b* 1940; *m* 1967 *Angus Hugh Gilroy, memb Roy Co Archers, of Grainfold, Five Oaks, Billingshurst, W Sussex, and has issue:

1a *Fergus Hugh; *b* 1969

1a *Margaret Cecilia; *b* 1970

(2) *Cecilia Barbara; *b* 1944; *m* 1968 *Alastair Robertson Goodlad, PC, MP, of Common Farm, Rhuddal Heath, Tarporley, Cheshire, and has issue:

1a *Magnus James; *b* 1972; *educ* Eton and Oriel Coll Oxford

2a *William Duff; *b* 1974; *educ* Eton and Pembroke Coll Oxford

(3) *Katharine Constance [Mrs Noel Gibbs, Combend Manor, Elkstone, Cheltenham, Glos GL53 9PT]; *b* 1948; *m* 1st 8 Oct 1975 Donald M Corbett (*d* 1987), yst son of R A Corbett, and has issue:

1a *Alexander James; *b* 1977

1a *Clare Barbara; *b* 1978

(3) (cont.) Mrs Katharine Corbett *m* 2nd 1991, as his 2nd w *(Peter) Noel Houldsworth Gibbs (*see* ALDENHAM and HUNSDON OF HUNSDON, B)

The 27th/10th EARL's er s,

DAVID ALEXANDER ROBERT LINDSAY, **28th Earl of Crawford** and **11th Earl of Balcarres**, KT (1955), GBE (1951), DL (Fife 1953); *b* 20 Nov 1900; *educ* Eton and Magdalen Coll Oxford (BA 1922); MP (U) Lonsdale 1924–40, PPS to Min Ag and Fisheries 1924 and Min Health 1931–40; Tstee: Tate Gallery 1932–37, Nat Gallery 1935–41, 1945–52 and 1953–60 (Chm 1938–41 and 1945–49) and Br Museum 1940–73; memb Standing Commn Museums and Galleries 1937–52, Chm Tstees Nat Galleries Scotland 1952–72, Chm Roy Fine Arts Commn 1943–57 and Tstees Nat Library Scotland 1944, Rector St Andrews U 1952–55, Chm Nat Trust, Chm Nat Art Collections Fund 1945, Dep Govr Bank of Scotland, Tstee Pilgrim Trust 1949–75, Hon LLD St Andrews and Cambridge, Hon LittD: Manchester, Exeter 1956 and Amherst Coll USA, Hon DCL Oxon, Hon FRIBA, Hon FRSA, Hon FRSE, Hon RA, Hon Memb Faculty Advocates 1956; *m* 9 Dec 1925 Mary Katherine (*d* 20 Nov 1994), 3rd dau of Lord Richard Cavendish (*see* DEVONSHIRE, D), and *d* 13 Dec 1975, leaving issue:

1 ROBERT ALEXANDER LINDSAY, **29th and present Earl of Crawford and 12th and present Earl of Balcarres**

2 Patrick; *b* 14 Nov 1928; *educ* Eton and Magdalen Coll Oxford; 2nd Lt Scots Gds; dir Christie, Manson & Woods (head Old Masters dept); *m* 16 Dec 1955 *Lady Amabel Mary Maud Yorke [The Lady Amabel Lindsay, 12 Lansdowne Rd, London W11], est dau of 9th Earl of Hardwicke (*qv*), and *d* 1986, leaving issue:

(1) +(Alexander) Ludovic; *b* 16 Sept 1957; *m* 10 Dec 1994 *Lucy, er dau of Richard Davenhill, of Belbroughton, Stourbridge, Worcs, and has

1a +Merlin Edward; *b* 29 Dec 1997

(2) +James Richard; *b* 4 March 1961; *m* 14 Feb 1995 *Arabella, dau of Gavin Tait and Mrs Humphrey Swire, and has issue:

1a +Luke; *b* 24 Aug 1996

(3) +Valentine; *b* 6 Oct 1962; formerly bass guitarist with pop group The Business Connection, now with Viz (promotional company); *m* 1990 *Hayley, dau of Rex Whittome, of Peterborough, and has issue:

1a +Patrick Andrew; *b* Oct 1995

(1) *Laura Mary; *b* 10 Oct 1956

3 +Thomas Richard [The Hon Thomas Lindsay, The Old Rectory, Ashmore, Salisbury, Wilts SP5 5AG]; *b* 18 Feb 1937; *educ* Eton; 2nd Lt Scots Gds; *m* 20 April 1961 *(Sarah) Virginia (*see* BARRY, Bt), only dau of George Nigel Capel Cure, TD, JP, DL, of Blake Hall, Ongar, Essex, and has issue:

(1) +Ivan James; *b* 8 June 1962; *m* 1992 (*divorce* 1994) Julie, dau of Mads Gad, of Denmark, and has:

1a Maximilian James; *b* 9 Sept 1993; *d* 7 Sept 1995

(2) +Constantine David; *b* 14 Aug 1966; *m* 20 Jan 1996 *Samantha, dau of Harry Asprey

(3) +Jason Richard; *b* 9 July 1968

(1) *Alexandra Mary; *b* 10 March 1964; *m* 26 May 1990 *Marcus Basil Ziani de Ferranti (*see* TEMPLE OF STOWE, E) and has:

1a *Thomas Ziani; *b* 5 May 1994

2a *Augustus Ziani; *b* 24 Jan 1997

1a *Polly; *b* 25 May 1992

(2) *Sophia Victoria; *b* 8 Oct 1971

CRAWLEY-BOEVEY

Arms: Erm. on a fess az., between three cranes ppr. a saltire couped between two cross crosslets fitchée or (for CRAWLEY); on a chief erm. a bend gu., charged with three gouttes d'or, between two martlets sa. (for BOEVEY). **Crest:** On a mount vert a crane ppr., collared, beaked and holding in the dexter foot a saltire or.
Motto: *Esse quam videri* ('To be rather than seem').
Creation: Bt. (GB) 22 Jan 1784.

SIR THOMAS MICHAEL BLAKE CRAWLEY-BOEVEY, 8TH BT, of Highgrove, Co Glos [Sir Thomas Crawley-Boevey Bt, Trebanau, Cilycwm, Llandovery, Dyfed SA20 0HP]; *b* 29 Sept 1928, *s* f 1968; *educ* Wellington and St John's Coll Cambridge (MA); 2nd Lt Durham LI 1947–48, with Shipping Agents 1952–61 and Consumer Assoc 1961–82, ed: *Money Which?* 1968–76, *Which?* 1978–82, ed-in-ch *Which?* magazines 1980–82, memb cncl Insur Ombudsman Bureau 1985–, author: *Buying, Selling and Owning Shares* (1987), *Finance your Future* (1989); *m* 16 Feb 1957 Laura (*d* 1979), est dau of Jan Pouwels Coelingh, of Wassenaar, Holland, and has issue:

1 +THOMAS HYDE; *b* 26 June 1958
2 +William Walstan; *b* 30 May 1960

Lineage (of Barrow): THOMAS BARROW, of Awre and Field Court, Hardwicke, Glos; living 1641; f of:

THOMAS BARROW, of Field Court; *m* Margaret, widow of John Pope, of Bristol, sis of Sir John Knight, Sheriff Bristol 1681, and dau of John Knight, Mayor Bristol, and had, with other issue:

1 THOMAS BARROW, of Field Court; *m* Ann dau of William Hayward, of Quedegeley, Glos, and *d* 1736, leaving an only dau and heiress:
(1) ELEANOR; *m* Rev Thomas Savage, MA (descended from the SAVAGEs of Rock Savage, Cheshire), Rector Standish, Glos, and *d* 1760 aged 60, leaving:
1a ANN, 2nd dau but eventually heir; *m* **Sir Thomas Crawley-Boevey, 2nd Bt** (*see below*)
2 CHARLES BARROW, of St Christophers; *m* Elizabeth Harris, and, *d c* 1743, leaving, with a dau Elizabeth (*d* unm):
(1) **Sir Charles Barrow, 1st Bt** (GB), so *cr* 22 Jan 1784, with remainder, failing his issue male, to his kinsman Thomas Crawley-Boevey (*see below*); MP Gloucester 1751–89); *m* Mary (*d* 1778), dau of Daniel Randall, of Gloucester, and *dsp* 10 Jan 1789

Lineage (of Crawley): JOHN CRAWLEY, of Luton, Beds, *s* his bro Edward on or after 20 Dec 1544; *d* shortly afterwards, leaving issue:

1 Richard, of Stoppisley, Luton; ancestor of the CRAWLEYs of Nether Crawley, Luton, and Northaw and Stockwood Pk, Beds
2 William; living 1544
3 Thomas, of Dunstable Lane, Luton; *m* Elizabeth widow of — Parett, and *d* 1581/2, having had issue (with three daus, Mary, Elizabeth and Judith, and two other sons, Richard and Abraham):
(1) Thomas, of Preston, King's Walden, Herts; *m* Anne — and *d* at a great age 1648, leaving:
1a Thomas, of King's Walden; *m* 28 June 1593 Sarah Basshope and *dvp* Nov 1647, having had issue (with two daus, Mary *d* unm 1669, and Sarah *m* 1647 John Hirst, also two est s and a yst s):
1b Robert; *b c* 1601; London grocer 1655; *m* Dec 1629 Elizabeth, dau of John Shipton, London grocer, and *d* in or after 1668, having had (with two daus, Sarah *m* — Hilton, and Mary living unm 1668, also two yr sons John and William):
1c Thomas, of St Dunstan's in-the-East, London, merchant; *b* 1638; *m* 1667 Mary, dau of David Bonnell, of Isleworth, Middx (s of David Bonnell, of Norwich, and cousin of James Bonnell, Accountant-Gen Ireland), by Ann, dau of Andrew Boevey and sis of James Boevey, of Flaxley Abbey, Glos, and *d* March 1714, leaving (with a dau Cornelia *m* Petley Ley, of Deptford, and an er s John, *d* unm in or after 1718):
1d Thomas CRAWLEY later CRAWLEY-BOEVEY (added 1726 on inheriting the Flaxley Abbey estate from his cousin's w Katherine, widow of William Boevey (only s of James Boevey above-mentioned), under William Boevey's will 1692); *m* 2 Feb 1701/2 Susanna (*d* July 1739), dau of John Lloyd, of London, merchant, by Susanna, dau of Thomas Holier, and *d* Feb 1741/2, leaving an est s:
1e Thomas, of Flaxley Abbey; *b* 11 Sept 1709; *m* 14 May 1743 his 1st cousin Susanna (*bur* 5 March 1762), dau and coheir of John Lloyd by Susanna (only child of John White, of Trelogas, Cornwall, by his 2nd w Susanna, dau of John Alway and Anne, dau and heiress of Sir Henry Hastings, of Newington Butts, Surrey, gs of 4th Earl of Huntingdon (*qv*)) and *d* 28 Nov 1769, having had issue:
1f THOMAS (Sir), **2nd Bt**
2f Charles (Rev), LLB, Rector Stowe, Northants; *b* 25 April 1756; *m* 12 Aug 1784 Mary (*d* 31 Oct 1819), dau of George Abraham Gibbs (*see* ALDENHAM and HUNSDON OF HUNSDON, B), and *d* 4 Jan 1849, leaving issue
1f Susanna; *m* 1st Edmund Bastard, of South Warnford, Devon; *m* 2nd 1777 Sir Thomas Hyde Page, RE, and *dsp*. He *d* 20 June 1821, leaving issue
2f Catharina; *m* 12 March 1777 Rev Duke Yonge, of Cornwood, Devon, and had issue

The er son,

Sir Thomas Crawley-Boevey, 2nd Bt; *b* 14 Feb 1745; *m* 20 Feb 1769 Ann Savage (*d* Sept 1816; *see* above) and had (with nine daus):

1 THOMAS (Sir), **3rd Bt**
2 John Lloyd CRAWLEY (Rev), Rector Heyford and Holdenby, Northants; *b* 21 Feb 1775; *m* 21 April 1806 Anne (*d* 2 May 1863), dau of Rev Charles Crawley, BCL, and *d* 18 Oct 1850, having had issue:
(1) John Lloyd (Rev), Vicar Arlingham; *b* 10 June 1808; *m* 25 June 1839 Mary Elizabeth (*d* 11 May 1880), dau of Rev John Sayer, of Arlingham, and *d* 30 Aug 1848, leaving issue:
1a John Lloyd; *b* 1 Nov 1845; *d* 11 Feb 1922
1a Mary Elizabeth Sayer
2a Ellen Sayer; *d* unm 17 June 1920
3a Selina Charlotte Sayer; *d* unm 11 Feb 1919
(2) George; *b* 8 Nov 1810; *m* 8 Aug 1850 Emily Ann Frances, 2nd dau of Rt Rev William Grant Broughton, DD, Bp Sydney, and *dsp* 2 Sept 1854
(3) Chares Gibbs, Cdr RN; *b* 17 April 1812; *dsp* 19 Dec 1892
(4) Henry (Rev), MA, Rector Stowe Nine Churches, Northants; *b* 7 July 1813; *m* 1st 15 Jan 1857 Emma (*d* 6 May 1858), dau of John Tollington, of Leicester; *m* 2nd 4 Oct 1870 his cousin Mary (*d* 1892), dau of Rev Charles Crawley, and *d* 1895 having by his 1st w had issue:
1a Emma Anne; *m* 1894 Fleet-Surgn Charles Francis Newland, RN, and had issue
(5) Thomas William (Rev) MA, Rector Heyford, Northants; *b* 21 Aug 1815; *m* 5 May 1853 Hannah Elizabeth (*d* 1892), dau of Jeffrey Carter, of Heyford, and *d* 1897, leaving, with other issue:
1a Thomas William, Clerk FO; *b* 12 Feb 1854; *m* 23 Sept 1875 Emily (*m* 2nd 1888 Rev George Nedham, Rector Kirkbride, Cumberland; *d* 1927), est dau of Walter Mingay Rochfort, of Acton, Middx, and *d* 1885, leaving issue:
1b Thomas Charles Rochfort; *b* 1882; Lt Pembroke Artillery W Div RA; *m* 1 June 1914 Margaret, 2nd dau of Charles McKerrow, MB, of Croft House, Workington, Cumberland, and *d* 25 May 1963, leaving issue:
1c Thomas Bryson; *b* 29 March 1918; *m* 26 July 1947 *Christina, only dau of H Vollweiter, of Toronto, Canada, and *d* 1996, leaving:
1d +Thomas Henry; *b* 8 Oct 1958
2d +Christopher John; *b* 1963
1d *Gilda Caroline; *b* 26 Jan 1951
2d *Carla Susan; *b* 18 May 1953
3d *Lisa Marlene; *b* 21 May 1956
2c +James Bryan [James Crawley Esq, 139 Kingston Row, Winnipeg 8, Manitoba R2M 0S7, Canada]; *b* 8 Feb 1921; *educ* U of Toronto; RAF and RCAF WW II; *m* 1964 *Edith Janice Doreen, dau of Charles Player Halls, of Regina, Saskatchewan, and has:
1d +Devin Charles Bryan; *b* 19 May 1968; *educ* U of Manitoba (BA); *m* 1993 *Heather Cullen
1c *Margery [Miss Margery Crawley, 1910–70 Garry St, Winnipeg, Manitoba R3C 1E9, Canada]; *b* 19 April 1915
2b John Lloyd (Rev Canon); *b* 1884; *educ* Selwyn Coll Cambridge (MA); Rector Harrington, Cumberland, 1945–48 and Kirkandrews on Eden 1948–51, Sr CF WW I (wounded, despatches); *m* 18 Oct 1921 Marion (*d* 12 March 1961), 3rd dau of Charles McKerrow, MB, of Croft House, Workington, and *d* 30 Sept 1951, having had issue:
1c +John Lloyd Rochfort (Rev) [The Rev John Crawley, Cove, Tarbert, Argyll PA29 6SX]; *b* 31 July 1922; *educ* Selwyn Coll Cambridge (MA) and Cuddesdon Theological Coll Oxford; served WW II MN, Vicar St Anthony's Newcastle 1953–59, Chaplain RAF 1959, Vicar Longhoughton and Rector Howick 1959, Master St Thomas the Martyr Newcastle and Chaplain Newcastle U 1969–74, Rector Cockermouth 1974–86; *m* 1947 *Isabell, 2nd dau of William Robson, of Reaveley Powburn, Alnwick, and has issue:
1d +Michael John; *b* 9 March 1949; *educ* Duke's Sch and Edin U; PhD, DIC; *m* 1971 *Greer Annie, only dau of George Williams, of New London, Conn, USA
2c Michael; *b* 14 Nov 1923; Trooper RTR WW II; *ka* Normandy 27 June 1944
1c *Margaret [Mrs William Dickinson, The Grange, 8 Osborne Terrace, Edinburgh 12]; *b* 6 Nov 1924; *m* 5 March 1946 Maj William Vivian Dickinson, MBE, RA (*d* 1994), and has issue:
1d *John [John Dickinson Esq, 16 Conduit Rd, Sheffield]; *b* 19 May 1948; *m* 1st (*divorce* 1973) Dianne Warby; *m* 2nd 1981 *Christine Gregory
2d *Michael [Michael Dickinson Esq, 16a Horsebrook Park, Calne, Wilts SN11 8EY]; *b* 19 Dec 1955; *m* 1982 *Rachel Garson

3d *Richard; *b* 30 May 1960

1d *Susan (Rev) [The Rev Susan Hope, The Vicarage, 23 Housley Park, Sheffield S35 2UE]; *b* 29 Dec 1949; Priest 1994; Priest-in-charge St Margaret and St Thomas Brightside, Vicar St Margaret and St Thomas Brightside with Wincobank 1995 and St John the Baptist Chapeltown, Sheffield 1997; *m* 1971 (*divorce* 1974) Kenneth Hope

1b Cecilia Emily Augusta Elizabeth; *d* unm 10 March 1955

2a Antony Frazer Hughes Reddall; *b* 1 Aug 1855; *d* 19 Jan 1931

3a Henry Hughes (Rev), Rector Stowe Nine Churches, Northants, RD Weedon 1904–13, MA Oxon; *b* 7 Aug 1856; *m* 18 June 1896 Mary Louisa (*d* 17 March 1912), dau of George Carter, of Stone Hall, Wallingford, and *d* 1921, leaving issue:

1b Rosa Mary Edith; *b* 30 June 1900; *m* 4 April 1929 Norman Horace Leach (*d* 24 July 1960), est s of Norman Leach, of Newport Pagnell, and had issue:

1c *Henry Norman Richard; *b* 21 April 1932; *m* 31 July 1964 *Caroline, dau of C W G Lacey, of Solis 1282, Hurlingham, Argentina, and has issue:

1d *Anthony Norman; *b* 1965

2c *Allan Lloyd; *b* 18 Jan 1936; *m* June 1963 *Denise Merle, dau of Eric G Finlay, of Chaconne, East Horsley, Surrey

3c *Simon Marshall; *b* 8 March 1937

1c *Frances Rosalind; *b* 14 Feb 1930; *m* 26 Nov 1955 Thomas only son of Hubert Smith, of Great Harwood, Lancs, and has issue:

1d *Gavin Mark Crawley; *b* 1960

1d *Janet Frances Crawley; *b* 25 Aug 1956

2d *Karen Rosanna Crawley; *b* 24 Feb 1958

3d *Deirdre Mary Anne Crawley; *b* 9 Dec 1962

2b Violet Sylvia Bathurst; *b* 16 Aug 1903; *m* 21 Dec 1946 Stanley Rutherford Gibson, only son of John Gibson, of Bishopwearmouth, Sunderland, Co Durham

4a George Burridge; *b* 10 March 1858; Lt-Col late IA; *m* 1st 1882 (*divorce* 1887) Kate Ouseley, dau of Surg-Maj Henry Sherlock, and had issue:

1b George Ouseley; *b* 1883

2b Thomas Henry Ouseley, Capt 4th Bn Worcs Regt; *b* 19 Feb 1885; *m* 6 Feb 1915 Meta Janette Steel (*m* 2nd 20 Dec 1917 Maj Graeme F Raper RFA; *d* 30 July 1953), dau of Robert Grant, of Bengarth, Blairgowrie, and was *ka* 6 May 1915

4a (cont.) Lt-Col George Crawley-Boevey *m* 2nd 1892 Adelaide (*d* 1946), dau of Charles Bell Syer, and *d* 26 Nov 1932

5a Charles Purrier; *b* 20 Aug 1859; *m* 18– Emily Kent, dau of — Hooper, and *d* 1896, leaving issue:

1b Charles Robert Thomas Edmund; *b* 10 Dec 1880

2b Noel George; *b* 1888

1b Lily; *d* young

2b Winifred Ella; *d* 1904

3b Albinia; *b* 18–

4b Hannah Dorothy; *b* 1887

6a John Sayer; *b* 8 March 1867; *m* 1st 1892 Constance Emily (*d* 1919), dau of T Wathen Thompson, of Bedford Park; *m* 2nd Nov 1922 Mary Ward, dau of John Bacon Holton, of Mason, Kentucky, and *d* 19–, having by his 1st w had issue:

1b Constance Elizabeth Vere; *b* April 1893; *d* 1919

(6) Antony Gibbs; *b* 10 Dec 1819; *d* unm 17 Sept 1851

(7) Alfred; *b* 4 Aug 1824; *d* unm 5 Sept 1905

(1) Eleanora; *m* 26 Sept 1833 Henry Norris, of Swalcliffe Park, Banbury, and *d* 14 Feb 1893, leaving issue. He *d* 19 Oct 1889

3 Charles (Rev), Vicar Hartpury, Glos; *b* 28 Nov 1870; *m* 30 Aug 1811 Catherine (*d* 2 Jan 1857), 3rd dau of Rev Duke Yonge, of Cornwood, Devon, by Katherine, dau of Thomas Crawley-Boevey, of Flaxley Abbey (*see* above), and *d* 17 Jan 1856, having had, with other issue:

(1) Charles Yonge (Rev), Rector Taynton Glos, Minor Canon Gloucester; *b* 2 March 1813; *m* 3 June 1845 Harriet (*d* 1889), only dau of James Wintle, of Gloucester, and *d* 5 June 1876, leaving issue:

1a Charles James; *b* 2 March 1850; *m* 4 Oct 1880 Maude Cameron (*d* 4 Dec 1945), dau of Roe Buck, of Cobourg, Ontario, Canada, and *d* 6 April 1920, having had issue:

1b Charles Yonge; *b* 16 Oct 1881; *d* an infant

2b (Charles) Alan; *b* 23 Aug 1887; barrister Manitoba; *m* 19 June 1915 Jean Nairn, only child of David Horn, of Winnipeg, and *d* 1975 leaving issue:

1c +(Charles) David [David Crawley, 1757 N Stanley Ave, Los Angeles, Calif 90046, USA]; *b* 2 July 1916; *educ* U of Manitoba and U of BC (BA 1939); served WW II as F/O RCAF; Im 1st 18 May 1942 (*divorce* 1960) Lois Kathleen, only dau of Francis Ritchie, of Vancouver, BC; *m* 2nd 1965 *Dorothy Fern Friend, of Los Angeles, Calif, and has issue by his 1st w:

1d +(Charles) Peter [Peter Crawley Esq, c/o 830 Sayward Rd, Victoria, BC Canada V8Y 1R4]; *b* 13 Oct 1943; *m* 1st 1963 (*divorce* 1971 Carole Cavalier, of Los Angeles, Calif; *m* 2nd 1987 *Janet Lesley King, of Victoria, BC, and has issue by 1st w:

1e *Theresa Lynn; *b* 1963

2e *Brandi Michelle; *b* 1969

3e *Trista; *b* 1971

2d +(Christopher) David; *b* 10 March 1947; *m* 1st 1972 (*divorce* 1977) Erin McMartin, of Sidney, BC, and has issue:

1e *Aleta; *b* 1974

2d (cont.) David Crawley *m* 2nd 1980 *Victoria Jean Miller, of Ottawa, and has further issue:

1e +Andrew; *b* 1973

2c +Michael [Michael Crawley Esq, 830 Sayward Rd, Victoria, BC, Canada, V8Y 1R4]; *b* 4 July 1919; *educ* Ravenscourt Sch Winnipeg; RCASC WW II

3b Jack, 1st Canadian Mounted Rifles 1st Canadian Expdy Force WW I; *b* 7 Oct 1893; *ka* France 2 June 1916

1b Mary; *b* 27 May 1886; *d* an infant

1a Harriet Maria; *m* 6 April 1875 O H A Nicholls, RA, and had issue

4 George, Capt RN; *b* 25 Dec 1781; *m* Aug 1806 Charlotte (*m* 2nd Thomas Collier Jones, DD, Rector Exeter Coll Oxford), 2nd dau of Rev Duke Yonge, of Cornwood, Devon, by Katherine, dau of Thomas Crawley-Boevey, of Flaxley Abbey (*see* above), and *d* 5 March 1810, leaving an only child:

(1) Georgina; *m* Rev Hugh Polson, of Bourton-on-the-Water

5 William (Rev), Perpetual Curate Flaxley, Glos; *b* 14 Dec 1790; *m* 8 Oct 1822 Charlotte (*d* 9 Aug 1892), 7th dau of Rev Charles Crawley, BCL, and *d* 17 Dec 1858, having had issue:

(1) William Savage; *b* 27 July 1823; *m* 30 April 1857 Clara Marianne (*d* 17 Jan 1913), dau of John Dennil Maddock, DL, of Liscard Manor, Cheshire, and *d* 1892, leaving issue:

1a William Evelyn Maddock; *b* 20 Jan 1859; *m* 1st 29 March 1894 Fanny Gertrude (*d* 8 March 1911), yst dau of Arthur Wellesley Critchley, and had issue:

1b William Asheton; *b* 23 May 1897; Lt RAF WW I; *das* 1917

1a (cont.) William Crawley *m* 2nd 6 Dec 1913 Harriet Gladys, yr dau of Robert Chambres Chambres, and *d* 27 Nov 1926, having by her had further issue:

2b +Evelyn Myles Chambres; *b* 1915

2a John Dennil Maddock; *b* 20 Jan 1861; *m* 28 Oct 1913 Flora (*d* 27 Dec 1928), widow of James Edward Horne and dau of Col R H Beddome, and *d* 17 April 1932

3a Alured Geoffrey Maddock; *b* 1863; *m* 1913 Amelia Kellett, and *d* 12 Dec 1936

4a Francis Herbert Maddock; *b* 1865; *d* 23 March 1916

1a Clara Cecilia Maddock; *m* 10 Dec 1901 Cdr Edmund F Talbot, RN, and *d* 29 Dec 1922. He *d* 2 July 1922

(1) Charlotte Sybella; *m* 18 Sept 1849 John Sayer, barrister, of Arlingham, Glos, and had issue. He *d* 1886

(2) Mary Catherine; *d* unm 1851, aged 22

(3) Joanna Gibbs; *d* unm 21 March 1906

(4) Margaret Susanna; *d* unm 11 Jan 1918

Sir THOMAS *d* 11 Aug 1818; his son,

Sir Thomas Crawley-Boevey, 3rd Bt; *b* 28 Nov 1769; *m* 28 Oct 1807 Albinia (*d* 16 Feb 1835 aged 50), dau of Sir Thomas Hyde Page, RE, by Mary Albinia (his 2nd w), only dau of Capt J Woodward, 70th Regt, and gdau of Rev R Monins, of Ringswould and Charlton, Kent, of the Moninses of Waldershare Park, Kent, and had had issue:

1 Thomas Lloyd; *b* 19 Feb 1811; *d* 15 Feb 1820

2 MARTIN HYDE (Sir), **4th Bt**

3 William John; *b* and *d* 1813

4 John Savage; *b* 23 June 1820; *d* 11 Nov 1835

1 Albinia Anne; *m* 14 Sept 1843 Rev George Barnston Daubeny, est son of Rev George William Daubney, of Seend Ho, Wilts, and *d* 21 Jan 1850, in her 40th year. He *d* 9 March 1869 aged 57

2 Susanna Elizabeth; *d* 16 Sept 1856

3 Matilda Blanche; *m* 1 Aug 1839 William Gibbs, of Tyntesfield, Wraxall, Somerset, and Clyst St George, Devon, and *d* 24 Sept 1887, leaving issue (*see* ALDENHAM and HUNSDON OF HUNSDON, B)

Sir THOMAS *d* 10 Jan 1847; his est surv son,

Sir Martin Hyde Crawley-Boevey, 4th Bt, JP, Verderer Forest of Dean 1847, Capt Glos Yeo Cav 1854, Capt 12th Glos Rifle Vol 1860; *b* 25 May 1812; *m* 9 June 1836 Elizabeth (*d* 9 Aug 1892), est dau of Rev George William Daubeny, of Seend House, Wilts, and had issue:

1 THOMAS HYDE (Sir), **5th Bt**

2 John; *b* 1, *d* 29 July 1838

3 Francis Gibbs; *b* 15 July 1839; *d* unm 16 Dec 1865

4 Walter Daubeny; *b* 13 April 1841; *d* unm 1 Sept 1896

5 Edward Barnston, Lt RA; *b* 29 March 1844; *m* 11 June 1884 Katherine (*m* 2nd 28 Nov 1893 Francis Grinham Howell), 2nd dau of Rev Henry Bolton Power, Vicar Bramley, Surrey, and *dsp* 5 May 1888

6 Arthur William, MA, Oxford, barrister, Bombay CS 1868–93, Fell Bombay U; *b* 12 Aug 1845; *m* 16 Sept 1873 Anna Maria (*d* 23 April 1924), 2nd dau of Gen Sir Robert Phayre, GCB, and 8 July 1913, leaving issue:

(1) Martin, DSO (1918), MC; *b* 17 Sept 1883; *educ* Trin Coll Oxford (BA); Capt and Brev-Maj DCLI, served Somaliland 1908–10 and WW I (despatches); *m* 3 June 1919 Elizabeth Adela (*d* 23 July 1972), dau of Capt Roger Hall, DL, of Narrow Water Castle, Co Down, and widow of Lt-Col Neville Reay Daniell, DSO, DCLI, and *d* 4 Jan 1954, leaving issue:

1a Antony, MBE (1964); *b* 10 Jan 1921; *educ* Repton; Maj 17th/21st Lancers, served WW II with 7th Hus, Palestine 1947–48 and Cyprus 1956–58, DAA and QMG Singapore Mil Forces 1961–64, GSO(2) HQ Scottish Cmd 1964, Fortress Gibraltar 1966–68, Dep Offr i/c RAC Recorders 1968–69, ret 1969; *m* 1st 22 July 1950 (*divorce* 1957) Cynthia Louise (*d* 1988), yst dau of William Hugh Neville Bagot, of Haut de Mont, La Haule, Jersey, CI, and has issue:

1b *Susan Elizabeth Mary [Mrs Peter Hard, Upper Street House, Pulborough, W Sussex RH20 1AF]; *b* 17 Aug 1951; *m* 1980 *Dr Peter Laurence Stanley Hard, est s of Lt Col L F Hard, MBE, MC, and has issue:

1c *Georgina Susan; *b* 1981

2c *Emily Alice; *b* 1984

1a (cont.) Maj Antony Crawley-Boevey *m* 2nd 17 Dec 1960 *Josephine (Josie) Beryl [Mrs Antony Crawley-Boevey, Sunny Cottage, Piddletrenthide, Dorchester, Dorset DT2 7QX], only child of Lt-Col

Nathaniel Henry Kindersley, of Sunny Cottage, Piddletrenthide, and *d* 17 Oct 1996, leaving by her:
1b +Martin Henry; *b* 4 May 1963
2b +Simon Antony; *b* 29 June 1967
2b *Katherine Lucy [Mrs Nicholas Walters, White House Farm, Holnest, Dorset DT9 6HX]; *b* 12 July 1964; *m* 1991 *Nicholas J Walters, er son of Dr P J R Walters, of Clifden, Co Galway, and has:
1c *Charlotte Lucy; *b* 1994
2c *Rebecca Sophie; *b* 16 May 1997
2a Thomas Roger (Tim), Sub-Lt RN WW II; *b* 1 Feb 1922; *ka* in HMS *Tigris* March 1943
3a +Arthur Martin, Capt RA WW II (despatches); *b* 28 May 1924
7 Octavius Charles; *b* 24 Nov 1846; *m* 2 Sept 1871 Maria Francesca, dau of Bernardino de Marga, Judge Corte Superior, Arequipa, Peru, and *d* 15 Feb 1897, having had issue:
(1) Santiago Carlos; *b* 25 July 1872; *m* 18– —, dau of Alamos Cuadra, of Valparaiso, and *d* 1913, leaving issue:
1a Charles; *b* 1897
1a Mary; *b* 1899
(2) Edwardo Maximo; *b* 18 Nov 1875
(3) Alfred Martin; *b* 26 April 1879; *d* 3 March 1880
(1) Maria Margarita Elisa; *d* young
(2) Mary Isabel; *b* 1878; *m* 1904 Frederico de la Fuenta and has ussue:
1a Frederico Francisco; *b* 1906
1a Hilda Carmela; *b* 1911
(3) Rose Agnes; *b* 1880
(4) Victoria; *d* young
(5) Lilian Maude Antonia; *b* 1882
(6) Leonora Octavia; *b* 1884
(7) Blanche Josephita; *b* 1889; *m* 1910 Gerald Bingham, of Arequipa, Peru, and has issue:
1a *Norah Frances; *b* 1912
2a *Dorothy Blanche; *b* 1913
3a *Eileen Gertrude; *b* 1915
4a *Elizabeth Hilda; *b* 1918
(8) Ella Margaret; *b* 1894
(9) Hilda Ines; *b* 1896
8 James Henry; *b* 2 July 1848; *m* 7 Dec 1878 Frances Georgina Hayes (*d* 5 Feb 1929), yst dau of Charles Edmund Hayes Newington, of Ticehust, Sussex, and *d* 18 March 1898, having had issue:
(1) Charles Arthur, Maj RASC (MT) WW I 1914–17 (despatches); *b* 8 Dec 1879; *m* 7 April 1906 Elisabeth Winifred (*d* 24 Oct 1962 aged 87), only surv dau of W Hartley King, of Wollescote Hall, Stourbridge, and *d* 5 Dec 1962, leaving issue:
1a Winifred Daphne; *b* 23 July 1908; *d* unm 14 March 1968
(2) Leslie, Capt Green Howards WW I; *b* 17 Sept 1884; *m* 28 July 1920 Janet Marjorie, 2nd dau of Henry Howard Middleditch, JP, formerly of Tamworth Ho, Derbyshire, and *dsp* 25 July 1945
(3) Richard Owen; *b* 27 Sept 1883; *d* 9 Oct 1888
(1) May Frances; *b* 22 Sept 1881; *m* 14 Oct 1933 Thomas William Goad, est son of Thomas William Goad, FRSA, FRGS, CE, and *dsp* 22 March 1961
9 Richard Lloyd (Rev), Vicar Kirkby St Chad, Liverpool 1906–15; *b* 22 March 1852; *educ* Univ Coll Oxford (MA); *d* 26 April 1928
10 Antony Page; *b* 26 July 1855; *m* 1st 2 July 1889 Agnes Charlotte Mary (*dsp* 8 April 1890), 2nd dau of Sir Samuel White Baker, FRS; *m* 2nd 23 Feb 1904 Blanche (*d* 11 Jan 1939), 3rd dau of Edmund Probyn, of Huntley Manor, Glos, and *d* 16 July 1924
1 Martina Elizabeth; *m* 3 Sept 1868 Rev William Cotton Risley, and *d* 29 May 1891
2 Sybella Mary; *d* unm 12 Aug 1911
Sir MARTIN *d* 14 Oct 1862; his est son,
Sir Thomas Hyde Crawley-Boevey, 5th Bt, JP Glos, High Sheriff 1882, Lt 69th Foot; *b* 2 July 1837; *m* 25 July 1865 Frances Elizabeth (*d* 24 Nov 1905), only dau of Rev Thomas Peters, Rector Eastington, Glos, and had issue:
1 FRANCIS HYDE (Sir), **6th Bt**
2 Edward Martin, Capt Roy Sussex Regt; *b* 26 March 1873; *m* 31 Oct 1905 Rosalie Winifred (*d* Sept 1966), yst dau of Col George Conrad Sartorius, CB, and was *ka* 24 Dec 1914, having had issue:
(1) George Martin; *b* 18 Oct 1906; *d* 7 June 1907
(2) Richard Martin; *b* 31 July 1908; *educ* Chillon Coll Switzerland and St John's Coll Cambridge; citrus grower, apiarist, dir Muden Co-op Co, memb S Africa Citrus Exchange; *m* 1 Sept 1945 Gladys Frances Farrar Young (*d* 14 Dec 1955), and *d* 1977 leaving issue:
1a +Timothy Martin [Timothy Crawley-Boevey Esq, 38 Balfour Rd, Pinetown, Natal 3610, S Africa]; *b* 31 Jan 1949; *m* 1975 *Agnes Avelene Peché and has issue:
1b +Richard Martin; *b* 1979
1b *Karin; *b* 1976
3 Arthur Curtis (Rev), Rector Grendon, Warwicks, 1913–52, Hon Canon Birmingham; *b* 10 July 1874; *educ* New Coll Oxford (MA); *m* 26 Sept 1906 Evelyn Rosalie (*d* 19 Nov 1962), yst dau of Robert Carnegie, of Terenure, Dublin, and *d* 13 Feb 1965, having had issue:
(1) +Robert Arthur (Rev) [The Rev Robert Crawley-Boevey, 3 St Michael's Close, Urchfont, Devizes, Wilts SN10 4QJ]; *b* 22 Oct 1912; *educ* Hertford Coll Oxford (BA 1934, MA 1938); vicar Cuddington with Dinton Bucks 1952–59 and Seer Green, Bucks, 1959, Chaplain RNVR, Rector Waltham on the Wolds Leics 1947–52; *m* 11 April 1947 *Josephine Mary Storrs, yst dau of Joseph Howard, of Holbeache, Trimpley, Worcs, and has issue:
1a +David Alexander [David Crawley-Boevey Esq, Lewins, Shurlock Row, nr Reading, Berks RG10 0PR]; *b* 14 Feb 1948; *m* 1977 *Isabelle Frances Lee, dau of Donald Eyre, of Torquay, and has issue:
1b *Catherine Rosanna; *b* 1979
2b *Sarah Frances; *b* 1982
3b *Julia Alexandra; *b* 1985
2a +Peter Robert [Peter Crawley-Boevey Esq, 25 Elizabeth St, Mentone 3194, Victoria, Australia]; *b* 12 July 1957; *m* 1991 *Joanne Margaret, dau of Ian Kurrle, of Somers, Australia, and has issue:
1b +Robert Ian; *b* 1993
1b *Natasha Margaret; *b* 20 May 1996
1a *Juliet Ann [Mrs Andrew Dean, St Margarets, Willand Rd, Cullompton, Devon EX15 1AP]; *b* 18 June 1950; *m* 1975 *Andrew Dean, and has issue:
1b *Kelvin John; *b* 1985
1b *Jamie Lee; *b* 1986
(1) *Nancy Albinia [Miss Nancy Crawley-Boevey, Sceapea, Sheepy Magna, Atherstone, Warwicks]; *b* 7 Jan 1910
(2) Juliet Blanche; *b* 1 July 1911; *m* Rev Arthur John Ernest Green, RNVR, yst son of H J Green, of Hanwell, and *d* 23 March 1948, leaving issue:
(3) *Marjorie Evelyn [Miss Marjorie Crawley-Boevey SRN, Sceapea, Sheepy Magna, Atherstone, Warwicks]; *b* 2 April 1916; SRN, SCM, HV
(4) *Elizabeth Jocosa [Miss Elizabeth Gatehouse, Sceapea, Sheepy Magna, Atherstone, Warwicks]; *b* 17 May 1918; *educ* Girton Coll Cambridge (BA)
4 Thomas Russell, MA Oxford, T/Capt Glos Regt; *b* 22 March 1880; *d* 30 Aug 1916 of wounds recd in action
1b Albinia Frances; *m* 15 June 1892 Rev Canon William Hartley Carnegie, Sub-Dean Westminster, Rector St Margaret's, Westminster, s of Robert Carnegie, of Terenure, Dublin, and *d* 12 May 1902, leaving five daus.
He *d* 18 Oct 1936
Sir THOMAS *d* 15 March 1912; his est s,
Sir Francis Hyde Crawley-Boevey, 6th Bt, JP, Verderer Forest of Dean; *educ* Ch Ch Oxford (BA); *b* 25 April 1868; *m* 18 March 1896 (Eliza) Barbara Blake (Id 9 Oct 1962 aged 87), only dau of William Valentine Blake McGrath, formerly of Hope Hall, Manchester, and *d* 6 Oct 1928, leaving issue:
1 **Sir Launcelot Valentine Hyde Crawley-Boevey, 7th Bt**, Verderer Forest of Dean; *b* 26 April 1900; *m* 24 Sept 1927 Elizabeth Goodith, dau of Herbert d'Auvergne Innes, late Indian Police, and *d* 4 July 1968, leaving issue:
(1) Sir THOMAS MICHAEL BLAKE CRAWLEY-BOEVEY, **8th and present Bt**
(2) +Anthony Francis d'Auvergne [Anthony Crawley-Boevey Esq, 4 Station Rd, Lydney, Glos]; *b* 2 Jan 1932; *educ* RNC Dartmouth; accountant; *m* 26 Sept 1968 *Ilse Gertrud, 2nd dau of Dr Johannes Felix Potrykus, of Soerabaya, Java

CRAWSHAW

Arms: Arg. three bars wavy az. a cross flory erminois, in chief a fountain. **Crest:** A demi-lion arg., charged on the shoulder with a fountain, holding in the paws a harpoon in bend sinister ppr. **Supporters:** Dexter, a stag; sinister, a horse; both arg. and gorged with a collar wavy az., pendant therefrom an escutcheon erminois charged with a fountain ppr. **Motto:** *Finem respice* ('Consider the end'). **Creations:** Bt. (UK) 9 Feb 1891, B. (UK) 25 Aug 1892.

THE 5TH BARON CRAWSHAW OF CRAWSHAW, Co Lancaster, **AND OF WHATTON**, Co Leicester, and a **Baronet** (David Gerald Brookes) [The Rt Hon The Lord Crawshaw, Little Riste Farm, Long Whatton, Loughborough, Leics]; *b* 14 Sept 1934; *s* bro 1997; *educ* Eton and RAC Cirencester; High Sheriff Leics 1985–86; *m* 27 Oct 1970 *Belinda Mary, dau of George Burgess, of 14 Kirkwood Ave, Sandringham, Melbourne, Australia, and Mrs Joan Allen, of Birling's Colemans Hatch, Sussex, and has:
1 *Susanna; *b* 5 Feb 1974
2 *Amanda; *b* 17 Feb 1975
3 *Elisabeth; *b* 1976
4 *Katharine; *b* 1978

Lineage: THOMAS BROOKS, of Langho, Lancs; living 1610; had, with a yr s (Thomas, *b* 1646):

SAMUEL BROOKS, of Billington, Lancs; *b* 1641; had, with an ers (Edmund, *b* 1693):

THOMAS BROOKS, of Billington; *b* 1696; had, with a dau (Elizabeth, *b* 1730):

JOHN BROOKS, of Waddington, Lancs; *b* 1727; had:

WILLIAM BROOKS, of Whalley, Lancs; banker; *b* 1763; *m* 29 Dec 1785 Sarah (*d* 18 June 1810), dau of Richard Greenall, of Langho, Lancs, and *d* 3 Oct 1846, leaving, with other issue:

1 JOHN, of whom presently

2 Samuel, of Whalley, Lancs; *b* 12 Aug 1793; *m* 1 Feb 1818 Margaret (*d* 29 Feb 1840 aged 48), dau of Thomas Hall, of Blackburn, Lancs, and *d* 7 June 1864, having had, with other issue:

(1) Sir WILLIAM CUNLIFFE BROOKS, 1st and last Bt (UK), so *cr* 4 March 1886, DL (Lancs and Aberdeenshire); MP E Cheshire 1869–85 and Altrincham 1886–92; *b* 30 Sept 1819; *m* 1st 25 July 1842 Jane Elizabeth (*d* 10 Oct 1865), er dau of Ralph Orrell, of Stockport, and had, with other issue:

1a Amy; *m* 14 July 1869 11th Marquess of Huntly (*qv*), and *d* 13 May 1920

2a Edith; *m* 1st 11 Oct 1874 Lord Francis Horace Pierrepont Cecil, and had issue (*see* EXETER, M); *m* 2nd 26 April 1892 Adml Philip Francis Tillard, DL, JP, of Alford Ho, Somerset, and Aberdeenshire, and *d* 9 May 1923, leaving further issue. He *d* 23 Feb 1933

(1) (cont.) Sir WILLIAM *m* 2nd 5 Nov 1879 Jane, dau of Col Sir David Davidson, KCB, and *dspm* 9 June 1900, when the btcy expired

1 Nancy; *bapt* 29 Sept 1796; *m* 2 March 1829 Rev Sandford John Cyril Adamson, of Padiham, Lancs

The est son,

JOHN BROOKS, of Crawshaw Hall, Lancs; *b* 23 Nov 1788; *m* 15 June 1814 Alice (*d* 7 June 1852), dau of James Marshall, and *d* 27 Oct 1849, leaving, with other issue:

1 John, of Crawshaw Hall; *b* 29 April 1819; *m* 4 Nov 1844 Mary (*d* 8 May 1860), dau of Ralph Orrell, and *d* 27 June 1864, leaving issue:

(1) John, of Portal, Cheshire; *b* 20 Oct 1850; *m* 8 Jan 1874 Louisa Annette Edla (*d* 30 June 1902), dau of Sir John Drummond-Hay, PC, GCMG, KCB (*see* KINNOULL, E), and had issue:

(1) Alice; *b* 17 Aug 1845; *m* 22 April 1868 James Tertius Dugdale, and had issue. He *d* 1915

(2) Mary; *b* 1 Nov 1847; *m* 31 Aug 1870 Samuel Taylor Mendel, and *d* 14 June 1881, leaving issue

2 THOMAS, **1st Baron**

The 4th son,

Sir Thomas Brooks, 1st Bt, and **1st Baron Crawshaw of Crawshaw**, Co Lancaster, **and of Whatton**, Co Leicester (both UK), so *cr* 9 Feb 1891 and 25 Aug 1892 respectively, JP (Lancs and Lancs), DL (Lancs); High Sheriff 1884; *b* 15 May 1825; *m* 7 Aug 1851 Catherine (*d* 26 June 1917), dau of John Jones, of Kilsall Hall, Salop, and had issue:

1 WILLIAM, **2nd Baron**

2 Marshall Jones, JP (Lancs and Cheshire); *b* 30 May 1855; *educ* Rugby and BNC Oxford (MA); *m* 29 April 1889 Florence, CBE (1918), JP Cheshire (*d* 2 Feb 1934), est dau of Frederick Freeman Thomas, MP, of Ratton, Sussex (*see* 1970 edn WILLINGDON, M), and *d* 5 Jan 1944, leaving issue:

(1) Thomas Marshall, MC, TD, Lt-Col and Brev-Col Cheshire Yeo, Res of Offrs (TA), DL and JP for Chester, served WW I 1914–19 (Croix de Guerre with palms); *b* 23 Feb 1893; *educ* Eton and New Coll Oxford (BA); *m* 14 April 1920 Evelyn Sylvia (*d* 17 Dec 1967), yst dau of Preb Hon Archibald Parker, MA (*see* MACCLESFIELD, E), and *d* 15 Sept 1967, having had issue:

1a +Ronald Marshall [Ronald Brooks Esq, Heath Hill, Wyck Rissington, Bourton-on-the-Water, Glos], late Lt Queen's Bays, served WW II; *b* 6 July 1924; *educ* Eton; *m* 9 May 1950 *Dorothy Valery, only child of Geoffrey Hubert Freer, of Ditchford Hill, Moreton-in-Marsh, Glos

1a Iris Dorothy; *b* 20 April 1921; *d* May 1941

(2) Noel Brand, MC, TD, Maj Cheshire Yeo, served WW I 1914–19, formerly chm Bolsover Colliery Co Ltd; *b* 17 Dec 1896; *educ* Eton and New Coll Oxford; *m* 29 Sept 1921 Joan Margaret, JP (*d* 1984), 2nd dau of Brig Gen Sir Edward Thomas Le Marchant, 4th Bt KCB, CBE (*qv*), and *d* 1984, leaving issue:

1a Robert Noel Brand; *b* 17 Dec 1927; *m* 8 Oct 1955 *Caroline Diana [Mrs Robert Brooks, Castle Barn, Churchill, Oxon], only dau of Brig George Herbert Norris Todd, MC, DL, of Court Ho, Stretton-on-Fosse, Moreton-in-Marsh, Glos, and *d* 1976, leaving issue:

1b +Christopher George; *b* 30 March 1959; *m* 1989 *Miranda, est dau of John Sergeant, of Phoenix Farm, Widford, nr Ware, Herts

2b +Charles Patrick Evelyn; *b* 3 March 1963

1b *Annabel Joan; *b* 4 Jan 1958; *m* 1981 *Damian David Harris (*see* OGMORE, B)

1a *Anne; *b* 7 Feb 1923

2a *Betty Rosamond [Mrs Nigel Kearsley, The Old Vicarage, Asthall, nr Burford, Oxon]; *b* 9 Dec 1924; *m* 7 Dec 1950 *Maj Nigel Steuart Kearsley, late Welsh Gds (*see* RAMSAY, Bt), only son of Maj Edward Reginald Kearsley, DSO, late RWF, of Rose Hill, Erbistock, nr Wrexham, Denbighs, and has issue:

1b *Rosamond Joanna; *b* 8 March 1955

2b *Grania Anne; *b* 11 June 1957; *m* 1983 *Maj Patrick John Tabor, The Blues and Royals, and has issue, two s and one dau

(1) Dorothy; *b* 22 Mar 1890; *m* 11 Jan 1911 Maj Charles Hugh Gregory-Hood, DL, 2nd son of Hon Alexander Frederick Gregory and has issue (*see* HOOD, V)

(2) Marjorie Nell, JP (Glos 1949); *b* 11 Dec 1901; *m* 10 June 1925 2nd Baron Ashton of Hyde (*qv*), and *d* 1993, having had issue

1 Alice Catherine; *b* 23 Aug 1852; *m* 1 July 1875 Robert Millington Knowles, of Colston Bassett Hall, Notts, and *d* March 1892, leaving issue

2 Anne Ellen; *b* 23 Feb 1859; *m* 20 Oct 1880 Capt Harry Leigh Townshend, of Caldecote Hall, Warwicks, and *d* 19 March 1938, leaving issue. He *d* 30 April 1924

3 Ruth Adamson; *b* 31 Aug 1864; *m* 18 Nov 1886 Maj Charles Richard Tennant, late 2nd Life Gds, of St Anne's Manor, Sutton, Loughborough, and *d* 20 Nov 1943. He *d* 9 Dec 1937

The 1st BARON *d* 5 Feb 1908; his er son,

WILLIAM BROOKS, **2nd Baron Crawshaw of Crawshaw and of Whatton**, JP Leics, JP and DL Lancashire; *educ* Ch Ch Oxford (MA); Ld of the Manor of Long Whatton, late Hon Col 5th Bn Leics Regt; *b* 16 Oct 1853; *m* 12 Oct 1882 Mary Ethel (*d* 1 Oct 1914), dau of Sir Michael Hicks-Beach, 8th Bt (*see* ST ALDWYN, E), and had issue:

1 GERALD BEACH, **3rd Baron**

2 Herbert William, JP (Salop 1942–57), late 1st Sec Dipl Serv; *b* 1 March 1890; *educ* Eton and Ch Ch Oxford (BA and MA 1926); *m* 12 July 1922 Hilda Muriel (*d* 1967), dau of Allen Gibson Steel, KC, and *d* 24 Nov 1974, leaving issue:

(1) Allan William Ivo, Lt The Queen's Bays, served WW II; *b* 14 April 1923; *ka* in Italy 25 Nov 1944

(2) Christopher John, Capt late Coldstream Gds, served WW II; *b* 13 Oct 1925; *m* 1st 2nd June 1951 (*divorce* 1957) Patricia Evelyn Beverly (*d* 1992), er dau of John William Matthews, FRCS, of Heathcroft, Hertford Heath, and had issue:

1a *Sarah Jane; *b* 1956; *m* 1988 *Maj Harry St John Holcroft, The Blues and Royals, yst son of Oliver Holcroft, of Upton-on-Severn, Worcs, and has issue:

1b *Harry Christopher Esmond; *b* 1990

2b *Christopher Nicholas; *b* 1991

(2) (cont.) Christopher Brooks *m* 2nd 24 Dec 1958 *Gwendoline Helen [Mrs Christopher Brooks, 10 Tonsley Rd, London SW18 1BG], est dau of Louis D Evans, and *d* 1991, having by her had issue:

1a +Timothy Allan William; *b* 23 March 1962; *m* 1986 *Christine, dau of Leonard Pugh, of Adelaide, Australia

2a *Georgina Helen [Mrs Peter Myrtle, 115 Golfers Dve, Covington, LA 70433, USA]; *b* 18 Nov 1960; *m* 1985 *Peter Myrtle, son of Giles Myrtle, of Dalreagle, Wigtownshire, and has issue:

1b *Frederick Giles Christopher; *b* 1988

2b *Christopher Thomas John; *b* 1992

1b *Victoria Gwendoline Virginia; *b* 1987

(3) +Timothy Gerald Martin, JP (Leics 1960), DL (1984) [Timothy Brooks Esq JP DL, Wistow Hall, nr Great Glen, Leicester LE8 0QF]; *b* 20 March 1929; *educ* Eton and RAC (NDA 1951); farmer, dir: Wistow Hall Gardens Ltd, Thomas Tapling and Co Ltd; memb Harborough DC 1975–89 (chm 1983–84), chm of govrs: Brooksby Ag Coll 1986–89, Wyggeston's Hosp, Leicester 1988–, High Sheriff 1979–80, Ld Lt 1989–, KStJ (1991); Hon LLD De Montfort U (1997), Hon DLitD Loughborough U (1997); *m* 29 Nov 1951 *Hon Ann Fremantle, only dau of 4th Baron Cottesloe, GBE (*qv*), and has issue:

1a +Richard Allan Halford; *b* 22 Nov 1958; *m* 1985 *Diana Elizabeth, yr dau of Sir Godfrey Michael David Thomas, 11th Bt (*see* THOMAS, Bt, of Wenvoe), and has issue:

1b +Charles John Halford; *b* 1989

2b +Michael; *b* 1994

1b *Sabrina; *b* 1991

2a +Andrew Herbert John; *b* 3 June 1966

3a +Michael Julian; *b* 27 June 1969

1a *Lucinda Jane; *b* 25 May 1953; *m* 1978 *Keith Charlton and has three sons and two daus

2a *Nicola Frances; *b* 3 Sept 1955; *m* 1978 *Gerald A Michel and has two daus

1 Ethel Laura, JP Leics; *m* 1st 5th Sept 1912 Capt Lawrence Peel, Yorks Regt, 3rd son of William Peel, of Knowlmere Manor, Yorks, and had issue. He was *ka* 23 or 24 Oct 1914. She *m* 2nd 19 Nov 1925 Lt-Col Sir Robert Edmund Martin, CMG, VL, JP, of The Brand, Loughborough, Leics, and *d* 28 April 1967, leaving further issue. He *d* 13 June 1961

2 Cicely Kate, JP (Lancs 1934); *d* unm 10 Feb 1975

The 2nd BARON *d* 19 Jan 1929; his er son,

GERALD BEACH BROOKS, **3rd Baron Crawshaw of Crawshaw and of Whatton**; *educ* Ch Ch Oxford (MA); *b* 1 April 1884; *m* 4 March 1930 Marjory Sheila (*d* 5 Sept 1964), only dau of Lt-Col Percy Robert Clifton, CMG DSO, TD, of Clifton Hall, Nottingham, and gdau of Sir Hervey Juckes Lloyd Bruce, 4th Bt, of Downhill (*qv*), and *d* 21 Oct 1946, having had issue:

1 WILLIAM MICHAEL CLIFTON BROOKS, **4th Baron Crawshaw of Crawshaw and of Whatton**, DL (Leics 1992); *b* 25 March 1933; *educ* Eton and Ch Ch Oxford; Jt Master Oxford U Draghounds 1952–53, chm Quorn Hunt ctee 1971–97, Treas Loughborough C Assoc 1954–58, Co Commr Leics Boy Scouts 1958–97, Treas Smith's Charity, Pres Leics Assoc for Disabled, *dsp* 7 Nov 1997

2 DAVID GERALD BROOKES, **5th and present Baron Crawshaw of Crawshaw and of Whatton**

3 +JOHN PATRICK [The Hon John Brooks, 25 Cadogan St, London SW3]; *b* 17 March 1938; heir presumptive; *educ* Loughborough Coll; *m* 17 June 1967 *Rosemary Vans Agnew, only dau of C Vans Agnew Franks, of Greenways, Hunmanby, E Yorks, and has issue:

(1) +Edward Samuel; *b* 1969

(1) *Caroline Miranda; *b* 1972

1 *Mary Aletheia; *b* 12 March 1931

CRICKHOWELL

Creation: B. (LP, UK) 1987.

THE BARON CRICKHOWELL, of Pont Esgob in the Black Mountains and Co of Powys ((Roger) Nicholas Edwards, PC (1979)) [The Rt Hon The Lord Crickhowell PC, Pont Esgob Mill, Fforest Coal Pit, nr Abergavenny, Mon NP7 7LS; 4 Henning St, London SW11 3DR]; *b* 25 Feb 1934; *educ* Westminster and Trin Coll Cambridge (MA 1968); memb Lloyd's 1965–; MP Pembroke (C) 1970–87, Oppn Spokesman Welsh Affrs 1975–79, Sec State Wales 1979–87; dir Wm Brandts Sons & Co 1974–76, ch exec Brandts Insur Div, chm NRA 1989–96 (chm Advsy Ctee 1988–89), dir HTV Gp 1987–, Associated Br Ports Holdings 1988–, Anglesey Mining 1988– (v-chm); dir WNO 1988–92, chm: ITNet Ltd 1997–, pres: Contemporary Art Soc Wales 1988–93, SE Arts Assoc 1988–94, Cardiff U of Wales 1988; Memb Ctee AA 1988–; Hon Fell UCW Cardiff 1985; *m* 1963 *Ankaret, dau of William James Healing, of Kinsham House, nr Tewkesbury, Glos, and has:

1 *Rupert Timothy Guy; *b* 1964; *educ* Radley and Trin Coll Cambridge; *m* 1990 *Olivia Grizel Kirkwood, yr dau of Capt David Colin Kirkwood Brown (*see* CAITHNESS E), and has issue:
(1) *Joshua James; *b* 1991
(1) *Camilla Sophie; *b* 1994
(2) *Eliza Nicola; *b* 1996
1 *Sophie Elizabeth Ankaret; *b* 1966
2 *Olivia Caroline; *b* 1970

Lineage: (HERBERT CECIL) RALPH EDWARDS, CBE, FSA, of Suffolk House, Chiswick Mall, London W4; *m* Marjorie Ingham Brooke and had:
1 David William Wood
2 Cecil Ralph Timothy
3 (ROGER) NICHOLAS, *cr* a **Baron**

CRISP

Arms: Paly of four erm. and gu., on a chevron or five horse shoes sa. **Crest:** A camelopard sejant or, gorged with a collar with chain reflexed over the back gu., supporting with the dexter foreleg an oar of the Royal State barge ppr. **Motto:** *Res non verba* ('Deeds not words'). **Creation:** Bt. (UK) 5 Feb 1913.

SIR (JOHN) PETER CRISP, 4TH BT, of Bungay, Suffolk [Sir Peter Crisp Bt, Crabtree Cottage, Drungewick Lane, Loxwood, Billingshurst, W Sussex RH14 0RP]; *b* 19 May 1925; *s f* 1950; *educ* Westminster; slr 1951, with Ashurst, Morris, Crisp and Co; *m* 5 June 1954 *Judith Mary, yst dau of Herbert Edward Gillett, FRICS, of Marlborough, Wilts (*see* GILLETT, Bt), and has issue:

1 +JOHN CHARLES; *b* 10 Dec 1955; *educ* Radley; *m* 1992 *Mary Jo, est dau of Dr Daniel J MacAuley, of Belfast, and has issue:
(1) +George Peter Daniel; *b* 17 Sept 1993
2 +Michael Peter; *b* 29 Oct 1957; *m* 1988 *Pauline Sarah, only dau of Sydney Gold, of Pinner, Middx, and has issue:
(1) +Alexander Samuel; *b* 1990
(2) +Joshua Peter; *b* 1993
3 +Charles Frank; *b* 26 Aug 1960; *m* 1992 *Susan Jennifer, er dau of Deryck Scrase, of Rudgwick, W Sussex, and has issue:
(1) +Frederick; *b* 1993
(2) +Henry James; *b* 1995
(3) +William; *b* 1997
1 *Catherine Mary; *b* 30 Sept 1962

Lineage: JAMES CRISPE, of Linstead Parva and afterwards of Bramfield, both in Suffolk, is named in the will of his kinsman William Crispe, of Bramfield, as heir to his lands in Bramfield, 28 May 1687. He *m* 11 Feb 1657/8 Sarah Kent (*bur* 13 April 1700), of Chediston, Suffolk, and was *bur* 9 Feb 1715/6, leaving a yr s:

WILLIAM CRISPE, of Bramfield; *bapt* 24 Feb 1666/7; *m* 26 March 1695 Susannah Smith, of Sibton (*bur* 2 Dec 1748) and was *bur* 25 Aug 1719, leaving a yr s:

JAMES CRISP, of Bramfield; *m* 1 Aug 1731 Mary Ellis, of Bramfield, and was *bur* 13 Nov 1757, leaving an est s:

JAMES CRISP, of Bramfield; *bapt* 3 June 1732; *m* Elizabeth (*bur* 13 Oct 1811 aged 74) and was *bur* 1 May 1805, having had a 2nd s:

WILLIAM CRISP, of Bramfield; *bapt* 1 Sept 1771; *m* 1st 4 Dec 1798 Elizabeth (*d* 20 Aug 1812), 3rd dau of Jacob Shalders, of Peasenhall, and had a 3rd s:
1 JOHN SHALDERS, of whom presently

WILLIAM CRISP *m* 2nd 12 May 1817 Rachel (*d* 7 Nov 1837), only dau of Robert Haward, of Bramfield, and by her had further issue

WILLIAM CRISP *d* 1830; his 3rd son,

JOHN SHALDERS CRISP, of Bramfield, Suffolk, FRMS; *b* 22 April 1811; *m* 1st 2 June 1842 Harriet (*d* 9 March 1846), only dau of John Childs, of Bungay, Suffolk, and Anna Maria, his w, est dau of Charles Brightly; *m* 2nd 8 June 1870 Jane (*d* 30 Oct 1894) dau of Benjamin Jackson, of Kennington, Surrey, and widow of John Smith, and *d* 22 Jan 1896, having by his 1st w had issue:

Sir Frank Crisp, 1st Bt (UK), so *cr* 5 Feb 1913, JP (Oxon); BA, LLB, London; *b* 25 Oct 1843; sr ptnr Ashurst, Morris, Crisp and Co, slrs; Hon Sec Roy Microscopical Soc 1878–89, Hon Treas and V-Pres of Linnean Soc of London 1881–1906, ktd 1907; *m* 27 Aug 1867 Catherine (*d* 2 Jan 1931), only child of George Durrant Howes, of Stoven, Suffolk, and *d* 29 April 1919, leaving:

1 **Sir Frank Morris Crisp, 2nd Bt**, of Friar Park, Henley; *b* 13 March 1872; *d* unm 5 April 1938
2 JOHN WILSON (Sir), **3rd Bt**
3 Bernard Woodward; *b* 31 March 1875; *m* 31 March 1901 Elsa Florence (*d* 28 Sept 1938), dau of Robert Schwartz, and *d* 28 April 1963, leaving issue:
(1) *Joan Veronica [Mrs John Broome, 4 Sprimont Place, London SW3]; *b* 3 March 1904; *m* 1st 7 Dec 1927 (*divorce* 1951) Trevor Gayer Fetherstonhaugh, MC, MB, ChB; *m* 2nd 5 Feb 1953 Capt John Egerton Broome, DSC, RN (*d* 19–)
(2) Daphne; *b* 21 May 1908; *m* 15 April 1931 Gerald H Pinckney, yr son of W Percy Pinckney, of Shawford Close, Shawford, Winchester, and has issue:
1a *Jeremy Gerald [Jeremy Pinckney Esq, 45 Black Lion Lane, London W6]; *b* 17 Oct 1935; *m* 21 Dec 1960 *(Helen) Belinda, 2nd dau of Maj Harcourt Michael Scudamore Gold, MC, TD, of West Stratton Ho, nr Winchester, Hants, and has issue:
1b *Charles William; *b* 1962
2b *Simon Philip; *b* 1964
1b *Emily Belinda; *b* 5 July 1967
1a *Julie Ann; *b* 11 March 1933; *m* 23 Sept 1955 Capt David Kentish Barnes, son of A J Kentish Barnes, of Caldecot, Caldy, Cheshire, and has issue:
1b *Timothy James; *b* 26 Jan 1961
1b *Nicola Jane; *b* 23 Oct 1963
4 Charles Oak, admitted a Slr 1905; *b* 11 April 1878; *educ* Univ Coll Oxford (BA); *m* 1 June 1929 Mabel, widow of J F Cooper of Old Westover, Milford-on-Sea, Hants, and dau of William Thompson, and *d* May 1946
1 Catherine Childs; *m* 15 Oct 1891 William Hocken Paterson, of 24a Kensington Park Gdns, W, and *d* 1 June 1952
2 Eleanor Howes; *m* 10 May 1905 Edward John Bullard, 2nd son of Sir Harry Bullard, MP, and *d* 9 July 1962, leaving issue. He *d* 1950

The 2nd Bt's bro,

Sir John Wilson Crisp, 3rd Bt, slr 1906, memb legal firm Ashurst, Morris, Crisp and Co, of 17 Throgmorton Avenue, EC; *b* 28 May 1873; *m* 10 April 1920 Marjorie, only dau of Joseph Shriver, and *d* 11 Oct 1950, having had issue:
1 Sir (JOHN) PETER CRISP, **4th and present Bt**
1 Susan Leila; *b* 20 Dec 1921; *m* 15 May 1943 Rev John Harold Stanley Burton, MA, Chaplain RAFVR, 1943–46, only son of John Stanley Burton, Gren Gds, and *d* 27 May 1960, leaving two daus

CRITCHETT

Arms: Az. a fire chest arg. fired ppr. between three crickets or. **Crest:** In front of an iris erect a starling, both ppr. **Motto:** *Suivez raison* ('Follow right'). **Creation:** Bt. (UK) 28 Nov 1908.

SIR IAN GEORGE LORRAINE CRITCHETT, 3RD BT, of Harley Street, London [Sir Ian Critchett Bt, Uplands Lodge, Pains Hill, Limpsfield, Surrey RH8 0RF]; *b* 9 Dec 1920; *s* f 1941; *educ* Harrow and Clare Coll Cambridge (BA); served WW II as F/Lt RAFVR (1942–46), For Serv 1948–80 (3rd Sec (Commercial) Vienna 1950–51, 2nd Sec (Commercial) Bucharest 1951–53, 2nd Sec Cairo 1956, 1st Sec, later Counsellor, FCO; ret 1980); *m* 1st 9 Oct 1948 Paulette Mary Lorraine (*d* 4 May 1962), er dau of Col Henry Brabazon Humfrey, IA, of North Lodge, Filgrave, Newport Pagnell, Bucks; *m* 2nd 10 Feb 1964 *Jocelyn Daphne Margaret, est dau of Cdr Christopher Mildmay Hall, RN, of Boswarva, Penzance, by his w Agnes Laura Margaret, only dau of Lt-Col Legh Harley Delves Broughton, DSO, RA (*see* BROUGHTON, Bt), and by her has issue:

1 +CHARLES GEORGE MONTAGUE; *b* 2 April 1965

1 *Xanthe Clare Lorraine; *b* 13 Feb 1968

Lineage: RICHARD CRITCHETT, of Cheltenham, Glos; *b* 1753; *m* Jane Billingsley, and *d* Oct 1839, having had, with other issue, an only son:

RICHARD CRITCHETT, of Queen's Sq, Bloomsbury; *b* March 1777; *m* Eliza Slack, and *d* June 1865, having had issue:

1 GEORGE, of whom presently

2 Charles; *b* 1827; *dsp* 7 March 1906

The er son,

GEORGE CRITCHETT, of 21 Harley St, London W, FRCS, Surgn London Hosp and Roy London Ophthalmic Hosp, memb of Cncl of Roy Coll of Surgeons; *b* 25 March 1817; *m* Martha, dau of Capt Brooker, RN, of Bosham, Sussex, and *d* 1 Nov 1882, having had issue:

1 (GEORGE) ANDERSON (Sir), **1st Bt**

2 Richard Claude (R C Carton, the dramatist); *b* 1853; *m* Katherine Compton, and *d* 1 April 1928

1 Amy Eliza; *m* 1st Edward Boursot; *m* 2nd Thomas O'Brien, and *d* 8 July 1928

The er son,

Sir (George) Anderson Critchett, 1st Bt (UK), so *cr* 28 Nov 1908, KCVO (1919, CVO 1905), ktd 1901; *b* 18 Dec 1845; *educ* Harrow and Caius Coll Cambridge (BA 1867, MA 1873), MRCS Eng 1872, FRCS Edin 1880; Surgn-Oculist to TM EDWARD VII 1901–10 and GEORGE V 1910–25, Sr Ophthalmic Surg to King George's Hosp, Consulting Ophthalmic Surg St Mary's Hosp, London, KGStJ; *m* 4 Aug 1883 Agnes Anne (*d* 9 Feb 1943), dau of Charles James Dunphie, and had issue:

1 GEORGE MONTAGUE (Sir), **2nd Bt**

1 Dora Sybil Mary; *m* 3 July 1913 William Moon Upjohn, Welsh Gds, er son of William Henry Upjohn, KC, and had issue. He was *ka* 24 Aug 1918

2 Violet Nita; *m* 24 June 1915 Andrew Sinclair Buchanan, MVO, late Capt 9th Co of London Regt, only son of Andrew Archibald Buchanan (*see* BUCHANAN, Bt)

Sir ANDERSON *d* 9 Feb 1925; his son,

Sir (George) Montague Critchett, 2nd Bt, MVO (5th Cl 1932); *b* 7 June 1884; *educ* Harrow and Clare Coll Cambridge; served WW I 1914–19, Capt late TA Res, formerly Lt 3rd Bn Oxf and Bucks LI; was in Ld Chamberlain's Office, St James's Palace from 1912, and was State Invitation Assist; OStJ; *m* 27 Oct 1914 Innes (*d* 20 Nov 1982), 3rd dau of Col Francis George Archibald Wiehe, late 68th Durham LI, and *d* 30 May 1941, having had issue:

1 Sir IAN GEORGE LORRAINE CRITCHETT, **3rd and present Bt**

CROFT

Arms: Quarterly per fess indented az. and arg., in the first quarter a lion passant guardant or. **Crests:** 1 A lion passant guardant arg., 2 A wyvern sa., vulned in the side gu. **Supporters:** Dexter, a lion rampant quarterly per fess indented az. and arg.; sinister, a wyvern sa. vulned in the side gu. **Motto:** *Esse quam videri* ('Being rather than seeming'). **Creations:** Bt. (UK) 28 Feb 1924, B. (UK) 28 May 1940.

THE 3RD BARON CROFT, of Bournemouth, Co Southampton, and a **Baronet** (Sir Bernard William Henry Page Croft, Bt) [The Rt Hon The Lord Croft, Croft Castle, Kingsland, Herefs HR6 9PW; 5 Comeragh Mews, Comeragh Rd, London W14 9HW]; *b* 28 Aug 1949; *s* f 1997; *educ* Stowe and U of Wales (BSc Econ); *m* 1993 *Mary Elizabeth, only dau of James Richardson, of Co Tyrone

Lineage: RICHARD BENYON CROFT, RN (*see* CROFT, Bt, of Croft Castle), of Fanhams Hall, Ware, Herts, had a 2nd s:

Sir Henry Page Croft, 1st Bt, and **1st Baron Croft**, of Bournemouth, Co Southampton (both UK), so *cr* 28 Feb 1924 and 28 May 1940 respectively, PC (1945), CMG (1915), TD, DL Herts; *b* 22 June 1881; *educ* Eton, Shrewsbury and Trin Hall Cambridge; memb Herts TAA, MP (C) Christchurch 1910–18 and Bournemouth 1918–40, Chllr and Prior of The Primrose League 1928–29, Jt Under-Sec War and V-Pres Army Cncl 1940–45, Lt-Col and Brevet Col Herts Regt (TA), Hon Brig-Gen 1924, T/Brig-Gen cmdg 1916, served WW I (despatches twice); *m* 10 July 1907 Hon Nancy Beatrice Borwick, CStJ (*d* 24 Jan 1949), yst dau of 1st Baron Borwick (*qv*), and *d* 7 Dec 1947, having had issue:

1 MICHAEL HENRY GLENDOWER PAGE CROFT, **2nd Baron Croft**; *b* 20 Aug 1916; *educ* Eton and Trin Hall Cambridge (BA 1938); Capt RASC WW II, barrister Inner Temple 1952, dir Henry Page 1946–57 Ware Properties 1958–65, memb: exec ctee Contemporary Arts Soc 1960–68 and 1970–81 (v-chm 1980–81), Br Museum Soc 1969–76 and Hereford and Worcester Preservation Tst 1986–97, Hon Keeper Contemporary Art Fitzwilliam Museum Cambridge 1984–97; OStJ, FRSA; *m* 30 Oct 1948 Lady Antoinette Fredericka Conyngham (*d* 15 June 1959), only dau of 6th Marquess Conyngham (*qv*), and *d* 11 Jan 1997, leaving:

(1) BERNARD WILLIAM HENRY PAGE CROFT, **3rd and present Baron Croft**

1 *Charlotte Elizabeth Ann [The Hon Mrs Devonald, Enderley, Stony Lane, Little Kingshill, Great Missenden, Bucks]; *b* 4 June 1952; *educ* Benenden; *m* 5 April 1975 *Emrys Thomas Devonald, yr son of Glyn Devonald, and has issue:

(1) *James Emrys; *b* 1979

(1) *Jennifer Ann; *b* 22 Sept 1977

1 *Hilda Elizabeth Mary [The Hon Mrs Bayford, The Coombe House, Streatley, Berks]; *b* 11 Feb 1909; *m* 16 May 1934 Richard Hayter Bayford (*d* 1982), barrister, est son of Robert Frederick Bayford, OBE, KC, of Netley Hill, Botley, Hants, and has issue:

(1) *Robert Michael Croft; *b* 1936

(1) *Gillian Sara Carolyn; *b* 1935; *m* 1958 F/Lt Michael Holmes, RAF

(2) *Mary Elizabeth; *b* 1944

2 *Nancy Diana Joyce [The Hon Mrs Nancy Uhlman, Croft Castle, Leominster, Herefs HR6 9PW]; *b* 31 March 1912; *m* 4 Nov 1936 Dr Manfred Uhlman (*d* 1985), son of Ludwig Uhlman, of Stuttgart, Germany, and has issue:

(1) *Francis Raymond Croft; *b* 1943

(1) *Caroline Ann; *b* 1940; *m* 1966 (*divorce* 19–) Albert Charles Compton, and has issue:

1a *Tristram Ludovic Archer; *b* 1968

1a *Sarah Harriet; *b* 1972

3 *Anne Rosemary Dorothea [The Hon Mrs Poole, Dower House, 17A Knight St, Sawbridgeworth, Herts]; *b* 2 April 1918; *m* 20 Nov 1946 (Herbert) Edmund Poole (*d* 1984), son of Herbert Poole, and has issue:

(1) *Herbert Benyon; *b* 1947

(2) *Jeremy Henry Borwick; *b* 1949

(3) *Hugo Edmund; *b* 1952; *m* 1st 1977 (*divorce* 1992) Christina Susan de Jong Cleyndert; *m* 2nd 1992 *Anne Margaret Lovell, and by 1st w has issue:

1a *Charlotte Annalika; *b* 1979

2a *Jessica Margery Anne; *b* 1981
3a *Kate Antonia; *b* 1982

Seat: Croft Castle, Croft, Herefs. Since 1957 the National Trust has owned the actual estate, but by agreement the family have continued to lived there (the **2nd Baron** was reported shortly after his death to have safeguarded its future). Between 1746 and 1923 the property was in other hands entirely. In the latter year the trustees of Sir James Croft bought back the Castle and some of the adjoining land, Sir James later willing it to his cousin the 1st Baron. In 1949, however, owing to death duties, the 2nd Baron Croft sold the place on to his cousin Maj Owen Croft (*see* CROFT, Bt, of Croft), though it was placed in the hands of the National Trust only eight years later.

Croft is a four-sided structure with corner towers originating in the late 14th/early 15th century. In the mid-18th century, some 20 years after the CROFTs had sold it to Thomas Johnes, it was prettily gothicised under the supervision of Thomas Farnolls Pritchard, an architect from Shrewsbury.

CROFT, Bt, of Cowling Hall

Arms: Quarterly, per fess indented or and gu., in the first quarter a lion passant-guardant of the second. **Crests:** 1 A lion passant-guardant or supporting a shield with the arms of St George, 2 Not shown (*see* 1970 edn). **Supporters:** Dexter, a lion guardant or, gorged with a wreath of laurel vert, therefrom pendent an escutcheon gu. charged with a tower gold; sinister, a bull sa., horned, crined, unguled and gorged with a ducal crown or, pendent therefrom an escutcheon arg. **Motto:** *Esse quam videri* ('Being rather than seeming'). **Creation:** Bt. (UK) 17 Dec 1818.

SIR THOMAS STEPHEN HUTTON CROFT, 6TH BT, of Cowling Hall, Yorkshire [Sir Thomas Croft Bt, The Barn House, Rayham Rd, Whitstable, Kent CT5 3DZ]; *b* 12 June 1959; *s f* 1990; *educ* King's Sch Canterbury, UCL (BSc) and RCA London (MA); architect with Richard Meier and Ptnrs New York 1985–86, project architect Rick Mather, Architects, London 1986–88, pncpl Thomas Croft, Architect, 1988–

Lineage: RALPH CROFT, of East Wilton, Yorks, though of Lancashire descent; had:

CHRISTOPHER CROFT, of Cottescue Park, Yorks, in 1611; *m* — Clapham, of Beamsley, Yorks, and had:

Sir CHRISTOPHER CROFT; Sheriff York 1618, Ld Mayor York 1629 and 1641, when he entertained CHARLES I at home and was ktd; *m* Elizabeth, dau of Sir T Harrison, and *d* 5 July 1649, leaving an est s:

THOMAS CROFT, of Stillington, Yorks; *m* Olive, only dau and heir of John Dunstey, of Bramhope, Yorks, and *d* 1654, leaving:

THOMAS CROFT, of Stillington; *m* Frances, dau of Sir Stephen Thompson, and *d* 1711, leaving:

STEPHEN CROFT, of Stillington; *m* Elizabeth, dau of Sir Edmund Anderson, Bt, of Broughton, and *d* 1733, leaving, with an er s (Stephen, ancestor of the CROFTs of Stillington):

THOMAS CROFT, of London; *b* 15 Oct 1717; *m* Lucy, dau and heir of Henry Thompson, of Kirby Hall, and *d* 1783, leaving:

JOHN CROFT; *m* 14 June 1775 Henrietta Maria (sis of the w of Sir Everard Home, MD, Serjeant-Surgn to GEORGE III, and of Catherine Tunstall, w 1st of Rev Edward Chamberlayne and 2nd of 2nd Earl of Orford; *see* WALPOLE, B), dau and coheir of Rev Dr James Tunstall, and had issue:

Sir John Croft, 1st Bt (UK), so *cr* 17 Dec 1818, of Cowling Hall, Yorks, and Doddington Place, Sittingbourne, Kent, DL, JP Kent; a Portuguese Commnr, 1st Baron da Serra da Estrella in Portugal, Hon Chargé d'Affaires Lisbon 1815, Kt of Tower and Sword Portugal 1821, DCL, FRS; *m* 1st 1 Aug 1816 Amelia Elizabeth (*d* 20 Oct 1819), dau of James Warre, and had, with another dau:

1 Elizabeth Anne; *m* 26 Aug 1843 Sir Harry Stephen Meysey-Thompson, 1st Bt (*qv*), of Kirby Hall, Co York, and *d* 28 March 1910, leaving issue

Sir John *m* 2nd 24 July 1827 Anne Knox (*d* 5 March 1887 aged 82), dau of Rev John Radcliffe, Rector Limehouse, and by her had, with a dau:

1 JOHN FREDERICK (Sir), **2nd Bt**

He *d* 5 Feb 1862; his only son,

Sir John Frederick Croft, 2nd Bt, of Doddington Place, Kent, JP Kent, High Sheriff 1872, 2nd Baron da Serra da Estrella in Portugal; *b* 31 Aug 1828; *m* 4 June 1856 Emma (*d* 28 April 1919), dau of John Graham (*see* GRAHAM, Bt, of Larbert), and *d* 24 May 1904, having had:

1 John Radcliffe; *b* 4 April 1857; *dvp* unm 1 June 1903

2 **Sir Frederick Leigh Croft, 3rd Bt**, and 3rd Baron da Serra da Estrella in Portugal; *b* 14 Feb 1860; *d* unm 31 March 1930

3 Francis Edgar; *b* 19 Oct 1861; *m* 1891 Zoë Bromley (*d* 29 June 1948), step-dau of A Stuart-Wortley, and *d* 18 June 1910, leaving issue:

(1) Lilian Mary; *m* 28 Jan 1915 (*divorce* 1939) Capt Nigel Graham, late Coldstream Gds, son of Donald Graham, CIE (*see* GRAHAM, Bt, of Larbert), of Airthrey Castle, Stirling, and *d* 1965, leaving issue. He *d* 25 Nov 1976

(2) Cynthia; *m* 7 Oct 1916 Wilfrid Holland, of Hartford, son of Sir Arthur Holland, and had issue. He *d* 1945

(3) Eleanor; *m* 10 June 1925 Lt-Cdr Thomas Hyde Villiers, RN, son of Sir Thomas Lister Villiers, and *d* 12 May 1958, leaving issue (*see* CLARENDON, E)

4 William Graham; *b* 26 Dec 1862; *m* 23 June 1909 Marjorie, dau of Rev Thomas Guppy Sarsfield Hall, Vicar of Dodington, Kent, and *d* 6 July 1928, leaving issue:

(1) **Sir John William Graham Croft, 4th Bt**, 4th Baron da Serra da Estrella in Portugal; *educ* Stowe; Lt RA; *b* 30 May 1910; *d* 1979

(2) William Noble, late Capt RE; *b* 9 Oct 1915; *d* unm 10 July 1953

5 Percy Hutton; *b* 27 Oct 1872; *d* 14 Feb 1935

6 Tom Radcliffe, OBE; *b* 1878; *m* 15 July 1909 Louise (*d* 9 April 1964), dau of Francis Sales, of Charlton, Kent, and *d* 21 March 1964, leaving issue:

(1) **Sir John Archibald Radcliffe Croft, 5th Bt**, Maj W Yorks Regt (PWO) WW II (wounded twice); *b* 27 March 1910; *m* 26 Sept 1953 *Lucy Elizabeth [Lady Croft, The Barn House, Rayham Rd, Whitstable, Kent CT5 3DZ], Lt ATS, Hon Col WRAC (TA), er dau of Maj William Dallas Loney Jupp, OBE, and *d* 1990, leaving issue:

1a Sir THOMAS STEPHEN HUTTON CROFT, **6th and present Bt**

(2) +CYRIL BERNARD [Cyril Croft Esq, Rayham Meadow, Whitstable, Kent CT5 3DZ], late Lt The Buffs; *b* 6 June 1918; heir presumptive; *m* 1st 18 Sept 1957 Sheila Maisie (*d* 1979), dau of Henry Clark Cox, of Whitstable, Kent; *m* 2nd 1980 *Anne Heather Newbatt, dau of Howard Cormack Bessant, and by 1st w has issue:

1a *Diana Louise; *b* 29 Jan 1959; *m* 19– *Neil Frederick Crumbie

2a *Wendy Jane; *b* 3 June 1961

(1) Rosalind Editha Louise; *b* 2 Oct 1914; *d* 4 Jan 1991

1 Elizabeth Graham; *d* 14 Feb 1862

2 Constance Margaret Graham; *m* 14 July 1877 Col Gilbert Charles Bourne, DL, JP, DSc, FRS, Emeritus Linacre Prof of Comparative Anatomy at Oxford, er surv son of Lt-Col R Bourne, DL, JP, of Cowarne Court, Herefordshire, and *d* 1954, leaving issue. He *d* 9 March 1933

3 Gertrude Mary; *m* 31 Aug 1893 Arthur John Chitty, barrister, est son of Sir Joseph Chitty, PC, and *d* 6 May 1912, leaving issue. He *d* 6 Jan 1908

4 Elinor Violet; *m* 13 Oct 1896 Walter Graham Crum, est son of William Graham Crum, of Thornliebank, Glasgow, and *d* leaving issue. He *d* 19 Feb 1947

5 Ethel Mary; *m* 1st 17 April 1890 Hubert Hedworth Grenville-Wells, of Kingsdown Ho, Sittingbourne, Kent, 2nd son of Capt Grenville Grenville-Wells, JP, of Holmewood, Hunts, and had issue. He *d* at Tenerife, 17 April 1904. She *m* 2nd 30 Sept 1906 Alfred Benjamin, and *d* 8 Oct 1935. He *d* 4 Nov 1944

6 Editha; *m* 6 March 1906 Bateman Lancaster Rose, 5th son of Sir Philip Rose, 1st Bt (*see* ROSE, Bt, of Rayners), and *d* 28 Dec 1963, aged 89, leaving issue

7 Lucy; *m* 17 Oct 1905 Donald Hatt Noble Graham, T/Capt Black Watch, 2nd son of Donald Graham, CIE, of Airthrey (*see* GRAHAM, Bt, of Larbert), and *d* 3 July 1940, leaving issue. He was *ka* France 25–27 Sept 1915

8 Jessie Graham Mildred; *d* unm 4 March 1923

CROFT, Bt, of Croft Castle

Arms: Quarterly per fess indented az. and arg, in the 1st quarter a lion passant guardant or. **Crests:** 1, A lion passant guardant arg., 2 A wyvern sa. vulned in the side gu. **Mottoes:** 1 *Esse quam videri* ('To be rather than to seem'); 2 *Tryumphe o trespas* ('Victory over death') **Creation:** Bt. (E) 18 Nov 1671.

SIR OWEN GLENDOWER CROFT, 14TH BT, of Croft Castle, Co Hereford [Sir Owen Croft Bt, Salisbury Court, Uralla, NSW 2358, Australia]; *b* 26 April 1932; *s* f 1984; *educ* Armidale Sch, NSW; grazier; memb NSW state advisory ctees; *m* 1959 *Sally Patricia, dau of Dr Thomas Montagu Mansfield, of Brisbane, Qld, and has issue:

1 +THOMAS JASPER; *b* 3 Nov 1962; *educ* Armidale Sch Armidale and Darling Downs Inst (Assoc Dip Mech Eng); *m* 1989 *Catherine Fiona, dau of Graham William White

1 *Patricia Alice; *b* 1960; *m* 1993 *Peter James Rasmussen

2 *Georgiana; *b* 1964

Lineage: BERNARD de CROFT; mentioned in Domesday Book as holding lands in Croft, Wharton, and Newton, Herefs; gave the tithes of Waverton to, and became a monk of, Thetford Priory, Norfolk; had:

GILBERT de CROFT; feudal Ld of Waverton, confirmed his f's grant of tithes to Thetford Priory; had:

HUGH de CROFT; with his bro Robert made a final disposition of the tithes of Wharton to the monks at Thetford; had:

HUGH de CROFT; in 1191 confirmed a grant of the tithes of Wharton by the Prior of Thetford to the Abbot of Oseney made 6 Nov 1189; had:

HUGH de CROFT; held a Kt's fee of the honour of Brechengog in the hundred of Webtree, Herefs, 1212; *m* Christina — and had:

Sir HUGH de CROFT; *m* Isabel, dau and coheir of Robert Longberch, and had:

Sir JOHN de CROFT; summoned to serve beyond the seas 7 July 1297; *m* Catherine — and had:

Sir HUGH de CROFT, KB (1305); present at a tournament at Dunstable, Beds, 1308; Sheriff Salop and Staffs, Constable Bruges and Shrewsbury Castle 1311, MP Herefs 1312; summoned 1313 and 1315 to raise troops against the Scots; present at a tournament in Stepney; *m* 1st Perená, dau of Sir John de Havering; *m* 2nd Eleanor (who survived him and *m* 2nd John Trummayn) and was murdered 1317 by the Lacys, to whom he was sent to treat for peace in Ireland, having by his 2nd w had:

HUGH de CROFT; *b* 29 Sept 1306; *m* Maud, dau and coheir of Sir Brian de Brampton, of Brampton Brian, Herefs, and had:

JOHN de CROFT; MP Herefs 1357; had:

Sir JOHN de CROFT, of Croft Castle, Herefs; Capt of Merk Castle, near Calais; frequently employed in negotiations in Flanders 1402–04; *m* Janet, dau and coheir of the celebrated Welsh patriot Owen Glendower, and had:

WILLIAM de CROFT; pardoned 9 April 1419 for the death of Thomas Lyngeyn at Leominster; summoned to serve in the wars in France 1428, Sheriff Herefs 1425; *m* Margaret, dau and coheir of Thomas Walwyn, and had an est surv s:

Sir RICHARD CROFT, KB (1487, following Battle of Stoke), of Croft Castle; High Sheriff and MP Herefs; fought with Yorkists at Mortimer's Cross 1461, the battle being fought on his own estate; captured Prince Edward, s of HENRY VI, at the Battle of Tewkesbury 1471 but was not responsible for the Prince's murder; Treasurer Household to HENRY VII; *m* Eleanor, widow of Sir Hugh Mortimer, of Kyre Wyard, Worcs, and dau of Sir Edmund Cornwall, of Burford, Salop, and *d* 29 July 1509, having had:

Sir EDWARD CROFT, of Croft, High Sheriff Herefs; ktd by 1513; *m* Joyce, dau and heir of Sir Walter Skull, of The Holt, Worcs, and *d* 1547, leaving with other issue (including a yr s George, in holy orders, of Oriel Coll Oxford, indicted in 1539 for saying the Pope was Supreme Head of the Church and executed 1540):

RICHARD CROFT, of Croft; *m* Katherine, dau of Sir Richard Herbert, of Montgomery, and *d* 1 Jan 1562, leaving:

Sir JAMES CROFT, of Croft, PC; MP Herefs, ktd 1547, Govr Haddington 1549, Ld Dep Ireland 1551, Dep Constable of the Tower 1552; convicted of high treason and committed to the Tower 21 Feb 1554 but escaped with being bound to good bearing and fined £500 18 Jan 1555; a Ld of (Welsh?) Marches 1557, Govr Berwick 1560, Comptroller Household, one of the PCs appointed to try MARY QUEEN OF SCOTS 1586; Commr Treaty of Bourbourg 1588; *m* 1st Alice (*d* 1573), widow of William Wigmore, of Shobdon, and dau of Richard Warncombe, of Ivington, Leominster; *m* 2nd Catherine, dau of Edward Blount, and *d* 4 Sept 1590, leaving by his 1st w:

EDWARD CROFT, of Croft; MP Leominster 1571 and 1580; *m* Ann, dau and heir of Thomas Browne, of Attleborough, Norfolk, and *d* 29 July 1601, leaving an est surv s:

Sir HERBERT CROFT; MP Herefs 1592–1617; turned RC 1607 and became a lay-brother of the Benedictine monastery of Douai, where he *d* 10 April 1622, having *m* Mary, dau and heir of Anthony Bourne, of Holt Castle, Worcs, and having had, with another s:

1 William (Sir), MP Malmesbury 1623 and 1625, royalist Col Civil War; shot at Battle of Stokesay Castle, near Ludlow, 9 June 1645 but rode his horse home before he collapsed and died on reaching his park palings; *d* unm

2 James (Sir), Col; *d* unm 9 Aug 1659

3 HERBERT, of whom we treat

The 3rd son,

Rt Rev HERBERT CROFT; turned RC, ordained priest 1626, but later reverted to C of E and after studying at Ch Ch Oxford became an Anglican parson; Dean Hereford, Bp Hereford 1662, Dean of the Chapel-Royal 1667 and Chaplain to CHARLES II; *b* 18 Oct 1603; *m* Ann, dau of Very Rev Jonathan Brown, DD, Dean Hereford, and *d* 18 May 1691, leaving an only s:

Sir Herbert Croft, 1st Bt (E), so *cr* 18 Nov 1671; MP Herefs 1679 and 1690–98; *m* Elizabeth (aunt of 1st Lord Archer, Baron of Umberslade; she *d* 1709), dau of Thomas Archer, of Umberslade, Warwicks, and *d* 3 Nov 1720, having had, with other issue:

1 **Sir Archer Croft, 2nd Bt**; MP Leominster 1722–27, Winchelsea 1728 and Deeralston 1728–34; *bapt* 3 March 1683/4; *m* 10 Jan 1723 Frances (*d* 6 May 1767), dau of Brig-Gen Richard Waring, and *d* 10 Dec 1753, leaving an est s:

(1) **Sir Archer Croft, 3rd Bt**; in 1746 sold the Croft estate (*see* CROFT, B, **Seat**) to Richard Knight, Recorder of Ludlow; *m* 24 April 1759 Elizabeth Charlotta, 2nd dau and coheir of Ashley Cowper, and great-niece of 1st Earl Cowper (*see* LUCAS OF CRUDWELL, B), and *dspm* 30 Nov 1790, leaving:

1a Elizabeth; *m* James Woodcock later Croft

2a Frances; *m* Harry Mount, of Wasing

3a Harriet; *m* Richard Ryland

(2) **Sir John Croft, 4th Bt**; *dspl* 4 Dec 1797

2 Francis, of London; *b* 1687; *m* Grace, dau and heir of Thomas Bramston, of Waterhouse, Essex, and had an only son:

(1) Herbert, of Waterhouse, Essex; *b* 14 June 1718; *m* 1st Elizabeth, dau of Richard Young, of Midhurst, Sussex, and had by her, with other issue:

1a **Rev Sir Herbert Croft, 5th Bt**, BD, author *Love and Madness*; *b* 1748; *m* 1st Sophia (*d* 8 Feb 1792), dau and coheir of Richard Cleave, and had three daus; *m* 2nd 25 Feb 1795 Elizabeth (*d* Sept 1815), dau of David Lewis, of Malvern Hall, Warwicks, and *d* 27 April 1816, having by her had no issue

2a RICHARD (Sir), **6th Bt**

(1) (cont.) Herbert Croft *m* 2nd Mary, dau of Thomas Chawner, of Sudbury Wood, Derbys, and *d* 7 July 1785, having had further issue:

1a Elizabeth

The 5th Bt's bro,

Sir Richard Croft, 6th Bt; *b* 9 Jan 1762; MD, Physician to GEORGE III; *m* 3 Nov 1789 Margaret (*d* 4 Sept 1847), dau of Thomas Denman, MD, and sis of 1st Baron Denman (*qv*), and *d* 13 Feb 1818, having had issue:

1 **Sir Thomas Elmsley Croft, 7th Bt**, FSA, Lt 2nd Bn 1st Foot Gds, severely wounded at Quatre Bras; *b* 2 Sept 1798; *m* 9 Sept 1824 Sophia Jane Lateward (*m* 2nd 7 Nov 1835 Col William Lyster and *d* 10 Dec 1890), only child of Richard Lateward, of Grove Ho, Ealing, and Perivale, Middx, and *d* 29 Oct 1835, leaving:

(1) Grace; *m* 5 March 1846 Edward Murray (*see* MURRAY, Bt, of Ochtertyre) and *d* 13 Jan 1898, leaving three sons

2 ARCHER DENMAN (Sir), **8th Bt**

3 Richard (Rev), Vicar of Hillingdon; *b* 22 Aug 1808; *m* 1st 15 Oct 1839 Charlotte Leonora (*d* 9 Nov 1854), dau of Lt-Col Russell, EICS, and had issue:

(1) Richard Benyon, of Fanhams Hall, Ware, DL, JP, High Sheriff 1892, Lt-Col Herts Imp Yeo, late Lt RN; *b* 9 July 1843; *m* 22 Sept 1869 Anne Elizabeth (*d* 6 Oct 1921), dau and heir of Henry Page, of Ware, and *d* 28 Jan 1912, leaving issue:

1a Richard Page, of Fanhams Hall, DL, JP Herts, High Sheriff 1911, Col late 4th Bn Beds Regt, served in S African War 1900–01 as ADC to Lord Methuen (despatches, wounded, medal, Hon Capt in the Army), and WW I 1914–17 (despatches); *b* 4 Nov 1872; *m* 19 Aug 1908 Eva Pansy Melicent Philippa Stanhope (*d* 1940), dau of William Sharp Waithman, DL, JP, of Merlin Park, Co Galway, and *d* 27 Feb 1961, leaving issue:

1b Richard Arthur Fitzroy Page, late Maj RASC, served WW II (despatches); *b* 25 Aug 1910; *educ* Shrewsbury and Trin Hall Cambridge; *m* 1st 14 Oct 1939 (*divorce* 1956) Felice Amy Peggy, dau of Douglas Irvin McClymont, of Buenos Aires, and has issue:

1c +Richard Nicholas Page; *b* 6 Dec 1941; *m* 1st June 1967 Teresa Mary (*d* 1971), formerly w of Sverre Wilberg, of Fredrickstadt, Norway, and dau of Donald Jewell, of Burry-Port, Carmarthenshire; *m* 2nd 1973 *Bruna Campesato

2c +Hugo Douglas Page; *b* 23 May 1944; *educ* Shrewsbury; *m* 1969 Dawn Pryde and has:

1d +Richard Page; *b* 1973

2d +Edward Page; *b* 1976

3d +James Craggs Page; *b* 1979

1d *Arabella; *b* 8 April 1971

1c *Miriam Anne Page; *b* 31 Oct 1948; *educ* Cobham Hall; *m* 1974 *Piers Rogers, of Castlebury, Ware, Herts, and has issue:

1d *Samuel Bennett; *b* 1978

1d *Scarlett Alice; *b* 1980

1b (cont.) Maj Richard Page Croft *m* 2nd 12 June 1956 Daphne (*d* 1978), formerly w of Jack Frye, of Alswick Hall, Buntingford, Herts, and dau of Eugen Aron, of Hillside, Hunton Bridge, Herts; *m* 3rd 1981 *(Maria) Isabel (*née* De Eguidazu) [Mrs Richard Page Croft, The Round House, Ware, Herts SG12 7PR], formerly w of Count Aymon de Roussy de Sales

2a HENRY PAGE CROFT (Sir), 1st Bt, and 1st BARON CROFT (*qv*)

1a Joyce Margaret Page; *m* 6 Jan 1897 Geoffrey de Mountney Gerard Hoare, of Meadham Haslow, and *d* 23 March 1925, leaving issue. He *d* 5 April 1943

2a Maud Elizabeth; *m* 28 Sept 1898 Spencer James Langton, of Little Hadham Place, Little Hadham, Herts, and *d* 14 July 1946, leaving issue. He *d* 16 April 1935

3a Anne Page, JP (Herts); OStJ; *m* 27 Oct 1928 1st Baron Brocket (*qv*), and *d* 18 Oct 1949

4a Helen Charlotte; *m* 5 May 1898 Maj Robert Mervyn Richardson, late 14th Hus, and *d* 2 Dec 1942, leaving issue. He *d* 6 March 1917

5a Violet Mary; *m* 24 Nov 1910 William Frank Gardiner Baird, 2nd son of Sir William James Gardiner Baird, 8th Bt (*see* BAIRD, Bt, of Saughton Hall), and *d* 17 Oct 1947, leaving issue. He *das* 5 Nov 1914 from wounds received in action

6a Susannah Grace; *m* 8 Sept 1904 Sir Edward Ernest Pearson, of Brickendonbury, Hertford, and has issue. He *d* 19 Nov 1925

(2) Thomas Denman (Rev), MA, Oxford, late Vicar of Kimpton, Herts; *b* 2 March 1845; *m* 6 May 1891 Eleanor Fraser (*d* 4 April 1944), er dau of Rt Rev George Tomlinson, DD, 1st Anglican Bishop of Gibraltar, by his w Eleanor Jane, dau of Col Charles Mackenzie Fraser, of Castle Fraser, and *d* 21 June 1913, leaving issue:

1a Thomas Fraser CROFYT later CROFT-FRASER (added 1906 on inheriting estate of his maternal great uncle, Col Frederick Mackenzie Fraser, of Castle Fraser and Inverallochy); RC priest; *b* 9 Jan 1893; *d* 4 Nov 1956

3 (cont.) The Rev Richard Croft *m* 2nd 1856 Louisa (*dsp* 9 Dec 1898), dau of Samuel Holland, of Dunbleton, and *d* 17 Feb 1869

1 Frances Elizabeth; *m* 19 Sept 1822 Louis Adolphe Marie de Chanteau, chev Legion of Honour, and *dsps* 2 Aug 1877

The 7th Bt's bro,

Sir Archer Denman Croft, 8th Bt, Master of the Court of Queen's Bench; *b* 7 Dec 1801; *m* 31 Aug 1837 Julia Barbara (*d* 17 Nov 1864), widow of Athelstan Corbet, of Ynys-y-Maengwyn, and dau of Maj-Gen John Garstin, HEICS, and had:

1 HERBERT GEORGE DENMAN (Sir), **9th Bt**

1 Julia Helen; *m* 14 June 1866 Rev Athelstan Corbet, MA, Rector of Adderley, Salop (*see* 1970 edn CORBET, Bt), and *d* 30 May 1885 aged 45, leaving issue. He *d* 27 April 1926

Sir ARCHER *d* 10 Jan 1865; his son

Sir Herbert George Denman Croft, 9th Bt, DL, JP, CA, MA Oxford, barrister, Inspr Constabulary N of England 1892–1902, MP Herefs 1868–74, Lt Herefs Militia; *b* 25 July 1838; *m* 10 Jan 1865 his cousin Georgiana Eliza Lucy (*d* 7 July 1925), est dau and coheir of Matthew Marsh, MP, of Ramridge Ho, Hants, and *d* 11 Feb 1902, having had, with other issue:

1 **Sir Herbert Archer Croft, 10th Bt**, DL, JP, High Sheriff 1911, Capt 1st Bn Herefs Regt (TF), late 4th Bn Shropshire LI; *b* 5 Sept 1868; *m* 1st 20 June 1892 Kathleen (*d* 25 Sept 1898), 2nd dau of John Hare, of Invercargill, NZ, and had:

(1) Dorothy Glendower; *b* 18 Nov 1893; *m* 18 Jan 1918 Capt Ossian Roy Cormack, 33rd Bn Australian IF, son of Donald Cormack, of Sydney, NSW and had issue

(2) Anna Joyce Helen; *b* 26 May 1895; *m* 22 April 1926 Geoffrey de Mounteney Gerard Hoare, of Meadham, Harlow, 3rd son of Henry Gerard Hoare, and *d* 12 July 1948, leaving issue. He *d* 5 April 1943

(3) Nancy Barbara Kathleen; *b* 6 Sept 1898; *m* 12 July 1928 W/Cdr John Sever Phillips, RAF, er s of Rev Philip Richard Phillips, Rector of Hildersham, Cambridge, and *d* 10 Oct 1970, leaving issue

1 (cont.) **Sir Herbert** *m* 2nd 3 Feb 1903 Katherine Agnes (*d* 1 Dec 1966), est dau of Joseph Charlton Parr, of Grappenhall Heyes, Warrington, and was reported missing believed *k* Gallipoli 11 Aug 1915, having by her had issue:

(1) **Sir James Herbert Croft, 11th Bt**; *b* 24 May 1907; *educ* Eton and BNC Oxford; Capt Herefs Regt (TAR) WW II in No 1 Commando Special Serv Bn; *kas* 15 Aug 1941

(4) Elinor; *b* 14 Jan 1904; *m* 24 Oct 1928 (*divorce* 1934) Henry Charlton Parr, only son of Roger Charlton Parr, of Grappenhall Heyes, Warrington, and had issue

2 Bernard Harley; *b* 23 July 1871; *d* 28 April 1889

3 HUGH MATTHEW FIENNES (Sir), **12th Bt**

4 William Denman, CB (1935), CMG (1919), DSO (1917, three bars, 1916, 1917 and 1918), Hon Brig-Gen (ret 1934), Lt-Col Cameronian Scottish Rifles, T/Lt-Col cmdg 11th Bn Roy Scots 1915–17, T/Brig-Gen Bde Cdr 1917–19, Lt-Col Roy Tank Corps India 1923, Col AHQ India 1925, Instructor Sr Offrs' Sch Sheerness 1927–29, T/Brig and Cmdt Roy Tank Corps Centre 1929–31, T/Brig and Bde-Cdr India 1931, served WW I (despatches ten times, Legion of Honour) and Mohmand operations 1933 (despatches), raised HG for Cornwall May 1940, Co Commr Boy Scouts Cornwall; *b* 15 March 1879; *educ* Oxford Mil Coll; *m* 23 May 1912 Esmé (*d* 1977), only dau of Sir Arthur Edwin Sutton, 7th Bt (*qv*), and *d* 14 July 1968, having had issue:

(1) William Owen Glendower, T/Capt IA; *b* 12 March 1913 *m* March 1944 *Margaret, dau of Maj Tobin, IA, and *das* 13 Nov 1946, leaving issue:

1a +Richard Owen Glendower [Richard Croft Esq, Barnesfield, South St, Boughton, Faversham, Kent]; *b* 29 Nov 1944; *educ* Kent U; Lt The Cameronians; *m* 1967 *Elizabeth Jillian Allen, and has issue:

1b +James Owen; *b* 1972

1b *Emma Kate; *b* 1974

(2) +John Armentières (Rev), MC (1944) [Maj The Rev John Croft MC, Vine House, The Common, Wincanton, Somerset]; *b* 1 Jan 1915; *educ* Stowe; late Maj RA, and IA, served on NWF 1935 (despatches), and WW II (wounded), ret 1956, ordained 1957, Vicar of Gwinear, Cornwall from 1960; *m* 19 July 1948 *Sheila Kathleen, yr dau of Maj JA Ford, of Pengreep, Ponsanooth, Cornwall, and has issue

1a +Edmund Hugh Glendower; *b* 8 Dec 1954

1a *Patricia Lucy; *b* 17 June 1951; *m* 1973 *Maj Robert Rowe, Roy Irish Rangers, and has issue:

1b *Victoria Lucy; *b* 1977

2b *Harriet Alice; *b* 1979

(1)*Violet Lorna; *b* 1917; *m* 28 March 1942 *Lt-Cdr Thomas Charteris Black, RNVR, son of J S Charteris Black, of Tudor Hotel, Fortis Green, NZ, and has issue:

1a *Peter Michael; *b* 20 Aug 1952

1a *Jane Margaret; *b* 18 Jan 1943

2a *Susan Mary; *b* 18 Sept 1945

(2) *Angela Desirée [Mrs Walter Carlson, 14A Upper Glenburn Rd, Bearsden, Glasgow G61]; *b* 1923; *m* 1st 6 May 1955 Roland Grievson (*d* 1974); *m* 2nd 1984 *Walter Carlson

5 Owen George Scudamore, JP (Herefs 1909), High Sheriff 1943, Ld of the Manors of Croft and Bircher, Maj Shropshire Yeo, WW I 1914–18; *b* 14 May 1880; *m* 4 Aug 1909 Stella Isabel (*d* 27 Aug 1972, aged 87), dau of Nicholas Bouwer, of Buenos Aires, and *d* 29 Feb 1956, having had issue:

(1) A son; *b* and *d* 7 Sept 1924

6 Jasper Brodie, Lt Australian RFA; *b* 27 April 1884; *m* 7 Aug 1907 Catherine Harriett (*d* 1975), 5th dau of Frederick G Taylor, of Terrible Vale, NSW, and *d* 11 Oct 1950, leaving issue:

(1) +Jasper Thomas, JP (1958) [Jasper Croft Esq JP, 50 Sandstone Crescent, Lennox Head, NSW 2478, Australia]; F/Lt RAAF; *b* 4 June 1924; *m* 1948 *Editha Deirdre, dau of George Westgarth, of Scone, NSW, and has issue:

1a +Jasper David, JP [Jasper Croft Esq JP, c/o NSW Agriculture and Fisheries, Wagga Wagga, NSW, Australia]; *b* 31 Jan 1949; BA, MSc; *m* 1977 *Frances Ellen, dau of Francis Hamilton, of Condobolin, and has issue:

1b +Jasper Brett Frank; *b* 1983

1b *Amanda Kate; *b* 1980

1a *Bettina Kay [Mrs David Leslie, Beverley, Nevertire, NSW Australia]; *b* 1 Oct 1951; *m* 1973 *David Peter Leslie, and has issue:

1b *Andrew David; *b* 1978

1b *Karina Jodi; *b* 1976

2b *Kristy Peta; *b* 1987

2a *Kerrie Leigh; *b* 11 May 1954

(1) *Kitty McLeod [Mrs Peter Assheton, Unit 49/45 Cook St, St David's Retirement Village, Forestville, NSW, Australia]; *b* 29 Dec 1909 *m* Feb 1938 Peter Assheton (*d* 1970), and has issue:

1a Pedir Raif Orme; *b* 26 June 1941; *m* 1972 *Nancy Shaw, of Sydney, NSW, and *d* 1992, leaving issue:

1b *Olwen Annaliese; *b* 1975

1a *Rowena Tydwr [Mrs Joseph Lisak, Lorne House, Kingsland, Herefs HR6 9RU]; *b* 21 Aug 1939; *m* 1966 *Joseph (Zbigniew) Lisak and has:

1b *Tamara; *b* 1967

2b *Nadezhda; *b* 1968

(2) *Ana Lucy McLeod, QAIMNS (R); *m* 1942 Claude Wallace Grievson, Staff Cdr Orient Line (*d* 26 Feb 1969, aged 67), and has issue:

1a *Jasper Wallace; *b* 21 Dec 1944

1a *Barbara Jasmine; *b* 22 June 1949

(3) *Isabel McLeod [Mrs Bassett Care, 16 Beaumetz St, Sandgate 4017, Qld, Australia]; *b* 6 April 1911; *m* 27 Feb 1947 *Bassett Frederick Care, and has issue:

1a *Frederick McLeod, RAN; *b* 6 March 1948; *m* 1969 *Jennifer Dianne, dau of Arthur Silas Faulk, and has issue:

1b *Thomas Lachlan; *b* 1986

1b *Amanda; *b* 1970

2b *Sally; *b* 1972

(4) *Marjorie McLeod [Mrs Cecil Lowe, 32 North Rd, Woodridge, Qld, Australia]; *b* 17 Dec 1912; *m* 1943 *Cecil Gordon Lowe, RAAF, and has issue:

1a *Benjamin John; *b* 1944; *m* 1st 1962 (*divorce* 1975) Gloria Daphne, dau of W Williams, of W Australia, and has issue:

1b *Dallas Gordon; *b* 1969

1a (cont.) Benjamin Lowe *m* 2nd 1979 *Patricia Lee Florian, and has further issue:

2b *Jason McLeod; *b* 1979

2a *William James; *b* 1951; *m* 1974 *Caroline, dau of Kenneth Watson, and has issue:

1b *Daniel William; *b* 1975

2b *Drummond Murray; *b* 1978

3b *Benjamin Gordon; *b* 1979

1a *Catherine Jane [Mrs Brian Finnigan, 65 Ashton St, Kingston, Qld, Australia]; *b* 1946; *m* 1971 *Brian Finnigan and has:

1b *Matthew Brian; *b* 1976

2b *David Joseph; *b* 1980

1b *Joanne Maree; *b* 1972

2b *Anna; *b* 1987

2a *Susanne Barbara; *b* 1950; *m* 1971 *Kenneth Murray, of Tieri, Qld, and has:

1b *Rachel Susanne; *b* 1976

2b *Deanne Gai; *b* 1978

3b *Alaina Alexandrea; *b* 1981

3a *Elizabeth; *b* 1953; *m* 1975 *Peter Anthony of Qld, and has issue:

1b *Jodie Alisha; *b* 1980

2b *Melissa Jane; *b* 1983
4a *Mary-Anne; *b* 1955; *m* 1977 *Denis Townsend, of Qld, and has issue:
1b *Shane Andrew; *b* 1980
2b *Timothy Neil; *b* 1983
(5) *Enid Barbara McLeod; *b* 6 March 1915; *m* 26 Sept 1959 George Ronald Hyde (*d* 1975)
(6) *Nancy Perena McLeod [Mrs Eric Adams, Balnabeen, Silver Leigh Rd, Kingsthorpe, Qld 4400, Australia]; *b* 7 Jan 1921; *m* 1950 *Eric W Adams, and has two adopted children
1 Janet Georgiana; *m* 21 Jan 1891 Edward Archer Greathed, of Chandlers Ford, Hants, est son of Maj-Gen William Wilberforce Harris Greathed, CB, and *d* 19 April 1921, leaving issue. He *d* 11 Nov 1921
2 Sybil Helen, OBE (1918); *m* 24 Sept 1902 Sir John Rumney Nicholson, CMG, only son of Isaac Nicholson, and *d* 11 Aug 1959, leaving issue. He *d* 22 Nov 1939
3 Lucy Barbara; *m* 1 June 1899 Frederick Evelyn Cairnes, of Bettyglen, Raheny, Dublin, 2nd son of Prof John Elliot Cairnes, and *d* 2 Feb 1957, leaving issue. He *d* 12 March 1944

The 11th Bt's uncle,

Sir Hugh Matthew Fiennes Croft, 12th Bt; *b* 10 May 1874; *m* 18 April 1900 Lucy, est dau of Frederick G Taylor, of Terrible Vale, NSW, and had issue:
1 BERNARD HUGH DENMAN (Sir), **13th Bt**
2 +Herbert Frederick [Herbert Croft Esq, Bareena, Uralla, NSW, Australia]; *b* 2 July 1906; *m* 20 Jan 1932 Marjorie Valmai (*d* 1990), dau of R Evans, and has issue:
(1) +Peter Herbert [Peter Croft Esq, Wongalee, Uralla 2358, NSW, Australia]; *b* 21 Feb 1933; *m* 1965 *Ann dau of LG Carpenter, of Toll-bar, Cooma, NSW, and has issue:
1a +Guy Herbert; *b* 2 Aug 1966
2a +Andrew Peter; *b* 14 Sept 1968; *m* 26 Nov 1994 *Sally Maree, dau of M J Holcombe, of Burren Junction, NSW, and has:
1b +Lyndon Murray; *b* 20 Aug 1996
(2) +Robert Ryland [Robert Croft Esq, PO Box 1586, Armidale, NSW 2350, Australia]; *b* 19 Sept 1937; *m* 21 Jan 1966 *Helen Magnus Fraser, and has issue:
1a +Quentin Stewart; *b* 10 Aug 1967
2a +Carlisle Robert; *b* 1974
3a +Sinclair Fraser; *b* 1976
(3) +James Phillip [James Croft Esq, Weebaree, Uralla 2358, NSW, Australia]; *b* 20 Jan 1950; *m* 1972 *Elaine, dau of S K Wall, of Cowra, and has issue:
1a +Michael James; *b* 1977
1a *Rowena Jane; *b* 1974
(1) *Shirley Anne [Mrs David Gill, 3 Buckingham Dve, Pottsville Beach, NSW 2489, Australia]; *b* 12 Oct 1934; *m* 1954 *David Gill and has issue:
1a *Michael David [Michael Gill Esq, 7 Gigas Ct, Rochedale, Qld 4123, Australia]; *b* 1957; *m* 1982 *Kim Elizabeth, dau of R R Crutcher, of Wee Waa, NSW, and has issue:
1b *Nichole May; *b* 1986
2b *Samantha Jane; *b* 1992
1a *Philippa Shirley [Mrs James Page, Boolneringbar, Copmanhurst, NSW, Australia]; *b* 1955; *m* 1975 *James Douglas Page, and has issue:
1b *Robert James; *b* 1975
1b *Rachelle Philippa; *b* 1978
2b *Jacqueline Frances; *b* 1982
2a *Katrina Anne [Mrs John Kerrison, Osprey St, Kingscliff 24, NSW, Australia]; *b* 1958; *m* 1988 *John Douglas Kerrison, and has issue:
1b *Dean Andrew; *b* 1993
1b *Anna Maree; *b* 1991
3 Frederick James, formerly F/O RAAF; *b* 2 March 1909; *m* 25 Feb 1943 *Barbara [Mrs Frederick Croft, Lugwardine, Barraba, NSW 2347, Australia], dau of Howard Carter, of Barraba, NSW, and *d* 1993, leaving issue:
(1) +Edward Hugh Wynford; *b* 5 Feb 1944; *m* 20 June 1969 *Jennifer Mary, dau of Thomas Shirton, of Armoobilia, Cheepie, Qld, Australia, and has issue:
1a +Edward James Wynford; *b* 1971
2a +Andrew John Wynford; *b* 1974
1a *Amanda Jane; *b* 1978
2a *Lucinda Jennifer; *b* 1981
4 Richard Marsh; *b* 6 Aug 1910; *m* April 1941 *Mary, dau of F Ewing, of Walcha, NSW
5 Archer John, formerly F/O RAAF; *b* 31 Aug 1913; *m* 13 Feb 1939 Marcie Issell Heathfield (*d* 1976), dau of Clifton Hazelwood Eliott (*see* ELIOTT, Bt), and *d* 1971, leaving issue:
(1) +Antony John [Antony Croft Esq, Vale St, Tamworth, NSW 2340, Australia]; *b* 10 May 1940; *m* 16 April 1966 (*divorce* 1978) Kathleen Frances, dau of RF Kelsall, of Round Hill, Tamworth, NSW, and has issue:
1a +Michael John; *b* 1967
1a *Tania Jane; *b* 1968
(2) +David Archer [David Croft Esq, 12 Hambledon Hill Rd, Singleton, NSW, Australia]; *b* 9 June 1946; *m* 1971 *Violeta, only child of V Deikus, of 6 Albert St, Cabramatta, NSW, and has issue:
1a +Justin Damian; *b* 1973
2a +Nathan David; *b* 1975
1a *Rebecca Lee; *b* 1978
(3) +Stephen Hugh; *b* 15 June 1953
1 Phyllis Lucy; *b* 25 April 1901; *m* 24 Nov 1923 *George Stuart Robertson Park, and *d* 1996, leaving:
(1) *Walter Stuart [Walter Park Esq, Wongabindi, New Winton Rd, Tamworth, NSW 2340, Australia]; *b* 1925; *m* 1950 *June Coates, and has issue:
1a *Elizabeth; *b* 1951; *m* 1973 *Robert John Nicoll, and has issue:
1b *Brett Robert; *b* 1975
1b *Sharon Elizabeth; *b* 1977
2a *Wendy; *b* 1954; *m* 1985 *John Stephen Dobis, and has issue:
1b *John Steven Walter; *b* 1990
1b *Jessica June Katalin; *b* 1993
3a *Deborah [Mrs Gary Craig, Baronia, Duri, NSW 2416, Australia]; *b* 1957; *m* 1979 *Gary Craig
(2) *Ian Croft [Ian Park Esq, 7 Asher Court, Upper Coomera, 4210 Qld, Australia]; *b* 1936; *m* 1960 *Kay, only dau of A Shaw, of Lammermoor, Wee Woa, NSW, and has issue:
1a *Kenneth Ian; *b* 1963
2a *Geoffrey Steven; *b* 1964; *m* 1990 *Kerry Leanne, est dau of John Compton, of Eden, NSW, and has:
1b *Brendan Stuart; *b* 1992
2b *Daniel John; *b* 1995
1b *Nikola Margaret; *b* 1997
3a *Nicholas David; *b* 1970
1a *Janine Maree [Mrs Darryle Brusnahan, Gainsborough Lodge, Hersley Rd, Toowoomba, Qld, Australia]; *b* 1968; *m* 1992 *Darryle Brusnahan and has:
1b *Taylor Kay; *b* 1997
(1) *Phyllis Joan [Mrs Roger Rankine, 100 Upper St, Tamworth, NSW, Australia]; *b* 1924; *m* 1949 Roger L'Estrange Rankine, Capt AIF (*d* 1982), and has issue:
1a *Timothy Roger; *b* 1951; *m* 1975 *, er dau of G Forté, and has issue:
1b *Dean Roger Forté; *b* 1978
2b *David Forté; *b* 1979
1b *Alexandra Forté; *b* 1987
2a *Andrew Stuart; *b* 1954; *m* 1981 *Mary-Alice, est dau of John Lloyd, of Delungra, NSW, and has issue:
1b *Roger Angus; *b* 1984
2b *Maxim John; *b* 1989
1b *Prudence Lucy; *b* 1986
3a *Steven John; *b* 1960; *m* 198– *Belinda Jan, er dau of Richard Boden, of Mt Ousley, NSW, and has issue:
1b *Thomas; *b* 1987
1b *Sophie Catherine; *b* 1990
2b *Eloise Claire Alice; *b* 1992
(2) *Mary Isabel [Mrs John Wilshire, 41 Hyman St, Tamworth 2340, NSW, Australia]; *b* 1928; *m* 1949 *John Mervyn Wilshire, and has issue:
1a *Malcolm John; *b* 1958; *m* 1984 *Fiona Anne Slattery, and has issue:
1b *Julie Kathryn; *b* 1986
1a *Marilyn Mary [Mrs Timothy O'Keefe, 13 Napier St, Tamworth, NSW, Australia]; *b* 1950; *m* 1973 *Timothy John O'Keefe, and has issue:
1b *George Alexander; *b* 1974
2b *Adam Timothy; *b* 1975
2a *Christine Linda [Mrs Lowell Reardon, 156 Green Point Dve, Green Point, via Forster, NSW 2428, Australia]; *b* 1953; *m* 1972 *Lowell Reardon, and has issue:
1b *Melissa Louise; *b* 1973
2b *Rebecca Gai; *b* 1976

Sir HUGH *d* 15 June 1954; his est son

Sir Bernard Hugh Denman Croft, 13th Bt; *b* 24 Aug 1903; *m* 8 April 1931 *Helen Margaret [Helen Lady Croft, 133 Dangar St, Armidale, NSW 2350, Australia], dau of H Weaver, and *d* 1984, leaving issue:
1 Sir OWEN GLENDOWER CROFT, **14th and present Bt**.
2 +Hugh Fiennes Denman [Hugh Croft Esq, Callemondah, Duri, NSW 2344, Australia]; *b* 5 Oct 1942; *m* 1972 *June Alison Cairnes, dau of John Wauch Johnston, of Straban, Walchan, NSW, and has issue:
(1) *Edwina Alexandra Cairnes; *b* 1974
(2) *Katrina Alison Cairnes; *b* 1976
(3) *Philippa Ann Cairnes; *b* 1977
(4) *Lucinda Anna Cairnes; *b* 1983
3 +Bernard John [Bernard Croft Esq, Westview, PO Box 253, Guyra, NSW 2365, Australia]; *b* 21 Oct 1943; *m* 1977 *Janet Madeleine, dau of Lloyd Alfred Streader, of Melbourne, Victoria, and has issue:
(1) +David William; *b* 1977
(2) +Ian Archer; *b* 1981
(1) *Briony Elizabeth; *b* 1979
(2) *Alice Madeleine; *b* 1985
1 *Margaret [Mrs David Wright, Wallamumbi, Armidale, NSW 2350, Australia]; *b* 7 May 1935; *m* 1960 *David Arundel Wright, and has issue:
(1) *Phillip Arundel; *b* 1963
(2) *David Andrew; *b* 1965
(1) *Charlotte May; *b* 1961
(2) *Catherine Arundel; *b* 1969
2 *Camilla; *b* 30 Sept 1947

CROFTON

Arms: Per pale indented or and az. a lion passant guardant counterchanged. **Crest:** A stalk of wheat (seven ears on one stalk) or. **Supporters:** Dexter, a lion az.; sinister, a stag ppr., armed and hoofed or. **Mottoes:** *Dat Deus incrementum* ('God gives the increase') and over the crest: *Pro patria et rege* ('For King and Country'). **Creations:** Bt. (I) 12 June 1758, B. (I) 9 March 1798.

THE 7TH BARON CROFTON OF MOTE, Co Roscommon, and a **Baronet** (Sir Guy Patrick Gilbert Crofton, Bt) [Lt-Col The Rt Hon The Lord Crofton, c/o Drummond's Bank, 49 Charing Cross, London SW1A 2DX]; *b* 17 June 1951; *s* bro 1989; *educ* Theresianistische AkademieVienna and Midhurst GS; Lt-Col 9th/12th Roy Lancers (PWO), Defence Attaché Berne 1995–; *m* 1985 *Gillian Susan Burroughs, only dau of Harry Godfrey Mitchell Bass, CMG, of Reepham, Norfolk, and has issue:

1 +(EDWARD) HARRY PIERS; *b* 23 Jan 1988

2 +(Charles) Marcus George; *b* 23 Jan 1988

Lineage: JOHN CROFTON, of Ballymurray, Co Roscommon; Auditor and Escheator-Gen Ireland 1584; accompanied Sir Henry Sidney, KG, Ld Dep of Ireland, when latter posted there, and was granted large tracts of land in Cos Roscommon, Leitrim and Sligo; *m* Jane, sis of Sir Henry Duke, of Castlejordan, Co Meath, and *d* 1610, having had issue:

1 EDWARD

2 John, of Lisdorne, Co Roscommon, MP Co Sligo 1633; *m* Sarah, dau of Richard Maypowder, of Killinboy, Co Roscommon, and was with her ancestor of the CROFTONs of Lisdorne, CROFTONs of Lakefield and the CROFTON-ATKINSes; *d* 16 Sept 1639, leaving, with other issue :

(1) Richard; *m* Anne, dau of Sir Basil Brooke, of Brooke Manor, Co Donegal, and *d* 1667, leaving issue

(2) Edward, of Grange-Godden, Co Meath, High Sheriff Co Leitrim 1658; *m* Katharine, yr dau of Brian Jones, of Burnells Court, Co Dublin, and Headfort Castle, Co Leitrim

(3) William, Capt in Lord Roscommon's Royalist Horse 1646

(4) Very Rev Thomas, Dean of Elphin in 1667

(5) Duke, Capt in Sir Oliver St George's Dragoons; *dsp* 1669

(1) Katherine; *m* Joseph Ware, Dean of Elphin, 3rd son of Sir James Ware, and *dsp* 1650

3 William, of Temple Ho, Co Sligo, Auditor-Gen of the Provinces of Ulster and Connaught 1617, MP Co Donegal 1613, High Sheriff Co Sligo 1606; *m* Mary, dau of Sir William Usher, of Donnybrook, Clerk PC, and had, with a dau (Mary, *m* 1st Silvester Kennedy, *m* 2nd Sir Paul Davis, Sec of State):

(1) William, of Temple Ho, High Sheriff Co Sligo 1613, MP Donegal 1634; *m* Rose, dau of John Newman, of Dublin, and had:

1a Mary; *m* 1st George Perceval, ancestor of the PERCEVALs of Temple House; *m* 2nd Richard Aldworth, of Stanlake, Berks, and *d* 15 Oct 1705

4 Henry, of Mohill, Co Leitrim; *b* 3 April 1643; ancestor of CROFTON, Bt, of Mohill (*qv*)

1 Sarah; *m* Gerald Dillon, of Freemore, son of Capt Garrett Dillon and nephew of 1st Viscount Dillon (*qv*)

2 Joan; *m* Edward Brabazon

JOHN CROFTON's est son,

EDWARD CROFTON, of Ballymurray; *m* Elizabeth, dau of Capt Robert Mostyn and widow of William Clifford, of Tullycastle, and had issue:

1 GEORGE

2 Thomas, of Longford Ho, Co Sligo, ancestor of CROFTON, Bt, of Longford House (*qv*)

3 John; *d* unm

4 William, of Clonsilla, Co Roscommon; *m* Mary, dau of Richard Maypowder, of Kilteevan, Co Roscommon, and *d* 1665

EDWARD CROFTON *d* 19 Jan 1627; his est son,

GEORGE CROFTON, of Ballymurray; MP Askeaton, Co Limerick, 1639; built the Castle of The Mote, Co Roscommon; *m* Elizabeth, dau of Sir Francis Berkeley, PC, of Askeaton, by Katherine, dau of Most Rev Adam Loftus, DD, Archbishop of Dublin (*see* ELY, M), and had issue:

1 EDWARD (Sir), **1st Bt**

2 John, of Kilbryan, Co Roscommon; *m* Elizabeth, dau of Hamond L'Estrange, of Castle Strange, Co Roscommon, and was ancestor of the CROFTONs of Kilbryan

3 Thomas, of Askeaton; *m* Christian, dau of Henry Lee, of Clanderlaw, Co Clare, and left two daus

1 Mary; *m* Philip Ormsby

GEORGE CROFTON's est son,

Sir EDWARD CROFTON, 1st Bt (I), so *cr* 1 July 1661 for his services to CHARLES II during the Civil War, of The Mote; *m* 1st 12 Oct 1647 Mary (*d* 1651), dau of Sir James Ware, Auditor-Gen of Ireland, and had a s (*dvp*); *m* 2nd by licence 11 Jan 1661/2 Susanna (*m* 2nd by licence 24 Feb 1676/7 Gerald Dillon, Recorder of Dublin), dau of Thomas Clifford, and *d* 1675, having by her had:

Sir EDWARD CROFTON, 2nd Bt, of The Mote, PC (1714); attainted by JAMES II's I Parl May 1689; MP Boyle 1695; *m* 2 Feb 1684 Katherine, dau of Sir Oliver St George, 1st Bt, of Carrickdrumrusk, Co Leitrim, and *d* 24 Nov 1729, having had:

1 Sir EDWARD CROFTON, 3rd Bt, of The Mote, MP Co Roscommon; *b* 25 May 1687; *m* 4 March 1711 Mary (*d* 10 Feb 1756), dau of Anthony Nixon, of Dublin, and *d* 11 Nov 1739, leaving:

(1) Sir EDWARD CROFTON, 4th Bt, of The Mote; MP Co Roscommon; *b* 12 April 1713; *m* 17 June 1741 Martha (*m* 2nd Ezekiel Nisbett, MD), dau of Joseph Damer, of Came, Dorset, and sis of 1st Earl of Dorchester (*see* PORTARLINGTON, E), and *dsp*, *ka* near Tournai 26 March 1745

(1) KATHERINE, of whom hereafter, as heiress of the family

2 Oliver, of Lissanarre, Co Limerick; *m* Katherine Armstrong (*d* 6 May 1750) and *d* 1709, having had:

(1) Sir OLIVER CROFTON, 5th and last Bt, of The Mote; lived at Galbally and Lissanarre, Co Limerick; *m* 6 Dec 1737 Abigail Jackson Buckley, heiress of estates in Cumberland, Yorks, Lancs and Co Dublin (*dsp* Dec 1763), and *dsp* 9 Nov 1780, when the btcy expired

The 4th Bt's sis,

KATHERINE Crofton; *m* 9 Sept 1743 Marcus LOWTHER later LOWTHER-CROFTON (added 1745), alias **Sir Marcus Lowther-Crofton, 1st Bt** (I), so *cr* 12 June 1758, MP Ratoath 1753–60 and 1769–76 and Roscommon borough 1761–68 (2nd s of Gorges Lowther (*d* 11 June 1716), of Kilrue, Co Meath, MP Ratoath, by Jane, sis of 1st Earl of Tyrone of the 1673 *cr*, and a distant cousin of the Earls of Lonsdale, and *d* 9 April 1767, having had, with other issue:

1 EDWARD (Sir), **2nd Bt**

2 John Frederick Lowther, Capt 32nd Regt; *b* 13 Oct 1758; *m* Mary Thorney (*d* 1799), and had, with two daus and four other s:

(1) Edward Lowther, CB, Capt RN; *b* 24 Nov 1783; *m* 23 April 1816 Mary, dau of William Leader, MP Camelford, and had issue

(2) Frederick Lowther, Lt RM, formerly Coldstream Gds; *m* 1810 Anne, dau of Stephen Smith, and *d* aboard the *Semiramis* 1819, leaving, with a dau:

1a Frederick Charles Edward Lowther; *b* 10 Feb 1813; *m* 1st 2 Sept 1837 Miriam, dau of Capt William White; *m* 2nd 17 Aug 1865 Mrs Helen Grimes (*d* 29 Aug 1893), and *d* 11 Oct 1883, having by his 1st w had issue:

1b George Lowther, 6th Dragoon Gds, Maj 1st Devon Rifles; *b* 24 March 1841; *educ* Exeter Coll Oxford (BA); *m* 27 April 1865 Ellen Mary (*d* 7 June 1911), dau and heir of Thomas George Norris, JP, of Gorphwysfa, Denbighs, and *d* 15 April 1915, leaving issue:

1c Frederick Norris Lowther; *b* 27 May 1870; *m* 1896 Edith (*d* 7 Oct 1951), dau of Hastings Cuningham (*see* FAIRLIE-CUNINGHAME, Bt), and *d* 28 Dec 1947, leaving issue:

1d George Lowther; *b* 15 Dec 1905; *m* 17 Oct 1928 Nea (*d* 1981), er dau of Rev A P Cameron (Moderator of Presbyterian Ch of NSW 1928), of The Manse, Glen Innes, NSW, and *d* 1976, leaving issue:

1e *Judith Mary [Mrs Edgar Allen, M/S 305 Windermere Rd, Bundaberg, Qld 4670, Australia]; *b* 1932; *m* 1st 1965 (*divorce* 1968) Les Hayna and has:

1f *Christine Nea [Mrs Wayne Olsen, PO Box 620, Bundaberg, Qld 4670, Australia]; *b* 1957; *m* 1977 *Wayne Olsen, of Bundaberg, Queensland, and has issue:

1g *Timothy Malcolm; *b* 1981

2g *Daniel Christopher; *b* 1985

1g *Kerri-Ann; *b* 1979

1e (cont.) Mrs Judith Hayna; *m* 2nd 1970 *Edgar Allen and by him has:

1f *Geoffrey Edgar Howell; *b* 1971; *m* 1996 *Angela Heloise Giess

2f *William George John (twin); *b* 1971

2e *Edith Clare [Mrs Desmond Fourro, 3/1A Kennedy St, Bundaberg, Qld, Australia]; *b* 4 April 1936; *m* 1st 1956 (*divorce* 1982) Alex Barry Mitchell; *m* 2nd 1986 *Desmond Fourro, of Bundaberg, Qld, and by 1st husb has issue:

1f *Steven George; *b* 1957; *m* 1989 *Lynette Mary Baker, of Mackay, Qld, and has issue:

1g *Kirsty Leeanne; *b* 1982

2g *Kylie Marie (twin); *b* 1982

2f *Brian Alec; *b* 1961; *m* 1985 *Jacqueline Davies, of Mackay, Qld, and has issue:

1g *Hayden Rhys; *b* 1992

1g *Kylie Nicole; *b* 1986

2g *Leah Suzanne; *b* 1988

3f *Glenn Cameron; *b* 1965; by Sharon Dawn McLean, of Cookton, Qld, and has:

1g *Jias Nathan Braid; *b* 1993

2g *Joel Aley Barry; *b* 1994

1f *Jennifer Jeanie; *b* 1959; *m* 1st 1984 (*divorce* 1986) Guus Hoogland, of Mackay, Qld; *m* 2nd *Wayne Robert King, of Mackay, Qld, and by him has:

1g *Michelle Cori; *b* 1991

1d Ellen Marjorie Lowther; *b* 11 Feb 1897; *d* unm 1969

2d Bettine Lowther; *b* 21 Dec 1900; *d* unm 14 Feb 1955

2c Edward George Lowther, DSO (1900), V-Adml, served in China; *b* 9 Aug 1873; *m* 1st 25 Feb 1911 (*divorce* 1925) Magdalen Sinclair, er dau of Duncan Anderson, of Eaton Sq, SW, and had issue:

1d Edward Duncan; *b* 12 Nov 1912; *d* 26 Sept 1932

2c (cont.) Edward Crofton *m* 2nd 4 Aug 1931 Rosalind Mabel Eaton CROFTON-SMALLEY (*m* 2nd 1 Oct 1947 Arthur Smalley (*d* 14 June 1948)), and *d* 19 July 1942

1c Miriam Ellen; *m* 8 April 1891 Hugh Brabazon Grant, and had issue

2c Cecil Florence; *d* unm 27 Feb 1933

3c Amy Georgiana; *m* 10 Sept 1892 Maj Henry Cornwall Cotton Gibbings, formerly Roy Inniskilling Fus, and *d* 24 April 1953, leaving issue. He *d* 28 Aug 1936

4c Violet Helen; *d* unm 25 July 1942

5c Rose Irene; *m* 2 Nov 1912 Alexander Graham Speirs, of Meeria Cotta, Ceylon, and *d* 8 Jan 1914

2a Stephen Smith, V-Adml; *b* 9 Nov 1818; *m* 1st 1849 Eliza (*d* 1855), dau of Senhor Fomm, of Rio de Janeiro, and had issue:

1b Marian Eliza; *d* unm 4 July 1944, aged 94

2b Rose Sophia; *d* unm 7 Jan 1945, aged 92

3b Eliza Ann; *d* unm 25 April 1951, aged 96

2a (cont.) V-Adml Stephen Crofton *m* 2nd 13 Feb 1868 Agnes (*d* 18 Jan 1927), only dau and heir of Sir John Reid, 6th Bt, of Barra, and *d* 27 Dec 1899

3 William Henry, Lt in the Army; *b* 28 Feb 1762; *m* Jane, dau of James Kelly, and *d* 21 Aug 1794, leaving, with two daus, a son:

(1) Marcus Lowther

1 Catherine; *m* 16 June 1770 Sir James Quaile Somerville, 3rd Bt, and *d* 1775, leaving issue (*see* 1970 edn SOMERVILLE, Bt). He *d c* 1800

2 Sophia Jane; *m* Peter Metge, MP for Boyle, afterwards Baron of the Exchequer in Ireland, and *d* Dec 1777, leaving issue

Sir MARCUS *d* 16 Jan 1784; his est son,

Sir Edward Crofton, 2nd Bt; MP Co Roscommon, Col Roscommon Militia; *m* 13 April 1767 ARMIDA/ANNE (*d* 12 Aug 1817), **Baroness Crofton of Mote**, Co Roscommon (I), so *cr* 8 March 1798 (in compensation for the ennoblement intended for her husb had he lived), with remainder to heirs male of the body of her late husband, only dau and heir of Thomas Croker, of Baxtown, Co Kildare; Sir Edward *d* 30 Sept 1797, having had, with other issue:

1 **Sir Edward Crofton, 3rd Bt**; *b* 23 Oct 1778; *m* 12 Sept 1801 Lady Charlotte Stewart (*d* May 1842), 5th dau of 7th Earl of Galloway (*qv*), and *dvm* 8 Jan 1816, having had, with other issue (a bro and the sisters of the 2nd Baron Crofton were granted 11 July 1837 rank of baron's daus/yr s):

(1) EDWARD (Sir), **4th Bt**, and **2nd Baron**

(1) Susannah Anne; *m* 17 Aug 1830 St George Francis Caulfeild, of Donamon Castle, Co Roscommon, and *d* 10 Jan 1894 aged 92, leaving issue (*see* CHARLEMONT, V)

(2) Charlotte; *m* 12 Jan 1832 Gibbs Crawford Antrobus, of Eaton Hall, Co Chester, and *d* 29 Sept 1839, leaving issue (*see* ANTROBUS, Bt)

(3) Frances; *m* 3 March 1825 Daniel Bunbury-Tighe, of Rossana, Co Wicklow, and *d* 20 Dec 1881, leaving issue. He *d* 26 March 1874

(4) Sophia; *m* 6 Dec 1837 Eyre Evans, of Ash Hill Towers, Co Limerick, and *d* 18 Dec 1885, leaving issue (*see* CARBERY, B)

(5) Frederica; *m* 24 Sept 1835 Rev Hubert McLaughlin, MA, Preb of Hereford, and Rector of Burford, Salop, and *d* 28 May 1881, leaving issue. He *d* 15 Dec 1882

1 (Harriet) Louisa; *m* 1803 Gen Sir Peregrine Maitland, GCB, C-in-C Madras Army, Govr of Cape of Good Hope (*m* 2nd 9 Oct 1815 Lady Sarah Gordon Lennox, 2nd dau of 4th Duke of Richmond and Lennox (*see* RICHMOND and GORDON, D)), son of Thomas Maitland, of Shrubs Hall, New Forest, by Eliza, er dau of Maj-Gen Edward Mathew, Govr of Grenada, Equerry to GEORGE III, and Lady Jane Bertie, sis and coheir of 5th and last Duke of Ancaster (*see* WILLOUGHBY DE ERESBY, B), and *d* 1805

2 Charlotte; *m* 12 Jan 1832, as his 2nd w, Gibbs Crawford Antrobus, DL, JP, of Eaton Hall, Cheshire, and *d* 29 Sept 1839, leaving issue (*see* ANTROBUS, Bt)

3 Frances; *m* 1802 St George Caulfeild, of Donamon Castle, Co Roscommon, and *d* 1831, leaving issue. He *d* 1810

4 Harriet; *m* 22 May 1806 James Caulfeild, of Drumcairne, and *d* 6 July 1837, leaving issue (*see* CHARLEMONT, V)

5 Augusta; *m* 8 May 1823 James Caulfeild, of Benown, RN, and *d* 29 Sept 1832, leaving issue (*see* CHARLEMONT, V)

The 3rd Bt's son,

Sir Edward Crofton, 4th Bt, and **2nd Baron Crofton of Mote**; *s f* as 4th Bt 1816 and grandmother as 2nd Baron 1817; rep I peer, Ld-in-Waiting Feb-Dec 1852, 1858–59 and 1866–68; *b* 1 Aug 1806; *m* 19 Oct 1833 Lady Georgiana Paget (*d* 9 Nov 1875), dau of 1st Marquess of Anglesey (*qv*), and *d* 27 Dec 1869, having had issue:

1 EDWARD HENRY CHURCHILL CROFTON, **3rd Baron Crofton of Mote**, DL Co Roscommon; rep I peer, State Steward to Ld Lt Ireland 1880 and Gentleman-in-Waiting 1886–92; *b* 21 Oct 1834; *d* unm 22 Sept 1912

2 Charles St George, Lt RN (ret); *b* 1 Feb 1836; *m* 19 Oct 1864 his cousin, Theresa Augusta (*d* 14 Aug 1867), 3rd dau of Daniel Bunbury-Tighe, of Rossana, Co Wicklow (*see* above), and *d* 2 Feb 1895, leaving issue (his daus were granted by roy licence 25 April 1913 rank of baron's daus):

(1) ARTHUR EDWARD LOWTHER, **4th Baron**

(1) Mabel Georgiana; *d* unm 27 July 1956 aged 90

(2) Theresa Diana; *m* 28 Dec 1912 Maj Reginald de Blaquiere Chichester (*see* DONEGALL, M), and *d* 26 March 1923

3 Alfred Henry; *b* 2 April 1837; *d* 29 Oct 1881

4 Francis George, Capt RN; *b* 7 June 1838; *m* 1st 18 Aug 1864 Gertrude Caroline (*d* 19 Aug 1869), widow of John Talbot, of Mount Talbot, Co Roscommon, and dau of Col Edward Symes Bayly, of Bally Arthur, Co Wicklow (*see* ANGLESEY, M), and had issue:

(1) Gertrude Catherine Georgiana; *b* 25 Dec 1867; *d* unm 4 Aug 1955

4 (cont.) Capt Francis Crofton *m* 2nd 7 Feb 1878 Emily Augusta (*d* 2 Jan 1924), est dau of Lt-Col William Montgomerie Stewart Caulfeild, of Monkstown, Co Dublin (*see* CHARLEMONT, V), and *d* 30 Sept 1900, having by her had issue:

(1) Ernest Alfred; *b* 6 Dec 1878; *m* 1st 10 Jan 1901 Mary Susanna (*d* 11 July 1948), only dau of Rev George Martin Bullock, BD; *m* 2nd 24 June 1949 Grace Elizabeth (*d* 30 March 1960), widow of Arthur Ward, of Ganges, BC, and dau of Hyla Elkington, and *dsp* 23 Dec 1961

(2) George; *b* 23 March 1881; *m* 19 Feb 1910 Elinor, dau of K Smith, of Natal, and *d* 1943, leaving issue:

1a +Francis George; *b* 6 April 1915

(3) Alfred Gerald; *b* 18 June 1882; *m* 17 Sept 1903 Frances Nora (*d* 19 Jan 1951), dau of Rev Edward Wilson, and *d* 3 Oct 1942, leaving issue:

1a +Dermott Kenneth [Dermott Crofton Esq, Winfrith, Ganges, Salt Spring Island, BC, Canada]; *b* 17 May 1904; *m* 2 Oct 1934 *Doris Livingstone, dau of J W Taylor, of Belfast, and has issue:

1b +Patrick Dermott [Lt-Cdr (S) Patrick Crofton CAF, Ballymurry Farm, 4010 Prospect Lake Rd, RR7, Victoria, BC V8X 3X3, Canada], Lt-Cdr (S) CAF; *b* 29 May 1935; *m* 9 Aug 1958 *Patricia Judith Mary, only dau of Capt Trevor Williams, of Folly, The Walled Garden, Wargrave, Berks and has issue:

1c *Marietta Susan Annette; *b* 29 Oct 1959

2c *Virginia Margaret Adele; *b* 8 March 1961

3c *Susanna Catherine Mary; *b* 1 Aug 1962

4c *Tessa Penelope Sarah *b* 14 April 1965

2b +Marcus Livingstone, Lt-Cdr CAF; *b* Nov 1937; *m* 20 Aug 1966 *Elizabeth Jane, dau of Lt-Col Geoffrey Churchill, of Victoria, BC, and has issue:

1c +Dermot Marcus Churchill; *b* 1970

2c +Geoffrey Patrick; *b* 1973

1c *Laura Elizabeth; *b* 3 Dec 1967

2c *Jenny Livingstone; *b* 13 May 1969

1b *Sharron Diana; *b* 17 July 1940; *m* 22 Aug 1964 (*divorce* 1970) Lt Robert Montagu Scott, RCN, and has issue:

1c *Ian Dermot Montagu; *b* 16 April 1967

1c *Andrea Gillian; *b* 13 May 1966

2a Desmond Gerald, ED, Lt Col cmdg 1st Bn Canadian Scottish Regt in France and NW Europe 1944–45 (wounded 1945, despatches), had Netherlands Bronze Lion; *b* 10 July 1904; *m* 1st 22 Jan 1925 Ida (*d* 1970), widow of Maj Frank Harvey Corbett, MC, RFA, and dau of Frank Hardcastle, JP, DL, MP, of Lancashire; *m* 2nd 1971 *Dorothea Herriet, yst dau of Arthur George Wilson, and widow of Keith Edward Hook, and *d* 1977, leaving by 1st w issue:

1b +John Edward, CD, S/Ldr RCAF; *b* 12 Dec 1925; *m* 9 June 1950 *Marie White, and has issue:

1c +Desmond; *b* 6 May 1951

2c +Kevin; *b* 26 Jan 1954

3c +Neil Arthur; *b* 6 Dec 1956

1b *Sylvia Ida; *b* 27 Aug 1928; *m* 15 Dec 1954 *Maj Arthur Leake Gale, CD, Princess Patricia's Canadian LI, and has issue:

1c *Reginald Derek Leake; *b* 4 June 1956

2c *Rupert Arthur Leake; *b* 3 Dec 1962

1c *Deirdre Sylvia Leake; *b* 23 Aug 1957

3a +Patrick Donavan [Maj Patrick Crofton, 10672 Madrona Dve, RR1, Sidney, BC V8L 3R9, Canada], Maj cmdg a coy of Princess Patricia's Canadian LI in Italy and NW Europe 1943–45 (despatches), served as a mil observer with UN India-Pakistan-Kashmir Dispute 1955–56; *b* 20 Jan 1915; *m* 1 June 1946 *Anne B, dau of Harry Marshall Erskine Evans, OBE, of Edmonton, and has issue:

1b +Cameron P L; *b* 17 April 1947; *m* Oct 1974 Sylvia Marielle Evans, dau of H G V Evans, of Edmonton

2b +Barry Gerald; *b* 22 Jan 1953

1b *Catherine Anne; *b* 18 April 1949

1a Diana Patricia; *b* 12 Dec 1906; *m* 17 Dec 1932 Graham Frederick Shove, and had issue:

1b *Nona Diana; *b* 12 May 1936; *m* 12 March 1960 *Lt-Cdr Richard Edgar Stone, RCN, and has issue:

1c *Richard Charles Edgar; *b* 11 June 1962

1c *Diana Louise; *b* 17 Feb 1961

2c *Naomi Elizabeth; *b* 8 May 1965

2a *Augusta Sheila Doreen; *b* 23 July 1911; *m* 26 Nov 1938 *Frederick Arthur Ernest Morris, and has issue:

1b *Robert Desmond Frederick; *b* 24 May 1942

2b *James Richard; *b* 23 Oct 1950

1b *Wendy Patricia; *b* 19 March 1940

3a *Denise Frances; *b* 27 May 1913

4a Dulcie Ruth Hart; *b* 5 Nov 1920; *m* 7 Jan 1955 Edward Wallace Bell

(4) Francis Lowther *b* 23 May 1883; *m* 1st 24 July 1917 Annie Rebecca, MM (*d* 1956), 3rd dau of Robert Colhoun, of Buncrana, and had issue:

1a +Francis David, MD, Capt Roy Canadian Army Medical Corps 1943–46; *b* 1919; *educ* McGill Univ; *m* 1948 Marguerite (*d* 15 Oct 1994), dau of Earl Hines, of Halifax, NS, and has issue:

1b *Catherine Elizabeth Ellen; *b* 1950

1a (cont.) Dr Francis Crofton adopted:

Keven Christopher Drew; *b* 1953; *d* 1955

*Jaice David Lowther; *b* 12 July 1960

*Tighe Francis Lowther; *b* 22 Sept 1962
*Ainsley Anne; *b* 12 Sept 1955
*Leslie Anne (twin); *b* 12 Sept 1955
(4) (cont.) Francis Crofton *m* 2nd 25 May 1957 Nancy Ester, widow of Arthur Inglis, of Salt Spring Island, BC, and dau of Harry H Nash, of Victoria, BC; *m* 3rd 17 Jan 1996 *Joan Anthea Maciejewski, of Sydney, dau of John Ernest Crofton, of Nottingham, and widow of Stephen Crofton formerly Maciejewski, and *d* 1971
1 Augusta Caroline, OBE (1920); *m* 18 July 1866 4th Baron Clonbrock, KP (*see* 1926 edn), and *d* 5 Sept 1928, leaving issue. He *d* 13 May 1917

The 3rd BARON's nephew,

ARTHUR EDWARD LOWTHER CROFTON, **4th Baron Crofton of Mote**, DL, JP Co Roscommon; rep I peer, Lt-Col late cmdg 12th Bn Roy Fus, formerly Capt Northumberland Fus, served WW I (despatches); *b* 7 Aug 1866; *m* 14 April 1893 Jessie Castle (ld 19 Jan 1923), widow of Neville Paddon and dau of James Hewitson, and had issue:

1 Edward Charles, T/Lt 14th Bn Northumberland Fus; *b* 18 Jan 1896; *m* 5 March 1925 (Cecilia) Mabel (*d* 7 Oct 1972), widow of Alexander Francis Macdonald, of Glenaladale, and dau of John T Day, of Hayeswood, Streatham Park, and *d* 25 Nov 1936, leaving issue:
(1) (EDWARD) BLAISE, **5th Baron**
(1) *Diana Faith; granted 1948 rank of baron's dau; *b* 13 Oct 1927; *m* 1st 1 Jan 1949 (*divorce* 1961) Cdr Hugh Seaburne May, RN, only son of Capt Archibald Seaburne May, of Hownam, Kelso, and has issue:
1a *Peter Seaburne; *b* 2 April 1952; *educ* Belmont Abbey Herefs
1a *Antonia Kinbarra; *b* 22 April 1950; *m* 8 June 1974 *Michael David Rayment, er son of David Rayment, of Newlands, Orchard End, Weybridge, Surrey
(1) (cont.) The Hon Mrs Diana Seaburne *m* 2nd 30 March 1963 *Cdr Edward Michael George Hewitt, RN, son of Capt John Graham Hewitt, DSO, RN, of 16 Royston Court, Kew, Richmond, Surrey, and has further issue:
2a *David Edward; *b* 5 June 1965
2a *Gemma Francis; *b* 13 Sept 1963
2 (Arthur) Marcus Lowther, Maj Irish Gds; *b* 7 Sept 1898; *educ* Wellington; *m* 1st 26 Nov 1919 (*divorce* 1923) Marguerite, only dau of Maj Deffield Welchman, of Camberley; *m* 2nd 17 July 1929 (*divorce* 1946) Ursula Augusta Jane, dau of Sir William Henry Mahon, 5th Bt (*qv*), and had issue:
(1) Francis Marcus, Midshipman RN; *b* 18 Jan 1940; *d* as the result of a motor accident at Dartmouth 15 July 1960
2 (cont.) Maj Marcus Crofton *m* 3rd 1946 Clive de Lacy Tainton (*d* 23 April 1950); *m* 4th Oct 1951 *Mrs Madeleine Barbara Pratt [The Hon Mrs Marcus Crofton, 401 1430 Newport Ave, Victoria, BC, Canada], dau of William James Heath, of Surrey, and *d* 23 May 1962
1 Eileen Mabel Lowther; *b* 24 March 1894; *m* 23 Sept 1918 Cdr Sir Geoffrey Henry Hughes-Onslow, KBE, DSC, JP, RN (*see* ONSLOW, E), and *d* 1972, having had issue

The 4th BARON *d* 15 June 1942; his gs,

(EDWARD) BLAISE CROFTON, **5th Baron Crofton of Mote**; Sub-Lt RN (ret 1947), served WW II; *b* 31 May 1926; *m* 1st 10 June 1948 (*divorce* 1963) Ann, er dau of G/Capt Charles Herbert Tighe, OBE, DFC, of Ballina Park, Co Wicklow, and had issue:

1 (CHARLES EDWARD) PIERS CROFTON, **6th Baron Crofton of Mote**; *b* 27 April 1949; *educ* in Vienna and Merchant Navy Coll; master mariner with Buries Markes (Ship Management) Ltd, MNI; *m* 1976 *Maureen Jacqueline [The Rt Hon Maureen Lady Crofton, Briscoe Cottage, Fort St, nr Wellington, Somerset], dau of Stanley James Bray, of Taunton, and *d* 1989, leaving:
(1) *Freya Charlotte; *b* 1983
2 Brian St George; *b* 8 May, *d* 26 Aug 1950
3 GUY PATRICK GILBERT CROFTON, **7th and present Baron Crofton of Mote**
4 (Arthur Blaise) Adrian; *b* 20 Jan 1957; *d* 1987
1 *Georgiana Ann [The Hon Georgiana Crofton, c/o The Red House, Inistioge, Co Kilkenny, Ireland]; *b* 27 Aug 1955; *m* 1980 (*divorce* 1986, resumed maiden name) Brent Hutchinson, son of Ivan Hutchinson, and has issue:
(1) *Blaise; *b* 1982
(1) *Louisa; *b* 1981

The **5th Baron** *m* 2nd 19 Dec 1964 *Mary [The Rt Hon Mary Lady Crofton, Flat 1, 123 Gloucester Terrace, London W2], formerly w of Robert W Flach and est dau of Maj James Irvine Hatfield Friend, OBE, MC, DL, of Northdown, Thanet, Kent, and *d* 13 June 1974

CROFTON, Bt, of Longford House

Arms: Per pale indented or and az., a lion passant guardant counterchanged. **Crest:** Seven ears of wheat on one stalk ppr. **Motto:** *Dat Deus incrementum* ('God gives the increase'). **Creation:** Bt. (UK) 18 Aug 1838.

SIR MALBY STURGES CROFTON, 5TH BT, of Longford House, Co Sligo [Sir Malby Crofton Bt, 12 Caithness Rd, London W14 0JB; Longford House, Co Sligo, Ireland]; *b* 11 Jan 1923; *s f* 1962; *educ* Eton and Trin Coll Cambridge; Capt Life Gds WW II, memb London Stock Exchange 1957–, ptnr Fenn and Crosthwaite; memb: Kensington BC 1962 (Leader 1968–77), GLC 1970–73 and 1977–81, Mayor Kensington and Chelsea 1978, Freeman Borough of Kensington and Chelsea 1983, Hon Fell Chelsea Coll; *m* 14 Jan 1961 (*divorce*1966) Elizabeth Madeline Nina, est dau of Maj Rhys Clavell Mansel, of Ropley Manor, Alresford, Hants (*see* MANSEL, Bt)

Lineage: This is now the senior male branch of the Crofton family in Ireland.

THOMAS CROFTON, of Longford House, Co Sligo; MP 1633–66, yr bro of George Crofton, of Mote, MP 1639 (whose s was made a Bt 1661, the title expiring with Sir Oliver Crofton, the 5th Bt); *m* Honora, dau of Roger O'Conor (the O'Conor Don), of Clonalis, Co Roscommon, and left, with three yr s and a dau (Elizabeth, *m* Thomas Nugent, of Colamber):

HENRY CROFTON, of Longford Ho; Capt in the Army, High Sheriff Co Sligo 1687, MP 1689; *m* Sarah, dau of Anthony Brabazon, son of Sir Anthony Brabazon by Ursula, dau of Sir Nicholas Malby, and had, with other issue:

EDWARD CROFTON, of Longford Ho, DL Co Sligo 1691; *m* 1680 his cousin Ann, dau of John Crofton, of Lisdorne, and had, with other issue (*d* unm):

JAMES CROFTON, of Longford Ho; turned Protestant 1731 and eventually inherited the estates, his father and brothers having been attainted as Catholics; *m* Elizabeth, dau of Capt Edward Robinson, and *d* 1755, leaving, with three er s and a dau (Ann, *m* Capt Edward Mapother, of Kilteevan, Co Roscommon, and had issue):

MALBY CROFTON, of Longford Ho; Capt 90th Regt, High Sheriff Co Sligo 1770, MP Co Sligo; *b* 1741; *m* July 1772 Elizabeth, second dau of Ignatius Kelly, of Cargins, Co Roscommon, and *d* 1838, leaving an only s:

Sir James Crofton, 1st Bt (UK), so *cr* 18 Aug 1838, DL Co Sligo, of Longford House; Maj Sligo Militia; *b* 8 Aug 1776; *m* 13 Oct 1794 Marion, dau of Rev John Lyster, DD, of Rocksavage, Co Roscommon, Rector of Clonpriest, and had issue:

1 MALBY (Sir), **2nd Bt**
2 James (Sir), MA, Rector of Dunleer, Co Louth; *b* 6 May 1803; *m* 1 Dec 1834 Barbara, dau of Peter North, of Kilduff, and *d* 1876, leaving, with other issue:
(1) James; *b* 12 Dec 1838
(1) Barbara Georgina
(2) Kathleen Barbara; *m* David McCormack, and had issue
(3) Maria Honora; *m* Patrick Deegan, and *d* 9 April 1881
1 Elizabeth Marion; *m* William Norcott, of Springfield, Co Cork, and *dsp* 1849
2 Maria Lucy; *m* Rev William F Black, DD, Rector of Newchurch, Warrington, Lancs, and left issue

Sir JAMES *d* 1849; his est son,

Sir Malby Crofton, 2nd Bt; *b* 21 Dec 1797; *m* 24 Jan 1821 Sarah Jane (*d* 14 April 1867), 4th dau of Andrew Parke, Maj 8th Regt, bro of Roger Parke, of Dunnally, Lt-Col Sligo Mil, and had issue:

1 Henry Bliss, Capt Sligo Mil Rifles; *b* 29 July 1833; *m* 24 Oct 1856 Sophia (*d* 23 July 1901), est dau of Thomas Horsfall, of Burley Hall, Yorks, and *d* 1868, having had, with other issue:
(1) MALBY (Sir), **3rd Bt**
(1) Emmeline; *m* 10 Feb 1886 Reginald Somers Yorke, of Dame Lys, Watlington, 2nd son of James Charles Yorke, Capt 5th Dragoon Gds, and *d* 23 April 1935, leaving issue (*see* HARDWICKE, E)

2 Frederick Robert Cameron, Maj-Gen, late Col cmdg 2nd Bn Roy Irish Rifles, served with 9th Lancers in Indian Mutiny; *b* 13 Sept 1837; *m* 19 Sept 1868 Louisa Maria Susannah (*d* 26 Jan 1934), 2nd dau of Richard Graves Brinkley, of Fortland, Co Sligo, and *d* 5 Dec 1909, leaving issue:

(1) Nora Marion; *d* unm

3 Malby Edward, Brev Col late cmdg 2nd Bn, King's Own Roy Regt, served in S Africa 1879 (medal with clasp) and 1899–1900 (wounded, medal with two clasps); *b* 25 Jan 1847; *m* 12 May 1880 Henrietta (*d* 2 March 1932), dau of Rev John Lewis Moore, DD, Vice-Provost of Trin Coll Dublin, and *d* 14 Jan 1929, leaving issue:

(1) Malby, DSO (1916, bar 1918), Col late RA, served in S Africa 1901–2 (medal with five clasps), and WW I 1914–18 (despatches six times, 1914 Star, Brev Lt-Col); *b* 19 March 1881; *m* 27 Sept 1911 Sarah Dorothy Beatrice, JP (*d* 9 Dec 1976), er dau of Col William Frederick Noel, late RE, of Stardens, Newent, Glos (*see* GAINSBOROUGH, E), and *d* 30 Dec 1948, leaving issue:

1a *(Ursula) Doryne Elizabeth [Mrs William Cleary, 64 Pelham Ct, Fulham Rd, London SW3], late Sect Offr WAAF, served WW II 1939–44; *b* 7 Oct 1921; *m* 3 Nov 1951 *William Robert Castle Cleary, RIBA, only son of Sir William Castle Cleary, KBE, CB, of 29, Denbigh Gdns, Richmond, Surrey

(2) Roger, CIE (1942), MC (1918), Brig IA (ret), served WW I with RA (despatches twice, Brevet Maj), Dir of Armaments and Mechanization, India 1938–42; *b* 13 March 1888; *educ* Rossall; *m* 1st 28 Nov 1914 Stella Clifton (*dsp* 11 Feb 1916), yst dau of His Honour Judge Thomas Gilbert Carver, KC, MA; *m* 2nd 6 Dec 1921 Dorothy Frances (*d* 8 Oct 1953), only child of Col Henry Melville Hatchell, DSO, late Roy Irish Regt, and had issue:

1a +(HENRY EDWARD) MELVILLE, MBE (1970) [Melville Crofton Esq MBE, Haldon, St Giles Hill, Winchester SO23 8JH]; *b* 15 Aug 1931; heir presumptive; *educ* Hilton Coll, Natal, and Trin Coll Cambridge (BA Eng 1954); formerly Prin Admin Offr, HM Overseas Civil Serv, Malawi; *m* 10 Dec 1955 *(Mary) Brigid, twin dau of Gerald K Riddle, of Buttercombe, Ogwell, Newton Abbot, Devon, and has issue

1b +Julian Malby; *b* 6 Nov 1958; *m* 1989 *Hilary, dau of Thomas James Twort, of 35 Sompting Ave, Worthing, Sussex, and has issue:

1C +William Robert Malby; *b* 5 May 1996

1c *Harriet Sophie; *b* 1992

2b +Nigel Melville; *b* 10 June 1964

1b *Nicola Dorothy; *b* 8 Jan 1961; *m* 1990 *Julian D P George, er son of John George, of Bridge Ho, Castle Eaton, Wilts, and has issue:

1c *Henry Dacre Malby; *b* 1994

(2) (cont.) Brig Roger Crofton *m* 3rd 26 July 1954 Agnes Marjorie (*d* 1982), yst dau of Samuel Osborn, of Halifax, Yorks, and widow of (a) Capt Cyril Oswald Denman-Jubb, Duke of Wellington's Regt, (b) John Johnson May, of 7 Park Lane, W1, and *d* in Cape Town 4 May 1972

1 Elizabeth Sarah; *m* 24 July 1843 Henry Laurence Cotton, est son of Ven Henry Cotton, DD, Archdeacon of Cashel, and *d* 11 Sept 1852, leaving issue. He *d* 1861

2 Marion Louisa; *m* 31 Oct 1878 Charles Philip Cotton, son of Ven Henry Cotton, Archdeacon of Cashel, and *d* 15 Jan 1908. He *d* 1904

3 Isabella Charlotte; *d* unm 26 Sept 1910

4 Frances Caroline; *m* 4 Aug 1870 Charles Capel Chapman, yst son of Rev William Herbert Chapman, Vicar of Basingbourne, and *d* 23 Nov 1889, leaving issue. He *d* 16 Oct 1920

Sir MALBY *d* 15 Dec 1872; his gs,

Sir Malby Crofton, 3rd Bt; *educ* Univ Coll Oxford (BA), DL, JP; *b* 20 Aug 1857; *m* 18 Aug 1880 Louisa Margaret, pres Women's Br British Legion, Co Sligo (*d* 20 June 1941), est dau of Richard John Verschoyle, JP, of Tanrago, Co Sligo, and had issue:

1 MALBY RICHARD HENRY (Sir), **4th Bt**

2 Thomas Horsfall, MC, Capt Connaught Rangers; *b* 3 Oct 1889; *ka* 21 March 1918

1 Louisa Emmeline; *d* unm 29 Nov 1964

2 *Dorothy [Miss Dorothy Crofton, Arva, Upper Glenageary Rd, Glenageary, Dublin, Ireland]

Sir MALBY *d* 17 Sept 1926; his only surv son,

Sir (Malby Richard) Henry Crofton, 4th Bt, DSO (1916) and bar (1917), Maj RA (ret), served WW I as Lt-Col (despatches twice, wounded four times); *b* 18 Sept 1881; *m* 17 Sept 1918 Katharine Beatrix (*d* 28 Feb 1961), only dau of George Sturges Pollard, JP, formerly of Scarr Hall, nr Bradford, Yorks, and *d* 21 Jan 1962, having had issue:

1 Sir MALBY STURGES CROFTON, **5th and present Bt**

1 *(Beatrix) Katharine [Miss Katharine Crofton, 2 Caithness Rd, London W14]; *b* 1921, late Jr Cdr ATS

Seat: Longford House, Beltra, Co Sligo. The principal part of the house, built in the late 18th century, burnt down in the first part of the following one. The only wing ever built of a planned twin-flank extension was subsequently converted to the chief living quarters and the shell of the main block reroofed and turned into a repository.

CROFTON, Bt, of Mohill

Arms: Per pale indented or and az., a lion passant guardant counterchanged, a crescent for difference. **Crest:** Seven ears of wheat on one stalk ppr. **Motto:** *Dat Deus incrementum* ('God gives the increase'). **Creation:** Bt. (UK) 10 Aug 1801.

(Sir) Hugh Denis Crofton [Hugh Crofton Esq, 34 Rhinefield Close, Brockenhurst, Hants SO42 7SU]; *b* 10 April 1937; *s* n 1987 but does not use title; *educ* Eton, Worcester Coll Oxford (BA) and Bristol U (BA)

Lineage: HENRY CROFTON, of Mohill Castle, Leitrim (yst son of John Crofton, of Ballymurry, Escheator-Gen, in the time of ELIZABETH I, ancestor likewise of the Lords Crofton), upon whom his father settled the castle and lands of Mohill, Co Leitrim, 2 June 1607, obtained a patent from CHARLES I erecting Mohill into a manor; *m* Ursula Moore and *d* 3 April 1643, leaving:

HENRY CROFTON, of Mohill; *b* 1630; *m* Frances, dau of Robert Morgan, of Cottestown, Co Sligo, and had, with seven s and three daus (all *d* young):

THOMAS CROFTON, of Mohill; *m* Nov 1707 Bridget, dau of Hugh Morgan, of Cottestown, and *d* 24 Sept 1738, having had, with an er s (Thomas, *dsp* 1729) and a dau (Elizabeth):

HUGH CROFTON, of Mohill; MP Co Leitrim; *m* 10 Aug 1730 Anne, dau of George Crofton, of Lisnadern, and *d* 20 Oct 1767, having had, with two other s (including a 2nd surv s,

Thomas, of Mohill, *m* Rachel, dau of Robert Sandford, of Castlerea, Co Roscommon, by Lady Henrietta O'Brien, dau of 3rd Earl of Inchiquin (*see* INCHIQUIN, B), and *dsp*) and a dau (Elizabeth, *m* Rev William Percy), a 3rd s:

Sir Morgan Crofton, 1st Bt (UK), so *cr* 10 Aug 1801; *b* 25 March 1733; *m* 19 Aug 1761 Jeanne (*d* July 1797), yst dau of Lt-Col Henri d'Abzac, Seigneur d'Abzac, in Périgord, Dordogne, 18th RI Regt and formerly Capt Roy Gd, and had, with two daus:

1 HUGH (Sir), **2nd Bt**

2 Henry (Rev); Chaplain Kilmainham Hosp, Dublin; *b* 26 July 1764; *m* 1st 1791 Susan (*d* 10 Aug 1797), only dau of Duke Crofton, of Lakefield, Co Leitrim, and had, with other issue:

(1) Mary; *m* 1821 Most Rev and Rt Hon Joseph Henderson Singer, PC, DD, Bishop of Meath 1852–66, Premier Bishop of Ireland, 3rd son of Commissary-Gen James Singer, 47th Regt, by his w Elizabeth, dau of Capt Joseph Henderson, of Carrick's Ho, Lifford, Co Donegal, and *d* 25 April 1869, leaving issue. He *d* 16 July 1866

2 (cont.) The Rev Henry Crofton *m* 2nd 1799 Frances (*d* 1850), dau of Capt Francis ffolliott, of Holybrook, Co Sligo, and *d* 23 April 1834, having by her had issue:

(1) John ffolliott, Gen in the Army, Col of the 6th Regt; *b* 9 Oct 1800; *educ* Trin Coll Dublin (BA); *m* 15 Oct 1845 Anne Agnes (*d* 14 Feb 1900), only child of John Addison, of Preston, and *d* 17 July 1885, leaving, with other issue:

1a Addison (Rev), MA Oxford; *b* 13 July 1846; *m* 7 Aug 1873 Mary Pilkington (*d* 7 May 1903), dau of John Hall, of Baldingstone, Lancs, and *d* 12 Jan 1904, leaving issue:

1b Annie; *d* unm 28 May 1947

2b Sydney d'Abzac; *m* 20 June 1910 Lt-Col Michael Balfour Hutchison Ritchie of Craigdhu, DSO, OBE, late 6th QO Cameron Highrs (TA), yst son of Rev Robert Ritchie, of Inverurie, Scotland

2a Henry Thomas, slr; *b* 23 July 1848; *m* 7 Sept 1871 Martha Pilling (*d* 22 Nov 1931), dau of Joseph McKeand, and *d* 17 April 1928, having had issue:

1b John ffolliott Frederick, Slr, late Capt 3rd Vol Bn Cheshire Regt, served in S African War 1900–01 (Queen's medal with four clasps); *b* 1 Jan 1877; *m* 26 Feb 1913 Frederica Fanny, widow of W F Allen, and yst dau of Frederick Nicholls, of Whitstable, Kent, and *dsp* 3 July 1927

1b Josephine Christie; *m* 7 Sept 1897 Hermon Barker-Hahlo, only son of George Hahlo, JP, of Victoria Park S, Manchester, by his w Fanny, dau of Nathaniel Barker of Westbourne, Manchester, and *d* 20 May 1906, leaving issue

2b Alice Addison; *d* 24 March 1938

3b Gladys Noelle; *m* 1st Jan 1913 Walter Ellis Williams, Capt 4th Bn Middx Regt; *m* 2nd 16 Sept 1920 William Henry Cleland. He *d* 8 Jan 1926

3a William d'Abzac (Rev), *b* 3 June 1854; *educ* Worcester Coll Oxford (MA); Vicar of Codicote, Herts, 1908–35, Chaplain TF (1st class), attached to 1st Hertford Regt, served WW I; *d* 18 Nov 1936

1a Caroline Anne Agnes; *m* 21 Jan 1879 Ralph Cririe Clayton, and *d* 2 Jan 1880, leaving issue

(2) Charles Stanhope; *b* 7 May 1810; *m* 30 Sept 1846 Mary (*d* 2 Nov 1889), est dau of Duke Crofton, DL, of Lakefield, and *d* 6 Dec 1868, leaving issue:

1a Henry, Maj RA; *b* 18 July 1847; *m* 18 July 1872 Ann Maria (*d* 7 Feb 1933), dau of Thomas Foster, MD, of Manchester, and *d* 8 Jan 1893, leaving issue:

1b Charles Stanhope Foster, ICS, BA Cambridge; *b* 16 April 1873; *m* 28 Nov 1903 Lilian (who *m* 2nd 17 June 1911 Capt William Lister Newcombe, late Worcs Regt (*d* 1949), 3rd son of W Lister Newcombe, of Gosforth, Newcastle-on-Tyne, and *d* 23 July 1976, having had further issue), yst dau of Lt-Gen James Crofton (*see* below), and *d* April 1909, leaving issue:

1c Delia Anne; *b* 27 Sept 1904; *m* 17 July 1929 Cdr Gage Duncan Saffery Johnson, RN, son of Gordon Johnson, of Rosway, Deal, and *d* 3 July 1969. He *d* 17 Sept 1966

1b Matilda Kathleen; *d* unm 25 Jan 1945

2b Charlotte Anne ffolliott; *d* unm 13 April 1931

1a Alice Frances; *m* 13 March 1888 Claude St Maur Williams, AMICE, of Harrow, son of Philip Penry Williams, DL, of Stoke Ho, Tenbury, and *d* 9 Aug 1920, leaving issue. He *d* 15 Feb 1921

(1) Sarah Frances; *m* 1827 Rev Robert Staveley, MA, and *d* leaving issue. He *d* June 1854

(2) Letitia; *m* 1829 Gen Robert Burn, RA, and *d* 1842, leaving issue. He *d* 18 Dec 1878

3 Morgan, barrister; *b* Oct 1766; *m* 19 Sept 1791 Mary (*d* Oct 1846), dau of William Dunn, and *d* 10 Jan 1831, leaving, with other issue:

(1) Morgan, Capt, RN; *b* 11 Oct 1793; *m* 18 Jan 1818 Helen Elizabeth (*d* July 1866), dau of Col Henry O'Hara, of O'Harabrook, and *d* 21 June 1871, leaving, with other issue:

1a Morgan (Rev); *b* 1 June 1819; *m* 30 July 1847 Rebecca (*d* 1887), widow of Capt Nicholas Palmer, and dau of William Carter Barrett, and *d* 16 May 1859, leaving issue:

1b Morgan Samuel, CB, DSO, Col S Staffs Regt, served in Zululand, on Nile, in Sudan, and in S Africa; *b* 2 Jan 1850; *m* 20 June 1894 Julia Ruperta (*d* 30 March 1949), widow of William Hale Willats, and dau of Charles Edward Gostling Murray (*see* ATHOLL, D), and *dsp* 9 Jan 1916

1b Mary Elizabeth; *m* 20 July 1870 John Henry Augustus Schneider, son of Henry William Schneider, of Furness, Lancs, and *d* 19 May 1913, leaving issue. He *d* 1912

2a James, Lt-Col RE; *b* May 1826; *educ* HEIC Mil Coll Addiscombe; *m* 1st 1 March 1858 Mary Susan (*dsp* 22 Dec 1860), dau of Sir Robert Montgomery, KCB; *m* 2nd 5 March 1867 Clara Elizabeth (*d* 16 Dec 1890), dau of Capt Edward Lake, RN, and *d* 22 Nov 1908, leaving issue:

1b Robert Benjamin, Maj RAOC, formerly RGA; *b* 19 Sept 1873; *m* 8 Sept 1904 Helena Chute (*d* 27 Oct 1974), est dau of Richard Grubb Ridgway, late of Riverview Ho, Waterford, and *d* 23 Nov 1923, leaving issue:

1c Robert Denis, BSc, MIEE, F/Lt RAF, served WW II; *b* 1 March 1907; *kas* 12 July 1942

1c Kathleen

2c Helen Norah

2b Charles D'Arcy, late ICS; *b* 19 April 1879; *m* 17 March 1910 Mary Helen Elizabeth (*d* 3 Dec 1960), est dau of H G Gearing, of Coonoor, Nilgris, S India, and *d* 24 Dec 1955, leaving issue:

1c Patience D'Arcy; *b* 3 Feb 1911; *m* 2 April 1936 Lt-Col Joseph Richard Waters, OBE, RA (*d* 6 Aug 1993), 2nd son of Henry Waters, and *d* 10 Dec 1991, leaving:

1d *Prudence D'Arcy [Mrs Harry Waugh, 14 Camden Sq, London NW1 9UY]; *b* 5 Jan 1937; *m* 5 Sept 1970 *Harry Waugh and has:

1e *Jamie Horsburgh; *b* 1973

2e *Harriet D'Arcy (twin); *b* 1973

2d *Ann Gillian; *b* 31 July 1938; *m* 30 Oct 1961 *Peter Llewellyn Sheldon, 2nd son of H D Sheldon, of Washington, DC, and has:

1e *Mark Valentine D'Arcy; *b* 4 Jan 1969; *m* 6 Sept 1997 *Karim (Luis) Grunauer Repetito

1e *Clare Helen Alexandra; *b* 21 March 1966

2c Beatrix Barratt]; *b* 28 Aug 1915; *m* 25 Sept 1938 Brig Anthony John Le Grand Jacob, MBE (*d* 24 Dec 1983), RE, s of Lt-Col Rupert Montague Jacob, MC, IA, of Fritton Old Rectory, Long Stratton, Norfolk, and *d* 7 March 1996, leaving:

1d *John Anthony; *b* 1 Oct 1940; *educ* Sherborne; *m* 1st 31 May 1963 Angela Hilda Mary, dau of Col E P Blake, AMIEE, of Gateways, Shiplake, Oxon, and has issue:

1e *Alaric Justin; *b* 15 Oct 1964

1e *Cyrilla Catherine; *b* 14 April 1966

2e *Esther Sybil; *b* 20 June 1968

1d (cont.) John Jacob *m* 2nd 28 Aug 1981 *Karen and by her has:

2e *Robin; *b* 13 Sept 1982

2d *Rupert; *b* 11 Sept 1948; *educ* Wellington; *m* 25 July 1986 *Lynne White and has:

1e *Thomas Alexander; *b* 25 July 1986

1e *Claudia Harriet; *b* 5 Aug 1992

1d *Rosemary; *b* 27 Dec 1944

2d *Alice Mary; *b* 14 April 1950

3b John Hutchinson, MRCS, LRCP, London; *b* 1 Dec 1883; *educ* Pembroke Coll Cambridge (MB, BCh); *m* 15 April 1914 Alice (*d* 10 June 1943), 2nd dau of Arthur Charles Humphreys-Owen, DL, of Glansevern, Montgomeryshire, and *d* 11 Dec 1953, leaving issue:

1c *Anne Dorothy; *b* 24 May 1915

2c Ruth Margaret; *b* 15 June 1919; *m* 7 July 1949 Norman Renshaw Sharpe, er son of F H Sharpe, of Peru, and 64 St Leonard's Court, St Leonard's Rd, East Sheen, SW14

1b Marion; *b* 5 April 1870; *d* unm 19 Feb 1951

2b Norah; *b* 4 Jan 1878; *d* unm 13 Sept 1959

3b Lilian; *b* 20 Sept 1880; *m* 1st 28 Nov 1903 Charles Stanhope Foster Crofton, only son of Maj Henry Crofton, and has issue (*see* above); *m* 2nd 17 June 1911 Maj William Lister Newcombe, late Worcs Regt, 3rd son of W Lister Newcombe, of Gosforth, Newcastle-on-Tyne, and *d* 23 July 1976, leaving further issue. He *d* 1949

(2) William (Rev), Rector of Skreene, Co Sligo; *b* 31 July 1795; *m* May 1825 Melisina (*d* 24 Jan 1881), dau of Rev Henry Woodward, and *d* 25 Dec 1851, leaving, with other issue:

1a Morgan William, FRS, DSc, MA, Dublin, late Prof of Mathematics RMA Woolwich; *b* 27 June 1826; *m* 1st 31 Aug 1857 Julia Agnes Cecilia (*d* 27 March 1902), dau of J B Kernan; *m* 2nd Catherine Charlotte (*d* 13 Jan 1945), dau of Holland Taylor, of Manchester, and *d* 13 May 1915, having by 1st w had, with other issue:

1b William John Camille; *b* 15 July 1858

2b John Louis; *b* April 1863

1b Mary Robertine

1a (cont.) Morgan Crofton

2a Henry Woodward (Rev); *b* 10 Sept 1827; *m* 1st 1856 Janette Barberie (*d* 1872), dau of Charles Butler, and had, with other issue:

1b Henry Francis (Rev), Rector of Somersby and Bag Enderby from 1929; *b* 6 Dec 1859; *educ* Univ Coll Durham (MA); *m* 26 Oct 1886 Catherine Louise (*d* 1948), dau of H N Chipman, MD, and *d* 12 Feb 1943, having had issue:

1c Harold Mowatt Maxwell, Lt and Acting-Paymaster, RN; *b* 13 Aug 1896 (twin); *d* 29 Nov 1918

2c Hubert Oliver Woodward; *b* 13 Aug 1896 (twin); *d* 30 June 1950

3c Charles Cyril Robarts; *b* 2 Jan 1898; *d* unm 2 Dec 1943

1c Janette Melesina; *b* 1887; *m* 1918 Albert J Perry, and *d* 2 March 1963

2c Isabel Ona; *b* 1892; *m* 28 Sept 1967 Rev Walter Herbert Symonds, MA Queen's Coll Cambridge, Vicar of N Shoebury, yst son of Rev Septimus Symonds, MA, Vicar of St Mark's Cambridge

3c Cecilia Francisca; *b* 3 Sept 1893; *m* 1 June 1955 George Rochford Porter, son of Frank Porter, of Benington, Boston, Lincs, and *dsp* 1968

2b Charles Woodward, Maj 9th Bn Worcs Regt, late Maj N Staffs Regt; *b* 8 Nov 1866; *m* 1901 Catherine Mary (*d* 1944), dau of C F W Stowell, and was *ka* 10 Aug 1915, leaving issue:

1c Hugh Charles Henry, Maj (ret) RA; *b* 1915; *educ* Wellington and RMA Woolwich; *m* 1949 *Margery, dau of T Summerson, of Sunderland, and *d* 1986, leaving issue:

1d +John Hugh, of Arkengarthdale, N Yorks; *b* 1954; *educ* Giggleswick Sch; *m* 1981 *Martha June, dau of William Thomas Holbert, of 435 Bluebird Lane, Delray Beach, Fla 33445, USA, and has issue:

1e *Emma Zoe; *b* 1983

2e *Chloe Alexandra; *b* 1986

1d *Kathleen Louisa

1b Katharine Melesina Mowatt; *d* 10 May 1938

2b Isabel Jane; *m* 1891 Joseph Ward, and *d* 12 July 1955, leaving issue. He *d* 1917

2a (cont.) The Rev Henry Crofton *m* 2nd 29 April 1875 Jane Inglis (*d* 22 May 1925), dau of E W H Schenley, and *d* 1894, having by her had issue:

1b Geoffrey Hugh Schenley, late Maj E Surrey Regt (SR), Temp Major att Suffolk Regt, and Capt 3rd Bn W Yorks Regt (formerly 3rd Hus), served with Imp Yeo in Africa 1900; *b* 5 Nov 1880; *m* 30 Dec 1908 Monica (*d* 19 March 1977, aged 96), yst dau of A W Hall, JP, of Barton Abbey, Steeple Aston, Oxon, and *d* 16 Dec 1954, leaving issue:

1c +Henry Horatio, Capt W Yorks Regt; *b* 4 Aug 1910

1c *Monica Melesina Nem; *b* 15 Aug 1915

2c *Angela Catherine; *b* 20 Nov 1917

3b Mary Evelyn; *m* 19 June 1901 (*divorce* 1922) Henry Frank Ward Farquharson, of Eastbury Park, Blandford, Dorset, and *d* 4 June 1965, leaving issue. He *d* 15 Nov 1950

4b Edrica Alice; *m* 16 Feb 1904 Capt Herbert Cyril Foster, late Roy Fus, and *d* 4 Aug 1951

5b Hermione Jane; *m* 15 Oct 1908 Maj Thomas Cunningham Cunningham, DSO, RA, er son of David Cunningham, JP, of Dalachy, Aberdour, Fife, and *d* 20 July 1965, leaving issue. He *d* 1952

6b Violet Rhoda; *d* unm 22 July 1973

3a Francis Blake, BA, TCD; *b* 17 July 1842; *m* 12 Dec 1872 Emma Katherine (*d* Nov 1920), dau of James Foster Bradshaw, and *d* 23 Oct 1911, leaving issue:

1b Algernon Francis Blake; *b* 20 Oct 1873; *m* 1893 Edith (*d* 1954), dau of James Hall, of Peterborough, Ontario, and *d* 1940, leaving issue:

1c Katherine; *m* 1st 21 April 1919 Louis de Laveaga Cebrian (*d* 1937), and had issue:

1d John Crofton; *b* 6 Dec 1923; *d* unm 2 June 1945

2d *Luis Enrique; *b* 2 May 1934

3d *José Maria Anthony; *b* 4 June 1935; *m* 1 Sept 1958 *Celia King McNear, and has issue:

1e *José Algernon Crofton; *b* 7 July 1959

2e *Luis Miguel Crofton; *b* 1962

1c (cont.) Mrs Louis Cebrian *m* 2nd 1937 Douglas Lindsay Pringle. He *dsp* Nov 1960

2b Arthur Molesworth, JP; *b* 5 Dec 1874; *m* 1897 Gwendolyn (*d* 1950), dau of Col Forrest, of Quebec, and *d* 1945, having had issue:

1c Eric Blake; *b* 14 Feb 1898; served WW I; *kas* 19 April 1917

2c +Brian Forrest [Brian Crofton Esq, 409 Kent St, Whitby, Ontario, Canada]; *b* 14 Oct 1905; *m* 1930 *Violet, dau of Thomas Janes, RCMP (Marine Section), and has issue:

1d +Ralph Janes; *b* 1931; *m* 1954 *Marcella, dau of James Billard, and has issue:

1e +Ralph Kevin; *b* 1958

1e *Heather Cavelle; *b* 1956; *m* 1979 *Jeffery Mitchell, and has issue:

1f *Alicia Violet; *b* 1982

2d +Ross Blake; *b* 1935; *m* 1961 *Claire, dau of Frederick Burke, and has issue:

1e *Sandra Jane; *b* 1962

2e *Karen Eileen; *b* 1964

3d +Brian Eric; *b* 1944; *m* 1970 *Helen, dau of James Seto, and has issue:

1e +Brian James; *b* 1971

2e +David Andrew; *b* 1973

1d *Gwendolyn Patricia; *b* 1939; *m* 1965 *Harvey Thompson, and has issue:

1e *Paul Gregory; *b* 1970

2e *David Harvey; *b* 1975

2d *Edith Jane; *b* 1941; *m* 1966 *Gary Carman Jones, and has issue:

1e *Jeffery Carman Blake; *b* 1973

3d *Brenda Faye; *b* 1943; *m* 1965 *Clive Orville Garlow Denyke, and has issue:

1e *Sean Forrest; *b* 1968

2e *Arthur Anslem; *b* 1972

3c +Henry Desmond; *b* 21 Jan 1907; *m* 1st 1935 Frances Veron Borgeest, of Shanghai (*d* 1942); *m* 2nd 1951 *Marie Jeanne, widow of S/Ldr Oliver J Gaboury, RCAF, and dau of Joseph Muloin

4c +Charles Patrick; *b* 15 July 1913; *m* 1943 *Catherine Kennedy, and has issue:

1d +David Ian; *b* 1944

2d +Arthur Blake; *b* 1946

3d +Alan; *b* 1953

4d +Terence (twin); *b* 1953

1d *Catherine Patricia; *b* 1948

2d *Joan; *b* 1949

5c +Francis Terence; *b* 26 Jan 1915; organist

1c *Ona Muriel; *b* 15 May 1904

1b Alice Muriel Woodward; *m* 4 June 1902 Capt Henry William Simms, late RN, and *d* 2 June 1955, leaving issue. He *d* 12 Oct 1951

2b Kathleen Maude; *b* 20 Jan 1887; *m* 27 Aug 1907 Percy Gillespie Shallcross, son of Richard Shallcross, of Capenhurst Grange, Capenhurst, Cheshire, and *d* 27 Nov 1967, leaving issue. He *d* 17 Nov 1953

Sir MORGAN *d* 12 Feb 1802; his est son,

Sir Hugh Crofton, 2nd Bt; *b* 17 July 1763; *m* June 1787 Frances (*d* 27 March 1847), yst dau of Ralph Smyth, of Barbavilla, Co Westmeath, and had, with other issue:

1 MORGAN GEORGE (Sir), **3rd Bt**

2 Ralf, Lt 81st Regt; *m* 1813 Elizabeth (who *m* 2nd Dec 1823 Daniel Massavey, of St Helier, Jersey), dau and coheir of Thomas Pipon, of St Peter's, Jersey, Jurat of the Royal Court, and *dsp*

3 Henry William (Rev), of Inchinappa, Co Wicklow; *m* 1st Marcia Anastasia, dau and coheir of Mathias Earbery, MP; *m* 2nd 1840 Marianne Amelia (*d* 1847), dau of Rev James Cazalet, of Paddock, Sussex, and had, with other issue:

(1) Henry Morgan Earbery, of Inchinappa, JP; *b* 31 May 1840; *m* 20 June 1865 Henrietta (*d* 13 Oct 1878), dau of Henry Townsend, and *d* 7 Sept 1878, having had issue:

1a Henry William George, of Inchinappa, Co Wicklow, Maj 3rd Bn E Surrey Regt; *b* 14 July 1866; *m* 3 Sept 1889 Marianne Gertrude (*d* 17 Dec 1945) (who *m* 2nd 31 Aug 1905 Maj James Logan Ellis, OBE, 4th W Yorks Regt (*d* 9 March 1936), only son of James Walter Ellis, of Cranstonhill, Stirling), dau of Drummond B Wingrove, and *dsp*, *k* in S Africa, 5 Feb 1902

2a Hugh Arthur; *b* 30 July 1873; *d* unm 16 Jan 1953

1a Henrietta Annabella Mary; *d* unm Dec 1943

2a Eva Annabella Jane; *m* 4 Nov 1892 Capt Vere Henry Birch-Reynardson (*d* 25 Jan 1941), of Rushington Manor, Hants, only surv son of Col Edward Birch Reynardson, CB, JP, of Rushington Manor, and *d* 29 April 1955, having had issue (*see* WESTMORLAND, E)

3a Lilian Elizabeth; *m* 5 Aug 1908 Riversdale Sampson French, MB, 2nd son of Ven Thomas Fitzgerald French, Archdeacon of Killaloe, and *d* 4 April 1952. He *d* 13 Nov 1932

(2) James Cazalet, of Broomfield, Co Wicklow, Maj 3rd Bn E Surrey Regt; *b* 24 Jan 1847; *m* 1st 16 Aug 1868 Henrietta Anne (*d* 26 Feb 1870), 3rd dau of John Edwards, JP, of Knockrobin, Wicklow, and had issue:

1a Nettie Elise; *d* unm May 1944

2a Myra Henrietta (twin); *d* unm 13 March 1951

(2) (cont.) Maj James Crofton *m* 2nd 1876 Charlotte (*d* 4 July 1894), widow of Capt Carpendale, Ind Marine, and *d* 3 July 1894, having by her had further issue:

3a Norah Gertrude Charlotte; *m* 25 Sept 1906 Capt Bertram Langford Farmer, RA, son of Dep Surg-Gen William Langford-Farmer, and had issue

4a Ada Bertha Catharine; *d* unm 22 Aug 1959

(1) Marianne Amelia (twin with James Cazalet); *m* 20 Jan 1870 Rev John Joseph Knox Fletcher, Rector of Whittlebury, and *d* 21 April 1916, leaving issue. He *d* 1891

3 (cont.) The Rev Henry Crofton *m* 3rd 1852 Frances (who *m* 2nd 18 Jan 1866 George Smith, and *d* 1879), 4th dau of Robert Westropp, of Fort Anne, Co Clare, and *d* 2 April 1862, having by her had issue:

(3) Edward Hugh Robert; *b* 5 Oct 1853, late 5th Lancers; *m* 19 June 1885 Mina Francis Westropp Harrison (*d* 1897), dau of William John Harrison Moreland, JP, of Raheen Manor, Co Clare, and *d* 26 March 1935, having had issue:

1a Edward Vivian Morgan, Lt RE; *b* 24 June 1889; *ka* 1917

1a Mina Aileen Emily; *d* unm 11 March 1966

(2) Frances Barbara; *m* 28 Aug 1895 Frank Hyde Maberly, MD, of Rockville, Glenbrook, Co Cork, and *d* 2 June 1949

4 Augustus (Rev); *b* 1798; *m* 7 April 1828 Charlotte (*d* 11 Feb 1861), dau of John Kirwan, of Moyne, Co Galway, and *d* 24 Feb 1861, leaving issue:

(1) Hugh Augustus, formerly 6th and 10th Regts, and Lt-Col 1st Sussex Vol; *b* 6 June 1829; *m* 1st 7 Feb 1856 Amelia Harriet (*d* 24 June 1890), est dau of Capt Charles Farquharson, RN, and had issue:

1a Alys Maud; *m* 19 Feb 1884 Maj Maxwell Robertson Hyslop, late Leics Regt, and *d* 21 July 1924, leaving issue. He *d* 2 June 1915

2a Kathleen Ruth; *m* 1st 2 July 1878 (*divorce* 1881) Col Edward Reginald Courtenay, CB, late 11th Hus (*see* DEVON, E); *m* 2nd 22 Nov 1881 (*divorce* 1888) Capt Ernest James Robinson; *m* 3rd 6 Feb 1889 Capt James Montgomerie Caulfeild, CBE, RN (*see* CHARLEMONT, V), and *d* 30 Aug 1951

(1) (cont.) Lt Col Hugh Crofton *m* 2nd 20 July 1892 Joan Ruby, dau of Donald Mackintosh, of Inverness, and *d* 7 April 1901

(2) Edward, MA, barrister; *b* 6 June 1832; *m* 10 Aug 1859 Sarah (*d* 19 Nov 1904), 2nd dau of William Tanner, DL, of Patcham, and *dsp* 12 March 1900

(1) Emily Frances; *m* 11 Oct 1860 Watson Scatcherd, HEICS, and *d* 26 Aug 1901, leaving issue

5 Parsons; *b* 1805; *m* 2 Aug 1831 Anne Palmer (*d* 12 March 1884), dau of Edward Westby, of High Park, Co Wicklow, and *d* 23 Oct 1884, leaving issue:

(1) Hugh Westby; *b* 3 April 1832; *d* unm 29 Dec 1918

(1) Fanny Palmer; *d* unm 6 April 1923

1 Anne Digby; *m* 17 Aug 1836 V-Adml Robert Jocelyn Otway, of Castle Otway, Co Tipperary, and *d* 14 Dec 1899, leaving issue. He *d* 16 Oct 1884

Sir HUGH *d* 6 Jan 1834; his est son,

Sir Morgan George Crofton, 3rd Bt, Lt RN, fought at Trafalgar; *b* 21 Dec 1788; *m* 21 May 1812 Emily (*d* 16 Feb 1876), dau of Rt Hon Denis Daly, of Dunsandle, Co Galway, and sis of 1st Baron Dunsandle and Clanconnel, and *d* 24 June 1867, having had issue:

1 Hugh Denis, Col, cmded 20th Regt at the Alma and was severely wounded while leading a Wing of that Regt at Inkerman, Chevalier Legion of Honour, Kt Order Medjidie; *b* 7 Jan 1814; *m* 26 May 1849 Georgiana Lucy, dau of Hon Peter Boyle de Blaquiere, and *d* 15 Sept 1861 after being shot by a soldier of the 32nd Regt at Preston, having had issue:

(1) **Sir Morgan George Crofton, 4th Bt**, DL, Co Leitrim, High Sheriff 1874, late Lt N Som Yeo Cav; *b* 5 April 1850; *m* 1 June 1897 Mabel Earle (*d* 16 Nov 1945), yst dau of Burton Archer-Burton, of Rockstone Place, Southampton, and *dsp* 26 Feb 1900

(2) Arthur Mark, Maj 8th Hus; *b* 25 April 1852; *m* 7 Nov 1881 Charlotte, dau of Col Charles Henry Hall, BSC, and *dsp* 13 April 1887

(3) Edward Hugh, Capt Rifle Bde; *b* 7 Sept 1854; *m* 1877 Isabel Annie Julia (*d* 8 July 1919), yst dau of Gen John Miller, late 13th Hus, and *d* 15 May 1882, leaving issue:

1a **Sir Hugh Denis Crofton, 5th Bt**, JP Leitrim and Roscommon; *educ* Trin Coll Cambridge (BA); *b* 11 Nov 1878; *d* unm 4 Feb 1902

2a **Sir Morgan George Crofton, 6th Bt**, DSO (1918), JP Cos Leitrim and Hants, Gold Staff Offr at Coronation of HM GEORGE VI, High Sheriff Hants 1925, CC Hants 1922–31; Lt-Col 2nd Life Gds, formerly Lt Irish Gds, Provost Marshal E African Expdny Force HQ Staff of Gen Smuts 1917, Maj Gds MGR 1918–19; served Boer War 1899–1902 (severely wounded, Queen's medal with five clasps) and WW I in France, E Africa and Italy (despatches twice, Legion of Honour, Order of Leopold); Col Cmdt on Staff of Mil Advsr to Govt NI 1922; raised and cmded 28th Bn Hants HG WW II; *b* 27 Nov 1879; *m* 1st 12 Dec 1905 (*divorce* 1910) Frances Margaret (*d* 4 Jan 1950), only dau of Lt-Col Leonard Howard Lloyd Irby (*see* BOSTON, B), and *d* 8 Dec 1958, having had issue:

1b Morgan George, Capt Hampshire Regt, Maj Gen List, WW II with 14th Army in Burma (despatches twice); *b* 18 April 1907; *m* 1st 28 June 1934 (*divorce* 1940) Rosalie [Mrs George Vigor, 27 Park St, Windsor, Berks] (who *m* 2nd 1947 Lt Col George St Vigor J Vigor, OBE, late Welsh Gds (*d* 1979)), yr dau of John Lever Tillotson, of Bidston Court, Cheshire, and Lady (William) Alexander, and had issue:

1c **Sir (Hugh) Patrick Simon Crofton, 7th Bt**; *educ* Eton; 2nd Lt Welsh Gds; *b* 2 Dec 1936; *m* 7 Feb 1967 *Lene [Lady Crofton, Foxleys Farm, Holyport, nr Maidenhead, Berks], formerly w of Michael Eddowes and dau of Kai Augustinus, of Copenhagen, and was k in a car crash 1987, leaving issue:

1d *Atlanta Chloë Majken; *b* 3 Jan 1969

1b (cont.) Maj Morgan Crofton *m* 2nd 31 July 1945 *Joan St John (*m* 2nd 24 June 1950 Dr Hugh Lestyn Williams, son of Lestyn Rhys Williams, of St Cyres, Penarth, Glam), er dau of William St John Inman, of Sunderland, gs of William Inman, of Upton Manor, Birkenhead, and *d* 31 March 1947

2a (cont.) **Sir Morgan** *m* 2nd 19 Nov 1919 Adèle Violet Blanche (*d* 9 Dec 1931), 3rd dau of Sir George Donaldson; *m* 3rd 20 June 1933 *Margaret Amelia [Margaret Lady Crofton, 34 Rhinefield Close, Brockenhurst, Hants SO42 7SU], 2nd dau of Judge Morris Dallett, of Philadelphia, USA, and by her had issue:

2b Sir HUGH DENIS CROFTON, **8th and present Bt**

3 +EDWARD MORGAN [Maj Edward Crofton, Long Durford, Upper Durford Wood, Petersfield, Hants], Maj Coldstream Gds (ret), memb Gentlemen-at-Arms 1996–; *b* 26 July 1945; heir presumptive; *educ* Eton and RMA Sandhurst; *m* 26 March 1977 *Emma Victoria Mildred, only dau of Sir Henry George Massy Dashwood, 8th Bt, DL, JP (*see* DASHWOOD, Bt, of Kirtlington Park), and has issue:

(1) +Henry Morgan; *b* 12 March 1979

(2) +George Edward; *b* 13 March 1981

CROHAM

Arms: Argent on a base checky or and azure an oak tree proper fructed or, the trunk supported by two crows respectant proper, beaked and legged gold. **Crest:** An alaunt proper gorged with a crown or, reposing its dexter paw upon a purse azure corded and tasselled, the cords tied over the paw in a bow or. **Supporters:** Dexter, a griffin azure semée of roundels or and argent, winged, beaked, legged and tufted or; sinister, a pegusus azure semée of mullets of six points or and argent, winged and hooved or. **Motto:** *Semper paratus* ('Ever ready') **Creation:** B. (LP, UK) 1977.

THE BARON CROHAM, of the London Borough of Croydon (Sir Douglas Albert Vivian Allen , GCB (1973, KCB 1967, CB 1963)) [The Rt Hon The Lord Croham CGB, 9 Manor Way, South Croydon, Surrey CR2 7BT; Ashcroft, Crowborough Rd, Nutley, Sussex]; *b* 15 Dec 1917; *educ* Wallington County GS and LSE (BScEcon 1938); WWII Capt AA Command RA; Cabinet Office 1947, Treasury 1948–58, Under Sec: Min Health 1958–60, Treasury 1960–62; Third Sec 1962–64, Dep Under-Sec DEA 1964–66 (Second PUS 1966, PUS 1966), Perm Sec Treasury 1968–74, Head Home Civ Serv and Perm Sec CSD 1974–77; Industl Advsr to Govr Bank England 1978–83, Pres Inst Fiscal Studies 1979–92; dir: Pilkington 1978–92, Guiness Mahon 1989–92, dep chm BNOC 1978–82 (chm 1982–85), chm: Anglo-German Fndn 1982– (tstee 1977–), BNOC 1982–86, Guiness Peat Gp 1983–89, Trinity Insur 1988–92; Pres Br Inst Energy Economies 1985–94; CIMgt, Hon Fell LSE 1969, FRSA 1975, Hon DSc Southampton 1977; *m* 1941 Sybil Eileen (*d* 18 Sept 1994), dau of John Marco Allegro, and has issue:

1 *John Douglas [The Hon John Allen, Westfields, 23 Quaker Rd, Sileby, Leics LE12 7SA]; *b* 1945; *m* 1969 *Sheila, only dau of Dr A J Ward, of Hemingford Grey, Cambs, and has:

(1) *Gregory John; *b* 1972

(2) *Alexander Richard; *b* 1975

(1) *Sarah Yvette; *b* 1979

2 *Richard Anthony [The Hon Richard Allen, 2 Mount Close, Kenley, Surrey CR8 5DP]; *b* 1950; *m* 1st 1980 (*divorce* 1986) Karen, only dau of F Hughes, of Whetstone, London; *m* 2nd 1988 (*divorce* 1995) Gillian, only dau of R Harraway, of Huddersfield, Yorks

1 *Rosamund Sybil [The Hon Mrs Sulyák, 8A Harewood Rd, S Croydon, Surrey CR2 7AL]; *b* 1942; *m* 1974 *Stephan Sulyák, s of Laszló Sulyák, of Kunszentmarton, Hungary, and has issue:

(1) *Veronica Claire; *b* 1976

Lineage: ALBERT JOHN ALLEN had:

DOUGLAS ALBERT VIVIAN, *cr* a **Baron**

CROMARTIE

Arms: Quarterly, 1st, a mountain az. in flames ppr. (for MACLEOD of Lewis); 2nd, az. a buck's head cabossed or (for MACKENZIE); 3rd, gu. three legs of a man armed ppr., conjoined in the centre at the upper part of the thighs, flexed in triangle, garnished and spurred or (for ISLE OF MAN); 4th, arg. on a pale sa. an imperial crown ppr. within a double tressure flory counterflory gu. (for ERSKINE of Innertiell). **Crest:** The sun in his splendour. **Supporters:** Dexter, a wild man wreathed about the loins with oak, holding a club resting on the exterior shoulder ppr.; sinister, a greyhound arg, collared gu. **Motto:** *Luceo non uro* ('I shine but do not burn'). **Creation:** E., V., Bs. (UK) 21 Oct 1861.

THE 5TH EARL OF CROMARTIE, **Viscount Tarbat** of Tarbat, Co Cromartie, **Baron Castlehaven** of Castlehaven, Co Cromartie, and **Baron Mcleod of Castle Leod**, Co Cromartie (John Ruaridh Grant Mackenzie) [The Rt Hon The Earl of Cromartie, Castle Leod, Strathpeffer, Ross-shire IV14 9AA]; *b* 12 June 1948; *s f* 1989; *educ* Rannoch Sch and Strathclyde U; explosives engr; recognized by Lord Lyon as Chief of Clan Mackenzie; dropped forename and surname BLUNT 1962; author *Selected Climbs in Skye* (1982), MIExpE (memb cncl); *m* 22 Dec 1973 (*divorce* 1983) Helen, dau of John Murray, steelworker, of Lanarks, and has had:

1 Kenneth; *b* 19 Jan 1980; *d* 6 March 1980

The 5th EARL *m* 2nd 1985 *Janet Clare, dau of Christopher James Harley, of Strathpeffer, and by her has:

2 +COLIN RUARIDH; *Viscount Tarbat*; *b* 7 Sept 1987

3 +Alasdair Kenelm Stuart; *b* 1989

Lineage: According to Celtic genealogies the MACKENZIEs of Kintail stem from Gillian Og ('The Younger'), s of Gillian of the Air, ancestor also of the Earls of Ross (*see* MACDONALD, B). Ninth in descent from Gillian, and the first of these MACKENZIEs for whose existence there is documentary evidence, was:

ALEXANDER MACKENZIE of Kintail, called 'Ionriac'; imprisoned 1427 by JAMES I; *d* 1488, having had, with two yr sons (Duncan, ancestor of the MACKENZIEs of Hilton; Hector, living 1511, ancestor of the MACKENZIEs of Gairloch, *see* INGLIS, Bt):

KENNETH MACKENZIE of Kintail; *m* 1st Margaret, dau of John, 11th of Ross and 1st Lord of the Isles (*see* MACDONALD, B), and had a s (Kenneth, of Kintail, *dspl c* 1499); *m* 2nd Agnes Fraser and *d* 7 Feb 1491/2, having by her had, with two yr sons (Alexander, ancestor of the MACKENZIEs of Davochmaluach (*see* also MACKENZIE, Bt, of Coul); Rhoderick, ancestor of the MACKENZIEs of Achilty) and a dau (Katherine, *m* Hector Munro of Foulis; *see* MUNRO, Bt, of Foulis-Obsdale):

JOHN MACKENZIE of Kintail, to which served heir 1500; had a Crown Charter 1508 erecting the same into the territorial Barony of Eileandonnan; *m* Elizabeth, dau of John Grant, 2nd of Freuchie (*see* STRATHSPEY, B), and *d* 1561, having had:

KENNETH MACKENZIE of Kintail, called *na Cuire*; *m* Jean, dau of 2nd Earl of Atholl (*see* MORAY, E), and *d* 6 June 1561, leaving, with an est s (Murdoch, *d* young) and two yst sons (Roderick, of Redcastle; Dugald), a 2nd s:

COLIN MACKENZIE of Kintail, called *Cam* ('one-eyed'); served heir to his f 1574; *m* his cousin Barbara, dau of John Grant of Grant and Freuchie, and *d* 14 June 1594, leaving, with an illegitimate s (*see* MACKENZIE, Bt, of Coul):

1 KENNETH MACKENZIE, 1st LORD MACKENZIE OF KINTAIL (S), so *cr* 17 Nov 1609, PC (S Feb 1595/6 and 1602), JP (Cromarty, Elgin, Fife, Inverness-shire and Nairne 1610); became Hereditary Constable of the castle of the Bp of Ross 1595 on acquisition of various Church lands; *m* 1st Jean, dau of George Ross of Balnagowan, and had, with two yr sons (*d* young):

(1) COLIN MACKENZIE, 2nd LORD MACKENZIE OF KINTAIL and 1st EARL OF SEAFORTH (S), so *cr* 3 Dec 1623, with remainder to heirs male whatsoever, PC (S 1628 and 1631); *m* 5 June 1614 Margaret, 4th dau of 1st Earl of Dunfermline (*see* EGLINTON and WINTON, E), and *dspm* 15 April 1633, leaving:

1a Jean; *m* 1st *c* Dec 1633 John, Master of Berriedaile (*see* CAITHNESS, E); *m* 2nd 1st Lord Duffus (*see* SUTHERLAND, D) and *d* in childbirth 31 March 1648, having by him had allegedly four sons (*dsp*)

2a Anne; *m* 1st c April 1640 1st Earl of Balcarres (*see* CRAWFORD and BALCARRES, E) and had issue; *m* 2nd 28 Jan 1670, as his 2nd w, 9th Earl of Argyll (*see* ARGYLL, D) and *d* 2 May 1707 *sp* by him

(1) Sybilla; *m* 1st Ian *Mor* Macleod, 16th Chief, and had issue (*see* BOSVILLE MACDONALD, Bt); *m* 2nd Alexander Fraser (*see* LOVAT, L)

(3) Barbara; *m* as his 1st w 1st Lord Reay (*qv*) and had issue

(3) Janet; m Sir Donald Macdonald of Sleat, 1st Bt (*see* BOSVILLE-MACDONALD, Bt)

1 (cont.) The 1st LORD MACKENZIE OF KINTAIL *m* 2nd by 12 March 1607 Isabel, dau of Sir Gilbert Ogilvy of Powrie, and *d* 27 Feb 1610/1, leaving by her, with an er s (*d* young):

(2) GEORGE MACKENZIE, 2nd EARL OF SEAFORTH, PC (S 1637 and 1641), JP (Elgin, Forres, Inverness-shire and Nairn); originally a Covenanter but later supported CHARLESes I and II, by latter of whom while in exile made Sec State Scotland; *m c* Jan 1627/8 Barbara, est dau of 10th Lord Forbes (*qv*), and *d* Aug 1651, leaving:

1a KENNETH MACKENZIE, 3rd EARL OF SEAFORTH, PC (S 1674); *educ* King's Coll Aberdeen; royalist, fought Battle of Worcester 1651, hence his estates confiscated 1654 and he imprisoned 1656–60; Sheriff Ross 1662 and 1675; *m c* 1660 his cousin Isabel, sis of 1st EARL OF CROMARTY (*see* below), and *d* 16 Dec 1678, leaving:

1b KENNETH MACKENZIE, 4th EARL OF SEAFORTH, KT (1687), PC (S 1686); *bapt* 8 Dec 1661; RC, accompanied JAMES II to France and Ireland, where assisted at Siege of Londonderry, accordingly *cr c* 1690 by JAMES after his deposition titular Marquess of Seaforth, Earl of Fortrose, Viscount Fortrose and Baron [*sic*] Fortrose (S), attempting a Jacobite rising in the N of Scotland the same year and being imprisoned Edinburgh and Inverness Castles till March 1696/7, when he was allowed to leave the country and settle in France after charges of high treason were preferred but not proceeded with; *m* Lady Frances Herbert, dau of 1st Marquess of Powis (*see* POWIS, E), and *d* Jan 1700/1, leaving:

1c WILLIAM MACKENZIE, 5th EARL OF SEAFORTH; imprisoned Edinburgh Castle March 1707/8 on suspicion of involvement with abortive pro-Jacobite French invasion that year; led more than 3,000 men in Jacobite Uprising 1715, when present at Sheriffmuir 13 Nov, following which apptd Jacobite Lt-Gen of Northern Counties, hence attainted 1716 and deprived of his titles and lands; fled to France July 1716, apptd titular KT by Old Pretender by Dec 1716; assisted in failed Jacobite rising 1719, when wounded at encounter of Glenshiel 10 June 1719, and again fled to France; pardoned all personal punishments by British Govt 1726 and his disabilities under the attainder removed by Act of Parl 1736 (though his titles remained under forfeiture); *m* 22 April 1715 Mary, dau of Nicholas Kennet, of Coxhow, Northumberland, and *d* 8 Jan 1740, leaving:

1d Kenneth, *Lord Fortrose*; *b* 1717; MP Inverness burghs 1741–47 and Ross-shire 1747–61, Burgess Edinburgh 1741, remained loyal to Hanoverians during 1745 Uprising; *m* 11 Sept 1741 Mary, dau of 6th Earl of Galloway (*qv*), and *d* 18 Oct 1761, leaving:

1e KENNETH MACKENZIE, 1st and last EARL OF SEAFORTH, so *cr* 3 Dec 1771, as also earlier 18 Nov 1766 BARON ARDELVE, Co Wicklow, and VISCOUNT FORTROSE, Co Wicklow (all I); *b* 15 Jan 1744; MP Caithness 1768–74; Lt-Col Seaforth Highrs (a regt he raised 1771) 1777–81; *m* 1st 7 Oct 1765 Caroline, dau of 2nd Earl of Harrington (*qv*); *m* 2nd clandestinely Harriet Lamb *alias* Powell, described by a contemporary source as a courtesan, dau of an apothecary, and *dspm* Aug 1781, when his titles expired, leaving by his 1st w:

1f Caroline; *b* 7 July 1766; *m* as his 2nd w Louis Pierre Francis Malcolm Drummond, Count de Melfort (*see* PERTH, E), and *d* 1847

2c Alexander; *m* Elizabeth, dau of John Paterson, Bp Ross, and had:

1d William; Maj; *m* Mary, dau of Matthew Humberston, of Humberston, Lincs, and *d* 12 May 1770, leaving:

1e Thomas Frederick MACKENZIE later MACKENZIE-HUMBERSTON (*c* 1775); *b* by 1754; bought 1779 the Seaforth estates from his cousin the 1st and last EARL OF SEAFORTH of the 1771 *cr*; Cornet 1st Dragoon Gds 1771, Capt 1777, exchanged into Seaforth Highrs 1778, Maj 1778, Lt-Col cmdg 100th Foot 1780, served Campaign against Hyder Ali in India 1782, *s* cousin as Lt-Col Seaforth Highrs 1782; *d* unm 30 April 1783 of wounds recd in a naval encounter with the Mahrattas off Bombay 23 days earlier

2e FRANCIS HUMBERSTON MACKENZIE, 1st and last LORD SEAFORTH, BARON MACKENZIE OF KINTAIL, Co Ross (GB), so *cr* 26 Oct 1797; *b* 9 June 1754; MP (Whig to 1794, Pittite thereafter) Ross-shire 1784–90 and 1794–96, Ld Lt Ross-shire 1794–1815, Lt-Col cmdg 78th Foot (Ross-shire Buffs) 1793–96, Col 2nd N British Militia 1798, Maj-Gen 1802, Lt Gen 1808, Govr Barbados 1800–06; *m* 22 April 1782 Mary, dau of Very Rev Baptist Proby, DD, Dean Lichfield, and *dspms* 11 Jan 1815, when his titles (including the Jacobite ones) expired, having had, with five yr daus:

1f William Frederick; *d* unm *vp*

2f George Leveson Boucherat; *d* unm *vp*

3f William Frederick; MP Ross-shire 1812–14; *d* unm & *vp* 25 Aug 1814

4f Francis John; Midshipman RN; *d* 1813

1f Mary Frederica Elizabeth; *b* 27 March 1783; *m* 1st 6 Nov 1804 V-Adml Sir Samuel Hood, 1st Bt (*dsp* 24 Dec 1814, *see* 1970 edn ST AUDRIES, B); *m* 2nd 21 May 1817 Rt Hon James Alexander STEWART later STEWART-MACKENZIE of Glasserton, Govr Ceylon and HC Ionian Islands, and *d* 28 Nov 1862, leaving by him:

1g Keith William; *m* Hannah Charlotte, est dau of James Joseph Hope-Vere (*see* LINLITHGOW, M), and *d* 18 June 1881, leaving:

1h JAMES ALEXANDER FRANCIS HUMBERSTON STEWART-MACKENZIE, 1st and last BARON SEAFORTH, of Brahan in Urray, in the Co of Ross and Cromarty (UK), so *cr* 19 Jan 1921; *b* 9 Oct 1847; *educ* Harrow and RMC Sandhurst; joined 9th Lancers 1867, Afghan War 1878–80 (despatches twice, wounded), Bevet Maj, Mil Sec to Govr Madras 1886–88, Lt-Col cmdg 9th Lancers 1891, ret 1896, V-Lt Ross and Cromarty, Hon Col 4th Bn Seaforth Highrs; *m* 18 July 1899 Mary Margaret, CBE, JP, LGStJ, only child of Edward Steinkopf, of Lydhurst, Haywards Heath, Sussex, and *dsp* 3 March 1923, when the Barony expired

1h Julia Charlotte Sophia; *b* 21 June 1846; *m* 1st 8 Oct 1873, as his 2nd w, 9th Marquess of Tweeddale (*qv*); *m* 2nd 24 June 1887 Sir John Rose, 1st Bt, of Montreal (*qv*); *m* 3rd 3 Feb 1892 Maj Sir William Evans Gordon, MP, and *d* 17 May 1937

1c Mary; apparently *m* titular 10th Lord Sempill (*see* SEMPIL, L)

2b John, of Assynt; had an only s:

1c Kenneth; had an only s:

1d William; Prior Scots Monastery Wurzburg

2a George; *m* and left male issue

3a Colin; *m* and had issue

4a Roderick

1a Jean; *m* 1st 1647, as his 2nd w, 20th/4th Earl of Mar (*qv*); *m* 2nd, as his 2nd w, 3rd Lord Fraser (*see* SALTOUN, L)

(2) Thomas; *m* twice and had two sons; his male issue died out by 1829

2 RODERICK

3 Colin, of Killin; ancestor of the MACKENZIEs of Kinnock

4 Alexander; ancestor of the Mackenzie Bts of Kilcoy (*see* 1902 edn)

5 Murdoch

1 Katherine; *m* as his 1st w 6th Lord (Fraser of) Lovat (*qv*)

2 Jennette; *m* Hector *Og* Maclean of Dowart and had issue (*see* MACLEAN, Bt, of Dowart)

3 Mary; *m* as his 2nd w Donald *Gorm Mor*, 7th of Sleat (*see* BOSVILLE-MACDONALD, Bt)

COLIN MACKENZIE's 2nd son,

Sir RODERICK MACKENZIE of Castle Leod, Cogeach and Tarbat, Co Cromarty; *b* 1579; *m* (contract 6 May 1605) Margaret (*m* 2nd (contract 17 Feb 1629) Thomas Fraser of Strichen, *see* LOVAT, L), dau and heiress of Torquil Macleod of Lewis, and *d* Sept 1626, leaving:

1 Sir JOHN MACKENZIE, 1st Bt, of Tarbat

2 KENNETH

3 Colin, of Tarvey; *m* his cousin —, dau of Alexander Mackenzie of Gairloch and widow of John Mackenzie of Inverlawe, and *d* 1645, leaving issue

4 Alexander, of Balone; *m* —, dau of Hugh Fraser of Culbockie and widow of Kenneth Mackenzie of Inverlawe, and *d* 1645, leaving issue

1 Margaret; *m* as his 1st w Sir James Macdonald of Sleat, 2nd Bt, (*see* BOSVILLE-MACDONALD, Bt)

Sir RODERICK *d* Sept 1626; his est son,

Sir JOHN MACKENZIE, 1st Bt (NS), of Tarbat, so *cr* 21 May 1628, with remainder to his heirs male whatsoever; *m* (contract 25 July 1629) Margaret (*m* 2nd 1661 Sir James Foulis, 2nd Bt (*qv*)), dau and coheir of Sir George Erskine of Innerteil, Senator Coll of Justice and bro of 1st Earl of Kellie (*see* MAR and KELLIE, E), and had, with other issue:

1 GEORGE (Sir), 2nd Bt

2 Roderick, of Prestonhall; Ld of Session as Lord Prestonhall; *m* 1st 28 April 1674 Mary, dau of Alexander Burnet, Archbp St Andrews, and had:

(1) Alexander MACKENZIE later FRASER of Fraserdale; *m* Æmilia, dau of 10th Lord Lovat (*qv*), and *d* 3 June 1775, leaving issue

2 (cont.) Lord Prestonhall *m* 2nd Margaret (*dsp* Jan 1713), widow of Sir George Mackenzie of Rosehaugh and dau of Halyburton of Pitcar, and *d* 4 Jan 1712

3 Alexander, of Ardloch and Kinnellan; ggf of:

(1) Sir Alexander Mackenzie; *b* 16 May 1802; Lt-Col HEIC's serv; assumed the 1704 btcy (*see* below) despite its being subject to attainder after the '45 Rising; *d* 28 April 1841

(2) Sir James Sutherland Mackenzie; also assumed the btcy; *d* unm 24 Nov 1858

4 Kenneth; *bapt* 26 Nov 1648; *m* Isabel Auchinleck, and had issue

1 Margaret; *m* 1st Roderick MacLeod of that Ilk; *m* 2nd Sir James Campbell of Lawers

2 Anne; *m* 1659 8th Lord Lovat (*qv*)

3 Isabel; *m* 3rd Earl of Seaforth and had issue

4 Barbara; *m* (contract 4 March 1670) Alexander Mackenzie of Gairloch and had issue (*see* INGLIS, Bt)

5 Catherine; *m* (contract 19 Aug 1667) Sir Colin Campbell, 1st Bt, of Aberuchill (*qv*), and had issue

Sir JOHN *d* 10 Sept 1654, his est son,

Sir GEORGE MACKENZIE, 2nd Bt, 1st EARL OF CROMARTY [*sic*], so *cr* 1 Jan 1702/3, as also VISCOUNT OF TARBAT and LORD MACLEOD AND CASTLEHAVEN, and earlier 15 April 1685 VISCOUNT OF TARBAT, LORD MACLEOD AND CASTLEHAVEN (all S), PC (S 1662); *b* 1630; *educ* Aberdeen U and King's Coll Aberdeen; raised and maintained a royalist force 1654–55 to restore CHARLES II but defeated by Gen Morgan, following which he lived on the Continent till 1660; Ld of Session 1661–Feb 1663/4 and 1681, Ld Justice Gen 1678–80 and 1705–10, Ld Clerk Register 1681–89 and 1692–95, FRS 1692, a Pncpl Sec State (S) 1702–05, Capt Gen Roy Co Archers 1705–10; resigned his btcy 1704 in favour of his 2nd s; *m* 1st (contract 6 July 1654) Anne (*d* 1699), dau of Sir James Sinclair, 1st Bt, of Mey, and had, with other issue:

1 JOHN, 2nd Earl

2 Sir KENNETH MACKENZIE, 1st Bt (NS), of Grandvale and Cromarty, so *cr* 29 April 1704, with remainder to heirs male whatsoever, and the precedence (1628) of his gf's patent; MP Cromarty 1710–13 and 1727; *m* 1st Mary, sis of David Kinnear of that Ilk; *m* 2nd 1701 Anne Campbell; *m* 3rd (contract 14 Jan 1726) Elizabeth Edwards, widow of (a) Charles Graydon and (b) Alexander Sutherland of Kinminitie, and *d* 13 Sept 1728, having by his 2nd w had, with other issue:

(1) Sir GEORGE MACKENZIE, 2nd Bt, of Cromarty, which he sold to William Urquhart of Meldrum; MP Cromarty; *m* 1742 Elizabeth (*d* 24 Aug 1807), sis of Capt John Reid, and *dsp* 20 May 1748

(2) Sir KENNETH MACKENZIE, 3rd Bt of the 1704 *cr* and 2nd of the (Roystoun; *see* below) Feb 1703/4 *cr*; *d* unm 14 Sept 1763, when both btcies fell under the attainder passed against the 3rd EARL, though both were later assumed by descendants of Alexander, 3rd son of the 1st Bt of the 1628 *cr* (*see* above), and on the extinction of that line by the descendants of Kenneth, next bro of the 1st Bt of the 1628 *cr* (*see* above)

(1) Katherine, *m* 1st James Callander and had issue; *m* 2nd Dr Adam Murray, and *d* 17 June 1755

3 Sir JAMES MACKENZIE, 1st Bt, of Roystoun (NS), so *cr* 8 Feb 1703/4; *b* 1671; Ld of Session 1710; *m* Elizabeth (*d* July 1717), widow of Sir Archibald Cockburn of Langton and dau of Sir George Mackenzie of Rosehaugh, and *d* 9 Nov 1744, having had issue:

(1) George, of Farnese, *b* 18 Oct 1708; *m* 20 Jan 1743 Isabella, dau of Archibald Stewart, and *dsp* 15 May 1744, *vp*

(1) Anne; *m* Sir William Dick, Bt, of Prestonfield

(2) Elizabeth; *m* 13 Jan 1725 Sir John Stewart, Bt, of Grandtully, and had issue

1 Elizabeth; *m* 1692 Sir George Broun, 2nd Bt, of Colstoun (*qv*), and *d* 5 May 1703, leaving issue

2 Jean; *m* Sir Thomas Stewart, Bt, of Balcaskie, and had issue

3 Anne; *m* Hon John Sinclair of Murkle, bro to 9th Earl of Caithness (*qv*) and a Ld of Session, and *dsp* 21 Oct 1740

The 1st EARL *m* 2nd 29 April 1700 Margaret, Countess of Wemyss in her own right (*see* WEMYSS and MARCH, E), by whom he had a dau, and *d* 27 Aug 1714

His est son,

JOHN MACKENZIE, 2nd EARL OF CROMARTY; *b c* 1656; MP Ross-shire 1685 though this annulled on account of his noble parentage, tried for murder 1691 but acquitted following death of a Frenchman in a Leith tavern brawl; became insolvent and his estates sequestrated 1724; *m* 1st (contract 10 Jan 1685; *divorce* 1698) Lady Elizabeth Gordon, dau of 1st Earl of Aboyne (*see* HUNTLY, M), but by her had no issue; *m* 2nd 25 April 1701 Mary, dau of 3rd Lord Elibank (*qv*), by whom he had, with other issue:

1 GEORGE MACKENZIE, 3rd EARL OF CROMARTY; *b c* 1703; Jacobite 1745, led 400 of his clan Battle of Falkirk 18 Jan 1745/6, captured with his s by a detachment of Lord Sutherland's Militia at Dunrobin Castle 15 April 1746, confined in the Tower of London, tried by his Peers, found guilty of high treason and attainted and sentenced to death 1 Aug 1746, his estates and honours being forfeited; got a remission for life 4 Oct 1749; *m* 23 Sept 1724 Isabel (*d* 23 April 1769), dau of Sir William Gordon of Invergordon, Bt, and *d* 28 Sept 1766, leaving, with other issue:

(1) John, Lord Macleod; *b* 1727; convicted of high treason but pardoned 22 Jan 1748; served Swedish mil forces from 1749, ADC to King of Sweden, who *cr* him Count Cromarty and made him a Cioomandant of the Order of the Sword of Sweden; returned to GB 1777, raised two Bns of Highrs and became Col of the 73rd Foot (MacLeod's Highlanders, renumbered 71st Foot 1782, later HLI), serving with them also in India; Maj-Gen 1782; returned from India 1784, when his forfeited estates restored him on payment of a £19,000 fine; MP (Tory) Ross-shire 1780–84; *m* 4 June 1786 Margery (*m* 2nd 11 April 1794 4th Duke of Atholl (*qv*) and *d* 3 Oct 1842, leaving issue), est dau of 16th Lord Forbes (*qv*), and *dsp* 2 April 1789

(2) William; *d* 1736 aged 3

(3) George Mackenzie, Lt-Col 71st Foot; *d* 1787

(1) ISABELLA Mackenzie; inherited the Cromarty estates from her cousin Kenneth in 1796; *m* 8 Jan 1760 George MURRAY, 6th Lord Elibank (*qv*), and *dspm* 28 Dec 1801, leaving, with another dau:

1a MARIA, for whom *see* further below

(2) Mary; *m* 1st 23 June 1750 Capt Clarke; *m* 2nd Aug 1757 Thomas Drayton, of S Carolina; *m* 3rd 17 June 1762 John Ainslie (*d* 10 Jan 1774); *m* 4th Henry Middleton, of S Carolina

(3) Anne; *m* 1st Hon Edmond Atkins, Pres of Cncl of S Carolina (*d* 8 Oct 1761); *m* 2nd 16 Feb 1764 John Murray, MD, and *d* 18 Jan 1768

(4) Caroline; *b* 6 May 1736; *m* 1st 5 Sept 1760 Capt Drake; *m* 2nd Walter Hunter, of Polmood (*d* 15 Jan 1796), and *d* 3 Oct 1791, leaving:

1a Elizabeth; *m* 14th Lord Forbes (*qv*)

2a Caroline; *m* 1 Sept 1799 James Elliot, of Woollie, WS, and *d* 25 April 1824

(5) Margaret; *m* 21 March 1769 John Glassford, of Dougalston, and *d* 29 March 1773, leaving issue

(6) Augusta; *m* 6 March 1770 (*divorce* 1791) Sir William Murray, Bt, of Ochtertyre (*qv*), and had issue

2 Roderick; Capt RN; present Siege of Gibraltar 1726; later Lt Royal Dragoons; Capt of Foot 1740; served Flanders 1745; *m* and had an only son:

(1) Kenneth, of Cromarty; *s* to the Cromarty estates on the death of his cousin Lord Macleod 1789; *dspm* 4 Nov 1796 (when the states passed back to Lord Macleod's sis; *see* above), leaving:

1a Mary Ann

3 William; in Dutch mil service, offr HEIC's mil service 1737; *d* off Angria in a hurricane

The 2nd EARL *m* 3rd 11 Nov 1716 Anne, dau of 9th Lord Lovat (*qv*) and widow of Peter Fotheringham, Yr. of Powrie, and *d* 20 Feb 1731, having by her had, with other further issue:

4 Norman; Offr in Dutch serv; *d* at sea

5 Hugh, Offr in Dutch serv; raised a company in Montgomery's Bn of Highrs 1757

1 Æmilia; *m* 22 Sept 1740 Archibald Lamont of that Ilk and *d* 19 Jan 1801, having had issue

The 3rd EARL's gdau,

MARIA Murray; *m* 3 May 1790 Edward HAY (*d* 5 Dec 1814), of Newhall, bro of 7th Marquess of Tweeddale (*qv*), who added the name and arms of MACKENZIE, and *d* 8 Oct 1858, leaving:

1 JOHN HAY-MACKENZIE of Newhall and Cromarty; sportsman and agricultural reformer; *m* 23 April 1828 Anne (*d* 8 Sept 1869), 3rd dau of Sir James Gibson-Craig, 1st Bt (*see* GIBSOB-CRAIG-CARMICHEL, Bt), and *d* 9 July 1849, leaving issue:

(1) ANNE Hay-Mackenzie, **Countess of Cromartie**, so *cr* 21 Oct 1861, as also VISCOUNTESS TARBAT of Tarbat, Co Cromartie, BARONESS MACLEOD OF CASTLE LEOD, Co Cromartie, and BARONESS CASTLEHAVEN of Castlehaven, Co Cromartie (all UK), with remainer to her 2nd surv son Francis and heirs male of his body, then each of her other yr sons by primogeniture, failing whom to Francis and the heirs of his body (*i.e.*, including females), failing whom to her other yr sons by primogeniture and the heirs of their bodies and finally to her dau Florence and the heirs of her body, failing whom to each of her other daus in order of primogeniture and the heirs of their bodies, with a proviso that if Francis 'or any other person taking under the said letters patent shall succeed to the Earldom of Sutherland, and there shall upon or at any time after the occurrence of such event be any other younger son or any other daughter of the said Anne, Duchess of Sutherland, or any heir of the body of such other son or daughter, then, and so often as the same may happen, the succession to the honours and dignities thereby created shall devolve on the son or daughter of the said Anne, or their heirs, who would be next entitled to succeed to the said honours if the person so succeeding to the Earldom of Sutherland were dead without issue'; in other words this remainder was drawn up so as to ensure that as far as possible the Earldoms of Sutherland and Cromartie would always be held separately; VA 3rd Cl; *b* 21 April 1829; Mistress of the Robes to HM QUEEN VICTORIA 1870–74; *m* 20 June 1849 3rd Duke of Sutherland (*qv*) and had issue:

1a George Granville, *Earl Gower*; *b* 27 July 1850; *d* 5 July 1858

2a CROMARTIE SUTHERLAND-LEVESON-GOWER, 4th DUKE OF SUTHERLAND (*qv*)

3a FRANCIS, **2nd Earl**

1a Florence; *m* 15 Nov 1876 1st Viscount Chaplin, PC, MP, DL, JP (*see* 1970 edn), and *d* 10 Oct 1881, leaving issue. He *d* 29 May 1923

2a Alexandria; *d* unm 16 April 1891

1 Dorothea; *m* 2 July 1813 Sir David Hunter Blair, 3rd Bt (*qv*), and *d* 22 May 1820, leaving issue

2 Isabella; *m* 1 Nov 1817 John Buckle (*d* 1863), of Wharton House, Edinburgh, and had issue

3 Georgina Ann; *m* 4 Aug 1821 5th Earl of Glasgow (*qv*) and *d* 14 March 1895

The COUNTESS *d* 25 Nov 1888; her 3rd son,

FRANCIS SUTHERLAND-LEVESON-GOWER, **2nd Earl of Cromartie**, V-Lt Ross and Cromarty, DL Sutherland, Maj 2nd Vol Bn Seaforth Highrs; *b* 3 Aug 1852; *m* 2 Aug 1876 Hon Lilian Janet (*m* 2nd 7 Oct 1895 Reginald Frederick Cazenove, late 6th Dragoon Gds (*dsp* 5 Sept 1905), and *d* 20 Nov 1926), 2nd surv dau of 4th Lord Macdonald, Baron of Slate (*qv*), and *dspms* 24 Nov 1893, when his titles fell into abeyance between his two daus, leaving:

1 SIBELL LILIAN Sutherland-Leveson-Gower; *s* as **Countess of Cromartie** in her own right on termination of abeyance by letters patent 25 Feb 1895; *b* 14 Aug 1878; author: *The Golden Guard, Temple of the Mind, Sons of the Milesians, The Decoy*, etc; *m* 16 Dec 1899 Lt-Col Edward Walter BLUNT later BLUNT-MACKENZIE (added 1905), DL, late RA (*d* 31 July 1949; *see* BLUNT, Bt), and *d* 20 May 1962, leaving:

(1) RODERICK GRANT FRANCIS BLUNT-MACKENZIE, **4th Earl of Cromartie**, MC (1945), TD (1964), JP (Ross and Cromarty 1937); *b* 24 Oct 1904; *educ* Charterhouse and RMC Sandhurst; commnd 1st Bn The Seaforth Highrs 1924, tfd to 2nd Bn 1925, served on NW Frontier of India 1925 and 1930–31 (medal), commnd 4th Bn The Seaforth Highrs TA 1935, Maj 1939, served WW II (POW 1940), Sec Scottish Peers Assoc, memb Ross and Cromarty CC 1964 (Convener 1971–89), Hon Sheriff Ross and Cromarty, FSA Scot; *m* 1st 11 March 1933 (*divorce* 1945) Mrs Dorothy Downing Porter, dau of Grant Butler Downing, of Kentucky, USA, and had issue:

1a +(Sibell Anne) Julia; *b* 15 Feb 1934; *m* 1st 16 June 1953 (*divorce* 1961) Francis Edward Lascelles Hadwen, er son of Edward Hubert Lascelles Hadwen, Levant Consular Service, and has issue:

1b +James Brian Mackenzie; *b* 23 July 1957

1b +Georgina Frances; *b* 19 Sept 1959

1a (cont.) Lady Julia Hadwen *m* 2nd 1974 *Apputhurai Jeyarama Chandran and has further issue:

2b +Anita Anne Dorothy; *b* 1977

2a +Gilean Frances; *b* 25 Feb 1936; *m* 30 Oct 1959 (*divorce* 1973) René Eugène Welter, only son of Prof Georges F Welter, Consul-Gen for Luxembourg, of Montreal, Canada, and has issue:

1b +Michael George; *b* 8 Feb 1964

1b +Nadia Christine; *b* 26 Dec 1960

(1) (cont.) The **4th Earl** *m* 2nd 30 Jan 1947 (*divorce* 1962) Olga (*d* 26 Sept 1996), dau of Stuart Laurance and Mme Ziv, of 27 Rue des Sablons, Paris, and formerly w of Peter Mendoza, and by her had issue:

1a JOHN RUARIDH (BLUNT) GRANT BLUNT-MACKENZIE later MACKENZIE, **5th and present Earl of Cromartie**

(1) The **4th Earl** *m* 3rd 1 Dec 1962 *Lilias Janet Garvie [The Rt Hon The Dowager Countess of Cromartie, Castle Leod, Strathpeffer, Ross and Cromarty], MB, ChB Leeds 1942, Co Pres BRCS, dau of Emeritus Prof James Walter Macleod, OBE, FRS, LLD, of Edinburgh, and formerly w of Lt-Col D S Richard, and *d* 1989

(2) Walter Osra, served WW II in RNVR 1941–43; *b* 6 Dec 1906; *m* 1st 21 March 1934 (*divorce* 1940) Pamela Leslie Ursula, dau of Mr Justice Oliver; *m*

2nd 16 Feb 1946 *Mary [Mrs Sijbren Tijmstra, PO Box 14, White River, E Transvaal, S Africa] (*m* 2nd 2 May 1964 Maj Clement Victor Palmer (*d* 1969); *m* 3rd 1982 *Sijbren Tijmstra), dau of Theophilus D Hix, of Holbeach, Lincs, and *d* 8 Jan 1951, having by her had issue:

1a +Roderick [Roderick Blunt-Mackenzie Esq, 21 Crowned Eagle Way, Oak Park, Pietermaritzburg 3201, S Africa]; *b* 1947; *m* 1969 *Yvonne, dau of Bernard Arthur (Bill) Lemmon, of White River, S Africa, and has issue:

1b +Craig Walter; *b* 1973

1b +Jacquelyn; *b* 1970

2b +Lara; *b* 1971

3b +Sarah Jane; *b* 1978

(1) Janet Frances Isobel; *b* 24 Nov, *d* 19 Dec 1900

(2) +Isobel [The Lady Isobel Linda, Assynt House, Evanton, Ross-shire]; *b* 22 March 1911; *m* 22 Nov 1947 *Capt Oscar Linda, son of Gen Maximilian Linda, of Zakopane, Poland

2 Constance; *m* 1st 19 April 1904 Sir Edward Stewart-Richardson, 15th Bt (*qv*), and had issue. He *d* 28 Nov 1914 from wounds received in action. She *m* 2nd 4 Aug 1921 Dennis Luckie Matthew, son of Hubert Denison Matthew, and *d* 24 Nov 1932. He *d* 26 Sept 1935

CROMER

Arms: Quarterly, 1st and 4th, az. a fess or, in chief a bear's head ppr., muzzled and ringed gold; 2nd and 3rd, gu. a cross pattée fitchée or between three fish haurient arg., within an orle of eight cross crosslets of the second. **Crest:** A mullet erminois, between two wings arg. **Supporters:** Two bears ppr., muzzled or, the dexter collared checky arg. and az. and charged on the shoulder with a lion's head erased or, the sinister collared gemel az. and charged on the shoulder with an escallop or. **Motto:** *Probitate et labore* ('By probity and industry'). **Creations:** B. (UK) 20 June 1892, V. (UK) 25 Jan 1899, E. and V. (UK) 8 Aug 1901.

THE 4TH EARL OF CROMER, Co Norfolk, **Viscount Errington**, of Hexham, Co Northumberland, **Viscount Cromer**, and **Baron Cromer** of Cromer, Norfolk (Evelyn Rowland Esmond Baring) [The Rt Hon The Earl of Cromer, Drayton Court, Drayton, Somerset]; *b* 3 June 1946; *s* f 1991; *educ* Eton; md Inchcape (China) Ltd 1979–94 and Inchcape Vietnam Ltd 1987–94, dep chm Motor Tport Co of Guangdong & Hong Kong Ltd (China) 1979–94 and Land-Ocean Inchcape Container Tport Co Ltd (China) 1985–94, memb St John's Cncl (Hong Kong) 1980–85; *m* 1st 25 Oct 1971 (*divorce* 1992) Plern Isarangkul Na Ayudhya, est dau of Dr Charanphat Isarangkul Na Ayudhya, of Thailand; *m* 2nd 1993 *Shelly Hu Cheng-Yu, dau of Hu Guoquin, of Shanghai, and has:

1 +ALEXANDER ROWLAND HARMSWORTH, *Viscount Errington*; *b* 5 Jan 1994

1 *A dau; *b* 22 Feb 1998

Lineage: HENRY BARING, MP (*see* NORTHBROOK, B); had a 9th s:

EVELYN BARING, **1st Earl of Cromer**, so *cr* 8 Aug 1901, as also VISCOUNT ERRINGTON OF HEXHAM, Northumberland, and earlier 20 June 1892 BARON CROMER OF CROMER, Norfolk, and 25 Jan 1899 VISCOUNT CROMER, PC (1900), GCB (1895, KCB 1887, CB 1885), OM (1906), GCMG (1888), KCSI (1883, CSI 1876), CIE (1880), Order of the Medjidie 1st Cl, FRS, DCL Oxford 1904, LLD Cambridge 1905; *b* 26 Feb 1841; *educ* RMA Woolwich; RA 1858, ret as Maj 1879, Commr Egyptian Public Debt 1877–79, Comptroller-Gen Egypt 1879–80, Financial Memb Cncl to Viceroy India 1880–83, Consul-Gen and Min Plen Egypt 1883–1907; Freedom City London 1907, Albert Medal of RSA 1908; *m* 1st 28 June 1876 Ethel (*d* 16 Oct 1898), dau and coheir of Sir Rowland Stanley Errington, 11th Bt (*qv*), and had issue:

1 ROWLAND THOMAS, **2nd Earl**

2 Windham; md Baring Bros, dir Buenos Aires Gt Southern Railway, WW I as Lt RNVR; *b* 29 Sept 1880; *m* 10 July 1913 Lady Gweneth Frida, JP (Kent 1942), Order of Mercy (*m* 2nd 4 Feb 1926 Col Ralph Henry Voltelin Cavendish, CBE, MVO, DL (*d* 21 June 1968), and *d* 1984) (*see* DEVONSHIRE, D)), dau of 8th Earl of Bessborough (*qv*), and *d* 28 Dec 1922, leaving issue:

(1) Robin Windham,TD, Capt 97th (Kent Yeo), Field Bde, RA (TA), OStJ, served WW II, memb London Stock Exchange; *b* 30 April 1914; *educ* Eton and Trin Coll Cambridge; *m* 15 Dec 1954 *Anne Elizabeth, JP [Mrs Robin Baring JP, Went House, W Malling, Kent], est dau of Maj William Frederick Husband, of Waterside Ho, Headbourne Worthy, Winchester, and *d* 6 Sept 1994, leaving:

1a +James Windham; *b* 24 Feb 1957; *educ* Eton; *m* 1st 1985 Suzy, dau of John Barry Prendergast, of Oyster Bay, NY; *m* 2nd 1991 *Mrs Angela P Clarke, est dau of Peter Halstead, of Cranmer Ct, London SW3, and has:

1b *Clementine (Clemmie) Lara; *b* 1992

1a *Clarissa Mary; *b* 22 Sept 1955; *m* 1987 *Michael Charles David Pilkington, est son of Ronald Charles Leslie Pilkington, of Stanstead Abbots, Herts, and has issue:

1b *Grace Cristabel Alice; *b* 1987

2b *Eleanor Scarlett Rose; *b* 1989

3b *Silvy Emerald Isabelle; *b* 1993

2a *Rosemary Anne [Mrs Anthony Standing, The Old Rectory, Sharrington, Melton Constable, Norfolk NR24 2PG]; *b* 19 Aug 1960; *m* 1980 *Anthony M Standing, son of Michael Frederick Cecil Standing, CBE, and has:

1b *Michael Frederick Oliver; *b* 1990

2b *Archie Jonathan Guy; *b* 1992

3a *Katherine Claire; *b* 11 March 1963; *m* 1992 *Alexander T H Slack, yr son of Tom Slack, of Mousehole, Cornwall

(2) Mark (Sir), KCVO, High Sheriff Gtr London 1975, Maj Gren Gds (Supp Res of Offrs) WW II, Mil Liasion Offr Br Embassy Rome 1945–46, dir Seccombe, Marshall and Campion Ltd, discount brokers; *b* 9 June 1916; *educ* Eton and Trin Coll Cambridge; *m* 9 Feb 1949 *Victoria Winifred (Vita) (*m* 2nd 2 July 1997 *Lord Michael Fitzalan Howard; *see* NORFOLK, D), only dau of Col Reginald Edmund Maghlin Russell, CVO, CBE, DSO, of Hurst Ho, Church Crookham, Hants, and *d* 1988, having had issue:

1a *Lavinia Gweneth; *b* 1 Aug 1951; Extra Lady in Waiting to HRH THE PRINCESS OF WALES 1981–92; *m* 1974 +Hon Vivian John Rowland Baring (*see below*)

2a *Juliet Victoria [Mrs Gavin Henderson, 22 Chester Sq, London SW1]; *b* 18 Feb 1953; *m* 1984 Gavin Adrian Alexander Henderson (*d* 1991; *see* FARINGDON, B)

(3) Patrick, 2nd Lt Gren Gds (Supp Res of Offrs) WW II; *b* 10 Jan 1919; *ka* nr Brussels 19 May 1940

The **1st Earl** *m* 2nd 22 Oct 1901 Lady Georgiana Louisa Thynne (*d* 4 March 1933), dau of 4th Marquess of Bath (*qv*), and *d* 29 Jan 1917, having by her had issue:

3 EVELYN, *cr* BARON HOWICK OF GLENDALE (*qv*)

His est son,

ROWLAND THOMAS BARING, **2nd Earl of Cromer**, PC (1922), GCB (1932), GCIE (1922, KCIE 1921), GCVO (1927, CVO 1920, MVO 4th Cl 1908); *b* 29 Nov 1877; *educ* Eton; Dip Serv 1900–11: Cairo, Teheran, St Petersburg and FO from 1906, Priv Sec to PUS For Affrs 1907–11; md Baring Bros 1913–14, Lt Gren Gds (SR) 1914–20, ADC to Viceroy India 1915–16, Equerry in Ordinary to HM GEORGE V and Assist Priv Sec 1916–20, Ch Staff to TRH THE DUKE OF CONNAUGHT India 1920–21 and PRINCE OF WALES India 1921–22, Ld Chamberlain 1922–38, Perm Ld-in-Waiting 1938–53, Receiver Gen OStJ 1943–47, Roy Victorian Chain 1935, Bailiff Grand Cross OStJ, WW II in HG, Br Govt dir Suez Canal Co 1926, dir: London and Lancashire Insur, The Marine Insur Co (dep chm 1938, chm 1939), P&O, BI Steam Navigation Co, Nat Provincial Bank, Lloyds and Nat Provincial Foreign Bank, chm: BRC and StJ (WO) 1939–40 and King George's Pension Fund for actors and actresses; v-pres Gordon Memorial Coll; pres MCC 1934–35; *m* 4 April 1908 Lady Ruby Florence Mary Elliot, GCStJ (*d* 5 Nov 1961), 2nd dau of 4th Earl of Minto (*qv*), and had issue:

1 GEORGE ROWLAND STANLEY, **3rd Earl**

1 *Rosemary Ethel [The Lady Rosemary Hills, 15 Hanover Ct, Dulverton, Somerset TA22 9HZ]; *b* 17 Dec 1908; FRGS; *m* 8 Oct 1932 Lt-Col John David Hills, MC, MA, Head Master Bradfield 1940–55 (*d* July 1975), est son of Rev Henry Gardner Hills, of Bryn Eglwys, Criccieth, and has issue:

(1) *John Evelyn Baring, TD, DL (1989) [Col John Hills TD DL, Stagg Mill, Uplowman, Tiverton, Devon EX16 7LY], Maj 17th/21st Lancers, Col Roy Wessex Yeo (TA), Hon ADC to HM THE QUEEN 1990–, High Sheriff Glos 1990; *b* 16 May 1939; *educ* Eton; *m* 6 March 1964 *Katherine Adrian, yr dau of G F Alderson-Smith, of Horsham, and has:

1a *John George Baring; *b* 24 March 1966; *educ* Bradfield

1a *Veronica Adrian Harriet; *b* 23 Aug 1968

(1) *Jean Adini [Mrs Jean Willoughby, Buckhold Farm, Pangbourne, Berks RG8 8QB]; *b* 22 Aug 1933; *m* 7 May 1955 (*divorce* 1990) Brig Hon (Henry Ernest) Christopher Willoughby, Coldstream Gds, yr son of 11th Baron Middleton, KG (*qv*), and has issue

(2) *Margaret Ruby; *b* 25 Sept 1934; *m* 27 Jan 1960 *Michael Giles Neish Walker, only son of Sir William Giles Newsom Walker, TD, of Pitlair, Cupar, Fife (*see* NAIRN, Bt), and has issue:

1a *Simon Giles David; *b* 9 March 1961; *educ* Eton; *m* 1991 *Corinne Rawstorne, and has issue:

1b *A dau; *b* 1993

2a *Geordie Michael; *b* 6 July 1966; *educ* Strathallan

1a *Nicola Margaret; *b* 17 July 1965

2 Violet Mary; *b* 17 Dec 1911; *m* 28 July *m* 28 Jan 1937 Maj Mervyn Sydney Bobus Vernon, MVO, Gren Gds, 2nd son of Rupert Robert Vernon, of Bowldown Farm, Tetbury (*see* LYVEDEN, B), and *d* 2 July 1978, leaving issue

The 2nd EARL *d* 13 May 1953; his only son,

GEORGE ROWLAND STANLEY BARING, **3rd Earl of Cromer**, KG (1977), PC (1966), GCMG (1974), MBE (1945), DL (Kent 1968); Lt City London 1961; *b* 28 July 1918 (HM GEORGE V stood sponsor); *educ* Eton and Trin Coll Cambridge, Hon DL New York U 1966, Page of Honour to TM. GEORGE V 1931–35 and QUEEN MARY at Coronation 1937; Lt-Col Gren Gds WW II (despatches), md Baring Bros 1948–60 and 1966–71, dir: Roy Insur, Liverpool London and Globe

Insur 1951–58, Daily Mail and General Tst Ltd 1948–58, Anglo-Newfoundland Devpt Co 1950–58, Harris and Ptnrs Toronto 1956–58 (Hon Chm) and Lewis's Investment Tst 1957–58, Fin Advsr and Ec Min Embassy Washington, DC, and Head UK Treasury and Supply Delegn Washington 1959–Jan 1961, Amb USA 1971–74, UK Exec Dir IMF, Internat Bank for Reconstruction and Development and Internat Finance Corp 1959–61, Govr Bank of England 1961–66, dir Bank of Internat settlements 1961–66, chm IBM (UK) 1967–70 and 1974–79, dir Union Carbide Corpn NY, Shell Transport and Trading Co 1974–91, chm London Multinat Bank 1974–91, dir Compagnie Financière de Suez, P&O Steam Navigation Co; *m* 10 Jan 1942 *Hon Esme Mary Gabriel Harmsworth, CVO (1980) [The Hon Mrs van der Woude CVO, Heronden, Eastry, Sandwich, Kent CT13 0ET; 1 Douro Place, London W8], Lady of the Bedchamber to HM THE QUEEN 1967–71 (Extra Ldy Bedchamber 1974–93 and Extra Woman Bedchamber 1993–) (*m* 2nd 1993, as his 2nd w, (Reinier) Gerrit Anton van der Woude, late Capt Gren Gds), yr dau of 2nd Viscount Rothermere (*qv*), and *d* 1991, having had:

1 EVELYN ROWLAND ESMOND BARING, **4th and present Earl of Cromer**

2 +Vivian John Rowland [The Hon Vivian Baring, The Stone House, Lower Swell, Stow-on-the-Wold, Glos GL54 1LQ]; *b* 12 June 1950; dir: Northcliffe Newspapers Gp and Northern Star Insur Gp; chm St John Ambulance Cncl Kent 1985–87 and Glos 1989–93; *m* 11 Dec 1974 his cousin *Lavinia Gweneth, er dau of Maj Sir Mark Baring, KCVO, JP (*see* above), and has issue:

(1) +Rowley Mark Thomas; *b* 5 Sept 1977; Page of Hon to HM THE QUEEN 1989–91

(2) +Thomas Patrick Vivian; *b* 8 June 1979

(1) *Camilla Rose; *b* 1985

1 Lana Mary Gabriel; *b* 1 March 1943; *m* 11 July 1963 *Anthony James Gray [Anthony Gray Esq, 5 Ranelagh Ave, London SW6], adopted son of Prof Sir James Gray, CBE, MC, FRS, of Cambridge, and *d* 17 Oct 1974, leaving:

(1) *Ashley James Rowland; *b* 12 May 1964; *educ* Grenville Coll, Devon; formerly with CCO, now media rels consultant; *m* 1990 *Annabel, yst dau of John Ludovici, of E Woodhay, Berks, and has issue:

1a *Theodore; *b* 10 Aug 1995

2a *Louis; *b* July 1997

1a *Lily Lana Patricia; *b* 1993

(1) *Tamara Mary Gabriel; *b* 29 Nov 1966; *m* July 1996 *Adam Thomas

CROMWELL

Arms: Quarterly, 1st and 4th, arg. a chief gu., over all a bend az. (for CROMWELL); 2nd and 3rd, chequy or and gu., a chief erm. (for TATSHALL); on an escutcheon of pretence, quarterly, 1st and 4th, arg. a cross moline sa. (for COPLEY); 2nd and 3rd, arg. five lozenges in fess gu., each charged with a mullet of the field, between three bear's heads erased sa. (for BEWICKE). **Crests:** 1 Issuant from a ducal coronet or a plume of five ostrich feathers arg. (for COPLEY), 2 A goat's head erased arg., armed, maned and gorged with a mural crown gu. (for BEWICKE). **Supporters:** Two lions sa., each charged on the shoulder with a representation of the Treasurer's purse or (badge of Ralph, 4th Lord Cromwell). **Motto:** *In cruce vinco* ('I conquer by the cross'). **Creation:** B. (E) 28 Dec 1375.

THE 7TH LORD (BARON) CROMWELL (Godfrey John Berwicke-Copley) [The Rt Hon The Lord Cromwell, House of Lords, London SW1A 0PW]; *b* 4 March 1960; *s f* 1982; *educ* Eton and Cambridge; *m* 23 June 1990 *Elizabeth Ann, dau of John Hawksley, and has:

1 +DAVID GODFREY; *b* 21 Sept 1997

1 +Helen Tatiana; *b* 18 March 1995

Cromwell, other creations: Thomas Cromwell, the architect of HENRY VIII's Dissolution of the monasteries and royal supremacy in ecclesiastical matters, was created Baron Cromwell in July 1536, four years before his promotion to the Earldom of Essex. Shortly after the conferring of the Earldom he was attainted and his honours forfeited but the Barony of Cromwell was revived for his son Gregory in December 1540. Whether this posthumous gesture by HENRY towards the family of his old servant was belated regret at having liquidated so useful a minister or whether it arose from the fact that Gregory had become his brother-in-law by marrying JANE SEYMOUR's sister Elizabeth is a matter for conjecture. Possibly it was a combination of both.

Gregory's son, the 2nd Baron, was the subject of an important milestone in English law. He was was arrested in 1572 for contempt of court (an injunction in the Court of Chancery), but the House of Lords insisted on his being freed since as a peer he was immune from arrest in civil actions. His son the 3rd Baron was involved in the abortive putsch of 1600 by the Earl of Essex of a completely different *cr* (*see* HEREFORD, V) but was pardoned soon afterwards. He sold his English estates and bought one in northern Ireland instead. His son the 4th Baron, another Thomas, was promoted Earl of Ardglass in January 1644/5, just at the time his more famous cousin Oliver was becoming the leading Parliamentary general. The Barony of Cromwell expired with the Ardglass Earldom in 1687, although the 4th and last Earl of Ardglass's daughter styled herself Baroness Cromwell in her own right under the misapprehension (widely shared at the time) that the Barony created in 1540 had been by writ rather than by patent.

Lineage: HALDANE; living *temp* HENRY II; had:

HUGH; had:

RALPH; had:

RALPH (I) de CROMWELL, of Cromwell, Notts, and West Hallam, Derbys; had:

RALPH (II) de CROMWELL; summoned for mil service under EDWARD I in Wales 1276–March 1282/3; *m* 1st Macerie/Mazere, yr dau and in her issue coheir of Philip Marmion, 8th of Scrivelsby, Lincs, and had a dau (Joan, of Tamworth Castle, Staffs; *m* Alexander de Friville and with him was ancestor of the FREVILLEs of Tamworth); *m* 2nd by 26 Jan 1270/1 Margaret, widow of Ralph Basset, of Drayton, Staffs, and est dau of Roger de Somery, of Dudley, Worcs, by his 1st w Nicole (3rd dau and eventually coheir of William d'Aubigny, Earl of Arundel; *see* NORFOLK, D), and *d* a little while before 18 Sept 1289, leaving by her:

1 RALPH (III) de CROMWELL; *d* just before 2 March 1298/9, leaving:

(1) RALPH (IV), for whom *see* further below

2 JOHN de CROMWELL (not definitely s of RALPH (II) but probably so), 1st and last LORD (Baron) CROMWELL of the putative 10 March 1307/8 *cr*, being called to Parl by writ of summons on that date, which according to later doctrine conferred a peerage; of age by 1305; Constable Chepstow Castle 1307–08 and Tower of London 1307/8, 1310–23 and 1326/7–(?)35; fought on EDWARD II's side Battle of Boroughbridge March 1321/2; Adml of the Fleet 1324; *m* by 25 June 1302 Idoine, widow of Roger de Leyburne and 2nd dau and coheir of Robert de Vipont, of Brougham Castle, Westmorland, and *d* apparently *sp* by 8 Oct 1335

RALPH (III)'s s,

RALPH (IV) de CROMWELL; *b c* 1291; *m* Joan de la Mare (probably the Joan who *m* as his 2nd w Henry de Grey; *see* GREY, B) and had:

RALPH (V) de CROMWELL, of Cromwell and W Hallam; *m* Anice, dau and coheir of Roger de Bellers, and *d* by 28 Oct 1364, leaving:

RALPH (VI) de CROMWELL, **1st Lord** (Baron) **Cromwell**, so *cr* by writ of summons (according to later doctrine) to Parl 28 Dec 1375; *m* by 20 June 1366 Maude (*d* 10 April 1419), with whom he obtained March 1366/7 the Tattershall estate, Lincs, dau of John Bernake, of Tattershall, by Joan,dau and coheir of John, 2nd Lord (Baron) Marmion, and *d* 27 Aug 1398, leaving issue:

1 RALPH (VII) de CROMWELL, **2nd Lord** (Baron) **Cromwell**; *b c* 1368; Constable of Castle Rising, Norfolk, 1404–17; *m* Joan — (*d* 1434) and *d* 1417, leaving:

(1) RALPH (VIII) de CROMWELL, **3rd Lord** (Baron) **Cromwell**, PC (1422); *b c* 1403; Ld High Treas 1433–43, fndr of the college of Tattershall and builder of the Castle there 1440, Master King's Mews and Falcons 1436; a suspected Yorkist; *m* by 4 July 1424 Margaret (*dsp* 15 Sept 1454), dau of John, Lord Deincourt, and *dsp* 4 Jan 1454/5, when the Barony fell into abeyance (according to later doctrine) between his two nieces and coheirs

(1) MAUD de Cromwell; *m* as his 2nd w Sir Richard STANHOPE, of Rampton (*d* 1436), and had:

1a Maud; *m* 1st by 9 Jan 1448/9, as his 2nd w, 6th Lord (Baron) Willoughby de Eresby (*qv*; *dspm* 25 July 1452); *m* 2nd Aug 1453 Sir Thomas Nevill(e), 2nd s of Richard Nevill(e), Earl of Salisbury (*see* ABERGAVENNY, M); *m* 3rd by 20 March 1462/3 Sir Gervase Clifton and *dsp* 30 Aug 1497

2a JOAN; *m* 1st by 14 Feb 1455/6 Sir Humphrey Bourchier (3rd s of 1st Earl of Essex of the 1461 *cr* (*see* ESSEX, E, preliminary remarks); *dsp*, *ka* fighting on EDWARD IV's side Battle of Barnet 14 April 1471), who was called to Parl 25 July 1461 by writs made out to 'Bourchier de Cromwell' or 'Cromwell' whereby he has been deemed to have been either 1st and last LORD (Baron) CROMWELL of a new (1461) *cr* or **4th Lord** (Baron) **Cromwell** in right of his w; she *m* 2nd Sir Robert Radclyffe, of Hunstanton, Norfolk, and *dsp* 10 March 1490

1 Amice/Anice/Hawise; *m* by 8 July 1382 Thomas Bardolf, 5th Lord (Baron) Bardolf, and *dspm* 1 July 1421

2 Maud; *m* Sir William Fitzwilliam, of Sprotborough, Yorks (*see* 1970 edn FITZWILLIAM, E), and was mother of:

(1) JOHN (Sir), for whom *see* further below

3 Elizabeth; *m* 1st Sir John Clifton and with him was ancestor of the KNEVITTs of Buckenham; *m* 2nd Sir Edward Benstead

LADY FITZWILLIAM's s,

Sir JOHN FITZWILLIAM, of Sprotborough; *m* Eleanor, dau of Sir Henry Green, of Drayton, Northants, and *d* July 1418, leaving:

Sir JOHN FITZWILLIAM, of Sprotborough and Elmley; *m* Margaret, dau of Sir Thomas Clarell, of Aldwark, and *d* at Rouen 1421, leaving:

Sir WILLIAM FITZWILLIAM, of Sprotborough; *m* Elizabeth, dau of Sir Thomas Chaworth, and *d* 1 Dec 1474, leaving an only s:

Sir WILLIAM FITZWILLIAM; *m* Elizabeth, dau of Sir John Conyers, of Sockburn, Co Durham, and *d* 1 Dec 1494, having had:

1 John; *m* Elizabeth, dau of Richard FitzWilliam of Aldwarke, and *dvp*, leaving an only s:

(1) William, of Sprotborough; *dsp* 1517

1 Margery; *m* Thomas Suthill and left an only child

2 DOROTHY Fitzwilliam; *m* Sir William COPLEY and *d* by 1529, leaving:

(1) Philip, of Sprotborough; *m* Mary (*d* 1597), dau and heir of Sir Bryan Hastings, of Fenwyke, and *d* 19 Oct 1577, leaving, with other issue:

1a William, of Sprotborough; *m* Elizabeth, dau of Godfrey Bosville, and *d* 1598, leaving two sons and a dau

2a Alverley, of Warren Hall, Yorks; *b* 1545; *m* Joan, dau of Simon Gunby, of Swinfleet, Lincs, and had an est s:

1b William; *m* Dorothy (*d* 1638), dau of William Booth, of Romley, Derbys, and *d* 1644, leaving:

1c Sir GODFREY COPLEY, 1st Bt (E), so *cr* 17 June 1661, of Sprotborough; *b* 21 Feb 1623; *m* 1st Eleanor (*d* Nov 1649), dau of Sir Thomas Walmesley, of Dunkenhalgh, Lancs, and had issue; *m* 2nd Elizabeth (ld Sept 1682), dau of William Stanhope, of Linby, Notts, and *d* Feb 1677/8; his est son by his 1st w:

1d Sir GODFREY COPLEY, 2nd and last Bt; MP, FRS (fndr Copley Medal); *b* 1653; *m* 1st 1681 Catherine, yr dau and coheir of John Purcell, of Nantriba, Montgomeryshire, and had issue; *m* 2nd Gertrude, dau of Sir John Carew, Bt, but had no issue by her and *d* 9 April 1709, when the btcy expired; his only surv child by his 1st w:

1e KATHERINE Copley; *m* Joseph MOYLE (2nd son of Sir Walter Moyle, of Blake, Cornwall); their est s:

1f Sir JOSEPH MOYLE later COPLEY (Act of Parl 1768), 1st Bt (GB), so *cr* 15 Aug 1778; *m* 23 Sept 1756 Mary, dau of John Buller, of Morval, Cornwall, and *d* 16 April 1781, having had, with other issue:

1g Sir LIONEL COPLEY, 2nd Bt; *b c* 1767; MP Tregony 1796–1802; *d* unm 4 March 1806

2g Sir JOSEPH COPLEY, 3rd Bt; *b c* 1769; *educ* Ch Ch Oxford; *m* 23 May 1799 Lady Cecil (*d* 19 June 1819), dau of Rev Hon George Hamilton (*see* ABERCORN, D) and divorced w of 1st Marquess of Abercorn, and *d* 21 May 1838, leaving issue:

1h Sir JOSEPH WILLIAM COPLEY, 4th and last Bt; *b* 27 July 1804; *educ* Ch Ch Oxford; *m* 19 Nov 1831 Lady Charlotte Anderson-Pelham, dau of 1st Earl of Yarborough (*qv*), and *dsp* 3 Jan 1883, when the btcy expired

1h Elizabeth Mary; *d* unm 12 Jan 1887

2h Maria; *m* 9 Aug 1832 3rd Earl Grey (*qv*) and *dsp* 14 Sept 1879

1g Catherine; *m* 20 June 1779 1st Marquess of Abercorn and *d* 13 Sept 1791, leaving issue (*see* ABERCORN, D)

2g JULIANA, of whom later

3g Anne; *m* 4 Nov 1803 1st Baron Manners (*qv*) and *dsp* 5 Aug 1814

Sir JOSEPH COPLEY, 1st Bt's 2nd dau,

JULIANA Copley; *m* 16 July 1789 Sir Charles WATSON, 1st Bt, of Fulmer (*d* 26 Aug 1844), and *d* 24 May 1834, leaving an only surv s:

Sir CHARLES WAGER WATSON, 2nd Bt; *b* 4 Jan 1800, *m* 19 June 1827 Jemima Charlotte (*d* 16 April 1877), dau of Charles Garth Colleton, of Haynes Hill, Berks, and *d* 30 Dec 1852, leaving an est s:

Sir CHARLES WATSON later WATSON-COPLEY (added with arms on inheriting the Sprotborough estate), 3rd Bt; *b* 6 April 1828; *m* 12 May 1854 Georgina (*d* 27 Jan 1892), dau of Rev Robert Tredcroft, and *d* April 1888, having had, with two s (*d* in infancy):

1 SELINA FRANCES

2 Caroline Selina; *m* 3 April 1893 John Home Adam Peebles-Chaplin, of Colliston, Forfarshire, and *d* 1 May 1914, leaving issue. He *d* 19 Jan 1927

3 Amabel Jemima; *m* 19 April 1887 Edward Lygon Somers-Cocks (*d* 18 Nov 1923), and *d* 10 July 1938, leaving issue (*see* McGRIGOR, Bt)

The est surv child,

SELINA FRANCES Watson-Copley; *b* 1856; declared by resolution of Ho of Lds 10 March 1922 a coheir of the Barony of Cromwell; *m* 2 Feb 1886 Brig-Gen Sir Robert Calverley Alington BEWICKE later BEWICKE-COPLEY (roy licence 5 April 1892), KBE, CB, DL, JP, late KRRC, and *d* 23 June 1923, having had issue (her daus were granted rank of baron's daus 15 Oct 1923):

1 Redvers Lionel Calverley, Capt Coldstream Gds, *b* 17 Sept 1890; *ka* 21 Dec 1916

2 ROBERT GODFREY WOLSELEY, **5th Lord**

1 Gladys; *m* 16 Nov 1909 Maj Hubert Francis Fitzwilliam Brabazon Foljambe, KRRC (*ka* 14 Sept 1914), and *d* 13 Jan 1957, having had issue:

(1) John Savile; *b* 6 Oct 1911; *d* 14 Aug 1943

2 Sybil; *d* an infant 20 April 1888

3 Dorothy Albreda; *m* 26 Nov 1926 Lt-Col Philip Albert Meldon, DSO, MA, late RA, son of Sir Albert Meldon, DL, of Vevey Ho, Bray, Co Wicklow, and had issue. He *d* 8 April 1942

LADY BEWICKE-COPLEY's only surv son,

ROBERT GODFREY WOLSELEY BEWICKE-COPLEY, **5th Lord** (Baron) **Cromwell**, abeyance terminated and he summoned to Parl by writ 16 July 1923, DSO (1944), MC, DL, JP, CA Leics, Ld Lt Leics 1949–66, Pres Leics TAA 1950–66, Chm Leicester Advsy Ctee Nat Assistance Bd, dir Martins Bank, chm Co Ag Exec Ctee, Memb Court Farmers' Co (Master 1960), Nat Treas Br Legion, Patron BRRC (Leics), Pres: Leics County Playing Fields Assoc, Cncl of OStJ Leics, Col RARO, late KRRC, Col Cmdt Leics Cadets 1945–66, served WW I (wounded, despatches), WW II (wounded, POW), KStJ; *b* 23 May 1893, *educ* Eton; *m* 12 Feb 1925 Freda Constance, dau of Maj Sir Frederick William Beresford Cripps, DSO, of Ampney Park, Cirencester (*see* WESTMORLAND, E), and had issue:

1 DAVID GODFREY, **6th Baron**

1 +Philippa Selina [The Hon Lady Mather, Oddington House, Moreton-in-Marsh, Glos GL56 0UP]; *b* 5 Dec 1925; *m* 13 Jan 1951 *Lt-Col Sir (David) Carol MacDonell Mather, MC, MP (C) Esher 1970–87, late Welsh Gds, yr son of Loris Emerson Mather, CBE, of Wimbledon, and has:

(1) +Nicholas David; *b* 22 Oct 1958; *m* 1985 *Susan Alexandra, dau of H B Thomas, of The Old Rectory, Harnhill, Glos, and has issue:

1a +Toby Montgomery William; *b* 1993

1a +Leila Isabella Nadezhda; *b* 1990

2a +Alexandra Hélène Selina; *b* 1995

(1) +Selina Jane; *b* 28 March 1952; *m* 1980 *Maj Alastair Alexander Linton Watson, The Black Watch, er son of Maj-Gen Andrew Linton Watson, CB, of Roy Hospital, Chelsea, and has issue:

1a +Harry William George; *b* 1988

1a +Sophia Arabella; *b* 1981

2a +Alice Selina; *b* 1985

(2) +Rose Amabel; *b* 10 Sept 1954; *m* 1986 *David Benjamin Shepherd-Cross, er son of Maj Peter Shepherd-Cross, of Compton Bassett, Wilts, and has issue:

1a +Max Peter; *b* 1989

2a +George Alexander; *b* 1991

(3) +(Alice) Victoria; *b* 28 July 1960; *m* 1988 *Edward Mortimer Harley, er son of Christopher Charles Harley, of Brampton Bryan Hall, Herefs, and has issue:

1a +(Leonora) Brilliana; *b* 1992

2a +Imogen Freda; *b* 1994

3a +Alice Ianthe; *b* 1997

The 5th LORD *d* 21 Oct 1966; his only son

DAVID GODFREY BEWICKE-COPLEY, **6th Lord** (Baron) **Cromwell**; *b* 29 May 1929; *educ* Eton and Magdalene Coll Cambridge; 2nd Lt KRRC, barrister Inner Temple 1956, Govt Broker; *m* 16 Jan 1954 *(Doris) Vivian [The Rt Hon The Dowager Lady Cromwell, The Oranges, Sherborne, Northleach, Glos], yst dau of Hugh de Lisle Penfold, of Isle of Man, and *d* 18 Aug 1982 following a riding accident, having had issue:

1 GODFREY JOHN BEWICKE-COPLEY, **7th and present Lord** (Baron) **Cromwell**

2 +Thomas David; *b* 6 Aug 1964; *educ* Eton; actor (as Percy Copley)

1 +Anne Elizabeth; *b* 15 June 1955; *m* 1982 *David James McNaught Runciman, yst son of Dr J B M Runciman, of Langbank, Renfrewshire, and has issue:

(1) +Findlay Redfers; *b* 1990

(1) +Ruth Vivian; *b* 1987

2 +Davina Mary; *b* 19 June 1958; *m* 1991 *Anthony William Savile-Birkbeck, and has issue (*see* SOMERLEYTON, B)

CROOK

Arms: Or, on a bend vert between in chief two Tudor roses barbed and seeded ppr. and in base a sprig of oak slipped and fructed of the second, a shepherd's crook of the field. **Crest:** Two shepherd's crooks in saltire or, surmounted by a Tudor rose barbed and seeded ppr. **Supporters:** Dexter, an antelope gorged with a chaplet of Tudor roses barbed and seeded ppr.; sinister, a greyhound arg., gorged with a collar or, thereon three cross crosslets, with a line reflexed over the back gu. **Motto:** *Crux scutum* ('The cross a shield'). **Creation:** B (UK) 3 July 1947.

THE 2ND BARON CROOK, of Carshalton, Surrey (Douglas Edwin Crook) [The Rt Hon The Lord Crook, Ridgehill Barn, Etchinghill, Folkestone, Kent CT18 8DF]; *b* 19 Nov 1926; *s f* 1989; *educ* Whitgift Middle Sch, Croydon, and Imp Coll, London (BSc (Eng) 1947, DIC, ACGI); MICE; *m* 15 Feb 1954 *Ellenor, dau of Robert Rouse, of Sunderland, and has issue:

1 +ROBERT DOUGLAS EDWIN [The Hon Robert Crook, 12 Fairfax St, Redhill, Qld 4059, Australia]; *b* 19 May 1955; *educ* Sir William Borlase's, Marlow and Newcastle U (BSc); *m* 1981 *Suzanne Jane, dau of Harold Robinson, of Farnsfield, Notts, and has issue:

(1) +Matthew Robert; *b* 28 May 1990

(2) +James Nicholas; *b* 1992

1 *Catherine Hilary [The Hon Catherine Crook, Foinavon, Church Rd, Compton, Berks RG20 6PP]; resumed maiden name 1993; *b* 26 May 1960; *educ*

Newcastle U; *m* 1984 *Christopher John Ramsdale, son of C Ramsdale, of Coventry

Lineage: GEORGE CROOK; *m* Louisa — (*d* 1901) and *d* 1932, leaving issue:

PERCY EDWIN CROOK; *b* 28 April 1876; *m* 7 Aug 1898 Charlotte Edith (*d* 29 June 1952), dau of Micklethwaite Rainey, and *d* 27 Jan 1920, leaving issue:

1 REGINALD DOUGLAS, **1st Baron**

1 Violet Elizabeth

2 Ethel Margaret; *m* A Smith

His only son,

REGINALD DOUGLAS, **1st Baron Crook**, of Carshalton, Co Surrey (UK), so *cr* 3 July 1947, JP (Surrey 1948); *educ* Strand Sch; Gen Sec Min of Labour Staff Assoc 1925–51, memb Civ Serv Nat Whitley Cncl 1925–51, offr Civ Serv Alliance 1939–51, Hon Sec Lab Party Assoc 1945–49, Organising Sec Poor Law Offrs' Union 1919–25, chm Interdepartmental Ctee on Registration of Opticians (Min of Health) 1949–52, UK Del 5th Assembly UN Sept-Dec 1950, memb UN Admin Tbnl 1951–71 (v-pres 1952–69), chm Nat Dock Labour Bd 1951–65, memb Police Cncl 1951, Freeman and Apothecary, memb Court of Assistants and Master Spectacle Makers' Co 1963–65, Warden and Life Memb Court of Guild of Freemen of City of London, pres Br Assoc of Industrial Editors 1954–61, a v-pres of RoSPA, pres The Pre-Retirement Assoc 1964–67, pres and fndr tstee The Cystic Fybrosis Fndn 1964–89, ed *Civil Service Argus* 1928–51, KStJ 1955, memb Chapter Gen OStJ 1956–89; *b* 2 March 1901; *m* 2 Oct 1922 Ida Gertrude (*d* 1985), dau of Joseph George Haddon, and *d* 1989, leaving issue:

1 DOUGLAS EDWIN CROSS, **2nd and present Baron Crook**

CROSS

Arms: Gu., a cross flory arg., charged with five passion nails sa., a bordure of the second. **Crest:** A griffin's head erased arg., gorged with a double chain gold, therefrom pendant a mullet pierced sa., in the beak a passion nail also sa. **Supporters:** On either side a pegasus arg., holding in the mouth a passion nail sa., the dexter gorged with a chain or, therefrom pendant a cross flory gu., the sinister gorged with a double chain or, therefrom pendant a mullet pierced sa.

Motto: *Crede cruci* ('Trust in the cross').

Creation: V. (UK) 19 Aug 1886.

THE 3RD VISCOUNT CROSS, of Broughton-in-Furness, Co Lancaster (Assheton Henry Cross) [The Rt Hon The Viscount Cross, Wildwood, Itchenor, Sussex]; *b* 7 May 1920; *s* f 1932; *educ* Shrewsbury and Magdalene Coll Cambridge; Lt Scots Gds WW II, former racing driver; *m* 12 Jan 1952 (*divorce* 1958) Patricia Mary, est dau of Edward Pearson Hewetson, MA, JP, of The Craig, Windermere, Westmorland; *m* 2nd 24 May 1972 (*divorce* 1977) Mrs Victoria Webb (*d* 20 July 1997), dau of John William Stoward; *m* 3rd Dec 1983 (*divorce* 1983) Mrs Patricia J Rossiter, widow of John Rossiter, and by his 1st w has:

1 *Venetia Clare [The Hon Mrs Hill, 10 The Hill, Gt Walsingham, Norfolk NR22 6DP]; *b* 6 April 1953; *m* 1986 *Rev Norman Hill, son of Charles Hill, of Sheffield, and has:

(1) *Gregory; *b* 24 June 1989

2 *Nicola; *b* 14 Dec 1954; *m* 1992 *Audley George Parry Burnett, son of Lt-Col G P Burnett, of Winchester, Hants

Lineage: HENRY CROSS, of Barton, Lancs; *m* 1691 Joan, dau of Henry Hall, of Woodplumpton, and *d* 1728, leaving a 3rd s:

WILLIAM CROSS, of Barton; *b* 1702; *m* Ellen, dau of George Beesley, of Ingolhead, and *d* 1783, leaving a 2nd s:

JOHN CROSS, of Preston and Cottam, Lancs; Dep Prothonotary; *b* 1742; *m* Dorothea, dau of Richard Assheton, of Preston (*see* CLITHEROE, B), and *d* 1799, leaving an only s:

WILLIAM CROSS, of Cottam and Red Scar, Lancs, DL, JP, Dep Prothonotary; *b* 1771; *m* 24 June 1813 Ellen, dau and coheir of Edward Chaffers, of Everton and Liverpool, and *d* 1827, having had, with other issue:

1 William Assheton, of Red Scar, DL, JP; *b* 19 May 1818; *m* 19 Aug 1846 Katherine Matilda (*d* 16 April 1871), dau of Charles Winn, of Nostell Priory, Yorks (*see* SAINT OSWALD, B), and *d* 25 Jan 1883, leaving issue

2 John Edward (Rev), MA Oxford, JP, Preb of Lincoln, Vicar of Appleby, near Brigg; *b* 1821; *m* 1854 Elizabeth (*d* 17 Oct 1923) dau of Adml Sir Phipps Hornby, GCB, and *d* 28 Feb 1897

3 RICHARD ASSHETON, **1st Viscount**

1 Ellen Dorothea; *m* 17 Jan 1837 Rev William Hornby, Archdeacon of Lancaster, and *d* 13 March 1840, leaving issue. He *d* 20 Dec 1899

The 3rd son,

RICHARD ASSHETON CROSS, **1st Viscount Cross** (UK), of Broughton-in-Furness, Co Lancaster, so *cr* 19 Aug 1886, PC, GCB, GCSI, DCL, LLD, FRS, DL and JP Lancs, and JP Cheshire, sometime chm Lancs QS, BA Cambridge, Hon LLD Cambridge, St Andrews, and Leeds, Hon DCL Oxford, barrister Inner Temple 1849, Bencher 1876, Treas 1895, MP (C) Preston 1857–62, SW Lancs 1868–85 and Newton 1885–86, Home Sec 1874–80 and 1885–86, Sec State India 1886–92, Ld Privy Seal; *b* 30 May 1823; *m* 4 May 1852 Georgiana, CI (*d* 20 Jan 1907). 3rd dau of Thomas Lyon, DL, of Appleton Hall, Cheshire, and had, with other issue:

1 William Henry, MP Liverpool; *b* 22 Aug 1856; *m* 19 Aug 1880 Mary (*d* 8 Nov 1946), dau of William Lewthwaite, of Broadgate, Cumberland (*see* LEWTHWAITE, Bt), and *d* 11 Dec 1892, leaving issue (his daus granted by roy warrant 29 July 1914 rank of viscount's daus):

(1) RICHARD ASSHETON, **2nd Viscount**

(1) Dorothy Mary, JP Cumberland, ARRC, served WW I; *d* unm 31 Aug 1962

(2) Georgiana Marjorie, ARRC, FSA, served WWs I and II; *d* unm 4 Feb 1958

(3) Katharine; *d* unm 10 Nov 1969

(4) Ellinor Frances

2 John Edward, of West Hall, High Legh, JP Cheshire, CC 1904–07; *b* 5 Sept 1858; *m* 1st 31 July 1889 Katherine Ellen (*d* 9 Dec 1891), 2nd dau of Rev Francis Haden Cope, MA, Vicar of N Malvern, and had issue:

(1) Katherine Madge; *b* 18 Nov 1891; *m* 24 May 1923 Capt Basil Richard Brooke, DSO, RN, son of John Townshend Brooke, of Haughton Hall, Salop. He *d* 8 Oct 1929

2 (cont.) John Cross *m* 2nd 18 April 1895 Sophy Katherine Mary (*d* 22 May 1946), yr dau of Henry Robertson Sandbach, DL, of Hafodunos, Denbighs, and *d* 26 June 1921, having by her had issue:

(2) Elizabeth Sophy, MM; *b* 27 Jan 1896; assumed by deed poll 14 March 1933 the name POWYS; *m* 1st 14 March 1923 (*divorce* 1938) Alexander Douglas, KAR, son of John Douglas, and had issue; *m* 2nd 12 July 1938 William Edward Powys, son of Rev Charles Francis Powys, of Montacute, Somerset, and *d* Aug 1963, leaving further issue

(3) Mary Georgiana; *b* 14 March 1901; *m* 29 Aug 1923 Rev Aubrey William Hooper, MC, MA, 2nd son of Rev Samuel Fry Hooper, late Rector of Lydlinch, Blandford, and had issue

3 Charles Francis (Rev), Vicar of Stretton, nr Warrington, formerly Vicar of Shotwick, Cheshire, Hon Canon Chester Cathedral 1921; *b* 22 Sept 1860; *educ* Trin Coll Cambridge (MA); *d* 28 March 1937

1 Georgiana Harriet; *m* 8 Jan 1895 Edward Wentworth Bowyer, yr son of Rev William Henry Wentworth Bowyer, Rector of Clapham, and *d* 15 March 1957 having had issue (*see* DENHAM, B)

2 Anne Margaret; *m* 3 Jan 1901 Lt-Col Henry Finch Dawson, late RA, of Barrow Hill, Rocester, Staffs, and *d* 8 July 1962, leaving issue. He *d* 28 Nov 1939

The 1st VISCOUNT *d* 8 Jan 1914; his gs,

RICHARD ASSHETON CROSS, **2nd Viscount Cross**; *b* 28 Jan 1882; *educ* Eton and Univ Coll Oxford (MA); Pncpl Treasury; *m* 11 Feb 1918 Maud Evelyn Inigo (*m* 2nd 18 April 1944 Guy Hope Coldwell (*d* 10 Oct 1948), son of Maj Robert Hanson Coldwell, and *d* 30 April 1976), yst dau of Maj-Gen Inigo Richmond Jones, CB, CVO, of Kelston Park, Som, by Elinor, dau of Hon Richard Charteris (*see* WEMYSS and MARCH, E), and *d* 14 March 1932, having had issue:

1 ASSHETON HENRY CROSS, **3rd and present Viscount Cross**

2 Richmond Gilfrid, Lt RE WW II; *b* 6 Jan 1922; *ka* in Italy May 1944

3 John Michael Inigo; *b* 23 March 1923; *m* 15 April 1950 *Sybil Anne [Mrs James Parker-Jervis, Templewood, Brechin, Angus DD9 7PT] (*m* 2nd 7 April 1956 Lt-Cdr James Parker-Jervis, RN, est son of George Parker-Jervis, of 20 Great Hampden, Bucks (*see* ST VINCENT, V)), only dau of Maj Thomas Prain Douglas Murray, MBE, TD, DL, of Templewood, Brechin, by Sybil Enid, 4th dau of Maj Thomas Clayton Toler, DL, JP, of Swettenham Hall and Saltersford Hall, Cheshire, and *d* 2 Feb 1951, leaving issue:

(1) *Mary Beatrice [Lady Jardine of Applegirth, Ash House, Millom, Cumbria]; *b* posthumously 18 April 1951; *m* 1982 *Sir Alexander Maule Jardine of Applegirth, 12th Bt (*qv*), and has issue

1 Idonea Mary Ellice; *b* 30 Nov 1918; *m* 19 Nov 1946 Lt-Col William Preston Ashton Shuttleworth, RCT, Roy Norfolk Regt (*d* 1994), only s of Capt William Gabbett Ashton Shuttleworth, RN, of Oak Lodge, Aylsham, Norfolk, and *d* 1994, leaving:

(1) *Hugh Ashton John; *b* 4 May 1948; *educ* Radley

(2) *William Richard Ashton; *b* 1 March 1958

(1) *Celia Mary Ashton; *b* 16 Feb 1951

(2) *Rosamond Ashton; *b* 30 Dec 1953

CROSSLEY

Arms: Az. a chevron between in chief two crosses tau and in base a hind statant all or. **Crest:** A hind's head or holding in the mouth a cross tau az. **Motto:** *Credo et amo* ('I believe and love'). **Creation:** Bt. (UK) 26 Nov 1909.

SIR NICHOLAS JOHN CROSSLEY, 4TH BT, of Glenfield, Dunham Massey, Co Chester [Sir Nicholas Crossley Bt, 331 Pen St #1, El Segundo, CA 90245, USA]; *b* 10 Dec 1962; *s f* 1989

Lineage: The CROSSLEYs of Scaitcliffe, Lancs, were settled at Todmorden *temp* EDWARD III; reputed ancestors of:

JOHN CROSSLEY, of Stansfield in Rochdale; *b* 1474; living 1524; had:

RICHARD CROSSLEY, of Scaitcliffe; *m* Alice — and *d* 1548, leaving a 2nd s:

RICHARD CROSSLEY, of Scaitcliffe; *b* 1537; *m* Elizabeth — and *d* 1588, leaving:

ANTHONY CROSSLEY, of Scaitcliffe; bought Hollinrake Holme 1586; *m* Mary — and *d* 1624, leaving an est s:

JOHN CROSSLEY, of Scaitcliffe; *m* 1615 Dorothea, dau of Richard Lorde, of Hundersfield, and had, with other issue:

JOHN CROSSLEY, of Frailcroft in Todmorden; *b* 1620; *m* 1640 Mary, dau of Cæsar Jackson, of Worsthorne, Lancs, and *dvp* 1646, having had, with other issue:

ANTHONY CROSSLEY, of Scaitcliffe; *m* 1st 1664 Anne Eastwood, of Ouldroyd, Yorks; *m* 2nd 1702 Grace, widow of John Ramsden, of Broadhalgh, Scotland, and *d* April 1707, leaving by his 1st w, with other issue:

ANTHONY CROSSLEY, of Further Scaitcliffe and Dromore, Ireland; fought Battle of the Boyne 1690; *d* Aug 1757; his 2nd s:

ANTHONY CROSSLEY; *m* — Brown and had, with an er s (William, of Lisburn, Co Antrim, *bapt* 7 April 1745, *m* Margaret Johnston and had issue):

JOHN CROSSLEY, of Lisburn; *bapt* 29 Jan 1746; *m* Elizabeth Alcott and *d* between 27 Dec 1826 and 8 April 1830, leaving a yr s:

FRANCIS CROSSLEY, of Glenburn, Dunmurry, Co Antrim, Maj HEICS, Govr the Banda Spice Islands; *b* 1787; *m* 1st — Stewart, of Lisburn; *m* 2nd 20 April 1837 Elizabeth Helen (*d* 9 Feb 1891), dau of William Irwin, of Mount Irwin, Co Armagh, and *d* 17 Sept 1846, having by her had issue:

1 Francis William; *b* 27 Nov 1839; *m* 1 June 1871 Emily (*d* 15 April 1928), dau of Archibald Kerr, of Lancaster Gate, London, and *d* 25 March 1897, leaving surv issue four s and a dau

2 WILLIAM JOHN (Sir), **1st Bt**

3 Thomas Hastings Henry, MA, LittD, Prof Greek Bristol and Belfast Us; *b* 8 Aug 1846; *m* Agnes, dau of Col Frederick Chidley Irwin, Govr W Australia, and *d* 23 March 1926, leaving issue:

(1) Guy Hastings Irwin; *d* 28 June 1959, aged 75

1 Emmeline; *b* 30 March 1842; *m* 13 Sept 1871 Alexander McLaren, of Edinburgh, and *d* 25 Dec 1917, leaving issue

The 2nd son,

Sir William John Crossley, 1st Bt (UK), so *cr* 26 Nov 1909, of Glenfield, Dunham Massey, Cheshire, JP Cheshire, Freeman and JP Manchester, MP (Lib) Altrincham 1906–10, chm Crossley Bros of Manchester, dir Manchester Ship Canal; *b* 22 April 1844; *m* 20 April 1876 Mabel Gordon, JP (Lancs) (*d* 30 April 1943), dau of Francis Anderson, Inspr-Gen Hosps, son of Drummond Anderson, of Belfast, by Margaret Crossley (*see* above), and had:

1 KENNETH IRWIN (Sir), **2nd Bt**

2 Eric, OBE (1919), WW I in 11th Hus (SR); *b* 23 May 1878; *m* 30 June 1903 Janet Boyd (*d* 22 July 1968 aged 85), dau of Frank Merriman, of Church Ho, Knutsford, Cheshire (*see* 1963 edn MERRIMAN, B), and *d* 23 May 1949, having had issue:

(1) Nigel John, Lt-Cdr RN WW II; *b* 29 May 1904; *m* 1st 1 Feb 1931 Iris (*d* 29 Sept 1931), dau of Rev Ewart Barter, and had issue:

1a CHRISTOPHER JOHN (Sir), **3rd Bt**

(1) (cont.) Lt-Cdr Nigel Crossley *m* 2nd 17 March 1932 *Marjorie (*m* 3rd 27 July 1957 Capt Richard William Ravenhill, CBE, DSC, RN, son of Capt Harold William Ravenhill, RHA, of Scaftworth Hall, Bawtry, Notts), formerly w of William Rodney Winterbottom and dau of John Gilley, and *d* of wounds received while in command of HMS *Gipsy* 27 Nov 1940

(2) John Richard Irwin, WW II as Lt-Cdr (E) RNVR; *b* 17 Oct 1908; *educ* Eton

(3) Michael Nicholson, DSO (1940), OBE (1946), DFC, W/Cdr RAF, served WW II (despatches); *b* 29 May 1912; *educ* Eton; *m* 1st 1940 (*divorce* 1945) Doreen Maud, only dau of George Tibbitt, of 59 Albert Court, SW7; *m* 2nd 27 April 1957 Sylvia Constance (*d* 1975), only dau of Cdr P A Heyder, RN; *m* 3rd 1977 *Moyra Louisa Margaret (*née* Hewitt) [Mrs Michael Crossley, Loughrigg, Box 379, White River, E Transvaal, S Africa], widow of Maj-Gen Theodore Henry Birkbeck, and *d* 1987, leaving by his 2nd w issue:

1a +Sloan Nicholas; *b* 20 March 1958

1a *Claudia Bettine; *b* 12 Sept 1959

2a *Alison; *b* 12 March 1964

(1) *Barbara Katharine; *b* 29 Oct 1905; *m* 27 Sept 1938 Lt-Col Humphrey Graham DSO, RA, yst son of Frank F Lambert, of Langholm, Beverley, Yorks. They adopted a son and a dau. He *d* 8 Oct 1959

(2) Mary Bettine; *b* 10 Jan 1910; *m* 11 April 1950 (George) Ronald Hamilton, OBE, TD, yr son of G C Hamilton, of Compton, nr Winchester, and *dsp* 20 July 1956

3 Brian, Lt 3rd Bn HLI; *b* 5 April 1886; *m* 1 July 1913 Margaret Lilian (*d* 8 April 1914), dau of Joseph Watson Sidebotham, of Merlewood, Bowden, Cheshire, and was *ka* 18 May 1915

1 Lettice; *b* 21 May; *d* 25 June 1879

2 Cicely; *b* 23 Aug; *d* 9 Dec 1880

Sir WILLIAM *d* 12 Oct 1911; his est son,

Sir Kenneth Irwin Crossley, 2nd Bt, JP (Cheshire); *b* 17 Feb 1877; *educ* Eton and Magdalen Coll Oxford (BA); High Sheriff Cheshire 1919; *m* 1st 25 June 1901 Florence Josephine (*d* 23 Feb 1954), dau of Joseph Nash Field, of Chicago, USA, and had issue:

1 Anthony Crommelin, MP Oldham 1931–35, and Stretford 1935–39, PPS to Sir C M Headlam, DSO, OBE, Min of Tport 1932–34, and Capt Austin Hudson 1935–39; Lt Shrops Yeo (TA); *b* 13 Aug 1903; *m* 7 Feb 1927 *Clare Frances Fortescue, er dau of Brig Alan Fortescue Thomson, DSO, late RA, of Craig Hall, Kennethmont, Aberdeenshire, and was *k* in a plane crash off the coast of Denmark 15 Aug 1939, leaving issue:

(1) Francis Patrick Irwin, Lt Gren Gds; *b* 17 March 1929; *educ* Ampleforth; *d* unm 26 Aug 1953

(1) *Penelope [The Rt Hon Penelope Countess of Lindsay, Stewards Cottage, Combermere, Whitchurch, Salop SY13 4AY]; *b* 22 March 1928; *m* 1st 3 Oct 1951 (*divorce* 1969) Maj (Henry) Ronald Burn-Callander, MC, late Coldstream Gds, yst son of Maj William Henry Burn-Callander, MBE, DL, 7th of Preston Hall, Ford, Midlothian, and has issue:

1a *Sarah Alexandra Mary; *b* 30 March 1952; *m* 1993 *Peter Thomas Beckett, est son of Thomas Beckett, and Mrs John Armitage, of Hall O'Coole, Cheshire

2a *Victoria; *b* 2 Jan 1954; *m* 1993, as his 2nd w, *(Morland Herbert) Julian Agnew (*see* AGNEW, Bt, of Great Stanhope Street)

3a *Emma Georgina (Gigi); *b* 20 March 1959; *m* 1992 *William Henry Salomon, only son of Sir Walter Hans Salomon, and has issue:

1b *A dau; *b* 1994

(1) Mrs Penelope Burn-Callander *m* 2nd 9 June 1969 15th Earl of Lindsay (*d* 1989) (*qv*)

(2) *Theresa Charlotte [The Marchesa d'Ayala Valva, 12 Selwood Place, London SW7; Camporempoli, Pietrafitta, Castellina in Chianti, Tuscany, Italy]; *b* 20 Aug 1936; *m* 1st 21 July 1956 (*divorce* 1973) Alain R E Camu, er son of Louis Camu, CBE, of Chateau de Ronsevaal, Alost, Belgium, and has had issue:

1a *Adrien Bonaventure; *b* 8 Sept 1957; *m* 1989 *Melanie J, est dau of Roger Worboys, of Putney, and has issue:

1b *Helena Claire; *b* 1991

2a François Henri; *b* 4 Oct 1958; *d* 1990

3a *Nicolas Pascal; *b* 3 April 1961; *m* 1991 *Mrs Rebecca Compton, only dau of Sir Alan Lewis Wigan, 5th Bt (*qv*), and has issue:

1b *Marguérite; *b* 1993

1a *Virginie Charlotte; *b* 14 Sept 1959; *m* 1986 *Napier Anthony Sturt Marten, son of Lt-Cdr George Gosselin Marten, LVO, DSC, by Hon Mary Anna Sibell Elizabeth, dau of 3rd Baron Alington (*see* 1935 edn), and has issue:

1b *Maximilian Augustus; *b* 1988

2b *Tobias; *b* 1991

1b *Constance Dorothea; *b* 1987

(2) (cont.) Mrs Theresa Camu *m* 2nd 1973 *Marchese Francesco d'Ayala Valva and by him has:

4a *Tancredi Simone; *b* 1975

5a *Sebastiano Vittorio; *b* 1978

1 Fidelia Josephine; *b* 1 June 1905; *m* 14 Sept 1949 Geza Schubert, son of Dr Ernst Schubert, of Bratislava

2 Ruth Irwin; *b* 17 Sept 1909; *m* 1st 1 July 1931 (*divorce* 1938) Brig James Michael Stewart Wardell, son of Harold Piper Wardell, and had issue; *m* 2nd 9 Nov 1944 Lt Konstanty Scheunert, MBE, former Assist Mil Attaché Polish Embassy London. He *d* 27 March 1970

3 Catherine Pamela Field; *b* 30 Dec 1913; *m* 1st 2 Sept 1944 W/Cdr Donald Geoffrey Simmons, RAF, yr son of Arthur Thomas Simmons, of Parkstone, Dorset. He was *k* in an aircraft accident in the Middle East, March 1945. She *m* 2nd 21 July 1950 Rev Canon Frank Hay Gillingham, BA, 2nd son of J Gillingham. He *d* 1 April 1953

Sir Kenneth *m* 2nd 16 Dec 1954 *Elizabeth Joyce [Elizabeth Lady Crossley, The Old Bakery, Milton Lilbourne, Pewsey, Wilts SN9 5LQ], dau of Enoch Shenton, of Boxmoor, Herts, and *d* 22 Nov 1957

His great-nephew,

Sir Christopher John Crossley, 3rd Bt; *b* 25 Sept 1931; *educ* Canford; Lt-Cdr RN (ret); *m* 28 Nov 1959 (*divorce* 1969) Carolyne Louise Grey, dau of Leslie Grey

Sykes, of Sandbanks, Dorset; *m* 2nd 1977 *Lesley A [Lady Crossley, 6B Laverton Mews, London SW6], er dau of Dr K A J Chamberlain, and *d* 1989, leaving by his 1st w:

1 Sir NICHOLAS JOHN CROSSLEY, **4th and present Bt**
2 +JULIAN CHARLES; *b* 11 Dec 1964; heir presumptive

CUCKNEY

Arms: Vert on each of two flaunches argent cotised rayonny on the outer edge or a flaunch vert. **Crest:** Two dragons' heads addorsed the necks entwined and conjoined in base the whole winged or. **Supporters:** On either side a seadragon vert supporting atrident or. **Motto:** Whither the fates call. **Creation:** B. (LP, UK) 11 June 1995.

THE BARON CUCKNEY, of Millbank, City of Westminster (Sir John Graham Cuckney) [The Rt Hon The Lord Cuckney, House of Lords, London SW1A 0PW]; *b* 12 July 1925; *educ* Shrewsbury and St Andrews; Roy Northumberland Fus and KAR WW II, attd War Office to 1957; chm: Thomas Cook Gp 1978–87, Brooke Bond Gp 1981–84 (dir 1979–84), John Brown 1983–86 (dir 1981–86, dep chm 1982–83), Westland Gp 1985–89, Roy Insur Hldgs 1985–94 (dir 1979–89, dep chm 1983–85), 3i Gp 1987–92 (dir 1986–92), Orion Publishing Gp 1994–97; dep chm: TI Gp 1985–90, v-chm Glaxo 1993–95 (dir 1990–95), dir: Lazard Bros 1964–70 and 1988–90, Midland Bank 1978–88, Brixton Estate 1985–96, ; Ch Exec PSA 1972–74; Chm PLA 1977–79, Internat Maritime Bureau, Internat Chamber Commerce 1981–85; Controller ROH Devpt Land Tst 1993–96, Tstee RAF Museum 1987–, Freeman City London 1977, Er Bro Trin Ho 1980; *m* 1st 1950 (*divorce* 1956) Elizabeth Mitchell (*née* Baleman); *m* 2nd 1960 *Muriel, dau of Walter Scott Boyd

Lineage: E J CUCKNEY, CB, CBE, DSC; AVM RAF; *m* Lilian Williams and had:

JOHN GRAHAM, *cr* a **Baron**

CULLEN OF ASHBOURNE

Arms: Arg. three cocks gu., beaked, combed, wattled and membered sa. **Crest:** A cock's head erased gu., beaked, combed and wattled sa. **Supporters:** Dexter, a lion guardant party per fess or and arg.; sinister, an ostrich arg., holding in its beak a horseshoe ppr., each gorged with a collar or, pendant therefrom an escutcheon arg., charged with two bars vert. **Motto:** *Virtus in arduis* ('Courage in adversity'). **Creation:** B. (UK) 21 April 1920.

THE 2ND BARON CULLEN OF ASHBOURNE, of Roehampton, Co Surrey (Charles Borlase Marsham Cokayne, MBE (1945)) [The Rt Hon The Lord Cullen of Ashbourne MBE, 75 Cadogan Gdns, London SW3 2RB]; *b* 6 Oct 1912; *s f* 1932 ; *educ* Eton; Maj Roy Sigs (TA) WW II, won Tennis Amateur Championship 1947 and 1952; a Ld in Waiting 1979–82, Dep Chm Ctees Ho Lds 1982–91, Lt City London 1976–, pres: Fedn of Ophthalmic and Dispensing Opticians 1983–96, Gen Cncl and Register of Osteopaths 1987–89; *m* 1st 2 July 1942 (*divorce* 1947) Valerie Catherine Mary, only dau of William Henry Collbran, and has:

1 *Julia Collbran [The Hon Mrs Wigart, Dock Lane, Beaulieu, Hants SO42 7YS; 20 St Luke's St, London SW3 3RP]; *b* 2 Oct 1943; *m* 1st 22 June 1968 (*divorce* 1989) Don Francesco Costa Sanseverino, yr son of Don Edoardo Costa Sanseverino, Principe di Bisiguano, of Rome; *m* 2nd 1991 (*divorce* 1994) Michael G M Groves; *m* 3rd 14 Dec 1994 *Sture Wigart and by her 1st husb has issue:

(1) *Edoardo; *b* 26 May 1969
(2) *Alessandro; *b* 1971
(3) *Sveva; *b* 16 Oct 1973

The 2nd BARON *m* 2nd 21 June 1948 Patricia Mary (*d* 23 June 1996), er dau of Lt-Col S Clulow-Gray, of 105 Marsham Ct, London SW1

Lineage: JOHN COKAYNE, of Ashbourne, Derbys; living 1150; had:

JOHN COKAYNE, of Ashbourne; had, with an er s (John, of Ashbourne and Cokayne, Allesford, Essex, *dspm* after 1279, leaving a dau and heiress who *m* Benedict de Cokefield, of Cokefield):

ANDREW COKAYNE; living 1277; had:

WILLIAM COKAYNE, of Ashbourne; *m* Sarah — and had:

WILLIAM COKAYNE, of Ashbourne; *m* Alice, dau of Hugh de Dalbury, and had, with a yr s (John, living 1311, *m* Matilda, dau of Robert de Alderney, and had a s (Andrew, *dsp* 1319) and dau, Margaret):

ROGER COKAYNE, of Ashbourne; living 1284; *m* Elizabeth — and had:

WILLIAM COKAYNE, of Ashbourne; *b* 1299; *m* Sarah, dau of Adam/Alexander de Mercaston, of Mercaston, Derbys, and heiress of her bro Thomas de Mercaston, of Ashbourne, and *d* 1323, leaving, with a yr s (Robert, *m* Elizabeth — and had a s (William) and dau, Elizabeth):

JOHN COKAYNE, of Ashbourne Hall; MP Derbys; *m* —, dau of Sir William Kniveton, of Bradley, and *d* 1332, leaving:

Sir JOHN COKAYNE, of Ashbourne Hall; MP Derbys; *m* Cecilia — (*m* 2nd Robert de Ireton, of Ireton Parva; *see* also FERRERS, E) and *d* 1373, leaving:

1 EDMUND (Sir)
2 John (Sir), of Hatley Cokayne, Beds; Ch Baron Exchequer; *m* Ida, dau of 3rd Lord (Baron) Grey (of Ruthin) (*see* GREY, B), and *d* 1429, leaving:
(1) Reginald/Reynold, of Hatley Cokayne; *m* Beatrice — (*m* 2nd William Melchet) and had:
1a Philip, of Hatley Cokayne; ancestor of:
1b Thomas, of Ickleford, Beds; had a dau and heiress:
1c Marian Charlotte Emily; *m* 14 Aug 1839 Hon Frederick Dudley Ryder (*see* HARROWBY, E)

The er s,

Sir EDMUND COKAYNE; *m* Elizabeth, dau and heiress of Richard de Harthill, of Harthill Hall and Pooley Hall, Polesworth, Warwicks, thus acquiring those properties, and was *ka* Battle of Shrewsbury 1403, having had:

1 George; *dsp* & *vp*
2 JOHN (Sir)
3 Thomas, of Harthill Hall; *d* 1447, leaving:
(1) Thomas, of Harthill Hall; had:
1a John, of Harthill Hall and Ballidon; *d* 1492, leaving:
1b John, of Harthill Hall
2b Francis; had:
1c Thomas, of Harthill; *b* 1522; *d* in or after 1539, leaving:
1d Francis, of Ballidon; *dsp* in or after 1595
2d Edward, of Ballidon, which with Harthill he sold 1599; had:
1e Nicholas; *m* Joan, dau of John Fulwood, of Middleton-by-Youlgreave
4 Edmund
1 Elizabeth

The 2nd s,

Sir JOHN COKAYNE, of Ashbourne Hall; MP Derbys, Ch Baron Exchequer; *m* 1st Jane (*dsp*), dau of Sir John Dabridgecourt, of Stratfield Saye, Hants; *m* 2nd Isabel, dau of Sir Hugh Shirley, of Staunton Harold, and *d* 1447, leaving, with two yst sons (Reginald; Roger) and two daus (Beatrice, *m* Sir Thomas Tyrell; Alice, *m* 1417 Roger Shirley):

1 John (Sir?), of Ashbourne Hall; *m* Agnes, dau of Sir Richard Vernon, of Haddon (*see* VERNON, B), and *d* 1504, having had, with a yr s (Roger):
(1) Thomas, of Ashbourne Hall; *m* Agnes, dau of Robert Barlow, of Barlow, and was *k* in a duel *vp* 1488, leaving:
1a Thomas (Sir); ktd *c* 1513, High Sheriff Derbys 1521 and 1530, author: *A Treatise on Hunting*; *m* Barbara, dau of John FitzHerbert, of Ash and Ewall, one of the FitzHERBERTs of Tissington (*see* FitzHERBERT, Bt), and *d* 1537, leaving:
1b Francis, of Ashbourne Hall; *m* Dorothy, dau and heiress of Thomas Marrow, Serjeant-at-law, and *d* 1538, leaving:
1c Thomas (Sir), of Ashbourne Hall; ktd 1544; *m* Dorothy, dau of Humphrey Ferrers, of Tamworth, Staffs, and *d* 1592, leaving, with seven daus:
1d Francis, of Ashbourne Hall; *m* Anne, dau of Sir Valentine Knightley, and *dsp* 1594
2d Thomas; *dsp* & *vp* 1587
3d Edward, of Ashbourne Hall; *m* Jane, dau of Nicholas Ashby, of Willoughby (Leics?) and Challaston, and *d* 1606, leaving:

1e Thomas, of Ashbourne Hall; *b* 1588; lexicographer; *m* Anne, half-sis of 1st Earl of Chesterfield (*see* HARRINGTON, E, also 1967 edn CHESTERFIELD and STANHOPE, E), and *d* 1638, leaving, with another s (Thomas, *dsp* 1628):

1f Sir ASTON COKAYNE, 1st and last Bt (E), so *cr c* 10 Jan 1641/2, of Ashbourne Hall, which he sold 1671 after getting into financial difficulties from its being sequestrated 1648 for non-payment of fines as not only a royalist in the Civil War but as a papist; *bapt* 20 Dec 1608; *educ* Trin Coll Cambridge; poet, author of among other works the 'Tragedy of Ovid'; *m* by 1635 Mary, dau of Sir Gilbert Kniveton, 2nd Bt, of Mercaston, and dspms and was bur 18 Feb 1683/4, having had:

1g Thomas; *b* 8 May 1636; *m* 14 Jan 1657/8 Rachel, dau and coheir of Carew Sturry, of Rossall, Salop, and *dsp* & *vp c* 1680

1g Mary; *m* 1st Thomas Hounslow; *m* 2nd William Lacy and *dsp*

2g Isabella; *b* 1654; *m* William Turville, of Aston, Leics, and had issue

2e George, of Ballidon; *m* Anne, dau of Vincent Lowe, of Park Hall, Derbys, and had:

1f Francis, of Ballidon; had:

1g George, of Ballidon; *dsp* 1698

1g Grace; *m* George Coke, of Derby

2g Elizabeth; *m* James Blore, of Ashbourne

2f George; *m* Elizabeth, sis and heiress of Thomas Angell, of Chaddesden, Derbys, and was ancestor of the COKAYNEs of Chaddesden and London

1f Anne; *m* Ralph Barker, of Burton-on-Trent

2f Jane; *m* John Booth

3e Francis; *m* Frances Cresswell and had, with three daus:

1f John, of Matlock, Derbys; living 1672

1e Dorothy; m William Fleetwood, of Calwich, Staffs

2e Jane; *m* Thomas Powell

3e Barbara; *d* unm

2c Francis; *m* — Browne, of Warwicks, and had a s (Thomas, of Derby) and dau (Dorothy)

3c William; living 1591

1c Alice; *m* Sir Edward Littleton (*see* HATHERTON, B)

2c Barbara; *m* John Ferrers, of Tamworth

2a Henry, of Little Chester; *m* Elizabeth, dau of Thomas Meverell, of Throwley, and was *bur* 9 March 1559/60

1a Margaret; *m* Humphrey Lowe, of Derby

2 WILLIAM, of Sturston Hall, Ashbourne

ROGER, of Sturston, and Baddesley Ensor, Warwicks; *m* Katherine — and had:

WILLIAM, of Baddesley Ensor and Clapham, Surrey; merchant adventurer and skinner in London; *m* 1st Elizabeth, dau of Roger Medcalfe, of Wensleydale, Yorks, and *d* 18 Nov 1599, leaving, with other issue (extinct in the male line), a 2nd s:

Sir WILLIAM COKAYNE, Ld Mayor of London 1619–20; bought Rushton Hall, Northants, the principal seat of the family for over two centuries, also of Elmesthorpe Manor, Leics; *m* 22 June 1596 Mary (*d* 8 Jan 1648/9), dau of Richard Morris, Master Ironmongers' Co, and *d* 20 Oct 1626, leaving, with an est s and two er daus:

1 CHARLES COKAYNE, 1st BARON AND VISCOUNT CULLEN, Co Tipperary (I), so *cr* 11 Aug 1642, with remainder, failing heirs of his body, to his sister Martha's four yr sons, Peregrine, Richard, Vere and Charles Bertie, and the heirs male of their bodies (*see* below and LINDSEY and ABINGDON, E); *b* 4 July 1602; MP Reigate 1628–29, High Sheriff Northants 1636, raised a troop of royalist horse Civil War; *m* 24 June 1627 Lady Mary O'Brien (*m* 2nd George Blount, of Sodington, Worcs (*see* BLOUNT, Bt), and *d* 1686), er dau and coheir of 5th Earl of Thomond (*see* INCHIQUIN, B), and *d* 1661, having by her had issue:

(1) William; *d* an infant 1629/30

(2) BRIEN, 2nd Viscount

(3) Charles; *d* an infant 1657

(1) Mary; *m* Robert Pierson, of Bishop's Middleham, Co Durham, and *d* 1682, leaving issue

1 Martha; *bapt* 26 May 1605; *m* 1st *c* July 1624, as his 2nd w, 1st and last Earl of Holderness (*dsps* 28 Feb 1625/6) of the Jan 1620/1 *cr*; *m* 2nd 18 April 1627 2nd Earl of Lindsey (*see* LINDSEY and ABINGDON, E) and *d* July 1641

The second son,

BRIEN COKAYNE, 2nd BARON AND VISCOUNT CULLEN; *b* 1631; *m* by 1 April 1657 Elizabeth (*d* 30 Nov 1713), Lady of the Bedchamber to CHARLES II's QUEEN CATHERINE, dau and heir of Francis Trentham, of Rocester Priory, Staffs, and *d* July 1687, having had an est s:

CHARLES COKAYNE, 3rd BARON AND VISCOUNT CULLEN; *b* 15 Nov 1658; *m* 26 Dec 1678 Katherine (*d* of the smallpox 11 Feb 1688/9), 5th dau of 6th Baron Willoughby of Parham (*see* WILLOUGHBY DE ERESBY, B), and *d* of the smallpox at Oxford (while forming part of the escort of PRINCESS ANNE at the time of her f's flight from England and WILLIAM III's arrival) 30 Dec 1688, leaving only surv issue:

1 CHARLES, 4th Viscount

1 Catherine; *b* 5 Jan 1687/8; *m* 13 March 1711/2 William Dowdeswell, of Pull Court, Worcs, and *d* Nov 1716, leaving issue

His son,

CHARLES COKAYNE, 4th BARON AND VISCOUNT CULLEN; *b* 4 Jan 1686/7; *m* 11 July 1706 Anne (*d* 1714), er dau of Arthur Warren, of Stapleford Hall, Notts, by Anne, dau of Sir John Borlase, Bt, and *d* 6 April 1716, leaving an only surv s:

CHARLES COCKAYNE/COKAYNE, 5th BARON AND VISCOUNT CULLEN; *b* 2 Sept 1710; *educ* Eton; *m* 1st 18 April 1732 Ann (*d* 28 June 1754), est surv dau of his maternal uncle, Borlase Warren, and had, with five other daus (*d* in infancy):

1 Charles; *b* 31 July 1736; *d* unm 1765

2 BORLASE COCKAYNE, 6th BARON AND VISCOUNT CULLEN; *b* 30 Sept 1740; *d* unm 11 Aug 1810, when the peerage was deemed to have expired but according to the remainder (*see* above) would only have become dormant; the patent however, was never enrolled and has long been lost

3 John; *b* 25 June 1745; *d* unm 1768

1 Anna Maria; *b* 16 April 1739; *m* 28 July 1768 Rev Nathaniel Mapletoft, Rector of Broughton, Northants, and *d* 3 April 1825, leaving issue

The 5th VISCOUNT *m* 2nd 16 Dec 1754 Sophia (*d* 13 July 1802), yr dau and coheir of John Baxter, Storekeeper Ordnance Gibraltar, and *d* 7 June 1802, having by her had an only child:

4 William; *b* 16 April 1756; Comptroller Ld Lt's Household Dublin Castle 1790; Govr Limerick Castle; *m* 11 Oct 1777 Barbara (added name and arms of MEDLYCOTT by Act of Parl 42 GEO III under terms of will of her gf Thomas Medlycott, of Cottingham, and *d* 2 June 1838), 2nd dau and eventually sole heir of George Hill, of Rothwell Manor, Northants, Serjeant-at-Law, and *d* 8 Oct 1809, leaving, with four other daus (*d* unm):

(1) Matilda Sophia; *b* 13 Feb 1779; granted with her surv sisters rank of viscount's daus by roy warrant 23 Sept 1836; *m* 31 Dec 1804 Rev Robert Austen, LLD, and *dspms* 23 Feb 1869

(2) Georgiana; *b* 17 Nov 1784; *m* 11 Oct 1824 John Edmund Maunsell, RHA, and *dsp* 19 Dec 1864

(3) Caroline Eliza; *b* 17 Oct 1787; *m* 6 April 1811 Thomas Philip Maunsell, of Thorpe Malsor, Northants, and *d* 12 March 1860, leaving issue

(4) Frances Annabella; *b* 21 July 1795; *m* 9 Aug 1816 William Assheton, of Downham and Cuerdale, Lancs, and *d* 25 July 1835, leaving issue (*see* CLITHEROE, B)

(5) Elizabeth Charlotte; *b* 9 June 1798; *m* 14 Feb 1825 Hon Edmond Sexton Pery, of Bury Ho, Cottingham, Northants (*see* LIMERICK, E), and *d* 21 April 1883, leaving issue

(6) Mary Anne; *b* 11 Dec 1781; *m* 6 April 1811, as his 2nd w, William Adams, LLD, of Eastley End, Thorpe, Surrey, and Dummer Grange, Hants (*d* 11 June 1851), and *d* 16 June 1873, having had issue:

1a William Cockayne (Rev), MA, Rector of Dummer, Hants; *b* 11 Nov 1813; *d* unm 17 Aug 1875

2a Borlase Hill, MA, barrister, JP Middx; *b* 4 April 1817; *m* 1st 10 May 1855 Harriet Anne Rose (*née* Cobbold), widow, who *d* 20 Nov 1864; *m* 2nd Mary Anne Staveley, and *d* 29 April 1885, having by her had issue

3a Henry Willoughby (Rev), MA, Rector of Great Parndon, Essex; *b* 15 June 1820; *d* unm 2 Aug 1906

4a GEORGE EDWARD, of whom presently

1a Barbara Margaretta; *b* 18 May 1812; *d* unm 29 Dec 1903

2a Georgiana Catherine; *b* 29 Jan 1815; *m* 4 June 1839 Rev George Adams, BD, Rector of Chastleton, Oxon, and E Farndon, and *d* 27 Sept 1879, leaving issue

3a Louisa Anne; *b* 10 Sept 1818; *m* 6 May 1845 1st Baron Aldenham, and *d* 17 April 1897, leaving issue (*see* ALDENHAM and HUNSDON OF HUNSDON, B)

4a Eliza; *b* 31 Aug 1822; *d* unm 2 March 1911

William Cockayne's gs,

GEORGE EDWARD ADAMS later COKAYNE (roy licence 15 Aug 1873 under terms of mother's will), of Exeter Ho, Roehampton, Surrey; *b* 29 April 1825; *educ* Exeter Coll Oxford (MA); barrister Lincoln's Inn; Rouge Dragon Pursuivant of Arms 1859, Lancaster Herald 1870, Norroy King of Arms 1882, Clarenceux King of Arms 1894, genealogical author, including *The Complete Peerage* and *The Complete Baronetage*, FSA; *m* 2 Dec 1856 Mary Dorothea (*d* 11 March 1906), yr dau of George Henry Gibbs, of Aldenham, Herts (*see* ALDENHAM and HUNSDON OF HUNSDON, B), and *d* 6 Aug 1911, having had issue:

1 Borlase Warren; *b* 3 Aug 1860; *d* 14 March 1875

2 BRIEN IBRICAN, **1st Baron**

3 Morton Willoughby (Rev), Curate of Carshalton, Surrey; *b* 11 Oct 1866; *educ* Oriel Coll Oxford (MA); *d* unm 8 Nov 1894

4 Francis Stewart; *b* 7 Aug 1871; *educ* Oriel Coll Oxford (BA); *m* 30 Dec 1909 Dorothy Emily (*d* 10 Dec 1963), yr dau of Sir Leslie Probyn, KCMG, and *d* 31 March 1945, having had issue:

(1) Thomas Probyn, Lt RHA WW II; *b* 27 April 1920; *d* in Italy, 6 Oct 1943

(1) Elizabeth; *b* 12 Sept 1913; *m* 31 Jan 1939 Peter Duke Doulton, late Maj RA, est son of Orrok Mills Doulton, and gn of Sir Henry Doulton, and had:

1a *Antony Cokayne [Antony Doulton Esq, 41 Hans Place, London SW1]; *b* 27 March 1940; *educ* Eastbourne Coll; memb Vintners' Co 1962, Freeman City London 1962; *m* 4 Oct 1968 *Sylvia Rosalind (Judy), only dau of Maj Amyas Henry Stafford Northcote, MC (*see* IDDESLEIGH, E), and has issue:

1b *Amyas John Stafford; *b* 13 Oct 1977

1b *Natasha Ophelia Stafford; *b* 28 Feb 1971

2a *Ian Duke; *b* 27 May 1941; *educ* Eastbourne Coll; *m* 2 Aug 1969 *Caroline Margaret, est dau of Michael Anthony Walker, of Digby Ho, Ebrington, Glos (*see* WALKER, Bt, of Sand Hutton), and has issue:

1b *Lucy Catherine; *b* 19 Jan 1971

(2) *Anne; *b* 2 Aug 1916; *m* 4 Feb 1937 Walter Arbuthnot Prideaux, est son of Walter Treverbian Prideaux, of Elderslie, Ockley, Surrey, and has issue:

1a *Walter Michael Cokayne; *b* 19 Nov 1937; *educ* Eton and Trin Coll Cambridge (BA 1960); *m* 19 Sept 1964 *Lenore Mary Jacqueline, dau of Brig Richard Hugh Rossiter Cumming, of Abbotswood Lodge, Walton-on-Thames, Surrey, and has issue:

1b *Rebecca Lenore; *b* 20 Aug 1965

2b *Belinda; *b* 20 June 1969

2a *Francis Martin; *b* 17 Oct 1945; *educ* Eton and Trin Coll Cambridge

1a *Sarah; *b* 7 Jan 1940; *educ* LMH Oxford (BA 1962); *m* 21 July 1962 David Marcus Knight, er son of Very Rev Marcus Knight, of The Deanery, Exeter, Devon, and has issue:

1b *Marcus Simon Prideaux; *b* 16 Aug 1963

2b *Jacob Thomas; *b* 17 July 1968

1b *Teresa Jane; *b* 28 April 1965

2b *Susannah Mary; *b* 6 Jan 1967

2a *Lucy Caroline; *b* 21 July 1947; *educ* St Mary's Coll Durham

(3) *Susan; *b* 14 Sept 1923; *educ* King's Coll London (STh 1950)

1 Blanche Dorothea; *b* 27 June 1858; *m* 10 Aug 1882, as his 1st w, Rev W F J Romanis, MA, and *d* 17 Sept 1883, leaving issue, an only dau, who *d* an infant. He *d* 31 Aug 1913

2 Caroline Louisa; *b* 20 July 1859: *d* unm 4 Sept 1929

3 Mary Beatrice Georgiana; *b* 11 Dec 1861; *d* 23 Oct 1862

4 Sylvia Beatrice; *b* 18 May 1863; *m* 26 April 1909 Francis Lomax Gibbs, 4th son of Rev John Lomax Gibbs, of Speen Ho, Newbury (*see* ALDENHAM and HUNSDON OF HUNSDON, B), and *dsp* 21 Aug 1949

The est surv son,

BRIEN IBRICAN COKAYNE (Sir), **1st Baron Cullen of Ashbourne**, of Roehampton, Co Surrey (UK), so *cr* 21 April 1920, KBE (1917); Lt City London, ptnr Antony Gibbs and Sons, Dir Bank of England 1902 (Dep-Govr 1915–18, Govr 1918–20); Grand Cordon Sacred Treasure Japan, Order Leopold Belgium; *b* 12 July 1864; *m* 29 Sept 1904 Grace Margaret (*d* 1971), 4th dau of Rev Hon John Marsham (*see* ROMNEY, E), and *d* 3 Nov 1932, having had:

1 CHARLES BORLASE MARSHAM COKAYNE, **2nd and present Baron Cullen of Ashbourne**

2 +EDMUND WILLOUGHBY MARSHAM [The Hon Edmund Cokayne, RR1, #15–1901 Maxwell Ave, Merritt, BC V1K 1LN, Canada]; *b* 18 May 1916; heir presumptive; *educ* Eton; F/Lt RAF WW II; retd mining engr; *m* 18 May 1943 *Janet Manson, dau of William Douglas Watson and Mrs Louis Lauritson, of Calgary, Canada, and adopted:

*Jean Charlotte Bell; *b* 28 March 1935

3 +John O'Brien Marsham (does not use courtesy title) [John Cokayne Esq, 14 St Omer Rd, Cowley, Oxford OX4 3HB]; *b* 11 Oct 1920; *educ* Eton; *m* 1 May 1948 Anne Frances (*d* 1971), er dau of Bertram Clayton, of 78 Saville St, Wakefield, Yorks, and has issue:

(1) +Michael John; *b* 28 Nov 1950; *educ* City of Oxford High Sch; *m* 1st 1976 (*divorce* 1985) Baudilia Medina Negrin, of Caracas, Venezuela; *m* 2nd 1986 *Yvette Santana

1 *Barbara Mary [The Hon Mrs Vandermoot, Oak Cottage, Hartley Wintney, Hants]; *b* 28 Nov 1905; *m* 7 Feb 1929 Maj Gilbert Edgar Francis Vandernoot, late Irish Gds (*d* 1981), er son of Rev Edgar F C Vandernoot by Constance Mary, only dau of Sir Algernon West, PC, GCB, and has issue:

(1) *Anthea Caroline [Mrs Michael Ryan, 22 Byfields Rd, Kingsclere, Newbury, Berks RG20 5TG]; *b* 15 Jan 1936; *m* 18 June 1963 John Michael Ryan (*d* 1990), son of Timothy John Ryan, of Hove, Sussex

2 Dorothy Grace; *b* 17 Feb 1907

3 Ruth Margaret, served WW II 1941–43 as Ferry Pilot ATA; *b* 8 Nov 1909; *m* 1st 17 Oct 1939 Capt Robert William Alfred Moore, RA (*ka* at Dunkirk, 30 May 1940), yr son of Richmond Moore, of Hill Ho, Spencer's Wood, Reading; *m* 2nd 21 Nov 1949 Rev David Henry Aitcheson Williams (*d* 20 Nov 1955), er son of Col Henry David Williams, CMG, of The Friary, Lichfield, Staffs and *d* 19 Jan 1997, having had issue by 1st husb:

(1) *(Elizabeth) Virginia; *b* posthumously 27 Nov 1940; *m* 21 April 1973 *Donald Franklin Hoover, of Telkwa, BC, Canada

CULME-SEYMOUR

Arms: Azure a pair of wings conjoined in pale and surmounted of a naval crown or, on a canton argent an anchor sable. **Crest:** On a naval crown or two brands in saltire, inflamed at the ends, proper, thereon an eagle rising, also proper, looking at a sun gold. **Supporters:** Dexter, a sailor in the Royal Navy; sinister, a soldier of the Royal Marines holding in his exterior hand a rifle, the butt resting upon the ground, all proper. **Motto:** *Foy pour devoir* ('Faith for duty'). **Creation:** Bt. (UK) 31 May 1809.

SIR MICHAEL CULME-SEYMOUR, 5TH BT, of High Mount, Co Limerick, JP (Northants 1948), DL (1958) [Cdr Sir Michael Culme-Seymour Bt JP DL RN (ret), Wytherston, Powerstock, Bridport, Dorset DT6 3TQ]; *b* 26 April 1909; *s* f 1925 (and on death 5 July 1925 of Rev Wentworth Watson (*see* 1970 edn SONDES, E) to the Rockingham estate, which he made over to his n Cdr Michael Saunders Watson 1967); ADC to Govr Gen Canada 1934–36, Cdr RN WW II (despatches), ret 1947, IDC 1946–47, Northants CC 1948–55, High Sheriff Northants 1966; *m* 18 March 1948 Lady (Mary) Faith (*d* 16 Feb 1983), er dau of 9th Earl of Sandwich (*qv*) and former w of Philip Booth Nesbitt, and has had:

1 Michael; *b* 25 Nov, *d* 28 Nov 1950

2 Francis Michael; *b* 27 July; *d* 25 Oct 1953

Sir MICHAEL adopted his step-dau:

*(Caroline) Gemma Nesbitt [Mrs Gemma Best, The Studio, 14 Priory Rd, London W4]; *b* 1 June 1939; *m* 1964 (*divorce* 1976) Andrew H Best and has issue (*see* SANDWICH, E)

Lineage: EDWARD SEYMOUR; *m* —, dau of Alderman William Hartwell, Mayor Limerick 1659, and had:

JOHN SEYMOUR; Alderman Limerick (Sheriff 1708, Mayor 1720); *m* Jane, dau of Seymour Wroughton, and had issue:

1 John; ancestor of the SEYMOURs of Castletown, Queen's Co

2 WILLIAM

3 James; Sheriff Limerick 1728; *m* a dau of Ezekiel Holland; *dsps*

4 Richard; Sheriff Limerick 1730

5 Walter; Sheriff Limerick 1742; *m* Margaret, dau of David Bindon, and *dsp*

JOHN SEYMOUR's 2nd s,

WILLIAM SEYMOUR; *m* Jane, 2nd dau of Edward Wight, Mayor Limerick 1694 and 1711, and had:

Rev JOHN SEYMOUR; Rector Palace, Co Limerick; *m* Grizel (*d* 17 Sept 1822), yst dau and coheir of William Hobart, of High Mount, and *d* July 1795, leaving:

Sir Michael Seymour, 1st Bt (UK), so *cr* 31 May 1809, KCB; cmded HMS *Amethyst*, frigate, 1806–09, capturing the French frigate *Niémen* (which he subsequently cmded and which action won him his btcy), Commr Portsmouth Dockyard 1829–32, R-Adml and C-in-C S America 1832–34; *m* 20 Jan 1789 Jane (*d* 12 March 1852), dau of Capt James Hawker, RN, and had issue:

1 JOHN HOBART (Sir), **2nd Bt**

2 James; *b* 17 July 1801; Capt 38th Regt; *d* 1827

3 Michael (Sir), GCB (1859, KCB 1855); *b* 3 Dec 1802; Adml, V-Adml UK, C-in-C E Indies Station and Canton, C-in-C Portsmouth; MP Devonport 1859–63; *m* 22 June 1829 Dora (*d* 1875), dau of Sir William Knighton, 1st Bt, GCH, and *d* 23 Feb 1887, having had, with other issue:

(1) Michael Francis Knighton; *b* 1841; *m* 7 Nov 1863 Elizabeth Georgina Frederica (*d* 1 July 1876), only dau of Capt William Henry Kennedy, RN, and gdau of Adml Hon Sir Charles Paget (*see* ANGLESEY, M), and *d* 1909, having had issue:

1a William Arthur; *b* 1864; Lt Warwicks Regt; *m* 1887 Florence Beatrice (*d* 1910), dau of John George Bilton, and *d* 9 Jan 1894, leaving issue:

1b Vere Hugh; *b* 15 May 1889; *educ* Wellington and Trin Hall Cambridge (BA 1910); Lt RNVR WW I France and Min Shipping, Lt-Cdr RNVR WW II France, UK, N Africa, India and Germany; *m* 1st 31 Dec 1910 Anne, 2nd dau of Frederick Gooch, and had issue:

1c Evan Hugh; *b* 13 Oct 1913; *d* 18 July 1914

1b (cont.) Lt-Cdr Vere Seymour *m* 2nd 17 Aug 1917 Margaret Letitia ('Rita') (*d* 17 June 1955), dau of William Irvine, BCS, and *dsps* 21 Oct 1955

1a Grace Frances Susan; *m* 1st 19 Oct 1887 Arthur John Cromwell (*d* 1897) and had issue; *m* 2nd 16 Jan 1901 (*divorce* 1906) Capt C S F Ferrers and *d* 27 April 1912

(1) Dorothea; *m* 20 April 1865 V-Adml Donald McLeod Mackenzie (*d* 25 Jan 1894), s of Sir George Stewart Mackenzie, 7th Bt, of Coul (*qv*), and *dsp* 26 May 1901

4 Edward; *b* 5 Oct 1804; Capt RN; *d* 13 June 1837

5 Richard (Rev); *b* 2 March 1806; MA, Rector Kinwarton, Warwicks, Canon Worcester; *m* 30 Oct 1834 Frances (*d* 27 April 1871), 3rd dau of Charles Smith, MP (*see* HAMILTON-SPENCER-SMITH, Bt), and *d* 9 July 1880, having had issue:

(1) Walter Richard; *b* 9 Dec 1838; *m* 30 Oct 1913 Hilda (*d* 29 Feb 1916), dau of Charles Irwin Grant, 6th Baron De Longueil, and *d* 16 March 1922

(2) Edward Hobart (Sir), GCB, OM, GCVO, PC; *b* 30 April 1840; RN: served Black Sea in Crimean War 1854–55, China War 1857–60, against Chinese rebels 1862, African coast 1870 (wounded), Egypt 1881, Naval ADC to HM QUEEN VICTORIA 1887–89, cmded Allied Naval Expdn Peking 1900, C-in-C: China Station 1897–1901 and Plymouth Station 1903–04, Adml of the Fleet, 1st and Pncpl Naval ADC to HM EDWARD VII 1902–03, 3rd Cl Osmanieh, Grand Cross Red Eagle, Spanish Naval Merit, Rising Sun Japan, Alexander Nevsky Russia, Roy Humane Soc's Medal, Hon LLD Cantab; *d* unm 2 March 1929

(3) Albert Eden (Ven); *b* 3 Oct 1841; MA Oxon, Archdeacon Barnstaple, Vicar Ilfracombe, Preb Exeter, Provost King's Coll Taunton; Im 14 Oct 1873 Hester Emily (*d* 17 July 1913), est dau of Rev Hon John Fortescue (*see* FORTESCUE, E), and *d* 24 Dec 1908, leaving issue:

1a Richard (Rev); *b* 23 July 1877; *educ* Keble Coll Oxford (BA 1900, MA 1915); Vicar Otterton, Budleigh Salterton, 1910–19, Rector Coombe Martin 1919–37, Vicar Chittlehampton, N Devon, 1937–46; *m* Annie Louisa Mary (*d* 20 Sept 1909), est dau of William Creswell Ernest Arthur, JP, and *d* 1959, leaving issue:

1b John Richard Arthur, OBE (1954), DSC; *b* 14 May 1905; Cdr RN WW II; *m* 1 Oct 1941 Helen Augusta, only child of Lt-Col Richard Edmund Coryndon Luxmoore-Ball, DSO, DCM, Welsh Gds, and *d* 19 Sept 1957, leaving issue:

1c +Richard Paul, AFC [Cdr Richard Seymour AFC RN, Sunnybrook Cottage, Lyatts Hill, Hardington Mandeville, Yeovil, Somerset BA22

9NR]; *b* 19 Sept 1943; *educ* Allhallows and RNC Dartmouth; Cdr RN; *m* 1971 *Valerie Ann, dau of P L Foulsham, and has issue:

1d +Alexander John; *b* 1974

2d +Mark Richard; *b* 1980

2c +(Anthony) John; *b* 22 May 1946; *educ* Allhallows

2b Michael Ernest; *b* 2 Nov 1906; *m* 1931 Gwendoline Arran, dau of William Stuart Gore, and had:

1c *Eleanor; *b* 9 Oct 1932; *m* 20 June 1953 *John Andrew Ferrari, s of Walter Leo Ferrari, and has:

1d *Timothy John [Timothy Ferrari Esq, 45 Tenth Ave, Oyster Bay, NSW 2225, Australia]; *b* 20 June 1954; *m* 1980 *Christine Elizabeth Hanson and has issue:

1e *Jillian Elizabeth; *b* 1984

2e *Emma Elise; *b* 1988

1d *Michele Jane; *b* 4 Sept 1958; *m* 1979 *Ronald Arthur Adam and has issue:

1e *Mathew James; *b* 1985

1b Alma Hester; *b* 28 April 1904; *d* 2 March 1908

2b *Ruth Mary [Mrs Ruth Gillard, 18 Wilder Park, Horne Rd, Ilfracombe, Devon EX34 8HH]; *b* 20 Aug 1909; *m* 1939 (*divorce* 1949) Wilfred Harold Gillard and has issue:

1c *John Patrick; *b* 1940

2a John; *b* 23 July 1877; *d* 11 Feb 1878

3a Hugh, DSO (1917) and bar (1918); *b* 22 Jan 1879; Capt RN WW I (despatches); *m* 1908 Florence Louisa (*d* 6 Dec 1926), dau of George White, of Clifton, and *dsp* 27 Nov 1950

4a Michael Richard; *b* 9 July 1880; Mayor Bethnal Green 1927–28; *d* 24 Dec 1936

5a Edward Albert; *b* 15 June 1884; MB, MRCS, LRCP; *m* 22 April 1914 Gwendolen Emily (*d* 25 March 1978), est dau of Rev William Gascoigne, Rector Woodeaton, Oxon, and *d* 16 March 1946, leaving issue:

1b Edward Richard Fortescue; *b* 7 May 1915; *educ* Blundells and King's Coll Cambridge; *m* 4 Jan 1943 *Margaret Eileen [Mrs Edward Seymour, 48 Military Rd, Rye, Sussex TN31 7NY], dau of Maj Grantham Dodd, TD, RAMC, and *d* 1981, having had issue:

1c Michael; *b* and *d* 7 July 1944

2c +Edward Grantham [Edward Seymour Esq, 4 Rue du Pont, L-5355 Oetrange, Luxembourg]; *b* 14 Nov 1945; *educ* Christ's Hosp and BNC Oxford (BA 1968); *m* 20 Sept 1969 *Philippa Rosalie Jane, BA (Oxon), only dau of Geoffrey Gerald Holman Mollett, of Henley-on-Thames, and has issue:

1d +Edward Hugo; *b* 1979

1d *Guinevere Jane; *b* 1974

2d *Susanna Rosalie; *b* 1977

3d *Augustina Maria; *b* 1981

3c +Charles Adrian [Charles Seymour Esq, 3 Stocklands Cl, Cuckfield, Sussex]; *b* 4 March 1947; *educ* Christ's Hosp; *m* 25 April 1970 *Sylvia Ellen, dau of Alfred Kimber, of Hurstpierpoint, Sussex, and has issue:

1d +Brendan Charles; *b* 1980

2d +Richard Edward; *b* 1982

4c +(Michael) Shaughan [Shaughan Seymour Esq, 4 Chelsham Rd, London SW4]; *b* 3 Aug 1949; *educ* De La Salle Coll and RADA; part in *The Rocky Horror Show*; *m* 1975 *Jane Constance Madeleine, dau of James Lytton, and has issue:

1d +Toby James Edward; *b* 1982

1d *Zoë Jane; *b* 1978

2d *Lucy Margaret; *b* 1980

5c +Gervais Richard Hugh [Gervais Seymour Esq, 179 Oundle Rd, Woodston, Peterborough PE2 9QZ]; *b* 12 Jan 1952; *educ* Ardingly; *m* 1st 1973 (*divorce* 1984) Ann Shirley Trowbridge and has issue:

1d *Rebecca Ann; *b* 1980

5c (cont.) Gervais Seymour *m* 2nd 1984 *Victoria Louise, dau of Robert Brewer, of Newborough, Cambs, and has issue:

1d +Thomas Christopher Gervais; *b* 1984

2d *Ellena Victoria; *b* 1986

5c (cont.) Gervais Seymour has two adopted daus:

*Joanna Claire Marie; *b* 1978

*Michaella Jayne; *b* 1980

6c +James Quentin [James Seymour Esq, Shephards Arms, Coates, nr Cirencester, Glos GL7 6JY]; *b* 1 June 1953; *educ* Ardingly; *m* 1979 *Rosemary Yvonne, dau of Lt-Cdr Peter Hampson Wailes, RN (ret), of Thetford, Norfolk, and has issue:

1d +Michael James; *b* 1980

1d *Alice Victoria; *b* 1982

1b Hester Mary; *b* 1 April 1917; SRN, QARNNS (Res); *d* unm 28 Dec 1995

2b *Joyce Eleanor [Miss Joyce Seymour, 52 Lombard Court, Old Portsmouth, Hants PO1 2HU]; *b* 1 July 1918

6a Algernon Giles (Very Rev); *b* 1 Sept 1886; *educ* Jesus Coll Cambridge (MA); Chaplain RN 1915–20, Provost St Mary's Cathedral Glasgow 1927–33; *m* 21 July 1921 Ida Grace, dau of V-Adml Robert Frederick Hammick (*see* HAMMICK, Bt), and *d* 22 Oct 1933, having had issue:

1b Maurice Robert Giles; *b* 19 May 1922; *d* 27 Feb 1932

2b Christopher Hugh; *b* 31 March 1926; *d* 6 Dec 1951

3b Timothy Maurice Barnabas; *b* 16 June 1932; *educ* RNC Dartmouth; Lt-Cdr RN; *m* 7 June 1954 *Monica [Mrs Timothy Seymour, 5 Tarleton Gdns, London SE 23], dau of Rt Rev Wilfrid Arthur Edmund Westall, BA, Suffragan Bp Crediton, and *d* 8 Feb 1975, leaving issue:

1c +Michael Nicholas; *b* 14 March 1960

2c +Charles Richard; *b* 22 Jan 1963; *m* 1992 *Deborah Miller

1b *Mary-Gracer [Lady Hutchison, Melton Mead, nr Woodbridge, Suffolk]; *b* 6 Feb 1924; *m* 16 July 1949 *Sir Peter Hutchison, 2nd Bt, of Thurle (*qv*), and has issue

7a Arthur (Rev); *b* 22 March 1888; *educ* Queens' Coll Cambridge (MA); *m* 7 Aug 1917 Emily Grace (*d* 20 April 1929), yst dau of Samuel Doidge, of Torrington, and *d* 6 Dec 1935

1a Eleanor Frances, JP; *d* as result of an accident 12 Nov 1944

2a Hester Sophia; *d* unm 12 Feb 1949

3a Alice Mary; *d* unm

(4) Richard Arthur Hamilton; *b* 28 June 1843; *m* 25 June 1878 Charlotte Elizabeth (*d* 4 Jan 1931), yr dau of Adml Cospatrick Baillie-Hamilton (*see* HADDINGTON, E), and *d* 8 April 1906, leaving issue:

1a Marjorie Elizabeth; *m* 10 April 1899 Col Henry Cecil Petre, CMG, OBE (*see* PETRE, B), and *d* 11 Aug 1928

2a Iris Mary; *m* 16 July 1912 Col Gerald Montagu Spencer-Smith, DSO, RA (*d* 9 Oct 1951), er s of Rev Orlando Spencer-Smith, and *d* 4 May 1967, leaving issue (*see* HAMILTON-SPENCER-SMITH, Bt)

3a Muriel Jane

(5) John Le Marchant; *b* 25 Sept 1845; served 41st Regt; *d* Agra 4 Oct 1866

(1) Augusta Frances; *m* 14 July 1875 Capt Hervey George St John-Mildmay, RN (*d* 21 May 1882), of Hazelgrove, Somerset (*see* 1970 edn ST JOHN-MILDMAY, Bt), and *dsp* Feb 1910

(2) Emma Jane; *d* unm 19 Feb 1927

(3) Frances Mary; *d* unm 8 Oct 1946

6 William Hobart; *b* 11 Aug 1820; Capt 99th Regt; *m* 11 Aug 1820 Sarah Mary Avory, of Sydney, NSW (*m* 2nd 1858 Henry Pleydell-Bouverie (*see* RADNOR, E); *d* 17 Feb 1859), and *d* 3 March 1857, leaving issue:

(1) Jane; *m* 23 May 1876 Charles Edward Hawker, RN (*d* 1913), and *d* 17 Nov 1934, leaving issue

1 Jane Ward; *d* 30 Aug 1862

2 Frances Anne; *m* 3 Sept 1836 Spencer Smith (*d* 2 May 1882), of Brooklands, Hants, and *d* 22 Feb 1897, leaving issue (*see* HAMILTON-SPENCER-SMITH, Bt)

3 Dora; *m* 1st 29 Aug 1837 Rev William H Clinton Chester, est s of Gen Chester; *m* 2nd 3 Sep 1845 Arthur Currie (*d* 1875) and *d* 5 Feb 1888 aged 78

4 Mary Dorothea; *m* 22 June 1830 Capt Orlando George Gunning-Sutton, RN (*d* 5 May 1852), 4th s of Sir George Gunning, 2nd Bt (*qv*), and *d* 31 March 1900, leaving issue:

(1) Mary Diana; *m* 8 Dec 1852 2nd Earl of Ravensworth and *d* 8 Dec 1890, having had issue (*see* RAVENSWORTH, B)

5 Caroline; *m* 15 March 1841 Capt George Carr, only s of Rt Rev Robert James Carr, DD, Bp Worcester, and *d* 1843

6 Elizabeth; *m* 29 Aug 1839 Lt-Col George Charles Ernest Adolphus Richard Howard-Vyse, JP, 2nd Life Gds (*d* 29 May 1890), and *dsp* 4 Dec 1892

7 Ellen; *m* 15 March 1841 Rev Henry B Forster, MA, Hon Canon Gloucester (*d* 1890), and *d* 28 Jan 1903, leaving issue

Sir MICHAEL *d* Rio de Janeiro 9 July 1834; his est s,

Rev Sir JOHN HOBART SEYMOUR later CULME-SEYMOUR (roy licence 6 May 1842), **2nd Bt**; *b* 24 March 1800; Canon Gloucester, Rector Berkhamstead St Mary and Northchurch, Herts, Chaplain-in-Ordinary to HM QUEEN VICTORIA, Preb Lincoln; *m* 1st 12 April 1833 Elizabeth (*d* 6 March 1841), er dau and coheir of Rev Thomas Culme, of Tothill, Devon, and had issue:

1 MICHAEL (Sir), **3rd Bt**

2 John Hobart; *b* 1 Oct 1837; Lt-Col, Clerk Cheque and Adj Gentlemen-at-Arms; *m* 15 March 1870 Mary Eliza (*d* 6 March 1925), only surv dau of Richard Hall, of Hillingdon Furze, Uxbridge, and *dsp* 10 Nov 1887

1 Elizabeth Culme; *m* 16 June 1874 Rev Henry John Rawlinson, MA, rector Bicton, Devon, and *d* 5 Oct 1911

Sir JOHN *m* 2nd 10 Feb 1844 Maria Louisa (*d* 24 July 1887), yst dau of Charles Smith, MP, of Suttons, Essex, and sis of Sir Charles Joshua Smith, 2nd Bt, of Tring Park, Herts (*see* HAMILTON-SPENCER-SMITH, Bt), and had further issue:

3 Henry Hobart, JP (Hants); *b* 5 April 1847; *educ* New Coll Oxford (MA); Maj 4th Bn Beds Regt, Hants CC; *m* 24 Sept 1878 Kate (*d* 10 Jan 1931), dau of William Charles Lucy, JP, FGS, and *d* 3 Feb 1920, having had issue:

(1) Reginald Hobart; *b* 28 Aug 1879; *d* unm 5 Nov 1901

(2) Evelyn; *b* 19 Sept 1881; Cdr RN, WWs I and II; *m* 29 May 1908 Laura Maud Amy (*d* 23 Sept 1958), yr dau of Sir Steuart Macnaghten, DL (*see* MACNAGHTEN, Bt), and *d* 9 April 1970, having had issue:

1a Gerald Henry Hobart; *b* 8 April 1914; Lt-Cdr RN WW II; *m* 1st 4 Feb 1939 Constance Helen (*d* 20 July 1959), only dau of Alfred Rendell Street (*see* DASHWOOD, Bt), of Sydney, Australia, and had issue:

1b *Victoria; *b* 7 Jan 1949; *m* 1963 Manuchehr Haeri, s of Sadreddin Haeri, of Teheran, and has issue:

1c *David; *b* 19 April 1967

1c *Mina; *b* 12 Nov 1965

2c *Sophia Helen; *b* 1978

2b *Anne Evelyn [Mrs Michael Allen, Kidmore House, Kidmore End, Oxon]; *b* 1 Sept 1941; *m* 1st 10 July 1961 (*divorce* 1970) John L M Denham, only s of Capt Henry M Denham, CMG, RN, and has issue:

1c *James Henry Seymour; *b* 27 March 1964

1c *Alexandra Sophia; *b* 5 Dec 1966

2b (cont.) Mrs Anne Denham *m* 2nd 1972 *(David) Michael (Richard Cecil) Allen and has issue:

2c *Louisa Chelsea; *b* 1975

3b *Catherine; *b* 21 April 1945; *m* 13 Jan 1972 *Christopher James Munro Hartley, s of W R Hartley, and has issue:

1c *Melissa Charlotte Victoria; *b* 1974

2c *Victoria Elizabeth Anne; *b* 1978

4b Elizabeth Rosemary; *b* 20 Feb 1947; *d* 25 March 1948

5b *Alexandra Jane; *m* 1975 *Simon Webb and has issue:

1c *Rowland Henry; *b* 1978

1c *Clementine Laura; *b* 1982

1a (cont.) Lt-Cdr Gerald Culme-Seymour *m* 2nd 15 Oct 1960 *Patricia Mary [Mrs Gerald Culme-Seymour, Sturdys, Wood Broughton, Cartmel, Cumbria LA11 6SJ], est dau of Edward Pearson Hewetson, JP, and formerly w of 3rd Viscount Cross (*qv*), and *d* 1973, leaving issue:

6b *Caroline Eve; *b* 3 Oct 1961

1a Katharine Rosemary Letitia; *b* 20 Feb 1909; *m* 5 Sept 1935 Charles Fuller Stanwood, s of Prof D C Stanwood, of Cambridge, Mass, and *d* 1 March 1963, leaving issue

2a *Patience Ann; *b* 1 March 1912; chm Holloway Prison Visitors Assoc; *m* 17 March 1939 (*divorce* 1951) Lt-Cdr David Robert Fremantle, RNVR (*d* 1989), yr s of Adml Sir Sydney Robert Fremantle, and has issue (*see* COTTESLOE, B)

3a Marjorie Rachel Maud; *b* 17 Feb 1916; *d* 21 Jan 1934

(3) Arthur Granville; *b* 10 April 1884; *educ* Radley and Wye Ag Coll; land agent, ARICS; Maj Norfolk Regt and MGC WW I (despatches); *d* unm 29 Jan 1955

(4) Ernest Victor; *b* 11 Feb 1887; *educ* Radley and New Coll Oxford (BA 1911, MA 1920); master RNC Dartmouth 1912–47; *d* unm 20 Sept 1949

(1) Violet Katharine Maria; *b* 26 Jan 1891; *m* 23 Oct 1926 Charles de la Cour Le Maistre, CBE (*d* 5 July 1953), s of Rev George John Le Maistre, MA, of Jersey

2 Laura Maria; *m* 1 Jan 1867 George Lewis Watson (*see* MONSON, B), and *d* 21 March 1893

3 Jane Eliza; *d* unm 20 Dec 1905

4 Caroline Mary; *d* young 1857

5 Charlotte Augusta Mary; *m* 6 Oct 1894 Farndon Groom Tuck, BA (*d* 3 Jan 1930), and *d* 1940, leaving issue

Sir JOHN *d* 17 Sept 1880; his est s,

Sir Michael Culme-Seymour, 3rd Bt, GCB, GCVO; *b* 13 March 1836; C-in-C Pacific 1885–87, cmded Channel Sqdn 1890–92, C-in-C: Mediterranean Fleet 1893–96, Portsmouth 1897–1900, Adml, First and Pncpl Naval ADC to TM QUEEN VICTORIA and EDWARD VII, V-Adml UK and Lt Admlty 1901–21, Kt Medjidie 1st Cl; *m* 16 Oct 1866 Mary Georgiana (*d* 6 March 1912), er dau of Hon Richard Watson (*see* MONSON, B), and had issue:

1 MICHAEL (Sir), **4th Bt**

2 John Wentworth, JP; *b* 13 Oct 1876; *educ* Winchester; Lt RNVR and Capt RAF WW I; *m* 2 April 1918 Evelyn Mary (*d* 15 Aug 1977), 2nd dau of Charles Alston Smith-Ryland, of Barford Hill, Warwicks, and *d* 6 July 1962, leaving issue:

(1) John Dennis; *b* 3 Dec 1923; *educ* Winchester; Capt Rifle Bde WW II; *m* 14 Sept 1957 (Elizabeth) Jane (*d* 1989), dau of Lt-Col Kenneth Mackessack, of Ardgye, Elgin, Moray, and *d* 1982, leaving issue:

1a *Caroline; *b* 9 May 1959

(1) (Mary) Primrose; *b* 9 Nov 1921; 3rd Offr WRNS WW II; *d* 1988

(2) *Jane [Mrs John Joughin, Flat 2, 11 St Fimbarrus Rd, Fowey, Cornwall PL23 1JJ]; *b* 4 Oct 1925; *m* 25 July 1959 Cdr John Hocken Joughin, DSC, RN (*d* 26 June 1986), s of John Clague Joughin, CBE, of Onchan, IoM

3 George; *b* 8 March 1878; Capt KRRC, Adj Queen Victoria's Rifles; *m* 7 Dec 1909 Janet Beatrix (*m* 2nd 8 July 1918 Rev Geoffrey Harold Woolley, VC, MC), er dau of Charles Lindsay Orr Ewing (*see* ORR EWING, Bt), and was *ka* Ypres 7 May 1915, leaving issue:

(1) Mark Charles; *b* 20 Dec 1910; *educ* Wellington and New Coll Oxford; Maj Rifle Bde WW II (wounded); *m* 1st 26 June 1935 (*divorce* 1938) Babette, only child of David Llewelyn Patric-Jones; *m* 2nd 5 April 1941 (*divorce* 1949) Princess Hélène Marie de la Trémoïlle, 3rd dau of Prince Louis Charles Marie, Prince and 11th Duke de la Tr33moïlle, 12th Duke de Thouars, Premier Duke of France, 12th Prince de Tarente and 15th Prince de Talmond, formerly w of Sir Campbell Mitchell-Cotts, 2nd Bt (*see* COTTS, Bt); *m* 3rd 6 Oct 1956 (*divorce* 1966) Patricia June, dau of Charles Reid-Graham and widow of Geoffrey Edward Ansell, and by her had issue:

1a +MICHAEL PATRICK [Michael Culme-Seymour Esq, 6 St Andrew's Rd, Henley-on-Thames, Oxon]; *b* 28 April 1962; heir presumptive; *m* 1986 *Karin Fleig and has issue:

1b +Michael; *b* 1986

2b +Julian; *b* 1988

1a *Miranda; *b* 26 March 1959; *m* 1990 *Jonathan Fuller, of Hollywood, LA

2a *Sarah Louise [Mrs Laurence Treloar, 30 Canoon Rd, S Turramurra, NSW 2074, Australia]; *b* 4 Feb 1961; *m* 1990 *Laurence Stewart Treloar and has issue:

1b *Hugh Michael James; *b* 15 March 1995

1b *Alice Patricia; *b* 1991

(1) (cont.) Maj Mark Culme-Seymour *m* 4th 1 Jan 1973 *Mary Darrall, only dau of Leander Armistead Riely, of Oklahoma City, and widow of Philip Kidd

(1) Angela Mary; *b* 3 Aug 1912; *m* 1st 13 May 1934 (*divorce* 1938) John George Spencer-Churchill, er s of Maj John Strange Spencer-Churchill, DSO, and has issue (*see* MARLBOROUGH, D); *m* 2nd 11 Feb 1938 (*divorce* 1942) 3rd Baron Kinross (*qv*; he *dsp* 4 June 1976); *m* 3rd 20 March 1948 (*divorce* 19–) Count René Guillet de Chatellus, 2nd s of Count Pierre de Chatellus; *m* 4th 1977 Mehmet Ali Bulent Rauf (*d* 1987)

1 Mary Elizabeth; *b* 10 Feb 1871; *m* 17 Aug 1899 V-Adml Sir Trevylyan Dacres Willes Napier, KCB, MVO (*d* 30 July 1920), s of V-Adml Gerard John Napier, and *d* 16 Oct 1944, leaving issue

2 Laura Grace; *b* 18 July 1873; *d* 22 Nov 1895

Sir MICHAEL *d* 11 Oct 1920; his est s,

Sir Michael Culme-Seymour, 4th Bt, KCB, MVO; *b* 29 Aug 1867; WW I: cmded HMS *Centurion* Battle of Jutland 1916 (despatches), R-Adml 1916, Dir Mobiln Admlty 1916–18, cmded Br E Mediterranean Sqdn 1918, Black Sea, Caspian and Sea of Marmora 1919, 2-i-c Mediterranean 1920, V-Adml 1920, C-in-C N America and W Indies Station 1923–24, 2nd Sea Ld and Ch Naval Personnel 1924, Order St Vladimir Russia 4th Cl with swords, St Stanislas Russia 1st Cl, Rising Sun Japan 2nd Cl, Legion Honour, Grand Cdr Order Redeemer Greece; *m* 9 April 1896 Baroness Florence Agnes Louisa (*d* 17 Jan 1956), dau of 3rd Baron Nugent (*see* WESTMEATH, E), and *d* 2 April 1925, leaving issue:

1 Sir MICHAEL CULME-SEYMOUR, **5th and present Bt**

1 Elizabeth; *b* 27 Oct 1904; *m* 11 March 1933 Capt Leslie Swain Saunders, DSO, RN, est s of James Swain Saunders, of Dolphinton House, Cramond Bridge, Linlithgow, and *d* 23 Oct 1963, leaving issue:

(1) *(Leslie) Michael MacDonald SAUNDERS later SAUNDERS WATSON, CBE (1993), DL (Northants 1979) [Cdr Michael Saunders Watson CBE DL RN, Rockingham Castle, Market Harborough, Leics LE16 8TH]; *b* 1934; *educ* Eton; Cdr RN (ret), chm Br Library 1990–93, High Sheriff Northants 1978, Hon DLitt Warwick and Leicester; *m* 1958 *Georgina Elizabeth Laetitia, dau of Adml Sir William Wellclose Davis, GCB, DSO (*see* NORMANBY, M), and has issue:

1a *James Michael Ross; *b* 1961; *m* 1990 *Elizabeth, dau of Dr Christopher Brown, and has:

1b *Eleanor Liebe Grace; *b* 1995

2b *Beatrice Elizabeth Rose; *b* 7 April 1997

2a *David William Wentworth; *b* 1968

1a *Fiona Jane Liebe; *b* 1965

(2) *Alasdair James Hew [Alasdair Saunders Esq, 17 The Little Boltons, London SW10]; *b* 1938; *educ* Eton; *m* 1974 *Joanna Christina, dau of Col John Offley Crewe-Read, OBE, and formerly w of Capt John Anthony Frank Morton, RHA, and has issue:

1a *Thomas Alasdair; *b* 1978

1a *Alice Elizabeth; *b* 1975

(3) *Iain Ogilvy Swain [Iain Saunders Esq, 10 Brunswick Gdns, London W8]; *b* 1947; *educ* Radley; *m* 1976 *Roberta Ann Phoenix, of Laguna Beach, California, and has issue:

1a *Christina Ann Swain; *b* 1983

(1) *Elizabeth Christina [Mrs Lawrence Banks, Ridgebourne, Kington, Herefs HR5 3EG]; *b* 1941; *m* 1963 *(William) Lawrence Banks and has issue:

1a *Richard Michael; *b* 1965; *m* 1992 *Chloë Berenice Josephine Macaskie and has issue:

1b *William Ferdinand; *b* 1995

2a *Edward Joseph; *b* 1967

CUMBERLEGE

Creation: B. (LP, UK) 1990.

THE BARONESS CUMBERLEGE, of Newick, East Sussex (Julia Frances Camm, CBE (1985)) [The Rt Hon The Baroness Cumberlege CBE, Vuggles Farm, Newick, Lewes, E Sussex BN8 4RU]; *b* 27 Jan 1943; *educ* Convent of the Sacred Heart, Kent; E Sussex: V-Ld Lt 1991 (DL 1986–91), memb: CC 1974–85 (Chm Social Servs Ctee 1979–82) and AHA 1977–81, JP 1973–85; memb Lewes Dist Cncl 1966–79 (Leader 1977–78), Chm Brighton HA 1981–88, Nat Assoc of HAs 1987–88 and SW Thames RHA 1988–92; Memb: NHS Policy Bd 1989–, Cncl St George's Med Sch, Press Cncl 1977–83 and Appointments Commn 1984–, Social Security Advsy Ctee 1980–82, DHSS Expert Advsy Gp on Aids 1987–89, Cncl UK Central Cncl for Nursing, Midwifery and Health Visiting 1989–92, Cncl Brighton Poly 1987–89; Chm Review of Community Nursing for England 1985; V-Pres RCN 1988–; Parly Under-Sec Health 1992–97; Pres Age Concern Brighton 1984–; Tstee Princess Roy Tst for Carers 1992–93; Governor Chailey and Ringmer Comprehensive Schs 1972–86 and 1979–85 respectively, also Newick Primary Sch 1977–85 and Chailey Heritage Sch and Hosp 1982–88; Founder: Newick Playgp and Newick Youth Club, FRSA 1989; *m* 1961 *Patrick Francis Howard Cumberlege (*see* GIBBONS, Bt), and has issue:

1 *(Christopher) Mark; *b* 1962; *educ* Sutton Valence

2 *Justin Francis; *b* 1964; *educ* Haileybury

3 *Oliver Richard; *b* 1968; *educ* Lancing

Lineage: Dr L U CAMM; *m* *M G G — and had issue:

JULIA FRANCES, *cr* a **Baroness**

CUNINGHAME

Arms: Argent a shakefork sable, a crescent azure for difference.
Crest: A unicorn's head erased proper. **Motto:** Over fork over.
Creation: Bt. (NS) 26 Feb 1671/2.

SIR JOHN CHRISTOPHER FOGGO MONTGOMERY CUNINGHAME, 12TH BT, of Corsehill, Co Ayr [Sir John Montgomery Cuninghame Bt, The Old Rectory, Brightwalton, Newbury, Berks RG20 7BL]; *b* 24 July 1935; *s* bro 1959, claims Earldom of Glencairn (dormant 1794); *educ* Fettes and Worcester Coll Oxford (MA); late Lt Rifle Bde; dir Ronald A Lee PLC 1986–, Euromax Electronics 1985–, Artemis Energy Co 1981– (ptnr), Purolite International Ltd 1984–, Ryobi Lawn and Garden Ltd, Bedford Capital Financial Corp; *m* 9 Sept 1964 *Laura Violet, 2nd dau of Sir Godfrey Nicholson, 1st Bt, of Winterbourne (*see* NICHOLSON OF WINTERBOURNE, B), and has issue:

1 *Christian Elizabeth; *b* 4 June 1967
2 *Georgiana Rose; *b* 22 July 1969
3 *Elizabeth Clara; *b* 6 Dec 1971

Lineage: VERNEBALD; living W Scotland *c* 1100; had:

ROBERT Fitz VERNEBALD; living 1153; *m* Richenda, dau of Sir Humphrey de Barclay of Gairntully, and had:

ROBERT Fitz ROBERT Fitz VERNEBALD; living shortly before 1189; ggf of:

HERVEY de CUNINGHAME; living 1264, fndr collegiate church Kilmaurs, Ayrshire; leading participant Battle of Largs against Danes 1263; *m* —, heiress of Riddell of Garnock, and had:

Sir WILLIAM de CUNINGHAME of Kilmaurs; *d* 1285, leaving an est s:

EDWARD de CUNINGHAME of Kilmaurs; had an est s:

GILBERT de CUNINGHAME of Kilmaurs; *d* 1292, leaving:

Sir ROBERT de CUNINGHAME of Kilmaurs; swore fealty to EDWARD I but later supported ROBERT I (THE BRUCE), who granted him as tenant-in-chief of the Crown the lands of Lambrachtoun and Grugere, in Cunningham; *d* 1330; possibly f of:

HUGH CUNINGHAME; probably f of:

Sir WILLIAM CUNINGHAME, 1st and last EARL OF CARRICK (S), so *cr c* 1362, but seemingly resigned the title to the Crown by 1369; *m* Margaret — and *d* after Dec 1396 but before July 1399, having had, with an est son (*d* young):

1 WILLIAM (Sir)
2 Thomas
3 Alexander
4 John

The est s,

Sir WILLIAM CUNINGHAME; got a regrant 1400 to him and his heirs male, failing whom his bros then to other close kin of the name of Cuninghame, of the lands and (territorial) Baronies of Kilmaurs, Kilbryde, Lambrachtoun, Polquharne and Skelmorlie, Ayrshire; the lands and (territorial) Barony of Redhall, Edinburgh; the lands of Nevy, Forfarshire; the (territorial) Barony of Hessenden, Roxburghshire; and the lands of Ranfurley, (territorial) Barony of Renfrew; *m* Margaret, er dau and coheir of Sir Robert de Danyelston, through whom he acquired the (territorial) Baronies of Glencairn (Nithsdale, Dumfriesshire) and Finlayston, and had:

Sir ROBERT CUNINGHAME; living *temp* JAMES I; *m* Anne, only dau of Sir John Montgomerie of Ardrossan (*see* EGLINTON and WINTON, E), and *d* between 1447/8 and 1450/1, leaving:

ALEXANDER CUNINGHAME, 1st EARL OF GLENCAIRN, so *cr* 28 May 1488, as also earlier between 8 Feb 1462/3 and 13 Jan 1463/4 LORD KILMAURS (both S); *b* after 1425; crushed an uprising against JAMES III at the Battle of Blackness; *m* Margaret, sis of Patrick Hepburn, 1st Lord Hailes (*see* BUCHAN-HEPBURN, Bt), and was *k* fighting for JAMES III against the latter's own son (subsequently JAMES IV) at the Battle of Sauchieburn early June 1488, leaving:

1 ROBERT, 2nd Earl
2 William; ancestor of the FAIRLIE-CUNINGHAME, Bts (*qv*), and allegedly the CUNYGHAME Bts of Milncraig (*qv*)
3 Alexander
4 Edward

The 1st EARL's est s,

ROBERT CUNINGHAME, 2nd (and last of the 1488 *cr*?) EARL OF GLENCAIRN 11 June–17 Oct 1488 (on which latter date, the rebel party now being in power, he was stripped of the title by Act of Parl), and 2nd LORD KILMAURS (which title he retained); *m* by 19 July 1476 Christian, widow of John Seton, Master of Seton, and est dau of 1st Lord Lindsay of the Byres (*see* LINDSAY, E), and *d c* 1490, leaving:

CUTHBERT CUNINGHAME, 3rd EARL OF GLENCAIRN, apparently so recognised (hence presumably restored as, though according to some sources *cr* by the ancient ceremonial custom known as belting) 13 Aug 1503; granted a charter 24 July 1511 of the Earldom and Barony of Glencairn; made abortive attempt to wrest custody of JAMES V from the Douglas faction and was beaten by them at encounter of Linlithgow 4 Sept 1526; *m c* 24 June 1492 Lady Marion/Mariot Douglas, est dau of Archibald, Earl of Angus (*see* HAMILTON and BRANDON, D), by his 1st w Elizabeth, dau of Robert, Lord Boyd (*see* KILMARNOCK, B), and *d* after 23 May 1540 but before May 1541, leaving:

WILLIAM CUNINGHAME, 4th EARL OF GLENCAIRN, PC (S 1545); *b c* 1493; ktd by summer 1509, High Treasurer Scotland June-Oct 1526, Envoy to France 1538, captured by English Battle of Solway Moss 1542 but ransomed and the next year was one of the Scots Ambs sent to negotiate peace with the English, being bribed by them to agree favourable terms and promote English interests in Scotland generally, but later ratted and was pardoned by the Scots Parl 1544; an enthusiastic Protestant; *m* 1st by 10 July 1509 Katherine (*d* in or after 17 Jan 1527/8), dau of 3rd Lord Borthwick and widow of Alexander Home/Hume; *m* 2nd after Jan 1535/6 Elizabeth, dau and heiress of John Campbell of West Loudon and widow of 4th Lord Crichton of Sanquhar (*see* BUTE, M), and *d* March 1547/8, leaving, with other issue (though whether by his 1st or 2nd w is unclear except in the case of the est s, who was by the former):

1 ALEXANDER CUNINGHAME, 5th EARL OF GLENCAIRN ('The Good Earl'), PC (S 1561); enthusiastic Presbyterian during Reformation, smashing altars and supposedly idolatrous objects in Holyrood Chapel; leading opponent of MARY QUEEN OF SCOTS Battles of Carberry Hill 1567 and Langside 1568, Jt Lt W of Scotland; *m* 1st *c* 26 Nov 1526 (*divorce* 1545) Lady Janet/Joan Hamilton, dau of 1st Earl of Arran (*see* ABERCORN, D), and had:

(1) WILLIAM CUNINGHAME, 6th EARL OF GLENCAIRN; *m* by 24 Aug 1549 Janet, dau of Sir John Gordon of Lochinvar, and *d* after 1576 but before 24 Feb 1579/80, leaving, with another s and two daus:

1a JAMES CUNINGHAME, 7th EARL OF GLENCAIRN, PC (S 1604); *b c* 1552; *m* 1st 5 Sept 1574 Mariot/Margaret, 3rd dau of Sir Colin Campbell of Glenorchy (*see* ARGYLL, D); *m* 2nd by 14 July 1612 Agnes, sis of James Hay, Earl of Carlisle, and widow of Sir George Preston of Craigmillar, and *d* in or after March 1630, leaving by his 1st w, with another s and two daus (one of whom, Jean, *m* Roger Kirkpatrick of Closeburne; *see* KIRKPATRICK, Bt):

1b WILLIAM CUNINGHAME, 8th EARL OF GLENCAIRN; *m c* 1609 Lady Janet Kerr, dau of 1st Earl of Lothian (*see* LOTHIAN, M), and *d* Oct 1631, leaving, with other issue:

1c WILLIAM CUNINGHAME, 9th EARL OF GLENCAIRN, PC (S 1641 and Feb 1660/1); *b c* 1610; royalist Civil War, cmdg an uprising on behalf of CHARLES II 1653, Ld Chllr Scotland 1661–64; *m* 1st *c* 5 April 1637 Lady Anne Ogilvy, dau of 1st Earl of Findlater (*see* SEAFIELD, E) by his 1st w Elizabeth, dau of 5th Earl of Rothes (*qv*); *m* 2nd Margaret, dau of Alexander Montgomerie, Earl of Eglinto(u)n (*see* EGLINTON and WINTON, E), and widow of 1st Earl of Tweeddale (*see* TWEEDDALE, M), and *d* 30 May 1664, leaving no issue by her, but by his 1st w having had, with two er sons and two other daus:

1d ALEXANDER CUNINGHAME, 10th EARL OF GLENCAIRN; *m c* 1660 Nicol, dau of Sir James Stewart of Kirkhill, Linlithgowshire, and *dspm* 26 May 1670, leaving:

1e Margaret; *m* 5th Earl of Lauderdale (*qv*) and *d* 12 May 1742, leaving issue (*see* also FERGUSSON, Bt; Lady Margaret's ggs Sir Adam Fergusson, 3rd Bt, in 1796 claimed the Earldom of Glencairn as heir general of his gggf the 10th Earl but the House of Lords in 1797 disallowed his claim, since back in 1670 the title had passed to an heir male (the 10th Earl's younger brother) without opposition and the House of Lords Privileges Committee had not the power to settle whether this had been right, that is to say whether the title was only heritable by heirs male, as the 1670 episode would suggest, or whether it could pass to heirs general (which could include females); if the Earldom of Glencairn was ever shown or judged to be descendible to heirs general, all living descendants of the original grantee would be in remainder)

2d JOHN CUNINGHAME, 11th EARL OF GLENCAIRN, PC (S 1689); *m* 1st 5 Aug 1673 Lady Jean Erskine, dau of John, Earl of Mar (*qv*); *m* 2nd by 1695 Margaret, dau of John Napier of Kilmahew, Dunbartonshire, and widow of Patrick Maxwell of Newark, and *d* 14 Dec 1703, leaving by his 1st w:

1e WILLIAM CUNINGHAME, 12th EARL OF GLENCAIRN, PC (S); Govr Dumbarton Castle 1715–34; *m* 20 Nov 1704 Lady Henrietta Stewart, dau of 3rd Earl of Galloway (*qv*) and *d* 14 March 1733/4, having had, with seven other sons (ldsp):

1f WILLIAM CUNINGHAME, 13th EARL OF GLENCAIRN; Lt-Col 9th Foot 1747, Maj-Gen 1770; *m* 6 Aug 1744 Elizabeth, est dau of Hugh Maguire, fiddler, of Drumdow, Ayrshire, and *d* 9 Sept 1775, having had, with two other sons (*dsp*) and another dau:

1g JAMES CUNINGHAME, 14th EARL OF GLENCAIRN; *b* 6 June 1749; *educ* Ch Ch Oxford; Capt W Fencibles 1778, rep S peer 1780–84; sold the Kilmaurs estate 1786; *d* unm 30 Jan 1791

2g Rev JOHN CUNINGHAME, 15th EARL OF GLENCAIRN; *b* May 1750; Offr 14th Dragoons before being ordained as C of E parson, prolix playwright and patron of the poet Burns; *m* 23 April 1785 Isabella, dau of Henry David, Earl of Buchan (*qv*), and widow of William Leslie Hamilton, and *dsp* 24 Sept 1796, when the Earldom became dormant

1g Henrietta; *m* Sir Alexander Don, 5th Bt, and had issue (*see* DON-WAUCHOPE, Bt)

1f Margaret; *m* 2 April 1732 Nicol Graham and was ancestor of the BONTINE-CUNINGHAME[*sic*]-GRAHAMs of Ardoch (*see* JAUNCEY OF TULLICHETTLE, LP)

2f Henrietta; *m* 20 April 1735 John Campbell of Shawfield, Lanarks, and was ancestor of the CAMPBELLs of Islay and Shawfield and the CAMPBELLs of Skipness

1d Jean; *m* 1st Earl of Kilmarnock (*see* KILMARNOCK, B)

2d Margaret; *m* 2nd Lord Bargeny

1c Marion; *m* 1st as his 2nd w 1st Earl of Findlater (*see* SEAFIELD, E); *m* 2nd 29 Oct 1660, as his 2nd w, Alexander, Master of Saltoun (*see* SALTOUN, L), and *dsp* by Jan 1660/1

1b Catherine; *m* her cousin Sir James Cuninghame of Glengarnock

2b Anne; *m* 2nd Marquess of Hamilton and had issue (*see* HAMILTON and BRANDON, D)

3b Mary; *m* John Crawfurd of Kilbirnie (*d* 1629) and had:

1c Sir JOHN CRAWFORD, 1st Bt (NS), so *cr* 14 May 1628, with it would seem remainder to heirs male whatsoever; cmded a royalist regt Civil War, MP (S Parl) Ayrshire1644 and 1661–62; *m* 1st Margaret (*dsp*), dau of Margaret, Lady Balfour of Buirleigh (*qv*) in her own right; *m* 2nd Magdalen, widow of Sir Gideon Baillie of Lochend and dau of David, Lord Carnegy, s of 1st Earl of Southesk (*see* FIFE, D), and *dspm* 1662 (when the btcy became dormant till assumed 1765 by a distant cousin, only to become dormant again 1885 on the death *sp* of the 5th Bt), leaving:

1d Ann; *m* Sir Archibald Stewart, 1st Bt, of Blackhall, and had issue (*see* SHAW-STEWART, Bt)

2d Margaret; *m* 27 Dec 1664 Patrick LINDSAY later CRAWFORD, 2nd s of 17th Earl of Crawford (*see* CRAWFORD and BALCARRES, E) and 1st Earl of Lindsay (*qv*), and *d* 1680, leaving:

1e JOHN CRAWFURD or LINDSAY-CRAWFORD , 1st VISCOUNT OF GARNOCK (*see* LINDSAY, E)

1a Margaret; *m* Sir Lachlan Maclean (*see* MACLEAN, Bt, of Dowart)

2a Elizabeth; *m* 1st James Crawford of Auchinames; *m* 2nd her cousin Alexander Cuninghame of Craigends

(2) Andrew; Prior Lesmahago

(1) Margaret; *m* John Wallace of Craigie

1 (cont.) The 5th EARL *m* 2nd *c* 22 Jan 1549/50 his cousin Janet, dau of Sir John Cunningham of Caprington (*see* below), and *d* 23 Dec 1574, leaving by her, with another s:

(2) Janet; *m* 1st 5th Earl of Argyll (*see* ARGYLL, D); *m* 2nd Humphrey Colquhoun of Luss (*see* COLQUHOUN, Bt)

2 Andrew, 1st of Corsehill, Stewarton, Ayrshire, which his f made over to him 1532; active Protestant convicted of heresy by the Lds Spiritual 1538 and his estate forfeited; later pardoned and his property restored, in confirmation of which he was granted a charter of the same lands to him, his w and heirs male; *m* Margaret Cunningham, of the CUNINGHAMEs of Polmaise, and *d* 1544, leaving an est son:

(1) Cuthbert, 2nd of Corsehill; *m* Mauld, dau of John Cuninghame of Aitket, and obtained on his f-in-law's resignation a new roy charter to him, his w and their heirs, and *d* 1575, leaving issue (who were for some time under the guardianship of their great-uncle Hugh Cuninghame of Watterson):

1a Patrick, 3rd of Corsehill; *k* 1588 in a CUNINGHAME *versus* MONTGOMERIE (*see* EGLINTON and WINTON, E) feud

2a ALEXANDER, for whom *see* further below

1a Jean

2a Margaret

3 Hugh, of Watterson; ancestor of the CUNINGHAMs of Carlung

4 Robert; ancestor of the CUNNINGHAMs of Mountgrenan

5 William, Bp Argyll

1 Elizabeth; *m* Sir John Cunningham of Caprington

PATRICK CUNINGHAME of Corsehill's bro,

ALEXANDER CUNINGHAME, 4th of Corsehill; *m* Marion, dau of William Porterfield, of Duchal, and *d* 1646, having had issue:

1 Alexander; *m* Mary, dau of John Houstoun of Houstoun and *d c* 1667, having had:

(1) Alexander; *m* Anne, dau of John Crawford of Kilbirnie, and *dvp c* 1646, leaving an er son:

1a ALEXANDER (Sir), **1st Bt**

2 Cuthbert

1 Elizabeth; *m* James Dunlop of Dunlop

2 Margaret; *m* James Stuart of Torrance

The gs,

Sir Alexander Cuninghame, 1st Bt (NS), so *cr* 26 Feb 1671/2, on whom and his affianced w his gf settled the family estate 1663, reserving to himself the life-rent; settlement confirmed by crown charter in favour of **Sir Alexander**, his w and their heirs; *b c* 1643; ruined by having guaranteed the credit of his cousin Sir David Cunigham, 4th Bt (*see* FAIRLIE-CUNINGHAME, Bt); *m c* 1665 Mary, sis of Sir Archibald Stewart, 1st Bt (*see* SHAW-STEWART, Bt), and *d* by March 1685, having had, with two daus (Mary, *m* Craufurd of Dalegle; Elizabeth):

Sir Alexander Cuninghame, 2nd Bt; *m* 1686 Margaret Boyle, sis of 1st Earl of Glasgow (*qv*), and *d* 1730, having had issue:

1 DAVID (Sir), **3rd Bt**

1 Jean; *m* William Newall of Barskeoch and Earlston, s of Adam Newall by his 2nd w Elizabeth (dau of James Chalmers of Waterside), and had, with an er s (John):

(1) James, JP, DL (Kirkcudbrightshire); *m* Agnes Montgomerie McCulloch (*d* 1825) and had, with other issue:

1a Mary; *bapt* 20 Jan 1770; *m* 10 Oct 1785 Rev Alexander Macgowan (*d* 1826), Minister of Dalry, and *d* 21 June 1867, leaving:

1b Thomas, MD; had:

1c Alexander Thorburn, MRCS, LRCP, LSA; *m* 7 May 1862 Elizabeth Yorstoun (*d* 17 Sept 1882), dau of William Stuart by Julia Moore, and had, with other issue:

1d William Stuart (Rev); *b* 1864; *educ* Neuwied, Prussia, Paris, Bristol GS and King's Coll Cambridge; Pncpl St Andrew's Grahamstown 1902–09, memb cncl U of Cape of Good Hope and Rhodes U Coll Cncl, LLD, Chev Legion Honour, chm Modern Language Assoc 1913–16 and 1920 and Educn Ctee French Instutute S Kensington, author: *The Religious Philosophy of Rudolf Eucken* (1914); *m* 1st 24 April 1889 Inez Ansell, dau of George Augustus Passingham by Catherine Amy Staples; *m 2nd* 1937 Emily Amelia, dau of John Coles, of Kensington Pk Gdns, and *d* 6 July 1939, having by his 1st w had, with other issue:

1e George Moore Stuart; *b* 29 Oct 1891; *m* 1925 Elizabeth Marjorie Ross and had:

1f *(Elizabeth) Rosemary; *b* 14 Sept 1929; *m* 1956 *Christopher (Kim) Buttery, MD, sometime USN, and has:

1g *Alexander Kevin; *b* 8 May 1958

2g *Nigel Christopher; *b* 20 July 1959

2f *(Kathleen) Shirley; *b* 27 Nov 1932; *m* 22 March 1958 Tom Moore (*d* 199–) and has issue

2e William Stuart; *b* 12 Feb 1898; *m* 1st 2 May 1918 Dorothy Gladys Cooke; *m* 2nd 25 April 1959 Audrey Joyce Darch and by his 1st w had:

1f Geraldine Dulcie; *b* 25 Feb 1919; *m* Ralph Brooking Thomas and had:

1g *Ian; *b* 19 June 1944

2g *Nigel William; *b* 29 Jan 1959

1g *Dena; *b* 9 March 1946

1e Beatrice Elizabeth Inez; *b* 31 July 1894; *m* 1st 1 March 1916 George Gordon Mosley (*d* 7 Aug 1918); *m* 2nd 22 Feb 1930 Thomas (Tommy) Percy Stewart (*d* 17 Jan 1952) and *d* 27 Aug 1988, leaving by her 1st husb:

1f George Gordon; *b* 15 Sept 1918; *educ* Charterhouse, King's Coll Cambridge, U of Zurich and The Sorbonne; with BBC 1947–65; *m* 23 March 1945 Christine Daisy Ord (*d* 7 April 1963), er dau of Lt-Col Roy Dowland (formerly Church), MC, ICS, and *d* by his own hand 26 Aug 1993, leaving:

1g *Charles Gordon [Charles Mosley Esq, Château de Mauprévoir, Mauprévoir 86460, France]; *b* 14 Sept 1948; *educ* Eton and King's Coll Cambridge; edtl staff *Encyclopaedia Britannica* 1971–73 and 1983–87 (London Ed 1985–87), IRD FCO 1974–77, ed *Debrett's Handbook* (1st edn 1981, subsequently retitled *Debrett's People of Today*), ed *Burke's Peerage and Baronetage* 1994–, author: *Lichfield in Retrospect* (1988), *American Presidential Families* (with Hugh Brogan, 1994), *Debrett's Guide to Entertaining* (1994) and *Debrett's Guide to Bereavement* (1995); *m* 17 March 1981 (*divorce* 1990) Alice Jean, er dau of John B Hyde, of Marshall, Texas

1g *Frances Christine [Ms Frances Mosley, 9 Lower St, Stroud, Glos GL5 2HT]; *b* 21 Jan 1951; *educ* Wycombe Abbey, Sussex U and Lady Spencer-Churchill Coll, Wheatley, Oxon; mathematics teacher ILEA, writer/ed ILEA Publishing Centre 1981–90, commissioning editor BEAM Project Islington 1990–, therapeutic counsellor 1996–, co-ed *Self and Society* (periodical) 1994–, author: *Count Me In* (1985), *Everybody Counts — Looking for Bias and Insensitivity in Mathematics Materials* (1985), *Help Your Child with Number Skills* (1990), *Cards on the Table* (1992) and *Calculators in Their Hands* (1995)

2d Alexandra Elizabeth Isabel; *m* Wilfred Becker and had issue

3d Julia Hamilton; *b* 9 May 1873; *m* 1st Dr Spence Reid and had issue; *m* 2nd Sir (Fenwick) Shadforth Watts (*d* 15 March 1926), chm Shipping Fedn and pres Chamber Shipping UK; by her 1st husb she had:

1e Leslie; *ka* WW I

2e Pat(rick); *educ* Harrow; had issue several daus

3e (Violet) Mary (Mollie); *m* 9 Dec 1919 Geoffrey Holland Gilbey (*see* GILBEY, Bt) and had issue

The 2nd Bt's only s,

Sir David Cuninghame, 3rd Bt; *m* Penelope, dau of Alexander Montgomery of Assloss, Ayrshire, and niece and heiress of Sir Walter Montgomery, Bt, of Kirktonholm (descended from the Montgomerys of Skelmorlie), and *d* 4 July 1770, having had issue:

1 Alexander CUNINGHAME later MONTGOMERY-CUNINGHAME (added under terms of entail on inheriting the Kirktonholm estate); Army Capt, served wars in Flanders; *m* Elizabeth, est dau and eventual heiress of David Montgomery of Lainshaw, Ayrshire (descendant of Sir Neil Montgomerie of Lainshaw and rep of the LYLEs, Lords Lyle), and *dvp* Jan 1770, leaving issue:

(1) **Sir Walter Montgomery-Cuninghame, 4th Bt**; claimed Earldom of Glencairn 1797; *d* unm March 1814

(2) **Sir David Montgomery-Cuninghame, 5th Bt**; Lt N Br Dragoons; *d* unm Nov 1814

(3) Eglinton; *d* young

(4) Alexander; Army offr American War; *d* unm

(5) JAMES (Sir), **6th Bt**

(6) Henry Drumlanrig; Lt RN aboard the *Alfred* Battle (Br victory over French) of the Saints 12 April 1782; *d* unm

(1) Anne; *d* young

(2) Elizabeth; *d* young

2 David; *d* Jamaica, and left issue

3 Walter

1 Margaret; *m* — Craig

The 5th Bt's only surv bro,

Sir James Montgomery-Cuninghame, 6th Bt; *m* 1802 Janet, 2nd dau of Thomas Cuming, Edinburgh banker and rep of the CUMINGs of Earnside, Nairnshire, and *d* March 1837, having had issue:

1 **Sir Alexander David Montgomery-Cuninghame, 7th Bt**; *d* 8 June 1846

2 THOMAS (Sir), **8th Bt**

3 James; *d* unm 1835

4 George; RN

5 Henry; 29th Regt; *d* 26 May 1883

1 Jessie Jean; *m* 1830 Sir James Boswell, 2nd and last Bt, of Auchinleck (*d* 4 Nov 1857), and *dspm*, leaving issue

2 Grace Matilda; *d* unm 11 Oct 1842

The 7th Bt's yr bro,

Sir Thomas Montgomery-Cuninghame, 8th Bt; Lt-Col Roy Ayrshire Rifles 1850–58; *m* 1832 Charlotte Niven (*d* 25 June 1902), only child and heir of Hugh Hutcheson, of Southfield, Renfrewshire, and *d* 30 Aug 1870, having had issue:

1 WILLIAM JAMES (Sir), **9th Bt**

2 Arthur Hugh; RN; *d* May 1850

3 Walter; *d* 1856

1 Jessie Augusta; *m* 22 May 1866 Hon Augustus Anthony Frederick Irby (*d* 5 April 1870), 3rd son of 3rd Baron Boston (*qv*), and *d* 13 July 1908, leaving issue

2 Eleanor

3 Edith Jane; *d* 1855

The 8th Bt's only surv s,

Sir William James Montgomery-Cuninghame, 9th Bt, VC, DL; *b* 20 May 1834; *educ* Harrow; Maj 4th Bn Roy Scots Fus, served Crimea; MP Ayr Burghs 1874–80; *m* 22 April 1869 Elizabeth (*d* 12 Feb 1936), yst dau of Edward Bourchier Hartopp, JP, DL, of Dalby Hall, Leics, and *d* 11 Nov 1897, having had issue:

1 THOMAS ANDREW ALEXANDER MONTGOMERY (Sir), **10th Bt**

2 Edward William Montgomery, DSO (1919); *b* 30 May 1878; Lt-Col RA; *m* 16 Nov 1909 Mary (*d* 13 Dec 1947), yst dau of James Stewart, of Blackhouse, Ayrshire, and *d* 6 April 1935, leaving issue:

(1) *Olive Bridget; *b* 12 Sept 1910; *m* 1st 5 June 1934 (*divorce* 1939) Alexander James Houison-Craufurd, Scots Gds, yr son of Brig-Gen John Archibald Houison-Crauford of Craufurdland, CMG, CBE; *m* 2nd John Sweeney

1 Edith Honoria; *b* 26 April 1870; *m* 7 Sept 1901 Rt Hon Sir John Anthony Cecil Tilley, PC, GCMG, GCVO, CB (*d* 5 April 1952), son of Sir John Tilley, KCB, and *d* 8 March 1949, leaving issue

2 Lilian Margaret; *b* and *d* 1871

3 Marjory Eva Charlotte; *b* 25 April 1873; *d* unm 1 Sept 1952

4 Elizabeth; *b* and *d* 1874

5 Violet Jessie; *b* 11 March 1876; *d* unm 5 June 1947

6 Letitia Margaret; *b* 26 June *d* 24 Dec 1880

7 Bridget Anne; *b* 20 Sept 1886; *m* 27 Jan 1914 Capt Henry Gilbert Smith-Rewse, son of Canon Smith-Rewse, of St Margaret's Rectory, South Elmham, Suffolk, and *d* 22 Jan 1960, leaving issue

The 9th Bt's s,

Sir Thomas Andrew Alexander Montgomery-Cuninghame, 10th Bt, DSO (1900); *b* 30 March 1877; *educ* Eton and RMC Sandhurst; Col Rifle Bde Boer War 1899–1901 (wounded, despatches twice), DAQMG 5th Div Irish Cmd 1909–12, Mil Attaché Vienna and Cetinje 1912–14, Athens 1915–16, WW I Gen Staff (despatches twice), GSO(1) 1916–17, Br Rep American Staff Coll France 1918, Br Mil Rep Austria 1919–20, Mil Attaché Vienna 1920–23, American DSM, Maria Theresa Medal Austria, Kt Grand Cross Order of George I Greece, Cdr Legion of Honour, Cdr Greek Order of The Redeemer, Czecho-Slovakian Croix de Guerre; *m* 1st 1 Nov 1904 (*divorce* 1925) Alice Frances Denison (*d* 9 June 1966), er dau of Sir George William des Voeux, GCMG (*see* 1940 edn DES VOEUX, Bt), and had issue:

1 Alexander William Henry James, DSO; *b* 28 Oct 1905; Lt-Col Roy Scots Fus WW II; *m* 23 Oct 1934 *Barbara Susanne, MBE (1964), granted rank of bt's widow 15 Nov 1948, 2nd dau of Col Hugh Annesley Gray-Cheape, DSO, JP, of Carse Gray, Forfar, and was *ka* July 1944

1 Pamela Richenda Cubitt; *b* 10 March 1910; *m* 1st 20 June 1932 (*divorce* 1941) Thomas Abdy Combe, late Gren Gds, er son of John Abdy Combe, and had issue; *m* 2nd 20 June 1942 Desmond FitzGerald Underwood (*d* 1 Nov 1968), son of Charles Frederick Weston Underwood, of Brigg, Lincs, and had further issue

Sir Thomas *m* 2nd 24 Nov 1925 Nancy Macaulay (*m* 2nd 1946 Johan Frederick Christian Killander, son of Lennart Killander, of Stockholm), dau of W Stewart Foggo, of Aberdeen, and Coldstream, BC, and *d* 5 Jan 1945, having by her had issue:

2 **Sir (William) Andrew Malcolm Martin Oliphant Montgomery Cuninghame, 11th Bt**; *b* 14 July 1929; *educ* Fettes and Worcester Coll Oxford (Pres Union 1953); Lt Rifle Bde; Dip Serv; *m* 7 Dec 1956 *Sara Carolyn [Lady Fergusson, c/o Coutts & Co, 440 Strand, London WC2R 0QS] (who *m* 2nd 19 Dec 1959 Sir Ewen Alastair John Fergusson, GCMG, GCVO, er son of Sir Ewen MacGregor Field Fergusson, of Singapore), only dau of Brig-Gen Lord Esmé Charles Gordon-Lennox, KCVO, CMG, DSO, JP, DL (*see* RICHMOND and GORDON, D), and *dsp* 18 Feb 1959

3 Sir JOHN CHRISTOPHER FOGGO MONTGOMERY CUNINGHAME, **12th and present Bt**

CUNLIFFE, Baron

Arms: Per chevron or and sa. three conies courant, counter-changed.
Crest: Upon a rock ppr. a greyhound sejant sa., collared or.
Supporters: On either side a figure habited as a gate porter of the Bank of England, supporting in the exterior hand his staff of office.
Motto: *Fideliter* ('Faithfully').
Creation: B. (UK) 14 Dec 1914.

THE 3RD BARON CUNLIFFE, of Headley, Surrey (Roger Cunliffe) [The Rt Hon The Lord Cunliffe, The Broadhurst, Brandeston, Woodbridge, Suffolk IP13 7AG]; *b* 12 Jan 1932; *s* f 1963; *educ* Eton, Trin Coll Cambridge (BA 1954, MA 1958), AA Sch of Architecture (AA Dipl), and OU; RIBA, MIMgt, dir Architectural Assoc 1969, consulting architect in own practice 1977–, dir Exhibition Consultants Ltd 1981–, govr: Goldsmith's Coll 1972–78 and Lancing College 1967–85, bd memb Coll of Estate Mgt 1992–; *m* 27 April 1957 *Clemency Ann, er dau of Maj Geoffrey Benyon Hoare, of Clover Ho, Aldeburgh, Suffolk, and has issue:

1 +HENRY; *b* 9 March 1962; *educ* Eton; Freeman Goldsmiths' Co

2 +Luke; *b* 29 June 1965; *educ* Eton and Bransons Coll; Freeman Goldsmiths' Co; *m* 1992 *Penelope A, dau of Cdr P S Wilson, RN, of Chipstead, Surrey

1 *Rachel Henrietta; *b* 14 Feb 1960; *educ* N London Collegiate Sch, Felsted Sch, Cambridge U (BA), Manchester U, Minnesota U (MEd), and Arizona U; Freeman Goldsmiths' Co; *m* 1987 *Roger David Hardesty, son of R D Hardesty, of Belle Mead, NJ, USA, and has:

(1) *Rolf Daniel; *b* 30 Nov 1994

Lineage: JAMES CUNLIFFE, of Blackburn, Lancs, and later 1 Upper Hyde Park St, W, at Great Harwood, Lancs; *b* 4 Jan 1798; *m* 14 May 1823 Mary (*d* 14 May 1873), dau of John Ostle, of Newcastle-on-Tyne, and *d* 4 Feb 1854, having had an est s:

ROGER CUNCLIFFE, of Tyrrells Wood, Leatherhead, Surrey; *b* 4 April 1824; *m* 1 Sept 1852 Ann (*d* 24 May 1912), est dau of John Edge, of Rusholme, Lancs, and *d* 6 Oct 1895, leaving, with three yr s and two daus:

WALTER CUNLIFFE, **1st Baron Cunliffe**, of Headley, Surrey (UK), so *cr* 14 Dec 1914, GBE (1917); *b* 4 Dec 1855; *educ* Harrow and Trin Coll Cambridge (MA 1882); Lt City London, High Sheriff 1913, Dir Bank of England 1895 (Dep Govr 1911–13, Govr 1913–18), Grand Cross Order Crown of Italy, Orders of Redeemer of Greece and St Anne of Russia 1st Cl, Grand Cordon of the Order of the Rising Sun of Japan, Cdr of the Legion of Honour and of Leopold of Belgium, Hon LLD Columbia U, USA; *m* 1st 10th June 1890 Mary Agnes (*dsp* 39 Nov 1893), yst dau of Robert Henderson, of Randalls Park, Leatherhead, Surrey; *m* 2nd 8 July 1896 Edith Cunningham (*d* 22 Nov 1965 aged 98), dau of Col Robert Tod Boothby, of St Andrews, Fife (*see* 1970 edn BOOTHBY, B), and by her had issue:

1 ROLF, **2nd Baron**

2 Geoffrey, Memb I&E Cncl, Bd of Trade from 1941; *b* 26 Aug 1903; *educ* Eton and Trin Coll Cambridge; *m* 1st 16 Aug 1922 Patrick Sidney (*d* Oct 1940), only dau of Robert Benjamin Frend, of Ardsallagh, Co Tipperary, and had issue:

(1) Robert George; *b* 20 June 1923; F/Lt RAFVR, served WW II; *ka* during air operations over Germany 14 Feb 1945

(2) Peter; *b* 29 May 1925; *educ* Eton; *m* 27 April 1955 *Barbara Marion [Mrs Peter Cunliffe, 5 Grouville Park, Jersey, CI], dau of H F Phillips, of Sous-la-Hogue, Jersey, and *d* 1987, leaving issue:

1a +Robert; *b* 4 March 1958

2a +Christopher; *b* 18 Aug 1960

3a +Oliver; *b* 15 March 1966

2 (cont.) Geoffrey Cunliffe *m* 2nd Sept 1941 (*divorce* 1947) Gavrelle (*d* 1 May 1959), dau of William Arthur Thomas, and widow of Christopher Hobhouse, barrister; *m* 3rd 1947 Barbara Waring (*d* 1990), formerly w of Laurence A Evans, and dau of Dr J A Gibb, of Maidstone, and *d* 1982, having by 2nd w had issue:

(3) +Adam [Adam Cunliffe Esq, 17 Dorset Rd, Leeds 8, W Yorks]; *b* 2 Feb 1946; *educ* Wellington

(1) *Carol [Mrs Jay Dilley, 7 Orchard St, Mendham, NJ 07945, USA]; *b* 8 March 1944; *m* 1st 1966 Joseph Francis Logan; *m* 2nd 1992 *Jay K Dilley

3 Maurice; *b* 30 Aug 1905; *d* 27 Feb 1909

1 Mary Betty; *m* 5 Oct 1921 Lt-Col Otho Stuart Irwin Northcote, only surv son of W H Northcote, of 6, Earls Court Square, and Bridford, Devon, and has issue. He *d* 12 Jan 1966

2 Ann Madeline; *m* 27 April 1922 Brig John Wedderburn-Maxwell, DSO, MC, RA, of Dalbeattie, Kirkcudbrightshire, er son of Maj James Andrew Colvile Wedderburn-Maxwell, and has issue (*see* OGILVY-WEDDERBURN, Bt)

3 Ethel Peggy; *m* 1st 5 Dec 1932 Brig Bernard Lorenzo de Robeck, MC, RA, yr son of Baron de Robeck, of Gowran Grange, Naas, Co Kildare, and had issue. He *d* 3 June 1957. She *m* 2nd 1964 Lt-Col Sir (Archibald) Richard Southby, 2nd Bt, OBE (*qv*), and *d* 3 Aug 1978

The 1st BARON *d* 6 Jan 1920; his est son,

ROLF CUNLIFFE, **2nd Baron Cunliffe**, W/Cdr RAFVR; *b* 13 May 1899; *educ* Eton and Trin Coll Cambridge (BA 1921, MA 1927), served WW I 1917–19 with RNAS and RAF(despatches), and WW II; chm Guy's Hosp 1947; *m* 1st 5 Nov 1925 (*divorce* 1952) Joan Catherine (*d* 21 June 1980), 2nd dau of Cecil Lubbock, of 17 Cranley Gdns, SW (*see* AVEBURY, B); *m* 2nd 24 Dec 1952 Kathleen Elsie (*d* 1990), widow of Capt Philip Robinson, RAMC, and dau of Ernest Brownfield Pope, of Wargrave, Berks, and *d* 24 Nov 1963, having by his 1st w had issue:

1 ROGER CUNLIFFE, **3rd and present Baron Cunliffe**

2 +Merlin [The Hon Merlin Cunliffe, Wills Rd, Dixon's Creek, Vic 3775, Australia]; *b* 29 April 1935; *educ* Eton; *m* 1st 23 April 1960 (*divorce* 19–) Deborah Rutherford, yst dau of Harold Thornton Grimwade, MBE, of Urara, Lismore, Victoria, Australia; *m* 2nd 11 March 1978 *Mrs Amanda June Foster, dau of Sam Rogers, and by 1st w has had issue:

(1) Tamsin Elizabeth; *b* 8 Dec 1963; *d* 1982

(2) *Sophia Catherine; *b* 17 May 1966

1 *Shirley Cynthia [The Hon Mrs Wilson, Ashbrook, Aston Tirrold, Didcot, Oxon OX11 9DL]; *b* 20 Sept 1926; *m* 21 Nov 1959 *Alan Desmond Wilson, son of James Morton Wilson, of 12, Valleyside Rd, Hastings, Sussex, and has issue:

(1) *Matthew Crispin; *b* 23 Jan 1961

(2) *Richenda Catherine; *b* 31 May 1963

2 *Corinna [The Hon Mrs Corinna Wildman, The Applehouse, RR1 Box 979, Dorset, VT 05251, USA]; *b* 18 April 1929; *m* 18 May 1957 (*divorce* 1965) Frederick Starr Wildman, son of Col Frederick Wildman, of 215 E 69th St, New York City, and Stonebrook, Colebrook, Conn, and has issue:

(1) *Tarik Charles; *b* 26 Nov 1959; *m* 1993 *Susan O'Reilly

CUNLIFFE, Bt

Arms: Sa. three conies courant arg. **Crest:** A greyhound sejant arg., collared sa. **Motto:** *Fideliter* ('Faithfully'). **Creation:** Bt. (GB) 26 March 1759.

SIR DAVID ELLIS CUNLIFFE, 9TH BT, of Liverpool [Sir David Cunliffe Bt, Sunnyside, Burnthouse Lane, Needham, Harleston, Norfolk IP20 9LN]; *b* 29 Oct 1957; *s f* 1969; *educ* St Albans GS; business development manager; *m* 1983 *Linda Carol, dau of John Sidney Batchelor, of 12 Marquis Lane, Harpenden, Herts, and has:

1 *Emma Mary; *b* 1986

2 *Katherine Alice; *b* 1990

3 *Bridget Carol; *b* 1991

Lineage: ROBERT CUNLIFFE, of Hollins, Lancs, 1560; ancestor of:

JOHN CUNLIFFE, of Hollins; Parliamentarian Civil War but opposed OLIVER CROMWELL; *m* 1st —, dau of — Hartley, of Winewell; *m* 2nd Mary, dau of Ralph Cheatham, of Castleton, and had (presumably by his 1st w), with an est s (Nicholas; *m* the yr dau and coheir of — Foster, of Airton, and was ancestor of the CUNLIFFEs of Wycollar):

ELLIS; Rector Newmarket and Etwall; *m* —, er dau and coheir of — Foster, of Airton, and had:

FOSTER; Liverpool merchant and MP; *m* Margaret, dau of Robert Carter, of Lancs, and had, with a yr s and two daus:

1 **Sir Ellis Cunliffe, 1st Bt** (GB), so *cr* 26 March 1759, with remainder, in default of his own male issue, to his bro Robert; ktd, MP Liverpool; *b* 12 April 1717; *m* 19 Dec 1760 Mary (*d* 8 Oct 1814), dau of Henry Bennet, of Moston, Cheshire, and *d* 16 Oct 1767, having had two daus

2 **Sir Robert Cunliffe, 2nd Bt**; *b* 17 May 1719; *m* 1752 Mary (*d* 19 Feb 1791), dau of Ichabod Wright, of Nottingham, banker, and had issue:

(1) FOSTER (Sir), **3rd Bt**

(1) Elizabeth; *m* April 1782 Clement Stafford Courtney

(2) Mary; *m* 2 May 1780 Sir Richard Brooke, 5th Bt, of Norton Priory (*qv*)

(3) Margaret; *m* Thomas Brooke, of Minshull, and *d* a widow in 1826

Sir ROBERT *d* 1778; his only son,

Sir Foster Cunliffe, 3rd Bt; *b* 8 Feb 1755; *m* 1 Oct 1781 Harriet (*d* 9 Sept 1830), dau of Sir David Kinloch, 5th Bt, of Gilmerton (*qv*), and had, with other issue:

1 Foster CUNLIFFE-OFFLEY of Madeley, Staffs; *b* 17 Aug 1782, assumed the name and arms of OFFLEY 1829; *m* 21 April 1809 Elizabeth Emma (*d* 15 Feb 1850), only dau of 1st Baron Crewe, and *dsp* 19 April 1832

2 ROBERT HENRY (Sir), **4th Bt**

3 Ellis Watkin; *b* 5 Sept 1787; *m* 13 June 1822 Caroline (*d* 1856), dau of John Kingston, and 20 Dec 1866, having had issue:

(1) Ellis Brooke, of Petton Park, Salop, late Capt 6th Dragoons; *b* 6 July 1832; *m* 17 July 1867 Emma Florence (*d* 13 May 1925), dau and heiress of Rev John Sparling, of Petton Park, and *d* 4 March 1915, leaving issue:

1a Ellis Sparling, of Petton Park, Lt-Col 4th Bn Shropshire LI, JP Salop; *b* 13 May 1868; *d* 12 June 1925

2a John Brooke, Maj Northamptonshire Yeo, Lt Shropshire Yeo Cav, served in S African War 1900 (medal with two clasps), and WW I; *b* 9 Oct 1869; *d* of illness contracted on active service 20 April 1917

3a William Noel, Dist Offr, Remount Depot, Capt 3rd Bn Shropshire LI; *b* 25 Dec 1877; *m* 12 July 1910 Nellie Phyllis (*d* 1976), er dau of Sir John Aird, 2nd Bt (*qv*), and *d* 30 July 1933, having had issue:

1b *Gundred [Mrs Mervyn Cunliffe-Fraser, 3 West Halkin St, London SW1X 8JJ]; *b* 13 Feb 1913; *m* 24 July 1937 *Mervyn Cunliffe-Fraser, yst son of Herbert Charles Fraser, and has:

1c *Valerie [Mrs Mark Thomasin-Foster, Moulsham Hall, Gt Leighs, Chelmsford, Essex CM3 1PZ]; *b* 24 July 1942; *m* 27 June 1972 *Mark Treanor Thomasin-Foster, and has issue:

1d *Nicholai Charles; *b* 1975

2d *Christopher William; *b* 1976

3d *David James; *b* 1979

2b Philae; *b* 22 Jan 1918; *d* 26 July 1919

4a Legendre Watkin; *b* 1878; *d* unm 24 Oct 1906

1a Catherine Violet; *m* 1st 1890 John Frederick Grant Hodgson-Roberts, and had issue; *m* 2nd 1905 Percival Ayton Onley Whitaker, only son of Herbert Whitaker, of Stone House, Southwood, and *d* Nov 1954, leaving further issue

2a Emma Veronica; *m* 1st 23 July 1890 Lt-Col Henry Jessop Stone, JP, of Bedfords, Havering-atte-Bower, Essex, and Bedfords Lodge, Windsor, and had issue. He *d* 26 Dec 1931. She *m* 2nd 17 Aug 1932 Maj Henry Siward Balliol Surtees, DL, JP, of Redworth Hall, Darlington, and *d* 13 Aug 1965, aged 93. He *d* 9 Feb 1955

3a Florence Vanda; *m* 1st 2 April 1891 Robert D'Oyly Freeman Thomas, only son of Col Henry John Thomas, RA (*see* 1970 edn WILLINGDON, M), and had issue. He *d* 9 June 1911; *m* 2nd 4 Feb 1919 J Hubert Fleming, and *d* 18 Sept 1936

4a Vebena; *m* 1st 1893 (*divorce* 1901) Capt Masterman Stanley Williams, RHA, and had issue; *m* 2nd 5 Nov 1902 Lt-Col Edwin James Fell, late 8th Hus, and *d* 1955. He *d* 1948

5a Caroline Muriel Valencia; *m* 16 Oct 1894 Loftus de Launay Mollerus-le-Champion, and *d* 1896, leaving issue

6a Mabel Virginia; *m* 18 Feb 1901 Maj Arthur Toward Watson, KRRC, of Bishopthorpe Garth, York, and Burnopfield, Durham, only surv son of Henry William Watson, of Burnopfield, Co Durham, and *d* 29 Jan 1974, leaving issue. He *d I*5 Aug 1917 of wounds received in action the same day*

(2) Arthur; *b* 20 Feb 1826; *d* unm 29 May 1876

(1) Caroline; *m* 23 Dec 1850 W F Foster, and had issue

(2) Gertrude; *m* 4 June 1868 Edmund Swettenham, and *d* 24 June 1876, leaving issue

4 Brooke, HEICS, of Erbistock Hall, Denbigh; *b* 23 July 1790; *m* 1st 1814 Mary (*d* 11 Sept 1825), dau of John Pirrie, and had issue:

(1) Brooke; *b* 6 Sept 1815; *m* 12 May 1847 Diana Wentworth (*d* 1897), dau of Stair Hathorn Stewart, of Physgill and Glasserton, Wigtownshire, and *d* 1897, leaving issue:

1a Brooke Stewart, Ch Constable of Wigtownshire, formerly Lt 93rd Highrs; *b* 12 June 1848; *m* 1883 Grace Amey (*d* 1 May 1914), dau of Thomas Gordon, and *d* 23 April 1936, leaving issue:

1b Brooke Foster Gordon, Capt Scottish Horse Yeo and RAF, served WW I; *b* 1889; *m* 1 March 1921 Catherine Hay (*d* 24 Dec 1962), yr dau of Col H R Peake, and *d* 1981, leaving issue:

1c +Brooke Malcolm, Supt Rhodesian Police; *b* 19 July 1928

1c *Diana Hay, TD [Miss Diana Cunliffe TD, 50 Corstorphine Hill Gdns, Edinburgh]; *b* 1923

1b Mary Grace Hamilton; *d* unm 7 Aug 1967

2b Gladys Egerton; *m* 23 Nov 1915 Henry Gerard Eley, MBE, T/Maj RE, er son of Capt Henry Eley, late 8th Regt

1a Helen Edith; *d* unm 7 April 1926

2a Gwenydd; *d* unm 23 Jan 1927

3a Lettice Frederica; *d* 19 Oct 1937

(2) Foster; *b* 6 April 1825; *d* unm 10 Nov 1845

(1) Louisa; *m* 11 March 1840 Rev W H Egerton, and *d* June 1902, leaving issue (*see* GREY EGERTON, Bt)

(2) Mary; *m* 9 April 1849 Maj-Gen Frederic Conyers Cotton, CSI (*see* COMBERMERE, V), and *dsp* 1886

4 (cont.) Brooke Cunliffe *m* 2nd 1827 Elizabeth (*d* 4 Aug 1833), dau of John Rayson, and by her had issue, with two daus (*d* unm):

(3) George Gordon, Maj-Gen; *b* 24 Sept 1829; *m* 22 May 1858 Pauline, dau of Capt J Lumsdaine, and *d* 29 Jan 1900, leaving issue:

1a Frederick Hugh Gordon, CB (1916), CMG (1916), Col and Hon Brig-Gen late Seaforth Highrs, R Inniskilling Fus, and Middx Regt, Cmdt Nigeria Regt 1914–17, Bde Cdr attached HQ Unit 1917–19, served Hazara Exped 1891 (medal with clasp), Chitral 1895 (medal with clasp), Boer War 1902 (despatches, medal with three clasps), WW I (despatches four times), Cdr of Legion of Honour, Offr Order of St Maurice and St Lazarus of Italy; *b* 6 Sept 1861; *m* 1895 Ella Sophie (*d* 1950), dau of David Gaussen, of Marton Hall, Salop, and *d* 13 June 1955, leaving issue:

1b Cecile Gertrude, MBE (1959)

1a Gertrude Mary Blanche; *m* 8 Dec 1881 Lewis Gordon Mortimer. He *d* 1928

2a Mary Dora; *d* unm 20 Oct 1956

3a Ethel Brooke; *d* unm 28 March 1954

4a Louise Egerton; *m* 1895 John William Rogerson, and *d* his widow, 23 March 1936, leaving issue

(4) Robert Henry, Maj-Gen Madras Army; *b* 6 July 1832; *d* unm 18 Oct 1903

4 (cont.) Brooke Cunliffe *m* 3rd 12 Sept 1850 Frances (*d* 16 Jan 1865), dau of Rev James R Lyon, and *d* 11 Dec 1857, having by her had further issue:

(5) Foster Lionel, Brev Col late RHA, cmdg Art TF 1908–11, served in Afghan War 1878–79 (medal), and Tirah Expdn 1897 (medal with clasp); *b* 20 April 1854; *m* 1st 10 April 1894 Alice Mary (*d* 30 Dec 1907), dau of Edward Lyon, of Windlesham Hall, Bagshot; *m* 2nd 7 Aug 1912 Rose Nannette (*d* 13 Nov 1950), widow of J Dowling, and dau of G J Fenwick, and *d* 15 April 1927, having by 1st *w* had issue:

1a Robert Lionel Brooke, CBE (1944), Capt RN, served WW II (despatches), Admlty Rep and Naval Assist to High Commnr for UK in Canada 1946–48, Chev Order of Leopold of Belgium; *b* 15 March 1895; *m* 1st 14 Sept 1926 Barbara Eleanor (*d* 1970), dau of Col Harry Cooper, of Pakenham Lodge, Pakenham, Suffolk; *m* 2nd 19 April 1971 Christine Cooper (*d* 1989), dau of Rev Canon Sydney Cooper, and *d* 1990, having by 1st *w* had issue:

1b *Bridget Eleanor Ailsie [Mrs Hugh Sackville-West, Knole, Sevenoaks, Kent TN15 0RP]; *b* 2 Oct 1927; *m* 29 June 1957 *Hugh Rosslyn Inigo Sackville-West, MC, yr son of Hon Bertrand George Sackville-West, of Knole, Sevenoaks, Kent (*see* SACKVILLE, B), and has issue

2b *Nicolette Anne [Mrs Robert Cotton, The Cherry Orchard, Badgemore, Henley on Thames, Oxon RG9 4NR]; *b* 2 Dec 1929; *m* 30 Oct 1954 *Robert Charles Cotton, 2nd son of Col Vere Egerton Cotton, CBE, TD, JP, of Langdale, Grassendale Park, Liverpool (*see* COMBERMERE, V), and has issue

3b *Barbara Clare [Barbara Lady Beevor, The Garden House, Pakenham, Bury St Edmunds, Suffolk]; *b* 7 May 1936 (*divorce* 1965) Sir Thomas Agnew Beevor, 7th Bt (*qv*), and has issue

1a Frances Alice Clare; *b* 1 July 1900

(3) Frances Brooke; *m* 29 April 1876 Col George Le Mesurier Gretton, and had issue

Sir FOSTER *d* 15 June 1834; his est serv son,

Sir Robert Henry Cunliffe, 4th Bt, CB, Gen Bengal Army; ktd 1829; *b* 22 April 1785; *m* 1st 15 Dec 1805 Louisa (*d* 4 May 1822), widow of Maj Arthur Forest, and had, with other issue:

1 Robert Ellis, Indian Service; *b* 27 March 1808; *m* 2 May 1837 Charlotte (*d* 1856), est dau of Ilted Howel, and *d* 31 March 1855, leaving, with other issue:

(1) **Sir Robert Alfred Cunliffe, 5th Bt**, of Acton Park, Wrexham, Denbighs, DL, JP, CC Denbighs, High Sheriff 1868, MP Flint 1872–74, Denbigh Boroughs 1880–85, formerly Capt Scots Gds, Hon Col 3rd Bn RWF; *b* 17 Jan 1839; *m* 1st 5 Aug 1869 Eleanor Sophia Egerton (*d* 13 March 1898), dau of Col Egerton Leigh, MP, of West Hall, High Leigh, and Jodrell Hall, Cheshire; *m* 2nd 5 Jan 1901 Hon Cecilie Victoria Sackville-West, CBE (*d* 10 March 1955), yr dau of Lt-Col Hon William Edward Sackville-West, and sis of 3rd Baron Sackville (*qv*), and *d* 18 June 1905, having by his 1st *w* had issue:

1a **Sir Foster Hugh Egerton Cunliffe, 6th Bt**; *educ* New Coll Oxford (MA); Fell of All Souls and sometime Lecturer in Military History at Oxford, T/Maj 12th Bn Rifle Bde; *b* 17 Aug 1875; *d* unm, *ka* 13 July 1916

2a **Sir Robert Neville Henry Cunliffe, 7th Bt**; *educ* Rugby and Hertford Coll Oxford; T/Lt Gen List; *b* 8 Feb 1884; *d* unm 1 May 1949

1a Violet Eleanor; *b* 4 July 1876; *d* 15 Feb 1878

2a Mary Evelyn; *b* 21 Nov 1878; *d* unm 22 Sept 1961

3a Kythe; *b* 25 Aug 1881; *d* unm 27 Sept 1928

(2) Walter Howell, Lt-Col late Oxfordshire LI, JP Berks; *b* 8 Sept 1850; *m* 1st 14 Sept 1875 Gertrude (*d* 12 Oct 1908), dau of William Fry Foster, *m* 2nd 30 Sept 1914 Annie Catherine (*d* 12 March 1923), dau of George Meakin, of Collingworth Hall, Burton-on-Trent, and *d* 6 Sept 1932, having by his 1st *w* had issue:

1a Gwynedd Sybilla; *m* 1902 Waller Gason FitzGerald, of Grenfell, Saskatchewan, Canada, and *d* July 1963, having had issue. He *d* 12 Aug 1934

2 George; *d* in India, 18 Oct 1834

3 David, BCS; *b* 14 Feb 1815; *m* 24 Oct 1837 Fanny Priscilla, dau of Samuel Davies, MD, and *d* 19 Sept 1873, leaving issue:

(1) David Arthur; *b* 1850; *d* unm March 1907

(2) Foster Kinlock, late DPW India; *b* 1851; *m* 1st 2 Nov 1881 Henrietta (*d* 3 March 1889), dau of J H Worthington, of Oxton, Cheshire; *m* 2nd 1890 Adele (*d* 24 Feb 1953), 2nd surv dau of Capt Horatio Gillmore, late 23rd RWF, and *d* 2 Oct 1912, having by 1st *w* had issue:

1a David Foster, Lt IA; *b* 5 May 1884; *d* unm 2 July 1903

1a Helen Brooke; *b* 21 Nov 1882; *m* 5 Sept 1906 Lt-Col Edmund Walter, CIE, late IA, son of Maj Frederic Edward Walter, MVO, and *d* 24 Oct 1966, leaving issue. He *d* 12 April 1951

2a Norah Dorothy; *b* 22 Nov 1885; *m* 17 April 1906 Lt-Col Norman Dunbar Walker, OBE, late RAMC, son of A Dunbar Walker, of Hampstead, and *d* 19 Sept 1960, leaving issue. He *d* 23 May 1953

3a Phylis Rowena; *b* 12 Dec 1886; *m* 16 July 1919 Thomas Steel Downie, OBE (*d* 14 Nov 1931), and had:

1b James Cunliffe; *b* 16 July 1920; *ka* 15 April 1944

1b *Cynthia Rowena; *b* 29 Nov 1922; *m* 29 Nov 1947 Maj Alastair William Mitchell Gauld, Argyll and Sutherland Highrs, and has issue:

1c *Andrew James Mitchell; *b* 1 Oct 1955

1c *Fiona Rowena; *b* 22 June 1949

4a Cecily Agnes; *b* 10 Aug 1888; *m* 1909 Lt-Col Cecil Julius Hamilton Lyster, MC, late IA, and *d* 31 Dec 1957, leaving issue. He *d* 30 Dec 1961

(3) Alfred Edward; *b* 5 July 1853; *m* 28 April 1886 Agnes (*d* 20 Jan 1955), dau of Dr J M Comley, of Calcutta, and *d* 5 June 1920, leaving issue:

1a Robert Ellis, temp 2nd Lt Roy Berks Regt; *b* 17 Oct 1893; *ka* 9 May 1915

2a CYRIL HENLEY (Sir), **8th Bt**

1a Ruth Agnes; *b* 20 Oct 1887; *d* 11 March 1889

2a Muriel Hyde; *b* 1 July 1890; *m* 22 April 1908 Percival Leo Falkner, FRGS, Indian Police, and *d* 22 Sept 1966, leaving issue. He *d* 14 Sept 1931

(4) Ernest William, Col IA; *b* 24 Feb 1857; *m* 1st 1885 Mary Adeline (*d* 1899), dau of Maj-Gen David Limond, CB, and had issue:

1a David Robert; *b* 1887; *m* Etta Fullerton (*d* 1959), and *dsp* June 1930

1a Ethel Laura; *b* 1886; *m* 1917 Cdr William Vesey Hamilton Harris, MVO, DSC, RN, and *d* leaving issue. He *d* 1949

2a Thelma Clemence; *b* 1890; *m* 1920 Lt-Col Colin Walter Johnstone Smith, DSO, son of Johnstone Smith, and *d* 4 Jan 1953, leaving issue

(4) (cont.) Col Ernest Cunliffe *m* 2nd 1900 Isabella Fergusson (*d* 25 Sept 1940), dau of John Bradford, and *d* 12 Nov 1912, having by her had issue:

2a William Lockhart, formerly chm of Bd, Int Standard Brands, Inc, of NY, USA, served WW I 1918, with Gren Gds; *b* 5 Feb 1902; *educ* Wellington; *m* 21 Oct 1923 Maude Ethel (*d* 1983), dau of Henry Suthers, of New York, and *d* 1982, leaving issue:

1b Bruce Fergusson, Lt-Col US Marine Corps, served WW II, in Korea and in Vietnam 1965, Bronze Star Medal, Korea (1950), 2nd Bronze Star Medal, Vietnam (1965); *b* 17 Oct 1925; *educ* Dartmouth Coll USA; *m* 23 Aug 1947 *Joanne [Mrs Bruce Cunliffe, 481 State St, Portsmouth, NH, USA], dau of Richard L Holbrook, of Keene, New Hampshire, and *d* 1989, leaving issue:

1c +Taylor Fergusson; *b* 6 Nov 1950

1c *Orinda [Mrs Edward Jerue, 53 Western Ave, Westfield, MA 01085, USA]; *b* 28 Jan 1949; *m* 1970 *Edward Andrew Jerue, late Capt US Marine Corps, and has issue:

1d *Tristan Aubrey; *b* 1975

2d *Brook Kai; *b* 1977

3d *Seth Orion; *b* 1979

1d *Summer Alia; *b* 1974

2c *Catherine Suthers; *b* 2 March 1956; *m* 1978 *Lawrence Samuel Muller, of Tallahassee, Florida, USA, and has issue:

1d *Randi Michelle; *b* 1981

2b Douglas Malcolm; *b* 1 Nov 1927; *d* 15 March 1928

3b +Stuart Owen [Mr Stuart Cunliffe, Lebanon Towers, 97 Hanover St, Apt 104, Lebanon, NH, USA], served with US Marine Corps during Korean War; *b* 23 July 1931; *educ* Kimball Union Acad, Meriden, NH, USA; *m* 13 April 1957 *Mary, dau of David Berglund, of Albany, NY, and has issue:

1c +Fred Owen [Mr Fred Cunliffe, 43 Chestnut St, Southington, CT 06489–4509, USA; *b* 1 April 1958; *educ* U of Massachusets; US Army 1977–80; *m* 10 Oct 1985 *Kathleen Theresa, dau of Richard Raymond Burbank, of Southington, CT, and has issue:

1d +Joshua Owen; *b* 1988

2d +Ian Richard; *b* 1991

1d *Hannah Leigh; *b* 1994

2c +David William; *b* 29 Feb 1960

1b *Lorna Margaret [Mrs Amos Gile, Wyeth Rd Circle, W Lebanon, NH, USA]; *b* 15 April 1929; *m* 10 Sept 1949 *Amos Webster Gile, son of Dr John F Gile, of Hanover, NH, and has issue:

1c *John Lockhart; *b* 16 June 1952

1c *Joanne Lorna; *b* 22 April 1951; *m* 1972 *Svein Michaelsen, of Bergen, Norway

2c *Pamela Jean; *b* 1 Dec 1954

3a +Colin Fergusson [Maj Colin Cunliffe, Torlundy, 71 Windermere Rd, London SW16], late Inspector, Staffs Constabulary, served WW II 1939–45, with Gren Gds and Maj N Staffs Regt; *b* 5 Jan 1909; *m* 1st 2 Jan 1934 Muriel Constance Gore (*d* 15 Oct 1953); *m* 2nd 22 March 1954 *Sally Marion Mackay

3a Audrey Roma; *b* 10 Sept 1903; *m* 1931 John Howard Tunley

4a Lorna Winifred; *b* 6 Oct 1905; *d* Feb 1906

5a *Sonia [Mrs Eric Skead, 60 Victoria St, Orillia, Ontario, Canada]; *b* 6 June 1911; *m* 1st 1935 (*divorce* 1948) Frank Shaw, and has issue:

1b *Sandra; *b* 1936

5a (cont.) Mrs Sonia Shaw *m* 2nd 1948 Eric Skead (*d* 1968), and has further issue:

1b *Howard; *b* 1949

(1) Ada Frances; *m* 2 April 1865 Charles Tweedie, late of Jessore, Bengal, 2nd son of Thomas Tweedie, of Quarter, Rachan, Peeblesshire, and had issue. He *d* 22 April 1928

(2) Emma Charlotte; *m* 30 Sept 1863 James Tweedie, and *d* 25 Oct 1910, having had issue. He *d* 25 Oct 1909

(3) Laura

Sir Robert *m* 2nd 2 April 1825 Susan Emily (*d* 11 Nov 1856), 2nd dau of Col John Paton, Commissary-Gen of the Bengal Army, and *d* 10 Sept 1859, having by her had further issue, with seven other daus:

4 Henry (Rev), MA, Vicar of Shifnal, Salop; *b* 16 March 1826; *m* 16 Nov 1853 Mary Augusta (*d* 2 Dec 1879), only dau of Sir James Milles Riddell, 2nd Bt, and

had a dau (Mary Susan, *d* 1857); *m* 2nd 20 April 1887 Lady Alexandrina Victoria Murray (*d* 21 Nov 1911), dau of 6th Earl of Dunmore (*qv*), and *d* 1 Aug 1894

5 Charles Watkin, Bengal CS; *b* 6 April 1833; *k* by mutineers at Byram Ghat June 1857

6 Foster John, Lt Bengal Art; *b* 14 Oct 1834; *d* at Lucknow 22 Sept 1857

7 Frank, Capt 58th Regt; *b* 8 July 1839; *d* unm 24 March 1878

The 7th Bt's cousin,

Sir Cyril Henry Cunliffe, 8th Bt; *b* 3 March 1901; *educ* Dulwich Coll and Faraday House; REME; *m* 1956 *Eileen M [Mrs Frederick Moore, 17 Gurney Court Rd, St Albans, Herts] (*m* 3rd 1970 Frederick Henry Moore (*d* 1987)), dau of Frederick William Parkins, and widow of Charles Clifford, and *d* 12 Feb 1969, having had issue:

1 Sir DAVID ELLIS CUNLIFFE, **9th and present Bt**

2 +ANDREW MARK; *b* 17 April 1959; heir presumptive; *m* 1980 *Janice Elizabeth, dau of Ronald William Kyle, and has issue:

(1) +Mark Ellis; *b* 1982

(1) *Sarah Nicolette; *b* 1984

(2) *Danielle Juliette; *b* 1989

(3) *Rachael Eileen Margaret; *b* 1992

1 *Susan Nicolette (twin); *b* 1959

CUNLIFFE-OWEN

Arms: Quarterly, 1st and 4th, sable a lion rampant between three crosses couped, a bordure all or (for OWEN); 2nd and 3rd, sable three conies courant in pale, within two flaunces argent (for CUNLIFFE). **Crests:** 1 A lion rampant sable, charged with three crosses couped in pale or (for OWEN), 2 A greyhound sejant argent, collared sable, in front of a flag-staff proper, flowing therefrom a banner also argent, charged with a cross gules (for CUNLIFFE). **Motto:** *Honestas optima politia* ('Honesty is the best policy'). **Creation:** Bt. (UK) 2 Feb 1920.

SIR HUGO DUDLEY CUNLIFFE-OWEN, 3RD BT, of Bray, Co Berks; *b* 16 May 1966; s f 1983; *educ* King William's Coll IoM and RNC Dartmouth

Lineage: WILLIAM OWEN, of Sheffield, Yorks; *b c* 1590; *m* 7 Oct 1619 Rose Broxsopp and had:

WILLIAM OWEN, of Sheffield; *b* Dec 1621; *m* 20 Sept 1647 Anne, dau of Edward Dickson, and had:

JOHN OWEN, of Sheffield; *b* Oct 1653; had:

JOSEPH OWEN, of Sheffield; Master Cutlers' Co 1754; *b* June 1698; *d* Dec 1773; his est son:

JOSEPH OWEN, of Crookes Moor, Sheffield; *b* Oct 1726; *m* 2 Jan 1746 Sarah, dau and coheir of Samuel Skargell by Elizabeth, dau of John Cunliffe, of Hollings, and eventual representative of that family, and *d* May 1800; his 2nd son:

CHARLES OWEN, of Chelsea, Middx, JP; *m* 1st 3 April 1784 Mary Newman (*d* 17 Aug 1793); *m* 2nd 3 Sept 1801 Mrs Mary Ann Kettlewell (*d* 19 April 1857), and *d* 23 Feb 1805, leaving by his 1st w an est surv s:

CHARLES CUNLIFFE-OWEN, of Wycoller Hall, Lancs; *b* 12 May 1786; Capt RN; *m* 9 Jan 1821 Mary Peckwell (3 May 1841), dau of Sir Henry Blossett, Ch Justice of Bengal, and *d* 20 Feb 1872; his 3rd son:

Sir FRANCIS PHILIP CUNLIFFE-OWEN, KCB, KCMG, CIE, Grand Offr Legion of Honour, Dir V&A; *b* 8 June 1828; *m* 12 May 1854 Jenny (*d* 24 Sept 1894), est dau of Baron Fritz von Reitzenstein, Cdr Roy Prussian Horse Gds, ADC Gen to FREDRICK WILLIAM IV OF PRUSSIA, and had issue:

1 Frederick Philip Lewis, CBE (1920); *b* 30 Jan 1855; *educ* Lancing; *m* 22 Nov 1877 (*divorce* Switzerland 1887) Emma Pauline de Couvreu de Deckersberg, of Vevey (*d* Dec 1918), and *d* 30 June 1926, having had issue:

(1) Philip, of Calgary, Alberta; *b* 1878

(1) Violet; *b* 1880

2 Alfred Mark; *b* 5 April 1858; *d* 8 Feb 1875

3 Charles Fowke; *b* 19 Nov 1859; *d* 26 Feb 1860

4 HUGO (Sir), **1st Bt**

1 Gertrude Agnes Cunliffe; *m* 10 Aug 1880 Maj Gilbert Edward Wyndham Malet, RHA (*d* 15 Oct 1918), and *d* 13 Nov 1923, leaving issue (*see* MALET, Bt)

2 Mary Monica Cunliffe, DBE (1925), DGStJ; *m* 29 April 1886 Henry Herbert Wills, of Barley Wood, Wrington, Somerset, son of Henry Overton Wills (*see* WILLS, Bt, of Blagdon), and *d* 2 April 1931

3 Emma Paulina; *m* 1st 18 April 1882 her cousin Edward Cunliffe-Owen, CMG (*d* 27 Dec 1918), only son of Col Charles Cunliffe-Owen, CB, and had issue: *m* 2nd Dr Robert Stamford

4 Grace Elise Cunliffe; *d* 1909

5 Olga Cunliffe; *b* 26 Sept 1866; *m* Oct 1891 Albert Hopkinson (*d* July 1949), and *d* Jan 1940, leaving issue

6 Victoria Mary Louise Adelaide Cunliffe; *b* 12 Dec 1875; *m* 1st (*divorce*) Otto Kyllman, and had issue; *m* 2nd 19 June 1919 William Hector Prior-Pitt (*d* 1933)

Sir FRANCIS *d* 23 March 1894; his 4th son,

Sir Hugo Cunliffe-Owen, 1st Bt (UK), so *cr* 2 Feb 1920; *b* 16 Aug 1870; *educ* Brighton and Clifton; pres BAT, dir: Midland Bank and Eagle Star Insur, chm Cunliffe-Owen Aircraft Ltd, Controller Eastern Propaganda Min Info 1918; *m* 1st 31 Dec 1918 Helen Elizabeth (*d* 14 Jan 1934), dau of James Oliver, of New York; *m* 2nd 20 April 1935 Mauricia Martha, Order of Mercy, dau of Herbert Shaw, of San Francisco, and by his 1st w had issue:

1 Hugo Leslie, Sub-Lt (A) RNVR WW II; *b* 17 July 192l; *ka* 12 Aug 1942

2 DUDLEY HERBERT(Sir), **2nd Bt**

1 *Philippa Helen; *b* 29 May 1926; *m* 1st 27 Sept 1945 (*divorce* 1952) Denis Macduff Burke, only son of Alfred George Burke, of Sheffield, and has issue:

(1) *David Macduff; *b* 17 July 1948; *educ* Uppingham

(1) *Alexandra Yvette [Mrs Edward Butler, Wynd-in-the Willows, Maidenhead Rd, Windsor, Berks]; *b* 7 Sept 1946; *m* 9 March 1968 *Edward Maurice Pierce Butler, son of Maurice Butler, of The Hill, Fethard on Sea, Co Wexford

1 (cont.) Mrs Philippa Burke *m* 2nd 16 Sept 1952 (*divorce* 1962) Archie Alistair Baring, son of Reginald Baring; *m* 3rd 4 July 1966 Peter William Thorn Warren (*d* 1973), yr son of Arthur Owen Warren, of 14 Dawson Place, London W2; *m* 4th 1979 *Gilbert Hugh Sandbach Toller and by her 2nd husb has further issue:

(2) *Adrian Alistair; *b* 10 May 1957

(2) *Sarah Elizabeth; *b* 15 June 1954

2 *Diana Elizabeth [Mrs Diana Hanbury, Queen's Lodge, Beldam Bridge Rd, Chobham, Surrey]; *b* 1 Aug 1928; *m* 1st 28 Oct 1947 (*divorce* 1955) William Gavin Buchanan, only son of E V Buchanan, of London, Ontario; *m* 2nd 1955 (*divorce* 1956) Michael Stoop; *m* 3rd 1964 (*divorce* 1967) Cdr Richard O'Brien, RN; *m* 4th 1967 (*divorce* 1991) Antony Hanbury, and by her 1st husb has issue:

(1) *Gray Hugo; *b* 2 Aug 1948

(2) *Diana Victoria; *b* 6 April 1951

Sir HUGO *d* 14 Dec 1947; his only surv son,

Sir Dudley Herbert Cunliffe-Owen, 2nd Bt; *b* 27 March 1923; Lt RN WW II, md Palace and Derby Castle Ltd, Palace Hotel and Casino Ltd, Palace Entertainments Ltd and Palace Services (Bahamas) Ltd; *m* 1st 3 Dec 1947 Mary Maud (*d* 31 March 1956), est dau of Robin Roy Redgrave, of Withington, Oatlands Chase, Weybridge, Surrey; *m* 2nd 3 July 1956 (*divorce* 1962) Hon Juliana Eveline (*m* 4th 1962 (*divorce* 1972) as his 2nd w, John Roberts, *see* ROBERTS, Bt of Milnerfield), formerly w of (a) George Derek Stanley Smith and (b) Frederick Nettlefold, and 3rd dau of 2nd Viscount Scarsdale, TD (*qv*), and by her had issue:

1 *Juliana Diana; *b* 29 June 1957; *m* 1980 *Stephen Markeson, and has issue:

(1) *Oliver James; *b* 1984

(1) *Lucy Juliana; *b* 1982

Sir Dudley *m* 3rd 10 March 1964 *Jean, only dau of Surgn-Cdr A N Forsyth, RN, and *d* 17 July 1983, having by her had further issue:

1 Sir HUGO DUDLEY CUNLIFFE-OWEN, **3rd and present Bt**

2 *Sophia Jean; *b* 26 Feb 1965

CUNYNGHAME

Arms: Argent a shakefork sable between three fleurs-de-lys azure, one in chief and two in flank. **Crest:** A unicorn argent, unguled, maned and armed or, resting on a mount vert. **Supporters:** Dexter, a knight in complete armour, holding in his exterior hand a lance in pale proper; sinister, a knight in the disguise of a countryman with a bonnet, habited azure, his thighs armed proper and in his exterior hand a cornfork in pale of the last. **Motto:** Over fork over.
Creation: Bt. (NS) 3 Feb 1701/2.

SIR ANDREW DAVID FRANCIS CUNYNGHAME, 12TH BT, of Milncraig, Ayrshire [Sir Andrew Cunynghame Bt, 12 Vicarage Gdns, London W8 4AH; The School House, Williamscot, Banbury, Oxon]; *b* 25 Dec 1942; *s f* 1978; *educ* Eton; FCA; *m* 1st 1972 Harriet Ann, dau of Charles Thomas Dupont, of Montreal, Canada, and has issue:

1 *Ann Marie Albinia; *b* 1978

2 *Tania Albinia Pamela Jean; *b* 1983

Sir ANDREW *m* 2nd 1989 *Isabella, dau of Edward Everett Watts, Jr

Lineage: The CUNYNGHAMEs of Milncraig claim descent from the CUNINGHAMs of Craigends (*see* FAIRLIE-CUNINGHAME, Bt).

JAMES CUNINGHAM of Polquhairn, Parish of Ochiltree; living 1578; may have been f of:

WILLIAM CUNYNGHAM of Polquhairn; living 1585; *m* 1st Janet McAdam; *m* 2nd Agnes Muir; his son:

(WILLIAM) CUNYNGHAM, 1st of Milncraig, in Coylton, Ayr, which he acquired by his w, dau of William Cathgart of Corbieston; had:

(WILLIAM) CUNYNGHAME of Milncraig; *m* —, dau of David Crawford of Kerse, Ayrshire, and had:

DAVID CUNYNGHAM of Milncraig; *m* Margaret, dau of John Masoun, of Rosebank, Burgh Clerk of Ayr, and *d* Dec 1659, leaving issue:

Sir David Cunynghame, 1st Bt (NS), so *cr* 3 Feb 1701/2, of Milncraig and Livingstone, Linlithgowshire; lawyer, MP (S Parl); *m* 1st Isobell, yst dau of 1st Viscount Stair (*see* STAIR, E); *m* 2nd 16 March 1698 Elizabeth, dau of Sir Robert Baird, 1st Bt, of Saughton Hall (*qv*), and *d* 28 Jan 1708, leaving:

1 **Sir James Cunynghame, 2nd Bt**; MP Linlithgowshire 1715–22; *d* unm 1 Feb 1747

2 **Sir David Cunynghame, 3rd Bt**; *b* 1 Aug 1700; Lt-Gen, Col 57th Regt 1757; *m* May 1731 Lady Mary Montgomerie (*d* June 1777), dau of 9th Earl of Eglinton and Winton (*qv*), and *d* 10 Oct 1767, having had, with other issue:

(1) WILLIAM AUGUSTUS (Sir), **4th Bt**

(1) Margaret; *m* 8 June 1767 Hon James Stuart Wortley Mackenzie, 2nd son of 3rd Earl of Bute (*see* WHARNCLIFFE, E)

The 3rd Bt's son,

Sir William Augustus Cunynghame, 4th Bt; MP Linlithgowshire 1774–90; *m* 1st 21 Oct 1768 Frances (*d* 14 Oct 1771), dau and eventual heir of Sir Robert Myrton, 2nd Bt, of Gogar, and had issue:

1 DAVID (Sir), **5th Bt**

2 Robert; *m* 8 April 1813 Maria, dau of George Dundas of Dundas, and left issue:

(1) Caroline Stirling; *m* 1st 9 Dec 1833 Capt Leinster John Henry Bulkeley, 40th Foot (*d* 1853); *m* 2nd 1855 Rollo James Bulkeley, barrister, and *d* 12 May 1895

(2) Frances Jane Myrton; *m* 19 July 1844 Adolphe Le Croix, Br Consul Nice

(3) Mary Montgomerie; *m* July 1846 Alexander Woodford, 3rd son of Lt-Gen Sir Alexander Woodford

3 Francis; Col; *m* 8 July 1805 Jane (*d* 19 Sept 1817), yst dau of Sir John Whiteford, 3rd Bt, of Whiteford, and *dsp* 19 Sept 1816

Sir William *m* 2nd 22 June 1785 Mary, only dau and heir of Robert Udney of Udney, and by her had four sons and a dau; he *d* 17 Jan 1828

His son by his 1st w,

Sir David Cunynghame, 5th Bt; *b* 14 Aug 1769; Col; *m* 1st 1801 Maria (*d* 21 Feb 1816), illegitimate dau of 1st Baron Thurlow (*qv*), and had issue, with two daus:

1 Edward Thurlow; *b* 23 Sept 1801; *d* 1825

2 **Sir David Thurlow Cunynghame, 6th Bt**; *b* 16 Sept 1803; Capt 12th Lancers; *m* 1st 15 July 1833 Annie (*d* 10 June 1864), dau of Gen Hon Robert Meade, son of 1st Earl of Clanwilliam (*qv*), and had issue:

(1) **Sir Edward Augustus Cunynghame, 7th Bt**; *b* Jan 1839; Capt 32nd Foot; *d* unm 24 Jan 1877

(1) Mary Louise; *m* 25 Aug 1858 Capt Thomas Henry Evans (*d* 1896), 2nd surv son of Thomas Browne Evans, of Dean House, Oxon, and Tuddenham, Norfolk, and *d* Oct 1913, having had issue, one child (*d* an infant)

(2) Augusta Theodosia Mary; *m* 11 Sept 1866 HH Prince Edward de Ligne (*d* 17 Oct 1911), and *dsp* 25 Oct 1872

1 (cont.) **Sir David, 6th Bt**, *m* 2nd 27 April 1866 Louisa Mary (*dsp* 7 Nov 1906), dau of William Baker, and *d* 12 Nov 1869

3 Robert S Thurlow; *b* 27 March 1807; *d* unm 13 April 1829

4 FRANCIS THURLOW (Sir), **8th Bt**

5 Arthur Augustus Thurlow (Sir), GCB; *b* 12 Aug 1812; Gen cmdg Dublin Div, Lt-Govr and Cdr forces Cape of Good Hope, Col 60th Rifles, served Crimea; *m* 13 Sept 1845 Frances Elizabeth, CI (*d* 9 July 1894), dau of 1st Viscount Hardinge (*qv*), and *d* 10 March 1884, leaving issue:

(1) Henry Hardinge Samuel (Sir), KCB (1908); *b* 8 July 1848; *educ* St John's Coll Cambridge (MA); Lt RE; barrister 1875, Special Commr Br Guiana 1880, Assist Commr under City of London Charities Acts 1884, Sec to Parnell Special Commn 1888, Bering Sea Arbitration 1892 and Featherstone Riots Commn 1894, Legal Assist to Under-Sec Home Dept 1894–1913; author works on law, electricity, fine arts; *m* 21 June 1893 Emily Harriette (*d* 15 April 1951), dau of Col Arthur Prescott, 2nd Bombay Cav (*see* PRESCOTT, Bt), and *d* 3 May 1935

(2) Arthur Hardinge David; *b* 17 Nov 1853; *educ* Trin Coll Dublin (BA); Dist Auditor Hampshire; *m* 24 June 1892 Alexandra Isabel (*d* 18 July 1938), dau of Alexander Scott, and *d* 14 Nov 1917, leaving issue:

1a Charles Hardinge; *b* 22 May 1893; *d* 1958

2a David Hardinge; *b* 25 April 1897; *educ* Cheltenham; Maj Roy Signals WW I 1915–19 (wounded); *m* 2 Oct 1934 *Ruth Ilon Ismay, dau of Rev A E Phillips, and *d* 1986, leaving issue:

1b +Francis Arthur David; *b* 1 July 1935

Mary Isabel Maud; *d* unm March 1963

1 Emily Caroline Thurlow; *m* 4 Aug 1888 Charles Walter Oddie (*d* 1920)

2 Mary Sarah Hardinge; *d* unm

3 Lavinia Augusta Charlotte; *m* 17 Oct 1883, Capt George Charles Peere Williams-Freeman (*d* 27 Dec 1905), late Roy Sussex Regt, and *d* 31 March 1922, leaving issue

Sir David *m* 2nd 31 March 1817 Gertrude Henrietta (*d* 1842), dau of William Kimpton, of Ampthill, and *d* 19 May 1854, having by her had issue, with three daus:

6 Henry Sydney Myrton; *b* 6 Aug 1819; *m* 1852 Mary Ann (*d* 1898), dau of Pryce Bostock, of Welshpool, Montgomeryshire, and *d c* 1900

7 William Augustus Charles Myrton; *b* 6 Jan 1824; Capt Roy Canadian Rifles; *d* 11 Dec 1892

8 Augustus Myrton; *b* 8 Jan 1829; Surveyor-Gen GPO for Scotland; *m* 27 April 1864 Anna Eliza (*d* 26 Oct 1899), er dau of Baron Molesworth de Mallet, and *d* 9 Aug 1904, leaving issue:

(1) Francis James de Mallet; *b* 25 July 1884; Maj 7th Bn London Regt WW I 1914–16, poet and biographer; *m* 6 July 1912 Joan, dau of Joseph Augustus Masterton, of Fairlie, Ayshire, and *d* 5 Dec 1958, having had issue:

1a David Augustus Francis de Mallet; *b* 17 April, *d* 25 May 1924

(1) Gertrude Marie; *d* unm 25 May 1961

(2) Anna Bertha de Mallet; *b* 1874; *d* 17 Jan 1973 aged 99

9 James Joseph Myrton (Rev); *b* 21 April 1832; MA; Rector Horseheath, Cambs; *m* 2 March 1871 Annie Constance (*d* 1889), only surv dau of Thomas Lane, JP, DL, of Moundsley Hall, Worcs, and *d* 20 July 1885, having had issue:

(1) Ida Constance Louisa; *d* unm 1 March 1933

(2) Alice Ethel; *d* unm 11 April 1898

(3) Florence Olivia Violet; *m* 7 Nov 1899 Charles Herbert Judkin (*d* 1926), and *d* 19 Jan 1952, leaving issue

(4) Cicily Rose Muriel; *m* 22 Dec 1910 Harold d'Albiac Lane (*d* 18 May 1922), est surv son of Rev James William Lane, Rector of Redruth, Cornwall, and *d* 31 March 1956, leaving issue

(5) Georgina Maud Evelyn; *d* unm Sept 1944

The 7th Bt's unc,

Sir Francis Thurlow Cunynghame, 8th Bt; *b* 11 Aug 1808; *m* 3 Aug 1830 Hannah Caroline (*d* 25 June 1902), dau of William Robertson Eyrn, MD, of Kindrocket, Perthshire, and *d* 27 Oct 1877, having had issue:

1 David Thurlow; *b* 21 Nov 1831; *d* 12 June 1832

2 William; *b* 1 June 1833; *d* unm 28 Feb 1876

3 FRANCIS GEORGE THURLOW (Sir), **9th Bt**

4 James Robertson Thurlow; *b* 24 Dec 1840; *m* 1878 Alice, dau of Josiah Carter, of Melbourne, and *d* 21 Jan 1890, leaving issue:

(1) Francis Thurlow Hardinge; *b* 1880; *m* 1909 Frances Anne (*d* 6 May 1954), dau of Nicholas Murnane, of Brisbane, and *d* 1940, leaving issue:

1a +Frank Vincent; *b* 1910; AIF 1940–45; *m* 1949 *Mary Terese, dau of John Joseph Hennessy, of Sydney, and has issue:

1b *Helen Ann; *b* 24 Nov 1949

2b *Diane Frances; *b* 6 Sept 1952

3b *Jennifer Ann; *b* 27 Jan 1955

4b *Frances Mary; *b* 21 Sept 1957

(1) Helene Emily Thurlow; *m* 1910 Arcalayus James Opie and had issue

(2) Blanche Thurlow Forster; *m* 1914 Harold Charles Daymond, and *d* 28 Sept 1963, leaving issue

5 Arthur Edward; *b* 8 Jan 1844; *d* 2 Dec 1850

Mary Sophia Thurlow; *m* 20 July 1858 Col Robert Broome Baker, late 39th Regt, and *d* 8 March 1904, leaving issue
2 Elizabeth Millicent Thurlow; *m* 12 Aug 1865 Maj-Gen Charles James Hughes (*d* 1903), late Bengal Staff Corps, and had issue
3 Caroline Georgina Thurlow; *m* 8 June 1871 Capt Robert Hoare Dwyer (*d* 1881), Roy Marine Light Inf, and *d* 21 Dec 1924, having had issue
4 Augusta Zuhlche Thurlow; *m* 5 Sept 1867 George Robertson, MD, RN, and *d* 21 Feb 1882, having had issue
5 Beatrice Geraldine Thurlow; Sister of Mercy St Mary's, Wantage; *m* her bro-in-law George Robertson
6 Georgina Frances Thurlow; *d* 30 Aug 1853
7 Louisa Annie Thurlow; *d* 15 April 1860

The 8th Bt's est surv son,

Sir Francis George Thurlow Cunynghame, 9th Bt; *b* 19 April 1835; Maj 3rd Bn Middx Regt, and 5th Bn Rifle Bde; *m* 1st 15 July 1863 Jessica (*d* 13 April 1884), dau of Rev William Henry Bloxsome, Rector of Stanton, Glos, and had issue:
1 PERCY FRANCIS (Sir), **10th Bt**
2 Stuart; *b* 18 Aug 1874; Maj late Cmdt Sarawak Rangers; *m* 2 June 1915 Helen Dorothy (*d* 31 Jan 1944), dau of Rev R Holland Taylor, DD, and *d* 10 Jan 1962, having had issue:
(1) Willfrid Bertram Stuart; *b* 1917; P/O RAF, WW II; *ka* over Germany 31 Aug 1940
(2) +Colin Kenneth; *b* 1918; Maj IA
(3) +David Francis; *b* 1920; Capt IA; Airline Sales Rep BOAC; *m* 1st 1947 (*divorce* 1957) Ruth Murray, and has issue:
1a *Diana Patricia; *b* 1950
(3) (cont) David Cunynghame *m* 2nd 1964 (*divorce* 1975) Renate Maria Dietrich, and has further issue:
1a +Christopher Daniel; *b* 1966
2a *Deborah Avril; *b* 1968
(3) (cont) David Cunynghame *m* 3rd 1984 *Leslie Stokoe (*née* Anderson)
(1) Derita Marion; *b* 1916; *m* 6 Feb 1942 W/Cdr Peter James Channer, DSO, DFC, RAFVR, son of Luther James Channer, of Hollywood, Cranbrook, Kent, and *dsp* May 1969
1 Annie Beatrice; *m* 31 July 1889 William Innes Stuckey, and *d* June 1921, having had issue
2 Jessie Mabel; *m* 29 Sept 1891 Rev Harry Gilbert Dickinson, Vicar of Long Houghton, and *d* 16 May 1893, leaving issue
3 Caroline Edith; *d* unm 11 March 1890
4 Gertrude Marion; *d* unm 17 March 1954

Sir Francis *m* 2nd 9 March 1886 Elizabeth Anne (*dsp* 2 Jan 1909), dau of William Yeo, of Appledore, Devon, and widow of J F Walton, and *d* 12 Nov 1900

His er son,

Sir Percy Francis Cunynghame, 10th Bt, OBE (1919), JP and DL (Co London); *b* 21 Feb 1867; Lt-Col 5th Bn Middx Regt, attd Staff of HH THE RAJAH OF SARAWAK as Resident of 1st Div Sarawak to 1909, when ret; served WW I 1914–19; *m* 16 Dec 1903 Maud Albinia Margaret Selwyn (*d* 2 Dec 1948), only child of Maj John Handcock Selwyn-Payne, JP, of Badgeworth Court, Glos, and *d* 7 Jan 1941, having had issue:
1 (HENRY) DAVID ST LEGER BROOKE SELWYN (Sir), **11th Bt**
2 Ian Francis Rowland Selwyn; *b* 19 March 1910; *educ* Eton; Ch Assist Min of Production and attached to Br Raw Materials Mn, Washington, USA 1943–46; *m* 1st 17 Dec 1938 Cicely Mary (*d* 12 Sept 1945), er dau of Francis Chayter Starkey, and had issue:
(1) +Michael Ian Francis Starkey [Michael Cunynghame Esq, Dury Stores, N Nestling, Shetland]; *b* 6 Sept 1945; *educ* Chilton Cantelo House, Yeovil; *m* 20 July 1970 *Penelope Mary, yr dau of Allan Mortimer, of Ballinger, Bucks, and has issue:
1a +Ian Michael; *b* 1979
1a *Daisy Albinia; *b* 1981
(1) *Sarah Albinia Starkey; *b* 23 May 1940; *m* 28 Nov 1964 Felco Jan Leemhuis, of 429 Lansdown Ave, Westmount, Quebec Prov, Canada, est son of S Leemhuis, and has issue:
1a *Adrian Samuel; *b* 8 April 1969
1a *Cicely Toosje; *b* 1974
(1) (cont.) Mr and Mrs Felco Leemhuis also adopted:
*Ian; *b* 1971
(2) *Caroline Mary Albinia Starkey [Mrs Caroline Lloyd, 31 Ridgemount, Guildford, Surrey], BA, PhD; *b* 22 July 1943; *m* 16 Aug 1968 *Barry Lloyd, M Phil, BSc, only son of Jack Lloyd, of Burpham, Arundel, Sussex, and has issue:
1a *Hannah Cicely; *b* 1973
2a *Leila Kate; *b* 1975
2 (cont.) Ian Cunynghame *m* 2nd 25 Jan 1947 Eugenie Beatrice Gwendolen (*d* 11 Oct 1962), dau of James Howard Allport and widow of R-Adml John Uniacke Penrose-Fitzgerald, CB, and *d* 1988, having by her had further issue:
(3) *Moira Janet Albinia Allport [Mrs Konstantin Stramentov, Gurrington House, Woodland, nr Ashburton, Devon TQ13 7JS]; *b* 10 Oct 1947; *m* 1969 Konstantin Andreevich Stramentov, of Rhicarn, Lochinver, Sutherland, only son of Andrei Evenevich Stramentov, of Moscow, and has issue:
1a *Bruce Sergei Cunynghame; *b* 1977
2a *Andrew Nikita Cunynghame; *b* 1979
1a *Alexandra Eugénie Cunynghame; *b* 1973
2a *Darya Esme Cunynghame; *b* 1983

The 10th Bt's er son,

Sir (Henry) David St Leger Brooke Selwyn Cunynghame, 11th Bt; *b* 7 Feb 1905; *educ* Eton; WW II 1940–44 as S/Ldr RAFVR; dir of several Br Film Producing and Distributing Cos; *m* 7 Oct 1941 Hon Pamela Margaret Stanley, 2nd dau of 5th Baron Stanley of Alderley (*see* STANLEY OF ALDERLEY, SHEFFIELD and, B), and *d* 6 Aug 1978, leaving:
1 Sir ANDREW DAVID FRANCIS CUNYNGHAME, **12th and present Bt**
2 +JOHN PHILIP HENRY MICHAEL SELWYN [John Cunynghame Esq, 26D Belgrave Rd, London SW1V 1RG]; *b* 9 Sept 1944; heir presumptive; *educ* Eton; *m* 1981 *Marjatta, 2nd dau of Martti Markus, of Muhos, Finland, and has issue:
(1) +Alexander David Martti; *b* 1985
(1) *Niina Kaarina; *b* 1983
3 +Arthur James Augustus [Arthur Cunynghame Esq, Grange Farm, Grange Lane, Alvechurch, Worcs B48 7DJ]; *b* 16 Feb 1951; *educ* Westminster; *m* 16 July 1977 *Rachel-Claire, er dau of Guy Baines, of Cattespoole, Tardebigge, Worcs, and has issue:
(1) +Richard George Arthur Selwyn; *b* 1980
(2) +Edward David Lyulph; *b* 1983

CURRIE

Arms: Gu. a saltire couped arg., in the centre chief point a rose of the last, barbed and seeded ppr. **Crest:** A cock ppr., resting its foot upon a rose arg., barbed and seeded ppr.
Creation: Bt. (UK) 11 Jan 1847.

SIR DONALD SCOTT CURRIE, 7TH BT [Sir Donald Currie Bt, 9061 WCR 34, Platteville, Colorado 80651, USA]; *b* 1930; *s* unc 1987; rancher and farmer 1949–75, Chief of Maintenance, Nat Park Serv, US Dept of the Interior; *m* 1st 1948 (*divorce* 1951) Charlotte, dau of Charles Johnstone, of Mesa, Arizona, USA, and has issue:
1 +DONALD MARK; *b* 1949; *m* 1st 31 May 1969 (*divorce* 1969) Gloria, dau of A Price, of California; *m* 2nd 1969 (*divorce* 1971) Inga Mae Rouse and by her has issue:
(1) +Mark Donald; *b* 1970
1 *Julia Ann; *b* 1950; *m* 1969 *Eugene R Gangaware, USAF, and has issue:
(1) *Elizabeth Ann; *b* 1970
(2) *Tiffany Sue; *b* 1974
(3) *Wendy Opal; *b* 1976
(4) *Jeanette Mae; *b* 1978
2 *Janet Sue (twin); *b* 1950; *m* 1st 1970 (*divorce* 1970) Jack D Hawkins, of Idaho, USA; *m* 2nd 1973 *Robert Eugene Buck, of Nebraska, USA, and has issue by 2nd husb:
(1) *Todd Allen; *b* 1973
(2) *Terry Lee; *b* 1975

Sir DONALD *m* 2nd 30 April 1952 *Barbara Lee, dau of A P Garnier, of Calif, and by her has issue:
2 +Gary Dwayne [Gary Currie, Box 116, Vona, CO, USA]; *b* 26 Sept 1953; *m* 1970 *Wilma Kathleen, dau of Tom Wyatt, of Colorado, USA, and has issue:
(1) +Bradley Wayne; *b* 1973
(1) *Brandy Sue; *b* 1971
3 *Tina Marie [Mrs Tina Linnerman, 19750 8th Ave, Fort Morgan, CO 80701, USA]; *b* 20 Dec 1955; *m* 1974 (*divorce* 1992) Ricky Lee Linneman, of Gillette, Wyoming, USA, and has issue:
(1) *Shawn Michael; *b* 1976
(2) *Tye Rae; *b* 1985
3 (cont.) Mrs Tina Linneman also has an adopted dau:
*Shayne Michelle; *b* 1973
4 *Kathren Evelyn; *b* 31 May 1959; *m* 1973 *Earl Avara, and has issue:
(1) *Scott William; *b* 1979
(1) *Jennifer Marie; *b* 1981

Lineage: WILLIAM CURRIE, held lands called 'Currie Parks'; living 1609; had, with another s (Cuthbert, *m* Elizabeth Little, *dsp* 1663):

WILLIAM CURRIE; *m* Agnes Nisbet and *d* 1681, leaving, with a yr s (James, ancestor of Dr Currie, of Liverpool, biographer of Burns):

WILLIAM CURRIE; *b* 1628; *m* Katherine Monielaws and *d* 1695, leaving:

WILLIAM CURRIE; *b* 1653; settled in Berwick-upon-Tweed; *d* 1728, leaving:

MARK CURRIE; *b* 1682; *m* his cousin Magdalen Anderson and *d* 1761, leaving, with a dau, (Mary, *m* William Riddell):

WILLIAM CURRIE; *b* 10 April 1721; London banker; *m* 17 May 1753 Madeleine (*d* 20 Oct 1801), dau of Isaac Lefevre, ggf of Viscount Eversley, GCB (*see* 1928 edn), and *d* 10 Nov 1781, leaving, with two daus:

1 William, of East Horsley Park, Surrey, ancestor of the CURRIEs of Rushden House

2 MARK, of whom hereafter

3 Isaac, of Bush Hill, Middx, ancestor of the 1st and last BARON CURRIE OF HAWLEY (*see* 1906 edn) and the CURRIEs of Minley Manor

4 John, of Bedwell Park, Herts, ancestor of the CURRIE-BLYTHs of Sandown House

5 Peter, of Richmond, Surrey; *b* 18 May 1765; *m* Elizabeth Caroline Hubbard (*d* 27 Oct 1828)

6 Leonard, ancestor of the CURRIEs of Seafield Park

The 2nd son,

MARK CURRIE, of Upper Gatton, Surrey, and later Hayes, Middx; *b* 13 May 1759; *m* 8 Jan 1789 Elizabeth (*d* 12 Jan 1856), dau of John Close, of Easby, Yorks, and *d* 1 March 1835, leaving, with two daus:

1 William; *b* 1 Aug 1791; *dsp* 16 Dec 1869

2 Mark John, V-Adml RN; *b* 21 June 1795; *m* 14 Jan 1829 Jane (*d* 17 May 1876), dau of Charles Boynton Wood, of Hayes, Middx, and *d* 2 May 1874, leaving issue

3 FREDERICK (Sir), **1st Bt**

4 Charles (Rev), Vicar of Tilney; *b* 3 Oct 1800; *m* 5 June 1839 Diana Elizabeth, dau of the Rev Charles Eusebius Isham

5 Edward, of Pickford, Sussex, HEICS; *b* 2 Feb 1804; *m* 3 March 1831 Georgiana, dau of John Macrae, and had issue

6 Alfred Peter, of Deans, Caversham, HEICS; *b* 8 Jan 1806; *m* 22 June 1835 Jane Latham (*d* 13 April 1900), dau of George Mainwaring, and *d* 3 Feb 1847, leaving issue

The 3rd son,

Sir Frederick Currie, 1st Bt (UK), so *cr* 11 Jan 1847; *b* 3 Feb 1799; Sec to Govt of India 1842, Memb Supreme Council of India 1846; *m* 1st 7 Aug 1820 Susannah (*d* 14 Jan 1832), est dau of John Pascal Larkins, EICS, and had issue:

1 **Rev Sir Frederick Larkins Currie, 2nd Bt**, MA Cambridge, Rector of Old Alresford, Hants; *b* 18 April 1823; *m* 1st 18 Sept 1849 Eliza Reeve (*d* 14 April 1861), only dau of Matthew Rackham, of Thorpe Hamlet, Norwich; *m* 2nd 24 April 1866 Mary Helen (*dsp* 24 Oct 1894), dau of Edgar Corrie, of Arlington Manor, Berks, and *d* 13 Nov 1900, having by his 1st w had issue:

(1) **Sir Frederick Reeve Currie, 3rd Bt**; *b* 13 May 1851; *d* unm 27 Feb 1930

(2) **Sir Walter Louis Rackham Currie, 4th Bt**; *b* 16 March 1856; *m* 28 June 1892 Bertha (*d* 15 June 1951), dau of Thomas Anthony Mitford Freeman, MD, of Brighton, and *d* 5 Feb 1941, having had issue:

1a **Sir Walter Mordaunt Cyril Currie, 5th Bt**; *educ* Sherborne; memb Performing Rights Soc, poet and dramatist, served WW I 1915–16 with RAOC; *b* 3 June 1894; *d* 1978

1a (Lenore Consuelo) Marguerite; *b* 24 April 1893; *m* 8 Sept 1917 Sir Forster Gurney Goring, 12th Bt (*qv*), and *d* 24 Jan 1941

(3) Percy George Colin, late India Postal Serv, Dep Postmaster-Gen, Bengal 1912; *b* 24 Dec 1857; *m* 1885 Agnes Grace Johnstone, dau of Charles Paterson, of Dumfries, and *d* 26 July 1932, leaving issue:

1a Frederick Charles Colin; *b* 1886; *d* 1922

1a Muriel Helen; *b* 1887; *m* 1911 Edgar Green, late Indian Tel Dept, and had issue:

1b *Richard Colin; *b* 1914

1b *Agnes Muriel Rachel; *b* 1915

2b *Margaret Suzanne; *b* 1919

2a Ethel Lilian Adelaide; *b* 1893

(4) Arthur Edward; *b* 17 March 1859; *d* 1919

(5) Cecil Edmund, BA Cambridge, slr; *b* 4 April 1861; *m* 6 Feb 1894 Louisa Fanny, 3rd dau of Maj-Gen George Drury, RMLI, of The Manor Ho, North Huish, Ivybridge, Devon, and *d* 2 Jan 1937

(1) Eliza Kate; *d* unm 11 Nov 1916

(2) Susannah Louisa; *d* unm 2 Sept 1935

2 Mark Edward, Maj RA; *b* 10 Sept 1824; *m* 1st 4 Nov 1847 Jane, est dau of Rev T T Upwood, of Lovells Hall, Norfolk; *m* 2nd 21 Oct 1867 Catherine Louisa (*dsp* 7 July 1879), only dau of Maj-Gen H M Graves, and *d* 14 Dec 1868, having by 1st w had issue:

(1) Frederick Alexander, Lt-Col, 1st Bn Norfolk Regt; *b* 23 Sept 1851; *m* 11 Aug 1874 Geraldine Lucy (*d* 3 Dec 1926), 2nd dau of R W Graves, and *d* 13 June 1902, leaving issue, with two daus, *d* in infancy:

1a Ryves Alexander Mark, CMG (1919), DSO (1916), Maj and Brevet Col (temp Brig-Gen) Somerset LI, Bde Maj 1914–15, GSO (1) 1915, Cmdt Offs Staff Course, Cambridge 1917; served on NW Frontier of India 1897–98 (medal with clasp), and WW I (despatches twice, brevet), Legion of Honour, Croix de Guerre of Belgium; *b* 18 June 1875; *m* 21 Sept 1908 Ida Melville (*d* 28 March 1923) dau of Joseph H Hatchell, FRCPI, and *d* 30 March 1920

1a Maud Geraldine; *m* 1st 18 Nov 1902 Maj Edgar Brandreth, IA (*d* 1908), yst son of Col Ashton Brandreth, RE, *m* 2nd 20 Sept 1928 Lt-Col Henry Rundle Lawrence, CIE, IA (*d* 4 Feb 1949), only son of Lt-Col H J Lawrence, IA, and by 1st husb had issue:

1b Elizabeth; *m* 12 Sept 1929 Col Gerald Brian Thatcher, DSO, RA, and *d* 30 Dec 1973, leaving:

1c *Gerald David Brandreth, Maj RHA; *b* 14 March 1932; *educ* Cheltenham; *m* 18 Dec 1965 *Aurea Anne, only dau of Lt-Col Lionel Heathcote Landon, RA, son of Geoffrey Edward Landon, by his w Helen Mary Caroline, sis of Rt Rev Sir Francis Heathcote, 9th Bt, DD (*qv*), and has issue:

2c *William Ryves, Lt RHA; *b* 17 Jan 1944; *educ* Allhallows

1c *Alix Mary Rose; *b* 13 Nov 1938; *m* 29 July 1961 *Christopher John Robinson, and has issue:

1d *David Allan; *b* 7 May 1963

1d *Julia Ann; *b* 29 Dec 1964

2b *Madeline Alix; *b* 2 June 1906; *m* 1st 14 June 1928 Brig Basil Hildebrand Hopkins, late RWF (took name RYVES HOPKINS by deed poll Dec 1951 and *d* 5 Jan 1960); *m* 2nd 17 Feb 1975 *Col Gerald Brian Thatcher, DSO, RA, and by her 1st husb has issue:

1c *Kenneth Michael Alexander; *b* 29 Sept 1929; *educ* Cheltenham and Trin Coll Oxford (BA Agric)

1c *Armorel Brandreth [Mrs David Nelson, Old Gledstone, nr Skipton-in-Craven, Yorks BD23 3JR]; *b* 13 July 1941; *m* 27 Feb 1965 *David George Hargraves Nelson, OBE, DL, yst son of Sir Amos Nelson, JP, of Gledstone Hall, nr Skipton, Yorks, and has issue:

1d *James Matthew Ryves; *b* 20 May 1971

1d *Lucinda Harriet; *b* 5 Oct 1966; *m* 30 May 1992 *Andrew Oliver Mullins, yst s of Col Gerald Oliver Mullins, and has:

1e *Benjamin George; *b* 16 Dec 1995

2d *Victoria Jane; *b* 28 April 1968

2a Clare Affice; *d* an infant, 23 April 1878

3a Violet Heathercote; *d* an infant, 29 May 1884

3 William Close; *b* 9 Dec 1826; *m* 9 Oct 1851 Harriet Gardiner (*d* 6 July 1904), 2nd dau of John Browne, of Hall Court, Hereford, and *d* 10 Jan 1865, having had issue:

(1) William John Frederick; *b* 28 Aug 1852; *m* 1 Jan 1887 Minnie Euphemia Henrietta McMillan (*d* 5 May 1953), 2nd dau of G H Catania, and *d* 2 Sept 1923, leaving issue:

1a William George Cubitt; *b* 29 Feb 1888; *m* 22 March 1952 Mrs Ellen May Thornton

2a Edward John Charles, served with Malayan Def Force at Singapore 1942 (prisoner) ; *b* 28 March 1892; *m* 8 Aug 1935 Mrs Doris Melrose

1a Marie Effie Georgie; *b* 9 Feb 1890; *m* 1913 Lt-Col Arthur Donovan Young, IA, and *d* 1951, leaving issue

(2) Edward Larkins; *b* 8 Feb 1854; *educ* Rugby; *m* 6 Dec 1919 Mary (*d* Feb 1945), dau of James Neal, MD, of Sandown, IoW, and *d* 23 Dec 1942

(3) Charles Ernest; *b* 8 Aug 1856; *m* 1888 Annie (*d* 1927), est dau of Isaac Hardy, of Stoney Hill, Co Antrim

(4) Robert Browne Vincent; *b* 6 Sept 1859; *m* 6 Jan 1923 Florence Alice Harvey (*m* 2nd 28 April 1950 Bert Thomas, who *d* 6 Sept 1966), and *d* 13 Dec 1944

(1) Mary Cymbriana; *d* unm 6 Sept 1929

(2) Harriett Susan; *d* unm 10 Jan 1943

4 Charles, Bengal CS; *b* 1 July 1829; *m* 8 Jan 1852 Marian (*d* 22 Jan 1903), 3rd dau of Rev T T Upwood, MA, and *d* 3 Sept 1878, leaving issue:

(1) Stanley Charles Cuthbert; *b* 21 Aug 1856; *m* 24 April 1889 Anita Cornelia, dau of R P Rundle, of New York, and *d* 25 Jan 1916

(2) Harry Augustus Frederick, CMG, Manager of the Uganda Railway, Br E Africa; *b* 3 Jan 1866; *m* 16 Aug 1906 Maud Hobson (*d* 14 Nov 1913), widow of Capt A J R Greene, RA, and dau of Capt H T Sheppard and *d* 2 July 1912

(1) Lucy Marian Alexander; *m* 5 Jan 1892 Arthur Byrom Gordon, of Portland Lodge, Lyme Regis, and *d* 1962, leaving issue. He *d* 1914

Sir Frederick *m* 2nd 3 Sept 1834 Lucy Elizabeth (*d* 25 July 1835), dau of Robert M Bird, of the Civil Service, and by her had issue:

5 Robert George, Bengal CS; *b* 4 July 1835; *m* 1st 26 April 1866 Fanny Catherine Ouseley (*d* 17 Sept 1870), est dau of Alexander C Macrae, MD, and had issue:

(1) Robert Alexander, Commnr Chinese Maritime Customs, FRGS, had Chinese Orders of the Excellent Crop and Double Dragon; *b* 1867; *m* 14 Sept 1904 Eleanor Mary (*d* 1967), 3rd dau of T W Richardson, of Swatow, China, and 27, Roland Gadens, SW, and *d* 14 Feb 1939

(1) Lucy Alexa Heathcote; *m* 19 Jan 1895 John Orlando Summerhayes, DSO, Lt-Col RAMC, MRCS, LRCP, of Saxonholme, Newhaven, Sussex, and *d* 19 Dec 1957, leaving issue. He *d* 1942

(2) Ida Mary; *d* unm 16 Jan 1937

5 (cont.) Robert Currie *m* 2nd 5 Aug 1872 Annie Flora (*d* June 1876), dau of A K MacKinnon, and *d* 13 June 1880, having by her had issue:

(2) Alick Charles, JP E Sussex, late ICS; *b* 1873; *m* 27 Nov 1902 Dorothea (*d* 1958), only dau of Arthur Crickitt, of Eastbourne, and *d* 1953

(3) George Hugh (twin with his bro Alick Charles), Forest Serv of USA; *m* 1st 1897 Grace, dau of A Miller, of Farmington, New Mexico; *m* 2nd 29 Aug 1925 Adelaide Caroline (*d* 1962), 3rd dau of Gore Ouseley, CSI, HEICS, and *d* 20 Jan 1951, having by 1st w had issue:

1a **Sir Alick Bradley Currie, 6th Bt**, US Govt (ret), formerly in radio communications US Navy and Federal Aviation 1923–50, US Rep ICAO 1945–50; *b* 1904; *d* 1987

2a George Donald; *b* 1907; *m* 1928 *Janet, dau of James Scott, of Bayfield, Las Animas, Colorado, USA, and *d* 1980, leaving issue:

1b Sir DONALD SCOTT CURRIE, **7th and present Bt**

2b +James Davidson; *b* 1932; *m* 6 Jan 1956 *Olga Mary, dau of Miguel Otero, of Tampa, Florida, and has issue

1c *Lila Jane; *b* 16 April 1957; *m* 1979 *Justin Chase Estep, and has issue:

1d *Crystal Lila; *b* 1980

3b +George Robert [George Currie, 3631 Columbia Ave, Palmdale, CA 93550, USA]; *b* 1943; *m* 1st 22 Sept 1962 (*divorce* 1972) Lucy Lavonne, dau of S M Gilliam, of Charlotte, N Carolina; *m* 2nd 19– *Judith Hoffman, and by 1st w has issue:

1c *Michael Todd; *b* 21 Aug 1963

2c *Richard Eric; *b* 11 March 1967

1a Annie Flora; *b* 1897; *m* 1920 Clinton B Fisk Harsh (*d* 1974), of Silver City, New Mexico, USA, and had issue:

1b *George Clinton [George Harsh, Box 134, Cliff, New Mexico, USA]; *b* 1920; *m* 1948 *Julia Cecelia, dau of Mathew John Retmiller, of Utica, Michigan, and has issue:

1c *Rhett Mathew; *b* 1954; *m* 1980 *Cinde Lu Ball, of Mesa, Arizona, and has issue:

1d *Mathew Clinton; *b* 1980
2d *Joshua Lee; *b* 1983
3d *Jason Earl; *b* 1985
1c *Diane Elizabeth; *b* 1949; *m* 1st 1968 (*divorce* 1971) Charles D Mannino, and has issue:
1d *Meridee Francis; *b* 1968
1c (cont.) Mrs Diane Mannino *m* 2nd 1971 (*divorce* 1983) Tamás Elemér Belá Kikovay, and has further issue:
1d *Stephen Tamás; *b* 1981
1d *Estike; *b* 1975
2d *Erzsebet (twin); *b* 1975
3d *Julia Etelka; *b* 1979
1c (cont.) Mrs Diane Kikovay has further issue:
4d *Clinton George; *b* 1991
2b *Robert Currie [Robert Harsh, 1916 Yucca Dve, Silver City, NM 88061, USA]; *b* 1922; *m* 1948 *Marjorie Ruth, dau of James E Shean, of Silver City, NM, USA, and has issue:
1c *Mathis Brayton; *b* 1955; *m* 1975 *Leona Rae, dau of James Dudley Messer, of New Mexico, and has issue:
1d *Brayton Bradley; *b* 1978
2d *Robert Cole; *b* 1981
1c *Alice Anne Thadia; *b* 1949
2c *June Margil; *b* 1950; *m* 1975 *James Monroe Foster, of New Mexico
3c *Alexis Mary; *b* 1958
4c *Cecily Louise; *b* 1960; *m* 1984 *Lt-Cdr Julio Jesus Gutierrez, US Navy
3b *Glenn Ray; *b* 1925; *m* 1949 *Jeanne, dau of Theophilus M Prator, of New Orleans, Louisiana, USA, and has issue:
1c *Glenn Ray; *b* 1958; *m* 1982 *Cheryl Ann Harty
1c *Sandra; *b* 1951; *m* 1977 *Davis Carea Dixon, of New Orleans, and has issue:
1d *Katherine Jean; *b* 1982
2c *Christine Elizabeth; *b* 1954
3c *Nancy Jeanne; *b* 1956
(4) Edward Mark; *b* 1875; *m* 1898 Agnes Fanny (*d* June 1967), dau of A F Miller, of Farmington, New Mexico, and *d* 18 Dec 1900
(3) Fanny Katherine (twin); *d* unm 9 Aug 1953
(4) Marie Eliza (twin); *m* 18 May 1918 Lt-Col Penton Shakespear Lowis, CMG, DSO, RA, and *dsp* 30 March 1960. He *d* 10 Oct 1931

Sir Frederick *m* 3rd 10 Feb 1841 Katherine Maria (*d* 30 Jan 1909), dau of George Powney Thompson, BCS, and *d* 11 Sept 1875, having by her had issue:
6 Fendall, Maj-Gen Bengal Cav, late Commr in Oudh, barrister; *b* 24 Nov 1841; *m* 1st 1 March 1866 Susan Elizabeth (*d* 30 June 1868), yst dau of Rev James R Pears, MA, of Woodcote Ho, Windlesham, and had issue:
(1) Fendall James Pears; *b* 1 Jan 1867; *m* 2 Sept 1890 Christina (*d* Nov 1942), dau of David Anderson, of Hamilton, Auckland, NZ, and *d* 1946, having had issue:
1a Fendall Anderson Reid; *b* 1904
1a Veda Mary Fendall; *b* 1891; *m* 1922 Thomas Scott MacMillan, son of Archibald MacMillan, of Otago, NZ, and had issue:
1b *Mary Christina; *b* 6 May 1924
2b *Elizabeth Scott; *b* 25 Oct 1925
(1) Kate ffolliott Fendall; *m* 30 Oct 1890 Lt-Col William Rowney, MD, RAMC, and had issue
6 (cont.) Maj-Gen Fendall Currie *m* 2nd 28 Dec 1869 Julia (*d* 18 April 1920), dau of Frederick Pole Buller, BCS, and *d* 4 Dec 1920, having by her had issue:
(2) Ivor Bertram Fendall, DSO (1919), Lt-Col RA; *b* 2 Aug 1872; *m* 30 Oct 1906 May Constance (*d* 7 Feb 1937), 2nd dau of Field Marshal Sir George White, VC, GCB, OM, GCSI, GCMG, GCIE, GCVO, and *d* 1 April 1924, leaving issue:
1a *Sylvia Constance [Mrs Nigel Burgess, 52 Cornwall Gdns, London SW7]; *b* 2 Oct 1910; *m* 17 July 1937 *Nigel George Kingsford Burgess, yr son of Cdr Malcolm Burgess, RN, and has issue:
1b *Anthony Malcolm Kingsford; *b* 28 Aug 1941; *educ* Winchester and King's Coll Cambridge (MA); *m* 24 April 1965 *Patricia Carol, dau of Maj Charles Gibson, of 10, Pengelly Ave, Northbourne, Bournemouth, and had issue:
1c *Irina Jane; *b* 17 Nov 1966
2c *Lucy Kate; *b* 24 May 1968
2b *Simon George Fendall; *b* 30 April 1945; *educ* Winchester
2a *Eleanor Frances; *b* 13 June 1918; *m* 5 Dec 1941 Charles Edward Brill (*dec*), and has issue:
1b *Caroline Frances; *b* 18 Dec 1953
(3) Harold Erskine Fendall, Lt ISC; *b* 10 Sept 1877; *d* unm 24 July 1900
(4) Cyril Amiand Fendall; *b* 15 Nov 1878; *d* young
(2) Ethel Mayne Fendall; *m* 4 Jan 1892 Lt-Col James John Pratt, FRCS, late IMS, Oudh, and *d* 5 Jan 1962, leaving issue. He *d* 1937
(3) Maud Julia Fendall; *m* 5 Aug 1905 John Bernard Lethbridge Stilwell, TD, Hon Col 4th Hampshire Regt, son of John Pakenham Stilwell, of Hilfield, Yateley, Hants, and *d* 13 Jan 1956, leaving issue. He *d* 4 Nov 1945
(4) Sybil Beatrice Fendall; *m* 3 March 1900 Walter James Edwin Lupton, OBE, ICS, and *d* 21 Dec 1932, leaving issue
(5) Hilda Katherine Fendall; *m* 28 Dec 1895 Bernard Montagu Champion Hamilton, Indian Police, and had issue
7 Hugh Penton (Rev), Prebendary of Wells; *b* 31 May 1854; *d* unm 20 March 1903
8 Rivers Grenfell; *b* 8 June 1857; *m* 6 Nov 1889 Alice Theresa Disney (*d* 1947), est dau of Arthur Disney Dunne, and *d* 3 May 1934, having had issue:
(1) Disney Rivers, MC, Maj, Roy Scots WW I (wounded, despatches, Croix de Guerre of Belgium), WW II (despatches); *b* 8 April 1894; *m* 12 March 1919 Ethel Jeanette (Joan) (*d* 1981), only dau of Arnold Bryce-Smith, of Preston Mountford Hall, Shrewsbury, and *d* 23 Oct 1964, leaving issue:
1a +Frederick Disney Rivers [Frederick Currie Esq, Whitehayes, 93 Church St, Willingdon, Eastbourne, Sussex], Capt Roy Scots, served WW II, Burma 1943 (wounded); *b* 24 June 1921; *educ* Wellington and Trin Hall Cambridge (MA); *m* 9 Aug 1949 *Jean Alison, yr dau of Lionel Westrop Jardine, CIE, of Englewood, Chobham, Surrey (*see* JARDINE, Bt, of Godalming), and has issue:
1b +Peter Frederick Rivers [Peter Currie Esq, 85 Bouverie Rd, London N16]; *b* 21 Dec 1950; *educ* Wellington; *m* 1973 *Mary Rose Veronica, dau of E J Goodman, and has had issue:
1c +Philip Simon Rivers; *b* 1977
2c +Francis William Mordaunt; *b* and *d* 1980
1c *Morag Claire Rowan; *b* 1981
1b *Jennifer Jean [Mrs Jeffrey Smith, 3 Ridge Rd, Falmer, E Sussex]; *b* 9 May 1953; *m* 1st 1972 (*divorce* 19–) Alan Sayers; *m* 2nd 19– *Jeffery R Smith, and by 1st husb has issue:
1c *Jonathan Alan; *b* 1974
2c *Daniel William; *b* 1976
2b *Fiona Alexandra [Miss Fiona Currie, 134 Wannock Lane, Lower Willingdon, E Sussex]; *b* 23 Jan 1958
2a Arnold William Rivers, OBE (1966), Lt-Col Roy Scots, served WW II (wounded); *b* 25 July 1923; *educ* Wellington; *m* 26 March 1960 *Daphne Valerie Helen, yr dau of Cdr Reginald Nash, DSC, RN, of Busta Ho, Eversley, Hants
(2) Frederick Rivers, Lt 3rd Bn (att 1st Bn) King's Shropshire LI; *b* 1896; *ka* 8 Aug 1915
(1) Mabel Rivers; *b* 1898; *m* 19 Dec 1924 Lionel Wilfred Harford, yr son of Rev Dundas Harford, Rector of Sculthorpe, Fakenham, and *d* 14 May 1967, leaving issue
1 Harriet Sophia; *m* 2 Sept 1865 Col Sir John Underwood Bateman-Champain, KCMG, RE, and *d* 14 Aug 1905, leaving issue. He *d* 1 Feb 1887
2 Susan Mary; *m* 9 July 1863 Edmund Elliot Lowis, late BCS, 2nd surv son of John Lowis, of Plean, and *d* 1910, leaving issue
3 Katherine Louisa; *m* 22 Nov1870 Rev Edwin Francis Dyke, Rector of Marsham, Kent, and Hon Canon of Canterbury (*see* DYKE, Bt), and *d* 26 March 1914
4 Mabel Thornton; *d* unm 30 Oct 1954, in her 92nd year

CURRIE OF MARYLEBONE

Creation: B. (LP, UK) 1997.

THE BARON CURRIE OF MARYLEBONE, of Marylebone, City of Westminster (David Anthony Currie) [The Rt Hon The Lord Currie of Marylebone, House of Lords, London SW1A 0PW]; *b* 9 Dec 1946; *educ* Battersea GS, Manchester U and Birmingham U; economist: Hoare Govett 1971–72, Economic Models 1972; Lecturer, Reader and Prof Economics Queen Mary Coll London U 1972–88, Research Fell Centre Ec Policy Research 1983–, Houblon-Norman Research Fell Bank England 1985–86, Visiting Scholar IMF 1987, Dir Centre Ec Forecasting 1988–95, Prof Economics London Business Sch 1988– (Res Dean 1989–92, Govr 1989–, Dep Pncpl 1992–95); dir Charter 88 1993–(chair of Exec 1993–97); memb: ABRC 1992–93, Retail Price Index Advsy Ctee 1992–95, Treasury's Panel Independent Forecasters 1992–95; Dir: Internat Schs of Business Management 1992, Joseph Rowntree Reform Tst (Investments) Ltd 1989, Joseph Rowntree Reform Tst (Properties) Ltd 1991; Tstee Joseph Rowntree Reform Tst 1991; author: *Advances in Monetary Economics* (1985), *The Operation and Regulation of Financial Markets* (with Charles Goodhart and David Llewellyn, 1986), *Macroeconomic Interactions between North and South* (with David Vines, 1988), *Rules, Reputation and Macroeconomic Policy Co-ordination* (1994), *North-South Linkages and International Macro-economic Policy* (1995), *The Pros and Cons of EMU* (1997), *Will the Euro Work? The Ins and Outs of EMU* (1998); *m* 1st 1975 (*divorce* 1992) Shaziye Gazioglu — and has two sons; *m* 2nd 1995 *Angela Mary Piers Dumas

Lineage: KENNEDY MOIR CURRIE; *m* Marjorie Thompson and has:
DAVID ANTHONY, *cr* a **Baron**

CURTIS

Arms: Paly of six or and az. a fess chequy arg. and sa., on a canton gu. a dragon's wing erect of the third, in base a sword ppr., pommel and hilt of the first, surmounting a key in saltire of the second. **Crest:** A ram's head couped arg., surmounted by two branches of oak in saltire ppr. **Motto:** *Gradatim vincimus* ('We conquer step by step'). **Creation:** Bt. (UK) 23 Dec 1802.

SIR WILLIAM PETER CURTIS, 7TH BT, of Cullands Grove, Middlesex [Sir William Curtis Bt, Oak Lodge, Bank St, Bishop's Waltham, Hants SO3 1AN]; *b* 9 April 1935; *s* f 1976; *educ* Winchester, Trin Coll Oxford (MA) and RAC Cirencester; late 16th/5th Lancers

Lineage: JOSEPH CURTIS, of London; *b* 1715, son of James Curtis, of Wanstead, Essex, who *d* 1731, and Sarah Clowden, his first w; *m* Mary (*d* 1759), dau of Timothy Tennant, and *d* 21 March 1771, having had with other issue:

1 Timothy, of Hackney; *b* 1743; *m* his cousin, Elizabeth (*d* 1769), dau of Cornelius Wildbore, of Nottingham, and Elizabeth, his w, dau of James Curtis, of Wanstead, and *d* 8 Aug 1804, leaving issue

2 WILLIAM (Sir), **1st Bt**

3 George, of Cardington, Beds, Capt HEICS; *m* 3 July 1787 Anna Delicia (*d* Feb 1795), dau of Edward Windsor, of Tottenham, and *d* 4 June 1819, leaving issue

4 Charles (Rev), Rector of St Martin's, Birmingham, and of Solihull, Warwicks; *b* 1756; *m* 1st 1780 Dorothy (*d* 1 Jan 1795), dau of John Wylde, of Bell Broughton, Worcs, and had issue; *m* 2nd 1797 Sarah, dau of Thomas Wilkinson, of London, and *d* 12 Jan 1829, having by her had further issue

The 3rd son,

Sir William Curtis, 1st Bt (UK), so *cr* 23 Dec 1802; Ld Mayor London 1794–95, MP City London 1790–1818 and 1820, Bletchingley 1819 and Hastings 1826; *b* 25 Jan 1752; *m* 9 Jan 1776 Anne (*d* 7 Aug 1833), yst dau and coheir of Edward Constable (and with her er sis, Mary, w of Rev Thomas Roberts, coheir of the Austens of Tenterden, Bts, of Bexley), and had, with another s:

1 WILLIAM (Sir), **2nd Bt**

2 Timothy Abraham; *b* 30 Jan 1786; *m* 1st 25 April 1809 Margaret Harriet (*d* 8 June 1847), yst dau of Young Green, of Poole, Dorset; *m* 2nd 17 May 1851 Frances Pitt (*dsp*), dau of L B Constable, and *d* 13 May 1857, having had, with other issue:

(1) William Frederick, Maj-Gen in the Army, late 21st Hus; *b* 4 May 1810; *m* 7 Feb 1842 Joanna Jacobina de Hubbenet (*d* 1 Aug 1845), and *d* 2 Sept 1882, leaving issue:

1a William Frederick de Hubbenet, Brig-Gen late RA; *b* 2 Dec 1842; *m* 11 Nov 1880 Mary Owen (*d* 13 Sept 1934), dau of John Ward Nicholls, and *d* 27 April 1906, leaving issue:

1b Frederick, Lt-Col 19th Lancers (Fane's Horse), IA; *b* 3 Dec 1882

2b Oscar Owen, Maj IA; *b* 8 Jan 1889; *m* 1939 *Mabel Frances Isobel, dau of Edward King-Frazer, of Co Sligo

1b Freda Isabella

2b Olga Bijou Dinah; *m* 29 Dec 1928 Alfred Edye Manning Foster, yst son of Thomas Gregory Foster, barrister (*see* FOSTER, Bt)

3b Joceline Sophia Lilian; *m* 2 May 1925 Paul Stutfield, est son of C H Stutfield

(2) James Charles, Col late Bengal Staff Corps; *b* 8 Jan 1820; *m* 25 April 1854 Harriet (*d* 15 Sept 1913), dau of Col George William Hamilton, CSI, and *d* 10 Oct 1889, leaving, with other issue:

1a George Arthur Hamilton, Lt RNR (ret), and Capt RAN (ret); *b* 28 Oct 1859; *m* 1891 Elizabeth Mary (*d* Nov 1941), yr dau of Edmund MacDonnell, of Dublin, and *d* 14 Aug 1933, leaving issue, with a dau:

1b Cecil Arthur Hamilton, late RAN, served WW I; *b* 1895; *m* 30 March 1929 Constance May (*d* 28 July 1968), dau of Aubrey E Webb, of Melbourne, Australia, and *d* 1970, leaving issue:

1c +Geoffrey Cecil Hamilton; *b* Aug 1932; *m* 1960 *Barbara Ellen, dau of Peter Angus, of Newmarket, Brisbane, Qld, and has issue:

1d *Fiona Madeline Hamilton, *b* 1962

2d *Helen Mary Hamilton; *b* 1964

1c *Anne Eleanor Hamilton; *b* 28 April 1935

2a Alfred William Hamilton; *b* 27 July 1864; *m* 1901 Euphemia Hilda McCluny (*d* in Br Columbia), widow of Henry Cooperthwaite, and dau of William A C Reynolds, and *d* 25 Feb 1918, leaving issue:

1b +James Percy Alfred Hamilton; *b* 1907; Lt 2nd Bn Rocky Mountain Rangers; *m* 1939 *Barbara Milsom, dau of Frank Weldon Russell, of Dartmouth, NS, and has issue:

1c +James Russell Hamilton [James Curtis Esq, 650 Beachview Dve, N Vancouver, BC VFG 1R1, Canada]; *b* 1941; *educ* U of BC (BCom), MBA; *m* 1966 *Marion Eileen, BEd, dau of George B Moore, of Vancouver, BC, and has issue:

1d +James David Hamilton; *b* 1974

2d +Russell Andrew Hamilton; *b* 1975

2c +Alfred William Hamilton; *b* 1945; *m* 1971 *Barbara Joan, dau of Benjamin Earl Tompkins, of Terrace, BC, and has issue:

1d +James William Hamilton; *b* 1973

1b *Annette Harriet Hamilton

2b *Grace Anna Delicia Florence Hamilton; *b* 1903; *m* 1923 *Laurie E Wiren, and has issue:

1c *John; *b* 1930

2c *James; *b* 1934

1c *Margaret; *b* 1926

2c *Leonore; *b* 1928

3b *Dorothy Gladys Claremont Hamilton

4b *Margaret Euphemia Ceclia Hamilton; *b* 1909; *m* 1940 *Lloyd E Kindleysides

1a Grace Frances Hamilton

(1) Emma Charlotte; *m* 10 Feb 1835 Charles James Bevan, and had issue

3 Charles Berwick; *b* 18 March 1795; *m* 30 Nov 1822 Henrietta (*d* 6 April 1884), 2nd dau of Rev J Battridge Pearson, of Croxall, Derbys, and *d* 26 Oct 1876, having had, with other issue:

(1) Charles William, of Kearsney Abbey, Dover, JP Kent and Wilts; *b* 13 Jan 1824; *m* 15 June 1850 Henrietta Francisca (*d* 18 May 1914), yst dau of William R Robinson, and *d* 5 May 1905, leaving, with other issue:

1a Charles Herbert, Lt-Col and Hon Col late 4th Bn E Surrey Regt, JP Middlesex; *b* 15 March 1852; *m* 29 April 1879 Frances Edith (*d* July 1945), dau of Capt P Pinckney, and *d* 15 Sept 1939, leaving issue

1b Timothy Herbert William, Maj late E Surrey Mil and 19th Roy Hus, served in S Africa 1901, Somaliland 1908, WW I 1914–15, and 1940–47 as Assist Ch Constable, War Dept Constabulary; *b* 3 Aug 1882; *educ* Harrow and Trin Coll Cambridge; *m* 11 Jan 1913 Edith Marjorie (*d* 29 Dec 1968, aged 81), yr dau of F Aldcroft Kay, and *d* 11 June 1966, leaving issue:

1c Pamela Kay, late J/Cdr ATS; *b* 10 Oct 1913; *m* 1 Jan 1944 *Maj John Howard Nickson, RA, only son of Howard Nickson, of The White Ho of Speen, Princes Risborough, and *d* 22 Sept 1995, leaving:

1d Simon John Curtis; *b* 1945; *d* 14 Sept 1995

2d *Jeremy David; *b* 1947

1d *Cecelia Anne [Mrs Cecelia Magee, The Glebe Cottage, East End, Chadlington, Oxon OX7 3LX]; *b* 1953; *m* 1984 *Sean Magee and has:

1e *Freddie Nicholas; *b* 28 Sept 1988

2e *Julia Claire; *b* 24 March 1986

2c *Mary Kay [Mrs Alexander Readman, 15 Victoria Sq, London SW1]; *b* 24 July 1917; *m* 10 June 1939 *Col Alexander George Jeffrey Readman, DSO, late Roy Scots Greys, est son of Lt-Col John Jeffrey Readman, DSO, of Broadholm, Lockerbie, Dumfriesshire, and has had issue:

1d *Timothy Christopher George; *b* 20 Nov 1944; *educ* Harrow; *m* 1st 12 Jan 1971 (*divorce*) Rosalind, er dau of Peter Trehearne, and has issue:

1e *Alexander

1d (cont.) Timothy Readman *m* 2nd *Christine, formerly w of —, and by her has issue:

2e *Harry Nicholas James; *b* 24 April 1977

1d Sally Kay; *b* at Jerusalem, 30 June 1941; lost at sea by enemy action, 13 Sept 1942

2d *Teresa Mary; *b* 23 June 1947; *m* 1973 *Hon Christopher Charles Lyttelton, 2nd son of 10th Viscount Cobham, KG (*qv*), and has issue, one son and one dau

2b Philip Pinckney (Toby), MC (1916), Maj late 15th The King's Hus, and 99th (Bucks and Berks Yeo) Bde, RFA, served WW I 1914–19 (despatches three times), GSO (2) (1918); *b* 21 Sept 1884; *m* 1st 16 April 1925 (*divorce* 1933) Hélène Ellinor Clare, 2nd dau of Capt Glen Kidston, and had issue:

1c *Cherry April Ellinor [Mrs Terence Gossage, Flexford House, Sway, Lymington, Hants SO41 6DP]; *b* 24 May 1926; *m* 28 Dec 1949 *Maj Terence Leslie Gossage, MBE, late KOYLI, son of Air Marshal Sir Leslie Gossage, KCB, CVO, DSO, MC, of Abbotswood, Buxted, Sussex, and has issue:

1d *Philip Leslie; *b* 8 April 1951; *educ* Cheltenham; ARICS, FAAV; *m* 1st 1983 (*divorce* 1986) Deborah Ann Darrell; *m* 2nd 1991 *Nicola Jane, day of Sir Nigel Frederick Althaus, of Swallowcliffe, Wilts, and has issue:

1e *James Peter; *b* 1993

1e *Sophie Harriet; *b* 1994

2d *Andrew Alexander; *b* 17 Jan 1963; maj Army Air Corps; *m* 1988 *Jessica Lucy, dau of Cdr Gresham Vaughan, RN, and has issue:

1e *Thomas Edmund Gresham; *b* 1994

1e *Henrietta Ellinor; *b* 1993

1d *Julia April Ellinor; *b* 21 Oct 1954; *m* 1982 *Christopher Jenkin, and has issue:

1c *Annabel Louise; *b* 1985

2c *Camilla Rose; *b* 1988

2c *Alison Audrey Primrose [Mrs William Windham, Parc Gwynne, Glasbury-on-Wye, via Hereford HR3 5LL]; *b* 23 Feb 1928; *m* 9 June

1956 *William Ashe Dymoke Windham, yr son of Lt-Col Henry Steuart Windham, of Priory Cottage, Chicksands, Shefford, Beds (*see* BOWYER-SMYTH, Bt), and has issue

3c Glenda Kidston; *b* 1 March 1931; *m* 1st 4 May 1953 (*divorce* 1969) Maj Colin Butchard, 1st/2nd KEO Gurka Rifles, er son of P Butchard, of Woodlands, Frinton, Essex; *m* 2nd Oct 1969 Rodney Frederick Hedderley Ward, late Coldstream Gds, yst son of D J H Ward, of Matching Green, Harlow, Essex and *d* 11 Aug 1982, having by her 1st husb had issue:

1d *William James Langrishe; *b* 7 Oct 1956

1d *Victoria Annabelle Ellinor [Mrs Victoria Spendlove, 88 Kings Court Rd, Streatham, London SW16 1JB]; *b* 2 Aug 1954

2d *Henrietta Matilda; *b* 17 Oct 1957

2b (cont.) Maj Toby Curtis *m* 2nd 21 Oct 1941 Marion (*d* 13 May 1997), only child of George Berkeley Wilson, of Long Barn, Ringwood, and *d* 11 March 1974, having by her had issue:

1c +Timothy Malise [Timothy Curtis Esq, Street Farmhouse, Vernham St, nr Andover, Hants SP11 0EL]; *b* 9 Aug 1942; *educ* Eton, Trin Coll Cambridge (BA 1964), and Harvard Business Sch (MBA); *m* 1st 1 June 1968 (*divorce* 1982) Sally Elizabeth, er dau of Ambrose S Higgins, of 191 Broadway, Bangor, Maine, USA; *m* 2nd 1986 *Cecilia Leueen, dau of Maj Peter Brown, of Longworth, Oxon, and by 1st w has issue:

1d +Timothy George; *b* 21 Nov 1972

2d +Edward Ambrose (twin); *b* 21 Nov 1972

1d *Katherine Pinckney; *b* 9 Sept 1970

2c +Giles Philip [Giles Curtis Esq, Walnut Tree Cottage, Upper Wootton, Basingstoke, Hants]; *b* 5 March 1945; *educ* Eton and St Andrews U (BSc); *m* 24 July 1971 *Sarah Anne, est dau of Lt-Col Walter George Finney, TD, of The Old Vicarage, Iford, Lewes, Sussex, by his wife Jean, yr dau of V-Adml Edmund Rupert Drummond, CB, MVO, DL (*see* PERTH, E), and has issue:

1d *Rowena Mary; *b* 30 May 1972

2d *Arabella Jean; *b* 18 Nov 1975

3d *Camilla Sarah; *b* 1979

4d *Lavinia Frances; *b* 1982

1b Gwendolen Edith; *m* 23 Nov 1908 Maj John Orr Ewing, MC, 16th Lancers, son of Hugh Moody Robertson Ewing (*see* ORR EWING, Bt), and *d* 20 July 1964, leaving issue

2a Percy Falconer, late Capt 1st Wilts RV; *b* 11 Aug 1859; *m* 8 Aug 1893 Alice Gertrude, dau of Richard Lea, late of Pembina Crossing, Manitoba, and *d* 8 March 1936

3a Thomas Reginald, late Lt Roy Wilts Yeo Cav; *b* 29 March 1862; *m* 22 April 1897 Dorcas Stewart (*d* 24 Aug 1939), dau of William Johnston, of Cowhill Tower, Dumfries-shire, and *d* 7 Sept 1932, leaving issue:

1b Jocelyn Stewart, Lt Rifle Bde; *b* 23 Jan 1898; *ka* 21 March 1918

2b William Patrick Stewart, OBE (1945), DL (Hants 1952), Col late Rifle Bde, Adjt Artists Rifles (TA) 1937–40, ADC to Govr-Gen and Cdr-in-Chief, Canada 1924–25, Commr St John Amb Bde for Hants 1954; *b* 9 April 1899; *m* 7 Feb 1929 Margaret Pamela Adderley (*d* 1979), er dau of Lt-Col Hartopp Francis Charles Adderley Cradock, of Knighton, Twyford, Hants, and *d* 12 Feb 1965, leaving issue:

1c *Jill Elizabeth; *b* 20 Feb 1930; *m* 1 Nov 1952 *Frederick Michael Pelly, yst son of Sir Harold Alwyne Pelly, 5th Bt, MC (*qv*), and has issue

2c *(Dorcas) Sara [Mrs Robert Ross, 15 York and Albany Close, Walmer, Deal]; *b* 20 May 1932; *m* 15 May 1965 *Capt Robert Jeremy Ross, RM, only son of Lt-Col Gerald Whitehill Ross, of Kilmacanogue, Co Wicklow, and has issue:

1d *Edward Patrick; *b* 27 Feb 1966

1d *Annabel Margaret; *b* 17 Jan 1968

3c *Jocelyn Patricia [Mrs Mark Tress, 19 Finlay St, London SW6 6HE]; *b* 2 June 1936; *m* 10 Sept 1960 *Mark Julian Cecil Tress, only son of Cecil William Boulton Tress, of Hyde Cottage, Willingale, Essex, and has issue:

1d *Oliver James Mark; *b* 8 May 1968

1d *Amanda; *b* 10 June 1961

2d *Camilla; *b* 17 Aug 1963

4c *Victoria Anne Dorothea Adderley [Mrs Denis Gamberoni, 43 Chepstow Place, London W2S]; *b* 20 March 1939; *m* 18 June 1965 *Denis Charles Pasquale Gamberoni, only son of I F Gamberoni, of Hayes, Kent, and has issue:

1d *Tobias Felix; *b* 8 Jan 1970

1d *Justine Louise; *b* 7 May 1967

5c *Tessa Evelyn Cecilia; *b* 1943

4a Eustace Henry; *b* 30 April 1863; *m* 16 Feb 1904 Laura, yst dau of Alfred Ibbotson, of Hill St, W, and *d* 1948, leaving issue:

1b +John Eustace; *b* 3 Aug 1910

1b *Corinna Laurel Mary; *b* 21 Aug 1908

5a Harold William; *b* 13 March 1875; *d* unm

1a Adela Henrietta; *m* 1st 5 Oct 1871 Archibald Godfrey Hope, and had issue (*see* HOPE, Bt). He *d* 17 June 1881. She *m* 2nd 1889 Perceval Kingsford, and *d* 15 Sept 1923, leaving further issue

2a Alice Francisca; *m* 1 Aug 1876 Maj John Thomas Browne, late 20th Hus, and *d* 3 July 1928, leaving issue

3a Isabel Lucy; *m* 1884 William Hugh Fowle, JP, of Chute Lodge, Andover, and *d* 30 March 1949, leaving issue. He *d* 1942

4a Dora Margaret; *m* 1st 1889 John Ball Forman, of Setley Ho, Brockenhurst, Hants, and had issue. He *d* 14 Sept 1900. She *m* 2nd 27 April 1904 Herbert T W Bowell, son of Rev William Bowell, MA, Vicar of Sissinghurst. She resumed the name FORMAN by deed poll 1906 and *d* 11 Jan 1931

5a Eveline Jane; *d* unm 195–

(2) James Falconer; *b* 2 Aug 1827; *m* 1st 7 Feb 1861 Josephina Adelaide (*d* 24 Aug 1868), dau of Col Samuel Mangin, and had issue:

1a Falconer Charles; *b* 30 Oct 1864; *m* 19 Jan 1893 Muriel Eva (*d* 30 June 1953), dau of F J Hammond, MD, FRCS, of Indianapolis, USA, and *d* 31 Aug 1931

1a Julia Augusta; *d* unm 18 Aug 1942

(2) (cont.) James Curtis *m* 2nd 5 Dec 1872 Mary Helen (*d* 23 Oct 1910), dau of Rev J Brown, and *d* 28 Dec 1879, having by her had issue:

2a Sybil Mary; *d* unm 13 Dec 1947

3a Gertrude Madeline; *b* 1875; *m* 25 Sept 1913 Imre Knopp, artist, of Damyanich Itea, Budapest, and *d* 16 March 1968, having had issue, one dau. He *d* 30 Jan 1946

(3) Reginald, Maj-Gen late RA; *b* 1 Feb 1829; *m* 10 Jan 1863 Marianne Emma (*d* 26 Dec 1874), er dau of James Salmond, of Waterfoot, Cumberland, and Langton Hall, Notts, and *d* 1894, leaving issue:

1a Reginald Salmond (Sir), KCMG (1917), CB (1915), DSO (1900), Maj-Gen late RE, Maj-Gen in charge of Admin, Aldershot 1917, served in Sudan, Ashanti, and S Africa; *b* 21 Nov 1863; *m* 28 March 1894 Hon Hilda Margaret Barrington (*d* 10 March 1929), dau of 9th Viscount Barrington (*see* 1970 edn), and *d* 11 Jan 1922, leaving issue:

1b Diane; *b* 1895; *m* 4 Aug 1914 Brig Robert Albany Boger, late RE and RFC, son of Capt H T Boger, RN, of Ryde, IoW, and *d* 10 May 1968, leaving issue, one son and two daus. He *d* 19 Sept 1957

2b Rosdew Maud; *b* 24 March 1908; *m* 1st 21 June 1932 (*divorce* 1947) Capt John Shields, DCM, late Scots Gds. He *d* 10 Jan 1964. She *m* 2nd May 1947 René Regnier, late Belgian Air Force, of Namur, Belgium and *d* 5 May 1966, leaving issue, one son

3b Ivy Agnes; *b* 25 March 1908 (twin); *m* 10 May 1933 John Malebisse Beckwith (*d* 26 July 1969), only son of Lt-Col William Malebisse Beckwith, DSO, and had issue:

1c *William John Malabisse, Capt 4th RGJ (TAVR), late Gordon Highrs, memb Br Computer Soc; *b* 24 Dec 1934; *m* 5 Oct 1968 *Flavia Rosamond, dau of Dr Norman George Hulbert, of Bentinck Mansions, W1

2a Harcourt Taylor; *b* 11 April 1865; *m* 11 May 1903 Ethel Emma, widow of F Elliot, and est dau of John Beattie, and *d* 19 Sept 1932, having had issue:

1b Reginald Derek; *b* 16 Sept 1908; *d* 10 Dec 1909

3a Edward George, CMG (1916), Col late Northants Regt TF, formerly Maj Bedf Regt, served WW I 1914–19 (despatches six times); *b* 26 Nov 1868; *m* 10 Sept 1903 Ethel (*m* 2nd 2 Oct 1926 Capt Norman Hornsby, who *d* 1957), yr dau of Walter Coote, FRGS, and *d* 7 March 1923, leaving issue:

1b David Sacheverell, memb Inst of Petroleum, Lt-Col Roy Fus, served WW II 1939–45 (despatches four times); *b* 7 March 1913; *m* 1st 12 July 1935 (*divorce* 1945) Annora Beatrice, yr dau of Frederick Rowland Williams-Wynn, CB (*see* WILLIAMS-WYNN, Bt), and has issue:

1c +Edward Peregrine Sacheverell [Edward Curtis Esq, Oak House, The Green Richmond, Surrey TW9 1NA], late Lt 8th Hus; *b* 7 Dec 1937; *educ* Stowe; *m* 1970 *Marie-Adèle, dau of Francis Le Baron Smoot, of Georgetown, Washington DC, and has issue:

1d +Charles Edward Peregrine; *b* 1971; *educ* Eton

2d +William Francis Peregrine; *b* 1974; *educ* Eton and Bristol U (BA)

3d +Robert Frederick Peregrine; *b* 1978; *educ* Stowe and London U

1d *Caroline Annora Adèle; *b* 1980; *educ* Godolphin and Latymer Sch

2c +Hugh Frederick [Hugh Curtis Esq, 58 The Vineyard, Richmond, Surrey TW10 6AT]; *b* 14 March 1941; *educ* Stowe; *m* *Maija Kaarina, dau of Aulis Samuli Pyy, of Helsinki, and has issue:

1d *Victoria Ann; *b* 1971; *educ* Westonbirt, St Paul's and Somerville Coll Oxford (BA)

2d *Natasha Kaarina Helena; *b* 1973; *educ* Godolphin Latymer Sch and Manchester U (BA Hons)

3d *Annabel Mary; *b* 1981

1b (cont.) Lt-Col David Curtis *m* 2nd 18 May 1948 (*divorce* 1957) Pamela Ruth, BA Columbia U, USA, dau of Reginald Walter Preston; *m* 3rd 7 Oct 1957 *Monica Sarah Anne [Mrs David Curtis, 20 Pembridge Crescent, London W11], dau of N Payne, of Athens, Greece, and *d* 11 Jan 1990, having by her had issue:

1c *Isabella Alexandra Nina [Mrs Isabella Curtis, 4 Odos Plutarchou, Athens, Greece]; *b* 11 Feb 1959; *m* 1984 (*divorce* 1992) Goulven Courtaigne, of 9 rue de l'Amiral Mouchez, Paris, son of Pierre Courtaigne, of Versailles, and has issue:

1d *Emma Louise Marie; *b* 1985

4a Arthur Evelyn Scott, Maj late 3rd Bn Suffolk Regt, served WW I 1914–19 (Mons Star, despatches); *b* 21 Jan 1870; *m* Margaret Emma (*d* 22 Aug 1940), dau of John Mackintosh, of Inverness, and *d* 6 June 1944, leaving issue:

1b Arthur Evelyn Scott, Lt late 4th Bn Suffolk Regt (SR), served with RE Signals in BEF WW I; *b* 12 May 1897; *m* 26 June 1930 *Elspeth Helen Margaret Cammell, dau of Percy H Jacobs, and *d* 9 May 1963, leaving issue:

1c +William Scott, ACII (1960), late 2nd Lt RA [William Curtis Esq, The Old Manor House, Radcliffe-on-Trent, Notts]; *b* 18 June 1931; *m* 2 July 1960 *Mary Florence, dau of G L Wilks, and has issue:

1d +Reginald James Scott; *b* 17 Nov 1963

1a Linda; *m* 8 Nov 1890 Vincent Biscoe Tritton, and *d* 3 July 1952, leaving issue (*see* TRITTON, Bt)

(4) Spencer Henry, JP Middx and Herts; *b* 11 July 1833; *m* 17 Aug 1864 Margaret Tupper (*d* 16 Nov 1899), est dau of De Vic Carey, of Le Vallon, Guernsey, and *d* 26 Feb 1913, having had issue:

1a Spencer Carey, FRIBA, Capt and Hon Maj (TD) 8th City of London Bn, London Regt (PO Rifles), and Capt and Hon Maj Roy Guernsey Engrs (Mil), served S Africa 1900–01, WW I as T/Maj cmdg RE Guernsey and Alderney Dist (despatches); *b* 23 July 1865; *m* 4 Feb 1902 Edith Mabel (*d* 10 Sept 1931), dau of T J Eaton, of Droogvlei, Malmesbury, Cape Colony, and *d* 28 March 1945, leaving issue:

1b *(Sylvia) Rosamond D'Urban Carey [Mrs Thomas Pyke, 11 Sycamore Ct, Hoskins Rd, Oxted, Surrey RH8 9JQ]; *b* 14 Sept 1908; *m* 22 Dec 1932 Thomas Musgrave Pyke, OBE, TD (*d* 1992), Schs Inspr, only s of F C Pyke, of Mullion, Cornwall, and has issue:

1c *Susan Musgrave [Mrs John Monaghan, 10 Wilton Close, Street, Somerset]; *b* 17 Oct 1935; *m* 1966 *John Leo Monaghan, and has issue:

1d *David John; *b* 29 Nov 1968

2d *Benjamin Musgrave; *b* 1970

2c *Anne Curtis [Mrs John Turner, The Old Vicarage, Church Rd, Combe Down, Bath BA2 5JJ], MB, BS (Lond 1962); *b* 25 Jan 1939; *m* June 1962 *John Ferens Turner, MB, BS, son of Maj Sidney Claud Turner, of Catchbells, Stanway, Colchester, Essex, and has issue:

1d *Edward Thomas; *b* 13 April 1966

1d *Sophia Jane; *b* 22 May 1964

2d *Jessica Charlotte; *b* 23 July 1968

2a Wilfried Henry, late chm Grand Union Canal Co, memb of Cncl of Inst of Tport; *b* 15 Nov 1866; *educ* Winchester; *m* 21 July 1897 Augusta (*d* 1945), dau of Rev E T Carey, and *d* 1943, leaving issue:

1b Anthony Edmund Spencer; *b* 17 July 1906; *m* 3 Oct 1931 Nancy M (*d* 1986), only child of R Nesbit Taylor, of Meadow Bank, Epsom, and *d* 29 July 1962, leaving issue:

1c *Jean Anna [Mrs Brian Humphreys, Jalna, St Johns Rd, Crowborough, E Sussex TN6 1RT]; *b* 18 Sept 1933; *m* 1st 24 Aug 1960 (*divorce* 1978) John Richard Aley; *m* 2nd 1980 *Brian James Humphreys

2c *Brenda Carey [Mrs Malcolm Upstone, Hermitage End, Treblers Rd, Crowborough, E Sussex]; *b* 24 June 1936; *m* 1st April 1960 William John Stickland Budd; *m* 2nd 1979 *Malcolm Cecil Upstone, and by 1st husb has issue:

1d *Duncan Spencer; *b* 1962

2d *Roger Alastair; *b* 1964

1d *Caroline Carey; *b* 1965

3a Bertram De Vic Carey; *b* 11 July 1873; *m* 25 Sept 1902 Edith Maude, dau of Frederick Chapman, of Cape Town and Liverpool, and *dsp* 8 Jan 1904

1a Margaret Helen; *b* 5 April 1871; *d* unm 20 Dec 1945

2a Catherine Louisa, OStJ; *b* 6 Nov 1876; *d* unm 14 Oct 1965

(5) Henry Downing; *b* 2 Dec 1836; *m* 20 Oct 1874 Ada Harriett (*d* 8 Feb 1939), dau of R Amadeus Baron Heath, of Croydon, and *d* 13 Sept 1914, leaving issue:

1a Berwick, CB (1919), CMG (1920), DSO and bar (1917), V-Adml, ADC to HM GEORGE V 1927, R-Adml-in-Charge and Adml Supt, Gibraltar 1929–31, V-Adml (ret) 1932, served WW I (despatches, promotion, Order of St Stanislaus of Russia, 2nd Cl with Swords), and WW II as Cdre of Convoys; *b* 9 Oct 1876; *m* 1st 24 July 1907 Mildred Henrietta (*d* 21 Sept 1927), er dau of Frank John Constable Curtis, of Merrivale, Ross, and had, with other issue:

1b *Janet Henrietta [Mrs Albert Cowell, Marrett Cottage, Hoarwithy, Hereford]; *b* 10 June 1908; *m* 1st 23 July 1927 (*divorce* 1936) Cdr William Kenneth Ramsden Cross, RN (lost in HMS *Hood*, 1941), er son of Thomas Cross, of The Cottage, Dunhampstead, Worcs, and has issue:

1c *Giles Berwick [Lt Cdr Giles Cross RN, Halfpenny House, Common Hill, Fownhope, Hereford], Lt-Cdr RN, served in Korea; *b* 28 Aug 1928; *m* 1st 27 Jan 1953 (*divorce* 1971) Sonia, dau of E Welsby-Williams, of Hove, Sussex; *m* 2nd 1971 *Lavinia, dau of Gp Capt P C Thomson, and by 1st w has issue:

1d *Piers William; *b* 3 Nov 1955

1d *Belinda Jane; *b* 10 Oct 1954

1c *Henrietta Caroline [Mrs Christopher Pratt, The Clergy House, Marlston, Newbury]; *b* 1931; *m* 20 Sept 1957 *Christopher Jermyn Pratt (*see* BATH, M), yr son of Col Edward Roger Pratt, MC, DL, JP, of Ryston Hall, Norfolk, and has issue:

1d *Roderick Jermyn; *b* 7 June 1959

2d *James Berwick; *b* 24 March 1963

1b (cont.) Mrs Janet Cross *m* 2nd 9 April 1943 (*divorce* 1950), as his 2nd w, Maj Arthur Christopher John Congreve (*d* 1992), late Rifle Bde, of Congreve, Staffs; *m* 3rd 1951 Albert Russell Cowell. He *d* 10 July 1964

2b Susan Berwick; *b* 6 Sept 1909; *d* unm 17 Dec 1962

1a (cont.) V-Adml Berwick Curtis *m* 2nd 21 March 1929 Violet Penelope Munro (*d* 1973), widow of Lt-Cdr George Francis Cholmley, RN, and dau of Robert J B Thompson, ICS, and *d* 9 May 1965

1a Nora Heath; *m* 11 Feb 1902 Cecil Thomas Gladstone, and *d* 8 Feb 1959, leaving issue. He *d* 1 April 1924

2a Cecil Mary; *m* 23 Jan 1908 Capt Phillip Colquhoun Pearson, RN, est son of Col George Falconer Pearson, of Kington, Herefs, and *d* 10 March 1961. He *d* 11 Sept 1933

3a Joan; *m* 16 April 1914 Francis Norton Gammidge, yr son of Henry Gammidge, of Chislehurst, Kent, and *d* Aug 1960, leaving issue

(1) Henrietta Mary Anne; *m* 1 Aug 1851, her cousin, Capt Constable Curtis, late 12th Roy Lancers, son of Capt Timothy Curtis, RN (*see below*), by his w Rebecca Mary, yr dau of Sir William Curtis, 1st Bt, and had issue. He *d* 30 March 1909

(2) Frances Anne; *m* 6 Aug 1850 Henry Toogood, of Torquay, and had issue. He *d* 27 Aug 1872

(3) Emma Cornelia; *m* April 1861 William Hall Eccles, late Capt Rifle Bde, of Davenham, Cheshire, and *d* 7 April 1919, leaving issue. He *d* 18 April 1900

1 Emma; *m* 18 June 1803 Henry Cadwallader Adams, DL, JP, of Anstey Hall, Warwicks, and *d* 22 June 1857, leaving issue. He *d* 31 Aug 1843

2 Rebecca Mary; *m* 29 March 1828 Capt Timothy Curtis, RN, son of Rev Charles Curtis, bro of Sir William Curtis, 1st Bt, and *d* 11 May 1848, leaving issue

Sir WILLIAM *d* 18 Jan 1829; his est son,

Sir William Curtis, 2nd Bt; *b* 2 March 1782; *m* 19 Nov 1803 Mary Anne (*d* 13 Nov 1865), only child of George Lear, of Leytonstone, Essex, and *d* 16 March 1847, having had, with other issue:

1 **Sir William Curtis, 3rd Bt**; *b* 26 Aug 1804; *m* 18 May 1831 Georgina Maria (*d* 29 March 1892), est dau of John Stratton, of Farthinghoe Lodge, Northants, and *d* 7 Nov 1870, having had issue:

(1) William Edmund, late Lt 1st Roy Dragoons; *b* 26 Oct 1833; *m* 10 Feb 1859 Emily Ariana (*m* 2nd 25 June 1868 George Berney Charleton, only son of Rev John K Charleton, Vicar of Elberton, Glos, and *d* 4 Sept 1928, leaving further issue), yst dau of Lt-Col William Chester Master, of Knole Park, Glos, and *dvp* 11 May 1860, leaving issue, an only child:

1a **Sir William Michael Curtis, 4th Bt**, Adj and QM Roy Def Corps, late Capt 4th Bn Glos Regt, JP Salop; *b* 11 Nov 1859; *m* 1st 14 April 1887 Mabel (*d* 26 April 1888, aged 22), 4th dau of Sir Somerville Arthur Gurney, KCVO, of North Runcton Hall, King's Lynn, and had issue:

1b Constance Mabel; *b* 14 April 1888; *m* 15 April 1914 Lionel George Everson Harrisson, of Easton Hall, Stamford, only son of Capt George Alexander Harrisson, 79th Highrs, and had issue. He *d* 28 Nov 1953

1a (cont.) **Sir William** *m* 2nd 16 Oct 1895 Georgina Mary (*d* 18 Nov 1943), widow of Capt Arthur B Mesham, Roy Dragoons, and dau of Col John Stanley Howard, of Ballina Park, Co Wicklow, and *d* 19 Dec 1916, having by her had issue:

2b Victoria Margaret; *b* 19 Jan 1897; *m* 29 April 1920 Lt-Col Richard Robinson Curling, DSO, late RA, yst son of Rev Joseph James Curling, of Hamble, Hants, and *d* 16 March 1965, leaving issue. He *d* 10 Sept 1953

3b Bettine Ariana; *b* 20 Dec 1898; *m* 1st 1924 (*divorce* 1931) John William Robert Elphinstone (*see* ELPHINSTONE, Bt, of Logie); *m* 2nd 22 Oct 1931 Capt Henry Brierley, CBE, MC, late Rifle Bde, yst son of J W Brierley, and *d* 5 May 1969, leaving issue

4b Mary; *b* 3 Dec 1901; *m* 16 Oct 1923 Capt James William Douglas Evans, late 21st Lancers, and had issue

(2) Philip Julian, late Capt 60th Rifles; *b* 20 March 1838; *m* 7 Dec 1875 Margaret Helena Marie (*d* 11 Dec 1932), yst dau of Charles Candy, and *d* 19 July 1900, leaving issue:

1a Margaret Kathleen; *b* 6 Oct 1876

2a Evelyn Renée Venetia; *b* 1 April 1879; *d* unm 5 Feb 1904

(3) John Egerton, Lt 45th Foot; *b* 6 Dec 1844; *m* 21 Nov 1871 Mary Ella (*d* 1897), yst dau of Marshall Wallace, of Halifax, NS, and *d* 19 April 1879, leaving issue, with a dau:

1a **Sir (Edgar) Francis Egerton Curtis, 5th Bt**, Maj, employed on Staff 1918, served in S Africa 1900 with Strathcona's Horse, and WW I in Egypt and Palestine 1916–17, Mil Govr of Hebron 1917; *b* 18 Dec 1875; *m* 1st 1903 Madeline Cairns (*d* 5 Oct 1941), 3rd dau of C W Alexander, ICS, of Lahore, India, and had issue:

1b *Winifred Lotus [Mrs Allen Dolby, Rush Court, Shillingford Rd, Wallingford, Oxon]; *b* 1904; *m* 8 Dec 1927 Capt Allen Walter Dolby, Royal Berks Regt (*d* 9 Oct 1943), and has issue:

1c *John Horatio Curtis [John Dolby Esq, Highway Cottage, Whitchurch, Pangbourne, Berks RG68 7DB]; *b* 30 Oct 1928; *educ* St Paul's; *m* 24 Oct 1958 *Anthea Louise, dau of Capt E O Whitamore, and has issue:

1d *Timothy William Curtis; *b* 24 Oct 1965

1d *Caroline Lurleen Curtis; *b* 2 Oct 1960

2c *Robert Francis [Capt Robert Dolby, 11 Oldfield Rd, Bath BA2 3ND], Master Mariner Merchant Navy; *b* 10 Oct 1933; *educ* Christ's Hosp; *m* 1st 30 April 1960 (*divorce* 1967) Jean Patricia, dau of Sidney Clark; *m* 2nd 1981 *Priscilla Jane, dau of Percy Ridley, OBE, DSC, Bengal Pilot Serv, and has issue:

1d *Simon Francis Curtis [Simon Dolby Esq, 520 Athlone Ave, Ottawa, Canada]; *b* 1962; *m* 1989 *Faye Tough, and has issue:

1e *Alan Curtis; *b* 1989

1d *Louise Winifred [Mrs Richard Kracher, 2208–133A Ave, Edmonton, Alberta T5A HJ9, Canada]; *b* 1964; *m* 1985 *Richard Kracher, and has issue:

1e *James Richard; *b* 1992

1e *Holly Louise; *b* 1989

2e *Christina Ellen; *b* 1990

1a (cont.) **Sir Francis** *m* 2nd 4 July 1942 Ethel (*d* 31 Aug 1943), widow of Arthur Leonard Warlow and dau of Edward Charles Barlow, of Fernbank, Fountayne Rd, Stoke Newington, N16, and *d* 9 Aug 1943

(1) Georgina Henrietta; *m* 27 Oct 1868 Henry Tichborne Hinckes (formerly Davenport), of Longport Hall, Staffs, MP South Staffs, and *d* 1892. He *dsp* 19 March 1895

(2) Madeline Harriet Louisa; *m* 23 Feb 1861 Col William Charles Chester Master, CB, late 5th Fus, son of Lt-Col William Chester Master, of Knole Park, Glos, and *d* 1889, leaving issue. He *d* 19 March 1913

2 George Lear; *b* 15 Sept 1805; *m* 21 Jan 1832 Augusta Elizabeth (*d* 1895), dau of Charles B Cotton, of Kingsgate, Kent, and *d* 11 Oct 1853, leaving, with other issue:

(1) William Cotton; *b* 20 June 1834; *m* 14 July 1859 Caroline Louisa (*d* 11 March 1903), dau of Edward Thornewill, of Dove Cliff, Staffs, and *d* 6 Oct 1905, leaving, with other issue:

1a Edward Beaumont Cotton, JP Northumberland; *educ* Trin Coll Oxford (MA); *m* 18 Jan 1905 Constance Mary, JP Salop (*d* 22 June 1958), yst dau of Lt-Col George Henry Grey, and sis of 1st Viscount Grey of Fallodon, KG (*see* GREY, Bt, of Fallodon), and *d* 18 March 1939, having had issue:

1b PETER (Sir), **6th Bt**

2b Gerald Edward, Colonial Admin Serv, T/Maj Civil Affairs, E Africa Cmd 1941–45; *b* 18 March 1909; *educ* Winchester and Trin Coll Oxford (BA 1930, MA 1935); *m* 15 Aug 1939 Philippa (*d* 27 Aug 1975, aged 58), 2nd dau of Captain Philip Clayton Alcock, DL, JP, of Overton Lodge, Ludlow, Salop, and *d* 1975 leaving issue:

1c +EDWARD PHILIP [Maj Edward Curtis, Lower Court, Bitterley, Ludlow, Salop SY8 3HP]; *b* 25 June 1940; heir presumptive; *educ* Bradfield and RMA Sandhurst; Maj 16th/5th The Queen's Roy Lancers (ret), stockbroker; *m* 1978 *Catherine Mary, dau of Henry J Armstrong, of Christchurch, NZ, and has issue:

1d +George Edward; *b* 31 Oct 1980

2d +Patrick James; *b* 1986
1d *Henrietta Rose; *b* 1979
2d *Clementine Zita; *b* 1983
1c *Sonia Mary; *b* 29 June 1944; *m* 1971 (*divorce* 1976) Charles Hamilton Ewart, of Sydney, Australia, and has issue:
1d *Gabrielle Alice Anne; *b* 1972
1b Louisa Harriet, JP Richmond, Yorks; *b* 27 May 1910; *m* 9 June 1938 John Gerald Frederick Milbank, 2nd son of Sir Frederick Richard Powlett Milbank, 3rd Bt (*qv*), and *d* 1974, having had issue
2a Hubert Montagu Cotton, DSO (1918, two bars, 1918 and 1919), Lt-Col late 6th Bn N Staffs Regt TF Res, was acting Lt-Col 7th Serv Bn, E Kent Regt in 1918; *b* 1 Feb 1876; *m* 1st 31 July 1915 (*divorce* 1929) Lilian Susette (*d* July 1931), widow of Alfred Stephen Broadwood, and dau of Louis Watson; *m* 2nd 4 May 1929 Marcella Olive Penrose (*d* 4 July 1969), dau of Peter Robinson, of Potton, Beds, and *d* 11 July 1948, having by her had issue:
1b +William Richard [William Curtis Esq, Whitewold, Mill Hill, Weston Colville, nr Cambridge CB1 5NY]; *b* 2 March 1933; *educ* Eton and RMA Sandhurst; *m* 27 April 1961 *Janice Clare, yr dau of William Yates Duckworth, of Myerscough Ho, Garstang, Lancs, and has issue:
1c +William Giles; *b* 13 March 1962; *educ* Ampleforth and RMA Sandhurst; commnd 13th/18th Hussars 1985
2c +Mark Edward; *b* 31 July 1964
3c +Timothy David; *b* 9 Oct 1968
1c *Anna Clare; *b* 28 April 1963
1b *Hilda Lucy Penrose [Mrs Hilda Anderson, 7 Lyston Lane, Long Melford, Suffolk]; *b* 7 March 1930; *m* 22 Oct 1955 (*divorce* 1968) Capt Charles Henry Anderson, Roy Inniskilling Fus, son of Henry Anderson, of Villa Les Annorelles, Cap d'Antibes, S France, and Dawlish, Devon, and has issue:
1c *Lucie Rose; *b* 1956
2c *Arabella Joan Louisa; *b* 1960
3c *Caroline Rebecca; *b* 1961
1a Mary Louisa Cotton; *m* 24 April 1906 Walter Parrott, of Woodeaton Ho, Islip, Oxon and 75, Eaton Place, SW, yst son of George Parrott, of Cavendish Sq, and *d* 12 Aug 1947. He *d* 21 June 1938
2a Ethel Cotton; *m* 23 Jan 1904 Maj Hugh Ferrers Courage, Shrops Yeo, son of Henry Courage, of Gravenhurst, Sussex, and *d* 8 Oct 1933
3a Florence Lucy Cotton, JP Herts; *d* unm 28 June 1954
4a Hilda Evelyn Cotton; *m* 22 Oct 1910 Rev Hugh Richard Anson, Vicar of Sandridge, nr St Albans 1906–19, son of Rev Canon Frederick Anson, and *d* 8 June 1924. He *d* 16 Aug 1935
5a Violet Mabel Cotton; *d* unm March 1941
6a Rosamond Augusta Cotton; *d* unm 12 Aug 1943
(2) Arthur Cecil, R-Adml; *b* 27 Feb 1836; *m* 18 Oct 1886 Arabella Augusta (*d* 10 Sept 1934), dau of W C Drury, of New Brunswick, and *d* 10 July 1895, leaving issue:
1a Arthur Drury, Col (Hon Brig), late RA, served WW I 1914–18, and WW II 1939–45, Cdr Fixed Defences, Malaya 1939–42; *b* 28 Feb 1888; *m* 1st 24 March 1915 Margery May (*d* Oct 1943), er dau of Robert Barlow, of Bombay; *m* 2nd Feb 1946 Evelyn Muriel (*d* 1951), dau of Murray Simmons, of Whitton, Middlesex, and *d* 2 Aug 1950, having by 1st w had issue:
1b +Arthur Derek Edward, MC [Lt-Col Arthur Curtis MC, Oak Covert, Kingsley Ave, Camberley, Surrey GU15 2NA], Lt-Col RE, served WW II; *b* 7 Dec 1917; *educ* St Catharine's Coll Cambridge (MA); *m* 15 May 1943 *Katherine Mary, dau of Thomas Hadfield, of Sheffield, and has issue:
1c +(Arthur) Richard Edward [Capt Richard Curtis, Stable House, 10 Sambourne Rd, Warminster, Wilts BA12 8LJ]; *b* 13 July 1947; *educ* RMA Sandhurst; Capt RA (ret); *m* 1983 *Georgina Carolyn, dau of James Michael Arnott, of Woodmylne, of Bailey Cottage, Old Bursledon, Hants, and has issue:
1d *Harriet Arabella; *b* 1986
2d *Imogen Elizabeth; *b* 1988
3d *Florence Helena; *b* 1990
1c *Katherine Margaret [Mrs M A Langdon, Worth Cottage, Worth, Wookey, Wells, Somerset BA5 1LW]; *b* 15 Oct 1944; *m* 1969 *Lt-Col M A Langdon, RM, and has issue:
1d *Julian Charles Anthony; *b* 1972
1d *Mathilda Mary; *b* 1974
2d *Eliza Katherine; *b* 1979
2b Robert Cecil, Lt-Col RA, served WW II; *b* 17 April 1922; *m* 2 Feb 1952 *Pamela Margaret [Mrs Robert Curtis, Yew Tree, Little Coxwell, Faringdon, Oxon SN7 7LP], yst dau of Oliver S Sedgwick, of Chislehurst, Kent, and *d* 1992, leaving issue:
1c *Carol Frances Margaret; *b* 29 Dec 1956; *m* 1979 *Maj Rowland Charles John Woollven, BSc, FRGS, RE, and has issue:
1d *Virginia Alexandra Frances; *b* 1989
1b *Joan Mary Lavie [Mrs Edward Lewis, Worcester Cottage, Beaufort West, Bath]; *b* 29 March 1916; *m* Jan 1940 *Col Edward Raymond Lewis, CBE, MA, son of William Raymond Lewis, of Stonelaw, Alberta, Canada, and has issue:
1c *Robert Edward Curtis; *b* 16 Dec 1941
1c *Penelope Alison; *b* 12 June 1947
2a Cecil Montagu Drury, OBE (1919), Capt late S W Borderers; *b* 30 July 1889; *m* 15 April 1933 *Rosa Marion [Mrs Cecil Curtis, 3 Church Close, Evercreechy, Somerset], dau of R H Woodley, and *d* 7 June 1966, leaving issue:
1b +Christopher Francis; *b* 25 Sept 1939; *educ* Oxford (BA, DPhil 1961) and Edinburgh U (PhD); *m* 1970 *Jill Pickup, PhD
1b Hazel Rosemary; *b* 22 Feb 1934; *m* 4 June 1960 *Sidney Edward Smith [Sidney Smith Esq, 8 Blunts Wood Rd, Haywards Heath, Sussex], son of P A Smith, of Frognal, Hampstead, NW3, and *d* 1993, leaving issue:
1c *David Edward; *b* 1965
1c *Rosalind Margaret; *b* 5 April 1961
2c *Alison Claire; *b* 1963
3c *Stephanie Jane; *b* 13 Aug 1968
3a Francis Augustus Drury; *b* 10 July 1891; *m* 13 Nov 1916 Gwendolen Angelo Taylour (*d* 18 Oct 1961), dau of Edwin Taylour English, of Toronto, Canada, and *d* 9 March 1927, leaving issue:
1b *Ada Harriette Drury [Mrs John Scowcroft, Roseland, Cubert, Newquay, Cornwall]; *b* 16 Dec 1918; *m* 23 Aug 1958 John Bernard Scowcroft (*d* 1989), Ch Engineer, Merchant Navy, son of Bernard Scowcroft, of King's Sterndale, Buxton, Derbyshire, and Waroonah, W Australia and has issue:
1c *Sarah Jane; *b* 23 June 1960
1a Ada Arabella Drury; *b* 18 Aug 1894; *m* 30 April 1924 Rev Thomas Hartley Jackson, MA, Hon CF, and *d* 19 May 1961, leaving issue. He *d* 1964
(3) Ernest Henry, Capt late Bengal Cav; *b* 12 April 1842; *m* 30 March 1875 Emily (*d* 11 Dec 1920), dau of Rev M W F Thurby, Rector of Abingdon, Northants, and *d* 15 Aug 1924, having had, with other issue:
1a Charles Nevill, MC, Capt late 3rd King's Shropshire LI; *b* 17 Dec 1880; *d* unm 30 Nov 1943
2a Edgar Ralph; *b* 8 Feb 1883; *m* 8 Jan 1921 Ellen Annie (*d* 1963), widow of Percival Wadhams, and dau of Thomas Underdown, of Tonbridge, and *d* 6 Nov 1950, leaving issue:
1b Montague Ralph, slr and commr for oaths, late Capt E Yorks Regt; *b* 30 March 1922; *educ* Malvern, and Trin Coll Oxford (MA); *m* 25 March 1964 *Margaret Winifred Welsby [Mrs Montague Curtis, La Fougere, Rozel Hill, St Martin, Jersey, CI JE3 6AN], only dau of Thomas Welsby Holland, of Chester and *d* 18 Jan 1992
1a Beatrice; *d* unm Sept 1963
2a Cecile Constance Thursby; *d* unm Nov 1964
(1) Constance Laura; *m* 28 Sept 1870 Henry Cecil Gunston, and *d* 20 March 1931. He *d* Dec 1905
(2) Georgie Florence Louisa; *m* 30 Oct 1888 C A Hopwood, CB, and *d* 27 April 1934. He *d* 21 March 1922
3 Henry Charles, an Offr of 85th Regt; *b* 27 June 1812; *m* 15 July 1852 Emma Jane (who *m* 2nd 28 April 1863 Rev C G Hill (*d* 1894), and *d* 1899), est dau of William Scott Binny, of Bryanston Sq, and *d* 7 March 1861, leaving issue:
(1) Stuart Edward; *b* 18 Aug 1853
(2) Henry Alexander Dyer, Lt-Col late RA; *b* 22 Nov 1854
4 Augustus John, Lt Madras Cav; *b* 27 March 1815; *m* 10 April 1838 Charlotte (*d* 1891), dau of Col Thomas Nuttall, Madras Cav, and *d* 31 Aug 1845, leaving, with other issue:
(1) Augustus Frederick, Maj Madras Cav; *b* 8 Aug 1840, and had issue
(2) Charles James; *b* 23 Oct 1842
(3) William Alexander; *b* 9 Sept 1845
5 Alexander Kyd, barrister; *b* 9 Jan 1822; *m* 30 July 1868 Charlotte, widow of Thomas Featherstone, and *d* 1897, leaving issue:
(1) Frances
(2) Florence
1 Emma; *m* 1st 13 Aug 1826 George Savage Curtis, of Teignmouth, Devon, and had issue; *m* 2nd 1848 William Winthrop (*dsp* 3 July 1869), of Massachusetts, and *d* 19 Jan 1897
2 Sabine Louisa; *m* 29 June 1839 Charles Barnett, DL Glos, and *d* 4 Nov 1884, aged 77, leaving issue
3 Charlotte; *m* 14 Dec 1842 Thomas Carew, of Marley Ho, 3rd son of Sir Henry Carew, 7th Bt (*qv*), and *d* 3 June 1884, leaving issue
4 Louisa Anne; *m* 29 Aug 1832 Rev Montagu James Taylor, and had issue. He *d* 1896
5 Julia Henrietta; *m* 1st 11 Jan 1848 Henry Charles Scott, and had issue; *m* 2nd 18 June 1866 M Barthelemy
6 Guilhermina; *m* 27 Nov 1849 Peter Burnett, of Elrich, Aberdeenshire, and *d* 5 July 1889, leaving issue
7 Agnes Cecilia; *m* 11 Jan 1848 Josias Bracken Canning Alexander, son of Josias du Pré Alexander, and had issue. He *d* 1882
8 Anne Augusta; *m* 22 Feb 1848 Col Sir Henry Atwell Lake, KCB, ADC, 3rd son of Sir James Samuel William Lake, 4th Bt (*qv*), and *d* 20 Dec 1877, leaving issue
9 Jessie Isabel; *m* 6 March 1860 Capt Robert George Tufnell, RN, 2nd son of Rev George Tufnell, of Uffington, Berks, and *d* 9 May 1876, leaving issue

The 5th Bt's cousin,

Sir Peter Curtis, 6th Bt; 16th/5th Lancers and Shropshire Yeo WW II (Armoured Corps, ADC, Pioneer Corps); *b* 9 April 1907; *m* 7 July 1934 *Joan Margaret [Joan Lady Curtis, Little Manor, Bishop's Waltham, Hants], only dau of Reginald Nicholson (*see* NICHOLSON OF WINTERBOURNE, Bt), and *d* 28 Sept 1976, having had issue:
1 Sir WILLIAM PETER CURTIS, **7th and present Bt**
2 Anthony Charles; *b* 14 Sept 1937; *d* Dec 1943
1 *Rosemary Antonia Joan [Mrs John Spink, Poplars Farm, Rotherwick, Basingstoke, Hants RG27 9BH]; *b* 3 Sept 1943; *m* 2 July 1966 *John Clarkson Spink, only son of Capt J C Spink, of 64 Vanbrugh Park, Blackheath, SE3, and has issue:
(1) *Jonathan Peter Charles; *b* 26 Oct 1976
(2) *Timothy Mark Christopher; *b* 1981
(1) *Annabel Louise; *b* 1970
2 *Fiona Mary [Mrs Anthony Littlejohn, Lythe Farm, Steep, Petersfield, Hants]; *b* 6 Nov 1946; *m* 4 May 1968 *Anthony David Findon Littlejohn, only son of Derrick Littlejohn, of, 9, Connaught Ho, Mount Row, Berkeley Sq, W1, and had issue:
(1) *Patrick David; *b* 1979
(1) *Ruth Hermione; *b* 20 Feb 1971
(2) *Georgina Clare; *b* 1973

DACRE

Creation: B. (E) 15 May 1321.

THE BARONESS DACRE (Rachel Leila Brand) [The Rt Hon the Lady Dacre, Derry House, Kilmeston, nr Alresford, Hants SO24 0NR]; *b* 24 Oct 1929; *s f* 1970 on termination of abeyance; *m* 26 July 1951 Hon William DOUGLAS-HOME (*d* 1992), 3rd s of 13th Earl of Home (*qv*), and has had:

1 +JAMES THOMAS ARCHIBALD; *b* 16 May 1952; *m* 1979 *Christine, dau of William Stephenson, of The Ridings, Royston, Herts, and has issue:
(1) +Emily; *b* 7 Feb 1983
1 +Sarah; *b* 4 July 1954; *m* 1977 *Nicholas Charles Dent and has issue:
(1) +A dau; *b* 1982
2 Gia Leila; *b* 23 June 1958; *d* 19–
3 +Dinah Lilian; *b* 22 Jan 1964; *m* 1989 *Harry Marriott and has issue:
(1) +A son; *b* 1994

Dacre, other creations: The chief of these are covered below, but the Earl of Carlisle (*qv*) possesses as a subsidiary title the Barony of Dacre of Gillesland, created with the superior peerage in 1661.

Lineage: WILLIAM de DACRE (*i.e.*, of Dacre, Cumberland); Sheriff Cumberland 1236–48 and 1268 and Yorks 1248–50; *d* 1258, leaving:

RALPH de DACRE; Sheriff Cumberland 1268–70 and Yorks 1278–80; *m* 1st Geva —; *m* 2nd Joan, dau of Alan de Multon by Alice, 2nd dau and coheir of Richard de Lucy, of Egremont, and *d* 3 May 1286, leaving by his 1st w:

Sir WILLIAM de DACRE; *b* 12 March 1265/6; served against Scots 1304 and 1311; granted charter of freewarren in all his demesne lands at Dacre and Halton, Lancs, and licence 1307 to crenellate his mansion at Dunwallog ht, Cumberland; *m* Joan (*d* 28 Nov 1324), dau and heir of Benet Gernet, forester of Lancaster Forest, of Halton, Fishwick and Eccleston, Lancs, and *d* just before 24 Aug 1318, having had:

Sir RANDOLF de DACRE, **1st Lord** (Baron) **Dacre** (E), so *cr* by writ of summons 15 May 1321, KB (May 1336/7); *b c* 1290; Sheriff Cumberland 1330–35/6, Constable Carlisle Castle 1330; *m* by 1315 Margaret (*d* 10 Dec 1361), only dau and heir of Thomas de Multon, Lord (Baron) Multon, of Gilsland, Cumberland, and *d* just before 20 April 1339, leaving issue:

1 WILLIAM de DACRE, **2nd Lord** (Baron) **Dacre**; *b c* 1319; fought Battle of Neville's Cross 1346, Sheriff Dumfriesshire Jan 1346/7; *m* by 20 April 1339 Katherine, 2nd dau of 2nd Lord (Baron) Nevill(e) (of Raby) (*see* ABERGAVENNY, M), and *dsp* July 1361
2 RANDOLF de DACRE, **3rd Lord** (Baron) **Dacre**; *b c* Oct 1322; in holy orders as priest of Prescot, Lancs; Warden W Marches 1366–71 and Feb 1371/2; murdered in his bed (possibly by or at the instigation of his bro the **4th Lord**, who was certainly imprisoned in the Tower of London as a suspect) 17 or 18 Aug 1375
3 HUGH DE DACRE, **4th Lord** (Baron) **Dacre**; *b c* 1335; Warden W Marches 1379–March 1381/2; *m* between 8 Oct 1354 and 1 July 1355 Elizabeth, widow of 1st and last Earl of Atholl of the 1341 *cr*, and possibly dau of Sir John Maxwell of Carlaverock, (*see* MAXWELL, Bt) and *d* 24 Dec 1383, leaving:
(1) WILLIAM de DACRE, **5th Lord** (Baron) **Dacre**; *b c* 1357; *m* allegedly Joan Douglas and *d* 20 July 1399, leaving:
1a THOMAS de DACRE, **6th Lord** (Baron) **Dacre**; *b* 27 Oct 1387; Ch Forester Inglewood Forest, Cumberland, Feb 1420/1 and 1422; *m* by 20 July 1399 Philippa, dau of Ralph Nevill(e), Earl of Westmorland (*see* ABERGAVENNY, M), and *d* 5 Jan 1457/8, having had issue:
1b Thomas (Sir); *m* Elizabeth, dau and heir of Sir William Bowett, of Horsford, Norfolk, and *dvp*, leaving:
1c JOAN, **Baroness Dacre**
2c Philippa; *m c* June 1446 her sister's husb's bro Robert Fiennes and *dsp* by 20 July 1499
2b RANDOLF DACRE, 1st and last LORD (Baron) DACRE (of Gilsland), so *cr* (according to later doctrine) by writ 9 Oct 1459; *m* Eleanor, dau of 5th Lord (Baron) FitzHugh (*see* WILLOUGHBY DE ERESBY, B), and was *k* fighting on the Lancastrian side at the Battle of Towton 29 March 1461, when any Barony he held expired; posthumously attainted 1461 or 1462
3b HUMPHREY DACRE, 1st LORD (Baron) DACRE (of Gilsland), so *cr*, it would seem with remainder to heirs male of his body (but *see* below), 8 April 1473 in an arbitration under the Gt Seal by EDWARD IV which allotted him Gilsland, Halton and the Cumberland and Westmorland estates (in fact the lion's share) of the Dacre property disputed between the aforesaid HUMPHREY (heir male) and Sir Richard Fiennes, **7th Lord** (Baron) **Dacre** (*see* below), husb of the heir general, with a peerage (frequently referred to as that of LORD DACRE OF THE NORTH) thrown in as sweetener; had been attainted with his er bro RANDOLF 1461 or 1462 but was pardoned *c* 1473; *m* Mabel, dau of Sir Thomas Parr, of Kendal, Westmorland, and great-aunt of HENRY VIII's 6th w Catherine Parr, and *d* 30 May 1485, leaving:
1c THOMAS DACRE, 2nd LORD (Baron) DACRE (of Gilsland), KG (1518), KB (Feb 1503/4); *b* 25 Nov 1467; *m c* 1488 Elizabeth, Baroness Greystoke in her own right according to later doctrine, dau and sole heir of Sir Robert Greystoke (s of 7th Lord (Baron) Greystoke) by Elizabeth, dau of 1st Earl of Kent of the 1465 *cr* (*see* GREY, B), and *d* 24 Oct 1525 in a fall from his horse, leaving:
1d WILLIAM DACRE, 3rd LORD (Baron) DACRE (of Gilsland) and 9th LORD (Baron) GREYSTOKE as which *s* mother 1516; *b* 29 April 1500; *m c* 1 Dec 1517 Elizabeth, dau of 4th Earl of Shrewsbury and Waterford (*qv*), and *d* 18 Nov 1563, leaving:
1e THOMAS DACRE, 4th LORD (Baron) DACRE (of Gilsland), though never called to Parl; *b c* 1526; *m* 1st Elizabeth (*dsp*), dau of 4th Earl of Westmorland of the 1397 *cr* (*see* ABERGAVENNY, M); *m* 2nd Elizabeth (*m* 2nd after 9 Sept 1566, as his 3rd w, 4th Duke of Norfolk (*qv*)), 2nd dau of Sir James Leyburne, and *d* 1 July 1566, having had, with an er s (*d* young):
1f GEORGE DACRE, 5th LORD (Baron) DACRE (of Gilsland); *b c* 1562; *d* 17 May 1569 (like his ggf in a fall from his horse, only this one was a toy one of wood and the accident occurred in the nursery), when the Barony was declared by the Earl Marshal's commrs to have been *cr* by writ, hence as falling into abeyance between his sisters
1f Anne; *b* 12 April 1557; *m* 1571 20th/13th Earl of Arundel (*see* NORFOLK, D), and had issue
2f Mary; *b* 4 July 1563; *m* by 9 May 1577, as his 1st w, 1st Earl of Suffolk (*see* SUFFOLK and BERKSHIRE, E) and *dsp* 7 April 1578
3f Elizabeth; *b* 12 Nov 1564; *m* Lord William Howard, s of 4th Duke of Norfolk (*qv*; *see also* CARLISLE, E), and had issue
2e Leonard; assumed title of 6th Lord (Baron) of Dacre (of Gilsland); *dsp* 12 Aug 1573
3e Edward; assumed title of 7th Lord (Baron) Dacre (of Gilsland); *dsp* 1584
4e Francis; assumed title of 8th Lord (Baron) Dacre (of Gilsland); *m* 1st by Jan 1573/4 Dorothy, dau of John Radcliffe or Rowell, of Derwentwater; *m* 2nd 17 June 1607 Avice, dau of Thomas Tyrrell, and *d* 19 Feb 1632/3, leaving by her:
1f Randolf; assumed title of 9th Lord (Baron) Dacre (of Gilsland); *bapt* 8 March 1607/8; *d* unm 10 Dec 1634, when the title, if it had been judged in 1569 as with remainder to heirs male, would have expired
1e Dorothy; *m* Sir Thomas Windsor, 2nd s of 2nd Lord (Baron) Windsor (*see* PLYMOUTH, E)
1d Mary; *m* by 30 Nov 1523, as his 1st w, 5th Earl of Shrewsbury and Waterford (*qv*)
1b Joan

The 6th LORD's gdau,

JOAN Dacre, **Baroness Dacre** in her own right according to later doctrine; *b c* 1433; *m c* June 1446 Sir Richard FIENNES, PC (who in right of his w was recognised as **7th Lord** (Baron) **Dacre**, Constable Tower London, *d* 25 Nov 1483), and *d* 8 March 1485/6, leaving:

Sir JOHN FIENNES; *m* Alice, est dau and coheir of 6th Lord (Baron) FitzHugh, and had issue:

THOMAS FIENNES, **8th Lord** (Baron) **Dacre**, KB (1494); Constable Calais 1493, helped defeat Cornish rebels Blackheath 1497; *m c* 1492 Anne, sis of Lord (Baron) Berners (*qv*), and *d* 9 Sept 1533, having had:

Sir THOMAS FIENNES; *m* 1514 Jane (*d* Aug 1539), dau of 2nd Lord (Baron) Dudley (*qv*), and *dvp* 26 Oct 1528, leaving:

THOMAS FIENNES, **9th Lord** (Baron) **Dacre**; *b c* 1516; *m* 1536 Mary, dau of 5th Lord (Baron) Bergavenny (*see* ABERGAVENNY, M), and was hanged 29 June 1541 for murder of a game keeper during a deer hunt at Laughton Park, Sussex (even though he was elsewhere in the park at the time and the fatal blow struck by a third party), when the Barony was judged forfeited, having had, with an er s (*d* aged 15):

1 GREGORY FIENNES, **10th Lord** (Baron) **Dacre**; *bapt* 25 June 1539; restored in blood and honours 1558; *m* by Nov 1558 Ann (*d* 14 May 1595), sis of 1st Earl of Dorset (*see* SACKVILLE, B), and *dsp* 25 Sept 1594
1 MARGARET Fiennes, **Baroness Dacre** in her own right, recognised as such 8 Dec 1604; *b* 1541; *m* just before 10 Nov 1564 Sampson LENNARD (*d* 20 Sept 1615), of Chevening, High Sheriff Kent 1590–91, and *d* 16 March 1611/2, having had, with two other sons (*dsp*):
(1) HENRY, **12th Lord**
(2) Gregory; *m* 1614 Maud, dau of Richard Llewellyn, and *dsps* 1620
(1) Ann; *m* Herbert Morley, of Glynde, Sussex
(2) Mary; *m* Sir Ralph Bosville, of Sevenoaks, Kent
(3) Margaret; *m* Sir Thomas Waller and had:
1a William (Sir); Parly Gen Civil War
(4) Elizabeth; *m* Sir Francis Barnham, of Boughton, Kent
(5) Frances; *m* Sir Robert More

The est son,

HENRY LENNARD, **12th Lord** (Baron) **Dacre**; *bapt* 25 March 1569/70; ktd 1596, MP W Looe 1597; *m* 1589 Chrysogona (*bur* 30 Sept 1616), dau of Sir Richard Baker, of Sissinghurst, Kent, and *d* 8 Aug 1616, having had:

1 RICHARD, **13th Lord**
2 Fynes; *m* M Prude and had issue (line now extinct)
3 Edward; *dsp*
1 Margaret; *m* Sir Anthony Wildgoose, of Edridge Court, Sussex
2 Philadelphia; *m* Sir Thomas Parker, of Ratton, Sussex
3 Pembroke; *m* Sir John Brooks, of Cowling Castle, Kent
4 Barbara; *m* Sir Philip Stapleton

The est son,

RICHARD LENNARD, **13th Lord** (Baron) **Dacre**; *b* April 1596; *m* 1st 14 July 1617 Elizabeth (*d* Feb 1621/2), dau and coheir of Sir Arthur Throckmorton, of Paulersbury, Northants, and had, with other issue:

1 FRANCIS, **14th Lord**

The **13th Lord** *m* 2nd 4 Jan 1624/5 Dorothy (*m* 2nd 28 Oct 1650 Challoner Chute (*see* 1956 edn CHUTE, Bt) and *d* 21 April 1698 aged 93), dau of 3rd Lord (Baron) North (*see* 1970 edn), and by her had:

2 Richard LENNARD later BARRETT (under terms of will of his 2nd cousin once-removed Sir Edward Barrett, 1st and last Lord Barrett of Newburgh, who left him the manor of Belhus and other land in Essex, also Horsford, Norfolk); *m* Anne, dau and heiress of Sir Robert Loftus (*see* ELY, M), and *d* 1696, having had issue:

(1) Dacre; *m* 1st Jane, dau of 2nd Earl of Donegall (*see* DONEGALL, M); *m* 2nd Elizabeth, dau and coheir of Thomas Moore, of Monaghan; *m* 3rd Sarah, dau of Sir Capell Luckyn, 2nd Bt (*see* VERULAM, E), and *d* 1733, leaving, with other issue by his 1st w

1a Richard; *m* ANNE, **Baroness Dacre** (*see* below)

1a Jane; *m* John Ranby, Serjeant Surgn to GEORGE II

2a Dorothy; *m* 1722 Hugh Smyth, of Weald Hall

(2) Richard; *d* unm 26 June 1682 in a fall from his horse

(1) Anne; *m* 1 May 1688 Carew Hervey Mildmay, of Marks, Essex, and *d* 18 Jan 1718, leaving issue

(2) Dorothy; *d* unm Dec 1713

The 13th LORD's est son,

FRANCIS LENNARD, **14th Lord** (Baron) **Dacre**; *b* 11 May 1619; *educ* Merton Coll Oxford; claimed Gilsland estate on death of Randolf Dacre (self-styled 9th Lord (Baron) Dacre (of Gilsland), *see* above) but the Howard family then in possession obliged him to accept merely the Manor of Dacre and certain Cumberland properties; Parliamentarian Civil War but objected to trial of CHARLES I; MP Sussex CROMWELL's Parl 1654; *m* 1641 Elizabeth (*cr* 6 Sept 1680 COUNTESS OF SHEPEY [*sic*] (E) for life; *m* 2nd David Walter, Lt-Gen Ordnance and Groom Bedchamber *temp* CHARLES II), dau and eventually coheir of 1st Viscount Bayning of Sudbury, and *d* 12 May 1662, leaving, with two yr sons and three daus (one of whom *m* 3rd Viscount Clare; *see* INCHIQUIN, B):

THOMAS LENNARD, **15th Lord** (Baron) **Dacre** and 1st EARL OF SUSSEX (E), so *cr* 5 Oct 1674; *b* 13 May 1654; *m* 16 May 1674 Lady Anne Fitzroy (*b* 29 Feb 1661; *d* 16 May 1722), illegitimate dau of CHARLES II by Barbara, Duchess of Cleveland (*see* JERSEY, E), and *dsp* 30 Oct 1715, when the Earldom expired while the Barony of Dacre fell into abeyance between his two daus, terminating on the death *sp* of the er, having had issue:

1 Charles, *Lord Dacre*; *b* 3 June 1682; *d* 13 March 1683/4

2 Henry; *d* an infant

1 Barbara; *b* 12 July 1676; *m* Lt-Gen Charles Skelton, of the French Service, Kt Grand Cross Order of St Louis, and *dsp* 1741

2 ANNE Lennard, **Baroness Dacre** in her own right; *b* 17 Aug 1684; turned RC 1698, a gambler who sold the Chevening estate, Kent (to Lord Stanhope in 1717 for £28,000; some £790,000 in late 1990s terms), also Dacre Castle and much of the Cumberland property; *m* 1st 15 June 1716 her cousin Richard BARRETT (*see* above) and had:

(1) THOMAS BARRET later BARRETT-LENNARD, **17th Lord** (Baron) **Dacre**; *b* 20 April 1717; *educ* Harrow; *m* 15 May 1739 Anna Maria (*d* 11 Aug 1806), dau of 1st Earl Camden (*see* CAMDEN, M), and *dsps* 12 Jan 1786, having had:

1a Anna Barbara; *d* unm 14 March 1749

1 (cont.) The **17th Lord** also had an illegitimate s (*see* BARRETT-LENNARD, Bt)

2 (cont.) **Baroness Dacre** *m* 2nd March 1717/8 8th Baron Teynham (*qv*) and had, with other issue:

(2) Charles, Capt of Dragoons; *b* 21 May 1721; *m* 27 June 1744 Gertrude (*d* 13 July 1780), sis and coheir of John Trevor, of Glynde, Sussex, and *dvm* 4 Feb 1754, having had issue:

1a TREVOR CHARLES ROPER, **18th Lord** (Baron) **Dacre**; *b* 14 June 1745; *m* 2 March 1773 Mary, only dau and heir of Sir Thomas Fludyer, and *dsp* 4 July 1794

2a Henry; *d* unm, *k* in a duel

1a GERTRUDE Roper, **Baroness Dacre** in her own right; *b* 25 Aug 1750; *m* 20 April 1771 Thomas BRAND (*d* 21 Feb 1794), of The Hoo, Herts, and *d* 3 Oct 1819, having had issue:

1b THOMAS BRAND, **20th Lord** (Baron) **Dacre**; *b* 25 March 1774; barrister 1800, MP (Whig) Helston Jan–April 1807 and Herts 1807–19; *m* 4 Dec 1819 Barbarina (*d* 17 May 1854), widow of Valentine Wilmot (*see* SULLIVAN, Bt), and dau of Adml Sir Chaloner Ogle, 1st Bt, of Worthy (*see* 1940 edn), and *dsp* 21 March 1851

2b HENRY OTWAY, **21st Lord**

1b Gertrude

2 (cont.) **Baroness Dacre** *m* 3rd 16 Oct 1725 Hon Robert Moore, MP (*d* 3 July 1728), son of 3rd Earl of Drogheda (*qv*), and *d* 26 June 1755, having had, with other issue:

(3) Henry, of West Dean Manor, Wilts; *d* unm

The 20th LORD's bro,

HENRY OTWAY BRAND later TREVOR (roy licence 18 Nov 1824 under terms of will of his cousin John Trevor-Hampden, 3rd and last Viscount Hampden of the 1776 *cr*), **21st Lord** (Baron) **Dacre**, CB (1815); *b* 27 July 1777; Gen 1851, served Copenhagen 1807, cmded 1st Bn Coldstream Gds Peninsular War 1808–12 (cmded Regt Salamanca, also fought Talavera and Busaco), Col 31st Foot 1847–53; *m* 24 July 1806 Pyne (*d* Jan 1844), 2nd dau of Hon Very Rev Maurice Crosbie, Dean of Limerick, sis and coheir of 4th Baron Brandon and formerly w of Sir John Gordon, 6th Bt (marriage *annulled* 1806), and *d* 2 June 1853, having had issue:

1 THOMAS CROSBIE WILLIAM TREVOR, **22nd Lord** (Baron) **Dacre**; *b* 5 Dec 1808; Ld Lt Essex 1865–69; *m* 12 Jan 1837 Susan Sophia (*d* 13 Aug 1896), est dau of 1st Baron Chesham (*qv*), and *dsp* 26 Feb 1890

2 HENRY BOUVERIE WILLIAM, **23rd Lord**

1 Pyne Jesse; *m* 1st 1828 John Henry Cotterell (*d* 1834); *m* 2nd 22 Nov 1845 Granville Harcourt Vernon, MP (*see* VERNON, B), and *d* 3 March 1872

2 Julia; *m* 28 June 1824 Samuel Charles Whitbread, JP, DL, FRS (*d* 27 May 1879), of Southill, Beds, and *d* 13 Oct 1858, leaving issue

3 Gertrude; *m* 21 July 1831 Sir George Hamilton Seymour, GCB, and *d* 30 Aug 1883 (*see* HERTFORD, M)

4 Frederica Mary Jane; *d* 21 Jan 1873

The 22nd LORD's bro,

HENRY BOUVERIE WILLIAM TREVOR later BRAND, **23rd Lord** (Baron) **Dacre** and 1st VISCOUNT HAMPDEN OF GLYNDE (*qv*); *b* 24 Dec 1814; *m* 16 April 1838 Eliza (*d* 9 March 1899), dau of Gen Robert Ellice, and had issue:

1 HENRY ROBERT, **24th Lord**

2 Thomas Seymour, of Glynde Place, Lewes, Sussex; *b* 20 Sept 1847;, CA, R-Adml; *m* 4 Dec 1879 Annie Blanche (*d* 18 Nov 1946), yst dau of Henry Lomax Gaskell, of Kiddington Hall, Woodstock, Oxon, and *d* 12 Nov 1916, leaving:

(1) Humphrey Ranulph, JP, DL Sussex, of Glynde Place; *b* 24 Feb 1895; Capt Sussex Yeo, RFA (TA), and Cdr RN, served WW I (despatches) and WW II, CA E Sussex; *m* 24 Jan 1940 *Aimee Gwendolyn, formerly w of Col Charles Robert Tolver Michael Gerard, DSO, OBE (*see* GERARD, B), and dau of Sir Rupert Turner Clarke, 2nd Bt, of Rupertswood (*qv*), and *dsp* 5 Feb 1953

(1) Phoebe; *b* 19 Oct 1893; *m* 27 July 1914 Lt-Col (Edward) Anthony (Mark) Fielden, MC (*d* 26 Aug 1972), 10th Hus, son of Edward Brocklehurst Fielden, of Condover Hall, Salop, and *d* following a car crash 17 Aug 1972, leaving issue:

1a +David Edward [David Fielden Esq, PO Kilifi, via Mombasa, Kenya]; *b* 1915; *educ* Eton; E African Forces WW II; *m* 1942 *Kathleen, dau of Thomas Grant, of Silverbridge, Co Down, and widow of Robert Sturge Ball, and has:

1b +Joshua Anthony [Joshua Fielden Esq, 283 Bowen Terrace, New Farm, Brisbane, Qld 4005, Australia]; *b* 1944; *educ* Queens' Coll Cambridge (BA)

1b +Sarah Brand [Mrs Antony Seth-Smith, Half-a-Hill, PO Box 24818, Nairobi, Kenya]; *b* 1947; *m* 1971, as his 2nd w, *Antony Martin Donald Seth-Smith, late Kenya Regt, and has issue:

1c +Tana; *b* 1977

2a +Philip Brand, MC [Lt-Col Philip Fielden MC, Manor Farm House, Adlestrop, Glos GL56 0YW]; *b* 1919; *educ* Eton and Magdalen Coll Oxford; Lt-Col Roy Dragoons WW II; *m* 1955 *Caroline Mary, yr dau of Sir John Henry Burder, of Swinbrook Manor, Burford, Glos, and has issue:

1b +Mark Philip [Mark Fielden Esq, 182 Holland Rd, London W14 8AH]; *b* 1956

1b +Nicola [Mrs Terence Stratton, Lower Farm, Gt Wolford, Shipston-on-Stour, Warwicks]; *b* 1957; *m* 1986 *Terence Edward Stratton and has:

1c +Edward Albert; *b* 1988

2c +George Frederick; *b* 1991

3a +John Anthony [John Fielden Esq, Court of Hill, Ludlow, Salop SY8 3AL]; *b* 1921; *educ* Eton; Lt (E) RNVR WW II; *m* 1953 *Helen Mary, 2nd dau of Charles Wakefield Christie-Miller, of Swyncombe House, Henley-on-Thames, and has issue:

1b +Samuel John; *b* 1956

1b +Lucy Anne [Mrs David Aspin, Southover, Burwash, E Sussex TN19 7JB]; *b* 1954; *m* 1993 *David William Aspin

3 Arthur George, JP, DL Sussex; *b* 1 May 1853, MP Wisbech 1891–95 and 1900–06, Treasurer Household 1894–95; *m* 15 April 1886 Edith (*d* 8 April 1903), yst dau of Joseph Ingram, JP, of Brooklands, Cheshire, and *d* 9 Jan 1917, leaving:

(1) Henry Arthur Trevor; *b* 15 March 1890, Capt 12th Lancers WW I (despatches); *m* 17 July 1920 *Elsie, widow of Maj Harold Frank Senior, RAF, and dau of William James, and *dsp* 4 Dec 1938

4 Charles, JP Sussex; *b* 1 May 1855; Maj Sussex Yeo, Lt Coldstream Gds; *m* 15 Aug 1878 Alice Emma Sturgis (*d* 4 Feb 1926), dau of His Excellency Sylvain van de Weyer, and *d* 25 Aug 1912, leaving issue:

(1) John Charles, DSO (1918), MC; *b* 24 Nov 1885; Lt-Col Coldstream Gds WW I (despatches, Legn Hon); *m* 20 May 1916 Rosabelle Millicent (*d* 12 Dec 1956), widow of David Cecil Bingham (*see* LUCAN, E) and dau of 5th Earl of Rosslyn (*qv*), and *d* 28 Dec 1929, leaving:

1a Robin; *b* 29 Oct 1917; Lt Rifle Bde WW II; *m* 29 Aug 1944 *Joyce, er dau of J Duncan, of Barnsley, Yorks, and *d* 13 Jan 1945 from illness contracted on active service

2a +Michael Charles; *b* 13 April 1925; *educ* Eton; Lt Coldstream Gds WW II (wounded); *m* 27 July 1953 *Hon Laura Caroline Beatrice Smith, er dau of 3rd Viscount Hambleden (*qv*), and has had:

1b +Charles David William; *b* 1 July 1954 (HRH PRINCESS MARGARET, COUNTESS OF SNOWDON, stood sponsor); *educ* Bryanston; *m* 1st 1985 Kirsten Margaret, dau of John Baillie Hamilton Leckie, of Gerrards Cross, Bucks; *m* 2nd 1992 *Hon Virginia Leslie Bonham Carter, 2nd dau of Baron Bonham-Carter (*see* OXFORD ASQUITH, E), and by her has:

1c +Henry Joshua Mark; *b* 26 June 1995

1c +Violet Laura; *b* 15 Dec 1992

1b A dau; *b* 10 June, *d* 11 June 1958

2b +Charlotte Katharine; *b* 5 Oct 1961; *m* 5 June 1997 *Gordon Ring, s of Brian Ring

3b +Rosabelle Patricia [Mrs Robert Batt, Chaucers Farm, Gresham, Norfolk]; *b* 28 Sept 1965; *m* 17 June 1995 *Robert Batt

1a +Patience [Mrs Patience Henderson, Oxleaze Farm, Uffington, Berks]; *b* 1 Jan 1922; *m* 16 Feb 1945 (*divorce* 1955) Capt Ian Alexander Henderson, RHG (*see* FARINGDON, B), and has issue

(1) Betty; *d* 11 Sept 1935

(2) Ruth; *b* 1882; *m* 19 Aug 1911 2nd Baron Monk Bretton (*qv*) and *d* 5 Aug 1967, leaving issue

(3) Evelyn; *m* 27 April 1916 Sir James Crerar, KCSI, CIE, ICS, (*d* 29 Aug 1960), and *d* 23 Dec 1954, leaving:

1a David James; *b* 1922; F/Lt RAFVR; *m* 1949 Eileen Ismay (*d* 1974), est dau of Henry Francis Chester Walsh, OBE, of Williamstown House, Castlebellingham, Co Louth, and *d* 1974, leaving issue:

1b +Peter John [Peter Crerar Esq, Rathdaniel, Cellon, Co Louth, Ireland]; *b* 1955; *m* 1982 *Patricia Anne, dau of John Alexander Kennedy, of Yamba, NSW, and has:

1c +James Henry Alexander; *b* 1988

1c +Marnie Eileen; *b* 1984

2c +Eileen; *b* 1991

2b +Rory James [Rory Crerar Esq, 21 Springfield Rd, Templeogue, Dublin, Ireland]; *b* 1958; *m* 1983 *Margaret Mary, dau of Thomas Paul Marsh, of Glebe House, Stackallan, Co Meath, and has issue:

1c +David James; *b* 1987

1c +Carla Catherine; *b* 1988

3b +Jonathan David; *b* 1963

1b +Catherine; *b* 1953; *m* 1978 *Edward Anthony Boland

1a Elizabeth Jean; *b* 1918; *m* 1946 Sir Hugh Evelyn Lockhart-Mummery, KCVO (*d* 1988), and *d* 1981, leaving:

1b +Christopher John, QC (1986) [Christopher Lockhart-Mummery Esq QC, 78 Lansdowne Rd, London W11 2LS]; *b* 1947; *educ* Stowe and Trin Coll Cambridge (BA); barrister Inner Temple 1971, Crown Court Recorder, Bencher Inner Temple 1991, Dep High Ct Judge 1995; *m* 1st 1971 (*divorce* 1992) Hon (Elizabeth) Rosamund Elles, dau of Baroness Elles (*qv*); *m* 2nd 1993 *(Mary) Lou Putley and by his 1st w has:

1c +Edward; *b* 1975

1c +Clare; *b* 1973

2c +Alice; *b* 1980

5 Richard; *d* an infant 1858

1 Alice; *m* 8 July 1862 Sir Henry Thomas Farquhar, 4th Bt (*qv*), and *d* 20 March 1925, leaving issue

2 Gertrude; *m* 2 Sept 1869 William Henry Campion, CB (*d* 4 Dec 1923), of Danny Park, Sussex, and *d* 21 Dec 1927, leaving issue

3 Mabel; *m* 18 June 1863 Frederick Freeman Thomas (*d* 1 Dec 1868), of Ratton Sussex, and *d* 29 May 1924, leaving issue

4 Mary Cecilia; *m* 2 Oct 1872 Henry Parkman Sturgis, son of Russell Sturgis, and *d* 24 June 1886 aged 35, leaving issue

5 Maud Elizabeth, DBE (1918), JP Herts; *m* 22 Oct 1885 David Augustus Bevan, JP (*d* 26 April 1937), 4th son of Richard Lee Bevan, JP, of Brixworth Hall, Northants, and *d* 8 Jan 1944, leaving issue

The 23rd LORD *d* 14 March 1892; his est son,

HENRY ROBERT BRAND, **24th Lord** (Baron) **Dacre** and 2nd VISCOUNT HAMPDEN OF GLYNDE; *b* 2 May 1841; *m* 1st 21 Jan 1864 Victoria Alexandrina Leopoldine (*dsp* 20 July 1865), dau of Sylvain van de Weyer, Belgian Min to UK; *m* 2nd 14 April 1868 Susan Henrietta (*d* 16 Oct 1909), yr dau of Lord George Henry Cavendish (*see* DEVONSHIRE, D), and had issue:

1 THOMAS WALTER, **25th Lord**

2 Hubert George (Hon Sir), GCB (1932, KCB 1927, CB 1918), KCMG (1919), KCVO (1922); *b* 20 May 1870; Naval Attaché Tokyo 1912–14, Naval Assist to 2nd Sea Ld 1914–16, Ch Staff Battle Cruiser Fleet 1916–17, Cdre 1917, R-Adml 1919, V-Adml 1924, Adml 1928, cmded HM's yachts 1919–22 and 1st Light Cruiser Sqdn 1922–24, Sec to 1st Ld Admlty 1925, Ch Naval Personnel 1925–27, C-in-C Atlantic Fleet 1927–29 and Plymouth 1929–32, Extra Equerry to TM GEORGE V 1922–36, EDWARD VIII 1936 and GEORGE VI 1937–52, 1st and Pncpl Naval ADC to HM GEORGE V 1931–32, R-Adml of the UK 1939, Order Rising Sun Japan 2nd Cl, Offr Legn Hon; *m* 28 Jan 1914 Norah Conyngham (*d* 5 March 1924), yr dau of Rt Hon Sir William Conyngham Greene, GCMG, KCB, PC, Amb Extrdy and Min Plen Japan, and *d* 14 Dec 1955, having had:

(1) +Elizabeth Norah [Mrs John Seymour, Edgedell Cottage, Martyr Worthy, Hants]; *b* 29 Aug 1915; *m* 17 Aug 1940 Maj John Edward Seymour (*see* HERTFORD, M), and has issue

(2) Mary Kathleen; *b* 26 Jan, *d* 6 March 1921

3 Richard; *b* 8 Aug 1871; *d* 18 Jan 1880

4 ROBERT HENRY BRAND, 1st and last BARON BRAND, of Eydon, Co Northampton (UK), so *cr* 17 July 1946, CMG (1910); *b* 30 Oct 1878; *educ* Marlborough and New Coll Oxford (BA 1901, MA 1905, Hon Fellow 1948); Hon DCL Oxford 1937, md Lazard Bros to 1944, chm N Br and Mercantile Insur to 1957, dir Lloyds Bank to 1958 and Times Publishing Co Ltd to 1960, Fell All Souls, pres Royal Ec Soc 1952, Sec Inter-Colonial Cncl S Africa 1902–09, memb Imperial Munitions Bd of Canada 1916–18, v-pres Internat Fin Conf Brussels 1920, represented S Africa as Ec Advsr Internat Conf Genoa 1922, Head Br Food Mission Washington 1941–44, Rep Treasury in USA 1944–46, chm Br Supply Cncl Washington 1945–46, Cdr Order Crown Belgium; *m* 9 June 1917 Phyllis (*d* 20 Jan 1937), dau of Chiswell Dabney Langhorne, of Mirador, Greenwood, Va., and *d* 23 Aug 1963, having had:

(1) Robert James; *b* 16 June 1923; Lt Coldstream Gds WW II; *ka* W Europe March 1945

(1) Virginia; *b* 31 Aug 1918; *m* 1st 9 Dec 1939 John Metcalfe Polk (*d* 12 Jan 1948), s of Frank Polk, of USA, and had issue; *m* 2nd 1 Dec 1949 *Sir Edward William Spencer Ford, KCB, KCVO, ERD [Sir Edward Ford KCB KCVO ERD, Canal House, 23 Blomfield Rd, London W9 1AD] (*see* SHREWSBURY and WATERFORD, E), and *d* 23 Dec 1995, leaving

(2) +Dinah; *b* 8 Sept 1920; *m* 1st 6 March 1943 (*divorce* 1950) Lyttleton Fox, BA, LLB, Cdr USNR, son of Lyttleton Fox, of New York, and has issue:

1a +James Lyttleton; *b* 19 Nov 1945; *educ* Eton

1a +Phyllis Langhorne; *b* 20 April 1944

(2) (cont.) The Hon Mrs Dinah Fox *m* 2nd 21 Sept 1953 Christopher Charles Cyprian Bridge, only son of Brig Charles Edward Dunscombe Bridge, CMG, DSO, MC, of Elmenteita, Kenya, and by him has:

2a +Charles Robert; *b* 11 Jan 1956

2a +Joanna; *b* 3 Aug 1954

5 Roger, CMG (1919), DSO (1916) and bar (1917); *b* 23 Nov 1880; Capt and Brevet Lt-Col Rifle Bde (SR), Hon Brig-Gen 1920, Boer War 1900–02 (two medals, five clasps) and WW I (despatches, two brevets), Legn Hon; *m* 21 Nov 1913 Muriel Hectorina Lillian (*d* 1988), dau of Henry Boyle Montgomery, and *d* 23 Oct 1945, leaving:

(1) +Patricia Helen Winifred; *b* 11 Dec 1926; *m* 1st 7 Dec 1950 (*divorce* 1957) John Ralph Lubbock (*see* AVEBURY, B) and has issue; *m* 2nd 5 July 1957 *Pierre Micheletto

6 Geoffrey; *b* 3 Oct 1885; *d* 25 Feb 1899

1 Margaret; *m* 21 April 1897 Brig Gen Algernon Francis Holford Ferguson, DL (*d* 5 Nov 1943), 2nd Life Gds, of Polebrooke Hall, Oundle, and *d* 27 Sept 1948, leaving issue:

(1) Andrew Henry; *b* 1899; Col; *m* 1927 Marian Louise (*m* 2nd 1968 Air Marshal Sir Thomas Walker Elmhirst, KBE, CB, AFC (*d* 1982), and *d* 11 Dec 1996), dau of Lt-Col Lord Herbert Montagu Douglas Scott, CMG, DSO (*see* BUCCLEUCH and QUEENSBERRY, D), and *d* 1966, leaving issue:

1a +Ronald Ivor [Maj Ronald Ferguson, Dummer Down House, Dummer, Basingstoke, Hants]; *b* 1931; *educ* Eton; Maj Life Gds, Dep Chm Gds Polo Club to 1989, with Roy Berks Polo Club to 1993; *m* 1st 1956 (*divorce* 1974) Susan Mary (*m* 2nd 1975 Hector Barrantes (*d* 1990), of Argentina), dau of FitzHerbert Wright (*see* POWERSCOURT, V), and has issue:

1b +Jane Louise; *b* 1957; *m* 1st 1976 (*divorce* 1991) William (Alex) Makim, of Australia, and has:

1c +Seamus; *b* 1981

1c +Ayesha; *b* 1986

1b (cont.) Mrs Jane Makim *m* 2nd Jan 1994 *Reiner Hans Luedecke and by him has:

2c +Heidi Olivia; *b* by 24 June 1996

2b +Sarah Margaret; *b* 15 October 1959; Chllr Salford U 1991–94, newspaper columnist, author *My Story* (with Jeff Caplan) and *Dining with the Duchess* (1998); *m* 23 July 1986 (*divorce* 30 May 1996) HRH THE PRINCE ANDREW ALBERT CHRISTIAN EDWARD, DUKE OF YORK, CVO, ADC, 2nd s of HM THE QUEEN, and has issue (*see* ROYAL FAMILY)

1a (cont.) Maj Ronald Ferguson *m* 2nd 1976 *Susan Rosemary, dau of Frederick Deptford, and by her has:

3b +Andrew Frederick John; *b* 1978

3b +Alice Victoria; *b* 1980

4b +Eliza; *b* 1986

(1) Margaret Susan; *b* 1906; *m* 1931, as his 1st w, Lt-Col Frederick Edwin Barton Wignall (*see* TATE, Bt), and *d* 1939, leaving issue:

1a +Ann Margaret [Mrs James Verner, The Dormers, Stembridge, Somerset TA12 6BL]; *b* 1932; *m* 1968, as his 3rd w, James William Hay Verner (*d* 1995) and has:

1b +James Frederick Guy; *b* 1967

2b +Alexander Louis; *b* 1968

(2) Jane Charlotte; *b* 1912; *m* 1934 Capt Sir William Albemarle Fellowes, KCVO (*d* 6 April 1986), and *d* 26 February 1986, leaving issue:

1a +Robert ('Bertie') (Sir), GCB (1998, KCB 1991, CB 1987), KCVO (1989, LVO 1982), PC (1990); *b* 1941; *educ* Eton; Assist Priv Sec to HM THE QUEEN 1977–85, Dep Priv Sec 1985–90, Priv Sec 1990–99; *m* 1978 *Lady (Cynthia) Jane Spencer, 2nd dau of of 8th Earl Spencer (*qv*), and has issue:

1b +Alexander Robert; *b* 1983; *educ* Eton

1b +Laura Jane; *b* 1980

2b +Eleanor Ruth; *b* 1985

2a +Thomas William [Thomas Fellowes Esq, The Old Rectory, Barking, Suffolk IP6 8HH]; *b* 1945; *educ* Eton; *m* 1st 1968 (*divorce* 1972) Caroline Moira, dau of Capt Richard Ker, MC, DL (*see* SUFFOLK and BERKSHIRE, E); *m* 2nd 1975 *Rosamund Isabelle, dau of Bernard van Cutsem (*see* FORTESCUE, E), and by her has:

1b +Catherine Margaret Jane; *b* 1977

2b +Mary Eleanor; *b* 1979

1a +Susan Mary [Mrs Michael Cole, Poplar Farm, Marlesford, Suffolk]; *b* 1936; *m* 1960 *Michael Cole and has:

1b +Henry Michael; *b* 1968

2b +Matthew Benjamin; *b* 1970

1b +Clare Jane; *b* 1963

2b +Sarah Marguerite; *b* 1964

2a +Rachel; *b* 1939; JP; *m* 1959 *Joseph Gilfred Studholme and has issue (*see* STUDHOLME, Bt)

2 Alice; *d* unm 11 July 1945

3 Dorothy Louisa, JP Oxon; *m* 11 Nov 1902 Maj Percy Henry Guy Feilden, DL, KRRC (*d* 25 March 1944), of Cokethorpe Hall, Witney, Oxon, yst son of Lt-Gen Randle Joseph Feilden, CMG, of Witton Park, Lancs, and *d* 21 July 1958, leaving issue:

(1) Randle Guy (Sir), KVCO, CB, CBE; *b* 1904, Maj-Gen; *m* 1929 *Mary Joyce [Lady Feilden, Cot Farm, Minster Lovell, Oxon OX8 5RS], dau of Sir John Frecheville Ramsden, 6th Bt (*qv*), and *d* 1981, leaving issue:

1a +Randle Joseph [Randle Feilden Esq, Home Farm, Cokethorpe, nr Witney, Oxon]; *b* 1931; *educ* Eton; *m* 1st 1958 (*divorce* 1970) Lady Caroline Victoria Wood, er dau of 2nd Earl of Halifax (*qv*); *m* 2nd 19– *Mary Francesca, dau of G/Capt Henry William Pearson-Rogers, CBE, JP, of Tostock, Suffolk, and formerly w of John Valentine Gosling, and by his 1st w has had issue:

1b +Randle Charles Roderick; *b* 1961

1b Virginia Mary; *b* 1959; *d* 1994 following a ski-ing accident in France

2b +Fiona Caroline; *b* 1965; *m* 1991 *James D E Bryant and has issue:

1c +Sarah Elizabeth; *b* 1993

2a +Andrew James [Andrew Feilden Esq, The Old Manor House, Minster Lovell, Oxon]; *b* 1941; *educ* Eton; *m* 1977 *Rowena Jane, LVO, dau of Hon Peter Esmé Brassey (*see* BRASSEY OF APETHORPE, B), and has issue:

1b +James William Guy; *b* 1980

1b +Emma Jane; *b* 1979

(2) Cecil Henry; *b* 1907; Maj; *m* 1st 1941 Olivia Constance Leonora (*d* 1975), dau of Lt-Col Hon Guy Victor Baring (*see* ASHBURTON, B); *m* 2nd 1976 *Tessa Eirene [Mrs Cecil Feilden, Manor Farm, Bramdean, Hants SO24 0JS], dau of Denis Griffiths, of Orlingbury Hall, Northants, and *d* 1983, leaving by his 1st w:

1a +Victoria Rose; *b* 1942; *m* 1971 *Gerald Hugo Cropper Wakefield and has issue (*see* WAKEFIELD, Bt)

2a +Mary Henrietta [Miss Mary Feilden, 10 Gertrude St, London SW10 0JN]; *b* 1944

(1) Dorothy Priscilla; *b* 1909; *m* 1941 *Lt-Col John Wilson Seton Galbraith, 11th Hus, and *d* 1983, leaving:

1a +Jonathan Charles [Jonathan Galbraith Esq, Blackburn Cottage, St Ann's, Lockerbie, Dumfriesshire, Scotland]; *b* 1942

2a +(Arthur) Guy [Guy Galbraith Esq, Newbold Revel, Haddington, E Lothian EH41 4HF]; *b* 1947; *m* 1975 *Sarah Jane, dau of Maj Robert Philip Henry Elwes, MBE, MC (*see* ANNANDALE AND HARTFELL, E), and has:

1b +Rowena Mary; *b* 1978

2b +Alice Katherine; *b* 1980

1a +Joanna Katherine [Mrs John Mitchell, Foxwood, Parkgate, Dumfries]; *b* 1943; *m* 1967 *Capt John William Nelson Mitchell and has:

1b +Mark Alastair Nelson; *b* 1969

1b +Katrina Mary; *b* 1972

2b +Miranda Janet; *b* 1973

The 24th LORD *d* 22 Nov 1906; his est son,

THOMAS WALTER BRAND, **25th Lord** (Baron) **Dacre** and 3rd VISCOUNT HAMPDEN OF GLYNDE, GCVO (1935), KCB (1921, CB 1917), CMG (1915); *b* 29 Jan 1869; *educ* Eton and Trin Coll Cambridge; Ld Lt, JP and CC Herts, Lt-Col 1st Bn Herts Regt TF 1913–15, Col and Hon Brig-Gen TFR 1919–21, Hon Col Herts Regt TA 1930, Col 10th Roy Hus (Prince of Wales's Own) 1935–39, ADC to HM GEORGE V 1920–31, a Lord-in-Waiting 1924–36, Maj 10th Hus, Bde Maj 2nd Cav Bde Boer War 1899–1901 (despatches, Brevet, Queen's Medal, six clasps), and WW I cmdg 1st Hertfordshire Regt and as a Bde Cdr (despatches eight times, Legion of Honour), KStJ; *m* 29 April 1899 Lady Katharine Mary Montagu-Douglas-Scott, JP Herts (*d* 7 March 1951), dau of 6th Duke of Buccleuch and (8th Duke of) Queensberry (*qv*), and *d* 4 Sept 1958, leaving:

1 THOMAS HENRY BRAND, **26th Lord** (Baron) **Dacre** and 4th VISCOUNT HAMPDEN, CMG; *b* 30 March 1900; *educ* Eton; Lt Rifle Bde, Page of Honour to HM GEORGE V 1913–16, Br Ch Exec Offr Combined Production and Resources Bd, Washington, USA, md Lazard Bros; *m* 26 July 1923 Leila Emily (*d* 27 Oct 1996), only dau of Lt-Col Frank Evelyn Seely, JP, DL (*see* SEELY, Bt), and *d* 17 Oct 1965, when the Barony of Dacre fell into abeyance between his two surv daus but was terminated in favour of the er 1970, having had:

(1) Sarah Eliza; *b* 7 July 1924; *d* 25 March 1937

(2) Gian Katharine; *b* 6 April 1927; *d* 23 Jan 1929

(3) RACHEL LEILA, **present Baroness Dacre**

(4) +Tessa Mary [The Hon Mrs Tessa Ogilvie Thompson, Froome, Froome Street, Athol Ext, Sandton 2196, Johannesburg, S Africa]; *b* 21 April 1934; *m* 24 July 1956 *Julian Ogilvie Thompson, son of Hon Mr Justice N Ogilvie Thompson, of Bilbury, Cotswolds, Kenilworth, Cape Town, S Africa, and has issue:

1a +Christopher William; *b* 31 Aug 1958; *m* 1984 *Kathleen Jean, dau of Alastair Blackstock, of Blairgowrie, Johannesburg, and has issue:

1b +James Alastair; *b* 1988

2b +Luke Julian; *b* 1991

2a +Anthony Thomas [Anthony Ogilvie Thompson Esq, 148th Ave, Lower Haughton 2193, Johannesburg, S Africa]; *b* 21 May 1964; *m* 24 Jan 1991 *Meredith Jensen and has:

1b +Nichols; *b* 13 June 1996

2b +Theodore; *b* 13 June 1996

1a +Rachel Amanda [Mrs Richard Keene, The Oast House, Mill Court, Upper Froyle, Hants]; *b* 12 Oct 1960; *m* 1985 *Richard Miles Keene and has:

1b +Harold Thomas; *b* 1988

2b +Justin Frederick; *b* 1989

3b +Oliver Stephen; *b* 1993

1b +Tessa Emily; *b* 29 March 1995

2a +Leila Katharine; *b* 17 Nov 1965; *m* 1990 *Hilton A Barnett, son of G G Barnett, of Bryanston, Johannesburg, and has:

1b +Thomas; *b* 1 March 1995

2 DAVID FRANCIS, 5th VISCOUNT HAMPDEN (*qv*)

3 Ranulph William; *b* 9 Dec 1909; *d* 6 Oct 1912

4 Charles Andrew; *b* 14 July 1920; *educ* Eton; Capt Irish Gds WW II (despatches)

1 +Joan Louisa [The Hon Lady Hill-Wood, Glebe Cottage, Knipton, Grantham, Lincs]; *b* 7 Dec 1904; *m* 18 Feb 1925 Sir Basil Samuel Hill Hill-Wood, 2nd Bt (*qv*), and has issue

2 +Barbara Constance; *b* 1 April 1907; *m* 19 Dec 1934 Ronald Harry Higham (*d* 29 Oct 1966) and has:

(1) +Robin David; *b* 1939; *m* 1978 *Janet Emily, yst dau of Michael Edward Gibb, of Forge House, Taynton, Oxon, and has issue:

1a +Jessica Barbara; *b* 1982

2a +Edwina; *b* 1987

(1) +Caroline [The Hon Mrs Grosvenor, Bennets, Grafton, Oxon OX18 8JE]; *b* 1936; *m* 1959 Hon Robert Victor Grosvenor (*d* 1993) and has issue (*see* EBURY, B)

3 +Elizabeth Margaret; *b* 21 Sept 1911; *m* 3 June 1935 Maj Cecil Chadwick Lomax (*d* 1988), 9th Lancers, and has issue:

(1) +Fiona Valerie; *b* 1936; *m* 1957 *Simon Hildebrand Melville Bradley and has issue:

1a +David Charles; *b* 1960

2a +Mark William; *b* 1964; *m* 1993 *Emily, dau of Anthony Skinner

1a +Sarah Elizabeth [The Hon Mrs Paul Chetwynd-Talbot, Gunville House, Grateley, nr Andover, Hants SP11 8JQ]; *b* 1961; *m* 1982 *Hon Paul Alexander Anthony Bueno Chetwynd-Talbot, son of 21st Earl of Shrewsbury and Waterford (*qv*), and has issue

(2) +Dinah Patricia [Mrs Pascal Voisin, 12 Ave du Cap de Nice, 06300 Nice, France]; *b* 1946; *m* 1977 *Pascal Voisin and has issue:

1a +Thomas Gregoire; *b* 1979

2a +Blaise Noël; *b* 1982

1a +Camille Aimée; *b* 1977

(3) +Camilla Elizabeth; *b* 1948

4 +Monica Dorothy [The Hon Mrs Lambton, Saxon House, Shottisham, Woodbridge, Suffolk]; *b* 3 March 1914; *m* 9 Oct 1933 D'Arcy Lambton and has issue (*see* DURHAM, E)

DACRE OF GLANTON

Arms: Quarterly, 1st and 4th per fesse azure and or, a pale and three roebucks' heads erased counterchanged (for ROPER); 2nd and 3rd, per bend sinister ermine and ermines a lion rampant or, and for distinction a canton sanguine, thereon an escallop argent charged with a cross flory of the fourth (for TREVOR). **Crests:** 1st, a lion rampant sanguine holding in his right paw a ducal coronet or (ROPER); 2nd, on a chapeau gules turned up ermine a wyvern wings elevated sanguine and for distinction on the breat an escallop charged as in the arms. Supporters: Dexter, a bull gules ducally gorged armed and unguled or; sinister a lion sable ducally gorged or langued gules. **Motto:** *Spes mea in Deo* ('My hope is in God'). **Creation:** B. (LP, UK) 1979.

THE BARON DACRE OF GLANTON, of Glanton, Co Northumberland (Prof Hugh Redwald Trevor-Roper) [The Rt Hon The Lord Dacre of Glanton, The Old Rectory, Didcot, Oxon OX11 7EB]; *b* 15 Jan 1914; *educ* Charterhouse and Ch Ch Oxford; Research Fell Merton Coll Oxford 1937–39; Student Ch Ch Oxford 1946–57 (Censor 1947–52, Hon Student 1979); Regius Prof Modern History Oxford 1957–80; Dir Times Newspapers Ltd 1974–88; Master Peterhouse Cambridge 1980–87; Hon Fell: Merton Coll Oxford 1980, Oriel Coll Oxford 1980, Peterhouse Cambridge 1987; Chevalier Legion of Honour 1975; author: *Archbishop Laud* (1940), *The Last Days of Hitler* (1947), *The Gentry 1540–1640* (1953), *Hitler's Table Talk* (ed, 1953), *The Poems of Richard Borgett* (ed with J A W Bennett, 1953), *Historical Essays* (1957), *Hitler's War Directives 1939–45* (ed, 1964), *Essays in British History presented to Sir Keith Feiling* (1964), *The Rise of Christian Europe* (1965), *Religion, The Reformation and Social Change* (1967), *The Age of Expansion* (ed, 1968), *The Philby Affair* (1968), *The European Witch-Craze of the 16th and 17th Centuries* (1970), *The Plunder of the Arts in the 17th Century* (1970), *Princes and Artists* (1976), *A Hidden Life* (1970), *The Goebbels Diaries* (ed, 1978), *Renaissance Essays* (1985), *Catholics, Anglicans and Puritans* (1987), *From Counter-Reformation to Glorious Revolution* (1992); *m* 1954 Lady Alexandra Henrietta Louisa (*d* 15 Aug 1997), dau of 1st Earl Haig (*qv*), and formerly w of R-Adml Clarence Dinsmore Howard-Johnston, CB, DSO, MC

Lineage: *See* TEYNHAM, B

DAHRENDORF

Creation: B. (LP, UK) 1993.

THE BARON DAHRENDORF, of Clare Market in the City of Westminster (Sir Ralf Dahrendorf, KBE (1982)) [The Rt Hon The Lord Dahrendorf KBE, House of Lords, London SW1A 0PW]; *b* 1 May 1929; *educ* Hamburg U (DPhil 1952) and LSE (PhD 1956); Lecturer Saarbrücken U 1957; Fell Center for Advanced Study in Behavioral Science USA 1957–58; Prof Sociology: Hamburg U 1958–60, Tübingen U 1960–64, Konstanz U 1964–66; Visiting Prof Columbia U 1960; Parly Sec of State Foreign Office W Germany 1969–70; Memb EEC Commn Brussels 1970–74; Dir LSE 1974–84 (Govr 1986–); memb: Hansard Soc Commn on Electoral Reform 1975–76, Roy Commn Legal Services 1976–79, Ctee to Review Functioning of Financial Issues 1977–80; Tstee Ford Fndn 1976–88; Chm Bd Freidrich Naumann 1982–88; Prof Social Science Konstanz U 1984–87; non-exec dir Glaxo Hldgs plc 1984–92, dir and chm Newspaper Publishing plc 1992–93; Warden St Antony's Coll Oxford 1987–97; Chm Commission on Wealth Creation and Social Cohesion 1994–; Hon DLitt: Reading 1973, Dublin 1975; Fell St Antony's Coll Oxford 1976; Hon Fell: Imperial Coll, LSE: Hon LLD Manchester 1973, Wagner Coll NY 1977, York Ontario 1979, Columbia NY 1989; Hon DSc: Ulster 1973, Bath 1977, Bologna 1991; Hon DHL: Kalamazoo Coll

1974, Johns Hopkins U 1982; Hon DUniv: OU 1974, Maryland 1978, Surrey 1978; Hon Dr Université Catholique de Louvain, Hon DSSc: Queen's U Belfast 1977, Birmingham 1991; Hon Dr Laws U of Westminster 1996; Hon MRIA 1974; FBA 1977; FRSA 1977; Hon FRCS 1982; Grand Croix de l'Ordre du Mérite: du Sénégal 1971, du Luxembourg 1974; Grosses Bundesverdienstkreuz mit Stern und Schulterband (Germany) 1974; Grosses goldenes Ehrenzeichen am Bande für Verdienste (Austria) 1975; Grand Croix de l'Ordre de Léopold (Belgium) 1975; Cdr's Cross Order of Civil Merit (Spain) 1990; author: *Marx in Perspective* (1953), *Industrie- und Bertriebssoziologie* (1956), *Soziale Klassen und Klassenkonflikt* (1957), *Homo Sociologicus* (1959), *Die Angewandte Aufklärung* (1963), *Gesellschaft und Demokratie in Deutschland* (1965), *Pfade aus Utopia* (1967), *Essays in the Theory of Society* (1968), *Konflikt und Freiheit* (1972), *Plädoyer für die Europäische Union* (1973), *The New Liberty* (1975), *Life Chances* (1979), *On Britain* (1982), *Die Chancen der Krise* (1983), *Reisen nach innen und aussen* (1984), *Law and Order* (1985), *The Modern Social Conflict* (1988), *Reflections on the Revolution in Europe* (1990), *LSE: A History of the London School of Economics and Political Science 1895–1995* (1995); *m* 1980 *Ellen Joan, dau of James Krug, of New York

Lineage: GUSTAV DAHRENDORF; *m* Lina Witt and had:

RALF, *cr* a **Baron**

DALHOUSIE

Arms: Argent an eagle displayed sable, beaked and membered gules. **Crest:** A unicorn's head couped at the neck argent, armed, maned and tufted or. **Supporters:** Dexter, a griffin argent; sinister, a greyhound argent, gorged with a collar gules, charged with three escallops of the first. **Motto:** *Ora et labora* ('Pray and labour'). **Creations:** L. (S) 25 Aug 1618 (Ramsay of Dalhousie), E. and L. (S) 29 June 1633, B. (UK) 12 June 1875 (Ramsay of Glenmark).

THE 16TH EARL OF DALHOUSIE, Co Midlothian, **Lord Ramsay of Dalhousie**, **Lord Ramsay and Carrington** and **Baron Ramsay of Glenmark**, Co Forfar (Sir Simon Ramsay, KT (1971), GCVO (1978), GBE (1957), MC (1944), JP (Angus 1967), DL (Angus 1951)) [The Rt Hon The Earl of Dalhousie KT GCVO GBE MC JP DL, Brechin Castle, Brechin, Angus DD9 6SH; 199 Cranmer Court, Sloane Ave, London SW3 3HG]; *b* 17 Oct 1914; *s* bro 1950; *educ* Eton and Ch Ch Oxford; late Maj 4/5th Bn Black Watch (TA), WW II (MC 1944, POW); MP (C) Forfarshire 1945–50, C Whip 1946–48, Ld Lt Angus 1967–89, Chllr Dundee U 1977–92, Govr-Gen Fedn Rhodesia and Nyasaland 1957–63, Ld Chamberlain to HM QUEEN ELIZABETH THE QUEEN MOTHER 1965–92, Kt Cdr Commandery Centl Africa OStJ 1957; *m* 26 June 1940 Margaret Elizabeth Mary (*d* 9 Feb 1997), er dau of Brig-Gen Archibald Stirling of Keir, JP, DL, MP (*see* HERON-MAXWELL, Bt), and has issue:

1 +JAMES HUBERT, *Lord Ramsay*, DL (Angus 1993) [Lord Ramsay DL, Brechin Castle, Brechin, Angus DD9 6SH]; *b* 17 Jan 1948; *educ* Ampleforth; 2nd Lt Coldstream Gds 1968–71, RARO 1971; *m* 3 Oct 1973 *Marilyn Davina, 2nd dau of Maj Sir David Butter, KCVO, MC, DL, of Cluniemore, Pitlochry, Perthshire, and has issue:

(1) +Simon David; *b* 18 April 1981; Page of Honour to HM THE QUEEN to 1996

(1) *Lorna Theresa; *b* 6 Feb 1975

(2) *Alice Magdalene; *b* 10 Aug 1977

2 +Anthony [The Hon Anthony Ramsay, 37 Anhalt Rd, London SW11 4NZ]; *b* 2 March 1949; *educ* Ampleforth; *m* 1st 3 Nov 1973 (*divorce* 1979) Georgina Mary, yr dau of Hon Michael Langhorne Astor (*see* ASTOR, V), and has issue:

(1) +Alexander; *b* 12 Jan 1977

2 (cont.) The Hon Anthony Ramsay *m* 2nd 1984 *Vilma, dau of Raphael Salcedo, of Santa Martha, Colombia, and has further issue:

(1) *Zoë Mary; *b* 1984

(2) *Isabella; *b* 1986

3 +John Patrick [The Hon John Ramsay, 1 Kassala Rd, London SW11]; *b* 9 Aug 1952; *educ* Ampleforth; *m* 25 July 1981 *Louisa Jane, only dau of Robert Edward Erland Nicholai d'Abo, of West Wratton Pk, Cambs, by Lady Ursula Isabel Manners, er dau of 9th Duke of Rutland (*qv*), and has issue:

(1) +Christopher; *b* 18 Feb 1984

(1) *Lucy Emma; *b* 1985

1 *Elizabeth Anne [The Rt Hon The Countess of Scarbrough, Sandbeck Park, Maltby, Rotherham S66 8PF]; *b* 16 Sept 1941; *m* 9 July 1970 *12th Earl of Scarbrough (*qv*), and has issue

2 *Sarah Mary [The Lady Sarah Keswick, 1A Ilchester Pl, London W14 8AA]; *b* 18 Oct 1945; *m* 23 April 1966 *Sir (John) Chippendale (Chips) Keswick, 2nd s of Sir William Johnston Keswick, of Theydon Priory, Theydon Bois, Essex, and has:

(1) *David; *b* 25 Feb 1967; *educ* Harrow and St Andrews

(2) *Tobias; *b* 2 Sept 1968; *educ* Eton

(3) *Adam Philip Charles; *b* 1 Feb 1973; *educ* Eton and Edinburgh U

Lineage: The RAMSAYs settled in the Lothians in the 12th century. Simundius (Simon) de Ramsay, first of the name on record in Scotland, witnessed a charter to the monks of Holyrood 1140 and another between 1189 and 1196; Sir Nessus de Ramsay (probably a cousin) put his seal to a charter by ALEXANDER II in 1217; and a brother or cousin of Sir Nessus, Nicholas de Ramsay, witnessed a charter between 1250 and 1270. Nearly two centuries later a presumed member of the family, Robert Ramsay of Dalhousie, witnessed charters by the Earl of Douglas in 1414, 1416 and 1417.

WILLIAM de RAMSAY witnessed the Coldinghame Charter 1198 and another 1236; had:

WILLIAM de RAMSAY; memb Cncl of Magnates of the Realm 1255; witnessed a charter 1260; *d* by 1262, leaving, with two yr sons (Malcolm; John):

WILLIAM de RAMSAY; witnessed a charter 1 Sept 1262 and another May 1274; *d c* 1295, leaving:

Sir WILLIAM RAMSAY de DALWOLSY (*i.e.*, Dalhousie, in Lothian); signed the Ragman Roll at Berwick 1296, supported ROBERT I (THE BRUCE); signed the letter to the Pope asserting the independence of Scotland 1320; seems to have had two sons:

1 Alexander (Sir), of Dalhousie; Warden Middle March, Constable Roxburghe Castle, Sheriff Teviotdale, cmded the men of Lothian July 1335, one of the Regent's ch cdrs at Borough Muir where the English-paid Flemish Army was defeated, helped capture Leuchars and St Andrew's Castles 1336, relieved Dunbar Castle June 1338, led 20 Scottish knights against 20 English knights under HENRY OF LANCASTER (later HENRY IV) in a joust at Berwick (at which his cousin, Sir William Ramsay, was *k*) autumn 1338, took Roxburghe Castle Easter Eve 1342 (for which the King made him Sheriff of Teviotdale), but was captured by Sir William Douglas (then Sheriff) 20 May 1342 and was starved to death in Hermitage Castle

2 William (Sir), of Inverleith; led a raid in the environs of Norham Castle, Northumberland, and lured its English garrison into an ambush at Battle of Nesbitt Moor 1355; had:

(1) Patrick (Sir), of Dalhousie; made over his estates to his er gs 1367; *d c* 1377, having had:

1a Alexander, of Carnock; *dvp*, leaving:

1b Alexander (Sir), of Dalhousie; held Dalhousie Castle against the English under HENRY IV 1400; *k* Battle of Homildon Hill 14 Sept 1402

2b James; living 1367

(2) William (Sir), of Inverleith, which he inherited 1357; had:

1a David; had a charter of Inverleith 1384

A presumed kinsman,

Sir ALEXANDER RAMSAY of Dalhousie, of which he had a charter (as Dalwolsy), along with Keringtoun, Co Edinburgh, and Foulden, Berwicks, to himself and his heirs 1456 (confirmed to his gs by JAMES III 1473); witnessed a charter by the 4th Earl of Douglas 1420; Auditor of the Exchequer 1450; *d* by 1464, having by his 2nd w Margaret had issue:

1 Alexander; Sheriff Edinburgh; *d* by 1456, leaving (with a dau Jouet):

(1) ALEXANDER

2 Robert, of Swynisdene; living 1456; ancestor of the RAMSAYs of Whitehill

3 David; Minister of Foulden

4 George, of Halhouse and Likbernard, Edinburgh, of which he had charter 1459

5 William

Sir ALEXANDER RAMSAY's gs,

ALEXANDER RAMSAY of Dalhousie; MP (S Parl) 1471–80; *m* Elizabeth/Isabel (*m* 2nd Thomas Livingstone), dau of George Douglas, 4th Earl of Angus, and *d* by 16 March 1482/3, leaving, with a dau (Elizabeth, *m* Sir Alexander Boswell of Balmuto):

Sir ALEXANDER RAMSAY of Dalhousie; *m* 1st (*divorce*) Elena Home; *m* 2nd *c* 1508 Nicola, dau and heir of George Ker of Samuelston and widow of Alexander, 2nd Lord Home (*see* HOME, E), and was *ka* Flodden 9 Sept 1513, having by her had, with a yr s (George) and a dau (Margaret):

NICOLAS RAMSAY of Dalhousie, Carnock, Foulden and Keringtoun; *m* 1st Isabella, dau of Robert Livingstone of Drumry and widow of John Ramsay, Lord Bothwell (*forfeited* 1488); *m* 2nd 5 Nov 1552 Christian, dau of Ninian, 3rd Lord Ross of Halkhead (*extinct* 1754), and widow of John Mure of Caldwell, and *d* by 9 May 1555, having had an est s:

GEORGE RAMSAY of Dalhousie; had charters of his lands 1528, 1536 and 1564; Justiciary over his lands 1555; supported MARY QUEEN OF SCOTS 1568; *m* Elizabeth (*d* Dec 1571), dau of Hepburn, Laird of Waughton, and *d* 2 Dec 1580, having had, with six daus:

1 John, of Dalhousie; had a charter of his lands 1589; *m* (contract 5 Oct 1574) Marion (*m* 2nd Patrick Murray of Falahill), dau of Sir John Bellenden of Auchnoull, Ld Justice, but *dsp* by 12 April 1592

2 James, of Cockpen, of which had a charter 1569 (confirmed 1580); *m* 5 April 1570 Elizabeth, est dau and heir of David Ramsay of Clatty, and *dvp* Nov 1580, leaving issue:

(1) GEORGE, **1st Lord**

(2) David; living 1580

(1) Elizabeth; *m* 1st 30 Nov 1591 Thomas Edingtoun of Edingtoun; *m* 2nd 1598 Lawrence Howburn

3 Alexander, of Edglaw

4 William; living 1570

GEORGE RAMSAY's gs,

GEORGE RAMSAY, **1st Lord Ramsay of Dalhousie**, so *cr* 5 Jan 1619 with precedence of an earlier *cr* 25 Aug 1618 as LORD RAMSAY OF MELROSE, which title he exchanged for the newer one; *b* after 1570; ktd by 1603, MP Kincardineshire 1617; *m* 1593 Margaret (living 12 Sept 1615), only dau of Sir George Douglas bro of 6th Earl of Morton (*qv*), and *d* by 22 July 1629, leaving issue:

1 WILLIAM, **1st Earl**

2 John, of Edington; had a charter of his lands from his f 1628; *m* (contract 19 Feb 1628, confirmed 10 Dec 1631) Egidia (Grills) (will confirmed 1 Oct 1692), dau of William Kellie, WS

3 James

4 David; living 27 July 1622

1 Janet; *b* 8 Nov 1608

2 Margaret; *m* 16 Dec 1626 Sir William Livingston of Kilsyth and had issue (*see* OXFUIRD, V)

The 1st LORD's est s,

WILLIAM RAMSAY, **1st Earl of Dalhousie**, so *cr* 29 June 1633, as also LORD RAMSAY OF CARRINGTON (*i.e.*, the long-held family property of Keringtoun); MP Montrose 1617 and 1621; raised and cmded a regt of horse in the Covenanter army, helping defeat the English royalists at Marston Moor 1644 and Philliphaugh 1645, but later supported CHARLES II; *m* 1st (contract 3 Oct 1617) Margaret (*d* April 1661), est dau of 1st Earl of Southesk (*see* FIFE, D); *m* 2nd Jocosa (*d* 28 April 1663), dau of Sir Alan Apsley and widow of Lister Blount, s of Sir Richard Blount, of Mapledurham, Oxford; *d* Nov 1672, having by his 1st w had, with three daus:

1 GEORGE RAMSAY, **2nd Earl of Dalhousie**; *m* (contract 10 Dec 1644) Lady Anne Fleming (*d* 20 April 1661), dau of 2nd Earl of Wigtown and widow of 8th Lord Boyd (*see* KILMARNOCK, B); *d* by 8 May 1674, having had, with three daus (including Jean; *m* 1st George, Lord Ross, and 2nd *c* 26 Dec 1684 2nd Viscount of Oxfu(i)rd, *qv*):

(1) WILLIAM RAMSAY, **3rd Earl of Dalhousie**, PC (S 1672); Sheriff Co Edinburgh 1672, Capt Edinburgh Militia 1678, 2nd i/c Earl of Mar's Regt at Bothwell Brig 23 Dec 1678; *m* Lady Mary Moore (*m* 2nd 2nd Lord Bellenden of Broughton (*see* ROXBURGHE, D) and *d* 17 March 1725), dau of 1st Earl of Drogheda (*qv*); *d* after 28 Feb 1682, having had issue:

1a GEORGE RAMSAY, **4th Earl of Dalhousie**; *d* unm 1696 (*k* in The Netherlands by a Mr Hamilton)

2a WILLIAM RAMSAY, **5th Earl of Dalhousie**; Col 3rd Gds Regt, Brig-Gen Jan 1710, sent 1705 to help the Archduke Charles, the candidate of the British, Austrians and Dutch for the crown of Spain in the War of the Spanish Succession; *d* unm Oct 1710 in Spain

3a James; Col; *ka* Battle of Almanza, Spain, 1707

1a Elizabeth; inherited her er bro the 5th Earl's personal property; *m* 3 Feb 1696/7 2nd Baron Hawley and *d* 1712

(2) John; Capt Scots regt in Dutch serv 1694

(3) George, of Carriden, Linlithgow; Lt-Gen, cmded Wauchope's Foot Battle of Killecrankie and Scots Gds Battles of Steenkirk and Landen; C-in-C forces Scotland 1702; *m* — Buckson, a Dutch woman, and was *bur* 12 Sept 1705, leaving a dau (Jean, *d* unm)

(4) Robert; will confirmed 23 Jan 1678

2 John, Capt Scots regt in Dutch service 1694; *m* 1660 — Sinclair and had:

(1) WILLIAM, **6th Earl**

3 James

4 William; living 1670; Capt Army; had:

(1) Ernest William

The 5th EARL's kinsman,

WILLIAM RAMSAY, **6th Earl of Dalhousie**; *bapt* Dundee 2 Dec 1660; Col; *m* 1st *c* 1700 Jean, dau of George, 10th Lord Ross; *m* 2nd Janet Martin; *d* 8 Dec 1739, having by his 1st w had, with other issue:

1 George, *Lord Ramsay*; *m* (contract 16 Nov 1726) Jean (*m* 2nd John Stroker Kerr and *d* 27 April 1769), 2nd dau of Hon Harry Maule of Kellie (bro of 4th Earl of Panmure, a title which was forfeited by attainder 1716), and *dvp* 25 May 1739, having had, with other issue (*d* young):

(1) CHARLES RAMSAY, **7th Earl of Dalhousie**; Capt 3rd Foot, Lt-Col 1753; *das* unm 29 Jan 1764

(2) GEORGE, **8th Earl**

(3) Malcolm; Lt-Col Roy Scots Fus and 83rd Foot, DAG Scotland; *d* unm 18 July 1783

The 7th EARL's bro,

GEORGE RAMSAY, **8th Earl of Dalhousie**; advocate 1757, a Ld of Police 1775–82, High Commr Gen Assembly Ch Scotland, rep S peer 1774–87; *s* to the Maule estates (settled on him for life, with remainder to his 2nd s (*see* below)) on death of his maternal unc 4th Earl of Panmure 1782; *m* 30 July 1767 Elizabeth (*d* 17 Feb 1807), dau of Andrew Glen and n and heir of James Glen, of Longcroft, Co Linlithgow, Govr Carolina, and *d* 4 Nov 1787, having had, with other issue:

1 GEORGE RAMSAY, **9th Earl of Dalhousie**, GCB (1815, KB 1813); *b* 23 Oct 1770; Gen 1830, Col 26th Regt 1813–28, cmded 2nd Foot W Indies, Ireland, Holland and Egypt 1795–1801, cmded 7th Div Peninsular War 1809, Lt-Govr Nova Scotia 1816, Govr Canada 1819–28, C-in-C India 1829–32, Capt-Gen Roy Co Archers 1830–38, rep S peer 1796–1815, *cr* 11 Aug 1815 BARON DALHOUSIE OF DALHOUSIE CASTLE, Co Edinburgh (UK); *m* 14 May 1805 Christian (*d* 22 Jan 1839), only child and heir of Charles Broun, of Colstoun, Haddingtonshire; *d* 21 March 1838, leaving issue:

(1) George, *Lord Ramsay*; *b* 3 Aug 1806; Capt 26th Foot; *dvp* unm 25 Oct 1832

(2) Charles; *b* 20 Oct 1807; *d* 8 July 1817

(3) JAMES ANDREW RAMSAY, **10th Earl of Dalhousie** and 1st and last MARQUESS OF DALHOUSIE OF DALHOUSIE CASTLE, Co Edinburgh, AND OF THE PUNJAUB (UK), so *cr* 25 Aug 1849, KT (1848), PC (1843); *b* 22 April 1812; *educ* Harrow and Ch Ch Oxford (MA); MP (C later Peelite) Co Haddington 1837–38, V-Pres BOT 1843–47 and Pres 1845–46, Viceroy India 1847–56, Ld Clerk Registrar of Scotland 1845, Pres Cncl Roy Co of Archers 1848, Ld Warden Cinque Ports 1853; *m* 21 Jan 1836 Lady Susan Georgina Hay (*d* 6 May 1853), est dau of 8th Marquess of Tweeddale (*qv*), and *dspm* 22 Dec 1860, when the Marquessate and 1815 Barony expired, leaving issue:

1a Susan Georgina, CI (1878); *m* 1st 21 Nov 1863 (*divorce* 1890) 1st and last Baron Connemara (*dsp* 3 Sept 1902); *m* 2nd 10 Oct 1894 Surg-Lt-Col William Hamilton Briggs, afterwards Broun, and *dsp* 22 Jan 1898

2a Edith Christian; *m* 9 Aug 1859 Rt Hon Sir James Fergusson, 6th Bt (*qv*) (*d* 14 Jan 1907), and *d* 28 Oct 1871, having had issue

2 WILLIAM RAMSAY later MAULE-RAMSAY (1782), 1st BARON PANMURE, of Brechin, and Navar, Forfar (UK), so *cr* 10 Sept 1831; *b* 27 Oct 1771; MP Forfar 1796–1831; *m* 1st 1 Dec 1794 Patricia Heron (*d* 11 May 1821), dau of Gilbert Gordon, of Halleaths; *m* 2nd 4 June 1882 Elizabeth (*m* 2nd 26 April 1856 Bonamy Mansell Power and *dsp* 25 June 1867), dau of John William Barton; *d* 13 April 1852, having by his 1st w had issue (with six daus):

(1) FOX MAULE later MAULE-RAMSAY (1861), **11th Earl of Dalhousie**, KT (1853), GCB (1855), PC (1841); *b* 22 April 1801, Keeper Privy Seal Scotland, Ld Lt Forfarshire, Ld Rector Glasgow U, MP Perthshire 1835–37 and 1841–52 and Edinburgh 1838–41, Parly U-Sec Home Dept 1835–41, V-Pres BOT 1841, Sec State for War 1846–52 and 1855–58; *m* 4 April 1831 Montagu (*d* 11 Nov 1853), est dau of 2nd Baron Abercromby (*see* 1924 edn), and *dsp* 6 July 1874, when the Barony of Panmure expired

(2) Lauderdale; *b* 27 March 1807; Lt-Col 79th Highrs, MP Forfar 1852; *das* unm Varna, Crimea, 1 Aug 1854

(3) William, of Fearn; *b* 29 March 1809; *m* 16th April 1844 Elizabeth (*d* 11 Feb 1905), est dau of William Binny; *d* 17 Feb 1859, leaving issue:

1a William Thomas; *b* 1845; *d* 1848

2a Lauderdale William; *b* 1854; *d* 1857

1a Elizabeth Patricia; *b* 1846 *m* 22 June 1880 Rev George Wingate, Vicar Stratton, N Cornwall (*d* 16 Dec 1898); *d* 24 Jan 1941, having had issue

2a Mary Christiana; *d* 1886

3a Clara; *d* unm Feb 1903

4a Alice; *d* 22 Jan 1890 aged 36

3 James; *b* 4 Oct 1772; Lt-Col 2nd Foot; *d* unm 15 Nov 1837

4 John; *b* 21 April 1775; Lt-Gen, Gen Staff India, Col-in-Ch 79th Highrs, Mil Sec to **9th Earl of Dalhousie** as Govr-Gen Canada 1819–28 and Viceroy India 1829–32; *m* 19 April 1800 Mary (*d* 28 Oct 1843), dau of Philip Delise, of Calcutta; *d* 28 June 1842, leaving issue:

(1) William; *b* 20 May 1804; Maj-Gen Bengal Army; *d* 13 Dec 1871

(2) GEORGE, **12th Earl**

(3) James; *b* 3 Oct 1808; Maj-Gen Bengal Army; *m* 3 Feb 1840 Florence Harriet Charlotte (*d* 13 Dec 1889), dau of William Robert Burlton Bennet, Bengal CS; *d* 26 Dec 1868, leaving issue:

1a James Andrew; *b* 23 June 1850; *d* 21 March 1871

1a Harriet Charlotte; *m* 15 Dec 1864 Maj Thomas Young, of Lincluden (*d* 1896), having had issue

2a Eliza Monckton; *m* 30 Nov 1867 Sir Edward J D Paul, 4th Bt (*qv*) (*d* 18 Nov 1895); *d* 29 May 1886, having had issue

3a Anne Montagu; *d* unm 1865

4a Patricia; *m* 24 Feb 1876 Gen Alfred Leitenitz, of the King of Italy's Army (*d* 1895), and had issue

(4) John; *b* 14 Jan 1811; Lt-Col HEICS; *m* 28 Dec 1852 Kate Sinclair (*d* 18 April 1880), dau of David Laing, of Thurso, Caithness, and *dsp* 23 Aug 1856

(5) Henry (Sir), KCSI, CB; *b* 25 Aug 1816; Gen Bengal Army, Commr Kumaon, raised to the rank of an Earl's s 1864; *m* 11 Nov 1850 Laura (*d* 29 July 1914), dau of Sir Henry Lushington, 3rd Bt (*qv*); *d* 16 Dec 1893, leaving issue:

1a Henry Lushington; *b* 15 Sept 1854; Lt-Col Indian Political Serv, served Afghan War 1878–79 (despatches, clasp); *m* 1 June 1893 Sophia (*d* 8 Feb 1946), dau of J P Thomas, of Warneford Place, Wilts, and Calcutta; *d* 16 Aug 1928, leaving issue:

1b Archibald Henry Maule; *b* 4 May 1894; Capt Coldstream Gds WW I 1914–16 (wounded), memb Roy Co Archers, MP (C) Midlothian and Peebles S 1931–45, Parly memb Potato Mktg Bd 1934; *m* 30 April 1917 Hon Ismay Lucretia Mary (*d* 16 Feb 1975), only dau of 14th Viscount Gormanston (*qv*) and widow of Lord Ninian Crichton-Stuart, MP (*see* BUTE, M); *d* 11 March 1955, leaving issue:

1c Alexander Henry Richard Maule; *b* 20 Feb 1918; Capt Scots Gds (Supp Res of Offrs), WW II; *das* unm 19 Aug 1943

2c Robert John Maule; *b* 17 May 1920; *educ* Cheltenham; *m* 1st 5 June 1948 (*divorce* 1961) Theodora Jean [Mrs Theodora Ramsay, 2 Cliffield, Shalford, Essex CM7 5HP], yr dau of Martyn Hewlett, of Little Waltham, Essex; *m* 2nd 30 Sept 1961 Elizabeth Frances (*d* 1972), est dau of A F Bultitude, of Sussex, Dir of Music, and *d* 12 May 1978 having by 1st w had issue:

1d *Theodora Alice Maule [Miss Theodora Ramsay, 8-2 Hailsland Grove, Wester Hailes, Edinburgh EH14 3BW]; *b* 18 Feb 1950

2d *Christian Ismay Maule [Miss Christian Maule-Ramsay, 2 Cliffield's, Shalford, Essex CM7 5H6]; *b* 2 Nov 1951; *m* 1972 (*divorce*, resumed maiden name) Juan Carlos Torres, of Santiago de Compostella, Spain, and has:

1e *Aaron; *b* 23 June 1976

3d Charlotte Maule; *b* 6 Oct 1954; *m* 1976 *John Gentry [John Gentry, 275 Peach Tree Lane, Newnan, GA 30263, USA], and *d* 1992, leaving:

1e *Nathan *b* 1975

2e *Mathew; *b* 1982

3e *Andrew; *b* 1989

3c +George Patrick Maule [Col George Ramsay, The Old School Ho, The Square, Elham, Canterbury, Kent CT4 6TJ]; *b* 15 Nov 1922; *educ* Eton; Col (ret) Scots Gds (Lt-Col cmdg 1964–67), WW II (wounded, despatches), psc, jssc, memb Royal Archers; dir Hill, Samuel & Co Ltd 1968–; *m* 1st 9 April 1947 (*divorce* 1977) Patricia Mary, dau of Dr John Joseph Morrin, of Chelsea, and has:

1d +Alexander John Patrick Maule [Alexander Ramsay Esq, Flat A 38 Dafforne Rd, London SW17]; *b* 5 Feb 1948; *educ* Ampleforth; Capt Scots Gds

2d +Patrick William Maule [Patrick Ramsay Esq, 40 Elmbourne Rd, London SW17]; *b* 17 May 1951; *educ* Ampleforth; *m* 1984 *Fiona, dau of Peter Stoddart, of N Rye Ho, Moreton-in-Marsh, Glos, and has:

1e +Nicholas George; *b* 1992

1e *Emily May; *b* 1986

2e *Katie Olivia; *b* 1988

1d *Catherine Mary Maule [Catherine Lady Walker-Okeover, The Stone House, Wyck Rissington, Glos GL54 2PN]; *b* 14 May 1950; *m* 5 Feb 1972 (*divorce* 1991) Capt Sir Peter Ralph Leopold Walker-Okeover, 4th Bt (*qv*), and has issue

2d *Diana Mary Maule [Mrs Timothy Coghlan, Weedon Lodge Cottage, Everdon, Northants NN11 6BQ]; *b* 4 Feb 1957; *m* 1983, as his 2nd w, *Timothy J P Coghlan, son of A F Coghlan, of Ludwell Grange, Horsted Keynes, Sussex, and has:

1e *Andrew Peter Monro; *b* 22 May 1978

2e *Patrick Ralph; *b* 6 May 1982

1e *Louise Mary; *b* 1985

2e *Elizabeth Mary; *b* 1987

3e *Georgina Elizabeth; *b* 30 March 1976

3d *Fiona Elizabeth Maule; *b* 29 June 1964 *m* 1987 *Maj Robert Algernon Radcliffe Boyle (*see* SHANNON, E)

3c (cont.) Col George Ramsay *m* 2nd 1980 *Bridget, dau of Ronald Thomas Dyson Hornby and formerly w of Capt Edward Kelly

4c John Charles Maule (Rev); *b* 24 Nov 1926; *educ* Eton and Pontifical Beda Coll Rome; late Maj Scots Gds, Malaya 1948–50; ordained RC priest 14 March 1959; *d* 15 Oct 1997

1b Maude Evelyn; *m* 12 Sept 1925 Col Richard Augustus Spencer, DSO, OBE, RA and *d* 1990, having had issue (*see* CHURCHILL, V)

2b Vera Edith; *b* 5 Aug 1900; *d* unm Dec 1997

2a John (Sir), KCIE (1915) CSI (1911); *b* 5 Dec 1862; Lt-Col IA, Political Resident Baghdad 1906–09 and Kashmir 1909–11, Ch Commr and Agent to Govr-Gen Baluchistan 1911–17; *m* 9 March 1889 Margaret, OBE (1917) (*d* 2 Jan 1946), est dau of Frederick Henvey, late Bengal CS; *d* 2 March 1942, leaving issue:

1b Mary Isabel; *m* 4 Jan 1916 Col Victor Wellesley Roche, Somerset LI (*d* 18 Dec 1970), s of Surgn-Lt-Col Arthur Wellesley Roche; *d* 11 Dec 1970, having had issue

1a Mary Louisa; *m* 13 Oct 1870 Col John Birney, RE (*d* 14 Oct 1901), of Red Castle and Glenswinton, Kirkcudbright; *d* 3 July 1918, having had issue

2a Lilian; *m* 18 April 1882 Lt-Col William St Pierre Bunbury and *d* 12 June 1936, having had issue (*see* BUNBURY, Bt)

3a Annie; *d* unm 2 Feb 1927

(6) Robert Anderson; *b* 5 Feb 1820; Lt-Col; *d* unm 5 Nov 1897

(1) Anne Finlay Anderson; *b* 9 Feb 1815; *m* 15 June 1848 Col David Ewart, Bengal Artillery (*d* 1880); *d* 13 May 1891

The 11th EARL's cousin,

GEORGE RAMSAY, **12th Earl of Dalhousie**, CB (1856); *b* 26 April 1806; Adml, C-in-C S American Station 1866–69, *cr* 12 June 1875 BARON RAMSAY OF GLENMARK, Co Forfar (UK); *m* 12 Aug 1845 Sarah Frances (*d* 1 May 1904), only dau of William Robertson, of Logan Ho; *d* 20 July 1880, leaving issue:

1 JOHN WILLIAM, **13th Earl**

2 George Spottiswoode; *b* 29 Oct 1848; Lt RA; *d* 1873

3 Arthur Dalhousie; *b* 6 July 1854; *d* 5 Dec 1857

4 Charles Maule, JP; *b* 29 Jan 1859; MP Forfarshire 1894–95, Lt-Col cmdg Forfar and Kincardine Artillery, Lt RA; *m* 28 May 1885 Martha Estelle (*d* 18 July 1964), dau of William R Garrison, of New York, and *dsp* 7 April 1936

The 12th EARL's est s,

JOHN WILLIAM RAMSAY, **13th Earl of Dalhousie**, KT (1881), PC (1886); *b* 29 Jan 1847; Cdr RN, MP (Lib) Liverpool 1880, Ld-in-Waiting in Ordinary to HM QUEEN VICTORIA 1880–85, Equerry to HRH THE DUKE OF EDINBURGH 1874–76 (Extra Equerry 1876–80), Sec State Scotland 1886; *m* 6 Dec 1877 Lady Ida Louisa Bennet (*d* 24 Nov 1887), yr dau of 6th Earl of Tankerville (*qv*), and *d* 25 Nov 1887, leaving issue:

1 ARTHUR GEORGE MAULE, **14th Earl**

2 Patrick William Maule (Sir), KCMG (1932); *b* 20 Sept 1879; *educ* Winchester and Univ Coll Oxford; Cnsllr Emb Dip Serv 1922, Envoy Extrdy and Min Plen Athens 1929–33, Budapest 1933–35, Copenhagen 1935–39, Consul-Gen Hungary 1933, ret 1939; *m* 15 Oct 1917 Dorothy Cynthia (*d* 5 Oct 1957), dau of Brig-Gen Sir Herbert Conyers Surtees, CB, CMG, DSO, MVO, Coldstream Gds, of Mainsforth Hall, Durham, and widow of Christopher Cecil Tower, of Weald Hall, Essex, and *d* 19 June 1962, having had issue:

(1) David Patrick Maule; *b* 31 Jan 1919; *m* 5 April 1948 (*divorce* 19–) Hélène (*m* 2nd John Tod Horton and *d* 1980), dau of Leonidas Arvanitidi, of 4 Avenue du Docteur Brouardel, Paris, and *d* 21 Jan 1978, leaving issue:

1a *Silvia Patricia [Miss Silvia Ramsay, 5617 S Dorchester Ave, Chicago, 60637–1749 Illinois, USA]; *b* 19–

(2) James Surtees Maule; *b* 22 Oct 1923; Lt Scots Gds WW II; *ka* Holland 26 Oct 1944

3 Alexander Robert Maule (Sir), GCVO (1938), KCB (1937), DSO (1916); *b* 29 May 1881; Naval Attaché Paris 1919–22, cmded HMS *Dunedin* 1922, Cdre RN Barracks Portsmouth 1929–31, R-Adml cmdg aircraft carriers 1933–36, V-Adml 1936, C-in-C E Indies 1936–38, Adml 1938, 5th Sea Ld and Ch Naval Air Servs 1938–39, Naval ADC to HM GEORGE V 1931, served WW I (despatches twice, Legion of Honour); *m* 27 Feb 1919 HRH PRINCESS (VICTORIA) PATRICIA HELENA ELIZABETH, CI, GCStJ (by roy licence 25 Feb 1919 dropped HRH and title of Princess, granted by roy warrant same date style of Lady Victoria Patricia Helena Elizabeth Ramsay, with precedence immediately before Marchionesses in the peerage of England; *d* 12 Jan 1974), 2nd dau of FM HRH THE DUKE OF CONNAUGHT AND STRATHEARN (3rd s of HM QUEEN VICTORIA), and *d* 8 Oct 1972, leaving issue:

(1) +Alexander Arthur Alfonso David Maule [Capt Alexander Ramsay of Mar, Cairnbulg Castle, Fraserburgh, Aberdeenshire, AB4 5TN; 25 Onslow Sq, London SW7 3NJ; Inverey House, Braemar, Aberdeenshire]; *b* 21 Dec 1919 (HRH THE DUKE OF WINDSOR and KING ALFONSO XIII OF SPAIN stood sponsors); *educ* Eton and Trin Coll Oxford (MA 1955); Page of Honour Coronation 1937; Capt Gren Gds WW II (wounded N Africa 1943), ADC to HRH THE DUKE OF GLOUCESTER 1944–47, ret 1947; FRICS, chartered surveyor (retd) and estate factor, Chm Exec Ctee Scottish Life-Boat Cncl RNLI 1965–84; *m* 6 Oct 1956 *Lady Saltoun (*qv*) and has issue

4 Ronald Edward Maule; *b* 5 March 1885; Lt Scots Gds; *d* unm 24 April 1909

5 Charles Fox Maule, MC (1917) and bar (1919); *b* 5 March 1885 (twin); Lt Northumberland Yeo, Interpreter 1914–15, WW I (despatches); *m* 14 Nov 1919 Aline Rose (*m* 2nd 15 May 1929 Maj Hon Arthur Michael Bertie, DSO, MC (*see* LINDSEY and ABINGDON, E); *d* 5 July 1948, leaving issue), dau of George Arbuthnot Leslie, and *d* Oct 1926

The 13th EARL's est s,

ARTHUR GEORGE MAULE RAMSAY, **14th Earl of Dalhousie**, JP (Forfar); *b* 4 Sept 1878; *educ* Eton and Univ Coll Oxford; Capt Scots Gds, Res of Offrs, Fife and Forfar Yeo, Boer War 1901–02 (medal with four clasps), WW I (wounded), Hon Col N Scottish RGA (TF); *m* 14 July 1903 Lady Mary Adelaide Heathcote-Drummond-Willoughby (*d* 23 May 1960), yst dau of 1st Earl of Ancaster (*see* HEATHCOTE, Bt, of London), and *d* 23 Dec 1928, leaving issue:

1 JOHN GILBERT RAMSAY, **15th Earl of Dalhousie**, DL (Angus); *b* 25 July 1904; *educ* Ch Ch Oxford (BA); Scots Gds 1925–30; Hon Pres Angus U Assoc 1937; *d* unm 3 May 1950

2 SIMON RAMSAY, **16th and present Earl of Dalhousie**

1 Ida Mary; *b* 29 Jan 1906; *m* 4 Jan 1938 Maj-Gen Sir George Frederick Johnson, KCVO, CB, CBE, DSO, Scots Gds, of Castlesteads, Brampton, Cumberland, and had issue:

(1) *Peter David; *b* 12 July 1940; *educ* Eton

(2) *Robert George; *b* 23 Sept 1946; *educ* Eton

(1) *Sheena Margaret; *b* 28 Dec 1938

2 Jean Maule; *b* 16 April 1909; *m* 28 April 1945 *Lt-Col David McNeil Campbell Rose, DSO, Black Watch [Lt-Col David Rose, Jezreel, 17 Leegomery Rd, Wellington, Shropshire TF1 3BP], s of Brig-Gen John Latham Rose, CIE, and *d* 16 Jan 1997, leaving:

(1) *Hugh Ramsay; *b* 4 July 1946; *educ* Trin Coll Glenalmond; *m* 5 March 1977 *Flora Margaret, est dau of Lt-Col William John Campbell Adamson, TD, JP, DL, FLAS, of Careston Castle, Nathro, Angus

(1) *Mary Janet; *b* 22 April 1948; *m* 1976 *Maj Anthony James Herbert Davies, RE (ret)

Seat: Brechin Castle, Brechin, Angus. It has been claimed that the oldest part of Brechin is no earlier than the 14th century and that some of it was incorporated in the southern flank of the present house. Another account maintains that Brechin was in existence by the end of the 13th century but that nothing from that time has survived. Its exact shape in the Middle Ages is unknown, though it presumably looked out over the River Southesk just as today's building does, dominating the little town of the same name, and by the 17th century seems to have consisted of longer and shorter wings at right angles to each other, though these are thought not to have been erected much more than 100 years before.

Patrick Maule was granted the territorial Barony of Brechin in 1634 and it was probably at the same time that he acquired the Castle. In 1647 he was also granted the lands of the Bishopric of Brechin, having been ennobled as Earl of Panmure the year before and commemorating his new property in the subsidiary title of Lord Brechin and Navar. One of his younger grandsons, Henry Maule, had a daughter who married into the RAMSAYs, being mother of the **7th Earl of Dalhousie**. It was through this connection that Brechin came to be owned by the present family, though the MAULEs continued in occupation till 1782. That was under a lease, however, since Henry's elder brother, the 4th Earl of Panmure, was a steadfast Jacobite, hence attainted after the failure of the 1715 Uprising and his directly held property confiscated. To forestall this fate for Brechin his wife let it to a Lady Orbistoun in May 1716, just before the act of attainder was passed, and the freehold later passed to the York Building Company.

The 4th Earl of Panmure had on inheriting the title in 1686 called in James Bain or Baine to advise on modernisation. Baine(e) was one of the most distinguished Scottish architects of the day, being King's Master Plasterer and Master Wright. (He also worked on Holyrood House in Edinburgh, THE QUEEN's official Scottish residence.) Whatever plans he submitted were not used and Lord Panmure, who seems to have been more fickle in architecture than politics, turned to Alexander Edward. The latter built him in 1696 a large house adorned by two pavilions, facing west and surrounding a courtyard. Another outer courtyard has not survived but this part of Brechin generally is of interest as the only piece of work of any size by Edward known still to exist. Externally it consists of a 13-bay block some 120 feet long, the middle three bays thrust slightly foward of their fellows, all under a pediment enclosing the family coat of arms. Four outer bays to either side of the central block are set in a flat-fronted facade but the two outermost ones are in round turrets capped by 'witch's hat' conical roofs.

Robert Adam is known to have been called in to advise on improvements in the late 1750s and John Gourley carried out some alterations in 1777. In the last few years of the 18th century Alexander Laing added an entrance hall in which twin files of ionic columns guide the visitor to a broad shallow-stepped staircase. He may also be responsible for the stable court, which dates from 1806. Lauderdale Maule-Ramsay, the younger brother of the **11th Earl**, became Brechin's owner in preference to his elder brother and during his tenancy started on modifications to designs by John Henderson. On his death in the Crimea the house was inherited by the future **11th Earl**, who had, as we have seen, originally been passed over but who on coming into the title six years later spent three years remodelling Alexander Edward's work on the east flank, extending the north flank and reshaping the south one to accommodate a long gallery. The square turret on this side dates from 1903–04 and is by Keeble of London. A notable feature of the grounds is the Image Bridge, by James Burn of Haddington.

DALRYMPLE-HAY

Arms: Quarterly, 1st and 4th, or on a saltire az., nine lozenges of the field, all within a bordure gu.; 2nd and 3rd, arg. in chief an ox yoke in fess ppr., three escutcheons gu. **Crests:** 1 A rock per pale az. and or, 2 Between two piles or issuant from the torse a falcon ppr., charged on the breast with an escutcheon gu. **Mottoes:** Above crest 1 'Firm', above crest, 2 *Servo jugum* ('I serve the yoke'). **Supporters:** Two volunteers belonging to the Corps of Wigtown in their uniforms of the year 1800, all ppr. **Creation:** Bt. (GB) 27 April 1798.

SIR JAMES BRIAN DALRYMPLE-HAY, 6TH BT, of Park Place, Co Wigtown [Sir James Dalrymple-Hay Bt, The Red House, Church St, Warnham, Horsham, W Sussex RH12 3QW]; *b* 19 Jan 1928; *s* kinsman 1952; *educ* Blundell's; Lt RM Commandos 1946–49, estate agent; *m* 12 April 1958 *Helen Sylvia, only dau of Stephen Herbert Card, of Reigate, Surrey, and has issue:

1 *Fiona Louise; *b* 15 Nov 1963; *m* 1993 *Richard M Norcross and has:

(1) *Rylan Daniel; *b* 19 March 1995

(2) *Briony Laura; *b* 5 Dec 1996

2 *Charlotte Ann; *b* 16 April 1966

3 *Lucie Helen; *b* 25 July 1969

Lineage: JAMES DALRYMPLE of Stair and Drummurchie; *m* 9 Sept 1617 Janet, dau of Fergus Kennedy, of Knockdaw, and had, with an er s (*see* STAIR, E):

JOHN DALRYMPLE; *b* 1621; acquired the estate of Dunragit 1682; *m* Agnes Cathcart and had:

JAMES DALRYMPLE; *m* Margaret Blair, of Dunskey (*d* 24 April 1747 aged 75) and had, with a yr s (John, Capt 21st Foot, *b* 1710, *m* 1741 Mary Niven,and *dsp k* Battle of Falkirk 17 Jan 1746):

JAMES DALRYMPLE, MD; *b* 18 Oct 1706; *m* 15 Jan 1740 Grace, dau of Patrick McDouall of Freugh, and *d* 14 May 1776, having had, with three other daus (*d* young):

1 James; *b* 1742; *d* 15 June 1746

2 JOHN (Sir), **1st Bt**

1 Grace; *b* 1747; *m* Sir Alexander Gordon of Culvennan

The 2nd son,

Sir JOHN DALRYMPLE later DALRYMPLE-HAY (roy licence 4 April 1798 after inheriting Park from his bro-in-law Sir Thomas Hay, 4th Bt (*d* 1794)), **1st Bt** (GB), so *cr* 27 April 1798; *b* 1749; Col War American Independence; *m* 15 April 1779 Susan, sis of Sir Thomas Hay, 4th Bt, of Park (*qv*), and had, with other issue:

1 JAMES (Sir), **2nd Bt**

1 Jean; *m* 1813 Vans Hathorn, of Garthlan, and *d* 1822, leaving issue

2 Elizabeth; *m* 1808 Lt Leveson Douglas Stewart, RN (*see* GALLOWAY, E)

Sir JOHN *d* 12 May 1812; his son,

Sir James Dalrymple-Hay, 2nd Bt; *b* 8 July 1788; *m* 1st 1 Sept 1819 Elizabeth (*d* 14 Feb 1821), est dau of Lt-Gen Sir John Shaw Heron-Maxwell, 4th Bt (*qv*), and had, with other issue:

1 **Sir John Charles Dalrymple-Hay, 3rd Bt**, PC, GCB, FRS, DCL, LLD, DL, JP Wigtownshire, a Public Works Loan Commr 1862–74, Ld Admlty 1866–69, MP (C) Wakefield 1862–65, Stamford 1866–80 and Wigtown Burghs 1880–85, Hon DCL Oxford 1872 and Hon LLD Glasgow 1904, served First Kaffir War 1835, W Coast Africa 1835–36, S America and Pacific 1836–39, Syrian War 1840, E Indies and China 1843–50, Borneo 1845, cmded squadron Bias Bay Sept 1849, Gulf Tonkin Oct 1849, HMS *Hannibal* Crimean War 1855–56, present capture Kertch, Kinburn and Sebastopol; *b* 11 Feb 1821; *m* 18 Aug 1847 Hon Eliza Napier (*d* 2 April 1901), 3rd dau of 9th Lord Napier and Ettrick (*qv*), and *d* 28 Jan 1912, having had issue:

(1) James Francis, Maj 3rd Bn Royal Scots Fus, DL, JP, CC Ayrshire and JP Wigtownshire; *b* 31 May 1848; *m* 15 April 1873 Ellen Douglas (*d* 2 April 1901), est dau of Robert Hathorn Johnston-Stewart of Physgill and Glasserton, and *d* 1 May 1908, having had with two s (*d* unm):

1a Eleanor Louisa, Headmistress Westonbirt Sch 1928–31, Prncpl Downham Sch 1932–50, V-Pres Girl Guides Assoc; *m* 27 Aug 1903 Brig-Gen John Archibald Houison Craufurd of Craufurdland, CMG, CBE, IA and RAF, and *d* 15 Dec 1950, leaving issue. He *d* 27 July 1933

(2) **Sir William Archibald Dalrymple-Hay, 4th Bt**; *b* 30 Jan 1851; *m* 2 June 1906 Mary (*d* 27 April 1933), only child of William McChlery, Bengal CS, and *dsp* 5 Feb 1929

(3) **Sir Charles John Dalrymple-Hay, 5th Bt**, CVO (1928, MVO 1924); *b* 21 March 1865; FO 1887–1895, PC Off 1895–1928; *m* 17 April 1906 Rose (*d* 21 April 1927), dau of Capt W T Hickman, 50th Regt, and *d* 22 March 1952

(1) Evelyn Eliza; *d* unm 23 April 1933

(2) Clara Georgiana; *d* unm 17 April 1946

(3) Mary Elizabeth, OBE (1920); *d* unm 9 Feb 1928

(4) Mabel Lucy; *d* unm 24 Jan 1900

(5) Ellinor Alice; *d* unm 19 Nov 1913

(6) Violet Susan; *m* 18 July 1899 Frederick Howard Marsh, MA, DSc, FRCS, Master Downing Coll and Prof Surgery Cambridge, and *dsp* 27 July 1953. He *d* 24 June 1915

Sir James *m* 2nd Anne (*d* 10 July 1838), dau of George Hathorn, and *d* 19 March 1861, having by her had issue:

2 George James, Col BSC; *b* 25 Sept 1829; *m* 11 May 1855 Amelia Emily (*d* 5 Aug 1912), dau of Col Henry Daniel Maitland, and *d* 30 Aug 1881, having had issue:

(1) James Reginald Maitland, CB (1910), DSO (1900), Col WI Regt, Brig-Gen cmdg Forces Jamaica 1910–14, served Transvaal, W Africa, Sierra Leone and on Staff WW I; *b* 30 July 1858; *m* 20 April 1892 Catherine Margaret (*d* 28 Dec 1949), dau of Henry Billinghurst, of Stedham Hall, Sussex, and *d* 6 Nov 1924

(2) Charles Vernon, Madras CS, Kaisar-i-Hind medal for public service in India, served WW I (despatches, three medals); *b* 8 Jan 1860; *m* 1888 Lina (*d* 30 Dec 1950), dau of F Hambley, and *d* 19 April 1936

(3) Harley Hugh (Sir), civil engr (esp London Underground and PO London rlwy), MCICE, ktd 1933; *b* 7 Oct 1861; *m* 1 Sept 1891 Agnes Yelland (*d* 6 April 1956), dau of Frederick Waters, of Clarence House, Gosport, and *d* 17 Dec 1940, leaving issue:

1a Alison Hathorn; *b* 10 Jan 1909; *m* 19 Feb 1938 John Berger and has issue:

1b *John Harley, slr 1966, ptnr Broomhead and Saul, Taunton; *b* 4 Aug 1942; *educ* Sherborne

1b *Ann Priscilla Dalrymple, ALAM; *b* 11 Dec 1938

(4) John Barstow Mackenzie; *b* 17 Aug 1863; *educ* Merchiston; *m* 30 Jan 1895 Frances Marion (*d* 18 Dec 1962), dau of Edward J Walker, of Upton-on-Severn, and *d* 8 May 1943, leaving issue:

1a James Erroll, Lt-Col Roy Scots Fus WW I (wounded), and WW II ; *b* 30 Aug 1896; *educ* Malvern and RMC Sandhurst; *m* 20 June 1928 Gladys Mary Fitzmaurice Crawford (Beryl) (*d* 8 June 1960), dau of Lt Col Charles Edward Daliel Oldham Rew, OBE, of Ixworth, Suffolk, and *dsp* 11 Dec 1946

(5) George Houston; *b* 9 Sept 1865; *m* 26 Nov 1894 Alice Kathleen (*d* 3 May 1963 aged 89), dau of Col Sir William Brereton Hudson, KCIE, and *d* 10 March 1948, having had issue:

1a Brian George Rowland, Col Indian Cav WW I, and WW II; *b* 31 Jan 1898; *m* 1st 1925 Beatrice (*d* Dec 1935), dau of A W Inglis, of Behar, and had issue:

1b Sir JAMES BRIAN DALRYMPLE-HAY, **6th and present Bt**

2b +JOHN HUGH [John Dalrymple-Hay Esq, Little Meadow, Forty Green Rd, Knotty Green, Beaconsfield, Bucks HP9 1XL]; *b* 16 Dec 1929; heir presumptive; *educ* Blundell's; Capt Roy Scots Fus, Korea with 1st Bn KOSB (despatches); *m* 6 Oct 1962 *Jennifer Phyllis Roberta, only dau of Brig Robert Johnston, CBE, of 44 Exeter House, Putney Heath, London SW15, and has issue:

1c +Malcolm John Robert; *b* 1 April 1966; FRCS

3b +Ronald George Inglis [Ronald Dalrymple-Hay Esq, Glenluce, Lee's Gully Rd, Tetoro RD4, Waiuku, Auckland, New Zealand]; *b* 3 March 1933; *educ* Blundell's; *m* 1973 *Anne Valerie, dau of Bernard James Dawson, and has issue:

1c +Russell James; *b* 1977

1a (cont.) Brian Dalrymple-Hay *m* 2nd 14 Dec 1937 *Elizabeth, only dau of Tennent Alton, of Behealing, Dibrugarh, Assam, and *das* 17 Oct 1943, having by her had issue:

4b +Christopher Hamish [Christopher Dalrymple-Hay Esq, Klein Constantia, PO Box 160, Letsitele, 0885, N Transvaal, S Africa]; *b* 26 Feb 1941; *m* 1968 *Margarte Linda Smith and has:

1c +Hamish Ian; *b* 1971

1c *Amanda Jane; *b* 1975

2a Hugh Brereton, DSO (1945), Lt-Col IA WW II (POW); *b* 15 Dec 1900; *m* 28 Aug 1939 *Gwendyth Margaret (*m* 2nd 1994 — Blake) [Mrs Blake, 1A Moorfield Rd, Woodbridge, Suffolk IP12 4JN], dau of Lt-Col Norman L Callard, and *d* 1987, leaving issue:

1b *Janet Margaret [Mrs Janet Stericker, Brownings, Pytches Rd, Woodbridge, Suffolk]; *b* 2 Sept 1941; *m* 29 June 1963 (*divorce* 1986) Anthony David Stericker and has issue:

1c *Johanna Margaret; *b* 26 Jan 1966

2c *Sophia Harriett; *b* 22 June 1968

3c *Lucinda Jean; *b* 15 July 1969

1a Lorna Alice Emily; *b* 14 Oct 1899; *m* 1 Dec 1922 Alexander Izat Walker, MC, and had issue

(6) Stair Francis Barton, Lt-Col IA Chitral Relief Force 1895 (medal and clasps), CP India famine 1899 (services brought to the notice of Govt of India), NW Frontier 1908 (medal with clasp), WW I (despatches, three medals), E Persia 1919–20 (despatches, medal and clasp), CD WW II; *b* 21 Jan 1872; *educ* St Paul's and RMC Sandhurst; *m* 1st 27 Sept 1893 Laura Mary Edith Catherine de Bouillion (*d* 1 Jan 1955), dau of Col Edmund Hill Wickham, RA, of Horsington, Somerset, by Princess Eugenie Palaeologue; *m* 2nd 20 Aug 1957 Dorothea Aimee Ellen (*d* 7 Sept 1962), only dau of Maj 51 Dighton-Probyn, RHA, and *d* 1 July 1963, having by his 1st w had:

1a Christopher Montague Vernon Francis, DSC (1944), Lt-Cdr RN WW I with submarines and anti-submarines (despatches, three medals), Roy Humane Soc medal for saving life at sea 1917, served WW II 1939–44 (despatches three times), cmded HMS *Mistral* Western Approaches 1942; *b* 9 Nov 1896; *m* 1st 27 Feb 1919 (*divorce* 1929) Mary Teresa (*d* 1977), twin dau of Lt-Col Edward Henry Joseph Mostyn (*see* MOSTYN, Bt); *m* 2nd 30 Nov 1929 Helen Violet, dau of H K Grierson, of Castle Douglas, and *das* 20 Dec 1944, having by his 1st w had:

1b *Mary Cecily Edith Teresa; *b* 8 March 1920; *m* 11 April 1947 *John Walter Ferlex Lloyd-Johnes, yr son of Herbert Thomas Lloyd-Johnes, MC, of Dolaucothy, Carmarthenshire

(1) Anne Susan; *m* 22 Nov 1880 Col Henry Townsend Butcher, Bde Cdr RFA, son of Maj-Gen Arthur Butcher, and *d* 14 May 1934, leaving issue. He was *ka* in France 20 Sept 1915

(2) Mary Emily; *d* unm

3 Houston Stewart; *b* 12 April 1833; *m* 26 March 1859 Mary Louisa, dau of William Richard King, magistrate Port Mackay Queensland, and *d* 5 Feb 1873, leaving, with other issue:

(1) James Stewart; *b* 21 Feb 1860; *m* 18 June 1886 Emily (*d* 16 June 1938), dau of William Irving, and *d* 31 March 1931, leaving issue:

1a John Charles Houston, District Forester in Forestry Commn of NSW, AIF WW I; *b* 7 July 1890; *m* 1st 10 Sept 1921 (*divorce* 1945) Vera May, dau of William Earl, of Dungog, NSW; *m* 2nd 28 Nov 1946 *Coral Elizabeth, dau of William Henry Richards Coats, of Mount Lofty, S Australia, and *d* 31 July 1960

1a Mary Grace; *b* 9 Sept 1888

(2) Richard Tycho, Commr Forests NSW, ret 1926; *b* 3 Oct 1861; *m* 22 Dec 1888 Bessie (*d* 1941), dau of J W Cheesbrough, of Tareela, Barraba, NSW, and *d* 9 Dec 1943, having had, with other issue:

1a Charles Stewart, MC, Lt Australian Artillery WW I (despatches); *b* 13 Oct 1891; *m* 1922 Barbara, dau of Warwick Chambers, of Sydney, and *d* 1972, leaving issue:

1b +John Warwick; *b* 16 Aug 1928; author and lecturer; *m* 31 Oct 1953 *Barbara Deirdre, dau of M J Moir, architect, of Canberra, Australia, and has issue:

1c *Heather Nan; *b* 1954

2c *Ann Louise; *b* 28 June 1956

1b *Ann [Mrs David Thompson, 41 Bundabah Avenue, St Ives, Sydney, NSW, Australia], served WW II 1942–45 in WRANS; *b* 10 Jan 1924; *m* 30 April 1947 *David Gordon Thompson, stockbroker, and has had issue:

1c Warwick Angus; *b* 3 July 1948; *d* 1964

1c *Jennifer Ann; *b* 22 Dec 1950

2c *Barbara Ann; *b* 28 Jan 1952

3c *Sally Ann; *b* 13 Nov 1958

2a +Kenneth Houston, OBE, memb Br Solomon Islands Advisory Cncl from 1953, WW I as Lt Australian MGC and WW II as Lt RANVR (Coast-watcher); *b* Aug 1896; *m* 1st 23 July 1932 (*divorce* 1947) Sylvia, dau of Dr L Conroy, of Blayney, NSW; *m* 2nd 30 March 1954 *Marjorie Susan, formerly w of — Georgetti and dau of Erwin Charles Hennell, of Pallinghurst, Worthing, Sussex

1a Margaret Fordyce, JP, Coronation Medal; *b* 24 Dec 1889

2a Kathleen Alice; *b* 12 Oct 1894; *m* 1st 1919 (*divorce* 1934) William Hay, of Yass, NSW; *m* 2nd 1945 Cdr Walter de Burgh Thomas, RNR. He *d* 1963

3a Bessie; *b* 20 Aug 1899; *m* 1921 (*divorce* 1927) Arthur Grigson, son of Dr R Grigson, of Muswellbrook, and *d* 7 April 1935

4a Ellinor Mary; *b* 2 July 1904; *m* 1928 (*divorce* 1937) Richard Clarence Kirby, son of C Kirby, of Cairns, Queensland, and *d* 18 May 1968

(3) Claude Thomas Hugh Vans; *b* 11 Aug 1865; *m* 1898 (*divorce* 1921) Isobel Ellen (*d* 18 Feb 1967), dau of Francis Wheelhouse, CE, and *d* 17 March 1953, leaving, with other issue:

1a Houston Francis Wilfred, Assoc of Australian Soc of Accountants; *b* 24 July 1907; *m* 1st 7 Jan 1938 (*divorce* 1943) Marie, dau of James Thomas Hawke, of Hamilton, NZ; *m* 2nd 11 March 1967 *Olive May [Mrs Houston Dalrymple-Hay, 5/55 King St, Wollstonecraft, NSW 2065, Australia], dau of John Jacob Worner, of Young, NSW, and *d* 22 July 1995

1a *Isobel Ellen Ruby [Mrs Arthur Hall, Unit 2, Retirement Village Lauriton, NSW 2443, Australia]; *b* 28 Oct 1904; *m* 29 Nov 1924 Arthur John Peverly Hall (*d* 1975), LLB, RAF, and has issue:

1b *Isobel Wendy Anne; *b* 1928

(4) Houston Stewart, Manager Commercial Bank, Penrith, NSW; *b* 27 Aug 1871; *m* 16 July 1906 Daisy Annie (*d* 6 Sept 1928), dau of David Davis, of Christchurch, NZ, and *d* 11 July 1956, having had, with other issue:

1a +Houston Stewart [Houston Dalrymple-Hay Esq, 96 Raglan St, Mosman, NSW, Australia], served WW II as Capt 2nd Australian Imp Force; *b* 6 July 1909; *m* 19– Peggy Fitzmaurice (*d* 1982), dau of Argyle Charles Charleston Loftus, of Brighton, Victoria, and has issue:

1b +Charles Stewart; *b* 1949

1b *Holene Fitzmaurice [Mrs Christopher Bell, 181 Rymans Rd, Eltham North, Vic 3095, Australia]; *b* 1951; *m* 1975 *Christopher James Bell, and has issue:

1c *Simon Christopher; *b* 1981

2c *James Stewart; *b* 1983

1a *Barbara [Mrs Charles Leleu, 4 Howell Avenue, Lane Cove, Sydney, NSW, Australia]; *b* 9 June 1913; *m* 1938 Charles John Newhill Leleu (*d* 1961), OBE, late RAF, and has issue:

1b *John Stewart Newhill; *b* 1939

1b *Antonia Blanche Newhill [Mrs Melchor Scribani, 38 Lady St, Mt Colan, NSW, Australia]; *b* 1945; *m* 1971 *Melchor Puig Scribani, of Caracas, Venzuela, and has issue:

1c *Damian Antonio; *b* 1972

1c *Natalia Daniela; *b* 1975

2a *Nancy Stair [Mrs Frank Fletcher, 6 Beauty Point Rd, Beauty Point, NSW, Australia]; *b* 6 June 1915; *m* 1940 *Frank Lawrence Fletcher, and has issue:

1b *James Lawrence; *b* 1941

1b *Susan Stair [Mrs Peter Pollock, 26 Ryeburn Ave, E Hawthorn, Victoria, NSW, Australia]; *b* 1945; *m* 1970 *Peter Brian Barton Pollock, and has issue:

1c *Peter James; *b* 1972

2c *Simon Stewart; *b* 1974

3c *Robert Lawrence; *b* 1978

2b *Josephine Daisy [Mrs Timothy Harpur, 22 Suffolk Ave, Collaroy, NSW, Australia]; *b* 1948; *m* 1972 *Timothy Martin Harpur and has:

1c *Richard Sydney Frank; *b* 1978

1c *Sophie Irene; *b* 1974

2c *Elizabeth Nancy; *b* 1974

3a *Elizabeth Mary [Mrs Roy Cooper, Unit 12, Coronation Towers, 24 Dunmore Terrace, Auchenflowe, Qld 4066, Australia]; *b* 1 Nov 1921; *m* 1947 *Roy Charles Cooper, CBE, and has issue:

1b *Peter Charles; *b* 1951; *m* 1984 *Catherine Black, and has issue:

1c *Elizabeth Marie; *b* 1985

2c *Zoe Catherine; *b* 1987

2b *Donald Stewart; *b* 1957; *m* 1987 *Heather-Mary —

1b *Sally Victoria; *b* 1948; *m* 1969 *John Neale Sturrock, and has issue:

1c *Angus John; *b* 1973

1c *Kate Elizabeth; *b* 1975

(1) Emma Annie; *b* 27 July 1863; *m* 22 April 1884 Thomas Burton Dibbs, only son of Sir Thomas Allwright Dibbs, and *d* 26 May 1956, leaving issue. He *d* 1921

(2) Ellen Moret; *b* 27 Aug 1871; *d* unm

1 Sarah Georgina; *m* 20 Nov 1849 James Stewart, and *d* 27 Sept 1910, leaving issue (*see* GALLOWAY, E)

2 Susan; *m* 18 Aug 1853 Hastings McDouall and *d* 8 May 1911, leaving issue (*see* BUTE, M)

3 Grace Maria; *m* 8 June 1854 Rev William Sutherland McDouall and *d* 3 April 1923, leaving issue (*see* BUTE M)

4 Mary Heron Maxwell; *m* 28 April 1864 Lt-Gen Charles Francis Fordyce, CB, and *d* 23 July 1914. He *dsp* Sept 1887

5 Anne Wilhelmina; *m* 24 April 1878 Ven Edwin Price, MA, Archdeacon of Auckland, Rector of Sedgefield, Co Durham, and Hon Priest-in-Ordinary to HM, and *d* 9 Nov 1932. He *d* 16 March 1914

DALRYMPLE-WHITE

Arms: Quarterly, 1st and 4th, vert a naval crown or between three roses argent, charged with a representation of the gold medal presented to Sir John Chambers White for his services in Egypt in 1801 pendent from a riband tenné (for WHITE); 2nd and 3rd, or, on a saltire azure between two water bougets in pale sable nine lozenges of the field (for DALRYMPLE). **Crests:** 1 Issuant from a coronet composed of four roses set upon a rim or, a lion's head argent (for WHITE), 2 In front of a rock proper a water bouget sable (for DALRYMPLE). **Motto:** *Virtus sibi munus* ('Virtue is its own reward'). **Creation:** Bt. (UK) 28 July 1926.

SIR HENRY ARTHUR DALRYMPLE DALRYMPLE-WHITE, 2ND BT, of High Mark, Wigtownshire, DFC (1941) and bar (1942)) [Sir Henry Dalrymple-White Bt DFC, c/o Aero Club of E Africa, PO Box 40813, Nairobi, Kenya]; *b* 5 Nov 1917; *s* f 1954; *educ* Eton, Magdalene Coll Cambridge and U of London; W/Cdr RAFVR WW II; *m* 17 Sept 1948 (*divorce* 1956) Mary, only dau of Capt Robert Henry Cunliffe Thomas, 8th Roy Hus, by Cynthia, 2nd dau of Capt Francis Sandford, and has issue:

1 +JAN HEW DALRYMPLE-WHITE; *b* 26 Nov 1950; *educ* Stowe, Huddersfield Poly and Stirling U; *m* 1st 23 June 1979 (*divorce*) Elizabeth —; *m* 2nd 1986 (*divorce*) Angela —; *m* 3rd 1990 *Betty Smith

Lineage: V-Adml Sir JOHN CHAMBERS WHITE, KCB; C-in-C Sheerness; *m* 1816 Charlotte Elizabeth (*d* 1830), est dau of Gen Sir Hew Whiteford Dalrymple, 1st Bt (*see* HAMILTON-DALRYMPLE, Bt), and *d* 4 April 1845, having had, with other issue:

Sir HENRY DALRYMPLE WHITE, KCB, of Marden Ash, Bournemouth; *b* 5 July 1820; Crimea 1854–56, cmded 6th (Inniskilling) Dragoons, Col 6th (Inniskilling) Dragoons, Gen, Kt Legion of Honour, 4th Cl Medjidie; *m* 1st 12 May 1858 Louisa Mary (*d* 25 April 1860), dau of Martin Tucker Smith, of Shirley, Surrey, and had a dau (Maud Mary; *d* unm 20 June 1952 aged 93); *m* 2nd 14 Feb 1863 Alice Elizabeth (*d* 28 April 1925), dau of Neil Malcolm of Poltalloch, Argyllshire, and *d* 27 March 1886, having by her had, with an er s (Arthur Dalrymple, *b* 29 Dec 1863, *d* 6 Jan 1882):

Sir GODFREY DALRYMPLE WHITE later DALRYMPLE-WHITE (deed poll 9 July 1926), **1st Bt** (UK), so *cr* 28 July 1926; *b* 6 July 1866; *educ* Wellington and RMC Sandhurst; Lt-Col Gren Gds, Ensign Gren Gds 1885, ADC GOC Br N America 1892–93, ADC GOC Home Dist 1899–1900, S African War 1899–1902 (despatches), WW I cmded 5th (Res) Bn Gren Gds 1914–16, staff France 1916–18 (despatches thrice, brevet Lt-Col); MP (C) Southport 1910–1923 and 1924–1931; FZS; Govr Wellington 1936; *m* 3 June 1912 Hon Catherine Mary Cary (*d* 16 Oct 1972), est dau of 12th Viscount Falkland (*qv*), and *d* 1 April 1954, leaving issue:

1 Sir HENRY ARTHUR DALRYMPLE-WHITE, **2nd and present Bt**

1 Merial Catherine Dalrymple; *b* 14 Nov 1913; *m* 15 April 1936 Lt-Col William Reeve, OBE, JP, DL, Gren Gds (ret) (*d* 11 Jan 1993), only son of Capt John Sherard Reeve, of Leadenham, and *d* 25 Feb 1989, leaving issue:

(1) *John [John Reeve Esq, West Chase Farm, Bower Chalke, Salisbury, Wilts SP5 5LR]; *b* 12 Jan 1937; *educ* Eton; *m* 1st 25 April 1964 (*divorce*) Penelope Anne, dau of AVM Alan Hunter Cachemaille Boxer, CB, DSO, DFC, RAF, of 19 Queen's Gate Place, London SW, and has issue:

1a *Philip John; *b* 11 July 1967

1a *Alexandra Penelope; *b* 3 Aug 1965; *m* 1992 *Charles — and has issue:

1b *A son; *b* 1993

(1) (cont.) John Reeve *m* 2nd 26 June 1973 (*divorce*) Priscilla, dau of David Harding, of Cirencester, Glos, and has further issue:

2a *Matthew; *b* 12 Aug 1976

3a *Jonathan Sherard; *b* 4 Dec 1979

2a *Merial; *b* 1 Sept 1974

3a *Nicola Mary-Claire; *b* 6 Dec 1977

(1) (cont.) John Reeve *m* 3rd 8 Aug 1988 *(Esmé) Jane, dau of William Briggs, and has further issue:

4a *Harry William; *b* 8 Jan 1990

4a *Francesca Jane Briggs; *b* 17 Nov 1994

(2) *Christopher William [Christopher Reeve Esq, Falkland Cottage, Oddington Rd, Stow-on-the-Wold, Glos GL54 1AN]; *b* 2 April 1944; *educ* Gordonstoun and Mons OCS; Gren Gds 1964–67; *m* 1st 19 Dec 1970 (*divorce*) Margaret Patricia, dau of William Brian Godfrey, OBE, KSG, CA, of Wimbledon, and has issue:

1a *Catherine Jane; *b* 4 Feb 1972; *educ* St Antony's Leweston Sch and Reading U

(2) (cont.) Christopher Reeve *m* 2nd 31 Jan 1975 (*divorce* 1983) (Patricia) Anne, dau of Ven Evan James Gwyn Rogers, Archdeacon Doncaster 1967–79, and by her has:

2a *Alice Eleanor; *b* 17 April 1975

3a *Lucy Harriet Isobel; *b* 17 July 1980

(2) (cont.) Christopher Reeve *m* 3rd 8th April 1991 *Linda Patricia, dau of Gordon Newell Done, of Kinnerley, Shropshire

(3) *Peter Richard [Peter Reeve Esq, Leadenham House, Lincs LN5 0PU]; *b* 15 June 1947; *educ* Gordonstoun; *m* 8 Sept 1978 *Henrietta Mary Louise, only dau of Maj (Francis) James Johnston, Coldstream Gds (ret), of Shamley Wood, Shamley Green, Surrey, by his 1st w Caroline Louise (*d* 21 Oct 1974), only dau of Sir Gerald Wills (*see* WILLS, Bt, of Blagdon), and has issue:

1a *William Francis; *b* 22 May 1980; *educ* Eton

2a *James Henry; *b* 6 Oct 1981; *educ* Eton

1a *Caroline Mary Louise; *b* 18 Nov 1983; *educ* Heathfield

2a *Eleanor Susan Katharine; *b* 4 June 1985; *educ* Heathfield

DALYELL

Arms: Quarterly, 1st and 4th, sable a naked man with his arms extended proper, on a canton argent a sword and pistol disposed in saltire, also proper (for DALYELL OF THE BINNS); 2nd, or a saltire engrailed sable between two swans proper naiant in lochs undy azure and argent and in chief point a mullet gules for difference (for LOCH); 3rd, or a bend chequy sable and argent betwixt three buckles azure (for MENTEITH OF AULDCATHIE); over all an intra-escutcheon additament of a Baronet of Nova Scotia. **Crest:** A dexter arm issuant from a wreath, the hand grasping a scimitar proper, hilted and pommelled or. **Supporters:** Two lions sejant guardant gules, armed and langued azure, each supporting with its inferior forepaw a pavilion pole sable with rosette and pennon spike garnished or, the pennon argent with forks of the same and sable, charged with a sword and pistol in saltire proper. **Mottoes:** Right is reason; (above the crest) I dare. **Creation:** Bt. (NS) 7 Nov 1685.

Thomas (Tom) Dalyell of the Binns, 11th Bt [Tam Dalyell Esq MP, The Binns, Linlithgow EH49 7NA]; *b* 9 Aug 1932; *s* mother 1972 but does not use title; *educ* Eton, King's Coll Cambridge and Moray House Teachers' Training Coll Edinburgh; claim to Btcy allowed by PC 1973; Trooper Roy Scots Greys 1950–52; Teacher Bo'ness High Sch 1956–60; fought (Lab) Roxburgh, Selkirk and Peebles 1959, Dep-Dir Studies Br India ship-sch *Dunera* 1961–62, MP (Lab) W Lothian 1962–83 and Linlithgow 1983–, memb Public Accounts Ctee H of C 1963–66, PPS to Rt Hon R H S Crossman MP 1964–70, Chm PLP Educn Ctee 1964–66, memb Ho of C Select Ctee Science and Technology 1967–69, Chm Lab Parly for affrs gp 1974075, political columnist *New Scientist* 1967–, author; *The Case for Ship-Schools* (1960), *Ship-School Dunera* (1963), *Devolution: the end of Britain?* (1977), *One Man's Falklands* (1982), *A Science Policy for Britain* (1983), *Thatcher's Torpedo* (1983), *Misrule* (1987), *Dick Crossman: a portrait* (1989); *m* 26 Dec 1963 *Kathleen Mary Agnes, Nat Tst for Scotland Administrator The Binns 1972–, memb Roy Fine Art Commn for Scotland 1992–, memb Historic Bldgs Cncl for Scotland 1975–87, author: *House of The Binns* (1973), only dau of Baron Wheatley (LP, *d* 1988), of Braemar House, Whitehouse Terrace, Edinburgh 9, and has issue:

1 +GORDON WHEATLEY; *b* 26 Sept 1965

1 +Moira Eleanor; *b* 25 May 1968

Lineage: THOMAS DALYELL/DALZELL, of Edinburgh (allegedly s of John Dalzell, of Edinburgh, living 2 April 1574, est son of Robert Dalzell of Dalzell and Elliock by his 2nd w Christine, dau of James Dundas, of Newliston; *see* 1939 edn CARNWATH, E); *b* 1572; Steward to Lord Bruce of Kinloss (*see* ELGIN and KINCARDINE, E); bought the estate of Binns, Linlithgowshire, 1629; *m* 8 Oct 1601 Janet Bruce, possibly dau of Edward Bruce, 1st Lord Bruce of Kinloss, and *d* 1642, leaving, with other issue:

Gen THOMAS DALYELL, of the Binns, PC (S, 1667); Col in Ireland 1642, had charge of the customs Carrickfergus 1649, royalist Gen Battle of Worcester 1651, captured and imprisoned Tower London, escaped to the Continent 1652, took part in royalist uprising 1654, Lt-Gen Russian service against Poles and Turks 1655; helped suppress Covenanters 1666, C-in-C Scotland 1666–85; MP Linlithgowshire 1678–85, raised Scots Greys 1681; *m* Agnes, dau of John Ker, of Cavers, and *d* 1 Oct 1685, leaving:

Sir Thomas Dalyell, 1st Bt (NS), so *cr* 7 Nov 1685, with remainder to his est son and heirs male and tailzie succeeding him in the estate of Binns; Army Capt; *m* Katharine, dau of Sir William Drummond of Riccaton by Magdalen, dau of Thomas Dalyell of the Binns, and had issue:

1 **Sir Thomas Dalyell, 2nd Bt**; *d* unm 4 May 1719, when the btcy became dormant till 1723–28

1 Magdalen; *m* 1688 James Mentheith of Auldcathy, a cadet of the MENTEITHs of Rusky and Kerse, descended from Sir John Menteith of Rusky, bro of 6th Earl of Menteith, and had, with other issue (including Janet, *m* Col Walter Shairp of Houston):

(1) Sir JAMES MENTEITH later DALYELL (1719, when also inerited the Binns), **3rd Bt**, of the Binns; *b c* 1690; Ensign in Cadogan's Regt; assumed btcy as heir of tailzie in possession of Binns (though not heir male) between

1723 and 1728; *m* Helen (*d* 29 Jan 1774), dau of Robert Campbell of Netherplace, Ayrshire, and *d* 28 Feb 1747, having had:

1a ROBERT (Sir), **4th Bt**

2a James; ADC to Sir Jeffrey Amherst; *dsp*, *k* nr Fort Detroit 1763

3a Thomas; RN; *d* 1765

1a Magdalen; *m* Robert Stewart of Binny and had issue (*see* KINTORE, E)

The 3rd Bt's est son,

Sir Robert Dalyell, 4th Bt, of the Binns; Army offr, served on the Continent; *m* 22 Sept 1773 Elizabeth (*d* 31 July 1825), dau of Nicol Graham of Gartmore by Lady Margaret Cunningham, 12th Earl of Glencairn (*see* CUNINGHAME, Bt), and *d* 10 Oct 1791, having had surv issue:

1 **Sir James Dalyell, 5th Bt**, of the Binns; *b* 7 July 1774; Army Offr Flanders 1793; *d* unm 1 Feb 1841

2 **Sir John Graham Dalyell, 6th Bt**, of the Binns; *b c* 1778; advocate Scottish Bar 1797; V-Pres Soc of Antiquaries Scotland, historical and scientific author, ktd 1836; *d* unm 7 June 1851

3 Robert; Gen; *dsp* 1848

4 **Sir William Cunningham Dalyell, 7th Bt**, of the Binns; *b* 27 April 1787; Capt RN, wounded over sixteen times in various actions, many years a prisoner in France; Govr Greenwich Hosp; *m* 19 Sept 1820 Maria (*d* 20 Oct 1871), dau of Anthony Teixeira Sampayo, of Peterborough House, Fulham, and sister of Anthony Sampayo, French Min to Hesse, and *d* 16 Feb 1865, having had issue:

(1) **Sir Robert Alexander Osborne Dalyell, 8th Bt**, of the Binns, DL (Linlithgowshire); *b* 1821; *educ* Trin Coll Cambridge (MA); barrister Inner Temple; Br Consul: Erzerum 1859, Jassy 1862 and Rustchuk 1865–79; *d* unm 21 Jan 1886, when the btcy became dormant (until allowed to the 9th Bt by Privy Cncl 1914), and the Binns estate passed to his only surv sis

(2) Osborne William; Cdr RN; severely wounded Sebastopol; *dsp* & *vp* 22 Dec 1862

(1) Maria Christina; *m* 1855 Maj-Gen Sir Charles Taylor Du Plat, KCB (*d* 2 Nov 1900), and *dsp* 7 April 1867

(2) Elizabeth Grace; *m* 11 April 1861 Gustavus Charles CORNWALL later CORNWALL-DALYELL (which name he assumed with his w 1886 after she had inherited the Binns; he *d* 22 July 1903) and *dsp* 1913

1 HARRIET Dalyell; *m* 1804 James WILKIE (*dvp* 1814), est son of Capt James Wilkie, of Foulden, Berwicks (*d* 8 Sept 1817), son of John Wilkie, of Foulden (*d* Sept 1780), son of James Wilkie, of Foulden (*d* Sept 1732), son of John Wilkie, of Broomhouse, Lanarks, MP 1654–55, son of Rev Robert Wilkie, Rector Glasgow U (*d* 1640), 2nd son of William Wilkie, MP Burgh of Lanark 1581–93, and had an only child:

(1) John, of Foulden, DL (Berwicks); *b* 1806; *m* April 1864 Henriette Eleanor (*d* May 1872), dau of Thomas Bruce of Arnot, Kinross-shire, and *d* 21 June 1884, having had issue:

1a JAMES BRUCE WILKIE-DALYELL (Sir), **9th Bt**

2a John Dalyell; *b* 20 Sept 1870; *m* Margaret Butterwick (*d* 1928), and *dsp* 11 June 1930

1a Henrietta Eleanor Maria; *d* unm 24 Feb 1900

2a Harriet Charlotte; *d* unm 29 Sept 1941

3a Eleanor Bruce; *d* unm 27 March 1964

The 8th Bt's cousin,

Sir JAMES BRUCE WILKIE later WILKIE-DALYELL (added 1913), **9th Bt** (claim to btcy allowed by PC 1 July 1914), of the Binns (which he inherited fom his cousin Mrs Gustavus Cornwall-Dalyell), JP (Berwicks); *b* 1 May 1867; *educ* Eton and Trin Coll Cambridge; Maj 3rd Bn KOSB Boer War and WW I (despatches); memb Roy Co of Archers; *m* 6 Feb 1894 Mary Marjoribanks (*d* 27 Nov 1947), 2nd dau of Watson Askew-Robertson, of Pallinsburn and Ladykirk, and *dspm* 12 Dec 1935, when the title again became dormant and the Binns estate passed to his dau:

Eleanor Isabel (Nora) Dalyell, *de jure* Baronetess of The Binns (10th holder of the title); *b* 3 Oct 1895; *m* 12 Sept 1928 Lt-Col Gordon LOCH later DALYELL of the Binns (decree of the Ld Lyon 1938), CIE, DL (W Lothian) (*d* 15 Sept 1953), Unicorn Pursuivant of Arms, Indian Pol Serv, memb Roy Co Archers, s of Lt-Col William Loch, CIE, and *d* 5 Feb 1972, leaving:

1 Sir THOMAS (TAM) DALYELL of the Binns, **11th and present Bt**

DARCY DE KNAYTH

Arms: Per pale azure and gules three lions rampant argent.
Supporters: Dexter, an heraldic tiger proper; sinister, a bull sable.
Motto: *Ung je serviray* ('One only will I serve').
Creation: B. (E) 27 Jan 1331/2.

BARONESS DARCY DE KNAYTH (Dame Davina Marcia Herbert, DBE (1996)) [The Rt Hon The Lady Darcy De Knayth DBE, Camley Corner, Stubbings, Maidenhead, Berks SL6 6QW]; *b* 10 July 1938; *s f* 1943; *m* 1 March 1960 Rupert George Ingrams (*k* in a car crash 28 Feb 1964), 3rd s of Leonard St Clair Ingrams, OBE, of 18 Cheyne Row, London SW3, by his w Victoria Susan Beatrice, yr dau of Sir James Reid, 1st Bt, of Ellon (*qv*), and has issue:

1 +CASPAR DAVID; *b* 5 Jan 1962; *m* 14 Sept 1996 *Catherine, er dau of Bryan Baker, of Abingdon, Berks

1 +Miranda; *b* 23 Oct 1960

2 +Catriona; *b* 18 Nov 1963

Lineage: (*Note:* This section of the article should be studied together with the section on the Barony of Conyers in the article YARBOROUGH, which it complements.)

NORMAN d'ARECI; feudal Ld of Nocton, Coningsby, Dunston, Stallingborough and Cawkwell, Lincs; living 1115; had issue:

ROBERT d'ARCY, of Nocton etc; living 1130; had issue:

THOMAS d'ARCY; had issue:

THOMAS d'ARCY, of Nocton; *m* Alice (*d* 1183), dau of Ralph d'Eyncourt, and *d* 2 July 1180, having had, with two yr s (Robert, William):

THOMAS d'ARCY; *b c* 1168; with RICHARD I in Normandy; *m* Joan — and *d c* 1206, leaving issue:

NORMAN d'ARCY, of Nocton; *m* Agnes — and *d* by 16 Oct 1254, leaving issue:

Sir PHILIP d'ARCY, of Nocton; *m* Isabel (living 15 June 1281), 2nd dau of Sir Roger Bertram, of Mitford, Northumberland, sis and coheir of Sir Roger Bertram, of Mitford, and *d c* 28 May 1264, leaving issue:

1 Sir NORMAN d'ARCY or DARCY; joined baronial war against HENRY III, pardoned 30 June 1267, served EDWARD I's wars Wales 1277, 1282 and 1287 and in Scotland 1291, kt banneret by Feb 1283/4; *m* 1st Julian — (*d* by 15 June 1281); *m* 2nd by 20 Jan 1292/3 Margery (living 19 Feb 1302/3), widow of (a) Barnaby de Stiucele (Stukeley), of Warden, Beds, and Gt Stukeley, Hunts (*dsp* 1257/8), (b) William de Swineford, Sheriff Norfolk and Suffolk, and (c) Ralph Rastel, and *d c* 6 Jan 1295/6, having had issue by his 1st w:

(1) PHILIP DARCY, 1st LORD (Baron) DARCY (E), so *cr* (according to later doctrine) by writ of summons to Parl 29 Dec 1299; had livery of his f's lands 9 Feb 1295/6, summoned for mily serv 15 May 1297 to 5 April 1327, Constable Durham Castle 1301, kt banneret by 16 March 1321/2, taken prisoner at the Battle of Boroughbridge 16 March 1321/2 where he had fought with Thomas, Earl of Lancaster, against EDWARD II's forces; *d c* 24 Nov 1333, leaving:

1a NORMAN DARCY, 2nd LORD (Baron) DARCY; captured with his f at Battle of Boroughbridge, lands in Cawkwell restored to him 31 Oct 1322, summoned for mily serv 30 June 1314 to 6 Oct 1337, MP Lincs 1327, 1335/6 and 1336; *m* Isabel — (*d* 16 Sept 1350) and *d* 31 March 1340, leaving issue:

1b PHILIP DARCY, 3rd LORD (Baron) DARCY; *b c* 1331; *dsp* by 16 Sept 1350, when any barony that may have been *cr* by the writ of 1299 would have fallen according to later doctrine into abeyance between his aunts Julian and Agnes or their issue

1a Julian; allegedly *m* 1st Philip de Nevill(e), of Scotton, Lincs (*see* ABERGAVENNY, M); *m* (?)2nd(?) Sir John de Limbury, of Limbury, Beds, and *d* between 1346 and 1350, leaving issue:

1b Philip (Sir), of Limbury and Ickleton, Cambs; *b c* 1320; *m* Joan (*m* 2nd 3rd Lord (Baron) Clinton (*qv*) and *d* 21 Feb 1387/8) and *d* 6 July 1367, leaving issue:

1c Philip; *dsp*

1c Elizabeth; *b c* 1360; *m* 1st Sir Thomas Trivett (*d* 6 Oct 1388), of Otterhampton, Somerset; *m* 2nd Sir Thomas Swinbourne (*d* 9 Aug

1412), Sire de Hammes, Mayor Bordeaux, and *dsps* 30 Nov or 2 Dec 1433, leaving issue by her 1st husb:

1b Anne; *m* 4th Lord (Baron) Clinton (*qv*)

2a Agnes; *b c* 1300; *m* 1st (possibly) Robert de Friskeneye; *m* 2nd Sir Roger de Pedwardine (*d* 10 Feb 1368/9), of Burton Pedwardine, Lincs, and *d* by 13 Sept 1359

(2) Robert, of Gt Sturton; Ld manors of Dunston and Stallingborough; *m* Joan, dau of Thomas Fitz Eustace, of Caswick and Woolsthorpe, Lincs, and *d* 1342/3, leaving issue:

1a Margaret; *m* John d'Argentine (*dspm* 18–26 Nov 1382) and *d* 1 Sept 1383

(3) John, of Coningsby Pk; *m* Pernell — and had issue

2 Roger (Sir), of Oldcotes and Styrrup, Notts; *m* Isabel, dau of Sir William d'Aton, of W Ayton, Yorks, and *d* by 12 May 1284, leaving issue:

(1) JOHN DARCY, **1st Lord** (Baron) **Darcy** (of Knaith, Lincs) of the 1332 *cr*, for whom *see* further below

3 Thomas (Sir); Ld manor of Scottlethorpe, Lincs; *dsp c* 1301

The 1st LORD (Baron) DARCY of the 1299 *cr*'s n,

JOHN DARCY, **1st Lord** (Baron) **Darcy** (E), so *cr* by writ of summons to Parl 27 Jan 1331/2 , of Knaith, Kexby and Upton, Lincs; *b* after 15 June 1271; outlawed for felony 1306 but pardoned 19 May 1307; Constable Norham Castle 1317, Sheriff: Derbys and Notts 1319–22, Lancs 1323 and Yorks 1327–28, MP Notts 1320, Justiciar Ireland 1323–27, 1328–31, 1332–7 (for life 1340 but resigned 1344), Steward King's Household 1337–40, Chamberlain 1341–46, Constable Nottingham Castle 1344 and Tower of London 1346 (both for life), fought Battle of Crécy 1346; *m* 1st Emmeline, dau and heir of Walter Heron, of Silkstone, Yorks, and had issue (with two other sons and a dau):

1 JOHN DARCY, **2nd Lord**

The **1st Lord** *m* 2nd 3 July 1329 Joan de Burgh (*d* 23 April 1359), 4th dau of 2nd Earl of Ulster of the 1264 *cr* and widow of 2nd Earl of Kildare (*see* LEINSTER, D), and *d* 30 May 1347, having by her had:

2 Aymer; living *c* 1333

3 Roger; living *c* 1333

4 William (Sir); living *c* 1333

1 Elizabeth; *m* 1st 2nd Earl of Ormonde (*see* MOUNTGARRET, V) and had issue; *m* 2nd Sir Robert de Hereford

The 1st LORD (Baron) DARCY (of Knaith)'s est s,

JOHN DARCY, **2nd Lord** (Baron) **Darcy de Knayth**; *b c* 1317; present Battle of Crécy and Siege of Calais 1346–47, Constable Tower of London 1347 (for life), when called to Parl (which he was 20 Nov 1348 to 15 March 1353/4) was addressed by writs made out to 'John Darcy de Knayth', almost certainly so as to make a distinction between him and three similarly named relatives (f, s and gs) known as 'John Darcy of (Coningsby) Park'; *m* 1st by 8 July 1332 Alianore de Holand (*dspm* before 21 Nov 1341), dau of 1st Lord (Baron) Holand of the 1314 *cr* (*see* ZOUCHE, B); *m* 2nd (dispensation 7 Jan 1344/5) Elizabeth (*m* 2nd before 18 Nov 1356 as his 1st w 3rd Lord (Baron) Mauley of the 1295 *cr* and *d* 9 July 1368), only child and heir (hence according to later doctrine *de jure* Baroness Menille) of 1st Lord (Baron) Menille of the 1336 *cr*, and *d* 5 March 1355/6, leaving by her:

1 JOHN DARCY, **3rd Lord** (Baron) **Darcy de Knayth**; *b* 24 June 1350; *d* 6 or 26 Aug 1362

2 PHILIP DARCY, **4th Lord** (Baron) **Darcy de Knayth**; *b* 21 May 1352; served Hundred Years War Picardy and Caux campaigns July–Nov 1369 and Brittany campaign July 1380–April 1381, Adml Thames northwards 1386; *m* Elizabeth (*d* 11 Aug 1412), 2nd dau of Sir Thomas Gray, of Heton, Norhamshire (an area of Northumberland), and *d* 24 April 1399, leaving issue:

(1) JOHN DARCY, **5th Lord** (Baron) **Darcy de Knayth**; *b c* 1376/7; *m* Margaret Grey (*m* 2nd by 12 July 1421, as his 2nd w, Sir Thomas Swinford (*d* 2 April 1432), of Kettlethorpe, Lincs, and *d* 1 June 1454), dau of 5th Lord (Baron) Grey (of Wilton) (*see* GREY, B), and *d* 9 Dec 1411, leaving issue (with four daus):

1a PHILIP DARCY, **6th Lord**

2a John; *m* Joane de Greystock, dau of 6th Lord (Baron) Greystock of the 1295 *cr*, and *d* 1458, having had issue:

1b Richard; *m* Eleanor le Scrope, dau of John Lord (Baron) Scrope (of Upsal), and *dvp*, leaving issue:

1c William (Sir); *m* (licence 23 Jan 1460/1) Euphemia, dau of John Langton, of Farnley, Yorks, and *d* 1488, leaving issue:

1d THOMAS DARCY, 1st LORD (Baron) DARCY, so *cr* by writ of summons to Parl possibly from 25 Jan 1503/4 but certainly from 17 Oct 1509 to 3 Nov 1529, KG (1509), PC; *b c* 1467; ktd 1489, kt banneret 1497, Constable Bamburgh Castle 1498, Capt Berwick 1498–1515, Treasurer Berwick 1501, Warden: E Marches 1505, E and Middle Marches 1511 and Forests N of Trent 1509, joined Pilgrimage of Grace 1536 and delivered up Pontefract Castle to the rebels, for which he was convicted of high treason and attainted; *m* 1st Dowsabel (living 1503), dau and heir of Sir Richard Tempest, of Giggleswick, Yorks (*see* LONDONDERRY, M); *m* 2nd by 1520 Edith (*d* 22 Aug 1529), dau of Sir William Sandys, of the Vyne, Hants, sis of 1st Lord (Baron) Sandys of the 1529 *cr*, and widow of Ralph Nevill(e), only s of 3rd Earl of Westmorland (*see* ABERGAVENNY, M), and was beheaded 30 June 1537, leaving by his 1st w:

1e GEORGE DARCY, 2nd LORD (Baron) DARCY; ktd 14 Oct 1513, Sheriff Yorks 1535–36, restored in blood by Act of Parl 1548 and to the dignity of LORD (Baron) DARCY to him and the heirs male of his body, ranked in Parl as a junior baron and allowed the precedence of this date only, but his successors were allowed the precedence of his f's barony; *m* (indentures 26 March 1511) Dorothy (*d* 21 Sept 1557), dau of Sir John Melton, of Aston, Yorks, and *d* 28 Aug 1558, having had issue, with three yr sons who *d* young and six daus:

1f JOHN DARCY, 3rd LORD (Baron) DARCY; *b c* 1530; ktd 15 Jan 1558/9; *m* by 25 Jan 1561/2 Anne, dau of Thomas Babington, of Dethick, Derbys, and *d* 18 Oct 1602, having had issue:

1g Michael; *m* Margaret, dau of Thomas Wentworth, of Wentworth Woodhouse, Yorks, and *dvp* 13 Dec 1588, leaving issue:

1h JOHN DARCY, 4th LORD (Baron) DARCY and (?)LORD (Baron) MEINILL(?); *b c* 1579; called to Parl by writ 5 Nov 1605 made out to 'John Darcy and Meinill [*sic*]'; *m* 1st Rosamund (*d* 18 April 1607), dau of Peter Frescheville, of Staveley, Derbys; *m* 2nd 7 May 1617 Isabel (*dsp* 27 Jan 1621/2), dau of Sir Christopher Wray, of Glentworth, Lincs, and widow of (a) Sir William Bowes (*d* 30 Oct 1611) and (b) Godfrey Foljambe, of Walton, Derbys (*d* 14 June 1595); *m* 3rd 7 Nov 1624 Mary Belasyse (*d* 14 Sept 1625), dau of 1st Visount Fauconberg of Henknowle of the 1643 *cr*; *m* 4th Elizabeth (*m* 2nd Sir Francis Fane, KB (*d* 1680) (*see* WESTMORLAND, E), and was *bur* 24 July 1669), dau of William West, of Firbeck, Yorks, and *dsps* 5 July 1635, having had by his 1st w:

1i John; *b c* 1602; *d* unm 21 April 1624

1i Rosamund; *bapt* 9 Feb 1605/6; *d* young

2i Elizabeth; *bapt* 10 April 1607; *d* unm 18 June 1624

1h Margaret; *d* unm

2h Anne; *m* Henry Savile, of Copley, Yorks

2f George; *k* Lewis and Edmund West

2e Richard; *dsp*

3e Arthur (Sir); Lt Tower of London; *m* Mary, dau of Sir Nicholas Carew, KG, of Beddington, Surrey, and *d* 1561, having had issue, with three sons (*dvp*) and five daus (of whom Elizabeth *m* 3rd Lord (Baron) Mordaunt; *see* MORDAUNT, Bt):

1f Henry (Sir), of Bremham, Yorks, and Leighton; *m* 1st Katherine (*dsp* & *vp* 1567), dau of Sir Robert Tyrwhitt; *m* 2nd Katherine, dau of Sir John Fermor (*see* HESKETH, B) and widow of Michael Pulteney (*d* 1567), and had issue:

1g Katherine Darcy; *m* 1st Lord (Baron) Clifton (of Leighton Bromswold) (*see* DARNLEY, E, also MORAY, E)

2f Thomas, of Hornby Castle, Yorks; Lt Tower of London; *m* Elizabeth Conyers, 2nd dau and coheir of 3rd Lord (Baron) Conyers, and had issue (*see* below)

3f Edward (Sir), of Dartford Place, Kent; *m* Elizabeth, dau of Thomas Astley, and had 15 children

4f Arthur, of Aldrington

5f Nicholas

6f John, of Potter Newton

7f Francis, of Gysborne; *m* Catherine, dau of Edward Leigh, of Rushall, Staffs

The 5th LORD (Baron) DARCY De KNAYTH's est s,

PHILIP DARCY, **6th Lord** (Baron) **Darcy de Knayth**; *b c* 1398; *m* by 28 Oct 1412 Alianore FitzHugh (*m* 2nd Sir Thomas Tunstall, of Thurland, Lancs, and had further issue; *m* 3rd 1st and last Lord (Baron) Vessy of the 1449 *cr* and *d* 30 Sept 1457), dau of 4th Lord (Baron) Fitz Hugh of the 1278 *cr*, and *d* 16 Jan 1468/9, when the Barony of Darcy de Knayth fell into abeyance between his two daus and their descendants (as did any entitlement to the putative Barony of Meinill), leaving issue:

1 Elizabeth Darcy; *b c* May 1417; *m* as his 1st w before 20 Nov 1431 Sir James Strangways, of W Harlsey, Yorks, Speaker H of C (*d c* 20 Aug 1480), and *d* between 1 Sept 1458 and Nov 1461, leaving issue:

(1) Richard (Sir); *m* Elizabeth Nevill(e), er dau and coheir of 1st Earl of Kent of the 1461 *cr* and 6th Lord (Baron) Faucomberge or Fauconberge in right of his w, and *d* 13 April 1488, leaving issue (*see* YARBOROUGH, E, and ABERGAVENNY, M)

2 MARGERY, for whom *see* further below

The 6th LORD (Baron) DARCY De KNAYTH's 2nd dau,

MARGERY Darcy; *b* posthumously 1 Sept 1418; *m* by 20 Nov 1431 Sir John CONYERS, KG (*d* 14 March 1489/90), of Hornby, Yorks (*see* YARBOROUGH, E), and *d* between 20 March 1468/9 and 20 April 1469, leaving issue:

JOHN CONYERS; *m* Joan or Alice Nevill(e), 3rd dau and coheir of 1st Earl of Kent and looked on as 6th Lord (Baron) Faucomberge or Fauconberge in right of his w (*see* YARBOROUGH, E, and ABERGAVENNY, M), and *dvp* 1470, leaving issue:

1 John; *d* after 4 July 1472

2 WILLIAM CONYERS, 1st LORD (Baron) CONYERS (E), so *cr* by writ of summons 17 Oct 1509; *b* 21 Dec 1468; *m* 1st (contract 21 June 1479) his 4th cousin Mary Scrope, dau of 5th Lord (Baron) Scrope (of Bolton) of the 1371 *cr*; *m* 2nd Anne (*m* 2nd licence 29 April 1525 Anthony Saltmarsh, of Hornby), dau of 3rd Earl of Westmorland (*see* ABERGAVENNY, M), and *d* 1524, leaving issue:

(1) CHRISTOPHER CONYERS, 2nd LORD (Baron) CONYERS; *m* 28 Sept 1515 Anne, dau of 3rd Lord (Baron) Dacre (*qv*) (of Gilsland), and *d* 14 June 1538, leaving issue:

1a JOHN CONYERS, 3rd LORD (Baron) CONYERS; ktd 11 May 1544; *m* by 28 Oct 1539 Maud, dau of 1st Earl of Cumberland (*see* DE CLIFFORD, B), and *d* 30 June 1557, when the Barony of Conyers fell into abeyance between his surv daus and their descendants, having had issue (with three other daus who either *dsp* or had issue who themselves *dsp* within at most two generations):

1b ELIZABETH Conyers; *m* Thomas DARCY (*d* 6 Nov 1605), of Hornby Castle, Yorks, Lt Tower of London, 2nd s of Sir Arthur Darcy (*see* above), and *d* 6 June 1572, leaving issue:

1c CONYERS DARCY, **7th Lord** (Baron) **Darcy de Knayth** and 4th LORD (Baron) CONYERS; *bapt* 27 Aug 1570; as coheir of the 1st Lord (Baron) Darcy of the 1331/2 *cr* and heir male of the 4th Lord (Baron) Darcy of the 1504 or 1509 *cr* (but not heir general) petitioned the King in the Parl of 3 Nov 1640 that he and 'the heirs male of his body' be restored to the dignity of LORD (Baron) DARCY, which was done 10 Aug 1641 (he was also restored to the dignity of LORD (Baron) CONYERS 12 Aug 1641), took seat 20 Jan 1641/2 as LORD DARCY and CONYERS, both being deemed new creations until 27 July 1903, when the Ho of Lds Privileges Ctee declared that the effect of the instruments of Aug 1641 and Jan 1641/2 was to terminate the abeyance in the much older Barony of Darcy of the Jan 1331/2 *cr* (and by implication that of Conyers) and that both dignities could thus descend to heirs general (which could include females and their issue); *m* (licence 1594) Dorothy, dau of Sir Henry Bellasis, Bt, and *d* 3 March 1653/4, having had,with seven daus:

1d CONYERS, **8th Lord**

2d William (Sir), of Witton Castle, Co Durham; *b* 1608; *m* Dorothy, dau of Sir George Selby, of Newcastle, and had, with two daus:

1e George

2e Thomas

3e Arthur

3d Henry, of New Pk, Yorks; *m* Mary, dau of William Scrope, of Highley, Durham, and was ancestor of the DARCYs of Colburne

4d Thomas, of Winkburne, Notts; *b* 1613

5d Marmaduke; MP Richmond, Gentleman Usher to CHARLES II; *d* unm 1687

6d James, of Sedbury Pk, Richmond, Yorks; *b* 1617; *m* Isabel, dau of Sir Marmaduke Wyvill, 2nd Bt, of Constable Burton, and had an only surv s:

1e JAMES DARCY, 1st BARON DARCY OF NAVAN, Co Meath (I), so *cr* 13 Sept 1721, with remainder to the son of his dau by his 1st w; *b c* 1650; MP (Tory) Richmond 1698–1701 and 1702–05; *m* 1st Bethia (*d* 19 Nov 1671), dau of George Payler, of Nun Monkton, Yorks, and had issue:

1f MARY Darcy; *m* 1697 William JESSOP, of Broomhall, Yorks, MP Aldborough, and *d* 17 June 1737, leaving, with other issue:

1g JAMES JESSOP later DARCY, 2nd and last BARON DARCY OF NAVAN; *d* unm 15 June 1733, when this Barony expired

1g Barbara Jessop; *m* Andrew Wilkinson, MP Boroughbridge, and had issue

2g Isabella Jessop; *m* John Eyre later Gell, of Hopton, Derbys

1e (cont.) The 1st LORD DARCY OF NAVAN *m* 2nd Anne Stawell, dau of 1st Baron Stawell of Somerton of the 1683 *cr*; *m* 3rd (licence 19 Oct 1693) Mary (*d* 1710), dau of Sir William Hicks, 2nd Bt; *m* 4th 6 April 1725 Margaret Garth (*d* 9 Aug 1758) and *dspm* 19 July 1731, having had by his 2nd w:

2f Anne; *m* John Yorke, of Richmond, and *dsp*

3f Elizabeth; *m* 5 March 1726 John Hutton (*d* 16 Jan 1768), of Marske, and *d* 1739, leaving issue

4f Isabel; *d* unm

The 7th LORD (Baron) DARCY De KNAYTH's est s,

CONYERS DARCY, **8th Lord** (Baron) **Darcy de Knayth**, also 1st EARL OF HOLDERNESSE (E), so *cr* 5 Dec 1682, and 5th LORD (Baron) CONYERS; Constable Middleham Castle, called to Parl by writ 8 May 1661 made out to 'Conyers Darcie de Darcie' and by writs 7 Oct 1678 and 1 March 1679/80 made out to 'Conyers Darcie de Darcie and Meynill [*sic*]', which might be supposed to have *cr* him LORD (Baron) MEINILL or MEYNILL in addition to the two Baronies he already held, but when his descendants the Countess of Yarborough and her sis the Countess of Powis claimed the Baronies of Fauconberg, Darcy de Knayth and Meinill in 1901 the Ho of Lds Privileges Ctee declared that no one had ever sat in Parl as Lord Meinill and the Countesses' petition on this point was rejected; *m* Grace, only dau of Thomas Rokeby, and *d* 14 June 1689, having had (with other issue):

1 CONYERS DARCY, **9th Lord**

1 Ursula; *m* Sir Christopher Wyvill, 3rd Bt, of Constable Burton, and had issue

2 Elizabeth; *m* 18 Oct 1650 Sir Henry Stapylton, 1st Bt, of Myton, and had issue

3 Grace; *m* 18 Oct 1655 Sir John Legard, 1st Bt, of Ganton, Yorks (*qv*), and *d* 1658, leaving issue

4 Margaret; *m* 19 May 1658 Sir Henry Marwood, 2nd Bt, and *dspm* 1660

5 Anne; *d* unm

The 8th LORD's only s,

CONYERS DARCY, **9th Lord** (Baron) **Darcy de Knayth**, 2nd EARL OF HOLDERNESSE and 6th LORD (Baron) CONYERS; *m* 1st Catharine, dau of 1st Earl of Westmorland (*qv*); *m* 2nd Frances, dau of 1st Earl of Berkshire (*see* SUFFOLK and BERKSHIRE, E); *m* 3rd Frances, dau of 2nd Duke of Somerset (*qv*); *m* 4th Elizabeth, dau of 1st Baron Frescheville of Staveley of the 1664 *cr*, and *d* 13 Dec 1692, having had by his 2nd w:

JOHN DARCY; *m* and *dvp* 7 June 1688, having had, with other issue:

1 ROBERT, **10th Lord**

2 Conyers (Sir), of Aske, KB, PC, Ld Lt N R,Yorks; *m* 1st 2 Aug 1714 Mary (*d* 20 Aug 1726), dau of 1st Earl of Portland (*qv*) and widow of 2nd Earl of Essex (*qv*); *m* 2nd 11 Sept 1728 Elizabeth, dau of John Rotherham and widow of (a) Sir Theophilus Napier, 5th Bt,

of the 1612 *cr*, and (b) 6th Baron Howard of Effingham (*see* EFFINGHAM, E), and *dsp* 1 Dec 1758

1 Elizabeth; *m* May 1708 Sir Ralph Milbanke, 4th Bt (*d* 1949 edn), and *dspm* Oct 1720

2 Charlotte; *m* Wardell George Westby

The 9th LORD's er s,

ROBERT DARCY, **10th Lord** (Baron) **Darcy de Knayth**, 3rd EARL OF HOLDERNESSE and 7th LORD (Baron) CONYERS; *b* 24 Nov 1681; *m* 26 May 1715 Frederica, dau of 3rd Duke of Schomberg, and *d* 20 Jane 1721/2, having had:

1 George Schomberg; *d* young

2 ROBERT, **11th Lord**

1 Caroline; *m* 6 Nov 1735 4th Marquess of Lothian (*qv*) and *d* 15 Nov 1778, leaving issue

The 10th LORD's yr s,

ROBERT DARCY, **11th Lord** (Baron) **Darcy de Knayth**, 4th and last EARL OF HOLDERNESSE and 8th LORD (Baron) CONYERS; *b* 17 May 1718; *m* 29 Oct 1743 Mary, dau of Francis Doublet, and *dspms* 16 May 1778, when the Earldom expired but right to the Baronies of Darcy de Knayth and Conyers passed to his only surv dau, having had (with two sons, *d* young):

1 AMELIA, *de jure* BARONESS DARCY DE KNAYTH and *de jure* BARONESS CONYERS, both in her own right; *b* 12 Oct 1754; *m* 1st 29 Nov 1773 (*divorce* May 1779) 5th Duke of Leeds (*see* 1963 edn) and had:

(1) GEORGE WILLIAM FREDERICK OSBORNE, *de jure* 13th LORD (Baron) DARCY DE KNAYTH, 6th DUKE OF LEEDS and 10th LORD (Baron) CONYERS (for recognition as which successfully petitioned 27 April 1798); *b* 21 July 1775; *m* 17 Aug 1797 Lady Charlotte Townshend (*d* 30 July 1856), dau of 1st Marquess Townshend (*qv*), and *d* 10 July 1838, having had issue:

1a FRANCIS GODOLPHIN OSBORNE later DARCY-OSBORNE (roy licence 6 Aug 1849), *de jure* 14th LORD (Baron) DARCY De KNAYTH, 7th DUKE OF LEEDS and 11th LORD (Baron) CONYERS; *b* 21 May 1798; *m* 24 April 1828 Louisa Catherine (*d* 8 April 1874), 3rd dau of Richard Caton, of Maryland, USA, and widow of Sir Felton Elwell Hervey-Bathurst, 1st Bt (*qv*), and *dsp* 4 May 1859, when the Barony of Conyers and right to that of Darcy de Knayth passed to his n while the Dukedom of Leeds and all his other titles passed to his cousin

2a Conyers George Thomas William; *dsvp* 16 Feb 1831

1a CHARLOTTE MARY ANNE GEORGIANA Osborne; *b* 16 July 1801; *m* 22 June 1826 Walter Sackville LANE-FOX, MP (*d* 18 Aug 1874), and *d* 17 Jan 1836, having had issue:

1b SACKVILLE GEORGE LANE-FOX, *de jure* 15th LORD (Baron) DARCY DE KNAYTH and 12th LORD (Baron) CONYERS, for whom *see* further below

2b Charles Pierrepoint Darcy; *b* 25 Aug 1830; granted with his sisters rank of baron's dau/ yr s 9 July 1859; *m* 22 June 1859 Louisa Emma (*d* 30 Jan 1870), dau of Thomas Fairfax, of Newton Kyme, Yorks, and *d* 13 Sept 1874, leaving issue (*see* YARBOROUGH, E)

1b Elizabeth Catherine; *m* 7 July 1864 Rev Robert Wentworth Cracroft (*d* 22 March 1905) and *dsp* 26 Oct 1879

2b Lora Mary; *d* unm 12 Feb 1908

(2) Francis Godolphin, ancestor of the last Duke of Leeds (*see* 1963 edn)

(1) Mary Henrietta Juliana; *m* 16 July 1801 2nd Earl of Chichester (*qv*) and *d* 21 Oct 1862, leaving issue

1 (cont.) AMELIA DUCHESS OF LEEDS and *de jure* BARONESS DARCY DE KNAYTH *m* 2nd 9 June 1779 John Byron (*see* BYRON, B) and *d* 27 Jan 1784, leaving further issue

The 14th LORD (Baron) DARCY De KNAYTH's n,

SACKVILLE GEORGE LANE-FOX, *de jure* 15th LORD (Baron) DARCY DE KNAYTH and 12th LORD (Baron) CONYERS (as which took seat in Parl 9 June 1859); *b* 14 Sept 1827; Lt 87th Foot 1855; *m* 14 Aug 1860 Mary (*d* 12 Nov 1921), 1st dau of Capt Reginald Curteis, of Windmill Hill, Sussex, 1st Dragoons, and *dspms* 24 Aug 1888, when the Baronies of Conyers and Darcy de Knayth again fell into abeyance, having had:

1 Sackville FitzRoy Henry; *b* 9 May 1861; *d* unm 27 Aug 1879

1 MARCIA AMELIA MARY LANE-FOX, BARONESS CONYERS following termination of abeyance in that Barony in her favour 8 June 1892 (*see* YARBOROUGH, E)

2 VIOLET IDA EVELYN Lane-Fox, **Baroness Darcy de Knayth**, on termination of abeyance in her favour 29 Sept 1903; *b* 1 June 1865; *m* 21 Aug 1890 4th EARL OF POWIS (*qv*) and *d* 29 April 1929, having had:

(1) Percy Robert, *Viscount Clive*; *b* 2 Dec 1892; *d* unm 13 Oct 1916 of wounds recd in action at the Somme Sept 1916

(2) MERVYN HORATIO HERBERT, **17th Lord** (Baron) **Darcy de Knayth**; *b* 7 May 1904; *educ* Eton and Trin Coll Cambridge (BA), barrister Inner Temple, S/Ldr RAFVR WW II; *m* 18 Oct 1934 *Vida, OStJ (*m* 2nd 24 Oct 1945 Brig Derek Shuldham Schreiber, MVO (*see* MARLESFORD, B), only dau of Capt James Harold Cuthbert, DSO, Scots Gds, of Beaufront Castle, Hexham, Northumberland, and was *kas* March 1943, leaving issue:

1a DAVINA MARCIA HERBERT later INGRAMS, **present Baroness Darcy de Knayth**

(1) Hermione Gwladys; *b* 17 Sept 1900; *m* 6 Nov 1924 Count Roberto Lucchesi Palli, 11th Duke della Grazia, 13th Prince di Campofranco (*d* 1979), Bailliff Grand Cross SMO Malta, ggs of Maria Carolina Ferdinanda Luisa de Bourbon, Princess of the Two Sicilies, by her 2nd husb Ettore Lucchesi Palli, 9th Prince di Campofranco and 8th Duke della Grazia, and *d* 25 May 1995, leaving:

1a +Violet Maria Carolina Sidoni Henrietta [Princess Luchesi Palli, Villa Rovera Molina, via Lunga 57, 21020 Barasso, Varese, Italy]; *b* 27 Nov 1930

DARELL

Arms: Az. a lion rampant or, ducally crowned arg. **Crest:** Out of a ducal coronet or a man's head in profile couped at the shoulders ppr., bearded sa., wreathed round the temples or and az., on the head a cap of the last, fretty arg., tasselled or, doubled ermine.
Creation: Bt. (GB) 12 May 1795.

SIR JEFFREY LIONEL DARELL, 8TH BT, of Richmond Hill, Surrey, MC (1945) [Brig Sir Jeffrey Darell Bt MC, Denton Lodge, Harleston, Norfolk IP20 0AD]; *b* 2 Oct 1919; *s* cousin 1959; *educ* Eton; Brig Coldstream Gds, cmdg 1st Bn 1957–59, served WW II, ADC to GOC-in-C Southern Cmd 1942, Bde Maj Gds Bde 1951–53, AAG War Office 1959–61, College Cdr RMA Sandhurst 1961–64, Col cmdg Coldstream Gds and Regtl Dist 1964–65, Brig cmdg 56 Inf (Lond) Bde (TA) 1965–68, V-Pres Regular Commns Bd 1968–70, ADC to HM THE QUEEN 1973–74, High Sheriff Norfolk 1985; *m* 30 June 1953 *Bridget Mary, est dau of Major-Gen Sir Allan Henry Shafto Adair, 6th and last Bt, GCVO, CB, DSO, MC (*see* 1970 edn), and has issue:

1 +GUY JEFFREY ADAIR [Guy Esq, 5 Norland Sq, London W11 4PX]; *b* 8 June 1961; *educ* Eton and RMA Sandhurst; Coldstream Gds 1981–84, dir Fenchurch Gp Ltd 1993–; *m* 1988 *(Justine) Samantha, dau of Mr Justice T Reynolds, of Quambi Place, Sydney, NSW, and has:

(1) +Harry Thomas Adair; *b* 10 May 1995

(1) *Sophia Elizabeth Alexandra; *b* 1989

(2) *Amelia Flora Frances; *b* 1993

1 *Katherine Mary; *b* 25 Sept 1954; *m* 7 July 1977 *John Richard Astor (*see* ASTOR OF HEVER, B)

2 *Camilla Viola [Mrs Henry Adeane, 44 Sterndale Rd, London W14 0HU]; *b* 7 Dec 1956; *m* 28 Sept 1983 *Henry R T Adeane, only son of Charles R W Adeane, of Babraham, Cambs, and has issue:

(1) *Anthony Charles; *b* 1991

(1) *Madeline Bridget; *b* 1987

Lineage: WILLIAM DARELL, of Sesay, Yorks, living *temp* KING JOHN, had issue: WILLIAM DARELL, living 1270; *m* allegedly Ada, dau and heir of — Percy, and had, with a yr s (Geoffrey) and a dau (Beatrix, *m* Sir John Maleverer, of Allerton, Yorks):

Sir MARMADUKE DARELL, living *c* 1300; *m* Helenisa, dau of William de Insula, and had:

Sir WILLIAM DARELL, of Sesay; living *c* 1314; *m* Joan, dau of Sir William Holtby, and had:

Sir MARMADUKE DARELL; living 1358; *m* Cecilia (living 1353) and had:

Sir WILLIAM DARELL; living 1350; *m* Elizabeth (living 1356) and had:

Sir MARMADUKE DARELL, of Sesay; living 1365; *m* Alice, dau of Ranulph Pigot and sis of Geoffry Pigot (living 1371), and had:

Sir WILLIAM DARELL, of Sesay; living 1370; *m* Emma — and had, with two er sons (Marmaduke, ancestor of the DARELLs of Sesay; William, ancestor of the DARELLs of Littlecote and those of Pageham):

JOHN DARELL, of Calehill, Kent; *m* 1st Thomasin, dau and heir of Valentine Barret, of Perry Court, and was ancestor of the DARELLs of Calehill; *m* 2nd Florence (*d* 8 Dec 1465), widow of (a) Sir Nicholas Peche and (b) John Burton, dau of William Chicheley and n of Henry, Archbp Canterbury, and *d* 25 Oct 1438, leaving by her:

THOMAS DARELL, of Scotney, Sussex; *b* 24 July 1422; *m* Thomasine, dau of Sir John Gresley, and had:

HENRY DARELL, of Scotney; *m* Elizabeth, dau of James Horne, of Bethersden, Kent, and *d* 1558, leaving a 2nd surv s:

EDWARD DARELL, of Pageham, Clerk to ELIZABETH I; *m* Mary, dau of Marmaduke Darell, of Pageham, and *d* 1573, leaving issue:

1 Thomas (Sir), of Pageham, ancestor in the female line of the DARELLs of Trewornan

2 MARMADUKE (Sir), of whom presently

3 George, DD, Preb Westminster; *m* Anne (*d* 1634), dau of John Darell, of Calehill, and *d* between 24 April and 31 Dec 1631

1 Elizabeth; *m* George Shakerley

The 2nd son,

Sir MARMADUKE DARELL, of Fulmer, Bucks; *m* Anne, dau of John Leonard, of Knoll, Kent, and *d* 22 March 1631, leaving:

MARMADUKE DARELL, of Horston, Lincs; *m* Elizabeth, dau of Robert Fitch, and left:

EDWARD DARELL, of Whitechapel, Middx; *m* Anne, dau of George Phipps, and *d* 17 Dec 1707, leaving:

EDWARD DARELL; *m* Sabina, dau of Rev Richard Hall, Rector Philleigh, Cornwall, and had:

LIONEL DARELL, of Bedford Row; *b* 1708; *m* 13 June 1734 Honoria, dau of Humphrey Hardwick, of Lisbon, and *d* 19 Oct 1783, leaving an est s:

Sir Lionel Darell, 1st Bt (GB), so *cr* 12 May 1795, MP Lyme Regis 1780–84 and Hendon 1784–1802; *b* 25 Sept 1742; Chm Court Dirs HEIC, Col an India-House Vol Regt; *m* 30 July 1766 Isabella (*d* 6 May 1800), dau of Timothy Tullie, Dir HEIC, and had, with other issue:

1 HARRY VERELST (Sir), **2nd Bt**

1 Florentia Elizabeth; *b* 12 Aug 1777; *m* 13 Aug 1800 Lt-Col Sir Miles Nightingale

2 Clarissa; *m* 30 June 1807 Capt James Sharpe, 21st Regt Native Inf Bengal, Dir and Chm Court Dirs HEIC, and *d* 29 June 1812

Sir LIONEL *d* 30 Oct 1803; his son,

Sir Harry Verelst Darell, 2nd Bt; *b* 25th Dec 1768; sr merchant on the Bengal establishment and HEIC commercial resident Eatwah and Calpu; *m* 2 June 1809 Amelia Mary Anne (*d* 5 Jan 1878), only dau of William Beecher, and *d* in India 13 April 1828, leaving issue:

1 **Sir Harry Francis Colville Darell, 3rd Bt**, Major and Brevet Lt-Col 7th Dragoon Gds; *b* 17 Nov 1814; *d* unm 6 Jan 1853

2 WILLIAM LIONEL (Sir), **4th Bt**

1 Emily Mary; *m* 11 Oct 1842 Rev Anthony Berwick Lechmere (*dsp* 8 Oct 1878), 2nd son of Sir Anthony Lechmere, 1st Bt (*qv*), and *d* 18 March 1869

2 Isabella Martha; *m* 23 Jan 1837 Henry Shirley (*d* 1848), of Peppingford Lodge, Sussex, and *d* 4 Nov 1899, leaving issue

3 Eliza Anne; *m* 16 June 1835 Henry Brown, Bombay CS

The 3rd Bt's yr bro,

Rev Sir William Lionel Darell, 4th Bt, MA, Rector Fretherne, Glos; *b* 5 Feb 1817; *m* 1st 29 May 1840 Mary (*dsp* 9 March 1842), est dau of Sir Francis Ford (*see* ST CLAIR-FORD, Bt); *m* 2nd 18 April 1843 Harriet Mary (*d* 27 June 1873), only dau of Sir Edward Tierney, Bt, and by her had issue:

1 LIONEL EDWARD (Sir), **5th Bt**

2 Edward Tierney Gilchrist, Lt Glos Yeo; *b* 6 Aug 1847; *m* 1st 15 June 1869 (*divorce* 1878) Amy (*d* 1915), dau of Leo Schuster, of Roehampton, and had issue:

(1) Harry Francis, DSO (1916), Lt-Col Rifle Bde, served Tochi Expdn 1897–98 (medal with clasp) and WW I (despatches); *b* 18 Aug 1872; *m* 12 Aug 1915 Florence (*d* 2 June 1931), dau of Henry M Leavitt, of New York, and *d* 20 July 1934

(1) Mary Leonora Amy; *m* 11 Jan 1898 John Burgess Preston Karslake (*d* 3 Sept 1942), TD, MA, FSA, DL, JP, Lt-Col Berks Yeo, barrister, only son of Preston Karslake, of White Knights, nr Reading, Berks, and *d* 19 March 1958, leaving issue

(2) Alice Olivia; *m* 20 Jan 1897 Capt Roderick Willoughby MacLeod (*d* 4 April 1931), of Cadboll and Invergordon Castle, Ross-shire, and *d* 26 Jan 1968 aged 95, leaving issue

2 (cont.) Edward Darell *m* 2nd 1 June 1882 Florence (*d* 14 Jan 1939), dau of William Johnson, of London, and widow of Thomas Broadwood, of Holmbush, Sussex, and *d* 8 Feb 1898, having by her had issue:

(3) Florence Mary; *m* 1st 24 Jan 1903 13th Earl of Kinnoull (*qv*), and had issue; *m* 2nd 26 May 1919 Maj John Joseph Berington (*d* 19 Aug 1955), RMA, s of Charles Michael Berington, of Little Malvern Court, Worcs, and *d* 2 July 1941, leaving issue

1 Flora Mary; *m* 18 June 1872 Edward McDougall Stopford Claremont, RN, son of Gen — Claremont, CB, and *dsp* 22 Feb 1907

The **Rev Sir Lionel** *m* 3rd 7 Jan 1880 Fanny Julia (*d* 17 Jan 1894), widow of T Hyde Clarke, of The Firs, Frimley, Surrey, and *d* 1 June 1883

His est son,

Sir Lionel Edward Darell, 5th Bt, DL, JP, CC Glos, Capt Glos Yeo Cav, High Sheriff 1887; *b* 6 Sept 1845; *m* 26 June 1870 Helen Frances (*d* 25 Sept 1937), only child of Edward Marsland, of Henbury Park, Cheshire, and *d* 17 Feb 1919, having had:

1 **Sir Lionel Edward Hamilton Marmaduke Darell, 6th Bt**, DSO (1917), DL, JP, CA Glos, High Sheriff 1924, Maj 1st Life Gds, ADC to GOC Cape Colony 1909–12, Hon Col 5th Bn Glos Regt 1936, served WW I 1914–17 (despatches twice); *b* 2 April 1876; *m* 21 April 1903 Eleanor Marion (*d* 6 July 1953), dau of Capt Justinian John Edwards-Heathcote, of Apedale, Staffs, and *d* 27 May 1954, having had issue:

(1) Lionel Algernon Heathcote; *b* 30 Aug; *d* 12 Nov 1905

(1) Margaret Eleanor Phyllis; *m* 2 June 1930 Helmut William Bruno Schroder (*d* 18 June 1969), only surv son of Baron Bruno Schroder, and has issue:

1a *Bruno Lionel [Baron Bruno Schroder, 42 Lansdowne Rd, London W11 4LU]; Lt (Res) Life Gds, dir Schroders and J Henry Schroder Wagg; *b* 17 Jan 1933; *educ* Eton, Univ Coll Oxford and Harvard Business Sch; *m* 29 May 1969 *Patricia Leonie Mary, only dau of Maj Adrian Holt, and has issue:

1b *Leonie; *b* 1974

1a *Charmaine Brenda [Mrs George von Mallinckrodt, 64 Chelsea Sq, London SW3 6LE]; *b* 8 Nov 1935; *m* 31 July 1958 *George von Mallinckrodt, only son of Arnold von Mallinckrodt, of Cologne, and has issue:

1b *Philip Stephan Arnold; *b* 26 Dec 1962

2b *Edward Gustav Paul; *b* 29 June 1965
1b *Claire Louise [Mrs Henry Fitzalan Howard, 103 Abingdon Rd, London W8 6QU]; *b* 11 Aug 1960; *m* 1987 *Henry Julian Nicholas Fitzalan Howard (*see* NORFOLK, D) and has issue
2b *Nina Sophie; *b* 8 Aug 1967
(2) Nancy Brenda; *m* 16 July 1931 Lt-Gen Sir George Charles Gordon Lennox, KBE, CB, CVO, DSO, Gren Gds, er son of Lord Bernard Charles Gordon Lennox, and *d* 1993, leaving issue (*see* RICHMOND and GORDON, D)
2 William Harry Verelst, CB (1929), CMG (1918), DSO (1915), Brig-Gen Coldstream Gds, Lt-Col cmdg Irish Gds, Hon Brig-Gen 1929, Sword of Honour Sandhurst 1897, won Diamond Sculls 1907, Boer War 1899–1902 (medals, seven clasps), and WW I, on Staff (despatches five times, two brevets, Legion of Honour), Cdr Order of Mérite Agricole of France; *b* 23 Jan 1878; *educ* Eton and RMC Sandhurst; *m* 26 Oct 1907 Eva Jeffie, CBE (1922) (*d* 9 March 1966), dau of Emerson Muschamp Bainbridge, of Auchnashellach, Ross-shire, MP Gainsborough, and *d* 7 Feb 1954, leaving issue:
(1) **Sir (William) Oswald Darell, 7th Bt**; *educ* Eton, and RMC Sandhurst; WW II with Intelligence Corps; *b* 5 Nov 1910; *d* unm 10 Feb 1959
(1) Elizabeth Joy; *m* 16 May 1934 (*divorce* 1945) Peter Julian Clive, est son of Sir Robert Henry Clive, PC, GCMG, Dip Serv, and has issue:
1a *Colin George; *b* 6 Nov 1936; *educ* Eton
1a *Caroline Jeffie; *b* 8 May 1935; *m* 4 Jan 1961 *Hon Henry Leoline Thornhill Lumley-Savile, yr son of 2nd Baron Savile (*qv*)
3 Guy Marsland, MC, Lt-Col Coldstream Gds WW I (wounded twice, despatches four times, brevet); *b* 10 July 1883; *m* 27 July 1914 Esmée Violet (*d* 8 March 1968), dau of Capt Walter Stewart Savile, JP, of Middleton Holt, Banbury, Oxon, and *d* 15 April 1947, leaving issue:
(1) Sir JEFFREY LIONEL DARELL, **8th and present Bt**
(1) *Cynthia Mary [Mrs Michael Harrap, Marsh House, Bentley, Surrey GU10 5JF]; *m* 4 July 1940 *Michael Webster Harrap, son of Gilbert Ward Harrap, of Marsh House, Bentley, nr Farnham, Surrey, and has issue:
1a *Simon Richard [Simon Harrap Esq, Perryland, Bentley, Farnham, Surrey GU10 5JJ]; *b* 25 March 1941; *educ* Harrow; *m* 24 May 1969 *Diana, yr dau of Capt Ian Stanley Akers-Douglas (*see* CHILSTON, V), and has issue:
1b *Nicholas Guy; *b* 1975
1b *Louise Jane; *b* 1971
2b *Lara Sophie; *b* 1979
2a *John Michael Darell [John Harrap Esq, 35 Kenway Rd, London SW5 0RE]; *b* 1 Dec 1943; Ieduc Harrow; *m* 1973 *Elizabeth Helen Rodica, yr dau of Radu Tilea (*see* CARNARVON, E), and has issue:
1b *Peter Mark; *b* 1975
2b *Edward Michael; *b* 1983
3a *Giles Thresher [Giles Harrap Esq, Hill Farm, Bentley, Farnham Surrey GU10 5HB]; *b* 14 May 1948; *educ* Harrow; *m* 1981 *Sona Sophia, er dau of John Gladstone, TD, of Capenoch, Thornhill, Dumfriesshire, and has issue:
1b *Richard Thresher; *b* 1984
2b *Gilbert William Frederick; *b* 1987
1b *Isla Marie; *b* 1990
1 Violet Mary; *d* unm 30 Jan 1938
2 Evelyn May; *d* unm 18 Nov 1949
3 Marguerite Helen; *m* 16 Dec 1908 Brig-Gen Montgomery Lancelot Carleton (*d* 18 Aug 1942), CBE, 2nd son of Gen Henry Alexander Carleton, CB, of Clare, Co Tipperary, and *d* 15 Oct 1944, leaving issue
4 Dorothy Muriel, SSStJ; *m* 10 Aug 1910 (*divorce* 1930) Capt John Sturges Burrow Hill (*d* 8 Sept 1962), OBE, MC, son of Edward Burrow Hill, of Bristol, and *dsp* 10 July 1961
5 Barbara Gladys; *d* unm 25 Jan 1913

DARESBURY

Arms: Quarterly, 1st and 4th, or on a bend nebuly vert three bugle horns stringed of the field (for GREENALL); 2nd and 3rd, argent, five pallets sable, the centre pallet charged with an ermine spot of the field (for GRIFFITH). **Crest:** Between two wings or a pomme surmounted by a bugle horn as in the arms. **Supporters:** Dexter, a bull proper; sinister, a bay mare, mane and tail sable, charged on the shoulder with a sprig of two oak leaves or. **Badge:** A rose gules and two ears of wheat leaved and slipped in saltire proper, enfiled with a baron's coronet or. **Motto:** *Alta peto* ('I seek the heights').
Creations: Bt. (UK) 22 Feb 1876, B. (UK) 21 June 1927.

THE 4TH BARON DARESBURY, of Walton, Co Chester, and a **Baronet** (Sir Peter Gilbert Greenall, Bt, DL (Cheshire 1994)) [The Rt Hon The Lord Daresbury DL, Hall Lane Farm, Daresbury, Cheshire WA4 4RH]; *b* 18 July 1953; *s* f 1996; *educ* Eton and Magdalene Coll Cambridge (MA); High Sheriff Cheshire 1992, twice champion amateur jockey; *m* 11 Sept 1982 *Clare, only dau of Christopher Weatherby, of Whaddon House, Bletchley, Bucks (*see* ERNE, E), and has issue:
1 +THOMAS EDWARD; *b* 6 Nov 1984
2 +Oliver Christopher; *b* 1986
3 +Toby Peter; *b* 1988
4 +Jonathan James; *b* 1992

Lineage: THOMAS GREENHALGH, of Ashton, Winwick, Lancs; granted by Sir Thomas Gerard 1562 lands in Ashton-in-Makerfield, Lancs; *m* Jane — and *d* between 30 March and 22 May 1584, leaving, with other issue:

THOMAS GREENHALGH, of Ashton; *m* Elizabeth (*bur* 3 Dec 1638) and *d* between 10 Jan 1591/2 and April 1592, leaving, with other issue:

THOMAS GREENHALGH, of Ashton; *bapt* 1575; *m* 2 Nov 1607 Grace Marsh and had, with other issue:

THOMAS GREENHALGH, of Ashton and Parr, Prescot, Lancs; *bapt* 21 Oct 1621; *m* Cecilia (*bur* 16 March 1684/5), and *d* in or after 1684, having had, with other issue:

EDWARD GREENHALGH, of Parr; *bapt* 5 Nov 1664; had:
RICHARD GREENHALGH, of Parr and Sutton, Prescot; *bapt* 22 Nov 1702; *m* 1st 28 Feb 1729/30 Phoebe, dau and coheir of Gilbert Lyon, of Billing, by Sarah (*bur* 26 Feb 1750/1), dau of Thomas Gerard, of Hollinshey, Ashton-in-Makerfield; *m* 2nd Jane Howard and *d* between 18 Jan 1768 and 26 Feb 1768/9, leaving by his 1st w, with other issue:

THOMAS GREENHALGH later GREENALL, of Hardshaw Hall, Windle, and Parr; *bapt* 21 Sept 1733; *m* Mary (*d* 9 Nov 1816), dau of John Turton, of Parr, and *d* 18 Jan 1805 aged 71, leaving, with other issue:

EDWARD GREENALL, of Wilderspool, Cheshire; *b* 10 Aug 1758; *m* 9 June 1791 Betty (*d* 29 March 1836 aged 65), dau of John Pratt, of Liverpool, and *d* 20 Nov 1835, leaving, with other issue:
1 Thomas, of Grappenhall Hall, Cheshire; *m* 1819 Helen, dau of Samuel Haslehurst, and *d* 1848, leaving issue
2 Peter, of St Helens; MP Wigan; *b* 26 April 1796; *m* 6 March 1821 Eleanor (*d* 1 Aug 1846), dau of Dr William Pilkington, and *d* 18 Sept 1845, leaving issue
3 John, of Middleton Hall, Lancs; *b* 5 Dec 1802; *m* 25 Aug 1829 Elizabeth, dau of Rev William Hockenhull Molyneux, Minor Canon Chester, and *d* 25 Oct 1850, leaving issue
4 Richard (Ven), Archdeacon Chester; *b* 11 May 1806; *m* 27 Nov 1856 Eliza Mary (*d* 10 Nov 1878), dau of Thomas Lyon, and *dsp* 27 Nov 1867
5 **Sir Gilbert Greenall, 1st Bt** (UK), so *cr* 22 Feb 1876, JP Lancs and Cheshire, DL Lancs; *b* 11 May 1806; High Sheriff Cheshire 1873, MP Warrington 1847–1868, 1874–1880 and 1880–1892; Im 1st 6 Oct 1836 Mary (*d* 4 Dec 1861), dau of David Claughton, of Haydock, Lancs; *m* 2nd 7 June 1864 Susannah (*d* 30 Oct 1896), dau of John Louis Rapp, of Middx, and by her had issue:
(1) GILBERT, **1st Baron**

(1) Susannah, JP parts of Kesteven, Lincs; *m* 7 June 1898 Cyril Edward Greenall (*d* 10 Aug 1939), OBE, JP, of The Manor, Carlton Scroop, Grantham, son of Canon Thomas Greenall, of Grappenhall, Cheshire, and has issue

(2) Bertha; *m* 26 July 1898 Lt-Col Edward Waldegrave Griffith (*d* 14 April 1937), DSO, TD, DL, JP, RA, of Plasnewydd, Denbighshire, and *d* 4 Feb 1945, leaving issue

Sir GILBERT *d* 10 July 1894; his son,

Sir Gilbert Greenall, 2nd Bt, and 1st Baron Daresbury, of Walton, Chester (UK), so *cr* 21 June 1927, CVO (1911), DL and JP Cheshire; *b* 30 March 1867; *educ* Eton; High Sheriff Cheshire 1907, LLD Cambridge 1921, Lt Cheshire Yeo Cav, MFH Belvoir 18996–1912, Hon Dir Roy Ag Soc 1906–30 (Pres 1910 and 1925), Offr Crown Belgium; *m* 25 Oct 1900 Frances Eliza, OBE (1945), JP Cheshire, (*d* 19 Dec 1953), dau of Capt Edward Wynne Griffith, Royal Dragoons, of Plasnewydd, Trefnant, Denbighshire, and Tiresford, Tarporley, Cheshire, and *d* 24 Oct 1938, having had issue:

1 Gilbert, Lt Life Gds; *b* 2 Oct 1901; *educ* Eton; *m* 15 Sept 1924 *Betty Isobel (*m* 2nd 6 Feb 1933 Reginald Arthur Farquhar (*d* 15 Feb 1937), yst s of Sir Walter Randolph FitzRoy Farquhar, 5th Bt, *qv*), er dau of John Shields Crawford, of Thorpe Satchville Hall, Melton Mowbray, and *d* 27 July 1928

2 EDWARD GREENALL, **2nd Baron Daresbury**, JP (Cheshire 1945); *b* 12 Oct 1902; *educ* Eton, Lt Res Offrs Life Gds, Jt MFH Belvoir 1934–47, MFH Limerick 1947–90; *m* 1st 11 Aug 1925 Joan Madeline (*d* 15 March 1926), er dau of Capt Robert Thomas Oliver Sheriffe, of Goadby Hall, Melton Mowbray; *m* 2nd 12 Sept 1927 Josephine (*d* 13 Nov 1958), yst dau of Brig-Gen Sir Joseph Frederick Laycock, KCMG, DSO, TD, DL, JP, and had issue; *m* 3rd 16 June 1966 Lady Helena Albreda Marie Gabriella (*k* in a hunting accident 14 Sept 1970), yst dau of 7th Earl Fitzwilliam, KCVO, CBE, DSO (*see* 1970 edn), and formerly w of Chetwode Charles Hamilton Hilton-Green, and *d* 1990, leaving by his 2nd w:

(1) EDWARD GILBERT GREENALL; **3rd Baron Daresbury**; *b* 27 Nov 1928; *educ* Eton; *m* 1st 7 Feb 1952 (*divorce* 1986) Margaret Ada, yst dau of Charles John Crawford by Ella Frances Olive, est sis of Sir Denis George William Anson, 4th Bt (*qv*), and had issue; *m* 2nd 1986 *Mary Patricia [The Rt Hon Mary Lady Daresbury, Crossbow House, Trinity, Jersey, CI], dau of Lewis Parkinson, and *d* 9 Sept 1996, leaving by his 1st w:

1a PETER GILBERT GREENALL, **4th and present Baron Daresbury**

2a +Gilbert, CBE (1993) [Dr The Hon Gilbert Greenall CBE, Bromesberrow Place, Worcs HR8 1RZ]; *b* 16 Aug 1954; *educ* Eton and RMA Sandhust; MB, ChB, MBA, Lt RARO (ret); *m* 28 June 1983 *Sarah Elizabeth, er dau of Ian C Mouat, of Stetchworth, Suffolk, and formerly w of Robert Greville Kaye Williamson, and has issue:

1b +Gilbert Edward; *b* 1984

2b +Frederick John; *b* 1986

3b +Alexander; *b* 1988

1b *Amelia Frances; *b* 1990

3a +John Edward [The Hon John Greenall, Lullington House, Lullington, Staffs DE12 8EG]; *b* 22 July 1960; *educ* Fettes; BSc Econ; amateur champion jockey 1993/94; *m* 1985 *Gabrielle, dau of Stephen James, of Lymington, Hants, and has issue:

1b +James Edward; *b* 1988

1b *Katie Laura; *b* 1986

1a *Susan Rosemary; *b* 18 Aug 1956; *m* 1st 16 April 1978 (*divorce* 1989) David St Clair Oswald Bruton, est son of Charles Meddon Karslake Bruton, of Hockworthy House, Wellington, Somerset, and has issue:

1b *Alastair Edward Oswald; *b* 1985

1b *Natasha Charlotte; *b* 1983

1a (cont.) The Hon Mrs Susan Bruton *m* 2nd 1989 *Anthony St John Haden-Taylor, son of Frank Pacey Haden-Taylor, of Broughton Gifford, Wilts, and has had further issue:

2b Pandora Eleanor Christine; *b* 1989; *d* 1990

3b *Annabella; *b* Aug 1995

DARLING

Arms: Argent on a chevron engrailed between three fleshpots sable a stirrup leathered or. **Crest:** 0In front of a dexter cubit arm proper, holding in the hand a heart gules, a chaplet of laurel vert. **Supporters:** On either side a pegasus argent, charged on the wing with a chevron engrailed sable. **Badge:** A sprig of heather and a sprig of gorse in saltire proper, enfiled by a baron's coronet or. **Motto:** 1 Aye be honest, 2 (over the crest) *Dei donum* ('The gift of God'). **Creation:** B. (UK) 12 Jan 1924.

THE 2ND BARON DARLING, of Langham, Essex (Robert Charles Henry Darling, DL (Avon 1974, Somerset 1972–74 and 1996)) [The Rt Hon The Lord Darling DL, Puckpits, Limpley Stoke, Bath, Avon BA3 6JH]; *b* 15 May 1919; *s* gf 1936; *educ* Wellington and RMC Sandhurst; Maj Somerset LI WW II; *m* 15 Aug 1942 (Bridget) Rosemary Whishaw (*d* 29 March 1997), dau of Rev Francis Cyprian Dickson, Vicar Emery Down, Hants, and has issue:

1 +(ROBERT) JULIAN HENRY [The Hon Julian Darling, Intwood Hall, Intwood, Norwich NR4 6TG]; *b* 29 April 1944; *educ* Wellington and RAC Cirencester; FRICS; *m* 1 Oct 1970 *Janet, yr dau of John Mallinson, of Carlisle, and has:

(1) +Robert James Cyprian; *b* 6 March 1972

(2) +Henry Thomas Unthank; *b* 27 Aug 1978

(1) *Rachael Pollyanna Margaret; *b* 4 March 1974

1 *(Anna) Josephine Bridget [The Hon Mrs Pardoe, Sharow Cottage, Sharow, Ripon, N Yorks]; *b* 22 April 1946; *m* 18 Sept 1971 *Anthony Robert Pardoe, er s of Major Robert Pardoe, of Raff Yard House, Raby Park, Co Durham, and has:

(1) *David Hugh Charles; *b* 13 Dec 1974

(1) *Georgina Rosemary Jane; *b* 14 May 1977

2 *Lucinda Mary Joan; *b* 23 Dec 1958; *m* 1982 *Rory P A Macdiarmid, only son of Col Peter Macdiarmid, and has issue:

(1) *George Peter Robert; *b* 1985

(2) *Fergus Charles Ian; *b* 1987

(1) *Philippa Rosemary Kate; *b* 1990

Lineage: CHARLES DARLING, of Haddington, E Lothian; *m* Janet, dau of James Traill, of Dirleton, and had:

CHARLES DARLING, of Langham Hall, Langham, Essex; *b* 27 April 1806; *m* March 1849 Sarah Frances (*d* 8 Oct 1897), dau of John Tizard, of Dorchester, and *d* 8 June 1862, leaving:

1 CHARLES JOHN, **1st Baron**

2 William Littell; *b* 2 April 1851; *d* 6 Oct 1891

1 Janet Susan; *m* March 1882 John Rose (*d* 5 Feb 1926), barrister, Metropolitan Magistrate, and *d* 30 June 1938

The est son,

CHARLES JOHN DARLING, **1st Baron Darling**, of Langham, Co Essex (UK), so *cr* 12 Jan 1924, PC (1917), QC (1885); *b* 6 Dec 1849; barrister Inner Temple 1874, Bencher 1892, MP Deptford 1888–97, ktd 1897, High Court Judge King's Bench 1897–1923; *m* 16 Sept 1885 Mary Caroline (*d* 5 Nov 1913), er dau of Major-Gen William Wilberforce Harris Greathed, CB, RE, and *d* 29 May 1936, leaving:

1 John Clive, DSO (1916); *b* 15 June 1887; Maj 20th and 8th Hus (ret 1923), served WW I (wounded, despatches); *m* 17 Aug 1918 Eleanor Joan Martin (*m* 2nd 6 Nov 1945 Rev Francis Cyprian Dickson, Vicar Emery Down, Hants, son of Rev R H Dickson), est dau of Henry Martin Powell, JP, of Wilverley Park, Lyndhurst, Hants, and *d* 5 Feb 1933, leaving issue:

(1) ROBERT CHARLES HENRY DARLING, **2nd and present Baron Darling**

(2) James Weyland, Midshipman RN WW II; *b* 3 May 1922; *ka* off Crete May 1941

1 Lucia Frances Alice; *m* 18 Dec 1906 Keppel Pulteney (*d* 8 Dec 1944), MA, only son of John Granville Beaumont Pulteney, JP, of St Austin's, Lymington, Hants, and *d* 4 April 1962, leaving issue

2 Diana Janet, JP (Hants 1941), Hon Co Sec Hants Fedn WIs 1945–55, V-Chm Nat Fedn WIs 1957–61; *d* unm 25 Feb 1961

DARNLEY

Arms: Az. a griffin segreant or, armed and langued gu., between three crescents arg. **Crest:** A griffin's head erased or. **Supporters:** Two griffins wings expanded or, ducally collared and chained az. **Motto:** *Finem respice* ('Look to the end'). **Creations:**, B (E) 9 July 1608 (Clifton (of Leighton Bromswold) and (I) 14 Sept 1721, V. (I) 7 March 1723, E. (I) 29 June 1725.

THE 11TH EARL OF DARNLEY, **Viscount Darnley of Athboy**, Co Meath, **Baron Clifton of Rathmore**, Co Meath, and **Lord** (Baron) **Clifton** (of Leighton Bromswold), (Adam Ivo Stuart Bligh) [The Rt Hon The Earl of Darnley, Netherwood Manor, Tenbury Wells, Worcs WR15 8RT]; *b* 8 Nov 1941; *s* half-bro 1980; *educ* Harrow and Ch Ch Oxford; *m* 14 Oct 1965 *Susan Elaine, JP (Havant 1977), yst dau of Sir Donald Forsyth Anderson, of 55 Cranmer Court, Sloane Ave, London SW3, by Margaret Elaine, est dau of Sir David Richard Llewellyn, 1st Bt, of Bwllfa (*qv*), and has issue:

1 +IVO DONALD STUART, *Lord Clifton*; *b* 17 April 1968; *educ* Marlborough and Edinburgh U

1 +Katherine Amanda; *b* 29 May 1971; *educ* St Mary's Sch Calne, Marlborough and St Edmund Hall Oxford

Darnley, other creations: All these prior to the Bligh one were in the peerage of Scotland. The first, a lordship of Parliament rather than earldom, seems to have been created in 1460. It was bestowed on Sir John Stuart, who was later promoted Earl of Lennox (*see* also MORAY, E). The 4th Earl's son was known by the courtesy title of Lord Darnley. It is he who married MARY QUEEN OF SCOTS, doing so as her 2nd husband in 1565. Although promoted Duke of Albany, he remains best known to posterity as Lord Darnley. He was murdered two years after his marriage, predeceasing his father. His son JAMES VI OF SCOTS and I of England, who had acceded to the Scottish throne in 1567, inherited the Earldom of Lennox and Lordship of Darnley in 1571 on his paternal grandfather's death, whereupon they merged in the Crown.

The 4th Earl of Lennox had before his death been temporarily deprived of his titles, however. During his period of disgrace John Stewart, a bastard son of JAMES V KING OF SCOTS by Catherine, dau of Sir John Carmichael, was created Lord Darnley. This took place some time between Jan 1561/2 and Feb 1562/3, though he had been legitimated as early as 1550. As if to confuse matters further this Lord Darnley married the sister of the 3rd Earl of Bothwell, father of the Earl of Bothwell who was MARY QUEEN OF SCOTS's 3rd husband. To top it all, the 2nd Lord Darnley of the 1561/2–62/3 creation was promoted Earl of Bothwell in 1581, three years after his more famous namesake and cousin on his mother's side had died without legitimate issue. He was attainted and stripped of all his titles in 1593.

Four further creations involving a lordship of Darnley took place between 1572 and 1581. They were all subsidiary to earldom or dukedom of Lennox creations, however (*see* MORAY, E, also below).

Lineage (of Bligh): WILLIAM BLIGH, Plymouth merchant, had a 3rd s:

JOHN BLIGH, of London and Rathmore, Co Meath, agent of the Adventurers for the Forfeited Estates 1641, was assigned lands in Co Meath 1654, Commr for auditing arrears of Customs and Excise 1648–63, MP (I Parl) Athboy 1660, Commr Inland Excise 1665; *bapt* 23 Feb 1616/7; *m* Catherine (*d* by 8 Dec 1669), sis of William Fuller, Bp Lincoln, and *d* 3 Nov 1666, leaving an only surv son:

THOMAS BLIGH, PC, of Rathmore; allegedly a grazier by origin; by the terms of the Act of Settlement of 1668 was granted large tracts of land in Ireland, MP Co Meath 1695–1710; *b c* 1654; *m* 9 Dec 1682 Elizabeth (*d* 21 March 1736/7), dau of Col James Naper, of Loughcrew, Co Meath, and *d* 28 Aug 1710, leaving, with other issue (including at least two daus: Dorothy, *m* William Monck (*see* MONCK, V); Elizabeth, *m* George St George and had issue; *see* ST GEORGE, Bt):

JOHN BLIGH, **1st Earl of Darnley**, Co Meath, so *cr* 29 June 1725 by virtue of his marriage, as also earlier 14 Sept 1721 BARON CLIFTON OF RATHMORE, Co Meath, and 7 March 1722/3 VISCOUNT DARNLEY OF ATHBOY, Co Meath (all I); *b* 28 Dec 1687; MP Trim 1709–13 and Athboy 1713–218; *m* 24 Aug 1713 Lady Theodosia Hyde, **Baroness Clifton** (of Leighton Bromswold) in her own right (*d* 30 July 1722), only dau and heir of 3rd Earl of Clarendon of the 1661 *cr* (*d* CLARENDON, E, preliminary remarks) and descendant through her mother of the Dukes of Lennox (among whose subsidiary creations in 1581 had been an Earldom of Darnley; *see* MORAY, E; her descendants of both sexes are in remainder to the Barony of Clifton, hence the + against living females henceforward in this article), and *d* 12 Sept 1728, leaving, with three daus:

1 George; *b* 31 Oct 1714 (GEORGE I stood sponsor); *d* an infant

2 EDWARD BLIGH, **2nd Earl of Darnley** and (*s* mother 1722 as) **11th Lord** (Baron) **Clifton** (of Leighton Bromswold); *b* 9 Nov 1715; *educ* Westminster; Ld in Waiting to FREDERICK PRINCE OF WALES 1742; *d* unm 22 July 1747

3 JOHN BLIGH, **3rd Earl of Darnley**; *b* 28 Sept 1719; *educ* Westminster and Merton Coll Oxford; MP (I Parl) Athboy 1739–47 and (GB Parl, anti-Walpole Whig) Maidstone 1741–47; *m* 11 Sept 1766 Mary (*d* 27 March 1803), dau and heir of John Stoyte, of Street, Co Westmeath, barrister, and had, with four daus:

(1) JOHN, **4th Earl**

(2) Edward, Gen; *b* 19 Sept 1769; *dsp* 2 Nov 1840

(3) William, Col; *b* 25 Sept 1775; *m* 21 July 1806 Sophia (*d* 1809), dau of 7th Earl of Galloway (*qv*), and *d* 6 Aug 1845, having had issue:

(1) William Stoyte; *b* 28 May 1808; *d* 26 April 1821

(1) Sophia; *m* 28 May 1835 3rd Baron Congleton (*qv*) and *d* 5 April 1846, leaving issue

The 3rd EARL *d* 31 July 1781; his est son,

JOHN BLIGH, **4th Earl of Darnley**; *b* 30 June 1767; unsuccessfully petitioned Ho of Lds 1829 to be declared Duke of Lennox, on the grounds that he was the heir general of the 6th Duke (*d* 1672) and that, although CHARLES II had been the then heir, with the extinction of the Stuart line following the death 1809 of Cardinal Henry Duke of York, his own descent from the 6th Duke's sis Catherine validated his claim; *m* 26 Aug 1791 Elizabeth (*d* 22 Dec 1831), 3rd dau of William Brownlow, PC, of Lurgan (*see* 1970 edn LURGAN, B), and had:

1 John, *Lord Clifton*; *b* 22 May, *d* 3 June 1793

2 EDWARD, **5th Earl**

3 William; *b* 25 May 1797; *d* 18 Oct 1807

4 John Duncan (Sir), KCB, DCL, Envoy-Extrdy and Min Plen Hanover; *b* 11 Oct 1798; *m* 1st 19 Dec 1835 Elizabeth Mary (*d* 22 July 1837), only dau of Thomas Gisborne, MP, and had:

(1) Elizabeth Mary; *m* 18 June 1861 4th Earl of Chichester (*qv*), and *dsp* 7 Dec 1911

4 (cont.) Sir John Bligh *m* 2nd 28 Nov 1865 Anne Julia (*dsp* 19 July 1882), 4th dau of Rev Francis and Lady Catherine Brownlow (*see* 1970 edn LURGAN, B), and *d* 8 May 1872

1 Catherine; *b* 18 June 1792; *d* 10 Jan 1812

2 Mary; *m* 1 June 1822 1st Baron Lurgan (*see* 1970 edn) and *d* 18 June 1823, leaving issue

3 Elizabeth; *m* 19 July 1833 Rev John Brownlow (*d* 24 May 1882) and *d* 13 Nov 1872, leaving issue

The 4th EARL *d* 17 March 1831; his est surv son,

EDWARD BLIGH, **5th Earl of Darnley**, MP Canterbury 1818–30, Lt Co Meath; *b* 25 Feb 1795; *m* 26 July 1825 Emma Jane (*d* 15 March 1884), dau of 1st Baron Congleton (*qv*), and had issue:

1 JOHN STUART, **6th Earl**

2 Edward Vesey (Rev), of Fartherwell Hall, Kent, DL, JP, and CA, MA Cambridge, Dip Serv, Vicar Birling, Kent; *b* 28 Feb 1829; *m* 23 Feb 1854 Lady Isabel Mary Frances Nevill (*d* 18 Dec 1915), sis of 1st Marquess of Abergavenny (*qv*), and *d* 22 April 1908, having had:

(1) Lodovick Edward, Major 3rd Bn The Buffs, JP Kent; *b* 24 Nov 1854; *m* 1 June 1886 Marion Louisa (*d* 10 Feb 1925), dau of Rev Frederick Alexander Stewart Savile, MA, of Kilmorie, Devon, and *d* 16 May 1924, leaving:

1a Harroweton Lodovick; *b* 9 July 1887; *d* 19 May 1888

2a Algernon Stuart, Jt Master Minehead Harriers 1928–32; *b* 6 Oct 1888; *educ* Eton and RAC Cirencester; *m* 1st 25 Sept 1922 (*divorce* 1937) Dora Joan (*d* 23 Feb 1969), only dau of Thomas Lovelace, of Bratton Court, Minehead, and had issue:

1b +Noel Edward [Lt Noel Bligh RN, Weeks Park, High Bickington, Umberleigh, Devon]; *b* 2 April 1926; *educ* RNC; late Capt RASC, Lt RN; *m* 11 Nov 1961 *Jane Mary, dau of Trevor Seymour-Smith and formerly w of Geoffrey Stanley William Waite, and has issue:

1c +Victoria Joan; *b* 2 Nov 1962

1b +Audrey Diana [Mrs John Spencer-Hawkins, Osbornes, Upper Dicker, Hailsham, Sussex]; *m* 9 Aug 1947 *John Sefton Spencer-Hawkins, er son of Alfred Cyril Spencer-Hawkins, of Scott's Lodge, Knockholt, Kent, and has issue:

1c +Nigel Bligh Spencer; *b* 10 Oct 1954

2c +David Stuart; *b* 29 May 1956

2a (cont.) Algernon Bligh *m* 2nd 14 Nov 1938 *(Emily Mabel) Dorothy, dau of Frederick Vincent Larway, of Pendeen, Irnham Road, Minehead, and *d* 27 Dec 1952, having by her had:

2b +Jennifer Wendy [Mrs Peter Prior-Wandesforde, Bally Lanigan House, Mullinahone, Co Tipperary, Ireland]; *b* 1 Aug 1942; *m* 1st 2 Feb 1963 (*divorce* 1974) Ronald Colin Board Webber, Master Minehead Harriers 1961–, son of William John Webber, of Hindon Cottage, Minehead, Somerset, and has issue:

1c +Katrina Jane; *b* 14 Dec 1964; *m* 1991 *Capt J P Stanhope-White

2b (cont.) Mrs Jennifer Webber *m* 2nd 1975 (*divorce* 19–) Alan Thomas Wormell; *m* 3rd 1982 *Peter MacDonell Prior-Wandesforde

3b +Heather Rosalind [Mrs Christopher Dunn, Staple Fitzpaine Manor, Staple Fitzpaine, Taunton, Som]; *b* 15 Feb 1945; *m* 1st 1968 (*divorce* 1977) Arthur Keith Amor, and has issue:

1c +Jason Keith Bligh; *b* 1970

2c +Lucinda Jane Bligh; *b* 1969

3b (cont.) Mrs Heather Amor *m* 2nd 1983 *Christopher James Dunn, and has further issue:

2c +Harry James Bligh; *b* 1984

3a Ronald Edward; *b* 15 July 1890; *d* 2 July 1891

4a Jack Frederick, MC, Capt (Actg Maj) RFA WW I (despatches); *b* 19 Jan 1893; *ka* 1 July 1917

1a Rose Marion, Jt Master Minehead Harriers 1928–32, Master 1932–49; *b* 14 Jan 1896; *m* 8 Feb 1923 Stanley Hosegood, of Deer Acre, North Road, Williton, Somerset, son of Frederick Hosegood, of Bilbrook, Washford, Somerset, and had issue

(1) Rosalind Isabel, MBE (1920); *m* 12 Oct 1881 Brig-Gen Cecil Vernon Wingfield-Stratford (*d* 5 Feb 1939), CB, CMG, RE, and *d* 18 March 1953, leaving issue (*see* POWERSCOURT, V)

3 Henry (Rev), Vicar Holy Trinity Fareham 1893–1900; *b* 10 June 1834; *m* 1st 14 Oct 1858 Emma (*d* 27 Dec 1881), yst dau of Col Henry Armytage (*see* ARMYTAGE, Bt), and had issue:

(1) Gertrude Frances; *m* 6 Aug 1889 Rev Murdoch Charles Kirby, Vicar of Tidebrook, Wadhurst, Sussex, and *d* Feb 1914, leaving issue

(2) Eva; *m* 26 June 1890 William Jesse Cooper (*d* 4 Aug 1946) and *d* 29 Jan 1951, leaving issue

3 (cont.) The Rev Henry Bligh *m* 2nd 3 April 1883 Anne Elizabeth Dobrée (*d* 20 Jan 1948), dau of Lt-Col Edward Dobrée Butler, 36th Regt, and *d* 4 March 1905, having by her had issue

(1) Edward Henry Swinburne, barrister, Lt Drake Div RND; *b* 16 April 1884; *ka* 10 Sept 1915

1 Elizabeth Caroline; *m* 13 Dec 1855 Sir Reginald John Cust (*d* 11 June 1913), and *d* 10 April 1914, leaving issue (*see* BROWNLOW, B)

2 Emma Bess; *m* 6 June 1854 Very Rev Arthur Perceval Purey-Cust (*d* 23 Dec 1916), DD, Dean of York, and *d* 27 July 1917, leaving issue (*see* BROWNLOW, B)

The 5th EARL *d* 12 Feb 1835; his est son,

JOHN STUART BLIGH, **6th Earl of Darnley**, DL, CA, Lt-Col West Kent Yeo Cav 1863–74; *b* 16 April 1827; *m* 31 Aug 1850 Lady Harriet Mary Pelham (*d* 4 Sept 1905), est dau of 3rd Earl of Chichester (*qv*), and *d* 14 Dec 1896, having had issue:

1 EDWARD HENRY STUART BLIGH, **7th Earl of Darnley**; *b* 21 Aug 1851; *m* 26 Jan 1899 Jemima Adeline Beatrice (*m* 2nd 3 March 1902 Adml Sir Arthur Cavenagh Leveson, GCB, RN, who *d* 26 June 1929, and *d* 25 April 1964), only dau of Francis James Lindesay Price Blackwood, of Norton Court (*see* DUFFERIN AND CLANEBOYE, B), and *d* 31 Oct 1900, leaving issue:

(1) ELIZABETH ADELINE MARY, **Baroness Clifton** (of Leighton Bromswold) in her own right, barrister Lincoln's Inn 1926; *b* 22 Jan 1900; *d* unm 5 July 1937

2 IVO FRANCIS WALTER, **8th Earl**

3 Arthur Frederick Pelham; *b* 25 April 1865; *d* 29 Dec 1924

1 Edith Louisa Mary; *b* 22 Aug 1853; *m* 17 Aug 1882 George Burvill Rashleigh (*d* 7 April 1916), barrister, est son of Rev Henry Burvill Rashleigh, Vicar Horton Kirby, Kent, and *d* 20 June 1904, leaving issue (*see* HARINGTON, Bt)

2 Kathleen Susan Emma; *b* 31 Oct 1854; *m* 1 June 1904, as his 2nd w, Maj-Gen William Vesey Brownlow (*d* 15 March 1928), CB, son of William Brownlow, of Knapton House, Queen's Co, and *d* 13 Nov 1928

3 Alice Isabella Harriet; *b* 18 Dec 1860; *d* unm 15 June 1943

4 Mary Rose Florence; *b* 21 April 1868; *d* unm 5 July 1896

5 Constance Violet Lucy; *m* 28 June 1894 William Shakespear Childe-Pemberton (*d* 4 Jan 1924) and had issue

The 7th EARL's bro,

IVO FRANCIS WALTER BLIGH, **8th Earl of Darnley**, rep I peer; *educ* Trin Coll Cambridge (BA); DL, JP, and CA Kent, Hon Col 4th Vol Bn Roy West Kent Regt; *b* 13 March 1859; *m* 9 Feb 1884 Florence Rose, DBE (1919) (*d* 30 Aug 1944), dau of John Stephen Morphy, of Beechworth, Victoria, Australia, and had issue:

1 ESME IVO, **9th Earl**

2 Noel Gervase, DSO (1918), Lt-Col Rifle Bde, served WW I (despatches), and WW II 1940–45 Roy Pioneer Corps; *b* 14 Nov 1888; *educ* Eton; *m* 1st 24 July 1912 (*divorce* 1934) Mary Jack (*d* 9 June 1940), dau of Capt George Alfred Frost, RA, and had issue:

(1) Jasmine Lydia; BBC TV announcer-hostess 1936; *b* 21 May 1913; *m* 1st 2 Oct 1940 (*divorce* 1947) Lt-Col Sir John Paley Johnson, 6th Bt (*d* 14 Dec 1975; *see* JOHNSON, Bt, of New York), and had issue; *m* 2nd 20 May 1948 (*divorce* 1953) Frank Hugh Shirley Fox, son of Frank Hugh Fox, of 12 Havengren Court, London W5, and *d* 1991

(2) +Susan Rachel; *b* 12 Aug 1916; *m* 22 Nov 1940 Lt-Col William Joseph Stirling of Keir (*see* HERON-MAXWELL, Bt), and *d* 1983, leaving

2 (cont.) The Hon Noel Bligh *m* 2nd 18 Jan 1934 Dorothy Millicent Isabella (*d* 31 March 1972), formerly w of Caryl Henry Courthorpe Munroe and dau of Hubert Lee Bevan; *m* 3rd 1973 *Mrs Kathleen Weatherill Strickland [The Hon Mrs Noel Bligh, 5 Sloane Gate Mansions, D'Oyly St, London SW1] and *d* 1984

1 Dorothy Violet; *b* 8 Feb 1893; *m* 29 Feb 1916 Capt Daniel Spencer Peploe (*d* 15 May 1958), 20th Hus, son of Daniel Henry Theophilus Peploe, DL, JP, of Garnstone Castle, Herefordshire, and *d* 16 Jan 1976, leaving issue

The 8th EARL *d* 10 April 1927; his er son,

ESMÉ IVO BLIGH, **9th Earl of Darnley** and (s cousin 1937 as) **18th Lord** (Baron) **Clifton** (of Leighton Bromswold), Major RAF; *b* 11 Oct 1886; *m* 1st 25 June 1912 (*divorce* 1920) Daphne Rachel (*d* 18 Jan 1948), only dau of Hon Alfred John Mulholland (*see* DUNLEATH, B), and had issue:

1 PETER STUART BLIGH, **10th Earl of Darnley**; *b* 1 Oct 1915; *educ* Eton and RMC Sandhurst, Major 1st King's Dragoon Gds WW II (POW); *d* unm 15 June 1980

1 +Marguerite Rose [The Lady Marguerite Tangye, 52 Redcliffe Gdns, London SW10]; *b* 24 April 1913; *m* 1st 3 Aug 1934 (*divorce* Feb 1941) Claud Dobrée Strickland, F/O, AAF (*ka* Oct 1941), son of Claud Hugh Strickland, of Charing, Kent (*see* STRICKLAND-CONSTABLE, Bt); *m* 2nd 30 April 1942 (*divorce* 1951) W/Cdr Gordon Stanley Keigh Haywood, RAF, only son of Charles Henry Percy Haywood, of The Shrubbery, Willington, Derbys, and has issue:

(1) +Gareth Peter [Gareth Haywood Esq, Flat 2, 11 Islington Green, London N1]; *b* 4 March 1943; *m* 28 Oct 1965 (*divorce* 1969) Zehra Ipek, only dau of Prof Semseddin Talip Diler, of Taksim, Istanbul, and Mme Huriser Uner, of Laleli, Istanbul

(1) +Lucinda March (twin); *b* 4 March 1943; *m* 12 Dec 1964 (*divorce* 1983) James Hilary Glyn, only son of Hilary Beaujolais Glyn, of Oakum House, Albury, Much Hadham, Herts (*see* WOLVERTON, B)

1 (cont.) Lady Marguerite Haywood *m* 3rd 5 May 1951 (*divorce* 1964) as his 2nd wife Nigel Trevithick Tangye (*d* 1988), 2nd son of Lt-Col Richard Trevithick Gilbertstone Tangye, OBE, DL, JP (*see* 1970 edn TANGYE, Bt)

The **9th Earl** *m* 2nd 11 Oct 1923 (*divorce* 1936) Nancy, est dau of Capt Archibald Glen Kidston, and by her had:

2 +Rose Amanda [The Lady Rose Hare, Stow Bardolph, King's Lynn, Norfolk PE34 3HU]; *b* 30 July 1935; *m* 16 Sept 1961 Sir Thomas Hare, 5th Bt (*qv*), and has issue

The **9th Earl** *m* 3rd 4 Nov 1940 *Rosemary (*b* 30 July 1916) [Mrs Pierre Trasenster, Meadow House, Cobham, nr Gravesend, Kent] (*m* 2nd 18 April 1963 Pierre Trasenster (*d* 16 Sept 1968), son of James Trasenster, of Hauster, Vaux Sous Chevremont, Belgium), dau of Edmund Basil Potter, of Witherslack, Westmorland, and *d* 29 May 1955, having by her had:

2 ADAM IVO STUART BLIGH, **11th and present Earl of Darnley**

3 +Melissa Geraldine Florence [The Lady Melissa Levey, The Vicarage, Orton, Cumbria C10 3RQ]; *b* 3 Oct 1945 (HM QUEEN GERALDINE of Albania stood sponsor); *m* 1st 7 July 1965 Don Manuel Torrado y de Fontcuberta (*d* 1980), 2nd son of Don Manuel Torrado Varela, of Barcelona, and has:

(1) +Manuel Ivo [Manuel Torrado Esq, 4 Aldbourne Close, Park St, Hungerford, Berks RG17 0SQ]; *b* 21 July 1966; *m* 1991 (*divorce* 1994) Audrey Elizabeth, dau of Andrew Perratt; *m* 2nd 1997 *Alison Frances de Vroome

(1) +Maria Melissa Amancia Ignacia; *b* 16 Oct 1968

(2) +Victoria Irene; *b* 28 Feb 1973

3 (cont.) Lady Melissa Torrado y de Fontcuberta *m* 2nd 1985 *Rev Colin Russell Levey

4 +Harriet Esme Ghislaine [The Lady Harriet Bligh, Meadow House Cottage, Cobham, Gravesend, Kent DA12 3BZ]; *b* 27 April 1949; *educ* Cobham Hall and Somerville Coll Oxford

Lineage (of Clifton): Sir JOHN CLIFTON, of Barrington Court, Somerset; *m* Anne Stanley, dau of 2nd Lord (Baron) Monteagle (*see* MONTEAGLE OF BRANDON, B, preliminary remarks), and had:

GERVASE CLIFTON, **1st Lord** (Baron) **Clifton** (of Leighton Bromswold) (E), so *cr* by writ 9 July 1608, of Leighton Bromswold, Hunts; *educ* St Alban's Hall Oxford; ktd by 1597, MP Hunts 1597–98 and 1601; *m c* 25 June 1591 Katherine, dau and heir of Sir Henry Darcy, and *dspms* by his own hand 14 Oct 1618 while imprisoned in the Tower of London (for uttering threats against Lord Keeper Bacon), leaving:

KATHERINE Clifton, *de jure* BARONESS CLIFTON in her own right; *m* 1st *c* 1609 Lord Esmé STUART, Seigneur d' Aubigny in France, *cr* 7 June 1619 Earl of March and Baron Stuart of Leighton Bromswold, and (on *s* his bro 16 Feb 1623/4 as) 3rd Duke of Lennox (*d* 30 July 1624); *m* 2nd by 1632 2nd Earl of Abercorn (*see* ABERCORN, D) and was *bur* 17 Sept 1637, leaving by her 1st husb:

1 JAMES STUART, *de jure* 3rd LORD (Baron) CLIFTON, also 4th DUKE OF LENNOX and 1st DUKE OF RICHMOND (so *cr* 8 Aug 1641; *see* RICHMOND and GORDON, D, preliminary remarks, also MORAY, E), KG (1633), PC (S May 1633, E July 1633), ktd 1630, Warden Cinque Ports 1640–42, Ld Steward Household 1641, Pres Cncl of Prince of Wales 1644–45; *b* 6 April 1612; *m* 3 Aug 1637 Mary (*m* 3rd *c* 1664 Col Thomas Howard; *bur* 28 Nov 1685), widow of Lord Herbert of Shurland (*see* PEMBROKE and MONTGOMERY, E), and dau of George Villiers, 1st Duke of Buckingham (*see* JERSEY, E), and *d* 30 March 1655, having had:

(1) ESME STUART, *de jure* 4th LORD (Baron) CLIFTON, also 2nd DUKE OF RICHMOND and (5th of) LENNOX; *b* 2 Nov 1649; *d* unm 10 Aug 1660

(1) MARY Stuart, (*s* bro as) *de jure* BARONESS CLIFTON in her own right; *m*, as his 1st w, Richard Butler, 1st Earl of Arran of the 1662 *cr* (*see* ARRAN, E, preliminary remarks; he *d* Jan 1685/6), and *dsp* 4 July 1667

2 Henry, Seigneur d'Aubigny; *bapt* 2 April 1616; *d* Venice 1632

3 George, Seigneur d'Aubigny; *b* 17 July 1618; *m* Catherine (*m* 2nd 1st Earl of Newburgh (*qv*) and *d* 1650), dau of 2nd Earl of Suffolk (*see* SUFFOLK and BERKSHIRE, E), and was *ka* Edgehill 23 Oct 1642, having by her had issue:

(1) CHARLES STUART, (*s* cousin as) *de jure* 6th LORD (Baron) CLIFTON, also 3rd DUKE OF RICHMOND and (6th of) LENNOX, KG (1661), previously *cr* 10 Dec 1645 BARON STUART OF NEWBURY, Co Berks, and EARL OF LICHFIELD (both E) and subsequently 28 May 1666 BARON OF COBHAM (E), Ld Lt Dorset, Gentleman Bedchamber 1661, Amb Denmark 1671–72; *b* 7 March 1639; *m* 1st Elizabeth (*d* 21 April 1661), widow of Charles Viscount Mansfield and dau and coheir of Richard Rogers, of Bryanston, Dorset; *m* 2nd 31 March 1662 Margaret (*bur* 6 Jan 1666/7), widow of William Lewis and dau of Laurence Banaster, of Papenham, Bucks; *m* 3rd March 1666/7 Frances Teresa Stewart (*d* 15 Oct 1702), gdau of 1st Lord of Blantyre (*d* 1900 edn), and *dsps* 12 Dec 1672, when all his titles expired except the Barony of Clifton

(1) KATHERINE Stuart, **Baroness Clifton** in her own right (recognised as such by Ho Lds 7 Feb 1673/4); *bapt* 5 Dec 1640; *m* 1st *c* 1661 Henry O'BRIEN, Lord O'Brien (*dvp*; *bur* 9 Sept 1678), est s of 7th Earl of Thomond (*see* INCHIQUIN, B), and had issue; *m* 2nd 1679 Sir Joseph Williamson (*dsp* 3 Oct 1701) and *dspms* 2 Nov 1702, having by her 1st husb had, with a s (Donough, *dvm* 5 May 1682):

1a Mary; *b* 7 May 1662; *m* John FitzGerald, 18th Earl of Kildare (*see* LEINSTER, D), and *d* 24 Nov 1683, leaving an only child:

1b Henry; *d* an infant, 1683

2a KATHERINE O'Brien, **Baroness Clifton** in her own right; *b* 29 Jan 1673; *m* 10 July 1688 Edward HYDE, 3rd Earl of Clarendon of the 1661 *cr* (*d* 31 March 1723; *see* above), and *d* New York 11 Aug 1706, having had:

1b EDWARD HYDE, **9th Lord** (Baron) **Clifton**, styled *Viscount Cornbury*; *dvp* unm 12 Feb 1712/3

1b Catherine; *d* young

2b THEODOSIA Hyde, **Baroness Clifton** in her own right; *b* 9 Nov 1695; *m* 24 Aug 1713 **1st Earl of Darnley** (*see* above) and *d* 30 July 1722, leaving issue

4 Ludovic, Seigneur d'Aubigny, Canon Nôtre Dame; *b* 14 Oct 1629; *d* 11 Nov 1665
5 John, Gen of Horse; *b* 23 Oct 1621; *ka* Battle of Bramdene 29 March 1644
6 Bernard, Cdr King's Gds, designated Earl of Lichfield (a title subsequently bestowed on his n; *see* above) but *ka* skirmish of Rowton Heath 26 Sept 1645 before *cr* could take effect
1 Elizabeth; *b* 17 July 1610; *m* March 1626 Henry Frederick, Earl of Arundel (*d* 17 April 1652), and *d* 23 Jan 1673/4, leaving issue (*see* NORFOLK, D)
2 Anne; *b* 23 Nov 1614; *m* 16 Aug 1630 Archibald, Earl of Angus, est s of 1st Marquess of Douglas, and *d* 16 Aug 1646, leaving issue (*see* HAMILTON and BRANDON, D)
3 Frances; *b* 19 March 1617; *m* 10 June 1632 2nd Earl of Portland (*see* PORTLAND, E, preliminary remarks), and *d* 13 March 1693/4, leaving issue. He *d* 17 March 1662/3, leaving issue

DARTMOUTH

Arms: Az. a stag's head cabossed arg. **Crest:** Out of a ducal coronet or a plume of five ostrich feathers alternately arg. and az. **Supporters:** Dexter, a lion arg. semée of fleurs-de-lys sa., ducally crowned or, issuant therefrom five ostrich feathers as in the crest; sinister, a stag arg., unguled or, semée of mullets gu. **Motto:** *Gaudet tentamine virtus* ('Virtue rejoices in trial'). **Creations:** B. (E) 2 Dec 1682, V. and E. (GB) 5 Sept 1711.

THE 10TH EARL OF DARTMOUTH, Viscount Lewisham, of Co Kent, and **Baron Dartmouth,** of Dartmouth, Co Devon (William Legge) [The Rt Hon The Earl of Dartmouth, Blakelea House, Marsden, W Yorks HD7 5AU]; *b* 23 Sept 1949; *s* f 1997; *educ* Eton, Ch Ch Oxford (Sec Union 1969, BA 1971) and Harvard Business Sch; chartered accountant, FCA 1975, fought (C) Leigh, Lancs, Feb 1974 and Stockport S Oct 1974 gen elections, chm and fndr Kirklees Cable

Lineage: THOMAS LEGGE, Sheriff London 1343, Ld Mayor 1346 and 1353; in 1338 lent EDWARD III £300 (some £150,000 in late-1990s terms) to wage the Hundred Years War; allegedly *m* Lady Elizabeth Beauchamp, dau of Thomas, Earl of Warwick (*see* WARWICK, BROOKE and, E), and had, with a yr s (John, MP Surrey 1379, beheaded by Wat Tyler's rebels):

SIMON LEGGE, *m* Joan, dau of John Clavering, and had:

THOMAS LEGGE; *m* Margaret, dau of Sir John Blount, and had an est surv son:

WILLIAM LEGGE; settled Ireland; *m* Anne, only dau of John, son of Miles, Lord Bermingham, and *d* aged 90, leaving:

EDWARD LEGGE; V-Pres Munster during Ltcy of his kinsman Sir Charles Blount, Lord Mountjoy; *m* Mary, dau of Percy Walsh, of Moyvalley, and had issue, with five yr sons and seven daus:

WILLIAM LEGGE; sent by his godfather, Henry Danvers, Earl of Danby, to serve under GUSTAVUS ADOLPHUS OF SWEDEN in the Thirty Years War; later fought under PRINCE MAURICE OF ORANGE in the Low Countries; Keeper Wardrobe to CHARLES I, Groom Bedchamber, royalist in Civil War, wounded and taken prisoner at Battle of Worcester 1651 and would have been executed had his w not contrived his escape from Coventry gaol in her clothes; *m* Elizabeth, est dau and coheir of Sir William Washington (*see* AMERICAN PRESIDENTIAL FAMILIES, 1994, Morris Genealogical Books SA), and *d* 1672, leaving an est son:

GEORGE LEGGE, **1st Baron Dartmouth,** of Dartmouth, Devon (E), so *cr* 2 Dec 1682, with remainder, in default of his own male issue, to his brother William and the heirs male of his body; naval cdr at sea 1667–72, Lt-Govr Portsmouth 1672, Govr 1673, Master of the Horse and Gentleman Bedchamber to JAMES (later II), DUKE OF YORK; Col foot regt 1677, Lt-Gen and Master Ordnance; PC; Adml cmdg Tangier expedn, on his return being granted £10,000; appointed Adml to intercept the PRINCE OF ORANGE (WILLIAM III) 1688 and consequently sent to the Tower after WILLIAM's accession; *d* there 25 Oct 1691; *m* Barbara (*d* 28 Jan 1717/8), dau and sole heir of Sir Henry Archibald, of Abbot's Bromley, and had, with Mary (*m* 1st Philip Musgrave; *m* 2nd John Crawford) and four other daus:

WILLIAM LEGGE, **1st Earl of Dartmouth,** so *cr* 5 Sept 1711, as also VISCOUNT LEWISHAM, of Co Kent (both GB); *b* 14 Oct 1672; a Pncpl Sec State 1710, Ld Privy Seal 1713, a Ld Justice 1714; *m* July 1700 Anne (*d* 30 Nov 1751), dau of Heneage, Earl of Aylesford (*qv*), and had, with other issue:

1 George, *Viscount Lewisham*, *m* Elizabeth (*m* 2nd 24 Jan 1736 7th Baron North (*see* GUILFORD, E) and *d* 21 April 1745), dau and heir of Sir Arthur Kaye, Bt, of Woodsome, York, and *dvp* 29 Aug 1732, leaving, with other issue:
(1) WILLIAM, **2nd Earl.**
(1) Anne; *m* 23 Nov 1760 5th Earl of Cardigan (*see* AILESBURY, M), and *dsp* 12 Nov 1786
2 Heneage; Baron Exchequer 1749; *m* 2 June 1740 Catherine (*d* 12 Nov 1759), dau and coheir of Jonathan Fogg, and *d* 29 Aug 1759, leaving issue:
(1) Heneage; *b* 7 Jan 1747; *m* 1768 Elizabeth, dau of Sir Phillip Musgrave, Bt (*see* MUSGRAVE, Bt, of Hartley Castle, Westmorland), and *dsp* 1 Jan 1827.
(1) Catherine; *m* 5 Oct 1765 Charles Chester, bro of 1st Baron Bagot (*qv*), and *d* 31 May 1819, leaving issue. He *d* 2 April 1793.
3 Henry Bilson, PC; Chllr Exchequer, *b* 29 May 1708, *m* 11 Sept 1750 Mary Stawell, *cr* BARONESS STAWEL [*sic*] OF SOMERTON (*m* 2nd Sept 1768 1st Marquess of Downshire (*qv*) and *d* 29 July 1780), dau of 4th and last Baron Stawell of Somerton of the Jan 1682/3 *cr*, and *d* 23 Aug 1764, leaving issue:
(1) HENRY, 2nd BARON STAWEL OF SOMERTON; *b* 22 Feb 1757, *m* 1 July 1779 Mary (*d* 12 Sept 1804), dau of Viscount Curzon, and *d* 25 Aug 1820, when the Barony expired, leaving issue:
1a Mary, *m* 11 Aug 1803 John, Baron Sherborne (*see* 1970 edn)
1 Barbara, *m* 27 July 1724 Sir Walter Bagot, 5th Bt, of Blithefield, and *d* 29 Oct 1765, leaving issue (*see* BAGOT, B)
2 Anne, *m* Oct 1739 Sir Lister Holte, 5th Bt, and *dsp* July 1740

The 1st EARL *d* 15 Dec 1750; his grandson,

WILLIAM LEGGE, **2nd Earl of Dartmouth,** PC, Recorder Lichfield; *b* 20 June 1731; *m* 11 Jan 1755 Frances Catherine (*d* 24 July 1805), only dau and heir of Sir Charles Gounter Nicoll, KB, by Elizabeth Blundell, afterwards Duchess of Ancaster (*see* LINDSEY and ABINGDON, E), and had issue:

1 GEORGE, **3rd Earl.**
2 Henry, barrister; *b* 23 Jan 1765, *d* 19 April 1844.
3 Arthur Kaye (Sir), KCB, Adml of the Blue, *d* unm 21 May 1835.
4 Edward (Rt. Rev); Bp Oxford, *d* 27 Jan 1827.
5 Augustus George (Rev), MA, Rector Wonston and N Waltham, Hants, Preb Winchester, *b* 21 Aug 1773, *m* 15 Dec 1795 Honora (*d* 2 Oct 1863), est dau of Rev Walter Bagot, brother of 1st Baron Bagot (*qv*), and *d* 1828, leaving, with other issue:
(1) George Augustus (Rev), *b* 8 July 1801, *m* Aug 1825 Frances Augusta (*m* 2nd 1828 Rev S W Cobbe, Rector Ightham, Kent, who *d* 23 Dec 1856), est dau of William Bowyer Atkins, of Braywick Grove, Berks, and *dsp* 16 June 1826
(2) William (Rev), of Mareland, Hants; Rector of Ashtead, *b* 29 July 1802; *d* 6 Nov 1872
(3) Henry (Rev), of Mareland, Surrey, and Bramdean, Hants, Rector of East Lavant, Sussex, *b* 29 June 1803, *m* 4 May 1830 Elizabeth Louisa (*d* 28 Oct 1840), est dau of R-Adml Stair Douglas (*see* QUEENSBERRY, M), and *d* 8 Nov 1879, leaving, with other issue:
1a Augustus George (Rev), MA Oxford, Vicar N Elmham, Norfolk, *b* 20 Jan 1835, *m* 25 Aug 1864 Alice Mary (*d* 21 Feb 1885), est dau of John Greenwood, QC, of Broadhanger, Hants, and *d* 9 Jan 1906, leaving, with other issue:
1b Walter Douglas, *b* 31 Oct 1865, *m* 24 Sept 1907 Rebecca Lang, 3rd dau of Theophilus Hoskin, of Gellings Park, Calstock, Cornwall, and *dsp* 14 Jan 1946
1b Honora Alice Charlotte, *b* 31 July 1867; *d* unm 10 Jan 1947
2b Beatrice Louisa, *b* 7 Dec 1870; *d* unm 29 Aug 1949
3b Frances Mary, *b* 4 Nov 1873; *d* unm 15 July 1965
4b Alice Georgina, *b* 10 June 1875, *m* 12 April 1923 Rev William Arthur Douglas-Hamilton (*see* HAMILTON and BRANDON, D), and *d* 1 Feb 1958
2a Charles Egerton, DL, JP Sussex, High Sheriff 1901, *b* 22 May 1840; *d* 19 March 1913
(1) Charlotte Anne, *m* 15 Dec 1825 Rev Hon Arthur Phillip Perceval, and *d* 21 June 1856, leaving issue (*see* EGMONT, E)
(2) Honora Augusta, *m* 1855 Gen. William Cowper Coles and *d* 27 Dec 1897. He *d* 27 Aug 1867
(3) Louisa Frances Catherine, *m* 4 April 1866 Rev Alfred Bishop, Rector of Martyr Worthy, Hants, and *d* 4 June 1893. He *d* 29 Sept 1885
1 Charlotte, *m* 24 Sept 1795 1st Baron Feversham (*qv*) and *d* 5 Nov 1848, leaving issue

The 2nd EARL *d* 15 July 1801; his est son,

GEORGE LEGGE, **3rd Earl of Dartmouth,** KG (1805; invested but never installed) who had been called up to Ho Lds *vp* in his f's Barony, *b* 3 Oct 1755, *m* 24 Sept 1782 Frances (*d* 21 Nov 1838), dau of 3rd Earl of Aylesford (*qv*), and had five sons and seven daus, of whom:

1 WILLIAM, **4th Earl.**
2 Heneage, Commr Customs, *b* 29 Feb 1788, *m* 19 July 1821 Mary (*d* 4 June 1848), dau of Maj — Johnstone, and *d* 12 Dec 1844, leaving issue:
(1) Mary, *m* 31 March 1846 F W Mackenzie, MD, Fell Univ Coll
3 Arthur Charles, DL Kent; Gen, Hon Col 1st Vol Bn South Staffs Regt; *b* 25 June 1800; *m* 1st 1 June 1827 Anne Frederica (*d* 31 Aug 1829), dau of 1st Earl of Sheffield (*see* STANLEY OF ALDERLEY, SHEFFIELD and, B), and had a son; *m* 2nd 29 Aug 1837 Caroline (*d* 7 March 1882), 4th dau of James Charles P Bouwens, and *d* 18 May 1890, having by her had issue:
(2) Alfred Arthur Kaye (Rev), MA Oxford, barrister; *b* 31 July 1839, *m* 9 Oct 1888 Lydia Annie Georgiana (*d* 25 Nov 1931), dau of Hon Oliver Lambart, RN (*see* CAVAN, E), and *dsp* 22 Jan 1906
(1) Alice Mary, *m* 6 Jan 1880 Rev Edward Samson, Rector Armitage, Vicar Pipe Redware, and *d* 31 Jan 1914, having had issue
4 Henry, DCL. (Rev), Vicar Lewisham 1831–79, *b* 1803, *m* 12 May 1842 Marian (*d* 10 July 1890 aged 75), dau of Sir Frederick L Rogers, 7th Bt, and *d* 13 Feb 1887

1 Louisa, *m* 17 Feb 1807 2nd Baron Bagot (*qv*) and *d* 13 Aug 1816, leaving issue
2 Charlotte, *m* 1816 Very Rev Hon G Neville Grenville, Master Magdalene Coll Cambridge, Dean Windsor, and *d* 15 June 1877, leaving issue
3 Harriet, *m* 1815 Gen Hon Sir Edward Paget, GCB, and *d* 11 March 1855, leaving issue (*see* ANGLESEY, M)
4 Barbara Maria, *m* 1820 Francis Newdegate and *d* 22 April 1840, leaving issue

The 3rd EARL *d* 10 Nov 1810; his son,

WILLIAM LEGGE, **4th Earl of Dartmouth**, DCL, FRS, FSA, *b* 29 Nov 1784, *m* 1st 5 April 1821 Frances Charlotte (*d* 4 Oct 1823), dau of 2nd Earl Talbot (*see* SHREWSBURY and WATERFORD, E), and had an only surv s:

1 WILLIAM WALTER, **5th Earl**

The 4th EARL *m* 2nd 25 Oct 1828 Frances (*d* 12 Aug 1849), 2nd dau of 5th Viscount Barrington (*see* 1970 edn), and by her had six sons and nine daus, of whom:

2 George Barrington (Rev), Capt Rifle Bde, afterwards Vicar of Packington, Warwicks, 1860–64, and Vicar of Whittington 1878–82, *b* 19 Dec 1831, *m* 9 Oct 1860 Sophia Frances Margaret (*d* 15 Oct 1895), only dau of John Levett, of Wichnor Park, Staffs, and *d* 9 Dec 1900, having had, with other issue:

(1) Arthur Edward John, Capt and Brevet Maj Worcs Regt WW I (despatches), *b* 25 May 1863, *m* 23 Aug 1918 Lucy Isabel (*d* 7 Oct 1940), widow of Maj J C Arthington Walker, Queen's Bays, and 3rd dau of Sir Stuart Saunders Hogg (*see* HOGG, Bt), and *d* 21 May 1934

(2) Robert George, BA Oxford, *b* 3 Aug 1864, *m* 11 July 1896 Margaret Emily Agnes (*d* 27 Aug 1925), dau of Frederick Evans, and *dsp* 10 Dec 1905

(3) Hugh (Rev), Rector Newbold de Verdun, Leicester, CF 1916, served WW I with Ambulance Corps, Serbian Army 1915, subsequently as gunner RGA; *b* 27 April 1870; *educ* Trin Coll Oxford (MA), *m* 26 April 1917 Bessie (*d* 27 May 1950), yst dau of Richard Pether, of Sandford-on-Thames, and *d* 9 Oct 1944, leaving issue:

1a John Barrington, Hon Major RA WW II (wounded); *b* 2 Sept 1918, *educ* Haileybury, *m* 4 Dec 1940 *Gertrude Sarah [Mrs John Legge, The Porch House, Dodford, Northants], dau of Frederick Wood, of Little Preston, Capes, Northants, and *d* 1989, leaving issue:

1b +Hugh; *b* 22 Aug 1945, *educ* Haileybury and RMA Sandhurst, Lt RA. *m* 5 Feb 1977 (*divorce* 1995) Julia, dau of J H Taylor, of Newcastle, Staffs, and has:

1c +Robin Francis, *b* 13 Nov 1980

2c +Colin Brendan, *b* 3 Nov 1982

1b *Jane [Mrs John Day, c/o Porch House, Dodford, Northants NN7 4SX]; *b* 31 May 1941; *m* 23 July 1977 *John Grace Day, son of K F G Day, of Walsall

2b Hannah, *b* 29 May 1947; *d* 7 May 1987

(1) Margaret, *b* 22 Aug 1872; *d* unm 3 April 1957

3 Edward Henry, Assist Serjeant-at-Arms H of C, MA, Lt-Col Coldstream Gds, *b* 23 April 1834, *m* 15 Jan 1873 Cordelia Twysden (*d* 19 March 1915), 3rd dau of Walter Hele Molesworth (*see* MOLESWORTH-ST AUBYN, Bt), and *d* 16 Aug 1900, having had, with other issue:

(1) Walter Traversari, Papal Chamberlain and Kt SMO Malta, Grand Cross Order of St Sylvester; ctee clerk H of C, Pncpl Treasury, Capt Coldstream Gds (SR) WW I (despatches, 1914 star), *b* 17 Oct 1874, *educ* Trin Coll Oxford (BA), *m* 18 July 1905 Jane Agnes Maud (*d* 19 Oct 1953), widow of Major Henry Anstruther Kinloch (*see* KINLOCH, Bt, of Gilmerton), and dau of Sir Reginald Robert Bruce Guinness (*see* GUINNESS, Bt) and *dsp* 19 Aug 1949

(2) Montague George Bentinck, DSO (1916), R-Adml, ADC to HM EDWARD VIII 1936, served WW I (despatches), *b* 16 Dec 1883; *d* unm 11 Feb 1951

(3) John Douglas, MC, Capt Coldstream Gds (SR), served WW I (despatches) and WW II 1940–43, *b* 5 Dec 1886, *m* 30 July 1917 Haroldine (*d* 30 Oct 1970), dau of Harold S Peck, of Chicago, and *d* 30 Dec 1954, leaving:

1a *Virginia Lois [The Hon Mrs Nial O'Neill, Crowfield House, Crowfield, Ipswich, Suffolk IP6 9TP], *b* 5 May 1922, *m* 21 June 1966 Hon Nial Arthur Ramleh O'Neill (*d* 1980), yst son of 1st Baron Rathcavan (*qv*)

(4) Heneage Cecil, DSC (1919), Capt RN, served WW I and WW II, *b* 17 Aug 1890; *d* unm 28 Sept 1956

(1) Lois Marjorie, *b* 18 Nov 1881, *m* 7 Nov 1906 Maj Ernest Wriothesley Denny, DSO, DL, of Garboldisham Manor, Diss, Norfolk, 19th Hus, son of Thomas Anthony Denny, of Connaught Place, London W, and *d* 9 March 1961, leaving issue. He *d* 20 Oct 1949

(1) Cecilia Katharine, *b* 27 Aug 1895, *m* 30 Dec 1916 Capt Reginald Hugh Errington, RN (ret), of Tostock Old Hall, Bury St Edmunds, Suffolk, son of George Henry Forbes Errington, of Chadwell, Essex, and *d* 19–, leaving issue (*see* HUNTINGFIELD, B). He *d* 15 April 1976

4 Augustus (Rt Rev), DD Oxford, Bp Lichfield 1891–1913, *b* 28 Nov 1839, *m* 3 Jan 1877 Fanny Louisa (*d* 23 Dec 1911), 2nd dau of William Bruce Stopford-Sackville (*see* COURTOWN, E), and *d* 15 March 1913, leaving:

(1) Francis Augustus, AMICE, *b* 2 Jan 1880, *educ* Charterhouse and King's Coll Lond, *m* 3 June 1909 Mabel Clara Arden (*d* 17 March 1963), only child of Charles Lucena, of Westwick, Easthampstead, Berks, and *d* 2 June 1966, leaving issue:

1a +Christopher Augustus Sackville [Christopher Legge Esq, c/o 1013 Mass Ave NE, Washington DC 20002, USA], barrister Inner Temple 1936, MS in Library Service, Columbia U, New York (1954), Head Librarian American U of Beirut 1954–57, Librarian Bradford (Mass.) Junior Coll 1957–66, Base Librarian RAF Bentwaters, Woodbridge, Suffolk 1966, *b* 27 Sept 1911, *educ* Eton and Worcester Coll Oxford (BA 1938, MA 1939), *m* 1st 5 Oct 1952 Kari (*d* 1971), dau of Senatspräsident Walther Brebeck, of Eutin, Holstein; *m* 2nd 1979 *Signe White and has had by his 1st w:

1b Robert Augustus, *b* 29 May 1953; *d* 19–

2b +Christopher Walter, *b* 24 July 1955

1b *Barbara Ingrid, *b* 13 June 1960

1a Fanny Angela Mary; *b* 18 Dec 1912, *m* 4 April 1940 Lt-Col Philip Lewis (*d* 1968), Somerset LI, son of Egbert Lewis, of Bath, and *d* 19 April 1997, leaving issue:

1b *Christopher Julian Arden [Christopher Lewis Esq, Lone Barn, E Garston, Berks RG17 7EU], *b* 1941; *m* 1972 *Caroline Dyson

1b *Lavinia Zaria [Mrs Neville Howard, Deer Park Lodge, Jolunby, Cumbria CA11 0UU]; *b* 1943; *m* 1969 *Lt-Col (Murray Bernard) Neville Cyprian Howard (*see* NORFOLK, D) and has issue

(2) George Stopford, *b* 5 April 1882; *d* unm 24 April 1952

(1) Beatrice Mary Caroline *b* 18 Dec 1883, *m* 2 Jan 1919 Rev Thomas Sidney Goudge, DSO, MA. He *d* 15 Oct 1954

(2) Rhoda Stephanie *b* 28 June 1887; *d* unm 28 Sept 1973

5 Charles Gounter; *b* 9 May 1842, Inspr Constabulary Midland Dist, Lt Rifle Bde, Ch Constable Lancs; *m* 2 June 1868 Mary (*d* 13 Dec 1896), est dau of Very Rev Thomas Garnier, Dean Lincoln, and *d* 15 Nov 1907, having had, with other issue:

(1) William Kaye, CMG (1918), DSO (1917), Col Essex Regt, Hon Brig-Gen 1926, served Boer War 1899–1902 (despatches) and WW I (despatches, two brevets, Croix de Guerre), *b* 13 June 1869; *m* 9 June 1902 Constance Adeline (*d* 1 Jan 1964), est dau of Hon James David Palmer, MLC, of Bloemfontein, Orange Free State Prov, S Africa, and *d* 29 March 1946, having had issue:

1a Paul Keppel, Australian Cwlth Serv, Capt IA WW II (despatches twice), *b* 25 Jan 1906, *educ* Wellington, *m* 18 Nov 1948 *Nellie Ruth, dau of Percy Edwin Dewey, of Norfolk Island, Australia, and *d* 19–

2a Charles James, *b* 16 Aug 1908, *d* 1911

3a +Peter; W/Cdr RAF, Maj RA WW II (wounded, despatches twice), *b* 28 Jan 1910, *educ* Wellington; *m* 1st 14 Dec 1937 (*divorce* 1953) Mary Claire, est dau of William Dwyer, of Elmville, Rushbrooke, Co Cork, and has issue:

1b +Michael William [Michael Legge Esq, 20 Fitzwilliam Place, Dublin, Ireland], *b* 15 Nov 1938, *educ* Downside; *m* 1965 (*divorce* 19–) Kim Hoang and has issue:

1d +Julian, *b* 1969

1d *Nicola, *b* 1967

2b +David Anthony, *b* 24 Jan 1941, *educ* Downside; *m* 1966 *Mary, dau of Dr D Roden, of 81 Wellington Road, Dublin, and has issue:

1d +Dermot, *b* 1970

2d +Thomas David, *b* 1974

3d +Andrew, *b* 1976

1d *Jennifer Claire, *b* 1968

2d *Anna Constance, *b* 1972

1b *Susan Noelle Ann, *b* 25 Dec 1943, *m* 1966 *Paul and has issue:

1c *Karen Jane, *b* 1967

2c *Joanna Ruth, *b* 1969

3c *Sophie Ann, *b* 1972

4c *Emma Claire, *b* 1973

5c *Rachel, *b* 1978

3a (cont.) Peter Legge *m* 2nd 31 Dec 1955 *Violet Bertha, only dau of George Wallace, of Alexandra House, Alresford, Essex

(2) John Augustus, RD, Lt-Cdr RNR, offr P&O Co 1892–1901, Master Attendant and Jt Police Magistrate Colombo, Ch Offr Naval Exam Serv Ceylon 1902–15, WW I as Naval Tport Offr (1st Grade) 1915–20 (despatches) and Ch Naval Exam Off Shipping, Ceylon (despatches), WW II 1940045 as Welfare Offr Wincanton Dist; Yr Bro Trin Ho, Liveryman Master Mariners' Co, dir Bukit Selangor Rubber Estates and Kampong Kuanton Rubber, FRGS, AINA, FRES and NGS of USA, *b* 31 July 1871; *m* 4 Jan 1908 Grace Margaret (*d* 28 Jan 1957), 2nd surv dau of Alexander Henderson Dunsmure, FRGS, of 46 Egerton Crescent, London SW3, and *d* 21 March 1945, leaving issue:

1a +(John) Michael Derek [Michael Legge Esq, Homefield, Nunney, Somerset TA11 4LG]; *b* 21 July 1913, *educ* Eton, *m* 8 June 1945 *Esme Edith, 2nd Offr WRNS, est dau of V-Adml Cyril St Clair Cameron, CBE, and has:

1b Derek Rupert Spicer; *b* 22 March 1949; *m* 1990 *Jacqueline Ann Hollaway [Mrs Derek legge, Strumble Cottage, 4 Primrose Hill, Bath BA1 2US], and *d* 5 Feb 1996, leaving:

1c +Henry Rupert Cameron, *b* 1993

1c *Victoria Alice, *b* 1990

1b *Elizabeth Angela, *b* 29 Sept 1946

2a +David Alexander Keppel, CBE (1970, MBE 1953) [Col David Legge CBE, Sandwell, Marston Magna, Yeovil, Somerset], Col Roy Fus WW II (wounded), *b* 7 Jan 1916, *educ* Eton, *m* 2 Dec 1944 *Patria, 3rd dau of Lt-Col Charles Bernard Raphael Hornung, DL, JP, of Ivorys, Cowfold, Sussex, and has issue:

1b +Richard Charles Gounter [Richard Legge Esq, Furneaux Farmhouse, Whatfield, Ipswich, Suffolk], *b* 21 May 1948, *educ* Oakham Sch; *m* 1972 *Lesley Mayfield Finch, dau of Frederick Ledger, of Brompton House, Malvern, and has issue:

1c +Jonathan Alexander Heneage, *b* 1979

2c +Thomas Henry Finch, *b* 1983

1b *Anthea Frances [Mrs Richard Roundell, Dorfold Hall, Nantwich, Cheshire], *b* 15 May 1946; *m* 4 Oct 1969 *Richard Charles Roundell, est son of C W Roundell, of Dorfold Hall, Nantwich (*see* 1970 edn DYSART, E), and has issue:

1c *Charles Henry, *b* 1975

1c *Laura Ann, *b* 1972; *m* 1996 *Hon Orlando William Montagu (*see* SANDWICH, E)

1a *Margaret Elizabeth [Miss Margaret Legge, Tutton Hill House, Colerne, Chippenham, Wilts]; *b* 19 Oct 1908

(3) Thomas Charles, Hon Lt 3rd Bn Imp Yeo Boer War 1901–02, Forest Dept Transvaal, *b* 11 Sept 1872, *m* 22 April 1903 Ivy Emily (*d* 1 Aug 1961), yst dau of J Reed, of Zeerust, Transvaal, and *d* 1949, having had issue:

1a Gounter Heneage Hugh, FICE, FASCE, MSA, ICE, MSAACE, BScEng Witwatersrand U, ptnr Watermeyer Legge Piesold and Uhlmann, Consulting Engrs, Johannesburg and London, Chm SA Assoc Consulting Engrs 1957–58, *b* 2 Jan 1909, *m* 9 Jan 1936 *Joyce Kathleen, BA, yst dau of Thomas Angus Brown, and *d* 1992, leaving:

1b +Trevor later Traver Francis Hugh [Traver Legge Esq, 20 Cherry Glebe, Mersham, Ashford, Kent TN25 6NL]; *b* 7 Aug 1942; *educ* Witwatersrand U (BSc (Eng)) and Imperial Coll, London (DIC, MSc); *m* 1972 *Helen Dorothy, dau of John Downie, of Johannesburg, and has issue:

1c *Angela Claire; *b* 1975

2c *Janet Helen; *b* 1980

2a Ronald Derek Barrington, *b* 15 Feb 1918, *d* 22 Feb 1925

1a *Mary Charlotte Lois [Mrs George Low, Cramond, Vipingo, via Mombasa, Kenya], *b* 1905, BCom Witwatersrand U; *m* 8 Sept 1934 *George Wilson Low, MBE, Colonial Veterinary Service, Kenya, only son of McNaughton Low, of Edinburgh

(4) Francis Cecil, CBE (1919), *b* 14 Sept 1873; *d* unm 24 Oct 1940

(5) Ronald George, Capt Devon Regt, Adj 1st Herefs Regt, Boer War with Imp Yeo 1900–01, *b* 4 July 1878, *m* 19 Nov 1910 Phyllis Mildred Harriet (*m* 2nd 17 April 1922 Lt-Col Richard Romer Claude Baggallay, DSO, MC, son of Claude Baggally, KC, of Wilderwick, East Grinstead, Sussex, and *d* 13 Aug 1967), dau of Rev Mortimer Ford, of Yarcombe, Devon, and was *ka* 18 Dec 1914, leaving issue:

1a Rupert Mortimer, Maj Roy Fus WW II, *b* 8 Sept 1911, *educ* Malvern, *m* 24 Feb 1940 Anne (*d* 1982), dau of Sir James Adam, CBE, KC, of Colne Park, Essex, and was *ka* Italy 5 Sept 1944, leaving issue:

1b +Rupert James [Rupert Legge Esq, Woodend Gdn Cottage, Thirsk, Yorks YO7 4DP], Lt 3rd Bn Roy Regt Fus, *b* 29 March 1944, *educ* Wellington and RMA Sandhurst, *m* 2 Nov 1968 *Jacqueline Hope, yr dau of Maj E T H Ubsdell, Somerset LI, and Mrs R E R Robinson, of Windmill Cottage Little Chesterton, Bicester, Oxon, and has:

1c +Edward James, *b* 15 April 1971

1c *Philippa Georgina, *b* 23 April 1972

1b *(Christian Anne) Victoria, *b* 4 Jan 1942; *m* 1973 (*divorce* 1993) Christopher T Sharman and has issue:

1c *Matthew Rupert Derek, *b* 1975

2c *Thomas Christopher James, *b* 1977

3c *Patrick William Adam, *b* 1979

(1) Helen Beatrice, *b* 18 July 1870; *d* unm 4 Sept 1934

6 Heneage, MP 1900–06, Col cmdg 9th Lancers, Capt Coldstream Gds; *b* 3 July 1845; *d* unm 1 Nov 1911

1 Frances Elizabeth, *m* 22 April 1862 Maj-Gen George Bruce Michell and *d* 13 March 1922 aged 92, leaving issue. He *d* 11 Feb 1866

2 Katharine, *m* 9 April 1863 Col Robert Jameson Eustace ROBERTSON later EUSTACE (roy licence 1875), 60th Rifles, and *d* 1 July 1914, leaving issue. He *d* 1 April 1889

3 Florence, *m* 11 Feb 1858 Nathaniel Barnardiston, DL, of The Ryes, Sudbury, Suffolk, and *d* 27 March 1917, leaving issue. He *d* 23 Feb 1916

4 Barbara Caroline, *m* 24 Nov 1875 Rt. Rev Huyshe Wolcott Yeatman-Biggs, DD, Bp Worcester 1905–18, Bp Coventry 1918–22, and *d* 5 Jan 1909, leaving issue. He *d* 14 April 1922

5 Wilhelmina, *m* 30 June 1874 John Townsend Brooke, of Haughton Hall, Shifnal, and *d* 31 Dec 1928, leaving issue. He *d* 31 Jan 1899

The 4th EARL *d* 22 Nov 1853; his son,

WILLIAM WALTER LEGGE, **5th Earl of Dartmouth**, Ld Lt Staffs, MP S Staffs 1849–53, Hon Col 1st Vol Bn S Staffs Regt; *b* 12 Aug 1823; *m* 9 June 1846 Lady Augusta Finch (*d* 1 Dec 1900), dau of 5th Earl of Aylesford (*qv*), and had, with four daus (*d* unm):

1 WILLIAM HENEAGE, **6th Earl**

2 Henry Charles (Sir) GCVO (1920), Col Coldstream Gds, Groom-in-Waiting 1889–93 and Equerry-in-Waiting to TM QUEEN VICTORIA 1893–1901, EDWARD VII 1901–10 and GEORGE V 1910–15, Extra Equerry 1915, Paymaster Household 1915–20, Registrar and Sec Order Merit from 1907, served Suakim campaign 1885 (despatches, brevet Maj), Orders of Jesus Christ of Portugal, Isabella of Spain, St Stanislas of Russia, St Maurice and St Lazarus of Italy and Redeemer of Greece, *b* 4 Nov 1852, *m* 25 Oct 1884 Amy Gwendoline Lambart (Maid of Honour to HM QUEEN VICTORIA 1877–84; *d* 28 Jan 1927), dau of Gustavus William Lambart, of Beau Parc (*see* 1970 edn LAMBART, Bt), and *d* 20 June 1924, having had issue:

(1) Nigel Walter Henry LEGGE later LEGGE-BOURKE (roy licence 26 April 1911), of Hayes, Beau Parc, Co Meath, Lt Coldstream Gds, Page of Honour to HM EDWARD VII 1902–06, *b* 13 Nov 1889, *m* 3 June 1913 Lady Victoria Alexandrina Wynn-Carrington (*d* 28 March 1966, having *m* 2nd 10 April 1916 Maj Hon Edric Alfred Cecil Weld-Forester (*d* 24 Sept 1963), son of 5th Baron Forester, *qv*), yst dau of 1st and last Marquess of Lincolnshire KG (*see* CARRINGTON, B), and was *ka* 30 Oct 1914, leaving:

1a (Edward Alexander) Henry (Harry) (Sir), KBE (1960), DL (Cambs 1955); Page of Honour to HM GEORGE V 1924–30, Maj RHG (Blues) WW II (wounded), ADC to Br Amb Cairo 1941–42, MP (C) Isle of Ely 1945–73, chm Conservative Party Def, Science and Technology Ctees 1922; *b* 16 May 1914 (HM QUEEN ALEXANDRA stood sponsor), *educ* Eton, *m* 10 June 1938 *Catherine Jean [Lady Legge-Bourke, 121 Dovehouse St, London SW3 6JZ], 3rd dau of Col Sir Arthur Grant, of Monymusk, 10th Bt (*qv*), and *d* 21 May 1973, leaving issue:

1b +William Nigel Henry [William Legge-Bourke Esq, Penmyarth, Glanusk Park, Crickhowell, Powys NP8 1LP]; *b* 12 July 1939; *educ* Eton and Magdalene Coll Cambridge (MA); Capt RHG, sometime Adj, Dep Lt Powys 1997; *m* 2 June 1964 *Hon (Elizabeth) Shân (Josephine) Bailey, LVO, Ld Lt Powys 1998–, only child of 3rd Baron Glanusk (*qv*), and has issue:

1c +Harry Russell, *b* 20 Feb 1972; Page of Honour to HM THE QUEEN 1985–87; commissioned Welsh Gds 1992 (despatches NI 1994)

1c *Alexandra ('Tiggy') Shân, *b* 1 April 1965; personal assistant to HRH THE PRINCE OF WALES 1994–97

2c *Zara Victoria, *b* 26 May 1966; *m* 1985 (*divorce* 1997) Capt Richard Grosvenor Plunkett-Ernle-Erle-Drax and has issue (*see* DUNSANY, B)

2b +Heneage [Heneage Legge-Bourke Esq, c/o 121 Dovehouse St, London SW3 6JZ]; *b* 13 March 1948; *educ* Eton; Page of Honour to HM THE QUEEN 1963–64; *m* 1978 *Maria Clara, dau of Vasco de Sá-Carneiro, of Lisbon, and has:

1c +Edward Alexander Heneage; *b* 1984

1c *Eleanor Jean Maria; *b* 1980

1b *Victoria Lindsay, LVO (1986) [Miss Victoria Legge-Bourke LVO, 21 Eccleston Sq, London SW1V 1NS]; *b* 12 Feb 1950; Extra Lady-in-Waiting to HRH THE PRINCESS ROYAL 1977–

(1) Victoria Alexandrina Stella; *b* 31 July 1885 (HM QUEEN VICTORIA stood sponsor); *m* 1st 27 Aug 1909 Maj Richard Gerard Wellesley Williams-Bulkeley, Welsh Gds, only son of Sir Richard Henry Williams-Bulkeley, 12th Bt (*qv*), and had issue. He *d* 28 March 1918 of wounds recd in action. She *m* 2nd 28 Sept 1921 (*divorce* 1944, resumed 1st husb's name by deed poll 1946) Roland Frank Holdway Norman, Capt Leics Regt and RAF, and *d* 22 April 1965, having had further issue. He *d* 2 June 1958

The 5th EARL *d* 4 Aug 1891; his son,

WILLIAM HENEAGE LEGGE, **6th Earl of Dartmouth**, GCVO (1928), KCB (1917), PC (1885), CA and JP Staffs, JP Salop; *b* 6 May 1851; *educ* Eton and Ch Ch Oxford; MP (C) W Kent 1878–85 and Lewisham 1885–91, V-Chamberlain Household 1885–86 and 1886–91, Hon LLD Dartmouth Coll USA, Hon Col 5th S Staffs Regt (VD), Hon Col 46th N Midland Div Trg RASC (TD; *m* 18 Dec 1879 Lady Mary Coke, CBE (*d* 28 Dec 1929), 4th dau of 2nd Earl of Leicester (*qv*), and *d* 11 March 1936, leaving:

1 WILLIAM LEGGE, **7th Earl of Dartmouth**, GCVO (1934), TD, DL, JP Staffs, LCC 1907, MP (C) W Bromwich 1910–18, High Bailiff Westminster 1930–42, Lt-Col Staffs Yeo, hon Col 1943–51, formerly hon Col 7th Bn WR Regt, 4th Cl Order of the Nile, executed by roy warrant 18 Oct 1928 office of Ld Gt Chamberlain 1928–36, *b* 22 Feb 1881, *m* 7 Dec 1905 Lady Ruperta Wynn-Carrington (*d* 26 June 1963), 3rd dau of 1st and last Marquess of Lincolnshire, KG (*see* CARRINGTON, B), and *d* 28 Feb 1958, leaving:

(1) William, *Viscount Lewisham*, Capt Staffs Yeo (TA) WW II 1939–42, *b* 23 Jan 1913, *educ* Eton and Hertford Coll Oxford, *ka* El Alamein Oct 1942

(1) *Mary Cecilia [The Lady Mary Findlay, 2 South Close, The Precincts, Canterbury, Kent CT1 2EJ]; *b* 27 Oct 1906, *m* 17 Oct 1929 Cdr Noel Charles Mansfeldt Findlay (*d* 9 April 1976), RN, s of Sir Mansfeldt de Cardonnel Findlay, GBE, KCMG, CB (a descendant of the DUKE OF MONMOUTH via his illegitimate dau Mary Hicks, w of James de Cardonnel), and has issue:

1a *Jonathan Mansfeldt [Cdr Jonathan Findlay RN (ret), Eden Lodge, Droxford, Hants]; *b* 1933; *m* 1962 *Jutta, dau of Gen Karl von Graffen, and has:

1b *Christopher Mansfeldt Karl; *b* 1967

1b *Caroline Ilse; *b* 1962

2b *Angela Mary; *b* 1964

2a *Martin Charles [Martin Findlay Esq, Ledburn Manor, Leighton Buzzard, Beds]; *b* 1935; *m* 1966 *Davina Margaret, dau of Maj Sir Thomas Calderwood Dundas, 7th Bt, MBE (*see* 1970 edn), and has issue:

1b *Mark Simon, *b* 1967

2b *Adam James, *b* 1969

1a *Jane Elizabeth [Mrs Jeremy Debenham, Reeds Farm, Sayers Common, Hassocks, W Sussex BN6 9JQ], *b* 1930; *m* 1961 *Jeremy Debenham and has:

1b *Catherine Mary; *b* 1962

2b *Henrietta Jane; *b* 1965; *m* 1991 *Oliver George Curtis and has:

1c *Job Thomas; *b* 1995

1c *Grace Rebecca; *b* 1996

3b *Susannah Elizabeth; *b* 1968

(2) *Elizabeth, DCVO (1989 CVO 1976) [The Lady Elizabeth Basset DCVO, 67 Cottesmore Court, Stanford Rd, London W8], Extra Woman of the Bedchamber to HM QUEEN ELIZABETH THE QUEEN MOTHER 1959–; *b* 5 March 1908; *m* 31 Oct 1931 Ronald Lambert Basset (*d* 1972), only son of Arthur Francis Basset, of 7 Carlos Place, London W1 (*see* SALUSBURY–TRELAWNY, Bt), and has issue:

1a *Bryan Ronald, CBE [Bryan Basset Esq CBE, Quarles, Wells-next-the-Sea, Norfolk NR23 1RY]; *b* 1932; *m* 1960 *Lady Carey Elizabeth Coke, dau of 5th Earl of Leicester (*qv*), and has issue:

1b *David Francis; *b* 1961

2b *Michael James; *b* 1963; *m* 7 Sept 1996 *Caroline, er dau of Philip Bailey, late of Bristol

3b *James Bryan; *b* 1968; formerly a Page of Honour to HM THE QUEEN

(3) Diana, CStJ, one of HM QUEEN ELIZABETH (later THE QUEEN MOTHER)'s train-bearers at the Coronation 1937; *b* 14 Nov 1910; *m* 1st 27 Sept 1937 Maj Hon John Hamilton-Russell, MC, The Royals, 3rd son of 9th Viscount Boyne (*qv*), and has issue. He was accidentally *kas* Sicily 19 Aug 1943. She *m* 2nd 2 June 1946 Brig Adrian Lewis Matthews, OBE, MC, JP, RA, son of Maj Barbran Henry Matthews, of 14 St James's Square, Bath, and *d* 25 Feb 1970, leaving further issue. He *d* 28 Oct 1976

(4) *Barbara [The Lady Barbara Kwiatkowski, The Bothy, Patshull Park, Burnhill Green, Wolverhampton, Staffs], WW II in FANY; *b* 24 June 1916; *m* 4 Feb 1945 *Lt Adam W Kwiatkowski, BSc, Polish Army, son of Judge Witold Jan Kwiatkowski, of Krakow, Poland, and has issue:

1a *Jan Witfold; *b* 17 Nov 1945; *m* 25 July 1968 *Sarah Hope, dau of Christopher Challis, of Pineways, Grays Park, Stoke Poges, Bucks, and has issue:

1b *Adam Witold; *b* 1972

2b *Daniel Christopher; *b* 1974

3b *William; *b* 1977

4b *Alexander George; *b* 1979

2a *Marek William; *b* 28 May 1947; *m* 1977 *Belinda Mary Graham, dau of Maj John Cecil Graham Moon (*see* MOON, Bt, of Portman Sq, Middx), and has issue:

1b *Stefan Marek; *b* 1981

3a *Christopher [Christopher Kwiatkowski Esq, The Stables, Patshull, Albrighton, Salop]; *b* 28 March 1951; *m* 1978 *Allison Porter, dau of R P Yates, of Hinnington Grange, Shifnal, Salop, and has issue:

1b *Marek; *b* 1987
1b *Anna; *b* 1989
4a *Michael Andrew Adam; *b* 17 Dec 1955; *m* 1978 (*divorce* 1981) Scylla Nina Antoinette, yst dau of Roderick W Parkyn, of Pen-y-Lan, Hardwicke, Herefs
(5) *Josceline Gabrielle; WW II in FANY; *b* 22 May 1918; *m* 16 Sept 1946 *7th Marquess of Donegall (*qv*) and has issue
2 Gerald, Capt 7th Bn S Staffs, Lt 4th Bn Lincs Regt; *b* 30 April 1882; *ka* 9 Aug 1915
3 HUMPHRY, **8th Earl**
1 Dorothy, OBE (1945), JP Staffs, Pres Staffs Branch BRCS to 1945; *b* 24 June 1883; *m* 3 Oct 1907 Col Francis Hugo Lindley Meynell, DSO, RFA (TF), of Hoar Cross, Burton on Trent, est son of Hon Frederick George Lindley Meynell (*see* HALIFAX, E), and *d* 28 July 1974, leaving issue
2 Joan Margaret, JP Staffs; *b* 21 Feb 1885; *d* unm 4 July 1939

The 7th EARL's brother,

HUMPHRY LEGGE, **8th Earl of Dartmouth**, CVO (1947), DSO (1919), KPM, DL (Staffs 1927–39); Cdr RN Staffs, Assist Ch Constable Staffs 1928–32, Ch Constable Berks 1932–53, served WW I (despatches), Grand Offr Order of Orange-Nassau Netherlands; *b* 14 March 1888; *m* 10 April 1923 *Roma Ernestine [The Rt Hon Roma Countess of Dartmouth, 15B The Bedford Towers, Cavendish Place, Brighton, Sussex], er dau of Sir Ernest Burford Horlick, 2nd Bt (*qv*), and *d* 16 Oct 1962, leaving:

1 GERALD HUMPHRY LEGGE, **9th Earl of Dartmouth**; *b* 26 April 1924; *educ* Eton; Capt Coldstream Gds WW II 1942–45 (despatches), FCA 1951, dir Rea Bros 1958–89, Chm: Roy Choral Soc 1970–92, Anglo-Brazilian Soc 1975–94, Hon LLD Dartmouth Coll USA 1969, Grand Official Order Cruzeiro Do Sul Brazil 1994; *m* 1st 21 July 1948 (*divorce* 1976) Raine (*m* 2nd 1976 8th Earl Spencer (*qv*); *m* 3rd 8 July 1993 (*divorce* Jan 1995) Count Jean-François de Chambrun), memb GLC Richmond-upon-Thames 1967–72, Chm: GLC Historic Bldgs Bd 1968–97, UK exec ctee European Architectural Heritage year 1975, Ocean Wilsons Hldgs 1977–97, memb English Tourist Bd 1971–73, only dau of Alexander George McCorquodale, of the White Lodge, Speen, Berks (*see* 1970 edn McCORQUODALE OF NEWTON, B); *m* 2nd 1 Oct 1980 *Gwendoline May formerly [The Rt Hon The Countess of Dartmouth, The Manor House, Chipperfield, Herts WD4 9BN], w of — and dau of Charles René Seguin, and *d* 14 Dec 1997, leaving by his 1st w:
(1) WILLIAM LEGGE, **10th and present Earl of Dartmouth**
(2) +RUPERT [The Hon Rupert Legge, Hamswell House, nr Bath, S Glos BA1 9DG]; *b* 1 Jan 1951; heir presumptive; *educ* Eton and Ch Ch Oxford (MA); barrister Inner Temple 1975; author: *The Children of Light* (1986), *Fashionable Circles* (1991), *Playing with Fire* (1993) and *A Dangerous Age* (1995); *m* 1984 *M Victoria S, dau of Lionel Edward Bruce Ottley (*see* AVEBURY, B), and has:
1a +Edward Peregrine; *b* 1986
1a *Claudia Rose; *b* 1989
(3) +Henry; *b* 28 Dec 1968; *educ* Eton; *m* 21 Dec 1995 *Cressida, yr dau of Sir Christopher Hogg, of Mayfair, and Lady Hogg, of Holland Pk
(1) *Charlotte [The Duchess Castello di Cárcaci, 25 Holland Park Gdns, London W14]; *b* 16 July 1963; *m* 1990 *Don Alexander Paternò Castello di Cárcaci, 13th Duke di Cárcaci
1 *Heather Margaret Mary [The Rt Hon The Lady Herschell, Westfield House, Ardington, Wantage, Berks]; *b* 12 Aug 1925; *m* 1 May 1948 *3rd Baron Herschell (*qv*), and has issue

DARWEN

Creation: B. (UK) 12 Feb 1946.

THE 3RD BARON DARWEN, of Heys-in-Bowland, in the West Riding of Yorkshire (Roger Michael Davies) [The Rt Hon The Lord Darwen, The Labourer's Rest, Green St, Pleshey, Chelmsford, Essex CM3 1HT]; *b* 28 June 1938; *s* f 1988; *educ* Bootham Sch York; *m* 16 Sept 1961 *Gillian Irene, dau of Eric G Hardy, of Valley View, Leigh Woods, Bristol, and has issue:
1 +PAUL; *b* 20 Feb 1962; *educ* Helena Romores Sch, Great Dunmow, Essex
2 +Benjamin; *b* 16 Dec 1966; *educ* Helena Romores Sch
1 *Sarah; *b* 17 Aug 1963
2 *Naomi; *b* 2 Feb 1965
3 *Mary; *b* 17 Nov 1969

Lineage: DAVID DAVIES, of Newport, Mon; *m* — Morgan and had issue:

THOMAS DAVIES (Rev), of Woodside Bank, Darwen; *b* 26 Nov 1815; *m* 7 April 1847 Sarah, dau of Rev James Brightwell Pearce, and *d* 6 May 1892, leaving issue:

THOMAS PEARCE DAVIES, of Heatherfield, Darwen, and Pengarth, Grange-over-Sands; *b* 29 July 1852; *educ* Crawford Coll; *m* 1st 1882 Lucy Dora (*d* 1924), dau of John Stubbins Webb, and had issue; *m* 2nd 1926 Constance, dau of Dr Thorpe, and *d* 9 April 1934; his s by his 1st w:

JOHN PERCIVAL DAVIES, **1st Baron Darwen**, of Heys-in-Bowland, West Riding of Yorks (UK), so *cr* 12 Feb 1946; *b* 28 March 1885; *educ* Sidcot, Bootham and Manchester U; cotton mfr, Quaker, adult educn worker, Ld-in-Waiting to HM GEORGE VI 1949–50; *m* 18 March 1914 (Mary) Kathleen (*d* 26 Jan 1964), dau of Alfred Kemp Brown, MA, BD, of Broxholme, Golders Green, and had issue:
1 CEDRIC PERCIVAL, **2nd Baron**
2 Thomas Barratt; *b* 4 June 1916; *educ* Sidcot, Bootham and Liverpool Sch of Art; Art Teachers Dip, lecturer art educn Reading U 1948–65; *m* 8 March 1941 *Doreen, dau of Arthur James Allen, of Portsmouth, and *d* 19–, leaving:
(1) +Alan John Barry; *b* 1949
(1) *Barbara Jean; *b* 22 June 1944
(2) *Frances Hilary; *b* 4 Feb 1947
(3) *Judith Anne (twin); *b* 1949
3 +(Francis) Ronald [The Hon Ronald Davies, 39 Parkside, Mill Hill, NW7]; *b* 29 March 1920; *educ* Bootham and Queen's Coll Oxford (BA 1943; MA 1946); barrister Gray's Inn 1948; *m* 1942 *Margaret Phyllis, MA, dau of John George Cocksworth, of London, and has:
(1) +Daniel Watson; *b* 22 June 1948
(2) +John Russell; *b* 12 June 1950
(1) *Helen Bronwen; *b* 21 March 1954; *m* 1979 *Peter Johnson
1 *Joan Kathleen [The Hon Mrs Brindle, 27 Abbotsford Court, Colinton Rd, Edinburgh EH10 5EH]; *b* 26 Oct 1917; *m* 1940 *Walter Higham Brindle, MBE, TD, son of Walter Brindle, of Lytham St Anne's, and has issue:
(1) *Michael Patrick [Michael Brindle Esq, 6 Nunnery Drive, Thetford, Norfolk IP24 3EN]; *b* 6 July 1943; *m* 13 Aug 1966 *Corinne, dau of G Hayward, of Stroud, Glos, and has:
1a *Thomas James; *b* 21 March 1974
1a *Elizabeth Jennifer; *b* 14 July 1971
(1) *Alison Lesley [Mrs Alan Cameron, 6 Braid Crescent, Edinburgh EH10 6AU]; *b* 19 June 1947; *m* 24 Aug 1968 *Alan Cameron, s of Ian Cameron, of Colintrave, Argyll, and has:
1a *Gavin Ian [Gavin Cameron Esq, 3/67 Sweetland Ave, Ottawa, Canada]; *b* 25 June 1972; *m* 1997 *Maureen, dau of Justice J F McCartney, of Thunder Bay, Ontario
2a *David William; *b* 12 Jan 1982
1a *Catherine Alison; *b* 17 Feb 1975
2 *Marjorie Heather, JP (Ilkeston, Derbys); *b* 27 Oct 1923; *m* 9 Aug 1944 *Frederick Joseph Adams, MA, son of Joseph Stephen Adams, of Hillcot, Grindley Lane, Blythe Bridge, Staffs, and has issue:
(1) *Christopher Stephen [Christopher Adams Esq, 4 Beechcroft, Madeley, Crewe, Cheshire]; *b* 26 Feb 1946; *m* 1968 *Julia Helena, dau of — Phipps

The 1st BARON *d* 26 Dec 1950; his est son,

CEDRIC PERCIVAL DAVIES, **2nd Baron Darwen**, Warden Letchworth Adult Educational Settlement 1948–51, Educn Sec Nat Assoc Mental Health 1951–53, md Darwen Finlayson, publishers, 1954–73, chm Hollybank Engrg 1957–70, dep chm Literary Periodicals Ltd 1960–62, Pres Ind Publisher's Guild 1973–88, Hon Treasurer Nat Peace Cncl 1954–88; *b* 18 Feb 1915; *educ* Sidcot Sch and Manchester U (BA 1947); *m* 14 July 1934 *Kathleen Dora [The Rt Hon Kathleen Lady Darwen, White Lodge, Sandelswood End, Beaconsfield, Bucks], dau of George Sharples Walker, of Pendleton, Manchester, and *d* 1988, leaving issue:
1 ROGER MICHAEL DAVIES, **3rd and present Baron Darwen**
2 +Stephen Humphrey [The Hon Stephen Davies, 111 Southend, Garsington, Oxon]; *b* 3 Oct 1945; *educ* Roy GS High Wycombe; *m* 3 Aug 1968 *Kathleen, dau of Richard Harold Prestwood, of Beaconsfield, Bucks, and has issue:
(1) +Timothy Prestwood; *b* 20 Feb 1970
(2) +Peter; *b* 1980
(1) *Ruth Margaret; *b* 25 March 1972
(2) *Rachel Mary; *b* 24 Feb 1976
3 +Phillip Cedric Mark [The Hon Phillip Davies, White Lodge, Sandelswood End, Beaconsfield]; *b* 2 Oct 1951; *educ* Sibford Sch
1 *Catharine Joy [The Hon Mrs Tipping, Coombe Cottage, 44 Worcester Rd, Droitwich, Hereford and Worcester]; *b* 10 July 1948; *educ* Cardiff U (BA, PGCE); lecturer Eng Lit and Lang; *m* 1st 5 Sept 1970 (*divorce* 1976) Robert Nienhuis, son of William Nienhuis, of Droitwich; *m* 2nd 18 Dec 1976 *Richard George Tipping, son of Percival George Tipping, and has issue:
(1) *Damian Richards George; *b* 1 Nov 1977
(2) *Gregory Luke Darius; *b* 1980

DASHWOOD of Kirtlington Park

Arms: Argent, on a fess double-cotised gules three gryphon's heads erased or. **Crest:** A gryphon's head erminois erased gules. **Supporters:** (specially granted by roy warrant 15 Sept 1883 to Sir Henry Dashwood, 3rd Bt, with limitation to the heirs male of his body holding the btcy) On either side a male gryphon argent, gorged with a collar flory counterflory gules. **Motto:** *Virtuti nihil invium* ('Nothing is inaccessible to virtue') **Creation:** Bt. (E) 16 Sept 1684.

SIR RICHARD JAMES DASHWOOD, 9TH BT, of Kirtlington Park, Oxfordshire, TD (1987) [Maj Sir Richard Dashwood Bt TD, Ledwell Cottage, Sandford St Martin, Oxon OX7 7AN]; *b* 14 Feb 1950; *s* f 1972; *educ* Eton; Lt 14th/20th King's Hus T&AVR 1973, Maj 1992; *m* 1984 (*divorce* 1993) Kathryn Ann, er dau of Frank Mahon, of Barretts Farm, Eastbury, Newbury, Berks, and has issue:

1 +FREDERICK GEORGE MAHON; *b* 29 Jan 1988

Lineage: Alderman GEORGE DASHWOOD, of Hackney, Middx (*see* DASHWOOD, Bt, of West Wycombe), Commr Excise and Hearth Tax; *b* 1617; *m* Margaret (granted rank of Bt's widow in her s's patent; *d* 7 May 1714), dau of William Pery, of Thorpe, Surrey, and *d* 8 March 1682, leaving issue:

1 ROBERT (Sir), **1st Bt**

2 Richard, of Cockley Cley, Norfolk, High Sheriff of Oxon 1706; *b* 1665; *m* 16 May 1697 Mary Jarrett, of St Olave's, London, and was ancestor of the DASHWOODs of Cockley Cley; gggf of:

1a Charles John (Rev), of Billingford, Norfolk, *d* 1890, leaving issue:

1b Charles Horace Pettus; had:

1c Horace Raikes, of Caldecott Hall, Fritton, Suffolk; *b* 1885; *m* 1912 Jessie Nina (*d* 1978), dau of Walter Cassels, of Buenos Aires, and *d* 1967, leaving issue:

1d +John Horace Cassels [John Dashwood Esq, 2 The Mariners, Sea View Rd, Milford-on-Sea, Hants]; *b* 1913; Maj (ret) RASC; *m* 1941 *Christina Fitzgibbon and has:

1e *Elizabeth Patricia; *b* 1942

2e *Annette Diana [Mrs Peter Goulden, Beechings, Water St, Hampstead Norreys, Newbury, Berks RG18 0SB]; *b* 1947; MB, BS, MRCPsych; *m* 1975 *Peter Anthony Goulden, and has:

1f *Michael John Toby; *b* 1979

2f *Nicholas James; *b* 1981

3e *Rosemarie; *b* 1950

2d +Donald Cassels [Donald Dashwood Esq, Long Acre, Cley, Holt, Norfolk]; *b* 1914; *m* 21 Dec 1940 *Rachel, dau of Rev James Mortimer La Fontaine McAnally, Rector Hethersett, Norfolk, and has issue:

1e +Timothy James [Timothy Dashwood Esq, 43 Wood Lane, Fleet, Hants]; *b* 1947; *educ* Marlborough, King's Coll Cambridge (scholar) and Trin Coll Oxford; *m* 1983 *Katherine Ruth, dau of John Oliver Harris, of Epsom, Auckland, NZ, and has issue:

1f +Peter James Oliver; *b* 1985

1f *Anne Jennifer Raven; *b* 1987

1e *Margaret Jessie [Mrs Neil Sconce, 11 Cromer Villas Rd, London SW18 1PH]; *b* 1942; *m* 1983 *Neil Douglas Sconce, only son of Maj Douglas Sconce, and has issue:

1f *Francisca Barbara; *b* 1985

1d *Elizabeth Cassels [Mrs Owen Davies, Shepperd's Hill, Toowoomba, Qld 4350, Australia]; *b* 1916; *m* 1st 1941 Antony Josiah Boek Gimson (*ka* 1942) and has had:

1e Josiah Jeremy Dashwood Boek; *b* 1942; d 1995

1d (cont.) Mrs Antony Gimson *m* 2nd 1944 Owen Lloyd Davies (*d* 1996), and by him has:

1e *Elizabeth Anne; *b* 19–

2c Richard Raikes; *b* 1890; *m* 1918 Rachel Mary Windham, dau of Rev Alfred Charles Lowth, Rector Colden Common, Winchester, and *d* 1967, leaving issue:

1d +Roland Pettus [Roland Dashwood Esq, 110 Tourist Rd Toowoomba, Qld 4350, Australia]; *b* 1922; *m* 1946 *Helen Theresa, dau of Leslie Armitage, of La Mimosa, Buena Esperanza, Argentina, and has issue:

1e +John Richard; *b* 1959

2e +Alan Roland; *b* 1960

3e +Paul Charles; *b* 1962

4e +Ray James; *b* 1964

1d *Jean Mary: *b* 1919; *m* 1941 her cousin John Stuart Michael Dashwood (*see* below)

2d *Edith Rachel [Mrs Ian McCulloch, 48 Tourist Rd, Toowoomba, Qld 4350, Australia]; *b* 1920; *m* 1948 Ian McCulloch (*d* 1971)

3d *Molly Frances; *b* 1925; *m* 1946 *George Locke Smiles, and has issue:

1e *Dorothy June; *b* 1957

2b Edmund Samuel, surgn; had issue:

1c John Rawdon; *b* 1889; *m* 1918 Marian (*d* 1965), dau of Robert Kohlhoff Clark, tea-planter, of Ceylon, and *d* 1961, leaving issue:

1d +John Stuart Michael [John Dashwood Esq, 10 Curtis St, Toowoomba, Qld, 4350, Australia]; *b* 1917; *m* 1941 his cousin Jean Mary, dau of Richard Raikes Dashwood, and has:

1e +Geoffrey Richard [Geoffrey Dashwood Esq, 27 rue de l'Etang de la Tour, 78120 Rambouillet, France]; *b* 1942; *m* 1966 *Eliane Michèle, dau of Kleber Barrassé, of Colombes, Seine, France, and has issue:

1f *Sophie Michèle; *b* 1968

2f *Valerie Mary; *b* 1971

3f *Annabel Anne; *b* 1973

2e +Oliver Michael; *b* 1947; schoolmaster Toowoomba GS; *m* 1983 *Ann, dau of Joseph Waxman, of Merricks North, Vic, Australia, and has issue:

1f +Robert Michael; *b* 1983

2f +Timothy Kester Paul; *b* 1985

1d *Mary Elizabeth Anne [Mrs Patrick Moss, 18 Crofton Lane, Hill Head, Fareham, Hants PO14 3LP]; *b* 1921; *m* 1942 Lt-Cdr Patrick Hugh Moss (*d* 1989), RN, and has issue:

1e *Nigel Patrick Stringer [Nigel Moss Esq, Henhurst Lodge, Beare Green Rd, Ockley, Dorking, Surrey RH5 4PX]; *b* 1946; *educ* King's Coll Taunton, Guildford and Lancaster Gate Law Colls and Kingston U; *m* 1971 *Linda, dau of Reginald Alfred Baillie, of 26 Green Lane, Copnor, Portsmouth, and has issue:

1f *James Robert; *b* 1975; *educ* Kings Sch Macclesfield, Reigate GS and Edinburgh U

2f *Jonathan Mark; *b* 1977; *educ* Reigate GS, Plymouth U and U of N Carolina

1e *Jane Elizabeth [Mrs Jane Moss, 14 Maizemore Walk, Lee-on-Solent, Hants PO13 8HL]; *b* 1943; *m* 1st 1969 (*divorce* 1974) Roger Sowerby; *m* 2nd 1976 (*divorce* 1980, resumed maiden name) Brian James Maby

3 George, Lt-Col; *b* 1669; *m* Algerina, 2nd dau of Sir Algernon Peyton, 1st Bt (*see* 1959 edn)

1 Elizabeth; *m* Sir Thomas Hare, 2nd Bt (*d* 1 Jan 1693) of the 1641 *cr*, and had issue

2 Anne; *m* 17 July 1701 Sir Sewster Peyton, 2nd Bt (*d* 28 Dec 1717), and left issue (*see* above)

The est son,

Sir Robert Dashwood, 1st Bt (E), so *cr* 16 Sept 1684, with remainder to the male issue of his f, of Northbrook, Oxon; High Sheriff 1683, MP Banbury 1689–1700; *bapt* 6 Nov 1662; *m* 9 June 1682 Penelope (*d* Feb 1734/5), dau and coheir of Sir Thomas Chamberlayne, 2nd Bt, of Wickham, Oxford, and had:

1 Chamberlayne; *d* unm 8 Sept 1743

2 Robert; *m* Dorothy (*d* 21 April 1753), dau and coheir of Sir James Read, 2nd Bt (*qv*), of the March 1641/2 *cr*, and *dvp* 29 Sept 1728, leaving:

(1) JAMES (Sir), **2nd Bt**

3 Richard, of Ledwell, Oxon, High Sheriff Norfolk 1705; *b* 1690; *m* 4 May 1710 Elizabeth (*m* 2nd June 1738 Maj-Gen Sir Charles Armand Powlett (*see* WINCHESTER, M), and *d* Sept 1756), dau of Thomas Lewes, of Stanford, Notts, and *d* April 1737, having had issue:

(1) Robert; *m* Anne, dau and coheir of Frances Lewes, of Stanford, Notts, and *d* 15 Oct 1757, leaving issue:

1a Charles Vere, of Stanford, Notts; High Sheriff 1780; *b* 1745; *m* 8 July 1765 Diana, dau of Samuel Dashwood, of Well Vale, Lincs, and had, with other issue:

1b Charles Armand; *m* 1st Harriet, dau of William Middleton, of Crowfield, Suffolk; *m* 2nd Anna Marie, dau of Very Rev W Shipley, Dean Asaph, and *dsp* 1812

2b Phillip; *b* 1770; *d* unm 6 April 1791

3b Samuel Francis, of Stanford, Notts; *b* 1773; *m* Lydia Boughton, widow of Thomas Tipping, of Lancs, and dau of Matthew Dymoke, of Burwell Park, Lincs, and had issue:

1c Samuel Vere (Rev), of Stanford Park; *b* 3 Nov 1803; *m* 1st 24 Oct 1828 Caroline (*d* 28 May 1840), dau of Philip Hammond, of Westacre, Norfolk, and had issue:

1d Charles Lewes, of Stanford Park, Notts, Capt 5th Fusiliers, JP; *b* 8 May 1833; *d* unm 15 Jan 1891

2d Richard Lewes, Maj-Gen 15th Foot; *b* 18 Feb 1837; *d* unm 12 June 1905

3d Robert Lewes (Rev), MA Cambridge; *b* 9 Feb 1840; *m* 15 Aug 1866 Edith Theresa (*d* 26 May 1920), dau of Rowland E Cooper, of Pain's Hill, Surrey, and *d* 23 June 1912, leaving:

1e Robert Vere Lewes (Rev), Rector N Perrott Somerset 1908–36; *b* 6 Sept 1869; *educ* Pembroke Coll Cambridge (MA); *m* 8 Oct 1901

Agnes (*d* 9 Jan 1957), dau of William S Nicholson, of Eastmore, Yarmouth, IoW and *dsp* 11 March 1949

2e Claude Burrard Lewes, BA Cambridge, Maj 9th Bn Northumberland Fus; *b* 30 Oct 1872; *m* 3 April 1907 Letitia (*m* 2nd 1929 Capt Thomas Harry Lockley Turner (*d* 1948), The Buffs, and *d* 7 Feb 1963), est dau of Henry le Sueur, ISO, JP, of Wynberg, Cape Colony, and *d* 26 April 1916 of wounds received in action, leaving issue:

1f Robert Armand Lewes, WW II as Capt Army Catering Corps; *b* 22 April 1916; *educ* Canford; *m* 23 July 1938 Peggy Violet (*d* 21 Aug 1963), only dau of Herbert Reeves, of Bournemouth, and *d* 1986, leaving issue:

1g +Ian Burrard Lewes [Ian Dashwood Esq, Camelot, 1 Groeneveld Rd, Rondesbosch 7700, Cape Town, S Africa]; *b* 25 Feb 1947; *educ* Homefield GS Southbourne, Hants; *m* 9 Nov 1968 *Marlene Dolores, er dau of P D Kruger, of Sea Point, Cape Town, S Africa, and has issue:

1h +Paul Burrard Lewes; *b* 1972

1h *Annemarie; *b* 1969

1g *Anne; *b* 2 April 1956

1f Joyce Viola; *b* 26 Jan 1908; *m* 17 Dec 1935 Henry Vernon de Burgh (*d* 10 Jan 1960)

2f Sheila Ianthe; *b* 2 May 1909

3f *Diana Mary; *b* 15 Aug 1913; *m* 1935 Ronald Hugh Foster (*d* 16 May 1973) and has:

1g *William Ronald [William Foster Esq, 50 Pauntley Rd, Mudeford, Dorset] *b* 1 Oct 1940; *m* 12 June 1971 *Susan Mary, dau of Garfield Wilkins, of Orchard Ave, Cambridge, and adopted:

*Lisa Jane; *b* 12 Oct 1974

3e Cuthbert William Lewes; *b* 29 Jan 1874; *educ* Radley and Keble Coll Oxford; *d* unm 17 Nov 1960

4e Sidney Lewes, MBE (1918), Capt RE (TA) and RAF WW I (despatches twice); *b* 25 Nov 1882; *educ* Radley and Ch Ch Oxford (BA); *m* 19 April 1922 Joan (*d* 17 Oct 1963), dau of Col Sir Sidney Burrard, 7th Bt, KCSI (*see* 1963 edn), and *d* 25 Dec 1966, leaving issue:

1f *Mary Edith Burrard [Mrs John Simmons, 24 Lovelace Close, Abingdon, Oxon OX14 1XW], BSc; *b* 27 March 1923; *m* 29 June 1946 John Harry Walrond Simmons (*d* 1994), MBE, BSc, and has had:

1g *Geoffrey Philip; *b* 16 March 1952; *educ* Wycliffe Coll; *m* 1976 *Wendy Jean, dau of Maurice Aylen, of Barton-on-Sea, and has issue:

1h *Heather Julie; *b* 1988

2g Julian Charles; *b* 20 Dec; *d* 31 Dec 1955

3g *Roland Paul; *b* 31 May 1957

1g *Rosemary Jane; *b* 28 Oct 1949

2g *Pamela Anne; *b* 28 April 1959

1e Theresa Emma Charlotte; *d* unm 19 July 1953

2e Edith Caroline; *d* unm 7 Jan 1958

3e Constance Alice; *d* unm 22 June 1966 aged 89

1d Caroline Maria; *m* 2 Oct 1849 Rev Richard Surtees (*d* 20 Oct 1899), MA, Rector Holtby, Yorks, and *d* 22 Feb 1906, leaving issue

2d Matilda Katherine; *m* 25 Oct 1854 Rev Charles Snell, MA, Rector Oulton, Suffolk, and *d* 3 Aug 1909, leaving issue

3d Sophia Diana; *m* 6 Feb 1866 Rev George H Davenport, MA of Foxley, Herefs, and *d* 12 March 1915, leaving issue

4d Lydia Charlotte; *m* 19 Sept 1871 Capt Hugh Bateman (*d* 3 May 1906), 43rd Regt, and *d* 14 Jan 1902 leaving issue

1c (cont.) The Rev Samuel Dashwood *m* 2nd 25 Jan 1844 Edith Elizabeth (*d* 22 July 1911) dau of Col — Hawkshaw, of Clifton, nr Bristol, and *d* 10 Nov 1876, having by her had:

4d Edward Vere, County Treasurer Hants; *b* 25 June 1846; *m* 1888 Laura Frederica Penelope (*d* 12 March 1931), dau of Maj Edmund Crofts, Rwelch Fus, and *d* 15 May 1919, leaving issue

1e Vere Edmund Crofts, MC; Lt-Col Roy Sussex Regt WW I (despatches twice); *b* 10 March 1889; *m* 7 April 1956 *Kathleen Ethel [Mrs Vere Dashwood, The Clachan, Newtonairds, Dumfries], widow of Norman Edward Douglas-Menzies, of Newtonairds, Dumfries, and dau of Crawford Logan, of Dumfries, and *dsp* 9 May 1967

1e Diana Penelope; *b* 13 June 1891; *m* 17 Jan 1923 Maj Alexander James Fraser, MC, JP, Roy Berks Regt (*d* 30 June 1962), er son of Col Alexander Henry Hugh Fraser, and has issue:

1f *Alexander Hugh, Maj Duke of Edinburgh's Royal Regt; *b* 8 Feb 1924; *educ* Imp Service Coll Windsor; *m* 12 March 1949 *Dorothy Mabel, dau of Reginald Edward Mitchell, of Seend Row Houses, Seend, and has issue:

1g *Penelope Angela; *b* 19 May 1950

2g *Fiona; *b* 19 July 1953

2f *James Gerald, late 4th WO Hus; *b* 31 Dec 1929; *educ* King's Sch Bruton; *m* May 1968 *Anne, only dau of Capt R Morton, MN, of Midford, Bath

2e Iris Laura, MBE (1948); *b* 29 Oct 1893; *m* 27 July 1921 James Christopher Bull, MC, BA, Maj 10th Duke of Wellington's Regt, and had issue:

1f Martin Christopher Dashwood, Lt The Buffs WW II; *b* 9 Jan 1924, *ka* Italy 1944

2f *Nicholas Vere [Nicholas Bull Esq, 12 Lomond Rd, Edinburgh 5]; *b* 18 Jan 1928; *educ* Clifton and King's Coll Cambridge; *m* 8 Sept 1962 *Cynthia Mary Sefton, dau of James Sefton Bickers, of Hovingham, Yorks, and has issue:

1g *Christopher Martin Sefton; *b* 9 May 1967

1g *Diana Mary Sefton; *b* 24 Sept 1964

5d Samuel Francis; *b* 3 April 1848; *m* 13 Dec 1877 Alice Lucy, dau of Rev W Buller, and *dsp* 2 May 1897

6d Frederick; *b* 10 Oct 1849; *d* 24 Feb 1897

7d Francis Henry; *b* 11 Feb 1855

8d Alfred Henry; *b* 8 Sept 1856; *m* 19 May 1892 Evelyn Maydwell (*d* 14 Dec 1928), dau of Rev John Henry Holditch, and *d* 23 Aug 1937, having had issue:

1e John Maydwell; *b* 6 June 1893; *d* 15 Nov 1902

9d Edmund William, CBE (1919); Col Northumberland Fus Boer War 1899 (wounded, despatches, brevet), and WW I; *b* 9 Sept 1858; *m* 23 Jan 1908 Geva Vereker, MBE (*d* 19 March 1942), dau of Cdr H J Stanley, RN, of Cavers Carre, Melbourne, and *dsp* 5 Oct 1946

10d Philip Wilmot; *b* 1 Oct 1862; *m* 21 Sept 1904 Katherine Mary Adelaide (*d* 21 April 1953), dau of Rev Edward John Harford, Canon Residentiary of Wells, and *d* 8 July 1956, leaving issue:

1e Millicent Katherine; *b* 12 Sept 1906; *d* unm 14 March 1963

5d Edith Helen; *d* unm 22 Jan 1935

6d Alice; *m* 15 July 1873 Col Thomas Tryon, of Bulwick Park, Northants, and *d* 2 May 1932, leaving issue (*see* TRYON, B)

7d Emily Laura; *m* 1st 13 Dec 1881 G H Colmore and had issue; *m* 2nd 1890 Edward Gordon Linzee, of Brambridge Lodge, Bishopstoke, and *d* 14 Dec 1945

1c Sophia; *m* Rev Banks Wright, of Shelton, Notts

2c Lydia Diana; *m* 15 June 1831 Major George Birch (*d* 23 Feb 1855), HEICS, of Clare Park, Surrey, only son of Rev Thomas Birch, DD, and *d* 10 Jan 1837, leaving issue

3c Maria

1 Penelope; *m* 29 Aug 1706 Sir John Stonhouse, 3rd Bt (*qv*)

2 Catherine; *m* 12 June 1718, Sir Robert Banks Jenkinson, 4th Bt (*qv*)

3 Anne; *m* 23 June 1737 Anthony Cope, brother of Sir Jonathan Cope, 1st Bt (*qv*)

Sir ROBERT *d* 14 July 1734; his gs,

Sir James Dashwood, 2nd Bt, LLD, MP Oxford, High Sheriff 1738, built the mansion at Kirtlington; *m* 17 Feb 1738/9 Elizabeth, dau and coheir with her sister, Anne Duchess of Hamilton (*see* HAMILTON and BRANDON, D), of Edward Spencer, of Rendlesham, Suffolk, and had with other issue:

1 HENRY WATKIN (Sir), **3rd Bt**

2 Thomas, HEICS; *b* 25 Dec 1749; *m* 23 Feb 1782 Charlotte Louisa (*d* 10 Jan 1833), dau of J Auriol, and *d* 20 Dec 1825, leaving issue:

(1) Thomas John, sr merchant Bengal establishment, Judge of Tirhost; *b* 27 Nov 1792; *m* 13 June 1822 Susan (*d* 2 Nov 1834), dau of Thomas Wodehouse, and *d* 17 June 1836, leaving with four daus (*d* unm):

1a Thomas Alexander, JP (Herts); BA Oxon; barrister; *b* 22 Feb 1826; *m* 3 Oct 1866 Charlotte Eliza (*d* 23 April 1931), dau of Rev Charles Knyvett, and *d* 9 Jan 1909, leaving:

1b Thomas Henry Knyvett, Maj RASC; *b* 3 Jan 1876; *m* 5 April 1910 Florence Kathleen (*m* 2nd 28 Oct 1937 Capt John Maurice Figgis, of Farnborough Grange, nr Banbury, and *d* 2 July 1939), er dau of Thomas Frederick Hugh Smith, FRCS, of Farningham, Kent, and *d* 24 Jan 1929, leaving issue:

1c Thomas John Russell, OBE (1952); Colonial Admin Service 1933–55, served Tanganyika, South African High Commr Territories and Nigeria, Sec Public Schools Club 1955; *b* 19 Jan 1911; *educ* Wellington and BNC Oxford (BA 1932, MA 1954); *m* 18 April 1936 *(Edith) Mary, dau of William Thomas, of Newport, Monmouthshire, and *dsp* 1 July 1979

1b Mary Susan; *m* 19 Jan 1892 Arthur Geoffrey Robins (*d* 1910) and had issue

2b Maud; *d* unm 8 May 1956

3b Florence; *d* unm 30 April 1937

4b Blanche Wodehouse; *d* young 6 Feb 1878

5b Rose; *d* unm 1947

6b Cecily; *d* young 13 Jan 1878

7b Alice Katharine; *d* unm 31 July 1954

2a Henry Wodehouse; *b* 30 Nov 1830; *dsp* 11 June 1892

(2) Alexander Wilton, of The Grange, Shenley, Herts, Lt-Col 19th Lancers and 71st Highrs; *b* 25 Sept 1796; *m* 15 May 1827 Marian (*d* 26 July 1887), dau of Peter Still, of Harley Street, London, and *d* 15 March 1877, leaving, with other issue:

1a Alexander John, 48th Bengal Inf; *b* 28 March 1830; *m* 13 July 1854 Emma Blanche (*m* 2nd 1894 Lt-Col AR Garrett (*d* 27 May 1903) and *d* 25 Oct 1907), dau of Capt J B Garrett, RN, and *d* 9 July 1857, leaving issue:

1b Alexander Thomas; *b* 4 April 1855; *m* 27 Aug 1904 Annie (*m* 2nd 1915 Albert Banister, of Rhoden, Paddock Wood, Kent, and *d* 1941), yst dau of Henry Morris, and *d* 18 Oct 1911, leaving issue:

1c Alexander John; Capt RA WW II; *b* 2 Nov 1905; *m* 1947 *Mary Whitburn [Mrs Alexander Dashwood, 3 Ladwill Sq, Ashburton, nr Newton Abbott, Devon], dau of Reginald Frank Thorne, of Southborough, nr Tunbridge Wells, and *d* 24 May 1979, leaving issue:

1d +Alexander Thomas Whitburn [Alexander Dashwood Esq, 9 Bradley Rd, Mannamead, Plymouth, Devon]; *b* 1950; *m* 1977 *Christine Ellen, dau of Lewis Badge, of 20 Ocean View Rd, Bude, Cornwall, and has issue:

1e +Benjamin Alexander John; *b* 1979

2d +Jeremy Charles Whitburn; *b* 1957

1d *Sophia Ann Whitburn; *b* 1954

2b Arthur Frederic; *b* 31 Aug 1857; *m* 1897 Etta (*d* 1919), dau of Warden Payne, of Fall River, Mass., USA, and widow of George Fox, DL, JP, of Elmhurst Hall, Lichfield, Staffs, and *dsp* 26 Oct 1944

2a George Lionel, of Wilton House, Shenley, Herts, JP; *b* 2 Aug 1843; *m* 1 Aug 1866 Avice Frances Anne (*d* 22 March 1893), dau of Thomas Part, of Aldenham Lodge, Herts, and *d* 7 March 1913, leaving issue:

1b Montague George, Capt RAF, JP Herts; *b* 26 Aug 1872; *m* 25 June 1903 Maud Isabella (*d* 6 April 1937), only dau of Rev Evan Henry Hopkins, of Woburn Chase, Addlestone, Surrey, Vicar St Luke's, Redcliffe Sq, London SW5, and *d* 21 April 1952

2b Henry Thomas Alexander (Sir), ktd 1952, JP Middx and Herts, Lt Gren Gds; *b* 9 July 1878; *educ* Harrow and Clare Coll Cambridge (BA 1899, MA 1913); *m* 29 April 1909 Norah Creina Bruce (*d* 19 Nov 1948), dau of Henry Arthur Whately, of Dancer's Hill, Barnet, by Hon Norah Creina Blanche, dau of 1st Baron Aberdare (*qv*), and *d* 25 May 1959, having had:

1c A son; *d* an infant 11 Jan 1913

2c George Henry Whately; *b* 15 Nov; *d* 28 Nov 1919

3c +Robert Henry Neville , JP, DL (Northants) [Robert Dashwood Esq JP DL, Farthinghoe Lodge Farm, Brackley, Northants NN13 5NX]; High Sheriff Northants 1980, late Capt RA; *b* 19 Sept 1921; *educ* Harrow and Magdalene Coll Cambridge (BA 1942, MA 1946); *m* 18 April 1959 *Ruth Mary, er dau of William Black Rankin Monteith, MA, MRCS, LRCP, of Purston Manor, Brackley, Northants, and has issue:

1d +David Henry William [David Dashwood Esq, The Farm House, Farthinghoe, Brackley, Northants]; *b* 29 Aug 1960; *educ* Harrow and Reading U; *m* 3 June 1994 *Katherine Elizabeth, dau of Walter Connies-Laing, of Cyncoed, Cardiff, and has:

1e +Henry Charles Napier; *b* 14 Sept 1995

1e *Sophia Ruth; *b* 11 Feb 1998

2d +(Ian) Bruce Robert Bruce Dashwood Esq, Grounds Farm, Hockliffe, Beds]; *b* 26 April 1962; *educ* Bradfield and Seale Hayne; *m* 25 Jan 1997 *Janet Catherine, dau of Peter Broadhead

1c *Norah Creina Frances [Mrs William Nell, Farthinghoe Lodge, Farthinghoe, Brackley, Northants]; *b* 26 March 1910; *m* 1 Aug 1958 William Nell (*d* 15 Feb 1971)

1b Marion Avice Frances; *d* unm 20 Sept 1932

2b Edith Georgina; *d* unm 28 Feb 1956

3b Ethel Isabelle; *m* 7 Sept 1899 Rev John MacInnes (*d* 1917), Hon Assist Sec CMS, Rector of Watton, Herts, and has issue

4b Constance Harriet Eleanor; *m* 7 June 1904 Rev Evan James Hopkins (*d* Aug 1955), and *d* 29 March 1953, leaving issue

5b Avice Charlotte; *d* unm 16 Nov 1944

1a Charlotte Still; *m* 20 May 1856 Richard Durant, of Sharpham, Devon, and *d* 23 April 1863, leaving issue

2a Selina Georgina; *m* 5 July 1854 Rev GW Watson, and *d* 10 Nov 1879, leaving issue

3a Louisa Charlotte; *m* 27 Dec 1859 Rev Alfred Child (*d* 1888), and had issue

4a Emma Marian; *m* 23 Sept 1868 His Hon Judge Lawford Yate-Lee (*d* 17 May 1901), and *d* 31 Jan 1927, leaving issue

(1) Charlotte Sophia; *m* 1st Hon Charles Andrew Bruce; *m* 2nd 1813 James Alexander, of Somerhill, Kent

(2) Anne Amelia; *b* 1789; *m* 1st 1806 Charles Murray (*see* ATHOLL, D); *m* 2nd George Warde and *d* 1851

(3) Louisa Hay; *m* 12 Jan 1811 William Fane (*d* 7 March 1839), HEICS, gs of 8th Earl of Westmorland (*qv*), and *d* 14 Nov 1855, leaving issue

1 Elizabeth; *m* 22 Oct 1762 4th Duke of Manchester (*qv*), and *d* 26 June 1832

2 Anne; *m* 13 June 1764 7th Earl of Galloway, KT (*qv*), and *d* 8 Jan 1830

3 Catherine; *m* Lucy Knightly (*d* 14 April 1764), MP Fawsley

Sir JAMES *d* 10 Nov 1779; his er son,

Sir Henry Watkin Dashwood, 3rd Bt, DCL, MP; *b* 1 Sept 1745; *m* 17 July 1780 Mary Helen, dau of John Graham, of Supreme Court, Calcutta, and Kinross, Scotland, by Helen, sister of William Mayne, Viscount Newhaven, and had issue:

1 Henry George Mayne; *b* 26 June 1782; *dvp* 24 Oct 1803

2 GEORGE (Sir), **4th Bt**

3 Charles, Lt-Col Fus Gds, CB; *b* 9 Dec 1787; *m* 27 Feb 1822 Caroline (*d* 29 April 1860), 4th dau of Adml Sir Robert Barlow, GCB (*see* BARLOW, Bt, of Fort William), and *dsp* 20 April 1832

4 Augustus (Rev); *b* 25 Feb 1795; Rector Thornage, Norfolk; *m* 16 June 1825 Hester (*d* 31 Aug 1867), 4th dau of Sir Jacob Henry Astley, 5th Bt (*see* HASTINGS, B), and *d* 12 July 1863, having had issue:

(1) Augustus Astley George, Maj 108th Foot, served Indian Mutiny; *b* 9 May 1827; *m* 19 March 1874 his cousin Edith Flora Caroline, est dau of J L Marshall, and gdau of Col Thomas Potter Macqueen, MP, by Anne, dau of Sir Jacob Henry Astley, 5th Bt (*see* above), and *dsp* 20 July 1882

(2) Charles Henry, Barrister; *b* 1833; *d* 1901

(1) Georgina Helen; *d* unm 18 Jan 1910

1 Anna Maria; *m* 22 May 1810 2nd Marquess of Ely (*qv*), and *d* 6 Sept 1857

2 Georgina Caroline; *m* 22 March 1819 Sir Jacob Astley, 6th Bt (*see* HASTINGS, B), and *d* 1836

Sir HENRY *d* 10 June 1828; his est surv son,

Sir George Dashwood, 4th Bt; *b* 17 Sept 1786; *m* 8 Sept 1815 Marianne Sarah (*d* 24 March 1877), dau of Sir William Rowley, 2nd Bt, of Tendring Hall (*qv*), and had issue:

1 HENRY WILLIAM (Sir), **5th Bt**

2 George Astley Charles, Capt 71st LI; *b* 3 June 1820; *m* 23 Feb 1854 Harriet Anne (*m* 2nd 14 Feb 1867 Lord Montague William Graham (*d* 21 June 1878; *see* MONTROSE, D), and *d* 18 April 1884), est dau of 1st Baron Bateman, and *d* 26 July 1863, having had issue:

(1) Charles Edmund, JP, Lt 4th Bn Shropshire LI; *b* 20 June 1857; *educ* Eton; *m* 1881 Emma, dau of Richard Baker, and *d* 29 April 1935

(2) Arthur George Frederick, of Thurlow House, Folkestone, Lt 4th Bn North Staffs Regt; *b* 28 May 1860; *m* 1st 12 June 1882 Caroline Isabella (*d* 19 June 1920), dau of Capt Arthur Owen Lord, 72nd Highrs, and had issue:

1a Iris Harriet; *m* 1st 30 Oct 1906 Capt Cecil Fyffe Pryce Hamilton (*ka* at Ypres 26 Oct 1914), Scots Gds; *m* 2nd 1922 Maj Percival Alexander Wilson, Royal West Kent Regt

(2) (cont.) Arthur Dashwood *m* 2nd 17 March 1921 Alice (*m* 2nd 19 Feb 1924 Lt-Cdr Harold Owen Joyce, DSC, RN, and *d* 1954), twin dau of Lt-Col Henry Green-Wilkinson, and *d* 10 Feb 1922

(1) Agnes Henrietta; *d* young 1863

(2) Marianne Caroline; *m* 5 Dec 1876 2nd Baron St Leonards (*see* 1970 edn), and *d* 12 Nov 1947, leaving issue

(3) Emma Sophia; *d* young 1863

3 Frederick Loftus, JP Oxon; *b* 13 Oct 1824, Maj 16th Lancers; *m* 7 Feb 1871 Lucy Amelia Clinton, and *dsp* 12 Oct 1902

1 Marianne Georgiana; *m* 11 Feb 1847 Sir Edmund Antrobus, 3rd Bt (*qv*) and *d* 3 Feb 1903, leaving issue

2 Emma Philadelphia; *m* 18 Aug 1857 Granville Robert Henry Somerset (*dsp* 23 March 1881), DCL, QC, est son of Lord Granville Somerset (*see* BEAUFORT, D), and *d* 9 March 1906

3 Susan Caroline; *m* 31 Oct 1854 Charles George Cholmondeley (*dvp* 7th Dec 1869), est s of 3rd Marquess of Cholmondeley (*qv*), and *d* 1891, leaving issue

Sir GEORGE *d* 22 Sept 1861; his est son,

Sir Henry William Dashwood, 5th Bt; Ld Lt and Custos Rotulorum Oxon; *b* 17 Oct 1816; *m* 18 Sept 1845 Sophia (*d* 15 Oct 1894), only dau of John Drinkwater, of Sherborne House, Warwicks, and had issue:

1 GEORGE JOHN EGERTON (Sir), **6th Bt**

2 Henry William Spencer; *b* 15 June 1854; *d* 15 June 1855

1 Ellen Louisa; *m* 27 Aug 1872 Hon Conrad Adderley Dillon (*d* 4 Nov 1901), 2nd son of 16th Viscount Dillon (*qv*), and *d* 2 June 1917, leaving issue

2 Florence; *d* unm 18 Jan 1917

3 Susan Alice; *d* unm 17 Dec 1922

4 Mary Sophia; *d* unm 28 Oct 1909

Sir HENRY *d* 25 Jan 1889; his son,

Sir George John Egerton Dashwood, 6th Bt, DL JP Oxfon, High Sheriff 1903, Lt and Capt Scots Fus Gds, Hon Maj 4th Bn Oxon LI; *b* 12 Sept 1851; *m* 12 Aug 1875 Lady Mary Margaret Seymour (*d* 29 Dec 1948), yst dau of 5th Marquess of Hertford (*qv*), and had issue:

1 ROBERT HENRY SEYMOUR (Sir), **7th Bt**

2 Ernest George, Capt 4th Bn Oxon and Bucks LI; *b* 18th Jan 1880; *ka* 12 May 1915

3 (Arthur) Paul, OBE (1919), Maj RE, AMICE; *b* 17 July 1882; *m* 17 July 1919 Edmée Elizabeth Monica (the novelist E M Delafield; *d* 2 Dec 1943), er dau of Count Henry Ducarel de la Pasture, and *d* 4 April 1964, having had issue:

(1) Lionel Paul; *b* 13 Aug 1920; *d* during his military training 4 Nov 1940

(1) *Rosamund Margaret [Mrs Leslie Truelove, 44 Victoria Crescent, St Vitel, Winnipeg 9, Manitoba, Canada]; *b* 1923; *m* 3 Jan 1948 *Leslie Harold Truelove, MA, MRCP, and has:

1a *Paul Alexander; *b* 30 Nov 1948

2a *Leslie Simon; *b* 6 June 1950

3a *Patrick Peter; *b* 22 May 1955

4a *Michael Andrew; *b* 18 April 1961

4 Wilfred James, Lt Gren Gds; *b* 3 Dec 1883; *d* 2 Aug 1917 of wounds recd in action

5 Lionel Albert, 2nd Lt Oxon and Bucks LI; *b* 3 Aug 1887; *ka* France 15 May 1915

6 Henry Godfrey, Lt (actg Capt) 3rd Bn Oxon and Bucks LI; *b* 16 Nov 1889; *educ* Cheltenham; *m* 1st 12 June 1918 Helen Gladys (*d* 24 Oct 1946), only child of Rev James William Cartmell, MA, Fell Christ's Coll Cambridge; *m* 2nd 6 March 1947 *Dora, yst dau of Lt-Col Henry Holmes, MVO, and *dsp* 2 Feb 1970

7 Edward John, F/O RAF; *b* 6 May 1902; *ka* NWF India 21 March 1925

1 Emily Sophia; *b* 8 May 1878; *m* 17 July 1913 Alfred Rendell Street (*d* 8 July 1938), son of John Rendell Street, of Sydney, NSW, and *d* 8 March 1962, having had issue

2 Dorothy Constance; *b* 17 March 1881; *d* unm 9 Nov 1950

3 Margaret Frances; *b* 9 July 1885; *m* 20 July 1909 Capt Robert Ronald Henderson (*d* 16 Jan 1932), MP S Oxon, 3rd KO Hus, of Studley Priory, Oxon, son of John Henderson, DCL, JP and *d* 28 May 1959, leaving issue

4 Muriel Helen; *b* 30 July 1892; *d* unm 12 Jan 1983

Sir GEORGE *d* 1 Sept 1933; his est son,

Sir Robert Henry Seymour Dashwood, 7th Bt , DL Oxon; *b* 19 July 1876; Maj 3rd Bn Oxon and Bucks LI, Bde Maj 1914, Capt 1st Bn Roy Irish Rifles WW I (despatches twice, wounded twice); *m* 14 Jan 1903 Margaret Helen (*d* 13 March 1952), only dau of Lt-Gen George Henry, CB, RE, and had issue:

1 HENRY GEORGE MASSY (Sir), **8th Bt**

2 John Arthur; *b* 17 July 1910; *m* 1952 *Patricia Maud, only dau of Frederick Burrows

1 Barbara Helen; *b* 18 June 1904; *m* 25 Oct 1928 Thomas Kitchingman Bower, er son of Thomas O Bower, of The Manor House, Wickhambrook, Suffolk, and had issue

Sir ROBERT *d* 3 July 1947; his er son,

Sir Henry George Massey Dashwood, 8th Bt, DL (1972) JP (1949); *b* 11 May 1908; *m* 9 Dec 1948 Susan Mary (*d* 1985), er dau of Maj Victor Robert Montgomerie-Charrington, OBE, 2nd Life Gds, of Hunsdon House, Herts, and *d* 5 Nov 1972, leaving issue:

1 Sir RICHARD JAMES DASHWOOD, **9th and present Bt**

1 *Emma Victoria Mildred [Mrs Edward Crofton, Long Durford, Upper Durford Wood, Petersfield, Hants GU31 5AW]; *b* 27 Feb 1955 *m* 26 March 1977 *Capt Edward Morgan Croftont (*see* CROFTON, Bt, of Mohill)

DASHWOOD of West Wycombe

Arms: Argent on a fess double cotised gules three griffin's heads, erased or. **Crest:** A griffin's head erased per fess erminois and gules. **Motto:** *Pro magna charta* ('For the great charter'). **Creation:** Bt. (GB) 28 June 1707.

SIR FRANCIS JOHN VERNON HEREWARD DASHWOOD, 11TH BT, of West Wycombe, Buckingham, [Sir Francis Dashwood Bt, West Wycombe Park, Bucks HP14 3AJ]; *b* 7 Aug 1925; *s f* 1966, also as Premier Baronet of Great Britain; *educ* Eton, Ch Ch Oxford (BA 1948, MA 1953) and Harvard Business Sch; CC Bucks 1951–52, High Sheriff Bucks 1976, memb Lloyd's 1956, SBStJ, author: *The Dashwoods of West Wycombe* (1987), *The Great Lloyd's Robbery* (1992); *m* 1st 3 May 1957 Victoria Ann Elizabeth Gwynne (*d* 26 June 1976), only dau of John Frederick Foley, Baron de Rutzen, DL, JP, Maj Welsh Gds, of Slebech Park, Pembs (*see* 1959 edn FOLEY-PHILIPPS, Bt), and Lady Dunsany (*qv*), and has issue:

1 +EDWARD JOHN FRANCIS; *b* 25 Sept 1964; *educ* Eton and Reading U (BSc), ARICS; *m* 10 April 1989 *Lucinda Nell, only dau of Gerrard Herman Francis Miesegaes, of 14 St Queen's Elm Sq, London SW3, and has:

(1) +George Francis; *b* 17 June 1992

(2) +Robert Edward; *b* 1993

(1) *Victoria Lucinda; *b* 1991

1 *Emily Jane; *b* 1 June 1958; *m* 1981 *Charles William Lennox Naper (*see* VALENTIA, V), and has issue:

(1) *Nicholas; *b* 1984

(2) *Edward; *b* 1986

(3) *John; *b* 1990

2 *Georgina Helen; *b* 22 Jan 1960; *m* 1991 *Charles Humphrey Joseph Weld, of Chideock Manor, Dorset, and has issue (*see* LOVAT, L)

3 *Caroline Sarah; *b* 20 June 1962; Dr; *m* 30 Aug 1997 *Michael Wade, only s of Peter Wade of Sutton Green, Surrey, and has:

(1) *Alexander Francis Neville; *b* 1 Jan 1998

Sir FRANCIS *m* 2nd 24 Sept 1977 *Marcella Teresa, dau of Marcellino Scarafina, formerly w of Giuseppe Sportoletti Baduel and widow of Jack Frye, CBE

Lineage: The DASHWOODs originated in Dorset but moved to Somerset, settling at Vellow Wood, Stogumber, *temp* ELIZABETH I.

SAMUEL DASHWOOD, of Rowdon, Stogumber; *m* 2 Sept 1590 Elizabeth Sweeting and *d* 1640, leaving:

1 John, ancestor of the DASHWOODs of Essex and Suffolk

2 FRANCIS, of whom presently

3 Richard; *m* 12 July 1657 Lydia Skinner

4 William, London merchant; *m* 19 April 1629 Elizabeth, dau of John Hawes, of London, and had issue

5 George, of Hackney, Middx, Alderman London, ancestor of DASHWOOD, Bt, of Kirtlington Park (*qv*)

The 2nd son,

FRANCIS DASHWOOD, of Vellow Wood and London, merchant; *b* 1603; *m* 1st Alice (*d* 6 Feb 1693/4), sis of Edmund Sleigh, Alderman London, and had issue; *m* 2nd Jan 1658/9 Martha —, widow, and *d* 23 April 1683, leaving by his 1st w, with four daus and a yst s (George, *d* Sept 1706):

1 Samuel (Sir), ancestor of the BATEMAN DASHWOODs of Well Vale, Lincs; ktd 1684, Ld Mayor London 1702–03, MP City London 1685 and 1689–90; *m* 17 May 1670 Anne (*d* 16 June 1721), dau of John Smith, of Tedworth, and *d* 14 Sept 1705, leaving issue (*see* SEBRIGHT, Bt)

2 Thomas; *m* Penelope, dau of — Hellersdon, and had issue

3 **Sir Francis Dashwood, 1st Bt** (GB), so *cr* 28 June 1707, of West Wycombe, Bucks; MP Winchelsea 1708–12; *b* 1658; *m* 1st *c* 13 April 1683 May (*d* 6 Feb 1693/4), only dau of John Jennings, of Westminster, and had, with two sons (*d* in infancy):

(1) Mary; *m* 19 Aug 1703 Sir Fulwar Skipworth, 2nd Bt (*d* 13 May 1728), and left issue

(2) Susannah; *m* 15 April 1702 Sir Orlando Bridgeman, 3rd Bt (*see* BRADFORD, E)

3 (cont.) **Sir Francis** *m* 2nd *c* 30 May 1705 Mary (*d* 19 Aug 1710), dau of 4th Earl of Westmorland (*qv*) and ultimately a coheir to the Barony of Le Despenser (*see* FALMOUTH, V, for the Barony's descent, including its period with the DASHWOOD Bts), and by her had issue:

(1) **Sir Francis Dashwood, 2nd Bt**, PC; *b* Dec 1708; Treas Chambers, Master Wardrobe, Chllr Exchequer 1762–63, Jt PMG 1766–81, Col Roy Bucks (King's Own) Militia, Ld Lt Bucks; *m* 19 Dec 1745 Sarah (*d* 19 Jan 1769), widow of Sir Richard Ellys, 3rd Bt, of Wyham, Lincs, and dau and coheir of George Gould, of Iver, Bucks, and *dsp* 11 Dec 1781

(3) Rachel; *m* 13 July 1738 Sir Robert Austin, 4th Bt, MP, and *dsp* 16 May 1788. He *d* 1743

3 (cont.) **Sir Francis** *m* 3rd 17 June 1712 Mary, dau of Maj — King, and by her had:

(2) JOHN (Sir), **3rd Bt**

(3) Charles, MA Oxon; *b* 4 Nov 1717; *d* unm

(4) Henrietta; *d* unm

(5) Mary; *m* 15 May 1732 John Walcott, of Bittersley Court, Salop

3 (cont.) **Sir Francis** *m* 4th 21 July 1720 Lady Elizabeth Windsor (*dsp* 16 Oct 1737), dau of 1st Earl of Plymouth (*qv*), and *d* 4 Nov 1724

The 2nd Bt's half bro,

Sir JOHN DASHWOOD later DASHWOOD-KING (added by Act of Parl 1742), **3rd Bt**, BCL, MP Bishop's Castle 1753–56; *b* 4 Aug 1716; *m* 1761 Sarah (*d* 9 April 1777), dau of Blundell Moore, of Byfleet, and *d* 6 Dec 1793, having had, with other issue, including a yst s (George, Im 21 March 1794 Elizabeth Callender, *dsp* 22 June 1801):

1 Francis; *dvp* 9 Nov 1779

2 **Sir John Dashwood, 4th Bt**, MP Wycombe 1796–1831; *m* 29 Aug 1789 Mary Anne (*d* 19 Jan 1844), dau of Theodore Henry Broadhead, of Monk Bretton, Yorks, and *d* 22 Oct 1849, having had, with two daus:

(1) **Sir George Henry Dashwood, 5th Bt**, DCL, MP Bucks 1832–35 and Wycombe 1837–62; *b* 1790; *m* 17 March 1823 his cousin Elizabeth (*d* 24 May 1889), dau of Sir Theodore Henry Broadhead later Brinckman, 1st Bt (*qv*), and *dsp* 4 March 1862

(2) Francis; *d* May 1817

(3) **Sir John Richard Dashwood, 6th Bt**; *b* 1792; *d* unm 24 Sept 1863

(4) Edwin Sandys, Capt RHG; *m* 1821 Emily, dau of Rev Robert Hare, of Hurstmonceux, Sussex, and *d* 1846, leaving issue:

1a EDWIN HARE (Sir), **7th Bt**

1a Amelia Caroline; *m* Capt Henry Storey, RN

(5) Henry (Rev); *m* 19 Sept 1826 Anne (*d* 1 Feb 1822), 3rd dau of W Leader, of Putney Hill, and *d* 6 Feb 1846, leaving issue

The 6th Bt's nephew,

Sir Edwin Hare Dashwood, 7th Bt, Capt 10th Regt; *b* 7 Sept 1825; *m* 25 Oct 1853 Roberta Henrietta (*d* 11 Nov 1901), dau of Sir Robert Abercromby, 5th Bt, of Birkenbog (*qv*), and *d* 8 May 1882, having had, with other issue:

1 **Sir Edwin Abercromby Dashwood, 8th Bt**; *b* 28 Oct 1854; *m* 24 Aug 1889 Florence (*m* 2nd 2 June 1894 Maj William Selby-Lowndes, OBE, TD, DL, NP of Whaddon Chase, Bucks (*d* 1952) and *d* 9 Feb 1923, leaving further issue), only dau of Frederick Norton, of Mangantare, NZ, and had issue:

(1) Florence Emily; *b* 11 Aug 1890; *m* 1st 28 April 1910 (*divorce* 1925) Alfred Ronald Gilbey, est s of Alfred Gilbey, of Wooburn House, Bucks, and had issue (*see* GILBEY, Bt); *m* 2nd Sept 1947 Otto Lerwill, yst s of W H Lerwill, and *d* 17 April 1969

2 George Julius Hare; *b* 19 Aug 1856; *d* unm 30 Nov 1878

3 ROBERT JOHN (Sir), **9th Bt**

4 Francis; *b* 18 Aug 1863; *d* 12 Aug 1932

Sir EDWIN *d* 7th April 1893; his brother,

Sir Robert John Dashwood, 9th Bt, DL, JP, CC Bucks; *b* 3 June 1859; *m* 25 July 1893 Clara Adelaide Ida Conyers (*m* 2nd 29 Jan 1913 Capt Alexander Robert Fraser, of 23 Alexander Sq, London SW3, est son of Major-Gen A R Fraser, MSC, and *d* 20 April 1945), est dau of Major William Bayford Lindsay, 14th Regt, and had issue:

1 Robert Francis Lindsay; *b* 17 Sept 1894; *d* 16 March 1895

2 JOHN LINDSAY (Sir), **10th Bt**

3 Robert Henry Lindsay, Capt 2nd Bn West Yorkshire Regt; *b* 27 Nov 1897; *d c* 27 May 1918 of wounds received in action

4 Richard Lindsay; *b* 25 Jan, *d* 29 Jan 1900

1 Ida Helen Lindsay; *b* 2 Dec 1903

Sir ROBERT *d* 9 July 1908; his er surv son,

Sir John Lindsay Dashwood, 10th Bt, CVO (1951), High Sheriff Bucks 1934; *educ* Wellington and Magdalen Coll Oxford, 2nd Sec Dip Serv 1923–27, Assist Marshal Dip Corps 1933–66, T/Lt 10th Service Bn Argyll and Sutherland Highrs, Actg Maj Tank Corps, served WW I, F/Lt No 902 (Middx) Balloon Sqdn AAF, Counsellor For Serv 1942–46; *b* 25 April 1896; *m* 20 Dec 1922 Helen Moira (*d* 1989), dau of Lt-Col Vernon Eaton, Royal Canadian Horse Artillery, and *d* 9 July 1966, leaving issue:

1 Sir FRANCIS JOHN VERNON HEREWARD DASHWOOD, **11th and present Bt**

2 +John [John Dashwood Esq, 27 Matham Rd, East Molesey, Surrey]; *b* 16 April 1929; *educ* Eton and Ch Ch Oxford; *m* 1st 12 Nov 1959 (*divorce* 1964) Susan Boyter Duncombe, er dau of Major Ernest Duncombe Shafto, KRRC (ret) and Sybil, Dowager Countess Howe (*qv*); *m* 2nd 17 Jan 1965 *Harriet Louise, er dau of John Philip Spencer, of Norbury Park, Mickleham, Surrey, and has issue:

(1) *Thomas; *b* 2 April 1973

(1) *Rebecca Louise; *b* 30 July 1971

1 *Maud Helen Sarah [The Rt Hon the Lady Aberdare, 32 Elthiron Rd, London SW6]; *m* 1 June 1946 *4th Baron Aberdare (*qv*) and has issue

Seat: West Wycombe Park, West Wycombe, Bucks. Although very much the creation of **Sir Francis Dashwood, 2nd Bt**, West Wycombe came about through an unusually strong set of family factors. **Sir Francis** had inherited a three-storey house from his father, who had put it up early in the century, probably about the time of his second marriage, the one that produced **Sir Francis** himself. The latter inherited when still under age and was brought up by his uncle and guardian the 7th Earl of Westmorland (*qv*), who had hired Colen Campbell to design Mereworth (it eventually passed to **Sir Francis**) in close emulation of the Villa Capra at Vicenza. But whereas neither Campbell nor his employer ever crossed the Alps to see the original, Sir Francis completed the Grandest of Grand Tours in the 1730s, visiting not only Italy but the Levant.

The young baronet might have travelled more than uncle Westmorland, but he was deeply influenced by him, in particular the Earl's devotion to the Classical World. Initially **Sir Francis** intended to rebuild his father's house completely. Yet the project hung fire till 1748, almost ten years after his return from what to 18th-century Britons were distant lands. He did not forget them, however, and instead of rebuilding the family home extended it, in effect commemorating his itinerary with a series of architectural references. The ionic order western portico is copied from the Temple of Dionysos at Teos, in Greece; the hall ceiling from that in Hadrian's Villa at Tivoli; another ceiling motif from one in the Temple of the Winds at Palmyra, in what is now northern Syria. The same hall has a hypocaust, or under-the-floor heating system, based on a system at Lincoln built by the Romans during their occupation of Britain.

The odd thing is that these most powerful testimonies to the far-flung nature of **Sir Francis**'s youth are late features. The north facade came earlier, in around 1751, probably executed by Isaac Ware; the easterly one some four years afterwards and that on the south side a little later still, just conceivably to the designs of Giovanni Servandoni, though the on-site project manager was John Donowell. Perhaps **Sir Francis** was his own architect on this occasion. The chief aspect of this last remodelling, a double-storeyed elevation of twin colonnades, one on top of the other, was the first of its kind in England — at any rate since its evacuation by the Emperor Honorius's legions in 410. That Sir Francis's reverence for the Ancients was deep and true is shown by his use of doric columns running straight to the ground without plinths to support them, a practice in actual use among the Romans of Antiquity but attacked by Renaissance pundits onwards as unsightly. True, the Renaissance is represented by the murals inside the house after Raphael and Annibale Carracci, but the subject matter, mythical scenes, is Ancient enough.

Not everything is high seriousness. The sphinx on the left as one faces the interior of the house in the entrance hall is said to bear **Sir Francis**'s features. He was after all not just a Chancellor of the Exchequer but a leading figure in the Society of Dilettanti. The climax to his astounding building programme came in late summer 1771 with a ceremony of dedication according to decidedly pagan rites.

DAVENTRY

Arms: Quarterly, 1st and 4th, gules three lion's gambs two and one argent (for NEWDEGATE); 2nd and 3rd grand quarters quarterly, 1st and 4th, France and England quarterly; 2nd, Scotland, 3rd, Ireland, the whole debruised by a baton sinister compony argent and azure (for FitzROY). **Crests:** 1 A fleur-de-lys argent (for NEWDEGATE), 2 On a chapeau gules, doubled ermine, a lion statant guardant or, ducally crowned azure and gorged with a collar counter compony argent and azure (for FitzROY). **Supporters:** Dexter, a lion rampant guardant or crowned azure; sinister, a greyhound argent, both gorged with a collar gobony ermine and azure, a mullet argent in the azure, each collar edged also azure. **Motto:** *Et decus et pretium recti* ('Both the reward and price of rectitude'). **Creation:** V. (UK) 6 May 1943.

THE 3RD VISCOUNT DAVENTRY, of Daventry, Co Northampton (Francis Humphrey Maurice FitzRoy Newdegate, JP (Warwicks 1960)) [The Rt Hon The Viscount Daventry JP, Temple House, Arbury, Warwicks CV10 7PT]; *b* 17 Dec 1921; *s* unc 1986; *educ* Eton; Capt Coldstream Gds WW II (wounded), ADC to Viceroy India 1946–47, Warwicks: High Sheriff, Ld Lt 1990–96 (V-Ld Lt 1974–90, DL 1970–74), KStJ 1991; *m* 20 Oct 1959 *Hon Rosemary Norrie, est dau of 1st Baron Norrie (*qv*), and has issue:

1 +JAMES EDWARD [The Hon James FitzRoy Newdegate, 17 Rosenay Rd, London SW11 4QN; *b* 27 July 1960; *educ* Milton Abbey and RAC Cirencester; *m* 10 Sept 1994 *Georgia, yr dau of John Lodge, of Daglingworth Place, Cirencester, and has:

(1) +Humphrey John; *b* 23 Nov 1995

(1) A dau; *b* 31 Dec 1997

2 +Hugh Francis; *b* 4 Oct 1962; *educ* Eton

1 *Joanna Norrie; *b* 8 Feb 1964; *m* 1990 *Nicholas Yvone John Kirkpatrick and has issue (*see* LODER, Bt)

Lineage: Lt-Col Hon ARCHIBALD CHARLES HENRY DOUGLAS-PENNANT (*see* PENRHYN B), of Daventry, Northants, had issue:

MURIEL Dougls-Pennant, **1st Viscountess Daventry**, of Daventry, Co Northampton (UK), so *cr* 6 May 1943 with special remainder to heirs of her body, CBE (1918), DGStJ; *b* 8 Aug 1869; *m* 19 Nov 1891 Capt Rt Hon Edward Algernon FitzROY, MP, Speaker H of C 1928–43 (*d* 3 March 1943) (*see* SOUTHAMPTON, B), and had issue:

1 (ROBERT) OLIVER, **2nd Viscount**

2 Michael Algernon, Capt 4th Bn Seaforth Highrs; *b* 27 June 1895; *ka* 15 April 1915

3 John Maurice FitzROY later FitzROY NEWDEGATE (roy licence 11 Nov 1936), Cdr RN, served WW I 1914–19 and WW II; *b* 20 March 1897; *educ* RNCs Osborne and Dartmouth; Im 19 May 1919 Lucia Charlotte Susan (*d* 1982), OBE (1957), JP (Warwicks 1949), CStJ, er dau and coheir of Sir Francis Alexander Newdigate Newdegate, GCMG (*see* BAGOT, B), and *d* 7 May 1976, leaving issue:

(1) FRANCIS HUMPHREY MAURICE FitzROY NEWDEGATE, **3rd and present Viscount Daventry**

(1) *Lucia Anne [The Hon Mrs Lewis, Inchdura House, North Berwick]; *b* 28 March 1920; granted with her sis 1988 rank of viscount's dau; *m* 4 July 1942 *Maj Timothy Stuart Lewis, RSG, s of Col William Herbert Lewis, DSO, MC, of Wynberg, S Africa, and has had:

1a Michael Humphrey Stuart; *b* 8 Aug 1943; *educ* Trin Coll Glenalmond; *d* as the result of a car accident 20 April 1963

1a *Caroline Anne; *b* 15 Aug 1946; *m* 29 April 1st 1967 (*divorce* 1994) Sir (Frederick Douglas) David Thomson, 3rd Bt, and had issue (*see* THOMSON, Bt, of Glendarroch); *m* 2nd as his 2nd wife, James Henry Denison-Pender (*see* PENDER, B)

(2) *Jocelyne; *b* 13 July 1929; *m* 1st 26 July 1952 (*annulled* 1953) Richard John Barton, 16th/5th Lancers, only son of Col John Seddon Barton, OBE, MC, DL, TD, of Glan-y-Wern Hall, Denbigh, N Wales; *m* 2nd 18 May 1957 (*divorce* 1980) Maj Henry John Allfrey, OBE, RA (ret), er son of Major Henry Sydney Allfrey, DL, JP of Bishops Acre, Upton Bishop, Ross-on-Wye, Herefs, and has issue:

1a *Henry David, 2nd Lt Scots Dragoon Gds; *b* 27 Feb 1959; *educ* Wellington and RMA Sandhurst; Maj Scots DG; *m* 1985 *Fiona Jean Hamilton, only dau of Gen Sir Edward Burgess, KCB, OBE, and has issue:

1b *Henry Edward; *b* 1991

1b *Olivia; *b* 1988

2a *Charles John; *b* 19th May 1963; *educ* Eton; Capt The Royal Hus (Prince of Wales's Own) (ret); *m* 1989 *Caroline Margaret Violet, er dau of Sir Alastair Sturgis Aird, KCVO (*see* AIRD, Bt) and has:

1b *Helena Idina; *b* 5 July 1996

1a *Lucia Susan [Mrs David Homer, 3 New Cottages, Furzedown Lane, Amport, Hants SP11 8BD]; *b* 2 June 1961; *m* 1988 *Maj David St John Homer, MBE, RGJ, er son of G/Capt Derek Homer, MVO, of Harpenden, Herts, and has issue:

1b *Thomas David William; *b* 1990

2b *Charles St John; *b* 1995

3b *William Richard John; *b* 1996

1 Nancy Jean, BEM; *b* 31 May 1894; Sgt-Dispenser VAD 1916–18 and 1939–46; *d* unm Feb 1984

The VISCOUNTESS *d* 8 July 1962; her est son,

(ROBERT) OLIVER FitzROY, **2nd Viscount Daventry**, High Sheriff Rutland 1956; *educ* RNCs Osborne and Dartmouth, Capt RN, served WW I and WW II (despatches), Dir Minesweeping 1940–43, cmded HMS *Rodney* 1943–46; *b* 10 Jan 1893; *m* 5 Sept 1916 Grace Zoe (*d* 14 Jan 1978), dau of Claude Hugh Campbell Guinness (*see* GUINNESS, Bt), and *d* 1986, leaving issue:

1 Mary Angela; *b* 4 Nov 1919; *m* 1st 2 Nov 1940 Maj (Anthony) Dermot Melloney Musker (*k* in a motor racing accident 8 Aug 1959), Coldstream Gds, yr son of Maj Herbert Musker, of Rushford Rall, Thetford, Norfolk, and had issue:

(1) *Charles Dermot FitzRoy; *b* 10 Oct 1941; *educ* Eton; *m* 18 Dec 1963 *Caroline Theresa, only dau of Hon Robert Henry Digby, of Berrow Lodge, Bury St Edmunds, Suffolk, son of 10th Baron Digby (*qv*), and has issue:

1a *Dermot Henry; *b* 9 Nov 1964; *educ* Milton Abbey

2a *Rupert Anthony; *b* 14 June 1975

1a *Emily Mary; *b* 16 Sept 1972

2a *Chloe Diana Leopoldine; *b* 12 June 1979

(2) *(Herbert) Oliver FitzRoy [Oliver Musker Esq, Malcolm House, Batsford, Moreton-in-Marsh, Glos]; *b* 21 Nov 1948; *educ* Eton; *m* 1st 1974 (*divorce* 1979) Victoria, former wife of Lionel Brooke; *m* 2nd 22 Jan 1979 *Lady Diana Rose Lambton, 3rd dau of Viscount Lambton (formerly 6th Earl of Durham (*qv*)), and has issue:

1a *Claud James FitzRoy; *b* 1977

2a *Sam; *b* 1982

2a *Lily; *b* 1981

(3) *Robert Anthony FitzRoy [Robert Musker Esq, Valley Farm, Brancaster Staithe, Norfolk]; *b* 14 June 1952; *educ* Milton Abbey; *m* 16 Oct 1976 *Charlotte Brownlow, er dau of W/Cdr Richard Cecil Cochrane Patrick, DFC, AFC, of Town Farm House, Brancaster, King's Lynn, Norfolk

(1) *Belinda Mary [Mrs Stuart Murray Threipland, Trafalgar House, Salisbury, Wilts]; *b* 27 Nov 1942; *m* 1st 13 Dec 1966 (*divorce* 1972) John Aspinall, son of Dr Robert Stavali Aspinall; *m* 2nd 10 Oct 1972 *Stuart Wyndham Murray Threipland , yst son of Maj Patrick Wyndham Murray Threipland, of Dale and Toftingdall, TD, and has issue:

1a *Alexander Patrick; *b* 17 Aug 1972

2a *Robert Wyndham; *b* 1 July 1978

1a *Alice Cassia; *b* 17 Aug 1972

(2) *Fiona Zoe [Mrs James McIntyre, Hempnells Hall, Colton, Stowmarket, Suffolk]; *b* 23 Oct 1945; *m* 22 Oct 1966 *James Robert McIntyre, son of John Andrew McIntyre, of Sydney, Australia, and has issue:

1a *Simon James; *b* 23 Aug 1969

1a *Zoe Claire; *b* 12 May 1967

1 (cont.) The Hon Mrs Musker *m* 2nd 22 Oct 1962 *Dr Richard Mayon Mayon-White, FRCP [Dr Richard Mayon-White, Baylham House, Baylham, Ipswich, Suffolk], son of Richard Hubert White, of Humberdoncy House, Ipswich, Suffolk

2 Olivia Gwyneth Zoe, authoress, served WW II as 3rd Offr WRNS; *b* 27 May 1921; *m* 31 July 1957, as his 2nd wife, Capt Sir Geoffrey Voltelin Bates, 5th Bt, MC, of Bellefield, Gryn Castle and Manydown (*qv*), and *d* 24 Dec 1969, having had:

(1) *Celina Zoe; *b* 29 Jan 1958

(2) Sarah Rose; *b* 4 Jan 1960; *d* following an accident 5 March 1977

3 *Katherine Susan [The Hon Mrs Boardley, PO Box 1284, Kelvin 2054, Transvaal, S Africa], WW II in FANY; *b* 24 Aug 1923; *m* 1st 13 Oct 1945 (*divorce* 1958) Phil John Turner, est son of Phil Turner; *m* 2nd 12 June 1958 Anthony Woodington Boardley (*d* 1967), yr son of Bertie Welton Boardley, and has issue:

(1) *Kevin Anthony FitzRoy; *b* 19 Dec 1961 *educ* St John's Coll Johannesburg

4 *Barbara Helen [The Hon Mrs Ormrod, Bridge Lodge, Pen-y-Lan, Ruabon, Wrexham, LL14 6HS]; *b* 19 Dec 1928; *m* 18 April 1952 *Col Peter Charles Ormrod, MC, 8th KRI Hus, JP 1958, DL (1972), High Sheriff Clwyd 1962, son of Maj James Ormrod, Royal Welch Fus, by Winifred Selina, dau of Col Charles Rivers Bulkeley, CB, of Clewer Lodge, Windsor, and has:

(1) *Emma Jane Caroline [Mrs Emma Holloway, Pen-y-Lan, Ruabon, Wrexham LL14 6HS]; *b* 29 Jan 1958; *m* 4 Oct 1980 (*divorce* 1997) Julian Pendrill Warner Holloway, yr son of A G W Holloway, of Boscobel, Minchinhampton, Glos, and has:

1a *James Oliver Pendrill; *b* 1986

2a *Thomas Henry Charles; *b* 1988

3a *Alexander Hugh George; *b* 1991

1a *Lavinia Sophie Olivia; *b* 1984

(2) *Alice Amelia [Mrs James Hedley, The Gronwen, Pen-y-Lan, Ruabon, Wrexham LL14 6HS]; *b* 18 Dec 1964; *m* 1991 *(Roger) James St George Hedley; BA (Hons), MSc (Wales), MSI (Dip), s of Maj Roger St George Hedley, Roy Fus, of Corton, Wilts, and has issue:

1a *Barbara Jane; *b* 1992

2a *Lilian Grace; *b* 1994

3a *Hermione Aurora; *b* 1996

5 *Amelia Grace [The Hon Mrs Amelia Jessel, Bridge Cottage, Stoke Charity, Winchester, Hants SO21 3PP]; *b* 26 March 1930; *m* 26 April 1950 (*divorce* 1978) Capt David Charles George Jessel (*see* JESSEL, Bt), and has:

(1) *Richard James [Richard Jessel Esq, Holly Acres, 34 Jennings Rd, Smith FL03, Bermuda]; *b* 5 Jan 1954; *m* 3 Sept 1982 (*divorce* 1997) Harriet, dau of W J de St Pierre Bunbury and has:

1a *David Hugh Joseph; *b* 1986

2a *George FitzRoy; *b* 1990

1a *Edwina Mary-Grace; *b* 1984

(1) *Davina Jane [Mrs Charles Phillips, Ashlands House, N Sydmonton, Berks]; *b* 6 April 1952; *m* 1st 7 Oct 1970 (*divorce* 1977) Hon Richard Tyrell-Kenyon (*d* 1982), 2nd son of 5th Baron Kenyon (*qv*), and has issue:

1a *Vanessa Zoë; *b* 1970

(1) (cont.) Mrs Davina Tyrell-Kenyon *m* 2nd 14 Dec 1977 (*divorce* 1984) James Remington-Hobbs, er son of Courtenay Remington-Hobbs, of La Rose de Vents, Fairmanville, France 50840, and has further issue:

1a *Max Hugh; *b* 31 Dec 1979

(1) (cont.) Mrs Davina Remington-Hobbs *m* 3rd 1988 *Charles Richard Markham Phillips, and has further issue:

2a *Richard David Markham; *b* 1988

3a *David Charles; *b* 1991

DAVID

Creation: B. (LP, UK) 1978.

THE BARONESS DAVID, of Romsey in the City of Cambridge (Nora Ratcliff Blakesley, JP (Cambridge 1975)) [The Rt Hon The Baroness David JP, 50 Highsett, Cambridge CB2 1NZ; Cove, New Polzeath, Cornwall PL27 6UF]; *b* 23 Sept 1913; *educ* Ashby-de-la-Zouch Girls' GS, St Felix Southwold and Newnham Coll Cambridge (MA); Cncllr: Cambridge City 1964–67 and 1968–74, Cambs CC 1974–78; Memb Bd Peterborough Devpt Corp 1976–78; Baroness-in-Waiting 1978–79, Oppn Whip 1979–82, Dep Ch Oppn Whip 1982–87, Oppn Spokesman Educn; Pres Inst for Study and Treatment of Delinquency 1987–96; Hon Fell Newnham Coll Cambridge 1986; Fell Anglia Poly U 1989; *m* 1935 Richard William David, CBE (*d* 1993), and has issue:

1 *Nicholas Christopher [The Hon Nicholas David, Dept of Archaeology, U of Calgary, Canada]; *b* 1937; *m* 1st 1962 (*divorce* 1975) Hilke Hennig; *m* 2nd 1977 (*divorce* 1982) Iva Williams; *m* 3rd 1985 *Judy Sterner

2 *(Richard) Sebastian [The Hon Sebastian David, Box 820, Fort Macleod, Alberta, Canada]; *b* 1940; *m* 1963 *Eva Ross

1 *Teresa Katherine [The Hon Mrs Davies, 50 Clarence Rd, Moseley, Birmingham B13 9UH]; *b* 1944; *m* 1967 *Llewelyn Anthony Davies

2 *Elizabeth Sarah; *b* 1947; *m* 1st 1966 (*divorce* 1977) Martin Anthony Potter; *m* 2nd 1979 *John Forder

Lineage: GEORGE BLOCKLEY BLAKESLEY, JP; *m* Annie Edith — and had issue:

NORA RATCLIFFE, *cr* a **Baroness**

DAVIDSON

Arms: Argent on a fess sable between in chief two pheons azure, and in base a boar's head erased of the second, a portcullis chained or. **Crest:** A lion passant gules charged on the shoulder with a pheon or, and holding in the dexter paw a torch inflamed proper. **Supporters:** Dexter, a horse argent, charged on the shoulder with a rose gules, barbed and seeded proper; sinister, a horse sable, charged on the shoulder with a martlet or. **Motto:** *Lux ex tenebris* ('Light from darkness'). **Creation:** V. (UK) 11 June 1937.

THE 2ND VISCOUNT DAVIDSON, of Little Gaddesden, Co Hertford (John Andrew Davidson) [The Rt Hon The Viscount Davidson, House of Lords, London SW1A 0PW]; *b* 22 Dec 1928; *s f* 1970; *educ* Westminster and Pembroke Coll Cambridge (BA); Black Watch and 5th Bn KAR 1947–49, memb cncl CLA 1965–75, chm Management Ctee Roy E County Hosp 1966–75, memb E Anglia Ec Planning Cncl 1971–75, Ld in Waiting (Govt Whip) 1985–86, Capt Yeomen Gd (Dep Ch Whip) 1986–91; *m* 1st 30 June 1956 (*divorce* 1974) Margaret Birgitta, only dau of Maj-Gen Cyril Henry Norton, CB, CBE, DSO, of Dunn House, Long Melford, Suffolk, and has issue:

1 Alexandra Frances Margaret; *b* 13 April 1957; *m* 14 Dec 1983 *Richard John Oldfield, son of C C B Oldfield and Mrs B R P Brooks, and *d* 1995, leaving:

(1) *Christopher; *b* 1986

(2) *Henry; *b* 1991

(1) *Leonora; *b* 1985

2 *(Georgina) Caroline; *b* 16 May 1958; *m* 2 Oct 1982 *Lord Edward Alexander Somerset, 2nd son of 11th Duke of Beaufort (*qv*)

3 *Camilla Birgitta; *b* 17 Feb 1963; *m* 1st 1988 (*divorce* 1991) Simon Guthrie McNair Scott (*see* CAMROSE, V); *m* 2nd 2 June 1995 *Mark Gibson (*see* GIBSON, Bt, of Linconia)

4 *Kristina Louise (twin); *b* 17 Feb 1963

The 2nd VISCOUNT *m* 2nd 1975 *Mrs Pamela Joy Dobb, dau of John Vergette

Lineage: JOHN DAVIDSON, of Estancia Santo Domingo, Varela, Buenos Aires, Argentina; *b* 11 Feb 1808; *d* April 1893, leaving issue:

Sir JAMES MACKENZIE DAVIDSON, ktd 1912, MB and CM Aberdeen, Fell Physical Soc, Hon Consultant Radiographer Mil Hosps London Dist, Consulting Surgn X-Ray Dept Roy Lond Ophthalmic Hosp 1909–19, memb Roy Inst; *b* 6 Dec 1856; *m* 6 April 1883 Georgina Barbara Watt (*d* 15 Jan 1927), dau of Rev William Henderson, of Aberdeen, and *d* 2 April 1919, leaving, with a dau (Marjorie Isobel MacKenzie, *m* 26 Sept 1917 Bernard Elwell Potter, MB (*d* 21 Oct 1962)):

JOHN COLIN CAMPBELL DAVIDSON, **1st Viscount Davidson**, of Little Gaddesden, Co Hertford (UK), so *cr* 11 June 1937, CB (1919), CH (1923), GCVO (1935), PC (1928); *b* 23 Feb 1889; *educ* Westminster and Pembroke Coll Cambridge (BA 1911), barrister Middle Temple 1913; MP (U) Hemel Hempstead 1920–23 and 1924–37, Priv Sec to: Colonial Sec 1910–16, Chllr Exchequer 1916–19, Ld Privy Seal 1919–21, PPS to Pres BOT 1921–22 and PM 1922–23, Chllr Duchy Lancaster 1923–24 and 1931–37, Parly and Fin Sec Admlty 1924–26, chm C and Unionist Pty Orgn 1926–30, chm Indian States Enquiry Ctee 1932, chm Depl Ctee revision Ordnance Survey Maps 1935, Patron Maida Vale Hosp Nervous Diseases, Pres Inst Industl Admin, pres Hispanic and Luso-Brazilian Cncls, Anglo-Argentine Soc and Engrg Industs Assoc 1944, Grand Cross Dominican Order Merit Duarte, Sanchez y Mella 1957, Grand Cross Sun: Peru 1960, Order Merit de Mayo Argentina 1960, Order Merit Chile 1960; *m* 10 April 1919 Hon Frances Joan Dickinson, DBE (1950) (*d* 1985), MP Hemel Hempstead 1937–59, *cr* 1963 BARONESS NORTHCHURCH (LP; *d* 1985; *see* 1970 edn), yr dau of 1st Baron Dickinson (*qv*), and *d* 11 Dec 1970, leaving issue:

1 (JOHN) ANDREW DAVIDSON, **2nd and present Viscount Davidson**

2 +MALCOLM WILLIAM MACKENZIE [The Hon Malcolm Davidson, Las Cuadras, Monte de la Torre, Los Barrios, Prov de Cadiz, Spain]; *b* 28 Aug 1934; heir presumptive; *educ* Westminster and Pembroke Coll Cambridge; Black Watch 1953–55; *m* 1970 *(Evelyn) Ann Carew, yr dau of William Blackmore Storey (*see* QUEENSBERRY, M), and previously wife of Alan Perfect, WS (*d* 19–) and has issue:

(1) *John Nicolas Alexander; *b* 1971

(1) *Sophie Ann Frances; *b* 1973

1 *Margaret Joan [The Hon Mrs Fox, Quin House, Arundell, Ely, Cambs CB6 1BQ]; *b* 24 June 1922; *m* 13 Feb 1943 Ven Benjamin George Burton Fox (*d* 1978), MC, TD, CF, Archdeacon Wisbech, only son of James Benjamin Fox, of the Manor Farm, Erpingham, and has issue:

(1) *Colin George [The Rev Colin Fox, The Rectory, Church St, Pewsey, Wilts SN9 5DL]; *b* 28 July 1946; *educ* Millfield; *m* 1975 *Bridget Andrea Louise Willan, and has issue:

1a *George Hugh; *b* 1977

2a *Henry Benjamin Andrew; *b* 1983

1a *Alice Frances; *b* 1979

(1) *Elizabeth Angela [Mrs Anthony Mellows, 22 Devereux Court, Temple Bar, London WC2R 3JJ]; *b* 21 Dec 1943; CStJ; *m* 28 July 1973 *Prof Anthony R Mellows, TD, GCStJ, LLD, s of L B Mellows, of Croydon

(2) *Catherine Anne [Mrs James Lemon, 23 Mulberry Close, Cambridge CB4 2AS]; *b* 8 Dec 1950; *m* 1st 1977 (*divorce* 19–) Lt Donovan O'Brien Wright, est s of Rev B G Wright, of St Margaret's Rectory, Kingston, Jamaica; *m* 2nd 19– James Lemon (*d* 12 May 1992)

(3) *Penelope Margaret [Mrs Jonathan Marland, The Cottage, Morlys Lane, Gislingham, nr Eye, Suffolk]; *b* 21 Aug 1953; *m* 1979 *Jonathan Hay Marland

(4) *Rosemary Marjorie; *b* 21 Aug 1953; *m* 1978 *Michael Swiney

2 *Jean Elizabeth [The Hon Mrs Charles Strutt, Berwick Place, Hatfield Peverel, Chelmsford, Essex], late Capt WRAC (TA); *b* 19 June 1924; *m* 17 Dec 1952 Hon Charles Richard Strutt (*d* 1981), MA, 2nd s of 4th Baron Rayleigh (*qv*), and has issue

DAVIES

Arms: Or, a lion rampant gules between two fleurs-de-lys in fess azure, on a chief azure two pickaxes fesswise. **Crest:** An arm embowed proper, vested to the elbow argent, holding in the hand a miner's safety lamp proper. Motto: *Goreu bonedd rhinwedd* ('The highest nobility is virtue'). **Creation:** B. (UK) 21 June 1932.

THE 3RD BARON DAVIES, of Llandinam, Co Montgomery (David Davies) [The Rt Hon The Lord Davies, Plas Dinam, Llandinam, Powys SY17 5DQ]; *b* 2 Oct 1940, *s f* 1944; *educ* Eton and King's Coll Cambridge (BA 1961, MA 1965); CEng, MiCE, MBA, Chmn Welsh Nat Opera 1975–; *m* 24 July 1972 *Beryl, dau of William James Oliver, of Harborne, Birmingham, and has issue:

1 +DAVID DANIEL; *b* 23 Oct 1975

2 +Benjamin Michael Graham; *b* July 1985

1 *Eldrydd Jane; *b* 24 Oct 1973

2 *Lucy Medina; *b* 31 Dec 1978

Lineage: DAVID DAVIES, of Llandinam, Montgomeryshire; *d* 29 July 1890, leaving:

EDWARD DAVIES, of Plas Dinam, Llandinam; *b* 16 June 1852; *m* 15 Aug 1877 May (*d* 28 April 1888), er dau of Rev Evan Jones, of Brynhafren, Llandinam, and *d* 1 Jan 1898, leaving:

1 DAVID, **1st Baron**

1 Gwendoline Elizabeth, CH (1937); *d* unm 3 July 1951

2 Margaret Sidney; *d* unm 1963

The only son,

DAVID DAVIES, **1st Baron Davies**, of Llandinam, Co Montgomery (UK), so *cr* 21 June 1932, JP Montgomeryshire; *b* 11 May 1880; *educ* King's Coll Cambridge (MA); Hon LLD, FRGS, MP (Lib) Montgomeryshire 1906–29, KGStJ, Pres King Edward VII Welsh Nat Memorial Assoc, Chm and Hon Treas The New Cwlth Soc, Pres Nat Library of Wales, U Coll of Wales (Aberystwyth) and Welsh Cncl League of Nations Union, chm Ocean Coal and Wilsons Ltd, dir Midland Bank and GWR, cmded 14th Bn Royal Welsh Fus 1914–16 ; *m* 1st 1910 Amy (*d* 1918), dau of L T Penman, JP, of Broadwood Park, Lanchester, and had issue:

1 DAVID, **2nd Baron**

The **1st Baron** *m* 2nd 9 Dec 1922 Henrietta Margaret (*d* 27 Oct 1948), yr dau of James Grant Ferguson, of Baledmund, Pitlochry, Perthshire, and by her had issue:

2 Edward David Grant; *b* 30 Jan 1925; *educ* Gordonstoun and King's Coll Cambridge; *m* 1st 12 March 1949 Patricia, yr dau of Clifford Roberts Musto, of Salisbury, Rhodesia, and *d* 26 Oct 1997, leaving:

(1) +David Edmund Clifford; *b* 17 Jan 1958; *m* 1988 *Nicola D M, yst dau of John Walter Maxwell Miller Richard, of Edinburgh

(1) *Mary Ann Margaret [Mrs Martin Lovegrove, Boarden House, Hawkenbury, Headcorn, Kent]; *b* 30 Dec 1949; *m* 1971 *Martin Lovegrove, yst son of Capt Herbert Lovegrove, CBE, RN, of Nesbit, Winchester, Sussex, and has issue:

1a *Thomas; *b* 1983

1a *Amy; *b* 1979

(2) *Patricia Jean [Mrs Toby Everett, Woodhill Farm, Frensham, Farnham, Surrey]; *b* 27 Nov 1951; *m* 22 Jan 1977 *Toby Douglas Everett, son of R Everett, of Roeburn Soar, Wray, nr Lancs, and has issue:

1a *James Douglas; *b* 1980

1a *Emma Patricia; *b* 1978

2a *Polly Victoria; *b* 1986

(3) *Penelope Eldrydd; *b* 31 March 1955; *m* 1983 *Maj Peter Geoffrey Scrope, 13th/18th R Hus (Queen Mary's Own) (*see* MEXBOROUGH, E), and has issue:

1a *Edward Ralph William; *b* 1989

2a *Thomas (Tom) Henry Aloysius; *b* 31 Aug 1994

1a *Alexandra Beatrice Mary; *b* 1985

2a *Victoria Emily Louise; *b* 1986

3a *Henrietta Perpetua Agnes; *b* 1991

2 (cont.) The Hon Edward Davies *m* 2nd 12 Sept 1975 *Shirley, dau of Le Greur Harrison and formerly wife of John Gaze and *d* 26 Oct 1997

3 +Islwyn Edmund Evan, JP (Montgomeryshire), DL (Powys) [The Hon Islwyn Davies JP DL, Perth-y-bu, Sarn, Newtown, Powys SY16 4EP]; late RNVR; *b* 10 Dec 1926; *educ* Gordonstoun; *m* 15 Dec 1959 *Camilla Ann, er dau of Col Lawrence William Coulden, of 14 Portsea Place, London, and has issue:

(1) +Robin David; *b* 4 Jan 1961; *m* 1988 *Julie Hughes and has issue:

1a +Ruport; *b* 1988

1a *Daisy; *b* 1990

(2) +Christopher William; *b* 15 April 1963; *m* 1988 *Wendy Jones and has issue:

1a *Tara; *b* 1991

2a *Zoe; *b* 1993

(3) +Richard Edward; *b* 26 Oct 1965; *m* 1992 *Jessica Willey and has issue:

1a +Harry; *b* 1994

1a *Kitty; *b* 1996

1 *Mary Myfanwy [The Hon Mrs Mary Noble, 3/3 East Champanyie, Edinburgh EH9 3EL], CStJ, formerly in WRCNS; *b* 20 Nov 1923; *m* 1958 (*divorce* 1979) Hugh MacAskill Noble and has:

(1) *Robert David; *b* 29 June 1961

(2) *Andrew Jonathan; *b* 1962; *m* 1992 *—

(3) *Hugh James; *b* 1965

2 *Gwendoline Rita Jean [The Hon Mrs Gwendoline Cormack, Fethom View, Glen Estate, Borders, Scotland EH44 6PX]; *b* 1 May 1929; *m* 1 July 1950 (*divorce* 1979) John McRae Cormack, AFC, MA, est son of Lt-Col H S Cormack, MC, IMS (ret), of Felpham, Sussex, and has issue:

(1) Michael John; *b* 9 Sept 1962, *d* as a result of an accident 1980

(1) *Shara Jane [Mrs Anthony Leonard, 5 Montana Rd, London SW20]; *b* 7 March 1955; *m* 1983 *Anthony J Leonard, son of Hon Sir John Leonard, and has issue:

1a *Olivia Mary; *b* 1985

2a *Stephanie Emma; *b* 1989

(2) *Amanda Caroline [Mrs Edward Weston, The Malt House, Coln St Aldwyns, Glos]; *b* 14 June 1957; *m* 1982 *Edward John Weston, and has issue:

1a *Ruth Medina; *b* 1984

2a *Ella Jane; *b* 1986

(3) *Teresa Mary [The Hon Mrs Henry Tennant, The Glen, Innerleithen, Peeblesshire]; *b* 29 May 1959; *m* 1983 Hon Henry Lovell Tennant (*d* 1990), 2nd son of 3rd Baron Glenconner (*qv*), and has issue

The 1st BARON *d* 16 June 1944; his est son,

DAVID DAVIES, **2nd Baron Davies**; *b* 16 Jan 1915; *educ* King's Coll Cambridge (BA), Maj Roy Welch Fus WW II; *m* 21 Dec 1939 Ruth Eldrydd, OStJ (*d* 22 July 1966), 3rd dau of Maj William Marshall Dugdale, CB, DSO, TD, of LLanfyllin, Montgomeryshire, and was *ka* NW Europe Sept 1944, leaving issue:

1 DAVID DAVIES, **3rd and present Baron Davies**

2 +Jonathan Hugh [The Hon Jonathan Davies, Stonehill House, Abingdon, Oxon]; *b* 25 Jan 1944; *educ* Eton and Univ Coll Oxford; memb Museums and Galleries Commn 1985–; *m* 15 Oct 1966 *Mary Veronica, est dau of Sir (William) Godfrey Agnew, CVO, of Pinehurst, South Ascot, Berks, and has issue:

(1) +Michael; *b* 28 May 1968

(2) +Alexander William; *b* 1972; *m* 1994 *Sophia Mary Clare, only dau of (John) Robin Thistlethwayte, of Sorbrook Manor, Adderbury, Oxon

(1) *Ruth Gwendoline; *b* 1969

(2) *Gwendoline Christianne Mary; *b* 1975

(3) *Christianne Eldrydd; *b* 1976

(4) *Mary Theresa Ruth; *b* 1982

DAVIES OF COITY

Creation: B. (LP, UK) 2 Aug 1997.

THE BARON DAVIES OF COITY, of Penybont, Co Mid Glamorgan (David Garfield Davies, CBE (1996), JP (1972)) [The Rt Hon The Lord Davies of Coity CBE JP, House of Lords, London SW1A 0PW]; *b* 24 June 1935; *educ* Heolgam Secondary Sch and Bridgend Tech; RAF 1956–58; jr operator, electrical apprentice and electrician BSC Port Talbot 1950–69; USDAW Area Organiser 1969–73, Dep Divnl Offr 1973–78, Nat Offr 1978–85, Gen Sec 1986–97; memb: TUC Gen Cncl 1986–, Employment Appeal Tbnl 1991–; Chm TUC Internat Ctee 1992, JP (1972–79); *m* 1960 *Marian Jones and has four daus

Lineage: DAVID JOHN DAVIES; *m* Lizzie Ann — and had:

DAVID GARFIELD, *cr* a **Baron**

DAVIES OF OLDHAM

Creation: B. (LP, UK) 2 Aug 1977.

THE BARON DAVIES OF OLDHAM, of Broxbourne, Co Herts (Bryan Davies) [The Rt Hon The Lord Davies of Oldham, 28 Churchfields, Broxbourne, Herts EN10 7JS]; *b* 9 Nov 1939; *educ* Redditch High Sch, UCL Inst Educn and LSE; teacher Latymer Sch 1962–65, lecturer Middx Poly Enfield 1965–74; MP (Lab) Enfield 1974–79, Oldham Centl and Royton 1992–, Sec PLP 1979–92, Assist Govt Whip 1979, memb Select Ctees: Public Expenditure 1975–79, Overseas Devpt 1975–79, Nat Heritage 1992–93, Oppn Spokesman Higher Educn 1993–97; memb MRC 1977–79; *m* 1963 *Monica Rosemary Mildred Shearing and has two sons and a dau

Lineage: GEORGE WILLIAM DAVIES; *m* Beryl — and had:

BRYAN, *cr* a **Baron**

DAVSON

Arms: Arg. on a chevron sa. between two stags lodged gu., attired of the second in chief, and a representation of the sailing ship *Santa Maria* ppr. in base, three pheons inverted or. **Crest:** A dove ppr. gorged with an antique crown or, standing upon a branch of oak, fructed ppr. **Motto:** *Vis in consilio* ('Strength in counsel'). **Creation:** Bt. (UK) 21 Jan 1927.

SIR CHRISTOPHER MICHAEL EDWARD DAVSON, 3RD BT [Sir Christopher Davson Bt, 4 Mermaid St, Rye, Sussex TN31 7ET]; *b* 26 May 1927; *s* bro 1998; *educ* Eton; FCA (1953), Capt Welsh Gds, Liveryman Musicians Co; *m* 1st 2 June 1962 (*divorce* 1971) Evelyn Mary, only dau of James Wardrop, of 47 Cheniston Gardens, London W8; *m* 2nd 1975 *Kate, dau of Ludovic Foster, of Greatham Manor, Pulborough, Sussex, and has issue by his 1st w:

1 +GEORGE TRENCHARD SIMON; *b* 5 June 1964; *educ* Eton and Magdalen Coll Oxford; *m* 13 July 1985 (*divorce* 1996) Joanna, er dau of Dr James Bentley, of Domme, France, and has:
(1) *James; *b* 23 Dec 1990
(1) *Emma Louise; *b* 17 Sept 1988

Lineage: SIMON DAVSON, of Berbice, Br Guiana; *d* 7 June 1856, leaving:

Sir HENRY KATZ DAVSON; *b* 31 Jan 1830; memb Court of Policy Br Guiana, head Henry K Davson & Co London; *m* 2nd 15 Aug 1871 Ann Helen, only dau of Thomas Miller, MA, LLD, FRSE, of Perth, and *d* 21 Feb 1909, leaving:

1 Harry Miller, CMG, DSO; *b* 4 June 1872, Lt-Col RA S African War, WW I (despatches six times) and WW II; *m* 19 Jan 1910 Hon Georgina Violet St Clair (*d* 28 Dec 1957), 3rd dau of 15th Lord Sinclair (*qv*), and *d* 10 Nov 1961, leaving issue:
(1) Evelyn Arthur St Clair; *b* 24 Feb 1912; *educ* Eton; *m* 1st 20 May 1947 (*divorce* 1948) Helena Norah, only dau of Arthur Lambton, of 32 Argyll Mansions, London SW3; *m* 2nd 10 June 1950 *Nancy Elizabeth [Mrs Evelyn Davson, 27e Bramham Gardens, London SW5], dau of Geoffrey C Payne, of Hobart, Tasmania, and *d* 14 July 1997, leaving:
1a *Philip James St Clair; *b* 30 Jan 1960
1a *Elizabeth Jane St Clair; *b* 15 Oct 1954
2a *Prudence Anne Lindsay; *b* 2 Feb 1957
2 EDWARD RAE (Sir), **1st Bt**
3 Ivan Buchanan (Sir), OBE (1919), TD (1919); *b* 1884; Lt-Col RAF, Chm West India Ctee 1936–45, ktd 1942; *d* 27 Jan 1947
4 Thomas Gordon; *b* 31 May 1888; Lt RHG; *k* Ypres 13 May 1915

Sir HENRY's 2nd s,

Sir Edward Rae Davson, 1st Bt (UK), so *cr* 21 Jan 1927, KCMG (1934); Chm West Indies Conf, memb Empire Marketing Bd, Tstee Imp Inst, Govr Imp Coll of Tropical Ag, Govt Advsr Colonial Tde Ottawa Conf 1932; *b* 14 Feb 1875; ktd 1919; *m* 7 April 1921 Margot Elinor OBE (1920) (*d* 9 Sept 1966), er dau of Clayton Louis Glyn (*see* GLYN, Bt, of Ewell and Gaunt's), and *d* 6 Aug 1937, leaving:

1 Sir GEOFFREY later ANTHONY GEOFFREY LEO SIMON DAVSON later GLYN, **2nd Bt**, of Berbice, Br Guiana; *b* 13 March 1922; *educ* Eton, assumed by deed poll 1957 surname GLYN in lieu of DAVSON and the additional christian name ANTHONY; Capt Welsh Gds WW II, author: *Romanza* (1953), *The Jungle of Eden* (1954), *Elinor Glyn, a Biography* (1955), *The Ram in the Thicket* (1957), *I Can Take it All* (1959), *Kick Turn* (1963), *The Terminal* (1965), *The Seine* (1966), *The Dragon Variation* (1969), *The Blood of a Britishman* (1970), *The Companion Guide to Paris* (1985); *m* 2 Oct 1946 *Susan Eleanor [Lady Glyn, Marina Baie des Anges, Ducal Apt U-03, 06270 Villeneuve-Loubet, Alpes Maritimes, France], barrister Inner Temple 1950, Jr Cdr ATS, er dau of Col Sir Rhys Rhys Williams, 1st Bt, DSO, QC (*see* 1956 edn), and *d* 20 Jan 1998, having had:
(1) Caroline Mary; *b* 27 Aug 1947; novelist; *d* 1981
(2) *Victoria Anne; *b* 22 Jan 1951; barrister Inner Temple 1978
2 Sir CHRISTOPHER MICHAEL EDWARD DAVSON, **3rd and present Bt**

DAWSON

Arms: Azure on a chevron ermine between three bird-bolts argent a rose gules, leaved and slipped, between two daws respectant proper. **Crest:** Out of a naval crown or a daw proper. **Motto:** *Facta non verba* ('Deeds not words'). **Creation:** Bt. (UK) 5 Feb 1920.

SIR HUGH MICHAEL TREVOR DAWSON, 4TH BT, of Edgewarebury House, Co Middlesex [Sir Hugh Dawson Bt, 11 Burton Court, Franklin's Row, London SW3]; *b* 28 March 1956; *s* f 1983

Lineage: HUGH DAWSON, barrister; had:

Sir (Arthur) Trevor Dawson, 1st Bt (UK), so *cr* 5 Feb 1920, ktd 1909; *b* 1 May 1866; Cdr RN WW I, MICE, MIME, dir Vickers Ltd and Vickers-Armstrongs Ltd, chm Whitehead Torpedo Co, silver medal RSA, Gustave Canet gold medal, Kt Grand Cross Order Naval Merit Spain, Rising Sun and Sacred Treasure Japan; *m* 6 Jan 1892 Louise (*d* 30 Jan 1935), dau of John Miller Grant, and had issue:

1 HUGH TREVOR (Sir), **2nd Bt**
2 Arthur Trevor; *b* 20 Oct 1906; *d* 24 Sept 1908
1 Iris; *m* 17 March 1917 Brig-Gen John Micklem (*d* 26 Feb 1952), DSO, MC, Rifle Bde, and *d* 11 May 1966, leaving issue
2 Eva May; *m* 1 Sept 1917 Brig Ralph Micklem (*d* 21 March 1977), CMG, CBE, RE, and had issue

Sir TREVOR *d* 19 May 1931; his son,

Sir Hugh Trevor Dawson, 2nd Bt, CBE (1950); *b* 17 Jan 1893; dir: Decca Navigator Co 1945–75, Br Tyre and Rubber Co 1924–69, formerly with Dawson & Forbes Ltd (investment bankers), Cdr RN; *m* 30 March 1918 Vera Anne Loch, dau of Sir Frederick Loch Halliday, CIE, MVO, and *d* 3 April 1976, leaving issue:

1 (HUGH HALLIDAY) TREVOR (Sir), **3rd Bt**
1 *Ursula Anne Trevor; *b* 1919

2 *Avice Louise Trevor (twin); *m* 30 May 1942 (*divorce* 1964) Maj Edwin Inigo Lloyd Mostyn, MC, Scots Gds (*see* MOSTYN B), and has issue

3 *Patricia Elinor Trevor (twin) [Mrs John Menzies, Kames, Duns, Berwickshire]; *m* 1st 17 April 1943 (*divorce* 1953) Maj Raymond Alexander Carnegie, Scots Gds (*see* FIFE, D), and has issue; *m* 2nd 4 June 1953 *John Maxwell Menzies, only son of John Francis Menzies, of Westerdunes, N Berwick, and has further issue:

(1) *Miranda Jane; *b* 27 Oct 1954; *m* 1979 *Dermot Julian Jenkinson, and has issue (*see* JENKINSON Bt)

(2) *Sarah Jane; *b* 8 Dec 1955; *m* 1980 (*divorce* 19–) Nigel Rawlence

(3) *Cynthia Emma; *b* 1958; *m* 1986 *Ian C L Harrison, son of J T C Harrison, of Little Stream, Ascot, Berks

(3) *Katherine Patricia; *b* 11 April 1960

Sir HUGH *d* 14 Feb 1983; his er son,

Sir (Hugh Halliday) Trevor Dawson, 3rd Bt; *b* 6 June 1931; *educ* Harrow and RMA Sandhurst, Maj Scots Gds, chm all cos of Arbuthnot Gp, md Dawson and Forbes; *m* 7 July 1955 *Caroline Jane [Lady Dawson, 11 Burton Court, Franklin's Row, London SW3], only child of William Antony Acton, of 115 Eaton Square, London SW1 (*see* COWDRAY, V), and *d* 1983, leaving issue:

1 Sir HUGH MICHAEL TREVOR DAWSON, **4th and present Bt**

2 +NICHOLAS ANTONY TREVOR; *b* 17 Aug 1957; heir presumptive

DEAN OF BESWICK

Creation: B. (LP, UK) 1983.

THE BARON DEAN OF BESWICK, of W Leeds, Co W Yorks (Joseph Jabez) [The Rt Hon The Lord Dean of Beswick, House of Lords, London SW1A 0PW]; *b* 3 June 1922; Leader Manchester City Cncl; MP (Lab) Leeds West 1974–83, PPS to Min State CSD 1974–77, Assist Govt Whip 1978–79, Lab Party Pairing Whip 1982–83, 1985–; *m* 1945 *Helen, dau of Charles Hill, and has issue

Lineage: JOHN DEAN, of Manchester; had issue:

JOSEPH JABEZ, *cr* a **Baron**

DEAN OF HARPTREE

Creation: B. (LP, UK) 1993.

THE BARON DEAN OF HARPTREE, of Wedmore, Co Somerset (Sir (Arthur) Paul Dean, PC (1991)) [The Rt Hon The Lord Dean of Harptree PC, Archer's Wyck, Knightcott, Banwell, Weston-super-Mare, BS24 6HS]; *b* 14 Sept 1924; *educ* Ellesmere Coll and Exeter Coll Oxford (MA, BLitt); WWII: Capt Welsh Gds, ADC to Cdr 1 Corps BAOR; farmer 1950–56; resident tutor Swinton C Coll 1957, CRD 1957–64 (Assist Dir 1962–64), MP (C) N Somerset 1964–83 and Woodspring 1983–92, Parly U-Sec DHSS 1970–74, Chm C Health and Social Security Ctee 1979–82, Dep Chm Ways and Means Ctee 1982–87 (1st Dep Chm 1987–92), Dep Speaker 1987–92; memb: exec ctee UK Branch CPA 1975–92, H of C Chm's Panel 1979–82, Commons Servs Select Ctee 1979–82, exec ctee Assoc C Peers 1995; ktd 1985; dir Charterhouse Pensions, Watney Mann and Truman Hldgs; Govr: Cwlth Inst 1981–89, BUPA; *m* 1st 1957 Doris Ellen (*d* 1979), dau of Frank Webb, of Sussex; *m* 2nd 1980 *Peggy Parker

Lineage: ARTHUR PERCIVAL DEAN; *m* Jessie Margaret Gaunt and had:

(ARTHUR) PAUL, *cr* a **Baron**

DEAN OF THORNTON-LE-FYLDE

Creation: B. (LP, UK) 1993.

THE BARONESS DEAN OF THORNTON-LE-FYLDE, of Eccles, Co Greater Manchester (Brenda Dean, PC (1998)) [The Rt Hon The Baroness Dean of Thornton-le-Fylde PC, House of Lords, London SW1A 0PW]; *b* 29 April 1943; *educ* St Andrews Eccles and Stretford GS; SOGAT: Admin Sec 1959–72, Assist Sec Manchester Branch 1971–76 (Sec 1976–83), Memb Nat Exec Cncl 1977–83, Pres SOGAT 1983–85, Gen Sec 1985–91; Dep Gen Sec GPMU 1991–92; Co-Chm Women's Nat Commn 1985–87; Gen Advsy Cncl BBC 1985–89; TUC Gen Cncl 1985–92, TUC Ec Ctee 1987–92, NEDC 1989–92; memb Cncl City U 1991–96; Govr Ditchley Foundation 1992–; Chm ICSTIS 1993– (memb 1991–); memb: Printing and Publishing Trng Bd 1974–82, Supplementary Benefits Commn 1976–80, Price Commn 1977–79, Occupational Pensions Bd 1983–87, Employment Appeal Tbnl 1991–, Cncl ABSA 1990, Bar Cncl Legal Educn 1992–, Press Complaints Commn 1993–, Broadcasting Complaints Commn 1993–; non exec dir Inveresk plc 1994–; Hon MA Salford 1986, Hon Fellow Lancs Poly 1991, Hon DCL City U 1993, FRSA 1992; *m* 1988 *Keith Desmond McDowall

Lineage: HUGH DEAN; *m* Lillian — and has issue:

BRENDA, *cr* a **Baroness**

DEARING

Creation: B. (LP, UK) 1998.

THE BARON DEARING, of Kingston upon Hull, Co of E Riding of Yorks (Sir Ron(ald) Ernest Dearing, CB (1979)) [The Rt Hon The Lord Dearing CB, c/o Sheila Hussein, 45 Notting Hill Gate, London W11 3JB];*b* 27 July 1930; *educ* Doncaster GS, Hull U and London Business Sch; with Min Lab and Nat Serv 1946–49, Min Power 1949–62, Treasury 1962–64, Mins Power and Technology and DTI 1965–72 (Regnl Dir N Regn and U-Sec 1972–74), U-Sec Dept Industry 1975–76, Dep Sec Dept Industry 1976–80, Post Office Corp: Dep Chm 1980–81, Chm 1981–87; Chm: NICG 1983–94, Accounting Standards Review Ctee CCAB 1987–88, CNAA 1987–88, Co Durham Devpt Corp 1987–90, PCFC 1988–93, London Educn Business Ptnrship 1989–92, Fin Reporting Cncl 1990–93, Northern Devpt Co 1990–94, UFC 1991–93, HEFCE 1992–93, Northern Sinfonia Appeals Ctee 1993–94, Camelot Gp 1993–95, Sch Curriculum and Assessment Authority 1993–96; dir: Whitbread 1987–90, Prudential 1987–91, IMI 1988–95, Br Coal 1988–91, Erisson Ltd 1988–93, English Estates 1988–90; memb cncl Industl Soc 1985–, Pres Inst Direct Mktg 1994–97, non-exec dir Business Systems 1997–, Chllr Nottingham U 1993–, Freeman City London 1982, ktd 1984; *m* 1954 *Margaret Patricia Riley and has two daus

Lineage: E H A DEARING; *m* M T Hoyle and had:

RON(ALD) ERNEST, *cr* a **Baron**

DEBENHAM

Arms: Sable a bend cotised between two crescents or. **Crest:** In front of a garb or a sickle erect proper, the blade pointing to the sinister.
Creation: Bt. (UK) 28 Jan 1931.

SIR GILBERT RIDLEY DEBENHAM, 3RD BT, of Bladen, Dorset [Sir Gilbert Debenham Bt, Tonerspuddle Farm, Dorchester, Dorset]; *b* 28 June 1906, *s* bro 1964; *educ* Eton and Trin Coll Cambridge (BA 1928, BChir 1935); DPM 1946, MRCPsych 1971, former consultant psychiatrist NHS; *m* 1 April 1935 Violet Mary (Mollie) (*d* 1994), er dau of Judge George Herbert Higgins, and has had issue:

1 George Andrew; *b* 10 April 1938; *educ* Bryanston and Trin Coll Cambridge (BA); *m* 1969 *Penelope Jane, dau of John David Armishaw Carter, and *d* 1991, leaving issue:

(1) +THOMAS ADAM; *b* 28 Feb 1971

(1) *(Anna) Rose; *b* 1972

2 +William Michael [William Debenham Esq, Cowper Lane Farm, Crich, Derbyshire]; *b* 30 June 1940; *educ* Bryanston and Trin Coll Cambridge (BA), MSC; *m* 1974 *Gunnel Birgitta, dau of Holger Elis Valfrid Holmgren, and has issue:

(1) +Oliver William; *b* 1976

(2) +Martin Ellis; *b* 1980

3 +Paul Edward [Paul Debenham Esq, Tonerspuddle Farm House, Dorchester, Dorset]; *b* 20 March 1942; *educ* Bryanston and Trin Coll Cambridge (BA, MB, BChir); *m* 16 Nov 1968 *Dr Jennifer Mary, MB, ChB, yr dau of G W Rees, and has issue:

(1) +Edward James; *b* 1970

(2) +Michael John; *b* 1973

(1) *Clare Elizabeth; *b* 1977

1 *Virginia Mary [Mrs Nigel Purchon, 54 Gondar Gdns, London NW6]; *b* 25 April 1936; *m* 1st 28 April 1960 (*divorce* 19–) Graham Leslie Nicol, of 53 Upper Park Rd, London NW3, and has issue:

(1) *Stephen Leslie; *b* 7 Oct 1961

(2) *Alan Leslie; *b* 21 Nov 1966

(1) *Lucy Jean; *b* 7 Aug 1963

1 (cont.) Mrs Virginia Nicol *m* 2nd 1982 *Nigel Denison Purchon, FLS

Lineage: FRANK DEBENHAM, of Fitzjohn's Avenue, Hampstead, JP; *b* 3 Nov 1837; *m* 8 April 1863 Emma Folkhard (*d* 9 Oct 1909), dau of Frederick Henry Ridley, and *d* 15 Jan 1917, leaving, with other issue:

Sir Ernest Ridley Debenham, 1st Bt (UK), so *cr* 28 Jan 1931, JP; *b* 26 May 1865; *educ* Trin Coll Cambridge (MA); chm Debenhams, dir Lloyds Bank; *m* 8 Nov 1892 Cecily (*d* 31 Oct 1950), dau of William Kenrick, PC, of The Grove, Harborne, Staffs, by Mary, sis of Joseph Chamberlain, PC, MP, and *d* 25 Dec 1952 leaving:

1 **Sir Piers Kenrick Debenham, 2nd Bt**, JP; *b* 28 July 1904; *educ* Eton and Trin Coll Cambridge (BA); Training Bn Coldstream Gds WW II, Control Commn Germany; *m* 24 May 1928 Angela Sibell (*d* 16 June 1965), 3rd dau of Sir Richard Arthur Surtees Paget, 2nd Bt, of Cranmore Hall (*qv*), and *dspm* 14 Sept 1964, leaving issue:

(1) *Caroline Susan; *b* 9 Jan 1930; *m* 24 April 1954 *Baron Neill of Bladen (*qv*), and has had issue:

1a *Timothy Piers Patrick; *b* 13 Feb 1955

2a *Robin Charles Richard; *b* 28 July 1956

3a *Jonathan Francis Kenrick; *b* 19 Feb 1960; *m* 1991 *Lucy, yr dau of Frank Mullens, of Mcmahon's Point, Sydney, Australia

4a Matthew Piers Thomas; *b* 26 April 1965; *m* 1990 *Kirstin R, dau of Ian Tegner, of 44 Norland Sq, London W11 and *d* 1993, leaving issue:

1b *Cecilia; *b* 199–

1a *Harriet Susan Anne; *b* 16 March 1962; *m* 1987 *Douglas Michael Free

2a *Emma Charlotte Angela; *b* 12 Nov 1967; *m* 6 July 1996 *Christopher Geidt, only s of late M B Geidt and Mrs Mackenzie Geidt, of Clapham, London

(2) *Anne Charlotte [Mrs Peter Horsfield, 24 Liverpool Rd, Kingston Hill, Surrey]; *b* 12 Aug 1932; *m* 9 June 1962 *Peter Muir Horsfield, QC, and has issue:

1a *Andrew Piers; *b* 17 March 1963; *m* 1991 *Gigi, yr dau of Dr Yvon Carignan, of Basking Ridge, NJ, USA

2a *Charles Peter; *b* 10 Nov 1964

3a *Thomas Martin; *b* 23 March 1966

2 Sir GILBERT RIDLEY DEBENHAM, **3rd and present Bt**

3 Martin Ridley, JP (1966); *b* 16 Oct 1909; *educ* Eton and Trin Coll Cambridge (BA); CC Dorset 1964, memb St Pancras Borough Cncl 1934–52, Capt Rifle Bde WW II, memb: Met Water Bd 1946–49, Wareham and Purbeck RDC 1964–77; *m* 19 May 1937 *Beatrice Sydney [Mrs Martin Debenham, Dairy House, Affpuddle, Dorset], yst dau of Ven Harry Sydney Radcliffe, Archdeacon Lynn, and *d* 17 March 1977, leaving issue:

(1) +James Martin Robert [James Debenham Esq, East Farm, Affpuddle, Dorset DT2 7HH]; *b* 14 Oct 1951; *educ* Bryanston; *m* 1982 *Jean Veronica, dau of Maj Royston Eric Acres, MBE, and has issue:

1a +Bosworth Ridley Oriole Acres; *b* 1982

2a +Branwell George Kenrick Acres; *b* 1985

1a *Bathsheba Alice Maisie; *b* 1989

(1) (cont.) James Debenham also adopted his stepchildren:

*Circe Alexandra Acres; *b* 1970

Salome Gabriella Pilkington Acres; *b* 1975; *d* 1995

(1) *Susanna Elizabeth; *b* 20 Sept 1943; *m* 2 June 1964 *Alexander Surtees Chancellor, yr son of Sir Christopher John Howard Chancellor, CMG (*see* PAGET, Bt, of Cranmore Hall), and has issue

1 Marjorie Cecily; *b* 3 Dec 1893

2 Hester Mary; *b* 17 Sept 1895; *m* 8 July 1937 Wolmer Marlow (*d* 22 Nov 1963), Govr Svalbard, Norway

3 Joan Millicent; *b* 24 Feb 1897; *m* 10 Dec 1919 Kenneth Murray Hutton (*d* 1950), of Murital, Bonne Nuit, St John's, Jersey, CI, and *d* a German POW 4 April 1943, leaving issue

4 Alison Edith; *b* 18 Feb 1903; *m* 4 Dec 1930 Rene Jules Lepiat (*d* 1958) and *d* 24 Nov 1967, leaving issue

5 *Cecil Audrey [Mrs Charles Bielby, 43 High St, Amersham, Bucks], F/O WAAF WW II (despatches); *b* 28 June 1906; *m* 22 June 1953 Charles Robert Bielby (*d* 28 Oct 1967)

DECIES

Arms: Quarterly, 1st and 4th, arg. crusilly fitchée three fleurs-de-lys within a bordure engrailed all sa.; 2nd and 3rd, arg. a chief indented sa.; over all a mullet for difference. **Crest:** A dragon's head erased az. transfixed in the neck with a broken tilting spear or, the point broken off arg., thrust through the upper jaw, charged with a mullet for difference. **Supporters:** Two angels ppr., vested arg., winged and crined or, each holding in the exterior hand a sword erect also arg., pommel and hilt gold and charged on the breast with a mullet for difference. **Motto:** *Nil nisi cruce* ('Nothing without the Cross'). **Creation:** B. (UK) 22 Dec 1812.

THE 7TH BARON DECIES, of Decies, Co Waterford (Marcus Hugh Tristram de la Poer Beresford) [The Rt Hon The Lord Decies, Straffan Lodge, Straffan, Co Kildare, Ireland]; *b* 5 Aug 1948; *s* f 1992; *educ* St Columba's Coll and Dublin U (MLitt); *m* 11 April 1970 (*divorce* 1974) Sarah Jane, only dau of Col Basil Gunnell, of Gun House, New Romney; *m* 2nd 1981 *Edel Jeannette, dau of Vincent Ambrose Hendron, of Dublin, and has issue:

1 +ROBERT MARCUS DUNCAN De La POER; *b* 14 July 1988

2 +David George Morley Hugh de la Poer; *b* 1991

1 *Louisa Katherine de la Poer; *b* 1984

2 *Jessica Laragh de la Poer; *b* 16 Nov 1996

Title of Decies: A Viscountcy of this name was created in January 1568/9 in favour of Maurice FitzGerald, whose family held the area called the Decies in Co Waterford. (The lands of Decies were later subject to various acquisitive ploys and counterploys by other peers connected with the title Decies.) On this first Viscount's death in 1572 the 16th-century title expired. A subsequent Viscountcy of Decies, together with an Earldom of Tyrone, was granted in 1673 to Richard Power, 6th Baron Le Power and Coroghmore. As a Catholic he fell victim to Titus Oates's inventions about a so-called Popish Plot and was incarcerated in Dublin Castle and the Tower of London at various times between late 1679 and early 1684. Under JAMES II he fared rather better, becoming Lord Lieutenant of Co Waterford, for which he had already sat as an MP in the Irish Parliament. With the collapse of the Jacobite cause in Ireland he was again sent to the Tower, where he died a few months later.

His son the 2nd Earl was a Protestant and accordingly attainted by JAMES II's Irish Parliament in 1689. He attempted to secure the Decies estates, which had previously been granted his father by the Crown although the grant was later nullified, by forcibly marrying the daughter of the former owner, John FitzGerald, of Dromana, a relative of the Maurice FitzGerald who had been ennobled as Viscount of Decies in 1568/9. She was in any case the 2nd Earl's cousin since John FitzGerald had married the 5th Lord Power's daughter. The marriage was annulled and she subsequently married the son and heir of the 4th Viscount Grandison of Limerick. Their descendant Henry Villiers-Stuart was created in 1839 Baron Stuart de Decies of Dromana (*see* BUTE, M).

With the death of the 2nd Earl's younger brother the 3rd Earl in 1704 the Viscountcy of Decies (as also the Earldom of Tyrone) expired. They were revived in 1720 and 1746 respectively for his son-in-law, Marcus Beresford, ancestor of both the current Lords Decies and the Marquesses of Waterford (*qv*).

Lineage: The 1st EARL OF TYRONE (*d* WATERFORD, M) had a 3rd s:

WILLIAM BERESFORD, **1st Baron Decies**, of Decies, Co Waterford (I), so *cr* 22 Dec 1812, PC (I 1794); *b* 16 April 1743; *educ* Trin Coll Dublin (BA 1763, MA 1766, DD 1780); Rector Urney, Co Derry, Bp: Dromore 1780, Ossory 1782, Archbp Tuam 1794; *m* 16 June 1763 Elizabeth, 2nd dau of John FitzGibbon and sis of 1st Earl of Clare of the 1795 *cr*, and had, with three er s (*d* young):

1 JOHN, **2nd Baron**

2 George (Rev); *b* 21 May 1776; *m* 21 May 1798 Susan, 3rd dau of Hamilton George, of Kilbrew, Co Meath, and *d* 10 Aug 1842, having had issue:

(1) William (Rev), Incumbent of St Chad's, Stafford; *b* 25 May 1799; *m* 15 May 1830 Sarah, widow of David Simpson and dau of John Bull, and *d* 1881, leaving issue

(2) Marcus, Gen-Col 20th Foot, Cmdt Bangalore; *b* 28 July 1800; *m* 1st Oct 1828 Isabella (*d* Aug 1836), dau of Thomas Bermingham Daly Henry Sewell, and had issue:

1a Harriet Louise; *d* 26 Feb 1876

2a Isabella Eliza; *m* 21 Jan 1856 Lt-Gen George Brydge-Rodney (*d* 8 July 1895), CB, and *d* 1 Aug 1915, leaving issue (*see* RODNEY, B)

(2) (cont.) Gen Marcus Beresford *m* 2nd 22 Jan 1838 Caroline (*d* 8 Jan 1895), 2nd dau of William Fane, HEICS (*see* WESTMORLAND, E), and *d* 16 March 1876, having by her had:

1a Marcus de la Poer, Capt and Hon Major 4th Bn Royal Warwicks Regt; *b* 20 Sept 1847

3a Ethel Louisa; *m* 7 Sept 1880 Henry Montagu Spencer (*d* 26 Oct 1924), of Blockley, Worcs, and *d* 5 Nov 1925, leaving issue (*see* CHURCHILL V)

(3) George Hamilton (Rev); *b* 1801; *m* 1st Nov 1829 Elizabeth (*d* Nov 1847), dau of Matthew Nisbet, of Derrycarn, Co Leitrim, and had, with other issue:

1a George de la Poer, Maj-Gen Madras Staff Corps; *b* 16 Aug 1830; *m* 16 Feb 1865 Hester Beatrice (*d* 9 May 1913), widow of Capt Francis Fox and dau of Rev Robert Bury, of Clogrenane, and *d* 7 Oct 1913, having had issue:

1b George de la Poer; *b* 3 Nov 1865; *d* unm 1896

1b Olivia Mary, OBE; *m* 9 Dec 1886 Sir Joseph Henry Greer (*d* 24 Aug 1934), KCVO, Capt Highland LI, of The Grange, Moy, Co Tyrone, and had issue

2b Hester Caroline; *m* 7 July 1900 Brig-Gen Robert Seymour Vandeleur (*d* 20 June 1956), CB, CMG, Seaforth Highrs, yr son of Capt Crofton Toler Vandeleur, 7th Dragoon Gds, and *d* 5 May 1940, leaving issue

2a Henry Tristram de la Poer; *b* 29 July 1841; *m* 1884 Louisa Margaret (*d* 1 Oct 1933), dau of William Coventry, of Lyndhurst, Armidale, NSW, and *d* 12 Aug 1930, leaving issue:

1b George de la Poer (Sir), CB (1938), MC (1918), Maj-Gen IA, T/Brig and Bde Cdr 1935, Maj-Gen 1938, DA and QMG N Command India 1938–40, Dist Cdr 1940 (despatches), ret 1942, ktd 1949, Order Nile 3rd Cl; *b* 21 July 1885; *m* 15 Nov 1916 Margaret Ethel Granville (*d* 30 Dec 1963), yst dau of Rev Canon Arthur Christopher Thynne (*see* BATH, M), and *d* 29 Sept 1964, leaving issue:

1c Benedict Henry de la Poer; WW II with RAC; *b* 2 Sept 1917; *m* 1949 *Dorothy Kate [Mrs Benedict de la Poer Beresford, 36 Cole Park Rd, Twickenham, Mddx TW1 4SI], dau of George Cooper, of Hillcrest, Gt Bedwyn, Wilts, and *d* 7 April 1997, leaving issue:

1d *Margaret Jane; *b* 18 Aug 1963; *m* 19– *— and has:

1e *Oliver Benedict

1e *Luchia Portia

2c Stephen Marcus de la Poer, DSC; Lt-Cdr RN WW II; *b* 18 Dec 1920; *m* 1952 Susan Wendy (*d* 13 March 1998), dau of Maj Tom Lees Dearbergh, of Stockhold Green, Suffolk, and *d* 1982, leaving:

1d *Diana Margaret; *b* 24 April 1953; *m* 1976 *Henry James Harmer, and has issue:

1e *Nicholas Benjamin; *b* 1983

1e *Claire Susan; *b* 1981

2e *Amy Diana; *b* 1986

2d *Angela Susan; *b* 24 April 1953

2b William Coventry de la Poer; *b* 2 June 1887; *m* 31 March 1921 Jessie (*k* in a motor accident 30 Sept 1930), only dau of Edgar Lindeman Rowling, of Wingham, NSW, and *d* 10 July 1938, leaving issue:

1c +Charles Marcus Tristram de la Poer [Charles de la Poer Beresford Esq, Deepdene, Coonabarabran, NSW, Australia]; WW II 1942–46 in RAAF; *b* 9 Nov 1923; *m* 1st 29 June 1948 Mary Frances (*d* 1972), dau of Hugh Buckingham Loveband, of Blenheim, Coonabarabran, NSW, and has issue:

1d *Roslyn de la Poer; *b* 11 Nov 1949

2d *Julie de la Poer; *b* 30 Sept 1952

1c (cont.) Charles Beresford *m* 2nd 1973 *Gwen Cornwell

1c *Patricia de la Poer [Mrs R S Meares, 51 Bishop St, Goulburn, NSW, Australia]; *b* 5 May 1922; *m* 1953 *R S Meares and has issue:

1d *Richard Grant; *b* 1955

2d *Philip Marcus; *b* 1960

3b Marcus Gervais de la Poer; Lt RFA WW I, Lt Australian Garrison Forces WW II; *b* 22 Oct 1888; *educ* Sydney U (BA 1913); *m* 27 Oct 1927 Susan Mildred Blomfield, er dau of Edward Charles Close Campbell, of Duntroon, NSW, and *d* 6 Oct 1967, leaving issue:

1c +Barrington Henry de la Poer; *b* 11 Oct 1928; *m* 8 March 1952 *Fleur Marie, yr dau of John Chrisp, of Corowa, NSW, and has issue:

1d +Sean Anthony de la Poer; *b* 31 July 1962

1d *Amanda de la Poer; *b* 31 Oct 1956

1a Mary; *m* Sept 1854 Antoine Butler, 3rd son of Sir Thomas Butler, 8th Bt, of Cloughgrenan (*qv*), and *d* 22 Nov 1862, leaving issue

2a Elizabeth; *m* 1857 Gen James Maurice Primrose (*d* 25 Nov 1892), CSI, and *d* 13 June 1925, leaving issue

(3) (cont.) The Rev George Beresford *m* 2nd 8 March 1853 Marianne Sarah (*d* 1 Feb 1884), dau of Robert Saunderson, of Dromkeen, Co Cavan, and widow of Rev John Delap, and *d* 2 March 1869

(4) John Gorges, EICS; *b* 3 June 1805; *m* 21 Oct 1826 Matilda Anne (*d* 25 Feb 1886 aged 76), dau of Maj Francis Russell Eagar, and *d* 24 Dec 1879, having had, with other issue:

1a Hamilton de la Poer, Maj RMA; *b* 20 Sept 1849; *m* 24 April 1879 Charlotte Sophia (*d* 1929), dau of Capt Cockburn, 18th Regt, and *d* 3 March 1942

1a Susan Georgina; *m* 6 Feb 1877 Rev G G Bird, Vicar Hollinwood, and *d* March 1906

(5) Henry, Capt 71st Regt; *m* 7 July 1838 Dora (*dsp* 1858), dau of W Watson, of North Seaton, and *d* 15 March 1842

(1) Elizabeth Anne; *m* 16 June 1829 Myles John O'Reilly (*d* 24 Oct 1857), of The Heath House, Queen's Co, and *d* 27 March 1838

(2) Susan Anne; *m* 1st 8 Feb 1830 Matthew O'Reilly (*d* 10 June 1841), of Thomastown, Co Louth; *m* 2nd 2 June 1842 Rev Gerald Stephen FitzGerald, Rector Wanstead, of Ophaley, and *d* 27 Dec 1881

3 William (Rev); *b* 20 Nov 1780; *m* 19 July 1804 Lady Anna Bennet (*d* Sept 1836), dau of 4th Earl of Tankerville (*qv*), and *d* 27 June 1830, leaving issue:

(1) William Henry, Capt Rifle Bde; *b* 1810; *m* 10 July 1850 Emma Catherine Lawrence, of Montreal, and *d* 26 Feb 1875, leaving issue:

1a Henrietta; *d* 20 Feb 1920

(1) Alicia; *m* 12 Sept 1834 Horace Hamond, KH, Consul at Cherbourg, and *d* 27 March 1882, leaving issue

1 Catherine Eleanor; *m* 1791 Rev William Armstrong, of Mealiffe, Co Tipperary, and *d* 1837

2 Araminta Anne; *m* 1794 Very Rev Arthur John Preston, DD, Dean of Limerick, and *d* 1816

3 Harriet; *m* Jan 1796 Col Thomas Bermingham Daly Henry Sewell (claimed the Barony of Athenry) and *d* 11 June 1834

4 Frances; *m* 1797, as his 2nd w, Col Thomas Burrowes, of Dangan Castle, Co Meath, and *d* his widow 7 Oct 1864

5 Louisa; *m* 1st 10 April 1806 Thomas Hope (*d* 2 Feb 1831), of Deepdene, Surrey, and had issue; *m* 2nd 29 Nov 1832 1st and last Viscount Beresford of Beresford (*dsp* 8 Jan 1854) and *d* 21 July 1851

The 1st BARON *d* 6 Sept 1819; his son,

JOHN BERESFORD later HORSLEY-BERESFORD (added on marriage), **2nd Baron Decies**; *b* 20 Jan 1773; *educ* Emmanuel Coll Cambridge; *m* 26 July 1810 Charlotte Philadelphia (*d* 9 March 1852), only dau and heir of Robert Horsley, of Bolam, Northumberland, and had issue:

1 WILLIAM ROBERT JOHN, **3rd Baron**

1 Georgina Catherine; *b* 21 Aug 1812; *m* 1st Aug 1831 William Watson, of North Seaton, Northumberland; *m* 2nd 25 Sept 1845 Henry Edward Brown

2 Louisa Elizabeth; *b* April 1814; *m* 25 Nov 1834 3rd Marquess of Ailesbury (*qv*) and *d* 14 Oct 1891, leaving issue

3 Caroline Agnes; *m* 1st 15 Oct 1836 4th Duke of Montrose (*qv*) and had issue; *m* 2nd 22 Jan 1876 William Stuart Stirling-Crawford (*d* 23 Feb 1883), of Milton, Lanark; *m* 3rd 26 July 1888 Marcus Henry Milner (*d* 16 Jan 1939), DSO, MVO (*see* MILNER, Bt), and *d* 16 Nov 1894

The 2nd BARON *d* 1 March 1865; his only son,

WILLIAM ROBERT JOHN HORSLEY-BERESFORD, **3rd Baron Decies**, Capt 10th Hus and Gren Gds; *b* June 1811; *m* 31 July 1860 Catherine Anne (*d* 27 Feb 1941), 2nd dau of Cdr William Dent Dent, RN, of Shortflatt Tower, Northumberland, and *d* 3 July 1893, having had issue:

1 WILLIAM MARCUS De La POER HORSLEY-BERESFORD, **4th Baron Decies**, DL, JP (Northumberland and Cinque Ports); *b* 12 Jan 1865; *m* 12 March 1901 Maria Gertrude (*d* 4 April 1939), yr dau of Sir John Pollard Willoughby, 4th Bt, and *dsp* 30 July 1910

2 JOHN GRAHAM HOPE De La POER, **5th Baron**

3 Seton Robert de la Poer, war correspondent Boer War, Lt 4th Bn Sherwood Foresters; *b* 1868; *m* 1st 1899 (*divorce* 1909) Delia Dorthy (*d* 28 Sept 1966), dau of Daniel John O'Sullivan, of The Grange, Killarney, Co Kerry; *m* 2nd 28 June 1915 Joan Rosemary (*m* 2nd 28 Feb 1929 Col Ralph Patterson COBBOLD later SAWLE (roy licence 1932), DSO (*d* 5 Dec 1965)), dau of R-Adml Sir Charles John Graves-Sawle, 4th Bt, MVO (*see* 1932 edn), and *d* 28 May 1928

4 Henry William Walter, Capt 4th Bn Sherwood Foresters, Lt 13th Hus, served Boer War 1901–02 and WW I; *b* 22 April 1876; *m* 6 Oct 1904 Constance, widow of Michael Levenston, and *d* 28 Jan 1924

5 William Arthur de la Poer, T/Lt RASC 1917, served Boer War 1899–1900; *b* 9 Aug 1878; *m* 1st 17 June 1901 (*divorce* 1919) Florence (*d* 1969), dau of Gardner L Miller, of Providence, RI, USA, and had issue:

(1) Charles William Marcus de la Poer; *b* 30 Nov 1902; *m* 1929 Barbara, dau of Dr Louis Scott, of Boston, Mass., and *dsp* 11 Feb 1968

(2) George Graham de la Poer; *b* 28 Oct 1903; *m* 1938 *Sherman [Mrs George Horsley-Beresford, Box 1085, Frederiksted, Isle of St Croix, US Virgin Islands], dau of Frank Olmsted, of New York, and *d* 1974, leaving issue:

1a +Marcus Hughes de la Poer [Marcus Horsley-Beresford, Box 1085, Frederiksted, Isle of St Croix, US Virgin Islands 00841]; *b* 1943; late Capt USAF, pilot Eastern Airlines; *m* 1st 1962 (*divorce* 19–) Lynne, dau of Linden Green, of E Millstone, NJ, and has issue:

1b +Marcus Tyler de la Poer; *b* 1963

1b *Teresa Leigh; *b* 1965

1a (cont.) Marcus Horsley-Beresford *m* 2nd 1979 *Diane Armstrong, and has further issue:

2b *Julia Victoria de la Poer; *b* 1983

2a +Peter Graham de la Poer [Peter Horsley-Beresford, 4501 15th St N, Arlington, Va 22207, USA]; *b* 1 Dec 1956; *m* 19– *Carrie, dau of John Peterson, of Naples, Florida

1a *Holly Audrey de la Poer; *b* 1939

(3) John Duncan de la Poer; *b* 24 Nov 1904; *m* 1934 Aina (*d* 1974), dau of Blaine R Richard, of Miami Beach, USA, and *d* 24 Jan 1998 having had:

1a Sheila Kathleen; *b* 1941; *d* 1986

(1) Audrey Catherine de la Poer; *d* 24 May 1922

(2) Sheila Kathleen de la Poer; *d* 31 March 1913

5 (cont.) William Horsley-Beresford *m* 2nd 22 July 1919 (*divorce* 1928) Laura (*d* 1958), dau of Capt St John Halford Coventry, Gren Gds (*see* COVENTRY, E), and by her had issue:

(4) +Patrick George; *b* 9 Nov 1924; *m* 1st 13 Feb 1953 (*divorce* 1956) Miriam Morton, of Philadelphia; *m* 2nd Nov 1959 Leslie Yvonne (*d* 1985), yst dau of Leslie Robert McCaskey, of Crawford House, Wellington, NZ, and Mrs Yvonne Taylor, of Parris End, Kent, and by her had issue:

1a +Marcus Dominic St John [Marcus Horsley-Beresford Esq, Buena Vista, Via dei Tirreni 16, 01015 Sutri (VT), Italy]; *b* 1960; *m* 1984 *Rossana, dau of Angelo Zeppo, of Viterbo, and has issue:

1b +Morgan J R; *b* 1985

2b +Jordan M L; *b* 1988

(3) *Hazel [Mrs Gerald Incledon, Springfield, 32 Park Ave, Old Basing, Basingstoke, Hants RG24 0HT]; *b* 1920; *m* 4 May 1940 Gerald Herbert Incledon (*d* 1990), and has issue:

1a *Jonathan Guy; *b* 19 July 1963

1a *Margaret-Anne [Mrs Anthony Hodson, Spring Lanes, Holly Hill Lane, Bracknell, Berks RG12 2JL]; *b* 16 Feb 1941; *m* 29 April 1961 *Anthony Edward Hodson and has issue:

1b *Christopher James; *b* 26 Nov 1963

1b *Lucy Alice [Mrs Stephen Head, 97 Lily Hill Rd, Bracknell, Berks RG12 2RY]; *b* 26 Aug 1967; *m* 22 April 1995 *Stephen David Head and has:

1c *Louise Catherine; *b* 18 Sept 1997

2a *Heather [Mrs Christopher Stamford, Grassmere, Mid St, S Nutfield, Surrey]; *b* 30 March 1943; *m* 9 April 1966 *Christopher Charles Edward Stamford, AIB, and has issue:

1b *Daniel Charles; *b* 10 Oct 1967

1b *Charlotte Anne; *b* 23 April 1970

2b *Louisa Emma; *b* 1975

3a Susan Amber; *b* 15 Nov 1945; *m* 1st 11 May 1968 (*divorce* 1976) David Ellis Green, MBE, 1st Bn Roy Fus, and *d* March 1993, leaving issue:

1b *Rebecca Claire; *b* 1973

3a (cont.) Mrs Susan Green *m* 2nd 1979 *Christopher Norman [Christopher Norman Esq, Merton House, 7 Bath Rd, Camberley, Surrey], and *d* 1993, leaving further issue:

2b *Annabel Sarah; *b* 1983

4a *Amanda Elizabeth [Mrs Richard Bailey, 38 Robert Cecil Ave, Swaythling, Southampton, Hants SO18 2NA]; *b* 10 July 1947; *m* 1983 *Richard Bailey

5a *Moya Catherine [Mrs Charles Mellor, 5 Sandpiper Close, Marchwood, Hants SO40 4XN]; *b* 2 April 1956; *m* 1976 *Charles Mellor, and has issue:

1b *Stephen Andrew; *b* 1981

1b *Gillian Leigh; *b* 1984

2b *Joanna (twin); *b* 1984

5 (cont.) William Horsley-Beresford *m* 3rd 18 Aug 1933 (*divorce* 1940) Georgina Leonora (*d* 30 April 1969), only dau of Richard Frederick Hendrick Mosselmans and formerly wife of (a) — Barnard, (b) Lord Sholto George Douglas (*see* QUEENSBERRY, M), (c) HIH Prince Mehmed Burhameddin of Turkey and (d) Count Fernand de Saurigny; *m* 4th 1941 *Ida Kaye [Mrs William de la Poer Beresford, 53 Overstrand Mansions, Prince of Wales Drive, London SW11], and *d* 11 July 1949, having by her had issue:

(5) +Peter; *b* 1945; *educ* Emanuel Sch and Univ Coll Oxford (BA 1967)

(4) *Maureen *b* 1942

1 Caroline Catharine; *b* 11 Oct 1861; *m* 14 July 1886 Col George Alexander Eason Wilkinson (*d* 13 Jan 1941), CBE, DSO, of Middlethorpe Hall and Dringhouse Manor, Yorks, and *d* 9 Feb 1929

2 Louisa; *b* 20 March 1863; *d* 5 Dec 1866

3 Catherine Elizabeth Ellen; *b* 9 May 1870; *m* 16 Sept 1902 Lt-Col Edward Machell Lumb, JP, 2nd Life Gds, of Homeward, Cumberland, and *dsp* 11 March 1948

4 Charlotte Ernestine; *b* 3 Sept 1871; *m* 8 Oct 1892 Maj Cameron Barclay (*d* 3 Aug 1954), 10th Hus, of The Orchard, York, 4th son of Henry Ford Barclay, DL, of Markham, Essex, and *d* 28 Sept 1923, leaving issue

The 4th BARON's bro,

JOHN GRAHAM HOPE De La POER BERESFORD, **5th Baron Decies**, PC (1918), DSO; *b* 5 Dec 1866; *educ* Eton; rep I peer 1912–44; Col Res of Offrs 7th Hus 1886–1910, Adj 1892, served Matabeleland Relief Forces 1896–97 (despatches), Boer War 1902 and Somaliland 1903–04 (despatches), Col S Irish Horse 1911–16, AQMG 39th Divn 1915–16, Ch Press Censor Ireland 1916–19, Dir Income Taxpayers' Soc; *m* 1st 7 Feb 1911 Vivien (*d* 3 Feb 1931), dau of George Jay Gould, of New York, and had issue:

1 ARTHUR GEORGE MARCUS DOUGLAS De La POER, **6th Baron**

1 Eileen Vivien de la Poer; *b* 17 Aug 1912; *m* 21 April 1931 Maj Robert Alfred O'Brien, MVO, TD, KStJ, and *d* 10 May 1975, leaving issue

(1) Michael, chartered accountant; *b* 23 Nov 1937; *d* unm 26 Sept 1968

(1) *Maureen [Mrs Richard Bickford, Tinkers Cottage, Waldron, Heathfield, Sussex]; *b* 19 Jan 1932; *m* 24 April 1954 *Richard Francis Bickford, 4th son of Cdr John Edmund Power Bickford, RN, and has issue:

1a *Christopher Richard; *b* 10 July 1956

1a *Sarah Mary; *b* 8 Feb 1955

2a *Bernadette Eileen; *b* 21 Feb 1960

3a *Nicola Frances; *b* 21 Aug 1962

(2) *Shelagh; *b* 5 Aug 1934; *m* 28 Dec 1961 *Lt-Cdr John Penny, RN, only son of Frederick Charles Penny, MBE, and has issue:

1a *Timothy Charles; *b* 15 Sept 1964

2a *Edward Robert Tristram; *b* 7 June 1968

2 Catherine Moya de la Poer; *b* 21 Sept 1913; *m* 1st 16 April 1936 (*divorce* 1946) Hon Patrick Herbert Bellew, yst brother of 5th Baron Bellew (*qv*), and had issue; *m* 2nd 1946 Dr Max Wilhelm Johannsen (*d* Feb 1965), Associate Clinical Prof of Medicine, and *d* 26 May 1967, leaving further issue

The **5th Baron** *m* 2nd 25 May 1936 Elizabeth Wharton (*d* June 1944), dau of Joseph Wilhelm Drexel, of Philadelphia, and widow of Henry Symes Lehr, and *d* 31 Jan 1944

His only son,

ARTHUR GEORGE MARCUS DOUGLAS De La POER BERESFORD, **6th Baron Decies**; *b* 24 April 1915; F/O RAFVR WW II, American DFC; *m* 1st 21 Oct 1937 Ann Christina Margo (*d* 28 March 1945), dau of Sidney Walter Trevor, of Camperdown, Victoria, Australia; *m* 2nd 12 Sept 1945 *Diana [The Rt Hon Diana Lady Decies, Little Barwick, Stanhoe, King's Lynn, Norfolk], dau of W/Cdr George Turner-Cain, of Marsh House, Wells, Norfolk, and widow of Maj David W A Galsworthy, Roy Fus, and *d* 1992, leaving issue:

1 MARCUS HUGH TRISTRAM De La POER BERESFORD, **7th and present Baron Decies**

1 *Sarah Ann Vivien de la Poer [The Hon Mrs McMeekan, 12A Malcolm Rd, London SW19 4AS]; *b* 23 June 1949; *m* 1st 1975 (*divorce* 1982) Joerg B Schnapka, son of Dr Herbert Schnapka, of Bochum, W Germany, and has issue:

(1) *Roland Rufus; *b* 1976

1 (cont.) The Hon Mrs Sarah Schnapka *m* 2nd 1992 *Andrew McMeekan

2 *Clare Antoinette Gabrielle de la Poer [The Hon Mrs Koechlin, c/o Coutts & Co, 1 Old Park Lane, London W1]; model; *b* 31 Dec 1956; *m* 1986 (*divorce* 1997) Jorge Koechlin, son of Jose Edmondo Koechlin, of Lima, Peru, and has:

(1) *Michael Joseph Tristram; *b* 1986

DE CLIFFORD

Arms: Argent a lion rampant gules, on a chief sable three escallops of the first. **Crest:** A goat statant argent, armed and unguled or. **Supporters:** Dexter, a wyvern gules; Sinister, a monkey proper, ringed round the loins and lined or. **Motto:** *Che sara sara* ('What will be will be'). The shield and motto are the same as those of the Russells Dukes of Bedford and derive from the marriage of Lord William Russell's son to the Coussmaker heiress in the 19th century. **Creation:** B. (E) 29 Dec 1299.

THE 27TH LORD (BARON) **DE CLIFFORD** (John Edward Southwell Russell) [The Rt Hon The Lord De Clifford, Riggledown, Pennymoor, Tiverton, Devon EX16 8LR]; *b* 8 June 1928; *s f* 1982; *educ* Eton and RAC Cirencester; *m* 27 June 1959 *Bridget, yst dau of Duncan Robertson, of Llantysilio Hall, Llangollen, Denbigh (*see* WILLIAMS-WYNN, Bt)

Lineage: RICHARD Fitz PONZ; had:

WALTER Fitz RICHARD later de CLIFFORD; living *temp* HENRY II; *m* Margaret, dau and heir of Ralph de To(s)ny, through her acquired Clifford Castle, nr Hay-on-Wye, Herefs, from which he took his surname, and had issue:

1 WALTER

2 Richard, ancestor of the CLIFFORDs of Frampton, Glos

1 Rosamond; mistress of HENRY II, known as 'Fair Rosamond' and quite possibly mother by him of William Longespee, Earl of Salisbury (*see* SALISBURY, M, preliminary remarks)

2 Lucia; *m* 1st Hugh de Say, of Richards Castle; *m* 2nd Bartholomew de Mortimer

WALTER's er s,

WALTER de CLIFFORD; Sheriff Herefs, living *temp* KING JOHN; *m* Agnes, only dau and heir of Roger de Cuni, and *d* 1222, having had issue:

1 Walter, living *temp* HENRY III; *m* Margaret, dau of LLEWELYN, PRINCE OF WALES, and widow of John de Braose, feudal Ld of Bramber and Gower (*d* by 18 July 1232), and *d* 1263, leaving issue:

(1) Maud; *m* 1st 1254 her cousin(?) Sir William de Longespee (*d* 1257), gs of William Earl of Salisbury (*see above*); *m* 2nd 1st Lord (Baron) Giffard of the 1295 *cr* (*d* 28 May 1299), and *d* between Dec 1282 and 9 May 1285, leaving issue

2 Roger; *m* Sibill, dau and coheir of Robert de Ewyas and widow of Robert de Tregoz, feudal Ld of Tregoz, and left issue:

(1) ROGER

3 Giles

4 Richard

WALTER de CLIFFORD's gs,

ROGER de CLIFFORD; Justice Forest S of Trent Aug 1265, feudal Ld of Kingsbury, Warwicks; *d* by 3 April 1286, leaving issue:

ROGER de CLIFFORD; *m* Isabel, dau and coheir of Robert de Vipont, of Brougham Castle, Westmorland, by Isabel, 2nd sis and coheir of 1st and last Lord (Baron) FitzJohn of the 1295 *cr*, and *dvp* 6 Nov 1282, leaving issue:

ROBERT de CLIFFORD, **1st Lord** (Baron) **Clifford** (E), so *cr* by writ of summons to Parl 29 Dec 1299 according to later doctrine (which held that the title was heritable by heirs general, *i.e.*, including females and their issue, hence the + against each living female and her issue, while descendants of the original grantee by females married into other families can also inherit); *b* 1274; in 1291 inherited Brougham Castle and the Hereditary Shrievalty of Westmorland on the death of his mother, Justice in eyre N of Trent 1297–1307/8, Govr Nottingham Castle July 1298; Capt Gen Marches of Scotland 1299, Marshal of England 1307, Justice S of Trent 1307–07/8, Warden Scottish Marches 1308; *m* by 21 Jan 1299/1300 Maud (*m* 2nd by 16 Dec 1315 2nd Lord (Baron) Welle of the 1299 *cr* and *d* between 4 March 1326/7 and 24 May 1327), dau of Thomas de Clare, Ld of Thomond in Connaught, 2nd s of 5th Earl of Hertford and 2nd Earl of Gloucester, and *d* 25 June 1314, leaving issue:

1 ROGER de CLIFFORD, **2nd Lord** (Baron) **Clifford**; *b* 21 Jan or 2 Feb 1299/1300; joined rebellion of Thomas, Earl of Lancaster, against EDWARD II and his favourites and was taken prisoner at the Battle of Boroughbridge 16 March 1321/2; *dsp*, being executed at York 23 March 1322

2 ROBERT de CLIFFORD, **3rd Lord** (Baron) **Clifford**; *b* 5 Nov 1305; *m* June 1328 Isabel de Berkeley (*m* 2nd just before 9 June 1345 1st Lord (Baron) Musgrave (*see* MUSGRAVE, Bt, of Hartley) and *d* 25 July 1362), dau of 2nd Lord (Baron) Berkeley (*qv*), and *d* 20 May 1344, leaving issue:

(1) ROBERT de CLIFFORD, **4th Lord** (Baron) **Clifford**; *b c* 1328–31; *m* 1 or 20 April 1343 Eufeme or Eupheme de Nevill(e) (*m* 2nd Reynold Lucy, 2nd s of 2nd Lord (Baron) Lucy of the 1321 *cr*; *m* 3rd Sir Walter de Heselarton and *d* Oct–Nov 1393), dau of 2nd Lord (Baron) Neville (of Raby) (*see* ABERGAVENNY, M), and *dsp* by 7 Nov 1354

(2) ROGER de CLIFFORD, **5th Lord** (Baron) **Clifford**; *b* 10 July 1333; Sheriff Cumberland 1377, Govr Carlisle Castle, kt banneret, Warden E and W Marches; *m* by 1363 his 3rd cousin Maud de Beauchamp (Id Jan–Feb 1402/3), dau of 3rd Earl of Warwick (*see* WARWICK, BROOKE and, E), and *d* 13 July 1389, leaving, with four daus:

1a THOMAS, **6th Lord**

2a William (Sir); *m* Anne Bardolf (*m* 2nd *c* 1427 3rd Lord (Baron) Cobham of the 1347 *cr* and *dsp* 6 Nov 1453), est dau of 5th Lord (Baron) Bardolf of the 1299 *cr*, and *dsp c* 1419

(3) John

(4) Thomas, ancestor of Richard de Clifford, Bp of Worcester

(5)(?) Lewis (Sir), KG (probably bro of 5th Lord); allegedly ancestor of the Barons Clifford of Chudleigh (*qv*)

The 5th LORD's est s,

THOMAS de CLIFFORD, **6th Lord** (Baron) **Clifford**; *b c* 1363; Govr Carlisle Castle (for life) 1384; *m* Elizabeth (*d* March 1424), dau of 5th Lord (Baron) Ros (of Helmsley) (*see* DE ROS) and *d* 18 Aug 1391, leaving:

1 JOHN, **7th Lord**

1 Maud; *m* 1st by 24 July 1406 (*divorce* because of his impotence) 6th Lord (Baron) Latimer (of Corby) (*see* ABERGAVENNY, M); *m* 2nd *c* 1414 1st Earl of Cambridge of the 1414 *cr* (gs of EDWARD III) and *dsp* 26 Aug 1446

The 6th LORD's s,

JOHN de CLIFFORD, **7th Lord** (Baron) **Clifford**, KG (1421); *b c* 1389; *m* between Aug 1403 and Nov 1412 Elizabeth Percy (*m* 2nd (contract 7 May 1426) as his 1st w 2nd Earl of Westmorland (*see* ABERGAVENNY, M) and *d* 26 Oct 1437), dau of Sir Henry 'Harry Hotspur' Percy, KG (*see* NORTHUMBERLAND, D), and *d* 13 March 1421/2, leaving issue:

THOMAS de CLIFFORD, **8th Lord** (Baron) **Clifford**; *b* 25 March 1414; *m* after March 1424 Joan Dacre, dau of 6th Lord (Baron) Dacre (*qv*), and was *k* fighting on the Lancastrian side at the Yorkist victory of St Albans 22 May 1445, leaving issue:

1 JOHN de CLIFFORD, **9th Lord** (Baron) **Clifford**; *b* 8 April 1435; like his f a Lancastrian in Wars of Roses, Govr Penrith Castle, Commissary Gen Scottish Marches, ktd 31 Dec 1460 at Battle of Wakefield (Lancastrian victory); *m* Margaret (*m* 2nd Sir Lancelot Threlkeld, of Threlkeld, Cumberland, and *d* 12 April 1483), dau and heir of 1st and last Lord (Baron) Vessy of the 1449 *cr*, and was *k* 28 March 1461 by a stray arrow on the eve of the Battle of Towton (Yorkist victory), being on 4 Nov following attainted posthumously and his peerage forfeited, having had issue:

(1) HENRY, **10th Lord**

(2) Richard; *k* Netherlands

(3) Thomas (Sir); *m* Ellen, dau and coheir of John Swarby, of Brakenburgh, Lincs

(1) Elizabeth; *m* Robert Aske and had issue (*see* GALWAY, V)

1 Maud; *m* Sir John Harington, of Hornby Castle, Lancs, a Yorkist *k* at Battle of Wakefield 1460, and had:

(1) Anne; *b c* 1455; *m* as his 1st w 1st Lord (Baron) Mo(u)nteagle (*see* DERBY, E)

2 Joan; *m* Richard Musgrave (*see* MUSGRAVE, Bt, of Hartley)

The 9th LORD's est s,

HENRY CLIFFORD, **10th Lord** (Baron) **Clifford**, KB (1509) 'The Shepherd Lord', so called because his mother is said to have concealed his very birth owing to the family's Lancastrian sympathies and had him brought up as a shepherd; *b c* 1454; ktd and his attainder reversed 9 Nov 1485 following the triumph of the ultimate Lancastrian claimant to the throne HENRY VII at Bosworth; fought at Battle of Flodden 9 Sept 1513; *m* 1st by 1493 Anne, dau of Sir John St John, of Bletso, Beds (*see* ST JOHN OF BLETSO, B), and had, with five daus:

1 HENRY, **11th Lord**

2 Thomas; *m* Lucia, dau of Anthony Brown

The **10th Lord** *m* 2nd by 11 July 1511 Florence (*m* 3rd Richard Grey, yr s of 1st Marquess of Dorset of the 1475 *cr*), dau of Henry Pudsey, of Berforth, Yorks, and widow of Sir Thomas Talbot, and *d* 23 April 1523, having had further issue three s (*d* young) and a dau; either she or one of her half-sisters *m* Sir Hugh Lowther (*see* LONSDALE, E)

The 10th LORD's est s,

HENRY CLIFFORD, **11th Lord** (Baron) **Clifford** and 1st EARL OF CUMBERLAND (E), so *cr* 18 June 1525, KG (1509); *b* 1493; Sheriff Yorks 1522, had large grants of monastic lands in Yorks, successfully defended Skipton Castle against rebels during the Pilgrimage of Grace 1536, Warden W Marches, Capt Carlisle 1525–28 and 1534–42, Constable and Steward Knaresborough and Penrith; *m* 1st Lady Margaret Talbot (*dsp*), dau of 4th Earl of Shrewsbury and Waterford (*qv*); *m* 2nd *c* 1516 Margaret Percy (*bur* 25 Nov 1540), dau of 5th Earl of Northumberland (*see* NORTHUMBERLAND, D), and *d* 22 April 1542, having had issue by his 2nd w:

1 HENRY, **12th Lord**

2 Ingeram (Sir); *m* Anne, dau and heiress of Sir Henry Ratcliff, and *dsp*

1 Catherine; a celebrated beauty; *m* 1st 8th Lord (Baron) Scrope (of Bolton) of the 1371 *cr* and had issue; *m* 2nd as his 2nd w Sir Richard Cholmondeley, of Roxby, Yorks, and had further issue

2 Maud; *m* by 28 Oct 1539 3rd Lord (Baron) Conyers (*see* DARCY DE KNAYTH, B, and YARBOROUGH, E) and had issue

3 Elizabeth; *m* Sir Christopher Metcalf, of Nappa, Yorks

4 Jane; *m* Sir John Huddlestone, of Millom Castle, Cumberland

The 11th LORD's er s,

HENRY CLIFFORD, **12th Lord** (Baron) **Clifford** and 2nd EARL OF CUMBERLAND, KB (1523); *b c* 1517; Constable and Steward Knaresborough 1542, Ld Lt Westmorland 1553–59, High Steward Duchy of Lancaster estates Yorks 1557; *m* 1st 1537 Lady Eleanor Brandon (*dspsm* 27 Sept 1547), yst dau and coheir of 1st Duke of Suffolk of the 1514 *cr* by his w Mary, sis of HENRY VIII (who in 1544 was given statutory authority by Act of Parl to devise the succession to the crown by will, which he did 1546, bequeathing it to his children EDWARD (VI), MARY and ELIZABETH (I) and in the event of their deaths without issue to the descendants of his sis Mary Duchess of Suffolk (in preference to the issue of Mary's er sis Margaret, ancestress of the Stuart kings of England), so that the Countess of Derby (the Countess of Cumberland's dau) was during her lifetime a potential successor to ELIZABETH I), and had issue (with two sons who *d* young):

1 Margaret; *m* 7 Feb 1555 4th Earl of Derby (*qv*) and *d* 29 Sept 1596, leaving issue

The **12th Lord** *m* 2nd 1552/3 Anne Dacre (*bur* 31 July 1581), dau of 3rd Lord (Baron) Dacre (*qv*), and *d* 2 Jan 1569/70, having had further issue, with two daus who *d* young:

1 GEORGE CLIFFORD, **13th Lord** (Baron) **Clifford** and 3rd EARL OF CUMBERLAND, KG (1592), PC (1603); *b* 8 Aug 1558; *educ* Peterhouse and Trin Coll Cambridge (MA 1576); Cncllr of the N 1582, ktd 1588, Constable and Steward Knaresborough 1597, Adml 1598, Lt-Gen in London 1599 and 1601, Col London Trained Bands 1599, High Steward Honour of Grafton and Ranger Salcey Forest 1602, Warden W and Middle Marches, Govr Carlisle and Harbottle Castle, Custos Rotulorum Cumberland 1603, mathematician and navigator (made nine voyages to the W Indies 1589–98, capturing the town of Fiall in the Azores and the fort of Puertorico 1598); *m* 24 June 1577 Lady Margaret Russell (*d* 22 May 1616), yst child of 2nd Earl of Bedford (*see* BEDFORD, D), and *dspms* 29 Oct 1605, having had issue:

(1) Francis, *Lord Clifford*; *b* 1584/5; *d* Dec 1589

(2) Robert, *Lord Clifford*; *d* 24 May 1591

(1) ANNE, *de jure* Baroness Clifford, for whom *see* further below

2 FRANCIS CLIFFORD, 4th EARL OF CUMBERLAND, KB (1604/5); *b* 1559; MP Westmorland 1584–87, Yorks 1604–05, Sheriff Yorks 1600, Jt Constable and Steward Knaresborough 1604, Custos Rotulorum Cumberland 1606–39, Ld Lt 1607–41, Ld Lt Northumberland, Westmorland and Newcastle-on-Tyne 1611–39; *m* soon after March 1589 Grisold (*d* 15 June 1613), dau of Thomas Hughes, of Uxbridge, Middx, and widow of 7th Lord (Baron) Bergavenny (*see* ABERGAVENNY, M), and *d* 21 Jan 1640/1, having had issue:

(1) HENRY CLIFFORD, 1st LORD (Baron) CLIFFORD of the 1627/8 *cr* and 5th and last EARL OF CUMBERLAND, KB (1610); *b* 28 Feb 1591/2; *educ* Ch Ch Oxford (BA 1608/9); MP Westmorland 1614 and 1621–22, Cncllr of the N 1619, called to Parl *vp* by writ 17 Feb 1627/8 in the (subsequently) 'mistaken' (though at the time generally accepted) belief that the Barony of Clifford was held by his f (in which case he could indeed have been called up to the Ho of Lds in one of his f's lesser peerages), but the effect was to create a new peerage by writ which was heritable by heirs general (these could include females and their issue), Jt Ld Lt Westmorland 1626–41, Ld-Lt 1641and 1642, Ld-Lt Yorks July 1642, Gen royalist forces in N of England during early stages of Civil War 1642 and 1643; *m* 25 July 1610 Frances Cecil (*d* 14 Feb 1643/4), dau of 1st Earl of Salisbury (*see* SALISBURY, M), and *dspms* 11 Dec 1643, when the Earldom expired, but the Barony *cr* in Feb 1627/8 descended to his dau:

1a Elizabeth, *de jure* BARONESS CLIFFORD (of the 1627/8 *cr*) in her own right; *b* 18 Sept 1613; *m* 3 July 1634 1st Earl of Burlington and had issue (*see* CORK and ORRERY, E)

1 Frances; *m* 3rd Lord (Baron) Wharton of the 1545 *cr* and had issue

The 13th LORD's dau,

ANNE CLIFFORD, justly (according to subsequently evolved doctrine) BARONESS CLIFFORD in her own right (unsuccessful claims to the title were entered by her mother 3 Nov 1606 and by herself 1628 and 1663); *b* 30 Jan 1589/90; inherited 11 Dec 1643 the huge estates of the Earls of Cumberland, together with the hereditary shrievalty of Westmorland, on the death of her unc the 5th and last Earl; *m* 1st 25 Feb 1608/9 3rd Earl of Dorset (*see* SACKVILLE, B); *m* 2nd 3 June 1630 4th Earl of Pembroke and (1st Earl of) Montgomery (*qv*) and *d* 22 March 1675/6 (when right to the Barony fell into abeyance between her er dau and her gdau Lady Alathea/Alethea Hungerford), having had surv issue by her 1st husb:

1 MARGARET Sackville; *b* 2 July 1614; *m* 21 April 1629 John TUFTON, 2nd EARL OF THANET (*d* 6 May 1664), and *d* 14 Aug 1676, leaving issue:

(1) NICHOLAS TUFTON, 3rd EARL OF THANET; *b* 7 Aug 1631; imprisoned in Tower of London 1655 and 1656–58 for alleged conspiracy to restore CHARLES II, Capt of Horse 1666, on the death of his cousin Lady Alathea/Alethea Hungerford 14 Oct 1678 became the sole representative of his grandmother hence *de jure* 15th LORD (Baron) CLIFFORD; *m* 11 April 1664 his cousin Lady Elizabeth Boyle (*d* 1 Sept 1725), 2nd dau of 1st Earl of Burlington (*see* CORK and ORRERY, E), and *dsp* 24 Nov 1679

(2) JOHN TUFTON, *de jure* 16th LORD (Baron) CLIFFORD and 4th EARL OF THANET; *b* 7 Aug 1638; *educ* Eton and Queen's Coll Oxford; MP (Tory) Steyning, Sussex, 1679; *d* unm 27 April 1680

(3) RICHARD TUFTON, *de jure* 17th LORD (Baron) CLIFFORD and 5th EARL OF THANET; *b* 30 May 1640; Capt Col Russell's Regt of Gds (Gren Gds) 1673–81, MP (Tory) Appleby 1679–80; *d* unm 8 March 1683/4

(4) THOMAS, **18th Lord**

(5) Sackville; *b c* 1647; Col Gds; *m* Elizabeth, dau of Ralph Wilbraham, of Newbottle, Northants, and *d* 30 March 1721, having had issue:

1a John; *b* 25 May 1687; *d* 23 Feb 1689/90

2a SACKVILLE TUFTON, 7th EARL OF THANET; *b* 11 May 1688; MP (Tory) Appleby 1722–29; *m* 11 June 1722 Mary Saville (*d* 30 July 1751), 4th dau of 2nd Marquess of Halifax of the 1682 *cr* (*see* HALIFAX, E, preliminary remarks), and *d* 4 Dec 1753, having had issue:

1b John, *Lord Tufton*; *b c* 1724; *d* 2 June 1734

2b SACKVILLE TUFTON, 8th EARL OF THANET; *b* Aug 1733; *educ* Westminster; *m* 30 July 1767 his cousin Lady Mary Sackville (*d* 30 Sept 1778), sis of 3rd Duke of Dorset (*see* SACKVILLE, B), and *d* 27 March 1786, leaving issue:

1c SACKVILLE TUFTON, 9th EARL OF THANET; *b* 30 June 1769; *m* 28 Feb 1811 Anne Charlotte de Bojanovitz (*d* 15 Feb 1819), and *dsp* 24 Jan 1825

2c CHARLES TUFTON, 10th EARL OF THANET; *b* 10 Sept 1770; *educ* Mil Sch Angers, France; Ensign 68th (Durham) Regt of Foot 1787 and 7th (Roy Fus) Regt of Foot 1788, Capt Balfour's Regt of Foot 1793; *d* unm 20 April 1832

3c John; *b* 22 Nov 1773; MP Appleby 1796–99; *d* unm 28 May 1799

4c HENRY TUFTON, 11th and last EARL OF THANET; *b* 2 Jan 1775; *educ* Westminster and Mil Sch Angers; Ensign 26th (Cameronian) Regt of Foot 1790, Capt Ind Co of Foot 1793, MP (Whig) Rochester 1796–1802 and Appleby 1826–32, Ld Lt Kent 1841–46; *d* unm 12 June 1849, when the Earldom expired

1c Elizabeth; *b* 2 May 1768; *d* 16 Sept 1849

2c Caroline; *b* 8 Oct 1771; *m* 26 July 1792 Joseph Foster Barham, MP (*d* 28 Sept 1832), and *d* 3 Nov 1832, leaving issue

1b Mary; *m* Sir William Duncan, 1st and last Bt of the 1764 *cr* (*dsp* Sept 1774), and *d* 1806

2b Charlotte; *d* 1803

(1) Anne; *b c* 1654; *m* by 1674, as his 2nd w, Sir Samuel Grimston, 3rd and last Bt (*see* VERULAM, E), and *dspm* 22 Nov 1713

2 Isabella; *m* 5 July 1647 James Compton, 3rd Earl of Northampton (*see* NORTHAMPTON, M), and *d* 14 Oct 1651, leaving issue:

(1) Alathea/Alethea Compton; *b* 14 March 1661; *m* Edward Hungerford, of Farleigh, Somerset, s and heir of Sir Edward Hungerford, KB, and *dsp* 14 Oct 1678

The *de jure* BARONESS CLIFFORD's gs,

THOMAS TUFTON, **18th Lord** (Baron) **Clifford**, so declared by a resolution of the Ho of Lds 12 Dec 1691, and 6th EARL OF THANET, PC (1702/3–07 and 1711–14); *b* 30 Aug 1644; MP Appleby 1668–79, Ld Lt Westmorland and Cumberland 1685–87 and 1712–14, Capt Troop of Horse and Col Regt of Horse (5th Horse) 1685; *m* 14 Aug 1684 Lady Catherine Cavendish (*d* 20 April 1712), dau of 2nd Duke of Newcastle-upon-Tyne of the 1664 *cr* (*see* DEVONSHIRE, D), and *dspms* 30 July 1729, when the Earldom passed to his nephew and the Barony of Clifford fell into abeyance between his daus until 13 Aug 1734, when it was terminated in favour of the 3rd dau:

1 John; *b* and *d* 29 April 1686

2 Thomas; *b* and *d* 19 Nov 1690

3 John; *b* and *d* 23 Sept 1691

1 Katherine; *b* 24 April 1693; *m* 21 March 1708/9 Edward Watson, Viscount Sondes (*dvp* 20 March 1721/2; *see* MONSON, B), s of the 1st Earl of Rockingham of the 1714 *cr*, and *d* 13 Feb 1733/4, leaving issue:

(1) LEWIS WATSON, 2nd EARL OF ROCKINGHAM; *b c* 1714; *educ* Eton; Ld Lt Kent 1737–45; *m* 10 April 1736 Catherine (*m* 2nd 13 June 1751 1st Earl of Guilford of the 1752 *cr* and *dsp* 17 Dec 1766), dau of Sir Robert Furnese, 2nd Bt of the 1707 *cr*, and *dsp* 4 Dec 1745

(2) THOMAS WATSON, 3rd EARL OF ROCKINGHAM; *b* 30 Dec 1715; *educ* Eton and Lincoln's Inn; MP Canterbury 1741–46, Ld Lt Kent 1745–46; *d* unm 26 Feb 1745/6

(3) Edward; *d* unm

(1) Katherine; *m* 21 Aug 1729 Edward Southwell (*see* SOUTHWELL, V) and *d* April 1765, leaving:

1a EDWARD, **20th Lord**

2 Anne; *m* 12 Feb 1708 5th Earl of Salisbury (*see* SALISBURY, M) and *d* 22 April 1750, leaving issue

3 MARGARET TUFTON, **Baroness Clifford** (19th holder of the title), the abeyance in which was terminated in her favour 3 Aug 1734; *b* 16 June 1700; *m* 3 July 1718 1st Earl of Leicester of the 1744 (*see* LEICESTER, E) and *dspms* 28 Feb 1775, when the Barony fell into abeyance until terminated 1776 in favour of her gn Edward Southwell

4 Mary; *m* 1st 17 April 1718 Anthony Grey, Earl of Harold, est s of 1st and last Duke of Kent (*see* LUCAS OF CRUDWELL, B); *m* 2nd 16 May 1736 1st Earl Gower (*see* SUTHERLAND, D) and *d* 19 Feb 1785, leaving issue

5 Isabella; *m* 1st 1731 Sir Nassau Powlett, KB (*d* 24 Aug 1741), yst s of 2nd Duke of Bolton (*see* WINCHESTER, M) of the 1689 *cr* by his 3rd w Henrietta, illegitimate dau of the Duke of Monmouth (himself illegitimate s of CHARLES II) by his mistress Eleanor Needham, and had issue; *m* 2nd Sir Francis Blake Delaval, KB (*dsp* 1771), and *d* 10 Jan 1764

The 18th LORD's ggs,

EDWARD SOUTHWELL, **20th Lord** (Baron) **Clifford** on the abeyance being terminated in his favour and his being called to Parl 17 April 1776; *b* 6 June 1732; MP (Tory) Bridgwater 1761–63 and Glos; *m* 29 Aug 1765 Sophia (*d* 3 Aug 1828), Governess to PRINCESS CHARLOTTE OF WALES, 3rd dau of Samuel Campbell, of Mount Campbell, Co Leitrim, and *d* 1 Nov 1777, leaving issue:

1 EDWARD SOUTHWELL, **21st Lord** (Baron) **de Clifford**; *b* 23 June 1767; the first to add the particule 'de' to the title; *m* 19 Feb 1789 Lady Mary Elizabeth Bourke (*d* 28 May 1845), 2nd dau of 3rd Earl of Mayo (*qv*), and *dsp* 30 Sept 1832, when the Barony fell into abeyance between the issue of his deceased sisters

1 CATHERINE Southwell; *m* 13 Nov 1790 Col George Kein Hayward COUSSMAKER, 1st Gds (*d* 11 July 1801), and *d* 19 July 1801, leaving issue:

(1) George; *d* unm 1821

(1) SOPHIA, **Baroness de Clifford**

2 Sophia; *m* 12 April 1790 2nd Viscount Sydney of St Leonards (*see* TOWNSHEND, M) and *d* 9 Nov 1795, leaving issue

3 Elizabeth; *m* 9 April 1792 4th Earl of Albemarle (*qv*) and *d* 14 Nov 1817, leaving issue

4 Henrietta; *m* 22 Dec 1799 Frederick Delme and *dsp*

The 21st LORD's niece,

SOPHIA Coussmaker, **Baroness de Clifford**; *b* 4 Nov 1791; abeyance terminated in her favour 4 March 1833; *m* 21 Aug 1822 Cdr John RUSSELL, RN (*d* 27 April 1835), s of Lord William Russell, bro of 6th Duke of Bedford (*qv*), and *d* 3 Jan 1874, leaving issue:

1 EDWARD SOUTHWELL, **23rd Lord**

1 Katherine Sarah Georgina; *m* 12 Sept 1850 Charles Robert Colville (*d* 10 March 1886), of Lullington, and *d* 5 April 1912, leaving issue

2a Mary Russell; *m* 10 April 1860 William Edward Oakeley (*d* 1 Feb 1912), of The Plâs, Tan-y-bwlch, Merioneth, and *d* 13 Sept 1914, leaving issue (*see* OAKELEY, Bt)

BARONESS DE CLIFFORD's only s,

EDWARD SOUTHWELL RUSSELL, **23rd Lord** (Baron) **de Clifford**; *b* 30 April 1824; *educ* Trin Coll Cambridge; MP (Lib) Tavistock 1847–52; *m* 31 March 1853 Harriet Agnes (*d* 17 Feb 1896), est dau of Adml Sir Charles Elliot, KCB (*see* MINTO, E), and *d* 6 Aug 1877, leaving issue:

1 EDWARD SOUTHWELL, **24th Lord**

2 Charles Somerset; *b* 10 Sept 1857; *d* unm 1886

1 Maud Clara; *d* unm 13 April 1947

2 Katherine, MBE (1918), DGStJ; *m* 23 April 1891 Reginald Corbet (*d* 9 Dec 1945), of Adderley Hall, Market Drayton, Salop, and *d* 6 March 1950, leaving issue (*see* 1970 edn CORBET, Bt)

The 23rd LORD's only s,

EDWARD SOUTHWELL RUSSELL, **24th Lord** (Baron) **de Clifford**, JP Leics; *b* 5 April 1855; *m* 16 April 1879 Hilda (*d* 7 Feb 1895), yst dau of Charles Balfour, of Bracknell, Berks, and *d* 6 April 1894, leaving issue:

JACK SOUTHWELL RUSSELL, **25th Lord** (Baron) **de Clifford**; *b* 2 July 1884; Lt Shropshire Imperial Yeo; *m* 16 Feb 1906 Evelyn Victoria Anne (stage name Eva Carrington, a 'Gibson Girl' at the Vaudeville Theatre; *m* 2nd 17 April 1913 Capt Arthur Roy Stock (*d* 12 Dec 1915), of Glenapp Castle, Ballantrae, Ayrshire; *m* 3rd 22 Sept 1922 George Vernon Tate, MC (*d* 30 Sept 1955), s of George Booth Tate (*see* TATE, Bt)), dau of Walter Robert Chandler, of Dalgan Park, Shrule, Tuam, Co Galway, and *d* 1 Sept 1909, leaving issue:

1 EDWARD SOUTHWELL, **26th Lord**

1 Diana Katherine; *b* 28 Feb 1909; *m* 1st 9 Dec 1933 (*divorce* 1948) Mervyn Hesseltine Taylor, only s of L H Taylor, of Hullavington House, Chippenham, Wilts; *m* 2nd 29 July 1948 His Hon Judge Thomas Elder-Jones, MA, Hon Maj Roy Glos Hus, of Somerford Heynes House, Cirencester, Glos, s of David Jones, JP, of Foxcote Grange, Andoversford, and *d* 16 March 1978, leaving by her 1st husb:

(1) +Christopher John [Christopher Taylor Esq, East Cottage, Bourton on the Hill, Moreton-in-Marsh, Glos]; *b* 11 Nov 1934; *m* 1st 1959 (*divorce* 1971) Sarah Mary, only dau of Ewan Mews; *m* 2nd 1972 *Jane Seymour, yst dau of George Macdonald Brown, and has issue by his 1st w:

1a +Vernon Edmund Christopher; *b* 24 June 1965

1a +Clare Virginia Mary; *b* 16 July 1962

(1) +Virginia Carol ELDER-JONES (adopted by her stepfather and took his surname 1956); *b* 14 Oct 1945

The 25th LORD's only s,

EDWARD SOUTHWELL RUSSELL, **26th Lord** (Baron) **de Clifford**, OBE (1955); *b* 31 Jan 1907; Col REME, Lt 21st (Roy Glos Hus) Armoured Car Co (TA), Capt RAC (TA) 1939, transferred RAOC then REME 1942, then to Regular Army 1947; *m* 1st 11 March 1926 (*divorce*1973) Dorothy Evelyn, dau of Ferdinand Richard Holmes Meyrick, MD, of 59 Kensington Court, London W8, by his w Kate, the nightclub proprietress (*see* also CRAVEN, E, and KINNOULL, E); *m* 2nd 4 Dec 1974 *Mina Margaret, only dau of George Edward Sands, by his w Countess Sands de Sainte Croix (dau of Ralph Noel Philippe le Roy, Count de Sainte Croix), and *d* 3 Jan 1982, leaving issue by his 1st w:

1 JOHN EDWARD SOUTHWELL RUSSELL, **27th and present Lord** (Baron) **de Clifford**

2 +WILLIAM SOUTHWELL [The Hon William Russell, Gilboa Farmhouse, Brokenborough, Malmesbury, Wilts SN16 OHX]; *b* 26 Feb 1930; heir presumptive; *educ* Eton, King's Coll Cambridge (BA) and Princeton; *m* 12 April 1961 *Jean Brodie, only dau of Neil Brodie Henderson, of Glebe House, Little Hormead, Buntingford, Herts, by Conn, est dau of Adml of the Fleet Sir Charles Edward Madden, 1st Bt (*qv*), and has issue:

(1) +Miles Edward Southwell; *b* 7 Aug 1966

(1) +Mary-Jane Sophia; *b* 13 March 1963; *m* 1991 *Matthew G er s of Philip Howe, of Sydney, Australia

(2) +Joanna Clare; *b* 23 Jan 1965

DEEDES

In 1653, during the Interregnum, Edward Bysshe, Garter King of Arms, granted arms to Robert Deedes in the form 'Per fess nebulée gu. and arg. three martlets counterchanged', with for crest 'an eagle's head erased per fess nebulée gu. and arg. between two wings expanded sa.' After the Restoration all such grants were declared null. They nevertheless appear to have been displayed by the family treated of below (who are not the grantee's direct descendants) into the 20th century. **Creation:** B. (LP, UK) 1986.

THE BARON DEEDES, of Aldington, Co Kent (William (Bill) Francis Deedes, MC (1944), PC (1962), DL (Kent 1962)) [The Rt Hon The Lord Deedes MC PC DL, New Hayters, Aldington, Kent TN25 7DT]; *b* 1 June 1913; *educ* Harrow; journalist *Morning Post* 1931–37; WWII Maj KRRC (TA); MP (C) Ashford 1950–74; Parly Sec Min Housing and Local Govt 1954–55, Jt Parly U-Sec Home Office 1955–57, Min without Portfolio 1962–64; ed *Daily Telegraph* 1974–86, author: *Dear Bill* (autobiography, 1997); Hon DCL Kent U 1988; *m* 1942 *Evelyn Hilary, dau of Clive Branfoot, of Stonegrave, Yorks, and has had issue:

1 *Jeremy Wyndham [The Hon Jeremy Deedes, Hamilton House, Compton, Newbury, Berks]; *b* 1943; *educ* Eton; jnlst, edtl dir *Daily Telegraph* 1986–96, md The Telegraph plc 1996–; *m* 1973 *Anna Rosemary, dau of Maj Elwin Clive Gray, Seaforth Highlanders, of Aldington, Kent, and has issue:

(1) *George William; *b* 1976

(2) *Henry Julius; *b* 1978

2 Julius Brook; *b* 10 Aug 1947; jnlst; *d* unm 1970

1 *Juliet Evelyn Mary [The Hon Mrs Means, 92 North Rd, Hythe, Kent]; *b* 22 Oct 1948; *m* 1990 *Robert Dale Means, est s of Robert Means, of Blythe, Calif

2 *Victoria Frances Jill [The Hon Mrs Southey, Maben House, Llaneast St, Malvern 3144, Victoria, Australia]; *b* 28 Feb 1950; *m* 1982 *Jonathan Edward Southey, 3rd s of Sir Robert Southey, AO, CMG, of Mount Eliza, Australia, and has issue:

(1) *Samuel William Robert; *b* 1984

(2) *Simon Raymond Julius; *b* 1986

3 *Lucy Rose [The Hon Mrs Crispin Money-Coutts, Church House, Stopham, W Sussex]; *b* 12 March 1955; *m* 1978 (*divorce* 19–), as his first w, *Hon Crispin James Alan Nevill Money-Coutts, s of 8th Lord (Baron) Latymer (*qv*), and has issue

Lineage: THOMAS DEEDES; *m* Elizabeth, sis of Robert Glover, Somerset Herald, and widow of Henry Quested, and was *bur* 20 April 1603, having had, with other issue:

JULIUS DEEDES; *b* 1565; *m* 1595 Elizabeth Hull and *d* 22 Oct 1628, having had, with other issue:

WILLIAM DEEDES; *b* 1604; Mayor Hythe four times; *m* 1st 1631 Bennett Smith and had two sons and a dau; *m* 2nd 2 Jan 1644 Eleanor Rucke and *d* 1653; his er s by his 1st w:

JULIUS DEEDES; *b* Aug 1635; Mayor Hythe three times; *m* Anne Bate and *d* Sept 1693, having had, with three yr sons and four daus:

WILLIAM DEEDES, of Ruffins Hill and Canterbury, Kent; *b* 28 April 1660; *educ* Merchant Taylors' and Lincoln Coll Oxford; *m* 1687 Mary, dau and coheir of Rev Henry Gregory, of Middleton Stoney, Oxon, and *d* 1738, having had, with an est and yst s and two daus:

Rev JULIUS DEEDES; *b* 16 Nov 1693; Rector Dymchurch, Kent, Preb and Canon Canterbury; *m* 9 April 1732 Dorothy, dau of Nathaniel Denew, of Canterbury, (by Mary, dau of Sir Abraham Jacob), and widow of Rev Richard Ibbotson, and *d* 1752, having had, with a yr s and two daus (including an er one, Dorothy, *b* 1735, *m* April 1757 Sir John Filmer, 4th Bt (*see* 1916 edn), and *dsp*):

WILLIAM DEEDES; *b* 1733; *educ* Corpus Christi Coll Oxford; Chm E Kent QS; *m* 1758 Mary, dau of Thomas Branston, of Skreens, Essex, and *d* 16 Nov 1793, leaving, with three yr sons and three daus:

WILLIAM DEEDES, of Sandling Park and Saltwood Castle; *b* 1 June 1761; *educ* Corpus Christi Coll Oxford; MP Hythe 1807–12, Col S Kent Vols; *m* 29 Dec 1791 Sophia, 2nd dau of Sir Brook Bridges, 3rd Bt (*see* 1899 edn, also this edn FitzWALTER, B), and *d* 1834, having had, with nine other sons (including Rev Charles, *b* 9 Oct 1808, *educ* Winchester, *m* 1843 Letitia Anne, est dau of Hon Philip Pleydell-Bouverie (*see* RADNOR, E); and *d* 25 Dec 1875) and five daus:

WILLIAM DEEDES, JP, DL, of Sandling; *b* 17 Oct 1796; MP E Kent 1845–March 1857 and Dec 1857–62; *m* 30 May 1833 Emily Octavia, n of Sir Herbert Taylor, GCB, and *d* 30 Nov 1862, leaving, with an est s (*dsp*), three yst sons and seven daus:

HERBERT GEORGE DEEDES, JP, of Sandling Park and Saltwood Castle; *b* 28 Sept 1836; *educ* Harrow; Col 60th Rifles, served Indian Mutiny, Assist U-Sec War 1878; *m* 5 Dec 1870 Rose Elinor, MBE, dau of Maj-Gen L Barrow, CB, and *d* 5 May 1891, leaving, with a yr s (Sir Wyndham Henry, CMG, DSO, *b* 10 March 1883, *educ* Eton, Ch Sec Palestine Admin 1920–23, *d* unm 2 Sept 1956) and two daus:

HERBERT WILLIAM DEEDES; *b* 27 Oct 1881; *educ* Eton; sold Sandling 1897 and Saltwood 1925; Lt 1st Bn 60th Rifles Boer War 1902; *m* 3 July 1912 Melesina Gladys, 2nd dau of Philip Francis Chenevix Trench (*see* ASHTOWN, B), and *d* 2 Aug 1966, having had, with an est dau (*d* unm):

1 WILLIAM FRANCIS, *cr* a **Baron**

1 *Hermione Gladys; *b* 23 Sept 1918; *m* 23 April 1965 *John Constantine Phipps, s of Sir Edmund Bampfylde Phipps, CB

2 *Margaret Melesina; *b* 7 Jan 1923; *m* 29 Sept 1951 *21st Lord (Baron) FitzWalter (*qv*) and has issue

DE FREYNE

Arms: Ermine a chevron sable. **Crest:** A dolphin embowed proper. **Supporters:** Dexter, an ancient Irish warrior, habited, supporting with his dexter hand a battle-axe, head downwards, and bearing on his sinister arm a shield, all proper; sinister, a female figure, vested, scarf flowing argent, all proper. **Motto:** *Malo mori quam foedari* ('I prefer to die than be dishonoured'). **Creation:** B. (UK) 5 April 1851.

THE 7TH BARON DE FREYNE OF COOLAVIN, Co Sligo (Francis Arthur John French) [The Rt Hon The Lord De Freyne, House of Lords, London SW1A 0PW]; *b* 3 Sept 1927; *s f* 1935; *educ* Glenstal; Kt SMO Malta; *m* 1st 30 Jan 1954 (*divorce* 1978) Shirley Ann Bradbury, only child of Douglas Rudolph Pobjoy, of Box Farm House, Woodmancote, Glos, and has issue:

1 +(FULKE) CHARLES ARTHUR JOHN [The Hon Charles French, 14 Langside Ave, London SW15 5QT]; *b* 21 April 1957; *educ* Downside; *m* 12 April 1986 *Julia Mary, only dau of Dr James H Wellard, of Hampstead, and has issue:

(1) +Alexander James Charles; *b* 22 Sept 1988

(2) +(William) Rory Francis; *b* 12 March 1991

2 +Patrick Dominick Fitzstephen Jude [The Hon Patrick French, 2 The Westbourne, 1 Artesian Road, London W2]; *b* 27 Nov 1969

1 *Vanessa Rose Bradbury [The Hon Mrs Phillips, Oak Farmhouse, Stradsett, Norfolk PE33 9HH]; *b* 19 Sept 1958; *m* 1991 *Richard Leslie Phillips, and has:

(1) *Toby Richard French; *b* 16 Sept 1994

(2) *Hugo Francis French; *b* 16 Sept 1994

(1) *Emma Elizabeth French; *b* 10 March 1998

The 7th BARON *m* 2nd 18 July 1978 *Sheelin Deirdre, yst dau of Lt-Col Henry Kane O'Kelly, DSO, of Co Wicklow, and widow of William Walker Stevenson

Lineage: WALTER FFRENCH, of Galway, living by *c* 1425, Ch Magistrate Galway 1444–45, was ancestor of the FFRENCHes Barons Ffrench as well as the FRENCHes Barons De Freyne.

STEPHEN FRENCH, of Galway, living late 16th Century; had:

PATRICK FRENCH; *b* 1583; Burgess Galway; bought or mortgaged large estates in Cos Sligo and Roscommon by 1636, though much of them confiscated by the Ld Dep Ireland 1636; allotted 6,000 acres in Co Roscommon by Cromwellian Commrs 1656/7; *d* 1669, leaving, with an est s (Stephen) and four yst ones (Edmond, Robert, Francis, Anthony):

DOMINICK FRENCH, of French Park and Boyle, Co Roscommon; Jt Govr and Conservator of the Peace Cos Roscommon and Sligo; *m* Anne, dau of John King, of Boyle (*see* KING, Bt, of Charlestown), and *d* between 3 May and 20 Sept 1670, leaving, with two yr sons (Dominick, Patrick) and four daus (Mary, *m* Gilbert

King, of Charlestown (*see* KING, Bt); Margaret, *m* J Folliott, of Co Sligo; Sarah; Anne):

JOHN FRENCH, called *'Tierna More'* ('the great landowner'), of French Park; attainted by JAMES II's Dublin Parl 1690, cmded a Williamite troop of Enniskillen Dragoons in the victory over the Jacobites of Aughrim 1691; bought 1703 from Tstees of Fofeited Estates most of the estate of Maj Owen O'Connor, of Ballinagar; MP Carrick-on-Shannon 1695, Co Galway 1703 and 1710 and Tulsk 1715 and 1722; *m* Anne (*d* between 8 May 1734 and 22 June 1756), dau of Sir Arthur Gore, Bt, of Newtown (*see* ARRAN, E), and had:

1 ARTHUR

2 Robert, MP Jamestown, Judge Common Pleas Ireland; *m* Frances Hull and *d* 29 May 1772 aged 82

3 John, of High Lake, Co Roscommon; *m* Judith (*m* 2nd Rev Rees Saunders, of Whitechurch, Salop), dau of John King, of Charlestown (*see* KING, Bt, of Charlestown), and *d* between 14 April 1733 and 1756, leaving issue (Isee 1970 edn YPRES, E)

4 William (Rev), Dean of Ardagh, of Abbey Boyle and Oak Port, Co Roscommon; *m* Arabella Frances, dau of Very Rev Jeremy Marsh, Dean of Kilmore, and had issue

1 Mary; *m* Francis Ormsby, of Willybrooke, Co Sligo, and had issue

2 Olivia; *m* Rev William Digby, of Lackan, Co Roscommon, cousin of 1st Baron Digby (*qv*)

3 Catherine; *m* 14 Sept 1728 John Crofton, of Lissadern

4 Sarah; *m* Gilbert King (*see* KING, Bt, of Castletown)

JOHN FRENCH *d* 1734; his est son,

ARTHUR FRENCH, of French Park, MP Co Roscommon 1721; *m c* 6 Feb 1722 Jane (*d* 1755), dau of John Percival, of Knightsbrook, Co Meath, and *d* by 15 April 1769, leaving:

1 John, known as *Shane Dhu* ('Black John'), of French Park; MP Co Roscommon 1745–75; *m* Alicia, dau of Ralph Crawford, of Snowhill, Co Fermanagh, and *dsp* (when on the point of being ennobled as Baron Dungar), drowned together with his brother Robert travelling from Dublin to Parkgate 1775

2 Robert, Army Maj; *m* 1775 Frances Donellan and was drowned with his bro John

3 ARTHUR

4 George, of Innfield, Co Roscommon; *m* Martha, dau of William Lennox, of Dublin, and was *k* in a duel by Sir Edward Crofton, Bt, 1770, leaving issue

1 Martha; *m* Very Rev Dean Walsh

ARTHUR FRENCH's 3rd son,

ARTHUR FRENCH, of French Park, MP Co Roscommon 1783–90, Col Castlereagh Vols, allegedly refused the reversion of the offer of the barony made originally to his er bro John; *b* 2 Aug 1728; *m c* 25 June 1764 Alicia, dau of Richard Magennis, of Dublin (*see* IVEAGH, E), and *d* between 24 April and 24 May 1799, leaving, with other issue:

1 ARTHUR

2 Richard, Commr Bd Works Dublin; *d* unm 28 Aug 1832

3 John (Very Rev), Dean Elphin; *m* Emily, dau of Richard Magennis, of Waringstown, Co Down, and left issue

4 George, QC; *b* 23 Nov 1771; *m* 18 Feb 1802 Anna (*d* April 1856), dau of David Jones, of Bensforth, Co Meath, and *d* 26 Oct 1860, leaving issue

5 Robert Henry, of Dublin; *m* 1798 Charlotte (*d* 1853), dau of John Reynell, of Castle Reynell, Co Westmeath, and *d* 28 Nov 1847, leaving issue:

(1) Arthur; *b* 1 Nov 1802; *m* 1 Feb 1828 his cousin Emily Eleanor Wilhelmina (*m* 2nd Rev John Charles William Leslie), only surv dau of Charles Albert Leslie, and *d* 6 March 1843

ARTHUR FRENCH's est son,

ARTHUR FRENCH, of French Park, MP Roscommon 1785–1820, allegedly propositioned into backing the Union of I and GB Parls with an earldom, and later offered a barony with no strings attached; *m c* 8 Oct 1784 Margaret, dau of Edmond Costello, of Edmonstown, Co Mayo, and *d* 24 Nov 1820, having had, with other issue:

1 ARTHUR FRENCH, **1st Baron De Freyne of Coolavin**, Co Sligo, so *cr* 5 April 1851, with remainder to his bros and their male issue, as also earlier 16 May 1839 BARON DE FREYNE OF ARTAGH, Co Roscommon (both UK); *b c* 1786; Co Roscommon: MP (Whig) 1821–32, Lt 1854–56; *m* 1818 Mary, dau of Christopher McDermott, of Cregga, and *dsp* 29 Sept 1856, when the Artagh Barony expired

2 JOHN FRENCH, **2nd Baron De Freyne of Coolavin**; *b* 1788; *educ* Trin Coll Dublin; Rector Grane Sylvae, Co Kilkenny; *dsp* 22 Aug 1863

3 CHARLES, **3rd Baron**

4 Patrick later Fitzstephen (FRENCH), of Lough Erritt, PC (I 1886), JP Cos Sligo and Roscommon; *b* 7 Dec 1801; *educ* Trin Coll Dublin; MP Co Roscommon (1832–73, Col Co Roscommon Militia 1854–73; *m* 24 Nov 1839 Charlotte Emma Georgina, dau and coheir of Hon Henry Grey Bennet (*see* TANKERVILLE, E), and *d* 4 June 1873, having had issue:

(1) Arthur Foulke Augustus; *b* 27 Aug 1840; *d* young

(1) Louisa Emma Corisande; *m* 18 June 1868 Capt George Henry Bridges, ADC

(2) Augusta Sarah

The 2nd BARON's brother,

CHARLES FRENCH, **3rd Baron De Freyne of Coolavin**; *b* 22 Oct 1790; *m* 13 Feb 1851 in an RC ceremony which under the laws of Ireland at the time was held invalid, and again in the C of I church of Grange Gorman, Dublin, 17 May 1854 Catherine (*d* 13 Oct 1900), dau of Luke Maree, and had:

1 Charles, JP Co Roscommon; *b* 21 Oct 1851; *educ* Downside; held with his two immediately yr bros to be illegitimate hence incapable of inheriting the title, which accordingly passed on their f's death to the 4th s; Co Roscommon: MP 1873–80, High Sheriff 1887; *m* 1880 Constance, dau of Lt-Col Charles Raleigh Chichester, of Runnamoat, Co Roscommon, and *d* 27 Oct 1925, leaving:

(1) Charles Henry; *b* 7 Nov 1891; *educ* Downside; Lt 13th Bn Roy Warwicks Regt WW I; *d* unm 1 May 1961

(1) Hilda Mary; *b* 29 Feb 1884; *d* unm 8 June 1970

(2) Amy Mary; *b* 6 June 1885; *m* 2 Nov 1927 Percy John Vincent MacDermot (*d* 7 June 1955), 2nd s of The MacDermot of Coolavin, and had a dau

(3) Eva Mary; *b* 13 Jan 1887; *d* unm 2 Jan 1962

(4) Muriel Mary; *b* 7 April 1888; *d* unm 8 Oct 1973

(5) Barbara; *b* 12 Sept 1892; *d* unm 17 Sept 1963

2 John, of Miramar, Queenstown (now Cobh), Co Cork, JP Co Roscommon; *b* 13 March 1853; *educ* Downside; RM Cos Kerry 1892–98 and Limerick 1898; *m* 26 July 1877 Nannie (*d* 3 Feb 1947), dau of Valentine B Dillon, and *d* 23 May 1916, having had, with three yst sons and an est dau (all *d* unm):

(1) Charles John; *b* 13 Oct 1878; Lord Longford's Yeo Boer War, Maj 5th Bn KSLI WW I, ADC 1914, attd RE 1916; *m* Oct 1914 Enid, dau of George Hudson, Br Resident Transvaal, and was *ka* 2 July 1916

(2) John Cyril; *b* 2 Aug 1883; Capt S African Scottish Regt WW I, Laison Offr WW II; *m* 1st 17 Sept 1915 (*divorce* 1926) Cecilia dau of Isaac Goldinger (*see* also STRATHMORE AND KINGHORNE, E), and had:

1a John Valentine Terence; *b* 30 Oct 1918; Lt SAAF; *m* 26 Aug 1940 *Nanette, est dau of Alfred William Ogilvie, and was *k* in a flying accident 21 April 1943, leaving:

1b *Diane Terry; *b* 30 Sept 1943; *m* 19 Jan 1963 *Kenneth Ross and has issue

1a Pamela Ismay [Mrs Wilfred Eadon, 122 Clarence Gate Gdns, Glentworth St, London NW1 6AL]; *b* 13 July 1917; *m* 25 May 1940 *Wilfred Myles Eadon and has:

1b *Nicholas Piers [Nicholas Eadon Esq, 122 Clarence Gate Gdns, Glentworth St, London NW1 6AL]; *b* 18 Oct 1941; *educ* Harrow

2b *Simon Dominic [Simon Eadon Esq, 26 Whitehall Gdns, London W3 9RD]; *b* 14 May 1952; *educ* Harrow; *m* 5 Sept 1981 *Susan Clare, dau of Basil Warren and great-niece of FM Sir Claude Auchinleck, and has:

1c *Alexander Chenevix; *b* 1 May 1983; *educ* King's Coll Sch Cambridge

2c *Benjamin Myles; *b* 20 June 1985; *educ* King's Coll Sch Cambridge

(2) (cont.) John French *m* 2nd Sept 1926 (*divorce* 19–) Winifred, dau of Thomas Eastwood, of Yorks, and by her had:

2a Sean de Freyne; *b* 3 June 1936; *m* 9 March 1963 *Denise Shirley, dau of Norman Robinson, of Johannesburg, and has:

1b *Lance de Freyne; *b* 22 Dec 1963

1b *Kerynne Diane; *b* 9 Nov 1965

2a *Maureen; *b* 7 Aug 1927; *m* *Owen Burdon

3a *Antonia; *b* 24 Dec 1930; *m* 11 June 1955 *Charles Mackintosh Flood, VRD, MD, FRCOG, and has had:

1b Nicola Marie; *b* 18 July 1957; *d* 13 Nov 1996

2b *Rosemarie Jane; *b* 6 May 1960

3b *Diana Marie; *b* 12 April 1967

(2) (cont.) John French *m* 3rd *Christine Botha and *d* 30 March 1955, leaving by her:

3a *John

4a *Christine

5a *Coleen

(3) Valentine Douglas; *b* 1888; 2nd Lt 5th Bn Roy Munster Fus and KSLI WW I; *ka* 16 June 1916

(1) Laura; *b* 19 Jan 1881; *m* 7 April 1907 Charles O'Hara, RIC, s of Thomas O'Hara, of Portarlington, Queen's Co, and *d* 10 March 1919

(2) Mabel Elizabeth; *b* 6 July 1885; *m* 8 Sept 1909 Cdr William Uvedale Hambro Parry Okeden, RN, of Hermon Estate, Grenada, WI, est s of Lt-Col Uvedale Edward Parry Okeden, of Turnworth, Dorset, and *dsp* 23 May 1957

(3) Lucinda Mary Stanley; *b* 1888; *m* 26 Nov 1914 Cdr Arthur Beauchamp St John, RN (*see* SAINT JOHN OF BLETSO, B)

3 William John; *b* 21 April 1854; *educ* Downside; Capt Wexford Militia

4 ARTHUR, **4th Baron**

5 Richard Patrick, Maj and Hon Lt-Col 5th Bn Connaught Rangers; *b* 30 April 1857; *d* 19 June 1921

6 Robert, Maj and Hon Lt-Col 2nd Bn Glos Regt; *b* 22 Oct 1858; *m* 29 July 1885 Mary Cassandra (*m* 2nd 5 Feb 1921 Capt Cyril Richards, RFC, s of D T Richards, MD, JP), only dau of Hugh Mair, of Phyllis Court, Oxon, and *d* 27 Sept 1920, leaving issue:

(1) Hugh Ronald, Capt 7th Dragoon Gds (SR); *b* 23 May 1886; *m* 17 June 1909 (*divorce* 1913) Ida Marcella, dau of Robert J Wynne, US Consul-Gen London, and *d* 5 July 1929, having had issue:

1a Valerie Marie; *b* 18 Feb 1911; *m* 2 Dec 1933 George Knowles, only son of Maj — Knowles, of Jamaica

1 Mary Josephine; *m* 1 Sept 1880 Valentine Joseph Blake (*d* 3 Oct 1912), 3rd son of Valentine O'Connor Blake, of Tower Hill, Co Mayo, and *d* 20 Feb 1919, leaving issue (*see* BLAKE, Bt, of Menlough)

The 3rd BARON *d* 28 Oct 1868; his est legitimate son,

ARTHUR FRENCH, **4th Baron De Freyne of Coolavin**, Hon Col 5th Bn Connaught Rangers; *b* 9 July 1855; *m* 1st 8 Feb 1877 Lady Laura Octavia Dundas (*d* 19 Jan 1881), sister of 1st Marquess of Zetland (*qv*), and had:

1 ARTHUR REGINALD FRENCH, **5th Baron De Freyne of Coolavin**, Capt 3rd Bn S Wales Borderers, previously Lt Roy Fus; *b* 3 July 1879; *m* 18 Nov 1902 Annabel, dau of William Angus, and was *ka* 9 May 1915

1 Gwendolen Mary; *b* 18 May 1878; *d* 17 May 1893

The **4th Baron** *m* 2nd 28 Sept 1882 Marie Georgiana (*d* 20 Feb 1923), only dau of Richard Westbrook Lamb, of West Denton, and *d* 22 Sept 1923, having by her had issue:

2 FRANCIS CHARLES, **6th Baron**

3 William Joseph, Lt RASC (TF), Adj and Actg Capt MGC, Lt 6th Bn Worcs Regt, High Sheriff Co Roscommon 1915, served WW I and WW II 1940–42 as Capt Gen List; *b* 5 Aug 1885; *educ* Oratory Sch; *m* 12 April 1920 Victoria Louise (*d* 1989), yst dau of William Dalglish Bellasis, JP, and *d* 4 Sept 1974, having had issue:

(1) Patrick George; *b* 9 May 1921; *d* 2 June 1926
(1) *Marie Isobel [The Rt Hon The Countess Cathcart, Moor Hatches, West Amesbury, Wilts SP4 7BH]; *m* 1st 21 July 1942 Capt Sir Thomas Brian Weldon, 8th Bt (*d* 5 Aug 1979; *qv*), and has issue; *m* 2nd 1984, as his 2nd w, 6th Earl Cathcart (*qv*)
(2) *Eleanor Mary [Mrs Munro of Foulis, Foulis Castle, Evanton, Ross-shire IV16 9UX]; *m* 11 Jan 1946 Capt Patrick Munro of Foulis, Seaforth Highrs (*d* 24 Feb 1995; *see* MUNRO, Bt, of Foulis-Obsdale), and has issue
(3) Cecily Marie Gabriel; *d* unm 5 July 1947
4 Edward Fulke, electrical engr, 2nd Lt RFA WW I; *b* 13 July 1886; *d* a POW 13 Nov 1918
5 Louis Richard, JP, Lt RASC(TF) WW I; *b* 6 Sept 1888; *m* 27 April 1922 Margaret Eleanor (*d* 1 June 1972 aged 72), dau of Capt Maurice Kirk, 4th King's Own Regt, and *d* 5 Feb 1952, leaving issue:
(1) Peter John Maurice; *b* 26 Feb 1923; *d* 15 Dec 1990
(1) *Sheila Mary, MBE (1987) [Mrs John Stilwell MBE, Casa dos Arcos, Tapada da Penina, CX3, 8500 Portimão, Portugal]; *b* 21 Oct 1924; *m* 18 Sept 1948 *John Benedict Stilwell MBE (1997), KSG (1994), Lt Coldstream Gds, and has issue:
1a *Mark Andrew [Mark Stilwell Esq, Quinta de Alcalar, Alvor, Portimão, Portugal]; *b* 29 July 1949; *m* 1974 *Viviane de Ghelderе, and has issue:
1b *John Philip; *b* 1975
2b *Alexandra Mary; *b* 1978
2a *Christopher John [Christopher Stilwell Esq, 21 Monte da Bemposta, Portimão, Portugal]; *b* 3 July 1952; *m* 1982 *Dr Ana Luiza Mendes Victor, and has issue:
1b *John William; *b* 1983
3a John William; *b* 27 March 1954; *d* 1983
4a *Charles Louis [Charles Stilwell Esq, Brackenwood, 5 Plymouth Rd, Barnt Green, Worcs B45 8JE]; *b* 16 May 1957; *m* 1986 *Mary Elizabeth Baker, and has:
1b *Simon Benedict; *b* 1989
2b *Christian Louis; *b* 1992
3b *Andrew Charles (twin); *b* 1992
1a *Philippa Anne [Mrs João Zilhão, 41 Avenida do Restelo, Lisbon, Portugal]; *b* 23 Nov 1950; *m* 1973 *João Carlos Zilhão, and has issue:
1b *João Miguel; *b* 1974
2b *Antonio Carlos; *b* 1976
3b *Francisco; *b* 1989
1b *Ana Felipa; *b* 1981
(2) Eleanor Georgina; *b* 23 Jan 1928; *m* 1 Jan 1954 *Robert Macalaster Symington, yr son of M M Symington, OBE, of Oporto, and *d* 23 Aug 1986, leaving issue:
1a *Nicholas Maurice; *b* 23 Dec 1954
2a *Richard Andrew; *b* 30 Dec 1955
3a *Anthony Macalaster [Anthony Symington Esq, Pond House, Lt Coxwell, nr Faringdon SN7 7LW]; *b* 17 June 1958
6 George Philip, Lt 3rd Bn S Wales Borderers; *b* 7 Jan 1890; *ka* 9 May 1915, the same day as his half-bro, the **5th Baron**
7 Ernest Aloysius, Lt 5th Bn S Wales Borderers; *b* 4 July 1894; *d* 16 Aug 1917 of wounds recd in action
8 Hubert John; *b* 11 March 1896; *educ* Trin Coll Cambridge (Ag Dip); *m* 19 Jan 1937 *Mary Frances [Mrs Hubert Stychfield, Stychens Lane, Bletchingley, Redhill, Surrey], 3rd dau of Charles Hasslacher, of 3 Kensington Park Gdns, London W11 and *d* 7 Dec 1961, leaving issue:
(1) +Christopher John [Christopher French Esq, Brewerstreet Farm, Bletchingley, Surrey]; *b* 18 Jan 1943; *educ* Oratory Sch Reading and Seale Hayne Ag Coll Devon; *m* 17 Sept 1966 *Sacha, 2nd dau of Robert Wild, and has issue:
1a +Philip John; *b* 15 Feb 1968
1a *Julia Winfred; *b* 1971
(2) +Richard Charles [Richard French Esq, 24 Detillens Lane, Limpsfield, Oxted, Surrey RH8 0DJ]; *b* 17 Oct 1945; *educ* Oratory Sch Reading and St Andrews U; *m* 18 Feb 1969 *Hilda Felicity, er dau of Lt-Col John James Pearson, of Vicarage Close, Tandridge, Oxted, Surrey, and has issue:
1a *Charles Peter; *b* 1974
1a *Helen Mary Louise; *b* 25 Nov 1969; *m* 1996 *Benjamin Moore
2a *Suszanna Frances (twin); *b* 1974
(1) *Jane Mary [Mrs Donald Lawlor, 2 Elsenwood Crescent, Camberley, Surrey]; *b* 28 March 1938; *m* 8 Jan 1966 *Donald John Lawlor and has issue:
1a *Bernard John; *b* 1969
2a *Timothy Charles; *b* 1970
3a *Stephen Andrew; *b* 1976
1a *Elizabeth Mary; *b* 1967
(2) *Sarah Anne [Mrs Clement Lutterodt, 6281 Lightpoint Place, Columbia, Md 21045, USA]; *b* 31 May 1940; *educ* Oxford (BA 1961), MPhil, MEd, PhD; *m* 19– *C H Lutterodt, PhD, and has issue:
1a *Tobias Henry; *b* 1973
1a *Isabelle Anne; *b* 1975
2a *Justine Frances; *b* 1979
9 Bertram Leo, 2nd Lt Coldstream Gds (SR); *b* 15 Feb 1900; *educ* Trin Coll Cambridge (BA); *m* 18 Jan 1927 Maud Mary (*d* 17 April 1974), only dau of Edmund Dease, of Levington Park, Mullingar, Co Westmeath, and *d* 11 May 1941, leaving issue:
(1) +Maurice Aloysius, MBE (1976) [Maj Maurice French MBE, 71 East St, Warminster, Wilts]; Maj Roy Fus Korea 1952–53 (despatches); *b* 5 March 1930; *educ* Ampleforth; *m* 1st 4 Sept 1958 (*divorce* 1965) Heather Stewart, yr dau of Arthur Charles Tarbutt, MC, of Jantar, Jos, Nigeria, and has issue:
1a +Dominic Arthur; *b* 5 June 1959; *m* 1987 *Miranda, dau of Philip Howden, and has issue:
1b +Richard Maurice; *b* 1988
2b +James Philip (twin); *b* 1988
1a *Nicola Anne; *b* 22 June 1960; *m* 1984 *David Stogdale, and has issue:
1b *Sam Patrick; *b* 1987
2b *Will Benedict; *b* 1994
1b *Abigail Gaynor; *b* 1990
(1) (cont.) Maurice French *m* 2nd 17 Aug 1965 *Lavinia Mary, 2nd dau of Maj (Patrick Henry) Anthony Burke, of Stackallan, Co Meath, and by her has issue:
2a +Patrick Rollo; *b* 28 May 1966; MA, FRGS; *m* 1992 *Abigail Digna Joanna, dau of Cdr Eoin Ashton-Johnson, of East Orchard, Dorset, and has issue:
1b +Thomas Tenzin; *b* 1994
3a +Gerald Hugh; *b* 1975
2a *Claudia Rosemary; *b* 1973
3a *Emily Mary Lucia (twin); *b* 1975
(2) +Arthur Edmund [Arthur French Esq, 38 Belfield Rd, Didsbury M20 6BH]; *b* 10 Jan 1933; *educ* Trin Coll Cambridge (BA 1957), Lt Irish Gds (res), barrister Inner Temple 1962; *m* 1986 *Charlotte Mary, 2nd dau of Sir Simon Peter Edmund Cosmo William Towneley, KCVO, of Dyneley, Burnley, Lancs (*see* LINDSEY and ABINGDON, E), and has issue:
1a +Edmund Peter; *b* 1989
2a *Alice Cecilia; *b* 1987
(1) *Lavinia Marie [Mrs John Watson, Pannett's, Shipley, Horsham, Sussex RH13 8PP]; *b* 28 Oct 1928; *m* 1st 8 Oct 1968 (*annulled* 1970) Michael Francis Vandeleur Cubitt, est son of Maj Charles Cyril Cubitt, MC, of Edge of the Hill, Crowthorne, Berks; *m* 2nd 1971 *Maj John Norman Pembroke Watson, RHG
2 Lily Marie; *b* 4 Aug 1887; *d* unm 4 June 1967
3 Muriel May; *b* 1 May 1891; *m* 7 April 1920 (*divorce* 1947) Maj William Alexander Wilkinson, MC, Coldstream Gds, and *d* 1980
4 Eileen Agnes; *b* 23 Dec 1892; *m* 19 Nov 1917 Maj John William Fitzherbert-Brockholes, CBE, MC, (*d* 21 July 1963), of Claughton Hall, Lancs, and *d* 28 Dec 1971, leaving issue (*see* QUINTON, B)

The 5th BARON's half-bro,

FRANCIS CHARLES FRENCH, **6th Baron De Freyne of Coolavin**, DL Co Roscommon, High Sheriff 1912; *b* 15 Jan 1884; *m* 28 Feb 1916 (Lina) Victoria (*d* 25 Oct 1974), dau of Sir John Alexander Arnott, 2nd Bt (*qv*), and *d* 24 Dec 1935, leaving issue:

1 FRANCIS ARTHUR JOHN FRENCH, **7th and present Baron De Freyne of Coolavin**
1 *Patricia Mary [The Hon Mrs Johnson, 4 Linley Court, Rouse Gdns, London SE21 8AQ]; *b* 3 Nov 1917; *m* 24 March 1941 Reginald Johnson (*d* 29 Oct 1958), and has issue:
(1) *Michael Reginald [Michael Johnson Esq, 56 Pymers Mead, London SE21]; *b* 1 Nov 1943; *m* 1982 *Marta Jablonska and has issue:
1a *Patrick Martin; *b* 1983
2a *Mark Conrad Eric; *b* 1986
(1) *Diana Mary [Mrs Frederick Robinson, 111 Gatley Ave, Westewell, Surrey]; *b* 31 March 1942; *m* 1972 *Frederick Robert Robinson and has issue:
1a *Nicholas Frederick; *b* 1980
1a *Victoria Jane; *b* 1977
2 Jeanne Victoria; *b* 25 July 1919; *d* unm 5 Nov 1960
3 Patience Veronica; *b* 11 Oct 1922; *m* 5 June 1952 *Lt-Cdr Arthur Rickards, RN, only son of Cdr Arthur Scott Horace Pitt Rickards, RNR (ret), of Glenburn House, N Berwick, and *d* 4 Jan 1985, leaving issue:
(1) *Luana Veronica; *b* 30 July 1957; *m* 4 June 1988 *Robert King, of Melbourne, Australia and has issue:
1a *Victoria; *b* 19 Oct 1995
(2) *Edwina [Mrs Anthony Collinson, The Coach House, Capernwray, Carnforth, Lancs]; *b* 13 Sept 1958; *m* 31 Dec 1996 *Anthony Collinson
4 Faith Gabriel; *b* 28 March 1925; *m* 15 Jan 1951 Richard Archdale Morris (*d* 18 Nov 1992), est son of Michael Archdale Morris, of Clonmore House, Pilltown, Co Kilkenny, and *d* 21 April 1962, leaving issue:
(1) *Maxwell Charles [Maxwell Morris Esq, Irenk, Piltown, Co Kilkenny, Ireland]; *b* 29 Nov 1951; *m* 3 Jan 1987 *Isobel Ryan
(2) *Michael Lauriston Francis [Michael Morris Esq, New Rath, Waterford, Ireland]; *b* 19 April 1959; *m* 13 June 1987 *Susannah Curran and has issue:
1a *Richard Arthur Archdale; *b* 12 May 1995
1a *Faith Victoria Mary; *b* 12 Oct 1989
2a *Susannah Elizabeth; *b* 13 May 1991
(3) *Victoria Gabriel Mary [Mrs Norman Moane, PO Box 1854, Sharigh, United Arab Emirates]; *b* 21 Sept 1954; *m* 3 May 1984 *Norman Moane
(4) *Alicia Mary Frances [Miss Alicia Morris, PO Box 53526, Dubai, United Arab Emirates]

De Hoghton

Arms: Sable three bars argent. **Crest:** A bull passant argent, the ears, tip of the horns, mane, hoofs and point of the tail sable. **Supporters:** Two bulls argent. **Motto:** *Malgré la tort* ('In spite of wrong'). **Creation:** Bt. (E) 22 May 1611.

SIR (RICHARD) BERNARD CUTHBERT DE HOGHTON, 14TH BT, of Hoghton Tower, and Walton le Dale, Co Lancaster, DL (Lancs 1988) [Sir Bernard de Hoghton Bt DL, Hoghton Tower, Hoghton, nr Preston, Lancs PR5 0SH]; *b* 26 Jan 1945; *s* half bro 1978; *educ* Ampleforth, McGill U (BA) and Birmingham U (MA); PhD (USA), Kt SMO Malta 1980, Constantinian Order St George Naples 1984; *m* 1974 *Rosanna Stella Virginia, dau of Terzo Buratti, of Florence, and has issue:

1 +THOMAS JAMES DANIEL ADAM; *b* 11 April 1980

1 *Elena Susannah Isabella; *b* 1976

Lineage: HERVEY WALTER (*see* ORMONDE, M); had a yst s:

HAMO PINCERNA; had:

RICHARD; had

ADAM de HOGHTON; held land in Hoghton, Lancs, 1203; *m* —, dau of Warin Bussel (*d c* 1150), and was gf or ggf of:

Sir ADAM de HOGHTON; *m* Agnes — and *d c* 1290, leaving, with other issue:

Sir RICHARD de HOGHTON; MP Lancs 1322, 1326–7 and 1337; *m* Sibilla de Lea and *d* after 1345, leaving:

ADAM de HOGHTON; MP Lancs 1348, 1363 and 1365; accompanied EDWARD III's invasion of France 1359; *d* 1385, leaving:

RICHARD de HOGHTON; MP Lancs 1383 and 1402, High Sheriff 1410, fndr Ribchester Chantry 1406, Commr Array for defence against Scots 1400, Ch Steward Lancs 1399–1422; *d* 1422, leaving issue:

Sir WILLIAM de HOGHTON; *dvp*, leaving issue:

Sir RICHARD de HOGHTON; *d* 1468, leaving issue:

Sir HENRY de HOGHTON; *d* 1479, leaving, with other issue, including an er s (Sir Alexander, KB 1482, *dsp* 1498):

Sir WILLIAM de HOGHTON; *d* 1501, leaving:

RICHARD de HOGHTON, deputised for Earl of Surrey as Steward of Amounderness; Lancs: High Sheriff 1540, MP 1553; *m* four times and *d* 1559, leaving, with other issue, including two er sons (Thomas, rebuilt Hoghton Tower, recusant, fndr Douai Seminary, *dsp* Liege 1580; Alexander, *d* 1581):

THOMAS; *m* Anne, dau of Henry Kighley, and was *k* in an affray at Lea 21 Nov 1589, leaving:

Sir Richard Hoghton, 1st Bt (E), so *cr* 22 May 1611, of Hoghton Tower; *b* Sept 1570, ktd Jan 1589/90, Lancs: Sheriff 1599, MP; *m* Katharine (*d* 17 Nov 1617), dau of Sir Gilbert Gerard, of Gerard's Bromley, Staffs, and ld 12 Nov 1630, having had, with four other sons and eight daus:

Sir Gilbert Hoghton, 2nd Bt, MP Lancs, ktd 1604; *m* Margaret (*d* 23 Dec 1657), est dau and coheir of Sir Roger Aston, and *d* April 1647, having had, with three other sons and four daus:

Sir Richard Hoghton, 3rd Bt, MP Lancs, Extrdy Gentleman Privy Chamber 1661; *m* Lady Sarah Stanhope (*d* May 1698), dau of 1st Earl of Chesterfield (*see* 1967 edn CHESTERFIELD and STANHOPE, E), and *d* 3 Feb 1677/8, having had, with other issue:

Sir Charles Hoghton, 4th Bt, MP Lancs; *m c* 8 March 1676 Mary (*d* 30 April 1732), dau of 2nd Viscount Massereene (*see* MASSEREENE and FERRARD, V), and had, with other issue:

1 **Sir Henry Hoghton, 5th Bt**, MP Preston, Col Militia; *m* 1st Oct 1710 Mary (*d* 23 Feb 1719), dau of Sir William Boughton, 1st Bt, of Lawford, Warwick (*see* 1963 edn ROUSE BOUGHTON, Bt); *m* 2nd 14 April 1721 Elizabeth Lloyd (*d* 1 Dec 1736), widow of Lord James Russell, yr son of 1st Duke of Bedford (*qv*); *m* 3rd Susanna (*d* 16 Oct 1772), est dau of Thomas Butterworth, of Manchester, but by her had no issue

2 Philip; *m* 1st 8 Jan 1724 Elizabeth (*d* March 1731), dau of Thomas Sclater, of Denham, Lancs, and *d* 10 June 1710, having had, with two daus:

(1) HENRY (Sir), **6th Bt**

2 (cont.) Philip Hoghton *m* 2nd Margaret (*d* Feb 1795), dau of Edward Rigby, of Middleton, Yorks, and by her had issue:

(1) Anne; *m* 28 Feb 1744 Rev Humphrey Shuttleworth, Vicar Preston and Kirkham, and *d* Nov 1783, leaving issue

1 Cordelia; *m* Robert Davie, of York, and *d* 8 Feb 1768

2 Anna; *m* 9 Oct 1721 Samuel Crook, of Coppull, Lancs

3 Margaret; *m* 27 Aug 1716 Samuel Watson and *d* 1775

4 Elizabeth; *m* 14 Feb 1715 Thomas Fenton, of Hunslet, Yorks, and *d* 15 May 1733

5 Lucy; *m* 6 Feb 1721 Thomas Lutwidge, of Whitehaven

Sir HENRY *d* 23 Feb 1768; his nephew,

Sir Henry Hoghton, 6th Bt, MP Preston; *b* 22 Oct 1728; *m* 1st 1761 Elizabeth (*d* 1762), only dau and heir of William Ashurst, of Hedingham Castle, Essex, and had an only dau; *m* 2nd 8 July 1766 Fanny (*d* April 1803), est dau and coheir of Daniel Booth, of Hutton Hall, Essex, and *d* 9 March 1795, having by her had, with a yr s (Daniel, Maj-Gen, *ka* Albuera 16 May 1811):

Sir Henry Philip Hoghton, 7th Bt, MP Preston, Col 3rd Roy Lancs Militia; *b* 12 June 1768; *m* 13 Nov 1797 Susannah (*d* 8 Dec 1852), only dau and heir of Peter Brooke, of Astley Hall, Lancs, and widow of Thomas Townley Parker, and had, with a dau:

Sir HENRY HOGHTON later BOLD-HOGHTON (roy licence 15 Feb 1825), **8th Bt**, JP, DL (Lancs); *b* 3 Jan 1799; High Sheriff Lancs 1829, Col 3rd Roy Lancs Militia; *m* 1st 23 May 1820 Dorothea (*d* 7 Dec 1840), 2nd dau and (on the death of her er sis Mary, w of Prince Eustace Saphieha, of Poland), est coheir of Peter Patten Bold, of Lancaster, and had issue:

1 Sir HENRY HOGHTON later BOLD-HOGHTON later still De HOGHTON (roy licence for him and siblings 6 Aug 1862), **9th Bt**, DL, JP Lancs, Cards: JP, High Sheriff 1849; *b* 2 Aug 1821; fndr memb Sunday League; *m* 1st 14 Aug 1845 (*divorce* 1849) Louisa Josephine, 4th dau and coheir of Joseph Sanders, and had issue:

(1) Cecil; *b* 5 Feb 1849; *d* 24 July 1874

1 (cont.) The **9th Bt** *m* 2nd 1 July 1851 Aline (*d* 29 Dec 1852), 3rd dau of Sir Henry Jervis-White-Jervis, Bt, of Bally Ellis, Co Wexford (*see* 1940 edn), and by her had issue:

(1) Aline Marian; *b* 8 Dec 1852; *m* 4 Jan 1875 Gerald John Fitzgerald and *d* 1886, leaving issue

1 (cont.) The **9th Bt** *m* 3rd 6 Sept 1854 Ellen Ann (*d* 27 Dec 1909), dau of Ralph Harvey, and *d* 2 Dec 1876, having by her had issue:

(2) Elinor Isabel; *b* 14 May 1860; *d* unm 23 Dec 1935

2 **Sir Charles de Hoghton, 10th Bt**; *b* 20 Nov 1823; Capt Army; *m* 1863 Florence (*d* 31 Dec 1873), dau of Louis Moyard, of Morges, Canton de Vaud, Switzerland, and *dsp* 12 April 1893

3 Richard, Lt 9th Lancers; *b* 20 May 1828; *m* 17 Sept 1863 Martha, 3rd dau of Septimus Miller, and *dsp* 17 Aug 1892

1 Mary; *b* 7 June 1825; *m* 12 Nov 1846 Col John Ireland Blackburne (*d* 5 Sept 1893), DL, JP, of Orford Hall, and Hale Hall, Lancs, and *d* 30 April 1855, leaving issue

2 Dora; *b* 12 Sept 1826; *m* 10 Nov 1857 Priestley Birch (*d* 9 June 1867) and *d* 10 Jan 1902, leaving issue

Sir HENRY *m* 2nd 13 Nov 1847 Harriet Sarah (*d* 25 Oct 1866), est dau of John Smith, of Norwich, and *d* 19 July 1862, having by her had, with other issue:

4 JAMES (Sir), **11th Bt**

5 Daniel, MBE, Maj Loyal N Lancs Regt; *b* 13 Aug 1853; *m* 1888 Mary (*d* 22 Nov 1933), dau of Henry Jones, and *d* 5 Jan 1929, leaving issue:

(1) Sybil

3 Frances; *d* unm 23 Aug 1948

The 10th Bt's half-bro,

Sir James de Hoghton, 11th Bt, CBE (1919), DL, JP; *b* 2 Feb 1851; Hon Col and Col Cmdt Lancs Vol Corps, Maj Lincs Regt, Maj and Hon Lt-Col 4th Bn; *m* 27 June 1878 Aimee Jean (*d* 1 July 1919), only dau of John Grove, 2nd son of John Grove, of Ferne, Wilts (*see* GROVE, Bt), and had issue:

1 Guy; *b* 12 May 1879; *d* 27 Dec 1880

2 CUTHBERT (Sir), **12th Bt**

3 Vere, Maj Lincs Regt, Adj 5th Bn 1913–15; *b* 6 March 1882; *m* 9 Nov 1911 Alice Dorothy Patience (*d* 14 Feb 1968) (*m* 2nd 14 May 1921 Joseph Eccles (*d* 18 March 1944), son of Joseph Eccles, of Myerscough House, Garstang, Lancs), yr dau of Sir Frank Hollins, 1st Bt, JP (*see* 1963 edn), and was *ka* France Oct 1915, leaving:

(1) *Diana; *b* 3 Sept 1913; *m* 6 July 1937 Maj Brian Peirson Doughty-Wylie (*d* 1982), MC, Royal Welch Fus, 2nd son of Hon Wilfred Gilbert Thesiger, DSO (*see* CHELMSFORD, V), and has issue

4 Guy, DSO (1918), MC, Lt-Col KOYLI WW I (wounded, despatches twice); *b* 21 Nov 1886; *educ* Harrow; *m* 1st 11 Feb 1915 (*annulled* 1918) Violet Caroline Townley, only child of Capt Gerald Townley Parker, of Bridge House, Dawlish, Devon; *m* 2nd 1 Nov 1922 (*divorce* 1938) Marian Barnard, yst dau of John Barnard Hankey, of Fetcham Park, Surrey, and formerly w of Frederick Gordon Colman, and *d* 4 April 1965

1 Dorothy; *b* 29 April 1883; *m* 24 Nov 1908 Col Sir Archibald Moir Park Lyle, 2nd Bt (*d* 4 Dec 1946; *qv*), and *d* 27 May 1967, leaving issue

2 Cicely; *b* 27 Dec 1884; *m* 29 Sept 1908 Piers Cecil Le Gendre Starkie (*d* 2 June 1947), 3rd son of Le Gendre Nicholas Starkie, DL, of Huntroyde, Lancs, and had issue

3 Joan; *b* 21 Sept 1891; *m* 12 July 1921 Maj Charles Robert Thropp Thorp (*d* 14 Jan 1935), MC, KOYLI, and had issue

4 Barbara; *b* 2 May 1894; *m* 1st 8 Dec 1914 Robert Myles Heywood (*d* 15 Feb 1915 from wounds recd in action), 2nd Lt 3rd Bn E Kent Regt, only son of Robert Heywood, of Hales Hall, Staffs; *m* 2nd 4 Oct 1926 Richard Leveson Vernon, son of Walter Bertie William Vernon, JP, of Hilton Park, Staffs, and had issue

Sir JAMES *d* 4 Nov 1938; his son,

Sir Cuthbert de Hoghton, 12th Bt, JP Lancs; *educ* Harrow and Magdalen Coll Oxford, Lt Coldstream Gds WW I, RNVR and RNAS; *b* 27 Aug 1880; *m* 1st 12 Feb 1917 Helen (*d* 15 Oct 1943), only dau of Major Duncan Macdonald, of Glencoe, and had issue:

1 **Sir (Henry Philip) Anthony Mary de Hoghton, 13th Bt**; *b* 19 April 1919; *educ* Beaumont and Magdalen Coll Oxford; Coroner for Manor of Walton-le-Dale; *d* unm 20 Feb 1978

2 Charles James Gilbert; *b* 5 July 1930; *educ* Ampleforth and Trin Coll Cambridge; *m* 27 Sept 1957 (Winifred) Valerie Maud, yr dau of William Richard Glynn Thomas, of Cefn Coed, Breconshire, and *d* 25 Sept 1971, leaving issue:

(1) *Katherine Anne; *b* 1959

1 Iseult Mary; *b* 25 April, *d* 1 May 1921

Sir Cuthbert *m* 2nd 31 Jan 1944 *Philomena (*m* 2nd 10 Feb 1960 Richard Grahame Adams (*d* 1985), Colonial Admin Service, Nigeria, est son of Godfrey Adams, of Radlett, Herts, and has further issue) [Mrs Richard Adams, Dower House, Bourton on the Water, Cheltenham, Glos], dau of Herbert Simmons, of Walton le Dale, Lancs, and *d* 5 Dec 1958, having by her had issue:

3 Sir (RICHARD) BERNARD CUTHBERT De HOGHTON, **14th and present Bt**

2 Mary Philomena Cecilia; *b* 13 Oct, *d* 31 Oct 1946

Seat: Hoghton Tower, nr Preston, Lancs. The word Hoghton signifies 'hill-top house' and when the Lancashire weather permits the place can indeed be seen from miles around. It dates from the mid-16th century, although the ancestors of the Baronets had been living there in other structures for several hundred years previously. Because the North was still subject to a degree of lawlessness unknown in the softer South the lay-out harks back to medieval times, chiefly the importance of defence, rather than expressing the Renaissance ideals of openness and ornamentation for their own sake. The plan is designed around two courtyards, the outer one dominated by a crenellated gatehouse. A massive tower that separated the outer and inner courtyards was demolished at the time of the Civil War, but the great hall still stands. It is probably there, if anywhere in the house, that JAMES I dubbed a side of beef 'Sir Loin' on that legendary occasion during his visit in 1617.

De la Bere

Arms: Argent on a fess between three crescents sable a lizard of the field. **Crest:** Issuant from an ancient crown or a plume of five ostrich feathers argent charged with a ladybird proper. **Motto:** *Prest pour le Roy* ('Ready for the King'). **Creation:** Bt. (UK) 18 Nov 1953.

SIR CAMERON DE LA BERE, 2ND BT, of Crowborough Place, Crowborough, Sussex [Sir Cameron de la Bère Bt, 1 Avenue Théodore Flournoy, 1207 Geneva, Switzerland]; *b* 12 Feb 1933; *s* f 1978; *educ* Tonbridge; Intell Corps 1951–53, Liveryman Skinners' Co; *m* 20 June 1964 *Clairemonde, only dau of Casimir Kaufmann, of 26 Avenue William Favre, Geneva, Switzerland, and has issue:

1 *Réjane; *b* 1 Oct 1965

Lineage: REGINALD de la BERE, of The Croft, Addlestone, Surrey, *m* Lillian Margaret and had, with a dau (Esme, *d* unm 23 Sept 1965):

Sir Rupert De La Bère, 1st Bt (UK), so *cr* 18 Nov 1953, KCVO (1952); *b* 16 June 1893; *educ* Tonbridge; WW I: Capt E Surrey Regt, seconded to RFC and RAF, graduated at Aboukir, Egypt, MP (C) Evesham 1935–50 and S Worcs 1950–55, City London: Sheriff 1941–42, Alderman Tower Ward, Ld Mayor London 1952–53, Past Master Skinners' and Bakers' Cos, KStJ 1953, Kt Cdr Orders Dannebrog and N Star Sweden, ktd 1952; *m* 30 April 1919 Marguerite (*d* 26 April 1969), est dau of Lt-Col Sir John Humphrey, of Walton Leigh, Addlestone, Surrey, and *d* 25 Feb 1978, leaving issue:

1 Sir CAMERON De La BERE, **2nd and present Bt**

2 +ADRIAN; *b* 17 Sept 1939; heir presumptive

1 Pamela; *b* 1920

2 *Valerie; *b* 1923

3 *Camilla [Mrs Camilla Bourcier, 6 Quarry Hill, Sevenoaks, Kent]; *b* 1926, *m* 11 Sept 1953 (*divorce* 1959) Louis Georges Bourcier and has issue:

(1) *Andrew Charles; *b* 19 April 1954

(1) *Yolande; *b* 19 April 1954

Delacourt-Smith of Alteryn

Creation: B. (LP, UK) 1974.

THE BARONESS DELACOURT-SMITH OF ALTERYN, of Alteryn, Co Gwent (Margaret Rosalind Hando) [The Rt Hon The Baroness Delacourt-Smith of Alteryn, House of Lords, London SW1A 0PW]; *b* 5 April 1916; *educ* Newport High Sch and St Anne's Coll Oxford (MA); Cncllr Windsor 1962–65, JP 1962–65; *m* 1st 1939 Charles Smith (Baron Delacourt-Smith LP, *d* 1972; *see* 1970 edn) and has issue:

1 *Stephen [The Hon Stephen Delacourt-Smith, 73 Athenlay Rd, London SE15]; *b* 1946

1 *Carolyn [The Hon Mrs Pudney, Tanglewood, Manor Park, Hazlemere, Bucks]; *b* 1944; *m* 1969 *Roger Martin Pudney, and has issue:

(1) *A son; *b* 1977

(1) *A dau; *b* 1975

2 *Lesley [The Hon Lesley Delacourt-Smith, 6 Herrick Rd, London N5]; *b* 1948

BARONESS DELACOURT-SMITH OF ALTERYN *m* 2nd 1978 *Prof Charles Stuart Blackton

Lineage: FREDERICK JAMES HANDO, of Newport, Mon; had:

MARGARET ROSALIND, *cr* a **Baroness**

Delamere

Arms: Gules two esquire's helmets in chief proper, in base a garb or. **Crest:** A demi-griffin sejeant sable, beaked and membered or, ducally gorged and wings elevated or, holding between the claws a helmet, as in the arms. **Supporters:** On either side a griffin sable, beaked, membered, wings elevated, ducally gorged, chain reflexed over the back or. **Motto:** *Cassis tutissima virtus* ('Virtue is the safest helmet'). **Creation:** B. (UK) 17 July 1821.

THE 5TH BARON DELAMERE OF VALE ROYAL, Co Chester (Hugh George Cholmondeley, JP (Cheshire 1937)) [The Rt Hon The Lord Delamere JP, Sugoni Farm, Soysambu, Elmenteita, Kenya; 26 Holland Park Rd, London W14]; *b* 18 Jan 1934; *s* f 1979; *educ* Eton and Magdalene Coll Cambridge (BA 1955, MA 1959); *m* 11 April 1964 *Ann Willoughby, only dau of Sir Patrick Muir Renison, GCMG, of Freeman's Farm House, Mayfield, Sussex, and formerly wife of Michael Patrick Tinné, and has issue:

1 +THOMAS (Tom) PATRICK GILBERT; *b* 19 June 1968; *educ* Eton; *m* 16 May 1998 *Dr Sally, dau of Prof Derrick Brewerton, of Westminster

Lineage: Sir HUGH CHOLMONDELEY; *m* Mary, only dau and heir of Christopher Holford, of Holford, and had, with other issue (including an er s Hugh, ancestor of the Marquesses Cholmondeley, *qv*):

THOMAS CHOLMONDELEY, deeded by his mother the estate of Vale Royal, Cheshire; *m* Elizabeth, dau and heir of John Minshull, of Minshull, and *d* 1652; his est s:

THOMAS CHOLMONDELEY, of Vale Royal; *b* 1627; MP Cheshire *temp* CHARLES II; *m* 1st Jane, dau of Sir Lionel Tollemache, Bt (*see* DYSART, E), and had, with three daus:

1 Robert; *m* 1675 Elizabeth, dau of Sir Henry Vernon, 1st Bt (*see* VERNON, B), and *d* 1679, having had:

(1) Elizabeth; *m* John Atherton, of Atherton

THOMAS CHOLMONDELEY *m* 2nd Anne, dau of Sir Walter St John, by whom he had, with two daus:

2 Charles, of Vale Royal, MP Cheshire; *b* 1684; *m* 1714 Essex, est dau of Thomas Pitt, of Blandford, and sis of 1st Earl of Londonderry of the 1726 *cr* (*see* LONDONDERRY, M, preliminary remarks), and had issue:

(1) THOMAS

(1) Jane; *m* Richard Meyrick and had issue (*see* TAPPS-GERVIS-MEYRICK, Bt)

2 Mary; *m* 25 July 1732 Rev William Wannup, of Walden

CHARLES CHOLMONDELEY *d* 1759; his son,

THOMAS CHOLMONDELEY, of Vale Royal, MP Cheshire; *b* 1726; *m* 1764 Dorothy (*d* 25 May 1786), dau and coheir of Edmund Cowper, of Overleigh, Cheshire, and had, with other issue:

1 THOMAS, **1st Baron**

2 Charles, of Overleigh; *b* 6 June 1770; *m* 13 Jan 1794 Caroline Elizabeth (*d* 1818), sister and coheir of Nicholas Owen Smyth Owen, of Condover, and *d* 5 Dec 1846, leaving:

3 Hugh (Rev), Dean Chester; *b* 18 Dec 1772; *d* unm 25 Nov 1815

1 Hester; *m* 11 June 1789 John Drummond (*d* 28 May 1833), of Stanmore, and *d* 30 Sept 1802, leaving issue (*see* PERTH, E)

2 Dorothy; *m* 14 Sept 1795 Thomas Parker, of Astie, Cheshire, and *d* 18 March 1853

THOMAS CHOLMONDELEY *d* 2 June 1779; his est son,

THOMAS CHOLMONDELEY, **1st Baron Delamere of Vale Royal**, Chester (UK), so *cr* 17 July 1821; *b* 9 Aug 1767; Sheriff Cheshire 1792–93, MP (Tory) Cheshire 1796–1812; *m* 17 Dec 1810 Henrietta Elizabeth (*d* 18 Aug 1852), yst dau of Sir Watkin Williams Wynn, 4th Bt (*qv*), and had issue:

1 HUGH, **2nd Baron**

2 Thomas Grenville, Capt 43rd Regt, Hon Col cmdg 3rd Bn Cheshire Regt; *b* 4 Aug 1818; *m* 8 Aug 1850 Katherine Lucy (*d* 6 March 1921), 2nd dau of Sir Tatton Sykes, 4th Bt, of Sledmere (*qv*), and *d* 9 Feb 1883, having had, with other issue:

(1) Hugh Cecil, CB (1900), CBE (1919), Hon Brig-Gen, Col Cmdt 1st London VRC, Capt Rifle Bde, DL, JP Salop, V-Chm Salop TAA, served Afghan War 1878–79 (medal, clasp), and Boer War 1900 (despatches twice, medal with six clasps); *b* 1 Dec 1852; *m* 1st 24 March 1885 Mary Stewart (*d* 5 April 1929), yr dau and coheir (with her sister Charlotte Frances, w of George Bernard Shaw, the dramatist and publicist (*see* SHAW, Bt, of Bushey Park)) of Horace Payne Townshend, DL, JP, of Derry, Co Cork, and had issue:

1a Cecily Charlotte; *b* 27 Feb 1886; *m* 2 Aug 1911 (*divorce* 1927) Capt Richard St John Jefferyes Colthurst (*d* 18 Feb 1955), later Sir Richard Colthurst, 8th Bt (*qv*), and *d* 1 Jan 1958, leaving issue

(1) (cont.) Gen Hugh Cholmondeley *m* 2nd 10 Feb 1931 Violet Maud, JP (*d* 26 May 1993), est dau of Preb Hon Archibald Parker (*see* MACCLESFIELD, E), and *d* 13 Dec 1941, having by her had issue:

2a *Violet Essex [Mrs James Pinney, Lee Old Hall, Ellesmere, Salop SY12 9AE]; *b* 4 Dec 1932; *m* 23 May 1964 *Maj (William) James Pinney, 11th Hus, son of Col George Ambrose Pinney, MC, TD, DL, JP, of Horn Park, Beaminster, Dorset, and has issue:

1b *Hugh Charles William; *b* 11 Nov 1966

(2) Henry Arthur; *b* 15 Sept 1855; *m* 7 Jan 1920 Helen Mary (*d* 18 April 1923), yr dau of Harold Wrigley, of Ganton Hall, Scarborough, and *d* 18 Jan 1952, having had issue:

1a Henry Pakenham Grenville, Lt Gren Gds WW II; *b* 5 March 1923; *ka* Nov 1943

1a *Essex Lucy [The Rt Hon the Countess of Cavan, The Glebe House, Stockton, Shifnal, Salop T11 9EF]; *b* 7 Oct 1921; *m* 10 April 1947 12th Earl of Cavan (*qv*) and has issue

(1) Beatrice Sarah; *m* 13 May 1880 Maj Francis Hibbert (*d* 1882), 7th Fus, and *d* 5 Feb 1928

(2) Essex Mary; *m* 6 Feb 1877 Thomas Egerton Tatton (*d* 2 Dec 1924), of Wythenshawe, Cheshire, and *d* 23 Nov 1942, leaving issue

(3) Mildred Henrietta; *m* 29 Oct 1896 Edward Lee Townshend (*d* 19 June 1914), of Gorstage Hall and Wincham Hall, Cheshire, and *d* 12 Feb 1938, leaving issue

3 Henry Pitt (Rev), Fell All Souls, Rector Broadwell-cum-Adlestrop, Glos, Hon Canon Gloucester, RD Stow; *b* 15 June 1820; *educ* Ch Ch Oxford (MA); *m* 4 May 1848 Mary (*d* 24 Aug 1906), dau of 1st Baron Leigh (*qv*), and *d* 14 April 1905, leaving issue:

(1) Francis Grenville (Rev), Fell All Souls, Rector Broadwell-cum-Adlestrop; *b* 23 March 1850; *educ* Ch Ch Oxford (MA); *d* 26 July 1937

(2) Lionel Berners (Rev), Vicar Edge, Painswick, Glos (ret 1931), Missionary Tokyo, Chaplain Embassy there; *b* 11 Dec 1858; *educ* Oriel Coll Oxford (MA); *d* unm 21 Jan 1945

(3) Edward Chandos, barrister, JP Worcs, Pncpl Holkar Coll Indore; *b* 28 March 1860; *educ* Corpus Christi Coll Oxford (MA); *m* 21 Nov 1895 Ethel Elizabeth (*d* 2 Sept 1935), dau of Sir Robert Joseph Crosthwaite, KCSI, and *d* Jan 1957, having had issue:

1a Hugh Grenville, 2nd Lt 16th Bn KRRC; *b* 25 July 1897; *d* unm 23 May 1931

2a Rupert Wynn; *b* 2 Nov 1902; *d* unm 12 July 1927

(4) Henry Reginald, DSO, Maj 10th Bn Devon Regt, Capt Cheshire Regt, served Burma 1887–89 (medal), Boer War 1900–01 (despatches, medal, four clasps) and WW I; *b* 11 June 1862; *m* 17 Nov 1903 Cordelia Mercy (*d* 19 Aug 1949), dau of James Cross Ormrod, of Wyresdale Park, Garstang, Lancs, and *d* 20 Dec 1947, leaving:

1a Anthony Pitt, Maj Glos Regt WW II (POW); *b* 11 Feb 1908; *m* 29 Dec 1936 Monica Irene, dau of Rev Albert Ernest Snow, vicar Watlington, Oxon, and *d* 1986 leaving issue:

1b *Anne; *b* 16 Oct 1938

2b *Gillian; *b* 19 Oct 1951

3b *Faith; *b* 15 Dec 1953; *m* 1978 *Nicholas John Vann

1a Diana Mercy, horse breeder; *b* 13 Aug 1904; *m* 18 Dec 1934 Henry Laurence Gill and has issue:

1b *John Laurence [John Gill Esq, Chastleton Hill, Moreton-in-Marsh, Glos], Capt late 17th/21st Lancers; *b* 13 Sept 1938; *m* 3 June 1967 *Juliet Flora, 2nd dau of Capt Alan Joseph Macdonald Richardson, of Southrop Manor, Lechlade, Glos

2b *Anthony Henry [Anthony Gill Esq, 2/20 High St, Upton-on-Severn, Worcs]; *b* 12 April 1940; MRCVS

(5) Charles Fiennes (Rev), Vicar Adderbury Oxon 1913–35; *b* 26 Nov 1863; *educ* New Coll Oxford (MA); *m* 27 July 1897 Katharine (*d* 28 Feb 1959), dau of William John Courthope, CB, and *dsp* Dec 1959

(1) Alice Margarette; *m* 3 Sept 1884 Rev Harrison Goodenough Hayter (*d* 21 May 1934), MA, Rector Elmdon, Warwicks, Hon Canon Birmingham, and *d* 12 Jan 1937, leaving issue

(2) Mary Louisa *m* 24 April 1878 Sir Charles Mordaunt, 10th Bt (*qv*), and *d* 10 June 1947, leaving issue

(3) Rose Evelyn; *d* unm 15 April 1907

(4) Eleanor Caroline; *d* unm 10 Nov 1947

4 Charles Watkin Neville; *b* 27 May 1826; *d* 18 March 1844

1 Henrietta Charlotte; *m* 21 July 1857 6th Baron Berners (*qv*) and *d* 13 Aug 1874

The 1st BARON *d* 30 Oct 1855; his est son,

HUGH CHOLMONDELEY, **2nd Baron Delamere of Vale Royal**, Hon Col 3rd Bn Cheshire Regt, Lt 1st Life Gds, MP Denbighshire 1840–41 and Montgomeryshire 1841–47; *b* 3 Oct 1811; *m* 1st 23 March 1848 Lady Sarah Hay (*d* 17 Feb 1859), 2nd dau of 11th Earl of Kinnoull (*qv*); *m* 2nd 27 Dec 1860 Augusta Emily (*d* 25 Feb 1911), est dau of Sir George Hamilton Seymour, GCB, PC, GCH, gs of 1st Marquess of Hertford (*qv*), and by her had:

1 HUGH, **3rd Baron**

1 Sybil; *b* 29 Dec 1871; *m* 13 April 1896 (*divorce* 1902) Algernon Edwyn Burnaby (*d* 13 Nov 1938), of Baggrave, Leics, only son of Maj-Gen Edwin Sherard Burnaby, of Baggrave, Leics, and *d* 26 May 1911, leaving issue

The 2nd BARON *d* 1 Aug 1887; his son,

HUGH CHOLMONDELEY, **3rd Baron Delamere of Vale Royal**, KCMG (1929), Lt 3rd Bn Cheshire Regt, Capt Cheshire Yeo Cav, unofficial memb Exec Cncl Kenya 1931, MLC and MEC Kenya; *b* 28 April 1870; *m* 1st 11 July 1899 Lady Florence Anne Cole (*d* 17 May 1914), dau of 4th Earl of Enniskillen (*qv*), and had issue:

1 THOMAS PITT HAMILTON, **4th Baron**

The **3rd Baron** *m* 2nd 28 May 1928 Gwladys Helen (*d* 22 Feb 1943), formerly wife of Sir Charles Markham, 2nd Bt (*qv*), and est dau of Hon Rupert Evelyn Beckett (*see* GRIMTHORPE, B), and *d* 13 Nov 1931

His only son,

THOMAS PITT HAMILTON CHOLMONDELEY, **4th Baron Delamere of Vale Royal**; *b* 19 Aug 1900; *educ* Eton; Capt Welsh Gds WW II, chm Everitts Advertising Ltd, dir Proved Securities Ltd; *m* 1st 14 June 1924 (*divorce* 1944) Phyllis Anne (*d* 9 March 1978), est dau of Lord George William Montagu-Douglas-Scott (*see* BUCCLEUCH and QUEENSBERRY, D), and has issue:

1 HUGH GEORGE CHOLMONDELEY, **5th and present Baron Delamer of Vale Royal**

1 Elizabeth Florence Marion; *b* 26 Dec 1925; *m* 1st 28 Jan 1947 (*divorce* 1953) Sir Evelyn Delves Broughton, 12th Bt (*qv*); *m* 2nd 27 Aug 1953 *Peter Alexander Barrington, and *d* 1988

2 *Anne Jeannetta Essex [The Hon Mrs Garnett, Burnside House, Easter Balgedie, Kinross-shire KY13 7HQ]; *b* 2 Sept 1927; *m* 30 Nov 1951 *Conrad Peter Almeric Garnett, er son of Donald Goddard Garnett, MB, MRCS, of Fairfield House, Leiston, Suffolk, and has had issue:

(1) *Jeremy Paul; *b* 11 May 1953

(2) David Michael; *b* 2 Sept 1956; *d* 1981

The **4th Baron** *m* 2nd 15 June 1944 (*divorce* 1955) Hon Ruth Mary Clarissa, yr dau of 1st and last Baron Mount Temple (*see* SHAFTESBURY, E) and formerly w of (a) Capt Alec Stratford Cunningham-Reid, DFC, and (b) Maj Ernest Laurie Gardner; *m* 3rd 26 March 1955 Diana, yr dau of Seymour Caldwell, of The Red House, Hove, Sussex, formerly w of Gilbert de Preville Colvile and previously widow of Sir Henry John Delves Broughton, 11th Bt (*qv*), and *d* 13 April 1979

De la Rue

Arms: Or three bars gules, each charged with as many estoiles of the first, in chief an increscent and a decrescent of the second. **Crest:** A brazier gules fired between two branches of laurel, issuant from the flames thereof a serpent nowed and erect proper. **Motto:** *Cherche la verité* ('Seek the truth'). **Creation:** Bt. (UK) 17 June 1898.

SIR ANDREW GEORGE ILAY DE LA RUE, 4TH BT, of Cadogan Square, Chelsea, Co London [Sir Andrew de la Rue Bt, 27 Kersley St, London SW11 4PR; Stragglethorpe Grange, Brant Broughton, Lincs LN5 0QZ]; *b* 3 Feb 1946; *s f* 1988; *educ* Millfield; *m* 1984 *Tessa Ann, er dau of David Dobson, of Stragglethorpe Grange, and has issue:

1 +EDWARD WALTER HENRY; *b* 25 Nov 1986

2 +Harry William; *b* 1989

Lineage: THOMAS de La RUE, of Guernsey; *m* Ann (*d* 20 May 1799), dau of François Pelley, of Guernsey, and had issue:

ELEAZAR de la RUE, of Guernsey; *b* 5 April 1774; *m* Rachael Allez, of Guernsey, and *d* 12 Nov 1816, leaving, with other issue:

THOMAS de la RUE, of 84 Westbourne Grove, Paddington, and The Hazels, Sandy, Beds; *b* 24 March 1793; *m* 21 March 1814 Jane (*d* 22 Sept 1858), dau of William Warren, of Bishop's Nympton, Devon, and *d* 7 June 1866, having had, with other issue:

WARREN de la RUE, MA, DCL, PhD, FRS, of Portland Place, London W, Kt Legion of Honour, Cdr Order of St Maurice and St Lazarus, corresponding memb St Petersburg Imp Acad Sciences, PRAS, PRCS; *b* 18 Jan 1815; *m* 17 Feb 1840 Georgiana (*d* 25 May 1918 aged 98), dau of Thomas Bowles, of Guernsey, and *d* 1889, having had a 2nd s:

Sir Thomas Andros de la Rue, 1st Bt (UK), so *cr* 17 June 1898; *b* 26 May 1849; *educ* Cambridge (MA); chm Thomas de la Rue & Co; *m* 1 Feb 1976 Emily Maria (*d* 11 Oct 1904), dau of William Speed, QC, and had issue:

1 EVELYN ANDROS (Sir), **2nd Bt**

2 Ivor Andros, Lt Service Bn Royal Fus; *b* 2 Dec 1880; *m* 16 Jan 1912 Lilian Blanche Mary (*d* 19 Oct 1968), er dau of Hon FitzRoy Somerset Keith Stewart (*see* GALLOWAY, E), and *d* 16 June 1927

3 Stuart Andros, JP Herts; *b* 29 May 1883; *m* 9 July 1912 Margaret Griselda (*m* 2nd 17 March 1928 Air-Marshal Sir Bertine Entwisle Sutton (*d* 1946), KBE, CB, DSO, and *d* 1987), only dau of Alexander Dundas Ogilvy Wedderburn, KC, of The Hoo, Willingdon, Sussex (*see* OGILVY-WEDDERBURN, Bt), and *d* 26 Oct 1927, leaving issue:

(1) Thomas Alexander; *b* 11 May 1913; *m* March 1952

(2) +Wedderburn Anthony [Wedderburn de la Rue Esq, Long Meadow, North End, Newbury, Berks]; *b* 18 Aug 1914; *m* 1st 20 May 1937 Jean Roberts; *m* 2nd 1948 *Mrs Marjorie Holland Marsh, dau of William Holland Harris

(3) Christopher Arthur; *b* 24 July 1916; *d* 28 July 1939

(4) Patrick Andrew; *b* 8 Feb 1920; *d* 5 Feb 1939

(1) *Ann Griselda [Mrs John Norwood, Old Coach House, Cannon St, Lymington, Hants]; *b* 23 Nov 1918; *m* 2 July 1938 G/Capt John Norwood (*d* 1978), RAF, er son of Capt John Norwood, VC, 5th Dragoon Gds, and has:

1a *Janet; *b* 1939

2a *Jill; *b* 1941

1 Sybil; *m* 17 July 1897 William Wilson Grantham (*d* 18 Feb 1942), KC, of Balneath Manor, nr Lewes, and 5 Crown Office Row, Temple, London EC, Recorder of Deal, and *d* 13 Feb 1952, leaving issue

Sir THOMAS *d* 10 April 1911; his est son,

Sir Evelyn Andros de la Rue, 2nd Bt, Capt RAF, Roy East Kent Yeo, JP Herts; *b* 5 Oct 1879; *m* 17 Feb 1903 Mary Violet (*d* 22 Oct 1959), est dau of John Liell Francklin, of Gonalston, Notts, and had issue:

1 Warren James St Vincent; *b* 23 March, *d* 23 April 1905

2 ERIC VINCENT (Sir), **3rd Bt**

3 Ian Hector; *b* 22 July 1910; *m* 14 Nov 1936 Violet Bertha (*d* 1983), dau of T Despard Bridges, and *d* 1991 leaving issue:

(1) +Anthony St Vincent [Anthony de la Rue Esq, PO Box Ch 760, Chisipite, Harare, Zimbabwe]; *b* 13 Jan 1947; *educ* Peterhouse; *m* 1st 1971 (*divorce* 1985) Ann Wyndham, dau of Frederic Roberts Blair, of Lloyds Neck, Long Island, NY, and has:

1a +Thomas Edward; *b* 1973; *educ* Peterhouse

2a +Michael Alexander; *b* 1975; *educ* Peterhouse

1a *Diana Alexandra; *b* 1982

(1) (cont.) Anthony de la Rue *m* 2nd 1986 *Merry, dau of Lt-Col Sir Edward Hugh Dudley Thompson, MBE, TD, of Culland Hall, Brailsford, Derbys, and has further issue:

2a *Justine Andrea; *b* 1987

4 Victor St George, Lt 60th Rifles WW II; *b* 20 Aug 1918; *ka* Burma April 1943

1 Ruby, CStJ; *m* 7 Jan 1930 Gen Sir George Watkin Eben James Erskine (*d* 29 Aug 1965), GCB, KBE, DSO, KRRC (*see* BUCHAN, E), and *d* 19 Jan 1974, leaving issue

2 Mona Ruth *m* 11 April 1935 Maj Edward Copleston Radcliffe, 9th Lancers (*d* 2 July 1967), 2nd son of Pollexfen Colmore Copleston Radcliffe, JP, of Derriford, Crown Hill, Devon, and *d* 2 May 1974, leaving issue:

(1) *Mark Colmore Copleston; *b* 14 March 1942; *educ* Diocesan Coll, Cape Town

(1) *Alice Fiona; *b* 18 Feb 1941; *m* 25 Nov 1960 her cousin *Maj Philip Neil Erskine, Scots Gds, and has issue (*see* BUCHAN, E)

3 Diana Beryl; *b* 1914; *d* unm 16 Feb 1998

Sir EVELYN *d* 30 Nov 1950; his er surv son,

Sir Eric Vincent de la Rue, 3rd Bt; *b* 5 Aug 1906; *educ* Oundle; Capt Notts Yeo WW II; *m* 1st 5 June 1945 Cecilia Lenella Beva, Subaltern ATS (*d* 17 March 1963), yr dau of Maj Walter Waring, 1st Life Gds, DL, JP, of Lennel, Coldstream, Berwickshire, and had:

1 Sir ANDREW GEORGE ILAY de la RUE, **4th and present Bt**

2 +John Vincent Francis [John de la Rue, PO Box 485, Elizabethtown, NY 12932, USA]; *b* 4 Dec 1953; *educ* Eton; *m* 15 Sept 1994 *Barbara Catherine, only dau of Joseph Sainton, of 5945 Flanders Rd, Sylvania, Ohio 43560, USA

Sir Eric *m* 2nd 13 Feb 1964 *Christine [Christine Lady de la Rue, Ayton Castle, Eymouth, Berwickshire TD14 5RD], dau of Kurt Schellin, MD, of Greenwich, Conn., and *d* 1988, leaving:

3 +Vincent St George; *b* 20 April 1965; *educ* Stowe

De la Warr

Arms: Quarterly, 1st, argent a fess dancettée sable (for WEST); 2nd, azure three leopard's heads reversed jessant de lys or (for CANTELUPE); 3rd, gules crusilly and a lion argent (for LA WARR); 4th, quarterly or and gules a bend vaire (for SACKVILLE). **Crests:** 1 Issuant from a ducal coronet or a griffin's head azure beaked and eared gold (for WEST), 2 Upon a coronet composed of fleurs-de-lys or an estoile argent (for SACKVILLE). **Supporters:** Dexter, a wolf coward argent gorged with a plain collar or; sinister, a cockatrice or, wings azure. **Badge:** A crampet or the inside per pale azure and gules charged with the letter R. **Motto:** *Jour de ma vie* ('Day of my life'). **Creations:** B.(E) 5 Feb 1569/70 (Delaware) and (UK) 27 April 1864 (Buckhurst of Buckhurst), V. and E. (GB) 18 March 1761.

THE 11TH EARL DE LA WARR, Viscount Cantelupe, Baron Delaware, and **Baron Buckhurst of Buckhurst**, Co Sussex (William Herbrand Sackville) [The Rt Hon The Earl De La Warr, Buckhurst Park, Withyham, E Sussex TN7 4BL; 14 Bourne St, London SW1W 8JU]; *b* 10 April 1948; *s f* 1988; *educ* Eton; dairy farmer and stockbroker with Credit Lyonnais Laing 1980–; *m* 10 Aug 1978 *Anne, est dau of Arthur Edmund Leveson, OBE, of Hall Place, Ropley, Hants, and formerly w of 4th Marquess of Linlithgow (*qv*), and has issue:

1 +WILLIAM HERBRAND THOMAS, *Lord Buckhurst*; *b* 13 June 1979 (HRH PRINCESS MARGARET COUNTESS OF SNOWDON stood sponsor)

2 +Edward Geoffrey Richard; *b* 6 Dec 1980

Lineage (of La Warre): JOHN La WARRE, granted manor of Brislington, Somerset, *c* 1207 by John Count of Mortain, who at that time held the Honour of Gloucester; *d c* 1213, leaving issue:

JORDAN La WARRE; opposed KING JOHN, but readmitted to favour on paying a fine, with two palfreys; *m* Emma — and *d* between 23 Aug and 6 Sept 1231, leaving issue:

Sir JOHN La WARRE, of Wickwar, Glos, and Brislington; Sheriff Herefs *c* 1275; *m* by 20 Jan 1242/3 Olimpia (living Aug 1265), dau of Sir Hugh de Fokington, of Fokington, Sussex, and had issue:

Sir ROGER La WARRE, 1st LORD (Baron) LA WARRE (E), so *cr* by writ (according to later doctrine) 6 Feb 1298/9; Capt Bourg-sur-Mer 1297/8 while on service with EDWARD I in France, present Siege Carlaverock July 1300, being then a banneret, Envoy to the Pope July 1304; *m* by Sept 1276 Clarice de Tregoz (*dvp* by 28 Aug 1300), er dau and coheir of 1st Lord (Baron) Tregoz of the 1299 *cr*, and *d* 20 June 1320, leaving:

JOHN LA WARRE, 2nd LORD (Baron) LA WARRE, KB; *b c* 1276/7; present Siege Carlaverock, ktd 1306, called to Parl by writs 26 Aug 1307–25 Aug 1318 made out to 'John la Warre, de la Warre or le Warre' thus apparently by later doctrine undergoing the absurdity of being *cr* LORD (Baron) LA WARRE during his f 's lifetime and by the same title, though his possession of the castle and manor of Ewyas Harold, Herefs (inherited through his mother) as a tenant in chief of the Crown may by contemporaries have been deemed to justify his summons to Parl as a lord baron of Parl (*see* ABERGAVENNY, M, for a discussion of the concept of barony by tenure); *m* shortly after 19 Nov 1294 Joan de Grelle/Grelley (*d* 20/1 March 1352/3), er dau of Sir Robert de Grelle, of Manchester and Cuerdley, Lancs, and sis and heir of 1st Lord (Baron) Grelle of the 1308 *cr*, thus acquiring the great possessions of the Gresleys, and *d* 9 May 1347, leaving issue, with a dau (Catherine, *m de jure* 2nd Lord (Baron) Latimer (of Braybrook); *see* LATYMER, B):

JOHN La WARRE; *m* Margaret de Holand (*d* 20/22 Aug 1349), dau of 1st Lord (Baron) De Holand of the 1314 *cr*, and *dvp* just before 24 June 1331, leaving issue:

1 ROGER, 3rd LORD, for whom *see* further below

2 John (Sir); Ld of Manor of Bockampton, Berks, which he held by Serjeanty (*i.e.*, the performance of a service, in this case keeping the King's harriers), and *dsp* 23 Oct 1358, leaving his estates to his bro

1 Catherine; *m* 2nd Lord (Baron) Latimer, of Braybrooke, of the 1299 *cr*, and had issue

The 2nd LORD (Baron) LA WARRE's gs,

ROGER La WARRE, 3rd LORD (Baron) LA WARRE; *b* 30 Nov 1326; in the retinue of The Black Prince at Battle of Crécy and Siege of Calais 1346–47, served Gascony Sept 1355 and again 1364, 1366, 1368, 1368/9 and 1370, present Battle of Poitiers 1356, served Picardy and Caux July-Nov 1369 under John of Gaunt, Duke of Lancaster; *m* 1st Elizabeth de Welle, 2nd dau of 3rd Lord (Baron) Welle of the 1299 *cr*, and *d* 27 Aug 1370, leaving issue:

1 JOHN La WARRE, 4th LORD (Baron) LA WARRE; *b c* 1345; served Gascony with The Black Prince Feb 1368/9, accompanied EDWARD III on his attempted invasion of France Sept 1372; *m* by 8 May 1368 Elizabeth —; *m* 2nd by 20 Jan 1388/9 Elizabeth (*dsp* 18 Dec 1393), dau and heir of Sir Gilbert de Nevill(e), of Grimsthorpe, Lincs, and widow of Simon Simeon, of Gosberton, Lincs (*dsp* 18 Dec 1387), and *dsp* 27 July 1398

2 THOMAS La WARRE, 5th LORD (Baron) LA WARRE; *b c* 1358; Rector Ashton-under-Lyne 1372–73, Preb New Lafford (Cathedral Church of Lincoln) and Vicar W Sleaford *c* 1376, Rector Swineshead 1378–82, 1394–1400 and 1422–27, Preb Grindall (York Minster) 1381–97, Rector Manchester 1382, Preb Oxton and Cropwell (Collegiate Church of Southwell) 1397–1407, Preb Riccall (York Minster) 1407–27, Preb Leighton Ecclesia 1417–18 and Ketton (both Cathedral Church of Lincoln) 1418–27; *dsp* unm 7 May 1427, when the Barony of La Warre passed to his half-sis's s Reynold West (*see* below)

The 3rd LORD (Baron) LA WARR *m* 2nd Alianore de Mowbray (*m* 2nd by 12 Feb 1372/3 Sir Lewis de Clifford (*d* 1404) and *d* by 18 June 1387), dau of Lord (Baron) Mowbray (*see* MOWBRAY, SEGRAVE and STOURTON, B) and *d* 27 Aug 1370, leaving further issue:

1 JOAN la Warre; *m* 1st Ralph de Welyngton/Wilington, of Sandhurst, Glos (*dsp* a minor 16 Aug 1382); *m* 2nd 1st LORD (Baron) WEST (*see* below) and *d* 24 April 1404, having had issue

Lineage (of West): Sir THOMAS WEST; granted 1322 the manor of Sharnbrook, Beds, for life by Aymer de Valence, Earl of Pembroke; MP Warwicks 1324, ktd 1326, in Oct 1330 took an active part in the arrest of Roger de Mortimer, Earl of March, the favourite of QUEEN ISABELLA (w of EDWARD II); Keeper Christchurch and Southampton Castles 1330–43, Keeper King's Stannary Devon 1337–43; *m* by 1321 Eleanor (living 27 April 1344), dau and heir of Sir John Cantelupe, of Hempston Cantelupe, Devon, and Snitterfield, Warwicks, and *d* 1 Nov 1343, leaving, with a yr s (John, served Crécy-Calais campaign of 1346–47 with his er bro):

Sir THOMAS WEST, of Hempston Cantelupe; *b c* 1321; fought at Battle of Crécy 1346 in 2nd division under the command of the Earl of Arundel, present Siege of Calais 1346–47, MP Wilts 1364/5, during the Peasants' Revolt received commns to suppress and punish the rebels in Hants and Wilts 1381–82 but reprimanded for his leniency; *m* Alice (*d c* 1 Sept 1395), dau of Reynold Fitzherbert, of Midsomer Norton, Somerset, and sis and heir of Sir Edmond Fitzherbert, and *d* 3 Sept 1386, leaving issue:

THOMAS WEST, 1st LORD (Baron) WEST (E), so *cr* by writ (according to later doctrine) 19 June 1402; *b* 1365; ktd by 15 Oct 1386, served wars in France 1387; *m* by 2 May 1384 Joan la Warre (*see* above), only dau of 3rd Lord La Warre, and *d* 19 April 1405, leaving issue:

1 THOMAS WEST, 2nd LORD (Baron) WEST; *b* 1392; ktd 1413, in HENRY V's retinue for the campaign of 1415 and fought at Agincourt; *m* by 2 July 1406 Ida de St Amand (*d* 6 Nov 1416), yr dau and coheir of 3rd Lord (Baron) St Amand of the 1313 *cr*, and *dsp* 29/30 Sept 1416 from injuries received in a sea battle

2 REYNOLD/REGINALD WEST, 3rd LORD (Baron) WEST and 6th LORD (Baron) LA WARRE; *b* 7 Sept 1395; ktd by 22 Nov 1416, Capt of St Lô in the Côtentin, France, 1417/8 and 1421, petitioned King and cncl Oct 1427 for right to sit in Parl with precedence held by his ancestors the Lds La Warre, had licence 13 Dec 1448 to visit the Holy Land; *m* 1st by 17 Feb 1428/9 Margaret (*d c* 24 Nov 1433), dau of Robert Thorley, of Tybeste, Cornwall; *m* 2nd by 19 Nov 1443 Elizabeth (*m* 2nd after 10 June 1451 as his 2nd w 1st Earl of Worcester of the 1449 *cr* and *d* 1 Sept 1452), dau and heir of Robert Greyndour, of Micheldean and Abenhall, Glos, and *d* 27 Aug 1450, leaving issue:

(1) RICHARD WEST, 4th LORD (Baron) WEST and 7th LORD (Baron) LA WARRE; *b* 28 Oct 1430; *m* by 10 June 1451 Katherine Hungerford (*d* 12 May 1493), dau of 2nd Lord (Baron) Hungerford of the 1426 *cr* (*see* SAINT DAVIDS, V), and *d* 10 March 1475/6, having had issue, with three other sons and a dau:

1a THOMAS, 5th/ 8th LORD

2a Richard; Franciscan monk at Greenwich

1a Margery; nun at Syon, Middx

(1) Elizabeth; *m* 1466 (*divorce* 1467), as his 1st w, 2nd Lord (Baron) Berkeley (*qv*)

The 7th LORD (Baron) LA WARRE's er s,

THOMAS WEST, 5th LORD (Baron) WEST and 8th LORD (Baron) LA WARRE, KG (1510); *b c* 1457; ktd 18 Jan 1477/8, granted by HENRY VII 5 March 1485/6 the estates in Sussex of the attainted Duke of Norfolk (*k* Battle of Bosworth 1485); helped quell the Cornish uprising 1497 in support of Perkin Warbeck; Kt Banneret 18 Aug 1513; *m* 1st Elizabeth, dau of Hugh Mortimer, of Mortimer's Hall, Hants, and sis and heir of Sir John Mortimer, and *d* 11 Oct 1525, having had issue, with four daus:

1 THOMAS WEST, 6th LORD (Baron) WEST and 9th LORD (Baron) LA WARRE, KG (1549), KB (1489), PC (1553); Kt Banneret 14 Aug 1513, Sheriff Surrey and Sussex 1524–25, granted large tracts of monastic lands, including Wherwell Abbey, Hants; Jt Ld Lt Sussex 1551; *m* by 24 Aug 1494 Elizabeth, dau and coheir of Sir John Bonville, of Halnaker, Sussex, and *dsp* 25 Sept 1554, when the Baronies of La Warre and West (according to later doctrine) fell into abeyance between his half-nieces Anne and Mary, daus of Sir Owen West

2 William; *dsp*

1 Eleanor; *m* Sir Edward Guilford and had, with other issue:

(1) Jane; *m* John Dudley, 1st Duke of Northumberland of the 1551 *cr*, and had with other issue:

1a Guilford Dudley; *m* LADY JANE GREY

2a Robert Dudley, 1st Earl of Leicester of the 1564 *cr*

3a Catherine; *m* 3rd Earl of Huntingdon (*qv*)

2 Dorothy; *m* Sir Henry Owen and had issue

The 8th LORD (Baron) LA WARRE *m* 2nd Eleanor (*d* between 10 May and 14 Nov 1536), dau of Sir Roger Copley, of Roughway, Sussex, and *d* 11 Oct 1525, having had further issue:

3 Owen (Sir); *m* Mary — and *d* 18 July 1551, leaving issue:

(1) Mary; *m* 1st Sir Adrian Poynings, illegitimate s of Sir Edward Poynings, KG, and bro of 1st and last LORD (Baron) POYNINGS of the 1545 *cr*, and had three daus and coheirs; *m* 2nd Sir Richard Rogers

(2) Anne

4 George (Sir), of Warbleton, Sussex; *m* Elizabeth, est dau and coheir of Sir Robert Morton, of Lechlade, Glos, and *d* Sept 1538, leaving issue:

(1) WILLIAM, **1st Baron Delaware**

5 Leonard; ancestor of the WESTs of Alscot Park, Glos

The 9th LORD (Baron) LA WARRE's n,

WILLIAM WEST, **1st Baron Delaware** (E), so *cr* by letters patent 5 Feb 1569/70; *b* by 1520; adopted by his unc the 9th LORD LA WARRE but tried to poison him, even though at the time another unc, Sir Owen West, was the next heir, nevertheless was as a result disbarred from all honours by Act of Parl 1 Feb 1549/50; restored in blood 10 April 1563; Capt in Army at Siege of St Quintin in Picardy July 1557; Jt Lt Sussex 1569; ktd; *m* 1st by 1555 Elizabeth, dau of Thomas Strange, of Chesterton, Glos; *m* 2nd Anne (*m* 3rd Richard Kemish, of Andover (*d* 6 Oct 1611)), dau of Henry Swift, of Andover, Hants, and widow of Thomas Oliver, and *d* 30 Dec 1595, leaving, with a dau (Elizabeth, *m* Sir Richard Blount, 2nd s of Sir Richard Blount, of Maple Durham):

THOMAS WEST, **2nd Baron Delaware**; *b* 1556; MP: Chichester 1571, E Looe 1572–83, Yarmouth (IoW) 1586–87, Hants 1588–89 and Aylesbury 1592–93, Sheriff Hants 1585–86, ktd 1587, granted 14 Nov 1597 the precedence of the Barony of LA WARRE *cr* 1299; *m* 19 Nov 1571 Anne, dau of Sir Francis Knollys, KG, and gdau of Mary, sis of ANNE BOLEYN (*see* ORMONDE, M), and *d* 24 March 1601/2, leaving issue:

THOMAS WEST, **3rd Baron Delaware**; *b* 9 July 1577; *educ* Queen's Coll Oxford (MA 1605); Govr and Capt-Gen Virginia 28 Feb 1610, residing there 1610–11 and giving his name to Delaware Bay and the state of Delaware; *m* 25 Nov 1596 Cecily (*bur* 31 July 1662), yst dau of Sir Thomas Shirley, of Wiston, Sussex, and *d* 7 June 1618, leaving, with at least one yr s (Robert, *m* as her 2nd husb Elizabeth Coch; *see* RAMSAY-FAIRFAX-LUCY, Bt) and at least one dau (Lucy, *m* Sir Robert Byron, yr bro of 1st and 2nd Barons Byron; *qv*):

HENRY WEST, **4th Baron Delaware**; *b* 3 Oct 1603; Capt Earl of Oxford's Regt of Foot 1624; *m* March 1624/5 Isabella (*d* between 15 Nov 1670 and 1679), dau and coheir of Sir Thomas Edmunds, Treasurer Household, and *d* 1 June 1628, leaving issue:

CHARLES WEST, **5th Baron Delaware**; *b* Feb 1625/6; Commr from Parl to treat with the Scots in 1646 during their invasion of England, imprisoned Aug 1659 on suspicion of being implicated in Sir George Booth's plot to restore CHARLES II; *m* 25 Sept 1642 Anne (*bur* 18 May 1702/3), dau and heir of John Wild, of Droitwich, Worcs, and *d* 22 Dec 1687, having had issue:

1 Charles; *m* 26 Dec 1678 Elizabeth, 2nd dau and coheir of Sir Edmund Pye, 1st and last Bt of the 1641 *cr*, and *dsp*

2 JOHN WEST, **6th Baron Delaware**; *b c* 1663; Treasurer of the Chamber 1713–14, Teller of Exchequer 1714015; *m* June 1691 Margaret (*d* 31 Jan 1737/8), dau and heir of John Freeman, of London, merchant, and widow of Thomas Salwey, 3rd s of Richard Salwey, of Richard's Castle, Herefs, MP, and *d* 26 May 1723, leaving:

(1) JOHN WEST, **7th Baron** and **1st Earl De La Warr**, so *cr* 18 March 1761, as also VISCOUNT CANTELUPE (both GB), KB (1725), PC (1731); *b* 4 April

1693; MP (Whig) Grampound 1715–22, Guidon and 1st Maj 1st Troop of Horse Gds 1715 (Lt-Col 1717), Lt-Col 1st Regt Foot Gds 1730, Col 1st Troop Horse Gds 1737–66, Brig Gen 1743, fought at Battle of Dettingen 1743, Maj-Gen 1745, Lt-Gen 1747, Gen of Horse 1765, Govr: Levant Co 1736–66, NY 1737, Gravesend and Tilbury Fort 1747–52 and Guernsey 1752–66, FRS 1728; *m* 1st 25 May 1721 Lady Charlotte Maccarty (*d* 7 Feb 1734/5), dau of 4th Earl of Clancarty of the 1658 *cr* (a prominent Jacobite, Ld of the Bedchamber to JAMES II in Ireland 1689, cmded a Regt of Infantry in the Irish Jacobite Army there and a Troop of Horse in France 1697, attainted 1691); *m* 2nd 15 June 1744 Anne (*d* 26 June 1748), dau of Nehemiah Walker, sea captain, and widow of 11th Lord (Baron) Abergavenny (*see* ABERGAVENNY, M), and *d* 16 March 1766, leaving, with other issue:

1a JOHN, **2nd Earl**

2a George Augustus; *m* 24 Feb 1764 Lady Mary Grey (*dsp* 1 March 1783), dau of 4th Earl of Stamford (*see* 1970 edn), and *dsp* 1776

The 1st EARL's er s,

JOHN WEST, **2nd Earl De La Warr**; *b* 1729; served 3rd Regt of Foot Gds 1746, Lt-Col 1st Troop Horse Gds 1755, Col 1758, ADC to GEORGE III, Maj-Gen 1761, Col 1st Troop Horse Gren Gds 1763–66, Col 1st Troop of Horse Gds 1766–77, Lt-Gen 1770, V-Chamberlain to QUEEN CHARLOTTE 1761–66, Master of the Horse 1766 and Ld Chamberlain 1768–77; *m* 8 Aug 1756 Mary (*d* 27 Oct 1784), dau of Lt-Gen John Wynyard, and *d* 22 Nov 1777, having had, with other issue (including a dau Georgiana, *m* Rev Henry Buckley and had issue; *see* JOHNSTONE, Bt):

1 WILLIAM AUGUSTUS WEST, **3rd Earl De La Warr**; *b* 27 April 1757; *educ* Eton; Lt-Col Goldstream Gds 1774; *d* unm Jan 1783

2 JOHN RICHARD, **4th Earl**

3 Frederick; *b* 1767; *m* 1st 17 April 1792 Charlotte (*d* 13 June 1795), dau and coheir of Richard Mitchell, of Culham Court, Berks, and had issue:

(1) Charlotte Louisa; *d* 27 Jan 1869

3 (cont.) The Hon Frederick West *m* 2nd 31 May 1798 Maria (*d* 23 Oct 1843), yr dau and coheir of Richard Myddelton, of Chirk Castle, Denbighshire, and *d* 22 March 1852, having had, with other issue:

(1) Frederick Richard, of Ruthin Castle, Denbighshire; *b* 1799; *m* 1st 14 Nov 1820 Lady Georgiana Stanhope (*dsp* 14 Aug 1824), dau of 5th Earl of Chesterfield (*see* 1967 edn CHESTERFIELD and STANHOPE, E); *m* 2nd 11 Sept 1827 Theresa (*d* 18 Sept 1886), only dau of Capt John Whitby, RN, and *d* 1 May 1862, leaving, with other issue:

1a William Cornwallis WEST later CORNWALLIS-WEST (deed poll 1895), VD, JP (Hants and Denbighshire), of Ruthin Castle and Newlands Manor, Lymington, Hants; barrister Lincoln's Inn 1862, Ld Lt Denbighshire, High Sheriff 1872, Hon Col 4th Bn Roy Welch Fus, pres Denbighs TFA, MP (Lib) Denbighs 1885–86 and (Lib U) 1886–92; *b* 20 March 1835; *m* 3 Oct 1872 Mary (*d* 21 July 1920), est dau of Rev Frederick FitzPatrick by Lady Olivia, dau of 2nd Marquess of Headfort (*qv*), and *d* 4 July 1917, leaving issue:

1b George Frederick Myddelton; *b* 14 Nov 1874; Maj Scots Gds, served Boer War, WW I, author of memoirs, novels and plays; *m* 1st 28 July 1900 (*divorce* 1913) Jennie, CI, RRC, DGStJ (*d* 29 June 1921), dau of Leonard Jerome, of NY, and widow of Lord Randolph Churchill (*see* MARLBOROUGH, D); *m* 2nd 6 April 1914 Beatrice Stella (the actress Mrs Patrick Campbell; *d* 9 April 1940), dau of John Tanner and widow of Patrick Campbell; *m* 3rd 15 April 1940 Georgette (*d* 21 Nov 1972), widow of Adolph Hirsch, of S Africa, and *dsp* 1 April 1951

1b Mary Theresa Olivia; *m* 8 Dec 1891 (*divorce* 1923) Hans Heinrich, Prince of Pless (*d* 3 Feb 1938), and *d* 29 June 1943, leaving issue (*see* ASHTOWN, B)

2b Constance Edwina, CBE (1918); *m* 1st 16 Feb 1901 (*divorce* 1919) 2nd Duke of Westminster (*qv*) and had issue; *m* 2nd 14 Jan 1920 W/Cdr John FitzPatrick Lewis, RAF (*d* 17 Dec 1965), s of John Hughes Lewis, and *d* 21 Jan 1970 aged 92

1b Georgiana Theresa Ella; *m* 30 Sept 1875 Warren W R Peacocke (*d* 5 March 1877), of Efford Park, Hants, and *d* 8 Feb 1915

The 3rd EARL's yr bro,

JOHN RICHARD WEST, **4th Earl De La Warr**; *b* 28 July 1758; *educ* Eton; Lt 2nd Foot Gds; *m* 22 April 1783 Catherine (*d* 27 May 1826), dau of Henry Lyell, of Bourn, Cambs (Memb Swedish House of Nobles), and *d* 28 July 1795, leaving, with a dau (Catherine Georgiana, *m* 16 Oct 1817 Lt-Col Joseph d'Arcy, RA, and *d* 7 March 1824, leaving issue):

GEORGE JOHN WEST later SACKVILLE-WEST (roy licence 30 Nov 1843), **5th Earl De La Warr**, PC (1841); *b* 26 Oct 1791; *educ* Harrow and BNC Coll Oxford (BA 1812, MA 1819, DCL 1834); LLD Cambridge 1828; *m* 21 June 1813 Lady Elizabeth Sackville (*b* 11 Aug 1795; *cr* 27 April 1864 **Baroness Buckhurst of Buckhurst**, Co Sussex (UK), with a 'jumping' or 'shifting' remainder to her 2nd surv s, Reginald, worded in such a way as to try and ensure that the Barony was always held by a yr bro, nephew or some other male relative of the Earl De La Warr of the time who was not directly heir to that Earldom itself, the risk being that because of possible deaths of intervening heirs the Barony of Buckhurst might jump from one holder to another in the lifetime of both as the Earldom became inherited by persons nearer and nearer in blood to the holder of the Barony; *d* 9 Jan 1870), yr dau and coheir of 3rd Duke of Dorset (*see* SACKVILLE, B), and *d* 23 Feb 1869, having had issue:

1 George John Frederick, *Viscount Cantelupe*; *b* 26 April 1814; *educ* Ch Ch Oxford; Lt Gren Gds, MP (C) Helston 1837–40 and Lewes 1840–41; *d* unm 25 June 1850

2 CHARLES RICHARD WEST later SACKVILLE-WEST, **6th Earl De La Warr**, KCB (1871, CB 1855); *b* 13 Nov 1815; *educ* Harrow; served 43rd Regt Foot 1833, Lt 15th Foot 1835, Capt 21st Foot 1842, ADC and Mily Sec to Lord Gough in India 1845, fought at Battle of Sobraon (Sikh War) 1846, Maj 21st Foot 1852, present at Battles of Alma, Balaclava and Inkerman Crimean War, Lt-Col 21st Foot Siege of Sebastopol, Maj-Gen 1864, Offr Legion of Honour France 1856, 3rd Class Medjidie Turkey 1858; *d* unm 23 April 1873, having drowned himself in the river Cam

3 REGINALD WINDSOR, **7th Earl**

4 MORTIMER SACKVILLE-WEST, 1st BARON SACKVILLE (*qv*)

5 LIONEL SACKVILLE-WEST, 2nd BARON SACKVILLE (*qv*)

6 William Edward; *b* 27 Oct 1830; *educ* Oxford (MA); Capt and Lt-Col Gren Gds; *m* 7 Aug 1860 Georgina (*d* 23 Feb 1883), yst dau of George Dodwell, of Kelvinsfort, Co Sligo, and *d* 30 Sept 1905, having had issue (*see* SACKVILLE, B)

1 Elizabeth; Extra Lady of the Bedchamber to HM QUEEN VICTORIA; *m* 18 Jan 1844 9th Duke of Bedford (*qv*) and *d* 22 April 1897

2 Mary Catherine; *m* 1st 29 April 1847 2nd Marquess of Salisbury (*qv*); *m* 2nd 5 July 1870 15th Earl of Derby (*qv*) and *d* 6 Dec 1900, leaving issue

3 Arabella Diana; *m* 25 Sept 1860 Sir Alexander Bannerman, 9th Bt (*qv*), and *d* 10 Feb 1869, leaving issue

The 6th EARL's yr bro,

REGINALD WINDSOR WEST later SACKVILLE-WEST later still SACKVILLE, **7th Earl De La Warr**, DL (Cambs and Sussex); *b* 21 Feb 1817; *educ* Balliol Coll Oxford (BA 1838, MA 1840); Rector Withyham, Sussex, 1841–65, Chaplain to HM QUEEN VICTORIA 1846–65; *s* mother 9 Jan 1870 as **2nd Baron Buckhurst of Buckhurst** despite the wording of the patent and by roy licence 24 April 1871 dropped the surname WEST, High Steward Stratford-on-Avon 1871–96; *m* 7 Feb 1867 Constance Mary Elizabeth Cochrane-Baillie (*m* 2nd 12 July 1902 Rev Paul Williams Wyatt, MA (*d* 29 Dec 1935), and *d* 19 July 1929), dau of 1st Baron Lamington (*see* 1949 edn), and *d* 15 Jan 1896, having had issue:

1 Lionel Charles Cranfield, *Viscount Cantelupe*; *b* 1 Jan 1868; Capt 3rd Bn Queen's RW Surrey Regt; *m* 24 June 1890 Dorothy, Ch Cmdt ATS 1938–41 (*m* 2nd 28 Feb 1905 1st Baron Jeffreys (*qv*) and *d* 21 May 1953), dau of John Postle Heseltine, of Walhampton, Lymington, Hants, and *dsp* 7 Nov 1890

2 GILBERT GEORGE REGINALD, **8th Earl**

1 Edeline; *b* 10 Sept 1870; LJStJ; *m* 26 Aug 1890 1st Baron Strickland, Count Della Catena (Malta), GCMG (*d* 22 Aug 1940) (*see* 1956 edn Foreign Titles section), and *d* 15 Dec 1918, leaving issue

2 Leonore Mary; *m* 10 July 1906 Maj John McClean Griffin, RFA (*d* 8 Jan 1957), of Bourn Hall, Cambs, est s of Robert Griffin, of Court Gdn, Marlow, and *d* 18 July 1939

3 Margaret; *d* unm 18 April 1963

The 7th EARL's only surv s,

GILBERT GEORGE REGINALD SACKVILLE-WEST later SACKVILLE, **8th Earl De La Warr**, JP, DL; *b* 22 March 1869; CA Sussex, Mayor Bexhill 1903 and 1904, Maj 2nd Cinque Ports Div RA and T/Lt RNVR (1914), served S Africa 1900 (wounded) and WW I 1914; *m* 1st 4 Aug 1891 (*divorce* 1902) Muriel Agnes (*d* 8 Aug 1930), dau of 1st Earl Brassey (*see* BRASSEY OF APETHORPE, B); *m* 2nd 20 Sept 1903 Hilda Mary Clavering (*m* 2nd 18 April 1922 John William Dennis (*d* 1949) s of William Dennis, of Kirton, Lincs, and *d* 1963), 3rd dau of Col C Lennox Tredcroft, of Glenancrum, Guildford, and *das* 16 Dec 1915, leaving issue by his 1st w:

1 HERBRAND EDWARD DUNDONALD BRASSEY, **9th Earl**

1 (Myra) Idina; *b* 26 Feb 1893; *m* 1st 26 Nov 1913 (*divorce* 1919) Capt David Euan Wallace, MC, PC, MP (*d* 9 Feb 1941), 2nd Life Gds Reserve, s of John Wallace, of Glassingall, Dunblane, and had issue; *m* 2nd 27 March 1919 (*divorce* 1923) Capt Charles Gordon, of Park Hill, Aberdeen, yst s of Alexander Gordon of Pitburg, JP; *m* 3rd 22 Sept 1923 (*divorce* 1930) 22nd Earl of Erroll (*qv*) and had issue; *m* 4th 22 Nov 1930 (*divorce* 1938) Donald Carmichael Haldeman, JP, s of John Haldeman; *m* 5th 1939 (*divorce* 1946) F/Lt Vincent William Soltau, RAF (Res) (*d* 1 Aug 1964), and *d* 5 Nov 1955

2 Avice Ela Murial; *b* 25 July 1897; *m* 1st 28 Nov 1918 (*divorce* 1931) Maj-Gen Sir Stewart Graham Menzies, KCMG, KCB, DSO, MC, 2nd Life Gds (*d* 29 May 1968), s of John Graham Menzies; *m* 2nd 22 July 1931 Capt Frank Fitzroy Spicer, DSO (*d* Oct 1973), of Spye Pk, Chippenham

The 8th EARL's only s,

HERBRAND EDWARD DUNDONALD BRASSEY SACKVILLE, **9th Earl De La Warr**, GBE (1956), PC (1936), JP (1925), DL (Sussex 1956); *b* 20 June 1900; *educ* Eton and Magdalen Coll Oxford; served RNR, Ld-in-Waiting to HM GEORGE V 1924 and 1929–31, Mayor Bexhill 1932, 1933 and 1934, V-Pres Army Cncl and Parly U-Sec: War Office 1929–30, Min Ag and Dep Minister Fisheries June 1930–Aug 1931, Min Ag and Fisheries 1931–35, Bd Educn 1935–36, Colonies 1936–37; Ld Privy Seal 1937–38, Pres Bd Educn 1938–40, 1st Commr Works April–May 1940, memb Empire Marketing Bd 1930, memb Cncl Duchy Lancaster 1931, PMG 1951–55, Govt Rep to negotiate with Emperor of Ethiopia 1944, Chm: Nat Lab Party 1931–43, Ag Res Cncl, Estates Ctee Nat Trust 1949–51 and 1955–69, Jt E and Centl African Bd 1956–59, Roy Cwlth Soc 1957–61 and Uganda Co, dir: Home Flax Production (Min of Supply) 1943–49 and Standard Bank; Legion of Honour; *m* 1st 30 Dec 1920 Diana (*d* 29 March 1966), dau of Capt Henry Gerard Leigh, 1st Life Gds; *m* 2nd 1 March 1968 Sylvia Margaret, DBE (1957), dau of William Reginald Harrison, of Liverpool, and widow of 1st and last Earl of Kilmuir, PC, GCVO (*see* 1967 edn), and *d* 28 Jan 1976, having by his 1st w had:

1 WILLIAM HERBRAND, **10th Earl**

2 Thomas Henry Jordan; *b* 13 Nov 1922; F/O RAFVR WW II 1941–43; missing presumed *k* on air operations 1943

1 *Katharine (Kitty) Pamela [The Lady Katharine Giles, 42 Blomfield Rd, London W9 1AH]; *b* 4 March 1926; *m* 29 June 1946 *Frank Thomas Robertson Giles, ed *Sunday Times* 1981–83, only s of Col Frank Lucas Netlam Giles, DSO, OBE, of Barn Close, Finchampstead, Berks, and has issue:

(1) *(Henry Frank) Sebastian; *b* 16 July 1952; *educ* Westminster; *m* 1988 *Sarah, er dau of Brian Palmer, of Highgate Village, London N6, and has issue:

1a *Maxwell Joseph W; *b* 1989

2a *Lucas Charles O; *b* 1992

(1) *Sarah Elizabeth; *b* 22 Feb 1950; *m* 8 July 1972 (*divorce* 1976) Rodolphe Frederic s of Leo Frederic Albert d'Erlanger, of 44 Upper Grosvenor St, London W1

(2) *Belinda Susan Mary; *b* 9 June 1958; *educ* Girton Coll Cambridge; *m* 25 Sept 1983 (*divorce* 1997) Christopher Simon Sykes, 3rd s of Sir Richard Tatton-Sykes, 7th Bt (*qv*), of Sledmere House, E Yorks, and has issue

The 9th EARL's er s,

WILLIAM HERBRAND SACKVILLE, **10th Earl De La Warr**, DL (E Sussex 1975); *b* 16 Oct 1921; *educ* Eton; Capt Parachute Regt WW II, chm: London YCs 1946 (pres 1947–49), INL and Reclamation and Disposal, Argus Press Hldgs, The Argus Press and Re-Chem Internat, Redifon 1978–79, Sussex Co Playing Fields Assoc 1956–71, dir: Mondtype Corp, Portals Hldgs, BET 1970–79, Wembley Stadium Ltd 1972–79, Portal Holidays 1974–88, Redifon Flight Simulation 1976–88, md Rediffusion Ltd 1974–79, Hon Col Sussex ACF 1969–88, V-Chm SE TAVR Assoc 1968–74 and 1978–88; *m* 18 May 1946 *Anne Rachel, only dau of Geoffrey Charles Devas, MC (*see* CAWDOR, E), of Hunton Court, Maidstone, Kent, and *d* by his own hand 1988, leaving issue:

1 WILLIAM HERBRAND SACKVILLE, **11th and present Earl De La Warr**

2 +Thomas (Tom) Geoffrey; *b* 26 Oct 1950; *educ* Eton and Lincoln Coll Oxford (BA); merchant banker, MP (C) Bolton W 1983–97, Parly Under Sec: Health 1992–95, Home Office 1995–97; *m* 22 Sept 1979 *Catherine Theresa, yr dau of Brig James C Windsor Lewis, DSO, MC, and formerly w of Simon Marsden, and adopted:

*Arthur Michael; *b* 1983

*Savannah Elizabeth; *b* 1986

1 *Arabella Avice Diana; *b* 20 June 1958; *m* 12 Oct 1981 (*divorce* 1988, resumed maiden name) Count Giovanni Emo Capodilista Maldura, of Palazzo Grazioli, Rome (*see* NEWBURGH, E)

DE L'ISLE

Arms: Quarterly, 1st and 4th, or a pheon az. (for SIDNEY); 2nd and 3rd, sa. on a fess engrailed between three whelk shells or, a mullet for difference (for SHELLEY). **Crests:** 1 A porcupine statant az., quills, collar and chain or, 2 A gryphon's head erased arg., ducally gorged or. **Supporters:** Dexter, a porcupine az., quills, collar and chain or; sinister, a lion, queue fourchée vert. **Motto:** *Quo fata vocant* ('Whither the Fates summon me'). **Creations:** Bt. (UK) 3 March 1806 and 12 Dec 1818, B. (UK) 13 Jan 1835, V. (UK) 12 Jan 1956.

THE 2ND VISCOUNT DE L'ISLE, Baron de L'Isle and Dudley of Penshurst, Kent, and a **Baronet** (Sir Philip John Algernon Sidney, 10th Bt, of Castle Goring, and 8th Bt, of Penshurst Place, Kent, MBE (1977)) [The Rt Hon The Viscount de L'Isle MBE, Penshurst Place, Tonbridge, Kent TN11 8DG]; *b* 21 April 1945; *s* f 1991; *educ* Tabley House, RMA Sandhurst; Maj Gren Gds 1966 (ret 1979), Hon Col 5th Bn Princess of Wales's Roy Regt 1992–, Freeman City London, Liveryman Goldsmiths' Co; *m* 15 Nov 1980 *Isobel Tresyllian, yst dau of Sir Edmund Gerald Compton, GCB, KBE, of 53 Evelyn Gdns, London SW7, and has issue:

1 +PHILIP WILLIAM EDMUND; *b* 2 April 1985

1 *Sophia Jacqueline Mary; *b* 1983

Title of (De) Lisle: A native of the Isle of Wight known for that reason as John de L'Isle was called to Parliament by writ in 1299, thereby becoming according to later doctrine Lord (Baron) Lisle. His son was briefly called to Parliament also, but not for every Parliament in his lifetime, while his successors in what was later to be thought of as the peerage were not called to Parliament at all. With the death of John's seven-times great-granddaughter Mary in March 1538/9 any barony created by the writ of 1299 would in any case by later doctrine be deemed to have fallen into abeyance.

In 1311 a Robert de Lisle, whose ancestors had been known as de Insula from a probable origin in the Isle of Ely, was called to Parliament and by later doctrine is therefore deemed to have been created Lord (Baron) Lisle. He seems to have fought against the Scots at Bannockburn in 1314 and certainly did so against the rebellious Thomas Earl of Lancaster on behalf of EDWARD II in March 1321/2. He eventually became a Franciscan and may even have taken holy orders as a priest. The 2nd Lord Lisle of this creation was made a Knight of the Garter and fought at Crécy. He was killed, still on active service in the Hundred Years War, some nine years later. The Barony seems to have fallen into abeyance in about 1428, or at any rate according to later doctrine would have been deemed to have done so.

Meanwhile in 1357 a Gerard de Lisle, second cousin of the Robert mentioned above and grandson of another Gerard who had acquired the Berkshire manor of Kingston Lisle from his mother, was called to Parliament by writ. He thus became according to later doctrine Lord (Baron) Lisle. As has been remarked elsewhere, the absurdity of two peers of Parliament with identical titles existing simultaneously is one of the strongest arguments for supposing early writs of summons were not intended to create heritable titles of honour. This 1st Lord Lisle of the 1357 creation also fought at Crécy, as well as in other battles of the Hundred Years War. The 1357 peerage descended to two sole heiresses in succession, who by a later doctrine would have been deemed baronesses in their own right. With the death of the second sole heiress any barony created by the writ of 1357 would have been deemed by later doctrine to have fallen into abeyance. In 1823 a descendant of this second sole heiress, Sir John Shelley Sidney, 1st Bt (*see* below), unsuccessfully petitioned the House of Lords to terminate the abeyance in his favour.

Long before that, however, the second sole heiress's eldest daughter's grandson in the female line, John Talbot (*see* SHREWSBURY and WATERFORD, E, and WARWICK, BROOKE and, E), was created Lord and Baron of Lisle with a curious remainder to heirs as lords of the manor of Kingston Lisle accompanied by a tendentious claim that Talbot's de Lisle ancestors had possessed the manor time out of mind. This creation took place in 1444 and was in effect a completely new peerage, even though it claimed to fix on John Talbot the descent of the old 1357 one. Seven years later Talbot was promoted Viscount Lisle. When the new Viscount's son and successor was killed in a skirmish in March 1469/70 the Viscountcy expired too, though the Barony creation of 1444 either fell into abeyance or was suspended pending a clarification of the terms under which it could be transmitted.

The 2nd and last Viscount's sole surviving heiress and sister, Elizabeth, married Sir Edward Grey, who in March 1474/5 was created Lord and Baron of Lisle, thus overcoming any doubts in the matter. In 1483 he too moved up a step in the peerage, becoming Viscount Lisle. This Viscountcy also expired after only one more generation, but the Barony creations of 1444 and 1474/5 eventually passed to an heiress, who married first Edmund Dudley, Henry VII's notoriously extortionate minister, and second Arthur Plantagenet, a bastard of EDWARD IV's by an unknown mother (the King's best-known mistress Jane Shore is only one of the possibilities). Arthur was created Viscount Lisle in 1523, though with such limitations as to ensure that the title would continue, if at all, in his wife's male issue. As it happened, he died without male issue and the Viscountcy was revived yet again in favour of the heiress's son by her first husb Edmund Dudley. This was John Dudley, who later became the celebrated Duke of Northumberland of EDWARD VI's reign.

John Dudley's fourth son Lord Ambrose Dudley was the next connection of the original grantees to enjoy a revived Viscountcy of Lisle, being so created in 1561. The Robert Sydney mentioned below who was created Viscount Lisle in 1605 was Lord Ambrose's nephew through his mother Lady Mary, *née* Dudley.

The Barony of Lisle of Mountnorth (*qv*), created in the Irish peerage in 1758 for John Lysaght, is still in existence. There appears to be no connection between the Lysaghts and the previously mentioned holders of the various peerages involving the name Lisle, L'Isle or De L'Isle.

Lineage of Sydney: JOHN de SYDENIE; yeoman, farmed at Alford, Surrey, *c* 1280; f or gf of:

JOHN de SYDENYE; of age by 26 May 1338, held lands in Sussex as well as Surrey; ancestor of:

Sir WILLIAM SYDNEY; Cdr Battle of Flodden 1513, Chamberlain and Steward Household to HENRY VIII, granted Penshurst Place by EDWARD VI; *m* Anne, dau of Hugh Pakenham (*see* LONGFORD, E) had:

Sir HENRY SYDNEY; Ld Pres Marches Wales, Ld Dep Ireland *temp* ELIZABETH I; *m* Mary, dau of John Dudley, Duke of Northumberland, and sister of Robert Dudley, Earl of Leicester, KG, and *d c* 1 May 1586, leaving:

1 Philip (Sir); the soldier and poet; *b* 30 Nov 1554; *m c* March 1583 Frances, dau of Sir Francis Walsingham, and *dspm* 16 Oct 1586 at Arnhem from a wound received at the Battle of Zutphen 22 Sept 1586

2 ROBERT (Sir), 1st EARL OF LEICESTER of the 1618 *cr*

3 Thomas; *dsp*

1 Mary; *m* 2nd Earl of Pembroke (*see* PEMBROKE and MONTGOMERY) and *d* 25 Sept 1621, leaving issue

Sir HENRY's 2nd son,

ROBERT SYDNEY, 1st EARL OF LEICESTER, so *cr* 2 Aug 1618, as also earlier 13 May 1603 BARON SYDNEY OF PENSHURST, Co Kent, and 4 May 1605 VISCOUNT L'ISLE, KG (1616); *b* 19 Nov 1563; *educ* Ch Ch Oxford; MP Glam 1584–86 and 1593 and Kent 1597–98, ktd 1586, Govr Flushing 1588–1616; *m* 1st 23 Sept 1584 Barbara (*d* May 1621), dau and heir of John Gamage, of Coity, Glam; *m* 2nd 25 April 1625 Sarah (*d* 1656), dau and heir of William Blount and widow of Sir Thomas Smythe, of Bidborough, Kent, and *d* 13 July 1626, leaving by his 1st w, with other issue:

ROBERT SYDNEY, 2nd EARL OF LEICESTER, KB (1610), PC (1639 and 1660); *b* 1 Dec 1595; *educ* Ch Ch Oxford; MP Wilton 1614, Kent 1620–22 and Mon 1624–25, Amb: Denmark July-Nov 1632, Holstein 1632, Paris 1636–41, Ld Lt: Ireland 1641–43 and Kent 1642; *m c* Jan 1615 Lady Dorothy Percy (*d* 19 Aug 1650), dau of 3rd Earl of Northumberland (*see* NORTHUMBERLAND, D), and *d* 2 Nov 1677, leaving, with other issue:

1 PHILIP, 3rd EARL

2 Algernon; *b* 1622; Parliamentarian Civil War, Govr Chichester 1645, MP Cardiff 1646, Govr and Lt of Dover 1648, memb Cncl State 1653 and 1659, author: *Discourses Concerning Government* (1698), arrested 26 June 1683 on suspicion of involvement in the Rye House Plot; executed 7 Dec 1683

3 HENRY SYDNEY, 1st and last EARL OF ROMNEY, Co Kent, so *cr* 14 May 1694, as also earlier 9 April 1689 BARON MILTON, Co Kent, and VISCOUNT SYDNEY of Shepey [*sic*], Co Kent (all E), PC (Feb 1688/9 and again 1702); *b* 1641; Envoy France 1672, Master Robes 1675–78, MP (Whig) Bramber 1679–81 and Tamworth Jan-April 1689, Gen cmdg English regts fighting on behalf of Holland 1681–85, Gent Bedchamber 1689–1700, Kent: Ld Lt 1689–92 and 1694–1704, V-Adml 1689–1702, Sec State N Dept 1690–92, Maj-Gen 1691, Lt-Gen 1694, Ld Warden Cinque Ports 1691–1702, a Ld Justice Ireland 1690, Ld Lt Ireland 1692–95, Master-Gen Ordnance 1693–1702, Groom Stole 1700–02; *d* unm 8 April 1704 when his titles expired

1 Dorothy (Waller's 'Sacharissa'); *m* 1st 20 July 1639 1st Earl of Sunderland (*see* MARLBOROUGH, D); *m* 2nd 8 July 1652 Robert Smythe, of Bidborough, Kent, and was *bur* 25 Sept 1683/4

2 Lucy; *m* 20 Jan 1647 Sir John Pelham, 3rd Bt, and was *bur* 19 Aug 1685, leaving issue (*see* CHICHESTER, E)

3 Isabella; *m* 22 Aug 1656 2nd Viscount Strangford and *d* June 1663, leaving issue

The est son,

PHILIP SYDNEY, 3rd EARL OF LEICESTER; *b* 10 Jan 1618/9; MP Yarmouth IoW March-April 1640 and Nov 1640–53, Kent 1653 and (I Parl) Co Louth 1642–44; republican, Ld Lt Ireland 1646–47, Memb: Cncl State Feb 1648/9, Feb 1649/50 and July 1653 (Pres Feb-March 1651/2), Cromwell's House of Lords, Cncllr to LORD PROTECTOR 1653; *m* 9 May 1645 Lady Catherine Cecil (*d* 18 Aug 1652), dau of 2nd Earl of Salisbury (*qv*), and *d* 6 March 1697/8, leaving:

ROBERT SYDNEY, 4th EARL OF LEICESTER, called up to Ho of Lds *vp* in his f's Barony of Sydney of Penshurst by writ 11 July 1689; *b* 1649; *m* 1672 Lady Elizabeth Egerton (*d* 1709), dau of 2nd Earl of Bridgwater (*see* GREY EGERTON, Bt), and *d* 11 Nov 1702, leaving, with other issue:

1 PHILIP SYDNEY, 5th EARL OF LEICESTER; *b* 8 July 1676; MP (Whig) Kent 1695–98; *m* 17 Dec 1700 Anne, dau and coheir of Sir Robert Reeve, 2nd Bt, of Thwaite, Suffolk, but *dsp* 24 July 1705

2 JOHN SYDNEY, 6th EARL OF LEICESTER, KB (1725), PC (1731); *b* 14 Feb 1680; Lt-Col 1st Foot Gds, MP (Whig) Brackley May-July 1705; *d* unm 27 Sept 1737

3 Thomas, Col; *m* Mary, yr dau and coheir of Sir Thomas Reeve, 2nd Bt, and *d* 1728, leaving issue:

(1) Mary; *m* 16 July 1738 Sir Brownlow Sherard, 4th Bt, and *dsp* 27 March 1758

(2) ELIZABETH, of whom presently

4 JOCELYN SYDNEY, 7th EARL OF LEICESTER; *b c* 1692; *educ* Univ Coll Oxford; *m* Feb 1717 Elizabeth (*d* 14 Nov 1747), dau and coheir of Lewis Thomas, of Gwernllwynwith, Glam, and *dspl* 7 July 1743, when all his titles expired

1 Elizabeth; *m* Sir Harcourt Masters

Col THOMAS SIDNEY's yr dau,

ELIZABETH Sydney; inherited the Sydney estates; *m* William PERRY, of Turville Park, Bucks, and left an only surv dau:

ELIZABETH JANE Perry; *m* 1769, as his 2nd w, Sir Bysshe SHELLEY, 1st Bt, of Castle Goring, Sussex (*d* 6 Jan 1815), and was *bur* 17 May 1781, leaving with other issue (*see* below):

Sir JOHN SHELLEY later SHELLEY SIDNEY (added by sign manual 1793), **1st Bt** (GB), so *cr* 12 Dec 1818, of Penshurst Place, Kent; *b* 18 Dec 1771; *m* 29 April 1799 Henrietta (*d* 5 Feb 1811), dau of Sir Henry Hunloke, 4th Bt, of Wingerworth Hall, Derbys, and *d* 14 March 1849, having had, with a dau (Emily Elizabeth, *m* 26 March 1826 Col William Wakefield and *d* 12 Aug 1827, leaving issue):

Sir PHILIP CHARLES SHELLEY SIDNEY later (by 1820) SIDNEY, **2nd Bt**, and **1st Baron De L'Isle and Dudley of Penshurst**, Co Kent, so *cr* 13 Jan 1835, GCH (1831, KCH 1830); *b* 11 March 1800; *educ* Eton and Ch Ch Oxford; Capt 1st Foot Gds, MP (Tory) Eye 1829–31, Equerry to his f-in-law WILLIAM IV 1830–35, Surveyor-Gen Duchy Cornwall 1833–49, Surveyor-Gen Duchy of Cornwall; *m* 13 Aug 1825 Lady Sophia FitzClarence (*d* 10 April 1837), est sister of 1st Earl of Munster (*qv*) and illegitimate dau of WILLIAM IV, and had, with other issue:

1 PHILIP, **2nd Baron**

1 Adelaide Augusta Wilhelmina; *m* 2 Dec 1856 her cousin Hon F C G FitzCLARENCE later HUNLOKE (1865) (*see* MUNSTER, E) and *d* 20 Sept 1904

2 Ernestine Wellington; *m* 9 Jan 1868 Philip Perceval (*d* 28 March 1897) and *d* 20 Sept 1910, leaving issue

3 Sophia Philippa; *m* 20 April 1871 Count Alexander Kielmansegg (*d* Aug 1914), est son of Count Edward Howe Kielmansegg, Min State to King of Hanover, and *dsp* 12 May 1907

The 1st BARON *d* 4 March 1851; his son,

PHILIP SIDNEY, **2nd Baron De L'Isle and Dudley of Penshurst**, DL, Lt RHG; *b* 29 Jan 1828; *educ* Eton; *m* 1st 23 April 1850 Mary (*d* 14 June 1891), only child of Sir William Foulis, 8th Bt (*see* 1877 edn), and had issue:

1 PHILIP SIDNEY, **3rd Baron De L'Isle and Dudley of Penshurst**, Maj Rifle Bde; *b* 14 May 1853; *m* 12 June 1902 Hon Elizabeth Maria (*d* 19 July 1958), 4th dau of 4th Viscount Gort (*qv*) and widow of William Harvey Astell, DL, of Woodbury Hall, Beds, and *dsp* 24 Dec 1922

2 ALGERNON SIDNEY, **4th Baron De L'Isle and Dudley of Penshurst**, Col RFA Boer War 1901–02; *b* 11 June 1854; *d* unm 18 April 1945

3 Henry; *b* 17 Jan 1858; *d* 13 April 1896

4 WILLIAM, **5th Baron**

1 Mary Sophia; *d* unm 25 Nov 1903

The **2nd Baron** *m* 2nd 25 Jan 1893 (Emily) Frances, LGStJ (*m* 2nd 21 Feb 1903 (*divorce* 1909) Sir Walter George Stirling, 3rd Bt (*d* 7 June 1934) and *d* 3 Nov 1926), er dau of William Fermor Ramsay, and *d* 17 Feb 1898

The 4th BARON's bro,

WILLIAM SIDNEY, **5th Baron De L'Isle and Dudley of Penshurst**, JP London, barrister, Mayor Chelsea 1906–08, memb LCC 1922–34; *b* 19 Aug 1859; *m* 5 Dec 1905 Winifred Agneta Yorke (*d* 11 Feb 1959), er dau of Roland Yorke Bevan by Hon Agneta Olivia, 4th dau of 10th Lord Kinnaird (*qv*), and *d* 18 June 1945, leaving issue:

1 WILLIAM PHILIP, **1st Viscount**, for whom *see* further below

1 Mary Olivia; *b* 20 Nov 1906; *m* 3 June 1939 Walter Hugh Stewart Garnett, of Radmore, Dorrington, Shrewsbury, son of Frank Nasmyth Garnett, JP, of Adsett Court, Westbury-on-Severn, and *d* 24 Nov 1959, leaving issue

Lineage of Shelley: JOHN SHELLEY; *m* Elizabeth, dau and heiress of John Michelgrove, of Michelgrove (*see* SHELLEY, Bt), and had a 2nd s:

EDWARD SHELLEY; settled Worminghurst, Sussex; had an est s:

HENRY SHELLEY; *m* Anne, dau and heiress of Richard Sackville, great uncle of 1st Earl of Dorset (*see* SACKVILLE, B), and had:

HENRY SHELLEY, of Worminghurst; *m* Barbara, dau of Sir William Cromer, of Tunstall and had, with a dau (Frances, *m* 1st William Holland and 2nd 1st Vicount Lumley of Waterford *see* SCARBOROUGH, E) a 3rd s:

RICHARD SHELLEY; *m* Joan, dau and coheir of John Fuste, of Ichingfield, Sussex, and had an est s:

JOHN SHELLEY, of Ichingfield; gf of:

JOHN SHELLEY; *m* Helen, yr dau and coheir of Roger Bysshe, who brought him Fen Place, and had:

TIMOTHY SHELLEY, of Fen Place; *b* 1700; *m* Mrs Johanna Plum, of New York, and had:

Sir Bysshe Shelley, 1st Bt (UK), so *cr* 3 March 1806, of Castle Goring, Sussex; *b* 21 June 1731; *m* 1st 30 June 1752 Mary Catherine (*d* 7 Nov 1760), only child of Rev Theobald Michell, of Horsham, and had issue:

1 TIMOTHY (Sir), **2nd Bt**

1 Helen; *m* Robert Parker, of Maidstone

Sir Bysshe *m* 2nd 1769 Elizabeth Jane (*bur* 17 May 1781), only dau and heiress of William Perry, of Turville Park (*see* above), and by her had issue:

2 **Sir John Shelley-Sidney, 1st Bt** of the 1818 *cr* (*see* above)

3 Philip SHELLEY later SIDNEY (roy licence 10 April 1799), Capt 4th Foot; *bapt* 20 Feb 1778; *d* unm Aug 1799

4 Robert, Maj Army; *d* 31 March 1849

2 Ariana; *m* Francis Aikin

3 Jane Caroline; *m* Rev Joseph Harris and had issue

Sir BYSSHE *d* 6 Jan 1815; his est son,

Sir Timothy Shelley, 2nd Bt; *b* 7 Sept 1753; *m* Oct 1791 Elizabeth, dau of Charles Pilfold, of Effingham, Surrey, and *d* 24 April 1844, having had, with three daus (*d* unm):

1 PERCY BYSSHE; *b* 4 Aug 1792; *educ* Eton and Univ Coll Oxford; the poet, novelist and political pamphleteer: *Zastrozzi* (novel, 1810), *Original Poetry by Victor and Cazire* (with his sister Elizabeth, 1810), *St Irvine, or, the Rosicrucian* (novel, 1811), *The Necessity of Atheism* (with Thomas Jefferson Hogg, 1811), *An Address to the Irish People* (1812), *A Letter to Lord Ellenborough* (1812), *Queen Mab* (1813), *The Assassins* (novella fragment, 1814), *Alastor* (1816), *An Address to the People on the Death of Princess Charlotte* (1817), *The Revolt of Islam* (1818), *The Cenci* (1819), *The Mask of Anarchy* (written 1819), 'To a Skylark', 'The Cloud' and 'Ode to the West Wind' (all written 1819), *Peter Bell the Third* (written 1819), 'To Liberty', 'To Naples' (both written 1820), *A Philosophical View of Reform* (1820), *Swellfoot the Tyrant* (1820), *Essay on the Devil* (1821), *The Defence of Poetry* (written 1821, published by his widow 1840), *Adonais* (1821), *Epipsychidion* (1821), *Hellas* (verse drama, 1822), *The Triumph of Life* (1822), *Poetical Pieces* (collected poems, 1823), *Posthumous Poems* (1824), *Julian and Maddalo, A Conversation* (1824), *The Poetical Works* (4 vols., ed Mary Shelley, 1839); *m* 1st Aug 1811 Harriet (drowned herself 1816), dau of John Westbrook, of London, and had issue:

(1) Charles Bysshe; *b* 1814; *d* 1826

(1) Ianthe Eliza; *m* 27 Sept 1837 Edward Jeffries Esdaile (*d* 14 Feb 1881), of Cothelstone, Somerset, and *d* 16 June 1876, leaving issue

1 (cont.) PERCY BYSSHE SHELLEY *m* 2nd 30 Dec 1816 Mary Wollstonecraft (*b* 1797; author: *History of a Six Weeks' Tour* (memoirs, 1817), *Frankenstein* (1818), *Valperga* (1823), *The Last Man* (1826), *Lodore* (1835), *Faulkner* (1837), *Rambles in Germany and Italy, in 1840, 1842 and 1843* (1844), *Mathilde* (begun 1819; not published till 1959); *d* 1 Feb 1851), dau of William Godwin, philosopher and novelist, by Mary Wollstonecraft, feminist, and was drowned in the Bay of Spezia, Italy, 8 July 1822, having by her had issue (he also may have had an illegitimate child Elena Adelaide Shelley by an unknown woman):

(2) William; *b* 1816; *d* young

(3) **Sir Percy Florence Shelley, 3rd Bt**, Capt Sussex Militia, DL and JP, High Sheriff 1865; *b* 12 Nov 1819; *m* 22 June 1848 Jane (*d* 24 June 1899), dau of Thomas Gibson and widow of Hon Charles Robert St John (*see* BOLINGBROKE and ST JOHN, V), and *dsp* 5 Dec 1889

2 John, of Avington House, Hants; *b* 15 March 1806; *m* 24 March 1827 Elizabeth (*d* 28 Nov 1889), est dau of Charles Bowen, of Kilnacourt, Queen's Co, Ireland, and *d* 11 Nov 1866, having had issue:

(1) **Sir Edward Shelley, 4th Bt**, Capt 16th Lancers; *b* 10 Dec 1827; *m* 25 June 1866 Mary (*d* 1886), dau of Henry Mitchell Smyth, of Castle Widenham, Co Cork, and *dsp* 17 Sept 1890

(2) CHARLES (Sir), **5th Bt**

(3) George Ernest, Capt Gren Gds; *b* 15 May 1840; *m* 1889 Janet (*d* 10 Sept 1955), dau of E Andrewes, and *d* 29 Nov 1910, having had issue:

1a George Edward, MBE (1938); *b* 2 Feb 1891; *educ* Harrow, Trin Coll Cambridge (BA 1912) and RMC Sandhurst; Maj Gren Gds WW I (wounded) and WW II, Gold Staff Offr Coronation 1937 and marriage of HM THE QUEEN 1947, OStJ, Silver Jubilee medal 1935, Coronation medal 1937, Coronation medal 1953; *m* 1st 8 Dec 1920 (*divorce* 1935) Cicely Alice Colquhoun (*d* 22 Feb 1954), dau of Lt-Col Lionel Arthur Bosanquet, of Gleddon, and had issue:

1b Rosemary Eveline, Subaltern ATS and WRAC 1941–50; *b* 10 Oct 1921

2b *Iris Gwendolin [Mrs Philip Tanner, 43 Victoria Rd, Cirencester, Glos GL7 1ES]; *b* 4 Jan 1927; *m* 30 Jan 1954 Maj Philip Gordon Tanner, RA (*d* 30 Dec 1994), only son of Charles Gordon Tanner, of Oaklands, Hasketon, nr Woodbridge, Suffolk, and has issue:

1c *Nicholas Shelley [Nicholas Tanner Esq, The Coach House, Ampney Crucis, Cirencester, Glos GL7 5RY]; *b* 7 Jan 1955; *educ* Harrow; *m* 21 June 1980 *Melanie Anne, er dau of A F Challis, and has had issue:

1d George William; *b* 4 July 1982; *d* 26 May 1989

2d *William Archie Bowen; *b* 4 June 1988

1d *Olivia; *b* 16 March 1990

2d *Isabel; *b* 10 June 1993

1c *Clare Theresa; *b* 29 Jan 1958; *m* 1987 *Keith Evans, er son of L Evans, and has issue:

1d *Christopher; *b* 1990

2d *Daniel; *b* 1992

1a (cont.) George Shelley *m* 2nd 6 July 1935 (*divorce* 1941) Hon Lucy Gwen (*d* 22 Aug 1957), est dau of Baron Atkin (LP; *see* 1940 edn) and formerly w of Col Stuart Low, DSO, TD, RA (TA); *m* 3rd 28 July 1951 Freda Victoria (*d* 1977), yr dau of Frederick Lincoln Jefferey, of Bloemfontein, and formerly wife of A M Ohlson, and *d* 7 Nov 1961

2a Ernest Bowen, Lt (acting Capt) Gren Gds; *b* 27 Feb 1896; *ka* 12 Sept 1918

1a Gwendolen Evelyn; *b* 4 Aug 1892; *m* 1st 23 Feb 1913 (*divorce* 1930) Rev Frank Mills, yst son of George Jonathan Mills, of Colville, Worthing, and had issue; *m* 2nd 24 June 1930 Eric Tregear Williams, Malayan CS and had further issue

(1) Elizabeth Emily; *m* 12 Aug 1857 Sir Frederick Peel (*dsp* 6 June 1906), KCMG (*see* PEEL, E), and *d* 30 July 1865

1 Mary; *m* 1819 D F Haynes, of Onesome, Surrey, and had issue

The 4th Bt's bro,

Sir Charles Shelley, 5th Bt, JP Hants; *b* 14 May 1838; Lt-Col Scots Fus Gds; *m* 3 Aug 1869 Lady Mary Jane Jemima Stopford (*d* 17 Nov 1937), 3rd dau of 5th Earl of Courtown (*qv*), and *d* 20 July 1902, having had issue:

1 Sir JOHN COURTOWN EDWARD SHELLEY later SHELLEY-ROLLS (roy licence 19 May 1917), **6th Bt**, JP Hants, DL Mon, High Sheriff 1928; *b* 5 Aug 1871; *educ* Wellington and RMC Sandhurst; Capt Scots Gds, Lt-Col 3rd Queen's Westminsters Cadet Bn, ADC to GOC Lond Dist, served S African War 1900; *m* 2 3 April 1898 Hon Eleanor Georgiana Rolls (*d* 15 Sept 1961), dau and eventually sole heiress of 1st and last Baron Llangattock, and *dsp* 18 Feb 1951

2 **Sir Percy Bysshe Shelley, 7th Bt**; *b* 24 June 1872; *educ* Wellington; *d* unm 24 Sept 1953

3 Cecil William Charles, Lt Scots Gds; *b* 5 Sept 1873; *m* 11 Nov 1903 Sybil Bertie (*d* 30 July 1906), 2nd dau of Lawrence Richard Peel, of Nuwara Eliya, Ceylon, and was *ka* 17 Oct 1915, leaving issue:

(1) Eileen Sybil; *b* 10 July 1906; *d* unm 11 Feb 1963

4 **Sir Sidney Patrick Shelley, 8th Bt**; *b* 18 Jan 1880; *educ* Wellington; Capt Hants Yeo Boer War 1900–01 (medal with four clasps) and WW I; *d* unm 25 July 1965

5 Hubert, Capt Hampshire Yeo, Lt 6th Bn Rifle Bde Boer War 1900–01 and WW I; *b* 10 Oct 1881; *educ* Wellington; *d* unm 26 April 1951

1 Ernestine Elizabeth; *d* unm 20 Dec 1952

2 Maud; *d* unm 8 March 1952

3 Nora Kathleen; *m* 25 Aug 1907 Adml Fausto M de Leva, Italian Navy, est son of Cavaliere Edoardo Leva, of Rome, and Elvira Leva-Travostini, and *d* 10 Dec 1963, leaving issue

4 Amy; *b* 8 Jan *d* 16 Nov 1878

The 5th BARON's s and 8th Bt (of the 1806 *cr*)'s distant cousin,

Sir WILLIAM PHILIP SIDNEY, **9th Bt** (in which s cousin 1965), and **1st Viscount De L'Isle**, of Penshurst, Co Kent (UK), so *cr* 12 Jan 1956, VC (1944), KG (1968), GCMG (1961), GCVO (1962), PC (1951), DL (Kent 1949); *b* 23 May 1909; *educ* Eton and Magdalene Coll Cambridge (Hon Fell 1955); Capt (T/Maj) Gren Gds WW II, MP (C) Chelsea 1944–45, PPS Min Food May 1945, Parly Sec Min Pensions May–July 1945, Sec State Air 1951–55, Govr-Gen and C-in-C Australia 1961–65, Chllr Order St Michael and St George 1968–91, Tstee: Br Museum 1950–64, Nat Portrait Gallery 1965–72, RAF Museum, 1st Chmn Bd Tstees Armories 1983–91, KJStJ, MInst FCA; *m* 1st 8 June 1940 Hon Jacqueline Corinne Yvonne Vereker (*d* 15 Nov 1962), only dau of 6th Viscount Gort (*qv*), and had issue:

1 PHILIP JOHN ALGERNON SIDNEY, **2nd and present Viscount De L'Isle**

1 *Elizabeth ('Libba') Sophia [The Hon Mrs Abel Smith, The Old Hall, Langham, Oakham, Rutland]; *b* 12 March 1941; *m* 1st 10 Oct 1959 (*divorce* 1966) (George Silver) Oliver Annesley Colthurst, yr son of Sir Richard St John Jeffreyes Colthurst, 8th Bt (*qv*), and has issue; *m* 2nd 1 July 1966 (*divorce* 1971), as his 2nd w, Sir (Edward) Humphrey Tyrrell Wakefield, 2nd Bt (*qv*), and has further issue; *m* 3rd 1972 (*divorce* 1989) Capt James Silvester Rattray, 28th Chief, only son of Col Paul Burn-Clerk-Rattray of Craighall-Rattray, CBE, and has issue:

(2) + Robert; *b* 11 Oct 1972; *educ* Milton Abbey

(2) *A dau *b* 25 March 1983

1 (cont.) The Hon Mrs Rattray *m* 4th 1989 *(Robert) Sam(uel) Clive Abel Smith (*see* BUXTON, Bt)

2 *Catherine Mary, OBE [The Hon Mrs Villiers OBE, St Leonard's Grange, Beaulieu, Hants SO42 7XF]; *b* 20 Oct 1942; *m* 1st 1 Dec 1964 (*divorce* 1983) Martin John Wilbraham, only son of Maj Edward Jack Wilbraham, MC, of 60 Cadogan Square, London SW1, and has issue:

(1) *Alexander John; *b* 22 Oct 1965; *educ* Eton; *m* 3 Aug 1996 *Fernanda Amaral, est dau of Arnaldo Valentini, of Sao Paulo, Brazil

(2) *Rupert Edward Robert; *b* 26 Feb 1967; *educ* Eton

(3) *Jocelyn Thomas Ralph; *b* 30 April 1970; *educ* Eton

2 (cont.) The Hon Mrs Catherine Wilbraham *m* 2nd 9 May 1983 *Nicholas Hyde Villiers (*see* CLARENDON, E)

3 *Anne Marjorie [The Hon Mrs Harries, Lower Woolwich, Rolvenden, Kent]; *b* 15 Aug 1947; *m* 3 June 1967 *Lt-Cdr David Alexander Harries, RAN, er s of R-Adml David Hugh Harries, CB, CBE, RAN (ret), of Sydney, NSW, and has issue:

(1) *David Henry; *b* 4 May 1970; *educ* Eton

(2) *James Hugh; *b* 28 June 1972; *educ* Eton

(1) *Alexandra Victoria Corinna; *b* 12 July 1968; *educ* Benenden and Somerville Coll Oxford

4 *Lucy Corinna Agneta [The Hon Mrs Michael Willoughby, North Crimston House, Malton, N Yorks YO17 8AX]; *b* 21 Feb 1953; *m* 26 Jan 1974 *Hon Michael Charles James Willoughby, est s of 12th Baron Middleton (*qv*), and has issue

The **1st Viscount** *m* 2nd 24 March 1966 *Margaret Eldrydd, JP (Breconshire 1958), CC (1955–61) [The Rt Hon Margaret Viscountess De L'Isle, Glanusk Park, Crickhowell, Powys NP8 1LP], only dau of Maj-Gen Thomas Herbert Shoubridge, CB, CMG, DSO, widow of Col 3rd Baron Glanusk (*qv*) and sister of Lt-Col Patrick Herbert Lort Phillips, DSO, and bar, DL, FRGS, Gren Gds, of Lawrenny Park, Pembs, and *d* 1991

Seat: Penshurst Place, Tunbridge Wells, Kent. When Penshurst was first built towards the end of the first half of the 14th century it was by a prosperous bourgeois, Sir John Pulteney, though his descendants several centuries later included the Pulteney Earls of Bath (*see* BATH, M, preliminary remarks) and the Earls of Harborough and Crewe (*see* 1940 edn CREWE, M). At that time Penshurst seems to have been relatively undefended. It was only towards the end of the 14th century that some attempt seems to have been made at fortification, of which the present 'Garden' Tower is the sole survivor in its entirety. Some two generations later the property was bought by the Duke of Bedford, one of HENRY IV's younger sons. Bedford added a more intimate extension to the original Great Hall, although he gets little credit for it since it is now called after the Stafford Duke of Buckingham, who did not own Penshurst till much later. Nevertheless, although the Great Hall was clearly seen as inconvenient as early as the 1430s from the point of view of those who had to sit and eat there, it remains the gem of the entire place, being 60 feet high at its apex and a little more than 60 feet long, with splendidly generous windows set high up in the end walls — a radical departure from common practice at the time, when windows were still thought of as first and foremost slits to fire arrows out of.

The Sir Henry Sidney who was father of the 1st Earl of Leicester more or less completed the medieval structure as it is seen today, erecting the King's Tower which dominates the entrance to the north. The 1st Earl's tenancy saw the building of the long gallery. Further alterations, chiefly internal, were carried out by Sir John Shelley Sidney, 1st Bt, the claimant to the 1357 Barony of Lisle.

DE MAULEY

Arms: Gules a chevron between three combs argent. **Crest:** Out of a ducal coronet or three arrows, points downwards, one in pale, two in saltire, entwined at the intersection by a snake, proper.
Supporters: Dexter, a lion regardant proper; sinister, a bull sable, armed, unguled and gorged with a ducal coronet or.
Motto: *Pro rege, lege, grege* ('For king, law and people').
Creation: B. (UK) 10 July 1838.

THE 6TH BARON DE MAULEY OF CANFORD, Co Dorset (Gerald John Ponsonby) [The Rt Hon The Lord de Mauley, Langford House, Little Faringdon, Lechlade, Glos GL7 3QN]; *b* 19 Dec 1921, *s* f 1962; *educ* Eton and Ch Ch Oxford (BA 1941, MA 1947); barrister Middle Temple 1949, Lt Leics Yeo, Capt RA, WW II (wounded); *m* 16 Nov 1954 *Helen Alice, only dau of Hon Charles William Sholto Douglas (*see* MORTON, E) and widow of Lt-Col Brian Lynch Leslie Abdy Collins, OBE, MC

Lineage: The 3rd EARL OF BESSBOROUGH (*qv*) had a 3rd s:

WILLIAM FRANCIS SPENCER PONSONBY, **1st Baron de Mauley of Canford**, Co Dorset (UK), so *cr* 10 July 1838; *b* 31 July 1787; MP (Whig) Poole 1826–31, Knaresborough June-Dec 1832 and Dorset 1832–37; *m* 8 Aug 1814 Lady Barbara Ashley Cooper (coheir of the medieval Barony of Mauley; *d* 5 June 1844), only dau and heir of 5th Earl of Shaftesbury (*qv*) by Barbara, dau and heir of Sir John Webb, Bt, of Odstock House, Wilts, by Mary (sis and eventually sole heir of Thomas Salvain, of Easingwold, Yorks, descended from George Salvain by his w Elizabeth, sis and coheir of Piers de Mauley, 5th Lord (Baron) Mauley (deemed to have been *cr* by writ of summons 1295, although the assembly held in that year was subsequently judged not to have constituted a Parliament), who *dspm* 1415, when the Barony fell according to later doctrine into abeyance between his sisters), and had issue:

1 CHARLES FREDERICK ASHLEY COOPER, **2nd Baron**

2 Ashley George John, Capt Gren Gds, DL, JP, MP Cirencester 1852–57 and 1859–65; *b* 24 June 1831; *m* 21 July 1857 Hon Louisa Frances Charlotte Gordon, Maid of Honour to HM QUEEN VICTORIA (*d* 12 Feb 1910), 2nd dau of Lord Henry Gordon (*see* HUNTLY, M), and *d* 12 Jan 1898, leaving issue:

(1) Claude Ashley Charles; *b* 16 Aug 1859; *educ* Trin Coll Cambridge (BA); *m* 28 Jan 1891 (*divorce* 1907) Haller (*d* 2 Feb 1932), yst dau of Orville Horwitz, of Baltimore, USA, and *d* 3 Feb 1935, having had issue:

1a Harold Ashley Curzon; *b* 6 Oct 1891; *m* 23 Aug 1941 Ruth Margaret, only dau of James Miller, of Chippenham, Wilts, and *d* 22 July 1950, leaving issue:

1b +John Ashley Charles; *b* 2 Sept 1948

1b *Sarah Haller [Mrs Phillip Hilton, Winishill, Nibley Lane, Yate, Bristol]; *b* 12 Oct 1944; *m* 1971 *Philip James Hilton

2b *Jane Caroline; *b* 10 Aug 1946; *m* 1966 (*divorce* 1969) Stephen Thornton Parr, and has issue:

1c *Sally Jane Thornton; *b* 1965

2a Eric; *b* 28 April 1893; *d* 17 Oct 1894

1a Moyra Blanche May Diana; *b* 3 Dec 1901; *m* 1st 11 Feb 1932 (*divorce* 1945) Hans Henning and had issue:

1b *Peter Ronald [Peter Knapp-Fisher Esq, 2 Wilby Mews, London W11], assumed name KNAPP-FISHER 1947; *b* 17 March 1933

1b *Jacqueline Haller [Mrs Carl Vidal, 1475 Kendall Dve, Boulder, Colorado 80302, USA]; *b* 22 March 1935; *m* 2 Sept 1967 *Dr Carl Rudolf Vidal, physicist, and has issue:

1c *Martin Andreas; *b* 21 May 1968

2b *Moyra Christine [Mrs Alexander Hendry, 76B St James's Lane, London N10]; *b* 6 March 1938; *m* 30 Sept 1964 *Alexander Hendry

1a (cont.) Mrs Moyra Henning *m* 2nd 14 May 1947 Maurice Heriot Nicolls (*d* 24 March 1954)

(2) Eustace Ashley William; *b* 30 Dec 1863; *m* — and *d* 15 April 1924

(1) Florence; *b* 27 June, *d* 20 July 1858

1 Frances Anne Georgiana; *m* 14 Dec 1937 9th Lord Kinnaird (*qv*), and *d* 20 March 1910, leaving issue

The 1st BARON *d* 16 May 1855; his er son,

CHARLES FREDERICK ASHLEY COOPER PONSONBY, **2nd Baron de Mauley of Canford**, MP (Lib) Poole 1837–47 and Dungarvan 1851–52; *b* 12 Sept 1815; *m* 9 Aug 1838 his cousin Lady Maria Jane Elizabeth (*d* 13 Sept 1897), dau of 4th Earl of Bessborough (*qv*), and *d* 24 Aug 1896, having had, with other issue:

1 WILLIAM ASHLEY WEBB PONSONBY, **3rd Baron de Mauley of Canford**, Lt Rifle Bde; *b* 2 March 1843; *d* unm 13 April 1918

2 MAURICE JOHN GEORGE, **4th Baron**

3 Frederick John William, DL Oxon; *b* 28 Aug 1847; *m* 1 Feb 1877 Margaret Fanny (*d* 1919), 2nd dau of Frederick John Howard, of Compton Place, Eastbourne (*see* CARLISLE, E), and *d* 25 Aug 1933, leaving issue:

(1) Mary Fanny Louisa; *b* 21 April 1879; *d* unm 1 June 1955

(2) Evelyn Margaret; *b* 24 Oct 1887; *d* unm 4 April 1969

4 Edwin Charles William, DL, JP, Oxon; *b* 13 Oct 1851; *m* 1st 10 Dec 1878 Emily Dora (*d* 3 Oct 1897), dau of Octavius Edward Coope, DL, JP, MP, and had issue:

(1) Sir CHARLES EDWARD PONSONBY, 1st Bt, so *cr* 1956 (*qv*)

(2) Maurice George (Rev Canon), MC, Rector Much Hadham, Herts, 1930–43, and St Mary's Pro-Cathedral Johannesburg 1919–24, Dean Johannesburg 1923–24, Hon Canon St Albans 1924, Chaplain to Archbp York 1914, Hon CF WW I (despatches); *b* 10 Sept 1880; *educ* Eton and Trin Coll Oxford (MA); *m* 23 Sept 1918 Lady Phyllis Sydney Buxton, OBE (*d* 27 Jan 1942), est dau of 1st Earl Buxton, GCMG (*see* BUXTON, Bt), and *d* 27 Feb 1943, having had issue:

1a John Ashley, Lt Coldstream Gds WW II; *b* 21 Aug 1920; *ka* Dec 1942

1a Constance Mary Louis; *b* 6 July 1919; *d* 7 June 1932

2a *Elizabeth [Mrs John Clay, Newtimber Place, Hassocks, Sussex]; *b* 30 April 1922; *m* 30 Aug 1952 *His Honour John Lionel Clay, TD, MA, Circuit Judge, and has issue:

1b *Andrew John Buxton; *b* 29 Nov 1962

1b *Fiona Elizabeth; *b* 4 Jan 1954; *m* 1982 *Rev John Alexander Taylor

2b *Catriona Mary; *b* 23 April 1955; *m* 1983 *John Kendall Bush

3b *Joanna Penelope; *b* 7 Jan 1958

3a Barbara Doreen; *b* 4 Nov 1924; *d* unm 16 Dec 1959

4a *Mary Veronica [Mrs William Barnes, 21 Rona Rd, London NW3 2HY]; *b* 15 April 1927; *m* 27 May 1961 *William Peter Ward Barnes, yr son of Rt Rev Ernest William Barnes, ScD, DD, LLD, FRS, Bp Birmingham, and has issue:

1b *Peter Denis Ponsonby; *b* 15 April 1962

2b *Thomas William Ponsonby; *b* 18 Dec 1965

1b *Susanna Barbara [Mrs Ian Hardy, 25 Farringford Close, Chiswell Green, Herts]; *b* 18 Aug 1963; *m* 1987 *Ian Hardy, and has issue:

1c *James William Barnes; *b* 1992

1c *Christina Louise; *b* 1990

(3) Ashley William Neville, Capt Oxon and Bucks LI, ADC to Govr Natal 1907 and Mil Sec to Govr-Gen S Africa 1914; *b* 1 March 1882; *ka* 8 Sept 1915

(4) Victor Coope, MC, Capt Herts Yeo WW I; *b* 21 June 1887; *educ* Eton; *m* 1 Feb 1923 Gladys Edith (*d* 15 Oct 1964), er dau of Godfrey Walter, of Malshanger, Basingstoke, and *d* 22 April 1966, leaving issue:

1a +Myles Walter, CBE (1966); *b* 12 Sept 1924; *educ* Eton; Capt KRRC WW II 1943–45 (wounded), FCO: Consul-Gen Hanoi 1964–65, Amb Mongolia 1974–77; *m* 20 May 1950 *Ann Veronica Theresa, dau of Brig Francis Herbert Maynard, CB, DSO, MC, and has issue:

1b +John Maurice Maynard; *b* 8 Aug 1955; S/Ldr RAF; *m* 1980 *Marie Jose (Cé) Antoinette, est dau of W M Van Huizen-Husselson, of Knoll House, Kilmersdon, nr Radstock, Bath, and has issue:

1c +Luke Myles William; *b* 1986

1c *Charlotte Emma; *b* 1982

2c *Francesca Sarah (twin); *b* 1986

1b *Belinda Mary [Mrs Edward Mitchell, 28 Lancaster Grove, London NW3]; *b* 5 May 1951; *m* 1973 *Edward John Mitchell and has issue:

1c *Jonathan Myles; *b* 20 Sept 1976

2c *Charles Edward; *b* 1978

2b *Emma Christina; *b* 29 Oct 1959; *m* 1981 *Capt Bryn St Pierre Parry, RGJ, er son of Lt-Col R G R Parry, MC, and has issue:

1c *Thomas Robin St Pierre; *b* 1985

1c *Sophie Laura; *b* 1983

2c *Louisa Mary; *b* 1987

1a *Sheila Mary [Mrs Giles Cartwright, Bathurst Cottage, Teffont Magna, Salisbury, Wilts SP3 5QP]; *b* 25 Sept 1927; *m* 1st 9 Aug 1952 Cdr Michael Edward St Quintin Wall, RN (*see* PEEL, E), er son of Capt Richard Bernard St Quintin Wall, of Burpham House, nr Arundel, Sussex, and has issue:

1b *Hugo St Quintin; *b* 18 Feb 1954

1b *Sarah Fenella; *b* 4 June 1955; *m* 1981 *Michael Hugh Warwick Bampfylde, and has issue (*see* POLTIMORE, B)

1a (cont.) Mrs Wall *m* 2nd 1976 Giles Aubrey Cartwright (*d* 1988) (*see* BUXTON, Bt)

(1) Diana Helen, JP; *b* 2 Sept 1891; *m* 14 Sept 1917 Lt-Col Henry Thomas Birch-Reynardson, CMG, Oxon and Bucks LI, son of William John Birch-Reynardson, of Adwell House, Tetsworth, Oxon, and *d* 26 Nov 1962, leaving issue (*see* POWERSCOURT, V)

4 (cont.) The Hon Edwin Ponsonby *m* 2nd 17 Feb 1906 Hilda Marion (*d* 15 Oct 1943), 4th dau of Robert Smith, of Goldings, Hertford, and *d* 15 Oct 1939

1 Emily Priscilla Maria; *m* 2 June 1870 Rev Charles William Norman Ogilvy (*d* 7 June 1903), MA, Vicar Oswestry, and *d* 12 May 1926, leaving issue (*see* OGILVY, Bt)

2 Helen Geraldine; *m* 25 July 1877 19th Earl of Morton (*qv*), and *d* 5 Jan 1949, leaving issue

The 3rd BARON's brother,

MAURICE JOHN GEORGE PONSONBY, **4th Baron de Mauley of Canford**; *b* 7 Aug 1846; *educ* Ch Ch Oxford (MA); Vicar Wantage 1903–18, Hon Canon Bristol 1890–1918; *m* 29 Dec 1875 Hon Madeleine Hanbury-Tracy (*d* 28 Jan 1938), yst dau of 2nd Baron Sudeley (*qv*), and *d* 15 March 1945, having had issue:

1 Gerald Maurice, Capt Roy Inniskilling Fus Boer War 1902, WW I (despatches); *b* 16 Oct 1876; *d* of wounds recd in action 31 Aug 1914

2 HUBERT WILLIAM PONSONBY, **5th Baron de Mauley of Canford**, JP (Oxon 1924); *b* 21 July 1878; Capt 2/1st Glos Yeo WW I, Legn Honour, Croix de Guerre; *m* 11 Oct 1920 Elgiva Margaret (*d* 1987), dau of Hon Cospatrick Thomas Dundas (*see* ZETLAND, M), and *d* 13 Sept 1962, leaving issue:

1 GERALD JOHN PONSONBY, **6th and present Baron de Mauley of Canford**

2 +THOMAS MAURICE, TD, JP (Oxon 1958), DL (Glos 1972) [Lt-Col The Hon Thomas Ponsonby TD JP DL, The Common, Little Faringdon, Lechlade, Glos]; *b* 2 Aug 1930; heir presumptive; *educ* Eton and RAC Cirencester; 2nd Lt 11th Hus 1950–51, Lt-Col Wessex Yeo, Brevet Col TA, High Sheriff Glos 1978; *m* 12 July 1956 *Maxine Henrietta, yr dau of William Dudley Keith Thellusson, of 39 Draycott Place, London SW3, and has:

(1) +Rupert Charles; *b* 30 June 1957; *educ* Eton

(2) +(Ashley) George; *b* 17 Nov 1959 *educ* Eton

1 *June Mary [The Rt Hon The Lady Grimston of Westbury, The Old Rectory, Westwell, Burford, Oxon]; *b* 9 March 1924; *m* 21 June 1949 *2nd Baron Grimston of Westbury (*qv*) and has issue

2 (Elizabeth) Winifred; *b* 4 Jan 1928; *m* 19 Jan 1950 *Christopher Boot Holman [Christopher Holman Esq, Northfield Farm, Evenlode, Moreton-in-Marsh GL56 0YT], yr son of Alexander McArthur Holman, of Hyes, Rudgwick, Sussex, and *d* 8 Oct 1982, leaving:

(1) *Sarah Charlotte; *b* 9 July 1951

(2) *Serena Jane; *b* 30 June 1952

(3) *Alice Elgiva Marie Gabrielle; *b* 28 July 1956

(4) *Catherine Rose; *b* 22 Feb 1963

DE MONTMORENCY

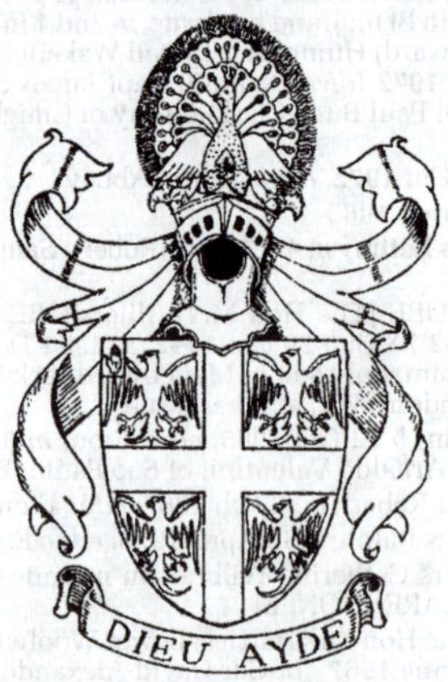

Arms: Or a cross gules, between four eaglets displayed azure. **Crest:** A peacock in its pride proper. **Motto:** *Dieu ayde*. ('May God help'). **Creation:** Bt. (I) 28 March 1631.

SIR ARNOLD GEOFFROY DE MONTMORENCY, 19TH BT, of Knockagh, Co Tipperary; *b* 27 July 1908; *educ* Westminster and Peterhouse Cambridge (BA 1930, LLB 1931, MA 1934); *s* cousin 1979; barrister Middle Temple 1932, Maj RASC and Staff WW II; *m* 20 April 1949 (*annulled* 1953 and re *m* 29 Sept 1972) Nettie Hay, only dau of William Anderson

Lineage: REDMOND MORRES, of Knockagh, Co Tipperary; *m* Elinor Cantwell, of Lahagres, Co Tipperary, and *d* 31 Aug 1624, leaving:

Sir John Morres, 1st Bt (I), so *cr* 28 March 1631; *b c* 1573; *m* by 1601 Katharine, dau of Sir Edmond Walsh, of Owney Abbey, also known as Abington, Co Limerick, and Grange, Co Kilkenny, and *d* on or after 29 Jan 1647/8, leaving an er s:

Sir Redmond Morres, 2nd Bt, of Knockagh; *b c* 1595; *m c* 1620 Ellice, dau of Garret Wall, of Coolnamucky Castle, Co Waterford, and *d* by 1656, having had issue:

1 **Sir John Morres, 3rd Bt**; *b* 29 Aug 1620; poet; *m c* 1665 Ellin Butler (*d* 27 May 1721), dau of 3rd Baron Caher, and *d* 26 Oct 1720, having had issue:

(1) Redmond, Col French Army; *m* Mary Tracy and *dvp* 1704, having had issue:

1a **Sir John Morres, 4th Bt**; *m c* 1717 Margaret, dau of Edmund O'Shee, of Cloran, Co Tipperary, and *d* on or after 4 Feb 1723, having had issue:

1b **Sir Redmond Morres, 5th Bt**; *b c* 1717; *d* unm 11 Oct 1740, having willed his entire property to his cousin Hervey Morres, 1st Viscount Mountmorres of Castle Morres, after falling out with his unc, later the 6th Bt

2b Edmund, living 25 Nov 1725; *d* unm before 1740

2a **Sir Simon Morres, 6th Bt**; *m* Jane, dau of Rev — Gregory, and *d* after 5 July 1747, having had an only s:

1b **Sir George Morres, 7th Bt**, of Maine, Co Louth; *m* — (*d* 24 April 1758) and *dsp* 26 April 1758 (two days later)

(2) Nicholas, of Seafield, Co Dublin; *b* 1676; *m* Susanna, dau of Richard Talbot, of Malahide, and *d* 23 March 1742, having had issue:

1a John; *d* unm *dvp* by 1744

2a Nicholas, Brig-Gen French Army, Kt of St Louis; *m* — Fraser but *dsp* 1745

3a **Sir Richard Morres, 8th Bt**, Col French Army; *d* unm 1774, *k* by a scaffold falling at the coronation of LOUIS XVI

(3) James, of Rosetown, Co Tipperary; *m* Anne, dau of Edward Morres, and *d* 1718, having had issue:

1a John; *d* unm

2a **Sir Nicholas Morres, 9th Bt**, Col French Army, Kt of St Louis; *b c* 1710; *m* Isabel, est dau of Donald Cameron of Lochiel, 19th Chief of Clan Cameron, and *dsp* 1795

2 Hervey, of Castle Morres, Co Kilkenny; *b c* 1633; Capt of Horse in CROMWELL's Regt in Ireland, MP (I Parl) Knocktopher, Co Kilkenny; *m* as his 3rd w Frances, 3rd dau of Pierce Butler, of Barrowmount, and sis of Edward, 2nd Viscount of Galmoye (*see* ORMONDE, M), and *d* 1722/3; his only surv s:

(1) Francis, of Castle Morres; *m* Catharine, dau and heiress of Sir William Evans, Bt, of Kilkreene, Co Kilkenny, by Jane, gdau of 1st Earl of Mountrath (*see* COOTE, Bt), and had:

1a HERVEY MORRES, 1st VISCOUNT MOUNTMORRES OF CASTLEMORRES, so *cr* 29 June 1763, as also earlier 4 May 1756 BARON MOUNTMORRES OF CASTLEMORRES (both I); *b c* 1706; *educ* Trin Coll Dublin; MP Irishtown (*alias* Canice) 1734–56, Mayor Kilkenny 1752–53; *m* 1st 3 Nov 1742 Letitia (*d* 9 Feb 1754), 4th dau of 1st Earl of Bessborough (*qv*), and had issue:

1b **Sir Hervey Redmond Morres, 10th Bt**, as which s cousin 1795, and 2nd VISCOUNT MOUNTMORRES OF CASTLEMORRES; *b c* 1743; blew his brains out 17 or 18 Aug 1797, leaving his entire property to his sisters and cutting his half-bro and successor in the titles from his will

1b Letitia; *m* 1st 27 Feb 1762 Hon Arthur Hill Trevor (*dsp* 19 June 1770), MP, only son of 1st Viscount Dungannon (*see* TREVOR, B), and had issue; *m* 2nd 3 July 1774 6th Marquess of Antrim (*see* ANTRIM, E), and *d* 7 Dec 1801

2b Sarah; *m* 1770 Rev Joseph Pratt, of Cabra Castle, Co Cavan, and had issue (*see* PIERS, Bt)

1a (cont.) The 1st VISCOUNT *m* 2nd July 1755 Mary (*d* Sept 1779), dau of William Wall, of Coolnamuckty Castle, Co Waterford, and widow of John Baldwin, of Curralanty, King's Co, and *d* 6 April 1766, having by her had:

2b Sir FRANCIS HERVEY MORRES later De MONTMORENCY (roy licence 17 June 1815, in the genuine but mistaken belief that his family descended from the distinguished medieval French family of that name), **11th Bt**, and 3rd VISCOUNT MOUNTMORRES OF CASTLEMORRES; *b* 31 Aug 1756; *educ* Trin Coll Dublin; *m* 4 April 1794 Anne (*d* 21 July 1823), dau of Joseph Reade, of Castle Hoyle, and Mount Pleasant, Co Kilkenny, and *d* 23 March 1833, having had, with three daus:

1c **Rev Sir Hervey de Montmorency, 12th Bt**, and 4th VISCOUNT MOUNTMORRES OF CASTLEMORRES; *b* 20 Aug 1796; Dean Cloyne 1845–50 and Achonry 1850–72, Chaplain to Ld Lt Ireland 1853; *m* 5 July 1831 Sarah (*d* 22 Feb 1877), dau of William Shaw, of Temple Mills, Co Kildare, and *d* 23 Jan 1872, leaving:

1d **Sir William Browne de Montmorency, 13th Bt**, and 5th VISCOUNT MOUNTMORRES OF CASTLEMORRES; *b* 21 April 1832; *m* 12 Nov 1862 Harriet (*d* 20 Feb 1923), 2nd dau of George Broadrick, of Hamphall Stubbs, Yorks, and gdau of Sir Richard Fletcher, 1st Bt, of Carrow, and was murdered at Rusheen, nr Clonbur, Co Galway, 25 Sept 1880 during the Land War, leaving issue:

1e Hervey Raymond; *b* 26 March, *d* 2 June 1865

2e **Rev Sir William Geoffrey Bouchard de Montmorency, 14th Bt**, and 6th VISCOUNT MOUNTMORRES OF CASTLEMORRES; *b* 23 Sept 1872; *educ* Radley, Paris U and Balliol Coll Oxford; Lt RNVR, Dir Tropical Inst Liverpool U 1904–08, Deacon 1913, Priest 1914, Vicar Swinton Lancs 1917–25 and St Mark's S Farnborough 1925–33, Rector St Paul's, Wokingham, 1935, Chaplain RNVR; *m* 1st 27 Sept 1893 Bessie Louise Cameron (*d* 15 Oct 1931), 4th dau of Sampson Taylor Rowe, of Trecarrel, Redruth, and had issue:

1e Marjorie Evelyn Louise; *b* 15 Oct 1897; *m* 24 Oct 1918 Sir Roger Braddyll Hulton, 3rd Bt (*d* 23 April 1956; *see* 1970 edn), and had issue

2e (cont.) **Sir William** *m* 2nd 10 April 1934 Tempe Irene (*d* 14 March 1937), only dau of Charles Frederick Cross, of The Hermitage, Totland Bay, IoW, and *dspm* 2 Dec 1936

3e Arthur Alberic, midshipman RN; *b* 25 Oct 1874; drowned 15 July 1891

1e Victoria; *d* unm 21 April 1953

2e Harriet Evelyn; *d* unm 11 Feb 1942

2d Francis Raymond, barrister; *b* 6 May 1835; *m* 1 June 1865 Elizabeth Hester (*d* 1 Nov 1903), yst dau of Lt-Col John Echlin Mathews, of White Abbey, Co Antrim, and *dsp* 27 Sept 1910

3d Albert Bouchard, Col RA; *b* 18 March 1840; *d* unm 19 May 1899

4d Arthur Hill Trevor, BA Dublin, MD, LRCSI; *b* 19 Feb 1846; *m* 28 March 1878 Caroline (*d* July 1937), yr dau of Rev George Kemmis, of St Helen's, Blackrock, Dublin, and *d* 1 Jan 1910, leaving issue:

1e **Rev Sir Arthur Hervé Alberic Bouchard de Montmorency, 15th Bt**, and 7th and last VISCOUNT MOUNTMORRES OF CASTLEMORRES; *b* 6 Feb 1879; *educ* Trin Coll Dublin (BA 1907, MA 1912); Rector Omeath, Co Louth, 1914–22, St Modoc's, Doune, Perthshire 1922–39 and Lasham, Vicar Herriard, Hants, 1939–48, memb Alton RDC 1939–43, served South African War (medal with two clasps) and as CF WW I, Hon CF 1916–51; *m* 15 April 1914 Katharine Sophia Clay, 2nd dau of Thomas Alexander Warrand, of Lentran, Bridge of Allan, Scotland, and *d* 15 Oct 1951, when his peerages expired, leaving issue:

1f *Sheila Marguerite Evelyn; CD WW II; *m* 9 Dec 1950 *Robert Vernon Smith, only son of W Smith, of Nailsea, Bristol, and has issue:

1g *Alastair Vernon Bouchard de Montmorency; *b* 19 Dec 1951

2g *Robert Hervé William de Montmorency; *b* 11 Aug 1953

2f *Carole Madge Warrand, MCSP, WAAF WW II; *m* 6 Dec 1947 *Douglas Osmond Morris, er son of W O Morris, of Beacon Lodge, Exmouth, Devon, and has issue:

1g *Andrew John; *b* 21 Feb 1957

2g *Diana Pauline; *b* 4 June 1954

1e Caroline Lucia Marguerite; *d* unm 24 Feb 1942

2e Alix Bertrude Ruby Wilhelmina; served WW I 1914–15

3e Anna Victoria Stephanotis Kemmis

1d Victoria; *m* 16 July 1878 Evory Carmichael (*d* 1890), of Eaton Square, Monkstown, Dublin, and *d* 10 July 1893 aged 56

2d Sarah Anna, *m* 7 Oct 1868 Richard D Pennefather (*d* 7 Sept 1881), DL, of Kilbracken, Co Leitrim, and *d* 22 June 1912 leaving issue

3b William Mary; *b* 1760; *m* Anne Clarke and was drowned in 1809, leaving a dau

2a Sir WILLIAM EVANS MORRES, 1st Bt (I), so *cr* 24 April 1758; MP (I Parl) Kilkenny 1752–68 and Newtown 1768–74; *m* 1st 2 June 1737 Margaret (*d* 22 Aug 1753), dau of Josias Haydock, of Beaulick, and had:

1b Sir HEYDOCK EVANS MORRES, 2nd Bt; MP Kilkenny 1769–76; *m* 23 July 1772 Frances Gorges (*m* 2nd 10 Feb 1778 William Gorr, of Woodford, Co Leitrim), dau and heiress of Ralph Gore, of Barrowmount, and *dsp* Dec 1776

1b Mary; *m* Clayton Bayley, of Gowran

2 (cont.) Sir WILLIAM *m* 2nd 1 July 1755 Mary Juliana (*d* 1812), dau and coheir of William Ryves, of Upperwood, and *d* 11 Oct 1774, having by her had issue:

(2) Sir WILLIAM EVANS RYVES MORRES later De MONTMORENCY (roy licence 17 June 1815), 3rd and last Bt, MP Newtown 1785–90; *b* 7 Nov 1763; *d* unm 14 April 1829, when the btcy expired

3 Redmond/Reymond, Barrister, MP Thomastown 1755–60, Newtown 1761–68 and Dublin 1773–76; *m* 27 March 1740 Elizabeth, only dau and heiress of Francis Lodge, of Dublin, and *d* Aug 1784, having had with three daus, issue:

(1) LODGE EVANS MORRES later De MONTMORENCY (roy licence 17 June 1815), 1st VISCOUNT FRANKFORT DE MONTMORENCY (I), so *cr* 22 Jan 1816, as also earlier 31 July 1800 BARON FRANKFORT OF GALMOYE, Co Kilkenny (both I), PC (I 1796), MP Innistioge 1768–70, Bandon Bridge 1776–96, Ennis 1796–7 and Dingle 1798–1800, Ch Sec to Ld Lt 1795–1800, a Ld Treasury I 1796–1806; *b* 26 Jan 1747; *m* 1 Jan 1777 Mary (*dsp* 7 Feb 1787), dau and heiress of Joseph Fade, of Dublin; *m* 2nd 6 Aug 1804 Catharine (*d* 12 Nov 1851), dau of George White, of Castle Bellingham, Co Louth, and *d* 21 Sept 1822, having by her had issue:

1a LODGE RAYMOND De MONTMORENCY, 2nd VISCOUNT FRANKFORT DE MONTMORENCY, Lt 10th Hus; *b* 26 Nov 1806; *m* 12 Jan 1835 Georgiana Frederica (*d* 16 April 1885), dau of Peter FitzGibbon Henchy, QC, LLD, and *d* 25 Dec 1889, having had:

1b RAYMOND HERVEY De MONTMORENCY, 3rd VISCOUNT FRANKFORT DE MONTMORENCY, KCB (1898); *b* 21 Sept 1835; *educ* Eton; Maj-Gen 1889, Hon Col 4th London Rifles, rep I peer 1900–02; *m* 25 April 1866 Rachel Mary Lumley Godolphin (*d* 10 March 1936), dau of FM Sir John Michel, PC, GCB, JP, of Dewlish House, Dorset, and *d* 7 May 1902, having had issue:

1c Reymond Hervey Lodge Joseph, VC, Capt 21st Lancers Sudan 1898 (despatches); *b* 5 Feb 1867; *kas vp* S Africa 23 Feb 1900

2c WILLOUGHBY JOHN HORACE De MONTMORENCY, 4th and last VISCOUNT FRANKFORT DE MONTMORENCY, Capt DCLI, served Burma 1891–92, Tirah 1897–98 and Nile Expdn 1899; *b* 3 May 1868; *m* 1 Feb 1916 Mrs Mabel Augusta Pearson (*d* 13 Dec 1946), yst dau of C L Throckmorton, and *dsp* 5 July 1917, when his titles expired

1c Caroline Blanche Fane; *b* 6 April 1871; *d* 18 Oct 1892

2c Kathleen Louisa Michel, served WW I, Order of Leopold with bar; *b* 21 Sept 1873; *d* 4 Oct 1927

3c (Lily) Rachel Mary, served WW I (two medals), had Order of Leopold and Medaille de la Reine Elisabeth of Belgium and Reconnaissance Française; *b* 13 April 1875; *d* unm 15 April 1967

1b Caroline Georgina; *d* young, 30 April 1844

1a Catherine Penelope; *m* 11 April 1822 Very Rev Hon Henry Montagu Browne (*d* 24 Nov 1884), Dean of Lismore, and *d* 24 June 1858, leaving issue (*see* KILMAINE, B)

2a Emilia Elinor; *m* Oct 1826 Richard Wordsworth Cooper (*d* March 1850), and had issue

3a Mary Elizabeth; *m* April 1833 Joseph Ormsby Radcliff (*d* 18 Oct 1862), QC, LLD, and *d* 10 June 1838

(2) Redmond/Reymond (Rev); *m* 21 May 1774 Mary Eyre (*d* 1798), only dau and heiress of Edward D'Alton, of Deer Park, Co Clare, and *d* 1794, having had issue:

1a Reymond Hervey MORRES later De MONTMORENCY (roy licence 1815), MP Dingle, Lt-Col 9th Light Dragoons, vol 13th Light Dragoons Peninsular War (POW 1811 in advance to Badajoz); *m* Laetitia (*d* 1822), dau of Rev Narcissus Charles Proby, of Boughton, Cheshire, and *d* 4 Oct 1827, having had issue:

1b Hervey Francis, Capt Madras Cav; *b* 20 July 1802; *m* 7 Sept 1832 Dorothea Anne, dau of Edward FitzGerald, of Carigoran, and widow of Robert Leigh, of Rosegarland, and *d* 8 Aug 1883, having had, with a dau (*d* unm):

1c William Bouchard, Lt 8th Regt; *b* 1 May 1834; *dsp* 30 Sept 1878

2c Charles Anne Law, Lt-Col RE; *b* 17 March 1835; *m* 19 May 1861 Elise Christine (*d* 13 Jan 1901), dau of James Motz, of Quebec, Canada, and *d* 26 Aug 1882, leaving issue

1d Hervey Guy Francis Edward, DSO (1917), Maj RFA, Lt RA, served in S African War 1900 (medal and three clasps) and WW I 1914 (despatches, Croix de Guerre with palm and two stars, Legion of Honour); *b* 5 Nov 1868; *m* 12 Nov 1907 Evelyn (*d* 11 May 1973 aged 96), dau of Rev Alexander Buchanan, MA of The Old Rectory, Finchampstead, and *dsp* 2 Sept 1942

1d Geraldine Dora; *d* unm 23 Feb 1926

2b Reymond Henry, Maj 65th Bengal NI; *b* 26 Aug 1808; *m* 8 Oct 1830 Anna Matilda (*d* 14 Jan 1895), dau of Henry Revell, and *d* 10 May 1847, having had issue:

1c Reymond Hervey, Maj BSC; *b* 19 Sept 1835; *m* 1st 24 May 1863 Eliza (*dsp* 23 Dec 1868), dau of Teignmouth Sandys, BCS; *m* 2nd 27 Aug 1870 Marion Ellen (*d* 8 Jan 1923), dau of George Coles, and *d* 15 July 1880, leaving issue:

1d Reymond Hervey; assist master Eton; *b* 6 Oct 1871; *educ* Keble Coll Oxford (MA); *m* 26 April 1905 Gwynedd Maud (*d* 24 April 1936), only dau of Lt-Col George T Thomas, IMS, MRCS (Eng), LRCP Lond, DPH, and *d* 19 Dec 1938, leaving issue:

1e Reymond Hervey, F/O RAF WW II; *b* 11 June 1916; *kas* May 1940

1e Kathleen; *b* 10 Feb 1906; *m* 1st 19 Dec 1929 (*divorce* 1935) Robert Hugh Swan Corbett; *m* 2nd 1935 Ralph R Prest, and *d* June 1959, leaving issue

2e *Anne Marion [Mrs Ernest Swanton, Delf House, Sandwich, Kent]; *b* 2 July 1911; *m* 1st 6 Feb 1935 George Henry Carbutt (*d* 1956), and has issue:

1f *Francis (Billy) [Francis Carbutt Esq, The White House, Langham, Colchester, Essex]; *b* 1936; *m* 1958 *Sally Fenella, dau of James Cole Harris, and has issue:

1g *George Henry de Montmorency [George Carbutt Esq, The Old Rectory, Salcott, Maldon, Essex]; *b* 1963; *m* 1991 *Camilla Lucy, dau of Hon Mr Justice (Sir Peter Edlin) Webster, of Bratton, Wilts, and has issue:

1h *Jack Francis; *b* 1994

1h *Rosanna Madeleine; *b* 1996

1g *Emma Louise; *b* 1961; *m* 1987 *Alexander Harold Swinton, son of Maj-Gen Sir John Swinton, KCVO, OBE, DL, of Kimmerghame, Duns, Berwickshire

2f *Edward Reymond [Edward Carbutt Esq, Mount Hall, Gt Horkesley, Colchester, Essex CO6 4BZ]; *b* 1940; *m* 1966 *Susan Elizabeth, twin dau of Robert Peter Healing (*see* PETRE, B), and has issue:

1g *James Michael Edward; *b* 1972

1g *Laura Frances Victoria; *b* 1981

2e (cont.) Mrs George Carbutt *m* 2nd 11 Feb 1958 Ernest William (Jim) Swanton, cricket correspondent *Daily Telegraph*, author, s of William Swanton, of Upper Welland, Worcs

1d Lily Margaret

1c Emily Frances; *d* unm 14 May 1909

2c Anna Matilda; *m* 24 Oct 1868 Gen Sir James Abbott, KCB (*d* 1896), and *d* 17 May 1870, leaving issue

2a Edward D'Alton, Lt RN; *b* 3 Feb 1782; *m* 7 April 1802 Mary Anne (*d* 23 Jan 1848), only child of John Peat, and *d* 28 Nov 1843, leaving issue:

1b William Reymond; *b* 21 May 1818; *m* 1st 13 March 1843 Mary (*d* 29 May 1865), only dau of John James Bristow, of Great Coram Street, London, and had issue:

1c Elizabeth Frances; *d* 18 June 1846

2c Mary Georgina Caroline; *m* 18 June 1863 Reuben James Browning, and had issue

1b (cont.) William Morres *m* 2nd 7 March 1866 Amelia, dau of W Logan, and *d* 4 Nov 1889, having by her had issue:

1c William Geoffrey; *b* 22 Jan 1867; *d* unm 8 March 1894

2c Edward D'Alton; *b* 1 May 1870; *m* 4 Aug 1894 Jane (*d* 23 Aug 1895), dau of Alexander Cumming, and *d* 28 Feb 1942, leaving issue:

1d Florence Eleanor; *b* 30 April 1895

3c Mabel Elizabeth Amelia; *b* 19 March 1873; *d* unm 14 Feb 1946

2b James Lodge; *b* 5 May 1821; *m* 9 Oct 1849 Susan (*d* 28 March 1913), only dau of John Kiddell, HEICS, and *d* 22 Nov 1886, having had issue:

1c Hervey Lodge; *b* 15 July 1854; *m* 2 June 1886 Elizabeth Nicolls (*d* 6 Sept 1937), dau of Capt Archibald Douglas William Fletcher, RN, and was drowned 30 March 1899, leaving issue:

1d **Sir (Hervey) Angus de Montmorency, 16th Bt**, OBE (1918); *b* 27 Sept 1888; *educ* Winchester and BNC Coll Oxford; with Min of Health 1919–44, Sec UGC 1944–51; *m* 20 Aug 1918 Eleanor Katharine, dau of Rev Edward Richard Heffreys Nicolls, rector Saxelby, Leics, and *dsp* 14 Oct 1959

2d **Sir Miles Fletcher de Montmorency, 17th Bt**; *b* 3 March 1893; *educ* Dover Coll; Lt (A/Capt) Kent Cyclist Bn (TF), artist (painter), memb Royal Soc of British Artists 1935, Hon Librarian 1947, painted portraits for National War Records 1940–41, author: *A Short History of Painting in England* (1943); *m* 5 Aug 1931 Rachel Marion (*d* 15 Nov 1961), yr dau of Rev Charles Coverdale Tancock, DD, of Winchester, Headmaster of Rossall and Tonbridge, and *dsp* 22 Dec 1963

2c John Kiddell; *b* 24 Feb 1860; *m* 5 Dec 1889 Ada Kate Margaret Ligonier (*d* 14 Jan 1929), 3rd dau of Capt George Macintosh Balfour, RN, and *d* 21 Aug 1916, leaving issue:

1d John Hervey Balfour, Admin Offr S Nigeria, Capt 18th Bn London Regt; *b* 30 July 1890; *m* 18 June 1925 Estelle (Stella) Georgiana (*d* 4 Dec 1977), er dau of George Gammon Adams, sculptor, of Chelsea and Acton, and *dsp* 29 May 1947

2d Reymond Ligonier; *b* 22 Jan 1892; *ka* WW I 3 Oct 1916

3d **Sir Reginald D'Alton Lodge de Montmorency, 18th Bt**; *b* 13 March 1899; HAC and RHA WW I, manager in Bombay of Bell, Russ and Co (E India Merchants) 1925–33, on staff *The Times* 1936–67; *m* 11 Aug 1928 Dorothy Victoria, 2nd dau of Gilbert Walter Robinson, and *dsp* 1979

1d Kathleen Letitia; *b* 6 Nov 1894; *m* 1 Nov 1924 Paul George Shore Phillipps-Treby, yst son of Maj-Gen Paul Winsloe Phillipps-Treby

3c James Edward Geoffrey, MA, LLB Cambridge; barrister, Quain Prof Comparative Law London U 1920–32; *b* 6 Dec 1866; *m* 15 Aug 1899 Caroline Maud Saumarez (*d* 17 Dec 1973, aged 100), 3rd dau of Maj-Gen James de Havilland, RA, and *d* 9 March 1934, having had:

1d Geoffrey James Brooke; *b* 9 June 1905; *d* 3 Sept 1906

2d Sir ARNOLD GEOFFROY De MONTMORENCY, **19th and present Bt**

1d Geraldine Susan Maud, FLA, Unesco Travelling Fellowship 1952; *b* 20 July 1900; *m* 29 Jan 1957 Sir (William) Hawthorne Lewis, KCSI, KCIE (*d* 19 Oct 1970), son of Thomas Crompton Lewis, Dir Public Instruction, UP, India

2d Eleanor Evelyn Saumarez; *b* 8 May 1903; *d* unm 7 Sept 1941

4c George Reymond; *b* 21 Feb 1870; *dsp* 22 Feb 1899

1c Eleanor Eyre; *d* unm 28 Nov 1916

2c Susan; *d* unm 27 May 1941

3c Bertha; *d* 4 June 1962

4c Ada D'Alton; *m* 18 Oct 1881 Septimus Croft (*d* 25 Feb 1928), of St Margaret's Bury, Herts, and *d* 7 Dec 1937, leaving issue

5c Constance Helen; *m* 3 June 1890 Walter William Hewitt (*d* 1910), Capt Fife Art Militia, and *d* 23 March 1952, having had issue

1b Jane Frances; *m* 1st 1829 Henry Hodder, RN; *m* 2nd 1 Jan 1839 W H Bessy

2b Elizabeth Holden; *m* Feb 1838 John Taylor Bracey, and *d* 13 Dec 1882, leaving issue

3b Adelaide Antoninette; *m* 1st 1834 John Brabazon Madden; *m* 2nd 24 June 1846 Rev Charles Dowson, and had issue

1a Elizabeth Dorothea; *m* Maj Edward Molesworth (*d* 14 June 1842), and *d* 8 Oct 1812, leaving issue (*see* MOLESWORTH, V)

DENBIGH and DESMOND

Arms: Arg. on a fess az. three lozenges or. **Crest:** A nuthatch with a hazel branch, fructed, all ppr. **Supporters:** Two bucks ppr., attired and unguled or. **Motto:** *Virtutis praemium honor* ('Honour is the reward of virtue'). **Creations:** E. (Denbigh) (E) 14 Sept 1622 and (Desmond) (I) 22 Nov 1622, V (Feilding) (E) 30 Dec 1620 and (Callan) (I) 22 Nov 1622, B (of Newnham Paddockes) (E) 30 Dec 1620, (Feilding of Lecagh) (I) 22 Nov 1622 and (St Liz) (E.) 2 Feb 1664/5.

THE 12TH EARL OF DENBIGH and **11TH EARL OF DESMOND, Viscount Feilding, Viscount Callan, Baron of Newnham Paddockes**, Co Warwick, **Baron Feilding of Lecagh**, Co Tipperary, and **Baron St Liz** (Alexander Stephen Rudolph Feilding) [The Rt Hon The Earl of Denbigh and Desmond, Newnham Paddox, Monks Kirby, Rugby CV23 0RX]; *b* 4 Nov 1970; *s* f 1995; *m* 27 Jan 1996 *Suzanne Jane, yr dau of Gregory R Allen, of Brixham, Devon

Earlier creations: Robert Dudley, the favourite of ELIZABETH I who is better known as Earl of Leicester, was the day before having the latter title conferred on him *cr* Baron of Denbigh. A Barony of Callan was briefly held by a member of the Agar family, Earls of Normanton (*qv*), between 1790 and 1815.

The Earldom of Desmond has a longer (and more distinguished) history as a separate entity. It was in 1329 conferred on Maurice Fitz Thomas (*see* FITZGERALD, Bt, of Valencia), descended from a certain Thomas Fitz Anthony, Seneschal of Leinster *temp* KING JOHN and presumably a Norman or hanger-on of the Normans who pushed into Ireland from S Wales in the 12th century. These Earls of Desmond later took the surname FitzGerald, intermarried with the old Irish nobility and like so many of the Normans 'went native'. The last Earl of Desmond of the 1329 creation was a constant thorn in the side of ELIZABETH I in her attempts to control Ireland and was eventually in 1583 attainted and killed while on the run in Co Kerry from the Elizabethan forces.

The title was revived for his son, who died unmarried, assumed illicitly by the said son's half-brother and his descendants till the early 1630s and conferred in 1619 on Lord Dingwall (*see* LUCAS OF CRUDWELL and DINGWALL, B) through the influence of the Duke of Buckingham (*see* below and JERSEY, E) in the expectation that Dingwall/Desmond's dau would marry his (Buckingham's) nephew George Feilding. Feilding later became 1st Earl of Desmond of the present creation.

Lineage: GEFFERY FEILDING, son of Sir Geffery (who served HENRY III in his wars, and whose name was variously spelt Felden, Fieldeng, Fyilding, or Filding), *m* Agnes, dau and heir of John de Napton, by whom he acquired the Lordship of Misterton, Leics, and had:

WILLIAM FEILDING, who acquired by marriage with Joan, dau of William Prudhome, and gdau and heir of Robert de Newnham, the Manor of Newnham Paddox, Warwicks, and had issue:

Sir JOHN FEILDING; ktd in the French Wars, *m* 1st Margaret, dau of William Purefoy, of Drayton, Warwicks; *m* 2nd Jane, dau of Sir William Bellair; had:

Sir WILLIAM FEILDING; Lancastrian in Wars of Roses; *m* Agnes, dau and heir of John St Liz, a branch of the St Lizes, Earls of Northampton and Huntingdon, through whom he acquired the Lordship of Martinsthorpe, Rutland, and was *k* Battle of Tewkesbury 4 May 1471, leaving an est surv son:

Sir EVERARD FEILDING, KB; Sheriff Warwicks and Leics *c* 1481, cdr in HENRY VII's army Battle of Stoke 1487; had an est son:

Sir WILLIAM FEILDING; *m* Elizabeth, dau of Sir Thomas P(o)ultney, and *d* 1547, leaving issue:

Sir BASIL FEILDING; *m* Goodith, dau and coheir of William Willington, of Barcheston, Warwicks, and left issue:

Sir WILLIAM FEILDING; *m* Dorothy, dau of Sir Ralph Lane by Magdalen, dau and coheir of William, Lord Parr of Horton, and cousin to HENRY VIII's w KATHARINE PARR, and left issue:

Sir BASIL FEILDING; Sheriff Warwicks *c* 1612; *m* Elizabeth, dau of Sir Walter Aston, of Tixall, Staffs, and had an est s:

Sir WILLIAM FEILDING, **1st Earl of Denbigh**, so *cr* 14 Sept 1622, as also VISCOUNT FEILDING and earlier 30 Dec 1620 BARON OF NEWNHAM PADDOCKES, Co Warwick; *b c* 1582; *educ* Emmanuel Coll Cambridge; ktd March 1606/7; *m c* 1607 Susan, dau of Sir George Villiers, of Brokesby, Leics, and sis of George, 1st Duke of Buckingham (*see* JERSEY, E), and *d* 8 April 1643 from a wound sustained in a skirmish near Birmingham 3 April 1643 during the early stages of the Civil War (in which he was a royalist), leaving issue:

1 BASIL FEILDING, **2nd Earl of Denbigh**, KB (Feb 1625/6); *b c* 1608; *educ* Emmanuel Coll Cambridge; called up *vp* to Ho Lds 21 March 1627/8 in his f's Barony of Newnham Paddockes; Parliamentarian in Civil War, Ld Lt Denbighshire and Flintshire 1642 and Warwicks 1643, Maj-Gen Coventry and several Midland counties, Parly commr to CHARLES I 1644, Speaker Ho Lds 1648, Memb Cncl State 1649–51, acquiesced in Restoration 1660 and accordingly *cr* 2 Feb 1664/5 BARON ST LIZ, with remainder to the heirs male of his father; *m* 1st Lady Anne Weston, dau of Richard, Earl of Portland (*see* PORTLAND, E, preliminary remarks), Ld High Treasurer; *m* 2nd 12 Aug 1639 Barbara (*d* 2 April 1641), dau of Sir John Lamb, of Rothwell, Northants; *m* 3rd 8 July 1641 Elizabeth (*d* 22 Sept 1870), dau and coheir of Edward Bourchier, Earl of Bath (*see* BATH, M, preliminary remarks); *m* 4th Dorothy, dau of Francis Lane, of Glendon, Northants, but *dsp* 28 Nov 1675

2 GEORGE, **1st Earl of Desmond**, so *cr* 22 Nov 1622 by reversion of the terms under which the title in question was conferred on his intended f-in-law (though the marriage never took place) with precedence dating from 7 Nov 1622 (*see* preliminary remarks above), as also BARON FEILDING OF LECAGH, Co Tipperary, and VISCOUNT CALLAN, Co Kilkenny (all I), KB (1661); *m* Bridget, dau and coheir of Sir Michael Stanhope, and *d* 31 Jan 1665, leaving, with other issue:

(1) WILLIAM, **2nd Earl of Desmond** and **3rd Earl of Denbigh**

(2) George, of St Edmundsbury, *m* —, dau of Sir John Lee, and was ancestor of the extinct FEILDINGs of Bebside, Northumberland

(3) Charles (Sir), Col. King's Regt of Gds, PC (I), *m* 1674 Ursula (*d* 30 Oct 1720), widow of Sir William Aston and dau of Thomas Stockton, Judge King's Bench Ireland, and *d* 24 April 1722, having had two daus

(4) John (Rev), DD; Canon Salisbury, Chaplain to WILLIAM III, *m* Bridget, dau of Scipio Cokayne, of Weybred, Suffolk, and *d* 1697, having had, with three daus:

1a John, Govr Jamaica; *m* 1st Susan, dau of Sir Richard Booth, Ch Justice Common Pleas Ireland, and had:

1b Charles, Capt RM; *m* Maria, dau of John Johnson, of Bebside, Northumberland, and *d* March 1746, having had issue

2b William, R-Adml; *m* Mary, dau of Capt William Cormack, and *d* 1773, having had, with other issue:

1c Sarah; *m* 1764 Capt Thomas Farrell, 65th Regt, and had issue

1a (cont.) John Feilding *m* 2nd Dorothea, dau of Lord Barry of Santry, and *d* 4 Jan 1715, having by her had:

1b Elizabeth; *m* 1727 Richard Gorges, of Kilbrew, Co Meath

2a George, Lt-Col RHG (Blues), Groom Bedchamber to QUEEN ANNE and GEORGE I; *m* Anne, dau and coheir of Bazaleel Sherman, and left an only child:

1b Sarah; *m* 1733 John Willis, est s of Richard Willis, DD, Bp Winchester, and had issue

3a Edmund (Lt-Gen); *m* 1st Sarah, dau of Sir Henry Gould, Judge King's Bench 1698, and had, with other issue:

1b Henry Fielding (as which all his male-line descendants spell their surname); author: *Tom Jones, Joseph Andrews, The History of Jonathan Wild the Great, Amelia*, dramatist (especially the burlesque *Tom Thumb*), barrister Middle Temple, a magistrate, journalist, *b* 22 April 1707, *educ* Eton and Leyden, *m* 1st 28 Nov 1734 Charlotte Craddock (*d* 1744) and had issue; *m* 2nd 27 Nov 1747 Mary Daniel (*d* 1802) and *d* 8 Oct 1754, having had, with other issue:

1c William; barrister, magistrate at Queen's Square; *b* 10 Feb 1748; *dsp* 1 Oct 1820

2c Allen (Rev), Vicar Shepherdswell and St Stephen's, Canterbury; *b* 3 Oct 1754; *m* 23 Oct 1783 Mary Ann Whittingham (*d* 1820), adopted dau of Sir John Feilding, and *d* 9 April, 1823, leaving, with other issue:

1d Henry (Rev), Vicar Blean Kent 1816–63; *b* 12 Jan 1786; *m* 6 Dec 1827 Augusta, dau of Rev Sir John Fagge, 6th Bt (*qv*), and *d* 7 Feb 1863, leaving, with other issue:

1e Allen; *b* 23 Nov 1828; *m* 1st 27 June 1857 Ellen Spencer (*d* 5 March, 1872), dau of Rev W E Chapman, and had issue:

1f Henry, MBE (1920), Town Clerk Canterbury; *b* 1 July 1861; *m* 1892 Amy Emma Cooper (*d* 1947), and *d* 7 Feb 1926, leaving issue:

1g Thora; *m* 14 Feb 1925 Lt-Col Sir William Villiers Leonard Prescott-Westcar, 7th Bt, DSO, and *d* 18 March, 1970, leaving issue (*see* 1956 edn). He *d* 3 Feb 1959

2g Barbara; *m* 12 July 1927 James Evelyn Thoresby, of 14 Lincoln House, Basil Street, SW3, son of James Thoresby Jones, MD, JP, of 103 Sutherland Avenue, W9, and *d* 19–, leaving issue:

1h *Henry Fielding [Henry Thoresby Esq, 71 Hamilton Terrace, London NW8], late Royal Tank Regt; *b* 11 Sept 1936; *educ* Harrow and LSE (BSc)

3g Mary; *m* 5 May 1933 Maj Reginald Horace MOULD later FIELDING-MOULD, RA (deed poll 31 July 1935), of Prestbury House, Smarden, nr Ashford, Kent, son of Rev H R Mould, Rector of Holy Cross and St Peter's Canterbury, and *d* 1950

2f John; *b* 5 July 1864; *d* 11 April 1927

1f Gertrude Ellen, *m* Aug 1882 Richmond Beauchamp Halhed, of Chemainus, Vancouver, and *d* 20 Sept 1828, leaving issue

2f Augusta Elizabeth; *m* 1893 James Kilvington Worsfold, of Victoria, BC, and *d* 9 Oct 1943, having had issue. He *d* 1917

3f Mildred Emerson, *d* unm 8 Aug 1960

1e (cont.) Allen Fielding *m* 2nd 29 Sept 1877 Helena Augusta (*d* 30 Dec 1923), widow of Robert Arthur-Elliott, 95th Regt, and *d* 1895, having by her had issue:

3f Allen, Cdr RNR; *b* 31 Oct 1878; *das* 1917

4f Geoffry Kenmil, Lt East Surrey Regt; *b* 25 June 1884; *m* 25 Aug 1917 Elsie (*d* 1986), dau of John Edward Watkins, of Kingsland, Shrewsbury, and *d* 9 Aug 1960, leaving issue:

1g +Allen Henry, ARIBA, ARAIA [Allen Fielding Esq, 5/60 Pennington Terr, N Adelaide, S Australia 5006], Capt Royal Sussex Regt 1939–46; *b* 28 June, 1919; *m* 7 Jan 1944, *Laura Estelle, dau of Harold Teague, of The Old Hall, Builth Wells, Brecon, and has issue:

1h +David Henry; *b* 12 Oct 1944

1h *Barbara Anne [Mrs William Henderson, PO Box 38, Clare, South Australia 5453]; *b* 25 July 1950; *m* 1972 *William Henderson and has issue:

1i *Andrew William Fielding; *b* 1987

2g +John Henry [John Fielding Esq, 113 Woodland Rd, Sidmouth, Devon], Lt Leeds Rifles, Capt RA 1939–46; *b* 28 June 1919; *m* 1st 18 June 1948 Pamela Mary (*d* 1986), dau of John Alfred Spurdel Barnard, of 6 Hillside Road, Streatham, London SW, *m* 2nd Grace McInnes, dau of William Collins, of Glasgow, and by his 1st w has:

1h +Simon Henry [Simon Fielding Esq, 100 Beaconsfield Rd, Leicester]; *b* 3 March 1949

2h +Geoffrey John [Geoffrey Fielding Esq, The Old Farmhouse, St Mary's Rd, Wrotham, Kent]; *b* 26 June 1950

4f Margery; *b* 1880; *d* unm 18 Oct 1961

1e Mary Anne Frances; *m* G Ingham and *d* 12 May 1907. He *d* March 1904

2d Charles (Rev), LLB, Vicar of Headcorn; *b* 12 June 1791; *m* 27 April 1825 Elizabeth Oakley (*d* 6 Jan 1849), dau of Capt John Boyce, HEICS, and *d* 25 Nov 1866, leaving, with three other sons and six daus:

1e George, JP; Mayor Dover 1877, Registrar County Court Dover; *b* 29 March 1827; *m* 20 March 1850 Rosa (*d* 22 Nov 1907), dau of Dr Thomas J Hammond, of Eton, and *d* 3 Oct 1910, having had issue:

1f George Frederick Marshall (Rev) MA Cantab, Rector Stoke Wake, Dorset, 1905–11; *b* 19 Jan 1851; *m* 25 Aug 1888 Elizabeth (*d* 1950), dau of John Armitage, and *d* 14 June, 1914, leaving issue:

1g George Basil, rlwy engr Havana, Cuba, Lt RAF; *b* 26 July 1889; *m* 1st 10 Aug 1918 (*divorce* 1932) Esme (*d* 1961), dau of Outram Kellie McCallum, and had issue:

1h George Geoffrey Pharamond, Lt York and Lancs Regt; *b* 31 July, 1919; *d* as a result of enemy action 2 Aug 1944

1h *Cecil Dolores [Mrs Charles Auchmuty, 53 Shepherd's Way, Liphook, Hants GU30 7HH]; *b* 9 June, 1922; *m* 28 Oct 1944 *Maj Charles William Auchmuty, Rajputana Rifles, son of Rev James Wilson Auchmuty, MA, Canon of St Patrick's Cathedral, Armagh, and has issue:

1i *Susan Anne Esmé [Mrs David Wavre, Swevenings, Linersh Wood Rd, Bramley, Surrey GU5 0EF]; *b* 19 Sept 1950; *m* 1972 *David André Wavre and has issue:

1j *Robert André Auchmuty; *b* 1975

2j *Thomas Marc; *b* 1978

1j *Natalie Chantal; *b* 1982

2i *Jane Dolores [Mrs Richard Crowe, 1450 Old Coach Rd, Kernersville, NC 27284-8961, USA]; *b* 3 Oct 1955; *m* 1977 *Richard David Lee Crowe and has issue:

1j *David William; *b* 1979

2j *James Andrew; *b* 1981

1g (cont) George Fielding *m* 2nd 1932 Gertrude (*d* 1983), widow of G A Vickers, and *d* 1959

2g Henry Armitage, Lt RASC; *b* 22 Oct 1892; *m* 1914 Ethel May Baldock (*d* 1975), and *d* Nov 1965, leaving:

1h +Henry George [Henry Fielding Esq, 89 Chapel Lands, Alnwick, Northumberland NE66 1ES]; *b* 1916; *m* 1st 1940 Anne Scargill (*d* 22 April 1965) and has issue:

1i +Henry Michael Clive, BSc, MSc [Henry Fielding Esq, 33 Woodstock Rd, Carlingford, Sydney, NSW 2188, Australia]; *b* 1944; *m* 1971 *Lorraine Patricia Kirton, and has issue:

1j *Zoë Anne Clare; *b* 1977

2j *Sorrel Elizabeth May; *b* 1979

3j *Imogen Olivia Heather; *b* 1981

2i +George Peter Keith [Lt-Cdr George Fielding RN (ret), 20 Ashwell Rd, Bygrave, Baldock, Herts SG7 5DT]; *b* 1945; *m* 1968 *Gillian Margaret Stearn and has:

1j +James Marcus; *b* 1977

1j *Sarah Anne; *b* 1970

2j *Emma Jade; *b* 1972

3i +John David Barry [John Fielding Esq, 19 Arnold Ave, Camden, Sydney, NSW 2570, Australia]; *b* 1946; *m* 1968 *Pamela Margaret Cann, and has issue:

1j *Maxine Anne; *b* 1969

2j *Chelsea Louise; *b* 1974

4i +Anthony Robert Max; *b* 1948; Lt RN (ret); *m* 1st 1977 (*divorce* 1978) Stephanie Ann Johnson, *m* 2nd 1980 *Mrs Rachael Jane Thompson, dau of Frederick Dodge, of Somerset, and by her has issue:

1j +Henry Lawrence Max; *b* 1983

1j *Amelia Ann; *b* 1981

1h (cont) Henry Fielding *m* 2nd 27 Sept 1965 *Eirene Helen, dau of George Sydney Sell, of Northumberland

1h Barbara Jean; *b* 1917; *m* 1st 1940 (*divorce* 1952) Frank St Omer and had:

1i *Judy Mary [Mrs Judy Moseling, 91 Hitchin Hatch Lane, Sevenoaks, Kent TN13 3BD]; *b* 1942; *m* 1970 (*divorce* 1984) Martin Moseling; and has issue:

1j *Mark Christian; *b* 1973

1j *Emma Jane; *b* 1972

1h (cont) Mrs Barbara St Omer *m* 2nd 1952 *Godfrey Walter Allen Sweet and *d* 18 Dec 1994, leaving by him:

1i *John Simon [John Sweet Esq, 171 Tuckers Rd, Loughborough, Leics LE11 2PH]; *b* 1954; *m* 1981 *Kathleen Susan Cornell and has issue:

1j *Robbie Dylan John; *b* 1993

1g Rosa; *m* 11 June 1918 George Harold Whiteman, Chief Officer of London Salvage Corps (ret 1946) (*d* 9 July, 1957), son of Frank Gilbert Whiteman, and had issue:

1h *Angela Beatrice; *b* 16 June 1919; *m* 1952 *Lt-Col Clement Swetenham, RE, s of Charles Condon Swetenham, of Sherborne, Dorset, and has:

1i *Richard Clement; *b* 1953

1i *Elizabeth Angela; *b* 1954

2f Ernest Charles, Dist Registrar of the High Court and Registrar of County Court, Dover; *b* 1 July 1853; *m* 1885 Florence Maria (*d* 5 June 1920), dau of Rev Joshua Ground, and *d* 17 Dec 1937, having had issue:

1g Walter Lionel, Lt RN; *b* 1885; *d* 17 March 1914

3f Arthur Gregory; *b* 13 Nov 1860; *m* 19 Sept 1898 Annie Louisa (*d* 31 May, 1936), dau of George Wallace, of Waterford

4f Percy; *b* 16 Nov 1866; *m* 1889 Alice (*d* 1935), dau of George Webber, and *d* 1950, having had issue:

1g George Rudolph, of 5th Avenue, Prince George, BC, Canada, served in 49th Bn Canadian Overseas Expdn Force; *b* 1889; *m* 1926 (*divorce* 1937) Marya Nagadzina (*d* 1973), and *d* 1969, leaving issue:

1h +Ernest Rudolph [Ernest Fielding Esq, 439 Willowdale Crescent SE, Calgary, Alberta, Canada T2J 1K2]; *b* 1927; *m* 26 May 1956 *Audrey Madge, dau of Alex Mackie, of Calgary, Alberta, Canada, and has issue:

1i +Douglas Ernest [Douglas Fielding Esq, 204 Woodmont Court SW, Calgary, Alberta, Canada T2W 4X1]; *b* 31 Oct 1957; *m* 1985 *Mary Ann Dibulski, and has issue:

1j +Mark Antantas; *b* 1989

2i +Grant Alexander; *b* 1964

1h *Karen Lea; *b* 1962

1h *Rosa Alice [Mrs John Boyd, Box 843, Rosedale, Alberta, Canada TOJ 2VO]; *b* 1926; *m* 1944 *John Boyd and has issue:

1i *Bryan Alexander; *b* 1955

1i *Kathleen Anne; *b* 1945

2i *Gloria Jean; *b* 1947

2h *Vera Marie [Mrs John Adamson, 3213 19th Av SE, Calgary, Alberta, Canada, T2B OA4]; *b* 1929; *m* 1946 *John McKenzie Adamson and has issue:

1i *Gary Wesley [Gary Adamson Esq, 50 Sandringham Way NW, Calgary, Alberta, Canada T2B OA4]; *b* 1951; *m* 1986 *Catherine Elizabeth Kirkham

1i *Carol Anne [Mrs Larry Jones, 2815 Dover Edge Drive SE, Calgary, Alberta, Canada T2B 2L2]; *b* 1948; *m* 1968 *Larry Alexander Jones

1g Vera; *d* 19 Feb 1892

2g Rosa Dorothy Mary; *b* 26 April 1893; *m* Jan 1915 Edmund John Golledge, of N Long Beach, California, USA, and had issue

1f Edith Margaret; *m* 3 April 1875 Walter Jeken Stride and *d* 15 May 1920, leaving issue. He *d* 26 Nov 1899

2f Rosa Beatrice; *m* 1880 John Benjamin Andrews, and *d* 15 Sept 1940. He *dsp* 1881

3f Lilian; *m* 1883 Rev Alfred Lloyd Coates, MA, and *d* 20 Aug 1935, leaving issue

4f Florence; *m* 18 July 1907 Rev Edmund John Ingle Dredge, Rector Horsington, Lincs, and *d* 18 Nov 1944

2e Thomas Mantell; *b* 19 Nov 1834; *m* 24 Sept 1856 Jean Eleanora (*d* May 1898), dau of William Leckie Ewing, and *d* 4 July 1914, leaving issue:

1f Charles William (Sir), KBE (1917), Dir-Gen Food Production; *b* 4 Oct 1863; *m* 15 Aug 1899 Florence (*d* 28 Feb 1958), dau of James Willis Dixon, of Hillsborough Hall, Sheffield, and *d* 9 April 1941, leaving issue:

1g Rudolph Burton, JP (1936), CC (1926), CA (1946–63) W Sussex, Chm Horsham Div W Sussex War Ag Ctee 1939–46, Maj 4th Bn Sussex HG WW II, underwriting memb Lloyd's 1946; *b* 16 March 1902; *educ* Charterhouse and Downing Coll Camb (Dip Ag 1924); *m* 16 Aug 1939 Frances Adelaide Graham (*d* 4 May 1996), yr dau of George Greene, of Dublin, and *d* 29 Oct 1970, leaving issue:

1h *Daphne Claire, MRCS, LRCP, MA, BA Oxon, MA Cantab [Mrs Timothy Drabble, Okehurst, Billinghurst, W Sussex RH114 9HS]; *b* 30 Aug 1942; *m* 1st 14 Feb 1970 Dr Peter Macdonald Tow, of Oakhurst, Billingshurst, Sussex; *m* 2nd 1980 *Timothy Hugh Drabble and by him has issue:

1i Oliver John Fielding; *b* 24 April 1981; *d* 22 Jan 1994

2h *Jean Eleanora Leckie [Mrs Terence O'Flynn, Wyneshore House, West Lavington, Devizes, Wilts SN10 4LW;, *b* 25 Sept 1946; *m* 23 March 1966 *Terence Michael O'Flynn and has issue:

1i *Caspar Michael; *b* 1969

1i *Emma Frances; *b* 31 Oct 1966; *m* 27 April 1996 *Logan Vijayaratnam

1g Jean Kathleen Mary; *b* 2 July 1900; *m* 1st 5 Sept 1925 Hugh Neville Clegg, RN, only son of Henry Gordon Clegg, of Wormington Grange, Broadway. He *d* 23 Nov 1929. She *m* 2nd 12 July 1944 Windsor Holden White, of 10 Lowndes Court, London SW1, and Polo Cottage, Midhurst, Sussex (*d* 1976), s of Windsor T White, of Chagrin Falls, Ohio, USA, and *d* 24 Jan 1986

2g Pamela; *b* 19 March 1906; *m* 25 Sept 1937, as his 2nd w, Maj William Walter Brough Scott (*d* June 1980), (*see* SCOTT, Bt, of Beauclere) and *d* 2 May 1992, leaving issue

1f Eleanora Ewing; *m* 9 Nov 1875 Rev A J Rogers, and *d* 16 May 1878, leaving issue

2f Matilda Amelia Henrietta; *m* 11 April 1896 Robert Forrester, JP, of Annfield, Stirling, and *d* 17 June 1968, leaving issue. He *d* Sept 1940

3f Isabel Leckie Ewing; *m* 16 May 1895 Aubrey Llewellyn Coventry Fell, CBE, and *d* 24 April, 1925. He *d* 4 Oct 1948

3d George (Rev), Vicar N Ockendon, Essex; *b* 27 March 1793; *educ* St John's Coll Camb (MA); *m* 17 Oct 1825 Mary Rebecca (*d* 7 Dec 1881), dau of E Hanbury Williams, and *d* 25 May 1869, leaving issue:

1e George Hanbury (Rev), Rector Knill, Herefs; *b* 22 Nov 1828; *educ* Lincoln Coll Oxford (MA); *m* 23 Nov 1880 Minna Emily Elizabeth (*d* 5 Jan 1934), dau of Ernest Neumann, and *d* 10 Oct 1898, leaving issue:

1f George Rudolf, Capt Sherwood Foresters and T/Maj 9th Bn; *b* 5 Oct 1881; *m* 30 Sept 1914 Evelyn Carlota (*d* 6 Jan 1961), dau of Edward Jewell, of Clifton Court, Bournemouth, and was *ka* 24 July 1915, leaving issue:

1g +George Rudolf Hanbury, DSO (1945) [Maj George Fielding DSO, Grevière D'Amont, 1837 Château d'Oex, Vaud, Switzerland], Maj 3rd KOH WW II (wounded); *b* 3 July 1915; *educ* Shrewsbury; *m* 10 May 1940 Beatrice Georgina (*d* 15 March

1997), dau of Major Maurice Pope, 17th Lancers, of Ashwicke Hall, Marshfield, Chippenham, Wilts, and has:

1h +Martin George Rudolf [Martin Fielding Esq, East Hall Gate Cottage, Middleton Tyas, nr Richmond, N Yorks DL10 6RE], Capt QOH (BFPO 30), ARICS, FAAV; *b* 2 Dec 1945; *educ* Eton; *m* 1992 *Erica MacKay Agace, yr dau of Acland Mackay Geddes, of Cuesta de la Villa, Tenerife, Canary Islands

1h *Sarah Georgina [The Hon Mrs Guy Norrie, Old Church Farm, Broughton, nr Stockbridge, Hants SO20 8AA]; *b* 10 May 1947; *m* 10 Feb 1968 *Lt-Col Hon Guy Bainbridge Norrie, Roy Hus (PWO), yr s of Lt-Gen 1st Baron Norrie (*qv*), and has issue

1g Mary Dorothea; *b* 10 April 1883; *d* 15 May 1893

2e Henry Johnes; *b* 30 Sept 1834; *educ* Exeter Coll Oxford (MA); *d* 25 Nov 1921

4d Allen (Rev); Chaplain Chatham Dockyard; *b* 2 Feb 1801; *m* 1 Feb 1844 Jemima (*d* 19 Feb 1894), dau of Rev Sir John Fagge, Bt (*qv*), and *dsp* 7 May 1808

1b Sarah; author: *David Simple* and other works; *b* 1708; *d* 1768

3a (cont) Lt-Gen Edmund Feilding *m* 2nd Eleanor Blanchfield or Rasa, perhaps a widow, and by her had, with other issue:

2b John (Sir); *b* 1721; ktd 1761; blind from birth, magistrate at Bow Street; *m* 1st 17 Oct 1751 Elizabeth, dau of Dr Whittingham, but *dsp* 4 Sept 1780

(1) Frances; *m* 1675 Sir Edward Gage, 1st Bt, of Hengrave (*see* GAGE, V), and *d* 1680, leaving issue

(2) Mary; *m* Sir Charles Gawdy, 2nd Bt, and was *bur* 8 Sept 1691, leaving issue

(3) Bridget; *m* Arthur Parsons (*see* ROSSE, E)

1 Mary; *m* 1620 1st Duke of Hamilton and *d* 10 May 1638, leaving issue (*see* HAMILTON and BRANDON, D)

2 Anne; *m* 25 Dec 1632 3rd Viscount Campden and *dsps* 24 March 1636 (*see* GAINSBOROUGH, E)

3 ELIZABETH Feilding; *cr* COUNTESS OF GUILDFORD, Co Surrey (E), for life; *m* 26 Dec 1639 Lewis BOYLE, Viscount Kinalmeaky (*dsp* 3 Sept 1642; *see* CORK and ORRERY, E), and *dsp* 3 Sept 1667

The 2nd EARL OF DENBIGH's n,

WILLIAM FEILDING, **3rd Earl of Denbigh** and **2nd Earl of Desmond**; *b* 29 Dec 1640; *m* 1st Mary (*d* 1669), dau of Sir Robert King and widow of Sir William Meredyth, and had two sons and a dau (Mary, *m* Evelyn Pierrepont, Marquess of Dorchester); *m* 2nd Mary (*d* 9 Dec 1719), dau and coheir of Henry Carey, Earl of Monmouth, and *d* 23 Aug 1685, having by her had no issue; his er s by his 1st w:

BASIL FEILDING, **4th Earl of Denbigh** and **3rd Earl of Desmond**; *b* 1668; Ld Lt Leics and Denbighs; *m* 22 June 1695 Hester (*d* 1 Jan 1725/6), dau and eventually sole heir of Sir Basil Firebrace, Bt (son of the devoted Royalist Sir Henry Firebrace, who attended CHARLES I to the scaffold and was given CHARLES's miniature set in diamonds in a small ring, which descended to subsequent Earls of Denbigh and Desmond), and had, with another s and three other daus:

1 WILLIAM, **5th/4thEarl**

2 Charles; *m* 28 Aug 1737 Anne (*d* 1743), widow of Sir Brook Bridges, Bt, and dau and coheir of Sir Thomas Palmer, Bt, of Wingham, Kent, and had, with other issue:

(1) Charles, Cdre RN; *m* July 1772 Sophia, 2nd dau of William Finch and sister of George, Earl of Winchilsea (*see* WINCHILSEA and NOTTINGHAM, E), and had issue:

1a Charles, R-Adml; *b* 1780; *m* 24 April 1804 Lady Elizabeth Theresa, widow of William Davenport Talbot and dau of 2nd Earl of Ilchester (*qv*), and *d* 2 Sept 1837, leaving issue:

1b Caroline, VA (2nd Cl); *m* 6 Dec 1831 3rd Earl of Mount Edgcumbe (*qv*) and *d* 2 Nov 1881, leaving issue

2b Horatia; *m* 1 Jan 1850 Thomas Gaisford, of Offington, Sussex, and *d* 8 Aug 1851, leaving issue. He *d* 26 Feb 1898

1a Sophia Charlotte; *m* Lord Robert FitzGerald (*see* LEINSTER, D) and *d* 19 Sept 1834

2a Matilda

3a Augustus Sophia; *m* 8 March 1813 George Hicks. He *d* 1 Aug 1820

(1) Elizabeth; *m* 1st Earl Digby (*see* DIGBY, B)

1 Diana; *m* Rev Randolph Marriott and had issue

2 Frances; *m* 1720 8th Earl of Winchilsea and (3rd Earl of) Nottingham (*qv*) and was *bur* 3 Oct 1734, leaving issue

The 4th/5th EARL *d* 18 March 1716/7; his est s,

WILLIAM FEILDING, **5th Earl of Denbigh** and **4th Earl of Desmond**; *b* 26 Oct 1697; *m* Isabella (*d* 16 May 1769), dau of Peter de Jonge, of Utrecht, and sister of the Marchioness of Blandford (*see* MARLBOROUGH, D), and *d* 2 Aug 1755, leaving an only s:

BASIL FEILDING, **6th Earl of Denbigh** and **5th Earl of Desmond**; *b* 3 Jan 1719; *m* 1st 12 April 1757 Mary (*d* 14 Oct 1782), 3rd dau and coheir of Sir John Bruce Cotton, Bt, of Connington, Hunts (the last male heir of the great antiquary Sir Robert Cotton, Bt, after whom the Cottonian Library is named), and had, with another s:

WILLIAM ROBERT BASIL, *Viscount Feilding*, Major-Gen; *b* 15 June 1760; *m* 20 April 1791 Anne Catherine (*d* Jan 1852), est dau of Thomas Jelf Powys, of Berwick House, Salop, and Moreton Hall, Cheshire, and *dvp* 8 Aug 1799, leaving:

1 WILLIAM BASIL PERCY, **7th/6th Earl**

2 Henry Wentworth FEILDING later POWYS (roy licence 1832), of Berwick House, Salop; *b* 31 July 1798; *d* 14 March 1875

3 Everard Robert Bruce (Rev); *b* 30 Oct 1799; *m* 21 June 1832 Anne Henrietta (*d* 21 Aug 1879), dau of Sir John Fenton Boughey, 2nd Bt (*qv*), and *d* 14 Sept 1854

1 Catherine Frances; granted 1813 with her sisters rank of earl's daus; *d* unm 21 Feb 1818

2 Marianne; *d* 13 Feb 1814

3 Emily; *m* 11 Oct 1827 Rev Henry Harding and *d* 8 Oct 1883 aged 86, leaving issue

The **6th/5th Earl** *m* 2nd 21 July 1783 Sarah (*d* 2 Oct 1814), widow of Sir Charles Halford, Bt, and dau of Edward Farnham, of Quorndon House, Leics, and *d* 14 July 1800

His gs,

WILLIAM BASIL PERCY FEILDING, **7th Earl of Denbigh** and **6th Earl of Desmond**, PC; *b* 25 March 1796, DCL; *m* 8 May 1822 Mary Elizabeth Kitty (*d* 16 Dec 1842), est dau of 1st Earl of Ducie (*qv*), and had, with other issue:

1 RUDOLPH WILLIAM BASIL, **8th/7th Earl**

2 Percy Robert Basil (Sir), KCB, of Broome Park, Betchworth, Surrey, Gen Coldstream Gds, Col Suffolk Regt, cmded Inf Bde at Malta 1879–84 and SE Dist 1885–87, served Crimea, present The Alma, Balaclava, Inkerman and Siege of Sebastopol, Order Medjidie 5th Cl; *b* 26 June 1827; *m* 29 April 1862 Lady Louisa Isabella Harriet Thynne (*d* 26 June 1919), dau of 3rd Marquess of Bath (*qv*), and *d* 9 Jan 1904, leaving issue:

(1) Geoffrey Percy Thynne (Sir), KCB (1919, CB 1916), KCVO (1920), CMG (1917), DSO (1900), Coldstream Gds, Maj-Gen, GOC 56th 1st London Div (TA) 1923–27, Registrar and Sec Order of Bath, served Boer War 1899–1902 (despatches twice, two medals, six clasps), WW I (despatches seven times, star, brevet of Col, promoted Maj-Gen), Cdr Orders of Leopold of Belgium and St Maurice and St Lazarus Italy, Legion of Honour, Croix de Guerre and Orders of the White Eagle of Serbia and Rising Sun of Japan 2nd Cl, KGStJ; *b* 21 Sept 1866; *d* unm 21 Oct 1932

(2) Percy Henry; *b* 23 Dec 1867; *m* 3 May 1904 Clotilde (*d* 25 Feb 1937), only dau of Henry Brewster, of Rome, and *d* 29 June 1929, leaving:

1a Basil Percy Terence Henry; *b* 18 April 1907; *m* 30 June 1932 Margaret Mary (*d* 1989), 3rd dau of Lt-Col Rowland Charles Feilding, DSO, of Stoke House, Slough (*see* below), and *d* 1986, leaving issue:

1b +Jocelyn Rupert Rowland Geoffrey [Jocelyn Feilding Esq, 37 Elvaston Place, London SW7]; *b* 12 May 1940; *educ* Downside; *m* 27 April 1963 (*divorce* 1983) Rowena Marion, only dau of Capt Simon Harvey Combe, MC (*see* LEICESTER, E), and has:

1c *Emma Mary Clothilde; *b* 20 March 1964

2c *Lucy Silvia Margaret; *b* 19 Feb 1966

1b (cont.) Jocelyn Feilding *m* 2nd 27 Feb 1998 *Harriet, dau of James Earle, of Pattingham, Staffs

1b *Julia Felicity Maria Gabrielle [Mrs Donald Morrison, Bridge End House, Dorchester on Thames, Oxon], Dip Arch Oxford, ARIBA; *b* 12 Sept 1933; *m* 1st 4 May 1957 (*divorce* 1963) Leslie Rebanks, ARIBA, son of John Rebanks, of Lytham St Annes, Lancs, and has issue:

1c *Leander Piers John; *b* 15 Jan 1960

2c *Alexander Basil; *b* 30 Sept 1961

1b (cont.) Mrs Julia Rebanks *m* 2nd 1963 *Donald Rhind Morrison, ARIBA, and has further issue:

3c *Justin Guy Stuart Feilding; *b* 1964

1c *Zuleika Jane Feilding; *b* 1963

2b *Chloë Mary Antonia [Mrs Chloë Coombes, 16 London Pl, Oxford]; *b* 24 June 1936; *m* 1962 (*divorce* 1973) David Coombes, of Victoria Cottage, East Street, Oxford, and has issue:

1c *Rowland William Sebastian; *b* 1967

1c *Victoria Roque-Rebecca; *b* 1963

2c *Connemara Alice Mary; *b* 15 Feb 1965

3b *Amanda Claire Marian [Lady Neidpath, Beckley Park, Oxford OX3 9SY; Stanway, Cheltenham, Glos GL54 5PQ]; *b* 30 Jan 1943; artist, known professionallly as Amanda Feilding; *m* 1st (*divorce* 1993) Joseph Chase Hurt Mellen, s of William Mellen; *m* 2nd 29 Jan 1995 *James Donald Charteris, Lord Neidpath, est surv s of 12th Earl of Wemyss (*qv*), and by her 1st husb has:

1c *Rock Basil Hugo FEILDING MELLEN; *b* 10 April 1979

2c *Cosmo Birdie FEILDING MELLEN; *b* 25 Jan 1985

1a Susan Louisa Mary; *b* 31 Jan 1906; *m* 31 May 1926 Maj-Gen Hugh Hibbert, DSO, KOYLI, of Sunton House, Collingbourne Ducis, Wilts, son of Adm Hugh Thomas Hibbert, CBE, DSO, of Longparish, Hants, and had issue

(1) Alice Augusta; *b* 9 March 1863; *d* unm 6 Feb 1940

(2) Louisa Mary; *b* 11 Feb 1864; *d* unm (accidentally *k*) 23 Jan 1918

(3) Grace; *b* 15 June 1865; *m* 21 April 1898 Frederick Keppel North and *d* 11 May 1946, leaving issue (*see* GUILFORD, E)

(4) Margaret Agnes, DBE (1918); *b* 21 April 1871; DGStJ; *m* 21 Oct 1907 Sir Walter Edward Davidson, KCMG, Govr NSW, and *d* 14 Oct 1964, leaving issue. He *d* 15 Sept 1923

3 Charles William Alexander (Rev); *b* 28 April 1833; MA Cantab, Rector Stapleton, Salop; *m* 1st 27 Sept 1866 Lucy (*d* 16 Jan 1875), 4th dau of John Grant, of Kilgraston, Perthshire, and had issue:

(1) John Basil, JP Flints; *b* 27 Dec 1868; Capt Roy Welch Fus (T), in service of Sultan of Johore, Tech Advsr Fisheries Dept Ontario; Dir Fisheries Research Conservation Commn, Dominion Food Control and Scientific Research Council, Canada; *m* 24 Feb 1897 Emily Margaret (*d* 15 Aug 1955) dau of Ewen Monteith Tod, and *d* 3 Aug 1942, having had issue:

1a Charles Rudolph (Rev); *b* 16 Jan 1902; *educ* Upper Canada Coll, McGill, King's Coll Nova Scotia (BA 1926) and Gen Theological Seminary New York (STD); Fell and Tutor of General Theological Seminary 1929–35, Rector St Mary's Staten Island NY 1935–40, Professor Moral Theology 1940 and Dean Divinity 1947–61 Trin Coll Toronto, Visiting Fell Divinity Sch Yale 1961–62; *m* 20 Aug 1935 *Ann [Mrs Charles Feilding, c/o 550 Gilmore St, Peterborough, ONT K9H 2K2, Canada], only dau of Ernest Truslow, of Southport, Conn., and *d* 10 Sept 1978, leaving issue:

1b +Geoffrey Truslow [Geoffrey Feilding Esq, 655 Grosvenor Av, Westmount, Quebec, Canada]; *b* 21 April 1939; *educ* U of BC (BA); *m* 28 May 1966 *Martha Anne, dau of John S Corrigan, of Toronto, and has issue:

1c +Charles Corrigan; *b* 1968
2c +Jonathan Corrigan; *b* 29 Jan 1971
1b *Goodith Mary [Mrs Brian Heeney, 550 Gilmour St, Peterborough, Ont K9H 2K2, Canada]; *b* 26 Aug 1936; *m* 2 June 1956 Rev William Brian Danford Heeney, DPhil Oxon, Prof History U of Alberta, V-Pres Trent U Peterborough, Ontario (*d* 1983), only s of Arnold Danford Patrick Heeney, Canadian Amb USA, and has had issue:
1c *Michael Feilding; *b* 4 Sept 1957; *m* 1982 *Hilary Meredith and has:
1d *Henry Meredith; *b* 1988
2d *Mark Meredith; *b* 1997
1d *Frances Meredith; *b* 1991
2c John Danford; *b* 7 Aug 1963; *d* 30 Jan 1965
3c *Timothy Charles; *b* 15 Feb 1966; *m* 1991 *Shuna Baird and has:
1d *Duncan Patrick; *b* 1995
1d *Emma Margaret; *b* 1997
4c *Matthew Macleod; *b* 10 Oct 1968
1c *Ann; *b* 24 March 1961; *m* 1987 *Richard Johnston and has issue:
1d *Rachel Margaret Heeney; *b* 1991
1a Frances Elizabeth; *b* 19 Jan; *d* 4 April 1898
(2) Bertram Francis Percy; *b* 15 Feb 1870; Lt Wilts Regt; *ka* Uganda 19 Oct 1897
(3) Rowland Charles, DSO (1917), Lt-Col Coldstream Gds (SR), Associate Royal School of Mines, Matabele War 1896 in Gifford's Horse (wounded), WW I (despatches twice); *b* 18 May 1871; *m* 29 April 1903 Edith Mary (*d* 31 July 1961), dau of Frederick Stapleton-Bretherton, of The Hall, Rainhill, Lancs, by Hon Isabella Mary, 2nd dau of 12th Baron Petre (*qv*), and *d* 5 Sept 1945, having had issue:
1a Joan May; *b* 1904; *m* 1 June 1926 Brig Ian Robert Craufurd George Mary Bruce (*d* 1956), DSO, MBE, 2nd son of Eric Henry Stuart Bruce, MA and *d* 1991, leaving issue (*see* BRUCE, Bt, of Stenhouse)
2a Anita Mary; *b* 1907; *m* 10 June 1931 (*divorce* 1949) Basil Antony Trevor Mostyn, later 13th Bt (*qv*), and *d* 19–, leaving issue
3a *Margaret Mary; *b* 1908; *m* 30 June 1931 Basil Percy Terence Henry Feilding (*d* 1986), son of Percy Henry Feilding, and has issue (*see* above)
4a Edith Mary; *b* and *d* 18 April 1909
5a *Prunella Mary Patricia [Mrs Charles Howard, The Cottage, Lodge Farm, Stowood, Beckley, Oxon], Jr Cdr ATS WW II; *b* 23 Oct 1916, *m* 7 Sept 1942 Maj Charles Neil Howard, MC (*d* 1975), Black Watch, yr s ;f George Percy Howard, and has issue:
1b *Simon Neil [Simon Howard Esq, 11 Crescent Mansions, 122 Elgin Crescent, London W11 2JN]; *b* 7 July 1951; *educ* Stonyhurst
1b *Caroline Edith Mary [Mrs Simon Gordon-Duff, Lodge Farm, Stowood, Oxon OX3 9SR]; *b* 29 April 1947; *m* 1st 1976 (*divorce* 1979) David Hugh Craig, MA; *m* 2nd 1990 *Simon Lachlan Gordon-Duff (*see* BAIRD, Bt) and by her 1st husb has:
1c *Nicholas Charles David; *b* 1977; *educ* Eton and Oriel Coll Oxford
2b *Harriet Prunella Mary; *b* 14 Dec 1948
(1) Adelaide Mary; *b* 10 Oct 1872; *m* 22 Aug 1907 Col Michael James Sweetman, OBE, BA, JP, E Yorks Regt, s of Walter Sweetman, of Clohamon, Co Wexford, and *dsp* 27 June 1934. He *d* 24 Sept 1922
(2) Lucy Constance; *b* 15 Jan 1875; *d* unm 20 May 1935
3 (cont.) The Rev C W A Feilding *m* 2nd 21 Sept 1882 Emily Margaret (*dsp* 19 March 1894), dau of Edward Christopher Egerton, MP (*see* 1956 edn EGERTON OF TATTON, B), and *d* 30 Nov 1893
5 William Henry Adelbert, Gen, Col Coldstream Gds, Inspr-Gen Recruiting HQ 1891–94, Chevalier Legion of Honour; *b* 6 Jan 1836; *m* 7 April 1893 Charlotte (*d* 28 June 1928), dau of Sir Baldwin Leighton, 7th Bt (*qv*), and *dsp* 24 March 1895
1 Jane Lissy Harriott; *m* 10 Jan 1856 Theophilus John Levett, of Wychnor Park, Capt 1st Life Gds, and *d* 26 April 1912, leaving issue. He *d* 27 Feb 1899
2 Adelaide Emily; *m* 27 April 1865 Charles Archibald Murray and *d* 24 May 1870, leaving issue (*see* MANSFIELD and MANSFIELD, E)
3 Ida Matilda Alice; *m* 30 July 1872 Malcolm Low, BCS, of Cupar, Fife, and *d* 16 Dec 1915, leaving issue. He *d* 14 June 1923
4 Katherine Elizabeth Mary Julia; *m* 10 Jan 1867 Charles Mersey Bolton Clive, JP, of Whitfield, Herefs, and *d* 10 July 1882, leaving issue. He *d* 11 Aug 1883

The 7th/6th EARL *d* 25 June 1865; his eldest son,

RUDOLPH WILLIAM BASIL FEILDING, **8th Earl of Denbigh** and **7th Earl of Desmond**; Hon Col 2nd Vol Bn Roy Welch Fus; *b* 9 April 1823; *educ* Eton and Trin Coll Cambridge; *m* 1st 18 June 1846 Louisa (*d* 1 May 1853), only child of David Pennant, of Downing, Flintshire, (gs of Thomas Pennant, antiquary and naturalist, author: *Pennant's London*); *m* 2nd 29 Sept 1857 Mary (*d* 3 June 1901), yst dau of Robert Berkeley, DL, JP, of Spetchley Park, Worcs (*see* BERKELEY, B), and by her had issue:

1 RUDOLPH ROBERT BASIL ALOYSIUS AUGUSTINE, **9th/8th Earl**
2 Francis Henry Everard Joseph, OBE (1919), barrister, T/Lt RNVR 1914, RN, served Egypt 1882, Intell Staff Egypt and Palestine WW I, 4th Cl Order Nile and El Nahda of Hedjaz; *b* 6 March 1867; *educ* Trin Coll Cambridge (BA, LLB); *m* 27 Nov 1919 Stanislawa Janina (Stasia) (*d* 2 April 1975), dau of Eustachiusz Tomczyk, of Warsaw, and *d* 8 Feb 1936
3 Basil George Edward Vincent (Very Rev Monsignor), PhilD, DD (Rome), Chaplain Boer War (medal and clasp); *b* 13 July 1873; *d* 31 July 1906, drowned in the Rhine
4 Philip; *b* and *d* 5 Dec 1877
1 Clare Mary Henrietta; *d* unm 26 May 1895
2 Edith Mary Frances; Sister of Charity in China; *d* 22 April 1918
3 Hilda; *d* an infant 14 April 1866
4 Winefride Mary Elizabeth, Nat Pres Catholic Women's League, Mem Nat Adoption Soc; *m* 11 May 1889 Gervase Henry Elwes, DL, of Billing Hall, Northants, and The Manor House, Brigg, Lincs, and *d* 24 Feb 1959 aged 90, leaving issue. He *d* 12 Jan 1921
5 Agnes Mary Pia; *m* 15 Oct 1892 Charles Edmund de Trafford, of Hothorpe, Theddingworth, Rugby, and *d* 20 July 1921, leaving issue (*see* DE TRAFFORD, Bt)

The 8th/7th EARL *d* 10 March 1892; his son,

RUDOLPH ROBERT BASIL ALOYSIUS AUGUSTINE FEILDING, **9th Earl of Denbigh** and **8th Earl of Desmond**, GCVO (1933, KCVO 1927, CVO 1903), TD, DL, JP (Warwicks), CC City of London LCC 1896–98, Ld-in-Waiting 1897–1901 and 1901–05, ADC to HM GEORGE V 1911–26, Col-Cmdt HAC 1893–1933, V-Chm City London TFA, Capt RHA, served in Egypt 1882 (medal with clasp, bronze star) and WW I, CRA 2nd Mounted Div Egypt 1915–16, Artillery Staff Southern Army E Cmd 1916, ADC to Ld Lt Ireland, Grand Cross Portuguese Order of Christ and Spanish Order of Charles III, Order Nile 3rd Cl; *b* 26 May 1859; *m* 1st 24 Sept 1884 Hon Cecilia Mary Clifford (*d* 8 Dec 1919), dau of 8th Baron Clifford of Chudleigh (*qv*), and had issue:

1 Rudolph Edmund Aloysius, *Viscount Feilding*, CMG, DSO, Lt-Col Res Offrs Coldstream Gds (SR), JP Warwicks, served WW I (despatches, brevet, Legion of Honour); *b* 12 Oct 1885; *educ* Oratory Sch and Ch Ch Oxford (BA); *m* 28 Feb 1911 Agnes Imelda Mary (*d* 6 May 1937), 2nd dau of Francis Egerton Harding, of Old Springs, Staffs, and *d* 10 Jan 1937, leaving issue:
(1) WILLIAM RUDOLPH STEPHEN, **10th/9th Earl**
(2) David Charles, BSc, Assoc Roy Sch of Mines, portrait painter, Hon Lt RE WW II 1939–40 (POW); *b* 1 Aug 1913, *educ* Oratory Sch; *m* 19 Oct 1938 *Elizabeth Alice, 2nd dau of William Fletcher, of Arlecdon, Cumberland, and *d* 25 Nov 1966, leaving issue:
1a +WILLIAM DAVID [William Feilding Esq, Oristano Great House, Bluefields, PO Box 1, Westmoreland, Jamaica]; *b* 12 Aug 1939; heir presumptive; *educ* Downside; artist; *m* 1980 *Lydia Sarah, dau of Martin Harding, of Chelsea
2a +Michael Henry [Michael Feilding Esq, 107 Hartfield Rd, London SW19 3TJ]; *b* 26 Jan 1946; *educ* Downside and Oxford (BSc); *m* 4 July 1970 *Linnet I A, dau of William Hale, of the Island, Hurstbourne Priors, Hants, and has issue:
1b *Emily Linnet; *b* 18 Aug 1973
2b *Melissa Anne; *b* 1976
3a +Charles Richard [Charles Feilding, 47 Vista Barranca, Rancho Santa Margarita, California 92688, USA]; *b* 17 March 1949; *educ* Downside and Fordham U NY; *m* 3 June 1972 *Jeanne, yst dau of Eugene Tanzillo, of New York
(3) Basil Egerton, Capt Coldstream Gds, P/O RAF WW II (wounded); *b* 14 May 1916; *educ* Oratory Sch and Ampleforth; *m* 14 Sept 1939 *Rosemary [The Hon Mrs Basil Feilding, The Park Cottage, Monk's Kirby, Rugby, Warwicks], only dau of Cdr Neville Eardley-Wilmot, RN, of East Lodge, Ascot, Berks (*see* EARDLEY-WILMOT, Bt), and *d* 3 Oct 1970, leaving issue:
1a +Peter Rudolph [Peter Feilding Esq, Highfields, 11 Marlow Rd, High Wycombe, Bucks HP11 1TA]; *b* 27 Nov 1941; *educ* Ampleforth, FCA; *m* 9 Nov 1968 *Diana Mourne, only dau of C C Cox, TD, of 16 Albany House, Albany Court, Lansdown Rd, Cheltenham, Glos, and has issue:
1b +Basil James; *b* 17 Dec 1974
1b *Chloë Louise; *b* 1972
2a +Giles Anthony [Giles Steuart-Feilding, The Manor House, Arnesby, Leics]; *b* 4 March 1950; *educ* Ampleforth; added by deed poll 1981 STEUART; *m* 17 March 1977 *Sara Jane, dau of Cdr D E Barton, MVO, DSC, of 47 St Mary Abbot's Terrace, London W14, and has issue:
1b +Thomas Assheton Henry; *b* 1980
1b *Imogen Clare; *b* 9 Feb 1978
3a +Crispin Everard; *b* 2 March 1960
1a *Jennifer Mary; *b* 6 June 1947; *m* 1st 9 March 1968 (*divorce* 1971) Graham F Bond, son of Major Gerald Bond, MC, of Woolstone Mill Farm, nr Faringdon, Berks; *m* 2nd 30 March 1974 *Charles Eliot Crawley, est s of Kenneth Eliot Crawley, of Brightsleigh Meadow Cottage, Milles Lane, Outwood, Surrey, and has issue:
1b *Tobias; *b* 1978
2a *Imelda Jane [Mrs Piers Rendell, Little Thatch, Woolage Green, Canterbury, Kent CT4 6SF]; *b* 9 July 1958; *m* 1981 *Piers L Rendell, son of Brig D B Rendell, of West Street House, Selsey, Sussex, and has issue:
1b *Hugo Anthony; *b* 1983
2b *Sebastian James; *b* 1985
(4) Hugh Richard; FCA, S/Ldr RAFVR WW II (despatches); *b* 15 July 1920; *educ* Ampleforth; *m* 28 March 1944 *Sheila Katherine [Mrs Hugh Feilding, Home Farm, Bainton, E Yorks YO25 9NJ], only dau of Brig Charles Arthur Bolton, CBE, and *d* 3 April 1996, leaving:
1a +John Henry; *b* 6 Oct 1945; *educ* Ampleforth; *m* 1971 *Veronica, 2nd dau of John Farmer, of 36 Iverna Gdns, London W8, and has issue:
1b +Michael John Richard; *b* 1975
2b +Andrew Francis Alexander; *b* 1977
1b *Natasha Frances Katherine; *b* 1973
2b *Alexandra; *b* 1981
(5) Henry Anthony, MC (1945), JP (1967) Warwicks, Capt Coldstream Gds WW II; *b* 27 Feb 1924; *educ* Ampleforth and King's Coll Cambridge (MA 1952); *m* 2 Aug 1950 *Dunia Maureen [The Hon Mrs Henry Feilding, Manor House, Pailton, nr Rugby, Warwicks], yr dau of Gordon Spencer, MD, of Putley, nr Ledbury, Herefs, and *d* 1994, leaving issue:
1a +Jasper Simon [Jasper Feilding Esq, Falstaff House, 33 Sheep St, Shipston-on-Stour, Warwicks]; *b* 3 May 1953; *educ* Ampleforth and RAC Circencester; *m* 1980 *Diana Margaret, dau of Maj E D Lloyd-Thomas, of Maes-y-Crochan House, St Mellons, Cardiff, and has issue:
1b *Katherine Louisa; *b* 1982
2b *Tessa Caroline; *b* 1985
1a *Penelope Dunia [Mrs Robert Goodwin, 6 Church Rd, Apsley Heath, Woburn Sands, Beds MK17 8TA]; *b* 13 Sept 1954; *m* 11 Dec 1976 *Maj Robert H P Goodwin, yst son of Lt-Gen Sir Richard Elton Goodwin, KCB, CBE, DSO, of Barrow House, Barrow, Bury St Edmunds, and has issue:
1b *Lucy Dunia; *b* 1980

2b *Clare Penelope; *b* 1982
3b *Alice Elizabeth; *b* 1985
2 Hugh Cecil Robert; Lt-Cdr RN; *b* 30 Dec 1887; *ka* Battle of Jutland 31 May 1916
3 Henry Simon, Capt Coldstream Gds; *b* 29 June 1894; *d* 9 Oct 1917 of wounds recd in action in Flanders
1 Mary Alice Clare; *b* 31 March 1888; *m* 25 Feb 1915 Sir Cecil Francis Joseph Dormer, KCMG, MVO, son of Hon Hubert Francis Dormer (*see* DORMER, B), and *dsp* 7 March 1973
2 Dorothie Mary Evelyn; Ambulance Corps WW I (British Mil Medal, 1914 Star, Order of Leopold of Belgium, Croix de Guerre); *b* 6 Oct 1889; *m* 5 July 1917 Capt Charles Joseph Henry O'Hara Moore, MC, Irish Guards, of Mooresfort, Co Tipperary, and *d* 24 Oct 1935, leaving issue. He *d* 25 April 1965
3 Agnes Mary Mabel, nun; *b* 13 Sept 1891; *educ* Lond U (BA 1936); *d* 31 Aug 1938
4 Marjorie Mary Winifrede; *b* 4 Sept 1892; *m* 1st 18 Jan 1915 (*divorce* 1923) Capt Edward Dudley Hanly, Roy Inniskilling Fus, est s of Lt-Col E A Hanly, of Avonmore House, Co Wicklow, and had issue. He *d* 17 Dec 1951. She *m* 2nd 8 Feb 1923 Capt Robert Arthur Heath, MC, son of Col Arthur Howard Heath, of 22 Bryanston Sq, London W, and *d* 19–, having had further issue. He *d* 4 Sept 1943
5 Clare Mary Cecilia; *b* 23 Nov 1896; *m* 22 Dec 1919 G/Capt Joseph Ruscombe Wadham Smyth-Pigott, CBE, DSO, RAF, s of Cecil Hugh Smyth-Pigott, JP, of Brockley Hall, Somerset, and *d* 31 March 1966, having had issue. He *d* 8 Oct 1971
6 Bettie Mary; *b* 22 Aug 1899; *m* 26 July 1926 Eric George Sherbrooke Walker, MC, late RAF, of Majorca, son of Rev George Sherbrooke Walker, of March, Cambs, and *d* 19–, leaving issue
7 Victoria Mary Dolores; *b* 29 March 1901; *m* 31 Jan 1933 Walter Miles Fletcher, of Ngobit, Kenya, s of Christopher Denton Fletcher, of Launceston, Tasmania, and *d* 19–, leaving issue

The **9th/8th Earl** *m* 2nd 12 Feb 1928 Kathleen (*d* 13 Feb 1952), yst dau of Thomas Addis Emmet, of New York, and *d* 25 Nov 1939

His grandson,

WILLIAM RUDOLPH STEPHEN FEILDING, **10th Earl of Denbigh** and **9th Earl of Desmond**, JP Warwicks; *educ* Oratory Sch; Capt Coldstream Gds WW II; *b* 17 April 1912; *m* 17 May 1940 Verena Barbara (Betty) (*d* 28 Feb 1995), widow of Lt-Col Thomas Paget Fielding Johnson and dau of William Edward Price, of Hallgates, Cropston, Leics, and *d* 31 Dec 1966, leaving issue:

1 WILLIAM RUDOLPH ('ROLLO') MICHAEL FEILDING, **11th Earl of Denbigh** and **10th Earl of Desmond**; *b* 2 Aug 1943; *educ* Eton; advertising exec, pop group promoter (including The Animals), in pirate radio broadcasting, Rolls-Royce dealer, pres Motorcycle Industry Assoc, sponsor TT Riders Assoc, Lib spokesman Ho Lds arts and tport and chm Standing Ctee Drug Abuse, chm Warwicks NSPCC Centenary Appeal; *m* 2 Sept 1965 *(Caroline) Judith Vivienne, only dau of Lt-Col Geoffrey Cooke, of Little Orchard, Sunningdale, Berks, and *d* 23 March 1995, leaving issue:
(1) ALEXANDER STEPHEN RUDOLPH FEILDING, **12th and present Earl of Denbigh** and **11th Earl of Desmond**
(1) *Samantha Clare Barbara; *b* 28 Nov 1966; *m* 1990 *Guy John Desmond Hurley, er s of David Hurley, of Ballydaheen, Port Salon, Co Donegal, and has issue:
1a *Charlotte Lauren Sasha; *b* 1992
2a *Constance Cora Anne; *b* 19 Aug 1994
3a *Cora Lucy Vivienne; *b* 4 Dec 1995
(2) *Louisa Helen Sonia; *b* 5 Feb 1969; *m* 16 Sept 1995 *Richard H R Barton, er s of Brian Barton
1 *(Imelda) Clare [The Lady Clare Simonian, Grounds Farm, Monks Kirby, Rugby CV23 0RH]; *b* 29 Nov 1941; *m* 26 Feb 1966 (*divorce* 1979) David Rodney Doig, eldest son of Lt-Col Alec Doig, of Karundas, Kiganjo, Kenya, and has issue:
(1) *Andrew William David; *b* 10 March 1969
(1) *Rowena Helen; *b* 24 Aug 1967
(2) *Zoe Claire; *b* 21 Feb 1971
1 (cont) Lady Clare Doig *m* 2nd 1984 *Jack Levon Simonian, of Harrogate

DENHAM

Arms: Or a bend vaire cotised sable. **Crest:** A falcon rising belled or. **Supporters:** Dexter, a golden retriever; sinister, a black greyhound proper, each charged on the shoulder with a portcullis chained or. **Motto:** *Contentement passe richesse* ('Contentment surpasses riches'). **Creations:** Bt. (E) 25 June 1660 and (UK) 21 Jan 1933 (UK), B. (UK) 24 May 1937.

THE 2ND BARON DENHAM, of Weston Underwood, Co Buckingham, and a **Baronet** (Sir Bertram (Bertie) Stanley Mitford Bowyer, 2nd Bt, of Weston Underwood, and 10th Bt, of Denham, KBE (1991), PC (1980)) [The Rt Hon The Lord Denham KBE PC, The Laundry Cottage, Weston Underwood, Olney, Bucks MK46 5JZ]; *b* 3 Oct 1927; *s* f in barony and 1933 btcy 1948 and kinsman in 1660 btcy 1950; *educ* Eton and King's Coll Cambridge (BA 1950); joined Gren Gds 1945, late Lt Oxon and Bucks LI, HAC 1955, Ld-in-Waiting 1961–64 and 1970–71, Oppn Jr Whip 1964–70, Capt Yeomen Gd 1971–74, Oppn Dep Ch Whip 1974–78, Oppn Ch Whip 1978–79, Capt Gentlemen-at-Arms (Govt Ch Whip Ho Lds) 1979–91, Countryside Commr 1993–, author: *The Man Who Lost His Shadow* (1979), *Two Thyrdes* (1983), Foxhunt (1988) and *Black Rod* (1997); *m* 14 Feb 1956 *Jean, only dau of Maj Kenneth McCorquodale, MC, TD, of Fambridge Hall, White Notley, Essex, and Dunach, Oban, Argyll (*see* 1970 edn McCORQUODALE OF NEWTON, B), and has issue:
1 +RICHARD GRENVILLE GEORGE; *b* 8 Feb 1959; *educ* Eton; *m* 1988 (*divorce* 19–) Eleanor, only dau of A Sharpe; *m* 2nd 17 Aug 1996 *Dagmar, only dau of Kavel Hugo Bozek, of Breslau, Czech Republic
2 +Henry (Harry) Martin Mitford; *b* 9 May 1963; *educ* Eton; *m* 10 Sept 1994 *Barbara, dau of J H Strachan, of Ednaston, Derbys and has:
(1) +Edmond Hunter Mitford; *b* 5 Aug 1997
3 +George Philip Paul; *b* 13 Dec 1964; *educ* Eton
1 *Jocelyn Jane; *b* 18 Oct 1957; *m* 1995 *Kenneth Roland George and has:
(1) *Diana Jean; *b* 1995

Lineage: THOMAS BOWYER; living *c* 1379; *m* Katherine de Knypersley, who brought him that estate; had

WILLIAM BOWYER; *m* Margaret, dau of Nicholas Trubshawe, and left, with other issue:

WILLIAM BOWYER; *m* Elizabeth, dau of — Erdiswick, of Sandon, and had, with other issue:

THOMAS BOWYER; *m* Janet, dau of William Cotton, of Chester, and had:

RICHARD BOWYER, of Petworth, Sussex; *m* Jane Gunter, of Racton, and had:

WILLIAM BOWYER, of Petworth; *m* Eliza, dau of Robert Tredcroft, of Billingshurst, and *d* 1528; his second s:

ROBERT BOWYER, Mayor Chichester 1532 and 1546; *m* Margaret — (*bur* 30 Aug 1563) and *d* between 1 July 1547 and 22 June 1552, leaving a 2nd s:

FRANCIS BOWYER, London merchant, Sheriff 1577, Alderman; *m* Elizabeth (*bur* 30 Oct 1606), dau and heiress of William Tillesworth, of London, and *d* 24 June 1581, having had, with three yr sons and three daus:

Sir WILLIAM BOWYER, bought Denham Court, Bucks; Teller Exchequer *temp* JAMES I; *m* Mary (*m* 2nd 13 Feb 1617 1st Earl of Marlborough of the Feb 1625/6 cr (*see* MARLBOROUGH, D, preliminary remarks)), dau and coheir of Thomas Pierson, of Westminster, Usher Court Star Chamber, and *d* Aug 1616, having had, with another s (Robert):

Sir HENRY BOWYER; *m* Anne, dau and heiress of Nicholas Salter, of London, and *dvp* 27 Dec 1613, having had, with a yr s (Henry, royalist, *k* Civil War):

Sir William Bowyer, 1st Bt (E), so *cr* 25 June 1660, of Denham Court; *bapt* 29 June 1612; helped the poet Dryden (*see* DRYDEN, Bt) translate Virgil; MP Bucks 1659–79; *m* 29 May 1634 Margaret (*d* 8 Jan 1678), dau of Sir John Weld, of Arnolds, Middx, and *d* 2 Oct 1679, leaving, with two yr sons and several daus:

Sir William Bowyer, 2nd Bt, MP Bucks; *b* 1639; *m c* 24 Dec 1679 Frances Cecil (*d* 15 June 1723), gdau of 2nd Earl of Salisbury (*see* SALISBURY, M), and *d* 13 Feb 1721/2, having had, with other issue, including a yr s (William, *m* Elizabeth, dau of Richard Parker, of Hedsor, and had issue):

CECIL BOWYER; *m* 22 July 1707 Juliana, dau of Richard Parker, of Hedsor, Bucks, and *d* 5 Dec 1720, leaving, with three other s and two daus:

Sir William Bowyer, 3rd Bt; *b* 1710; *m* 21 Aug 1733 Anne (*d* 22 May 1785), dau of Sir John Stonhouse, 3rd Bt (*qv*), and had, with other issue:

1 **Sir William Bowyer, 4th Bt**; *b* 1736; *m* 26 Aug 1776 Anne (*d* 25 Dec 1802), dau of — Carey and widow of Capt James Baker, RN, and *dsp* April 1799

2 **Sir George Bowyer, 5th Bt**, and 1st Bt (GB), so cr 8 Sept 1794 in recognition of his conduct at the Glorious First of June naval victory under Earl Howe (*qv*) three months earlier, of Radley, Berks (an estate inherited 1795 from his unc Sir James Stonhouse, Bt), Adml the Blue, MP Queenborough 1784–90; *m* 1st 11 Nov 1768 Margaret (*dsp* 18 Sept 1778), dau of Rev — Price and widow of Sir Jacob Downing, 4th Bt; *m* 2nd 4 June 1782 Henrietta (*d* Nov 1845), only dau and heir of Sir Piercy Brett, MP, Adml the White, and *d* 6 Dec 1799, leaving, with other issue:

(1) **Sir George Bowyer, 6th Bt**, and 2nd Bt, MA Oxon, MP Malmesbury 1807–10 and Abingdon 1811–18; *b* 3 March 1783; *m* 19 Nov 1808 Anne Hammond (*d* 1844), dau of Capt Sir Andrew Snape Douglas, RN, and *d* 1 July 1860, leaving, with other issue:

1a **Sir George Bowyer, 7th Bt**, and 3rd Bt, DCL, barrister, MP Dundalk 1852–68 and Wexford 1874–80, Kt Justice SMO Malta, Grand Cross Order St Gregory, Grand Collar Constantinian Order St George, Chamberlain to the Pope; *b* 8 Oct 1811; *d* unm 7 June 1883

2a **Sir William Bowyer, 8th Bt**, and 4th Bt, barrister; *b* Oct 1812; *m* 16 June 1857 Ellen Sarah (*d* 7 Dec 1899), dau of Shirley Foster Woolmer, barrister, and *dsp* 30 May 1893

3a Henry George, Schs Inspr; *b* 3 Jan 1813; *m* 20 Feb 1855 Katherine Emma (*d* 2 Jan 1926), only child of Rev George Sandby, and *d* 26 Sept 1883, leaving surv issue:

1b **Sir George Henry Bowyer, 9th Bt**, and 5th and last Bt, Lt Staff and 4th Bn Cheshire Regt; *b* 9 Sept 1870; *m* 4 May 1899 (*divorce* 7 Nov 1900) Ethel, dau of Francis Hawkins, and *dsp* 27 Sept 1950, when the 1794 btcy expired and the 1660 one passed to the **2nd Baron Denham** (*see* below)

1b Beatrice Mary; *b* 19 Oct 1867; *m* 1890 James Frederick Shaw (*d* 21 Dec 1946), of Bourton Hall, nr Rugby, and *d* 18 March 1947, having had issue

2b Helen Gertrude (Mother Rita Maria), nun Order of The Assumption; *b* 14 Nov 1871; *d* 31 Jan 1954

(1) Henrietta; *m* 10 Oct 1812 Charles Sawyer, of Heywood Lodge, Berks, and had issue

3 RICHARD, of whom presently

Sir WILLIAM *d* 12 July 1768; his 3rd son,

RICHARD BOWYER later ATKINS-BOWYER (added under terms of will of Sir Richard Atkins, Bt, of Clapham, Surrey); *m* 3 Feb 1773 Elizabeth, dau of C Brady, of Dublin, and *d* 21 Nov 1820, leaving, with other issue:

WILLIAM ATKINS-BOWYER, of Braywick Grove, Berks, and Clapham, Surrey, Brevet Maj 59th Regt, Bde Maj Forces Halifax, Nova Scotia; *b* 11 Jan 1779; *m* 13 April 1803 Frances (*d* 24 Jan 1856), dau of Hon Behning Wentworth, Sec Nova Scotia, of Canon Bridge, Madley, Herefs, by Anne, 2nd dau of William Bird, JP, of Drybridge House, Herefs, and had, with other issue:

1 WILLIAM HENRY WENTWORTH, of whom presently

1 Frances Augusta; *m* 1st 20 Aug 1825 Rev George Augustus Legge (*d* 16 June 1826), est s of Rev Hon Augustus George Legge, MA (*see* DARTMOUTH, E); *m* 2nd 1828 Rev Samuel Wyatt Cobb (*d* 23 Dec 1856), Rector Ightham, and *d* 4 Dec 1869, leaving issue

2 Penelope Maria; *m* Rev William Frankelin, and *d* 1859, leaving issue

3 Anne Elizabeth; *m* 13 June 1851 Rev Henry Hodgson, Rector Ashwell, Herts, and had issue

4 Eleanor Catherine; *m* 2 May 1846 Beaumont Hankey, and had issue

William ATKINS-BOWYER *d* 9 Feb 1844; his son,

Rev WILLIAM HENRY WENTWORTH ATKINS-BOWYER, Rector Clapham 1847–72; *b* 1807; *educ* BNC Oxford (MA, BCL 1859); *m* 1st 12 May 1831 Emily (*d* 3 June 1840), dau of Henry Harpford, of Downe Place, Maidenhead, and had, with other issue:

1 Frances Emily; *m* 26 Aug 1865 Edward Till, of Clapham Common, Surrey, and had issue

The Rev WILLIAM *m* 2nd 18 April 1844 Charlotte (*d* 3 May 1864), yr dau of Capt William Wells, RN, of Holmewood, Hunts, and by her had, with other issue:

1 WENTWORTH GRENVILLE, of whom presently

2 Edward Wentworth; *b* 23 Jan 1862; *m* 8 Jan 1895 Hon Georgiana Harriet Cross (*d* 15 March 1957), est dau of 1st Viscount Cross (*qv*), and *d* 29 Dec 1914, leaving issue:

(1) Richard Wentworth, Assist Master Cranleigh Sch, Surrey; WW I (wounded twice) as Capt 9th Service Bn Sherwood Foresters; *b* 27 Dec 1895; *educ* Univ Coll Oxford (MA, BMus); *d* unm 15 Aug 1943

(1) Helen Georgiana; *b* 1 Nov 1898; *m* 8 Oct 1919 Charles Whitby Vickers, and *d* 20 Sept 1921

2 Beatrice Anne; *m* 16 Nov 1878 Rev Henry Ley Greaves (*d* 27 Dec 1899), Rector Trinity, Midlothian, and *d* 23 Oct 1907, leaving issue

3 Lilian; *m* 11 July 1876 Henry Charles Zerffi (*d* 1915), and *d* 4 Aug 1926, having had issue

The Rev WILLIAM *d* 25 Feb 1872; his er son,

Lt-Col WENTWORTH GRENVILLE BOWYER, RE, DL, JP; *b* 10 Nov 1850; *m* 29 Oct 1883 Eva Mary (*d* 22 May 1954), dau of Major-Gen Charles Stuart Lane, CB, and had issue:

1 GEORGE EDWARD WENTWORTH, **1st Baron**

2 Aldred William; *b* 15 March 1889; *d* 10 Jan 1890

3 Richard Grenville, Lt RN; *b* 18 May 1890; *ka* 17 March 1917

4 John Francis, CB (1966), Lt-Cdr RN (Emergency List), barrister Inner Temple 1928, Bencher Lincoln's Inn 1952, Registrar High Court Bankruptcy 1953 (Ch Registrar and Clerk Restrictive Practices Court 1957); *b* 11 Jan 1893; *m* 3 July 1919 Violet, 3rd dau of Maj-Gen George Robert James Shakespear, IA, and widow of Maj Egerton Lowndes Wright, MC, and *d* May 1974, leaving issue:

(1) Peter George Grenville, F/Lt RAF; *b* 22 March 1920; *m* 21 Dec 1951 Mary Bayliss, of Toronto, and *d* 31 Dec 1991, having adopted:

*John Robert; *b* 24 Oct 1953

(2) Hugh Edward Wentworth, Maj The Rifle Bde, barrister Inner Temple 1947; *b* 11 Oct 1921; *m* 22 Sept 1942 *Suzette [Mrs Hugh Bowyer, The Pantiles, 12 Fountain Hill, Budleigh Salterton, Devon EX9 6AR], dau of Capt Peter Longton, MC, of Heatherwold, nr Newbury, Berks, and *d* 1985 leaving issue:

1a +James David Ross [James Bowyer Esq, 9 Fairview Gdns, Woodford Green, Essex G98 7DG]; *b* 28 Sept 1949; *educ* Harrow; *m* 1993 *Susan Rymond

1a *Sally Anne [Mrs Robert Tailyour, Boxfield, 15 Knowle Rd, Budleigh Salterton, Devon EX9 6AR]; *b* 10 Sept 1945; *m* 28 Oct 1967 *Lt Robert Stewart Tailyour, RM, and has issue:

1b *Helen Caroline; *b* 1971

2b *Georgina Anne; *b* 1977

(3) +John Robert Patrick [John Bowyer Esq, Rectory Farmhouse, West Hanney, Wantage, Berks]; *b* 24 May 1924; *m* 1948 *Diana, dau of J P Longland, of Meadow View, Olney, Bucks, and has issue:

1a +David Hugh; *b* Feb 1950

1a *Sabrina Violet Jane; *b* July 1949

2a *Sarah Joy; *b* 1958

3a *Diana Jane; *b* 1965

(4) Michael Christopher, Rifle Bde 1945–47, Kenya Police 1953–63; *b* 26 Oct 1926; *m* 12 July 1952 *Elizabeth Anne [Mrs Michael Bowyer, 14 Exeter House, Putney Heath, London SW15 3SU], dau of Cdr Stuart Layton Bennett, RN (ret), and *d* 5 Sept 1996

(1) Penelope Rosemary Joy MOUNTLANGEN (assumed by deed poll 1968), twin with Michael; *m* 1953 (*divorce* 1963) Derek Langenberg and *d* 19 Dec 1994

1 Margaret Anne; *b* 15 Sept 1884; *d* 19 Dec 1887

2 Hilda Mary; *m* 15 Sept 1913 1st Baron Spens (*qv*) and *d* 5 March 1962, leaving issue

3 Mildred Elizabeth; *m* 27 Nov 1917 (*divorce* 1924) Lt-Cdr Geoffrey Bateman Hope (*d* 31 March 1929), RN, and *d* 1966, having had issue

The est son,

Sir George Edward Wentworth Bowyer, 1st Bt, so *cr* 21 Jan 1933, and **1st Baron Denham**, of Weston Underwood, Co Buckingham, so *cr* 24 May 1937 (both UK), MC, DL Bucks; *b* 16 Jan 1886; *educ* Eton and New Coll Oxford (BA 1908); WW I (wounded, despatches) as Capt Oxon and Bucks LI, barrister Inner Temple 1910, MP (C) Buckingham 1918–37, PPS to Pres BOT 1921–23, Pres UDC Assoc 1923–26 and 1929–48, V-Chm C and U Pty Orgn 1930–36, C Whip 1925–35, Jr Ld Treasury 1927–29, Comptroller Household June-Dec 1935, Parly Sec Min Ag and Fisheries 1930–40, C Whip Ho Lds 1945–47, ktd 1929; *m* 27 Feb 1919 Hon Daphne Freeman-Mitford (*d* April 1996), 4th dau of 1st Baron Redesdale (*qv*), and *d* 30 Nov 1948, having had issue:

1 Richard Laurence Grenville, F/O RAFVR WW II; *b* 17 Feb 1920; *ka* Jan 1943

2 BERTRAM STANLEY MITFORD BOWYER, **2nd and present Baron Denham**

1 *Peggy [The Hon Mrs Repard, Bridleway Cottage, Leafy Lane, Tring, Herts HP23 6JS]; *b* 18 May 1925; *m* 24 April 1947 *Cdr (John) David Latimer Repard, OBE, DSC, RN, and has issue:

(1) *Jennifer Ann; *b* 12 Feb 1948; *m* 27 June 1970 (*divorce* 1998) Peter William Allen, er s of R K Allen, of Headlands, Berkhamsted, and has:

1a *William John Kenneth; *b* 1974

2a *John Peter Clarkson; *b* 1977

(2) *Susan Elizabeth; *b* 27 Feb 1950; *m* 1976 *Richard G Algeo, s of Sir Arthur Algeo, CBE, and has:

1a *Nicholas Arthur; *b* 1981

2a *Jonathon Henry; *b* 1985

1a *Lucy Catharine; *b* 1978

(3) *Melinda Louise; *b* 29 June 1955; *m* 1993 *Gerald Stone

DENINGTON

Creation: B. (LP, UK) 1978.

THE BARONESS DENINGTON, of Stevenage, Co Herts (Dame Evelyn Joyce Bursill, DBE (1974, CBE 1966)) [The Rt Hon The Baroness Denington DBE, Flat 3, 29 Brunswick Sq, Hove BN3 1EJ]; *b* 9 Aug 1907; *educ* Blackheath High Sch and Bedford Coll London; jnlst 1927–31, teacher 1933–50; Gen Sec Nat Assoc Lab Teachers 1938–47; memb: St Pancras Borough Cncl 1945–59, LCC 1946–65 (chm New and Expanding Towns Ctee 1960–65), GLC 1964–77 (chm Housing Ctee 1964–67, Dep Leader (Lab) Oppn 1967–73, chm Tport Ctee 1973–75, Chm 1975–76); memb Stevenage Devpt Corp 1950–80 (Chm 1965–80); Chm New Towns Assoc 1973–75; memb: Minister's Centl Housing Advsy Ctee 1955–73, Sutton Dwellings Housing Tst 1976–82, Sutton (Hastoe) Housing Assoc 1981–88, N Br Housing Assocn 1976–88; govr schs in St Pancras and Islington 1945–73, Chm Govrs Coll for the Garment Trades (renamed Coll of Fashion), Ardale Sr Boys Approved Sch; V-Chm Town and Country Planning Assoc; Freeman City London, Hon FRIBA, Hon MRTPI; *m* 1935 Cecil Dallas Denington, son of Richard Denington, of Wanstead

Lineage: PHILIP CHARLES BURSILL, of Woolwich; *m* Edith Rowena — and had issue:

EVELYN JOYCE, *cr* a **Baroness**

DENMAN

Arms: Argent on a chevron between three lion's heads erased gules, three ermine spots or. **Crest:** A raven rising proper, in the beak an annulet or. **Supporters:** On either side a lion gules, charged on the body with five ermine spots in cross or. **Motto:** *Prudentia et constantia* ('Prudence and constancy'). **Creations:** Bt (UK) 2 July 1945, B. (UK) 28 March 1834.

THE 5TH BARON DENMAN OF DOVEDALE, Co Derby, and a **Baronet** (Sir Charles Spencer Denman, 2nd Bt, CBE (1976), MC (1942), TD (1947)) [The Rt Hon The Lord Denman, House of Lords, London SW1A 0PW]; *b* 7 July 1916; *s* cousin as 5th Baron 1971 and f as 2nd Bt 1957; *educ* Shrewsbury; WW II Middle East, DCLI (TA) Maj 1943; *m* 11 Sept 1945 Sheila Ann (*d* 1987), er dau of Col Algernon Bingham Anstruther Stewart, DSO (*see* GALLOWAY, E), and has issue:

1 + RICHARD THOMAS STEWART, ACA; *b* 4 Oct 1946; *educ* Milton Abbey; *m* 1984 *(Lesley) Jane, dau of John Stevens, of 2 Shakespeare Drive, Hinckley, Leics, and has issue:

(1) *Natasha Anne; *b* 1986

(2) *Philippa Jane; *b* 1987

(3) *Louisa Clare; *b* 1993

2 +James Stewart [The Hon James Denman, 14 Prairie St, London SW8 3PU]; *b* 7 Oct 1954; *educ* Stowe; *m* 1989 *Philippa Jane Emma, dau of Lewis Ronald Frederick Trowbridge, of Falfield, Winchester, Hants, and has:

(1) *Olivia Anne Stewart; *b* 1991

3 +(Christopher) John [The Hon John Denman, Hurston Street Farm, Hurston Lane, Storrington, W Sussex RH20 4HF]; *b* 5 Sept 1955; *educ* Millfield; *m* 1984 *Jenny Bridget, MVO, only dau of Rupert Allen, of Head Hedgeside, Headley, Hants, and has issue:

(1) +Nicholas Thomas Stewart; *b* 1988

(2) +Charles Rupert Pendarves; *b* 1990

(3) +Thomas Oliver Pelham; *b* 1993

1 *Gillian Patricia [The Hon Mrs McCall, Upper Old Park Farm, Farnham, Surrey GU9 0AR]; *b* 2 Sept 1944; *m* 3 April 1971 *William Kenneth McCall (*see* LAURIE, Bt) and has issue

Lineage: WILLIAM DENMAN; living *c* 1392; *m* Joane, dau and coheir of William Bolyngbrok; 5th in descent from him was:

NICHOLAS DENMAN; *m* 1st Elizabeth, dau of Roger Eyre, of Holme, Escheator Notts 1516 (and was gggf of Nicholas Denman, Mayor Kingston-upon-Hull 1634 and 1644, memb Ctee Defence Civil War; the line expired in the 6th generation with Thomas Denman, of Walcot, Lincs (*dsp* 1701; left his estates to his cousin Thomas Goulton); *m* 2nd Ann, 7th dau of Humfrey Hercy and sis and coheir of Sir John Hercy, of Grove, Notts; 9th in descent from the 2nd marriage was:

THOMAS DENMAN, of Bevercotes, Notts; agent to the Earl of Clare; *bapt* 20 Oct 1650; *m* 27 Nov 1688 Anne, dau of William Nicholson, of W Retford, Notts, and *d* 1741; his 2nd s:

JOHN DENMAN, of Bakewell, Derbys; *b* 1693; *m* 6 May 1726 Elizabeth (*d* July 1760), dau of Anthony Buxton, and *d* 25 Sept 1752, leaving issue:

1 Joseph, MD, of Buxton, DL, JP Derbys; *b* 1731; *m* 22 March 1761 Elizabeth (*d* 5 March 1803), dau and coheir of Richard Finney, and *dsp* 20 July 1812

2 Thomas, MD, of Mount Street, London W1, physician; *b* 27 June 1733; *m* 1 Nov 1770 Elizabeth (*d* 19 Jan 1833), dau of Alexander Brodie, and *d* 26 Nov 1815, leaving:

(1) THOMAS, **1st Baron**

(1) Margaret; *m* 3 Nov 1789 Sir Richard Croft, 6th Bt, of Croft Castle (*qv*), and *d* 24 Sept 1847

(2) Sophia; *m* 5 May 1791 Matthew Baillie, MD (*d* 23 Sept 1823), and *d* 6 Aug 1845

The only son,

THOMAS DENMAN, **1st Baron Denman of Dovedale**, Co Derby (UK), so *cr* 28 March 1834; *b* 23 Feb 1779; Slr-Gen to QUEEN CAROLINE, whom he defended at her trial, Common Serjeant City London 1822, Attorney-Gen to WILLIAM IV 1830–1832, Ld Ch Justice 1832–50; *m* 18 Oct 1804 Theodosia Anne (*d* 28 June 1852), est dau of Rev Richard Vevers, Rector of Saxby, Leics, by Theodosia Dorothy, 3rd dau of Rev Sir William Anderson, 6th Bt, of Lea, Lincs, and *d* 22 Sept 1854, having had issue:

1 THOMAS DENMAN later AITCHISON-DENMAN (roy licence 20 Dec 1876), **2nd Baron Denman of Dovedale**, DL Haddington and Derbys; *b* 30 July 1805; *m* 1st 12 Aug 1829 Georgina (*d* 25 April 1871), est surv dau of Rev Thomas Roe; *m* 2nd 10 Oct 1871 Marion (*d* 27 Feb 1902), est dau of James Aitchison, of Alderston, Haddington, and *dsp* 9 Aug 1894

2 Joseph, V-Adml, C-in-C Pacific; *b* 23 June 1810; *m* 12 Feb 1844 Grace (*d* 18 Dec 1902), yst dau of Jesse Watts-Russell, of Ilam Hall, Staffs, and Biggin House, Northants, and *dsp* 26 Nov 1875

3 Richard, of Westergate, Arundel; barrister; *b* 13 Jan 1814; *educ* Trin Coll Cambridge (MA); *m* 28 Oct 1840 Emma (*d* 2 Jan 1904), dau of Hugh Jones, of Lark Hill, Lancs, and *d* 19 March 1887, having had issue:

(1) Richard; *b* 3 Jan 1842; *m* 31 May 1871 (*divorce* 1878) Helen Mary (*d* 11 June 1919, having *m* 2nd 1888 Sir Henry Primrose, KCB, CSI, ISO, PC; *see* ROSEBERY, E), est dau of Gilbert McMicking, of Miltonise, Wigtownshire, and *d* 5 April 1883, having had issue:

1a THOMAS DENMAN, **3rd Baron Denman of Dovedale**, PC (1907), JP Sussex; *b* 16 Nov 1874; Ld-in-Waiting 1905–07, Capt Gentlemen-at-Arms 1907–11, Dep Speaker Ho Lds 1909, Govr Gen and C-in-C Australia 1911–14, Hon Capt Army, Maj Middx Hus Imp Yeo, Lt Roy Scots, Hon Col Middx Yeo, Boer War 1900–01 (wounded), WW I as Lt-Col cmdg 2nd Bn Middx Yeo; *m* 26 Nov 1904 Hon Gertrude Mary Pearson, GBE, JP Sussex, Chm Nat Fedn WIs 1917–46, Hon Dir WLA 1939–45, Life Tstee and Memb Exec Ctee Carnegie UK Tst (*d* 2 June 1954), only dau of 1st Viscount Cowdray (*qv*), and *d* 24 June 1954, leaving:

1b THOMAS DENMAN, **4th Baron Denman of Dovedale**; *b* 2 Aug 1905; *d* unm 21 March 1971

1b Anne Judith, OBE (1947), Chm WLA W Sussex; *b* 20 Aug 1907; *educ* Newnham Coll Cambridge (BA 1929); *m* 6 Aug 1931 Lt-Col Sir Walter Raymond Burrell, 8th Bt (*qv*), and *d* 1987, leaving issue

2a **Sir Richard Douglas Denman, 1st Bt** (UK), so *cr* 2 July 1945, JP Cumberland; *b* 24 Aug 1876; *educ* Westminster and Balliol Coll Oxford (BA), MP Carlisle 1910–18 and Leeds Centl 1929–45, Priv Sec to PMG 1906–10 and PPS to Pres BOT 1910, Pres Bd: Ag 1917, Educn 1917, Sec State Air 1931, 2nd Church Estates Commr 1931–43, Memb Ho Laity Ch Assembly 1939–58, Treasurer Queen Ann's Bounty 1939–44, Chm: Nat Lab Orgn 1943–44, Marine and Gen Mutual Life Assur Soc 1939–44, Lt RFA WW I; *m* 1st 11 Feb 1904 (*annulled* 1913) Helen Christian, only dau of Sir Thomas Sutherland, GCMG; *m* 2nd 10 June 1914 Mary Radley (*d* 1 April 1974), dau of James Spencer, of Murrah Hall, Greystoke, Penrith, Cumbria, and *d* 22 Dec 1957, leaving:

1b CHARLES SPENCER DENMAN, **5th and present Baron Denman**

2b +Harold [Harold Denman Esq, East Heath Barn, Stream Lane, Hawkhurst, Kent TN18 4RD]; WW II 1941–46 in RA; *b* 26 Jan 1922; *educ* Repton and Balliol Coll Oxford (BA); *m* 26 March 1976 *Lady Frances Esmé Curzon, 2nd dau of 5th Earl Howe (*qv*) and formerly wife of Derek Alan Whiting, and has issue:

1c +Roland Sebastian Richard; *b* 1977

3b +George [George Denman Esq, Stratton House, Stoney Stratton, Shepton Mallet, Somerset BA4 6EA], served WW II 1943–45, cmded Border Regt 1945, attd 16th Punjab Regt 1945–47; *b* 3 June 1925; *educ* Westminster; *m* 5 Oct 1960 *Linda Louise, 2nd dau of David Fortune Landale, of Dalswinton, Dumfries, and has:

1c *Louisa Anne; *b* 29 Oct 1961

2c *Carola Jane; *b* 22 April 1963; *m* 6 Feb 1993 *Sir James Alexander Moffat Bain Campbell, Bt, of Aberuchill (*qv*)

3c *Davina; *b* 10 March 1968

1b *Phyllis [Miss Phyllis Denman, Penberth, 41 Oakfield Rd, Ashtead, Surrey KT21 2RD]; *b* 13 April 1919; MRCS Eng, LRCP London 1945

2b *Catherine [Mrs Philip Cowburn, Cherwell House, Old Kidlington, Oxford OX5 2EG]; *b* 10 June 1920; *m* 28 Dec 1957 Philip Musgrave Cowburn (*d* 1989), son of Maj Arthur Basil Cowburn, MC, TD, of Graceholme, Lorton, Cumberland, and has issue:

1c *Stephen Denman; *b* 7 May 1959

1c *Anne Clare; *b* 3 April 1962; *m* 1986 *Ieuan D Hemlock

1a Anna Maria Heywood; granted rank of baron's dau 1896; *m* 13 July 1895 Sir John Emmott Barlow, 1st Bt, of Bradwall Hall, Cheshire (*qv*), and *d* 28 May 1965, aged 91, leaving issue

(2) Thomas Hugh Anderson, barrister; *b* 16 Jan 1855; *educ* Trin Coll Cambridge (BA); *m* 28 Jan 1890 Margaret Evelyn (*d* 31 May 1933), 4th dau of Charles Watson Townley, of Fulbourn Manor, Cambridge, and *d* 9 Dec 1918, having had issue:

1a Richard Charles, 2nd Lt Gren Gds; *b* 16 Aug 1896; *ka* 1 Dec 1917

2a John Evelyn Thomas, For Serv, barrister Inner Temple; *b* 21 Dec 1901; *educ* Trin Coll Cambridge (MA); *d* unm 8 Oct 1948

1a Margaret Cecil; *b* 21 June 1898; *m* 12 Jan 1927 Charles Seymour Eastwood, MC, and had issue

(1) Theodosia Anne; *d* 3 June 1852

(2) Emma Sophia Georgiana; *m* 1st 31 Oct 1872 Maj Oswin Cumming Baker-Cresswell (*d* 26 Feb 1886), JP Cresswell and Harehope, Northumberland, and had issue; *m* 2nd 7 Sept 1892 2nd Earl of Ravensworth (*see* RAVENSWORTH, B); *m* 3rd 30 April 1904 James William Wadsworth and *d* 31 Jan 1939

(3) Elizabeth Margaret; *m* 20 Jan 1870 Sir Peniston Milbanke, 9th Bt (*see* 1949 edn), and *d* 31 Oct 1929, leaving issue

(4) Anna Maria; *m* 16 July 1867 Reginald Garton Wilberforce (*d* 19 Jan 1914), DL, of Bramlands, Henfield, Sussex, est son of Rt Rev Samuel Wilberforce, DD, Bp Winchester, and *d* 21 Oct 1938, leaving issue

(5) Eleanora; *m* 11 Feb 1907 Richard Patrick Boyle Davey (*dsp* 25 Nov 1911), of Palazzo Vendramin, Venice, and *d* 5 Jan 1932

4 George (Rt Hon), PC (1893), MA, QC (1861), MP Tiverton 1859–65 and 1866–72, Justice Common Pleas 1872–75, High Court Judge 1875–92; *b* 23 Dec 1819; *m* 19 Feb 1852 Charlotte (*d* 19 Dec 1950), 5th dau of Samuel Hope, of Liverpool, and *d* 21 Sept 1896, leaving issue:

(1) George Lewis, barrister, Metropolitan Police Magistrate 1890–1922; *b* 5 May 1854; *educ* Trin Coll Cambridge (LLM); *m* 13 Jan 1921 Mary Forbes (*d* 28 June 1928), dau of John G Chancellor, of Shieldhill, Lanarks, and widow of John F Cobbett, of Saddington Grange, Leics, and *d* 26 May 1929

(2) Arthur (Sir), FSA, barrister, Clerk Assize SE circuit 1887; *b* 1 May 1857; *educ* Trin Coll Cambridge (MA); *m* 1st 17 Dec 1884 Catherine Agnes (*d* 10 Feb 1917), 7th dau of Edward Nathaniel Conant, DL, JP, of Lyndon Hall, Rutland (*see* CONANT, Bt), and had issue:

1a Roderick Peter George, AMIEE, AFRAcS, Lt-Col Signals WW I (despatches), and WW II; *b* 1 Dec 1894; *educ* Trin Coll Cambridge (MA); *m* 28 Nov 1922 Charlotte Marie Mathilde, MBE (*d* 1980), dau of Baron Raphael d'Erlanger, and was *ka* Libya 20 Nov 1941, leaving issue:

1b +Peter Frederick Arthur [Peter Esq, Dukes House, 23 Lawrence St, London SW3], served WW II in Intell Corps; *b* 12 Dec 1923; *educ* Eton and Trin Coll Cambridge (BA); *m* 6 Sept 1957 *Cornelia, est dau of Maj Hon Oscar Montague Guest, of Cabalva House, Whitney-on-Wye, Herefordshire (*see* WIMBORNE, V), and formerly wife of Hugh Dearman Janson, and has issue:

1c +Philip Roderick; *b* 14 June 1961

2c +Benedict Raphael; *b* 1 Sept 1970

1c *Francesca Marie-Carola; *b* 30 Dec 1959

1b *Carol Antonia Rosaline; *b* 1928

1a Edith Kate; *b* 12 Oct 1885; *d* unm 20 Aug 1958

2a Violet Victoria; *b* 14 Oct 1887; *m* 2 June 1926 Cyril Clarke Prescott, and had issue:

1b *Valentine Crystal [Mrs Michael Stephenson, Pumpkin Cottage, Easton, Nr Wells, Somerset]; *b* 21 Aug 1928; *m* 20 Aug 1953 *Michael Champness Stephenson, and has issue:

1c *Jennifer Sarah; *b* 27 Feb 1956

2c *Elizabeth Anne; *b* 20 Dec 1958

(2) (cont.) Sir Arthur Denman *m* 2nd 4 Oct 1917 Marie Françoise Marcelle Clothilde Louise (*d* 30 May 1934), 3rd dau of Count Henry du Bourg, and *d* 15 Dec 1931, having by her had issue:

2a Henry du Bourg; *b* 16 Sept 1918; *m* 1936 *Joy (*m* 2nd 1947 William Herbert Hooper (*d* 1974), barrister) [Mrs William Hooper, 75 Mill Lane, Herne Bay, Kent], dau of George Henry Hatton, and *d* 18 May 1938, leaving issue:

1b +Carol Julian du Bourg [Carol Denman Esq, 70 Fiddlers Folly, Fordham Heath, Colchester, Essex]; *b* 1938

3a Antony du Bourg; *b* 13 July 1923; *ka* France 1944

(3) Launcelot Baillie, Cdr RN; *b* 15 Jan 1861; *m* 27 April 1892 Blanche Isabella Pauline, 3rd dau of William Ernest de Veulle, of Jersey, and *d* 29 Aug 1935

(4) Francis Richard Amory, Sub-Lt RN; *b* 5 Dec 1862; *m* 12 Jan 1889 Minne Fredericka May (*d* 27 July 1947), dau of William Ernest de Veulle, of Jersey, and *d* at Bulawayo, Rhodesia, 5 May 1900

(1) Charlotte Edith; *m* 19 June 1883 Rev William Henry Draper, MA, Master of the Temple, and *d* 29 Dec 1884

(2) Grace; *m* 6 Nov 1890 Sidney Gambier Parry (*d* 1948), of The Old Rectory, Duntisbourne Rous, Cirencester, and *d* 16 April 1935, leaving issue

5 Lewis William (Rev), MA Cambridge; *b* 23 March 1821; *m* 1st 18 June 1850 Frances Marianne (*d* 25 April 1862), dau of Thomas Eden, of The Bryn, nr Swansea (*see* EDEN OF WINTON, B), and had, with other issue:

(1) Lewis William Eden; *b* 9 May 1857; *m* 5 Aug 1889 Emma (*d* 2 March 1936), dau of Charles Rainbow, and *d* 19 May 1947, leaving issue:

1a Joseph Alban; *b* 17 June 1890; *m* 26 March 1919 Annie Mary (*d* 27 March 1954), dau of Thomas Spicer, of Tilney, Saskatchewan, and *d* 21 April 1965, leaving issue:

1b +George Lewis [George Denman Esq, Cartin, RR1 Sorrento, Canada]; *b* 1920; *m* 1st 7 Dec 1949 Emily (*d* May 1956), dau of — Woodgate, of Prince George, BC, Canada, and has issue:

1c +Robert John; *b* 22 Sept 1952

2c +Ronald Dean; *b* 20 Dec 1954

1c *Dorothy Louisa; *b* 30 Aug 1951; *m* 1971 *Robert Honeyman

1b (cont.) George Denman *m* 2nd 4 April 1963 *Catherine Rose Batchelor Woodgate, dau of A A E Batchelor, of Water Valley, Alberta, Canada

2b +David Keith; *b* 3 March 1937; *m* 27 Dec 1957 *Helen, dau of Fred Balko, of Gilsome, BC, Canada, and has issue:

1c +Stephen Lawrence; *b* 14 July 1961

2c +Stacey Eldon; *b* 12 April 1968

3c +Shaun Lewis Eden; *b* 1973

1c *Debra Ann; *b* 9 Nov 1958

2c *Denise Josephine; *b* 21 April 1965

1b *Joan Gwendoline [Mrs Maurice Parfitt, RR8, Site 5, Comp 3A9, Prince George, BC, Canada V2N 4M6]; *b* 1925; *m* 21 Nov 1959 *Maurice Parfitt

1c *Dennis Lee; *b* 1946; *m* 1966 *Lynn Stoddard, and has issue:

1d *Michelle Lee; *b* 1970; *m* 1991 *Jacques Pelletier, and has issue:

1e *Brandon Dennis Rudolphe; *b* 1993

1e *Kristen Lynne; *b* 1996

2c *Sydney Robert; *b* 1947; *m* 1969 *Susan Strom, and has issue:

1d *Rachael Andrea; *b* 1971

2d *Kirsten Jane; *b* 1973

3c *Lee Roy; *b* 1949

4c *Gordon Douglas; *b* 1952; *m* 1973 *Brenda Erickson, and has issue:

1d *Spencer James; *b* 1976

2d *Amy Olan; *b* 1978

1a Theodosia Victoria; *b* 8 June 1897

5 (cont.) The Rev Lewis Denman *m* 2nd 22 Aug 1865 Frances Starkie Mary (*dsp* 24 *d* 1893), est dau of Col Henry Armytage, Coldstream Guard (*see* ARMYTAGE, Bt), and *d* 6 May 1907

1 Theodosia; *b* 16 Sept 1806; *m* 21 Nov 1825 Ichabod Charles Wright (*d* 14 Oct 1871), of Mapperley Hall, Notts, and *d* 20 May 1895 aged 88, leaving issue

2 Elizabeth; *b* 21 Nov 1807; *m* 3 May 1838 Ven Francis Hodgson (*d* 29 Dec 1852), BD, Provost Eton, Archdeacon Derby, and *d* 2 Aug 1880, leaving issue

3 Frances; *b* 17 Sept 1812; *m* 8 July 1846 Adml Sir Robert Lambert Baynes, KCB (*d* 7 Sept 1869), and *d* 29 April 1890 aged 77, leaving issue

4 Margaret; *b* 8 Aug 1815; *m* 1st 23 Nov 1841 Henry William Macaulay (*d* 24 Sept 1845), brother of Lord Macaulay, and had issue; *m* 2nd 10 Aug 1848 Edward Cropper (*d* 23 May 1877), of Swaylands, Kent, and had further issue (*see* ROSSLYN, E); *m* 3rd 22 April 1879 Col John Owen (*d* 1 or 2 Dec 1890), 2nd son of Sir Hugh Owen, 2nd Bt, of Orielton (*qv*), and *d* 11 June 1899

5 Anne; *b* 26 June 1822; *m* 18 Aug 1846 Cdr Frederick Holland (*d* 21 July 1860), RN, and *d* 23 Aug 1913, leaving issue

6 Caroline Amelia; *b* 26 Aug 1823; *m* 3 Feb 1846 Rev John George Beresford (*d* 17 July 1899), and *d* 23 May 1911, leaving issue (*see* BERESFORD-PEIRSE, Bt)

DENNING

Arms: Per bend or and gules a bar wavy between two lion's heads erased in chief and a lion's face in base all counterchanged. **Crest:** On a chapeau gules, doubled ermine, a dexter glove argent grasping a scroll fesswise proper. **Supporters:** On either side a representation of a Chief Justice of the King's Bench in judicial robes, the dexter *c* 1780 and the sinister *c* 1580. **Motto:** *Fiat justitia* ('Let justice be done'). **Creation:** B. (LP, UK) 1957.

THE BARON DENNING, of Whitchurch, Co Southampton (Sir Alfred Thompson Denning, OM (1997), PC (1948), DL (Hants 1978)) [The Rt Hon The Lord Denning OM PC DL, The Lawn, Whitchurch, Hants RG28 7AS]; *b* 23 Jan 1899; *educ* Andover GS and Magdalen Coll Oxford; WWI: RE (BEF France); barrister Lincoln's Inn 1923, KC 1938, Bencher 1944, ktd 1944; Chllr: Diocese of Southwark 1937–44, London 1942–44; Recorder of Plymouth 1944; Nominated Judge for War Pensions Appeals 1945–48; High Court Judge 1944–48, Ld Justice of Appeal 1948–57, Ld of Appeal in Ordinary 1957–62, Master of the Rolls 1962–82; conducted Profumo Inquiry 1963; Chm: Ctee Procedure in Matrimonial Causes 1946–47, Br Inst of Internat and Comparative Law 1959–86, Ctee Legal Educn Students from Africa 1960, Roy Commn on Historical MSS 1962–82; Pres Birkbeck Coll 1952–83; Treas Lincoln's Inn 1964; Hon Bencher: Middle Temple 1972, Gray's Inn 1979, Inner Temple 1982; Hon Fell: Magdalen Coll Oxford 1948, Nuffield Coll Oxford 1982; Hon LLD Ottawa 1955, Glasgow 1959, Southampton 1959, London 1960, Cambridge 1963, Leeds 1964, McGill 1967, Dallas 1969, Dalhousie 1970, Wales 1973, Exeter 1976, Columbia NY 1976, Tilburg (Netherlands) 1977, W Ontario 1979, Br Columbia 1979, Sussex 1980, Buckingham 1983 and Nottingham 1984; Hon DCL Oxford 1965, Hon FBA 1979; author: *Smith's Leading Cases* (jt ed, 1929), *Bullens and Leake's Precedents* (jt ed, 1935), *Freedom Under the Law* (1949), *The Changing Law* (1953), *The Road to Justice* (1955), *The Discipline of Law* (1979), *The Due Process of Law* (1980), *The Family Story* (1981), *What Next in the Law* (1982), *The Closing Chapter* (1983), *Landmarks in the Law* (1984), *Leaves from my Library* (1986); *m* 1st 1932 Mary (*d* 1941), dau of Rev F N Harvey, R of Fawley, Hants, and has issue by 1st w

1 *Robert Gordon; *b* 1938; *educ* Winchester and Magdalen Coll Oxford (Fellow 1968); *m* 1967 *Elizabeth Carlyle Margaret, dau of E R Chilton, of Oxford, and has issue

BARON DENNING *m* 2nd 1945 Joan Daria (*d* 1992), dau of John Vinings Elliott Taylor and widow of John Matthew Blackwood Stuart, CIE

Lineage: CHARLES DENNING; *m* Clara — and had:

ALFRED THOMPSON, *cr* a **Baron**

DENNY of Castle Moyle

Arms: Gules, a saltire argent between twelve cross-crosslets or. **Crest:** A cubit arm vested azure, turned up argent, holding five wheatears or. **Motto:** *Et mea messis erit* ('The harvest also shall be mine'). **Creation:** Bt. (I) 12 May 1782. NB 'Castle Moyle' is an error in the patent of the baronetcy for 'Castle More', *i.e.*, the 'Great Castle' of Tralee.

SIR ANTHONY CONINGHAM DE WALTHAM DENNY, 8TH BT, of Castle Moyle, Co Kerry [Sir Anthony Denny Bt, The Priest's House, Muchelney, Somerset TA10 0DQ]; *b* 22 April 1925; *s* f 1953; *educ* Clayesmore Sch and Anglo French Art Centre and Regent St Poly Sch of Architecture; FRSA, MCSD, Hereditary Freeman City of Cork, F/Sgt RAF 1943–47, designer, ptnr Verity and Beverley, architects and designers; *m* 1 Sept 1949 *Anne Catherine, er dau of Samuel Beverley, FRIBA, of Wilmead, Linslade, Bucks, and 32 Old Burlington St, London W1, and has issue:

1 +PIERS ANTHONY De WALTHAM [Piers Denny Esq, Gilletts Farm, James Lane, Yarcombe, Devon EX14 9AZ]; *b* 14 March 1954; *educ* King Alfred Sch and Westfield Coll London U; *m* 1987 *Ella Jane, only dau of Peter P Huhne, and has issue:

(1) *Matilda Ann; *b* 1988

(2) *Isabel Margaret; *b* 1990

2 +Thomas Francis Coningham [Thomas Denny Esq, Lower Cross Cottage, Hinton St Mary, Sturminster Newton, Dorset]; *b* 12 May 1956; *educ* King Alfred Sch and Edinburgh Coll of Art; *m* 1985 *Benita Jane, yr dau of S/Ldr Simon Hugh Kevill-Davies, RAF (*see* LEES, Bt, of S Lytchett), and has issue:

(1) *Madeline Anne; *b* 1987

Sir ANTHONY and Lady Denny also adopted 3 Feb 1975:
*Sophy Elinor Sisophanh; *b* 1974; *educ* U of West of England; *m* 3 Jan 1988 *Harvey Layzell, s of Peter Layzell

Lineage: GEOFFREY DENNY; *m* Cecily, dau of Hugh de Waltham, MP City London 1319, and had:

Sir ROBERT DENNY, MP Cambridge 1391–93, Lt to Ld High Constable at time of Siege of Rouen; *m* Amy, widow of John (s and h of Sir John Furneux, of Bergham), and *d* 1420; ggf of:

Sir EDMUND DENNY, of Cheshunt, Herts; King's Remembrancer to HENRY VII, Baron of the Exchequer 1513–20; *d* 1520, having had, with other issue:

1 Thomas (Sir), of the Great House, Cheshunt, whose son, John of Howe Hall, Norfolk, one of the Privy Chamber of HENRY VIII, was ancestor of the extinct DENNYs of Howe

2 ANTHONY (Sir)

1 Joice; *m* 1st William Walsingham and had issue; *m* 2nd Sir John Cary and had issue (*see* FALKLAND, V)

2 Mary; *m* Sir John Gates, KB, PC, Chllr Duchy Lancaster, Capt Gd to EDWARD VI

3 Martha; *m* Sir Wymond Carew, KB, of Antony, Devon

The yr son,

Sir ANTHONY DENNY, PC; MP Herts 1547; *b* 1500; Ch Gentleman Privy Chamber, Comptroller Household, an executor HENRY VIII's will and a guardian of EDWARD VI; *m* Joan, dau of Sir Philip Champernowne, of Modbury, and *d* 1549, having had issue:

1 Henry, of Cheshunt, Herts, and Waltham Abbey, Essex (godson of HENRY VIII); *m* 1st Honora, dau of 13th Lord (Baron) Grey (of Wilton) by Lady Mary Somerset, dau of 1st Earl of Worcester (*see* BEAUFORT, D), and had, with other issue:

(1) Robert; *d* 12 Aug 1576

(2) EDWARD DENNY, 1st LORD (Baron) DENNY, so *cr* by writ of summons 27 Oct 1604, also 1st and last EARL OF NORWICH, so *cr* by letter patent 24 Oct 1626 (both E); MP Westmorland 1592–93 and Essex; *b* 15 Aug 1569; *educ* St John's Coll Cambridge; ktd 1589, MP Westmorland 1593 and Essex 1604, High Sheriff Herts 1602–03; *m c* 1590/1 Lady Mary Cecil, dau of 1st Earl of Exeter (*see* EXETER, M), and *dspm* 24 Oct 1637, when the Earldom expired, although the Barony, having been *cr* by writ of summons, passed to his deceased dau's s, having had issue:

1a Honora; *m* 6 Jan 1608 James Hay, 1st Earl of Carlisle of the 1622 *cr* (*see* CARLISLE, E, preliminary remarks), and *dvp* 1614, leaving:

1b JAMES HAY, 2nd and last LORD (Baron) DENNY and 2nd and last EARL OF CARLISLE, KB (Feb 1626/6); *b c* 1612; ktd 1623, hereditary proprietor of Barbados (at that time known as the Carlile [*sic*] Islands), where he rode out the Civil War years though a Col of royalist Horse; *m* 21 March 1631/2 Lady Margaret Russell, dau of 4th Earl of Bedford (*see* BEDFORD, D) and *dsp* 30 Oct 1660, when his peerages expired

1 (cont.) Henry Denny *m* 2nd Elizabeth, dau of Lord John Grey, and *d* 1574, having by her had issue:

(3) Henry; *d* unm

2 Edward (Sir), KB, of Stortford Manor, Herts (godson of EDWARD VI), Gentleman Privy Chamber to ELIZABETH I, memb Cncl of Munster, MP Liskeard 1584 and Tregony 1597, High Sheriff Co Kerry 1588, ktd 1589, served against the Earl of Desmond, the Irish and the Spaniards in Ireland and was granted 6,000 acres of Desmond's forfeited estates, including the town and the Earl's chief castle of Tralee; *m* Margaret, Maid of Honour to ELIZABETH I, dau of Pierce Edgcumbe, of Mount Edgcumbe, MP Cornwall (*see* MOUNT EDGECUMBE, E), and had, with other issue:

(1) ARTHUR (Sir)

(2) Henry, of Bishops Stortford Manor, whose line became extinct when his ggs Lt-Col William Denny, of Cheshunt, BA Oxon 1730, Lt-Govr Pennsylvania 1756–59, *dsp* 1765

(3) Anthony, of Bishops Stortford Manor; *m* Mary, dau of Thomas Aldrich, of Swadeston, Norfolk, and *d* April 1662, leaving issue:

1a Edward, of Bishops Stortford; *m* Cordelia, dau of Adam Hill, of Spaldwick, Hunts, and *d* 14 March 1720 in his 90th year, leaving issue:

1b Elizabeth

2b Anne; *m* John Sandford and *d* 10 Sept 1747, leaving issue

Sir EDWARD *d* 12 Feb 1599/1600; his est son,

Sir ARTHUR DENNY, of Tralee Castle and Carrignafely Manor, nr Tralee; *b* 1584; *m* Elizabeth (*m* 2nd 26 May 1639 Sir Thomas Harris), sis of Sir Anthony Forest, and *d* 1619, having had:

Sir EDWARD DENNY, of Tralee Castle, High Sheriff Co Kerry 1634, MP 1639, Constable Castle Magne 1641, a royalist cdr Ireland; *b* 1605; *m* 1625 Ruth, est dau and eventually heir of Sir Thomas Roper, Viscount Baltinglass, and had, with other issue:

1 ARTHUR (Sir)

2 Edward, of Castle Lyons, Co Cork; *b* 1630; *m* Lady Catherine Barry, dau of 1st Earl of Barrymore, and *d* 1695, leaving issue:

(1) Barry, MP Tralee 1696–99; *m* 1691 Catherine, dau and eventual coheir of Sir Boyle Maynard, MP Curryglass, Co Cork, and had issue:

1a Edward, MP; *m* Angell, dau of Digby Foulkes, of Youghall, Co Cork, and *dsp*

1a Anne; *m* Rev Maurice O'Connor, Rector of Tralee (*see* below)

Sir EDWARD *d* 1646; his est son,

Sir ARTHUR DENNY, of Tralee Castle; High Sheriff Co Kerry 1656, MP 1661, V-Adml Munster 1669, memb Cncl of Munster, MA Dublin; *b* 21 Sept 1629; *m* 1st Lady Ellen Barry, dau of 1st Earl of Barrymore; *m* 2nd Frances, dau of Sir Richard Kyrle, Govr Carolina, and *d* 1673, leaving by his 1st w:

EDWARD DENNY, of Tralee Castle; Col, MP Co Kerry 1695–99, Provost Tralee; *b* 10 Feb 1652; *m* 1673 Mary, dau and eventual coheir of Sir Boyle Maynard (*see* above), and had issue:

1 EDWARD

1 Catherine; *m* 1708 William Sprigge, of Clonevoe, King's Co, MP Tralee, and had issue

2 Jane; *m* Col John Blennerhasset, MP Ballyseedy (*see* BLENNERHASSET, Bt), and had issue

Col DENNY *d* 1709; his only son,

EDWARD DENNY; Col, MP Doneraile 1695–99, Co Kerry 1703–14 and Askeaton 1715–28, Provost Tralee; *m* 1700 Lady Letitia Coningsby, 2nd dau and coheir of Thomas, Earl of Coningsby, and *d* 1728, leaving, with other issue:

1 Arthur, Col, MP Co Kerry 1727–42, High Sheriff 1741, Provost Tralee; *m* Lady Arabella FitzMaurice, 2nd dau of Thomas, Earl of Kerry (*see* LANSDOWNE, M), and *dsp* 1742

2 Thomas (Sir), of Tralee Castle, Dep Govr Co Kerry, ktd 1743, Col Regt of Dragoons 1745, Provost Tralee; *m* 1740 his cousin Agnes, dau of John Blennerhasset, MP Ballyseedy (*see* BLENNERHASSET, Bt), and *d* 1761, having had, with four sons (*dsp*):

(1) Letitia; *m* Lt-Col Rowland Bateman, MP, of Killeen or Oak Park, Co Kerry, and had issue

(2) Jane; *m* her cousin **Sir Barry Denny, 1st Bt**, and had issue (*see* below)

3 Barry (Rev), of Ballyvelly; Treasurer Cathedral of Ardfert, Provost Tralee, Rector Tralee 1738, JP; *m* Jane, dau and eventual heir of Rev Maurice O'Connor, Rector Tralee (*see* above), and *d* Sept 1751, leaving with other issue:

(1) Arthur; *d* unm 1767

(2) BARRY (Sir), **1st Bt**

(3) Edward; Col of Carabineers, MP Tralee 1769–75, Provost of Tralee, LLD; *m* 1769 Mary (*d* 1774), dau and heiress of David Rynd, of Derryvullan, and Drumlone, Co Fermanagh, and *d* Feb 1775, leaving issue

(4) Maynard (Rev), BA, of Churchill, Co Kerry; *b* 1749; *m* Penelope, dau of Anthony Stoughton, of Ballyhorgan, Co Kerry, and *d* 27 June 1812, leaving issue:

1a Jane; *m* Rev Arthur Herbert

The Rev BARRY DENNY'S 2nd son,

Sir Barry Denny, 1st Bt (I), so *cr* 12 Jan 1782, MP Co Kerry 1769–76, 1783–90 and 1790094, High Sheriff Co Kerry 1774, Col of the Tralee Corps Irish Vol and Gen for the County, Major Kerry Militia, Provost of Tralee; *m* 1767 his cousin

Jane (*d* 30 Oct 1811), yr dau and coheir of Sir Thomas Denny, of Tralee Castle, and *d* April 1794, having had, with other issue:

1 **Sir Barry Denny, 2nd Bt**; MP Co Kerry, High Sheriff 1794, Maj Kerry Militia; *m* 12 Jan 1794 Anne (*m* 2nd 29 July 1805 Gen Sir John Floyd, 1st Bt (*qv*), and *d* 4 Dec 1844), dau of Crosbie Morgell, MP Mount Morgell, Co Limerick, and *dsp* 20 Oct 1794 (when about to be raised to the peerage as Baron Castlemore)

2 EDWARD (Sir), **3rd Bt**

1 Agnes; *m* Richard Francis Blennerhassett, of Blennerville (*see* BLENNERHASSETT, Bt)

2 Arabella; *m* her cousin Rowland Bateman, of Oak Park, Co Kerry

3 Letitia; *m* William Rowan, of Arbela, Co Kerry

4 Charlotte; *m* 18 Oct 1796 Rev John Day, of The Manor and Keelballylahive, Co Kerry

5 Diana; *m* Thomas Collie, of Barrow House, Tralee

6 Sophia; *m* Daniel MacGillycuddy, of Tralee (*see* below)

The 2nd Bt's bro,

Sir Edward Denny, 3rd Bt, of Tralee Castle, Co Kerry, DL; High Sheriff 1794, MP 1828–29, Provost of Tralee; *m* 26 May 1795 Elizabeth (*d* 27 April 1828), only child of Hon Robert Day, MP, Judge King's Bench in Ireland, and Id 1 Aug 1831, having had, with other issue:

1 **Sir Edward Denny, 4th Bt**; MP Tralee 1818–19, High Sheriff Co Kerry 1827; *b* 2 Oct 1796; *d* unm 13 June 1889

2 Robert Day (Rev), MA Oxon, Vicar Shedfield, Hants; *b* 21 Aug 1800; *m* 1st 14 June 1833 Sarah (*d* 23 Sept 1839), dau of Thos Grant, of Soberton, Hants, and had issue:

(1) **Sir Robert Arthur Denny, 5th Bt**, Lt 22nd Regt; *b* 23 July 1838; *m* 1872 Jane (*d* 7 Feb 1935), dau of Thomas Kirton, and *dsp* 24 Nov 1921

(1) Arabella Elizabeth; *m* 16 Nov 1864 Rev Frederick Thomas Salmon (*d* 18 May 1906), Rector Gittisham, Devon, and *d* 11 June 1914, leaving issue

2 (cont.) The Rev Robert Denny *m* 2nd 30 Jan 1849 Frances (*m* 2nd 7 Aug 1863 Very Rev Archibald Boyd, Dean of Exeter, and *d* 6 Jan 1877), only dau of Thos Waller, of Ospringe, and *d* 12 July 1864, having by her had:

(2) **Sir Cecil Edward Denny, 6th Bt**; *b* 14 Dec 1850; fndr City of Calgary, Canada, sometime Archivist and Keeper Records to Govt of Alberta, Capt and Inspr Roy NWMP, Commr and Police Magistrate, Canada, served in suppression of Riel Rebellion 1885; *d* unm 24 July 1928

(3) Herbert Champernowne; *b* 22 Feb 1852; *d* unm 17 Feb 1900

(2) Gertrude Honora Frances; *m* 1883 Archibald Henry Boyd, DL, of Bellevue, Westward Ho, N Devon, and *d* 3 July 1921, leaving issue

(3) Frances Flora; *m* 28 Oct 1879 Rev James Arthur Kempe, Rector Abbotsham, Devon, JP, Hon Canon Truro, and *d* 19 March 1937, leaving issue

(4) Constance Mary Sophia; *m* 1883 Johann Josef Weller (*d* 1924), of 111 Krumgasse 2, Vienna, and *d* 17 May 1929, leaving issue

3 Henry (Rev), of Churchill, BA Oxford, Rector Union of Ballynahaglish, Cloherbrien and Annagh, Co Kerry; *b* 20 June 1802; *m* 22 May 1834 his cousin Sophia Catherine (Id 17 Jan 1890), dau of Daniel MacGillycuddy, JP, of Day Place, Tralee, and *d* 25 Sept 1877, leaving, with other issue:

(1) Edward (Rev), Rector Ballyheigue Co Kerry 1878–81 and Laracor, nr Trim, Co Meath 1881–97; *b* 17 Aug 1835; *educ* Trin Coll Dublin (MA); *m* 18 Oct 1877 Marion Georgina (*d* 27 Feb 1940), est dau and eventually sole heir of Lyttelton H Lyster, late 1st Royal W Surrey Regt, of Union Hall, Co Cork, and of Dublin, and *d* 13 Feb 1909, having had issue:

1a HENRY LYTTELTON LYSTER (Rev Sir), **7th Bt**

(2) Henry, Dist Inspr RIC; *b* 1 Jan 1837; *m* 1 Dec 1864 Jane (*m* 2nd 18 May 1875 Joseph Keatinge (*d* 1904), of Lismore, Co Waterford, and *d* 16 Oct 1913), dau of Joseph Armstrong, of Coote Hill, and *d* 9 Nov 1872, leaving:

1a Henry Arthur Francis; *b* 8 March 1868; *d* unm 17 June 1916

2a Edward Ernest Armstrong; *b* 21 July 1873; *d* unm 17 March 1891

1a Kathleen Elizabeth; *m* 23 Oct 1890 George Washington Smith (*d* 10 June 1939), and *d* 19 March 1955, leaving issue

(3) Arthur MacGillycuddy, Lt-Col 13th Regt; *b* 3 March 1838; *d* unm 30 Aug 1898

(4) De Courcy Daniel; *b* 24 Dec 1840; *m* 17 April 1873 Clementina (*d* 10 March 1932), dau of Richard Leahy, of Ballycarty House, Co Kerry, and *d* 16 Dec 1875, leaving issue:

1a Henry De Courcy, Capt 5th Bn Roy Inniskilling Fus, DC Ashanti; *b* 28 May 1874; *d* unm 23 March 1910

(5) Richard, Brevet Lt-Col RMLI, Cmdt Barnstaple VTC 1914–15; *b* 8 Aug 1848; *m* 24 Aug 1881 Mary (*d* 25 Nov 1939), dau of Thomas Stokes Guppy, MD, and *d* 6 July 1915, leaving issue:

1a Richard Brougham, Maj Somerset LI, GSO War Office 1915–17, 1919–22, Assist Mil Attaché Peking 1917–19, Orders of Rising Sun of Japan and St George of Russia, served WW I 1915 (wounded, despatches), Garrison Adj Aldershot 1939–40; *b* 24 June 1889; *educ* Haileybury; *m* 1st 21 April 1928 (*divorce* 1963) Sybil Nina (*d* 1977), er dau of Francis N Evans-Freke (*see* CARBERY, B), barrister, of Newtown Park, Doneraile, Co Cork, and had:

1b *Diana Brougham [Mrs Ronald Macintosh, 77 Oriel Ave, Tawa, Wellington, NZ]; *b* 14 Dec 1930; *m* 21 May 1960 *Ronald Herbert Macintosh, CEng, AMIME, MRINA, and adopted:

*Claire Diana [Mrs Peter Ball, 17 Lake Apex Drive, Gatton, Queensland, Australia]; *b* 20 Aug 1965; *m* 1st 1985 (*divorce* 1988) Steven Charles Marshall, and has issue:

1d *Kylie Deanna; *b* 1987

(cont.) Mrs Claire Marshall *m* 2nd 1988 *Peter John Ball, and has further issue:

1d *Benjamin Peter; *b* 1989

*Fiona Juliet; *b* 19 Nov 1966; *m* 1993 *Nyoman Putra Abriawan, of Bali, Indonesia

2b *Juliet Oldfield [Mrs Peter Taylor, The Chipping Croft, Tetbury, Glos GL8 8EY]; *b* 18 July 1932; *m* 22 Nov 1952 *Peter Walter Taylor, ARSM, BScLond, MA and PhD Queens' Coll Cambridge, and has issue:

1c +Christopher Richard de Courcy; *b* 1957

1c *Caroline Mary Louise; *b* 26 Sept 1954; *m* 1988 *Douglas Wagstaff, MA, and has:

1d *James Douglas; *b* 1989

2d *Adam; *b* 1990

2c *Catherine Jane; *b* 1961; *m* 1988 *Anthony Nicholas Dickinson, and has issue:

1d *Piers Anthony Brougham; *b* 1993

1a (cont.) Maj Richard Denny *m* 2nd 10 May 1967 *Edith Winifred [Mrs Richard Denny, 2 Ashdown Rd, Bexhill-on-Sea, Sussex], er dau of George Arthur Winstone, of Worcester, and *d* 31 Aug 1967

1a Eileen; *educ* Trin Coll Dublin (BA); *m* 4 Feb 1913 Col Francis Crofton Molesworth (*d* 27 June 1955), RE, 4th son of Lt-Col Anthony Oliver Molesworth, and *d* 27 May 1951, leaving issue (*see* MOLESWORTH, V)

2a Joan; *educ* Trin Coll Dublin (BA); *d* unm 20 April 1963

3a Geraldine; *m* 13 July 1918 Col George ThomasIA (ret), and had issue:

1b *Michael Denny, Capt Royal Fus; *b* 1921; *m* 1959 *Sylvia Lorna, dau of V-Adml Lawson

2b *Brian Denny [Brian Johnson Esq, Springvale School, Marandellas, Zimbabwe], MA, served in RAF Coastal Cmd; *b* 1923; *m* 1958 *Truda Neale, and has issue:

1c *Fiona Patricia

1b *Jacqueline Naomi; *m* 1952 (*divorce*) Cdr Richard Arthur Fogwill, RN, and has issue:

1c *Robert Michael

2c *John Richard

(6) Roland John, LRCSI; *b* 30 Sept 1849; *d* unm 17 Sept 1913

(7) Edmund Barry, LRCSI, LRCPE, JP (Lincs); *b* 29 Nov 1860; *m* 18 Sept 1884 Emily Barclay (*d* 1957 aged 99), dau of Henry Colclough Allen, of Dublin, and *d* 21 Oct 1945, having had issue:

1a Henry Allen Maynard, Capt 6th Bn Lincs Regt WW I (wounded); *b* 28 March 1887; *m* 1st 22 May 1926 (*divorce* 1950) Kathleen Mary, 2nd dau of Walter Werden Goddard, of Stroud, Glos, and has issue:

1b *Norah Peta; *b* 11 April 1928; *m* 19 Nov 1949 *Robert Addison King, RCAF, son of John Addison King of 201 10th Ave, S Port Albernal, Vancouver Island, BC, and has issue:

1c *Keith Alan; *b* 31 March 1951; *m* 1974 *Heather Ann, dau of William Farquharson

1c *Katharine Diane; *b* 28 Sept 1953

2c *Rachel Anne; *b* 15 May 1955

2b *Kathleen Wendy Elizabeth; *b* 28 Sept 1930; *m* 1st 12 April 1952 (*divorce* 1963) James Palmer Lee, and has:

1c *Randal James; *b* 23 Jan 1953

1c *Teresa Gayle; *b* 2 Nov 1955; *m* 1975 *Michael Farup, of Salt Spring Island, BC, and has issue:

1d *Jodie Lee; *b* 1975

2b (cont.) Mrs Kathleen Lee *m* 2nd 1965 *William Ernest Smith

1a (cont.) Capt Henry Denny *m* 2nd 23 Feb 1950 *Elsi Margaret, widow of J Ryall, and dau of R O Williams

2a Robert Edmund Barry, 16th Bn Canadian Scottish; *b* 19 March 1891; *d* unm 22 May 1915 of wounds received in action

3a (Thomas) Hamilton, MBE (1942), Capt 7th Gurkha Rifles, 2nd Lt 6th Bn Devon Regt WW I, WW II as Maj 8th Bn Suffolk (HG); *b* 16 June 1893; *m* 8 Jan 1920 Muriel Mary (*d* 1974), yst dau of Edward Doncaster, of Silk Willoughby, Sleaford, and *d* 21 June 1959, leaving issue:

1b *Pamela Diana [Mrs Pamela Denny, Daphne Cottage, 55 High St, Aldeburgh, Suffolk IP15 5AU], WW II 1943–45 with FANY; *m* 28 June 1952 (*divorce* 1969) Lionel Percy Denny, Capt RE (ret), only son of Sir (Jonathan) Lionel Percy Denny, MC, JP, and has issue:

1c *Patrick Jonathan Hamilton; *b* 20 Oct 1956; *m* 1981 *Bridget Anne Meneer, and has:

1d *Samuel Patrick; *b* 1988

1d *Lucy Anne; *b* 1982

2d *Kate Joanna; *b* 1985

1c *Caroline Peta; *b* 21 Jan 1955; *m* 1st 1982 (*divorce* 1983) Errol Currie; *m* 2nd 1986 *Kevin Clive Arthur Hollyoak and has issue:

1d *Rory Clive Anthony; *b* 1987

2d *Liam; *b* 1992

4a +Arthur de Courcy MacGillycuddy, late Lt RFA, and RAF, served WW I, WW II in Roy Canadian Artillery and RCAF, Coronation Medal 1953; *b* 10 Jan 1899; *educ* Sutton Valence Sch; *m* 1st 25 Aug 1924 (*divorce* 1934) Marie Cecilia, dau of Herbert Brooke, and has issue:

1b Maynard de Courcy Barry; RA 1945–48, HAC (TA) 1959–67; *b* 23 June 1927; *educ* Magdalen Coll Sch Oxford and Trin Coll Dublin (BA 1952); *m* 26 March 1966 *Christine Mary [Mrs Maynard Denny, 35 Walpole St, London SW3], yr dau of Walters S Browne, of Ipswich, Suffolk, and *d* 1993, leaving issue:

1c +Anthony de Courcy Edmund; *b* 1973

4a (cont.) Lt Arthur Denny *m* 2nd 27 March 1937 *Mary Evelyn, only dau of Brig-Gen Noel Ernest Money, CMG, DSO and two bars, of Vancouver Island

1a Norah Creina, nurse WW I (despatches ARRC, Jubilee medal), Freeman City of Duncan, Headmistress and co-fndr Queen Margaret's Sch, Duncan; life memb Canadian Girl Guides; *b* 3 Aug 1885

2a Iris, driver RAF WW I, Section Offr WAAF WW II; *d* unm 15 Jan 1978 aged 88

(1) Arabella Jane; *m* 16 Feb 1874 Richard Hungerford Townsend (*d* 1922), MD, of Queenstown, Co Cork, and *d* 13 June 1908, leaving issue

4 Anthony (Ven), MA Oxon, Archdeacon Ardfert, Rector Tralee and Kilgobbin; *b* 1 July 1807; *m* 1st 18 Sept 1830 Catherine (*d* 16 Feb 1866), dau of James Magill, and had, with other issue:

(1) Edward, Lt RN; *b* 17 March 1833; *m* 1st 15 Aug 1869 Florence Annette (*d* 1886), dau of Charles Condell, and had a s and dau (both *d* unm); *m* 2nd 1889 Jane, dau of John Brannan Quick, and *d* 1893
(2) George Herbert; *b* 1851; *m* 1876 Ellen (*d* 26 Jan 1937), dau of Nathan Jarvis, and *d* 30 Jan 1937, having had, with other issue:
1a Edward Jarvis; *b* 1879; *m* 1903 Clara Elizabeth, dau of August Will, and had issue:
1b *Ellen Elizabeth
2b *Catharine Antoinette
2a Anthony George; *b* 1882; *m* 1910 Mathilda Henrietta, dau of Claus Dargeloh
1a Catharine; *m* 1900 Curtis Le Roy Sleeper, of Chicago
(1) Mary Jane; *m* 28 Jan 1857 Rev W H Disney and *d* 31 Aug 1864, leaving issue
(2) Gertrude Alice; *m* J W Neligan (*d* 1924), MD, and *d* 1896, leaving issue
(3) Antoinette Helen; *d* unm 28 Jan 1951
4 (cont.) Archdeacon Anthony Denny *m* 2nd 24 March 1868 Charlotte (*dsp* 5 Jan 1914), dau of George Coare, of Heavitree, Exeter, and *d* 30 Dec 1890
5 William, DL, JP, Provost Tralee; *b* 29 Oct 1811; *m* 25 July 1832 Marianne (*d* 1860), dau of Thomas Trueman, of Exeter, and *d* 27 Jan 1871, having had, with other issue:
(1) Edward Coningsby; *b* 1839; *m* 22 July 1863 Louisa Mary (*d* 1916), dau of Augustus Callaway, and *d* 1888, leaving issue:
1a William Coningsby; *b* 1867; *m* 1892 Rose Elizabeth (*d* 1947), dau of Joseph Ingram, of Wellington Square, Hastings, and *d* 18 Aug 1935, leaving issue:
1b William; *d* young
2b Charles; *d* young
1b Marjorie Ethel; *b* 1896
2a Edmund Henry; *b* 1873; *m* 1909 Beatrice Mary Louisa (*m* 2nd 15 March 1933 Maj William Alfred Charles Denny, OBE (*see* below), and *d* 21 Aug 1942), dau of Alfred Boydell Golborne, of Chester, and *dsp* 14 June 1932
3a Charles Edward; *b* 1875; *m* 1902 Alice, dau of Samuel Grantham Baker, of Brighton, and *d* 1946, leaving:
1b *Letitia Ivy Coningsby [Mrs Woolmore Duncan, Bowersbury, Bowers Heath, Harpenden, Herts]; *b* 1904; *m* 1 Sept 1936 *Woolmore Stewart Duncan
2b *Ethel Mildred Coningsby; *b* 1907; *m* 9 Sept 1933 *Sydney Walter Stubbs, AMIEE, and has issue:
1c *Brian Maurice Denny; *b* 26 May 1936
2c *Colin Anthony, BCom, ACA; *b* 8 Sept 1939
3c *Richard Ivan; *b* 30 July 1949
3b *Kathleen Mary Coningsby; *b* 1910; *m* 25 July 1936 *Joseph Henry Smith, and has issue:
1c *Peter Nigel Coningsby [Peter Smith Esq, 19 Redding Dve, Amersham, Bucks]; *b* 12 April 1948; *m* 1978 *Susan Spriggs, and has issue:
1d *Oliver James Coningsby; *b* 1980
1d *Victoria Clare Coningsby; *b* 1982
1c *Kathleen Hazel Coningsby; *b* 26 Nov 1940; *m* 1964 (*divorce* 1979) Peter James Guile, and has issue:
1d *Christopher James; *b* 1968
1d *Moyra Elizabeth; *b* 1970
2c *Yvonne Coningsby [Mrs Stanley Ritter, Tophams, Brays Lane, Hyde Heath, Bucks]; *b* 15 Nov 1944; *m* 1965 *Stanley Ritter, and has issue:
1d *Martin Neill; *b* 1976
1d *Michelle Clare; *b* 1973
4b *Geraldine Coningsby [Mrs Stuart Clarke, 44 Swakeleys Drive, Ickenham, Middlesex]; *b* 1917; *m* 1939 *Stuart Robson Clarke, and has issue:
1c *Barry Ian Charles; *b* 6 Sept 1946
1c *Diana Susan Coningsby; *b* 14 Jan 1948
4a Horace; *b* 1877; *m* 1904 Mabel, dau of Adml Arthur De Bellin, Royal Italian Navy, and had issue:
1b +John; *b* 19–
1b *A dau; *b* 19–
1b *A dau; *b* 19–
1a Ethel May Army; staff nurse; *d* unm Nov 1938
2a Constance Frances; *m* Arthur Vaughan Treherne and *dsp* 1929
3a Ada Louisa; *m* 1901 Herbert Barraclough, and *d* 8 May 1947, leaving issue
(2) Henry Arthur, Lt RA; *b* 1841; *m* 23 Aug 1870 Emma Florence (*d* 1886), dau of Abraham Denny, JP, and *d* 1888, leaving issue:
1a Frederick Wootton, Lt Wilts Regt; *b* 1881; *m* 1913 Rose, widow of — Cramp and dau of Charles T G Bright, of Toronto, and had issue:
1b *Shirley Geraldine; *b* 17 March 1915
1a Beatrice Winifred; *m* 1910 James Hugh Sims, CBE, Dep Resident Commr and Govt Sec, Basutoland, and *d* 1943
2a Florence Geraldine; *d* unm 11 Nov 1930
(3) George Anthony, MB Dublin; *b* 1843; *m* 21 Sept 1871 Clara (*d* 8 Oct 1873), dau of R A Thomson, and *d* March 1873, leaving issue:
1a Ethel; *m* 1895 Lewin Henry Dell Hayman, son of Rev Canon Hayman, Head Master of Rugby, and *dsp* 26 Nov 1943
(4) Alfred Edward, Lt RN; *b* 1844; *m* 26 Feb 1870 Mary Harriet Scott (*d* 13 Nov 1914), dau of Henry Grout Stokes, of Swilly Manor, Plymouth, and *d* 22 Feb 1903, leaving issue:
1a William Alfred Charles, OBE (1919); *b* 20 April 1871; Maj RASC, Leinster Regt DAAG, S China 1902–03, Dir-Gen Mil Intell and Col Cmdg Corps of Guides Canadian Militia Forces 1903–05, Dep Controller Welfare Supervision Dept Roy Arsenal Woolwich 1917, Freeman and Liveryman City of London; Boer War 1899–1900 with Natal Field Force (wounded three times, despatches, brevet and medal with six clasps); *m* 1st 1896 Lucy Florence (*d* 15 Feb 1931), dau of Maj-Gen Herbert Coningham, and had issue:
1b Joan Lucy Dorothy; *m* 1st 3 July 1924 her cousin **Rev Sir Henry Lyttelton Lyster Denny, 7th Bt** and had issue (*see* below); *m* 2nd 8 Dec 1956 Victor Salvador Levy (*d* 27 April 1969), son of Salvador Marco Levy, and *d* 7 May 1976
2b *Eileen Mary Diana; *b* 1903; *m* 10 June 1933 William Samuel Sandes Boxwell (*d* 1961), only son of Samuel Boxwell, of Dublin
1a (cont.) Maj William Denny *m* 2nd 15 March 1933 Beatrice Mary Louisa (*d* 21 Aug 1942), widow of Edmund Henry Denny (*see* above) and dau of Alfred Boydell Golborne, of Chester, and *d* 9 July 1934
1a Ethel Mary; *m* 10 Aug 1905 Rev Henry Herbert Leeper (*d* 11 March 1946), BA, Rector Fincham, Norfolk, and had issue
(1) Elizabeth; *m* 1860 Capt Adolphus George Eyde (*d* 1901), RN, JP, and *d* 1908, leaving issue
(2) Joan Frances; *m* 6 Aug 1885 John Thomas (*d* 1913), harpist to TM QUEEN VICTORIA, EDWARD VII and GEORGE V, and *d* 8 Nov 1926, leaving issue
1 Elizabeth; *m* 1832 Rev George Bellett, MA, and *d* 1889, leaving issue

The 6th Bt's cousin,

Rev Sir Henry Lyttelton Lyster Denny, 7th Bt; *b* 10 Sept 1878; MA Dublin, Fell Soc Genealogists, hon dir London TSB, V-Pres and Hon Sec Co Kerry Soc, Hon Memb and Laureate Institut Historique de France, Hon Minor Canon St Patrick's Cathedral Dublin 1907–08, priest-in-charge St Jude's Chelsea 1912–16, Chaplain Duke of York's HQ Chelsea 1914–15, Chelsea VTC and Metro Spec Constabulary 1915–16, Vicar Winslow Bucks 1916–18, Rector Horsted Keynes Sussex 1918–20, Vicar St Mark's Myddelton Sq London, Fell Sion Coll 1920–25, Rector W Wickham Kent 1925–30, Rector Abinger Surrey and memb Chllr's Advsy Ctee Diocese of Guildford 1930–36, Rector and Vicar Burwash Sussex 1936–53, CD WW II, 19th Sussex HG 1940–45, Officiating CF 1940–46, memb Cncl Empire Settlement 1928–37, ed *The Genealogists' Magazine* 1925–31; *m* 3 July 1924 his cousin Joan Lucy Dorothy (*m* 2nd 8 Dec 1956 Victor Salvador Levy (*d* 27 April 1969), s of Marco Salvador Levy, and *d* 7 May 1976), er dau of Major William Alfred Charles Denny, OBE, and *d* 1 May 1953, leaving issue:
1 Sir ANTHONY CONINGHAM DE WALTHAM DENNY, **8th and present Bt**
2 +Barry Francis Lyttelton, LVO (1979) [Barry Denny Esq LVO, Tudor House, Broadwindsor, Dorset DT8 3QP]; *b* 6 June 1928; *educ* Clayesmore and RMA Sandhurst; IA Cadet 1946–47, 2nd Lt RA 1949, ret as T/Major 1960, Dip Serv 1962–89, Counsellor FCO Cret, Cdr Order of St Olav Norway 1981; *m* 1st 8 Dec 1951 (*divorce* 1968) Gertrude Tamara, yr dau of Harry Carnet Jex, of Hong Kong, and formerly wife of Clifford Crofton, and has issue:
(1) +James Barry Lyster; *b* 24 April 1958; *m* 1979 *Susan Elizabeth, dau of Derek Scholfield, of Dummer, Hants, and has issue:
1a +Thomas James Lyttelton; *b* 1988
2a +James Henry Lyttelton; *b* 1994
(1) *Shelagh Joan Lyttelton; *b* 12 Aug 1959; *m* 1989 *Paul Nigel Wickman and has:
1a *Edward Guy Denny; *b* 1991
1a *Eleanor Katherine Denny; *b* 1994
2 (cont.) Barry Denny *m* 2nd 9 April 1969 *Anne Rosemary Jordon, only dau of Col James Frederick White, MC, Roy Warwicks Fus, of Claypit Hill, Foxearth, W Suffolk, and has further issue:
(2) *Emma Harriet Lyttelton; *b* 1970
3 +Edward Maurice FitzGerald (Robyn) [Robyn Denny Esq, Unit 4B, 20/30 Wilds Rents, London SE1 4QG]; artist and designer, RNAS; *b* 3 Oct 1930; *educ* Clayesmore and RCA (ARCA 1957); *m* 1st 1953 (*divorce* 1975) Anna Rose Frances, only dau of Geoffrey Teasdale, of Rye, Sussex; *m* 2nd 4 Feb 1995 *Marjorie May, dau of George Abéla, of Mercues, France, and by his 1st w has:
(1) +Dominic Charles FitzGerald; *b* 1963
(2) +Edward Drouet Coningham; *b* 1975
(1) *Lucy Anna Dando; *b* 1966
4 +Richard William Geoffrey [Richard Denny Esq, Foxcote Court, Moreton-in-Marsh, Glos GL56 0NJ]; *b* 4 Feb 1940; *educ* Royal Masonic Sch; *m* 1st 25 Feb 1961 (*divorce* 1978) Andrée Suzanne Louise, est dau of Marcel Louis Parrot, of Paris; *m* 2nd 24 Aug 1984 *Linda May, dau of Maximilian Magnun, of Calcutta, and by his 1st w has:
(1) +Lyster Richard Henry; *b* 15 Aug 1961
(2) +Walter Victor Marcel; *b* 12 April 1963; *m* 1990 *Lorna Caroline, er dau of Maurice Statham, of Aylesbury, Bucks
(3) +Giles Anthony William; *b* 18 Nov 1964
(4) +Julius André Geoffrey; *b* 5 June 1966

DENNY of Dumbarton

Arms: Azure three suns in their splendour in chief or, and in the honour point a martlet of the last for difference. **Crest:** A dexter hand erect pointing with two fingers at a sun in his splendour, all proper. **Motto:** *Fortis et benignus* ('Brave and kind'). **Creation:** Bt. (UK) 16 June 1913.

SIR CHARLES ALISTAIR DENNY, 4TH BT [Sir Charles Denny Bt, Farthing Cottage, The Down, Lamberhurst, Kent TN3 8HD]; *b* 7 Oct 1950; *s* f 1995; *educ* Wellington and Edinburgh U; *m* 1981 *Belinda M J, yr dau of J P McDonald, of Dublin, and has issue:

1 +PATRICK CHARLES ALISTAIR; *b* 2 Jan 1985

1 *Georgina Mary; *b* 1989

Lineage: WILLIAM DENNY, of Woodyard House, Dumbarton, shipbuilder; *b* 19 June 1779; *m* 13 Jan 1801 Christian (*d* 9 March 1838), dau of James McIntyre, and *d* 27 Dec 1838, leaving:

PETER DENNY, of Helenslee, Dumbarton, DL, JP Dunbartonshire, LLD Glasgow; *b* 29 Oct 1821; *m* 26 Jan 1846 Helen (*d* 5 March 1905), dau of James Leslie, of Greenfield, Dumbarton, and *d* 22 Aug 1895, leaving a 4th s:

Sir Archibald Denny, 1st Bt (UK), so *cr* 16 June 1913, JP, Hon LLD Glasgow and Camb, Lt-Col 1st Dunbartonshire Rifle Vols and 1st Vol Bn Argyll and Sutherland Highrs, dir William Denny & Bros, shipbuilders and engrs (builders of the *Cutty Sark*); *b* 7 Feb 1860; *m* 1885 Margaret (*d* 16 Feb 1951), dau of John Tulloch, engr, of Dumbarton, and had issue:

1 MAURICE EDWARD (Sir), **2nd Bt**

2 William Murray; *b* 20 June 1887; *m* 6 Nov 1913 Margaret de Hertel (*m* 2nd —; *d c* 1954), er dau of J F Cunningham, of Ottawa, and *d* 2 July 1914

3 Peter Archie, Capt 1st Argyll and Sutherland Highrs; *b* 11 Nov 1892; *m* 23 Aug 1933 Lillian Vera, dau of Alfred Hurst, of Lincoln, and *d* 14 Feb 1938

4 James Murray Tulloch, Capt RE, IWT; *b* 15 Sept 1896; *m* 3 Nov 1934 Ivy Rose, dau of Henry Pottle, of Bournemouth

5 Walter Brock; *b* 16 Feb 1898; *d* 25 Aug 1902

1 Eileen Margaret; *b* 10 March 1891; *m* 18 July 1917 Alexander Muir McGrigor, OBE (*d* 28 Nov 1963), Capt Glos Yeo, son of Alexander McGrigor of Balnacoil, Aboyne, Aberdeenshire, and Cairnoch Lodge, Stirlingshire, by Margaret, dau of Sir John Muir, 1st Bt (*qv*), and had issue

Sir ARCHIBALD *d* 29 May 1936; his est son,

Sir Maurice Edward Denny, 2nd Bt, KBE (1946), DL, JP; *b* 11 Feb 1886; BSc, LLD 1949; pres William Denny & Bros (liquidation 1963), Chm Air Registration Bd, PIME 1935–36, Pres Jr Inst Engrs 1943–44, V-Pres Inst Naval Architects; Im 23 Nov 1916 Marjorie, er dau of William Royse Lysaght, CBE, of Castleford, Chepstow, and *d* 2 Feb 1955, leaving:

1 **Sir Alistair Maurice Archibald Denny, 3rd Bt**, *b* 11 Sept 1922; *educ* Marlborough; Fleet Air Arm 1944–46; *m* 18 April 1949 *Elizabeth Hunt [Elizabeth Lady Denny, Crombie Cottage, Abercrombie, Fife KY10 2DE], yst dau of Major Sir (Ernest) Guy Richard Lloyd, 1st Bt (*qv*), and *d* 29 Aug 1995, leaving issue:

(1) Sir CHARLES ALISTAIR MAURICE DENNY, **4th and present Bt**

(2) Nigel Peter; *b* 12 Dec 1952; *educ* Wellington; *d* 1977

(3) +Mark Richard Leslie; *b* 20 Feb 1955; *educ* Wellington; *m* 1983 *Junemary, 2nd dau of R E Jameson, of Durban, S Africa, and has issue:

1a +James William Leslie; *b* 1986

2a +Michael; *b* 1991

1a *Suzannah Caroline; *b* 1988

2 +Graham Royse [Graham Denny Esq, Ash Cottage, Balfron Rd, Killearn, Glasgow G63 9NJ]; *b* 26 Nov 1927; *educ* Marlborough and King's Coll Cambridge (BA 1948, MA 1952)

1 *Rosamund Margaret [Mrs John Churchill, Sunhill House, Mayford, nr Woking, Surrey]; *b* 28 Dec 1917; *m* 8 March 1941 *Lt Col John Malcolm Thorpe Fleming Churchill, DSO, MC, Seaforth Highrs, and has issue:

(1) *Malcolm John Leslie; *b* 11 Nov 1942; *educ* Wellington and Woodberry Forest, Va, USA

(2) *Rodney Alistair Gladstone; *b* 4 July 1947; *educ* Wellington

2 *Patricia Leslie [Mrs Thomas Jones, The House on The Hill, Dunblane, Perthshire]; *b* 30 July 1931; *m* 1 Nov 1952 *Thomas Dunlop Bruce Jones, MC, only son of John Cumming Bruce Jones, of Glenbervie, Larbert, Stirlingshire, by Dorothy Euphemia Mitchell, 2nd dau of Sir Thomas Dunlop, 1st Bt (*qv*), and has issue:

(1) *Veronica Margaret; *b* 1953

(2) *Victoria Leslie; *b* 1956

(3) *Claire Patricia; *b* 1958

(4) *Juliet Mary; *b* 1966

DENTON OF WAKEFIELD

Creation: B. (LP, UK) 1991.

THE BARONESS DENTON OF WAKEFIELD, of Wakefield in West Yorkshire (Jean Moss, CBE (1990)) [The Rt Hon The Baroness Denton of Wakefield CBE, House of Lords, London SW1A 0PW]; *b* 29 Dec 1935; *educ* Rothwell GS and LSE (BScEcon); Communications Exec Proctor & Gamble 1959–61; Marketing Consultant EIU 1961–64; IPC 1964–66; Hotel and Catering Dept Surrey U 1966–69; professional racing and rally driver 1969–72; mktg dir Huxford Gp 1972–78 and Heron Motor Gp 1978–80, md Herondrive 1980–85; Govr LSE 1982–91; Dir External Affairs Austin Rover Gp 1985–86; Dep Chm Black Country Devpt Corp 1987–91; Tstee Brooklands Museum 1987–89; Dir: Ordnance Survey 1985–88, Br Nuclear Fuels 1987–92, Burson-Marsteller 1987–, London and Edinburgh Insur Gp 1989–92, Triplex Lloyd 1990–92, Think Green 1989–92; Baroness-in-Waiting 1991–92; Parly U-Sec: DTI 1992–93, DoE 1993–93, NI 1994–97, Oppn Spokesman NI 1997–; Chm: FORUM UK 1989–1992 (Pres 1992), Marketing Gp GB 1987 and 1988, Woman on the Move against Cancer 1979–92; Memb: Bd UK 2000 1986–88, Engrg Cncl 1986–91, School Teachers Review Body 1989–, Teachers Pay Review 1989, 1990 and 1991, RSA Cncl 1991, Bd NW TV 1991–; Memb Marketers' Co; Freeman City of London 1982, FCInstM 1972, FIMI 1974, FRSA 1987, CBIM 1988; *m* 1958 (*divorce* 1974) Dr A A Denton

Lineage: CHARLES J MOSS; *m* Kathleen Tuke and had:

JEAN, *cr* a **Baroness**

DERAMORE

Arms: Quarterly, 1st and 4th grand quarters, 1st and 4th, argent three bat's wings erect sable, on a chief gules a lion passant or (for BATESON); 2nd and 3rd, per pale argent and azure a chevron between three chaplets counterchanged (for DE YARBURGH); 2nd and 3rd grand quarters, argent three lions dormant in pale sable between two flaunches of the last, each charged with three mullets palewise of the first (for LLOYD). **Crests:** 1 A bat's wing erect sable (for BATESON), 2 A falcon close or, belled gold, preying upon a duck proper (for DE YARBURGH). **Supporters:** Dexter, a lion or, gorged with a collar gemel gules, pendant therefrom an escutcheon ermine, charged with a bat's wing erect sable; sinister, a like lion or, gorged with a collar gemel gules, pendant therefrom an escutcheon ermine charged with a raven proper. **Motto:** *Nocte volamus* ('We fly by night'), *Non est sine pulvere palma* ('The prize is not won without dust'). **Creations:** Bt. (UK) 18 Dec 1818, B. (UK) 18 Nov 1885.

THE 6TH BARON DERAMORE OF BELVOIR, Co Down, and a **Baronet** (Sir Richard Arthur de Yarburgh-Bateson, 7th Bt) [The Rt Hon The Lord Deramore, Heslington House, Aislaby, Pickering, North Yorks, YO18 8PE]; *b* 9 April 1911; *s* bro 1964; *educ* Harrow and St John's Coll Cambridge (BA 1932, MA 1938); F/Lt RAFVR WW II, ARIBA; *m* 28 Aug 1948 *Janet Mary, est dau of John Ware, MD, of Nether Close, Askam-in-Furness, Lancs, and has issue:

1 *Ann Katharine [The Hon Mrs Peel, Sturdy Cottage, High St, Thornborough, Bucks MK18 2DF]; *b* 10 Aug 1950; *m* 15 May 1982 *Jonathan Henry Maconchy

Peel, er son of Walter Peel, of Knockdromin, Lusk, Co Dublin (*see* RUGGE-PRICE, Bt), and has issue:

(1) *Nicholas Richard Yarburgh; *b* 1987

(1) *Katharine Diana; *b* 1985

Lineage (of Yarburgh): WILLIAM de YERBURGH (er s of Robert de Yerburgh, of Cockerington and Grimoldby, Lincs; *see* ALVINGHAM, B); *m* a dau of Thomas Anguine, and had, with a yr s (John, had a s, Walter):

RICHARD de YERBURGH, of Kelstern and Yarburgh, both Lincs; *m* Joan, dau and heiress of John Atwell and had, with a yr s (Robert/Thomas, may have had a s, William):

WILLIAM de YERBURGH; *m* Isabel, dau and heiress of Sir John Billing, had, with six yr sons:

RICHARD de YERBURGH; *m* Elizabeth, dau of Thomas Moyne, and had, with five yr sons and a dau (Margaret, *m* Thomas Barde, of N Kelsey):

CHARLES de YERBURGH; Ld Manors of Kelstern, Legbourne and Yarburgh; *m* 1st Agnes, dau of Sir John Skipwith (*see* SKIPWITH, Bt), and had issue, who appear to have sunk in the world, being obliged to alienate Yarburgh after some two generations, though it would seem that the property was later bought back by the more prosperous Yorkshire branch of the family, descended from CHARLES's 2nd w; *m* 2nd Elizabeth, dau of Martyn Newcomen, and *d* on or after 15 March 1544/5, leaving by her a 2nd s:

EDMUND YARBURGH; *b c* 1529; settled at Lincoln; *m* Margaret, dau of Sir Vincent Grantham, and *d* 20 Feb 1590/1, leaving, with a yr s (Charles, whose male line issue failed after another generation):

FRANCIS YARBURGH, of Northorpe, Lincs; Serjeant-at-law; *m* 1st Elizabeth, dau of John/Robert Farmour, and had:

1 Robert; *m* a dau of Sir Gervase Elwes, and had:

(1) Mary; *m* Thomas Saville and *dsp*

FRANCIS YARBURGH *m* 2nd Frances, dau of Leonard Wray, of Cusworth, and niece of Sir Christopher Wray, Ld Ch Justice Queen's Bench, and *d* between 13 July and 29 Oct 1595, leaving by her, with another dau (Elizabeth, *m* Martin Glydon):

2 Edmund; not yet of age 1595; *m* 28 May 1611 Sarah, dau of Thomas Wormsley, of Cusworth and Hatfield, Yorks, and *d* 6 May 1631, leaving:

(1) NICHOLAS (Sir)

(2) Thomas, Serjeant-at-law

(3) Edmund, of Doncaster, MD

(1) Frances; *m* 1st Sir John Reresby, 1st Bt, of Thrybergh; *m* 2nd James Moyser

The est son,

Sir NICHOLAS YARBURGH, of Snaith Hall, Yorks, JP, Commr Array for CHARLES I; *m* Faith (*d* 1657), dau of John Dawnay, of Cowick, son of Sir Thomas Dawnay, and *d* Aug 1655, having had, with five yr sons and two daus:

Sir THOMAS YARBURGH, of Baine Hall and Snaith Hall, High Sheriff Yorks 1676, MP Pontefract; *m* Henrietta Maria, est dau and coheir of Col Thomas Blague, of Hollinger, Suffolk, Govr Wallingford, by Mary, dau of Sir Dudley North, and had an est s:

JAMES YARBURGH, of Snaith Hall, godson and Page Honour to JAMES II, Lt-Col Gds, Ld of Manors of Yarburgh, Snaith, Cowick and part of Heslington; *m* Anne (*d* April 1717), dau and coheir of Thomas Hesketh, of Heslington, by Mary, dau of Sir Walter Bethell, of Aine, Yorks, and gdau of Sir Henry Slingsby, Bt, and *d* 1728, leaving, with other issue:

1 Thomas, of Heslington and Snaith; *bapt* 16 Feb 1696; *m* Anne (*d* 27 March 1753), dau of Rev Thomas Thwaites, and *dsp* 1741

2 Henry, of Heslington and Snaith, *dsp*

3 Hesketh, of Heslington and Snaith; *d* unm 1754

4 CHARLES, of whom presently

1 Henrietta Maria; *m* Sir John Vanbrugh, Clarenceux King of Arms

JAMES YARBURGH's yst son,

CHARLES YARBURGH, of Heslington and Snaith and Yarburgh, Lincs; *m* 1st Mary Griffin (*d* 26 Nov 1757 aged 40), of Wirksworth, Derbys, and *d* 13 Aug 1789 aged 73, having had, with a dau:

1 Henry, of Heslington, Capt 20th Light Dragoons; *m* Anne (*dsp* 14 Feb 1817), dau of E Agar, of Canterbury, and *d* 28 Oct 1825 aged 77

CHARLES YARBURGH *m* 2nd Sarah Griffin, of Wirksworth, and by her had, with five other daus:

2 Charles, Capt RN (joined 1779); *b* 19 Oct 1763; served HMS *Britannia* and HMS *Hero*; *d* 1781 East Indies

3 Nicholas Edmund, of Heslington, DL, Maj 3rd Regt Provisional Militia, High Sheriff Yorks 1836; *d* unm

1 A dau; *m* — GREAME and had issue:

(1) — GREAME later YARBURGH, of Sewerby House, E R Yorks; *dsp*

(1) — Greame; *m* — LLOYD and had issue:

1a GEORGE JOHN LLOYD later YARBURGH (roy licence 1857), of Heslington, JP; *b* 28 July 1811; *m* 23 July 1840 Mary Antonia, 3rd dau of Samuel Chetham Hilton, of Pennington Hall, Lancs, by Martha, dau of Samuel Clowes, of Broughton Hall, and *d* 16 March 1875, having had:

1b MARY ELIZABETH Lloyd later Yarburgh; *m* 8 May 1862 **2nd Baron Deramore of Belvoir** (*see* below)

2b Susan Anne; *m* 25 Jan 1865 Charles Lethbridge, est son of Rev Thomas P Lethbridge, of Combe Florey, Somerset, and *d* 21 May 1908, having had issue (*see* LETHBRIDGE, Bt)

Lineage (of Bateson): THOMAS BATESON, of Lancs; *d* 1630, leaving, with a yr s and dau:

ROBERT BATESON; *d* 1663, leaving an only s:

ROBERT BATESON; had:

1 THOMAS

2 Richard, High Sheriff Co Donegal 1761, settled Londonderry, bought estates in Cos Antrim, Donegal and Tyrone; *m* 1st Sarah, dau of John McClintock (*see* RATHDONNELL, B), and had issue; *m* 2nd 16 Oct 1740 Elizabeth (*d* 1787), dau of Robert Harvey, of Londonderry, and *d* by 1767, leaving issue

The er son,

THOMAS BATESON, of Orange Field House, Co Down; *b* 1705; *m* 1747 Margaret, widow of William Hartley, of Dublin, and dau and coheir of — White, of Whitehall, Co Antrim, and *d* 1791; his est s:

THOMAS BATESON; *b* 1752; *m* 1780 Elizabeth, yst dau of George Lloyd, FRS, of Hulme Hall, Lancs, by Susannah, sis of Sir William Horton, 1st Bt, of Chadderton, and *d* 15 May 1811; his only s:

Sir Robert Bateson, 1st Bt (UK), so *cr* 18 Dec 1818; *b* 13 March 1782; MP Co Londonderry 1830–32; *m* 27 April 1811 Catherine (*d* 21 Jan 1874), dau of Samuel Dickson, of Ballynaguile, Co Limerick, and *d* 21 April 1863, having had, with other issue:

1 Robert; *b* 29 March 1816; MP Co Londonderry; *d* unm 23 Dec 1843

2 **Sir Thomas Bateson, 2nd Bt**, and **1st Baron Deramore of Belvoir**, Co Down (UK), so *cr* 18 Nov 1885, with remainder, in default of male issue, to his only surv bro George, DL; *b* 4 June 1819; Capt 13th Light Dragoons, MP (C) Co Londonderry 1844–57 and Devizes 1864–85, Jr Ld Treasury Feb-Dec 1852; *m* 21 Feb 1849 Hon Caroline Elizabeth Anne Rice-Trevor (*d* 12 Aug 1887), 2nd dau and coheir of 4th Baron Dinevor (*qv*), and *d* 1 Dec 1890, leaving:

(1) Eva Frances Caroline; *m* 4 March 1871 David Alfred Ker (*d* 8 Dec 1777), est son of David Stewart Ker, of Montalto, Co Down, and *d* 18 May 1940, having had issue

(2) Kathleen Mary; *m* 29 May 1877 Walter Randolph Farquhar (*d* 26 Aug 1901), 2nd son of Sir Walter Rockcliff Farquhar, 3rd Bt (*qv*), and *d* 20 July 1935, leaving issue

3 Samuel Stephen, barrister; *b* 13 Oct 1821; *m* 25 July 1854 Florinda (*d* 26 April 1908), dau of 3rd Baron Castlemaine (*qv*), and *dsp* 9 March 1879

4 GEORGE WILLIAM BATESON (1823–76) later (Feb-15 April 1876) BATESON-YARBURGH later still (roy licence 15 April 1876–92) BATESON De YARBURGH and last of all (roy licence 1892–93) De YARBURGH-BATESON, **2nd Baron Deramore of Belvoir**; *b* 2 April 1823; *educ* Rugby; *m* 8 May 1862 Mary Elizabeth (*d* 22 Oct 1884), est dau and coheir of George John Yarburgh (*see* above), of Heslington Hall, Yorks, and *d* 29 April 1893, leaving:

(1) ROBERT WILFRED BATESON (1865–76) later (Feb-15 April 1876) BATESON-YARBURGH later still (by roy licence 15 April 1876–92) BATESON De YARBURGH and last of all (by roy licence 1892–1936) De YARBURGH-BATESON, **3rd Baron Deramore of Belvoir**, TD, Ld Lt E R Yorks, Chm CC E R, JP W R Yorks, DL, JP Co Down, Hon LLD Leeds, Hon Er Bro Hull Trin House, Pres TAA E R Yorks, Lt-Col Yorks Hus; *b* 5 Aug 1865; *m* 1st 15 July 1897 Lucy Caroline (*d* 26 Oct 1901), est dau of William Henry Fife, of Lee Hall, Northumberland, and had issue:

1a Moira Faith Lilian; *b* 9 June 1898; *m* 1st 24 Oct 1919 (*annulled* 1923) John Robert Rankin Fullerton (*d* 14 Jan 1966), Lt 15th/19th Hus, est s of John Skipworth Herbert Fullerton, of Thrybergh Park; *m* 2nd 5 June 1924 (*divorce* 1935) Sir Edward George Chichester, 10th Bt (*qv*), and *d* 21 Dec 1982, having had issue

(1) The **3rd Baron** *m* 2nd 26 June 1907 Violet Blanche (*d* 30 Dec 1972), est dau of Col Philip Saltmarshe, JP, RA, of Saltmarshe, Yorks, and *dspm* 1 April 1936

(2) GEORGE NICHOLAS, **4th Baron**

(3) Eustace, Capt RASC (TF); *b* 13 Oct 1884; *educ* Trin Coll Cambridge (BA); *m* 1 June 1927 Elsie Florence, widow of Capt Charles Cottam, MC, Hampshire Regt, and dau of Henry Josiah Julius Jones, of St Anne's House, King's Lynn, and *dsp* 5 March 1958

(1) Mary Lilla; *d* unm 12 Feb 1939

(2) Katherine Hylda; *d* unm 27 Nov 1955

The 3rd BARON's bro,

GEORGE NICHOLAS BATESON (1870–76) later (Feb-15 April 1876) BATESON-YARBURGH later still (roy licence 15 April 1876–92) BATESON De YARBURGH and last of all (roy licence 1892–1943) De YARBURGH-BATESON, **4th Baron Deramore of Belvoir**, JP E R Yorks; *b* 20 Nov 1870; *m* 12 Dec 1900 Muriel Katharine (*d* 21 March 1960), dau of Arthur Grey (formerly Duncombe), of Sutton Hall, Easingwold (*see* FEVERSHAM, B), and *d* 4 Nov 1943, having had issue:

1 STEPHEN NICHOLAS De YARBURGH-BATESON, **5th Baron Deramore of Belvoir**; *b* 18 May 1903; *educ* Harrow and St John's Coll Camb; S/Ldr RAFVR WW II (despatches); *m* 14 Nov 1929 Nina Marion (*d* 1979), OBE (1955), CStJ, Patron BRCS E R Yorks, est dau of Alastair Macpherson-Grant (*see* 1970 edn MACPHERSON-GRANT, Bt), and *d* 23 Dec 1964, leaving issue:

(1) Jane Faith; *b* 20 March 1933; *m* 28 June 1952 *26th Baron Mowbray, (27th Baron) Segrave and (23rd Baron) Stourton (*qv*), and *d* 2 April 1998, leaving issue

2 RICHARD ARTHUR De YARBURGH-BATESON, **6th and present Baron Deramore of Belvoir**

1 Judith Katharine; *b* 22 March 1909; *d* unm 23 May 1988

DE RAMSEY

Arms: Azure, a fess dancettée ermine between three lion's heads erased or, murally crowned argent. **Crest:** A lion's head erased and crowned as in the arms charged with a fess dancettée ermine. **Supporters:** Two rams proper, each gorged with a chain or, thereupon pendant an escutcheon ermine charged with a ram's eye, also proper. **Motto:** *Patientia et perseverantia cum magnanimitate* ('Patience and perseverance with magnanimity'). **Creation:** B. (UK) 8 July 1887.

THE 4TH BARON DE RAMSEY OF RAMSEY ABBEY, Co Huntingdon (John Ailwyn Fellowes, DL (Cambs 1993)) [The Rt Hon The Lord De Ramsey DL, Abbots Ripton Hall, Huntingdon, Cambs PE17 2PQ]; *b* 27 Feb 1942; *s* f 1993; *educ* Winchester and Essex Inst of Ag; Chm Environment Agency 1994–; Pres CLA 1991–93, Crown Estate Commr 1994–, Pres Assoc Drainage Authorities 1992–94; *m* 7 July 1973 (*divorce* 1983) Phyllida Mary, yr dau of Dr Philip Forsyth, MRCS, LRCP, of Wickhambrook, Suffolk, and has:

1 +FREDDIE JOHN; *b* 31 May 1978; *educ* Eton

The 4th BARON *m* 2nd 1984 *Alison Mary, er dau of Sir Archibald Birkmyre, 3rd Bt (*qv*), and has further issue:

2 +Charles Henry; *b* 1986

1 *Daisy Lilah; *b* 1988

2 *Flora Mary; *b* 1991

Lineage: WILLIAM FELLOWES, of London; *m* Ann, dau of Thomas Worfield, of Leigh, Worcs, and had:

WILLIAM FELLOWES, of London; *m* 27 Sept 1653 Susannah (*d* 14 Dec 1676), sister and eventual coheir of Thomas Coulson, MP Totnes, Dir HEIC, and had, with other issue:

WILLIAM FELLOWES, of Eggesford, Devon; Sr Master in Chancery; *b* 4 Oct 1660; *m* 8 Oct 1695 Mary (*d* 28 Dec 1759), only dau and heir of Joseph Martin, of London, and *d* 19 Jan 1723/4, having had, with other issue:

1 COULSON

2 Martin; *b* 20 July 1702; *m* Jane Clarke (*m* 2nd Charles Bowles, of N Ashton, Oxon, and *d* 1780) and *dsp* 19 July 1731

3 William, of Shotesham Park, Norfolk, ancestor of the FELLOWESes, of Shotesham Park, among whom is Sir Robert Fellowes, KCB, KCVO, PC, Priv Sec to HM THE QUEEN (*see* also DACRE, B)

The est son,

COULSON FELLOWES, of Hampstead, Park Place, Hunts, Ramsey Abbey, Hunts, and Eggesford, Devon; *b* 12 Oct 1696; *m* 20 April 1725 Urania (*d* 6 Feb 1779), dau of Francis Herbert, of Oakley Park, Salop, and sis of 1st Earl of Powis (*qv*) of the 1748 *cr*, and had, with three daus:

1 WILLIAM

2 Henry Arthur, of Eggesford; *d* unm 29 Jan 1792, leaving Eggesford to his n 4th Earl of Portsmouth (*qv*)

1 Urania; *m* 27 Aug 1763 2nd Earl of Portsmouth (*qv*) and *d* 29 Jan 1812, leaving issue

COULSON FELLOWES *d* 23 Feb 1769; his er son,

WILLIAM FELLOWES, of Ramsey Abbey and Nacton, Suffolk, MP Sudbury and Andover; *m* 17 May 1768 Lavinia (*d* 6 Dec 1827), dau and coheir of James Smyth, of St Audries, Somerset, and *d* 4 Feb 1804, having had, with two daus and two yr sons (*dsp*):

WILLIAM HENRY FELLOWES, of Ramsey Abbey and Haverland, MP Huntingdon; *b* 15 July 1769; *m* 23 July 1805 Emma (*d* 27 Jan 1862), 4th dau of Richard Benyon, of Gidea Hall, Essex, and had issue:

1 William Henry; *b* 11 July 1806; *d* unm 17 March 1836

2 EDWARD, **1st Baron**

3 Richard FELLOWES later BENYON (roy licence 1854 on inheriting the estates of his maternal uncle, Richard Benyon de Beauvoir), of Englefield House, Berks (also inherited from his unc Richard); *b* 17 Nov 1811; *m* 25 March 1858 Elizabeth Mary, dau of Robert Clutterbuck, of Watford House, Herts, and *d* 26 July 1897, leaving three daus

4 James, of Kingston House, Dorset, JP, DL, High Sheriff 1859; *b* 31 July 1813; *m* 19 July 1847 Gertrude Charlotte (*d* 25 April 1906), dau of Nathaniel Micklethwaite, of Taverham Hall, Norfolk, and *d* 8 July 1889, leaving issue

1 Emma; *m* 9 Aug 1842 3rd and last Baron Bayning of Foxley (*dsp* 5 Aug 1866) and *d* 13 Nov 1887

WILLIAM HENRY FELLOWES *d* 23 Aug 1837; his son,

EDWARD FELLOWES, **1st Baron De Ramsey of Ramsey Abbey**, Co Huntingdon (UK), so *cr* 8 July 1887, JP, DL (Hunts and Norfolk); *b* 14 April 1809; *educ* Charterhouse; MP (C) Huntingdon 1837–80, Lt 15th Hus; *m* 22 July 1845 Hon Mary Julia Milles (*d* 10 April 1901), est dau of 4th Baron Sondes (*see* MONSON, B), and *d* 9 Aug 1887, having had, with a yr s (AILWYN EDWARD FELLOWES, *cr* BARON AILWYN, *see* 1970 edn) and two daus:

WILLIAM HENRY FELLOWES, **2nd Baron De Ramsey of Ramsey Abbey**, Custos Rotulorum Isle of Ely, DL, JP Hunts, Ld-in-Waiting 1890–92, Hon Col 4th Vol Bn Beds Regt, Capt 1st Life Gds, MP (C) Hunts 1880–87; *b* 16 May 1848; *m* 12 July 1877 Rosamond Jane Frances (*d* Dec 1920), 2nd dau of 7th Duke of Marlborough (*qv*), and had:

1 Coulson Churchill, Capt 1st Life Gds WW I; *b* 8 Feb 1883; *m* 1st 9 July 1906 (*divorce* 1912) Gwendolen Dorothy, est dau of Harry Wyndham Jefferson, of Stoke Rochford Hall, Lincs, and had:

(1) AILWYN EDWARD, **3rd Baron**

(1) Diana Rosamond; *b* 30 May 1907; granted 9 March 1933 with her half-bro rank of baron's dau/yr s; *m* 28 June 1932 2nd Baron Fairhaven (*qv*) and *d* 12 May 1937, leaving issue

1 (cont.) The Hon Coulson Fellowes *m* 2nd 12 Sept 1914 Hon Lilah O'Brien (*m* 2nd 6 March 1925 Nobile Riccardo Assanti (*d* 1957), Cdr Crown Italy, Kt St Maurice and St Lazarus, SMO Malta, Capt Reserve Alpine Regt, son of Gen Damiano Assanti, Senator and Equerry to King of Italy, and *d* 12 Aug 1968), dau of 14th Baron Inchiquin (*qv*), and *d* 22 Oct 1915 of illness contracted on active service, having by her had issue:

(2) +(John) David Coulson [The Hon David Fellowes, Flat 3, 117 Elgin Cres, London W11], 2nd Lt Rifle Bde WW II (wounded, despatches, POW); *b* 1 May 1915; *educ* Eton and Univ Coll Oxford (BA 1936); *m* 1st 31 May 1946 (*divorce* 1962) Louise (*d* 27 Sept 1975), yr dau of Sir James Henry Domville, 5th Bt (*see* 1970 edn), and formerly w of Leslie Alexander Mackay, and has had:

1a +Peter Reginald [Peter Fellowes Esq, 134 Belsize Rd, London NW6]; *b* 11 April 1948; *educ* privately and Army Sch (Jr Leaders); *m* 1980 *Alison Elizabeth, 2nd dau of Dr John Vance, of Fulham, and has:

1b +Charles Oliver Vance; *b* 1983

1b *Daisy Louise; *b* 1984

1a A dau; *b* and *d* 8 Oct 1953

2a *Jacqueline Denise; *b* 10 Dec 1955; *m* 1982 *Michael Humfrey

(2) (cont.) The Hon David Fellowes *m* 2nd 4 April 1963 Joan Lynette (*d* 22 Jan 1965), formerly w of Richard Dewar Neame and only dau of Edgard George Rees, of Llanelly; *m* 3rd 1977 *Mervyn, dau of Reinold de Toll and formerly wife of Peter Sherwood

2 Reginald Ailwyn, JP Hunts, Capt 4th Vol Bn Beds Regt, Hon F/Lt RAFVR; *b* 20 Jan 1884; *m* 9 Aug 1919 Marguerite Severine Philippine (*d* 13 Dec 1962), widow of Prince Jean de Broglie and dau of 4th Duke Decazes and Glucksberg, and *d* 19 March 1953, leaving issue:

(1) *Rosamond Daisy [Mrs Rosamond Fellowes, 7 Eliza St, Thornhill, Ontario L3T 2E3, Canada]; *b* 16 Jan 1921; *m* 1st 29 Oct 1941 (*divorce* 1945) Capt James Gustavus Gladstone, TD, KOSB, yr son of Sir Hugh Gladstone of Capenoch, Dumfriesshire, and has issue:

1a *James Reginald [James Gladstone Esq, Marsh Benham House, Newbury, Berks], journalist; *b* 17 Jan 1943; *educ* Eton; *m* 1st 29 Sept 1965 Mary Valentine, dau of L A Chiodetti, of Crondall, Surrey, and has:

1b *Alexander; *b* 1969

2b *Benedict Hugh; *b* 1973

1a (cont.) James Gladstone *m* 2nd 1993 *Jane Doxford

(1) (cont.) Mrs Rosamond Gladstone *m* 2nd 3 March 1952 (*divorce* 19–, resumed maiden name by deed poll) Tadeusz Maria Wiszniewski, MA, s of Dr Maria Ludwik Wiszniewski, of Horyhiady, Poland, and has further issue:

1a *Diana Marguerite Mary [Ms Diana Wiszniewski, 106 Coon's Rd, Station B, Oak Ridges, Ontario L4E 2R2, Canada]; *b* 2 July 1953; *m* 1978 (*divorce* 1995, resumed maiden name) Robert Shaw, and has:

1b *James Robert; *b* 1983

1b *Jennie Marguerite; *b* 1981

1 Alexandra Frances Anne; *b* 29 June 1880; *m* 15 Feb 1904 Brig-Gen Hon Ferdinand Charles Stanley (*d* 17 March 1935), CMG, DSO, son of 16th Earl of Derby (*qv*), and *d* 16 Sept 1955, leaving issue

2 Gladys Cecil Georgina; *b* 4 Jan 1885; *m* 11 June 1907 Heneage Greville, Lord Guernsey (*dvp ka* 14 Sept 1914), est son of 8th Earl of Aylesford (*qv*), and *d* 4 Aug 1952, having had issue

3 Hermione Frances Caroline; *b* 31 July 1886; *m* 1st 8 June 1909 (*divorce* 1923) Brig-Gen Lord Esme Charles Gordon-Lennox (*d* 4 May 1949), KCVO, CMG, DSO, Scots Gds, 2nd son of 7th Duke of Richmond and Gordon (*qv*), and had issue; *m* 2nd 14 Nov 1923 Baron Rolf Cederstrom (*d* 24 Feb 1947), son of Baron Edward Cederstrom, of Stockholm, Sweden, and *d* Jan 1972, leaving further issue

4 Sybil Inna Mildred; *b* 24 Oct 1888; *m* 23 Feb 1915 5th Marquess of Ormonde (*see* MOUNTGARRET, V), and *d* 18 May 1948, leaving issue

The 1st BARON *d* 8 May 1925; his gs,

AILWYN EDWARD FELLOWES, **3rd Baron De Ramsey of Ramsey Abbey**, KBE (1974), TD; *b* 16 March 1910; *educ* Oundle; Capt RA (TA) WW II (POW), Ld Lt Hunts 1947–65, Huntingdon and Peterborough 1965–68 (DL 1973), Pres CLA 1963–65; *m* 27 July 1937 Lilah Helen Suzanne (*d* 1987), JP (Hunts), dau of Francis Anthony Labouchere, of 15 Draycott Ave, London SW, by Evelyn Mary, dau of Sir Walter Stirling, 3rd Bt, of Faskine (*qv*), and *d* 1993, leaving issue:

1 JOHN AILWYN FELLOWES, **4th and present Baron De Ramsey of Ramsey Abbey**

2 +Andrew Edward [The Hon Andrew Fellowes, 36 Charolais Crescent, Ben Owa, Qld 4217, Australia]; *b* 24 March 1950; *educ* Rannoch and Yanco Ag Coll, NSW; *m* 19– *Anne, est dau of Roy Tweedy, of Mungle, North Star, Australia, and has issue:

(1) +Robert Andrew; *b* 1978

(1) *Katherine Jane; *b* 18 May 1976

(2) *Rachael Julie; *b* 1982

1 *Sarah [The Hon Mrs Shelton, E3 Moli Nou De Canet, Es Glayeta, Majorca, Spain]; *b* 28 March 1938; *educ* Essex Inst of Ag; *m* 27 Nov 1972 *Peter Alfred Shelton and has issue:

(1) *David Patrick; *b* 24 Jan 1977

(1) *Fay Lilah; *b* 31 July 1973

2 *Jennifer Julia [The Hon Jennifer Fellowes, Hall Farm, Abbots Ripton, Cambs PE17 2PG]; *b* 30 April 1940; *m* 6 June 1964 (*divorce* 1986, resumed maiden name) John Frederick Moxon and has issue:

(1) *Simon John; *b* 15 Jan 1965; *educ* Uppingham

(2) *Matthew Sebastian; *b* 9 Dec 1967

(3) *Christian Frederick; *b* 19 Jan 1974

(1) *Alice Lavinia [Mrs Anthony Cripps, 4 Machbridge Ave, Hunteys Hill, Sydney 2110, NSW, Australia]; *b* 13 Dec 1966; *m* 1989 *Anthony Cripps and has issue:

1a *William John; *b* 1990

2a *Henry Anthony; *b* 1992

3a *Charles Frederick; *b* 25 Feb 1996

1a *Daisy Jennifer Elizabeth; *b* 14 Aug 1997

(2) *Emily Faith Martha; *b* 8 July 1972

DERBY

Arms: Argent on a bend azure three stag's heads cabossed or. **Crest:** On a chapeau gules doubled ermine an eagle, wings extended or, preying on an infant in its cradle proper, swaddled gules, the cradle laced or. **Supporters:** Dexter, a griffin, wings elevated or, ducally collared and line reflexed over the back azure; sinister, a stag or, collared and lined as the dexter. **Motto:** *Sans changer* ('Unchanging'). The armorial bearings are said to have been first assumed by William (II) de Stanley in the late 13th century. The origin of the crest is more problematical and the subject of two legends (both of which, however, are almost certainly only legends). One tells of how the Isabel who married Sir John Stanley (*see* below) was dau of a foundling discovered in an eagle's nest and made by the childless octogenarian Thomas, Lord of Lathom (*d* 1370), his heir. The other tells of how Thomas had an illegitimate son who was discovered under a tree near an eagle's nest and subsequently bequeathed a trifling part of the Lathom properties, the lion's share going to the aforesaid Isabel and her Stanley descendants, who commemorated the picturesque incident in their own adoptive crest. Actually the crest in question was used by two members of the Lathom family a couple of generations before Isabel's time. **Creations:** E. (E) 27 Oct 1485, B. (Stanley of Bickerstaffe) 22 Dec 1832 and (Stanley of Preston) 27 Aug 1886 (both UK), Bt. (E) 26 June 1627.

THE 19TH EARL OF DERBY, Baron Stanley of Bickerstaffe, Baron Stanley of Preston and a **Baronet** (Sir Edward Richard William John Stanley, Bt) [The Rt Hon The Earl of Derby, Knowsley, Prescot, Merseyside L34 4AF; 1 Netherton Grove, London SW10 9TQ]; *b* 10 Oct 1962 (HRH THE DUKE OF WINDSOR stood sponsor); *s* unc 1994; *educ* Eton and RAC Cirencester; served Gren Gds 1982–85, merchant banker with Robert Fleming & Co; *m* 21 Oct 1995 *Hon Caroline Neville, dau of 10th Baron Braybrooke (*qv*), and has:

1 +EDWARD JOHN ROBIN, *Lord Stanley*; *b* 21 April 1998; *christened* 24 July 1998 (HRH THE DUKE OF YORK stood sponsor)

1 *Henrietta Mary Rose; *b* 6 Feb 1997

Earldom of Derby: Robert de Ferrieres, whose father Henry had been Lord of Ferrières in Normandy (so-called from its iron works) and had held around 210 lordships or manors at the time of the Domesday Survey of 1086, inherited most of his father's English properties and commanded troops on KING STEPHEN's behalf at the Battle of the Standard 1138 during the period of anarchy when the EMPRESS MATILDA and STEPHEN struggled for the throne. In his gratitude STEPHEN created him Earl of Derby.The title remained with successive members of the same family (latterly known as de Ferrers) till a few years before 1279, when Robert de Ferrers, 6th Earl of Derby, died. In 1266, following rebellion by Robert against HENRY III, his lands had been forfeited and since at that time the existence of an earldom without lands attached for its upkeep was unheard of, he was effectively deprived of the title (*see* also NORTHUMBERLAND, D, and RUTLAND, D, preliminary remarks, for a discussion of the concept of earldoms as quasi-appointive posts inseparable from territorial possessions).

The Ferrers possessions were then granted to Edmund, HENRY III's younger son, who is occasionally referred to as Earl (of) Ferrers or in Latin 'Ferrariis'. Edmund was executed and his titles forfeited in March 1331/2. His grandson was created Earl of Derby anew in March 1336/7. On the latter Earl's death without male issue in March 1360/1 his son-in-law John Duke of Lancaster (4th son of EDWARD III), who had married the late Earl's daughter Blanche, took the title Earl of Derby in right of his wife, as was the custom then. John and Blanche's son Henry sat in Parliament as Earl of Derby from 1385 but later ascended the throne as HENRY IV, when the Earldom merged with the Crown.

Descendants of the original de Ferrerses through various female lines eventually became Earls Ferrers (*qv*). In addition the last Ferrers Earl of Derby had a granddaughter Alianore who married Sir Thomas de Lathom or Lathum in around 1329. Their granddaughter Isabel, who has already been mentioned in the legends surrounding the Derby crest recounted above, married Sir John de Stanley (for both of whom *see* below).

Lineage: ADAM de STANLEY, bro of Liulf de Audley (f of Adam de Audley (*see* 1970 edn AUDLEY, B)), living *temp* STEPHEN and HENRY II, had issue:

1 WILLIAM (I) de STANLEY

2 Adam

3 Thomas

ADAM de STANLEY's est s,

WILLIAM (I) de STANLEY; granted Stanley (on what are now the northeasterly outskirts of Stoke-on-Trent) and half of Balterley, Staffs, by his 1st cousin Adam de Audley; had, with a yr s (John, Rector Astbury, Cheshire, *d* by 1292/3):

WALTER de STANLEY; recognitor (one exercising certain kind of action for debt) for Staffs 1271–72; sued for wrongful dispossession over a wood that was part of his holding at Stanley 1282; *d* by Trinity term 1285, leaving:

WILLIAM (II) de STANLEY; Ld of Manor and Bailiwick of Wyrall (modern Wirral) Forest; went to law with the Prior of Trentham, Staffs, 1292/3 over land in Over Elkeston, Staffs; *m* 27 Sept 1282 Joan (living 1326), est dau and coheir of Philip de Baumvile, hereditary Forester of Wirral, by Agnes, dau and coheir of Alexander de Storeton (cognate(?) with Stourton, Staffs) by Anabilla, dau and heir of Ranulph de Silvester, s of Allan Silvester, Ld of Storeton, and had issue:

JOHN de STANLEIGH or STANLEY; Ld of Manor of Stourton (Storeton?) etc; allegedly (but it may have been he who *m* Alice, dau of Hamon Massey/de Mascy (*see* below)) *m* Mabel, dau of Sir James Hawkset, of Stourton Parva, and had, with a yr s (John, of Greswithin, Cumberland, MP Carlisle *c* 1347, ancestor of Edward Stanley, of Ponsonby Hall, MP Cumberland 1832–52, whose own descendants were living there as late as the the first half of the 20th century):

WILLIAM de STANLEY; Ld of Manor of Stourton etc, Hereditary Forester Wirral Forest 1361/2; allegedly *m* Alice, dau of Hugh Massey/de Mascy (*see* above), of Timperley, and sis of Sir Hamon Massey/de Mascy, of Dunham Massey, and *d c* 1398, having had issue, with a dau:

1 William (Sir), of Hooton, Cheshire; *m* Margery, dau and heir of William de Hooton, and was ancestor of the Stanley Bts (later called Errington) of Hooton

2 JOHN (Sir)

3 Henry

WILLIAM de STANLEY's 2nd s,

Sir JOHN de STANLEY, KG (*c* 1405), SOVEREIGN LORD OF THE ISLE OF MAN; Ld Dep Ireland for Robert de Vere, Marquess of Dublin, 1386–88, Justiciary Ireland 1389–91, Justice Chester 1394, Controller Roy Household 1399, Lt Ireland 1399–1401, Steward Household to Henry Prince of Wales (later HENRY V) *c* 1403, Steward Macclesfield and Surveyor Forests of Macclesfield, Mare and Mondrem, Cheshire, 1403, Master Forester and Ranger of same 1403, Govr City and County of Chester 1403, granted by HENRY IV (it having been forfeited by the Earl of Northumberland (*see* NORTHUMBERLAND, D)) the Isle, Castle, peel and Ldship of Man 1406, Constable Windsor Castle 1409, Lt Ireland 1413–19; *m* by 1385 his 3rd cousin Isabel, dau and heir of Sir Thomas Lathom, of Lathom and Knowsley, Lancs (descended from Robert Fitz Henry, whose s, Robert, took the name Lathom from the place where he lived); *d* by 28 Jan 1413/4, having had issue, with three yr sons (Henry; Sir Thomas, of Elford, Staffs, ancestor of the STANLEYs of Elford Pipe; Sir Ralph) and two daus:

JOHN de STANLEY, SOVEREIGN LORD ISLE OF MAN; Steward Macclesfield Feb 1413/4; *m* Isabel (or possibly Elizabeth), dau of Sir John Haryngton, of Hornby Castle, Lancs, and *d* 27 Nov 1437, having had issue, with two yr sons (Richard; Edward; both Archdeacon Chester) and two daus:

THOMAS STANLEY, KG (1457); 1st LORD (Baron) STANLEY (E), so *cr* (according to later doctrine) by writ of summons to Parl 15 Jan 1455/6, and although this Barony, together with that of Strange (*see* below), has passed to another family, yet descendants of both sexes of the grantee are in remainder to it according to the later doctrine as to heritability of baronies by writ of summons — a fact reflected in the + sign against the names of living females and the issue of females, who are, however, not in remainder to those titles still held by the Earls of Derby; ktd *c* 1431, Lt of Ireland 1432–36, Constable Chester Castle, Controller Roy Household and Chamberlain N Wales 1439, Justice Cheshire, Flintshire and N Wales 1443, Ch Steward Duchy Lancaster 1448, Warden Calais; *m* Joan, dau and coheir of Sir Robert Goushill, of Hoveringham, Notts, by Elizabeth FitzAlan (widow of Sir William de Montagu and 1st Duke of Norfolk of the 1396 *cr*), and dau and coheir of 11th/4th Earl of Arundel by Elizabeth Bohun, gdau of EDWARD I, and *d* 20 Feb 1458/9, leaving issue, with three daus:

1 THOMAS, 2nd LORD

2 William (Sir), of Holt; present Battle of Bosworth where he played a decisive role in the victory of HENRY VII over RICHARD III; executed 16 Feb 1494/5 for supporting Perkin Warbeck

3 John (Sir); *m* Elizabeth, dau and heir of Sir Thomas Weever, of Weever, Cheshire; ancestor of the Barons Stanley of Alderley (*see* STANLEY OF ALDERLEY, SHEFFIELD and, B)

4 James, Archdeacon Carlisle

The 1st LORD (Baron) STANLEY's est s,

THOMAS STANLEY, 2nd LORD (Baron) STANLEY and **1st Earl of Derby** (E), so *cr* 27 Oct 1485, KG (1483), PC (1471); *b c* 1435; Esq of the Body to HENRY VI 1454, ktd 1460, Ch Justice Chester, Steward of the Household to EDWARD IV and RICHARD III 1471–85, Constable England 1483 for life, at Battle of Bosworth 22 Aug 1485 betrayed RICHARD III at a decisive moment and allegedly set the crown on HENRY VII's head afterwards, Ch Steward Duchy of Lancaster (Northern parts) 1485–1504; *m* 1st after 10 May 1457 Eleanor Nevill(e), 4th dau of 5th Earl of Salisbury of the 1337 *cr* (*see* ABERGAVENNY, M); *m* 2nd Margaret Beaufort (*d* 29 June 1509), dau and heir of 1st Duke of Somerset of the 1442/3 *cr* (*see* BEAUFORT, D) and widow of (a) 1st Earl of Richmond of the 1452 *cr* (by whom she was mother of HENRY VII) and (b) Sir Henry Stafford (*see* STAFFORD, B), and *d* 29 July 1504, having had by his 1st w:

1 GEORGE STANLEY, LORD (Baron) STRANGE (of Knokyn), as which called to Parl by writ 15 Nov 1482 in right of his w, KG (1487), KB (1475), PC; *b c* 1460; Constable: Pontefract Castle 1485, Knaresborough Castle 1485 and Wicklow Castle 1486, Ch Steward Duchy of Lancaster N of Trent 1486; *m* by 26 Feb 1480/1 Joan Lestrange, who according to later doctrine was Baroness Strange (of Knokyn) in her own right (*see* SAINT DAVIDS, V), and *dvp* 4/5 Dec 1503, allegedly poisoned at a banquet, having had, with two daus (including Jane; *m* as his 1st w Sir Robert Sheffield and had issue; *see* SHEFFIELD, Bt):

(1) THOMAS STANLEY, **2nd Earl of Derby**, 10th LORD (Baron) STRANGE (of Knokyn) and 6th LORD (Baron) MOHUN (in which two Baronies he *s* his mother (according to later doctrine) 20 March 1513/4), KB (1494), PC (1520); also assumed the titles VISCOUNT KYNTON and LORD (Baron) BASSETT, BURNAL and LACY (none of which he was entitled to); *b* by 1485; *m* by 1503 Anne Hastings (*bur* 17 Nov 1550), dau of 2nd Lord (Baron) Hastings of Hastings and sis of 1st Earl of Huntingdon (*qv*), and *d* 23 May 1521, having had issue:

1a John; *d* young

2a EDWARD STANLEY, **3rd Earl of Derby**, 11th LORD (Baron) STRANGE (of Knokyn) and 7th LORD (Baron) MOHUN, KG (1547), KB (1533), PC (1553 and 1558); *b* 10 May 1509; Ld Lt Lancs 1552–72, Ld High Steward 1553, V-Adml Lancs and Chester 1553–69, Chamberlain Chester 1559–65, Ld Lt Cheshire 1569–72; *m* 1st *c* 21 Feb 1530 Lady Dorothy Howard, dau of 2nd Duke of Norfolk (*qv*); *m* 2nd Margaret (*d* 19 Jan 1558/9), dau of Ellis Barlow, of Barlow, Lancs; *m* 3rd by 1 Jan 1561/2 Mary (*m* 2nd 6th Earl of Kent of the 1465 *cr* (*see* GREY, B) and *dsp* 16 Nov 1580), dau of Sir George Cotton (*see* COMBERMERE, V), and *d* 24 Oct 1572, having had:

1b HENRY STANLEY, **4th Earl of Derby**, KG (1574), 12th LORD (Baron) STRANGE (of Knokyn) and 8th LORD (Baron) MOHUN, KB (1547), PC (1585); *b* Sept 1531; called up to Ho Lds 23 Jan 1558/9 *vp* in his f's Barony of Strange, Ld Lt Lancs and Cheshire 1572–93, V-Adml Lancs and Cheshire 1573–87, Ld High Steward trial of the Earl of Arundel 14 April 1589 (*see* NORFOLK, D), Chamberlain Chester 1588–93; *m* 7 Feb 1555 Margaret Clifford (*d* 29 Sept 1596), only surv child of 2nd Earl of Cumberland (*see* DE CLIFFORD, B), and *d* 25 Sept 1593, having had issue:

1c Edward; *d* young

2c FERDINANDO STANLEY, **5th Earl of Derby**, 13th LORD (Baron) STRANGE (of Knokyn), 9th LORD (Baron) MOHUN and SOVEREIGN LORD OF THE ISLE OF MAN; *b c* 1559/60; *educ* St John's Coll Oxford (MA 1589); called up to Ho Lds 28 Jan 1588/9 *vp* in his f 's Barony of Strange, Ld Lt Lancs and Cheshire 1594, V-Adml Lancs and Cheshire 1594; *m c* 1580 Alice (*m* 2nd 20 Oct 1600, as his 3rd w, 1st Viscount Brackley (*see* GREY EGERTON, Bt) and *d* 26 Jan 1637), dau of Sir John Spencer, of Althorp, Northants (*see* SPENCER, E), and *d* 16 April 1594, when the Baronies of Stanley (*see* LOUDOUN, E), Strange (*see* ST DAVIDS, V) and Mohun fell into abeyance between his daus, while the Earldom passed to his bro, leaving issue:

1d Anne; *b* 1580; *m* 1st 28 Feb 1607/8 5th Baron Chandos of Sudeley (*see* TEMPLE OF STOWE, E); *m* 2nd 22 July 1624 2nd Earl of Castlehaven (*see* 1970 edn AUDLEY, B) and was *bur* 11 Oct 1647

2d Frances; *b* May 1583; *m c* 1601 1st Earl of Bridgwater (*see* GREY EGERTON, Bt, also SUTHERLAND, D), s of 1st Viscount Brackley (*see* above) by his 1st w, and *d* 11 March 1635/6, leaving issue

3d Elizabeth; *m* 15 Jan 1601 5th Earl of Huntingdon (*qv*) and *d* 20 Jan 1623, leaving issue

3c WILLIAM STANLEY, **6th Earl of Derby** and SOVEREIGN LORD OF THE ISLE OF MAN, KG (1601); *b c* 1561; *educ* St John's Coll Oxford and Lincoln's Inn; Chamberlain Cheshire 1603–20 and jointly with his s 1626–42, Ld Lt Lancs and Cheshire 1607–26 and jointly with his s 1626–42, bought out his nieces as to the rights to the Ldship or Admlty of the IoM and confirmed in his possession 7 July 1609, V-Adml Lancs and Cheshire 1619–38; *m* 26 June 1594 Lady Elizabeth de Vere (*d* 10 March 1626/7), est dau of 17th Earl of Oxford (*see* ST ALBANS, D), and *d* 29 Sept 1642, having had issue, with four daus:

1d JAMES STANLEY, **7th Earl of Derby**, SOVEREIGN LORD OF THE ISLE OF MAN and 1st LORD (Baron) STRANGE, being called to Parl 7 March 1627/8 in what was mistakenly thought to be his f 's Barony of Strange (of Knokyn) and was given that Barony's precedency of 1299, although the Barony in question had in fact fallen into abeyance (according to a doctrine which only came to fruition in the late 17th century) between his female cousins on his unc's death so that in effect a new Barony of Strange was now *cr*, KG (1650), KB (1626); *b* 31 Jan 1607; MP Liverpool 1625, Jt Ld Lt (with his f) Lancs and Cheshire and Jt Chamberlain Chester 1626–42, sole Ld Lt and Chamberlain 1642–47, Ld Lt N Wales 1642; held the IOM for CHARLES I during the Civil War; *m* 26 June 1626 Charlotte (who conducted a spirited defence of Lathom House 1644 and 1646 against Parly troops; *d* 21 March 1663/4), dau of Claude de la Trémoïlle, Duke of Thouars, by Charlotte, dau of William of Nassau, Prince of Orange, and Charlotte de Bourbon, and was beheaded 15 Oct 1651 for supporting CHARLES II's attempt to regain his crown, having had issue, with four daus:

1e CHARLES STANLEY, **8th Earl of Derby**, SOVEREIGN LORD OF THE ISLE OF MAN and 2nd LORD (Baron) STRANGE; *b* 19 Jan 1628; joined Sir George Booth's uprising 1659 on behalf of the exiled CHARLES II, Ld Lt Lancs and Cheshire 1660–72, Jt Chamberlain Chester 1660–72, V-Adml Lancs and Cheshire 1661–72; *m* 1650 Dorothea Helena (*d* 6 April 1703), dau of Jan van den Kerckhove, Ld of Heenvliet in Zeeland, by Catherine, Countess of Chesterfield (*see* 1967 edn CHESTERFIELD and STANHOPE, E), Maid-of-Honour to ELIZABETH, QUEEN OF BOHEMIA, and *d* 21 Dec 1672, leaving issue:

1f WILLIAM GEORGE RICHARD STANLEY, **9th Earl of Derby**, SOVEREIGN LORD OF THE ISLE OF MAN and 3rd LORD (Baron) STRANGE; *b* 18 March 1656; V-Adml Lancs and Cheshire 1673–1702, Ld Lt Lancs and Cheshire 1676–87 and 1688–89 and Lancs June–Nov 1702, Chamberlain Chester 1677–1702, Ld Lt N Wales (except Denbighshire) 1702; *m* 10 July 1673 Lady Elizabeth Butler (*d* 5 July 1717), sis of 2nd Duke of Ormonde (*see* MOUNTGARRET, V), and *dspms* 5 Nov 1702, when the Barony of Strange *cr* 1628 fell into abeyance between his two daus, having had issue:

1g James, *Baron Strange*; *b* 28 June 1680; *dvp* unm Oct 1699

1g HENRIETTA MARIA, *de jure* BARONESS STRANGE in her own right on death of her yr sis 1714; *b c* 1687; *m* 1st 21 May 1706 4th Earl of Anglesey (*dspms* 18 Sept 1710 (*see* VALENTIA, V)) and had issue:

1h Elizabeth; *d* unm by 1718

1g (cont.) The *de jure* BARONESS STRANGE *m* 2nd 24 July 1714 1st Earl of Ashburnham (*d* 10 March 1736/7; *see* 1924 edn) and *dspm* 26 June 1718, leaving further issue:

2h HENRIETTA BRIDGET ASHBURNHAM, *de jure* BARONESS STRANGE in her own right; *d* unm 8 Aug 1732

2g Elizabeth; *d* unm 23 April 1714

2f JAMES STANLEY, **10th Earl of Derby**, SOVEREIGN LORD OF THE ISLE OF MAN and 6th LORD (Baron) STRANGE of the 1628 *cr* (as which s great-niece 1732), PC (1706); *b* 3 July 1664; MP (Whig): Clitheroe 1685–87, Preston 1689–90 and Lancs 1690–1702, Lt Col Foot Gds, Col 16th Foot 1692–1705, Maj-Gen 1704, Ld Lt Lancs 1702–10 and 1714–36, V-Adml Lancs 1702–12, Chamberlain Chester 1702–36, Chllr Duchy of Lancaster 1706–10; *m* Feb 1705 Mary (*d* 29 March 1752), dau and sole heir of Sir William Morley, KB, of Hainaker, and *dspms* 1 Feb 1735/6, when the Ldship or Admlty of the IOM with the Barony of Strange passed to the heir general 2nd Duke of Atholl (*see* below), having had issue:

1g William, *Lord Stanley*; *b* 31 Jan, *d* 4 March 1709/10

1e Amelia Sophia; *m* 5 May 1659 1st Marquess of Atholl (*see* ATHOLL, D) and *d* 22 Feb 1702/3, leaving issue (their gs the 2nd Duke of Atholl inherited the sovereignty of the IOM on the death of the 10th Earl of Derby and was called to Parl 14 March 1736/7 as 7th Lord (Baron) Strange)

2d Robert (Sir); *m* Elizabeth, dau of Sir Arthur Gorges, and had issue, with a dau:

1e Charles (Sir), of Chelsea, Middx, whose issue became extinct

2e James, whose two sons *d* young

3e Ferdinand; *d* young

4c Francis; *educ* St John's Coll Oxford

2b Thomas (Sir), of Winwick; *m* Margaret, dau and coheir of Sir George Vernon (*see* VERNON, B), and *d* 1576, leaving issue:

1c Edward (Sir), KB, of Tong Castle, Salop, and Eynsham, Oxon; *m* Lucy, dau of 1st Earl of Northumberland of the 1557 *cr* (*see* NORTHUMBERLAND, D), and had:

1d Frances; *m* Sir John Fortescue, 1st Bt of the 17 Feb 1635/6 (NS) *cr*

2d Venetia; *m* Sir Kenelm Digby, of Gothurst (*see* DIGBY, B)

1b Anne; *m* 8th Lord (Baron) Stourton (*see* MOWBRAY, SEGRAVE and STOURTON, B)

2b Jane; *m* 1566/7 4th Lord (Baron) Dudley (*qv*) and was *bur* 4 Sept 1569, leaving issue

3b Mary; *m* by 23 Nov 1566 3rd Lord (Baron) Stafford of the 1547 *cr* (*see* STAFFORD, B) and *d* 3 Sept 1609, leaving issue

4b Elizabeth; *m* 2nd Lord (Baron) Morley of the 1299 *cr* and had issue

(2) John; *d* young

(3) James (Sir), of Crosshall, Lancs; Marshal of Ireland; *m* Anne, dau of John Hart by Elizabeth, sis and heir of Sir John Peache, of Lullingstone Castle, Kent, and widow of Edmund Talbot de Bashall, Yorks, and had issue:

1a George (Sir), of Crosshall; known as 'The Black Knight'; Marshal of Ireland, Capt IOM; had two sons (*dsp*) and at least one dau (Mary, *m* Robert Hesketh; *see* HESKETH, B)

2a Henry, of Aughton; *b* 1515; *m* 26 Sept 1563 Mary, dau and heir of Peter Stanley, of Bickerstaff, 3rd s of Sir William Stanley, of Hooton, and *d* 23 July 1598, leaving, with another s James:

1b **Sir Edward Stanley, 1st Bt** (E), so *cr* 26 June 1627, of Bickerstaff, Lancs; *m* 1st Catherine (*d* Nov 1613), dau of Sir Randal Mainwaring, of Over Peover, and had three daus; *m* 2nd Isabel, dau and coheir of Sir Peter Warburton, of Arley, and was *bur* 4 May 1640, leaving issue, with six other sons:

1c **Sir Thomas Stanley, 2nd Bt**; *bapt* 22 Oct 1616; *m* Mary (*m* 2nd Henry Hoghton), dau of Peter Egerton, of Shaw, and *d* May 1653, leaving issue:

1d **Sir Edward Stanley, 3rd Bt**; *educ* Oxford (MA); *m* 25 Dec 1663 Elizabeth, dau and coheir of Thomas Bosvile, of Warmsworth, Yorks, and *d* 16 Oct 1671, leaving issue:

1e **Sir Thomas Stanley, 4th Bt**; *b* 27 Sept 1670; *m* 1st 16 Aug 1688 Elizabeth (*d* 1694), only dau and heir of Thomas Patten, of Preston, MP; *m* 2nd Margaret (*d* 14 Oct 1735), dau of Thomas Holcroft, of Holcroft, Lancs, and widow of Sir Richard Standish, 1st Bt of the 1677 *cr*, and *d* 7 May 1714, leaving issue by his 1st w:

1f EDWARD, **11th Earl**

2f John (Rev), DD; Rector Liverpool, Bury and Winwick; *m* 1st Alice, dau of Edward Warren; *m* 2nd May 1753 Sarah (*d* Feb 1807), dau of John Earle, of Liverpool (*see* EARLE, Bt), and *dsp* 1781

1e Barbara; *m* Rev Zachary Taylor

2d Peter; *m* 19 April 1683 Catherine (*m* 2nd Paul Amyas), dau of Col Alexander Rigby, and was *bur* 27 Jan 1686, leaving issue:

1e Thomas, of Cross Hall; High Sheriff Lancs 1718; *m* Catherine, dau of Anthony Parker, of Bradkirk, Lancs, and was *bur* 18 April 1733, leaving, with other issue:

1f Charles; *dspm*

2f Thomas (Rev), DD; *bapt* 2 Jan 1717; *m* Betty (*d* 4 Dec 1780), dau and coheir of John Shaw, of York, and was *bur* 30 June 1764, leaving, with other issue:

1g James; *b* 26 Dec 1750; *m* May 1786 Augusta, dau of John Cornwall, and *d* 28 Sept 1810, leaving, with other issue:

1h Edward, of Cross Hall, JP, DL; *b* 1789; *m* 3 Sept 1819 Lady Mary Maitland (*d* 8 Nov 1877), dau of 8th Earl of Lauderdale (*qv*), and *d* 8 March 1870, leaving issue:

1i Edward James, of Cross Hall, JP, DL (Lancs and Somerset); *b* 16 Dec 1826; *educ* Oxford (MA); MP W Somerset 1882–85 and Bridgwater 1885–1907; *m* 19 Sept 1872 Hon Mary Dorothy Labouchere (*d* 15 March 1920), dau and coheir of 1st Baron Taunton, and *d* 28 Sept 1907, having had issue:

1j Henry Thomas; *b* 20 Aug 1873; Lt W Somerset YC; *ka* Hekpoort, S Africa, 16 Sept 1900

2j Edward Arthur Vesey; *b* 30 Aug 1879; *educ* Eton and Ch Ch Oxford; Capt 21st Lancers, Master Quantock Staghounds, Devon and Somerset Staghounds, MFH Pytchley, memb Cncl Nat Greyhound Racing Soc, chm Greyhound Betting Arbitration Ctee; *m* 1st 11 June 1919 (*divorce* 1932) Sybil Agnes (*d* 1972), dau of Maj Heathfield Butler Dodgson, DSO, of Handborough, Oxford (*see* VIVIAN, B), and had issue:

1k +Peter Vivian; *b* 3 Jan 1921; *educ* Eton; late Lt RA; *m* 30 Aug 1960 (*divorce* 1974) Kay, dau of R S Wybrow, of Valley Wood Place, Cobbham, Surrey, and has had issue:

1l Camilla; *b* 4 July 1964; *d* in infancy

2k Michael Edward; *b* 21 July 1923; Lt RN; *k* 29 Aug 1951 in a flying accident

3k David Norman Sidney; *b* 20 July 1926; *d* 19–

2j (cont.) Edward Stanley *m* 2nd 30 Jan 1936 *Marjorie Beatrice [Mrs Charles Sidey, 8 Ash Court, Stanway Close, Taunton, Somerset] (*m* 2nd 28 April 1942 Charles Langford Sidey (*d* 1993), only *s* of James Walker Sidey, of Longcroft, Rotherfield, Sussex), only child of Alexander Reid Booth, and *d* 11 June 1941, leaving further issue:

4k +John Alexander; *b* 9 July 1938; *educ* Repton; *m* 1983 *Susan, dau of Dennis Brown, and has issue:

1l +Thomas Charles Edward; *b* 1984

1j Evelyn Mary; *m* 1 Nov 1898 Lt-Col Henry William Ludovic Heathcoat-Amory (*d* 22 Dec 1945), Coldstream Gds, of Hele Manor, Dulverton, Somerset (*see* HEATHCOAT-AMORY, Bt), and *d* 16 Nov 1929

1i Eleanor Julian; Maid of Honour to HM QUEEN VICTORIA; *m* 11 Dec 1866 Lt-Col Samuel Long, DL (*d* 31 Aug 1881), of Bromley Hill, Kent, and *d* 21 Jan 1903, leaving issue

2i Augusta; *m* 12 July 1841 1st Earl of Dartrey of the 1866 *cr* (*d* 12 May 1897; *see* 1933 edn), and *d* 9 Aug 1887, leaving issue

1d Mary; *m* John Bradshaw, of Pennington

2c Henry; *bapt* 3 Sept 1617; *m* 1st Eleanor Dutton; *m* 2nd Mary, dau of Hamlet Cropper, of Bickerstaff, and had issue:

1d Edward, of Preston, Lancs; *bur* 4 Jan 1755 aged 103, leaving issue, with six other sons:

1e Henry, whose gs Henry Stanley was named in the will of the **11th Earl of Derby** as heir in remainder but *d* unm Jamaica before 17 Jan 1799, when this line became extinct

2e Charles, of Balla Cagan, IOM; *b* 16 Sept 1702; *m* Elizabeth, dau and coheir of Christopher Parker by Katherine, dau of John Stanley, of IOM, and had issue, with three sons who *d* unm:

1f Charles; *b* 3 April 1745; heir to the Manx estates, of which he signed away the reversion; had:

1g James (Rev); *b* 30 Oct 1768; Vicar Ormskirk; *m* 11 July 1797 Sarah (*d* 12 Feb 1853), dau of John Edleston, and was *bur* 17 June 1812, leaving, with other issue:

1h (Adml) Edward, RN; *b* 10 May 1798; *m* 1st 5 July 1834 Elizabeth (*dsp* 20 April 1848), dau of John Snell; *m* 2nd 18 Oct 1855 Caroline Cordelia (*d* 4 Oct 1876), dau of Edward Hancorne, and *d* 19 Feb 1878, leaving, with other issue:

1i Edward James; *b* 12 Dec 1857; *m* 1st 8 July 1885 Catherine Mary Maud (*d* 5 Oct 1896), dau of William Kidger, of Cradock; *m* 2nd 15 Sept 1902 Annie Clifford (*d* 1949), dau of Richard Cawood, of Ganna Hoek, Cradock, S Africa, and *d* 15 Oct 1933, leaving issue by his 1st w:

1j Irene; *b* 28 Sept 1886; *m* 5 March 1916 (Frederick) Charles Pope (*d* 1948) and had issue

2j Joan Arundel; *b* 23 Oct 1893; *m* 5 March 1916 John Samuel Wainwright, of Hopewell, Stenysburg, CP, S Africa, and *d* 25 May 1954, leaving issue

3j Kate Dorothy; *b* 18 Sept 1896; *m* 16 April 1917 Arthur Charles Levey, of Fairview, Tarkastad, CP, S Africa, and had issue

2i Montagu Nevill; *b* 5 Sept 1861

3i Henry Harrington; *b* 14 Dec 1862; *m* 3 Sept 1887 Jane, dau of George Thorneloe, and *dsp* 17 March 1949

4i Ferdinand Charles Nelson; *b* 11 April 1865; *m* 1st 25 Dec 1891 Hannah (*d* 13 Oct 1910), dau of Robert Jaggs, of Ware, Herts; *m* 2nd 1924 Martha, widow of Herbert Peter Barrow Rigby, and had issue by his 1st w:

1j Montague Ernest; *b* 20 Jan 1893; *m* 1940 *Augusta, dau of Herbert Klugman

5i Alphonse Frederick; *b* 1869; *m* his sis-in-law Ruth, dau of Robert Jaggs, and had issue:

1j Dorothy; *b* 1894

2j Constance; *b* 1900

2 EDWARD STANLEY, 1st LORD (Baron) MO(U)NTEAGLE (E), so *cr* (in reward for cmdg the left wing of the English Army in its rout of the Scots at Flodden 1513) 21 May 1514 (the choice of title commemorating his occupation of a strategic mount on the field of Flodden and the eagle in the Stanley crest), KG (1514), JP (Kent 1484, Yorks and Westmorland 1509), Kt Banneret 1482; Sheriff Lancs 1485; *m* 1st Anne (*b c* 1455; *dsp* 5 Aug 1460), dau of Sir John Harington, of Hornby Castle, Lancs, by Maud, dau of 8th Lord (Baron) Clifford (*see* DE CLIFFORD, B); *m* 2nd by 25 Nov 1501 Elizabeth (*d* 15 Jan 1514/5), dau of Sir Thomas Vaughan, of Tretower, Brecon, and widow of (a) 8th Lord (Baron) Grey (of Wilton) of the 1295 *cr* (*see* GREY, B) and (b) Sir Thomas Cokesey (*alias* Greville/Grevile), and *d* 6/7 April 1523, leaving:

(1) THOMAS STANLEY, 2nd LORD (Baron) MO(U)NTEAGLE, KB (1533); *b* 25 May 1507; helped his cousin the Earl of Derby crush the Pilgrimage of Grace 1536; *m* 1st between 2 June 1527 and 1529 Lady Mary Brandon (*d* between 1540 and 1544), dau of 1st Duke of Suffolk of the 1514 *cr* by his w Anne Browne, gdau of 1st Marquess of Montagu (*see* ABERGAVENNY, M); *m* 2nd Helen (*d* by 14 Nov 1571), dau of Thomas Preston, of Levens, Westmorland, and widow of Sir James Leybourne (*see* below), and *d* 25 Aug 1560, leaving by his 1st w:

1a WILLIAM STANLEY, 3rd LORD (Baron) MO(U)NTEAGLE; *m* 1st Anne (living Nov 1571), dau of Sir James Leybourne, of Conswyke, Westmorland; *m* 2nd *c* 15 Sept 1575 Anne (*m* 2nd 1st Lord Compton (*see* NORTHAMPTON, M); *m* 3rd 4 Dec 1592 2nd Earl of Dorset of the 1603 *cr* (*see* SACKVILLE, B) and *d* 22 Sept 1618), 5th dau of Sir John Spencer, of Althorp, Northants (*see* MARLBOROUGH, D), and *dspm* 10 Nov 1581, leaving:

1b Elizabeth; *m* 7th Lord (Baron) Morley of the 1299 *cr* and had issue

2 (cont.) The 1st LORD (Baron) MO(U)NTEAGLE also had illegitimate issue:

(2) Edward; living 1514

(3) Thomas; Parson Baddisworth; living 1523

(1) Mary; *m* — Radcliff (*d* by 7 April 1522) and *d* 7 April 1522

3 James; Bp Ely

The 10th EARL OF DERBY's 6th cousin,

Sir Edward Stanley, 5th Bt, and **11th Earl of Derby**; *b* 17 Sept 1689; V-Adml Lancs 1712–76, High Sheriff Lancs 1723, MP (Whig) Lancs 1727–36, Ld Lt Lancs 1742–57 and 1771–76; *m* 14 Sept 1714 Elizabeth (*d* 24 Feb 1776), only dau and heir of Robert Hesketh (*see* HESKETH, B), and *d* 22 Feb 1776, having had, with six daus:

JAMES STANLEY later SMITH-STANLEY (Act of Parl 21 GEORGE II), incorrectly styled *Lord Strange*, PC (1762); *b* 7 Jan 1716/7; *educ* Westminster and Leyden U; MP (Tory) Lancs 1741–71, Ld Lt Lancs 1757–71, Chllr Duchy of Lancaster 1762–71; *m* 17 March 1746/7 Lucy (*d* 5 Feb 1759), 2nd dau and coheir of Hugh Smith, of Weald Hall, Essex, by Dorothy, dau of Dacre Barrett Lennard (*see* HAMPDEN, V), and *dvp* 1 June 1771, having had, with other issue (including Lucy, *m* Rev Geoffrey Hornby, Rector Winwick, Lancs, and had issue; *see* below):

EDWARD STANLEY later SMITH-STANLEY, **12th Earl of Derby**, PC (1783); *b* 12 Sept 1752; *educ* Eton and Trin Coll Cambridge (MA 1773); MP (Whig) Lancs 1774–76, Ld Lt Lancs 1776–1834, Col 1779, Chllr Duchy Lancaster 1783 and 1806–07, V-Adml Lancs 1809–31; *m* 1st 23 June 1774 Lady Elizabeth Hamilton (*d* 14 March 1797), only dau of 6th Duke of Hamilton and Brandon (*qv*); *m* 2nd 1 May 1797 Elizabeth, actress (*d* 23 April 1829), dau of George Farren, of Cork, surgeon and apothecary, later an actor, and *d* 21 Oct 1834, having had issue by his 1st w:

1 EDWARD, **13th Earl**

1 Charlotte; *m* 22 Aug 1796 her cousin Edmund Hornby (*d* 18 Nov 1857), of Dalton Hall, Westmorland, and *d* 25 Nov 1805, leaving issue

2 Elizabeth Henrietta; *m* 15 Jan 1795 Stephen Thomas Cole (*d* 1835), of Twickenham, and *d* Nov 1857, leaving issue

The 12th EARL OF DERBY's *s*,

EDWARD SMITH-STANLEY, **13th Earl of Derby**, KG (1839); *b* 21 April 1775; *educ* Eton and Trin Coll Cambridge (MA 1795); Col 1798, MP: (Whig) Preston 1796–1812, Lancs 1812–32, V-Adml Lancs 1831, *cr* 22 Dec 1832 BARON STANLEY OF BICKERSTAFFE, Co Lancaster (UK), Pres Linnaean Soc 1828–33 and Zoological Soc 1831, Tstee Br Museum 1834–51; *m* 30 June 1798 his cousin

Charlotte Margaret (*d* 16 June 1817), 2nd dau of Rev Geoffrey Hornby, and *d* 30 June 1851, leaving, with other issue:

1 EDWARD GEOFFREY, **14th Earl**

2 Henry Thomas; *b* 9 March 1803; MP Preston 1832–37; *m* 1 Sept 1835 Anne, dau of Richard Woolhouse, and *d* 2 April 1875, having had issue:

(1) Edward Henry; *b* 5 Jan 1838

(2) Charles Geoffrey; *b* 5 Sept 1839; Capt 32nd Regt; *m* 11 April 1861 Agnes Nina, yst dau of Honoratus Leigh Rigby, and *d* 22 April 1877, having had issue:

1a Charles Henry, DSM; *b* 25 March 1863; WW I RNVR; *m* 1st 23 April 1883 Mary Massy, dau of Charles Nason, of Cork, and had issue:

1b Charles Geoffrey Nason (Very Rev); *b* 10 Nov 1884; *educ* Trin Coll Dublin (BA 1906); Dean and Rector Lismore, Co Waterford, 1934–61, RD Waterford 1957–61; *m* 1st 1914 Eileen Chapman (*d* 19 June 1928) and had:

1c Desmond Geoffrey; *b* 23 Sept 1917; WW II RAF; *ka* 7 Dec 1940

2c +Eric William (Rev) [The Rev Eric Stanley, Cuanbeg, Ballycotton, Co Cork, Ireland]; *b* 22 May 1922; *educ* Trin Coll Dublin (BA 1945, MA 1948); *m* 28 April 1949 *Phoebe Elizabeth Mary Pollard and has issue:

1d +Joy; *b* 7 July 1950

2d +Katherine; *b* 11 July 1953

1b (cont.) The Very Rev Charles Stanley *m* 2nd 1931 *Violet Claire Baldwin [Mrs Charles Stanley, Glendonagh House, Dungourney, Midleton, Co Cork, Ireland] and *d* 1977, leaving further issue:

3c +Arthur Patrick (Rev) [The Rev Arthur Stanley, Route 1, Box 212, 2081 S Avenue, Stanton, Iowa 51573, USA]; *b* 24 June 1932; *educ* Trin Coll Dublin (MA); Army Chaplain; *m* 1st 16 July 1958 Kathleen Marjorie Ethel (*d* 1981), dau of Harold Victor Earl, of Waterford; *m* 2nd 1983 *Jessie Ernestine Fisher, *née* Tombleson, and has issue by his 1st w:

1d +Stephen Patrick; *b* 19 May 1961

1d +Belinda Susan; *b* 10 Sept 1959; *m* 4 May 1990 *Timothy Sykes and has:

1e +Richard Andrew Stanley; *b* 16 May 1996

1e +Elizabeth Claire Stanley; *b* 23 Feb 1995

1c +Sylvia Penelope [Mrs William Spence, RR2, Box 20, Parker Rd, Nanoose Bay, BC VOR 2RO, Canada]; *b* 22 Nov 1936; *m* 1956 *Rev William George Stanley Spence, MSc, and has issue:

1d +Peter Edward; *b* 15 June 1959; PhD Cantab

1d +Janet; *b* 14 April 1962; *m* 1982 *Robert Kellow and has:

1e +Robyn Tara; *b* 1992

2c +Hazel Claire [Mrs Richard Armstrong, Nedre Markveg 1, 9011 Tromsø, Norway]; *b* 9 April 1940; *m* 1963 *Richard John Armstrong, PhD, and has issue:

1d +Geoffrey James; *b* 1966

2d +Charles Ivan; *b* 1969

3d +Niall John; *b* 1974

1d +Claire Winifred; *b* 1964; *m* 1989 *Stein-Halvar Støver and has:

1e +Eva; *b* 1996

2b Frederick George; *b* 1888; *m* 8 Aug 1931 Grace Evelyn Thrower (*d* 1988) and *d* 1979, leaving issue:

1c +Helen Audrey [Mrs George Watts, 12 Greenways, Abbots Langley, Watford, Herts]; *m* 1st 20 June 1959 (*divorce* 1966) Roger Laurence, s of Charles Laurence, of Croydon, Surrey; *m* 2nd 27 Aug 1966 *George Watts, s of George Watts, of Muswell Hill, London

1b Edith Mary; *m* 1916 Kingsmill Barnes Williams (*d* Dec 1966) and *d* Aug 1967, having had two sons (the er *das* WW II) and two daus

1a (cont.) Charles Stanley *m* 2nd Belinda Ottley and had further issue:

3b Henry William Valentine; *b* 1903; *m* 16 June 1930 Kathleen May Hardwick (*d* 1981) and *d* 1977, leaving:

1c +Leslie Hugh [Leslie Stanley Esq, 18 Heather Avenue, Bearsden, Glasgow G61 3JE]; *b* 5 Nov 1931; *m* 13 Nov 1957 *Marjorie Mary Green and has:

1d +Christopher John; *b* 2 Sept 1958; *m* 1991 *Sally Ann Morrison and has:

1e +Tessa Morrison; *b* 30 April 1994

2d +Geoffrey Hugh Desmond, BSc; *b* 4 March 1962; *m* 1989 *Catherine Anne Sheehan, BSc

1d +Lissa Rachel; *b* 1 Oct 1963; *m* 1984 *Mark Stephen Ferguson and has:

1e +Geoffrey Christopher; *b* 1990

2c +Norman Edward [Norman Stanley Esq, Carraghan, Church St, Alcombe, Minehead, Somerset]; *b* 26 Feb 1937; *m* 23 Dec 1961 *Maxine Wyness and has:

1d +Adam; *b* 1969; *educ* Cambridge (BA)

1d +Dominique; *b* 10 April 1965

2d +Mia; *b* 1966; *educ* Edinburgh Coll of Art (BA)

1a (cont.) Charles Stanley *m* 3rd Mabel Johnson

2a Henry Edmund; *b* 8 July 1868; *m* Poppy Ferguson and had:

1b Beatrice; *m* 1st Maj — West; *m* 2nd F C Cashel and *d* *c* 1950

1a Mary Kathleen Fanny; *m* 22 Oct 1894 Francis Horatio Lloyd (*d* 1920), s of Sir Horatio Lloyd, County Ct Judge, and *dsp*

(3) Henry Edmund; *b* 27 Dec 1840; Capt 23rd Regt; *d* 15 Nov 1867 at Jubbulpore after a fall from his horse

(1) Charlotte Margaret Sidney Anne; *d* 26 Oct 1872

3 Charles James Fox; *b* 25th April 1808; Lt-Col Gren Gds, Col 3rd Bn Lancs Militia; *m* 10 Dec 1836 Frances Augusta (*d* 29 May 1878), dau of Sir Henry Frederick Campbell, KCB, and *d* 13 Oct 1884, leaving:

(1) Charles Edward Henry; *b* 28 April 1843; Lt-Col Gren Guards; *m* 30 July 1874 Frederica Lucy Phipps (*d* 9 June 1936), er dau of Capt Phipps John Hornby, RE, and *d* 16 Dec 1909, leaving:

1a Charles Douglas; *b* 9 April 1878; *educ* Eton; *m* 27 April 1909 Adela Grace (*d* 2 Jan 1950), 3rd dau of Francis Alexander Walker-Jones, JP, of Beddgelert, Gwynedd, and *d* 1975, leaving:

1b +Charles John Geoffrey [Charles Stanley Esq, 5 Shoreham Place, Shoreham, Sevenoaks, Kent TN14 7RX]; *b* 10 Oct 1918; *educ* Eton and St John's Coll Cambridge (BA 1940); Capt RAC WW II France 1940 NW Europe 1944–45; *m* 21 March 1942 *Marjorie Laura Awdry, only dau of John Frederick Awdry Ball, of Tardebigge, Worcs, and has:

1c +Christopher Geoffrey Awdry [Christopher Stanley Esq, The Old Rectory, Knighton on Teme, Worcs WR15 8LY]; *b* 18 March 1949; *educ* Radley and London U (BSc Econ); *m* 1974 *Anita Jane Keogh and has:

1d +Thomas Edward Christopher; *b* 1983

1d +Ruth Mary Frances; *b* 1987

2c +Martin John Llewelyn [Martin Stanley Esq, Ruard, Neb Lane, Oxted, Surrey]; *b* 19 June 1952; *educ* Radley and St John's Coll Oxford; *m* 1979 *Philippa Alison Beauvais, yst dau of W Beric Southwell, of Ide Hill, Sevenoaks, Kent, and has:

1d +Charles Douglas Llewelyn; *b* 1982

2d +Max Wilfred Southwell; *b* 1988

1d +Isobel Beauvais; *b* 1984

2a Phipps Edward; *b* 21 April 1881; *m* 3 Sept 1920 Elsie (*d* 1991), only dau of J C Piddock, of Altenburg Gardens, London SW, and *d* 10 April 1924

3a John William; *b* 10 March 1886; 2nd Lt Lancs Fus; *ka* 7 June 1917

1a Frances Ellinor; *b* 1 May 1882; *d* unm 25 Jan 1945

2a Alice Margaret; *b* 6 June 1884; *d* unm 20 Sept 1944

(2) Douglas James George; *b* 8 March 1847; Lt RA; *d* unm 10 July 1877

(3) Albert Hamilton; *b* 9 July 1849; Capt Durham LI; *d* unm 3 Jan 1900

(4) Edmund Phipps (Rev); *b* 13 Oct 1855; Preb Wells Cathedral, Rector Wootton Courtenay, Somerset, 1884–1926; *m* 9 Sept 1885 Catherine Stewart (*d* 8 April 1905), dau of John Stewart Browne, of Port Lincoln, S Australia, and *d* 6 Sept 1929, having had issue:

1a Edmund Stewart; *b* 3 Sept 1891; *educ* Eton and King's Coll Cambridge (BA 1913, MA 1917); T/Lt RGA WW I (wounded); *d* unm 23 Aug 1968

(1) Evelyn Emma; *d* unm 4 Jan 1926

(2) Margaret Alice; *d* unm 24 Sept 1935

(3) Mary Louisa; *d* unm 18 March 1921

(4) Constance Emily; *d* unm 16 April 1933

The 13th EARL OF DERBY's est s,

EDWARD GEOFFREY SMITH-STANLEY, **14th Earl of Derby**, KG (1859), GCMG (1869), PC (E 1830, I 1831); *b* 19 March 1799; *educ* Eton and Ch Ch Oxford; MP: (Whig) Stockbridge 1822–26, Preston 1826–30, Windsor 1831–32, N Lancs 1832–35 and (C) 1835–44, Under Sec Colonies 1827–28, Ch Sec Ireland 1830–33 with a Cabinet seat from June 1831, Sec of State Colonies 1833–34 and 1841–45, Ld Rector U of Glasgow 1834–36, called up to Ho of Lds *vp* 4 Nov 1844 in his f's Barony of Stanley of Bickerstaffe, PM Feb-Dec 1852, March 1858–Jan 1859 and July 1866–Feb 1868, Chllr Oxford U 1852–69, DCL 1852, trans Homer's *Iliad*; *m* 31 March 1825 Hon Emma Caroline Bootle-Wilbraham (*d* 26 April 1876), 2nd dau of 1st Baron Skelmersdale (*qv*), and *d* 23 Oct 1869, leaving issue:

1 EDWARD HENRY STANLEY, **15th Earl of Derby**, KG (1884), PC (1858); *b* 21 July 1826; *educ* Rugby and Trin Coll Cambridge (MA 1848); MP (C) King's Lynn 1848–69 (Lib in Ho of Lds 1879 and U 1886), U-Sec For Affrs 1852, 1866–68 and 1874–78, Sec State Colonies 1858 and 1882–85, India 1858–59, Pres Bd of Control 1858, DCL Oxford 1853, LLD Cambridge 1862, Ld Rector Glasgow U 1868–71 and Edinburgh U 1874–77, Chllr London U 1891–93, FRS 1859; *m* 5 July 1870 Lady Mary Catherine West (*d* 6 Dec 1900), dau of 5th Earl De La Warr (*qv*) and widow of 2nd Marquess of Salisbury (*qv*), and *dsp* 21 April 1893

2 FREDERICK ARTHUR, **16th Earl**

1 Emma Charlotte; *m* 11 Oct 1860 Col Hon Sir Wellington Patrick Manvers Chetwynd Talbot, KCB (*d* 23 Sept 1898), bro of 18th Earl of Shrewsbury (*see* SHREWSBURY and WATERFORD, E), and *d* 23 Aug 1928, leaving issue

The 15th EARL OF DERBY's yr bro,

FREDERICK ARTHUR STANLEY, **16th Earl of Derby**, KG (1897), GCB (1886), PC (1878); *b* 15 Jan 1841; *educ* Eton; Lt Gren Gds 1858, Capt 1862–65, MP: (C) Preston 1865–68, N Lancs 1868–85 and Blackpool 1885–86, a Ld of Admlty 1868, Constable Castle Rising 1870–1908, Fin Sec War Office 1874–77 and Treasury 1877–78, Militia ADC to TM QUEEN VICTORIA 1877–1901 and EDWARD VIII 1901–08, Sec of State War 1878–80 and Colonies 1885–86, Pres BOT 1886–88, *cr* 27 Aug 1886 BARON STANLEY OF PRESTON, Co Lancaster (UK), Govr Gen Canada 1883–93, Ld Mayor Liverpool 1895–96 and Preston 1901, Ld Lt Lancs 1897–1908, Chllr Liverpool U 1903–08; *m* 31 May 1864 Lady Constance Villiers (*d* 17 April 1922), est dau of 4th Earl of Clarendon (*qv*), and *d* 14 June 1908, having had issue:

1 EDWARD GEORGE VILLIERS, **17th Earl**

2 Victor Albert (Sir), KCB, MVO; *b* 17 Jan 1867 (HM QUEEN VICTORIA stood sponsor); Adml, Naval Attaché Russia 1905–09, Cmdt RNC Dartmouth 1912–14, R-Adml 1st Battle Sqdn Atlantic Fleet 1919–20, V-Adml cmdg Reserve Fleet 1924–26, served Egypt War 1882 and WW I 1914 (despatches), Orders: St Anne of Russia 2nd Cl, Redeemer of Greece, Sword of Sweden, St Olaf of Norway and Rising Sun of Japan, Offr Legion of Honour; *m* 25 Nov 1896 Annie Bickerton (*d* 14 April 1962), dau of Hon Charles Edward Pooley, KC, Pres Cncl of Br Columbia Cabinet (*see* 1963 edn POOLEY, Bt), and *d* 9 June 1934, having had issue:

(1) Godfrey Victor; *b* 18 Jan 1902; *d* 9 March 1903

(1) Violet Alice; *b* 11 Oct 1897; *m* 7 Oct 1924 (*divorce* 1932) Capt Booker Milburn, DSO, MC (*d* 11 March 1941), Coldstream Gds, s of William Milburn (*see* MILBURN, Bt)

(2) Rosemary Constance; *b* 9 Oct 1905; *m* 29 April 1943 George Pelham Ritchie, s of H A Ritchie

3 Arthur (Sir), GCVO (1944), GBE (1917), CB (1916), JP, DL (Lancs); *b* 18 Nov 1869; 2nd Sec Dip Serv, MP Ormskirk Lancs 1898–1918, Treasurer St Thomas's Hosp 1917–43, Hon LLD Leeds, Hon FRCP Edinburgh, Cdr Legion of Honour, KGStJ, chm BRRC and Roy Auto Club 1905–36; *d* unm 4 Nov 1947

4 Geoffrey; *b* 18 Nov 1869; *d* 16 March 1871

5 Ferdinand Charles, CMG (1918), DSO (1900); *b* 28 Jan 1871; Hon Brig-Gen, Capt Gren Gds, served Nile Expdn 1898 (medal with clasp, Egyptian medal), S African War 1899–1901 (despatches, Queen's medal with three clasps, King46s medal with two clasps) and WW I (despatches, brevet), Cdr Legion of Honour; *m* 15 Feb 1904 Hon Alexandra Frances Anne Fellowes (*d* 16 Sept 1955), est dau of 2nd Baron De Ramsey (*qv*), and *d* 17 March 1935, leaving issue:

(1) Frederick Arthur, OBE (1945), TD (1964); *b* 3 March 1905; *educ* Wellington; Col QO Cameron Highrs (TA) WW II; *m* 6 April 1932 *Ann Jane [Mrs Frederick Stanley, Bramshott Lodge, Liphook, Hants], only dau of Col William Fellowes Collins, DSO, by Lady Evelyn Innes-Ker, 4th dau of 7th Duke of Roxburghe (*qv*), and *d* 1978, leaving issue:

1a +Peter Henry Arthur [Peter Stanley Esq, Cundall Hall, Helperby, Yorks]; *b* 17 March 1933; *educ* Eton; 2nd Lt Gren Gds; *m* 9 May 1965 (*divorce* 1985) Countess Gunilla Margaretha Antonia Sophie Douglas, dau of Count Wilhelm Douglas, of Schloss Langenstein, Baden, Germany, *m* 2nd 1990 (*divorce* 1992) Mrs Lucy Barnett Campbell, dau of James A Barnett, of Bel Air, California, USA, and formerly w of Clifford Smith Jr and Colin Guy Napier Campbell (*see* CAMPBELL, Bt, *cr* 1815), and has issue by his 1st w:

1b +Robin James Axel; *b* 20 April 1968

1b +Louisa Charlotte Ann; *b* 17 Nov 1966

1a +Sarah [Mrs Simon Creswell, Markers, Cattistock, Dorset DT2 0JH]; *b* 29 Sept 1935; *m* 7 May 1962 *Simon Hawkshaw Creswell, s of Capt John Creswell, RN (ret), of Ellerslie, Cattistock, Dorset, and has:

1b +Alexander John Peter; *b* 21 July 1965; *m* 1 July 1995 *Katherine Louise Reid

1b +Miranda Ann Louise [Mrs Rory Carnegie, 269A Portobello Rd, London W11]; *b* 27 June 1963; *m* 1994 *Rory D A Carnegie and has:

1c +Sholto Hector Hawshaw; *b* 28 Feb 1995

2c +Lorcan Fred Andrew; *b* 5 Nov 1996

1c +Cloudy Ann Hardy; *b* 26 July 1993

2b +Sophia Alice Chrystal; *b* 21 March 1969

(2) John; *b* 9 July 1907; *d* unm 17 Feb 1964

(3) +Henry Ferdinand, MC [Maj Henry Stanley MC, Binfield Priory, Bracknell, Berks]; *b* 4 April 1911; *educ* Wellington; Maj Gren Gds WW II; *m* 1 Feb 1949 *Grizel Sophie, er dau of AVM Sir Norman Duckworth Kerr MacEwen, CB, CMG, DSO, and formerly w of Maj Humphrey Hugh Sykes

6 George Frederick (Sir), GCSI, GCIE, CMG, PC; *b* 14 Oct 1872; Lt-Col RHA, MP Preston 1910–22 and E Willesden 1924–29, PPS to Ldr of Opposition 1912–13, Oppn Whip 1913–14, PPS to Sec of State War 1916–17, Comptroller Household 1919–21, Fin Sec War Office and memb Army Cncl 1921, Parly U-Sec Home Office 1922–23, Parly Sec Min of Pensions 1924–29, memb E India Assoc 1919, Govr Madras 1929–34, Viceroy and Actg Govr-Gen India 1934, served S Africa 1899–1900, and WW I (despatches twice), Legion of Honour and Offr Order of the Crown of Belgium; *m* 26 Nov 1903 Lady Beatrix Taylour, CI, CBE (*d* 3 May 1944), yst dau of 3rd Marquess of Headfort (*qv*), and *d* 1 July 1938, leaving issue:

(1) Barbara Helen; *b* 6 March 1906; *m* 23 Feb 1932 Maj Sir Charles James Buchanan, 4th Bt (*d* 1984), of Dunburgh, Stirlingshire (*qv*), and left issue

7 Algernon Francis, DSO (1914), JP (Wilts); *b* 8 Jan 1874; Col 2nd Life Gds 1916, Col cmdg 195th Inf Bde 1923–27, served Boer War 1899–1900 and WW I (despatches); *m* 18 April 1918 Lady Mary Cavendish (*d* 14 Jan 1959), 3rd dau of 1st Duke of Westminster (*qv*) and widow of Viscount Crichton (*see* ERNE, E), and *d* 10 Feb 1962, having had issue:

(1) Anthony Hugh; *b* 20 Feb 1923; F/O RAFVR WW II; *ka* 11 March 1943

(1) +Constance Mary Stanley [Mrs Malcolm Weaver, Center, Texas, USA]; *b* 24 Jan 1919; *m* 18 Feb 1946 *Lt Malcolm Weaver, US Army, s of Marion Martin Weaver, of Center, and has issue:

1a +Mark Marion; *b* 13 Sept 1960

1a +Mary Constance; *b* 31 Dec 1954; *m* 1978 *Thomas Milton Crain and has issue:

1b +Allison Mary; *b* 1982

8 Frederick William, DSO (1917); *b* 27 May 1878; Capt 10th Hus, Capt and Brevet Lt-Col Lancs Hus Yeo, served Boer War 1899–1902 (severely wounded, Queen's medal, six clasps, King's medal, two clasps) and WW I (despatches); *m* 17 June 1905 Lady Alexandra Louise Elizabeth Acheson (*d* 21 Jan 1858), est dau of 4th Earl of Gosford (*qv*), and *d* 9 Aug 1942, leaving issue:

(1) David William; *b* 9 Aug 1906; *educ* Wellington and Trin Coll Cambridge (BA); Maj REME WW II Middle East N Africa and Italy; *m* 5 June 1937 *Marjorie [Mrs David Stanley, Amberfield, Howick, Natal, S Africa], only dau of Douglas Knox Homan, Indian Police, and *d* 14 Jan 1997, leaving:

1a +William Douglas [William Stanley Esq, PO Box 318, Hilton 3245, S Africa]; *b* 25 April 1938; *educ* St Andrew's Coll Grahamstown and Trin Coll Cambridge (BA); *m* 7 Dec 1963 *Sally Avory, est dau of Stanley Harold Read, of Sugarbush, Morningside, Johannesburg, S Africa, and has:

1b +David Andrew; *b* 19 Dec 1964; *m* 19– *Nicole, dau of Ross Bush, of Christchurch, NZ, and has:

1c +Daniel; *b* 5 Sept 1996

1b +Clare Alexandra; *b* 10 March 1967

2b +Nicola Avory; *b* 13 March 1969

3b +Fiona Anne; *b* 1972

2a +David Patrick [David Stanley Esq, Besltone Cottage, Badgworth, Somerset]; *b* 6 Feb 1943; *educ* St Andrew's Coll Grahamstown and Trin Coll Cambridge (BA 1965); *m* 5 Sept 1968 *Margaret Jane, er dau of Denis Evers, of Four Winds, Wolverley, Worcs, and has issue:

1b +Andrew Mark; *b* 15 July 1969

1b +Deborah Rebecca; *b* 1973

1a +Caroline Alexandra [Mrs Nigel Proddow, 27 Hertford Av, London SW14 8EF]; *b* 22 May 1940; *m* 25 May 1968 *Nigel Norman Proddow, MA, FIA, ACIS, s of William Norman Proddow, of The Bourne, Bourne End, Bucks, and has issue:

1b +Charles William Nigel; *b* 18 Oct 1969

2b +Guy Edward Stanley; *b* Oct 1971

(1) Olivia Mary Beatrice; *b* 1 Jan 1908; *m* 1st 8 April 1937 John Galloway Rankin (*ld* 31 March 1949), only s of Edwyn Christopher Rankin (*see* RANKIN, Bt); *m* 2nd 3 Oct 1950 Brig Archer Francis Lawrence Clive, DSO, MC, DL, JP, Gren Gds, est s of Lt-Gen Sir George Sidney Clive, GCVO, KCB, CMG, DSO, DL, JP, Hon FRAM, of Perrystone, Herefs

(2) Diana Margaret, FIAL; *b* 18 Feb 1909; *m* 5 Jan 1954 Prof Charles Aubrey Pannett, FRCS, MD, BS, BSc (*d* 28 July 1969), s of Charles Yeatman Pannett

1 Katharine Mary; *d* young 21 Oct 1871

2 Isobel Constance Mary, DCVO (1945); *b* 2 Sept 1875; Woman of the Bedchamber to HM QUEEN MARY; *m* 10 Dec 1898 Gen Hon Sir John Francis Gathorne-Hardy, GCB, GCVO, CMG, DSO (*d* 21 Aug 1949), 2nd s of 2nd Earl of Cranbrook (*qv*), and *d* 30 Dec 1963, leaving issue

The 16th EARL OF DERBY's s,

EDWARD GEORGE VILLIERS STANLEY, **17th Earl of Derby**, KG (1915), GCB (1920, CB 1900), GCVO (1908, KCVO 1905), PC (1903), JP; *b* 4 April 1865; *educ* Wellington; Lt Gren Gds 1885–95, ADC to Govr-Gen Canada1888–91, MP (C) W Houghton 1892–1906, Ld of Treasury 1895–1900, served S African War 1899–1900, Priv Sec to C-in-C S Africa 1900, Fin Sec War Office 1900–03, PMG 1903–05, Chllr Liverpool U 1909 (Hon LLD), Ld Mayor Liverpool 1911–12, Dir-Gen Recruiting 1915–16, U-Sec for War and V-Pres Recruiting 1915–16, V-Pres Army Cncl 1916, Sec State War and Pres Army Cncl 1916–18, Amb Extrdy and Plen France 1918–20, Pres Army Cncl 1922, Sec State War 1922–24, Chm W Lancs TAA, Ld Lt Lancs 1928, Hon LLD Birmingham U 1934, Hon DCL Oxon 1934, Hon LLD Cantab 1935, Hon Col 4th Bn Manchester Regt, 4th and 5th Bns Loyal N Lancs Regt, 5th Bn The King's (Liverpool Regt), W Lancs Divl Trg RASC, 106th (Lancs Yeo) Bde RFA (TA) (TD), and 5th Bn Lancs Fus TA, Hon Col Inns of Court OTC, Hon Col 62nd Searchlight Regt RA, Hon Capt RNVR, KGStJ, Roy Victorian Chain 1935, Grand Cordon Legn Hon and Order of Charles XII of Spain; *m* 5 Jan 1889 Lady Alice Maude Olivia Montagu, DJStJ, Hon LLD Liverpool, Extra Ldy Bedchamber to HM QUEEN ALEXANDRA (*d* 23 July 1957), yst dau of 7th Duke of Manchester (*qv*), and *d* 4 Feb 1948, having had:

1 Edward Montagu Cavendish, *Lord Stanley*, PC (1934), MC (1919), DL, JP (Lancs); *b* 9 July 1894; *educ* Eton and Magdalen Coll Oxford; Capt Res of Offrs Gren Gds, ADC to GOC 2nd Army Corps 1914, Adj Household Bn 1916–17, Staff Capt 1917–18, Brig-Maj 1918, MP Abercromby 1917–18 and Fylde 1922–24, Jr Ld Treasury Nov 1924–27, dep chm Conservative Pty Organisation 1927–29, Parly and Fin Sec Admlty 1931–35, Parly Under-Sec Dominion Affrs 1935, Parly and Fin Sec Admlty 1935–37, Parly Under-Sec India and Burma 1937–38, Sec of State Dominion Affrs 1938, Chm Jr Imperial League 1927–33 and pres 1933, memb Imperial War Graves Cmmn, Hon Col 9th Bn Manchester Regt 1936, Croce di Guerra Italy; *m* 17 July 1917 Hon Sibyl Louise Beatrix Cadogan, Maid of Honour to HM QUEEN MARY (*d* 21 June 1969), est dau of Viscount Chelsea, s of 5th Earl Cadogan (*qv*), and *dvp* 16 Oct 1938, leaving:

(1) EDWARD JOHN, **18th Earl of Derby**, MC (1944); *b* 21 April 1918; *educ* Eton and Magdalen Coll Oxford; Ld Lt Lancs 1951–68 (DL 1946–51), Constable Lancaster Castle 1972–94, Maj Gren Gds Res of Offrs, served WW II, Lt-Col King's Regt TA 1947, Hon Col: 5th/8th (Vol) Bn King's Regt (Comdg) 5th Bn TA 1947–51, 4th (Vol) Bn Queen's Lancashire Regt TAVR 1951–67, 1st Bn The Liverpool Scottish (TA) 1964 and 1st and 2nd Bn Lancastrian Vols 1967–75, Hon Capt Mersey Div RNVR 1955, Hon LLD Liverpool and Lancaster Us 1949, pres: Liverpool Chamber of Commerce 1948–71, Merseyside and dist Chambers of Commerce 1972–94, Br Cotton Growing Assoc 1946–94, Empire Cotton Growing Corp 1957, Bath and W and Southern Counties Soc, Pro-Chllr Lancaster U 1964–71, NW Provincial Area Cncl of Nat Union of C Assocs 1969–72, Hon Freeman City of Manchester 1961, dir Martins Bank, CStJ; *m* 22 July 1948 Lady Isabel Milles-Lade (*d* 1990), sis of 4th Earl Sondes (*see* MONSON, B), and *dsp* 28 Nov 1994

(2) Richard Oliver; *b* 29 Jan 1920; *educ* Eton and Trin Coll Cambridge; Capt Gren Gds, MP N Fylde 1950–66, PPS to 1st Ld of Admlty 1951–55, Hon Col 9th Manchester Regt, Jt Hon Treasurer Conservative Pty 1962–66, underwriting memb Lloyd's; *m* 5 Jan 1965 Susan Mary Fynvola (found dead in her bath 29 Feb 1976), only dau of John Henry Lancelot Aubrey-Fletcher (*see* AUBREY-FLETCHER, Bt); *m* 2nd *Mary [The Hon Mrs Richard Stanley, Barn House, Ledwell, Oxon OX7 7AN], dau of Maj Vyvian Alfred Tylor, MC, and formerly w of W/Cdr P H M Richey, DFC, and widow of William Herbert Harrison, and *dsp* Nov 1983

(3) Hugh Henry Montagu; *b* 26 Oct 1926; *educ* Eton; ARICS, QALAS, AAI; Lt Gren Gds; *m* 7 Nov 1961 *(Mary) Rose [Mrs William Spiegelberg, Oulton Park House, Tarporley, Cheshire CW6 9BL] (*m* 2nd July 1973 *A William Spiegelberg MBE, TD, DL, est s of F E F Spiegelberg), 2nd dau of Charles Francis Birch, of Rhodesia, and *d* 8 Dec 1971, leaving issue:

1a EDWARD RICHARD WILLIAM STANLEY, **19th and present Earl of Derby**

2a +Peter Hugh Charles [The Hon Peter Stanley, New England Stud, Newmarket, Suffolk CB8 OXB]; *b* 4 March 1964; *educ* Eton; *m* 1990 *Hon Frances Caroline Burke Roche, only dau of 5th Baron Fermoy (*qv*), and has issue:

1b +Richard Hugh Edward; *b* 1 May 1993

1b +(Portia Ruth) Isobel; *b* 19 April 1995

2 Oliver Frederick George, MC, PC (1934); *b* 4 May 1896; barrister Gray's Inn, MP (C) Westmorland 1924–45 and Bristol W 1945–50, PPS to Pres Bd Educn Dec 1924–29, Parly Under-Sec Home Office 1931–33, Min Transport 1933–34, Min Labour 1934–35, Pres Bd Educn 1935–37 and Tde 1937–40, Sec of State War 1940, Sec of State Colonies 1942–45, Pres Nat Union of C and U Assocs 1946–50, Chllr Liverpool U 1949–50, Hon Col Roy Signals (TA) and Manchester Regt 1940–50, Maj Lancs Hus, formerly T Capt RFA, Croix de Guerre; *m* 4 Nov 1920 Lady Maureen Helen Vane-Tempest-Stewart (*d* 20 June 1942), est dau of 7th Marquess of Londonderry (*qv*), and *d* 10 Dec 1950, leaving issue:

(1) Michael Charles, MBE (1945), DL (1964); *b* 11 Aug 1921; *educ* Eton and Trin Coll Cambridge (BA, MA); CEng, MIEE, V-Lt (1965), High Sheriff 1959, Capt Roy Signals (TA) WW II; *m* 26 Jan 1951 *(Aileen) Fortune Constance Hugh [Mrs Michael Stanley, Halecat House, Witherslack, Grange-over-Sands, Cumbria LA11 6RU], er dau of Owen Hugh Smith, JP, of

Old Hall, Langham, Oakham, Rutland, bro of 1st Baron Bicester (*qv*), and *d* 1990, leaving issue:

1a +Oliver Hugh [Dr Oliver Stanley, Halecat House, Witherslack, Grange-over-Sands, Cumbria LA11 6RT]; *b* 30 Jan 1952, *educ* Eton and Cambridge (MA, MD); *m* 1982 *Bernadette, dau of John McMullen, of Middlesbrough, and has issue:

1b +John Michael; *b* 1982

2b +Aidan; *b* 1986

1b +Naomi Isabel; *b* 1989

2a +Nicholas Charles [Nicholas Stanley Esq, Halecat House, Witherslack, Grange-over-Sands, Cumbria LA11 6RT]; *b* 28 April 1954; *educ* Eton; *m* 1986 *Sarah Louise Gilroy, only dau of George Henry Gilroy Williams, of Warwick Rd, Maperley Park, Nottingham, and has issue:

1b +Thomas Michael Henry; *b* 1990

2b +Jack William Oliver; *b* 1993

(1) +Kathryn Edith Helen, DCVO (1984, CVO 1973), JP (1963), DL (Salop 1995) [Lady Dugdale DCVO JP DL, Tickwood Hall, Much Wenlock, Salop TF13 6NZ]; *b* 4 Nov 1923; T/Woman Bedchamber to HM THE QUEEN 1955–60, Extra Woman Bedchamber 1960–72, Woman Bedchamber 1972–, Cdr Roy Order of N Star Sweden 1956, WRNS WW II; *m* 25 July 1956 Sir John Robert Stratford Dugdale, KCVO (*see* DUGDALE, Bt), and has issue

1 Victoria Alice Louise; *b* 24 June 1892; *m* 1st 7 April 1915 Rt Hon Neil James Archibald Primrose, MC, MP (*d* 18 Nov 1917 of wounds recd in action), yr s of 5th Earl of Rosebery (*qv*), and had issue; *m* 2nd 10 June 1919 Capt Malcolm Bullock, MBE, MP, Scots Gds, barrister (later Sir Malcolm Bullock, 1st and last Bt (*see* 1963 edn); *d* 20 June 1966), and *d* as the result of a hunting accident 26 Nov 1927, leaving further issue

Seat: Knowsley Hall, Knowsley, Lancs. The oldest surviving part of this enormous house, which has been knit this century into a reasonably coherent whole from a muddle of structures of various dates and styles, is the north facade of the west wing. Here the work is essentially late 17th-century, though crenellated by the Liverpudlian architect John Foster during the Regency. Foster also embellished the back in like manner. His masterpiece, however, is the State Dining Room (though it was altered 70 years later). The doors alone rise to an altitude of 30 feet. Not surprisingly, another of Foster's creations was the Liverpool railway station at Lime Street.

The next oldest part would appear to date from the 1730s, the result of an expansion programme carried out by the **11th Earl** after deciding to abandon Lathom. The latter had been largely destroyed in the Civil War following its defence against Parliamentarians by the **7th Earl**'s Countess (*see* above). Possibly the fact that the new Earl was from a different branch of the family influenced his decision.

Another early 19th-century architect brought in to remodel Knowsley was William Burn, a Scot who was also responsible for the New Club in Edinburgh and who worked on Bowhill for the Duke of Buccleuch (*see* BUCCLEUCH and QUEENSBERRY, D). He was actually born almost the same year as Foster but his alterations to Knowsley are nearly 20 years later, though he too used crenellation to enliven the 17th-century rear of the west wing. He also designed the separate structure known as the Dynamo Tower.

The first attempt at synthesising Knowsley occurred in the second decade of the 20th century, when Romaine-Walker imposed a neo-William and Mary appearance on the entrance front and substituted an exceptionally adroit pastiche of the same period for a 19th-century cupola on the garden side. A further tidying-up was carried out in the 1950s by the late Lord (4th Baron) Phillimore (*qv*), especially to the entrance front already remodelled by his colleague some 40 years earlier. The most imposing aspects of the interior other than Foster's are by Romaine-Walker, though they fall far short of the kind of Adam creation of which the old Derby town house in Grosvenor Square would have furnished an example. (Another Derby town house, now the Oriental Club, in Stratford Place, off Oxford Street, is still standing.)

But it was Phillimore who planned the smaller neo-Georgian house in which the late (**18th**) **Earl** lived, half the main building being leased to the Lancashire Police Force. It is a good strategic position from which to patrol the motorways that hem in Knowsley from almost every side, though its actual use till 1998, when the **19th Earl** took partial repossession, was as a training centre, dog-handling unit and police band accomodation and centre for covert operations in drug and fraud cases. In spring 1998 the **19th Earl** announced plans to redecorate Knowsley and mount pop and classical concerts in the grounds.

DE ROS

Arms: Quarterly,1st and 4th, argent a saltire gules (for FitzGERALD); 2nd and 3rd, gules three water-bougets argent (for DE ROS). **Supporters:** Two falcons, wings expanded and inverted, proper. **Motto:** *Crom a boo* ('I will burn'). **Creation:** B. (E) 6 Feb 1298/9 with precedence of 14 Dec 1264.

THE 28TH LORD (BARON) **DE ROS OF HELMSLEY** (Peter Trevor Maxwell) [The Rt Hon The Lord De Ros, Old Court, Strangford, Co Down]; *b* 23 Dec 1958; *s* mother 1983; premier baron in the peerage of England; *educ* Headfort Co Meath, Stowe, Down High School Co Down; upholsterer and furniture-maker; *m* 5 Sept 1987 *Angela Siân, dau of Peter Campbell Ross, and has issue:

1 +FINBAR JAMES; *b* 14 Nov 1988

1 +Katherine Georgina; *b* 26 Oct 1990

2 +Jessye Maeve; *b* 8 July 1992

Lineage: PIERS de ROS (a name that seems to have been taken from Ros, Holderness, E Riding of Yorks); steward to Count d'Aumale (feudal Ld of Holderness); *m* Adeline, 3rd and yst sis and coheir of Walter Espec, feudal Ld of Helmsley, Yorks, and Wark, Northumberland, and *d* by 1130, leaving, with an er s (Everard, *m* Eustache — and *d* by 1153):

ROBERT de ROS; Constable to the Count d'Aumale *c* 1153–62/3; *m* Sibyl de Valognes (*m* 2nd *c* 1166, as his 2nd w, William de Percy (*d* 1174/5; *see* NORTHUMBERLAND, D); *m* 3rd 1181/2 Ralph d'Aubigny (*d* by autumn 1192) and *d c* 1212–18), and had:

EVERARD De ROS; *m* Roese, dau and coheir of William Trussebut, feudal Ld of Warter (eventually inherited by her Ros descendants), E R Yorks, and *d* by early autumn 1183, leaving, with another s:

ROBERT ('Furfan' or 'Furson') de ROS; Bailiff of the district organised to defend the royal Castle of Bonneville sur Toques, Normandy, *temp* RICHARD I; served with KING JOHN in Ireland 1210; Sheriff Cumberland 1213–15; one of the 25 barons (magnates rather than lords of Parl) chosen to oversee implementation of Magna Carta's provisions; *m* 1191 Isabel, illegitimate dau of WILLIAM THE LION, KING OF SCOTS, and widow of Robert de Brus, and probably *d* by 23 Dec 1226, leaving:

1 WILLIAM, of whom presently

2 Robert (Sir), of Wark on Tweed, Northumberland; gf of:

(1) ROBERT de ROS, putative 1st and last LORD (Baron) ROS OF WARK, so *cr* (according to later doctrine) by writ of summons 24 June 1295; opposed EDWARD I and was stripped of his lands for treason; *m* Laura — and *dspm* in or shortly following 1296, the notional Barony of 1295 expiring

The er s of ROBERT 'Furfan/Furson',

WILLIAM de ROS (Sir), of Helmsley (often known as Hamlake), Yorks; opposed KING JOHN; *m* Lucy, possibly dau of Piers FitzHerbert, feudal Ld of the Honour of Brecknock, and *d* probably 1264, having had:

1 ROBERT (Sir)

2 Piers

3 William (Sir); ancestor of the de ROSes of Ingmanthorpe, Kirk Deighton, Yorks (part of the Trussebut inheritance)

The est s,

Sir ROBERT de ROS, of Belvoir; summoned 24 Dec 1264 to a 'Parliament' convened by Simon de Montfort, an event which prompted the legal decision of 1616 (also accepted 1806) assigning precedence in the barony of DE ROS OF HELMSLEY to 1264, although the 'Parliament' in question was convoked not by the King but by a noble in opposition to him; by subsequent evolutions in peerage law doctrine no sitting in what can only be termed a council of that date could be held to confer a peerage; Ch Commr to investigate excesses in Herefs 1258; sided with Simon de Montfort in the Barons' War, surrendering Northampton to HENRY III April 1264 and Gloucester to PRINCE EDWARD (later EDWARD I) June 1265; pardoned 14 Aug 1265 for his opposition to HENRY III; Commr in North of England 1268 to ensure Aid (a tax) was yielded up to the King; *m* after 5 June 1243 but by 17 May 1244 Isabel (*d* 15 June 1301), dau and heiress of William d'Aubigny, feudal Ld of Belvoir, Leics, through whom he acquired that manor, and *d* 17 May 1285, leaving, with at least one dau (Isabel, *m* as his 1st w 2nd Lord (Baron) Faucomberge; *see* YARBOROUGH, E) an est s:

WILLIAM de ROS, **1st Lord** (Baron) **De Ros of Helmsley** (E), so *cr* according to later doctrine by writ of summons 6 Feb 12989/9 (but *see* above for an earlier precedence assigned the title in later centuries); candidate for the Crown of Scotland 1291 by reason of his descent from WILLIAM THE LION, albeit illegitimate; granted 1301 Wark Castle on its forfeiture for rebellion by his cousin Robert De Ros of Wark; Jt Warden Northumberland 1307, Jt Lt and Warden in Scotland 1308; *m* Maud, yr dau and coheir of John de Vaux (*see* VAUX OF HARROWDEN, B), and *d* after 12 May but by 16 Aug 1316, leaving an er s:

WILLIAM de ROS, **2nd Lord** (Baron) **De Ros of Helmsley**; Sheriff Yorks 1326, one of the two Barons, representing the entire class of Barons or magnates of the realm, who at Kenilworth Jan 1326/7 informed EDWARD II of his deposition; memb Cncl Regency Feb 1326/7; *m* by 25 Nov 1316 Margery (*m* 2nd *c* 6 March 1350/1 Sir Thomas de Arundel; *m* 3rd Sir John Avenel; *d* 18 Oct 1363), est sis and coheir of Giles, 2nd Lord (Baron) Badlesmere, of Leeds Castle, Kent, and *d* 3 Feb 1342/3, having had, with other issue (including a dau Maud, *m* John, 4th Lord (Baron) Welles (*d* 1361) and Elizabeth, *m* 2nd Lord (Baron) Zouche, *qv*), an er s:

1 WILLIAM de ROS, **3rd Lord** (Baron) **De Ros of Helmsley**; *b* 19 May 1329; ktd 1346, helped defeat the Spaniards in the naval battle off the Sussex coast at Winchelsea 1350; *m* by 8 May 1341 Margaret Nevill(e) (*m* 2nd, as his 1st w, 1st and last Earl of Northumberland of the 1377 *cr*; *see* NORTHUMBERLAND, D), dau of 2nd Lord (Baron) Neville (of Raby) (*see* ABERGAVENNY, M), and *dsp* by 3 Dec 1352

2 THOMAS de ROS, **4th Lord** (Baron) **De Ros of Helmsley**, KB (by 1372); *b* 13 Jan 1336/7; Jt Warden W March of Scotland 1367 and E March 1371; *m c* 1 Jan 1358/9 Beatrice (*m* 3rd Sir Richard Burley, KG, and *d* 14 April 1415), widow of Maurice FitzMaurice, 2nd Earl of Desmond (*see* DENBIGH and DESMOND, E, preliminary remarks), and dau of 1st Earl of Stafford (*see* STAFFORD, B), and *d* 8 June 1384, having had:

(1) JOHN De ROS, **5th Lord** (Baron) **De Ros of Helmsley**; *b c* 1368; Jt Warden W March of Scotland 1389; *m* by 22 June 1382 Mary (*d* 1394), dau of Henry, Lord (Baron) Percy (*see* NORTHUMBERLAND, D), went on pilgrimage to Jerusalem and *dsp* on his way home at Paphos, Cyprus, 6 Aug 1393

(2) WILLIAM, **6th Lord**

(3) Thomas

(4) Robert

(1) Elizabeth; *m* 6th Lord (Baron) Clifford (*see* DE CLIFFORD, B)

(2) Margaret; *m* 3rd Lord (Baron) Grey (of Ruthin) (*see* GREY, B)

The 5th BARON's bro,

WILLIAM de ROS, **6th Lord** (Baron) **De Ros of Helmsley**, KG (1404), PC *temp* RICHARD II and HENRY IV; *b c* 1369; Ld Treasurer 1403–04; *m* (licence 9 Oct 1394) Margaret (*d* 3 July 1438), sis of 13th/6th Earl of Arundel (*see* NORFOLK, D), and *d* 1 Sept 1414, leaving:

1 JOHN de ROS, **7th Lord** (Baron) **De Ros of Helmsley**; *b c* 1397; was at Agincourt 1415, Siege Rouen 1417–19 and Siege Melun 1420; *m* Margery (*m* 2nd by 2 March 1422/3 Roger Wentworth and was ancestor with him of the Lords Wentworth (*see* LYTTON, E); *d* 20 April 1478), dau and heir of Philip, Lord (Baron) Le Despenser (*see* FALMOUTH, V), and *dsp, ka* Battle of Beaugé 22 March 1420/1

2 THOMAS de ROS, **8th Lord** (Baron) **De Ros of Helmsley**, PC (1429); 26 Sept 1406; ktd 1426; *m* Eleanor (*m* 2nd by 7 March 1437/8 Edmund Beaufort, 1st Duke of Somerset (*see* BEAUFORT, D)), dau and coheir of Richard Beauchamp, Earl of Warwick (*see* WARWICK, BROOKE and, E), and *d* 18 Aug 1430, leaving:

(1) THOMAS de ROS, **9th Lord** (Baron) **De Ros of Helmsley**; *b* 9 Sept 1427; ktd 1452, Lancastrian in Wars of Roses: fought 1st Battle of St Albans 1455, Battle of Wakefield 1460, 2nd Battle of St Albans Feb 1460/1, Battle of Hedgley Moor 1464, following which he was captured and beheaded 17 May 1464, having been attainted by EDWARD IV's Parl 4 Nov 1461 when the Barony was forfeited; *m* Philippe Tiptoft (*m* 2nd, as his 2nd w, Sir Thomas Wingfield (*see* POWERSCOURT, V); *m* 3rd 26 Aug 1471, as his 3rd w, Edward Grimston; *see* VERULAM, E), sis of 1st Earl of Worcester of the 1449 *cr* (*see* BEAUFORT, D, preliminary remarks), and had, with three daus (two of whom, including Isabel, *m* Sir Thomas Lovel(l), *dsp*) an only s:

1a EDMUND de ROS, **10th Lord** (Baron) **De Ros of Helmsley** on restoration of his Barony after HENRY VII's accession 1485, although HENRY kept the **9th Lord**'s forfeited estates by reason ultimately of the **10th Lord**'s incapacity; *dsp* unm 15 Oct 1508, when the Barony fell into abeyance between his three sisters and coheirs

1a ELEANOR; *m* Sir Robert MANNERS, of Etal (*see* RUTLAND, D, and for further details of Manners holders of Barony of De Ros below), and had:

1b GEORGE MANNERS, **11th Lord** (Baron) **De Ros of Helmsley**; had:

1c THOMAS MANNERS, **12th Lord** (Baron) **De Ros of Helmsley** and 1st EARL OF RUTLAND; had:

1d HENRY MANNERS, **13th Lord** (Baron) **De Ros of Helmsley** and 2nd EARL OF RUTLAND; had:

1e EDWARD MANNERS, **14th Lord** (Baron) **De Ros of Helmsley** and 3rd EARL OF RUTLAND; *dspm* 14 April 1587, when the Earldom of Rutland passed to his bro, leaving an only dau:

1f ELIZABETH Manners, **Baroness De Ros of Helmsley** in her own right; *b c* Jan 1575/6; *m* 13 Jan 1588/9, as his 1st w William CECIL, 2nd Earl of Exeter (*see* EXETER, M), and *d* 11 May 1591, leaving:

1g WILLIAM CECIL, **16th Lord** (Baron) **De Ros of Helmsley**, confirmed as such 22 July 1616; *b* May 1590; *m* 13 Feb 1615/6 Anne (*m* 2nd George Rodney and had issue; *see* RODNEY, B), dau of Sir Thomas Lake, of Cannons, and *dsp* & *vp* 27 June 1618

2e JOHN MANNERS, 4th EARL OF RUTLAND: had issue:

1f ROGER MANNERS, 5th EARL OF RUTLAND

2f FRANCIS MANNERS, **17th Lord** (Baron) **De Ros of Helmsley**, 6th EARL OF RUTLAND and 1st and last LORD (Baron) ROOS OF HAMLAKE (E), so *cr* 22 July 1616 in compensation for failing in his claim to the Barony of De Ros of Helmsley on the death of the 14th Lord in 1587, though he inherited it anyway in 1618 on the death of his cousin the 16th Lord; *b* 1578; *m* 1st 6 May 1602 Frances, widow of Sir William Bevill and 3rd dau and coheir of Sir Henry Knyvett, and had issue; *m* 2nd after 26 Oct 1608 Cecily (*dsps*), dau of Sir John Tufton, 1st Bt, and widow of Sir Edward Hungerford, and *dspm* 17 Dec 1632, when the Barony of Roos of Hamlake expired, but that of De Ros of Helmsley passed to his only dau by his 1st w:

1g KATHERINE Manners, **Baroness De Ros of Helmsley** in her own right; *m* 1st 16 May 1620 George VILLIERS, 1st Duke of Buckingham (assassinated 23 Aug 1628; *see* JERSEY, E); *m* 2nd by 12 April 1635, as his 2nd w, Randal Mac Donnell, 1st Marquess of Antrim (*dsp* 3 Feb 1682; *see* ANTRIM, E), and *d* late Oct 1649, leaving an est surv s:

1h GEORGE VILLIERS, **19th Lord** (Baron) **De Ros of Helmsley**, his right to succeed as which was allowed 5 Feb 1666/7, and 2nd DUKE OF BUCKINGHAM, KG (1649), PC (1650, 1662–Feb 1666/7 and 1667–73/4); *b* 30 Jan 1627/8; *educ* Trin Coll Cambridge; condemned to death by H of C 7 July 1648, fought as royalist Col of Horse Battle of Worcester 1651, Ld Lt W R Yorks 1661–Feb 1666/7 and Nov 1667–74, FRS 1663, Master of the Horse 1668–74, Amb Paris 1670 and 1671 and Jt Amb 1672, Lt-Gen the Forces 1672–73, a Ld of Admlty 1673–74, memb CABAL (acronym standing for first letters of five ministers' names, his (Buckingham) providing the B), the Zimri of Dryden's 'Absalon and Achitophel'; *m* 15 Sept 1657 Mary Fairfax (*d* 20 Oct 1704), dau and heir of 3rd Lord Fairfax of Cameron (*qv*), and *dspl* 16 April 1687, when his other titles became extinct or dormant but the Barony of De Ros of Helmsley fell into abeyance between the heirs of the **17th Lord** (Baron) **De Ros of Helmsley** (and 6th EARL OF RUTLAND)'s sisters Bridget (*b* 21 Feb 1572, *m* secretly Aug 1594 Robert Tyrwhitt, of Kettleby, Lincs; *d* Sept 1604) and Frances (*see* immediately below)

1f FRANCES Manners; *b* 22 Oct 1588; *m* 4 Feb 1602/3 3rd Baron Willoughby of Parham (*d* 28 Aug 1617) and *d c* 1643, leaving, with an er s (4th Baron Willoughby of Parham):

1g FRANCIS WILLOUGHBY, 5th BARON WILLOUGHBY OF PARHAM; *b* 1613/4; *educ* Eton; pro-Parl Civil War, Parly Ld Lt Lincs 1642, surrendered Gainsborough to royalists 1643, voted an earldom by H of C 1645, Speaker Ho Lds 1647, impeached of high treason by H of C 1647, when escaped to the Dutch Republic and joined royalists in exile there; *m c* 1628/9 Elizabeth Cecil, dau of Viscount Wimbledon, and *dspms c* 23–24 July 1666 when his ship was lost at sea with all hands in a hurricane off Guadeloupe, leaving:

1h ELIZABETH Willoughby; *m* 28 Oct 1662, as his 1st w, Richard JONES, 1st Earl of Ranelagh (*dspms* 5 Jan 1711/2), and *d* 1 Aug 1695, leaving, with an er dau:

1i FRANCES Jones; *b* 1674; *m* 23 April 1698, as his 2nd w, Thomas CONINGSBY, 1st Earl of Coningsby of the 1719 *cr*, and *d* 19 Feb 1714/5, leaving a yst dau:

1j FRANCES Coningsby; *m* July 1732 Sir Charles HANBURY-WILLIAMS, KB (*see* SUDELEY, B), and had, with an er dau:

1k CHARLOTTE Hanbury-Williams; *m* Cdre The Hon Robert BOYLE later BOYLE-WALSINGHAM (*see* SHANNON, E) and *d* 1790, leaving:

1l CHARLOTTE, *née* Boyle later (by marriage) FitzGerald later still FitzGERALD-De ROS (roy licence 6 Oct 1806), **Baroness De Ros of Helmsley** in her own right on the abeyance in the peerage being terminated in her favour 1806; *b* 24 May 1769; *m* 4 Aug 1791 Lord Henry FitzGerald (*d* 9 July 1829), 4th s of 1st Duke of Leinster (*qv*), and *d* 9 Jan 1831, having had, with other issue:

1m HENRY WILLIAM FitzGERALD later FitzGERALD-De ROS, **21st Lord** (Baron) **De Ros of Helmsley**; *b* 12 June 1793; *educ* Eton; MP W Looe 1815–18; *d* unm 29 March 1839

2m WILLIAM LENNOX LASCELLES, **22nd Lord**

1m Olivia Cecilia; *m* 22 Oct 1833 1st Earl Cowley (*qv*) and *d* 21 April 1885, leaving issue

2m Geraldine; *m* 25 Nov 1830 Rev Frederic Pare and *d* 28 Sept 1881

3m Cecilia; *m* 10 Dec 1835 Hon John Boyle (*see* CORK and ORRERY, E) and *d* 6 Oct 1869, leaving issue

(1) Margaret; *m* 1st by 1458, as his 2nd w, 3rd Lord (Baron) Botreaux (*see* LOUDOUN, E); *m* 2nd 1462–64 Sir Thomas Burgh (*see* BURGH, B)

1 Margaret; *m* (papal dispensation March 1415), as his 1st w, 5th Lord (Baron) Audley (*see* 1970 edn, also WAKE, Bt)

The 21st LORD's bro,

WILLIAM LENNOX LASCELLES FitzGERALD later FitzGERALD-De ROS, **22nd Lord** (Baron) **De Ros of Helmsley**, PC (1852); *b* 1 Sept 1797; *educ* Westminster and Ch Ch Oxford; Gen 1868, Col 4th Hus 1865, Lt-Govr Tower of London 1852; *m* 7 June 1824 Lady Georgiana Lennox (*d* 15 Dec 1891 aged 96), 3rd dau of 4th Duke of Richmond (*see* RICHMOND and GORDON, D), and had:

1 DUDLEY CHARLES, **23rd Lord**

1 Frances Charlotte; *d* 21 Feb 1851

2 Blanche Arthur Georgiana; *m* 11 July 1865 James Rannie Swinton (*d* Dec 1888), 2nd son of John Campbell Swinton, of Kimmerghame, Berwick, and *dsp* 10 March 1910

The 22nd LORD *d* 6 Jan 1874; his only son,

DUDLEY CHARLES FitzGERALD-De ROS, **23rd Lord** (Baron) **De Ros of Helmsley**, KP (1902), KCVO (1897), DL, JP Co Down; *b* 11 March 1827; *educ*

Eton; Lt-Gen 1881, Col 1st Life Gds 1861–72, Equerry to HRH THE PRINCE CONSORT 1853–61, Extra Equerry to HM QUEEN VICTORIA 1862–68, Equerry 1868–74 and a Ld-in-Waiting 1874–80, 1885 and 1886–92; *m* 1st 12 Oct 1853 Lady Elizabeth Egerton (*d* 14 March 1892), dau of 2nd Earl of Wilton (*qv*), and had issue:

1 MARY FRANCES, **Baroness De Ros of Helmsley**

The **23rd Lord** *m* 2nd 14 Jan 1896 Mary Geraldine (*d* 28 Dec 1921), est dau of Rev Sir William V R Mahon, 4th Bt (*qv*), and *d* 29 April 1907

His only child,

MARY FRANCES FitzGerald-de Ros, **Baroness De Ros of Helmsley** in her own right; *b* 31 July 1854; *m* 2 Oct 1878 Anthony Lucius DAWSON, 3rd and last Earl of Dartrey (*d* 9 Feb 1933; *see* 1933 edn), and had issue:

1 UNA MARY, **Baroness De Ros of Helmsley**

2 Maude Elizabeth; *b* 21 Jan 1882; *d* unm 17 June 1970

3 Eleanor Charlotte Augusta; *b* 1 Feb 1885; *m* 1st 18 July 1906 (*divorce* 1920) Aubrey Nugent Wade-Palmer, of Borough Marsh, Twyford, Berks, yst son of Fairfax Bloomfield Wade-Palmer, JP, of Holm Park, Berks, and had:

(1) Barbara Madeline; *b* 21 March 1907; *m* 1923 (*divorce* 1936) Béla Domjan de Domjanszeg, of Hungary, and *d* 1992, having assumed the name DOMJAN WADE-PALMER, leaving issue:

1a +Robert [Robert Domjan, Dene Hill, Beechenlea Lane, Swanley Village, Kent BR8 7PR], chemical engr Technical U Budapest; *b* 6 Dec 1924; *m* 11 Sept 1956 *Countess Heilwig Freda Anna Helene Christa Hildegard, dau of Count Gerhart von Budingen, of Bergstrasse, Jugenheim, and has issue:

1b +Nicholas Charles Robert; *b* 11 May 1960; *educ* Dulwich; *m* 1st 1985 (*divorce* 1991) Margaret Mitchell; *m* 2nd 1995 *Deborah Hamilton and by her has:

1c +Charlotte Rose; *b* 19 July 1995

2c +Holly Eleanor; *b* 7 Oct 1996

(2) +Ismé Ruth [Mrs Ismé Satzger de Bálványos, 21 Northumberland Court, 62-64 Marine Parade, Brighton, Sussex]; *b* 30 Aug 1908; *m* 2 June 1934 (*divorce* 1941) Christian Satzger De BALVANYOS later WADE-PALMER (*d* 1995)

3 (cont.) Mrs Eleanor Wade-Palmer *m* 2nd 8 July 1920 János Orsolya Kiss (*d* 12 March 1932), of Balantonalmádi, Öreghegy, Kastely, Hungary; *m* 3rd 7 May 1934 Dr Frigyes Szántó (*d* 18 March 1947); *m* 4th 26 Nov 1951 Syed Waris Ameer Ali (*d* 1975), CIE, ICS, er s of Syed Ameer Ali, CIE, PC, of 2 Cadogan Place, London SW1, and *d* 15 Sept 1974

The BARONESS De ROS OF HELMSLEY *d* 4 May 1939, when the title fell into abeyance between her three daus, until terminated May 1943 in favour of the est,

UNA MARY Dawson, **Baroness De Ros of Helmsley**; *b* 5 Oct 1879; *m* 30 July 1904 Arthur John ROSS, of Old Court, Strangford, Co Down (*ka* Aug 1917), er son of Charles J Ross, of Grosvenor Street W, and had issue:

1 Peter, Lt-Cdr (E) RN; *b* 8 Aug 1906; *m* 10 Sept 1929 *Hon Angela Ierne Evelyn Dixon [The Hon Mrs Horn, Luckington Court, Chippenham, Wilts] (*m* 2nd 12 Nov 1943 Lt-Col Trevor Langdale Horn, MC, 16th/5th Lancers (*d* 26 Dec 1966), and has further issue), est dau of 1st Baron Glentoran (*qv*), and was *ka* Oct 1940, leaving issue:

(1) GEORGIANA ANGELA, **Baroness De Ros of Helsmley**

(2) +Rosemary [The Hon Mrs Osborne, 36 Queensdale Rd, London W11 4SA]; *b* 14 Jan 1937; *m* 1973 *Beresford George Edward Osborne, MIPA, and has issue:

1a +Joanna Elizabeth; *b* 1975

2 Charles Dudley Anthony, Lt Seaforth Highrs; *b* 5 Oct 1907; *educ* Shrewsbury and Cambridge; *m* 1st 31 Aug 1940 (*divorce* 1949) Lady Elizabeth (*d* 1982), er dau of 8th Earl of Roden (*qv*) and formerly w of Gerald Francis Annesley (formerly Sowerby), and had issue:

(1) +Anthony Arthur; *b* 28 July 1941; *educ* Winchester; ACA, CASA; *m* 1969 *Joan, dau of Herbert Cahn, of Highlands North, Johannesburg, and has issue:

1a +Zara Gail; *b* 1971; *m* 1994 *Stephen Mark Sanders

2a +Deborah Kim; *b* 1972

2 (cont.) Charles Ross *m* 2nd 1953 Mary Margaret (*d* 1994), dau of Thomas Graham, of Monaghan, and *d* 1976

The BARONESS *d* 9 Oct 1956, when the title fell into abeyance between her two gdaus until terminated Aug 1958 in favour of the elder,

GEORGIANA ANGELA Ross, **Baroness De Ros of Helmsley**; *b* 2 May 1933; *educ* Wycombe Abbey and Studley Ag Coll; *m* 24 July 1954 *Cdr John David MAXWELL, DL, RN (*m* 2nd 1984 Mrs Patricia Carolyn Coveney (*née* Ash)) [Cdr John Maxwell DL RN (ret), Old Court, Strangford, Co Down BT30 7NG], High Sheriff Co Down 1981, yst son of Capt Thomas Kennedy Maxwell, RN, of Strangford, Co Down, by Zoë, 2nd dau of Lt-Col Thomas John de Burgh, DL, JP, of Oldtown, Co Kildare, and *d* 21 April 1983, leaving issue:

1 PETER TREVOR MAXWELL, **27th and present Lord** (Baron) **De Ros of Helmsley**

1 +Diana Elizabeth; *b* 6 June 1957; *m* 1st 29 Nov 1976 (*divorce* 1978) Jonathan Watkins; *m* 2nd 1978 (*divorce* 1981) Don Richard Bell, son of Naple Christopher Bell, of Fort Worth, Texas; *m* 3rd 1987 (*divorce* 1992) Eric Ford, resumed her maiden name and by him has:

(1) +Nisha; *b* 1988

DERWENT

Arms: Quarterly, 1st and 4th, argent a saltire sable, in base a human heart ensigned with a regal crown proper, on a chief gules three cushions or (for JOHNSTONE); 2nd and 3rd, per fess the chief or, the base per pale gules and vert, a demi-eagle with two heads displayed issuing in chief sable, the dexter base charged with a tower, the sinister with five towers in saltire gold, the gate and portcullis of each proper (for VANDEN-BEMPDÉ). **Crests:** 1 A winged spur erect or, leathered gules, buckle argent (for JOHNSTONE), 2 Out of the battlements a tower argent, issuant therefrom a demi-eagle with two heads displayed sable (for VANDEN-BEMPDÉ). **Supporters:** Dexter, a lion ermine crowned or, charged on the breast with an escutcheon also or, thereon a winged spur gules; sinister, a horse ermine, bridled and saddled gules, charged on the shoulder as the dexter. **Motto:** *Nunquam non paratus* ('Never unprepared'). **Creations:** Bt. (GB) 6 July 1795, B. (UK) 10 Oct 1881.

THE 5TH BARON DERWENT, of Hackness, in the North Riding of Co York, and a **Baronet** (Sir Robin Evelyn Leo Vanden-Bempdé-Johnstone, Bt, LVO (MVO 1957), DL (N Yorks 1991)) [The Rt Hon The Lord Derwent LVO DL, Hackness Hall, nr Scarborough, Yorks YO13 0BL; 9 Queen St, London W1X 7PH]; *b* 30 Oct 1930; *s* f 1986; *educ* Winchester and Clare Coll Cambridge (MA); late Lt Queen Victoria's Rifles (TA) and 2nd Lt KRRC; 3rd Sec Dip Serv 1954–55, Paris 1955, 2nd Sec 1957, FO 1958, Mexico City 1961, 1st Sec 1962, Washington 1965, FCO 1968–69; dir NM Rothschild 1969–85, md Hutchison Whampoa (Europe) Ltd 1985–, dir Foreign & Colonial (Pacific) Investment Tst and Scarborough Bldg Soc, Chev Legn Hon 1957, Officier de l'Ordre Nationale du Mérite 1978; *m* 12 Jan 1957 *Sybille Marie Louise Marcelle, dau of Vicomte de Simard de Pitray and Mme Jeanine Hennessy, and has:

1 +FRANCIS PATRICK HARCOURT; *b* 23 Sept 1965; *educ* Eton and Edinburgh U; *m* 1990 *Cressida E, only dau of Christopher Bourke

1 *Emmeline Veronica Louise [The Hon Mrs Winterbotham, 48 Oakley Rd, London N1 3LS]; *b* 3 Nov 1958; *m* 4 Sept 1982 *James Winterbotham, s of Richard Winterbotham, of The Hall, Wittersham, Kent, and has:

(1) *Alexander William Harcourt; *b* 1988

(2) *Frederick Charles Leo; *b* 1990

(1) *Héloïse Sophie Laura; *b* 1990

2 *Joanna Louise Claudia; *b* 1 March 1962; *m* 1991 *Timothy Matthews, yr son of Rev Canon John Matthews, of Walberswick, Suffolk, and has issue:

(1) *Leopold Kai Maximilian; *b* 1993

3 *Isabelle Catherine Sophie; *b* 26 Nov 1968

Lineage: Lt-Col JOHN JOHNSTONE, yr son of Sir William Johnstone of Westerhall; *m* Charlotte Van Lore (*d* 23 Nov 1762), dau and heir of John Vanden-Bempdé, of Hackness, and widow of 1st Marquess of Annandale (*see* ANNANDALE AND HARTFELL, E), and was *ka* Cartagena 1741, having had, with a yr s (*see* JOHNSTONE, Bt, of Westerhall):

Sir RICHARD JOHNSTONE later VANDEN-BEMPDÉ (Act of Parl 1793) later still VANDEN-BEMPDÉ-JOHNSTONE (roy licence 1795), **1st Bt** (GB), *so cr* 6 July 1795, with remainder, in default of his own male issue, to his bro Charles John Johnstone; *b* 21 Sept 1732; *m* 1st Nov 1756 Catherine (*dsp* 1790), dau of James Agnew, of Bishop Auckland, Co Durham; *m* 2nd 26 Feb 1795 Margaret (*m* 2nd William Gleadowe and *d* 7 Dec 1853), dau of John Scott, of Charterhouse Sq, London, and *d* July 1807, having by her had issue, with three daus:

1 JOHN (Sir), **2nd Bt**

2 Charles (Rev); *b* 24 Aug 1800; MA; Canon of York; *m* 13 Sept 1827 Amelia (*d* 1862), 2nd dau of Rev Richard Hawksworth, and *d* 15 May 1882 having had with other issue:

(1) William John; *b* 31 Oct 1833; *d* May 1855

(1) Charlotte Frances; *m* 8 Feb 1866 Edmund Walker (*d* 17 May 1873), of Mount St John, Thirsk, and *d* 14 March 1888, leaving issue

(2) Louisa Maria; *d* 1855

(3) Alicia Margaret; *d* 1871
(4) Caroline; *d* 30 May 1934

The 1st Bt's er son,

Sir John Vanden-Bempdé-Johnstone, 2nd Bt; *b* 28 Aug 1799; *educ* Rugby and Trin Coll Cambridge (MA 1821); DCL Oxford 1841; MP Co York 1830–31 and 1831–32, Scarborough 1832–37, 1841–53 and 1857–69; *m* 14 June 1825 Louisa Augusta Venables Vernon (*d* 4 Aug 1869), 2nd dau of Most Rev Edward Harcourt, Archbp of York, 2nd son of 1st Baron Vernon (*qv*), and *d* 24 Feb 1869, having had, with other issue:

1 HARCOURT, **1st Baron**

2 Henry Richard JOHNSTONE later JOHNSTONE-SCOTT (roy licence 1860), of Wood Hall, Yorks; *b* 7 March 1830; (BA Cambridge); *m* 4 Oct 1866 Cressida Elizabeth (*d* 6 May 1937), 3rd dau of William Selby-Lowndes, of Whaddon Hall, Bucks, and *d* 29 Jan 1912, having had issue:

(1) Henry Lister, of Wood Hall, JP (WR Yorks); *b* 18 Oct 1869; *m* 9 Aug 1910 Marjorie (*d* 1948), 4th dau of W Paton, of Scarborough, and *dsp* 14 Feb 1946

(2) Charles; *b* 30 Oct 1870; Def Force U of S Africa, Matabeleland 1893 (medal), Rhodesia 1896 (clasp), Mashonaland 1897 (clasp), S African War (despatches twice, two medals and five clasps) and German SW Africa 1915 during WW I; *m* 22 April 1907 Elizabeth Irvine (*d* 15 Sept 1957), dau of Matheson-Warrack, of Aberdeen, and *d* 7 March 1948, leaving issue:

1a Ronald; *b* 26 Feb 1911; *educ* Wellington; RAF 1934–46; *m* 11 Sept 1937 *Winifred Joan [Mrs Winifred Johnstone-Scott, 19 Boleyn Drive, Eastcote, Ruislip, Middx], er dau of Edgar Reginald Peck, of Selsey, W Sussex, and *d* 17 Nov 1967, leaving issue:

1b +Richard Anthony [Richard Johnstone-Scott Esq, 124 Miladi Farm, Longueville, St Saviours, Jersey, CI]; *b* 9 Oct 1946; *m* 10 Oct 1968 *Jennifer, er dau of Donald Le Lerre, of St Helier, Jersey, CI, and has issue:

1c +Ian Richard; *b* 1972
2c +Giles Edward; *b* 1978
1c *Emma Louise; *b* 1970; *m* 1990 *Robert John Paul Thomas, and has issue:
1d *Oliver Robert; *b* 1991

2b +Bruce Roger [Bruce Johnstone-Scott Esq, 97 Mount Park Rd, Old Eastcote, Pinner, Middx]; *b* 8 May 1956

1b *Gillian Fenton [Mrs David Kimsey, Squirrels Leap, 94 Broadwood Ave, Ruislip, Middx HA4 7XT]; *b* 7 April 1938; *m* 11 June 1960 *David Godfrey Kimsey, Det Ch Supt, est son of Arthur Ernest Kimsey, of Ruislip, and has:

1c *Stephen David [Stephen Kimsey Esq, 70 Collins Drive, Eastcote, Middx]; *b* 27 May 1962; *m* 1985 *Sharon Ivy Elaine Crick, and has issue:
1d *Alyse Louise; *b* 1991

2c *Mark Fenton [Mark Kimsey Esq, 12 Elliott Ave, Ruislip, Middx HA4 9LY]; *b* 23 July 1967; barrister (LLB); *m* 1994 *Emma Jane Sykes

1c *Deborah Gillian [Mrs Michael Hennessey, 46 Hatherleigh Rd, Ruislip, Middx]; *b* 2 Aug 1964; *m* 1987 *Michael John Hennessey and has issue:
1d *Callum Michael Charles; *b* 1992
1d *Emily Kate; *b* 1989

2c *Sarah Cressida; *b* 2 April 1972; ALCM

2b *Sandra Elizabeth Louise [Mrs Ivor Tormley, Dellside, Dibden Hill, Chalfont St Giles, Bucks]; *b* 17 Jan 1952; *m* 1974 *Ivor Owen Tormley, and has issue:
1c *Hannah Jane; *b* 1977
2c *Charlotte Louise; *b* 1979

2a +Charles Hugh, MBE (1957) [Charles Johnstone-Scott Esq MBE, Apartado de Correos 25, Alhaurin el Grande, Malaga, Spain]; *b* 23 March 1913; *educ* Wellington; joined Colonial Police Force 1930, Br section Palestine Police 1930–48, Colonial Police Medal 1948; *m* 5 Aug 1946 *Denise McShetty, Subaltern ATS Roy Corps Signals, Jerusalem, and has had:
1b Nicholas Hugh William; *b* 3 June 1947; *d* 11 March 1971

1a *Aline; *b* 26 Feb 1908; *m* 1934 Errol Chapman Houston (*d* 1977), and has issue:

1b *Anthony Charles [Anthony Houston Esq, 225 Bree St, Vryheid, Natal]; *b* 1935; *educ* Capetown U (BCom, CA); *m* 1960 *Ryvés Dawn, only child of Joseph Geber, of Parktown, Johannesburg, and has issue:
1c *Murray James; *b* 1964; *educ* Capetown U (BCom)
1c *Andrea Leigh; *b* 1961; *m* 1984 *Bruce John Murray-Reinders, and has issue:
1d *Scott Charles; *b* 1986
1d *Nicola Brigid; *b* 1967

2a *Margaret Cressida [Mrs Richard Brooker, Waverley, Lauriston Rd, Gatehouse-of-Fleet, Castle Douglas, Kirkcudbrightshire]; *b* 2 Jan 1915; *m* 16 Jan 1947 *Richard Melville Brooker, son of Richard William Brooker, of Mill Hill, London NW, and has issue:

1b *Robin Nicholas; *b* 18 Feb 1948; *m* 1971 *Roberta Cope, and has issue:
1c *Caroline; *b* 1972

2b *Richard David [Richard Brooker Esq, 31 Oldaker Rd, Newick, E Sussex BN8 4LN]; *b* 19 June 1949; *m* *Vivienne Smith, and has issue:
1c *Julian Charles; *b* 1981
2c *Jonathan; *b* 1984

1b *Sally Patricia [Mrs Edward Meyer, 9 Wood Rd, Rondesbosch, Cape Town, S Africa]; *b* 1942; *m* 1965 *Edward Carl William Meyer, and has issue:
1c *Graham Carl; *b* 1966
2c *Craig Carl Anthony; *b* 1973
1c *Susan Belinda; *b* 1968

(3) Egerton; *b* 24 May 1873; *d* unm 30 Jan 1910
(1) Lucy Cressida; *b* 2 April 1878; *d* unm 8 July 1954

1 Caroline; *m* 2 May 1848 1st Marquess of Abergavenny (*qv*) and *d* 23 Sept 1892, leaving issue

2 Elizabeth Margaret; *m* 6 June 1855 Sir Thomas Erskine Perry (*d* 22 April 1882), Ch Justice Bombay 1847–52, and *d* 11 April 1913, leaving issue

3 Blanche Maria; *m* 23 Aug 1859 Robert Swann, of Askham Hall, and *d* 11 Jan 1878, leaving issue

The 2nd Bt's est son,

HARCOURT VANDEN-BEMPDÉ-JOHNSTONE, **1st Baron Derwent**, of Hackness, in the North Riding of Co York (UK), so *cr* 10 Oct 1881, JP and DL (NR Yorks); *b* 3 Jan 1829; *educ* Eton; Lt 2nd Life Gds and Maj E R Artillery Vols; MP (Lib) Scarborough 1869–80; *m* 2 May 1850 Charlotte (*d* 22 Aug 1903), 2nd dau of Sir Charles Mills, 1st Bt, and sis of 1st Baron Hillingdon (*see* 1970 edn), and *d* 1 March 1916, having had issue:

1 FRANCIS VANDEN-BEMPDÉ-JOHNSTONE, **2nd Baron Derwent**, JP (N R Yorks); *b* 26 May 1851; Capt 2nd Life Gds; *m* 23 Sept 1880 Ethel (*d* 2 Oct 1891), est dau of Henry Strickland-Constable, JP, of Wassand, Yorks (*see* STRICKLAND-CONSTABLE, Bt), and *dspm* 20 April 1929, having had issue:

(1) Sibell, OBE; *b* 4 Aug 1881; *m* 1st 17 Dec 1910 Brig-Gen Walter Long, CMG, DSO (*ka* 27 Jan 1917), est son of 1st Viscount Long (*qv*), and had issue; *m* 2nd 25 April 1921 1st and last Baron Glyn DL (*d* 1 May 1960; *see* 1959 edn), and *d* 23 March 1958

(2) Freda; *b* 9 April 1885; *m* 1 Dec 1904 4th Earl of Listowel (*qv*) and *d* 10 March 1968, leaving issue

2 Edward Henry; *b* 27 Nov 1854; *m* 27 June 1896 Hon Evelyn Mary Agar-Ellis (*d* 8 June 1952), dau of 5th Viscount Clifden (*see* 1970 edn), and *d* 29 April 1903, leaving issue:

(1) Leopold Edward; *b* 6 April 1897; Sub-Lt RN; *ka* Battle of Jutland 31 May 1916

(2) GEORGE HARCOURT VANDEN-BEMPDÉ-JOHNSTONE, **3rd Baron Derwent**; *b* 22 Oct 1899; *educ* Charterhouse and Merton Coll Oxford (BA 1920, Newdigate Prize); WW II in RAF; FRSA, Fell Roy Asiatic Soc, Hon Attaché Dip Serv (Warsaw 1923, Brussels 1928, Madrid 1929 and Berne 1939), Pres Yorks Lib Fedn and Co-Treas Br Lib Internat Cncl, author: IFifty Poems, *Before Zero House*, *Return Ticket*, and essays on Prosper Merimée, Goya and Rossini; *m* 21 Dec 1929 Countess Sabine Czaykowska (*d* 18 May 1941), dau of Gen D Iliesco, formerly ADC to KING FERDINAND OF ROMANIA and Ch of Gen Staff Romanian Army, and *dsp* 12 Jan 1949

(3) PATRICK ROBIN GILBERT, **4th Baron**

3 Cecil; *b* 26 Dec 1856; CE; *d* 29 Jan 1933

4 Alan (Sir), GCVO (1908); *b* 31 Aug 1858; entered Dip Serv 1879, Sec Legation Copenhagen 1895, Darmstadt 1900, Sec Emb Vienna 1903, Envoy Extrdy and Min Plen Copenhagen 1905, The Hague 1910 (ret 1919), Grand Cross Dannebrog; *m* 21 Dec 1892 Antoinette (*d* 1 July 1934), only dau of J W Pinchot, of New York, and *d* 31 July 1932, leaving issue:

(1) Harcourt; *b* 19 May 1895; *educ* Eton and Balliol Coll Oxford (MA); WW I with Rifle Bde and on Gen Staff; MP E Willesden 1923–24, S Shields 1931–35 and Middlesbrough W 1940–45, Assist Govt Whip 1931–32, Sec Dept Overseas Trade 1940–45; *d* unm 1 March 1945

5 Louis; *b* 25 Feb 1862; *m* 8 Jan 1891 Gwendoline Mary Elizabeth (*d* 16 Nov 1969) er dau of Maj Henry Charles Talbot, late 43rd Regt (*see* SHREWSBURY and WATERFORD, E), and *d* 12 Dec 1922, leaving issue:

(1) Granville Henry, DSO (1918); *b* 18 Dec 1891; *educ* Eton; Lt-Col RA (Ret), WW I (despatches three times, 1914 star, Croix de Guerre); *m* 7 June 1923 Margarita Ruby (*d* 1972), dau of Arthur Vernon O'Connell, of Buenos Aires, and *d* 21 July 1969, leaving issue:

1a +John Louis [John Vanden-Bempdé-Johnstone Esq, 61 Salisbury Rd, Farnborough, Hants]; *b* 9 Aug 1928; *educ* Eastbourne Coll; Capt RA (ret); *m* 4 Nov 1964 *Eltis, dau of W Robinson, of Ashington, Northumberland, and has:
1b *Louise Dorothy Ann; *b* 1967

1a *Elizabeth Mary [Mrs Richard McCaig, 15 Gorselands, Andover Rd, Newbury, Berks]; *b* 22 July 1924; *m* 24 March 1945 *Lt-Col Richard McCaig, MC, RA (ret), son of William McCaig, of Dunedin, NZ, and has issue:
1b David John; *b* 13 Feb 1949; *educ* Wellington; *d* 1977
2b *Mark Richard; *b* 28 Sept 1959
1b *Susan Mary; *b* 2 Nov 1951; *m* 1974 *Maj Jeremy Turner, RIR, of 1 Holly Villas, Salisbury Rd, Shipton Bellinger, Hants

(2) Robin Talbot, JP; *b* 7 Aug 1901; *m* 1st 27 July 1927 (*divorce* 1936) Peggy, dau of Rupert Marais, of Brooklyn, Pretoria; *m* 2nd 1936 Louise, only dau of Guy Chalkley, of Transvaal, and adopted a dau:
*Robin Louise; *b* 6 June 1945

(2) (cont) Robin Vanden-Bempdé-Johnstone *m* 3rd 26 April 1951 (*divorce* 1959) Betty van Zwanenberg (taken by deed poll March 1959), dau of Michael Cooper and widow of Frank van Zwanenberg; *m* 4th 1960 *Mrs Elsa Ann Zillah Mann, dau of Maj James Eland Buchanan, of Hales Hall, Market Drayton, Salop

(1) Dorothy Ethel; *b* 25 Nov 1892; *d* unm 23 April 1967

(2) Joan Gwendoline; *b* 30 Dec 1895; *m* 1st 7 April 1915 (*divorce* 1923) William Robert Younger (afterwards 2nd Bt; *d* 23 May 1973), er son of Sir William Younger, 1st Bt, of Auchen Castle (*qv*), and had issue; *m* 2nd 1923 Capt Hubert Lachlan Pelham-Burn, Gordon Highrs (*d* 21 July 1927), est son of Ven William Pelham-Burn, Archdeacon of Norwich, and had further issue; *m* 3rd 8 Aug 1931 Dennis Yates Wheatley, author, only son of Albert David Wheatley

6 Gilbert; *b* 25 Sept 1865; *m* 21 Jan 1897 Rachel (*d* 15 July 1968), dau of Col Hon Archibald Charles Henry Douglas Pennant (*see* PENRHYN, B), and *d* 5 Jan 1949, leaving issue:

(1) Mark; *b* 1 Sept 1900; Lt-Col late Intell Corps; stockbroker; *m* 25 Jan 1928 Susan (*d* 1993), only dau of Geoffrey Head, OBE, of Berkeley Sq, London (*see* HEAD, V), and *d* 3 March 1956, leaving issue:

1a *Virginia Susan [Miss Virginia Vanden-Bempdé-Johnstone, 127 Cranmer Ct, Whiteheads Grove, London SW3 3HE]; *b* 26 Oct 1928

(2) Felix Gilbert; *b* 31 July 1904; Cdr RN (ret), WW II; *m* 1st 8 April 1938 (*divorce* 1945) Jessie Helen June, only dau of Herbert William Looker, of Sussex, and formerly w of Lt-Col Edward Noel Keith Estcourt, DSO, OBE, RA, and had issue:

1a *Sarah June [Mrs Peter Glossop, The White House, 68 East St, Coggeshall, CO61 1SL]; *b* 17 June 1939; *m* 19 Oct 1961 *Peter George Glossop, er son of George Charles William Glossop, of Duxford, Cambs, and has issue:

1b *Nicholas George; *b* 1971

2b *Georgemma Sarah; *b* 1963; *m* 1990 *Richard Morgans and has:

1c *Max Christopher; *b* 1993

1c *Polly; *b* 1994

3b *Lucy Maria; *b* 1966; *m* 1992 *James Patrick Atherton, only son of Brig Maurice Alan Atherton CBE, of Barnham, Kent and has issue:

1c *Alexander; *b* 1997

4b *Camilla June; *b* 1969; *m* 1997 *Graham Vernon Appleyard

(2) (cont.) Cdr Felix Vanden-Bempdé-Johnstone *m* 2nd 23 May 1945 *Frances Elizabeth [Mrs Felix Vanden-Bempdé-Johnstone, 6 Orchard Thatch, Scotney Manor, Sutton Scotney, Hants SO21 3JX], est dau of Charles McIntyre Brown, and *d* 26 Nov 1964, having by her had:

1a +Nicholas Gilbert; *b* 17 Oct 1948; *d* 14 Dec 1966

2a Philippa Rachel; *b* 4 Aug 1946; *m* 1976 *Patrick Ramsey Andrew and *d* 8 Feb 1988, leaving:

1b *Edwina; *b* Sept 1981

2b *Emily; *b* Dec 1983

(1) Gwyneth Ella; *b* 19 July 1908; *d* 25 Oct 1918

1 Hilda; *d* young March 1853

2 Edith; *b* 7 June 1860

3 Mary; *d* young 1865

The 3rd BARON's bro,

PATRICK ROBIN GILBERT VANDEN-BEMPDÉ-JOHNSTONE, **4th Baron Derwent**, CBE (1974); *b* 26 Oct 1901; *educ* Charterhouse and RMC Sandhurst; granted rank of baron's yr s 14 Aug 1929, Maj KRRC; Jr Oppn Whip Ho Lds 1950–51, Chm Br Rd Fedn 1954–62, Min State: BOT 1962–63 and Home Off 1963–64, Dep Speaker Ho of Lds 1970–86,; *m* 7 Dec 1929 *Marie-Louise Henriette, dau of Albert Picard, of Paris, and formerly w of Brig Philip Stafford Myburgh, CBE, DSO and bar, MC, and *d* 1986, leaving:

ROBIN EVELYN LEO VANDEN-BEMPDÉ-JOHNSTONE, **5th and present Baron Derwent**

DESAI

Creation: B. (LP, UK) 1991.

THE BARON DESAI, of St Clement Danes in the City of Westminster (Meghnad Jagdishchandra Desai) [The Hon The Lord Desai, LSE, Houghton St, London WC2A 2AE]; *b* 10 July 1940; *educ* Bombay U (BA Hons, MA) and Pennsylvania U (PhD 1964); Associate Specialist Dept Ag Ec UCA Berkeley 1963–65; LSE: Lecturer1965–77, Sr Lecturer 1977–80, Reader 1980–83, Prof Economics 1983–; Head Devpt Studies Inst 1990–95; Dir Centre for the Study of Global Governance 1992–; Chm Islington S and Finsbury Constituency Lab Party 1986–92; Pres Assoc U Teachers in Economics 1987–90; Memb: Cncl Roy Ec Soc 1988, Exec Ctee Fabian Soc 1990–92; Hon DSc Kingston 1992, Hon DSc (Ec) E London 1994; D Univ Middlesex 1993; author: *Marxian Economic Theory* (1974), *Applied Econometrics* (1976), *Marxian Economics* (1979), *Testing Monetarism* (1981), *The Cambridge Economic History of India 1757–1970* (assist ed to Prof Dharma Kumar, 1983), *Agrarian Power and Agricultural Productivity in South Asia* (1984), *Lenin on Economics* (ed, 1987), *Selected Essays: Macroeconomics and Monetary Theory* (vol 1, 1995), *Poverty Famine and Economic Development* (vol 2, 1995), *Global Governance* (jt ed, 1995), *On Inequality* (ed, 1995); *m* 1970 *Gail Graham, dau of George Ambler Wilson, CBE, of Brandon House, N End Ave, London NW3, and has issue.

1 *Sven; *b* 1975

1 *Tanvi; *b* 1972

2 *Nuala; *b* 1974

Lineage: JAGDISHCHANDRA CHANDULAL DESAI; *m* Mandakini — and had:

MEGHNAD JAGDISHCHANDRA, *cr* a **Baron**

DE SAUMAREZ

Arms: Argent on a chevron gules between three leopard's faces sable as many castles triple-towered or. **Crest:** A falcon displayed proper. **Supporters:** Dexter, a unicorn argent, the tail cowarded, gorged with a naval crown azure and charged on the shoulder with a castle triple-towered gules; sinister, a greyhound argent, collared gules, ring and rim or, charged on the shoulder with an anchor erect sable, encircled with a wreath of laurel vert. **Motto:** *In deo spero* ('My hope is in God'). **Creations:** Bt. (UK) 13 June 1801, B. (UK) 15 Sept 1831.

THE 7TH BARON DE SAUMAREZ, in the Island of Guernsey, and a **Baronet** (Sir Eric Douglas Saumarez Bt) [The Rt Hon The Lord de Saumarez, Shrubland Park, Coddenham, Suffolk IP6 9QQ]; *b* 13 Aug 1956; *s* f 1991, premier Bt UK; *educ* Milton Abbey, Nottingham U and RAC Cirencester; *m* 1st 14 July 1982 (*divorce* 1990) Christine, yr dau of B N Halliday OBE, of Woodford Green, Essex, and has issue:

1 *Claire; *b* 23 Feb 1984

2 *Emily; *b* 14 June 1985

The 7th BARON *m* 2nd 4 Sept 1991 *Susan, dau of Joseph Hearn

Lineage: The family of Samares/Samersq/Saumarez/Sausmarais/Sausmarez descends from a Norman family of St Hilaire du Harcouet, who held a castle built by WILLIAM I (THE CONQUEROR) on the borders of Brittany. The name derives from the Fief de Saumareys, or salt marsh, in the parish of St Clement, Jersey, which was allegedly given to Ralph de St Hilaire by WILLIAM II (RUFUS) in 1096. The family's Jersey estates were forfeited in 1333 and they appear to have left the island about that time.

GUILLAUME de SALINELLES, Seigneur of Saumareys; *fl* 1180; had a s:

—, Seigneur of Saumareys; *fl* 1221; had, with an est s (Sir William Samerals, Seigneur of Saumareys, *fl* 1254, twice Justice of Assize Channel Islands *temp* HENRY III and EDWARD I) and a yst s (Ralph):

NICOLAS de SAUMARAIS; *b c* 1205; *m* —, est dau and chief heir of Jordan de Lucy or de Barneville, with whom he acquired the Seigneurie of the Fief, situated at Jerburg, Guernsey, which later became known as the Fief de Sausmarez, and *d* 1250, leaving:

MATHIEU de SAUSMAREZ, Seigneur 1267; *m* Alice de St Rémy and had, with two daus (Johanna; Philippa, *m* Jean de Barentyn, later Seigneur Samarès, Jersey):

MATHIEU de SAUSMAREZ; did homage in 1299 for his holdings in Guernsey; fortified Jerburg; in 1330 his rights to the fief and castle were confirmed; he held them in chief from the King as his third cup-bearer when the King was on Guernsey; his s:

NICOLAS de SAUSMAREZ; *m* Avice de St Martin; putative f of:

COLLIN de SAUSMAREZ, Seigneur 1390; putative ancestor (f?) of:

NICOLAS de SAUSMAREZ, Jurat Royal Court, Seigneur 1438; putative ancestor (f?) of:

NICOLAS de SAUSMAREZ, Seigneur; *m* Collenette Henry and *d* in or after 1469, leaving:

THOMAS de SAUSMAREZ, Seigneur, had:

1 THOMAS

2 Michel; *m* Colliche Fouaschim and had, with seven daus:

(1) Nicolas; *m* Anne de la Marche and *d* 1583, having had Jean and Matthieu

(2) John

3 William; *dsp*

The est son,

THOMAS de SAUSMAREZ; of age 1520, Seigneur; *m* Isabel d'Yscart and had issue:

1 GEORGE de SAUSMAREZ, Seigneur; *m* Collette Baudouin (*dsp*) and was succeeded in the Seigneurie by

1 JUDITH; *m* Jean Andros. It remained in the Andros family until 1748

A presumably connected family is as follows:

JEAN de SAUSMAREZ; *m* Marguerite, dau of Jacques Guille, Bailiff, and had issue:

THOMAS de SAUSMAREZ; *b* 1573; *m* 1598 Rebecca Hancock, of Poole, and had issue:

MICHEL de SAUSMAREZ; *b* 1599; *m* 1623 Bertrame Fautrat and had issue:

THOMAS de SAUSMAREZ; *b* 1631; *m* Marthe Nicolle and had:

MICHEL de SAUSMAREZ; *b* 1655; *m* 1681 Charlotte Le Marchant and had:

MATTHEW de SAUSMAREZ, of Guernsey; Col of Militia; *b* 4 June 1685; *m* Anne, dau of John Durell, Attorney Gen Jersey, and had, with other issue:

1 John, King's Procureur, Seigneur of Sausmarez 1748–74, bought the fief from John Andros 1748; *b* 1706; *m* 1st Martha de Lisle and had issue:

(1) Matthew, Seigneur 1774–1820, *dsp*

1 (cont.) John Saumarez *m* 2nd Martha Le Marchant and by her had issue:

(2) Thomas, Attorney-Gen Guernsey and Seigneur of Sausmarez 1820–1837; *m* 1st 20 Oct 1780 Martha, 2nd dau of Isaac Dobrée, of Guernsey, merchant, and sister of Isaac Dobrée, who *m* Anne, sister of 1st Baron de Saumarez (*see* below); *m* 2nd Catherine, dau of Sir Peter de Havilland, Bailiff of Guernsey, and by his two marriages had 28 children, including:

1a John Thomas, Attorney-Gen Guernsey; *b* 1790; *m* 1829 Mary Anne (*d* 1877), est dau of Hellier Dobrée, of Hauteville Guernsey, and *d* 1870, leaving issue:

1b Thomas John; *b* 1832; *m* March Malloch and had issue:

1c Arthur St Vincent; *m* Olive Fisher and had issue:

1d Hugh John, Lt Col Gurkha Regt; *m* Lydia Gibson and had:

1e *Peter; *m* *Caroline V F, dau of Maj J F Mundy, of Crondall, Herts, and has issue:

1f *A son; *b* 3 April 1976

2e *James

1e *Jennifer; *m* —

2e *Susan (twin with Jennifer); *m* —

3e *Diana; *m* —

4e *Sara

2d *Thomas; *m* *Georgina —

1d *Damaris; *m* Col — Wingfield

2a Philip, ancestor of Maurice Saumarez, RA, who *d* 27 Oct 1969 aged 54

3a Havilland (Rev), Rector of St Peter's Northampton; *b* 1813; *m* 1st 23 July 1850 Hon Elizabeth Spencer (*d* 12 Sept 1858), dau of 1st Baron Churchill (*see* CHURCHILL, V), and had issue:

1b George Spencer (Rev), Rector Acton, Middx; *b* April 1855; *m* Fanny Maria, dau of Capt H Temple, RN, and *d* Jan 1927, leaving, with nine daus (*unm*):

1c Havilland George Temple, Lt-Col RA; *b* 8 Nov 1894; *educ* Queen's Coll Oxford (BA 1915); *m* Alice, dau of Lt-Col E R Howell, IA, and had issue:

1d *John Havilland Russell (Rev); Vicar of St Peter-in-Thanet; *b* 1 Nov 1926; *m* 17 March 1956 *Maureen F, only dau of Mr Justice C R Hemeon, ICS, and has issue:

1e *Philip Matthew Hemeon; *b* 30 Aug 1957

2e *Havilland James; *b* 6 Dec 1958

3e *Jonathan Mark; *b* 29 Feb 1960

1e *Mary Elizabeth Frances *b* 4 Oct 1965

2d *Nicolas Spencer; *b* 15 Oct 1933; *m* 1961 *Anne Gillian, dau of Percival Kingsley Davis, of Barnet, Herts, and has issue:

1e *Charlotte Louise; *b* 9 July 1961

2e *Hester Mary; *b* 13 July 1962

3e *Sophie Rose; *b* 4 July 1965

3d *Michael George, slr MAFF 1967; *b* 14 Sept 1934; *educ* King's Coll London (LLB); *m* 21 Nov 1964 *Pauline Belinda, dau of Cdr P M Latham, RN, of 1 Old Palace Lane, Richmond, Surrey, and has issue:

1e *Nicholas Havilland; *b* 18 Sept 1965

2e *Alexander Michael; *b* 27 Jan 1967

3e *Matthew Peter; *b* 27 Aug 1970

1d *Elizabeth Ann [Mrs Donald Murton, Wayside, Wadhurst, Sussex]; *b* 6 June 1931; *m* 27 Feb 1954 *Donald Eric Whitehead Murton and has issue:

1e *Andrew Charles; *b* 23 May 1956

2e *Richard David Henry; *b* 31 Dec 1959

1e *Susan Elizabeth; *b* 2 Feb 1958

2e *Anna Kathryn; *b* 12 Oct 1966

3a (cont.) The Rev Havilland Saumarez *m* 2nd Anne Priaulx, dau of Rev Nicholas Walters, and *d* 17 April 1882, having by her had issue

2b Sir HAVILLAND WALTER SAUMAREZ, 1st and last Bt (UK), so *cr* 26 June 1928, of Jerburg, Seigneur of the fief de Sausmarez and Châtelain of Jerburg; *educ* Trin Coll Cambridge (BA 1883), Hon Docteur of Law U of Caen 1927, barrister Inner Temple 1884, entered FO Judicial Serv 1892; Assist Judge Zanzibar 1892–97, Assist Judge Supreme Consular Court for Ottoman Empire 1898–1903 (full Judge 1903–05), Judge Supreme Court for China 1905–21, 1912–20 presided Court of Appeal Hong Kong (ret 1921), Bailiff of Guernsey 1922–29; *b* 30 May 1861, ktd 1905; *m* 1st 2 June 1892 Dora Beatrice (*d* 13 July 1893), 2nd dau of Maj-Gen Gother Mann, CB, RE; *m* 2nd 9 April 1896 Annie Elizabeth, GBE, Medaille de la Reine Elisabeth, Pres and Hon Sec of Br Women's Work Assoc in China during WW I (*d* 15 March 1947), 2nd dau of Rev F W Mann, Rector of St Mary de Castro, Guernsey, and *dsp* 5 March 1941,when the btcy expired

3b Philip d'Arcy, Capt RN; *d* 6 May 1935

4b Cecil, CB (1924), CMG (1918), DSO (1900), Brig-Gen RA, served Boer War 1899–1902, Expdn against Zakha Kul Afridis 1908 (Brevet Major), WW I (Brevet Lt-Col 1915, Brevet Col 1919), Inspr Demobilisation 1919–20, Seigneur of Sausmarez March 1947; *b* 29 Sept 1870; *m* 7 Dec 1905 Mary Mildred Gainor (*d* 21 April 1937), dau of Rev J P Morgan, and *d* 20 Aug 1966, leaving issue:

1c *Cecil Havilland, MBE (1946) [Cecil Saumarez Esq MBE, Saumarez Manor, St Martin's, Guernsey CI]; People's Deputy States of Guernsey 1961, Rep of Br Cncl in Belgium 1946–48, Tutor at Wilton Park 1951–58; *b* 20 Nov 1907; *m* 9 April 1938 Christian Elizabeth Anne (*d* 20 July 1997), dau of Col Sir Coote Hedley, KBE, CB, CMG, and adopted:

*Janice Christine (Jennie) [Mrs John Lintell, c/o Saumarez Manor, St Martins, Guernsey, CI]; *b* 26 April 1949; *m* 8 April 1972 *John Lintell, 2nd son of R B Lintell, of Cliffe House, Village de Putron, Guernsey, CI

*Louisa Jillian; *b* 4 Aug 1953

1c Cecily Mildred Rosemary; *b* 15 March 1909; *m* William Ashley and *d* 28 Feb 1997

2c *(Hazel) Carterette [Miss Hazel Saumarez, 24 Mount Durand, St Peter Port, Guernsey, CI]; *b* 5 Jan 1911; adopted:

*Keith

*Josephine [Mrs Philip Courtil de Rigeaux, St Saviours, Guernsey, CI]; *m* *Philip de Garis

*Evelyn [Mrs Michael Thorp, Erin, St John's Rd, St John's, Guernsey CI]; *m* *Michael Thorp

1b Evelyn; *d* unm 14 July 1956

4a George, Seigneur of Sausmarez 1873–90, General in IA; *b* 1816; *m* 1st Annie de Lisle; *m* 2nd Louise d'Arcy, dau of Rev Nicholas Walters, and *dsp* 4 July 1890

2 Philip; *b* 17 Nov 1710; sailed with Cdre Anson (*see* LICHFIELD, E) on his voyage round the world 1743; *ka* Battle of Finisterre 14 Oct 1747

3 Thomas, Capt RN; *b* 20 April 1720; *m* Catherine Mountstevens and *dsp* 1764

1 Anne; *m* Philip Dumaresq

2 Elizabeth; *m* George Durell, Capt RN

3 Madeleine; *m* Adml Philip Durell

The 4th son,

MATTHEW SAUMAREZ; *b* 10 Oct 1718; *m* 1st Susannah, dau of Thomas Dumaresq, of Jersey, and had issue:

1 Susannah; *m* Henry Brock, of Jersey;

MATTHEW SAUMAREZ *m* 2nd Carteret, dau of James le Marchant, and was drowned in his passage to England March 1778, having had, with other issue:

1 John *b* 1755; *m* Judith, dau of William Brock, and *d* 2 Feb 1832

2 JAMES, **1st Baron**

3 Thomas (Sir), Gen; *b* 1 July 1760; served War of American Independence, Equerry and Groom of Chamber to DUKE OF KENT 1790, C-in-C New Brunswick 1813; *m* Harriet (*d* 18 Feb 1858), dau of William Brock, and *dsp* 4 March 1845

4 Richard, of Newington, Surrey; surgn, FRS and FSA; *b* 13 Nov 1764; *m* 9 Jan 1786 Martha, dau of John Le Mesurier, and *d* 27 Jan 1835, leaving issue:

(1) Richard, Adml, Order of Leopold of Austria; *b* 11 Sept 1791; *m* 12 Feb 1825 Anne Ellson and *d* 18 Jan 1864, having had issue:

1a Richard; *b* 25 Nov 1825; *d* 28 March 1846

2a Thomas, CB, Adml; *b* 21 March 1827; *m* 1st 31 Nov 1854 Agnes Jean, dau of S Block, and had issue:

1b Richard James, CMG, Lt-Col RM; *b* 12 July 1864; *m* 10 July 1902 Elliot Mabel (*d* 18 Feb 1936), dau of Alexander Milne Ogston, of Ardoe, Aberdeen, and *d* 26 Feb 1943, leaving issue:

1c Philip Lionel, DSC and bar; Capt RN; *b* 18 Sept 1904; *m* 14 March 1933 *Elizabeth Patricia, dau of Capt Thomas Reginald Gill O'Connor, RN, of 13 Tryon St, London SW3, and had issue:

1d *James Philip de Havilland [Lt-Cdr James Saumarez RN (ret), Olive Farm, Orchard Hill, Devon EX39 2RA]; *b* 6 June 1937; Communications Offr 1964, ret from RN 1968; *m* 24 April 1965 (*divorce* 1986) Teresa Mary, dau of Wallace Grant Edwards, MBE, TD, of Caterham, Surrey; *m* 2nd 1 Oct 1988 *Carol Jane, dau of Robert Ashton Aspinwall, of Mystic, Conn., and has by his 1st w:

1e *William Thomas; *b* 22 Feb 1966; *m* 19– *Claire, dau of Paul Lewis, of Marnhull, Dorset, and has:

1f *Victoria Elizabeth; *b* 28 Dec 1967

1e *Victoria Elizabeth; *b* 28 Dec 1967

2d *Richard Charles; *b* 9 March 1948

1d *Susanna Elizabeth Carteret; *b* 27 April 1934; *m* 19– *Campbell Coningsby Heinemann and has issue:

1e *Edward Anthony; *b* 10 Jan 1958

1e *Caroline Anne; *b* 10 July 1960

1c *Lesley Elliot [Mrs Norman Finlinson, Waterhouse Residential Home, Limpley Stoke, Bath BA2 7JB]; *b* 28 Sept 1903; *m* 10 July 1931 Col Norman West Finlinson, DSO, S Staffs Regt, and has:

1d *Penelope Ann [Mrs Richard Dawnay, Courtside, Richmond Rd, Bath BA1 5PU]; *b* 9 Jan 1933; *m* 1st 8 Dec 1956 (*divorce* 1962) Harry Douglas Smith, and has issue

1e *Emma Charlotte; *b* 23 Nov 1958

1d (cont.) Mrs Penelope Smith *m* 2nd 1 Sept 1962 *Lt-Col Richard William Dawnay (*see* DOWNE, V) and has further issue:

2d *Joanna Lesley [Mrs John Hutton, Well House, Crockerton, Wilts BA12 8AD]; *b* 27 June 1936; *m* 21 May 1966 *Maj John Michael Coats Hutton, KOYLI, s of Lt-Cdr Peter Coats Hutton, DSC, RN, and has:

1e *Guy Peter Coats; *b* 3 July 1970

1e *Nicola Gay; *b* 21 June 1967; *m* 3 Sept 1994 *Tobias George Minter, s of Frederick George Minter, of London, and has:

1f *Frederick George; *b* 11 Oct 1995

1b Agnes Margaret; *b* 14 Jan 1866; *m* Col Charles Daniel (*d* 3 July 1949), Loyal N Lancs Regt, and *d* 7 Jan 1937

2a (cont.) Adml Thomas Saumarez *m* 2nd 1868 Eleanor, dau of Benjamin Scott Riley, and by her had issue:

2b Edith Eleanor; *m* 6 April 1891 William Luther Watson (*d* 8 Feb 1896), S Lancs Regt, and *d* 19 Jan 1961, leaving issue

1a Martha; *b* 6 Sept 1828; *m* Rev S Sowden, and *d* 27 Oct 1879

(2) Frederick; *b* 19 Oct 1794; *d* 20 Jan 1886

(3) Thomas, Capt RN; *b* 8 June 1796; *d* 19 May 1823

(4) Basil (Rev), Rector Gt Easton; *b* 22 March 1798; *d* 15 Nov 1876

(1) Carterette; *b* 4 April 1789; *m* 5 Feb 1827 John Gimmingham, and *d* 4 Jan 1867

(2) Martha; *b* 5 Sept 1797; *m* 7 Oct 1819 Maj Charles de Havilland (*d* 23 Nov 1844), yr son of Sir Peter de Havilland, Bailiff of Guernsey, and *d* 26 Dec 1864, having had issue

1 Anne; *b* 3 July 1752; *m* 22 Dec 1782 Isaac Dobrée (*d* 9 June 1792), only son of Isaac Dobrée, of Guernsey, merchant, and *d* 9 Feb 1846, having had issue

2a Charlotte; *b* 22 Feb 1763; *m* July 1789 Rev Nicholas Peter Dobrée (*d* 5 Feb 1843), MA, Rector of St Mary-de-Castro, Guernsey, yst s of Col Nicholas Dobrée, of Belle Vue, Guernsey, and *d* 22 Oct 1860, having had issue

The 3rd son,

Sir James Saumarez, 1st Bt, and **1st Baron de Saumarez**, in the Island of Guernsey, so *cr* 13 June 1801 and 15 Sept 1831 respectively (both UK), GCB (1815, KB 1801); *b* 11 March 1757; Col RM 1799–1801, R-Adml 1801, V-Adml 1806, Adml of the Blue 1814, the White 1819 and the Red 1830, R-Adml of the UK 1819–21, V-Adml of UK 1821–32, Gen Marine Forces 1832, ktd 1793, Grand Cross Swedish Order of the Sword, DCL Oxon 1814; *m* 27 Oct 1788 Martha (*d* 17 April 1849), dau and heir of Thomas Le Marchant, of Guernsey, by Mary, dau of Peter Dobrée, and *d* 9 Oct 1836, having had, with other issue:

1 **Rev 2nd Baron de Saumarez**; Rector Huggate, Yorks; *b* 9 Oct 1789; *m* 5 Oct 1814 Mary (*d* May 1849), dau of V-Adml William Lechmere, of Steeple Aston, Oxon (and niece of Sir John Dashwood King, 3rd Bt; *see* DASHWOOD, Bt, of West Wycombe), and *dsp* 9 April 1863

2 Thomas Le Marchant; *b* 30 Oct 1803; *m* 1 Oct 1829 Catherine Spencer A Beresford (*m* 2nd 8 Feb 1841 Rev Eardley Wilmot Marshall, of Bury, Sussex), dau of Lt-Col Spencer Vassall, and was *ka* Montevideo 4 July 1834

3 JOHN ST VINCENT, **3rd Baron**

1 Amelia; *m* 3 Sept 1822 William Young Herries (*d* 12 Feb 1872), of Spottes, Kirkcudbridht, and *d* 7 Dec 1838

The 2nd BARON's bro,

JOHN ST VINCENT SAUMAREZ, **3rd Baron de Saumarez**; Col; *b* 28 May 1806; *m* 1st 2 June 1838 Caroline Esther (*d* 15 July 1846), est dau of William Rhodes, of Kirskill and Bramhope Halls, Yorks, and had:

1 JAMES ST VINCENT, **4th Baron**

2 John St Vincent, Capt 14th Hus; *b* 6 March 1845; *d* unm 12 Jan 1877

1 Caroline Amelia; *m* 30 July 1861 4th Baron Boston (*qv*), and *d* 20 Dec 1922, leaving issue

2 Augusta Caroline; *m* 1st 27 Oct 1859 5th Baron Boston (*qv*), and had issue; *m* 2nd 16 April 1883 Sir Henry Percy Anderson (*d* 19 July 1896), KBC, KCMG, and *d* 16 Feb 1929

The **3rd Baron** *m* 2nd 13 April 1850 Margaret Antoinette (*d* 10 May 1904), 4th dau of William Richard Hopkyns Northey, JP, of Oving House, Bucks, and by her had issue:

3 Arthur, Priv Sec to 1st Earl of Iddesleigh (*qv*) 1881–87; *b* 21 July 1852; *m* 3 Aug 1881 Hon Edith Mary McGarel-Hogg (*d* 31 Aug 1939), only dau of 1st Baron Magheramorne (*see* HOGG, Bt), and *d* 14 Aug 1933, leaving issue:

(1) Michael; *b* 26 Aug 1884 ; *d* 1 Nov 1897

(2) Reginald Stafford, MC, Capt 22nd Bn London Regt (The Queen's), Staff Capt BEF; *b* 11 Jan 1886; *ka* in France 23 March 1918

(1) Muriel Antoinette, Deaconess Church of Ascension, Pollards Hill, Mitcham; *b* 15 July 1882; *d* unm 15 March 1954

(2) Rosalind Edith; BRC WW II; *b* 15 May 1899; *d* unm 29 April 1970

4 Gerald Le Marchant; *b* 23 June 1859; *d* unm 16 June 1941

3 Antoinette Elizabeth; *m* 20 Sept 1880 Piers Egerton-Warburton (*d* 24 March 1914), DL, JP, of Arley Hall, Northwich, and *d* 24 Sept 1918, leaving issue (*see* GREY EGERTON, Bt)

4 Eleanor Mary; *m* 11 May 1903 Rev Charles J Walbrand Evans, Rector of Burstow, Surrey, and *d* 18 Dec 1937, leaving issue

The 3rd BARON *d* 8 Jan 1881; his est son,

JAMES ST VINCENT SAUMAREZ, **4th Baron de Saumarez**; *b* 17 July 1843; *educ* Eton and Trin Coll Cambridge (MA); Capt Gren Gds, Dip Serv 1867–83; *m* 10 Oct 1882 Jane Anne, OBE (1918) (*d* 17 Jan 1933), est dau of Capt Charles Acton Vere-Broke, RE, and had:

1 JAMES ST VINCENT BROKE, **5th Baron**

1 Evelyn; *b* 13 Aug 1883; *m* 30 June 1919 Lt Sir John Arthur Haigh Wood, 2nd Bt, MC, DSC, RNVR (*see* 1970 edn), and *d* 2 May 1934, leaving issue

2 Marion; *b* 29 June 1885

3 Gladys; *b* 21 March 1887; *d* unm 21 Feb 1975

The 4th BARON *d* 25 April 1937; his son,

JAMES ST VINCENT BROKE SAUMAREZ, **5th Baron de Saumarez**, DL (Suffolk 1937–64); *b* 29 Nov 1889; *educ* Harrow and Trin Coll Cambridge; Capt Scots Gds WW I (wounded), ADC to Air Marshal 1st Viscount Trenchard 1918–19, High Sheriff Suffolk 1932, WW II as Assist Zone Cdr Merioneth and Montgomeryshire HG, fndr Rhodesia Fairbridge Coll 1946; *m* 30 April 1914 Gunhild (*d* 1985), yr dau of Maj-Gen Sir Victor Gustaf Balck, KCMG, of Stockholm, and had issue:

1 Philip St Vincent; *b* 17 Nov 1917; *d* 15 Dec 1935

2 JAMES VICTOR BROKE, **6th Baron**

1 *Veronica [The Hon Mrs Palmer, Clos du Menage, Sark, CI]; BRC and ATS WW II; *b* 21 June 1915; *m* 12 July 1945 Brig Anthony William Allen Llewellen Palmer (*d* 1990), DSO, MC, King's Dragoon Gds, cmded NI Horse, 9th Lancers, er surv son of Col William Llewellen Palmer, MC, of Great Somerford, Chippenham, Wilts

2 Christine; *b* 31 July 1916; WRNS WW II; *m* 15 April 1944 *Lt-Col Sir Henry Morton Llewellyn, 3rd Bt, CBE, DL, JP, of Bwllfa, Glam (*qv*), and *d* 20 April 1998, leaving issue

The 5th BARON *d* 16 Jan 1969; his only surv son

JAMES VICTOR BROKE SAUMAREZ, **6th Baron de Saumarez**; *educ* Eton and Magdalene Coll Cambridge (BA 1949, MA 1952); Life Gds WW II, BAOR, dir Shrubland Health Clinic Ltd; *b* 28 April 1924; *m* 28 April 1953 *Joan (Julia) [The Rt Hon Joan Lady de Saumarez, Shrubland Park, Coddenham, Ipswich, Suffolk IP6 9QQ], dau of Douglas Raymond Charlton, of Holland-on-Sea, Essex, and *d* 1991, leaving issue:

1 ERIC DOUGLAS SAUMAREZ, **7th and present Baron de Saumarez**

2 +VICTOR THOMAS (twin) [The Hon Victor Saumarez, 22 Taeping Rd, Isle of Dogs, London]; *b* 13 Aug 1956; heir presumptive; *educ* Milton Abbey and Exeter U (BA); MBA; jazz musician; *m* 9 Sept 1995 *Bing Chen, of Taiwan

1 Louisa; *b* 7 March 1955; *m* 4 Sept 1982 (*divorce* 1989) Duncan W Macgregor and *d* 1994, having resumed her maiden name

Seat: Shrubland Park, Barham, Suffolk. An Italianate palace (the gardens were indeed inspired by those of the Villa d'Este), Shrubland defiantly straddles the Suffolk flatlands a few miles north of Ipswich. It was originally a Bacon property (*see* BACON, Bt), and by one of the whimsicalities in which English country-house history abounds is still involved in the curing process — as a health hydro. James Paine, architect also of Brocket Hall, Herts, and Wardour Castle, Wilts, erected the centre block in the early 1770s. Over half a century later J P Gandy-Deering extended the building to include a stepped entrance. Then Sir Charles Barry put up the campanile at one end of the garden front (it has been suggested that Barry's taste for towers dated from his successful plan to rebuild Parliament), topped off the elevations with a balustrade and finally, and most audaciously, jumped back both a hundred years and six hundred miles north in style (from Rome, that is) to round his creation off with two saloons in Louis Quinze. The result is reminiscent of a landlocked Osborne.

DE TRAFFORD

Arms: Argent a griffin segreant gules. **Crest:** A thresher proper, his hat and coat per pale argent and gules, sleeves counterchanged, breeches and stockings of the second and third, his flail of the first, over the flail a scroll with the motto 'Now Thus.' **Motto:** Gripe griffin; hold fast. **Creation:** Bt. (UK) 7 Sept 1841.

SIR DERMOT HUMPHREY DE TRAFFORD 6TH BT, of Trafford Park, Lancashire VRD (1961) [Sir Dermot de Trafford Bt VRD, The Old Vicarage, Appleshaw, Andover, Hants SP11 9BH]; *b* 19 Jan 1925; *s* f 1983; *educ* Harrow and Ch Ch Oxford (MA); Lt-Cdr RNR, FRSA, CIMgt; *m* 1st 26 June 1948 (*divorce* 1973) Patricia Mary, MA Oxford, only dau of Francis Mycroft Beeley, of Long Crumples, nr Alton, Hants, and has:

1 +JOHN HUMPHREY [John De Trafford Esq, 30 Norland Square, London W11 4 PU]; *b* 12 Sept 1950; *educ* Ampleforth and Bristol U (BSc); *m* 1975 *Anne M M, dau of J Faure de Pebeyre, of 134 rue de Courcelles, Paris 17, and has issue:

(1) +Alexander Humphrey; *b* 28 June 1978

(1) *Isabel June; *b* 1980

2 +Edmund Francis; *b* 9 Dec 1952; *educ* Worth and Ch Ch Oxford

3 +Gerard Thomas Joseph; *b* 12 June 1968; *educ* Harrow and Ch Ch Oxford

1 *Mary Annette; *b* 18 March 1949

2 *Elizabeth Eugenie [Mrs John Langdon, 50 Chepstow Rd, London W2]; *b* 26 Dec 1951; *m* 1975 *John Augustin Langdon, and has issue:

(1) *Tobias Hector; *b* 1985

(2) *Frederick George; *b* 1989

3 *(Patricia) Clare; *b* 5 Feb 1955; *m* 1975 *(Patrick) William Uvedale Corbett, and has issue:

(1) *Edmund Uvedale; *b* 1983

(1) *Laura; *b* 1985

4 *Victoria Mary; *b* 4 Feb 1958; *m* 22 Oct 1983 *Andrew Roberts and has issue:

(1) *Mark Lonsdale; *b* 1985

(1) *Katherine; *b* 1987

5 *Cynthia Joan Bernadette; *b* 7 June 1959; *m* 1990 *Nicolas C Kirkman, est son of Maj Charles Kirkman, of Lymington, Hants, and has issue:

(1) *Christopher Chevalier; *b* 1991
(2) *James Alexander; *b* 1994
6 *(Antonia) Lucy Octavia; *b* 12 May 1966; *m* 1994 *David Carotti and has:
(1) *Thomas Raymond Barton; *b* 1997
Sir DERMOT *m* 2nd 22 Dec 1973 *Sandra Carandini, only dau of Lt-Col Geoffrey Trollope Lee and formerly w of Roderick Walter

Lineage: RANULPH/RANDOLPH; had:

RALPH de TRAFFORD, of Lancs; had:

ROBERT de TRAFFORD; had:

HENRY de TRAFFORD; *d c* 1221, leaving:

RICHARD de TRAFFORD; *d c* 1272, having had issue:
1 HENRY (Sir)
2 Geoffrey de Chaderton
1 Anabilla; *m* Robert de Radcliffe

The er son,
Sir HENRY de TRAFFORD, of Trafford; ktd by 1284; *d c* 1288, leaving:

Sir HENRY de TRAFFORD, of Trafford; ktd by 1309; *d c* 1334, leaving a gs:

JOHN de TRAFFORD; *dvp*, leaving:

Sir HENRY de TRAFFORD, of Trafford; of age 1336; *m* Agnes — and had issue:

Sir HENRY de TRAFFORD, of Trafford; *m* Margery, dau of Robert Ince, and *d* 1386, leaving:

HENRY de TRAFFORD, of Trafford; *m* Elizabeth, dau of Sir Ralph Radcliffe, and had, with an er s (Henry, of Trafford, *m* Agnes — (*m* 2nd Sir Robert Sturley) and *dsp c* 1415) and three daus:

Sir EDMOND TRAFFORD, of Trafford; ktd 1426; *m* Alice, est dau and coheir of Sir William Venables, of Bolyn, and *d* 1457, leaving an est s:

Sir JOHN TRAFFORD, of Trafford; ktd 1444; *m* Elizabeth, dau of Sir Thomas Ashton, of Ashton, and had:
1 EDMOND (Sir), his heir
2 William; *d* 1518
1 Dulcia; *m* Hugh Bulkeley, of Whatcroft

Sir JOHN *d* 1488; his est son,
Sir EDMOND TRAFFORD, of Trafford, KB (1495); *m* Margaret, dau of Sir John Savage, of Clifton, and had, with three daus:
1 EDMOND (Sir), his heir
2 William, Under Sheriff Cheshire 1540; *m* Margery, dau of Sir Ralph Longford, of Longford, Derbys
3 Henry, DD, Chllr of York 1528; *d* 1557

Sir EDMOND *d* 1514; his est son,
Sir EDMOND TRAFFORD, of Trafford; *m* Elizabeth, dau of Sir Ralph Longford, of Longford, and had, with five daus:
1 EDMOND (Sir), his heir
2 George, *dsp*
3 Thomas, of Langham, Rutland; *m* Elizabeth, dau of James Fawkener, of Rutland, and was ancestor of the TRAFFORDs of Low Leyton, Essex, and Wroxham Hall, Norfolk
4 Henry, in holy orders
5 Richard

Sir EDMOND *d* 28 June 1533 aged 48; his est son,
Sir EDMOND TRAFFORD, of Trafford; ktd 1544; *m* Anne, dau of Sir Alexander Radcliffe, of Ordsall, Lancs, and *d* 1564, leaving, with other issue:
1 Sir EDMOND TRAFFORD, of Trafford; *b* 3 June 1526; *m* 1st Mary (*dsp*), dau of Lord Edmond Howard (*see* NORFOLK, D); *m* 2nd Elizabeth, dau of Sir Ralph Leicester, of Toft, and had issue:
(1) EDMOND (Sir)
(1) Margaret; *m* Sir Urian Leigh, of Adlington
(2) Elizabeth; *m* Sir John Michel

Sir EDMOND *d* 1590; his son,
Sir EDMOND TRAFFORD, of Trafford; ktd 1603, thrice High Sheriff Lancs; *m* 1st Mary, dau and heir of John Booth, of Barton, Cheshire, and had, with other issue, a dau (Elizabeth, *m* Richard Fleetwood, of Penwortham, Lancs); *m* 2nd Lady Mildred Cecil, dau of 1st Earl of Exeter (*see* EXETER, M) and widow of Sir Thomas Read, and *d* May 1620, leaving:

Sir CECIL TRAFFORD, of Trafford; *b* 15 Aug 1599; ktd 1617; *m* Penelope, dau of Sir Humphrey Davenport, of Sutton, Cheshire, Lord Ch Baron Court of Exchequer, and had, with other issue:
1 Humphrey, of Trafford; *m* 1st — Holland, of Clifton, Lancs; *m* 2nd Katherine, dau of Sir George Warburton, 1st Bt, of Arley, Chester, by whom he had issue:
(1) Humphrey, of Trafford; *m* 15 Aug 1701 Anne, dau and coheir of Sir Ralph Assheton, 2nd Bt, of Middleton, Lancs, and had, with three s (*dsp*) and four daus:
1a Humphrey, of Trafford; *m* Elizabeth, dau of Sir Oswald Mosley, 1st Bt, of Rolleston, Stafford (*see* RAVENSDALE, B), and *dsp* 1 July 1779
2 John, of Croston, Lancs; *m* Anne, dau and coheir of Richard Ashton, of Croston, and *d* 28 Feb 1686, leaving, with other issue:
(1) John, of Croston; *m* 10 Feb 1688 Katherine, dau and coheir of Thomas Culcheth, of Culcheth, Lancs, and *d* 25 Aug 1727, leaving, with other issue (*dsp*):
1a John, of Croston; *b* 18 Feb1689; *m* 1st Elizabeth Thornbury; *m* 2nd 18 Aug 1756 Alice, dau of James Sharrock, of Preston and Fulwood, and *d* 5 Dec 1760, leaving issue:
1b John, of Croston, *dsp* 10 March 1761
1b Katherine Eloisa; *m* Laurence Nihell
2a Humphry, of Croston; *b* 15 Nov 1698; *m* Frances, dau of John Dalton, of Thurnham, Lancs, and *d* 11 Dec 1773, leaving issue:
1b John, of Trafford, previously of Croston; *m* 21 Sept 1773 Elizabeth, dau of Stephen Walter Tempest, of Broughton, Yorks, and *d* 29 Oct 1815, leaving issue:
1c THOMAS JOSEPH, (Sir), **1st Bt**
1c Maria; *m* John Clifton, 2nd son of John Clifton of Lytham

JOHN TRAFFORD's son,
Sir THOMAS JOSEPH TRAFFORD later De TRAFFORD (roy licence Oct 1841), **1st Bt** (UK), so *cr* 7 Sept 1841, of Trafford Park; *b* 22 March 1778; *m* 17 Aug 1803 Laura Anne (*d* 22 Oct 1852), dau and coheir of Francis Colman, of Hillersdon, Devon, and had, with seven daus (including Jemima; *m* Henry Tempest, of Heaton, Lancs, *see* LONDONDERRY, M):
1 HUMPHREY (Sir), **2nd Bt**
2 Thomas William; *b* 23 Aug 1813; *d* unm 7 May 1844
3 John Randolphus, of Croston Hall, Preston, JP; *b* 11 April 1820; *m* 13 July 1850 Lady Adelaide Cathcart (*d* 15 Feb 1871), dau of 2nd Earl Cathcart (*qv*), and *d* 3 Feb 1879, leaving:
(1) Sigismund Cathcart, of Croston Hall, JP (Lancs); Lt 14th Foot; *b* 31 July 1853; *m* 20 Nov 1879 Clementina Frances (*d* 4 June 1937), 4th dau of Sir Pyers Mostyn, 8th Bt (*qv*), and *d* 1 Aug 1936, having had issue:
1a Geoffrey Edmond, of Croston Hall, Lancs, MC (1918), JP; Capt RFA (SR), served WW I (wounded); *b* 12 Dec 1891; *d* unm 29 Nov 1960
2a Reginald Francis; Lt 3rd Bn KOR Lancs Regt; *b* 12 Dec 1891 (twin); *d* 9 May 1915 of wounds received in action
1a Ermyntrude Frances; ARRC; *b* 10 Aug 1883; *d* unm 13 Jan 1964
2a Elfrida Adelaide; *b* 8 June 1886; *m* 23 May 1914 Lord Edward Beauchamp Seymour (*d* 5 Dec 1917 of wounds received in action), Lt Canadian Cav, 3rd son of 6th Marquess of Hertford (*qv*), and *d* 10 Nov 1965
(2) Galfrid Aloysius Cathcart; Lt 2nd Bn Roy Hus; *b* 4 Aug 1865; *m* 20 Aug 1887 Cecile Elizabeth Margaret (*d* 20 May 1945), only child of Count Hubert de Stacpoole, and *d* 12 Feb 1924, having had issue:
1a Cecil Noel; T/2nd Lt Roy W Surrey Regt; *b* 24 Dec 1888; *m* 1st 20 Sept 1917 Mona (*d* 4 April 1920), dau of William Major; *m* 2nd 30 Aug 1929 *Amelie, dau of Pierre Chateau, of Angers, France
2a Ralph Eric Galfrid Antony; Lt Royal Fus; *b* 30 April 1892; *ka* 30 April 1915
1a Daphne Ruth Elizabeth Adelaide Mary; *b* 25 Sept 1903; *d* 10 Feb 1996
(3) Randolphus Cathcart; *b* 4 Sept 1857; *d* unm 31 March 1900
(4) Charles Alan Cathcart, JP Warwickshire; Lt-Col 16th Service Bn Roy Warwicks Regt, V-Consul Brest, WW I in France, HG WW II; *b* 8 Feb 1871; *m* 29 May 1900 Lady Victoria Seymour (*d* 23 April 1960), dau of 6th Marquess of Hertford (*qv*), and *d* 9 May 1950, leaving issue:
1a Joan Agnes Mary Seymour; memb Southam RDC 1961, Subaltern ATS
(1) Henrietta Cathcart; *m* 2 Aug 1877 Hon Henry Robert Orde-Powlett (*d* 9 Feb 1915), and *d* 14 Feb 1934, leaving issue (*see* BOLTON, B)
4 Charles Cecil; *b* 28 Dec 1821; *d* unm 15 Dec 1878
5 Augustus Henry, of Haselour Hall, Tamworth; late 1st Dragoons; *b* 12 April 1823; *m* 19 Sept 1876 Gertrude Mary (*d* 25 Feb 1922), dau of Herman Walmesley, of Gidlow, nr Wigan, and *d* 19 Jan 1895, leaving issue
(1) Henry Joseph, BA Oxon; barrister, Capt 3rd Bn S Staffs Regt; *b* 30 July 1877; *ka* 25 Sept 1915
(2) Augustus Francis, DSO; Lt 1st Bn S Staffs Regt; *b* 27 Oct 1879; *d* unm 1 June 1904
(3) Thomas Cecil; Capt 2nd Bn Roy Fus WW I (wounded); *b* 3 Jan 1881; *m* 7 Sept 1914 Mary Winefride (Freyda) (*m* 2nd 5 June 1924 7th Baron Vaux of Harrowden (*qv*), and *d* 14 Dec 1944), only dau of Sir Joseph Radcliffe, 4th Bt (*qv*), and *d c* 11 Nov 1914, of wounds received in action
(4) Herman St Michael, JP Staffs; Lt 3rd Bn S Staffs Regt WW I (wounded); *b* 1882; *d* unm 10 Feb 1954
(5) Oswald; Maj 2nd Bn S Staffs Regt WW I; *b* 26 July 1885; *m* 23 April 1923 Mary, widow of William Grahame-Jones and dau of Henry Hartley Vale, of Calthorpe Hall, Yorks, and *d* 9 Aug 1942
(6) Robert Ashton (Rev), SJ; RC priest, Lt OTC; *b* 27 Jan 1887; *educ* Stonyhurst and London U (BA); *d* 18 Jan 1969
(7) Edward Aloysius, MC; Capt 3rd Bn S Staffs Regt WW I, silver medal of Savoy; *b* 13 Jan 1892; *d* unm 7 Jan 1960
(1) Mary Hermione; *m* 30 April 1900 George Trevor Basil Mostyn (*d* 17 April 1913), of Haunton Hall, Tamworth, 2nd son of Sir Pyers Mostyn, 8th Bt (*qv*), and *d* 14 March 1955, leaving issue
(2) Jane Seymour Mary; *m* 11 April 1907 Francis Joseph Scott-Murray (*d* 13 Feb 1925), er surv son of Charles Aloysius Scott-Murray, JP Hambledon, and *d* 12 Jan 1957
(3) Gertrude Mary; *m* 28 Sept 1909 Lt-Col William Erdeswick Ignatius Butler-Bowdon (*d* 30 March 1956), DSO, DL, of Southgate House, Derbys, and had issue
(4) Agnes Mary; *d* unm 6 Sept 1978

Sir THOMAS *d* 10 Nov 1852; his est son,
Sir Humphrey de Trafford, 2nd Bt; *b* 1 May 1808; High Sheriff of Lancs 1861; *m* 17 Jan 1855 Lady Mary Annette Talbot (*d* 1 July 1922), est sister and coheir of 17th Earl of Shrewsbury (*see* SHREWSBURY and WATERFORD, E), and had:
1 HUMPHREY FRANCIS (Sir), **3rd Bt**
2 Charles Edmund, of Hothorpe, Theddingwoth, Rugby, DL, JP Northants, and JP Leics; High Sheriff 1893, Kt SMO Malta; *b* 21 May 1864; *m* 15 Oct 1892 Lady Agnes Mary Pia Feilding (*d* 20 July 1921), dau of 8th Earl of Denbigh (*see* DENBIGH and DESMOND, E), and *d* 11 Nov 1951, leaving issue:
(1) Hubert Edmund Francis, Capt 1st Dragoons, Kt Honour and Devotion SMO Malta (Cross of Merit 1st Cl 1959), served WW I (wounded) with 1st Dragoons, WW II with King's Own Malta Regt; *b* 27 Nov 1893; *educ* Downside; *m* 18 Oct 1927 Hon Cecilia Victoria Strickland, 2nd dau of 1st and last Baron Strickland (*see* 1970 edn), of Sizergh Castle, Westmorland, and Villa Bologna, Malta, and *d* 21 March 1974, having had issue:
1a +Gerald Edmund Hubert [Gerald de Trafford Esq, Villa Bologna, Attard, Malta, GC], Kt SMO Malta 1959; *b* 23 Dec 1929; *educ* McGill U Montreal

(BA 1951) and Oxford; *m* 1971 *(Helena Catherina) Charlotte, only dau of Herman Sybrand Hallo, former Dutch Amb, and has issue:

1b +Jasper Peter Paul Sybrand; *b* 1975

1b *Aloisia Cecilia Mary; *b* 1973

2a +Anthony Charles Everard [Anthony de Trafford Esq, Apricot Cottage, Upper Slaughter, Glos GL54 2JQ]; *b* 17 Oct 1935; *educ* Beaumont; *m* 24 Sept 1966 *Gabrielle Frances, only dau of Maj Ronald Edward Boone, of Rockcliffe House, Upper Slaughter, Glos, by Susan Margaret Rose, er dau of Capt Howard John Kennard, RN (*see* KENNARD, Bt)

3a (Hubert) George Joseph; *b* 18 Jan 1937; *m* 1st 7 Jan 1966 (*divorce* 1973) Christine Elizabeth, only dau of Lt-Cdr Maurice Sydney Adams, RN (ret), of Kingswood, Surrey, and has issue:

1b *Rachel Samantha [Mrs Bengt Sjöberg, Tjurgränd 4, 175 45 Järfälla, Stockholm, Sweden]; *b* 2 March 1967; *m* 1991 *Bengt G Sjöberg, and has issue:

1c *Rebecca Linnéa Christine; *b* 10 Sept 1993

2c *Matilda Emma Cecilia; *b* 24 April 1995

2b *Martha Christine Joanna; *b* 7 Nov 1969

3a (cont.) George de Trafford *m* 2nd 1975 *Mary Kate Willis, dau of Lt-Col Edward C A Willis Fleming, and *d* 1993 having had further issue:

1b +John Oliver George; *b* 1976

2b +George Jonathon Augustus; *b* 1980

3b *Fleur Cecilia Kate; *b* 1978

4a John; *b* 9 Oct 1941; *d* 17 March 1943

1a Margaret Annette; *b* 9 Oct 1928; *m* 23 April 1952 Cdr William John Macnamara Faulkner, RN, est s of R-Adml Hugh Webb Faulkner, CB, CBE, DSO, of The Close, Hatch Beauchamp, Taunton, and *d* 18 May 1997, leaving:

1b *Hugh Edmund Brooke [Hugh Faulkner Esq, 77 Laurel Way, London N20 8HT]; *b* 27 Aug 1953; *educ* Ampleforth; *m* 1992 *Hon Mrs Sarah Louise Walsh, er dau of Baron Wedderburn of Charlton (LP, *qv*), and has:

1c *Lucy Grace; *b* 1993

2c *Amy; *b* 1995

2b *Mark William Bingham [Lt-Col Mark Faulkner, Hollintree House, Newsham, Thirsk, N Yorkshire YO7 4DH]; *b* 13 April 1955; *educ* Ampleforth; Lt-Col 5th Royal Dragoon Gds; *m* 1979 *Hon Deborah Jane MacAndrew, only dau of 2nd Baron MacAndrew (*qv*), and has issue:

1c *James William MacAndrew; *b* 21 May 1983

2c *Alexander Charles MacAndrew; *b* 2 April 1987

3c *Patrick Mark MacAndrew; *b* 28 Sept 1992

1b *Rosalinda Mary; *b* 30 March 1958; *m* 1986 *(Francis) Michael Willis, and has issue:

1c *Francis Edmund Hugh; *b* 1989

2c *Robert William Peter; *b* 1991

3c *Matthew Henry Michael; *b* 1993

2b *Catharine Frances [Mrs Andrew Scott, 49 Telford Ave, London SW2 4XL]; *b* 6 April 1961; *m* 1984 *Andrew Templer Scott, and has issue:

1c *Rory David Templer; *b* 1993

1c *Alice Emily Cecilia; *b* 1989

2a *Elizabeth Clare Hilda Melita [Lady Turner, Plantation House, Ockham Rd South, East Horsley, Surrey KT24 6SG]; *b* 4 July 1932; *m* 19 Sept 1963 Adml Sir Arthur Francis Turner, KCB, DSC (*d* 1991), Ch Fleet Support and 4th Sea Ld, s of R-Adml Arthur William John Turner, of Abbotsford, Elie, Fife, and has:

1b *Francis Christopher Neale; *b* 9 June 1966; *m* 1992 *Rebecca Jane Thompson and has:

1c *Jack Francis George; *b* 8 May 1995

2b *Michael Paul Charles; *b* 1969

3a Mary Roma Pia Goditha; *b* 7 March 1934; *m* 19 Sept 1964 *Philip James Gooding [Philip Gooding Esq, The Barn, Sarratt, Herts] and *d* 1983, leaving:

1b *Edward; *b* 18 Feb 1974

1b *Louise Alexandra Mary; *b* 27 May 1967; *m* 1994 *Ryan Oliver

2b *Elizabeth Victoria; *b* 16 July 1969; *m* 1995 *Richard Fenton

(1) Clare Mary Annette; *b* 22 Dec 1895; *m* 19 Aug 1916 Sir Edric Charles Joseph Wolseley, 10th Bt (*qv*), and *d* 27 June 1978, having had issue

(2) Hilda Mary Bartha Clare; *b* 22 Sept 1898; *d* unm 29 Nov 1967

3 Gilbert Talbot Joseph; *b* 20 May 1871; *d* 14 July 1890

1 Mildred Mary Josephine; *b* 27 March 1856; *m* 8 Aug 1883 3rd Baron Bellew (*qv*) and *d* 29 Dec 1934

2 Gundrede Annette Teresa; *b* 9 Oct 1860; *m* 22 Sept 1885 Sir Timothy Carew O'Brien , 3rd Bt (*qv*), and *d* 17 Dec 1952, leaving issue

3 Mary Annette; *b* 9 Sept 1865; *m* 27 Sept 1905 Samuel Sproston (*d* 2 May 1950), and *d* 3 Sept 1934

4 Sicele Agnes; *b* 22 Feb 1867; *m* 2 June 1892 Charles William Clifford (*d* 21 Sept 1939), of the Red House, Market Drayton, son of Sir Charles Clifford, 1st Bt (*qv*), and *d* 5 Feb 1948, leaving issue

5 Mary Hilda; *b* 11 Feb1875, *d* unm 1965

Sir HUMPHREY *d* 4 May 1886; his er son,

Sir Humphrey Francis de Trafford, 3rd Bt; Maj and Hon Lt-Col Lancs Hus; *b* 8 July 1862; *m* 9 Aug 1886 Violet Alice Maud (*d* 20 July 1925), dau of James Franklin, Lt 2nd WI Regt and 77th Regt (The Royals), and *d* 10 Jan 1929, leaving:

1 **Sir Humphrey Edmund de Trafford, 4th Bt**, MC, DL (Herts 1946), JP (Herts 1944); *b* 30 Nov 1891; *educ* Oratory Sch and RMC Sandhurst; High Sheriff Herts 1945, racehorse owner and breeder, Sr Steward Jockey Club 1936 and 1942–53, Capt Coldstream Gds WW I (despatches); *m* 2 Oct 1917 Hon Cynthia Hilda Evelyn (*d* 13 March 1966), 3rd dau and coheir of Viscount Chelsea, 2nd son of 5th Earl Cadogan (*qv*), and *dspm* 6 Oct 1971, leaving:

(1) Ann (Dame), DCVO (1977), Ch Commr Cwlth Girl Guides Assoc; *b* 14th July 1918; *m* 14 Feb 1939 Derek Henry Parker Bowles, only surv son of Eustace Bowles, of Far Croft, Market Drayton, Salop, and had issue (*see* MACCLESFIELD, E)

(2) *Mary [Lady Bowes-Lyon, Beltingham House, Bardon Mill, Hexham, Northumberland]; *b* 23 Feb 1920; *m* 22 April 1941 Maj-Gen Sir James Bowes-Lyon KCVO, CB, OBE, MC (*d* 1977), and has issue (*see* STRATHMORE AND KINGHORNE, E)

(3) *Violet [Lady Aitken, Mickleham Downs House, Dorking, Surrey]; *b* 17 June 1926; *m* 1 Jan 1951 Gp Capt Sir (John William) Maxwell Aitken, 2nd Bt (*d* 1985), DSO, DFC (briefly 2nd Baron Beaverbrook, *qv*), and has issue

(4) *Catherine [Mrs Fulke Walwyn, Saxon House Stables, Lambourn, Berks]; *b* 5 Nov 1928; *m* 24 June 1952 Fulke Thomas Tyndall Walwyn, CVO (*d* 1991), racehorse trainer, son of Lt-Col Fulke James Walwyn, DSO, Roy Welch Fus, of Plas Hendy, Raglan, Mon, and has issue:

1a *Jane; *b* 1957

2 RUDOLPH EDGAR FRANCIS (Sir) , **5th Bt**

3 Raymond Vincent; *b* 28 Jan 1900; Lt Coldstream Gds; *m* 1st 22 Feb 1932 (*divorce* 1938) Alice (*d* 19 March 1943), formerly wife of Count Frederick de Janzé, of Paris, and dau of William Edward Silverthrone, of Riverside, Ill., USA; *m* 2nd 19 May 1951 *Eve, est dau of George Henry Drummond, of Mount Rule, IoM (*see* PERTH, E), and *dsp* 14 May 1971

1 Violet Mary; *b* 8 May 1893; *m* 1st 29 Jan 1919 (*annulled* 1921) Capt Hon Rupert Oswald Derrick Keppel (*d* 7 May 1964), Coldstream Gds, 3rd son of 8th Earl of Albemarle (*qv*); *m* 2nd 3 Oct 1922 Col Keith Graham Menzies (*d* 7 Dec 1952), OBE MC, Welsh Gds, and *dsp* 28 Feb 1968

The 4th Bt's bro,

Sir Rudolph Edgar Francis de Trafford, 5th Bt, OBE; *b* 31 Aug 1894; *educ* Downside and Trin Coll Cambridge (BA 1915); Capt WW I (despatches twice), dir Roy Exchange; *m* 1st 6 Feb 1924 (*divorce* 1938) June Isabel, MBE (*d* 1977), only dau of Lt-Col Reginald Chaplin, and had issue:

1 Sir DERMOT HUMPHREY DE TRAFFORD, **6th and present Bt**

Sir Rudolph *m* 2nd 2 Feb 1939 Mrs Katherine Lo Savio, eldest dau of W W Balke, of Cincinnati, USA, and *d* 1983

DE VESCI

Arms: Or on a cross sable a patriarchal cross of the field. **Crest:** A dexter hand erect in armour holding a laurel branch, all proper. **Supporters:** Two figures of Hercules each holding in his exterior hand a club over his shoulder, habited about the middle, all proper. **Motto:** *Sub hoc signo vinces* ('Under this sign thou shalt conquer'). **Creations:** Bt. (I) 28 Sept 1698, B. (I) 10 April 1750, V. (I) 19 July 1776.

THE 7TH VISCOUNT DE VESCI OF ABBEY LEIX, Queen's Co, **Baron Knapton**, of Queen's Co, Ireland, and a **Baronet** (Sir Thomas (Tom) Eustace Vesey, Bt) [The Rt Hon The Viscount de Vesci, 14 Rumbold Rd, London SW6 2JA]; *b* 8 Oct 1955; *s* f 1983; *educ* Eton and Univ Coll Oxford; Lt Irish Gds (SR); *m* 1987 *Sita-Maria Arabella, dau of Brian de Breffny, of Castletown Cox, Co Kilkenny, and Maharaj Kumari Jyotsna Dutt, dau of Maharajadhiraja Bahadur Sir Uday Chand Mahtab of Burdwan, KCIE, and has issue:

1 *Damian Brian John; *b* 1985

2 +OLIVER IVO; *b* 16 July 1991

1 *Cosima Frances; *b* 1988

Lineage: Ven THOMAS VESEY, Rector Ballinascullen and Maghera, Diocese of Derry, 1629; Rector Coleraine 1635, Archdeacon Armagh 1655; had:

1 JOHN (Most Rev)

2 Theodore (Rev); *b* 1641; scholar Trin Coll Dublin 1660, Prev Kilnaglory, Co Cork; *d* 1682, leaving:

(1) Theodore; *b* 1672

1 Lettice; *m* Merrick Hart, of Crobert, Co Cavan

Archdeacon VESEY *d* 1662; his er s,

Most Rev JOHN VESEY; *b* 1638; DD, Archbp Tuam, PC, Ld Justice Ireland; *m* 1st (licence 1662) Rebecca Wilson and had:

1 THOMAS (Sir), **1st Bt**

1 Mary; *m* 13 March 1682 Sir Robert Staples, 4th Bt (*qv*) and had issue

JOHN VESEY *m* 2nd Anne, dau of Col Agmondisham Muschamp, and by her had:

2 Agmondisham, of Lucan, Co Dublin, ancestor of the VESEYs of Lucan

3 John (Rev); his gdau, Catherine Vesey, w of Rt Hon James FitzGerald, was *cr* 31 July 1826 BARONESS FitzGERALD AND VESEY OF CLARE AND INCHICRONAN, Co Clare (I)
4 William; *m* Mrs Mary Ormsby and *d* between 13 March 1734/5 and 19 July 1735, leaving issue
5 George, of Hollymount, Co Mayo; *m* Frances, dau of Archibald Stewart, of Ballintoy, Co Antrim, and was ggf of Samuel Vesey, of Derrabard House, Co Tyrone, DL, JP
6 Muschamp, Archdeacon of Leighlin; *m* 1735 Elizabeth, yst dau of Mathew Forde, of Seaforde, and *d* between 9 Aug 1761 and 4 Feb 1762
2 Elizabeth; *m* 1723/4 Richard Dawson, MP Co Monaghan, and had:
(1) THOMAS DAWSON, 1st VISCOUNT CREMORNE (*see* 1933 edn DARTREY, E)
3 Leonora; *m* Rev Archibald Stewart, of Ballintoy
4 Elizabeth, Mrs Walker
5 Catherine; *m* Ven James Smyth, Archdeacon of Meath
6 Anne; *m* Rt Hon Henry Bingham, MP

JOHN VESEY *d* 28 March 1716; his est son,

Rev Sir Thomas Vesey, 1st Bt (I), so *cr* 28 Sept 1698; Bp Killaloe 1711 and Ossory 1712; *m* Mary, dau and heir of Denny Muschamp, of Horsley, Surrey, Muster-Master-Gen of Ireland, by Elizabeth, est dau of Dr Michael Boyle, Archbp Armagh, and had issue:
1 JOHN DENNY (Sir), **1st Baron**
1 Frances Muschamp; *m* 20 Jan 1717, as his first wife, Caesar Colclough (*d* 15 April 1766), of Duffrey Hall, MP Co Wexford, and *dsps* 1719
2 Elizabeth; *m* 1st William Handcock (*see* CASTLEMAINE, B); *m* 2nd her cousin Agmondisham Vesey, MP Lucan, Accountant-Gen of Ireland

Sir THOMAS *d* 6 Aug 1730; his son,

Sir John Denny Vesey, 2nd Bt, and **1st Baron Knapton**, of Queen's Co (I), so *cr*10 April 1750; *m* 1732 Elizabeth, dau of William Brownlow (*see* BROWNLOW, B), and had:
1 THOMAS, **1st Viscount**
1 Elizabeth; *m* 1st 1751 Robert Handcock (*see* CASTLEMAINE, B); *m* 2nd 1762 Edmund, Viscount Pery (*see* LIMERICK, E), and *d* 1821
2 Anne; *m* 23 Aug 1753 Thomas, Viscount Northland, and *d* 21 Oct 1803, leaving issue (*see* RANFURLY, E)
3 Jane; *m* 1776 Sir Robert Staples, 7th Bt (*qv*), and *d* 1822

Sir JOHN *d* 25 July 1761; his son,

THOMAS VESEY, **1st Viscount de Vesci of Abbey Leix**, Queen's Co (I), so *cr* 19 July 1776; *m* 24 April 1769 Selina Elizabeth, est dau and coheir of Sir Arthur Brooke, 1st and last Bt (*see* BROOKEBOROUGH, V), and had, with other issue:
1 JOHN, **2nd Viscount**
2 Arthur (Rev); *b* 3 March 1773; Rector Abbeyleix, Chllr Diocese of Killaloe; *m* 1810 Sydney (*d* 13 July 1860), only dau of Edward Johnstone, of Woodpark House, Co Armagh, and *d* 5 Dec 1832, leaving issue:
(1) John Thomas; *b* 10 Oct 1815; *d* 1881
(2) Arthur George; *b* 20 Nov 1818; Col 46th Regt; *m* Aug 1854 Helena Augusta (*m* 2nd 19 Dec 1872 William Agnew Pope (*d* Dec 1890), Capt 101st Regt, and *d* 5 March 1925), dau of Col J Dawson, and *d* 18 Oct 1868, leaving:
1a Arthur Sydney; *b* 29 May 1856; Maj Essex Regt; *m* Marie Leon (*d* 26 Oct 1925), dau of Joseph Adshead, and *dsp* 24 July 1890
1a Constance Lucinda Irene; *d* unm 30 Dec 1947
2a Alexandrina Maude; *m* 1st 19 June 1877 Count Richard Bethell Metaxa (*d* 5 July 1888) and had issue; *m* 2nd 14 Aug 1890 Col Frederick George Steuart (*d* 12 May 1912), s of Col Thomas David Steuart, Bombay Cav, gs of John Steuart, 7th of Dalguise, and *d* 14 July 1923
(3) Edward; *b* 24 Jan 1821; Dep Paymaster-Gen CS; *m* 16 Jan 1854 Anne Julia (*d* 2 Jan 1900), yst dau of Samuel Page, of Hadley, and *d* 5 Jan 1916, having had:
1a Arthur Henry; *b* 13 Jan 1859; AMICE; *d* unm 6 Jan 1899
2a Edward Darby; *b* 14 April 1862; barrister; *d* unm
3a Herbert Charles; *b* 17 Jan 1864; Capt IA; *ka* Somaliland 17 April 1903
4a William; *b* 1 May 1868; *d* 2 April 1928
1a Geraldine Louisa; *m* 4 April 1888 Frederick Beard, MB, MRCS, and *d* 11 Jan 1945, leaving issue
2a Kathleen Frances, *d* unm 1 April 1946
(4) Charles, Adml RN, ADC to Ld Lt Ireland; *b* 4 March 1823; *m* 20 Dec 1860 Harriet (*dsp* 10 Oct 1897), est dau of Sheffield Grace, KH, of the Knole, Sussex (*see* 1970 edn GRACE, Bt), and *dsp* 18 Feb 1904
(5) George Henry, Maj-Gen RA; *b* 29 Dec 1824; *m* 18 Oct 1966 Constance (*d* 25 Dec 1927), 2nd dau of George Marshall, and *d* 29 Jan 1893, leaving issue:
1a John Fraser Gore; *b* 26 Dec 1867; *d* 11 March 1871
2a Charles Edward Gore, Lt-Col RE, served Ashanti Expdn 1895–96 and WW I (despatches twice, 1914 star); *b* 27 May 1871; *m* 16 Dec 1920 Mary Dorothea (*d* 21 June 1966), dau of Arthur Henry Loring, and *d* 17 April 1958, having had issue:
1b Thomas George, Lt RA WW II; *b* 12 Dec 1921, *ka* Italy Oct 1944
1b *Claudine Mary Rosalind [Mrs William Brown, Red Wing, South Park, Sevenoaks, Kent TN13 1EL], MB, ChB, MRCS Eng and LRCP Lond 1950, DCH Eng 1954; *m* 12 Dec 1959 *William Anthony Barry Brown, LDSRCS, MS, yr s of Col Patrick Edward Brown, and has had:
1c *Martin Thomas Vesey; *b* 25 Sept 1960; *m* 1996 *Caroline Gray
2c James Benedict; *b* 15 Sept 1961; *d* 1990
3c *Adrian Walter; *b* 13 Feb 1963
1c *Susan Mary Loring; *b* 15 Jan 1965; *m* 1993 *Nicholas Stephen Wiltshire and has:
1d *Reuben; *b* 1996
1d *Martha Constance; *b* 1992
3a Ivo Lucius Beresford (Sir), KBE (1923), CMG (1919), DSO (1917); *b* 11 Aug 1876; *educ* Wellington; Gen Queen's Royal Regt, Dir Organisationn War Office 1919–22, AVM, Dir Organisation and Staff Duties Air Ministry 1923–29, Cdr 48th (S Midland) Div (TA) 1930–31, Dir Staff Duties War Office 1931–34, GOC Western Command India 1935 and Southern Command 1936–37, CGS India 1937–39, ret 1939, cmded Bn HG 1940–42, Dep Regl Commnr Southern Region 1942; served S Africa 1899–1902 (severely wounded, despatches) and WW I (despatches four times), Offr Legion of Honour, Order Crown Belgium, Croix de Guerre, Order St Maurice and St Lazarus Italy, Col The Queen's Regt 1939–45; *m* 28 Jan 1913 Geraldine (*d* 16 Sept 1963), er dau of V-Adml Francis John Foley (*see* FOLEY, B), and *d* 19 Feb 1975, having had issue:
1b Desmond Ivo; *b* 27 Nov 1913; *educ* Wellington and Corpus Christi Coll Cambridge
2b Christopher Thomas, MC; Maj RHA WW II (wounded); *b* 8 March 1916; *educ* Wellington; *m* 29 Nov 1952 *Helen Cynthia Mary (*m* 2nd 15 Dec 1969 Brig Ferdinand Shaw Eiloart OBE (*d* 1993)) [Mrs Ferdinand Eiloart, Vinesse Farm, Little Horkesley, Essex CO6 4DT], dau of Brig Wilfrid Algernon Ebsworth, CB, CBE, of Camberley, Surrey, and *d* 30 Aug 1956, leaving issue:
1c +Nicholas Ivo [The Rev Nicholas Vesey, 2 Tudor Court, Tunbridge Wells, TN2 5Q8]; *b* 7 Sept 1954
2c +Thomas Wilfrid; *b* 17 July 1956; *m* 1981 *Marie-Christine Joaiane Renée, yst dau of Roger Landon, of Pamiers, France, and has issue:
1d +Alexander Thomas Ferdinand; *b* 1981
2d +Sebastien Guillaume; *b* 1989
1d *Olivia Denise Helen; *b* 1984
1a Isabel Constance, OBE (1920); Cmdt Empress Eugenie's Hosp for Offrs Farnborough WW I, *d* unm 7 Sept 1966 aged 97
2a Dorothea Claudine Rothe; *m* 19 April 1913 Wilfrid Fowke (*d* 7 April 1951), son of Maj — Fowke, of St Martin's, Guernsey, and *d* 17 June 1948, leaving issue
3a Rose Mildred Stewart; *d* 11 April 1919
(6) William Muschamp, of Upton House, Co Carlow, JP; *b* 23 June 1827; *m* 16 Oct 1871 Anne Henrietta (*d* 26 Feb 1927), 2nd dau of Philip Jocelyn Newton, DL, of Dunleckney, Co Carlow, and *d* 24 Sept 1880, leaving issue:
1a Sydney Philip Charles, CBE (1918), JP Co Carlow; T/Capt KRRC; *b* 9 March 1873; *educ* Ch Ch Oxford (MA); *m* 24 April 1902 Blanche Edith, dau of Edmund Nicholas Power, of Tranmore House, Co Waterford, and *d* 29 Oct 1932
2a Charles; *b* 10 Feb 1874; *d* unm 1 Nov 1911
(1) Jane; *m* 30 Sept 1841 Very Rev Henry Barry Knox, co-Dean Bocking, and *d* 13 Nov 1846
(2) Selina Elizabeth, *d* unm 6 Oct 1902
(3) Frances Sydney; *m* 3 May 1838 Thomas FitzHerbert (*d* 29 April 1879), of Black Castle, Co Meath, and *d* 20 Sept 1908, leaving issue
(4) Louisa Catherine; *d* 19 Dec 1920 aged 91
1 Selina; *m* 1800 Andrew Savage Nugent (*d* Feb 1846), of Portaferry, Co Down

The 1st VISCOUNT *d* 13 Oct 1804; his est son,

JOHN VESEY, **2nd Viscount de Vesci of Abbey Leix**; Ld Lt Queen's Co; *b* 15 Feb 1771; *m* 25 Aug 1800 Frances Letitia (*d* 6 June 1840), dau of William Brownlow (*see* LURGAN, B), and had issue:
1 THOMAS, **3rd Viscount**
2 William John; *b* 12 Aug 1806; *m* July 1837 Isabella Elizabeth (*d* 8 March 1900), dau of Rev Francis Brownlow (*see* LURGAN, B), and *d* 3 Aug 1863
1 Catherine; *m* 30 April 1833 her cousin Lt-Col Patrick John Nugent (*d* Nov 1857), of Portaferry House, Co Down, and *d* 27 Feb 1882, leaving issue

The 2nd VISCOUNT *d* 19 Oct 1855; his er son,

THOMAS VESEY, **3rd Viscount de Vesci of Abbey Leix**; *b* 21 Sept 1803; rep I peer; *m* 19 Sept 1839 Lady Emma Herbert (*d* 10 Oct 1884), dau of 11th Earl of Pembroke and (8th Earl of) Montgomery (*qv*) and *d* 23 Dec 1875, leaving:
1 JOHN ROBERT WILLIAM VESEY, **4th Viscount de Vesci of Abbey Leix** and 1st and last BARON DE VESCI OF ABBEY-LEIX, Queen's Co (UK), so *cr* 8 Nov 1884; Lt and Custos Rotulorum Queen's Co, Lt-Col Coldstream Gds and HAC London; *b* 21 May 1844; *m* 4 June 1872 Lady Evelyn Charteris (*d* 18 June 1939), est dau of 10th Earl of Wemyss (*qv*), and *dspm* 6 July 1903, when the UK Barony expired, leaving:
(1) Mary Gertrude; *b* 10 April 1889; *m* 20 Oct 1910 Hon Aubrey Nigel Henry Molyneux Herbert (*d* 26 Sept 1923), MP, 2nd s of 4th Earl of Carnarvon (*qv*), and *d* 28 Nov 1970, leaving issue
2 Eustace, MA; Capt 9th Lancers; *b* 31 Jan 1851; *m* 19 June 1877 Hon Constance Mary Lawley (*m* 2nd 7 July 1892 Hon Edward William Berkeley Portman (*dsp* 27 April 1911), est s of 2nd Viscount Portman (*qv*), and *d* 4 May 1951), 3rd dau of 2nd Baron Wenlock (*see* 1932 edn), and *d* 18 Nov 1886, having had:
(1) Eustace Thomas Beilby; *b* 18 Aug 1878; *d* 9 April 1882
(2) YVO RICHARD VESEY, **5th Viscount de Vesci of Abbey Leix**, JP, DL Queen's Co; rep I peer, Maj Irish Gds, with BEF 1918, cmded 6th Bn Shropshire HG WW II (SR), Dep Assist Dir Forestry; *b* 15 Dec 1881; *m* 1st 24 April 1906 (*divorce* 1919) Georgiana Victoria (*d* 22 April 1930), only dau of Gerald Edward Wellesley (*see* COWLEY, E); *m* 2nd 15 May 1920 (Frances) Lois, widow of 5th Earl of Rosse (*qv*) and 2nd dau of Sir Cecil Edmund Lister-Kaye, 4th Bt (*qv*), and *dsp* 16 Aug 1958
(3) Osbert Eustace (Sir), KCVO (1956, CVO 1953), CMG (1950), CBE (1919); Lt-Col Reserve of Offrs 9th Lancers, served WW I (despatches thrice) and WW II, Legion of Honour, memb Gentlemen-at-Arms 1922 (Clerk of the Cheque and Adj 1948–53, Standard Bearer1953–57); *b* 20 Feb 1884; granted with yr bro rank 14 April 1904 of viscount's yr s; *educ* Eton and RMC Sandhurst; *m* 3 Feb 1910 Dorothy (*d* 24 June 1961), yst dau of William Morison Strachan, of Strood Park, Horsham, and *d* 20 July 1957, leaving issue:
1a Elizabeth; *b* 6 Nov 1910; *m* 26 March 1931 Lt-Col William Dudley Henry Charles Forbes of Callendar, Coldstream Gds (*d* 13 Aug 1977), and had issue
2a Anne; *b* 22 Aug 1914; *m* 7 Jan 1937 (*divorce* 1949) Maj Lord Roderic Armyne Gordon, MBE, TD (*see* HUNTLY, M), and *d* 6 Jan 1997, leaving issue

(4) Thomas Eustace; Lt-Col Reserve of Offrs Irish Gds WW I (wounded twice, 1914 Star, Croix de Guerre); *b* 21 Dec 1885; *educ* Eton and Ch Ch Oxford; *m* 28 Oct 1911 Lady Cecily Kathleen Browne, dau of 5th Earl of Kenmare (*see* 1949 edn), Ldy-in-Waiting to HRH THE DUCHESS OF GLOUCESTER 1947–51, Woman Bedchamber to HM QUEEN MARY 1951–53, Extra Lady-in-Waiting to HRH DUCHESS OF GLOUCESTER 1953, and *d* 1 Feb 1946, leaving:

1a JOHN EUSTACE, **6th Viscount**

1a *Margaret Constance [Mrs Herbert Quinton, 6 Forest Field, Horsham, Sussex]; *b* 9 Nov 1912; *m* 24 Aug 1946 Maj Herbert William Quinton and has:

1b *Thomas William; *b* 4 July 1947; *m* 1975 *Beverley Eileen, dau of H Lestor Price

2b *Christopher John *b* 16 Dec 1948; *m* 1969 *Carol, dau of Clifford H Green, and has:

1c *William Alan John; *b* 1972

2c *Thomas Henry Alexander; *b* 1973

3c *Michael Patrick James; *b* 1979

1c *Catherine Sarah; *b* 1969

3b *Peter Valentine; *b* 21 May 1953; *m* 1979 *Deborah Helen, dau of Bernard Boucher

1b *Caroline Mary; *b* 15 June 1950; *m* 1976 *John Grinsted and has:

1c *Matthew John; *b* 1981

1c *Sarah Margaret; *b* 1979

2a *Bridget Georgiana [Lady Airey, The White Cottage, Hempnall, Norwich NR15 2NG]; *b* 6 Feb 1915; *m* 1 July 1947 Lt-Gen Sir Terence Sydney Airey, KCMG, CB, CBE (*d* 1983)

1 Frances Isabella Catherine; *m* 20 Aug 1861 4th Marquess of Bath (*qv*) and *d* 31 Oct 1915, leaving issue

2 Georgiana Mary, *d* unm 7 Nov 1923

3 Beatrice Charlotte Elizabeth; *m* 5 Nov 1874 1st Baron Stalbridge (*see* WESTMINSTER, D) and *d* 15 Jan 1876, leaving issue

The 5th VISCOUNT's nephew,

JOHN EUSTACE VESEY, **6th Viscount de Vesci of Abbey Leix**; served WW II (wounded, POW), FLAS(O); *b* 25 Feb 1919; *m* 20 May 1950 Susan Anne (*d* 1986), only dau of Ronald Owen Lloyd Armstrong-Jones, MBE, QC (*see* SNOWDON, E), and the Countess of Rosse (*qv*), and *d* 13 Oct 1983, having had:

1 THOMAS EUSTACE VESEY, **7th and present Viscount de Vesci**

1 *Emma Frances [The Hon Mrs Zalkind, 186 Highland Ave, Newtonville, MA 01260, USA]; *b* 17 March 1951; *m* 1986 *Norman Zalkind and has:

(1) *Susan; *b* 1987

2 *Catherine Anne [The Hon Mrs Cretton, Le Plot, 74570 Groisy, France]; *b* 19 May 1953; *m* 1984 *Bruno Cretton and has issue:

(1) *Matthew John; *b* 1985

(2) *Alexis Pierre; *b* 1988

(1) *Cecily Anne; *b* 1986

(2) *Madeleine; *b* 1991

3 Georgina Mary; *b* 2 Sept 1963; *d* 14 March 1965

De Villiers

Arms: Azure a bend enhanced argent, on a mount in base a paschal lamb proper. **Crest:** Issuant from a circlet of gold embellished with nine pearls raised upon points, a dexter arm in armour embowed, grasping in the hand a seax argent. **Supporters:** On either side a springbok proper gorged with a circlet of gold embellished by nine pearls raised upon points. **Motto:** *La main à l'œuvre* ('All hands to work'). **Creation:** B. (UK) 21 Sept 1910.

THE 3RD BARON DE VILLIERS, of Wynberg, in the Province of the Cape of Good Hope, in the Union of South Africa (Arthur Percy de Villiers) [The Rt Hon The Lord de Villiers, PO Box 66, Kumeu, Auckland 1250, NZ]; *b* 17 Dec 1911; *s* f 1934; *educ* Magdalen Coll Oxford (BA. 1936); barrister Inner Temple 1938 and Auckland Supreme Court 1949; *m* 9 Nov 1939 (*divorce* 1958) Edna Alexis Lovett, est dau of Rev Dr Alexander D Mackinnon, of Williams Lake, British Columbia, Canada, and has issue:

1 +ALEXANDER CHARLES; *b* 29 Dec 1940; *m* 1966 (*divorce* 19–) —

1 *Celia Yvonne Lovett; *b* 7 Nov 1942; *m* 1st 23 March 1968 (*divorce* 1978) Robin Hastings Sancroft Beck, son of Hastings Beck, of Cape Town, and has issue:

(1) *Donovan Henry; *b* 27 April 1968

(2) *Robert Arthur; *b* 5 Oct 1974

(1) *Honor Alexa Catherine; *b* 12 Oct 1970

1 (cont.) The Hon Mrs Celia Beck *m* 2nd 1979 *Alan McCallum, and has further issue:

(2) *Georgina Kay Lovett; *b* 1983

2 *Rosemary Aletta; *b* 20 March 1946; *m* 1st 1967 (*divorce* 1979) Robin Anderson Elliott, TD, and has issue:

(1) *Robert Alexander Blyth; *b* 14 Oct 1970

(2) *Hector de Villiers James; *b* 1 March 1973

(3) *Conrad Lovat Johnston; *b* 6 April 1974

Lineage: PIERRE de VILLIERS, a Huguenot refugee from La Rochelle, France, settled in South Africa 6 May 1689; *m* Elizabeth, dau of Isaac Tallefer, a Huguenot refugee from Château Thierry, France, and left issue:

PIERRE de VILLIERS; *b* 26 Dec 1695; *m* Hester Roux, and left issue:

PIETER de VILLIERS; *b* 1 July 1725; *m* Johanna de Villiers, and left issue:

JACOB NICOLAS de VILLIERS, of Paarl, Cape of Good Hope; *b* 26 Nov 1786; *m* Susanna Bernhardi, and left:

CHARLES CHRISTIAN de VILLIERS, of Paarl; *b* 26 Oct 1811; *m* 8 Dec 1830 Dorothea Elizabeth (*d* 2 July 1857), dau of Johannes Hendrik Retief, and *d* 8 May 1854, leaving issue:

1 Jacob Nicolas Peter; *b* 27 Sept 1837; *m* 10 Dec 1873 Annie, dau of David P Marais

2 JOHN HENRY, **1st Baron**

3 Charles Christian; *b* 22 May 1847; *m* 21 Oct 1873 Lily, dau of Paul Zacharias de Villiers, and *d* Aug 1837

4 Melius; *b* 5 Sept 1849; *m* 1883 Adelaide, dau of Rev John Holmes-Orr, and *d* 6 July 1938, leaving issue

1 Helena Alida

2 Susanna Magaretha; *m* 1870 Rev Jacobus Pieter Jordaan and *d* 3 May 1881, leaving issue

3 Catharina Maria

4 Johanna Emerentia

The 2nd son,

Sir JOHN HENRY DE VILLIERS, **1st Baron de Villiers**, of Wynberg, in the province of the Cape of Good Hope, in the Union of South Africa (UK), so *cr* 21 Sept 1910, KCMG (1882), PC (1896); *b* 15 June 1842; *educ* South African Coll and Utrecht and Berlin Us; barrister Inner Temple 1865, Memb Cape Parliament for Worcester 1866–73, Attorney-Gen Cape Colony 1872–74, Ch Justice Cape Colony and Pres of Legislative Cncl 1874–1910, Ch Justice Supreme Court of the Union of South Africe 1910–14, Acting Govr-General Union 1914, a Roy Commr for the settlement of the Transvaal 1881, Delegate to the Colonial Conference 1894, Pres of the Convention for drafting the Constitution for United South Africa 1909, Member Cncl U of Cape of Good Hope, Hon LLD 1901, ktd 1877, Memb Judicial Ctee; *m* 7 March 1871 Aletta Johanna (*d* Aug 1922), dau of Jan Pieter Jordaan, of Worcester, Cape Colony, and had issue:

1 CHARLES PERCY, **2nd Baron**

2 Jean Henry Tallefer; *b* 30 Nov 1879; *m* 18 June 1910 Minnie, dau of Manuel Daniel Urtel, of Hoelenhof, Cape of Good Hope, and *dsp* 1944

1 Alida Johanna; *b* 1 Jan 1873; *m* 11 March 1897 Phillippus Albertus Myburgh Cloete, of Oosterzee, Wynberg, and *d* 17 Oct 1918, leaving issue

The 1st BARON *d* 2 Sept 1914; his son,

CHARLES PERCY De VILLIERS, **2nd Baron de Villiers**; *b* 24 Nov 1871; *m* 14 Jan 1911 Adelheid Selma Hélene (*d* 28 Jan 1968), dau of Henri Christian Koch, of Pietermaritzburg, Natal, and *d* 10 Feb 1934, leaving issue:

1 ARTHUR PERCY De VILLIERS, **3rd and present Baron de Viliers**

2 John Maurice; *b* 13 June 1915; *educ* U of Cape Town (BA 1947); slr 1950, F/Lt RAF; *m* 1946 *Christine Mary [The Hon Mrs John de Villiers, 61 Berg'n See, Hermanus 7200, Cape, S Africa], dau of A C Buller, of Dwarsriviershoek, Stellenbosch, and *d* 1988, leaving:

(1) *Jeanne Clair [Mrs Patrick Grierson, 228 Erskine Ave, Toronto, Canada M4P 1Z4] ; *b* 23 March 1947; *m* 1st 1968 Peter Puttick; *m* 2nd 1972 *Patrick Grierson

(2) *Michèle Jacqueline; *b* 12 Sept 1950

1 *Yvonne Aletta [The Hon Mrs Hill, 2/7 Tyndall St, Surrey Hills, Vic 3127, Australia]; *b* 25 Aug 1913; *educ* LMH Oxford; *m* 3 Oct 1939 James Kenneth Hill (*d* 9 April 1997), and has:

(1) *Antony James de Villiers; *b* 1 Aug 1940; *educ* Sydney U (BA)

(2) *Richard Lansley; *b* 6 Jan 1946

(3) *Hamish Robert; *b* 23 April 1949

(1) *Susan Felicity; *b* 27 Oct 1942

DEVITT

Arms: Per pale gules and azure a bascule argent chained, or, in chief, a fountain. **Crest:** A merman azure, pointing with the index finger of the dexter hand, and holding in the sinister a rudder gold. **Motto:** *De vita vis* ('Strength as to life'). **Creation:** Bt. (UK) 4 July 1916.

SIR JAMES HUGH THOMAS DEVITT, 3RD BT, of Chelsea, in the County of London [Sir James Devitt Bt, The Old Rectory, Ford Lane, Alresford, Essex CO7 8AX]; *b* 18 Sept 1956; *s* f 1995; *educ* Sherborne and Corpus Christi Coll Cambridge (MA), Govr Pangbourne Coll; *m* 20 April 1985 *Susan Carol, er dau of Dr (Adrian) Michael Campbell Duffus, of Woodhouse Farm, Thelbridge, Crediton, Devon, and has:

1 +JACK THOMAS MICHAEL; *b* 29 July 1988
2 +William James Alexander; *b* 1990
1 *Gemma Florence; *b* 1987

Lineage: ANDREW DEVITT, of Newry, Co Down; *m* Elizabeth — and *d* 29 Oct 1833, leaving issue:

THOMAS HENRY DEVITT, of Hackney, Middx; *b* 25 March 1800; *m* 6 Feb 1838 Margaret (*d* 1 March 1876), 2nd dau of Barzillai Lane, of Lansdown Place, Hackney, and *d* 17 Feb 1860, having had an est s:

Sir Thomas Lane Devitt, 1st Bt (UK), so *cr* 4 July 1916; *b* 28 March 1839; Pres Inst of Shipbrokers, Fndr and Chm of Shipping Fedn, Fndr Devitt and Moore Nautical Coll, Pangbourne, sr ptnr Devitt and Moore, Master Skinners' Co 1885–86 and 1896–97, Chm Lloyd's Register of Shipping 1909–20; *m* 26 Feb 1863 Fanny Theodora (*d* 5 Feb 1917), dau of Ebenezer Pye-Smith, FRCS, and *d* 8 Dec 1923, leaving issue:

1 Arthur; *b* 29 Dec 1867; *educ* Trin Hall Cambridge (BA); *m* 8 Dec 1897 Florence Emmeline (*m* 2nd 14 Sept 1932 Rev Arthur Lloyd Phillips, Vicar of Ware, and *d* 5 Aug 1951), est dau of William Forbes Gordon, of Manar, NSW, and *d* 16 June 1921, leaving issue:

(1) **Sir Thomas Gordon Devitt, 2nd Bt**; *b* 27 Dec 1902; *educ* Sherborne and Corpus Christi Coll Cambridge (BA 1926, MA 1931); served WW II 1940–45 as Lt-Col Seaforth Highrs and Officer Cmdg Raiding Support Regt, late Lt 1st Bn Seaforth Highrs, Govr Sherborne 1967–75, Offr Royal Order of the Phoenix with swords Greece; *m* 1st 21 June 1930 (*divorce* 1936) Joan Mary, 2nd dau of Charles Reginald Freemantle, of Hayes, Barton, Pyrford, Surrey; *m* 2nd 25 Jan 1937 (*divorce* 1953) Lydia Mary (*d* 1995), dau of Edward Milligen Beloe, of King's Lynn, Norfolk, and by her had issue:

1a *Georgina Jane [The Hon Mrs Nigel Parker, Combe Lane Farm, Wormley, Godalming, Surrey]; *b* 6 Oct 1937; *educ* Benenden and Open U (BA); *m* 23 April 1965 *Hon Nigel Geoffrey Parker, yst son of Hon John Holford Parker, of Pound House, Yelverton, S Devon, and has issue (*see* MORLEY, E)

2a *Stephanie Gordon [Mrs Dudley Lucas, Becketts, Chilmark, Salisbury, Wilts SP3 5BD]; *b* 11 Aug 1942; *educ* Benenden; *m* 7 Jan 1966 *Col (James Norman) Dudley Lucas, The Cameronians (Scottish Rifles) and Royal Scots, son of Maj Harold Norman Lucas MBE, of Sutton, Surrey, and has issue:

1b *Timothy James Stephen; *b* 14 Dec 1968
1b *Chloe Henrietta; *b* 2 May 1967

(1) (cont.) **Sir Thomas** *m* 3rd 12 Dec 1953 *Janet Lilian [Janet Lady Devitt, 5 Rembrandt Close, Holbein Place, London SW1W 8HS], only dau of Col Hugh Sidney Ellis, CBE, MC, of Shirley Lodge, Ashstead, Surrey, and *d* 23 Dec 1995, leaving by her:

1a Sir JAMES HUGH THOMAS DEVITT, **3rd and present Bt**
3a *Angela Susan [Mrs Iain Morpeth, 32 Alleyn Rd, London SE21 8AL]; *b* 18 Oct 1954; *m* 30 June 1979 *Iain Cardean Spottiswoode Morpeth and has:

1b *Richard Douglas Gordon; *b* 1985
2b *Duncan Hugh Sinclair; *b* 1987
3b *James Rutherford Thomas; *b* 1992
1b *Catherine Louise Nicholl; *b* 1990

(1) Mary Gordon; *m* 21 June 1924 Dennis John Alsen Fletcher (*ka* March 1942), RAFVR, of Nether Hall, Widford, Herts, and had issue

2 Howson Foulger; chm Howson F Devitt and Sons Ltd, underwriting memb Lloyd's, memb Ctee Roy Merchant Navy Sch Bear Wood 1938–49 (Chm 1943–47); *b* 8 July 1869; *educ* Sherborne; *m* 2 May 1908 Winifred Lina (*d* 1972), est dau of Richard Woolicombe, of Starmead, Wokingham, and *d* 13 March 1949, having had issue:

(1) Howson Charles, OBE (1941), WW II as W/Cdr RAFO, memb Lloyd's, chm Howson F Devitt and Sons Ltd, Howson Devitt (Agents) Ltd, Douglas Cox Tyler and Co Ltd, dir Devitt, Langton and Downay Day Ltd, Devitt (DA Insurance) Ltd, AA Insurance Services Ltd, Govr of Pangbourne Coll; *b* 30 Jan 1909; *educ* Sherborne and Trin Hall Cambridge (MA); *m* 2 Sept 1939 *Elizabeth Carola, yr dau of Edward George Fairholme, OBE, of Burke's Corner, Beaconsfield, Bucks, and *d* 9 Feb 1996, leaving:

1a +Richard Howson; *b* 12 Aug 1940; *educ* Nautical Coll Pangbourne and Trin Hall Cambridge (MA); Govr Pangbourne Coll 1972–89; *m* 9 April 1992 his cousin *Mrs Lucy Clare Hulme (*see* below)

1a *(Carola) Waveney [Mrs Peter Jenkins, Pages, Shalford, Essex]; *b* 25 Nov 1942; *m* 29 May 1962 *Peter John Laidlaw Jenkins and has:

1b *Mark Alan Laidlaw; *b* 14 Jan 1964
1b *Carola Rosemary; *b* 9 Sept 1965
2b *Tamsin Elisabeth; *b* 7 Oct 1970

(2) Peter Kenneth, DL (Surrey 1959–67); W/Cdr RAuxAF WW II (despatches), Air memb Surrey T&AFA, memb Lloyd's, Govr Roy Merchant Navy Sch, dir Devitt Langton and Dawnay Day, and Howson Devitt (Agencies) Ltd, memb Court Skinners' Co; *b* 4 June 1911; *educ* Sherborne; *m* 1st 12 Sept 1935 (*divorce* 1950) Eunice Stephanie, yst dau of Sir Charles Sheriton Swan, of Broomley Grange, Stocksfield, and had:

1a +Jeremy Peter [Cdr Jeremy Devitt RN, 2 Chelfham Barton Cottages, Chelfham, Barnstaple, N Devon EX31 4RP]; *b* 3 Nov 1937; *educ* Sherborne; *m* 29 July 1961 *Elspeth, est dau of Brig William Edward Guest, MBE, and has issue:

1b +Mark Edward Peter; *b* 31 Aug 1962
2b +Simon Charles Guest; *b* 3 May 1964; BSc, MBA London
3b +Nicholas Jeremy James; *b* 5 Feb 1968; BA Newcastle; *m* 23 June 1995 *Allison Walker and has:

1c +Thomas Kane; *b* 14 June 1996

4b +Timothy William Guy; *b* 5 Feb 1968; BA Mddx; *m* 26 July 1996 *Vanessa Pickford

1a *Lorna Stephanie [Mrs Geoffrey Glynn-Jones, Leaf House, Sowton, Exeter EX52 2AD]; *b* 22 Feb 1942; *m* 24 Aug 1963 *Geoffrey Glynn-Jones and has issue:

1b *Timothy Patrick *b* 24 May 1965
1b *Lavinia Mary; *b* 27 April 1969

2a *Jacquetta Anne [Mrs Robert Pease, 12 Elm Grove Rd, London SW13 0LD]; *b* 21 April 1946; *m* 1st 21 Sept 1968 (*divorce* 1974) Christopher David Legge; *m* 2nd 1976 *Robert Patrick Pease and has:

1b *Tanya Jacquetta; *b* 1977
2b *Sophie Claire; *b* 1980

3a *(Vivien) Gay [Mrs Gay Devitt, 33A Buckingham Terr, Edinburgh EH43 3AF]; *b* 1948

(2) (cont.) W/Cdr Peter Devitt *m* 2nd 20 Jan 1950 (*divorce* 1953) Joan Elizabeth, only dau of T Forbes Robertson, of Santa Barbara, Calif.; *m* 3rd 1953 (*divorce* 1965) his 1st wife Eunice Stephanie (*see* above); *m* 4th 19–*June Baines and *d* 29 March 1997

(1) *Ursula Helen; *b* 19 Dec 1912; *m* 25 Oct 1935 *Michael Alastair Spencer-Nairn, 2nd son of Maj Sir Robert Spencer-Nairn, 1st Bt (*qv*), and has issue

(2) *Sheila Winifred [Mrs Edward Harrison, Barn House, Otterton, Budleigh Salterton, Devon]; *b* 19 Dec 1912, Long Service WRVS Medal 1969; *m* 24 July 1936 *Edward Michael Harrison, and has issue:

1a *Hugh Michael James [Hugh Harrison Esq, Ringcombe Farm, West Anstey, Devon EX36 3NZ]; *b* 26 July 1942; *m* 1st 23 March 1968 (*divorce* 1974) Joanna Mary, est dau of Col W R Healing, of Budleigh Salterton, Devon, and has issue:

1b *James Edward; *b* 1969

1a (cont.) Hugh Harrison *m* 2nd 1974 *Stephanie Christine, er dau of the Rev Peter Haslewood Shaw, of Greatworth, Northants, and has further issue:

1b *Camilla Rose; *b* 1975
2b *Zoë Grace; *b* 1977

1a *Juliet Mary [Mrs Tuckerman Moss, The Old Vicarage, W Anstey, S Molton, N Devon]; *b* 7 Dec 1937; *m* May 1964 *Tuckerman Moss, PhD, and has issue:

1b *Michael Duval; *b* 17 July 1965
2b *Jeremy Gilbert; *b* 4 Nov 1968
1b *Rebecca Alice; *b* 4 Nov 1968

2a *Lucy Clare; *b* 21 March 1950; *m* 1971 (*divorce* 1987) Paul Robert Hulme; *m* 2nd 9 April 1992 her cousin *Richard Howson Devitt (*see* above), and by her 1st husb has had:

1b *Richard Jeremy; *b* 1973
1b Emma Catherine; *b* 1971; *d* 31 Oct 1995

(3) Lorna Mary; *d* 24 Nov 1921

3 Herbert Pye-Smith, MRCS, LRCP London, Visiting Apothecary to St George's Hosp; *b* 18 May 1873; *educ* Trin Coll Cambridge (BA); *m* 1st 7 Nov 1903 Roberta Mary Cornelia (*d* 25 July 1934), er dau of Maj James George Anderson, Roy Irish Fus, and had issue:

(1) Philip Eyre, Maj Dorsetshire Regt WW II, Headmaster Falconbury School Bexhill 1948; *b* 7 Jan 1907; *educ* Sherborne and Gonville and Caius Coll Cambridge (BA 1929); *m* 20 Dec 1947 *Patricia Melicent [Mrs Philip Devitt, Whydown Lodge, Little Common, Bexhill-on-Sea], dau of Walter Edward Leslie, of Bath, and *d* 1992 leaving issue:

1a +Desmond Philip; *b* 20 Nov 1950; *educ* Sherborne

1a *Ann Patricia; *b* 11 July 1954

(2) (Herbert) Lionel; *b* 15 March 1910; *educ* Sherborne and Trin Hall Cambridge; *m* 1st 26 Aug 1939 (*divorce* 1948) (Myfanwy Rina) Doreen, 2nd dau of Alwyn H Holman, of 7 Holland Villas Rd, London W14, and had issue:

1a +Michael Wyn; *b* 3 June 1943; *educ* Stowe; *m* 2 Sept 1967 *Susan Gundreda de Warrenne, only dau of Walter Kingsley Brett, of Ballacowie Farm, Agneash, Isle of Man, and has issue:

1b +Roland; *b* 4 May 1972

1b *Madeleine; *b* 31 Oct 1969

2a David Anthony; *b* 11 May 1946; *d* unm 31 Aug 1966

1a *Judith Anne Mary; *b* 1 July 1940; *m* 14 Dec 1963 *Edward David Beresford Tebbs, only son of Edward Andre Tebbs, of Withdean House, Bulkington, Devizes, Wilts, and has issue:

1b *Andrew; *b* 1971

1b *Lucy Jane; *b* 26 April 1965

2b *Amanda Elizabeth; *b* 24 Oct 1967

(2) (cont.) Lionel Devitt *m* 2nd 25 Jan 1949 (*divorce* 1954) Sheila Mary, dau of Edmund Ironside Bremner, of North Acres, Streat, Sussex; *m* 3rd 1954 *Fleur Agnes Trehern-Thomas [Mrs Lionel Devitt, 11B Bina Gdns, London SW6], and *d* 27 Dec 1964

(3) John Desmond, MRCS, LRCP, Lt RAMC, served WW II (wounded), US Silver Star; *b* 30 July 1917; *educ* Sherborne and Trin Hall Cambridge; *m* 28 Dec 1957 *Pamela Ruth, dau of Leonard Bruce Foot, of Egbury, Hants, and *d* 13 Nov 1973, leaving issue:

1a +Timothy John Herbert [Timothy Devitt Esq, Ground Floor Flat, 5 Carden Rd, London SE15]; *b* 1958

2a +Jonathan Stephen [Jonathan Devitt Esq, 31 Ryedale, London SE22]; *b* 1960; *m* 1992 *Maria Soledad Fidalgo Suarez, and has issue:

1b +Calum John; *b* 1993

3a +Andrew James [Andrew Devitt Esq, 25 Milford Ct, Huddersfield, W Yorks]; *b* 1962

(1) *Dorothea [Mrs Harry Clarke, Windrush, 30 Wealden Way, Little Common, Bexhill-on-Sea]; *b* 9 Sept 1904; *m* 23 April 1930 Harry Martin Ward Clarke (*d* 1963), and has issue:

1a *Rosemary [Mrs Michael Herzig, 56 Farnham Rd, Guildford, Surrey]; *b* 18 Dec 1932; *m* June 1958 *Michael Leopold Herzig, son of Leopold Herzig, of Osterley, Middx, and has:

1b *Andrew Michael; *b* 12 Sept 1960

2b *Peter John; *b* 13 Aug 1962

3b *Martin Robert; *b* 6 July 1966

1b *Catherine Jane; *b* 1969

2a *Jennifer Jane; *b* 20 June 1935

(2) *Margaret Mary [Mrs Cedric Bramley, Windrush, 30 Wealden Way, Little Common, Bexhill-on-Sea, Sussex]; *b* 13 Dec 1915; *m* 19 April 1944 *Cedric Bramley, and has issue:

1a *Roberta [Mrs Jean-Louis Joly, 114 Elphinstone Rd, Hastings, E Sussex]; *b* 16 Oct 1949; *m* 1981 *Jean-Louis René Daniel Joly, and has issue:

1b *Claire Margaret; *b* 1981

2b *Kathryn Mary; *b* 1982

3 (cont.) Herbert Devitt *m* 2nd 12 April 1935 Muriel (*d* 15 Sept 1951), dau of Reginald M Snow, of Bideford, and widow of F-Lt G E Blake, RAF; *m* 3rd 6 Sept 1952 Carola Evelyn (*d* 1984), er dau of E Howard May, of Bournemouth, and widow of W W Brownlee, and *d* 1958

4 Sir PHILIP HENRY DEVITT, 1st and last Bt (UK), so *cr* 25 June 1931, JP (Herts), of Pangbourne, Berks; *b* 26 Jan 1876; *educ* Trin Hall Cambridge (MA); Chm Bd Govrs and fndr Devitt and Moore Nautical Coll Pangbourne, Dep Chm Roy Alfred Aged Merchant Seamen's Inst, V-Pres Marine Soc, V-Chm Bd Sailors' Home, Dock Street; Chm Annual Nat Service for Seafarers, Tstee and Hon Memb Master Mariners' Co; *m* 22 Feb 1919 Dorothy Maud (*d* 25 Feb 1969), dau of Rev Frederick John Hall, of St Just, Northaw, Herts, and *dspm* 5 June 1947, when the btcy expired, leaving issue:

(1) *Theodora Joan [Miss Theodora Devitt, St Just, Northaw, Potters Bar, Herts]; *b* 15 Dec 1919

(2) *Elizabeth Anne [Lady Koelle, Pippins, Long Burton, Dorset DT9 6ES]; *b* 31 Aug 1921; *m* 28 April 1948 V-Adml Sir Harry Philpot Koelle, KCB (*d* 1980), and has issue:

1a *Victoria Anne; *b* 6 Nov 1949; *m* 1980 *Andrew James Carter and has:

1b *Philip Harry; *b* 1976

2b *Jack Edward; *b* 1981

3b *Timothy Robert; *b* 1985

2a *Philippa June; *b* 21 June 1951; *m* 1979 *Hugo C Woolley, and has issue:

1b *Giles Thomas; *b* 1984

1b *Emily Anne; *b* 1981

(3) Jennifer Margaret; *b* 9 March 1923; *d* 13 May 1997

(4) Dorothy Susan; *b* 7 Aug 1931; *d* April 1985

(5) *Bridget Helen (twin) [Mrs Michael Greenwood, Tyn y Waen, Glasfryn, Corwen LL21 0RY]; *b* 1931; *m* 10 Oct 1952 Capt (Oliver) Michael Robin Greenwood (*d* 1992), Coldstream Gds, yst son of Col R N Greenwood, of Hatfield, Herts, and has issue:

1a *Simon Nelson; *b* 5 Jan 1954; *m* 1984 *Sara A Johnston

2a *Christopher Philip; *b* 8 June 1957; *m* 1988 *Tara Simonis

3a *James William Dickon; *b* 11 June 1964

1a *Nicola Jane; *b* 29 Dec 1954; *m* 1979 *Robert C Atkinson

1 Mary Theodora; *d* an infant 24 Aug 1864

2 Helen Margaret, *d* unm 13 Sept 1932

3 Emily Ruth; *d* unm 21 Dec 1950

4 Lilian Dorothea; *m* 31 Oct 1903 Herbert Stringfellow Pendlebury (*d* 22 April 1953), MB, FRCS, of 44 Brook St, London W, and *d* 8 Sept 1921, leaving issue

5 Katherine Rutherford; *m* 28 June 1906 Rev William Francis Eliot (*d* 7 Aug 1922), Rector Upton St Leonard, Glos, and *d* 27 Jan 1964, leaving issue

DEVON

Arms: Quarterly, 1st and 4th, or three torteaux (for COURTENAY); 2nd and 3rd, or a lion rampant azure (for De REVIERS or De VERNON). **Crests:** 1 Out of a ducal coronet or a plume of seven ostrich feathers, four and three, argent, 2 A dolphin embowed proper. **Supporters:** Two boars argent, bristled, tusked and unguled or. **Mottoes:** 1 *Quod verum tutum* ('What is true is safe') 2 *Ubi lapsus, quid feci* ('Where have I fallen; what have I done?'). **Creation:** E. (E) 3 Sept 1553, Bt. (E) Feb 1644/5.

THE 17TH EARL OF DEVON and a **Baronet** (Sir Charles Christopher Courtenay, Bt, JP (Devon 1950)) [The Rt Hon The Earl of Devon JP, Stables House, Powderham Castle, Exeter EX6 8JQ]; *b* 13 July 1916; *s* f 1935; *educ* Winchester and RMC Sandhurst; Capt Coldstream Gds (RARO) WW II (wounded despatches); *m* 29 July 1939 *(Sybil) Venetia, Order of Mercy, only dau of Capt John Vickris Taylor, Welsh Gds, of N Aston Manor, Oxon, and formerly w of 6th Earl of Cottenham (*qv*), and has issue:

1 +HUGH RUPERT, *Lord Courtenay*, DL (Devon 1991) [Lord Courtenay DL, Powderham Castle, Devon EX6 8JQ]; *b* 5 May 1942; *educ* Winchester and Magdalene Coll Cambridge (BA 1964); ARICS, Capt Roy Devon Yeo (W Yeo) 1972, chm Devon branch CLA 1987–89; *m* 9 Sept 1967 *Dianna Frances, er dau of Jack Watherston, of Menslaws, Jedburgh, Roxburghshire, and has issue:

(1) +Charles Peregrine; *b* 14 Aug 1975

(1) *Rebecca Eildon; *b* 8 April 1969

(2) *Eleonora Venetia; *b* 24 May 1971

(3) *Camilla Mary; *b* 23 Jun 1974

1 *Katherine Felicity [The Lady Katherine Watney, 1 Playhatch Cottages, Playhatch, nr Reading RG4 9QX]; *b* 22 Oct 1940; *m* 8 Jan 1966 Antony Stephen Pope Watney (*d* 1986), yr s of John Lewis Watney, TD, of Little Nowers, Spinney Lane, Itchenor, Sussex, and has issue:

(1) *Michael Hugh Sanders; *b* 26 Nov 1966; *educ* Stowe and RAC Cirencester; *m* 25 Nov 1995 *Louise, er dau of Anthony Winsborough, of Hindhead, Surrey

Earldom of Devon: Baldwin de Reviers, son of Richard de Reviers, Lord of Reviers, Vernon and Néhou (all in Normandy), supported the EMPRESS MAUD against KING STEPHEN in the period known as the Anarchy following the death of HENRY I and was by her created Earl of Devon *c* 1141. The name de Reviers was subsequently corrupted to Redvers. As well as holding the Earldom of Devon the de Revierses were Lords of the Isle of Wight. The 7th Earl of the 1141 creation died without surviving issue in 1262, leaving a sister, whose children also died without issue. A cousin of the last Earl, one Hugh de Courtenay (*see* below), was created Earl of Devon in Feb 1334/5. His great-grandfather had married Mary de Vernon (the other name the de Revierses were known by, from their fief in Normandy) in the early 13th century, she being dau and in her issue ultimately sole heir of William de Reviers/de Vernon, 5th Earl of Devon of the 1141 creation.

The 6th Earl of Devon of this second (Feb 1334/5) *cr* was attainted as a Lancastrian after the defeat of that house by the Yorkists in the Wars of the Roses at the Battle of Towton in 1461. Subsequently a member of the Stafford family who were for a while Dukes of Buckingham (*see* STAFFORD, B) was created Earl of Devon in 1469 by EDWARD IV. On joining an uprising in the North of England, however, he was executed later the same year, having held the title exactly three months. For further creations in favour of members of the Courtenay family *see* **Lineage**.

From 1556, the year of the death of the 1st Earl of the 1553 and current creation, till 1831, the title was in effect dormant. In the latter year a remote cousin, William Courtenay, 3rd Viscount Courtenay of Powderham Castle, successfully claimed the Earldom of 1553 on the grounds that the wording of its remainder was to 'heirs male for ever' rather than the usual 'heirs male of his body for ever' and that this accordingly allowed the title to pass to a descendant of a common ancestor such as himself even though he was not a direct descendant of the Earl of the 1553 creation. But in the intervening three centuries it had been regarded as extinct and titles involving the same county were conferred in 1603 on Charles Blount, Lord Mountjoy (*dspl* 1606), and in 1618 on William Cavendish, Lord Cavendish of Hardwick, whose descendants became Dukes of Devonshire (*qv*). Fortunately the dual form of wording of 'Earl of Devon or Devonshire' has meant that the Courtenays came to be known as Earls of Devon and the predecessors of the Dukes of Devonshire as Earls of Devonshire, rather as the county itself is sometimes referred to as Devon and sometimes as Devonshire.

Lineage: ATHON de COURTENAY, Lord of Courtenay and castellan of Château-Renard, fortified Courtenay, in Gâtinais in the Isle de France, *c* 1010; f of:

JOSSELIN de COURTENAY, Lord of Courtenay, living 1060; *m* 1st Hildegarde, dau of Geoffrey, Count of Gâtinais (ancestor of the PLANTAGENETs), and had issue:

1 Stephen; took part in the First Crusade; *m* Hersent, dau of — , Seigneur de Montereau, and *d* 1101, leaving:

(1) Adam, of Chailly; *m* 1st — , heiress of the Vicomtes de Melun, and had issue:

1a Giles, Vicomte de Melun; *d* 1138, leaving issue:

1b Adam, Vicomte de Melun; *dsp* by 1150

2b Josselin, Vicomte de Melun; *m* Alpais and *d* 1157, being ancestor of the Vicomtes de Melun, among whom was William III, Vicomte de Melun and Count of Corsica, who *dsp* 1278, and William IV, Count of Tancarville and Vicomte de Melun, Constable and Chamberlain of Normandy and Grand Butler of France, who was *k* Battle of Agincourt 1415

(1) (cont.) Adam de Courtenay, of Chailly, *m* 2nd Aveline, Dame de Yerres, dau of Baldwin de Corbeuil, and had further issue:

2a Thierry, Sire de Yerres, ancestor of the COURTENAYs, Lords of Yerres, who died out in the male line 1415

1 Hodierne; *m* 1080 Geoffrey de Joinville, Count of Joigny (*d* 1100)

JOSSELIN de COURTENAY *m* 2nd 1065 Elizabeth, dau of Guy de Montlhéry, aunt of Baldwin II, Count of Edessa, and had further issue:

2 MILES

3 Josselin; held various fiefs in the Crusader kingdoms in and around the Holy Land, becoming Prince of Galilee (1112–18), Count of Edessa (1118–31), both principalities in what is now northern Syria, and Lord of Turbessel in the County of Edessa (enfeoffed by his cousin BALDWIN II of Edessa), Tiberias and Nazareth; *m* 1st a sis of Leo, Prince of Armenia; *m* 2nd a sis of Roger, Prince of Antioch, and *d* 1131 after being injured by falling masonry while sapping the tower of a castle he was besieging, leaving issue by his 1st w:

(1) Josselin, Count of Edessa 1131–44 (in the latter year its capture by the Saracens was a factor in bringing about the Second Crusade); besieged Caesarea 1138; *m* Ic 1132/3 Beatrice, widow of William of Sahyun, Lord of Zerdana (*d* 1132), and *d* 1156 a prisoner of the Saracens at Aleppo, leaving issue:

1a Josselin, Seneschal of the Kingdom of Jerusalem 1176, where he held great estates by the service of 50 knights, captured by the Saracens 1165 but ransomed by his sis the Princess of Sidon 1175, fought against Saladin at Battle of Ascalon 1176; Amb to EMPEROR MANUEL II COMNENUS at Byzantium 1180, guardian of his infant gn BALDWIN V KING OF JERUSALEM 1183, and *d* in the siege of that city 1187

1a Agnes; *b c* 1133; *m* 1st Renaud, 4th Crusader Lord of Maresh (*d* 1148); *m* 2nd *c* 1157 (*divorce* 1162 on grounds of consanguinity) her 3rd cousin AMAURY I KING OF JERUSALEM (half-bro of Geoffrey Count of Anjou, ancestor of the Plantagenet Dynasty) and had issue; *m* 3rd 1167 Hugh de Ibelin, Castellan of Cairo; *m* 4th Reynold, Lord of Sidon

4 Geoffrey; *k* in battle with the Saracens nr Mont Ferrand 1137

JOSSELIN de COURTENAY's 2nd s,

MILES de COURTENAY, Lord of Courtenay; living 1127, fndr Cistercian Abbey of Fontaine-Jean; *m c* 1095 Ermengarde, dau of Renaud, Count of Nevers, and had issue:

1 William, Lord of Courtenay; living 1147; *dsp*

2 RENAUD de COURTENAY, Lord of Courtenay; accompanied LOUIS VII OF FRANCE on Second Crusade but quarrelled with him so that LOUIS seized his French possessions and bestowed them, with Renaud's dau in marriage, on his own yr bro Pierre; RENAUD subsequently threw in his lot with the English kings and was granted the lordship of Sutton (now Sutton Courtenay), on the Berks-Oxon borders, by HENRY II 1161; accompanied HENRY II to Wexford in the Irish expedition of 1172; *m* 1st Hedwige (living 1148–58), sis of Guy du Donjon; *m* 2nd Maud, Dame du Sap (*dsp* 1224), dau of Robert Fitz Roy (illegitimate s of HENRY I OF ENGLAND) by his w Maud d'Avranches, and *d c* 1192, leaving issue by his 1st w:

(1) Robert, Lord of Sutton Courtney; *m* Alice de Rumeli, widow of Gilbert Pipard and sis and coheir of the 'Boy of Egremont', last heir male of DUNCAN II, KING OF SCOTS, and *dsp* 1209

(2) RENAUD, for whom *see* further below

(1) Elizabeth; *m c* 1150 Peter/Pierre de Courtenay (took his w's name and the arms of Courtenay, *viz.* or three roundlets gules (to which his descendants sometimes added an escutcheon of France), and *d* 1183), 7th s of LOUIS VI OF FRANCE, and *d* in or after 1205, having had, with other issue (including Eustachie, *m* William, 2nd s of Erard II Count of Brienne, *see* BEAUMONT, Bt; and Alice, *m* Aymer, Count of Angoulême, and had issue; *see* GREY, B):

1a PETER de COURTENAY, EMPEROR-elect OF BYZANTIUM, Lord of Courtenay, Marquis de Namur and Count of Nevers, Auxerre and Tonnerre; took part in the Third Crusade 1190, present at Battle of Bouvines 1214 when PHILIP AUGUSTUS OF FRANCE defeated an army sent by KING JOHN to reconquer the lands previously held by the Angevins, elected Latin EMPEROR OF BYZANTIUM by the Frankish nobles of that city 1216 and crowned by the Pope in Rome, but captured on his way to the East 1217 by order of Theodore Angelus, Despot of Epirus, and put to death 1219, having never set foot in the city, let alone reigned there; *m* 1st Agnes de Nevers and had issue:

1b Maud, Countess of Nevers

1a (cont.) The EMPEROR *m* 2nd Yolande (who did, however, reach Constantinople and even reigned there), dau of Baldwin VIII, Count of Flanders, and sis of BALDWIN I and HENRY, successively Latin EMPERORS OF BYZANTIUM, leaving further issue:

1b Philip de COURTENAY, Marquis de Namur; fought against PHILIP AUGUSTUS OF FRANCE at Battle of Bouvines 1214, remained in France when his f was elected Emperor, and *d* Siege of Avignon 1226

2b ROBERT de COURTENAY, Latin EMPEROR OF BYZANTIUM (the imperial Courtenays bore for arms gules a cross between four annulets, in each quarter five crosslets potent in saltire, or); *m* — , dau of Baldwin de Neufville, and *dsp* 1228

3b Henry, Marquis de Namur; *d* 1229

4b BALDWIN II, Latin EMPEROR OF BYZANTIUM 1228–61; subsidised 1244 by LOUIS IX OF FRANCE, to whom he had presented 'a choice selection of relics, including the rod of Moses, the jawbone of John the Baptist, and Our Lord's crown of thorns'; escaped in a Venetian galley from his burning capital when Byzantine troops recaptured the city in the name of the EMPEROR MICHAEL VIII PALAEOLOGUS July 1261; *m* Mary, dau of JOHN OF BRIENNE, CO-EMPEROR OF BYZANTIUM and previously KING OF JERUSALEM (*see* BEAUMONT, Bt), and *d* 1273 in exile, leaving issue:

1c PHILIP, titular Latin EMPEROR OF BYZANTIUM; pawned by his f to Venetian bankers to fund the defence of his empire but redeemed by LOUIS VII OF FRANCE; *m* Beatrice of Anjou, dau of CHARLES I, KING OF NAPLES (who was prevented by the 'Sicilian Vespers' from attempting to restore his son-in-law to the throne of Byzantium 1282), and *d* 1286, leaving an only dau:

1d CATHERINE, titular Empress of Byzantium in her own right; *m* Charles, Count de Valois, bro of PHILIP IV OF FRANCE, and had issue

1b Margaret; *m* 1st Raoul d'Issodun (*d* 1212); *m* 2nd Henry, Count of Vianden (*d* 1252/3), with whom she ruled Namur 1229–37, and *d* 1270

2b Elizabeth; *m* 1st Gaucher (*d* Siege of Damietta, Egypt, 1219), s of Miles III, Count of Bar; *m* 2nd Eudes, Seigneur de Montagu

3b Yolande; *m* ANDREW II, KING OF HUNGARY, and *d* 1233

4b Mary; *m* THEODORE LASCARIS, GREEK EMPEROR OF NICAEA (*d* 1222)

5b Agnes; *m* GEOFFREY II de VILLEHARDOUIN, PRINCE OF ACHAIA

6b Eleanor; *m* Philip de Montfort, Seigneur de Ferté Aleps, cousin of Simon de Montfort, Earl of Leicester (*see* LEICESTER, E, preliminary remarks)

2a Robert, Seigneur de Champignelles, Butler of France 1223, took part in the French campaign against the Albigensian heretics 1210 under the leadership of Simon de Montfort, present at Sieges of Niort and Rochelle 1224; *m* Maud, dau and heiress of Philip, Seigneur de Mahun-sur-Yevre, and *d* in the Holy Land 1239, leaving:

1b Pierre, Seigneur de Conches; *m* Perronelle, dau of Gaucher de Joigny, Seneschal de Nivernois, and was *k* in Egypt 1250, leaving an only dau:

1c Amice; *m* 1262 Robert, Count of Artois, and *d* 1275

2b Philip, Seigneur de Champignelles; *d c* 1245

3b Raoul, Count of Chieti in Italy; took part with CHARLES OF ANJOU in the conquest of Naples and was granted Chieti, the chief city of the Abruzzi, in 1269; *d* 1271, leaving an only dau:

1c Maud, Countess of Chieti; *m* Philip, yst s of Guy, Count of Flanders, and *d* 1300

4b Robert; Bp of Orleans; accompanied LOUIS IX OF FRANCE on Crusade and *d* 1279

5b John; Archbp of Rheims; *d* 1271

6b William, Seigneur de Champignelles; with 6 of his own knights accompanied LOUIS IX OF FRANCE on Crusade; *m* Margaret, dau of John I, Count of Châlon, and *d* 1282, leaving issue:

1c Robert, Archbp of Rheims; *d* 1323

2c John; *d* 1395, leaving issue: ancestor of the COURTENAYs, feudal Lds of La Ferté, Loupière and Chavillon, extinct in the male line 1733

3a William, Seigneur de Tanlai, whose male issue died out 1383

4a John, Seigneur de Yerre, whose issue male apparently died out in the 15th century

1a Alice; *m* 1st William I, Count of Joigny; *m* 2nd Aymer Taillefer, Count of Angoulême, by whom she had a dau:

1b Isabelle; *m* JOHN, KING OF ENGLAND

RENAUD de COURTENAY's yr s,

RENAUD de COURTENAY; Sheriff Devon and Castellan Exeter; *m* by 1178 Hawise (*d* 31 July 1219), feudal Ldy of Okehampton, dau and coheir of William de Crucy (or Geoffrey de Crunes (Craon)) by his w Maud d'Avranches (*see* above), the latter being heiress of Baldwin Fitz Gilbert's family, which had held the Honour of Okehampton and the Shrievalty of Devon 1080–1142, and *d* 27 Sept 1194, leaving issue:

ROBERT de COURTENAY; feudal Lord of Okehampton and Sutton Courtenay; Sheriff Devon and Oxon, Castellan Exeter and Oxford, inherited 31 July 1219 from his mother the great Honour of Okehampton in Devon, amounting to 92 knights' fees; KING JOHN granted him the right to coin tin in Devon and Cornwall in 1215; *m* Mary, yst dau of William de Reviers or de Vernon, 5th Earl of Devon of the 1141 *cr* and Lord of the Isle of Wight (*d* preliminary remarks above), and widow of Pierre de Preaux; *d* 26 July 1242, leaving issue:

JOHN de COURTENAY, feudal Lord of Okehampton; *m* Isabel de Vere (living Feb 1298/9), dau of 4th Earl of Oxford (*see* ST ALBANS, D), and *d* 3 May 1274, leaving issue:

HUGH de COURTENAY, feudal Lord of Okehampton; *b* 25 March 1248/9 or 1250/1; *m* Eleanor (*d* 30 Sept 1328), dau of Sir Hugh le Despenser (*see* FALMOUTH, V), and *d* 28 Feb 1291/2, leaving issue:

1 HUGH de COURTENAY, 1st LORD (Baron) COURTENAY, so *cr* by writ of summons to Parl 6 Feb 1298/9 according to later doctrine and 1st EARL OF DEVON, so *cr* by letters patent 22 Feb 1334/5; *b c* 1276; *s* his f in the Okehampton estates 1292 and such of the Reviers estates as had not been alienated 1293; present Siege of Carlaverock 1300, ktd 1306, kt banneret 1308, a Lord Ordainer 1313 (one of 20 magnates chosen to restrict EDWARD II, particularly in his habit of advancing his favourites), Warden Devon and Cornwall Coast 1324 and 1336; *m* 1292 Agnes (*d* 11 June 1345), dau of John St John (*see*

SAINT JOHN OF BLETSO, B), and *d* 23 Dec 1340, leaving (with another putative dau, alleged 1st w of Henry de Grey; *see* GREY, B):

(1) HUGH de COURTENAY, 2nd EARL OF DEVON; *b* 12 July 1303; served in Scottish and French Wars, kt banneret 1327, repulsed a French descent on Cornwall 1339, called to Parl 23 April 1337 in what would under modern doctrine have been his f 's Barony, Jt Warden Devon and Cornwall 1352, Ch Warden Devon 1373; *m* 11 Aug 1325 Margaret de Bohun (whose dowry included Powderham; she *d* 16 Dec 1391), 1st surv dau of Humphrey, Earl of Hereford and Essex, Ld High Constable of England, by his w Elizabeth, dau of EDWARD I, and *d* 2 May 1377, having had issue, with eight daus (including Elizabeth, *m* John de Vere, est s of 7th Earl of Oxford; *see* SAINT ALBANS, D):

1a Hugh (Sir), KG (1348); *b* 22 March 1326/7; fought at Battle of Crécy 1346, present at Siege of Calais 1347; *m* 1341 Elizabeth (*m* 2nd as his 2nd w 3rd Lord (Baron) Mowbray (*see* MOWBRAY, SEGRAVE and STOURTON, B) and 3rd 18 Jan 1368/9 Sir William de Cosynton and *d* Aug or Sept 1375), dau of 7th Earl of Oxford (*see* ST ALBANS, D), and *dvp* by 2 Sept 1349, leaving issue:

1b HUGH de COURTENAY, 3rd LORD (Baron) COURTENAY; ktd 1367, present Battle of Nájera 1367 (when an Anglo-Gascon army under the Black Prince defeated a Franco-Castilian one, thereby temporarily securing the restoration of PEDRO THE CRUEL OF CASTILE), called to Parl 8 Jan 1370/1 in his gf 's Barony; *m* 1st by May 1361 Margaret de Bryan (*d c* 1361), dau of 1st Lord (Baron) Bryan of the 1350 *cr*; *m* 2nd (papal dispensation 5 Sept 1363) Maud de Holand (*m* 2nd Waleran de Luxemburg, Count of Ligny and St Pol, and *d* by 13 April 1392), dau of 1st Earl of Kent of the 1360 *cr* by his w Joan, 'the Fair Maid of Kent', gdau of EDWARD I, and *dsp* 20 Feb 1373/4

2a Thomas; MP Devon; *dvp*

3a Edward, of Goodrington; *m* Emmeline (*d* 1372 by 20 Sept), dau and heiress of Sir John Dawnay, and *dvp* between 1364 and 1372, leaving issue:

1b EDWARD de COURTENAY, 3rd EARL OF DEVON, known as 'The Blind Earl'; *b c* 1357; ktd 1380, Adml in the West 1383–85, memb King's Cncl 1395; *m* Maud Camoys, allegedly dau of 1st Lord (Baron) Camoys (*qv*), and *d* 5 Dec 1419, having had with other issue:

1c Edward, *Lord Courtenay*; *b c* 1388; ktd 13 Oct 1399 at the coronation of HENRY IV, Warden King's Forests Devon and Cornwall, fought at Battle of Agincourt 1415, Adml of the Fleet May-Aug 1418; *m* between 13 May 1406 and 20 Nov 1409 Alienor Mortimer (living Jan 1413/4), dau of 4th Earl of March of the 1328 *cr*, gs of EDWARD III, and *dsp* & *vp c* Aug 1418

2c HUGH de COURTENAY, 4th EARL OF DEVON; *b c* 1389; ktd 13 Oct 1399 coronation of HENRY IV, Capt of a Fleet to guard the sea March-Aug 1418, Lt of the King at sea April-Nov 1419; *m* his 3rd cousin Anne Talbot (*d* 16 Jan 1440/1), sis of 1st Earl of Shrewsbury and Waterford (*qv*), and *d* 16 June 1422, leaving issue:

1d THOMAS de COURTENAY, 5th EARL OF DEVON, PC; *b* 1414; ktd 1426, Ld High Steward at coronation of HENRY VI's w MARGARET OF ANJOU 1445, campaigned in France towards end of Hundred Years War; *m* Margaret Beaufort, 2nd and yst dau of 1st Earl of Somerset of the 1397 *cr* (*see* BEAUFORT, D), and *d* 3 Feb 1458, leaving, with other issue:

1e THOMAS COURTENAY, 6th EARL OF DEVON; *b* 1432; Keeper Exmoor Forest 1459; beheaded 3 April 1461 after Battle of Towton, when all his honours became forfeited

2e Henry, of Topsham, Devon; had restored to him the manor of Topsham and other parts of the Devon estates by EDWARD IV 1461, but subsequently beheaded at Salisbury for treason 4 May 1466

3e JOHN COURTENAY, 7th EARL OF DEVON; ktd 29 Dec 1460 by his bro Thomas, 6th Earl of Devon; on the restoration of HENRY VI 9 Oct 1470 restored to the family honours, but after Battle of Barnet 14 April 1471 all his honours once more became forfeit; *d* unm 4 May 1471 at Battle of Tewkesbury

1e Joan; *m* 1st Sir Roger Clifford (beheaded 1485); *m* 2nd Sir William Knyvett

2e Elizabeth; *m* Sir Hugh Conway

2b Hugh (Sir), of Goodrington and Stancombe, Devon; *m* 1st by 11 Feb 1392/3 Elizabeth (*dsp* 29 Oct 1397), dau of Sir William Cogan, of Bampton, Devon, and widow of 5th Lord (Baron) FitzWarine; *m* 2nd Philippe, dau and coheir of Sir William Arcedekene, and *d* 5/6 March 1424/5, leaving by his 2nd w, with other issue:

1c Joan; *m* 1st Sir Nicholas Carew (*see* CAREW, Bt); *m* 2nd Sir Robert Vere and by him was grandmother of 15th Earl of Oxford (*see* SAINT ALBANS, D)

2b (cont.) Sir Hugh *m* 3rd Maud, dau of Sir John Beaumont, of Sherwell, Dorset, and had further issue:

1c Hugh (Sir), of Boconnock, Cornwall, MP; *m* Margaret, dau and coheir of Thomas Carminow, of Carminow, and *d* between May 1471 and Aug 1472 as a result of wounds received at the Battle of Tewkesbury, having had:

1d EDWARD COURTENAY, 1st and last EARL OF DEVON or DEVONSHIRE (E), so *cr* 26 Oct 1485, with remainder to the heirs male of his body (and by Act of Parl 1485 was restored to the supposed honours lost by 'his' [*sic*] attainder in the Parl of 1483, though it is unclear what honours are thereby meant), having been attainted and banished by RICHARD III 1484; KG (1494); present at Battle of Bosworth 1485, ktd 1485 by HENRY VII; Constable Restormel Castle, Cornwall, 1486/7; defended Exeter against Perkin Warbeck during his invasion of England and subsequently defeated same at Blackheath 22 June 1497; *m* his cousin Elizabeth, 1st dau of Sir Philip Courtenay, of Molland (bro of Sir William Courtenay, of Powderham, *see* below), and *d* 28 May 1509, when the Earldom became forfeited owing to the attainder then in force of his son and heir, leaving issue:

1e WILLIAM COURTENAY, 1st EARL OF DEVON of the 1511 *cr*, KB (1487); *b c* 1475; imprisoned 1503–09 for alleged complicity in the rebellion of Edmund de la Pole, Earl of Suffolk, n of EDWARD IV and RICHARD III, attainted Feb 1504 and so incapable of inheriting his f 's Earldom, restored by HENRY VIII 9 May 1511 to the powers, privileges and rights of an English subject that had been lost by the attainder of 1504 but since he was subsequently (10 May 1511) *cr* EARL OF DEVON (E) such rights etc can hardly have been deemed to include the Earldom; *m c* Oct 1495 Katherine (*d* 15 Nov 1527), 6th dau of EDWARD IV, and *d* 9 June 1511 before his investiture could be completed, though *bur* with an earl's honours, leaving, with other issue:

1f HENRY COURTENAY, 2nd and last EARL OF DEVON of the 1511 *cr*, 3rd and last EARL OF DEVON of the 1485 *cr* on his successfully petitioning for the reversal of the 1504 attainder and 1st and last MARQUESS OF EXETER (E), so *cr* 18 June 1525, KG (1521), PC (1520); *b c* 1498; High Steward Duchy of Cornwall and Warden Stannaries 1523, Constable Windsor Castle 1525, Lt Order of the Garter 1528, Seneschal Duchy of Cornwall June 1528, helped put down the Pilgrimage of Grace 1536; *m* 1st after June 1515 Elizabeth Grey, Baroness Lisle in her own right (*dsp*), dau of 2nd Viscount Lisle of the 1483 *cr* (*see* also NORFOLK, D); *m* 2nd 25 Oct 1519 Gertrude Blount (*d* 25 Sept 1558), dau of 4th Lord (Baron) Mountjoy of the 1465 *cr*, and was beheaded on Tower Hill 9 Jan 1538/9 for treasonable correspondence with Cardinal Pole (*see* ABERGAVENNY, M), his honours and lands being forfeited, having had issue by his 2nd w:

1g Henry; *d* young

2g EDWARD COURTENAY, **1st Earl of Devon** (E), so *cr* 3 Sept 1553 (and restored in blood but not his forebears' honours by Act of Parl 10 Oct 1553), KB (1553); *b* 1526; prisoner in Tower of London nearly 15 years till released 3 Aug 1553 shortly after accession of MARY I; allegedly involved in Sir Thomas Wyatt's conspiracy against MARY and apparently entertained the notion of marrying Princess Elizabeth (subsequently ELIZABETH I), as a result of which he was again imprisoned in the Tower 15 March 1553/4–25 May 1554 and then at Fotheringhay till 6 April 1555; on his release he went abroad and *d* unm 18 Sept 1556

1f Margaret; *m* as his 1st w (papal dispensation 15 June 1514) her cousin 2nd Earl of Worcester (*see* BEAUFORT, D) and *dsp* by 15 April 1526

2d Walter (Sir); took part with his bro and his cousin Piers Courtenay, Bp of Exeter, in the Duke of Buckingham's rising against RICHARD III 1484 and fled abroad on its failure; *d* unm

1d Maud; *m* Sir John Arundell (*see* 1939 edn ARUNDELL OF WARDOUR, B), and had issue

2d Elizabeth; *m* John Trethurffe and had issue

3d Isabel; *m* William Mohun, of Hall, Lanteglos, Cornwall, ancestor of the MOHUNs of Boconnock, extinct 1712

4d Florence; *m* John Trelawny, of Trelawny (*see* SALUSBURY-TRELAWNY, Bt)

2c Margaret; *m* Sir Theobald Grenville

4a William; Chllr Oxford 1367, Bp: Hereford 1370 and London 1375, Ld High Chllr England 1381, Archbp Canterbury 1381–96, officiated at marriage of RICHARD II to Anne of Bohemia 1382, afterwards crowning the Queen, but publicly rebuked the King for extravagance 1385 and was forced to take refuge among the Courtenay vassals and retainers in Devon; a commr appointed by Parl to reform the roy household and kingdom 1386; acted as mediator between RICHARD and his enemies 1387; *d* 31 July 1396

5a John; MP Devon; *dsp*

6a Philip (Sir), of Powderham Castle; Lt of Ireland 1383–93, inherited Powderham Castle from his mother the Countess of Devon, ktd 1367; *m* Anne, dau of Sir Thomas Wake (*see* WAKE, Bt), and *d* 1406, leaving with other issue:

1b Richard, PC; Bp Norwich 1413–15, *s* to Powderham Castle and considerable estates 1406; Chllr Oxford 1407, Amb to France 1414 to demand the French crown for HENRY V; *d* 15 Sept 1415 of dysentery at Siege of Harfleur

2b John (Sir); predeceased his bro, leaving issue:

1c Philip (Sir), of Powderham; *m* Elizabeth Hungerford, dau of 1st Lord (Baron) Hungerford (*see* ST DAVIDS, V), and *d* 1463, having had issue, with two daus:

1d William (Sir), of Powderham Castle; High Sheriff Devon 1483; *m* Margaret Bonville, dau of 1st Lord (Baron) Bonville of the 1449 *cr*, and *d* 1485, leaving:

1e William (Sir); *m* Cecily, dau of Sir John Cheney, of Pincourt, and *d* 1512, leaving issue:

1f William 'The Great' (Sir); *m* 1st Margaret, dau of Sir Richard Edgcombe, of Cothele (*see* MOUNT EDGCUMBE, E); *m* 2nd Mary, dau of Sir John Gainesford, had further issue, and *d* 24 Nov 1535, having had issue by his 1st w, with three other sons and a dau:

1g George; *m* Catherine, dau of Sir George St Leger, and *dvp*, leaving issue:

1h WILLIAM COURTENAY, *de jure* 2nd EARL OF DEVON of the 1553 *cr*, for whom *see* further below

1e Elizabeth; *m* Sir John Rogers and had issue (*see* ZOUCHE, B)

2d Philip (Sir), of Molland; *m* —, dau of Robert Hingeston, and had with other issue:

1e Elizabeth; *m* her cousin the 1st EARL OF DEVON of the 1485 *cr* (*see* above)

3d Piers, Bp Winchester 1487–92 and Exeter 1478–87; *educ* Oxford and Padua; joined in the Duke of Buckingham's unsuccessful plot against RICHARD III 1484, fled abroad with his cousins Walter and

Edward Courtenay (husband of his niece and later Earl of Devon, *see* above); one of the magnates who corresponded with HENRY VII prior to his arrival in England, joining him when he landed in 1485; Ld Privy Seal 1485–87; *d* 1492

4d Edmund (Sir), of Devlock, ancestor of the Cornish COURTENAYs

5d Walter (Sir)

6d John (Sir)

7d Humphrey; *m* and had issue:

1e A dau; *m* Thomas Carew

7a Piers (Sir), KG; Standard-Bearer to EDWARD III, Castellan Windsor, Capt Calais, Chamberlain to RICHARD II; *d* unm 1409

8a Humphrey

1 Margaret; *m* 1332/3 3rd Lord (Baron) Cobham of the 1312/3 *cr* and *d* 2 Aug 1385, leaving issue

The 1st EARL (of the 1553 *cr*)'s 6th cousin once-removed,

WILLIAM COURTENAY, *de jure* 2nd EARL OF DEVON (according to the decision of the House of Lords 1831); *b c* 1529; *s* his gf in the Powderham estate 1535, ktd 20 Oct 1553, MP Plympton 1555; *m* (licence 28 Nov 1545) Lady Elizabeth Paulet (*m* 2nd Sir Henry Oughtred and *d* 4 Nov 1576), dau of 2nd Marquess of Winchester (*qv*), and was *k* Siege of St Quintin, France, leaving issue:

WILLIAM COURTENAY, *de jure* 3rd EARL OF DEVON; *b c* 1553; ktd 25 March 1576, Sheriff Devon 1579–80, MP Devon 1584–86, 1588–89 and 1601; *m* 1st 18 Jan 1572/3 Lady Elizabeth Manners, dau of 2nd Earl of Rutland (*see* RUTLAND, D); *m* 2nd Elizabeth (*dsp* 9 June 1598), dau of Sir George Sydenham, of Combe Sydenham, and widow of Sir Francis Drake, and *d* 24 June1630, having had, with other issue by his 1st w:

1 William (Sir); ktd 1599; *dvp* unm 1603

2 FRANCIS, *de jure* 4th EARL

3 Sir GEORGE OUGHTRED COURTENAY, 1st Bt (I), so *cr* apparently Jan 1621/2, of Newcastle, Co Limerick; *b c* 1580–85; *m* by 1616 Catharine, dau of Francis Berkeley, of Askeaton, Co Limerick, and had:

(1) Sir WILLIAM COURTENAY, 2nd and (last?) Bt; *b c* 1616; *dspm c* 1651, when the btcy expired or became dormant

(2) Francis; *b c* 1617; may have had issue

(3) Morris; *dsp*

1 Elizabeth; *m* Sir William Wrey, 1st Bt (*qv*), and had issue

The *de jure* 3rd EARL OF DEVON's 2nd s,

FRANCIS COURTENAY, *de jure* 4th EARL OF DEVON; *b c* 1576; MP Devon 1625 and Grampound 1626; *m* 1st 7 Nov 1606 Mary (*dsp*), dau of Sir William Pole, of Colcomb, Devon, and widow of Nicholas Hurst; *m* 2nd Elizabeth (*m* 2nd as his 1st w Sir Amos Meredith, 1st Bt, of Marston, Devon, who *d* 3 Sept 1669; she *d* by 6 Feb 1664), dau of Sir Edward Seymour, 2nd Bt, of Berry Pomeroy (*see* SOMERSET, D), and *d* 3 June 1638, leaving:

Sir William Courtenay, 1st Bt (E), so *cr* by writ of Privy Seal Feb 1644/5, though he never bothered to have the patent enrolled, allegedly through contempt for the title; nevertheless styled as a Bt in communications from CHARLES I; also *de jure* 5th EARL OF DEVON; *bapt* 7 Sept 1628; ktd 9 April 1644, Sheriff Devon 1664–65, MP Devon 1679–81; *m* Margaret (*bur* 9 Jan 1693/4), dau of Sir William Waller, Parly Gen, and *d* 4 Aug 1702, having had:

Francis; *m* Mary, dau of William Boevey, of Flaxley, Glos and London, merchant, *dvp* and was *bur* 12 May 1699, leaving issue:

Sir William Courtenay, 2nd Bt, and *de jure* 6th EARL OF DEVON; *b* 4 March 1675; MP: (Tory) Devon 1700/1–10 and 1712–35 and Honiton 1715, Ld Lt Devon 1714–16; *m* 20 July 1704 Lady Anne Bertie (*d* 31 Oct 1718), dau of 1st Earl of Abingdon (*see* LINDSEY and ABINGDON, E), and *d* 10 Oct 1735, having had, with other issue:

1 **Sir William Courtenay, 3rd Bt**, and *de jure* 7th EARL OF DEVON; *b* 11 Feb 1709/10; *educ* Magdalen Coll Oxford (MA 1730/1, DCL 1739); MP (Tory) Honiton 1734–41, Devon 1741–62; *cr* 6 May 1762 VISCOUNT COURTENAY OF POWDERHAM CASTLE, Co Devon (GB); *m* 2 April 1741 Frances Finch (*d* 19 Dec 1761), dau of 2nd Earl of Aylesford (*qv*), and *d* 16 May 1762, having had, with five daus:

(1) **Sir William Courtenay, 4th Bt**, and *de jure* 8th EARL OF DEVON; *b* 30 Oct 1742; *m* 7 May 1762 Frances (*d* 25 March 1782), dau of Thomas Clack, of Wallingford, Berks, and *d* 14 Oct 1788, having had, with 13 daus (including Frances, *m* Sir John Honywood, 4th Bt (*qv*), and an 8th dau, Anne, *b* 2 July 1774, *m* 3 Sept 1790 9th Viscount Valentia (*qv*) and *d* 6 Jan 1835):

1a **Sir William Courtenay, 5th Bt**, and **9th Earl of Devon**; *b* 30 July 1768; on 15 March 1831 the Ho of Lords declared his right to the Earldom; *d* unm 26 May 1835, when the Viscountcy of Courtenay of Powderham Castle expired

2 Henry Reginald; MP, *b* 8 June 1714; *m* 14 April 1737 Lady Catherine Bathurst (*d* 1783), dau of 1st Earl Bathurst (*qv*), and *d* 30 April 1763, leaving issue:

(1) William (Rev); Rector Kenn, Devon; *b* 1738; *m* 31 Dec 1764 Anne, dau of John Downes, of Otterbury, Hants, and *dsp* 27 Nov 1783

(2) Henry Reginald (Rt Rev); Bp Exeter; *b* 1741; *m* 26 Jan 1774 Lady Elizabeth Howard (*d* 31 Oct 1815), dau of 2nd Earl of Effingham (*qv*), and *d* 9 June 1803, leaving issue:

1a WILLIAM, **10th Earl**

2a Thomas Peregrine; *b* 31 May 1782; *m* 5 April 1805 Anne (*d* Dec 1860), dau of Mayow Wynell-Mayow, of Sydenham, Kent, and *d* 8 July 1841, having had issue:

1b Thomas Peregrine; *b* 24 Feb 1810; Clerk Treasury; *d* 7 June 1861

2b Reginald (Rt Rev), DD (Oxon), Bp Kingston, Jamaica, 1856–79; *b* 26 Feb 1813; *m* 23 July 1842 Georgiana (*d* 7 Sept 1870), 2nd dau of Adml Sir John de la Poer Beresford, 1st Bt (*see* BERESFORD-PEIRSE, Bt), and *d* 13 April 1906, having had issue:

1c John Peregrine Charles; *b* 1843; *d* unm

2c Reginald Edward; *b* 7 Nov 1844; *d* 5 June 1873

1c Georgiana Harriet Anne; *b* 31 Jan 1846; *m* 11 Aug 1869 Rev George Thomas Ryves, MA (*d* 30 Jan 1897), and *d* 14 Feb 1932

2c Evangeline Claudette; *b* 22 April 1855; *m* 28 May 1880 Col Charles John Blake, RA, er s of Charles Blake

3c Mabel; *b* 24 Dec 1857; *d* 4 Nov 1936

3b George Henry; *b* 23 Dec 1814; Maj 60th Rifles; *m* 22 Sept 1852 Laura (*d* 28 June 1892), yst dau of David Samuda, and *d* 2 Jan 1910, having had issue:

1c Edward Reginald, CB; *b* 27 June 1853; Col (ret), T/Brig-Gen and DAG 2nd Army, Central Force, 1914, Lt-Col 11th Hus, served Zulu War 1870 (despatches twice, medal with clasp), Nile Expdn 1884–85 (medal with clasp and star), Sudan Expdn 1885–86 (despatches) and NW Frontier India 1897–98 (medal with clasp); *m* 1st 2 July 1878 (*divorce* 1881) Kathleen Ruth (*d* 30 Aug 1951), dau of Lt-Col Hugh Augustus Crofton (*see* CROFTON, Bt, of Mohill); *m* 2nd 5 Aug 1891 Mary Emily (*d* 20 Dec 1928), est dau of Maj-Gen F Hammersley, of Ashe Grange, Surrey, and *d* 29 March 1919, leaving issue:

1d Mary Catherine Natalie; *b* 14 Dec 1892; *m* 10 Aug 1922 George Gilbey Riviere (*d* 18 Sept 1937), of 93 Gloucester Place, London W1, 2nd s of Henri Riviere, and *d* 2 Sept 1933, leaving issue

2c Peregrine George; *b* 1855; *d* 1865

3c Thomas Peregrine (Rev); *b* 21 Feb 1856; Rector Down St Mary, N Devon, 1908–17, Vicar Hewish, Bristol, 1917–20; *m* 24 Jan 1883 Elizabeth (*d* 1920), dau of William Gittoes, and *dsp* 30 Aug 1941

1c Catherine Laura; *b* 13 March 1857; *d* unm 23 March 1934

2c Anne Henrietta; *b* 12 Nov 1858; *d* unm 22 Feb 1917

3c Elizabeth Frances; *b* 5 Jan 1860; *d* unm 2 Dec 1950

4c Laura Georgina; *b* 26 April 1861; *m* 1st 31 March 1880 (*divorce* 1884) her cousin Hon Hugh Leslie Courtenay (*see* below); *m* 2nd 7 Feb 1885 Reginald Latham Workman and *d* 1947

4b Francis (Rev); *b* 1816; *d* 25 Dec 1850

5b Edward; *b* 26 July 1818; *d* 7 Dec 1848

6b Richard William; *b* 11 March 1820; V-Adml RN, Kt of the Medjidie 5th Cl; *d* unm 4 May 1904

7b Henry Reginald; *b* 11 March 1823; Maj-Gen RA; *m* 1893 Elizabeth (*d* 18 Nov 1941), dau of Thomas Booth, of Plas Madoc, N Wales, and *dsp* 9 March 1911

8b Josceline; *b* 22 Dec 1824; *d* unm 7 Feb 1908

1b Anne Mayow; *b* 10 Feb 1807; *m* 31 March 1833 Edward Ross (*d* 1840) and *d* 14 July 1837

2b Elizabeth Howard; *b* 1 Aug 1808; *m* 18 Aug 1853 Rev John Hughes, MA, and *d* 23 Dec 1883

3b Mary; *b* 27 Aug 1811; *m* 1st Rev Henry James Wharton (*d* 1858), Vicar Mitcham; *m* 2nd Maj — Agnew and *d* 8 Feb 1902

4b Catherine; *b* 17 Feb 1827; *m* 3 June 1851 Rev George Carter, MA (*d* 1890), Rector Compton Beauchamp, Berks, and *d* 12 June 1914, leaving issue

5b Caroline Wynell; *b* 26 Oct 1829; *d* unm 4 March 1898

1a Elizabeth; Maid-of-Honour to QUEEN CHARLOTTE; *b* 5 Aug 1779; *d* unm 27 June 1852

2a Catherine; *b* 7 Jan 1781; *m* 30 Dec 1805 Ven Archdeacon Edward Berens and *d* 21 Nov 1865

3a Anne; *b* 31 March 1784; *d* unm 1818

4a Frances Charlotte; *b* 7 Sept 1790; *m* 20 Nov 1811 Rev Edward Bouverie (*see* RADNOR, E) and *d* 29 March 1854, leaving issue

3 Peregrine; *b* 11 May 1720; *m* 1st 1751 Lucy Incledon (*d* 2 Dec 1778); *m* 2nd 18 Feb 1780 Augusta Beaumont (*d* 1785), widow of Sir John Glynne, and *d* 2 Dec 1786

The 9th EARL's 2nd cousin,

WILLIAM COURTENAY, **10th Earl of Devon**; *b* 19 June 1777; *educ* Westminster and Ch Ch Oxford (BA 1798, MA 1801); barrister Lincoln's Inn 1799, Commr of Bankrupts 1802–17, MP (Tory) Exeter 1812–26, Master in Chancery 1817–26, DCL Oxford 1837, High Steward Oxford U 1838–59, Ecclesiastical Commr 1842–50; *m* 1st 29 Nov 1804 Lady Harriet Leslie (*d* 16 Dec 1839), dau of Sir Lucas Pepys, 1st Bt (*see* COTTENHAM, E), by his w Jane Elizabeth, Countess of Rothes (*qv*) in her own right; *m* 2nd 30 Jan 1849 Elizabeth Ruth (*d* 17 March 1914), dau of Rev John Middleton Scott and n of 10th Earl of Meath (*qv*), and *d* 19 March 1859, having had issue by his 1st w:

1 WILLIAM REGINALD COURTENAY, **11th Earl of Devon**, PC (1866); *b* 14 April 1807; *educ* Westminster and Ch Ch Oxford (BA 1828, BCL 1831, DCL 1838), Fell All Souls 1828–31, MP (C) S Devon 1841–49, Chllr Duchy Lancaster July 1866–May 1867, Hon Col Roy 1st Devon Yeo Cav; *m* 27 Dec 1830 Lady Elizabeth Fortescue (*d* 27 Jan 1867), 7th and yst dau of 1st Earl Fortescue (*qv*), and *d* 18 Nov 1888, having had:

(1) William Reginald; Lt Roy S Devon Yeo Cav; *b* 28 Oct 1832; *educ* Ch Ch Oxford; *dvp* 21 Nov 1853

(2) Hugh; *b* 10 Nov 1833, *d* 13 March 1835

(3) EDWARD BALDWIN COURTENAY, **12th Earl of Devon**; *b* 7 May 1836; *educ* Westminster and Ch Ch Oxford; MP (C) Exeter 1864–68 and E Devon 1868–70; *d* unm 15 Jan 1891

(1) Agnes Elizabeth; *m* 22 April 1869 2nd Viscount Halifax (*see* HALIFAX, E) and *d* 4 July 1919, leaving issue

2 HENRY HUGH, **13th Earl**

3 Edward; *b* 3 May 1813; *d* 16 Jan 1814

4 Charles Leslie (Rev), MA; *b* 31 March 1816; Canon Windsor, Vicar Bovey Tracey, Devon, Chaplain-in-Ordinary to HM QUEEN VICTORIA; *m* 20 June 1849 Lady Caroline Margaret Cocks (*d* 14 Nov 1894), est dau of 2nd Earl Somers (*see* SOMERS, B), and *dsp* 29 Oct 1894

1 Harriet Elizabeth; *b* 30 May 1809; *d* unm 3 Oct 1826

The 12th EARL's unc,

Rev HENRY HUGH COURTENAY, **13th Earl of Devon**; *b* 15 July 1811; *educ* Westminster and Merton Coll Oxford (BA 1833, MA 1844); Rector: Mamhead, Devon, 1845–77, Powderham 1877–1904, Preb Exeter 1876–1904; *m* 6 Jan 1835

Lady Anna Maria Leslie (*d* 18 Feb 1897), dau of Henrietta Anne, Countess of Rothes (*qv*) in her own right, and *d* 29 Jan 1904, having had issue:

1 Henry Reginald, *Lord Courtenay*, JP, DL Devon; *b* 20 Jan 1836; *educ* Westminster and Merton Coll Oxford (BA 1859); barrister Inner Temple 1864, Hon Col Roy Devon Yeo Cav; *m* 12 June 1862 Evelyn (*d* 7 Oct 1910), yst dau of 1st Earl of Cottenham (*qv*), and *dvp* 27 May 1898, leaving issue:

(1) CHARLES PEPYS COURTENAY, **14th Earl of Devon**, JP (Devon); *b* 14 July 1870; Inspector Bd of Ag 1895–1904, Maj Somerset LI (ret 1908), T/Major 1914–15; *d* unm 4 Feb 1927

(2) Rev HENRY HUGH COURTENAY, **15th Earl of Devon**; *b* 1 Aug 1872; Rector Powderham 1904–27; *d* unm 8 Feb 1935

(3) FREDERICK LESLIE, **16th Earl**

(1) Amy Evelyn; *b* 22 Feb 1865; *m* 18 Oct 1892 Col Hon Reginald Henry Bertie, CB, yst s of 6th Earl of Abingdon (*see* LINDSEY and ABINGDON, E), and *dsp* 21 Dec 1948

(2) Caroline Elizabeth; *b* 3 Jan 1867; *d* unm 5 June 1935

2 Hugh Leslie, MA (Oxford); *b* 1 Aug 1852; *m* 31 March 1880 (*divorce* 1884) his cousin Laura Georgina (*d* 1947), yst dau of Maj Geo Henry Courtenay (*see* above), and *d* 24 Nov 1907, leaving issue:

(1) Anna Maria Laura (Nita); *b* 26 Feb 1881; *m* 14 Sept 1909 Maj Edward Osborne Armstrong Newcombe, DSO, RE (*d* 15 May 1941), and *d* 30 Nov 1964, leaving issue

The 15th EARL's yr bro,

Rev FREDERICK LESLIE COURTENAY, **16th Earl of Devon**; *b* 31 Aug 1875; *educ* Exeter Coll Oxford; Rector Honiton, Devon, 1907–35, 2nd Lt late 1st Vol Bn Devonshire Regt, Mayor Honiton 1929–33, RD Honiton 1928–33; *m* 9 Jan 1907 Marguerite (*d* 4 May 1950), dau of John Silva, of Itchen Abbas, Hants, and *d* 19 June 1935, having had issue:

1 Henry John Baldwin; *b* 1 April, *d* 4 April 1915

2 CHARLES CHRISTOPHER COURTENAY, **17th and present Earl of Devon**

1 Evelyn Frances; *b* 30 June 1908; *m* 17 Oct 1936 *Maj Thomas Anstey, TD, MA, 4th Bn Devonshire Regt (RA), est s of Maj Alfred Anstey, of Matford House, Exeter, and *d* 198–, leaving issue:

(1) *Thomas Michael Courtenay [Thomas Anstey Esq, Cross Cottage, Bovey Tracey, Devon]; *b* 28 Sept 1937; *educ* Clifton; Capt The Devonshire Regt (TA), served Rifle Bde 1955–57 and London Rifle Bde, Rangers (TA) 1957–63, slr 1963; *m* 12 Aug 1961 *Margaret, LLB, er dau of Dudley Woodman, of Stratford-on-Avon, Warwicks, and has issue:

1a *Thomas Dudley; *b* 5 Oct 1965

2a *Henry Michael; *b* 5 Oct 1965

1a *Angela Margaret; *b* 25 Feb 1964

(2) *Patrick John; *b* 5 Dec 1942; *educ* Clifton

(1) *Anne Caroline; *b* 10 May 1939; *m* 30 May 1964 *Maj David Lionel Scott Langley, MC, RM, yr s of Lionel Scott Langley, of Hedgerow, Budleigh Salterton, Devon, and has issue:

1a *Jeremy David; *b* 24 Oct 1967

(2) *Evelyn Margaret [Mrs Philip Penfold, Craigend House, Stirling FK7 9QW]; *b* 25 May 1941; *m* 19 Feb 1966 *Philip James Bedford Linzee Penfold, s of Lt-Col Richard John Linzee Penfold, RA (ret), Mil Kt Windsor, of 18 Lower Ward, Windsor Castle and has:

1a *Jonathan Michael Falkner Linzee; *b* 16 July 1969; *educ* St Edward's Oxford

1a *Victoria Susan Linzee; *b* 1 Nov 1967; *educ* St Mary and St Anne's Abbots Bromley

2 *Mary Elizabeth, SRN, SCM [The Lady Mary Courtenay, The Briary, Exton, nr Exeter, Devon]; *b* 15 Jan 1910

3 *(Marguerite) Kathleen [The Lady Kathleen Birnie, The Cottage, Longparish, Hants]; *b* 15 Feb 1911; *m* 22 Nov 1933 Col Eugene St John Birnie, OBE, IA (*d* 1976), er s of Cyril Montague Birnie, of Melbourne, Australia, and has issue:

(1) *Marguerite Susan [Mrs Jasper Clutterbuck, Mottisfont House, nr Romsey, Hants]; *b* 19 Oct 1934; *m* 21 June 1958 *Jasper Meadows Clutterbuck, s of Hugh Meadows Clutterbuck, of Wootton Place, Woodstock, Oxon, and has issue:

1a *Hugh Meadows; *b* 31 July 1959

1a *Nichola Marguerite; *b* 17 March 1961

(2) *Angela Patricia Jane [Mrs Michael Joly de Lotbinière, Rougham House, Bury St Edmunds, Suffolk]; *b* 13 Aug 1936; *m* 7 Sept 1956 *Michael Edmund Joly de Lotbinière, yr s of Lt-Col Sir Edmond Joly de Lotbinière, of Horringer Manor, Bury St Edmunds, Suffolk (*see* HYLTON, B), and has issue:

1a *Christopher David; *b* 26 Dec 1957; *m* 1991 *Victoria C, dau of Graham Harvey Evers, of Domaine de la Rose, Opio, France AM

2a *Giles Anthony; *b* 3 Dec 1959; *m* 1990 *Veronica J, er dau of John Egerton Levett-Scrivener, of Sibton Abbey, Peasenhall, Suffolk

1a *Tessa Jane Joly; *b* 27 March 1962; *m* 1984 *Nigel N V Raywood

4 (Camilla) Gabrielle [The Lady Gabrielle Courtenay, The Briary, Exton, nr Exeter, Devon]; *b* 8 April 1913

5 *Angela Leslie [The Lady Angela Horsley, Marwood House, Offwell, Devon EX14 9RW]; *b* 7 Sept 1918; *m* 18 Jan 1947 Harold Cecil Moreton Horsley, MBE (*d* 9 Nov 1969), Malayan CS, only s of Harold Richard Horsley, of Harpenden, Herts, and has issue:

(1) *Richard Geoffrey Courtenay [Richard Horsley Esq, Elliotts Farmhouse, Adstone, Northants NN12 8DY]; *b* 26 Nov 1947; *educ* Westminster and Ch Ch Oxford; *m* 1983 *Susan Philippa, only dau of E A Trotman, of Lower Twinhoe Cottage, Midford, Bath, and has issue:

1a *Moreton William Edward; *b* 1985

1a *Anna Gabrielle Susan; *b* 1987

(2) *William Frederick Moreton [William Horsley Esq, 30 Bina Gardens, London SW5 0LA]; *b* 28 Jan 1949; *educ* St Edward's Sch Oxford and Pembroke Coll Oxford; *m* 1979 *Noriko, er dau of Tetsuo Makuuchi, of Tokyo

Seat: Powderham Castle, Kenton, Devon. The Sir Philip Courtenay who was Lieutenant of Ireland between 1383 and 1393 erected a building at Powderham about the same time. In his day the courses of the Rivers Exe and Kemm brought their waters right up to the house, which was fundamentally a narrow oblong surrounding a courtyard with towers at intervals. A walled courtyard and garden dating from this time survived till the mid-18th century.

Powderham, which remains basically a fortified manor house despite its name, has six towers still, the three main ones being at the northwest corner and half way along the east and west flanks. The latter two, which are of brick and built or rebuilt fairly late (in one case in 1766), are punctuated at their base by porches. The rest are of stone and probably of medieval origin, though greatly restored.

Internally Powderham is predominantly 18th-century rather than medieval. The Great Staircase in particular, with lavish plasterwork beneath the stairs as well as on the walls above, has been called one of the half-dozen best examples of its kind in the baroque style in the country. The chief executant was John Jenkins, whose putative father, Howell Jenkins, was responsible for the ceiling in the Library. The Music Room, which is domed and has a splendid white marble chimney piece, is by James Wyatt. In the 1790s Richard Westmacott the Elder also worked on the interior.

The **10th Earl** restored Powderham in the then fashionable baronial style, employing a Devonian architect, Charles Fowler. The principal entrance was shifted from the west side to the eastern one and embellished with a courtyard and mock-fortified gatehouse set in a curtain wall with more towers. A banqueting hall was inserted in the west front between two of the pre-existing towers. This, which was only completed in the **11th Earl**'s time, has as its main feature a huge Gothic fireplace copied from the one installed in his Palace by the two Earls' collateral ancestor Piers Courtenay, Bishop of Exeter in the 1470s and great-grandson of the Sir Philip who built Powderham.

The grounds, which have been called the best example of forest landscape in the country, contain a delicious neo-Gothick folly. This was put up by the 2nd Viscount Courtenay of Powderham Castle, who held that title between 1762 and 1788 (*see* against **Sir William Courtenay, 4th Bt**). It had the lead stolen from its roof during World War II and was twice damaged by vandal arsonists before being restored from the 1960s onwards.

DEVONPORT

Arms: Azure, in chief two mitres argent garnished or, and in base a square tower of the second. **Crest:** An ancient ship or, the mainsail azure charged with a sea lion gold. **Supporters:** On either side a sea lion argent, crined, finned and tufted or, each gorged with a collar gules charged with three roses gold and each supporting a spear erect proper. **Motto:** *Fit via vi* ('Life is made by strength').

Creations: Bt. (UK) 22 July 1908, B. (UK) 15 July 1910, V. (UK) 22 June 1917.

THE 3RD VISCOUNT DEVONPORT, Baron Devonport, of Wittington, Co Buckingham, and a **Baronet** (Sir Terence Kearley, Bt) [The Rt Hon The Viscount Devonport, Ray Demesne, Kirkwhelpington, Northumberland NE19 2RG]; *b* 29 Aug 1944; *s* f 1973; *educ* Aiglon Coll Switzerland and Selwyn Coll Cambridge (MA, BArch 1967, Dip Arch 1970); ARIBA 1973, architect London Borough of Lambeth, chartered architect with Barnett Winskell 1972–, BPhil (Landscape Design) of U of Newcastle 1975–77, farmer and forester; *m* 7 Dec 1968 (*divorce* 1979) Elizabeth Rosemary, 2nd dau of John Gordon Hopton, slr, of Chute Manor, Chute, Andover, Hants, and has:

1 *Velvet Jane; *b* 17 July 1975

2 *Idonia Clare; *b* 6 Nov 1977

Lineage: GEORGE EWBANKE KEARLEY, of Uxbridge Middx; *b* 29 April 1814 (s of William Kearley, of Tarrant Gunville, Dorset); *m* 30 Aug 1840 Mary Ann (*d* 20 Jan 1892), widow of Josiah John Barrow and dau of Charles Hudson, of Old Ford, Essex, and *d* 1 March 1876, having had a yst s:

Sir Hudson Ewbanke Kearley, 1st Bt, and 1st Viscount Devonport (UK), so *cr* 22 July 1908 and 22 June 1917 respectively, as also 15 July 1910 BARON DEVONPORT, of Wittington, Co Buckingham (all UK), DL, JP (Bucks) and JP (Surrey), PC (18 Oct 1909); *b* 1 Sept 1856; MP (Lib) Devonport 1892–1910, Parly Sec BOT 1905–09, Chm PLA 1909–25, Food Controller 1916–17, sr ptnr Kearley and Tonge, of London, Calcutta and Ceylon; *m* 18 Jan 1888 Selina (*d* 28 Sept 1931), only dau of Edward Chester, of Blisworth, Northants, and had:

1 GERALD CHESTER, **2nd Viscount**

2 Mark Hudson; *b* 3 March 1895; *educ* Eton, Magdalen Coll Oxford and on the Continent; Civil Prisoner of War Ruhleben 1914–18, sometime officially designated war artist in HMCS Naden, Esquimalt, BC, co-fndr Art Gallery of Greater Victoria BC 1944; *m* 26 May 1928 Mabel Florence (*d* 10 June 1967, est dau of John Francis Dagley, and *d* 1977, leaving issue:

(1) +CHESTER DAGLEY HUGH [Chester Kearley Esq, S Patos 466, Denia, Alicante, Spain]; *b* 29 April 1932; heir presumptive; *m* 1974 *Josefa, only dau of Nadal Mezquida, of Denia and has:

1a +David; *b* 18 Jan 1982

1a *Melanie; *b* 24 Aug 1978

(2) +Patrick Richard Hudson [Patrick Kearley Esq, 9 Chemin Tavarnay, 1218 Geneva, Switzerland]; *b* 20 July 1935; *educ* Selwyn Coll Cambridge; *m* 25 Aug 1962 *(Birgitta) Susanne, est dau of Director Karl-Erik Ringberg, of Bangergatan 43, Stockholm, and has:

1a *Selina Anna-Karin Georgiana Dayley; *b* 19 Aug 1967

2a *Cecilia Laura Anthea; *b* 29 Jan 1974

(1) *Anthea [Sigra Luigi Triossi, via del Babuino 141, Rome 00187, Italy]; *b* 25 May 1929; *m* 28 Nov 1959 *Luigi Triossi, Cav Dott Ing Gr Uff, only s of Raniero Triossi, of Rome, and has:

1a *Amanda Consuelo Fiorenza; *b* 11 June 1963

1 Beryl Kathleen; *d* unm 10 April 1965

The 1st VISCOUNT *d* 5 Sept 1934; his est son,

GERALD CHESTER KEARLEY, **2nd Viscount Devonport**; *b* 16 Sept 1890; *educ* Eton and Exeter Coll Oxford; WW I in Scots Gds and Remount Service, WW II as Head Observer Roy Observer Corps 1939–43 and CD 1943–45, memb LLoyd's; *m* 12 March 1938 *Sheila Isabel [The Rt Hon Sheila Viscountess Devonport, The Old Vicarage, Peasmarsh, Rye, E Sussex TN31 6XB], est dau of Col Charles Hope Murray, of Morishill, Beith, Ayrshire, and *d* 29 March 1973, leaving issue:

1 TERENCE KEARLEY, **3rd and present Viscount Devonport**

1 *Marilyn Whitson [The Hon Marilyn Kearley, Hermitage Farm, Peasmarsh, E Sussex TN31 6XL]; *b* 11 Sept 1939

DEVONSHIRE

Arms: Sable, three buck's heads cabossed argent. **Crest:** A serpent nowed proper. **Supporters:** Two bucks proper, each wreathed round the neck with a chaplet of roses alternately argent and azure. **Motto:** *Cavendo tutus* ('Safe by being careful'). **Creations:** B. (E) 4 May 1605 (Cavendish of Hardwick), E. (E) 7 Aug 1618, M. and D. (E) 12 May 1694, B. and E. (UK) 10 Sept 1831 (Cavendish of Keighley, Burlington).

THE 11TH DUKE OF DEVONSHIRE, Marquess of Hartington, Co Derby, **Earl of Devonshire**, **Earl of Burlington**, **Baron Cavendish of Hardwick**, Co Derby, and **Baron Cavendish of Keighley**, Co York (Andrew Robert Buxton Cavendish, KG (1996), MC (1944), PC (1964)) [His Grace The Duke of Devonshire KG MC PC, 4 Chesterfield St, London W1X 7HG; Chatsworth, Bakewell, Derbyshire DE45 1PP]; *b* 2 Jan 1920; *s f* 1950; *educ* Eton and Trin Coll Cambridge (BA 1943); Maj Coldstream Gds WW II, Mayor Buxton 1952–54, V-Lt Derbyshire 1957–87 (DL 1953–57), Cwlth Rels: Parly Under Sec 1960–62 and Min State 1962–64, Pres: Chesterfield C Assoc, Bldg Socs Assoc 1954–61, Royal Hosp and Home for Incurables and Nat Deaf Children's Soc, Chm: Roy Cwlth Soc 1966–69 (Pres 1969–) and Grand Cncl Br Empire Cancer Campaign 1956–81, Steward Jockey Club 1966–69, Patron in Chief Polite Society 1991–, KStJ , Chllr Manchester U 1965, Hon LLD Liverpool 1981, Hon Dr of Law Memorial U Newfoundland, author: *Park Top: A Romance of the Turf* (1976); *m* 19 April 1941 *Hon Deborah Vivien (Freeman-)Mitford, yst dau of 2nd Baron Redesdale (*qv*), and has had:

1 A son; *b* and *d* 14 Nov 1941

2 +PEREGRINE ANDREW MORNY, *Marquess of Hartington*, CBE (1997) [Marquess of Hartington CBE, Beamsley Hall, Bolton Abbey, Skipton, N Yorks BD23 6HD]; *b* 27 April 1944; *educ* Eton, Exeter Coll Oxford and RAC Cirencester; Sr Steward Jockey Club, dir Sotheby's, HM's Rep Ascot 1998–; *m* 28 June 1967 *Amanda Carmen, only dau of Cdr Edward Gavin Heywood-Lonsdale, DSC and bar, JP, RN, and has:

(1) +William, *Earl of Burlington* [Earl of Burlington, Beamsley Hall, Bolton Abbey, Skipton, N Yorks BD23 6HD]; *b* 6 June 1969; *educ* Eton

(1) *Celina Imogen; *b* 4 Oct 1971; *m* 3 June 1995 *Alexander Corfield Key Carter, only s of W G K Carter, CBE, FCA, of The Old Rectory, Elmley Lovett, Worcs, and has:

1a *A son; *b* 7 Dec 1997

(2) *Jasmine Nancy; *b* 4 May 1973

3 Victor; *b* and *d* 22 May 1947

1 *Emma; *b* 26 March 1943; chm Nat Tst Gdns Advsy panel 1984–; *m* 3 Sept 1963 *Hon Tobias William Tennant, yst son of 2nd Baron Glenconner (*qv*), and has issue

2 Mary; *b* and *d* 5 April 1953

3 *Sophia Louise Sydney [The Lady Sophia Morrison, The Quadrangle, Tisbury, Wilts]; *b* 18 March 1957; *m* 1st 20 Oct 1979 (*divorce* 1987) Anthony William Lindsay Murphy; *m* 2nd 1988 *Alastair John Morrison (*see* MARGADALE, B)

Earldom of Devonshire: For the ambiguous wording of titles concerning Earldoms of Devon or Devonshire, *see* DEVON, E, preliminary remarks.

Earldom of Burlington: The first creation of this title was in March 1663/4 in favour of Richard ('Richard the Rich') Boyle, who had succeeded his father as 2nd Earl of Cork in 1643. The latter (but earlier) Earldom was in the peerage of Ireland; the newer one brought a seat in the Westminster House of Lords as it was a creation in the English peerage. Boyle helped suppress the 1641 uprising in Ireland on CHARLES I's behalf. Later he was active in the Civil War as a royalist, so that he was fined and obliged to go into exile when the Parliamentarians triumphed. It is his great-grandson, the 3rd Earl (on whose death in 1753 this first creation of the Burlington Earldom expired), who was the celebrated amateur architect. 'Amateur' in this context is a relative term. None but a handful of professionals could have designed Chiswick House, the 3rd and last Earl of Burlington's testament to mankind, designed by him in 1723 on the lines of Palladio's Villa Capra near Vicenza. Lord Burlington was also a connoisseur of paintings and a patron of literature. The title Burlington is a corruption of Bridlington, in Yorkshire.

Lineage: Sir JOHN CAVENDISH; Ld of the Manor of Cavendish Overhall, Suffolk; Ch Justice King's Bench 1366, 1373 and 1377, Chllr Cambridge U *c* 1381; during the Peasants' Revolt he was given the responsibility of suppressing unrest in York; back in Suffolk he was unpopular both generally as a lawyer and particularly as father of the man who had allegedly killed Wat Tyler and he was accordingly dragged by a mob into the market place of Bury St Edmunds and beheaded; *m* Alice, dau and heiress of John de Odyngseles, and had, with a dau:

1 Andrew (Sir), of Cavendish Overhall; MP Suffolk *c* 1378, Sheriff Norfolk and Suffolk *c* 1385; *m* Rose — and *d* 1396, leaving issue:

(1) William, of Cavendish Overhall; conveyed his manor to his cousin William *c* 1412

2 John (Sir); Esq of the Body to RICHARD II; supposedly the killer of Wat Tyler during the Peasants' Revolt; ktd in consequence; *m* Joan, dau of Sir William Clopton, of Clopton, and had issue:

1 WILLIAM

2 Robert; Serjeant-at-Law; *dsp* 1439

3 Walter; living *c* 1433

The est son,

WILLIAM CAVENDISH, of Cavendish Overhall; *m* Joan Staventon and *d* 1433, having had, with a yr s (William):

THOMAS CAVENDISH, of Cavendish Overhall; *m* Katherine Scudamore (*d* 15 Sept 1499) and *d* 1477, leaving:

THOMAS CAVENDISH, of Cavendish Overhall; *m* 1st Alice (*d* 12 Nov 1515), dau and coheir of John Smith, of Podbrook Hall, Suffolk; *m* 2nd Agnes —, by whom he had a dau (Mary) and *d* shortly after 13 April 1523, leaving by his 1st w:

1 George, of Cavendish Overhall; attendant on Cardinal Wolsey with such fidelity that HENRY VIII later took him into his own service; *d c* 1562, leaving issue:

(1) William, of Cavendish Overhall, which he sold to William Dones 1569

(2) Ralph

2 WILLIAM

The 2nd son,

Sir WILLIAM CAVENDISH, PC; Gentleman-Usher to Cardinal Wolsey, later commissioner for suppressing various religious houses, as a result of which he built up huge territorial holdings; Treasurer of the Chamber to HENRY VIII, EDWARD VI and QUEEN MARY; *m* 1st Margaret, dau of Edmund Bostock, of Walcroft, Cheshire, and had issue; *m* 2nd Elizabeth, dau of Thomas Conyngsby, and had further issue; *m* 3rd 1547 Elizabeth ('Bess' or 'Building Bess' of Hardwicke; *b* 1518; *m* 3rd Sir William St Loe; *m* 4th 6th Earl of Shrewsbury (*see* SHREWSBURY and WATERFORD, E), and *d* 13 Feb 1607/8), widow of Robert Barley and dau and heir of John Hardwick, of Hardwicke, Derbys, and *d c* 1562; by his 3rd w he had:

1 Henry; MP Derbys; *m* Lady Grace Talbot, 3rd dau of 6th Earl of Shrewsbury (*see* SHREWSBURY and WATERFORD, E), and *dspl* 12 Oct 1616; his illegitimate s Henry was ancestor of the Barons Waterpark (*qv*)

2 WILLIAM, **1st Earl**

3 Charles (Sir), of Stoke, Derbys, and Welbeck Abbey, Notts; *b c* 1553; *m* 1st —; *m* 2nd Catherine, Baroness Ogle (*d* 18 April 1629) in her own right according to the then evolving doctrine (confirmed as such by letters patent 4 Dec 1628), yr dau and coheir of 7th Lord (Baron) Ogle, and *d* 4 April 1617, leaving:

(1) WILLIAM CAVENDISH, 1st DUKE OF NEWCASTLE-UPON-TYNE and EARL OF OGLE, both Co Northumberland, so *cr* 16 March 1664/5, as also earlier 29 Oct 1620 VISCOUNT MANSFIELD, Co Nottingham, ((?)and(?) BARON OGLE OF BOTHAL, Co Northumberland?), 7 March 1627/8 BARON CAVENDISH OF BOLSOVER, Co Derby, and EARL OF NEWCASTLE-ON-TYNE, and 27 Oct 1643 MARQUESS OF NEWCASTLE-ON-TYNE (all E); *s* mother as 9th LORD (Baron) OGLE 1629, KG (Jan 1649/50), KB (1610), PC (1639); *bapt* 16 Dec 1593 or perhaps *b* 1595; *educ* St John's Coll Cambridge; MP E Retford 1614, Ld Lt Notts 1626–42 and 1660–76 and Derbys

1628–38, royalist cdr in the N of England during Civil War, beating Parly forces at Piercebridge 1 Dec 1642 and Adwalton 1643, also taking Wakefield, Rotherham, Sheffield, Halifax, Leeds and, in Lincs, Gainsborough and Lincoln; in addition raised siege of York; advised beforehand against joining battle at the decisive royalist defeat of Marston Moor 1644, thereafter in exile till Restoration; Ld Lt Notts 1660, Jt Ld Lt Northumberland 1670–76; one of the best horsemen of his day, author of two books on equitation as well as some plays and poems on miscellaneous subjects and a work of political philosophy called *Treatise on Government*; *m* 1st *c* 1618 Elizabeth (*d* 17 April 1643), dau of William Bassett (*see* BOOTHBY, Bt) and widow of Henry Howard (*see* SUFFOLK and BERKSHIRE, E); *m* 2nd *c* Dec 1645 Margaret (*b* 1617; an extravagant and eccentric dresser, with pretensions to being a bluestocking, also a poet and playwright, author of what contemporaries described as an absurd encomium of her husb (though later views are more friendly), but known accordingly in her own time as 'Mad Madge of Newcastle'; *dsp* 15 Dec 1673), sis of 1st Baron Lucas of Shenfield (*see* LUCAS OF CRUDWELL, B), and *d* 25 Dec 1676, having had, with other issue, including three er sons and at least two daus (Elizabeth, *m* 2nd Earl of Bridgwater, *see* GREY EGERTON, Bt; Frances, *m* 6th Baron Saint John of Bletso, *qv*):

1a HENRY CAVENDISH, 2nd and last DUKE OF NEWCASTLE-UPON-TYNE, KG (1677), PC (1670–Feb 1668/9; *b* 24 June 1630; MP Derbys 1660 and Northumberland 1661–76; was against the declaration of WILLIAM and MARY as sovereigns after the departure of JAMES II and declined to take oath of loyalty to them; accordingly retired from public life after the Glorious Revolution of 1688; *m* by 1652 Frances, dau of William Pierrepont (2nd s of 1st Earl of Kingston-upon-Hull) and *dspms* 26 July 1691, when all his peerages save the Barony of Ogle expired, leaving five daus (of whom the 1st, Elizabeth, *m* 1st 2nd Duke of Albemarle (*see* MONCK, V); *m* 2nd 1st Duke of Montagu; the 3rd, Lady Margaret Cavendish, *m* John Holles, Earl of Clare, afterwards Duke of Newcastle, from whom descended the Dukes of Portland (*see* PORTLAND, E) and Newcastle (*see* LINCOLN, E); the 5th, Lady Arabella Cavendish, *m* the 3rd Earl of Sunderland (*see* MARLBOROUGH, D))

1 Frances; *m* Sir Henry Pierrepont, ancestor of the extinct Earls and Dukes of Kingston

2 Elizabeth; *m* 1574 Charles Stuart, Earl of Lennox (*see* MORAY, E), paternal uncle of JAMES I, and was mother of Lady Arabella Stuart, who allegedly was the cause of he 1st Earl being given his first step in the peerage as a baron

3 Mary; *m* 9 Feb 1567/8 7th Earl of Shrewsbury and Waterford (*qv*), and had issue

Sir WILLIAM's 2nd son,

WILLIAM CAVENDISH, **1st Earl of Devonshire**, so *cr* 7 Aug 1618, as also earlier 4 May 1605 BARON CAVENDISH OF HARDWICK [*sic*], Co Derby (both E), KB; *b* 27 Dec 1552; *educ* Eton and Gray's Inn; ktd 1580, MP Liverpool 1586–87 and Newport, Cornwall, 1587–88, Sheriff Derbys 1595–96, involved in transatlantic schemes of land devpt, including Virginia and Bermuda; *m* 1st (licence 21 March 1580/1) Anne, dau and coheir of Henry Keighley, of Keighley, Yorks, and had issue:

1 WILLIAM, **2nd Earl**

1 Frances; *m* William, 1st Baron Maynard

The **1st Earl** *m* 2nd by 1619 Elizabeth, dau and heir of Edward Boughton, of Causton, Warwicks, and widow of Sir Richard Wortley, of Wortley, by whom he had issue:

2 John (Sir), KB

The 1st EARL *d* 3 March 1625/6; his 2nd but er surv son,

WILLIAM CAVENDISH, **2nd Earl of Devonshire**; *b* 1590; *m* 10 April 1608 Christian Bruce (*d* 16 June 1674), dau of 1st Lord Kinloss (*qv*), and had:

1 WILLIAM, **3rd Earl**

2 Charles; royalist Civil Wars; *ka*

1 Anne; *b c* 1612; *m* 9 April 1632, as his 1st w, Robert Rich, 3rd Earl of Warwick of the 1618 *cr* (*see* WARWICK, BROOKE and, E), and *d* 24 Aug 1638

The 2nd EARL *d* 20 June 1628; his est son,

WILLIAM CAVENDISH, **3rd Earl of Devonshire**, KB (Feb 1625/6); *b* 10 Oct 1617; *m* (licence 4 March 1638/9) Lady Elizabeth Cecil (*d* 19 Nov 1689), 2nd dau of 2nd Earl of Salisbury (*see* SALISBURY. M), and *d* 23 Nov 1684, having had, with a dau (Anne, *m* 5th Earl of Exeter; *see* EXETER, M):

WILLIAM CAVENDISH, **1st Duke of Devonshire** and MARQUESS OF HARTINGTON, Co Derby (both E), so *cr* 12 May 1694, KG (1689), PC (1689); *b* 25 Jan 1640/1; one of the seven magnates who signed the invitation to William of Orange to come to England and among the first to take up arms on his behalf on his arrival, Ld Steward Household 1689–1707; *m* 26 Oct 1662 Lady Mary Butler (*d* 31 July 1710), 2nd dau of 1st Duke of Ormonde (*see* MOUNTGARRET, V), and had:

1 WILLIAM, **2nd Duke**

2 Henry, MP; *b* 1673; *m* Rhoda (*d* 24 Jan 1729/30), sis of Thomas Cartwright, of Aynhoe, Oxon, MP Northants, and *d* 10 May 1700, having had issue:

(1) Mary; *m* 7th Earl of Westmorland (*qv*) and *dsp* 29 July 1778

3 James, MP, of Staveley, Derbys, and Latimer, Bucks; *m* Anne (*d* 27 June 1734), dau of Elihu Yale, Govr Fort St George, and *d* 14 Dec 1751, having had:

(1) William; *m* Barbara, dau of Edward Chandler, Bp Durham, and *dsp* July 1751

(1) Elizabeth *m* Feb 1722 Richard CHANDLER later CAVENDISH, er s of the Bp of Durham

1 Elizabeth; *m* Sir John Wentworth, 1st Bt, of North Elmsal

The 1st DUKE *d* 18 Aug 1707; his est son,

WILLIAM CAVENDISH, **2nd Duke of Devonshire**, KG (March 1709/10); *b c* 1673; MP (Whig) Derbys 1695–1701, Castle Rising Feb-July 1702 and Yorks 1702–07, Ld Steward Household 1707–10, Ld Pres Cncl 1716–17 and 1725–29; *m* 21 June 1688 Rachel (*d* 28 Dec 1725), sister of 2nd Duke of Bedford (*qv*), and had, with other issue (including a dau Elizabeth, *m* Sir Thomas Lowther, 2nd Bt; *see* LONSDALE, E):

1 WILLIAM, **3rd Duke**

2 James, MP; *d* unm 14 Dec 1741

3 Charles; MP Heytesbury 1725, Westminster 1727 and Derby 1734; *m* 9 Jan 1727 Lady Ann Grey (*d* 20 Sept 1733), dau of Henry, Duke of Kent (*see* LUCAS OF CRUDWELL, B), and had issue:

(1) Frederick

(2) Henry, FRS; the chemist

The 2nd DUKE *d* 4 June 1729; his est son,

WILLIAM CAVENDISH, **3rd Duke of Devonshire**, KG (1733), PC (1731); *b* 1698; *educ* New Coll Oxford; MP (Whig) Lostwithiel 1721–24, Grampound 1724–27 and Hunts 1727–29, Ld Privy Seal 1731–33, Ld Steward Household 1723–37 and 1745–49, Ld Lt Ireland 1737–45; *m* 27 March 1718 Catherine (*d* 8 May 1777), only dau and heir of John Hoskins, of Oxted, Surrey, Steward to Duke of Bedford, and had, with three daus:

1 WILLIAM, **4th Duke**

2 George Augustus, of Holker, Lancs, which he inherited from his cousin, Sir William Lowther, 3rd and last Bt, of Marske (*see* LONSDALE, E); *d* unm 2 May 1794

3 Frederick; FM, Col 34th Foot; *b* 1729; *d* unm 21 Oct 1803

4 John; *b* 1734; Chllr Exchequer 1782 and 1783

1 Elizabeth; *m* 22 Sept 1743 John Ponsonby (*see* BESSBOROUGH, E) and *d* 1796

The 3rd DUKE *d* 5 Dec 1755; his est son,

WILLIAM CAVENDISH, **4th Duke of Devonshire**, called up to Ho Lds 13 June 1751 *vp* in his f's Barony of Cavendish of Hardwick, KG (1756), PC (1751–62); *b* 1720; MP (Whig) Derbys 1741–51, Ld High Treas Ireland and Govr Co Cork 1754–64, Ld Lt Ireland 1755–56, 1st Ld Treasury and PM 16 Nov 1756–June 1757, Ld Chamberlain 1757–62; *m* 27 March 1748 Charlotte Elizabeth, Baroness Clifford (*see* DE CLIFFORD, B) in her own right (*d* 24 Dec 1754), only dau and heir of Richard Boyle, 3rd Earl of Burlington (of the March 1663/4 *cr*) and (4th Earl of) Cork (*see* CORK and ORRERY, E), and *d* 2 Oct 1764, having had:

1 WILLIAM CAVENDISH, **5th Duke of Devonshire**, KG (1782); *b* 14 Dec 1748; *m* 1st 5 June 1774 Georgina (*b* 7 June 1757; the fashionable beauty who canvassed for Charles James Fox (*see* ILCHESTER, E) in the Westminster election by trading kisses for votes; *d* 30 March 1806), dau of 1st Earl Spencer (*qv*), and had, with two daus:

(1) WILLIAM SPENCER CAVENDISH, **6th Duke of Devonshire**, KG (1827), PC (1827); *b* 21 May 1790; *educ* Harrow and Trin Coll Cambridge; Amb Russia, Ld Chamberlain 1827–28 and 1830–34, Ld Lt and Custos Rotulorum of Derbyshire 1811–58, High Steward of Derby; *d* unm 17 Jan 1858

1 The **5th Duke** *m* 2nd 19 Oct 1809 Lady Elizabeth (*d* 20 March 1824), dau of 4th Earl of Bristol (*see* BRISTOL, M) and widow of John Thomas Foster and *d* 29 July 1811

2 Richard; *d* unm 1781

3 GEORGE AUGUSTUS HENRY CAVENDISH, **1st Earl of Burlington** of the (10 Sept) 1831 *cr*, also *cr* that day BARON CAVENDISH OF KEIGHLEY, Co York (both UK); *b* 31 March 1754; MP (Whig) Knaresborough 1775–80, Derby 1780–96 and Derbyshire 1797–1831; *m* 27 Feb 1782 Lady Elizabeth Compton (*d* 7 April 1835), dau and heir of 7th Earl of Northampton (*see* NORTHAMPTON, M), and *d* 4 May 1834, having had issue:

(1) William, MP; *b* 10 Jan 1783; *m* 18 July 1807 Louisa O'Callaghan (*d* 18 April 1863), est dau of 1st Baron Lismore (*see* 1898 edn), and *dvp* 14 Jan 1812, leaving issue:

1a WILLIAM CAVENDISH, **2nd Earl** and **7th Duke**

2a George Henry; MP N Derbyshire; *b* 19 Aug 1810; granted 1858 with his sis and yr bro rank of duke's dau/yr s; *m* 4 July 1835 Lady Louisa Lascelles (*d* 10 March 1886 aged 73), yst dau of 2nd Earl of Harewood (*qv*), and *d* 23 Sept 1880, leaving issue:

3a Richard; *b* posthumously 3 July 1812; *d* unm 19 Nov 1873

1a Fanny; *m* 1 July 1837 Frederick John Howard (*d* 28 Feb 1897), gs of 5th Earl of Carlisle (*qv*), and *d* 30 Dec 1885 aged 76, leaving issue

(2) George Henry Compton; *b* 14 Oct 1784; *d* 22 Jan 1809

(3) Henry Frederick Compton; Gen, Col 2nd Dragoon Gds; *b* 5 Nov 1789; *m* 1st 24 Oct 1811 Sarah (*d* Nov 1817), dau of William Augustus Fawkener, and had issue:

1a William Henry Frederick; Groom-in-Waiting to HM QUEEN VICTORIA, Lt-Col Chatsworth Rifles; *b* 31 Oct 1817; *m* 19 Aug 1843 Lady Emily Lambton (*d* 2 Nov 1886), dau of 1st Earl of Durham (*qv*), and *d* 11March 1881, having had, with other issue:

1b Henry Frederick Compton, DL, JP Derbyshire; Capt (emergency list) RN; *b* 6 May 1854; *m* 10 July 1888 Lady Harriet Castalia Godolphin Osborne (*d* 16 June 1922), dau of 9th Duke of Leeds (*see* 1963 edn), and *d* 21 Jan 1928, leaving issue:

1c Henry James Francis, DSC; Cdr RN WW I (despatches); *b* 17 Aug 1893; *m* 1928 (*divorce* 1934) Dola Frances (*d* 9 Dec 1966), dau of Hon James Dunsmuir, Premier of British Columbia, and *dsp* 30 June 1956

2c George Sidney Godolphin; Lt-Cdr RN WW I (despatches); *b* 3 Dec 1895; *m* 11 Jan 1933 *Mary Stuart, widow of Samuel Grey Dayton and dau of Charles Stewart Wurts, of Philadelphia

1c Emily Georgiana Harriet; *b* 22 Dec 1890; *m* 17 Nov 1938 Sir Pryse Loveden Saunders-Pryse, 5th and last Bt (*d* 5 Jan 1962; *see* 1956 edn), and *dsp* 23 Dec 1976

2c Evelyn Alice Beatrix; *b* 30 July 1892; *m* 14 July 1924 Brig James Erskine Stirling, DSO, HML, Seaforth Highrs (*d* 20 Dec 1968), son of Maj William Stirling, of Fairburn, Ross-shire, and had issue:

1d *William Henry [William Stirling Esq, 3 Woodsford Sq, Addison Rd, London W14]; *b* 12 Dec 1926; *m* 1st 28 Nov 1959 (*divorce* 1967) Mariota, yst dau of Col Ronald Menzies of Menzies, DL, JP, of Arndilly House, Craigellachie, Banffshire; *m* 2nd 4 April 1968 *Primrose, yst dau of Maj William Francis Butler, 13th/18th Hus, and has issue

1d *Bridget Mary [The Hon Mrs David Rollo, 30 King St, Nairn, Scotland]; *b* 20 June 1925; *m* 30 Sept 1948 Capt Hon David Ian Rollo (*d* 1981), MBE, MC, Gren Gds, yst son of 12th Lord Rollo (*qv*) of Duntrub, and has issue

2d *Ann Evelyn [Mrs Claude Kelway-Bamber, Oakhill House, Frensham, Surrey]; *b* 5 July 1929; *m* 12 Jan 1951 *Lt-Col Claude Glen Kelway-Bamber, MBE, Argyll and Sutherland Highrs, son of Cdr Herbert Roderick Kelway-Bamber, RN (ret), and has issue:

1e *Roderick James; *b* 8 July 1952

2e *Martin Charles; *b* 31 March 1955

3e *Euan Glen; *b* 8 May 1958; Capt Scots Gds; *m* 1984 *Laura Isabel Hester Morgan-Grenville (*see* KINLOSS, L)

1e *Emma Clare; *b* 8 Sept 1960

3d *Sarah Caroline [Mrs Patrick Doyne, Northend Manor, Leamington Spa, Warwicks]; *b* 24 June 1933; *m* 7 Dec 1963 *Capt Patrick Robert Doyne, The Rifle Bde, son of Col Robert Harry Doyne, of Barrow Court, Galhampton, and has issue:

1e *Timothy Robert Hamish; *b* 28 March 1966; *educ* Eton

2b Cecil Charles; Maj 2nd Bn Highland LI; *b* 14 May 1855; *m* 4 March 1890 Maud Henrietta (*d* 5 March 1955), dau of Lt-Gen George Thomas Halliday, ISC, and *d* 21 Jan 1931, having had issue:

1c Frederick George, DSO (1919), MC; Maj Highland LI WW I (despatches twice, wounded); *b* 2 Nov 1891; *m* 29 Nov 1919 Milla Jean (*d* 28 June 1976 aged 83), only dau of William St Clair Grant, of Bhagalpur, Bengal, India, and *d* 10 April 1936, leaving issue:

1d Ann; *b* 30 Nov 1920; *d* 24 Feb 1995

2d *(Jean) Caroline [Mrs George Lassalle, Kapodistrias 46a, Limassol 3032, Cyprus]; *b* 3 April 1932; *educ* LMH Oxford; *m* 1st 14 July 1954 (*divorce* 1959) Anthony Richard Champion de Crespigny, 3rd son of AVM Hugh Vivian Champion de Crespigny, CB, DFC, MC, of Vierville, Natal, S Africa, and has issue:

1e *Camilla Georgiana; *b* 1955

2d (cont.) Mrs Caroline Champion de Crespigny *m* 2nd 1974 George Charles Denis Lassalle (*d* 17 April 1997)

2c Bruce Alwynne; *b* 27 April; *d* 5 June 1894

3c Ronald Valentine Cecil, OBE (1940), MC; Brig Sherwood Foresters, Maj Notts and Derbyshire Regt, T/Staff Capt British Troops Sudan 1935, served WW I (despatches twice, wounded twice) and WW II (despatches); *b* 14 Feb 1896; *m* 20 Dec 1923 (Violet) Helen (*d* 7 Feb 1974), est dau of Arthur Sackville Boucher, of Sharpcliffe Hall, Staffs, and was *ka* whilst cmdg 6th Inf Bde on Mayu Peninsula, Burma, 6 April 1943, leaving:

1d +Peter Boucher, CB (1981), OBE (1969) [Brig Peter Cavendish CB OBE, The Rock Cottage, Middleton, Bakewell, Derbyshire]; Brig-Col cmdg 14th/20th King's Hus, late 3rd King's Own Hus, Chm NATO Mil Agency for Standardisation, MBIM; Ib 26 Aug 1925; *educ* Winchester; *m* 12 June 1952 *Marion Loudon, 2nd dau of Robert Alfred Constantine, TD, JP, of Tanton Grange, Stokesley, Yorks, and has:

1e +(Ronald) Simon Constantine [Simon Cavendish Esq, 191 Annie St, New Farm, Brisbane, Qld 4005, Australia]; *b* 19 March 1954; *educ* Wellington; *m* 1990 *Rosemary Alexandra, yr dau of P G F Lancaster, of Aston Flamville, Leics, and has issue:

1f +Nicholas Peter Lancaster; *b* 1993

1f *Maia Marita; *b* 20 March 1995

2e +Mark Francis; *b* 3 Nov 1955; *educ* Wellington

3e +Rupert William; *b* 5 April 1962; *m* 1986 *Lesley, er dau of J K Buckle, of Harlow, Essex, and has issue:

1f *Sarah Frances; *b* 1991

2d Robin Francis, MBE (1975); Capt KRRC; *b* 12 March 1930; *educ* Winchester; *m* 29 June 1957 *Diana Mary [Mrs Robin Cavendish, Furlongs, Drayton St Leonard, Oxon OX10 7AU], yr dau of Lt-Col Latham Valentine Stewart Blacker, OBE, of Coldhayes, Liss, Hants (*see* PEEL, E), and *d* 1994, leaving issue:

1e +Jonathan Stewart; *b* 4 Feb 1959; *educ* Eton and Oxford; *m* 1992 *Lesley A, dau of Eric Rogers and has:

1f +Theodore Robin; *b* 30 March 1996

1f *Polly Elinor; *b* 30 March 1996

2f *Willow Alice; *b* 30 March 1996

4c Charles Vernon Balfour; *b* 14 Oct 1902; *educ* Haileybury; *m* 1st 17 April 1937 (*divorce* 1950) Nancy Cranswick Neal (*d* 1986), dau of Ernest William Redstone, of Wellington, NZ, and has issue:

1d Susan; *b* 10 Aug 1939

2d *Rosalind [Mrs Alan Davidson, 16A Clarendon Rd, Colliers wood, London SW19 2DU]; *b* 29 May 1945; *m* 1971 *Alan Hugh Davidson

4c (cont.) Charles Cavendish *m* 2nd 27 July 1963 Eve (*d* 1986), widow of Athelstan Douglas Dempster Bonnor, and *d* 1981

1a Elizabeth Georgina Harriet; *m* 1st 3 Feb 1837 William Bernard Harcourt (*d* 25 May 1846), of St Leonard's, Berks (Marquis d'Harcourt in France), and had issue; *m* 2nd 30 June 1852 Lt-Gen James R Crauford (*d* 24 March 1888), and *d* 3 Jan 1892, leaving issue

2a Sarah Mary; *m* 28 June 1842 2nd Earl Cawdor (*qv*), and *d* 21 April 1881, leaving issue

(3) (cont.) Gen The Hon Henry Cavendish *m* 2nd 16 June 1819 Frances Susan (*d* 23 Nov 1840), widow of Col Hon Frederick Howard (*k* 1815 at Waterloo) and sister of 1st Earl of Durham (*qv*), and by her had issue:

2a Francis William Henry; FO; *b* 6 Feb 1820; *m* 1st 24 April 1856 (*divorce* 1866) Lady Elinor Sophia Diana FitzGibbon (*d* 1915), 3rd dau and coheir of 3rd Earl of Clare, and had:

1b Reginald Richard Frederick; *b* 25 Feb 1857; *m* 1st 11 Sept 1880 Mary Constance (*d* 14 July 1914), dau of Rev Harry Dupuis, Vicar Richmond, Surrey, and had issue:

1c George Francis Compton; *b* 23 Aug 1881; *d* 3 Feb 1884

2c Godfrey Lionel John, Capt IA; *b* 30 March 1884; *m* 22 March 1911 Cora Grace Graham (*m* 2nd 24 Sept 1919 Douglas Moor Horsford, Lt Gren Gds (SR), yr son of Col Thomas Moor Alphonse Horsford, of Bosvathick, Falmouth, Cornwall, and *d* 5 June 1962), yr dau of Joseph Alphonsus Horsford, MRCS, LRCP Edin, of Long Melford, Suffolk, and *d* of wounds received in action 22 Dec 1914, leaving issue:

1d Godfrey Herbert Richard; memb London Stock Exchange, Capt Royal Wilts Yeo, served WW II in Middle East and on Br Mil Mission to Egyptian Army; *b* 14 Jan 1912; *m* 15 April 1950 *Angela Margaret Jervis [Mrs Godfrey Cavendish, 9 Oakhill Place, London SW15 2QN], only dau of Lt-Col William Gerald Officer, Duke of Wellington's Regt, by Winifred Margaret Mylne, only dau of Sir Alfred Kensington, ICS, and *d* 25 Aug 1958, leaving issue:

1e *Diana Grace Angela [Mrs John Reeves, Kilmichael House, Kilmichael Glassary, by Lochgilphead, Argyll PA31 8QA]; *b* 30 Jan 1954; *m* 15 May 1975 *(Frederick) John Reeves, er son of Lt-Col N R Reeves, and has:

1f *Henry Frederick Godfrey; *b* 1981

1f *Georgina Caroline Angela; *b* 1984

2f *Olivia Clare Lucy; *b* 1989

2e *Caroline Elizabeth Clare [The Hon Mrs Philip Remnant, Ham Farm House, Ramsdell, Hants RG26 5SD]; *b* 16 June 1956; *m* 14 July 1977 *Hon Philip John Remnant, est son of 3rd Baron Remnant (*qv*), and has issue

2d (Hubert) Gordon Compton; Capt RASC WW II E Africa; *b* 26 Feb 1913; *m* 17 April 1942 *Beaujolois Inez [Mrs Gordon Cavendish, Bosvathick, Constantine, Falmouth, Cornwall TR11 5RD], er dau of Capt Philip George Wodehouse, DSO, RN (*see* KIMBERLEY, E), and *d* 1993, leaving issue:

1e +Richard Gordon John [Richard Cavendish Esq, 10 Basil Close, Earley, Reading, Berks]; *b* 13 April 1949; *educ* Sherborne; Capt BA; *m* 1st 1973 (*divorce* 1980) Jill Dare, dau of Frank D Baker, of Sunbury on Thames, and has issue:

1f +Charles William Gordon; *b* 1975

1f *Susanna Lucy; *b* 1974

1e (cont.) Richard Cavendish *m* 2nd 1981 *Mrs Susan Denton, dau of John Glyndwr Thomas, and has further issue:

2f *Theresa Louise; *b* 1983

1e *(Beaujolois) Katharine [Mrs Stephen Smyth-Tyrrell, Bosvathick, Constantine, Falmouth, Cornwall TR11 5RD]; *b* 1 April 1947; *m* 1978 *Stephen Charles Smyth-Tyrrell and has issue:

1f *Philip Charles; *b* 1981

1f *Eleanor Katherine Beaujolois; *b* 1979

2f *Josephine Clare; *b* 1983

3c Richard Charles Alexander, CBE (1939), KPM (1927); Inspr-Gen Kenya Police, CStJ; *b* 6 Aug 1885; *m* 26 May 1936 Margaret, OBE (1966), DGStJ (*d* 28 July 1977), widow of F O Lyon and dau of Lt-Col Duncan Johnstone, and *dsp* 29 April 1941

1c Rachel Muriel Constance Evelyn; *b* 13 Oct 1882; *d* unm 24 June 1939

2c Diana Violet Gladys; *b* 6 Feb 1887; *m* 16 April 1914 James Shuckburgh Carter (*ka* 27 Sept 1918), Capt Gren Gds, 3rd son of J P Carter, of Eton College, and *d* 27 July 1962, leaving issue

3c Beatrix Frances Dupois; *b* 8 March 1888; *m* 16 April 1914 Hugh Molyneux Miller (*d* 1944), son of Robert Miller, of Wimbledon, Surrey, and had issue

4c Dorothy Alice Georgina; *b* 1891; *m* 28 Aug 1918 Capt Hilliary Ralph Hood (*d* 1960), MC, RGA, and *d* 1965, leaving issue

1b (cont.) Reginald Cavendish *m* 2nd 4 July 1922 Martha Douglas (*d* 26 Jan 1963), widow of Col Richard Leigh, HLI, and dau of Thomas Henry Reynolds, and *d* 3 Nov 1941

2b Alfred Edward John, CMG (1900); Col and Hon Brig-Gen Argyll and Sutherland Highrs, served Japan and China War 1894–95, S African War 1899–1902 (despatches), WW I on Staff (despatches); *b* 19 June 1859; *m* 18 May 1886 Alice Isabella (*d* 26 Dec 1944), yr dau of Hon John Van der Byl, of Cape of Good Hope, and *d* 2 Feb 1943, leaving issue:

1c Ralph Henry Voltelin, CBE (1945), MVO (1910), DL (1952) Kent; Capt Gren Gds WW I (despatches), WW II as Col HG; *b* 27 March 1887; *educ* Eton; *m* 4 Feb 1926 Lady Gweneth Frida (*d* 1984), JP, widow of Hon Windham Baring (*see* CROMER, E), and dau of 8th Earl of Bessborough (*qv*), and *d* 21 June 1968, having had:

1d Edward Simon Myles; *b* 4 Aug 1928; *d* unm 4 Jan 1947 while serving in the ranks (Offr Cadet) Gren Gds

3b Ernest Lionel Francis, served Madras Police and Prisons Depts 1883–1900, and Prisons Service UK 1900–22; *b* 2 Feb 1863; *m* 23 Feb 1886 Jessie (*d* 29 Oct 1930), 2nd dau of William Jenkins, of West House, Fishguard, and *d* 10 May 1946, having had issue:

1c Alwyn Lionel Compton, Sudan Political Service, Maj Rifle Bde WW I (despatches, severely wounded twice); *b* 26 March 1890; *m* 18 Aug 1917 Muriel Cecil Harriott (*m* 3rd 20 Aug 1946 2nd Baron Forteviot (*qv*) and *d* 1975), widow of Richard Charles Graves-Sawle, Coldstream Gds (*see* 1932 edn GRAVES-SAWLE, Bt), and dau of Lt-Col Sir Charles Henry Brabazon Heaton-Ellis, CBE, DL, of Wyddiall Hall, Herts, and *d* 28 Aug 1928, leaving:

1d +Charles Francis Alwyn Compton [Charles Cavendish Esq, Cider Cottage, Hemyock, Cullompton, Devon]; *b* 29 May 1919; *educ* Eton and Fettes; served WW II (wounded) in Middle East and NW Europe, Intell Corps and 2nd Lt 8th Hussars, Lt KOSB; *m* 1st 22 July 1943 (*divorce*1946) Margaret Savage, MB, BS, Sect Offr WAAF (*d* 22 Aug 1961), 4th dau of Capt Philip Clayton Alcock, DL, JP, of Overton Lodge, Ludlow Salop; *m* 2nd 19 July 1947 *Esther Marion Patricia, only dau of Col Chichester de Windt Crookshank, DL, JP, KGStJ, FSA, 7th of Drumhairy, Co Longford, and of Johnstounburn, Humble, E Lothian, and by her has issue:

1e +William Alwyn Charles Chichester; *b* 27 Nov 1956; *m* 1985 *Margaret Josephine, dau of Joseph Benedict MacDonald, of Antigonish, Nova Scotia, and has issue:

1f +Myles Joseph Charles; *b* 1991

1f *Monica Josephine Patricia; *b* 1988

2e +Mark Andrew Lionel Compton; *b* 1 Aug 1958; *m* 1988 *Sarah Jane, er dau of Richard Formby, of Chartley Hall, Staffs, and has issue:

1f +George Andrew Francis Stuart; *b* 1989

2f +Edward Charles Robert Pitcairn; *b* 14 Nov 1994

1f *Katharine (Kitty) Mary Louise; *b* 1991

2a (cont.) Francis Cavendish *m* 2nd 14 Oct 1876 Ianthe Florence (*d* 20 July 1917), est dau of Maj-Gen Charles Francis Skyring, RE, and *d* 12 Jan 1893, having by her had issue:

4b Nigel Frederick Rupert; *b* 22 Jan 1879; *educ* Bedford; *d* unm 16 Sept 1949

3a Henry Charles Lambton; *d* 6 Oct 1839

4a Charles William; *b* 24 Sept 1822; *m* 1st 27 Oct 1847 Felicia Susan (*dsp* 29 Oct 1848), est dau of 4th Earl Beauchamp (*see* 1970 edn); *m* 2nd 25 June 1863 Louisa Cockburn (*d* 25 April 1869), and by her had issue:

1b Louis Francis John, Lt RMLI; *b* 24 Oct 1864; *d* unm 31 Dec 1890

4a (cont.) Charles Cavendish *m* 3rd 16 June 1873 Mary (*d* 26 Aug 1900), adopted dau of Ivie Gregg, and *d* 21 Dec 1890, leaving issue:

2b Charles George; *b* 5 July 1874; *m* 27 July 1895 Virginia, dau of Otto Hoz, and *dsp* 29 Nov 1946

5a George Henry; Capt 1st Life Gds; *b* 9 Jan 1824; *m* 16 Oct 1848 (*divorce* 1866) Emily Victorine Elizabeth (*d* 11 Sept 1904), only dau of Sir William Rumbold, 3rd Bt (*qv*), and *d* 21 Jan 1889, leaving issue:

1b William Henry Alexander George Delmar; Queen's Messenger 1881–85, Consul Stettin 1885–87; *b* 3 Oct 1849; *m* 15 Sept 1874 Edith Louisa (*d* 1 June 1902), dau of Edmund Chivers, and *d* Jan 1919, leaving issue:

1c Charles Alfred William Delmar; *b* 28 July 1878; *m* 1st 30 March 1914 (*divorce*1926) Ruth Madeline, yst dau of Henry Smith, of NSW, and had issue:

1d +Richard Blake Delmar; *b* 22 March 1916

1d Sheelah Mary Elizabeth; *b* 21 Feb 1917; *m* 26 July 1949 *Keith Cavendish Harris, yst s of Douglas Stuart Harris, of Ganges, BC, by Alice Lucy Caroline Cavendish (*see* below), and *d* 1965

1c (cont.) Charles Cavendish *m* 2nd 4 Dec 1926 Marguerite Florence (*d* 12 Oct 1943), est dau of Henri Moreau, of Paris and Sydney, and *d* 22 Sept 1939

2c William Henry George; *b* 11 July 1886; *m* 18 Sept 1907 Beatrice (*d* 7 Nov 1914), 3rd dau of Edwin P Pearson, of Toronto, and *d* 10 Aug 1965, leaving issue:

1d Edwin Pearson Delmar; WW II as Capt RCA (despatches, Croix de Guerre); *b* 28 July 1908; *educ* Bedford Sch and Jesus Coll Cambridge; *m* 11 Dec 1943 *Daphne Joan [Mrs Edwin Cavendish, Banchory Cottage, Hinton St George, Somerset], widow of S/Ldr John Pink, RAF, and 2nd dau of Maj William John van de Weyer, MVO, of Clyffe, Dorchester, and *d* 5 Aug 1970, leaving issue:

1e +Adrian Delmar; *b* 9 June 1947; *educ* Sherborne; late Life Gds; *m* 1982 *Louise Russell, dau of Thomas Allison Ray, Sr, of Ramona, California, USA, and has issue:

1f +John Spencer; *b* 1987

2d +William Delmar [William Cavendish Esq, via Gramsci 36, 00197 Rome]; *b* 5 July 1911; *educ* Bedford Sch; WW II as Capt Middx Regt (wounded twice), Pres John Cabot Internat Coll Rome; *m* 1943 *Louisa, dau of Antonio Fusco, of Catania, Sicily, and has:

1e +William Anthony [William Cavendish Esq, Via Privata Maria Teresa 8, Milan, Italy]; *b* 29 April 1952; *educ* San Leone Magno Sch and Columbia U, New York; Kt Order of SS. Maurice and Lazarus; *m* 1979 Liliana Delabarbara, of New York, and has issue:

1f +Edward William Henry Delmar; *b* 1987

1f *Georgiana Beatrice; *b* 1985

1e *Jessica Luisa; *b* 23 Aug 1946

1c Georgina Edith Bessie; *b* 26 July 1875; *m* 12 Aug 1897 Winsloe Hall (*d* 29 April 1936), of Adelaide U, S Australia, and had issue

2c Edith Emily Ida; *b* 27 March 1881; *m* 12 Sept 1906 Richard Lucas Chaldecott (*d* 1933), and had issue

3c Louisa Anna Grace; *b* 27 March 1882; *m* 30 April 1914 Henry Augustus Norie, of Cowichan Station, Vancouver Island, BC, and had issue

4c Alice Lucy Caroline; *b* 2 Nov 1884; *m* 23 July 1912 Douglas Stuart Harris, of Ganges, BC, and had issue

1b Emily Frances Ida; *m* 11 April 1877 Prince Luigi Pignatelli d'Aragon (*d* 8 Dec 1930), of the Pavilion de la Rochefoucauld, Biarritz, and *d* 12 Sept 1922, leaving issue

3a Caroline Fanny; VA, sometime Maid of Honour and Extra Woman of the Bedchamber to HM QUEEN VICTORIA; *b* 11 Nov 1826; *d* unm 25 Jan 1910

(3) (cont.) Gen The Hon Henry Cavendish *m* 3rd 28 Jan 1873 Susanna Emma (*d* 1910), dau of William Byerlie, and *d* 5 April 1873

(4) CHARLES COMPTON CAVENDISH, *cr* BARON CHESHAM (*qv*)

(1) Anne; *m* 25 Oct 1825 Lord Charles FitzRoy (*see* GRAFTON, D) and *d* 27 May 1871

(2) Caroline; *d* 9 Jan 1867

1 Dorothy; *m* 8 Nov 1766 3rd Duke of Portland (*see* PORTLAND, E) and *d* 3 June 1794, leaving issue

The 6th DUKE's cousin,

WILLIAM CAVENDISH, **7th Duke of Devonshire**, KG (1858), PC (1878); *b* 27 April 1808; *educ* Eton and Trin Coll Cambridge (2nd Wrangler, 1st Smith's Prizeman and 8th Classic, BA and MA 1829, LLD 1835); MP (Lib) Cambridge U 1829–31, Malton July-Sept 1831, Derbys 1831–32 and N Derbys 1832–34, DCL, FRS, Ld Lt Derbys, High Steward Cambridge, Chllr Cambridge U, Chllr London and Victoria Us; *m* 6 Aug 1829 Lady Blanche Georgiana Howard (*d* 27 April 1840), dau of 6th Earl of Carlisle (*qv*), and *d* 21 Dec 1891, having had issue:

1 SPENCER COMPTON CAVENDISH, **8th Duke of Devonshire**, KG (1892), GCVO (1907), PC (GB 1866, I 1871), DL, JP Lancs; *b* 23 July 1833; *educ* Trin Coll Cambridge (MA 1854); MP (Lib) N Lancs 1857–68, Radnor 1869–80, NE Lancs 1880–85 and Rossendale 1885–91, a Ld Admlty March-April 1863, Under-Sec War 1863–66, Sec State War Feb-July 1866 and 1882–85, PMG 1868–71, Ch Sec Ireland 1871–74, Sec State for India 1880–82, Lord Pres Cncl 1895–1903, Pres Bd Educn 1900–02, Rector U of Glasgow 1877–80, Chllr Cambridge U 1892 and Victoria U Manchester 1907, Ld Lt Derbys and Co Waterford; *m* 16 Aug 1892 Louise Fredericke Auguste, LJStJ (*d* 15 July 1911), widow of 7th Duke of Manchester (*qv*), and dau of Count von Alten, of Hanover, and *dsp* 24 March 1908

2 Frederick Charles, PC (1882); MP NWR Yorks, Jnr Ld Treasury 1873–74, Fin Sec 1880–02, Ch Sec Ireland 1882; *b* 30 Nov 1836; *m* 7 June 1864 Lucy Caroline (*d* 22 April 1925), Maid-of-Honour to HM QUEEN VICTORIA, 2nd dau of 4th Baron Lyttelton (*see* COBHAM, V), and was murdered in the Phoenix Park, Dublin, a few hours after his arrival from England 6 May 1882

3 Edward, DL, MP W Derbyshire, previously E Sussex 1865–68, Lt Rifle Bde 1860–65, Lt Col 1st Vol Bn Royal Lancaster Regt; *b* 28 Jan 1838; *m* 3 Aug 1865 Emma Elizabeth (*d* 24 Sept 1920), 4th dau of Rt Hon William Lascelles (*see* HAREWOOD, E), and *d* 18 May 1891, leaving issue:

(1) VICTOR CHRISTIAN WILLIAM, **9th Duke**

(2) Richard Frederick, PC, (1912), CB (1919, CMG (1915), TD, DL, JP Lancs; *educ* Trin Coll Cambridge (BA), Hon Col of the 4th Bn R Lancaster Regt, MP Lonsdale 1895–1906, Chm Devpt Commrs, Priv Sec to Sec of State India, served WW I (wounded, despatches), Hon Col 56th (King's Own Reg) AT Regt; *b* 31 Jan 1871; granted Nov 1908 with yr bro rank of duke's yr s; *m* 31 July 1895 Lady Moyra de Vere Beauclerk (*d* 7 Feb 1942), dau of 10th Duke of St Albans (*qv*), and *d* 7 Jan 1946, having had issue:

1a John Edward Compton; *b* 10 Oct 1907; *d* 29 May 1908

2a Richard Edward Osborne, DL (1946), JP (1953) Lancs; Capt Sherwood Foresters and RHG WW II; *b* 23 Nov 1917; *educ* Eton and Trin Coll Cambridge; *m* 16 Dec 1937 *Pamela [Mrs Richard Cavendish, The Dower House, Holker, Cark-in-Cartmel, Cumbria], dau of Hugh Lloyd Thomas, CMG, CVO, Br Min Paris , and *d* 14 Aug 1972, leaving issue:

1b +(RICHARD) HUGH CAVENDISH, *cr* (LP) BARON CAVENDISH OF FURNESS (*qv*)

2b +Edward Osborne [Edward Cavendish Esq, Butley Priory, nr Woodbridge, Suffolk IP12 3NR]; *b* 31 Aug 1955; *m* 1st 1977 (*divorce* 1980) Kirsten, est dau of Dr Ronald T St Blaize-Molony, of Fordwich, Kent; *m* 2nd 1983 *(Anna) Frances, yr dau of Spencer Shelley, of Mayhill Lodge, Mayhill, Glos (*see* SHELLEY, Bt), and has:

1c *Elizabeth Angelica; *b* 1985

2c *Georgiana Rose; *b* 1988

1b *Georgiana Elizabeth [Mrs Andrew Clowes, 52 Bowerdean St, London SW6]; *b* 2 May 1939; *m* 8 July 1968 *Capt Andrew Henry Clowes, late Scots Gds, only son of Col Henry Nelson Clowes, DSO, OBE, of 30 Burnsall St, London SW3, and has issue (*see* LOTHIAN, M)

2b *Harriet Moyra Aline [Mrs Anthony Sykes, Bellamont House, Long Bredy, Dorset DT2 9HN; 27 Fawcett St, London SW10 9EY]; *b* 25 Sept 1944; *m* 12 Aug 1972 *Capt Anthony Peter Coote Sykes, late R Scots Greys, yr son of Lt-Col Peter Thomas Wellesley Sykes, OBE, of Chilterne House, Warminster, Wilts, and has issue:

1c *Eyre William; *b* 1975

1c *Nina Aline; *b* 1973

2c *Evelyn Harriet; *b* 1980

3b *Susan Anne; *b* 31 Aug 1949; social ed *Harpers & Queen* 1991–92, ed *House & Gardens* 1993–; *m* 1st 5 March 1970 (*divorce* 1983) Quentin Hugh Crewe, son of Col Hugh and Lady Annabel Crewe (*see* 1940 edn CREWE, M), and has issue:

1c *Nathaniel Richard; *b* 22 April 1971

1c *Charity; *b* 1972

3b (cont.) Mrs Susan Crewe *m* 2nd 10 May 1984 *(Christopher) Nigel John Ryan, CBE, est son of Brig Charles Edmond Ryan, MC, of Uckfield, Sussex

1a Elizabeth Vere; *b* 22 Jan 1897; *m* 8 Dec 1915 5th Marquess of Salisbury (*qv*) and *d* 1982, leaving issue

2a Alix *b* 5 Aug 1901; *d* unm 29 June 1925

3a Mary Katharine; *b* 20 July 1903; *m* 9 Dec 1925 28th Earl of Crawford and Balcarres (*qv*) and *d* 20 Nov 1994, leaving issue

4a Diana; *b* 15 Sept 1909; *m* 1st 21 March 1935 (*divorce* Court of Session, Edinburgh 1937) Baron ('Bob') Boothby (LP) (*d* 1986), only son of Sir Robert Tuite Boothby, KBE, of Beechwood, Murrayfield, Edinburgh; *m* 2nd 7 July 1942 Lt-Col Hon Ian Campbell-Gray, RE (*d* 21 March 1946), yr son of Henry Tufnell Craig-Campbell and Lady Gray (*see* GRAY, L); *m* 3rd 14 Jan 1971 6th Viscount Gage (*qv*) and *d* 1992

5a *Sybil Moyra [Mrs Lawrence Dykes, The Garden House, Holker Hall, Cark-in-Cartmel, Cumbria]; *b* 10 Aug 1915; *m* 3 June 1941 Rev Lawrence Gregson Fell Dykes (*d* 1993), son of Rev Ernest Huntington Dykes, MA, Vicar Holy Trinity, Leeds, and has issue:

1b *Michael; *b* 1942

1b *Rose; *b* 1946

2b *Catherine Mary; *b* 1948

(3) John Spencer, DSO, Maj 1st Life Gds, served Boer War 1899–1900 (despatches, medal) and WW I; *b* 25 March 1875, *ka* 20 Oct 1914

1 Louisa Caroline; *m* 26 Sept 1865 Adml Hon Francis Egerton, 2nd son of 1st Earl of Ellesmere, KG, and *d* 21 Sept 1907, leaving issue (*see* SUTHERLAND, D)

The 8th DUKE's n,

VICTOR CHRISTIAN WILLIAM CAVENDISH, **9th Duke of Devonshire**, KG (1916), GCMG (1916), GCVO (1912), PC (1905), DL, JP Lancs; *b* 31 May 1868; *educ* Trin Coll Cambridge (BA), Hon LLD 1911, Ld Lt Derbys, Pres Derbys TAA, High Steward Derby, High Steward U and Borough of Cambridge, Chllr U of Leeds 1909, V-Pres Navy League 1909, Hon Col 5th Bn Sherwood Foresters (TD), Hon Col 24th (Derby Yeo), Armd Car Co, Royal Tank Regt, Col Derbyshire Vol Regt, Maj Derbyshire Yeo, Mayor Eastbourne 1909–10 and Chesterfield 1911–12, MP (Lib U) W Derbyshire 1891–1908, Treasurer Household 1900–03, Fin Sec to Treasury 1903–05, Civil Lord Admlty 1915–16, Govr-Gen and C-in-C Canada

1916–21, Sec State Colonies 1922–24, KJStJ; *m* 30 July 1892 Lady Evelyn FitzMaurice (*d* 2 April 1960), GCVO, DJStJ, JP Derbyshire, Hon LLD Leeds, Mistress of the Robes to HM QUEEN MARY 1910–53, er dau of 5th Marquess of Lansdowne (*qv*), and had issue:

1 EDWARD WILLIAM SPENCER, **10th Duke**

2 Charles Arthur Francis; Lt Royal Tank Regt; *b* 29 Aug 1905; *m* 9 May 1932 Adele (*m* 2nd 29 April 1947 Kingman Douglass, of 41 Biltmore Estates, Phoenix, Arizona, USA, and *d* 19–), dau of Frederick E Astaire, of USA, and sister of Fred Astaire the dancer, and *d* 23 March 1944, having had issue:

(1) A dau; *b* and *d* 8 Oct 1933

1 Maud Louisa Emma, CBE (1941), JP Derbys; Controller ATS, former Hon Col 540 LAA Regt, RA; *b* 20 April 1896; *m* 1st 3 Nov 1917 Capt Angus Alexander Mackintosh (*d* 13 Oct 1918), RHG, only son of The Mackintosh of Mackintosh Chief of the Clan Chattan, and had issue; *m* 2nd 15 Nov 1923 Brig Hon George Evan Michael Baillie (*d* 6 June 1941), MC, RA, er son of Col James Baillie, of Dochfour, and Baroness Burton (*qv*), and *d* 30 March 1975, leaving further issue

2 Blanche Katharine; DStJ, Sr Cmdt ATS; *b* 2 Feb 1898; *m* 30 April 1919 Lt-Col Ivan Murray Cobbold, Scots Gds, DL (*k* by enemy action 18 June 1944), son of John Dupuis Cobbold, DL, of Holywells, Ipswich, and *d* 1987, leaving:

(1) John Cavendish; Lt Welsh Gds, dir Tollemache Cobbold Breweries, Chm Ipswich Town Football Club; *b* 30 June 1927; *educ* Eton; *d* 1983

(2) Patrick Mark; *b* 20 June 1934; *educ* Eton; commissioned Scots Gds, ADC Govr Bahamas 1957–60, dir Tolly Cobbold to 1989, Pres Ipswich Football Club 1990–94 (Chm 1976–90); *d* unm 1994

(1) Pamela Maud; *b* 1 March 1920; *m* 1st 27 March 1943 (*divorce* 1950) Maj (William August Ludwig) Vernon Alexander Hope-Johnstone (*see* ANNANDALE AND HARTFELL, E), and had issue; *m* 2nd 7 Dec 1955 (*divorce* 1971) Ambrose Alec Patrick George Cadogan (*see* CADOGAN, E) and *d* 1994

(2) *Jean [Mrs Roger Paul, Brundish Lodge, Woodbridge, Suffolk]; *b* 7 Oct 1921; *m* 3 Nov 1951 *Roger Hewitt Paul and has issue:

1a *Ivan Robert Hewitt; *b* 23 Feb 1953

2a *David Victor Hewitt; *b* 29 May 1957

1a *Henrietta Catherine; *b* 2 Aug 1955

2a *Lavinia Christine; *b* 11 Sept 1962

3 Dorothy Evelyn, GBE (1964); *b* 28 July 1900; *m* 21 April 1920 1st Earl of Stockton (*qv*) and *d* 21 May 1966, leaving issue

4 Rachel, OBE (1946); *b* 22 Jan 1902; *m* 4 Aug 1923 1st Viscount Stuart of Findhorn (*qv*) and *d* 2 Oct 1977, leaving issue

5 Anne, MBE (1952); *b* 30 Aug 1909; *m* 1st 28 Nov 1929 (*divorce* 1945) Lt-Col Henry Philip Hunloke, only son of Maj Sir Philip Hunloke, GCVO, of Cowbridge, Malmesbury, and had issue:

(1) *Timothy Henry; *b* 30 Dec 1932; *educ* RNC Dartmouth; late Gren Gds

(2) *Nicholas Victor [Nicholas Hunloke Esq, The Old Rectory, Poulshot, Devizes, Wilts]; *b* 22 April 1939; *educ* Eton; late Gren Gds; *m* 15 July 1965 *Lady Katharine Victoria Montagu, 4th dau of 10th Earl of Sandwich (*qv*), and has issue:

1a *Edward Perceval; *b* 1969

1a *Henrietta Yvery; *b* 14 May 1968

2a *Matilda Anne; *b* 1972

(1) *Philippa Victoria; *b* 10 Dec 1930; *m* 26 April 1955 (*divorce* 1960) 3rd Viscount Astor (*qv*) and has issue

5 (cont.) Mrs Anne Hunloke *m* 2nd 27 July 1949 Christopher John Holland-Martin (*d* 5 April 1960), MP, yst s of Robert Martin Holland-Martin, CB, FSA, of Overbury Court, Tewkesbury; *m* 3rd 7 June 1962 (*annulled* 1965) 10th Earl of Sandwich (*qv*) and *d* 1981

The 9th DUKE *d* 6 May 1938; his er son,

EDWARD WILLIAM SPENCER CAVENDISH, **10th Duke of Devonshire**, KG (1941), MBE, TD, JP (Derbys); *b* 6 May 1895; *educ* Eton and Trin Coll Cambridge; Ld Lt Derbyshire, High Steward Cambridge U, Chllr Leeds U 1938, Hon LLD Cambridge 1938, Mayor of Buxton 1919 and 1920, Maj and Brev Lt-Col Derbyshire Yeo, Hon Col Notts and Derbyshire Regt (TA), Hon Col 24th (Derby Yeo) Armoured Car Co, Royal Tank Regt (TA), memb: Nat Assembly C of E, Roy Commn on Historical Monuments, Br Delegn Peace Conf Paris 1919, MP (U) W Derbyshire 1923–38, Assist Priv Sec to his f the 9th Duke 1923, Parly Under-Sec Dominion Affrs 1936–40, India and Burma 1940–42 and the Colonies 1942–45, Grand Master United Grand Lodge of England, Warden Fishmongers' Co 1940, Chm Overseas Settlement Bd, served WW I (despatches twice), Legion of Honour; *m* 21 April 1917 Lady Mary Alice Gascoyne-Cecil (*d* 1988), GCVO (1955), CBE (1946), Hon LLD Leeds (1954), Mistress of the Robes to HM THE QUEEN 1953–66, Chllr Exeter U 1956–71 (Hon LLD 1956), dau of 4th Marquess of Salisbury (*qv*), and *d* 26 Nov 1950, having had issue:

1 William John Robert, *Marquess of Hartington*; Maj Coldstream Gds WW II (despatches); *b* 10 Dec 1917; *educ* Eton; *m* 6 May 1944 Kathleen (*k* in a flying accident in France 13 May 1948), 2nd dau of Joseph P Kennedy (*see* AMERICAN PRESIDENTIAL FAMILIES, Morris Genealogical Books SA, 1994), and was *ka* Belgium 10 Sept 1944

2 ANDREW ROBERT BUXTON CAVENDISH, **11th and present Duke of Devonshire**

1 Mary; *b* 6 Nov, *d* 17 Nov 1922

2 *Elizabeth Georgiana Alice, CVO (1997, LVO 1976) [The Lady Elizabeth Cavendish CVO, 19 Radnor Walk, London SW3], Extra Lady-in-Waiting to HRH PRINCESS MARGARET Oct 1954–; *b* 24 April 1926

3 *Anne Evelyn Beatrice [The Lady Anne Tree, 29 Radnor Walk, London SW3]; *b* 6 Nov 1927; *m* 3 Nov 1949 *Michael Lambert Tree and adopted:

*Isabella Elizabeth Nancy; *b* 1964; *m* 1993 *Charles Raymond Burrell, est son of Sir (John) Raymond Burrell, 9th Bt (*qv*)

*Esther Anne Mary; *b* 14 Oct 1966; *m* 1992 *James Michael Beale Cayzer-Colvin (*see* CAYZER, B)

Seats: Chatsworth, Bakewell, Derbys; Bolton Abbey, Yorks; Lismore Castle, Lismore, Co Waterford, Ireland.

The site of the present house of Chatsworth was first selected by Bess of Hardwicke and her husband of five years Sir William Cavendish when in 1552 they started to transform a wild Derbyshire valley. The plan was conventional enough: a courtyard enclosed by four wings. It was the **1st Duke** who transformed their structure into something more closely resembling what the visitor sees today. Employing William Talman, WILLIAM III's Comptroller of the Works and the man who completed Wren's planned alterations to Hampton Court, he initially remodelled the south front. He then turned to the east wing. Between 1687, when he started, and his death in 1707 he transformed almost all the Tudor exterior, though some internal features remained. It was at this time too that the grounds were laid out, in particular the spectacular water features, notably the canal pond and the stepped waterfall issuing from a temple.

Some fifty years after the **1st Duke**'s death Capability Brown carried out substantial alterations to the grounds, even changing the course of the river facing the south front, over which James Paine built the bridge. In the early 19th century Sir Jeffry Wyatville extended the main house to encompass a new set of state rooms, a theatre, a library and a sculpture gallery. He also carried out alterations to the private apartments. Sir Joseph Paxton undertook similarly extensive remodelling of the grounds.

The Bolton Abbey property was acquired through marriage with the Cliffords. It is fundamentally a shooting box rather than palatial country mansion like Chatsworth, though the box in question is the converted gatehouse to a dissolved Augustinian priory. It is surrounded by 30,000 acres of some of the best grouse shooting in the British Isles, kept on after the **10th Duke**'s death despite the depredations of inheritance tax and his successor's giving up shooting altogether.

The Lismore Castle estate came into the family through marriage with the Boyles, Earls of Cork and Burlington, who had in turn bought it from Sir Walter Raleigh in 1602. Lismore is of medieval origins, built by the Bishops of Waterford, but was a ruin when Lord Cork/Burlington acquired it. He restored it, however, only to see its destruction during the Civil War. It was again restored by his son but the aspect it wears today dates from the **6th Duke**'s time, who 'reigned' from 1811 to 1858. He employed William Atkinson between 1812 and 1822 as architect and in the 1850s Augustus Welby Pugin and Frederick Crace on the internal features. Paxton also carried out work on Lismore — to perhaps a surprising degree considering the scale of his commitments at Chatsworth and elsewhere, such as the Crystal Palace.

DEWEY

Arms: Quarterly, 1st and 4th, per fess sable and or three cinquefoils within two barrulets between three dragon's heads erased counterchanged, in each of their mouths a sword in bend proper, pommel and hilt of the second (for DEWEY); 2nd and 3rd, sable a griffin segreant ermine, armed or, the wings erminois, a bordure compony argent and gules (for BALLARD). **Crest:** A dragon's head erased sable, holding in the mouth a sword in bend proper, pommel and hilt or, between two dragon's wings of the last, on each a bend of the first charged with a cinquefoil of the third.
Motto: *Vir sapiens fortis est* ('The wise man is strong').
Creation: Bt. (UK) 20 Feb 1917.

SIR ANTHONY HUGH DEWEY, 3RD BT, of South Hill Wood, Bromley, Kent, JP (Somerset 1961) [Sir Anthony Dewey Bt JP, The Rag, Galhampton, Yeovil, Somerset BA22 7AJ]; *b* 31 July 1921; *s* gf 1948; *educ* Wellington and RAC Cirencester; served WW II as Capt RA, Maj N Som Yeo (ret); *m* 22 April 1949 *Sylvia Jacqueline Rosamund, only dau of John Ross MacMahon, MB, CM, of Branksome Manor, Bournemouth, by Emily, only dau of William Wilkinson Marshall, MA, BCL, FRSL, and has issue:

1 +RUPERT GRAHAME; *b* 29 March 1953; *educ* Wellington; slr; *m* 23 Nov 1978 *Suzanne Rosemary, dau of Andrew Lusk, of Fordie, Comrie, Perthshire, and has:

(1) +Thomas Andrew; *b* 27 Jan 1982

(2) +Oliver Nicholas; *b* 1984

(1) *Laura Kate; *b* 1988

2 +Charles Ross [Charles Dewey Esq, Manor Cottage, Egford, Frome, Som BA11 3JQ]; *b* 25 May 1960; *m* 1982 *Melinda Ruth, dau of Peter Marriott, and has:

(1) +Fabian Peter Christopher; *b* 1993
(1) *Isobel Hope; *b* 1995
1 *Delia Mary [Mrs Nicholas Wingfield Digby, Lanwades, Moulton, Newmarket]; *b* 14 Sept 1951; *m* 1977 *Nicholas John Wingfield Digby, 2nd son of Archdeacon Stephen Basil Wingfield Digby, MBE, of The Vicarage, Sherborne, Dorset, and has:
(1) *James; *b* 1988
(1) *Emily Clare; *b* 1981
(2) *Julia Mary; *b* 1985
2 *Carola Jane [Mrs Robert Sutton, The Manor House, Newton Valence, Hants]; *b* 17 Aug 1955; *m* 1981 *Robert Hiles Sutton and has issue:
(1) *Patrick William; *b* 1984
(2) *Jonathan David Ormerod; *b* 1990
(1) *Joanna Kate; *b* 1987
3 *Angela Rosamund [Mrs Ivan Hicks, Garden Cottage, Stansted Park, Rowlands Castle, Hants]; *b* 16 Sept 1957; *m* 1992 *Ivan Hicks, and has:
(1) *Miles Anthony; *b* 1992
(1) *Alice Rosamund; *b* 1986
(2) *Lydia Jane; *b* 1987

Lineage: LEWIS DOUE/ DOUEY/DEWAY, of Cheshunt, Herts, *m* Elizabeth — (*bur* 12 Feb 1775) and was *bur* 31 Oct 1760, leaving, with two er sons and two daus:

LEWIS DOUEY/DEWEY; *bapt* 23 Nov 1729; *m* 1st 16 July 1758 Elizabeth Bird (*bur* 16 Nov 1758); *m* 2nd 13 July 1760 Mary Logsden (*bur* 20 April 1806 aged 76) and by her had, with an er s and four daus:

LEWIS DEWE(Y); *bapt* 25 Dec 1776; *m* Martha — (*d* 29 Jan 1849 aged 72) and *d* 29 May 1840 aged 63, leaving five s and three daus; the 4th s:

CHARLES DEWEY, of Cheshunt; *b* 9 Sept 1813; *m* June 1837 Caroline (*d* 15 Oct 1882), only dau of Thomas Ballard, of High Halden, Kent, by Mary Anne, dau of Nathaniel Fiske, and had, with two daus:
1 THOMAS CHARLES (Sir), **1st Bt**
2 George Nathaniel, of Herne Hill, Surrey; *b* 20 Nov 1844; *m* 11 Oct 1871 Mary, only dau of — Stewart, of Edinburgh, and *d* 7 Aug 1916, leaving issue
3 Edwin Ballard, of Toronto; *b* 20 Feb 1847; *m* 14 Jan 1871 Louisa Elizabeth, dau of Frederick George Johnson, of Camberwell, and had issue

CHARLES DEWEY *d* 19 Jan 1892; his est son,

Sir Thomas Charles Dewey, 1st Bt (UK), so *cr* 20 Feb 1917, JP Kent; Hon Col 4th Lond (Howitzer) Bde RFA (TA), pres Prudential Assur Co; *b* 31 Aug 1840; *m* 29 Aug 1866 Clara (*d* 1913), dau of Thomas Daws, of Pyrford Place, Surrey, and had issue:
1 STANLEY DAWS (Rev Sir), **2nd Bt**
2 Marshall; *b* 14 Oct 1874; *m* 15 June 1897 Ethel Julia (*d* 8 May 1925), 3rd dau of Charles Harvey, of Bromley, and *d* 25 Nov 1919, leaving issue:
(1) Kenneth Marshall; Capt Argyll and Sutherland Highrs; *b* 17 Sept 1900; *m* 3 Oct 1925 Mabel Barratt Jones (*d* 1944), dau of T Maddison, of South Bailey, Durham, and *d* 9 March 1937
(2) Sidney Maurice; *b* 8 May 1902; *educ* Repton and Trin Coll Cambridge (MA); *m* 6 June 1931 Dorothy Catherine (*d* 10 Dec 1968), yst dau of J D Holt, and *d* 18 Nov 1968, leaving issue:
1a +Anthony Guy [Anthony Dewey Esq, Mallards, Hook-by-Warsash, Hants]; late Capt Berks and Westminster Dragoons (TA), 2nd Lt RA; *b* 7 July 1932; *educ* Repton; *m* 9 Oct 1968 *Mrs Caroline Rose Hardie, dau of Lionel Martin Hanbury-Bateman, and has issue:
1b +Martin Guy; *b* 13 May 1969
2b +Nicholas George; *b* 1971
(3) +Roy Marshall [Roy Dewey Esq, 69 Harrington Gdns, London SW7]; *b* 11 March 1910; *educ* Repton and St Catharine's Coll Cambridge (BA); *m* 20 June 1945 (*divorce* 1953) Davina Alexandra, yst dau of David Alexander Davidson
(1) Phyllis Muriel; *b* 28 May 1904; *m* 30 March 1936 *Leonard Gilbert, son of Rev T H Gilbert, and had issue
(2) Ethel Kathleen Clare; *b* 26 July 1906; *m* 14 Dec 1929 Lt-Col Kenneth Dalrymple Gairdner (*d* 18 May 1959), Argyll and Sutherland Highrs, and *d* 18 Sept 1956
1 Violet; *b* 30 Sept 1869; *m* 3 Aug 1904 Rev Edmund Francis Edward Wigram (*d* 15 Sept 1933), MA, Hon Sec CMS, and *d* 8 Dec 1918, leaving issue (*see* WIGRAM, Bt)
2 Lilly; *b* 8 April 1873; *m* 22 June 1898 Arthur Willoughby Harvey, and *d* Dec 1939, leaving issue
3 Daisy; *b* 28 June 1877; *m* 26 April 1905 Rev Lewis James Elwin (*d* Dec 1910), Vicar of All Souls', Cheriton, and *d* 21 March 1932, leaving issue
4 Ivy Muriel; *b* 29 Oct 1883; *m* 1st 12 May 1914 Rev Arthur Howe Stevenson (*d* 29 Nov 1923), MA, Vicar St Mary Cray, Kent; *m* 2nd 10 July 1929 Ven Donald Tait (*d* 24 Sept 1932), Archdeacon and Canon Rochester, s of Rev Canon — Tait, Rector Hilperton, Preb Salisbury, and *d* 30 April 1962
5 Daphne Dorothy; *b* 31 Jan 1888; *d* unm 16 Jan 1956

Sir THOMAS *d* 13 July 1926; his son,

Rev Sir Stanley Daws Dewey, 2nd Bt; High Sheriff Devon 1935; *educ* Dulwich and Pembroke Coll Cambridge (MA 1894); Fell Roy Meteorological Soc, Rector Moretonhampstead Devon 1901–27, RD Moreton 1920–27, Preb Exeter Cathedral 1935–43, WW I as 2nd Lt 4th Vol Bn Devon Regt, Silver Jubilee Medal 1935; *b* 12 Aug 1867; *m* 1st 1 Dec 1891 Emily Rose (*d* 23 June 1940), dau of Rev Hugh Lewis Pryce, BA, Rector Llanfairynghornwy, Anglesey, and had issue:
1 Hugh Grahame, MC, Maj RA WW I (despatches); *b* 8 Jan 1895; *educ* Winchester and Pembroke Coll Cambridge; *m* 9 June 1920 Marjorie Florence Isobel (*m* 2nd 19 Oct 1940 Sir Robert Duncan Bell, KCSI, CIE (*d* 24 May 1953), and *d* 1988), only dau of Lt-Col Alexander Hugh Dobbs, IA, formerly of Co Antrim, N Ireland, and *d* 14 May 1936, leaving issue:
(1) Sir ANTHONY HUGH DEWEY, **3rd and present Bt**
(2) Michael Grahame, Maj The Queen's Own Hus; *b* 15 Jan 1928; *educ* Wellington; *m* 24 April 1954 *Anne Cecilia [Mrs Michael Dewey, Warden Grange, Chipping Warden, Banbury, Oxon], er dau of Brig Edward Thomas Arthur Boylan, CBE, DSO, MC, of Hilltown, Drogheda, Co Meath, by Eileen Mary Frances, 5th dau of Sir Timothy Carew O'Brien, 3rd Bt (*qv*), and *d* 20 June 1973 as the result of a motor accident, leaving issue:
1a +Christopher Grahame; *b* 3 July 1963
1a *Philippa Mary [Mrs Stephen Neel, Langleys Farm, Charlton, Malmesbury, Wiltshire]; *b* 31 Aug 1955; *m* 1980 *Stephen William George Neel, and has issue:
1b *George; *b* 1983
2b *Henry William; *b* 1988
1b *Jessica Anais; *b* 1985
2a *Amanda Julia; *b* 7 March 1957; *m* 1978 *Col Richard Neville Brayley Quicke, Light Dragoons, and has:
1b *Edward James; *b* 1983
2b *Michael Charles; *b* 1985
3b *Thomas William; *b* 1987
4b *Jonathan Alexander; *b* 1992
(1) *Hilary Mary [Mrs Paul Morgan, Hollin Old Hall East, Grimshaw Lane, Bollington, Macclesfield, Cheshire SK10 5LY], BSc London 1944, MSc London 1947; *b* 30 July 1923; *m* 13 June 1953 *Paul Faulconer Morgan, only s of Lt-Col Charles Robert Faulconer Morgan, DSO, RASC, of Redcourt, Odiham, Hants, and has:
1a *Hugh Faulconer; *b* 21 Aug 1960; *m* 1988 *Rebecca Susan Kate, dau of Dr John Alfred Humphrey Waterhouse, of Birmingham, and has issue:
1b *Elsa Charlotte; *b* 1990
2b *Sophia Myfanwy; *b* 1992
3b *Corinna Daloni; *b* 1996
1a *Clare Anne; *b* 16 Feb 1954; *m* 1980 *Derek Crosby Coleman and has:
1b *Ben Richard; *b* 1987
1b *Catherine Helen; *b* 1984
2a *Stella Margaret; *b* 11 March 1956
3a Patricia Hilary; *b* 12 Sept 1957; *m* 1992 *Mark Andrew Wood and *d* 1994
2 Norman Strafford, MC; Lt RFA WW I; *b* 14 Sept 1896; *educ* Winchester and Pembroke Coll Cambridge (MA); *m* 5 May 1925 Ursula Marguerite (*d* 30 Aug 1994), dau of H D D Barman, of Helensburgh, and *d* 1985, leaving issue:
(1) +Thomas Norman [Thomas Dewey Esq, High View, 4 Beadon Rd, Bromley BR2 9AT]; *b* 16 Aug 1926; *educ* Radley, Pembroke Coll Cambridge (BA 1947, MA 1951) and Brunel U (MTech); MIEE (1958), MI Mech E (1962); *m* 14 Aug 1964 *Janet Mary, dau of Bert Candlet Baxter, of Enfield, Middx, and has issue:
1a +Stephen Thomas; *b* 4 June 1965; *educ* Brighton Coll and Sheffield U (B Eng, PhD); *m* 1992 *Elizabeth Ann, dau of J Cartledge, of Sheffield
1a *Claire Margaret; *b* 1966; *educ* Bromley High Sch and City of London U (BA); *m* 1994 *Timothy Michael Corum
(2) +David Lewis [Dr David Dewey, Happs Edge, 60 Box Lane, Bovingdon, Herts HP3 0DJ]; *b* 17 Nov 1927; *educ* Radley and Pembroke Coll Cambridge (BA 1949, MA 1951); PhD Lond 1953, 2nd Lt RAEC 1947–48, Research Staff Br Empire Cancer Campaign Research Unit in Radiobiology 1956; *m* 30 July 1960 *Jacqueline Anne, dau of Lewis F Curtis, of Dartford, Kent, and has issue:
1a +Nigel Lewis; *b* 14 March 1967
1a *Fiona Jane [Mrs Andre Mook, Douw van der Kraplaan 23, 2252 Bt Voorschoten, Netherlands]; *b* 25 June 1961; *educ* Southampton U (BSc); Sr Geophysicist Wintershall, Netherlands; *m* 1989 *Andre Mook, and has issue:
1b *Christopher Benjamin; *b* 25 April 1992
1b *Emily Louise; *b* 11 Oct 1994
2a *Helen Gay [Mrs Ross Heath, 6 Berry Court, Maddington 6109, Perth, Australia]; *b* 11 March 1964; *m* 1988 *Ross Heath, and has issue:
1b *David Russell; *b* 1993
2b *James Michael; *b* 1994
(3) +Martin Ross [Martin Dewey Esq, Terra Cotta, Llandevaud, Gwent NP6 2AE]; *b* 2 May 1933; *educ* Radley; *m* 25 Jan 1964 Barbara (*d* 1990), dau of David Sharpe, of Wokingham, Berks, and has issue:
1a +Ross Meredith [Ross Dewey Esq, 96 Warwick Rd, Kenilworth, Warwicks CV8 1HL]; *b* 14 Oct 1966
(1) *Olive Rosemary [Mrs Peter Wilson, Holywater House, Rembrandt Way, Bury St Edmunds, Suffolk IP33 2LR], BSc Lond 1955; *b* 11 Oct 1931; *m* 17 Feb 1962 *Peter Gordon Hiam Wilson, yst son of Capt R G M Wilson, MC, of Gardone, Seaton, Devon, and has had:
1a Alan Richard Hiam; *b* 7 Oct 1964; *d* 18 Oct 1997
1a *Carol Tania; *b* 1966; *m* 1st 1987 Adam Edward Grainger Simpson; *m* 2nd 1994 *Garry Bushnell
3 Thomas Lewis, served WW I; *b* 27 Feb 1900; *educ* Winchester and Pembroke Coll Cambridge (Scholar, MA); *m* 15 April 1936 *Josephine May Sadler (*m* 2nd 1957 Andrew Mackenzie Ross, MD, DLO) [Mrs Andrew Ross, Cherry Tree Cottage, Nether Compton, Sherborne, Dorset], dau of Joseph Sadler Stockton, of Whitely Woods, Sheffield, and *d* 18 May 1951, leaving issue:
(1) +Peter Lewis [Peter Dewey Esq, 39 Harvard Rd, Isleworth, Middx]; 2nd Lt Royal Signals 1957–59, Cncllr Roy Borough of Kensington and Chelsea 1968–70, Ordained C of E 1971, Chaplain to Bp of Kensington 1973–75, Curate in Charge All Saints Isleworth 1975–; *b* 5 July 1938; *educ* Lancing and Wycliffe Hall, Oxford; *m* 5 March 1977 *Hilary Elizabeth, yr dau of George Dudley Ricketts, of Grassholm, Blackmore Way, Wheathampstead, Herts
(1) *Jennifer Ann; *b* 3 Feb 1937; *m* 6 Dec 1966 *Lt-Col David John Younger (*see* YOUNGER OF LECKIE, V) and has issue
4 Theodore Stanley; *b* 7 Feb 1902; *educ* Rugby and Pembroke Coll Cambridge (Scholar, MA, MB BCh); *m* 16 May 1929 *Monica, dau of Vincent Daniel, of Coppings, Leigh, Knt, and has issue:
(1) +Terence Charles; commnd RNVR 1954 ; *b* 30 April 1933; *educ* Ampleforth and Pembroke Coll Cambridge (BA 1957, MA 1961, Mech Sciences)

(2) +Timothy Hugh [Timothy Dewey Esq, The Cottage, Kelston, Bath, Somerset], 2nd Lt Royal Signals 1955–57; *b* 16 June 1935; *educ* Ampleforth; *m* 12 May 1962 *Margaret Mia, er dau of Dr Thomas Rodbard Dixon Aubrey, of The Croft, Bitton, Glos, and has issue:

1a +Adrian Charles; *b* 23 March 1963

1a *Annabel Mary [Mrs Peter Mosse, 115 Park Ave, Barking, Essex IG11 8QY]; *b* 22 Feb 1965; *m* 1987 *Peter Vernon Mosse

2a *Laura Rose; *b* 20 April 1967

3a *Jessica Mia; *b* 18 Aug 1968

(1) *Amanda Jane, SRN (1954); *b* 12 Feb 1931; *m* 1st 5 Sept 1956 (*divorce* 1966) John Robin Millner and has issue:

1a *Julian John; *b* 25 Oct 1958

2a *Piers Theodore; *b* 18 July 1960

3a *Giles William; *b* 16 April 1961

1a *Susanna Jane; *b* 16 April 1964

(1) (cont.) Mrs Amanda Millner *m* 2nd 1966 *Peter Michael Lloyd Wenham, and has further issue:

2a *Arabella Monica; *b* 15 April 1966

(2) *Caroline Mary [Mrs Julian Clist, Woodbury Old Farm, Shelsley Beauchamp, Hereford and Worcester]; *b* 3 June 1938; *m* 15 July 1961 *Julian Reginald Brinton Clist, MBE, son of H A Clist, of Kidderminster, and has:

1a *Sophia Ann Brinton; *b* 23 May 1963

2a *Samantha Gëbriella Chaytor Brinton; *b* 16 Oct 1964; *m* 1992 *Andrew M Coates

3a *Imogen Cecilia Brinton; *b* 9 March 1969

(3) *Corinne Rose [Mrs Keith Knowles, 9 St Omer Rd, Guildford, Surrey]; *b* 3 June 1938; *m* 28 May 1960 *Keith Stanley Knowles and has issue:

1a *Tobias Sebastian; *b* 15 June 1961

2a *Hugh Stanley Keith; *b* 19 June 1962

3a *Benedict Caradoc; *b* 23 May 1968

1a *Miranda Vivian; *b* 6 Oct 1964

5 Meredith Ballard (Rev); Fell and Dean of Pembroke Coll 1936, Assist Tutor 1945, WW II as T/Chaplain RNVR; *b* 10 March 1907; *educ* Rugby and Pembroke Coll Cambridge (Scholar, MA); *d* 24 Oct 1983

1 Elayne Veronica; *b* 10 Feb 1893; *educ* Newnham Coll Cambridge (MA); *m* 24 Feb 1927 Alexander John Scott Scott-Gatty (*d* 6 Nov 1937), son of Sir Alfred Scott-Gatty, KCVO, Garter Principal King of Arms, and *d* 17 June 1970

2 (Rose) Myfanwy, OBE (1957); Inspr DES 1931–64; *b* 27 Aug 1898; *d* unm 11 Nov 1976

Sir Stanley *m* 2nd 31 Oct 1940 Mary Violet (*d* 19 Oct 1962), dau of Rev William Jones, Rector of Llansoy, Monmouth, and *d* Jan 1948

DHOLAKIA

Creation: B. (LP, UK) 1997.

THE BARON DHOLAKIA, of Waltham Brooks, Co W Sussex (Navnit Dholakia OBE (1994), JP) [The Rt Hon The Lord Dholakia OBE JP, 76 Penland Rd, Haywards Heath, W Sussex RH16 1PH]; *b* 4 March 1937; *educ* Home Sch and Inst Sci Bhavnager, Gujarat, and Brighton Tech Coll; medical lab technician Southlands Hosp Shoreham-by-Sea 1960–66, Devpt Offr Nat Ctee Cwlth Immigrants 1966–68, Sr Devpt Offr 1968–74, Pncpl Offr and Sec 1974–76, Community Relations Commn; CRE 1976–94 (Pncpl Fieldwork, Admin and Liaison Offr 1976–78, Pncpl Off Management 1978–81, Head Admin Justice Section 1984–94); V-Chm NACRO 1995–; Chm Brighton Lib Assoc 1962–64, Sec Race and Community Rels Panel Lib Pty 1969–74; memb: Lib Dem Fedl Exec and Fedl Policy Ctee 1996–, Police Complaints Authority 1994–; *m* *1967 *Ann McLuskie and has two daus

Lineage: PERMANANDDAS MULJI DHOLAKIA; *m* Shantabi — and had:

NAVNIT, *cr* a **Baron**

DIAMOND

Creation: B. (LP, UK) 1970.

THE BARON DIAMOND, of the City of Gloucester (John Diamond, PC (1965)) [The Rt Hon The Lord Diamond PC, Aynhoe, Doggetts Wood Lane, Chalfont St Giles, Bucks HP8 4TH]; *b* 30 April 1907; *educ* Leeds GS; accountant 1931; MP (Lab) Blackley 1945–51 and Gloucester 1957–70; PPS Min of Works 1947; Chm Gen Nursing Cncl Finance Ctee 1947–53; Hon Treas Fabian Soc 1950–64; Dir Sadler's Wells Tst 1957–64; Hon Treas Lab Ctee for Europe 1961–64; Ch Sec Treasury 1964–70 (Memb Cabinet 1968–70), Dep Chm Ctees Ho Lds 1974; Chm Roy Commn: Distribution of Income and Wealth 1974079, Industry and Parly Tst 1976–81; Tstee SDP 1981–82, Leader SDP Ho Lds 1982–88; FCA; Hon LLD Leeds 1978; author: *Socialism the British Way* (jt author, 1948), *Public Expenditure in Practice* (1975); *m* 1st 1932 (*divorce* 1947) — and has issue:

1 *Derek; *b* 1933

2 *Martin; *b* 1935

1 *Ruth; *b* 1937

The BARON DIAMOND *m* 2nd 1948 *Julie — and by her has issue:

2 *Joan; *b* 1949

Lineage: Rev SOLOMON DIAMOND of Leeds; *m* Henrietta — and had:

JOHN, *cr* a **Baron**

DICK-LAUDER

Arms: Gu. a griffin salient within a bordure arg. **Crests:** A tower, portcullis down, the head and shoulders of a sentinel appearing above the battlements in a watching posture ppr. **Supporters:** Two lions rampant arg. **Motto:** *Ut migraturus habita* ('Dwell as if about to depart'). **Creation:** Bt. (NS) 25 Jan 1690.

SIR PIERS ROBERT DICK-LAUDER, 13TH BT, of Fountainhall, Co Haddington [Sir Piers Dick-Lauder Bt, 91 Womerah Ave, Rush Cutters Bay, Sydney, NSW, Australia]; *b* 3 Oct 1947; *s f* 1981; *educ* Stowe, Edinburgh Acad and Warwick U

Lineage: ROBERT LAUDER (allegedly descended from LAUDER of that Ilk); *m* — Inglis, of the INGLISes, later Bts, of Cramond, and had:

ANDREW LAUDER, of Edinburgh; merchant; *m* Janet, dau of David Ramsay of Hillhead, of the RAMSAYs of Polton, and had:

Sir John Lauder, 1st Bt (NS), so *cr* 25 Jan 1690, with remainder to the heirs male of his body and his heirs male 'successive'; *bapt* 17 Aug 1595; merchant and burgess Edinburgh (Treas 1652, Baillie 1657–61); bought the Newington estate, nr Edinburgh, 1672, and the Woodhead, Templehall and other estates in Cos Edinburgh and Haddington, which were erected in his favour into the Barony of Fountainhall 1681; *m* 1st 20 Nov 1639 Margaret/Marion Speirs (*d* 1643) and had two sons (*d* young); *m* 2nd 17 July 1645 Isabel, dau of Alexander Ellis of Mortonhall, by whom he had 14 sons; *m* 3rd 15 Feb 1670 Margaret, dau of George Ramsay of Idington, Berwicks, and *d* 1692, having by her had a further three sons and a dau (Elizabeth, *m* John Cunningham, of Woodhall, Co Edinburgh); his est s by his 2nd w:

Sir John Lauder, 2nd Bt, of Fountainhall, Pencaithland, Haddingtonshire, PC 1683; *b* 2 Aug 1646; advocate 1668, ktd *c* 1680, MP (S Parl) Haddington Constabulary 1685–86, 1690–1702 and 1702–07, Ld of Session as Lord Fountainhall 1689, Ld of Justiciary 1690–1707; *m* 1st 21 Jan 1669 Janet (*d* 1686), dau of Sir Andrew Ramsay of Abbotshall, Ld of Session and Ld Provost Edinburgh, and had a s; *m* 2nd 26 March 1687 Marion, dau of Rev John Anderson, Minister Dysart, and *d* 20 Sept 1722, having by her had further issue; his er s by his 1st w:

Sir John Lauder, 3rd Bt; *bapt* 5 Dec 1669; *m* 10 Aug 1696 Margaret, dau of Sir Alexander Seton, 1st Bt, of Pitmedden (*qv*), and *d* Feb 1728, having had issue:

1 **Sir Alexander Lauder, 4th Bt**; *b* 6 Nov 1698; *d* unm 17 May 1730

2 **Sir Andrew Lauder, 5th Bt**; *bapt* 8 May 1702; *m* his cousin Isobel (*d* 7 Nov 1758), only child and heiress of William Dick, of Grange, Co Edinburgh, by Anne (dau of Sir Alexander Seton, 1st Bt), and *d* 6 March 1769, having had a 3rd and yst but only surv son:

(1) Sir ANDREW LAUDER-DICK (later probably DICK-LAUDER after mother's death 7 Nov 1758), **6th Bt**, of Fountainhall and Grange; *m* 25 Oct 1783 Elizabeth, dau of Thomas Broun, of Johnstonburn, Haddingtonshire, and *d* 16 Dec 1820, leaving, with other issue:

1a **Sir Thomas Dick-Lauder, 7th Bt**; *b* 13 Aug 1784; *m* 8 Feb 1808 Charles [*sic*] Anne (*d* 22 Nov 1864), only child and heiress of George Cumin, of Relugas, by Susanna Judith, est dau of Col — Craigie-Halkett, of Hall Hill, Fife, and *d* 29 May 1848, having had, with other issue:

1b JOHN DICK (Sir), **8th Bt**

2b George, of Huntley Wood; *b* 1820; *m* 28 Jan 1850 Antoinette Amelia Barclay (*m* 2nd 18 Dec 1851 Gilbert Mitchell-Innes, of Inverleith Place, Edinburgh, and *d* 22 April 1910, leaving issue), dau of James Macpherson, of Amsterdam, and *dsp* 23 Feb 1851

1b Charlotte Gordon; *m* 23 Sept 1840 Alexander Mitchell-Innes, of Ayton Castle, and *d* 17 July 1848

2b Julia Jane; *m* 20 Jan 1841 Thomas Shairp Mitchell-Innes (*d* 8 March 1892), of Ayton Castle, and *d* 29 Jan 1911, having had issue

3b Maddalena; *m* 31 Aug 1848 Col W J Wilson, Police Magistrate Madras, and *d* 24 April 1885

4b Beatrice Ambrosia; *m* 20 July 1870 George Ramsay (*d* 11 Sept 1887), and *d* March 1903

The er son,

Sir John Dick-Lauder, 8th Bt; *b* 21 April 1813; served HEIC Bengal Army; *m* 22 May 1845 Lady Anne Dalrymple (*d* 10 Aug 1919), 2nd dau of 9th Earl of Stair (*qv*), and *d* 23 March 1867, having had issue:

1 **Sir Thomas North Dick-Lauder, 9th Bt**; *b* 28 April 1846; Lt 60th Rifles; *d* unm 19 June 1919

2 John Edward Arthur, FZS, FRGS; *b* 28 July 1848; *m* 14 Oct 1873 Rosa (*d* 28 Sept 1932), dau of C H Caldecott, MLC, of King Williamstown, S Africa, and *d* 27 June 1913, leaving issue:

(1) Zella Evelyn, OBE (1918); *b* 20 Oct 1875; *m* 22 Oct 1904 George Leather-Culley (*dsp* 20 July 1910), Coldstream Gds, of Northumberland, and *d* 8 Sept 1957

(2) Norma Anne; *b* 26 Aug 1878; *m* 15 Oct 1898 Sackville Alick Payne-Gallwey (*d* 3 Oct 1923), of Bransby Lodge, Yorks, and *d* 31 Dec 1924, leaving issue (*see* FRANKLAND-PAYNE-GALLWEY, Bt)

(3) Marguerita Maud Elizabeth; *b* 1 March 1883; *m* 6 Jan 1914 Capt Thomas Charles Carpenter Bolster, DSO, RN (*d* 19 Aug 1955), and *d* 11 Feb 1949, leaving issue

3 GEORGE WILLIAM DALRYMPLE (Sir), **10th Bt**

4 Stair; *b* 4 Nov 1853; *m* 3 Dec 1878 Eleanor Alma (*d* 27 Feb 1942), yst dau of George Gordon Browne Leith, of Ancaster, Canada, and gdau of Maj-Gen Sir George Leith, 2nd Bt, KCB (*see* LEITH-BUCHANAN, Bt), and *dsp* 23 June 1945

1 Margaret Louisa; *m* 29 Oct 1878 Capt Arthur Charles Van Notten Pole, 13th Hus (*d* Lucknow 14 Dec 1879), and *d* 18 April 1928, having had issue (*see* POLE, Bt, of Wolverton)

2 Charlotte Anne; *m* 1st 1 March 1875 Lt-Col John Fletcher Hathorn (*d* 18 Nov 1888), of Castle Wigg, Wigtownshire, and had issue; *m* 2nd 16 April 1891 Francis Somerville Head (*see* HEAD, Bt), and *d* 14 March 1936

3 Catherine Seton; *m* 2 Aug 1871 Steuart James Charles Duckett, DL (*d* 1915), of Russellstown Park, Co Carlow, and *d* 3 April 1932, leaving issue

Sir THOMAS's bro,

Sir George William Dalrymple Dick-Lauder, 10th Bt; *b* 4 Sept 1852; *m* 1st Jane Emily Clifford (*d* 22 Aug 1921), dau of W P Woodward, ICS, and had issue; *m* 2nd 30 April 1923 Alice Elfride (*d* 2 Dec 1973), dau of Francis John Collinson, barrister, and widow of Lt Malcolm Douglas McNeile, RN, and *d* 7 May 1936; his only s (by his 1st w):

Sir John North Dalrymple Dick-Lauder, 11th Bt; *b* 22 July 1883; *educ* Malvern and RMC Sandhurst; V-Lt Ross and Cromarty 1945–58, Lt-Col 6th DCO Lancers IA WW I (despatches), and NWF 1930 (despatches), cmded 1st Bn Ross-shire HG WW II, Hon Col 412th Coast Regt RA (TA) 1948–51; *m* 24 Feb 1914 Phyllis Mary (*d* 5 April 1976), dau of Brig-Gen Herbert Augustus Iggulden, CIE, and *d* 19 Sept 1958, having had issue:

1 David John; *b* 10 Feb 1915; *d* unm 14 Jan 1943

2 GEORGE ANDREW (Sir), **12th Bt**

1 *Patricia Mary [Mrs Patricia Davy, 51 Princes Gate Mews, London SW7]; *b* 20 April 1920; FANY 1939–40; *m* 11 June 1940 (*divorce* 1970) Maj Ian Alastair George Davy, TD, QO Cameron Highrs, only son of Maj George Alastair Charles Davy, JP, of Owthorpe, Notts, and has:

(1) *Alastair John George; *b* 30 Aug 1944; *educ* Charterhouse; Lt QO Highrs; *m* 30 Aug 1968 *Olivia Joanna, dau of Noel Butler-Madden, and has issue:

1a *Catriona Noel; *b* 1970

(1) *Charlotte Jane; *b* 21 March 1942

(2) *Jean Patricia [Miss Jean Davy, 51 Prince's Gate Mews, London SW7]; *b* 13 June 1947

(3) *Lila Christabel [Miss Lila Davy, 51 Prince's Gate Mews, London SW7]; *b* 2 Jan 1950

(4) *Alice Lorna Mary [Miss Alice Davy, 51 Prince's Gate Mews, London SW7]; *b* 27 May 1961

Sir GEORGE's only son,

Sir George Andrew Dick-Lauder, 12th Bt, of Fountainhill; *b* 17 Nov 1917; *educ* Stowe and RMC Sandhurst; Maj Black Watch (RHR) WW II in Palestine, Somaliland, 52nd Middle E Commandos, Sudan, Crete (POW), 2ic 2nd Bn Black Watch 1955–56 and 11th Bn KAR 1957; *m* 13 Nov 1945 *Hester Marguerite [Lady Dick-Lauder, 17 Vine Court Rd, Sevenoaks, Kent TN13 3UV], yst dau of Lt-Col George Cecil Minett Sorell-Cameron, CBE, of Gorthleck House, Gorthleck, Inverness-shire, and *d* 1981, having had issue:

1 Sir PIERS ROBERT DICK-LAUDER, **13th and present Bt**

2 +Mark Andrew [Mark Dick-Lauder Esq, 3 Sunnymead Terr, Totnes, Devon]; *b* 3 May 1951; *m* 1970 (*divorce* 1982) Jeanne Mullineaux, and has issue:

(1) +Martin; *b* 1976

1 *Georgina Jane; *b* 5 Jan 1949; *m* 1973 her cousin *Nicholas Ernest Kerr-Smiley, and has issue (*see* SMILEY, Bt)

2 *Selina Rose; *b* 29 May 1955; *m* 1978 *Piers Henry Chandler, and has issue:

(1) *Rory George; *b* 1988

(1) *Isobel Marguerite; *b* 1995

DICKINSON

Arms: Or a bend cotised between two lions passant gules. **Crest:** Issuant from clouds a dexter cubit arm erect, the hand holding an olive branch fructed, all proper. **Supporters:** Dexter, a falcon proper, collared and lined or; sinister, a dove holding in the beak an olive branch fructed, both proper. **Motto:** Seek agreement. **Creation:** B. (UK) 18 Jan 1930.

THE 2ND BARON DICKINSON, of Painswick, Co Gloucester (Richard Clavering Hyett Dickinson) [The Rt Hon The Lord Dickinson, Painswick House, Stroud, Glos GL6 6TH]; *b* 2 March 1926; *s* gf 1943; *educ* Eton and Trin Coll Oxford; late Capt Coldstream Gds; *m* 1st 31 Aug 1957 (*divorce* 1980) (Margaret) Ann, er dau of Brig-Gen Gilbert Reader McMeekan, CB, DSO, OBE, of Greenacres, Painswick, Glos, and has issue:

1 +MARTIN HYETT; *b* 29 Jan 1961; *educ* Shrewsbury; *m* 6 May 1995 *Caroline, dau of Nigel Edwards and Mrs Jill Edwards

2 +Andrew; *b* 15 Feb 1963; *educ* Shrewsbury

The 2nd BARON *m* 2nd 1980 *Mrs Rita Doreen Moir

Lineage: JOHN DICKINSON; Capt RN, Elder Bro of Trinity House; *b* 1723 at Alnwick; *m* 26 Sept 1745 Alice Quin and *d* 1783, leaving:

THOMAS DICKINSON; Capt RN, Supt Shipping Bd of Ordance; *b* 1754; *m* Frances Cossé de Brissac (*d* 1854) and *d* 1828; his s:

THOMAS DICKINSON; Gen RE; *b* 1784; *m* 1811 Catherine Deane and *d* 1861; his s:

SEBASTIAN STEWARD DICKINSON, of Brown's Hill, Stroud, Glos; MP Stroud, Chm QS; *b* 25 March 1815; *m* 15 May 1856 Frances Stephana (*d* 1893), dau of William Henry Hyett, of Painswick House, Painswick, and *d* 24 Aug 1878, leaving issue:

1 WILLOUGHBY HYETT, **1st Baron**

1 Frances May; *b* 22 April 1857; *m* 5 Aug 1891 Sir James Berry (*d* 17 March 1946), BS, FRCS, of Kirby Gate, Westmead, Roehampton, and *d* 15 April 1934

2 Annie Josephine; *b* 15 Oct 1864; *d* umn 5 Aug 1953

The only son,

WILLOUGHBY HYETT DICKINSON, **1st Baron Dickinson**, of Painswick, Co Gloucester (UK), so *cr* 18 Jan 1930, PC (1914), KBE (1918), DL and JP Co London; *b* 9 April 1859; *educ* Eton and Trin Coll Cambridge (BA); barrister Lincoln's Inn 1884, memb LCC 1889–1907 (Dep Chm 1892–96 and Chm 1899–1900), MP (Lib) N St Pancras 1906–18, a Commr Bd of Control Min of Health 1913–21, Br Delegate to Assembly of League of Nations 1924, Pres Internat Fedn League of Nations Societies 1925; *m* 12 Dec 1891 Minnie Elizabeth Gordon Cumming (*d* 11 May 1967 aged 102), dau of Gen Sir Richard John Meade, KCSI, CIE, and *d* 31 May 1943, having had issue:

1 Richard Sebastian Willoughby, DSO (1916); *b* 15 Jan 1897; *educ* Eton; Assist Ch Sec to Govt of N Rhodesia, Lt Coldstream Gds and RAF, formerly RNAS served WW I 1915–19 (despatches,Croix de Guerre); *m* 15 May 1924 *May Southey, JP (Bucks 1951 and Glos 1957) [The Hon Mrs Richard Dickinson JP, The Poultry Court, Painswick, Glos], dau of Charles Lovemore, of Melsetter Schoombie, Cape Province, and *d* 27 July 1935, leaving issue:

(1) RICHARD CLAVERING HYETT DICKINSON, **2nd and present Baron Dickinson**

(2) +Peter de Brissac [The Hon Peter Dickinson, Bramdean Lodge, Wood Lane, Bramdean, Hants SO24 0JN]; *b* 16 Dec 1927; granted with yr bros May 1944 rank of baron's yr sons; *educ* Eton and King's Coll Cambridge; *m* 1st 25 April 1953 Mary Rose (*d* 1988), er dau of V-Adml Sir Geoffrey Barnard, KCB, CBE, DSO, of Bramdean, Alresford, Hants, and has issue:

1a +John Geoffrey Hyett; *b* 24 June 1962; *m* 1992 *Philippa Ann, dau of Michael Thomson, and has issue:

1b +George Ellis; *b* 1997

1b *Rosemary Clare; *b* 1994

2a +James Christopher Meade; *b* 28 Dec 1963; *m* 1988 *Sarah Ann, dau of John Reid, and has issue:

1b +Samuel George Lambourne; *b* 1992

2b +Andrew Francis Southey; *b* 1994

1a *Philippa Lucy Anne; *b* 7 March 1955; *m* 1983 *Stephen West, son of Reginald West, and has issue:

1b *Nicholas Oliver; *b* 1988

2a *Polly (taken instead of her baptismal names Dorothy Louise); *b* 12 April 1956; *m* 19 – (*divorce*) — and has:

1b *David Adelman; *b* 1988

(2) (cont.) The Hon Peter Dickinson *m* 2nd 1992 *Jennifer Carolyn Robin McKinley, of Blue Hill, Maine, USA

(3) +Hugh Geoffrey (Very Rev) [The Very Rev and Hon Hugh Dickinson, 22 St Peter's Rd, Cirencester Glos GL7 1RG]; *b* 17 Nov 1929; *educ* Westminster and Trin Coll Oxford (MA 1956); ordained 1956, Assist Curate St Michael and All Angels, Melksham, Wilts 1956–58, Chaplain Trin Coll Cambridge 1958–63 and Winchester Coll 1963–69, Bishop's Adviser for Adult Educn Coventry Diocese 1969–77, Vicar St Michael's St Albans 1977–86, Dean of Salisbury 1986–96; *m* 29 June 1963 *Jean Marjorie, only dau of Arthur Storey, of 25 Woodbourne Ave, Leeds, Yorks, and has issue:

1a +Benjamin Mark; *b* 28 June 1966

1a *Teresa; *b* 17 July 1964

(4) +David Christopher [The Hon David Dickinson, Nanneys Bridge, Church Minshull, Nantwich, Cheshire CW5 6DX]; *b* 29 Jan 1935; *educ* Eton and Trin Coll Oxford; *m* 1970 *Caroline Mary, dau of Arthur Denton Toosey and widow of Peter Yeoward

1 Agnes Désirée, OBE (1966), JP (Bucks 1941); *b* 30 Dec 1892; *m* 8 April 1922 James Cyril Butterwick (*d* 23 Feb 1966), only son of Rev James Butterwick, Rector of Kirby-in-Ashfield, and had issue

2 FRANCES JOAN Dickinson, BARONESS NORTHCHURCH, of Chiswick, Co Middlesex (UK, LP), so *cr* 13 Jan 1964, DBE (1952); MP (C) Hemel Hempstead 1937–59; *b* 29 May 1894; *m* 10 April 1919 1st Viscount Davidson (*qv*) and *d* 1985, leaving issue

DIGBY

Arms: Azure a fleur-de-lys argent. **Crest:** An ostrich, holding in the beak a horse-shoe, all proper. **Supporters:** Two monkeys proper, environed about the middle and lined or. **Motto:** *Deo non fortuna* ('From God not Fortune'). **Creations:** B. (I) 29 July 1620 and (GB) 19 Aug 1765.

THE 12TH BARON DIGBY OF GEASHILL, King's Co, and **Baron Digby of Sherborne**, Co Dorset (Edward Henry Kenelm Digby, JP (Dorset 1959)) [The Rt Hon The Lord Digby JP, Minterne, Dorchester, Dorset DT2 7AU]; *b* 24 July 1924; *s* f 1964; *educ* Eton, Trin Coll Oxford and RMC Sandhurst; Capt Coldstream Gds, served WW II and Malaya 1948–50, ADC to: C-in-C Far East Land Forces 1950–51 and C-in-C BAOR 1951–52, memb Dorchester RDC 1962, Dorset: CC Dorset 1966, Ld Lt 1984 (V-Lt 1965–84, DL 1957–65), KStJ 1985 (Pres Cncl Dorset), Hon Col 4th Bn Devonshire & Dorset Regt, Patron Dorset Red Cross, Hon Fell Roy Ag Soc Cwlth, Dep chm SWEc Planning Cncl 1972–79; *m* 18 Dec 1952 *Dione Marian, DBE, DL (Dorset), yr dau of R-Adml Robert St Vincent Sherbrooke, VC, CB, DSO, JP LLD, of Oxton, Notts, and has issue:

1 +HENRY NOEL KENELM; *b* 6 Jan 1954; *educ* Eton; ACA; dir Jardine Fleming Investment Management; *m* 12 July 1980 *Susan E, er dau of Peter Watts, of 6 Albert Terrace Mews, London NW1, and has issue:

(1) +Edward St Vincent Kenelm; *b* 5 Sept 1985

(1) *Alexandra Jane Kira; *b* 1987

2 +Rupert Simon [The Hon Rupert Digby, Rookwood Farmhouse, Stockcross, Berks RG16 8JX]; *b* 21 Aug 1956; *educ* Eton and Southampton U; *m* 1986 *Charlotte Fleury, yr dau of Robert Hirst, of Durford Mill, nr Petersfield, Hants, and has:

(1) *Arabella Dione; *b* 26 Sept 1989

(2) *Olivia; *b* 1991

1 *Zara Jane [The Hon Mrs Percy, 82 Horder Rd, London SW6 5EE]; *b* 27 May 1958; dress designer; *m* 1993 as his 2nd wife *James Edward Caulfeild Percy (*see* NORTHUMBERLAND, D)

Lineage: EVERARD DIGBY, High Sheriff Rutland 1434, MP Rutland; *m* Jaquetta, dau and coheir of Sir John Ellys, of Devon, and was *k* Battle of Towton 1460 fighting on the Lancastrian side, leaving, with other issue:

1 Everard (Sir), feudal Ld of Tilton and Drystoke, ancestor of:

(1) Everard (Sir), beheaded 1606 for complicity in the Gunpowder Plot; f of:

1a Kenelm (Sir); celebrated royalist Civil War; *m* the renowned beauty Venetia, dau and coheir of Sir Edward Stanley, KB, of Tonge Castle, Salop, by Lady Lucy Percy, dau and coheir of 1st Earl of Northumberland of the 1557 *cr* (*see* NORTHUMBERLAND, D), and *d* 11 June 1665, leaving, with another s (*d* young) and a dau:

1b John, of Goathurst, Bucks; had:

1c Margaretta Maria; *m* Sir John Conway, 2nd Bt (*see* LANGFORD, B)

2c Charlotte Theophila; *m* Richard Henry Mostyn, of Penbeddw

2 SIMON (Sir)

3 John (Sir), of Eye Kettleby, Rutland; ancestor of:

(1) Simon, of North Luffenham; *m* Margaret Saunderson and *d* 1729, having had:

1a Kenelm, of N Luffenham

2a James, of Red Hall, Lincs; *dsp* 1811

1a Mary; *m* John Fowell, of Blackhall, Devon

2a Henrietta; *m* 12 Jan 1769 Maj George Pauncefort (*d* 8 Oct 1786), of Witham, and had issue (*see* PAUNCEFORT-DUNCOMBE, Bt)

The 2nd son,

Sir SIMON DIGBY, of Col(e)shill; Lancastrian Battle of Bosworth; *m* Alice, dau and heir of John Walleys, of E Haddon, Devon, and *d* 1519, leaving issue:

1 REGINALD, of whom presently

2 Thomas, of Mansfield Woodhouse, Notts; ancestor of:

(1) John, MP E Retford *temp* GEORGE I; had a dau (Frances, *m* Sir Thomas Legard, 4th Bt)

1 Agnes; *m* William Tracy (*see* SUDELEY, B)

The elder son,

REGINALD DIGBY, of Col(e)shill; *m* Anne, dau and coheir of John Danvers, of Calthorpe, Oxon, and had:

JOHN; *m* Anne, est dau of Sir George Throgmorton, and had issue:

Sir GEORGE DIGBY; *m* Abigail, dau of Sir Arthur Heveningham, of Ketteringham, Norfolk, and had, with other issue:

1 ROBERT (Sir), his successor

2 JOHN DIGBY, 1st EARL OF BRISTOL, so *cr* 15 Sept 1622, as also earlier 25 Nov 1618 BARON DIGBY OF SHERBORNE, Co Dorset (both E), PC (1616–25 and Feb 1640/1); *b* Feb 1586; *educ* Magdalen Coll Oxford, Gentleman Privy Chamber 1605, ktd 1606, MP Hedon 1610–11, Amb Spain 1610–18, V-Chamberlain Household 1616–25, temporarily imprisoned Tower of Londomn 1626 for impeaching Duke of Buckingham (*see* JERSEY, E), initially Parliamentarian Civil War but soon joined royalists and fought with them Battle of Edge Hill 1642; his estates subsequently confiscated and he himself proscribed by Parl and a resolution passed that he be condemned to death March 1648(?)/9; *m* 31 May 1609 Beatrice, dau of Charles Walcott, of Walcott, Salop, and widow of Sir John Dive or Dyves, and *d* exiled in France 31 Jan 1651/2, leaving:

(1) GEORGE DIGBY, 2nd EARL OF BRISTOL, though called up to Ho Lds *vp* in f's barony 1641, KG Jan 1652/3 (not installed till 1661), PC (1643); *b* Oct 1612; *educ* Magdalen Coll Oxford; MP Dorset 1640–41, Sec State 1643–45 and 1657 till his political career cut short by his turning RC, royalist Civil War; *m* Lady Anne Russell, 2nd dau of 4th Earl of Bedford (*see* BEDFORD, D) and *d* 20 March 1676/7, leaving:

1a JOHN DIGBY, 3rd and last EARL OF BRISTOL; *b c* 1635; MP (Tory) Dorset 1675–77, Ld Lt Dorset 1679–89; *m* 1st 26 March 1656 Alice, dau of Robert Bourne, of Blake Hall, Bobbingworth, Essex; *m* 2nd Aug 1663 Rachael, yr dau of Sir Hugh Wyndham, of Stilton, Dorset, Judge Court Common Pleas, and *dsp* 18 Sept 1698, when his titles expired

1a Anne; *m* 10 June 1665 2nd Earl of Sunderland and *d* 26 April 1715, leaving issue (*see* MARLBOROUGH, D)

1 Abigail; *m* 11 Nov 1600, as his 1st w, Sir Baldwin Wake, 1st Bt (*qv*), and *d* 6 Feb 1630/1

The er s,

Sir ROBERT DIGBY, of Col(e)shill, PC; MP Athy, Co Kildare, 1613; *m c* April 1598 Lettice Baroness Offaly in her own right (I) (*see* LEINSTER, D) and had, with five yr sons (George; Gerald; John; Symon; Philip):

1 ROBERT, **1st Baron**

2 Essex (Rt Rev), DD, Bp of Dromore; *m* 1st Thomasine, dau of Sir William Gilbert, of Kilminchy, Queen's Co; *m* 2nd Lettice Brereton, and *d* 12 May 1683, leaving issue:

(1) Simon (Rt Rev), MA Dublin, DD Oxford, Bp of Elphin; *m* Elizabeth, dau of Warner Westenra, of Dublin, and *d* 7 April 1720, having had, with six daus:

1a John, of Landenstown, Co Kildare, MP; *m* 20 March 1717 May (*d* 17 March 1731), only child of Very Rev Jeremy Marsh, DD, and was gf of:

1b Kenelm Henry; author: *The Broadstone of Honour*; *m* 1833 Jane Mary, dau of Thomas Dillon, of Mount Dillon, Co Dublin, descended from Edmund Dillon, er brother of 1st Viscount Dillon (*qv*), and *d* 22 March 1880, leaving issue

2a William (Rev), of Lackan; *m* Olivia, dau of John French, of French Park, and had:

3a Benjamin (Rev), of Osbertstown, Co Kildare; Vicar of Geashill; *m* 26 Sept 1734 Mary (*d* 1768), dau and heir of Lewis Jones, of Osbertstown, and *d* 1769, having had issue

1a Jane; *m* 1713 Patrick ffrench (*d* 3 June 1744), of Monivea Castle, and had issue

Sir ROBERT *d* 24 May 1614; his est son,

ROBERT DIGBY, **1st Baron Digby of Geashill**, King's Co (I), so *cr* 29 July 1620, with remainder to his brothers, PC (I 1641); royalist Civil War; *m* 1st Sarah (*d* 14 July 1633), widow of Thomas Moore and dau of 1st Earl of Cork (*see* CORK and ORRERY, E), and had a s; *m* 2nd Elizabeth (*m* 3rd Sir Robert Bernard, Bt, and *d* 3 Jan 1662/3), widow of Sir Francis Astley, of Hill Morton, Warwicks, and dau of Sir James Altham, of Oxhey, Herts, and *d* 7 June 1642; his only s by his 1st w:

KILDARE DIGBY, **2nd Baron Digby of Geashill**; Govr King's Co; *b c* 1631; *m* by 1652 Mary (*d* 23 Dec 1692), dau of Robert Gardiner, of London, and *d* 11 July 1661, leaving issue:

1 ROBERT DIGBY, **3rd Baron Digby of Geashill**; *b* 30 April 1654; MP Warwick May-Dec 1677; *d* unm 29 Dec 1677

2 SIMON DIGBY, **4th Baron Digby of Geashill**; *b* 18 July 1657; MP (Tory) Warwick 1685–86; *m* 27 Aug 1683 Lady Frances Frances Noel (*d* 29 Sept 1684), dau of 1st Earl of Gainsborough (*qv*) of the 1682 *cr*, and *d* 19 Jan 1685, having had issue:

(1) Frances; *m* 3rd Viscount Scudamore and *d* 3 May 1729, leaving issue (extinct 1820)

3 WILLIAM, **5th Baron**

The 4th BARON's yr bro,

WILLIAM DIGBY, **5th Baron Digby of Geashill**; *b* 1661; MP (Tory) Warwick 1689–98; *m* 22 May 1686 Jane (*d* Sept 1733), dau of 1st Earl of Gainsborough (*qv*) of the 1682 *cr*, and *d* 29 Nov 1752, having had, with other issue:

1 Edward; MP Warwick; *m* 5 July 1729 Charlotte (*d* Nov 1778), dau of Sir Stephen Fox (*see* ILCHESTER, E), and *dvp* 2 Oct 1746, leaving issue:

(1) EDWARD DIGBY, **6th Baron Digby of Geashill**; *b* 5 July 1730; MP (Tory) Malmesbury 1751–54 and Wells 1754–57; *d* unm 30 Nov 1757

(2) HENRY DIGBY, **7th Baron Digby of Geashill** and 1st EARL DIGBY, Co Lincoln, so *cr* 1 Nov 1790, as also VISCOUNT COLESHILL, Co Warwick, and earlier 13 or 19 Aug 1765 **Baron Digby of Sherborne**, Co Dorset (all GB), with in the last case remainder, failing issue male of his own, to the issue male of his father; *b* 21 July 1731; MP Ludgershall 1755–61 and Wells 1761–65, Under Sec for South 1755–56, a Ld Admlty 1763–65; *m* 1st 5 Sept 1763 Elizabeth (*dsp* 19 Jan 1765), dau of Hon Charles Feilding, son of 4th Earl of Denbigh and Desmond (*qv*); *m* 2nd 10 Nov 1770 Mary (*d* 26 Feb 1794), dau and heir of John Knowler, of Canterbury, and *d* 25 Sept 1793, having by her had, with other issue:

1a EDWARD DIGBY, **8th Baron Digby of Geashill**, **2nd Baron Digby of Sherborne** and 2nd and last EARL DIGBY; Ld-Lt and custos rotulorum Dorset; *b* 6 Jan 1773; *d* unm 12 May 1856, when the Earldom and Viscountcy expired

2a Robert (Rev); *b* 10 April 1775; *d* 25 Sept 1830

1a Charlotte Maria; *m* 22 July 1796 William Wingfield-Baker, MP, Master in Chancery, and *d* 15 May 1807, leaving issue

(3) Robert, Adml RN; *b* 20 Dec 1732; *m* 19 Aug 1784 Eleanor (*d* 28 July 1830), widow of James Jauncey, of New York, and dau of Andrew Elliot, Govr of New York and *dsp* 25 Feb 1815

(4) William (Very Rev), LLD, Dean Durham; *b* 21 Jan 1733; *m* 14 April 1766 Charlotte (*d* 27 June 1791), dau of Joseph Cox, and *d* 18 Sept 1788, leaving, with other issue:

1a Henry (Sir), GCB, Adml RN, C-in-C at Sheerness, cmded HMS *Africa* Battle of Trafalgar 1805; *b* 20 Jan 1770; *m* 17 April 1806 Jane Elizabeth (*d* 29 April 1863), widow of Charles, Viscount Andover (*see* SUFFOLK and BERKSHIRE, E), and dau of 1st Earl of Leicester (*qv*), and *d* 19 Aug 1842, having had issue:

1b EDWARD ST VINCENT, **9th/3rd Baron**

2b Kenelm Henry (Rev), MA, Hon Canon of Norwich, and Rector of Tittleshall, Norfolk; *b* 18 Aug 1811; granted 1859 rank of baron's yr s; *m* 13 May 1835 Caroline (*d* 12 Dec 1866), 5th dau of Edward Sheppard, of Firgrove, Salop, and *d* 4 April 1891, leaving:

1c Kenelm Edward (Sir), GCB, JP Essex, barrister 1865, Bencher Lincoln's Inn 1891, KC 1904, County Court Judge 1892–95, PUS Home Dept 1895–1903; *b* 9 Sept 1836; *m* 30 Aug 1870 Caroline (*d* 23 July 1926), 2nd dau of 1st Baron Belper (*qv*), and *d* 21 April 1916, leaving issue:

1d Arthur Kenelm, DSO (1915), MBE (1961), DL (1961) Lincs, Major RA (ret) (Hon Lt-Col), served Boer War 1901–02 (Queen's medal with five clasps), WW I (despatches, wounded twice) and WW II 1939–41, Army Welfare Offr, Lincs, and Hon Co Sec SSAFA; *b* 19 May 1879; *educ* Harrow, and Corpus Christi Coll Oxford (BA 1903); *m* 22 Feb 1911 Violet Mary (*d* 27 April 1978 aged 92), yr dau of Lt-Col Sherbrooke Augustus John Keating, of Lenham Court, Lenham, and *dsp* 7 Oct 1966

2d Edward Aylmer, JP Essex, barrister 1909, KC 1927, Bencher 1934, Cdr RN; *b* 3 Oct 1883; *m* 30 May 1911 Winifred Digby (*d* 14 June 1967 aged 83), yst dau of Arthur George Watson, DCL, JP, of Uplands, Wadhurst, and *d* 14 Nov 1935, having had issue:

1e +Kenelm Hubert [Kenelm Digby Esq, 3 Mount St, Kelburn, Wellington, NZ], barrister Middle Temple 1934; *b* 10 March 1912; *educ* St John's Coll Oxford (BA); *m* 21 Feb 1946 *Mutal Agnes Helen, only dau of Bertram E Fielder, of Romsey, formerly of Hong Kong, and has issue:

1f +Noel Kenelm [Noel Digby Esq, 3400 Alsten Lane, Plano, Dallas, Tx, USA]; *b* 8 Dec 1946

2f +Geoffrey Aylmer; *b* 2 Nov 1957

1f *Rosalind Clare [Mrs Rosalind Broadmore, 85 Weld St, Wadestown, Wellington, NZ]; *b* 15 May 1948; *m* 19– (*divorce* 19–) — Broadmore

2e Robert Arthur; *b* 9 June 1913; *d* unm 14 Sept 1963

3e Noel Aylmer; *b* 25 Dec 1914; *d* 20 March 1935

1e Fiona; *b* 6 July 1917; *d* unm 13 April 1994

2e Monica; *b* 2 Jan 1920; *d* unm 1981

1d Emily, MBE (1920); *d* unm 30 June 1957

2d Lettice *b* 1877; *d* aged 95 27 Nov 1972

2c Henry Almarus, JP, Norfolk, Capt RN; *b* 9 Feb 1843; *m* 24 Sept 1874 Leonora Sabrina (*d* 9 March 1920), dau of Rev G L Wasey, and *dsp* 18 Sept 1913

3c William FitzGerald; *b* 24 July 1844; *m* 26 Oct 1869 Charlotte Mary (*d* 16 Feb 1930), 3rd dau of Rev Henry T Lee, and *d* 18 Nov 1898, leaving issue:

1d Kenelm William; *b* 20 Jan 1872; *m* 9 June 1915 Eve (*d* 29 May 1926), dau of E J Gross, Fell Gonville and Caius Coll Camb, and *dsp* 2 Oct 1919

1d Alice; *b* 28 Aug 1874; *d* unm 12 Nov 1938

2d Catherine Lucy; *b* 28 Jan 1877; *d* unm 30 April 1924

3d Bertha Emily; *b* 15 Aug 1883; *m* 26 July 1913 James Glen Harley, MA, and *d* 24 May 1967, leaving issue

4c Charles Tilton (Rev), Rector Warham Norfolk 1874; *b* 24 Nov 1845; *educ* Corpus Christi Coll Oxford (MA); *d* 5 Nov 1923

5c Reginald, JP; *b* 30 April 1847; *m* 7 Nov 1872 Caroline Grace (*d* 28 Dec 1943), 2nd dau of Rev Thomas Fremeaux Boddington, MA, Rector Badger, Salop, and *d* 29 Sept 1927, leaving issue:

1d Lionel Kenelm (Rev), Rector Tittleshall Norfolk 1915–18, WW I with Norfolk Regt; *b* 15 Nov 1883; *educ* Corpus Christi Coll Oxford (MA); *d* 18 Oct 1918, of wounds recd in action

1d Ethel Margaret; *b* 7 Dec 1873

2d Edith; *b* 5 Jan 1878; *d* unm 9 Aug 1965

3d Mabel; *b* 5 April 1880; *d* unm 14 Dec 1962

6c Algernon; *b* 23 May 1849; *educ* Corpus Christi Coll Oxford (MA); *m* 30 Dec 1888 Richenda Catherine (*d* 25 Jan 1940), est dau of Capt Philip Hamond, 34th Regt, and *d* 24 Sept 1936, having had issue:

1d John Kenelm, Lt 7th Service Bn Norfolk Regt; *b* 21 Nov 1890; *ka* 4/5 Aug 1915

2d Thomas Hankinson; 4th Dragoon Gds, Capt Battery of Light Armoured Cars EEF 1919, served WW I (despatches); *b* 5 Feb 1892; *educ* Marlborough; *m* 5 Jan 1938 *Diana Broughton, only dau of Lt-Col Frederick Guy Knight, MC, Queen's Bays, and *d* Nov 1985, leaving:

1e +Simon Kenelm [Simon Digby Esq, 12 Busby House, Aldrington Rd, London SW16 1TZ]; *b* 23 Dec 1938; *educ* Marlborough, and London U (BA); *m* 1st 4 April 1961 (*divorce* 1965) Ann, only dau of Rev Geoffrey Kitson Walton, of Hereford; *m* 2nd 1965 (*divorce* 1978) Sylvia Josephine, dau of John Cheers, and has issue:

1f +Oliver Francis; *b* 1966

2f +Roland Anthony; *b* 1969

2e +Patrick Timothy [Patrick Digby Esq, Bryngwyn, Llandissilio, Clunderwen, Dyfed SA66 7UR]; *b* 14 Sept 1941; *educ* Bradfield; *m* 1973 *Lyneth Anne, dau of David Clee, and has issue:

1f +Huw Timothy; *b* 15 Feb 1975

1f *Catrin Elizabeth; *b* 1 Sept 1978

3e +Robin Paul [Robin Digby Esq, Ramlösavägen 124A, 25656 Helsingborg, Sweden]; civil engr; *b* 29 July 1944; *educ* Radley and Trin Coll Dublin (BA); *m* 1966 *Marja Birgitta, dau of Helmer Hägglöf, of Njurunda, Sweden, and has issue:

1f *Christina Ruth; *b* 4 May 1967

2f *Joanna Isabella; *b* 7 Jan 1971

3f *Rebecca Alice; *b* 14 April 1987

1d Almeria Catharine; *b* 14 March 1894; *d* unm 1 Dec 1934

2d Bridget Mary; *b* 19 Feb 1899; *m* 5 Jan 1931 Pandia Andrew Scaramanga (*d* 15 Sept 1952), and *d* 15 Dec 1950, leaving issue

3d Noel Richenda; *b* 13 Sept 1904; *d* unm 23 Dec 1935

1c Caroline Jane; *m* 15 Dec 1864 Arthur George Watson (*d* 21 Oct 1916), DCL, of Uplands, Wadhurst, Sussex, and had issue

2c Lucy Georgiana; *d* unm 3 Jan 1877

3c Emily; *m* 23 Jan 1862 Edward North Buxton, of Knighton Buckhurst Hill, 3rd son of Sir Edward North Buxton, 2nd Bt (*qv*), and *d* 26 Oct 1929, leaving issue

3b John, of Prince's Gate, London SW7, Sec London Dock; used name DIGBY-JOHNSON; *m* 26 Jan 1834 Anne (*d* 1873), dau of James Kelso, of Diamond, Co Londonderry, and *d* 1857, having had issue:

1c John Digby; *b* 30 Aug 1839; *d* 9 March 1844

2c Thomas Hyde; *b* 9 April 1841; *d* 21 May 1874

3c James Kelso; *b* 16 Dec 1842; *d* 10 Aug 1863

4c John, of Branksome, nr Buxton, Derbys; *b* 20 June 1844; *m* 25 July 1877 Ada (*d* 13 March 1927), dau of John Hirst, of Lindley, W R Yorks, and Southport, Lancs, and *d* 17 May 1908, leaving issue:

1d Arthur; *b* June 1878; *educ* Marlborough; *d* 1903

2d Harold; *b* Sept 1880; *d* 1882

3d Donough Noel, Lt RARO 1920–36, Lt Offrs' Emergy Res 1937–39, Lt RASC WW I 1916–18 (attd RGA) Flanders; *b* 26 May 1886; *educ* Harrow and Jesus Coll Cambridge (BA) 1905); *d* 21 Oct 1953, having adopted:

Peter Sprague; *b* 28 Dec 1920

4d Eric, AFC, A/Cdre RAF, Lt E Surrey Regt and Capt RFC, served WW I (despatches) and WW II (despatches three times); *b* 25 Dec 1892; *educ* Harrow; *m* 16 July 1921 Marjorie Alice Maud, est dau of Harold Beeching, MA, and *d* Jan 1971, leaving issue:

1e Coral Alisha, memb CSP; *b* 1 Aug 1924; *m* 6 April 1946 S/Ldr William Anthony Brenard, RAF, and had:

1f *Simon Nicholas; *b* 2 July 1951; *educ* Caterham Sch

1f *Sarah Penelope; *b* 4 Nov 1955

2e Patricia June; *b* 10 Oct 1928; *m* 20 Sept 1958 *Peter Gavin Davy, BSc, and had:

1f *Thomas Digby; *b* 21 Oct 1959

2f *Daniel Brereton; *b* 25 July 1962

1d Ada Anne Muriel; *b* Aug 1881; *d* 1890

5c Sidney; *b* 12 Sept 1847; *d* 7 Aug 1853

1c Annie Elizabeth; *b* 30 Jan 1846: *d* 15 March 1872

1b Jane Elizabeth; *m* 1st 18 Sept 1824 Baron Ellenborough (*divorce* 1830 for adultery with Prince Schwarzenberg, Ch Min Austria, by whom she had an illegitimate s, Adolf, whose descendants are still extant); *m* 2nd

10 Nov 1832 Baron Venningen, of Bavaria; *m* 3rd Sheikh Medjuel el Mazrab and *d* 11 Aug 1881

2a William (Rev), Preb of Worcester; *b* 25 Feb 1774; *m* 1st 1800 Almeria Augusta, dau of Hon Lucius Ferdinand Cary (*see* FALKLAND, V); *m* 2nd 1803 his cousin Charlotte Elizabeth (*d* 13 Sept 1820), only dau of Col Hon Stephen Digby (*see* below), and *dsp* 2 Jan 1848

3a Charles George, Capt RN; *b* 14 Dec 1780; *m* 13 Sept 1821 Elizabeth (*d* 26 Dec 1855), only dau of Sir John Benn Walsh, 1st Bt (*see* 1953 edn), and *d* 14 Jan 1829, leaving issue:

1b George Walsh; *b* 1824; *d* 1847

2b John Almarus, of Chalmington House, Dorchester; Lt-Col Gren Gds; *b* 29 May 1826; *m* 13 June 1861 Diana Alicia (*d* 6 May 1878), est dau of Rev Hon William Hugh Scott (*see* POLWARTH, L), and *d* 13 July 1885, leaving issue:

1c George Hugh, of Chalmington House, JP Dorset, Maj Dorset Yeo Boer War 1901–02; *b* 21 Sept 1867; *m* 5 Aug 1903 Lady Muriel Augusta Fox-Strangways (*d* 7 Jan 1920), only dau of 5th Earl of Ilchester (*qv*), and was accidentally *k* 20 Oct 1914

2c Lionel William John, Lt Dorset Regt Boer War; *b* 31 March 1870; *d* unm 23 Dec 1945

3c Henry Montagu, of Chalmington, Maj 3rd Bn W R Regt Boer War 1900–02; *b* 4 March 1874; *d* 7 Oct 1934

1c Katharine Diana; *b* 24 Aug 1864; *d* unm 6 Dec 1932

1b Charlotte; *d* 1837

(5) Stephen; Col; *b* 10 May 1742; *m* 1st 1 Oct 1771 Lucy (*d* 16 Aug 1787), dau of 1st Earl of Ilchester (*qv*), and had issue:

1a Charles (Rev), Canon Windsor; *b* 31 May 1775; *m* Mary (*d* 28 April 1834), dau of Hon Hugh Somerville, and *d* 23 June 1841, leaving, with other issue:

1b Charles Wriothesly, of Meriden Hall, Warwicks, and Manor House, Studland, nr Wareham; *b* 2 May 1802; *m* 1st 21 July 1831 Elizabeth (*d* 18 July 1834), only dau of Rev William Floyer, and had issue:

1c Elizabeth Mary; *m* 2 Aug 1854 Henry Maitland Wilson, and *d* 12 July 1856, leaving issue (*see* 1970 edn WILSON, B)

1b (cont.) Charles Digby *m* 2nd 9 July 1840 Frances Anna Margaret (*d* 22 Aug 1849), widow of Rev George Bingham, of Melcombe Bingham, and dau of Anthony Blagrave, and by her had issue:

2c Frances Rachel; *m* 1st 14 Feb 1865 Rev Richard Henry Wingfield Digby (*d* 31 Oct 1876), and had issue; *m* 2nd 21 Feb 1882 Charles Thomas Palmer (*dsp* 18 Dec 1916), of Newland House, Coleford (*see* PALMER, Bt, of Wanlip), and *d* 11 Dec 1930

1b (cont.) Charles Digby *m* 3rd 17 June 1856 Adelaide (*d* 19 May 1878), 3rd dau of Rt Hon George Bankes, 7th of Kingston Lacy and Studland Manor, Dorset, and *d* 29 Dec 1873, having by her had issue:

1c Charles Wriothesly, of Meriden Hall, JP Warwicks, BA Cantab; *b* 31 Jan 1859; *m* 1st 15 Feb 1881 Dora Adelaide (*d* 20 Nov 1898), dau of Rupert Pennefather Fetherstonhaugh-Frampton, of Moreton, Dorset, and Balrath, Co Westmeath, and had issue:

1d Lettice Adelaide; *b* 17 June 1882; *m* 19 Feb 1906 Capt Edward Nugent Banes (*ka* in Flanders shortly before 1 May 1915), Roy Dublin Fus, Queen's Bays, yst son of Henry Hyde Nugent Bankes, DL, of Wraysbury, Bucks, and *d* 21 June 1953, leaving issue

2d Margery Frances; *b* 14 Oct 1883; *m* 29 April 1911 her cousin John Walter Somerville Wingfield-Digby (*d* 10 Sept 1914), 2nd son of Rev Richard H Wingfield-Digby, Rector Thornford, and *d* 8 Aug 1951, having had issue

1c (cont.) Charles Digby *m* 2nd 26 Oct 1904 Evelyn Frances Adams (*m* 2nd 27 April 1911 Maj Cecil Edward George Woollcombe-Adams, DL, JP, RHA, of Anstey Hall, Warwicks (*d* 8 June 1926), only son of Lt-Col Edward Woollcombe-Adams, DL, JP, RHA, and *d* 8 Feb 1936), 2nd dau of Ralph Coker Adams Beck, of Bookham Lodge, Cobham, and *d* 9 Feb 1908

3c Georgina Emily; *d* 1900

4c Adelaide Mabel; *m* 27 April 1892 Rev Claude Samuel Homan (*d* May 1947), BA, Rector Stockton, Codford St Mary, Wilts, and *d* 27 Feb 1947, having had issue

5c Augusta Henrietta Sophia; *m* 7 June 1892 Harry William Buddicom (*d* 29 Dec 1925), of Penbedw, Mold, Flintshire, and *d* 1 May 1943, leaving issue

6c Ethel Octavia; *d* unm 9 Jan 1945

7c Katharine Vera; *m* 29 June 1893 Cuthbert Lionel Fetherstonhaugh (*d* 27 Feb 1939), of Studmore, Parkstone, Dorset, s of Rupert Pennefather Fetherstonhaugh-Frampton, of Moreton and Balrath, and *d* 12 April 1955, leaving issue

2b George Somerville, Capt Gren Gds; *b* 27 Sept 1805; *m* 6 Sept 1836 Lady Emily Jane Butler-Danvers (*d* 28 March 1895), sister of 5th Earl of Lanesborough (*qv*), and *d* 16 Nov 1864, leaving, with other issue:

1c Henry Somerville; *b* 21 Oct 1837; *dsp* 10 Jan 1870

2c Noel Stephen Fox, V-Adml; *b* 2 Oct 1839; *m* 1st 9 July 1879 Ethel Dorothea (*dsp* 3 Feb 1881), dau of Rev William Webb Spicer, of Itchen Abbas, Hants; *m* 2nd 28 Nov 1893 Isabella Frances (*d* 12 March 1944), est dau of Henry Drake, of Reading, and *d* 18 Jan 1920, having by her had issue:

1d Noel Somerville, Lt-Cdr RN; *b* 20 Feb 1899; *m* 22 Nov 1923 Margaret Kathleen Abbott, and *d* 1 Jan 1934

1d Emily Frances; *b* 12 Oct 1894; *m* 7 Jan 1922 Ernest Gathorne Wood (*d* 6 April 1948), son of John Gathorne Wood, DL, JP, of Thedden Grange, and *d* 8 Jan 1938

3c Charles Robert (Rev), Vicar Meriden 1902–15; *b* 3 Nov 1850; *educ* St Peter's Coll Cambridge (MA); *d* 9 June 1919

2a Stephen Thomas, Capt RN; *d* 1820

1a Charlotte Elizabeth; *m* 1803 her cousin Rev William Digby (*d* 2 Jan 1848), 2nd son of Very Rev Hon William Digby, LLD (*see* above), and *dsp* 13 Sept 1820

(5) (cont.) Col The Hon Stephen Digby *m* 2nd 6 Jan 1790 Charlotte Margaret (*d* 1794), est dau of Sir Robert Gunning, 1st Bt (*qv*), and *d* 30 May 1800, having by her had further issue

(6) Charles (Rev), MA, Canon Wells; *b* 22 April 1743; *m* 5 Jan 1775 Priscilla (*d* 14 Dec 1837), dau of William Mellier, of Castle Cary, Somerset, and *d* 10 Sept 1810, having had:

1a Mary Charlotte; *m* 22 Sept 1810 Rev John Dampier (*d* 16 Jan 1841), of Bulow, Somerset

2 Wriothesly; *m* Mary, dau of John Cotes, of Woodcote, Salop, and had issue (*see* AUBREY-FLETCHER, Bt)

The 8th/2nd BARON's cousin,

EDWARD ST VINCENT DIGBY, **9th Baron Digby of Geashill** and **3rd Baron Digby of Sherborne**; Lt 9th Lancers; *b* 21 June 1809; *m* 27 June 1837 Lady Theresa Anna Maria Fox-Strangways (*d* 2 May 1874), est dau of 3rd Earl of Ilchester (*qv*), and had issue:

1 EDWARD HENRY TRAFALGAR, **10th/4th Baron**

2 Almarus Kenelm; *b* 5 Sept 1850; *d* 13 Dec 1886

3 Everard Charles, Col Gren Gds; *b* 6 Sept 1852; *m* 2 June 1886 Lady Emily Louisa Anne FitzMaurice (*d* 2 Dec 1939), dau of 4th Marquess of Lansdowne, KG (*qv*), and *d* 16 Jan 1915, leaving issue:

(1) Almarus Edward Henry, Lt RM; *b* 16 Dec 1889; *d* unm 8 Nov 1950

(2) Giles Stephen FitzMaurice; *b* 10 April 1894

(1) Theresa Emily Margery; *b* 11 July 1888; *m* 26 Nov 1912 Capt Albert Oscar Hood (*d* 31 Jan 1952), JP, Irish Gds and Rifle Bde, 2nd son of Hon Albert Hood (*see* HOOD, V), and *d* 31 Dec 1970, leaving issue

4 Gerald FitzMaurice, Capt RN; *b* 20 Dec 1858; *m* 26 July 1906 Lady Lilian Mary Harriet Diana Liddell, MBE (1918), ARRC (*d* 18 March 1962), yr dau of 2nd Earl of Ravensworth (*see* RAVENSWORTH, B), and *d* 8 Dec 1942 having had issue:

(1) Theresa Mary, served in ATS 1939–40; *b* 1 May 1907; *d* unm 2 June 1940

1 Victoria Alexandrina; *m* 6 June 1865 Richard Marker (*d* 1916), of Combe House, Devon, and *d* 21 May 1917, leaving issue

2 Leonora Caroline; *m* 5 Jan 1864 4th Baron Ashburton (*qv*), and *d* 19 Aug 1930, leaving issue

3 Mary-Theresa; *d* unm 12 Oct 1896

The 9th/3rd BARON *d* 16 Oct 1889; his son,

EDWARD HENRY TRAFALGAR DIGBY, **10th Baron Digby of Geashill** and **4th Baron Digby of Sherborne**, JP and CA Dorset, Col Coldstream Gds, Hon Col Dorsetshire RGA, MP (C) Dorset 1876–85; *b* 21 Oct 1846; *educ* Harrow; *m* 19 Sept 1893 Emily Beryl Sissy (*d* 28 Nov 1938), er dau of Hon Albert Hood (*see* HOOD, V), and had issue:

1 EDWARD KENELM, **11th/5th Baron**

2 Robert Henry; *b* 24 Nov 1903; *m* 1st 11 Dec 1928 Diana Mary (*d* 17 July 1969), only dau of Sir Berkeley Digby George Sheffield, 6th Bt (*qv*), and *d* 4 April 1959, having had issue:

(1) Henry Berkeley; *b* 1 March 1933; *educ* Eton; *m* 1st 31 Dec 1960 (*divorce* 1983) Jacqueline Winifred, er dau of Charles A Hussey, of Barking, Essex, and had issue:

1a *Jane Diana; *b* 21 Sept 1962; *m* 1987 *Christoph D Auer, est son of Ernst Auer, of Grunwald, Munich, and has issue:

1b *Charles Felix Ernst; *b* 1991

2b *Hugo Henry Berkeley; *b* 2 Feb 1995

2a *(Charlotte) Sophia; *b* 27 March 1964

(1) (cont.) Henry Digby *m* 2nd 25 Aug 1983 *Mrs S Rosalie McLaren, er dau of Maj Richard Atkinson-Turner, of Worlington, Suffolk, and formerly w of Andrew McLaren, of Coughton, Warwicks, and *d* 1992

(2) A son; *b* 14 Feb 1942; *d* in infancy

(1) *Caroline Theresa; *b* 15 Sept 1943; *m* 18 Dec 1963 *Charles Dermot FitzRoy Musker (*see* DAVENTRY, V), est son of Capt Anthony Dermot Melloney Musker, of Bardwell Hall, Bury St Edmunds, Suffolk, and has issue

3 (Albert) Elmar; *b* 26 July 1911

1 Lettice Theresa, JP Sussex; *b* 16 April 1896; *m* 19 March 1921 Eric Tillyer Tatham, and *d* 6 Sept 1967, leaving issue

2 Geraldine Margot; *b* 21 March 1989; *m* 10 Jan 1918 (*divorce* 1946) Sir Michael Albert James Malcolm, 10th Bt (*qv*), Scots Gds, and *d* 1 June 1965, leaving issue

3 Venetia Jane; *b* 3 Nov 1900; *m* 6 Dec 1923 Capt Hon Oswald Wykeham Cornwallis, OBE, RN, 3rd son of 1st Baron Cornwallis, CBE (*qv*), and *d* 16 March 1956, leaving issue

The 10th/4th BARON *d* 11 May 1920; his est son,

EDWARD KENELM DIGBY, **11th Baron Digby of Geashill** and **5th Baron Digby of Sherborne**, KG (1960), DSO (1919), MC (1916) and bar (1918), TD (1945); Dorset: Ld Lt 1953–64, JP and CA, V-Chm CC 1951–55, Chm 1955–62; Col Coldstream Gds, Adj 1st Bn 1915–18, Actg Maj and 2ic 1918–19, ADC to GOC Aldershot Command 1919–20, Mil Sec to Govr-Gen Australia 1920–23; Hon Col RA (Dorset TA) 1929–60, served WW I 1914 (despatches twice, wounded twice, Croix de Guerre 1917), memb Gentlemen-at-Arms 1939–62; Freeman City of London 1952; Assist Inspr Inf War Office 1939–42, Inspr Inf Trg Estabs War Office 1942–44, KJStJ 1961; *b* 1 Aug 1894; *m* 1 July 1919 Hon (Constance) Pamela Alice Bruce (*d* 15 March 1978), OBE (1944), JP (1934) Dorset, Ch Cdr ATS 1940–45, CC Dorset 1944046 and 1952–78, CA 1957, Pres Dorset Branch BRCS 1964–78, yst dau of 2nd Baron Aberdare (*qv*), and *d* 29 Jan 1964, leaving issue:

1 EDWARD HENRY KENELM DIGBY, **12th and present Baron Digby of Geashill and 6th Baron Digby of Sherborne**

1 Pamela Beryl; *b* 20 March 1920; US Amb to Paris 1993–97, Cdr Order Arts and Letters France, Grand Cross Legion Honour 1997; *m* 1st 4 Oct 1939 (*divorce* 1946) Maj Hon Randolph Frederick Edward Spencer Churchill (*d* 6 June 1968), MBE, 4th Hus (SR), only son of Sir Winston Leonard Spencer Churchill, KG, PC, CH, and Baroness Spencer-Churchill, OBE, and had issue (*see* MARLBOROUGH D); *m* 2nd 4 May 1960 Leland Hayward (*d* March 1971), theatrical producer and chm Pacific Airways; *m* 3rd 28 Sept 1971, as his 2nd w, Averell Harriman (*d* 1986), US diplomat, and *d* 5 Feb 1997

2 *Constance Sheila [The Hon Mrs Moore, Bearforest, Mallow, Co Cork, Ireland]; *b* 20 Sept 1921; ATS WW II and with Br Security Co-ordination 1943–45;

m 27 Nov 1945 Charles Arthur Moore (d 1989), est son of Charles Arthur Moore, of Greenwich, Conn., USA

3 *Jaquetta Mary Theresa [The Hon Mrs Guthrie-James, Little Torosay Craignure, Isle of Mull, Argyllshire PA65 6AY]; *b* 28 Oct 1928; memb Mid-Sussex Hosp Ctee 1960–68 and Dorset AHA 1974–81, chm Hamilton Lodge Sch for Deaf Children Brighton 1962–80; *m* 20 May 1950 David Pelham JAMES later GUTHRIE-JAMES (added 1979; *d* 1986), MBE, DSC, MP (C) Brighton Kemp Town 1959–64 and Dorset N 1970–79, est s of Sir Archibald William Henry James, KBE, MC, of Bita, Marendella, Rhodesia, and has issue:

(1) *Peter Edward; *b* 1 April 1951; *educ* Downside

(2) *Michael David Ashworth; *b* 15 July 1955; *educ* Downside; *m* 1996 *Namrata Rai

(3) *Christopher Leslie Donan; *b* 17 April 1957; *educ* Downside and Edinburgh U; *m* 1997 *Sarah MacDonald, *née* Finlayson

(4) *Kenelm Henry Thomas; *b* 10 April 1962; *educ* Downside

(1) *Patricia Bridget Edwina [Mrs Ian Maxwell, 5 St Marks Place, Edinburgh]; *b* 13 April 1952; *educ* Mayfield and York U; *m* 1989 *Ian Maxwell, and has issue:

1a *Rowan; *b* 1992

1a *Anna; *b* 1989

(2) *Diana Mary [Mrs Diana Guthrie-James, 104 High St, Grantown on Spey, Morayshire]; *b* 7 Sept 1953; *educ* Mayfield and Lancaster U; *m* 1972 (*divorce* 1980, resumed maiden name) Alan Fry and has:

1a *Daniel; *b* 1972

2a *Adam; *b* 1975

1a *Susannah; *b* 1974; *educ* Grantonn and Imperial Coll

(2) (cont.) Mrs Diana Guthrie-James has further issue:

2a *Marina; *b* 1991

DILHORNE

Arms: Quarterly, 1st and 4th, sable on a cross argent quarterly, pierced of the field, four eagles displayed of the first (for BULLER); 2nd and 3rd, sable a fess ermine, in chief three griffin's heads erased or (for MANNINGHAM). **Crests:** 1 A Saracen's head affrontée, couped, proper (for BULLER), 2 Out of a ducal coronet gules a talbot's head or, collared gules, therefrom a line terminating in a knot sable (for MANNINGHAM). **Supporters:** Dexter, an eagle, wings elevated and addorsed erm., beaked and legged or, gorged with a ducal coronet gu., therefrom a line reflexed over the back and terminating in a knot sa.; sinister, a pegasus, winged, crined, unguled and queued arg; both charged on the shoulder with a portcullis chained gold. **Motto:** *Aquila non capit muscas* ('The eagle does not catch flies'). **Creation:** Bt. (UK) 20 Jan 1866, B. (UK) 17 July 1962, V. (UK) 7 Dec 1964.

THE 2ND VISCOUNT DILHORNE, of Greens Norton, Co Northampton, **Baron Dilhorne**, of Towcester, Co Northampton, and a **Baronet** (Sir John Mervyn Manningham-Buller, Bt) [The Rt Hon The Viscount Dilhorne, 164 Ebury St, London SW1W 8UP; 4 Breams Bldgs, London EC4A 1AQ]; *b* 28 Feb 1932; *s* f 1980; *educ* Eton and RMA Sandhurst; memb Wilts CC 1967–70, Lt Coldstream Gds RARO 1957, barrister 1979, Fell and memb Cncl Inst of Taxation, md Stewart, Smith (LP & M) Ltd, dir Stewart, Smith (Southern) Ltd, Crawley; *m* 1st 8 Oct 1955 (*divorce* 1973) Gillian Evelyn, JP (Wilts 1964), er dau of Col George Cochrane Stockwell, Seaforth Highrs, of Roquebrune, Cap Martin, France, by Evelyn Dorothy, only dau of Richard Heywood, JP, of Pentney House, Narborough, Norfolk, and has issue:

1 +JAMES EDWARD [The Hon James Manningham-Buller, Ballymote House, Downpatrick, Co Down]; *b* 20 Aug 1956; *educ* Harrow and RMA Sandhurst; formerly Capt Welsh Gds, Maj NI House, sr ptnr Heritage Insur Servs; *m* 4 May 1985 *Nicola Marion, est dau of Sven Mackie, of Ballydugan House, Downpatrick, and has issue:

(1) +Edward John; *b* 25 Jan 1990

(1) *Camilla Mary; *b* 1 July 1992

2 +Mervyn Reginald [The Hon Mervyn Manningham-Buller, 126 Hurlingham Rd, London SW6 3NF]; *b* 11 July 1962; *m* 7 Oct 1989 *Lucy Meriel, dau of George Thurstan

1 *Mary Louise; *b* 8 March 1970; *m* 1992 *Capt James M Cowan, Black Watch, and has:

(1) Fergus Edward Napoleon; *b* 8 Feb 1996

The 2nd VISCOUNT *m* 2nd 17 Dec 1981 *Dr Susanna Jane Gilchrist, MB, BSc, FRCPath, formerly w of Colin Gilchrist and dau of Cdr W C Eykyn, RN

Lineage: The 1st BARON CHURSTON (*qv*) had a bro:

Sir EDWARD YARDE-BULLER later MANNINGHAM-BULLER (roy licence 1866), **1st Bt** (UK), so *cr* 20 Jan 1866, of Dilhorne Hall, Staffs; *b* 19 July 1800; MP N Staffs 1833–42 and Stafford 1842–47, 1865 and 1874; *m* 1st 12 Aug 1824 Mary Anne (*d* 20 June 1860), dau and heiress of Maj-Gen Coote Manningham, and had, with other issue:

1 **Sir Morton Edward Manningham-Buller, 2nd Bt**, DL, JP Staffs; Hon Col cmdg 3rd Bn Prince of Wales's North Staffs Regt, BA Oxford; *b* 31 May 1825; *m* 12 Feb 1863 Mary (*d* 12 Oct 1923), dau of William Davenport, of Maer Hall, Staffs, and *d* 27 April 1910, having had:

(1) Hilda Mary Adelaide; *d* an infant 1867

(2) Evelyn Mary; *b* 12 April 1869; *s* to Dilhorne Hall on her f's death 1910; *m* 22 April 1891 Sir William Henry Feilden, 4th Bt (*qv*), and *d* 11 Feb 1946, leaving issue

(3) Adelaide Marianne; *b* 1871; *m* 4 April 1894 John Mountford Wood (*d* 23 Jan 1927), JP, of Barton Hall, Neatishead, Norwich, and *d* 29 Dec 1948

(4) Lilian; *b* 14 Feb 1874; *m* 8 Aug 1894 Charles Edward Stuart Cockburn (*d* 12 Dec 1917), 2nd s of Col George William Cockburn, Black Watch, and *d* 23 Nov 1943, leaving issue (*see* COCKBURN, Bt)

2 Edmund Manningham, Maj-Gen 1st Bn Rifle Bde; *b* 1 June 1828; *m* 16 Jan 1874 Lady Anne Coke (*d* 23 Jan 1876), 2nd dau of 2nd Earl of Leicester (*qv*), and *d* 14 Feb 1897, leaving:

(1) MERVYN EDWARD (Sir), **3rd Bt**

(1) Julia; *b* 4 Jan 1875; *m* 4 July 1894 Col Herbert Francis Smith (*d* 20 Dec 1948), JP, est s of Frederic Chatfield Smith, of Bramcote Hall, Notts, and *d* 25 April 1961, leaving issue

3 Frederick Charles, Col Coldstream Gds; *b* 9 June 1837; *m* 28 July 1881 Alice Jessie (*d* 10 Jan 1942), dau and coheir of William Davenport, of Staffs, and *dsp* 9 Jan 1884

1 Giulietta Romana; *m* 2 Feb 1848 Sir Thomas Sutton Western, 2nd Bt (*d* 20 June 1877), and *d* 20 Sept 1850, leaving issue

Sir EDWARD *m* 2nd 2 June 1863 Georgina Charlotte (*d* 7 Dec 1875), only dau and heiress of Adml of the Fleet Sir Charles Edmund Nugent, GCH, KCB, and widow of Rt Hon George Bankes, 7th of Kingston Lacy and Studland Manor, Dorset, and *d* 22 Sept 1882

The 2nd Bt's nephew,

Sir Mervyn Edward Manningham-Buller, 3rd Bt, JP (Northants); Lt-Col the Rifle Bde, Capt Northamptonshire Imp Yeo Boer War (despatches), T/Lt-Col cmdg 12th Bn Rifle Bde 1914, MP Kettering 1924–29 and Northampton 1931–40; *b* 16 Jan 1876; *m* 8 July 1903 Hon Lilah Constance Cavendish, OBE (*d* 27 April 1944), only surv dau of 3rd Baron Chesham (*qv*), and had issue:

1 REGINALD EDWARD, **1st Viscount**

1 Evelyn Constance, MBE (1947); *b* 22 June 1904; *m* 30 Aug 1972 Capt Patrick Mervyn Archdale, RN

2 *Myra [Mrs Percy Snatt, The Stone House, Chelwood Gate, Sussex], WW II as Jr Cdr ATS; *b* 15 May 1909; *m* 21 Dec 1940 Lt-Col Percy Cyril Snatt (*d* 27 Dec 1961), MC, Royal Signals

3 Helen Marjorie, WW II as VAD 1940–43, India 1944–46 with Br Red Cross, memb Red Cross Soc 1930–72; *b* 18 Feb 1913; *d* unm 29 Jan 1972

4 *Pamela Lilah; *b* 20 May 1919; *m* 2 May 1951 Norman Wilkinson-Cox (*d* 22 Aug 1969) and has:

(1) *Gavia Lilah; *b* 25 July 1952

Sir MERVYN *d* 22 Aug 1956; his only son,

Sir Reginald Edward Manningham-Buller, 3rd Bt, and **1st Viscount Dilhorne**, of Greens Norton, Co Northampton, so *cr* 7 Dec 1964, as also earlier 17 July 1962 BARON DILHORNE, of Towcester, Co Northampton (both UK), PC (1954), KC (1946), DL (Northants 1967); *b* 1 Aug 1905; *educ* Eton and Magdalen Coll Oxford (BA 1926); Hon DCL McGill, Hon DL SMU Dallas, Texas, MP (C) Daventry 1943–50 and Northants S 1950–62, Parly Sec Min Works May–July 1945, Slr-Gen 1951–54, Attorney-Gen 1954–62, Ld Chllr 1962–64, Ld of Appeal in Ordinary 1969, Dep Leader Oppn Ho Lords 1964–66, barrister Inner Temple 1927, Recorder Kingston-upon-Thames 1962, Reader Inner Temple 1974, Treas 1975, ktd 1951; *m* 18 Dec 1930 *Lady Mary Lilian Lindsay, 4th dau of 27th Earl of Crawford and Balcarres (*qv*), and *d* 1980, leaving issue:

1 JOHN MERVYN MANNINGHAM-BULLER, **2nd and present Viscount Dilhorne**

1 *Marian Cynthia [The Hon Mrs Brudenell, 18 Laxford House, Ebury St, London SW1]; *b* 26 Nov 1934; *m* 8 Nov 1955 *Edmund Crispin Stephen James George Brudenell, only son of George Lionel Thomas Brudenell, of Deene Park, Corby, Northants (*see* AILESBURY, M), and has issue

2 *Elizabeth (Eliza) Lydia [The Hon Elizabeth Manningham-Buller, 11 Ursula St, London SW11]; *b* 14 July 1948; *educ* Benenden and LMH Oxford; Dep Dir-Gen MI5 1997–; *m* 1991 *David —

3 *Anne Constance; *b* 13 Aug 1951 *m* 20 Feb 1982 *John Christopher Parsons (*see* ROSSE, E) and has issue

DILKE

Arms: Quarterly of nine, 1st, gules a lion rampant per pale argent and or; 2nd, argent a mullet gules; 3rd, sable a chevron between three leopard's faces or; 4th, argent a cross grady throughout sable; 5th, paly or six argent and gules a bend counterchanged; 6th, gules, on a bend argent three escallops azure; 7th, paly of six argent and sable on a bend gules three mullets argent; 8th, quarterly, or and gules on a bend sable, between two frets or, three escallops of the first; 9th, ermine two chevrons sable. **Crest:** A dove proper. **Motto:** *Leo inimicis, amicis columba* ('A lion to my enemies, to my friends a dove') **Creation:** Bt. (UK) 22 Jan 1862.

(REV) SIR CHARLES JOHN WENTWORTH DILKE, 6TH BT, of Sloane Street, Chelsea; *b* 21 Feb 1937; *s* f 1998; *educ* Winchester and King's Coll Cambridge (BA); Provost Brompton Oratory to 1996

Lineage: RICHARD DILKE, of Kirkby Mallory, Leics, had, with other issue:

Sir THOMAS DILKE, of Maxstoke Castle, Warwicks; *m* 5 Jan 1588 Anne, est dau of Sir Clement Fisher, of Packington, Warwicks, and *d* 1618, leaving issue:

1 Thomas, of Maxstoke Castle; *b* 11 June 1590, ancestor of the DILKEs of Maxstoke Castle

2 FISHER

1 Lettice; *bapt* 21 July 1597

The 2nd son,

FISHER DILKE, of Shustock, Warwicks; *bapt* 27 Feb 1591; *m* Sybyl, dau of Nicholas Wentworth, of Lillington Lovell, Oxon, and sister of Sir Peter Wentworth, KB, MP, and *d* 1660, leaving, with a yr s (Fisher, *d* unm):

SAMUEL DILKE; Fell Commoner Peterhouse Cambridge 1650; *b* 1631; *m* 1st Elizabeth, dau of Sir Edward Zouche, of Woking, Surrey, Kt Marshal to JAMES I, and had three sons and a dau; *m* 2nd Chrysogon Draper, of Salop, and *d* 1701, having by her had issue:

WENTWORTH DILKE; *b* 26 Dec 1676; *m* Mary (*d* 24 March 1743), dau of Jonathan Gumbleton, and *d* 5 March 1726, leaving:

WENTWORTH DILKE later DILKE WENTWORTH (added under terms of will of his great-great-uncle Sir Peter Wentworth); *b* 4 April 1698; *m* Winifred Street (*d* 20 March 1762) and *d* 18 Nov 1781, leaving an only s:

CHARLES WENTWORTH DILKE; *b* 25 Nov 1742; *m* 17 Feb 1783 Sarah Blewford (*d* 27 Oct 1825) and *d* 25 March 1826, leaving, with two daus and a yr s (William, *m* Mary, widow of Henry Silverlock, of Lincoln's Inn, and dau of Richard Grant, and *d* 30 Aug 1885 aged 90, having had issue):

CHARLES WENTWORTH DILKE; *b* 8 Dec 1789; *m* Maria Dove Walker (*d* 12 Nov 1850) and *d* 10 Aug 1864, having had, with two daus:

Sir Charles Wentworth Dilke, 1st Bt (UK), so *cr* 22 Jan 1862; Chm Soc of Arts and of Royal Horticultural Soc, took a prominent part in the Internat Exhibitions of 1851 and 1862, MP Wallingford 1865–68; *b* 18 Feb 1810; *educ* Trin Hall Cambridge; *m* 30 March 1840 Mary (*d* 16 Sept 1853), dau of William Chatfield, Capt Madras Cav, and *d* 11 May 1869, having had:

1 **Sir Charles Wentworth Dilke, 2nd Bt,** PC (1882); MP (Lib) Chelsea 1868–86 and Forest of Dean 1892–1911, Under Sec For Affrs 1880–82, Pres Local Gov Bd 1882–85, barrister, LLM Cambridge, Scholar Trin Hall Cambridge; *b* 4 Sept 1843; *m* 1st 30 Jan 1872 Katherine Mary Eliza (*d* 20 Sept 1874), only dau of Capt Arthur Gore Snell, 49th Foot, and had issue:

(1) **Sir Charles Wentworth Dilke, 3rd Bt;** *b* 19 Sept 1874; *m* 17 July 1915 (Florence) Pearl (*d* 9 May 1955), dau of Henry Montague Faithfull, MA, of Sydney, NSW, and *dsp* 7 Dec 1918

1 (cont.) **Sir Charles** *m* 2nd 3 Oct 1885 Emilia Frances (*dsp* 24 Oct 1904), widow of Rev Mark Pattison, Rector Lincoln Coll Oxford, and dau of Major Henry Strong, HEICS, and *d* 26 Jan 1911

2 Ashton Wentworth, MP Newcastle-on-Tyne, scholar Trin Hall Camb; *b* 11 Aug 1850; *m* 10 April 1876 Margaret Mary (*m* 2nd 19 Sept 1891 William Russell Cooke (*d* 30 Jan 1903) and *d* 19 May 1914), est dau of Thomas Eustace Smith, of Gosforth House, Northumberland, MP, and *d* 12 March 1883, leaving:

(1) FISHER WENTWORTH (Sir), **4th Bt**

(2) Clement Wentworth, 2nd Lt Surrey Yeo; *b* 16 Jan 1878; *educ* King's Coll Cambridge (BA); *m* 14 Dec 1901 Marie Hilda Jessie (*d* 24 June 1944), only child of William Phelps, MD, and *d* 14 Sept 1944, leaving issue:

1a Oswald Ashton Wentworth; *b* 26 April 1915; *educ* Stowe and King's Coll Cambridge (BA 1938, MA 1945); DLitt and DPhil U of S Africa 1963, Capt Intell Corps WW II, lecturer in classics U Coll Hull 1946–50, lecturer humanities U of Glasgow 1950, Sr Lecturer 1964, Prof Classics Rhodes U Grahamstown 1961 and 1962, Prof Latin U of Leeds 1967, Visiting Prof Classics Ohio State U 1969; *m* 9 Aug 1949 *Margaret Sterndale, MA (Manchester) [Mrs Oswald Dilke, 6 Winniford Close, Chideock, Dorset DT6 6SA], only dau of George Williamson, of Ashton-under-Lyne, and *d* 10 July 1993, leaving:

1b Stephen Wentworth; *b* 31 March 1951; *educ* Manchester GS, Winchester, New Coll Oxford (MA) and Sheffield U (MSc); *m* 30 July 1990 *Dr Lucilla Maria Antonietta, dau of Umberto Costantini, and *d* 15 Oct 1992

1a Muriel Mary Wentworth; *b* 17 Feb 1903; *m* 25 June 1930 Herbert Fraser STANDEN later STANDEN-McDOUGAL (deed poll 1952) and had:

1b Peter Douglas; *b* 25 July 1932; *m* 21 May 1955 *Sally Ann (*m* 2nd 2 March 1968 Peter Michell, of Estoril, Portugal), dau of John Stewart, of Bolivia Mount, Lezaure, IoM, and *d* 30 Sept 1964, leaving issue:

1c *Andrew John; 2nd Lt Royal Signals; *b* 27 April 1958; *educ* All Hallows and RMA Sandhurst

2c *James Stewart; *b* 17 May 1960

1c *Caroline Susan; *b* 10 July 1956

2b *John Anthony Phelps (Rev) [The Rev John Standen-McDougal, Silverbridge Cottage, N Chideock, Dorset DT6 6LG], AKC, Deacon 1959, Priest 1960; *b* 23 Dec 1933; *educ* King's Coll London and Warminster Theological Coll; *m* 18 Sept 1965 *Susan Eleanor, dau of Edward George Kent, of Church Farm House, Angmering, Sussex, and has issue:

1c *Anthony Peter; *b* 4 Aug 1966

2a Sybil Iris Wentworth; *b* 19 April 1904; *m* 21 July 1945 Arthur Sidney Kellaway Knight (*d* 15 Aug 1961)

3a Celia Wentworth; *b* 30 Oct 1908; *m* 1933 *Otto Rene Gottleib Vervuurt and has:

1b *Reinhardt James; *b* 12 Jan 1934; *m* 1965 *Anita Douwes and has issue:

1c *Melvin Michael; *b* 1966

2c *Norbert Calmon; *b* 26 Sept 1967

2b *Gerard Michael; *b* 4 Oct 1938

1b *Celia Wentworth [Mrs Anton Smit, Box 1449, Paramaribo, Surinam]; *b* 1 July 1936; *m* 1962 *Anton F Smit, and has issue:

1c *Willem Otto Anton; *b* 11 Aug 1968

1c *Audrey Elizabeth; *b* 11 June 1965

2c *Jeanine Annette; *b* 21 Feb 1967

(1) Sybil Mary Wentworth; *b* 21 Feb 1879; *m* 12 Feb 1901 John Roskill (*d* 19 Aug 1940), KC, of 33A Montague Square, London, and Newtown Common, Newbury, and *d* 14 Feb 1931, leaving issue:

1a Stephen Roskill, DSC; Capt RN, CTSE, naval historian; *d* 4 Nov 1982 aged 79

1 Mildred; *d* an infant 31 Jan 1853

The 3rd Bt's cousin,

Sir Fisher Wentworth Dilke, 4th Bt; *b* 5 Jan 1877; *educ* Trin Hall Cambridge (BA); *m* 7 June 1905 Ethel (*d* 14 Dec 1959), er dau of W K Clifford, FRS, and *d* 25 March 1944, leaving:

1 Sir JOHN FISHER WENTWORTH DILKE, **5th Bt;** *b* 8 May 1906; *educ* Winchester and New Coll Oxford; For Serv 1929–32, Head Br Official Wireless News 1942–45, formerly with *The Times* Foreign Dept, Govt Information Servs and BBC External Serv; *m* 1st 15 Sept 1934 (*divorce* 1949) Sheila, only dau of Sir William Seeds, KCMG, and *d* 28 June 1998, leaving:

(1) Sir CHARLES JOHN WENTWORTH, **6th and present Bt**

(2) +TIMOTHY FISHER WENTWORTH [Dr Timothy Dilke, 15 Wemyss Rd, London SE3 0TG]; *b* 1 Aug 1938; heir presumptive; *educ* Winchester and New Coll Oxford (MA, BM, BCh); MRCP 1969, FRCP 1986; *m* 4 Sept 1965 his cousin *Caroline Sophia, est dau of Christopher Wentworth Dilke (*see* below), and has:

1a +Felix Wentworth [Felix Dilke Esq, 75 Crimsworth Rd, London SW8]; *b* 2 Aug 1967

1a *Rosemary Frances [Miss Rosemary Dilke, 152c Coldharbour Lane, London SE5]; *b* 5 July 1970

1 (cont.) Sir JOHN *m* 2nd 28 Dec 1951 *Iris Evelyn, only child of Ernest Clark

2 Michael Clifford Wentworth; *b* 22 March 1909; *m* 9 March 1940 Rosemary Blanche (*d* 25 June 1974), widow of Capt Roderick Kilgour Mackenzie, Seaforth Highrs, and yr dau of Sir Thomas Troubridge, 4th Bt (*qv*), and *d* 25 March 1944, leaving issue:

(1) *Lucilla Rose [Mrs Gareth van den Bogaerde, 42 Bennerley Rd, London SW11]; *b* 17 April 1941; *m* 1970 *Gareth Ulric van den Bogaerde, and has issue:

1a *Ulric Michael Amadeus Landrover; *b* 1970

2a *Alice Rosemary Patience Lucilla; *b* 1973

3 Christopher Wentworth, Hon Lt-Col RA, served WW II, memb of Lloyd's, a novelist, Manager of BBC's English by Radio Dept; *b* 15 Dec 1913; *educ* Winchester; *m* 15 Aug 1939 *Alice Mary [Mrs Christopher Dilke, Valehouse Farm, Whitchurch Canonicorum, Bridport, Dorset], er dau of Hon James William Best, OBE, of Hincknowle, Melplash, Dorset (*see* WYNFORD, B), and *d* 2 Nov 1987, leaving issue:

(1) +Fisher William Wentworth [Dr Fisher Dilke, 142 Iffley Rd, London W6]; *b* 14 June 1948; *educ* Westminster, Sussex U (BA) and Darwin Coll Cambridge (PhD); *m* 1985 *Diana Madelaine, dau of Dr Raymond John Adie, and has issue:

1a +Thomas Wentworth; *b* 1991

1a *Stella Maye; *b* 1987

2a *Athene Elizabeth; *b* 1988

(1) *Caroline Sophia; *b* 28 May 1940; *m* 4 Sept 1965 her cousin *Dr Timothy Fisher and has issue (*see* above)

(2) *Annabel Mary [Mrs Georgi Markov, 23 Lynette Ave, London SW4]; *b* 28 April 1942; *m* 1975 Georgi Markov (*assassinated* 1978) and has issue:

1a *Alexandra Raina; *b* 1976

(3) *Lucy Catherine [Mrs Anthony Pinney, Egremont Farm, Payhembury, Devon]; *b* 25 July 1952; *educ* York U (MA); *m* 1975 *Anthony Charles Pinney, and has issue:

1a *Samuel Charles; *b* 1980

2a *Nathaniel Henry; *b* 1994

1a *Katharine Elizabeth; *b* 1979

DILLON

Arms: Quarterly: 1st and 4th, arg. a lion passant between three crescents gu. (for DILLON); 2nd and 3rd, arg. a fess between three crescents sa. (for LEE). **Crest:** A demi-lion gu., holding between the paws an estoile arg. **Supporters:** Two angels ppr., vested arg., winged and crined or, each with a sash over the shoulder az. and holding in the exterior hand a palm branch, also ppr. **Motto:** *Dum spiro spero* ('While I breathe I hope'). **Creations:** V. (I) 16 March 1621/2, Count (France) 1711.

THE 22ND VISCOUNT DILLON OF COSTELLO-GALLIN, Co Mayo and **Count Dillon** in France (Henry (Harry) Benedict Dillon) [The Rt Hon The Viscount Dillon, 28 Canning Cross, London SE5 8BH]; *b* 6 Jan 1973; *s* f 1982

Lineage: Sir HENRY de LEON, a cadet of the Vicomtes de Leon, of Brittany, accompanied Prince (later KING) JOHN to Ireland 1185 and acquired extensive land grants in Cos Longford and Westmeath which he held as a tenant in chief by service of 60 knights' fees, he and his heirs thereby being called to the Irish Parliament. These lands were called Dillon's county till shired and divided into the barony of Kilkenny West and others by statute 34th HENRY VIII; he was afterwards styled 'Premier Dillon, Lord Baron of Drumrany'. He completed the Franciscan Monastery at Kilkenny West; *m* —, dau of Sir John de Courcy, and was *bur* 1244, leaving with other issue:

Sir THOMAS DYLON; *m* Maud, dau of Sir Edmond Butler, Ld Justice of Ireland 1215 (*see* ORMONDE , M), and had, with two yr sons (Dominick, Bp of Ossory; James, a canon regular):

HENRY DYLON, *m* Olivia, dau of Maurice FitzGerald, ancestor of the Earls of Kildare (*see* LEINSTER, D), and had, with other issue, including a yr s (Sir Maurice, *m* Letitia, dau of Sir Richard Tuite, and was *k* by insurgents in the N of Ulster):

Sir HENRY DYLON, Ld of Drumrany; fndr Abbey of St Frances Athlone 1343, granted Manor of Kilkenny West 15 May 1343; *m* Bridget, dau of Peter de Bermingham, Ld of Thetmoy/Totemoy, and sis of 1st Earl of Louth of the 1319 *cr*, and had, with other issue:

ROBERT DYLON, Ld of Drumrany; *m* Anne, 2nd dau of Sir Eustace le Poer, Baron of Kells in Ossory (*d* 1311), and had, with other issue:

GERALD DILLON, Ld of Drumrany; *m* Lady Emily FitzGerald, dau of Earl of Desmond, and had issue, with two daus:

1 MAURICE (Sir)

2 Henry, Prior St John's, Newtown, nr Trim, Co Meath

3 James (Sir), of Proudstown; *m* Honora, dau of Sir John Darcy, and was ancestor of the DILLONs, Earls of Roscommon, DILLONs, Barons Clonbrock, DILLONS, Bts and Barons of the Holy Roman Empire 1782, and DILLONs of Proudstown and Skrine, Barons of the Holy Roman Empire 1767, all now extinct

4 John, coroner Meath 1407

GERALD DILLON's est s,

Sir MAURICE DILLON, of Drumrany; *m* 1st Lady Anne FitzGerald, dau of Earl of Desmond, and had, with other issue:

1 THOMAS

Sir MAURICE *m* 2nd Margaret, dau of — MacCoghlan, chief of his name, by whom he had, with other issue:

2 Maurice, of Low-Baskin; *m* Mary, dau of Sir George FitzGerald, of Tecroghan, Co Meath, and was ancestor of the DILLONs of Mount Dillon, Strokestown, Co Roscommon

3 Edmund, of Kilcornan Castle; ancestor of the DILLONs *cr* Count Dillon in France (*see* 1970 edn)

Sir MAURICE DILLON's est s,

THOMAS DILLON, of Drumrany; *m* Jean, dau of Sir Robert Dillon, and had issue:

EDMUND DILLON, of Drumrany, *m* 1st Anne, dau of William Pettyt, Baron of Mullingar, and had six sons and two daus; *m* 2nd — , dau of Sir Christopher Plunkett, and had issue:

GERALD DILLON, of Dunimoney; Custos Brevium Court of Common Pleas 12 Sept 1532; *m* Ismay, dau of Sir Edward Tuite, of Tuitestown, Co Westmeath, when his f settled on him the lands of Dunimoney, by which his family was subsequently known, and had, with other issue:

1 Robert, of Dunimoney; *m* — , dau of — O'Farrell, of Longford, and was ancester of the DILLONs of Dunimoney, now extinct

2 James (Sir), of Ballynakill; *m* Catherine, dau of Sir Christopher Dalton, of Dalton's Country, and had, with other issue:

(1) Thomas, of Ballynakill; *m* Mary, dau of Christopher Dillon, of Kilmore, and had issue, with three daus:

1a Gerald; *m* Mary, dau of Pierce Dillon, of Highbaskin, and had issue:

1b Margaret; *m* — Dillon

2b Joan; *m* — Dillon

2a Edmund, of Ardnegragh, Co Westmeath, and Urdoghill, Co Longford; *m* Sarah, dau of — O'Ferrall, Ld of Carlow, and *d* by 16 June 1629; ancestor of John Moore-Dillon, of London and Widdington, Newport, Essex

3a THEOBALD, **1st Viscount**

4a Garrett, of Portlick; Capt of an independent company *temp* ELIZABETH I; *m* Margaret, dau of — MacCostello, Baron of Costello; his ggs Gerald Dillon, Prime Sergeant to JAMES II with Col John Browne (ancestor of the Marquess of Sligo), drafted the Articles of Limerick 16 Oct 1691

5a James, of Carrownegarry, Co Roscommon; left issue

THOMAS DILLON's 3rd s,

THEOBALD DILLON, **1st Viscount Dillon of Costello-Gallin**, Co Mayo (I), so *cr* 16 March 1621/2; cmded an independent troop *temp* ELIZABETH I, ktd 1599, Ch Serjeant and Gen Collector and Receiver taxes Connaught and Thomond 1582 (confirmed 1604), helped suppress the native Irish under Earl of Tyrone 1598–1601; Ld Pres Connaught; *m* Eleanora (*d* 8 April 1638), dau of Sir Edward Tuite, of Tuitestown, and widow of William Tuite, of Monilea, and *d* 15 March 1624, leaving, with numerous other issue:

1 Christopher (Sir), of Ballylagham, Co Mayo; *m* Nov 1604 his cousin Lady Jane Dillon, est dau of 1st Earl of Roscommon, and *dvp* 28 Feb 1623/4, leaving with other issue:

(1) LUCAS DILLON, **2nd Viscount Dillon of Costello-Gallin**; *b* March 1610; *m* 1625 Lady Mary MacDonnell (*m* 2nd 6th Baron Louth (*qv*)), 2nd dau of 1st Earl of Antrim (*qv*), and *d* 13 April 1629, leaving issue:

1a THEOBALD DILLON, **3rd Viscount Dillon of Costello-Gallin**; *b* July 1629; *d* 13 May 1630

(2) THOMAS DILLON **4th Viscount Dillon of Costello-Gallin**; *b* March 1615; Jt Govr Mayo Nov 1641, Jt Ld Pres Connaught, Govr Fort of Athlone 27 April 1645, exiled and his estates sequestrated during the Commonwealth but recovered them at the Restoration, Custos Rotulorum Co Westmeath 1662; *m* 1635 Frances, dau of Nicholas White, of Leixlip, and *d* 1673/4, having had, with other issue:

1a Charles; *b* 1636; Gen French and Spanish Armies, Govr Tournai; *dvp*

2a Rupert; Page to CHARLES II; *kas*

3a THOMAS DILLON, **5th Viscount Dillon of Costello-Gallin**; *m* Elizabeth (*m* 2nd Sheffield Grace, of Courtstown, Kilkenny), est dau of Sir John Burke, of Derymaclaghtny, Co Galway, and *dsps* 1674, having had:

1b Thomas; *d* young

1b Elizabeth; *d* young

(3) Theobald; *m* Sarah, illegitimate dau of Hon David Bourke, 2nd s of 1st Viscount Mayo, and had issue:

1a LUCAS DILLON, **6th Viscount Dillon of Costello-Gallin**; *m* 1st Ursula Dungan (*d* by 11 Feb 1680/1), dau of 1st Earl of Limerick (*qv*); *m* 2nd 1681 Anne Nugent (*m* 2nd Sir William Talbot, 3rd Bt, and *d* shortly after 14 July 1710), est dau of 2nd Earl of Westmeath (*qv*), and *dsp* Sept/Oct 1682

2 Lucas (Sir), of Loughglynn, Co Roscommon; High Sheriff Mayo 1662; *m* Jane, dau of John Moore, of Brees, Balla, and Cloghan, Co Mayo, and had, with other issue:

(1) Robert, of Loughglynn; *m* Rose (*m* 2nd Gen John O'Farrel, of Tyrlekin, and *d* 1681), est dau of John Dillon, of Streamstown, and had, with other issue:

1a THEOBALD, **7th Viscount**

3 William, of Tolchan; *m* Margery, dau of James Magawly, of Ballylohlor, Co Westmeath, and had issue

4 Thomas, of Brackloon; *b* Tower of London 1592; *m* Katharine, dau and ultimate heiress of Maurice FitzGerald, of Laccagh (6th in descent from Thomas, 7th Earl of Kildare; *see* LEINSTER, D), by Ellen Butler, dau of 11th Baron Dunboyne (*qv*), by Margaret, dau and heir of Barnaby FitzPatrick, Baron of Upper Ossory; and had:

(1) Theobald, of Brackloon; *m* Sarah, dau of Capt Anthony Brabazon (*see* MEATH, E), and left issue

(2) John, of Lissiane; *m* Frances, dau of Capt Anthony Brabazon, ggs of Sir William Brabazon, Ld Justice Ireland 1543, and was ancestor of:

1a Martin (Sir), GCB, CSI; Gen; *d* 18 Aug 1913

2a Luke; had issue:

1b Charles Blake; had issue:

1c Luke Gerald, OBE, JP; *b* 24 April 1862; MD, FSA, Maj RAMC(T) WW I, mentioned for services, OStJ; *m* 6 Feb 1900 Elizabeth Mary (*d* 29 Nov

1949), 4th dau of Hon Hubert Dormer (*see* DORMER, B), and *d* 27 April 1937, leaving issue:

1d Gerald Dormer FitzGerald; *b* 1 April 1901; *educ* Downside and Balliol Coll Oxford (BA 1922); *m* 6 Aug 1940 Maureen (*d* 4 Feb 1992), dau of Thomas Stewart, of Cowdenbeath, Fifeshire, and *d* 25 Dec 1979, leaving issue:

1e +Martin Luke Gerald [Martin Dillon Esq, The Red House, Much Hadham, Herts SG10 6BU]; *b* 8 Nov 1942; *educ* Downside and Queen's Coll Oxford (BA); *m* 1965 *Diana Mary, dau of Rev Arthur Robert Botting, BA, and has:

1f +Anthony Hugh Patrick Martin; *b* 1965

1f *Clare Elizabeth Teresa; *b* 1968; *m* 1988 *Robert James Ashcroft and has issue:

1g *Thomas Alexander; *b* 1989

2g *Matthew Robert; *b* 1991

3g *William James; *b* 1994

4g *Hugo Oliver; *b* 1995

4 (cont.) Thomas Dillon was also ancestor in the sixth generation of:

(1) Martin (Rev); had issue:

1a John Monro; had issue:

1b Arnold Michael; *b* 1892; Capt; *m* 1915 Esther Dorothy, dau of William Currie Allen, of London, Ontario, Canada, and *d* 1955, leaving issue:

1c +Arnold Charles; *b* 1920; *m* 1947 *Donalda Ruth, dau of Arthur J Cowie, of Caledonia, Ontario, and has:

1d +John Michael; *b* 1956

1d *Dorothy Nina; *b* 1954

1c *Mary Louie Margarette; *b* 1917; *m* 1944 *Dennis Bishop, F/O RAFVR, and has issue:

1d *Dennis John; *b* 1945

1d *Caroline Mary Beverley Anne; *b* 1952

2a Maurice Ashurst; had issue:

1b Marmaduke Murray, MC, ED; *b* 1894; Brig; *m* 1st 1919 Muriel, dau of Rev Canon Richard Hicks; *m* 2nd 1956 *Mildred Whitley [Mrs Marmaduke Dillon, 842 Wellington St, London, Ontario, Canada], widow of Col Charles W Jeffers, US Army, and *d* 1976, leaving issue by his 1st w:

1c +Richard Maurice, MC, ED; *b* 1920; BA; Lt-Col (ret) Canadian Mil, Dean Faculty of English Science W Ontario U, served WW II Sicily and Italy (Coronation medal); *m* 1945 *Mary Elizabeth, dau of Harry H Dempsey, of Stratford, Ontario, and has issue:

1d *Kelly Elizabeth; *b* 1949

2d *Ann Dempsey; *b* 1952

3d *Katherine Talbot; *b* 1955

2c +Michael Talbot, CD [Michael Dillon Esq CD, Unit 73, 2 Cadeau Terrace, London, Ontario N6K 4K7, Canada]; *b* 1926; BA, MA; Lt-Col (ret) RCAMC; *m* 1959 *Margaret, dau of Roy Kirk Hamilton, of Arthur, Ontario, and has issue:

1d +Timothy Arthur; *b* 1960

2d +Kirk FitzGerald; *b* 1961; *m* 1989 *Julie Anne, dau of Charles Duncan, of London, Ontario, and has issue:

1e +Eoghan Charles Michael; *b* 11 Aug 1994

1e *Rebecca Anne; *b* 1990

2e *Kate Elizabeth Margaret; *b* 1992

3d +David Morgan; *b* 1963; has issue by Lisa Westulaken:

1e *Morgan Jane; *b* 1986

1c *Shelagh Muriel [Mrs Neil Watters, 172 Rosedale Heights Drive, Toronto, Canada]; *b* 1924; *m* 1945 *Neil Archibald Watters, MD, FRCS (Canada), and has issue:

1d *Douglas Bruce; *b* 1948

2d *James Murray; *b* 1952

3d *Michael Grant; *b* 1955

1d *Louise Shelagh; *b* 1959

2c *Diana Mary Morgan; *b* 1926; *m* 1956 *Rev Gerald Cecil Johnson, BA, BTh, and has issue:

1d *Patrick Bruce; *b* 1965

2d *Kevin Sean; *b* 1965

1d *Michele Ann Jean; *b* 1958

2d *Margaret Rebecca Morgan; *b* 1962

(1) Margery; *m* Pierce Dillon, of Ballinloghduff

(2) Mary; *m* — Brown

(3) Bridgett; *m* Col Luke Dowell, of Roscommon

5 James (Sir), the yr; joined Irish uprising of 1640s, excepted from gen pardon by OLIVER CROMWELL, Maj-Gen French and Spanish Armies, raised 16 June 1653 the Dillon Regt (disbanded 29 Feb 1664); *m* 1st Elizabeth, dau of Thomas Plunket, of Rathmore; *m* 2nd by 1653 Mary (*dsp* 1664), dau of Roger Jones, of Sligo, and had issue by his 1st w:

(1) Ulick; *d* young

(2) James; *d* young

The 6th VISCOUNT's cousin,

THEOBALD DILLON, **7th Viscount Dillon of Costello-Gallin**; Lt-Col Clanricarde's Regt of Gds in army of JAMES II, reformed the Dillon Regt in two Bns 1688, attainted 11 May 1691 (reversed 20 June 1694); *m* Mary (*k* by a shell at the Siege of Limerick 7 Sept 1691), dau of Sir Henry Talbot, of Templeogue, Co Dublin, and Mt Talbot, Co Roscommon, and was *k* Battle of Aughrim 12 July 1691, having had, with other issue:

1 Robert; *dvp* unm

2 HENRY DILLON, **8th Viscount Dillon of Costello-Gallin**; MP Co Westmeath in JAMES II's I Parl, Ld Lt Co Roscommon 1689, Col Regt of Foot in JAMES's army, Govr Galway; *m* July 1687 Frances (*m* 2nd Patrick (*dvp* 12 June 1720), er s of Sir John Bellew, Bt (*see* BELLEW, B), and *d* 16 Nov 1751), 2nd dau of Count Sir George Hamilton by Frances Jennings, later Duchess of Tyrconnel (*see* ABERCORN, D), and *d* 13 Jan 1713/4, leaving:

(1) RICHARD DILLON, **9th Viscount Dillon of Costello-Gallin**; *b* 1688; *m* 1720 Lady Bridget Bourke (*d* 16 July 1779), 2nd dau of 9th Earl of Clanricarde (*see* SLIGO, M), and *d* Feb 1737, leaving:

1a Frances; *m* 16 Jan 1734/5 her 1st cousin **10th Viscount Dillon of Costello-Gallin** (*see* below) and *d* 17 Jan 1738/9, leaving issue

(1) Bridget; *m* as his 3rd w 8th Earl of Clanricarde (*see* SLIGO, M)

3 ARTHUR DILLON, COUNT DILLON, so *cr* 1711 by LOUIS XIV; *b* 1670; entered French Mil Serv 1690, Col proprietor Dillon Regt, Maréchal de Camp 1705, Govr Toulon, Lt-Gen French Army 1706, Cdr Order of St Louis, titular KT 1715, *cr* 1722 titular Earl Dillon by the titular James III; *m* Christina (*d* 5 Aug 1757), Maid of Honour to MARY OF MODENA, w of JAMES II, dau of Ralph Sheldon, and *d* 5 Feb 1732/3, leaving with other issue:

(1) CHARLES DILLON, **10th Viscount Dillon of Costello-Gallin**; *b* 1701; Col Proprietor Dillon Regt 1730–41; *m* 16 Jan 1734/5 his 1st cousin Frances Dillon (*d* 17 Jan 1738/9), only child of **9th Viscount Dillon of Costello-Gallin**, and *d* 24 Oct 1741, having had issue:

1a Charles; *b* 10 Nov 1738; *d* May 1739

(2) HENRY DILLON, **11th Viscount**

(3) James Denis; *bapt* 21 Nov 1718; Kt SMO Malta, Col Dillon's Regt; *k* leading his men to victory over the British Battle of Fontenoy 30 April 1745

(4) Edward; *b* 1720; *s* his bro in the command of Dillon's Regt; *k* Battle of Laufeld 1747

(5) Arthur Richard; RC priest; *b* St Germains 1721; Bp Evreux 1753, Archbp Toulouse 1758, Archbp Narbonne 1762, Cdr Order of Holy Ghost 1776, Primate of the Gauls, Pres States of Languedoc; *d* London 5 July 1806

The 10th VISCOUNT's yr bro,

HENRY DILLON, **11th Viscount Dillon of Costellò-Gallin**; *b* 1705; Col Proprietor Dillon Regt 1741–44 and 1747–72; *m* 26 Oct 1744 Lady Charlotte Lee (*d* 19 June 1794), est dau and eventual coheir of 2nd Earl of Lichfield (*see* LICHFIELD, E, preliminary remarks) and ggdau of CHARLES II by Barbara, Duchess of Cleveland (*d* JERSEY, E); *d* 15 Sept 1787, leaving, with other issue:

1 CHARLES, **12th Viscount**

2 Arthur; *b* 3 Sept 1750; Lt-Gen French Army, Govr Tobago, Kt of St Louis 1780, last Col proprietor of the Dillon Regt 1772–94; *m* 1st 1769 his cousin Lucie (*d* 1782), dau of Edward, Count de Rothe, and was guillotined 13 April 1794, having had, with a s (*d* an infant):

(1) Henrietta-Lucy; *b* 1770; *m* Frédéric Séraphin de la Tour du Pin, Count de Gouvernet (*d* 1837), and *d* 1853, leaving issue

2 (cont.) Arthur Dillon *m* 2nd 1784 Marie-Françoise Laure, dau of M de Girardin and widow of Count de la Touche, and had further issue:

(1) Fanny; with her husb accompanied NAPOLEON into exile on St Helena; *m* Henri, Count Bertrand, and *d* 1836

3 Henry; *b* 28 June 1759; Major-Gen French and English Armies, Col Dillon Regt 1794–98, when after the surrender of the 2nd Bn at San Domingo it was absorbed into the Br Army; *m* 1st 27 April 1790 Frances (*d* 12 Oct 1828), dau of Dominick Henry Trant, of Easingwold; *m* 2nd 23 May 1829 Lucinda Matthews and *d* 7 July 1837, having had issue by his 1st w:

(1) Frederick; *b* 28 Aug 1798; RN; *d* unm 1826

(2) Charles Henry; *b* 1808; Page to CHARLES X OF FRANCE, Col 10th Cuirassiers; *d* unm Paris 14 May 1890

(1) Maria; *b* 10 March 1796; *m* 5 Nov 1821 HSH AUGUSTUS PHILIP, DUKE OF CROY DULMEN, and *d* 1827

(2) Charlotte; *b* 1 Aug 1797

1 Frances; *m* 16 June 1767 Sir William Jerningham, 6th Bt, and *d* 1 March 1825, leaving issue (*see* STAFFORD, B)

The 11th VISCOUNT's est s,

CHARLES DILLON later DILLON-LEE (added 1776 under terms of will of his uncle, 3rd Earl of Lichfield), **12th Viscount Dillon of Costello-Gallin**, KP (1798), PC (I 1784); *b* 6 Nov 1745; conformed to C of E 1767, MP Westbury, Wilts, 1770, High Sheriff Co Mayo 1787 and Govr 1788, Constable Athlone 1805, FRS, MRIA; *m* 1st 19 Aug 1776 Henrietta Maria Phipps (*d* 1 Aug 1782), only dau of 1st Baron Mulgrave (*see* NORMANBY, M), and had issue:

1 HENRY AUGUSTUS, **13th Viscount**

1 Frances Charlotte; *m* 14 March 1799 Sir Thomas Webb, Bt, and *d* 17 April 1819

The **12th Viscount** *m* 2nd 1787 Marie Rogier (*d* 28 Aug 1833), of Malines, Netherlands (subsequently Belgium), and *d* 9 Nov 1813, having had further issue:

2 James William; *b* 1792; Ensign Gren Gds; *d* 10 Oct 1812

2 Henrietta; *d* 11 April 1811

3 Charlotte; *m* 1813 Rev Ld Frederick Beauclerk DD, 4th s of 5th Duke of Saint Albans (*qv*), and *d* 26 Sept 1866

The 12th VISCOUNT's est s,

HENRY AUGUSTUS DILLON-LEE, **13th Viscount Dillon of Costello-Gallin**; *b* 28 Oct 1777; MP Harwich 1799 and Co Mayo 1802, 1806, 1807 and 1812, Col Surrey Yeo, Capt Oxford Militia 1798, raised 1807 on his f 's Irish estates the 101st Regt, Duke of York's Irish Regt of LI (disbanded 1817); *m* 9 Feb 1807 Henrietta (*d* Paris 18 March 1862), sis of 1st Baron Oranmore and Browne (*qv*), and *d* 24 July 1832, leaving, with other issue:

1 CHARLES HENRY DILLON-LEE, **14th Viscount Dillon of Costello-Gallin**; *b* 20 April 1810; served Scots Fus Gds; *m* 1 Feb 1833 Lydia Sophia (*d* 4 Nov 1876), dau of Philip Laycock Story, of Tusmore House, Oxford, and *dspm* 18 Nov 1865, leaving issue:

(1) Ethelred Florence; *d* unm 17 March 1910

(2) Geraldine Lee Frances; *m* 13 July 1859 Capt Charles Augustus Drake Halford (*d* 25 April 1907), of East Bergholt, Suffolk, and *d* 14 Jan 1920, leaving issue

2 THEOBALD DOMINICK GEOFFREY DILLON-LEE, **15th Viscount Dillon of Costello-Gallin**, DL; *b* 5 April 1811; ensign 60th Rifles 1828, Lt 1833; *m* 28 Sept 1856 Sara Augusta (*d* 17 July 1890), dau of Alexander Hanna, of Paris, and *dsp* 30 Nov 1879

3 ARTHUR EDMUND DENIS, **16th Viscount**

4 Constantine Augustus; *b* 14 Sept 1813; served RN, 7th Dragoon Gds and 17th Lancers; *m* 10 Feb 1842 Fanny Dorothea (*d* 20 Feb 1896), 3rd dau of P L Story, and *d* 16 April 1853, leaving issue:

(1) Henry Philip Constantine, JP (Oxon); *b* 2 Jan 1843; Lt-Col RE; *m* 1 Oct 1872 Emily Blanche Mary Courtenay (*d* 13 Sept 1903), dau of Mountifort Longfield, of Castle Mary, Co Cork, and *d* 6 Feb 1911, leaving:

1a Constantine Theobald Francis, DSO (1902); *b* 9 Sept 1873; Capt 3rd Bn Worcs Regt Boer War 1900–01 (despatches, wounded); *d* 27 April 1920

2a Henry Mountifort, DSO; *b* 20 Jan 1881; Lt-Col Oxon and Bucks LI, Boer War 1900, N Nigeria 1906 and WW I 1914; *d* 13 Jan 1918 of illness contracted on active service

1a Kathleen Nora; *d* unm Nov 1958

(2) Philip Gerald; *b* 23 Jan 1848; *m* June 1876 Constance Charlotte (*d* 31 March 1910), dau of Sir David Monro, MD, and *d* 4 March 1890, leaving issue:

1a Francis Noel; *b* 1878; *m* 1909 Mildred Edith (*d* 1962), dau of A G Fell, of Wellington, NZ, and *d* 9 Aug 1938, leaving issue:

1b Patrick Philip Lee; *b* 1912; *educ* Stowe; *m* 1937 *Joan Elfie [Mrs Patrick Dillon, Leefield, Blenheim, NZ], dau of G C Williams, of Masterton, NZ, and *d* 1993, leaving issue:

1c +Patrick Francis Lee [Patrick Dillon Esq, Waikirikiri, RD3, Leeston, Canterbury, NZ]; *b* 11 Jan 1946; *m* 1974 *Susan Lee, dau of Dr Peter Thodey, of Timaru, NZ, and has issue:

1d +Jonathan Patrick Lee; *b* 1977

2d +Mark Peter Lee; *b* 1981

1d *Lisa Frances; *b* 1975

2d *Brigid Louise Lee; *b* 1982

2c *Rachel Anne [Mrs Robert Bengeo Hall, Hertford, Herts]; *b* 16 Feb 1939; *m* Aug 1966 *Robert Lionel Savory, s of Christopher Savory, and has issue:

1d *Charlotte Katharine Anne; *b* 29 Sept 1968

2d *Victoria Lucy Lee; *b* 1970

3d *Josephine Elizabeth; *b* 1972

3c *Joanna Lee [Mrs David Cameron, Waituma, Waikari, N Canterbury, NZ]; *b* 27 May 1941; *m* 3 April 1963 *David Cameron, er s of Clifford C Cameron, and has issue:

1d *Timothy Charles; *b* 27 April 1967; *m* 9 Dec 1995 *Jo-Ann Mirrielle McKean and has:

1e *Archibald Charles; *b* 19 May 1997

2d *Andrew Lee; *b* 25 June 1970

1d *Nicola Jane; *b* 10 Oct 1965; *m* 1994 *Andrew Robert Davie, of Wellington, NZ

2b Michael Lee; *b* 1913; *educ* Stowe; F/Lt RNZAF WW II; *m* 1939 *Gwyndoline Reay [Mrs Michael Dillon, The Tummil, Blenheim, NZ], dau of J W Trolove, of The Shades, Marlborough, NZ, and *d* 26 Dec 1968, leaving:

1c +Richard Lee [Richard Dillon Esq, The Tummil, Blenheim, NZ]; *b* 17 Jan 1941; *m* 17 July 1965 *Elizabeth Campbell, dau of James Browning Hay, of Glenralloch, Pigeon Bay, Banks Peninsula, NZ, and has issue:

1d +Nicolas Lee; *b* 18 Aug 1966

2d +Samuel Hay; *b* 9 Nov 1967

1d *Sarah Elizabeth; *b* 1971

2c +James Michael Lee [James Dillon Esq, Box 284, Picton, NZ]; *b* 13 Feb 1947; *educ* Christ's Coll Christchurch; *m* 1st 1974 (*divorce* 1990) Maling Eve, dau of Michael Joseph Nathan, of Wellington, NZ; *m* 2nd 26 Nov 1994 *Julie Constance, dau of George Arthur Hutton, of Christchurch, NZ, and by his 1st w has:

1d *Olivia Michal; *b* 1976

2d *Amber Maling; *b* 1978

3d *Honor Louisa; *b* 1982

1c *Sarah Christine [Mrs Peter Coy, Salt Creek, Woorndoo, Victoria, Australia]; *b* 1942; *m* 7 May 1965 *Peter Wallace Coy, s of Francis William Coy, and has had issue:

1d Benjamin William, *b* 19 Nov, *d* 21 Nov 1967

2d *Edward Francis Dillon; *b* 1974

1d *Rosa Susan; *b* 28 Sept 1966

2d *Sally Amanda; *b* 11 Dec 1968

3d *Georgina Anne; *b* 1971

2c *Rosa Lee [Mrs Michael Davison, Kaiwara, Culverdon, NZ]; *b* 29 Jan 1949; *m* 1975 *Michael John Hawdon Davison and has issue:

1d *Frederick Michael Dillon; *b* 1980

1d *Antonia Frances Alice; *b* 1979

2d *Georgina Constance Lee; *b* 1982

3b Gerald Francis Lee; *b* 1917; *educ* Stowe; Maj NZ Forces WW II 1940–45; *m* 1946 *Mary Ritson [Mrs Gerald Dillon, Spelsbury, Blenheim RD1, Marlborough, NZ], dau of Cdr T S Critchley, RN, of Tirohunga, Blenheim, NZ, and *d* 1983, leaving issue:

1c +David Sandford Lee [David Dillon Esq, The Throne, Blenheim, NZ]; *b* 26 Nov 1946; Lt NZ Army, farmer; *m* 1973 *Susan Hamilton, dau of P D Reid, of Blenheim, NZ, and has issue:

1d +Henry Gerald Lee; *b* 1976

2d +Thomas Patrick Lee; *b* 1979

1d *Hannah Frances; *b* 1982

1c *Susan Ann Lee [Mrs Richard Macfarlane, Winterholme, Kekerengu, Marlborough, NZ]; *b* 1947; *m* 1974 *Richard John Macfarlane and has issue:

1d *Sandford Samuel; *b* 1975

2d *Winston William; *b* 1977

3d *Clive Charles; *b* 1978

1d *Alexandra Augusta; *b* 1981

1a Marion Geraldine; *m* 8 Aug 1904 Thomas William Rowley, Malay CS, 2nd s of Thomas Rowley, of Christchurch, NZ, and *d* 4 Jan 1937, leaving issue

2a Constance Helen; *m* 26 Sept 1906 Everard Aloysius Weld (*d* 1 June 1956), of Flaxbourne, Marlborough, NZ, 2nd s of Sir Frederick Weld, of Chideock Manor, Dorset, and *d* 27 June 1934, leaving issue

3a Beatrice Eugenie; *m* 13 April 1905 Charles Gordon Teschemaker (*d* 6 Nov 1946), 2nd s of Charles de Vere Teschemaker-Shute, of Marlborough, NZ, and *d* 2 Feb 1957, leaving issue

4a Ethel Georgiana; *b* 1885; *m* 5 Dec 1914 Lt Col Michael John Furnel (*d* 10 March 1958), Irish Fus, of Ballyclough and Caberelly Grange, Co Limerick, and *d* 27 April 1954, leaving issue

(3) Constantine Francis Arthur (Rev); *b* 24 Dec 1851; *m* 19 Oct 1886 Adela (*d* 1 Dec 1935), dau of Maj Arthur Ogle, and *d* 8 Aug 1925

(1) Constance Louisa; *m* 19 March 1878 Capt Philip Henry Massie Wynter (*d* 1915), of The Hays, Charlbury, Oxon, and had issue

(2) Marion Henrietta; *d* 21 March 1895

(3) Lydia Eliza; *d* unm 22 May 1915

5 Robert George Lee; *b* 7 Oct 1817; *d* Sept 1822

6 Gerald Normanby DILLON-LEE later FitzGIBBON (roy licence 8 Nov 1873), of Mt Shannon, Co Limerick, DL, JP; *b* 21 Nov 1823; Capt Oxford Militia; *m* 22 May 1847 Lady Louisa FitzGibbon (*m* 2nd May 1882 Gen the Marquis della Rochella, of Palermo, and *d* 4 June 1898), dau and coheir of 3rd Earl of Clare and ultimately heiress to the estates of her unc, 2nd Earl of Clare, and *d* 3 Jan 1880, having had issue, with a dau:

(1) Charles Richard George; *b* 5 Oct 1849; *d* 30 July 1870

(2) Augustus Henry; *b* 6 Dec 1850; *m* 17 Feb 1874 Adele (*d* 31 May 1928), 4th dau of Baron Ernest Poellnitz, of Babenwohl Bregenz, Austria, and *d* 26 July 1918, leaving issue:

1a Gerald Ernest George, MC; *b* 4 Feb 1883; Capt Rifle Bde WW I 1914–19; *m* 1st 20 Aug 1908 (*divorce* S Rhodesia 1912) Mary Monica (*d* 1930), only child of Lt-Col Hugh Marshall Hole, CMG, of 2 London Wall Buildings, London EC2, and had issue:

1b Doreen Adele Monica Clare; *b* 24 Dec 1910; Im 1st 14 Jan 1928 (*divorce* 1937) James Edward Stuart-Lyon (later W/Cdr RAF (ret)), s of Maj Claude Stuart-Lyon, MC; *m* 2nd 1938 Francis Prideaux Allbutt (*d* 26 Dec 1965), slr; *m* 3rd 12 June 1968 her former husb W/Cdr James Edward Stuart-Lyon, RAF (ret), of Hurst-on-Clays, East Grinstead, Sussex, and had issue by her 1st (and 3rd) husb:

1c *James Alastair Garry STUART-LYON later ALLBUTT (deed poll 1951); *b* 12 Dec 1934; *educ* Bradfield; late RN; *m* 2 Jan 1960 *Gillian Mary, dau of Donald Arthur Dawes, of New Milton, Hants, and has issue:

1d *Steven Alastair; *b* 9 Sept 1960

2d *James Alexander; *b* 1962

3d *Jonathan Michael; *b* 1964

4d *Angus Edward; *b* 13 Sept 1965

2b *Elizabeth Rosemary; *b* 29 Nov 1912; *m* 5 May 1934 Henry Brockholst Livingston, CBE (*d* 4 June 1968), s of Edwin Brockholst Livingston, and has issue:

1c *Nicholas Henry [Nicholas Livingston Esq, Valfond, Chemin du Moulin Vieux, 84210 St Didier, Vaucluse, France]; *b* 7 June 1942; *educ* King's Canterbury and King's Coll Cambridge; joined For Serv 1964, 3rd Sec Buenos Aires 1968–68, 2nd Sec Moscow 1970–72; *m* 1968 *Ana Maria, only dau of Dr Idilio Oneto, of Buenos Aires, and has issue:

1d *Barnaby; *b* 1973

1d *Emma Sophie; *b* 1976

1a (cont.) Capt Gerald FitzGibbon *m* 2nd 1914 Helene (*d* 23 June 1969), widow of Strentham Forde, of Cape Town, and *d* 8 Jan 1929, having had further issue:

3b Diana Clare; *b* 16 July 1924; *m* 10 March 1952 Derek Harry Johnson (*d* 1977), of Boden Hall, Scholar Green, Cheshire, s of Col Harry Johnson, DSO, TD, DL, JP, of Boden Hall, and *d* 1993, leaving issue:

1c *Gerald Harry [Gerald Johnson Esq, c/o Withers, 12 Gough Sq, London; PO Box 232, Malindi, Kenya]; *b* 5 Dec 1952; *educ* Harrow and St Columba's Coll Dublin; *m* 1st 1980 (*divorce* 1985) Jasmine Violet, dau of Victor Wild, of Shenley Hill, Shenley, Herts; *m* 2nd 1987 (*divorce* 1996) Claire, dau of Francis Rooney, of St Peter Port, Guernsey, and has by her:

1d *Harry Francis FitzGibbon; *b* 1989

1c *Mary Clare Hélène [Mrs Robert Rodwell, Lamyatt Lodge, nr Shepton Mallet, Somerset BA4 6NP]; *b* 28 Feb 1958; *m* 1st 1985 (*divorce* 1989) Robin Bailey Hamilton Vetch; *m* 2nd 1990 *Robert Edward Hunter Rodwell and has by her 1st husb:

1d *Annabel Susannah Clare; *b* 10 Dec 1987

1a Elizabeth Louisa Theobaldina; *m* 1898 George Norman Douglas (*d* 9 Feb 1952) and *d* 11 Sept 1916, leaving issue

2a Violet; *m* 14 Sept 1905 James Louis Fairholme (*d* 1944), of Bregenz, Austria, 3rd s of G K E Fairholme, of Old Melrose, Roxburghshire, and *d* 19–, leaving issue

(3) John Arthur; *b* 12 Oct 1854; *m* 1st 17 Oct 1882 Louisa Bosville (*dsp* 1883), dau of Sir Balford Hinton Wilson, KCB; *m* 2nd 4 June 1890 Katherine Maude (*d* 1939), 2nd dau of Rev W C Randolph, of Yate House, Glos, and *d* 29 April 1908, leaving issue by his 2nd w:

1a Brian Normanby; *b* 14 April 1894; Lt 6th Service Bn Roy Irish Regt, *ka* Aug 1916

(4) Clare Valentine; *b* 14 Feb 1859; *m* 13 Aug 1882 Mary Agnes, dau of Richard Barrett Bernard, and had issue:

1a Agnes

(5) Louis Theobald; *b* 6 Dec 1859; Lt Oxford LI; *m* 10 March 1884 Maria Dolores (*d* 1909), dau of Robert Maxwell, and *d* 17 June 1913, leaving issue:

1a Robert Francis FitzGIBBON later LEE-DILLON (resumed 1925; styled Comte Robert F Lee-Dillon in France); *b* 21 Sept 1884; Lt French Army and Lt-Cdr (emerg list) RN, served WW I 1914–19, Order of Sacred Treasure Japan, ; *m* 1st 5 Feb 1908 (*divorce* 1923) Georgette (*d* 23 June 1972 aged 89), dau of George Winthrop Folsom, of Lenox, Mass, USA, and had issue:

1b (Robert Louis) Constantine FitzGIBBON; *b* 8 June 1919; *educ* Wellington, Munich U, Sorbonne and Exeter Coll Oxford; Maj US Army 1942–46, Lt Oxf and Bucks LI WW II 1939–42, author: *The Arabian Bird* (1949), *The Iron Hoop* (1950), *Dear Emily* (1952), *Miss Finningan's Fault* (1953), *Norman Douglas* (1953), *The Holiday* (1953), *The Little Tour* (1954), *The Shirt of Nessus* (1955), *In Love and War* (1956), *The Blitz* (1957), *Paradise Lost and More* (1959), *When the Kissing had to Stop* (1960), *Going to the River* (1963), *Random Thoughts of a Fascist Hyena* (1963), *The Life of Dylan Thomas* (1965), *Selected Letters of Dylan Thomas* (ed, 1966), *Through the Minefield* (1967), *Denazification* (1969), *High Heroic* (1969), *Out of the Lion's Paw* (1969), *Red Hand: The Ulster Colony* (1971), *The Devil at Work* (play, 1971), *A Concise History of Germany* (1972), *In the Bunker* (1973), *The Life and Times of Eamon de Valera* (1973), *The Golden Age* (1976), *Secret Intelligence* (1976), *Man in Aspic* (1977), *Teddy in the Tree* (1977), *Drink* (1979), *The Rat Report* (1980) and *The Irish in Ireland* (1982), memb Irish Acad Letters, FRSL, Fell Guggenheim Meml Fndn; *m* 1st 1939 (*divorce* 1944) Margaret Aye Moung; *m* 2nd 1944 (*divorce* 1960) Theodora Rosling (*m* 2nd George Morrison, film archivist, and *d* 1991); *m* 3rd 27 Aug 1960 (*divorce* 196–) Marion Gutmann, and by her had issue:

1c +Francis George Herbert [Francis FitzGibbon Esq, 46 Brondesbury Rd, London NW6]; *b* 18 July 1961; *m* 1986 *Camilla G Beresford and has:

1d +Sam; *b* 24 June 1997

1d *Lily Theodora; *b* 1987

1b (cont.) Constantine FitzGIBBON *m* 4th 1967 *Marjorie, formerly w of (a) Huntington Hartford and (b) Dudley Sutton, actor, and dau of Harold Wright Steele, of California, and *d* 23 March 1983, leaving further issue:

1c *Oonagh Louisa Dillon; *b* 1968

1b *Frances Geraldine [Mrs Harry Colville, Beau Chêne, Chemin de la Souque, Aix-en-Provence, France]; *b* 4 Dec 1908; *m* 17 Oct 1942 *Harry Morton Colvile and has issue

2b Maria Dolores; *b* 16 July 1909; *d* 6 Sept, 1910

3b *Frances Hastings [Miss Frances Dillon, 10 The Close, Addington Park, Maidstone, Kent]; *b* 10 Sept 1911

4b Georgette Winifred; *b* 23 April 1915; *m* 19– (*divorce* 19–) Claude Mounsey and *d* 21 Feb 1957

1a (cont.) Robert Lee-Dillon *m* 2nd 1924 Kathleen Clare (*d* 29 Dec 1950), widow of Hon Harry Lee-Dillon (*see* below), and *d* 24 Feb 1954, leaving issue:

2b +Louis Theobald Dillon LEE-DILLON later FitzGIBBON (deed poll 1962) [Louis FitzGibbon Esq, Flat 2, 8 Portland Place, Brighton, Sussex BN2 1DG]; *b* 6 Jan 1925; *educ* St Augustine's Abbey Sch and RNC Dartmouth; Lt RN (ret, served 1942–54), dir De Leon Properties 1954–72 and 1994–, personal assist to (Lord) Duncan(-)Sandys, MP, 1967–68, gen sec Br Cncl Aid to refugees 1968–72, exec offr Nat Assoc Freedom 1977–78, area pres St John Ambulance Bde E Hants 1974–76, Kt Honour and Devotion SMO Malta 1985, Kt Cdr Polonia Restituta 1976, Polish Gold Cross of Merit 1969, Cross of Merit 1st Class Germany, author: *Katyn — A Crime without Parallel* (1971), *The Katyn Cover-up* (1977), *Unpitied and Unknown* (1975), *The Katyn Memorial* (1976), *The Betrayal of the Somalis* (1982), *Straits and Strategic Waterways in the Red Sea* (1984), *Ethiopia Hijacks the Hijack* (1985), *The Evaded Duty* (1985); *m* 1st 6 Jan 1950 (*divorce* 1962) Josephine Miriam Maud (*d* 1979), dau of John Herbert Webb and formerly w of (a) Donald Andrew McDonald, (b) S/Ldr Alan Charles Triptree, RAF; *m* 2nd 15 Aug 1962 Madeleine Sally (*d* 1980), dau of Peter Hayward-Surry; *m* 3rd 1980 (*divorce* 19–) Mrs Joan Elizabeth Jevons and has issue by his 3rd w:

1c +James Augustus; *b* 7 Nov 1963

1c *Simone Frances; *b* 16 Nov 1962

2c *Michele Clare; *b* 24 April 1965

2a Harold Constantine Dillon, MC; *b* 20 July 1890; Capt 13th Hus (SR), Silver Medal of Italy for military valour; *ka* Southern Kurdistan 13 Jan 1922

1a Olive Geraldine Emma; Polish Gold Cross of Merit; *m* 1st 1911 Jordon Dumaresq (*d* 1915), of Boston, USA; *m* 2nd 29 Nov 1919 Sir Philip Humphrey Antrobus, 6th Bt (*qv*)

The 15th VISCOUNT's yr bro,

ARTHUR EDMUND DENIS DILLON-LEE, **16th Viscount Dillon of Costello-Gallin**, JP, DL; *b* 10 April 1812; BA, FSA, FRGS, FZS; *m* 22 April 1843 Ellen (*d* 10 Feb 1896), dau of James Adderly, 95th Rifles, now Rifle Bde (*k* Battle of Badajoz 1812), and *d* 12 Jan 1892, leaving issue:

1 HAROLD ARTHUR DILLON-LEE later LEE-DILLON, **17th Viscount Dillon of Costello-Gallin**, CH (1921); *b* 24 Jan 1844; *educ* Oxford (MA, DCL); Maj 4th Bn Oxford LI, formerly of the Rifle Bde, Pres Soc of Antiquaries 1897–1904, Tstee Br Museum, Nat Portrait Gallery and Wallace Collection, Curator Tower Armouries, FBA; *m* 1st 3 Nov 1870 Julia, memb League of Mercy (*d* 6 June 1925), est dau of Isaac Brock Stanton, Canadian CS; *m* 2nd 15 June 1926 Margaret Louisa Everard (*d* 12 July 1954), dau of Rev Henry Edward Browne Ffolkes (*see* FFOLKES, Bt) and widow of Rev John Erasmus Philipps, MA, and *dspms* 18 Dec 1932, having had issue by his 1st w:

(1) Harry Lee Stanton (Comte Henri Lee de Dillon in France), JP (Co Roscommon); *b* 25 July 1874; Lt Rifle Bde, FSA; *m* 1st 5 Aug 1904 (*divorce* 1912) Brenda Mary, er dau of Thomas Smith, MRCS; *m* 2nd 9 Sept 1913 Kathleen Clare (*m* 2nd 1924 Lt-Cdr Robert Francis Lee-Dillon, RN (*see* above), and *d* 29 Dec 1950), 2nd dau of James Aitchison, CE, of Marly, Strathavon, Lanarks, and Sydney, NSW, and *d* 7 Feb 1923, leaving by his 1st w:

1a *Charlotte Henriette Eleanor Florence Lee de Leon; *b* 21 June 1907; *m* Sept 1929 Leonard Cundell (*d* 26 July 1952) and has issue

2 Conrad Adderly DILLON-LEE later DILLON; *b* 2 Sept 1845; *m* 27 Aug 1872 Ellen Lousia (*d* 2 June 1917), est dau of Sir Henry William Dashwood, 5th Bt, of Kirtlington Park (*qv*), and *d* 4 Nov 1901, leaving issue:

(1) ARTHUR HENRY DILLON, **18th Viscount Dillon of Costello-Gallin**, JP, DL (Oxon); *b* 5 Jan 1875; Maj QO Oxford Hus WW I, High Sheriff 1931; *m* 5 Jan 1907 Hilda (*d* 23 May 1966), 3rd dau of Rt Hon Sir John Tomlinson Brunner, 1st Bt (*qv*), and widow of Charles Harold Broadbent, JP, and *dsp* 25 May 1934

(2) ERIC FitzGERALD, **19th Viscount**

(1) Hilda Ellen; granted with her sisters rank of viscount's dau 7 Sept 1934; *d* unm 16 March 1957

(2) Margaret Sophia; Head of Talbot Settlement 1918–26, memb Nat Assembly of C of E for Southwark 1925–45; *m* 19 Oct 1907 Rev Charles Taylor, DD, LLD (*d* 12 Aug 1908), Master St John's Coll Cambridge, and *dsp* Feb 1962

(3) Evelina Victoria; *m* 6 May 1919 Maj Robert Pentland Mahaffy (*d* 8 May 1943), TA, barrister, Legal Advsr to Govt and Forces at Malta 1921–29, 2nd s of Rev Sir John Mahaffy, GBE, and *d* 17 Feb 1959, leaving issue

(4) Vere Mary; *m* 27 July 1911 Reginald Edward Marsden (*d* 30 July 1960), Imperial Forest Serv, er s of Reginald Godfrey Marsden, barrister, and had issue

The 18th VISCOUNT's yr bro,

ERIC FitzGERALD DILLON, **19th Viscount Dillon of Costello-Gallin**, CMG (1919), DSO (1915); *b* 4 April 1881; *educ* Rugby and Staff Coll Camberley; memb Gentlemen-at-Arms, Brig Roy Munster Fus, formerly RASC, served S Africa 1900–01 (medal with four clasps) and WW I (despatches seven times), Offr Legion of Honour and Leopold of Belgium, Croix de Guerre with Palm, Croix de Guerre Belgium, 1914 star, two medals, and in WW II 1939–41; *m* 4 July 1907 Nora Junatia Muriel, served in France and England Army Auxiliary Hospitals, 1915 star, two medals (*d* 9 Sept 1962), only child of Brig-Gen Charles Edward Beckett, CB, by Louisa Augusta, yr dau of FM Rt Hon Sir John Michel, GCB, of Dewlish, Dorchester, and *d* 6 April 1946, leaving issue:

1 MICHAEL ERIC, **20th Viscount**

1 Pamela Louisa Eleanor, JP (Guildford 1950); *b* 26 Aug 1915; *m* 4 Aug 1936 (*divorce* 1962) 6th Earl of Onslow (*qv*) and *d* 1992, leaving issue

The 19th VISCOUNT's s,

MICHAEL ERIC DILLON, **20th Viscount Dillon of Costello-Gallin**; *b* 13 Aug 1911; *educ* Eton and RMC Sandhurst; Lt-Col RHG, 15th/19th Hus, local Capt Transjordan Frontier Force 1935–37, served WW II, v-pres Roy Stuart Soc, Kt SMO Malta, Offr Order of Orange Nassau with Swords; *m* 4 Dec 1939 *Irène Marie France [The Rt Hon Irène Viscountess Dillon, The Grange, Manor Rd, Goring-on-Thames, Oxon RG8 9DY], yr dau of René Merandon du Plessis, of Whitehall, Mauritius, and *d* 30 Nov 1979, leaving issue:

1 CHARLES HENRY ROBERT, **21st Viscount**

2 +RICHARD ARTHUR LOUIS [The Hon Richard Dillon, Brook House, Sudborough, nr Kettering, Northants NN14 3BX], heir presumptive; *b* 23 Oct 1948; *educ* Downside and RAC Cirencester; FSVA; *m* 24 May 1975 *Hon Priscilla Frances Hazlerigg, yr dau of 2nd Baron Hazlerigg (*qv*), and has issue:

(1) +Thomas Arthur Lee; *b* 1 Oct 1983

(1) *Charlotte Frances, *b* 1978

3 +Patrick Dominic; *b* 9 March 1956; *educ* Downside and Trinity Coll Dublin

4 +Michael Edmond [The Hon Michael Dillon, 8 Keslake Rd, London NW6 6DL]; *b* 29 Oct 1957; *educ* Glenstall and Hants Coll of Ag; painter; *m* 1 Oct 1983 *Henrietta Catherine, yr dau of Charles Elwell, of Bottnells Close, Chalfont St Giles, Bucks, and has issue:

(1) +Charles Augustus Henry; *b* 1985

(1) *Emily Madeleine; *b* 1987

(2) *Catherine Elizabeth; *b* 1989

(3) *Henrietta Sophie; *b* 1993

1 *Isabelle Anne Marie Henrietta [The Hon Mrs Cobbe, The Manor House, Yattenden, Newbury, Berks RG16 OUH]; *b* 6 Sept 1942; *m* 25 July 1970 *Richard Alexander Charles Cobbe, 2nd s of Francis Charles Cobbe, of St Margaret's, Co Dublin, and has issue:

(1) *Thomas Alexander Michael; *b* 1973

(2) *Henry Frederick Hugh; *b* 1975

(1) *Frances Henrietta; *b* 1971

(2) *Rose Eleanor; *b* 1973

2 *Inés Marie Jeanne; *b* 1 Jan 1952

3 Rosaleen Marie Carmel; *b* 2 Feb 1953; *d* as the result of an accident 16 Sept 1960

4 *Madeleine Marie CVO (1997) [The Hon Mrs Louloudis, Flat 2, 66 Westbourne Terrace, London W2 3UJ]; *b* 29 Oct 1957; Ldy in Waiting to HRH THE PRINCESS ROYAL; *m* 1989 *Leonard Constantine Louloudis, only s of Constantine Louloudis, and has issue:

(1) *Constantine Michael; *b* 1991

(1) *Theodora Catherine Lily; *b* 1993

The 20th VISCOUNT's est s,

CHARLES HENRY ROBERT DILLON, **21st Viscount Dillon of Costello-Gallin**; *b* 18 Jan 1945; *educ* Downside and Furniture Sch RCA; designer; *m* 13 May 1972 *(Mary) Jane, furniture designer [The Rt Hon The Viscountess Dillon, 28 Canning Cross, London SE5 8BH], dau of John Young, of Castle Hill House, Birtle, Lancs, designer, and *d* 15 Sept 1982, leaving issue:

1 HENRY BENEDICT DILLON, **22nd and present Viscount Dillon of Costello-Gallin**

1 *Beatrice Inès Renée; *b* 28 Dec 1978

DILLWYN-VENABLES-LLEWELYN

Arms: Quarterly, 1st and 4th, argent gutté de poix three chevronels gules, in base a lamb passant proper (for LLEWELYN); 2nd, azure two bars each cotised between five mullets, three in chief and two in base, all argent, and for difference a cross-crosslet or (for VENABLES); 3rd, gules on a chevron nebuly argent five trefoils slipped of the first (for DILLWYN); on an inescutcheon of pretence the arms of Venables without distinction. **Crests:** 1 Upon the trunk of a tree fesswise, eradicated and sprouting, a lamb passant proper, supporting a staff or, therefrom flowing a banner gules charged with three chevronels argent (for LLEWELYN), 2 A wyvern, wings expanded gules, each wing charged with a fess argent, issuant from a wicker basket proper, the dexter claw resting on a mullet azure, charged for difference as in the arms (for VENABLES), 3 In front of a stag's head couped proper, three trefoils slipped vert (for DILLWYN). **Motto:** *Craignez honte* ('Dread shame').

Creation: Bt. (UK) 20 March 1890.

SIR JOHN MICHAEL DILLWYN-VENABLES-LLEWELYN, 4TH BT, of Penllergaer, and of Ynis-y-gerwn, Co Glamorgan [Sir John Dillwyn-Venables-Llewelyn Bt, Llysdinam, Newbridge-on-Wye, Llandrindod Wells, Powys LD1 6NB]; *b* 12 Aug 1938; *s f* 1976; *educ* Eton and Magdalene Coll Cambridge; *m* 1st 20 April 1963 (*divorce* 1972) Nina (*d* 1995), dau of Lt J S Hallam, KRRC, and Mrs Edward Llewelyn Thomas, of Cefndyrys, Builth Wells, Breconshire, and has issue:

1 *Georgina Katherine; *b* 7 Dec 1964; *m* 1989 *Anthony H Mead, 2nd son of Humphrey Mead, of Moyaux, Normandy

2 *Emma Susan; *b* 23 Nov 1967

Sir JOHN *m* 2nd 1975 Nina Gay Richardson Oliver (*d* 10 April 1995), and has had further issue:

3 A dau; *b* 1981; *d* 1982

Lineage: Towards the close of the 17th century most of the descendants of JEFFREYS DILWYN, of Langorse, adopted the Welsh custom of taking the surname JEFFREYS. About the year 1699 WILLIAM DILWYN, presumably one of these descendants, migrated from Breconshire with his friend William Penn to Philadelphia; had:

JOHN DILLWYN, of Philadelphia; *m* Susanna, dau and heiress of George Painter, of Haverford, Pa., and formerly of Broomhill, Dale, Pembs, and had:

WILLIAM DILLWYN, of Higham Lodge, Walthamstow, Essex; *m* Nov 1777 Sarah, dau and heiress of Lewis Weston, of High Hall, Essex, and *d* Sept 1824 aged 81, leaving:

LEWIS WESTON DILLWYN, of Burrough Lodge and Sketty Hall, Glamorgan, JP and DL; *b* 21 Aug 1778; FRS; High Sheriff 1818, MP Glamorgan 1832; *m* 13 July 1807 Mary (*d* 1865), dau of John Llewelyn, of Penllergaer and Ynys-y-gerwin, Glamorgan, and had surv issue:

1 JOHN

2 Lewis Llewelyn, of Hendrefollan, Glam, JP and DL; *b* 19 May 1814; Lt-Col cmdg 3rd Glam RV; MP Swansea 1855–92; *m* 16 Aug 1838 Elizabeth (*d* 1866), dau and heiress of Sir Henry Thomas de la Beche, CB, and *d* 19 June 1892, leaving issue

1 Fanny Llewelyn; *m* 1836 Matthew Moggridge, of Woodfield, Mon, JP, and *d* 7 Aug 1894. He *d* 1882

2 Mary; *m* 1857 Rev Montague Earle Welby, MA, Rector Uffington, Stamford (*see* WELBY, Bt), and *dsp* 29 Nov 1906

LEWIS DILLWYN *d* 1855; his est son,

JOHN DILLWYN later DILLWYN-LLEWELYN, of Penllergaer, JP, DL; FRS; *m* 10 June 1833 Emma-Thomasina, dau of Thomas Mansel Talbot, of Margan Abbey and Penrice Castle, Glam, and had issue:

1 JOHN TALBOT (Sir), **1st Bt**

1 Theresa Mary; *m* 29 June 1858 Mervin Herbert Nevil Story-Maskelyne, DL, MP, of Basset Down, Wilts, er s of Anthony M R Story-Maskelyne, FRS, and had issue. He *d* 20 May 1911

2 Emma Charlotte; *m* Henry Benyon Crichton (*d* 1889)

3 Ellinor Amy

4 Lucy Catharine; *d* 1 April 1920

JOHN DILLWYN-LLEWELYN *d* 24 Aug 1882, his only son,

Sir John Talbot Dillwyn-Llewelyn, 1st Bt (UK), so *cr* 20 March 1890, JP and DL (Glam), JP (Carmarthenshire and Breconshire); *b* 26 May 1836; *educ* Ch Ch Oxford (MA); High Sheriff Glam 1878; MP Swansea 1895–1900, Mayor Swansea 1891; *m* 7 May 1861 Caroline Julia (*d* 3 March 1917), est dau of Sir Michael Hicks Beach, 8th Bt, MP (*see* ST ALDWYN, E), and had issue:

1 William; *b* 1 April 1868; *d* unm 25 Aug 1893

2 CHARLES LEYSHON (Sir), **2nd Bt**

1 Gwendoline Harriet; *d* unm 2 Jan 1944

2 Gladys Mary; *m* 13 April 1910 Capt Francis Mount (*ka* 13 Oct 1915), 5th Bn Berks Regt, yst s of William George Mount, DL, of Wasing Place, Berks, and had issue (*see* MOUNT, Bt)

Sir JOHN *d* 6 July 1927; his son,

Sir CHARLES LEYSHON DILLWYN-LLEWELYN later DILLWYN-VENABLES-LLEWELYN (roy licence 27 June 1893), **2nd Bt**, CB (1947), TD, JP and DL (Breconshire), JP (Radnorshire); *b* 29 June 1870; *educ* Eton and New Coll Oxford; Col, Lt-Col cmdg Glam Yeo, Pres Radnorshire TAA; MP Radnorshire Jan–Dec 1910, High Sheriff Radnorshire 1924; HM's Lt Radnorshire 1929–49; *m* 23 Aug 1893 Katharine Minna (*d* 29 Jan 1956), er dau and coheir of Rev Richard Lister Venables, MA, of Llysdinam, Brecon, and had issue:

1 John Lister; Capt Coldstream Gds; *b* 20 March 1897; *ka* 10 July 1917

2 (CHARLES) MICHAEL (Sir), **3rd Bt**

3 George William, MICE; Lt RE, WW II; *b* 20 Aug 1910; *educ* Eton and Ch Ch Oxford; *ka* Norway 26 May 1940

1 Agnes Barbara, CVO (1967, MVO 1960); Ldy-in-Waiting to HRH THE DUCHESS OF GLOUCESTER 1951–69, Extra Ldy-in-Waiting 1969–; *b* 18 July 1894; *m* 15 June 1925 V-Adml Cedric Swinton Holland, CB (*d* 11 May 1950), only s of Adml Swinton-Colthurst Holland, of Dial Ho, Seaford, Sussex, and had issue

Sir CHARLES *d* June 1951; his only surv son,

Sir (Charles) Michael Dillwyn-Venables-Llewelyn, 3rd Bt, MVO (1937), JP (1946), DL (both Radnorshire); *b* 23 Feb 1900; *educ* Eton and RMC Sandhurst; Brig Gren Gds; Ld Lt Radnorshire 1949–74, CC Radnorshire, V-Lt Powys 1974–76, CStJ; *m* 3 Dec 1934 *Lady Delia Mary Hicks-Beach [The Lady Delia Dillwyn-Venables-Llewelyn, Llysdinam, Newbridge-on-Wye, Llandrindod Wells, Powys LD1 6NB], only dau of Viscount Quenington and sis of 2nd Earl St Aldwyn (*qv*), and *d* 15 March 1976, having had issue:

1 Sir JOHN MICHAEL DILLWYN-VENABLES-LLEWELYN, **4th and present Bt**

1 *Mary Julia [Mrs Michael Elster, Gwaracae, Llanddew, Brecon, Powys]; *b* 31 Jan 1936; *m* 1971 *Michael B Elster and has issue:

(1) *Jake; *b* 1972

(1) *Caitlin; *b* 1974

DIXON

Creation: B. (LP, UK) 19 April 1997.

THE BARON DIXON, of Jarrow, Co Tyne and Wear (Don(ald) Dixon, PC (1996), DL (Tyne and Wear (1997)) [The Rt Hon The Lord Dixon PC DL, 1 Hillcrest, Jarrow NE32 4DP; 35 Park Road, Jarrow NE32 5JL]; *b* 6 March 1929; *educ* Ellison St Elementary Sch Jarrow; shipyard worker 1947–74; GMWU Branch Sec 1974–79; Cncllr South Tyneside MDC 1963; MP (Lab) Jarrow 1979–97, memb H of C Servs Select Ctee, Dep Oppn Ch Whip 1987–96, Chm PLP Shipbuilding Gp; Freeman Jarrow 1972; *m* *Doreen Morad and has a s and dau

Lineage: CHRISTOPHER ALBERT DIXON; *m* Jane — and had:

DON(ALD), *cr* a **Baron**

DIXON, Bt

Arms: Gules a fleur-de-lys or, on a chief argent three ermine spots sable. **Crest:** A demi-lion rampant gules, holding between the paws a fyflot or. **Motto:** *Mores componunt hominem* ('Manners maketh man'). **Creation:** Bt. (UK) 15 May 1919.

SIR JONATHAN MARK DIXON, 4TH BT, of Astle, Chelford, Chester [Sir Jonathan Dixon Bt, 19 Clyde Rd, Redland, Bristol BS6 6RJ]; *b* 1 Sept 1949; *s* unc 1990; *educ* Winchester and Univ Coll Oxford (BA 1972, MA 1987); *m* 1978 *Patricia Margaret, dau of James Baird Smith, and has issue:

1 +MARK EDWARD; *b* 29 June 1982

2 +Timothy Nigel; *b* 1987

1 *Katherine Anne; *b* 1980

Lineage: JOHN DIXON; *b* 1696 (4th in descent from William Dixon, of Heaton Royds, Yorks, living 1564); *m* Frances, dau of Thomas Gower, of Hutton, nephew of Sir Thomas Gower, Bt, of Sittenham, Yorks (*see* SUTHERLAND, D), and *d* 1749, leaving an only s:

JEREMIAH DIXON, of Gledhow Hall, Yorks, DL, JP, FRS 1726; *m* Mary, dau of Rev H Wickham, Rector Guiseley, and had, with other issue:

1 JOHN, his heir

2 Jeremiah, Mayor Leeds 1784; *m* Mary, dau of John Smeaton (who built the Eddystone Lighthouse), and *dsp*

3 Henry, of Brooke Farm, Liverpool; *m* Catherine Townley, dau of Thomas Plumber, of Tong Hall, Yorks, and *d* 1819

JEREMIAH DIXON *d* 7 June 1782; his son,

JOHN DIXON, of Gledhow Hall and Weating Hall, Suffolk, DP, JP Yorks, Col 1st West York Militia; *b* 27 June 1753; *m* 1784 Lydia (*d* 1844), 3rd dau of Rev John Parker, of Astle Hall, Cheshire, and sister and coheir of Thomas Parker, of Astle, and *d* 18 April 1824, having had, with other issue:

1 Henry, of Gledhow Hall and Astle Hall, DL, JP, Lt 15th Hus; *b* 19 Nov 1794; *m* 24 Dec 1822 Emma Matilda, dau of Rev E Sacheverell Wilmot, of Chaddesden, and *dsp* 3 Aug 1838

2 JOHN

3 George, Gen, Col 104th Regt, cmded 2nd Bn Scots Fus Gds; *b* 5 Aug 1801; *m* Mary Frances, widow of Rev E Sacheverell Wilmot, of Chaddesden, Co Derby, and *dsp* 1874

The 2nd s,

JOHN DIXON, of Astle and Gledhow, DL, JP; Capt and Brevet Lt-Col 1st Royals; *b* 13 Feb 1799; *m* 14 May 1840 Sophia (*d* 1885), dau of Thomas William EGERTON later TATTON, of Wythenshawe, Cheshire, and had:

1 GEORGE (Sir), **1st Bt**

2 Charles Egerton, OBE (1920), DL, JP Co Anglesey, County Cmdt Caernarvs Vols, Lt-Col 18th Roy Irish Regt; *b* 12 Dec 1848; *m* 4 Feb 1899 Susan, widow of Capt Adam Park, Roy Irish Regt, and dau of John Lloyd Blood, of Monkstown, Co Dublin, and *d* 17 Feb 1922

3 Henry Grey (Sir), KCB (1902); ADC 1901, Col Hon Brig-Gen KSOB; *b* 14 Aug 1850; *m* 1st March 1885 Helen Mary (*d* May 1893), est dau of L J Frost, of Copenhagen; *m* 2nd 28 Nov 1900 Constance Ethel (*d* 16 Aug 1955), dau of Capt William Mitchell-Innes, 13th Hus, of Ayton Castle and Whitehall, Berwicks, and *d* 13 Nov 1933, leaving issue

4 Frederick Parker; *b* 17 Aug 1852; *m* 1885 Olivia Blanche (*d* 20 Oct 1910), widow of William George Clayton Wade and dau of Anthony O'Reilly, of Beltrasna, and *d* 14 Feb 1926, leaving issue

5 William Arthur Tatton

6 Edward Wilbraham, JP Cheshire; *b* 2 Nov 1860; *m* 15 July 1890 Alice Isobel Hardcastle (*d* 18 March 1936), dau of Thomas Hardcastle Sykes, DL, of Cringle House, Cheadle, Cheshire, and *d* 28 Feb 1936, leaving issue:

(1) Noel Wilbraham, OBE, Cdr RN, served submarines WW I and Naval Staff WW II 1939–44 (invalided); *b* 24 Dec 1891; *m* 1st 18 July 1917 Frances Mary Hester, Sr Cmdt ATS (*das* 3 March 1941), dau of Capt Francis Alan Richard Bowles, RN, of Dully House, Sittingbourne, Kent, and had issue:

1a Bridget Wilbraham; *b* 27 April 1918; *educ* Oxford (MA); *m* 28 Oct 1939 Lt-Col John Aylmer Christie-Miller, CBE, TD, DL, JP, 2nd son of Col Sir Geoffrey Christie-Miller, KCB, DSO, MC, DL, of Acton Grange, Nantwich, Cheshire, and has issue:

1b *Caroline Aylmer [Mrs Peter Cannon-Brookes, Keele House, 33 St Mary's Rd, Harborne, Birmingham, 17]; *b* 4 Feb 1942; *educ* Courtauld Inst (BA 1965); *m* 13 April 1966 *Peter Cannon-Brookes, and has issue

2b *Lydia Wilbraham; *b* 15 May 1947; *m* 9 Aug 1969 *Lt Ian A M McClure, RN, er son of Lt-Cdr J A Maclure, of Buckleigh House, Milford, Godalming, Surrey

3b *Charlotte Hardcastle; *b* 31 May 1949

(1) (cont.) Cdr Noel Dixon *m* 2nd 28 March 1942 *Maud Vera Rosebud (*m* 3rd 1 Jan 1965 Frank Perkins) [Mrs Frank Perkins, 9 Pembroke House, 7–9 Chesham St, London SW1], widow of Cdr C E C Robinson, RN, and dau of R L Andrewes, of the Old House, Coombe, Oxon, and *d* 13 May 1960

(1) Alice Kathleen Mary; *b* Feb 1894; *m* 1st Jan 1931 Col George Elliot Llewhellin (*d* 20 Sept 1940), CBE, of Camlad House, Bishop's Castle, Salop, s of George William Llewhellin; *m* 2nd 1 Feb 1961 Brig Sir Francis William Crewe Fetherston-Godley, OBE, er son of Maj Harry Crewe Godley, DSO, 48th Regt

1 Anna Louisa; *m* 4 Feb 1874 Rev William Reinfred Arundell Harris Arundell (*d* 17 Oct 1901), Rector Cheriton Fitzpaine, Devon, and *d* 1 Oct 1902, leaving issue

2 Sophia Lydia; *m* 1st 1 Aug 1872 Richard Grahame (*d* 26 Jan 1874) and had issue; *m* 2nd 11 Sept 1877 Col William Lisle Blenkinsopp Coulson (*d* 1 June 1911), of Newbrough Park, Fourstones, Northumberland, and *d* 6 Oct 1925, leaving issue

3 Jessie Maria; *m* 13 Oct 1885 Henry G Seaman (*d* 2 June 1922), of Vines Gate, Brasted, Kent

4 Eleanor Georgina; *m* 19 Aug 1885 Rev Alfred Littledale Royds (*d* 15 June 1929), Rector Brereton, Cheshire, 1895–1919

Lt-Col JOHN DIXON *d* 7 March 1873; his est son,

Sir George Dixon, 1st Bt (UK), so *cr* 15 May 1919; V-Lt Cheshire, DL, JP, High Sheriff 1881, Ld Manor Astle, Col Cmdt Cheshire Vol Regt, which he raised 1915, Capt 25th KOSB, Maj and Hon Lt-Col 5th Cheshire Rifle Vols; *b* 23 May 1842; *m* 1 July 1885 Emily Katherine (*d* 1 Oct 1925), 2nd dau of George Beauchamp Cole, of Heatham House, Twickenham, and widow of John Baskervyle Clegg, of Withington Hall, Cheshire, and *d* 1 April 1924, leaving, with a dau (Sophia Evelyn, *b* 9 April 1888, *d* unm 22 Aug 1949):

Sir John Dixon, 2nd Bt; *b* 13 June 1886; *educ* Eton; *m* 24 Nov 1910 Gwendoline Anne, (*d* 2 April 1974), 2nd dau of Sir Joseph Layton Elmes Spearman, 2nd Bt (*qv*), and *d* 7 Aug 1976, leaving:

1 **Sir John George Dixon, 3rd Bt**; *b* 17 Sept 1911; *educ* Cranleigh; Capt 4th Hus SR of Offrs; *m* 1 May 1947 *Caroline, er dau of Charles Theodore Hiltermann, of 31 Melbury Court, London W8, and *d* 1990, leaving:

(1) *Mary Jane [Mrs Olav Ek, Blijdensteinlaan 11, 1217 PD, Hilversum, The Netherlands]; *b* 16 May 1951; *m* 1976 *Olav Alexander Ek

2 Nigel, Capt RN; *b* 28 Feb 1920; *educ* RNC Dartmouth; *m* 31 March 1948 *Margaret Josephine [Mrs Nigel Dixon, 3 Abbots Quay, Wareham, Dorset BH20 4LY], dau of Maurice John Collett, of Aston Lodge, Malvern Wells, Worcs, and *d* 1978, leaving issue:

(1) Sir JONATHAN MARK DIXON, **4th and present Bt**

1 *Beryl; *b* 1916

DIXON-SMITH

Creation: B. (LP, UK) 1993.

THE BARON DIXON-SMITH, of Bocking, Co Essex (Robert William Dixon-Smith, DL (Essex 1986)) [The Rt Hon The Lord Dixon-Smith DL, Lyons Hall, Braintree, Essex CM7 6SH]; *b* 30 Sept 1934; *educ* Oundle and Writtle Ag Coll; 2nd Lt King's Dragoon Gds 1955–57; farmer; memb: Essex CC 1965–93 (Chm 1986–89), Assoc of CCs 1983–93 (v-chm 1989–92, chm 1992–93), Local Govt Management Bd 1991–93, Cncl Essex U 1991–94; Chm Govrs Anglia Poly U 1992–93; Memb: Ho Lds EC Ctee sub-ctee C (Environment) 1994–, Ho Lds Select Ctee on Science and Technology 1994–; Govr Writtle Ag Coll 1967–94 (Chm 1973–85, Fell 1993); Freeman City London 1988 and Farmers' Co 1988 (Liveryman 1991); *m* 1960 *Georgina Janet, dau of George and Kathleen Cook of Halstead, Essex, and has issue:

1 *Adam William George; *b* 1962; *m* 19– *Anna Hogg, and has issue:

(1) *Guy; *b* 1994

(2) *Kit; *b* (twin) 1994

1 *Sarah Jane [The Hon Mrs Hoare, 130 Kensington Park Rd, London W11 2EP]; *b* 1960; *m* 1986 *Christopher Henry St John (Toby) Hoare, s of J Michael Hoare, and has issue:

(1) *Oscar; *b* 1988

(2) *Giles; *b* 1990

(1) *Camilla; *b* 1994

Lineage: DIXON SMITH, of Lascelles, Braintree, Essex; *m* Winifred Stratton and had:

ROBERT WILLIAM DIXON later DIXON-SMITH, *cr* a **Baron**

DODDS

Arms: Azure, issuant from a chief argent and out of a sunburst a dexter hand proper between two crab's heads downwards argent, each transfixed by a sword or, on the chief a steer's head cabossed sable, armed gold, between two capons proper. **Crest:** A demi-woman affronty proper vested azure, holding an open book proper inscribed with the chemical formula for stilboelstrol sable. **Motto:** Deeds not thoughts. **Creation:** Bt. (UK) 10 Feb 1964.

SIR RALPH JORDAN DODDS, 2ND BT, of West Chiltington, Co Sussex [Sir Ralph Dodds Bt, 49 Sussex Square, London W2 2SP]; *b* 25 March 1928; *s f* 1973; *educ* Winchester and RMA Sandhurst; commissioned 13th/18th Hus 1948, ret as Capt 1958, underwriting memb Lloyd's 1964–97; *m* 9 Oct 1954 *Marion, dau of Sir Daniel Thomas Davies, KCVO, of 36 Wimpole St, London W1, and has issue:

1 *Caroline; *b* 10 March 1956; *m* 1st 1981 James George Ball; *m* 2nd 1987 *David Pegg

2 *Arabella; *b* 24 July 1961; *m* 1982 *Maj Philip Henry Marmion Dymoke, WG, son of Lt-Col John Lindley Marmion Dymoke, MBE, 34th Hereditary Queen's Champion

Lineage: RALPH EDWARD DODDS, of Darlington and London; *b* 5 Aug 1868; *educ* privately; *m* 2 Sept 1897 Jane (*d* 29 Jan 1939), dau of Charles Pack, of London, and *d* 11 Jan 1932, leaving issue:

Sir (Edward) Charles Dodds, 1st Bt (UK), so *cr* 10 Feb 1964; *b* 13 Oct 1899; *educ* Harrow County Sch and Middx Hosp Medical Sch, PhD, MD (Lond 1926), DSc (Lond 1932), Hon MD: Melbourne 1952 and Birmingham, Hon DSc Cambridge 1954, Bologna and Chicago, FRS 1942, FRSE, FRIC, FRCP Lond 1933, Hon FRCOG, Hon FRCPS (Canada), Hon LLD Glasgow, Hon FRACP, Hon FACP, Hon Fell Coll Pathologists, Hon Memb Assoc Physicians, Emeritus Prof Biochemistry Lond, Dir Courtauld Inst Biochemistry Middx Hosp 1927–65, Pres RCP 1962–66, Pres 4th Internat Congress in Endocrinology 1968, Sims Travelling Prof RCS 1952, Chm: Planning Sub-Ctee Arthritis and Rheumatism Cncl, Science Advsy Ctee Br Empire Cancer Campaign; memb Governing Body: Lister Inst, Science Ctee Br Heart Fndn, Management Ctee Cancer Research Inst, Roy Cancer Hosp, Food Additives and Contaminants Sub-Ctee MAFF, Tropical Products Inst Ctee DSLR, Advsy Ctee Poisonous Substances used in Ag and Food Storage MAFF, SAC of Fleming Memorial Fund for Medical Research, Advsy Cncl Scientific Research and Tech Devpt War Office, biological research Advsy Bd MOD, memb Cncl and V-Pres Roy Soc 1957–59, Master Soc of Apothecaries, Goulstonian Lecturer RCP 1934, Harvey Lecturer New York U 1935, Cantor Lecturer RSA 1939, Bertram Louis Abrahams Lecturer RCP 1950, Purser Lecturer Trin Coll Dublin 1950, Sanderson-Wells Lecturer Middx Hosp 1953, Dorothy Platt Lecturer King's Coll Hosp 1953, Cavendish Lecturer W Lond Med Chir Soc 1955, Guiteras Lecturer American Urology Soc Boston 1956, Lane Lecturer Stanford U 1956, Crookshank Lecturer RCS 1959, Addison Lecturer Guy's Hosp 1946 and 1960, Linacre Lecturer St John's Coll Cambridge 1960, Comfort Crookshank Lecturer Middx Hosp 1960, Wallace Lecturer U of Hawaii 1968, Gold Medal Therapeutics W London Medical Soc 1938, Cameron Prizeman U of Edin 1940, William Julius Mickle Fellowship U of Lond 1943, Charles L Meyer Prize 1946, Walker Prize, RCS 1946, Garton Prize and Medal Br Empire Cancer Campaign 1948, Berzelius Medal Swedish Medical Soc, Medals U of Ghent and Brussels, Gold Medal Therapeutics Soc of Apothecaries 1951, Gold Medal Soc of Chem Industry 1951, Harben Medal Royal Inst Public Health 1952, memb Heberden Soc, Fell Inst Biology, author: *Recent Advances in British Medicine* (with G E Beaumont), *Chemical and Physiological Properties of Internal Secretions* (with F Dickens), *The Laboratory in Surgical Practice* (with L E H Whitby), KStJ, ktd 1954; *m* 6 Dec 1923 Constance Elizabeth (*d* 22 Nov 1969), only dau of John Thomas Jordan, of Darlington, Co Durham, and *d* 16 Dec 1973, leaving issue:

Sir RALPH JORDAN DODDS, **2nd and present Bt**

DONALDSON OF LYMINGTON

Arms: Sable two bars or, in chief three pegasi argent winged gold. **Crest:** A sealion erect sable, scales, fins and tail or, holding a lymphad also or, the mainsail displaying the arms, each mast ensigned by a cross formy gules. **Motto:** *Pro libertate per leges* ('For liberty through law'). **Creation:** B. (LP, UK) 1988.

THE BARON DONALDSON OF LYMINGTON, of Lymington, Co Hants (Sir John Francis Donaldson, PC (1979)) [The Rt Hon The Lord Donaldson of Lymington PC, House of Lords, London SW1A 0PW]; *b* 6 Oct 1920; *educ* Charterhouse and Trin Coll Cambridge (MA 1941); WWII: commd Roy Signals 1941, Gds Armoured Divnl Signals 1942–45, Mil Govt Schleswig-Holstein 1945–46, Hon Lt-Col 1946; barrister Middle Temple 1946, Jr Counsel to Registrar Restrictive Trading Agreements 1959–61, QC 1961, Dep Chm Hants QS 1961–66, Bencher 1966, ktd 1966, High Court Judge Queen's Bench 1966–79, Ld Justice of Appeal 1979–82, Master of the Rolls 1982–92, Treas Middle Temple 1986; memb: Croydon Borough Cncl 1949–53; Pres: Nat Industrial Relations Court 1971–74, Cncl Inns of Court 1987–90, Carthusian Soc 1978–82, Br Maritime Law Assoc 1979– (V-Pres 1969–78), Br Insur Law Assoc 1979–81 (Dep-Pres 1978–79), Br Records Assoc 1982–92; memb: Gen Cncl Bar 1956–61 and 1962–66, Cncl on Tbnls 1965–66; Chm: Advsy Cncl Public Records 1982–92, Magna Carta Tst 1982–92, Financial Law Panel 1993–, Inquiry into prevention of pollution from merchant shipping 1993–94; FCIArb 1980 (Pres 1980–83); Govr Sutton's Hosp Charterhouse 1981–84; Visitor: Nuffield Coll Oxford 1982–92, UCL 1982–92, London Business Sch 1986–92; MA Oxon 1982; Hon Freeman Drapers' Co 1984; Hon Fell Trin Coll Cambridge 1983, Hon DU Essex 1983, Hon LLD: Sheffield 1984, Nottingham Trent 1992; author: *Lowndes and Rudolf on General Average and the York-Antwerp Rules* (jt ed, 8th edn 1955, 9th edn 1964, 10th edn 1975); *m* 1945 *(Dorothy) Mary, GBE, dau of Reginald George Gale Warwick, of Wickham, Hants, and has issue:

1 *Michael John Francis [The Hon Michael Donaldson, The Old Coach House, Westwood Rd, Windlesham, Surrey GU20 6LT]; *b* 1950; chm Marquis & Co, surveyors, Twickenham, 1975–; *m* 1972 *Judith Margaret, only dau of Edgar William Somerville, FRCS, of Stone House, Garsington, Oxford, and has issue:

(1) *William Michael Somerville; *b* 1977

(2) *James John Francis; *b* (twin) 1977

1 *Margaret-Ann Michelle [The Hon Mrs Tompson, 736 University Dve, Saskatoon, Saskatchewan S7N 0J4 Canada]; *b* 1946; *educ* St Paul's Girls' Sch, London Sch of Occupational Therapy (Dip OT) and U of Saskatchewan (MCEd and PhD); *m* 1969 *Conal Tompson, and has issue:

(1) *Douglas Conal; *b* 1974

(1) *Caroline Margaret; *b* 1975

2 *Jennifer Mary; *b* 1946; *m* 1970 *Michael Lodwig Williams and has issue

Lineage: MALCOLM DONALDSON, FRCS, FRCOG; *m* Evelyn Helen Marguerite Maunsel and had:

JOHN FRANCIS, *cr* a **Baron**

DONEGALL

Arms: Quarterly, 1st and 4th, checky or and gu., a chief vair (for CHICHESTER); 2nd and 3rd, az. fretty arg. (for ETCHINGHAM). **Crest:** A stork ppr., wings expanded, holding in its beak an eel arg., head or. **Supporters:** Two wolves gu., ducally gorged and chained or. **Motto:** *Invitum sequitur honor* ('Honour follows him who does not seek it'). **Creations:** B. (Chichester of Belfast) and V. (I) 1 April 1625, E. (I) 30 March 1647 (Donegall), E. (Belfast) and M. (I) 4 July 1791, B. (GB) 3 July 1790 (Fisherwick) and (UK) 1831 (Templemore).

THE 7TH MARQUESS OF DONEGALL, Earl of Belfast, Viscount Chichester of Carrickfegus, Co Antrim, **Baron Chichester of Belfast**, Co Antrim, **Baron Fisherwick**, Co Stafford, and **Baron Templemore**, of Templemore, Co Donegal (Dermot Richard Claud Chichester, LVO (1986)) [The Most Hon The Marquess of Donegall LVO, c/o Dunbrody Park, Arthurstown, Co Wexford, Ireland]; *b* 18 April 1916; *s f* as Baron Templemore 1953 and cousin as Marquess etc 1975; *educ* Harrow and RMC Sandhurst; Hereditary Lord High Adml of Lough Neagh and Govr Carrickfergus Castle, 2nd Lt 7th Hussars 1936, Lt 1939, served WWII in Middle East and Italy (POW), Maj 7th QO Hus, Standard Bearer Gentlemen at Arms 1984–86; *m* 16 Sept 1946 Lady Josceline (Josephine) Gabrielle Legge (*d* 19 June 1995), yst dau of 7th Earl of Dartmouth (*qv*), and has issue:

1 +(ARTHUR) PATRICK, *Earl of Belfast* [Earl of Belfast, Dunbrody, Campile, Co Wexford, Ireland]; *b* 9 May 1952; *educ* Harrow; Lt Coldstream Gds; *m* 1989 *Caroline Mary, er dau of Maj Christopher Roland Philipson, Life Gds, of Lofts Hall, Saffron Walden, Essex, and has issue:

(1) +James, *Viscount Chichester*; *b* 19 Nov 1990

(1) *Catherine Gabrielle; *b* 1992

1 *Jennifer Evelyn [The Lady Jennifer Fowler, Rahinston, Enfield, Co Meath, Ireland]; *b* 3 April 1949; *m* 1971 *John Robert Henry Fowler, and has issue:

(1) *Robert Henry; *b* 1975

(2) *Charles James; *b* 1977

2 *Juliet Clare [The Lady Juliet Frazer, Hillmount, Cullybackey, Co Antrim, N Ireland]; *b* 2 Nov 1954; *m* 1983 *Andrew David Frazer and has issue:

(1) *William John Andrew; *b* 1985

(1) *Mary Emma (twin); *b* 1985

Donegall, other creations: A Barony of Donegall was conferred wth the Earldom of Tyrconnell on Rory O'Donnell in 1603 but became forfeited with the higher creation some years later after Rory and the Earl of Tyrone's departure from Ireland in 1607 in the episode known as 'The Flight of the Earls'.

Lineage: RICHARD de CICESTER (*i.e.*, Chichester, Sussex), granted lands in Sussex by KING JOHN; had issue:

ROBERT de CICESTER; living 1263; *m* Petronilla — and had:

RICHARD de CICESTER; living 1272; *m* Elizabeth — and had issue:

ROGER de CICESTER; did mil serv in Wales and Gascony *temp* EDWARD I; had:

ROGER de CICESTER; served Hundred Years War in France, also in Scotland, *temp* EDWARD III; had:

Sir ROGER de CICESTER; ktd *c* 1347; fought Poitiers 1356; had:

Sir JOHN CHICHESTER, of Donwer, Somerset; *m* 1384 Thomasine, dau and heir of Sir John Raleigh, of Raleigh, Devon, which he acquired through her and by which the CHICHESTERs became one of the most important families in N Devon; had:

JOHN CHICHESTER, of Raleigh; High Sheriff Devon; *m* Alice, dau and heir of John Wotton, of Widworthy, and *d* 14 Dec 1437, having had, with a yr s (John, *m* Elizabeth, dau and heir of Richard Dymock, and was ancestor of the CHICHESTERs of Hall):

RICHARD CHICHESTER, of Raleigh; High Sheriff Devon 1469 and 1475; *m* 1st Margaret, dau of Nicholas Kaynes, of Winkley, and had issue; *m* 2nd Elizabeth, dau of Sir John Sapcott, and *d* 24 Dec 1498, having by her had no issue; one of his children by his 1st w:

NICHOLAS CHICHESTER; *b* 1452; *m* Christina (*m* 3rd Sir William Martin, of Okehampton; *m* 4th James Chudleigh, of Asheton), widow of Henry Hall and dau of Sir William Paulet (*see* WINCHESTER, M), and *dvp*, having had, with two other sons:

JOHN CHICHESTER, of Raleigh; *m* 1st Margaret, dau and heir of Sir Hugh Beaumont, of Youlston, Devon, and had, with two other sons:

1 Edward, of Hounditon Sampton and Braunton, Devon; *m* Elizabeth (*d* 23 Aug 1548), dau of John Bourchier, Earl of Bath (*see* BATH, M, preliminary remarks), and *dvp* July 1522, having had, with other issue:

(1) JOHN (Sir)

JOHN CHICHESTER *m* 2nd Joan, sis of Robert Brett, of Whitstaunton, Som, and *d* 22 Feb 1537, having by her had issue:

2 John, ancestor of the CHICHESTERs of Widworthy

3 Amyas, ancestor of the CHICHESTERs of Arlington

The gs,

Sir JOHN CHICHESTER, of Raleigh and Youlston, Devon, High Sheriff 1552 and 1557, MP 1553 and 1562, ktd 1556; *m* Gertrude (*d* April 1566), dau of Sir William Courtenay, of Powderham Castle, Devon (*see* DEVON, E), and had, with other issue:

1 Sir ARTHUR CHICHESTER, 1st and last BARON CHICHESTER OF BELFAST, Co Antrim (I), so *cr* 23 Feb 1612, PC (I 1603); Ld Dep Ireland 1604–10 and 1613–15, Ld High Treasurer Ireland 1616; *m* Letitia (*d* 27 Nov 1620), widow of Vaughan Blackham and dau of Sir John Perrott, of Haroldston, Pembs, Ld Dep Ireland, and *dsp* 19 Feb 1624/5, when the Barony expired

2 Sir EDWARD CHICHESTER, **1st Viscount Chichester of Carrickfergus**, of Co Antrim, so *cr* 1 April 1625, as also BARON CHICHESTER OF BELFAST, Co Antrim (both I); *m* 1st 4 July 1605 Anne (*d* 8 March 1616), dau and heir of John Coplestone, of Eggesford, Devon, who brougt him a large estate, and had, with two daus:

(1) ARTHUR CHICHESTER, **1st Earl of Donegall** (I), so *cr* 30 March 1647, with remainder to the male descendants of his father; *b* 16 June 1606; MP Co Antrim 1639; Govr of Carrickfergus; *m* 1st Dorcas (*d* 10 April 1630), dau of John Hill, of Honiley, Warwicks, and had:

1a Mary; *m* 1655 John St Leger, of Doneraile, Co Cork, and had issue (*see* DONERAILE, V)

(1) (cont.) The **1st Earl** *m* 2nd Lady Mary Digby (*d* 5 Nov 1648), dau of 1st Earl of Bristol (*see* BRISTOL, M, preliminary remarks, also DIGBY, B), but by her had no surv issue; *m* 3rd 13 Aug 1651, as her 1st husb Letitia, only surv dau of Sir William Hicks, 1st Bt, of Beverston (*see* SAINT ALDWYN, E), and *d* 18 March 1674/5, having by her left issue:

1a William; *d* young 24 Dec 1660

2a Anne; *m* 1st Jan 1674 1st and last Earl of Gowran (*see* MOUNTGARRET, V); *m* 2nd 1st Earl of Longford (*dsp* 22 Dec 1700) of the 1677 *cr* (*see* LONGFORD, E, preliminary remarks) and *dsp* 14 Nov 1697

(2) John, MP Dungannon 1639, royalist Col Civil War, Sergeant-Maj 1647; *b* 22 Feb 1609; *m* Mary Jones (*m* 2nd Col Christopher Copley and *d* by 3 Nov 1673), dau of 1st Viscount Ranelagh, and *d* between 1 Nov 1643 and 4 Feb 1647/8, leaving, with three daus:

1a ARTHUR, **2nd Earl**

2a John, ancestor of the BARONs O'NEILL (*qv*), who with their male issue and male line kin are in remainder to the Earldom of Donegall, Viscountcy of Chichester of Carickfergus and Barony of Chichester of Belfast

(3) Edward, Lt-Col; *b* 1 Sept 1611; *m* Elizabeth, dau and coheir of Sir Edward Fisher, of Fisher's Prospect, Co Wexford, and had issue:

1a Edward; *m* Agnes, dau of Dr William Bulkeley, Archdeacon Dublin, and *dsp* 1673

2a John, High Sheriff Co Wexford 1701; sold his manor of Chichester 1711 to James Stopford, of Courtown, f of 1st Earl of Courtown (*qv*)

2 (cont.) The **1st Viscount** *m* 2nd Mary (*d* 2 Feb 1637), widow of Othwell Hill and dau of — Denham, of Wortham, and *d* 8 July 1648

3 John (Sir); *d* Sept 1569; gf of 1 Sir John Chichester, Bt (*qv*)

4 Thomas, to whom JAMES I granted lands in Wicklow. He had a grant of 1,000 acres of Rathdonnell, Co Donegal, 8 Dec 1610

5 John (Sir), the yr; Sgt-Major of the Army in Ireland and Govr of Carrickfergus in 1597, captured by Randal MacSorley Macdonnell (*see* ANTRIM, E) in a sally from that town 4 Nov 1597 and beheaded on a stone at the head of the Glynns, Co Antrim

1 Susanna; *m* as his 2nd w, John Fortescue, MP, of Buckland Filleigh, Devon, and was ancestor of the extinct Earl of Clermont, Viscounts Clermont and Barons Clermont of Dromisken (who were also Barons Clermont of Clermont Park and briefly held the Barony of Carlingford, all also equally extinct; *see* 1898 edn)

2 Elizabeth; *m* Hugh Fortescue, of Filleigh, ancestor of Earl Fortescue (*qv*)

3 Eleanor; *m* Sir Arthur Bassett

4 Dorothy; *m* Sir Hugh Pollard, of Mymett

5 Bridget; *m* Sir Edward Prideaux, of Farway

6 Urith; *m* John Trevelyan and had issue (*see* TREVELYAN, Bt, of Nettlecombe)

The 1st EARL's nephew,

ARTHUR CHICHESTER, **2nd Earl of Donegall**, PC (I 1672); ktd 1660, MP Dungannon 1661–66; *m* between 30 Nov 1660 and 9 March 1660/1 Jane (*m* 2nd Richard Booth, of Epsom, s of Sir Richard Booth, of Butler's Grove), dau and heir of John Itchingham, of Dunbrody, Co Wexford, and d 26 Oct 1678, having had, with other issue:

1 ARTHUR, **3rd Earl**

2 John, of Dunbrody

3 Edward (Rev) BA Oxon; Rector Clonenagh; *m* his cousin Elizabeth, dau of Capt John Chichester, and had:

(1) Arthur (Rev); *b* 5 Jan 1716; Vicar Tullynisk

The 2nd EARL's est son,

ARTHUR CHICHESTER, **3rd Earl of Donegall**; *b* 1666; Maj-Gen Spanish forces War of Spanish Succession 1704; *m* 1st Lady Barbara Boyle (*d* 16 Nov 1682), dau of 1st Earl of Orrery (*see* CORK and ORRERY, E), by whom he had no surv issue; *m* 2nd 1685 Lady Catherine Forbes, dau of 1st Earl of Granard (*qv*), and was *k* 10 April 1706 at Fort Monjuich, having by her had:

1 ARTHUR CHICHESTER, **4th Earl of Donegall**; *b* 28 March 1695; *m* 3 Oct 1716 Lady Lucy Ridgeway (*d* 16 July 1732), dau and coheir of 4th Earl of Londonderry of the 1622 *cr* (*see* LONDONDERRY, M, preliminary remarks), and *dsp* 30 Sept 1757

2 John, MP Belfast; *b* 1700; *m* 13 Sept 1726 Elizabeth, dau of Sir Richard Newdigate, 3rd Bt, of Arbury, Warwicks, and *d* 1 June 1746 leaving issue:

(1) ARTHUR, **1st Marquess**

(2) John; *b* 26 Dec 1740

1 Katherine; *m* 9 Sept 1713 4th Viscount Massereene (*see* MASSEREENE and FERRARD, V)

2 Jane; *d* with her two next yr sisters in a fire in her f's house in Belfast caused by a servant's carelessness

3 Frances

4 Henrietta

5 Mary, *d* unm

6 Anne; *m* 12 July 1716 4th Earl of Barrymore

The 4th Earl's nephew,

ARTHUR CHICHESTER, **1st Marquess of Donegall**, so *cr* 4 July 1791, as also EARL OF BELFAST (both I), and earlier 3 July 1790 BARON FISHERWICK, Co Stafford (GB), PC (I 1766); *b* 13 June 1739; MP Malmesbury 1768–74; *m* 1st 16 Nov 1761 Lady Anne Hamilton (*d* 11 Nov 1780), est dau of 5th Duke of Hamilton and Brandon (*qv*), and had issue:

1 GEORGE AUGUSTUS CHICHESTER, **2nd Marquess of Donegall**, KP (1821), PC (I 1803); Ld Lt Co Donegal 1831–44; *b* 13 Aug 1769; MP Carrickfergus 1798–99; *m* 8 Aug 1795 (discovered 20 years later to be invalid since the bride was under age and the wedding took place by special licence rather than after the calling of banns, the fact of the bride's illegitimacy rendering the consent to the marriage granted by the couple who had brought her up insufficient; accordingly Lord Donegall had to get an Act of Parl passed to legalise the marriage) Anna May (*d* 6 Feb 1849), illegitimate dau of Sir Edward May, 2nd Bt, and *d* 5 Oct 1844, having had:

(1) GEORGE HAMILTON CHICHESTER, **3rd Marquess of Donegall**, KP (1857), GCH (1831), PC (GB 1830); *b* 10 Feb 1797; *educ* Eton and Ch Ch Oxford; MP (Tory) Carrickfergus 1818–20, Belfast 1820–30 and 1837–38 and Co Antrim 1830–37; *cr* 18 Aug 1841 BARON ENNISHOWEN AND CARRICKFERGUS, of Ennishaven, Co Donegall, and Carrickfergus, Co Antrim (UK), Capt Yeomen Gd, ADC to HM QUEEN VICTORIA, Ld Lt and Custos Rotulorum Co Antrim, Col Antrim Militia, FRS, Col 4th Bn Royal Irish Rifle Vol; *m* 1st 8 Dec 1822 Harriet Anne (*d* 14 Sept 1860), dau of 1st Earl of Glengall, and had issue:

1a George Augustus, *Viscount Chichester*; *b* 26 May 1826; *d* 18 June 1827

2a Frederick Richard, *Earl of Belfast*; *b* 25 Nov 1827; *d* unm at Naples 11 Feb 1853

1a Harriet Augusta Anna Seymourina; *m* 22 Aug 1857 8th Earl of Shaftesbury (*qv*), and *d* 14 April 1898, leaving issue

(1) The **3rd Marquess** *m* 2nd 26 Feb 1862 Harriet (*dsp* 6 March 1884), widow of Lt-Gen Sir Frederick Ashworth, KCB, and est dau of Sir Bellingham R Graham, 7th Bt, of Norton Conyers (*qv*), and *d* 20 Oct 1883, when the UK Barony expired

(2) EDWARD CHICHESTER, **4th Marquess of Donegall**, Dean of Raphoe 1832–73; *b* 11 June 1799; *educ* Eton and Trin Coll Dublin; *m* 21 Sept 1821 Amelia Spread Deane (*d* March 1891), 3rd dau of Henry Deane Grady, of Stillorgan Castle, Co Dublin, and *d* 20 Jan 1889, having had issue:

1a GEORGE AUGUSTUS HAMILTON CHICHESTER, **5th Marquess of Donegall**, Lt 6th Foot; *b* 27 June 1822; bankrupt 1889; *m* 1st 31 Aug 1865 Mary Anne Williams (*dsp* 11 Nov 1901), yst dau of Edward Cobb, of Kensington, and Arnold, Kent; *m* 2nd 23 Dec 1902 Violet Gertrude, FRSA, Order of Mercy (*d* 8 Oct 1952), only dau of Henry St George Twining, of Halifax, Canada, and *d* 13 May 1904, leaving:

1b EDWARD ARTHUR DONALD ST GEORGE HAMILTON CHICHESTER, **6th Marquess of Donegall**; *b* 7 Oct 1903; *educ* Eton and Ch Ch Oxford; jnlst (gossip columnist), war correspondent WW II, Capt HG; Lt-Col Army Cadet Force 1945–75, radio commentator, BBC disc jockey 1949; *m* 1st 24 April 1943 (*divorce* 1968) Gladys Jean, yr dau of Capt Christian Combe, of Strathconon, Scotland; *m* 2nd 17 Aug 1968 *Maureen, formerly wife of Douglas McKenzie and dau of Maj Geoffrey C Scholfield, MC, of Birkdale, Lancs, and *dsp* Switzerland 24 May 1975

2a Henry FitzWarrine, Capt Royal Antrim Rifles; *b* 11 Sept 1834; *m* 14 July 1860 Elizabeth Julia (*d* 15 June 1902), only child and heiress of Samuel Amy Severne, of Poslingford, Suffolk, and *d* 7 Nov 1928, leaving issue:

1b Severne Edward Spencer FitzWarrine; *b* 16 April 1861; *d* unm 8 March 1951

2b Forester Augustus Harold; *b* 30 Nov 1864; *d* 20 Jan 1865

1b Amelia Laura Flora; *b* 17 Nov 1865; *d* Dec 1865

2b Caroline Lizzie Henrietta; *d* unm 17 Oct 1947

3b Louisa Jean Amelia; *m* 22 June 1896 Maj Samuel Pearson Yates, 11th Hus, of Broughton Grange, Banbury, and *d* 28 March 1952

4b Lizzie Frances Augusta; *m* 16 Dec 1895 Capt George Stanley Cary (*d* 4 April 1896), Royal Irish Rifles, and *dsp* 14 March 1953

5b Marie Jeanette Amelia; *m* 1st 21 Sept 1897 (*divorce* 1914) William Henry Cleland, of Rook's Nest Hall, Banstead, Surrey, and had issue; *m* 2nd 17 June 1914 Capt Archibald Alastair McLeod (*ka* 1914), Glos Regt, son of Lt-Gen W K McLeod; *m* 3rd 1919 John Llewelyn Owen, of Meon Holt, Catisfield, Hants

3a Adolphus John Spencer Churchill, of Moyola Park, Castledawson, Co Londonderry, DL, JP Co Londonderry and Co Antrim, High Sheriff Co Londonderry 1882, Maj and Hon Lt-Col 4th Bn Roy Irish Rifles, Lt 12th Lancers; *b* 18 Dec 1836; *m* 9 Oct 1872 Mary (*d* 19 June 1924), only child of Col Robert Peel Dawson, MP, of Moyola Park, and *d* 5 March 1901, leaving:

1b Robert Peel Dawson Spencer, of Moyola Park, DL, JP Cos Londonderry, Antrim and Donegal, High Sheriff Co Londonderry 1907 and Co Antrim 1911–12, Lt-Col Roy Irish Rifles and Maj Res of Offrs Irish Gds, served Br Centl Africa 1897–1900 (medals and clasp) and Boer War (medal and clasp); *b* 13 Aug 1873; *m* 11 Dec 1901 Dehra Ker, PC (NI) 1949, GBE (1957, DBE 1949, OBE 1918), JP Co Londonderry, MP City of and Co Londonderry 1921–29 and S Londonderry 1933–60 NI Parl, Parly Sec Min Educn NI 1937–44, Min Health and Local Govt 1949–60 (*m* 2nd 4 June 1928 Adml Henry Wise Parker, CB, CMG, who *d* 1 Aug 1940, and *d* 28 Nov 1963), only child of James Ker Fisher, of The Manor House, Kilrea, Ireland, and *d* 10 Dec 1921, having had issue:

1c Robert James Spencer; *b* 30 Sept 1902; *d* 5 Jan 1920

1c Marion Caroline Dehra; *m* 1st 10 May 1922 Capt James Lenox-Conyngham Chichester-Clark (*d* 31 Jan 1933), DSO and bar, RN, DL, JP, MP, and had:

1d *JAMES DAWSON CHICHESTER-CLARK, BARON MOYOLA (LP, *qv*)

1c (cont.) Mrs James Chichester-Clark *m* 2nd 22 Nov 1938 Charles Edward Brackenbury

2b Edward Brownlow Dawson, Capt 4th Bn Royal Irish Rifles; *b* 20 March 1876; *d* unm 4 March 1909

3b Augustus John Bruce Macdonald Dawson, Lt RFA; *b* 7 Sept 1878; *d* unm 11 June 1902

1a Augusta Annabella; *m* 1st 23 July 1844 9th Earl Ferrers (*qv*), and had issue; *m* 2nd 15 June 1864 Frederick Henry Walsh, Capt 78th Highrs, and *d* 9 Oct 1914, leaving further issue

2a Dorcas Juliana Fanny; *d* unm 6 March 1980

(3) Spencer Augustus; *b* 27 Nov 1805; *d* 27 May 1825

(4) Arthur, MP Belfast 1832–34; *b* 30 Sept 1808; *d* 25 June 1840

(5) Hamilton Francis, Army Offr; *b* 9 March 1810; *m* 7 Dec 1837 Honoria Anastatia (*d* 7 Feb 1878), dau of Col Henry James Blake, of Ardfry, Co Galway, and sister of Baron Wallscourt (*see* 1917 edn) and *d* 1 Jan 1854

(6) John Ludford, MP Belfast 1845–52; *b* Nov 1811; *m* 27 July 1844 Caroline (*d* 11 Dec 1883), dau of Henry Bevan, and *d* 22 April 1873

(7) Stephen Algernon; *b* 1814; *m* 30 Dec 1843 Alphonsine Louise Laura de Narbonne (*d* 5 July 1881) and *d* 14 Jan 1890

2 Arthur; *b* 1771; *d* 1788

3 Spencer Stanley Chichester, of Dunbrody Park, Co Wexford; *b* 20 April 1775; *m* 8 Aug 1795 Lady Harriet Stewart (*d* 30 Jan 1850 aged 80), dau of 7th Earl of Galloway, KT (*qv*), and *d* 22 Feb 1819, having had, with two daus (*d* unm):

(1) ARTHUR CHICHESTER, **1st Baron Templemore**, of Templemore, Co Donegal (UK), so *cr* 10 Sept 1831; *b* 1797; MP (Whig) Milborne Port 1826–30 and Co Wexford 1830–31, Lt-Col, Ld Bedchamber to WILLIAM IV and Ld-in-Waiting; *m* 1820 Lady Augusta Paget (*d* 1872), dau of 1st Marquess of Anglesey (*qv*), and had issue:

1a HENRY SPENCER, **2nd Baron**

2a Augustus George Charles, Lt-Gen; 77th Foot; *b* 20 May 1822; *m* 26 Aug 1868 Jane (*d* 29 Aug 1929), widow of Major H A Macdonald, 77th Regt, and dau of William Townend, and *dsp* 26 July 1896

3a Frederick Arthur Henry, Gentleman Usher of the Scarlet Rod; *b* 22 Feb 1824; *m* 7 Aug 1852 Frances Marianne (*d* 6 Jun 1912), eldest dau of Daniel Tighe, of Rossana, Co Wicklow, and *d* 18 May 1863, having had, with three daus (*d* young or unm):

1b Spencer Frederick, JP Hants, Maj Roy Scots Fus, served S Africa 1879–81, Zulu War (medal with clasp) and Transvaal (despatches); *b* 27 Sept 1854; *educ* Marlborough; *m* 21 April 1892 Helen Elizabeth (*d* 4 Jan 1948), est dau of Archibald Coats, of Woodside, Paisley (*see* COATS, Bt), and *d* 29 Jan 1931, leaving issue:

1c Charles Frederick Spencer, Lt 4th Hus WW I, Capt WW II, Assist Mil Attaché Bucharest 1919–20, Romanian Star with swords; *b* 18 Jan 1893; *educ* Winchester and abroad; *m* 31 Oct 1924 (*annulled* 1928) Pamela Georgiana (*d* following a car crash 17 Sept 1962), er dau of Horace Peel, of 22 Ovington Sq, London SW (*see* PEEL, E), and *dsp* 1 March 1971

1c Doreen Margaret Helen; *b* 25 Sep 1897; *m* 1st 29 April 1920 (*divorce* 1925) Thomas Peter Murray, yr s of R Stuart Murray, of Wool Wool, Sandringham, Australia; *m* 2nd 8 Aug 1925 (*divorce* 1940) Maj Lewis Coker, and had issue; *m* 3rd 19 Oct 1940 (*divorce* 1946) Thomas Edmund Fenlon

2c *Verena Frances Elizabeth [Mrs Derek Secker, Les Chomettes, Ave Font-de-Veyre, 06150 Cannes, La Bocca, France AM]; *b* 1906; *m* 1931 Cdr Derek Howard Secker (*d* 1988), LVO, RN, and has issue:

1d +Malcolm Chichester [Malcolm Secker Esq, Flat 9, 10 Porchester Terr, London W2]; *b* 1934; *educ* Eton

2b Alan George, OBE (1924), DL Hunts, Lt-Col 18th Royal Irish Regt, Ch Constable Hunts 1901–27, served Egyptian Campaign 1882 (severely wounded, medal with clasp, bronze star, 5th Cl Medjidie) and Boer War 1899–1900 (despatches, medal with six clasps); *b* 8 April 1857; *educ* Felsted; *m* 1st 27 April 1882 Hon Georgiana Charlotte Morgan (*dsp* 22 April 1886), widow of Lord Francis Conyngham, 2nd son of 2nd Marquess Conyngham (*qv*), and dau of 1st Baron Tredegar (*see* 1959 edn); *m* 2nd 2 June1909 Beatrice, dau of Edmund Snow, of Franklyn, Exeter, and *dsp* 6 March 1947

3b Ernest William; *b* 21 Sept 1858; *d* unm 21 April 1917

4b Athol Augustus, Colonial CS, Commr S Nigeria (Africa medal with three clasps), served WW I; *b* 9 May 1861; *m* 14 Jul 1910 Caroline Ethel Gertrude (*d* 28 Aug 1947), 7th dau of Adm Hon Keith Stewart, CB (*see* GALLOWAY, E), and *dsp* 19 Nov 1937

5b Reginald de Blaquiere, Maj Border Regt, served Waziristan Campaign 1894–95 (medal with clasp), Boer War 1900–02 (Queen's medal with three clasps, King's medal with two clasps) and WW I; *b* 15 Aug 1862; *m* 28 Dec 1912 Hon Theresa Diana Crofton (*d* 26 March 1923), sis of 4th Baron Crofton (*qv*), and *d* 11 Sept 1923

4a Adolphus William; *b* 24 May 1825; *d* 26 Aug 1855

5a Francis Algernon James, JP, Capt 7th Hus; *b* 17 Nov 1829; *m* 1st 21 Feb 1855 Elizabeth Ann (*d* 24 March 1871), 2nd dau of George Dixon, and had, with a s (*d* an infant):

1b Augusta Jane; *b* 15 April 1862; *d* unm 12 May 1914

5a (cont.) Capt Francis Chichester *m* 2nd 4 Feb 1875 Lady Emily Octavia Stewart (*d* 7 July 1929), 5th dau of 9th Earl of Galway (*qv*), and *d* 15 Feb 1885, having by her had issue:

1b Shane Randolph, OBE (1919); Irrigation Dept PWD Egypt 1905–10 (invalided), served RN Div (1914 star), Min Munitions 1916–18, Inspr Engr Rolls Royce Ltd 1913–42 (except during WW I), V-Pres Shaftesbury Homes and Arethusa Trg Ship; *b* 24 Feb 1883; *educ* Wellington and Pembroke Coll Camb (BA 1905, MA 1942); *m* 26 Dec 1914 Madeline Herschel (*d* 14 Aug 1977 aged 86), dau of Henry Arthur Whately, of Midford Castle, Bath, and *d* 6 April 1969, leaving issue:

1c +(Oscar) Richard Herschel [Major Richard Chichester, Wiscombe Park, Southleigh, Colyton, Devon EX13 6JE]; *b* 17 Oct 1915; *educ* Wellington and Trin Coll Cambridge (BA 1937); Maj Rifle Bde (Prince Consort's Own); ADC to High Commr for Palestine 1946–48, Palestine 1936 (medal), WW II (African Star); *m* 29 Sept 1951 Margaret Edmondson, dau of Charles Edgar Farr, JP, of Weston Bury, Weston, Herts, and has:

1d +Timothy Arthur Shane; *b* 23 April 1956; *m* 1983 *Mary Frances, yr dau of Frank Sebastian Cooksey, CBE, MD, FRCP, of Aldeburgh, Suffolk, and has issue:

1e +John Francis Shane; *b* 6 Nov 1985

1d *Jane Caroline Sheelah; *b* 13 Oct 1952; *m* 1980 (*divorce*) Richard Philip Palmer, and has issue:

1e *Daniel; *b* 7 Sept 1981

2e *Thomas; *b* 12 Sept 1983

2d *Sara Kathleen Arabella; *b* 6 June 1958; *m* 1988 *Michael Constant John Raynor, and has issue:

1e *Madeline Jacqueline Kathleen; *b* 29 July 1989

2c +Desmond Shane [Desmond Chichester Esq, Holway House, Whatcombe, Blandford, Dorset]; *b* 7 Aug 1919; *educ* Wellington and Trin Coll Cambridge (BA 1948, MA 1951); agent to Earl of Radnor, FRICS, Capt 80th HAA Regt RA and NI Horse WW II N Africa and Italy; *m* 11 Aug 1951 Patricia (*d* 1987), yr dau of Lt-Col Henry George Moreton Pleydell-Railston, DSO (*see* MANSEL, Bt), and has issue:

1d +Piers Desmond Herschel [Piers Chichester Esq, Kingston Farmhouse, Winterborne Kingston, Blandford, Dorset DT11 9AX]; *b* 20 Feb 1954; *educ* Wellington and RAC Cirencester; FRICS, FAAV; *m* 1989 *Charlotte Anne, only dau of Lt-Col Peter Richard Heaton-Ellis, OBE, of The Coach House, Chitterne, Wilts, and has issue:

1e +Harry Pleydell Whately; *b* 26 Aug 1992

1e *Sophia Patricia; *b* 9 Sept 1990

2d +Jonathan Morton [Jonathan Chichester Esq, 46 Redway Drive, Whitton, Middx]; *b* 20 Feb 1954; *educ* Wellington; *m* 1982 *Caroline Margaret, dau of Peter Douglas Bird, of W Kirby, Wirral, and has issue:

1e +Peter Shane; *b* 18 May 1983

2e +Benjamin Charles; *b* 12 May 1986

1e *Eleanor Madeline Patricia; *b* 29 Oct 1987

3d +(Adrian) George [George Chichester Esq, The Mount, Chieveley, Newbury, Berks]; *b* 23 Dec 1955; *educ* Wellington and Keble Coll Oxford (MA); FRICS, FAAV; *m* 1988 *Caroline Ann, only dau of Dr John Richard Storer, of Westfield House, Blewbury, Oxon, and has issue:

1e +Hugh Edmund; *b* 16 March 1991

1e *Tessa Ann; *b* 18 Nov 1989

2e *Camilla Emily; *b* 30 Dec 1993

3e *Iona Madeline; *b* 3 Oct 1995

1d *Morna Rosemary [Mrs Andrew Partridge, 6 Beavers Rd, Farnham, Surrey GU9 7BD]; *b* 30 June 1952; *educ* Westonbirt and LMH Oxford (MA); *m* 1982 *Andrew David Wood Partridge, son of Simon Harry Wood Partridge, OBE, of Kilndown, Kent, and has issue:

1e *Katharine Mary Emily; *b* 17 Jan 1986

2e *Verena Frances Herschel; *b* 4 Oct 1987

2b Evangeline Blanche; *b* 4 Feb 1876; *m* 15 July1897 Major Hubert Alcock Nepean Fyers, MVO (*d* 1 Aug 1951), Rifle Bde, Equerry to HRH THE DUKE OF CONNAUGHT, s of Lt-Gen Sir William Fyers, KCB, and *d* 5 May 1959, leaving issue

3b Kathleen Mary; *b* 23 March 1877; *d* unm 19 June 1966

4b Sheelah Maud Emily; *b* 17 Feb 1878; *m* 1st 11 April 1901 Essex Edgeworth Reade (*d* 11 Oct 1908), of 27 Eaton Place, London SW, and had issue; *m* 2nd 6 June 1933 Sir Evelyn John Ruggles-Brise, KCB (*d* 18 Aug 1935; *see* RUGGLES-BRISE, Bt), and *d* 11 March 1953

5b Morna Sybil; *b* 24 Feb 1879; *m* 23 April 1914 Henry Arthur Whately (*d* 2 May 1957 aged 102), s of Canon William Joseph Whately, and *d* 13 April 1951, leaving issue

6b Margaret Rosa; *b* 20 July 1880; *d* unm 14 Oct 1966

1a Caroline Georgiana; *m* 27 April 1848 Sir Charles Lennox Peel GCB (*d* 19 Aug 1899), s of Laurence Peel, of Kemp Town, Brighton (*see* PEEL, E), and *d* 26 April 1892, leaving issue

2a Augusta; *m* 1st 18 July 1854 7th Earl of Kingston (*qv*) and had issue; *m* 2nd 14 Nov 1872 Alfred Henry Caulfeild (*see* CHARLEMONT, V) and *d* 1 April 1873

(2) George Augustus Frederick (Rev); *d* unm 8 June1829

(1) Elizabeth; *m* 16 Aug 1822 1st Baron Bateman and *d* 19 Sep 1882, leaving issue. He *d* 22 July 1845

The 1st BARON *d* 26 Sept 1837; his est son,

HENRY SPENCER CHICHESTER, **2nd Baron Templemore**, DL, JP Co Wexford; *b* 14 June 1821; *educ* Eton and Ch Ch Oxford; Hon Col 3rd Bn Royal Irish Regt; *m* 1st 3 Aug 1842 Laura Caroline Jane (*d* 9 Dec 1871), 3rd dau of Rt Hon Sir Arthur Paget, GCB (*see* ANGLESEY, M), and had issue:

1 ARTHUR HENRY, **3rd Baron**

1 Flora Augusta; *b* 7 July 1856; *d* 5 Oct 1874

The **2nd Baron** *m* 2nd 8 Jan 1873 Lady Victoria Elizabeth Ashley (*d* 15 Feb 1927), dau of 7th Earl of Shaftesbury (*qv*), and had further issue:

2 Hilda Caroline; Extra Lady in Waiting to HRH PRINCESS BEATRICE 1912–44; *b* 17 Dec 1875; *m* 2 Dec 1913 Sir Victor George Seymour Corkran, KCVO (*d* 10 March 1934), Comptroller Household to HRH PRINCESS BEATRICE, and had issue

The 2nd BARON *d* 10 June 1906; his only son,

ARTHUR HENRY CHICHESTER, **3rd Baron Templemore**, DL, JP Co Wexford; *b* 16 Sept 1854; *educ* Eton; Major 3rd Bn Roy Irish Regt, High Sheriff Co Wexford 1890; *m* 1st 14 Aug 1879 Evelyn (*d* 3 Dec 1883), dau of Rev William James Stracey (*see* STRACEY, Bt), and had:

1 ARTHUR CLAUD SPENCER, **4th Baron**

1 Evelyn Laura Mary; *b* 23 Nov; *d* 20 Dec 1883

The **3rd Baron** *m* 2nd 15 July 1885 Alice Elizabeth (*d* 30 Sept 1954), dau of Clinton George Augustus Dawkins, and had further issue:

2 Gerald Henry Crofton (Hon Sir), KCVO; Attaché Copenhagen 1916 and Paris 1918, Priv Sec to Lords Derby 1919, Hardinge of Penshurst 1920 and Crewe 1923, Assist Priv Sec to HM QUEEN MARY 1926–35, Priv Sec 1935–39, Groom-in-Waiting to HM GEORGE V 1931–36; *b* 22 June 1886; *educ* Eton and Trin Coll Cambridge; *d* unm 8 Oct 1939

3 Richard Cecil Frederick; *b* 4 Apr 1889; *educ* Harrow and Ch Ch Oxford (BA 1910); *d* Serbia 31 July 1915

The 3rd BARON *d* 28 Sept 1924; his est son,

ARTHUR CLAUD SPENCER CHICHESTER, **4th Baron Templemore**, KCVO (1938), DSO (1918), OBE (1919), PC (1943), DL (Hants and Co Wexford); *b* 12 Sept 1880; *educ* Harrow and RMC Sandhurst; Col TA cmdg 5th/7th Bn Hants Regt, Maj Irish Gds, Capt Roy Fus; S Africa 1902, Tibet Mission 1904 (present Gyantse and march to Lhasa), WW I, Priv Sec to Parly U-Sec War 1927–28 and Paymaster-Gen 1928–29, Ld-in-Waiting 1929 and 1931–34, Capt Yeomen Gd 1934–45, Ch Whip Lds 1940–45; *m* 10 Jan 1911 Hon Clare Meriel Wingfield (*d* 1969), dau of 6th Viscount Powerscourt (*qv*), and *d* 1953, having had:

1 Arthur Patrick Spencer; *b* 23 March 1914; *educ* Harrow and RMC; Maj Coldstream Gds; *d* of wounds recd in action N Africa Dec 1942

2 DERMOT RICHARD CLAUD CHICHESTER, **5th and present Baron Templemore and 7th and present Marquess of Donegall**

3 +Desmond Clive, MC [The Lord Desmond Chichester MC, Preston Hill, Preston, Hitchin, Herts SG4 7UH]; *b* 27 Jan 1920; *educ* Harrow and Ch Ch Oxford (BA 1944, MA 1945); granted 1977 rank of marquess's yr s, Maj Coldstream Gds (ret), ADC to Govr-Gen Canada 1948–50, WW II N Africa and Italy (despatches), dir Colne Valley Water Co 1956–91 (Chm 1983); *m* 1st 7 March 1946 Lorna Althea (*d* 9 April 1948), dau of Capt Montagu Hamer Ravenhill (*see* 1938 edn COLLETON, Bt), and widow of (a) Geoffrey Christopher Appleby Holt, P/O RAF and (b) Capt Richard Cecil Twining, Welsh Gds, and has issue:

(1) +(Desmond) Shane Spencer [Shane Chichester Esq, Cygnet House, Martyr Worthy, Hants SO21 1DZ]; *b* 9 April 1948; *m* 1976 *(Isabel) Jane, dau of Michael George Thomas Webster, of The Vale, Windsor Forest, Berks, and has issue:

1a +Patrick Michael Desmond; *b* 1980

2a +Henry Richard; *b* 1981

1a *Louisa Clare; *b* 1978

2 (cont.) Lord Desmond Chichester *m* 2nd 12 April 1951 *Felicity Stella, dau of Maj John Fenwick Harrison (*see* BURNHAM, B), and has further issue:

(2) +Dermot Michael Claud [Dermot Chichester Esq, Lowick House, Lowick, Northants NN14 3BL]; *b* 22 Nov 1953; *m* 1st 1975 (*divorce* 1980) Frances Jane Berners, dau of Michael Edward Ranulph Allsopp (*see* HINDLIP, B); *m* 2nd 1982 *Shan, dau of Alastair Ros McIndoe, of Heythrop Cottage, Wyck Rissington, Glos, and has issue:

1a +Rory Alastair St Clair; *b* 1985

1a *Ottilie Georgia; *b* 1988

2a *Sapphira Rose; *b* 1990

The **1st Marquess** *m* 2nd 24 Oct 1788 Charlotte (*d* 19 Sept 1789), widow of Thomas Moore, of Barn, Co Tipperary, and dau and coheir of Conway Spencer, of Tremary Co Down; *m* 3rd 12 Oct 1790 Barbara (*d* 28 Dec 1829), dau of Rev Luke Godfrey, DD, Rector Middleton, Yorks, and *d* without further issue 5 Jan 1799

DONERAILE

Arms: Arg. fretty argent, a chief or. **Crest:** A griffin passant or. **Supporters:** Two griffins or, wings elevated az. fretty arg. **Motto:** *Haut et bon* ('Great and good'). **Creations:** B. (I) 2 July 1776, V. (I) 22 June 1785.

THE 10TH VISCOUNT DONERAILE, of Doneraile, Co Cork, and **Baron Doneraile**, of Doneraile, Co Cork (Richard Allen St Leger); *b* 17 Aug 1946; *s* f 1983; *educ* Rancho Alamitos High Sch and Orange Coast Coll, Coasta Mesa, California; *m* 1969 *Kathleen Mary, er dau of Nathaniel Simcox, of Church town, Mallow, Co Cork, and has issue:

1 +NATHANIEL WARHAM ROBERT ST JOHN; *b* 13 Sept 1971

1 *Maeve Isobel Melva; *b* 1974

Lineage: RALPH ST LEGER, of Ulcombe, Kent; Ld Manor Harbleton, Kent; *m* Anne, dau of Sir Edward Hart, and had, with other issue:

1 ANTHONY (Sir)

2 George; *m* Thomasin, dau of John Heath, of Herne, Kent, and had, with a dau:

(1) Anthony (Sir), Master of the Rolls Ireland 1603–09; *m* 1st Eleanor (*dsp* 2 Feb 1598), dau of Richard Markham, of Seggebrooke, Lincs; *m* 2nd Mary (*d* 19 Dec 1603), dau of Francis Southwell, of Wyndham Hall, Norfolk (*see* SOUTHWELL, V), and widow of (a) Thomas Sydney, (b) Nicholas Gorges and (c) Sir Conyers Clifford, Govr Connaught, and by her had issue:

1a Anthony (Sir), of Wierton House and Bobbing Court, Kent; ktd 1627

The er son,

Sir ANTHONY ST LEGER, KG (1541), PC (1538), of Ulcombe, Kent, Ld Manor Harbleton, Ld Dep Ireland 1540–53; *b c* 1496; *m* Agnes, dau and heir of Hugh Warham, of Malshanger, Hants, and *d* 1559, leaving issue:

1 WILLIAM, of whom we treat

2 Warham (Sir), PC (I); Sheriff Kent 1560, Ld Manor Harbleton; ancestor of the ST LEGERs of Ulcombe, Kent

The er son,

WILLIAM ST LEGER; *m* Isabel, dau of Thomas Keys, and had issue:

Sir WARHAM ST LEGER; Commr Govt Munster 1599; *m* Elizabeth Rothe, of Kilkenny (*d* 17 Jan 1620), widow of (a) Capt Humphrey Mackworth and (b) Henry Davells, and was *k* in single combat by Hugh Maguire, Chief of Fermanagh, leaving issue:

Sir WILLIAM ST LEGER, PC; Lord Pres of Munster 1627, MP Cork 1639, Sgt-Maj-Gen 1639; *m* Gertrude de Vries, of Lower Germany, and *d* 2 July 1642, leaving issue:

1 William (Sir), MP, *k* Battle of Newbury 1644

2 John, of Doneraile, Co Cork; *m* 1st 1655 Lady Mary Chichester, er dau and coheir of 1st Earl of Donegall (*see* DONEGALL, M), and *d* 31 March 1696, having had, with two daus:

(1) ARTHUR ST LEGER, 1st VISCOUNT DOWNERAYLE or DONERAILE, Co Cork, so *cr* 23 June 1703, as also BARON KILMAYDEN, Co Waterford (both I), PC (I 1715); MP Doneraile 1692–93; *m* 24 June 1690 Elizabeth, dau and heir of John Hayes, of Winchelsea, Sussex, and *d* 7 July 1727, leaving:

1a ARTHUR ST LEGER, 2nd VISCOUNT DONERAILE; *b c* 1695; MP Doneraile 1715–27; *m* 1st 8 June 1717 Mary, only child of 4th Baron Mohun of Okehampton, and had issue:

1b ARTHUR MOHUN ST LEGER, 3rd VISCOUNT DONERAILE; *b* 7 Aug 1718; *m* 1st 3 April 1738 Mary, heir of Anthony Sheppard, of Newcastle, Co Longford; *m* 2nd 3 June 1739 Catherine, est dau of 4th Viscount Massereene (*see* MASSEREENE and FERRARD, V), and *dsp* Aug 1750

1a (cont.) The 2nd VISCOUNT *m* 2nd March 1725 Catherine Sarah, dau of Capt John Conyngham, and *d* 13 March 1733/4, having by her had no surv issue

2a John; *k* 1741 in a duel

3a HAYES ST LEGER, 4th and last VISCOUNT DONERAILE of the 1703 *cr*, PC (I 1751), MP Doneraile 1728–50; *m* 1722 Elizabeth (*d* 4 Dec 1768), est dau and coheir of Joseph Deane, of Crumlin, Co Dublin, Chief Baron of the Exchequer, and *dsp* 25 April 1767, when his titles expired

1a Elizabeth; *m* Richard Aldworth, of Newmarket, Co Cork, MP, gs of Sir Richard Aldworth (*d* 25 April 1776), Provost Mareschal of Munster, and *d* 1773, leaving issue:

1b Boyle, of Newmarket, Co Cork, ancestor of the ALDWORTHs of Newmarket

2b ST LEGER, of whom presently

2 John St Leger *m* 2nd Afra, dau of Thomas Harflete, of Trapham, Ash, Kent, and had further issue, with a dau:

(2) William; *d* 1678

(3) John (Sir), MP Doneraile, Baron of the Exchequer in Ireland; *m* 2nd Lavina, dau of Kingsmill Pennefather, of Newpark, Co Tipperary, MP, and *d* at his seat, Grangemellan, Co Kildare, 14 May 1743, leaving issue

The 4th and last VISCOUNT ST LEGER (of the 1703 *cr*)'s nephew,

ST LEGER ALDWORTH later ST LEGER (took arms with surname 9 May 1767 on inheriting estates of his uncle, the last Viscount Doneraile of the previous *cr*), **1st Viscount Doneraile**, of Doneraile, Co Cork, so *cr* 22 June 1785, as also earlier 2 July 1776 BARON DONERAILE, of Doneraile, Co Cork (both I); MP Doneraile 1749–76; *m* Mary (*d* 3 March 1778), est dau of Redmond Barry, of Ballyclough, Co Cork, and *d* 15 May 1787, having had, with other issue (including a dau Louisa Anne, *m* Lt-Col Francis Leighton; *see* LEIGHTON, Bt):

1 HAYES ST LEGER, **2nd Viscount Doneraile**, MP Doneraile 1777–87; *b* 9 March 1755; *m* 3 Sept 1785 Charlotte Bernard (*d* 2 Sept 1835), sister of 1st Earl of Bandon (*see* 1970 edn), and *d* 8 Nov 1819, having had, with two daus:

(1) HAYES ST LEGER, **3rd Viscount Doneraile**, rep I peer, Col S Cork Militia; *b* 9 May 1786; *m* 14 June 1816 Charlotte Esther (*d* 7 Feb 1846), dau of 3rd Earl of Bandon (*see* 1970 edn), and *d* 27 March 1854, leaving:

1a HAYES ST LEGER, **4th Viscount Doneraile**, DL; rep I peer, Hon Col 9th Bn KRRC; *b* 30 Sept 1818; *m* 20 Aug 1851 Mary Anne Grace Louisa (*d* 24 Feb 1907), only dau of George Lenox Conyngham, and *dspms* 26 Aug 1887 from rabies contracted after being bitten by a fox the preceding Jan, having had issue:

1b Hayes Warham; *b* and *d* 1852

1b Ursula Clara Emily; *m* 23 April 1874 2nd and last Baron Castletown (*dsp* 29 May 1937; *see* 1937 edn), and *d* 11 March 1927

2b May; *d* young 6 May 1867

2 Richard, Col; *b* 12 July 1756; *m* 1st 20 July 1779 Anne (*d* 19 July 1809), est dau of Charles Blakeney, of Holywell, Co Roscommon, and had issue:

(1) Richard Thomas Arthur (Rev), Vicar Otterford, Somerset; *b* 1 April 1790; *m* 13 May 1824 Charlotte (*d* 2 Oct 1856), 2nd dau and in her issue coheir of Sir John Frederick, 5th Bt (*qv*), and *d* 28 Jan 1875, having had issue:

1a RICHARD ARTHUR ST LEGER, **5th Viscount Doneraile**; *b* 22 Feb 1825; *d* unm 1 Jan 1891

2a Edward Frederick (Rev), MA, Rector of Scotton, Lincs; *b* 23 July 1832; *m* 7 Jan 1864 Caroline Elizabeth (*d* 17 May 1913), dau of William Richard Bishop, of Exeter, and *d* 5 Dec 1881, having had issue:

1b EDWARD ST LEGER, **6th Viscount Doneraile** Temple, JP Co London; *b* 6 Oct 1866; *educ* New Coll Oxford (MA); barrister Inner, chm City of Westminster Bd of Guardians 1926–27, chm Metropolitan Asylums Bd 1928–30, Alderman City of Westminster May 1919 and 1920, Offr Legion of Honour; *d* unm 7 Sept 1941

2b Ralph; *b* 4 April 1868; *d* unm 12 April 1908

3b HUGH ST LEGER, **7th Viscount Doneraile**; slr High Court; *b* 6 Aug 1869; *m* 18 Dec 1919 Mary Isobel (*d* 1 Nov 1973 aged 83), est dau of Francis Morice, JP, of Whakapunake, Gisborne, NZ, and *dsp* 18 Dec 1956

4b Richard; *b* 19 June 1872; *d* 12 Jan 1879

1b Ethel; *d* unm 6 Feb 1942

2b Edith (twin with Ethel); *d* unm 2 May 1927

3b Ursula; *d* unm 19 Aug 1902

1a Elizabeth; *d* 28 Nov 1886

2a Frances; *d* 27 June 1867

3a Mary Anne; *m* 4 Jan 1854 John B Fellowes (*d* 12 May 1856), and *d* 18 June 1903, leaving issue

(2) Francis Barry Boyle, barrister; *b* 1790; *d* unm 20 Nov 1829

(1) Marianne; *m* 10 Feb 1807 Rev Hon Edward Taylor (*see* HEADFORT M) and *d* 22 March 1859

(2) Henrietta Frances; *d* 30 Nov 1878

2 (cont.) The Hon Richard St Leger *m* 2nd 1 Oct 1809 Elizabeth (*d* 29 April 1871), only child of Daniel Robert Bullen, of Old Connaught, Co Dublin, and *d* 30 Dec 1840, having by her had issue:

(3) John Gillis, of Rathmines House, Co Dublin; *b* 19 July 1811; *m* 12 Oct 1848 Charlotte Anne (*d* 1883), 2nd dau of William Salde Gully, of Trevennen House, Cornwall, and *d* 17 Jan 1867, having had, with other issue:

1a Richard William; *b* 9 Jan 1852; *m* 28 Aug 1877 Matilda Emma (*d* 1901), dau of Samuel Higgins Burroughs, and *d* 20 March 1925, having had issue:

1b ALGERNON EDWARD, **8th Viscount**

2b St John Richard, Lt London Regt; *b* 1885; *k* WW I 1916

1b Josephine Irene; *b* 1880; *m* 1899 Samuel Baker Weldon (*d* 1941), yst son of Rev Robert Smythe Weldon, and *d* 9 March 1958, leaving issue

2b Agnes Claire; *b* 1890; *d* 1900

3b (Charlotte) Hazel; *b* 1892; *m* 8 Oct 1913, as his 2nd w, Francis Boxwell (*d* 25 Jan 1950), est son of John Boxwell, of Butlerstown, Ballycogley, Co Wexford, and *d* 17 March 1875, leaving issue

2a William Fagan; *b* 18 Nov 1853; *m* 4 Nov 1886 Anne Leslie (*d* 16 Jan 1929), dau of M C Hendley, of Mount Rivers, Co Cork, and *dsp* 18 March 1916

3a St John James, Lt-Col 2nd Bn Leinster Regt; *b* 11 July 1856; *m* 8 Jan 1885 Agnes Mary Helyar (*d* 9 Aug 1919), dau of Rev William Nott, Rector Sutterton, Lincs, and *d* 22 Dec 1916

1a Josephine Eliza; *m* 14 July 1874 Charles G Perrins (*d* 1887), Cdr P&O Co's service, and *d* Nov 1931

(4) James Aldworth, Capt RN; *b* 20 Feb 1814; *m* 16 Aug 1853 Maria Emilia, 2nd dau of Rev W H Flemyng, and *d* 19 Nov 1877, leaving issue:

1a Richard Flemyng; *b* 9 Nov 1858
(5) William Henry, Co Inspr RIC; *b* 6 Jan 1816; *m* 1st Aug 1841 Emily, dau of Luke Davis; *m* 2nd 12 Oct 1848 Katherine Maria, dau of Major John Doyle, 72nd Regt, and *dsp* 3 May 1886
3 James (Ven), Archdeacon Cloyne, Rector Castletownroche; *b* 4 Oct 1757; *m* 2 March 1809 Catherine (*d* 12 March 1821), yst dau of Thomas Williams, of Epsom, Surrey, and *d* 22 Nov 1834, leaving issue:
(1) Charles Arthur; *b* 14 Feb 1817; *m* 25 July 1838 Jane Robina (*d* 30 Dec 1884), dau of William Hawksley, of 36 Lowndes St, London SW1, formerly 12th Lancers, and *d* 4 Dec 1874, leaving issue:
1a Arthur Hayes Francis; *b* 15 June 1846; *m* 15 Dec 1869 Ada Henrietta Maria (*m* 2nd 4 March 1905 Count de St Ferriol), 2nd dau of John Morison, of Bognie and Frendraught, Aberdeenshire, and *d* 31 July 1902, having had:
1b Valentine Aldworthy; *b* 14 Feb 1871; *d* 30 March 1873
2a Archibald William; *b* 11 April 1853; *d* 1934
(1) Caroline; *m* 11 Feb 1835 Thomas Netherton Langford, Post Capt RN, and had issue
(2) Catherine; *m* 23 Feb 1843 her cousin Rev Francis Knyvett Leighton (*d* 13 Oct 1881), DD, and *d* March 1811, leaving issue (*see* LEIGHTON, Bt)

The 7th VISCOUNT's cousin,

ALGERNON EDWARD ST LEGER, **8th Viscount Doneraile**; *b* 10 June 1878; *m* 27 Nov 1919 Sylvia Stephenson, dau of Alexander Mitchell, of Jarrow-on-Tyne, and *d* 18 Nov 1957, leaving:

RICHARD ST JOHN ST LEGER, **9th Viscount Doneraile**; *b* 29 Oct 1923; *m* 1945 *Melva Jean, dau of George W Clifton, of St Louis, Mo., and *d* 1983, leaving issue:
1 RICHARD ALLEN ST LEGER, **10th and present Viscount Doneraile**
2 +David Hugh; *b* 3 Nov 1950; *educ* California State U, Long Beach; communications and electronics engr
3 +Edward Hayes; *b* 1 Aug 1960; *educ* U of Calif, Riverside
1 *Elizabeth Adele; *b* 12 Jan 1953
2 *Karen Jean; *b* 6 Oct 1955; *m* 1977 (*divorce* 1981) Richard Lehman, and has issue:
(1) *Corey R; *b* 1980

DONOUGHMORE

Arms: Quarterly, 1st and 4th, per pale gu. and az. a lion rampant between eight cross-crosslets arg. (for HUTCHINSON); 2nd az. a fess between three stag's heads erased in chief arg. and a demi-lion rampant in base or (for HELY); 3rd, az. a garb or between three wolf's heads erased arg. (for NIXON). **Crest:** Out of a ducal coronet a demi-cockatrice, wings elevated az. **Supporters:** Two cockatrices, wings elevated or, collared sa., combs and wattles gu., each charged on the breast with a wreath of laurel vert. **Motto:** *Fortiter gerit crucem* ('He bravely bears the cross'). **Creations:** B. (I) 16 Oct 1783, V. (I) 20 Nov 1797, E. (I) 31 Dec 1800, V (UK) 14 July 1821 (Hutchinson).

THE 8TH EARL OF DONOUGHMORE OF KNOCKLOFTY, Viscount Hutchinson of Knocklofty, Co Tipperary, **Viscount Donoughmore of Knocklofty**, Co Tipperary, and **Baron Donoughmore of Knocklofty**, Co Tipperary (Richard Michael John Hely-Hutchinson) [The Rt Hon The Earl of Donoughmore, The Manor House, Bampton, Oxon OX18 2LQ]; *b* 8 Aug 1927; *s f* 1981; *educ* Winchester, Groton and New Coll Oxford (MA, BM, BCh 1952); late Capt RAMC; *m* 1 Nov 1951 *Sheila, only dau of Frank Frederick Parsons, and has issue:
1 +JOHN MICHAEL JAMES, *Viscount Suirdale* [Viscount Suirdale, 38 Thornton Ave, London W4 1QG]; *b* 7 Aug 1952; *educ* Harrow; *m* 8 Jan 1977 *Marie-Claire, er dau of Gerard van den Driessche, of Wondelgem, nr Ghent, Belgium, and has issue:
(1) +Richard Gregory; *b* 3 July 1980
(1) *Marie-Pierre Joanna; *b* 13 March 1978
(2) *Tatiana Louise; *b* 1985
2 +Timothy Mark [The Hon Timothy Hely-Hutchinson, 25 Royal Crescent, London W11 4SN]; *b* 26 Oct 1953; *educ* Eton and Magdalen Coll Oxford; with Macmillan 1975–82, md Macdonald & Co 1982–86 and Headline Book Publishing 1986–93, gp ch exec Hodder Headline 1993–
3 +Nicholas David; *b* 30 April 1955; *educ* Harrow; *m* 19 June 1982 *Fiona Margaret MacIntyre, yr dau of Maj W R Watson, of Wokingham, Berks, and has issue:
(1) +Seamus David; *b* 1987
(1) *Flora Clare; *b* 1984
4 +Ralph Charles; *b* 16 Dec 1961; *educ* Eton; *m* 3 Nov 1995 *Caroline, only dau of John Rylance and Mrs Colette Davis, of Shiplake, Oxon, and has:
(1) +Ranulph Edward; *b* 5 Aug 1996

Lineage: FRANCIS HELY, of Gortroe, Co Cork; *m* Prudence, dau of Mathias Earbury, and had:

JOHN HELY later HELY HUTCHINSON (on his w's inheriting the Hutchinson estates), PC (GB 1787); *educ* Trin Coll Dublin; barrister 1748, MP Lanesborough 1759–61, Cork 1761–90 and Taghmon 1790–94, Prime Serjeant 1761–64, Provost Trin Coll Dublin 1774–94, Pncpl Sec State Ireland and Keeper Privy Seal 1777–94; *m* 8 June 1751 Christiana, *cr* 16 Oct 1783 **Baroness Donoughmore of Knocklofty**, Co Tipperary (I) (*d* 24 June 1788), dau of Abraham Nickson, of Munny, Co Wicklow, and great-niece and heir of Richard Hutchinson, of Knocklofty, Co Tipperary, and had, with other issue:
1 RICHARD HELY HELY-HUTCHINSON, **1st Earl of Donoughmore of Knocklofty**, so *cr* 31 Dec 1800, with special remainder to the male descendants of his mother, as also earlier 20 Nov 1797 VISCOUNT DONOUGHMORE OF KNOCKLOFTY, Co Tipperary (both I), and 14 July 1821 VISCOUNT HUTCHINSON OF KNOCKLOFTY, Co Tipperary (UK); *b* 29 Jan 1756; Lt-Gen, Govr Co Tipperary and Lord Treasurer's Remembrancer Court of Exchequer Ireland; *d* unm 22 Aug 1825
2 JOHN HELY-HUTCHINSON, **2nd Earl of Donoughmore of Knocklofty**, GCB (1815, KB 1801); *b* 15 May 1757; *educ* Eton, Magdalen Coll Oxford and Trin Coll Dublin; joined Army 1774, Lt-Coll 77th Regt 1783, Col 94th Foot 1794–95, 2nd Bn 40th Foot 1799–1802, 74th Foot 1802–06, 57th Foot 1806–11 and 18th Foot 1811–32, Maj Gen 1796, Lt Gen 1803, Gen 1813, Govr Stirling Castle, C-in-C Egypt 1801, *cr* 5 Dec 1801 BARON HUTCHINSON OF ALEXANDRIA AND KNOCKLOFTY, Co Tipperary (UK), for mil servs with a pension of £2,000 p.a.; *d* unm 29 June 1832, when the Barony of Hutchinson of Alexandria and Knocklofty expired
3 Francis; *b* 26 Oct 1769; MP Dublin U and Naas; *m* Frances Wilhelmina (*d* 1 June 1830), dau and heir of Henry Nixon, of Belmont, Co Wexford, and *d* 16 Dec 1827, leaving issue:
(1) JOHN, **3rd Earl**
(2) Henry, of Weston, Northants; *b* 26 March 1790; Col; granted with his siblings rank of earl's daus/yr s; *m* 26 April 1825 Harriet (*d* 16 July 1864), widow of Hon Frederick Silvester North Douglas and est dau of William Wrightson, of Cudworth, Yorks, and *d* 2 July 1834, leaving issue:
1a Harriet Frances; *m* 2 Oct 1877 Sir Wyndham Edward Hanmer, 4th Bt, of Hanmer (*qv*), and *dsp* 17 May 1911
2a Frederica Katherine; *m* 28 Dec 1850 Col Arthur John Reynell Pack (*d* 16 Aug 1860), CB, of Avisford, Sussex, and *d* 7 Oct 1904, leaving issue
3a Georgina Mary; *m* 3 Aug 1848 Rev Charles Edward Thomas (*d* 12 April 1901) (*see* 1970 edn WILLINGDON, M), and *d* 1 Jan 1923, leaving issue
4a Louisa Lucy; *m* 20 Aug 1857 Sir Sitwell Reresby Sitwell, 3rd Bt, of Renishaw (*qv*), and *d* 31 Oct 1911, leaving issue
5a Marianne Christiana Isabella; *m* 13 March 1860 Arthington Worsley (*d* 3 June 1861), 2nd s of Sir William Worsley 1st Bt (*qv*), and *d* 11 Aug 1893, leaving issue
(3) Coote, Capt RN; *m* 26 Aug 1834 Sophia (*d* 30 April 1896), yst dau of Rev Sir Samuel Synge Hutchinson, 3rd Bt (*see* SYNGE, Bt), and *d* 6 May 1842, having had issue:
1a John, of Seafield, Donabate, Co Dublin, DL, JP, High Sheriff 1872; *b* 20 Nov 1836; *m* 25 Feb 1865 Mary Louisa (*d* 26 March 1915), est dau of Robert Tottenham, of Annamult, Co Kilkenny, and *d* 4 Sept 1919, leaving:
1b Coote Robert, OBE (1919), Lt-Col cmdg Res Bn Royal Fus; *b* 6 Feb 1870; *m* 10 Jan 1914 Julia Harriet Vere (*d* 10 June 1948), 8th dau of William Clayton Browne-Clayton, DL, of Browne's Hill, Co Carlow, and *d* 30 Sept 1930, leaving issue:
1c John; *b* 15 Oct 1914; *educ* St Columba's Coll; *d* 2 Jan 1985
2c +Michael [Maj Michael Hely-Hutchinson, Croft Cottage, New Marton, St Martins, Oswestry, Salop], Maj Royal Norfolk Regt WW II 1939–43 Malaya (POW); *b* 12 April 1916; *educ* Repton and RMC Sandhurst; *m* 29 Sept 1951 *Ruth Somerled, 2nd dau of Kenneth Mackenzie, MD, FRCS, of Auckland, NZ, and has issue:
1d *Caroline Anne [Mrs Timothy Harlow, Whitley House, Bradninch, Devon EX5 4LA]; *b* 26 Sept 1954; *m* 1979 *Timothy Neal Harlow, MB, ChB, and has issue:
1e *Alastair Michael; *b* 1984
1e *Jennifer Fiona; *b* 1985
3c David Coote ; *b* 5 Nov 1918; *educ* Bedford Sch; *m* 25 Sept 1948 *Geraldine Mary, yst dau of Donough Richard O'Brien (*see* INCHINQUIN, B), and *d* 26 April 1994, leaving:
1d *Fiona Kathryn O'Brien [Miss Fiona Hely-Hutchinson, Parteena-Lax, Co Limerick, Ireland]; *b* 2 Dec 1965
1c *Mary Caroline [Miss Mary Hely-Hutchinson, Newport House, Donabate, Co Dublin, Ireland]; *b* 15 Oct 1914
2c *Julia Louisa [Miss Julia Hely-Hutchinson, Newport House, Donabate, Co Dublin, Ireland]; *b* 13 March 1921
2b Richard George, DSO (1915), Col 1st Bn Roy Fus WW I (despatches, wounded twice); *b* 8 March 1871; *educ* Clifton and RMC Sandhurst; *m* 20 April 1899 Alice (*d* 29 Aug 1962), only dau of William Crozier Cunningham, of Dante House, Whiteabbey, Co Antrim, and *d* 10 June 1953, leaving issue:
1c Pamela; *b* 7 Jan 1909
1b Ethel Mary; *b* 3 March 1868; *d* unm 6 May 1886
2b Cecil Frances Katherine; *b* 3 March 1869; *d* unm 29 Jan 1950

3b Eleanor Blanche; *b* 27 July 1872; *d* unm 3 Oct 1946
2a Francis Henry, RN; *b* 5 Dec 1839; *m* 21 Jan 1882 Eliza (*d* 12 June 1928), dau of Joseph Stroud, and *d* 8 July 1905, leaving issue:
1b Samuel Arthur; *b* 26 Jan 1889; *d* unm 9 April 1967
1b Ruth; *b* 19 April 1884; *d* unm 25 May 1963
2b Frances Florence; *b* 8 March 1886; *d* unm 28 May 1952
1a Sophia Dorothy; *b* 9 Dec 1840; *d* unm 26 May 1927
(4) George; *m* 1826, Eugenie, est dau of Baron d'Angell de Kleinfeld, of Paris, and *dsp* 17 Nov 1845
(5) Richard; *d* Feb 1877 aged 74
(1) Anna Louisa; *m* 18 April 1811 Very Rev Thomas John de Burgh (*d* 4 Sept 1845), MA, of Oldtown, Co Kildare, Dean of Cloyne, and *d* 29 Dec 1857
(2) Catherine Henrietta; *m* 29 July 1814 Col Thomas Bernard (*d* 18 May 1834), of Castle Bernard, MP King's County, and *d* 1844, leaving issue
(3) Charlotte Sophia; 12 April 1831 Rev Richard Wolfe (*d* 29 July 1841), of Forenaghts, Co Kildare, nephew to Ch Justice Lord Kilwarden, and *dsp* 19 Jan 1870
(4) Louisa Frances; *m* 17 June 1824 Francis Hutchinson Synge (*d* 3 April 1833), only son of Rev Sir Samuel Hutchinson Synge, 3rd Bt (*qv*), and *d* 13 Jan 1876, leaving issue
4 Augustus Abraham, Commr Customs; *b* 20 March 1766; *m* Dec 1815 Catherine Maria (*d* 3 Nov 1824), dau of John Burke, of Clongowna, Co Tipperary, and widow of John Alexander Jones, and *d* 10 June 1834, leaving:
(1) Christopher; *dsp*
(1) Christiana Sophia Frances; *d* 11 March 1843

The 2nd EARL's nephew,

JOHN HELY-HUTCHINSON, **3rd Earl of Donoughmore of Knocklofty**, KP 1834), PC (I 1834); *b* 1787; Capt Army, served Peninsular War, MP (Whig) Co Tipperary 1826–30 and 1831–32; *m* 1st 15 June 1822 Hon Margaret Gardiner (*d* 13 Oct 1825), 7th dau of 1st Viscount Mountjoy, and had issue:
1 RICHARD JOHN, **4th Earl**
1 Margaret; *d* young 1828

The **3rd Earl** *m* 2nd 5 Sept 1827 Barbara (*d* 11 Dec 1856), 2nd dau of Lt-Col William Reynell, of Castle Reynell, Co Westmeath, by Jane, dau of Sir William Montgomery, 1st Bt, of Macbie Hill, and *d* 14 Sept 1851, having by her had another s (*d* unm) and four daus

His surv son,

RICHARD JOHN HELY-HUTCHINSON, **4th Earl of Donoughmore of Knocklofty**, PC (1858); *b* 4 April 1823; Offr 98th Foot, Lt-Col S Tipperary Militia 1849, V-Pres BOT 1858 (Pres 1859); *m* 7 April 1847 Thomasina Jocelyn (*d* 8 May 1890), est dau and heiress of Walter Steele, of Moynalty, Co Monaghan, by Mary Sophia, dau of Hon George Jocelyn (*see* RODEN, E), and had issue:
1 JOHN LUKE GEORGE **5th Earl**
2 Walter Francis (Sir), PC, GCMG; *b* 22 Aug 1849; *educ* Trin Coll Cambridge (BA), Hon LLD Edin, Lt-Govr Malta 1884–89, Govr and C-in-C: Windward Islands 1889–93, Natal and Zululand 1893–1901, Cape of Good Hope 1901–10, HC S Africa 1909; *m* 19 Feb 1881 May (*d* 15 Nov 1938), dau of Maj-Gen William Clive Justice, CMG, and *d* 23 Sept 1913, having had issue:
(1) John Walter *b* 14 Jan 1882; *educ* Eton and Trin Coll Oxford (BA 1905); *m* 23 Jan 1911 Sybil Katherine (*d* 10 Jan 1954), er dau of James Henderson, of 56 Cadogan Sq, London, and *d* 11 Sept 1955, having had issue:
1a Patrick Walter Richard, W/Sgt RA WW II; *b* 23 Nov 1913, *ka* Burma 17 March 1944
(2) Christopher Douglas, MC (1919), Capt RA WW I, pres Br S Africa Co, dir Westminster Bank; *b* 30 Jan 1885; *educ* Eton; *m* 3 Nov 1914 Gladys (*d* 21 Feb 1974), only dau of William Beachy Head, of Johannesburg, and *d* 7 Nov 1958, leaving:
1a *Frances Anne [Lady Stevens, East Worlington House, Crediton, Devon EX17 4JS]; *b* 20 May 1917; *m* 11 Oct 1940 Sir John Melior Stevens (*d* 27 Oct 1973), KCMG, DSO, OBE, md Morgan Grenfell, and has issue:
1b *John Christopher Courtenay [John Stevens Esq MEP, 39 St James's Place, London SW1A 1NS]; *b* 23 May 1955; *educ* Winchester and Magdalen Coll Oxford; merchant banker 1976–89, advsr St James's Place Capital plc 1989–, MEP (C) Thames Valley 1989–
1b *Jane Frances [Dr Jane Stevens, 3 Clarendon St, Cambridge]; *b* 12 April 1945; MD
2b *Mary Anne Victoria [Mrs John Myerscough, 39 Campden St, London W8]; *b* 1 April 1947; MA (London), art historian; *m* 1980 *John Myerscough, and has issue:
1c *John Claude; *b* 1982
1c *Catherine Anne; *b* 1986
(3) Maurice Robert, MC, Capt Irish Gds, MP Hastings 1937–45, served WW I 1916–18 (despatches); *b* 22 May 1887; *educ* Eton and Balliol Coll Oxford (BA 1908); *m* 11 Aug 1920 Melita Agnes Mary (*d* 1987), yr dau of Adml Sir Colin Keppel, GCVO, KCIE, CB, DSO (*see* ALBEMARLE, E), and *d* 11 Feb 1961, having had issue:
1a Dermot Arthur John; *b* 25 June; *d* 9 Sept 1922
2a +Henry Aymar [Henry Hely-Hutchinson Esq, 22 Kylestrome House, Cundy St, London SW1W 9JT]; Lt Coldstream Gds 1944–47, memb Lond Stock Exchange 1966, ptnr G S Herbert & Sons 1968; *b* 14 Nov 1925; *educ* Eton; *m* 27 April 1957 *Maria Anna, dau of Charles de Erney, of Budapest, and has issue:
1b +Nicholas Charles; *b* 28 March 1958; *m* 1986 *Kate Johanna, er dau of Timothy Connolly, of Knockholt, Kent, and has issue:
1c +Harry Thomas; *b* 9 April 1992
1c *Rose (Rosie) Millie; *b* 1990
2c *Lily Matilda; *b* 25 Oct 1994
2b +Colin Henry [Colin Hely-Hutchinson, Hopewell House, Marsh Green, Kent TN8 5QS]; *b* 9 Aug 1959; *m* 7 June 1983 *Emma (Pipi), er dau of Hugh Morton, of London and New York, and has issue:
1c +James Alexander; *b* 21 April 1986
2c +Nicholas Henry; *b* 3 Dec 1991
1c *Victoria Sarah; *b* 29 Oct 1984
2c *Alexandra Melita; *b* 26 Jan 1990
3c *Lucinda Catherine; *b* 19 July 1994
1b *Melita Louise [Mrs Stephen Glaister, Arlebury Park Cottage, Alresford, Hants SO24 9ES]; *b* 6 June 1962; *m* 1992 *Stephen Blair Glaister and has issue:
1c *Henry Augustus; *b* 1994
2c *Albert Constantine; *b* 1996
1c *Jessica; *b* 1993
3a +Colin Christopher [Colin Hely-Hutchinson Esq, c/o 22 Kylestrome House, Cundy St, London SW1W 9JT]; *b* 14 Nov 1925; *educ* Eton; late Lt Irish Gds
4a Robert Anthony Walter; *b* 14 Feb 1933; *d* 6 June 1950
1a *(Marie) Elizabeth [Miss Elizabeth Hely-Hutchinson, 35 Richmond Court, 200 Sloane St, London SW1X 9QU]; *b* 30 May 1921
2a Myrtle Melita; WW II 1942–46 in ATS; *b* 6 Aug 1924; *m* 17 July 1951 *Alexander Lindsay Aymer, only surv s of James Aymer, of Bervie, Kincardineshire, and *d* 1989
3a *Diana Margaret [Mrs Walter von Halle, 7 Condray Place, Battersea Church Rd, London SW11 3PE]; *b* 4 Aug 1928; *m* 8 Dec 1960 *Walter Franz Erich von Halle, son of Prof Dr Ernst Hermann von Halle, of Berlin-Grunewald
4a *Patricia May, JP, DL Co Antrim [Mrs George MacKean JP DL, Chapel Court, 51a Loughermore Rd, Co Antrim BT41 2HN]; *b* 11 Oct 1929; *m* 5 Sept 1950 Maj George Burrell MacKean (*d* 1983), DL, JP, s of Charles Louis MacKean, JP, of Loughanmore, Dunadry, and has had issue:
1b *William Muir; *b* 1 Dec 1954; *educ* Eton; *m* 1988 *Charlotte, yr dau of Paddy Davies, of Slinfold, Sussex, and has issue:
1c *George Louis; *b* 1992
2c *William Patrick; *b* 1996
1c *Emily Rose; *b* 1990
2b *Shane Charles Robert; *b* 5 Sept 1958; *m* 1983 *Elizabeth A Paul, of Maryland, USA, and has issue:
1c *William Muir; *b* 1987
2c *Cassian Donald Burrell; *b* 1988
3c *Milo David Feargus; *b* 1992
1c *India May Frances; *b* 1990
1b *Kirsten Henrietta; *b* 10 Dec 1951; *m* 1st 1972 (*divorce* 1986) Sir (Robert) Nicholas Oliver Couper, 6th Bt (*qv*); *m* 2nd 1987 *Michael J Tussaud
2b Claudia Margaret Diana; *b* 5 July 1953; *d* 23 April 1957
3b *Georgia Isabella; *b* 26 July 1961; *m* 1983 *Maj Michael B Stubington and has:
1c *Claudia Mary; *b* 1990
2c *Lucca Inez; *b* 1995
(4) Jocelyn Frederick Osbert; *b* 17 July 1891; *d* 18 Jan 1893
(5) (Christian) Victor Noel Hope; *b* 28 Dec 1901; *educ* Eton and Balliol Coll Oxford; D Mus 1941, lecturer music Cape Town U 1922–26, music staff BBC 1926–34, Prof Music Birmingham U 1934–44, Dir Music BBC 1944–47; *m* 20 June 1925 Marjory Anna (*d* 1988), yr dau of Dr Dirk de Vos Hugo, and *d* 11 March 1947, leaving:
1a +John Richard [Dr John Hely-Hutchinson, Moolmanshof, 217 Voortrek Str, Swellendam 6740, S Africa]; *b* 6 March 1929; *educ* Eton; PhD, CEng; *m* 27 April 1957 *Allison Joyce, only dau of Ernest Simpson, and adopted:
*John Andrew; *b* 7 Sept 1960
*Teresa Mary; *b* 16 May 1963
2a +Christopher Adrian [Lt-Cdr Christopher Hely-Hutchinson RN (ret), The Garden House, 3 Brand Lane, Ludlow, Salop], CEng, MIMechE, AMIMarE, AMBIM; *b* 20 Dec 1931; *educ* Eton; *m* 6 July 1963 *Beatrice Mary, yr dau of Stephen Reginald Albert Harris, of Parsons Hill, Barbon, Westmorland, and has issue:
1b +Adam Hugo; *b* 13 Aug 1968
1b *Henrietta Lucy; *b* 21 July 1973
(1) Violet La Vallette; *b* 26 July *d* 11 Dec 1883
(2) Natalie Leila Margaret; *b* 5 Aug 1894; *m* 9 May 1916 Gerard Mackworth Young, CIE, ICS, est s of Sir William Mackworth Young, KCSI (*d* 28 Nov 1965), and had issue (*see* YOUNG, Bt, of Formosa Place)
3 Patrick Maurice, Lt and Cdr RN, Torpedo Offr to Govr Victoria Australia 1883–88, served Zulu War 1877–79 (medal with clasp) and Egyptian War 1882 (medal with clasp and Khedive's Bronze Star); *b* 27 April 1855; *d* unm 27 Jan 1893
4 Granville William, JP Co Tipperary; *b* 24 Sept 1858; *m* 1st 14 July 1891 Grace (*d* 26 Jan 1893), widow of John Charters, of Petre Hall, Coventry, and dau of Major Clement Heigham, of Hunston Hall; *m* 2nd 7 Nov 1903 Eleanor Beatrice (*d* 25 March 1928), 3rd dau of Rev H Manning Richards, of Betchworth, Winchester, and *dsp* 11 June 1906
1 Mary Sophia; *m* 14 Aug 1879 Col Lewis Vivian Loyd (*d* 21 Sept 1908), DL, MP, and *d* 30 July 1936, leaving issue
2 Margaret Frances; *m* 6 July 1882 Col Douglas James PROBY formerly HAMILTON (*d* 18 March 1931), of Elton Hall, Peterborough, DL, JP, Irish Gds (*see* PROBY, Bt, and ABERCORN, D), and *d* 2 March 1937, leaving issue

The 4th EARL *d* 22 Feb 1866; his est son,

JOHN LUKE GEORGE HELY-HUTCHINSON, **5th Earl of Donoughmore of Knocklofty**, KCMG (1879), DL, JP Cos Tipperary and Waterford; *b* 2 March 1848; *educ* Eton and Balliol Coll Oxford; Assist Commr European Commn for the Organization of Eastern Roumelia 1878–79; *m* 19 May 1874 Frances Isabella (*d* 27 April 1924), dau of Gen William Frazer Stephens, HEICS, and had issue:
1 RICHARD WALTER JOHN, **6th Earl**
1 Nina Blanche Mary; *b* 1 Oct 1876; *d* 11 May 1877
2 Evelyn, Lady-in-Waiting to HRH PRINCESS ARTHUR OF CONNAUGHT 1920–22; *b* 27 Nov 1877; *m* 1st 27 April 1905 Col Francis Douglas Farquhar (*ka*

vp cmdg Princess Patricia's Canadian LI 20 March 1915), DSO, Coldstream Gds, son of Sir Thomas Henry Farquhar, 4th Bt (*qv*), and had issue; *m* 2nd 3 May 1923 Sir Dougal Orme Malcolm (*d* 30 Aug 1955), KCMG, and *d* 18 Sept 1962

3 Norah; *b* 26 Feb 1880; *m* 1st 25 July 1906 Lt-Col Harold Ernest Brassey (*ka* 16 July 1916), RHG, and had issue (*see* BRASSEY OF APETHORPE, B); *m* 2nd Aug 1917 (*divorce* 1934) Brevet Maj Alan Charles Douglas Graham, MC, son of Sir Henry John Lowndes Graham, KCB, of 4 Cadogan Gdns, London; *m* 3rd 9 Oct 1935 Geoffrey Wilfred Melson Smith (*d* 1 Jan 1949), and *d* 2 Aug 1964

4 Margarita Oonah Isabella; *b* 27 Nov 1888; *d* 1 July 1894

The 5th EARL *d* 5 Dec 1900; his only son,

RICHARD WALTER JOHN HELY-HUTCHINSON, **6th Earl of Donoughmore of Knocklofty**, KP, PC (1918), DL, JP Cos Tipperary and Waterford; *b* 2 March 1875; *educ* New Coll Oxford (MA, Hon Fellow 1931); Capt 3rd Bn Royal Irish Regt, Col Gen List, T/Col BRCS France 1916–17 (despatches twice); memb London School Bd 1903, Priv Sec to Govr of Hong Kong 1898–1900, Parly U-Sec War 1903–05, civil Memb Army Cncl 1904–05, chm ctees and Dep Speaker Ho Lds 1911–31, Memb Senate IFS 1921, chm Special Commn Ceylon Constitution 1927–28, memb Nat Radium Tst, chm Nat Radium Commn 1933, Orders of Leopold Belgium and Charles XIII Sweden, KJStJ; *m* 21 Dec 1901 Elena Maria (*d* 22 Feb 1944), 2nd dau of Michael Paul Grace, of New York, and 40 Belgrave Square, London, and had:

1 JOHN MICHAEL HENRY, **7th Earl**

2 David Edward, Lt-Col RE (TA), served WW II; *b* 12 Jan 1911; *educ* Winchester and New Coll Oxford (BA 1932, MA 1954); *m* 7 June 1934 *Barbara Mary, 3rd dau of Maj Hugh James Wyld, of Beverstone Old Rectory, Tetbury, Glos, and *d* 1984, leaving issue:

(1) *Rose Mary [Mrs William Fernie, Manor Farm, Tellisford, Bath BA3 6RL]; *b* 10 Aug 1935; *m* 15 July 1959 *William Mackinnon Fernie and has issue:

1a *James Mackinnon; *b* 17 April 1962; *m* 1987 *Fiona Elizabeth Swann

1a *Barbara Alison; *b* 1 July 1960; *m* 1988 *Colin Francis Smith

2a *Juliet Rose; *b* 14 June 1967; *m* 1993 *Burton Simon Persse and has:

1b *Jessica Rose; *b* 4 May 1995

3a *Deborah Mary; *b* 1971; *m* 1996 *Julian Murray Wakeham

(2) *Jean Elena [Mrs Bernard Kairn, Poplar Farm, Atworth, Melksham, Wilts]; *b* 2 Feb 1939; *m* 21 July 1972 *Bernard B D Kairn, son of Mrs Arthur King, of Rowley Grange, Farleigh Hungerford, Somerset

(3) *Pollyann Elise [Mrs Hamish Lochore, Burgie House, Forres, Moray]; *b* 20 Nov 1942; *m* 6 June 1970 *Capt Hamish J Lochore, RSG, and has issue:

1a *Alexander David; *b* 6 Aug 1971

2a *Hugh Mark; *b* 18 Feb 1974

1a *Clare Hermione; *b* 1977

(4) *Kathryn Gabriel [Mrs Christopher Amery, Flash Farm, Antrobus, Northwich, Cheshire]; *b* 25 March 1944; *m* 13 Sept 1973 *Christopher B Amery, Blues and Royals (ret), and has issue:

1a *Edward Mark Richard; *b* 24 March 1975

2a *Nicholas John David; *b* 21 July 1979

(5) *Deborah Jane [Mrs William Backhouse, Layer Marney Wick, Colchester, Essex CO5 9UT]; *b* 15 April 1949; *m* 4 Nov 1971 *William Backhouse and has issue (*see* BACKHOUSE, Bt)

1 Doreen Clare, Sr Area Offr NFS WW II; *b* 3 April 1905; *m* 11 July 1927 Hon Bartholomew Pleydell-Bouverie, 3rd s of 6th Earl of Radnor (*qv*), and *d* 21 Aug 1942 as the result of an accident, leaving issue

The 6th EARL *d* 19 Oct 1948; his er son,

JOHN MICHAEL HENRY HELY-HUTCHINSON, **7th Earl of Donoughmore of Knocklofty**, Col RAC (TA), MP Peterborough 1943–June 1945, kidnapped with his wife by IRA as political hostages June 1974, released after a week; *b* 12 Nov 1902; *educ* Winchester and Magdalen Coll Oxford; *m* 27 July 1925 Dorothy Jean, MBE (1947), SSStJ (*d* 29 Dec 1995), est dau of John Beaumont Hotham, of Milne Graden, Coldstream (*see* HOTHAM, B), and *d* 1981, leaving issue:

1 RICHARD MICHAEL JOHN HELY-HUTCHINSON, **8th and present Earl of Donoughmore of Knocklofty**

2 +Mark [The Hon Mark Hely-Hutchinson, Larch Hill, Coolock Lane, Dublin 17, Ireland]; *b* 19 May 1934; *educ* Eton, Magdalen Coll Oxford (BA and BSc 1958, MA 1961) and MIT (SM 1968); late 2nd Lt Irish Gds, Dir Bank of Ireland 1975–, md Guinness Ireland 1975–82; *m* 26 May 1962 *(Rosita) Margaret, yr dau of Dr Robert Rowan Woods, MB, BCH, FRCSI, of Dublin 2, and has issue:

(1) +Henry Peter [Henry Hely-Hutchinson Esq, 16 Friars Ave, Shenfield, Essex CM15 8HY]; *b* 22 Dec 1963; *educ* Eton and Trinity Coll Dublin; *m* 22 Dec 1993 *Susan, 3rd dau of Rudolph Essex, of Southend-on-Sea, and has:

1a *Laura Beth; *b* 24 April 1996

(2) +Walter James [Walter Hely-Hutchinson Esq, 64A Furley Rd, London SE15 5UQ]; *b* 17 Dec 1966; *educ* Eton and Magdalene Coll Cambridge

(1) *Anna Doreen [Mrs Andrew Maltzoff, Flat 5, 78 Redcliffe Sq, London SW10 9BN]; *b* 17 June 1969; *educ* Trinity Coll Dublin; *m* 28 June 1997 *Andrew Maltzoff, 3rd s of Serge Maltzoff, of Paris

1 *Sara Elena [The Lady Sara Collins, High Coodham, Symington, Ayrshire KA1 5SJ]; *b* 22 Aug 1930; *m* 2 Aug 1951 *William Janson Collins and has:

(1) *William Noel [William Collins Esq, 1 Dundonald St, Edinburgh, Scotland]; *b* 2 Sept 1952; *educ* Eton; *m* 7 April 1979 *Lucinda Rosemary, est dau of Michael Harper Gow (*see* GREENWELL, Bt), and has:

1a *Emily Lucinda Julian; *b* 1981

2a *Melissa Daisy; *b* 1984

(1) *Jane Margarita [Mrs Richard Oliphant, 77 Lexham Gdns London W8]; *b* 25 Nov 1954; *m* 29 July 1976 *Richard Eric Laurence Oliphant, er son of Maj Reginald Godfrey Oliphant, of Cranleigh, Surrey

(2) *Tiffany Anne; *b* 25 July 1964

(3) *Bryony Mary Pierre; *b* 9 April 1974

DONOUGHUE

Creation: B. (LP, UK) 1985.

THE BARON DONOUGHUE, of Ashton, Co Northants (Bernard Donoughue) [The Rt Hon The Lord Donoughue, 71 Ebury Mews E, London SW1W 9QA]; *b* 8 Sept 1934; *educ* Northampton GS and Lincoln and Nuffield Colls Oxford (MA, DPhil); Sr Research Officer PEP 1960–63; LSE: Lecturer, Sr Lecturer, Reader 1963–74; Sr Policy Advsr to PM 1974–79; Devpt Dir EIU 1979–81; assist ed *The Times* 1981–82; Kleinwort Grieveson Securities: Head Investment Policy and Research 1982–86, Head Investment Policy and Internat Research 1986–88; Exec V-Chm London, Bishopsgate Internat Investment Holdings 1988–91; Tstee Inst Policy Research 1991; Oppn Spokesman: Treasury 1991–92, energy 1991–93, National Heritage 1992–97, Parly U-Sec MAFF 1997–; memb: Sports Cncl 1965–1971, Commn Enquiry into Assoc Football 1966–68, Ct Govrs LSE 1968–1974 and 1982–, Civil Service Coll Advsy Cncl 1976–79, Advsy Bd Wissenschaftzentrum Berlin 1978–91, Bd Centre European Policy Studies Brussels 1982–87, London Arts Bd 1991–; Exec LSO 1979–91 (Patron 1989–96); Patron Inst Comtemporary Br History 1988–; v-Pres Newbury Music Festival 1993–; Assoc memb Nuffield Coll Oxford 1982–87; Hon Fell: Lincoln Coll Oxford 1986, LSE 1989; Hon LLD Leicester 1990; author: *Oxford Poetry* (jt ed, 1956), *Wage Policies in the Public Sector* (1962), *Trade Unions in a Changing Society* (1963), *British Politics and the American Revolution* (1964), *The People into Politics* (with W T Rogers, 1966), *Herbert Morrison: Portrait of a Politician* (with G W Jones, 1973), *Prime Minister* (1987); FRHistS; *m* 1959 (*divorce* 1989) Carol Ruth, dau of Abraham Goodman, and has issue:

1 *Paul Michael David; *b* 1969; *educ* William Ellis Sch

1 *Stephen Joel; *b* 1969; *educ* William Ellis Sch

1 *Rachel Anne; *b* 1965;

2 *Kate Miriam; *b* 1967;

Lineage: THOMAS JOSEPH DONOUGHUE; *m* Maud Violet Andrews and had:

BERNARD, *cr* a **Baron**

DON-WAUCHOPE

Arms: Quarterly, 1st and 4th, azure a crescent between two mullets in chief and a garb in base or (for WAUCHOPE of Edmonstone); 2nd, vert on a fess argent three mascles sable (for DON of Newton Don); 3rd, or a cross engrailed sable accompanied by an escutcheon gules in dexter chief and in sinister base a cinquefoil azure (for RAIT of Edmonstone); over all the badge of a Baronet of Nova Scotia on an inescutcheon surmounted of an imperial crown.
Crests: 1 (dexter) A garb or charged of a crescent vert (for WAUCHOPE of Edmonstone), 2 (sinister) a fruit of pomegranate vert, slit and seeded or (for DON of Newton Don).
Mottoes: 1 *Industria ditat* ('Industry enriches'), 2 *Non deerit alter aureus* ('Another golden fruit shall not be wanting').
Creation: Bt. (NS) 7 June 1667.

SIR ROGER HAMILTON DON-WAUCHOPE, 11TH BT, of Newton Don [Sir Roger Don-Wauchope Bt, Newton, 53 Montrose Dve, Pietermaritzburg 3201, Natal, S Africa]; *b* 16 Oct 1938; *s* f 1989; *educ* Hilton Coll Natal and Natal U (Higher Diploma Taxation); Chartered Accountant (SA) with Deloitte Touche; *m* 14 Dec 1963 *Sallee, yr dau of Lt Col Harold Mill-Colman, OBE, ED, AMICE, of Durban, and has:

1 +ANDREW CRAIG; *b* 18 May 1966; *educ* Hilton Coll and Witwatersrand U (MB, BCh); *m* 1990 *Louise Silvia, dau of John Crawford Johnstone-Dougall, of Durban

2 +John Hamilton; *b* 5 Jan 1969; *educ* Hilton Coll and Pietermaritzburg U (BCom); Chartered Accountant (SA); *m* 1995 *Despina Makris, dau of Antonius Makris of Ialysos, Rhodes

1 *Georgina Anne; *b* 20 Nov 1970; *educ* St John's DSG and Tech Natal (MDipHon); *m* 1994 *Nikolaos Makris, s of Antonius Makris of Ialysos, Rhodes, and has:

1a +Antonios John; *b* 9 Dec 1997

Lineage (of Don): Sir Alexander Don, 1st Bt (NS), so *cr* 7 June 1667, of Newton Don; *m* Isabella Smith of Duns and *d c* 22 July 1687, leaving, with four daus:

1 **Sir James Don, 2nd Bt**; *m* 3 July 1680 Marion Scot of Goranbery and had:

(1) **Sir Alexander Don, 3rd Bt**; *m* 1717 Margaret (*d* 24 Aug 1767), dau of John Carre of Cavers, and *d* 13 April 1749, leaving an only surv s:

1a **Sir Alexander Don, 4th Bt**; *m* 1750 Mary, dau of John Murray of Philiphaugh, and *d* 2 Oct 1776, leaving, with two daus:

1b **Sir Alexander Don, 5th Bt**; Capt Southern Fencibles 1778; *m* 1778 Henrietta (*d* 12 March 1801), sis of 15th Earl of Glencairn (see CUNINGHAME, Bt), and *d* 5 June 1815, leaving, with two daus (Elizabeth; Mary; both accidentally drowned 12 June 1795):

1c **Sir Alexander Don, 6th Bt**; *b* 1779; *educ* Eton; Offr Dumfries Militia, MP Roxburghs 1814–26; *m* 1st 1809 Lucretia (*dsp* 1815), 2nd dau of George Molineux Montgomerie, of Garboldisham Hall, Norfolk; *m* 2nd Aug 1824 Grace (*m* 2nd 1836 Lt Gen Sir James Maxwell Wallace, KH, and *dl* 13 March 1878), est dau of John Stein, of Edinburgh, MP Bletchingley, and d* 11 March 1826, leaving by her, with a dau (Alexina Harriet Elizabeth, *m* 18 Sept 1844 Sir Frederick Acclom Milbank, 1st Bt (*qv*), and *d* 22 Feb 1919, leaving issue):

1d **Sir William Henry Don, 7th Bt**; *b* 4 May 1825; *educ* Eton; Offr 5th Dragoon Gds 1842–45; sold Newton Don for £85,000 (over £3,400,000 in late–1990s terms) and became an actor; *m* 1st June 1847 Antonia (*d* 1869), dau of M Lebrun, of Hamburg, and had a dau (Alexina Mary); *m* 2nd 17 Oct 1857 Emily Eliza, actress (*d* 20 Sept 1875), dau of John Saunders, and *d* Hobart, Tasmania, 19 March 1862, leaving by her:

1e Harriette Grace Mary; *m* 1st 19 July 1887 Everett Gray (*d* 1891), yr s of George Gray, of Perth; *m* 2nd 10 Aug 1892 John Satterfield Sandars, CVO, PC, DCL (*d* 29 March 1934), only s of Charles Sandars, of Mackworth, Derbys

2 Alexander (Sir), of Rutherford; *m* Anna, dau of George Pringle of Torwood, and *dsp* 1712

3 Patrick, of Aldtouneburn; advocate; *m* 26 June 1683 Anne, dau of John Wauchope, a Ld of Session as Lord Edmonstone (*see* (**Lineage (of Wauchope)** below), and had:

(1) John DON later WAUCHOPE (on inheriting Edmonstone); *d* unm

(2) James DON later WAUCHOPE (on inheriting Edmonstone); *m* 1733 Christian, 2nd dau of Sir John Inglis, Bt, of Cramond, and had:

1a John; *b* 1742; *m* 1766 Anne (*d* 1811), est dau of John Erskine of Dunn and aunt of Margaret, Marchioness of Ailsa (*qv*), and *d* 1810, having had:

1b James; *dvp* unm

2b JOHN, for whom *see* further below

3b David (Rev); *b* 1770; Rector Warkton, Northants; *m* 1st Mary (*d* 24 Feb 1810), est dau of Sir William Dick, 3rd Bt, of Prestonfield (*see* 1940 edn DICK-CUNYNGHAM, Bt), and had a s (*d* young); *m* 2nd 15 Aug 1821 Anne (*d* 14 July 1877), 4th dau of Andrew Wauchope of Niddrie, and *d* 16 Feb 1826, having by her had, with a s and dau (*d* young):

1c David (Rev); *b* 16 April 1825; MA Oxon; Rector Church Lawford, nr Rugby; *m* 18 July 1861 Julia Caroline (*d* 27 Feb 1890), dau of Rev Charles Maitland, and *d* 3 Feb 1911, leaving:

1d David Maitland (Rev); *b* 4 March 1864; *educ* Keble Coll Oxford (MA); Rector Elstead Surrey 1905–07; *m* 17 July 1888 Ethel Sarah (*d* 5 March 1950), dau of Lewis Maxey Stewart, and *d* 1947, leaving:

1e Andrew Maxey; *b* 13 Dec 1890; *m* 6 March 1918 Mary Veronica (*d* 1986), dau of Daniel Fisher, of Elstead, and *d* 1987, leaving:

1f +Michael Andrew Anthony [Michael Wauchope Esq, Uplands Lodge, Old Lane, Mayfield, E Sussex TN20 6AU]; *b* 23 April 1925; *educ* Douai; late Lt Black Watch (RHR); *m* 26 Nov 1955 *Margaret Mary Eleanor Victoria, yst dau of Mrs I S Thomas, of Dublin, and has:

1g +Piers Andrew Charles; *b* 15 Oct 1956; *educ* Worth (BA); barrister; Kt SMO Malta

2g +Francis Alastair; *b* 22 Feb 1959; Maj Gren Gds; *m* 1987 *Jessica, dau of Lt-Gen Sir Peter Hudson, KCB, CBE, DL, of Frilsham, Newbury, Berks, and has:

1h +Alasdair William; *b* 1992

3g +Matthew Michael; *b* 8 Nov 1960; *educ* Douai; Kt SMO Malta; *m* *Elveira Ramos de Deus and has:

1h *Alice Margaret; *b* 1990

4g +James Jonathon; *b* 12 Oct 1962; *educ* Winchester (LLB); *m* *Helen, dau of Dr W Spiegel

1f *Deirdre Veronica; *b* 1921; *m* 3 April 1964 (*divorce*) Alan Harry Augustus Emery, s of William Thomas Every, of London

2e Oswald Stewart; *b* 2 July 1897; *educ* Tonbridge; *m* 23 Aug 1914 Dorothy Lettice, dau of James Chandos White, of London, and *d* 1956, leaving:

1f +James David; *b* 11 June 1924; *m* 23 June 1951 *Maria Sofia, dau of Col Pio Zanucolli, of Florence

1f *Estella Olive; *b* 4 Feb 1916; *m* 1943 Dr Michael Walter West (*d* 1946), s of Charles Frederick Marling West, of Malta, and has:

1g *Michael Tom; *b* 6 Oct 1948

1g *Sarah Avalon; *b* 14 Oct 1944; *m* 1968 *John Beddington and has:

1h *Francis John; *b* 1968

2g *Julia Jane; *b* 12 Jan 1946

2f *Anne Jean [Mrs Z Jaworski, 138b Golf Links, New Delhi 110003, India]; *b* 14 Jan 1922; *m* 1st 11 June 1943 (*divorce* 1953) Leon Zuckerman, s of Ari Zuckerman, and has:

1g *Selma; *b* 9 Aug 1944; *m* — Käfinger

2f (cont.) Mrs Anne Zuckerman *m* 2nd 7 Aug 1953 *Zbigniew Ernest Jaworski, Dip Ing, DIC, CEng, s of Zygmunt Sas Jaworski, of Lwow, Poland, and by him has had:

2g Helen Jean; *b* 25 May 1955; *d* 30 Oct 1961

1d Anne Julia; *d* unm 1963

2d Caroline; *d* unm 24 Dec 1914

1c Anne; *m* 30 Oct 1849 Capt John de Courcy Andrew Agnew, RN (*see* AGNEW, Bt, of Lochnaw), and *dsp* 13 July 1852

2a Patrick; *b* 26 Jan 1750; Gen; *ka* Rosetta 1807

(1) Anne; *m* 1708 James Durham of Largo

(2) Margaret; *m* 1702 John Carre of Cavers

JOHN WAUCHOPE's 2nd s,

JOHN WAUCHOPE; Lt-Col Edinburgh Militia; *m* 1815 Henrietta Cecilia (*d* 1826), 2nd dau of Sir James Gardiner Baird, 6th Bt, of Saughton Hall (*qv*), and *d* June 1837, having had, with three daus (including Henrietta Mary; *m* 13 May 1845 Sir James Gardiner Baird, 7th Bt, DL, of Saughton Hall (*qv*), and *d* 3 Nov 1896, having had issue):

Sir JOHN WAUCHOPE later DON-WAUCHOPE, **8th Bt**, DL (Midlothian); *b* 10 July 1816; *educ* Trin Coll Cambridge (MA); Capt Midlothian Yeo Cav; Chm Gen Bd Commrs in Lunacy Scotland 1863, Chm Bd Educn Scotland 1872; *m* 26 April 1863 Bethia Hamilton* (*d* 20 Feb 1911), est dau of Andrew Buchanan, JP, DL, and *d* 12 Dec 1893, having had:

1 **Sir John Douglas Don-Wauchope, 9th Bt**, JP (Midlothian); *b* 15 Sept 1859; *educ* Trin Coll Cambridge (BA 1891); Lt 3rd Bn Roy Scots; *d* unm 28 April 1951

2 Andrew Ramsay; *b* 29 April 1861; *educ* Fettes and Trin Coll Cambridge (BA 1883); internat rugby player; *m* 28 Oct 1903 Emma Margaret (Maizie) (*d* 14 Dec 1959), est dau of Maj-Gen Sir William Salmond, KCB , and *d* 16 Jan 1948, having had:

(1) John Andrew; *b* 24 March 1910; Lt HLI WW II; *m* 14 July 1931 Mrs Yona Marie Gillies (*m* 3rd 14 Dec 1941 Brig David Campbell Mullen, CBE, HLI (*d* 13 Sept 1968), and *d* 26 Jan 1958), yr dau of Ferdinand Plew, of Craigmount, Peebles, and was *ka* Dunkirk 30 May 1940

3 Patrick Hamilton, WS; *b* 1 May 1863; *m* 10 June 1897 Georgiana Renira Buchan (*d* 5 May 1928), dau of George Fitzjohn, and *d* 9 Jan 1939, leaving:

(1) **Sir Patrick George Don-Wauchope, 10th Bt**, of Edmonstone; *b* 7 May 1898; *educ* Edinburgh Acad; RFA WW I (wounded), Egypt and Italy WW II; horticulturist; *m* 15 Aug 1936 (*divorce* 1947) Ismay Lilian Ursula [Mrs G Shipman, 16 Elgarth, St Patrick's Rd, Pietermaritzburg 3209, Natal, S Africa] (*m* 2nd 1989 G W Shipman), dau of Sidney Richard Hodges, of Edendale, Natal, and *d* 15 Sept 1989, leaving:

1a Sir ROGER HAMILTON DON-WAUCHOPE, **11th and present Bt**

2a +Malcolm John [Malcolm Don-Wauchope Esq, P/BAG X23, Winterton 3340, Natal, S Africa]; *b* 14 Dec 1939; *educ* Kearnsey Coll, Botha's Hill, Natal; *m* 27 July 1968 *Rea Marion, est dau of Philip Mantague Adams, of Doonside, S Coast, Natal, and has:

1b +Keith John; *b* 1970

2b +Iain John; *b* 1975

1b *Jane Alice; *b* 1972

2b *Helen Louise; *b* 1977

4 David Buchanan; *b* 12 Feb 1865; *d* 24 April 1896

1 Bethia Hamilton; *d* unm 6 Nov 1944

2 Henrietta Cecilia; *m* 29 Nov 1882 Maj Ernest Digby Mansel (*see* MANSEL, Bt) and *dsp* 17 Feb 1939

3 Clotilde Georgina; *m* 29 Jan 1886 Hon Arthur Henry Browne, 6th s of 3rd Baron Kilmaine (*qv*), and *d* 24 Jan 1945, having had issue

4 Anne Erskine; *d* unm 19 Jan 1888

Lineage (of Wauchope): Sir JOHN WAUCHOPE of Niddrie; *m* Anne Hamilton of Redhouse and had a 2nd s:

JOHN WAUCHOPE; *bapt* 1633 (CHARLES I, who was present, took from his neck and put round that of the child a gold and enamel chain, which remained in the family till Oct 1931 when they presented it to Edinburgh Corporation, who placed it in the City Museum, Canongate); Ld of Session as Lord Edmonstone 1672–88, having acquired Edmonstone, of which he had a confirmatory charter 9 June 1671, through his w; *m* Anna, dau of James Rait of Edmonstone by his 2nd w Anna, dau of Alexander Hay of Monkton, and *d* 1709, leaving:

1 John; *d* unm 1720

2 Andrew; advocate; *d* unm 1730

1 Anne Patrick Don, 3rd s of **Sir Alexander Don, 1st Bt** (*see* (**Lineage of Don**) above)

DORMAN

Arms: Argent, two bars azure, each charged with as many roses of the field, barbed and seeded proper, over all a lozenge sable, charged with a lion's head erased or. **Crest:** Upon a rock proper a lion's paw erased sable, grasping a spear in bend sinister proper. **Motto:** *Virtus in arduis* ('Valour in difficulties'). **Creation:** Bt. (UK) 21 July 1923.

SIR PHILIP HENRY KEPPEL DORMAN, 4TH BT, of Nunthorpe, Co York [Sir Philip Dorman Bt, Belmont House, St George's Lane, Hurstpierpoint, W Sussex BN6 8QX]; *b* 19 May 1954; *s* cousin 1996; *educ* Marlborough and St Andrews; tax accountant; *m* 1st 1982 (*divorce* 1992) Myriam Jeanne Georgette, dau of René Bay, of Royan, France, and has:

1 *Megan Bay Keppel; *b* 1984

Sir PHILIP *m* 2nd 15 June 1996 *Sheena Alexandra Faro

Lineage: MARK DORMAN, of Ashford, Kent; *b* 7 Nov 1783; *d* 1 June 1860, leaving:

CHARLES DORMAN, of Ashford; *b* 30 Nov 1809; *m* 13 June 1844 Emma (*d* 30 Sept 1914), dau of Richard Wilson Page, and *d* 29 Aug 1885, leaving issue:

Sir Arthur John Dorman, 1st Bt (UK), so *cr* 21 July 1923, KBE, JP N R Yorks; Ld Manor Nunthorpe, fndr/chm Dorman, Long & Co, of Middlesbrough; *b* 8 Aug 1848; *m* March 1873 Clara Share (*d* 27 Jan 1933), dau of George Lockwood, of Stockton-on-Tees, and *d* 12 Feb 1931, having had:

1 Arthur Charles, JP, N R Yorks, High Sheriff 1918; *b* 21 April 1874; *m* 30 June 1909 Audrey Marguerite (*d* 2 Oct 1950), dau of George Frederick Moore Inman, of Monkstown, Co Dublin, and *d* 28 Feb 1929

2 **Sir Bedford Lockwood Dorman, 2nd Bt**, CBE (1948), JP N R Yorks; *b* 6 April 1879; barrister Inner Temple 1901, T/Cpt RAOC, chm N R Yorks War Ag Ctee, dep chm N R Yorks QS; *m* 26 March 1919 Constance Phelps (*d* 25 Aug 1946), dau of Alexander Sowerby Hay, of Sacombe, Ware, Herts, and widow of Cyril Webster, and *d* 5 Sept 1956, leaving issue:

(1) **Sir Charles Geoffrey Dorman, 3rd Bt** , MC (1942); *b* 18 Sept 1920; *educ* Rugby and BNC Oxford (BA 1941, MA 1947); served WW II in Egypt and Italy Kings Own Hus, 13th/18th Royal Hus (QMO): Capt 1947, Maj 1954, Lt-Col 1961, GSO(1) (ADSR) AORE 1961–64; *m* 22 Dec 1954 (*divorce* 1972) Elizabeth Ann, CStJ (*d* 1993), only dau of George Gilmour-White, OBE, JP, of Hammerton House, North Cerney, Cirencester, Glos, and *d* 2 Sept 1996, leaving:

1a *Eve Constance [Ms Eve Dorman, La Plenière, St Pierre du Chemin, 85120 La Chataigneraie, Vendée, France]; *b* 20 June 1962; has:

1b *Kean; *b* 14 July 1989

2b *Patrick; *b* Jan 1996

3 Arthur John, MA Cambridge, JP N R Yorks, Pres Iron and Steel Inst 1944–46; *b* 21 Sept 1881; *m* 5 Oct 1910 Dorothy Helen (*d* 6 March 1957), dau of Col Arthur Walter Patrick Inman, Army Medical Res, and *d* 8 Sept 1957, having had:

(1) John Geoffrey; *b* 13 April 1915; *d* 22 Aug 1917

(2) Richard, Capt Green Howards WW II; *b* 25 May 1918; *educ* Rugby; *m* 16 Aug 1947 *Lilian Diana Keppel [Mrs Richard Dorman, 14 FitzJohn Court, W Hassocks, W Sussex BN6 8QP], dau of Dr Henry Edward Barrett, of 33 Holland Park, London W11, and *d* 1976, leaving issue:

1a Sir PHILIP HENRY KEPPEL DORMAN, **4th and present Bt**

1a *Jane Elizabeth Keppel [Mrs Michael Orr, Selhurst, 119 Gordon Rd, Camberley, Surrey GU15 2JQ]; *b* 23 Oct 1950; MB, BS, LRCP, MRCS, DRCOG; *m* 1977 *Michael John Orr and has:

1b *Katherine Jane Keppel; *b* 5 March 1981

2b *Mary Elizabeth Keppel; *b* 18 Feb 1983

3b *Lucy Caroline Keppel; *b* 22 Aug 1984

(3) Arthur Michael; *b* 7 Dec 1924; *d* 22 Feb 1925

(1) Patricia Marguerite; *m* 5 Sept 1933 *John Bell Dixon, 2nd s of Maj Clive Dixon, 16th Lancers, and *d* 198–, leaving:

1a *Robert Clive; *b* 19 Nov 1936; *educ* St Edward's Sch Oxford and Southampton U

2a *Peter Richard John; *b* 3 June 1945; *educ* Brighton Coll

1a *Diana Margaret; *b* 24 Oct 1942; *educ* Leicester U

1 Clara Lilian; *d* unm 25 Oct 1940

2 Frances Mary; *m* 2 Oct 1900 Charles F H Bolckow (*d* 12 March 1934), of Wayside, Nunthorpe, Yorks, and *d* 13 Jan 1935, leaving issue

3 Alice; *m* 21 Oct 1902 Lt-Col George Trevor Roper Cook (*ka* 26 March 1918), CMG, DSO, 20th Hus, and *d* 3 April 1932, leaving issue (*see* TEYNHAM, B)

DORMAND OF EASINGTON

Creation: B. (LP, UK) 1987.

THE BARON DORMAND OF EASINGTON, Co Durham (John Donkin Dormand) [The Rt Hon The Lord Dormand of Easington, House of Lords, London SW1A 0PW]; *b* 27 Aug 1919; *educ* Bede Coll Durham, Loughborough Tech, St Peter's Hall Oxford and Harvard; teacher 1940–48; educn advsr 1948–52 and 1957–63, District Educn Offr Easington RDC 1963–70; MP (Lab) Easington 1970–87, Assist Govt Whip 1974, Ld Commr Treasury 1974–79, Chm PLP 1981–87, peers; rep Shadow Cabinet 1995–97; Dep Chm Teesside Devpt Corpn; Hon Fell St Peter's Hall Oxford 1993; *m* 1963 *Doris, dau of Thomas Robinson, of Hought-on-le-Spring, Co Durham

Lineage: BERNARD DORMAND; *m* Mary — and had:

JOHN DONKIN, *cr* a **Baron**

DORMER

Arms: Azure ten billets, four, three, two and one, or; on a chief of the second a demi-lion issuant sable. **Crest:** A falconer's righthand glove fesswise argent, thereon perched a falcon, wings displayed and inverted, also argent, belled and beaked or. **Supporters:** Two falcons, wings inverted argent, legged and beaked or, belled gules. **Motto:** *Cio che dio vuole io voglio* ('What God wills I will'). **Creations:** Bt. (E) 10 June 1615, B. (E) 30 June 1615.

THE 17TH BARON DORMER OF WYNG, Co Buckingham, and a **Baronet** (Lt-Cdr Sir Geoffrey Henry Dormer, Bt, RNR [The Rt Hon The Lord Dormer, Yew Tree Cottage, Dittisham, Devon TQ6 0EX]; *b* 13 May 1920; *s* second cousin 1995; *educ* Eton and Trin Coll Cambridge; Lt RNVR, Lt-Cdr RNR WW II; *m* 1st 20 Aug 1947 (*divorce* 1957) Janet, yr dau of James Forrest Alexander Readman, of Edinburgh, and has:

1 *Carol Susan [The Hon Mrs Lynn, Hockerwood Park, Southwell, Notts NG25 0PZ]; *b* 20 Feb 1949; *m* 1974 *Patrick Howard Lynn and has:

(1) *Iain Patrick; *b* 22 July 1978

(2) *Joshua Alexander; *b* 6 July 1980

(1) *Sarah Amy Janet; *b* 23 May 1986

2 *Sally Ann Vanessa; *b* 3 Feb 1951; *m* 3rd March 1973 Roger Arthur Skinner (*d* 27 Feb 1995) and has:

(1) *Timothy Roger; *b* 4 Aug 1977

(1) *Clare Vanessa; *b* 6 June 1975

The 17th BARON *m* 2nd 15 Dec 1958 *Pamela, dau of Wallace Levick Simpson, and by her has:

1 +WILLIAM ROBERT [William Dormer Esq, The Old Rectory, The High St, Lewknor, Oxon OX9 5TL]; *b* 8 Nov 1960; *educ* King Edward VI Comprehensive Sch, Totnes, U of Southampton and Cranfield U Sch of Management (MBA); *m* 27 Dec 1985 *Paula, only dau of Cecil Ingram Peter Robinson, of Stockport, Cheshire, and has:

(1) +Hugo Edward Geoffrey; *b* 7 July 1995

2 +Hugh Richard Cecil; *b* 20 April 1964; *educ* King Edward VI Comprehensive Sch, Totnes, U of Plymouth (BSc Hons, Dip HS); *m* 27 Oct 1996 *Denise, only dau of Peter Anthony Lunt

Lineage: RICHARD de DOREMERE; held lands at West Wycombe, Bucks, 1244.

HENRY de DORMERE granted lands at West Wycombe to Geoffrey de Everslegh 1276.

RICHARD and ADAM de DORMERE featured in the Bp of Winchester's Pipe Rolls between 1286 and 1305.

WILLIAM DORMERE, held land at W Wycombe 1324; possibly f of:

GEOFFREY DORMER; held lands at W Wycombe 1363; Lucy — and predeceased her

GEFFERY DORMER, of W Wycombe, possibly kin to the above; *m* Eleanor, dau and heir of Thomas Dorre *alias* Chobbs, and had:

GEFFERY DORMER, of W Wycombe; *m* Isabel, dau and coheir of Thomas Balldington, Ld Manors of Balldington, Thame, Oxon, and Adderbury, Oxon, by Agnes (dau of John Danvers, of Cothorpe, by Alice, dau and heiress of William Verney, of Byfield), and had:

GEFFERY DORMER, of W Wycombe; Ld Manor of Thame; *m* 1st Margaret (*d* 1454), dau and coheir of John Launcelyn, of Cople, Beds; *m* 2nd Ursula, dau and heir of Bartholomew Collingridge and gdau of Ranulf FitzAlan and ggdau of Sir William FitzAlan, KG (*d* 1 Aug 1400), and had, with other issue, including a yr s (Sir Michael, Sheriff London 1529, Ld Mayor 1541):

WILLIAM DORMER, of W Wycombe; *d* 1506, leaving an only s:

Sir ROBERT DORMER; High Sheriff Beds and Bucks *temp* HENRY VIII; *m* Jane, dau of John Newdigate, of Harefield, Middx, Serjeant-at-Law, and *d* 1552, leaving an est s:

Sir WILLIAM DORMER, KB, of Wing, Bucks; MP Bucks *c* 1515; *m* 1st Mary, dau of Sir William Sidney, and had:

1 Anne; *m* Sir William Hungerford

2 Jane; Maid-of-Honour to QUEEN MARY; *m* Don Gomez Suarez, Count of Feria

Sir WILLIAM *m* 2nd Dorothy (*d* 30 Sept 1613, having *m* 2nd, as his 2nd w, Sir William Pelham; *see* YARBOROUGH, E), dau of Anthony Catesby, of Whiston, Northants, and *d* 17 May 1575, having by her had, with other issue (including another dau, Catherine, *m* 2nd Baron Saint John of Bletso; *qv*):

1 **Sir Robert Dormer, 1st Bt**, and **1st Baron Dormer of Wyng**, Co Buckingham, so *cr* 10 June 1615 and 30 June 1615 respectively (both E); *bapt* 26 Jan 1551; MP Tregony 1571 and Bucks 1592–93, High Sheriff Bucks 1584–85, ktd 1591; *m* 1590 Elizabeth Browne, dau of 1st Viscount Montagu, and *d* 8 Nov 1616, having had, with daus:

(1) William (Sir); *m* Alice, dau of Sir Richard Molineux, Bt, of Sefton, Lancs (*see* 1970 edn SEFTON, E), and *dvp*, leaving:

1a ROBERT DORMER, **2nd Baron Dormer of Wyng** and 1st EARL OF CARNARVON, so *cr* 2 Aug 1628, as also VISCOUNT ASCOTT, Co Buckingham (both E); *b c* 1610; *educ* Eton and Exeter Coll Oxford; Ld Lt Bucks 1641; *m* 27 Feb 1625 Lady Anna Sophia Herbert, dau of 4th Earl of Pembroke and Montgomery (*qv*), and was *k* 1st Battle of Newbury 20 Sept 1643, leaving an only s:

1b CHARLES DORMER, **3rd Baron Dormer of Wyng** and 2nd and last EARL OF CARNARVON; *b* 25 Oct 1632; *m* 1st Elizabeth Capell, dau of 1st Baron Capell of Hadham (*see* ESSEX, E), and had issue:

1c Elizabeth; *m* 2nd Earl of Chesterfield (*see* 1967 edn CHESTERFIELD and STANHOPE, E)

2c Isabella; *m* Charles Coote, 3rd Earl of Mountrath (*see* COOTE, Bt)

3c Anna Sophia

1b (cont.) The 2nd EARL *m* 2nd Lady Mary Bertie (*dsp*), dau of 2nd Earl of Lindsey (*see* LINDSEY and ABINGDON, E), and *d* 29 Nov 1709, when the Earldom and Viscountcy expired

1a Elizabeth; *m* Edward Somerset, Marquess of Worcester (*see* BEAUFORT, D)

(2) Anthony, of Grove Park, Warwicks; *m* Margaret, dau of Sir Henry Terringham, of Terringham, Bucks, and had issue:

1a Robert; *m* Anne, dau of Rowland Eyre, of Hasop, Derbys, and had, with other issue:

1b ROWLAND DORMER, **4th Baron Dormer of Wyng**; *b c* 1651; *d* unm 27 Sept 1712

(3) Robert, of Peterley, Bucks; *m* Mary, dau of Edward Banester, of Idsworth, Hants, and had, with other issue:

4a Charles; *m* Mary Cellier and had issue:

1b CHARLES DORMER, **5th Baron Dormer of Wyng**; *m* 1st Catherine, dau and coheir of Edmond Fettiplace, of Swincombe, Oxon, and had:

1c Rev CHARLES DORMER, **6th Baron Dormer of Wyng**; RC priest; *d* 7 March 1761

2c JOHN, **7th Baron**

1b (cont.) The **5th Baron** *m* 2nd 7 June 1694 Elizabeth (*d* 29 Oct 1739), dau of Richard Biddulph, and *d* 2 July 1728, having by her had, with 5 er sons, 1 yst s, 2 er and 2 yst daus:

3c James, of Antwerp; had issue

1c Frances; *m* 1726 William Plowden (*see* PLOWDEN, B) and had issue

The 6th Baron's bro,

JOHN DORMER, **7th Baron Dormer of Wyng**; *b* 2 June 1691; *m* 1719 Mary (*d* 29 Oct 1739), dau of Sir Cecil Bisshopp, Bt, of Parham, and *d* 7 Oct 1785, having had, with two daus:

1 CHARLES DORMER, **8th Baron Dormer of Wyng**; *b* 30 April 1725; *m* 1st 9 Aug 1759 Mary Talbot (*d* 18 May 1753), sister of 15th Earl of Shrewsbury and Waterford (*qv*), and had issue:

(1) CHARLES DORMER, **9th Baron Dormer of Wyng**; *b* 10 Jan 1753; *d* unm 2 April 1819

1 (cont.) The **8th Baron** *m* 2nd 23 Jan 1768 Elizabeth (*d* 15 Sept 1797), widow of Gen John Mordaunt, bro of 6th Earl of Peterborough (*see* MORDAUNT, Bt), and dau of Samuel Hamilton, and *d* 30 March 1804, having by her had, with three daus:

(2) JOHN EVELYN PIERREPONT DORMER, **10th Baron Dormer of Wyng**; *b* March 1771; conformed to C of E, thereby becoming the first peer of this creation actually to take his seat in the House of Lords; *m* 20 Nov 1795 Lady Elizabeth Kerr (*dsp* 13 Aug 1822), dau of 5th Marquess of Lothian (*qv*), and *d* 9 Dec 1826

2 John; Gen Austrian serv; *b* 18 Feb 1730; *m* in Hungary 22 May 1755 Elizabeth (*d* 6 April 1824), 2nd dau of Gabriel, Count Buttler, and *d* 21 Nov 1795, leaving issue:

(1) JOSEPH THADDEUS, **11th Baron**

(1) Antonia; *m* Baron O'Brien, Gen Austrian serv; and *d* 1805, leaving issue

3 James; *b* 27 May 1735; *m* Mary (*d* 10 Aug 1797), dau of Patrick Purcil, of Cadiz, and *d* 1817, leaving issue:

(1) James; *b* 16 Feb 1765; *m* 1792 Lucy (*d* 1816), dau of Thomas Fitzherbert, of Norbury and Swynnerton (*see* STAFFORD, B), and *d* 1810, leaving issue:

1a Charles; *m* 1st Elizabeth Charlotte (*d* April 1832), dau of Charles Frederick de Coetlogon, of Ashford, Middx; *m* 2nd 25 Oct 1836 Jane (*d* 23 Feb 1855), yst dau of Rev R C Long, of Dunston Hall, Norfolk, and *d* 22 May 1852

2a Miles; *m* 1825 Susan, dau of W Randall

1a Catherine; *m* Dec 1826 Henry Williams, and *d* 13 July 1853

(2) Robert; *b* 1768; *m* 1816 Elizabeth (*m* 2nd 31 March 1834 Maj — Bisshopp), dau and sole heir of Richard Hill, of Kineton, and *d* 12 Dec 1823, leaving issue:

1a Anne

2a Mary; *d* 1831

The 10th BARON's cousin,

JOSEPH THADDEUS DORMER, **11th Baron Dormer of Wyng**; *b* 1 June 1790; Offr Austrian serv; *m* 5 May 1829 Elizabeth Anne (*d* 4 July 1883), est dau of Sir Henry Tichborne, 8th Bt (*see* 1967 edn DOUGHTY-TICHBORNE, Bt), and *d* 5 July 1871, having had issue:

1 JOHN BAPTIST JOSEPH DORMER, **12th Baron Dormer of Wyng**, DL, JP, CA Warwicks, served RHG, Gren Gds and 74th Foot Crimea and India; *b* 22 May 1830; *m* 1st 14 June 1866 Louisa Frances Mary (*d* 9 Sept 1868), er dau of Edward King Tenison, of Kilronan Castle, Co Roscommon, and gdau of 1st Earl of Lichfield (*qv*), and had issue:

(1) Henry Edward; *b* 4 March; *d* 24 Dec 1867

(1) Florence Edith Louise, ARRC; *b* 8 Sept 1868; *m* 20 July 1892 Henry Charles Vicars Hunter (*d* 20 June 1934), only son of Henry Frotheringham Hunter, of Kilbourne Hall, Derbyshire, and *d* 21 Dec 1956, leaving issue

1 (cont.) The **12th Baron** *m* 2nd 11 Feb 1871 Leonie (*d* 1 Sept 1883, aged 40), widow of Count Alfred de Bueren and dau of M Fortamps, Senator of Belgium; *m* 3rd 8 Jan 1885 Emily Constance Campbell (*d* 18 Sept 1919), dau of John Bald, of Monzie Castle, Perthshire, and *d* 22 Dec 1900

2 James Charlemagne (Sir), KCB, Lt-Gen, Ch of Staff army of occupation Egypt 1882–85, DAG auxiliary forces 1885–86, Maj-Gen cmdg Dublin Dist 1886–88, staff cmdg troops Egypt 1888–90, Lt-Gen cmdg Madras Army and memb Cncl Govt Fort St George 1891; *b* 26 Jan 1834; *m* 8 Oct 1861 Ella Frances Catherine (*d* 2 June 1906), widow of Robert Cutlar Fergusson, of Graigdarroch and Orroland, and only dau of Sir Archibald Alison, 1st Bt (*see* 1970 edn), and *d* 3 May 1893, leaving issue:

(1) ROLAND JOHN DORMER, **13th Baron Dormer of Wyng**, DL, JP Warwicks, Sub-Dir Secretariat Egyptian Finance, Order Medjidie 3rd Cl; *b* 24 Nov 1862; *m* 16 Aug 1897 Marie Hanem (*d* 1964), dau of F Eywaz, of Cairo, and *d* 9 Feb 1920, having had issue:

1a Rosa Mary Victoria Eugenie; *b* 30 July 1912; *d* 1913

(2) CHARLES JOSEPH THADDEUS DORMER, **14th Baron Dormer of Wyng**, CBE, DL Warwicks, Capt RN, Naval Attaché Tokyo 1906–08, 3rd Cl Sacred Treasure Japan, Gentleman Usher in Ordinary to HM GEORGE V 1919; *b* 24 Feb 1864; *m* 17 Feb 1903 Caroline May (*d* 18 March 1951), dau of Sir Robert Cavendish Spencer Clifford, 3rd Bt (*qv*), and *d* 4 May 1922, leaving:

1a CHARLES WALTER JAMES DORMER, **15th Baron Dormer of Wyng**; *b* 20 Dec 1903; *educ* The Oratory Sch and RMC Sandhurst; Capt Life Gds, ADC to Govr-Gen NZ 1939–41, Kt of Honour and Devotion SMO Malta; *m* 19 Feb 1944 *Lady Maureen Thérèse Josephine Noel (*m* 2nd, as his 2nd w, Peregrine Edward Launcelot Fellowes) [The Lady Maureen Fellowes, The Court, Chipping Campden, Glos GL55 6JQ], only dau of 4th Earl of Gainsborough (*qv*), and *d* 27 Aug 1975, leaving issue:

1b *Jane Maureen Thérèse [The Hon Mrs Glennie, 14 Langham Place, Burlington Lane, London W4 2QL]; *b* 20 Nov 1945; *m* 1st 21 July 1966 (Henry Alistair) Samuel Sandbach, er son of Cdr Ralph Maxwell Sandbach, RN, of Stantons, Kingsclere, nr Newbury, Berks, and has issue:

1c *James Peter Charles; *b* 1969

1c *Emma Pauline Jane; *b* 29 June 1967; *m* 1993 *Graham Defries

1b (cont.) The Hon Mrs Sandbach *m* 2nd 1980 S/Ldr Geoffrey E Meek (*d* 1984), RAF; *m* 3rd 1988 *Lt Cdr R N F Glennie, RN (ret)

2b *Catherine Mary [The Hon Mrs Stone, 81 Lakeside Rd, London N13]; *b* 2 April 1950; *m* 1st 14 Feb 1973 (*divorce* 1989) Christopher J G Bird, son of Brig Garth R G Bird, of Great Broadhurst, Broad Oak, Heathfield, Sussex (*see* VAVASOUR, Bt); *m* 2nd 1992 *Dr Michael Simon Stone, and has issue:

1c *Raphael Charles; *b* 1992

2a JOSEPH SPENCER PHILIP DORMER, **16th Baron Dormer of Wyng**; *b* 4 Sept 1914; *educ* Ampleforth and Ch Ch Oxford; Capt Scots Gds WW II, consultant Thomas Comely & Sons, memb Cncl W Midlands Area C Assoc; *dsp* and unm Dec 1995

1a Georgiana Mary, MBE (1943); *b* 1 Feb 1906 (HM GEORGE V stood sponsor); Chm and Organiser Cheshire WVS; *m* 28 Sept 1927 Col Geoffrey Egerton-Warburton (*d* 1 Aug 1961), DSO, TD, JP, DL, son of Piers Egerton-Warburton, JP, DL, of Arley Hall, Cheshire and *d* 23 Sept 1955, leaving issue (*see* GREY EGERTON, Bt)

2a Myrtle Emmeline Theresa; *b* 15 Oct 1907; *m* 23 Nov 1927 Robert George Wilmot Berkeley, DL, only son of Robert Valentine Berkeley, JP, DL, FSA, of Spetchley Park, Worcester (*see* BERKELEY, B), and had issue

3a Rosamund Jane, JP (Warwicks 1948); *b* 15 April 1911; Jr Cdr ATS WW II; *d* unm 27 May 1995

(1) Gwendeline Mary; *b* 11 July 1865; *m* 16 Oct 1883 7th Earl of Abingdon (*see* LINDSEY and ABINGDON, E), and *d* 16 Sept 1942, leaving issue

(2) Eveline Mary; *b* 30 July 1866; *m* 18 May 1892 James Logan Stewart (*d* 29 June 1898), late 7th Hus, and *d* 23 Oct 1929, leaving issue

(3) Mary Catherine; *b* 13 Oct 1867; *m* 9 Sept 1891 Sir John David Rees, 1st Bt (*see* 1970 edn), KCIE, CVO, MP E Nottingham 1912–22, and *d* 30 May 1943, leaving issue

(4) Ethel Mary; *b* 31 May 1870; *d* unm 7 July 1949

(5) Leonie Mary, a nun; *b* 2 Nov 1872

(6) Constance Mary; *b* 1 Dec 1874; *d* unm 5 March 1955

3 Hubert Francis; *b* 4 Nov 1837; *m* 11 Nov 1865 Mary Jane Elizabeth (*d* 15 Aug 1938), dau of Kenelm Henry Digby (*see* DIGBY, B), and *d* 16 April 1913, leaving issue:

(1) Edward Henry, Capt and RTO BEF, served Mashona campaign 1896, S African War 1900 (medal with four clasps) and WW I; *b* 13 Oct 1870; *m* 24 June 1903 Hon Vanessa Margaret Borwick (*d* 16 June 1962), 5th dau of 1st Baron Borwick (*qv*), and *d* 9 July 1943, leaving issue:

1a Robert Francis Edward Baptist, Lt RASC; *b* 27 June 1904; *educ* Eton; *m* 1st 9 March 1928 (*divorce* 1934) Ebba, dau of Niels Stockholm-Hestbeck, of Mors, Denmark; *m* 2nd 11 Oct 1934 (*divorce* 1949) Barbara, dau of Martin Reed Brierly; *m* 3rd 22 May 1951 Loris, yr dau of John Hardcastle Baines, of Hove, Sussex, and *dsp* 18 Jan 1980

2a GEOFFREY HENRY DORMER, **17th and present Baron Dormer of Wyng**

1a Cecilia Mary Margaret; *b* 22 Nov 1905; *m* 1st 24 Nov 1926 Lt-Col William Basil Wilberforce (*ka* 6 May 1943), DSO, 1st Bn KOYLI, of Markington Hall, Yorks, and had issue; lm 2nd 22 May 1950 Lt-Col Hugh de Neufville Lucas (*d* 2 July 1970), IA, yst s of Lt-Col Charles Arthur de Neuf Lucas, IA, and *d* 6 Aug 1974

(2) John Hubert Aloysius; *b* 13 Jan 1874; *m* 1900 Virginia Sinclair (*d* 24 June 1956), dau of Charles Tankerville-Chamberlaine Bey, of 65 Avenue D'Iena, Paris, and *d* 9 Aug 1946, having had issue:

1a John Hubert Charles; *b* 21 Jan 1901; *d* 3 Sept 1905

2a +Charles Herbert Aloysius [Charles Dormer Esq, 124 Upper McNaughton Ave, PO Box 423, Hudson, Quebec J0P 1H0, Canada]; *b* 6 June 1906; *m* 1st 1930 (*divorce* 1946) Mary Johnson, of Ottawa, Canada; *m* 2nd 1946 (*divorce* 1948) Jane Loutitt Ellis, and has issue:

1b +Anthony Fredrick Charles; *b* 1946; *m* 1966 *Anita Lusick, of Melbourne, Australia, and has issue:

1c +Aaron; *b* 1972

1c *Justine; *b* 1974

1b *Lynn Elizabeth Jane; *b* 1944

2b *Susan Ann Sturrock; *b* 1948; *m* 1973 *Peter James McNevern, of Qld, Australia

2a (cont.) Charles Dormer *m* 3rd 1948 (*divorce* 1991) Mary Johnson (his 1st wife)

3a +Richard Joseph Thaddeus, DSC [Richard Dormer Esq DSC, Flat 6, The Manor Park Lands Gdns, Inner Park Rd, London SW19], Lt RNVR; *b* 12 Feb 1913

1a Olivette Ferdinande Mary; *b* 23 June 1902; *m* 20 Feb 1928 F/Lt Eugene McLoughlin, RAF, and *d* 18 Nov 1938, leaving issue

2a Mary Louise; *b* 11 May 1904

3a *Hélène Venetia Anne [Mrs Frank Kelley, 7 Ridgewood Lane, Westport, Conn, 06880, USA]; *b* 23 Dec 1907; *m* 19 March 1937 Frank R Kelley (*d* 1985), son of Frank Kelley, of New York, and has had issue:

1b *Christopher Francis Valentine [Christopher Kelley, 531 Dakota Dve, Herndon, VA 20170, USA], served in US Army 1961–64; *b* 24 March 1939; *educ* Notre Dame Int Sch Rome and Villanova U, Villanova, Pa. (BSEcon 1961); *m* 1st 24 Aug 1963 (*divorce* 1976) Ruth Ellen, dau of Robert Jordan, of Washington, DC, USA, and has issue:

1c *Kevin Francis Dormer; *b* 7 June 1966

1c *Laura Anne; *b* 23 July 1964

1b (cont.) Christopher Kelley *m* 2nd 1978 (*divorce* 1996) Elizabeth Ann Bowser, of Norfolk, Va., and has further issue:

1c *Patrick David Christopher; *b* 1978

2c *Matthew John Martin; *b* 1980

2b *Peter John Dormer [Peter Kelley, 10 Cranbrook Drive, Centerport, NY 11721, USA], served USAF 1961–65; *b* 24 April 1943; *educ* The Oratory Sch, nr Reading, Fairfield Coll, Conn., and Columbia U (BA); *m* 30 Dec 1967 *Patricia F, dau of — Ruehle, of Chicago, and has issue:

1c *Peter John; *b* 1983

1c *Elizabeth Louise Estelle; *b* 1978

2c *Margaret Evelyn Venetia; *b* 1981

3b David Richard Paul; *b* 13 Dec 1946; *d* unm 3 June 1972

4a Pia Magdalen Virginia; *b* 16 April 1920; *m* 7 July 1945 *Col Henry Thomas Bernard Bellingham Rooke, MBE, IA and Colonial Serv, Gold Coast [Henry Rooke Esq, Pigeon's Piece, Wootton, Woodstock, Oxon OX20 1DR], and *d* 22 June 1995, leaving:

1b *Henry John Patrick Dormer [Maj Henry Rooke, c/o Yew Tree Cottage, Higher Holton, Somerset BA9 8AP]; *b* 9 May 1946; *educ* Ampleforth; Maj QRIH (ret); *m* 1969 *Helen Elizabeth, dau of William McLaren Howard, QC

5a *Louise Cecilia Mary [Mrs William Petrie-Hay, Lower Bouts Farm, Inkberrow, Worcs WR7 4HP]; *b* 1 Jan 1922; *m* 1st 13 Nov 1940 (*divorce* 1954) Maj Peter Bailward, RA (*d* 19 Jan 1964) and has:

1b *David John Aucher Michael; *b* 24 Sept 1941; *educ* Ampleforth; *m* 30 Aug 1969 *Charlotte Martha Petra, only dau of Herbert Frohberg, of Ottawa, and has issue:

1c *Alan; *b* 1975

1b *Sarah Jane Mary [Mrs Richard Showell, Old Schoolhouse, Bishampton, Worcs WR10 2LX]; *b* 23 Feb 1944; *m* 2 Jan 1965 *Capt Richard Grahame Dugard Showell, CEng, MIMechE, MIProdE, QO Warwicks and Worcs Yeo, and has issue:

1c *Jeremy Peter Dugard; *b* 22 Nov 1965; *d* 1974

2c *Alexander Geoffrey Dugard; *b* 1971; *educ* Belmont Abbey

1c *Claire Louise Dugard; *b* 26 Oct 1966

5a (cont.) Mrs Louise Bailward *m* 2nd 1954 *Maj William Goulding Petrie-Hay, RA, and has further issue:

2b *Rufus William; *b* Nov 1955; *educ* Stoneyhurst

(3) Kenelm Everard, Capt Irish Gds (SR) WW I; *b* 22 Feb 1879; *m* 14 April 1910 Josephine Sarah (*d* 23 May 1965), yst dau of Hon John T Toohey, MLC, of Sydney, NSW, and *d* 28 May 1935, leaving issue:

1a +John Kenelm [John Dormer Esq, Flat E, 36 Courtfields Gdns, London SW5 0PJ]; Capt KOYLI WW II; *b* 1 April 1915; *m* 1984 *Kathleen, dau of Frederick Rhys Michael, of Cairns, Australia

2a Hugh Everard, DSO (1943), Capt Irish Gds WW II; *b* 11 March 1919; *ka* Normandy 1 Aug 1944

(4) Robert Stanhope, Capt Scots Gds (SR) WW I (wounded), Cdr Order of St Olaf; *b* 18 Aug 1880; *m* 14 Feb 1927 Ebba (*d* 5 Nov 1961), widow of Sir Everard Alexander Hambro, KCVO (*see* HAMBRO, B), and dau of Charles Cecil Beresford Whyte, of Hatley Manor, Co Leitrim, and *d* 28 July 1960, leaving issue:

1a +Michael Henry Stanhope [Michael Dormer Esq, Bowdown House, Greenham, Newbury, Berks], Kt Honour and Devotion SMO Malta; *b* 8 Dec 1930; *m* 21 Jan 1959 *Daphne Margaret, er dau and coheir of Capt Oswald James Battine by Gwendolen Margaret Mary Grace (later Mrs Gerald Hamilton), est dau and coheir of Col Sir Colin MacRae of Feoirlinn, CVO, CBE, and has issue:

1b +Merlin Robert Colum Charles; *b* 5 Nov 1963

1b *Leanda Xenia Sophia Stanhope; *b* 24 Dec 1959; columnist 'Country Living' *Spectator*; *m* 1984 *Peter Andrew Paul Phillipps de Lisle, of Osbaston Hall, Osbaston, Leics, 2nd s of Gerard Arnaud March Phillipps de Lisle, of Quenby Hall, Hungarton, Leics, and has:

1c *Rupert Gerard Xavier; *b* 1986

2c *Christian Michael Frederick; *b* 1988

3c *Dominic Robert Peter; *b* 1990

2b *Athena Cecilia Stanhope; *b* 16 Jan 1961

(5) Cecil Francis Joseph (Sir), KCMG, MVO, Clerk FO 1905, 3rd Sec Dip Serv 1910, Actg 2nd Sec 1911, Assist Priv Sec to For Sec 1915, Chargé d'Affaires Caracas 1919–21, 1st Sec Legation Holy See 1921–26, Counsellor Tokyo 1926–30, Envoy Extrdy and Min Plen Bangkok 1930–34, Oslo 1934–41, Amb to Polish Govt in London 1941, ret 1943, Grand Cross St Olav Norway, Norwegian War Medal and Order White Eagle Serbia; *b* 14 Feb 1883; *m* 25 Feb 1915 Lady Mary Alice Clara Feilding (*d* 7 March 1973), dau of 9th Earl of Denbigh and Desmond (*qv*), and *dsp* 28 July 1979

(1) Gertrude Jane Mary; *m* 28 May 1885 (*annulled* 1896) Edmund Ward (*d* 2 Sept 1915), of North Wood Park, IoW, and *d* 31 March 1964, aged 97

(2) Mary Dolores; *d* unm 9 May 1878

(3) Isabel; *d* unm 24 Aug 1888, aged 19

(4) Elizabeth Mary; *m* 6 Feb 1900 Luke Gerald Dillon (*d* 27 April 1937), OBE, MD, JP, FSA, of Seaham, Durham, and *d* 29 Nov 1949, leaving issue (*see* DILLON, V)

(5) Alice Mary; *d* unm 19 March 1950

4 Henry Edward, Offr 60th Rifles; *b* 29 Nov 1844; *d* 2 Oct 1866

1 Mary Isabel Lucy, a nun; *d* 9 March 1932

DOWDING

Arms: Argent three bars gemel sable, over all a fleur-de-lys azure, on a chief of the second three doric columns of the first. **Crest:** Upon a catherine wheel azure a falcon rising or, belled and hooded gules. **Motto:** *Laborare est orare* ('To work is to pray'). **Creation:** B. (UK) 5 July 1943.

THE 3RD BARON DOWDING, of Bentley Priory, Co Middlesex (Piers Hugh Tremenheere Dowding) [The Rt Hon The Lord Dowding, House of Lords, London SW1A 0PW]; *b* 18 Feb 1948; *s f* 1992; *educ* Fettes and Amherst Coll, Mass. (BA); Assoc Prof of English Okayama Shoka U Japan 1977–; *m* 1973 *Noriko Shiho, of Japan, and has issue:

1 *Rosemary June; *b* 1975

2 *Yuki Elizabeth; *b* 1989

Lineage: The Rev B C DOWDING, Rector of Devizes; *m* — Caswall, and had issue:

ARTHUR JOHN CASWALL DOWDING, of St Ninian's, Moffat, and of Wimbledon; *educ* Winchester and New Coll Oxford; *m* 1880 Maud Caroline (*d* 20 Sept 1934), dau of Lt-Gen Charles Tremenheere, CB, and *d* 1932, leaving issue:

1 HUGH CASWALL TREMENHEERE, **1st Baron**

2 Arthur Ninian (Sir), KBE (1945), CB (1938), V-Adml (1940), Capt RN 1926, ADC to HM GEORGE VI 1936, Adml Supt Devonport Dockyard 1938–45, Offr US Legion of Merit; *b* 4 Jan 1886; *educ* Clifton; *m* 1 May 1915 Kathleen (*d* 2 Nov 1961), dau of Capt J H Drummond, Border Regt (34th), of California, and *d* 26 Nov 1966, having had a s (*ka* 1940)

ARTHUR DOWDING's er son,

HUGH CASWALL TREMENHEERE DOWDING, **1st Baron Dowding**, of Bentley Priory, Middlesex (UK), so *cr* 5 July 1943, GCB (1940, KCB 1933, CB 1928), GCVO (1937), CMG (1919); *b* 24 April 1882; *educ* Winchester and RMA Woolwich; ACM RAF (ret), Maj and Brevet Lt-Col RA WW I (despatches), Dir Trg Air Ministry 1926–29, Cdr Fighting Area Air Def GB 1929, memb Air Cncl (R and D) 1930, AOC-in-C Fighter Command 1936–40, Aircraft Advsr Br Purchasing Mission USA 1940, Pncpl Air ADC to HM GEORGE VI 1937–43, DCL 1946; *m* 1st 16 Feb 1918 Clarice Maud (*d* 28 June 1920), dau of Capt John Williams, IA, and widow of — Vancourt, and had issue; *m* 2nd 25 Sept 1951 Muriel (*d* 1993), dau of John Albino, and widow of P/O Jack Maxwell Whiting, RAFVR (*ka* 1944), and *d* 15 Feb 1970; his son by his 1st w:

DEREK HUGH TREMENHEERE DOWDING, **2nd Baron Dowding**; *b* 9 Jan 1919; *educ* Winchester and RAF Coll Cranwell; W/Cdr RAF 1951 (ret 1956), served WW II; *m* 1st 17 Feb 1940 (*divorce* 1946) Joan Myrtle, dau of Donald James Stuart, of Nairn, Scotland; *m* 2nd 7 May 1947 (*divorce* 1960) Alison Margaret (*m* 3rd 1963 David Hartnell-Beavis) [Mrs David Hartnell-Beavis, The Manor, Norwich Rd, Aylsham, Norfolk NR11 6BN], dau of James Bannerman, LRCP, LRCS, of Norwich, and widow of Maj R W H Peebles, BCS; *m* 3rd 17 Dec 1961 *Mrs Odette L M S Hughes [The Rt Hon Odette Lady Dowding, 501 Gilbert House, Barbican, London EC2Y 8BD], dau of Louis Joseph Houles and formerly w of Brian Hughes, and *d* 1992, leaving by his 2nd w:

1 PIERS HUGH TREMENHEERE DOWDING, **3rd and present Baron Dowding**

2 +MARK DENIS JAMES; *b* 11 July 1949; heir presumptive; *educ* Wymondham Sch, Norfolk; painter; *m* 1982 *Heather, dau of Stanley Arter, of S Africa, and has issue:

(1) +Alexander; *b* 1983

DOWNE

Arms: Argent on a bend cotised sable three annulets of the field. **Crest:** A demi-Saracen in armour, couped at the thighs, wreathed about the temples proper, holding in the dexter hand a ring or, stoned azure, and in the sinister a lion's jamb erased gold, armed gules. **Supporters:** Two lions or, ducally crowned argent, each gorged with a collar cotised sable, charged with three annulets of the second. **Motto:** *Timet pudorem* ('He fears shame'). **Creations:** V. (I) 19 Feb 1680/1, B. (UK) 24 July 1897.

THE 11TH VISCOUNT DOWNE and **Baron Dawnay of Danby** (John Christian George Dawnay, DL (N Yorks 1982)) [The Rt Hon The Viscount Downe DL, 5 Douro Place, London W8 5PH; Wykeham Abbey, Scarborough, N Yorks YO13 9QS]; *b* 18 Jan 1935 (HM GEORGE V stood sponsor); *s f* 1965; *educ* Eton and Ch Ch Oxford; 2nd Lt Gren Gds (Res) 1953–55, chm Brookdeal Electronics 1971–84 (v-chm 196871, md 1965–68), dir: Dawnay Faulkner Associated Ltd (conultants) 1968–, York Ltd 1980–, Yorkshire Bank 1990–, SensorDynamics 1990–, Aaston Ltd 1992–, Scarborough Theatre Tst 1981–, memb N Yorks CC 1969–85, Hon Col 150 (Yorks) Regt RLC (V) 1984–, Freeman Co of the Staple of England 1979, Liveryman Scientific Instrument Makers' Co 1991–; *m* 16 Sept 1965 *Alison Diana, est dau of Ian Francis Henry Sconce, OBE, TD, of Brasted, Kent, and has issue:

1 +RICHARD HENRY; *b* 9 April 1967; *educ* Eton

1 *Sarah Frances; *b* 2 April 1970

Downe, other creations: An Earldom of Downe in the Irish peerage was conferred in 1628 on William Pope, nephew of the Sir Thomas Pope who founded Trinity College Oxford. The title expired with the death of the 4th Earl, William's grandson, in 1668. It has been suggested that one of two younger brothers of the 2nd Earl might have been an ancestor of the poet Alexander Pope, but this is extremely doubtful and if so was through an illegitimate line.

A Viscountcy of Downe, also in the Irish peerage, was conferred in 1675 on William Ducie, who had inherited the family baronetcy (created 1620, extinct 1703) on his elder brother's death nearly twenty years earlier. It expired with the grantee in 1679. (*See* DUCIE, E.)

Lineage: Sir GUY DAUNAY, of Cowick, Yorks, *temp* HENRY VII and HENRY VIII; *m* Joan, sis and heir of John Darrell, of Sessay, and *d* 1552, leaving:

Sir JOHN DAUNAY, of Cowick; Sheriff Yorks *c* 1544; *m* Dorothy, dau of 2nd Lord (Baron) Latimer (*qv*), and *d* 2 March 1553, leaving an est s:

Sir THOMAS DAUNAY, of Sessay and Cowick; *m* Edith, est dau of George, 1st Baron D'Arcy (of Aston), and *d* 3 Sept 1566, leaving an er s:

Sir JOHN DAUNAY; *m* Elizabeth, dau of Sir Marmaduke Tunstall, of Thurland, Lancs, and had an est s:

Sir THOMAS DAWNAY, of Cowick; *m* Faith, dau and heir of Sir Richard Legard, of Ryse, and *d* May 1642, having had an est s:

JOHN DAWNAY, of Wormesley, Yorks; *m* Elizabeth, dau of Sir Richard Hutton, Judge King's Bench, and *dvp* 16 March 1629/30, having had:

1 George; *d* unm and *bur* 19 April 1639

2 Sir CHRISTOPHER DAWNAY, 1st Bt (E), so *cr* 19 May 1642, of Cowick; *m* Jane, dau and heir of Thomas Moseley, of Uskelf, Yorks, and *d* 13 July 1644, having had:

(1) Sir THOMAS DAWNAY, 2nd and last Bt; *d* an infant

3 Sir JOHN DAWNAY, **1st Viscount Downe** (I), so *cr* 19 Feb 1680/1; *bapt* 25 Jan 1624/5; ktd 1660, MP Yorks 1660 and Pontefract 1661–81, 1685–87 and 1689–90, attainted by JAMES II's I Parl May 1689; *m* 1st 4 Aug 1645 Elizabeth (*d* 21 Feb 1662), dau of Sir John Melton; *m* 2nd 14 May 1663 Dorothy, dau of William Johnson, of Wickham, Lincs, and *d* 1 Oct 1695, leaving an only s:

(1) HENRY DAWNAY, **2nd Viscount Downe**; *bapt* 7 June 1664; MP (Tory) Pontefract 1690–95 and Yorks 1698–1700 and 1707–27; *m* 29 Sept 1685 Mildred (*d* Aug 1725), dau of William Godfrey, of Thornock, Lincs, and was *bur* 21 May 1741, having had, with other issue:

1a John, MP Pontefract 1713–16; *b* 8 Dec 1686; *educ* Ch Ch Oxford (MA); *m* 10 Aug 1724 Charlotte Louisa (*bur* 19 April 1729), dau and heir of Robert Pleydell, of Ampney Crucis, Glos, and *dvp* 12 Aug 1740, having had:

1a HENRY PLEYDELL DAWNAY, **3rd Viscount Downe**, FRS; *b* 8 April 1727, MP (Whig) Yorks 1750–60; Ld Bedchamber to PRINCE OF WALES, Lt-Col 25th Foot Battles of Minden 1759 and Campen, nr Wesel, 16 Oct 1760; *d* unm 9 Dec 1760

2a JOHN DAWNAY, **4th Viscount Downe**; *b* 9 April 1728; MP (Whig) Cirencester 1754–68 and Malton 1768–74; *m* 20 May 1763 Laura (*d* 24 April 1812), only dau and heir of William Burton, of Luffenham, Rutland, by – Langley, and *d* 21 Dec 1780, having had, with other issue:

1c JOHN CHRISTOPHER BURTON DAWNAY, **5th Viscount Downe** and 1st and last BARON DAWNAY, of Cowick, Co York (GB), so *cr* 9 June 1796; *b* 15 Nov 1764; MP (Whig) Petersfield 1787–90 and Wootton Bassett 1790–96; *m* 1st —, yr dau of Maj John Scott of Balconie by Margaret, yst dau of Robert Dundas; *m* 2nd 9 Dec 1815 Louisa Maria (*dsp* 20 March 1867), dau of George Welstead, of Apsley, Sussex, and *d* 18 Feb 1832, when the GB Barony expired

2c WILLIAM HENRY, **6th Viscount**

3c Marmaduke DAWNAY later LANGLEY (roy licence 1824); *b* 26 July 1777; *d* unm 1 Oct 1851. (*See* also section **Seat** below.)

The 5th VISCOUNT's bro,

Rev WILLIAM HENRY DAWNAY, **6th Viscount Downe**; Rector Sessay and Thormanby, Yorks; *b* 20 Aug 1772; *m* 6 June 1811 Lydia (*d* 18 March 1848), only dau of John Heathcote, of Conington Castle, and *d* 23 May 1846, having had, with a yr s (Payan, of Beningbrough Hall, nr York, *b* 18 Nov 1815, *d* 17 June 1891) and dau:

WILLIAM HENRY DAWNAY, **7th Viscount Downe**; *b* 15 May 1812; *educ* Eton and Ch Ch Oxford; MP (C) Rutland 1841–46; *m* 25 July 1843 Mary Isabel (*m* 2nd 6 Jan 1863 Sidney Leveson Lane and *d* 14 April 1900), 4th dau of Rt Rev Hon Richard Bagot, Bp Bath and Wells (*see* BAGOT, B), and had issue:

1 HUGH RICHARD, **8th Viscount**

2 Lewis Payan, MP Thirsk and Thirsk and Malton 1880–93, Lt-Col Coldstream Gds, JP N R Yorks; *b* 1 April 1846; *m* 6 June 1877 Lady Victoria Alexandrina Elizabeth Grey (*d* 15 Jan 1922), sis of 4th Earl Grey (*qv*), and *d* 30 July 1910, leaving issue:

(1) Guy Payan, CB (1918), CMG (1918), DSO (1902), MVO (1907), Hon Maj-Gen Coldstream Gds, GSO(2) 1914, GSO(1) 1915, T/Brig-Gen 1916, T/Maj-Gen General Staff 1918, Hon Maj-Gen 1919, served Boer War 1899–1902 and WW I (despatches eleven times, two brevets), Legion of Honour, Croix de Guerre, Orders of St Anne of Russia, St Maurice and St Lazarus Italy and American DSM; *b* 23 March 1878; *m* 12 July 1906 Cecil (ld 13 Feb 1972) yst dau of Francis William Buxton (*see* BUXTON, Bt), and *d* 19 Jan 1952, having had issue:

1a Christopher Payan, CBE (1946), MVO (1944), Lt City London, Lt-Col Coldstream Gds WW II (despatches), pres Dalgety and Co to 1971 and Guardian Assur, md Lazard Bros, dir Martins Bank, 2nd Warden Fishmongers' Co 1972, Prime Warden 1973, 4th Warden 1975, Legion of Merit, Czechoslovakian Mil Cross; *b* 24 July 1909; *educ* Winchester and Magdalen Coll Oxford; *m* 6 Sept 1939 Patricia (*d* 1989), 3rd dau of Maj-Gen Sir Hereward Wake, 13th Bt (*qv*), and *d* 1989, leaving issue:

1b +Rupert Payan [Rupert Dawnay Esq, The Mill House, Longparish, Andover, Hants SP11 6QH]; *b* 4 Nov 1940; *educ* Eton; *m* 1982 *Carolyn, dau of Chapman Marshall, of Miami, Florida, and has issue:

1c +Nicholas Marshall; *b* 1986

2c +Lewis Payan (twin); *b* 1986

3c +Thomas Payan; *b* 1988

2b +Guy Payan [Guy Dawnay Esq, 10 Farm Place, London W8]; *b* 6 Oct 1944; *educ* Eton and Lausanne U; *m* 1975 (*divorce* 1990) Charmian Rose, dau of Lt-Col Alistair Neilson, of Dene House, Callaly, Northumberland, and has:

1c +Christopher Payne; *b* 23 March 1977

2c +Mark Payne; *b* 1979

1b *Gillian [Mrs Ian Butler, 18 Staverton Rd, Oxford OX2 0XJ], BA Oxford; *b* 13 April 1942; *m* 25 June 1966 *(Ian) Christopher Butler, Prof English Lang and Lit Oxford, and has:

1c *Sophie Rosalind; *b* 8 July 1968

2c *Josephine Laura; *b* 22 April 1970; *m* 29 June 1996 *Nicholas James Johnson

2b *Sarah [Mrs Jolyon Coombs, Firgo Farm, Whitchurch, Hants]; *b* 9 Aug 1947; *m* 1970 *Jolyon Coombs, Welsh Gds, son of W/Cdr Robin Coombs, and has issue:

1c *Charles T Hardy; *b* 1976

1c *Arabella Sarah; *b* 5 July 1971

2c *Victoria Margaret Daisy; *b* 1974

2a Oliver Payan, CVO (1953), Capt Coldstream Gds WW II (despatches), Priv Sec and Equerry to HM QUEEN ELIZABETH THE QUEEN MOTHER 1950–56, Extra Equerry 1956–62, memb London Stock Exchange, ptnr Grieveson Grant & Co; *b* 4 April 1920; *educ* Eton and Balliol Coll Oxford; *m* 1st 3 Feb 1944 (*divorce* 1963) Lady Margaret Dorothea Boyle, yst dau of 8th Earl of Glasgow (*qv*), and had issue:

1b +(Charles) James Payan [James Dawnay Esq, Symington House, nr Biggar, Lanarks ML12 6LW]; *b* 7 Nov 1946; *educ* Eton; *m* 1978 *Sarah, er dau of (Edgar) David Stogdon, of Witchampton, Dorset, and has issue:

1c +David Frederick Payan; *b* 1985

1c *Alice Britannia; *b* 1979

2c *Olivia Margaret; *b* 1981

3c *Fenella Christian; *b* 1988

2b +Ivo Nicholas Payan; *b* 9 Dec 1952 (HM QUEEN ELIZABETH THE QUEEN MOTHER stood sponsor); *educ* Eton; jnlst with *Sunday Telegraph*; *m* 1st 1980 (*divorce* 1986) Chantal Mary Beatrice, dau of Michael Rigby Bishop, of Combe House, Beckley, nr Rye, Sussex; *m* 2nd 1992 *Rachel S, dau of Stanley Patrick Johnson, of W Nethercote, Winsford, Somerset, and has issue:

1c +Ludo(vic) James Payan; *b* 1993

2c +Oliver Payan; *b* 28 Sept 1996

1c *(Charlotte) Milli(c)e(nt); *b* 1994

1b *Caroline Margaret; *b* 22 Jan 1950; literary agent; has issue:

1c *Hugo Ronald Alexander MacPherson; *b* 1980

2a (cont.) Oliver Dawnay *m* 2nd 25 March 1963 *Hon Iris Irene Adele Peake, LVO [The Hon Mrs Oliver Dawnay, Flat 5, 32 Onslow Sq, London SW7 3NS], est dau of 1st Viscount Ingleby (*qv*), and *d* 1988, having by her had:

2b *Emma Jane Clarissa; *b* 30 June 1964

1a Pamela; *b* 30 May 1907; *d* unm 20 Sept 1983

2a Frances Priscilla; *b* 25 April, *d* 28 May 1912

3a Elizabeth Lavender; *b* 29 June 1914; *m* 26 July 1938 Peter Noel Loxley (*k* in an aircraft accident while on an official mission 1 Feb 1945), Dip Serv, only s of Capt Noel Loxley, RN, and *d* 1996, leaving issue:

1b *David Noel; *b* 1941

1b *Elizabeth Patricia; *b* 1939; *m* 1963 *Baron Bingham of Cornhill (LP, *qv*) and has issue:

1c *Thomas Henry; *b* 1967

2c *Christopher Toby; *b* 1969

1c *Catherine Elizabeth; *b* 1965

(2) Alan Geoffrey Charles, CBE (1919), DSO (1917), Maj-Gen Coldstream Gds, GSO(1) War Office 1930–33, cmdg Irish Gds Regt and Regimental Dist 1935–36, T/Brig and Army Instr IDC 1936, Dir PR War Office 1937, Controller BBC (Programmes Div) 1933–35, served WW I (despatches eight times, brevet), Order Nile, Italian Silver Medal for Mil Valour, Legion Honour and Order El Nahda of Hadjaz; *b* 24 March 1888; *m* 3 Aug 1914 Elizabeth Sofia (*m* 2nd 9 Aug 1949 Col Sir Guy Shaw-Stewart, 9th Bt, MC (*qv*) and *d* 22 April 1968), yr dau of George Bulteel, of Pamflete, Devon, and *d* 28 Sept 1938, leaving issue:

1a Lewis, MBE, Maj Coldstream Gds; *b* 11 Sept 1917; *educ* Eton; *d* unm 30 Aug 1957

2a Denys; *b* 26 Jan 1921; *d* unm 9 Feb 1983

(1) Margaret (Hon), Maid of Honour to HM QUEEN ALEXANDRA 1905–08; *b* 8 April 1880; *m* 23 April 1908 Rev Canon Arthur Rowland Harry Grant (*d* 24 Oct 1961), CVO, MA, TD, DD, Chaplain to HM, Vicar Scalby, Yorks, s of Rev Charles Grant, Preb Wells, and *d* 27 Feb 1948, leaving issue

(2) Marion Vere; *b* 16 Feb 1884; *m* 5 Aug 1905 Col Henry Morris Pryce-Jones (*d* 5 Nov 1952), CB, DSO, MVO, MC, DL, Coldstream Gds, yst s of Sir Pryce Pryce-Jones, of Dolerw, Montgomeryshire (*see* 1956 edn PRYCE-JONES, Bt), and *d* 15 Feb 1956, leaving issue

3 Alan Charles; *b* 15 June 1847; *d* 3 March 1853

4 Guy Cuthbert, MP, NR Yorks 1852–85, DL Yorks; *b* 26 July 1848; *d* 28 Feb 1889

5 Eustace Henry, of West Helserton Hall, Yorks DL, JP, E R Yorks, JP Essex, T/Maj 1914, Lt Coldstream Gds, served Egypt 1882 (medal and star); *b* 15 April 1850; *m* 5 Sept 1883 Lady Evelyn de Vere Capel (*d* 14 Nov 1939), gdau of 6th Earl of Essex (*qv*), and *d* 15 Dec 1928, leaving issue:

(1) Cuthbert Henry, MC, DL, JP E R Yorks, High Sheriff Yorks, Capt Yorks Regt, Hon Lt-Col, WW I ; *b* 4 Nov 1891; *educ* Eton; *m* 10 Nov 1921 Marjorie Kathleen (*d* 1986), only dau of Maj Reginald Bernard Loder (*see* LODER, Bt), and *d* 18 March 1964, leaving issue:

1a *Eve Margaret [Miss Eve Dawnay, West Heslerton Hall, Malton, Yorks]; *b* 26 Oct 1926; *educ* Queen Margaret's Sch Castle Howard and LMH Oxford (BA 1948)

2a *Delia Mary [Lady Millar, The Cottage, Rays Lane, Penn, Bucks HP10 8LH]; *b* 18 Jan 1931; *educ* Queen Margaret's Sch Castle Howard and Courtauld Inst (BA 1953); *m* 21 Jan 1954 Sir Oliver Nicholas Millar, GCVO (*see* INCHYRA, B), and has:

1b *Charles James; *b* 1965; *m* 1990 *Alice Katherine, dau of John W P Martin, of E Molesey, Surrey

1b *Cynthia Mary; *b* 1956

2b *Lucy Anne; *b* 1958; *m* 1st 1977 (*divorce* 1982) John E L Porter and has:

1c *Roland Oliver; *b* 1979

2c *Max John; *b* 1981

2b (cont.) Mrs Lucy Porter *m* 2nd 1983 *Barnaby John Dickens and by him has:

3c *Archie; *b* 1994

1c *Marianna; *b* 1985

3b *Beatrix Jane; *b* 1961; *m* 1987 *Peter Andrew Flory and has:

1c *Oliver William; *b* 1990

2c *Nico Piers; *b* 1993

3a *Verena Joan [Mrs John de la Cour Elliott, 12 Cathcart Rd, London SW10 9NN]; *b* 16 Feb 1936; *educ* Queen Margaret's Sch, Escrick Park, York; *m* 19 April 1958 John Antony de la Cour Elliott and has:

1b *Davina Mary; *b* 1 May 1962

2b *Bridget Victoria [Mrs Charles Benthall, Rectory Farm, W Heslerton, Malton, N Yorks]; *b* 11 Nov 1964; *m* 1988 *Charles Holme Benthall, s of James Holme Benthall, of Benthall Hall, Broseley, Salop (2nd son of Sir (Arthur) Paul Benthall, KBE)

3b *Felicity Jane; *b* 7 July 1966; *m* 1990 Ronald Bourlet (*d* 1995), and has:

1c *Michael Lionel; *b* 1990

2c *Thomas Anthony; *b* 1995

3c *Christopher James; *b* 1995

1c *Rebecca Lucy; *b* 1993

(1) Dorothy Maud; *b* 12 June 1884; *m* 7 Nov 1912 Col Charles William Harry Crichton (*d* 8 Nov 1958), DSO, 10th Hus, est s of Col Hon Sir Henry Crichton, KCB, and *d* 16 April 1959, leaving issue (*see* ERNE, E)

(2) Leila Mary; *b* 12 March 1886; *d* unm Oct 1974

6 William Frederic, DL, JP N R Yorks, JP Northants, Capt Staffs Militia; *b* 14 Oct 1851; *m* 22 April 1875 Lady Adelaide Helen Parker (*d* 14 July 1941), 2nd dau of 6th Earl of Macclesfield (*qv*), and *d* 29 Sept 1904, leaving issue:

(1) Nigel William; *b* 21 Sept 1878; *m* 1st 2 June 1903 Daisy Rosalie Norman (*d* 3 July 1940), only dau of Harry Norman Dunnett, of Stratford St Mary, Suffolk, and had issue:

1a Frederick Cecil; *b* 9 Sept 1905; *educ* Radley and Oxford; *m* 1st 21 June 1929 (*divorce* 1955) Margaret Jean (*d* 11 March 1989), dau of William Coats Hutton, of Lexden Grange, Colchester, and *d* 24 April 1983, leaving:

1b +Richard William, OBE (1970) [Brig Richard Dawnay OBE, Courtside, Richmond Rd, Bath, Somerset BA1 5PU]; Dep Cdr 39th Inf Bde 1974, Brig Div Army Recruiting 1979; *b* 20 April 1930; *educ* Sherborne and RMA Sandhurst; *m* 1 Sept 1962 *Penelope Anne, formerly w of Harry Douglas Smith and dau of Col Norman West Finlinson, DSO, of Goldenfields, Liphook, Hants, by Lesley Elliot, dau of Lt Col Richard James Saumarez (*see* DE SAUMAREZ, B), and has issue:

1c +Rupert Charles Richard; *b* 29 Dec 1964

1c *Philippa Ruth; *b* 3 July 1963; *m* 1990 Peter Shepherd (*divorce* 1994), and has:

1d *Samuel Elliot; *b* 1992

1d *Jessica Kate; *b* 1991

2c *Deborah Kate; *b* 15 July 1966; *m* 1997 *Denis Colman Moloney

2b +Christopher Ronald [Christopher Dawnay Esq, 19 Asher Drive, Mill Ride, Ascot, Berks SL5 8LJ], Capt 10th Roy Hus (PWO); *b* 25 March 1933; *educ* Sherborne and RMA Sandhurst

1a (cont.) Frederick Dawnay *m* 2nd 10 July 1956 *Betty Thora [Mrs Frederick Dawnay, 2 Spring Grove, Sunningdale, Berks], dau of Samuel Henry Darling, of Wentworth, Surrey

2a William Richard; *b* 20 Dec 1910; *m* 1st 25 Oct 1940 (*divorce* 1961) Olive Margaret, dau of Arthur James Barratt, of Mile House, Owestry, and had:

1b *Diana Margaret; *b* 12 Nov 1947

2a (cont.) William Dawnay *m* 2nd 14 Sept 1963 *Pamela [Mrs William Dawnay, Crouch Farm, Whatfield, Ipswich, Suffolk], dau of Charles Lester, of Piper's Croft, Harpenden, Herts, and *d* 1977

3a +Eric Christopher, TD [Eric Dawnay Esq TD, Llyndir, Dolgellau, Gwynedd], Capt 104th (Essex Yeo) Regt RHA (TA) WW II 1939–41 (POW); *b* 28 May 1913; *educ* Radley; *m* 6 Oct 1945 *Vera Winifred, formerly w of James Hobbs, of Denbigh, and dau of Arthur James Barratt, of Mile House, Oswestry, and has issue:

1b +David Nigel [David Dawnay Esq, Llyndir, Dolgellau, Gwynedd]; *b* 24 Oct 1946; *educ* Clayesmore; *m* 1975 (*divorce* 1990) Hilary Jane, dau of James W Robins, MC, of Spinners, Lackford, Suffolk

2b +Michael William; *b* 14 April 1950; *educ* Radley and London U (BA)

1a Evelyn Adelaide; *b* 6 July 1904; *m* 1st 16 March 1927 Lt-Col James Archibald Innes (*d* 16 Aug 1948), DSO, of Horringer Mannor, Bury St Edmunds, Suffolk, and had issue (*see* STANLEY OF ALDERLEY, SHEFFIELD and, B); *m* 2nd 19 Jan 1954, as his 3rd w, Lt-Col Sir Edmond Joly de Lotbiniere, of Horringer Manor

2a *Daisy Isabel (St Margaret's, Dedham, Essex); *b* 25 Oct 1917

(1) (cont.) Nigel Dawnay *m* 2nd 25 Nov 1941 Violet Mary (*d* 7 March 1965), widow of Laurence Harrison and dau of Edward Robert Wilkinson, and *d* 3 Sept 1942

(1) Sybil Mary, OBE (1918); *b* 7 April 1876; *d* unm 9 Oct 1959

(2) Helen Louise; *b* 15 Sept 1877; *m* 20 Aug 1924 Sir Ernest Edward Fletcher (*d* 16 Dec 1940), of Saxlingham Hall, Norwich, and *d* 20 Jan 1974

(3) Hylda; *b* 18 Jan 1880; *m* 9 July 1919 Rev Valentine Pryor Powell (*d* 1948), 2nd son of Henry Pryor Powell, of Hale House, Oakwood, Surrey, and *d* 14 June 1963

(4) Olive; *b* 14 Feb 1886; *m* 15 Dec 1910 Maj Gerard Edmund Byng Stephens (*d* 8 Jan 1962), Rifle Bde, of Cagebrook, Eaton Bishop, Herefs, 4th s of Capt Frederick Stephens, of Bentworth, Hants, and *d* 8 May 1958, leaving issue

7 Geoffrey Nicolas, Capt York Hus; *b* 13 Dec 1852; *m* 18 Aug 1887 Emily Janie (*d* 8 Dec 1935), 4th dau of John Bulteel, JP, of Pamflete, Devon, and *d* 31 Dec 1941, leaving:

(1) Eric Geoffrey, Capt Yorks Hus WW I (despatches); *b* 6 June 1890; *educ* Eton; Im 18 July 1930 Daisy (*d* 26 Jan 1967), only dau of Lt-Col Lewis Butler, of The Wilderness, Earley, Reading, and *d* 12 Sept 1970, leaving issue:

1a *Diana Buttercup; *b* 13 Dec 1931; *m* 16 Feb 1957 *Hugh Rowland Murray Barran, only son of Capt Hugh Bradley Barran, MC, of Finghall, Leyburn, Yorks (*see* BARRAN, Bt), and has issue

(1) Marjorie Clare; *b* 12 Aug 1888; *m* 18 June 1918 Lt-Col Frederick Farrer Deakin, DSO, and *d* 16 Sept 1920, leaving issue

(2) Kathleen; *b* 6 Nov 1892

(3) Eileen; *b* 6 Nov 1892

(4) Joan; *b* 24 Jan 1902

8 Francis Herbert, of Easthorpe Hall, Malton, Yorks, barrister Inner Temple, Capt and Hon Maj Yorks Hus; *b* 11 Dec 1853; *d* unm 26 June 1914

1 Alice Isabel; *d* unm 8 Oct 1929

2 Edith Mary; *m* 2 Feb 1884 Robert Grant-Suttie (*d* 15 Sept 1933), of Ealgone, North Berwick, 4th s of Sir George Grant-Suttie, 5th Bt, of Balgone (*qv*), and *d* 15 July 1941, leaving issue

The 7th VISCOUNT *d* 26 Jane 1857; his est son,

HUGH RICHARD DAWNAY, **8th Viscount Downe** and **1st Baron Dawnay of Danby** (UK), so *cr* 24 July 1897, KCVO (Dec 1902, CVO Nov 1902), CB (1900), CIE (1886); *b* 20 July 1844; *educ* Eton and Ch Ch Oxford; Maj-Gen (ret 1902), Col 10th Hus, Lt-Col cmdg 1887–92, served Zulu War 1879 and Boer War 1899–1901; *m* 1st 12 July 1869 Lady Cecilia Maria Charlotte, VA, Lady of the Bedchamber to HM QUEEN VICTORIA (*d* 26 May 1910), only dau of 3rd Earl of Sefton (*see* 1970 edn), and had issue:

1 JOHN, **9th Viscount**

2 Hugh, DSO, Maj 2nd Life Gds, Capt Rifle Bde, ADC to C-in-C 1901–05, served Nile Expdn 1898, Boer War 1899–1900, Somaliland 1908–10 and WW I; *b* 19 Sept 1875; *m* 28 April 1902 Lady Susan de la Poer Beresford (*d* 31 Oct 1947), dau of 5th Marquess of Waterford (*qv*), and was *ka* 6 Nov 1914, leaving issue:

(1) David (Sir), KCVO, CB, (1952), DSO (1943) and bar (1945), Maj Gen 10th Hus, Hon Col NI Horse WW II, cmdg 1941–44, 21st Tank Bde 1944–45, 2nd Armoured Bde 1946–47 and 8th Armoured Bde 1948–50, Cmdt RMA Sandhurst 1951–54, Cdr 56 (London) Armoured Div TA 1954, Col 10th Royal Hus 1962–63; *b* 10 July 1903; *educ* Eton and RMC Sandhurst; *m* 14 Oct 1926 Lady Katherine Nora de la Poer Beresford, 2nd dau of 6th Marquess of Waterford (*qv*), and *d* 1971, leaving issue:

1a +Hugh [Major Hugh Dawnay, Whitfield Court, Co Waterford, Ireland], Maj The Royal Hus (PWO) (ret); *b* 17 Dec 1932; *educ* Eton; *m* 1971 *Maria Ines, dau of Dr D Cermesoni, of Salta, Argentina, and has issue:

1b +David Danton; *b* 15 Sept 1972

2b +Sebastian Hugo; *b* 3 Oct 1975

2a +Peter [Peter Dawnay Esq, Pendene, Kale St, Batcombe, Somerset]; dir Sidgwick and Jackson 1961–65, md Peter Dawnay, publishers, 1966; *b* 17 Dec 1932; *educ* Eton and Ch Ch Oxford (BA 1956); *m* 1980 *Caroline Mary, 2nd dau of Gp Capt Nicolas Henry Joseph Tindal, RAF, of Co Mayo, and has:

1b +Giles William; *b* 1981

1a Blanche; *b* 1 Feb 1928; *k* in car crash Copenhagen 22 Aug 1953

2a Rachel; *b* 25 Sept 1929; *d* 1983

(2) Peter (Sir), KCVO (1961, MVO 1939), CB (1958) , DSC (1944), DL (Hants 1975); V-Adml (ret 1962), served WW II, Dep Controller Admlty 1956–58, Flag Offr Royal Yachts 1958–61, Extra Equerry to HM THE QUEEN 1958, OStJ 1973, dir Morland and Co 1965, USA Legion of Merit; *b* 14 Aug 1904; *educ* RNCs Osborne and Dartmouth; *m* 28 April 1936 *Lady Angela Christine Rose Montagu Douglas Scott [The Lady Angela Dawnay, Flat 8, Sutton Manor Mews, Sutton Scotney, Hants], yst dau of 7th Duke of Buccleuch and (9th Duke of) Queensberry (*qv*), and *d* 1989, leaving:

1a +Charles John, Lt-Col Welsh Gds [Lt-Col Charles Dawnay, Fleet House, Eversley, Hants RG27 0QN]; *b* 29 Jan 1938; *educ* Eton; *m* 18 March 1968 *Adriana Louise, est dau of Maj-Gen Godfrey John Hamilton, CB, CBE, DSO (*see* COLTHURST, Bt), and has:

1b +Henry Marcus; *b* 4 Jan 1969

2b +George Edward; *b* 19 June 1970

3b +Nicholas St John; *b* 5 July 1978

1b *Sophia Penelope; *b* 23 May 1981

1a *Moyra Jane [Mrs Timothy de Zoete, 33 Pembridge Villas, London W11]; *b* 8 April 1946; *m* 2 July 1969 *Timothy Rupert de Zoete, only son of Rupert Edward de Zoete by Anna, er dau of Maj Guy Melvil Gibbs, TD (*see* ALDENHAM and HUNSDON OF HUNSDON, B), and has issue:

1b *Alexandra Margot; *b* 18 April 1973

(3) Ronald, Lt-Col Coldstream Gds WW II 1939–42 (despatches, POW); *b* 2 Feb 1908; *m* 1st 26 July 1932 Lady Elizabeth Katherine Grey (*d* 25 Feb 1941), yr dau of 5th Earl Grey (*qv*), and had issue:

1a +Andrew Charles, late 2nd Lt Coldstream Gds; *b* 8 Nov 1934; *educ* Eton and Ch Ch Oxford

2a John Alexander George; *b* 28 March 1938; *d* unm 14 March 1961

1a *Ann Josephine; *b* 13 Aug 1933; *educ* Somerville Coll Oxford

2a *Mary, LVO (1983), JP [Lady Carew Pole LVO JP, Antony House, Torpoint, Cornwall PL11 2QA]; Ldy-in-Waiting to HRH THE PRINCESS ANNE April 1970; *b* 15 April 1936; *m*, as his 2nd w, Sir (John) Richard Walter Reginald Carew Pole, 13th Bt (*qv*), and has issue

(3) (cont.) Lt-Col Ronald Dawnay *m* 2nd 23 June 1949 *Sibell Margaret [Mrs Ronald Dawnay, The Glen Ballingary, Co Limerick, Ireland], formerly w of Hon Archibald Edward Cubitt (*see* ASHCOMBE, B) and er dau of Ronald Collet Norman, JP, and *d* 1990

(4) Michael, W/Cdr RAF WW II; *b* 24 Oct 1912; *m* 29 March 1938 Julian Mary (*d* 1979), adopted dau of 1st Baron Brassey of Apethorpe (*qv*), and *d* 19 March 1946, leaving issue:

1a +Patrick Julian [Patrick Dawnay Esq,The Tower House, Sible Hedingham, Essex]; *b* 27 March 1939; *educ* Eton; *m* 21 May 1966 *Julie Katharine, yr dau of Lt-Col William Herbert Olivier, TD, DL, RA, of Ashford Hall, Bakewell, Derbys, and has issue:

1b +Michael William; *b* 17 July 1969

1b *Katherine Julian; *b* 31 March 1968

2b *Evelyn Mary; *b* 1974

2a *Romayne Julian; *b* 25 Aug 1940; *m* 1972 *Peter Rowland Timms, and has issue:

1b *Matthew Rowland Julian; *b* 1974

2b *Christopher Rowland Julian; *b* 1978

1b *Virginia Julian; *b* 1975

1 Beryl; *b* 20 Oct 1873; *m* 11 Jan 1905 Sir Archibald Henry Campbell (*d* 10 May 1948), of Commonwood Lodge, Chipperfield, Herts (*see* CAWDOR, E), and *d* 28 Dec 1950

2 Norah, OStJ; *b* 15 Oct 1874; *d* unm 27 June 1947

3 Faith, served WW I, Medaille Reconnaissance Françcaise, Croix de Guerre; *b* 25 Dec 1877; *d* unm 15 July 1952

The **8th Viscount** *m* 2nd 27 July 1911 Florence Faith (*m* 2nd 15 April 1931 Rev Arthur Maxwell Bury, Vicar Loose, Maidstone (*d* 29 Dec 1936), and *d* 23 Jan 1958), JP Northants, DGStJ, dau of Rev Thomas Henry Dening, Vicar Holy Trinity, Kilburn, and *d* 21 Jan 1924

His er son,

JOHN DAWNAY, **9th Viscount Downe**, CMG, DSO, DL, JP N R Yorks; Brev Lt-Col, Maj Norfolk Yeo, Capt 10th Hus, Staff Offr WW I, Mil Sec to Ld Lt Ireland 1918, Chevalier Legion of Honour, served Boer War 1899–1901 (despatches, Queen's medal with seven clasps); *b* 23 May 1872; *m* 24 July 1902 Dorothy, JP (Norfolk 1934) (*d* 23 March 1957), only dau of Sir William Hovell Browne ffolkes, 3rd Bt (*qv*), and had issue:

1 RICHARD, **10th Viscount**

2 George William ffolkes, MC (1945), JP (Norfolk 1961); Maj (ret 1959) Coldstream Gds WW II, dir Barclays Bank; *b* 20 April 1909 (HM GEORGE V stood sponsor); *educ* Eton; *m* 23 July 1945 Rosemary Helen (*d* 19 Sept 1969), dau of Lord Edward Grosvenor (*see* WESTMINSTER, D), and *d* 1990, leaving issue:

(1) +Valentine George; *b* 25 April 1948; *educ* Eton

(2) +Edward (Ned) William [Edward Dawnay Esq, Hillington Hall, King's Lynn, Norfolk PE31 6BW]; Ib 10 Feb 1950; *educ* Eton; with Lazards to 1993, bank dir; *m* 11 June 1996 his cousin Lady Jane Grosvenor, dau of 5th Duke of Westminster (*qv*) and formerly w of 10th Duke of Roxburghe (*qv*)

(1) *Elizabeth Rose; *b* 29 June 1946

(2) *(Mary) Isabel Dorothy; *b* 24 Nov 1955; *m* 25 Sept 1976 *Victor Anthony Cazalet, yr son of Peter Victor Ferdinand Cazalet, DL, and has issue:

1a *Catherine Rosemary; *b* 22 June 1979

2a *Clare Elizabeth; *b* 1983

1 Ruth Mary; *b* 29 Aug 1907; *m* 8 Dec 1937 Archibald Crawford Scott (*d* 15 Sept 1965), and *d* following a car crash 28 Nov 1962, leaving issue

The 9th VISCOUNT *d* 1 Dec 1931; his er son,

RICHARD DAWNAY, **10th Viscount Downe**, OBE (1945), DL (1947), JP (1933); *b* 16 May 1903; *educ* Eton; Col 5th Bn The Green Howards, Lt Res of Offrs Gren Gds, served WW II, Page of Honour to HM 1917–19, OStJ; *m* 28 Oct 1928 Margaret Christine (*d* 25 March 1967), dau of Christian Bahnsen, of Passaic, New Jersey, USA, and *d* 8 Dec 1965, leaving issue:

1 JOHN CHRISTIAN GEORGE DAWNAY, **11th and present Viscount Downe**

2 James Richard; *b* 8 Sept 1937; *m* 29 Nov 1976 *Gillian, yst dau of Maj James Cyril Aubrey George Dance, MP, of Moreton House, Moreton Morrell, Warwicks, and formerly w of Capt Simon George Melville Portal, 17th/21st Lancers (*see* PORTAL, Bt), and *d* 1991, leaving issue:

(1) +Thomas Payan; *b* 24 July 1978

Seat: Wykeham Abbey, Scarborough, N Yorks. The name derives from a Cistercian convent, which at the dissolution of the religious houses in the 1530s was granted to a certain Francis Poole. He sold it on a few years later to one Richard Hutchinson, apparently a prosperous local farmer. In the middle decades of ELIZABETH I's reign Richard's son Edward, or more likely his grandson Stephen, built a reasonably commodious house of steep gables, a main block with jutting wings and prominent chimney stacks. At least one of these last is thought to survive as part of the present structure and even the Elizabethan house was probably not a wholly fresh start inasmuch as it has been suggested the pre-Reformation prioress's lodgings were adapted to form part of what is now the southwest corner.

Some 150 years later the property appears still to have been in the hands of the HUTCHINSONs, for a Richard of that name was in possession at Wykeham, though later, on coming into landed property at North Grimston willed him by his uncle Thomas Langley, he adopted the latter's surname. His son, another Richard, carried out remodelling in the 1780s and 1790s which included the formation of the curved bay window on the south facade, a new coach house and stables and major repairs to the roof. He died in 1817, leaving Wykeham to his first wife for her life and then to his second cousin Marmaduke, who on the widow's death in 1824 accordingly took the name Langley too. (*See* the younger brother of the **2nd** and **3rd Viscounts** above.)

Date stones of 1835 and 1839 show that Marmaduke must have carried out his own remodelling programme on the house, possibly being responsible for the colonnade along the south flank. His architect, it has been suggested, was Henry Wyatt, who is known to have helped transform Scarborough, the nearest big town, into a resort of some elegance. But on Marmaduke's death the place was left alone for half a century, the next phase of building dating from the time of the future **9th Viscount**'s marriage, when his father employed Walter Mills of Banbury to add the three-storey two-bay extension and sweep away the twin front doors in the main facade, replacing them by a single porch. Internally Mills peopled the hallway with columns, thrusting the staircase up the entire height of the building and throwing out single-storey wings along the south front to create a large dining-room in the west wing. This was given a groined and vaulted plasterwork ceiling in pastiche Adam style by George Jackson in 1902. J H Bolton carried out further changes to the Green Drawing Room shortly after the last War, breaking the overhead space up into a series of panels and decorative bands which culminate in a single octagonal central medallion.

DOWNSHIRE

Arms: Quarterly, 1st, sable on a fess argent, between three leopards passant guardant or, spotted of the field, as many escallops gules (for HILL); 2nd, party per bend sinister ermine and ermines a lion rampant or (for TREVOR); 3rd, gules a quatrefoil or (for ROWE); 4th, argent a chevron azure between three trefoils, slipped per pale gules and vert, also (for ROWE). **Crest:** A reindeer's head, couped gules, attired and plain collared or. **Supporters:** Dexter, a leopard or, spotted sable, ducally gorged and chained gules; sinister, a reindeer gules, attired, unguled and plain collared, or. **Mottoes:** 1 *Per Deum et ferrum obtinui* ('I have won my possessions by God and the sword'), 2 *Ne tentes aut perfice* ('Triumph or do not attempt at all'). **Creations:** B. (Hill of Kilwarlin) and V. (Hillsborough) (I) 21 Aug 1717, E. (Hillsborough) and V. (Kilwarlin) (I) 3 Oct 1751, B. (Harwich) (GB) 17 Nov 1756, E. (Hillsborough) and V. (Fairford) (GB) 28 Aug 1772, M. (I) 20 Aug 1789.

THE 8TH MARQUESS OF DOWNSHIRE, Earl of Hillsborough, Viscount Hillsborough, Co Down, **Viscount Kilwarlin,** Co Down, **Baron Hill of Kilwarlin,** Co Down, **Earl of Hillsborough, Viscount Fairford,** Co Gloucester, and **Lord Harwich, Baron of Harwich,** Co Essex ((Arthur) Robin Ian Hill) [The Most Hon The Marquess of Downshire, Clifton Castle, Ripon, N Yorks HG4 4AB]; *b* 10 May 1929; *s* unc 1989; *educ* Eton; Hereditary Constable Hillsborough Fort, 2nd Lt RSG 1948–50, chartered accountant; *m* 1st 5 Oct 1957 Hon Juliet Mary Weld-Forester (*d* 1986), 2nd dau of 7th Baron Forester (*qv*), and has issue:

1 +(ARTHUR FRANCIS) NICHOLAS (NICK) WILLS, *Earl of Hillsborough* [Earl of Hillsborough, High Burton, N Yorks]; *b* 4 Feb 1959; *m* 1990 *(Diana) Jane (Janey), only dau of Gerald Leeson Bunting, of Otterington House, Northallerton, Yorks, and has issue:

(1) +Edmund Robin Arthur, *Viscount Kilwarlin*; *b* 21 May 1996

(1) *Isabella Diana Juliet; *b* 1991

(2) *Beatrice Hannah Georgina; *b* 1994

2 +Anthony Ian; *b* 20 Oct 1961; *m* 1992 *Annabel Priscilla Angela, yr dau of Hon David Lawrence Robert Nall-Cain (*see* BROCKET, B), and has issue:

(1) +Marcus Robert Francis; *b* 3 July 1994

(2) +Orlando Harry Wills; *b* 10 June 1997

2 *Georgina Mary; *b* 29 Dec 1964

The 8th MARQUESS *m* 2nd 1989 *Mrs Diana Marion Hibbert, 2nd dau of Rt Hon Sir Ronald Hibbert Cross, 1st and last Bt, KCMG, KCVO (*see* 1959 edn)

Lineage: Sir MOYSES HILL; offr in Ireland 1573 to suppress O'Neil's uprising, Govr Olderfleet Castle, MP Co Antrim 1613, 1st Provost Marshal of the forces in Carrickfergus, Provost Marshal Province of Ulster 1617; *m* 1st Alice, sis of Sorley Buie Macdonnel; *m* 2nd Anne Grogan and *d* Feb 1629/30, having had, with three daus:

PETER HILL; Provost Marshal and Sheriff Co Down 1641; *m* —, dau of Sorley Buie Macdonnel and sis of 1st Earl of Antrim (*qv*), and had issue:

1 Francis, of Hill Hall, Co Down; *m* Ursula, dau of Sir Francis Stafford, of Portglenone, Co Antrim, and had issue:

(1) Anne; *m* her cousin Moyses Hill and had issue (*see* below)

(2) Rose; *m* Sir Robert Colvil, of Newtown, Co Down

2 Randal; *d* unm

3 Arthur, of Hillsborough, PC; Constable Hillsborough Fort 1660, Col royalist regt Civil War, MP *temp* OLIVER CROMWELL and after the Restoration; *m* 1st Anne (*bur* 7 Jan 1636), dau of Sir Richard Bolton, Ld Chllr Ireland, and had, with two other sons:

(1) Moyses, of Hillsborough; Lt-Col, MP Drogheda 1661; *m* Anne (*m* 2nd Patrick Sheridan, Bp Cloyne, and *d* July 1683), est dau and coheir of Francis Hill, of Hill Hall (*see* above), and *d* 19 April 1664, having had issue

3 (cont.) Arthur Hill *m* 2nd Mary, dau of Sir William Parsons, Ld Justice Ireland (*see* ROSSE, E), and *d* April 1663, having by her had, with other issue:

(2) William, PC *temp* CHARLES II and JAMES II; Lt Cos Down and Antrim, MP Ballyshannon 1661–92; *m* 1st Eleanor, dau of Michael Boyle, Archbp Armagh, and had:

1a MICHAEL, of whom presently

(2) William Hill *m* 2nd Mary (*d* 9 July 1711), (est?) dau of 1st Viscount Dungannon of the 1662 *cr* and sis of 2nd and 3rd Viscounts of that *cr*, and *d* between 7 July 1692 and 20 Nov 1693, having by her had, with another s:

2a Marcus; bequeathed property he had inherited from his mother's Trevor relations to MICHAEL, his half-bro through his f, whence MICHAEL's yr s's choice of title (*see* below)

(1) Penelope; *m* 1666 Richard Coote, s of Sir Charles Coote, 2nd Bt (*qv*), 1st Earl of Mountrath, and had issue

His s by his 1st w,

MICHAEL HILL, of Hillsborough, PC; *b c* 1672; MP Saltash (E Parl) and Hillsborough (I Parl), Lt Co Down; *m* 1690 Anne, dau and eventual heir of Sir John Trevor, of Brynkinalt, Denbighs, Master of the Rolls, Speaker H of C, 1st Lord-Commr Gt Seal, and had issue, with a dau (Anne, *m* St John Brodnich; *see* MIDLETON, V):

1 TREVOR, **1st Viscount**

2 ARTHUR HILL later HILL-TREVOR (added by Act of Parl Jan 1759 on inheriting the Brynkinhalt estate), 1st VISCOUNT OF DUNGANNON, so *cr* 17 Feb 1766, as also BARON HILL OF OLDERFLEET (both I), of Belvoir, Co Down, and Brynkinalt, PC (I 1750); MP Hillsborough 1715–27 and Co Down 1727–65, Sheriff Co Down 1736, Chllr Exchequer I 1754–55 and Commr Revenue I 1755–71; *m* 1st Anne (*dsps*), 2nd dau and coheir of Joseph Deane, of Crumlin, Co Dublin, by Margaret Boyle, sis of 1st Earl of Shannon (*qv*); *m* 2nd 12 Jan 1737 Anne, dau of Edmund Stafford, of Brownstown, Co Meath, and *d* 30 Jan 1771, having had by her:

(1) Arthur; *b c* 1740; *m* Letitia (*m* 2nd 1st Marquess of Antrim (*see* ANTRIM, E) and *d* 7 Dec 1801), dau of 1st Viscount Mountmorres, and *dvp* 19 June 1770, leaving:

1a ARTHUR HILL-TREVOR, 2nd VISCOUNT OF DUNGANNON; *b* 3 Oct 1763; *m* 30 July 1795 Hon Charlotte FitzRoy, dau of 1st Baron Southampton (*qv*), and *d* 14 Dec 1837, leaving an only s:

1b ARTHUR HILL-TREVOR, 3rd and last VISCOUNT OF DUNGANNON; *b* 9 Nov 1798; *educ* Harrow and Ch Ch Oxford; MP (I) New Romney 1830–31 and Durham 1831–32, 1835–41 and April-July 1843, High Sheriff Flints 1855, rep I peer 1855–62; *m* 10 Sept 1821 Sophia, dau of Col Gorges Marcus Irvine, of Castle Irvine, Co Fermanagh, and *dsp* 11 Aug 1862, when his titles expired, leaving his estates to his cousin 1st Baron Trevor of Brynkinalt (*qv*; *see* also below)

(1) Anne; *b* 23 June 1742; *m* 1st Earl of Mornington, and *d* 10 Dec 1831, leaving issue (of whom the 3rd s, Arthur, was *cr* Duke of Wellington (*qv*))

(2) Prudence; *b* 17 March 1745; *m* 22 May 1765 Charles Powell Leslie (*see* LESLIE, Bt)

MICHAEL HILL *d* 1699; his er son,

TREVOR HILL, **1st Viscount Hillsborough**, Co Down, so *cr* 21 Aug 1717, as also BARON HILL OF KILWARLIN, Co Down (both I), with remainder, in default of heirs male of his body, to the heirs male of the body of his f; *b* 1693; *m* Mary (*d* 23 Aug 1742), widow of Sir Edmund Denton, 1st and last Bt, and est dau and coheir of Anthony Rowe, of Muswell Hill, and *d* 3 May 1742, having had, with two er sons and a dau (Anne, *m* 1st Earl of Moira; *see* SAINT DAVIDS, V):

WILLS HILL, **1st Marquess of Downshire** (I), so *cr* 20 Aug 1789, as also 3 Oct 1751 VISCOUNT KILWARLIN, Co Down, and EARL OF HILLSBOROUGH, Co Down (both I), with remainder in default of male issue to his uncle, Arthur Hill; also 17 Nov 1756 LORD HARWICH, BARON OF HARWICH, Co Essex (GB), and 28 Aug 1772 VISCOUNT FAIRFORD, Co Gloucester, and EARL OF HILLSBOROUGH (both GB), PC (1754), LLD; *b* 30 May 1718; MP Warwick 1741–56, 1st Commr of Trade and Plantations 1763, Jt PMG 1766, Sec State Colonies 1768–72 and 1779, Registrar High Court Chancery Ireland; *m* 1st 1 March 1747 Lady Margaretta Fitz Gerald (*d* 19 Jan 1766), sis of 1st Duke of Leinster (*qv*), and had sons and two daus; *m* 2nd 14 Oct 1768 Mary Baroness Stawel [*sic*] of Somerton in her own right (*b* 27 Jan 1725/6; *d* 29 July 1780), so *cr* 21 May 1760 (GB), with remainder to heirs male of her body by her 1st husb, dau and heir of 4th and last Baron Stawell of Somerton and widow of Rt Hon Henry Legge later Bilson-Legge, s of 1st Earl of Dartmouth (*qv*), and *d* 7 Oct 1793; his only surv s by his 1st w:

ARTHUR HILL, **2nd Marquess of Downshire**, PC (I 1793); *b* 3 March 1753; MP (Tory) Lostwithiel 1774–80, Malmesbury 1780–84 and (I Parl) Co Down 1776–93; *m* 29 June 1786 Mary, *cr* 19 June 1802 Baroness Sandys of Ombersley, Co Worcester, with remainder to her 2nd and yr sons successively (*d* 1 Aug 1836), dau of Hon Martyn Sandys by Mary, dau of William Trumbull, of Easthampstead Park, Berks, by Mary, dau of Montague Blundell, Viscount Blundell, and *d* 7 Sept 1801, having had, with other issue (*see* SANDYS, B):

ARTHUR BLUNDELL SANDYS TRUMBULL HILL, **3rd Marquess of Downshire**, KP, DCL, Ld Lt Co Down; *b* 8 Oct 1788; *educ* Eton and Ch Ch Oxford; *m* 25 Oct 1811 Lady Maria Windsor (*d* 7 April 1855), est dau of 5th Earl of Plymouth (*qv*), and had, with two daus:

1 ARTHUR WILLS BLUNDELL SANDYS TRUMBULL WINDSOR, **4th Marquess**

2 William Frederick Arthur Montagu, Capt Scots Greys; *b* 10 July 1816; *d* thrown from his horse while hunting 18 March 1844

3 ARTHUR EDWIN HILL TREVOR, 1st BARON TREVOR OF BRYNKINALT (*qv*)

The 3rd MARQUESS *d* 12 April 1845; his est son,

ARTHUR WILLS BLUNDELL SANDYS TRUMBULL WINDSOR HILL, **4th Marquess of Downshire**, KP (1859); *b* 6 Aug 1812; *educ* Eton and Ch Ch Oxford; MP (C) Co Down 1836–45, Col S Downshire Militia; *m* 23 Aug 1837 Caroline

Frances (*d* 10 May 1893), est dau of 1st Viscount Combermere (*qv*), and had, with an est s (*d* young):

1 ARTHUR WILLS BLUNDELL TRUMBULL SANDYS RODEN, **5th Marquess**

2 Arthur William, PC; Comptroller Household 1885–86, 1886–92 and 1895–98, Hon Col 5th Bn Roy Irish Rifles, Lt-Col 2nd Middx Art Vol, Lt 2nd Life Gds, JP Berks and Co Down, DL, MP Co Down 1880–85 and W Down 1885–98 and 1907–08; *b* 29 July 1846; *m* 1st 16 Jan 1873 Annie Nisida Denham (*d* 16 Jan 1874), only child of Lt-Col George Denham Cookes, 3rd KO Light Dragoons, and had issue:

(1) Arthur, MP W Down 1898–1905, Maj 5th Bn Royal Irish Rifles; *b* 30 Dec 1873; *m* 1908 Roberta Menges, formerly wife of Halsey Corwin, of Brooklyn, New York, and *dsp* 27 June 1913

2 (cont.) Col Lord Arthur Hill *m* 2nd 14 March 1877 Annie (*d* 12 Feb 1944), 3rd dau of James Fortescue Harrison, of Crawleywood Park, Sussex, MP Kilmarnock, and *d* 13 Jan 1931, having by her had issue:

(1) Nina; *b* 23 Dec 1877; *m* 25 June 1907 George Brooke (*dvp* 5 Oct 1914 of wounds received in action), Irish Gds, est son of Sir George Brooke, 1st Bt, of Summerton (*qv*), and *d* 3 Sept 1970, leaving issue

1 Alice Maria; *m* 9 Oct 1867 Thomas, Earl of Bective (*d* 15 Dec 1893), and *d* 25 Feb 1928, leaving issue (*see* HEADFORT, M)

The 4th MARQUESS *d* 6 Aug 1868; his er son,

ARTHUR WILLS BLUNDELL TRUMBULL SANDYS RODEN HILL, **5th Marquess of Downshire**; Offr 1st Life Gds; *b* 24 Dec 1844; *m* 26 July 1870 Georgiana Elizabeth (*d* 12 Jan 1919), 2nd dau of John Balfour, of Balbirnie, Fife, by Lady Georgiana, dau of 1st Earl Cawdor (*qv*), and *d* 31 March 1874, leaving an only s:

ARTHUR WILLS JOHN WELLINGTON TRUMBULL BLUNDELL HILL, **6th Marquess of Downshire**, DL, JP Co Down, Capt Berks Yeo, formerly Derbyshire Imp Yeo; *b* 2 July 1871; *m* 1st 22 June 1893 (*divorce* 1902) Katherine Mary (*d* 2 Feb 1959), 2nd surv dau of Hugh Henry Hare (*see* LISTOWEL, E), and had issue:

1 ARTHUR WILLS PERCY WELLINGTON BLUNDELL TRUMBULL SANDYS HILL, **7th Marquess of Downshire**; *b* 7 April 1894; *educ* Eton; Lt Berks Yeo, attd BRC France WW I; *m* 23 July 1953 *Noreen, only dau of William Barraclough and widow of (a) — Gray-Miller and (b) Maj Walter Fox and previously wife of — Allen, and *d* 28 March 1989

2 (Arthur) Francis Henry, Capt 2nd Dragoons, Scots Greys, WW I (despatches), ADC to Govr-Gen S Africa 1921–24; *b* 28 Aug 1895; *m* 15 Oct 1927 Ishabel Wilhelmina Sheila (*d* 29 March 1961), yst dau of Col Stewart MacDougall of Lunga, Argyll, and *d* 25 Dec 1953, leaving issue:

(1) (ARTHUR) ROBIN IAN HILL, **8th and present Marquess of Downshire**

(1) *Venice Marigold (Rosie) [Venice Lady Kindersley, Ramhurst Manor, Tonbridge, Kent]; *b* 21 July 1930; *m* 4 Sept 1954 (*divorce* 1989) 3rd Baron Kindersley (*qv*) and has issue

(2) *Caroline Sylvia [The Lady Caroline Borg, Telegraph House, 36 West Sq, London SE11 4SP]; *b* 21 March 1938; *m* 23 July 1976 *Dr Alan C N Borg, CBE, Dir V&A, and has:

1a *Leonora Ishbel; *b* 1980

2a *Helen Olivia; *b* 1982

1 Kathleen Nina, Co Assist ATS; *b* 15 Sept 1898; *m* 1st 14 Feb 1917 (*divorce* 1946) William Hereward Charles Rollo (*k* in a hunting accident 3 Oct 1962), son of Hon Eric Norman Rollo (*see* ROLLO, L), and had issue; *m* 2nd 12 Dec 1949 *Lt-Col Daniel Vincent Hanson Asquith, DSO, The Queens Bays, son of Bentley Asquith, of Tring, Herts, and Low Moor, Yorks, and *d* 30 Nov 1960

The **6th Marquess** *m* 2nd 16 May 1907 Evelyn Grace Mary (*d* 30 Dec 1942), est dau of Edmund Benson Foster, DL, of Clewer Manor, Windsor, and *d* 29 May 1918

D'OYLY

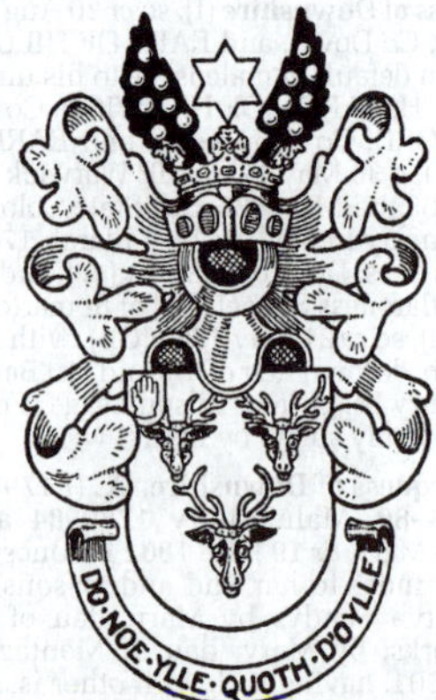

Arms: Gu. three buck's heads cabossed arg. **Crest:** Out of a ducal coronet two wings erect sa. bezantée, between which and resting on the strawberry leaf of the coronet an estoile of six points arg. **Motto:** *Do noe ylle, quoth D'Oylle* ('Do no ill, quoth Doyle'). **Creation:** Bt. (E) 29 July 1663.

SIR NIGEL HADLEY MILLER D'OYLY, 14TH BT, of Shottisham, Norfolk [Sir Nigel D'Oyly Bt, New Lodge, Crowhurst, E Sussex TN33 9AB]; *b* 6 July 1914; *s* half-bro 1986; *educ* Radley and RMC Sandhurst; Maj The Roy Scots WW II Hong Kong, France, War Office; *m* 27 Oct 1939 Dolores (*d* 1971), dau of R H Gregory, of New Lodge Crowhurst, Sussex, and has issue:

1 +HADLEY GREGORY [Hadley D'Oyly Esq, Flat B, 37 New North Rd, Islington, London N1 6JB]; *b* 29 May 1956; *educ* Milton Abbey; *m* 1st 1978 (*divorce* 1982) Margaret Mary Dent; *m* 2nd 1991 *Annette Frances Elizabeth, yst dau of Maj Michael White, of Farnham Royal, Bucks, and has issue:

(1) *India Dolores; *b* 1992

1 *Carol Dolores; *b* 7 April 1942; *m* 1st 1961 (*divorce* 1966) Robert Macvarish, and has:

(1) *Simon; *b* 1962

(1) *Robyn; *b* 1964

1 (cont.) Mrs Carol Macvarish *m* 2nd 1968 *Charles Pearce, and has further issue:

(2) *Carl; *b* 1970

2 *Sherry Angela [Mrs Ronald Mumford, The Smuggler Inn, Pett Level Rd, Pett Level, E Sussex TN35 4EH]; *b* 3 Nov 1946; *m* 1st 1969 (*divorce* 1981) Charles Coxsedge; *m* 2nd 23 Oct 1993 *Ronald Trevor Mumford and by her 1st husb has:

(1) *Benjamin John; *b* 1975

(1) *Hannah Ruth; *b* 1974

Lineage: Sir JOHN D'OYLY; living *temp* HENRY III; *m* Rose, dau and coheir of Sir William de Duston, of Duston, Northants, and was ancestor of:

THOMAS D'OYLY; had:

EDWARD D'OYLEY, of Pondhall, nr Hadleigh, Suffolk; *m* Anne, dau and heir of Helmin Legat, through whom he acquired the Pondhall estate, and had issue:

JOHN D'OYLY, of Pondhall; *m* Elizabeth — and *d* 1483, having had issue:

EDWARD D'OYLY, of Pondhall and Cosford Hall, Suffolk; *m* Anne, dau of Sir Thomas Cotton, of Longwade, Cambs, and *d* 25 Jan 1534, leaving issue:

Sir HENRY D'OYLY, of Pondhall; Sheriff Suffolk 1558, ktd Feb 1546/7; *m* 1st Jane, dau and heir of John Elwy, of Wignal St James, Norfolk, and *d* 13 Feb 1564, leaving:

HENRY D'OYLY, of Pondhall; Sheriff Norfolk 1572 and 1590; *m* Anne, dau of Edmund Whyte and heiress of her bro, Edmund Whyte, of Shottisham, Norfolk, and had an est s:

EDMOND D'OYLY, of Shottisham and Pondhall; Sheriff Norfolk 1602–03; *m* 2nd Catharine, dau of Sir Henry Neville, of Billingbere, Berks (*see* BRAYBROOKE, B), and *d* 1612, leaving:

1 Henry (Sir), of Shottisham; *m* Susan, dau of Sir Lionel Talmache, of Helmingham, ancestor of the Earls of Dysart (*qv*), and left an only s:

(1) Edmond, of Shottisham and Pondhall; *m* Bridget (*m* 2nd Sir Isaac Astley, 1st Bt (*see* HASTINGS, B)), dau of John Coke, of Holkham (s of Sir Edward Coke, Ld Ch Justice (*see* LEICESTER, E), and *d* 28 Sept 1638, leaving an only child:

1a Susuan, *d* a minor 1648

2 William, of Hadleigh, Suffolk; *m* Elizabeth, dau of Ven Richard Stocks, Archdeacon of Norfolk, by Anne, dau of Thomas Wodehouse, of Kimberley, ancestor of the Earls of Kimberley (*qv*), and *d* 1637, having had, with other issue:

(1) **Sir William D'Oyly, 1st Bt** (E), so *cr* 29 July 1663, of Shottisham; MP Norfolk 1654–59 and Yarmouth 1660–77, ktd 1641; *m* 1637 Margaret Randall (*d* May 1679), of Pulham, Norfolk, stepdau of Sir Robert Bacon, 3rd Bt (*qv*), and *d* Nov 1677, leaving an est s:

1a **Sir William D'Oyly, 2nd Bt**; ktd 1664, Teller Exchequer 1666–77; *m* 1666 Mary, dau of John Hadley by Anne, 1st wife of Earl of Torrington, and had:

1b **Sir Edmund D'Oyly, 3rd Bt**; *m* 13 Nov 1684 Dorothy (*d* Dec 1718), est dau of Philip Bedingf(i)eld, of Ditchingham, by Ursula, dau of Sir John Potts, 1st Bt, of Mannington, and was *bur* 24 Oct 1700, leaving issue:

1c **Sir Edmund D'Oyly, 4th Bt**; sold Shottisham and Pondhall and retired to Cossey, Norfolk; *d* unm 1763

2c William; *d* unm 1737

2b Hadley, of Holborn; *m* Elizabeth, dau of Charles Yallop, son of Sir Robert Yallop, of Bowthorpe Hall, nr Norwich, and had surv issue, with a dau:

1c HADLEY (Sir), **5th Bt**

2c Thomas, of Gray's Inn, gf of:

1d Edward, of Sion Hill, nr Thirsk, Yorks, DL, JP N R; Capt W R Yeo Cav; inherited the Burnell estates in the W R 1795; *d* by 23 July 1680

The 4th Bt's cousin,

Rev Sir Hadley D'Oyly, 5th Bt; MA Oxon, Rector Wotton and Felixstowe; *m* Henrietta Maynard (*d* Aug 1793), dau of Rev Henry Osborne, MA, of Nailworth, nr Salisbury, Wilts, Vicar Thaxted, Essex, and *d* 30 July 1764, leaving, with a yr s (Hadley, RM, *k* Bunker's Hill 1775) and five daus:

Sir John Hadley D'Oyly, 6th Bt, of Calcutta and D'Oyly Park, Hants; *b* 1754, Sr Merchant Bengal Establishment, Collector Calcutta, and of the twenty-four Pergunnahs; MP Ipswich 1790–96; *m* 1780 Diana (*d* 6 Sept 1803), widow of William Cotes, of Calcutta, dau of William Rochfort, niece of 1st Earl of Belvidere and gdau of Lady Elizabeth Rochfort, dau of 3rd Earl of Drogheda (*qv*), and *d* Jan 1818, having had, with other issue:

1 **Sir Charles D'Oyly, 7th Bt**; amateur artist; *b* 18 Sept 1781; *m* 1st his cousin Marian (*d* 1814), 3rd dau of William Greer, of Keyhaven, Hants; *m* 2nd Elizabeth Jane (*d* 1 June 1875), dau of Maj Thomas Ross, RA, by Isabella MacLeod, aunt of the Marchioness of Hastings (*see* LOUDOUN, E), and *dsp* 21 Sept 1845

2 **Sir John Hadley D'Oyly, 8th Bt**; served with HEIC Calcutta; *b* 29 Sept 1794; *m* 1st 1 Dec 1819 Charlotte, dau of George Nesbitt Thompson, and had issue:

(1) **Sir Charles Walters D'Oyly, 9th Bt**; Maj-Gen Bengal Army, JP Dorset, served Gwalior Campaign and suppression Indian Mutiny 1857; *b* 21 Dec 1822; *educ* Addiscombe; *m* 1st 25 Sept 1855 Emily Jane (*d* 12 May 1857), 2nd dau of Maj-Gen George Nott, Madras Army, and had issue:

1a Mary Lushington; *m* 4 April 1877 Lt-Col Arthur Francis Bernard (*d* 20 May 1915), of Combe Raleigh, Devon, took the name BERNARD-D'OYLY in lieu of BERNARD and *d* 31 May 1930, leaving issue

(1) (cont.) **Sir Charles** *m* 2nd 5 June 1867 Elinor (*d* 3 Dec 1914), 3rd dau of James Winter Scott, of Rotherfield Park, Hants (*see* SCOTT, Bt, of Rotherfield), and *d* 11 July 1900

(2) George Fendall, Capt 67th Bengal NI; *b* 3 Nov 1824; *educ* Addiscombe Mil Coll; *d* 10 Aug 1859

(1) Diana Rochfort; *d* unm 1840

2 (cont.) **Sir John** *m* 2nd 1830 Mary (*d* 26 May 1885 aged 91), est dau of Hon John Fendall, memb Supreme Cncl Calcutta, and *d* 21 March 1869, having by her had issue:

3 **Sir Warren Hastings D'Oyly, 10th Bt**; Bengal CS 1858–91; *b* 6 April 1838; *m* 1st 1 March 1859 Henrietta Mary (*d* 11 March 1904), dau of Sir Frederick Halliday, KCB, Lt-Govr Bengal, and had issue; *m* 2nd 20 Nov 1909 Amy Agnes (*d* 14 April 1922), widow of Sir George Cotton, KCIE, and dau of James George White, ICS, and *d* 16 Feb 1921, leaving by his 1st w:

(1) HASTINGS HADLEY (Sir), **11th Bt**

(2) Edward Halliday; Assist Dist Supt Police Bengal, Lt Roy Def Corps WW I; *b* 28 July 1865; *m* 1 Aug 1891 Laura, dau of Herbert George Yatman, and *d* 14 Dec 1957, leaving issue:

1a Mary Edith; *b* 1892

2a Mildred Dorothea; *b* 1893

(3) Warren Hastings, Lt RN 1891, Cdr 1902, Capt 1908, R-Adml 1919, V-Adml 1925, served Boer War 1899–1902 (despatches medal), Gambia Expdn 1901 (despatches, medal, clasp), Aro and Niger Expdns 1902 (despatches and clasp to medal), cmded Anglo-French Punitive Expdns New Hebrides 1905 (despatches, promotion), cmded Internat Force landing at Port-au-Prince during Haiti Revolution 1914, WW I (three medals, despatches); *b* 3 Aug 1867; *m* 1 Jan 1912 Sylvia Agnes Alicia (*d* 23 Oct 1966), only surv dau of Gen Sir Reginald Clare Hart, VC, GCB, KCVO, and *d* 22 March 1950, having had issue:

1a Reginald Clare Hastings, Lt (E) RN WW II; *b* 2 Oct 1918; *ka* on HMS *Bonaventure* 31 March 1941

(4) Henry Ralph Neville, Lt-Col RM, served China 1900 (medal), WW I (two medals); *b* 29 Nov 1878; *d* unm 25 Sept 1947

(1) Florence Mary; *m* 1885 Lt-Col Ernest Inglis (*d* 1910), IA, and *d* April 1929, leaving issue

(2) Alice Fanny; *m* 24 June 1886 Col Hugh Thomas Lyle (*d* 24 Jan 1942), CBE, DSO, Royal Welch Fus, of Knocktarna, Co Londonderry, and *d* 26 July 1943, leaving issue

(3) Etta Ellen; *m* 1st 1882 George K Lyon (*d* 1888), BCS, and had issue; *m* 2nd 2 June 1900 Francis Griffiths Swayne (*d* 1949), MA, MB, of Lyndhurst, Church Rd, Upper Norwood, and *d* Dec 1947

(4) Edith Maud Caroline; *d* unm 26 Aug 1891

(5) Margaret Howard; *m* 18 April 1900 Surgn-Capt Frederick Francis Mahon (*d* 27 Aug 1953), RN, and *d* Oct 1965

The 10th Bt's est son,

Sir Hastings Hadley D'Oyly, 11th Bt, Dep Commr Andaman and Nicobar Islands, Capt Roy Def Corps TF and Bihar Light Horse; *b* 26 Jan 1864; *m* 1st Aug 1897 Beatrice Alice (*d* 26 Feb 1906), dau of Francis Bingham Clerk, JP, of Mysore, and had issue:

1 **Sir Charles Hastings D'Oyly, 12th Bt**; *b* 3 July 1898; *d* unm 10 Jan 1962

2 **Sir John Rochfort D'Oyly, 13th Bt**; Cdr RN; *educ* HMS *Conway* and Caius Coll Camb, served WWs I and II; *b* 19 April 1900; *m* 9 Aug 1930 (*divorce* 1944) Kathleen, er dau of Robert Brown Gillespie, of Ceylon, and had:

(1) *Jill Rochfort [Mrs George Creighton, 31 Jalan Kampong Chantek, Singapore, 588612] ; *b* 11 June 1931; *m* 16 Feb 1952 *George Creighton, of Greenock, Renfrewshire, and has:

1a *Glen John; *b* 24 Jan 1953; *m* 1976 (*divorce* 1990) Catherine Heffernan, and has issue:

1b *Chay George; *b* 1982

2b *Keir James (twin); *b* 1982

1b *Maxine Leah; *b* 1979

2a *Ian Robert; *b* 26 June 1960; *m* 1988 (*divorce* 1991) Alexandra Mary Poxon

1a *Linden Gay; *b* 28 Sept 1954; *m* 1974 *Rolf Evans and has issue:

1b *Scott Jamie; *b* 1977

1b *Jacey Samantha; *b* 1979

(2) *Ann Hastings [Mrs Thomas James, Lambs Farm, Tanyard Lane, Danehill, E Sussex RH17 7JN]; *b* 26 Sept 1936; *m* 2 May 1959 Thomas Hepburn James (*d* 14 April 1997) and has:

1a *Shona Ann; *b* 14 Aug 1960; *m* 1986 (*divorce* 1994) Simon James Robert Thomas

2a *Karen Hepburn; *b* 4 April 1964; *m* 1987 (*divorce* 1997) David Leslie Ashby

3a *Tiffany Carterette; *b* 23 Oct 1965; *m* 1991 *Shaun Dudley Sizen

1 Marjorie Isobel; *b* 23 Dec 1901; *m* 18 Feb 1925 (*divorce* 1947) Cdr Godfrey Francis Evans, RN, s of C F Evans, and had issue:

(1) *David D'Oyly [David Evans Esq, Old Stones, Cronks Hill, Redhill, Surrey]; *b* 26 March 1926; *m* 2 June 1956 *Elizabeth Anne, dau of Raymond Austin, and has issue:

1a *Susan; *b* 27 Aug 1957

2a *Carol Jane; *b* 1959

Sir Hastings *m* 2nd 26 Dec 1910 Evelyn Maude (*d* 16 Dec 1962), only dau of George Taverner Miller, JP, and *d* 20 March 1948, having by her had issue:

3 Sir NIGEL HADLEY MILLER D'OYLY, **14th and present Bt**

2 Maude Ethelind Halliday; *b* 27 Dec 1912; *m* 1st 11 July 1934 (*divorce* 1947) Lt-Col John Evelyn Fairlie, The Baluch Regt, IA, est s of Lt-Col C E Fairlie, of Natal, S Africa; *m* 2nd 23 July 1948 Capt (Tom) Gordon Hemming, s of Capt F A Hemming

3 Beryl Evelyn; *b* 26 May 1916

DROGHEDA

Arms: Azure on a chief, indented or, three mullets, pierced gules. **Crest:** Out of a ducal coronet or a Moor's head in profile proper, wreathed about the temples argent and azure. **Supporter:** Two greyhounds argent. **Motto:** *Fortis cadere, cedere, non potest* ('A strong man may fall but cannot yield'). **Creations:** B. (I) 20 July 1616 (Moore of Mellefont) and (UK) 30 Jan 1954 (Moore), V. (I) 7 Feb 1621, E. (I) 14 June 1661.

THE 12TH EARL OF DROGHEDA, Viscount Moore of Drogheda, Baron Moore of Mellefont, Co Louth, and **Baron Moore**, of Cobham, Surrey (Henry Dermot Ponsonby Moore) [The Rt Hon The Earl of Drogheda, 40 Ledbury Rd, London W11 2AB]; *b* 14 Jan 1937; *s f* 1989; *educ* Eton and Trin Coll Cambridge (BA 1960); late 2nd Lt The Life Gds, photographer (as Derry Moore), dir Derry Moore (Photography) Ltd; *m* 1st 15 May 1968 (*divorce* 1972) Eliza, dau of Stacy Barcroft Lloyd, Jr, of Philadelphia, and St Croix, Virgin Islands, and Mrs Paul Mellon, of Upperville, Virginia, and Washington, DC; *m* 2nd 9 Dec 1978 *Alexandra, only child of Sir (John) Nicholas Henderson, KCMG, sometime Br Amb USA, and has:

1 +BENJAMIN GARRETT HENDERSON, *Viscount Moore*; *b* 21 March 1983

2 +Garrett Alexander; *b* 1986

1 *Marina Alice; *b* 1988

Lineage: Two bros and descendants of the MOOREs of Moore Place, Kent, Sir EDWARD and Sir THOMAS MOORE (ancestor of the Earls of Charleville (extinct 1764)), settled in Ireland temp ELIZABETH I

The er bro,

Sir EDWARD MOORE, of Mellefont, Co Louth; *m* 1st Elizabeth (*d* 30 Nov 1581), widow of (a) Sir William Brabazon, V-Treas Ireland, (b) Christopher Blunte and (c) Capt Humphrey Warren and dau and coheir of Nicholas Clifford, of Chart, Kent; *m* 2nd (licence 28 March 1589) Dorothy (*dsp*), widow of John Wentworth, of Gosfield, Essex, and dau of Sir Richard Southwell, and *d* 1602, having by his 1st w had, with an er s (Henry, *dvp*, having had a dau Lettice, who *m* Nicholas Arnold and left issue):

Sir GARRET MOORE, **1st Viscount Moore of Drogheda**, so *cr* 7 Feb 1621/2, as also earlier 20 July 1616 BARON MOORE OF MELLEFONT, Co Louth (both I), PC (I 1604); ktd 1599, Seneschal of Cavan 1601, MP Dungannon 1613, Pres Munster 1615; *m* Mary (*m* 2nd 1st Viscount Wilmot of Athlone and *d* 3 June 1654), dau of Sir Henry Colley, of Castle Carbery, Co Kildare, and had, with other issue:

1 CHARLES, **2nd Viscount**

2 James (Sir), of Ardee, Co Louth; *m* Jane (*m* 2nd Sir Robert Stirling), dau of Edward, 1st Lord Blayney, Baron of Monaghan, and *d* 1639, leaving issue

3 Arthur, of Drumoghan, Co Louth, and Drumbanagher, Co Armagh; *m* Dorothy, dau of Sir John King, of the Abbey of Boyle, Co Roscommon (*see* KINGSTON, E), and *d* 9 April 1635, having had, with another s (Charles, *dsp*):

(1) John, of Drumbanagher; *m* Elizabeth, dau of Sir Robert Honeywood, of Petts Place, Kent, and *d* Oct 1680, having had, with other issue (*dsp*):

1a John, of Drumbanagher; *b* May 1675; *m* 1st Catherine (*dspm*), dau of Patrick Savage, of Portaferry, Co Down; *m* 2nd July 1724 Hon Mary Caulfeild (*d* 26 Jan 1769), dau of 2nd Viscount Charlemont (*qv*), and *d* 1 May 1752, having by her had, with other issue:

1b John, of Drumbanagher; *b* 21 Dec 1726; *m* Nov 1752 Gertrude, dau and heir of Capt Francis Baillie, and *d* 24 Sept 1809, having had issue:

1c John, of Drumbanagher; *b* 1756; *m* Nov 1781 Mary, dau of Sir Annesley Stewart, 6th Bt (*see* STEWART, Bt, of Ramelton), and *dsp* 21 May 1834

2c Charles, Col Royal Irish Art; *m* —, and *d* 1848, leaving issue:

1d —; *m* Lt James Martin, 85th LI

3c Francis, Gen; *b* 1768; *m* 25 March 1802 Charlotte Stephens, widow of Capt J K Pulling, RN, and sis of Rev John Kingsmill (previously Stephens), of Sydmonton Court, Hants, and *d* 22 Aug 1861, having had issue:

1d Francis, Capt 1st Royal Dragoons; *b* 5 Sept 1810; *m* 29 April 1841 Susanna (*d* 28 Jan 1900), dau of Rev William Wilkieson, of Woodbury Hall, Cambs, and *d* 20 May 1864, having had issue:

1e Francis, Col 8th Regt and Royal Munster Fus; *b* 20 Sept 1843; *m* 7 April 1875 Eliza Cara (*d* 1939), dau of Thomas Mannix Cummins, JP, of Coolaha and Ballydulea, Co Cork, and *d* 18 Nov 1915, having had issue:

1f Francis, DSO (1915), OBE (1919), Col Roy Fus, served Boer War 1901–02 (Queen's medal with five clasps), WW I (despatches), Orders of St Anne of Russia with swords and St Vladimir of Russia with riband and swords; *b* 22 Dec 1879; *m* 26 Jan 1916 Anne Early (*d* 16 Jan 1964), dau of William Van Wyck, of New York, and *d* 13 June 1938, leaving issue:

1g Mary Van Wyck; *b* 5 Jan 1917; *m* 3 Feb 1951 Douglas Arden Lyon Camm

2g *Kathleen Clifford [Mrs Stephen Rose, Bradford House, Bradford Rd, Sherborne, Dorset]; *b* 31 July 1918; *m* 31 Oct 1942 *Lt-Col Stephen Murfin Rose, OBE, Roy Fus, s of Douglas Rose, TD, JP, of Banstead House, Woodstock Rd, Oxford, and has issue:

1h *Margaret Anne [Mrs Mark Roberts, Daisyfield Cottage, Rowledge, Farnham, Surrey]; *b* 20 June 1947; *m* 1975 *Col O Mark Roberts, OBE, Roy Regt of Wales, and has:

1i *Camilla Margaret Rose; *b* 1977

2i *Katharine Frances Rose; *b* 1980

2h *Mary Elizabeth [Mrs Jeremy Hurlbatt, The Grange, Ash, Martock, Somerset] *b* 12 Sept 1951; *m* 1979 *Cdr Jeremy G Hurlbatt, OBE, RN, and has issue:

1i *Charles Henry; *b* 1984

1i *Claire Alice Rose; *b* 1982

2f Charles Ronald, Lt Roy Munster Fus; *b* 12 Jan 1881; *ka* Transvaal 25 May 1901

1f Cara; *m* 17 Oct 1900 Col Frederick Scudamore, of Castle Carey, Guernsey, and *d* 28 Feb 1924

2f Mary; *m* 1st 7 June 1905 Capt Hugh Walters (*d* 29 April 1906), S Lancs Regt, and had issue; *m* 2nd 28 Nov 1922 Col John Poe (*d* 12 May 1941), CMG, DSO, MB, RAMC

3f Geraldine; *m* 3 Jan 1906, Lt-Col William Scrobie MacKenzie (*d* 1 Sept 1926), DSO, OBE, RAOC, and had issue

2e William Boyle, Capt Hampshire Regt; *b* 16 April 1846; *m* 1 May 1878 Alice (*dsp* May 1878), 2nd dau of Gordon Mainwaring, of Whitmore Hall, Staffs; *m* 2nd 15 Jan 1880 Ada Cecily (*d* 6 Dec 1880), dau of Rev Alfred John Edward Bowyer-Smythe, Rector Attleborough (*see* BOWYER-SMYTHE, Bt), and *d* 29 Aug 1902, having by her had issue:

1f Francis Cecil, Maj, Hants Regt, served Boer War 1900–01 (Queen's medal with four clasps) and WW I; *b* 2 Dec 1880; *d* unm

1c Mary; *m* 14 July 1775 Gustavus Handcock-Temple, of Waterstown, Co Westmeath

2c Sarah; *m* 22 May 1781 Sir John Craven Carden, 1st Bt (*qv*), and had issue

The 1st VISCOUNT MOORE OF DROGHEDA *d* 9 Nov 1627; his est surv son,

CHARLES MOORE, **2nd Viscount Moore of Drogheda**, PC (I Feb 1627/8); *b c* 1603; *m* Alice Loftus (*d* 13 June 1649), yst dau of 1st Viscount Loftus of Ely (*see* ELY, M), and *d* 7 Aug 1643, having had, with other issue:

HENRY MOORE, **1st Earl of Drogheda** (I), so *cr* 14 June 1661, PC (I 1660); MP Ardee 1639/40–43; *m* Alice Spencer (*d c* 1712), sis of 1st Earl of Sunderland (*see* MARLBOROUGH, D), and *d* 11 Jan 1675, having had issue:

1 CHARLES MOORE, **2nd Earl of Drogheda**; *m* 1669 Lady Letitia Isabella Robartes (*m* 2nd William Wycherley, the dramatist and poet), est dau of 1st Earl of Radnor (*qv*) of the 1679 *cr*, and *dsps* 18 June 1679

2 HENRY, **3rd Earl**

3 William; *m* Elizabeth, widow of 3rd Earl of Meath (*qv*) and dau of Francis Lennard, Lord (Baron) Dacre (*qv*), and *dspm*

1 Alice; *m* 1st May 1661 2nd Earl of Clanbrassil of the 1647 *cr*; *m* 2nd, as his 2nd w, 2nd Lord (Baron) Bargeny and *dsp* 25 Dec 1677

2 Mary; *m* 1st 3rd Earl of Dalhousie (*qv*); *m* 2nd 10 April 1683 2nd Lord Bellenden of Broughton (*see* ROXBURGHE, D)

The 2nd EARL's bro,

HENRY MOORE later HAMILTON-MOORE (on inheriting the estates of his bro-in-law the last Earl of Clanbrassil), **3rd Earl of Drogheda**, PC (I) 1680; *m* 3 July 1675 Mary (*d* 6 May 1826), dau of Sir John Cole, 1st Bt, of Newland (*see* ENNISKILLEN, E), and *d* 7 June 1714, having had, with other issue:

1 Charles, *Lord Moore*; *m* 24 Aug 1699 Jane Loftus, only dau and heir of 3rd and last Viscount Loftus of Ely (*see* ELY, M), and *dvp* 21 May 1714, leaving issue:

(1) HENRY MOORE, **4th Earl of Drogheda**; *b* 7 Oct 1700; inherited the Loftus estates, including Monasterevan (thereafter called Moore Abbey), Co Kildare, on his maternal gf's death 6 Nov 1725; *m* 11 Feb 1719/20 Charlotte (*d* 28 May 1735), dau of 1st Viscount Falmouth (*qv*), and *dsp* 28 May 1727

(2) EDWARD, **5th Earl**

2 Henry (Rev), Rector Malpas and Wilmslow, Cheshire; *m* Catherine, widow of Adml Sir George Rooke and only dau of Sir Thomas Knatchbull, 3rd Bt (*see* BRABOURNE, B), and had issue

3 John (Rev); *m* 1708 Elizabeth, widow of Edward Devonish and yst dau of Sir Charles Porter, Ld Chllr Ireland, and *d* 1 June 1716

4 William, of Moor Hall, Co Louth; *m* March 1717 Lucy, dau of Rev Edward Parkinson, of Ardee, and *d* 1 April 1732

5 Robert, MP Co Louth and Co Belfast; *m* 16 Oct 1725 Anne Lennard, Baroness Dacre in her own right (*qv*), widow of (a) Richard Barrett-Lennard and (b) 8th Baron Teynham (*qv*), and *d* 3 July 1728, leaving issue (*see* HAMPDEN, V)

6 Capel; *m* Lady Mary Paulet, dau of 2nd Duke of Bolton (*see* WINCHESTER, M) and widow of Henry O'Neill, of Shane's Castle

The 4th EARL's bro,

EDWARD MOORE, **5th Earl of Drogheda**, PC (I 1748); *b* 1701; MP Dunleer 1725–27; *m* 1st 1727 Lady Sarah Ponsonby (*d* 19 Jan 1736/7), dau of 1st Earl of Bessborough (*qv*), and had, with other issue:

1 CHARLES MOORE, **6th Earl of Drogheda** and 1st MARQUESS OF DROGHEDA (I), so *cr* 5 July 1791, as also 17 Jan 1801 BARON MOORE OF MOORE PLACE, Co Kent (UK), KP (1783); FM, Master-Gen Ordnance; *b* 29 June 1730; *m* 15 Feb 1766 Lady Anne Seymour (*d* 4 Nov 1784), dau of 1st Marquess of Hertford (*qv*), and *d* 22 Dec 1821, having had, with four daus:

(1) EDWARD MOORE, **7th Earl of Drogheda** and 2nd MARQUESS OF DROGHEDA; *b* 23 Aug 1770; *d* unm 6 Feb 1837

(2) Henry Seymour; *m* 28 Sept 1824 Mary Letitia (*m* 2nd 30 Dec 1830 Edward Henry Cole, of Stoke Lyne, Oxon, and *d* his widow 6 May 1881), 2nd dau of 1st Baron Congleton (*qv*), and *d* Aug 1825, leaving issue:

1a HENRY FRANCIS SEYMOUR MOORE, **8th Earl of Drogheda** and 3rd and last MARQUESS OF DROGHEDA, KP (1868), PC (I 1858); Ld Lt and custos rotulorum Co Kildare, V-Adml Leinster, Hon Col 3rd Bn Roy Dublin Fus, Ranger of the Curragh; *b* 14 Aug 1825; *educ* Eton and Trin Coll Dublin; *m* 25 Aug 1847 Hon Mary Caroline Stuart Wortley (*d* 3 April 1896), dau of 2nd Baron Wharncliffe (*see* WHARNCLIFFE, E), and *dsp* 29 June 1892, when the Marquessate and UK Barony expired

2 Ponsonby, of Moorefield, Co Kildare, and Ballyhale, Co Kilkenny; *b* by 1736; *m* 1st Nov 1768 Elizabeth, dau of 1st Viscount Mountcashell of the City of Cashell of the 1766 *cr*; *m* 2nd 3 April 1781 Catherine (*d* 1810), dau of Frederick Trench, of Woodlawn, Co Galway (*see* ASHTOWN, B), and *d* 9 Aug 1819, having by her had issue:

(1) Henry (Rev), of Ballyhale, Co Kilkenny; *b* 19 Oct 1784; *m* 15 Feb 1814 Lucie (*d* 15 June 1852), dau of James Currie, MD, of Liverpool and *d* 12 May 1856, having had, with other issue:

1a Ponsonby Arthur; *b* 4 Aug 1816; *m* 27 Aug 1844 Augusta Sophia (*d* 21 Sept 1903), 5th dau of Gen Hon William Henry Gardner (*see* 1970 edn GARDNER, B), and *d* 3 May 1871, having had issue:

1b PONSONBY WILLIAM, **9th Earl**

1b Agnes Alexandrina; granted rank of earl's dau 4 July 1893; *m* 4 March 1873 Sir Robert Anderson, KCB, LLD (*d* 15 Nov 1918), and *d* 7 Nov 1925, leaving issue

2b Alice Mary; *m* 6 Oct 1870 Rev T Russell Wade, and *dsp* 8 Oct 1871

2a Graham Currie; *b* 1820; *d* 4 May 1837

3a Henry, Lt RN; *b* 28 June 1828; *m* 1859 Mary Tatteshall, and *dsp* 6 Oct 1861

4a Edward Charles; *b* 14 March 1833; *m* 1857 Elizabeth Constance (*d* 1904), dau of Edmund Kidd, and *d* 9 Nov 1876, leaving issue:

1b Graham Ponsonby; *b* 14 April 1859; *m* 1882 Marie (*d* 28 Jan 1937), dau of W von Radsky, and *d* 9 May 1916, leaving issue:

1c Emily; *d* unm 18 Aug 1961

2c Florence Helena; *m* 25 Jan 1913 George Witherby

2b Henry; *b* 10 Oct 1860; *m* 1885 Esther Marion, dau of Louis Perrottet, and *d* 1895, leaving issue:

1c Henry Ponsonby; *b* 1892; *d* unm 3 April 1912

1c Kathleen Brenda

2c Nancy

3c Annesley

1b Beatrice Eleanor; *m* 1890 Edmund Joseph Keogh, of Wangrabel, Malvern, Victoria, Australia, and had issue

(2) Ponsonby, of Moorefield, Co Kildare; *b* 2 May 1786; *m* 9 Feb 1813 Barbara (*d* 15 Sept 1866), dau of John Maconchy, of Rathmore, Co Longford, and *d* 22 April 1868, leaving, with other issue:

1a Henry Edward, Capt 95th Regt; *b* 11 April 1826; *m* 3 Aug 1865 Hannah Elizabeth (*d* 16 May 1921), est dau of Joseph Pratt Tynte, of Tynte Park, Co Wicklow, and *d* 16 Feb 1868, having had issue:

1b Ponsonby; *b* 1 Aug 1866; *d* 14 Jan 1879

1a Mabel; *d* unm 2 Feb 1958

(3) Robert, of Lansdowne, Lt-Col Kildare Militia; *b* 15 Oct 1789; *m* 13 Nov 1809 Elizabeth (*d* 22 April 1875), dau of Rev Robert Warren, and *d* 3 March 1879, having had issue

(4) Charles (Rev), Incumbent Monasterevan, Co Kildare, Preb Harristown; *b* 20 Sept 1790; *m* 30 Sept 1815 Agnes (*d* 13 Jan 1872), dau and coheir of James Cleghorn, MD, Physician to the State in Ireland, and *d* 24 April 1857, having had, with five daus:

1a Ponsonby, barrister; *b* 1818; *d* unm 15 Sept 1851

2a James Cleghorn; *b* 10 May 1820; *m* 10 Feb 1847 Emily Jean (*d* 1901), dau of Rev Henry Moore, of Ballyhalde, and *d* 1894

(5) Frederic, Capt 12th Lancers; *d* unm 27 Oct 1856

(1) Catherine; *m* May 1818 Richard Molesworth Reynell (*d* 13 Sept 1824), of Reynella, and *d* 17 Dec 1859, leaving issue

3 Edward Loftus (Rev); *b* 29 Dec 1736; drowned unm 28 Oct 1758

The **5th Earl** *m* 2nd 13 Oct 1737 Bridget (*d* 27 July 1761), dau of William Southwell, bro of Thomas, 1st Lord Southwell (*see* SOUTHWELL, V), and was lost at sea with his s Edward while sailing from Holyhead to Dublin 28 Oct 1758, having by her had two other sons

The 8th EARL's cousin,

PONSONBY WILLIAM MOORE, **9th Earl of Drogheda**, DL and JP Devon and Queen's Co, JP Co Kildare; rep I peer; *b* 29 April 1846; *m* 16 Oct 1879 Anne Tower (*d* 21 Feb 1924), dau of George Moir, LLD, Sheriff Stirling, and *d* 28 Oct 1908, leaving, with a dau (Beatrice Minnie Ponsonby, *m* 1st 15 July 1909 Capt Struan Robertson Kerr-Clark (*ka* 25 Sept 1915), 7th Bn Seaforth Highrs, and had issue; *m* 2nd 15 Sept 1941 1st Baron Rankeillour (*qv*) and *d* 25 May 1966):

HENRY CHARLES PONSONBY MOORE, **10th Earl of Drogheda**, KCMG (1945, CMG 1919), PC (1951); *b* 21 April 1884; rep I peer 1913–57, Clerk FO 1907–17, Lt Irish Gds (SR), barrister Inner Temple 1935, chm Ctees and Dep Speaker Ho Lds 1946057, chm: Cinematograph Films Cncl 1944–54 and Home Office Advsy Cncl Treatment Offenders 1954, Dir-Gen Min Ec Warfare 1942–45; Grand Offr Order Orange-Nassau Netherlands; *cr* 30 Jan 1954 BARON MOORE, of Cobham,

Surrey (UK); *m* 1st 3 March 1909 (*divorce* 1922) Kathleen, CBE (1919) (*d* 18 March 1966), yst dau of Charles Maitland Pelham Burn; *m* 2nd 22 June 1922 Olive Mary (*d* 24 Nov 1947), formerly w of Lord Victor Paget (*see* ANGLESEY, M) and dau of George Meatyard, and *d* 22 Nov 1957, leaving by his 1st w:

1 CHARLES GARRETT PONSONBY MOORE, **11th Earl of Drogheda**, KG (1972), KBE (1964, OBE 1946); Capt RA (TA) 1940, on Staff Min Production 1942–45, md The Financial Times Ltd 1946–72, Ind Nat Dir Times Newspapers Hldgs Ltd 1983–89, dir: Economist Newspaper Ltd and S Pearson Publishers, chm: Newspaper Publishers' Assoc and Financial Times, Pres IOD 1974–89, author: *Double Harness* (memoirs, 1978), Chev Legion of Honour 1961, Order Merit Italy, Grand Offr Order Leopold II Belgium 1974; *b* 23 April 1910; *educ* Eton and Trin Coll Cambridge; *m* 16 May 1935 Joan Eleanor (*d* 16 Dec 1989), only dau of William Henry Carr, and *d* 1989, leaving issue:

(1) HENRY DERMOT PONSONBY MOORE, **12th and present Earl of Drogheda**

1 Patricia Doreen; *b* 20 Sept 1912; *m* 1st 29 June 1933 (*divorce* USA 1941, UK 1943) Sir Herbert Paul Latham, 2nd Bt (*qv*), and had issue; *m* 2nd 1943 Richard V K Aherne, son of William Aherne, JP, CC, of Ross, Co Meath, and *d* 3 March 1947, having had further issue

DRYDEN

Arms: Azure a lion rampant, in chief a sphere between two estoiles or. **Crest:** A demi-lion sustaining in the dexter gamb a sphere as in the arms or. **Creations:** Bt. (GB) 24 Aug 1733 and 2 May 1795.

SIR JOHN STEPHEN GILES DRYDEN, 8TH BT, of Canons Ashby, Northamptonshire, and **11TH BT**, of Ambrosden, Oxfordshire [Sir John Dryden Bt, Spinners, Fairwarp, Uckfield, East Sussex TN22 3BE]; *b* 26 Sept 1943, *s f* 1970; *educ* The Oratory Sch; *m* 10 April 1970 *Diana Constance, dau of Cyril Tomlinson, of Highland Park, Wellington, NZ, and has issue:

1 +JOHN FREDERICK SIMON; *b* 26 May 1976

1 *Caroline Diana Rosamund; *b* 1980

Lineage (of Turner): HUGH TURNER, of Sutton Coldfield, Warwicks; *m* Ellyn — and *d* between 7 Oct 1558 and 9 July 1560, leaving, with three daus:

1 John, of Sutton Coldfield; *m* Sybelle —, and had four sons (John; Richard; William; Hewe)

2 RICHARD, of whom presently

3 Nicholas; *m* Isobel — and *dsp*

4 Hugh, *dsp*

The 2nd son,

RICHARD TURNER, of Ashfurlong, Sutton Coldfield; barrister Middle Temple; *m* Mary (*bur* 17 May 1609), dau of Richard Masterson, of Winnington, Cheshire, and coheir of John Masterston, and *d* 15 Aug 1578, leaving, with three daus:

1 WILLIAM, of whom presently

2 John, of Hill, Sutton Coldfield; *m* — and *d* 1601, leaving issue

3 Robert

The est son,

WILLIAM TURNER, of Ashfurlong; *m* 10 Sept 1567 Margaret, dau of Christopher Breton, of Teeton, Northants, by Christian, dau of Thomas Saunders, of Sibbertoft, and *d* 1625, having had issue:

1 EDWARD, of whom presently

2 Richard, of Maston Trussell, Northants; *m* Beatrice — and *d* 1630, leaving a dau and three sons (John; William; Edward)

3 John, of Hothorpe, Northants; *m* Mary, dau of William Pell, of Hannington, and *dvp* 1619, leaving two sons (John; Benjamin) and two daus

1 Joyce; *m* Robert Tanfield

The est son,

EDWARD TURNER, of Leicester and Bramcote, Bulkington, Warwicks; *m* Joice (*bur* 28 Oct 1626), dau of Lybias Chamberlain, Mayor Leicester, and had, with four daus:

1 William, allegedly ancestor of the TURNERs of Brownhills, nr Walsall

2 Edward; *d* unm 1672

3 James

4 JOHN, of whom presently

EDWARD TURNER *m* 2nd Bridgit, widow of Sir Parr Lane, of Horton, and was *bur* 14 Sept 1628

His yst son,

JOHN TURNER, of London and Pritllewell, Essex; merchant, citizen and vintner; *bapt* 13 Oct 1622; *m* Mary (*bur* 2 March 1689), dau of — Cartwright, of Leicester, and was *bur* 1694, having had issue:

1 JOHN, of whom presently

2 Edward, of Gray's Inn; *d* unm 1737

3 Richard; *d* 1733

4 William, of Grosvenor Sq; *m* — and had issue

5 Elias, of Barking and Ilford, Essex; *m* Abigail — and *d* 1745, leaving issue

1 Elizabeth; *m* Capt Abraham Dawes

2 Mary; *m* Charles Atherstone

The est son,

JOHN TURNER, of London and Stepney; *bapt* 17 Oct 1650; *m* Elizabeth (*bur* 15 July 1747), dau of Nicholas Caplin, of Stanmore Magna and London, and was *bur* 20 Aug 1708, having had, with another dau:

1 John, of Sunbury, Ipswich; dir South Sea Co; *m* Ann Borough and *dsp* 1760

2 EDWARD (Sir), **1st Bt**

3 Joseph; *d* young

4 Samuel; *d* young

5 William; *educ* Balliol Coll Oxford (BA 1721); *m* — and *dsp*

1 Mary

2 Elizabeth

The 2nd son,

Sir Edward Turner, 1st Bt (GB), so *cr* 24 Aug 1733, of Ambrosden, Oxon; Dir and Chm HEICS, memb Lincoln's Inn; *bapt* 6 Oct 1691; *m* May 1718 Mary (*d* 5 Feb 1723), est dau and eventual heir of Sir Gregory Page, 1st Bt, of East Greenwich, and *d* 19 June 1735, having had, with two er sons (Gregory, *d* young; William, *d* young):

Sir Edward Turner, 2nd Bt, of Ambrosden, MP Gt Bedwin 1741–47, Oxon 1754 and Penrhyn 1761–66, memb Lincoln's Inn, inherited the fortune of his g-unc, Edward Turner, and the estates of his unc, John Turner, of Sunbury, Middx; *b* 28 April 1719; *educ* Balliol Coll Oxford (BA 1735, MA 1738, DCL 1744); *m* 8 Sept 1739 Cassandra (*d* 18 Oct 1770), dau of William Leigh, of Adlestrop and Longborough, Glos (*see* LEIGH, B), and *d* 31 Oct 1766, having had, with three other sons and another dau (*d* as infants):

1 GREGORY (Sir), **3rd Bt**

2 William; *b* 26 Sept 1750; *educ* Magdalen Coll Oxford (BA 1767); *d* 20 Nov 1819, leaving issue

3 Sir JOHN TURNER later DRYDEN (roy licence 16 Dec 1791), **1st Bt** (GB), so *cr* 2 May 1795; Sheriff Northants 1792, Capt 1st Foot, ktd 1793; *bapt* 11 Nov 1752; *educ* Harrow; *m* 14 May 1781 Elizabeth, est dau of Bevill Dryden, brother of Sir John Dryden, 7th Bt (*see* below, **Lineage (of Dryden)**), and *d* 14 Aug 1797, leaving issue

1 Elizabeth; *m* 14 Dec 1767 13th Baron Saye and Sele (*qv*) and *d* 1 April 1816, leaving issue

2 Cassandra; *m* 6 Feb 1771 2nd Baron Hawke (*qv*), and *d* 19 Nov 1813, leaving issue

The er son,

Sir GREGORY TURNER later PAGE-TURNER (roy licence 15 Nov 1775 on inheriting estate of his great-uncle Sir Gregory Page, 2nd and last Bt), **3rd Bt**, of Ambrosden; MP Wricklemarsh, Kent, High Sheriff Oxfordshire 1783, MP Thirsk, Yorks, 1784; inherited the Battlesden Park Estate, Beds, on the death 1780 of his great-aunt Hon Judith (Juliana), w of Thomas Page, of Battlesden, 2nd son of Sir Gregory Page, 1st Bt, of East Greenwich, and 2nd dau of 1st Viscount Howe (*see* HOWE, E); *b* 16 Feb 1748; *educ* Eton and Hertford Coll Oxford; *m* 2 Jan 1785 Frances (*d* 12 Feb 1828), dau of Joseph Howell, of Elm, nr Wisbech, Cambs, and *d* 4 Jan 1805, leaving issue:

1 **Sir Gregory Osborne Page-Turner, 4th Bt**, of Ambrosden, High Sheriff Beds 1810; *b* 28 Sept 1785; *educ* Harrow and BNC Oxford (BA 1805, MA 1809, DCL 1818); *m* 28 April 1818 Helen Eliza (*m* 2nd 15 Aug 1844 Joseph J G Cholmondeley and *d* 21 Nov 1858), only dau of John Wolsey Bayfield, and *d* 6 March 1843, having had:

(1) Gregory Osborne; *b* 23 Jan 1822; *d* 30 March 1823

(1) Helen Elizabeth; *b* 6 Feb 1820; *m* 22 Aug 1838 Rev Charles Gulliver FRYER later FRYER-PAGE (roy licence 27 April 1876) and *dsp* 2 Aug 1884

2 EDWARD GEORGE THOMAS (Sir), **5th Bt**

3 Francis William Martin, Capt 10 Royal Hus (PWO) Peninsular War; *b* 15 Feb 1794; *educ* Magdalen Coll Oxford (BA); *d* unm 28 April 1818

1 Frances Stacpole; *b* 15 Jan 1787; *d* unm 14 March 1804

2 Anna Leigh Guy; *m* 1 May 1822 Sir Henry Winston Barron, 1st Bt (*d* 19 April 1872), and *d* 22 Nov 1852, leaving issue

The 4th Bt's bro,

Sir Edward George Thomas Page-Turner, 5th Bt, of Ambrosden, Capt 10th Royal Hus (PWO) Peninsular War; *b* 12 Sept 1789; *m* 1 Dec 1818 Sophia (*d* 20 Jan 1854 aged 60), dau of Andrew Williams, Physician-Gen HEICS, and *d* 10 Oct 1846, leaving issue:

1 EDWARD HENRY (Sir), **6th Bt**

2 Arthur Augustus; *b* 18 April 1832; *d* 30 April 1835

1 Fanny Maria, *s* her er bro in his estates

2 Katherine Jane; *b* 7 May 1822; *m* 11 Oct 1862 Frederick St Vincent Ricketts (*d* 1891) and *dsp* 15 June 1906

3 Emily Mary; *b* 13 Aug 1824; *d* unm 13 Feb 1885

The er son,

Sir Edward Henry Page-Turner, 6th Bt, of Ambrosden; *b* 3 Oct 1823; *educ* Ch Ch Oxford (BA 1843, MA 1852); *m* 10 Aug 1872 Mary Ann (*m* 2nd 1881 Rev Thomas Isaac Guest, Curate Preston, Sussex, and *d* 25 Sept 1902), dau of Charles Otway, of Norwich, and *dsp* 24 March 1874, being *s* by his cousin **Sir Henry Edward Leigh Dryden, 4th Bt**, of Canons Ashby (*see* below)

Lineage (of Dryden): WILLIAM DRIDEN or DREYDEN, of Walton, Cumberland; had:

DAVID DRYDEN; *m* Isabel, dau and heir of William Nicholson, of Staffe Hill, Cumberland, and had an est s:

JOHN DRYDEN, of Canons Ashby, Northants; *m* Elizabeth, dau of Sir John Cope, and *d* 30 Sept 1584; his est s:

Sir ERASMUS DRYDEN, 1st Bt (E), so *cr* 16 Nov 1619, of Canons Ashby; BA Oxford, MP Banbury, High Sheriff Northants 1598 and 1619; *b* 20 Dec 1553; *m* Frances (*d* 16 Feb 1630/1), 2nd dau and coheir of William Wilkes, of Hodnell, Warwicks, and *d* 22 May 1632, having had:

1 Sir JOHN DRYDEN, 2nd Bt; MP Northants, High Sheriff 1634; *m* 1st Priscilla (*dsps*), sis of Sir Robert Quarles; *m* 2nd Anna (*dsp* 20 Feb 1630/1), dau of Henry Parvis, of Rockholts, Essex; *m* 3rd 3 July 1632 Honor, sis and coheir of Sir Robert Bevill, KB, of Chesterton, and *d* by 11 Nov 1658, having by her had, with a dau (*d* unm):

(1) Sir ROBERT DRYDEN 3rd Bt; High Sheriff Northants 1667 and WarwickS 1669; *d* unm 19 Aug 1708

2 William, of Farndon, Northants; *m* — Cave, of Leics, and was *bur* 24 Dec 1660, having had:

(1) Sir JOHN DRYDEN, 4th Bt; *m c* 1 June 1663 Elizabeth Luck and was *bur* 23 May 1710, having had:

1a John; *dvp* unm

3 Erasmus, of Tichmarsh, Northants; *m* 21 Oct 1630 Mary (*d* 1676), dau of Rev Henry Pickering, DD, and was *bur* 18 June 1654, having had, with daus:

(1) John; the poet; *b* 1631; *educ* Westminster and Trin Coll Cambridge (1650, MA at King's request 1668); *m* 1 Dec 1663 Lady Elizabeth Howard (*d* a lunatic 1714), dau of Thomas, Earl of Berkshire (*see* SUFFOLK and BERKSHIRE, E), and *d* 1 May 1700, having had issue:

1a Charles; *b* 1666; *educ* Westminster and Trin Coll Cambridge; Chamberlain to HH POPE INNOCENT XII; drowned in Thames nr Datchet and was *bur* Windsor 20 Oct 1704

2a John; *educ* Westminster and Ch Ch Oxford; held an appointment at the Papal court, poet; *d* unm 28 Jan 1701

3a Sir ERASMUS HENRY DRYDEN, 5th Bt; RC priest, Sub-prior Convent of the Holy Cross in Bournheim, Rome; *b* 2 May 1669; *educ* Charterhouse; *bur* Canons Ashby 14 Dec 1710

(2) Sir ERASMUS DRYDEN, 6th Bt; *m* 27 Aug 1667 Elizabeth, dau of Edward Martyn, of Westminster, and *d* 3 Nov 1718, having had, with two daus:

1a Edward; *m* Elizabeth, dau of Edward Allen, of Finchly, and gdau of Sir Thomas Allen, and *dvp* Nov 1717, leaving, with other issue:

1b Sir JOHN DRYDEN, 7th and last Bt; DCL, High Sheriff Northants 1727; *m* 1st June 1724 Frances (*bur* 30 Jan 1724/5), dau and heir of Thomas Ingram, of Barraby, Yorks; *m* 2nd 22 Sept 1726 Elizabeth (*d* 7 May 1791), dau of John Rooper, and *dsp* 21 March 1770, when the btcy expired and the estates passed to his niece

2b Bevill; *m* Mary, dau of William Dubber, of Cirencester, and left issue:

1c ELIZABETH, for whom *see* further below

2c Maria; *m* William Ramsay, of Inveresk, and left issue

3c Philippa; *m* Thomas Steele

4c Anne; *d* unm

3b Henry; had:

1c Richard; living 1708

4b James; *m* Elizabeth Dunch, of London, and *d* 1694, leaving issue

The 7th and last Bt's niece,

ELIZABETH Dryden; *b* 18 July 1753; *m* 1st 14 May 1781 Sir John TURNER later DRYDEN, **1st Bt**, of Canons Ashby (*see* above), and *d* 14 Aug 1797, leaving issue:

1 **Sir John Edward Dryden, 2nd Bt**; *b* 17 Sept 1782; *d* unm 29 Sept 1818

2 **Rev Sir Henry Dryden, 3rd Bt**, MA Oxford, Vicar Ambrosden, Oxon, and Leek Wootton, Warwicks; *b* 7 July 1787; *m* 31 July 1817 Elizabeth (*d* 22 Nov 1851), dau of Rev Julius Hutchinson, of Woodhall Park, Herts, and Owthorpe, Notts, and *d* 17 Nov 1837, leaving:

(1) **Sir Henry Edward Leigh Dryden, 4th Bt**, of Canons Ashby, and **7th Bt** (as which *s* kinsman 24 March 1874), of Ambrosden; MA, DL; *b* 17 Aug 1818; *m* 24 Jan 1865 Frances (*d* 4 Jan 1899), est dau of Rev Robert Tredcroft, Rector Tangmere, Sussex, and *d* 24 July 1899, leaving:

1a Alice; *m* 8 April 1913 John Marcon (*d* 13 April 1929), of Edgefield, Norfolk, son of Lt-Col John Marcon, of Wallington Hall, Norfolk, and *d* 4 Feb 1956 in her 90th year

(2) **Sir Alfred Erasmus Dryden, 5th Bt**, of Canons Ashby, and **8th Bt**, of Ambrosden; MA Oxford, barrister Middle Temple 1847; *b* 14 Oct 1821; *m* 16 May 1849 Frances Isabella (*d* 10 Feb 1901), only dau of Rev John Christian Curwen, Rector Harrington, Cumberland, and *d* 2 April 1912, having had issue:

1a Henry John Lawrence; *b* 21 Feb 1850; *d* 1867

2a **Sir Arthur Dryden, 6th Bt**, of Canons Ashby, and **9th Bt**, of Ambrosden; barrister Lincoln's Inn 1878; *b* 12 April 1852; *d* unm 15 March 1938

3a Alfred Curwen; *b* 7 March 1857; *m* 1887 Mary Josephine Swinburne (*d* 28 Aug 1916), only child of W G Waller, of Withington Lodge, Lancs, and *dsp* 28 Feb 1938

1a Ethel Marion; *d* young 1862

2a Clara Elizabeth Emma; *d* unm 27 March 1938

3a Louisa Isabella, of Canons Ashby, which she inherited from her bro Sir Arthur; *m* 16 Oct 1889 Maj Alfred Basset Pritchard, IA and *d* 28 Sept 1948, leaving issue

4 Mary Ethel Lawrence; *d* unm 29 May 1937

(1) Elizabeth Matilda; *m* 31 March 1859 Baron Frederick William Amelius Perger von Perglas (*d* 1902), Lt Roy Wurttemburg Inf, and *d* 16 Aug 1909, leaving issue

3 Leopold Erasmus (Rev); *b* 25 Sept 1792; *m* 12 June 1839 Emily, est dau of Rev Richard Frederick Vavasour, Rector Stow-on-the-Wold, and *d* 21 Jan 1846, leaving issue:

(1) Helen; *m* W Macfarlane, and left issue

4 Lempster George Gregory (Rev), Vicar Ambrosden, Oxon; *b* 24 Feb 1794; *d* 23 Jan 1866

5 Charles Beville; *b* 4 April 1796; *m* 28 Oct 1842 Eliza Barnard Skottowe, RN, and *d* 28 Dec 1883, leaving:

(1) John Erasmus Skottowe, Maj 3rd Bn Northampton Regt; *b* 13 March 1853; *m* 12 Oct 1904 Kate Mary (*d* 1 April 1923), dau of Charles John Gibb, MD, of Sandyford Park, Newcastle, and *d* 4 Feb 1925, leaving issue:

1a John Erasmus Charles Beville; *b* 19 June 1907; *educ* Eton; *d* unm 12 March 1933

2a NOEL PERCY HUGH (Sir), **7th/10th Bt**

1a Gladys Ethel Florence; *m* 12 July 1934 Maj Hartley N Butterworth, Staffordshire Regt, and had issue:

1b *Nigel Hartley Dryden [Nigel Butterworth Esq, c/o Hong Kong & Shanghai Bank, Hong Kong]; *b* 23 Aug 1936; *educ* Charterhouse; *m* 23 Jan 1965 (*divorce* 1983) Jane, dau of Geoffrey Dawson by Helen Amy, er dau of Rt Rev Bp Alfred Walter Frank Blunt, DD (*see* BLUNT, Bt), and has issue:

1c *Julian Richard Nigel [Julian Butterworth Esq, 16 Brandon Mansions, Queen's Club Gdns, London W14]; *b* 21 Nov 1970

1c *Fiona Catherine [Mrs Christopher Crace, Molens Cottage, Bures Rd, White Colne, Essex CO6 2QF]; *b* 1 Nov 1967; *m* 1992 *Christopher Gregory Crace and has issue:

1d *Jack Edward; *b* 19 April 1996

1d *Sasha Amy; *b* 14 March 1994

1b *Gillian Alison Joan; *b* 25 Feb 1939; *m* 23 May 1964 *Anthony Neville Adams, MSc London, son of Leonard Eustace Adams, of Uganda, and has issue:

1c *Philip Dawson; *b* 21 April 1966

1c *Kate Dawson; *b* 21 April 1966

2a Evelyn Kate Mary; *b* 1909; *m* 29 Aug 1931 Brig Gerald Ernest Thubron (*d* 1992), DSO, OBE, N Staffs Regt, only son of Ernest Blakelock Thubron, of Preston Park, Sussex, and had issue:

1b *Colin Gerald Dryden, FRSL (1969); *b* 14 June 1939; *educ* Eton; FRSL; writer (Hawthornden Prize 1987)

1b Carol Sheena; *b* 3 Sept 1937; *d* unm 18 Jan 1959

2a (cont.) Brig and Mrs Gerald Thubron also adopted:

*Sarah Elizabeth; *b* 1963

3a Honor Elizabeth Helen

(1) Caroline Helen Skottowe; *m* 21 Feb 1878 Cyril Percy Mundy (*d* 14 March 1913), of the Inner Temple, only surv s of Maj-Gen Godfrey Charles Mundy, and *d* 29 Nov 1938, leaving issue

1 Eliza Maria Cassandra; *d* unm

2 Harriott Eliza; *d* unm

3 Caroline Julia Eliza; *d* 9 Jan 1872

4 Matilda; *d* in infancy

Lady Dryden *m* 2nd Godfrey Scholey (*d* 4 Jan 1819), of London, and *d* 5 Nov 1824

The 6th/9th Bt's cousin,

Sir Noel Percy Hugh Dryden, 7th Bt, of Canons Ashby, and **10th Bt**, of Ambrosden; *b* 24 Dec 1910; *educ* Stowe; *m* 22 Aug 1941 Rosamund Mary (*d* 10 Nov 1994), est dau of Stephen Scrope, and *d* 23 March 1970, leaving issue:

Sir JOHN STEPHEN GYLES DRYDEN, **8th and present and 11th and present Bt**

DUBS

Creation: B. (LP, UK) 20 Aug 1994.

THE BARON DUBS, of Battersea, London Borough of Wandsworth (Alfred Dubs) [The Rt Hon The Lord Dubs, 56 Westbourne Park Villas, London W2 5EB]; *b* Dec 1932; *educ* LSE; local govt offr, memb Westminster CC 1971–78, Chm Westminster Community Rels Cncl 1972–77, memb Kensington, Chelsea and Westminster AHA 1975–78, Dir Refugee Cncl 1988–95, MP (Lab) Wandsworth, Battersea S, 1979–83, Batersea 1983–87 (fought Cities of London and Westminster 1970, Herts S Feb and Oct 1974), Oppn Front-Bench Spokemsan Home Affrs 1983–87, Chm Bdcasting Standards Commn 1997, Parly U-Sec NI 1997–; *m* *— and has a s and dau

DUCIE

Arms: Quarterly, 1st and 4th, argent a chevron gules, between three square buckles sable (for MORETON); 2nd and 3rd, or two lions passant guardant gules (for DUCIE). **Crest:** A moorcock's head or, combed and wattled gules, between two wings azure. **Supporters:** Two unicorns argent, armed, maned, tufted and unguled or, each gorged with a ducal coronet per pale gold and gules. **Motto:** *Perseverando* ('By persevering'). **Creations:** B. (GB) 27 April 1763 (Ducie), B. and E. (UK) 28 Jan 1837.

THE 7TH EARL OF DUCIE, Baron Ducie of Tortworth, Co Gloucester, and **Baron Moreton of Tortworth**, Co Gloucester (David Leslie Moreton) [The Rt Hon The Earl of Ducie, Talbots End Farm, Cromhall, Glos GL12 8AJ]; *b* 20 Sept 1951; *s f* 1991; *educ* Cheltenham and Wye Coll London (BSc Ag 1973); *m* 26 April 1975 *Helen, er dau of Martin Leslie Duchesne, of Langford, Bristol, and has issue:

1 +JAMES BERKELEY, *Lord Moreton*; *b* 6 May 1981

1 *Claire Alison; *b* 1984

Lineage: HENRY DUCIE, of London and Little Aston, Staffs; *m* 2 July 1571 Mary, dau and heir of Robert Hardy, of London, and *d* Nov 1587; his est surv s:

Sir ROBERT DUCIE, 1st Bt (E), so *cr* 28 Nov 1629; *bapt* 29 May 1575; Sheriff of London 1620 and Alderman, Lord Mayor 1631; accumulated great wealth and though he lost over £80,000 (just under £3m in late 1990s terms) by CHARLES I, whose banker he had been before the Civil War, he died allegedly worth £400,000 (*c* £15m in late 1990s terms); *m* Elizabeth (*bur* 9 Feb 1635/6), dau of Richard Pyott, and *d* 12 July 1634, leaving issue:

1 Sir RICHARD DUCIE, 2nd Bt; *d* unm 7 March 1656/7

2 Sir WILLIAM DUCIE, 3rd Bt, 1st and last VISCOUNT DOWNE, so *cr* 19 July 1675, as also BARON OF CLONEY (both I), KB (1661); *m* (by licence 23 June 1662) Frances (*bur* 20 Sept 1699), dau and coheir of Francis, 1st Baron Seymour of Trowbridge (*see* SOMERSET, D), and *dspm* 9 Sept 1679, when his titles expired, but his estates passed to his niece ELIZABETH (*see* below)

3 Hugh (Sir), KB; *d* 1662, leaving issue:

(1) Sir WILLIAM DUCIE, 4th Bt; *dsp* 1691

(2) Sir ROBERT DUCIE, 5th and last Bt; *d* unm 1703

4 Robert, of Little Aston; *m* — and had issue:

(1) ELIZABETH Ducie; *m* Edward MORETON, of Moreton and Ingleton, Staffs, and had:

1a MATTHEW DUCIE MORETON, 1st LORD DUCIE, BARON OF MORETON, Co Stafford (GB), so *cr* 9 June 1720, PC (I 1717); High Sheriff Staffs 1704–05 and Glos 1705–06, MP (Whig) Glos 1708–13 and 1715–20, V-Treas Ireland 1717–20; *m* 11 Jan 1689/90 Arabella (*d* 14 March 1750), est dau and coheir of Sir Thomas Prestwich, 2nd Bt, and *d* 2 May 1735, having had issue:

1b MATTHEW MORETON, 2nd LORD DUCIE, BARON OF MORETON and **1st Baron Ducie of Tortworth**, Co Gloucester (GB), so *cr* 27 April 1763, with remainder to his nephews, Thomas and Francis Reynolds; *b* by 1700; MP (Whig) Cricklade 1721–22, Calne 1723–27, Gloucester 1727–28, Tregony 1729–34 and Lostwithiel March-May 1735, Ld Lt Glos 1755–58; *d* unm 25 Dec 1770, when the Barony of Ducie of Moreton expired and that of Tortworth passed to his er nephew

2b Charles; *m* — and had issue:

1c Anne; *m* Mark Dyer

1b ELIZABETH Moreton; *m* 1st Richard Syms, of Blackheath (*dsp*); *m* 2nd Francis REYNOLDS, of Strangeways, Manchester, MP Lancaster 1745–73, and had issue:

1c THOMAS REYNOLDS later REYNOLDS-MORETON (Act of Parl 8 March 1771), **2nd Baron Ducie of Tortworth**; *b* 26 Oct 1733; Lt-Col Coldstream Foot Gds 1762–71, Clerk to Crown of Co Palatine of Lancaster 1761–80; *m* 20 Feb 1774 Margaret, dau of Sir John Ramsden, 3rd Bt (*qv*), and *dsp* 11 Sept 1785

2c FRANCIS, **3rd Baron**

1c Mary; *m* Thomas Legh, of Wincham, son and heir of Charles Legh, of Adlington, Cheshire, and *d* 26 March 1818

2c Arabella Penelope; *m* J Bettesworth, of East Hyde

2b Penelope; *m* Thomas Stourton

The 2nd BARON's bro,

FRANCIS REYNOLDS later REYNOLDS-MORETON (Act of Parl 1786), **3rd Baron Ducie of Tortworth**; *b* 28 March 1739; Capt RN, cmdg the *Monarch* in Adml Rodney's (*see* RODNEY, B) victory against the French 12 April 1782, MP (Whig) Lancaster 1784–85, FSA 1790; *m* 1st 10 Oct 1774 Mary (*d* May 1789), dau of Thomas Provis, of Shepton Mallet, Somerset, and had issue (including a yr s Augustus John Francis, Lt-Col Regt of Foot Gds, *b* 10 July 1777); *m* 2nd 18 June 1791 Sarah (*d* without issue by him 23 May 1793), widow of Robert Child, banker, of Osterley, Middx (*see* WESTMORLAND, E, and JERSEY, E), and dau of Gilbert Jodrell, of Ankerwycke, Bucks, and *d* 19 Aug 1808; his er s by his 1st w:

THOMAS REYNOLDS later REYNOLDS-MORETON, **4th Baron Ducie of Tortworth** and **1st Earl of Ducie**, so *cr* 28 Jan 1837, as also BARON MORETON OF TORTWORTH, Co Gloucester (both UK); *b* 31 Aug 1776; *educ* Eton and Exeter Coll Oxford; FSA 1814, FRS 1814, Lt-Col W Glos Militia 1800; *m* 5 Dec 1797 Lady Frances Herbert (*d* 22 Aug 1803), only dau of 1st Earl of Carnarvon (*qv*), and had, with five daus:

1 HENRY GEORGE FRANCIS, **2nd Earl**

2 Augustus Henry MORETON later MACDONALD-MORETON, of Largie, Argyll, MP; *b* 24 June 1804; *m* 15 Sept 1837 Mary Jane Lockhart Macdonald (*d* 10 Dec 1851), dau and heir of Sir Charles Macdonald-Lockhart, Bt, of Lee and Carnworth, a Count of the Austrian Empire, and *d* 14 Feb 1862, having had, with three daus (*see* SUTHERLAND, D):

(1) Charles, of Largie; *b* 12 July 1840; *m* 25 Oct 1870 Elizabeth Hume (*d* 1896), dau of Archibald Campbell, of Glendaruel, Argyll, and *d* 16 July 1879, leaving issue:

1a John Ronald, of Largie Castle, DL, JP; *b* 25 May 1873; *educ* Magdalen Coll Oxford (MA); *m* 30 April 1906 Daisy Maud (*d* 1966), twin dau of Brig-Gen Eyre Macdonnell Stewart Crabbe, CB, Gren Gds, of Glen Eyre, Hants, and *d* 10 Sept 1921, leaving issue:

1b +John [John Maxwell-Macdonald of Largie, Gortinanane House, Tayinloan, Argyll PA29 6XG], 19th of Largie, in Forestry Commn 1931, served WW II 1939–41 with 8th Bn Argyll and Sutherland Highrs (wounded); *b* 6 Jan 1908; *educ* Winchester and Magdalen Coll Oxford (BA 1929); *m* 22 April 1930 *Anne, only child of Sir John Maxwell Stirling-Maxwell, 10th Bt (*see* HERON-MAXWELL, Bt), and has:

1c +John Ronald [John Maxwell-Macdonald Esq, Gortinanane House, Tayinloan, Argyll PA29 6XG]; *b* 22 May 1936; *educ* Winchester; *m* 18 July 1964 *(Eleanor) Ruth, yr dau of T B Laird, of Taylor's Wynd, by Forfar, Angus, and has issue:

1d +John Ranald; *b* 16 Sept 1965

2d +Angus; *b* 30 July 1967

1d *Victoria Anne; *b* 1 Aug 1971

2d *A dau; *b* 14 July 1972

2c +Donald [Donald Maxwell-Macdonald Esq, 55 Park Walk, London SW10 0AZ], CA; *b* 9 Nov 1938; *educ* Winchester and Ch Ch Oxford (MA); *m* 1st 8 Sept 1962 (*divorce* 1976) Rosemary, yst dau of Robert Jenkins, of The Manor House, Hooton Roberts, Yorks, and has issue:

1d +James Donald; *b* 1 Sept 1965

1d *Harriet Caromy Anne; *b* 7 Feb 1967

2c (cont.) Donald Maxwell-Macdonald *m* 2nd 1977 *Margaret Anne, dau of Alfred Kingerley

2b Charles Angus, Maj Argyll and Sutherland Highrs WW II; *b* 22 June 1913; *educ* Winchester and Magdalen Coll Oxford; missing presumed *ka* March 1942

3b Simon Foster MACDONALD LOCKHART OF THE LEE (added by declaration 1946), DL (1950), JP (1950) Lanarks; served WW II in Lovat Scouts (wounded) and with Lanarks Yeo (TA) 1947–49; *b* 11 July 1916; *educ* Winchester and Magdalen Coll Oxford; *m* 28 Feb 1942 *Catriona [Mrs Simon Macdonald Lockhart of the Lee, Dunsyre House, Dunsyre, Lanarks], er dau of Seton Gordon, CBE, FZS, author and naturalist, of Upper Duntullim, Isle of Skye, and *d* 1991, leaving issue:

1c +Angus Hew [Angus Macdonald Lockhart of the Lee, Newholm, Dunsyre, Lanarks ML11 8NQ]; *b* 17 Aug 1946; *educ* Rannoch Sch and Aberdeen Ag Coll; *m* 1970 *Susan Elizabeth, dau of Hon William Normand (*see* 1956 edn NORMAND, B), and has issue:

1d +Ranald William Angus; *b* 1975

1d *Fiona; *b* 1972

2c +Simon James [Simon Macdonald Lockhart Esq, Crosshill House, Auchterader, Perthshire]; *b* 9 Aug 1949; *educ* Winchester; *m* 1973 *Lavinia, dau of Col Peter William Marsham, MBE (*see* ROMNEY, E), and has issue:

1d +James Seton Alexander; *b* 1976

2d +Andrew Peter Robert; *b* 1978

3d +Davina; *b* 1981

3c +Norman Philip; *b* 24 Dec 1954

1c *Mairi Susan [Mrs Ian Finlay, Shawfield, Dunsyre, Lanarks ML11 8NQ]; *b* 29 March 1943; *m* 1st 27 Oct 1962 (*divorce* 1965) Leslie Swan; *m* 2nd 19– (*divorce* 1989) Ian Hamilton Finlay and has by him:

1d *Alexander; *b* 14 March 1966

1d *Aileen; *b* 30 Oct 1967

1b Elizabeth; *b* 21 Sept 1909; *m* 5 Oct 1932 Rev Henry Richard Rogers, MA, only s of Rev Henry Rogers, MA, of Coltishall Hall, Norwich, and Ellary, Argyll, and had issue

2b Esther Mary; *b* 16 Nov 1920; *m* 23 Sept 1947 David Stewart Gladstone, 2nd s of Sir Hugh Gladstone, DL, JP, FZS, FRSE, FSA Scot, of Capenoch, Penpont, Dumfriesshire, and had issue

1a Esther; *m* 5 Jan 1898 Thomas William Westropp Bennett, of Ardvullen, Kilmallock, Co Limerick, and *d* 16 July 1920

(2) Augustus Henry, Maj and Lt-Col Coldstream Gds; *b* 3 Nov 1848; *m* 25 July 1874 Anna Harriet Mary (*d* 9 May 1924), est dau of Sir Richard Sutton, 4th Bt (*qv*), and *d* 6 Aug 1918, leaving issue:

1a Norman Charles Henry, MC; Capt 3rd Bn KRRC WW I (despatches); *b* 18 July 1888; *ka* 13 Oct 1915

1a Cara Mary Emily; *m* 28 March 1900 Keith Ronald Mackenzie (*d* 1 March 1928), of Bembridge, IoW, and *d* 16 Oct 1950

2a Hilda Maud; *m* 1st 14 Dec 1898 Col Sir Simon Lockhart, 5th Bt, MVO (*dsp* 25 March 1919); *m* 2nd 3 July 1922 Adml of the Fleet Sir John Michael de Robeck, 1st and last Bt (*d* 20 Jan 1928; *see* 1928 edn), GCB, GCMG, GCVO, and *d* 25 April 1944

3a Evelyn Geraldine; *d* unm 29 May 1960

4a Muriel Harriet Charles; *m* 6 Oct 1903 James Hainsworth Ismay (*d* 24 Jan 1930), of Iwerne Minster House, Blandford, Dorset, and *d* 19– , leaving issue

5a Margaret Aline; *m* 17 Aug 1909 Brig-Gen Lewis Francis Philips (*d* 23 Oct 1935), CB, CMG, CBE, DSO, KRRC, yst son of John William Philips, DL, of Heybridge, Staffs, and *d* 4 May 1971 aged 89, having had issue

6a Aubrey Beatrix; *m* 26 March 1913 Lt-Col Augustus Charles Oppenheim (*d* 30 Sept 1967), DSO, KRRC, yst son of Henry Oppenheim, DL, by Isabel Georgina, dau of Hon James Butler (*see* DUNBOYNE, B), and *d* 28 Nov 1971 aged 87, leaving issue

7a Islay Mary Cecil; *m* 27 Oct 1921 Brig-Gen Charles Richard Woodroffe (*d* 18 Nov 1965), CMG, CVO, CBE, and *d* 30 Dec 1968, leaving issue

3 Percy, Capt 10th Hus; *b* 18 June 1808; *m* 28 April 1846 Jane Frances (*d* 19 Aug 1903), yst dau of Sir Rose Price, 1st Bt, of Trengwainton (*qv*), and *d* 15 March 1886, having had:

(1) Francis; *b* 27 Feb 1847; *d* 22 Aug 1894

(2) Robert; *b* 8 June 1850; *m* 3 April 1880 Annabella Emily (*d* 30 Dec 1915), 6th dau of Edward Thornewill, of Dove Cliff, Staffs, and *d* 22 Feb 1884, leaving issue:

1a Maurice Fitzhardinge Reynolds; *b* 6 Feb 1884; *m* 5 June 1917 Anna Margaretta (*d* 1971), est dau of Rev Edward Brown Charlton, Rector Tatenhill, Staffs, and *d* 1976, leaving issue:

1b +Berkeley ('Jock') John Reynolds [Berkeley Reynolds-Moreton Esq, Wason House, Castle Cary, Somerset]; *b* 9 March 1918; *educ* Stowe; *m* 22 Dec 1945 *Lois, yr dau of Louis Hardaker, of Ackworth, Yorks, and has issue:

1c +Stephen Maurice; *b* 9 June 1950; *educ* Stowe; *m* 1972 *Lynn, dau of Thomas Milford, of Swansea

2c +John Evelyn [John Reynolds-Moreton Esq, Treetops, Leckhampton Hill, Glos]; *b* 6 Feb 1952; *educ* Stowe; *m* 1981 *Jennifer, yr dau of David Davis, of Cheltenham, and has issue:

1d +Robert Berkeley Reynolds; *b* 1983

1c *Jane Margaretta; *b* 1 Sept 1956

1b Evelyn Emily Margaretta; *b* 9 May 1921; Sch Sec King's Sch Bruton; *d* unm 26 Feb 1998

(3) Ernest; *b* 17 Jan 1852; *d* 31 July 1919

(4) Percy Dundas (Rev), Vicar Compton Dundon, Somerset; *b* 24 May 1855; *m* 17 Jan 1884 Alti Edith (*d* 4 Aug 1940), dau of Gen Sir William Anthony Gibb, KCB, and *d* 13 Feb 1939, leaving issue:

1a Percy Clifford Reynolds, DSO (1917), Maj RE WW I (wounded, despatches), DC Gold Coast; *b* 20 Jan 1886; *d* unm 8 Jan 1957

2a Claude Anthony, Capt KOSB, served WW I (wounded) and WW II; *b* 8 July 1897; *m* 24 Jan 1925 Mabel Helen (*d* 1947), only dau of Horace Theobold, and *d* 20 May 1954

1a Gwendolen; *m* Dec 1912 A E Faulkner (*d* 1939) and *d* 23 Nov 1960

2a Muriel Evelyn

(1) Edith; *d* unm 12 Sept 1929

(2) Florence; *d* unm 27 Dec 1945

(3) Rose; *d* unm 16 July 1950

The 1st EARL *d* 22 June 1840; his son,

HENRY GEORGE FRANCIS REYNOLDS-MORETON, **2nd Earl of Ducie**; *b* 8 May 1802; *educ* Eton and Trin Coll Cambridge; MP (Lib) Glos 1831–32 and E Glos 1832–35, Ld in Waiting 1846–47; *m* 29 June 1826 Elizabeth (*d* 15 March 1865), er dau of 2nd Baron Sherborne (*see* 1970 edn), and *d* 2 June 1853, having had issue:

1 HENRY JOHN REYNOLDS-MORETON, **3rd Earl of Ducie**, GCVO (1906), PC (1859), JP Oxon; *b* 25 June 1827; *educ* Eton; MP (Lib) Stroud 1852–53, Ld Lt Glos 1857–1911, FRS, Hon Col 2nd Vol Bn Gloucester Regt, Capt Yeomen Gd 1859–66, Ld Warden Stannaries Cornwall, memb Cncl of HRH THE PRINCE OF WALES 1888–1908; *m* 24 May 1849 his first cousin Julia (*d* 3 Feb 1895), dau of James Haughton Langston, MP Sarsden, Oxon, and *d* 28 Oct 1921, having had issue:

(1) Henry Haughton, *Lord Moreton*, MP (Lib) Glos W 1880–85, DL, JP Glos and Oxon; *b* 4 March 1857; *m* 18 Dec 1888 Ada Margarette (*d* 22 Jan 1944), dau of Dudley Robert Smith, and *dsp* & *vp* 28 Feb 1920

(1) Constance Emily; *m* 24 March 1874 1st and last Baron Eversley (*d* 19 April 1928), and *d* 27 Feb 1920

2 Herbert Augustus, Lt RN; *b* 13 July 1828; *d* 10 April 1863

3 Algernon Thomas, of Eastwood, Co Carlow, Capt 3rd Dragoons; *b* 10 Aug 1829; *m* 1st 10 Dec 1857 Annie Jane (*d* 27 Aug 1873), only dau of Thomas Paget, of Knockglass, Co Mayo, and had issue:

(1) Algernon Paget Reynolds; *b* 24 Nov 1858; *d* 13 Dec 1861

(2) Reginald Percy; *b* 22 July 1861; *d* an infant

3 (cont.) Capt Algernon Reynolds-Moreton *m* 2nd 1 April 1875 his cousin Emilia Olivia (*d* 17 Feb 1920), dau of Hon Augustus Henry Macdonald-Moreton, of Largie, Argyll (*see* above), and *dsps* 18 Jan 1880

4 BERKELEY BASIL, **4th Earl**

5 Reynolds, DL, JP Leics, Post Capt RN (ret); *b* 21 Dec 1835; *m* 1st 11 July 1860 Charlotte Constance (*d* 30 Aug 1865), only dau of Sir John Dunlop, MP, and had issue:

(1) Basil Hugh Reynolds; *b* 5 May 1861; *d* 14 Aug 1873

(2) Henry John; *b* 30 May 1862; *m* 1889 Carrie Cecelia Richards, widow of Col Charles Ball, US Army, and *d* 1942, leaving issue:

1a Theodore Reynolds; *b* 1 April 1890; *m* 10 Oct 1921 Marie Ann Josephine (*d* 1965), dau of David Oral Anderson, of Duluth, Minnesota, and *d* 1970, leaving issue:

1b +David Oral [David Reynolds-Moreton Esq, Highlands Rd, PO Box 32, Jackson, NH 03846-0032, USA]; *b* 25 Aug 1922; *m* 1948 *Barbara Colby, dau of L Graham Harris, of New York, and has had issue:

1c +Henry Packard [Henry Reynolds-Moreton, 140 Phillip Rd, Woodside, CA 94062, USA]; *b* 1958; *m* 1995 *Ann Woodward, dau of William J Sydeman, of Nevada City, Calif., and has:

1d *Emily Woodward; *b* 1996

1c Theodora; *b* 1954; *d* 1969

2a Hugh Berkeley; *b* 3 Dec 1891; *m* 1923 Phyllis Mott (*d* 1928), and *d* 1935, leaving:

1b +Henry John [Henry Reynolds-Moreton Esq, The Pas, Manitoba, Canada]; *b* 1926; *m* 1951 *Patricia, dau of William A Russell, and has issue:

1c +John Russell Berkeley; *b* 1956

2c +Richard Steven; *b* 1963

1c *Brenda Leigh; *b* 1952; *m* 1973 *Dennis Boiteau, and has issue:

1d *Mark Steven; *b* 1976

2d *Dereck Troy; *b* 1979

3d *Mathew Scott; *b* 1982

2c *Patricia Ann; *b* 1954; *m* 1983 *Colin Chopp

1b Carrie Ann; *b* 1924; *m* 1950 *Charles William Schmidt II, and has issue:

1c *Charles William; *b* 1951

2c *Stephen Berkeley; *b* 1957

1c *Susan Moreton; *b* 1953

2c *Karin Marie; *b* 1955

(3) Francis James; *b* 13 Nov 1863; *m* 1894 Clara Frances, dau of W Smith, of Iowa, and *d* 14 Feb 1915, leaving issue

1a Constance

2a Evelyn Jane

5 (cont.) Capt The Hon Reynolds Reynolds-Moreton *m* 2nd 18 Oct 1866 Margaret (*d* 19 March 1892), 2nd dau of Rev Denis Mahony, of Dromore Castle, Co Kerry, and by her had:

(4) Reginald; *b* 26 Jan 1869; *m* 8 Aug 1907 Mary Emily (*d* 6 March 1935), dau of Edward Beresford, of Aubawn Killshandra, Co Cavan (*see* WATERFORD, M), and *d* 1929, leaving:

1a Richard Beresford Reynolds; *b* 11 April 1909; *m* 15 Nov 1929 Irene Beatrice (*d* 1986), only dau of Maj — Donnithorne, of Torquay, Devon, and *d* 1984, leaving issue:

1b +David Buckland [David Reynolds-Moreton Esq, Cobb Cottage, 23 Fore St, Bovey Tracey, Devon]; *b* July 1931; *m* 1965 *Cecilie Margaret Elswood, dau of Lilian Elswood, of Isleworth, Middx

2b +Anthony Reynolds [Anthony Reynolds-Moreton Esq, 20 St George's Rd, W Harnham, Salisbury, Wilts]; *b* Nov 1938

1b *Jennifer Anne [Mrs John Wrigley, Manor Cottage, E Grimstead, Salisbury, Wilts]; *b* June 1941; *m* 1969 *John Wrigley

2a +Edward Havelock Erroll; *b* 6 May 1911

(5) Theodore; *b* 22 Dec 1869; *d* 11 March 1876

(1) Rose; *d* 12 April 1876

(2) Florence Lilian; *m* 30 April 1903 Edward Beresford (*d* 8 June 1939), of Aubawn, Co Cavan, and *d* 16 Dec 1940, leaving issue (*see* WATERFORD, M)

(3) Evelyn Mabel; *m* 10 July 1895 Arthur Cortlandt Macgregor, only s of Lt-Col R F H Macgregor, and had issue

(4) Grace Ruth Kathleen; *b* 10 April 1879; *d* 9 March 1880

5 (cont.) Capt The Hon Reynolds Reynolds-Moreton *m* 3rd 19 June 1894 Gertrude (*d* 22 Dec 1927), yst dau of Sir Percyval Hart Dyke, 6th Bt (*qv*), and *d* 19 June 1919

6 Howard, 7th Royal Fus; *b* 14 March 1837; *d* 24 Nov 1856

7 Wyndham Percy, Lt 7th Foot; *b* 10 May 1839; *d* 29 July 1877

8 Seymour; *b* 1 March 1841; *m* 23 Jan 1869 Mary Ellen (*d* 1945), dau of John Kent, and *d* 8 April 1905, having had issue:

(1) Albert Eliott Kingscote, JP Qld; *b* 10 Sept 1875

(2) Douglas Seymour Herbert, Manager of English, Scottish, and Australian Bank Ltd, Haymarket, Sydney, JP NSW and Qld; *b* 26 May 1878; *m* 18 Sept 1905 Winifred Josephine Hilda, dau of William Richards, JP, of Charters Towers, Qld, and *d* 1948, leaving issue:

1a Marjory Elizabeth Douglas; *m* 1932 John Albert Lane (*d* 5 Aug 1965)

2a Hilda Jeannette Douglas; *m* 1934 Clifford Ewing Spoule, and has issue

3a Ellen Evelyn Douglas *m* 1937 James Edward Neville Rolfe, and has issue

(1) Elizabeth Emily; *b* 8 Aug 1880; *d* unm June 1964

(2) Ida Jeanette; *b* 23 July 1883; *m* 2 June 1928 Lt-Col Edwin Mayhew Brissenden, MBE, KC, LLD (*d* 30 Oct 1930), Australian Forces

9 Richard Charles (Sir), KCVO, of Crookham House, Crookham, Hants, Marshal Ceremonies 1887–1913, formerly RN, DL Gloucester and Bristol; *b* 21 Jan 1864; *m* 15 July 1868 Janie (*d* 25 July 1929), Ldy-in-Waiting to HRH THE DUCHESS OF ALBANY, est dau of Thomas Ralli (*see* RALLI, Bt), and *d* 2 March 1928, leaving:

(1) Marie Evelyn, DGStJ, Order of Queen Elisabeth of Belgium; *b* 11 Jan 1870; *m* 30 April 1902 FM 1st and last Viscount Byng of Vimy (*d* 6 June 1935), and *dsp* 20 June 1949

10 Matthew Henry, Lt 78th Regt, Magistrate New Guinea; *b* 4 Aug 1847; *m* 1901 Kathleen Louisa, dau of John Seale, of Cork, and *dsp* 17 March 1909

1 Georgina Mary Louisa; *m* 29 Jan 1856 Rev Charles Edward Oakley (*d* 15 Sept 1865), MA, Rector Wickwar, Glos, and St Paul's Covent Garden, and *d* 20 Oct 1867, leaving issue

2 Alice; *m* 10 May 1865 Sir Henry Marsham Havelock-Allan, 1st Bt (*qv*), and *d* 22 Dec 1922, leaving issue

3 Eleanor; *m* 1 Jan 1869 Hugh Fife Ashley Brodie (*d* 2 Sept 1889), of Brodie, Morayshire, and *d* 1 Feb 1925, leaving issue

4 Evelyn, Ldy-in-Waiting to HRH THE DUCHESS OF ALBANY; *d* unm 15 Jan 1945

The 3rd EARL's bro,

BERKELEY BASIL REYNOLDS-MORETON later MORETON, **4th Earl of Ducie**; Min Public Instruction Qld 1885–86, Colonial Sec and Min Public Instruction Qld 1886–88; *b* 18 July 1834; *m* 13 Oct 1862 Emily Eleanor (*d* 7 June 1921), dau of John Kent, Commr Crown Lands, Qld, and *d* 7 Aug 1924, having had issue:

1 CAPEL HENRY BERKELEY REYNOLDS MORETON, **5th Earl of Ducie**; *b* 16 May 1875; *m* 1 Aug 1903 Maria Emma (*d* 5 June 1958), dau of Frederick Bryant, of Maryborough, Qld, and *dsp* 17 June 1952

2 Algernon Howard; *b* 2 May 1880; *m* 1913 Dorothy Edith Annie (*d* 13 April 1958), dau of Robert Bell, of Rockhampton, Qld, and *d* 23 June 1951, having had issue:

(1) BASIL HOWARD, **6th Earl**

(1) Dorothy Mildred; *m* 1945 R Sutherland Grant, MM

(2) May Reynolds; *b* 1919; *d* May 1997

(3) Joan Eleanor; *m* 1944 *S/Ldr Basil Bannister Daish, RAAF

1 Eleanor Alice; *d* unm

2 Evelyn Beatrice; *d* unm 14 Dec 1942

3 Constance Ethel; *d* unm 28 Aug 1952

4 May Isabel; *d* unm 14 Aug 1957

5 Cecil Agnes; *d* an infant 10 Sept 1871

6 Beatrice Lilian; *d* unm 1934

7 Ada Georgina; *d* unm Sept 1963

8 Irmengarde; *b* 1879; *m* 1924 Rev John Reginald Stotten, s of John Stotten, of Qld, and *dsp* 13 April 1977

The 5th EARL's nephew,

BASIL HOWARD MORETON, **6th Earl of Ducie** *b* 15 Nov 1917; *educ* C of E GS Brisbane, Qld; served 1941–45 with 62nd AI Bn and 2nd/3rd AI Bn (New Guinea and Islands) as Staff/Sgt; *m* 15 April 1950 *Alison May [The Rt Hon Alison Countess of Ducie, Church Cottage, Tortworth, Wotton-under-Edge, Glos], est dau of Leslie Aitken Bates, of Pialba, Qld, and *d* 1991, leaving issue:

1 DAVID LESLIE MORETON, **7th and present Earl of Ducie**

2 +Douglas Howard [The Hon Douglas Moreton, Tortworth, Wotton-under-Edge, Glos]; *b* 21 Oct 1958; *educ* Bredon Sch

3 +Robert Matthew [The Hon Robert Moreton, Crockleys Farm, Tortworth, Glos]; *b* 8 March 1964; *educ* Malvern and RAC Cirencester; *m* 1988 *Heather Elizabeth, only dau of Colin Lynton-Jenkins, of Alveston, Avon, and has:

(1) +Charles Henry Robert; *b* 23 Jan 1993

(1) *Olivia Alexandra Rose; *b* 5 Jan 1991

1 *(Alison) Jeannette [The Lady Jeanette Stewart, 1159 St Jerome Crescent, Orleans, Ontario K1C 2A7, Canada]; *b* 9 March 1954; *m* 1986 *Mark Allan Stewart, of Ottawa, and has:

(1) *Derek Allan; *b* 1987

(1) *Laura Jessica; *b* 1989

DUCKWORTH

Arms: Argent on a chevron engrailed azure between two leopard's faces in chief and a garb in base sable, three crosses patée or. **Crest:** Upon a mount between two palm branches vert a garb fesswise or, charged with two crosses patée in fess and surmounted by a duck sable. **Motto:** *Perseverantia* ('Perseverance'). **Creation:** Bt. (UK) 15 July 1909.

SIR EDWARD RICHARD DYCE DUCKWORTH, 4TH BT, of Grosvenor Place, City of Westminster [Sir Edward Duckworth Bt, Holly Cottage, Moreton Paddox, Warwicks CV35 9BU]; *b* 13 July 1943; *s* f 1997; *educ* Marlborough and Cranfield; *m* 9 Oct 1976 *Patricia, only dau of Thomas Cahill, of Datchet, Berks, and has:

1 +JAMES DYCE; *b* 1984

1 *Helen Dyce; *b* 1987

Lineage: ROBINSON DUCKWORTH, of Huddersfield; *b* 2 Aug 1794 (s of Robinson Duckworth, of Huddersfield); *m* 19 Aug 1828 Elizabeth Forbes (*d* 14 July 1868), dau of William Nicol, MA, MD, Surgn RN, of Stonehaven, and *d* 31 Jan 1875, leaving, with a dau:

1 William Nicol; *b* 8 Nov 1829; *m* 31 Oct 1861 Elizabeth, dau of Adam Paterson, WS, of Edinburgh, and *d* 16 March 1899, leaving issue

2 Robinson (Rev), CVO, VD, DD Oxon, Sub-Dean and Canon Westminster, Chaplain and Almoner OStJ; *b* 4 Dec 1834; *d* unm 20 Sept 1911

3 Henry, FLS, FGS, JP Liverpool; *b* 27 Aug 1836; *m* 12 Feb 1867 Mary Jane (*d* 1 Oct 1916), dau of T F Bennett, of Liverpool, and gdau of David Gladstone, of Liverpool, and *d* 14 Jan 1921, leaving issue:

(1) Henry Thomas Forbes (Rev), Prof Ancient History and Dean Trin Coll Toronto; *b* 29 Nov 1868; *educ* Merton Coll Oxford (MA); *m* 2 Sept 1908 Hope Holland, only dau of Wellington Hunt, of Brantford, Ontario, and *dsp* 7 Sept 1927

(2) Wynfrid Laurence Henry, MD and DSc Cambridge, Fell Jesus Coll Cambridge, Master 1940–45, Reader Human Anatomy 1920–45, Lecturer Physical Anthropology 1898–1920, U Rep GMC 1923–26; *b* 5 June 1870; *m* 16 Sept 1902 Eva Alice (*d* 14 Feb 1955), widow of Lt Charles Cheyne, 24th PI, Ind SC, and dau of Frederick Wheeler, and *dsp* 14 Feb 1956

(3) Francis Robinson Gladstone, CBE (1942, MBE 1918), Sr Ch Inspr Schs, ret 1943, master Eton, Dover Coll and Cheltenham, T/Maj RFA WW I (despatches twice), Croix de Guerre; *b* 21 Aug 1881; *educ* Rossall and Trin Coll Oxford (MA); *m* 2 Aug 1906 Ethelwyn, only child of Canon William Cookworthy Compton, Headmaster Dover College, and *d* 21 Sept 1964

(1) Evangeline Mary Elizabeth; *b* 27 Dec 1871; *d* unm 24 July 1962

(2) Mary Emmeline Theodora; *b* 15 Jan 1874; *m* 15 April 1903 Walter W Skeat (*d* 24 July 1953), MA, and *d* 26 July 1956, leaving issue

4 DYCE (Sir), **1st Bt**

The 4th son,

Sir Dyce Duckworth, 1st Bt (UK), so *cr* 15 July 1909; *b* 24 Nov 1840; MD Edin 1863, Hon LLD Edin 1890, Hon LLD Liverpool 1925, Hon MD Cincinnati 1879, Roy U Ireland 1887, Queen's U Belfast 1910, Hon FRCPI 1887, Consulting Physician St Bartholomew's Hosp, FRCP London 1870, Treasurer 1884, Sr Censor 1901, ktd 1886, Hon Physician to HRH THE PRINCE OF WALES 1890–1901, lecturer medicine St Bartholomew's Hosp, Assist-Surgn RN 1864–5, KJStJ; *m* 1st 26 April 1870 Annie Alicia (*d* 14 Sept 1889), widow of John Smith, of Mickleham Hall, Surrey, and dau of Alexander Hopkins, of Limavady, Co Antrim, and had issue:

1 EDWARD DYCE (Sir), **2nd Bt**

1 Elizabeth Dyce; *b* 14 Sept 1871; *d* 20 March 1884

2 Margaret Dyce; *b* and *d* 22 April 1873

Sir Dyce *m* 2nd 4 Nov 1890 Ada Emily (*d* 19 July 1953), yst dau of George Arthur Fuller, of The Rookery, nr Dorking, by Georgiana Craven, yr dau of Rev Loraine Loraine-Smith (*see* 1956 edn LORAINE, Bt), and by her had:

2 Christian Leslie Dyce, BSc (Glas), MInstCE, AMINA; *b* 19 Nov 1891; *m* 15 Sept 1925 Elspeth (*m* 2nd 9 Sept 1954 Rev Hywel Glyn Lewis, MA, Vicar Mortlake with E Sheen), dau of Charles John Macalister, MD, FRCP, DL, of Bourton on the Water, Glos, and *dsp* 18 June 1953

3 Arthur Dyce, Capt RN, Sec RINA 1945–63; *b* 6 March 1896; *m* 6 July 1927 Grace Ella Mary (*d* 1993), dau of Edmund Lionel Pontifex, of Bishops Court, Broadwater Down, Tunbridge Wells, and *d* 1973, leaving issue:

(1) +Geoffrey Loraine Dyce, CBE (1977) [Brig Geoffrey Duckworth CBE, Weir Cottage, Bickton, Fordingbridge, Hants SP6 2HA]; *b* 24 May 1930; *educ* Stowe; Brig RTR, ADC to HM 1982–85; *m* 16 Dec 1961 *Philippa Ann, dau of Sir (Edward) Percy Rugg, of Fulham, and has issue:

1a +Jeremy Dyce; *b* 1 May 1963; *m* 30 Aug 1997 *Christabel Elizabeth Ffynone Fordham

1a *Juliet Ann; *b* 26 Nov 1964; *m* 1992 *Christopher Brian Davidson Smith and has:

1b *Francesca Elizabeth; *b* 22 March 1994

2b *Isabella Louise; *b* 5 Dec 1995

3b *Emily Alice; *b* 5 Dec 1995

(1) Rosemary Margaret Dyce; *b* 13 Aug 1931; *m* 9 March 1957 *Brig Athelwold Colin Devereux Watts, AAC, RTR [Brig Athelwold Watts, Shearings, Rockbourne, Hants SP6 3NA], s of Lt-Col John Athelwold Iremonger Watts, of Alderton, Tewkesbury, Glos, and *d* 4 July 1995, leaving:

1a *Andrew Colin Iremonger [Maj Andrew Watts, Shearings, Rockbourne, Hants SP6 3NA]; *b* 9 June 1960; Maj AAC; *m* 23 Jan 1987 *Katherine Mary Gooch and has:

1b *Jonathon George Iremonger; *b* 16 Sept 1991

2b *Harry Andrew Devereux; *b* 17 March 1995

1b *Jessica Kay Devereux; *b* 13 April 1990

2a *Nigel John Iremonger; *b* 3 Feb 1962; *m* 10 Oct 1988 *Helen Ruth Debney and has:

1b *Matthew Edward Iremonger; *b* 11 March 1991

2b *Daniel Timothy Iremonger; *b* 9 Feb 1993

3b *Patrick Christopher Iremonger; *b* 12 Nov 1994

1a *Caroline Susan Devereux; *b* 4 Jan 1958; *m* 11 Aug 1979 *Gordon Scott Alexander Montgomery and has:

1b *Duncan Colin Gordon; *b* 23 June 1982

2b *Alistair James Scott; *b* 25 Sept 1989

1b *Jenna Mary Caroline; *b* 28 June 1984

2a *Kay Rosemary Devereux; *b* 10 Oct 1963; *m* 5 Nov 1988 *Hugh Lionel Wakefield Fox, of Wakes Colne, Essex, and has:

1b *Jamie Edward Devereux; *b* 25 May 1991

2b *Jonathan Hugh Devereux; *b* 18 Oct 1992

3b *Toby Christopher Devereux; *b* 9 March 1994

4b *Angus David Devereux; *b* 2 Aug 1997

Sir DYCE *d* 20 Jan 1928; his est son,

Sir Edward Dyce Duckworth, 2nd Bt, JP (Suffolk); *b* 10 July 1875; *educ* Pembroke Coll Oxford (BA); ICS, Puisne Judge High Court Rangoon, KGStJ; *m* 12 Nov 1913 Cecil Gertrude (*d* 9 March 1953), dau of Robert E Leman, of Bayswater, and *d* 5 Aug 1945, leaving:

1 **Sir Richard Dyce Duckworth, 3rd Bt**; *b* 30 Sept 1918; *educ* Marlborough; Maj RA WW II; *m* 5 Sept 1942 Violet Alison (*d* 1 June 1996), only dau of Lt-Col George Boothby Wauchope, DSO, of The Mount House, Highclere, Hants, and *d* 29 Dec 1997, leaving:

(1) Sir EDWARD RICHARD DYCE DUCKWORTH, **4th and present Bt**

(2) +Antony George Dyce; *b* 20 Nov 1946; *educ* Marlborough and Gonville and Caius Coll Cambridge; *m* 1974 *Geraldine, dau of Kevin Broderick, of Blackrock, Co Dublin, and has:

1a +Nathaniel James Dyce; *b* 1977

1 Phyllis Dyce; *b* 12 Nov 1914; *m* 5 Nov 1935 Sir Godfrey William Rowland Morley, OBE, TD, MA, slr, only son of Arthur Morley, OBE, KC, MA, of W Kensington, and *d* 16 June 1963, leaving issue

DU CROS

Arms: Quarterly, 1st, vert a greyhound courant argent, in chief a crescent or of the last; 2nd, azure an antique crown or; 3rd, azure a heart and crescent in pale argent, a chief of the last; 4th, azure a saltire or; all within a bordure argent; on an escutcheon of pretence argent a rose gules, slipped and leaved proper. **Crest:** Issuant from an antique crown or a demi-greyhound sable. **Creation:** Bt. (UK) 5 July 1916.

SIR CLAUDE PHILIP ARTHUR MALLET DU CROS, 3RD BT, of Canons, Co Middx [Sir Claude du Cros Bt, Long Meadow, Ballaugh Glen, Ramsey, Isle of Man]; *b* 27 Dec 1922; *s* f 1975; Capt Welsh Gds WW II; *m* 1st 20 June 1953 (*divorce* 1974) Christine Nancy (*d* 1988), yr dau of F E Bennett, of Spilsby, Lincs, and formerly w of George Tordoff, and has issue:

1 +JULIAN CLAUDE ARTHUR MALLET; *b* 23 April 1955; *educ* Eton; *m* 1984 *Patricia M, only dau of Gerald A Wyatt, of Littlefield Sch, Liphook, Hants, and has issue:

(1) +Alexander Julian Mallet; *b* 25 Aug 1990

(1) *Henrietta Mary; *b* 1988

Sir ARTHUR *m* 2nd 1974 (*divorce* 1982) Margaret Roy Cutler, dau of R J Frater, of Gosforth, Northumberland

Lineage: GUILLAUME Du CROS, Seigneur du Cros; had:

JEAN JACQUES Du CROS, Seigneur de la Combe, doctor and advocate of Montpellier; *m* 1st (banns 9 April 1606) Marie, dau of Jean de Fambon, procureur de la cour des Aydes, of Montpellier, and had issue; *m* 2nd (banns 15 Jan 1617) Jeanne, dau of Jacques d'Esterre (Estienne), Seigneur de Pradilles, of Montpellier, and *d* 15 Aug 1646 aged 62, having had further issue; his est s:

JACQUES Du CROS, of Montpellier; Conseiller du Roy, Auditor Chamber of Accounts; *b* 16 July 1607; *m* (banns 28 Dec 1630) Madeleine, dau and eventual heir of Jacques d'Estienne, Seigneur de Pradilles, Conseiller du Roy, Prof Medicine Montpellier, and *d* 6 Feb 1674 having had a 3rd s:

FRANÇOIS Du CROS, Seigneur de la Combe; Capt Regt Royal of Inf 1679, adjudged noble and entitled to arms by arrest de conseil 7 May 1697, served heir to his uncle Armerie d'Estienne, Seigneur de Pradilles, 16 Sept 1699; *b* 1660; *m* 15 July 1679 Suzanne, dau of Jean Donnadieu, Conseiller du Roy, and had:

JEAN PETER Du CROS, of Montpellier and Dublin; *b* 14 July 1680 and *bapt* Reformed Church at Montpellier 15 July 1680; Lt in Col La Barthe's Regt of Foot during the wars *temp* WILLIAM III and ANNE, left France in wake of Revocation of Edict of Nantes (which had established toleration for Huguenots) and settled Dublin by 10 May 1716; *m* Marie Sophie Gould (living 9 July 1756) and *d* by 11 May 1724, having had, with three er sons:

PIERRE SAMUEL Du CROS; *b* 10 Feb 1714/5; *m* Rachael — and *d* 18 April 1768, having had:

SAMUEL PETER Du CROS, of Dublin; *bapt* 28 March 1751; *m* 22 Feb 1778 Mary Dawson, of Dublin, and had:

WILLIAM HARVEY Du CROS, of Dublin; *bapt* 20 Dec 1778; *m* (licence 17 Aug 1804) Harriet Maria Williams (*bur* 8 July 1867), of Dublin, and was *bur* Sept 1836, having had:

EDWARD PETER Du CROS, of South Hill, Blackrock, Co Dublin; *bapt* 28 Dec 1828; *m* 16 Sept 1845 Anna Marie (*bur* 27 Sept 1892), dau of John Molloy, of Dublin, and *d* 14 June 1907, having had:

WILLIAM HARVEY Du CROS, of Howberry Park, Wallingford, Berks, and Inniscorring, Dalkey, Co Dublin, JP Sussex, Chev Legion of Honour, Kt Order of Isabella the Catholic Spain, MP Hastings 1906–08, fndr pneumatic tyre industry, pioneer Br motor industry; *b* 19 June 1846; *m* 20 May 1868 Annie Jane (*d* 5 May 1899), dau of James Roy, of Durrow, Queen's Co, and *d* 21 Dec 1918, having had a 3rd s:

Sir Arthur Philip du Cros, 1st Bt (UK), so *cr* 5 July 1916, JP; *b* 26 Jan 1871; Hon Col 8th Bn Roy Warwicks Regt, MP (C) Hastings 1908–18 and Clapham 1918–22, Associate Nat Gallery, fndr with f of pneumatic tyre industry, fndr and pres Dunlop Rubber Co, fndr Jr Imp League, formed Aerial Def Ctee H of C 1909; *m* 1st 31 Oct 1895 (*divorce* 1923) Maude (*d* 12 Dec 1938), dau of William Gooding, of Coventry, Warwicks, and had issue:

1 PHILIP HARVEY (Sir) **2nd Bt**

2 Arthur Roy Peter, barrister Inner Temple 1936, Maj RASC WW II; *b* 15 March 1913; *educ* Harrow and Magdalen Coll Oxford; *m* 27 July 1935 Myra Mary (*d* 18 Nov 1969), formerly w of John A McArevey and dau of Gerald Mooney, of Killiney, Dublin

1 Renée Maude; *b* 24 April 1897; *m* 16 Sept 1920 Lt-Col William Edward DENT later HEDLEY-DENT (deed poll 1 Nov 1926), of Shortflatt Tower, Belsay, Northumberland, and had issue

2 Denise Anne; *b* 3 Sept 1901; *m* 1 Jan 1923 (*divorce* 1927) Alan V Insole, FRGS, FZS, Hon Lt RA

Sir Arthur *m* 2nd 21 Oct 1928 Florence May Walton (*d* 4 June 1951), dau of James Walton King, of Walton, Bucks; *m* 3rd 22 Dec 1951 Mary Louise Joan Beaumont (surname assumed on naturalization 1934; *d* 13 July 1956), dau of William Buhman, of Hanover, and *d* 28 Oct 1955

His er son,

Sir Philip Harvey du Cros, 2nd Bt; Capt 3rd Hus, served WW I and II (despatches), chm Cheapside Land Devpt Co, dir St Martin's Le Grand Property Co; *b* 19 June 1898; *educ* Harrow; *m* 1st 27 Feb 1922 (*divorce* 1950) (Maltilde) Dita, dau of Sir Claude Coventry Mallet, CMG, and had:

1 Sir CLAUDE PHILIP ARTHUR MALLET Du CROS, **3rd and present Bt**

1 *Edome Dita Mallet [Miss Edome Quita Pena, Hinton St George, Somerset]

2 *Primrose Millicent Elaine Mallet [Mrs James Mallet-Harris, Mallet Court, Curry Mallet, Somerset]; *b* 1938; took by deed poll name MALLET-HARRIS on marriage; FLS, botanical artist; *m* 1978 *James Gordon Shute Harris (*see* 1970 edn AIREDALE, B)

Sir Philip *m* 2nd 3 Nov 1950 *Rosemary Theresa, MBE, only dau of Sir John David Rees, 1st Bt, KCVO, CIE (*see* 1970 edn), and *d* 11 Oct 1975

DUDLEY, Earl of

Arms: Checky or and az., a bend erm. **Crest:** Out of a ducal coronet or a lion's head az. **Supporters:** Two angels ppr., hair and wings or, under robes sanguine, uppermost az. **Motto:** *Comme je fus* ('As I was'). **Creations:** B. (E) 23 March 1643/4, V. and E. (UK) 17 Feb 1860.

THE 4TH EARL OF DUDLEY, of Dudley Castle, Co Stafford, **Viscount Ednam**, of Ednam, Co Roxburgh, **Baron Ward of Birmingham**, Co Warwick (William Humble David Ward) [The Rt Hon The Earl of Dudley, 6 Cottesmore Gdns, London W8 5PR; Vention, Putsborough, Devon EX33 1LD]; *b* 5 Jan 1920 (HRH THE DUKE OF WINDSOR stood sponsor); *s* f 1969; *educ* Eton and Ch Ch Oxford; Royal Hus (PWO) WW II (wounded), ADC to Viceroy India 1942–43; *m* 1st 10 Jan 1946 (*divorce* 1961) Stella (*see* also ASTOR, V), est dau of Dr Don Miguel Angel Carcano, KCMG, KBE, Argentine Amb to UK 1942–46, and has:

1 +(WILLIAM HUMBLE) DAVID JEREMY, *Viscount Ednam*; *b* 27 March 1947; *educ* Eton and Ch Ch Oxford; *m* 1st 3 July 1972 (*divorce* 1975) Sarah Mary, only dau of Sir Alastair Francis Stuart Coats, 4th Bt (*see* COATS, Bt, of Auchendrane); *m* 2nd 1976 (*divorce* 1980) Debra Louise, dau of George Robert Pinney, and has:

(1) *Bethany Rowena; *b* 1977

1 *Rosemary Millicent [The Lady Rosemary Cañedo, Jorge Juan 37, 28001 Madrid, Spain]; *b* 26 May 1955; *m* 26 April 1980 *Castor Cañedo, s of Castor Cañedo and Maria Del Carmen Angoso, of Madrid, and has:

(1) *Gabriela; *b* 1982

2 *Anne-Marie Ines [The Lady Anne-Marie Gimena, Plaza de Las Salesas 3, Madrid 28004, Spain]; *b* 26 May 1955; *m* 1978 *Laureano Perez-Andujar Gimena, son of Laureano Perez de Andujar y Andujar and Caridad Gimena de Manas, of Madrid

The 4th EARL *m* 2nd 24 Aug 1961 *Maureen, actress, dau of James Swanson, and by her has:

2 +William; *b* 21 Oct 1961

3 +Leander Grenville Dudley *b* 30 Oct 1971; *educ* Eton and U of S California; film production coordinator

3 *Susanna Louise; *b* 23 May 1963

4 *Melissa Eileen Patricia [The Lady Melissa Puxley, The Mansard, Vention, Putsborough, nr Georgeham, N Devon EX33 1LD]; *b* 18 July 1964; *m* 1991 *Dr Simon P Puxley, and has issue:

(1) *India Ward; *b* 1991

5 *Victoria Cecilia Larissa; *b* 28 May 1966

6 *Amelia Maureen Erica; *b* 5 Sept 1967

7 *(Emma Sophia) Cressida; *b* 7 Jan 1970; medical PR; *m* 29 June 1996 *Oliver Preston, cartoonist, s of Nicholas Preston, of Tetbury, Glos

Lineage: ROBERT WARD, of Kirby Bedon, Norfolk; *m* —, dau of Sir Giles Capell, of London, and had issue:

HENRY WARD, of Poswyke; *m* —, dau of William Ugge, of Peckthorpe, and had issue:

EDWARD WARD, of Poswyke, and Bixley, Norfolk; *m* Anne, dau of John Havers, of Winfarthing, and *d* 1583 aged 41, having had, with other issue:

1 Thomas, of Bixley; gf of Sir EDWARD WARD, of Bixley, *cr* a Baronet 19 Dec 1660, which title expired on the death *sp* of the 8th Bt *c* 1770

2 William, of Heal, Staffs, and Cheapside, London; goldsmith; paid off his dau-in-law's gf's mortgages in exchange for £10,000 (*c* £350,000 in late 1990s terms) and (probably) her hand in marriage for his own son; *m* Elizabeth, dau and in her issue heir of Richard Humble, of Goosehayes, Hornchurch, Essex, and Southwark, vintner, and had issue:

(1) HUMBLE WARD, **1st Baron Ward of Birmingham**, Co Warwick (E), so *cr* 23 March 1643/4; *b c* 1614; ktd 1643, High Sheriff Staffs 1658–59; *m* (settlement dated 17 Feb 1628) Frances, Baroness Dudley in her own right (*see* DUDLEY, B), and *d* 14 Oct 1670, having had, with a yst s (Humble, *d* young) and three daus:

1a EDWARD WARD, **2nd Baron Ward of Birmingham** and 7th BARON DUDLEY on succeeding his mother 1697; *b* 1631; *m* Frances (*bur* 21 Nov 1676), dau of Sir William Brereton, 1st Bt, of Handford, Cheshire (a Parly Gen in the Civil War), and sole heiress of her bro, Sir Thomas, and *d* 3 Oct 1701, having had, with three daus:

1b John; *d* young 1675

2b William; *m* Frances, dau of William Dilke, of Maxstoke Castle, Warwicks, and *dvp* (*bur* 16 May 1692 aged 32), leaving issue:

1c EDWARD WARD, **3rd Baron Ward of Birmingham** and 8th BARON DUDLEY; *bapt* 20 Dec 1683; *m* 9 April 1703 Diana (*d* 17 March 1709), dau of Thomas Howard (*see* SUFFOLK and BERKSHIRE, E) and *d* 28 March 1704, leaving:

1d EDWARD WARD, **4th Baron Ward of Birmingham** and 9th BARON DUDLEY; *b* 16 June 1704; *d* unm 6 Sept 1731

2c John; *bur* 29 July 1696

3c WILLIAM WARD, **5th Baron Ward of Birmingham** and 10th BARON DUDLEY; *d* unm 20 May 1740, when the Barony of Dudley passed to his n and heir general FERDINANDO DUDLEY LEA, s of his sis Frances, while the Barony of Ward with Dudley Castle and the Dudley estates passed to his cousin and heir male JOHN WARD, 1st VISCOUNT DUDLEY AND WARD OF DUDLEY (*see* below)

1c Frances; *m* William Lea, of Halesowen Grange, Salop, and had issue (*see* DUDLEY, B)

3b Ferdinando; *d* unm 1717

2a William; *m* Anne, dau and sole heir of William Parker, of Willingsworth, Staffs, acquired with her Willingsworth and other estates, and *d* 1713, having had issue:

1b William, of Willingsworth and Sedgeley Park, Staffs; MP Staffs 1710–13 and 1715–20; *m* Mary, sis of 3rd Earl of Stamford (*see* 1970 edn), and *d* 25 Oct 1720, leaving:

1c JOHN WARD, **6th Baron Ward of Birmingham** and 1st VISCOUNT DUDLEY AND WARD OF DUDLEY, Co Worcester (GB), so *cr* 21 April 1763; *b c* 1700; MP (Tory) Newcastle-under-Lyme 1727–34; *m* 1st 26 Dec 1723 Anna Maria (*d* 12 Dec 1725), dau of Charles Bourchier, of Clontarf, Co Dublin, and had issue:

1d JOHN WARD, **7th Baron Ward of Birmingham** and 2nd VISCOUNT DUDLEY AND WARD OF DUDLEY; *b* 22 Feb 1724/5; *educ* Oriel Coll Oxford (MA), LLD Cambridge; MP (Tory) Marlborough 1754–61 and Worcester 1761–74; *m* 15 July 1738 Mary (*m* 3rd 14 Aug 1790 Benjamin Jennings; *m* 4th 9 Dec 1791 Capt John Smith, RN, and was *bur* 24 May 1810), dau of Gamaliel Fair, of Norfolk, and widow of — Baker, and *dsp* 10 Oct 1788

1c (cont.) The **6th Baron** *m* 2nd 1 Jan 1744/5 Mary (*d* 31 May 1782), dau and heiress of John Carver, and *d* 6 May 1774, having by her had further issue:

2d Humble; *b* 11 March 1747; *d* an infant

3d WILLIAM WARD, **8th Baron Ward of Birmingham** and 3rd VISCOUNT DUDLEY AND WARD OF DUDLEY; *b* 21 Jan 1750; *educ* Eton and Oriel Coll Oxford; MP (Tory) Worcester 1780–88; *m* 1 Aug 1780 Julia (*d* 23 June 1833), 2nd dau of Godfrey Bosville, of Gunthwaite, Yorks, and *d* 25 April 1823, leaving:

1e JOHN WILLIAM WARD, **9th Baron Ward of Birmingham**, 4th and last VISCOUNT DUDLEY AND WARD OF DUDLEY and 1st and last EARL OF DUDLEY OF DUDLEY CASTLE, so *cr* 5 Oct 1827, as also VISCOUNT EDNAM, of Ednam, Co Roxburgh (both UK), PC (1827); *b* 9 Aug 1781; *educ* Oriel Coll Oxford (BA 1802, MA 1818); FRS, MP (Tory) Downton 1802–03, Worcs 1803–06, Petersfield 1806–07, Wareham 1807–12 and Bossiney 1819–23, For Sec 1827–28; *d* unm 6 March 1833, when the Earldom and both Viscountcies expired

2c William (Rev); Rector Himley and Kingswinford, Staffs; *m* Elizabeth, dau of John Hawkes, and *d* 21 July 1758, having had issue:

1d Humble; *bapt* 1 Dec 1755; *m* 1779 Susanna Beecroft and *d* 1785, having had:

1e WILLIAM HUMBLE, **10th Baron**

1d Frances; *m* 24 July 1781 8th Earl Ferrers (*qv*) and *d* 4 March 1812, leaving issue

1b Frances; *m* (settlement dated 15 May 1695) Robert Pigott, of Chetwynd, Salop, Sheriff of Salop 1697, and had, with other issue:

1c Honor; *m* (settlement dated 12 June 1731) John Harvey Thursby (*d* 1 June 1764), DCL, Oxon, was ancestress of THURSBY, Bt (*see* 1940 edn), and *d* 24 Sept 1781 aged 68

2b Jane; *m* Daniel Jevon

3b Rebecca; *d* unm

The 9th BARON's 2nd cousin,

Rev WILLIAM HUMBLE WARD, **10th Baron Ward of Birmingham**; *b* 9 Jan 1781; *educ* Eton and Queens' Coll Cambridge; Rector Himley; *m* 22 May 1816 Amelia (*d* 23 May 1882 aged 85), dau of William Gooch Pillans, of Bracondale, Norfolk, and had, with other issue:

1 WILLIAM, **1st Earl**

2 Humble Dudley; *b* 20 Dec 1821; *m* 17 Dec 1843 Eleanor Louisa (*m* 2nd 13 April 1812 John Gerard Leigh, of The Hoo, Luton, Beds (*d* 24 Feb 1875); *m* 3rd 4 Dec 1883 Christian Frederic de Falbe, Danish Amb to UK (*d* 1896) and *d* 16 Dec 1899), 3rd dau of Thomas Hawkes, MP, of Himley House, Staffs, and *d* 14 Dec 1870, leaving:

(1) William Humble Dudley; 14th Hus and Capt Herts Yeo Cav; *b* 19 Feb 1849; *m* 24 Oct 1876 Hon Eugenie Violet Adele (*d* 13 March 1938), dau of 1st Viscount Esher (*qv*), and *d* 29 May 1903, leaving issue:

1a William Dudley, PC (1922); barrister, Lt-Cdr RNVR, MP Southampton 1906–22, Treas Household 1909–12, PPS to Patronage Sec 1912–17, V-Chamberlain Household 1917–22; *b* 14 Oct 1877; *educ* Eton and Trin Coll Cambridge (BA); *m* 9 July 1913 (*divorce* 1931) Winifred May (*m* 2nd 1937 W/Cdr Marquis de Casa Maury (Spain) and *d* 1983), dau of Col Charles Wilfrid Birkin, CMG, of Lamcote, Notts (*see* BIRKIN, Bt), and *d* 11 Nov 1946, leaving issue:

1b Penelope (Pempy) Ann Rachel; *m* 1st 29 Dec 1939 (*divorce* 1944) Harry Anthony Compton Pelissier, s of H G Pelissier and Fay Compton, the actress, and had issue; *m* 2nd 24 Jan 1948 Sir Carol Reed (*d* April 1976) and had further issue

2b *(Clare) Angela Louise, JP (1968) [Lady Laycock JP, La Cañada Real, c/Avila, 11310 Soto Grande, Cadiz, Spain]; CC (1961) Notts, DStJ; *m* 24 Jan 1935 Maj-Gen Sir Robert Edward Laycock, KCMG, CB, DSO, JP, late RHG (*d* 10 March 1968; *see* LISTOWEL, E), est s of Brig-Gen Sir Joseph Laycock, KCMG, DSO, TD, DL, JP, of Wiseton, Doncaster, and has had:

1c Joseph William Peter; *b* 1938; *educ* Eton; *m* 1971 *(Eve) Lucinda (actress Lucy Fleming) (*m* 2nd 1986 as his 2nd wife Simon Williams, actor), yr dau of Lt-Col Peter Fleming, OBE, of Merrimoles House, Nettlebed, Oxon, by Dame Celia Johnson, DBE, actress, and was accidentally drowned 1980, leaving issue:

1d *Robert; *b* 1973

2d *Diggory; *b* 1975

1d Flora; *b* 1972; drowned with her father 1980

2c *Benjamin Richard [Benjamin Laycock Esq, Kingwell Farm House, Old Hill, Wincanton, Somerset]; *b* 1947; *m* 1971 *Rose Cuninghame, and has issue:

1d *Samuel Edward; *b* 1983

1d *Bonny Mary; *b* 1972

2d *Josephine Clare; *b* 1973

1c *Edwina Ottilie Jane [Mrs Sydney Davis, 217 E 61st St, NYC, New York, USA]; *b* 1936; *m* 1st 1955 (*divorce* 1963) Lt (Richard) Mark Walter Agnew, RN (*see* AGNEW, Bt, of Gt Stanhope St); *m* 2nd 1963 Sidney Davis (*d* 1988)

2c *Emma Rose [Mrs Richard Temple, Lower Spargrove Farm, Evercreech, Somerset]; *b* 1943; *m* 1964 *Richard Temple, est s of Sir Richard Antony Purbeck Temple, 4th Bt (*qv*)

3c *Katherine Martha [Mrs David Mlinaric, 61 Glebe Place, London SW3]; *b* 1949; *m* 1969 *David A Mlinaric, the interior decorator, and has issue:

1d *Nicholas Maximilian; *b* 1977

1d *Jessica Rose; *b* 1970

2d *Josepha Octavia; *b* 1972

2a Charles Humble, DSO (1919), MC; Maj Res of Offrs 1st Bn Welsh Gds (SR) WW I (despatches); *b* 5 Dec 1879; *m* 20 July 1901 (*divorce* 1918) Maidie Florence Frederica Kate Constance Hope (*d* 18 April 1937), and *dsp* 8 April 1945

1a Eugenie Sybil; *m* 1st 15 June 1901 Capt Dermot Howard Blundell-Hollinshead-Blundell (*d* 26 Oct 1910), MVO, KRRC, son of Maj-Gen Richard Blundell-Hollinshead, and had issue; *m* 2nd 30 Dec 1911 Lt-Col Maxmillian David Francis Wood (*ka* 22 Aug 1915), DSO, W Yorks Regt, s of Capt Charles Watkins Arthur Harcourt Wood; *m* 3rd 25 March 1919 Charles Evelyn Seymour (*see* HERTFORD, M) and *d* 1 Nov 1950

2a (Georgiana) Viola Eleanor; *m* 18 Feb 1908 Sir William Augustus Forbes Erskine (*d* 17 July 1952), PC, GCMG, MVO, 2nd son of 11th Earl of Mar and Kellie (*qv*), and *d* 14 May 1972 aged 91, leaving issue

3a Eugenie Fanny Eveline; *m* 11 April 1907 Capt Sir Bryan Godfrey-Faussett (*d* 20 Sept 1945), GCVO, CMG, RN, and *d* 6 April 1956, leaving issue

4a Enid Violet Ida; *m* 28 April 1919 Maj-Gen Sir Alan Henry Shafto Adair, 6th and last Bt, GCVO, CB, DSO, MC, Gren Gds (*see* 1970 edn), and had issue. He *d* 1988

(1) Amelia Alice Julia; *m* 10 June 1865 Lt-Gen James Keith Fraser (*d* 30 July 1895), CMG, late 1st Life Gds, and *d* 5 Sept 1929, leaving issue (*see* FRASER, Bt)

(2) Henrietta Maria; *m* 14 June 1869 George Stewart Forbes (*d* 8 July 1894), and *d* 30 March 1935, leaving issue (*see* FORBES, Bt, of Newe)

1 Julia Susannah; *m* 14 June 1842 Rt Rev Thomas Legh Claughton (*d* 25 July 1892), DD, Bp St Albans, and *d* 28 May 1902, leaving issue

The 10th BARON *d* 6 Dec 1835; his son,

WILLIAM WARD, **1st Earl of Dudley**, of Dudley Castle, Co Stafford, so *cr* 17 Feb 1860, as also VISCOUNT EDNAM of Ednam, co Roxburgh (both UK); *b* 27 March 1817; *educ* Eton and Ch Ch and Trin Coll Oxford; Col Worcs Yeo, Tstee Nat Gallery and Nat Portrait Gallery; *m* 1st 24 April 1851 Selina Constance (*d* 14 Nov 1851), est dau of Hubert de Burgh, of West Drayton, Middlesex; *m* 2nd 21 Nov 1865 Georgina Elizabeth, RRC, DJStJ (*d* 2 Feb 1929), 3rd dau of Sir Thomas Moncreiffe of that Ilk, 7th Bt (*see* ERROLL, E), and by her had:

1 WILLIAM HUMBLE, **2nd Earl**

2 John Hubert (Sir), KCVO, Brevet Maj Gen List, Lt Worcs Yeo, 4th Bn Worcs Regt, on HQ Staff Boer War 1899–1900 (despatches, medal with four clasps) and WW I (despatches twice), Assist Priv Sec to Fin Sec War Office 1901, Equerry in Ordinary to HM EDWARD VII 1902–10, Extra Equerry to TM GEORGE V 1910–36, QUEEN ALEXANDRA 1910–25, EDWARD VIII 1936 and GEORGE VI 1937–38, Cdr Orders of Isabella the Catholic Spain, Zahringer Lowen of Baden, Crown Prussia, Christ Portugal, Crown Italy, Our Saviour Greece and Dannebrog Denmark, Offr Legion of Honour, OStJ; *b* 20 March 1870; *educ* Eton; *m* 23 June 1908 Jean Templeton, CBE (1918), DGStJ (*d* 1 May 1962), dau of Whitelaw Reid, US Amb to UK, and *d* 2 Dec 1938, having had issue:

(1) (Edward) John Sutton, MVO (1952), MC (1944); CC (1958–64) Berks, Lt-Col cmdg Inns of Court Regt 1947–50 and The Life Gds 1950–53, Col cmdg Household Cavalry 1953–56 (ret 1956), Silver Stick-in Waiting, Jt Hon Col Inns of Court Regt 1959–90, served WW II, Chm Hungerford RDC 1961–64; *b* 24 March 1909 (HM EDWARD VII stood sponsor); *educ* Eton; *m* 1st 2 Aug 1934 Margaret Susan (*d* 1981), er dau of Geoffrey Robert Josceline Corbett, DSO, of Rossferry, Enniskillen, Co Fermanagh, and *d* Nov 1990, leaving:

1a +Gerald John [Gerald Ward Esq CBE, Chilton Park Farm, Hungerford, Berks RG17 0SY], Capt RHG; *b* 31 May 1938; *educ* Eton, RMA Sandhurst and RAC Cirencester; CBE (1989); *m* 30 March 1967 (*divorce* 1984) Rosalind Elizabeth, yr dau of Hon Richard Edward Lygon, of Pyndar House, Hanley Castle, Worcs (*see* 1970 edn BEAUCHAMP, E), and has issue:

1b *Sarah Patricia; *b* 3 Feb 1968; *m* 1993 *Adrian Richard Scrope (*see* SYKES, Bt, of Sledmere)

2b *Margaret Lucy; *b* 1970

1a (cont.) Capt Gerald Ward *m* 2nd 1984 *Mrs Amanda Mildred Dinan, only dau of Sir Lacey Eric Vincent, 2nd Bt (*qv*)

1a Patricia Elizabeth Marion; *b* 24 Oct 1935; *m* 1st 4 Sept 1956 (*divorce* 1964) Kenneth E Cooper and *d* May 1988, leaving:

1b *Susan Elizabeth Margaret; *b* 1957

2b *Laura Jean; *b* 21 Feb 1959

1a (cont.) Mrs Patricia Cooper *m* 2nd Dec 1965 (*divorce* 1966) John D Gray, of Los Angeles; *m* 3rd 1966 *Frederick Calvin Danner

(1) (cont.) Lt-Col John Ward *m* 2nd 1986 Marion Elizabeth Jessie (*d* 7 Sept 1997), dau of Charles M Clover, formerly w of Geoffrey Adams and widow of (a) Capt Lionel Cecil and (b) 4th Baron Romilly (*see* 1970 edn), and *d* 1990

(2) (Alexander) Reginald, JP Berks 1941–47, pilot with ATA 1941–46; *b* 27 Feb 1915 (HM QUEEN ALEXANDRA stood sponsor), *educ* Eton; *m* 1st 24 April 1946 (*divorce* 1959) Ilona (Ila), only dau of Maj B Hollos, of Budapest; *m* 2nd 10 Jan 1967 (*divorce* 1969) Zena Moyra (Zena Marshall, the actress), step-dau of Capt George W Tailby, of Sheffington, Lincs; *m* 3rd *Constance Cluett Sage, only dau of George Bywater Cluett II, of New York

3 Robert Arthur, OBE (1919), Capt Army, Lt Worcs Imp Yeo, served Matabeleland Rebellion 1896 (medal), Boer War with 4th Imp Yeo and as ADC to Gen Broadwood 1901–02 (Queen's medal with five clasps), Gen Staff WW I (despatches twice, Legion of Honour), MP Crewe 1895–1900; *b* 23 Feb 1871; *m* 24 July 1906 Lady Mary Acheson, 2nd dau of 4th Earl of Gosford (*qv*), and *d* 14 June 1942, leaving issue:

(1) Julian Humble Dudley, WW II as Maj RHG (despatches); *b* 27 March 1908; *educ* Eton and Magdalene Coll Cambridge; *m* 1st 14 Aug 1946 (*divorce* 1954) Ann Elisabeth, only child of Capt John Walter Wilson Bridges, of Ober House, Brockenhurst, Hants, and had:

1a *Patricia Ann; *b* 22 May 1947

2a *Georgina Mary; *b* 2 Aug 1950

(1) (cont.) Maj Julian Ward *m* 2nd 1962 *Mary Rebecca Jane, widow of Col Harry Latham, RHA, and dau of Albert Edward Morris-Hadwell, of Kidderminster, Worcs, and Ballarat, Victoria, and *d* 29 April 1971

(1) Lettice Mary; *b* 5 Dec 1909; *m* 15 Sept 1934 (*divorce* 1947) Arthur Thomas Wilson-Filmer, and *d* 17 April 1968

4 Reginald, DSO, Capt RHG Boer War 1899–1902; *b* 11 June 1874; *d* unm 7 March 1904

5 Cyril Augustus, MVO (1903), Capt RN, ADC 1919–21, cmded Div with Grand Fleet 1914–17; *b* 31 Jan 1876; *m* 14 April 1904 Baroness Irene de Brienen (*m* 2nd 6 Dec 1934 V-Adml Hon Arthur Charles Strutt, CBE who *d* 10 Feb 1973 (*see* RAYLEIGH, B), and *d* 21 April 1974 aged 90), dau of Baron de Brienen, and *d* 11 Jan 1930, leaving issue:

(1) Margaret Helene Edith; *b* 11 Jan 1905; *m* 10 Dec 1929 Count Paul William Alexander Munster (*d* 24 Jan 1968), 2nd s of Prince Alexander Munster, of Derneburg, Hanover, and had issue

(2) Helen Elizabeth; *b* 28 Dec 1907; *m* 27 April 1931 7th Earl of Ilchester (*qv*), and *d* 8 Nov 1970, leaving issue

(3) Nicolette Joan, JP (1942), Berks; *b* 28 Dec 1907; *m* 15 Nov 1928 Michael Charles St John Hornby (*d* 1987), of Pusey House, Faringdon, est s of Charles Harry St John Hornby, of Shelley House, Chelsea, and Chantmarle, Dorset, and *d* 1988, leaving, with other issue:

1a *Simon Michael (Sir) [Sir Simon Hornby, 8 Ennismore Gdns, London SW7 1NL; The Ham, Wantage, Oxon OX12 9JA]; *b* 29 Dec 1934; *educ* Eton, New Coll Oxford and Harvard Business Sch; 2nd Lt Gren Gds 1953–55, Freeman and Liveryman Goldsmiths' Co 1955, FBIM, FRSA, dir 1974–94 (chm 1982–94) WH Smith Gp, ktd 1988, Pres RHS; *m* 15 June 1968 *(Ann) Sheran, dau of Peter Victor Ferdinand Cazalet, of Fairlawne, Tonbridge, Kent

6 Gerald Ernest Francis, MVO, Lt 1st Life Gds, served Boer War 1899–1900 and WW I; *b* 9 Nov 1877; *m* 7 Nov 1899 Lady Evelyn Crichton (*d* 4 May 1955), dau of 4th Earl of Erne (*qv*), and was *ka* 30 Oct 1914

1 Edith Amelia, CBE (1918); *b* 16 Sept 1872; *m* 5 May 1895 4th Baron Wolverton (*qv*) and *d* 6 June 1956, leaving issue

The 1st EARL *d* 7 May 1885; his son,

WILLIAM HUMBLE WARD, **2nd Earl of Dudley**, PC (1902), GCB, GCMG, GCVO (1903), DL Worcs; High Steward Kidderminster, Hon Maj, Lt-Col TAR, Lt-Col Worcs Yeo (TD), DAAG Imp Yeo Boer War 1900, Mayor Dudley 1895 and 1896, Parly Sec BOT 1895–1902, Ld Lt Ireland 1902–05, Govr-Gen and C-in-C Australia 1908–11; *b* 25 May 1867; *m* 1st 14 Sept 1891 Rachel, CBE (*d* 26 June 1920), yst dau of Charles Henry Gurney, and had issue:

1 WILLIAM HUMBLE ERIC, **3rd Earl**

2 Roderick John, Lt-Col, WW I in the Buffs, WW II in KAR, Br Mil Mission Ethiopia, Br Mil Admin Malaya (wounded); *b* 13 April 1902; *educ* Eton; *m* 1st 28 Sept 1928 (*divorce* 1936) Eileen Patricia, only dau of Lt-Col Marcus Michael Hartigan, CMG, DSO; *m* 2nd 11 March 1940 (*divorce* 1947) Valerie Maud (*d* 1989), only dau of Robert Jeremiah Skelton, of Nairobi, and had issue:

(1) +Robert John Christopher WARD later BARWICK-WARD (deed poll 5 Feb 1952) [Robert Barwick-Ward Esq, Towton Hall, Tadcaster, N Yorks LS24 9PB]; *b* 25 Aug 1942; *educ* Millfield and Grenoble U; *m* 1st 2 March 1968 (*divorce* 1974) Frances Pauline (*d* 1975), er dau of S/Ldr Matthew Donald Einhorn, JP, of Cragg Hill House, Killinghall, nr Harrogate, Yorks, and has issue:

1a *Annabel Jane; *b* 27 July 1970

(1) (cont.) Robert Barwick-Ward *m* 2nd 1976 (*divorce* 1985) Laura Madeleine, dau of Henry J Sutcliffe, of W Yorks, and has further issue:

2a *Lucinda Marie Clare; *b* 1980

2 (cont.) Lt-Col Roderick Ward *m* 3rd March 1947 *Charlotte Anne Park (*d* 1971) dau of Capt Charles Frederick Osbourne, RD, RNR, of Broadstone, Dorset, and *d* 2 Oct 1952, having by her had issue:

(2) +Rupert Michael; *b* 4 May 1947; *educ* Aiglon Coll and Le Rosey; *m* 25 April 1970 *Frances Margaret Mary, er dau of J C Barry, of Adelaide House, Banff, Co Limerick, and has issue:

1a +Eric Roderick Humble; *b* 1973

3 Edward Frederick, G/Capt RAF, 2nd Lt 10th Hussars, WW II, Chm S Durham Steel and Iron Co; *b* 20 Nov 1907 (HM EDWARD VII stood sponsor); *educ* Eton; *m* 1st 30 Nov 1940 (*divorce* 1947) Pauline Katharine, er dau of Hon Charles Frederick Winn, of Nostell Priory, Wakefield (Isee ST OSWALD, B); *m* 2nd 2 July 1953 *Hon Alathea Gwendoline Alys Mary Fitzalan-Howard [The Hon Mrs Edward Ward, 21b Ave du Temple, Lausanne, CH 1012, Switzerland], er dau of 2nd Viscount FitzAlan of Derwent, OBE (*see* NORFOLK D), and *d* 1987

4 GEORGE REGINALD WARD, 1st and last VISCOUNT WARD OF WITLEY, so *cr* 1960; *b* 1907; *m* 1st 1940 (*divorce* 1951) Ann Diana France Ayesha, dau of Capt Arthur Edward Capel, CBE, and the Dowager Countess of Westmorland (*qv*), and had issue:

(1) Anthony Giles Humble; *b* 1943; *educ* Eton; *d* 1983

(1) *Georgina Anne [The Hon Mrs Tritton, Quintana 23, Gustavo A Madero, Mexico DF ZP14]; *b* 1941; *m* 1st 1966 (*divorce* 1971, resumed maiden name by deed poll 1972) Alastair Cameron Forbes; *m* 2nd 1978 Patrick Claude Henry Tritton (*d* 1 Feb 1998; *see* TRITTON, Bt)

4 (cont.) The 1st and last VISCOUNT *m* 2nd 1962 Barbara Mary Colonsay (*d* 1980), dau of Capt Ronald Frank Rous NcNeill, Irish Gds, and formerly w of Hon Michael Langhorne Astor (*see* ASTOR, V), and *d* 1988, when the Viscountcy expired

1 Gladys Honor; *m* 20 Feb 1923 (*divorce* 1932) Maj Percival Cunningham Allan Bridgeman, OBE, s of F Orlando Bridgeman, of Dunedin, NZ, and *d* 5 Dec 1961, having had issue. He *d* 23 Nov 1961

2 Morvyth Lillian; *m* 29 June 1921 A/Cdre Constantine Evelyn Benson (*d* 20 Sept 1960), CBE, DSO, RAuxAF, s of Robert Henry Benson, JP, of Buckhurst, Sussex, and *d* 11 March 1959, leaving issue

3 (Alexandra) Patricia; *b* 24 Aug 1904 (HM QUEEN ALEXANDRA and HRH THE DUKE OF CONNAUGHT stood sponsors); *d* unm 7 July 1964

The **2nd Earl** *m* 2nd 30 April 1924 Gertrude (*d* 25 April 1952), dau of John Millar and widow of Lionel Monckton (*see* MONCKTON OF BRENCHLEY, V).

He *d* 29 June 1932; his est son,

WILLIAM HUMBLE ERIC WARD, **3rd Earl of Dudley**, DL (1927–66) and JP Staffs; *b* 30 Jan 1894; *educ* Eton and Ch Ch Oxford; Maj Staffs Yeo (TA), Maj Res of Offrs 10th Hus, Col 51st (Midland) Med Bde 1933–36, Hon Air Cdre No 915 (Warwicks) Sqdn AAF 1939–49, Ld High Steward Kidderminster, High Sheriff Worcs 1930, MP Hornsey 1921–24 and Wednesbury 1931–32, PPS to U-Sec State India 1922–24, served WW I (wounded, Legion of Honour), KStJ; *m* 1st 8 March 1919 Lady Rosemary Millicent Leveson-Gower, RRC (*d* 21 July 1930), dau of 4th Duke of Sutherland (*qv*), and had issue:

1 WILLIAM HUMBLE DAVID WARD, **4th and present Earl of Dudley**

2 John Jeremy; *b* 7 May 1922; *d* 9 Dec 1929

3 +Peter Alistair [The Hon Peter Ward, Cornwell Manor, Chipping Norton, Oxon], served RCAF 1943–44 and Fleet Air Arm 1945–46; *b* 8 Feb 1926; *educ* Eton, U of BC and Ch Ch Oxford (MA); *m* 21 Nov 1956 (*divorce* 1974) Claire Leonora, only child of Amyas Evelyn Giles Baring (*see* ASHBURTON, B), and has issue:

(1) +Alexander Evelyn Giles; *b* 1 July 1961; *m* 1988 *Lucy Rose, est dau of Rupert Lycett Green (*see* GREEN, Bt), and has issue:

1a +Archibald Rupert William; *b* 1993

1a *Jasmine Carrie: *b* 1990

(1) *Rachel Claire; *b* 12 Sept 1957; actress (appearances include *Thornbirds*); *m* 1983 *Bryan Brown, actor, of Sydney, Australia, and has issue:

1a *Rosie; *b* 1985

2a *Matilda; *b* 1987

(2) *Tracy Louise [Marchioness of Worcester, Badminton House, Glos GL9 1DB]; *b* 22 Dec 1958; *m* 1987 *Henry John FitzRoy, Marquess of Worcester, est s of 11th Duke of Beaufort (*qv*), and has issue

3 (cont.) The Hon Peter Ward *m* 2nd 18 April 1974 *Elizabeth Rose, dau of Richard Victor Charles Westmacott, of Ascona, Switzerland, and has further issue:

(2) +Jeremy Christopher; *b* 13 Jan 1975

(3) +Benjamin Robin; *b* 16 Feb 1978

The **3rd Earl** *m* 2nd 25 Feb 1943 (*divorce* 1954) Frances Laura, formerly w of 2nd Viscount Long (*qv*) and 2nd dau of Hon Guy Lawrence Charteris (*see* WEMYSS and MARCH, E); *m* 3rd 17 July 1961 *Grace Maria, formerly w of Prince Stanislas Radziwill and er dau of Dr Michael Kolin, of Saint Jacob, Dubrovnik, and *d* 26 Dec 1969

DUDLEY, Baroness

Arms: Az. two bars nebuly arg., each charged with as many crescents sa., a chief or, issuant therefrom a demi-lion of the third. **Supporters:** Two lions rampant double-queued vert, armed and langued gu., ducally gorged and lined or. **Motto:** *Dieu donne* ('The Lord giveth'). **Creation:** B. (E) 15 Feb 1439/40.

THE BARONESS DUDLEY (Barbara Amy Felicity Lea Smith) [The Rt Hon The Lady Dudley, Hill House, Napleton, Kempsey, Worcs WR5 3PY]; *b* 23 April 1907, *s* bro 1972; artist; *m* 1st 22 Aug 1929 Guy Raymond Hill Wallace (*d* 16 March 1967), yst s of Gen Hill Wallace, CB, RHA, of Astley, Worcs, and has:

1 +JIM ANTHONY HILL [The Hon Jim Wallace, Little Grange, Kempsey, Worcs]; *b* 9 Nov 1930; *educ* Lancing; *m* 16 June 1962 *Nicola Jane, dau of Lt-Col Philip William Edward Leslie Dunsterville, and has issue:

(1) +Jeremy William Guilford; *b* 12 Sept 1964

(2) +Nicholas John Hill; *b* 31 Jan 1967

2 +Robin Guy Hill [The Hon Robin Wallace, Pond House, Ham Hill, Powick, Worcs WR2 4RD]; *b* 19 March 1936; *educ* Malvern; *m* 2 Jan 1959 *Jill Alexandra, dau of Herbert Williams, of High Tree House, Leintwardine, Herefs, and has:

(1) +Simon Alexander Hill; *b* 17 May 1962

(2) +Andrew George Hill; *b* 17 Nov 1964

3 +William John Sutton [The Hon William Wallace, Beechmount House, Shoulton, Worcs]; *b* 9 Jan 1938; *educ* Malvern; *m* 27 April 1962 *Jean Carol Ann, dau of Albert Edward Shipton, and has issue:

(1) +Guy Edward John Sutton; *b* 18 Dec 1963; *educ* Malvern

(2) +Piers William Somery; *b* 25 April 1965; *educ* Malvern

1 +Felicity Lilla [The Hon Mrs Faram, Heath Hill, Queen Hill, Upton-on-Severn, Hereford and Worcester]; *b* 14 Feb 1944; *m* 29 July 1967 *Philip Neil Faram, and has issue:

(1) +David Stephen; *b* 24 July 1968

(2) +Michael Guy; *b* 30 May 1970

(3) +Philip John; *b* 20 May 1976

BARONESS DUDLEY *m* 2nd 1980 *Charles Anthony Crosse Hamilton

Dudley, other creations: *See* DUDLEY, E. In addition, Alice, estranged w of the Sir Robert Dudley who was created Duke of Northumberland (*see* NORTHUMBERLAND, D, preliminary remarks) by the Holy Roman Emperor Ferdinand II, was made in 1644 Duchess Dudley for life.

Lineage (of Dudley/Sutton): HERVEY de SUTTON; feudal Ld of Sutton-upon-Trent, Notts; gave the Church of Sutton to the Canons of Radford, Notts; had, with two er sons (Robert, *dsp*; Richard, had five daus):

ROWLAND de SUTTON; *m* probably in 1215 Alice, dau of Richard de Lexinton and yst sister and coheir of Henry de Lexinton, Bp Lincoln, and had, with a yr s (Robert, ancestor of the Barons Lexinton of Aram):

WILLIAM de SUTTON, of Worksop, Notts; *b* 1217; *m* 1st Matilda — (living 1242) and had issue; *m* 2nd Eva — (*m* 2nd Robert Paynell and was living 1275/6), and *d* 1267; his s by his 1st w:

ROBERT de SUTTON, of Worksop; *b* 1240; *m* Johanna —, who had lands of Ekering and Allerton in dower *c* 1274, and *d* 1273/4 possessed of the Manors of Theydon and Montem, Essex, and those of Aston and Byfeld, Northants; his s:

RICHARD de SUTTON; *b* 29 Sept 1266; *m* Isobel (living 1289/90), dau and heir of William Patrick by Beatrice, dau and coheir of David de Malpas, and had:

Sir JOHN de SUTTON, of Dudley Castle, Staffs; made over the Castle and Manor of Dudley to Hugh le Despenser by deed 19 Oct 1325 but this grant, extorted from him while in prison, was cancelled 1327 and the property restored; *m* Margaret, dau of Roger de Somery, of Dudley Castle, and er sister and coheir of John, 1st and last Lord (Baron) Somery of the 1308 *cr*, and had, with a dau (Margaret, *m* Roger Hillary):

JOHN SUTTON, of Dudley Castle; summoned to a Roy Cncl by writ 25 Feb 1341/2, but not afterwards; *m* Isabella (*m* 2nd Sir Richard le Fisher later Dudley and *d* 10 April 1397, having outlived both her s and gs), dau of John, Lord (Baron) Cherleton, and *d* 23 Nov 1359, leaving:

Sir JOHN SUTTON; *m* 1st 25 Dec 1357 Catherine (*d* Dec 1361), dau of 1st Earl of Stafford (*see* STAFFORD, B), and had issue; *m* 2nd Joan (*m* 3rd by 1371 Sir Henry Griffith), widow of Sir John de Mountfort and dau and heir of John Clinton, of Coleshill, Warwicks, and *d* *c* 1370; his only s by his 1st w:

Sir JOHN SUTTON; *b* 6 Dec 1361; *m* 1st Alice (*d* 1392), probably dau of his guardian Philip le Despenser, of Carlington, and had issue; *m* 2nd Joan — (*d* 1408) and *d* 10 March 1395/6, leaving:

Sir JOHN SUTTON, of Dudley Castle; *b* *c* 1380; *m* by 10 Dec 1401 Constance (*d* Sept 1432), dau of Sir Walter Blount, of Barton, Derbys, and *d* 29 Aug 1406, leaving:

JOHN SUTTON or DUDLEY, **1st Lord** (Baron) **Dudley** (E), so *cr* by writ 15 Feb 1439/40, KG (1459); *b* 25 Dec 1400; Ld Dep Ireland 1428–30; served Hundred Years War in France, Constable Tower London 1473; *m* Elizabeth (*d* by 1479), widow of Edward, Lord (Baron) Cherleton, and dau of Sir John Berkeley, of Beverstone, and had, with other issue:

1 Edmund (Sir); *m* 1st Joyce, sis and coheir of Edward, Earl of Worcester (*see* BEAUFORT, D), and had, with other issue (including a dau):

(1) EDWARD, **2nd Lord**

(2) John (Sir), of Aston le Walls; *m* and had issue:

1a Margaret; *m* John Butler, and had issue

1 (cont.) Sir Edmund *m* 2nd Matilda, dau of Thomas, 8th Lord (Baron) Clifford (*see* DE CLIFFORD, B), and *dvp* after 6 July 1483, having by her had, with other issue (including, either by his 1st or 2nd w, Dorothy, *m* Richard Wrottesley, *see* WROTTESLEY, B):

(2) John, of Atherington, Sussex; ancestor of the Dudley Earls of Warwick and Leicester

(3) William, Bp Durham 1476–83

The 1st LORD *d* 30 Sept 1487; his gs,

EDWARD SUTTON or DUDLEY, **2nd Lord** (Baron) **Dudley**; *b* *c* 1459; ktd 1487; *m* Cicely, dau of Sir William Willoughby, and had, with other issue (including a dau, Joyce, *m* John Leighton and had issue; *see* LEIGHTON, Bt):

1 JOHN, **3rd Lord**

2 Arthur, Priest Lichfield, Preb Worcester

3 Geoffrey; *m* Eleanor, dau of Sir Gilbert Talbot (*see* SHREWSBURY and WATERFORD, E), and was ancestor of the DUDLEYs of Russell's Hall

4 Thomas; alleged ancestor of the DUDLEYs of Massachusetts

5 George

The 2nd LORD *d* 31 Jan 1508; his est son,

JOHN SUTTON or DUDLEY, **3rd Lord** (Baron) **Dudley**; ktd 1513, made over Dudley Castle and his estates to his cousin Sir John Dudley (later Duke of Northumberland) and was accordingly nicknamed 'Lord Quondam [Latin for 'formerly']'; *m* after 30 Oct 1519 Lady Cicely Grey (*bur* 28 April 1554), dau of 1st Marquess of Dorset, and had, with two daus (one of whom, Eleanor, *m* Henry Beaumont, of Wednesbury, Staffs):

1 EDWARD, **4th Lord**

2 Henry; *m* —, dau of Sir Christopher Ashton

3 George, a soldier in the garrison of Calais

4 Thomas; *b* 1539; *d* 1574, leaving a dau, Elizabeth

The 3rd LORD was *bur* 18 Sept 1553; his son and heir,

EDWARD SUTTON or DUDLEY, **4th Lord** (Baron) **Dudley**; served in campaign led by Protector Somerset (*see* SOMERSET, D) against Scots 1547; Govr Hume Castle after its surrender; by letters patent 31 Dec 1555 Dudley Castle, taken into the Crown's possession after the fall of John Dudley Duke of Northumberland, was given back to him; *m* 1st 1556 Katherine (*bur* 28 April 1566), dau of 1st Baron Chandos of Sudeley, and had issue:

1 Agnes; *m* 1st Francis Throckmorton; *m* 2nd Thomas Wylmer, barrister

The **4th Lord** *m* 2nd Lady Jane Stanley (*bur* 4 Sept 1569), dau of 3rd Earl of Derby (*qv*), and by her had issue:

1 EDWARD, **5th Lord**

2 John, of Compton, Staffs; *bapt* 30 Nov 1569; *m* Elizabeth, dau of Thomas Whorwood, of Compton, and had issue (all *dsp* in 1660 bar Anne, who *m* Edward Gibson, of York, and left issue)

The **4th Lord** *m* 3rd Mary (*m* 2nd Richard Mompesson and *d* 21 Aug 1600), dau of 1st Baron Howard of Effingham (*see* EFFINGHAM, E), but by her had no issue

He *d* 8 July 1586; his er son,

EDWARD SUTTON or DUDLEY, **5th Lord** (Baron) **Dudley**; *bapt* 17 Sept; *m* *c* 1586 Theodosia (*bur* 12 Jan 1649/50), dau of Sir James Harington, of Exton, Rutland (*see* HARINGTON, Bt), and *d* 24 June 1643, having had, with four daus:

FERDINANDO (Sir), KB (1610); *b* 1588; *m* 9 July 1610 Honora (*bur* 23 March 1620), gdau of 1st Earl of Hertford (*see* SOMERSET, D), and *dvp* 22 Nov 1621, having had issue:

FRANCES Sutton or Dudley, **Baroness Dudley** in her own right; *b* 23 July 1611; *m* (settlement 17 Feb 1628) 1st Baron Ward of Birmingham (*see* DUDLEY, E, also for further details of 7th to 10th Barons inclusive) and had, with other issue:

EDWARD WARD, **7th Lord** (Baron) **Dudley**; *m* Frances (*bur* 21 Nov 1676), dau of Sir William Brereton, 1st Bt, and *d* 3 Aug 1701, having had, with other issue:

WILLIAM; *b* 1660; *m* Frances, dau of William Dilke, but *dvp* (*bur* 16 May 1692), leaving, with other issue:

(1) EDWARD WARD, **8th Lord** (Baron) **Dudley**; *bapt* 20 Dec 1683; *m* 9 April 1703 Diana (*d* 1709), only dau and heir of Thomas Howard (*see* SUFFOLK and BERKSHIRE, E), and *d* 28 March 1704, leaving:

1a EDWARD WARD, **9th Lord** (Baron) **Dudley**; *b* posthumously 16 June 1704; *d* unm between 23 Feb 1729 and 7 Sept 1731

(2) WILLIAM WARD, **10th Lord** (Baron) **Dudley**; *b* 16 Oct 1685; *d* unm 21 May 1740

(1) FRANCES Ward; *b* 5 Dec 1687/8; *m* 12 Nov 1709 William LEA (*d* 31 Jan 1741 aged 64), of Halesowen Grange, Worcs, and *d* 24 Jan 1737, having had issue:

1a FERDINANDO DUDLEY LEA, **11th Lord** (Baron) **Dudley**; *bapt* 14 Sept 1710; *d* unm 21 Oct 1757, when the Barony of Dudley fell into abeyance between his five sisters and coheirs

2a William; *bapt* 15 May 1722; *bur* 29 March 1742/3

1a ANNE, of whom presently

2a Frances; *bapt* 12 April 1717; *m* 8 Dec 1740 Walter Woodcock, JP Salop, and *d* 9 March 1800, having had two sons (*dsp*) and six daus, eventually coheirs

3a Mary; *bapt* 19 June 1723; *m* 2 Aug 1741 Joseph Harvey, MD, of Stourbridge, and *dsp* (*bur* 14 April 1742), leaving issue:

1b William; *bapt* 13 April, *d* 15 May 1742

4a Catherine; *bapt* 8 Feb 1726/7; *m* 1st 16 Nov 1744 Thomas Jordan, of Birmingham; *m* 2nd Henry Turner and *d* 12 April 1756, leaving issue by both husbs

5a Elizabeth; *bapt* 23 Feb 1728/9; *m* 14 July 1759 Rev Benjamin Briscoe, Rector Staunton, Worcs, and was *bur* 29 July 1760, having had issue:

1b William Lea; *bapt* 20 April 1760; *dsp* 25 Aug 1834

The est sis and coheir,

ANNE Lea, upon whose heirs the estate of Halesowen was entailed by her bro's will; *bapt* 24 March 1714; *m* (settlement 18 May 1737) William SMITH (*d* 19 May 1784), of Stoke Prior and Ridgware, Worcs, and assumed the title BARONESS DUDLEY on her bro's death 1757, though the abeyance had neither been terminated nor, in the event that it was terminated, adjudicated in her favour, and had issue:

1 Harry Grey; *d* 21 March 1760

2 FERDINANDO

1 Frances; *m* her cousin Walter Woodcock (*dsp* and *bur* 1 March 1821), er s of Walter Woodcock and Frances, sis and coheir of **11th Lord** (Baron) **Dudley**

2 Anne; *m* Edward Baker, of Hill Court, Worcs

3 Mary; *d* unm, *bur* 19 Feb 1826

ANNE SMITH, the self-styled Lady Dudley, *d* 29 April 1762; her only surv son,

FERDINANDO SMITH, of Halesowen Grange; *bapt* 23 Jan 1747; *m* 27 Dec 1774 Elizabeth (*bur* 21 Sept 1805), dau of Humphrey Lyttelton, and was *bur* 13 Jan 1794, having had, with two yr s and eight daus:

FERDINANDO SMITH, of Halesowen Grange, DL, JP Worcs; Lt-Col Worcs Militia, served Ireland during 1798 Uprising, Freeman Worcester; *b* 26 March 1779; *m* 1st 1 July 1802 Elosia (*dsp* 14 Feb 1805), dau and coheir of Maj-Gen St George Knudson, HEICS; *m* 2nd 5 Oct 1830 Elizabeth (*d* 23 Jan 1875), 4th dau of Michael Grazebrook, of Audnam, Staffs, and *d* 20 July 1841, having by her had, with a yr s (William Lea, Lt 13th Regt; *b* 27 Feb 1836; *d* 5 Feb 1880):

FERDINANDO DUDLEY LEA SMITH, of Halesowen Grange, DL, JP Worcs; High Sheriff 1860, JP Staffs, barrister Inner Temple, Capt Queen's Own Worcs Yeo; *bapt* 15 June 1834; *m* 23 Feb 1865 Amy Sophia, 2nd dau of James Heath Leigh, of Belmont Hall, Cheshire, and *d* 8 Feb 1905, having had, with a yr s (Charles Edward Lea, *b* 23 Nov, *d* 6 Dec 1874) and dau (Lilian Amy Lea, *d* unm 27 May 1954):

FERDINANDO DUDLEY WILLIAM LEA, **12th Lord** (Baron) **Dudley** on termination of abeyance in his favour, summoned to Parl 9 May 1916, JP Worcs; Lt-Col 6th Bn Worcs Regt, served Boer War 1901–02 (Queen's medal with four clasps); *b* 4 April 1872; *m* 3 Feb 1904 Sybil Augusta (*d* 5 Nov 1958), dau of Rev Canon Henry Coventry, Rector Severn Stoke, Worcs (*see* COVENTRY, E), and *d* 5 Dec 1936, leaving:

1 FERDINANDO DUDLEY HENRY LEA, **13th Lord** (Baron) **Dudley**; *b* 18 June 1910; *educ* Repton; Lt 8th Bn Worcs Regt, S/Ldr RAFVR WW II; *m* July 1941 (*divorce* 1965) Kirsten Laura Hedvig, dau of Lars Anton Albrechtsen, of Vibsig, Denmark, and *dsp* 19 April 1972

1 BARBARA AMY FELICITY, **present Baroness Dudley**

Lineage (of Lea): WILLIAM LEA, of Lea Green, King's Norton, Worcs; *m* Joice (*d* after 24 Nov 1631), dau of John Ive, of King's Norton, and heiress of the Halesowen Grange estate, and *d c* 1612, having had a yst s:

JOHN LEA, of Halesowen; *m* Anne (*d* after 6 June 1685), sister of Robert Tibbots, and *d* after 5 Nov 1657, having had three sons and five daus; his 2nd s:

JOHN LEA, of Halesowen; *m* Mary (*d* 1720), dau of William Deely, of Warley-Wigorn, and had:

1 William, of Halesowen; *m* 12 Nov 1709 Frances, sister and in her issue heir of **10th Lord** (Baron) **Dudley** (*see* above)

1 Anne; *m* Alan Garway, Jr

2 Margaret; *m* 1706 John Shenstone

Lineage (of Smith): WILLIAM SMITH/SMYTH, of the Breach, Hunnington, and Stoke Prior, Worcs; *d* Dec 1684, having had issue:

WILLIAM SMITH, of the Breach; had:

1 William; ancestor of the SMITHs of Bourne Heath, Worcs, whose heir Mary; *m* William Clinton, of Belbroughton

2 Joseph; ancestor of the SMITHs of Hunnington, now extinct

3 JACOB, of whom presently

1 Eleanor; *m* 1693 William Cardale, surgeon, of Dudley

2 Sarah

The yst son,

JACOB SMITH, of Stoke Prior; *m* June 1709 Elizabeth (*d* May 1762 aged 86), dau of Humphrey Lowe, of Warley, by Joice, dau of John Lea, of Halesowen (*d* above), and had:

1 WILLIAM, of Stoke Prior; *m c* 18 May 1737 ANNE, est sister and coheir of **11th Lord** (Baron) **Dudley**

1 Mary; *m* 1746 Rev Richard Chambers, Rector Naunton Beauchamp, and *d* 1786, leaving issue

DUDLEY-WILLIAMS

Creation: Bt. (UK) 2 July 1964.

SIR ALASTAIR EDGCUMBE JAMES DUDLEY-WILLIAMS, 2ND BT, of the City and Co of Exeter [Sir Alastair Dudley-Williams Bt, 10 Lower Church Lane, Farnham, Surrey GU9 7PS]; *b* 26 Nov 1943; *s* f 1987; *educ* Nautical Coll Pangbourne; dir Wildcat Consultants 1986–; *m* 22 April 1972 *Diana Elizabeth Jane, twin dau of R H C Duncan, of The Old Rectory, Sutton Montis, Somerset, and has issue:

1 *Marina Elizabeth Catherine; *b* 13 May 1979

2 *Lorna Caroline Rachel; *b* 8 Aug 1977

Lineage: ARTHUR HENRY WILLIAMS, of Plymouth; *b* 1872; *m* Minnie Jane (*d* Oct 1922), dau of Samuel Edgcumbe, of Ermington, Devon, and *d* 1924, leaving issue:

1 **Sir Rolf Dudley Williams, 1st Bt** (UK), so *cr* 2 July 1964; *b* 17 June 1908; *educ* Plymouth Coll and RAF Coll Cranwell; F/O RAF 1934 (ret due ill health 1934), dir Power Jets 1936, md 1941; MP (C) Exeter 1951–66, PPS to: Sec State War 1958, Min Ag 1960–64, chm Tremletts, dir Amalgamated Investments and Property; *m* 20 May 1940 *(Margaret) Helen, er dau of Frederick Eaton Robinson, OBE, of Enfield, and *d* 1987, leaving:

(1) Sir ALASTAIR EDGCUMBE JAMES DUDLEY-WILLIAMS, **2nd and present Bt**

(2) +MALCOLM PHILIP EDGCUMBE [Malcolm Dudley-Williams Esq, 9 Bowerdean St, London SW6 3TN]; *b* 10 Aug 1947; heir presumptive; *educ* Nautical Coll Pangbourne; *m* 28 April 1973 *Caroline, twin dau of R H C Duncan, of The Old Rectory, Sutton Montis, Somerset, and has issue:

1a +Nicholas Mark Edgcumbe; *b* 2 July 1975

2a +Patrick Guy Edgcumbe; *b* 4 April 1978

1a *Clare Helen Colina; *b* 7 Sept 1982

DUFF GORDON

Arms: Quarterly; 1st and 4th, az. three boar's heads couped or, armed ppr. and langued gu., within a double tressure flory counteflory interchangeably with thistles, roses and fleurs-de-lys of the second (for GORDON); 2nd and 3rd, vert a fess dancetté erm. between a buck's head cabossed on chief and two escallops in base or (for DUFF). **Crests:** 1 (Dexter) Two arms from the shoulder naked, holding a bow, and ready to let fly an arrow, all ppr., 2 (Sinister) A demi-lion gu., holding in the dexter paw a sword erect ppr., hilted and pommelled or, charged on the shoulder with a mullet arg. **Supporters:** Dexter, a savage wreathed about the head and middle with laurel, holding in the dexter hand the branch of a tree, all ppr.; sinister, a stag ppr., unguled and attired or, gorged with a ducal coronet of the last and pendant therefrom an inescutcheon charged with the following arms: vert a fess dancetté erm. between a buck's head cabossed in chief and two escallops in base or, the fess charged with a mullet arg. **Mottoes:** *Fortuna sequatur* ('May fortune follow'), *Deo juvante* ('With God assisting'), *Virtute et opera* ('By virtue and deeds'). **Creation:** Bt. (UK) 12 Nov 1813.

SIR ANDREW COSMO LEWIS DUFF GORDON, 8TH BT, of Halkin, Co Ayr [Sir Andrew Duff Gordon Bt, Downton House, Walton, Presteigne, Powys LD8 2RD; 27 Cathcart Rd, London SW10 9JG]; *b* 17 Oct 1933; *s* f 1964; *educ* Repton; served Worcester Regt and 1st Bn 22nd Cheshire Regt Suez 1953–54, memb Lloyd's 1962–91; *m* 1st 2 Sept 1967 (*divorce* 1975) Grania Mary, only dau of Fitzgerald Villiers-Stuart, of Dromana, Villierstown, Co Waterford (*see* BUTE, M), and has issue:

1 +COSMO HENRY VIVIAN; *b* 18 June 1968

Sir ANDREW *m* 2nd 18 Dec 1975 *Eveline Virginia BA, yst dau of Lt-Col Samuel Soames, RA, of Boxford House, Newbury, Berks, and has further issue:

2 +William Andrew Lewis; *b* 12 Oct 1977

3 +Thomas Francis Cornewall; *b* 2 Aug 1979

4 +Frederick Samuel Douglas; *b* 1981

Lineage: WILLIAM DUFF, of Crombie; *m* Elizabeth, dau of Sir Robert Dalrymple, of N Berwick, and had issue:

1 **Sir James Duff, 1st Bt** (UK), so *cr* 12 Nov 1813, with remainder to his n; Br Consul Cadiz; *d* 20 Nov 1815

1 Janet; *m* Sir Hew Hamilton-Dalrymple, 3rd Bt (*qv*)

2 Anne; *m* 1st 5th Earl of Dumfries (*dsps* 27 July 1768; *see* BUTE, M); *m* 2nd 19 or 26 July 1769 Hon Alexander Gordon, a Ld of Session as Lord Rockville (*d* 13 March 1792), 3rd s of 2nd Earl of Aberdeen (*see* ABERDEEN AND TEMAIR, M), and *d* 21 Aug 1811, leaving, with other issue:

(1) Sir WILLIAM DUUF later DUFF GORDON (roy licence 9 Oct 1813), **2nd Bt**; *b* 8 April 1772; *m* 10 Feb 1810, Caroline (*d* 23 April 1875), dau of Sir George Amyand Cornewall, 2nd Bt, of Moccas Court, Herefs (*see* 1959 edn), and *d* 8 March 1823, having had, with two daus:

1a **Sir Alexander Cornewall Duff Gordon, 3rd Bt**; *b* 3 Feb 1811; Assist Gentleman Usher to HM QUEEN VICTORIA; *m* 16 May 1840 Lucie (*d* 13 July 1869), only child of John Austin, and *d* 27 Oct 1872, leaving:

1b **Sir Maurice Duff Gordon, 4th Bt**, of Fyvie; *b* 15 March 1849; *m* 1st 24 June 1872 Fanny (*d* 12 Feb 1890), widow of Seymour Ball Hughes and dau of Henry Waterton, of Woodland, Yorks, and had issue:

1c Caroline Lucie, OBE (1920); *m* 1 July 1902 Aubrey William Waterfield, of La Fortezza, Aulla, Italy, yst s of Ottiwell Charles Waterfield, of Nackington House, Canterbury, and *d* 27 Nov 1964 aged 90, leaving issue. He *d* 14 July 1944

1b (cont.) **Sir Maurice** *m* 2nd 12 Sept 1894 Sophia Mary (*m* 2nd 1898 Robert Nuttall, son of Col H Nuttall, and *d* 13 Jan 1927), dau of Charles Steer, Judge High Court Calcutta, and *d* 5 May 1896

1b Janet Ann; *m* 5 Dec 1860 Henry James Ross, of Alexandria, Egypt, and *d* 23 Aug 1927, leaving issue

2b Urania; *d* unm 22 Sept 1877

2a Cosmo Lewis; *b* 23 Feb 1812; *m* 8 Nov 1859 Anna Maria (*d* 26 Jan 1898), yst dau of Sir Edmund Antrobus, 2nd Bt (*qv*), and *d* 14 Aug 1876, leaving issue:

1b **Sir Cosmo Edmund Duff Gordon, 5th Bt**, DL (Kincardineshire); *b* 22 July 1862; *m* 24 May 1900 Lucy (*d* 20 April 1935), widow of James Stewart Wallace and er dau of Douglas Sutherland, of Toronto, and *dsp* 20 April 1931

2b HENRY WILLIAM (Sir), **6th Bt**

3b John Cornewall, MBE (1920); *b* 17 Aug 1869; *m* 22 Nov 1920 Ruth Mary (*d* 1977) dau of C F Dobson, of Nottingham, and *d* 31 May 1964, leaving issue:

1c +Cosmo John; *b* 7 April 1924

2c +Alexander Mostyn; *b* 10 Aug 1927

1b Flora; *m* 5 Oct 1887 Arthur Newton Streatfeild, son of Rev Newton Streatfield, MA, and *d* 31 July 1930, leaving issue. He *d* 9 May 1956

2b Evelyn; *m* 8 Nov 1883 Roger Cunliffe and *d* Nov 1964, having had issue. He *d* 1922

The 5th Bt's bro,

Sir Henry William Duff Gordon, 6th Bt, DL and JP (Radnorshire 1914–46); High Sheriff 1918; *b* 12 Jan 1866; *m* 26 Oct 1891 Maud Emily (*d* 5 May 1951), dau of Hugh Hammersley, and had issue:

1 DOUGLAS FREDERICK (Sir), **7th Bt**

2 Cosmo Lewis; Lt Hereford Regt and MGC; *b* 3 March 1897; *ka* 3 Sept 1916

1 Dulcibella; *b* 27 Sept 1894; *d* 20 March 1895

2 *Anne Maud [Mrs Richard Quincey, Blackaldern, Narberth, Dyfed]; *b* 3 Jan 1903; *m* 25 March 1926 Richard S de Q Quincey (*d* 1991)

Sir HENRY *d* 9 Jan 1953; his only surv son,

Sir Douglas Frederick Duff Gordon, 7th Bt; *b* 12 Sept 1892; *educ* Radley and Exeter Coll Oxford; WW I as Lt Montgomeryshire Yeo, Scots Gds 1918–19, WW II in HG; *m* 31 March 1932 Gladys Rosemary (*d* 18 Oct 1933), est dau of Col Vivian Henry, CB, and *d* 15 March 1964, leaving issue:

1 Sir ANDREW COSMO LEWIS DUFF GORDON, **8th and present Bt**

DUFFERIN AND CLANEBOYE

Arms: Azure a fess or in chief a crescent argent between two mullets of the second and in base a mascle of the third. **Crest:** On a cap of maintenance gules doubled ermine, a crescent argent. **Motto:** *Per vias rectas* ('By straight ways'). Sir John Blackwood, the 2nd Bt, made a neat allusion to the family arms on one occasion. In the run-up to the Act of Union of 1800 amalgamating the Irish and British Parliaments a Dublin Castle apparatchik called on Sir John and hinted at bribing him into acquiescence with a peerage, observing that though his host's dinner service was marked with a very pretty crest it would be improved by a coronet. Sir John replied that the motto had evidently escaped the functionary's notice. **Creations:** B. (I) 31 July 1800, Bt. (I) 1 July 1763 and (UK) 1 Sept 1814.

THE 11TH BARON DUFFERIN AND CLANEBOYE OF BALLYLEIDY AND KILLYLEAGH, Co Down, and a **Baronet** (Sir John Francis Blackwood, Bt) [The Rt Hon The Lord Dufferin and Claneboye, 169 Anson St, Orange, NSW 2800, Australia]; *b* 18 Oct 1944; *s* f 1991; *educ* Barker Coll Hornsby and U of NSW (BArch); *m* 1971 *Annette Kay, dau of Harold Greenhill, of Seaforth, Sydney, NSW, and has issue:

1 +FRANCIS SENDEN; *b* 6 Jan 1979

1 *Freya Jodie; *b* 1 Sept 1975

Lineage: The Blackwoods are of Scottish origin. It seems to have been the 1st Marquess of Dufferin and Ava (*see below*) who first traced the Poitiers branch of the family.

WILLIAM BLACKWOOD; *m* — (*d* soon after her husb), niece of Robert Reid, Bp Orkney (*d* 1558), and was *k* in battle before 1549, having had issue (not necessarily in the order given):

1 ADAM

2 Henry; *b* Dunfermline, Fife, 15–; *educ* U of Paris; instructor in philosophy *c* 1551, MD, memb College of Physicians Paris, Dean of Medical Faculty there, ed commentary on works of Aristotle and other medical writings, author of MSS. on the teachings of the ancient medical writers Galen (*c* AD 130-201), Hippocrates (*c* 460-377/359 BC) and Alexander Tralles (*fl* 6th century AD), also the miscellaneous writer Pliny the Elder (AD 23-79); *m* and *d* 1614, leaving issue:

(1) Henry; prof medicine and surgery Paris; *d* Rouen 17 Oct 1634

3 George; instructor in philosophy Paris *c* 1571, ordained priest and ministered in France

The (?)est s,

ADAM BLACKWOOD; *b* Dunfermline 1539; *educ* U of Paris; returned briefly to Scotland 1558 on his great-uncle Bp Reid's death but was soon back in Paris, where he enjoyed the patronage of MARY QUEEN OF SCOTS, then married to the Dauphin of France, who subsequently succeeded as FRANCIS II OF FRANCE; Blackwood published several works in praise of the Queen, who arranged his appointment as Judge of the Parlement of Poitiers; *m* Catherine Courtinier, dau of Poitiers' *procureur du roi* and *d* 1613, leaving four sons and seven daus

The male line of the French Blackwoods became extinct at the death of Simon Xavier de Blacvod, Chevalier, Seigneur des Frozes, in Poitou; his est dau and co-heiress:

Marie Thérèse Blacvod; *m* 1776 Jean Philippe Bellin de la Bontadière, Chevalier, Seigneur des Côtes. Harold Nicolson, nephew by marriage of the 1st Marquess of Dufferin and Ava, says in *Helen's Tower* (1937) that the last descendant of the French line died without issue in the late 19th century.

A member of a yr branch of this Fife family was:

JOHN BLACKWOOD, of Bangor, Co Down; *b* Scotland 1591; acquired considerable estates in Ireland, moving to Bangor and settling his landed property on his s on the latter's marriage; *m* Janet Clerke and *d* 22 May 1663, leaving, with three daus:

JOHN BLACKWOOD, of Ballyleidy, in the Upper Clandeboye (also spelled Claneboye, the name, in either of its forms, referring to an area straddling part of both Cos Antrim and Down), Co Down; attainted by JAMES II's Irish Parl 1689; *m* Anna Wauchope and *d* 1698, leaving issue:

1 JOHN

1 Isabella; *m* Alexander Hamilton (*b* 1648), of Ballyvernon, Co Down, er s of John Hamilton, of Ballymenoch and Ballyvernon, and *d* 12 Oct 1738, leaving issue:

(1) Alexander, of Ballyvernon; *dsp*

2 Margaret

3 Anne

JOHN BLACKWOOD's only s,

JOHN BLACKWOOD, of Ballyleidy; also attainted by JAMES II's Parl; *m* Ursula (*d* 12 Sept 1741), dau and coheir of his sister Isabella's f-in-law John Hamilton's yst bro Robert Hamilton, of Killyleagh, by Robert's w Jane Phillips, and had issue:

1 ROBERT (Sir), **1st Bt**

2 James; ancestor of the BLACKWOODs later PRICEs of Saintfield

1 Ursula; *m* Michael Cromie

The er s,

Sir Robert Blackwood, 1st Bt (I), so *cr* 1 July 1763, of Ballyleidy; *b* 5 Nov 1694; *m* 1st 1721 Joyce, dau of Joseph Leeson, a Dublin brewer, and sis of 1st Earl of Milltown (*see* 1970 edn), and had issue:

1 JOHN (Sir), **2nd Bt**

2 Leeson; *d* unm 1773

1 Margaret; *m* Stewart Banks

Sir Robert *m* 2nd 1729 Grace (*d* 30 Dec 1788), only dau of Isaac Macartney, Sheriff Co Antrim 1690, by Grace (sis and heir of John Haltridge, MP (I Parl) Killyleagh 1703–27), and aunt of Sir John Macartney, 1st Bt (*qv*), and *d* 1774, having had issue:

3 William; *m* Susannah, dau of Thomas Bateman Lane

2 Grace; *d* unm 1824

3 Dorcas; *d* unm 1833 aged 93

4 Sarah

5 Elizabeth

6 Ursula Harriot; *m* 1767 Arthur Johnston, of Redemon, Co Down, MP Killyleagh

Sir ROBERT's est s,

Sir John Blackwood, 2nd Bt; *b* 1722; MP (I Parl) Killyleagh 1761–68, 1776–90 and 1798–99, also Bangor 1769–76 and 1790–97, opposed the Union of British and Irish Parls; *m* (licence 22 May 1751) Dorcas (*b* 1726; *cr* 31 July 1800 **Baroness Dufferin and Claneboye of Ballyleidy and Killyleagh**, Co Down (I), with remainder to heirs male of the body of her late husb; *d* 8 Feb 1807), est dau and coheir (by Ann, dau of Gen Nicholas Price) of James Stevenson, of Killyleagh, only s of Col Hans Stevenson by Anne, dau and eventually sole heiress of James Hamilton, of Neilsbrook, Co Antrim, nephew and eventual heir (in property only; not to the titles) of James Hamilton, who was *cr* 4 May 1622 Viscount Claneboye (I) and was f of James Hamilton, *cr* 7 June 1647 Earl of Clanbrassil (I); both the Viscountcy and Earldom expired 12 Jan 1675, but the name Claneboye was resuscitated in the Barony *cr* in 1800; **Sir John** *d* 27 Feb 1799, having had issue, with four daus:

1 Robert; *k* in falling from his horse 31 Jan 1785

2 **Sir James Stevenson Blackwood, 3rd Bt**, and **2nd Baron Dufferin and Claneboye of Ballyleidy and Killyleagh**; *b* 8 July 1755; MP (I Parl) Killyleagh 1788–1800, granted £15,000 (just under £321,000 in late-1990s terms) compensation for the seat's being disenfranchised on the Union of British and Irish Parls 1800, a measure he supported (unlike his f) and as reward for which support his request that his mother be ennobled was granted, MP (Tory) Helston 1807–12 and Aldeburgh 1812–18, Sheriff Co Down 1804 and Govr Co Down 1808–31, rep I peer 1820–36, ADC to WILLIAM IV 1830–36; through his mother became sr rep and heir general of the family of the 1st Earl of Clanbrassil; *m* 15 Nov 1801 Hon Anne Dorothea Foster (*d* 28 March 1865 in her 92nd yr), only dau of 1st Baron Oriel of Ferrard (last Speaker I House of Commons) by his w Margaretta, *née* Burgh, who was *cr* 5 June 1790 Baroness Oriel of Collon, Co Louth (I), and 22 Nov 1797 Viscountess Ferrard, Co Louth (I) (*see* MASSEREENE and FERRARD, V), and *dsp* 8 Aug 1836

3 John (Rev); *b* 9 Oct 1757; *m* 1st 1778 Sophia (*d* 1803), dau of Hill Benson, Archdeacon Down; *m* 2nd 4 June 1803 Eliza (*d* 12 Dec 1860), est dau of Josias Dupré, of Wilton Park, Bucks, and widow of Col Brice, and *dsp* 5 Jan 1833

4 HANS BLACKWOOD, **3rd Baron Dufferin and Claneboye of Ballyleidy and Killyleagh**; *b* Oct 1758; MP (I Parl) Killyleagh 1799–1800, Commr Audit Ireland 1813–32; *m* 1st 19 June 1784 Mehetabel Hester (*d* 7 Feb 1798), 2nd dau and coheir of Robert Temple, of Ten Hills, Boston, Mass., er bro of John Temple, who styled himself Sir John Temple, (8th) Bt, although his and Robert's descent from the Temple Bts so *cr* in 1611 was through their mother (*see* TEMPLE OF STOWE, E), their own name of Temple being untraceable with full certainty further back than one Capt Robert Temple senior, their f, who emigrated from N Ireland to Boston 1717 aged 23; by his 1st w the **3rd Baron** had issue:

(1) Robert Temple, *b* 13 July 1788; offr 52nd Regt Peninsula Campaign (severely wounded Badajoz 1811), Capt 69th Foot; *ka* Waterloo 18 June 1815

(2) Hans; *b* 28 Sept 1792; *d* unm of fever at Naples

(3) PRICE BLACKWOOD, **4th Baron Dufferin and Claneboye of Ballyleidy and Killyleagh**; *b* 6 May 1794; joined RN 1803, Capt 1823, Cdr 1824, stood unsuccessfully for Parl in Chatham by-election 1841; *m* 4 July 1825 (HRH THE DUKE OF YORK giving away the bride) Helen Selina (*b* 1807; authoress (anonymously in her lifetime) of many poems and songs, the best known being 'The Irish Emigrant' (1845), 'The Charming Woman' (1835) and 'The Fine Young English Gentleman', also the burlesque novel *Lispings from Low Latitudes; or Extracts from the Journal of the Hon Impulsia Gushington* (1863) and the play *Finesse; or a Busy Day in Messina* (first performed 1863); *m* 2nd 13 Oct 1862 Earl of Gifford (s and heir apparent of 8th Marquess of Tweeddale (*qv*)) and *d* 13 June 1867), est of the trio of celebrated daus of T(h)om(as) Sheridan known as The Three Graces (for the other two *see* SOMERSET, D, and GRANTLEY, B) for their beauty, wit, fashion and intelligence, Tom being est s of Richard Brinsley Sheridan, the playwright and Parliamentarian; the **4th Baron** *d* 21 July 1841 on board a steamer off Belfast from an overdose of morphine after a local pharmacist, acting in haste because of the ship's imminent sailing, made up an overstrong prescription, leaving issue:

1a FREDERICK TEMPLE BLACKWOOD later HAMILTON-BLACKWOOD (roy licence 9 Sept 1862) and later still HAMILTON-TEMPLE-BLACKWOOD (roy licence 13 Nov 1872), **5th Baron Dufferin and Claneboye of Ballyleidy and Killyleagh** and 1st MARQUESS OF DUFFERIN AND AVA, so *cr* 17 Nov 1888, as also EARL OF AVA, Co Down and Burma (Ava being the ancient capital of the kingdom of Burma; it was Lord Dufferin who as Viceroy of India annexed Upper Burma), and previously 22 Jan 1850 BARON CLANDEBOYE, of Clandeboye, Co Down, also 13 Nov 1871 EARL OF DUFFERIN, Co Down, and VISCOUNT CLANDEBOYE, of Clandeboye, Co Down (all UK), KP (1863), GCB (1883, KCB 1861), GCSI (1884), GCMG (1876), GCIE (1887), PC (I, 1897), JP (Middx and Westminster); *b* 21 June 1826; *educ* Eton and Ch Ch Oxford (MA, Pres Union 1865); Liberal to 1886, Unionist thereafter, Ld-in-Waiting 1849–52 and 1854–58, attaché to Lord John Russell (*see* RUSSELL, E) at abortive Vienna conference called to end Crimean War 1855, Special Commr: Syria 1860–61 (investigating massacres in Lebanon) and Egypt 1882, Under-Sec of State: India 1864–66 and War Feb-June 1866, Chllr Duchy of Lancaster and Paymaster-Gen 1868–72, Chm Roy Commission on Mil Educn 1871, Govr-Gen Canada 1872–78, Amb: Russia 1879–81, Ottoman Empire 1881–84, Italy 1888–91 and France 1891–96, Viceroy India 1884–88, chm London and Globe Finance Corp 1897–1900 and 1901 on, Lt and Custos Rotulorum Co Down 1864–1902, V-Adml Province of Ulster, Chllr Roy U of Ireland 1886–1902, Ld Rector: St Andrews U 1890–92 and Edinburgh U 1899–1902, DCL Oxford (1879), Hon LLD: Cambridge (1891), Dublin (1879), Harvard (1878), Laval, Lahore, St Andrews, Toronto and Natal Us, Hon Col 3rd Bn Roy Irish Rifles, FRS (1865), PRGS 1878–79, Hon Freeman City of London 1889, Ld Warden Cinque Ports 1891–95, freedom of Edinburgh 1898, author: *Letters from High Latitudes* (travel book, 1856) and *Mr Mill's Plan for the Pacification of Ireland examined* (1868); *m* 23 Oct 1862 Harriet or Hariot Georgina, VA (3rd class 1889), CI, DBE (1917) (*b* 5 Feb 1843; Pres Girls' Friendly Soc Belfast, fndr Nat Assoc for suplying Female Medical Aid to the Women of India (Countess of Dufferin Fund) 1885, held Grand Crescent of the Turkish Order of the Chefakat and the Persian Order of the Sun; author: *Our Viceregal Life in India* (1889), *My Canadian Journal* (1891), *My Russian and Turkish Journals* (1916) and *A Record of Three Years' Work of the National Association for Supplying Female Medical Aid to the Women of India*; *d* 25 Oct 1936), est dau of Archibald Rowan-Hamilton, of Killyleagh Castle, Co Down (*see* section Taft in AMERICAN PRESIDENTIAL FAMILIES, 1994, Morris Genealogical Books SA), and *d* 12 Feb 1902, having had issue:

1b Archibald James Leofric Temple, *Earl of Ava*; *b* 28 July 1863; ADC to his f when latter Viceroy, Lt 17th Lancers; *dvp* Ladysmith, S Africa, 11 Jan 1900 from wounds recd in a sortie from that town during the Boer War

2b TERENCE JOHN TEMPLE HAMILTON-TEMPLE-BLACKWOOD, **6th Baron Dufferin and Claneboye of Ballyleidy and Killyleagh** and 2nd MARQUESS OF DUFFERIN AND AVA, JP, DL (both Co Down); *b* 16 March 1866; *educ* Harrow; FO/Dip Serv 1891–1918 (served Constantinople, Paris and Stockholm, reaching rank of 2nd Sec, later Sr Clerk FO); *m* 16 Oct 1893 Florence (*m* 2nd 11 Dec 1919 4th Earl Howe (*qv*) and *d* 14 April 1925), dau of John H Davis, of 24 Washington Sq, New York, and *d* 7 Feb 1918, leaving issue:

1c Doris Gwendoline; *b* 14 Dec 1895; *m* 19 Oct 1922 Capt Cecil Gunston, MC (*d* 9 Dec 1934), Gren Gds, s of Maj Bernard Hamilton Gunston and er bro of Sir Derrick Gunston, 1st Bt (*qv*), and *d* 198–, leaving issue

2c Ursula Florence; *b* 9 Feb 1899; *m* 10 Feb 1926 Arthur Swithin Newton Horne (*d* 18 March 1954), Federated Malay States Govt Serv and Capt Border Regt, s of Arthur Horne, and *d* 198–

3c Patricia Ethel; *b* 20 March 1902; *m* 11 June 1926 Henry Russell (*d* 10 Oct 1937) and *d* 198–

3b (Ian) Basil Gawaine Temple; *b* 4 Nov 1870; barrister, Dep Judge-Advocate S Africa 1900, Sec to High Commr 1902, Assist Colonial Sec Orange River Colony 1903, Colonial Sec Barbados 1907–09 and Assist Sec to Devpt Commn 1910–14, 2nd Lt 9th Lancers (wounded Nov 1914) and Intell Corps 1914–16, Priv Sec to Ld Lt Ireland 1916, Lt Gren Gds 1916, artist and illustrator; *ka* 3 July 1917

4b FREDERICK TEMPLE HAMILTON-TEMPLE-BLACKWOOD, **7th Baron Dufferin and Claneboye of Ballyleidy and Killyleagh** and 3rd MARQUESS OF DUFFERIN AND AVA, DSO (1900), PC (I 16 Sept 1921, NI 12 Dec 1922); *b* 26 Feb 1875; Capt 9th Lancers 1897–1913, served Boer War 1899–1900 (wounded, despatches twice 1900) and with Gren Gds WW I 1914–17 (DAQMG 1915, Staff Capt Gds Div 1916, Inspr QG as Maj, twice wounded), resigned commission 1920, Mil Sec to Govr-Gen Australia 1914, Capt RNVR and CO Ulster Div RNVR 1924, ADC to HM GEORGE V (RNVR), V-Adml Ulster, Speaker NI Senate 1921–30; *m* 20 June 1908 Brenda (*m* 2nd 28 Jan 1932 Henry Charles Somers Augustus Somerset (*d* 25 Nov 1945), s of Lord Henry Somerset (*see* BEAUFORT, D), and *d* 17 July 1946), only dau of Maj Robert Woodhouse, DL, of Orford House, Bishops Stortford, Herts, and *d* 21 July 1930 following a plane crash, leaving issue:

1c BASIL SHERIDAN HAMILTON-TEMPLE-BLACKWOOD, **8th Baron Dufferin and Claneboye of Ballyleidy and Killyleagh** and 4th MARQUESS OF DUFFERIN AND AVA; *b* 6 April 1909; *educ* Eton and Balliol Coll Oxford; memb Indian Franchise Ctee 1932, PPS to: Parly U-Sec India 1932 and Pres Bd Educn Nov 1932–June 1935, Sec State War 1935 and Ld Privy Seal 1935–36, Parly U-Sec Colonies 1937–40, Dir Empire Div Min Info 1941, Ld in Waiting 1936–37, Capt RHG WW II (HQ Staff, Mandalay Sector, Burma); *m* 3 July 1930, as her 1st husb, Maureen Constance (*d* 3 May 1998), 2nd dau of Hon Arthur Ernest Guinness (*see* IVEAGH, E), and *das* 25 March 1945, leaving:

1d SHERIDAN FREDERICK TERENCE HAMILTON-TEMPLE-BLACKWOOD, **9th Baron Dufferin and Claneboye of Ballyleidy and Killyleagh** and 5th and last MARQUESS OF DUFFERIN AND AVA; *b* 9 July 1938; *educ* Eton and Oxford; 2nd Lt RHG, Tstee Wallace Collection 1973–88; *m* 1964 *Serena Belinda ('Lindy') Rosemary [The Most Hon The Marchioness of Dufferin and Ava, 4 Holland Villas Rd, London W14; Clandeboye, Co Down], dau of Capt (Thomas) Loel Evelyn Bulkeley Guinness (*see* GUINNESS, Bt) and *dsp* 1988, when the Marquessate, two Earldoms, Viscountcy and Barony of Clandeboye expired

1d Caroline Maureen (Hamilton-Temple-)BLACKWOOD; *b* 16 July 1931; writer (as Caroline Blackwood): *For All That I Found There*, *The Stepdaughter* (David Higham Prize 1976), *Great Granny Webster* (1977, runner-up Booker Prize), *The Fate of Mary Rose*, *Good Night Sweet Ladies* (short stories), *On the Perimeter* (subtitled *Caroline Blackwood at Greenham Common*, 1984), *Corrigan*, *In the Pink*, *Darling, You Shouldn't Have Gone to So Much Trouble* (cook book); *m* 1st 9 Dec 1953 (*divorce* 1958) Lucien Michael Freud, the painter, s of Ernst Freud and gs of Sigmund Freud; *m* 2nd 15 Aug 1959 (*divorce* 19–) Israel Citkowitz, composer (*d* 1974), and had:

1e 1 Natalya; *b* 17 Aug 1960; *d* of postural asphyxia 22 June 1978

2e *Eugenia or Evgenia; *b* 1964; *m* 1990 *Julian Sands, actor, s of William Sands

3e *Ivana; *b* 1966

1d (cont.) By the American poet Robert Lowell (who she *m* 1972 as his 3rd w and who *d* 12 Sept 1977) Lady Caroline, who *d* 14 Feb 1996, was mother of:

1e *Robert Sheridan LOWELL; *b* Aug 1971

2d *Perdita Maureen [The Lady Perdita Hamilton-Temple-Blackwood, Cavallo Farm, Crawfordsburn Rd, Newtownards, Co Down]; *b* 17 July 1934; breeder of Arab horses

1c Veronica Brenda (Hamilton-Temple-)BLACKWOOD; *b* 13 Dec 1910; *m* 1st 17 Dec 1931 (*divorce* 1940), as his 1st w, (Roger) Anthony Hornby (*b* 5 Feb 1904; *educ* Winchester and New Coll Oxford; stockbroker, ktd 1960; *d* 1987), 2nd s of Charles Harry St John Hornby, of Shelley House, Chelsea and Chantmarle, Dorset, and had:

1d *Marie Antoinette ('Mariette') [Mrs Thomas Hall, Marylands Farm, Chiselhampton, Oxon OX44 7XD]; *b* 9 Nov 1932; *m* 24 Feb 1954 *Col Thomas Armitage Hall, OBE, memb Gentlemen-at-Arms 1980– and High Sheriff Oxon 1981, only child of Athelstan Argyle Hall, of Cricket St Thomas, Somerset, and has issue:

1e *Edward St John; *b* 10 Jan 1960; *m* 1 Oct 1988 *Lucinda Thring and has:

1f *Rupert Dyson; *b* 15 Jan 1991

1f *Phoebe Emma; *b* 18 March 1993

2f *Eliza Charlotte; *b* 20 March 1995

2e *John Anthony; *b* 7 Nov 1964; *m* 5 Dec 1990 *Anne Tytherleigh and has:

1f *Theodore Thomas; *b* 11 Oct 1996

1f *Amelia Rose; *b* 4 March 1994

1e *Jane; *b* 11 Feb 1955; *m* 7 Oct 1975 *Michael Wentworth-Stanley and has issue (*see* ERNE, E)

2e *Anna; *b* 24 June 1956; *m* 19 Dec 1981 (*divorce* 1989) Hon David Sharples (*see* SHARPLES, B); *m* 2nd 26 Oct 1993 *Nicholas Barley and has:

1f *Matilda Meysey; *b* 27 June 1996

3e *Lucy; *b* 10 Jan 1960; *m* 19 Sept 1987 *Simon Peter Taylor and has:

1f *Anthony James; *b* 24 Jan 1991

1f *Sophie Catherine; *b* 9 Oct 1993

4e *Catherine (twin with John); *b* 7 Nov 1964; *m* 14 July 1990 *Jean-Pierre Dutheil and has:

1f *Alice; *b* 15 June 1992

1c (cont.) Lady Veronica Hornby *m* 2nd Oct 1941 (*divorce* 1947) S/Ldr Ernest Henry Maddick, RAF, s of Ernest Robert James Maddick, of Putney, resumed her maiden name by deed poll 1964 and *d* 30 July 1971

1b Helen Hermione, GBE (1918), JP (Fife); *b* 1863; LLD; *m* 31 Aug 1889 Ronald (from 1914 Sir Ronald) Craufurd Munro-Ferguson, MP (Lib) Ross and Cromarty 1884–85 and Leith Burghs 1886–1914, *cr* 6 Dec 1920 (1st and last) Viscount Novar, KT, GCMG, PC (*d* 30 March 1934), and *d* 9 April 1941

2b Hermione Catherine Helen; *b* 1869; nurse WW I; *d* unm 19 Oct 1960 aged 91

3b Victoria Alexandrina; *b* 1873 (HM QUEEN VICTORIA stood sponsor); *m* 1st 4 June 1894 5th Baron Plunket (*qv*) of Newton and had issue; *m* 2nd 1 Oct 1920 Col Francis Powell Braithwaite, CBE, DSO, MC (*d* 23 Dec 1952), late RE, 2nd s of Rev John Masterman Braithwaite, Vicar Croydon (*see* 1956 edn BRAITHWAITE, Bt), and *d* 11 Feb 1968 aged 94

(1) Henrietta; *m* April 1807 William Stewart Hamilton, of Brown's Hall, Co Donegal

4 (cont.) The **3rd Baron** *m* 2nd 8 July 1801 Elizabeth (*d* July 1843 aged 65), est dau and coheir of William Henry Finlay by Mary Anne, dau and coheir of William Stear, of Ginnetts, Co Meath, and *d* 18 Nov 1839, leaving, with five daus:

(4) William Stear (Rev); *b* 27 April 1802; Vicar Ballinderry, Co Antrim; *m* 24 March 1832 Elizabeth (*d* 25 Sept 1877), dau of Robert Hamilton, of Clonsilla, Co Dublin, and *d* 28 May 1874, leaving issue:

1a Hans Stevenson; *b* 28 Nov 1833; *m* 1st 29 July 1862 Jane (*dsp* 1 Dec 1890), yst dau of Adml-of-the-Fleet Sir John West, GCB, himself gs of V-Adml Temple West, whose mother Maria was est dau of Sir Richard Temple, 3rd Bt (*see* TEMPLE OF STOWE, E); *m* 2nd 6 Jan 1892 Mary Emily, only dau of Henry Hunt, JP, of Hunningham, Warwicks, and *d* 25 Aug 1897, having had issue:

1b Henry Stear; *b* 9 March 1894; *educ* Eton; T/Capt 9th Bn London Regt WW I; *d* 1 May 1917 of wounds recd in action

2a Robert William; *b* 7 Jan 1840; Maj 2nd Bn Oxford LI, ret as Lt-Col; *m* 19 April 1879 Mary Elizabeth (*d* 26 March 1918), dau of Simon Watson Taylor, of Erlestoke Park and Urchfont, Wilts, and *d* 13 Sept 1909, having had:

1b William Stear; *b* 1880; *d* 16 March 1889

2b Robert Montagu; *b* 20 Nov 1881; Lt Sherwood Foresters, DC Nigeria 1905–18, Capt cmdg Sqdn RAF 1918–19; *m* 29 April 1925 Daisy, dau of Thomas Kitching Kelsey, and *d* 28 March 1951

3b Hans Frederick, MC; *b* 18 April 1887; Lt-Col Reserve of Offrs, formerly Green Howards, WW I (wounded); *d* 29 April 1936

1b Elizabeth Mary; *m* 21 April 1909 Marcus Leonard Theodore Hare (*d* 4 June 1929), of Forest House, Chigwell Row, Essex, gs of Lt Marcus Theodore Hare, RN, and Hon Lucy Anne Stanley, dau of 1st Baron Stanley of Alderley (*see* STANLEY OF ALDERLEY, SHEFFIELD and, B), and *d* 21 March 1956, leaving issue

3a Price Frederick, JP (Berks and Northants); *b* 11 Oct 1841; Maj RA; *m* 14 July 1880 Henrietta (*d* 16 Dec 1936), only child of Albemarle Bertie Cator, himself gs of Joseph Cator and Diana, sis of Adml Sir Albemarle Bertie, 1st and last Bt, KCB, and *d* 1 Dec 1930, having had issue:

1b Albemarle Price, DSO (1918); *b* 4 Nov 1881; Maj and Brevet Lt-Col Border Regt S Africa 1901–02 and WW I (despatches twice, Order of the Star of Romania, T/Brig-Gen and Brig-Gen General Staff 1919); *m* 28 April 1920 Kyra (*d* 16 Jan 1937), dau of Albert Llewelyn Hughes and widow of Serge de Boursac, and was drowned on service at Karachi 16 Oct 1921, leaving issue:

1c *Kyra Henrietta; *b* 28 Feb 1921; Sgt WAAF WW II; *m* 1st 4 May 1945 Samuel Junior Marshall, USAAF (*d* April 1948); *m* 2nd 28 April 1951 *Iain Gregor Finton Robertson, s of Don A Robertson, of Chiswick Village, London, and has issue:

1d *James Paul [James Robertson Esq, St Helier, 2 Harrowden Rd, Inverness]; *b* 1952; *m* 1982 *Judith Ellen Bull and has issue:

1e *Ian David; 1989

1e *Kyra Frances; *b* 1992

1b Ursula Henrietta, MBE (1928); *b* 10 Sept 1885; served War Office 1918–31, memb Roy Institution; *d* 197–

(5) Henry Stevenson; *b* 4 Aug 1819; Capt 17th Lancers; *m* 25 April 1857 Lady Amelia Capell (*d* 29 May 1892), sis of 6th Earl of Essex (*qv*), and *dsp* 25 Oct 1865

5 Price; *b* 24 Jan 1760; *m* 1st 29 Aug 1787 Louisa (*d* 20 Sept 1802), 2nd dau and coheir of William Southwell; *m* 2nd 21 Jan 1804 Anne (*d* 8 Oct 1836), 2nd dau of Richard Cox, of Castletown Cox, Co Kilkenny, only s of Michael Cox, Archbp Cashel, who commissioned from the Sardinian architect Davis Ducart the building 1767 of the celebrated mansion of Castletown Cox, and *dsp* 1816

6 Leeson; *d* 1804

7 **Sir Henry Blackwood, 1st Bt** (UK), so *cr* 1 Sept 1814, KCB (1819), GCH; *b* 28 Dec 1770; joined RN April 1781, Signal Midshipman 1790, Lt 3 Nov 1790, 1st Lt 1 June 1794, Capt 2 June 1795, cmded inshore sqdn under Nelson in the blockade of Cadiz 1805 and was witness with Hardy of the oral codicil to Nelson's will 21 Oct 1805 in which he commended the care of Emma Hamilton and Horatia, Nelson's dau by her, to his country (a request which was disregarded), Capt of the Fleet May 1814, R-Adml 4 June 1814, C-in-C E Indies 1819–22, V-Adml the Blue 1825, C-in-C The Nore 1827–30; *m* 1st 12 Jan 1795 Jane Mary (*dsp* 19 Jan 1798), 2nd dau of Launcelot Crosbie, of Tubrid, Co Kilkenny; *m* 2nd 3 June 1799 Eliza (*d* 30 Oct 1802), 4th dau of Capt Martin Waghorn, RN, and had issue:

(1) HENRY MARTIN (Sir), **2nd Bt**

7 (cont.) **Sir Henry** *m* 3rd 9 May 1803 Harriet (*d* 5 May 1851), dau of Francis Gore, Govr Grenada, and *d* 17 Dec 1832, having by her had, with other issue (including Harriette Anne, *m* Robert George Cecil Fare and had issue; *see* WESTMORLAND, E):

(2) Arthur Johnstone; *b* 25 April 1808; Gentleman Usher to HM QUEEN VICTORIA; *m* 2 March 1830 Cecilia Georgiana, widow of John Wright, of Lenton Hall, Notts, and *d* 2 Jan 1874, having had issue (with a dau, Harriet Cecilia, who *d* 1855):

1a Stevenson Arthur (Sir), KCB (1887, CB 1880); *b* 22 May 1832; Sec GPO; *m* 16 Dec 1858 (Harriet) Sydney (*d* 30 May 1907), dau of Conway Richard Dobbs, of Castle Dobbs, Co Antrim, and widow of 6th Duke of Manchester (*qv*), and *d* 2 Oct 1893, leaving issue:

1b Stevenson Arthur; *b* 30 Aug 1867; *m* 11 Dec 1911 Kate Lavinia, dau of Leonard Abbott, of Parkstone, Dorset, and *d* 16 June 1914, leaving issue:

1c Patrick Stevenson; *b* 5 Dec 1912; *m* 19 Nov 1945 *Ellen, dau of Wilfred Rupert Cave, of London

2b Algernon Henry, CBE (1949); *b* 14 March 1869; *educ* Moravian Sch Germany, Wellington, Edinburgh U and abroad; sometime hotelier, gold prospector, journalist and farmer, one of the first television writers (six stories broadcast 1950, Television Society Silver Medal for outstanding artistic achievement 1948), author: *The Empty House* (1906), *The Listener* (1907), *John Silence* (1908, reissued 1942), *The Education of Uncle Paul* (1909), *Jimbo* (1909), *The Human Chord* (1910), *The Lost Valley* (1910), *The Centaur* (1911), *Pan's Garden* (1912), *A Prisoner in Fairyland: Ten Minute Stories* (1913, dramatised as *The Starlight Express* 1916), *Incredible Adventures* (1914), *The Extra Day* (1915), *Julius Le Vallon* (1916), *The Wave* (1916), *Day and Night Stories* (1917), *The Promise of Air* (1918), *The Garden of Survival, Karma: A Reincarnation Play* (1918), *The Crossing* (with Bertram Forsyth, 1920), *Through the Crack* (children's play, with Violet Pearn, 1921, revised version 1922), *The Wolves of God* (short stories, with W Wilson, 1921), *The Bright Messenger* (1921), *Episodes Before Thirty* (1923, reissued 1950), *Tongues of Fire* (1924), *Full Circle* (1929), *Dudley and Gilderoy* (1929), *The Fruit-Stoners* (1934), *Shocks* (1935), *The Tales of Algernon Blackwood* (1938), *The Doll and One Other* (USA edn, 1946), *Tales of the Uncanny and Supernatural* (1949); *d* 10 Dec 1951

1b Cecilia Grace; *m* 18 March 1920 Arthur Ernest Hobart-Hampden (*d* 18 June 1952), s of Capt Hon Charles Hobart-Hampden (*see* BUCKINGHAMSHIRE, E), and *d* 18 March 1929

2b Beatrice Lucy; *d* unm 23 April 1911

3b Ada Sydney; *b* 1871; *d* 197–

Sir HENRY's s,

Sir Henry Martin Blackwood, 2nd Bt; *b* 11 June 1801; Capt RN; *m* 19 Aug 1826 Harriet Louisa (*d* 6 Feb 1873), yst dau of John Matthew Bulkeley, and *d* 7 Jan 1851, having had issue, with four daus:

1 **Sir Henry Blackwood, 3rd Bt**; *b* 7 May 1828; Lt RN; *d* unm 26 May 1854

2 FRANCIS (Sir), **4th Bt**

3 Percy; *b* 18 May 1840; Colonial Sec for Tobago; *d* 1 June 1866

The 3rd Bt's bro,

Sir Francis Blackwood, 4th Bt; *b* 11 Nov 1838; Capt RN; *m* 1st 17 Dec 1861 Laura Olivia (*d* 6 Nov 1865), 2nd dau of Robert Samuel Palmer, of Merrion Sq, Dublin, and had issue:

1 Henry Robert Temple; *b* 6 Oct 1862; *m* 13 July 1892 Rebecca Paffard (*m* 2nd 4 Oct 1930 Walter G C Stevenson, of Vancouver, BC, and *d* 3 March 1953), est dau of John Scullard, of Cosham, Hants, and *d* 3 June 1910, leaving issue:

(1) **Sir Henry Palmer Temple Blackwood, 5th Bt**; *b* 12 May 1896; served Canadian Expdny Force WW I; *m* 12 Aug 1926 Ethel Edith Mary, dau of Humphrey Grenfell Ratcliffe, of Deal, Kent, and *dsp* 1 Sept 1948

(2) **Sir Francis Elliot Temple Blackwood, 6th Bt**; *b* 11 March 1901; Assist V-Pres Crocker-Citizens' Nat Bank, Sacramento, Calif; *m* 1921 *Lilian Margaret, dau of H Fulton MacGougan, of Vancouver, and *dsp* 1979

(1) Laura Temple; *b* 24 April 1893; *m* 1912 Walter David Geoghegan and had issue

1 Laura Gwendoline; *m* 30 June 1887 Rev Louis Henry Bradford (*d* 1920), Rector Hunton, Maidstone, and *d* 18 April 1967, leaving issue

Sir Francis *m* 2nd 10 Aug 1871 Dorothea Frances (*d* 14 April 1919), est dau of Rev Edward Henry Quicke, Rector Newton St Cyres, Devon, and *d* 20 June 1924, having by her had issue:

2 Francis Edward; *b* 21 Aug 1874; Capt E Surrey Regt; *ka* N Nigeria 14 Feb 1906

3 Maurice Baldwin Raymond, DSO (1917); *b* 22 Sept 1882; Capt RN; *m* 16 Jan 1915 Dorothea (*d* 27 Nov 1967), dau of Hon G Bertrand Edwards, Memb House of Reps, of Huon Park, Sydney, Australia, and *das* 26 Aug 1941, leaving issue:

(1) FRANCIS GEORGE (Sir), **7th Bt** and **10th Baron**

(2) +George, OBE (1970), DSC [Cdr George Blackwood OBE DSC, c/o National Westminster Bank, Chichester, W Sussex]; *b* 1920; served RN; *m* 1950 *Diana, dau of Lt-Col A L A Flint, of Maidenhead, Berks, and has issue:

1a +Robert George Temple; *b* 3 Oct 1953

2a +Michael Francis; *b* 15 Aug 1959

1a *Clare Mary; *b* 24 Nov 1956

(3) +Henry [Henry Blackwood Esq, 37 The Crescent, Vaucluse, NSW 2030, Australia]; *b* 1922; *educ* Knox GS Wahroonga; Lt RANR(S), Capt Merchant Marine; *m* 1948 *Kathryn, dau of Donald Thomas Rankin, of Westwood, West Wyalong, NSW, and has:

1a +Maurice Henry [Maurice Blackwood Esq, 310 Moreton Park Rd, Douglas Pk 2569, NSW, Australia]; *b* 1954; *educ* Sydney C of E GS, NSW U and Sydney Tech Coll (Assoc Dip Metallurgy); *m* 1982 *Anne Edith, dau of M H L Macarthur, of Katoomba, NSW, and has issue:

1b +James Maurice Henry; *b* 1988

1b *Jennifer Anne Halley; *b* 1986

(1) *Mary [Mrs Edward Ifould, 317 Peninsula Gdns, Bayview, NSW, Australia]; *b* 11 Nov 1917; *m* 1st 1940 P/O John Frankcomb, RAAF (*kas* 1942), and has issue:

1a *Dorothy Pamela; *b* 1942

(1) (cont.) Mrs John Frankcomb *m* 2nd 1945 S/Ldr Edward Lister Ifould, DSO, DFC and bar, RAAF (*d* 1981), and has further issue:

1a *William Edward; *b* 1947; *educ* Sydney C of E GS

2a *Marian; *b* 1946

3a *Frances Gay Lister; *b* 1953

4 Neville Foster; *b* 26 Oct 1884; *educ* Haileybury; *m* 26 Nov 1919 Kathleen Nelly (*d* 18 June 1959), dau of Henry Sidney Mosenthal, and *d* 25 April 1964, having had issue:

(1) Guy Neville; *b* 16 April 1921; 2nd Lt Roy Berks Regt WW II; *das* at sea Jan 1942

(2) +Robin Henry [Robin Blackwood Esq, 5 Gurney Close, Caversham, Reading, Berks]; *b* 18 April 1926

2 Ida Dorothy; *m* 12 July 1898 Capt Cordell William Firebrace, JP, FSA (*d* 14 April 1934), late 7th Hus and late of Elmstone Court, Kent, only s of Robert Tarver Firebrace, JP, whose ggggggf was unc of Sir Basil Firebrace, 1st Bt (*cr* 1698; extinct 1759), and *d* 26 May 1968 aged 96, leaving issue:

(1) Robert Cordell (Rev); *b* 25 April 1899; *educ* Harrow and Trin Hall Cambridge; Vicar Raglan 1964; *m* 21 Sept 1922 Hazel, dau of Cornelius Gabriel Stafford Day, of Auckland, NZ, and had issue:

1a *Dorothy Mary Ruth; *b* 10 Aug 1924; *educ* Sydney U Medical Sch (BSc 1948); *m* 8 April 1950 *John Constant Hurst, s of Leslie Constant Hurst, of St Ives, NSW, and has issue:

1b *Jonathan Robert Constant; *b* 20 June 1957

2b *Edward Justin; *b* 13 Feb 1964

1b *Amanda Rosalind; *b* 3 Feb 1952

2b *Susan Mary; *b* 1 Sept 1953

3b *Deborah Frances; *b* 13 Dec 1954

4b *Joanna Elizabeth; *b* 15 March 1961

2a *Rosemary Anne; *b* 31 May 1926; *m* 21 Feb 1955 *Reginald Geoffrey Screen, s of Edward Screen, of London

3a *Elizabeth Gabriel; *b* 25 Sept 1928; *m* 1st 1952 (*divorce* 1959) Eric Charles Jessup; *m* 2nd 1960 *Bernard Francke

The 6th Bt's 1st cousin of the half-blood,

Sir Francis George Blackwood, 7th Bt; *b* 20 May 1916; *s* cousin as **10th Baron Dufferin and Claneboye of Ballyleidy and Killyleagh** and as **11th Baronet** of Ballyleidy 1988; *m* 1941 *Margaret, dau of Hector Kirkpatrick, of Lindfield, NSW, Australia, and *d* 1991, leaving issue:

1 JOHN FRANCIS BLACKWOOD, **11th and present Baron Dufferin and Claneboye of Ballyleidy and Killyleagh**

2 +Peter Maurice [The Hon Peter Blackwood, 2 Hawkins Court, Alice Springs, NT 0870, Australia]; *b* 1950; *educ* Knox GS Wahroonga and Macquarie U (BA); anthropologist; *m* 1979 *Kay Lynette, dau of William Maurice Winkle, of Brisbane, and has issue:

(1) +Alexander Francis Winkle; *b* 1986

(1) *Alice Kathleen Winkle; *b* 1982

1 *Angela Margaret [The Hon Mrs Barker, 141 Campbell Dve, Wahroonga, NSW 2076, Australia]; *b* 1942; *educ* Sydney (BSc) and Charles Sturt Us (DipEd); *m* 19 Jan 1965 *Clifton Elliott Barker, BSc, and has issue:

(1) *Stephen Michael; *b* 1969; *m* 1993 *Sally Ann, dau of Douglas Alan Farrington, and has:

1a *Emily Rose; *b* 16 April 1996

(1) *Zoe Frances; *b* 1971

(2) *Lucinda Alice; *b* 1975

(3) *Karina Emily; *b* 1980

DUGDALE

Arms: Quarterly, 1st and 4th, argent, a cross-moline gules charged in the centre with a Garter King of Arms' coronet or, and in the first quarter a torteau (for DUGDALE); 2nd and 3rd, barry of ten argent and azure, over all a lion rampant gules (for STRATFORD). **Crest:** A griffin's head, wings addorsed or, gorged with a coronet, as in the arms. **Badge:** An oak leaf slipped or. **Motto:** *Pestis patriæ pigrites* ('Sloth is the plague of the country'). **Creation:** Bt. (UK) 17 July 1936.

SIR WILLIAM STRATFORD DUGDALE, 2ND BT, CBE (1985), MC (1943), JP (Warwicks 1951), DL (Warwicks 1955), of Merevale and Blyth, Co Warwick [Sir William Dugdale Bt CBE MC JP DL, 24 Bryanston Mews West, London W1H 7FR; Merevale Hall, Atherstone, Warwicks CV9 2HG; Blyth Hall, Coleshill, W Midlands B46 2AD]; *b* 29 March 1922; *s* f 1965; *educ* Eton and Balliol Coll Oxford;

Capt Gren Gds WW II (despatches), slr 1949, Govr of Henry VIII Sch Coventry, chm Trent River Authority 1965, memb Cncl King George's Jubilee Tst 1965, chm Nat Water Cncl 1982–83, High Steward Stratford-upon-Avon 1976–, chm Gen Utilities plc 1988–, dir N Surrey Water 1989–; *m* 1st 13 Dec 1952 Lady Belinda Pleydell-Bouverie (*d* 29 July 1961), 2nd dau of 7th Earl of Radnor (*qv*), and has issue:

1 +(WILLIAM) MATTHEW STRATFORD [Matthew Dugdale Esq, Merevale Hall, Atherstone, Warwicks CV9 2LA]; *b* 22 Feb 1959; *m* 1990 *Paige Sullivan, dau of Thomas Haines Dudley Perkins, and has issue:

(1) +William Stratford; *b* 15 Aug 1992

(2) +Nathaniel Francis Stratford; *b* 29 Aug 1996

(1) *Clementine Alexandra Louise; *b* 1991

(2) *Fernanda Elizabeth Grace; *b* 1994

1 *Laura [The Hon Mrs Arthur Hazlerigg, Noseley Hall, Billesdon, Leics LE7 9EH]; *b* 20 Sept 1953; *m* 1986 *Hon Arthur Grey Hazlerigg, only son of 2nd Baron Hazlerigg (*qv*), and has issue

2 *Matilda [Mrs Marcus May, The Malthouse Farm, Bentley, Warwicks]; *b* 15 May 1955; *m* 1989 *Marcus May, s of Col R K May

3 *Charlotte [The Hon Mrs Gerard Noel, 29 Ingersol Rd, London W12]; (twin); *b* 15 May 1955; *m* 1985 *Hon Gerard Edward Joseph Noel, 2nd son of 5th Earl of Gainsborough (*qv*)

Sir WILLIAM *m* 2nd 17 Oct 1967 *Cecilia Mary, est dau of Sir William Michael Mount, 2nd Bt, ED, DL (*qv*), and by her has further issue:

2 +Thomas Joshua Stratford; *b* 20 Sept 1974

4 *Adelaide Margaret Victoria Jane; *b* 7 July 1970

Lineage: Sir WILLIAM DUGDALE; Garter King of Arms 1677–86, antiquary and genealogist, author: *The Monasticon Anglicanum, The Baronetage of England*, and many other well-known works; *b* 12 Sept 1605 (s of John Dugdale, of Shustoke, Warwicks (*d* 1624), by Elizabeth, dau of Arthur Swynfen, of Dunchurch, and gs of James Dugdale); bought Blyth Hall 1626; *m* Margery (*d* 1681), 2nd dau of John Huntbach, of Seawall, Staffs, and *d* 10 Feb 1685/6, having had, with other surv issue:

Sir JOHN DUGDALE, of Blyth Hall; Norroy King of Arms 1686–1700, Windsor Herald 1675–86; *b* 1 June 1628; *m* 1st 3 Dec 1662 Mary (*d* 9 Jan 1671), 2nd dau and coheir of Alexander Baker, of Windsor, and had issue:

1 WILLIAM, of whom later

1 Mary; *m* Anthony Townshend, of Hem, Denbighs

Sir JOHN *m* 2nd 1671 Elizabeth, only dau and heir of Thomas Pidgeon, Alderman Coventry, and had further issue:

2 Elizabeth, *m* 1st Thomas Skeffington, of Skeffington; *m* 2nd William Hyde, of Langtoft, Lincs

Sir JOHN *d* 31 Aug 1700; his son,

WILLIAM DUGDALE, of Blyth Hall; *b* 15 April 1664; *m* 1686 Judith (*d* 14 April 1743), yst dau of John Gough, of Bushbury, Staffs, and *d* 19 Feb 1714, having had, with other issue:

1 John, of Blyth Hall; *b* 2 May 1690; Blanch Lyon Herald Extrdy 1707–13, Mowbray Herald Extrdy 1713–49; *m* Mary (*d* 11 July 1746), dau of Joseph Wafforne, of Stoneleigh, Warwicks, and *dsp* 4 Aug 1749, leaving his estates to his n RICHARD

2 William; *b* 1702; *d* 1733

1 JANE Dugdale; *m* 19 April 1722 Richard GEAST, of Handsworth, Staffs, and had:

(1) RICHARD, for whom *see* further below

(2) Henry; *b* 1728; *m* Anne, 2nd dau of John Walford, and *d* 15 Jan 1793, having had, with four daus (three of whom *d* unm):

1a Richard, *dsp* 1797

2a Henry GEAST later DUGDALE (roy licence 1822), of Bordesley Park, Worcs; MA, barrister; *d* 15 May 1840

1a Ann; *m* Francis Dugdale Astley and *dsp* 1813

(1) Judith; *m* 1710 Francis Bickley, of Kingsbury, and had issue:

1a Mary; *m* William Francis Corbet Astley and was grandmother of Sir John Dugdale Astley, Bt (*see* 1970 edn)

JOHN DUGDALE's nephew,

RICHARD GEAST later DUGDALE (roy licence 1799 on inheriting unc's property); *b* 1724; barrister; *m* 1767 Penelope Bate (*d* 1819), est dau and coheir of Francis Stratford, of Merevale Hall, Warwicks, and *d* 1806, leaving issue:

1 DUGDALE STRATFORD, of whom presently

1 Penelope; *m* 25 Nov 1791 Charles James Packe, of Prestwold, and *d* 1841

2 Louise Anne; *m* William Dilke, of Maxstoke Castle, and *d* 1841, leaving issue

3 Emma; *d* unm 1826

The only son,

DUGDALE STRATFORD DUGDALE, of Merevale Hall; MP N Warwicks 1802–1830; *b* 1773; *m* 1st 27 June 1799 Hon Charlotte (*d* 30 Dec 1832), aunt to 1st Earl Howe (*qv*), and had issue; *m* 2nd 16 Sept 1834 Mary Elizabeth (*d* 26 Oct 1846), widow of Sir Mark Masterton Sykes, 3rd Bt, MP, of Sledmere (*qv*), and only dau of William Tatton Egerton, of Tatton Park and Wythenshawe, Cheshire, and *d* 5 Nov 1836; his only s by his 1st w:

WILLIAM STRATFORD DUGDALE, of Merevale Hall, DL, JP; *b* 1 April 1800; *educ* Westminster and Ch Ch Oxford; MP Bramber 1826, Shaftesbury 1830 and N Warwicks 1832–47; *m* 1 March 1827 Harriet Ella (*d* 17 April 1903), sister of 1st Viscount Portman (*qv*), and had issue:

1 WILLIAM STRATFORD, of whom presently

2 Richard Geast; *b* 23 June 1830; *d* 22 Sept 1836

3 John Stratford, KC, DL, JP Warwicks; Chm CC and QS, Recorder Birmingham, MP Nuneaton 1886–92; *b* 30 July 1835; *m* 21 Oct 1890 Alice (*d* 19 Aug 1949), dau of Gen Henry Alexander Carleton, CB, RA, of Clare, Co Tipperary, and *d* 27 Oct 1920, leaving issue:

(1) Joan Stratford; *b* 9 May 1892; *m* 3 April 1916 Sir Algernon Thomas Peyton, 7th and last Bt (*d* 14 March 1962; *see* 1959 edn), and had issue

4 Henry Charles Geast, of Bordesley, Worcs, Col Rifle Bde; *b* 30 April 1837; *m* 5 Sept 1878 Edith Cecil (*d* 22 March 1948), dau of Hugh Montgomery, of Grey Abbey, Co Down, and *d* 8 Sept 1911, leaving issue:

(1) Charles John Geast; *b* 24 Sept 1887; *m* 29 Oct 1915 Lucy Violet (*d* 22 April 1935), dau of Rt Hon Henry Cecil Raikes, MP, and *dsp* 16 June 1944

5 Arthur George, of Fifehead Nevill, Sturminster Newton, Dorset, DL, JP, Maj RA; *b* 12 Aug 1843; *m* 25 July 1878 Mary Eliza Cornwallis (*d* 2 Aug 1931), dau of James Whatman, MP, and *d* 17 Jan 1932

6 Edward Stratford, of Gordon Lodge, Aboyne, Cdr RN; *b* 10 May 1845; *educ* Eton and HMS *Britannia*; *m* April 1878 Alice Florence (*d* 13 Jan 1929), dau of Alfred Richards, barrister, and *d* 27 Jan 1931, leaving issue:

(1) Alfred Stratford; *b* 8 Nov 1882; *educ* Westminster and Merton Coll Oxford; *m* 1st 1916 Eileen (*d* 22 Nov 1917), est dau of H Gonne Browning, and *d* 22 April 1974, leaving:

1a George Stratford, Fell Library Assoc 1956, Assist London Museum 1947–52, Assist Librarian RGS 1957–66, Librarian 1966–, author: *Whitehall Through The Centuries* (1950); *b* 1 Nov 1917; *educ* Eton and King46s Coll Cambridge (BA 1939, MA 1946); *d* unm 28 June 1982

(1) (cont.) Alfred Dugdale *m* 2nd 25 Aug 1925 Phoebe Marianne (*d* 29 March 1971 aged 80), widow of Capt Thomas Humphrey Sneyd, of Basford Hall, nr Leek, Staffs, and 2nd dau of John Sharp Callender Brodie, of Angus

(1) Una Harriet Ella Stratford; *m* 13 Jan 1912 Victor D Duval (*d* 4 Oct 1945) and had issue

(2) Joan Frances Tara Stratford; *m* 5 July 1921 Fletcher Cecil Macdonald Cruickshank, ICS, er s of Alexander Walmesley Cruickshank, CSI, ICS, of Brooklands, Crowborough, Sussex, and had issue

(3) Marjory Georgina Philomela Stratford; *m* 7 Sept 1926 Alured Phayre Cunningham (*d* 27 July 1962), OBE, JP, s of Maj-Gen Charles Alexander Cunningham, IA

(4) Rosalind Colina Emma Stratford; *m* 27 June 1906 John Broadley Harrison-Broadley (*d* 29 Oct 1944), only s of Henry Broadley Harrison-Braodley, MP Welton, Yorks, and *d* 10 Aug 1977 aged 90, having had issue

7 Sidney; *b* 22 Oct 1846; *d* unm 29 Sept 1899

1 Harriet Ellen; *d* 5 Jan 1834

2 Adelaide; *m* 14 Aug 1862 1st Viscount Peel (*see* PEEL, E), and *d* 5 Dec 1890, leaving issue

3 Mary Louisa; *d* unm 17 Dec 1923

WILLIAM STRATFORD DUGDALE *d* 15 Sept 1871; his est son,

WILLIAM STRATFORD DUGDALE, of Merevale Hall, DL, JP, barrister, High Sheriff 1876; *b* 2 May 1828; *educ* Eton and Balliol Coll Oxford (MA); *m* 14 Dec 1871 Alice Frances (*d* 2 Jan 1902), yst dau of Sir Charles Edward Trevelyan, 1st Bt, of Wallington (*qv*), and left:

1 WILLIAM FRANCIS STRATFORD, **1st Bt**

2 Edgar Trevelyan Stratford, JP Leics, Cpt Leics Yeo, memb Aeronautical Commn of Control in Germany 1920, memb Lloyd's 1905–64, Hon Sec and later Treasurer of the Handel Soc 1936–38; *b* 22 July 1876; *educ* Eton and Balliol Coll Oxford; *m* 1st 18 Nov 1902 Blanche Elizabeth Campbell Balfour (*d* 16 May 1948), author, est dau of Col Eustace James Anthony Balfour (*see* BALFOUR, E), and had issue:

(1) Michael Arthur Stratford, FRIBA, Capt RE, served WW II ; *b* 24 Sept 1905; *educ* Eton and Balliol Coll Oxford; *d* unm 31 Oct 1970

(1) Louise Frances Balfour Stratford; *m* 17 July 1930 Sir James Fergusson, 8th Bt (*qv*), and *d* 1988, leaving issue

2 (cont.) Capt Edgar Dugdale *m* 2nd 21 Dec 1948 *Gladys Margaret, widow of Randall Davies, FSA, and yr dau of Lt-Gen Sir Herbert Scott Gould Miles, GCB, GCMG, GBE, CVO, of Satis House, Yoxford, Suffolk, and *d* 14 Oct 1964

WILLIAM STRATFORD DUGDALE *d* 9 May 1882; his er son,

Sir William Francis Stratford Dugdale, 1st Bt (UK), so *cr* 17 July 1936; *b* 20 Oct 1872; *educ* Eton and Balliol Coll Oxford; V-Lt Warwicks 1939–64, DL, JP, CA, High Sheriff 1911, FSA, chm Warwickshire CC 1933–47, chm and md Baddesley Collieries Ltd, Govr Rugby, dir Midland Bank Ltd; *m* 5 Aug 1920 Margaret, JP Warwicks (*d* 4 Oct 1965), 2nd dau of Brig-Gen Sir Robert Gordon Gilmour, 1st Bt (*qv*), and *d* 18 April 1965, leaving issue:

1 Sir WILLIAM STRATFORD DUGDALE, **2nd and present Bt**

2 John Robert Stratford (Sir), KCVO 1994; Ld Lt Salop 1975–94; *b* 10 May 1923; *educ* Eton and Ch Ch Oxford; *m* 25 July 1956 *Kathryn Edith Helen, JP (1936) Salop, DCVO [Lady Dugdale DCVO JP, Tickwood Hall, Much Wenlock, Salop TF13 6NZ], Woman of the Bedchamber to HM THE QUEEN 1955–60, Extra Woman of the Bedchamber 1960–, only dau of Oliver Frederick George Stanley, PC, MC, MP, of Witherslack Hall, Kendal (*see* DERBY, E), and *d* 13 Dec 1994, leaving issue:

(1) +Edward Stratford; *b* 17 Aug 1959; *m* 1995 *Anna Maria Ulrika Wiklund

(2) +Henry Stratford [Henry Dugdale Esq, 122 St Stephen's Ave, London W12]; *b* 12 Nov 1963; *m* 1991 *Adi Litia Cakobau Mara, dau of the President of Fiji and Paramount Chief of Lau, and Adi Lady Lala Mara, Paramount Chief of Rewa, and has issue:

1a +A son; *b* 1993

(1) *Elizabeth Alice; *b* 21 June 1957

(2) *Mary Kathryn; *b* 1 Aug 1961

1 *Susan [Mrs Neil Hughes-Onslow, 112 Swan Court, Chelsea Manor St, London SW3 5RU]; *m* 10 March 1950 (Timothy) Neil Hughes-Onslow (*d* 4 Aug 1995) and has issue (*see* ONSLOW, E)

2 *Judith Margaret [Mrs John Shirley, Ettington Park, Stratford-on-Avon, Warwicks]; *m* 17 Jan 1952 *Maj John Evelyn Shirley, 60th Rifles (ret), only son of Lt-Col Evelyn Charles Shirley, of Lough Fea, Co Monaghan, and Ettington Park, Stratford-on-Avon (*see* FERRERS, E), and has issue

Seat: Merevale Hall, Atherstone, Warwicks; Blyth Hall, Shustoke, Warwicks. Merevale is a very early-Victorian mansion, dating from the first years of Her Majesty's reign, and, as was frequently the case at that time, in a bogus Jacobean style. A post-Restoration 17th-century house stood on the site till demolished to make way for it.

Blyth Hall is a more modest and comelier affair. It is substantially the house the antiquary Sir William Dugdale knew (he lived and died there), though it was remodelled early the next century and again in Victorian times. A fine 17th-century staircase survives inside.

DULVERTON

Arms: Gules three suns in splendour fesswise between two gryphons passant, wings expanded and inverted, all or. **Crest:** Issuant from an annulet or a demi-gryphon gules charged with an estoile as in the arms, and holding in the dexter claw a battle-axe gold. **Supporters:** Dexter, a trumpeter of the Royal North Devon Yeomanry; sinister, a huntsman of the Dulverton Hunt, both proper. **Motto:** *Quo lux ducit* ('Wherever the light leads'). **Creations:** Bt. (UK) 15 Feb 1897, B. (UK) 8 July 1929.

THE 3RD BARON DULVERTON, of Batsford, Co Gloucester, and a **Baronet** (Sir (Gilbert) Michael Hamilton Wills, Bt) [The Rt Hon The Lord Dulverton, Batsford Park, Moreton-in-Marsh, Glos]; *b* 2 May 1944; s f 1992; *educ* Gordonstoun and RAC Cirencester; *m* 1980 *Rosalind Johnny Maria, only dau of J van der Velde, of Rozenburg, Holland, and has:

1 +ROBERT ANTHONY HAMILTON; *b* 20 Oct 1983

1 *Charlotte Alexandra Hamilton; *b* 1981

Lineage: HENRY OVERTON WILLS (*see* WILLS, Bt, of Blagdon), JP, of Bristol; *d* 23 Nov 1871, leaving, with other issue:

Sir Frederick Wills, 1st Bt (UK), so *cr* 15 Feb 1897, of Northmoor, Somerset, JP; MP (Lib U) N Bristol 1900–06; *b* 21 Nov 1838; *m* 3 July 1867 Annie (*d* 1910), est dau of Rev James Hamilton, DD, of Lanarks, and *d* 18 Feb 1909, having had:

1 Arthur James Hamilton; *b* 1 May 1868; *m* 15 July 1895 Evelyn McDonald (*d* 1 Feb 1940, having *m* 2nd Nov 1906 Bertram Douglas MacCulloch, Capt 16th Lancers), yst dau of Philip Albert Myburgh, QC, and had issue:

(1) Evelyn Irene Hamilton; *b* 30 May 1896; *m* 1st 26 July 1919 Wilfred Francis Herbert Watson (*d* 7 Dec 1929), s of Col Solomon Watson and gs of 17th Baron Teynham (*qv*), and had issue (*see* NALL, Bt); *m* 2nd 6 Nov 1933 Lt-Cdr William Bagwell, RN, of Marlfield, Clonmel, Co Tipperary, and *d* 6 Sept 1965, leaving further issue

2 GILBERT ALAN HAMILTON, **1st Baron**

3 Frederick Noel Hamilton, Capt Roy N Devon Yeo; *b* 25 Feb 1887; *educ* Magdalen Coll Oxford (BA); *m* 25 April 1912 Margery Hamilton (*m* 2nd 18 Aug 1942 W/Cdr Huntly Macdonald Sinclair, RCAF, of Dunrobin, Ontario, Canada, 2nd son of Rev Robert Colin Havelock Sinclair, of Aultsville, Ontario, Canada), est dau of Sir Hugh Fraser, High Court Judge, of Stromeferry House, Ross-shire, and *d* 11 Oct 1927, leaving issue:

(1) Michael Desmond Hamilton, MC, T/Maj Coldstream Gds WW II; *b* 4 Oct 1915; *m* 25 Aug 1939 *Mary Margaret (*m* 2nd 5 July 1947 Col Sir Martin St John Valentine Gibbs (*d* 1992), KCVO, CB, DSO, TD (*see* ALDENHAM and HUNSDON OF HUNSDON, B)), er dau of Lt-Col Philip Mitford, of Berryfield, Lentran, Inverness-shire, and was *ka* on the Mareth Line 16/17 March 1943, leaving issue (male line membs of which are in remainder to the btcy only):

1a +(Michael) Thomas Noel Hamilton, DL (Glos 1991) [Maj Thomas Wills DL, Misarden Park, Miserden, Stroud, Glos]; *b* 31 May 1940; *educ* Eton; Maj Coldstream Gds (ret), High Sheriff Glos 1985, Essex Yeomen Gd 1993, Pres Stroud Hosp League of Friends; *m* 1982 *Penelope A, er dau of Ben Howard-Baker, of Glascoed Hall, Llansilin, Salop, and has issue:

1b +Nicholas James Noel Hamilton; *b* 1983

1b *Camilla Jane Hamilton; *b* 1985

2a +Frederick Hugh Philip Hamilton [Frederick Wills Esq, The Old House, Rendcombe, Cirencester, Glos GL7 7EV], Capt R Yeo (R Wilts Yeo PWO Sqn), 11th Hus (PAO); *b* 31 May 1940; *educ* Eton and RAC Cirencester; Capt 11th Hus (PAO) and Roy Yeo, High Sheriff Glos 1995–96; *m* 2 Dec 1969 *Priscilla Annabelle, dau of Alec David Charles Francis, of The Grange, Malmesbury, Wilts, and has issue:

1b +Michael James Hamilton; *b* 1972

2b +Edward Hamilton; *b* 31 Oct 1974

1b *Clare Alexandra; *b* 31 Oct 1974

3a +(Peter) John Hamilton [John Wills Esq, Kirkham, Lower Slaughter, nr Cheltenham, Glos]; *b* 26 June 1941; *educ* Eton and Magdalen Coll Oxford; *m* 12 Sept 1970 *Elizabeth J, dau of Maj Jock Mann, of Oxleaze Farm, Filkins, Lechlade, Glos, and has issue:

1b *Richard Henry; *b* 1974

1b *Grania Sarah; *b* 1972

2b *Emily Jane; *b* 1975

(2) +(Hugh) David Hamilton (Sir), CBE (1971, MBE 1946), TD (1965), DL (Oxon 1967) [Sir David Wills CBE TD DL, Sandford Park, Sandford St Martin, Oxon]; *b* 19 June 1917; High Sheriff Oxon 1961, Maj QO Cameron Highrs (TA) WW II, ktd 1979; *m* 9 May 1949 *Eva Helen McMorrough, yst dau of Maj Arthur Thomas McMorrough Kavanagh, MC, 7th Hus, of Borris House, Co Carlow, and has had:

1a Martin David Hamilton; *b* 4 Oct 1952; *educ* Eton and Magdalen Coll Oxford; *d* 1992

1a *Catherine Mary Hamilton; *b* 23 Nov 1950

(1) Rosemary Theodora Hamilton; *m* 8 Dec 1938 Sir John MacLeod (*d* 1984), TD, QO Cameron Highrs, yst s of Duncan MacLeod, of Skeabost House, Isle of Skye, and *d* 1994, leaving issue

1a *David John Noel, Lt QO Cameron Highrs; *b* 12 Sept 1939; *educ* Gordonstoun; *m* 1972 *Wendy Joy, dau of E N Cookson, of Minshull Hall, Nantwich, Cheshire, and has:

1b *Fiona Carolyn; *b* 1976

2b *Kirsty Davina; *b* 1978

3b *Alison Wendy; *b* 1980

2a *Martin Michael Alan; *b* 14 April 1949; *educ* Haileybury

1a *Carolyn Margery Hamilton [Mrs Hugh Barclay, Box 7006, Nakuru, Kenya]; *b* 12 Sept 1939; *m* 23 Sept 1961 *Hugh Petre Barclay, only s of Capt Hugh Barclay, OBE, MC, of Kenya (*see* PETRE, B), and has issue:

1b *Edward Hugh; *b* 21 March 1963

2b *Jonti Peter; *b* 1967

1b *Karen Theodora; *b* 3 June 1962

2b *Camilla Patricia; *b* 1966

2a *Jocelyn Ishabel Ann; *b* 10 July 1946; Ldy-in-Waiting to HRH THE DUCHESS OF YORK 1986–96, thereafter SARAH DUCHESS OF YORK; *m* 1st 2 Feb 1967 David Algernon Fleming (*d* 1975) (*see* BORTHWICK, Bt), and has issue:

1b *Lara Kate; *b* 18 Jan 1968

2b *Annabel Theodora; *b* 28 Dec 1968

3b *Katrina Jane; *b* 1971

2a (cont.) Mrs David Fleming *m* 2nd 1978 *John Edmund Kincaid Floyd (*see* FLOYD, Bt)

3a *(Patricia) Mary-Rose Turkden [Mrs Nicholas Bosanquet, Lee Place Farm, nr Pulborough, W Sussex]; *b* 17 March 1951; *m* 1979 *Nicholas Gaston Ives Bosanquet and has:

1b *Emma Claire; *b* 1980

2b *Hermione Lucinda; *b* 1981

3b *Davina Jayne (twin); *b* 1981

(2) *Margery Angela Hamilton [Mrs Rodney Windsor, Mains of Warthill, Meikle Wartle, Inverurie, Aberdeenshire]; *b* 1922; *m* 1st 14 Oct 1948 (*divorce* 1971) Anthony Andrew Francis Tabor and has issue:

1a *(Adrian Andrew) Hamish; *b* 9 March 1960; *m* 1986 *Carolina Giovanna, dau of Count Massimiliano Magnaghi, of Le Martinet, Lausanne, Switzerland, and has issue:

1b *Francesca Giovanna Angela; *b* 1989

2b *Julia Aloisa Allegra; *b* 1992

1a *Marilyn Margery Hamilton; *b* 6 Oct 1949; *m* 4 May 1972 *Anthony Germain-Ribon

2a *Nicola Mary Hamilton; *b* 19 March 1952; *m* 1974 *Hugh Sherbrooke (*see* HERRIES, L)

(2) (cont.) Mrs Margery Tabor *m* 2nd 1 June 1972 Maj Anthony Stainton (*d* 1988); *m* 3rd 1994, as his 2nd w, *Col Rodney Francis Maurice Windsor, CBE, DL

(3) *Audrey Mackenzie Hamilton [Mrs Peter Gibbs, Hall's Grove, Elkstone, Glos GL53 9PU]; *m* 4 Dec 1946 *Capt Peter Houldsworth Gibbs, Scots Gds (*see* ALDENHAM and HUNSDON OF HUNSDON, B), and has issue:

1a *(Peter) Noel Houldsworth [Noel Gibbs Esq, Combend Manor, Elkstone, Cheltenham, Glos]; *b* 1948; *educ* Eton and Magdalen Coll, Oxford; *m* 1st 1976 (*divorce* 1989) Clare, dau of Nigel Viney, and has issue:

1b *Hugo Houldsworth; *b* 1984

1b *Chlöe Lucy; *b* 1982

2b *Amelia Emma (twin); *b* 1982

1a (cont.) Noel Gibbs *m* 2nd 1991 *Katharine, yst dau of Col Richard Lumley Hurst (*see* CRAWFORD and BALCARRES, E), and widow of Donald M Corbett

1a *Linda Hamilton; *b* 1951; *m* 1st 1973 Robert Bruce John Dunipace, and has issue:

1b *Aulden Malcolm Bruce; *b* 1975

2b *Fergus Roland Fraser; *b* 1981

1b *Imogen Larissa; *b* 1976

2b *Flavia Iona Churchill; *b* 1983

1a (cont.) Mrs Dunipace *m* 2nd 1991 *Lt-Col Anthony Singer, KRH, OBE

1 Edith Anne Hamilton; *b* 4 Jan 1871; *m* 20 July 1901 Percy Seymour Douglas-Hamilton (*d* 6 Feb 1940), only son of Algernon Douglas-Hamilton (*see* HAMILTON and BRANDON, D), and *d* 22 Aug 1927

2 Margaret Hamilton; *b* 14 July 1874; *m* 10 June 1903 (*divorce* 1910) Ernest Gaddesden Fellows, 1st Suffolk Regt, and *d* 3 Aug 1926, having had issue

3 Kathleen Mary Christine Hamilton, Govr St Bartholomew's, Westminster and Roy Northern Hospitals; *b* 26 June 1884; *m* 1st 21 Sept 1909 Edward Henry Douty (*d* 27 May 1911), MA, MD, FRCS, MRCP, of Cannes, and had issue; *m* 2nd 28 June 1922 Vet Lt-Col Graham Beauchamp Coxeter Rees-Mogg (*see* REES-MOGG, B) and *d* 12 March 1949

Sir FREDERICK *dvp* 20 Oct 1905; his 2nd son,

GILBERT ALAN HAMILTON WILLS, **1st Baron Dulverton**, of Batsford, Co Gloucester (UK), *so cr* 8 July 1929, OBE, TD, JP Somerset and Glos; *b* 28 March 1880; *educ* Magdalen Coll Oxford (MA); High Sheriff Glos 1928, MP (C) Taunton 1912–18 and Weston-super-Mare 1918–22, WW I:Lt-Col Roy No Devon Hus and Lt-Col cmdg a Bn MGC 1918–19 (despatches), Extra ADC to Ld Lt Ireland 1908–12, PPS to Assist PMG 1921, pres Imperial Tobacco, dir Br-American Tobacco Co and GWR to 1948; *m* 2 Dec 1914 Victoria May OBE (1951) (*d* 5 April 1968), dau of R-Adml Sir Edward Chichester, 9th Bt (*qv*), and had issue:

1 (FREDERICK) ANTHONY HAMILTON (Sir), **2nd Baron**

2 +(Edward) Robert Hamilton [Maj The Hon Robert Wills, Farmington Lodge, Northleach, Glos]; *b* 30 April 1918; *educ* Eton; Maj Gren Gds WW II (wounded); chm Farmington Tst

3 +(Victor) Patrick Hamilton, DL (Hants 1975) [The Hon Patrick Wills DL, Litchfield Manor, Whitchurch, Hants]; *b* 4 May 1926; *educ* Eton and Coll of Estate Management; FLAS 1957, Lt Gren Gds and Parachute Regt (ret), CC 1965–73, chm Hants Playing Fields Assoc 1969–79, Tstee Dulverton Tst 1949–81, Govr Internat Students Tst 1965 (v-pres 1979, chm 1984), v-chm Trident Tst 1972 (chm 1978–80), chm Atlantic Salmon Conservation Tst (Scotland) 1985–91; *m* 1st 28 July 1948 (*divorce* 1962) Felicity Betty, dau of Maj Aubrey Thomas Jonsson, Royal Irish Rifles, of Cranford, Winterskloof, Natal, S Africa, and has issue:

(1) +Christopher Aubrey Hamilton [Christopher Wills Esq, Litchfield Down, Whitchurch, Hants]; *b* 21 Feb 1953; *educ* Eton; Lt Gren Gds (ret); Tstee Dulverton Tst 1979; *m* 1987 Lady Katharine Anne Meade, 5th dau of 6th Earl of Clanwilliam (*qv*), and has issue:

1a +Thomas Robert Hamilton; *b* 1991

2a +George Edmund Hamilton; *b* 1993

1a *Laura Felicity Hamilton; *b* 1996

(2) +Jeremy Robert Hamilton [Jeremy Wills Esq, Bevis Farm, Charlbury, Oxon]; *b* 27 Jan 1955; *educ* Eton; Capt Gren Gds (despatches 1984); *m* 1982 *Alison Mary, dau of David Malkin, of Winnington Grange, Market Drayton, Salop, and has issue:

1a +Nicholas Patrick Hamilton; *b* 1986

2a +Benjamin James Hamilton; *b* 1988

(1) *Penelope Margaret Hamilton; *b* 14 Jan 1950; *m* 27 March 1975 (*divorce* 1986) David J Enthoven, and has issue:

1a *James John; *b* 1980

1a *Belinda Margaret; *b* 1977

3 (cont.) Patrick Wills *m* 2nd 10 Jan 1963 Jean Felicity (*d* 1984), formerly w of Hon Desmond Rupert Strutt (*see* BELPER, B) and yr dau of Hon Francis Walter Erskine (*see* MAR and KELLIE, E); *m* 3rd 1988 (*divorce* 1993) Mrs Elizabeth Gilmor Shaw

The 2nd BARON *d* 1 Dec 1956; his est son,

(FREDERICK) ANTHONY HAMILTON WILLS, **2nd Baron Dulverton**, CBE (1974), TD; *b* 10 Dec 1915; *educ* Eton and Magdalen Coll Oxford (BA 1937); WW II in Lovat Scouts (RA), Maj 1944, dir W Highland Woodlands and Lochaber Sawmills, pres Timber Growers' Assoc and Br Deer Soc, dir Imperial Tobacco Co, chm: The Dulverton Tst, Forestry Ctee of GB, Africa Ctee and Oxfam, Govr Rendcomb Coll; *m* 1st 2 Sept 1939 (*divorce* 1961) Judith Betty (*d* 1983), est dau of Lt-Col Hon Ian Leslie-Melville, TD (*see* LEVEN and MELVILLE, E), and had issue:

1 (GILBERT) MICHAEL HAMILTON WILLS, **3rd and present Baron Dulverton**

2 +(Robert) Ian Hamilton [The Hon Ian Wills, Soundborough Farm, Andoversford, Cheltenham, Glos]; *b* 28 June 1948; *educ* Harrow and Warwick U (BA); *m* Elizabeth Jane, est dau of Michael Downes, of The Old Parsonage, Lower Slaughter, Glos, and has issue:

(1) *Emma Elizabeth Hamilton; *b* 22 Dec 1982

1 Marion Hamilton; *b* 11 Sept 1940; *m* 15 June 1964 *John Glen Alexander Tulloch [John Tulloch Esq, Tundergarth House, Lockerbie, Dumfriesshire], est s of Alexander Rose Tulloch, MC, TD, JP, MA, of Gillesbie, Lockerbie, Dumfriesshire, and *d* 19–, leaving:

(1) *Andrew John Alexander; *b* 8 Sept 1965

(1) *Miranda Louise; *b* 26 Jan 1968; *m* 11 Oct 1997 *John Stainton, s of Andrew Stainton of Hastings-Leigh, Kent

2 *Sarah May Hamilton [The Hon Sarah Wills, 8 Montrose Court, Prince's Gate, London SW7]; *b* 31 March 1942

The **2nd Baron** *m* 2nd 28 April 1962 *Ruth Violet Mary [The Rt Hon Ruth Lady Dulverton, Barnbrook Cottage, Milton Lilbourne, Pewsey, Wilts SN9 5LQ], only dau of Sir Walter Randolph FitzRoy Farquhar, 5th Bt (*qv*), and formerly w of Maj Richard Gennys Fanshawe, 16th/5th Lancers, and *d* 1992

Seat: Batsford Park, Moreton-in-Marsh, Glos. A family called Freeman owned the Batsford estate from just after the accession of the TUDORs to the close of World War I. The earliest known house there of any size appears to have been a rambling multi-gabled structure whose principal facade pointed west. By about the end of the following century a more regular south-facing wing had been added. It had five bays on two storeys under a pediment and was built at a time when the Freeman of the day, Richard, had achieved something more than local squirearchical prominence by being appointed Lord Chancellor of Ireland. His son, another Richard, seems to have been keener on landscape gardening than bricks and mortar, for though he commissioned plans for a house of seven bays, with a more elaborate pediment than that of his father's time and even a cupola, there is no evidence that any of it got built.

His re-landscaping of the grounds, on the other hand, was finished well before the mid-century, by which time he had died and the property passed to his nephew Walter Edwards later Freeman. The latter's son Thomas succeeded in 1756 and in the mid-1760s employed Samuel Driver, a fairly prominent Gloucestershire architect, to extend the south front to seven bays, while the easterly one may have been given as many as nine. The park, which had been made somewhat formal in the time of Richard Freeman the Younger, was now rendered more 'natural' and 'wild' in the then fashion for Rousseau-esque unkemptness.

When Thomas Freeman died in 1808 he left the estate to his wife's sister's son John Mitford, 1st Baron Redesdale (*qv*) of Redesdale of the 1802 creation, who like Richard Freeman had been a Lord Chancellor of Ireland. The new owner was required to add the name Freeman under the terms of the will of his uncle-by-marriage. Towards the end of the Napoleonic Wars he carried out additions in the architectural field as well, erecting a service wing and Doric portico and remodelling the main entrance. On the death in 1886 of his only son and heir the 1st and last Earl of Redesdale, Batsford was demolished and entirely rebuilt over the next seven years in late Victorian Tudor-Gothic by the architectural partnership of Ernest George (the creator of those fanciful Flemish-style houses in Harrington Gardens, South Kensington) and Peto on behalf of the late owner's cousin, the 1st Baron Redesdale (*qv*) of the current creation. The present structure is an unusually artful example of its school of revivalism inasmuch as it deceives even the knowledgeable as to its true age. Its most interesting features are internal, namely the Great Hall and minstrel's gallery.

DUNALLEY

Arms: Per pale argent and gules three wolf heads erased, counterchanged. **Crest:** A wolf's head erased argent. **Supporters:** Dexter, a man in complete armour, holding in the exterior hand a tilting spear, all proper; sinister, a stag proper, armed, hoofed, ducally collared and chained or. **Motto:** *In omnia paratus* ('Prepared for all things'). **Creation:** B. (I) 31 July 1800.

THE 7TH BARON DUNALLEY OF KILBOY, Co Tipperary ((Henry) Francis Cornelius Prittie) [The Rt Hon The Lord Dunalley, 25 Stephen Road, Oxford OX3 9AY]; *b* 30 May 1948; *s f* 1992; *educ* Gordonstoun and Trin Coll Dublin (BA); *m* 1978 *Sally Louise, est dau of Ronald Vere, of Heaton Chapel, Cheshire, and has issue:

1 +JOEL HENRY; *b* 29 April 1981

1 *Rebecca Louise; *b* 1979

2 *Hannah Beatrice; *b* 1983

3 *Rachel Sarah; *b* 1987

Lineage: HENRY PRITTIE/PRETTY; Capt Kentish Regt of Horse New Model Army, Maj Cromwell's New Regt of Horse 1649, Govr Carlow 1652, High Sheriff Co Carlow 1650 and Co Tipperary 1659; granted Dunalley Castle and other estates in Cos Kerry and Tipperary 26 June 1678; *m* Honor, 5th dau of Richard Foley, of Stourbridge, Worcs, and *d* 1671, having had, with three daus (Honor; Elizabeth; Abigail, *m* Capt William Bolton, of Fatlock Castle, Co Waterford):

HENRY PRITTIE, of Kilboy and Dunalley; Capt of Horse; besieged at Dunalley Castle by disbanded soldiers of JAMES II's army after the Battle of the Boyne 1690 and thrown from the top of the castle, but miraculously escaped unhurt; *m* Elizabeth (*d* Feb 1701), sis of Charles Alcock, of Powerstown, Co Tipperary, and *d* Jan 1691, having had with a yr s (Richard, of Ballycrowley, Co Wexford; *b* 1691; *m* 1714 Barbara Bourchier) and five daus:

HENRY PRITTIE, of Kilboy, High Sheriff 1706; *b* 18 May 1683; *m* 1702 Elizabeth, only dau and heir of Col James Harrison, of Cloughjordan, Co Tipperary, MP Co Tipperary, and *d* 1738, leaving, with three daus:

HENRY PRITTIE, of Kilboy; MP Co Tipperary 1761–68; *b* 1708; *m* 1736 Deborah (*d* 3 Nov 1760), widow of John Bayly, of Debsborough, Co Tipperary, and dau of Ven Benjamin Neale, Archdeacon of Leighlin, and *d* 1768, having had, with five daus (including Margaret, *m* Michael Head (*d* 5 Nov 1812), of Derry Castle, Co Tipperary, and had issue):

HENRY PRITTIE, **1st Baron Dunalley of Kilboy**, Co Tipperary (I), so *cr* 31 July 1800; *b* 3 Oct 1743; MP Banagher 1767–68, Gowran 1769–76 and Co Tipperary 1776–90, High Sheriff Co Tipperary 1770; *m* 6 Jan 1766 Catherine (*d* 26 Feb 1821), widow of John Bury (f of 1st Earl of Charleville) and yr dau and coheir of Col Francis Sadleir, of Sopwell Hall, Co Tipperary, and *d* 3 Jan 1801, having had, with five daus:

1 HENRY SADLEIR PRITTIE, **2nd Baron Dunalley of Kilboy**; MP Carlow 1798–1801 and Okehampton 1819–24, rep I peer 1828–54; *b* 3 March 1775; *m* 1st 10 July 1802 Maria (*d* 15 Oct 1819), only dau of Dominick Trant, of Dunkettle; *m* 2nd 10 Feb 1826 Hon Emily Maude (*d* 10 Feb 1884), dau of 1st Viscount Hawarden (*qv*), and *dsp* 10 Oct 1854

2 Francis Aldborough, DL and Custos Rotulorum Co Tipperary, High Sheriff 1838, MP Doneraile 1800, Carlow 1801 and Co Tipperary 1807–31; *b* 4 June

1779; *m* 1st 10 Sept 1800 Martha (*d* March 1802), widow of George Hartpole, of Shrule Castle, Queen's Co, and only dau of Cook Otway, of Castle Otway, Co Tipperary, and had issue:

(1) Elizabeth Mary Martha; *m* 3 May 1827 Very Rev and Hon Robert Maude, Dean Clogher (*see* HAWARDEN, V), and *d* 25 July 1887 aged 85, leaving issue

2 (cont.) Francis Prittie *m* 2nd 16 July 1803 Elizabeth (*d* 11 Jan 1849), only dau of Rt Hon George Ponsonby (*see* BESBOROUGH, E), and *d* 8 March 1853, having had further issue:

(1) HENRY, **3rd Baron**

(2) George Ponsonby; *b* 4 Aug 1808; granted with his siblings rank of baron's dau/yr s 13 July 1855; *m* 10 Oct 1841 Henrietta Hester (*d* 10 May 1885), only dau of Lt-Col — Gregory, and *d* 15 Aug 1871, having by her had issue

(3) Francis Sadleir, of Glenview, nr Clonmel; Army Offr; *b* 25 Oct 1811; *m* 1st 1 Oct 1838 Mary (*d* 25 March 1844), dau of Hon P Rose, and had issue:

1a Francis William; 97th Foot; *b* 15 Dec 1839; *dsp*

2a Peter Rose; *b* Feb 1844; *d* 4 Sept 1860

1a Huntly Mary; *m* 16 Oct 1862 Henry Mervyn D'Arcy Irvine (*d* 1 July 1870), of Castle Irvine, Co Fermanagh, and *d* 2 March 1864, leaving issue

(3) (cont.) The Hon Francis Prittie *m* 2nd Nov 1846 Susanna (*d* 13 June 1856), dau of William Henry Carter, of Castle Martin, Co Kildare, and by her had issue:

3a Edward, Lt Rifle Bde; *b* Nov 1851; *d* 15 March 1882

2a Elizabeth Susan; *m* 18 June 1908 Alfred Gilley (*d* 1 July 1922), of the Rock, Castleconnell, Co Limerick, and *d* 13 Aug 1933

(3) (cont.) The Hon Francis Prittie *m* 3rd 3 Feb 1859 Janet (*d* 24 Sept 1900), dau of Edward Gonne Bell, of Streamstown, and *d* 26 July 1867, having by her had issue:

3a Geraldine Frances; *m* 1st 1 Oct 1889 Capt Frederick John Gough (*d* 26 Aug 1908), of Salisbury House, Clonmel, and left issue; *m* 2nd 27 July 1911 Lt-Col Reginald Anson Cartwright (*d* 12 May 1923), E Yorks and Northants Regts, and *d* 31 Aug 1923

(2) Mary; *d* 19 Feb 1853

(3) Catherine Charlotte; *m* 11 Nov 1830 Lt-Col William Leader Maberly, and *d* 7 Feb 1875

(4) Frances Eliza; *m* 21 June 1838 John Bagwell (*d* 10 March 1883), of Marlfield, Co Tipperary, MP Clonmel, and *d* 17 April 1901, leaving issue

The 2nd BARON's nephew,

HENRY PRITTIE, **3rd Baron Dunalley of Kilboy**; DL Co Tipperary, High Sheriff 1840; *b* Jan 1807; *m* 10 May 1841 Anne Marie Louisa O'Callaghan (*d* 6 July 1867), only dau of Cornelius, 1st Viscount Lismore of Shanbally, and *d* 10 Sept 1885, having had, with two daus (Eleanor Mary, *d* 30 Dec 1847; Cornelia Elizabeth, *d* 28 Dec 1888 aged 37):

HENRY O'CALLAGHAN PRITTIE, **4th Baron Dunalley of Kilboy**; *b* 21 March 1851; *educ* Harrow and Trin Coll Cambridge (BA); Lt Co Tipperary 1905, High Sheriff 1883, rep I peer 1891, Hon Col 3rd Bn Royal Irish Regt, Lt Rifle Bde; *m* 22 Aug 1876 Mary Frances MBE (1920) (*d* 18 May 1929) only dau of Maj-Gen Reginald Onslow Farmer, RA, and had:

1 HENRY CORNELIUS O'CALLAGHAN, **5th Baron**

2 Francis Reginald Dennis, Capt Rifle Bde, Assist Commr Uganda Boundary Commn 1910–14, served WW I (despatches, Legion of Honour); *b* 15 Oct 1880; *ka* 19 Dec 1914

1 Maura Geraldine Anne; *b* 2 Sept 1879; *d* 19 May 1880

2 Kathleen Everilda; *b* 13 April 1882; *d* unm 27 April 1910

3 Mary; *d* 24 Jan 1885

4 Irene Rose; *b* 24 April, *d* 2 Nov 1887

The 4th BARON *d* 5 Aug 1927; his only surv son,

HENRY CORNELIUS O'CALLAGHAN PRITTIE, **5th Baron Dunalley of Kilboy**, DSO (1916); Maj Rifle Bde, served S Africa 1901–02 and WW I (wounded, despatches), author: *Saddle and Steel* and *Khaki and Rifle Green*; *b* 19 July 1877; *m* 19 June 1911 Beatrix Evelyn (*d* 4 April 1967 aged 89), er surv dau of James Noble Graham, DL, of Carfin and Stonebyres, Lanarks, and had issue:

1 HENRY DESMOND GRAHAM, **6th Baron**

2 Terence Cornelius Farmer, MBE (1946); *b* 15 Dec 1913; Lt Rifle Bde (SR) WW II 1939–40 (POW, despatches), author: *South to Freedom*, correspondent *Manchester Guardian*; *m* 29 Aug 1946 Laura (*d* 1988), only child of G Dreyfus-Dundas, of Colombia, S America, and *d* 1988, leaving issue:

(1) +Oliver Alan Graham [Oliver Prittie Esq, 9 Blithfield St, London W8]; *b* 21 Oct 1948; *educ* Eton; *m* 1st 1973 (*divorce* 1983) Alison Victoria, er dau of Arnold Bertram Kingsley Tillie, of Chelsea, and has issue:

1a *Jemma Victoria; *b* 8 Dec 1975

2a *Kinvara Louise; *b* 18 May 1978

(1) (cont.) Oliver Prittie *m* 2nd 1986 *Krystyna Emilia, dau of Michael Wasiukiewicz, of Stratford-upon-Avon, and has further issue:

1a +Dominic Terence; *b* 1987

3a *Laura Zoe; *b* 1989

(2) +(James) Hugo Cameron [Hugo Prittie Esq, Le Breuilh, St Meard-de-Dronne, 24600 Riberac, France]; *b* 21 Sept 1950; *educ* Eton; *m* 1983 *Mrs Helga Isolda Lachnitt, est dau of Robert Werthenbach, of Siegen, W Germany

The 5th BARON *d* 3 May 1948; his er son,

HENRY DESMOND GRAHAM PRITTIE, **6th Baron Dunalley of Kilboy**; *b* 14 Oct 1912; *educ* Stowe and RMC Sandhurst; WW II with Rifle Bde, KAR and Staff E Africa, Middle East and Far East, ret Feb 1953 as Hon Lt-Col; *m* 23 April 1947 *(Mary) Philippa [The Rt Hon Philippa Lady Dunalley, Church End House, Swerford, Oxon OX7 4AX], only child of Maj Hon Philip Cary, Gren Gds (*see* FALKLAND, V), and had issue:

1 (HENRY) FRANCIS CORNELIUS PRITTIE, **7th and present Baron Dunalley of Kilboy**

2 +Michael Philip St John [The Hon Michael Prittie, PO Box 95871, Seattle, Washington 98145-2871, USA]; *b* 31 Oct 1961; *educ* Stowe

1 *Mary Rose Madeline [The Hon Mary Prittie, Athry, Recess, Co Galway, Ireland]; *b* 23 Nov 1953; has issue:

(1) *Thomas Benjamin; *b* 6 April 1996

(1) *Flora Tamsine JOYCE; *b* 18 Aug 1981

(2) *Pollyanna Felicity Rose JOYCE; *b* 1 May 1990

(3) *Lily Philippa JOYCE; *b* 31 May 1992

DUNBAR of Durn

Arms: Quarterly, 1st and 4th, gu. a lion rampant within a bordure arg., charged with eight roses of the first, barbed and seeded vert; 2nd and 3rd, or three cushions within the royal tressure gu., all within a bordure nebuly, quartered az. and gu. **Crest:** Two sprigs of laurel in saltire ppr. **Motto:** *Spes dabit auxilium* ('Hope will give help'). **Creation:** Bt. (NS) 29 Jan 1697/8.

SIR DRUMMOND COSPATRICK NINIAN DUNBAR, 9TH BT, of Durn, Banff, MC (1943) [Sir Drummond Dunbar of Durn Bt MC, Town Hill, Westmount, Jersey, CI JE2 3LP]; *b* 9 May 1917; *s f* 1949; *educ* Radley and Worcester Coll Oxford (BA 1938); Maj Black Watch (ret 1958), WW II (twice wounded); *m* 5 Jan 1957 *Sheila Barbara Mary, dau of John Berkeley de Fonblanque, and has issue:

1 +ROBERT DRUMMOND COSPATRICK, Yr. of Durn; *b* 17 June 1958; *educ* Harrow and Ch Ch Oxford (BA 1979); *m* 1994 *Sarah, dau of Robert Anthony Brooks, of Hattingley, Hants, and has issue:

(1) +A son; *b* 19–

Lineage: DAVID DUNBAR of Durris, Inverness-shire (5th s of Sir Alexander Dunbar of Westfield; *see* DUNBAR, Bt, of Mochrum); ancestor of:

MARK DUNBAR; sold Durris *c* 1592 and bought Grangehill, Morayshire; had:

NINIAN DUNBAR of Grangehill; *m* 1st Mary, dau of Walter Ogilvy of Dunlugas and Banff; *m* 2nd Christian Dunbar and had issue:

1 Robert (Sir), of Grange; *d* 1659, leaving issue (*see* MUNRO, Bt, of Foulis-Obsdale); male line now extinct

2 David, of Kirkhill; *m* 1st Margery, dau of Sir William Seton of Pitmedden (*see* SETON, Bt, of Pitmedden); *m* 2nd Janet Leslie, of Pitcaple, and *d* 14 Feb 1691, having had issue:

(1) John, of Kincourt; tutor of (guardian for) Grangehill; had, with other issue:

1a Robert (Rev), of Baddinspink, Fordyce, Banffshire; Minister Dyce 1727; had:

1b John (Rev); Minister Knockando 1764 and Dyce 1788; *m* Janet, dau of George Grant, of Aberdeen, and had:

1c **Sir Robert Dunbar, 5th Bt**; *b* 6 Jan 1780; *m* 22 Oct 1801 Elizabeth Margaret (*d* 14 Jan 1831), dau of William Fyfe, MD, of Jamaica, and *d* 11 Nov 1813, having had, with other issue:

1d WILLIAM (Sir), **6th Bt**

2d Hugh Grant; *d* unm 23 April 1831

2c William, of Elgin; left issue

3c George; *d* unm

3 **Sir William Dunbar, 1st Bt** (NS), so *cr* 29 Jan 1697/98, with remainder to the heirs male of his body and their heirs male for ever, of Durn; *m* Janet, dau of John Brodie, Dean of Aldearn, and had, with other issue:

(1) **Sir James Dunbar, 2nd Bt**; *bapt* 9 Jan 1665; *m* Margaret (*d* 11 Nov 1737), dau of Sir James Baird of Auchmedden, and *d* Nov 1737, having had issue:

1a **Sir William Dunbar, 3rd Bt**; *m* 1st 1737 Clementina (*d* 1 June 1765), dau of Sir James Grant of Grant; *m* 2nd 1737 Jane Bartlet, of Banff, and *d* 28 Jan 1786, leaving issue:

1b **Sir James Dunbar, 4th Bt**; *bur* 20 Jan 1812

2a James of Kincorth; male line *extinct*

(1) Anne; *m* 1687 1st Earl of Seafield (*qv*) and had issue

4 John, of Wellhead; issue now extinct

The 5th Bt's er son,

Rev Sir William Dunbar, 6th Bt; *b* 16 May 1804; Rector Dummer, Hants; *m* 9 Feb 1836 Ann (*d* 21 July 1889), est dau of George Stephen, and *d* 27 Nov 1881, having had, with other issue:

1 Alexander Stephen; *b* 12 May 1837; *m* 29 Dec 1863 Minnie, est dau of Joseph Rigby, of The Priory, Kew, and *dsp* & *vp* 29 Jan 1868
2 DRUMMOND MILES (Sir), **7th Bt**
1 Eleanor Duff Fyfe; *m* 1 March 1870 Richard Carrow (*d* 16 May 1905), of Johnston Hall, Pembs, and *d* 9 April 1924, leaving issue

Sir WILLIAM's only surv son,

Sir Drummond Miles Dunbar, 7th Bt; *b* 21 Nov 1845; *m* 24 July 1873 Maria Louisa (*d* 29 Nov 1922), 4th dau of John Hancorn Smith, of Lower Albany, S Africa, and *d* 4 Jan 1903, having had issue:

1 William; *b* 1 May 1876; *dvp* unm 19 May 1900
2 GEORGE ALEXANDER DRUMMOND (Sir), **8th Bt**
3 Hugh Stephen; *b* 25 Feb 1881; *m* 1910 Coralie Howard (*d* 1948), dau of William James Vere, of Johannesburg, and *d* 19 Dec 1936, leaving issue:
(1) Uthred Ninian Vere; *b* 27 Sept 1910; Sgt SAAF WW II; *m* 1942 *Susan Kathleen, dau of Arthur George Thompson, and *d* 1977, having had issue:
1a +Stephen Bruce; *b* 1949
1a *Eleanor Lynne; *b* 1947
(2) William Hancorn Vere; *b* 1 Aug 1912; SAAF WW II; *m* 8 Aug 1936 *Dorothy Christabel, dau of James Smith Gow, and *d* 1984, having had issue:
1a *Coral Lisette; *b* 21 June 1939; *m* 1964 *Henry William Walker, of Dunnottar, Transvaal, and has issue:
1b *Gordon Henry; *b* 1965
(3) Aldred Cospatrick; *b* 1916; *m* 1940 Isidoris Elliott (*d* 1986), dau of Maj William Harrison, and *d* 1971, leaving issue:
1a +Raymond Robert; *b* 1943
(4) Robert Fyfe; *b* 1920; Lt SA Artillery 1st Field Regt WW II; *m* 1941 *Eileen Mary [Mrs Robert Dunbar, 33 Julia Rd, Overport, Durban, Natal, S Africa], dau of Frederick Locke, and *d* 1991, leaving issue:
1a +George Drummond; *b* 14 Oct 1957; *m* 1990 *Lydia, dau of Gawie Grobbelaar, and has issue:
1b *Merissa Anne; *b* 1992
1a *Beverley Anne; *b* 1946; *m* 1974 John Derek Walters (*d* 1992)
2a *Gail Elizabeth; *b* 25 June 1953; *m* 1976 *Patrick Murphy
3a *Dianne Roberta; *b* 14 Feb 1959; *m* 1991 *Peter Riddle, of Oxon, and has issue:
1b *Robert Adam; *b* 1992
4 Patrick Martin Borlase; *b* 7 June 1884; *m* 27 Sept 1924 Mary (*d* 1983), est dau of Claude F Shoolbred, of Halstead, Essex, and *d* 17 Sept 1925, leaving issue:
(1) *Patricia Martin [Mrs William Groves, 2 Cumberland Ave, Vandia Grove, Randburg, Johannesburg, Transval, S Africa]; *b* posthumously 16 Jan 1926; *m* 24 March 1951 *William Harold Groves, of Johannesburg, s of Arthur W Groves, and has issue:
1a *Martin Westley; *b* 7 March 1960
2a *James Arthur; *b* 22 Sept 1967
1 Mary Annette; *m* 1st 1895 Douglas Kingsley ANDERSON later DUNBAR-ANDERSON, of Invergordon (*d* 30 Oct 1906), and had issue; *m* 2nd 1907 Cormack Grant, MB, and had further issue; *m* 3rd 1922 A McGlashan (*d* 1937); *m* 4th 1942 William Coulson Tregarthern (*d* 1942), Mus B, and *d* Jan 1956
2 Lisette Eleanor; *m* 1906 Edward Fitzgibbon Benson, of Johannesburg, and *d* 1918, leaving issue
3 Augusta Marjory; *d* unm 10 Aug 1896
4 Helen Mackenzie Edith; *m* 20 March 1912 Lt-Col Robert Fyfe King, S African Forces, Commr Oaths CP, and *d* 1 July 1962, leaving issue

Sir DRUMMOND's est surv son,

Sir George Alexander Drummond Dunbar, 8th Bt; *b* 10 May 1879; Capt Black Watch (SR), WW I in German SW Africa 1914–15 and France 1916–19; *m* 24 May 1916 Sophie Kathleen (*d* June 1936), dau of James Benson Kennedy, of New York, and *d* 25 June 1949, having had issue:

1 Sir DRUMMOND COSPATRICK NINIAN DUNBAR, **9th and present Bt**
1 Marjorie Frederica Anne; *b* 13 Dec 1919; *d* unm 24 April 1968

DUNBAR of Hempriggs

Arms: Quarterly, 1st, gu. a lion rampant within a bordure arg., charged with eight roses of the field (for DUNBAR); 2nd, gu. three mullets or, a crescent of the last for difference (for SUTHERLAND); 3rd, vert on a fess dancettée erm. between a buck's head cabossed in chief and two escallops in base or, a mullet of the first for difference (for DUFF); 4th, or three cushions within a double tressure flory counter-flory gu. (for RANDOLPH); all within a bordure vairy or and gu. **Crest:** A key and a sword in saltire ppr. **Supporters:** Dexter, a lion rampant arg.; sinister, a savage man holding a baton over his shoulder ppr. **Motto:** *Sub spe* ('Labouring under hope'). **Creation:** Bt. (NS) 10 Dec 1706.

SIR RICHARD FRANCIS DUNBAR OF HEMPRIGGS, 9TH BT [Sir Richard Dunbar of Hempriggs Bt, 732 Crossway Rd, Burlingame, CA 94010, USA]; *b* 8 Jan 1945; *s* mother 1997; *educ* Charterhouse; *m* 27 Dec 1969 *(Elizabeth Margaret) Jane, only dau of George Lister, of Gloucester, and has:

1 +EMMA KATHERINE; *b* 1977
2 +Fiona Blake; *b* 1981

Lineage: The 4th EARL OF SUTHERLAND (*qv*); had a 2nd s:

NICHOLAS SUTHERLAND; *m* Mary, dau and coheir of Reginald le Cheyne, who brought him the lands of Duffus, Morayshire; had:

HENRY SUTHERLAND of Torboll; apparently *dvp*; had:

ALEXANDER SUTHERLAND of Duffus; *m* 1433 Muriel, dau of John Chisholm of Chisholm, and *d c* 1484, having had:

WILLIAM SUTHERLAND of Berriedale; *dvp*, leaving:

WILLIAM SUTHERLAND of Duffus; *s* to Quarrelwood 1484 and had a charter of Duffus 1507; *m* 22 July 1484 Janet (*m* 2nd *c* 1517 Hugh Rose of Kilravock), dau of Berowald Innes, and *d* 1514, leaving issue:

WILLIAM SUTHERLAND of Duffus; had a charter of Torboll 1525; *m* Janet, dau of Sir James Innes, 12th of that Ilk (*see* ROXBURGHE, D), and was probably the laird of Duffus who was *k c* Sept 1530, leaving, with a dau (Elizabeth, *m* 3rd Earl of Caithness, *qv*):

WILLIAM SUTHERLAND of Duffus; *m* Elizabeth Stewart (*m* 2nd James Murray of Culbardie) and *d* 1543; his est son:

ALEXANDER SUTHERLAND of Duffus; *m* 1553 Janet (*m* 2nd 1577 James Dempster and *d* 1600), dau of James Grant of Freuchie (*see* STATHSPEY, B), and *d c* 1570, leaving:

WILLIAM SUTHERLAND of Duffus; *m* 1st 1579 Elizabeth/Margaret, dau of 4th Earl of Caithness (*qv*); *m* 2nd 1604 Margaret, dau of William Mackintosh of that Ilk, 15th Chief, and widow of (a) Duncan Grant of Freuchie (*see* STRATHSPEY, B), (b) Alexander Forbes, 7th of Pitsligo (*see* FORBES, Bt, of Newe), and (c) Alexander Gordon, 5th of Abergeldie, and *d* 1616; his est son:

WILLIAM SUTHERLAND of Duffus; *m* 1612 Jean (*m* 2nd Thomas Mackenzie), dau of John Grant of Freuchie (*see* STRATHSPEY, B), and *d* 21 Oct 1626; his est son:

ALEXANDER SUTHERLAND, 1st LORD DUFFUS (S), so *cr* 8 Dec 1650; *m* 1st Jean (*d* 31 March 1648), dau and coheir of 1st Earl of Seaforth (*see* CROMARTIE, E) and widow of John Sinclair, Master of Berriedale (*see* CAITHNESS, E), and had issue; *m* 2nd 13 Jan 1653 Jean (*d* 10 March 1653), dau of Sir Robert Innes of Innes, 1st Bt (*see* ROXBURGHE, D); *m* 3rd Margaret (*d* Jan 1667), dau of James Stewart, Earl of Moray (*qv*); *m* 4th Margaret, dau of 11th Lord Forbes (*qv*), and afterwards w of Sir Robert Gordon of Gordonstoun, 3rd Bt, and *d* 31 Aug 1674; his only surv son:

JAMES SUTHERLAND, 2nd LORD DUFFUS, PC; *m* 1674 Margaret (*d* Aug 1706), dau of 3rd Earl of Seaforth (*see* CROMARTIE, E), and *d* 24 Sept 1705, leaving, with other issue:

1 KENNETH SUTHERLAND, 3rd LORD DUFFUS; Capt RN; *m* (contract 30 March 1708) Charlotta Christina, dau of Eric Sioblade, Govr Gothenberg, Sweden; attainted 1716 for part in Jacobite Rising and *d* 18 March 1733/4, leaving an only son:

(1) Eric; *m* his cousin Elizabeth, 3rd dau of his unc Sir James Dunbar, 1st Bt (*see* below), and *d* 28 Aug 1768, leaving, with at least one dau (Elizabeth, *m* Alexander Sinclair, s of Sir William Sinclair, 2nd Bt, *qv*), an only surv son:

1a JAMES SUTHERLAND, 4th LORD DUFFUS; attainder reversed 25 May 1826; *b* 8 June 1747; *d* unm 30 Jan 1827, when the Ldship became dormant, it being uncertain what the original remainder had been (*e.g.*, to heirs general (which could include females and their issue), heirs male of the body or some other one such as heirs male whatsoever)

1a Anne; *m* 1776 Hon George Mackay of Skibo and had issue (*see* REAY, L)

2 JAMES (Sir), **1st Bt**

3 William, of Roscommon; *m* (contract 22 Oct 1702) Helen (*dsp* July 1740), est dau of William Duff, of Dipple, and sis of 1st Earl Fife (*see* FIFE, D)

The 2nd LORD DUFFUS's 2nd son,

Sir JAMES SUTHERLAND later DUNBAR, **1st Bt**, of Hempriggs (NS), so *cr* 10 Dec 1706, with remainder to heirs whomsoever; *m* 1705 Elizabeth (*d* 11 March 1756), only surv child of Sir William Dunbar, 1st Bt (*see* DUNBAR, Bt, of Northfield), and widow of Sir Robert Gordon of Gordonstoun, 3rd Bt, and *d* 1724, having had issue:

1 WILLIAM (Sir), **2nd Bt**

2 James; *k* Cartagena 1741

1 Janet; *m* 1st 1 Jan 1738 John Sinclair of Barrock; *m* 2nd Harry Innes of Borlum and Sandside, and by both husbs had issue

2 Charlotte; *m* 23 Dec 1731 William Sinclair of Keiss, and had issue

3 Elizabeth; *m* her cousin Eric Sutherland and *d* 21 July 1800, leaving issue (*see* above)

4 Rachel; *m* James Sutherland of Langwell and had issue

Sir JAMES's er son,

Sir William Dunbar, 2nd Bt; *m* 1st 6 Jan 1729 Elizabeth (*d* 3 June 1746), dau and heir of Alexander Dunbar of Westfield, and had a surv dau (Janet, *m* 26 Feb 1762 Thomas Dunbar of Grangehill and *d* 16 Sept 1769, leaving issue); *m* 2nd 21 March 1747 Jane (*dsp* 9 Aug 1749), dau of David Sinclair of Southdun; *m* 3rd 21 Oct 1749 Henrietta (*d* Sept 1795), 2nd dau of Hugh Rose, 16th of Kilravock, and *d* 12 June 1793, having by her had, with a further dau (Elizabeth, *d* unm):

Sir Benjamin Sutherland Dunbar, 3rd Bt; *b* 28 April 1761; called himself 1827 Lord Duffus as heir male of the body of the grantee and petitioned the Ho of Lds for formal recognition, but no further steps taken; *m* 10 Dec 1784 Janet (*d* 15 March 1857), dau of George Mackay of Bighouse, and *d* 27 Jan 1843, having had, with other issue:

1 **Sir George Dunbar, 4th Bt**; petitioned 1838 for recognition but did not assume the peerage title; *b* 6 Jan 1799; *d* unm 28 Aug 1875

2 Robert; *b* 12 April 1801; *dsp* 18 Aug 1857

1 Louisa; *b* 11 April 1788; *m* 17 Sept 1805 Garden Duff, JP, DL (*d* 15 March 1859), 8th of Hatton, Aberdeenshire (*see* 1949 edn DUFF, Bt, of Hatton), and *d* 10 June 1865, having had, with other issue:

(1) BENJAMIN, *de jure* 5th Bt

(2) Garden William, 9th of Hatton; *b* 10 June 1814; *m* 1st 1 June 1850 Douglas Isabella Maria (*d* June 1861), 3rd dau of Beauchamp Colclough Urquhart of Meldrum and Blyth, and had issue; *m* 2nd 14 Oct 1862 Jean, dau of William Cook, of Edinburgh, and *d* 17 Sept 1866, leaving further issue

(3) Robert George, DL Caernarvs; *b* Oct 1817; *m* 12 May 1847 Mary (*d* 4 Oct 1874), only surv child of William Buckler Astley, of Everleigh, Wilts, by Elizabeth, sis of Thomas Assheton-Smith, MP Vaynol, and *d* March 1890, leaving issue (*see* 1970 edn DUFF, Bt)

(4) James, of Knockleith; *b* 22 May 1820; Capt 74th Regt, Col Banff, Moray and Nairn Militia; *m* April 1835 Jane Bracken, dau of Alan Colquhoun Dunlop, and *d* 1898, leaving issue

(1) Jessie; *m* 1836 Alexander Morison (*dsp* 1874), of Bognie and Frendraught, Aberdeenshire, and *d* 1883

(2) Helen; *m* 12 June 1833 James Buchan, 14th of Auchmacoy, Aberdeenshire (*d* 28 Nov 1874), and *d* 20 Nov 1889, leaving issue

Sir GEORGE's nephew,

BENJAMIN DUFF, *de jure* 5th Bt; did not assume the title; *b* 1808; Offr 92nd Highrs; *m* 1832 Emma, dau of Gregory Haines, CB, Commissary-Gen Forces, and *d* 7 Dec 1897, having had:

1 GARDEN DUFF later DUFF-DUNBAR (under terms of will of his great-uncle **Sir George Dunbar, 4th Bt**) of Hempriggs and Ackergill, Caithness, JP; *b* 1838; Offr 79th Regt Cameron Highrs; *m* 26 Sept 1876 Jane Louisa (*d* 1947), est dau of Lt-Col James Duff, of Knockleith, and *dvp* 1 June 1889, leaving issue:

(1) Sir GEORGE DUFF-DUNBAR later DUFF-SUTHERLAND DUNBAR, **6th Bt**; *b* 29 May 1878; *educ* Harrow and RMC Sandhurst; Offr QO Cameron Highrs 1898, IA 1902–25, cmdg Mily Police Assam, served Abor Expdn (despatches, King's Police Medal), WW I, WO, France, Indian Frontier and WW II, special duty IO and WO; *m* 1st 8 July 1903 Sybil Hawtrey (*d* 28 June 1911), dau of Col Charles W H Tate, Army Ordnance Dept, and had issue:

1a **Sir George Cospatrick Duff-Sutherland Dunbar, 7th Bt**, DL (Caithness 1955); *b* 3 Aug 1906; *educ* Harrow and New Coll Oxford; barrister Middle Temple 1931, Hon Col WW II; *d* unm 4 Feb 1963

(1) (cont.) Sir GEORGE *m* 2nd 3 May 1921 Dorothy (*d* 30 Nov 1945), er dau of Col G G Hewlett, of E Cowes, IoW; *m* 3rd 2 Nov 1956 Dulcie Edith, dau of S Wescombe Joyce, of Winchester, and *d* 8 April 1962

(2) Kenneth James, DSO; *b* 16 Oct 1886; Lt-Cdr, RN; *m* 10 Feb 1915 Katherine Isabel Bennett, only dau of William Adams Daw, of Ealing, and was *kas* 19 Aug 1916 cmdg HM submarine E16, Harwich Patrol Flotilla, leaving:

1a Kenneth James; *b* posthumously 21 Nov 1916; *educ* Trin Coll Cambridge (BA), Capt Seaforth Highrs WW II; *ka* Normandy 6 Aug 1944

1 Louisa; *d* young

2 Helen Emma; *d* 25 Feb 1923

3 Jessie Mona; *b* 2 Sept 1843; *m* 15 April 1869 Rev Courtenay Moore, Rector Mitchelstown, Co Cork, and Canon Cloyne (*d* 9 June 1922), s of Alexander Moore, MD, of Roshnashene (*see* MOORE, Bt, of Moore Lodge), and *d* 31 Dec 1936, leaving issue:

(1) Courtenay Edward; *b* 26 June 1870; *m* 1897 Janie King, dau of Rev Canon Askins, Rector Dunleer, Co Louth, and *d* 9 June 1951, leaving issue:

1a Edward Francis Courtenay; *b* 17 Nov 1898; *ka* 24 March 1918

1a Dame MAUREEN DAISY HELEN Moore, **8th holder of btcy** on being recognised as Baronetess of Hempriggs by Lyon Court 1965; *b* 19 Aug 1906; *educ* Headington Sch and RCM (LRCM 1928); *m* 27 Aug 1940 Leonard James Blake (*d* 1989), Dir Music Malvern Coll, s of Robert Arthur Blake, of Hendon, took name DUNBAR instead of BLAKE 1963 and *d* 15 Feb 1997, leaving:

1b Sir RICHARD FRANCIS BLAKE later DUNBAR (deed poll 1965), **9th and present Bt**

1b +Eleanor Margaret [Mrs Michael Dunbar-Constable, 24 Stoke Rd, Bishops Cleeve, Glos GL52 4RP]; *b* 16 Nov 1949; *m* 1st 1973 (*divorce* 1987) David C Eldridge and has:

1c +Hannah Louise; *b* 1980

1b (cont.) Mrs Eleanor Eldridge *m* 2nd 1989 *Michael CONSTABLE later DUNBAR-CONSTABLE and by him has:

1c +Thomas Matthew; *b* 1987

(2) Alexander Duff; *b* 1872; *m* Harriet Nina Bourchier

(1) Harriet Emma; *b* 1874; *m* 1909 Lt-Col Hubert Bernard Tonson Rye, DSO, Roy Munster Fus (*d* 1950), and *d* 1957, leaving issue:

1a +Eudo John; *b* 1910; Maj Duke of Cornwall's LI; *m* 1940 *Rosemary Hilda, dau of Maj Guy Hughes, XIIth Bengal Cav, and has issue:

1b +Rohaise Harriet Julia [Mrs Christopher Everard, Broford Farm, Dulverton, Somerset]; *b* 1942; *m* 1966 *Christopher Thomas Everard, and has issue

1c +Guy Richard; *b* 1969

1c +Lucilla Damaris Mary; *b* 1966

2c +Adela Jessie Bridget; *b* 1974

2b +Caroline Mary Georgina; *b* 1947

3b +Amarylde Louise; *b* 1950; *m* 1972 *Richard Peter Eliot

(2) Jessie Louisa; *b* 1876; *m* 1st 1901 Robert Dudley Innes Ackland; *m* 2nd 1908 Lt-Col Victor George Howard Rickard (*ka* 1915); *m* 3rd 1916 (*divorce* 1935) Lt-Col Tudor Fitzjohn, DSO, and *d* 1963, having by her 2nd husb had:

1a +Justin Victor [Justin Rickard Esq, Swiftsden Farm, Hurst Green, Sussex]; *b* 1913; *m* 1939 *Joan, dau of Alexander William Haig, of Henley-on-Thames, and has issue:

1b +Alexander; *b* 1944

1b +Catherine; *b* 1949

2b +Patricia; *b* 1955

DUNBAR of Mochrum

Arms: Gu. a lion rampant arg., armed and langued az., within a bordure of the second charged with eight roses of the first, barbed and seeded vert, in a dexter canton arg. a saltire az., surmounted by an inescutcheon charged with a lion rampant gu. within a double tressure flory counterflory gu. **Crest:** A horse's head arg., bridled and reined gu. **Supporters:** Two white doves imperially crowned ppr. **Badge:** A lion sejant guardant arg., armed and langued az., upon a mount vert, grasping with his dexter paw the stem of a rosebush. **Mottoes:** (above) *In promptu* ('In readiness'), (below) *Candoris praemium honos* ('Honour is the prize of honesty'). **Creation:** Bt. (NS) 29 March 1694.

SIR JAMES MICHAEL DUNBAR, 14TH BT, of Mochrum [Col Sir James Dunbar Bt USAF, 211 Gardenville Dr, Yorktown, VA 23692, USA]; *b* 17 Jan 1950; *s* f 1993; *m* 1st 1978 (*divorce* 1989) Margaret Jacobs (*d* 1991) and has:

1 +MICHAEL JOSEPH; *b* 5 July 1980

2 +David Scott; *b* 1983

1 *Stacy Beth; *b* 1985

Sir JAMES *m* 2nd 1989 *Margaret, dau of Roger Gordon Talbot, and by her has:

2 *Cassandra Talbot; *b* 1991

Lineage: DUNCAN (*see* also O'NEILL, B), Lay Abbot (*i.e.*, protector of the Abbey) of Dunkeld (to the north of Perth in what subsequently became the Scottish county of Perthshire); *k* Battle of Duncrub *c* 965 (fighting for Colin, representative of a rival royal line of Aodh, when the latter was defeated by Duff, est s of MALCOLM I King of Scots), leaving an est s:

DUNCAN, Lay Abbot of Dunkeld; cmded the Scottish left wing at the battle of Luncarty (*c* 990), where the Danes were so crushingly defeated that their raids on that part of what subsequently became Perthshire, hitherto periodic and devastating, were terminated; had, with two yr sons (Grim, Thane (hereditary tenant of the Crown) of Strathearn (west of Perth) and Baillie (functionary with judicial powers) of Dule, *k* 1010 Battle of Mortlach, where MALCOLM II King of Scots (reigned 1005–34) defeated invading Norsemen; Duncan, ancestor of the IRVINGs of Dumfries and FORBES IRVINEs of Drum):

CRINAN; Lay Abbot Dunkeld; *m c* 1000 Bethoc, er dau of MALCOLM II, and was *k* 1045 in battle against MACBETH (the historic figure who murdered CRINAN's er s DUNCAN I, and subsequently is portrayed as having usurped the Scottish throne, most famously by Shakespeare), leaving, with an er s (DUNCAN I 'The Gracious', King of Scots 1034–40; ancestor of the Sovereigns of England and later England, Ireland, Scotland, Great Britain etc; *see* 1967 edn ROYAL LINEAGE):

MALDRED; *m* Aldgyth/Ealdgyth, dau of Uchtred/Ughtred, Earl of Northumberland or Northumbria, by his 3rd w Ælfgifu/Elgiva (dau of ETHELRED II 'The Unready', King of England 979–1013 and 1014–16), and had, with a probable yr s (Maldred; *see* ABERGAVENNY, M):

GOSPATRIC; *b* 1040–48; installed 1068/9 by WILLIAM I (THE CONQUEROR) as Earl (then still predominantly an administrative post; *see* NORTHUMBERLAND, D, preliminary remarks) of Northumberland after his payment of a heavy fine or what would now be thought of as an entrance fee (though his hereditary claim through his maternal gf also played a part), later (Oct or Nov 1072) deprived of the Earldom on a charge of having taken part in a massacre at Durham; fled to Scotland, where his cousin MALCOLM III granted him the Mormaorship of Dunbar; *m* —, sister of Edmund —, and was *bur* Ubbanford (modern Norham, Northumberland, on the border with Scotland) *c* 1075, leaving, with two er sons and several daus:

GOSPATRIC de DUNBAR, 1st EARL (OF DUNBAR); living *c* 1115, when he seems to have been a signatory to the Charter of Scone by which the Abbey of Scone was founded; *k* leading his men of Lothian in Scottish defeat by the English at the Battle of the Standard (nr Northallerton, N Yorks) 23 Aug 1138, having had, with an er s (Alan, *dspms* after 16 Aug 1139):

GOSPATRIC de DUNBAR, 2nd EARL (OF DUNBAR); *m* Derdere — and *d* between 1156 and 1166, having had:

WALTHEOF de DUNBAR, 3rd EARL (OF DUNBAR); hostage 1175 for WILLIAM I ('THE LION') OF SCOTS (then held captive by the English); *m* Aline — (*d* 20 Aug 1179) and *d* 1182, leaving:

PATRICK de DUNBAR, 4th EARL OF DUNBAR, the first fully so to style himself, though referred to by at least one contemporary source as Earl of Lothian; *b* 1152; Justiciar Lothian, Keeper Berwick; *m* 1st 1184 Ada, illegitimate dau of WILLIAM I ('THE LION'); *m* 2nd by 1214 Christine, widow of William Bruce of Annandale, eventually entered a monastery and *d* 31 Dec 1232, leaving by his 1st w:

PATRICK de DUNBAR, 5th EARL OF DUNBAR; led troops in suppression of the rebel Bastard of Galloway 1235; *m* by 1213 Eupheme, dau of Walter Stewart (*see* MORAY, E), 3rd Lord High Steward of Scotland, and *d* Marseilles 1248 en route to the Holy Land to join the Crusade of (ST) LOUIS IX OF FRANCE; his est son:

PATRICK de DUNBAR, 6th EARL OF DUNBAR; *b c* 1213; memb of a pro-English group among the Scots nobility, as which managed to get the boy King ALEXANDER III away from the dominance of the Comyn family, becoming in consequence 1255 Regent of Scotland and Guardian to ALEXANDER and his young consort (dau of HENRY III of England); cmded a div of the Scottish army in the victory over Norsemen at Largs 1263; *m* 1242 Cecil, dau of John (Fraser?) and *d* 24 Aug 1289, leaving:

PATRICK de DUNBAR, 7th EARL OF DUNBAR, also from *c* 1290 known as (1st) EARL OF MARCH from his possessions on the Border, or March, with England, and more familiarly as 'Black-Beard', *b c* 1242; a claimant to the vacant Scottish Crown 1291 but quite soon dropped the claim, allying himself with the English in their war against the Scots 1296 and being made King's (*i.e.*, EDWARD I's) Lt of Scotland 1298 and taking part with the English in the Siege of Carlaverock 1300 (on which occasion in one source the title is revived for him of Earl of Lothian; *see* also above against 4th EARL); *m* by 1282 Lady Marjory Comyn (apparently of completely opposite loyalties to those of her husband since she held out in Dunbar Castle on behalf of the Scots against the besieging English till obliged to capitulate in April 1296), dau of Alexander, Earl of Buchan (*see* BUCHAN, E, preliminary remarks), and *d* 10 Oct 1308, having had issue:

1 PATRICK de DUNBAR, 8th EARL OF DUNBAR/(2nd) EARL OF MARCH; *b c* 1285; initially pro-English, playing host at Dunbar Castle to the defeated EDWARD II after the rout of Bannockburn 1314 and facilitating his escape back to England; later supported Scottish independence and helped take Berwick 1318 (by which time Sheriff Lothian); cmded Scottish troops at defeats by English of Dupplin 1332 and Halidon Hill 1333, following which he again went over to the English but after a year or so ratted on them a second time, subsequently cmdg the Scottish left wing at the defeat by the English of Neville's Cross 1346; he appears to have deserted the Scots Crown yet a third time by Feb 1360/1 since in that month he is called a rebel and his lands are pronounced forfeited; *m* 1st by 1303 Ermengarde —; *m* 2nd just after Sept 1320 Agnes (known as 'Black Agnes'; held Dunbar Castle nearly five months against the English from Jan 1337/8 until they raised the siege entirely), dau of Thomas Randolph, 1st Earl of Moray (*see* MORAY, E, preliminary remarks), was *cr* in right of her EARL OF MARCH AND MORAY 1357/8, resigning his Earldom of Dunbar/March to the Crown for regrant 25 July 1368 to his great-nephew and heir male GEORGE (*see* below), and *dspms* 11 Nov 1368, by which time the Earldom of March and Moray appears to have reverted to the Crown, having had:

(1) Patrick; *b* 1304; *d* by 5 Sept 1351

(2) John; *d* by July 1368

(1) Agnes; *m* Sir James Douglas of Dalkeith (*see* MORTON, E)

2 Alexander (Sir); living 1331; had:

(1) Patrick (Sir); fought against the English at Neville's Cross 1346 and Poitiers 1356; *m* Isabel, sis of 'Black Agnes' (*see* above) and yst dau of Thomas Randolph, Earl of Moray, and *d* at Candia, Crete, 1356 en route to the Holy Land, leaving, with other issue (including a dau Agnes, *m* John Maitland; *see* LAUDERDALE, E):

1a GEORGE (de) DUNBAR, 9th EARL OF DUNBAR/MARCH; *b c* 1336; referred to in contemporary sources by 1370–90 as Ld of Annandale and the Isle of Man; Warden of the Marches 1372, took cmd of the Scots at Otterburn 1388 after the death of 'Black Douglas' (*see* below against Elizabeth, Countess of Moray); renounced his allegiance to ROBERT III 1400 on that King's est son and heir the Duke of Rothesay breaking off his engagement to the 9th EARL's dau Elizabeth, sided with the English and fought for HENRY IV at Battles of Homildon Hill (defeat of Scots by Harry Hotspur) 1402 and Shrewsbury (against Harry Hotspur, now in rebellion; *see* NORTHUMBERLAND, D) 1403; after ROBERT III's death 1406 the 9th EARL negotiated with the Regent a renewal of allegiance to the Scottish Crown, though at the price of the Ldship of Annandale among other possessions; *m* Christian, dau of Alan de Seton formerly Winto(u)n (*see* EGLINTON and WINTON, E), and *d c* 1416–20, leaving an est s:

1b GEORGE DUNBAR, 10th and last EARL OF DUNBAR/MARCH; *b c* 1370; ktd 1424; deprived 1434 of the Earldom by JAMES I on the pretext that the allegiance renewed by his (the 10th EARL's) f after 1406 had been invalid since negotiated with a Regent rather than King regnant, hence that the Earldom and estates remained forfeited because of the 9th EARL's treason (the real reason being JAMES's determination to end the power of the only intermittently loyal Earls of Dunbar once and for all); simultaneously fobbed off with the cosmetic title EARL OF BUCHAN (never assumed by GEORGE and conferred to another person altogether a few years after); in consequence GEORGE took flight to England, where he was paid a paltry sum from Scottish sources till his death; *m* Beatrice — (*d* by 1421); possibly *m* 2nd *c* 7 Aug 1421 Alice, dau of Sir William Hay of Yester (*see* TWEEDDALE, M), though the marriage may never have occurred at all, and *d* 1455–57, leaving descendants in the male line, the DUNBARs of Kilconquhar (*see* SPENS, B), who died out 1564

2a JOHN de DUNBAR, 1st EARL OF MORAY (S), so *cr* 9 March 1371/2; fought at Otterburn 1388 (*see* above); *m c* 11 July 1370 Marjorie, dau of ROBERT II, and *d* by 15 Feb 1391/2 from injuries sustained in a tournament where he was unhorsed by the Earl Marshal of England, leaving, with other issue:

1b THOMAS de DUNBAR, 2nd EARL OF MORAY; Sheriff Inverness *vp*; captured by English Battle of Homildon Hill 1402, set free 1405, Sheriff Banff by late 1405; *m* by Feb 1391/2 Margaret — and *d* in or after spring 1415, leaving, with a dau (Janet, *m* Hugh Fraser, 8th of Lovat; *see* LOVAT, L):

1c THOMAS DUNBAR, 3rd EARL OF MORAY; allegedly *m* Margaret, dau of Sir William Seton of Seton or 1st Lord Seton (*see* EGLINTON and WINTON, E), and *dspl* presumably autumn 1427 or later

2c JAMES DUNBAR, 4th EARL OF MORAY; allegedly *m* Janet/Katherine, dau of Sir Alexander Seton of Gordon, and *dspml* or was *k c* 10 Aug 1429, having by her had issue (in addition, by a woman alleged to have been Isobel of Innes, an illegitimate s ALEXANDER, for whom *see* further below):

1d Janet; *m* 1442–46 James, 2nd Lord Crichton, *cr* Earl of Moray 12 June 1452 by the ceremony known as belting (*d* Aug 1454); *m* 2nd by 17 Jan 1458/9 John Sutherland and *d* between 18 March 1493/4 and 1505/6, having by him had:

1e Alexander

2d Elizabeth; *m* 1st between Aug 1434 and 26 April 1442 Archibald (yr twin s of 7th Earl of Douglas (*see* QUEENSBERRY, M), who took his seat in Parl as Earl of Moray 3 July 1445 in supposed right of his w but in reality by virtue of the overpowering ascendancy just then of the DOUGLASes; *m* 2nd by forced contract 20 May 1455 (*divorce* by 10 March 1459/60) 2nd Earl of Huntly (*qv*); *m* 3rd Sir John Colquhoun of Luss (*see* COLQUHOUN, Bt) and *d* just prior to 17 Feb 1485/6

The 4th EARL OF MORAY's illegitimate son,

Sir ALEXANDER DUNBAR of Westfield, Morayshire, of which had possession by 1450; inherited the lands of Carnoustie, Cluny and others from his f; Hereditary Sheriff Moray; *m* (contract 3 Jan 1451/52) Isobel, dau of Alexander Sutherland of Duffus (*see* DUNBAR OF HEMPRIGGS, Bt), and *d* 10 March 1497/8, having had, with other issue (including Margaret, *m* Robert Munro of Foulis; *see* MUNRO, Bt of Foulis-Obsdale):

1 James (Sir), of Westfield; Sheriff Moray; *m* 1474 Eupheme, est dau and coheir of Patrick Dunbar of Cumnock and Mochrum, descended from David Dunbar, yst bro of 9th EARL OF DUNBAR/(3rd Earl of) MARCH (*see* above); the last of this line, Ludovic Dunbar, sold the heritable Shrievalty of Elgin to the Earl of Moray 1744 and *dsp*; Sir James *d* 20 April 1504, leaving issue, including a dau (Christian, *m* 1493 Alexander Innes, 13th of that Ilk (*see* ROXBURGHE, D))

2 John (Sir), of Mochrum, Wigtownshire (*see* HOPE-DUNBAR, Bt); ggf of:

(1) John (Sir), of Mochrum; had, with a yr dau:

1a Grizel; *m* 1564 Alexander Dunbar of Conzie and Kilbuyack (*see* below)

3 ALEXANDER

4 Gavin; Dean Moray, Bp Aberdeen 1518–32; *d* 9 March 1531/2

The 3rd son,

ALEXANDER DUNBAR of Conzie and Kilbuyack; *m* Oct 1480 Janet, dau of 7th Earl of Sutherland (*qv*), and was murdered *c* 31 March 1493, leaving:

JAMES DUNBAR of Conzie, of which had charter, with Aldcash, 12 March 1508; *m* Ellen Innes and had:

ALEXANDER DUNBAR of Conzie and Kilbuyack; *m c* 1554 Elizabeth (*d* Dec 1570), dau of 6th Lord Forbes (*qv*) and widow of Alexander Innes, 14th of that Ilk (*see* ROXBURGH, D), and *d* 27 Feb 1578/9, leaving:

1 ALEXANDER

2 David, of Kinstairie

3 Patrick, of Eastergrange

4 Gavin; Archdeacon Moray

5 William; *see* DUNBAR, Bt, of Northfield

The est s,

ALEXANDER DUNBAR, Yr. of Conzie; *m* (contract dated 17 Nov 1564) Grizel, er dau and coheir of Sir John Dunbar of Mochrum (*see* above), thereby acquiring Mochrum, and *d* 1585, having had issue:

1 John (Sir), of Mochrum; had:

(1) Alexander, of Mochrum; had:

1a Alexander; *d* 1656

2 Alexander, of Pankill; *m* Nicola, dau of Sir Alexander Stewart of Garlies, and had:

(1) John, of Mochrum, which he inherited from his cousin Alexander; *m* Marjory, dau of Thomas Urquhart of Burdsyards, and *d* 1661, leaving:

1a Thomas, of Mochrum; *m* Christian, dau of Maj James Ross, of Balneil, and *d* 1675, leaving:

1b **Sir James Dunbar, 1st Bt** (NS), so *cr* 29 March 1694; had charter of the lands and territorial Barony of Mochrum 1 June 1677; *m* 1st 11 Feb 1679 Isabella, dau and coheir of Sir Thomas Nicolson, 2nd Bt (*see* CARNOCK, B), who brought him the Plean estate, Stirlingshire, and had, with other issue:

1c GEORGE (Sir), **2nd Bt**

2c John; Cornet Scots Dragoons; *ka* Teniers

1b (cont.) **Sir James** *m* 2nd Jane, dau of — Kennedy of Minuchen, and *d* 1718, having had further issue

His est son,

Sir George Dunbar, 2nd Bt; became chief of his family on death of Ludovic Dunbar of Westfield 14 April 1744; sold Mochrum and Pankill and bought Woodside, Stirlingshire; Capt Roy Scots Dragoons War of Spanish Succession; *m* Janet (*d* 18 May 1764), dau of Sir John Young of Lenie, and *d* Oct 1747, leaving, with other issue:

1 **Sir James Dunbar, 3rd Bt**; Judge-Advocate Scotland 1768; *m* 31 Oct 1760 Jacobina (*d* 29 Jan 1792), dau and coheir of John Hamilton of Newton, yr s of William Hamilton of Wishaw (*see* BELHAVEN AND STENTON, L), and *d* 16 April 1782, leaving, with other issue:

(1) **Sir George Dunbar, 4th Bt**; Lt-Col 14th Light Dragoons; *m* Maria (*d* 31 Aug 1808), dau of Rev Gustavus Hamilton, gs of 1st Viscount Boyne (*qv*), and *dspm* 15 Oct 1799, having had:

1a Helen; *m* William Coplard of Colliston and had issue (*see* below)

2 Thomas, of Liverpool; *m* 1748 Tryphena, dau of J Pincock, of London, and had:

(1) GEORGE (Sir), **5th Bt**

(2) Thomas; Army Capt

(3) William; Maj War American Independence; *m* —, dau of Count de Chambaud, Canada, and had issue

The 4th Bt's cousin,

Sir George Dunbar, 5th Bt; *m* 1775 Jane (*d* 28 Dec 1830), dau and coheir of William Rowe, of Liverpool, and *d* 10 Oct 1811, having had, with other issue:

1 **Sir William Rowe Dunbar, 6th Bt**; *b* 19 Oct 1776; Capt 21st Light Dragoons; *m* 24 Aug 1798 his cousin Jacobina Anne (*d* 1807), only child of William Copland of Colliston by Helen, dau of **Sir James Dunbar, 3rd Bt** (*see* above), and *d* 22 June 1841, having had:

(1) Helen; *d* 1808

2 James; *b* 20 June 1778; Offr 21st Light Dragoons; *m* 11 April 1811 Anna Catharina (*d* 3 Nov 1860), dau of William Ferdinand, Baron van Reede d'Oudtshoorn, of Holland, and *d* 31 Jan 1840, leaving, with other issue:

(1) **Sir William Dunbar, 7th Bt**, JP, DL Wigtownshire; *b* 2 March 1812; MP Wigtown Burghs 1857–65, a Ld of Treasury, Keeper PRINCE OF WALES's Privy Seal 1859–65, memb Cncl Duchy Cornwall 1863–65, Comptroller-Gen Roy Exchequer and Auditor-Gen 1867–88, Keeper Gt Seal of PRINCE OF WALES for Scotland 1863–65; *m* 7 Jan 1842 Catherine Hay (*d* 2 April 1890), est dau of James Paterson of Carpow, Perthshire, by Jane, only dau of John Balfour Hay of Leys and Randerston, and *d* 18 Dec 1889, having had issue:

1a **Sir Uthred James Hay Dunbar, 8th Bt**, JP, DL; *b* 26 Feb 1843; *educ* Exeter Coll Oxford (BA); barrister; *m* 20 April 1882 Lucy Blanche Cordelia, est dau of Charles Thomas Constantine Grant of Kilgraston and Pitkeathly, and *dsp* 4 Sept 1904

2a **Sir William Cospatrick Dunbar, 9th Bt**, CB, JP, DL Wigtownshire, JP Perthshire; *b* 20 July 1844; FRGS (Scot), FSS; Home Office 1868–1909, Priv Sec to Under-Secs State 1876–85, Assist Under-Sec for Scotland 1885–1902, Registrar-Gen for England 1902–09; *m* 30 July 1878 Nina Susannah (*d* 19 Jan 1943), est surv dau of Alfred Douglas-Hamilton (*see* HAMILTON and BRANDON, D), and *dsp* 6 Feb 1931

(2) James Cospatrick Alexander; *b* 8 Dec 1813; Capt 98th Regt; *d* India Aug 1847

(3) George van Reede; *b* 6 Sept 1825; *m* 21 Aug 1858 Louise Agnes, dau of Henry William Marriott, of Bayswater and Clarendon Lodge, Elstree, Herts, and *d* 11 March 1872, leaving issue:

1a **Sir James George Hawker Rowland Dunbar, 10th Bt**; *b* 6 Sept 1862; *d* unm 23 Jan 1953

1a Jessie Anne Pauline Louise; *b* 16 May 1859; *m* 27 Jan 1886 Col Walter Ferrier Graham, RA, of Priory Kennels, Oxton, Notts, and *d* 13 April 1918, leaving issue

2a Anna; *b* and *d* 1860

3a Louise Clementina Jane; *b* 7 May 1861; *m* 26 June 1889 Rev Reginald Moseley, MA (*d* 18 April 1937), Vicar St Bartholomews-the-Less 1918–23, CF 1889–1918, and *d* 5 Jan 1940

4a Mary Vanderzee Sophia; *b* 27 June 1864

(4) Thomas Clement; *b* 6 Sept 1825; Lt-Col 75th Regt; *m* 24 July 1849 Caroline Adriana (*d* 1911), dau of Albert Matthews, of Bengal, and *d* 1896, leaving issue:

1a Richard Taylor; *b* 14 July 1855; *m* 1st 28 Jan 1873 Helen (*d* 2 June 1910), dau of Joseph Maas, and had issue:

1b **Sir Richard Sutherland Dunbar, 11th Bt**; *b* 7 June 1873; *m* 15 June 1911 Daisy, dau of John Kinman, of Anerley, and *d* 25 Jan 1953, having had issue:

1c *Joyce Marguerite; *b* 1 June 1912

2c *Vida Mary [Miss Vida Dunbar, 69 Grandison Rd, London SW11]; *b* 16 April 1916

1b Helen Gertrude Edith; *b* 30 June 1875; *d* unm 19 Dec 1960

2b Hilda Catherine; *b* 24 Sept 1876; *d* unm 20 Jan 1963

1a (cont.) Richard Taylor *m* 2nd in two ceremonies 11 March 1890 (to which legal objections were raised) and 5 Feb 1912 Grace Mary (*d* 23 Jan 1935), dau of William Stanton, Clerk of the Pilots; *m* 3rd 20 Feb 1935 Emma, widow of George Hollis Beetles, 7th Dragoon Gds, and *d* 1940, having by his 2nd w had issue:

2b William Henry George, of Kilconzie, OBE, TD; *b* 10 June 1893; legitimated with yr bro under Legitimation (Scotland) Act 1968, including as regards remainder to btcy, though claimed it unsuccessfully 1984; author: *Dunbars' 1000 Years*; Hon Lt-Col RA WWs I and II, raised TA Battery 1920 and HG Bn 1952; branch manager Nat Prov Bank, Assist Treas and Treas Southwark Diocesan Appeal; *m* 1st 17 Jan 1917 Stella Kathleen (*k* by enemy action 20 March 1941), dau of Henry Underdown, of Dover, and had issue:

1c *Graham William [Graham Dunbar Esq, Gibbs Close, Cheshunt, Herts]; *b* 2 March 1920; *m* 15 Oct 1955 *Alice Louise, dau of Joseph Lollee, of Stolzenberg, Uzwill, St Gall, Switzerland, and has issue:

1d *Andrew William [Andrew Dunbar Yr. of Kilconzie, Doorfstrasse 19, 4222 Zwingen, Basel, Switzerland]; *b* 18 Feb 1961; BSc

1d *Janet Marjorie [Miss Janet Dunbar, Moosmühle Strasse 20, 9112 Schachen, Herisau, Switzerland]; *b* 27 Feb 1964

1c Audrey Jean, AIMSW; *b* 23 Nov 1921; *d* unm 13 April 1976

2b (cont.) William Dunbar of Kilconzie *m* 2nd 25 Oct 1941 Joan Marguerite (*d* 23 June 1966), dau of Capt Sydney Church Leopard, TD, RAMC, of Easebourne, W Sussex; *m* 3rd 23 Sept 1967 *Irene Mary [Mrs Dunbar of Kilconzie, Greenways, Oxenden Sq, Herne Bay, Kent CT6 8TW], dau of Charles Edwin Frith, of Weeley, Essex, and widow of Harold Campbell Bromley, of Aden, and *d* 1987

3b Richard John Victor Michael; *b* 19 June 1897; served WW I (twice wounded); Fell Roy Cwlth Soc; *m* 24 Sept 1932 *Daffodil Helen [Mrs Richard Dunbar, 30 Kennet Court, Woosehill, Wokingham RG11 9DB], only dau of Rev Eardley Wilmot Michell, MA, Vicar Bolney, Sussex, and *d* 1983, leaving issue:

1c *Gavin Cospatrick Michell, RD [Cdr Gavin Dunbar RD RNR, Summer Place, London Drive, Wargrave, Berks RG10 8HH]; *b* 14 Feb 1936; *educ* St Catharine's Coll Cambridge (MA); *m* 3 Dec 1960 *Jean, only dau of Dr Roy Kemball Price, of Hove, Sussex, and has issue:

1d *Emma Claire; *b* 25 Nov 1961; *m* 1988 *James Harrison and has:

1e *Henry Douglas; *b* 3 July 1995

2d *Katrina Michelle; *b* 24 Oct 1964

3d *Lisa Carol; *b* 16 Dec 1966; *m* 1996 *Andrew Hosie

2c *David Randolph Michell [David Dunbar Esq, The Hermitage, 193 Lower Rd, Gt Bookham, Surrey]; *b* 31 Oct 1938; FCA; *m* 3 April 1965 *Brenda, yr dau of Maurice W Mitchell, of Ashtead, Surrey, and has issue:

1d *James Stuart Michell; *b* 25 May 1967

2d *Struan Gordon David; *b* 1970

3b Grace Maud Harriet; *b* 19 Oct 1891; BD (Lond)

2a Clement Adrian; *b* 20 March 1871; *m* 1890 Emily (*d* 1946), dau of Thomas Morgan, MRCS, and *d* 1940, leaving issue:

1b Thomas Clement; *b* May 1892; *dsp* 5 Aug 1922

2b ADRIAN IVOR (Sir), **12th Bt**

3b Frederick Ernest; *b* 1896; *m* — and *dsp* Australia 24 Sept 1955

4b William Uthred; *b* 1902; *m* 1924 Theresa Rose Della, dau of Jerome Cole, and had issue:

1c +William Thomas; *b* 1925

5b David Allan; *b* 1905; *d* 1988

1b Minnie Emily; *b* 1891; *m* 1910 Thomas Harvey, and had issue

2b Dorothy Joan; *b* 1894; *m* 1918 Alan Ashleigh, of Toronto, Canada, and had issue

3b May Hilda

1a Matilda; *m* 12 May 1874 Harry Pitt Napier Kennedy

2a Frances Ellen; *b* 16 Jan 1865; *d* unm 1897

The 11th Bt's cousin,

Sir Adrian Ivor Dunbar, 12th Bt; *b* 11 June 1893; WW I with AIF; *m* 1st 25 Sept 1917 Emma Marie (*d* 1 Sept 1925), dau of Jean Witvrongel, and had issue:

1 JEAN IVOR (Sir), **13th Bt**

Sir Adrian *m* 2nd 25 June 1930 Esther Naomi, dau of William Henry Robinson, and *d* 1977, having by her had issue:

2 +Rowland Adrian [Rowland Dunbar Esq, 1 Sandhurst Ave, Cullercoats, Tyne and Wear]; *b* 14 July 1934; US Med Corps (ret); *m* 14 Dec 1957 *Janet Lockhart, dau of George Heron, of Newton Stewart, Wigtownshire, and has issue:

(1) *Mary Naomi; *b* 12 Oct 1958; *m* 1983 (*divorce* 19–) Edward Thomas Lisle and has:

1a *Scott; *b* 1988

1a *Sarah Elizabeth; *b* 1985

2a *Joanna Marie; *b* 1986

(2) *Sylvia Katherine; *b* 10 June 1960; *m* 1984 *Derek Graham, and has issue:

1a *Ross Christopher; *b* 1985

2a *David Adrian; *b* 1989

1a *Laura Marie; *b* 1987

(3) *Shonna Janet; *b* 26 Feb 1962; *m* 1996 *Christopher Bowler and has:

1a *Daniel; *b* ;1992

3 +Donald Robert [Donald Dunbar Esq, 10 The Avenue, Brookville, Thetford, Norfolk]; *b* 24 July 1936; Sr Master/Sgt USAF, formerly US Med Corps; *m* 1st 27 July 1957 (*divorce* 1962) Marie Fowler, dau of Douglas Allan, of Newton Stewart, Wigtownshire, and has issue:

(1) +Allan William; *b* 6 May 1958

(1) *Roseanne; *b* 12 Dec 1960; *m* 15 Feb 1985 *William Graham McKie and has:

1a *Craig

2a *Allan (twin)

3 (cont.) Donald Dunbar *m* 2nd 5 Jan 1963 (*divorce* Oct 1987) Susan Elizabeth May, dau of William Radden Gates, of Newbury, Berks, and by her has:

(2) +David Wayne; *b* 24 Jan 1966

(2) *Linda Carol; *b* 28 March 1969; *m* 28 Aug 1993 *Mark — and has:

1a *Joseph William; *b* 26 Oct 1995

3 (cont.) Donald Dunbar *m* 3rd 29 Aug 1992 *Maureen Elizabeth, dau of Victor Spenser Watling

Sir ADRIAN's est son,

Sir Jean Ivor Dunbar, 13th Bt; *b* 4 April 1918; Sgt Mountain Engrs US Army; *m* 1st 1944 (*divorce* 1979) Rose Jeanne, dau of Henry William Hertsch; *m* 2nd 1987 (*divorce* 1988) Mrs Vivianna Patricia Arrow de Blonville, dau of Ernest Bloomfield and formerly w of (a) Francesco Enea and (b) Herman Arrow, and *d* 1993, having by his 1st w had:

1 Sir JAMES MICHAEL DUNBAR, **14th and present Bt**

2 +Dennis William; *b* 16 May 1952

1 *Anne Marie; *b* 12 Sept 1946; *m* 19– — Bickauskas

DUNBAR of Northfield

Arms: Quarterly, 1st and 4th, gu. a lion rampant arg. within a bordure of the last charged with eight roses of the field (for DUNBAR); 2nd and 3rd, or three cushions within the royal tressure gu. (for RANDOLPH); all within a bordure quartered az. and of the first. **Crest:** A dexter hand appaumée reaching at an astral crown ppr. **Motto:** *Spem vigilantia firmat* ('Vigilance strengthens hope'). **Creation:** Bt. (NS) 10 April 1700.

SIR ARCHIBALD RANULPH DUNBAR, 11TH BT, of Northfield [Sir Archibald Dunbar Bt, The Old Manse, Duffus, Elgin IV30 2QD]; *b* 8 Aug 1927; *s* f 1969; *educ* Wellington, Pembroke Coll Cambridge and Imp Coll Tropical Ag Trinidad; 2nd Lt Gordon Highrs RARO 1945–48, Colonial Serv 1953–70 (Ag Offr Uganda CS); Hon Sheriff, Sheriff Court Dist Moray 1989–, Kt Honour and Devotion SMO Malta 1989; author: *A History of Bunyoro-Kitara* (1965), *Omukama Chwa II Kabarega* (1965), *The Annual Crops of Uganda* (1969); *m* 1974 *Amelia Millar Sommerville, dau of Horace Campbell Davidson, of Currie, Midlothian, and has issue:

1 +EDWARD HORACE, Yr. of Northfield; *b* 18 March 1977

1 *Harriet Sophie; *b* 27 Sept 1974

2 *Stephanie Clare; *b* 19 Sept 1975

Lineage: WILLIAM DUNBAR (s of Alexander Dunbar, Yr. of Conzie (*dvp*), and gs of Alexander Dunbar of Conzie and Kilbuyack (*see* DUNBAR, Bt, of Mochrum) by Elizabeth, dau of 6th Lord Forbes, *qv*), 1st of Hempriggs, Caithness, of which had charter 30 March 1576; *m* Margaret Anderson and had:

JOHN DUNBAR, 2nd of Hempriggs; served heir to his f 30 Oct 1636; had:

1 John, 3rd of Hempriggs; *m* Anne, dau of Andrew Fraser, Commissary of Inverness, and *d c* 3 April 1666, having had, with other issue:

(1) **Sir William Dunbar, 1st Bt** (NS), so *cr* 10 April 1700, with remainder to heirs male, of Hempriggs; MP Caithness 1678; *m* Margaret, dau of Alexander Sinclair of Lathron, and *dspms* 1711, having had:

1a Benjamin; *m* Janet (*m* 2nd 3rd Lord Reay, *qv*), dau of John Sinclair of Ulbster (*see* THURSO, V) and *dsp & vp*

1a Elizabeth; *m* 1st Sir Robert Gordon, 3rd Bt, of Gordonstoun (*d* 1701); *m* 2nd *c* 1704 Hon James Sutherland (*d c* 1739), 2nd son of 2nd Lord Duffus (*see* DUNBAR OF HEMPRIGGS, Bt)

(2) **Sir Robert Dunbar, 2nd Bt**, of Northfield; *m* 1675 Mary, dau of Patrick Sinclair of Ulbster, and *d* 1742, leaving issue:

1a **Sir Patrick Dunbar, 3rd Bt**, of Northfield; *b c* 1676; MP Caithness 1727–34; *m* 1st —, dau of William Sinclair of Dunbeath; *m* 2nd 1722 Catherine, dau of Joseph Brodie of Mentoun, and *dspms* 5 April 1763, when the btcy became dormant till 1776, having had:

1b John; *b c* 1726; *dvp* unm April 1749

2 James (?); *b* 25 May 16–; had:

(1) Archibald, of Newton and Thunderton; *m* 1st 12 May 1666 Elizabeth (*d* 27 July 1678), dau and coheir of Walter Hacket, of Mayen (by Janet, er dau of George Leslie, of Burdsbank); *m* 2nd 28 April 1681 Katherine (*d* 4 Feb 1686), dau of Sir Walter Innes, 2nd Bt, of Balveny (*qv*), and *d* 3 May 1689, leaving by his 1st w:

1a Robert, of Newton and Thunderton; *b* Feb 1670; *m* 27 Nov 1690 Margaret, only dau of Colin Mackenzie of Pluscarden, and *d* Sept 1742, leaving, with other issue:

1b ARCHIBALD (Sir), **4th Bt**

2b William; Capt 43rd Regt; *d* March 1783

2a Archibald, of Thunderton; *b* 1671; Sheriff Moray, Provost Elgin; *m* 1st Aug 1703 Rebecca, only dau of Rev James Adamson and widow of Robert Mackenzie, WS, and had two daus; *m* 2nd Phillis Walker and *dspm* 16 April 1733

Sir PATRICK's cousin,

ARCHIBALD DUNBAR, *de jure* 4th Bt, of Northfield, though he neither assume nor claimed the title, of Newton, Thunderton and Duffus, Elginshire; *b* 15 Dec 1693; served heir male 1776 and directed by Lord Lyon to continue designation of Northfield; *m* 1st 1735 his cousin Helen (*d* 10 April 1748), dau of Archibald Dunbar of Thunderton, and had, with other issue:

1 ALEXANDER (Sir), **5th Bt**

ARCHIBALD DUNBAR *m* 2nd 1750 Anne Bayne (*d* 26 Nov 1780) and *d* 13 Jan 1769, leaving further issue:

2 William; *m* and left descendants in America

3 Thomas, Maj-Gen; *dsp* 20 Dec 1815

The *de jure* 4th Bt's est surv son,

Sir Alexander Dunbar, 5th Bt (as which served heir male to the 3rd Bt 8 Oct 1776), of Northfield; *b* 12 Jan 1742; advocate; *m* 21 April 1769 Hon Margaret Arbuthnott (*d* 8 June 1801), dau of 6th Viscount of Arbuthnott (*qv*), and *d* 20 Dec 1791, leaving issue:

1 ARCHIBALD (Sir), **6th Bt**

2 John; Lt 78th Highrs, Capt 6th Dragoon Gds; *d* unm 1812

1 Jean; *m* 1792 James Coull, of Ashgrove, Elginshire, and *d* 1857, leaving issue

Sir ALEXANDER's er son,

Sir Archibald Dunbar, 6th Bt, of Northfield, JP, DL; *b* 30 June 1772; Convenor Elginshire 1813–47, Lt-Col Elginshire Militia; *m* 1st 6 Nov 1794 Helen (*d* 16 March 1819), dau of Col Sir Alexander Penrose Cumming-Gordon, 1st Bt (*see* GORDON-CUMMING, Bt), and had, with other issue:

1 **Sir Archibald Dunbar, 7th Bt**, of Northfield, JP, DL; *b* 5 July 1803; Convenor Morayshire 1847–88, Lt 22nd Cheshire Regt; *m* 1st 12 June 1827 Keith Alicia (*d* 15 March 1836), dau of George Ramsay, of Barnton, Midlothian, by Hon Jean Hamilton, sis of 7th Lord Belhaven and Stenton (*qv*), and *d* 7 Jan 1898, having had, with other issue:

(1) **Sir Archibald Hamilton, 8th Bt**, JP, DL Elgin; *b* 5 April 1828; Capt 66th Berks Regt; *m* 1st 15 July 1865 Isabella Mary (*d* 17 June 1931), er dau of Charles EYRE formerly ARCHER-HOUBLON, of Welford Park, Berks, and *dsp* 6 June 1910

(2) George Ramsay; *b* 24 Nov 1831; *educ* Winchester and New Coll Oxford (Fell); advocate Edinburgh; *d* unm 30 April 1862

1 (cont.) **Sir Archibald** *m* 2nd 5 Nov 1840 Sophia (*d* 2 June 1909), dau of George Orred, of Tranmere Hall, Cheshire, and by her had issue:

(3) Randolph John Edward; *d* unm 1862

(4) **Sir Charles Gordon-Cumming Dunbar, 9th Bt**, of Northfield; *b* 14 Feb 1844; *educ* Winchester; DD Jena U, Chaplain to Bp Claughton 1867–75, Archdeacon Grenada 1875–77, Incumbent St James, Little Heath, Essex 1887–90; *m* 17 Oct 1872 Edith (*d* Jan 1891), yst dau of William Charles Wentworth, Pres Legislative Cncl, Sydney, and *d* 8 Jan 1916, leaving issue:

1a Beatrix Leyla Marjorie Wentworth; *m* 2 Oct 1897 John Spencer Ward, of Boreham Wood, Herts, 3rd s of John Francis Ward and gs of Dean of Lincoln, and *d* 8 Jan 1919, leaving issue

(5) William James Colquhoun; *b* 14 Jan 1850; Dep Conservator Forests Bombay; *m* 1883 Dora (*d* 1940), est dau of William Jennings, and *dsp* 4 Nov 1885

2 John; *b* 14 March 1805; Bengal CS; *m* 20 Dec 1825 Anna Sophia (*d* 17 May 1863), dau of Rev G Hagar, and *d* 1 Nov 1856, having had issue:

(1) Penrose John; *b* 2 Sept 1827; Maj The Buffs; *m* 1st 25 Sept 1858 Elizabeth Ann Clarinda (*dsp* 17 Jan 1867), dau of W W Sleigh, MD; *m* 2nd Emma (*d* 13 Dec 1917), dau of Charles Beddis, and *dsp* 14 April 1903

(2) Lennox Archibald; *b* 1830; *d* 1832

(3) Rothes Lennox; *b* 24 Oct 1834; Capt 42nd Highrs; *d* unm 1 Feb 1857

(4) Arbuthnott Pery Byng Sutherland; *b* 18 Nov 1847; Lt-Col 3rd Bn Gordon Highrs; *m* 16 April 1873 Catharina Hester (*d* 26 July 1915), dau of John Orred, of Ashwicke, Glos, and *d* 1 March 1890, having had issue:

1a Arbuthnott John; *b* 6 Sept 1885; Capt RFA; *ka* 17 March 1915

2a (ARCHIBALD) EDWARD (Sir), **10th Bt**

1a Catharina Agnes Sophie; *d* unm 11 June 1955

2a Ianthe Margaret; *m* 9 Jan 1902 Sandbach Percy Harrison (*dsp* 1910), and *d* 24 July 1938

3a Ethel Gordon; *d* unm 29 Dec 1929

4a Aileen Edith; *m* 27 April 1909 Robert Cecil Hunter (*d* 6 Nov 1921), est s of Robert Lewin Hunter, and *d* 15 April 1952, leaving issue

5a Hilda; *d* an infant

6a Marjorie Isabel; *d* unm 15 Sept 1941

7a Lilias; *m* 26 Oct 1921 Lt-Col Eustace Clementi Smith (*d* 26 Dec 1954), IA, yr s of Sir Cecil Clementi Smith, GCMG, PC

8a Helen Penuel; *m* 6 Sept 1911 Lt-Col Gerald Ponsonby Sneyd Hunt, CMG, DSO, Roy Berks Regt (*ka* 23 March 1918), and had issue
(1) Aileen Sophia; *b* 1828; *d* 1829
(2) Ianthe Aileen Bowes Lyon; *b* 1838; *d* 1840
3 Edward DUNBAR later DUNBAR-DUNBAR (roy licence24 Nov 1848), of Sea Park, nr Forres in Moray, and Glen of Rothes, nr Elgin in Moray, JP, DL Elgin; *b* 23 Aug 1818; Capt 21st/22nd Regts; *m* 17 Oct 1848 Phoebe (*d* 9 May 1899), sis and heir of John Dunbar, of Sea Park, and *d* 10 Jan 1898, having had, with other issue:
(1) John Archibald (Rev), of Sea Park and Kinloss, Forres, JP Elgin; *b* 8 Oct 1849; *educ* Oxford (MA); *m* 5 Nov 1875 Louisa (*d* 21 May 1934), 2nd dau of Thomas Cambray, of Oxford, and *dsp* 11 Nov 1905

Sir Archibald *m* 2nd 26 Sept 1822 Mary (*d* 5 May 1869), sis and heir of Lt-Col Brander, of Pitgaveny, Elgin, and *d* 23 March 1847, and by her had further issue:
4 James Brander DUNBAR later DUNBAR-BRANDER (roy licence 1869), of Pitgaveny, JP, DL Elgin; *b* 6 Jan 1825; Capt Scots Greys, Lt Madras Cavalry; *m* 22 Dec 1874 Alice (*d* 6 Dec 1936), dau of James Grant, Provost Elgin, and *d* 16 Nov 1902, leaving issue:
(1) James Brander DUNBAR-BRANDER later DUNBAR, of Pitgaveny, DL Elgin; *b* 10 Oct 1875; Superior Burgh of Lossiemouth, Capt Res of Offrs, QO Cameron Highrs, Br Centl Africa 1900 (medal with clasp), Boer War (despatches twice, medal with clasp), Sudan 1903–04, WW I with W African Forces Sierra Leone; *m* 8 Feb 1922 Noela (*d* 20 Aug 1975) dau of Matthew Noel Whiting, and *d* 25 Dec 1969, leaving issue:
1a Juliette; *b* 5 Jan 1923; *m* 9 Dec 1957 *Herbert Lawrence Miller, of S Lynstone, Bude, Cornwall, and *d* Dec 1987, leaving:
1b *Loveday; *b* 8 Sept 1958
2a Una; *d* 16 Nov 1987
(2) Archibald Alexander, OBE (1918); *b* 23 April 1877; Imp Forest Serv, FRGS, FZS; *m* 1st 1 Nov 1902 Elizabeth (*dsp* 22 May 1903), dau of Francis Edward Thompson; *m* 2nd 22 Sept 1919 Frances Emily (*d* 10 April 1954), widow of George Rowell, FRCS, and *d* 31 March 1953
1 Margaret Alice; *m* 7 Feb 1856 William A Stables (*d* 1890), banker, of Nairn, and *d* 23 July 1908, leaving issue

Sir CHARLES's cousin,
Sir (Archibald) Edward Dunbar, 10th Bt, MC (1916); *b* 17 Feb 1889; *educ* Wellington and Pembroke Coll Cambridge; Maj W Yorks Regt WW I (despatches); *m* 10 April 1926 Olivia Douglas Sinclair (*d* 26 Aug 1964), 5th dau of Maj-Gen Sir Edward Sinclair May, KCB, CMG, RA, of Devon, and *d* 15 June 1969, leaving:
1 Sir ARCHIBALD RANULPH DUNBAR, **11th and present Bt**
2 +Alexander Arbuthnott [Alexander Dunbar Esq, Pitgaveny, Elgin, Moray IV30 2PQ]; *b* 14 March 1929; *educ* Wellington and Pembroke Coll Cambridge; barrister Inner Temple 1953; *m* 16 Jan 1965 *Elizabeth Susannah, dau of Rev Edward Denzil Chetwode Wright, of Brattleby, Lincs, by Diana Blanche, 2nd dau of Maj Frederick Strickland (*see* STRICKLAND-CONSTABLE, Bt), and has:
(1) +Crinan James; *b* 6 Nov 1965
(1) *Clodagh Rebecca Helen; *b* 1 Nov 1968

DUNBOYNE

Arms: Or, a chief indented az, three escallops in bend counterchanged. **Crest:** Out of a ducal coronet or a plume of five ostrich feathers, therefrom a demi-falcon rising arg. **Supporters:** Dexter, a lion guardant arg.; sinister, a horse sa., mane, tail and hoofs or. **Motto:** *Timor Domini fons vitæ ('The fear of the Lord is the fountain of life').* **Creation:** B. (I) (by prescription) 1324, (by patent) 11 June 1541.

THE 18TH/28TH BARON DUNBOYNE, Co Meath (Patrick Theobald Tower Butler, VRD (1987)) [His Honour The Lord Dunboyne VRD, 36 Ormonde Gate, London SW3 4HA; The Flat, West Ilkerton Farm, Lynton, Devon EX35 6QA]; *b* 27 Jan 1917; *s* f 1945; *educ* Winchester and Trin Coll Cambridge (Pres Union 1939, BA 1938, MA 1947); barrister Middle Temple 1949 (Harmsworth Scholar), Inner Temple 1962 and King's Inn Dublin, 1966, Western Circuit 1949–51, SE Circuit 1951–71, Commissary-Gen Canterbury Diocese 1959–71, Recorder Hastings 1961–71, Dep Chm QS: Kent 1963–71, Middx 1963–65, Inner London 1971, Circuit Judge Inner London 1972–86, 2nd Lt (SR) Irish Gds 1939, Lt 1940–44 (POW, repatriated 1943, King's Badge), Lt RNVR 1958–60, Refugee Dept FO 1945–46, Pres Wireless Telegram Appeal Tbnl England and Wales 1967–70, Home Sec's Commr ward-boundaries 1960–70, author: *The Trial of J G Haigh* (1953), *Cambridge Union 1815–1939* (co-author 1953) and *Butler Family History* (1966), Pres Irish Genealogical Research Soc 1971–91 (Fellow), fndr-sec Bar Lawn Tennis Soc 1952–62 (v-pres 1963–) and Irish Peers Assoc 1963–71 (pres 1988–91), Pres: Internat Lawn Tennis Club of GB 1973–83 and Forty Five Club; *m* 29 July 1950 *Anne Marie, only dau of Sir Victor Alexander Louis Mallet, GCMG, CVO (*see* also BEAVERBROOK, B), of Wittersham House, Wittersham, Kent, and has issue:
1 +JOHN FitzWALTER [The Hon John Butler, Argos Hill House, Rotherfield, E Sussex TN6 3QG]; *b* 31 July 1951; *educ* Winchester and Trin Coll Cambridge (BA 1973, MA 1977); Sloan Fell London Business Sch 1979; *m* 26 April 1975 *(Diana) Caroline, yr dau of Sir Michael Sanigear Williams, KCMG, of Wentways, Waldron, Sussex, and has issue:
(1) +Richard Pierce Theobald; *b* 5 July 1983
(1) *Genevieve Synolda; *b* 7 Aug 1977
(2) *Imogen Katharine; *b* 7 July 1979
(3) *Cleone Isolde; *b* 15 July 1986
1 *Mary Synolda [The Hon Mrs Walton, 26 Paradise Walk, London SW3 4JL]; *b* 29 April 1954; *educ* Benenden and Girton Coll Cambridge (BA 1975, MA 1979); admitted to Inner Temple 1974, slr Supreme Court 1980; *m* 1984 *Alastair Henry Walton, only s of Sir Raymond Henry Walton, and has issue:
(1) *Alexandra Mary; *b* 1985
(2) *Christina Frances; *b* 1986
(3) *Stephanie Katharine; *b* 1988
(4) *Florence Lucy; *b* 1992
2 *Betty Quenelda [The Hon Mrs Perks, 4 Broomwood Road, London SW11 6HT]; *b* 23 June 1956; *educ* Benenden and Girton Coll Cambridge (BA 1978, MA 1983, PGCE Cantab); *m* 1985 *Edward Roland Haslewood Perks, yr s of His Honour Clifford Perks, MC, TD, FSA, and has issue:
(1) *Lawrence Patrick Haslewood; *b* 1989
(1) *Candida Anne Quenelda; *b* 1986
(2) *Sophie Maria Katherine; *b* 1994
3 *Victoria Morina [The Hon Mrs Eveleigh, West Ilkerton Farm, Lynton, Devon EX35 6QA]; *b* 19 Dec 1959; *educ* Benenden, St Andrews (BSc 1982) and Wye Ag Coll London U (MSc 1983); *m* 1986 *Christopher J P Eveleigh, est s of John Eveleigh, of Croyde, N Devon, and has issue:
(1) *George Jethro; *b* 1987
(1) *Sarah Victoria; *b* 1990

Lordship of Dunboyne: About 1192 William le Petyt or Petit, 1st feudal Lord of Dunboyne and Moymet, *s* Hugh de Lacy, Earl of Hereford, as Ld Justice of Ireland and was granted extensive lands in Cos Westmeath and Meath. Around 1207 he was called to an assembly and in 1239 Nicholas le Petit, 3rd Lord of Dunboyne and Molyngar (Mullingar), was summoned to attend HENRY III with 22 other of the great Barons of Ireland. These occasions cannot be regarded as Parliaments, however.
The Earls of Verulam (*qv*) hold a subsidiary Barony of Dunboyne, granted 1719 at a time when the Butler-held title was thought to be extinct.

Lineage: THEOBALD BUTLER or Le BOTILLER; *b c* 1242 (*see* MOUNTGARRET, V); *m* by 1268 Joan, dau of John Fitz Geoffrey, and *d* 26 Sept 1285, leaving issue a 3rd s:
Sir THOMAS BUTLER or Le BOTILLER, **1st Baron of Dunboyne**; called to the I Parl 1324 (as were intermittently his descendants in the succeeding two centuries before the creation of the Barony of Dunboyne as a lordship of Parl by patent 1541), whereby what in England might have been regarded as a feudal lordship became in some sense a lordship of Parl by prescription or repeated treatment as grounds for a summons to Parl; *m* Synolda le Petit (*m* 2nd Richard de Lacy, *m* 3rd Sir William FitzGerald and *d c* 1346), Lady of Dunboyne and Molyngar, only child and heiress of William le Petit, 6th Lord of Dunboyne and Molyngar (*see* above), through whom those lordships came to the Butler family and was *k* by the MACGHEOGHAN, at the Battle of Ardnurcher 9 Oct 1329, leaving:
PETER/PIERS BUTLER, **2nd Baron of Dunboyne**; called to Parl 1366; *m* by 1353 Katherine, dau of John de Bermingham, Lord of Kiltenian, and *d* 5 Aug 1370 leaving:
1 THOMAS *MacPiarais* ([*i.e.*, 'Pierson'] so-called in Irish, as had been his f before him and as his successors continued to be) BUTLER, **3rd Baron of Dunboyne**; *b* 1354; *dsp* by 7 Nov 1370
2 Nicholas; *dsp*
3 Richard; *dsp*
4 WILLIAM Le BOTILLER/BUTLER, **4th Baron of Dunboyne**; Seneschal Tipperary 1383–1405; *m* Elizabeth Plunket and *d* 1406, leaving:
(1) PIERS BUTLER, **5th Baron of Dunboyne**; *dsp* 28 Nov 1415
(2) EDMOND BUTLER, **6th Baron of Dunboyne**; *dsp* 1419
(3) JAMES, **7th Baron**
(4) John, of Ardmayle; Seneschal liberty of Tipperary 1429–34; *k* 1434 by Teig O'Shee, leaving:
1a Thomas fitz John, of Ardmayle; *d* after 1464, being probable ancestor of the BUTLERs of Ardmayle, sometimes styled feudal Barons of Ardmayle, and of Oughteragh, Co Tipperary
The 3rd s,
JAMES BUTLER, **7th Baron of Dunboyne**; Keeper Peace Co Tipperary 1425; *m* Mór Marina, dau of Donnchadh O'Brien, and d 1445, leaving:
1 EDMOND, **8th Baron**
2 William; unjustly (as he admitted to a priest in confession before battle) appropriated the Manors of Dunboyne and Moymet, Co Meath, from his er bro; *m* (divorce) Margaret, dau of 1st Baron Delvin (see WESTMEATH, E), and was k 1457 or 1458 while invading the Pale as part of a pro-Lancastrian operation in concert with O'Connor of Offaly, and was attainted, leaving issue
3 John; ancestor of the BUTLERs of Cabragh, Co Tipperary

4 Richard; ancestor of the BUTLERs of Ballykirren, Co Tipperary
5 Thomas; dsp by 1453
6 Theobald; ancestor of the BUTLERs of Brittas, Co Tipperary
The est s,

EDMOND BUTLER, **8th Baron of Dunboyne**; acquired the castle and feudal Barony of Kiltinan from his cousin Edmond fitz Thomas Butler 1452; entailed Manor of Drangan and other lands on his bros and cousin 1453; Seneschal liberty of Tipperary by 1457, being granted the office as a hereditary post by the 6th Earl of Ormonde (*see* MOUNTGARRET, V) 1462; attainted 1460 as part of the feuding arising from the Wars of the Roses but restored by the 1472 Parl; *m* Catherine, dau of Sir Edmond 'MacRichard' Butler (*see* MOUNTGARRET, V), and *d* 1498, leaving:
1 JAMES, **9th Baron**
2 William; Rector Kilbride, Co Meath; *d* 7 April 1499
3 Thomas; ancestor of the BUTLERs of Ballynard
4 Piers, of Knockakelly; *k* 1502 by James Tobin, leaving:
(1) Piers *Og* ('The Younger'), of Knockakelly; had:
1a Theobald; living 1575
1 Alice; *m* Christopher Barnewall (*see* BARNEWALL, Bt) and *d* 1501
The est s,

JAMES BUTLER, **9th Baron of Dunboyne**; *m* 1st (*divorce*) Eleanor Taaffe, of Braganstown, Co Louth; *m* 2nd Catherine, dau of McCarthy Reagh, feudal Ld of Carbery, Co Cork, and *d* 1508, leaving by her:
1 JAMES, **10th Baron**
2 John, of Derryluskan, Co Tipperary; *m* Ellen (*m* 2nd Sir Maurice FitzGerald, of Dromona, 1st and last Viscount Decies; *see* DECIES, B, preliminary remarks), dau of Sir John FitzGerald, who assumed the Earldom of Desmond on the death of his bro the 12th Earl of the 1329 *cr* (*see* DENBIGH and DESMOND, E, preliminary remarks), and *d* after 1535, leaving:
(1) Theobald *na Sidheáin* ('of the fairy-mound'), of Derryluskan; *m* 1st Catherine, widow of John Butler (by whom she was mother of 11th Earl of Ormonde; *see* MOUNTGARRET, V) and dau of Corma MacCartie, The MacCartie Reagh; *m* 2nd Catherine Bourke, widow of the native Irish leader James fitz Maurice FitzGerald, and had by his 1st w:
1a James, of Derryluskan; *m* Margaret, dau of 3rd Baron Le Power and Coroghmore (*see* WATERFORD, M), and *d* 1602
(2) Edmond, of Rathbrit; *d* by 1600, leaving issue
(1) Eleanor; *m* Gerrot FitzGerald, of Ballyheny, Co Waterford, bro of her stepf, and was mother of Sir John FitzGerald, of Dromana
The er s,

JAMES BUTLER, **10th Baron of Dunboyne**; *m* by 6 May 1519 Joan, dau of 8th Earl of Ormonde (*see* MOUNTGARRET, V), and *d* 28 Jan 1533/4, leaving:
1 EDMOND, **11th/1st Baron**
2 Peter or Pierce (known as *Pierce na Bulle* or 'Wild Peter'), of Grallagh, Co Tipperary, *m* 1st Elinor, dau of Oliver Grace; *m* 2nd Lady Honora FitzGerald, dau of 10th Earl of Desmond (*see* DENBIGH and DESMOND, E, preliminary remarks), and *d* 11 Jan 1571, being by her ancestor of the BUTLERs of Doon, Bunnahow, Walterstown and Ballyline, Co Clare, and leaving issue:
(1) James; gggf of:
1a James, of Doone, Co Clare; had:
1b James; *d* 1746; gggf of:
1c James Blake, JP; had a 6th son:
1d Theobald FitzWalter, JP, DL; had issue:
1e Theobald Blake; *b* 1888; *m* 1st 1921 (*divorce* 1930) Mary Gammell Stewart (*m* 2nd 1931, as his 2nd w, Norman Roy Fox-Andrews, QC), dau of William Smytton Davidson; *m* 2nd 1933 (*divorce* 1942) Catherine Dorothy, dau of Arthur Ashworth; *m* 3rd 1962 Elsie (*d* 1970), dau of Albert Edward Keen, and *d* 1965, leaving by his 1st w:
1f +James Roland Blake BUTLER later FOX-ANDREWS (took stepf's name 1939), QC (1968) [His Honour James Fox-Andrews Esq QC, 20 Cheyne Gdns, London SW3 5QT; Lepe House, Exbury, Hants SO4 1AD]; *b* 24 March 1922; *educ* Stowe and Cambridge (BA); FCIArb, RNVR 1940–46, barrister Gray's Inn 1949, Bencher 1974, Memb Middle Temple 1972, Recorder Winchester 1971 (Hon Recorder 1972), Dep Chm Devon QS 1970–71, Recorder Crown Court 1972–85, Leader Western Circuit 1982–84, Circuit Judge 1985–94, Memb General Cncl of Bar 1968–72, Senate of Inns of Court and Bar 1976–79, ed Inst of Arbitrators Jnl 1950–54; *m* 1950 Angela Bridget (*d* 1991), dau of Brig Charles Copley Swift, OBE, MC, and has:
1g +Jonathan Mark Piers [Jonathan Fox-Andrews Esq, 62 Redcliffe Rd, London SW109NQ]; *b* 1952; *educ* Eton and Trin Hall Cambridge (BA); *m* 1984 *Rosemary, dau of Dennis Jenks, and has issue:
1h +Maximilian George; *b* 1987
2h +Alfred James; *b* 1993
1h *Florence Ruth; *b* 1989
2h *Constance Augusta; *b* 1992
2g +Piers Norman James [Piers Fox-Andrews Esq, Farr Oak, Rogate, nr Petersfield, Hants]; *b* 1954; *educ* Eton and Bristol U; *m* 1985 *Elizabeth Keith, dau of Terence Allan, and has issue:
1h +Charles Adam; *b* 1986
2h +Guy James; *b* 1992
1h *Emma Mary; *b* 1988
2f John Stuart Blake Butler; *b* 1923; *m* 1947 Stephanie Elizabeth (*m* 2nd 1963 Guy Green and *d* 1970), dau of Thomas Swann, of The Old Vicarage, Thriplow, Cambs, and *d* 1957, leaving issue:
1g +Samuel Thomas Blake; *b* 1949
2e FitzWalter Butler; *b* 1889; *d* 1979, leaving issue:
1f +Theobald FitzWalter [Theobald Butler Esq, Little Croft, 7 Spooner Vale, Windermere, Cumbria LA23 1AU]; *b* 1921; *m* 1951 *Patricia Penelope, dau of Richard Lowe, of Donaghadee, Co Down, and has issue:
1h +Simon Blake FitzWalter [Dr Simon Butler, c/o Little Croft, Spooner Vale, Windermere, Cumbria LA23 1AU]; *b* 1958; *educ* U of Wales at Lampeter (BA) and Sheffield U (MA 1985, PhD 1992)
1h *Judith Margaret [Mrs Paul Evans, 20 Histons Drive, Codsall, Wolverhampton WV8 2ET]; *b* 1953; *educ* U Coll Cardiff (LLB) and Wolverhampton Teacher Training Coll (CertEd); *m* 1977 *Paul Llewelyn Evans, BSc, ACA, and has issue:
1i *Ian Llewelyn; *b* 1981
2i *Richard Theobald *b* 1984
3i *Edward Pierce; *b* 1988
2b Peter; had:
1c William, of Bunnahow, Co Clare; *b* 1759; had issue:
1d Walter; had:
1e Nicholas; had:
1f Walter Blake BUTLER later BUTLER-CREAGH (roy licence 1889); Lt-Col KOYLI; *b* 1859; *m* 1888 Clara (*d* 1928), dau and coheir of Cornelius Creagh, of Dangan, Co Clare, and *d* 1943, leaving issue:
1h Richard; *b* 1890; *m* 1919 Ada Murray (*d* 1949, and *d* 1955, leaving issue:
1i +Richard [Richard Butler-Creagh Esq, PO Box 8951, Nairobi, Kenya]; *b* 1922; *m* 1957 *Therese Agnes Spoorenberg, and has issue:
1j +Vincent; *b* 19–
2j +Walter; *b* 19–
1j *Michelle Edith; *b* 1957
2j *Simone Antoinette; *b* 1960
3j *Mary; *b* 19– ; *m* 19– *William Witham
4j *Shelia; *b* 19– ; *m* 19– *Michael Baines
5j *Maureen; *b* 19– ; *m* 19– *— Whittingham
1i *Clara; *b* 1929; *m* 1953 *William Craig, and has issue:
1j *Albert; *b* 1954
2j *William Richard; *b* 1956
3j *Robert; *b* 1958
2i *Ethanna; *b* 19– ; *m* 1957 *William Henry Harris, and has issue
3i *Jaon; *b* 19– ; *m* 19– *— Finn, and has issue:
1j *Anthony Richard; *b* 19–
2j *David; *b* 1956
1j *Linda; *b* 19–
2j *Bernadette Marie; *b* 1952
1h Mary Gertrude, of Dublin; *b* 1892
3 Thomas, of Boytonrath; *dsp* 1571
1 Joan; *m* Rowland Eustace, 2nd Viscount Baltinglas of the 1541 *cr*, and *d* in or after Sept 1585
2 Elaine; *m* 5th Lord (Baron, but sometimes ranked as a 'Viscount') Roche of Fermoy (*see* FERMOY, B, preliminary remarks)
3 A dau; *m* Sir Piers/Thomas Butler, later (10 Nov 1543) *cr* Baron Caher, Co Tipperary (I)
The 10th BARON (by prescription)'s est son,

Sir EDMUND BUTLER, **1st/11th Baron (of) Dunboyne**, Co Meath (I), so *cr* 11 June 1541 by a patent which regranted and confirmed the Barony to him and his heirs male for ever; ktd by 1541; *m* Cecilia, dau of Cormac Oge McCarty, of Muskerry, and *d* in prison 12/31 May 1567, leaving issue:
JAMES BUTLER, **2nd/12th Baron (of) Dunboyne**; *m* 1st *c* 1580 Margaret, dau and heir of Barnaby FitzPatrick, 2nd Baron Upper Ossory, by whom he had, with two other sons (*dsp*):
1 John; *m* Joan, dau of Florence, 3rd Baron Upper Ossory, and *dvp*, *k* by Richard Grace 7 Jan 1602, leaving:
(1) EDMOND BUTLER, **3rd/13th Baron (of) Dunboyne**; *m* 1st Margaret (*d* 1632), dau and heir of Thomas Butler, 2nd Baron of Caher (*see* MOUNTGARRET, V); *m* 2nd Ellen, dau of Gerald, Earl of Desmond, and *d* 17 May 1640, having had by his 1st w, with four yr sons (*dsp*):
1a JAMES BUTLER, **4th/14th Baron (of) Dunboyne**, *m* Ellen, dau of Pierce Butler, Viscount Ikerrin (*see* CARRICK, E), and *dspm* 1662, leaving issue:
1b Margaret; *m* Barnaby Fitzpatrick, Baron Upper Ossory
2a Pierce, of Ballydroghid, *m* Ellen, dau of Gerald Sutton, of Ballykyroe, and *d* 1626, having had, with two yr sons (Pierce, *dsp*; William, of Castletown, whose line is extinct):
1b Edmund, of Curragh; *m* Honora Gould, dau of William O'Mulryan, and *d* 1641, leaving an only son:
1c PIERCE BUTLER, **5th/15th Baron (of) Dunboyne**; *m* Catherine, dau of Sir Thomas Hurly, Bt, and *d* 3 May 1690, leaving issue:
1d JAMES BUTLER, **6th/16th Baron (of) Dunboyne**; *m* (articles 1 Nov 1686) Elizabeth, dau of Sir Redmond Everard, Bt, and *d* Jan 1701, leaving issue:
1e PIERCE BUTLER, **7th/17th Baron (of) Dunboyne**; *m* Anna, dau and heir of Robert Cadell, of Dublin, and *dsp* 1718
2e EDMOND BUTLER, **8th/18th Baron (of) Dunboyne**; *m* Anne, widow of Richard Nagle and dau of Oliver Grace, of Shanganagh, Ch Rememberancer Court of Exchequer in Ireland, and *d* 1732, having had issue:
1f JAMES BUTLER, **9th/19th Baron (of) Dunboyne**; *dsp* 12 Dec 1768

2f PIERCE BUTLER, **10th/20th Baron Dunboyne**; *m* 3 June 1773 Maria (*m* 2nd David Walsh, MP), dau of George Macnamara, of Cong, Co Mayo, and *d* 20 Aug 1773, leaving issue:

1g PIERCE EDMOND CREAGH BUTLER, **11th/21st Baron (of) Dunboyne**; *d* unm Dec 1785

3f Rt Rev JOHN BUTLER, DD, **12th/22nd Baron (of) Dunboyne**, Catholic Bp of Cork (resigned 1786); *b c* 1720; *m* 1787 Maria (*m* 2nd 1801 John Hubert Moore, of Shannon Grove, King's Co, barrister, and *d* Aug 1860), dau of Theobald Butler, of Wilford, Co Tipperary, and *dsp* 7 May 1800, leaving money for the foundation of Dunboyne House at Maynooth Coll

4f Edmond; *dsp* 1783

1f Catherine; *m* William O'Brien-Butler, of Bansagh, Co Tipperary

The **2nd/12th Baron (of) Dunboyne** *m* 2nd Margaret (*d* 20 Feb 1636/7), dau of Connor O'Brien, Earl of Thomond (*see* INCHIQUIN, B), and *d* 8 Feb 1624/5, having by her had, with other issue:

2 James, of Grellagh, Co Tipperary; *m* Lady Ellen Butler, dau of Walter, Earl of (Ossory and) Ormond (*see* MOUNTGARRET, V), and had, with a yr s (Walter, *dsp*):

(1) Thomas, of Kilconnell; *m* Ellen, dau of Philip O'Dwyer, and had an only s:

1a Richard (Count); offr in Imperial service; *dsp* Rearnstein, Bohemia, 1686

3 Edward, of Clare, Co Tipperary; *m* Elizabeth, dau of Alderman Nicholas Dobbin, of Waterford, and had an est s:

(1) James; *m* Janet, dau of Capt John Cantwell, and had an est s:

1a Edward; had:

1b James (Most Rev), DD; Archbp Cashel; *d* unm 1774

2b Michael; *m* Mary O'Leary and *d* 15 Aug 1776, leaving an only son:

1c James, of Cranagowra, Co Clare; *m* Bridget, dau of Bartholomew Sheehy, and *d* 22 May 1784, leaving an only son:

1d **JAMES, 13th/23rd Baron**

4 Theobald; *m* Margaret, dau of Sir Valentine Blake, 1st Bt of Menlough (*qv*), and widow of Sir Nicholas Arthur, of Limerick, and had issue:

(1) James; recovered his estate of Killoskehan and Drom *temp* CHARLES II; *m* Margaret Burke, and had issue:

1a James; *m* Marjory Dalton, and had issue:

1b Richard; *b c* 1710; *m* Margaret, dau of Morgan O'Brien, and had issue:

1c Theobald ('Big Toby'); *m* 1st 1751 Bridget, dau of Edmund Butler, of Wilton, and had issue; *m* 2nd Elizabeth, dau of Edward Lee, Archdeacon Waterford, and by her had, with other issue:

1d William, of Drom and Wildford; *m* Caroline (*d* 1837), dau of 1st Baron Massy (*qv*), and *d* 3 Jan 1812, leaving, with other issue:

1e Theobald; *b c* 1790; *m* 1815 Anne, dau of James Kearney, of Blancheville, Kilkenny, and *d* 1837, leaving, with other issue:

1f William; *b* 1819; *m* 1842 Catherine (*d* 1904), only dau of John Lloyd, of Lisheen, and *d* 1870, leaving, with other issue:

1g Charles James BUTLER later BUTLER-KEARNEY, of Three Castles, Kilkenny, DL, JP and High Sheriff Co Kilkenny 1903, Lt-Col Royal Munster Fus; *b* 1851; *m* 1873 Georgina Hannah (*d* 1919), dau of Robert Hare Clarke, of Bansha, Co Tipperary, and *d* 1933, leaving issue:

1h Charles James; *b* and *d* 1874

2h Theobald William; *b* 1876; *m* 26 Aug 1914 Hester Louisa Edith Davis (*d* 11 April 1972 aged 80), 4th dau of Carew Davies Gilbert, DL, JP, of Trelissick, Cornwall, and Eastbourne, Sussex and *d* 2 Jan 1936, leaving issue:

1i +James Davies Theobald [James Butler-Kearney Esq, 46 Ashdell Rd, Alton, Hants GU34 2TA]; *b* 16 April 1916; *educ* Nautical Coll Pangbourne; photographer; *m* 1st 31 March 1951 (*divorce* 1954) Gillian Mary Soltau, est dau of Major W H Anketell, of Mauton, West Brabourne, Ashford, Kent; *m* 2nd 9 April 1970 *Juliet Mary, dau of Rev Andrew Hunt, of 10B Edgar Road, Winchester, Hants

1i *Catherine Mary [Miss Catherine Butler-Kearney, Spring Cottage, Durcott Rd, Camerton, Bath]; WW II 1939–44 with Land Army, social welfare offr 1962; *b* 21 March 1918

3h Trench Frank, *b* 1877; Capt Army; *m* 1920 Shirley (*d* 1971), dau of John Bailey Sequeira, and *d* 7 Feb 1956, leaving issue:

1i *Jean [Miss Jean Butler-Kearney, 15 The Green, Burgh Heath, Surrey KT20 5NP]; *b* 1920

2i *Norma [Miss Norma Butler-Kearney, 15 The Green, Burgh Heath, Surrey KT20 5NP]; *b* 1924

1h Mary Violet; *b* 1884; *m* 1916 Mervyn Hampden Corsellis and *d* 1 March 1958, leaving issue. He *d* Jan 1961

1g Anne; *m* William Butler (*see* below)

2c Pierce; *d* 1774, leaving three daus

3c James, of Park; *m* Elizabeth Butler (*d* 1774) and *d* 1774, leaving, with other issue:

1d William; *m* Anne, dau of Theobald Butler (*see* above), and *d* 1800, leaving, with other issue:

1e James, of Park; Capt 4th Dragoon Gds; *b* 1785; *m* 1813 Gertrude, dau of Sir John Carden, 3rd Bt, of Templemore (*qv*), and had issue:

1f William, of Park; *b* 1814; *m* 1857 Mary (*d* 1901), dau of Major George Jackson, 1st Roy Scots, and *d* 1857, leaving, with other issue:

1g Charles Herbert Jackson; *b* 10 Nov 1870; *m* 20 Jan 1900 Margaret Daisy (*d* 21 May 1939), dau of Frederick Batten, of Durban, Natal, and *d* 22 May 1937, leaving issue:

1h George Herbert; *b* 21 Feb 1901; *m* 1 May 1929 Irene Rose, dau of Edward Sparnon, and *d* 1955, leaving:

1i John Charles Edward, *b* 23 April 1935; *d* 1993

1i *June Rose Margaret [Mrs June Brown, 31 Ellis Park Drive, Durban North 4051, S Africa]; *b* 10 Aug 1930; *m* 1961 Philip Clement Brown (*d* 1984), and has issue:

1j *Timothy Philip; *b* 1964; *educ* Natal U; *m* 1993 *Paula Claire, dau of John Raftesath, of Natal

1j *Rosalind Jane; *b* 1962; *m* 1984 *Dr Bruce Gummow, and has issue:

1k *Ian Andrew; *b* 1994

2i *Patricia Colleen [Miss Patricia Butler, 1103 Kensington, 311 North Ridge Road, Durban 4001, S Africa]; *b* 2 Oct 1938

2h Frederick William Webb; *b* 2 Sept 1903; *m* 24 May 1934 *Nancy Anne O'Mahony, and *d* 19 Nov 1946, leaving issue:

1i *Patrick Barry Webb; *b* 11 Aug 1941

2i *Michael Terence Webb; *b* 29 Dec 1943

2g Henry John BUTLER later BUTLER-LLOYD; *b* 1874; *m* 1st 1897 Catherine (*d* 1907), dau of James Davoran, and had issue:

1h William Francis; *b* 1899; *m* 1930 *Mary Margaret [Mrs William Butler-Lloyd, Killea, Templemore, Co Tipperary, Ireland], dau of Thomas Fitzgerald, and *d* 1956, leaving issue:

1i +Thomas Henry John [Thomas Butler-Lloyd Esq, Richmond, Templemore, Co Tipperary, Ireland]; *b* 1932; *m* 1966 *Veronica, dau of Patrick Harney, of Templemore, and has issue:

1j +William Francis; *b* 1969

1j *Audrey Veronica; *b* 1972

1i Catherine Mary *b* 1930; *d* unm 1940

2j (cont.) Henry Butler-Lloyd *m* 2nd 1908 Jane (*d* 1956), dau of Capt W Headech, 20th Regt, and *d* 1945, having by her had issue:

3h Henry John, of Granagh, Templemore; *b* 1910; *m* 1947 *Kathleen Leacky [Mrs Henry Butler-Lloyd, Castleleiny Cottage, Templemore, Co Tipperary, Ireland], and *d* 19–, leaving issue:

1i +Henry John [Henry Butler-Lloyd Esq, 57 Maundeby Walk, London NW10 2TG]; *b* 1948; *m* 19– *Florence, dau of Douglas Henry Lewis, of Burnt Oak, Edgware, Middx, and has issue:

1j *Jason James; *b* 1977

1j *Katherine Geraldine *b* 1973

2j *Jacqueline Caroline; *b* 1975

3j *Mary; *b* 19–

4j *Maggie-Jo; *b* 19–

5j *Caroline; *b* 19–

6j *Carmel; *b* 19–

7j *Geraldine; *b* 19–

1i *Ann; *b* 1956

4h +James [James Butler-Lloyd Esq, Lalors, Naas, Co Kildare, Ireland]; *b* 1912

5h +Charles; *b* 1913

1h *Anne [Mrs Walter Thompson, Tyn y Rhos Hall, Weston Rhyn, Oswestry, Salop]; *b* 1908; *m* 1930 *Walter Thompson, and has issue:

1i *Mervyn THOMPSON later THOMPSON-BUTLER-LLOYD (deed poll 1963) [Brother Demetrius AP, Eastern Orthodox Church, Tyn y Rhos Hall, Weston Rhyn, Oswestry, Salop]; *b* 1939

2i *Kenneth; *b* 1946; *educ* Salford U (BA); *m* 1969 *Carol, only dau of Sidney Shipton, of Liverpool

3i *Ivor, RN, *b* 1947; *m* 1969 *Catherine, dau of William Hunter Gardner Russell, of Bo'Ness, West Lothian, and has issue:

1j *Carol Anne; *b* 1970

1g Kathleen; *b* 1868; *m* 1894 Edmund Jacob, of Templemore, and *d* 1959, leaving issue. He *d* 1930

(2) Pierce, Rector Glenbeigh, *m* Alice, dau of Lt John Langton, and *d* 1710, leaving issue:

1a Theobald; *b c* 1690; *m* 1st Maria O'Hara (*dsp* 1714); *m* 2nd 14 Aug 1722 Mary, dau of Sir Nathaniel Whitwell, Ld Mayor Dublin 1727, and by her had issue:

1b James, of Priestown; *b c* 1746; *m* Dorothea, dau of Sir Richard Steele, 1st Bt, and had:

1c Richard, DD, Vicar Barnchurch, Kilkenny; *m* 1792 Martha (*d* 1855), 2nd dau of Richard Rothwell, of Rockfield, Co Meath, and *d* 1841, leaving, with other issue:

1d James (Rev), of Priestown; *b* 1793; *m* 1818 Isabella (*d* 1876), est dau of Thomas Rothwell, of Rockfield, and *d* 1872, leaving issue:

1e Richard; *d* 1851

2e Thomas, of Priestown; *b* 1822; *d* unm

3e James, of Brownstone Park, Co Meath; *b* 1825; *m* 7 June 1864 Mary Elizabeth (*d* 1906), only dau of Tottenham Alley, of Athboy, Co Meath, and *d* 1899, leaving issue:

1f James Tottenham, JP, of Priestown; Capt 5th Bn Leinster Regt; *b* 4 June 1868; *m* 1906 Geraldine (*d* 8 Jan 1966), yr dau of Henry St George Osborne, of Dardesdown Castle, Co Meath, and *dsp*

1f Frances Isabel, *b* 1875, *m* 22 July 1896 Ernest Pitman and *d* 25 Nov 1957, leaving issue. He *d* 7 Aug 1948

2f Augusta Madeline; *b* 1877; *d* unm 1 Feb 1960

1e Emma; *m* 3 Dec 1889 Vincent Gernon, of Hammondstown, Co Louth, and *dsp* 11 Nov 1899

2d Richard (Very Rev), Dean Clonmacnoise; *b* 14 Oct 1794; *m* 14 Aug 1826 Harriet (*d* 1889), dau of Richard Lovell Edgeworth, and *dsp* 17 July 1862

3d Thomas Lewis, Capt 79th Highrs; *dsp* 1868

4d Whitwell, of Staffordstown; carried the Colours at Waterloo; *b* 1798; *m* 1833 Elizabeth (*d* May 1865), dau of John Paine Garnet, of Arch Hall, Co Meath, and *d* 12 July 1877, leaving issue:

1e Whitwell, of Staffordstown; *d* 16 Nov 1881

2e Richard John; *b* 1840, *m* 1878 Georgina Eleanor (*d* 1888), dau of Charles Rothwell, of Staffordstown, and *d* 14 Oct 1908, leaving issue:

1f Richard John; *b* 1879; *m* 1 Sept 1909 Grace Pauline, dau of George Ernest Englehart, and *d* 28 April 1964

2f George Whitwell; *b* 1888; *m* 1918 Ada Isabel Deering (*d* 29 Sept 1961), dau of Arthur Lucius Cary, of Swords, Dublin, and *d* 7 Oct 1960, leaving issue:

1g John Radcliff, of Sutton Coldfield; *b* 18 Nov 1921; *d* March 1994

1g *Mary Isabel [Mrs Carass Topham, 25 Selwyn Crescent, Radley, Abingdon, Oxon OX14 3AL]; *b* 1919; *m* 1943 *Carass Frederick Bladon Topham and has issue:

1h *Ronald Bladon; *b* 4 May 1945; *educ* Radley

2h Michael George, of Oxford; *b* 24 March 1947; *d* 1980

3h *John Carass [John Topham Esq, 114 Mid St, S Nutfield, Surrey]; *b* 8 April 1951; *m* 1981 *Christine Allen, and has issue:

1i *Laurence James Carass; *b* 1982

2i *Ralph Lewis Bladon; *b* 1984

3i *Philip George Graham; *b* 1987

1h *Pamela Mary; *b* 8 April 1951

2g *(Eileen) Synolda [Miss Synolda Butler, 7 Fordhook Ave, London W5 3LS]; *b* 1926

1f Synolda Elizabeth; *b* 1881; *m* 5 Aug 1903 Rev Arthur Cowan Digby French, est s of Rev Robert Digby French, Vicar Market Wighton, Yorks, and had issue. He *d* 1950

2f Ethel Georgina; *b* 1884; *m* 23 Oct 1911 Edward Apsley Parker White, MRCVS, and *d* 1954, leaving issue. He *d* 1948

3f Harriet Cecilia; *b* 1886; *m* 1924 Thomas Coghlan, of Ontario, and *d* 15 March 1965. He *d* 1947

1e Mary

2e Elizabeth

5d Edward (Rev), of Llangoed Castle, Brecon; *b* 1800; *m* 1st 1830 Henrietta (*d* 1832), dau of Henry Skryne, of Warleigh, Somerset, and had issue:

1e Bagot; *b* and *d* 1832

5d (cont.) The Rev Edward Butler *m* 2nd 1835 Anne Elizabeth (*d* 1845), dau of William Woodville, and by her had issue:

2e Theobald William, Lt-Col 72nd Highrs; *b* 1838; *m* 1871 Anne Robina (*d* 1925), dau of Maj Richard Thomas William Brikenden, and *dsp* 1928

5d (cont.) The Rev Edward Butler *m* 3rd 1846 Blanche (*d* 1867), dau of Phillip Perring, and by her had issue:

3e Edward, of Llangoed Castle; *b* 1851; *m* 1887 Emily Frances (*d* 1951), dau of Arthur Battiscombe, and *d* 1928, leaving issue:

1f Emily Blanche; *b* 1889; *d* unm 19 Nov 1957

2f Judith Eileen, MBE (1966), of Aberllynfi, Glasbury, Brecon; *b* 1895

5d (cont.) The Rev Edward Butler *m* 4th 1868 Mary Elizabeth (*d* 1913), dau of Richard Rothwell, of Rockfield, Co Meath, and *d* Feb 1877, having by her had issue:

1e Katherine May Dorothea; *b* 1870; *m* 27 April 1899 Sir Ivor Algernon Atkins, FRCO, s of Frederick Atkins, of Cardiff, and *d* 15 Dec 1954, leaving issue. He *d* 26 Nov 1953

6d John, of Maiden Hall, Co Kilkenny; *m* 1863 Mary, dau of Robert Barton, of Greenhill, and *d* 1890, leaving, with other issue:

1e George, *b* 1859, *m* 25 Jan 1898 Harriet Neville (*d* 18 July 1939), dau of Marshal Neville Clarke, of Graiguenoe Park, Co Tipperary, and *d* 8 April 1941, leaving issue:

1f Hubert Marshal, of Maiden Hall, Bennettsbridge, Co Kilkenny, *b* 23 Oct 1900, *educ* Charterhouse and St John's Coll Oxford, *m* 2 June 1930 *Susan Margaret [Mrs Hubert Butler, Maiden Hall, Bennettsbridge, Co Kilkenny, Ireland], dau of Dr Thomas Clement Guthrie, of Annaghmakerrig, Co Monaghan, and *d* 1991, leaving:

1g *Julia Mary Synolda [Mrs Richard Crampton, 1106 Rugby Rd, Charlottesville, Va 22903-1610, USA], *b* 17 April 1935, *m* 6 June 1959 *Dr Richard Savington Crampton, s of Savington Warren Crampton, of Baltimore, Md, and has:

1h *Thomas William Butler, *b* 9 July 1967

1h *Anne Cordelia [Mrs James Gelly, 139 Liberty Corner Rd, Far Hills, NJ 07931, USA], *b* 13 Dec 1960; *m* 19 June 1988 *James Vaughan Gelly, and has issue:

1i *Piers George Crampton, *b* 30 July 1991

2i *Bennett Butler Vaughan, *b* 26 Feb 1993

3i *Clement Guthrie Estes; *b* 20 May 1995

2h *Suzanna Louise, *b* 21 Sept 1963

3h *Katherine Synolda, *b* 22 Feb 1966

2f +(George) Gilbert [Gilbert Butler Esq, Scatorish, Bennettsbridge, Co Kilkenny, Ireland], *b* 16 Feb 1910, *educ* Cheltenham and Trin Coll Cambridge, *m* 24 Feb 1940 Noreen Helen (*d* 11 Oct 1997), dau of George Pomeroy Arthur Pomeroy Colley (*see* HARBERTON, V), and has:

1g +James George; *b* 10 Aug 1942; *m* 8 April 1972 *Diana Gillian, dau of John Hedges Becher, of Bagenalstown House, Co Carlow, and has issue:

1h +Thomas George; *b* 1973

2h +John James; *b* 1974

1g *Jessica Harriet [The Rt Hon The Lady Rathdonnell, Lisnavagh, Rathvilly, Co Carlow, Ireland]; *b* 17 Dec 1940; *m* 2 Oct 1965 *5th Baron Rathdonnell (*qv*) and has issue

1f Cicely Marion; *b* 3 Feb 1899; *m* 15 Dec 1947 *Herbert Victor Atherton Doudney, of Lavistown House, Kilkenny, son of Raymond Pelly Doudney, of St James's, Carlisle, and Ceylon

2f *Joanna Vernon [Mrs Gerald Lenox-Conyngham, Anaverna, Ravensdale, Dundalk, Co Louth, Ireland]; *b* 22 Feb 1903; *m* 12 July 1938 *Gerald Lenox-Conyngham, and has issue:

1g *Edward Vere Gerald; *b* 10 Aug 1942

1g *Melosina Anne; *b* 22 Feb 1941

2g *Eleanor Elizabeth Rita; *b* 1 July 1946

2b Whitwell, of Waterville, JP; *b* 1743; *m* 1760 Belinda, dau of Richard Yeilding, of Rathkeale, Limerick, and *d* 1807, leaving, with other issue:

1c James, of Waterville, DL, JP, *b* 1780, *m* 1817 Agnes (*d* May 1839), est dau of Rev John Day, MA, Rector Kiltallagh, and *d* June 1863, leaving, with other issue:

1d James, of Waterville, JP; *b* 28 May 1820; *m* 28 Oct 1847 Anne Margaret (*d* 30 March 1903), only dau of Roger Green Davis, of Killeagh, and *d* 26 Oct 1887, leaving issue:

1e James Edward, of Waterville, JP, High Sheriff Co Kerry 1892; *b* 23 Jan 1856; *m* 24 Feb 1897 Mary Goyne, (*d* 25 April 1938), est dau of William Goyne Stevens, and *d* 20 Nov 1905, leaving issue:

1f James Whitwell, of The Precincts, Rosscarbery, Co Cork; Maj 8th King's Royal Irish Hus and Pioneer Corps, served WWs I and II; *b* 19 Oct 1897; *educ* Trent Coll and RMC Sandhurst; *m* 24 March 1927 Hilda Winifred (*d* 1978), dau of Charles Nason Haines, of Appian Way, Leeson Park, Dublin, and *d* 1971, leaving issue:

1g +James Charles MC (1951) [James Butler Esq MC, Belgrove, Cobh, Co Cork, Ireland], Lt 8th KRI Hus Korea; *b* 5 May 1928; *educ* Wellington and RMA Sandhurst; *m* 3 Oct 1959 *Margaret Perry, est dau of Harold Perry Goodbody, of The Glen, Cobh, Co Cork, and has issue:

1h +James Perry George; *b* 5 Sept 1960

1h *Corinna Margaret; *b* 28 May 1962

2g Edward Theobald, of Anner House, Cloneen, Fethard, Co Tipperary; *b* 9 May 1929; *educ* St Columba's and RAC Cirencester; *m* 8 Oct 1952 *Judith Valerie [Mrs Edward Butler, Tullow, Fethard, Co Tipperary, Ireland], dau of Otto Edward Webb, of Borris-in-Ossory, Co Laois, and *d* 1992, leaving issue:

1h *Jennifer Mary; *b* 17 June 1954

2h *Dianna Elizabeth; *b* 13 Feb 1956; *m* 1975 *John Aloysius Taylor, of Boyertown, Pa., USA, and has:

1i *Kerry Ann; *b* 1978

3h *Caroline Eve; *b* 7 Nov 1960; *m* 1984 *Hugh Christopher Stanhope Morshead, er s of Christopher William Trelawny Morshead, MC, TD, of Bellewstown House, Co Meath, and has issue:

1i *Christopher Edward; *b* 1986

2i *James Stanhope; *b* 1989

1g *Hilda Elizabeth [Mrs Julius Jameson, Shell Cove House, Teignmouth Road, Dawlish, Devon]; *b* 14 April 1932; *m* 3 Oct 1956 *Julius Pridden Jameson, only s of Robert Stanley Jameson, of Nether Compton, Sherborne, Dorset, and has issue:

1h *Robert Julius Whitwell; *b* 1957

2h *James Leander; *b* 1964

1h *Linda Rose; *b* 1959

2f Theobald Richard FitzWalter, of Highgate; barrister Inner Temple 1921 (Bencher 1960), Recorder Newark 1945, Chm Notts QS 1954, Dep Chm Middx QS 1960–65, Chm Gtr London (SE Area) QS 1965–67, Chllr Diocese Peterborough 1962, Dep Chm Kent QS 1963, sr ed *Archbold's Criminal Proceedings* 1973; *b* 24 May 1894; *educ* Charterhouse and Univ Coll Oxford; *m* 28 July 1948 *Laura Rachel Mary, dau of Sir Vincent Nash, DL, of Shannon View House, Castletroy, Co Limerick, and *dsp* 9 March 1976

1f Susan Elizabeth Aileen; *b* 1 Oct 1881; *m* 27 Nov 1927 Arthur King, MB, ChB, of Merlin, Ilfracombe, Devon, s of Rhees Benjamin King, of Rhymney, Mon, and *d* 19 May 1956

2f Arabella Agnes Muriel; *b* 29 Aug 1883; *m* 17 Oct 1911 Sir William Seeds, KCMG, Amb Brazil 1930–35 and USSR 1939–40, son of Robert Seeds, QC, of Dublin, and *d* 19– leaving issue. He *d* 2 Nov 1973

3f Mary Gwenda; *d* unm Sept 1904

4f Synolda; *d* unm 31 March 1906

3e John Edward; *b* 15 Nov 1858; *d* unm 2 Nov 1880

1e Elizabeth Agnes

2e Belinda Beatty; *m* 22 June 1875 Rev William Spottswood Green, CB, MA, only s of Charles Green, of Youghal, Co Cork, and had issue

3e Mary Pratt

4e Agnes Arabella; *d* unm 30 Jan 1909

5e Margaret Mackenzie John

2d John; *d* unm July 1854

1d Arabella Agnes

2d Belinda; *d* unm

2c Whitwell
1c Ellen
1b Ellen; *m* Robert Beatty, and *d* leaving issue
2b Synolda; *dsp*
(3) Thomas; *m* Catherine, dau of Edmund Butler, of Balacaring, and had issue
(4) Jasper
(1) Margaret; *m* Edmund Graham, of Bandon, Co Cork

The 12th/22nd BARON (OF) DUNBOYNE's cousin,

JAMES BUTLER, **13th/23rd Baron (of) Dunboyne**; *b* 25 July 1780; *m* 1st 17 Aug 1799 Ellen (*d* 15 March 1817), dau of David O'Connell, of Cork, and had issue:

1 Edward; *d* an infant
2 THEOBALD FitzWALTER, **14th/24th Baron**
3 St John, of Portrane and Walshestown, Co Dublin; High Sheriff Co Dublin 1856; *b* 24 June 1808; *m* 1st 14 Feb 1832 Anne Maria (*d* 7 Nov 1859), widow of James Fitzpatrick, of Spiddal, Co Galway, and only child of Walter Arcedeckne Burke, of Gortnamona, Co Galway, and had issue:
(1) James Henry Edward BUTLER later ARCEDECKNE-BUTLER (roy licence 1867); *b* 3 July 1838; *m* 20 June 1867 Minna (*d* 11 Aug 1925, having *m* 2nd 16 April 1872 Charles Thomas Lane, JP, of Dangstein, Petersfield (*d* 17 Sept 1912), 2nd s of Rev Charlton Lane, Vicar Hampstead), dau of Joseph Locke, MP Honiton, and *d* 5 Feb 1871, having had issue:
1a St John Henry; *b* 15 Oct 1868; *m* 7 Aug 1895 Maud Geraldine (*m* 2nd 2 Nov 1926 Henry Laycock, of Sherbourne, Nuwara Eliya, and *d* 17 Jan 1948), 2nd dau of Capt Albert William Money, of Little Stodham, Liss, and *d* 20 Nov 1914, leaving issue:
1b St John Desmond, CBE (1946); Maj-Gen Roy Signals and Lt Royal Munster Fus, served WWs I and II; *b* 30 Nov 1896; *m* 15 July 1929 Ethel Helen Nesbit (*d* 9 Aug 1953), only dau of Col Reginald Selby Walker, DSO, RE, and *d* 4 Feb 1959, leaving issue:
1c +(St John) Patrick [Maj Patrick Arcedeckne-Butler, Parker's Pound, Walton Lane, Old Bosham, W Sussex PO18 8QB], Maj (ret) Roy Signals; *b* 15 Sept 1930; *educ* Eton, RMA Sandhurst and Trin Col Cambridge; *m* 1st 28 Jan 1956 (Jane) Frances Elizabeth Mary (*d* 1983), dau of Lt-Col Frank Eric Massie, MC, of W Ayton, Scarborough, and has issue:
1d +St John Terence; *b* 13 Aug 1956
2d +Christopher Michael; *b* 10 June 1959
3d +John Patrick; *b* 30 Nov 1969
4d +Mark Piers; *b* 20 March 1972
1c (cont.) Maj Patrick Arcedeckne-Butler *m* 2nd 1991 *(Jacqueline) Jean, dau of H C Morris, of Dorchester, Dorset
2c Michael Francis Peel, Lt-Cdr RN; *b* 18 Sept 1933; *educ* Eton; *m* 7 Jan 1961 *Jacqueline [Mrs Michael Arcedeckne-Butler, Cutlers, Wickham, Hants PO15 5AN], only child of Col Leonard George Carpenter-Garnier, OBE, Devon and Dorset Regt, of Beverley, Wickham, Hants, and *d* 1993, leaving issue:
1d +Timothy Garnier; *b* 15 Aug 1962; *educ* Eton; *m* 3 June 1995 *Nathalie Catherine, dau of M M Rawoo, of London, and has:
1e *Emily Julia Garnier; *b* 5 June 1996
1d *Nicola Catherine [Ms Nicola Arcedeckne-Butler, c/o Corney and Barrow, 12 Helmet Row, London EC1]; *b* 3 July 1964; Master of Wine 1996; *m* 6 Jan 1996 *Jonathan James Longden, s of Capt John Longden RN
1c *Christal Synolda [Mrs Geoffrey Medcalf, Malt Square House, 15 High St, S Witham, Grantham, Lincs]; *b* 10 Feb 1938; *m* 23 Sept 1961 *Geoffrey William Medcalf, s of William Medcalf, of Tetford, Lincs, and has:
1d *Richard William Desmond; *b* 1966
2d *David Geoffrey; *b* 1969
1d *Sallie Jane; *b* 1969
2d *Helen Sheevaun Christal; *b* 1963
3d *Patricia Ann; *b* 1964
4d *Rosemary Janet Slaney; *b* 1970
2a James FitzWalter, Maj E Surrey Regt; *b* 23 Oct 1869; *d* 29 Aug 1928
(2) Charles Arcedeckne; *b* 6 Dec 1843; *d* 1 Nov 1865
(1) Maria Rosalinda; *m* 19 Oct 1887 William Henry Peters, of Harefield, Devon, and *d* 19 Oct 1923. He *d* 2 Jan 1896
(2) Emily Anne; *d* April 1862
3 (cont.) St John Butler *m* 2nd 9 Dec 1863 Anne (*d* 14 Oct 1869), widow of Robert George Parnther, Rifle Bde; *m* 3rd 21 April 1873 Marianne Jane (*d* 16 April 1874), sister of Rt Hon Thomas Edward Taylor, MP, of Ardgillan Castle, Co Dublin (*see* HEADFORT, M), and *d* 17 March 1878
4 Henry BUTLER later BUTLER-JOHNSTONE, of Corehead and Auchen Castle, Dumfriesshire, DL, Col Dumfries Militia, MP Canterbury; *b* 28 Aug 1809; *m* 14 May 1834, Isabella Margaret Munro-Johnstone (*d* 1873), only dau of Col Sir Alexander Munro, of Novar, Ross-shire, and *d* 1 April 1879, having had, with other issue:
(1) Henry Alexander BUTLER-JOHNSTONE later MUNRO-BUTLER-JOHNSTONE, DL (Ross-shire); MP Canterbury 1862–78, BA Oxford; *b* 7 Dec 1837; *m* 1st 17 Nov 1877 Maria Irma, Countess de Soyres (*dsp* 16 July 1880); *m* 2nd 29 Dec 1896 Elaine, widow of Joseph Skipp Lloyd, Clerk to the Cheque and Adj Gentlemen-at-Arms, and 2nd dau of Felix Johnson, of Somerton, Oxon, and *dsp* 17 Oct 1902
5 James, of Lamberton Park, Queen's Co, High Sheriff 1857 and JP Queen's Co; *b* 8 Nov 1810; *m* 3 Oct 1836 Emilia Mary (*d* 18 Nov 1897), only dau of Sir William FitzGerald, 2nd Bt, of Carrygoran, Co Clare, and *d* 11 Feb 1891, leaving, with other issue:
(1) James William FitzGerald, 72nd Highrs; *b* 10 Oct 1837; *m* 4 May 1858 Ada (*d* 10 May 1913), yst dau of Lawrence Gwynne, LLD, of Devon, and *d* 12 May 1873, having had issue:
1a James William FitzGerald; *b* and *d* 1865
1a Ada Emily Gwynne; *m* 22 Jan 1881 James Bower DUNN later BOWER (assumed 1881), 51st Regt, of Claremont, Devon , est s of R R Marsh Dunn, of Carlton Lodge, E Teignmouth, and *d* 11 Aug 1898, leaving issue. He *d* 1920
2a Synolda Ellen Le Petit; *m* 17 Jan 1884 Col John Winston Thomas SPENCER later MUNRO-SPENCER, RA, s of Lt-Col Hon George Augustus Spencer, and *d* 1890, leaving issue (*see* CHURCHILL, V)
3a Alexandra Amy Geraldine, RRC; *m* 1st 28 July 1887 William George Gould (*d* 21 Jan 1911), of 18 South St, Mayfair; *m* 2nd 21 July 1920, as his 2nd w, Henry Beaufort Wilmot Beaumont Inglefield, of 27 Cadogan Square, London SW, er s of Adml Sir Edward Augustus Inglefield, KCB, FRS, FRGS, and *d* 1 May 1931. He *d* 26 April 1926
(1) Emily Sarah FitzGerald; *m* 17 May 1865 Walter Harvey Thursby-Pelham, JP, of Cound Hall, Salop, and *d* 5 Jan 1925, leaving issue. He *d* 15 Dec 1874
(2) Isabel Georgina; *m* 16 April 1868 Henry Maurice William Oppenheim, DL, of Chipstead, nr Sevenoaks, Kent, and *d* 24 March 1933, leaving issue. He *d* 4 May 1912
(3) Rosalinda Eleanor; *m* 5 Sept 1875 Frederick Robert Knollys, of Brookfield House, Bucks, son of Gen Rt Hon Sir William Knollys, KCB, and *d* 17 Nov 1876, leaving issue (*see* KNOLLYS, V)
6 Edward (Sir), of Harefield, Hants, DL, JP, High Sheriff 1855, Lt Gentlemen-at-Arms 1839–45; *b* 29 Oct 1811; *m* 1st 16 March 1839 Emma Jane (*d* 4 Dec 1840), only child and heir of Arthur Baily, of London, and had:
(1) Arthur Francis Baily; *d* an infant 7 Jan 1841
6 (cont.) Sir Edward Butler *m* 2nd 1 Feb 1844 Urania Elizabeth (*d* 2 Dec 1858), dau of V-Adml Lord Henry Paulet, KCB, son of 12th Marquess of Winchester (*qv*), and *d* 22 Oct 1858, having by her had issue:
(2) Arthur Paulet; *b* 21 March 1845; *m* 6 Oct 1870 Emily Maria (*m* 2nd 7 July 1874 Sir Henry Bernhard Samuelson, 2nd Bt (*qv*), and *d* 5 July 1930), er dau of John Goodden, DL, JP, of Over Compton, Dorset, and Martock, Somerset, and *dsp* 23 Dec 1872
7 Charles Lennox, DL, JP Middx and Warwicks; High Sheriff Warwicks 1862, Maj Westminster Militia; *b* 29 Nov 1813; *m* 1st 24 Oct 1835 Eliza (*d* 31 Dec 1866), only child and heir of Thomas Lindsey Holland, of Cornwall Terrace, Regent's Park, and had issue:
(1) Lindsey Holland, 7th Fus; *b* 22 Aug 1836; *d* 13 July 1887
(2) Charles Lennox; *b* 5 Oct 1841; accidentally *k* by a fall on the Great Gable at Westdale, Cumberland, 8 Feb 1865
(3) Edward Arthur, of Winford Hall, Yarmouth, Norfolk; Lt-Col 1st Bn Roy Irish Rifles; *b* 3 July 1843; *m* 28 May 1872 Clara Maria (*d* 16 Oct 1912), 2nd dau of Major-Gen James Francis, Bombay Staff Corps, and *d* 16 April 1916, leaving issue:
1a Arthur Lennox, Sudan CS, 4th Cl Order Nile; *b* 22 Feb 1873; *m* 10 Sept 1908 his cousin Ada Rose (*d* 14 April 1962), 3rd dau of Edward Allesley Ward-Boughton-Leigh, DL, of Brownsover Hall, Rugby, and *dsp* 31 Dec 1939
2a Charles Edward; *b* 7 May 1874; *m* 25 Oct 1919 Alice Elizabeth (*d* 1984), 2nd dau of Thomas James Worship, of N Walsham, and *d* 17 Nov 1960, leaving issue:
1b +Clarence Francis [Clarence Butler Esq, West Winds, Baldhoon Rd, Laxey, IoM IM4 7QH]; F/Lt RAF WW II (wounded, despatches); *b* 29 Aug 1920; *m* 14 March 1944 Pamela Constance (*d* 1991), dau of Francis John Drakard, of Ingham House, Martlesham, Suffolk; *m* 2nd Nov 1996 *Annette Dolors, yr dau of Percy Herbert Froud, of Maidstone, Kent, and by his 1st w has:
1c *Julia Rosemary; *b* 11 April 1945; *m* 1967 *Dennis Curran, of Bishops Stortford, Herts
2c *Denise Angela [Mrs Christopher Simpson, Baldhoon, Laxey, Isle of Man]; *b* 6 June 1947; *m* 1988 *Christopher Bannister Simpson
2b Brian Charles, of Leigh House, Holcombe, Dawlish, Devon; *b* 24 Jan 1924; *m* 15 Sept 1952 *Joyce Caroline [Mrs Brian Butler, Little Leigh, Holcombe, Dawlish, Devon], dau of George Westley Hitchcock, of Kenton, Devon, and *d* 1992, leaving issue:
1c *Rosena Marie; *b* 17 Dec 1959
1b *Rosalinda Maria [Mrs Douglas Redgrave, Pantiles, Woodland Ave, Teignmouth, Devon TQ14 8UU]; served in WAAF; *b* 10 Dec 1921; *m* 20 Nov 1946 Douglas Kyrle Redgrave (*d* 9 Aug 1992), s of John Kyrle Redgrave, of Cofton, Devon, and has:
1c *Michael Kyrle; *b* 6 May 1950
1c *Diana Lynne; *b* 15 July 1952
3a Henry Francis, of Cowan Island, Auckland, NZ; *b* 30 May 1877; *m* 15 Sept 1908 Ethel Isabel Harriet Marion, 2nd dau of Allix Edward Pardoe, of Carinmona, Dawlish, Devon, and *d* 1969, leaving issue:
1b *Sheila Francis [Mrs Andrew Stevens, Sandspit Rd, RD2, Warkworth, Auckland, NZ]; *b* 31 Aug 1914; *m* 9 Jan 1940 *Andrew McKenzie Stevens and has issue:
1c *Mary Louise [Mary Stevens, Mulberry Grove School House, RD1 Tryphena, Gt Barrier Island, NZ]; *b* 28 April 1945; *m* 1966 (*divorce* 1979) Johnny Bindner, of Copenhagen, and adopted:
*Daniel; *b* 1975
(4) Cecil, barrister; *b* 15 Feb 1846; *m* 21 April 1887 Alice (added by roy licence 16 April 1910 the name WOOLSEY and *d* 21 Feb 1939), only child of Major-Gen O'Brien Bellingham Woolsey, RA, of Milestown, Castlebellingham, and *d* 6 Dec 1901, having had issue:
1a Cecilia Frances; *m* 17 Sept 1912 Maj Ronald Edmund Barrow, IA, s of Gen Sir Edmund George Barrow, GCB, GCSI, and *d* 31 Oct 1961, leaving issue. He *d* 30 June 1942
(1) Ellen Caroline; *m* 19 Dec 1867 Edward Allesley Boughton Ward-Boughton-Leigh, of Brownsover Hall, Warwicks, and *d* 10 Feb 1922, leaving issue. He 25 May 1894
(2) Eliza Emily; *m* 21 April 1858 Lt-Col James Hatherell, only son of Rev Dr James William Hatherell, DD, of Westend, Hants, and *d* 18 Dec 1928, leaving issue. He *d* 25 Dec 1887

7 (cont.) The Hon Charles Butler *m* 2nd 16 Oct 1872 Constance Isabel (*m* 2nd 14 May 1888 Lt-Gen George John Peacocke (*d* 1895) and *d* 17 Dec 1923), yst dau of Adml John Edward Wacot, MP, and *d* 5 March 1885, having by her had issue:

(3) Beatrice Constance Charlotte; *m* 5 Nov 1904 Lt Col Guy Bernard Campbell Ward, DSO, S Wales Borderers, s of Major-Gen Sir Edward Wolstenholme Ward, KCMG, and *d* 18 Jan 1959, having had issue (*see* BANGOR V)

1 Roselinda Eleanor, *m* June 1819 Lt-Col John Marshall, and *d* 19 June 1859

The **13th/23rd Baron (of) Dunboyne** *m* 2nd 19 Dec 1843 Mary Anne Vincent (*d* 1846), dau of — Vaughan, of Belle Hatch House, Oxon, and *d* 6 July 1850

His son,

THEOBALD FitzWALTER, **14th/24th Baron (of) Dunboyne**; right to title confirmed by Ho Lds 10 Aug 1860, rep I peer 1868; *b* 11 Feb 1806; *m* 14 Nov 1832 Julia Celestina Maria (*d* 25 Dec 1897), dau of William Brander, of Moreden Hall, Surrey, and *d* 22 March 1881, having had, with four daus:

1 JAMES FitzWALTER BUTLER later CLIFFORD-BUTLER (roy licence 13 Nov 1860), **15th/25th Baron (of) Dunboyne**, DL, JP (Mon and Devon); Col 2nd Monmouth Rifle Vols; *b* 20 May 1839; *m* 12 June 1860 Marion (*d* 15 June 1919), only surv child of Col Henry Morgan Clifford, of Llantillo, Mon, and *d* 17 Aug 1899, leaving issue:

(1) Rosalinda Catherine Sophia; *b* 25 April 1861; *m* 30 April 1883 Maj-Gen William Henry Brooke Peters, 4th Hus, of Harefield, Devon, and *d* 21 April 1953, leaving issue. He *d* 27 Oct 1913

2 Theobald FitzWalter, JP; Capt Clare Militia; *b* 19 July 1840; *d* unm 19 Nov 1877.

3 ROBERT ST JOHN FitzWALTER BUTLER, **16th/26th Baron (of) Dunboyne**, DL Middx, JP and DL Co Clare; rep I peer, barrister, Master Court of Judicature 1874–1905, King's Remembrancer to 1905, BA, TCD; *b* 20 Jan 1844; *m* 9 Feb 1869 Caroline Maude Blanche (*d* 11 Jan 1927), dau of Capt George Probyn, and had issue:

(1) FitzWALTER GEORGE PROBYN, **17th/27th Baron**

(2) Leslie James Probyn, CMG (1917), DSO (1916), DL (Devon 1930); Col cmdg 2nd Bn Irish Gds, T/Brig-Gen whilst Bde Cdr 1916, Hon Brig-Gen 1922, sec TAA Devon 1922–38, served S African War 1900 (medal with four clasps) and WW I 1914 (despatches 6 times, brevet); *b* 22 April 1876; *m* 24 July 1907 Mary Christal, JP (*d* as the result of a hunting accident 27 Feb 1951), yst dau of Sir John Heathcoat-Amory, 1st Bt (*qv*), and had issue:

1a James Dighton; *educ* Winchester and RMC Sandhurst; Lt-Col cmdg 15th /19th King's Roy Hus and previously Probyn's Horse IA, served Waziristan 1936–37 (despatches) and WW II Middle East, Persia and India (despatches); *b* 9 Jan 1911; *m* 23 Oct 1943 Pamela (*d* 1987), widow of Lt-Col Alfred James Frederick Sugden, RA, and dau of William Alfred Pickwood, OBE, of Bolivia, and *d* 1987, leaving issue:

1b +(Michael) James [James Butler Esq, Morgans Bradley, Templeton, Tiverton, Devon EX16 8BJ], late Lt 15th/19th King's Royal Hus; *b* 7 July 1944; *educ* Eastbourne Coll, RMA Sandhurst and RAC Cirencester (Dip Rural Estate Management), FRICS, Fellow Western Counties Assoc of Ag Valuers; *m* 1981 *Jennifer, dau of Percy Williams, of Dundee, and has issue:

1c *Elizabeth Mary; *b* 1985

2b +Robert Patrick; *b* 19 Oct 1947, *educ* Milton Abbey; late Queen's Royal Irish Hus; *m* 2 Dec 1972 *Nicola, yr dau of Philip W R Pope, of W Stafford, Dorchester, Dorset, and has issue:

1c +Alexander Philip Dighton; *b* 1975

2c +Edward Patrick; *b* 1978

1a *Anne Christal; *b* 6 Jan 1909; *m* 11 Dec 1948 *Gerald Frederic Wigram, est son of Loftus Edward Wigram, MB, of Sogota Naibor, Rumuruti, Kenya (*see* WIGRAM, Bt), and has issue

2a Bridget Mary; *b* 8 Dec 1912; *d* unm 13 June 1956

(3) Robert Thomas Rowley Probyn, DSO (1918), MC (1915), Maj IASC, joined PWD India 1905, served RE and RTC (despatches, wounded) WW I; *b* 8 Oct 1882; *educ* Winchester and Cooper's Hill; *m* 15 July 1913 Grace Theodosia Farquhar (*d* 6 April 1971), dau of Lt-Col George Kinloch, JP, 13th Somerset LI, of Clonaslee, Queen's Co, and *dsp* 14 Dec 1938

(4) Theobald Patrick Probyn, DSO (1918), Col (Hon Maj-Gen) RA, OC 1st Regt RHA 1935–37, Cmdt RA Depot and Woolwich Garrison (T/Brig) 1937–39, cmded Bombay Dist 1940–41, attd Egyptian Army 1914–24, WW I in France, Palestine and Sudan (despatches twice, Sudan medal with two clasps, 3rd Cl Order Nile), NWF India 1930, Brevet Lt-Col 1931; *b* 3 July 1884; *educ* Winchester and RMA Woolwich; *m* 6 Dec 1933 *Hon Vera Elizabeth Sanders, OBE (1955), er dau of 1st and last Baron Bayford (*see* 1940 edn), and *dsp* 18 Oct 1970

(1) Lavinia Alice Julia; *b* 17 Dec 1869; *m* 25 Aug 1891 Rev John Hutchinson Hindson, MA, of Bradwall Hall, Sandbach, Cheshire, and *d* 24 Sept 1965, leaving five sons and four daus. He *d* 1916

(2) Maude Celestina; *b* 9 June 1872; *m* 16 Oct 1895 Robert Charles Donner, of Bowden, Lacock, Wilts, est surv son of Julius Donner, of Priest Hill, Surrey, and *d* 10 Dec 1952, leaving issue. He *d* 28 Feb 1926

(3) Blanche Amy Charlotte; *b* 3 Aug 1878; *d* unm 28 Jan 1961

(4) Rosalinda Laetitia; *b* 24 Jan 1881; *m* 2 April 1910 Capt John Colthurst Bowen-Colthurst, of Terrace, BC, Canada, Roy Irish Rifles, er s of Robert Walter Travers Bowen-Colthurst, of Oakgrove, Co Cork, and *d* 1 Aug 1940, leaving issue

The 16th/26th BARON *d* 29 Aug 1913; his est son,

FitzWALTER GEORGE PROBYN BUTLER, **17th/27th Baron (of) Dunboyne**; Capt RN, served Vitu Expdn 1890 and WW I 1914; *b* 20 March 1874; *m* 26 July 1915 (Dora) Isolde Butler (*d* 26 May 1977), est dau of Francis Fitzpatrick Tower, OBE, Cdr RNVR, by Laura, only surv child of Thomas Butler (*see* BUTLER, Bt, of Cloughgrenan), and *d* 9 May 1945, leaving issue:

1 PATRICK THEOBALD TOWER BUTLER, **18th/28th and present Baron (of) Dunboyne**

1 *(Doreen) Synolda Tower [The Hon Mrs Duncan, 9 Marland House, 28 Sloane Street, London SW1X 9NE]; *b* 17 Feb 1918; *m* 16 June 1945 Maj John Atholl Duncan, MC (*d* 1983), RA, s of Walter Atholl Duncan, of 53 Cadogan Sq, London SW1, and has issue:

(1) *(Walter) Alastair; *b* 8 Oct 1947; *educ* Eton

(2) *Patrick Atholl; *b* 16 Nov 1957; Maj RHA; *m* 1987 *Margrit Victoria, dau of Franz Frefel, of Frampton, Dorchester, Dorset and has issue:

1a *Christopher Patrick; *b* 1991

2a *Alexander Edward; *b* 1993

1a *Charlotte Isabel; *b* 1989

(1) *Zara Synolda [Mrs David Firmin, 24 Ursula St, London SW11 3DW]; *b* 3 Feb 1950; *m* 1979 *David Firmin, FRIBA, son of E H Firmin, of Aldwick Bay Estate, Bognor Regis, W Sussex, and has issue:

1a *Philip Duncan; *b* 1981

2a *Robert Charles; *b* 1985

3a *Zoe Charlotte; *b* 1980

(2) *Lora Romayne [Mrs Bryan Elliott, 22 Pennard Road, London W12 8D5]; *b* 10 May 1956; *m* 1987 *Lt-Col Bryan M Elliott, MBE, s of Cdr Charles Elliott, RN

2 *Maureen Maude Tower [The Hon Mrs Price, 98 Old Church Street, London SW3 6EP]; *b* 12 June 1919; *m* 6 April 1946 Lt-Col Robert Caradoc Rose Price, DSO, OBE (*d* 1988), Welsh Gds, er s of Brig-Gen Thomas Rose Price, CMG, DSO, of Madron House, Hythe, Kent (*see* PRICE, Bt), and has issue

3 *Isolde Sheila Tower [The Hon Mrs Monck, Yaverland Manor, Sandown, IoW; Albany, Piccadilly, London W1]; *b* 24 April 1925; *m* 23 April 1949 Cdr Victor Robert Penryn Monk Monck, RNVR (*d* 1987), yr s of Maj Charles Sydney Goldman, MBE, by Hon Agnes Mary, RRC, 2nd dau of 1st Viscount Peel (*see* PEEL, E), and has:

(1) *Rory Penryn; *b* 14 Nov 1951; *educ* Harrow

(1) *Tasha Penryn [Mrs William Donald, 82 Forest View Rd, Tuffley, Gloucester GL4 OBY]; *b* 7 April 1950 *m* 1st 14 July 1976 Martin P A Travers, son of M V Travers, of Melhingar, and has issue:

1a *Isabel Eileen; *b* 1977

(1) (cont.) Mrs Travers *m* 2nd 1984 *Rev William Donald, and has further issue:

1a *Jesse Michael Penryn; *b* 1985

(2) *Fiona Penryn; *b* 22 May 1957; *m* 1981 *Andrew Pettinger, 2nd son of Eric J C Pettinger, of Watsons, Belsford, Harberton, Totnes, Devon TQ9 7SP

DUNDEE

Arms: Gules, a lion rampant or, armed and langued azure, holding in his dexter paw a broad-sword proper. **Supporters:** Two greyhounds argent, collared gules. **Crest:** A lion's gamb erased in bend or holding a cutlass argent all proper. **Motto:** *Dissipate* ('Disperse'). **Creations:** V. (S) 15 Nov 1641, L. (S) 15 Nov 1641 and Sept 1660, E. (S) Sept 1660, B. (UK) 30 July 1954.

THE 12TH EARL OF DUNDEE, Viscount Dudhope, Lord Scrymgeour, Lord Innerkeithing, and **Baron Glassary**, of Glassary, Co Argyll (Alexander Henry Scrymgeour of Dundee) [The Rt Hon The Earl of Dundee, Birkhill, Cupar, Fife KY15 4QP]; *b* 5 June 1949; *s f* 1983; *educ* Eton and St Andrews; Hereditary Roy Standard-Bearer for Scotland and Constable of Dundee; Page of Honour to HM THE QUEEN 1964–65; Ld in Waiting (Govt Whip) 1986–89; CStJ; *m* 1979 *Siobhan Mary, dau of David Llewellyn, of 41 Cleveland Sq, London W2, and has issue:

1 +HENRY DAVID WEDDERBURN OF THAT ILK, *Lord Scrymgeour*; *b* 20 June 1982

1 *Marina Patricia; *b* 21 Aug 1980

2 *Flora Hermione Vera; *b* 1985

3 *Lavinia Rebecca Elizabeth; *b* 1986

Viscountcy of Dundee: John Graham of Claverhouse, whose mother was daughter of the 1st Earl of Northesk (*qv*) and who descended from a female Scrymgeour (Maud, dau of one of the Sir James Scrymgeours who was Constable of Dundee), was created Viscount of Dundee and Lord Graham of Claverhouse in 1688. At this time the grantee of the Earldom of Dundee (*see* below) had been dead twenty years and his honours were thought to be dormant or extinct.

The Lord Dundee of the 1688 creation was called 'Bloody Clavers' for his repression of the Covenanters (extreme Presbyterians) on the restored Stuarts' behalf. It is this Dundee to whom Scott is referring in his famous lines 'To the Lords of Convention 'twas Claver'se who spoke,/ "Ere the King's crown shall fall there are crowns to be broke;/So let each cavalier who loves honour and me, Come follow the bonnet of Bonny Dundee."' He stood by JAMES II when practically everyone else had deserted him and raised the clans for the Jacobite cause in Scotland. He defeated the Williamite General Mackay at the Battle of Killiecrankie 1689 but was himself killed there.

His son survived him only a few months and the title became forfeited by his younger brother, the 3rd Viscount, for his continuing fidelity to the Stuarts. Nevertheless a cousin of theirs assumed the style 'Viscount of Dundee'. This latter gentleman's son and grandson continued the Jacobite family tradition, one in the '15, the other in the '45, and were accordingly both attainted. Meanwhile the titular James III created a brother of Cardinal Gualterio titular Earl of Dundee in 1705.

Lineage: Sir ALEXANDER SCRYMGEOUR; granted the lands of Dudhope, Forfarshire, and *cr* Constable of Dundee by charter from WILLIAM WALLACE 29 March 1298 as reward for services as Hereditary Standard-Bearer at victory over English of Stirling Bridge; joined ROBERT I (THE BRUCE) 1306; captured by English Battle of Methven and was hanged, drawn and quartered York 4 Aug 1306, leaving:

NICHOLAS SCRYMGEOUR, of Dudhope; bore Roy Standard of Scotland at Battle of Bannockburn 1314, recd lands in Inverkeithing and confirmation in his office by charter of ROBERT I (THE BRUCE) 12 March 1324; had:

Sir JOHN SCRYMGEOUR of Dudhope; *ka* Battle of Dupplin Moor 1332; had:

Sir ALEXANDER SCRYMGEOUR of Dudhope; negotiated ransom of DAVID II 1357; *m* Agnes, dau of Gilbert —, of Glassary, Co Argyll; *d* 1383, leaving issue:

Sir JAMES SCRYMGEOUR of Dudhope; *m* Egidia, dau of Sir John Maxwell of Pollok (*see* 1956 edn STIRLING-MAXWELL, Bt), and was *ka* Battle of Harlaw 24 July 1411, leaving:

1 John (Sir), of Dudhope; *m* 1st (?) Marion, widow of Sir Robert Maitland (*see* LAUDERDALE, E); *m* 2nd Isabella Oliphant; *d* 1465, leaving by her:

(1) James (Sir), of Dudhope; *m* Margaret Maitland; *d* 1478, leaving issue:

1a James (Sir), of Dudhope; *m* 1495 Isobel, dau of 2nd Lord Gray (*qv*), and *d* 1504, leaving issue:

1b James, of Dudhope; *m* Marion Stewart; *d* 1546, having had issue:

1c Elizabeth; *m* her kinsman James Scrymgeour of Kirkton (*see* above)

2c Agnes; *m* Sir W Bruce of Earlshall

1a Mariot; *m c* 1475, as his 2nd w, Robert Arbuthnott of that Ilk (*see* ARBUTHNOTT, V)

2a Elizabeth; *m c* 15 Oct 1481 John Sandilands, 6th of Calder (*see* TORPHICHEN, L)

(1) Elizabeth; *m* probably by 1450 3rd Lord Glamis (*see* STRATHMORE AND KINGHORNE, E)

2 John, of Glassary or Glastrie; bore the Roy Standard at Battle of Flodden 1513 as his n James was not of age to bear arms; *m* Janet Ogilvy and *d* Oct 1513 of wounds recd at Flodden, leaving issue:

(1) John, of Glassary; *s* cousin as Standard-Bearer of Scotland and Constable of Dundee and in the estates of Dudhope 1546; *m* Isobel Cunningham; *d* 1562, leaving issue:

1a John, of Dudhope; *m* Margaret, dau of Sir J Campbell of Lundle, and had issue:

1b James (Sir), of Dudhope; Provost Dundee 1588, MP Dundee 1600 and 1605, Forfarshire 1605 and 1607, ktd on return from Denmark with embassy which negotiated marriage of the Danish Princess Anne to JAMES VI 1589, confirmed by Act of Parl 1600 together with heirs-male as bearer of the King's standard on all occasions, both on horse and foot (which statute is still part of the laws of Scotland); *m* Margaret, dau of Sir Robert Carnegie of Kinnaird (*see* FIFE, D), and *d* 13 July 1612, having had an est s:

1c JOHN SCRYMGEOUR, **1st Viscount Dudhope**, so *cr* 15 Nov 1641, as also LORD SCRIMGEOUR (both S); *b* 1570; MP Forfarshire 1612, 1617 and 1621 and Argyllshire 1628–33; *m* Sept 1596 Margaret, dau of Sir David Seton of Parbroath, and *d* 7 March 1643, leaving an est s:

1d JAMES SCRYMGEOUR, **2nd Viscount Dudhope**; *m* 4 Aug 1618 Isabella Ker, dau of 1st Earl of Roxburghe (*see* ROXBURGHE, D), and was *k* at the royalist defeat Marston Moor 1644, leaving issue:

1e JOHN SCRYMGEOUR, **1st Earl of Dundee**, so *cr* Sept 1660, as also VISCOUNT OF DUDHOPE, LORD SCRIMGEOUR AND INNERKEITHING (S), with remainder to his heirs male whatsoever; raised a regt of 250 horse, served under Montrose 1645 and Hamilton 1648, carried the standard of CHARLES II on the march to Worcester 1651 and was wounded at Torwood, raised a regt of horse under Middleton 1654, was captured and had his estates sequestrated; *m* July 1644 Anne Ramsay (*m* 2nd 13 Oct 1670 Sir Henry Bruce of Clackmannan), dau of 1st Earl of Dalhousie (*qv*), and *dsp* 23 June 1668, when the er line of Dudhope expired but when he would normally have been *s* in his titles and estates by his heir-male

3 David, of Sonahard, Chamberlain of the King's revenues north of the Tay; *d* 1471, leaving issue:

(1) Alexander, of Sonahard; priest, recd a charter of Kirkton in Earlstradilty from Sir James Scrymgeour of Dudhope 21 June 1500; *d* 1505 and was *s* by his n

(2) David; *m* and *d* 1493, leaving issue:

1a James, of Kirkton; *m* Lily Lessilis and *d* March 1513, leaving issue:

1b James, of Kirkton; *m* 1539 his cousin Elizabeth Scrymgeour (*see* below) and *d* by 1555, leaving issue:

1c James, of Kirkton; *m* Agnes Bruce, of Earlshall; *d* 1580, leaving issue:

1d John, of Kirkton; *m* 3 May 1593 Marion, dau of Thomas Fothringham of Pourie; *d* June 1629, leaving issue:

1e John, of Kirkton; *m* 11 Oct 1624 Jean, dau of Rev John Makgill (*see* OXFUIRD, V); *d* 23 June 1656, leaving:

1f JOHN SCRYMGEOUR of Kirkton, *de jure* 2nd EARL OF DUNDEE, 4th VISCOUNT DUDHOPE and Hereditary Standard-Bearer of Scotland and Constable of Dundee, heir-male and of line, also heir of entail under two charters under Gt Seal 1541 and 1587; deprived of his right to *s* to the estates of Dudhope and to the Viscountcy and Earldom by the influence of the Duke of Lauderdale (*see* LAUDERDALE, E) with CHARLES II; *m* Magdalene, dau of Alexander Wedderburn of Kinggenny and Easter Powrie (*see* OGILVY-WEDDERBURN, Bt); *d* 1698, leaving, with other issue:

1g JAMES SCRYMGEOUR, *de jure* 3rd EARL OF DUNDEE; *dsp*

2g ALEXANDER SCRYMGEOUR, *de jure* 4th EARL OF DUNDEE; Lay Prof of Humanity, Philsosphy and Theology at St Andrews *temp* QUEEN ANNE; *m* Janet, only dau of David Falconer, Prof Divinity St Andrews, and had issue:

1h DAVID SCRYMGEOUR, of Birkhill, Fifeshire, *de jure* 5th EARL OF DUNDEE; Advocate and Sheriff Depute of Inverness; *m* Katherine, 3rd dau of Sir Alexander Wedderburn, 4th Bt, of Blackness, and had issue:

1i ALEXANDER SCRYMGEOUR later SCRYMGEOUR-WEDDERBURN (1788 after inheriting estates of David Wedderburn of Wedderburn (*dsp* 1761)), of Birkhill, *de jure* 6th EARL OF DUNDEE; *m* Elizabeth, dau of James Ferguson, of Pitfour, and *dsp* 1811

2i John, *d* 1791

3i David, *d* 1780

4i HENRY SCRYMGEOUR-WEDDERBURN of Wedderburn, *de jure* 7th EARL OF DUNDEE; attended GEORGE IV as standard-bearer on his visit to Holyrood Aug 1822; *m* 5 April 1793 Mary Turner, est dau of Capt Hon Frederick Lewis Maitland, of Rankeillour, RN (*see* LAUDERDALE, E); *d* 30 Dec 1841, leaving issue, with eight daus:

1j FREDERICK LEWIS SCRYMGEOUR-WEDDERBURN of Wedderburn, JP, DL, *de jure* 8th EARL OF DUNDEE; *b* 4 March 1808; *m* 1st 26 April 1839 Hon Helen Arbuthnott (*d* 23 April 1840), 5th dau of 8th Viscount of Arbuthnott (*qv*), and had issue:

1k HENRY SCRYMGEOUR-WEDDERBURN, *de jure* 9th EARL OF DUNDEE, for whom *see* further below

1j (cont.) The *de jure* 8th EARL OF DUNDEE *m* 2nd 31 Aug 1852 Selina Mary (*d* 18 Oct 1902), dau of Capt Thomas Garth, RN, of Haines Hill, Berks; *d* 16 Aug 1874, having by her had further issue, two sons and three daus

His est s,

HENRY SCRYMGEOUR-WEDDERBURN of Wedderburn, Angus, and Birkhill, Fife, JP and DL (Fife), and JP (Angus), *de jure* 9th EARL OF DUNDEE; *b* 18 April 1840; Capt 17th Regt; bore Standard of Scotland at Coronation of EDWARD VII as Hereditary Standard-Bearer of Scotland; *m* 31 March 1869 Juliana (*d* 28 May 1921), yst dau of Thomas Braddell, of Coolmelagh, Co Wexford, and *d* 1 Feb 1914, leaving issue:

1 HENRY SCRYMGEOUR-WEDDERBURN, *de jure* 10th EARL OF DUNDEE for whom *see* further below

2 Frederick Lewis, of Balhousie, Largo, Fife; *b* 27 June 1874; *m* 17 Dec 1913 Zaida Grace (*d* 27 Feb 1943), only dau of Sir Ffolliott William Erskine of Cambo, 3rd Bt (*qv*); *d* 22 May 1936, having had issue:

(1) William Alexander, DFC and Bar; *b* 22 Feb 1919; WW II as F/Lt; *m* 1st 1940 Mabel Kathleen, dau of F W Rowe, of Torquay; *m* 2nd 1951 Margaret Emily (*d* 1988), dau of William Henry Innes, of Largo, and *d* 7 May 1995, leaving:

1a +John Frederick [John Scrymgeour-Wedderburn Esq, The West Lodge, Craigtoun, St Andrews, Fife KY16 8NY]; *b* 1955; PhD; *m* 1984 *Sabine, yr dau of Hubert Schauten, of Essen, Germany, and has:

1b +Lewis Alexander; *b* 28 Dec 1994

1b *Georgina Emily; *b* 3 June 1997

1a *Caroline Sarah; *b* 1954; *m* 1986 *John Quentin Conway Ashton, er s of Conway Allen Ashton, of Blackburn, Lancs, and has:

1b *Chloe; *b* 1 Sept 1986

2a *Grace Marion [Mrs Jonathan Humphrey, Myrtle Cottage, Orton, by Fochabers, Moray IV32 7QB]; *b* 31 Aug 1959; *m* 1980 *Jonathan W Humphrey, er s of D W Humphrey, of Cross Farm, Styal, Cheshire

(1) Kathleen; *b* 17 Sept 1914; *d* 15 Jan 1920

(2) *Cecily Grace; *b* 17 Dec 1915; a Sis of Bethany

(3) Marion; *b* 19 Feb 1917; *d* 28 Aug 1996

3 Charles Kenneth; *b* 29 May 1887; *educ* Marlborough; WW I 1915–18 as Lt Special List; Min of Supply Timber Control 1940–41, Timber Production Dept 1941–45; *m* 24 Nov 1915 Gertrude Louisa Marie (*d* 12 Dec 1957), dau of James Carnegie Wemyss; *d* 13 Aug 1963, leaving issue:

(1) *Rosemary [Mrs William Roper-Caldbeck, Strowan, by Crieff, Perthshire]; *b* 29 Nov 1916; *m* 1st 14 July 1937 (*divorce* 1947) Lt-Col Christian Landale Melville, DSO, 2nd s of Col Edward Patrick Alexander Melville, and has:

1a *Robin Kenneth Christian [Robin Melville Esq, Woodborough Manor, nr Pewsey, Wilts]; *b* 1938; WS; *m* 1st 1961 (*divorce* 1984) Elizabeth Mary Melville, dau of Capt Melville Stewart Jameson, and has issue:

1b *James Landale; *b* 1963; Capt Roy Scots Dragoon Gds; *m* 1991 *Sophie E, yr dau of Brig Peter Marsh, of Camberley, Surrey

2b *Christian Kenneth Bowring; *b* 1965; Capt Roy Scots Dragoon Gds

1a (cont.) Robin Kenneth Christian Melville *m* 2nd 1985 *Loraine Sylvia Alice, widow of Benjamin Mark Weston Wells

2a *Edward Charles [Edward Melville Esq, Holydean, Melrose, Roxburghshire]; *b* 1940; WS; *m* 1966 *Alison Sinclair, dau of Thomas Sinclair Fraser, and has issue:

1b *Peter Charles Fraser; *b* 1970

1b *Rachel Anne Rosemary; *b* 1972

3a *Anthony [Anthony Melville Esq, 7 Hagbourne Clo, Woodcote, Oxon RG8 0RZ]; *b* 1942; *m* 1981 —

4a *Michael Landale [Maj Michael Melville, Strowan, Crieff, Perthshire]; *b* 1943; Maj Black Watch; *m* 1971 *Susan Louise Margaret, dau of Maj Edmund Robert Cox, TD, JP, and has issue:

1b *Neil Edmund Landale; *b* 1976

1b *Sarah Anne Louise; *b* 1974

2b *Julia Rosemary Susan; *b* 1983

(1) (cont.) Mrs Rosemary Melville *m* 2nd 10 June 1949 Brig William Noel Roper-Caldbeck, DSO (*d* 22 July 1965), est s of Maj William Caldbeck-Roper-Caldbeck, JP, of Moyle Park, Clondalkin, Co Dublin

(2) *Lorna Mabel [Mrs Ian Miskelly, Glenara, Methven, Perthshire]; *b* 7 Jan 1918; *m* 7 Dec 1966 Ian Miskelly, DSC, JP (*d* 1993), s of John Miskelly, of Ravenswood, Dunoon, Argyllshire

(3) *Aimée Elspeth Scrymgeour-Wedderburn [Mrs James Macfarlane, Appt 507, 3495 Mountain St, Montreal, Quebec,Canada H3G 2A5]; *b* 16 April 1920; *m* 21 April 1945 James Ferrier Macfarlane (*d* 1986), s of Clare MacFarlane, of Quebec, and has issue:

1a *Charles Ferrier; *b* 1946; *m* 1970 *Kathryn Anne Oppé and has issue:

1b *James Andrew; *b* 1973

2b *Ian Fraser Oppé; *b* 1975

1a *Jennifer Elizabeth; *b* 1948; *m* 1975 *William Lorne Lindsay, and has issue:

1b *Christopher Lorne Ferrier; *b* 1977

1b *Gillian Aimée; *b* 1980

(4) Susan Mary; *b* 28 March 1926; *m* 28 Jan 1950 (divorce 1970) Noel George Moore, 2nd s of Ernest Clement Moore, of 100 Mulgrave Rd, Sutton, Surrey, and had issue:

1a *Mary Louisa; *b* 21 Oct 1954

(4) (cont.) Mrs Susan Moore *m* 2nd 1970 John Frederick Ingleby and *d* 1981

4 William Ogilvy, DSC; *b* 22 Nov 1894; Capt RN (ret), Ch of Staff C-in-C Rosyth 1939–40, Ch Staff Offr Flag Offr Ceylon 1942–43, lent to RIN as Cdre Bay of Bengal 1943–44; *m* 16 Sept 1921 Joyce (*d* 1990), only dau of Col Robert Henry Jennings, CSI, RE; *d* 29 Oct 1958, leaving issue:

(1) +Ian Alexander [Cdr Ian Scrymgeour-Wedderburn RN (ret), Dunlichty Lodge, Farr, Inverness-shire IV1 2AN]; *b* 22 Jan 1923; Cdr RN (ret), FRIN; *m* 25 March 1947 *Pamela Desirée, dau of Lt-Col Richard White, of Church Farm House, Smarden, Kent, and has issue:

1a +James Ian [James Scrymgeour-Wedderburn Esq, 87 Howards La, London SW15 6NZ]; *b* 21 April 1951; *educ* Sherborne and Hertford Coll Oxford (MA); *m* 1981 *Sarah M A, dau of Col Michael Seys-Phillips, of The Malt House, Mereworth, Kent, and has issue:

1b +Charles Richard; *b* 1986

2b +Alexander James; *b* 1988

1b *Catherine Juliet; *b* 1984

(1) *Fiona Marigold Joyce [Mrs James Yates, 97 Grove Rd, Hitchin, Herts]; *b* 31 Dec 1925; *m* 30 June 1951 *Rev James Ainsworth Yates, yst s of Brevet Col James Ainsworth Yates, CIE, DSO, IA, and has issue:

1a *Katherine Fiona; *b* 12 Jan 1958

2a *Veronica Margaret; *b* 12 Jan 1958

*Susannah Elizabeth (adopted); *b* 6 Dec 1956

1 Helen Margaret; *m* 16 Oct 1901 Herbert Godsal (*d* 22 Sept 1932), yst s of Philip William Godsal, of Iscoyd Park, Flints; *d* 15 Feb 1942, leaving issue:

(1) Charles Philip Lloyd; *b* 22 Oct 1907

2 Mary Turner; *m* 3 Aug 1903 Brig-Gen James Dalgleish Heriot-Maitland, CMG, DSO (*d* 18 Jan 1958), er s of Maj-Gen Sir James Makgill Heriot-Maitland, KCB, RE, and *d* 11 March 1937, leaving issue (*see* LAUDERDALE, E)

3 Anne Grizel; SSB; *d* unm 20 Dec 1954

4 Katherine Elspeth; *d* unm 5 Nov 1940

5 Juliet; *d* unm 28 Feb 1956

6 Maud Kathleen; *m* 9 Aug 1910 Lt-Col James Charles Walter Connel, DSO, KOSB; *d* 31 Jan 1925, leaving issue

The *de jure* 9th EARL OF DUNDEE's est s,

HENRY SCRYMGEOUR-WEDDERBURN, of Wedderburn and Birkhill, *de jure* 10th EARL OF DUNDEE; *b* 28 June 1872; Lt-Col TAR, formerly Lt-Col cmdg 5th Bn Black Watch and Capt Gordon Highrs, OC 5th Bn Black Watch (RHR) in France WW I (despatches); carried Roy Standard of Scotland in place of his f Coronation of HM KING GEORGE V 1911; *m* 30 July 1901 Edith (*d* 16 Oct 1968 aged 91), only dau of John Moffat, CE, of Ardrossan, by his w Jessie Fulton, only dau of James Arthur, of Carlung, Ayshire (*see* GLENARTHUR, B); *d* 12 May 1924, leaving issue:

1 HENRY JAMES, **11th Earl**

2 David, DSO (1944); *b* 2 April 1912; *educ* Winchester and RMC Sandhurst; Lt-Col cmdg 1st Bn Scots Gds; *m* 9 Sept 1940 *Patricia Katherine (*m* 3rd 30 Oct 1946 her bro-in-law 11th Earl of Dundee), yr dau of Lord Herbert Andrew Montagu-Douglas-Scott, CMG, DSO (*see* BUCCLEUCH and QUEENSBERRY, D), and widow of Lt-Col Walter Douglas Faulkner, MC, Irish Gds; *d* of wounds Anzio 1 March 1944, leaving issue:

(1) *Janet Mary [Mrs Mervyn Fox-Pitt, Grange, Scrymgeour, Cupar, Fife]; *b* 14 Aug 1941; *m* 18 Jan 1962 *Capt (Edward Arthur) Mervyn Lane Fox-Pitt, Welsh Gds, yr s of Maj-Gen William Augustus Fitz-Gerald Lane Fox-Pitt, DSO, MVO, MC, DL, of Marsh Court, Sherborne, Dorset, and has issue:

1a *David William; *b* 19 Aug 1964

1a *Leonie Patricia; *b* 27 Oct 1962; *m* 1982 *Aidan Joseph Merry Gibbs (*see* ALDENHAM and HUNSDON OF HUNSDON, B)

2a *Miranda Mary; *b* 29 Dec 1968; *m* 1988 *Hon Peregrine David Euan Malcolm Moncreiffe of Moncreiffe and has issue (*see* ERROLL, E)

(2) *Elizabeth [The Rt Hon The Lady Teynham, The Walton Canonry, The Close, Salisbury, Wilts; Pylewell Park, Lymington, Hants]; *b* 5 Oct 1943; *m* 31 Oct 1964 *20th Baron Teynham (*qv*) and has issue

1 Janet; *d* 18 Aug 1926

The *de jure* 10th EARL OF DUNDEE's er s,

HENRY JAMES SCRYMGEOUR-WEDDERBURN later SCRYMGEOUR OF DUNDEE, **11th Earl of Dundee**, PC (1959), JP (Fife 1927), DL (Fife 1936); *b* 3 May 1902; *educ* Winchester and Balliol Coll Oxford (MA 1926) (Pres Oxford Union 1924); Capt 7th Black Watch 1939–41; MP W Renfrewshire 1931–45, PPS to Pres Bd of Edcn 1933–35, to Min of Ag 1935–36, to Sec of State Scotland 1936, Parly Under-Sec Scotland 1936–39, Jt Under-Sec 1941–42, memb Parly Delegation to China 1942, accepted by the Ctee for Privileges Ho of Lds 31 July 1952 as having made out his claim to the titles, honours and dignities of VISCOUNT DUDHOPE (S) and LORD SCRYMGEOUR (S) and 18 May 1953 to those of EARL OF DUNDEE (S) and LORD INNERKEITHING (S), *cr* 30 July 1954 BARON GLASSARY, of Glassary, Argyll (UK), Min without Portfolio 1958–61, Min of State FO 1961–64, Dep Ldr Ho of Lds 1962–64, Hon LLD St Andrews 1954, Order of Brilliant Star with Special Cravat China 1942; *m* 30 Oct 1946 his sis-in-law (*see* above) *Patricia Katharine [The Rt Hon Patricia Countess of Dundee, Coultra Farm House, Newport-on-Tay, Fife]; *d* 29 June 1983, leaving issue:

ALEXANDER HENRY SCRYMGEOUR OF DUNDEE, **12th and present Earl of Dundee**

DUNDONALD

Arms: Argent a chevron gules between three boar's heads erased azure. **Crest:** A horse passant argent. **Supporters:** Two greyhounds argent, collared and lined or. **Motto:** *Virtute et labore* ('By courage and labour'). **Creations:** L. (S) 26 Dec 1647 (Cochrane of Dundonald) and 12 May 1669 (Cochrane of Paseley and Ochiltrie), E. (S) 12 May 1669.

THE 15TH EARL OF DUNDONALD, Lord Cochrane of Dundonald, Lord Cochrane of Paseley and Ochiltrie and **Marquess of Maranham** in Brazil ((Iain Alexander) Douglas Blair Cochrane) [The Rt Hon The Earl of Dundonald, Lochnell Castle, Ledaig, Argyll PA37 1QT; Beacon Hall, Benenden, Cranbrook, Kent]; *b* 17 Feb 1961; *s f* 1986; *educ* Wellington and RAC Cirencester; dir Duneth Securities Ltd and Assoc Cos, Hon Consul in Scotland for Chile 1993–; *m* 1987 *M Beatrice L, dau of Adolphus Russo, of Cumberland Rd, Gibraltar, and has issue:

1 +ARCHIE IAN THOMAS BLAIR, *Lord Cochrane*; *b* 14 March 1991

1 *Marina Aphra Mariola; *b* 1992

Lineage: JOHN COCHRANE of Lincliff ; had:

ROBERT COCHRANE of Cochrane (or Lincliff), near Paisley, Renfrewshire; resigned the lands of Cochrane 5 March 1456/7 in favour of his s:

ALLAN COCHRANE OF THAT ILK; had a charter of the lands of Cochrane from JAMES II on the resignation of his f, witnessed a charter by Robert, Lord Lyle, to the Abbot of Paisley 25 Sept 1452, and a contract of marriage 8 May 1480; *m* and left , with an er s (James, living 10 May 1486, *dsps*):

ROBERT COCHRANE OF THAT ILK; had sasine of the lands of Cochrane 1488; living 2 Jan 1516/7, having resigned his lands in favour of his s:

JOHN COCHRANE OF THAT ILK; seised of the lands of Cochrane 10 Jan 1492, had a charter of these lands 13 Jan 1498; *m* Elizabeth Sempill and with her had a charter of the lands of Corsefoord 20 Jan 1486/7; his s:

JOHN COCHRANE OF THAT ILK; served heir to his gf in the lands of Wester Cochrane 8 May 1520; *m* Marion Stewart (*m* 2nd by 1556 John Gibson and *d* 12 May 1539) and had , with two yr sons (William, living 1 April 1565; David, living 28 May 1536):

JOHN COCHRANE OF THAT ILK; *m* Elizabeth Sempill of Fulwood and with her had a charter of the lands of Craigton 5 April 1529; had an only s:

WILLIAM COCHRANE OF THAT ILK; had a charter of confirmation of the lands of Cochrane 30 Nov 1556, added the Tower to his Manor House which was henceforward called Cochrane Castle; *m c* 1579 Elizabeth (*d* 15 Aug 1594), dau of Robert Montgomerie of Skelmorlie, and *d* 14 July 1603, having had, with two er daus (Dorothy, *d c* 1601; Margaret, *d c* 1601):

ELIZABETH Cochrane; *m* (contract 24 July 1593) Alexander BLAIR later COCHRANE (on whom the lands of Cochrane were settled 7 Feb 1601; also acquired the lands of Auchencreugh, Ayrshire, by 30 July 1618 and the Barony of Cowdown, Neilstone, Renfrewshire, by 23 April 1623; *d c* July 1641), 3rd s of John Blair of that Ilk by Grizel, dau of Robert, Lord Sempill (*qv*), and had, with other issue:

1 John (Sir), of Cochrane; royalist Civil War; resigned his estates to his bro William 1642; *m* Grace Butler and *dsp*

2 WILLIAM, **1st Earl**

3 Alexander, of Auchencreugh; royalist Col Civil War; *m* Agnes Richie and *d* 1673, leaving issue

4 Hugh, of Ferguslie; royalist Col Civil War; *m* Joan, dau of Henry Savage, of Ardken, Co Down, and had issue

5 Gavin, of Craigmure; *m* Margaret, dau of James Cleland, of Faskin, Lanarks, and *d* 1701, leaving issue

The 2nd s,

Sir WILLIAM COCHRANE, **1st Earl of Dundonald**, so *cr* 12 May 1669, as also LORD COCHRANE OF PASELEY AND OCHILTRIE, with remainder in default of male issue to the est heirs female of his body and without division and their heirs male who should bear or assume the name and arms of Cochrane, whom failing to his nearest heirs whomsoever, as also earlier 26 Dec 1647 LORD COCHRANE OF DUNDONALD, with remainder to the heirs male of his body (all S); had a charter of Cowdown on the resignation of his f 1634, acquired the lands of Dundonald 1638, ktd 1641, MP Ayrshire 1644; *m c* 14 April 1633 Eupheme, dau of Sir William Scott of Ardross, Fife, by Jean, dau of Sir John Skene of Curriehill, and *d* 1685, having had issue:

1 William, *Lord Cochrane*, PC; Capt of Horse; *m* 1653 Lady Catherine Kennedy (*bur* 15 Feb 1700), 2nd dau of 6th Earl of Cassillis (*see* AILSA, M), and *dvp* 25 Aug 1679, having had, with other issue:

(1) JOHN COCHRANE, **2nd Earl of Dundonald**; supported William of Orange; *m* Nov 1684 Susannah (*m* 2nd 3rd Marquess of Tweeddale (*qv*) and *d* 7 Feb 1737), 2nd dau of William, Duke of Hamilton (*see* HAMILTON and BRANDON, D), and *d* 17 May 1690, having had issue:

1a WILLIAM COCHRANE, **3rd Earl of Dundonald**; *b c* 1686; *d* unm 22 Nov 1705

2a JOHN COCHRANE, **4th Earl of Dundonald**; *b* 4 July 1687; rep S peer 1713–15, Col 4th Regt Horse Gds; *m* 1st 4 April 1706 Lady Anne Murray (*d* 30 Nov 1710), 2nd dau of 1st Earl of Dunmore (*qv*), and had, with three daus:

1b WILLIAM COCHRANE, **5th Earl of Dundonald**; left his unentailed property to his nephew, 4th Duke of Hamilton; *d* unm 27 Jan 1724/5

2a (cont.) The **4th Earl** *m* 2nd 15 Oct 1715 Mary (*d* 4 Feb 1721/2), dau of 2nd Duke of Leeds (*see* 1963 edn) and widow of 2nd Duke of Beaufort (*qv*), and *d* 5 June 1720, having by her had no issue

1a Anne; *bapt* 4 Sept 1685; *d* young

(2) William, of Kilmarnock; Jt-Keeper of the Signet 1711; *m* Lady Grizel Graham, 3rd dau of James, Marquess of Montrose (*see* MONTROSE, D), and *d* Aug 1717, having had, with other issue:

1a THOMAS COCHRANE, **6th Earl of Dundonald**; *b* 1702; *m* Oct 1727 Catherine (*d* 13 April 1779), 2nd dau of Lord Basil Hamilton, of Baldoon (*see* HAMILTON and BRANDON, D), and *d* 28 May 1737, having had, with other issue:

1b WILLIAM COCHRANE, **7th Earl of Dundonald**; mil offr; *ka* unm Siege of Louisburg America 9 July 1758

1b Katherine; *m* William Wood, of Nether Gallowhill, and *d* 4 Oct 1776, leaving issue

2b Charlotte; *bur* 10 May 1740

1a Catherine; *m* David Smythe, of Methven, Perthshire, and *d* 19 March 1772, leaving issue

2a Isabella; *m* John Ogilvy of Balbegno, and *d* 21 Dec 1770, leaving three daus

3a Grizel; *m* her cousin John Cochrane of Ferguslie, and *d* 12 Sept 1753

(3) Thomas, of Polkellie, Ayshire; *m* Diana, dau and heir of Sir David Cuningham of Robertland (*see* FAIRLIE-CUNINGHAME, Bt), and *dsp* by 4 Oct 1694

(4) Alexander, of Bollinshaw; *m* (contract 15 Sept 1698) Emilia, dau of James Murray, of Bolton, and *d* 1706, leaving:

1a Alexander, of Bollinshaw; *dsp c* 1709

2 John (Sir), of Ochiltree; Covenanter, MP Ayrshire 1669, suspected of complicity in the Rye House Plot 1683 and fled to Holland; returned to Scotland and took part in Argyll's rising 1685, was imprisoned and his lands confiscated but was restored to his estates 1690; *m* March 1656 Margaret, dau of Sir William Strickland, 1st Bt, of Boynton, Yorks, memb Cromwell's Ho of Lds, and *d* soon after 23 June 1707, having had, with two other s and another dau:

(1) William, of Ochiltree; *m* 19 April 1681 Lady Mary Bruce (who unsuccessfully claimed the Earldom of Kincardine 1705), est dau of 2nd Earl of Kincardine (*see* ELGIN and KINCARDINE, E), and *d* after 1739, having had, with other issue:

1a William, Yr. of Ochiltree; *bapt* 25 Jan 1682; *dvp c* 1716

2a Charles, of Ochiltree and Culross; *b* 25 Jan 1683; advocate, had sasine of Ochiltree 15 July 1717, *s* mother at Culross; *d* unm 19 Sept 1752

3a James, of Ochiltree and Culross; *b* 13 May 1690; Lt-Col 15th Foot; *m* Margaret Hawkison and *d* 29 June 1758, leaving:

1b Mary Anne; *m* Robert Sibthorne, and had issue

2b Betty; *m* 1st Henry Carey Hamilton, of Holycross; *m* 2nd 3 June 1759 Lt-Col Nathaniel Gould

4a THOMAS, **8th Earl**

(2) John, of Waterside; *bapt* 30 June 1662; imprisoned with f for his share in Argyll rising 1685, afterwards pardoned; *m* (contract 14 Sept 1687) Hannah de Werth and *d c* 7 Jan 1729, leaving, with other issue:

1a John, of Waterside; *m* (contract 11 Aug 1733) Elizabeth (*d* 4 Jan 1777), gdau of James Cairns, of Minniebutes; drowned 23 Nov 1752

2a James; Judge Advocate; *m* Jan 1731 Cecilia, dau of George Oliphant, of Edinburgh, and *d* 29 Aug 1762, leaving:

1b William; *s* f as Judge Advocate; *d* 20 Jan 1766

(1) Grizel; *m* 18 Feb 1686 John Ker of Moriestoun, Berwicks (*d* 27 Sept 1691), and *d* 21 March 1748, leaving issue

3 James; *d* by 13 Feb 1694

1 Grizel; *m* (contract 11 Oct 1653) 11th Lord Ross (*d* April 1682), and was *bur* 1 Feb 1665, leaving issue

The 7th EARL's cousin,

THOMAS COCHRANE, **8th Earl of Dundonald**; Capt 27th Foot, MP (Whig) Renfrewshire 1722–27, Commr for Excise Scotland 1730; *m* 1st *c* 1721 his cousin Elizabeth (*d* 1743), dau of John Ker of Moriestoun by Grizel, 2nd dau of Sir John Cochrane, of Ochiltree (*see* above), and had a s (*d* young) and dau; *m* 2nd 6 Sept 1744 Jane (*d* 21 May 1808), est dau of Archibald Stuart of Torrance, Lanarks, and *d* 27 June 1778, having had by her, with other issue:

1 ARCHIBALD, **9th Earl**

2 Charles; *b* 12 Jan 1749; Maj, ADC to Lord Cornwallis in America; *m* Catherine (*m* 2nd Charles Owen Cambridge and *d* 24 Oct 1835), dau of Maj Pitcairn, and was *ka* America 18 Oct 1781, having had a s and dau (both *d* young)

3 James Atholl (Rev); *b* 23 Oct 1751; Vicar Mansfield, Notts; *m* Mary Smithson (*d* 15 March 1867 aged 89) and *d* 1823

4 Basil; *b* 22 April 1753; Madras CS; *m* 13 Aug 1812 Caroline (*d* 14 Aug 1826), sis of George Gosling and widow of Rev S Lawry, and *d* 14 Aug 1826

5 Alexander Forrester (Sir), GCB; *b* 22 April 1758; Adml of the Blue, MP; *m* April 1788 Maria, dau of David Shaw and widow of Capt Sir Jacob Wheate, 5th Bt, RN, and *d* 29 June 1832, leaving, with other issue:

(1) Thomas John (Sir), GCB; *b* 5 Feb 1789; Adml of the Fleet; *m* 1st 6 Jan 1812 Matilda (added name Wishart and *d* 4 Sept 1819), est dau of Lt-Gen Sir Charles Ross, 7th Bt, and by her had, with other issue:

1a ALEXANDER DUNDAS ROSS COCHRANE-WISHART-BAILLIE, 1st BARON LAMINGTON, of Lamington, Co Lanark (UK), so *cr* 1880; extinct 1951 (*see* 1949 edn)

1a Maria Theresa; *m* 1st 24 March 1851 Alexander Robert Sutherland, of Silver Hill, Torquay, Devon (*d* 24 May 1861); *m* 2nd Sept 1864 Thomas Charles Ware Scott, of Beechwood, Forfarshire, and *d* 16 Sept 1897

(1) (cont.) Adml of the Fleet Sir Thomas Cochrane *m* 2nd 8 Jan 1853 Rosetta (*d* 27 May 1901), dau of Sir Jonah Denny Wheeler-Cuffe, 1st Bt, and *d* 19 Oct 1872, leaving, with other issue:

2a Thomas Belhaven Henry, MVO (1904); *b* 24 Nov 1856; Lt RN, Dep Govr IoW 1899–1910; *m* 1st 19 Feb 1887 Lady Adela Rous (*dsp* 18 May 1911), 3rd dau of 2nd Earl of Stradbroke (*qv*); *m* 2nd 1911 Beatrice, dau of William H Knight, and *d* 31 March 1925, leaving issue:

1b John; *b* 1909; RN; *m* 1937 Jocelyn Mary (*m* 2nd 1946 Col Brian Leslie Sundius-Smith and *d* 1988), dau of John Francis Robins, RN; *ka* 1941, leaving issue:

1c *Vivien Mary Grisell [Mrs Anthony Chappell, Croxton House, Fullmodeston, Norfolk NR21 0NJ]; *b* 31 July 1939; *m* 28 Sept 1962 *Anthony Courtlandt Richard Chappell, and has:

1d *Richard John Anthony; *b* 3 Oct 1967; *educ* Oundle and Bristol U; *m* 5 July 1997 *Caroline Jane Harding

2d *Andrew Thomas Robert; *b* 1 March 1969; *educ* Oundle and Leicester U

1d *Carol Margaret Joan; *b* 3 Feb 1966; *m* 17 March 1995 *Edward Tom Atkinson

2b +Thomas Dundonald Hugh [Thomas Dundonald Cochrane Esq, 157 Temelec Circle, Sonoma, Calif 95476, USA]; *b* 4 July 1912; *educ* Oundle; Lt RNVR 1940–46; *m* *Margery, dau of Norman Rowe, and has issue:

1c +Norman Thomas [Norman T Cochrane, 12398 Copenhagen Court, Reston, Va 22091, USA]; *b* 1938; *m* 1965 *Sarah Wills, and has issue:

1d +Thomas Alexander; *b* 1970

1d *Ann Lee; *b* 1972

1c *Sandra Ann [Mrs Graham Baker, 7417 Continental Trail, N Richmond Hills, Texas 76180, USA]; *b* 1946; *m* 1982 *Graham Baker

2a Anne Annette Minna, DCVO (1938), DGStJ, Ldy-in-Waiting to HRH PRINCESS BEATRICE; *d* unm 6 Jan 1943

(2) Andrew Coutts; *b* 5 April 1799; *m* 1835 Marie Teresa, est dau of Baron de Strack, Col in the Austrian serv, and *d* 22 June 1870, leaving, with other issue:

1a Adelaide Beaujolais Stuart; *m* 24 March 1860 Timothy Lewis O'Mahony, Capt 12th Uhlans, est s of Dennis O'Mahony, of Co Cork, and *d* 1920, leaving issue

(1) Anna Maria; *m* 19 Oct 1810 Sir Edward Thomas Troubridge, 2nd Bt, CB (*qv*), and *d* 14 May 1873, leaving issue

(2) Jane; *m* 6 Feb 1822 V-Adml Sir Henry W Bruce (*d* 14 Sept 1863), and *d* 22 June 1830, leaving issue (*see* BRUCE, Bt)

6 Andrew James COCHRANE later COCHRANE-JOHNSTONE; *b* 24 May 1767; Col, MP Stirling and afterwards Grampound, Govr Dominica, involved his nephew (**10th Earl**) in a fraud on the Stock Exchange for which they were both found guilty and imprisoned 1814; *m* 1st 20 Nov 1793 Lady Georgiana Hope-Johnstone (*d* 17 Sept 1797), dau and coheir of 3rd Earl of Hopetoun (*see* LINLITHGOW, M, and ANNANDALE AND HARTFELL, E), and had issue:

(1) Elizabeth *m* 28 March 1816 9th Lord Napier (*see* NAPIER and ETTRICK, L), and *d* 6 June 1883, leaving issue

6 (cont.) Col Andrew Cochrane-Johnstone *m* 2nd 21 March 1803 Amelia Constance Gertrude Etiennette, only child and heir of Baron de Clugny, Govr Guadaloupe, and widow of Reymond Godet, of Martinique

The 8th EARL's est surv s,

ARCHIBALD COCHRANE, **9th Earl of Dundonald**; *b* 1 Jan 1748; Cornet 3rd Dragoons 1764, transferred to RN, inventor; *m* 1st 17 Oct 1774 Anne (*d* 13 Oct 1784), 2nd dau of Capt James Gilchrist, RN, and had:

1 THOMAS, **10th Earl**

2 William Erskine; Maj 15th Hus Peninsular War; *m* Mary Anne (*d* 22 Oct 1860), dau of Alexander Manson, and *d* 16 March 1871, leaving issue:

(1) William Marshall; *b* 22 Dec 1817; Col 3rd Bn HLI; *m* 1st 14 Oct 1846 Mary (*d* 14 Aug 1868), dau of William Hussey and widow of Philip Bennett Marshall, and had issue:

1a William Francis Dundonald, CB (1896); *b* 7 Aug 1847; Hon Maj-Gen, Col DCLI, S Africa 1878–79, Egypt 1882, Sudan 1896–98; *m* 30 Dec 1893 Carola (*d* 10 Jan 1936), dau of Enrique Teodoro Möller, of Valparaiso de Chile, and *d* 23 Oct 1927, leaving issue:

1b Carola Maria Rosita Isabel; *b* 15 June 1896; *d* 10 Feb 1993

2a Thomas Erskine; *b* 12 Oct 1849; Cdr RN; *m* 24 March 1886 Mary (*d* 2 Oct 1937), 4th dau of John Bell-Irving, JP, of Whitehill, Lockerbie, Dumfries, and *d* 17 Oct 1906, leaving issue:

1b Mary; *b* 18 Nov 1889; *m* 6 May 1916 her cousin W/Cdr John Erichsen Blair Cochrane, RAFVR (*d* 28 June 1949) (*see* below), and *d* 28 April 1958, leaving issue

2b Jessie Edith; *b* 22 July 1891; *m* 2 Dec 1912 (*divorce* 1943) Maj Walter Peter Stewart, DSO, HLI (Res of Offrs) (*d* 1980), s of Charles Stewart, of Davo House, Fordoun, and had:

1c Kenneth Walter Hugh Cochrane; *b* 1916; *m* 1948 *Heather Nagel, of Brisbane, and has:

1d *Clarissa Cochrane; *b* 1950

2d *Jane Cochrane; *b* 1951

1c *Grizel Margaretta Cochrane DStJ [Mrs George Williams, Llanhavan House, Llanhavan, Mid Glam; 27 Broad St, Ludlow, Salop SY8 1NJ]; *b* 1914; *m* 1950 *George Mervyn Williams, CBE, MC, DL, and has:

1d *Owain Anthony Mervyn; *b* 1955; *m* 1983 *Bethan M, er dau of Dr Richard Watkins, of Mwyndy House, Mwyndy, Mid Glam, and has:

1e *Elizabeth Beatrice; *b* 1988

2e *Antonia Mary; *b* 1994

3b Daisy, of Koteri Lodge, Taupo, NZ; *b* 30 July 1894, *m* 9 Sept 1916 Edward Ernest Mizen (*d* 1972), Lt 5th Bn E Surrey Regt, and *d* 1975, leaving:

1c *Patrick Erskine Cochrane; *b* 1917; *m* 19– *Norma Margaret Ball and has:

1d *Gary Edward; *b* 1947

1d *Caroline Margaret; *b* 1948

2d *Linda Sue; *b* 1950

3d *Julie Loretta; *b* 1952

1c *Joan Louise; *b* 1919; *m* 1st 19– David Malpas Snow and has:

1d *Penelope June; *b* 1940; *m* 19– *David Paykel and has:

1e *Christopher David; *b* 1970

1c (cont.) Mrs David Snow *m* 2nd 19– Adrian Rhodes Delamore (*d* 1987) and by him has:

1d *Robin Cochrane Rhodes; *b* 1951; *m* 19– *Judith Pemberton and has:

1e *Thomas Cochrane; *b* 19–

1e *Chloe; *b* 19–

2d *Nicholas Edward; *b* 1953; *m* 19– — and has:

1e *Louis Edward; *b* 19–

2e *Samuel; *b* 19–

1e *Jessie; *b* 19–

3d *Adrian Michael; *b* 1955; *m* 19– *Vibusha Shreeve and has:

1e *Toby; *b* 19–

2e *David; *b* 19–

2c *Elizabeth Anne [Mrs Elizabeth Waymouth, 69 Queens Drive, Waiheke Island, Auckland, New Zealand]; *b* 1927; *m* 1951 John Hugh Newcombe Waymouth and has:

1d *Peter John Newcome [Peter Waymouth Esq, 11 Bouverie St, NE Valley, Dunedin, New Zealand]; *b* 1952; *m* 1970 *Mary Hamilton Livesey, of Timaru, and has:

1e *Benjamin Newcome; *b* 1971

2e *Nicholas Newcome; *b* 1975

1e *Emma Newcome; *b* 1972

2d *Christopher Simon Newcome [Christopher Waymouth Esq, 12 Brett Ave, Takapuna, Auckland, New Zealand]; *b* 1955; *m* 1973 *Lynette Joy Caites, of Auckland, and has:

1e *Samuel Newcombe; *b* 1973

3a John Palmer; *b* 28 March 1852; Maj Cape Mounted Rifles; *m* 19 June 1882 Frances (*d* 31 Oct 1934), dau of William Gilbert, of Canterbury, Kent, and *d* 30 Sept 1921, leaving, with other issue:

1b Basil William Dundonald; *b* 17 May 1891; Supt Kenya Police, Colonial Police Medal, Capt Cape Mounted Rifles and 13th Hus (SR), SBStJ; *m* 22 July 1920 Anne (*d* 1986), 2nd dau of William Robertson, of Edinburgh, and *d* 17 June 1953, having had issue:

1c Palmer Basil Dundonald; *b* 4 July 1922; Lt KRRC WW II; *ka* Italy 28 Nov 1943

2c John Robertson; *b* 4 Sept 1924; *d* as the result of an accident, 6 Oct 1938

1c *Elizabeth Ann [Mrs Peter Dodds, PO Box 318, Simon's Town 7995, S Africa]; *b* 2 Oct 1926; *m* 1951 *Peter Dodds, and has issue:

1d *Peter John Cochrane; *b* 13 July 1953; *educ* Gresham's; late Merchant Navy; *m* 1980 *Catherine, dau of John Stubbs, of Harare, Zimbabwe, and *d* 1993, leaving issue:

1e *Andrew John Cochrane; *b* 1984

1e *Richard David Cochrane; *b* 1986

2d *David Michael Cochrane [David Cochrane Esq, PO Box 130281, Bryanston 2021, S Africa]; *b* 10 Sept 1954; *educ* Gresham's; photographer

3d *Anthony Palmer Cochrane [Anthony Dodds Esq, Box 15, Rumuruti, S Africa]; *b* 14 Oct 1962; *educ* Falcon Coll, Zimbabwe; *m* *Mary Lucinda, only dau of Clive Aggett, of Kifuku Ranch, Rumuruti, Kenya, and has:

1e *George Ian; *b* 1996

1e *Chala Jane; *b* 1994

2b John Erichsen Blair; *b* 1894; Lt 1st S African Inf and W/Cdr RAFVR; *m* 6 May 1916 his cousin Mary (*d* 28 April 1958), dau of Cdr Thomas Erskine Cochrane, RN (*see* above), and *d* 28 June 1949, leaving issue:

1c John Erskine Dundonald; *b* 29 July 1920; *educ* Canford; Lt RA WW II; *m* 1st 15 June 1943 (*divorce* 1957) Elizabeth Mary (*d* 19 Jan 1995), dau of Capt Bertram Allgood, and had issue:

1d +Ian Michael Dundonald [Ian Cochrane Esq, 1 Spinning Mill Cottages, Goulds Ground, Frome BA11 3OW]; *b* 15 July 1950; *educ* Shiplake Coll; *m* 1973 (*divorce* 1995) Nicola Robina, dau of Eric Wood, of Stour Provost, Dorset, and has:

1e +Adam Thomas Dundonald; *b* 1977

1e *Katrin Emma; *b* 1975

2e *Lydia Rose; *b* 1983

2d +Alastair Charles Dundonald [Alastair Cochrane Esq, Nutters Cottage, Nutters Wood, Cleeve Hill, Glos]; *b* 4 Oct 1956; *m* 1978 *Julia, dau of George Alan Bedwell, MD, MRCP, of King's Stanley, nr Stroud, Glos, and has issue:

1e +Charles Alexander Dundonald; *b* 1985

1e *Victoria Louise; *b* 1978

2e *Rebecca Frances; *b* 1981

3e *Francesca Emily; *b* 1990

1d *Sarah Elizabeth [Sarah Bull, 36 Jessica Rd, London SW18 2QN]; *b* 8 Sept 1946; *m* 1971 (*divorce* 1981) Alastair John Milne Home (*see* MINTO, E), and has issue:

1e *Marcus John Hepburn; *b* 1975

1e *Camilla Marian Isobel; *b* 1973

1c (cont.) John Cochrane *m* 2nd 1958 *Bela — [Mrs John Cochrane, Lion Cottage, 24 Park Rd, Chislehurst, Kent, BR7 5AY] and *d* 1987, leaving by her:

3d +David John Dundonald; *b* 11 July 1959

4d +Peter John Dundonald; *b* 14 July 1963

5d +Anthony Albert Dundonald; *b* 2 Feb 1967

2c +Basil Thomas Dundonald [Basil Cochrane Esq, 8 Resthaven Dve, Tokai 7945, Cape, S Africa]; *b* 17 May 1924; *educ* Sevenoaks; late RAFVR; *m* 24 Sept 1955 (*divorce* 1972) Sally, only dau of Henry Edmund Housell, of Livingston, N Rhodesia; *m* 2nd 16 May 1974 *Daphne Maureen Joyce, dau of Lage Elliot Esmond Baxter, of Camberley, Surrey

3b Douglas Thomas Archibald Nelthorpe; *b* 1900; Lt RAF; *m* 1st 14 July 1926 Ivy (*d* 1928), est dau of G H Massdorp, of Queenstown, S Africa, and had issue:

1c +Edward Denzil Dundonald [Edward Cochrane Esq, 11 Linda Rd, Claremont 7700, Cape Town, S Africa]; *b* 28 April 1927; MSM, MSc, CEng; *m* 2 May 1953 *Janet Ainslie, dau of Robert Allan, OBE, MC, DCM, of Salisbury, Rhodesia, and had:

1d +Michael Allan Dundonald; *b* 1957; *m* 1980 *Fiona Jane, er dau of Norman McDonald, and has issue:

1e +Daniel Dundonald; *b* 1985

1e *Bridget Jane; *b* 1982

1d *Susan Elizabeth; *b* May 1954; *m* 1980 *David William Butcher, only son of James Butcher, and has issue:

1e *Joshua David; *b* 1988

1e *Sian Catherine; *b* 1982

2e *Clare Louise; *b* 1985

2c +Douglas Blair Hilliard [Douglas Cochrane Esq, Bonnyvale, PO Box 101, Karoi, Zimbabwe]; *b* 1928; *m* 1958 *Thea Jean, er dau of Norman R Stevenson, and had issue:

1d +Ian Dundonald; *b* 1959

2d +Robert Douglas Dundonald; *b* 14 Nov 1961

1d *Jennifer Mary; *b* 20 Aug 1965

2d *Sarah Alison Jane; *b* 1972

3b (cont.) Douglas Cochrane *m* 2nd 4 May 1935 *Marie Hammond [Mrs Douglas Cochrane, The Retreat, 4 Harris Rd, PO Highlands, Harare, Zimbabwe], and *d* 1988, having by her had further issue:

3c +John Robert Colly [John Cochrane Esq, PO Box 650, Harare, Zimbabwe]; *b* 28 Sept 1939; *m* 8 Oct 1960 *Rosemary Josephine Anne, dau of George William Robert Caine, of Salisbury, Rhodesia, and has issue:

1d +Jeremy Robert; *b* 10 May 1962

1d *Samantha Caroline; *b* 5 Aug 1965

4c +William Thomas [William Cochrane Esq, PO Box 650, Harare, Zimbabwe]; *b* 1943; *m* 1969 *Pamela Evelyn, dau of Van Setzcorn, of Amanzimtoti, Natal, and has issue:

1d +Richard William; *b* 1974

1d *Ingrid Margaret; b1971

2d *Lucille Pamela; *b* 1976

5c +Richard Bruce; *b* 1948; *m* 1975 *Pamela Brown and has issue:

1d +Douglas; *b* 1981

2d +Alexander Richard; *b* 1984
1d Jennifer Leigh; *b* 1983
6c +Steven David [Steven Cochrane Esq, 33 Court Rd, Greendale North, Harare, Zimbabwe]; *b* 1951; BSc (Ag); *m* 1st 1973 (*divorce* 1987) Penelope Jane Lutley, est dau of Denzil Awdry Randles, and has issue:
1d +William James Dundonald; *b* 1975
2d +Graham Douglas; *b* 1977
3d +James Denzil; *b* 1980
6c (cont.) Steven Cochrane *m* 2nd 1991 *Evelyn Judy, dau of John Rau, of Harare, and by her has further issue:
1d *Michelle Cecily; *b* 1993
1c *Cecily Mary Elizabeth [Mrs Kenneth Saywood, PO Box 177, Karoi, Zimbabwe]; *b* 1935; *m* 1959 *Kenneth Saywood, and has issue:
1d *Neil Frank; *b* 1960
2d *David; *b* 1961
3d *Peter John; *b* 1966
4d *Michael Anthony; *b* 1970
2c *Una Patricia Leowina Cochrane [Mme Una Cochrane, 8 Rue Cdt Mouchotte, 75014 Paris, France]; *b* 1937; *m* 1958 (*divorce* 1975 and resumed her maiden name) Kenneth Davies, and has issue:
1d *Patricia Clare Cochrane; *b* 1959; *m* 1981 *Roy Alexander Brooks, and has issue:
1e *William Sebastien; *b* 1981
2e *Lawrence Thomas; *b* 1983
2d *Andrea Jane; *b* 1962
1b *Marion Mary Erskine; *m* 1912 Louis J D Pare, of Rhodesia, and had issue
2b Cecily Sommerville; *m* 1st 1909 Ernest George Williams, of Johannesburg, Transvaal, and had issue; *m* 2nd 24 Feb 1922 Maj James Alexander MacDonald, DSO and bar, MC, MA, late RFA, and *d* 9 March 1933
3b Una Fairfax; *m* 1910 Louis R P Fennell, slr, of Butterworth, Transkei, S Africa, and *d* 4 Aug 1954, leaving issue
4b Carola Urquhart; *b* 1897; *m* 10 Sept 1934 Hubert Walpole Hilliard, and *d* 14 June 1964
4a Arthur Henry Douglas; *b* 19 Aug 1856; *m* 20 July 1882 Maria Josephine Clegg (*d* 19 May 1934), dau of George Killick, of Kirby Hall, Leics, and *d* 14 Jan 1925, having had issue:
1b Douglas Erskine; *b* 18 Jan 1885; *m* 1925 Ida Johanna Fechat (*d* 1953), dau of Capt H Becher, late 42nd Foot, and *d* 1950
2b Arthur Blair Dundonald; *b* 28 April 1888; Capt late Nigeria Regt; *m* 22 Oct 1918 Nancy (*d* 22 Dec 1985), only dau of Robert Barber, barrister, and *d* 18 June 1936, leaving issue:
1c John Blair; *b* 27 July 1923; P/O RAF WW II; *ka* 24 Sept 1943
2c +Hugh Benjamin [Hugh Cochrane Esq, Hope Cottage, 88 Newland, Sherborne, Dorset DT9 3DT]; *b* 8 April 1925; *educ* Radley and Queens' Coll Cambridge (MA); chartered engr, FInstCE, FInst, MechE, Lt RE 1945–47; *m* 5 Sept 1953 *Anne Deirdre, er dau of William Schoener Scott
3c +Nicholas Baillie [Nicholas Cochrane Esq, Old Oak Farm, Easthampstead Park, Wokingham, Berks RG11 3DL]; *b* 18 Jan 1929; late Capt KAR, formerly Roy Berks Regt; *m* 29 Nov 1958 *Diana Isabel, only dau of Norman Balfour Craig, of Port Said, and has issue:
1d *Amanda Elizabeth; *b* 9 Aug 1959; *m* 19– *Capt Jeremy Robert Shafto (AAC), and has issue:
1e *Hamish Alexander Cochrane; *b* 1993
2d *Susan Mary; *b* 1962
1b Grizel Olive; *b* 16 Feb 1884, *d* same year
2b Gladys Cochrane; *b* 14 April 1891; *m* 12 April 1916 (*divorce* 1930 and resumed her maiden name) Alexander Cockburn Robertson, of Sandhills, Monkton, Ayrshire, and *d* 12 Sept 1977
3b Ruby Stella; *b* 3 Jan 1887; *m* 1st 1918 Capt Ralph Mainwaring West; *m* 2nd 15 June 1923 (*divorce* 1935) Lt-Cdr Basil William Barrymaine Hallwood, DSC, late RN, only surv s of James Barrymaine Hallwood, and has issue; *m* 3rd 6 Nov 1936 Cyril Edmondson Coates, s of Andrew Crossley Coates, and *d* 7 July 1976, leaving further issue
1a Caroline Katherine Laura May; *m* 1st 7 Aug 1878 Arthur Octavius Bayly, and had issue; *m* 2nd 1896 Henry Herbert Lyde, of 7 Cranley Place, Onslow Sq, London SW, and *d* 13 July 1923, having by her 1st husb had:
1b Eric; *b* 1879; *d* 1898
2b Hugh Alexander; *b* 1882; *d* 1975
3b Erskine; *b* 1886; *d* 1916
1b Isobel Edith Cochrane; *b* 1884; *m* 1st 19– Bertram Allgood and had:
1c Elizabeth Mary Cochrane; *b* 1914; *m* 1st 15 June 1943 (*divorce* 1957) John Erskine Dundonald (*see* above) and had issue; *m* 2nd 19– Phillip Carrington
1b (cont.) Mrs Bertram Allgood *m* 2nd 19– Charles Richard Sherriff and had:
1c Guy William; *b* 1920; *d* 1921
2c *(Rosemary) June Christina [Miss June Sherriff, Lidgate Cottage, Lidgate, nr Newmarket, Cambs CB8 9JW]; *b* 1924
2a Edith Hamilton; *m* 13 April 1893 John Mathison Fraser, JP (*d* 11 Nov 1950), of Buckham Hill House, Uckfield, Sussex, and *dsp* 6 Aug 1949
(1) (cont.) Col William Cochrane *m* 2nd 14 Aug 1884 Elizabeth Mary Somerville (*d* 6 Nov 1917), dau of Sir Henry Fairfax, 1st Bt, of Maxton, and widow of James Liebig Gregory, and *d* 30 July 1898
4 Archibald, of Hetton Hall, Co Durham; *b* 1783; Capt RN; *m* 11 Jan 1812 Hannah Jane (*d* 8 Oct 1864), dau of Arthur Mowbray, of Sherburn Hall, Co Durham, and *d* 6 Aug 1829, having had, with other issue:
(1) Robert Alexander; *b* 18 March 1816; *m* 27 Oct 1847 Julia (*d* 23 March 1895), dau of Gen Denzil Onslow, of Stoughton House, Hunts, and *d* 19 Jan 1907, having had, with other issue:
1a Blair Onslow, OBE (1919), of Westhill, Bembridge, IoW, JP (Wilts); *b* 11 Sept 1853; Capt RHA; Dep Sheriff IoW; *m* 9 May 1881 Mary Evelyn (*d* 6 Feb 1934), 4th dau of Sir Richard Sutton, 4th Bt, and *d* 7 Dec 1928, having had:
1b Blair Sutton; *b* 24 Oct 1885; Midshipman RN; *d* 1 July 1904
1b Mary Evelyn; *b* 11 Feb 1883; *m* 27 Sept 1919 Col Duncan Gustavus Baillie, CMG, DSO (*d* 3 July 1968), TA Res of Offs, late Lovat Scouts, s of Lt-Gen Duncan James Baillie, and had issue
2b Joan; *b* 4 June 1884; *m* 3 March 1909 Bernard Norman Fraser, formerly Berks RHA (T) (*d* 19 Feb 1955), yst s of Alexander Casper Fraser, JP, DL, of Mongewell Park, Wallingford, and had issue:
1c Blair Alexander Fraser, of Dolphin House, North End, Bath, Avon; *b* 7 Dec 1909; *educ* Wellington and RAF Coll Cranwell; G/Capt RAF WW II; *m* 24 March 1937 *Margaret Mary, late Assist Section Offr WAAF, dau of Harry J Pilcher, and had issue:
1d *Ann Fraser; *b* 1 Feb 1943; *m* 9 Jan 1965 *Michael Norton-Griffiths, yr s of Sir Peter Norton-Griffiths, 2nd Bt (*qv*)
2c *Norman Cochrane Fraser [Maj Norman Fraser, Flat 2, 5 Kensington Pk Gdns, London W11]; *b* 24 Feb 1920; *educ* Harrow and RMA Sandhurst; Maj QO Highrs WW II
1c *Marjorie Constance, JP [Miss Marjorie Fraser JP, Little Copse House, Bucklebury, nr Reading, Berks]; *b* 9 Feb 1913
3b Jeanie Harriet Dorothy; *b* 30 Sept 1891; *d* unm 5 Sept 1947
1a Constance Amelia; *b* 3 June 1850; *d* unm 24 June 1936
2a Florence Amy; *b* 15 Jan 1852; *d* 1946
(2) Basil Edward Arthur, DL (Co Durham); *b* 21 Dec 1817; *m* 2 Oct 1839 Sally Caroline (*d* 3 Jan 1892), est dau of Lt-Col Edward FitzGerald, of Carrigoran, Co Clare, and niece of Sir William FitzGerald, Bt, and *d* 24 March 1895, having had, with other issue:
1a Basil Edward; *b* 24 Aug 1841; V-Adml; *m* 11 June 1873 Cornelia Ramsay (*d* 10 Feb 1925), yr dau of Capt John Robinson Owen, RN, of Windlesham House, Surrey, and *d* 4 May 1922, leaving, with other issue:
1b Archibald, CMG (1918); *b* 20 June 1874; R-Adml, ADC to HM GEORGE V 1929, served WW I (despatches), Legn of Honour and Order Redeemer of Greece; *m* 20 April 1904 Maye Amelie Lucile (*d* 10 Aug 1954), only child of Col Alured de Vere Brooke (*see* BROOKE Bt), and *d* 15 July 1952, leaving issue:
1c Marie Cecilia; *b* 3 Aug 1905; *m* 30 Oct 1944 Maj Reginald Joseph Vosser, MBE, Beds and Herts Regt (*d* 15 Sept 1967), 2nd s of Walter C Vosser, of Clapham Junction, and had issue:
1d *Michael Cochrane [Michael Vosser Esq, 1 Cobham Rd, Woodley, Reading RG5 4LB]; *b* 5 Aug 1945; *educ* Ampleforth; *m* Aug 1970 *Susan —
2d *Charles Brooke; *b* 25 March 1948
2c Grizel Rosemary; *b* 3 June 1907; *m* 1st 1941 Maj Thomas Lionel Ashburner Clapton, DLI (*ka* Normandy 12 July 1944), s of Lt-Cdr Thomas Clapton, RNVR, and has issue:
1d *Peter Thomas Archibald; *b* 8 Dec 1942; *educ* Ampleforth; 2nd Lt Scots Gds
2d *Thomas Robert [Thomas Clapton Esq, Balbeg, Straiton, nr Maybole, Ayrshire]; *b* 14 July 1944; *educ* Ampleforth and RMA Sandhurst; 2nd Lt 9th/12th Roy Lancers
2c (cont.) Mrs Thomas Clapton *m* 2nd 14 Sept 1948 Cdr Sir (Henry) Francis (Morton) Peto, 3rd Bt (*qv*), and has further issue
3c *Monica Frances Mary [Mrs George Worcester, Penny Cottage, Pound Lane, Windlesham, Surrey]; *b* 24 Sept 1908; *m* 17 Aug 1950 George Raleigh Grey Worcester (*d* 5 Jan 1969), s of Capt W Worcester, RNR
4c *Stella Dorothea [Mrs John Harrison, 102 Lytton Boulevard, Toronto, Canada]; *b* 26 Nov 1913; *m* 27 June 1951 *John Errington Rothwell Harrison, s of Eric Bothwell Harrison, of Lacombe, Alberta, Canada, and has issue:
1d *James Anthony Rothwell Harrison; *b* 20 April 1952; *m* 1975 *Louise Marie, dau of Louis Mantarazzo, of Thunder Bay, Ontario, Canada, and has issue:
1e *Neil Owen; *b* 1981
2e *Thomas Louis; *b* 1984
1e *Laura Catherine; *b* 1990
1d *Anne Lucille Rothwell Harrison; *b* 30 Sept 1953; *m* 1988 *Robert Wallis Sargallis
2b Edward Owen (Sir), KBE (1943); *b* 17 Aug 1881; *educ* HMS *Britannia*; R-Adml, WW I cmdg HMAS *Cairo*, E India Station 1924–26, cmded Devonport Gunnery Sch 1927–29, Dir Training and Staff Duties 1929–31, cmded HMS *Repulse* 1931–32, ADC to HM GEORGE V 1932–33, WW II as Convoy Cdre with rank of Cdre RNR (despatches); *m* 18 Jan 1908 Mary Lucy (Molly) (*d* 19 March 1955), only dau of Sydney King George, of The Brackens, Ascot, and *d* 27 Jan 1972, having had issue:
1c James Owen, MC (1943); *b* 21 July 1914; Actg Maj RA WW II; *m* 25 Jan 1941 Margaret Angela Clare (*m* 2nd 23 Feb 1950 Desmond Brian Pertwee, of Rookery House, Great Horkesley, nr Colchester, Essex), er dau of V-Adml Charles Wolfram Round-Turner, CB, CMG, and was *ka* N Africa 13 Feb 1943, leaving issue:
1d *Janet Owen (Jane) [Mrs Paul Moore, Flat 2, 391 Clapham Rd, London SW9]; *b* 31 Dec 1942; *m* 17 April 1965 *Paul Bernard John Moore, AA Dip, ARIBA, est s of Philip Moore, of Cheam, Surrey, and has issue:
1e *Thomas Owen; *b* 22 June 1966
1e *Amy Clare; *b* 13 Jan 1969
1c *Susanne Gloria [Mrs David Howell, 23 Ashley Court, Morpeth Terrace, London SW1P 1EN]; *b* 24 Oct 1918; *m* 24 Sept 1957 *David Logan Howell, DFC, yr s of Rev Alexander Rutherford Howell, of Pimlico
1b Grizel Martha Lily; *b* 11 March 1876; *d* unm 13 April 1948

2a Blair Hamilton; *b* 22 April 1853; *m* 18 Sept 1899 Beatrice Elizabeth Laura (*d* 12 March 1935), dau of John Henry Grant, and *d* 17 May 1926, having had issue:

1b Alwyne Archibald Hamilton; *b* 3 Aug 1902; *d* 11 May 1912

3a William Edward; *b* 8 Sept 1858; *m* 19 Feb 1887 Evelyn (*d* 28 May 1908), dau of Charles Lamb, of Ryton, Co Durham, and *d* 7 March 1929, leaving issue:

1b Arthur FitzGerald; *b* 9 Jan 1888; Cdr RN; *m* 10 Dec 1913 Beryl Irma (*d* 22 Aug 1954), dau of Gen Charles Frederick Thomas, of Excliff, Devon, and widow of Percy Hugh Druce, and *d* 12 Feb 1967, having had issue:

1c +Peter William FitzGerald [Peter Cochrane Esq, 761 London Rd, Sarnia, Ontario, N7T 4X7, Canada]; *b* 27 April 1916; *educ* Ampleforth and McGill U (B Eng McGill U, P Eng Ontario), MEIC; WW II with Alantic Ferry Command and as F/O RCAF; *m* 7 Oct 1944 *Margaret Eunice, only dau of Wesley William Rowley, of London, Ontario, Canada, and adopted:

*Richard Arthur Wesley Rowley; *b* 2 July 1948; *educ* Michigan State U (BA 1971); *m* 1986 *Adrina Maria, yst dau of Peter Rull, of Hong Kong and New York, and has issue:

1e *Marie Margaret Cochrane; *b* 1987

*Stephen Bryce Rowley; *b* 17 June 1952; *m* 1980 *Tracey, dau of R Gordon Henderson, of BC, Canada, and has issue:

1e *Sydney Margaret Cochrane; *b* 19–

2c Archibald Hamish FitzGerald; *b* 16 Jan 1920; A/Capt KOSB WW II; *d* of wounds received in action Burma 28 Jan 1944

3c Michael Owen FitzGerald; *b* 27 Nov 1920; *k* in a motor accident 15 Aug 1935

1c *Evelyn Jean FitzGerald; *b* 22 July 1914

2c *Sheila FitzGerald [Mrs John Stubbs, 10 Dorset Close, Oakdale, Harrogate, Yorks]; *b* 20 Nov 1917; *m* 30 Nov 1942 *Lt-Cdr John Aarvold Loughlin Stubbs, RNVR, s of William Cuthbert Stubbs, of Corby House, Carlisle, and has:

1d *Penelope Anne; *b* 4 Feb 1945; BSc; *m* 17 Aug 1966 Capt Patrick Joseph David Herberts, Parachute Regt, s of Maj David Herberts, of N Lancs, and has:

1e *Alison Philippa; *b* 22 July 1967

2e *Catherine Elizabeth; *b* 1972

2d *Gillian Mary [Miss Gillian Stubbs, 7 Spencer Hill, London SW19]; *b* 25 June 1947

3c *Cecilia Florence FitzGerald [Mrs John Robertson, Sunlaws, Parkhead, Dumfries]; *b* 13 Aug 1924; *m* 25 June 1955 *John Gray Robertson, s of John Wares Robertson, of Perth, and has issue:

1d *Peter Arthur Cochrane; *b* 15 Jan 1956; Bsc Glasgow; *m* 1982 *Shirley Margaret Bradford, and has issue:

1e *Andrew George Cochrane; *b* 1987

2e *David John; *b* 1991

2d *Philip John Cochrane; *b* 1 June 1962; *m* 1984 *Rhonda Eleanor Kelly

4a Charles FitzGerald Thomas; *b* 14 April 1863; Maj late Prince of Wales's Leinster Regt, WW I, RTO 1914; *m* 1st 17 April 1896 Maud Mary (*d* 24 Jan 1913), dau of Robert de Ros Rose, of Ardhu and Ahabeg, Co Limerick, and had issue:

1b Basil Robert; *b* 16 Feb 1898; Lt RN WW I; *d* 14 March 1919

2b Thomas FitzGerald; *b* 2 Sept 1899; Lt RAF; *d* 29 Dec 1922

3b Alexander Francis; *b* 29 March 1902; Cdr RN, served WWs I and II; *m* 8 Aug 1928 Osma Heather, er dau of Oswald Henry Cochrane, of Middlesbrough, and Melbury, Salcombe, and had issue:

1c Basil Alexander; *b* 12 Aug 1929; F/O RAF; missing and believed *k* through a premature explosion of ammunition while leading an anti-bandit strike Malaya 3 May 1952

4a (cont.) Maj Charles Cochrane *m* 2nd 21 July 1933 Nora Avice (*d* 12 Aug 1976), only dau of Charles Bernard Mervyn Drake-Cutliffe, of The Manor House, Lee, N Devon, and *d* 7 March 1952

1a Katherine Elizabeth Cochrane; *m* 1 May 1879 John Edward Leveson-Gower, of Bill Hill, Berks (*d* 21 Jan 1892), and *d* 20 April 1928, leaving issue (*see* SUTHERLAND, D)

2a Caroline Mary; *m* 25 Oct 1871 Rev Lionel Corbett (*d* 20 June 1905),Rrector Hampton Bishop, Herefs, and *d* 28 April 1915, leaving issue

3a Helen Frances; *d* unm 31 Oct 1940

4a Margaret Grizel; *m* 13 Feb 1884 Hugh Penry Powell (*d* 18 Nov 1910), of Castell Madoc, Brecon, and *d* aged 101, leaving issue

(3) Archibald Hamilton, of Dalnabreck, Blairgowrie, Scotland, and Brookfield, Weston, Bath, JP (Durham and NR Yorks); *b* 2 June 1819; *m* 22 May 1856 Rose (*d* 7 April 1907), yst dau of G P Hutchinson, of Eggleston Hall, Co Durham, and *dsp* 7 March 1907

(4) Arthur Mowbray, JP (Leics); *b* 2 Oct 1826; *m* 10 June 1850 Mary, yst dau of John Michael Malonek (*d* 16 May 1924), formerly Prussian Consul-Gen Liverpool, and *dsp* 5 Oct 1907

(1) Caroline Elizabeth Cochrane; *b* 15 June 1814; *m* 18 Nov 1835 Benjamin Holme WIGGON later MOWBRAY and *d* 25 Oct 1861, having had issue

The **9th Earl** *m* 2nd 12 April 1799 Isabella (*d* Dec 1808), dau of Samuel Raymond, of Belchamp Hall, Essex, and widow of John Mayne, of Teffont, Wilts; *m* 3rd April 1819 Anna Maria (*d* 19 Dec 1922), est dau of Francis Plowden, LLD, historian, and *d* Paris 1 July 1831, having by her had an only dau (*d* young)

His est s,

THOMAS COCHRANE, **10th Earl of Dundonald**, GCB (1847, KB 1809–14, reinstated 1847); *b* 14 Dec 1775; Capt 106th Foot 1794 but later joined RN; the most famous individualist naval cdr of the age after Nelson; his exploits have been resuscitated for the 20th century only lightly disguised in the novels of Mr C S Forester and Mr Patrick O'Brian; Actg Lt 1795 (substantive 1796), as Capt *Speedy* (brig of 158 tons, with 14 4-pounders and 54 men on board) took in 1801 the Spanish frigate *El Gamo* (over 600 tons, 32 guns, 319 men aboard), a feat said to be unmatched in the entire history of the RN; Capt Aug 1801; played a leading part in the defence of Rosas 1809 by garrisoning the fortress of Trinidad when others on the Allied side considered it indefensible, also the attempted crushing of a large part of Bonaparte's navy at the Basque Roads 1809, which, but for the want of support by his commanding offr Lord Gambier could, as Cochrane himself later pointed out (to the detriment of his professional advancement), have been completed; MP (Radical) Honiton 1806–07 and Westminster 1807–18; found guilty of rigging the Stock Exchange 1814 (the real culprit appears to have been his uncle Andrew Cochrane-Johnstone; *see* above), unseated and struck off the navy list and stripped of his KB, fined £1,000 and sentenced to stand in the pillory for an hour (this latter punishment was subsequently cancelled) and a year's imprisonment (from which he escaped, was recaptured and finally set free on payment of the £1,000; this he did with a banknote on the back of which he wrote a short apologia, ending with the statement that he submitted to robbery to avoid being murdered; he was pardoned 1832, R-Adml with seniority of 1830, V-Adml 1841, Adml of the Blue 1851, Adml of the White 1853, Adml of the Red 1857, R-Adml of GB 1854–60); served Govt of Chile (as Adml and C-in-C of the naval forces of the republic) and Peru in Wars of Independence from Spain 1817–22, capturing Valdivia and taking the Spanish frigate *Esmeralda* under the very guns of the fortress of Callao; during 1823–25 set up (with rank of First Admiral of the National and Imperial Navy) the Brazilian Empire as a naval power, hence *cr* Brazilian MARQUESS OF MARANHAM; subsequently cmded Greek Navy in Greek War of Independence 1827–28; C-in-C WI and N American Station 1848–51; like his f patented many inventions, being in particular quick to recognise the advantages of steam-propelled ships and doing much to improve naval architecture where steam boilers and screw propellers were concerned; Grand Cross Imp Brazilian Order of Cruzero, Kt Roy Order Saviour of Greece, Kt Order of Merit Chile; author *Narrative of Services in the Liberation of Chili, Peru, and Brazil, from Spanish and Portuguese Dominion* (1859); *m* 8 Aug 1812 (secretly) and 22 June 1818 (publicly) Katherine Frances Corbet (*d* Boulogne 26 Jan 1865 aged 69), dau of Thomas Barnes, of Romford, Essex, by Frances, dau of James Corbet, of Bridgnorth, Salop (*see* 1970 edn CORBET, Bt), and *d* 31 Oct 1860, having had issue:

1 THOMAS, **11th Earl**

2 William Horatio Barnardo; *b* 8 March 1818; 92nd Gordon Highrs; *m* 29 Oct 1844 Jacobina Frances (*d* 25 July 1881), widow of George J Carnegie, and *dsp* 6 Feb 1900

3 Arthur Auckland Leopold Pedro (Sir), KCB; *b* 24 Sept 1824; Adml, commended for gallantry at Acre, cmded HMS *Niger* destruction of Chinese fleet June 1857 (wounded); *d* unm 20 Aug 1905

4 Ernest Grey Lambton, JP and DL (Co Donegal); *b* 4 June 1834; Capt RN; High Sheriff Donegal 1879; *m* 1st 15 Sept 1864 Adelaide (*d* 3 Oct 1864), only dau of Col Samuel W Blackall, Govr Sierra Leone and Queensland, Australia; *m* 2nd 16 Oct 1866 Elizabeth Frances Maria Katherine (*d* 28 Dec 1928), only child of Richard Doherty, of Red Castle, Co Donegal, and *d* 2 Feb 1911, having by her had issue:

(1) Thomas Alfred Dundonald O'Degherty; *b* 23 Sept 1868; *d* unm

(2) Richard Francis Ernest, of Red Castle, Co Donegal, JP; *b* 18 Sept 1873; late Capt and Hon Maj 5th Bn Roy Inniskilling Fus, High Sheriff Donegal 1908; *d* unm 16 Feb 1959

(3) Ernest Algernon; *b* 11 May 1877; *d* unm 16 Sept 1959

(4) Horace Egerton Cochrane Egerton; *b* 16 March 1833; *m* 1907 Eva Avice Martha (*d* 11 Dec 1945), dau of — Clarke, of London, and *d* 1 May 1959, leaving issue:

1a Richard Ernest Horace; *b* 12 March 1906; *m* 21 Oct 1939 *Alma Josephine [Mrs Richard Cochrane, c/o Mrs James Creamer, 3309 Hopewell Rd, Valley, Alabama 36864, USA], er dau of Albert Helland, of Powell River, BC, Canada, and *d* 1985, leaving issue:

1b +David Lambton Grey [David Cochrane Esq, 61 Great Dover St, London SE1 4YF]; *b* 7 March 1957; *educ* Cambridge U and Ulster Poly; *m* 1991 *Gillian Christine, dau of Edwin O'Brien, of Salford, Lancs, and has issue:

1c +Robert Thomas; *b* 18 March 1997

1c *Rachel Katherine; *b* 6 Dec 1991

2c *Rose Frances; *b* 16 May 1994

1b *Gayle Patricia [Mrs James Creamer, 3309 Hopewell Rd, Valley, Alabama 36864, USA]; *b* 19 July 1941; *m* 1977 *James Creamer

2b *Myrna Avice Ruth [Mrs James Eddison, 565 Chantenay Drive, Mississauga, Ontario L5A 1G4, Canada]; *b* 30 March 1946; *m* 1971 *James Eddison and has:

1c *David James; *b* 1974

2c *John Richard; *b* 1976

(1) Elizabeth Rosetta Stewart; *b* 19 Oct 1867; *d* unm

(2) Adelaide Maria; *b* 19 Oct 1874; *d* unm 16 Nov 1958

(3) Frances Katherine; *b* 8 Nov 1875; *d* unm May 1951

(4) Blanche Edith; *b* 4 Oct 1879

(5) Mabel Alice Maria ; *b* 6 March 1884; *d* unm 3 Feb 1931

1 Elizabeth Katharine; *m* 27 Feb 1840 John Willis Fleming, of Stoneham Park, Hants (*d* 29 May 1872), and *d* Florence 25 Aug 1869

The 10th EARL's est s,

THOMAS BARNES COCHRANE, **11th Earl of Dundonald**; *b* 18 April 1814; Capt Army; rep S peer 1879–85; *m* 1 Dec 1847 Louisa Harriet (*d* 24 Feb 1902), 2nd dau of William Alexander Mackinnon of Mackinnon, 33rd Chief, JP, DL, FRS, FSA, and *d* 15 Jan 1885, having had issue:

1 Thomas Alexander; *b* 10 April, *d* 25 July 1851

2 DOUGLAS MACKINNON BAILLIE HAMILTON, **12th Earl**

3 THOMAS HORATIO ARTHUR ERNEST COCHRANE, 1st BARON COCHRANE OF CULTS (UK), so *cr* 1919 (*qv*)

1 Louisa Katherine Emma, DGStJ; *m* 30 June 1873 2nd Baron O'Neill (*qv*), and *d* 10 Aug 1942, leaving issue

2 Alice Laura Sophia; *m* 27 July 1878 George Onslow Newton, JP, DL, of Croxton Pk, Cambs (*d* 7 Dec 1900), and *d* 8 Dec 1914, leaving issue

3 Elizabeth Mary Harriet; *d* unm 30 March 1951

4 Esther Rose Georgina

The 11th EARL's er surv s,

DOUGLAS MACKINNON BAILLIE HAMILTON COCHRANE, **12th Earl of Dundonald**, KCB (1913, CB 1896), KCVO (1907, CVO 1901, MVO 4th Cl 1878); *b* 29 Oct 1852; Lt-Gen, Col 2nd Life Gds, Hon Col 91st Canadian Highrs, Camel Corps and Desert March Relief of Khartoum (despatches, promoted Lt-Col), cmded Mounted Bde Natal Army and 2nd Cav Bde 1899–1900 (despatches six times, promoted Maj-Gen), cmded Canadian Mil 1902–04, WW I overseas (medal), rep S peer 1886–1922; *m* 18 Sept 1878 Winifred, DGStJ (*d* 17 Jan 1924), only surv dau of Robert Bamford-Hesketh, formerly 2nd Life Gds, of Gwyrch Castle, Denbighshire, and *d* 12 April 1935, having had issue:

1 THOMAS HESKETH DOUGLAS BLAIR COCHRANE, **13th Earl of Dundonald**; *b* 21 Feb 1886; Capt Scots Gds and on Gen Staff BEF WW I, rep S peer 1941–55, Chm Anglo-Chilean Soc, Grand Offr Order por Servicios Distinguidos Peru, Order of Merit Chile; *d* unm 23 May 1958

2 Douglas Robert Hesketh Roger; *b* 24 June 1893; Lt 2nd Life Gds; *m* 16 Jan 1918 Enid Marion (*d* 29 Dec 1960), dau of Miles Leonard Davis, and *d* 19 May 1942, leaving issue:

(1) IAN DOUGLAS LEONARD, **14th Earl**

(2) Richard Thomas Mackinnon; *b* 6 Feb 1927; *k* in an air crash 25 Dec 1954

(1) *(Winifred) Anne Grizel [The Lady Anne Ashford, Clareholm, Highgate, Hawkhurst, Kent]; *b* 1 Oct 1923; granted rank of earl's dau Jan 1960; *m* 23 Sept 1967 Alfred Ashford (*d* 1981), only s of Alfred Ashford, of Bromley, Kent, and has issue:

1a *Alexis; *b* 12 March 1969

1 Grizel Winifred Louise; *m* 1 March 1904 Hon Ralph Gerard Alexander Hamilton, Master of Belhaven (*ka* 31 March 1918), only s of 10th Lord Belhaven and Stenton (*qv*), and *d* 5 Dec 1976

2 Jean Alice Elaine Cochrane; *m* 1st 29 Oct 1914 (*divorce* 1933) 5th Marquess of Bristol (*qv*) and had issue; *m* 2nd 15 Dec 1933 Capt Sir Peter Drummond MacDonald, KBE (*d* 2 Dec 1961), s of Ronald MacDonald, of Nova Scotia, and *d* 5 Jan 1955

3 Marjorie Gwendoline Elsie; *m* 1 June 1917 (*divorce* 1932) Owsley Vincent Fudell Rowley, BA (*d* 10 Jan 1941), er s of George Fydell Rowley, DL, of Priory Hill, St Neots, Hunts, and had issue

The 13th EARL's n,

IAN DOUGLAS LEONARD COCHRANE; **14th Earl of Dundonald**; *b* 6 Dec 1918; *educ* Wellington and RMC Sandhurst; Maj Black Watch WW II N Africa, Sicily, Italy and Greece, psc, GSO(2) Army Air Transport Devpt Centre 1947–49, DAQMG SHAPE 1951, GSO(2) Army Cncl Secretariat 1952–53; rep S peer 1960–86, Pres Ayr and Bute Assoc Youth Clubs, V-Pres Roy Caledonian Schs, Chm Secure Holdings Ltd and the de Jersey Gp of cos, Chm Anglo-Chilean Soc 1958–65, memb UK Delegation at Political Conference of NATO Nations Paris 1962; *m* 1st 30 Jan 1960 Aphra Farquhar (*d* 15 Jan 1972), dau of Cdr George Fetherstonhaugh, RNR, of The Beacon, Benenden, Kent, and had issue:

1 (IAIN ALEXANDER) DOUGLAS BLAIR COCHRANE, **15th and present Earl of Dundonald**

1 *Tanya Jean Farquhar [The Lady Tanya Peake, Stanton Waters Farm, Hannington, Highworth, Swindon, Wilts SN6 7RY]; *b* 9 July 1964; *educ* Benenden; *m* 1992 *Anthony J L Peake, yr s of Peter Lowsley Peake, of Chantry Dene, Guildford, Surrey, and has issue:

(1) *Patrick Ian Lowsley; *b* 1994

(1) *Francesca Mary Lowsley; *b* 20 Dec 1996

The **14th Earl** *m* 2nd 15 July 1978 *(Ann) Margaret [The Rt Hon The Dowager Countess of Dundonald, Beau Coin, La Haule, Jersey, CI JE3 8BY], only dau of Sir Joseph Welsh Park Harkness, CMG, OBE, MA, MB, BSc, DPH, CStJ, of Tenterden, Kent, and formerly w of Christian Frederick Edward Staib, and *d* 4 Oct 1986

DUNLEATH

Arms: Azure a stag's head erased argent, between three escallops or. **Crest:** An escallop gules. **Supporters:** On either side an elk proper, charged on the shoulder with an escallop or and holding in the mouth a trefoil slipped vert. **Motto:** *Semper præcinctus* ('Always girt'). **Creation:** B. (UK) 29 Aug 1892, Bt. (UK) 4 July 1945.

THE 6TH BARON DUNLEATH OF BALLYWATER, Co Down and a **Baronet** (Sir Brian Mulholland, Bt) [The Rt Hon The Lord Dunleath, Ballywater Park, Newtownards, Co Down BT22 2PA]; *b* 25 Sept 1950; *s f* 1997; *educ* Eton; *m* 1976 *Mary Joan, yst dau of Maj Robert John Fuller Whistler, of Achaeon, Middleton Rd, Camberley, Surrey, and has issue:

1 +ANDREW HENRY; *b* 15 Dec 1981

2 +William Alexander; *b* 1986

1 *Tara Miranda; *b* 1980

Lineage: THOMAS MULHOLLAND, of Belfast; *b* 1756; *m* 1784 Ann Doe (*d* 1858) and *d* 1820, having had, with other issue:

1 ANDREW, of whom hereafter

2 St Clair Kelburn, of Eglantine, Hillsborough, JP Co Down, High Sheriff Co Louth 1866, Order Leopold Belgium; *b* 1798; *m* 1829 Margaret (*d* 13 July 1887), dau of Rev Joseph Wright, Rector Killincoole and Haynestown, Co Louth, and *d* 27 Jan 1872, having had, with five daus:

(1) St Clair Kelburn; *d* Sorrento, Italy, April 1861

(1) Sarah; *m* 14 March 1865 Conway Edward Dobbs (*d* 18 April 1898), of Glenariff Lodge, Dublin, and had issue

The er son,

ANDREW MULHOLLAND, of Springvale (later Ballywater Park), DL, JP, Mayor Belfast 1845; *b* 15 March 1792; *m* 13 Feb 1818 Elizabeth, dau of Thomas McDonnell, of Belfast, and had, with other issue:

1 JOHN, **1st Baron**

1 Annie; *m* 8 Jan 1851 Nicolas de la Cherois, 2nd son of Nicholas de la Cherois Crommelin, of Carrowdore Castle, Co Down, and *d* 1888

2 Sarah Jane; *m* 12 Aug 1851 James Acheson Lyle, JP, of Portstewart House, Co Londonderry

3 Mary; *m* 1858 Henry Head (*d* 13 Jan 1910), JP, MD, er s of Col Henry Aldeburgh Head, and *dsps* 15 Feb 1859

4 Andrina; *m* 19 Oct 1865 Rev Edward Augustus Lyle (*d* 1897), MA, Perpetual Curate Kircubbin, Co Down, and *d* 1881

ANDREW MULHOLLAND *d* 24 Aug 1866; his est son,

JOHN MULHOLLAND, **1st Baron Dunleath of Ballywater**, Co Down (UK), so *cr* 29 Aug 1892, JP Co Antrim, DL, JP Co Down; LLD, MP Downpatrick 1874–1885, High Sheriff Co Down 1868 and Co Tyrone 1878; *b* 16 Dec 1819; *m* 2 April 1851 Frances Louisa (*d* 23 Feb 1909), dau of Hugh Lyle, of Knocktana, Co Derry, and had issue:

1 Andrew Walter; *b* 30 Sept 1852; *m* 15 March 1877 Hon Amy Harriet (*m* 2nd 18 March 1884 Ferdinand Suydam van Zandt (*d* 2 March 1892), of New York, and *d* 19 May 1929), dau of 1st Baron Avebury (*qv*), and *dsp* 2 June 1877

2 HENRY LYLE, **2nd Baron**

3 Alfred John; *b* 25 July 1856; *educ* Balliol Coll Oxford (BA); *m* 1 June 1889 Mabel Charlotte (*d* 29 Dec 1934), est dau of Llewellyn Traherne Bassett Saunderson, of Dromkeen, Co Cavan, and *d* 26 June 1938, leaving:

(1) John Llewellyn; *b* 1 June 1908; *m* 1st 1928 (*divorce* in Hungary 1930) Helen (*d* 1992), dau of V Moss, and had:

1a +John Peter [John Mulholland Esq, New Cottage, Painswick, Glos GL6 6UA]; *b* 2 Sept 1929; *educ* Berkhamsted, RMA Sandhurst, Trin Coll Dublin and London U Sch of Slavonic Studies (BA); barrister Middle Temple 1969 and Kings Inn Dublin 1975, Brazilian Programme Organiser BBC; *m* 1st 1962 (*divorce* 1970) Suelly, dau of Olympio Jose do Lindo; *m* 2nd 1973 *Rosemary Kathleen Vaughan, only dau of Charles Hawkins, MC, BDS, and has issue:

1b +John Charles; *b* 27 Feb 1975

2b +James Patrick; *b* 23 June 1977

(1) (cont.) John Mulholland *m* 2nd in Hungary 1930 (*divorce* 1937) Olga, dau of Nicolas Kuznetzov, and by her had:

2a +Alexander Anatol [Alexander Mulholland Esq, Rua Senador Vergueiro 237/501, 2230 Rio de Janeiro, Brazil]; *b* 15 April 1931; *educ* Colegio S Jose, Rio de Janeiro, Solihull Sch and Trin Coll Dublin (BA) (Mod)); *m* 17 Oct 1959 *Judith, dau of Domico Francisco de Azevedo, and has issue:

1b *Ines; *b* 16 March 1961

(1) (cont.) John Mulholland *m* 3rd in France 1937 (*divorce* 1938) Colette, dau of Georges Mounter, and by her had issue:

3a Christian; *b* 1938; *m* 1964 *Danielle Andrée (*m* 2nd 19– R A Turner) [Mrs R Turner, 17 Stoke Rd, Leighton Buzzard, Beds], dau of André Emile Bombail, of Relizane, Algeria, and *d* 1968, leaving issue:

1b *Valentine Marie Danielle; *b* 1964; BA

2b *Hélène Marie Christine; *b* 1965

(1) (cont.) John Mulholland *m* 4th in Brazil 1944 *Lucia, dau of Antonio Izaquirre, and *d* 23 June 1989

(2) +Alfred Ivo [Major Alfred Mulholland, 22 Avon Close, S Brent, Devon TQ10 9PR], Maj Beds and Herts Regt (ret) 1950), served WW II, psc Quetta 1942; *b* 10 Feb 1913; *m* 11 Oct 1946 *Monica Mary, dau of William Lowry Craig Knight, CMG, and has issue:

1a *Mary Rose Emma [Miss Mary Mulholland, Lantern Lodge, Aish, S Brent, Devon TQ10 9JQ]; *b* 10 July 1951

(1) Daphne Rachel; *m* 1st 25 June 1912 (*divorce* 1920) 9th Earl of Darnley (*qv*) and had issue; *m* 2nd 1921 Col Hugo Henry Chandor, OBE, of Worlingham Hall, Beccles, Suffolk, and *d* 18 Jan 1948

1 Helen Mary, CBE (1919), DGStJ, Medaille de la Reconnaissance Française; *m* 23 Sept 1879 Sir George Herbert Murray, GCB, GCVO, PC, and *d* 19 Feb 1932, leaving issue (*see* ATHOLL, D)

2 Louisa Frances; *m* 12 July 1881 Edward Roger Murray Pratt (*d* 20 Nov 1921), DL, JP, of Ryston Hall, Norfolk, and *d* 25 March 1943, leaving issue

3 Alice Elizabeth; *m* 22 Nov 1892 John George Massy-Beresford (*d* 25 July 1923), of St Hubert's, Co Fermanagh, and *d* 23 Nov 1948, leaving issue (*see* MASSY, B)

The 1st BARON *d* 11 Dec 1895; his er surv son,

HENRY LYLE MULHOLLAND, **2nd Baron Dunleath of Ballywater**; DL, JP Co Down; *b* 30 Jan 1854; *educ* Balliol Coll Oxford (BA); High Sheriff Co Down 1884, Lt RE and Maj 5th Bn Royal Irish Rifles, MP N Londonderry 1885–95; *m* 28 July

1881 Norah Louisa Fanny, OBE (*d* 23 July 1935), dau of Hon Somerset Ward (*see* BANGOR, V), and *d* 22 March 1931, having had:

1 Andrew Edward Somerset, Capt Irish Gds; *b* 20 Sept 1882; *educ* Eton and Ch Ch Oxford; *m* 10 June 1913 Lady (Hester) Joan Byng, DBE (*m* 2nd 27 Nov 1922 10th Earl of Cavan (*qv*) and *d* 31 Aug 1976), yst dau of 5th Earl of Strafford (*qv*), and was *ka* nr Ypres 1 Nov 1914, leaving issue:

(1) Daphne Norah, Sr Cdr ATS; *b* posthumously 11 March 1915; *m* 12 Dec 1942 Sir John Guthrie Ward, GCMG, Amb Rome, and *d* 18 Nov 1983, leaving issue

1a *Jane Mulholland; *b* 7 Dec 1943; *m* 27 Sept 1968 *Fabrice Gauguier

2a *Joanna Guthrie; *b* 29 Jan 1950

2 CHARLES HENRY GEORGE MULHOLLAND, **3rd Baron Dunleath of Ballywalter**, CBE (1921, OBE 1919), DSO (1915), DL, JP Co Down; High Sheriff 1931, Capt 11th Hus, Mil Sec to Ld Lt Ireland 1919–21 and Govr-Gen Australia 1923–25, served WW I (despatches, wounded), KStJ; *b* 19 Aug 1886; *m* 1st 26 Feb 1920 Sylvia Henrietta (*d* 19 May 1921), er dau of Sir Arthur Douglas Brooke, 4th Bt, DL, JP (*see* BROOKEBOROUGH, V); *m* 2nd 23 Aug 1932 Henrietta Grace (*d* 20 March 1959), OStJ, 2nd dau of Most Rev Charles Fredrick D'Arcy, DD, Archbp Armagh, and *d* 20 July 1956, having by her had issue:

(1) (CHARLES EDWARD) HENRY JOHN MULHOLLAND, **4th Baron Dunleath of Ballywalter**, TD, DL (Co Down); *b* 23 June 1933; *educ* Eton and Trin Coll Cambridge; 2nd Lt 11th Hus, Lt-Col cmdg NI Horse (TA) 1967–69 (disbandment), Lt-Col RARO (1974), memb Ulster Assembly N Down 1973–74, Nat Govr BBC NI, pres NI Assoc Care and Resettlement of Offenders, chm Carreras NI 1974–93, Pres Roy Ulster Ag Soc 1975–93; *m* 5 Dec 1959 *Dorinda Margery [The Rt Hon Dorinda Lady Dunleath, 9 Killyvolgan Rd, Ballywater, Newtownards, Co Down], Hon Col WRAC (Ulster) TA 1962–, only dau of Lt-Gen Arthur Ernest Percival, CB, CMG, DSO, OBE, MC, DL, of Ware, Herts, and *dsp* 1993

3 **Sir Henry George Hill Mulholland, 1st Bt** (UK), so *cr* 4 July 1945, DL (Co Down); *b* 20 Dec 1888; *educ* Eton and Trin Coll Cambridge (BA 1913), Lt Co Londonderry 1960–65, served WW 1 as Lt RM Cavalry and RAF, MP Co Down (NI Parl) 1921–29 and Ards (Co Down) 1929–45, Assist Parly Sec Min Fin NI 1926–29, Speaker Parl NI 1929–45, Govr BBC 1952–71; *m* 16 April 1914 Sheelah (*d* 1982), yr dau of Sir Arthur Douglas Brooke, 4th Bt, of Colebrooke (*see* BROOKEBOROUGH, V), and *d* 1971, leaving issue:

(1) **Sir Michael Henry Mulholland, 2nd Bt**, and **5th Baron Dunleath of Ballywater** (as which *s* cousin 1993); *b* 15 Oct 1915; *educ* Eton and Pembroke Coll Cambridge (BA); Maj Oxon and Bucks LI WW II Burma 1942–45; *m* 1st 1942 (*divorce* 1948) Rosemary, only dau of Maj David Alfred William Ker, OBE (*see* BARRINGTON, Bt); *m* 2nd 1949 Elizabeth M (*d* 1989), dau of Laurence B Hyde, and *d* 3 May 1997, leaving:

1a BRIAN HENRY MULHOLLAND, **6th and present Baron Dunleath of Ballywater**

(1) *Sylvia Patricia Norah; WW II as Co Assist ATS; *b* 13 June 1918; *m* 2 Oct 1939 *Maj Timothy Clephan Palmer, RA, and has issue:

1a *Richard Timothy Mulholland; *b* 7 Nov 1954

1a *Amanda Clare; *b* 13th Sept 1950

4 (Godfrey) John Arthur Murray Lyle, MC; dir Westminster Bank, ptnr Edward de Stein and Co, Capt RASC, Priv Sec to Govr S Australia 1914–15, served WW I (despatches); *b* 3 Oct 1892; *educ* Eton and Trin Coll Cambridge; *m* 29 Oct 1923 Hon Olivia Vernon Harcourt (*d* 1984), DCVO (1971, CVO 1958), Woman of the Bechamber to HM QUEEN ELIZABETH THE QUEEN MOTHER, 2nd dau of 1st Viscount Harcourt (*see* VERNON, B), and *d* 1 March 1948, leaving:

(1) +Martin Edward Harcourt [Martin Mulholland Esq, North Hall, East Chiltington, Sussex], High Sheriff Co Antrim 1961, Lt Irish Gds; *b* 23 Feb 1927; *educ* Eton; *m* 24 Feb 1953 *Lilian Diana Tindall, only dau of Maj John De Blaquiere Tindall Lucas, MC, and has issue:

1a +John Martin [John Mulholland Esq, Cautley Cottage, Slaley, Hexham, Northumberland]; *b* 1 Dec 1953; *educ* Eton; late Capt 5th R Inniskilling Dragoon Gds; *m* 1981 *Diana Margaret Sara, dau of Geoffrey Walter Wilson, of Garden Lodge, Ballygargvey, Co Antrim, and has issue:

1b +Charles John; *b* 1984

1b *Sara Juliet; *b* 1987

2a +Simon Edward, Page of Honour to HM QUEEN ELIZABETH THE QUEEN MOTHER 1969–71; *b* 26 March 1955; *educ* Eton; *m* 1991 *Catriona M, yst dau of J B C Darroch, of Sevenoaks, Kent

3a +Giles Alexander; *b* 2 Dec 1959

(1) *Mary Norah, WW II in WRNS; *b* 23 Oct 1924; *m* 1 April 1944 *Capt John William Owen Elliot, late Scots Gds, only s of Hubert William Arthur Elliot (*see* MINTO, E), and has issue

(2) Bridget Olivia; *b* 19 May 1930; *m* 14 Jan 1953 Gerald Cecil Williams, yr s of Henry Harcourt Williams, JP, of Penair, Truro, and had:

1a *Christopher Harcourt; *b* 28 March 1960

1a *Carolyn Mary; *b* 23 Oct 1953

2a *Anne Olivia; *b* 1 Nov 1955

(1) Eva Norah Helen; *b* 4 Nov 1884; *m* 12 Jan 1910 Capt John Vernon Saunderson (*d* 27 Aug 1960), yst s of Col Rt Hon Edward James Saunderson, of Castle Saunderson, Co Cavan, and had issue

Seat: Belle Isle, Lisbellaw, Co Fermanagh, Northern Ireland. The name states no more than the truth: Belle Isle is quite simply a beautiful island, or at least an island in a beautiful position, being on Upper Lough Erne. An earlier occupant, Sir Ralph Gore, 6th Bt (*qv*), even took the name of his Viscountcy from it. In his day the house was a simple affair on two floors with a canted bay at one end. After Gore's death the Rev John Grey Porter (*see* LUCAN, E) bought the place and during GEORGE IV's reign a wing was added to form an L. Late in the 19th century Belle Isle was substantially refaced in Tudor style, though the new wing and the old canted bay were left more or less alone. A further Tudor extension was put up in the early years of the 20th century. Descendants of the Rev John continued to live at Belle Isle into the last quarter of the 20th century.

DUNLOP

Arms: Argent a double-headed eagle displayed gules, armed and membered azure, on a chief of the last a three-masted galley under full sail proper, flagged of the second, at the stern the banner of Scotland, all between two garbs or. **Crest:** A dexter hand couped at the wrist grasping a dagger, all proper. **Motto:** *Merito* ('Deservedly'). **Creation:** Bt. (UK) 6 July 1916.

SIR THOMAS DUNLOP, 3RD BT, of Woodbourne, Co Renfrew [Sir Thomas Dunlop Bt, The Corrie, Kilmacolm, Renfrewshire PA13 4NY]; *b* 11 April 1912, *s* f 1963; *educ* Shrewsbury and St John's Coll Cambridge; Maj Roy Signals WW II, ptnr Thomas Dunlop and Sons, shipowners and insur brokers, 1938–86, chartered accountant, chm: Savings Bank of Glasgow, Assoc of Underwriters and Insurance Brokers in Glasgow, memb: Exec Ctee Savings Bank Assoc, Bd of Management Roy Hosp for Sick Children Glasgow, Commr: Princess Louise Scottish Hosp, Erskine, Royal Alfred Merchant Seamen's Soc, Govr Hutcheson's Educnl Tst, OStJ; *m* 15 Oct 1947 *Adda Alison Mary, yst dau of T Arthur Smith, of Lindsaylands, Biggar, Lanarks, and has issue:

1 +THOMAS [Thomas Dunlop Esq, Bredon Croft, Bredons Norton, Tewkesbury, Glos GL20 7HB]; *b* 22 April 1951; *educ* Rugby and Aberdeen U (BSc, MICF); *m* 1984 Eileen (*d* 1990), er dau of Alexander Henry Stevenson, of Hurlford, Ayrshire, and has issue:

(1) +Thomas; *b* 11 March 1990

(1) *Nicola Mary; *b* 1987

1 *Jennifer Margaret [Mrs David Johnson, High Gables, Bell Lane, Thelwall, Warrington, Cheshire WA4 2SX]; *b* 11 Aug 1948; *m* 1st 1978 (*divorce* 1983) Rupert V Bruce; *m* 2nd 1983 *David Johnson, and has issue:

(1) *James David; *b* 1992

(1) *Charlotte Mary; *b* 1991

2 *Alison Mary; *b* 8 Nov 1955; *d* 1982

Lineage: THOMAS DUNLOP, of Glasgow; shipowner and grain merchant, sr ptnr and fndr Thomas Dunlop and Sons; *b* 15 March 1831; *m* 22 Nov 1852 Robina (*d* 6 Feb 1891), dau of William Jack, merchant, of Glasgow, and *d* 30 Jan 1893, having had issue:

1 THOMAS (Sir), **1st Bt**

2 Robert Jack, of Barskimming, Mauchline, Co Ayr, VD, DL, JP, ptnr Thomas Dunlop and Sons, pres Chamber of Shipping; *b* 8 April 1857; *m* 1st 21 Sept 1882 Mary Louise (*d* 20 Feb 1929), dau of Alexander Mackenzie, and had issue:

(1) Louise; *m* 21 Sept 1911 Archibald Mackenzie, er s of George Mackenzie, of N Greenhill, Paisley

2 (cont.) Robert Dunlop *m* 2nd 7 Jan 1930 Mary Hastie (*d* 7 July 1956), widow of James Craig Gatheral, slr, Glasgow, and *d* 11 Sept 1938

1 Robina Jack; *m* 15 March 1881 Andrew Ross Scott, of New York, and *d* 27 Jan 1939

2 Anne Jack; *m* 9 Oct 1888 William Brodie Galbraith (*d* 23 Sept 1945), and *d* 12 July 1942, leaving issue (*see* STRATHCLYDE, B)

3 Alexandra Margaret Scott; *m* 23 June 1904 Thomas Purdie (*d* 3 April 1946), of Aucheneck, Killearn, Stirlingshire, and *d* 1958

4 Janet Agnes Scobie; *m* 31 March 1898 Thomas Chalmers McGuffie (*d* 1931) and *d* 1949, leaving issue

The est son,

Sir Thomas Dunlop, 1st Bt (UK), so *cr* 6 July 1916, GBE (1918), DL Lanarks, JP Renfrews, DL, JP Glasgow, LLD Glasgow U, sr ptnr Thomas Dunlop and Sons, dir Roy Bank Scotland, Bruce Peebles Ltd and Scottish Union and Nat Insur Co, Ld Provost Glasgow, Ld Lt Co of City of Glasgow 1914–17, Order Crown Belgium, Order St Sava Serbia 4th Cl, Russian Red Cross, Medaille du Roi Albert; *b* 2 Aug 1855; *m* 1st 12 June 1879 Dorothy Euphemia (*d* 22 Sept 1891), dau of Peter Mitchell, of Longniddry, E Lothian, and had:

1 THOMAS (Sir), **2nd Bt**

2 Peter Mitchell, Lt RNVR, ptnr Thomas Dunlop and Sons, Ag Labour Organiser for E Lothian 1941–45; *b* 15 May 1883; *m* 5 Jan 1915 Florence Leathard (*d* 1983), dau of John Gardner Brewis, of Newcastle-upon-Tyne, and *d* 9 Jan 1962, leaving issue:

(1) *Mary Mitchell [Mrs Walter Bishop, Larchfield, Old Rd, Buckland, Betchworth, Surrey]; *b* 12 April 1924; *m* 1 March 1963 Walter Albert Bishop (*d* 1983)

3 Robert Jack, Capt 1st/7th Highland LI, JP, Commr Income Tax; *b* 4 Sept 1891; *m* 8 Aug 1918 Maude Rowena, est dau of William C Teacher, of Cove, Dunbartonshire, and *d* 15 Nov 1952, having had issue:

(1) George Teacher; *b* 27 May 1923; *m* 9 June 1950 *Margaret Jane, dau of George Frederick Schoelles, and *d* 1992, leaving:

1a +Nicholas George Teacher; *b* 17 Sept 1956

1a *Rosalie Anne; *b* 5 Sept 1951

2a *Carolyn Jane; *b* 20 Jan 1954

3a *Philippa Christine; *b* 20 Sept 1961

4a *Sally Margaret; *b* 1963

(2) +Robert Jack [Robert Dunlop Esq, Glaiceriska Cottage, Appin, Argyll]; *b* 2 July 1927; *m* 9 Sept 1950 *Dorothy Shirley, dau of James Dodd Dixon, MD, CM, FRCS, of Quebec, and has issue:

1a +Robert Alastair; *b* 30 June 1951; *m* 1975 *Jane Christian Rankin

2a +Timothy Dixon; *b* 19 March 1953; *m* 1979 *Pauline Anne Paisley

3a +Andrew James; *b* 21 June 1959; *m* 1991 *Lucia Elizabeth Mary Campbell Murfitt

1a *Gillian Elizabeth; *b* 4 Jan 1956; *m* 1983 *David James Conway

(1) Rowena Margaret; *b* 12 April 1921; *d* 27 April 1933

(2) *Audrey Dorothy [Mrs Antony Cullen, Leighon, Manaton, Newton Abbot, S Devon]; *b* 4 Feb 1932; *m* 20 Sept 1952 *Antony Leonard Cullen, MC, TD, and has issue:

1a *Michael Robert Antony; *b* 14 Dec 1955; *m* 1991 *Julie Cox

2a *Roderick Leonard Dunlop; *b* 17 March 1958; *m* 1983 *Marianne Carlsen, and has issue

3a *John Hamish Charles; *b* 24 July 1965; *m* 1989 *Susan Flowers, and has issue

3a *David Alastair Thomas; *b* 1971

1a *Rowena Gay; *b* 12 Aug 1959

2a Audrey Hilary; *b* 12 Oct 1963; *m* 1989 *John Grigg, and has issue

1 Robina Stirling; *m* 6 Dec 1917 John Brownlie Somerville (*d* 2 April 1934) and had issue:

(1) *John Brownlie [John Somerville Esq, 65 Cornwall Gdns, London SW7], WW II as Lt RNVR; *b* 26 Sept 1919; *educ* Shrewsbury and Lincoln Coll Oxford

2 Dorothy Euphemia Mitchell; *m* 5 Oct 1917 John Cumming Bruce Jones (*d* 25 Dec 1953) and has issue:

(1) *Thomas Dunlop, MC [Thomas Jones Esq MC, The House-on-the-Hill, Dunblane, Perthshire], WW II as Capt RA; *b* 2 May 1920; *educ* Rugby and St John's Coll Cambridge; *m* 1 Nov 1952 *Patricia Leslie, yr dau of Sir Maurice Edward Denny, 2nd Bt, of Dumbarton (*qv*), and has issue:

1a *Veronica Margaret; *b* 13 Nov 1953

2a *Victoria Leslie; *b* 10 June 1956

3a *Claire Patricia; *b* 1 Nov 1958

4a *Juliet Mary; *b* 13 Jan 1966

(1) *Margaret Mitchell Dunlop [Mrs Benjamin Leslie, Kenlygreen, Boarhills, Fife]; *b* 21 Jan 1922; *m* 9 June 1945 *Benjamin Stewart Leslie and has issue:

1a *Michael Francis Bruce; *b* 25 March 1946; *educ* Rugby and RAC Cirencester

2a *Christopher Malcolm Stewart; *b* 8 April 1948; *educ* Rugby and St Andrews

3a *David Stewart; *b* 1 Feb 1964

(2) *Dorothy Mary Dunlop; *b* 19 April 1925; *m* 26 March 1946 (*divorce* 1971) Sir Hugh Ripley, 4th Bt (*qv*), and has issue

3 *Mary Boyd

Sir Thomas *m* 2nd 19 Oct 1893 Margaret (*d* 12 May 1952), dau of Peter Mitchell, and *d* 29 Jan 1938

His est son,

Sir Thomas Dunlop, 2nd Bt; Consular Service 1919–39, ptnr Thomas Dunlop and Sons; *b* 17 Nov 1881; *m* 28 June 1911 Mary Elizabeth, dau of William Beckett, slr, of Glasgow, and *d* 8 March 1963, leaving issue:

1 Sir THOMAS DUNLOP, **3rd and present Bt**

2 William Beckett, WW II as Capt RA, slr 1947; *b* 6 March 1915; *educ* Rugby and St John's Coll Cambridge; *m* 22 April 1947 *Charmian Katherine Chauncy [Mrs William Dunlop, 66 Novar Drive, Glasgow G12], dau of Col Gavin Charteris Towers Speirs, MC, TD, DL, BSc, and *d* 15 Oct 1970, leaving issue:

(1) +Anthony Charles Beckett; *b* 13 Feb 1948; *educ* Rossall

(2) +Michael William Beckett; *b* 4 May 1951; *educ* Rugby

(3) +Simon Speirs Beckett; *b* 24 March 1955; *educ* Millfield

1 *Dorothy Frances; *b* 21 Nov 1921; *m* 9 July 1948 Ernest Forrester Fortune (*d* 1993), MBE, TD, and has issue:

(1) *George Dunlop [George Fortune Esq, PO Box 707, 07080 Palma, Mallorca, Spain]; *b* 3 Oct 1953; *m* 1977 *Patricia Elise, dau of Eric Moore, of Cheadle, Lancs

(1) *Susan Elizabeth; *b* 21 Sept 1949

DUNMORE

Arms: Quarterly of six in three ranks, 1st (in dexter chief) azure, three mullets argent within a double tressure flory and counterflory of fleurs-de-lys or (for MURRAY OF ATHOLL); 2nd (in sinister chief) or a fess checky azure and argent (for STEWART); 3rd (in dexter fess) paly of six or and sable (for ATHOLL); 4th (in sinister fess) argent on a bend azure three buck's heads cabossed or (for STANLEY); 5th (in dexter base) gules three legs in armour proper garnished and spurred or, flexed and conjoined in triangle at the upper part of the thigh (for ISLE OF MAN); 6th (in sinister base) gules two lions passant in pale argent, armed and langued azure (for STRANGE); overall at the honour point a crescent sable. **Crest:** A demi-wild man wreathed about the loins and temples with laurel, charged on the breast of a crescent sable, holding in his dexter hand a sword proper, hilted and pommelled sable, and in his sinister hand a key also sable. **Supporters:** Dexter, a savage proper wreathed about the loins, charged on the breast of a crescent sable; sinister, a lion rampant gules, armed and langued azure, gorged of a collar argent, charged with three crescents sable. **Motto:** Furthward Fortune ('Go forward and make good'). **Creations:** L. V. and E. (S) 16 Aug 1686 (UK) 10 Sept 1831.

THE 12TH EARL OF DUNMORE, Viscount of Fincastle and Lord Murray of Blair, Moulin, and Tillemot, (Malcolm Kenneth Murray) [The Rt Hon The Earl of Dunmore, House of Lords, London SW1A 0PW]; *b* 17 Sept 1946; *s f* 1995; *m* 1970 *Joy Anne, dau of A Partridge, of Launceston, Tasmania, and adopted:

*Leigh Kenneth; *b* 1978

*Elisa Anne; *b* 1981

Lineage: The 1st MARQUESS OF ATHOLL (*see* ATHOLL, D) had a 2nd s:

CHARLES MURRAY, **1st Earl of Dunmore** (S), so *cr* 16 Aug 1686, as also VISCOUNT OF FINCASTLE and LORD MURRAY OF BLAIR, MOULIN, AND TILLEMOT, PC (1703); *b* 24 Feb 1661; Col Scots Greys 1685, Master of the Horse to PRINCESSES MARY and ANNE, imprisoned as suspected Jacobite 1689, 1692 and 1696; *m* 8 Dec 1682 Catharine (*d* by 22 Jan 1711), dau and heir of Richard Watts, of Great Munden, Herts, and *d* 19 April 1710, having had, with other issue:

1 James, *Viscount Fincastle*; *b* 7 Dec 1683; Capt Macartney's Regt of Scots Foot; *m* 29 April 1702 Janet, dau of Patrick Murray, of Livingstone, and *dsp* & *vp* 29 Sept 1704

2 JOHN MURRAY; **2nd Earl of Dunmore**; *b* 31 Oct 1685; Gen, Col 3rd (Scots) Foot Gds, Govr Plymouth, rep S peer 1713–15 and 1727–52; *d* unm 18 April 1752

3 Robert; *b* 7 Jan 1689; Brig-Gen, Col 38th Regt; MP Wootton Bassett 1722 and Gt Bedwyn 1734; *m* 1708 Mary, dau of Sir Charles Ralket, of Pitfirran, and *d* 9 March 1738, having had issue:

(1) Catherine; *bapt* Jan 1709

4 WILLIAM, **3rd Earl**

5 Thomas, of Dorney House, Weybridge; *b* June 1698 (twin); Lt-Gen, Col 40th Foot; *m* Elizabeth, sis of Lt-Gen Robert Arminger, and *d* 21 Nov 1764, leaving:

(1) Frances Maria

The 2nd EARL's bro,

WILLIAM MURRAY, **3rd Earl of Dunmore**; *b* 2 March 1696; Jacobite 1745, pleaded guilty of high treason 1746 but pardoned; *m* 1728 his cousin Catherine, dau of his unc Lord William Murray, later Lord Nairne (*see* MERSEY, V), and *d* 1 Dec 1756, having had, with other issue:

1 JOHN, **4th Earl**

2 William; *b* 1734; Capt RN; *m* 11 Aug 1783 Sarah Maese (*m* 2nd 1 Nov 1802 George Aust, U-Sec For Affairs, and *d* 5 Nov 1811), and *d* 25 Dec 1786

1 Elizabeth; *b* 1743; *m* 24 July 1763 Rev John Murray, Dean of Killaloe, and had issue (*see* ATHOLL, D)

The 3rd EARL's er s,

JOHN MURRAY, **4th Earl of Dunmore**; *b* 1730; rep S peer 1761–74 and 1776–90, last Br Govr Virginia; *m* 21 Feb 1759 Lady Charlotte Stewart (*d* 11 Nov 1818), dau of 6th Earl of Galloway (*qv*), and *d* 25 Feb 1809, having had, with other issue:

1 GEORGE MURRAY, **5th Earl of Dunmore**; *b* 30 April 1762; *cr* 10 Sept 1831 BARON DUNMORE in the Forest of Atholl, Co Perth (UK); *m* 3 Aug 1803 Susan (*d* 24 May 1846), dau of 9th Duke of Hamilton (*see* HAMILTON and BRANDON, D), and *d* 11 Nov 1836, having had issue:

(1) ALEXANDER EDWARD MURRAY, **6th Earl of Dunmore**; *b* 1 June 1804; Capt 9th Lancers, ADC to HRH THE 1st DUKE OF CAMBRIDGE; *m* 27 Sept 1836 Catherine (*d* 12 Feb 1886), dau of 11th Earl of Pembroke and (8th Earl of) Montgomery (*qv*), and *d* 15 July 1845, having had issue:

1a CHARLES ADOLPHUS MURRAY, **7th Earl of Dunmore**, VD, DL (Inverness-shire); *b* 24 March 1841; Capt Scots Fus Gds, Hon Col 1st Vol Bn Cameron Highrs; Ld-in-Waiting 1874–80, Ld Lt Stirlingshire; *m* 5 April 1866 Lady Gertrude Coke (*d* 28 Nov 1943), 3rd dau of 2nd Earl of Leicester (*qv*), and *d* 27 Aug 1907, having had issue:

1b ALEXANDER EDWARD MURRAY, **8th Earl of Dunmore**, VC (1897), DSO, MVO, DL (Inverness-shire); *b* 22 April 1871; Maj 16th Lancers, ADC to Viceroy India 1895–97 and Maj-Gen Sir H C Chermside 1899, Sudan Field Force 1896 (medal), Malakand Field Force 1897 (despatches three times, medal with clasp), Boer War 1899–1900 and 1902 (despatches, medal with four clasps), raised and cmded Fincastle's Horse 31st Bn Imp Yeo 1902, WW I 1914 (despatches four times, wounded twice, 1914 Star, two medals), Capt Gentlemen-at-Arms Jan-Nov 1924, Ld-in-Waiting 1930–36; *m* 5 Jan 1904 Dorothea (*d* 9 Feb 1966), est dau of Horace William Kemble, of Knock, Isle of Skye, and *d* 29 Jan 1962, having had issue:

1c Edward David, *Viscount Fincastle*; *b* 3 April 1908 (HM EDWARD VII stood sponsor); *educ* Winchester; Capt 4th Bn Cameron Highrs WW II; *m* 26 April 1938 Hon Pamela Kate Hermon-Hodge (*m* 2nd 27 June 1944 Capt Follett Watson Bell, RA, son of Frederick Norman Bell), est dau of 2nd Baron Wyford (*qv*), and was *ka* June 1940, leaving:

1d JOHN ALEXANDER MURRAY, **9th Earl of Dunmore**; *b* 3 April 1939; *educ* Eton; 2nd Lt QO Cameron Highrs 1958–59, Lt 4th/5th Bn 1959–65; PR exec Charles Barker and Sons, PRO Schweppes USA 1964–67, memb Inst Public Rels 1968; *m* 8 Dec 1967 *Anne Augusta [The Rt Hon The Countess of Dunmore, 14 Regent Terrace, Edinburgh EH7 5BN], er dau of Thomas Clouston Wallace, of Holodyke, Dounby, Orkney, and *d* 1980 when the 1831 UK Barony expired, leaving issue:

1e *Kate Rodel; *b* 9 May 1969

2e *Rebecca Moulin; *b* 11 Dec 1970; *m* 21 June 1997 *Ben Wightman

1c *Marjorie Hilda [The Lady Marjorie Stirling, 20 Kingston House South, Ennismore Gdns, London SW7], Order of Mercy; *b* 1 Nov 1904; *m* 27 Jan 1926 Duncan Alexander Stirling (*d* 1990), Chm Nat West Bank, Capt Coldstream Gds, 4th s of Maj William Stirling, JP, DL, of Fairburn, Ross-shire, and had issue:

1d *Alexander Murray [Alexander Stirling Esq, Hunterswood House Chipperfield, Herts WD4 9AY]; *b* 11 Aug 1927; *educ* Eton and New Coll Oxford (BA 1950); late Lt Coldstream Gds; late partner Thomas R Miller & Son; dir P&O Lines 1969–75, Exec Ctee City & Guilds London Art Sch 1990–, Chm London Assay Office 1991–95, Prime Warden Goldsmiths' Co 1993–94; *m* 1 Dec 1951 *Mary, 2nd dau of Neville Wakefield, DSO, and has issue:

1e *Robert Alexander; *b* 22 April 1959; *m* 16 Jan 1988 *Susan Mary, yr dau of R-Adml James Humphrey Walwyn, CB, OBE, and has issue:

1f *Alexander Humphrey; *b* 1994

2f *Rory James; (twin) *b* 1994

2e *Oliver John; *b* 28 Feb 1961; *m* 21 Dec 1991 *Susan Caroline Foster, and has issue:

1f *Rufus Alexander Algernon; *b* 14 Oct 1993

1f *Iona Grace Jean; *b* 25 Oct 1995

2f *Flora India Oriana; *b* 27 Aug 1997

1e *Annabel Mary Charlotte; *b* 14 April 1963; *m* 15 July 1995 *Richard Hugh Jolly

2d *Angus Duncan Æneas (Sir) [Sir Angus Stirling, 25 Ladbroke Grove, London W11 3AY]; *b* 10 Dec 1933; *educ* Eton and Trin Coll Cambridge; chm ROH 1991–96, Dir Gen Nat Tst 1983–95, Sr Policy Advsr Nat Heritage Meml Fund 1996–97, chm Greenwich Fndn for Roy Naval Coll 1996–, chm Jt Nature Conservation Ctee 1997–, Tstee Courtauld Collection 1983–, memb: Advsy Cncl LSO 1979–, Bd Tstees Heritage of London Tst 1983–95, Cncl RSCM 1996–; chm Policy Ctee CPRE 1996; ktd 1994; *m* 20 June 1959 *Armyne Morar Helen, est dau of William George Broadbent Schofield (*see* HASTINGS, B), and has issue:

1e *Duncan William Angus; *b* 10 Aug 1963

1e *Emma Elisabeth [Mrs Andrew Sutcliffe, Kildale Hall, Whitby, N Yorks]; *b* 18 June 1960; *m* 17 Dec 1988 *Andrew Harold Wentworth Sutcliffe, er s of John Harold Victor Sutcliffe, and has had:

1f Ralph Andrew Aeneas; *b* 26 June 1991; *d* 27 Nov 1992

1f *Rose Cecilia; *b* 18 Feb 1990

2f *Helena Morar; *b* 17 Oct 1993

3f *Laura Mary; *b* 9 June 1995

2e *Candida Helen; *b* 9 Feb 1966

2c *(Mary) Elisabeth [The Lady Elisabeth Oldfield, Ham Cottage, Sydmonton, Newbury, Berks]; *b* 28 Nov 1913; *m* 29 April 1937 Maj Peter Carlton Oldfield, OBE, Warwicks Yeo, yst s of Carlton Oldfield, and has issue:

1d *Sara Elisabeth [Mrs Sara Thomson, West Manor Stables, Standen, Hungerford, Berks RG17 0RB]; *b* 14 Feb 1939; *m* 16 Nov 1961 (*divorce* 1983) William Bennet Thomson, s of Norman Bennet Thomson, and has issue:

1e *Lucinda Elisabeth ; *b* 4 April 1965

1b Evelyn; *m* 23 April 1891 John Dupuis Cobbold, DL (*d* 12 June 1929), and *d* 25 Jan 1963, leaving issue

2b Muriel; *m* 16 July 1890, as his 2nd w, Col Harold Gore Browne (*d* 4 Jan 1938), KRRC, s of Col Sir Thomas Gore Browne, KCMG, CB, and *d* 27 Sept 1946

3b Grace, MBE (1919); *b* 17 Feb 1873; *m* 25 Jan 1896 William James Barry (*d* 2 July 1952), of Witchingham Hall, Norwich, and *d* 23 Sept 1960, leaving issue (*see* BARRY, Bt)

4b Victoria Alexandrina; *b* 17 May 1877 (HM QUEEN VICTORIA stood sponsor); *d* unm 13 Dec 1925

5b Mildred; *b* 13 Nov 1878; *m* 1st 30 June 1904 Brig-Gen Gilbert Burrell Spencer Follett, DSO, MVO, Coldstream Gds (*ka* 27 Sept 1918), only s of James Skirrow Follett, JP, and had issue; *m* 2nd 14 Oct 1919 Sir John Peter Gerald Maurice FitzGerald, 3rd Bt, Knight of Kerry (*qv*), and *d* 7 June 1969

1a Susan Catherine Mary; *m* 29 Nov 1860 9th Earl of Southesk (*see* FIFE, D) and *d* 27 April 1915, leaving issue

2a Constance Euphemia Woronzow; *m* 16 June 1864 15th Lord Elphinstone (*qv*) and *d* 16 March 1922, leaving issue

3a Alexandrina Victoria; *m* 20 April 1887 Rev Henry Cunliffe (*see* CUNLIFFE, Bt) and *dsp* 21 Nov 1911

(2) Charles Augustus (Sir), KCB, PC; *b* 22 Nov 1806; Master Household and Extra Groom in Waiting to HM QUEEN VICTORIA, Envoy-Extrdy and Min-Plen; *m* 1st 12 Dec 1850 Elizabeth (*d* 8 Dec 1851), dau of James Wadsworth, of New York, and had issue:

1a Charles James, DL, of Loch Carron, Ross-shire; *b* 29 Nov 1851; MP Hastings 1883 and Coventry 1895–1906, 3rd Sec Dip Serv, served Ross and Cromarty Mountain Bn RGA WW I France 1917–18, Officier de Merite Agricole; *m* 9 Aug 1875 Lady Anne Francesca Wilhelmina Finch (*d* 10 Jan 1933), dau of 6th Earl of Aylesford (*qv*), and *d* 25 Sept 1929, having had issue:

1b Alastair Heneage; *b* 24 April 1878; Lt Gren Gds; *d* of wounds recd nr Senekal, S Africa, 3 June 1900

2b Charles Wadsworth; *b* 15 July 1894; Sub-Lt RNVR; *m* 8 Jan 1924 Elizabeth (*d* 1993), 2nd dau of Frank Grant, of Knockie, Inverness, and *d* 22 March 1945, leaving issue:

1c *Helen Rosemary; *b* 25 April 1928; *m* 1966 Hubert Zipperlen

1b Sibyl Louise; *b* 23 June 1876; *m* 24 Oct 1904 Col Hon Claude Henry Comaraich Willoughby, CVO, 9th Lancers (*d* 22 Sept 1932), and *d* 8 Oct 1957, having had issue (*see* MIDDLETON, B)

(2) (cont.) The Hon Sir Charles Murray *m* 2nd 1 Nov 1862 Hon Edith Susan Esther FitzPatrick (*d* 1 Dec 1906), dau of 1st Baron Castletown (*see* 1937 edn), and *d* 3 June 1895, having by her had further issue:

2a Cecil Henry Alexander; *b* 4 April 1866; *d* at sea 3 June 1896

3a Henry Anthony; *b* 10 Jan 1810; R-Adml, Kt Gd Cross Bavarian Order St Michael of Merit; *d* 17 Feb 1865

2 Alexander; *b* 12 Oct 1764; Lt-Col; *m* 18 May 1811 Deborah (*d* 28 Jan 1870), dau of Robert Hunt, C-in-C Bahamas, and *d* July 1842, having had, with other issue:

(1) Augustus Charles; *b* 16 Dec 1815; Cdr RN; *m* 14 Aug 1851 Abbie, dau of David Lee, of New York, and *dsp* 1902

(2) Virginius; *b* 20 Sept 1817; Capt 94th Foot; *m* 23 Oct 1844 Elizabeth Alicia (*d* 27 Dec 1877), only dau of Col Charles Poitiers, 61st Regt, and *d* 25 Dec 1861, having had, with other issue:

1a Reginald Augustus Frederick; *b* 18 Feb 1846; *m* 1st 30 Jan 1869 Jane Louisa Otway (*d* 30 Nov 1887), dau of Henry Bayles Ford, of Melbourne, Australia, and had issue:

1b Virginius Henry Randolph; *b* 12 Nov 1872; *m* 16 March 1910 Alice (*d* 29 July 1966), dau of William Clarke, MD, of Banff, and *d* 18 Aug 1937, having had issue:

1c William Reginald; *b* 16 May 1912; *d* 10 Jan 1930

1c Virginia Margaret; *b* 26 Feb 1911; *m* 30 May 1942 Alfred Allen Gibbs (*d* 1982), chartered accountant, and *d* 24 July 1976, leaving:

1d Peter Murray; *b* March 1943; BDc (Melbourne) LDS (Victoria); FRACS, dentist; *m* 17 May 1969 *Susan Barrett [Mrs Peter Gibbs, 7 Morey St, Burwood, Victoria 3125, Australia]; and *d* 15 Oct 1985 leaving:

1e *Eleanor Ann; *b* 21 July 1971

2e *Elizabeth Denise; *b* 14 June 1973; *m* 22 April 1995 *Jamie Baker, of Bishops Stortford

3e *Megan Virginia; *b* 10 March 1978

2d *David Ian [David Gibbs, 4/24 Kensington Rd, South Yarra, VICT 3141, Australia]; *b* Dec1950; *educ* Melbourne U (B Comm), FCA

2c *Patricia Aimée [Mrs Peter Horne, 42 Musgrave St, Mosman 2088, NSW, Australia]; *b* 1916; *m* 1960 *Peter Bayard Horne

3c *Judith Dunmore [Mrs Ian Monk, 35a Raglan St, Mosman 2088, Sydney, NS W, Australia]; *b* 1918; *m* 1944 Ian Monk, MB, BS, MS, FRCS (*d* 31 July 1978), and has issue:

1d *Virginia Ann; *b* 10 Aug 1949; *m* 1977 *Neil Hersfield, of Vancouver, Canada, and has issue:

1e *Zach Dunmore; *b* 1983

2e *Gabriel Ian; *b* 1988

2d *Victoria Jane [Mrs Victoria Tan, 34 Bucknell st, Newtown, NSW 2042, Australia]; *b* 10 July 1952; *m* 1975 (*divorce*) Tan Choo Lim, economist

3d *Serena Dunmore [Mrs Christian Dubois, 11 Coachwood Ave, Dicton, NSW 2571, Australia]; *b* 1954; *m* 1983 *Christian Dubois, of Aigle, Switzerland, and has issue:

1e *Oriane Dunmore; *b* 1985

2e *Tamara Judith; *b* 1988

2b Arthur Charles; *b* 9 Sept 1882; Boer War 1901–02 (medal, four clasps); *m* 1st 1909 Susan Maud (*d* 1922), dau of Edward Richards, of Tasmania; *m* 2nd 31 Dec 1929 Ida Clara, dau of John Mallinson and widow of Alfred Dawe, of Gladstone, Tasmania, and *d* 5 Sept 1964, leaving issue by his 1st w:

1c REGINALD ARTHUR MURRAY, **10th Earl of Dunmore**; *b* 17 July 1911; *m* 1948 *Patricia Mary [Mrs Geoffrey Fitze, Kooringal, 27 Beach Road, Gravelly Beach 7276, W Tamar, Tasmania, Australia] (*m* 2nd 1984 Geoffrey Howard Fitze), dau of Frank Coles, of Robigana, W Tamar, Tasmania, and *d* 1981, leaving:

1d *Susan [The Lady Susan Price, 15 Wandoo Rd, Duncraig, W Australia 6023]; *b* 1949; *m* 1980 *Graham Price

2d *Elizabeth Mary [The Lady Elizabeth Parkinson, 882 Cambridge Rd, Cambridge, Tasmania 7170, Australia]; *b* 1951; *m* 1973 *John Michael Parkinson, and has issue:

1e *James Murray; *b* 1976

1e *Anna Louise; *b* 1978

2c KENNETH RANDOLPH MURRAY, **11th Earl of Dunmore**; *b* 6 June 1913; Sgt 12th/50th Bn Australian Inf; *m* 1938 Margaret Joy (*d* 1976), dau of P D Cousins, of Burnie, Tasmania, and *d* 25 Oct 1995, leaving:

1d MALCOLM KENNETH MURRAY, **12th and present Earl of Dunmore**

2d +GEOFFREY CHARLES [The Hon Geoffrey Murray, PO Box 2133, Launceston, Tasmania 7250, Australia]; *b* 31 July 1949; heir presumptive; *m* 1974 *Margaret Irene, dau of H Bulloch, of Blackwall, Tasmania

3c Alexander Edward; *b* 12 Sept 1917; WW II as Able Seaman RAN; *m* 1st 1943 (*divorce* 1968) June Caroline Lucy, dau of B Rabinovitch, of 6 Culloden Ave, E Moonah, Tasmania; *m* 2nd 1970 *Irene Maud Barwick, of Hobart, Tasmania, and *d* 30 June 1994, leaving by his 1st w:

1d +Stephen Alexander [Stephen Murray Esq, 36 Newlands St, Riverside, Launceston, Tasmania 7250, Australia]; *b* 14 May 1953; *m* 1979 *Marilyn Ann Rose and has had:

1e Mathew James; *b* 1982; *d* 7 July 1995

2e +Anthony Victor; *b* 1989

1d *Marilyn Joy [Mrs Brian Carson, 11 Leamington St Reservoir, Victoria 3073, Australia]; *b* 28 May 1947; *m* 1st 1964 (*divorce* 1971) Michael John Hankin and has issue:

1e *Brett Michael; *b* 1967

1e *Tania Marie; *b* 1965

2e *Sharon Louise; *b* 1971

1d (cont.) Mrs Marilyn Hankin *m* 2nd 1979 *Brian Carson

2d *Wendy Lorraine [Mrs Maxwell Upton, 122 Brent St, Glenorchy, Hobart, Tasmania]; *b* 29 May 1951; *m* 1969 *Maxwell Kevin Upton, and has issue:

1e *Jason Boaz; *b* 1971

1e *Natasha Ruby Marie; *b* 1976

1c *Lorraine Edith; *b* 1914; *m* 1st 1940 Hector Bird (*d* 20 July 1963); *m* 2nd 1 Oct 1966 Stanley Millwood Farquhar (*d* 3 April 1996), and has by her 1st husb:

1d *Grace Lucinda [Mrs Haydn Borella, c/o 62 Talbot Rd, Launceston, Tasmania 7250, Australia]; *b* 21 Feb 1950; *m* 1969 (*divorce* 1995) Haydn Peter Borella and has:

1e *Paul Andrew; *b* 1973

1e *Angela Jane; *b* 1971

1d (cont.) Mrs Borella also has:

2e*David John; *b* 19 Jan 1968

2c *Constance Margaret [Mrs John Mallinson, 12 Munford St, Kings Meadows, Launceston, Tasmania]; *b* 1922; *m* 1946 *John Mallinson and has had issue:

1d Brian Leslie; *b* 20 Sept 1952; *k* in a car crash 4 Jan 1960

2d *Edward Arthur John; *b* 5 Oct 1955; *m* 1979 *Janice Maree Shipp, and has issue:

1e *Damien Edward; *b* 1980

1e *Erin Elizabeth; *b* 1983

3d *David Andrew; *b* 27 Sept 1957

3b Malcolm Fincastle; *b* 26 April 1885; *m* 5 June 1915 Rhoda Dorothy (*d* 1970), dau of Richard Davies Hanson, and gdau of Sir Richard Davies Hanson, Ch Justice S Australia, and *d* 30 May 1935, leaving issue:

1c *Judith Hanson Fincastle; *b* 1923; *m* 1945 *Donald Munro Walker, Australian Trade Commr Serv, and has:

1d *Malcolm John Munro; *b* 1946; *m* 1973 *Margo Jill Chalmers, dau of J Chalmers, of Wagga Wagga, NSW, and has issue:

1e *Andrew John; *b* 1977

1e *Rebecca Lee; *b* 1975

1d *Pamela Murray; *b* 1952

1b Edith Louise; *m* 24 April 1895 Clyde B Norton, and *d* 6 Sept 1936, having had issue

2b Constance Mary; *d* unm 28 June 1965

1a (cont.) Reginald Murray *m* 2nd 4 July 1888 Ethel (*d* 15 Nov 1912), dau of Thomas Thompson Bates, of Melbourne, and *d* 5 Sept 1925, having by her had issue:

4b Reginald Herbert Earn; *b* 3 Oct 1893; FASA, FCIS; WW I (despatches); *m* 3 Oct 1928 Nina Clarendon (*d* 18 Dec 1975), dau of Clarendon James Seager and gdau of Lt-Gen Edward Seager, CB, 8th Hus, and *d* 1980, having had:

1c John Dunmore [John Murray Esq, Coonawarra, 2 Twin St, Stirling, S Australia 5152]; *b* 11 Aug 1929; *educ* St Peter's Coll S Australia and U of Adelaide (BE 1953), MIE Aust;*m* 14 Nov 1962 *Geraldine Marjorie, yr dau of Col Rupert Edward Fanning, DSO, of South Yarra, Victoria, Australia, and has issue:

1d *Catriona Dunmore Stewart [Mrs Michael Mills, 138 Mount Pleasant, Cockfosters, London EN4 9HG]; *b* 23 July 1965; *m* 1992 *Michael David Mills

2d *Bridget Dunmore Stewart; *b* 8 Aug 1967

3d *Vanessa Dunmore Stewart; *b* 12 May 1969

4d *Kirsten Dunmore Stewart; *b* 5 June 1971

3b Christina Dunmore; *b* 25 March 1889; *m* 16 March 1917 Dr WW McLaren, and had issue

4b Katrine Elizabeth Alice; *b* 10 June 1891; *m* 11 Nov 1913 Hon James Miller Balfour, JP, MLC (*d* 30 July 1943), of Warragul, Victoria, and has had issue:

1c *James Charles Murray; *b* 30 Sept 1914; MLA Victoria; *m* 1937 *Mary Emma, dau of Condah Savige, of Victoria, Australia, and has had issue:

1d Kenneth James; *b* 28 Dec 1937; *d* 16 June 1942

2d *Russell Miller; *b* 19 March 1939

3d *Peter Murray; *b* 9 April 1943

4d *David; *b* 14 June 1945

5d *Graeme Charles; *b* 14 Nov 1952

2c Alexander Jeffrey; *b* 28 June *d* 26 Sept 1918

1c Margaret Jane; *b* 17 March 1917; *d* 4 April 1921

2c *Daisy Miller [Mrs Geoffrey Mander-Jones, 153 Kooyong Rd, North Caulfield, Victoria, Australia]; *b* 29 Oct 1920; *m* 25 June1947 *Lt-Col Geoffrey Mander-Jones, York and Lancaster Regt (ret), s of Dr George Burnet Mander-Jones, of Wahroonga, NSW, and has issue:

1d *Robert; *b* 25 Jan 1949

1d *Angela Margaret; *b* 14 Jan 1953

2d *Susan Elizabeth; *b* 5 May 1958

3c *Beryl Miller; *b* 17 April 1922; BA (1942); *m* 10 Jan 1946 *Rev Ronald Ian Scott, min Presbyterian Church, Lilydale, Victoria, Australia, s of Archibald T Scott, of Devonport, Tasmania, and has issue:

1d *John Balfour; *b* 9 Nov 1946

1d *Katrine Elizabeth; *b* 18 Dec 1947

2d *Margaret Anne; *b* 10 May 1950

3d *Virginia Blanche; *b* 24 Oct 1956

5b Phyllis Ethel Sheila; *b* 2 Aug 1901; *m* 1938 Dr R Keenan

2a George Earn; *b* 11 Nov 1850; *m* 1889 Julia Mary McLeod (*d* 8 June 1933), 2nd dau of Gen C B Fuller, RHA, and *d* 1902, leaving issue:

1b Dudley Stewart; *b* 1892

1b Gladys; *b* 1890; *m* — Wyatt, and had one dau (*k* in motor accident)

2b Doris Vivienne; *b* 1894

3a Henry Alexander; *b* 6 June 1857; *m* 8 May 1889 Fannie Morris (*d* 1940), dau of Samuel D Babcock, of New York, and *d* 25 March 1934, leaving issue:

1b Henry Alexander; *b* 13 May 1893; MD Columbia, PhD Cambridge; Lt-Col USA Med Corps, Legn of Merit 1946; *m* 1st 1916 Josephine Lee (*d* 14 Jan 1962), dau of Neal Rantoul, of Boston, USA, and had issue:

1c *Josephine Lee Murray [Dr Josephine Murray, 41 Concord Ave, Cambridge, MA 02138, USA]; *b* 1921; MA 1954, MD New York U 1961, pediatrician Judge Baker Guidance Center Boston

1b (cont.) Lt-Col Henry Murray *m* 2nd 1969 *Caroline Fish [Mrs Henry Murray, 1010 Memorial Drive, Cambridge, MA 023138, USA], dau of Alfred Chandler, of Wilmington, Del., and *d* 1988

2b Cecil Dunmore; *b* 20 Dec 1897; Lt USNAF, Northern Bombing Gp, Navy Cross, Victory Medal with Aviation clasp; *m* 1921 Veronica (*d* 1988), dau of Kenneth Frazier, of Garrison, New York, and *d* 4 July 1935, leaving issue:

1c +Michael Hunt (Rev) [The Rev Michael Murray, 209 Tred Avon Ave, Oxford, MD 21654, USA]; *b* 1922; *educ* Harvard U (BA 1948) and Johns Hopkins U (MA 1950); late Lt USNAF, publisher of Editions Euros, Paris; *m* 1st 1943 (*divorce*) Gloria Caruso, and has issue:

1d +Eric Dunmore; *b* 25 March 1945; *m* June 1970 *Lynne Valeti

2d +Colin Duncan Alexander [Colin Murray Esq, 260 W 62nd St, Jacksonville, Florida, USA]; *b* 1949; *m* Dec 1971 *Elizabeth Kanfold

1c (cont.) The Rev Michael Murray *m* 2nd 1955 *Eliane, dau of Eugene Cadilhac, of Paris

1c *Julia Frazier; *m* 1953 *Robert Linfield Mackintosh, of Manchester, Mass, USA, and has issue:

1d *Amy Rogers; *b* 1954

2d *Louisa Linfield; *b* 1956

3d *Susan Frazier; *b* 1958

1b Virginia, OBE (1948); *b* 6 Sept 1890; Chm Fighting Funds for Finland 1939–40, Chm Br War Relief Washington, Amb Jubilee of Emperor Haile Selassie 1955, Amb Coronation of Mahandra of Nepal 1956, Legn Hon and Order White Rose of Finland; *m* 1913 Robert Low Bacon (*d* 12 Sept 1938), Col Field Art Res Corps, USA, memb Congress 1922–38, and had issue:

1c Alexandra Murray; *b* 4 March 1914; *dsp* Dec 1935

2c *Virginia Murray; *b* 7 June 1916; *m* 1949 *Byron Thomas, and has issue:

1d *Richard; *b* July 1951

1d *Virginia Murray; *b* 9 April 1950

2d *Mary Elizabeth; *b* 13 May 1953

3c Martha; *b* 30 Sept 1918; *m* 1st 1942 Capt Creighton Churchill, and has issue:

1d *Daniel; *b* 19 June 1948

1d *Alexandra; *b* 7 Sept 1946

3c (cont.) Mrs Churchill *m* 2nd 1953 *James L Farley and *d* 16 Nov 1990, leaving by him:

2d *Kevin Lawlor; *b* 7 Sept 1955

3d *Robert Bacon; *b* 23 Feb 1957

1d *Deirdre Murray; *b* 30 Oct 1953

2d *Sheila Sullivan; *b* 11 May 1958

(3) Alexander Henry; *b* 8 Oct 1829; Col RA, Brig-Gen; *m* 2 Oct 1856 Martha Frances Vincent (*d* 26 Nov 1911), dau of Thomas E Davenport, and *d* 4 April 1885, leaving issue:

1a Alexander Gerald; *b* 27 Nov 1857; *d* unm 28 Aug 1885

2a Charles Stewart, CIE; *b* 4 Dec 1858; Bengal Police; *m* Jan 1892 Laura Susan (*m* 2nd 31 July 1914 Maj-Gen Charles Edmund Layard (*d* 16 Jan 1920)), dau of Franklin Prestage, of Darjeeling, and *d* 4 May 1903, leaving:

1b Archie Alastair Stewart; *b* Dec 1892; Cdr RN WW I (wounded, medal), and WW II; *m* 31 Jan 1925 Marie Louise Ravend de Martainville (*d* 1990), 2nd dau of Alfred Taylor Pattison, of New Orleans, and *d* 7 Dec 1964, leaving:

1c +Hugh Archie Stewart [Hugh Murray Esq, Quinta Arca de Noé, Ferragudo, Algarve, Portugal]; *b* 11 Aug 1927; *educ* Stowe and Trin Coll Oxford (BA); late Lt Welsh Gds; *m* 1st 1955 (*annulled* 1964) Kathleen Mary, only dau of Clive Raymond Hargreaves; *m* 2nd 1967 *Eileen Alexandra Jane, dau of Charles Clements Ross, of Kildary, Ross-shire

2b Alastair Donald Stewart, MC; *b* 17 May 1898; Capt Res of Offrs RA, TA, WW I (despatches twice); *m* 1st 7 Nov 1922 Joan Ethel, yst dau of Robert Moore McMohan, of Hilly Mount, Carlow; *m* 2nd 3 Aug 1933 (*divorce* 1948) Marjory (*d* 1959), yst dau of Capt Anthony Standidge Thomson, CB, CBE, and formerly w of Capt Herbert Caryl Uniacke, RA; *m* 3rd 1951 *Oona Tighe, only dau of Thomas Tait, of Gatehouse of Fleet, Kircudbrightshire, and formerly w of — McKellar, and *d* 1966, having by her had issue:

1c +Alastair Stewart [Alastair Murray Esq, 31 Chater Hall, G/F 1 Conduit Rd, Mid-Levels, Hong Kong]; *b* 1952; MIExpE, MIABTI; Ch Inspr Roy Hong Kong Police; *m* *Sheila Garvie, and has issue:

1d +Struan Alastair Stewart; *b* 1977

2d +Ian Nairn; *b* 1980

3b Charles Stewart; *b* 10 Jan 1900; Lt IA, Afghan War 1919 (medal), WW II with RAF and RAAF; *m* 1st March 1926 (*divorce* 1933) Beryta, only dau of Roland Allport, of Sydney, NSW, and had issue:

1c *Diana Stewart; *b* 12 Sept 1930; *m* 1st 14 Aug 1948 (*divorce* 1960) Richard de Graaff Hunter, s of Dr James de Graaff Hunter, FRS, of Cottenham House, Cottenham, Cambs; *m* 2nd 7 May 1969 *Arthur Eustace Farmiloe and has issue by her 1st husb:

1d *Sarah Stewart; *b* 9 Aug 1949

3b (cont.) Charles Murray *m* 2nd 18 Dec 1937 *Alice Mary, 3rd dau of Robert Matthews, of Sydney, and *d* 1950

3a Cyril Francis Tyrrel, CB (1916), MVO (1911); *b* 19 Jan 1863; Lt-Col IA, Miranzai Expdn 1891 (medal with clasp), NWF India 1897–8, Tirah Expdn 1898 (despatches twice, medal, three clasps), special duty Delhi Coronation Durbar 1911, WW I (despatches); *m* 10 Feb 1887 Helen Edith (*d* 23 Oct 1945), dau of Rev George William Grogan, of The Priory, Prestbury, Glos, and *d* 2 July 1929, leaving issue:

1b Cyril Alexander George Octavius, DSO (1918); *b* 19 Nov 1887; Col KOSB WW I (wounded despatches, Croix de Guerre), Cdr 155 (E Scottish) Inf Bde (TA) (1936–39), Hon Brig 1945; *m* 4 May 1922 Marjorie Lilias (*d* 17 Sept 1965), yr dau of W Jennings Milles, MD, FRCS, of Shanghai, and *d* 15 June 1960, having had issue:

1c Alexander Donald Milles; *b* 6 April 1925; Lt KOSB (1st Airborne Div) WW II; *ka* Holland Sept 1944

2c Blair Cyril; *b* 28 March 1929; *educ* Winchester and Magdalene Coll Cambridge (MA 1957); Lt 10th Roy Hus; *d* 17 July 1982

1b *Anne Elizabeth [Miss Anne Murray, 2 Mansfield Place, Moffat, Dumfriesshire DG10 9DS]; *b* 4 July 1937

4a Malcolm Donald (Sir), GCVO, CB, CIE; *b* 9 July 1867; Maj and Brevet Lt-Col late Seaforth Highrs, Boer War 1899–1900 and WW I, Comptroller and Equerry to HRH THE DUKE OF CONNAUGHT, Dep Ranger Windsor Gt Park 1929–37, OStJ; *m* 12 April 1898 Lady Hilda Joanna Gwendoline Finch (*d* 13 Aug 1931), dau of 7th Earl of Aylesford (*qv*), and *d* 2 Aug 1938, leaving issue:

1b Iain Arthur, DSO (1944) and bar (1946); *b* 17 Sept 1904 (HRH THE DUKE OF CONNAUGHT stood sponsor); *educ* Eton; Page of Honour to HM GEORGE V 1917–21; WW II with Gren Gds, Lt-Col Glider Pilot Regt; *m* 1st 15 Dec 1932 (*divorce* 1946) Angela, est dau of Lt-Col Arthur Houssemayne Du Boulay, DSO, and had issue:

1c *Virginia Anne [Mrs Ricardo Saenz de Heredia, 45 Castle Rd, Isleworth, Middx TW7 6QR]; *b* 4 March 1936; *m* 1st 20 July 1955 (*divorce* 1963) Anthony Gordon Reid, yr s of Ven Ernest Gordon Reid, MA, Archdeacon Hastings, of Windmill Hill Place, Hallsham, Sussex, and has issue:

1d *Iain Malcolm Gordon; *b* 21 April 1956; *m* 1980 *Susan McLeod, and has issue:

1e *Philippa Susanna; *b* 1986

2e *Serena Madeleine; *b* 1994

1c (cont.) Mrs Virginia Reid *m* 2nd 1964 (*divorce* 1977) Ricardo Saenz de Heredia, yr s of D Angel Saenz de Heredia, of Madrid, Spain, and has further issue:

2d *Ricardo; *b* 8 April 1968

3d *Roberto; *b* 31 March 1969

4d *Pedro; *b* 30 Nov 1970

2c *Serena Jane [Sra Konradin Vidigal, Quinta das Galeotas, 2925 Azeitão, Portugal]; *b* 3 March 1939; *m* 6 May 1963 Konradin Goette Vidigal, est s of Dr Bernardo Jose de Silva Vidigal, of Carcavelos, Portugal

1b (cont.) Lt-Col Iain Murray *m* 2nd 16 Jan 1947 (*divorce* 1959) Anne (*d* 1985), er dau of Hon Rupert Drummond (*see* PERTH, E), and *d* 1986

(1) Augusta; *m* 12 Aug 1834 Prince Louis Stanislas de Koska de la Tremoille (*d* 20 July 1837) and *d* 22 Jan 1877, leaving issue

(2) Susan Emma; *m* 4 June 1863 Rev John Glover, MA, Vicar Brading, IoW (*d* 1884), est s of Col Glover, of Livingshayes, Devon, and *d* 18 July 1921

3 Leveson Grenville Keith; *b* 16 Dec 1770; Madras CS; *m* 1st Wemyss (*d* 14 Dec 1804), dau of Sir William Dalrymple, 3rd Bt, of Cousland (*see* STAIR, E), and had issue:

(1) Jane Wemyss; *b* 14 Oct 1804; *m* 1st Oct 1824 Maj C H Campbell, HEICS (*d* 1832), and had issue; *m* 2nd 17 May 1836 Lt-Col C S Maling, Bengal NI

3 (cont.) The Hon Leveson Murray *m* 2nd 24 Jan 1807 Anne, widow of John Thursby, Madras CS, and by her had:

(1) Jack Henry; *b* 26 July 1810; R-Adml; *m* 13 Jan 1845 Catherine (*d* 1899), dau of Sir Neil Menzies, 6th Bt, and *d* 1881, having had issue:

1a Jack George; *b* 27 June 1853

1a Emily Neil; *m* 26 Sept 1867 Arthur Edward Baird, and had issue

2a Frances Balfour

(2) Samuel Hood; *b* 27 Dec 1814; Lt-Col; *m* Oct 1840 Susan (*d* 18 Jan 1888), dau of H C Sempill, and *d* 17 Dec 1867, leaving issue

1a Hamilton George Dunmore; *b* 1841

2a Leveson Grenville Keith; *b* 1843

1a Susan Augusta; *m* 1878 Havilland le Mesurier, and had issue

(2) Augusta; *m* 24 Sept 1824 John Gunn Collins, of Belmont, King's Co, Capt 13th Light Dragoons, and *d* 1833, leaving issue

3 (cont.) The Hon Leveson Murray *m* 3rd 10 May 1834 Louisa Mitty (*m* 2nd 2 Jan 1836 Rev S J Lott; *m* 3rd 15 May 1851 George Wilson Grove, and *d* 29 March 1852), only dau of Thomas Abraham, of Chapel House, Surrey, and *d* 4 Jan 1935

1 Catherine; *m* 24 May 1782 Hon Edward Bouverie (*see* RADNOR, E), and *d* 7 July 1783, leaving issue

2 Augusta; *m* Rome 4 April 1793 in contravention of the Roy Marriage Act of 1772 HRH AUGUSTUS FREDERICK, DUKE OF SUSSEX, and again 5 Dec 1793 at St George's, Hanover Sq, London W1, and *d* 4 March 1830, leaving issue (who took the surname D'ESTE):

(1) Augustus (Sir), KCB; *b* 13 Jan 1794; *d* unm 18 Dec 1848

(1) Augusta Emma; *b* 11 Aug 1801; *m* 13 Aug 1845 Thomas Wilde, 1st Baron Truro (*d* 11 Nov 1858), and *dsp* 21 May 1866

3 Susan; *m* Joseph Tharp, of Chippenham, Cambs, and had:

(1) John; *m* 1815 Hannah Charlotte, dau of 7th Marquess of Tweeddale (*qv*), and *d* 2 Aug 1863

DUNN

Creation: B. (LP, UK) 1990.

THE BARONESS DUNN, of Hong Kong Island in Hong Kong and of Knightsbridge in the Royal Borough of Kensington and Chelsea (Dame Lydia Selina Dunn, DBE (1989, CBE 1983, OBE 1978), JP; retains maiden name) [The Rt Hon The Baroness Dunn DBE, John Swire and Sons Ltd, Swire House, 59 Buckingham Gate, London SW1E 6AJ]; *b* 29 Feb 1940; *educ* St Paul's Convent Sch Hong Kong and U of Calif at Berkeley (BS); Hong Kong: MLC 1976–88 (Sr Memb 1985–88); MEC 1982–95 (Sr Memb 1988–95); Chm Swire & Maclaine Ltd 1982–, Exec Dir Swire Pacific Ltd 1982–; Chm Hong Kong Trade Devpt Cncl 1983–9, Hong Kong/US Ec Co-op Ctee 1984–93; Hong Kong Seibu Enterprise Co Ltd 1989–; Dir: Cathay Pacific Airways Ltd 1985–, Volvo AB 1991–93 (Memb Internat Advsy Bd 1985–91), GEC 1997–; Dep-Chm: Hongkong & Shanghai Banking Corp 1992–96 (Dir 1981–92), HSBC Holdings 1992– (Dir 1990–92); Chm: Lord Wilson Heritage Tst 1993–95, Hong Kong/Japan Business Co-op Ctee 1988–95 (Memb 1983–88); Exec Dir John Swire and Sons 1996–; Prime Minister of Japan's Trade Award 1987; USA Sec of Commerce's Award To Peace and Commerce 1988; Hon LLD Chinese U of Hong Kong 1984, U of Hong Kong 1991, U of British Columbia 1991, Leeds U 1994; Hon DSc Buckingham U 1995; author: *In the Kingdom of the Blind* (1983); *m* 1988 *Michael David Thomas, CMG, QC

Lineage: YENCHEUN YEH DUNN; *m* Chen Yin Chu; and had:

LYDIA SELINA, *cr* a **Baroness**

DUNNING

Creation: Bt. (UK) 24 June 1930.

SIR SIMON WILLIAM PATRICK DUNNING, 3RD BT, of Beedinglee, Parish of Lower Beeding, Co Sussex [Sir Simon Dunning Bt, Low Auchengillan, Blanefield, by Glasgow G63 9AU]; *b* 14 Dec 1939; *s f* 1961; *educ* Eton; *m* 1975 *Frances Deirdre Morton, formerly w of Capt Nigel Edward Corbally Stourton (*see* MOWBRAY, SEGRAVE and STOURTON, B) and dau of Maj Patrick Lancaster, of Wapsbourne Manor, Sheffield Park, Sussex, and has:

1 *Mariota Kathleen Masika; *b* 30 Aug 1976

Lineage: SIMON DUNNING, of Townsend, Winkleigh, N Devon; *d* 28 March 1850, leaving:

SIMON DUNNING, of 2 Warwick Sq, London; *b* 11 Oct 1815; *m* 19 June 1856 Elizabeth Mary (*d* 5 Feb 1921), er dau of John Burder, of Burlington Lodge, Streatham Common, and *d* 25 April 1883, having had:

Sir Leonard Dunning, 1st Bt (UK), so *cr* 24 June 1930; *b* 17 June 1860; *educ* Eton and Exeter Coll Oxford (BA); Dist Inspr RIC 1882–95, Assist Head Constable Liverpool 1895–1902 and Head Constable 1902–12, Inspr Constabulary Home Office 1912–30, ktd 1917; *m* 19 Nov 1902 Edith Muriel (*d* 10 Nov 1965 aged 86), dau of William Tod, of Drygrange, Allerton, Liverpool, and *d* 8 Feb 1941, leaving:

Sir William Leonard Dunning, 2nd Bt; *b* 13 Nov 1903; *educ* Eton and Trin Coll Cambridge (BA 1925); AMIMechE; *m* 16 June 1936 Kathleen Lawrie (*d* 1992), only child of J Patrick Cuthbert, MC, of Barclayhills-by-Perth, and *d* 10 Sept 1961, leaving issue:

1 Sir SIMON WILLIAM PATRICK DUNNING, **3rd and present Bt**

1 Susan Mary; *b* 10 April 1938; *d* unm 25 Aug 1963

DUNNINGTON-JEFFERSON

Arms: Quarterly, 1st and 4th, gules a griffin sejant, wings addorsed argent, a bordure engrailed of the last charged with eight pellets (for JEFFERSON); 2nd and 3rd, paly of six argent and azure, on a chief gules a bezant between two annulets or (for DUNNINGTON). **Crests:** 1 A griffin as in the arms, gorged with a collar gemel azure, in the beak a lily slipped proper (for JEFFERSON), 2 A horse courant argent, gorged with a collar gules charged with a bezant between two annulets or (for DUNNINGTON). **Motto:** *A cruce salus* ('Salvation by the cross'). **Creation:** Bt. (UK) 7 July 1958.

SIR MERVYN STEWART DUNNINGTON-JEFFERSON, 2ND BT, of Thorganby Hall, Yorks [Sir Mervyn Dunnington-Jefferson Bt, 7 Bolingbroke Grove, London SW11 6ES]; *b* 5 Aug 1943; *s* f 1979; *educ* Eton; with Bass Charrington (brewers) 1962–68, fndr/ptnr Proprety Company 'Marldon' 1968–; *m* 4 March 1971 *Caroline Anna, only dau of John M Bayley, of Hillan Hall, Monk Fryston, Yorks, and has issue:

1 +JOHN ALEXANDER; *b* 23 March 1980

1 *Annabelle Mary; *b* 1 July 1973

2 *Emma Elizabeth; *b* 20 Aug 1978

Lineage: THOMAS DUNNINGTON, of Thorganby and W Cottingwith, E R Yorks, by 1685; *d* 1710, leaving:

JOHN DUNNINGTON; *b* 1697; *d* 1759, leaving:

JOHN DUNNINGTON; *b* 1735; *d* 1810, leaving (with an er s John DUNNINGTON later DUNNINGTON-JEFFERSON (roy licence 1812 after inheriting from a descendant of Peter Jefferson, of Hook and Howden, Yorks, who had owned an estate there 1664), *b* 1759, *d* 1840):

JOSEPH; *b* 1769; *m* 1805 Mary, dau of William Toutill, and *d* 1835, leaving:

Rev JOSEPH DUNNINGTON later DUNNINGTON-JEFFERSON (roy licence 1841 on inheriting his unc's estates), JP; *b* 17 July 1807; *educ* St John's Coll Cambridge (MA); Vicar Thorganby, Canon York; *m* 23 May 1837 Anna Mervinia (*d* 2 Nov 1808), est dau of Gen Sir Henry Maghull Mervin Vavasour, 2nd Bt, of Spaldington (*see* 1912 edn), and *d* 31 July 1880, having had issue:

1 Joseph John, of Thicket Priory, Yorks, JP (W R Yorks); *b* 19 Nov 1845; *educ* Eton and Trin Coll Cambridge (MA); Capt and Hon Maj Yorks Hus, barrister, CC E R; *m* 14 Sept 1870 Emma Sarah (*d* 1920), dau of Thomas Butler-Stoney, JP, of Portland Park, Co Tipperary, and *dsp* 21 March 1928

2 Mervyn, JP; *b* 10 Feb 1850; *educ* Eton; Capt 33rd Regt; *m* 1881 Louisa Dorothy (*d* 5 March 1951), est dau of Rev John Barry, Rector Gt Smeaton, Yorks, and *d* 21 March 1912, leaving issue:

(1) JOHN ALEXANDER (Sir), **1st Bt**

(2) Wilfrid Mervyn; *b* 2 April 1892; *educ* Radley; 2nd Lt 7th Bn Roy Fus WW I, *ka* France 26 April 1915

(1) Dorothy; *b* 25 March 1882; *d* unm 2 Nov 1965

(2) Hilda, MBE; *b* 1 Jan 1887

(3) Ella; *b* 23 May 1888; *d* unm 29 Nov 1934

3 Thomas Trafford; *b* 14 Dec 1852; *d* 1 April 1882

1 Mervinia Jane; *d* unm 31 May 1905

2 Caroline Emma; *d* Oct 1852

3 Mary Campbell; *m* — White and *d* 24 Feb 1889

4 Theodosia; *d* unm 19 Oct 1940

MERVYN DUNNINGTON-JEFFERSON's est s,

Sir John Alexander Dunnington-Jefferson, 1st Bt (UK), so *cr* 7 July 1958, ktd 1944, JP (1921), DL (1936), DSO (1917); *b* 10 April 1884; *educ* Eton and RMC Sandhurst; Hon LLD Leeds 1947, Hon DUniv York 1947, E R Yorks: V-Lt 1942–68, Chm CC 1936–68, War Ag Exec Ctee 1939–47, Lt-Col Roy Fus WW I (despatches six times), chm: York Co Savings Bank 1949–79, Derwent Valley Light Rlwy, Orders SSt Maurice and Lazarus Italy, Crown Belgium, Croix de Guerre Belgium, Legn Honour; *m* 1 Oct 1938 *(Frances) Isobel [Lady Dunnington-Jefferson, Rectory Cottage, Escrick, Yorks YO4 6LE], yr dau of Col Herbert Anderson Cape, DSO, of Thorganby, and *d* 12 April 1979, leaving issue:

1 Sir MERVYN STEWART DUNNINGTON-JEFFERSON, **2nd and present Bt**

1 *(Rosemary) Nicolette [Miss Nicolette Dunnington-Jefferson, 35 Horder Rd, Fulham, London SW6 5ED]; *b* 12 Feb 1941

DUNRAVEN and MOUNT-EARL

Arms: Quarterly, 1st and 4th, gules a hand couped below the wrist, grasping a sword all proper, between in base two serpents erect and respecting each other, tails nowed or; in chief two crescents argent (for QUIN); 2nd and 3rd, azure a chevron between three lions, heads erased or, with a mullet for difference (for WYNDHAM). **Crests:** 1 A wolf's head erased argent (for QUIN), 2 A lion's head erased within a fetterlock and chain or (for WYNDHAM). **Supporters:** Two ravens with wings elevated proper, collared and chained or. **Motto:** *Cenn natanac abu* ('Head of the serpent for ever'). **Creation:** Bt. (I) 8 June 1781, B. (I) 31 July 1800, V. (I) 5 Feb 1816 (Mount-Earl) and 5 Feb 1822, E. (I) 5 Feb 1822.

THE 7TH EARL OF DUNRAVEN and MOUNT-EARL, Viscount Mount-Earl, Viscount Adare, Baron Adare of Adare, and a **Baronet** (Sir Thady Windham Thomas Wyndham-Quin, Bt) [The Rt Hon The Earl of Dunraven and Mount-Earl, Kilcurley House, Adare, Co Limerick, Ireland]; *b* 27 Oct 1939, *s* f 1965; *educ* Ludgrove and Le Rosey; *m* 15 Feb 1969 *Geraldine, dau of A/Cdre Gerald Ward McAleer, CBE, of Poynings, Wokingham, Berks, and has issue:

1 *Ana; *b* 20 March 1972

Lineage: This is one of very few families of Celtic origin in the Irish peerage. Initially Chiefs of the Clan of Hy-Ifearnan, Co Clare, the O'Quins of Munster (the southwest province of Ireland) allegedly stem from Conn Mor, eldest of three sons of Deadha.

JAMES QUIN, of Kilmallock; had:

DONOGH QUIN; gf of:

DONOGH QUIN; *m* Judith O'Riordan, of Co Limerick, and *d* 1671, leaving:

THADY QUIN, of Adare, Co Limerick; *b* 1645; *m* 1st Bridget, dau and heir of Andrew Rice, of Dingle, Co Kerry; *m* 2nd Frances, dau of Maj Boyle Hull, s of Sir William Hull, of Leamcon, Co Cork; *m* 3rd Catharine, dau of Piers Morony, and by her had, with other issue:

1 VALENTINE

2 John, of Rosbrien; *b* 1692; *m* 1714 Mary, dau of Sir Walter Blake, 6th Bt (*see* BLAKE, Bt, of Menlough), and *d* 1729, leaving issue now extinct in the male line

THADY QUIN *d* 1726; his er s,

VALENTINE QUIN, of Adare; *m* 14 Oct 1707 Mary, est dau and coheir of Henry Widenham, of The Court, Co Limerick, and had, with five daus:

1 WINDHAM, his heir

2 George, of Quinsborough, Co Clare; *b* 23 Feb 1729; *m* Caroline, dau of Sir Henry Cavendish, 1st Bt, of Doveridge Hall, Derbys (*see* WATERPARK, B), and *d* 1791, leaving:

(1) Mary; *m* Dec 1778 1st Marquess of Headfort (*qv*) and *d* 12 Aug 1842, leaving issue

VALENTINE QUIN *d* 29 July 1744; his er son,

WINDHAM QUIN, of Adare; MP Kilmallock 1769–76; *b* 1717; *m* July 1748 Frances, dau of Richard Dawson, of Dawson's Grove, Co Monaghan, and *d* April 1789, leaving, with four daus:

1 (VALENTINE) RICHARD, **1st Earl**

2 Windham, Lt-Col; *m* 1783 Mary Anne (*d* 1831), est dau of Richard Dawson, of Ardee, and niece of Thomas, Viscount Cremorne

3 John (Rev); *m* 1784 Catherine (*m* 2nd George Gumbleton), dau of Standish O'Grady, of Cappercullen, Co Limerick, and *dsp* 1789

The est son,

Sir (Valentine) Richard Quin, 1st Bt, and **1st Earl of Dunraven** and **Mount-Earl,** so *cr* 8 June 1781 and 5 Feb 1822 respectively, also on the latter date VISCOUNT ADARE and previously 31 July 1800 BARON ADARE of Adare (all I);

b 30 July 1752; *educ* Magdalen Coll Oxford; MP (I Parl) Kilmallock 1799–1800; *m* 1st 24 Aug 1777 Lady Frances Muriel Fox Strangeways (*d* May 1814), dau of 1st Earl of Ilchester (*qv*), and had, with two daus:

1 WINDHAM HENRY, **2nd Earl**

2 Richard George; *b* 20 April 1789; *m* 7 Sept 1813 Amelia (*d* 18 May 1845), 2nd dau of Sir John Smith, 1st Bt (*see* SMITH-MARRIOTT, Bt), and *dsp* 5 Oct 1843

The **1st Earl** *m* 2nd 26 Feb 1816 Margaret Mary (*d* 6 Nov 1821), dau of James Coghlan, of Cloghan House, King's Co, and widow of (a) George L'Estrange (b) Col Arthur Blennerhasset, of Bath, and *d* 24 Aug 1824

His est son,

WINDHAM HENRY QUIN later WYNDHAM-QUIN (roy licence 7 April 1815), **2nd Earl of Dunraven** and **Mount-Earl**; *b* 24 Sept 1782; *educ* Eton and Magdalen Coll Oxford; MP (Whig) Co Limerick 1802–20, rep I peer 1839–50, Custos Rotulorum Co Limerick 1818–50; *m* 27 Dec 1810 Caroline (*d* 26 May 1870), dau and sole heir of Thomas Wyndham, of Dunraven Castle, Glam (hence the wording of the Earldom), and *d* 6 Aug 1850, having had:

1 EDWIN RICHARD WINDHAM WYNDHAM-QUIN, **3rd Earl of Dunraven** and **Mount-Earl**, KP (1866); *b* 19 May 1812; *educ* Eton and (Trin Coll?) Dublin; MP (Cl) Glamorgan 1837–51, Ld Lt Co Limerick 1864–71, *cr* 12 June 1866 BARON KENRY, Co Limerick (UK) by 1st Earl Russell (*qv*) after turning Lib; *m* 18 Aug 1836 Augusta (*d* 22 Nov 1866), 3rd dau of Thomas Goold, Master in Chancery, and had issue:

(1) WINDHAM THOMAS WYNDHAM-QUIN, **4th Earl of Dunraven** and **Mount-Earl**, KP (1872), PC (I 1899), CMG (1902), OBE, JP (Glam); *b* 12 Feb 1841; *educ* Ch Ch Oxford; Ld Lt Co Limerick 1896–22, Hon Capt RNR, Lt 1st Life Gds, Hon Col 5th Bn Roy Munster Fus, 23rd Armoured Car Co TA and Glamorgan RGA, served Abyssinian Expdn (medal) and S Africa 1900–01 (medal with two clasps), Parly Under Sec Colonies 1885–87; *m* 29 April 1869 Florence Elizabeth (*d* 21 Sept 1916), dau of Lord Charles Lennox Kerr (*see* LOTHIAN, M), and *d* 14 June 1926, when the Barony of Kenry expired, having had:

1a Florence Enid; *b* 13 June 1870; *d* July 1891

2a Rachael Charlotte; *b* 20 Feb 1872; *m* 28 Oct 1897 Desmond FitzJohn Lloyd FitzGerald (*d* 17 Sept 1936), 27th Knight of Glin, DL, JP, and *d* 30 Jan 1901, leaving issue

3a Aileen May; *b* 9 April 1873; *m* 12 Feb 1908 13th Earl of Meath (*qv*) and *d* 25 Feb 1962, leaving issue

(1) Caroline Adelaide; *d* unm 2 July 1853

(2) Augusta Emily; *m* 4 March 1867 Sir Arthur Pendarves Vivian (*d* 17 Aug 1926), KCB, MP, of Glanafon, Glam, and *d* 11 Feb 1877, having had issue (*see* SWANSEA, B)

(3) Mary Frances; *m* 17 Aug 1868 Arthur Hugh Smith Barry (*d* 22 Feb 1925), MP, DL, later 1st Baron Barrymore, and *d* 21 Sept 1884, leaving issue

(4) Edith; *d* unm 10 April 1885

(5) Emily Anna; *d* unm 21 Nov 1940

1 (cont.) The **3rd Earl** *m* 2nd 27 Jan 1870 Anne (*m* 2nd 26 April 1879 2nd Baron Hylton (*qv*) and *dsp* 30 Oct 1917), dau of Henry Lambert, DL, MP, of Carnagh, Co Wexford, and *d* 6 Oct 1871

2 Windham Henry, Capt Gren Gds; *b* 2 Nov 1829; *m* 24 Jan 1856 Caroline (*m* 2nd 5 March 1867 Lt-Gen N O S Turner, CB, RA (*d* 1884), and *d* 22 Oct 1898), 3rd dau of R-Adml Sir George Tyler, KH, DL, JP, of Cotterell, Glam, and *d* 24 Aug 1865, leaving, with two daus:

(1) WINDHAM HENRY, **5th Earl**

(2) Charles Frederick Talbot, OBE (1919), Lt-Col Glamorgan Yeo, Capt 3rd Bn Royal Lancaster Regt, RTO 1915; *b* 12 July 1864; *d* 2 April 1926

1 Anna Maria Charlotte Wyndham; *m* 11 Aug 1836 1st Baron Emly (*see* 1935 edn) and *d* 7 Jan 1855

The 4th EARL's cousin,

WINDHAM HENRY WYNDHAM-QUIN, **5th Earl of Dunraven** and **Mount-Earl**, CB (1903), DSO (1900), DL Co Glamorgan; MP S Glamorgan 1895–1906, High Sheriff Co Kilkenny 1914, Cmdt Line of Communications 1915, Lt-Col cmdg and Hon Col Glamorgan Yeo, Maj 16th Lancers, Hon Maj Roy Glos Hus, ADC and Mil Sec to Govr Madras 1886–89, served Boer Wars 1881 and 1899–1901 (despatches, Queen's medal with three clasps); *b* 7 Feb 1857; *m* 7 July 1885 Lady Eva Constance Aline Bourke (*d* 19 Jan 1940), dau of 6th Earl of Mayo (*qv*), and had issue:

1 RICHARD SOUTHWELL WINDHAM ROBERT, **6th Earl**

2 Valentine Maurice, Capt RN, served WWs I and II (despatches four times), Naval Attaché Argentina and Uruguay 1945–47; *b* 22 May 1890; *m* 21 July 1919 Marjorie Elizabeth (*d* 6 May 1969), 2nd dau of Ernest George Pretyman, PC, DL, JP, of Orwell Park and Bacton, Suffolk, and Riby Grove, Lincs, and *d* 27 Feb 1983, leaving:

(1) Ursula Eva; *b* 20 July 1921; *m* 17 Jan 1945 Lord Roderic Pratt (*d* 1997, *see* CAMDEN, M) and *d* 1993, leaving issue

(2) *Marjorie Olein (Mollie) [The Most Hon The Marchioness of Salisbury, Hatfield House, Hatfield, Herts AL9 5NF]; *b* 15 July 1922; *m* 18 Dec 1945 *6th Marquess of Salisbury (*qv*) and has issue

(3) *Pamela [The Rt Hon Pamela Lady Egremont, Cockermouth Castle, Cockermouth, Cumbria]; *b* 29 April 1925; *m* 24 July 1947 1st Baron Egremont (*see* EGREMONT, LECONFIELD, and, B) and has issue

1 Olein Eva Constance, MBE (1943), OStJ; *b* 5 March 1892; *d* unm 22 April 1969

2 Kathleen Sybil (Cathlin); *b* 12 Feb 1895; *d* 29 Dec 1907

The 5th EARL *d* 23 Oct 1952; his er son,

RICHARD SOUTHWELL WINDHAM ROBERT WYNDHAM-QUIN, **6th Earl of Dunraven** and **Mount-Earl**, CB (1923), CBE (1921), MC; *b* 18 May 1887; *educ* Winchester; Capt 12th Lancers, Mil Sec to Ld Lt Ireland, served WW I (wounded, despatches); *m* 1st 1915 (*divorce* 1932) Helen Lindsay (*d* 1 Jan 1962), dau of John Swire, of Hillingdon House, Harlow, Essex; *m* 2nd 7 March 1934 Nancy (*d* 1994), dau of Thomas B Yuille, of Virginia, USA, and *d* 23 Aug 1965, leaving by her:

1 THADY WINDHAM THOMAS WYNDHAM-QUIN, **7th and present Earl of Dunraven and Mount-Earl**

1 *Melissa Eva Caroline [The Lady Melissa Brooke, Glenbevan, Croom, Co Limerick, Ireland]; *b* 16 Feb 1935; MFH Limerick 1990–96; *m* 25 June 1959 Maj Sir George Cecil Francis Brooke, 3rd Bt, MBE (*d* 1982), of Summerton, and has issue

2 *Caroline Olein Geraldine; *b* 14 Sept 1936; *m* 23 July 1957 *8th Marquess of Waterford (*qv*), and has issue

DUNROSSIL

Arms: Per bend sinister gules and argent a demi-lion rampant issuant or, armed and langued azure, holding in his paws a battleaxe and shaft, curved or, the axehead azure, in chief, and in base, issuant from the sea undy vert and or, a tower sable windows and port or, over all a bend sinister embattled azure, charged with an open crown or, jewelled gules, between two fleurs-de-lys argent, within a bordure vert for difference. **Crest:** Issuant from waves of the sea azure crested argent, a mount vert, thereon an embattled wall azure masoned argent, charged with a portcullis or, and issuant therefrom a cubit arm naked proper, the hand grasping a dagger azure, hilted or. **Supporters:** Two lions regardant or, armed and langued gules, collared vert, supporting between their exterior forepaws and interior hind paws battleaxes azure, the shafts embowed. **Mottoes:** (above crest) *Teaghlach Phabbay* ('Hold on to Phabbay'); 2 (below shield) *An tighearna mo bhuachaille* 'The Lord is my Shepherd'). **Creation:** V. (UK) 12 Nov 1959.

THE 2ND VISCOUNT DUNROSSIL, of Vallaquie, Isle of North Uist, Co Inverness (John William Morrison, CMG (1981), JP (1994)) [The Rt Hon The Viscount Dunrossil CMG JP, Dunrossil House, Clachan Sands, Lochmaddy, Isle of N Uist, Western Isles HS6 5AY]; *b* 22 May 1926; *s* f 1961; *educ* Fettes and Oriel Coll Oxford (BA 1950, MA 1951, Hon Fell 1994); Ld Lt Islands Area Western Isles 1993– (DL Western Isles 1990–92); F/Lt RAF 1945–48, RAFVR 1948–53, CRO 1951–88: Priv Sec to Sec State 1952–54, 2nd Sec Canberra 1954–56, 1st Sec and Actg Dep HC E Pakistan 1958–60, 1st Sec Pretoria/Cape Town 1961–64, seconded to For Serv 1961 (Dip Serv Admin Office 1965), seconded to Intergovernmental Maritime Consultative Org 1968–1970, Counsellor and Head Chancery Ottawa 1970–74, Counsellor Brussels 1975–78, HC: Fiji 1978–82 and Barbados, Antigua, Barbuda, Dominica, Grenada, St Vincent and The Grenadines 1982–83, Govr and C-in-C Bermuda 1983–88, KStJ 1983, Liveryman Merchant Taylors' Co 1984; *m* 1st 3 July 1951 (*divorce* 1969) Mavis Dawn, dau of Arthur Llewellyn Spencer-Payne, MRCS, LRCP, LDS, of St Anthony, Somerset West, Cape, S Africa, and has issue:

1 +ANDREW WILLIAM REGINALD; *b* 15 Dec 1953; *educ* Eton and Univ Coll Oxford; *m* 1986 *Carla Brundage and has a s and three daus

2 +Ranald John [The Hon Ranald Morrison, 9 Hurlingham Rd, St Andrews, Bristol BS7 9BA]; *b* 19 Dec 1956; *educ* Westminster and UCL (BSc); *m* 8 Sept 1979 *Henrietta Frances, dau of John Hilary Wilson, of Addison Rd, London W8, and has issue:

(1) +Richard Donald; *b* 1983

(2) +Alexander Thomas; *b* 1988

(1) *Alison Catherine; *b* 1984

(2) *Rebecca Louise; *b* 1987

3 +Alasdair Godfrey [The Hon Alasdair Morrison, 81 Fifth Cross Rd, Twickenham TW2 5UJ]; *b* 4 April 1962; *educ* Eton; *m* 1987 *Tania M, only dau of J A Redman, of Minehead, Somerset

1 *Catriona Mary [Mrs John Galt, 3315 Linda Vista Rd, Glendale, CAL 91206, USA]; *b* 10 July 1952; *m* 1973 *John James Galt, and has issue:

(1) *Iain Robert; *b* 1978

(2) *Malcolm David; *b* 1982

(1) *Sarah Christine; *b* 1976

The 2nd VISCOUNT *m* 2nd 1969 *Diana Mary Cunliffe, dau of C M Vise, and by her has:

2 *Joanna Catherine; *b* 25 April 1971

3 *Mary Allison; *b* 12 Dec 1972

Lineage: JOHN MORRISON, of Ruchdi, N Uist, Outer Hebrides; *m* Ann Ross and had, with three other sons and three daus (all *d* unm):

JOHN MORRISON, of Uist and later Torinturk, Argyllshire; went to sea; diamond prospector S Africa; farmer Torinturk; *b* 1842; *m* Marion, dau of Ronald MacVicar, of Grenetote, N Uist, formerly of Boreray, and had issue:

1 John, of Ruchdi; MB, ChB Edin, Surg RN 1914–19; *b* 15 Aug 1883; *m* Dorothy Mary, dau of Rev William Swan, DD, Min of S Leith, and had issue:

(1) *Iain Martin MORRISON OF RUCHDI [Iain Morrison of Ruchdi, 26 Ham St, Ham Common, Richmond, Surrey], Ch of Clan Morrison, MB, BS; *b* 11 Nov 1938; *educ* Cheltenham and St Thomas's Hosp; *m* 4 Jan 1964 *Caroline Elizabeth, dau of George Lowe, FRCS Edin, of Horsdon Close, Tiverton, Devon, and has issue:

1a *John Ruairdh MORRISON OF RUCHDI, Yr.; *b* 8 Jan 1968

(1) *Mary [Mrs Michael Halliday, Old Malling Farm House, Lewes, Sussex]; *b* 23 Feb 1937; *educ* Cheltenham Ladies' Coll and Girton Coll Cambridge (MA); *m* 1 Oct 1958 *Michael Sebastian Halliday, MA, PhD, and has issue:

1a *Martin John; *b* 27 Jan 1963

2a *David Benedict; *b* 5 Jan 1965

1a *Donnet Jane; *b* 25 July 1961

2a *Mary Kate; *b* 27 Aug 1966

2 Donald; *b* 14 Dec 1884; *m* — and *d* 14 Dec 1934 leaving issue

3 Alexander, *ka* Battle of Loos 1915

4 Neil, slr, served WWI as Capt QO Cameron Highrs; *educ* George Watson's Coll Edinburgh and Edin U; *m* 1918 Margaret Grant (*d* 8 Aug 1935), dau of Angus Matheson, of Edinburgh, and *d* 23 May 1964, leaving issue:

(1) *John; *b* 23 May 1919; *m* 19– *Beatrice, dau of John Beates, of Queensland, Australia, and has issue

(2) *Angus Matheson; *b* 3 Nov 1920

(3) *Alexander; *b* 13 Oct 1922; *m* 19– *Edith Roger, dau of Alexander Mathers McLeod, of Edinburgh, and has issue:

1a *Roderick McLeod Matherson; *b* 4 Aug 1951

1a *Fiona Mary; *b* 28 April 1948

(4) Neil Roderick McLeod Matheson, MA; *b* 22 June 1926; *m* 19– *Patricia, dau of James Lynch, of Brisbane, Qld, and has issue

(5)*Ronald Cameron [Ronald Morrison Esq, 23 Davenport St, Ayr, Qld 4807, Australia] *b* 11 Jan 1931; *m* 19– *Elaine Halworth, of Cairas, Qld

5 Donald John; *b* 19 Feb 1890; *educ* George Watson's Coll Edinburgh and Edin U (MB, ChB 1920, DPH 1935); *m* 1926 Patricia Sinclair, dau of Peter Keith, DL, JP, of Olrig House, Caithness, and *d* 22 Dec 1963, leaving:

(1) *Peter Keith; Procurator Fiscal Depute W Fife; *b* 3 Jan 1928; *educ* Melville Coll Edinburgh and Edin U (MA, LLB); *m* 5 Oct 1963 *Mary Brown, dau of Alexander Osler, of Edinburgh, and has issue:

1a *Alastair Peter; *b* 8 March 1969

1a *Christine Jane; *b* 25 Dec 1964

2a *Catriona Mary; *b* 20 Dec 1966

(1) *Patricia Joy [Mrs George Philip, 66 Woodend Drive, Glasgow]; *b* 4 July 1933; *educ* Edin U (MA); *m* 26 April 1961 *Rev George Mackenzie Philip, MA, Min Sandyford-Henderson Memorial Ch, Glasgow, and has issue:

1a *John Morrison; *b* 25 March 1962

1a *Ruth Gillian; *b* 6 March 1964

6 WILLIAM SHEPHERD, **1st Viscount**

7 Cecil John Rhodes, LRCP, LRCS, LRFPS, DMRE Cambridge; *m* — and *d* Jan 1964, leaving issue

8 Roderick; *d* in infancy

The 6th son,

WILLIAM SHEPHERD MORRISON, **1st Viscount Dunrossil**, of Vallaquie, Isle of North Uist, Co Inverness (UK), so *cr* 12 Nov 1959, PC (1936), GCMG (1959), MC, QC (1934); *b* 10 Aug 1893; *educ* George Watson's Coll and Edin U (MA 1921); Capt RFA WW I (wounded, despatches three times), barrister Inner Temple 1923, Bencher 1951, Hon LLD Edinburgh 1938, Leeds 1939, St Andrews 1953 and London 1959, Hon FRCS Edin 1955, MP (C) Cirencester and Tewskesbury 1929–59, memb Medical Research Cncl 1932–35, Recorder Walsall Feb-Nov 1935, Priv Sec to Slr-Gen 1922–23 and 1924–27 and Attorney-Gen 1927–28, PPS to Attorney-Gen 1931–35, Fin Sec Treasury 1935–36, Min Ag and Fisheries 1936–39, Chllr Duchy Lancaster and Min Food 1939–40, PMG 1940–43, Min Town and Country Planning 1943–45, Speaker H of C 1951–59, Govr-Gen and C-in-C Australia 1960–61, KStJ; *m* 22 April 1924 (Catherine) Allison (*d* 26 March 1983), CStJ, dau of Rev William Swan, DD, Min of S Leith parish, and had issue:

1 JOHN WILLIAM MORRISON, **2nd and present Viscount Dunrossil**

2 +Alasdair Andrew Orr [The Hon Alasdair Morrison, Maisemore Lodge, Gloucester]; *b* 25 March 1929; *educ* Fettes, Balliol Coll Oxford (BA and MA 1960) and Chicago U (PhD 1965); High Sheriff Glos 1983; *m* 9 Aug 1958 *Frances Mary, dau of Wilfred Rippon Snow, of Adelaide, S Australia, and has issue:

(1) +William Alasdair Ewing; *b* 23 Sept 1960

(1) *Alexandra Mary; *b* 23 June 1962; *m* 1989 *David T M Young

(2) *Joanna Allison; *b* 28 April 1964

3 Nial Ranald (Rev), ordained 1956, Assist Curate St Catherine's Gloucester 1956–58, Stroud 1959–62, Vicar Randwick Glos 1962–1991; *b* 27 July 1932; *educ* Fettes and Jesus Coll Oxford (BA 1954, DipTheol 1955, MA 1957); *m* 27 Aug 1959 *Sheila Mary [The Hon Mrs Nial Morrison, 24 Fox Close, Stroud, Glos], MB, BS Lond 1953, MRCS Eng, LRCP Lond 1953, dau of Alexander Forbes, of Northernhay, 12 Denmark Rd, Gloucester, and *d* 1991 following a road accident, leaving issue:

(1) +Neil William Alexander; *b* 21 Nov 1961; *m* 1992 *Clare E, dau of John Molloy, of Haslemere, Surrey

(2) +John Forbes; *b* 2 Oct 1963

(3) +Hugh Robert Shepherd; *b* 17 Aug 1965

(1) *Alison Mary; *b* 30 July 1960; *m* 1992 *Paul A Broad

(2) *Elizabeth Iona; *b* 4 Aug 1969; *m* 1992 *Dr Mark W James

4 Godfrey Donald; *b* 11 April 1937; *educ* Stowe and Balliol Coll Oxford; *d* 1986

DUNSANY

Arms: Sable, a bend argent, in the sinister chief point a castle of the last. **Crest:** A horse passant argent. **Supporters:** Dexter, a pegasus per fess or and argent; sinister, an antelope argent, collared, chained, armed and hoofed or. **Motto:** *Festina lente* ('Make haste, but carefully'). **Creation:** B. (I) *c* 1462.

THE 18TH LORD (BARON) OF DUNSANY (Randal Arthur Henry Plunkett) [The Rt Hon The Lord Dunsany, Dunsany Castle, Dunsany, Co Meath, Ireland]; *b* 25 Aug 1906; *s f* 1957; *educ* Eton; Lt-Col Indian Cav (The Guides), NW Frontier 1930 (medal and clasp) and WW II, ret 1947; *m* 1st 23 Aug 1938 (*divorce* 1947) Vera (*d* 1986), yst dau of Dr Genesio de Sà Sottomaior, of Sao Paulo, Brazil, and formerly w of Ivar Bryce, and has:

1 +EDWARD JOHN CARLOS [The Hon Edward Plunkett, Dunsany Castle, Dunsany, Co Meath, Ireland]; *b* 10 Sept 1939; *educ* Eton, Slade Sch of Fine Art and Ecole des Beaux Arts, Paris; *m* 1982 *Maria Alice Villela de Carvalho and has:

(1) +Randal; *b* 9 March 1983

(2) +Oliver; *b* 26 Sept 1985

The 18th LORD *m* 2nd 8 Oct 1947 *Sheila Victoria Katrin, only dau of Sir Henry Erasmus Edward Philipps, 2nd Bt (*see* 1956 edn FOLEY-PHILIPPS, Bt), and widow of Maj John Frederick Foley, Baron de Rutzen, Welsh Gds, and by her has:

1 *Beatrice Mary; *b* 15 July 1948

Lineage: JOHN PLUNKET; living 1322; *m* Alice de Trim and had, with an er s (John, feudal Ld of Beaulieu, Co Louth; *see* LOUTH, B)

RICHARD PLUNKET(T); King's Serjeant-at-law; acquired Manors of Rathregan and Tullaghanogue, together with other lands in Meath, 1357–63; called to Parl 1375 on, Ch Justice Common Pleas Ireland 1388; *m* by 1364 Margaret, widow of Robert Burnell, of Balrothery, Co Dublin, and *d* by 4 Oct 1388, leaving:

1 John, of Stadalt, Co Meath; *d* by 1403, leaving:

(1) William, of Stadalt; *m* Alice, widow of Nicholas Woder, of Dublin, and *d* 9 Oct 1424, leaving:

1a Patrick; *dsp* after 1424

2a Philip, of Stadalt; *d* after 1439, leaving an heiress dau or sis (Elizabeth, *m* Sir Richard Tuite)

(2) Richard; *dsp* after 1403

2 CHRISTOPHER

1 Anne

The yr s,

Sir CHRISTPHER PLUNKET, of Rathregan and Tullaghanogue, JP Meath 1403; Sheriff Co Meath 1409, ktd by 1425; Ld Dep Ireland 1432–33; *m* by Oct 1399 Genet/Joan (*d* 8 March 1441/2), dau and heiress of Sir Luke de Cusack, thus acquiring Killeen and other lands, and *d* 1445, leaving:

1 JOHN PLUNKET; *m* Elizabeth Hollywood and *dvp* by 9 May 1434, leaving:

(1) CHRISTOPHER PLUNKET, 1st LORD (Baron) KILLEEN, (I), so *cr c* 1449; *m* by 1434 Joan/Genet Bellew (*m* 2nd Sir Roland Eustace, 1st and last Baron Portlester and had a dau Alison, *m* 8th Earl of Kildare; *see* LEINSTER, D) and *d* by 5 Jan 1462/3, leaving:

1a CHRISTOPHER PLUNKET, 2nd LORD (Baron) KILLEEN; of age by 1463; *m* by 5 Jan 1463/4 his cousin Elizabeth (*m* 2nd James Fleming, Lord Slane, and *d* 1508), dau and coheir of Sir William Welles, Ld Chllr Ireland 1461, and *dspm* of the plague by 1470, leaving:

1b Genet; *m* Nicholas, Lord Howth

2a EDMOND PLUNKET, 3rd LORD (Baron) KILLEEN; of age soon after Nov 1470; *m* 1st — FitzGerald (*dspm*); *m* 2nd Eleanor Fleming, dau of James, Lord Slane, and *d* 18 Aug 1510, leaving issue, of which the 9th LORD (Baron) KILLEEN was promoted EARL OF FINGALL (I) 26 Sept 1628 (*see* 1970 edn); the Earldom and Barony of Killeen expired 1984

2 CHRISTOPHER (Sir), **1st Lord**

The yr s,

Sir CHRISTOPHER PLUNKETT [*sic*], **1st Lord** (Baron) **Dunsany**, *cr c* 1462, of Dunsany; *b c* 1410; Constable Dublin Castle 1435; *m* 1st Anne (*d* 20 June 1459), dau and heir of Richard FitzGerald, illegitimate s of 5th Earl of Kildare (*see*

LEINSTER, D), by Julia, dau of Nicholas de Castlemartin and dau of Richard Wellesley; *m* 2nd Elizabeth, sis of 1st Viscount Gormanston (*qv*), and *d* 1467, having had by his 1st w, with other issue:

JOHN PLUNKET; *m* Thomasine, dau of Sir Christopher Barnewall (*see* BARNEWALL, Bt) and was *k* in battle 1455 by the O'REILLYs, leaving:

JOHN PLUNKETT, **2nd Lord** (Baron) **Dunsany**, Kt Irish Order of St George 1472; involved in Lambert Simnel's imposture but pardoned 1488; *m* Catherine, dau of — Hussey, feudal baron of Galtrim, and *d c* 1500, leaving:

EDWARD PLUNKETT, **3rd Lord** (Baron) **Dunsany**; *m* Anne (*m* 2nd Gerald Wellesley, of Dangan; *see* WELLINGTON, D), dau and heir of Philip de Bermingham, and was *k* 23 Jan 1520/1 attempting to crush resistance by the native Irish under the Chiefs O'Carroll and O'Connor, leaving:

ROBERT PLUNKETT, **4th Lord** (Baron) **Dunsany**; *m* 1st Eleanor, yst dau of Sir William Darcy, of Platten, V-Treasurer Ireland, and had four sons and nine daus including Elizabeth, *m* Walter FitzGerald; *see* LEINSTER, D); *m* 2nd Genet, widow of Alderman Robert Shillingford and dau of Alderman William Sarsfield of Dublin, and *d* 31 March 1558/9, having by her had two more sons; his 2nd but est surv s (by his 1st w):

CHRISTOPHER PLUNKETT, **5th Lord** (Baron) **Dunsany**; *m* Elizabeth, dau of Sir Christopher Barnewall, of Crickstown, and *d* between 29 May 1564 and 28 Aug 1565, leaving:

PATRICK PLUNKETT, **6th Lord** (Baron) **Dunsany**; of age after 1 July 1565; Govr Barony of Kells 1599, helped suppress the uprising of 1600; *m* Ismay, 11th dau of Sir Christopher Barnewall, of Turvey, Co Dublin, and *d* 17 March 1601/2, leaving an only s:

CHRISTOPHER PLUNKETT, **7th Lord** (Baron) **Dunsany**; *m* by 1595 Madeline/Maud, dau of Henry Babington, of Dethick, Derbys, and *d* 15 Dec 1603, leaving:

PATRICK PLUNKETT, **8th Lord** (Baron) **Dunsany**; *b* March 1595; *m* by 1634 Jane, dau of Sir Thomas Heneage, of Hainton, Lincs, and *d* in or after May 1668, having had, with an er s (Christopher, *m* apparently Mary (*m* 2nd by 1641 2nd Earl of Westmeath, *qv*), dau of Sir Thomas Nugent, 1st Bt, of Moyrath, and *dsp* or *dspm*):

EDWARD PLUNKETT; *m* Lady Catherine MacDonnell, 4th dau of 1st Earl of Antrim (*qv*), and *dvp* May 1668, leaving:

(1) CHRISTOPHER PLUNKETT, **9th Lord** (Baron) **Dunsany**; *d* unm 1690

(1) RANDALL PLUNKETT, **10th Lord** (Baron) **Dunsany**; supported JAMES II, hence outlawed 16 April 1691 on the triumph of the Williamite forces in Ireland; included in the articles of the Treaty of Limerick, however, so that his outlawry was reversed; but because he was RC he could not sit in Parl; *m* 1st between 1678 and 1681 Anne (*dsp*), widow of 1st Earl of Carlingford and dau of Sir William Pershall; *m* 2nd May 1711 Bridget, only dau of Richard Fleming, of Stahalmock, Co Meath, and *d* 16 March 1735, leaving by her:

1a EDWARD PLUNKETT, **11th Lord** (Baron) **Dunsany**; *b* 1713; conformed to C of I but made no attempt to establish his right to a seat in the I Ho of Lds; *m* Aug 1734 Mary, est dau of Francis Allen, of St Wolstan's, Co Kildare, MP, and *d* 9 June 1781, having had issue:

(1) RANDALL, **12th Lord**

(1) Bridget; *m* Hugh McGuire, of Kelston

(2) Rose; *m* Marquis de Carondelet

The only son,

RANDALL PLUNKETT, **12th Lord** (Baron) **Dunsany**; *b* March 1738/9; established 1785 right to seat in I Ho of Lds; *m* 1st 12 Aug 1771 Margaret (*d* 13 Sept 1791), widow of Edward Mandeville, of Ballydine, Co Tipperary, and dau of Edward Archdekin, of Co Kilkenny, and had, with four daus (including Anna Maria, *m* Philip Roche, of Donore, Co Kildare, and had issue; *see* TRIMLESTOWN, B):

1 EDWARD WADDING, **13th Lord**

2 Randall; *b* 1 Oct 1778; *d* 30 Oct 1835

The **12th Lord** *m* 2nd 24 April 1797 or 7 Aug 1800 Emma Mary (*dsp* June 1828), sis of Sir Drummond Smith, 1st Bt (*see* SPENCER-SMITH, Bt), and *d* 4 April 1821

His er son,

EDWARD WADDING PLUNKETT, **13th Lord** (Baron) **Dunsany**; *b* 7 April 1773; *educ* Westminster; Lt-Col Coldstream Gds, Ld Lt Co Meath 1835–48, rep I peer 1836–48; *m* 1st 20 June 1803 Hon Charlotte Louisa Lawless (*d* 10 June 1819), dau of 1st Baron Cloncurry (*see* 1929 edn), and had issue; *m* 2nd 23 March 1823 Hon Eliza Kinnaird (*dsp* 30 April 1864), est dau of 7th Lord Kinnaird (*qv*), and *d* 11 Dec 1848; his issue by his 1st w:

1 RANDALL EDWARD PLUNKETT, **14th Lord** (Baron) **Dunsany**; *b* 5 Sept 1804; *educ* Eton and Ch Ch Oxford; MP (C) Drogheda 1835–37, rep I peer 1850–52; *m* 29 Dec 1838 Elizabeth (*d* 2 April 1874), only dau and heir of Lyndon Evelyn, of Keynsham Court, Herefs, and *dsp* 7 April 1852

2 EDWARD, **15th Lord**

1 Emily Valentina; *m* 18 Oct 1839 George Price (*d* 29 Sept 1890), s of Sir Rose Price, 1st Bt (*qv*), and *d* at Ellerslie, Jamaica, 30 Sept 1864

The 14th LORD's yr bro,

EDWARD PLUNKETT, **15th Lord** (Baron) **Dunsany**, DL; *b* 29 Nov 1808; RN: Capt 1846, R-Adml 1864, V-Adml 1871, Adml 1877, rep I peer 1864–89; *m* 22 Sept 1846 Hon Anne Constance Dutton (*d* 27 June 1858), dau of 2nd Baron Sherborne (*see* 1970 edn), and had:

1 Randall Edward Sherborne, MP W Gloucester 1874–80; *b* 15 Nov 1848; *d* unm 25 Dec 1883

2 JOHN WILLIAM, **16th Lord**

3 Horace Curzon (Sir), KCVO (1903), PC (I 1897), JP Co Meath, DL Co Dublin; FRS, BA, Hon MA and Hon DCL Oxford, Hon Fell Univ Coll Oxford, Hon LLD Dublin, Commr Congested Districts Bd for Ireland 1891–1919, MP S Dublin 1892–1900, 1st V-Pres Dept of Ag Ireland 1899–1907, Chm Irish Convention 1917; *b* 24 Oct 1854; *d* unm 26 March 1932

4 Edward Reginald; *b* 10 Aug 1856; *d* 20 Dec 1864

1 Mary Sophia Eliza; *m* 22 Oct 1873 Chambré Brabazon Ponsonby (*d* 9 Oct 1884), 10th Hus, and *d* 5 July 1921, leaving issue (*see* BESSBOROUGH, E)

2 Constance Lavinia Harriet; *m* 7 April 1881 Capt Raymond Parr (*d* 6 April 1921) and *d* 23 Jan 1921, leaving issue

3 Julia Elizabeth; *d* 16 Nov 1866

The 15th LORD *d* 22 Feb 1889; his son,

JOHN WILLIAM PLUNKETT, **16th Lord** (Baron) **Dunsany**, JP Co Meath and Kent; *b* 31 Aug 1853; *educ* Trin Coll Cambridge; MP (C) S Glos 1886–92, rep I peer 1893–99; *m* 3 April 1877 Ernle Elizabeth Louisa Maria Grosvenor (added by roy licence 20 Dec 1905 names ERLE and DRAX after PLUNKETT-ERNLE and the arms of DRAX, ERLE and ERNLE and *d* 28 Feb 1916), only child of Col Francis Augustus Plunkett Burton, Coldstream Gds, by Sarah Frances Elizabeth, yr dau and coheir of John Samuel wanley Sawbridge-Erle-Drax, of Charborough Park, Dorset, and had issue:

1 EDWARD JOHN MORETON DRAX, **17th Lord**

2 Reginald Aylmer Ranfurly PLUNKETT later PLUNKETT-ERNLE-ERLE-DRAX (roy licence 4 Oct 1916) (Sir), KCB (1934), DSO, DL, JP Dorset; *b* 28 Aug 1880; Dorset CC 1924–32, served Grand Fleet WW I, present Battles of Heligoland, Dogger Bank and Jutland (despatches), Naval ADC to HM GEORGE V 1927–28, R-Adml 1st Battle Sqdn 1929–30, Dir Manning Dept Admlty 1930–32, C-in-C America and W Indies Stations May 1932–Oct 1934, C-in-C Plymouth June 1935–38 and the Nore 1939–41, 1st and Pncpl Naval ADC to HM GEORGE VI 1939–41, Cdre Ocean Convoys 1943–54; V-Adml 1932, Adml 1936; Grand Cross Order Orange-Nassau Holland, Russian Order of St Stanislas 2nd Cl with swords; *m* 15 April 1916 Kathleen (*d* 1980), only dau of Quintin Chalmers, MD, JP, and *d* 16 Oct 1967, leaving issue:

(1) +(Henry) Walter, JP and DL (Dorset) [Walter Plunkett-Ernle-Erle-Drax Esq JP DL, Charborough Park, Wareham, Dorset BH20 7EW]; High Sheriff Dorset 1988; *b* 18 March 1928; *educ* RNC Dartmouth; *m* 6 April 1957 *Hon Pamela Rose Weeks, er dau of Lt-Gen 1st and last Baron Weeks, KCB, CBE, DSO, MC, TD (*see* 1959 edn), and has issue:

1a +Richard Grosvenor; *b* 29 Jan 1958; *educ* Harrow; late Coldstream Gds; *m* 1985 (*divorce* 1997) Zara Victoria, yr dau of William Nigel Henry Legge-Bourke (*see* DARTMOUTH, E), and has, with another child:

1b +Toby Henry; *b* 1989

1b *Tamara Katherine; *b* 1987

2b *Natasha Shan; *b* 1993

2a +Jeremy Ryton; *b* 11 March 1960

3a +Charles Ranfurly [Charles Plunkett-Ernle-Erle-Drax Esq, High Fogrigg, Bardon Mill, Hexham, Northumberland]; *b* 8 June 1962; *m* 1990 *Camilla Mary, only dau of Christopher Robin St Quintin Wall (*see* CRAWFORD and BALCARRES, E), and has:

1b +Michael Oliver; *b* 12 Oct 1996

1b *Katherine Anne; *b* 18 Sept 1994

4a +Mark Wyndham; *b* 4 Aug 1967

5a +Edward Quintin; *b* 8 March 1971

(1) Kathleen Mary; *m* 18 April 1963 *Charles Owen George, s of Griffith Owen George, JP, of The Mount, Peterston-super-Ely, Cardiff, and *d* 19–

(2) *Patricia Doreen [Mrs Neil Maude, Priory Farmhouse, Wheathill, Somerton, Somerset TA11 7HG]; *m* 7 Jan 1953 Col Neil Stanley Eustace Maude (*d* 1987), RM, yr d of Lt-Col Eustace Arthur Maude, DSO, IA, of Staceys, Bentley, Hants, and has:

1a *Nicholas John Eustace; *b* 10 Oct 1953; *educ* Winchester; *m* 1993 *Alison, dau of Donald Sword, of Yarnhams, Upper Froyle, Hants

1a *Julia Jane [Mrs Thomas King, 37 Rodenhurst Rd, London SW4 8AE]; *b* 14 Nov 1954; *m* 1st 1986 (*divorce* 1988) Charles Miller; *m* 2nd 1994 *Thomas Walter Bullard King and has:

1b *Olivia Clare Victoria; *b* 2 Oct 1996

2a *Sarah Anne [Mrs Richard Parry, 72 Ritherdon Rd, London SW17 8QG]; *b* 20 July 1956; *m* 1981 *Richard William James Parry and has issue:

1b *William; *b* 1989

2b *Timothy; *b* 1997

1b *Sophie; *b* 1983

2b *Emily; *b* 1985

(3) Joan Elizabeth; *d* 1995

(4) Mary; *m* 1st 17 July 1948 Robert Gustaf Percy Hollond, only s of Maj-Gen Spencer Edmund Hollond, CB, CMG, DSO, of Chelsea, and had:

1a *Tom Robert; *b* 22 Sept 1950; *educ* Milton Abbey

2a *John Ernle; *b* 11 July 1953; *educ* Eton

3a *James Nicholas; *b* 15 Aug 1959; *m* 1985 *Beatrice Hannah Millicent, dau of Brian Entwhistle Hare, of Chartley, Fleet, Hants, and has issue:

1b *Phoebe Natasha Lara; *b* 1989

2b *Lara Blaise; *b* 1991

(4) (cont.) Mrs Hollond *m* 2nd 19– *Baron Robert Rothschild, KCMG (Hon), Grand Offr Order of Leopold of Belgium, Belgian Amb UK 1973–76, and by him has:

1a *Eliza Jane; *b* 7 May 1965

The 16th LORD *d* 16 Jan 1899; his er son,

EDWARD JOHN MORETON DRAX PLUNKETT, **17th Lord** (Baron) **Dunsany**, DL; *b* 24 July 1878; *educ* Eton; author and playwright, Hon LittD Dublin 1940, Capt Roy Inniskilling Fus, 2nd Lt Coldstream Gds, served South Africa 1899–1900 and WW I (wounded); *m* 15 Sept 1904 Lady Beatrice Child-Villiers (*d* 30 May 1970), yst dau of 7th Earl of Jersey (*qv*), and *d* 25 Oct 1957, leaving issue:

1 RANDAL ARTHUR HENRY PLUNKETT, **18th and present Lord** (Baron) **Dunsany**

Seat: Dunsany Castle, Dunsany, Co Meath, Ireland. The original castle dates back to shortly after the Normans arrived in Ireland, having been started around 1200. It came to the PLUNKETTs by marriage in the early 15th century. The castle as it was developed and enlarged grew to consist of two massive tower blocks. These the **12th Lord** connected in the late 18th century by a hall, the purpose being to cover over a court that lay between them. Happily the period coincided with the full flood of light-hearted Neo-Gothickry rather than the heavier-handed revival of the high 19th century. Less happily, many of these 'improvements', particularly the windows, were swept away a couple of generations later under the **13th Lord**'s tutelage (the 1780s windows survive at the rear of the castle, however). The **13th Lord** probably employed James Shiel, who put in mullioned windows in place of the ogival fantasies of the preceding age. The interior part, especially the hall, was left relatively untouched from its 1780s appearance. The drawing-room, which is on the first floor, retains its late 18th-century plasterwork. This is by Michael Stapleton, often called the Irish Adam. Shiel's interior work in the library combines gothic book cases and a graining effect simulating wood plus a remarkable groined ceiling to engender a quite magical atmosphere.

DUNTZE

Creation: Bt. (GB) 8 Nov 1774.

SIR DANIEL EVANS DUNTZE, 8TH BT, of Tiverton, Co Devon [Sir Daniel Duntze Bt, 8049 Gannon Ave, University City, Missouri 63130, USA]; *b* 4 April 1926; *s* cousin 1987; *educ* Washington U Sch of Fine Arts; commercial artist, in USAAF WW II; *m* 3 Dec 1954 *Marietta, dau of Ferdinand Welsh, of St Louis, and has issue:

1 +DANIEL EVANS; *b* 11 Aug 1960; *educ* U of Missouri

1 *Jill Alison [Mrs Eugene Pfeiffer, 7827 Greensfelder Lane, University City, Mo 63130, USA]; *b* 28 April 1957; *m* 1988 *Eugene Pfeiffer, and has issue:

(1) *William Thomas; *b* 1988

(2) *Benjamin Carl; *b* 1991

2 *Robin Evans [Dr Robin Wright, 8944 Powell, Brentwood, Mo 63144, USA]; *b* 3 Feb 1959; *m* 1987 *Dr Mark Wright and has issue:

(1) *Thomas Walker; *b* 1991

Lineage: JOHN DUNTZE, of Exeter; *m* Elizabeth, widow of Nicholas Munckly and dau of James Hawker, of Luppit, Devon, and had:

Sir John Duntze, 1st Bt (GB), so *cr* 8 Nov 1774, of Tiverton, Devon; MP Tiverton 1768–97; *m* 17– Frances (*d* 31 March 1801), dau of Samuel Lewis, and *d* 5 Feb 1795, leaving, with three daus:

1 **Sir John Duntze, 2nd Bt**; Receiver-Gen land and assessed taxes Devon; *m* 1st 5 June 1804 Dorothy (*d* 4 Nov 1806), dau of Sir Thomas Carew, 6th Bt (*qv*); *m* 2nd 1808 Elizabeth (*d* 1 June 1832), sis of his 1st w, and *d* 21 June 1830, having by her had:

(1) **Sir John Lewis Duntze, 3rd Bt**; *b* 16 Aug 1809; *m* 15 March 1834 Frances Elizabeth (*d* 23 Nov 1892), dau of Rev James Coles, Rector Michaelstone, Mon, and *dsp* 7 Sept 1884

2 James Nicholas, Paymaster-Gen to the Forces in Sicily; *m* 3 June 1794 Jane Harriot, dau of Sir James Cockburn, 5th Bt (*qv*), and *d* 22 Sept 1846, having had issue:

(1) Samuel Henry (Rev); *b* 10 Oct 1800; *m* 11 Oct 1827 Frances (*d* 12 March 1869), dau of Very Rev Joseph Palmer, MA, Dean of Cashel, niece and heiress of Sir Joshua Reynolds, the painter, also niece of Mary Palmer, Marchioness of Thomond (*see* INCHIQUIN, B), and *d* 15 Oct 1855, having had, with other issue:

1a **Sir George Alexander Duntze, 4th Bt**; *b* 27 Jan 1839; *m* 31 July 1869 Henriette Elizabeth Isabella (*d* 1 Aug 1908), est dau of R Lloyd Thomas, and *d* 2 May 1922, leaving:

1b **Sir George Puxley Duntze, 5th Bt**; S African Constabulary, served S African War 1900 (despatches) and WW I with S African Bde and Devon Regt; *b* 6 Dec 1873; *m* 16 June 1908 Violet May, dau of Henry Mark Sanderson, and *d* 20 May 1947, leaving:

1c **Sir George Edwin Douglas Duntze, 6th Bt**, CMG (1960); *b* 1 June 1913; *educ* Shrewsbury and Trin Coll Oxford (MA); joined Colonial Admin Serv 1936, Provisional Commr Uganda 1952–61; *m* 1st 30 July 1941 (*divorce* 1966) Joan, dau of Maj Frederick Edgar Bradstock, DSO, MC, and had issue:

1d *Elizabeth Joan [Mrs Nicholas Grove, Malden Lodge, Stone Cross, Bissington, Kent TN25 7JL]; *b* 6 March 1944; *m* 5 Nov 1966 *Nicholas Lowther James Grove, yr s of Lt-Col Michael Grove, of Wye, Kent, and has:

1e *Richard Nicholas Dougall; *b* 14 Aug 1970

2e *Iain Anthony Douglas; *b* 1973

1c (cont.) **Sir George** *m* 2nd 17 Sept 1966 *Nesta [Dowager Lady Duntze, 2 Amesbury Abbey Mews, Amesbury, Salisbury, Wilts SP4 7EX], dau of Thomas Richard Pendrell Herbert, of Newport, Mon, formerly w of Lt-Col Godfrey Ariel Evill, and *dsp* 1985

1c *Ivy Henriette; *m* 1940 Brian Dougherty (*d* 20 May 1962)

2c *Esme Ida; *m* 1937 Vyvyan Mackenzie, and has issue:

1d *Brenda Rosalind; *b* 20 July 1941

2d *Lorna Esmee; *b* 5 Sept 1943

1b Ethel Maud; *m* 5 May 1897 John Henry Whitehouse, and *d* 16 July 1940

2b Ida Rosario; *d* unm 12 Dec 1963

1a Jane Harriot Anne; *m* 1st 26 Feb 1867 Rev David Evans (*d* 9 June 1871), and had issue; *m* 2nd 6 Oct 1874 Rev David William Herbert, Vicar of Tremean

2a Isabel Theophilla Charlotte; *m* 1 Aug 1871 William Raynor Wood (*d* 20 Aug 1884), DL, of Singleton, Lancs, and had issue

3a Lucy Maria Emily; *m* 6 Jan 1870 Henry Travers Smyth, of The Gables, Tenby, Pembs, and had issue

(2) John Alexander, Adml; *b* 26 Aug 1896; *m* 28 May 1832 Maria del Rosario (*d* 8 April 1889), dau of Don Francisco le Paula Ramirez y Balasco, and *d* 15 May 1882, leaving issue:

1a John Alexander, CE, Lt 31st Regt and West India Regt; *b* 4 April 1855; *m* 9 Jan 1878 Irene Matilda (*d* 1923), dau of Ralph Nunes, of Kingston, Jamaica, and *d* 25 Oct 1909, leaving issue:

1b John Alexander Ralph; 22nd Regt Engineers NGNY, served US Army Spanish-American War 1898; *b* 16 Nov 1878; *m* 1st 15 Feb 1905 Carrie Fairchild (*d* 19 Aug 1927), dau of Edward J Godfrey, of St Paul, Minnesota, and had issue:

1c **Sir John Duntze, 7th Bt**; *b* 13 Nov 1909; mechanical engr with Perkin-Elmer Corp, Norwalk, Conn.; *m* 30 Dec 1935 *Emily Ellsworth [Emily Lady Duntze, c/o Linda F Greiner, PO Box 457, Washington, NJ 07882, USA], dau of Elmer Ellsworth Harlow, of New Bedford, Mass., and *dsp* 1987

1b (cont.) John Duntze *m* 2nd 14 March 1929 Louise Marie Berthelon, and *d* 5 May 1950

2b George Douglas, 2nd US Cavalry; *b* 23 Jan 1882; *m* 15 Dec 1920 Mabel Lillian, dau of Daniel Evans, of St Louis, Mo., and *d* 10 July 1946, leaving issue:

1c Sir DANIEL EVANS DUNTZE, **8th and present Bt**

1c *Dorothy Jane [Mrs Hal Roach, 9 Wood Hill Rd, Birmingham, Alabama, USA]; *b* 11 April 1923; *m* 25 Nov 1950 *Hal Roach, and has issue:

1d *Michael Todd; *b* 1952; *m* 19– (*divorce* 19–), and has issue:

1e *Chauncey Blane; *b* 1979

2d *Scott Evans [Scott Roach Esq, 3814 Old Leeds Rd, Mountain Brook, Alabama 35213, USA]; *b* 1953; *m* 1978 *Leigh Anne Sellers, and has issue:

1e *Katie Elizabeth; *b* 1979

2e *Hillary Anne; *b* 1981

3d *Brooke Normile [Brooke Roach Esq, 204 Fairmont Dve, Mountain Brook, Alabama 35213, USA]; *b* 1955; *m* 1983 *Susan Lynn Alford, and has issue:

1e *Keegan Wade; *b* 1984

1e *Sarah Savannah; *b* 1986

4d *Todd Douglas [Todd Roach Esq, 1454 Linkwood Lane, Decatur, Georgia 30033, USA]; *b* 1957; *m* 1986 *Daisy Cleveland, and has issue:

1e *Zachary Cleveland; *b* 1987

1b Irene Matilda Rosario; *m* 1904 George O Heffter, MD, PhD, of New York, and *d* 1955

1a Gertrudia Juana Antonia; *m* 5 June 1860 Capt Alexander Walter Armstrong Ogilvie (*d* 21 June 1865), RA, and *d* 10 May 1914, leaving issue

2a Jane Harriot; *m* 5 June 1860 Lt-Col Hugh Chetham Lyle (*d* 30 Aug 1897), late RA, and had issue

(1) Frances Lewis; *m* Rev John C Clarke (*d* 24 Dec 1847), Rector of Clayhidon, Devon, and *d* 28 Nov 1825, leaving issue

3 Samuel Lewis; Offr 62nd Regt of Foot; *m* Jane, dau of William Shaw, Sec to Govr Jamaica, and *d* Dec 1794, leaving issue

DUPREE

Arms: Vert on a bend between two calves passant or, three mullets of the field. **Crest:** A lion sejant ppr., supporting with the dexter fore-paw a flagstaff ppr., flowing therefrom a banner vert charged with a mullet or. **Motto:** *Le monde est mon pré* ('The world is my field'). **Creation:** Bt. (UK) 24 Jan 1921.

SIR PETER DUPREE, 5TH BT, of Craneswater, Portsmouth, Co Southampton [Sir Peter Dupree Bt, 15 Hayes Close, Chelmsford, Essex CM2 0RN]; *b* 1924; *s* f 1976; *m* 1 Feb 1947 *Joan, dau of Capt James Desborough Hunt

Lineage: WILLIAM DUPREE; had:

Sir William Thomas Dupree, 1st Bt (UK), so *cr* 24 Jan 1921, VD, TD, JP Portsmouth, DL Hants; *b* 4 Sept 1865; Hon Col 54th Bde RFA (TA), memb Hants TAA, served Vol Force and TA, cmded 2nd Hampshire Garrison Artillery and 1st Wessex Bde RFA, R-Cdre RAYC, Mayor Portsmouth 1901–03 and 1909–10, ktd 1902, Order Rising Sun and Sacred Treasure Japan; *m* 1st 26 March 1878 Mary (*d* 29 May 1907), dau of George Groves, of Selsey, Sussex, and had issue:

1 **Sir William Dupree, 2nd Bt**; *b* 5 March 1882; *educ* privately and Birmingham U; Maj Wessex Field Bde RA WW I, Pres Roy Ag Soc 1939–46, chm and md Portsmouth and Brighton Utd Breweries; *m* 7 Oct 1908 Edith Mary (*d* 14 Feb

1959), dau of Arthur Aloysius Mutimer, MA, of Egbaston, Warwicks, and *dsp* 30 Jan 1953

2 **Sir Vernon Dupree, 3rd Bt**; Capt Hon Maj 7th Roy Fus WW I (wounded); *b* 23 Dec 1884; *m* 1st 10 April 1912 Amy Marcella (*d* 18 Dec 1953), dau of John Price, of Askeaton, Co Limerick, and had issue:

(1) William Vernon John; Lt 10th Hus WW II; *b* 24 Oct 1917; *ka* Libya 28 May 1942

(1) *Mary Marcella Lucy [Mrs Terence Lawrence, Fawley Vicarage, Fawley, Berks]; *m* 18 Dec 1941 *Terence Patrick Lawrence, yst s of Sir Walter Lawrence, of Hyde Hall, Sawbridgeworth, Herts, and has issue

2 (cont.) **Sir Vernon** *m* 2nd 10 Nov 1955 *Louisa Jennie, dau of George Hillyard, and *d* 4 Sept 1971

3 VICTOR (Sir), **4th Bt**

4 Eric, MA Cantab; barrister, Capt 10th Bn Hampshire Regt WW I (despatches); *b* 8 March 1895; *m* 9 April 1928 Gwendoline Violet (*d* 1993), dau of Henry Harvey, and *d* 1 Nov 1932, leaving issue:

(1) *Monica Mary [Mrs Robin Morris, 43b York St, Broadstairs, Kent]; *b* 17 Jan 1930; *m* 22 May 1954 (*divorce* 1974) Robin Gordon Hazlitt Morris and has issue:

1a *Anthony John David; *b* 1955

2a *John Richard Hazlitt; *b* 1958

3a *Andrew Quentin Dupree; *b* 1963

(2) *Barbara Jane [Mrs Ronald Mitchell, 51 High St, Broadstairs, Kent]; *b* 26 Aug 1931; *m* 1st 4 Aug 1954 Lt John Richard Haward (*d* 1956), RN; *m* 2nd 1957 (*divorce* 1967) Ronald Mitchell and has issue:

1a *Terence Roger Anstey; *b* 1957

2a *Robert Killian; *b* 1959

3a *Simon Paul Adam; *b* 5 Jan 1966

5 James; Midshipman RNR WW I 1917–18, Lt-Cdr RNVR WW II; *b* 27 Oct 1899; *educ* Harrow and Reading U; *m* 20 Dec 1928 Mary Ethel Gillot (*d* 1 April 1949), widow of A Stuart Elsworth, of Sheffield, and dau of T W Reid, of Rockhall, Dumfriesshire, and *d* 1972, leaving issue:

(1) +(THOMAS WILLIAM JAMES) DAVID [David Dupree Esq, Little Fircliff, Whitworth Rd, Darley Dale, nr Matlock]; *b* 5 Feb 1930; heir presumptive

(1) *Jennifer Rosemary Gillott [Mrs Roberto Mercadaz, Plaza Mayor, 19, 4 Piso, Palma, Mallorca, Spain]; *b* 2 March 1933; *m* 20 Oct 1962 *Roberto Lorenzo Mercadaz, 2nd son of Bartolme Mercadal, of Palma, Mallorca, and has issue

1 Ethel Hannah Mary; *m* 20 Aug 1902 Henry Duncan Dormor (*d* 6 March 1958), MICE, and *d* 7 Aug 1955, leaving issue

2 Violet Isabel Mary; *m* 8 June 1910 Capt Brian Cameron Gourley (*d* 1 Sept 1964), RN (ret), and *d* 17 May 1952, leaving issue

3 Hilda Maud Mary; *b* 5 July 1883; *m* 3 July 1923 Harold Ernest Smith

4 Dorothy Ella Mary; *m* 3 March 1917 Theodore Carter (*d* 10 Feb 1942), late PWD, India, and *d* 18 July 1958, leaving issue

5 Olive Elise Mary; *m* 2 Oct 1918 Stanley Stallebrass, and *d* 21 Feb 1929, leaving issue

6 Nora Decima Mary; *b* 15 July 1893; *m* 10 Nov 1920 John Fulton Houston, and has issue

Sir William *m* 2nd 18 Sept 1909 Marion (*d* 23 May 1952), dau of John Price, of Askeaton, Co Limerick, and *d* 2 March 1933, having by her had further issue:

6 +Thomas William [Thomas Dupree Esq, Paradis Roc, Bloc D, Chemin de St Christophe, 06130 Grasse, France]; *b* 21 July 1913; *educ* Harrow; 1st Sec Embassy Paris and Priv Sec to Amb, 2nd Lt Gren Gds, Hon Attaché Madrid 1936038, News Dept FO 1938–43 and April–Oct 1946, Dep Assist to Br Resident Min Allied Force HQ Algiers 1943–44, Press Attaché (local rank of 1st Sec) Paris 1944–46, FO Observer (Press Relations) Trials War Criminals Nuremberg 1946 ; *m* 1st 11 July 1938 (*divorce* 1953) Anne, yst dau of Sir Henry Getty Chilton, GCMG, and has issue:

(1) *Delia [Mrs Delia Guy, 147 Homerton High St, London E9]; *b* 6 Dec 1939; *m* 6 Oct 1962 (*divorce* 19–) Peter Guy and has:

1a *Dominic William; *b* 29 Sept 1963

1a *Susannah; *b* 12 Nov 1965

(2) *Sarah Anne [Mrs Michael Wilkins, 47 St Johns Ave, London SW15 6AL]; *b* 23 May 1942; *m* 1977 *Michael Wilkins, and has issue:

1a *William Michael; *b* 1978

1a *Sarah Jeanne; *b* 1979

6 (cont.) Thomas Dupree *m* 2nd 16 Aug 1953 *Jacqueline, formerly w of Max Harari and dau of Commendatore Leo Goldschmid

7 John Rupert; Capt Irish Gds WW II, memb Lloyd's; *b* 21 May 1915; *educ* Harrow and Magdalene Coll Cambridge (BA Econ); *m* 7 March 1946 *Ann Margaret Frances (*m* 3rd 16 June 1965 Roger Thornycroft (*d* 1983), DSC, yst son of Sir John Edward Thornycroft, KBE, of Bembridge, IOW; *m* 4th 1984 *Stuart Warren Don) [Mrs Stuart Don, 113 Dovehouse St, London SW3], only dau of Lt-Col Robert George Barlow, Seaforth Highrs, of Little Stodham House, Liss, Hants, and formerly w of Hon William Gladstone Bethell (*see* BETHELL, B), and *d* 19 Jan 1965, leaving issue:

(1) +Michael John; *b* 29 April 1947; *educ* Harrow; *m* 1982 *Alexandra Columbia, dau of Michael Anthony Telfer Smollett, and has issue:

1a *Tamara; *b* 1985

7 *Irene Amy Marion [Mrs John O'Hagan, Upperton Cottage, Petworth, W Sussex GU28 9BE]; *b* 26 July 1910; *m* 15 April 1936 S/Ldr John Gerard Brendan O'Hagan, RAF (*d* 13 Oct 1986), only s of Joseph O'Hagan, of Newry, Co Down, and Dublin, and has:

(1) *Timothy David Brendan [Timothy O'Hagan Esq, The Old Rectory, 1 Mill Hill Rd, Norwich NR2 3DP]; *b* 4 Jan 1945; *educ* Westminster and Corpus Christi Coll Oxford (BA) (DPhil); *m* 1970 *Jennifer Kaue and has:

1a *Gabrielle; *b* 1973

2a *Rachel; *b* 1974

(1) *Elizabeth Mary Marion; *b* 30 Nov 1936; *m* 1st 24 June 1961 John Shelley Bevington; m 2nd 19– *—Burton and by her 1st husb has:

1a *Mark; *b* 1963

1a *Amanda; *b* 1967

2a *Catherine; *b* 1968

(2) *Jennifer Ann [Mrs Guy Liardet, The Downes Cottage, New Rd, Meonstoke, Hants SO32 3NN]; *b* 29 Aug 1938; *m* 17 Feb 1962 *R Adml Guy Francis Liardet, CB, CBE, s of Maj-Gen Henry Maugham Liardet, CB, CBE, DSO, DL, of Warningcamp House, Arundel, Sussex, and has:

1a *Patrick; *b* 1965

1a *Frances; *b* 1962

2a *Sophie; *b* 1969

8 Margaret Marcella Marion; *b* 11 Aug 1911; *m* 20 July 1939 Maj Donald Harris Browne, MBE, Roy Dragoons, s of Col Percival John Browne, CB, of Fifehead Magdalen, Gillingham, Dorset, and *d* 9 Jan 1991, leaving:

(1) *David [David Browne Esq, Woodview, Jenkins Lane, St Leonards, Tring, Herts]

(1) *Susan [Ms Susan Browne, Sandy Corner, Ogdens Nth, Fordingbridge, Hants SP6 2QD]; *b* 4 Aug 1940

The 3rd Bt's yr bro,

Sir Victor Dupree 4th Bt; Capt 3rd Dragoon Gds and Roy Tank Corps WW I (wounded, POW); *b* 19 Dec 1887; *m* 1st 5 March 1910 Gladys (*d* 9 Oct 1922), dau of Charles Henry Lawson; *m* 2nd 1922 *Margaret Cross and *d* 11 Aug 1976, leaving:

1 Sir PETER DUPREE, **5th and present Bt**

1 *Mary; *b* 1926; *m* 10 Aug 1948 *George Dutton Gibb and has issue:

(1) *Elizabeth; *b* 1951; *m* 1983 *Peter Glen

DURAND

Arms: Azure five fusils conjoined in fess or within a bordure of the last, on a chief embattled of the second a shack-bolt of the first. **Crest:** A rock proper surmounted by a crescent argent between two branches of laurel or. **Motto:** *Esperance en Dieu* ('Hope in God'). **Creation:** Bt. (UK) 8 April 1892.

SIR EDWARD ALAN CHRISTOPHER DAVID PERCY DURAND, 5TH BT, of Ruckley Grange, Salop [Sir Edward Durand Bt, Lisnalurg House, Sligo, Ireland]; *b* 21 Feb 1974; *s* f 1992; *educ* St Columba's Coll Dublin, Milltown Inst of Theology and Philosophy and U of Ulster Coleraine

Lineage: Maj-Gen Sir HENRY MARION DURAND, KCSI, CB, RE, memb Cncl of Sec State for India, Lt-Govr Punjab 1870; *b* 6 Nov 1812; *m* 1st Annie, dau of Maj-Gen Sir John McCaskill, KCB, KCH, 92nd Highrs, and had:

1 EDWARD LAW (Sir), **1st Bt**

2 Henry Mortimer (Sir), GCMG (1900), KCSI (1894), KCIE (1889), PC (1901), barrister Lincoln's Inn 1872, entered Bengal CS 1873, in FO and political dept; Amb Extrdy and Plen Teheran 1894–1900 and Madrid 1900–03, Amb Washington 1903–06; *b* 14 Feb 1850; *m* 1 March 1875 Ella Rebe (*d* 29 April 1913), dau of Teignmouth Sandys, BCS, and *d* 8 June 1924, leaving issue:

(1) Henry Marion, DSO (1914), Maj and Brevet Lt-Col 9th Lancers, served Boer War 1899–1902 (despatches) and WW I (despatches, brevet); *b* 23 Feb 1876; *d* unm 19 Dec 1954

(1) Amy Josephine; *b* 8 Oct 1881; *m* 19 Dec 1923 Arthur Clement Wilmot, of The Gate, Farnham Royal, Bucks, and *dsp c* 1968

3 Algernon George Arnold, CB (1892), CIE (1897), Col Indian Staff Corps, Mil Sec to Viceroy India 1894–99, memb Gentlemen-at-Arms 1902–23, served Afghan Campaign and march to Kandahar with Centl India Horse (medal, bronze star), ADC to Viceroy India, Br Resident Gilgit 1888, ch political offr and cdr troops expdn against Hunza and Nagar 1891 (medal); *b* 31 March 1854; *m* 17 July 1895 Elizabeth Marjorie (*d* 29 April 1929), er dau of Hon Thomas Charles Bruce (*see* ELGIN and KINCARDINE, E), and *d* 8 Oct 1923, having had:

(1) Algernon Thomas Marion, Maj 5th City of London Rifle Bde WW II; *b* 6 Jan 1900; *educ* Eton and Magdalen Coll Oxford (BA); *m* 10 March 1939 *Margery [Mrs Algernon Durand, 3 Kings Close, Henley-on-Thames, Oxon RG9 2DS], only dau of J S Underwood, and *dsp* 23 July 1961

(2) Robert Joceline; *b* 17 Jan 24 1902; *m* 24 Aug 1935 Claire (*d* 2 Dec 1983), dau of Warwick Brookes, and *d* 10 June 1980, leaving:

1a *Pamela Evelyn Theresa [Miss Pamela Durand, Flat 2, Weavers Court, Weavers Lane, Henfield, Sussex BN5 9DY]; *b* 9 Oct 1941; has:

1b *Julian Alan [Julian Durand Esq, 2 Albourne House, High St, Henfield, W Sussex BN5 9DE]; *b* 12 July 1967

(1) Marjorie Caroline Marion; *b* 10 April; *d* 12 May 1898

1 Annie Marion; *m* 28 Dec 1868 Col John Henry Rivett-Carnac (*d* 11 May 1923), CIE (*see* RIVETT-CARNAC, Bt), and *dsp* 13 Nov 1935

2 Emily Jane; *b* 20 May 1845; *m* 15 June 1871 Maj Frederick Bruce Prinsep, 21st Hus (*d* 1879), and *d* 18 Feb 1932, leaving issue

3 Eleanor Louisa; *m* 1st 27 April 1872 Col Joseph Oats Travers (*d* 23 July 1884), 17th Regt and had issue; *m* 2nd 1888 Maj Arthur Collingwood Denny (*d* Feb 1891), Connaught Rangers, and *d* 16 Dec 1924, leaving issue

4 Frances Mary; *b* 6 Oct 1851; *m* 23 Sept 1869 Maj-Gen Sir Charles Metcalfe Macgregor, KCB, CSI, CIE (*d* 5 Feb 1887), and *d* 9 May 1873, leaving issue

Sir HENRY *m* 2nd 23 Aug 1859 Emily Augusta (*d* 30 March 1905), widow of Rev Henry S Polehampton, Chaplin EICS, and dau of Charles Blake Allnatt, of Shrewsbury, and by her had:

4 Charles Henry Marion; *b* 6 June 1860; *d* unm 27 March 1912

5 Reginald; *b* 13 Feb 1862; *d* unm

5 Ethel; *b* 21 May 1864; *m* 1st 1885 James Sligo Jameson (*d* 17 Aug 1888), of Glen Lodge, Co Sligo, and had issue; *m* 2nd 16 July 1901 Roberto Henri Pres de Villamarina, Conte di Contadone (*d* 1916), 2nd son of Marquis Emanuel de Villamarina, and *d* 14 Oct 1933

6 Isabel; *b* 30 May 1866; *d* 30 Jan 1868

7 Muriel; *b* 18 Dec 1868; *d* unm 3 May 1930

Sir HENRY *d* 1 Jan 1871; his est son,

Sir Edward Law Durand, 1st Bt (UK), so *cr* 8 April 1892, CB (1887), Lt-Col Indian Staff Corps, formerly of 96th Regt, Assist Commr Afghan Boundary Commn 1884–86, Resident Nepal 1888–91; *b* 5 June 1845; *m* 18 Aug 1880 Maude Ellen (*d* 2 June 1953), 4th dau of Algernon Charles Heber-Percy (*see* NORTHUMBERLAND, D), and *d* 1 July 1920, having had issue:

1 **Sir Edward Percy Marion Durand, 2nd Bt**; Maj 8th Rajputs IA Mesoptamia 1915–17 and Waziristan Field Force 1920, Assist Political Agent Rajputana Indian Political Dept 1917–20; *b* 11 July 1884; *m* 29 July 1913 Vera Helen Lucas (*d* 23 Dec 1968), dau of Sir Robert Lucas-Tooth, 1st Bt (*qv*), and *dsp* 4 March 1955

2 Reginald Heber Marion, Capt Centl India Horse; *b* 5 April 1892; *d* 29 June 1917 of wounds recd in action

3 **Sir Alan Algernon Marion Durand, 3rd Bt,** MC (1919); *b* 14 Oct 1893; *educ* Cheltenham and RMA Woolwich; 2nd Lt RA WW I (despatches twice, wounded twice), Capt 1917, WW II Belgium and France 1939–40 (despatches) and Egypt 1944–46 (despatches), Col 1942, ret 1946, Hon Brig RA, chm Glos Co Br Legion 1947–53, pres 1966, V-Lt Glos 1957–71; *m* 1st 5 Feb 1924 (*divorce* 1936) Vivien Enid, dau of Herbert Chamberlain, and had:

(1) *Patricia Marion [Mrs Kenneth Booth, Fletching Cottage, Fletching St, Mayfield, E Sussex TN20 6TN]; *m* 1st 14 June 1960 W/Cdr Howard Rex English Rumsey (*d* 8 Aug 1964), s of Capt Reginald English Rumsey, of Shrewsbury, and has issue:

1a *Alan; *b* 16 March 1962

1a *Fiona Marion; *b* 31 Jan 1964

(1) (cont.) Mrs Howard Rumsey *m* 2nd 26 June 1969 Kenneth A J Booth (*d* 1981), MBE, FILA

3 (cont.) **Sir Alan** *m* 2nd 6 June 1944 *Evelyn Sherbrooke, CBE (1955), JP (1942) Glos, 2nd dau of Charles Anrold Crane, of The Reddings House, nr Cheltenham, and widow of Sir Stanley Tubbs, 1st Bt (*see* 1940 edn), and *d* 16 Feb 1971

4 Mortimer Henry Marion, Lt-Cdr RN, served WW I and WW II 1939–41; *b* 1898; *m* 1st 30 Aug 1922 (*divorce* 1930) Evelyn Mary, dau of Capt Carroll, USN; *m* 2nd 28 Jan 1931 Beatrice Garvan-Sheridan, dau of Judge Sheridan, of Sydney, NSW, by Beatrice Maude, Baroness de Tuyll, and *d* 18 Feb 1969, having by her had:

(1) HENRY MORTIMER DICKON MARION (Sir), **4th Bt**

(1) *Elizabeth Pamela Marion [Mrs George Bowden, Higher Shute Farm, Huish Champflower, Taunton, Somerset TA4 2HE]; *b* 12 March 1932; *m* 31 Aug 1957 *Maj George Naismith Bowden, Loyal (N Lancs) Regt, est son of Lt Col G T Bowden, MC, of Winsham, Somerset, and adopted:

*Alexander Dickon Naismith; *b* 1971

*Veronica Mary Patricia; *b* 1968

1 Marion Isobel; *b* 27 July 1881; *m* 27 Aug 1913 Lt-Col John Campbell (*d* 7 Feb 1928), of Kilberry, Argyll, DL, JP, and *d* 21 Nov 1945, leaving:

(1) John Edward Ian; *b* May 1918; *d* Oct 1919

(1) Maud Isobel Margaret; *b* Sept 1916; *d* April 1917

(2) *Marion [Miss Campbell of Kilberry, Druim A'Bhuinne, Kilberry, Tarbert Loch Fyne, Argyll PA29 6YD]; *b* 16 Dec 1919; 3rd Offr WRNS WW II; author

2 Everild Blanche Marion; *b* 10 Oct 1882; *m* 16 June 1908 Capt Selwyn Lucas Lucas-Tooth (*ka* 20 Oct 1914), est s of Sir Robert Lucas Lucas-Tooth, 1st Bt (*qv*), and *d* 18 Oct 1928, leaving issue

3 Beryl Marion; *b* 27 July 1887; *m* 13 Oct 1915 Capt Wilfred Pollen Haviland (*d* 9 May 1947), MBE, Argyll and Sutherland Highrs, s of Rev Arthur Coles Haviland, Rector Lilley, Herts, and *d* 15 July 1977, having had issue:

(1) David Reginald Ferrers; *b* 8 June 1918; *educ* Eton and Trin Coll Cambridge; P/O RAFVR WW II; *ka* 23 Dec 1940

(1) *Gwendolen Mary Beryl [Mrs Peter Sparks, The Old Vicarage, Compton Abdale, GL54 4DS]; *b* 1 Nov 1916; *m* 1946 *Maj Peter Hebert Sparks, King Edward's Own Gurkha Rifles, and has:

1a *Richard Peter Haviland [Richard Sparks, 942 Nth Alpine Drive, Beverly Hills, CA 90210, USA]; *b* 20 Aug 1951; *educ* Eton and Exeter Coll Oxford (MA); *m* 1983 *Jennifer Denise Okun, *neé* Klix, and has:

1b *Elizabeth Rose Haviland; *b* 11 Aug 1989

1a *Marigold Wendy Maude; [Mrs Jonathan Heron, Edwinsford Farmhouse, Talley, Llandeilo, SA9 7BX] *b* 3 Jan 1949; *educ* Westonbirt; *m* 1975 *Jonathan Crawford Heron

(2) *Daphne Marion [Mrs Edward Nicholson, The Lea, Upper Sapey, Worcs WR6 6XS]; *b* 13 Feb 1923; *m* 4 Feb 1950 Cdr Edward Adams Nicholson, RN (*d* 25 Dec 1994), s of Lt-Col Walter Adams Nicholson, and has:

1a *David Adams Pollen [David Nicholson Esq, 18 Unwin Mansions, Queens Club Gardens, London W14 9TH]; *b* 25 Dec 1950; *educ* Lord Treloar Coll Hants

2a *Michael Edward [Michael Nicholson Esq, Upper Vobster Farm, Upper Vobster, Bath BA3 5SA]; *b* 8 Oct 1952; *educ* Wellington and Magdalene Coll Cambridge (MA); ACA; *m* *Patricia Anne (Dunhill), 1st dau of Dr Michael Micallef and has:

1b *David Michael Adams; *b* 20 Dec 1981

2b *James Edward; *b* 6 March 1984

3a *Alexander Kerio William [Alexander Nicholson Esq, 157 Ravenslea Rd, London SW12 8RT]; *b* 21 Nov 1955; *educ* Wellington and Goldsmiths' Coll U of London (BA); *m* 1983 *Lucy Ann, yst dau of Henry Prince, and has:

1b *Samuel Kerio George; *b* 18 Jan 1986

1b *Molly Marion Slaney; *b* 31 May 1990

The 3rd Bt's nephew,

Rev Sir (Henry Mortimer) Dickon Marion St George Durand, 4th Bt; *b* 19 June 1934; *educ* Wellington, Sydney U and Salisbury Theological College; Bishop's Curate Kilbixy Union of Parishes Co Westmeath 1979–82; *m* 8 May 1971 *Stella [Stella Lady Durand, Lisnalurg House, Co Sligo, Ireland], dau of Capt Christopher Carleton L'Estrange, of Lisnalurg, and *d* 24 Oct 1992, leaving:

1 Sir EDWARD ALAN CHRISTOPHER PERCY DURAND, **5th and present Bt**

2 +DAVID MICHAEL DICKON PERCY; *b* 6 June 1978; heir presumptive; *educ* St Columba's Coll Dublin

1 *Rachel Elizabeth Marion; *b* 1972; *educ* St Columba's Coll Dublin, Heatherley Sch of Fine Art London and Nat Coll of Art and Design Dublin

2 *Madeleine Eleanor Marion; *b* 1980

DURHAM, Bt

Arms: Quarterly, 1st, sable a fess between three lambs passant argent (for LAMBTON); 2nd, argent a fess gules between three popinjays vert, collared of the second (for LUMLEY); 3rd, argent an escutcheon sable within an orle of cinquefoils gules (for HEDWORTH); 4th, argent three cinquefoils gules (for D'ARCY). **Crest:** A ram's head cabossed argent, attired sable. **Motto:** *Le jour viendra* ('The day will come'). **Creations:** B. (UK) 29 Jan 1828, V. and E (UK) 23 March 1833.

Antony Claud Frederick Lambton, JP (1931) [Lord Lambton JP, Villa Cetinale, Sovicille, Siena, Italy]; *b* 10 July 1922; *s f* 4 Feb 1970 in earldom and other peerages but disclaimed them for life 23 Feb 1970 though desiring still to be known as 'Lord Lambton' and being so known both as an MP and as a Minister of the Crown; MP (C) Berwick-on-Tweed Oct 1951–73, PPS to Min of Supply 1954 and For Sec 1955–57, Parly Under Sec Def 1970–73, author: *Snow and Other Stories* (1983), *Elizabeth and Alexandra* (1985), *The Abbey in the Wood* (1986), *The Mountbattens* (1989), *Pig and Other Stories* (1990); *m* 10 Aug 1942 *Belinda Bridget, dau of Maj Douglas Holden Blew-Jones, of Westward Ho!, N Devon, and has issue:

1 +EDWARD (NED) RICHARD, *Lord Durham*; *b* 19 Oct 1961; former lead guitarist with pop group The Frozen Turkeys; Referendum Party Parly candidate Berwick 1997 gen election; *m* 1st 1983 (*divorce* 19–) Christabel Mary, yst dau of Roderick (Rory) McEwen (*see* McEWEN, Bt), and has:

(1) +Frederick; *b* 23 Feb 1985

1 (cont.) *Lord Durham* *m* 2nd 19 Oct 1995 *Catherine, dau of Desmond FitzGerald, 29th Knight of Glin, of Glin Castle, Co Limerick, Ireland (*see* also WAKEFIELD, Bt)

1 *Lucinda [The Lady Lucinda Worsthorne, The Old Rectory, Hedgerley, Bucks SL2 3UY]; *b* 10 May 1943; writer, photographer and broadcaster: *Vanishing Victoriana* (1976), *Temples of Convenience* (1978), *Chambers of Delight* (1983), *Beastly Buildings* (1985), *An Album of Curious Houses* (1988), *Lucinda Lambton's A to Z of Britain* (1996), photographer and TV personality; *m* 1st 16 Jan 1965 (*divorce* 1973) Henry Mark Harrod, barrister, er s of Sir (Henry) Roy Forbes Harrod, FBA, of The Old Rectory, Holt, Norfolk, and has issue:

(1) *Henry Barnaby; *b* July 1965

(2) *Nathaniel; *b* 22 March 1967

1 (cont.) Lady Lucinda Harrod *m* 2nd 1986 (*divorce* 1989), as his 2nd w, Sir Edmund John William Hugh Ramsay-Fairfax-Lucy, 6th Bt (*qv*); *m* 3rd 1991, as his 2nd w, *Sir Peregrine Gerard Worsthorne, (*see* LINDSEY and ABINGDON, E)

2 *Beatrix Mary; *b* 23 July 1949; *m* 1st 1971 George William Bowdrey and has:

(1) *Honey; *b* 19–

(2) *Rose Violet; *b* 1973

2 (cont.) Lady Beatrix Bowdrey *m* 2nd 1982 Guy Rupert Gerard Nevill (*see* ABERGAVENNY, M)

3 *Rose Diana [The Lady Rose Musker, Malcolm House, Batsford, Moreton-in-Marsh, Glos]; *b* 26 Nov 1952; *m* 1979 (*divorce* 1989) (Herbert) Oliver FitzRoy Musker (*see* DAVENTRY, V), and has issue

4 *Anne Mary Gabrielle; *b* 4 July 1954; actress

5 *Isabella [The Lady Isabella Naylor-Leyland, The Ferry House, Milton Park, Peterborough, Cambs]; *b* 17 May 1958; *m* 1980 *Sir Philip Vyvian Naylor-Leyland 4th Bt (*qv*), and has issue

Lineage: ROBERT de LAMBTON; feudal Ld of Lambton Castle, Co Durham; *d* 1350; ancestor in the 8th generation of:

JOHN LAMBTON, of Lambton; *b* 1505; *m* Agnes, dau and coheir of Roger Lumley (*see* SCARBROUGH, E), and *d* 1582, leaving:

ROBERT LAMBTON, of Lambton; *m* Frances, dau of Sir Ralph Eure by Margaret (dau of Sir Ralph Bowes) and sis of William, Lord (Baron) Eure, and *d* 1583, leaving:

RALPH LAMBTON, of Lambton; *m* 1587 Eleanor, dau of Thomas Tempest, of Stanley, and *d* 1593, leaving:

Sir WILLIAM LAMBTON, of Lambton; ktd 1614, Col royalist infantry regt Civil War; *m* 1st Jane, 3rd dau and coheir of Sir Nicholas Curwen, of Workington, Cumberland, and had:

1 HENRY, of whom presently

Sir WILLIAM *m* 2nd Catherine, dau of Sir Henry Widdrington, of Widdrington, Northumberland, and had, with other issue:

2 William; royalist Civil War, in which *k*

3 Thomas (Sir); Col of Horse, Govr Leeward Islands; *m* —, dau of Nicholas Freville, of Hardwick, and *d* 1662, leaving issue:

(1) Freville; *m* thrice and *d* 1731, leaving issue:

1a Thomas, of Hardwick; *m* Dorothy, dau of Claverley Bewick, and left issue:

1b Barbara; *m* Robert Ord

2b Dorothy; *m* Robert Surtees

3b Thomasin; *m* — Rawling

4b Margaret; *m* Henry Ruddock

5b Philadelphia; *m* Charles Burne

6b Elizabeth; *m* Francis Mascal

1 Elizabeth; *m* Sir Thomas Davison

2 Eleanor; *m* Henry Anderson, of Long Cowton

Sir WILLIAM was *ka* Marston Moor 2 July 1644; his est s,

HENRY LAMBTON, of Lambton; *m* 1635 Mary, dau of Sir Alexander Davison, of Blakiston, and *d* 1693, having had, with other issue:

RALPH LAMBTON; *m* 1696 Dorothy, dau and coheir of John Hedworth, of Harraton (heir general and rep of the D'ARCYs of Harraton and Herrington), and 1717, leaving, with other issue:

JOHN LAMBTON, of Lambton Castle; Gen, Col 68th Foot, MP Durham; *m* Sept 1763 Susan (*d* 26 Feb 1769), est dau of Thomas, 8th Earl of Strathmore (*see* STRATHMORE AND KINGHORNE, E), and *d* 1794, leaving, with another s (Ralph John, MP Durham; *d* 29 July 1844) and two daus (Jane Dorothy; Susan Mary Anne, *m* 1790 John Wharton, MP):

WILLIAM HENRY LAMBTON, of Lambton, MP Durham; *b* 16 Nov 1764; *m* 19 June 1791 Lady Anne Barbara Frances Villiers (*m* 2nd Hon Charles William Wyndham and *d* 1832), dau of 4th Earl of Jersey (*qv*), and had issue:

1 JOHN GEORGE, **1st Earl**

2 William Henry, of Biddick Hall, Co Durham; *b* 27 March 1793; *m* 28 Jan 1824 Henrietta (*d* 20 March 1883 aged 75), 2nd dau and coheir of Cuthbert Ellison, DL, JP, of Hebburn, Co Durham, and *d* 3 April 1866, leaving issue

3 Hedworth, MP; *b* 26 March 1797; *m* 19 May 1835 Anna (*d* 23 June 1843), est dau of Gervase Parker Bushe, of Kilfane, and *d* 16 Sept 1876

1 Frances Susan; *m* 1st 16 Aug 1811 Col Hon Henry Frederick Howard (*ka* Waterloo); *m* 2nd 16 Jan 1819 Hon H F Compton Cavendish, MP (*d* 5 April 1873), and *d* 23 Nov 1840

WILLIAM LAMBTON *d* 30 Nov 1797; his est son,

JOHN GEORGE LAMBTON, **1st Earl of Durham**, so *cr* 23 March 1833, as also VISCOUNT LAMBTON and earlier 29 Jan 1828 BARON DURHAM OF THE CITY OF DURHAM AND OF LAMBTON CASTLE, Co Durham (all UK), PC (1830), GCB (1837); *b* 12 April 1792; *educ* Eton; served 10th Dragoons (later Hussars) 1809–11, MP (Whig) Co Durham 1813–28, Ld Privy Seal 1830–1833, Amb Russia 1835–37, Govr-Gen Canada Jan-Dec 1838 and was largely the author of the Durham Report which shaped Britain's policy towards the Colonies for the next century, High-Steward Hull, Kt Orders of St Andrew, St Alexander Nevsky, St Anne and the White Eagle of Russia, Leopold of Belgium and the Saviour of Greece; *m* 1st 1 Jan 1812 Harriet Cholmondeley (*d* 11 July 1815), illegitimate dau of 1st Marquess Cholmondeley (*qv*) by a Mme St Alban, and had issue:

1 Frances Charlotte; *m* 8 Sept 1835 Hon John George Brabazon Ponsonby (*d* 28 Jan 1880), later 5th Earl of Bessborough (*qv*), and *dsp* 18 Dec 1835

2 Georgiana Sarah Elizabeth; *d* 3 Jan 1833

3 Harriet Caroline; *d* 30 May 1832

The **1st Earl** *m* 2nd 9 Dec 1816 Lady Louisa Elizabeth Grey (*d* 26 Nov 1841), dau of 2nd Earl Grey (*qv*), and by her had issue:

1 Charles William ('Master Lambton' of Sir Thomas Lawrence's celebrated portrait); *b* 16 Jan 1818; *d* 24 Dec 1831

2 GEORGE FREDERICK D'ARCY, **2nd Earl**

4 Mary Louisa, CI; *b* 7 Nov 1846; *m* 8th Earl of Elgin and Kincardine (*qv*) and *d* 9 March 1898, leaving issue

5 Emily Augusta; *m* 19 Aug 1843 William Henry Frederick Cavendish (*d* 11 March 1881), only s of Gen Henry Frederick Compton Cavendish (*see* DEVONSHIRE, D), and *d* 2 Nov 1886, leaving issue

6 Alice Anne Caroline; *m* 7 July 1853 18th Earl of Morton (*qv*) and *dsp* 15 Jan 1907

The 1st EARL *d* 28 July 1840; his only surv son,

GEORGE FREDERICK D'ARCY LAMBTON, **2nd Earl of Durham**; *b* 5 Sept 1828; *m* 23 May 1854 Lady Beatrix Frances Hamilton (*d* 21 Jan 1871), 2nd dau of 1st Duke of Abercorn, KG (*qv*), and *d* 27 Nov 1879, leaving:

1 JOHN GEORGE LAMBTON, **3rd Earl of Durham**, KG (1909), GCVO (1911), PC (1911); Ld Lt and Custos rotulorum Co Durham, DCL, Chllr Durham U, Mayor Durham 1899, Lt Coldstream Gds, Hon Col Durham RATA and 8th Bn Durham LI (VD), pres Durham TAA, KJStJ, Ld High Steward to HM GEORGE V 9 Nov 1911–12; *b* 19 June 1855; *m* 28 Oct 1882 Ethel Elizabeth Louisa (*d* 28 Oct 1931), 2nd dau of Henry Milner, of W Retford House, Notts, 2nd s of Sir William Mordaunt Milner, 4th Bt (*qv*), and *dsp* 18 Sept 1928

2 FREDERICK WILLIAM, **4th Earl**

3 Hedworth LAMBTON later MEUX (roy licence 2 Sept 1911 under terms of will of Lady Meux, of Theobald's Park) (Sir), GCB, KCVO; *b* 5 July 1856; Adml of the Fleet, Extra Equerry to TM EDWARD VII 1902–10 and GEORGE V 1910, ADC 1901–02, Priv Sec to successive 1st Lds of the Admlty 1894–97, MP Portsmouth 1916–18, served Egyptian War 1882, cmded naval bde Siege of Ladysmith S Africa 1899–1900 and roy yacht *Victoria and Albert* 1901–02, 2ic Channel Fleet 1903–4, cmded 3rd Cruiser Sqdn 1904–06, C-in-C China Sqdn 1908–10 and Portsmouth 1912–16, Keeper Jewel House Coronation of HM GEORGE V, Grand Offr Legion of Honour and St Maurice of Italy, Kt Dannebrog Denmark; *m* 18 April 1910 Mildred Cecilia Harriet (*m* 3rd 4 Dec 1930 Lord Charles Montagu, CVO (*d* 10 Nov 1939), 2nd son of 7th Duke of Manchester (*qv*)), widow of Viscount Chelsea (*see* CADOGAN, E), and *d* 17 Sept 1942), 3rd dau of 1st Baron Alington (*see* 1940 edn), and *dsp* 20 Sept 1929

4 Charles, DSO (1898); *b* 3 Nov 1857; *educ* Eton and RMC Sandhurst; Brevet Col and Hon Brig-Gen, cmdg: 2nd Bn Northumberland Fus 1900–4 and 34th Inf Bde New Army 1914, T/Lt-Col and Cmdt Durham Vol Regt 1917, Hon Brig-Gen 1918, served Nile Expdn 1898 (despatches, two medals, six clasps); *m* 22 June 1912 Lavinia Marion (*d* 18 Aug 1976), er dau of William Henry Garforth, of Westow Hall, Yorks, by Hylda Maria Madeline, dau of 8th Baron Middleton (*qv*), and *d* 5 Dec 1949, leaving issue:

(1) +Charles William [Maj Charles Lambton, The Old Rectory, Calstone, Calne, Wilts SN11 8PZ], Maj (ret) Coldstream Gds; *b* 22 Aug 1921; *educ* Eton; *m* 27 July 1950 *Lady Elizabeth Mary FitzMaurice, yr dau of 6th Marquess of Lansdowne (*qv*), and has issue:

1a +William Henry Charles; *b* 10 April 1951; *educ* Eton; *m* 1st 1975 Elizabeth Susan Kingdom and has issue:

1b *Lucy Marion; *b* 1980

2b *Sarah Isabella; *b* 1982

1a (cont.) William Lambton *m* 2nd 14 Oct 1989 *Sorrel M G, dau of Michael Pym, of Canada, and Mrs Grace Pym, of Ballaghmore Castle, Borris-in-Ossory, Co Laois, Ireland, and has further issue:

1b +Theodore Charles Maurice; *b* 11 May 1990

2a +Julian Edward [Julian Lambton Esq, Pennybridge House, Pennybridge, Ulverston, Cumbria]; *b* 21 Nov 1955; *educ* Eton; *m* 1986 *Vanda Jane, yr dau of Lt Col Charles David Agnew, of Bilborough, York (*see* AGNEW, Bt, of Gt Stanhope St), and has issue:

1b +Patrick David Charles; *b* 1992

1b *Georgina Marion; *b* 1990

3a +Christopher John [Christopher Lambton Esq, 39 Bellevue Place, Edinburgh EH7 4BS]; *b* 21 July 1960; *educ* Eton and Edinburgh U; *m* 1991 *Julie, er dau of Dr James Kenneth Watt Morrice, of Aberdeen, and has:

1b +Alexander Maurice; *b* 1993

1b *Katherine Norah; *b* 1996

1a *Anne Elizabeth [Mrs Patrick Wintour, Weavers House, Sandridge Lane, Bromham, Chippenham, Wilts]; *b* 25 Nov 1952; *m* 1979 *Patrick J Wintour, yr son of Capt E R Wintour, and has:

1b *Adam Richard; *b* 1988

1b *Laura Katherine; *b* 1981

2b *Mary Rose Cecilia; *b* 1982

3b *Isabel Martha Grace; *b* 1994

(1) Diana Mary; *b* 26 June 1914; *m* 1st 10 Dec 1936 Maj William Hedworth Williamson (*ka* Middle East, Oct 1942), of Whitburn Hall, Durham, 2nd son of Frederick Charles Williamson (*see* WILLIAMSON, Bt), and had issue; Im 2nd 7 June 1945 1st Baron Hailes, PC, GBE, CH (*see* 1970 edn BUCHAN-HEPBURN, Bt)

5 George, Lt 3rd Bn Sherwood Foresters *b* 23 Nov 1860; *m* 7 Dec 1908 Cicely Margaret, er dau of Sir John Francis Fortescue Horner, KCVO, of Mells Park, Somerset, and *d* 23 July 1945, leaving issue:

(1) John, 2nd Lt Coldstream Gds, F/O RAFVR WW II; *b* 31 July 1909; *m* 15 March 1934 *Ethel Ruth (*m* 2nd E Ballard, of USA), only dau of Capt William Henry Nicholson, RN (*see* NICHOLSON, Bt, of Kensington), and was *ka* 11 Aug 1941, leaving issue:

1a +Peter John George; *b* 26 May 1935

(2) Edward George; Capt RHG WW II; *b* 29 April 1918; *educ* Eton; *m* 1st 24 Nov 1949 (*divorce* 1959) Anne, formerly w of David Rawnsley and only dau of Col Lawrence Lees, of Cheswardine, Salop; *m* 2nd 16 Dec 1959 Pauline Mary (*d* 2 Sept 1996), formerly w of Earl Jermyn (later 6th Marquess of Bristol (*qv*)) and dau of Herbert Coxon Bolton, and *d* 23 June 1983, leaving issue:

1a +George; *b* 6 March 1962; *m* 19– *Lise Blemmer and has:

1b +James; *b* 8 Dec 1994

2b +Thomas; *b* 6 May 1998

(1) *Ann Katharine Swynford, OBE (1943) [Prof Ann Lambton OBE, Gregory, Kirknewton, Wooler, Northumberland NE71 6XE]; *b* 8 Feb 1912; BA, PhD, DLitt, Hon DLitt Durham 1971 and Cambridge 1973, FBA 1964, Prof Persian Lond U 1953–79, Press Attaché Br Legation Teheran 1939–46, Hon Fell New

Hall Cambridge 1973, SOAS, U London 1983, Prof Emeritus Diocese of Newcastle 1988

(2) Sybil Frances Mary Diadem; *b* 7 Oct 1919; *m* 20 Oct 1953 *Maj William Jessop [Maj William Jessop, The Ovens, Harrington, Spilsby, Lincs], and *dsp* as a result of a fall in a point-to-point 22 April 1961

6 William (Sir), KCB (1918), CMG (1904), CVO (1914), DSO (1900); Maj-Gen, Mil Sec to Govr and C-in-C Transvaal 1900–04, Lt-Col and Col cmdg Coldstream Gds 1910–12, AA and QMG London Dist 1913–14, Mil Sec to C-in-C BEF 1914–15, Cdr Legion of Honour, Groom-in-Waiting to HM GEORGE V 1910–16; served Nile Expdn 1898 (despatches, medal with two clasps, Khedive's Star), S African War 1899–1902 (despatches, wounded, Queen's medal with four clasps, King's medal with two clasps) and WW I (despatches five times); *b* 4 Dec 1863; *m* 22 April 1921 Lady Katherine de Vere Somerset (*d* 31 Jan 1958), dau of 10th Duke of St Albans (*qv*), and *d* 10 Oct 1936

7 Claud; *b* 4 Jan 1865; *m* 27 April 1901 Lettice (*d* 15 Jan 1945), dau of Edward Wormald, and *d* 15 Feb 1945, leaving issue:

(1) Hedworth, DSC, Cdr RN WW II (despatches); *b* 20 March 1904; *m* 1st 14 Feb 1935 (*divorce* 1963) Iris Wynnfred Violet (*d* 21 Jan 1997), formerly w of Charles Caulfield Hewitt and dau of William Law Halpin, mining engr, and had issue:

1a *Rosemary Ann [Miss Rosemary Lambton, 20 Malvern Court, Onslow Square, London SW7 3HU]; *b* 27 May 1936

(1) (cont.) Cdr Hedworth Lambton *m* 2nd 17 June 1963 Olivia (*d* 1986), widow of Col Denys Redwood Vachell, MC, and dau of Reginald Monckton, and *dspm* 22 Sept 1983

(2) D'Arcy; *b* 10 July 1908; *m* 9 Oct 1933 *Hon Monica Dorothy Brand [The Hon Mrs D'Arcy Lambton, Saxon House, Shottisham, Woodbridge, Suffolk], yst dau of 3rd Viscount Hampden (*qv*), and *d* following a car crash 18 Nov 1938, leaving:

1a +Michael Charles [Michael Lambton Esq, 6 Rosenau Cres, London SW11 4RZ]; *b* 24 Nov 1934; *educ* Eton and Newcastle U; *m* 1969 *Nancy, dau of George Gillespie, and has:

1b +D'Arcy; *b* 1970; *educ* Eton and Newcastle U

1b *Monica Dorothy [Mrs Brian Dimitroff, Saxon House, Shottisham, Woodbridge, Suffolk]; *b* 1965; *m* 28 Sept 1996 *Brian Dimitroff, yr s of Paschanko Dimitroff, of Beaconsfield, Bucks, and has:

1c *Sebastian; *b* 14 April 1998

1a Lorna Katherine; *b* 23 April 1938; *d* 6 May 1995

(3) Gervase; *b* 4 March 1912; *d* 17 Oct 1937

(1) Angela Marjory; *b* 12 Oct 1902; *m* 9 June 1961 Hon Niall Greville Chaplin (*d* 8 Feb 1963), yr s of 2nd Viscount Chaplin (*see* 1970 edn)

8 D'Arcy, Cdr RN (emergency list), Capt 3rd Bn DCLI; *b* 3 June 1866; *m* 14 June 1888 (*divorce* 1899) Florence Ethel (*d* 1 Jan 1941), dau of Arthur Sproule, of Goulburn, NSW, and *d* 30 Dec 1954, leaving issue:

(1) Eileen, MBE (1948), JP (Surrey 1942); barrister Lincoln's Inn 1954, Nat Dip Ag 1918; *b* 19 March 1891; *m* 1st 6 Aug 1918 (*divorce* 1923) Alfred Trevor Barker (*d* 1942), est son of Edward Cecil Barker, of The Corner House, Roehampton; *m* 2nd 27 Aug 1931 Charles Leach (*d* 3 Sept 1952), yr son of Louis James Leach, of Melbourne, Australia, and *d* 19–

9 Francis, 2nd Lt RHG; *b* 18 Jan 1871; *ka* 31 Oct 1914

1 Beatrix Louisa; *m* 29 Aug 1877 14th Earl of Pembroke and Montgomery (*qv*) and *d* 12 March 1944, leaving issue

2 Katherine Frances; *m* 13 Feb 1884 10th Duke of Leeds (*see* 1963 edn) and *d d* 6 Dec 1952, having had issue

3 Eleanor; *m* 22 Jan 1859 1st and last Viscount Cecil of Chelwood (*d* 24 Nov 1958; *see* SALISBURY, M) and *dsp* 24 April 1959

4 Anne, JP Durham; *d* 24 Feb 1922

The 3rd EARL's twin bro,

FREDERICK WILLIAM LAMBTON, **4th Earl of Durham**, DL, MP S Co Durham 1880–85 and Co Durham SE 1900–10, Hon Col Northumberland Fus, Lt Coldstream Gds; *b* 19 June 1855; *m* 26 May 1879 Beatrix (*d* 27 April 1937), 2nd dau of John Bulteel, of Pamflete, Devon, and had issue:

1 JOHN FREDERICK, **5th Earl**

2 Geoffrey, Lt Coldstream Gds; *b* 13 Sept 1887; *m* 6 June 1914 Dorothy (*m* 2nd 5 Oct 1920 Lt-Col Graham Sidney Leventhorpe, DSO, RA (*d* 15 Dec 1963), and *d* 12 Feb 1965), er dau of Christopher John Leyland, of Haggerston Castle, Northumberland, and was *ka* 1 Sept 1914, leaving issue:

(1) Monica Helen, OBE (1946); *b* posthumously 26 March 1915; *m* 4 Oct 1934 Baron Kilmany (LP) and 1st Bt, MC, Coldstream Gds (*see* 1970 edn), and has issue

3 Claud, DSO (1918), JP (Northumberland 1927), Capt Lanarks Yeo WW I (wounded); *b* 3 Dec 1888; *m* 20 May 1916 Olive Eleanor Isobel (*d* 14 Oct 1955), dau of William Robert Percival Lockwood, DL, bro of 1st and last Baron Lambourne (*see* 1928 edn), and *d* 7 Sept 1976, leaving issue:

(1) Barbara Anne; *b* 16 Feb 1917; *d* unm 14 April 1998

1 Violet, LGStJ; *b* 3 July 1880; *m* 28 Oct 1905 4th Earl of Ellesmere (*see* SUTHERLAND, D), and has issue

2 Lilian; *b* 8 Dec 1881; *m* 14 July 1902 13th Earl of Home (*qv*) and *d* 26 Sept 1966, leaving issue

3 Joan Katherine; *b* 21 Sept 1893; *m* 19 July 1921 3rd Baron Joicey (*qv*) and *d* 4 Jan 1967, leaving issue

The 4th EARL *d* 31 Jan 1929; his est son,

JOHN FREDERICK LAMBTON, **5th Earl of Durham**; *b* 7 Oct 1884; *educ* Eton; Capt 3rd/7th Bn Northumberland Fus WW I (wounded); *m* 1st 12 Nov 1919 Diana Mary (*d* 28 Aug 1924), only dau of Granville Richard Frederick Farquhar, of Dalton Hall, Beverley (*see* FARQUHAR, Bt), and had:

1 John Roderick Geoffrey Francis Edward; *b* 6 Sept 1920; *d* unm 4 Feb 1941

2 ANTONY CLAUD FREDERICK LAMBTON, **briefly 6th Earl of Durham**

The **5th Earl** *m* 2nd 4 March 1931 Hermione (*d* 1990), only dau of Sir George Bullough, 1st and last Bt (*d* 1939 edn), and *d* 4 Feb 1970, leaving by her:

3 +John George [The Hon John Lambton, 39 Hill St, London W1]; *b* 10 June 1932

DURRANT

Arms: Or a cross-crosslet ermines between four spots of ermine sable. **Crest:** A boar passant per fess wavy argent and gules, bristled and tusked azure, and pierced through the body with a broken lance bendways sable, the head downwards gold. **Motto:** *Labes pejor morte* ('A dishonouring stain is worse than death').
Creation: Bt. (GB) 22 Jan 1784.

SIR WILLIAM ALEXANDER ESTRIDGE DURRANT, 8TH BT, of Scottow, Co Norfolk, JP (NSW 1957) [Sir William Bt JP, Red Hill, Nundle Rd, Nemingha, NSW 2340, Australia]; *b* 26 Nov 1929; *s* f 1995; Capt 12th/16th Hunter River Lancers 1958; *m* 7 Feb 1953 *Dorothy (BA), dau of Ronal Croker, of Quirindi, NSW, and has issue:

1 +DAVID ALEXANDER; *b* 1 July 1960

1 *Susan Elizabeth; *b* 9 July 1962

Lineage: WILLIAM DURRANT; *m* 1587 Catherine Steward and *d* 1606, leaving, with an er s (Thomas):

ROBERT DURRANT; *m* 1628 Margaret Rutland, and *d* 1647, leaving issue:

WILLIAM DURRANT, of Scottow, Norfolk; *m* Margaret Redford, and *d* 20 Jan 1700, having had issue:

1 Thomas, of Scottow; High Sheriff Norfolk 1715; *b* 1656; *m* 1st Sarah Hardingham; *m* 2nd Mary Randall; *m* 3rd Anne Coker and *d* Oct 1727, having by his 3rd w had:

(1) Margaret; *m* her 1st cousin Davy Durrant (*see below*) and *d* 1742, having had issue

2 Daniel; had:

(1) Davy, *s* his uncle Thomas at Scottow; *educ* Caius Coll Cambridge (BA1724, MA 1729); *m* his 1st cousin Margaret (*d* 1742), only child and heiress of Thomas Durrant, of Scottow (*see above*), and had issue:

1a THOMAS, **1st Bt**

1a Susannah; *m* Sir Randal Ward, of Bedey Park, Norfolk

1 Margaret; *b* 11 March 1653; *m* 1681 Robert Blake (*d* 7 Dec 1729), of Scottow Hall, Norfolk, and *d* 8 May 1742, having had issue

THOMAS DURRANT's gs,

Sir Thomas Durrant, 1st Bt (GB), so *cr* 22 Jan 1784, of Scottow, High Sheriff High Sheriff 1784; *m* 1773 Susannah (*d* 9 Dec 1833), est dau of Hambleton Custance, of Weston, Norfolk, High Sheriff 1753, and *d* 6 Sept 1790, having had, with other issue, including a yr s (William, of Wimpole St, London; *b* 14 Jan 1779):

Sir Thomas Durrant, 2nd Bt; *b* 1775; *m* 28 Sept 1799 Sarah Crooke (*d* July 1845), dau of Henry Steenbergen, of the Island of St Christopher, and *d* 22 May 1829, having had, with other issue, including a dau (Emily Mary Swinfen, *m* 18 June 1821 Rev Thomas Lovick Cooper, Rector Empingham, Rutland, and *d* 1 Aug 1838, leaving:

Sir Henry Thomas Estridge Durrant, 3rd Bt; *b* 4 May 1807; *m* 1st 23 June 1830 Angus Sophia Katherine (*d* 28 April 1831), dau of Robert Marsham, of Stratton Stawless, Norfolk; *m* 2nd 31 Jan 1833 Diana Julia Wildbrat (*d* 9 Feb 1867), dau of Sir Josias Henry Stracey, 4th Bt (*qv*), and *d* 16 May 1861, having by her had issue:

1 **Sir Henry Josias Durrant, 4th Bt**, DL; *b* 2 Sept 1838; *m* 30 April 1863 at Brussels Alexandrina Charlotte (Ina) (*m* 2nd 15 July 1884 Lt-Col Arthur Blundell and *d* 30 Jan 1919), dau of Gen Sir Robert Barton, KCH, and *d* 6 April 1876, leaving:

(1) Nathalie Julie Colette; *d* unm 24 Nov 1925

(2) Emily Amelia Massy; *d* unm 7 Jan 1943

(3) Adela Constance Alexandrina, CBE (1930), JP; *m* 27 July 1892 James Edward Shaw (*d* 14 Oct 1911), of the Manor House, Welburn, Kirby Moorside, Yorks, and *d* 16 Dec 1962 aged 93, leaving issue

2 WILLIAM ROBERT ESTRIDGE (Sir), **5th Bt**

1 Julia Agnes Pauline; *m* Brussels 4 Aug 1862 Lawrence Hare Finn, of Dresden

2 Louisa Mary Caroline; *m* 1st 10 Aug 1865 John Richard Fenwick (*d* 1874); *m* 2nd 20 March 1875 Sir Archibald Lamb, 3rd Bt (*dsp* 5 Nov 1921), and *d* 31 Jan 1927

The 4th Bt's bro,

Sir William Robert Estridge Durrant, 5th Bt, Lt 15th Regt; *b* 19 Aug 1840; *m* 3 June 1869 Emily Grace (*d* 1942), dau of John Street, of London, and *d* 17 Dec 1912, leaving, with a dau (Florence Elizabeth Wildbredt; *b* 1 Feb 1875; *m* 1st 18

May 1905 James Collier (*d* 21 June 1925); *m* 2nd 1925 George William Romany Lee Gaudie (*d* 24 April 1952)):

Sir William Henry Estridge Durrant, 6th Bt; *b* 23 Dec 1872; *m* 10 Aug 1900 Ethel May (*d* 2 May 1943), dau of Henry Robert Jeffress, of Sidney, Australia, and had issue:

1 WILLIAM HENRY ESTRIDGE (Sir), **7th Bt**

2 Reginald Walter Estridge; *b* 28 Oct 1905; *m* 6 March 1937 *Joy Minnie [Mrs Reginald Durrant, 42 Hayle St, St Ives, NSW 2075, Australia], dau of William George Smith, of Manly, NSW, and *d* 1986, leaving issue:

(1)*Beverley Joy; *b* 12 July 1938; *m* 1957 *Stanley Ross Ackers and has had issue:

1a *Geoffrey Ross; *b* 1965; *d* 1991

1a *Annette Ruth; *b* 1959

2a *Margaret Lynne; *b* 1963

(2) *Kaye Lorraine [Mrs Malcolm Bird, 384 Bobbin Head Rd, Turramurra, NSW, Australia]; *b* 10 Dec 1944; *m* 1966 *Malcolm Harvey Bird and has issue:

1a *Murray Scott; *b* 1969

1a *Julie Anne; *b* 1968

1 *Pearlie May Wildbredt; *b* 1 March 1903; *m* 1931 *Thomas Henry Downs, of Sydney, NSW, Australia

Sir WILLIAM *d* 22 July 1953; his er son

Sir William Henry Estridge Durrant, 7th Bt, JP (NSW 1940); *b* 1 April 1901; served WW II; *m* 15 Oct 1927 Georgina Beryl Gwendoline (*d* 13 July 1968), dau of Alexander Purse, of Kircubbin, Co Down, and *d* between 1 April and 30 June 1995, leaving:

1 Sir WILLIAM ALEXANDER ESTRIDGE DURRANT, **8th and present Bt**

1 *Beryl Elizabeth Wildbredt; *b* 9 May 1928; *m* 5 Jan 1952 *Douglas James Weaving and has issue:

(1) *John Laurence; *b* 31 Jan 1956

(2) *Peter Douglas; *b* 9 Feb 1958

(1) *Elizabeth Anne; *b* 18 April 1953

DYER

Arms: Or a chief indented gules. **Crest:** Out of a ducal coronet or a goat's head argent armed gold. **Motto:** *Terrere nolo, timere nescio* ('Unwilling to frighten, unacquainted with fear').
Creation: Bt. (E) 6 July 1678.

SIR (HENRY) PETER FRANCIS SWINNERTON DYER, 16TH BT, of Tottenham, Co of Middlesex, KBE (1987) [Sir Peter Dyer Bt KBE, The Dower House, Thriplow, Royston, Herts SG8 7RJ]; *b* 2 Aug 1927; *s* f 1975; *educ* Eton (Fell 1981) and Trin Coll Cambridge (Fell 1955, Dean 1963–73); FRS 1967, CC Salop, Master St Catharine's Coll Cambridge 1973–83, Prof Maths Cambridge 1971–88, lecturer Cambridge Mathmatical Lab 1960–67, V-Chllr Cambridge U 1979–81, chm ctee on Academic Organisation (Lond U) 1980–82, Visiting Prof Harvard 1971, Cwlth Fund Fell U of Chicago 1954–55 and Research Fell Trin Coll Cambridge 1950–54, chm UGC 1983–89, ch exec U Funding Cncl 1989–92, Chm: Sec of State for Nat Heritage's Advsy Ctee and Library and Information Servs Cncl 1992–95, Hon Fell Worcester Coll Oxford 1980, Hon DSc Bath 1981, Hon LLD Aberdeen 1991, sometime mem English Bridge Team; *m* 25 May 1983 *Dr Harriet Crawford, er dau of Rt Hon Sir Patrick Reginald Evelyn Browne, OBE, TD

Lineage: GEORGE DYER, of Heytesbury Park, Wilts; *bapt* 24 Oct 1596; *m* 1st 30 Oct 1616 Sara (*bur* 23 July 1630), dau of Thomas Rolfe, of Enford, Wilts, and had issue:

1 George, of Heytesbury; *m* Editha — (*bur* 9 Jan 1674/5) and *d* by 1661, leaving issue:

2 WILLIAM (Sir), **1st Bt**

3 John (Sir); *bapt* Heytesbury 12 Oct 1623; *m* — and had issue:

(1) Swinnerton; *bapt* 26 April 1686; *bur* 19 April 1687

1 Sarah; *bapt* 19 April 1626

GEORGE DYER *m* 2nd 27 Nov 1633 Constance (*bur* 3 July 1666), dau of Rev William Mervin, Rector Boyton, Wilts, and *d* after 13 Oct 1661, leaving by her, with other issue:

4 Richard; *bapt* 26 Sept 1634; *m* 11 Feb 1666 Sarah Symens (*bur* 4 Jan 1687/8), and was *bur* 3 Aug 1672, having had issue:

(1) Henrietta; *bapt* 24 July 1670

5 Ralph; *bapt* 29 Oct 1634; *m* — and had issue

6 Matthew; *bapt* 10 April 1638

7 William; *m* Mary — and was *bur* 16 Jan 1708, leaving issue

2 Margaret; *bapt* 16 Oct 1633

The 2nd son,

Sir William Dyer, 1st Bt (E), so *cr* 6 July 1678, of Tottenham, Middx, Newnham, Herts, and Newton Hall, Great Dunmow, Essex; barrister; *bapt* 15 April 1621; *m c* 1650 Thomasine (*m* 2nd 8 Aug 1683 John Hopwood and ld 13 April 1697), only dau and heir of Thomas Swinnerton, of Stanwey Hall, Essex (3rd s and eventual heir of Alderman Sir John Swinnerton, Ld Mayor of London, descended from the SWINNERTONs of Swinnerton), and had, with other issue:

1 JOHN SWINNERTON (Sir), **2nd Bt**

2 Edward Swinnerton; *m* Hannah — and was *bur* 14 Sept 1665, having had issue

3 William, of Newnham, High Sheriff 1694; *b* 1657; *m* 1st 27 June 1684 Mary Hayward (*d* 17 Nov 1685), and had issue:

(1) Thomasine; *bur* 17 Nov 1685

3 (cont.) William Dyer *m* 2nd 31 May 1687 Anne (*d* 1740), dau of Sir Thomas Hooke, 1st Bt, of Flanchford, and was *bur* 25 Feb 1736, having by her had further issue

Sir WILLIAM was *bur* 27 Jan 1680; his er surv son,

Sir John Swinnerton Dyer, 2nd Bt; *b* 1657; *m* (by licence 5 Sept 1683) Elizabeth (*d* 30 May 1727 aged 57), dau of Sir Rowland Johnson, of Gray's Inn, and *d* 17 May 1701, having had, with other issue:

1 **Sir Swinnerton Dyer, 3rd Bt**; *bapt* 15 Feb 1687/8; *m* 1st 16 Sept 1712 Anne (*d* 21 Aug 1714), 4th dau of Edward Belitha, of Kingston-on-Thames, Surrey, and had issue:

(1) Anne; *m* 1735 Paul Whitehead (*d* 20 Dec 1774 aged 64) and *d* 1768

1 (cont.) **Sir Swinnerton** *m* 2nd (by licence 21 Dec 1727) Mary, sis and coheir of John Kempe, of Spains Hall, Essex, and *dspm bur* 14 March 1735/6

2 **Sir John Swinnerton Dyer, 4th Bt**; *b c* 1692; *bur* 12 Feb 1754

3 William; *bapt* 24 Nov 1693; *m* 1st 31 Aug 1731 Catherine (*dsp bur* 28 Dec 1732), sis and coheir of John Kempe, of Spains Hall, Essex; *m* 2nd Susannah Bowles, who survived him, and was *bur* 16 Aug 1741, having by her had issue:

(1) Swinnerton; *bapt* 10 Dec 1741; *d* before 1754

4 THOMAS (Sir), **5th Bt**

The 4th Bt's bro,

Sir Thomas Dyer, 5th Bt; *bapt* 12 March 1695; *m* 2nd 25 Sept 1735 Elizabeth (*d* 1777), dau of Maj — Jones, and *d* 4 Oct 1780, having had, with other issue:

1 **Sir John Swinnerton Dyer, 6th Bt**; Col, Groom Bedchamber to THE PRINCE OF WALES; *bapt* 30 Nov 1738; *m* 9 Dec 1761 Susannah (*bur* 7 April 1773), dau of Henry Vicary, of Windsor, and *d* 21 March 1801, having had, with three daus:

(1) **Sir Thomas Richard Swinnerton Dyer, 7th Bt**; *b* 5 Feb 1768; Lt-Gen; *m* 14 April 1814 Elizabeth (*m* 2nd 30 May 1839 Frederick, Baron von Zandt (*d* 5 March 1842), Chamberlain to the King of Bavaria, of Seehof Castle, Bamburg, Bavaria, and *d* 27 May 1864), only dau and heir of James Standerwicke, of Ovington House, Hants, and *dsp* 12 April 1838

2 Thomas; *bapt* 14 July 1744; *m* 1st 20 Nov 1768 Mary (*d* Aug 1775), widow of William Berney, of Barbados, and dau of Richard Smith, of Islington (*see* SMITH-GORDON, Bt), and had issue:

(1) Richard Swinnerton; *b* 17 Oct 1769; *d* unm *bur* 24 Dec 1794

(2) **Sir Thomas Swinnerton Dyer, 8th Bt**; Capt RN; *b* 6 Oct 1770; *m* 11 April 1814 Mary (*d* 1855), dau of John Davis, and *dspm* 27 March 1854, having had, with other issue:

1a Matilda; *m* 31 Jan 1857 E R Davy, of Pilton

(3) John (Sir), KCB, Maj-Gen RA; *b* 5 Feb 1772; *m* 14 March 1795 Jane (*d* 11 March 1851), dau and heir of Simon Halliday, of Westcombe Park, Kent, and Brompton Hall, Middx, and was *k* 2 July 1816, having had, with other issue:

1a THOMAS (Sir), **9th Bt**

(4) Edward; *b* 20 July 1774; *m* 10 Oct 1801 Jane (*d* 1 April 1861), dau of James Hewett, and *d* 6 March 1816, leaving issue:

1a Edward, Capt Madras Army; *b* 5 Dec 1802; *m* 5 Feb 1824 Penelope Jane (*d* 1 June 1884), dau of Col John North Boydell, and *d* 29 April 1886, having had, with other issue:

1b Archibald Thomas Bergman; *b* 4 Dec 1838; *m* 8 March 1863 Mary Anne, dau of John Clark, and *d* 22 Dec 1914, having had, with other issue:

1c William Frederick; *b* 1864; *d* 1887, leaving issue:

1d A dau; *b* posthumously

2c Herbert Edward; *b* 1869; *m* 1901 Mildred Baldwin (*dsp* 1904)

3c Archibald; *b* 1874; *m* 1906 Louisa, dau of James Parsons, of Lyndhurst, Heaton Mersey

1c Mary Ellen

2c Elsie Lydia

2b Thomas Richard; *b* 16 June 1842; *m* 13 Oct 1897 his cousin Kate Constance Swinnerton (*d* 3 Aug 1945), dau of Frederick Swinnerton Dyer (*see* below), and *d* 26 Dec 1916, having had issue:

1c Frederick Thomas Swinnerton, MRST, served WW I as Lt Royal Hampshire Regt, and WW II as Maj RIAOC; *b* 15 Dec 1898; *educ* Haileybury and Gonville and Caius Coll Cambridge (BA 1922, MA 1946); *m* 26 April 1927 Beatrice Henrietta (*d* 1978), dau of Charles John Davies, and *d* 1982, leaving issue:

1d +John Frederick [John Dyer Esq, Holdens, Shipton Green, W Sussex PO20 7BZ]; *b* 13 Jan 1928; F/Lt RAFR 1946–53, Sr Trg Capt BA (ret; *m* 5 Aug 1950 Linda Mary (*d* 1996), dau of Thomas Rees James, and has issue:

1e +Martin John Swinnerton [Dr Martin Dyer, 36 Effingham Rd, Reigate, Surrey RH2 7JN]; *b* 8 Oct 1955; *educ* Worcester Coll

Oxford (MA, DPhil) and King's Coll Cambridge (MB, BChir), MRCP, Mere's Student St John's Coll Cambridge 1987–90; *m* 1982 *Sally Ann, dau of John Woodward, of Torquay, and has issue:

1f +Samuel John Swinnerton; *b* 1987

1f *Rebecca Ann Swinnerton; *b* 1984

2e +Richard Kenneth Swinnerton; *b* 9 July 1960; *educ* Hadlow Coll; *m* 1991 *Mary Finlay, dau of Timothy William Palmer, of Sevenoaks

2d +Julian Swinnerton [Julian Dyer Esq, The Mews, Rystwood, Forest Row, East Sussex]; *b* 1 May 1936; late P/O RAF, Co Sec Vickers Gp, Assist Sec Vickers Ltd, 1973–94; *m* 10 June 1961 *Patricia Newman and has:

1e +Jeremy Swinnerton; *b* 1964; *educ* Sheffield Hallam U (BA Hons)

1e *Ann-Louise; *b* 1966

1d *Jean Anne [Mrs Alexander Gransden, 23 Mavis Close, Ewell, Surrey]; *b* 26 Jan 1931; *m* 26 April 1952 Alexander William Gransden (*d* 1996) and has:

1e *Jonathan Kim; *b* 2 May 1953; *m* 1980 *Janice Ruth, dau of William Smith, of Beddington, Surrey

1e *Joanna Debra; *b* 23 April 1957; *m* 1992 *Christopher James Barker, s of G R Barker, of Ewell, and has:

1f *Clive Anthony; *b* 1995

1f *Sarah May; *b* 1994

2c Douglas John Swinnerton; *b* 11 Feb 1901

3c Hugh Swinnerton, JP, served WW II (1st Roy Berks Regt 1904–42, and RE 1942–45); *b* 6 March 1902; *educ* Hailbeybury and Reading U; *m* 1933 *Barbara Eileen Homewood, and *d* 1981, leaving issue:

1d +David Swinnerton; *b* 28 Sept 1934; Dept of Attorney-General, Prov Govt of BC; *m* 1971 *Beverley, dau of Robert W Steep

2d +Patrick Swinnerton [Patrick Dyer Esq, The Rookery, Benington Park, nr Stevenage, Herts]; *b* 3 March 1937; *educ* Haileybury; Assist Master Heathmount Sch, Hertford; *m* 1st 28 Aug 1960 (*divorce* 1970) Elizabeth Rule, yst dau of Air Marshal Sir Thomas Arthur Warne-Browne, KBE, CB, DSC, of Martins, Chilbolton, Stockbridge, Hants, and has issue:

1e *Thalia Elizabeth Swinnerton; *b* 6 Dec 1961

2e *Lucinda Jane Swinnerton; *b* 1 March 1963

3e *Susannah Swinnerton [Mrs Stuart Rand-Bell, Otta Leys, Murcott, Oxon OX5 2RE]; *b* 14 June 1966; *m* 1991 *Stuart D Rand-Bell, er s of John Sydney Bell, of The Manor House, Overthorpe, Oxon

4c Gordon Swinnerton, 2nd Lt RASC WW II (invalid); *b* 2 March 1907

1c *Ruth Penelope Swinnerton [Miss Ruth Dyer, Sunny Corner Kennels, Little Clacton, Essex]; *b* 25 Oct 1903

3b Frederick Campbell Spencer; *b* 25 Aug 1845; *m* 7 March 1867 Ellen (*d* 25 Feb 1908), 4th dau of Charles Weavings, of Salisbury, and *d* 3 Nov 1925, leaving issue:

1c Campbell Charles Frederick; *b* 29 Dec 1871; *m* 2 April 1902 Eleanor Augusta Louise (*d* 2 Sept 1935), dau of Samuel Bignell, of Andover, Hants, and had issue:

1d *Gweneth Mary Bignell [Mrs Charles Davine, 17 Bowen St, Warragul, Melbourne, Australia]; *b* 29 Aug 1905; *m* 1927 Charles Milo Davine, barrister, and has issue

2c Thomas Henry; *b* 11 July 1878; *m* 1904 Kate (*d* 25 Dec 1952), dau of John Willis, and *d* 24 Sept 1937, leaving issue:

1d John Arnold Swinnerton, WW II as Sgt RA; *b* 24 Jan 1905; *m* 1st 31 May 1930 Theresa Sylvester Stannard (*d* 23 July 1944), painter RA, dau of Henry Sylvester Stannard, RBA, RSA, and had issue:

1e +Thomas John Swinnerton; *b* 11 June 1931

1d John Dyer *m* 2nd 23 June 1949 *Elizabeth Mahala, dau of Edward Valentine Johnson, and *d* 1971, leaving further issue:

2e +Philip John; *b* 29 June 1953

1e *Linda Theresa; *b* 27 Jan 1950

1d *Nellie Kathleen [Mrs Francis Coyle, 141 Healdsburg Ave 13, Cloverdale, Calif 95425, USA]; *b* 31 Sept 1906; proprietor Nell Dyer's Hat Shop, William St, Dublin, to 1959, when emigrated to US, private and gen hosp nurse (ret); *m* 1957 Francis Coyle (*d* 1982), of Blackrock, Co Dublin

2d *Patricia [Mrs John Mackenzie, 2 Greenville Rd, Stradbrook, Blackrock, Dublin, Ireland]; *b* 31 Oct 1912; *m* 1 Nov 1940 *John Eric Mackenzie, late Royal Fus, attd E Africa Intelligence Corps, s of Alexander Mackenzie, of Bray, Co Wicklow, and has issue:

1e *Alan Donald; *b* 28 July 1946

1e *Jean Valerie; *b* 22 June 1950

3c Frank Stanley; *b* 15 Oct 1880; *m* 1910 Ellen Knight, and *d* 16 Feb 1961, leaving issue:

1d Benjamin Stanley; *b* 25 Feb 1914; *m* 11 Oct 1937 *Lillian Averina, dau of C H Gillan, and *d* 1993, leaving:

1e *Althea Dawn [Mrs Allen Millan, 939 Florimond St, Richmond, BC, Canada]; *b* 16 July 1938; *m* 1956 *Allen Francis Millan, and has issue:

1f *Montgomery Allan; *b* 1956

2f *Andrew Brian; *b* 1961

1f *Cynthia Dawn-Marie; *b* 1958

1d (cont.) Benjamin Dyer also adopted June 1951:

*Michael Edward Swinnerton; *b* 16 Jan 1948

2d +Frederick Douglas [Frederick Dyer Esq, 5287 Parker Ave, Cordova Bay, Victoria, BC, Canada]; *b* 24 April 1916; *m* 21 July 1941 *Myrtle Winifred Foster, and has issue:

1e *Barbara Louise [Mrs Barbara McDonell, R 1926 Crescent Rd, Victoria, BC, Canada]; *b* 16 Oct 1942; *m* Sept 1965 (*divorce* 1966) Derry Allan McDonell

2e *Carol Ann [Mrs Ronald Robb, Mount Gardner Rd, General Delivery, Bowen Island, BC, Canada]; *b* 21 April 1947; *m* 1967 *Ronald Douglas Robb

3e *Nancy May; *b* 4 March 1957

4c Benjamin Archibald, with HAC WW I (wounded); *b* 26 Nov 1882; *m* 14 July 1908 Mabel Maude, dau of William Moore, and has issue:

1d Benjamin Frederick Swinnerton, Maj RIASC, Mounted Palestine Police 1933–38; *b* 20 March 1910; *educ* Brighton Coll; *m* 4 May 1945 *Betty, dau of William Francis Smithies, of Worthing

1c Amelia Mary; *b* 7 May 1868; *m* 25 Feb 1895 Arnold William Clark (*d* 18 Aug 1931), of Andover, Hants, and *d* 29 Dec 1954, leaving issue

2c Ada; *b* 18 March 1870; *d* 13 Nov 1917

3c Nellie Penelope May; *b* 13 Dec 1873

4c Jennie Elizabeth; *b* 15 Jan 1876

2a Charles; *b* 15 Oct 1805; *m* 22 Sept 1829 Anna, dau of John Scott, and *dspm* 25 Jan 1844

3a John; *b* 2 Nov 1810; *m* 1st 30 Nov 1839 Eliza (*d* 5 Nov 1847), widow of — Bulmer, and had issue:

1b Frederick Swinnerton; *b* 2 May 1843; *m* 27 April 1876 Constance Josephine Minna, dau of Joseph Mackintosh Gordon, of Jamaica, and *d* 1896, leaving issue:

1c Kate Constance Swinnerton; *m* 13 Oct 1897 her cousin, Thomas Richard Dyer (*d* 26 Dec 1916) (*see above*), and *d* 3 Aug 1945, leaving issue

3a (cont.) John Dyer *m* 2nd 15 Oct 1851 Martha Elizabeth, dau of Charles White, and *d* 27 Aug 1855, having by her had, with other issue:

1b Nina Eliza Swinnerton; *m* 11 Sept 1872 Lt-Col William Poyntz Blandy, RA, and had issue

2b Annie Marguerite Swinnerton; *m* 15 July 1875 William Simonet, and had issue

1a Eleanor; *m* 3 June 1839 D C Hewitt, and *d* 19 Feb 1849, leaving issue

2a Frances; *b* 1814; *d* unm 2 June 1897

(1) Maria Elizabeth Charlotte; *m* 1805 Philip Neile, and *d* Nov 1805

2 (cont.) Thomas Dyer *m* 2nd 9 Nov 1779 Maria Letalia (*d* 1 Dec 1840), dau of Col Archibald Grant, of Manchester Sq and Pittencrieff, and was *bur* 16 Aug 1800, having by her had further issue

The 8th Bt's nephew,

Sir Thomas Swinnerton Dyer, 9th Bt, of Brompton Hall, Middx, and Westcroft Park, Chobham, Surrey, Capt RA, JP Surrey; *b* 10 Dec 1799; *m* 7 Feb 1832 Mary Anne (*d* 9 Feb 1880), dau of Col John Albeck Clement, RA, and *d* 2 Oct 1878, having had, with three daus:

1 **Sir Swinnerton Halliday Dyer, 10th Bt**, of Westcroft Park, Chobham, Surrey, Capt 8th Foot, served Crimea (medal and clasp, Order of the Medjidie); *b* 4 June 1833; *m* 29 July 1858 Helen Maria (*d* 12 Aug 1915), est dau of Rev Robert Croker, Rector of Athlacca, Co Limerick, and sis and coheir of Edward Croker, DL, JP, of The Grange, Co Limerick, and *d* 16 March 1882, leaving:

(1) **Sir Thomas Swinnerton Dyer, 11th Bt**; *b* 3 Oct 1859; *m* 21 Jan 1886 Dona Edith (*d* 3 Feb 1909), yst dau of Sir Charles Roderick McGrigor, 2nd Bt (*qv*), and *d* 23 Aug 1907, having had issue:

1a **Sir John Swinnerton Dyer, 12th Bt**, MC; Capt Scots Gds, Staff Capt 1916, DAQMG, Gds Division 1917, WW I (wounded, despatches); *b* 27 May 1891; *m* 21 Dec 1912 Maude (*m* 2nd 1 June 1928 Louis Collier and *d* 11 April 1938), dau of W H Turner, of Western Australia, and was *ka* 31 July 1917, leaving:

1b **Sir John Lodovick Swinnerton Dyer, 13th Bt**; *b* 20 Jan 1914; *d* unm 2 Aug 1940

1b *Jacqueline Christine Swinnerton [Mrs Vincent Paravicini, Nutley Manor, Basingstoke, Hants RG25 2HL], Section Offr WAAF; *b* posthumously 28 Jan 1918; *m* 1st 1943 (*divorce* 1949) Colin E C Campbell and has issue; *m* 2nd 7 May 1949 Col Vincent R Paravicini (*d* 1989), TD, only son of Charles Rudolf Paravicini, Swiss Minister London 1920–40, and has further issue

1a Dona Eva Swinnerton; *m* 19 July 1917 Capt Sir Richard Cameron Gull, 3rd Bt (*qv*), Rifle Bde, and *d* 19 Nov 1973, leaving issue

2a Helen Elizabeth Swinnerton; *m* 1st 5 May 1915 Capt Hon Ronald Ian Macdonald (*das* 17 Oct 1918), Cameron Highrs, yst s of 6th Baron Macdonald (*qv*); *m* 2nd 20 Jan 1932 Maj-Gen Charles John Wallace (*das* 20 Dec 1943), CB, DSO, OBE, MC, Highland LI, 3rd s of Lt-Col Hugh Robert Wallace, DSO, and *d* 30 April 1966

(1) Eva Helen Swinnerton; *b* 5 Oct 1860; *d* unm 20 Oct 1886

(2) Kathleen Maria Swinnerton, V-Pres League of Mercy; *b* 19 Sept 1862; *m* 11 Sept 1889 Richard Henry Gosling (*d* 4 Aug 1930), of Hawthorn Hill, Bracknell, Berks, and *d* 10 June 1948, leaving issue

2 Henry Clement Swinnerton, of Westhope, Craven Arms, Salop; Col RA, served Crimea (medal and clasp, Turkish Medal), India (medal with two clasps), Kt Cdr Crown of Italy, Charles VII of Spain, Rose of Brazil, Order Merit Spain; *b* 30 Dec 1834; *m* 6 April 1869 Amelia Susan (*d* 3 Jan 1903), only dau and heir of John Ward, of Otterington Hall, Hants, by Henrietta, 3rd dau of Sir John Lister-Kaye, 1st Bt (*qv*), and *d* 21 March 1898, leaving:

(1) LEONARD WHITWORTH SWINNERTON (Sir), **14th Bt**

(1) Evelyn Henrietta; *m* 16 Dec 1889 Col George Blake Napier Martin (*d* 20 Jan 1917), CB, RA, and *d* 12 Dec 1921

3 Frederick Carr Swinnerton, Capt 17th and 75th Regt and Hon Maj, served in the Crimea (medal and clasp and Medjidie); *b* 6 March 1837; *m* 1st 6 March 1861 Selenah Maria Ann (*d* 9 Nov 1867), 3rd dau of Rev Edward Windsor Richards, Rector St Andrew's, Glam, and had issue

(1) Frederick Stewart Hotham DYER later DYER-BENNET (1894); *b* Dec 1862; *m* 1885 Adelaide (*d* 1942), dau of George Taylor, and *d* 24 Dec 1923, leaving issue:

1a Richard Stewart, Maj Leicester Regt WW I (wounded twice); *b* 6 Oct 1886; *m* 1st 17 Feb 1912 (*divorce* 1955) Miriam Wolcott (*d* 1973), dau of Prof Edward Bull Clapp, of Berkeley, California, and had issue:

1b Richard; *b* 6 Oct 1913; folk singer; *m* 1st 1936 (*divorce* 1941) Elizabeth Hoar Pepper and had issue:

1c *Ellen Wood [Miss Ellen Dyer-Bennet, 7921 Millvale Rd, Chesterfield, VA 23832, USA]; *b* 1937

2c *Eunice [Mrs Hilary Davis, 11030 SW 42 Court, Davie, FL 33328, USA]; *b* 1939; *m* 1962 *Hilary Roche Davis, and has issue:

1d *Robert Hilary; *b* 1967

2d *Lance Bradshaw; *b* 1971

1d *Mary Ellen; *b* 1965; *m* — *Scott Vincent Smith

1b (cont.) Richard Dyer-Bennet *m* 2nd 1942 *Melvene Ipcar [Mrs Richard Dyer-Bennet, Star Route 62 Box 29, Great Barrington, MA 01230, USA], and *d* 1991, leaving further issue:

3c *Bonnie; *b* 1943

4c *Brooke; *b* 1946

2b +John [Prof John Dyer-Bennet, 907 Winona St, Northfield, Minn 55057, USA]; *b* 17 April 1915; Emeritus Prof of Mathematics Carleton Coll, Northfield, Minn.; *m* 1951 *Mary Abby, dau of George B Randall, and has issue:

1c +David; *b* 1954

1c *Barbara; *b* 1965

3b Frederick; *b* 24 May 1918; architect; *m* 1941 *Patricia Esther Arndt [Mrs Frederick Dyer-Bennet, 154 Hillcroft Way, Walnut Creek, CA 94596, USA], and *d* 1991, leaving issue:

1c +Oliver [Oliver Dyer-Bennet Esq, 5847 Sharpe Rd, Calistoga, CA 94515, USA]; *b* 1945; *m* 1984 *Linda Helen Specht and has issue:

1d +Colin Wesley; *b* 1988

1d *Katherine Elise; *b* 1985

2c +John [John Dyer-Bennet, 425 42nd Ave, Oakland, CA 94609, USA]; *b* 1947

1c *Cynthia [Mrs David Peoples, 634 King St, Santa Rosa, CA 95404, USA]; *b* 1949; *m* 1983 *David Karl Peoples

4b Christopher; *b* 1920; *m* 1st 1945 Peggy Friedman and had issue:

1c +Christopher; *b* 1946

2c +Matthew; *b* 1948

1c *Anne; *b* 1952

4b Christopher Dyer-Bennet *m* 2nd 1973 *Mrs Anna Louise Erben Baumhoff, and *d* 1985

1b *Miriam [Mrs Kenneth May, 10 Ross St, Toronto, Ont M5T 1Z9, Canada]; *b* 1922; *m* 1st 1945 (*divorce* 1962) Thomas Timothy Crocker, and has issue:

1c *Steven; *b* 1949

2c *Thomas; *b* 1952

3c *Cedric; *b* 1954

1c *Edith; *b* 1947

1b (cont.) Mrs Miriam Crocker *m* 2nd 1963 Kenneth O May (*d* 1977)

3 (cont.) Capt Frederick Dyer *m* 2nd 19 Nov 1868 Frances Margaret (*d* 1920), only child of Sir William Ogle Carr, Ch Justice of Ceylon, and *d* 12 Nov 1896

4 Stewart John, of Westcroft Park, Chobham, Surrey, Capt 3rd Buffs; *b* 10 March 1842; *m* 10 July 1873 Emily Mary Elizabeth (*d* 21 Dec 1912), only child and heir of Henry Edmund Bythesea, of Nettleton, Wilts, and *d* 21 Nov 1925, leaving issue:

(1) Stewart Barton Bythesea, DSO, Maj 3rd Bn Wilts Regt, Capt 2nd Life Gds, GSO 1914–16, Hon Attaché Madrid 1916, served with Kaduna, Bornu, Kano-Sokoto, and with Dukkakerri Expdns; *b* 26 Nov 1875; *m* 11 June 1906 Mai (*m* 2nd 1921 Baron A Pontenani (*d* 1937) and *d* 1969), only child of Capt S L Osborne, RN, of The Hermitage, Shanklin, IoW, and *d* 26 Jan 1917, leaving issue:

1a +Thomas Musgrave Swinnerton [Thomas Dyer Esq, 6 The Gardens, East Pennard, Shepton Mallet, Somerset]; WW II as Lt The Buffs ; *b* 5 July 1907; *educ* Oratory Sch, RMC Sandhurst and St Catharine's Coll Cambridge (BA 1934); *m* 1st 6 Oct 1936 (*divorce* 1948) Violet Elizabeth, dau of Ebenezer Cunningham, Roy Norfolk Regt; *m* 2nd 2 Sept 1948 *Renee Marie Davies and by her has issue:

1b *Georgina Musgrave Swinnerton; *b* 6 Dec 1950

(1) Mabel Charlotte; *b* 18 May 1874

(2) Florence Emily Mary Bythesea; *b* 3 Dec 1879; *d* unm 1 May 1933

The 13th Bt's cousin,

Sir Leonard Whitworth Swinnerton Dyer, 14th Bt; Sub-Lt RNVR WW I 1914–15; *b* 30 Oct 1875; *m* 12 June 1897 Lucy (*d* 4 Aug 1948), est dau of Hon Francis Schroeder, of New York, and *d* 19 Aug 1947, leaving:

Sir Leonard Schroeder Swinnerton Dyer, 15th Bt; Chm Salop CC 1969–75; *educ* Repton; Lt RFA WW I 1916–18, pres Br Chess Fedn 1956–58; *b* 30 March 1898; *m* 16 June 1925 Barbara, JP (Salop 1946; *d* 1990), only dau of Hereward Brackenbury, CBE, of Seaton Burn House, Northumberland, and *d* 10 June 1975, leaving issue:

1 Sir (HENRY) PETER FRANCIS SWINNERTON DYER, **16th and present Bt**

1 *Anne Winifred Swinnerton; *b* 17 Dec 1932

DYKE

Arms: Or three cinquefoils sable. **Crest:** A cubit arm in armour, the hand in a gauntlet sable, garnished or, holding a cinquefoil slipped, also sable. **Motto:** *Prest à faire* ('Ready to act'). **Creation:** Bt. (E) 3 March 1676/7.

SIR DAVID WILLIAM HART DYKE, 10TH BT, of Horsham, Sussex [Sir David Dyke Bt, 28 King St West, Apt 14B, Stoney Creek, Ont L8G 1H4, Canada]; *b* 5 Jan 1955; *s* f 1987; *educ* Ryerson Polytechnical Inst (BA)

Lineage: THOMAS DYKE, of Cranbrook, Kent; *m* Joane (*d* 1 Jan 1632), dau of Thomas Walsh, of Horsham, Sussex, and *d* 6 April 1632, having had, with two er s and four daus:

Sir THOMAS DYKE, of Horsham; *m* 7 Aug 1639 Catherine (*d* 28 May 1695), dau of Sir John Bramston, of Skreens, Essex, Ld Ch Justice King's Bench, and *d* 13 Dec 1669, having had, with an est s, a yst s and nine daus:

Sir Thomas Dyke, 1st Bt (E), so *cr* 3 March 1676/7; MP Sussex 1685–87 and E Grinstead 1689–98, Commr Public Accounts 1696; *m* 1695 Philadelphia, est dau and coheir of Sir Thomas Nutt, of Mays, Sussex, and *d* 31 Oct 1706, leaving issue:

1 THOMAS (Sir), **2nd Bt**

1 Philadelphia; *m* Rev Lewis Stephens, DD, Canon Residentiary of York

2 Elizabeth; *m* John Cockman, MD, and *d* Sept 1739, leaving issue

The only surv son,

Sir Thomas Dyke, 2nd Bt, of Horsham, later Lullingstone Castle, Kent; MA, DCL Oxford; *m* 23 May 1728 Anne (*d* 24 Nov 1763), widow of John Bluet, of Holcombe Regis, Devon, and dau and heir of Percyvall Hart, of Lullingstone Castle, descended from Sir John Peche, who bought Lullingstone 1361, and *d* 20 Aug 1756; his 3rd but only surv s:

Sir John Dixon Dyke, 3rd Bt; *b* 23 Nov 1732; *m* 3 May 1756 Philadelphia Payne (*d* 31 Jan 1781), dau of George Horne, of E Grinstead, and *d* 6 Sept 1810, having had, with three daus:

1 **Sir Thomas Dyke, 4th Bt**, High Sheriff Kent 1821, Col W Kent Militia; *b* 29 Dec 1763; *d* unm 22 Nov 1831

2 PERCIVAL HART (Sir), **5th Bt**

3 George Hart, Lt-Col Gds; *m* 22 April 1802 Louisa (*d* 8 Nov 1839), 3rd dau of Sir William Lemon, Bt, and *d* 6 Nov 1843, having had issue:

(1) Louisa Anne; *d* 28 May 1861

(2) Caroline Anne; *m* 15 Aug 1838 Richard Taylor, 2nd s of John Taylor, of Coed Du, and *d* 20 Aug 1913

The 4th Bt's bro,

Sir Percival Hart Dyke, 5th Bt, BA Oxon; *b* 27 Dec 1767; *m* 26 July 1798 Anne (*d* 27 Dec 1847), est dau of Robert Jenner, of Wenvoe Castle, Glam, and Chislehurst, Kent, and had, with other issue:

1 PERCYVALL HART (Sir), **6th Bt**

2 Thomas Hart (Rev), Rector of Long Newton, Co Durham, and Lullingstone; *b* 11 Dec 1801; *m* 4 Feb 1833 Elizabeth (*d* 6 Oct 1893 aged 92), 2nd dau of Thomas Fairfax, of Newton Kyme, and *d* 25 June 1866, having had:

(1) Thomas, of Beaumaris, Clifton, Bristol, MICE, JP; *b* 1 April 1834; *m* 26 Feb 1863 Georgina Isabella Russell (*d* 29 Jan 1933), yst dau of Robert Edward Fullerton, of Shuthonger Manor, nr Tewkesbury, and *d* 6 Aug 1906, leaving issue:

1a Percyvall Hart, DSO (1918), Col IA, served Uganda 1897–98 (despatches, medal, two clasps), NW Frontier India (despatches, medal with clasp), E Africa 1908–10 (medal with clasp), WW I (despatches, brevet) and Waziristan 1921–24 (clasp to Frontier medal), Order St Stanislas Russia 3rd Cl with swords; *b* 24 Aug 1872; *m* 10 Oct 1900 Louisa Catherine (*d* 22 Feb 1961), yst dau of Adml John Halliday Cave, CB, and *d* 14 Jan 1952, leaving:

1b Trevor Hart, DSO (1944), DL (Derbys 1981); *b* 19 Feb 1905; *educ* Marlborough; Brig Queen's Royal Regt WW II France and Burma; *m* 1st 19 April 1933 (*divorce* 1965) Eileen Joyce, er dau of John Herbert Niblock-Stuart, of Nairobi, and *d* 3 June 1995, leaving:

1c +Terence Percyvall Hart [Terence Dyke Esq, c/o Cavalry and Guards Club, 127 Piccadilly, London W1V 0PX]; Capt Roy Dragoons, dir John Hoskyns & Co; *b* 19 July 1934; *educ* Marlborough and RMA Sandhurst; *m* 4 April 1964 *Wanda Krystyna Hermione, only dau of Lt-Col Joseph Mostyn (*see* MOSTYN, Bt) and has:

1d +Paul Percyvall Hart; *b* 4 Jan 1965

2d +James Terence; *b* 8 Nov 1966

1c *Jennifer Hart; *b* 26 Aug 1939; *m* 12 Aug 1967 (*divorce* 1979) Lt Oliver Nicholas Vaudrey, RN (ret), 2nd s of John Randle Vaudrey, MBE, of Buckland Court, Buckland, Betchworth, Surrey, and has issue:

1d *David Clough Percyvall; *b* 4 April 1969

1d *Annabel; *b* 1972

1b (cont.) Trevor Dyke *m* 2nd 7 Aug 1965 *Mary Eliot, widow of Maj D E Lockwood, and dau of J A Roberts, of Brook Dean, Hope, Derbyshire

2b Eric Hart (Rev); *b* 28 July 1906; Rector Cowden Kent 1953–63, Cdr RN WW II (despatches twice), Deacon 1952, Priest 1953; *m* 7 Aug 1935 *Mary, only dau of Maj Robert Alexander (*see* SHAW-STEWART, Bt) and *d* 1 Nov 1971, having had:

1c +David Hart, CBE (Mil 1990), LVO (1980) [David Dyke Esq CBE LVO, Hambledon House, Hambledon, Hants PO7 4RU]; *b* 3 Oct 1938; *educ* St Lawrence Coll Ramsgate and Britannia RNC; Capt RN, ADC to HM THE QUEEN 1988–89, *m* 8 July 1967 *Diana Margaret, dau of Sir William Henry Tucker Luce, GBE, KCMG, and has:

1d *Miranda Katharine; *b* 14 Dec 1972

2d *Alice Louisa; *b* 12 Sept 1975

2c Robert Hart; *b* 3 Oct 1938; *educ* Haileybury and Selwyn Coll Cambridge; *d* in a car crash 1 Nov 1963

1c *Jane Hart [Mrs David Holland, Little Tye, Upper Hartfield, E Sussex TN7 4DX]; *b* 7 May 1936; *m* 3 Oct 1959 *David Charles Holland, ERD, and has issue:

1d *Charles Thurstan; *b* 30 Aug 1962; *m* 1987 *Rachael Margaret McCabe and has:

1e *Richard Oliver; *b* 1994

2e *Robert David; *b* 19 Oct 1996

1e *Catherine Jane; *b* 1992

1d *Caroline Mary; *b* 23 Aug 1960; *m* 1983 *Dr Stephen Cox and has:

1e *James Robert; *b* 1986

2e *Jonathan Richard Andrew; *b* 1992

3e *Rachel Elizabeth; *b* 1988

2d *Clare Lucinda; *b* 22 March 1966; *m* 26 Oct 1996 *David Jonathan Frances

2c *Sarah Alexander Hart; *b* 20 Jan 1946; *m* 1974 her cousin *(Oliver) Guy Hart Dyke (*see below*)

1b *Cicely Hart [Mrs John Dugmore, Storrs Hill, Windermere, Cumbria]; *b* 20 Dec 1907; *m* 24 April 1936 Lt-Col John William Radclyffe Dugmore (*d* 1992), KOYLI, son of Maj Arthur Radclyffe Dugmore, of Bournemouth, Hants, and has issue:

1c *William Radclyffe; *b* 18 Feb 1940; *educ* The Abbey Sch, Fort Augustus; *m* 1974 *Patricia Elizabeth, 2nd dau of F B Jarvis, of Hen Ard, Morya Bychan, Gwynedd, and has:

1d *Amy Tamsyn Elizabeth; *b* 1976

2d *Polly Louise; *b* 1978

3d *Daisy Catherine; *b* 1983

1c *Janet Elvyn Catherine [Mrs John Merrett, Bank End, Plumgarth, Kendal, Westmorland]; *b* 9 Jan 1938; *m* 27 June 1964 *John Peter Merrett, s of Rev Percival Cresswell Merrett, and has issue:

1d *Peter William; *b* 14 June 1965

1d *Sophie Catherine; *b* 23 Sept 1966

2d *Nicola Mary; *b* 1971

2a Thomas; *d* an infant

1a Ethel Frances; *d* unm 10 Jan 1955, aged 87

2a Winifred Evelyn; *d* unm 2 Jan 1911

3a Theophania Louisa; *d* unm 22 Feb 1921

4a Constance Maud; *d* an infant

(2) Percival Hart (Rev), Hon Canon of Salisbury; *b* 1 June 1835; *m* 12 Jan 1864 Margaret Isabella (*d* 10 April 1909), 4th dau of Robert J Peel, of Burton-on-Trent, and *d* 14 Dec 1910, leaving issue:

1a Robert Percyvall Hart; *b* 3 Nov 1864; *m* 30 Sept 1908 Mary Harriette Theodora (*d* 1974), dau of Rev Canon John Shephard, Vicar of Eton, and *d* 22 Nov 1954, leaving issue:

1b +Michael Percyvall Hart [Major Michael Dyke, 10 Goldney Ave, Clifton, Bristol BS8 4RA]; *b* 10 Sept 1909; *educ* Marlborough; Maj RASC Middle East 1940–45; *m* 4 June 1955 *Jean (*d* 1992), dau of Rupert MacGlashan, and has issue:

1c +Timothy Percyvall Hart; *b* 10 Jan 1959; *m* 1992 *Kate, only dau of C H G Proctor, of Teignmouth, Devon

2c +Jeremy Percyvall Hart; *b* 26 May 1963

1c *Jennifer Mary Hart; *b* 10 July 1956; *m* 1984 *Stephen Jeffrey Peacock, and has issue:

1d *Thomas Michael; *b* 1990

1d *Alice Felicity; *b* 1987

1a Mabel Louisa; *b* 20 March 1866; *m* 11 Feb 1892 Harold Gordon (*d* 18 May 1911), of Meddecombra, Ceylon, son of Charles William Gordon, of Wincombe Park, Wilts, and *d* 6 Jan 1960

2a Maud Cecilia; *m* 16 April 1891 Rev Walter Basil Broughton, MA, Vicar Brackley, Northants

(3) Francis Hart; *b* 1838; *m* 27 Aug 1887 Louisa, 2nd dau of J Turner, of Holgate, York, and *dsp* 27 Dec 1887

(1) Theophania Anne; *d* unm

3 John Dixon, Lt-Col HEIC; *b* 6 Jan 1803; *m* 10 Feb 1836 Millicent (*d* 5 Aug 1901), yst dau of Isaac Minet, of Baldwins, Kent, and *d* 1 Aug 1885, leaving, with other issue:

(1) John Dixon (Rev), RD Camberwell, Vicar St James's Camberwell 1870–1913; *b* 31 Oct 1836; *d* 15 Dec 1933

(2) Edward Hart, Col RA; *b* 11 Nov 1837; *m* 23 March 1893 Elizabeth Grace (*d* 14 May 1936), dau of Col Thomas Stannard MacAdam, of Blackwater, Co Clare, and *d* 17 March 1930, having had issue:

1a Francis Hart, 2nd Lt W Kent Regt; *b* 25 Jan 1898; *ka* 27 Sept 1917

2a Edward Hart; *b* 24 Oct 1899; *educ* Queens' Coll Cambridge (MA); *d* unm 8 April 1964

3a Charles Hart; *b* 27 May 1901; *m* 25 Oct 1958 *Kathleen Edith, dau of — Gregory, of Southampton

4a Percyvall Hart; *b* 15 Dec 1902; *m* 23 May 1931 Helen Leonora (*d* 1985), yr dau of Philip MacAdam, JP, Colonial Med Serv Br Guiana, and *d* 1982, leaving issue:

1b +Michael Percyvall Hart [Michael Dyke Esq, 37 St John's Rd, Farnham, Surrey]; *b* 3 May 1932

2b +Patrick Alan Hart [Patrick Dyke Esq, 48 Abbots Ride, Farnham, Surrey]; *b* 6 April 1938; *m* 1969 *Elzbieta Izabella, of dau of Eugeniusz Lotocki, Warsaw, and has issue:

1c +James Paul; *b* 1972

2c +Stephen Peter; *b* 1975

1a Millicent Grace; *d* unm 22 July 1974 aged 77

(3) Frederick Hotham, Lt-Col 69th Rgt, Prof Mil Studies Cambridge 1904–12, psc; *b* 6 Feb 1840; *m* 20 April 1871 Emily (*d* 17 April 1941), dau of Rev Charles Faunce Thorndike, and *d* 16 Aug 1934, leaving issue:

1a Agnese Millicent; *m* 16 Dec 1893 Richard Thomas Nicholson (*d* 26 April 1931) and *d* 6 Nov 1954, leaving issue

2a Winifred Amy; *b* 1881; *m* 8 July 1911 Cyril Arthur Mileham, slr (*d* 14 June 1958), and had issue:

1b Margaret Emmeline; *b* 29 April 1913; *m* 1st 18 May 1936 Richard Fieldsend Cartwright (*d* 11 Sept 1939), and had issue; *m* 2nd 1 Aug 1947 *Henry Robert Wildsmith and *d* 30 July 1961, leaving further issue

2b Barbara Dera; *b* 24 Aug 1918; *m* 12 Sept 1936 *Eric Adrian Milne, and has issue:

1c *Adrian Edward; *b* 3 June 1940

2c *Ian Hugh; *b* 6 April 1950

1c *Rosemary Faith; *b* 8 Nov 1941; *m* 1966 *Dr Christopher John Bretherton Hundleby, and has issue:

1d *Alison Mary; *b* 1967

(4) Augustus Hart, of Roy Mail Steam Packet Co; *b* 1843; *m* 8 July 1884 Mercy Constance Cecilia (*m* 2nd 7 Aug 1894 Ernest Homan), dau of W Anthony Hamilton Harris, and *dsp* 21 Sept 1889

(5) George Hart, Lt-Col Northumberland Fus; *b* 21 Jan 1847; *m* 26 July 1895 Edith Louise (*d* 15 Feb 1952 aged 93) yr dau of Thomas William Kinder, and *d* 30 June 1922, having had issue:

1a Edith Cecil; *d* an infant 1896

2a Helen Sandra Millicent; *b* 6 Dec 1897; *m* 6 Jan 1920 Lt-Col Esdaile Addison Burkitt Orr (*d* 1977), MC, Roy Berks Regt, and had issue:

1b *Elizabeth [Mrs William Moon, Old Timbers, Friday St, Henley-on-Thames, Oxon]; *b* 12 Oct 1923; *educ* St Mary's Wantage; *m* 12 April 1947 William Edward Penlygon Moon, BA, BA, MICE, (*d* 27 Aug 1965), and has:

1c *Sandra Anne; *b* 28 Feb 1953

(6) Henry Hart, V-Adml; *b* 26 March 1848; *m* 1st 10 Feb 1886 Louisa (*d* 1886), dau of William Covey, of Lee, Kent; *m* 2nd 3 July 1900 Mary Blanche (*d* 8 June 1905), dau of Rev Thomas Prater, and *dsp* 12 July 1912

(1) Julia; *d* unm May 1945

(2) Matilda; *d* unm 16 July 1954 aged 100 years and 11 months

4 Francis Hart, Queen's Proctor; *b* 28 Nov 1803; *m* 1 Dec 1835 Charlotte Lascelles (*d* 17 Dec 1899), yst dau of Rt Hon Sir Herbert Jenner Fust, and *d* 17 July 1876, leaving issue:

(1) Edwin Francis (Rev), Rector Mersham Kent 1896–1916, Hon Canon Canterbury 1892–1919; *b* 27 Sept 1842; *educ* Trin Hall Cambridge (MA); *m* 22 Nov 1870 Katharine Louisa (*d* 26 March 1914), dau of Sir Fredrick Currie, 1st Bt (*qv*), and *d* 26 Aug 1919

(1) Charlotte Elizabeth; *m* 9 June 1864 Hon Frederick Barnewall Best (*d* 5 Jan 1876), 2nd Bengal Fus, 2nd s of 2nd Baron Wynford (*qv*), and *d* 18 March 1865

(2) Evelyn Ellen; *d* 1944

(3) Alice Frances; *d* unm 15 July 1934

5 Peché Hart, Capt RN; *b* 21 Nov 1805; *m* 13 Jan 1853 Annette Augusta (*d* 6 Jan 1898), yst dau of Frederick Richard Coore, and *d* 27 Feb 1892

1 Harriet Jenner; *m* 11 June 1836 Rev Nicholas Fiott (*d* 1858), Vicar Edgware, and took the name LEE

2 Georgiana Frances; *m* 18 Oct 1842 William Fox, of Chester Terrace, Regent's Park, and *d* 19 Nov 1883

3 Laura; *m* 9 Feb 1847 Rev Thomas Prankerd Phelps, Hon Canon Rochester, Rector Ridley, Kent, and *d* 28 Feb 1900, leaving issue

4 Philadelphia; *m* 1st 11 May 1847 Rev James Mackenzie (*dsp* 20 Aug 1857), s of Sir George Steuart Mackenzie, 7th Bt, of Coul (*qv*); *m* 2nd 19 Oct 1858 William Knapp (*d* 1887) and *d* 27 Dec 1904

Sir PERCIVAL *d* 4 Aug 1846; his est son,

Sir Percyvall Hart Dyke, 6th Bt; *b* 9 June 1799; *m* 25 June 1835 Elizabeth (*d* 16 July 1888), yst dau of John Wells, DL, JP, MP, of Bickley Hall, Kent, and had issue:

1 Percyvall Hart, Lt Rifle Bde; *b* 18 Aug 1836; *d* unm 19 April 1855 in the Crimea

2 WILLIAM HART (Sir), **7th Bt**

3 George Augustus Hart; *b* 27 Sept 1847; *d* unm 19 Sept 1940

4 Reginald Charles Hart, Slr Duchy of Lancaster; *b* 1 May 1852; *m* 1st 22 Oct 1891 Guinevere Eva (*d* 26 Feb 1894), dau of Gen Lord Alfred Paget, CB (*see* ANGLESEY, M), and had issue:

(1) Wyndham Douglas Hart, Cdr RN; *b* 13 Aug 1892; *m* 1st Sept 1942 Margaret Reynolds (*d* 1956), dau of Arthur N Wyatt, of Hartford, Cheshire; *m* 2nd

1958 Elizabeth Creasy, dau of Christopher William Frederick Wheeler, FRIBA, of Horsham, Sussex, and *dsp* 10 June 1968

4 (cont.) Reginald Dyke *m* 2nd 10 June 1897 Millicent Ada (*d* 7 Aug 1946), dau of Robert Cooper Lee Bevan, of Trent Park, Herts, and Fosbury House, Wilts, and *d* 17 April 1943, having by her had issue:

(2) Ashley Francis Hart; *b* 16 Oct 1899; *educ* Eton; *m* 17 April 1940 *Marie, dau of Johan Voldengen, of Lier, Norway, and had issue:

1a *Margaretha Millicent; *b* 2 Nov 1946

1 Frances Julia; *m* 24 July 1877 Abel Smith (*d* 30 May 1898), MP, of Woodhall Park, Herts, and *d* 12 Feb 1925, leaving issue

2 Eleanor Laura; *d* unm 13 Jan 1942

3 Catherine Sybella; *d* unm 12 Aug 1890

4 Sybella Catherine; *d* unm 19 Jan 1919

5 Emily Anne; *d* unm 4 Feb 1880

6 Gertrude; *m* 19 June 1894 Hon Reynolds Moreton (*d* 19 June 1919), bro of 3rd Earl of Ducie (*qv*), and *dsp* 22 Dec 1927

Sir PERCYVALL *d* 12 Nov 1875; his est son,

Sir William Hart Dyke, 7th Bt, PC, DL, JP Kent; MA Oxon, MP W Kent 1865–68, Mid-Kent 1868–85 and NW Kent 1885–1906, Jt-Sec Treasury 1874–80, Ch Sec to Ld Lt Ireland 1885–86, V-Pres Ctee Cncl on Educn 1887–92; *b* 7 Aug 1837; *m* 30 May 1870 Lady Emily Caroline Montagu (*d* 8 Aug 1931), er dau of 7th Earl of Sandwich (*qv*), and had issue:

1 Percyvall Hart, barrister, JP Kent; *b* 27 Oct 1871; *educ* King's Coll Cambridge (BA); *m* 15 Aug 1908 Edythe (*d* 7 June 1937), dau of W G Harrison, QC, and *d* 26 June 1922, leaving:

(1) *Edythe Frediswide; *b* 18 July 1909; *m* 1st 16 Feb 1935 (*divorce* 1949) Frederic Andrew Milward, of Churt, Surrey; *m* 2nd 17 June 1950 (*divorce* 1956) Herbert Samuel Gallagher; *m* 3rd 1956 Maj Austin Edward Marsh (*d* 1963), RASC

2 William Montagu; *b* 10; *d* 29 April 1877

3 OLIVER HAMILTON AUGUSTUS HART (Sir), **8th Bt**

1 Lina Mary, OBE (1918), Order Elisabeth of Belgium; *m* 1st 10 Feb 1902 (*divorce* 1926) Alexander John Scott Gatty (*d* 6 Nov 1937), actor, est s of Sir Arthur Scott Gatty, KCVO, Garter Pncpl King of Arms, and had issue; *m* 2nd 7 Sept 1931 Capt Antonio Crivellari (*d* July 1954) and *d* 15 April 1964

2 Mary, Maid of Honour to HM QUEEN ALEXANDRA 1901–05; *b* 19 March 1875; *m* 11 July 1905 Lt-Col Matthew Gerald Edward Bell (*d* 8 May 1926), OBE, Rifle Bde, and *d* 7 Oct 1962, leaving issue

3 Sydney Margaret Eleanor; *b* 7 July 1881

Sir WILLIAM *d* 3 July 1931; his only surv son,

Sir Oliver Augustus Hart Dyke, 8th Bt; *b* 4 Sept 1885; *educ* Harrow; MIMechE; *m* 1st 29 July 1922 (*divorce* 1944) (Millicent) Zoe (*d* 12 Feb 1975), author: *So Spins the Silkworm* (autobiography, 1949), dau of Dr Mayston Bond, of Hammersmith, and had issue:

1 DEREK WILLIAM HART (Sir), **9th Bt**

2 +(Oliver) Guy Hart [Guy Hart Dyke Esq, Lullingstone Castle, Eynsford, Kent DA4 0JA]; *b* 9 Feb 1928; *educ* U of BC (BSc); *m* 1974 his cousin *Sarah Alexander Hart, yr dau of Cdre the Rev Eric Hart Dyke, RN, and has issue:

(1) +Thomas Guy; *b* 12 April 1976

(1) *Anya Elizabeth; *b* 16 March 1978

1 Rosemary June; *b* 27 Jan 1930; *m* 1st 12 June 1952 (*divorce* 1969) Jack Farr, and has issue:

(1) *Amanda Zoë Frances; *b* 1953

1 (cont.) Mrs Farr *m* 2nd 1969 *Michael Prince and *d* 1 Nov 1995

Sir Oliver *m* 2nd 9 Nov 1945 Mildred Turnour (*d* 9 June 1984), dau of James Blackwood and widow of Cecil Berens, JP, of Kevington Park, St Mary Cray, Kent, and *d* 9 July 1969

His er son,

Sir Derek William Hart Dyke, 9th Bt; *b* 4 Dec 1924; *m* 1st 4 Sept 1953 (1963) Dorothy Moses, of Hamilton, Ontario, Canada, and had issue:

1 Sir DAVID WILLIAM HART DYKE, **10th and present Bt**

1 *Diana Lynn [Mrs John McDonald, 52 Evelyn St, Brantford, Ontario, Canada]; *b* 15 Sept 1967; *m* 1986 *John Costellow McDonald

Sir Derek *m* 2nd 28 March 1964 *Margaret Dickson Elder, of Hamilton, Ontario, and *d* 1987

DYNEVOR

Arms: Quarterly, 1st and 4th, argent a chevron between three ravens sable (for RHYS); 2nd, gules a lion rampant within a bordure engrailed or (for TALBOT); 3rd, argent two chevronels between three trefoils slipped vert (for CARDONNEL). **Crest:** A raven sable. **Supporters:** Dexter, a griffin per fess or and argent, wings addorsed and inverted, the tail between the legs; sinister, a talbot argent, ears ermine, collared flory counter-flory gules and charged on the shoulder with a trefoil slipped vert. **Motto:** *Secret et hardi* ('Secret and bold'). **Creation:** B. (GB) 17 Oct 1780.

THE 9TH BARON DYNEVOR OF DYNEVOR, Co Carmarthen (Richard Charles Uryan Rhys) [The Rt Hon The Lord Dinevor, Penybanc Farm, Llandeilo, Carmarthens SA19 6SH]; *b* 19 June 1935; *s* f 1962; *educ* Eton and Magdalene Coll Cambridge; *m* 7 Jan 1959 (*divorce* 1978) Lucy Catherine King, only child of Sir John Knewstub Maurice Rothenstein, CBE, MA, PhD, LLD, of Beauforest House, Newington, Warborough, Oxon, and 8 Tryon St, London SW3, and has:

1 +HUGO GRIFFITH URYAN; *b* 19 Nov 1966; *educ* Bryanston

1 *Miranda Jane Caroline; *b* 17 Sept 1960; *m* 1986 *David Rule and has:

(1) *James Gareth; *b* 1986

(1) *Rhiannon; *b* 1987

2 *Sarah Sophia Rhiannon; *b* 8 March 1963; *m* 1987 *Dyfrug Williams and has:

(1) *Stefan Orlando; *b* 1988

(1) *Sophie Adeline; *b* 1993

3 *Susannah Mair Elizabeth; *b* 2 June 1964; *m* 1993 *Barnaby Stone and has:

(1) *Matthew Hugo Jonathan; b 16 Oct 1994

Lineage: The RICEs (later RHYSes) have in their time claimed descent from URIEN RHEGED, ruler of an area called Rheged on the English-Scottish borders in the late 6th century. But the known chronology does not fit. Indeed the descent may be from a much later Urien.

EINION Ap (*i.e.*, son of) LLYWARCHI; *b c* 1150; had:

GRONWY Ap EINION; had:

RHYS Ap GRONWY; had:

ELIDIR Ap RHYS; served on a jury at Llandeilo, Carmarths, 1326; had issue:

ELIDIR DDU ('Black'), of Y Crug, Llandeilo, Carmarths; fined 1302–03; said in 16th-century sources to have been a Kt of the Sepulchre; had issue:

PHILIP Ap ELIDIR, of Y Crug; witness 1362; in retinue of JOHN OF GAUNT (s of EDWARD III) 1386–87; had:

NICHOLAS Ap PHILIP; *m* Jonet, dau of Gruffudd ap Llywelyn *Foethus* ('The Luxurious'), of Llangathen, Carmarths, Constable Maenordeilo 1355–58, and had issue:

GRUFFUDD Ap NICHOLAS, of Newton, Dinefwr; living 1415; Sheriff Carmarthen 1426, Dep Constable Dinefwr Castle 1429, Dep Justiciar S Wales 1437 and 1447–56, Dep Chamberlain S Wales 1443–54, Escheator Carmarthen 1429–32 and 1454–55, Mayor-Escheator Carmarthen 1456–57; *m* 1st Mabli, dau of Maredudd ap Henry Dwnn, of Croesallgwyn, Carmarths; *m* 2nd Joan, dau of Sir Thomas Perrot, of Haroldston, Pembs; *m* 3rd *c* 1442 Jane, dau of Jenkin ap Rhys, of Gilfachwen, Llandysul, Cards, and *d c* 1460, having by his 1st w had issue:

THOMAS Ap GRUFFUDD, Dep Justiciar S Wales 1455, Dep Sheriff Cards 1442–43, Lancastrian supporter; *m* 1st Elsbeth, dau of Sir John Griffith, of Wichnor, Staffs, descended from Ednyfed Fychan, steward to LLYWELYN THE GREAT, and Dep Justiciar S Wales 1438 and 1457; *m* 2nd Jonet, dau of Henry Malephant, of Cydwell, Carmarths, and was *k* in a skirmish at Pennal, Merioneths, between 1472 and 1474, leaving by one of his ws a dau (Margaret, *m* Sir Richard Herbert, of Coldbrooke, Abergavenny, and had iisue; *see* POWIS, E), and by his 1st w:

Sir RHYS Ap THOMAS, KG (1505), KB (1497); *b c* 1449; ktd 1485, Justiciar S Wales 1496–1525, served French campaign 1513 and present Field of Cloth of Gold 1520; *m* 1st Efa, dau and heir of Henry ap Gwilym, of Glan-lais, Constable Dryslwyn Castle 1460–61; *m* 2nd Jonet (*d* 1535), dau of Thomas Mathew, of Radur, Glam, and widow of Thomas Stradling, and *d* 1525, leaving by his 1st w:

Sir GRUFFUDD Ap RHYS, KB (1501); courtier, present Field of Cloth of Gold; *m c* 1507 Catherine (*m* 2nd Sir Piers Edgcumbe, of Cotehele, Cornwall (*see* MOUNT EDGCUMBE, E) and *d* 1553), dau of John St John, of Bletso, Beds, and *d* 1521, having had:

RHYS Ap GRUFFUDD, of Newton, Carmarths; *b c* 1508; Mayor-Escheator Carmarthen 1529–30; *m* by 1522 Catherine (*m* 2nd, as his 2nd w, Henry Daubeny, Earl of Bridgwater, and was *bur* 11 May 1554), dau of 2nd Duke of Norfolk (*qv*), and was beheaded for treason 1531, having had, with another s (Thomas, *dsp*) and a dau (Agnes, *m* Sir Edward Bayntun but also had illegitimate issue by the 7th Baron Stourton; *see* MOWBRAY, SEGRAVE and STOURTON, B):

GRIFFITH RICE, of Newton; *b* 1526; Mayor Carmarthen 1571, High Sheriff Carmarths 1567–83; *m* Elinor, dau of Sir Thomas Jones, of Abermalais, High Sheriff Carmarths 1541, by his 2nd w Mary (dau of Sir James Berkeley), and had issue:

1 WALTER (Sir)

1 Mary; *m* Walter Vaughan, of Golden Grove, Carmarths, and with him was great-great-grandparent of Lucy Walter(s), CHARLES II's mistress (*see* BUCCLEUCH and QUEENSBERRY, D)

2 Barbara: *m* David Flude and *dsp*

GRIFFITH RICE *d* 1592; his son,

Sir WALTER RICE, of Newton; *b c* 1562; MP Carmarths 1584–85 and Carmarthen 1601 and 1604–11, High Sheriff Carmarths 1586, ktd 1603; *m* Elizabeth, er dau of Sir Edward Mansel, of Margam (*see* MANSEL, Bt), and *d c* 1636, having had an est s:

HENRY RICE, of Newton; *b c* 1590; *m* Margaret, dau of Sir Edward Lewis, of Y Fan, near Caerphilly, Glam, and *d c* 1651, having had, with an er s (Edward (Sir), High Sheriff Carmarths 1663, *dsp* by 1664):

WALTER RICE, of Newton; *m* 1st Elizabeth, widow of Richard Games, of Penderyn, and dau of Piers Deere, of Penderyn, Breconshire, and had, with other issue:

1 GRIFFITH, his heir

1 Elizabeth; *m* Richard Middleton, of Middleton Hall, Carmarths, High Sheriff 1701 (*d* by 1733)

WALTER RICE *m* 2nd 1673 Dorothy (*d* 6 Nov 1687), widow of Robert Brandling, of Leathley, Yorks, and dau of Sir William Vaughan, of Tor-y-coed, Carmarths, and *d* by 1681

His only surv son,

GRIFFITH RICE, of Newton; High Sheriff Carmarths 1694, MP Carmarths 1701–10; *b* 1664; *m* 1st 28 Aug 1690 Catherine (*d* 4 May 1717), dau and coheir of Philip Hoby, of Neath Abbey, Glam, and had, with other issue:

1 Edward, of Newton; MP Carmarthen; *m* Lucy, dau of John Morley Trevor, of Glynde, Sussex, and *dvp* 5 April 1727, having had, with two daus:

(1) GEORGE, of whom presently

2 Philip, of the Inner Temple *d* 1710

1 Elizabeth; *m* Thomas Lloyd (*d* by 1721), of Alltycadno and Gwaelod-y-maes, Carmarths

2 Catherine; *m* William Brydges (*d* 24 Sept 1764), of Tibberton, Herefs

GRIFFITH RICE *m* 2nd Eliza, dau of John Morgan, of Baily-Ficar, Llansawel and Upland, Carmarths, and *d* 27 Sept 1729.

His gs,

GEORGE RICE, of Newton, PC; Ld Lt and Custos Rotulorum Carmarths 1755–79, MP Carmarths 1754–79; *m* 16 Aug 1756 Cecil (*née* Talbot July 1735, but took her mother's maiden name De CARDONNEL by roy licence 21 May 1787 under terms of her mother's will, may have *m* 2nd Robert Wilson, of Trevallyn, Denbighs, and *d* 14 March 1793), **Baroness Dinevor of Dinevor** in her own right, only child of William Talbot, 1st Earl Talbot (*see* SHREWSBURY and WATERFORD, E) and **1st Baron Dinevor of Dinevor**, Co Carmarthen (GB) (*d* 27 April 1782), so *cr* 17 Oct 1780, with special remainder to his dau and the heirs male of her body, and *d* 3 Aug 1779, having had, with other issue:

1 GEORGE TALBOT RICE later De CARDONNEL (roy licence 30 April 1793) later still RICE (roy licence 4 Feb 1817), **3rd Baron Dynevor of Dynevor** (a spelling adopted *c* 1793 and adhered to ever since); *b* 8 Oct 1765; *educ* Ch Ch Oxford; MP (Tory) Carmarths 1790–93, Ld Lt Carmarths 1804–52; *m* 20 Oct 1794 Hon Frances Townshend (*d* 13 Aug 1854), 3rd dau of 1st Viscount Sydney of St Leonards (*see* TOWNSHEND, M), and *d* 9 April 1852, having had, with six daus (*d* unm):

(1) GEORGE RICE later RICE-TREVOR (roy licence 28 Oct 1824 on inheriting the Glynde estate, Sussex, from his paternal ggf's w's family), **4th Baron Dynevor of Dynevor**; MP (Tory) Carmarths 1820–31 and 1832–52, Hon Col Carmarths Militia, Militia ADC to HM QUEEN VICTORIA 1852–69, V-Pres Cambrian Instn; *b* 5 Aug 1795; *m* 27 Nov 1824 Frances (*d* 30 April 1878), est dau of Lord Charles FitzRoy (*see* GRAFTON, D), and *d* 7 Oct 1869, having had, with other issue:

1a Frances Emily; *m* 1 May 1848 Capt Edward ffolliott Wingfield (*d* 26 Sept 1865), 2nd Life Gds (*see* POWERSCOURT, V), and *d* 26 Nov 1863, leaving issue

2a Caroline Elizabeth Anne; *m* 24 Feb 1849 1st Baron Deramore (*qv*), and *d* 12 Aug 1887, leaving issue

3a Selina; *m* 12 Nov 1862 4th Earl of Longford (*qv*) and *d* 22 Jan 1918, leaving issue

2 Edward (Rev), DD, Dean of Gloucester; *b* 19 Nov 1779; *m* 9 July 1800 Charlotte (*d* 26 Feb 1832), illegitimate dau of Gen Francis Lascelles (*see* HAREWOOD, E) by the singer Anne Cateley, and *d* 15 Aug 1862, having had, with other issue:

(1) FRANCIS WILLIAM, **5th Baron**

(2) Henry (Rev), MA, Rector Gt Rissington, Glos; granted with siblings rank of baron's dau/yr s; *m* 12 Dec 1837 Emma (*d* 14 Sept 1907), dau of W F Lowndes Stone, of Brightwell Park, Oxon, and *d* 16 Sept 1896, having had issue:

1a Edward William; *b* 16 May 1855; *m* 1st 6 Dec 1877 Esther S (*d* 26 Dec 1901), yst dau of Edward Brown Kirton, and had issue:

1b Talbot Edward Kirton; *b* 6 April 1882; *m* 18 Feb 1910 Hilda Elizabeth (*d* 6 May 1951), dau of Julius Laurence, of Buffalo, USA, and *dsp* 1954

1a (cont.) Edward Rice *m* 2nd 23 July 1904 Helen (*d* 28 Nov 1936), yst dau of T Armstrong Roe, of Cork, and niece of N Flood-Davin, KC, and *d* 30 April 1924

2a Henry Charles Talbot, Capt 4th Bn Gloucestershire Regt; *b* 19 May 1862; *m* 9 Nov 1887 Cecil Mary (*d* 10 Jan 1940), yst dau of Edward Lloyd, of Lingcroft, nr York, and *d* 16 Aug 1931, leaving issue:

1b Harry Talbot, BA, Maj Welsh Gds (ret), OStJ; *b* 27 July 1889; *m* 12 July 1927 Hon Blanche Marion Devereux (*d* 13 Jan 1976), OStJ, er dau of 17th Viscount Hereford (*qv*), and *d* 29 April 1948, leaving issue:

1c +(David) Arthur Talbot [Arthur Talbot Rice Esq, Barnfield House, Cowfold, W Sussex RH13 8AT]; *b* 1 March 1931; *educ* Eton and Ch Ch Oxford; *m* 1st 5 Oct 1957 (*divorce* 1961) Annabella Frances Serena, yr dau of Maj Cyril Augustus Drummond, DL, JP (*see* PERTH, E); *m* 2nd 1961 *Sylvia Dorothea, yr dau of Platon Basil Metaxas, of Belgravia, and by her has:

1d +Robert Harry Talbot; *b* 19 Aug 1963; *educ* Eton and Durham U; Maj Welsh Gds; *m* 1991 (Alice) Elspeth Middleton, yr dau of David Middleton Lindsley, of Springfield House, Fremington, N Yorks

2d +Alexander Thomas Talbot; *b* 4 Aug 1969; *educ* Stowe and Durham U

1d *Victoria Penelope Helen Talbot; *b* 5 Oct 1961; *m* 1994 *Mark Thornley, yr s of H N Thorniley, of Johannesburg

1c Cecil Penelope Talbot; *b* 13 July 1928; *d* unm 16 June 1961

2b John Arthur Talbot, MC, Capt 5th Lancers, served WW I (Croix de Guerre); *b* 3 Jan 1892; *d* 14 April 1918, of wounds received in action

3b David Talbot, CBE, TD, FSA; *b* 11 July 1903; *educ* Eton and Ch Ch Oxford (BA 1925, BSc 1927, MA 1928, DLitt 1939); Prof History of Fine Art Edin U and V-Pncpl, Tstee Nat Gallery Scotland, memb Scottish Arts Cncl, UGC and Reviewing Ctee Export Works of Art, author: *The Birth of Western Painting* (1930), *Byzantine Painting* (1948) and other works, Lt-Col TA WW II; *m* 31 Dec 1927 Tamara (*d* 1993), adopted dau of Boris Abelson, of Paris, and *d* 12 March 1972, leaving issue:

1c +Nicholas Charles Talbot [Nicholas Talbot Rice Esq, Pigeon House, Coln Rogers, Glos GL54 3LB]; *b* 30 June 1944; *educ* Eton and Ch Ch Oxford; *m* 1973 *Jocelyn (Wiggy) Mary, dau of Maj R S W Higgens, of High Lands, Berden, Bishops Stortford, Herts, and has issue:

1d +David Henry Talbot; *b* 18 Jan 1975

1d *Sophia Elizabeth Talbot; *b* 13 Jan 1974

1c *Elizabeth Roussoudana Talbot, TD (1965); Capt RARO late WRAC (TA); *b* 10 June 1931; *educ* Edinburgh U (MA 1951)

2c *Nina Violet Tamara Talbot; *b* 15 Dec 1941; *m* 1 Sept 1966 *Hugh Bredin, son of George Richard Frederick Bredin, CBE, MA, of Rough Lea, Boar's Hill, Oxford, and has:

1d *Cosmo James; *b* 27 Oct 1970

1d *Zoë; *b* 1972

1a Frances Anna; *m* 23 April 1861 Cecil Charles Pole (*d* 17 Sept 1876), only son of Sir Peter Van Notten Pole, 3rd Bt (*see* POLE, Bt, of Wolverton), and *d* 5 Jan 1921, leaving issue

2a Katherine Emily; *m* 16 Feb 1881 Rev John Stevenson Lyle, Incumbent St Thomas, Martara, Ceylon, and *d* 2 Feb 1882

3a Cecil Louisa; *m* 5 Aug 1869 Col Arthur Price Jones, of Glanrannel Park, Carmarths, and *d* 5 March 1901, leaving issue

4a Florence Maria Caroline; *m* 17 July 1879 Harry Walter Cholmley (*d* 1901), of Howsham, Yorks, and *d* 7 March 1908

5a Georgiana Clara; *d* 21 Aug 1938

6a Amy Augusta Mary; *m* 2 Oct 1873 Rev William Patrick Lenard Hand (*d* April 1900), Vicar of Coln St Aldwyn, and *d* 30 March 1929, leaving issue

7a Beatrice Helen; *d* 24 April 1921

(3) John Talbot; *b* 16 April 1819; *m* 1st 13 Oct 1846 Clara Louisa (*d* 11 Aug 1853), 3rd dau of Sir John Chandos Reade, 7th Bt (*qv*); *m* 2nd 24 Oct 1855 Elizabeth Lucy (*d* 25 Oct 1914), dau of Robert Boyd, and *dsp* 12 May 1899

(1) Charlotte; *m* 1 Sept 1835 Rev Alexander Cameron, 2nd son of Donald Cameron of Lochiel, 22nd Chief of Clan Cameron, and *d* 8 Sept 1882, leaving issue

(2) Cecil; *m* 4 Jan 1837 Col Charles Augustus Arney and *d* 2 June 1852, leaving issue

(3) Maria; *m* 3 Sept 1839, as his 2nd w, Rev Edward Bankes (*d* 24 May 1867), of Soughton Hall, Flint, and *d* 17 April 1886 aged 77, leaving issue

(4) Lucy Horatia; *m* 7 June 1832 Rev William Sweet-Escott (*d* 2 March 1884), of Hartrow, Rector of Brompton-Ralph, Somerset, and *d* 1895, leaving issue

(5) Frances Emma; *m* 20 March 1842 Rev William Wiggin, Rector of Oddington, Glos, and *d* 1 May 1860, leaving issue

The 4th BARON's cousin,

Rev FRANCIS WILLIAM RICE, **5th Baron Dynevor of Dynevor**; *b* 10 May 1804; *educ* Westminster and Ch Ch Oxford; Vicar Fairford, Glos, 1827–78; *m* 1st 3 Feb 1830 Harriet Ives (*d* 22 July 1854), dau of Daniel Raymond Barker, and had issue:

1 ARTHUR DE CARDONNEL, **6th Baron**

1 Ellen, CBE (1920), LGStJ; *m* 20 Sept 1855 Rev James Gerald Joyce (*d* 28 June 1878), MA, Rector of Stratfield Saye, Berks, and *d* 21 May 1924, leaving issue

The **5th Baron** *m* 2nd 18 Nov 1856 Eliza Amelia (*d* 5 Aug 1896), dau of Rev Henry Carnegie Knox, Rector of Lechlade, and by her had, with other issue:

2 William Talbot (Rev), Vicar of All Saints Plumstead 1888–93, Rector St Peter-le-Bailey Oxford 1893–1902, Vicar Swansea 1902–19 and St Paul's Onslow Sq 1919–35, Preb St David's 1916–20; *b* 24 March 1861; *educ* Ch Ch Oxford (MA); *m* 10 Nov 1887 Marian (*d* 17 April 1950), dau of Henry Edmund Gurney, of Nutwood, Reigate, Surrey, and *d* 13 Nov 1945, having had issue:

(1) Francis Edmund Talbot; *b* 30 Dec 1889; *d* 2 Feb 1890

(2) Mervyn Gurney Talbot, FCA; *b* 4 July 1899; *educ* Charterhouse and Ch Ch Oxford (MA); Lt Coldstream Gds; *m* 1st 23 May 1929 Eleanor Butler Adair (*d*

17 May 1965), yr dau of Andrew Williamson, of 6 Wetherby Gdns, London SW5, and *d* 7 Nov 1979, leaving:

1a +Andrew Gurney [Andrew Talbot Rice Esq, 33 Cornwall Gdns, London SW7 4AP]; *b* 4 Aug 1930; *educ* Eton and Worcester Coll Oxford; *m* 23 Feb 1957 *Helen Lalage (Gay), only dau of Charles William Edmund Buchanan, of Chesterhill, Newport-on-Tay, Fife, and has:

1b +Richard Bruce Talbot [Richard Talbot Rice Esq, The Malthouse, Sheepscombe, Glos GL6 7RG]; *b* 4 Dec 1957; *m* 9 Dec 1995 *Kathryn Jane Elizabeth Owen and has:

1c +William David; *b* 1997

2b +Jonathan William Gurney Talbot [Jonathan Talbot Rice Esq, 13 Steeles Rd, London NW3 4SE]; *b* 14 July 1961; *m* 18 May 1996 *Martina Leonie Elizabeth Sprinz

1b *Julia Margaret Talbot [Mrs Nicholas Bannister, 6 Thomas Place, London W8 5UG]; *b* 30 May 1959; *m* 1990 *Nicholas W A Bannister and has:

1c *Harry Andrew Ayrton; *b* 1994

2c *Archibald William Rennie; *b* 1995

2b *Catherine Helen Talbot [Mrs William Gibson, 8 St Hildas Rd, London SW13 9JE]; *b* 20 Jan 1964; *m* 1991 *William H M Gibson and has:

1c *Dominic John Mulholland; *b* 1993

2c *Angus Michael Mulholland; *b* 1995

1c *Tessa; *b* 8 Feb 1998

2a +David Mervyn; *b* 3 Dec 1935; *educ* Charterhouse and Worcester Coll Oxford

3a +Nigel [Nigel Talbot Rice Esq, Summer Fields, Oxford]; *b* 14 May 1938; Headmaster of Summerfields Oxford 1975–; *b* 14 May 1938; *educ* Charterhouse and Ch Ch Oxford (BA 1960, MA, Dip Ed); *m* 20 July 1968 *(Rosfrith) Joanna Sarah, yst dau of A/Cdre Frederick John Manning, CB, CBE, and has:

1b *Samuel Peter Gurney; *b* 1982

1b *Sarah Kate; 6 24 Oct 1969

2b *Caroline Emma; *b* 26 Sept 1971

2b *Rebecca Mary; *b* 2 Sept 1973

4b *Helena Rachel; *b* 28 Jan 1977

1a *Margaret Adair Talbot [Mrs Edward Saunders, The Hensol, Shires Lane, Chorleywood, Herts WD3 5NH]; *b* 2 June 1932; *m* 3 Nov 1956 *Rev Edward George Humphrey Saunders, MA, son of Lt-Col George Muskett Saunders, OBE, of Littlewood House, Drayton, Norwich, and has issue:

1b *Hilary Margaret; *b* 1 Aug 1959; *m* 1996 *Rev David A McClay, Rector Kilkeel, Co Down

1a (cont.) The Rev and Mrs Edward Saunders also adopted:

*Mark Talbot; *b* 24 Aug 1964

*Jeremy George; *b* 20 June 1966

(2) (cont.) Mervyn Talbot Rice *m* 2nd 15 Sept 1969 Esther Lynette (*d* 1990), dau of Maj James Reay Sutherland Mackay, of Doune, Perthshire, and widow of Ronald David Stewart-Brown, QC

(1) Winifred Marian; *b* 21 Sept 1888; *m* 6 Dec 1918 Rt Rev George Alexander Chambers (*d* 5 Dec 1963), OBE, DD, Bp of Centl Tanganyika 1927–47, s of William Chambers, of Sydney, NSW, and has issue

(2) Dorothy Jean; *b* 22 Aug 1891; *d* unm 20 Dec 1974

(3) Katheryn Cecil; *b* 30 May 1893

(4) Muryell Gladys; *b* 26 March 1895; *m* 16 Jan 1917 Prof Patrick Alfred Buxton (*d* 13 Dec 1955), CMG, FRS, MRCS, LRCP, son of Alfred Fowell Buxton (*see* BUXTON, Bt), and had issue

(5) Victoria May; *b* 9 May 1897

(6) *Lettice Evelyn; *b* 6 July 1901; *m* 5 Oct 1960 *Robert Mathew Hale

2 Cecil Mina; *m* 19 Oct 1898 Rev Hubert Vaughan-Johnson (*d* 6 Feb 1936), Rector of Lullington, Frome, and *d* 15 Feb 1924, leaving issue

3 Alice Sophia; *m* 10 March 1897 Ven Leonard Rhys Hancock (*d* May 1943), Rector of Marston Bigot, Frome, Somerset, and *d* 15 Jan 1939, leaving issue

4 Mary Charlotte; *d* unm 10 July 1923

The 5th BARON *d* 3 Aug 1878; his est son,

ARTHUR De CARDONNEL RICE, **6th Baron Dynevor of Dynevor**, DL, JP Carmarths; *b* 24 Jan 1836; MA Oxford; *m* 4 Feb 1869 Selina (*d* 16 Dec 1889), 3rd dau of Hon Arthur Lascelles (*see* HAREWOOD, E), and had:

1 WALTER FitzURYAN, **7th Baron**

1 Gladys; *m* 16 June 1909 Lt-Col Elliott Beverley Steeds-Bird (*d* 16 May 1945), DSO, TD, RAMC (TA), and *d* 13 Aug 1950

2 Nest; *m* 25 July 1896 Sir (James) Reginald Lea Rankin, 2nd Bt (*qv*), and *d* 21 June 1943, leaving issue

3 Gwenllian Clare; *m* 26 Sept 1911 Capt Roger Dawson Dawson Duffield Brownson (*d* 21 Oct 1918), BA, MB, RAMC (SR), only son of Rev Frank Brownson, Rector of Compton Greenfield, Glos, and *d* 6 April 1969 aged 94, leaving issue

The 6th BARON *d* 8 June 1911; his only son,

WALTER FitzURYAN RICE later RHYS (roy licence 26 Dec 1916), **7th Baron Dynevor of Dynevor**, JP (Carmarths); *b* 17 Aug 1873; *educ* Eton and Ch Ch Oxford; Capt Carmarths Artillery, Ld Lt Carmarths 1928–49, CC 1919–35, Brighton 1910–11, Assist Priv Sec to Sec State India 1899–1903 and 1st Ld Admlty 1903–05, Assist Min Munitions 1916–18; *m* 12 Oct 1898 Lady Margaret Child-Villiers (*d* 1 April 1959), est dau of 7th Earl of Jersey (*qv*), and had issue:

1 CHARLES ARTHUR URYAN, **8th Baron**

2 Elwyn Villiers, Capt Welsh Gds; *b* 19 Dec 1900; *educ* Eton; *m* 14 July 1931 *Diana [The Hon Mrs Elwyn Rhys, Forest Home, Beechwood Lane, Burley, Hants], 2nd dau of Maj Roger Cyril Hans Sloane Stanley, of Paultons, Romsey, Hants, and *d* 10 Jan 1966, leaving:

(1) *Daphne Margaret [Mrs Maurice Brain, Tower Farm, Whiteparish, nr Salisbury, Wilts]; *b* 11 Jan 1933; *m* 1 May 1956 *Maurice Brain and has issue:

1a *Graham Stephen Maurice; *b* 16 March 1957

2a *Patrick John Elwyn; *b* 2 Sept 1959

3 David Reginald, Capt Welsh Gds WW II (wounded), became DUKE OF CIUDAD RODRIGO and a Grandee of Spain 1st Cl on succession of his 1st w to these titles 1943, ceded them 1947 to 7th Duke of Wellington (*qv*); *b* 18 March 1907; *educ* Eton; *m* 1st 23 March 1933 (*divorce* 1963) Lady Anne Maud Welles-ley, only dau of 5th Duke of Wellington (*qv*), and had issue:

(1) +Llewelyn Arthur [Llewelyn Rhys Esq, Hilliers, Bucklebury Common, Reading, Berks]; *b* 8 June 1935; *educ* Eton; *m* 23 Sept 1961 *Rosemary Martha Ann, er dau of Rev Canon Robert Victor Sellers, MA, DD, of The North Liberty, Wells, Somerset, and has issue:

1a +Robert David Arthur; *b* 26 July 1963

2a +Julian Nicholas James; *b* 16 Sept 1966

1a *Fiona Martha Alison; *b* 28 June 1962; *m* 1986 *Capt R D C James, and has issue:

1b *Charles Richard Arthur; *b* 1993

1b *Olivia Martha Alison; *b* 1987

2b *Lucinda Sophie Rose; *b* 1989

(1) *Elizabeth Maud [Mrs Peter Doran, 7 Killock, Martock Park, Canford Cliffs, Poole, Dorset BH13 7BA]; *b* 14 Aug 1937; *m* 10 Feb 1966 *Peter Matthew Doran, son of Patrick Doran

3 (cont.) David Rhys *m* 2nd 21 Oct 1963 *Sheila Mary [The Hon Mrs David Rhys, Southwick Court Chapel, Southwick, Trowbridge, Wilts BA14 9QB], served in American Ambulance GB 1944–46, formerly w of Christopher d'Ambrumenil and only dau of Douglas James Phillips, of Peopley Field, Basingstoke, Hants, and *d* 1991, leaving further issue:

(2) +George Dafydd; *b* 30 April 1965; *educ* Milton Abbey and Caen U; *m* 199– *Vanessa Jane, 2nd dau of Colin Donald, of Newbury, Berks, and has issue:

1a +Samuel David; *b* 5 May 1995

1 *Imogen Alice [The Rt Hon Imogen Viscountess Hampden, Trevor House, Glynde, Lewes, Sussex]; *b* 27 Aug 1903; *m* 14 July 1936 5th Viscount Hampden (*qv*) and has issue

The 7th BARON *d* 8 June 1956; his est son

CHARLES ARTHUR URYAN RHYS, **8th Baron Dynevor of Dynevor**, CBE (1962), MC, DL (Carmarths 1925), JP (1931); Capt Gen Gds Res of Offrs 1918–20 and WW II, MP (C) Romford 1923–29 and Guildford 1931–35, PPS to 1st Earl Baldwin of Bewdley (*qv*) 1927–29, chm Milford Haven Conservancy Bd, dep chm Sun and Life Offices, dir Sun Alliance and Richard Thomas and Baldwins, pres U Coll S Wales and Mon 1960–62, Govr Nat Museum Wales, chm Cities of London and Westminster C Assoc 1948–60, Order St Anne Russia 1919; *b* 21 Sept 1899; *educ* Eton and RMC Sandhurst; *m* 29 Sept 1934 Hope Mary Woodbine (*d* 1980), formerly w of Capt Arthur Granville Soames, OBE, Coldstream Gds, and dau of Charles Woodbine Parish, FRGS, of Ennismore Gdns, SW, and *d* 1962, leaving:

RICHARD CHARLES URYAN RHYS, **9th and present Baron Dynevor of Dynevor**

DYSART

Arms: Azure an Imperial Crown proper between three mullets argent within a double tressure flory counterflory or. **Supporters:** Two lions gules, collared azure, each collar charged with three mullets argent. **Creations:** L. and E. (S) 3 Aug 1643.

THE COUNTESS OF DYSART, Co Fife, and **Lady Huntingtower**, Co Perth, 11th holder of the titles (Rosamund Agnes Greaves) [The Rt Hon The Countess of Dysart, Bryn Garth Farm, Grosmont, Abergavenny, Gwent]; *b* 15 Feb 1914; *s* mother 1975

Lineage: The Rev WILLIAM MURRAY, MA (a cadet of the MURRAYS of Ochtertyre (*see* MURRAY, of Ochtertyre, Bt), and bro of Thomas Murray, Provost of Eton and Tutor and Sec to CHARLES I when PRINCE OF WALES); Minister of Dysart, Co Fife; had an only s:

WILLIAM MURRAY, **1st Earl of Dysart**, so *cr* 3 Aug 1643, as also LORD HUNTINGTOWER, Co Perth (both S; MP Fowey 1626 and E Looe 1628–29, leased manors of Ham and Petersham, Surrey; *m c* June 1636 Catherine, dau of Col Norman Bruce, of the BRUCEs of Clackmannan, and *d c* 11 Sept 1653, having had, with a yr dau (Margaret, *m c* 30 May 1662 William, 2nd Baron Maynard (*d* 3 Feb 1699), and *d* 4 June 1682):

ELIZABETH Murray, **Countess of Dysart** in her own right, which title she resigned, obtaining a regrant 5 Dec 1670 with precedence of 1643; *m* 1st *c* 22 May 1651 Sir Lionel Tollemache, 3rd Bt, of Helmingham, Suffolk (*cr* 1611) (*d* 1669); *m* 2nd 17 Feb 1672 2nd Earl of Lauderdale (*qv*), and *d* 4 June 1698, having had surv issue by her 1st husb:

1 LIONEL, **3rd Earl**

2 Thomas; Williamite Lt-Gen in Ireland; *d* of a wound received when C-in-C expdn against Brest and was *bur* 30 June 1694

3 William; Capt RN; *k* Hon William Carnegie in a duel at Paris 1681 (*see* FIFE, D); *d* unm W Indies 25 May 1691

1 Elizabeth; *m* 12 March 1677/8 1st Duke of Argyll (*qv*), and *d* 16 May 1735, leaving issue

2 Catherine; *m* 1st 2 Dec 1677 James Stuart, Lord Doune (*d* 1685), est son of 5th Earl of Moray (*qv*); *m* 2nd as his 2nd w 16th Earl of Sutherland (*qv*)

The COUNTESS's est son,

Sir LIONEL TOLLEMACHE, 4th Bt, and **3rd Earl of Dysart**; *b* 30 Jan 1648; MP (Tory) Suffolk 1698–1707; declined an English barony on the accession of QUEEN ANNE 1702; *m c* 1 Nov 1680 Grace (*d* 30 April 1740), est dau and coheir of Sir Thomas Wilbraham, 3rd Bt, of Woodhey, Cheshire (*see* SKELMERSDALE, B), and *d* 23 Feb 1727, having had, with other issue:

1 Lionel, *Lord Huntingtower*; *b* 6 June 1682; *m* 6 Dec 1706 Henrietta Cavendish (*d* 11 Jan 1717/18), illegitimate dau of 2nd Duke of Devonshire (*qv*), and *dvp* 26 July 1712, leaving issue:

(1) LIONEL, **4th Earl**

(1) Henrietta; *m* 4 May 1731 Thomas Clutterbuck (*d* 23 Nov 1742), and *d* 8 Dec 1772, leaving issue

1 Catherine; *m* 11 Sep 1724 John, Marquess of Carnarvon, est son of 1st Duke of Chandos, and *d* 1 Jan 1754, leaving issue

The 3rd EARL's gs,

Sir LIONEL TOLLEMACHE, 5th Bt, and **4th Earl of Dysart**, KT (1743); *b* 1 May 1708; *m* 22 July 1729 Lady Grace Carteret (*d* 23 July 1755), est dau of 1st Earl Granville (*qv*), and *d* 10 March 1770, having had, with seven other children (*d* young):

1 Sir LIONEL TOLLEMACHE, 6th Bt, and **5th Earl of Dysart**; *b* 6 Aug 1734; *m* 1st 2 Oct 1760 Charlotte (*dsp* 5 Sept 1789), dau of Hon Sir Edward Walpole, KB (*see* WALPOLE, B); *m* 2nd 19 April 1791 Magdalene (*d* 2 Feb 1823), dau of David Lewis, of Malvern Hall, Warwickshire, and *dsp* 22 Feb 1799

2 Sir WILBRAHAM TOLLEMACHE, 7th and last Bt, and **6th Earl of Dysart**; *b* 23 Oct 1739; Ld High Steward of Ipswich; *m* 4 Feb 1773 Anna Maria (*d* 14 Sept 1804), dau of David Lewis, of Malvern Hall, and *dsp* 9 March 1821, when the btcy expired

3 George; *b* 14 March 1744; Offr RN; drowned on a voyage to Lisbon 13 Nov 1760

4 John; *b* 30 March 1750; Capt RN; *m* 3 Dec 1773 Bridget (*d* 13 March 1796), est dau of 1st Earl of Northington and widow of Hon Robert Fox-Lane, MP; *k* in a duel 25 Sep 1777, leaving an only son:

(1) Lionel Robert; *b* 10 Nov 1774; Ensign Coldstream Gds; *ka* Valenciennes 14 July 1793

5 William; *b* 22 March 1751; Offr RN; lost in the frigate *Repulse* in a hurricane 16 Dec 1776

1 Frances; *b* 1738; *d* unm 18 Dec 1807

2 LOUISA, **Countess of Dysart**

3 Jane; *b* 26 March 1750; *m* 1st 23 Oct 1771 Maj John Delap Halliday, of the Leasowes, Salop (*d* 24 Oct 1794), and had four children (*see* TOLLEMACHE, B, also WOLSELEY, Bt, of Wolseley); *m* 2nd 4 March 1802 George David Ferry and *d* 28 Aug 1802

The 6th EARL's only surv sis,

LOUISA Tollemache, **Countess of Dysart** in her own right; *b* 2 July 1745; *m* 4 Sept 1765 John MANNERS, MP, of Hainby Hall, Lincs, and Grantham Grange, Lincs (illegitimate s of Lord William Manners, 2nd s of 2nd Duke of Rutland; *qv*) and *d* 22 Sept 1840, having had:

1 Sir WILLIAM MANNERS later TALMASH (roy licence 6 April 1821), 1st Bt, styled by courtesy *Lord Huntingtower* 1821–40; *b* 1766; *m* 12 Jan 1790 Catherine Rebecca (*d* 21 March 1852), dau of Francis Gray, of Lehena, Co Cork, and *dvm* 11 March 1833, having had, with other issue (*see* TOLLEMACHE, Bt):

(1) LIONEL WILLIAM JOHN, **8th Earl**

2 John; *m* 19 Aug 1806, as her 2nd husb, Mary (*d* 9 April 1838), dau of Capt Benjamin Bechnoe, RN (*see* SMITH-MARRIOTT, Bt), and widow of 4th Duke of Roxburghe (*qv*), and *dsp* 13 Feb 1837

3 Charles, of Harrington, Northants; *b* 2 Jan 1775; *m* 1st 4 Aug 1797 Frances (*d* 29 March 1808), only dau of Maj William Hay of Newhall (*see* TWEEDDALE, M), and had, with other issue:

(1)Wilbraham Francis; *b* 26 April 1800; Cdr RN; *m* 5 Oct 1841 Elizabeth (*d* 13 Oct 1830), est dau of Alexander Munro, and *d* 6 Jan 1862, leaving issue:

1a Charles Hay; *b* 20 Dec 1842; Lt 83rd Foot; *d* unm Gibraltar 22 April 1867

2a Lionel Alexander Arthur; *b* 24 July 1844; *m* 29 April 1869 Louisa (*d* 22 Nov 1909), yst dau of Maj-Gen Frederick Hope (*see* LINLITHGOW, M), and *dsp* 13 Nov 1887

3 (cont.) The Hon Charles Tollemache *m* 2nd 8 Aug 1803 Gertrude Florinda (*d* 27 Sept 1864), dau of Gen William Gardiner and widow of John Charles Clarke, and *d* 26 July 1850, having by her had further issue:

(2) William; *b* 7 Nov 1810; *m* 1st 13 Sept 1838 Anna Maria (*d* 23 Sept 1873), dau of 11th Duke of Somerset (*qv*); *m* 2nd 11 May 1875 Emma (*d* 28 Aug 1904), dau of James Sidney and widow of Maj-Gen Sir Herbert Edwardes, KCB, KCSI, and *d* 17 March 1886, having had issue by his 1st w:

1a Algernon Seymour; *b* 31 Jan 1842; Maj 108th Foot; *m* 3 Aug 1868 Caroline Marianne, dau of Gen Montriou, Bombay Army, and *d* 22 April 1904, leaving issue:

1b Algernon Montriou; *b* 2 July 1884; Lt Lancs Hus

1a Emma Maria; *m* 3 Oct 1875 4th Baron Forester (*qv*) and *d* 24 June 1898, leaving issue

2a Maltilda Jane; *m* 17 June 1873 Capt Marcus Augustus Stanley Hare, RN (*d* 24 March 1878), of Newton Abbot, Devon, and *d* 14 March 1918, leaving issue

3a Caroline Elizabeth; *m* 15 Oct 1890 Jerome Maurice Neuburger, and *d* 1911

(3) Henry Bertie; Scots Fus Gds; *m* 12 Aug 1837 Emilie Magdalen Louisa (*d* 19 Jan 1864), est dau of Sir George Sinclair, 2nd Bt (*qv*), and *d* 28 Oct 1886, having had issue:

1a Wilbraham Archibald; *b* July 1838; *m* Florence Mary, est dau of Alfred Trueman, and *dsp*

(1) Frances Louisa; *m* 1st 1850 George Richard Halliday, of Bridgefield, Lt RN (*d* 11 Nov 1855); *m* 2nd 28 Nov 1857 her cousin Hon Algernon Gray Tollemache (*d* 16 Jan 1892, *see* TOLLEMACHE, B), and *d* 15 April 1893

(2) Maria; *m* 20 Aug 1833 1st Marquess of Ailesbury (*qv*) and *d* 7 May 1893, leaving issue

1 Catherine Sophia; *m* 16 Aug 1793 Sir Gilbert Heathcote, 4th Bt (*qv*), and *d* 28 May 1825, leaving issue

2 Maria Caroline; *m* 9 Sept 1799 4th Earl of Fife (*d* 9 March 1857; *see* FIFE, D), and *dsp* 20 Dec 1805

3 Louisa Grace; *m* 15 Aug 1802 6th Duke of St Albans (*qv*) and *d* 19 Feb 1816, leaving issue

4 Laura; *m* 2 June 1808 (*divorce* 16 July 1811, resumed maiden name by roy licence 13 March 1821) 7th Earl of Stair (*qv*) and *dsp* 11 July 1834

The COUNTESS's gs,

Sir LIONEL WILLIAM JOHN TALMASH later TOLLEMACHE, 2nd Bt (as which *s* f 1833), and **8th Earl of Dysart**; *b* 18 Nov 1794; *m* 23 Sept 1819 his cousin Maria Elizabeth (*d* 15 Feb 1869), est dau of Sweeney Toone, of Keston Lodge, Kent, and *d* 23 Sept 1878, having had issue:

1 William Lionel Felix, *Lord Huntingtower*; *b* 4 July 1820; *m* 26 Sept 1851 his cousin Katherine Elizabeth Camilla (*d* 21 Nov 1896), yst dau of Sir Joseph Burke, 11th Bt, of Glinsk Castle, Galway, and *dvp* 21 Dec 1872, having had, with another dau (*d* young):

(1) Sir WILLIAM JOHN MANNERS TOLLEMACHE, 3rd Bt, and **9th Earl of Dysart**, JP (Leics); *b* 3 March 1859; Ld Lt Rutland 1881–1906; *m* 19 Nov 1885 Cecilia Florence (*dsp* 23 Dec 1917), dau of George Onslow Newton, of Croxton Park, Cambs (*see* 1939 edn ELTISLEY, B), and *d* 22 Nov 1935, when the btcy passed to a cousin (*see* TOLLEMACHE, Bt)

(1) Mary Louisa Napoleona Manners; granted with her sisters rank of earl's daus; *d* 20 June 1859

(2) Agnes Mary Manners; *b* 27 June 1855; *m* 4 Feb 1882 Charles Norman Lindsay Tollemache Scott, of Bosworth Park, Leics, DL (*d* 6 Sept 1938), est s of John Lindsay Scott, of Kirkcudbrightshire, and *d* 27 July 1912, leaving:

1a WENEFRYDE AGATHA Scott, **Countess of Dysart** in her own right; *b* 13 Nov 1889; *m* 4 Jan 1913 Maj Owain Edward Whitehead GREAVES, JP, DL, RHG (Blues) (*d* 18 Feb 1941), son of Edward Seymour Greaves, JP, of Glen Etive, Argyllshire, and *d* 2 June 1975, leaving:

1b ROSAMUND AGNES GREAVES, **present Countess of Dysart**

2b +KATHERINE [The Lady Katherine Grant of Rothiemurchus, Druminioul Lodge, Aviemore, Inverness-shire]; *b* 1 June 1918; heir presumptive; *m* 12 April 1941 Col John Peter Grant of Rothiemurchus, MBE (*d* 1987), est s of Col John Peter Grant of Rothiemurchus, CB, MC, TD, and has issue:

1c +John Peter Grant, Yr. of Rothiemurchus [John Grant Yr of Rothiemurchus, The Boat House, Rothiemurchus, Aviemore, Inverness-shire]; *b* 22 Oct 1946; *educ* Gordonstoun; *m* 8 May 1971 *(Wendy) Philippa, only dau of John Wybergh Chance, of Llanvapley Court, Mon, and has issue:

1d +James Patrick; *b* 14 Sept 1977

1d +Louisa Katherine; *b* 9 June 1975

2d +Alexander Rose; *b* 1985

1c +Jane Margery; *b* 2 Feb 1943; *m* 1 May 1965 *Andrew Robert Fowell Buxton, of Ipswich, Suffolk, er s of Joseph Gurney Fowell Buxton, and has issue (*see* BUXTON, Bt)

3b Mary; *b* 22 Sept 1921; *m* 14 April 1942 Bernard Albert Blanger, Sec French Legation, Lisbon, formerly Capt Free French Air Force (*d* 1950), s of Benjamin Henry Edward Blanger, of Amiens, France, and *d* 22 Feb 1955, leaving:

1c +Brigitte Mary; *b* 8 Feb 1943; *m* 1st 1964 (*divorce* 1967) John Fotheringham; *m* 2nd 1969 (*divorce* 1976) Pavlos Athanasacopoulos

2c +Beatrice Wenefryde; *b* 24 June 1945; *m* 1977 *Robin Evans, and has issue:

1d +Schuyler Benjamin; *b* 1978

1d +Beatrice Rosamund; *b* 19–

(3) Agatha Manners; *b* 16 Jan 1857; *m* 24 July 1882 3rd Baron Westbury (*qv*) and *d* 8 Jan 1941, having had issue

EAMES

Creation: B. (LP, UK) 1995.

THE BARON EAMES, of Armagh, Co Armagh (Most Rev Dr Robert Henry Alexander Eames) [The Most Rev The Archbishop of Armagh and Primate of All Ireland The Rt Hon The Lord Eames, The See House, Cathedral Close, Armagh, Co Armagh BT61 7EE]; *b* 27 April 1937; *educ* Belfast Roy Acad, Methodist Coll Belfast, Queen's U Belfast and Trin Coll Dublin (LLB, PhD); law tutor Queen's U Belfast 1960–63, Curate Assist Bangor 1963–66, Rector St Dorothea's Belfast 1966–74, Examining Chaplain to Bp Down 1973, Rector St Mark's Dundela 1974–75, Bp Derry and Raphoe 1975–80, Bp Down and Dromore 1980–86; Chm Commn: Communion and Women in the Episcopate 1988–, Inter-Anglican Rels 1988–; Govr Church Army 1985–, Archbp and Primate 1986–; Hon LLD Queen's U Belfast 1989, Trin Coll Dublin 1992–, Lancaster 1994–, Hon DD Cantab 1994; author: *A Form of Worship for Teenagers* (1965), *The Quiet Revolution — Irish Disestablishment* (1970), *Through Suffering* (1973), *Thinking Through Lent* (1978), *Through Lent* (1984), *Chains to be Broken* (1992); *m* 25 June 1966 *Ann Christine, LLB, MPhil, World-Wide Pres Mothers' Union 1995–, dau of Capt William Adrian Reynolds Daly by his w Olive Margaret, and has:

1 *Niall William Adrian; *b* 19 Aug 1967; FRCS, MD

2 *Michael Harvey Alexander; *b* 15 June 1969; FRCS

Lineage: WILLIAM EDWARD EAMES; *m* Mary Eleanor Thompson and had:

ROBERT HENRY ALEXANDER, *cr* a **Baron**

EARDLEY-WILMOT

Arms: Quarterly, 1st, sable on a fess or between three eagle's heads couped argent as many escallops gules (for WILMOT); 2nd, argent on a chevron azure three garbs or a canton gules charged with a fret or (for EARDLEY); 3rd, azure a fess engrailed or between three maiden's heads proper crined or (for MAROW); 4th, quarterly argent and sable a bend gules charged with three mullets of the first.
Crests: 1 An eagle's head couped argent, in his beak an escallop gules, 2 A buck courant gules attired and unguled or.
Creation: Bt. (UK) 23 Aug 1821.

SIR MICHAEL JOHN ASSHETON EARDLEY-WILMOT, 6TH BT, of Berkswell Hall, Co Warwick [Sir Michael Eardley-Wilmot Bt, 26 Arundel Gdns, London W11 2LB; c/o Beaufort Hotel, 33 Beaufort Gdns, London SW3 1PB]; *b* 13 Jan 1941; *s* f 1995; *educ* Clifton; *m* 1st 10 July 1971 (*divorce* 1987) Wendy, yr dau of A J Wolstenholme, of Clandon, Surrey, and Mrs C Chapman Pincher, of Ewhurst, Surrey, and has issue:

1 +BENJAMIN JOHN; *b* 24 Jan 1974

2 +Guy Assheton; *b* 1979

1 *Holly Joanna; *b* 27 June 1976

Sir MICHAEL *m* 2nd 1987 *Diana Margaret, dau of Robert Graham Wallis, and has further issue:

2 *Poppy Clementine; *b* 1987

Lineage: ROBERT WYLMOT, of Chaddesden (*see* WILMOT, Bt); had a 3rd s, to whom he bequeathed Osmaston and other Derbyshire estates:

Sir NICHOLAS WILMOT; Serjeant-at-law, Dep Recorder Nottingham; *b* 1611; *m* Dorothy (*d* 22 Jan 1682), dau of Sir Henry Harpur, of Calke, Derbys (*see* 1924 edn HARPUR-CREWE, Bt), and *d* 28 Dec 1682, leaving an est s:

ROBERT WILMOT; MP Derby 1689; *m* Elizabeth, dau and sole heiress of Edward Eardley, of Eardley, Staffs, and had, with other issue:

1 ROBERT

2 John; ancestor of the WILMOT-CHETWODEs of Woodbrook, Queen's Co

3 Charles (Rev); Rector Langley, Derbys; *m* Bridget, dau of Benjamin Blundell, and had issue

4 Christopher; *m* Anne Montague, sis of 1st Earl of Halifax of the 1715 *cr* (*see* MANCHESTER, D), and had issue

5 Henry, of Farnborough Pk, Hants; *m* Catherine Dowson

ROBERT WILMOT *d* 1722; his est s,

ROBERT WILMOT; *m* Ursula, 3rd dau and coheir of Sir Samuel Marowe, 1st and last Bt, of Berkswell, Warwicks, and *d* Sept 1738, having had, with two daus:

1 Sir ROBERT WILMOT, 1st Bt (GB), so *cr* 1772, with special remainder; *dsp*

2 John Eardley (Sir); Ld Ch Justice; said twice to have refused the Ld Chllrship and a peerage; *m* 3 April 1743 Sarah (*d* 27 July 1772), dau of Thomas Rivett (*see* RIVETT-CARNAC, Bt), and *d* 5 Feb 1792, leaving:

(1) JOHN WILMOT later EARDLEY-WILMOT (roy licence 1812), of Berkswell Hall; barrister, Master Chancery, MP Tiverton 1776–84; *b* 1750; *m* 1st Frances, only dau of Samuel Sainthill; *m* 2nd Sarah, dau of Col Haslam, and by his 1st w had, with four daus:

1a JOHN EARDLEY (Sir), **1st Bt**

(1) Maria Marowe; *m* 6 Dec 1766 Sir Sampson GIDEON later EARDLEY (roy licence 17 July 1789), 1st and last Bt, and 1st and last Baron Eardley of Spalding (*d* 25 Dec 1824), s of Sampson Gideon, of Stepney, a stockbroker of Portuguese Sephardic extraction, and *dspms* 1 March 1794

(2) Elizabeth; *m* Sir Thomas Blomefield, 1st Bt (*qv*), and had issue

JOHN EARDLEY-WILMOT *d* June 1815; his son:

Sir John Eardley Eardley-Wilmot, 1st Bt (UK), so *cr* 23 Aug 1821; FRS, Govr Van Diemen's Land, MP N Warwicks 1832–43; *b* 21 Feb 1783; *m* 1st 21 May 1808 Elizabeth Emma (*d* 22 March 1818), dau of Caleb Hillier Parry, MD, of Bath, and sis of Adml Sir Edward Parry, and had issue:

1 JOHN EARDLEY (Sir), **2nd Bt**

2 Frederick Marow, Maj-Gen RA; *b* 29 May 1812; *m* 19 June 1851 Frances Augusta (*d* 22 Jan 1951), dau of George James Pennington, of Cumberland St, and *d* 30 Sept 1877, having had, with another dau (*d* an infant):

(1) Kenred, with Bank of Montreal; *b* Sept 1853; *m* 1st 1880 Margaret (*d* 8 Nov 1892), dau of James Osborne, and had issue:

1a Trevor Kenred; *b* Oct 1889; *educ* McGill U (BSc 1913); *m* 1st 11 Feb 1914 (*divorce* April 1935) Louise Margaret, dau of William George Warner, of Montreal; *m* 2nd 15 June 1935 Frances Rebecca, dau of Alfred O Secord, of Montreal

1a Hilda Woodburn; *b* 19 April 1882; *m* 9 Sept 1911 Maj John Hennings Wright, 48th Highrs (*d* 1942), of Canada, and *d* 23 Dec 1964, leaving issue

2a Madge Pennington; *b* 1 March 1887; *m* 1st 19 Nov 1921 Sherman de Witt Enoch, civil engr (*d* 1934); *m* 2nd 1945 Dr Josef Heinrich Amrjem, of New York, and *d* 10 Jan 1966

(1) (cont.) Kenred Eardley-Wilmot *m* 2nd 1896 Beatrice (*dsp* 7 April 1909), dau of T C Chisholm; *m* 3rd June 1911 Ethel Grace (*d* 1954), dau of Henry Taylor, of Perth, Ontario, and *d* 28 April 1932

(2) Arthur, CMG (1917), Lt-Col and Brev Col RFA, served Mahsud Waziri Expdn 1881 and WW I (wounded); *b* 6 June 1856; *m* 2 April 1887 Mary Blanche (*d* 13 Aug 1942), only dau of Clement Thomas Sneyd-Kynnersley, JP, DL, of Loxley Pk and Highfields, Staffs, and *d* 9 March 1940, having had:

1a Frederick Lawrence, Lt Princess Patricia's Canadian LI; *b* 25 Feb 1895; *ka* 19 March 1915

1a Dorothy Revell; *b* 8 July 1888; *d* unm 21 Jan 1972

2a Margaret Stuart; *b* 17 Nov 1891; *d* unm 29 March 1971

3a Dulce; *m* 28 Oct 1920 Stanley Smith (*d* 1944), Prof Physics U of Alberta, Canada, and *d* 19 Jan 1960

(3) Irton, Col IA; *b* 8 April 1859; *m* 22 Oct 1885 Florence (*d* 25 Sept 1946), dau of Harry Corbyn Levinge (*see* LEVINGE, Bt), and *d* 17 July 1936, leaving:

1a Vere Levinge, ARSM, AIMM, Canadian Govt Mines Dept, Capt RE WW I; *b* 29 Oct 1886; *educ* Wellington; *m* 23 July 1815 Mary Cecil (*d* 1968), dau of H Moffatt, of Toronto, Canada, and *d* 23 April 1965, having had issue:

1b John Vere, Capt Canadian Armoured Corps WW II; *b* 18 March 1918; *ka* France 15 Aug 1944

2b +Hugh Irton [Hugh Eardley-Wilmot Esq, RR No 1, Norland, Ontario K0M 2L0, Canada]; *b* 19 Nov 1925; *educ* McGill U (BSc 1951); RCAF 1944–45

(1) Bertha; *m* 14 Nov 1878 George N Todd (*d* 1891), and *d* 1896, leaving issue

(2) Mabel; *m* 10 July 1890 Lt-Col Alexander Kenneth Gillespie, KGStJ (*d* 11 Sept 1934), Staff Paymaster APD, and *d* 29 Sept 1946

(3) Eva; *m* 10 Oct 1891 Rev George Herbert Aitken, BA (*d* 1919), Rector Lambeth, and *d* 27 March 1959

(4) Freda; *d* unm 24 March 1953

3 Edward Revell (Rev), Hon Canon Worcester; *b* 11 Feb 1814; *educ* Trin Hall Cambridge (MA); *m* 1st 4 Aug 1840 Frances Anne (*d* 11 April 1846), dau of Rev Charles Elkins, Canon Salisbury, and had issue:

(1) Hubert Frederick; *b* 29 April 1843; *d* unm 1877

(2) Edward Snowdon; *b* 13 Nov 1844; *d* unm 4 July 1875

(3) Francis, Lt RN; *b* 27 March 1846; *m* 10 Aug 1874 Lucy Mary Emily (*d* 18 Feb 1929), dau of Rev George Rundle Prynne, Vicar St Peter's, Plymouth, and *d* 23 Feb 1921, having had issue:

1a Kenred; *b* 29 April 1875; *d* 23 March 1878

2a Eric Hugh; *b* 28 May; *d* 29 July 1876

3a Hubert Valentine (Rev), Vicar Coggeshall Essex 1924–30, Proctor in Convocation 1929, Hon CF 1917 WW I (wounded); *b* 14 Feb 1878; *educ* St Paul's and Keble Coll Oxford (BA 1900, MA 1904); *m* 22 April 1908 Muriel Ivy Holloway (*d* 9 Sept 1966), dau of S William Lovett, of Norwich, and *d* 17 Jan 1963, leaving issue:

1b +Paul Revell [Paul Eardley-Wilmot Esq, Woodland View, New Rd, Cookham Rise, Berks SL6 9HB], RAF WW II; *b* 13 May 1917; *educ* St Paul's; *m* 27 March 1953 *Joan Violet, only dau of Herbert John William Shepherd, of High Wycombe, and has issue:

1c +David Revell; *b* 17 Aug 1954

1c *Susan Mary [Mrs Peter Rushton, Clare Cottage, 40 Hale Rd, Farnham, Surrey GU9 9QH]; *b* 20 Oct 1957; *m* 1978 *Peter William Rushton, and has issue:

1d *Oliver William; *b* 1983
2d *Morgan David; *b* 1988
3d *Theodore Alexander; *b* 1992
1b Hazel Mary; *b* 6 Feb 1910; *educ* St Anne's Coll Oxford (BA 1931); *d* unm 11 May 1998
2b Monica Germaine; *b* 18 June 1913; *d* unm April 1992
4a George Revell; *b* 10 June 1880; *m* 18 Nov 1909 Janet Mary (*d* 30 June 1964), dau of Rev Canon W Crisp, of Cape Town, and *dsp* 27 Sept 1910
5a Gerald Howard, Lt 9th Bn Devonshire Regt; *b* 14 March 1890; *d* of wounds recd in action 10 March 1916
1a Mabel Ernestine; *b* 22 March 1879; *m* 11 May 1907 Edward Fletcher Emmet (*d* 21 Nov 1967), slr, 4th s of Rev William Edward Emmet, and *d* 8 April 1964, leaving issue
2a Muriel; *b* 9 Jan 1883, *d* unm 14 June 1956
3 (cont.) The Rev Edward Eardley-Wilmont *m* 2nd 8 Feb 1848 Emma Hutchinson (*d* 14 Feb 1907), dau of William Lambert, BCS, and *d* 30 May 1899, having by her had:
(4) Ernest Augustus (Rev), Preb Wells, Vicar Broxbourne, Herts; *b* 9 Nov 1848; *educ* Clare Coll Cambridge (MA); *m* 1st 8 April 1875 Emily Dora (*d* March 1897), dau of Rev Charles Holland, Preb Chichester, and had:
1a Charles Revell (Rev), Rector Levis, Quebec, 1938–42, Canon Quebec Cathedral 1932–42 (Hon Canon 1942), Examining Chaplain to Bp Quebec 1932–42; *b* 24 Jan 1880; *educ* Haileybury and Clare Coll Cambridge (BA 1902, MA 1906); *m* 1914 Rose Meredith (*d* 1 Dec 1954), dau of C H Bowen, of Sherbroke, PQ, Canada, and *d* 1962, leaving issue:
1b +Robert Lloyd, Sgt RCAF WW II; *b* 1921; *m* 1949 *Joyce Ethel, dau of Delbert Dagles, of Three Rivers, Quebec, and has:
1c +David Robert; *b* 1952
1b *Barbara Rose [Mrs Geoffrey Constable, 36 Morewood Cres, Willowdale, Toronto, Ontario M2K 1L7, Canada], Nursing Sis RCAF WW II; *m* 1st 1 Aug 1942 John Franklin Carr, RCAF, of New Liskeard, Ontario (*kas* 26 Oct 1942); *m* 2nd Oct 1947 *Geoffrey Constable, s of Guy Constable, of Creston, BC, and by him has:
1c *Peter Geoffrey; *b* 1961
1c *Catherine Judith; *b* 1950
2c *Janet Meredyth; *b* 1953
3c *Susan Emily; *b* 1956
2b *Cecilia Torlesse; Canadian WAC 1942–45; *m* July 1946 *Eliot Albert Leyden, and has issue:
1c *Richard Harold; *b* 1950
2c *Michael Peyton; *b* 1952
3c *Andrew Charles; *b* 1954
1c *Sylvia Dawn; *b* 1947
2c *Elizabeth Rose; *b* 1957
3b *Sylvia Revell [Mrs Allan Saunders, RR2 Petitcodiac, New Brunswick, Canada]; *educ* McGill (BSc); *m* 18 Sept 1948 *Allan Adolphus Saunders, s of Adolphus Fulton Saunders, of Petitcodiac, New Brunswick, and has had:
1c Heather Anne; *b* 5 Nov 1949; *d* 8 March 1956
2c *Nancy Peyton; *b* 18 June 1951
3c *Sylvia Lee; *b* 12 Sept 1953
2a Ernest Lancelot, NZ Expdny Force WW I 1917–18 (wounded); *b* 13 Oct 1888; *m* 2 Dec 1919 Margaret (*d* 1966), dau of L Hanlon, of Auckland, NZ, and *d* 1975, leaving:
1b +Philip [Philip Eardley-Wilmot Esq, 8 Ballaret St, Ellerslie, Auckland, New Zealand], F/Sgt RNZAF WW II; *b* 1920; *m* 1948 *Joan Hazel, dau of G R Fox, of Auckland, and has:
1c +Ronald Ernest; *b* 10 Feb 1953; *m* 1972 *Gaylene Mildon, of Mt Wellington, Auckland, and has issue:
1d +Matthew Ronald; *b* 1973
2d +Jamie; *b* 1975
3d +Nicholas; *b* 1977
1c *Kay; *b* 1951; *m* 1972 *William James Chapman, of Roslyn, Dunedin, NZ, and has issue:
1d *Kirsten; *b* 1974
2d *Melanie; *b* 1977
1b *Eileen; *b* 1922; *m* 1943 *Richard Quentin Taylor and has:
1c *Peter Raymond; *b* 1945
1c *Lynne Carol; *b* 1946
1a Mary Dora; *b* 2 March 1877; *d* unm 5 April 1924
2a Maud Cecilia; *b* 28 Jan 1882; *d* unm 19 Feb 1967
3a Irene Mildred; *b* 15 March 1884; *d* unm 6 Sept 1976
4a Hilda Violet; *b* 13 July 1886; *m* 7 Feb 1912 Frederick Kingsmill Brownrigg, s of John Annesley Brownrigg, MD, and *d* Jan 1944, leaving issue
5a Christine; *b* 11 July 1893; *d* unm 19–
(4) (cont.) The Rev Ernest Eardley-Wilmot *m* 2nd 15 Aug 1906 Arthurina Jane Arabella (*d* Aug 1943), yst dau of Maj-Gen Arthur Butcher, and *d* 13 Dec 1932
(5) Robert, JP, MB, MRCSE; *b* 6 Nov 1849; *m* 3 May 1876 Frances Gwynne (*d* 18 May 1928), dau of Charles William Whitby, MB, MRCS, of Ottery St Mary, Devon, and *d* 3 Dec 1935, having had issue:
1a Edward Gwynne; *b* 1 Feb 1877; *educ* Tonbridge and Oriel Coll Oxford (BA 1899, MA 1903); barrister Lincoln's Inn 1908, Bencher 1939, assist master Harrow 1901–06, Master Skinners' Co 1922–23, T/Capt 7th Bn RWF and RTO 1916, Counsel to PO 1939–47; *m* 4 Aug 1904 Jane Millicent, OBE (1920) (*d* 11 Dec 1964), only dau of Sir James William Scott, 1st Bt, of Yews (*qv*), and *d* 12 Oct 1965, leaving issue:
1b Elizabeth Averil, MBE (1955); *b* 21 May 1905; *m* 26 June 1928 Maj Sir Cyril Holland Shakerley, 5th Bt (*qv*), and had issue
2b Mary Marow; *b* 18 May 1909; *m* 24 Oct 1933 Capt John de Bourbel Stansfeld, MC, JP, Gordon Highrs (*d* 1975), only s of Lt-Col John Raymond Evelyn Stansfeld, DSO, and *d* 1 Aug 1997, leaving:
1c *John Raoul Wilmot, JP, DL (Angus 1984) [John Stansfeld Esq JP DL, Dunninald, Montrose, Angus DD10 9TD]; *b* 1935; *m* 1965 *Rosalinde Rachel, dau of Desmond Gurney Buxton (*see* BUXTON, Bt), and has issue:
1d *Edward John Buxton; *b* 1966; *m* 27 Jan 1996 *Mary Katharine Margaret, only dau of Robert Graham Langton Brackenbury, and has:
1e *Katharine Elizabeth; *b* 2 April 1997
2d *Robert George Wilmot; *b* 1967
3d *Nicholas Desmond Morse; *b* 1972
2c *Martin Raymond Eardley; *b* 1937; *m* 1991 *Monica Ann Joseph, of Youngstown, Ohio
2a Theodore, DSO, Maj (T/Lt-Col) York and Lancs Regt; *b* 15 Dec 1879; *m* 29 July 1908 Mildred Clare (*d* 3 Feb 1956), dau of William Francis Reynolds, of Woodland Grange, nr Leamington, and was *ka* 22 March 1918, leaving issue:
1b Anthony Revell, Capt (T/Maj) Irish Gds WW II; *b* 9 Jan 1910; *educ* Downside and Trin Coll Cambridge (MA); *ka* Aug 1944
1b *Mildred Joan [The Rt Hon The Lady Cross of Chelsea, The Bridge House, Leintwardine, Craven Arms, Salop]; *b* 12 Jan 1912; *m* 1st 28 June 1939 Thomas Walton Davies (*d* 28 Jan 1948), only s of David Davies, MB, MRCS, LRCP, of Hurst View, Tunbridge Wells, Kent, and has issue:
1c *Caroline; *b* 1941
2c *Sophia; *b* 1946; *m* 1969 *Henning Rasmussen
1b (cont.) Mrs Thomas Davies *m* 2nd 23 Feb 1952 Baron Cross of Chelsea, PC (LP, *cr* 1971, *d* 1989), s of Arthur George Cross, and by him has:
1c *Julia; *b* 1953; *m* 1st 1973 (*divorce*) Barney Walker; *m* 2nd 19— *David Openshaw and has issue
(6) Henry, Maj ISC; *b* 3 March 1854; *m* 17 Nov 1883 Agnes Mary (*d* 11 June 1944), dau of Lt-Gen Edward Burgoyne Cureton, and *d* 18 Feb 1933, leaving:
1a Percy, OBE (1919), T/Capt Gen List (Staff Capt 1917); *b* 22 Oct 1886; *m* 1915 Maisie Loder and *d* May 1960
2a Lambert, OBE (1942), F/Lt RAF, Lt Roy Leics Regt and RFC, Assist Regnl Dir Home Office NE Regn (ret 1959); *b* 12 July 1894; *m* 14 July 1930 Angela Clare Gertrude (*d* 4 March 1955), 2nd dau of Col Arthur Hare Vincent, of Summerhill, Co Clare, and *d* 1989, having had issue:
1b +Charles Vincent Burgoyne [Charles Eardley-Wilmot Esq, Fir Tree House, Lower Morton, Thornbury, Avon BS12 1LF]; *b* 30 May 1932; *educ* Wellington; *m* 26 Aug 1961 *Sheila, only dau of George Frederick Broomfield, of Thornbury, and has issue:
1c *Jane Clare [Mrs Geoffrey Sprackman, 30 Severn Dve, Thornbury, Bristol]; *b* 24 Feb 1962; *m* 1984 *Geoffrey J Sprackman and has:
1d *Ben Charles; *b* 1991
1d *Katie-Jane; *b* 1988
2c *Sarah Elizabeth [Mrs Jeremy Northcott, Hazel Cottage, St Tudy, Wadebridge, Cornwall]; *b* 3 Oct 1963; *m* 1990 *Jeremy Northcott and has:
1d *Emma Claire; *b* 1993
1a Florence; *m* 5 Sept 1905 Rev George William Philips (*d* 16 Dec 1920), Rector Checkley, Staffs, and had issue
2a Eleanor; *m* 27 July 1914 William Taylor Loveday, s of John Edward Taylor Loveday (*d* 15 Aug 1955), of Williamscote, Banbury, Oxon, and *d* 29 Oct 1939
(1) Edith Augusta; *b* 26 April 1851; *m* 27 Sept 1877 Rev Walter Lancelot Holland, MA (*d* 11 April 1935), 2nd s of Rev Charles Holland, Rector Petworth, Sussex, and *d* 12 April 1935, leaving issue
(2) Louisa Caroline; *b* 2 Oct 1852; *m* 27 Sept 1877 Col Vincent Rivaz, CB, IA (*d* 1 March 1924), and *d* 25 June 1924, leaving issue
4 Arthur Parry, CB, V-Adml; *b* April 1815; *m* 28 July 1868 Charlotte Louisa Mackenzie (*d* 9 April 1870), dau of Richard Wright, JP, of Larriga Ho, Co Cork, and *d* 2 April 1886, leaving issue:
(1) Flora Cecilia; *m* 25 Nov 1897 Arthur John Frederick Dawson, and *d* 29 March 1907, leaving issue
5 Henry Robert, Maj RA; *ka* Kaffir War 1 Jan 1852
6 Augustus Hillier; *b* 12 March 1818; *m* 20 May 1845 Matilda Jessie (*d* 28 April 1904), dau of John Dunn, banker, of Hobart Town, and *d* 9 Jan 1892, leaving:
(1) Stuart; *b* 16 Sept 1847; *m* 1874 Rosa Cornelia (*d* 1 Aug 1924), dau of William Johnstone, of Launceston, Tasmania, and *d* 29 June 1932, having had:
1a Gerald Stuart; *b* 1876; *m* 1902 Vera Constance (*d* 19 June 1965, having *m* 2nd 2 Jan 1913 Capt William Henry Wake Ridley, RN; *see* RIDLEY, V), dau of Charles Walker, of Launceston, Tasmania, and *d* 12 Nov 1909, leaving:
1b Stuart Jeffery, Capt RASC WW II; *b* 4 Aug 1907; *educ* Geelong GS Australia and St Edward's Sch Oxford; *m* 11 Nov 1933 Isobel Mary (*d* 1994), dau of William Young Fleming, of Bexhill-on-Sea, Sussex, and has issue:
1c +Brian [Brian Eardley-Wilmot, 15 Fernglen Rd S, St Heliers, Auckland, New Zealand]; *b* 24 Oct 1939; *m* 1st 1960 (*divorce* 1972) Margaret Robyn, dau of A Doust, and has issue:
1d +Allen Stuart; *b* 8 Oct 1961
1d *Kathryn Anne; *b* 16 June 1966
1c (cont.) Brian Eardley-Wilmot *m* 2nd 1980 *Maureen Jean, dau of George Huddlestone, of Cambridge
1c *Gillian Mary [Mrs William Cook, 346 Vesuvius Dve, La Brea, CA, USA]; *b* 6 Aug 1935; *m* 12 Oct 1957 *William H Cook, and has issue:
1d *Victoria Mary; *b* 20 Aug 1961
2c *Valerie [Mrs R P Haley, 1160 W Farrington Dve, La Habra, California, USA]; *b* 20 Nov 1946; *m* 16 June 1968 (*divorce* 1978) Lowell Keith Eitzen; *m* 2nd 1981 *R P Haley
2a Trevor, DSO (1918), Cdr RN, served WWs I (despatches) and II, Offr Order St Maurice and St Lazarus Italy; *b* 2 Jan 1884; *m* 19 Sept 1912 Fran-

ces Isabel (*d* July 1969), dau of Dr Kenneth Cousens, of Honolulu, and *dsp* 24 May 1957

3a Arthur Parry; *b* 1888; *m* 14 Aug 1912 Amy, dau of Percy Reynolds, of Hobartville, Richmond, NSW, and had issue:

1b +A son

2b A son; *k* in motor cycle accident

(2) Trevor; *b* 23 Nov 1850; *m* 19 Feb 1898 Rosa Matilda (*d* 27 Oct 1945), widow of Arthur Bryden and dau of Sir Percy Cuninghame Fairlie, 10th Bt (*see* FAIRLIE-CUNINGHAME, Bt), and *d* 21 April 1922

(3) Sainthill (Sir), KCIE, Inspr-Gen Forests India 1903–08; *b* 17 July 1852, *m* 1st 1 Dec 1884 Emma Elizabeth (*d* 5 July 1890), dau of George Casey, of Winterbourne St Leonards, and had:

1a Helen Jessie, MBE (1955); *b* 22 Feb 1886; *d* unm 4 March 1963

(3) (cont.) Sir Sainthill Eardley-Wilmot *m* 2nd 12 Dec 1891 Mabel Boisragon (*d* 18 Aug 1958), dau of W H Winter, of Tunbridge Wells, and *d* 13 Nov 1929, having by her had further issue:

2a Mabel Iris; *b* 6 Aug 1893; *m* 21 Dec 1922 George H Dummett (*d* 12 Nov 1969), s of R Dummett, and had issue

(4) Hungerford Colston; *b* 7 Dec 1855; *m* Mary (*d* Feb 1941) and *d* 28 April 1919, leaving a dau

(5) Colville, Ceylon CS; *b* 5 Jan 1858; *m* 1st 27 Sept 1894 Frances Field (*d* 22 June 1902), only dau of James Bruyn Andrews, of Le Pijautier, Mentone, and has issue:

1a Irene Victoria; *b* 26 July 1897; *m* 5 June 1918 Maj John Wilberforce Hare, DSO, RA (*d* 28 Nov 1954), and *d* 1956, having had issue

(5) (cont.) Colville Eardley-Wilmot *m* 2nd 21 Sept 1903 Adèle Winifrede (*dsp* 7 Aug 1910), 2nd dau of John Arthur Locke, of Dulverton, Somerset; *m* 3rd 7 March 1916 Marian Constance (*d* 11 Aug 1962), dau of C E Hare, of Lee-on-Solent, and *d* 11 Nov 1934

(6) George; *b* 27 Nov 1862; *m* 1st 1896 Florence (*dsp* 18 Jan 1910), dau of Rev George B de Renzi; *m* 2nd 1 June 1911 Rose Suzanne, er dau of F Eden Waddington, and *dsp* 31 July 1946

(1) Katherine; *m* 1875 John R Binney, and *d* 1876, leaving issue

(2) Annie; *m* 28 May 1914 Frederick Edward Farrer, barrister

1 Elizabeth Emma Eardley; *m* March 1829 George Graham Blackwell (*d* 30 March 1838), of Ampney Park, Glos, and had issue

2 Selina Matilda Caroline; *m* 1st 11 June 1844 Wade Browne (*d* 2 Aug 1851), of Monkton Farleigh, Wilts, and had issue; *m* 2nd 15 Dec 1859 Rev Joseph Abbott (*d* 1896), Rector Wrentham, Suffolk, and *d* 20 March 1902

Sir John *m* 2nd 30 Aug 1819 Elizabeth (*d* 15 Dec 1869), dau of Sir Robert Chester, of Bush Hall, Master Ceremonies to GEORGE III, and by her had, with two daus:

7 Robert Charles Chester, Sec Prison Dept Home Office; *b* 4 June 1822; *m* 4 Dec 1849 Jeanie Louisa Stewart (*d* 19 March 1909), 2nd dau of John Dunn, banker, of Tasmania, and *d* 24 May 1910, having had issue:

(1) Arthur Denison; *b* 13 Feb 1858; *d* 11 Nov 1888

(1) Eliza Catherine; *m* 27 March 1878 Holland John Cotton, MD (*d* 25 June 1908), and *d* 14 Dec 1938, having had issue

(2) Constance; *m* 5 Sept 1907 William Tisdall Pilkington (*d* 29 Sept 1909), s of William Pilkington, of Carrick, Queen's Co, and *d* 23 Feb 1940

8 Charles Octavius, Capt 96th and 31st Regts; *b* 2 Oct 1824; *m* 1st 3 May 1849 Grace Sophia (*d* 30 Sept 1865), dau of John Dunn, and had, with another dau (*d* unm):

(1) Charles Herbert de Vere; *b* 13 Oct 1853; *d* unm 21 Feb 1888

(2) Cecil Francis de Lys, Commr Prisons England and Wales, Capt 2nd Bn Cheshire Regt; *b* 4 Aug 1855; *m* 25 April 1888 Alice Maule (*d* Jan 1930), er dau of Edmund Scott, of San Francisco, and *dsp* 14 July 1916

(1) Violet Agnes; *m* 12 Jan 1882 Henry Sydney Smith, of Chelsea, and *d* 26 July 1935, leaving issue

(2) Edith Mary; *m* 21 May 1885 Maj Jeffrey Charles Marston, RA (*d* 4 Oct 1899), and *d* 16 Sept 1951, leaving issue

8 (cont.) Capt Charles Eardley-Wilmot *m* 2nd 2 Oct 1866 Elizabeth (*d* 9 Feb 1924), 2nd dau of Charles Brooke, and *d* 26 July 1886, leaving by her:

(3) Charles Chester, MD; *b* 29 Oct 1867; *d* unm 8 April 1895

(4) Ernest, Capt ISC; *b* 27 Sept 1868; *d* unm 7 April 1900

Sir JOHN *d* 3 Feb 1847; his est s:

Sir John Eardley Eardley-Wilmot, 2nd Bt, DL; barrister, Recorder Warwick 1852–74, Co Ct Judge Bristol 1854–63 and Marylebone 1863–71, MP S Warwicks 1874–85; *b* 16 Nov 1810; *m* 27 April 1839 Eliza Martha (*d* 23 Oct 1887), sis of Sir Richard Bulkeley Williams-Bulkeley, 9th Bt (*qv*), and had, with another dau (*d* unm):

1 WILLIAM ASSHETON (Sir), **3rd Bt**

2 Revell, CB; Maj-Gen Bengal Inf, Col cmdg 14th Bengal Lancers, served Bhutan and Jowaki Expdns and Afghan War; *b* 29 Aug 1842; *m* 23 July 1906 Elizabeth, dau of J W Toone-Smith, MD, and *d* 14 June 1922

3 Edward Parry; *b* 23 Dec 1843; *m* 4 May 1872 Justine (*d* 21 Jan 1917), dau of M Klein, of Lorraine, and *d* 27 June 1898, having had two daus (*d* unm)

4 Frederick Henry, Lt RA; *b* 3 March 1846; *ka* Ashanti War 3 Nov 1873

5 Sydney Marow (Sir); R-Adml, Supt Naval Ordnance Stores 1902–09; *b* 3 Oct 1847; *m* 11 Oct 1877 Grace Maude (*d* 20 Feb 1946), dau of Thomas Rolls Hoare, and *d* 27 Feb 1929, leaving issue:

(1) Guy; *b* 29 Jan 1893; Lt RGA WW I; *d* unm 31 May 1966

(1) Kate; *b* 21 Feb 1879; *m* 10 Dec 1903 Norman Deakin, RFC, only s of G H Deakin, and *d* 8 Dec 1917, leaving issue

(2) May; *b* 15 Feb 1883; *educ* Heidelberg; lyricist; *d* unm 3 June 1970

(3) Nora; *b* 24 Feb 1885; *m* 19 Oct 1909 Edward Cleland Richardson, s of D Richardson, of Cove, Dunbartonshire and *d* 23 Nov 1976, leaving a s and two daus

6 Hugh Eden; *b* 7 Nov 1850; barrister 1871, Co Ct Judge (Circuit 33) 1891–1920; *m* 19– Elizabeth Ellen (*d* 14 April 1923) and *d* 10 March 1926

1 Selina Anne Mary; *m* 1st 19 April 1876 (*divorce* 26 Oct 1886) Capt St Aubyn Henry Player, Inniskilling Dragoons (*d* 1891), and had issue; *m* 2nd 18 Nov 1886 Chaloner Chute Ellis and *d* 20 May 1922, leaving issue

Sir JOHN *d* 1 Feb 1892; his est s:

Sir William Assheton Eardley-Wilmot, 3rd Bt; Col Northumberland Fus, DAAG HQ Ireland 1879–82, DJA Ireland 1882–85 and London 1885–96; *b* 16 May 1841; *m* 12 Dec 1876 Mary (*d* 22 Feb 1929), 3rd dau of David Watts Russell, of Biggin, Northants, and *d* 12 April 1896, leaving issue:

1 **Sir John Eardley-Wilmot, 4th Bt**; *b* 14 Oct 1882; *educ* Eton; Capt Rifle Bde S Africa 1902 (medal and two clasps) and WW I (wounded); *m* 14 June 1916 Amabel (*d* 20 Feb 1961), dau of Elverton R Chapman, of Long Island, NY, and *d* 9 Feb 1970, having had issue:

(1) *Mary Assheton Alexandra; *b* 9 Feb 1927; *m* 25 Nov 1950 *Gavin Douglas Don, only surv s of Capt William Gilbert Don, Fife and Forfar Yeo, of Angus, by Jeannette Elizabeth Edith Grizel, 2nd dau of Brig-Gen William Charles Douglas of Brigton, CB, DSO, JP, DL, and has issue:

1a *William Assheton Eardley Douglas; *b* 16 May 1958

2a *John Gavin Marow Douglas; *b* 11 Dec 1960

3a *Alexander John Wilmot Douglas; *b* 25 July 1964

1a *Susannah Mary Grizel Douglas; *b* 10 Jan 1952

2a *Sarah Amabel Douglas; *b* 31 March 1955

3a *Cecily Margaret Douglas; *b* 21 Jan 1970

2 (Frederick) Neville, Cdr RN; *b* 29 Jan 1885; *m* 5 July 1915 Dorothy (*d* 11 Nov 1959), er dau of Charles Carruthers Little, of Double Bay, Australia, and *d* 15 July 1956, having had issue:

(1) **Sir John Assheton Eardley-Wilmot, 5th Bt**, LVO (1957), DSC (1943); *b* 2 Jan 1917; *educ* RNC Dartmouth; RN WW II (Norwegian War Medal 1943), Cdr 1950, cmded HMS *Opossum* 1951–53, ret 1967 as Dep Dir Naval Admin Planning; Monopolies Commn 1967–82; MIMgt, FRSA 1970, Freeman City London; *m* 23 June 1939 his cousin *Diana Elizabeth [Diana Lady Eardley-Wilmot, 41 Margravine Gdns, London W6 8RN], yr dau of Cdr Aubrey Moore, RN, and *d* Dec 1995, leaving:

1a Sir MICHAEL JOHN ASSHETON EARDLEY-WILMOT, **6th and present Bt**

1a *Patricia Enid [Mrs Andrew McMeekan, 41 Margravine Gdns, London W6 8RN]; *b* 12 Oct 1944; *m* 30 July 1966 *Lt Andrew McMeekan, RN, s of Thomas McMeekan, of Earl's Court, and has issue:

1b *Emily Charlotte; *b* 1974

2b *Isabel Heloise; *b* 1978

(2) Anthony Neville, Maj Roy Northumberland Fus attd 6th Durham LI WW II (despatches); *b* 24 March 1918; *educ* St Paul's; *ka* N Africa 23 March 1943

(3) +Michael [Michael Eardley-Wilmot Esq, 2 Mittara Rd, Terrigal, NSW, Australia]; *b* 29 July 1924; *m* 10 Feb 1956 *Sylvia, dau of Arthur Irish, of Sydney, NSW

(1) Rosemary; *b* 17 July 1920; *m* 14 Sept 1939 Capt Hon Basil Egerton Feilding, Coldstream Gds (*see* DENBIGH and DESMOND, E), and *d* 3 Oct 1970, leaving issue

3 Stephen, T/Lt Northumberland Fus WW II; *b* 11 Aug 1887; *educ* Wellington; *m* 10 July 1923 Marguerite May (*d* 12 Feb 1958), dau of Edgar C Prettie, and *dsp* 23 March 1950

1 Cicely Marguerite; *b* 12 June 1878; *m* 14 June 1916 Cdr Ivor Francis Chichester, OBE, RN (*d* 22 March 1955), Naval Sec Ordnance Bd, 4th s of Maj Newton Charles Chichester, and *d* 10 Oct 1961

2 Sylvia Mary; *b* 24 Aug 1880; *m* 24 June 1913 Geoffrey Greenwood Pearson, RNVR (*d* 5 Feb 1951), s of George Pearson, and *d* 17 March 1964, having had issue

EARLE

Arms: Arg. three pallets ermine. **Crest:** A lion's gamb erased sa., holding a harpoon arg. **Motto:** *Servare modum* ('Maintaining the happy mean'). **Creation:** Bt (UK) 3 Nov 1869.

SIR (HARDMAN) GEORGE ALGERNON EARLE, 6TH BT, of Allerton Tower, Co Lancaster [Sir George Earle Bt, Abington Rectory, Murroe, Co Limerick, Ireland]; *b* 4 Feb 1932; *s* f 1979; *educ* Eton; Ensign Gren Gds, memb London Metal Exchange 1962–73; *m* 24 Jan 1967 *Diana Gillian Bligh, yst dau of Col Frederick Ferris Bligh St George, CVO (*see* ST GEORGE, Bt), and has:

1 +ROBERT GEORGE BLIGH; *b* 24 Jan 1970

1 *Katherine Susan; *b* 8 July 1968

Lineage: The E(A)RLEs, originally from the North of England, settled in the Stockton district of Cheshire *c* 1490

RICHARD ERLE, of Stockton; *fl c* 1460–1525; ancestor of:

1 ROBERT EARLE; *fl* at Stockton *c* 1550–1615

1 Ellen; *m c* 1575 Thomas Birchall, of Cuerdley, Lancs

The bro,

ROBERT EARLE; had, with two er sons:

GREGORY EARLE, of Stockham, Cheshire, and Warrington, Lancs; *m* 20 Oct 1625 Alis Holbrucke (*bur* 31 July 1666) and was *bur* 1 April 1650, leaving, with a dau and three yr sons:

JOHN EARLE, of Warrington; *bapt* 20 Feb 1626/7; *m* 1673 Sarah (*bur* 23 Feb 1709), dau of Thomas Warburton, of Partington, and was *bur* 14 Mar 1708, leaving an est s:

JOHN EARLE; Mayor Liverpool 1709; *bapt* 29 Oct 1674; *m* 1st 10 Dec 1700 Eleanor Tyrer, of Liverpool (*bur* 14 July 1702), and had a s (*d* an infant); *m* 2nd 16 Feb 1709/10 Mary (*d* 7 June 1751), only child and heiress of Ralph Finch, of Chester, and *d* 14 April 1749, having had, with two daus:

1 John; *b* 1713; *bur* 30 Oct 1737

2 Ralph EARLE later WILLIS (on inheriting the estates of his kinsman Daniel Willis); Mayor Liverpool 1769; *b* 1715; *m* Dorothy, 2nd dau of Richard Aldersley, and had two sons

3 Thomas, of Leghorn; *b* 1719; *m* June 1754 Mary (*d* 1785), only child and heiress of Adam Mort, of Wharton Hall, Tyldesley, Lancs, and *d* 1781, leaving:

(1) Mary; *m* her cousin Thomas Earle, DL, of Spekelands (*see* below)

(2) Jane Elizabeth; *m* Richard Gwillym, of Bewsey, Lancs

4 William, of W Derby, Lancs; *b* 1721; *m* Ann (*d* 9 Jan 1785), widow of John Winstanley and dau of Thomas Hesken, and *d* 28 April 1788, leaving, with other issue:

(1) THOMAS, of whom presently

(2) William, of Everton; *m* 8 May 1791 Ann (*d* 1 May 1819), dau of John Copland, of Liverpool, and *d* 10 Jan 1839, leaving:

1a Charles; *b* 1798; *d* 1881, leaving issue.

The er son,

THOMAS EARLE, of Spekelands, Lancs, JP, DL; Mayor Liverpool 1787; *b* 1754; *m* 20 April 1786 his cousin Mary (*see* above) and *d* 9 July 1822 aged 68, having had, with other issue:

1 William, DL, JP Lancs; Mayor Liverpool 1836; 7 Feb 1787; *m* 15 July 1829 Anne (*d* 15 Aug 1855), 6th dau of Joseph Bradish, of Kilkenny, and *dsp* 26 Sept 1864

2 HARDMAN (Sir), **1st Bt**

3 Richard, of Edenhurst, Lancs; barrister; *b* 26 April 1796; *m* 29 Sept 1829 Margaret (*d* 30 Nov 1871), yst dau of William Langton, of Kirkham, and *d* 21 April 1848, leaving:

(1) Frederic William, of Edenhurst, JP; *b* 22 July 1830; *m* 8 Jan 1868 Alice Louisa (*d* 15 Dec 1932), dau of Miles Henry Custance, of Brussels, and *dsp* 27 April 1891

1 Mary; *m* 18 Nov 1820 Sir W P de Bathe, Bt, and *d* 14 Sept 1854, leaving issue

2 Anne; *m* 24 May 1821 Joseph Langton and *d* 15 Aug 1875, leaving issue. He *d* 25 Oct 1855

3 Jane; *m* 4 April 1831 George Hall Lawrence, of Liverpool, and *dsp* 5 Feb 1883. He *d* 15 Jan 1869

The 4th son (2nd here mentioned),

Sir Hardman Earle, 1st Bt (UK), so *cr* 3 Nov 1869, of Allerton Tower, Lancs; *b* 11 July 1792; *m* 24 Aug 1819 Mary (*d* 25 March 1850), 2nd dau of William Langton, of Kirkham, Lancs, and had issue:

1 THOMAS (Sir), **2nd Bt**

2 Hardman; *b* 20 Jan 1825; *m* 19 Aug 1852 Harriet Matilda (*m* 2nd 15 Oct 1863 Maj James Legh Thursby, JP (*d* 31 July 1886), 2nd s of Rev William Thursby, of Ormerod House, Lancs), est dau of Edward Johnston, and *dsp* 28 May 1853

3 William, CB, CSI; *b* 18 May 1833; Maj-Gen Gren Gds, served Crimea and Egypt cmdg River Column Nile Expdn; *m* 21 July 1864 Mary (*d* 27 Jan 1928), 2nd dau of Gen Sir William John Codrington, GCB (*see* CODRINGTON, Bt, of Dodington (1876)), and was *k* Kirbekan, the Sudan, 10 Feb 1885, leaving:

(1) Rachel Mary; *d* unm 30 Dec 1935

(2) Grace Elizabeth; *m* 19 April 1893 John Russell Villiers and *d* 31 May 1962 aged 93, leaving issue (*see* CLARENDON, E)

4 Arthur, JP Lancs; *b* 14 Dec 1838; FRGS; *m* 19 Nov 1867 Ida Euphemia Bertie (*d* 1 April 1903), est dau of Sir George Buckley Matthew, KCMG, CB, and *d* 5 Feb 1919, having had issue:

(1) Cecil Arthur, Lt RA; *b* 19 Nov 1868; *m* 1891 Isabella, MBE (*d* 3 June 1944), dau of Fife John Scott, and *d* 15 July 1896, leaving issue:

1a Guy Fife, Capt Rifle Bde WWs I (wounded) and II in RAF; *b* 24 Aug 1891; *educ* Harrow and RMC Sandhurst; *m* 1st 6 June 1918 (*divorce* 1922) Isabel Bridget (*d* 1971), 2nd dau of Andrew Greville Rose Boughton-Knight, of Wormesley Grange, Herefs (*see* 1963 edn ROUSE-BOUGHTON, Bt), and had issue:

1b *Audrey Bridget [Miss Audrey Earle, Arnolds, Burnham Market, King's Lynn, Norfolk]; served WW II with No 3 Motor Ambulance Convoy, Br Red Cross, and Paris Sub-Commn Civilian Relief; *b* 29 June 1920

1a (cont.) Guy Earle *m* 2nd 10 Nov 1924 (*divorce* 1928) Helen Alice (*d* 1967), only dau of Ninian Elliot (*see* MINTO, E); *m* 3rd 26 April 1935 Bridget Joan (*d* 1993), only child of Peter Davis Sherston, of Hill House, Templecombe, Somerset, and *d* 30 Dec 1966, leaving by her:

1b +Michael Guy [Michael Earle Esq, 83 Fairview Ave, Newtown, Victoria 3220, Australia]; *b* 28 Sept 1942; *educ* Harrow and RAC Cirencester; *m* 1969 *Morrell Frances Armitage, dau of S/Ldr John Robert Nassau Molesworth, DFC (*see* MOLESWORTH, V), and has issue:

1c +Guy Robert; *b* 1973

2c +Nicholas Molesworth; *b* 1980

1c *Amanda Morrell; *b* 1971

2b *Susan Mary [Mrs Susan Searle, Taponecco 45, Tavernelle, MS54010, Italy]; *b* 14 Nov 1940; *m* 1978 (*divorce* 19–) Kenneth Searle, MBE, CMZS

3b *Virginia Ida [Mrs Virginia Jackson, Valley Barn, Hawkeslane, Colaton Raleigh, Devon EX10 0JA]; *b* 6 March 1945; *m* 1971 (*divorce* 1977) Frederick Jackson and has issue:

1c *Conrad Guy Frederick; *b* 1973

2a Eric Greville, DSO (1915), DL (Bucks 1950), CC Bucks 1949–65, High Sheriff 1953, Co Cmmr Boy Scouts 1951–61, memb Govr's Cncl Gibraltar 1944–45 (Actg Govr 1945), Brig RA, served WW I (despatches four times, wounded twice), Afghan War 1919 (medal and clasp) and WW II, Chev Order Leopold Belgium and Croix de Guerre; *b* 24 Feb 1893; *educ* Wellington; *m* 1st 17 Jan 1918 (*divorce* 1931) Noel (*d* 1975), yst dau of Capt Edward Downes-Martin, of Killoskehane Castle, Co Tipperary, and had issue:

1b Cecil Diccon, Capt RHA WW II; *b* 12 Nov 1919; *m* 30 Nov 1943 *Elizabeth Anne (*m* 2nd 10 Jan 1950 Maj A G F Mathers, RTR), er dau of E A Sainsbury, of Weston-super-Mare, and was accidentally *k* 15 Nov 1945

2b +David Eric Martin, OBE (1969) [David Earle Esq OBE, Shipways, Church Lane, Kington Langley, Wilts]; Capt RA Burma 1945, Palestine 1947–48, Cyprus 1955–56, Instructor Staff Coll 1956–60; *b* 14 Aug 1921; *educ* Stowe and Ch Ch Oxford; *m* 8 April 1947 *Betty Isabel, yst dau of Lawford Shield, of Cheltenham, Glos, and has:

1c +Charles Henry Diccon [Charles Earle Esq, Riseholme, Seven Hills Rd, Cobham, Surrey]; *b* 29 May 1951; *educ* Stowe and Ch Ch Oxford; *m* 1984 *(Margorie) Lucy, dau of Dr William Mervyn Jones, of Aberystwyth, and has:

1d +Guy Charles William; *b* 1985

2d +James Edward David; *b* 1987

2c +George Eric William [George Earle Esq, 15 Castello Ave, London SW15 6EA]; *b* 19 Aug 1953; *educ* Stowe; *m* 1985 *Clare, dau of Graeme Campbell-Johnston, and has issue:

1d +Graeme David Campbell; *b* 1988

2d +Andrew David Campbell; *b* 1993

1d *Rosemary Elizabeth Campbell; *b* 1990

1c *Victoria Lilian Gay (Tolla); *b* 29 July 1952; *m* 1977 (*divorce* 1989) Richard Walter Sutcliffe and has:

1d *Diccon Thomas George; *b* 1983

1d *Sophie Isobel Susan; *b* 1980

2c *Charlotte Mary [Mrs Anthony A'Hern, Lantern Cottage, High St, Lane End, Bucks HP14 3SF]; *b* 28 Nov 1959; *m* 1991 *Anthony N A'Hern, only s of Maj T A'Hern, of Sherborne, Dorset, and has issue:

1d *William David Anthony; *b* 1993

2d *Henry Thomas Edward; *b* 1995

3b Robin Denys Michael, OBE (1942), Lt (A) RNVR; *b* 15 Oct 1922; *educ* Wellington; *m* 1st 2 Nov 1946 (*divorce* 1962) Rosemary, dau of Maj F A Latter, of Birkdault, Lindfield, and has:

1c +Toby Dick [Toby Earle Esq, 54 Long Copse Lane, Emsworth, Hants PO10 7UR]; *b* 8 June 1951; *m* 1981 *Juliet Miranda, dau of Basil Peredur Jones, of Constantine, Cornwall, and has had issue:

1d Robin; *b* 1982; *d* 1984

2d +Joshua Robin; *b* 1984

3d +Barnaby Dicken; *b* 1988

1c *Penelope Jane [Mrs Kenneth Ward, 54 Langham Rd, Teddington, Middx TW11 9HQ]; *b* 8 Oct 1947; *m* 1977 *Kenneth Brunton Ward, s of James Alfred Ward, of Edinburgh, and has issue:

1d *Gemma Kate; *b* 1981

2c *Jemima Tamsin; *b* 20 Jan 1949; *m* 1st 1970 (*divorce* 1985) Robert Arthur Meads, s of Arthur Meads, and has had issue:

1d *Nicholas John; *b* 1972

2d *Andrew David; *b* 1975; *d* 1991

1d *Caroline Elizabeth; *b* 1977

2c (cont.) Mrs Jemima Meads *m* 2nd 1986 *Roland Wooding and by him has:

1d *David; *b* 1986

3c *Lucy Noel; *b* 3 Dec 1954; *m* 1st 19– (*divorce* 19–); *m* 2nd 19– *Stuart Wilson

3b (cont.) Robin Earle *m* 2nd 1963 Anne, dau of Capt — Lawford; *m* 3rd 19– *Ann — and *d* 1990

4b +Peter Desmond Noel [Peter Earle Esq, Chestnuts, Beckley, E Sussex]; Lt RNVR WW II Atlantic & SE Asia; *b* 20 Nov 1923; *educ* Wellington and Ch Ch Oxford (BA 1949, MA 1954); *m* 6 Sept 1952 Hope Shirley Raymond (*d* 1986), dau of Wallace Sinclair MacGregor, of Vancouver, BC, and has issue:

1c *Virginia Melanie; *b* 17 Jan 1963

4b (cont.) Mr and Mrs Peter Earle also adopted:

*Robert Henry Mathew; *b* 18 Oct 1956

*Heather Anne; *b* 15 Oct 1958

2a (cont.) Brig Eric Earle *m* 2nd 25 Nov 1931 Diana Mary (*d* 26 Dec 1964), er dau of Dr Vaughan Harley, of Walton Hall, Bletchley, and *d* 19 Oct 1965

(2) John Greville, JP Lancs; *b* 26 Oct 1869; *m* 21 April 1920 Jacobina Reid (*d* 7 July 1970), only dau of James Clark, of Kilmarnock, and *d* 15 Nov 1933, having had issue:

1a +John Arthur [John Earle Esq, 21 via Udine, 34132 Trieste, Italy], Capt Rifle Bde WW II (wounded); *b* 30 Jan 1921; *educ* Winchester and Trin Coll Cambridge (BA 1948); *m* 8 Jan 1947 *Anna Maria, only dau of Maj-Gen Lorenzo Tiziani, Italian Army, of Trecenta, and has:

1b +Lawrence Hardman [Lawrence Earle Esq, 8 via Tor S Piero, Trieste, Italy]; *b* 16 May 1948; *educ* Winchester and Malta U (BA); *m* 1984 *Rita Dougan and has issue:

1c +Mathew John; *b* 1986

1c *Martina Jacobina Paola; *b* 1988

1b *Arabella Ida [Mrs Paul Lizioli, 14 via Machiavelli, Milan, Italy]; *b* 2 Jan 1955; *m* 14 Sept 1996 *Paul Lizioli

2a Thomas Mathew; *b* 23 Dec; *d* 25 Dec 1921

3a +William Hardman [William Earle Esq, The Walnuts, Beanacre, Wilts SN12 7PT]; Capt RE SE Asia 1945; *b* 12 Jan 1924; *educ* Winchester and Trin Coll Cambridge (BA 1945, MA 1954); *m* 13 Sept 1958 Vera Charteris (*d* 1992), yr dau of Colin Charteris Black, of W Chiltington, Sussex, and has:

1b +Rupert Langton; *b* 16 Nov 1960; *educ* Winchester and Trin Coll Cambridge (BA)

2b +Greville Hoare; *b* 17 March 1963; *educ* Winchester and Edinburgh U

1b Melanie Charteris; *b* 6 May 1965; *d* 14 Dec 1971

2b *(Alice) Jacobina; *b* 19 June 1970; *educ* Edinburgh U

4a +Richard Greville, DL (Dorset 1984) [Richard Earle Esq DL, Frankham Farm, Ryme Intrinseca, Dorset DT9 6JT], Sub-Lt (A) RNVR; *b* 12 Nov 1925; *educ* Winchester and Trin Coll Cambridge (BA 1949, MA 1959); High Sheriff Dorset 1983; *m* 19 Jan 1956 *Joanna Mary, JP, yr dau of Cdr Henry Kelsall Beckford Mitchell, CBE, JP, DL, RN (ret), of Folke Manor, Sherborne, and has issue:

1b *Elizabeth Mary; *b* 9 Sept 1957; *educ* Manchester U (BA); *m* 19 July 1997 *Geoffrey William Kenton, s of Richard Kenton, of W Bexington, Dorset

2b *Susan Helen; *b* 6 May 1959; *educ* Sheffield U (BSc) and UCL (MSc); *m* 1993 *Neil S Ross, s of Leslie Ross, of Evesham, Worcs, and has:

1c *Duncan Edward; *b* 30 April 1997

1c *Fenella Jane; *b* 18 May 1995

(3) Ronald Hamilton, Capt Lancs Artillery; *b* 20 Feb 1874; *m* 24 June 1901 Louise Mary, CStJ (*m* 2nd 20 Dec 1927 Sir Henry Mulleneux Grayson, 1st Bt (*qv*), and *d* 4 June 1954), only dau of Richard John Delaney, and *d* 24 Aug 1919, leaving issue:

1a Arthur Herbert Greville; *b* 20 June 1906; *m* 17 July 1930 (*divorce* 1933) Marie Maurissen-Ruglioni, dau of Capt Ernest Maurissen, and *d* 25 Aug 1951

(4) Lawrence Matthew; FRGS, T/Lt RASC 1915–19, Assist Censor 1939–44; *b* 16 Sept 1881; *educ* Winchester and Trin Coll Cambridge (BA 1903, MA 1908); *m* 23 March 1916 Helen Elizabeth Dunkin (*d* 22 May 1963), dau of Capt Frederick Street, W Kent Regt, of Dulverton, Somerset, and *d* 8 July 1968, leaving issue:

1a +Adrian Mathew; *b* 23 May 1922; *educ* Winchester and Worcester Coll Oxford

2a +Nigel Lawrence; WW II 1944–45 in RAC; *b* 6 Jan 1926; *educ* Radley; *m* 9 June 1951 *Jean Roxburgh, only dau of Dr Hugh McClintock, of Dreghorn, Eastbourne, and has issue:

1b +Brian Lawrence; *b* 2 Dec 1953; *educ* Radley

2b +Patrick Nigel; *b* 12 July 1958; *m* 1981 *(Susan) Elizabeth, dau of Capt David Kenneth Bawtree, RN, of Portsmouth, and has issue:

1c +Guy; *b* 1993

1c *Amaryllis (Lily) Roxborough; *b* 1991

(1) Lillian Ida; *d* unm Feb 1958

1 Mary; *m* 11 Oct 1849 James Loxham Foster, barrister, and *d* 11 Dec 1911. He *dsp* 19 July 1902

2 Elizabeth; *d* unm 10 July 1905

3 Emily; *m* 24 Sept 1857 Hugh Perkins, DL, and *d* 22 Feb 1914, leaving issue. He *d* 1899

4 Harriet; *m* 23 Oct 1850 Archibald Tod, of The Grange, Woolton, Lancs, and *d* 17 Feb 1913, leaving issue. He *d* 19 Aug 1870

5 Georgina; *m* 30 June 1859 Hugh Longueville Jones, of Elmsall Lodge, Yorks, and *d* 10 Dec 1908. He *dsp* 1 Aug 1875

6 Caroline; *m* 1 July 1856 Francis John Johnston, of Westerham, Kent, and *d* 3 Dec 1875, leaving issue. He *d* 1911

7 Mary; *d* an infant 18 Nov 1821

Sir HARDMAN *d* 25 Jan 1877; his est s,

Sir Thomas Earle, 2nd Bt, DL, JP Lancs; *b* 30 June 1820; *m* 6 Sept 1853 Emily (*d* 2 June 1905), dau of William Fletcher, of Allerton, Lancs, and *d* 13 April 1900, having had issue:

1 **Sir Henry Earle, 3rd Bt**, DSO (1887); *b* 15 Aug 1854; *educ* Eton and Trin Coll Oxford (Jon MA Cantab); Lt-Col KOYLI, served Jowaki campaign 1877, Afghan War 1878–80, Egyptian campaign 1882, Burma 1886–87 (despatches), Tirah Expdn 1897–98 (severely wounded), S Africa 1899–1901 (severely wounded Modder River, despatches, promoted Lt-Col) and WW I 1914–16; *m* 17 Sept 1891 Evelyn Grace (*d* 20 July 1963), dau of Maj Charles Henry Boileau (*see* BOILEAU, Bt), and *dspm* 16 July 1939, leaving:

(1) Phyllis Audrey; *m* 29 April 1915 Capt Osbert Stephen COOPER later CUNDY-COOPER, MC, Roy Fus (*d* 9 July 1962), only s of Rev Thomas Stephen Cooper, MA, of Chiddingfold, Surrey, and had issue

2 Hardman Arthur; *b* 17 Jan 1859; *educ* Eton; *m* 1 July 1946 Edith Eugenie (*d* 19 Jan 1969), widow of Arthur Holland and dau of Charles Wixley, and *d* 19 Nov 1935

3 THOMAS ALGERNON (Sir), **4th Bt**

4 William Edward; *b* 27 Sept 1861; *educ* Eton; *d* 30 Jan 1925

5 Alfred; *b* 29 June 1864; *educ* Eton; *d* unm 2 Jan 1941

6 Charles Frederic; *b* 19 April 1867; *educ* Eton; *m* 30 Nov 1911 Alice Adelaide (*d* 22 May 1942), widow of Patrick Cumin Scott, MB, of Blackheath, and dau of Henry Cleveland, and *d* 17 Dec 1939, leaving issue:

(1) *Evelyn Alice [Miss Evelyn Earle, 16 Rectory Green, Hayne Rd, Beckenham, Kent]; *b* 30 Aug 1912

(2) *Josephine Noëlle [Mrs Douglas Swinscow, Everley, 24 Monmouth St, Topsham, Exeter, Devon EX3 0AJ]; *b* 25 Dec 1914; *m* 17 July 1941 Douglas Swinscow (*d* 1992), MB, BS, DSc, dep ed *BMJ*, s of William Sprague Swinscow, of Knebworth, Herts, and has issue:

1a *Louise Patricia; *b* 25 Feb 1947; *m* and has two sons

2a *Katherine Janet; *b* 12 April 1951; *m* and has two sons

3a *Rosemary Helen; *b* 26 Sept 1954; *m* and has five sons and a dau

(3) *Rosamond Cleveland [Mrs Eric Metcalfe, 14 Burnhill Rd, Beckenham, Kent]; *b* 14 Oct 1918; *m* 7 Jan 1939 Rev Canon Eric Albert Metcalfe (*d* 1984), s of Albert Metcalfe, of New Malden, and has issue

7 Reginald; *b* 10 Sept 1871; *educ* Eton; *m* 6 May 1913 Maude Isobel (*d* 22 Oct 1957), dau of Capt Willoughby Still, RN, and *d* 13 April 1951

8 John Wilfrid, Capt Lancs Hus WW I (despatches); *b* 14 June 1878; *educ* Eton; *m* 19 Oct 1915 Margaret Cecil, dau of Robert Gartside-Tipping, CB, and *d* 8 March 1965

1 Mary; *d* an infant 16 April 1856

2 Mary; *d* young 26 Sept 1870

3 Emily Josephine; *d* unm 12 Sept 1942

4 Caroline; *d* unm 19 Jan 1946

5 Constance; *d* an infant 1865

6 Evelyn Margaret; *m* 3 April 1900 Maj Francis Gordon Cardew, OBE, 10th Bengal Lancers, and *d* 4 April 1957, leaving issue. He *d* 1946

The 3rd Bt's bro,

Sir Thomas Algernon Earle, 4th Bt, TD; *b* 16 July 1860; *educ* Eton; Col Lancs Hus WW I; *m* 20 April 1901 Edith (*d* 20 July 1963), 3rd dau of General Disney Leith, CB (*see* BURGH, B), and had issue:

1 HARDMAN ALEXANDER MORT (Sir), **5th Bt**

1 *Rosemary; *b* 1904

2 *Myrtle Valentine; *m* 1st 22 July 1933 (*divorce* 1947) Robert Owen Symon, only s of Lt-Col Walter Conover Symon, CMG, RA, of Chelsea; *m* 2nd 1948 Sydney Vernon (*d* 1961); *m* 3rd 1962 Brig Maurice Robert Lonsdale, DSO, OBE (*d* 1989), s of Robert Lonsdale, and by her 1st husb has:

(1) *Mairi Edith; *b* 1935

Sir THOMAS *d* 5 Sept 1945; his only s,

Sir Hardman Alexander Mort Earle, 5th Bt, TD; *b* 19 Aug 1902; *educ* Eton; 99th (Bucks and Berks Yeo), Brigade RFA, TA, WW II (wounded); *m* 27 July 1931 Maie (*d* 1986), dau of John Drage, of The Red House, Chapel Brampton, and *d* 1979, leaving:

1 Sir (HARDMAN) GEORGE ALGERNON EARLE, **6th and present Bt**

1*Belinda Mary [Mrs Anthony Forbes, Wakerley Manor, Oakham, Rutland LE15 8PA]; *b* 31 Oct 1937; *m* 1st 12 Oct 1959 (*divorce* 1968) Capt Patrick John Boteler Drury-Lowe, Scots Gds (*d* 1993; *see* LINLITHGOW M); *m* 2nd 1973, as his 2nd w *Anthony David Arnold William Forbes (*see* FARINGDON, B) and by her 1st husb has issue:

(1) *Lucy Belinda; *b* 1961; *m* 1989 *David Charles Palmer and has issue (*see* CHURCHILL, V)

(2) *Candida Dorothy; *b* 1963, *m* 1990 *G Piers Bracher, only s of Peter Bracher, of The Old Rectory, Ashford, Kent, and has issue:

1a *Barnaby Alexander Patrick; *b* 1993

2a *Harvey Peter Garnett; *b* 1995

EATWELL

Creation: B. (LP, UK) 1992.

THE BARON EATWELL, of Stratton St Margaret, Co Wilts (John Leonard Eatwell) [The Rt Hon The Lord Eatwell, President's Lodge, Queens' College, Cambridge CB3 9ET]; *b* 2 Feb 1945; *educ* Headlands GS Swindon, Queens' Coll Cambridge (BA 1967, MA 1971) and Harvard (AM, PhD 1975); Teaching Fell Harvard 1968–69, Research Fell Queens' Coll Cambridge 1969–70, Fell and Dir Studies Economics Trin Coll Cambridge 1970–96, Assist Lecturer Economics Cambridge 1975–77, Lecturer 1977–; Visiting Prof Economics New Sch for Social Research NY 1982–; Ec Advsr to Leader Lab Party 1985–92; Oppn Spokesman Ho Lds Treasury and Trade and Industry 1992–93, Pncpl Oppn Spokesman Ho Lds Treasury and Ec Affairs 1993–97; Tstee and Sec Inst Public Policy Research 1988–97 and chm 1997–, non-exec dir: Anglia TV Gp 1994– and Cambridge Econometrics Ltd, Pres Queens' Coll Cambridge 1996–; Chm: Extemporary Dance Theatre 1990, Crusaid 1993–; Govr Contemporary Dance Trust 1991–95; Dir: Arts Theatre Trust Cambridge 1991–95 and dir and independent memb Bd Securities and Futures Authority; memb: Cambridge Constituency Lab Party, Roy Ec Soc, American Ec Assoc; author: *An Introduction to Modern Economics* (with Joan Robinson, 1973), *Whatever Happened to Britain?* (1982), *Keynes's Economics and the Theory of Value and Distribution* (ed with Murray Milgate, 1983), *The New Palgrave: A Dictionary of Economics* (ed with Murray Milgate and Peter Newman, 4 vols, 1987), *The New Palgrave Dictionary of Money and Finance* (3 vols, 1992), *Transformation and Integration: Shaping the future of Central and Eastern Europe* (with Michael Ellman, Mats Karlsson, Mario Nuti and Judith Shapiro 1995), *Global Unemployment: loss of jobs in the '90s* (edited 1996) and *Not 'Just Another Accession': The Political Economy of EU Enlargement to the East* (with Michael Ellman, Mats Karlsson, Mario Nuti and Judith Shapiro 1997); *m* 1970, Hélène, dau of Georges Seppain, of Marly-le-Roi, France, and has issue:

1 *Nikolai; *b* 1971

2 *Vladimir; *b* 1973

1 *Tatyana; *b* 1978

Lineage: HAROLD JACK EATWELL, of Swindon, Wilts; had:

JOHN LEONARD, *cr* a **Baron**

EBRAHIM

Arms: Arg. in base on waves of the sea a Chinese junk sailing to the sinister, in chief also on waves two dhows sailing to the dexter, all ppr.; in chief per pale gu. and or thereon a pale az. between a rose of the first and a lotus flower also ppr. and charged with a mullet issuant from a crescent above five mullets in crescent, also of the first. **Crest:** Above an Indian lily on water ppr., a mullet radiated or. **Motto:** *Deo ducente nil nocet* ('With God leading, nothing can do [us] harm'). **Creation:** Bt (UK) 20 July 1910.

SIR (MAHOMED) CURRIMBHOY EBRAHIM, 4TH BT, of Bombay [Sir Currimbhoy Ebrahim Bt, Baitullah 33, Bait-ul-Amen Mirza, Kalig Beg Rd, Jameshed Quarters, Karachi, Sind, Pakistan]; *b* 24 June 1935; *s* f 1952; BA, LLB, advocate, memb Standing Cncl Baronetage 1961–; *m* 15 Nov 1958 *Dur-e-Mariam, dau of Minuchehir Ahmud Ghulamaly Nana, of Karachi, and has issue:

1 +ZULFIQAR ALI CURRIMBHOY; *b* 5 Aug 1960; *educ* Habib Public Sch and DJ Science Coll; *m* 1984 *Adila, dau of Akhtar Halipota, and has issue:
(1) +Mustafa; *b* 22 Sept 1985
2 +Murthaza Ali; *b* 21 Jan 1963
3 +Raza Ali; *b* 15 Dec 1964
1 *Durre Najaf; *b* 10 May 1969

Lineage: EBRAHIMBHOY PABANEY, shipowner; f of:

Sir Currimbhoy Ebrahim, 1st Bt (UK), so *cr* 20 July 1910, JP, leading memb Khoja Community, Pres Anjuman-i-Islam and Mahomedan Educnl Conference Bombay, merchant and millowner India and China, fndr many charitable instns in India, ktd 1905; *b* 25 Oct 1839; *m* 1st 5 Feb 1854 Bai Foolbai (*d* 8 July 1875), dau of Asoobhay Gangji, of Bombay, and had (with other issue, *d* young):

1 Gulamhusenbhoy; *b* 24 May; *d* 22 Nov 1857
2 (MAHOMEDBHOY) CURRIMBHOY (Sir), **2nd Bt**
3 Rahimbhoy; *b* 1 Nov 1868; *d* 11 Sept 1869
4 Fazulbhoy (Sir), ktd 1913, CBE (1918), JP Bombay; *b* 11 July 1873; *m* 24 Feb 1889 Sakinabai (*d* 1930), dau of Datoobhoy Ebrahim, of Cutch Mandvi, India, and *d* 1970, leaving issue:
(1) Abdulla; *b* 12 Jan 1901; *d* 4 May 1905
(2) +Ahmedbhoy; *b* 31 Aug 1902; *m* Aug 1922 *Zarina, dau of Ahmedbhoy Currimbhoy (*see* below), and has issue,
1a +Ariff; *b* 17 Nov 1926
2a *Niamat; *b* 1928
(3) +Mohamedali; *b* 21 May 1904
(4) +Gulamali; *b* 13 Sept 1905; *m* 1928 *Hamida, dau of Rehemtullah Ebrahim (*see* below)
(5) +Hoosein; *b* 27 Oct 1910
(6) +Amir Ali; *b* 7 July 1913
1 Kulsumbai; *b* 20 Aug 1860; *m* 7 Feb 1873 Abdullabhoy Meherali Dharamsey and *d* 14 Dec 1912, leaving issue. He *d* 9 Sept 1897
2 Fatmabai; *b* 4 Dec 1862; *m* 24 May 1878 Jafferbhoy Khak Padamsey, of Bombay, and *d* 23 Aug 1890, leaving issue
3 Khanumbai; *b* 4 Nov 1870; *m* 2 Nov 1882 Noormahomed Jairajbhoy Peerbhoy and *d* 10 Nov 1913. He *dsp* 20 Aug 1897

Sir Currimbhoy *m* 2nd 28 Aug 1876 Bai Foolbia (*d* 2 May 1918), dau of Vishram Sajan, of Bombay, and by her had issue:

5 Gulamhusein; *b* 12 Jan 1879; *m* 10 Feb 1896 *Khanoobai, dau of Datoobhoy, of Cutch Mandvi, and *d* 16 Feb 1918, leaving issue:
(1) Ebrahim; *b* 1 May 1897; *m* 1923 *Zarina, dau of Ahmed Curmally Janmahomed, and *d* 1969, leaving:
1a Allen; *b* 1924; *m* 1958 *Pritee Misra and *d* 1960, leaving:
1b *Alia; *b* 1961
2a +Asif Currimbhoy [Asif Ebrahim, 43 Bakhtawar, 22 N Dabholkar Rd, Bombay 400 006, India]; *b* 1928; *m* 1951 his cousin *Suraiya Ismail, dau of Ismailbhoy Currimbhoy Ebrahim, and has issue:
1b +Tabrik; *b* 1952; *m* 1979 *Nelofar Hussain and has issue:
1c +Sharik; *b* 1980
2b +Tarek; *b* 1954
3b +Nahed; *b* 1959; *m* 1982 *Amit Moitra and has issue:
1c +Tahzeeb; *b* 1983
1c *Tahini; *b* 1991
1a *Zinet; *b* 1925
(2) +Ali Mahomed; *b* 8 July 1902
(3) +Aziz; *b* 22 July 1915
(1) Ahmeena; *b* 20 Dec 1898; *m* 1916 A O Jamal, of Calcutta
6 Ahmedbhoy; *b* 17 Sept 1885; *m* 24 Oct 1902 Shireen, dau of Dost Mahomed Allana, of Bombay, and *d* Oct 1925, leaving issue:
(1) Hooseinali; *b* 4 Jan 1908; *m* 1928 *Nazil, dau of Rehemtullah Ebrahim (*see* below), and *d* 1968, leaving issue:
1a *Ziba (Semine); *b* 1929
2a *A dau; *b* 1933
(2) +Habibbhoy; *b* 5 Jan 1910
(1) *Zarina; *b* 18 Sept 1904; *m* Aug 1922 her cousin Ahmedbhoy, est son of Sir Fazulbhoy Currimbhoy, and has issue (*see* above)
7 Rehemtullah; *b* 27 May 1887; *m* 11 Dec 1908 Sakinabai, dau of Jafferbhoy Ratansey, of Bombay, and *d* 1921, leaving issue:
(1) *Nazli; *b* 26 Sept 1909; *m* 1928 her cousin Hooseinali Ebrahim (*see* above)
(2) *Hamida; *b* 1912; *m* 1928 her cousin Gulamali, 4th son of Sir Fazulbhoy Ibrahim, CBE (*see* above)
8 Habibbhoy; *b* 5 Sept 1889; *m* 30 Mar 1913 Khatijabai, dau of Nensey Khairag, of Bombay, and *d* 22 Nov 1949, having had issue:
(1) Akbar; *b* 22 Jan 1914; *d* 1920
(2) +Nazim; *b* 30 June 1915; *m* 13 Jan 1941 *Zarina, dau of Ahmed S Moloobhoy, of Bombay, and has issue:
1a *Reisa; *b* 16 Sept 1944
(3) +Sultan; *b* 29 Dec 1921; *m* 16 Oct 1949 *Munira, dau of Sir Fazal Ibrahim Rahimtoola, CIE, and has issue:
1a +Habib; *b* 8 July 1950
(4) Husein; *b* 1924; *d* 1925
(5) +Aziz; *b* 1927
(1) *Munira; *b* 1926
9 Ismailbhoy; *b* 8 Mar 1906; *m* 1925 Zarina, dau of Gulam Husain Sachedina, and *d* 1975, leaving issue:
(1) A son; *b* and *d* 1926
(2) +Aziz; *b* 1927
(1) *Suraiya; *b* 1929; *m* 1951 her cousin *Asif Currimbhoy Ebrahim (*see* above) and has issue
4 Jenabai; *b* 19 Nov 1880; *m* 5 Feb 1896 Gulamhusen Ladhabhoy Ebrahim, of Bombay, and had issue
5 Sherbanubai; *b* 23 Oct 1882; *m* 25 Sept 1899 Gulamhusen Rehemtullah Khairaj, of Bombay, and had issue
6 Labai; *b* 23 Sept 1883; *m* 19 Oct 1902 Abdullabhoy Gulamhusen Allana, of Bombay, and had issue
7 Remibai; *b* 21 Sept 1884; *d* 13 Sept 1885
8 Shireenbai; *b* 10 April 1888; *m* 1911 Rahin Vali Mahomed Pirmahomed and had issue
9 Khairubai Khairunisha; *b* 17 Dec 1894; *m* 1916 Carrumbhoy Nensey Khairaz
10 Mariumbai; *b* 8 Aug 1896; *m* 1916 Cassumali Subjeally
11 Sharifabai; *b* 29 June 1899; *m* 1920 Suleiman Rahimtulla Syani
12 Khatijabai; *b* 9 Nov 1901; *m* 1923 Yusufali Moosabhoy Jafferbhoy Pradham

Sir CURRIMBHOY *d* 26 Sept 1924 and was *s* by his est son,

Sir (Mahomedbhoy) Currimbhoy Ebrahim, 2nd Bt, ktd, millowner and merchant, JP, memb Haj Ctee, tstee: Currimbhoy Ebrahim Khoja Orphanage and Port of Bombay 1908–23, Kaisar-i-Hind gold medal; *b* 11 Sept 1867; *m* 12 Feb 1882 Sakinabai, dau of Jairazbhoy Pirbhoy, of Bombay, and had:

1 HUSEIN ALI (Sir), **3rd Bt**
2 Kamarkhanum; *b* 11 Jan 1901; *d* 25 Sept 1914

Sir CURRIMBHOY *d* 31 March 1928; his son,

Sir (Husein Ali) Currimbhoy Ebrahim, 3rd Bt, of Pabaney Villa, Bombay, JP; MLC Bombay 1937, nominated memb Bombay Municipal Corp 1935; *b* 13 April 1903; *m* 1st 1921 (*m* diss 1924) Zainub, dau of Dawoodbhoy Fazulbhoy, and had issue:

1 *Mumtaz; *b* 1922; *m* 1941 *Ahmed Rahim Valimahomed Peermahomed
2 *Munira; *b* 1923; *m* 1941 *Fazal Rahemtulla Maherali Chinoy

Sir CURRIMBHOY *m* 2nd 1926 (*divorce* 1944, remarried 1949) Al-Hagja Amina Khanum, dau of Ali Haji Qassamali Zairajbhoy; of Guishan, Peddar Rd, Bombay, and by her had issue:

1 MAHOMED (Sir), **4th and present Bt**

Sir CURRIMBHOY *m* 3rd 1946 (*divorce* 1949) Khoorshidbanoo, formerly Kathleen Mary MacKenzie, only dau of Martin Thomas Smith, of London, and *d* 4 March 1952

EBURY

Arms: Az. a garb or, a mullet for difference. **Crest:** A talbot statant or. **Supporters:** On either side a talbot regardant or, collared az., charged on the shoulder with a mullet of the second. **Motto:** *Virtus non stemma* ('Virtue, not ancestry'). **Creation:** B. (UK) 10 Sept 1857

THE 6TH BARON EBURY OF EBURY MANOR, Co Middlesex (Francis Egerton Grosvenor) [The Rt Hon The Lord Ebury, PO Box 466, Mt Macedon, Vict 3441, Australia]; *b* 8 Feb 1934; *s f* 1957; heir presumptive to earldom of Wilton; *educ* Eton and U Melbourne; *m* 1st 10 Dec 1957 (*divorce* 1962) Gillian Elfrida (Elfin) Astley, only dau of Martin Roland Soames, of Knightsbridge, by Myra, er dau of Col Hon Sir Maurice Charles Andrew Drummond, KBE, CMG, DSO (*see* PERTH, E), and has issue:

1 +JULIAN FRANCIS MARTIN [The Hon Julian Grosvenor, 101 Barcom Ave, Rushcutters Bay, Sydney 2011, NSW, Australia]; *b* 8 June 1959; *educ* Gordonstoun; *m* 1987 (*divorce* 1990) Danielle, 6th dau of Theo Rossi, of Sydney

The 6th BARON *m* 2nd 8 Mar 1963 (*divorce* 1973) Kyra, only dau of L L Aslin; *m* 3rd 1974 *Suzanne Jean, dau of Graham Suckling, of Christchurch, New Zealand, and has further issue:

1 *Georgina Lucy; *b* 29 March 1973

Lineage: ROBERT GROSVENOR, **1st Baron Ebury of Ebury Manor**, Co Middx (UK), so *cr* 10 Sept 1857, PC, 3rd son of 1st Marquess of Westminster (*see* WESTMINSTER, D); Groom Stole to HRH THE PRINCE CONSORT, MP Chester 1826–47 and Middx 1847–57; *b* 24 April 1801; 17 May 1831 Hon Charlotte Arbuthnot Wellesley (*d* 21 Nov 1891), sis of 1st Earl Cowley (*qv*), and had, with two daus:

1 ROBERT WELLESLEY, **2nd Baron**

2 Thomas George, CB; Sec Legation Peking 1879–83, Chargé d'Affaires 1882–83, Sec Embassy St Petersburg 1885–86; *b* 6 Feb 1842; *m* 24 April 1877 Sophie (*d* 6 May 1938), having *m* 2nd 30 Nov 1895 Sir Albert Gray, KCB, KC, (*d* 27 Feb 1928), only dau of S Wells Williams, LLD, US Min China, and *dsp* 8 Oct 1886

3 Norman de l'Aigle, Capt Gren Gds, MP Chester 1869–74; *b* 22 April 1845; *m* 25 June 1881 Caroline Susan Theodora, CBE (*d* 7 Aug 1940), 4th dau of Rt Hon James Stuart-Wortley (*see* WHARNCLIFFE, E), and *d* 21 Nov 1898, leaving:

(1) Susan Charlotte, DGStJ; author: *The Lilac and the Rose, A Winter Bouquet, The Edwardian Lady, John Buchan, by his wife and friends* and children's books *Mice on Horseback* and *The Cat's Grandmother*; *m* 15 July 1907 1st Baron Tweedsmuir (*qv*) and *d* 1977, leaving issue

(2) Margaret Sophie Katherine; *m* 2 Dec 1916 Jeremy Peyton-Jones, s of Peyton Peyton-Jones, of Melbourne, and had issue. He *d* 30 Oct 1930

4 Algernon Henry JP, DL Middx; Lt Rifle Bde, Hon Lt-Col 13th Middlesex RV, and Capt Herts YC; *b* 2 July 1864; *m* 25 Oct 1887 Catherine Dorothea Mary (*d* 18 Feb 1917), dau of Sir John Simeon, 3rd Bt (*qv*), and *d* 27 March 1907, leaving:

(1) Rosamund Mary Dorothy; *b* 5 Sept 1888; *m* 10 March 1924 Lt-Col John Alexander Lynch, 4th/14th Punjab Regt, of Kensington, s of James Lynch, of Chiswick, and was *k* by a flying bomb 30 June 1944, leaving issue. He *d* 19 March 1956

5 Richard Cecil, barrister; *b* 7 Jan 1848; *m* 1 Nov 1898 Jessie Amelia (*d* 28 Oct 1926), dau of Rev Charles Clarke, of Esher, Surrey, and *dsp* 28 Oct 1919

The 1st BARON *d* 18 Nov 1893; his est s,

ROBERT WELLESLEY GROSVENOR, **2nd Baron Ebury of Ebury Manor**, Capt 1st Life Gds and Cheshire Yeo Cav, DL Northants, MP Westminster 1865–74; *b* 25 Jan 1834; *m* 20 July 1867 Hon Emilie Beaujolais White (*d* 18 Dec 1923), yr dau of 1st Baron Annaly (*qv*), and had issue:

1 ROBERT VICTOR, **3rd Baron**

2 Hugh; 2nd Sec Dip Serv; *b* 8 Oct 1869; *d* unm 6 Aug 1900

3 Gilbert; *b* 18 Sept 1878; *d* 16 Feb 1891

4 FRANCIS EGERTON, **4th Baron**

1 Maud; *b* 18 Aug 1874; *m* 6 Oct 1897 Maurice George Carr Glyn and *d* 2 June 1948, leaving issue (*see* WOLVERTON, B)

2 Alice Katherine Sibell; *b* 26 Sept 1880; *m* 10 Feb 1902 1st Viscount Wimborne (*qv*) and *d* 17 April 1948, leaving issue

The 2nd BARON *d* 13 Nov 1918; his est s,

ROBERT VICTOR GROSVENOR, **3rd Baron Ebury of Ebury Manor**, Govr Guy's Hosp, Capt 13th Middlesex RV, served S African War 1900–01 (despatches); *b* 28 June 1868; *m* 1 Feb 1908 Florence (*d* 20 Oct 1927), dau of Edward M Padelford, of Savannah, Ga., and *d* 5 Nov 1921

FRANCIS EGERTON GROSVENOR, **4th Baron Ebury of Ebury Manor**, DSO and bar (1918), MC and bar; Maj Canadian Forces, GSO2 1918, WW I (despatches, wounded, Croix de Guerre avec palme); *b* 8 Sept 1883; *m* 21 July 1902 Mary Adela (*d* 13 Oct 1960), dau of John Glasson, and had:

1 ROBERT EGERTON, **5th Baron**

2 +Hugh Richard [The Hon Hugh Grosvenor, River Ridge, Courtlands Park, Carmarthen, Wales]; served WW II as Capt KSLI *b* 25 Nov 1919; *educ* Radley and RMC Sandhurst; *m* 1st 20 Sept 1939 (*divorce* 1952) Margaret, dau of James L Jacobs, of St Ives, Cornwall, and has issue:

(1) *Margaret Elizabeth; *b* 18 May 1947

2 (cont.) The Hon Hugh Grosvenor *m* 2nd 1955 *Victoria, only dau of H Wright, of Newport, Salop, and by her has issue:

(1) +William Peter Wellesley; *b* 1959

(1) *Victoria; *b* 1975

1 *Maud Elizabeth [The Hon Mrs O'Shaughnessy, Bethavon, Duke St, Northam 6401, Western Australia]; *b* 8 April 1909; *m* 1st 1 June 1931 (*divorce* 1942) 2nd Viscount Harcourt and has issue (*see* VERNON, B); *m* 2nd 8 Sept 1942 *Lt-Col Edward O'Shaughnessy, s of E O'Shaughnessy, of Cahircaveen, Co Kerry, and has further issue:

(1) *Elizabeth Mary; *b* 17 June 1947

(2) *Caroline Margaret [Mrs Dan Thornton, 150 Graydon Hall Drive, Apt 1610, Don Mills, Toronto Canada]; *b* 17 June 1947; *m* 19— *Dan Thornton

The 4th BARON *d* 15 May 1932; his er s,

ROBERT EGERTON GROSVENOR, **5th Baron Ebury of Ebury Manor**, DSO (1944), TD (1954), Ld in Waiting to HM GEORGE VI 1939–40, Maj Berkshire Yeo, Capt and T/Major RA, served WW II; *b* 8 Feb 1914; *m* 1st 1 July 1933 (*divorce* 1941) Anne, only dau of Maj Herbert Walter Acland-Troyte, MC (*see* ACLAND, Bt, of Columb John), and had issue:

1 FRANCIS EGERTON GROSVENOR, **6th and present Baron Ebury of Ebury Manor**

2 (Robert) Victor; 2nd Lt Life Gds; *b* 18 Mar 1936; *educ* Eton and Gordonstoun; *m* 1959 *Caroline [The Hon Mrs Grosvenor, Bennets, Grafton, Oxon OX18 2RY], only dau of Ronald Harry Higham, of S Kensington, by Hon Barbara Constance, 2nd dau of 3rd Viscount Hampden (*qv*), and *d* 1993, leaving issue:

(1) *Rachel Egerton [Mrs Tobias Buckler, Llwyn-on Llanthony, Gwent NP7 7NW]; *b* 15 Aug 1963; *m* 1986 *Tobias S Buckler, s of Humphrey Buckler, of Bledington, Oxon, and has issue:

1a *Peregrine Humphrey; *b* 1988

2a *Valentine Robert; *b* 1993

1a *Kiloran Dorothea Anne; *b* 1989

(2) *Virginia; *b* 19 May 1965; *m* 1988 *Mark Quinton Graham, s of John Graham, of Newcastle-upon-Tyne, and has issue:

1a *Emily Charlotte; *b* 1990

The **5th Baron** *m* 2nd 21 Nov 1941 (*divorce* 1954) Hon Denise Margaret Yarde-Buller, 2nd dau of 3rd Baron Churston (*qv*), and by her had:

3 +William Wellesley [The Hon William Grosvenor, 6 Lloyds Ave, London EC3N 3ES]; md Osborne Mktg Communications 1977; *b* 12 Sept 1942; *educ* Eton, Perugia U, Italy, and Trin Coll Oxford (MA 1968); *m* 15 Sept 1966 *Ellen, only dau of Dr Gunther Ulrich Seeliger, of Harlaching, Munich, Dir-Gen For Affrs EC and German Amb Mexico, and has:

(1) +Alexander Egerton; *b* 22 Jan 1968

(1) *Petra Antonia Primrose; *b* 24 Dec 1969; *m* 26 July 1996 *Gavin Pinnock, of Northants, and has:

1a *Tara Primrose; *b* 1997

4 +Richard Alexander; antique dealer; *b* 5 July 1946; *educ* Milton Abbey and Us of Perugia, Montpelier, Lyons and Munich; *m* 24 Oct 1970 (*divorce* 1986) Gabriella, dau of Dr Xavier Speckert, of Bishopsgate House, Englefield Green, Surrey, and has:

(1) +Bendor Robert Gerard; *b* 1977

4 (cont.) The Hon Richard Grosvenor *m* 2nd 1989 *Frances Ann, dau of David Samuel Williams, of Newport, Gwent, and has further issue:

(1) *Letisah Emma; *b* 1989

1 *(Laura Georgina) Kiloran; *b* 5 July 1946; *m* 12 June 1969 (*divorce* 1979 resumed maiden name by deedpoll 1983) G R Mark Cross, only s of Geoffrey Cross, of Bray-on-Thames, and Mrs Peter de Lande Long, of Heatherson Green Farm, Cheshire; *m* 2nd 1993 *Brian Murrell

2 *Linda Denise [The Hon Mrs Vane Percy, Island Hall, Godmanchester, Cambs]; *b* 29 June 1948; *m* 17 May 1973 *Christopher D Vane Percy, s of Kenneth Vane Percy, of Biddenham, Beds, and has:

(1) *Maximilian Egerton; *b* 1979

(1) *Grace Dorothy Denise; *b* 1981

(2) *Tryce Mary Susanne; *b* 1991

The **5th Baron** *m* 3rd 12 Oct 1954 *Mrs Sheila Winifred Anker [The Rt Hon The Dowager Lady Ebury, 37 Linkside Avenue, Five Mile Drive, Wolvercote, Oxford OX2 8JE], yr dau of Arthur Edward Dashfield, of Oxford, and was *k* in a motor racing accident 5 May 1957

ECCLES

Arms: Chevronny arg. and sa. per pale counter-changed two torches erect or, enflamed ppr. **Crest:** A three-masted ship, sails furled, pennons and flags flying or, between two wings addorsed sa. **Supporters:** On either side a wolf sa, armed and langued gu, gorged with a plain collar, attached thereto a chain reflexed over the back and resting the interior hind paw on a portcullis chained or. **Motto:** Truth and beauty. **Creation:** B. (UK) 1 Aug 1962, V. (UK) 14 Jan 1964.

THE 1ST VISCOUNT ECCLES, of Chute, Co Wilts, so *cr* 14 Jan 1964, as also earlier 1 Aug 1962 **Baron Eccles**, of Chute, Co Wilts (both UK) (Sir David McAdam Eccles, CH, KCVO (1953), KBE (1984), PC (1951)) [The Rt Hon The Viscount Eccles CH KCVO KBE PC, Dean Farm, Upper Chute, nr Andover, Hants SP11 9ET; 6 Barton St, London SW1P 3NG]; *b* 18 Sept 1904; *educ* Winchester and New Coll Oxford; with Min Ec Warfare Sept 1939–40, Ec Advsr to Br Amb Lisbon and Madrid 1940–42, with Min Prodn 1942–43, MP (C) Chippenham 1943–62, Min: Works 1951–54, Educn 1954–57 and 1959–62, Pres BOT 1957–59, PMG and Min with Special Responsibility for Arts 1970–73, Chm Br Library Bd 1973–78, pres World Craft Cncl 1974–78, dir Courtaulds 1962–70, Tstee Br Museum 1963–70 (chm 1968–70), chm: W Cumberland Silk Mills 1964 and Anglo-Hellenic League 1967–70, hon FRIBA, SNR, Fell RCA 1962, author: *Half-Way to Faith* (1966), *Life and Politics: A Moral Diagnosis* (1967), *On Collecting* (1968), *By Safe Hand: Letters of Sybil and David Eccles 1939–42* (1983); *m* 10 Oct 1928 Hon Sybil Frances Dawson (*d* 2 June 1977), est dau of 1st and last Viscount Dawson of Penn, PC, GCVO, KCMG; *m* 2nd 26 Sept 1984 *Mary, widow of Donald Hyde, of Four Oaks Farm, 350 Burnt Mill Rd, Somerville, New Jersey, USA, and by his 1st w has issue:

1 +JOHN DAWSON, CBE (1985) [The Hon John Eccles CBE, Moulton Hall, Moulton, Richmond, Yorks; 6 Barton St, London SW1P 3NG]; *b* 20 April 1931; *educ* Winchester and Magdalen Coll Oxford; Capt TA, md Head Wrightson 1955–77, dir: Glynwed Int plc 1972–96, Investors in Industry plc 1974–88, Davy Int plc 1977–81, Courtaulds Textiles plc 1993 and chm 1995–, Garett Strategic Investment Tst 1995–, chm Chamberlin & Hill plc 1982–, memb Monolopies & Mergers Cmmn 1976–85 (dep chm 1981–85), memb Cwlth Devpt Corp 1982–85 (gen man 1985–94), chm Bd of Tstees Roy Botanical Gdns Kew 1983–91, The Georgian Theatre Roy Richmond Yorks, Hon DSc Silsoe Coll Cranfield Inst of Technology 1989; *m* 29 Jan 1955 *Diana (*cr* 1990 Baroness Eccles of Moulton; *qv*) and has issue:

(1) +William David [The Hon William Eccles, 111 Howards Lane, London SW15 6NZ]; *b* 9 June 1960; *educ* Winchester and St John's Coll Oxford; *m* 1984 *Claire Margaret Alison, dau of Brian Seddon, of 77 Lawn Rd, London NW3, and has issue:

1a +Peter David; *b* 1987

2a +Thomas Edward; *b* 1988

1a *Catherine Lucy; *b* 1991

(1) *Alice Belinda [The Hon Mrs Ward, 1 Hawthorn Villas, The Green, Wallsend-on-Tyne, Northumberland]; *b* 15 Jan 1958; *m* 1981 *Rev Robert Charles Irwin Ward, est *s* of John Ward, of The Old Vicarage, Salehurst, Robertsbridge, Sussex, and has issue:

1a *Samuel John; *b* 1982

2a *James Nicholas; *b* 1984

3a *David Christopher; *b* 1994

1a *Susanna Mary; *b* 1988

(2) *Catherine Sara [The Hon Mrs Gannon, 18 Lynton Rd, London NW6 6BL]; *b* 3 March 1963; *m* 1990 *Joseph Brendan Gannon, *s* of Patrick Gannon, of Dublin, and has issue:

1a *Sorcha Margaret; *b* 1993

2a *Ella Catherine; *b* 1996

(3) *Emily Frances; *b* 1970

2 +Simon Dawson [The Hon Simon Eccles, 27 Chestnut St, Boston, Mass 02108, USA]; *b* 11 Sept 1934; *educ* Repton; Capt Roy Fus; *m* 17 Oct 1961 (*divorce* 1986) Sheelin Lorraine, only dau of Henry Edmund Ryan, of Long Meadow, Goring-on-Thames, Oxon, and has issue:

(1) +Anthony James; *b* 15 April 1967

(1) *Annabelle Charlotte; *b* 29 June 1964; *m* 1988 *Leo Zinovieff (*see* NORTHUMBERLAND, D) and has issue

1 *(Selina) Polly Dawson [Polly Marchioness of Lansdowne, 29 Maunsel St, London SW1]; *b* 18 Jan 1937; *m* 1 June 1962 (*divorce* 1968) Robin Duthac Carnegie, only s of Hon James Duthac Carnegie, TD, JP, of Balloch, Alyth, Perthshire (*see* FIFE, D), and has issue; *m* 2nd 1969 (*divorce* 1978) 8th Marquess of Lansdowne (*qv*)

Lineage: Dr WILLIAM SOLTAU ECCLES, IMS; *m* his 1st cousin Anna Selina Campbell, er dau of George McAdam by Theresa dau of William Eccles, and had:

WILLIAM C McADAM ECCLES; MS, FRCS, consulting surgn St Bartholomew's Hosp; *b* 4 Aug 1867; *m* 12 June 1894 Anna Coralie (*d* 3 Nov 1930), dau of Edward Benjamin Anstie, JP, of Devizes, Wilts, by Suzanne Henriette, dau of Jean Marie Vaucher, architect, of Geneva, and *d* 30 May 1946, having had:

1 John Denison, MC; Capt Queen Victoria's Rifles WW I; *b* 1896 *educ* Winchester; *d* of wounds recd in action Sept 1916

2 Ronald Anstie; *b* 25 March 1897; *educ* Sherborne; *d* unm 1923

3 DAVID McADAM (Sir), **1st Viscount**

4 Philip Campbell, CBE (1957); *b* 29 July 1907; *educ* Winchester and Oriel Coll Oxford; *m* Beatrice Hodgman, of New York, and *d* 22 Dec 1960

1 Margaret Coralie; *b* 24 March 1900; *d* unm Sept 1939

ECCLES OF MOULTON

Creation: B. (LP, UK) 1990.

THE BARONESS ECCLES OF MOULTON, of Moulton in the County of N Yorkshire (Diana Catherine Sturge) [The Rt Hon The Baroness Eccles of Moulton, Moulton Hall, Moulton, N Yorks DL10 6QH; 6 Barton St, London SW1P 3NG]; *b* 4 Oct 1933; *educ* St James's Sch W Malvern and OU (BA); ptnr Gray Design Assocs 1963–77, dir Tyne Tees TV 1986–94, J Sainsbury 1986–95, Yorkshire Electricity Gp 1990–97, Nat & Provincial Bldg Soc 1991–96, memb Teesside Urban Devpt Corp 1987— and Unrelated Live Transplant Regulatory Authority 1990–, v-chm Durham U Cncl 1985–, Hon DCL Durham 1995, Chm Ealing, Hammersmith & Hounslow Health Authority 1993–, dir Times Newspaper Hldgs 1998–; *m* 1955 *Hon John Dawson Eccles, CBE, s of 1st Viscount Eccles (*qv*), and has issue

Lineage: RAYMOND WILSON STURGE, of Lords Mead, Ashmore, Salisbury, Wilts; *m* Margaret — and had a 2nd dau:

DIANA CATHERINE, *cr* a **Baroness**

ECHLIN

Arms: Quarterly, 1st and 4th, or an antique galley, sails furled sa, a forked pennon gu.; 2nd and 3rd, gu. a fess chequy arg. and az, in chief of the last a deer at full speed pursued by a dog, all ppr. **Crest:** A talbot passant ppr. **Motto:** *Non sine praeda* ('Not without prey'). **Creation:** Bt (I) 17 Oct 1721.

SIR NORMAN DAVID FENTON ECHLIN, 10TH BT, of Clonagh, Kildare [Sir Norman Echline Bt, Nartopa, 36 Marina Ave, Appley, Ryde, Isle of Wight PO33 1NJ]; *b* 1 Dec 1925; *s* f 1932; *educ* Masonic Boy's Sch, Clonskeagh, Co Dublin; Capt 14th/1st Punjab Regt IA (ret); *m* 8 Dec 1953 *Mary Christine, only dau of John Arthur, of Oswestry, Salop.

Lineage: Rt Rev HENRY ECHLIN, DD, moved fom Scotland to Ireland *temp* JAMES I, Bp Down and Connor 1613, made a free denizen of Ireland 18 May 1613; *m* Jane, dau of James Seaton, of Latrisse, Scotland, and had, with four daus:

1 JOHN (Rev)

2 Hugh; *m* Magdalen, dau of Robert Cowell, of Co Armagh

The Bishop *d* 17 July 1635; his er s,

Rev JOHN ECHLIN, of Templecranny alias Ballyphilip; made free denizen Ireland 9 Aug 1633; *m* Mary, dau of Sir Francis Stafford, of Mount Stafford, Co Antrim, and had, with two daus:

1 ROBERT

2 Francis, of Clonowen, Co Antrim, inherited the estate of his uncle, Sir Edmund Stafford, and took his surname; *m* Sarah, dau of Sir James MacDonnell, 2nd Bt, of Moyane, and had issue

The er s,

ROBERT ECHLIN, of Ardquin, Co Down, *b* 1628; *m* Mary (*m* 2nd Sir Robert Ward, 1st Bt) dau of Most Rev Henry Leslie, DD, Bp Meath, and had, with a dau:

1 John, his heir, ancestor of the ECHLINs of Ardquin (his est dau Elizabeth *m* George Hamilton, of Tyrella, Co Down, and had issue)

2 HENRY (Sir), **1st Bt**

3 Robert; Lt-Gen; *dsp*

ROBERT ECHLIN *d* 25 April 1657; his 2nd s,

Sir Henry Echlin, 1st Bt (I), so *cr* 17 Oct 1721, of Kenure Park, Rush, Co Dublin, Clonaugh Castle, Co Kildare, and Castle Hacker, Co Mayo, 2nd Baron Court Exchequer Ireland; *m* Agnes, dau of Rev William Mussen, of Belfast, and *d* 29 Nov 1725, leaving:

1 Robert, MP Downpatrick 1692–93 and Newry 1695–1706, barrister; *m* Penelope, dau of Sir Maurice Eustace, of Harristown, Co Kildare, and *dvp* Dec 1706, leaving:

(1) **Sir Robert Echlin, 2nd Bt**; *b* 13 Nov 1699; *m* 4 Dec 1725 Elizabeth (*d* Jan 1783), dau and coheir of William Bellingham, of Levens, Westmorland, and *dspm* 13 May 1757, leaving issue:

1a Elizabeth; *m* 15 June 1747 Francis Palmer, of Swords, Co Dublin, and had issue

(2) **Sir Henry Echlin, 3rd Bt**; *b* 22 Dec 1740; *m c* 28 Jan 1762 Emily La Roche, dau of the Govr of Martinique, and *dsp* 1799

(1) Mary; *m* Col Hamilton and had issue

2 Henry (Rev); DD, Vicar St Catherine's, Dublin, Vicar-Gen Diocese of Tuam, Dean Tua;, *m* Jane, dau of 5th Earl of Drogheda (*qv*), and *d* 4 Nov 1764, having had:

(1) Henry, of Clonaugh Castle, Co Kildare; *m c* 5 Dec 1765 Bridget Hickey and *d* between 27 Jan 1787 and 7 May 1789, leaving issue:

1a **Sir James Echlin, 4th Bt**; *b* 1769; *m* 2 Feb 1788 his first cousin Jane, dau of Chambré Echlin, and *d* 18 Feb 1833, having had, with three daus (*d* unm):

1b James Chambré; Capt 4th Regt; *b* 22 July 1801; *d* unm 1826

2b **Sir Frederick Henry Echlin, 5th Bt**; *b* 4 March 1795; *d* unm 27 May 1871

3b FERDINAND FENTON (Sir), **6th Bt**

(2) Chambré, of Dublin; *b* 18 March 1711; *m* 29 Feb 1759 Esther, dau of Frederick Newman, and *d* Nov 1776, leaving:

1a Henry Frederick, of New York; Army Capt; *m* 1787 Anne, dau of John Conklan, of Nova Scotia, and had issue

2a Chambré; left issue, now thought *extinct*

1a Jane; *m* 2 Feb 1788 her cousin **Sir James Echlin, 4th Bt**

(3) Chaworth

(4) Edward

(5) Robert

(1) Agnes; *m* Rev Philip Gayer, of Decryiaghy

3 William; Col, godson of WILLIAM III; *b* 14 June 1703; *m* Rachel, widow of Col Robert McCausland, and had two sons (*d* abroad) and three daus

1 Mary; *m* Rev — Duncan, of Kilmore, Co Meath

Sir FREDERICK's bro,

Sir Ferdinand Fenton Echlin, 6th Bt; *b* 10 March 1798; *m* 10 Nov 1841 Mary (*d* May 1869), only dau of William Cavanagh, of Grangebeg, Co Westmeath, and *d* 4 July 1877, having had:

1 **Sir Thomas Echlin, 7th Bt**; RIC; *b* 8 Nov 1844; *d* unm 16 Nov 1906

2 **Sir Henry Frederick Echlin, 8th Bt**; *b* 14 Aug 1846; *m* 14 April 1890 Mary Grace (*d* 3 Aug 1913), dau of John Dennis, and had:

(1) Margaret Daisy; *m* 1919 Charles Albert Chapman (*d* 1940)

3 John Fenton; *b* 20 June 1847; *m* 6 May 1869 Harriet Jane (*d* 31 Aug 1915), dau of George Kennedy, of Westport, Co Mayo, and *d* 23 March 1917, having had:

(1) Ferdinand George; *b* 25 June 1875; *d* 9 Sept 1897

(2) William Thomas; *b* 27 April 1877; *d* unm 17 Dec 1902

(3) Alfred Henry; *b* 10 Nov 1883; *d* unm 16 March 1919

(4) JOHN FREDERICK (Sir), **9th Bt**

(5) Richard Brabazon Moore; *b* 3 Oct 1894; *ka* Dec 1914

(1) Evelyn Marion; *m* 18 Sept 1896 Leopold Gabriel Berman and *d* Oct 1935, leaving issue. He *d* 14 Feb 1943

(2) Martha Emily; *m* 3 April 1899 Samuel Wilson Larminie and *d* Jan 1905

(3) Harriet Alice; *m* 17 July 1912 James Hoey, s of William Hoey, of Artnagullion, Kells, Co Antrim, and *d* 17 Nov 1964, leaving issue. He *d* 10 April 1943

(4) Victoria; *d* 23 July 1895

(5) Ethel Frances; *d* Oct 1933

(6) Aileen Alexandra; *m* 17 April 1919 John Atkinson (*d* 23 Aug 1922)

1 Mary

2 Bride Emily; *m* 1864 Bernard Norton, of Michigan

Sir HENRY *dspm* 8 Nov 1923; his nephew,

Sir John Frederick Echlin, 9th Bt; Sgt RUC; *b* 18 Sept 1890; *m* 5 Sept 1923 Ellen Patricia (*d* 2 Feb 1971), dau of David J Jones, JP, of Dublin, and *d* 25 Sept 1932, leaving issue:

1 Alfred Richard Moore; *b* 27 Sept; *d* 4 Oct 1924

2 Sir NORMAN DAVID FENTON ECHLIN, **10th and present Bt**

1 *Patricia Hazel; *b* 7 June 1928; *m* 9 July 1951 *Fred Tiller and has issue:

(1) *Fred; *b* 1 June 1966

(1) *Hazel Jean; *b* 11 June 1952

(2) *Heather Valerie; *b* 18 June 1956

EDEN OF WINTON

Arms: Gu. on a chevron arg. between three garbs or, banded vert, as many escallops sa. **Crest:** A dexter arm in armour, embowed, couped at the shoulder ppr., the hand grasping a garb as in the arms, the forearm encircled by an annulet gu. **Supporters:** Two lions rampant gu. about the mane of each a chain pendant therefrom a portcullis or, the dexter holding by the interior paw a cross patonce also or, the sinister holding by the interior paw a rose branch ppr., having three double roses arg. on gu. barbed and seeded ppr., the compartment comprising a mount rising in the centre, growing therefrom fir trees and beech trees, in the foreground a bay with cliffs ppr. and a rivulet wavy az. running across a sandy beach, also ppr., into the sea barry wavy of four az. and arg. **Motto:** *Si sit prudentia* ('If there be but prudence'). **Creations:** Bt. (E) 13 Nov 1672 and (GB) 19 Oct 1776, B.(LP, UK) 1983.

THE BARON EDEN OF WINTON, of Rushyford in the County Palatine of Durham, and a **Baronet** (Sir John Benedict Eden, Bt, PC (1972)) [The Rt Hon The Lord Eden of Winton PC, 41 Victoria Road, London W8 5RH]; *b* 15 Sept 1925; *s* f in btcies 1963; *educ* Eton and St Paul's Sch, USA; chm Gp Five Hldgs 1982–, Central and Sherwood 1984–; Lt Rifle Bde and 2nd KEO Gurkha Rifles, loaned Gilgit Scouts, 1943–47, MP (C) Bournemouth W Feb 1954–83, Oppn Front Bench Spokesman Power 1968–70, Min Indust 1970–72 and Posts and Telecommunications 1972–74, Chm H of C Select Ctee European Legislation 1976–79, memb Selective Ctee Estimates 1960–64, V-Chm Assoc of C Clubs 1964–67, C Parly Aviation Ctee 1964–66, C Parly Trade and Power Ctee 1966–68 and C Parly Def Ctee 1964–66, Chm C Air Sub-Ctee 1964–66, memb UK Delegn to Cncl of Europe and WEU 1960–62 and UK Delegn NATO Parliamentarians Conf 1962–66, Executive C Members' Ctee 1966–68, Pres Ind Schs Assoc 1969–71, Min State Technology June-Oct 1970, Pres Wessex Area Cs 1974–77, Pres Wessex Area YCs 1978–80, V-Pres Chamber Trade 1968–, Hon V-Pres Nat Assoc of Master Bakers, Confectioners and Caterers 1978–82, Memb H of C Expenditure Ctee 1974–76, Chm Select Ctee Home Affrs 1980–83 and Br-Lebanese Assoc 1990–, V-Pres Internat Tree Fndn, Chm Roy Armouries Museum 1986–94, chm Leslie and Godwin Ltd 1983–; *m* 1st 28 Jan 1958 (*divorce* 1974) Belinda Jane, only dau of Sir (Frederick) John Pascoe, of 8 Eaton Place, SW1, and has issue:

1 +ROBERT FREDERICK CALVERT; *b* 30 April 1964 (HRH THE DUCHESS OF KENT stood sponsor); *m* *Encarnacion Garrido and has:

(1) +Petrouchka; *b* 6 Sept 1997

2 +John (Jack) Edward Morton; *b* 25 Jan 1966; *m* 1991 *Joanna, est dau of Barrie D Spears, of Hong Kong, and has issue:

(1) +Nicholas Cazenac; *b* 1 May 1997

(1) *Madeleine Alexandra; *b* 1992

1 *Emily Rose [The Hon Mrs Brown, 2312-4 Mikado, Misaki-Machi, Isumi-Gun, Chiba 299-46, Japan]; *b* 26 Feb 1959; *m* June 1984 *Ronald Etienne Brown, yr s of James Brown, and has issue:

(1) *Nicholas James; *b* 1986

(1) *Charlotte Lucy; *b* 1985

2 *(Arabella) Charlotte [The Hon Mrs Mungo McGowan, Bragborough Farm, Braunston, Daventry, Northants]; *b* 1 Aug 1960; *m* 12 Feb 1983 *Hon Mungo Alexander McGowan, yst s of 2nd Baron McGowan (*qv*), and has issue

The BARON EDEN OF WINTON *m* 2nd 8 Jan 1977 *Margaret Ann, formerly w of Viscount Strathallan, er s of 17th Earl of Perth (*qv*), and dau of Robin Gordon

Lineage: ROBERT de EDEN; held of the Bp of Durham three messuages and ten oxgangs of land in Preston-on-Tees; *d* 1413; ancestor of:

ROBERT EDEN, of W Auckland, Co Durham and Windlestone; Col royalist army Civil War; had:

JOHN EDEN, of W Auckland; Col royalist army, raised a regt of foot; *m* Catherine, dau of Sir Thomas Layton, of Layton, Yorks, and *d* 1675, leaving:

Sir Robert Eden, 1st Bt (E), so *cr* 13 Nov 1672, of W Auckland; MP Co Durham 1679; *m* Margaret, dau and heir of John Lambton, of Durham, and was *bur* 17 May 1720, leaving an est s:

Sir John Eden, 2nd Bt; MP Co Durham 1713–27; *m* 31 Jan 1715 Catherine (*d* 2 July 1730), dau of Mark Shafto, of Whitworth, and *d* 2 May 1728, having had an only s:

Sir Robert Eden, 3rd Bt; *m* 8 May 1739 Mary (*d* 31 Jan 1794), yst dau of William Davison, of Beamish, Co Durham, and *d* 25 June 1755, having had, with three daus:

1 **Sir John Eden, 4th Bt**; *b* 16 Sept 1740; *educ* Cambridge (MA), MP Co Durham 1774–90; *m* 1st 26 June 1764 Catherine (*dsp* 12 March 1766), dau of John Thompson, of Kirby Hall, Yorks; *m* 2nd 9 April 1767 Dorothea (*d* 21 June 1792), only dau and heir of Peter Johnson, Recorder of York, and *d* 23 Aug 1812, having had, with six daus (including Eleanor, *m* 1 March 1813 Rev Thomas Fourness Wilson; *see* WILSON, Bt, of Eshton Hall):

(1) Sir ROBERT EDEN later JOHNSON-EDEN (roy licence 15 Feb 1811), **5th Bt**, MA Cantab; *b* 25 Oct 1774; *d* unm 4 Sept 1844

(2) Morton John EDEN later DAVISON (roy licence 26 Oct 1812), of Beamish Park, Co Durham; *b* 30 June 1778; *d* unm 28 June 1841

2 ROBERT (Sir), **1st Bt**, of Maryland (*see below*)

3 WILLIAM EDEN; *cr* 18 Nov 1789 BARON AUCKLAND (I) and 22 May 1793 BARON AUCKLAND of West Auckland, Co Durham (GB) (*qv*), and had issue

4 Thomas, of Wimbledon; Dep-Auditor Greenwich Hosp; *m* 7 July 1783 Mariana, dau of Arthur Jones, of Reigate, and *d* 1 May 1805, leaving issue:

(1) Thomas, of the Bryn, Glamorgan; Sec to Govr of Ceylon; *b* 29 Nov 1787; *m* 4 Jan 1810 Frances Eliza (*d* 5 Jan 1879), dau of Hon John Rodney (*see* RODNEY, B), and *d* 4 Nov 1845, leaving, with six daus:

1a John Patrick (Rev), Hon Canon Durham; *b* 6 July 1813; *m* 3 May 1850 Catherine Frances (*d* 6 May 1885), dau of Col Henry Stobart, and *d* 6 May 1885, leaving issue:

1b John Henry, Lt-Col 19th Regt (Green Howards), Ch Constable Co Durham 1892–1902, Inspr Constabulary Northern Dist 1902–16; *b* 10 May 1851; *educ* Marlborough; *m* 12 Oct 1893 Lady Florence Lowry-Corry (*d* 10 May 1943), dau of 4th Earl Belmore (*qv*), and *d* 8 Feb 1931, having had issue:

1c Robert John Patrick, Cadet RN; *b* 26 April 1896; *d* 19 Oct 1909

2c George Wilfrid, CBE (1952), Brig Green Howards, served Waziristan 1937 (despatches) and WW II (wounded), Brig A/Q HQ Southern Cmd 1949–52, Dep Dir Movements War Office 1952–55, Dir Pioneers and Labour War Office 1955–57, ADC to HM THE QUEEN 1955–57, Col Green Howards 1959–65, Cdr Order St Olav Norway 1963; *b* 13 Aug 1903; *educ* Charterhouse; *m* 14 Dec 1946 *Katherine Margaret Dorothy, MBE [Mrs George Eden MBE, Norchard Farm, Stanton St Gabriel, Morcombelake, Bridport, Dorset], 2nd dau of Rev Edward Henry Good, Chaplain RN, and *d* 1986, leaving issue:

1d +John Patrick Edward; *b* 24 March 1950; *educ* Charterhouse

1d *Philippa Catherine [Mrs Stephen McDonnell, 49 St Catherines Road, Winchester, Hants]; *b* 28 Oct 1948; *m* 1976 *Stephen Lawrence McDonnell and has issue:

1e *Catherine Claire; *b* 1981

1c Christian Florence; *d* unm 7 Sept 1983 aged 88

2c Norah Madeline

2b Arthur Francis; *b* 3 June 1852; *m* 1 July 1882 Frances (*d* 19 March 1933), dau of Rev Robert Springett, Vicar Brafferton, Yorks, and *d* 25 Sept 1936

3b George Rodney (Rt Rev), Canon and Archdeacon Canterbury, Bp Suffragan Dover 1890–97, Bp Wakefield 1897–1928; *b* 9 Sept 1853; *educ* Pembroke Coll Cambridge (MA 1879, DD 1891, Hon Fell 1906), dau of Rev Henry John Ellison, Rector Gt Haseley, and *d* 7 Jan 1940, leaving issue:

1c John Rodney, T/Capt Serv Bn S Wales Borderers, Assist Manager Sena Sugar Estates Ltd; *b* 4 July 1892; *educ* Winchester and Pembroke Coll Cambridge; *m* 28 Aug 1928 (*divorce* 1946) May, est dau of Thomas Taylor Poynton, of Durban, S Africa, and *d* 7 March 1963

2c Gerald Balfour, S/Ldr RAF, Capt KRRC; *b* 12 Aug 1896; *educ* Winchester; *m* 1 Aug 1929 Phyllis Anne (*d* 1977), dau of Maj Thomas Yarnold Macy, IA, and *d* 1970, leaving issue:

1d John Hamilton Rodney, Sgt Air Quartermaster RAF; *b* 26 Sept 1939; *educ* Nautical Coll Pangbourne; *m* 29 Aug 1964 *Sandra Anne [Mrs John Eden, 28 West End, Westbury, Wilts BA13 3HA], dau of Dennis Rowland Toms, of Westbury, Wilts, and *d* 1992, leaving issue:

1e +Anthony Winston Richard [Anthony Eden Esq, 3 Beech Park Court, Coolock Village, Dublin 5, Ireland]; *b* 12 Oct 1965; *m* 1993 *Catherine Mary, dau of B O'Connell, and has issue:

1f +John Anthony Bernhard; *b* 1994

2e +Jeremy Rodney Hugh; *b* 6 April 1967

1e *Françoise Geraldine [Mrs James Eden-Hamilton, c/o Milton of Ruthven Blairgowrie, Perthshire, Scotland]; *b* 28 Aug 1968; *m* 1993 *James McLaren HAMILTON later EDEN-HAMILTON and has issue:

1f *John Alexander; *b* 1993

2f *James Winston; *b* 2 Feb 1995

1d *Margaret Anne [Mrs John Kirkbride, 66 Swansfield Park Rd, Alnwick, Northumberland NE66 1AR]; *b* 21 Dec 1929; *m* 2 July 1955 *John William Howard Kirkbride, and has issue:

1e *Nicholas George; *b* 21 Sept 1959; *m* 1989 *Philippa Jane, dau of Julian Ross Smith, and has issue:

1f *Olivia Clare; *b* 1990

1e *Amanda [Mrs Adrian Hardwick, 7 Laverdene Ave, Sheffield, Yorks]; *b* 11 Feb 1957; *m* 1980 *Adrian Hardwick, and has issue:

1f *Mark Andrew; *b* 1986

2e *Katherine [Mrs Nicholas Clemo, 28 St Mark's Crescent, Maidenhead, Berks]; *b* 14 April 1961; *m* 1985 *Nicholas Graham Clemo

1c Margaret Agnes; *m* 5 June 1918 Geoffrey HOFFMANN later EDEN (roy licence; *d* 26 July 1959), MD, FRCP, and had:

1d *Anthony Rodney; *b* 14 Nov 1921, *m* 7 Feb 1955 *Manuella, yst dau of Baron Hubert d'Estreux de Beaugrenier, and has issue:

1e *Alexandra Marie Monique; *b* 7 Nov 1956

2e *Margaret Jeanne-Marie; *b* 3 Sept 1959

1d Joan Bridget Constance; *b* 26 March 1919; *m* 24 Aug 1957 Adml Sir Wilfrid John Wentworth Woods, GBE, KCB, DSO, s of Sir Wilfrid Wentworth Woods, KCMG, KBE, of Ceylon and Newfoundland, and *d* 9 Dec 1976. He *d* 1 Jan 1975

2d Cynthia Myrtle Margaret; *b* 22 Oct 1922; *m* 1st 1948 (*divorce* 1958) Maj Thomas Reynolds, MC, KOYLI; *m* 2nd 30 Sept 1969 *Maj-Gen John Evered Witt, CB, CBE, MC, and *d* 1982, having by her 1st husb had:

1e *Jane Caroline Margaret; *b* 4 March 1953

2c Dorothy Frances, WW I nursing in France (despatches 1916); *m* 17 Feb 1920 Rt Rev Clement Mallory Ricketts, Bp Suffragan Dunwich, and had issue (*see* RICKETTS, Bt)

3c Mary Catharine; *m* 9 April 1921 Aubrey Everard Hughes, MC, T/Maj RE, s of Rev Cecil Hughes, Vicar Southwater, Sussex, and *d* 6 June 1936

4b Charles Hamilton, OBE (1920); *b* 2 April 1855; *m* 27 Jan 1885 Caroline Sophia (*d* Aug 1936), dau of Rev Charles Henry Ford, Vicar Bishopton, Co Durham, and *d* 28 July 1921, leaving issue:

1c Henry Charles Hamilton, CBE (1945), MC and bar, Lt-Col RA cmdg 88th (2nd W Lancs) Field Bde 1936–38, served WW I, Army Staff Coll 1924, Navy Staff Coll 1931, GSO(1) 51st Highland Div 1939, CRA 51st Highland Div 1940, served WW II (despatches); *b* 12 March 1889; *educ* Rugby; *m* 1st 11 Nov 1916 Violet Alice (*d* 2 March 1956), only dau of Capt Henry Percy Pulleine, of Sandford House, Richmond, Yorks; *m* 2nd 8 April 1957 *Penelope Glynne [Mrs Henry Eden, Mortons, 48 Church Rd, Ferndown, Dorset BH22 9EU], widow of Lt-Col Raymond John Garmondsway Temple, RA, and 2nd dau of Hervey Wheler Sitwell, of The Manor, Leamington Hastings, Warwicks, and d 17 Nov 1963, having by his 1st w had:

1d +Robert John Pulleine [Robert Eden Esq, Badlake Farm, West Anstay, S Molton, Devon], memb: Essex CC 1961, Chelmsford RDC (chm Fin Ctee 1961), Capt TA WW II; *b* 16 Feb 1920; *educ* Rugby; *m* 1st 25 Jan 1947 (*divorce* 1969) Hon Rosemary Winifred Vivian (*d* 1981), 2nd dau of 3rd Baron Swansea (*qv*), and has issue:

1e *Sarah; *b* 7 March 1948; *m* 27 March 1982 *Robin Fasola, son of E J Fasola, of Paris

1d (cont.) Robert Eden *m* 2nd 1969 *Elizabeth Stanley, formerly w of — Cleverly and er dau of Alan Crowe Rawlinson, and by her has issue:

2e *Catherine; *b* 1969

3e *Emily Rose; *b* 1972

2d Michael Charles, Lt RE, 1st Airborne Div WW II; *b* 28 Dec 1921; *m* 9 Feb 1944 *Patricia (VAD) (*m* 2nd 26 Aug 1946 Robert Everett, FRCOG), yr dau of Lt-Col Reginald James Brook, CBE, DSO, ED, of The Ridding, Low Bentham, Lancs, and was *ka* Arnhem Sept 1944, leaving issue:

1e +Peter Michael [Peter Eden Esq, Quinta dos Penedos, Elvas, Portugal]; *b* posthumously 12 Dec 1944; *educ* Marlborough; *m* 7 Aug 1965 *Rosemary Frances, only dau of Kenneth Charles Bishop, MBE, TD, MA, of Evans House, Sedbergh, Yorks, and has issue:

1f *Rupert Michael; *b* 6 Dec 1972

1f *Caroline Rose; *b* 2 Aug 1967

2f *Claire Louise; *b* 2 March 1969; *m* 1992 *António Freire Dias da Costa, of Valvere, Evora, Portugal, and has issue:

1g *Sophie Alexandra; *b* 1993

2g *Lucy Catherine; *b* 1995

1c Frances Catherine; *m* 14 Sept 1921 Noel Ernest Little (*d* 11 March 1954), s of Knightley Little, CBE, JP, of Newbold Pacey Hall, Warwicks, and *d* 19–, leaving issue:

1d *John Ernest, MC, Lt-Col RA WW II; *b* 8 June 1922; *educ* Marlborough; *m* 1953 *Nancy Elizabeth, er dau of William J Smith, of Greenfields, Yorks, and has issue:

1e *William Jonathan Knightly; *b* 10 Aug 1958

1e *Catherine Elizabeth; *b* 8 April 1955

2e *Georgina Felicity; *b* 23 Feb 1964

2c Dulcibella; *m* 27 June 1931 Rev Charles Overton Rockett, and *d* 30 Jan 1958, leaving issue. He *d* 20 April 1960

5b Frederick Nugent (Rev), Hon Canon Rochester; *b* 3 Sept 1857; *educ* Pembroke Coll Cambridge (MA); *m* 29 Sept 1919 Katherine Mary (*d* 27 Oct 1928), est dau of Bryan Holme Holme, of Paull Holme, Yorks, and *d* 11 June 1926

6b Henry Culley (Rev); *b* 1 Nov 1858; *educ* Pembroke Coll Cambridge; *d* 18 May 1934

7b Robert Gerald Rodney; *b* 7 Jan 1860; *m* 11 April 1901 Elizabeth Anne (*d* 17 Dec 1932), 3rd dau of Rt Rev Thomas Bunbury, DD, Bp Limerick, Ardfert and Aghadoe, and *d* 22 Nov 1915

1b Frances Margaret; *m* 27 June 1893 Rev Richard Appleton, Master Selwyn Coll Cambridge, Hon Canon Durham, and *d* 4 March 1930. He *dsp* 28 Feb 1909

2b Mary Dulcibella; *d* unm 14 Feb 1942

2a William Frederick, Col; *b* 31 Aug 1814; *m* 1 Jan 1838 Marie Sidonie (*d* 1894), dau of Jean Isador Delaselle, and *d* 14 Nov 1867, leaving issue

(2) John, CB, Gen; *b* 25 March 1789; *m* 1st 1830 Anne (*d* Nov 1841), only dau of Sir John Caldwell, Bt, of Castle Caldwell, and had, with two sons (*dsp*):

1a William Thomas, Col Bombay SC; *b* 23 April 1838; *d* 15 Oct 1919

(2) (cont.) Gen John Eden *m* 2nd 4 July 1843 Charlotte Carse (*d* 11 Feb 1912), dau of E S Prentice, and *d* 6 Oct 1874, having by her had issue:

2a Frederick Morton, Maj RMLI; *b* 28 Dec 1847; *m* 6 Jan 1881 Minnie Pitts (*d* 23 June 1939), dau of Edward Allen, and *d* 6 Jan 1919, having had issue:

1b Lionel Morton; *b* 9 April 1888; *d* 24 April 1904

3a George Henry, Lt-Cdr RN; *b* 29 Oct 1849; *m* 1901 Miriam Sophia (*d* 21 Aug 1919), er dau of William Farnham, and had issue:

1b Hugh Morton; *b* 28 June 1903; *m* 26 Nov 1938 Monica, 2nd dau of Cdr Eustace William Clitherow Stracey-Clitherow, RN (*see* STRACEY Bt)

1a Frances Charlotte; *m* 18 Sept 1872 M StJ Maule, of Bath, and *d* 3 Jan 1911, leaving issue

2a Emily Elizabeth; *m* 3 Sept 1874 Ernest Wallace Rooke, of Stratton House, Bath. He *d* 4 July 1934

(3) Arthur; *b* 9 Aug 1793; *m* 1824 Frances (*d* 25 March 1877), widow of William Baring, MP (*see* NORTHBROOK, B), dau of J P Thomson, of Waverley Abbey, and sis of 1st and last Baron Sydenham, and *d* 1874, leaving issue:

1a Arthur John; *b* 1827; *d* unm 8 June 1917

2a Frederick; *b* 1828; *m* 28 Feb 1865 Caroline (*d* 6 Dec 1928), dau of of Capt Edward J L Jekyll, Gren Gds, and *d* 5 Dec 1916

1a Mabel; *m* 1861 Frederick Cox, DL, of Harefield, Uxbridge, and had issue

2a Dulcibella; *m* 1856 Hugh Hamersley, and had issue. He *d* 28 Sept 1882

(4) Henry, of Gillingham Hall, Suffolk, Adml RN; *b* 9 Aug 1797; *m* 8 Feb 1849 Elizabeth Harriet Georgiana (*d* 25 Jan 1889), dau of Gen Lord George Beresford (*see* WATERFORD, M), and *dsp* 30 Jan 1888

(5) Robert; *b* 13 May 1800; *m* 21 April 1829 Frances (*d* 11 Jan 1898), dau of Rev Rowland Egerton Warburton (*see* GREY EGERTON, Bt), and *d* 23 April 1879, leaving issue:

1a Morton Robert, Col 56th Regt; *b* 9 May 1830; *m* 31 March 1864 Frances Maria (*d* 11 Feb 1900), dau of Nathaniel Clarke Barnardiston, of The Ryes, Suffolk, and *d* 30 Aug 1900, having had issue:

1b Ethel Morton; *m* 16 April 1903 Maj Herbert Charles Selwyn Heath, MBE, Essex Regt, s of Cdr G P Heath, RN, and *d* 8 June 1953. He *d* March 1939

2a Charles Henry, RN; *b* 20 March 1839; *m* 11 May 1863 Georgina (*d* 22 Nov 1916), dau of Capt F W Hill, and *d* 16 Feb 1900, leaving issue:

1b Guy Ernest Morton, barrister Inner Temple 1901; *b* 6 May 1864; *m* 4 Dec 1897 Ethel (*d* 13 Dec 1956), dau of William Henry Holman, and *d* 5 Dec 1954, leaving issue:

1c Rodney Guy Morton, Lt Scots Gds (SR); *b* 4 May 1899; *educ* Eton; *d* 1979

2c Charles Egerton, barrister Inner Temple, 1930; *b* 5 Feb 1908; *m* 8 Feb 1936 *Eileen Antoinette, dau of H H Menzies, of Taplow, and *d* 20 Aug 1957, leaving:

1d +David Guy Egerton; *b* 21 June 1937

3c Adrian Arthur (Rev), Vicar N Elmham with Billingford 1958, Hon Lt-Col RARO, Maj RA WW II; *b* 12 April 1911; *educ* Eton; *m* 27 June 1939 Margaret Anne (*d* 1972), er dau of Harold Edgar Bushell, of Golborne Manor, Tattenhall, Cheshire, and *d* 1980, leaving issue:

1d +Robin Guy [Robin Eden Esq, 3 Othello Court, 50 Shakespeare Rd, Bedford MK40 2ED]; *b* 12 March 1943; *educ* King's Sch Canterbury; LTCL; schoolmaster

2d +John Kenneth [John Eden Esq, Little Wootton, Church Rd, Scaynes Hill, Haywards Heath, Sussex RH17 7NH]; *b* 8 Jan 1949; *educ* King's Sch Canterbury and Dundee U (MA); stockbroker; *m* 1st 1977 (*divorce* 1983) Margaret Elizabeth, dau of William Alfred Noy, of Rochester and has:

1e +Christopher Guy Eden; *b* 1978

1e *Kathleen Anne Elizabeth; *b* 1980

2d (cont.) John Eden *m* 2nd 1992 *Sophie Jane, dau of Timothy John Green, of Scaynes Hill, Sussex, and by her has:

2e +Nicholas Morton Eden; *b* 5 Dec 1996

2e *Charlotte Daisy; *b* 6 May 1998

1c Kathleen Ethel; *m* 14 Feb 1924 Charles Ronald Graham, OBE (*d* 19 Oct 1933), and *d* 1978

2b Arthur Henry; *b* 4 July 1866; *d* unm 1 Sept 1903

1b Victoria Beatrice Edith; *d* unm 1 Dec 1942

(1) Marianne; *m* 1st 19 Dec 1807 John Spalding, MP (*d* 26 Aug 1815); *m* 2nd 1 April 1819 1st Baron Brougham and Vaux (*qv*), and *d* 12 Jan 1865, leaving issue

(2) Dora; *m* Adml Sir Graham Moore, GCB, brother of Sir John Moore, the hero of Corunna

(3) Dulcibella, Maid of Honour to QUEEN ADELAIDE, *d* unm

5 MORTON EDEN, 1st BARON HENLEY (*qv*)

Sir ROBERT's 2nd s,

Sir Robert Eden 1st Bt (GB), so *cr* 19 Oct 1776; Govr Maryland, N America, 1776; *m* 26 April 1763 Caroline Calvert, sis and coheir of 7th and last Baron Baltimore, and *d* 2 Sept 1784, leaving an er s:

Sir Frederick Morton Eden, 2nd Bt; *educ* Ch Ch Oxford (MA); author: *State of the Poor*; *m* 10 Jan 1792 Anne (*d* 14 July 1808), dau and heir of James Paul Smith, of New Bond Street, London, and *d* 14 Nov 1809, leaving:

1 **Sir Frederick Eden, 3rd Bt**, Ensign 85th Foot; *ka* Battle of New Orleans 24 Dec 1814

2 WILLIAM (Sir), **4th Bt**

3 Robert (Rt Rev), DD, Bp Moray and Ross, Primus Episcopal Ch Scotland; *b* 2 Sept 1804; *m* 17 Sept 1827 Emma (*d* 24 Nov 1880), 3rd dau of Sir James Allan Park, Judge Common Pleas, and *d* 26 Aug 1886, having had:

(1) Frederick Morton, barrister, Fell All Souls; *b* 1 Nov 1820; *m* 1st 23 May 1857 Louisa Ann (*d* 9 March 1868), est dau of V-Adml Hyde Parker, CB (*see* PARKER, Bt), and had:

1a Morton; *b* 8 Sept 1859; *d* unm 26 March 1933

2a Frederick Charles; *b* 6 March 1864; *d* unm 15 July 1944

1a Alice; *d* 15 May 1920

(1) (cont.) Frederick Eden *m* 2nd 4 Oct 1870 Fanny Helen (*d* 14 April 1918), est dau of Edward Pomeroy Barrett-Lennard (*see* BARRETT-LENNARD, Bt), and *d* 11 March 1917, having by her had issue:

3a Rowland Frederick; *b* 17 Aug 1874; *m* 1900 Marie Bernadette Anita (*d* 23 June 1959), dau of Col Henry George Saunders, late Bengal SC, and *d* 8 Feb 1948, leaving issue:

1b Frederick Augustus Morton, Lt-Cdr RN, ARP 1939; *b* 1 May 1904; *m* 26 July 1929 Everil Mary (*d* 1993), est dau of John Stephen Lang Whiteaway, of Liddesdale, Gloucester Rd, Kingston Hill, Surrey, and *d* 1985, leaving:

1c +David Frederick Edward, MBE [David Eden Esq MBE, 31 Howard Court, Rutland Drive, Harrogate, N Yorks HG1 2PB]; *b* 10 Jan 1934; *educ* Ampleforth; W/Cdr RAF; *m* 1957 *Audrey Joan Wilson, and has issue:

1d *Audrey Mary Caroline; *b* 1958

2c +John Graham Walter [John Eden Esq, 16 East MacKenzie Park, Inverness IV2 3SR]; *b* 25 April 1948

1c *Mary Alexandra Morton [Mrs Robert Cameron, Gallowa' View, Dockhead, Dumfries DG1 2RX]; *b* 22 Oct 1945; *m* 1983 *Robert S Cameron, and has issue:

1d *Neil Robert David; *b* 1987

4a Algernon Graham, T/Maj RASC Boer War 1901–02 (Queen's medal), WW I; *b* 1877; *m* 1907 Georgina Edith, dau of G W de Tunzelmann, and *d* 24 Jan 1941

2a Dorothy Ione Helen; *m* 1 Jan 1902 Arthur Dalrymple Forbes-Gordon, of Greenknowe, Berwicks, and *d* 23 Jan 1964, leaving issue (*see* SEMPILL, L)

(2) Henley; *b* 8 March 1838; *m* 15 April 1871 Amy Frances (*d* 7 Aug 1939), yst dau of Lord Charles Lennox Kerr (*see* LOTHIAN, M), and *d* 21 Sept 1917, leaving issue:

1a Schomberg Henley, CMG (1919), DSO (1917), Col Black Watch (Roy Highrs), Boer War 1901–02 (Queen's medal with four clasps), WW I (despatches, Brevet Lt-Col), Legion of Honour and Order Crown Belgium; *b* 18 March 1873; *d* 31 Dec 1934

2a Charles William Guy, CMG (1929), Prov Commr Colonial CS Uganda 1899–1929; *b* 20 June 1874; *m* 1913 Hilda Marion, dau of R J Barton, of Dalkey, Co Dublin

(3) Robert Allan (Rev); *educ* Oxford (MA), Vicar Old St Pancras; *b* 27 Dec 1839; *d* 29 April 1912

(4) William Alexander, Col RA; *b* 16 June 1843; *m* 18 July 1885 Giovanna Anna Malvina (*d* 21 Sept 1931), widow of Col William Macbean, of Tomatin, Inverness-shire, and *dsp* 23 Dec 1915

(5) Charles John, Col Black, Watch (R Highrs); *b* 28 Jan 1846; *d* unm 15 March 1896

(1) Lucy; *m* 12 June Rev Herbert S Hawkins, Rector of Beyton, and had issue. He *d* 1893

(2) Caroline; *m* 11 Sept 1851 Col A A'Court Fisher, CB, RE, and *d* 2 April 1918, leaving issue. He *d* 1879

(3) Alice; *m* 5 Dec 1857 Rt Hon George Ward Hunt, MP, and *d* 24 Nov 1894, leaving issue. He *d* 29 July 1877

(4) Emma Selina; *m* 18 June 1861 Rev Canon Dacres Olivier, Rector Wilton 1867–1912, and *d* 10 Sept 1908, leaving issue. He *d* 7 Jan 1919

(5) Mary; *d* unm 7 Sept 1927

4 George Morton, Lt Gen; *b* 10 May 1806; *m* 18 Jan 1834 Louisa Anne (*d* 5 Nov 1878), dau of George Robert Eyres, of Norfolk, and *d* Nov 1862, having had issue:

(1) Morton Parker, Lt-Col RA; *b* 11 March 1835; *m* 4 April 1861 Georgina Louisa Helen (*d* 22 April 1890), yst dau of Gen H Pester, RA, and *d* 18 Sept 1880, leaving issue:

1a Morton Henry; *b* 24 Oct 1865; *d* unm

2a Robert John; *b* 6 Oct 1869; *d* unm

3a Frederick Schomberg; *b* 7 March 1872; *d* 10 March 1920

1a Beatrice Caroline; *m* 5 Oct 1889 Capt Charles Cockburn Talbot, RD, RNR, and *d* 1 June 1950, leaving issue. He *d* 4 March 1933

2a Georgina Clarice; *m* 1895 Rev W H Paine, (MA), and *d* Sept 1944. He *d* 15 Sept 1938

3a Lilian; *m* 16 May 1895 Cdr William Nicholson McGachen, RN, and *d* 1 Dec 1921, having had issue. He *d* 1912

(2) Charles Calvert, of The Grange, Kingston, Somerset; Dip Serv; *b* 5 Nov 1837; *m* 16 Dec 1862 Cecile (*d* 7 Feb 1931), dau of Freiherr von Sinner, of Marchligen, Switzerland, and *d* 10 March 1878, having had issue:

1a Morton Frederic, MBE (1919), served Boer War 1900–01 (medal with six clasps); *b* 16 June 1865; *m* Marie Therèse MacMahon (*d* 1962), and *d* 2 Jan 1948, having had issue:

1b +Robert Charles Frederick, MBE (1948) [Robert Eden Esq MBE, Märchligen, 3312 Allmendingen, Berne, Switzerland], Capt Intell Corps WWII; *b* 5 Aug 1916; *educ* Zuoz Coll Switzerland and Cambridge (BA 1940); *m* 26 April 1958 *Barbara, yr dau of Maj George Reginald Benson, of The Granary Mill Hamlet, Sidlesham, W Sussex, and has issue:

1c +Michael Anthony; *b* 14 March 1960

1c *Joanna Mary; *b* 25 Jan 1962

1b Marie Cecile Evelyn; *b* 28 Feb 1910; *d* 20 Sept 1927

1a Evelyn Louisa Cecile; *d* unm 24 June 1948

2a Violet Cecile; *m* 30 Aug 1899 Lt-Col Arthur Street, OBE, RASC, and *d* 1958, having had issue. He *d* 1949

(1) Fanny Evelyn Mary; *d* 1 July 1920

5 Charles (Sir), KCB, V-Adml, a Ld Admlty 1859–66; *b* 3 July 1808; *m* 1st 17 Aug 1828 Emma (*d* 8 Jan 1866), 2nd dau of Sir Robert Williams, 9th Bt (*see* WILLIAMS-BULKELEY, Bt); *m* 2nd 30 April 1866 Fanny Cecilia (*d* 18 July 1912), yst dau of V-Adml Henry Francis Greville, CB (*see* WARWICK, BROOKE and, E), and *dsp* 7 March 1878

1a Marianne; *m* Nov 1812 Francis Maller Spong, and *d* 13 May 1859. He *d* April 1857

2 Caroline; *m* 16 July 1821 V-Adml Hyde Parker, CB, and *d* 10 Nov 1854, leaving issue (*see* PARKER, Bt, of Long Melford)

The 3rd Bt's bro,

Sir William Eden, 4th Bt, of Maryland and **6th Bt** (as which *s* cousin 1844), of W Auckland; *b* 31 Jan 1803; *m* 23 April 1844 Elfrida Susanna Harriet (*d* 8 July 1882), yst dau of Col William Iremonger, of Wherwell Priory, Hants, and had, with other issue:

1 WILLIAM (Sir), **7th/5th Bt**

2 Morton; *b* 25 June 1859; *d* unm 31 March 1909

3 Charles; *b* 26 Nov 1862; *m* 1894 Laura, dau of John Compton Maul, and *dsp* 21 Sept 1902

1 Caroline; *d* 29 Feb 1860

2 Blanche; *d* 10 Aug 1865

3 Rose; *d* 11 Aug 1865

4 Helen; *m* 12 Aug 1871 William St Lo Malet, Capt 8th Hus, and *d* 26 May 1878, leaving issue (*see* MALET, Bt)

5 Edith; *m* 1st 20 July 1875 4th Baron Auckland (*qv*) and had issue; *m* 2nd 10 June 1879 Philip Symons, of Laddingford House, Yalding, Kent, and *d* 28 March 1931. He *d* 4 Jan 1926

The 4th/6th Bt *d* 21 Oct 1873; his est surv son,

Sir William Eden, 7th Bt, and **5th Bt**, DL, JP Co Durham, Hon Col 6th Bn Durham LI (TD), Lt 8th Hus; *b* 4 April 1849; *m* 20 July 1886 Sybil Frances, OBE (1920), DGStJ (*d* 17 June 1945), dau of Sir William Grey, KCSI (*see* GREY, E), and had issue:

1 John, Lt 12th Lancers; *b* 9 Oct 1888; *ka* France 17 Oct 1914

2 TIMOTHY CALVERT (Sir), **8th/6th Bt**

3 (ROBERT) ANTHONY EDEDN (Sir), 1st EARL OF AVON (*see* 1970 edn), KG (1954), MC , PC (1934)

4 William Nicholas, Midshipman RN; *b* 14 March 1900; *ka* Battle of Jutland 31 May 1916

5 A son; *b* and *d* 10 Feb 1904

1 Elfrida Marjorie, DGStJ, Mayor Warwick 1929–30 and 1931; *b* 5 June 1887; *m* 29 April 1909 6th Earl of Warwick (*see* WARWICK, BROOKE and, E), and *d* 10 Feb 1943, leaving issue

Sir WILLIAM *d* 20 Feb 1915; his est surv son,

Sir Timothy Calvert Eden, 8th Bt, and **6th Bt**; *b* 3 May 1893; *educ* Eton and Ch Ch Oxford; Yorks LI WW I (POW), WW II as Staff Capt, author: *The Tribulations of a Baronet*; *m* 30 Jan 1923 Edith Mary (Patricia) (*d* 1990), dau of Arthur Prendergast, and *d* 13 May 1963, leaving issue:

1 Sir JOHN BENEDICT EDEN, **9th and present Bt and Baron Eden of Winton**

1 *Ann Caroline [Mrs Peter Negretti, The Old Stables, Gracious St, Selborne, Hants GU34 3JD]; *b* 19 Oct 1923; *m* 27 Oct 1951 *Peter Noel Negretti and has had:

(1) *Alexandra Mary; *b* 3 March 1953; *m* 1981 *David C C Maule and has:

1a *Robert Alexander Carteret; *b* 1985

2a *Oliver Raymond Carteret; *b* 1990

1a *Emma Charlotte; *b* 1983

(2) Emma Frances; *b* 16 Dec 1954; *d* 1977

(3) *Cristina Gabrielle; *b* 28 Dec 1956; *m* 1982 *W Guy R Fearon and has:

1a *Christopher Nicholas; *b* 1991

1a *Camilla Frances; *b* 1989

(4) *Sarah Ann [Mrs Jonathan Asquith, 8 Colinette Rd, London SW15 6QQ]; *b* 29 Sept 1959; *m* 23 June 1984 *Jonathan Paul Asquith and has issue (*see* OXFORD AND ASQUITH, E)

2 *(Meriall) Rose [Mrs James Murray, 66500 Mosset, Prades, Pyrénées-Orientales, France]; *b* 15 June 1927; *m* 25 Sept 1959 James Dalton Murray, CMG (*d* 1984), only s of Dr James Murray, of Edinburgh, and has issue:

(1) *William Andrew Eden; *b* 16 May 1960

2 (cont.) Mrs James Murray also adopted:

*Hugo Felix; *b* 10 Jan 1963; *m* 1989 *Kaye Melanie Underhill, of Bridgwater, Somerset, and has issue:

1a *Matthew James; *b* 1993

3 *Amelia Mary [Mrs Giovanni Borrelli, Chapel Lane Cottage, Fritham, Lyndhurst, Hants SO43 7HL]; *b* 16 Jan 1933; *m* 7 Sept 1958 (*separated* 1971) Giovanni Borrelli and has:

(1) *Raffaelle Timoteo; *b* 9 Jan 1962

(2) *Matteo Francesco Antonio; *b* 13 March 1965

(1) *Chiara Maria Concetta; *b* 9 Dec 1959

4 Mary Clare; *b* 18 Jan, *d* 8 Feb 1938

5 *Elfrida Charlotte [Mrs Richard Fallowfield, 78 West Side, Clapham Common, London SW4]; *b* 17 June 1940; *m* 21 Sept 1963 *Richard Gordon Fallowfield, s of Capt Walter Herman Gordon Fallowfield, RN, and has:

(1) *Timothy Gordon; *b* 23 June 1965

(2) *Nicholas John; *b* 29 Sept 1967

(1) *Laura Louise; *b* 11 March 1974

EDGE

Arms: Sa. an eagle displayed arg. between four cinquefoils or. **Crest:** In front of a reindeer's head erased two rose sprigs in saltire ppr. flowered gu. **Motto:** *Officio egere nolo* ('I do not wish to fail in my duty'). **Creation:** Bt (UK) 9 June 1937.

(SIR) WILLIAM EDGE, 3RD BT, of Ribble Lodge, in the Borough of Lytham Saint Annes in the County Palatine of Lancaster [William Edge Esq, 66 Harrow Rd, Maidenhead, Berks]; *b* 5 Oct 1936; *s* f 1984 but does not use title; *educ* Shrewsbury, Trin Hall Cambridge (MA) and Harvard Business Sch (MBA); *m* 5 Sept 1959 *Avril Elizabeth, dau of Harold Denson, of Willingham, Cambridges, and has issue:

1 +EDWARD KNOWLES; *b* 6 June 1965

2 +Martin William; *b* 19 June 1968

1 *Christina Jane; *b* 29 June 1963

2 *Susannah Clare; *b* 1971

Lineage: WILLIAM EDGE, of Lyndene, Smithills, Bolton (est s of Thomas Edge, of Breighmet, 10th in descent from John Edge, of Middle Hulton, Deane, Lancs, assessed for subsidy 1526); *bapt* 27 Feb 1825; *m* 15 Dec 1850 Anne Byron (*d* 21 July 1885), dau of Edward Knowles, of Bolton, and *d* 25 Jan 1913, leaving issue:

Sir KNOWLES EDGE, of Great Marld, Smithills, Bolton, JP Lancs, Mayor Bolton 1916–17 and 1917–18, when he raised money to further WW I and for charities; *b* 7 Feb 1853; ktd 18 Aug 1919; *m* 7 April 1880 Mary Jane (*d* Oct 1932), dau of John Preston, of Bolton, and *d* 24 Jan 1931, leaving issue:

1 WILLIAM (Sir), **1st Bt**

2 John Harold, of Ivy House, W Beach, Lytham, Lancs; *b* 31 July 1888; *m* 4 Dec 1913 Elizabeth Tudor, dau of William Brown, of Llanfyllin, Montgomeryshire, and *d* Coonoor, S India, 18 Oct 1931

The er son,

Sir William Edge, 1st Bt (UK), so *cr* 9 June 1937, JP (Lancs 1941); *b* 21 Nov 1880; Staff-Capt War Office, MP Bolton 1916–23 and Bosworth 1927–45, PPS to Min of Nat Serv 1917–19, Min Nat Serv and Reconstruction 1919 and Min Lab 1919, Jr Ld Treasury 1919–22, Parly Charity Commr 1932–35; headed William Edge & Sons (mfg chemists of Bolton); ktd 10 Feb 1922; *m* 9 Aug 1904 Ada Jane, Mayor Lytham 1937–38, memb Lytham Borough Cncl 1929, Mayor Lytham St Annes 1937, Alderman 1940 (*d* 14 March 1973 aged 93), dau of Ira Ickringhill, JP, of Keighley, and had issue:

1 KNOWLES (Sir), **2nd Bt**

1 *Mary Margaret (Peggy), JP (Mid-Salop 1961); *b* 24 Feb 1917; *m* 1 June 1940 *Gilbert Roy Fletcher, s of Alfred Fletcher, of Upper Berwick, Shrewsbury, and has issue:

(1) *David Nicholas; *b* 17 Dec 1942; *educ* Malvern; *m* 16 Dec 1967 *Helen Elizabeth, est dau of Noel Spencer, of Hereford

(1) *Rosemary Ann; *b* 11 Sept 1945; *m* 23 Sept 1967 *Simon Honess, est s of T F Honess, of Wellington, Salop

(2) *Elizabeth Jane; *b* 1 March 1947

(3) *Gillian Mary *b* 7 April 1950

Sir WILLIAM *d* 18 Dec 1948; his only son,

Sir Knowles Edge, 2nd Bt, JP (1955); *b* 31 Dec 1905; *educ* Bolton Sch and Trin Hall Cambridge; chemical mfr, chm Br Fedn Music Festivals; *m* 31 Dec 1932 Dorothea Eunice (*d* 1976), yr dau of Robert Walker, of New Haven, Conn., and *d* 19 March 1984, leaving issue:

1 Sir WILLIAM EDGE, **3rd and present Bt**

2 +John Robert [John Edge Esq, 1 Seafield Rd, Lytham, Lancs]; *b* 7 June 1939; *educ* Shrewsbury; slr

EDMONSTONE

Arms: Or an annulet gu., stoned az., between three crescents of the second within a double tressure flory-counter-flory of the second. **Crest:** Out of a ducal coronet or a swan's head and neck, ppr. **Supporters:** Two lions rampant gu. **Motto:** *Virtus auget honorem* ('Virtue adds to honour'). **Creation:** Bt. (GB) 20 May 1774.

SIR ARCHIBALD BRUCE CHARLES EDMONSTONE, 7TH BT, of Duntreath, Co Stirling [Sir Archibald Edmonstone Bt, Duntreath Castle, Blanefield, Stirlingshire G63 9AJ]; *b* 3 Aug 1934; *s f* 1954; *educ* St Peter's Court and Stowe; 2nd Lt Roy Scots Greys 1954–56; *m* 1st 17 Jan 1957 (*divorce* 1968) Jane (*m* subsequently Bingham Hartley, of London, SW1), er dau of Maj-Gen Edward Charles Colville, CB, DSO, of Old Barton, Stroughton, nr Chichester, Sussex (*see* COLVILLE OF CULROSS, V), and has issue:

1 +ARCHIBALD EDWARD CHARLES [Archibald Edmonstone Esq, 2A Rhodesia Rd, London SW9 2EL]; *b* 4 Feb 1961; *educ* Stowe and RMA Sandhurst; 2nd Lt Scots Gds 1982; *m* 1988 *Ursula, est dau of Benjamin Worthington (*see* HOWARD-LAWSON, Bt)

2 +Nicholas (Nick) William Mark; *b* 16 April 1964; *m* 1st 1989 (*divorce* 19–) Mary M, dau of Malcolm Hall, of Gibraltar Farm, Jersey, CI, and has issue:

(1) *Emily Cari; *b* 1990

2 (cont.) Nicholas Edmonstone *m* 2nd 26 Nov 1994 *Arabella, dau of Richard Johnsen, of Shalden Manor, Shalden, Hants, and has further issue:

(1) +Jack William Charles; *b* 5 Sept 1996

1 *Philippa Carolyn; *b* 12 June 1958; *m* 15 Oct 1983 (*divorce* 1994) Peter William Huntington (*see* PALMER, Bt), 3rd s of Victor William Huntington, JP, of Bonawe House, Tayn, Argyll

SIR ARCHIBALD *m* 2nd 24 June 1969 *Juliet Elizabeth, only dau of Maj-Gen Cecil Martin Fothergill Deakin, CB, CBE (*see* GRANT, Bt, of Cullen), late Gren Gds, of Stocks Farm House, Beenham, Berks, by Evelyn Mary Frances, est dau of Col Sir Arthur Grant, of Monymusk, 10th Bt (*see* GRANT, Bt, of Cullen), and by her has issue:

3 +Dru Benjamin Marshall; *b* 26 Oct 1971

2 *Elyssa Juliet; *b* 11 Sept 1973

Lineage: The EDMONSTONEs of Duntreath may well be a junior line of the EDMONSTOUNEs of Edmonstoune and Ednam.

Sir ARCHIBALD EDMONSTOUNE (probably yr s of the 1st Sir John, of Edmonstoune); had (with a dau Janet, *m* 1st Earl of Montrose; *see* MONTROSE, D):

Sir WILLIAM EDMONSTONE of Culloden; *m* as her 4th husb Mary, dau of ROBERT III (*see* also HAMILTON and BRANDON, D; AILSA, M; MONTROSE, D) and was granted 1445 the lands of Duntreath, which long served as the chief seat of the family; had:

Sir WILLIAM EDMONSTONE, a Ld of Articles (memb Standing Ctee S Parl); *m* Matilda, gdau of the last Regent Duke of Albany (*see* MORAY, E), and had:

Sir ARCHIBALD EDMONSTONE; had:

Sir WILLIAM EDMONSTONE; *k* Battle of Flodden 1513, leaving:

Sir WILLIAM EDMONSTONE; *m* Lady Agnes Stewart, dau of Earl of Lennox (*see* MORAY, E), and had issue:

Sir JAMES EDMONSTONE; *m* Margaret, dau of Sir John Colquhoun of Luss (*see* COLQUHOUN, Bt) ancestor in the fourth generation of:

ARCHIBALD EDMONSTONE, of Duntreath and Red Hall, Co Antrim; *m* 1st Anne, dau of David, Lord Cardross (*see* BUCHAN, E), and had a dau; *m* 2nd Anne, dau of John Campbell, sis of 4th Duke of Argyll (*qv*), and had:

Sir Archibald Edmonstone, 1st Bt (GB), so *cr* 20 May 1774; MP Dumbartonshire and Ayr and Irvine 1761–95; *m* 1st Susanna Mary, dau of Roger Harenc, and had, with other issue:

1 CHARLES (Sir), **2nd Bt**

2 Neil Benjamin, HEICS India; *b* 1765; 1803 Charlotte Anne, dau of Philip Friell, and *d* 1841, leaving, with six daus:

(1) William Archibald; *d* unm

(2) Neil Benjamin, HEICS; *b* 13 June 1809; *m* 7 Feb 1840 Madalina Elinor (*d* 1898), only dau of William Henry Trant, MP, and *d* 1872, leaving issue:

1a Neil Benjamin, Lt-Col 4th Hus; *b* 20 June 1843; *m* 1 June 1886 Edith Isabella (*d* 25 Mar 1958), er dau of Col Henry Lumsden, JP, DL, FRGS, of Pitcaple Castle, Aberdeenshire, and *d* 29 Nov 1915, leaving issue:

1b Edith Meriel; *m* 1st 3 June 1909 (*divorce* 1913) Cdr Richard St John, RN (*see* SAINT JOHN OF BLETSO, B); *m* 2nd 25 March 1920 Maj (Lewis Aloysius) Macdonald Hastings, MC, RFA (*d* 1966), s of Stephen T G Hastings, and *d* 4 April 1971, leaving issue:

1c *Stephen Lewis Edmonstone (Sir), MC (1944) [Sir Stephen Hastings MC, Milton, Peterborough, Hunts PE6 7AA; Stibbington House, Wansford, Peterborough PE8 6JS]; Ensign Scots Gds 1939, sub Maj, served 2nd Bn Western Desert 1941–43 (despatches), 1st SAS Regt 1943, No 1 Special Force, Italy, FO 1948, Br Legation Helsinki 1950–52, Br Embassy Paris 1953–58, 1st Sec Political Office MEF 1957–60, MP (C) Mid-Beds Nov 1960–1983, dir FitzWilliam Estates 1980–, ptnr and manager Milton Park Stud 1985–, chm Br Field Sports Soc 1982–88, memb Cncl Thoroughbred Breeders Assoc 1989–91, Jt MFH Fitzwilliam; author: *The Murder of TSR 2* (1966), *The Drums of Memory* (1995); *b* 4 May 1921; *educ* Eton and RMC Sandhurst; *m* 1st 1948 (*divorce* 1971) Harriet Mary Elizabeth, dau of Col Julian Latham Tomlin, CBE, DSO, RE, and has issue:

1d *Aubrey Neil Edmonstone; *b* 30 March 1950; *educ* Eton

1d *Carola Ann; *b* 3 March 1952

1c (cont.) Sir Stephen Hastings *m* 2nd 1975 Hon Elizabeth Anne (*d* 20 March 1997), formerly w of Sir Vivyan Naylor-Leyland, 3rd Bt (*qv*), and yr dau of 2nd Viscount FitzAlan of Derwent (*see* NORFOLK, D)

1c *Edith Anne Edmonstone [Mrs Roger Kerrison, Sloley Lodge, Sloley, Norfolk NR12 8HE]; *m* 21 Sept 1942 *Roger Edmund Fulke Kerrison, yr s of Roger Fulke Kerrison, JP, of Burgh Hall, Aylsham, Norfolk, and has had:

1d Philip Roger Stephen; *b* 18 Feb 1950; *educ* Eton; *d* 1977

1d *Caroline Felicity; *b* 19 Sept 1943; *m* Nov 1968 *Peter Sandford Cox, s of Sir Geoffrey Sandford Cox, CBE, of Hampstead and has:

1e *Celia Anne; *b* 1974

2e *Susannah Meriel; *b* 1977

2d *Teresa Mary; *b* 2 April 1948; *m* Jan 1969 *William Marlborough Pryor, only s of Mark Gillachrist Marlborough Pryor, MA, PhD, of Cambridge, and has:

1e *Lydia; *b* 1970

2a William Henry; *b* 29 May 1850; *dsp* 19 June 1899

(3) Charles Welland (Rev), MA, Vicar Christ Church, Hornsey; *b* 19 March 1811; *m* 12 Jan 1842 Susanna Mary (*d* 26 March 1952), dau of Rev Philip H Douglas, and *d* 1897, having had, with three other daus:

1a Susanna Carnegie; *m* 20 June 1867 John Venn, FRS, MA, DSc, Pres Gonville and Caius Coll Cambridge, and *d* 25 March 1931, leaving issue. He *d* 3 April 1923

2a Charlotte Anne; *m* 16 Dec 1871 Rev Thomas Dalton, Eton maths master, and *d* 10 Feb 1925, leaving issue. He *d* 1894

3a Frances D'Oyley; *m* 30 June 1881 Rev Arthur Powys Woodhouse, Vicar Grendon, Northants, 1911–20, and *d* 4 Jan 1946, leaving issue

(4) George Frederick (Sir), KCB; Lt-Govr NW Frontier Province India; *b* April 1813; *m* Anne (*d* 1859), dau of T Turner, and *d* 24 Sept 1864, leaving:

1a George Frederick; *dsp*

2a Charles William; *d* unm 15 March 1878

1a Ellen Craigie; *d* unm 19 April 1942

(5) James; *d* unm

Sir Archibald *m* 2nd Hester, dau of Sir John Heathcote, Bt, of Normanton Park

He *d* July 1807; his er surv son,

Sir Charles Edmonstone, 2nd Bt; *b* 10 Oct 1764; MP Stirlingshire 1812–21; *m* 1st Emma, sis of 1st Baron Skelmersdale (*qv*), and had:

1 **Sir Archibald Edmonstone, 3rd Bt**; *b* 12 March 1795; *m* 10 Oct 1832 his cousin Emma (*d* 25 May 1891), dau of Randle Wilbraham, JP, of Rode Hall, Cheshire, and *dsp* 3 March 1871

1 Mary Emma; *d* unm 12 May 1885

Sir Charles *m* 2nd 5 Dec 1804 Hon Louisa Hotham (*m* 2nd Jan 1832 Charles Woodcock and *d* 30 Aug 1840), yst dau of 2nd Baron Hotham (*qv*), and *d* 1 April 1821, having by her had, with other issue:

2 WILLIAM (Sir), **4th Bt**

3 George; Bengal CS; *b* 25 Jan 1816; *m* 15 Nov 1838 Amelia Helen, widow of H Millet and dau of E M Hogg, and *dsp* 29 Feb 1888

4 Frederick Neil, Lt-Col Bengal Inf; *b* 7 Sept 1818; *m* 17 March 1863 Henrietta, yst dau of Lt-Col W Smith-Neill, of Barnweill and Swindrigemuir, and *dsp* 14 Aug 1865

2 Louisa Henrietta; *m* 15 Dec 1829 John Kingston, of London, and *d* 14 March 1840, having had issue

The 3rd Bt's half-brother,

Sir William Edmonstone, 4th Bt, CB, DL; MP Stirlingshire 1874–80, Adml ADC to HM QUEEN VICTORIA; *b* 29 Jan 1810; *m* July 1841 Mary Elizabeth (*d* 11 Aug 1902), dau of Lt-Col Parsons, CMG, and had surv issue:

1 ARCHIBALD (Sir), **5th Bt**

1 Louisa Ann; *m* 12 Oct 1872 Maj-Gen Henry Pipon, CB, RHA), Maj of Tower London, 2nd s of Col J K Pipon, of Jersey, and *d* 3 July 1921, leaving issue. He *d* 14 Jan 1924

2 Charlotte Henrietta; *m* 9 June 1866 Rev John Francis Kitson, Vicar Antony, Cornwall, and *d* 21 Oct 1931, leaving issue. He *d* 29 July 1907

3 Jessie; *m* 3 June 1884 Maj Edward John Winnington-Ingram (*see* WINNINGTON, Bt), and *d* 10 June 1837

4 Frances Euphemia; *m* 3 June 1873 Alexander R Duncan, of Parkhill, Forfar, and *d* 14 Feb 1921, leaving issue. He *d* 13 April 1927

5 Sophia; *m* 3 June 1880 James Edward Hope, and *d* 19 Feb 1924, leaving issue (*see* HOPE, Bt)

6 Susanna Emily; *m* 16 Feb 1885 Jonathan Bucknill and *d* 9 May 1886, leaving issue

7 Mary Clementina; *m* 1 Oct 1874 1st and last Viscount Dunedin, GCVO (*see* 1940 edn), and *d* 2 Dec 1922, leaving issue. He *d* 21 Aug 1942

8 Alice Frederica; *m* 1 June 1891 Lt-Col Hon George Keppel, MVO, s of 7th Earl of Albemarle (*qv*), and *d* 11 Sept 1947, leaving issue

Sir WILLIAM *d* 18 Feb 1888; his only son,

Sir Archibald Edmonstone, 5th Bt, CVO (1909), DL; Groom-in-Waiting to HM KING EDWARD VII 1907–10, Cdr Order Vasa of Sweden with star, Lt 3rd Bn Argyll and Sutherland Highrs; *b* 30 May 1867; *m* 30 Nov 1895 Ida Agnes Eleanor (*d* 21 Dec 1946), Woman Bedchamber to HRH PRINCESS CHRISTIAN, dau of George Stewart Forbes (*see* FORBES, Bt, of Newe), and had issue:

1 William George, Lt 2nd Bn Coldstream Gds; *b* 20 Oct 1896; *ka* Somme 15 Sept 1916

2 ARCHIBALD CHARLES (Sir), **6th Bt**

3 Edward St John; *b* 3 Nov 1901 (HM EDWARD VII stood sponsor); Cdr RN, served WWs I and II; *m* 30 Nov 1936 Hon Alicia Evelyn Browne (*d* 1992), only dau of 5th Baron Kilmaine (*qv*), and *d* 3 Dec 1983, leaving:

(1) +(William Henry) Neil [Neil Edmonstone Esq, Barcombe Old Rectory, nr Lewes, Sussex; 54 Warwick Sq, London SW1]; *b* 11 Aug 1942; *educ* Eton, FCA; *m* 1994 *Mrs Selma Patricia Deidre Rees, dau of S/Ldr Finan O'Driscoll

(1) *(Helen) Antonia [Mrs Michael Gibbs, 19 Caroline Place, London W2 4AN]; *b* 6 Oct 1937 (HRH THE late DUKE OF KENT stood sponsor); *m* 31 March 1960 *Michael Edmund Hubert Gibbs (*see* ALDENHAM and HUNSDON OF HUNSDON, B), and has:

1a *Patrick Michael Evans [Patrick Gibbs Esq, 75 Arlington Rd, London NW1 7ES]; *b* 1962; *m* 1989 *Catherine Barroll and has issue:

1b *Rufus; *b* 1994

1b *Clemency; *b* 1992

2a *Edward Michael John; *b* 1964

3a *Adrian Michael Philip; *b* 1967

1a *Arabella Marina Clare [Mrs Quintin Davies, 36 Winfield House, Vicarage Crescent, London SW11 3LN]; *b* 1969; *m* 1994 *Quintin John Davies, s of Thomas Davies

Sir ARCHIBALD *d* 1 April 1954; his er surv son,

Sir Archibald Charles Edmonstone, 6th Bt; *b* 16 June 1898; *educ* Wellington and RMC Sandhurst; Lt 9th Lancers WW I, ADC to Govr Madras; *m* 5 April 1923 Gwendolyn Mary (*d* 27 Nov 1989), dau of Marshall Field, of Chicago, and *d* 5 June 1954, having had issue:

1 Sir ARCHIBALD BRUCE CHARLES EDMONSTONE, **7th and present Bt**

2 Angus Ian Marshall; *b* 25 April 1936; *d* 11 April 1937

1 *Mary Bettine [Lady McGrigor, Upper Sonachan, by Dalmally, Argyll PA33 1BJ; 18 Cranmer Court, London SW3]; *b* 28 Sept 1927; *m* 7 June 1948 *Capt Sir Charles Edward McGrigor, 5th Bt (*qv*), and has issue

2 *Jane Fiona [Mrs Hugh Cameron-Rose, 25c Kelso Place, London W8; Hoopers Farm, Kings Sombourne, Hants SO20 6QG]; *b* 24 Aug 1931; *m* 1st 5 Oct 1950 (*divorce* 1975) Maj Sir Andrew Rupert John Buchanan-Jardine, 4th Bt (*qv*), and has issue; *m* 2nd 1976 Hugh Alastair Cameron-Rose (*d* 30 Dec 1994)

3 *Susan Morag; *b* 13 Jan 1941; *m* 27 June 1964 *Robert Keith Erskine (*see* BUCHAN, E) and has issue

4 (Anne) Sibylla; with Tredore & Harpers; *b* 18 Nov 1943; *m* 1970 (*divorce* 19–) James Manwering Robertson, restaurateur, yr s of David Robertson, and *d* 198–, leaving issue:

(1) *Dickon Manwering; *b* 1971

EDWARDS of Pye Nest

Arms: Azure on a bend nebuly argent, cotised or, a fleur-de-lys between two martlets of the field. **Crest:** Out of a crown vallery or a talbot's head argent, semée-de-lys azure. **Motto:** *Omne bonum Dei donum* ('All good is the gift of God'). **Creation:** Bt (UK) 3 Aug 1866.

SIR CHRISTOPHER JOHN CHURCHILL EDWARDS, 5TH BT [Sir Christopher Edwards Bt, 11637 County Club Drive, Westminster, Colorado 80234, USA]; *b* 16 Aug 1941; s f 1963; *educ* Frensham Heights Sch and Loughborough Coll; gen manager Kelsar Inc, American Home Products, San Diego, California 1979–84, v-pres Valley Lab Inc, Boulder, Colorado 1981–89, dir Ohmeda BOC Gp, Louisville, Colorado 1989–92; *m* 1972 *Gladys Irene Vogelgesang and has issue:

1 +DAVID CHARLES PRIESTLEY; *b* 22 Feb 1974

2 +Ryan Matthew Churchill; *b* 16 April 1979

Lineage: WILLIAM EDWARDS, of Warwick; *b* 1680; *m* — dau of James Dolphin, and *d* May 1748, leaving:

JOHN EDWARDS, of Warwicks; *b c* 1710; *m* 9 Aug 1737 Mary, dau of John Tompon, and *d* April 1740, leaving:

JOHN EDWARDS, of Pye Nest, Yorks, JP; *b* 6 Feb 1737; *m* 15 July 1762 Elizabeth (*d* 19 Aug 1803), dau of Samuel Lees, of Willow Hall, Skircoat, Halifax, and *d* 14 July 1823, having had, with four daus and a yr s (Thomas Grove, of Regent's Park, *b* 1 Nov 1783, *d* unm 14 March 1855):

HENRY LEES EDWARDS, of Pye Nest, DL; *b* 29 Nov 1775; *m* 10 May 1804 Lea (*d* 6 Sept 1853), dau of Joseph Priestley, of White Windows, Sowerby, and Goodgrave, Yorks, by Lydia, dau of John Lea, of Haugh End, Sowerby, Yorks, and *d* 2 May 1848, leaving, with other issue:

1 John Lea, of Darcey Hey, Halifax; *b* 11 Feb 1805; *m* 17 Oct 1833 Anne Elizabeth, dau of John Waterhouse, of Wellhead, Halifax, Yorks, and *d* 27 Dec 1835, leaving an only child:

(1) Catherine Frances; *m* Rev Canon Philip Robin, Rector Woodchurch, Cheshire

2 Charles, of Darcey Hey; *b* 2 April 1809; *m* 9 Nov 1836 Catherine (*d* 7 Sept 1842), dau of John Waterhouse, of Wellhead, Halifax, and *dsp* 19 Sept 1842

3 HENRY (Sir), **1st Bt**

4 Joseph Priestley, of Castle Carr and Fixby Park, Yorks, JP, DL; Ld Manor of Oxenhope, Capt W Yorks Yeo Cav; *b* 29 Dec 1818; *m* 16 Jan 1844 Margaret (*d* 17 June 1902), dau of James Edward Norris, of Savile Hall, Halifax, and *d* 20 Aug 1868, leaving issue

The 3rd son,

Sir Henry Edwards, 1st Bt (UK), so *cr* 3 Aug 1866, CB, of Pye Nest, JP, DL (W R Yorks); High Sheriff 1872, Provincial Grand Master Freemasons W Yorks, Col 2nd W Yorks Regt Yeo Cav, MP (C) Halifax 1847–52 and Beverley 1857–68; *b* 20 July 1812; *m* 19 April 1838 Maria Churchill (*d* 5 March 1906), est dau of Thomas Coster, of Regent's Park, London, and had, with other issue:

1 HENRY COSTER LEA (Sir), **2nd Bt**

2 Charles Grove, JP (W R Yorks and Berks), of Wicklesham, Faringdon, and Lambourn Place, Berks; MA Oxon, Col 2nd W Yorks Yeo; *b* 3 Sept 1843; *m* 10 Oct 1871 Beatrix (*d* 15 Jan 1928), dau of Henry Hippisley, of Lambourn Place, and *dsp* 5 Dec 1904

3 Arthur Hancock, of Pye Nest, Halifax, JP, DL W R Yorks, Maj 2nd W Yorks Yeo Cav; *b* 4 July 1847; *educ* Ch Ch Oxford (MA); *m* 22 Jan 1874 Eleanor Louisa (*d* 24 Aug 1911), 2nd dau of Lt-Col Joseph Walker Pease, of Hesslewood, Hull, Yorks, and *d* 19 Dec 1924, having had issue:

(1) Geoffrey Otho Charles, Lt 3rd Bn Duke of Wellington's W R Regt; *b* 2 Oct 1876; *educ* New Coll Oxford (BA); *ka* 7 July 1916

(2) Henry Arthur Rolleston; *b* 21 Jan 1881; *d* 8 Nov 1934

(1) Eleanor Churchill; *m* 25 June 1900 William Henry Boger, MRCS, LRCP, of The Gardens, Lambourn, Berks, and *dsp* 27 Dec 1968 aged 93

(2) Barbara Florence; *m* 12 Sept 1912 Capt Basil John Orlebar, 3rd Bn Beds Regt, er s of John Orlebar, of Silsoe, Ampthill, Beds, and *d* 27 Dec 1952. He was *ka* 15 Jan 1915

(3) Winifred Delia; *m* 1st 11 Dec 1902 Capt Spencer Allen Hickley, RN, s of Adml H D Hickley, of Oxford, and had issue. He *d* 27 Sept 1914. She *m* 2nd 20 March 1920 Lt-Cdr George William Seymour Seton, RN, s of Col Alexander David Seton, of Mounie Castle, Aberdeenshire, and *d* 20 Jan 1946, having had further issue

Sir HENRY *d* 23 April 1886; his son,

Sir Henry Coster Lea Edwards, 2nd Bt, JP; Lt 2nd W Yorks Yeo Cav; *b* 3 June 1840; *m* 1st 22 June 1872 (*divorce* 1886) Agnes Harcourt, dau of Edward Rawson Clark; *m* 2nd 29 Sept 1887 Laura Selina (*d* 24 March 1919), 2nd dau of John Capes Clark, of Bridgefoot House, Iver, Bucks, and *d* 5 Dec 1896, leaving by her:

1 **Sir John Henry Priestley Churchill Edwards, 3rd Bt**, T/Lt 4th Bn Rifle Bde, Lt 23rd Bn London Regt TF, served WW II with Australian Forces; *b* 7 July 1889; *das* unm 13 Nov 1942

2 **Sir (Henry) Charles Serrell Priestley Edwards, 4th Bt**; *b* 1 March 1893; *educ* Rossall; *m* 1st 23 June 1916 Margarita Ethlyn (*d* 1 April 1932), dau of John Brindahan King Kalvi, of Panama; *m* 2nd 26 April 1935 *Daphne Marjory Hilda (*m* 2nd 1972 Leonard Mallett), est dau of William George Birt, of Kensington, and *d* 3 April 1963, leaving issue:

(1) Sir CHRISTOPHER JOHN CHURCHILL EDWARDS, **5th and present Bt**

(2) +Peter Henry; *b* 11 Jan 1944; *educ* Frensham Heights Sch

EDWARDS of Treforis

Arms: Per chevron sa. and arg. in chief two lions rampant and in base a castle counterchanged. **Crest:** A stag's head erased ppr., gorged with a coronet composed of eight roses set upon a rim or, between the attires an escarbuncle gold. **Motto:** *Absque labore nihil* ('Nothing without labour'). **Creation:** Bt. (UK) 30 June 1921.

SIR (JOHN) CLIVE LEIGHTON EDWARDS, 2ND BT, of Treforis, Glamorgan [Sir Clive Edwards Bt, Milntown, Lezayre, Ramsey, Isle of Man IM7 2AB]; *b* 11 Oct 1916; *s* f 1922; *educ* Winchester; RASC and Capt Roy Pioneer Corps WW II

Lineage: RICHARD EDWARDS; *b* 1525; *d* 1566, leaving:

RICHARD EDWARDES; *b* 22 Nov 1566; had:

1 William; *b c* 1586; had:

(1) Thomas; *b c* 1610; emigrated July 1635 aboard the ship *Ye Merchants Hope* to Virginia, together with his two yr bros

(2) Robert

(3) William

(4) John; *d* in America, leaving property to kin still in England

2 Joshua; *b c* 1587; had:

(1)William; *b c* 1610; *m* 1st 1634 —; *m* 2nd — and by her had a s (Thomas Nathaniel); his s by his 1st w:

1a William; *b* 1635; had:

1b Thomas; *b* 1667; *m* 1st 1694 Margaret Saunders and had:

1c William, of Monmouth; *b* 1695; *m* 31 Dec 1714 Jennet Powell (*d* 4 Feb 1779)

1b (cont.) Thomas Edwards *m* 2nd 1718 Mary Scandrett and *d* 1722, leaving by her:

2c Thomas, of Bristol; *b* 1721; *d* 1765

3c JOHN

The yst s, JOHN EDWARDS, of Bristol; *b* 1719; *m* 1762 Mary — and had:

EBENEZER EDWARDS, of Morriston, Glam; had:

DANIEL EDWARDS, of Bedford House, Morriston, JP; had:

WILLIAM HENRY EDWARDS, of The Hill, Sketty, Glam, JP; *b* Dec 1860; *m* 17 April 1888 Margaret Hannah (*d* 23 Sept 1904), dau of William Williams, MP, JP, and *d* 27 May 1919, having had issue:

1 JOHN BRYN (Sir), **1st Bt**

2 William Armine, Lt Glamorgan Yeo WW I; *b* 3 May 1892; *d* 1 Nov 1917 from wounds recd in action in Palestine

The er son,

Sir John Bryn Edwards, 1st Bt (UK), so *cr* 30 June 1921, MA, LLB; *b* 12 Jan 1889; *m* 18 Jan 1911 Kathleen Ermyntrude (*d* 2 Dec 1975), dau of John Corfield, JP, and *d* 22 Aug 1922, leaving issue:

1 Sir JOHN CLIVE LEIGHTON EDWARDS, **2nd and present Bt**

1 Margaret Kathleen Valerie; *b* 21 Aug 1912; *m* 22 June 1935 Eric Davan Wetton, CBE, only s of Henry Davan Wetton, MusD, and *d* 14 Jan 1971, leaving issue:

(1) *Philip Henry Davan; *b* 21 Sept 1937; *educ* Westminster and Ch Ch Oxford

(2) *Hilary John Davan; *b* 23 Dec 1943; *educ* Westminster and BNC Oxford

EDWARDS-MOSS

Arms: Quarterly, 1st and 4th, quarterly erm. and erminois a cross patée az. between six billets, three in chief and three in base, gu. (for MOSS); 2nd and 3rd, arg. a lion rampant guardant sa., on a chief of the last dancetté two eagles displayed of the first (for EDWARDS). **Crests:** 1 Issuant from the battlements of a tower or, charged with a rose gu., slipped vert, a gryphon's head erm., on the neck a cross patée az. (for MOSS), 2 A rock ppr., therefrom rising a dove arg., holding in its beak an olive branch and surmounted by a rainbow ppr. (for EDWARDS). **Motto:** *En la rose je fleurie* ('I flourish in the rose'). **Creation:** Bt (UK) 23 Dec 1868.

David John Edwards-Moss, 5th Bt; *b* 2 Feb 1955; *s* f 1988 but does not use title; *educ* Cranleigh

Lineage: JOHN MOSS, of Otterspool, in Childwall, Lancs (s of Thomas Moss, of Whiston, Lancs, and gs of John Moss, of Hurst House, Lancs); *b* 18 Feb 1782; *m* 3 Sept 1805 Hannah (*d* 16 Dec 1872), dau of Thomas Taylor, of Blakeley, Lancs, and *d* 3 Oct 1858, having had issue:

1 Thomas; *b* 6 Jan 1810; *d* an infant

2 THOMAS (Sir), **1st Bt**

3 John James (Rev); MA, Rector E Lydford, Somerset; *b* 15 July 1822; *m* 27 Feb 1862 Louisa (*d* 12 Sept 1863), est dau of Gen Hon Sir Edward Cust, 1st Bt (*see* BROWNLOW, B), and *dsp* 1887

4 William Henry; *b* 11 April 1824; *d* 20 Dec 1859

5 Gilbert Winter, JP Lancs; *b* 31 March 1828; *m* 29 April 1852 Eliza Seilliere, dau of Emanuel Zwilchenbart, of Roselands, and *d* 5 July 1899, leaving issue:

(1) Gilbert Winter Zwilchenbart, Capt Roy Fus; *b* 13 Feb 1857; *m* 4 Feb 1885 Annie Norah, dau of M Thornhill, and *d* 4 July 1890, leaving issue

(1) Gertrude Emily; *d* 23 July 1920

(2) Edith; *m* 23 April 1884 Very Rev John William Diggle, DD, Bp Carlisle, and had issue

1 Margaret; *m* Jan 1829 Walker Ferrand, DL, JP, of Harden Grange, Yorks, and *dsp* 5 April 1846. He *d* 20 Sept 1835

2 Hannah; *d* 11 Jan 1858

3 Anne Jane; *d* unm

4 Harriet Eliza; *m* 15 April 1857 Rev G D Bourne, Rector Weston-sub-Edge, and *d* 13 Sept 1867, having had issue

The 2nd son,

Sir THOMAS MOSS later EDWARDS-MOSS (roy licence 26 March 1851), **1st Bt**, of Roby Hall (UK), so *cr* 23 Dec 1868; *b* 17 July 1811; *m* 18 May 1847 Amy Charlotte (*d* 7 May 1882), only child and heiress of Richard Edwards, of Roby Hall, Lancs, and *d* 26 April 1890, leaving issue:

1 JOHN EDWARDS (Sir), **2nd Bt**

2 Tom Cottingham, MA, MP Widnes 1885–92, Capt Lancs Hus; *b* 7 April 1855; *d* unm 16 Dec 1893

1 Minna Amy; *m* 26 June 1877 Osgood Hanbury Mackenzie, yst s of Sir Francis Alexander Mackenzie, 5th Bt, of Gairloch (*see* INGLIS, Bt), and *d* 19 Aug 1909, leaving issue

2 Mary Ethel; *d* 29 July 1920

Sir THOMAS's est son,

Sir John Edwards-Moss, 2nd Bt, MA Oxon; Priv Sec to Home Sec; *b* 25 Oct 1850; *m* 20 Feb 1873 Margaret Everilda (*d* 16 June 1942), yst dau of Col John Ireland Blackburne, of Hale Hall, Lancs, and *d* 26 June 1935, leaving:

1 **Sir Thomas Edwards-Moss, 3rd Bt**; *b* 17 Jan 1874; *educ* Eton; Capt 3rd Bn Loyal North Lancashire Regt; *m* 15 May 1926 Eda (*d* 30 Dec 1964), dau of Edward Goodison, of Bradford, and *dsp* 26 July 1960

2 John; Maj Cornwall RGA; *b* 28 Sept 1882; *educ* Eton and Trin Coll Cambridge; *m* 27 April 1911 Dorothy Kate Gwyllyam (*d* 12 Nov 1961), est dau of Ven Henry William Watkins, DD, Archdeacon Durham, and *d* 8 Nov 1958, having had issue:

(1) Thomas Cottingham; *b* 23 April 1912; *d* 23 March 1916

(2) JOHN HERBERT THEODORE (Sir), **4th Bt**

(3) Thomas Richard; Hon Capt Scots Gds WW II (ret 1948); *b* 24 Oct 1921; *educ* Eton; *m* 1st 18 Dec 1943 (*divorce* 1953) Bridget Doreen, dau of Maj Hon Richard Coke (*see* LEICESTER, E), and had:

1a +John Richard [John Edwards-Moss Esq, Glebe Farm House, E Leake, Leics LE12 6LE]; *b* 2 Feb 1947; *educ* Eton; *m* 18 Sept 1976 *Penelope F, only dau of Michael Horne, of Bath Villas, Mill Hill, Newmarket, Suffolk, and has issue:

1b +Thomas Michael; *b* 1980

1b *Rose Bridget; *b* 1981

2b *Letitia Patience; *b* 30 May 1983

(3) (cont.) Thomas Edwards-Moss *m* 2nd 6 Feb 1953 *Monica Hughes [Mrs Thomas Edwards-Moss, 4 Marlborough Buildings, Bow St, Langport, Som TA10 9PH], only dau of Maj H G Wilkinson, BSc, Burma Service of Engrs, and *d* 1974, leaving by her:

1a *Stella Lucy; *b* 3 April 1958

(1) Dorothy Margaret; *b* 7 June 1915; *d* 23 July 1922

(2) Rosemary Ethel Amy; *b* 1917; *d* 4 June 1997

3 William; *b* 24, *d* 28 June 1890

1 Margaret; *d* an infant

2 Amy; *m* 21 April 1915 Alfred Robert Maclean Camm, 2nd s of John B M Camm, of Deveron Lodge, Bournemouth, and *d* 12 May 1959. He *d* 16 March 1929

The 3rd Bt's nephew,

Sir John Herbert Theodore Edwards-Moss, 4th Bt; *b* 24 June 1913; *educ* Down House; served WW II; *m* 21 Nov 1951 *Jane Rebie [Lady Edwards-Moss, Ruffold Farm, Guildford Rd, Cranleigh, Surrey GU6 8LT], only dau of Carteret John Kempson, of Four Corners, Ewhurst, Surrey, and *d* 1988, leaving:

1 Sir DAVID JOHN EDWARDS-MOSS, **5th and present Bt**

2 +Peter Michael; *b* 26 Sept 1957; *m* 1988 *Jenifer Cadisch and has:

(1) +John Herbert Theodore; *b* 1992

(2) +Charles Anthony; *b* 1994

3 +Paul Richard; *b* 12 May 1960

4 +Christopher James; *b* 27 Jan 1963

5 +Jonathan Francis William; *b* 20 May 1967

1 *Penelope Anne; *b* 3 Feb 1956; *m* 1988 *Michael Geoffrey Jennings and has:

(1) *Johnnie Sam; *b* 1991

(1) *Kathrine Sarah; *b* 1989

(2) *Lucie Charlotte; *b* 1995

EFFINGHAM

Arms: Gu. on a bend between six cross-crosslets fitchée arg. an escutcheon of the field charged with a demi-lion rampant, pierced through the mouth with an arrow, within a double tressure flory-counterflory. **Crest:** On a chapeau gu. doubled erm. a lion stantant-guardant, his tail extended or, gorged with a ducal coronet arg. **Supporters:** Two lions arg., on the shoulder of each a mullet for difference. **Motto:** *Virtus mille scuta* ('Virtue is worth a thousand shields'). **Creations:** E. (UK) 27 Jan 1837, B. (E) 11 March 1554.

THE 7TH EARL OF EFFINGHAM, Co Surrey (David Mowbray Algernon Howard) and **Baron Howard of Effingham**, Co Surrey [Cdr The Rt Hon The Earl of Effingham RN (ret), Readings Farmhouse, Blackmore End, Essex CM7 4DH]; *b* 29 April 1939; *s* uncle 1996; *educ* Fettes; *m* 1st 10 Oct 1964 (*divorce* 1975) Anne Mary, dau of Harrison Sayer, of Cambridge; *m* 2nd 1992 *Elizabeth Jane, dau of Dennis Eccleston, of Gt Saling, Essex, and formerly w of Peter Robert Easton Turner, and by his 1st w has:

1 +EDWARD MOWBRAY NICHOLAS, *Lord Howard of Effingham*; *b* 11 May 1971

Lineage: Lord WILLIAM HOWARD, **1st Baron Howard of Effingham** Co Surrey (E), as which *cr* 11 March 1553/4, KG (1554), est s of 2nd Duke of Norfolk (*qv*) by the latter's 2nd w; *b c* 1510; *educ* Trin Hall Cambridge; Amb to Scotland Feb 1534/5 and March–May 1536, France 1537 and 1541; found guilty of treasonable activity in conjunction with his n QUEEN KATHERINE HOWARD 1542 (pardoned 1544), Ld Dep Calais 1552–53, Ld High Adml 20 March 1553/4, helped suppress Wyatt's rebellion 1554, Ld Chamberlain Household 1558–72, Ld Lt Surrey 1559–73, Ld Privy Seal 1572–Jan 1572/3; *m* 1st Katharine (*d* 23 April 1535), sister and coheir of John Broughton, and had:

1 Agnes; *m* 3rd Marquess of Winchester (*qv*)

The **1st Baron** *m* 2nd by 1536 Margaret (*d* 18 May 1531), 2nd dau of Sir Thomas Gamage, of Coity, Glam, and *d* 21 Jan 1572/3, having had by her (with other issue):

1 CHARLES HOWARD, **2nd Baron Howard of Effingham** and 1st EARL OF NOTTINGHAM (E) *cr* 22 Oct 1596, KG (1574); *b* 1536; C-in-C English Fleet against Spanish Armada 1588; *m* 1st July 1563 Catherine (*d* 25 Feb 1602/3), dau of Henry Cary, Lord Hunsdon (*see* FALKLAND, V), and had, with three daus (including Elizabeth, *m* Sir Robert Southwell; *see* SOUTHWELL, V):

(1) WILLIAM HOWARD; called up to Ho of Lds *vp* as **3rd Baron Howard of Effingham**; *m* 7 Feb 1596/7 Anne, dau of 2nd Baron Saint John of Bletso (*qv*), and *dspm* & *vp* 28 Nov 1615, having had at least one dau (Elizabeth, *b* 19 Jan 1602/3, a celebrated beauty and fervent anti-monarchist, *m* 2 March 1620/1 1st Earl of Peterborough (*see* MORDAUNT, Bt) and was *bur* 18 Nov 1671)

(2) CHARLES HOWARD, **4th Baron Howard of Effingham** and 2nd EARL OF NOTTINGHAM; *b* 17 Sept 1579; *m* 1st 19 May 1597 Charity (*d* 18 Dec 1618), widow of William Leche and dau of Robert Whit; *m* 2nd 22 April 1620 Mary (*d* 6 Feb 1650/1), sis of 1st Viscount Cullen (*see* CULLEN OF ASHBOURNE, B), and *dsp* 3 Oct 1642

1 (cont.) The **2nd Baron** *m* 2nd Sept 1603 Margaret (*m* 2nd 23 Oct 1625, as his 1st w, 1st and last Viscount Monson of Castlemaine (*see* MONSON, B), and *d* 4 Aug 1639), dau of 2nd Earl of Moray (*qv*), and *d* 14 Dec 1624, having by her had, with another son:

(3) CHARLES HOWARD, **5th Baron Howard of Effingham** and 3rd EARL OF NOTTINGHAM; *b* 25 Dec 1610; *m* Arabella (*d* 16 Jan 1681/2), sis of Sir Edward Smith, and *dsp* 26 April 1681, when the Earldom expired

2 William (Sir), of Lingfield, Surrey; *m* Frances, dau of William Gouldwell, of Gouldwell Hall, Kent; *d* 2 Sept 1600, leaving (with a yst s Charles (Sir)):

(1) Edward (Sir), cup-bearer to JAMES I; *dsp* 1620

(2) Francis (Sir), of Eastwick, Great Bookham, Surrey; *m* Jane, dau of Sir William Monson, of Kinnersley (*see* MONSON, B), and *d* 7 July 1651, leaving an est son:

1a Charles (Sir), of Eastwick; *m* Frances, dau of Sir George Courthope, of Wyleigh, Sussex, and *d* 20 March 1672/3, leaving issue:

1b FRANCIS HOWARD, **6th Baron Howard of Effingham**, of Great Bookham, Surrey; *bapt* 17 Sept 1643; Govr Virginia; *m* 1st 8 July 1673 Philadelphia (*d* 13 Aug 1685), dau of Sir Thomas Pelham, Bt (*see* CHICHESTER, E); *m* 2nd 20 Jan 1689/90 Susan (*d* 11 Dec 1726), widow of Philip Harbord, of Stanninghall, Norfolk, and dau of Sir Henry Felton, Bt, and *d* 30 March 1695, having by his 1st w had with another s and three daus:

1c THOMAS HOWARD, **7th Baron Howard, of Effingham**; *bapt* 7 July 1682; *m* 1st 25 Feb 1706/7 Mary (*d* 29 May 1718), dau and heir of Ruishe Wentworth, n of Thomas, Earl of Strafford; *m* 2nd 25 Jan 1722 Elizabeth (*m* 3rd Sir Conyers Darcy (*see* DARCY DE KNAYTH, B, and YARBOROUGH, E), and *d* 30 Nov 1741), widow of Sir Theophilus Napier, Bt, and dau of John Rotheram, and *dspm* 13 July 1725, having by his 1st w had:

1d Anne; *m* Sir William Yonge, 4th Bt, of Escot

2d Mary; *m* 1st Lord Vernon (*qv*), Baron of Kinderton

2c FRANCIS HOWARD, **8th Baron Howard, of Effingham** and 1st EARL OF EFFINGHAM, Co Surrey (GB), so *cr* 8 Dec 1731; *b* 20 Oct 1683; Dep Earl Marshal 1731; *m* 1st 23 Feb 1713 Diana, dau of Maj-Gen Fergus O'Farrell; *m* 2nd 23 May 1728 Anne (*dsps* 15 Nov 1774), sis of Robert Bristow, a Commr Bd Green Cloth, and *d* 12 Feb 1742/3, leaving by his 1st w:

1d THOMAS HOWARD, **9th Baron Howard of Effingham** and 2nd EARL OF EFFINGHAM; *b* 1714; Dep Earl Marshal; *m* 14 Feb 1744/5 Elizabeth (*m* 2nd 21 May 1771 FM Sir George Howard, KB (*see* below), and *d* 13 Oct 1791), dau of Peter Beckford, Speaker Jamaican Ho of Assembly and sis of William Beckford, of Fonthill, Ld Mayor and MP City of London, and *d* 19 Nov 1763, having had issue, with three daus:

1e THOMAS HOWARD, **10th Baron Howard of Effingham** and 3rd EARL OF EFFINGHAM; *b* 13 Jan 1746; Dep Earl Marshal; *m* 14 Oct 1765 Catherine (*d* at sea 14 Oct 1791), dau of Metcalfe Proctor, of Thorpe, near Leeds, and *dsp* 19 Nov 1791

2e RICHARD HOWARD, **11th Baron Howard of Effingham** and 4th EARL OF EFFINGHAM; *b* 21 Feb 1747/8; *m* 14 June 1785 Harriet Elizabeth, dau and coheir of John March of Waresley Park, Huntingdon, only surv son of Henry March by Elizabeth, est dau of Edward Lisle, of Wodyton, by Mary (*d* 7 March 1827), only dau of Sir Ambrose Phillipps, of Garendon Park, and *dsp* 10 Dec 1816, when the Earldom expired

2b George; *m* Anne, dau of Thomas Kidder, of Lewes, and *d* 1684, leaving:

1c Thomas; Govr Berwick; Lt-Gen; *m* Mary, yst dau of William Morton, Bishop of Meath, and *d* 1758, leaving issue:

1d George (Sir), KB; FM, MP, Govr Chelsea Hosp; *m* 1st Lady Lucy Wentworth, sis and coheir of William, Earl of Strafford and had:

1e Ann; *m* 1780 Gen Richard Vyse and *d* 1784, leaving:

1f Richard William VYSE later HOWARD-VYSE, of Stoke, Bucks; *d* 8 June 1853, leaving issue

1d (cont.) Sir George *m* 2nd Elizabeth, dau of Peter Beckford and widow of 2nd Earl of Effingham of the 1731 *cr*, but by her had no issue. He *d* 1796

2d Henry, of Tower House, Arundel; *m* 1st Catherine (*d* Dec 1762), dau of Rev John Carlton, DD, and had issue:

1e Catherine; *m* Rev Robert Blayney, Ld Manor Garlford, and *d* 12 April 1830

2e Mary; *d* unm 16 Dec 1833

2d (cont.) Henry Howard *m* 2nd Maria (*d* 29 Jan 1826), 2nd dau and coheir of Kenneth MacKenzie, Viscount Fortrose, and *d* 10 Sept 1811, leaving by her an only son:

1e KENNETH ALEXANDER, **1st Earl**

1d Mary; *m* Sir Francis Vincent, 7th Bt, and had a dau Mary, Countess of Rosebery (*qv*)

2d Catherine; *m* FM Studholme Hodgson, Col 7th Dragoon Gds, Ranger Windsor Forest, and had issue

1b Jane; *m* Thomas Methold, of Hale House, Kensington

1 Douglas (dau); *m* 1st *c* 1562 2nd Baron Sheffield (*see* SHEFFIELD, Bt); allegedly *m* 2nd 1573 Robert Dudley, Earl of Leicester (*see* LEICESTER, E, preliminary remarks); *m* 3rd (?) 29 Nov 1579 as his 2nd w, Sir Edward Stafford, Amb France 1583–90, and was *bur* 11 Dec 1608

The 11th BARON's cousin,

KENNETH ALEXANDER HOWARD, **1st Earl of Effingham** (UK), so *cr* 27 Jan 1837, KCB; *b* 29 Nov 1767; Gen, Col 70th Regt; *m* 27 May 1800 Lady Charlotte Primrose (*m* 2nd 30 April 1858 aged 82 Thomas Holmes and *d* 17 Sept 1864), dau of 3rd Earl of Rosebery (*qv*), and had, with other issue:

1 HENRY, **2nd Earl**

2 Charles; *b* 6 Dec 1807; 2nd Foot Gds; *d* 8 March 1882

3 William (Rev); *b* 23 April 1815; MA, Hon Canon York, Rector Whiston Yorks; *m* 12 Feb 1862 Barbara Frances Wilhelmina (*d* 26 April 1909), yst dau of Lt-Gen John Chester (*see* BAGOT, B), and *d* 12 May 1881, having had issue:

(1) A dau; *d* an infant 26 Sept 1864

1 Charlotte; *b* 30 Oct 1803; *d* unm 8 Mar 1886

2 Arabella Georgina; *b* 25 Jan 1809; *m* 31 Mar 1841 1st Baron Northbrook (*qv*) and *d* 10 Dec 1884, leaving issue

The 1st EARL *d* 13 Feb 1845; his est son,

HENRY HOWARD, **2nd Earl of Effingham**; *b* 23 Aug 1806; *m* 18 Aug 1832 Eliza (*d* 27 Feb 1894), only dau of Gen Sir Gordon Drummond, GCB, and *d* 5 Feb 1889, having had, with other issue:

1 HENRY HOWARD, **3rd Earl of Effingham**, DL; *b* 7 Feb 1837; *m* 31 Oct 1865 Victoria Francesca (*d* 20 June 1899), est dau of A Boyer, of Paris, and *d* 4 May 1898, leaving:

(1) HENRY ALEXANDER GORDON HOWARD, **4th Earl of Effingham**; *b* 15 Aug 1866; *d* unm 6 May 1927

2 Frederick Charles; *b* 21 June 1840; Capt Coldstream Gds; *m* 3 June 1871 Constance Eleanora Caroline (*d* 15 April 1910), est dau of 11th Earl of Winchilsea (*see* WINCHILSEA and NOTTINGHAM, E), and *d* 26 Oct 1893, leaving issue:

(1) GORDON FREDERICK HENRY CHARLES, **5th Earl**

(2) Algernon George Mowbray Frederick, MC (1919); *b* 15 Sept 1874; Capt Duke of Lancaster's Own Yeo, late 3rd Bn Roy Lancaster Regt; granted rank of earl's yr s 6 Dec 1929; *d* unm 7 May 1950

3 Kenneth; *b* 14 June 1845; clerk in FO; *d* unm 21 Jan 1903

The 4th EARL's cousin,

GORDON FREDERICK HENRY CHARLES HOWARD, **5th Earl of Effingham**; *b* 18 May 1873; *m* 1st 26 Jan 1904 (*divorce* 1914) Rosamond Margaret (*d* 25 Dec 1957), dau of Edward Harrison Hudson, of Scarborough; *m* 2nd 17 Jan 1924 Madeleine (*d* 27 June 1958), widow of James P Keleher, of San Francisco, and dau of William D Foshay, of the USA, and *d* 7 July 1946, leaving by his 1st w:

1 MOWBRAY HENRY GORDON HOWARD, **6th Earl of Effingham**; *b* 29 Nov 1905; *educ* Lancing; served WW II RA 1939–40 and 3rd Maritime Regt as gunner on convoy duty; *m* 1st 28 Oct 1938 (*divorce* 1946) Manci Maria Malvina, dau of Ferenc Joseph Gertler, of Hungary; *m* 2nd 12 Aug 1952 (*divorce* 1971) Gladys Irene, dau of Capt William Freeman, MN, and formerly w of Frederick Charles Kerry; *m* 3rd 19 May 1972 *(Mabel) Suzanne Mingay, dau of Maurice Jules-Marie Le Pen, of Paris, and widow of W/Cdr Francis Talbot Cragg, of London, and *d* 22 Feb 1996

2 John Algernon Frederick Charles; *b* 29 Dec 1907; *m* 1st 12 Jan 1938 (*divorce* 1942) Suzanna Patricia, dau of Edgar Macassey, of London, and had:

(1) DAVID PETER MOWBRAY ALGERNON HOWARD, **7th and present Earl of Effingham**

2 (cont.) The Hon John Howard *m* 2nd 9 Nov 1946 *Nadia Frances (*m* 3rd 1972 Geoffrey Gaskell Royal (*d* 1984)), formerly w of Hugh Boucher and dau of Henry Morden Guest, of The Elms, Keynsham, Somerset, and *d* 24 April 1970, Leaving by her:

(2) +Charles Anthony Frederick [Charles Howard Esq, 5 Wingate Rd, London W6 0UR]; *b* 7 March 1951; *educ* Sherborne and St John's Coll Cambridge (BA, MA); barrister Inner Temple 1975; *m* 1978 *Geraldine Margaret Theresa, er dau of Dr Thomas Dorman, of Holly Farm, Morley, Derbys, and has issue:

1a +Alexander Charles Frederick; *b* 1981

1a *Francesca Clare; *b* 1982

Eglinton and Winton

Arms: Quarterly, 1st and 4th, grand quarters counter quartered, 1st and 4th, azure three fleurs-de-lys or (for MONTGOMERIE); 2nd and 3rd, gules three annulets or, stoned azure (for EGLINTON), all within a bordure or charged with a double tressure flory-counterflory gules; 2nd and 3rd, grand quarters counter quartered, 1st and 4th, or three crescents within a double tressure flory-counterflory gules (for SETON); 2nd and 3rd, azure three garbs or (for BUCHAN); over all an escutcheon parted per pale gules and azure, the dexter charged with a sword in pale proper, pommelled and hilted or, supporting an imperial crown, the sinister charged with a star of twelve points argent, all within a double tressure flory-counterflory gold. **Crests:** 1 A lady dressed in ancient apparel azure, holding in her right hand an anchor or and in the sinister the head of a savage suspended by the hair couped, all proper (for EGLINTON), 2 A ducal coronet or, issuing therefrom a wyvern vomiting fire, his wings elevated proper. **Supporters:** Two wyverns vert, vomiting fire proper. **Mottoes:** 1 *Garde bien* ('Take good care'), 2 Hazard yet forward. **Creations:** L. (S) 3 July 1445, E. (S) 3–20 Jan 1506/7 (Eglinton), E. (UK) 17 June 1859 (Winton), B. (UK) 15 Feb 1806.

THE 18TH EARL OF EGLINTON and **6TH EARL OF WINTON**, **Lord Montgomerie** and **Baron Ardrossan**, of Ardrossan, Co Ayr (Archibald George Montgomerie) [The Rt Hon The Earl of Eglinton and Winton, Balhomie, Cargill, Perth PH2 6DS]; *b* 27 Aug 1939; *s f* 1966; *educ* Eton; Hereditary Sheriff Renfrewshire; Chm Edinburgh Investment Tst plc 1994–, memb London Stock Exchange, ptnr Grieveson Grant & Co, md Gerrard Hlds 1972–92, Chm Gerrard Vivian Gray Ltd 1992–94, Assist Grand Master United Grand Lodge of England 1989–95; *m* 7 Feb 1964 *Marion Carolina, twin dau of John Henry Dunn-Yarker, of Chateau de la Tour de Peilz, Vaud, Switzerland, and has:

1 +HUGH ARCHIBALD WILLIAM, *Lord Montgomerie* [Lord Montgomerie, 17 Ormiston Grove, London W12]; *b* 24 July 1966; RN (ret 1993); shipping ops manager; *m* 1991 *Sara Alexandra, est dau of Niel Redpath, of Fulham

2 +William John; *b* 4 Oct 1968

3 +James David; *b* 10 Jan 1972

4 +Robert Seton; *b* 21 March 1975

Lineage: ROBERT de MONTGOMERY obtained the lands of Eaglesham, Renfrewshire, from Walter, 1st High Steward of Scotland (*see* MORAY, E), in the latter half of the 12th century. His descendant:

JOHN MONTGOMERY, of Eaglesham; fought Battle of Otterburn 1388 and captured Sir Henry ('Harry Hotspur') Percy (*see* NORTHUMBERLAND, D), who had to build the Castle of Polnoon in the Barony of Eaglesham for his ransom; *m* Elizabeth, dau and heir of Sir Hugh Eglinton of that Ilk (descendant and representative of Bryce Eglinton, who acquired certain lands from the community of Irvine, which were re-granted to his gs Rodolph 1205) by Egidia (half-sis of ROBERT II and widow of Sir James Lindsay of Crawford; *see* CRAWFORD and BALCARRES, E), and by this marriage acquired the territorial Baronies of Eglinton and Ardrossan; had, with a dau (*m* Sir John Maxwell of Pollok, *see* HERON-MAXWELL, Bt):

1 JOHN (Sir), his successor

2 Alexander; acquired from his mother the lands of Bonnington in the Barony of Ratho 1387

3 Hugh; *ka* Otterburn (according to the ballad 'Chevy Chase')

The est son,

Sir JOHN MONTGOMERIE, of Eaglesham and Eglinton, more usually known as 'of Ardrossan'; hostage for the Earl of Douglas and JAMES I; *m* 1st Agnes of the Isles; *m* 2nd Margaret, dau of Robert Maxwell of Carlaverock, and *d* between 1426/7 and Nov 1429, having had issue:

1 ALEXANDER

2 Robert; ancestor of the MONTGOMERIEs of Giffen

3 Hugh

1 Anne; *m* 1425 Sir Robert Cunningham of Kilmaurs

2 Joan; *m* Thomas Boyd, 4th of Kilmarnock (*see* KILMARNOCK, B)

The est son,

ALEXANDER MONTGOMERIE, **1st Lord Montgomerie** (S), so *cr* just before 3 July 1445, PC (S); *b* by 1413; Commr to negotiate armistice with England 1437, 1449, 1451–52 and 1456; *m* Margaret, sis of 1st Lord Boyd (*see* KILMARNOCK, B), and *d c* 1470, having had issue:

1 Alexander, *Master of Montgomerie*; *m* Elizabeth, est dau of Sir Adam Hepburn of Hailes, and *dvp* 1452, leaving:

(1) Alexander, *Master of Montgomerie*; *b c* 1445; *m* by 1459 Catherine, dau of 1st Lord Kennedy (*see* AILSA, M), and *d* apparently in 1468, having had issue:

1a HUGH, **1st Earl**

2a John; *m* a dau of Ramsay of Monfode

3a James

1a Eupheme; *m* Sir Robert Bruce of Airth

(2) Robert, of Braidstane; ancestor of the Earls of Mount Alexander and the MONTGOMERYs of Grey Abbey and Blessingbourne

(3) Hugh, of Hazlehead, Ayr; had at least one dau (Marion, *m* 1st Thomas Crawford of Auchinames, 2nd, as his 3rd w, 2nd Lord Sempill (*qv*), and 3rd John Campbell of Skipnish); ancestor of the MONTGOMERYs of Beaulieu, Co Louth

2 George; ancestor of the extinct MONTGOMERIEs of Skelmorlie, Ayrshire

3 Thomas (Rev); Rector Eaglesham

1 Margaret; *m* 1438 10th Earl of Lennox and (1st Earl of) Darnley (*see* MORAY, E)

2 Elizabeth; *m* 2nd Lord Kennedy (*see* AILSA, M)

3 Agnes; *m* 1470 William Cunningham of Glengarnock

4 Margaret; *m* 1st Lord Home (*see* HOME, E)

The 1st LORD's ggs,

HUGH MONTGOMERIE, **1st Earl of Eglinto(u)n**, so *cr* between 3 and 20 Jan 1506/7, PC (S); *b* 1459/60; fought against JAMES III Battle of Sauchieburn 1488 on behalf of the rebellious Prince James, who as a result became JAMES IV and granted the Earl in 1488 the Island of Arran for life, also custody of Brodick Castle; Constable Rothesay Castle 1489, Bailie and Justiciary Bute 1489 and Cunningham 1499 (the latter formerly held by his gf); this caused a feud with the Cunninghams of Glencairn during which Eglinton Castle was burnt by the Master of Glencairn (*see* CUNINGHAME, Bt); *m* 21 April 1478 Helen, dau of 1st Earl of Argyll (*see* ARGYLL, D), and *d* June 1545, having had issue, with six daus:

1 John, *Master of Eglinton*; *m c* 1500 Elizabeth, dau of Sir Archibald Edmondstone (*see* EDMONSTONE, Bt), of Duntreath, and *dvp* 28 April 1520 (*k* in the affray in Edinburgh between the Earls of Arran and Angus known as the 'Battle of Cleanse the Causeway'), having had issue:

(1) Archibald, *Master of Eglinton*; *d* unm *c* late 1526

(2) HUGH, **2nd Earl**

(1) Christian; *m* as his 2nd w Sir James Douglas, 7th of Drumlanrig (*see* QUEENSBERRY, M)

2 William, of Greenfield; *m* Elizabeth, dau and heir of Robert Francis of Stane, and had issue

3 Neil, of Lainshaw; *m* Margaret, dau and heir of Quintin Mure of Skeldon and was ancestor of the MONTGOMERIEs of Lainshaw; a yr branch of this family settled in Sweden

4 Robert; Rector Kirkmichael, Bp Argyll 1531

1 Mariot; *m* 1st 2nd Lord Sempill (*qv*); *m* 2nd John Campbell, Provost of Kilmun

The 1st EARL's gs,

HUGH MONTGOMERIE, **2nd Earl of Eglinto(u)n**; *m* between 30 Jan and 8 Feb 1530/1 Mariot Seton (*m* 2nd Alexander, 2nd s of 2nd Earl of Montrose; *see* MONTROSE, D), dau of 3rd Lord Seton (*see* below **Lineage (of Seton)**), and *d* 3 Sept 1546, having had, with a yr s (*dsp*) and three daus:

HUGH MONTGOMERIE, **3rd Earl of Eglinto(u)n**; fought for MARY QUEEN OF SCOTS Battle of Langside 1568 but later made his peace with JAMES VI, involved in the affair called the 'Raid of Ruthven' 1582 (*see* CARLISLE, E); *m* 1st *c* 13 Feb 1554/5 (*divorce* 30 May 1562 on grounds of consanguinity) Lady Jean Hamilton (*dsp* Dec 1596), yst dau of James Hamilton, Earl of Arran (*see* ABERCORN, D); *m* 2nd by 10 Aug 1562 Agnes (*m* 3rd 1588 3rd Lord Drummond (*see* PERTH, E) and *d* 1589), dau of Sir William Drummond of Innerpeffray and widow of Sir Hugh Campbell, and *d* 3 June 1585, having by her had issue:

1 HUGH MONTGOMERIE, **4th Earl of Eglinto(u)n**; *b* 1563; *m* 1st *c* 13–20 May 1576 Giles/Gille, dau of 5th Lord Boyd (*see* KILMARNOCK, B), and had issue; *m* 2nd Helen (*m* 2nd John Graham of Knockdoliane and 3rd Alexander Kennedy of Craigneill), dau of Thomas Kennedy of Bargeny, and was shot dead 18 or 20 April 1586 by a party of Cunninghams as yet another episode in the feud between the two families; his only s by his 1st w:

(1) HUGH MONTGOMERIE, **5th Earl of Eglinto(u)n**; *b* 1584; bought the church Barony of Kilwinning 1594, which he made over 1611, as with his titles (*see* below), under the designation of the Lordshipof Kilwinning, though this is not regarded as a peerage honour by authorities on the subject; *m c* 3–9 May 1604 (separated 1608, *annulled* 11 March 1611/2), as her 1st husb, his cousin Margaret, er dau and heir of Robert Montgomerie of Giffen (*see* above), and arranged *c* 1606 that the Earldom with its estates should pass to her, but as the marriage began to sour revoked the plan and since he was childless directed by an instrument of 28 Nov 1611 that the Earldom and associated estates of Eglinto(u)n should pass to his first cousins Alexander, Thomas and John (three yr sons of his aunt Margaret, Dowager Countess of Winton) in that order, and the heirs male of their bodies bearing the name and arms of Montgomerie; *dsp* 4 Sept 1612

2 Robert, of Giffen, Ayrshire; *m* 1589 Jean (*m* 2nd, as his 2nd w, 2nd Duke of Lennox; *see* MORAY, E), dau of Sir Matthew Campbell of Loudoun, and *d* Aug 1596, having had issue:

(1) Margaret; *s f* in Giffen; *m* 1st her cousin Hugh Montgomerie, **5th Earl of Eglinto(u)n**; *m* 2nd by 24 March 1614/5, as his 1st w, 7th Lord Boyd (*see* KILMARNOCK, B) and *dsp*

(2) Agnes; *d* unm

(3) Isabel; *d* unm

1 Margaret; *m* 1582 1st Earl of Winto(u)n of the 1600 *cr* (*see* below, **Lineage (of Seton)**) and *d* 9 April 1624, leaving :

(1) ROBERT SETON, 2nd EARL OF WINTO(U)N; *b c* 1585; went mad on his wedding night, emptying a chamberpot down his bride's cleavage, and was kept shut away at the family property of Seton till his death, being accordingly prevailed upon to resign the Earldom in favour of his yr bro 26 June 1606, though this not put into effect till 12 May 1607; *m* 1 Feb 1602/3 Anna (petitioned for divorce on grounds of her husb's impotence; *d* 6 July 1609), sis of 1st Earl of Lauderdale (*qv*), but by her had no issue

(2) GEORGE SETON, 3rd EARL OF WINTO(U)N, PC (S); *b* Dec 1584; Justice-Gen St Andrews, Burgess Glasgow 1618, T/Pres Cncl Dec 1625–March 1625/6, Memb Cncl of War Feb 1627/8; *m* 1st 26 April 1609 Lady Anne Hay, est dau of 9th Earl of Erroll (*qv*), and had, with other issue:

1a George, *Lord Seton*; *b* 15 May 1613; royalist Civil War, captured Battle of Philiphaugh 1645; *m* (contract 25 March and 9 and 19 Oct 1639) Lady Henrietta Gordon (*m* 2nd 1649 2nd Earl of Traquair; *see* MORAY, E), dau of 2nd Marquess of Huntly (*qv*), and *dvp* 4 June 1648, having by her had, with other issue:

1b GEORGE SETON, 4th EARL OF WINTO(U)N; *b* 4 May 1642; jt-cdr with unc Lord Kingston (*see* below) of the men of E Lothian at Pentland 1666 and was with his unc at Bothwell Brigg 1679; recd a regrant of his titles 31 July 1686, with remainder to the heirs male of his body, failing whom, to any he cared to nominate with like remainder, failing which nomination, to his heirs male, failing whom to his nearest heirs and assigns, the daus to succeed by primogeniture; *m* 1st 4 Sept 1662 (separated by 24 June 1675) Lady Mary Montgomerie (*d* 18 Nov 1703), est dau of **7th Earl of Eglinto(u)n** (*see* below), by whom he had no surv male issue; *m* 2nd by 6 March 1679/80 his mistress of some years standing Christian, dau of George Hepburn of Addinstoun, Haddington, and *d* 6 March 1703/4, having by her had issue:

1c GEORGE SETON, 5th EARL OF WINTO(U)N; *b* a few years before his parents' marriage but by Scottish law was legitimated on their subsequent marriage; Jacobite 1715, captured at the Govt's victory of Preston 13 Nov 1715, convicted of high treason and condemned to death 19 March 1715/6, when his honours forfeited, but by apparently feigning madness, or at any rate extreme eccentricity (something his family history made more plausible than with most people) obtained a reprieve; after several unsuccessful attempts, including one in which he had nearly sawed through one of the iron bars to his cell with a watch spring, escaped from the Tower of London 4 Aug 1716 (possibly through the authorities turning a blind eye) and fled to join the titular James III, first at Avignon, then Rome, where he was Grand Master of the Masonic Lodge from 1736 till it was closed down by the papal authorities 1739 and *d* unm 19 Dec 1749

2c Christopher; *d* unm 1704

2a Christopher; *b* 2 March 1617; *d* 30 June 1618

3a ALEXANDER SETON, 1st VISCOUNT OF KINGSTON, so *cr* 6 Feb 1650/1; *b* 1621; ktd 1633; royalist Civil War; jt-cdr with nephew in the victory over the Covenanters at encounter of Pentland Hills 1666 and (under Monmouth, *see* BUCCLEUCH and QUEENSBERRY, D) over rebels at Bothwell Brigg 1679; *m* 1st Jean, dau of Sir Andrew Fletcher of Inverpeffer, and had three sons (*d* young); *m* 2nd *c* 1661 Elizabeth, dau of Sir Archibald Douglas of Whittinghame (*see* MORTON, E); *m* 3rd Elizabeth, dau of 1st Lord Belhaven and Stenton (*qv*); *m* 4th 3 Aug 1686 Margaret, gdau of 1st Marquess of Douglas (*see* HAMILTON and BRANDON, D), and *d* 21 Oct 1691, leaving by his 2nd w, with two intermediate sons (*d* young):

1b ARCHIBALD SETON, 2nd VISCOUNT OF KINGSTON; *b* 5 Oct 1661; *d* unm 1714

2b JAMES SETON, 3rd and last VISCOUNT OF KINGSTON; *b* 29 Jan 1667; Jacobite 1715, accordingly attainted 1716 and the title forfeited; *m* by 16 April 1714 Anne, dau of 3rd Earl of Balcarres (*see* CRAWFORD and BALCARRES, E) and widow of 4th Earl of Kellie (*see* MAR and KELLIE, E) and *dsp c* 1726 when the title expired anyway

1b Elizabeth; *m* 1695 William Hay of Drumezier (*see* TWEEDDALE, M)

1a Elizabeth; *m* 1637 7th Earl of Marischal (*see* KINTORE, E) and *d* 16 June 1650, having had issue

(2) (cont.) The 3rd EARL *m* 2nd by 1628 Elizabeth, dau of 6th Lord Herries of Terregles (*qv*), and *d* 15 or 17 Dec 1650, having by her had, with other further issue:

4a Christopher; *b* 28 June 1631; scholar; lost at sea off Dutch coast July 1648

5a William; *b* 8 Jan 1633; lost at sea with his bro

6a Sir JOHN SETON, 1st Bt (NS), so *cr* 9 Dec 1664, of Gairmiltoun (subsequently Garletoun), Haddington; *b* 29 Sept 1639; *m* Christian/Isabel, dau of Sir John Home of Renton, and *d* Feb 1685/6, leaving:

1b Sir GEORGE SETON, 2nd Bt; *m* by 1685 (*divorce* 1705) Barbara, dau of Andrew Wauchope of Niddrie Mareschal, Co Edinburgh, by Margaret, dau of Sir John Gilmour of Craigmillar (*see* GILMOUR OF CRAIGMILLAR, B), and *d* between June 1718 and May 1720, when the btcy was forfeited as a result of his son's attainder, leaving:

1c George; *b* 1685; Jacobite 1715, captured Battle of Preston 13 Nov 1715 and attainted 1716; seems to have become heir to the forfeited Earldom of Winton on death of 5th Earl 1749; *d* unm 9 March 1769

2b John, of Durham; *m* Frances, dau of Sir Richard Neale, of Pleny, and *d* 1715, leaving:

1c Ralph; *b* 27 June 1702; heir to btcy and Earldom of Winton from 1769, though both subject to forfeiture; *d* unm 31 Dec 1782

7a Sir ROBERT SETON, 1st and last Bt (NS), so *cr* 24 Jan 1670/1, of Windygoul; *b* 10 Nov 1641; *dsp* Nov 1671, when the btcy expired

2a Isabel; *m* 6th Lord Sempill (*qv*)

3a Anne; *m* 2nd Earl of Traquair (*see* MORAY, E) and had issue

4a Mary; *m* 10 Dec 1676 4th Earl of Carnwath (*see* 1940 edn) and had issue

(3) ALEXANDER (SETON) MONTGOMERIE, **6th Earl of Eglinto(u)n**, as which *s* under the 1611 settlement, though it was not till a royal charter of confirmation was wrung from JAMES VI (and I) on 24 March 1614/5 (following a formal resignation by ALEXANDER into the King's hands) that his right to assume the title was fully recognised; the King insisted that he himself was the sole fount of honour and objected to the prior alienation of a title of honour by the 5th Earl as if it were a mere tract of land (this was an important point, it having been orthodox thinking in Scotland hitherto that a title was so closely bound up with land that without land a man could have no title; but it could *mutatis mutandis* come to mean that if the land was alienable the title could be too; it was about this time that the more modern notion of a title as an inalienable honour began to take hold); the 'Lordship' of Kilwinning was in 1612 granted away from him to 1st Lord Balfour of Burleigh (*qv*) but later sold back to him by Lord Balfour for over £5,000 (over £200,000 in late-1990s terms); *b* 1588; Parliamentarian Civil War, in which fought Marston Moor 1644; later supported CHARLES II, to whom he was Capt of Horse Gds 1650, but was subsequently imprisoned 1651–60; dubbed 'Grey Steel' for his bravery; *m* 1st 22 June 1612 Lady Anne Livingstone (*d* Nov 1632), dau of 1st Earl of Linlithgow (*see* LINLITHGOW, M, preliminary remarks), and by her had issue; *m* 2nd between Nov 1642 and March 1643/4 Margaret (*d* 3 Oct 1651), dau of 1st Lord Scott of Buccleuch (*see* BUCCLEUCH and QUEENSBERRY, D) and widow of 6th Lord Ross, and *d* 7 Jan 1661, leaving by his 1st w:

1a HUGH MONTGOMERIE, **7th Earl of Eglinto(u)n**, PC (S Feb 1660/1); *b* 30 March 1613; *educ* Glasgow U and Paris; Covenanter 1639 but royalist Civil War (fought against own f Marston Moor); *m* 1st (contract 7–13 April 1631) Lady Anne Hamilton (*d* 16 Oct 1632), dau of 2nd Marquess of Hamilton (*see* HAMILTON and BRANDON, D), and *d* Feb 1669, having by her had issue:

1b Anne; *m* 1st Robert Seton, son of Sir George Seton of Hailes; *m* 2nd *c* 1658, as his 1st w, 3rd Earl of Findlater and had issue (*see* SEAFIELD, E)

1a (cont.) The **7th Earl** *m* 2nd (contract 17–24 Dec 1635) Lady Mary Leslie, est dau of 6th Earl of Rothes (*qv*), and had issue:

1b ALEXANDER MONTGOMERIE, **8th Earl of Eglinto(u)n**, PC (S 16789); *m* 1st Jan 1657/8 Elizabeth, est dau of 2nd Earl of Dumfries (*see* BUTE, M), and had, with two other sons:

1c ALEXANDER MONTGOMERIE, **9th Earl of Eglinto(u)n**, PC (S *temp* WILLIAM III and QUEEN ANNE); *b c* 1660; Commr Treasury 1702–04, rep S peer 1710–14; *m* 1st *c* Dec 1676 Margaret, gdau of 1st Earl of Dundonald (*qv*), and had, with three sons (*d* young):

1d Catherine; *m* 5th Earl of Galloway (*qv*), and *d* Dec 1757

2d Eupheme; *m* 13 April 1697 George Lockhart of Carnwath and *d* 1 Dec 1738

3d Grace; *m* 19 Jan 1710 6th Earl of Carnwath (*see* 1940 edn)

4d Jean; *m* 29 Dec 1711 Sir Alexander Maxwell of Monreith, 2nd Bt (*qv*)

1c (cont.) The **9th Earl** *m* 2nd Ann (*d* Dec 1708), dau of 1st Earl of Aberdeen (*see* ABERDEEN AND TEMAIR, M), by whom he had:

5d Mary; *m* Sir David Cunynghame of Milncraig, 3rd Bt (*qv*)

1c (cont.) The **9th Earl** *m* 3rd *c* June 1709 Susanna (*d* 18 March 1780), dau of Sir Archibald Kennedy, of Culzean, 1st Bt (*see* AILSA, M), and *d* 18 Feb 1729, having by her had, with further issue (including Susan, *m* John Renton of Lamerton and had issue; *see* MURRAY, Bt of Dunerne):

1d James, *Lord Montgomerie; dvp* 1 Sept 1724 aged six

2d ALEXANDER MONTGOMERIE, **10th Earl of Eglinto(u)n**; *b* 10 Feb 1722/3; *educ* Winchester; Govr Dumbarton Castle 1759–61, Ld Bedchamber 1760–67, rep S peer 1761–69; *d* unm 25 Oct 1769, shot by Mungo Campbell, an Excise Offr whom the Earl found trespassing on his lands; Campbell was convicted of murder at Edinburgh but hanged himself in prison 28 Feb 1770

3d ARCHIBALD MONTGOMERIE, **11th Earl of Eglinto(u)n**; *b* 18 May 1726; *educ* Eton; Col: 51st Foot 1767–95 and 2nd Dragoons 1795–96, Gen 1793, MP (Whig) Ayrshire 1761–68, Equerry to QUEEN CHARLOTTE 1761–69, Govr Dumbarton Castle 1764–82, Dep Ranger Hyde and St James's Parks 1766–68, rep S peer 1776–96, Govr Edinburgh Castle 1782–96, Ld Lt Ayrshire 1794–96; *m* 1st 30 March 1772 Lady Jean Lindsay (later w of Francis Moore, bro of Gen Sir John Moore), dau of 21st Earl of Crawford (*see* LINDSAY, E); *m* 2nd 9 Aug 1783 Frances (*dsp* 22 Jan 1778), only dau of Sir William Twisden, 6th Bt, of Raydonhall, Kent, and *d* 30 Oct 1796, having by her had issue:

1e Mary; *m* 28 March 1803 her kinsman Archibald Montgomerie, Lord Montgomerie, est s of **12th Earl of Eglinto(u)n** (*see* below)

2e Susanna; *d* unm 16 Nov 1805

6d Elizabeth; *m* 1749 Sir John Cunninghame, Bt, of Caprington, Ayrshire, and *d* 19 Feb 1800

7d Helen; *m* 4 Jan 1745 Hon Francis Stuart, 3rd son of 7th Earl of Moray (*qv*)

8d Margaret; *m* 24 April 1739 Sir Alexander Macdonald 7th Bt and had issue (*see* BOSVILLE MACDONALD, Bt)

1c Mary; *m* (contract 22 June 1683) Sir James Agnew, 4th Bt, of Lochnaw (*qv*), and *d* April 1742, having had 22 children

1b (cont.) The **8th Earl** *m* 2nd 2 Feb 1678/9 Grace (*d* 5 Dec 1675), dau of Francis Popeley, of Wooley Morehouse, and widow of Sir Thomas Wentworth, 1st Bt; *m* 3rd 6 Dec 1698 (he aged 70 and she 90 or 96) Katherine (*bur* 6 Aug 1700), dau of Sir William St Quintin, 1st Bt, and widow of (a) Sir John Kaye, of Woodsome, 1st Bt, and (b) Henry Sandys, of Doune Court, Kent, and *d* 1701

2b Francis, of Giffen; MP Ayrshire last S Parl and first Parl of GB; *m* 1st Margaret, Countess of Leven (*see* LEVEN and MELVILLE, E) in her own right; *m* 2nd Elizabeth, dau of Sir Robert Sinclair of Longformacus, Bt, and widow of Sir James Primrose of Barnbougle (*see* ROSEBERY, E), and had, with other issue:

1c John; Lt-Col; MP Ayrshire 1708–1722, Master of the Mint Scotland; *m* 1704 Lady Mary Carmichael, dau of 1st Earl of Hyndford (title dormant or extinct 1817), and had issue:

1d Beatrix; *d* unm

1c Elizabeth; *m* Hon Patrick Ogilvy, 2nd s of 3rd Earl of Findlater (*see* SEAFIELD, E), and *d* 1753

2b Mary; *m* 1662 4TH EARL OF WINTON (*see* below)

3b Margaret; *m* 2nd Earl of Loudoun (*qv*)

4b Christiana; *m* 4th Lord Balmerino (title forfeited 1746)

5b Eleanor; *m* 1674, as his 2nd w, David Dunbar of Baldoon (*dvp* 20 March 1682), son of Sir David Dunbar, 1st Bt, and had issue (*see* HOPE-DUNBAR, Bt)

6b Anne; *m* Sir Andrew Ramsay of Abbotshall, Bt

2a Henry (Sir), of Giffen; *b* 26 June 1614; *m* 21 Sept 1640 Lady Jane Campbell, dau of 7th Earl of Argyll (*see* ARGYLL, D) and widow of 1st Viscount of Kenmure and Lord Lochinvar (dormant 1847), and *dsp* 3 May 1643

3a James, of Coylsfield; Col; *m* June 1659 Margaret, dau of John Macdonald, in Kintyre, by Elizabeth, dau of Sir William Stewart, and *d* 18 Oct 1675, having had issue:

1b Alexander, of Coylsfield; *s* f; *d* unm 3 March 1679

2b Hugh, of Coylsfield; *m* 1st 29 April 1692/3 Jean, 2nd dau of Sir William Primrose, Bt (*see* ROSEBERY, E), and had three daus; lm 2nd 10 Sept 1708 Katharine Arbuckle, widow of John Hamilton of Letham, and had, with two daus:

1c Alexander, of Coylsfield; *m* 11 June 1735 Lillias (*d* 18 Nov 1783), dau of Sir Robert Montgomery of Skelmorlie, 5th Bt, and *d* 28 Dec 1783, having had, with other issue:

1d HUGH, **12th Earl**

2d Alexander, of Annick Lodge; *b* 24 May 1744; HEICS; *m* 20 Oct 1784 Elizabeth (*d* 13 Feb 1839), dau of Dr John Taylor, HEICS, and *d* 8 July 1802, leaving, with other issue:

1e William Eglinton, of Annick Lodge, Ayrshire, JP, DL; *b* 15 April 1789; *m* 7 Jan 1824 Susanna Fraser (*d* 1884), dau of John Anderson, and *d* 14 June 1852, having had issue:

1f Alexander, of Annick Lodge and Eaglesham, Wanganui, NZ; *b* 10 Nov 1824; Capt 10th Foot; *m* 1860 Elizabeth (*d* 1921), dau of Thomas Wright, and *d* 16 Nov 1890, leaving issue:

1g Alexander; *b* 1865; *m* 1892 Emily Bashford and *d* 1905, leaving issue:

1h Alexander James; *b* 1892; WW I with NZEF; *m* 1919 Winifred Jane (*d* 1993), dau of George Gifford, of Bulls, NZ, and *d* 1 July 1945, leaving issue:

1i +Alexander Kelvin [Alexander Montgomerie Esq, 35 Washington Ave, St Heliers, Auckland, New Zealand]; *b* 1922; WW II in NZ Scottish Regt and RNZN; *m* 1958 *Doreen Evelyn, dau of Capt G Price, of Farlington, Hants, and has:

1j +Alexander Andrew [Alexander Montgomerie Esq, Jurastrasse 16, 5406 Baden-Rutihof, Switzerland]; *b* 1962; *educ* Auckland U (BTP); *m* 1990 *Sandra, only dau of Edwin Baumann, of Burglen, Thurgau, Switzerland, and has:

1k *Kristina Katherine; *b* 1992

2k *Stephanie Kim; *b* 1994

3k *Jessica Grace; *b* 1996

2j +Stuart Hugh [Stuart Montgomerie Esq, Mathildevej 16 DK-2000, Frederiksberg, Copenhagen, Denmark]; *b* 1966; *educ* Auckland U (BA); *m* 1995 *Suzsanne Rehder, only dau of Benny Rehder, of Frederiksberg

2i +Seton Eglinton [Seton Montgomerie Esq, 18 Tongariro St, Castlecliff, Wanganui, New Zealand]; *b* 20 Dec 1924; *m* 27 Aug 1960 *Joan, dau of Harry Bladen, of 11 High St, Smethwick, Staffs, and has issue:

1j +Seton Bladen; *b* 27 Jan 1962

1j *Elsa Jane [Mrs Philip Belton, Te Huia, RD2, Ngutuwera, Waverley, New Zealand]; *b* 6 April 1964; *m* 1985 *Philip Keith Belton, yst s of John Keith Belton, and has:

1k *Christopher Reece; *b* 1986

1k *Sarah Jane; *b* 1988

2k *Emma Louise; *b* 1993

1i *Zona Winnifred [Mrs Norman Nicholson, Woodleigh, 19 Jocelyn Crescent, Pinehaven, Silverstream, Wellington, New Zealand]; *b* 1920; *m* 7 Jan 1943 *Norman Claude Nicholson, RNZAF, and has issue:

1j *John Montgomerie [John Nicholson Esq, 13B Beryl Grove, Birchville, Upper Hutt, New Zealand]; *b* 11 May 1947; *m* 1977 *Deborah Mary, dau of W J Evenson, of Upper Hutt, and has issue:

1k *Jonathan Montgomerie; *b* 1980

1k *Victoria Rose; *b* 1983

2j *Murray James [Murray Nicholson Esq, 132 Oberon Rd, Chittaway Bay, Wyong, NSW 2259, Australia]; *b* 4 Jan 1950; *m* 1971 *Joy Louise, dau of V Frampton, of Gosford, NSW, and has issue:

1k *Matthew James; *b* 1974

1k *Jodie Louise; *b* 1972

2k *Lisa Eileen; *b* 1975

1j *Claudia Michele [Mrs Peter Fitzsimmons, 6/22 Killarney St, Takapuna, Auckland, New Zealand]; *b* 26

July 1945; *m* 24 Dec 1966 *Peter William Fitzsimmons, OBE, and has issue:

1k *Timothy Peter; *b* 1974; *educ* Massey U (BEd)

1k *Megan Clare; *b* 1977

2i *Rana Maude [Mrs Jack Elder, Broadview, 279 Bellevue Heights, Tauranga, New Zealand]; *b* 1929; *m* 17 Feb 1951 *Jack Rogers William Elder, RNZAF, yst s of Thomas Lawson Elder of Tauranga, NZ, and has issue:

1j *David Lawson James [David Elder Esq, 74B Greerton Rd, Tauranga, New Zealand]; *b* 21 April 1959; *m* 1989 *Helen Margaret, dau of R A Pond, and has issue:

1k *Kevin Robert James; *b* 1992

1k *Rachel Kawa Bett; *b* 1995

1j *Raèwyn Janice [Mrs Stephen Allen, 2 Greerton Rd, Tauranga, New Zealand]; *b* 16 Aug 1955; *m* 1980 *Stephen Hugh Allen, and has issue:

1k *Matthew Stephen; *b* 1983

1k *Kimberley Jane; *b* 1981

3i Cynthia Beryl June Seton; *b* 1935; *d* 1983

2h Archibald William; *b* 1894; WW I with NZEF; *m* 1942 *Barbara Mary [Mrs Archibald Montgomerie, 36 Brookvale Rd, Havelock North, New Zealand], dau of Samuel Scott Linton, and *d* 1969, leaving issue:

1i +David William; *b* 1944; *educ* McGill (PhD)

2i +Roger Linton [Roger Montgomerie Esq, 5 Thomas Ave, Roseville, NSW 2069, Australia]; *b* 1946; *educ* Massey U NZ (B Tech, Dip BIA); *m* 1977 *Judith Loraine, dau of R A Holland, of Sydney, and has issue:

1j +Simon Holland; *b* 1980

2j +Andrew Scott; *b* 1987

1j *Kate Louise; *b* 1982

1i *Barbara Mary; *b* 1942; *m* 1973 (*divorce* 1982) Bernard Antoine Vollon, of Paris

2i *Jeanne Elizabeth; *b* 1945; *m* 1969 (*divorce* 1982) Griffith Powell Richards, and has issue:

1j *Nicholas Powell; *b* 1971

2j *Philip Powell; *b* 1972

3j *Michael Powell; *b* 1975

1j *Anna Elizabeth; *b* 1977

3i *Barbara Hylda; *b* 1950

3h John Eglinton; *b* 1899; *m* 1921 Irene Agnes (*d* 1959), dau of Thomas Ross Cameron, of New Plymouth, NZ, and *d* 1971, leaving issue:

1i Leighton John, DFC; *b* 1922; F/Lt RNZAF WW II; *ka* Italy 1944

2i Alexander Cameron; *b* 1926

3i +Archibald William; *b* 1931; *m* 10 Aug 1962 *Geraldine Anne, dau of Gerald Cecil Davy, of Tauranga, NZ, and has issue:

1j +Michael William; *b* 1966

1j *Donna Marie; *b* 1962

3i (cont.) Archibald Montgomerie also adopted:

*Christopher Edward; *b* 1958

*Stephen Brian; *b* 1959

4i +Robert Patrick [Robert Montgomerie Esq, 24 Ihaia St, Waitara, Taranki, New Zealand]; *b* 1934; *m* 17 Sept 1960 *Mhyre Laughton, dau of Arthur Harold Collins of Waitara, NZ, and has issue:

1j +Leighton John; *b* 12 June 1966

2j +Wilson Bruce; *b* 2 May 1968

1j *Patricia Ann; *b* 23 Aug 1961; *m* 1982 *Charles Patrick McAlister, and has issue:

1k *Charles Luke; *b* 1983

1k *Kayla Marie; *b* 1988

2j *Kerrie Lyn; *b* 23 May 1963

3j *Jillian Beth; *b* 28 Oct 1964

5i +Ian James; *b* 1935; *m* 20 May 1961 *Diana Margaret, dau of Alan Walter Long, of Waitara, NZ, and has:

1j +Paul Ian; *b* 24 Aug 1963

1j *Tracy Diana; *b* 12 Feb 1965

2j *Lisa Alayne; *b* 1967

1i *Anita Mary; *b* 1921; *m* 1944 *David Gordon Harrison, and has issue:

1j Errol John; *b* 14 July 1945; *m* 1970 *Shirley Doreen Elwin, and *d* 1993, leaving issue:

1k *Sheree Ann; *b* 1975

2k *Melanie Jane; *b* 1977

2j *Ira James [Ira Harrison Esq, 59b Manu Crescent, New Plymouth, New Zealand]; *b* 30 Sept 1948

3j *Peter David [Peter Harrison Esq, 17a Divon St, Oakuru, New Zealand]; *b* 15 March 1950; *m* 1970 Susan Wilson (*d* 1993) and has issue:

1k *Jason David; *b* 1970

1k *Kim Sheree; *b* 1973

4j *Patrick Vivian [Patrick Harrison Esq, 399 Main South Rd, Omata, Taranaki, New Zealand]; *b* 13 Nov 1959; *m* 1986 *Kay Walter, and has issue:

1k *Greer Sam Walter; *b* 1993

1j *Carrol Ann [Mrs Terry Jordan, 28 Joseph Banks Drive, Whitby, Wellington, New Zealand]; *b* 7 Sept 1948; *m* 1967 *Terry Arthur Jordan, and has issue:

1k *Rhys Craig; *b* 1968

1k *Carla Ann *b* 1970

2j *Shirley Mary; *b* 1 Feb 1953; *m* 1977 *Marco Grandacci, of Camerino, Italy, and *d* 1986, leaving issue:

1k *Marco; *b* 1977

1k *Natalie Anita; *b* 1978

3j *Yvonne Joan [Mrs Ronald Wood, 35 Matairo St, Titahi Bay, Wellington, New Zealand]; *b* 4 Jan 1956; *m* *Ronald Lance Wood, and has issue:

1k *Bianca Jay; *b* 1978

1k *Amber; *b* 1980

2k *Candice Skye; *b* 1987

2i *Nola Joan; *b* 1923; *m* 1941 *Eric Wiliam Hopson and has:

1j *Kevin Eric; *b* 1943; *m* 1966 *Shirley Anne Montague, and has issue:

1k *Trevor John; *b* 1968

2k *Warrick David; *b* 1972

3k *Gareth Andrew; *b* 1981

1k *Janelle Marie; *b* 1970

2j *Denis Michael; *b* 1946; *m* 1980 *Elizabeth Margaret Baker, and has issue:

1k *Tessa Elizabeth; *b* 1980

2k *Catherine Anne; *b* 1982

3k *Bridget Alice; *b* 1984

4k *Rebecca Clare; *b* 1985

3j *Graham Patrick; *b* 1950; *m* 1972 *Diane Elizabeth Hicks, and has issue:

1k *Craig Patrick; *b* 1975

1k *Susan Marie; *b* 1973

4j *Murray John; *b* 1953; *m* 1981 *Sandra Daphne Brooks, and has issue:

1k *Brendan Murray; *b* 1989

1k *Christine Sandra; *b* 1983

2k *Andrea Jane; *b* 1985

5j *Alan David; *b* 1956; *m* 1978 *Gillian Joy Christopher, and has issue:

1k *Tanya Kirstin; *b* 1978

2k *Rene Jade; *b* 1981

1j *Joan Frances; *b* 1941; *m* 1962 *Peter Bruce Donnison, and has issue:

1k *Bruce Stephen; *b* 1962; *m* 1987 *Adele Wilcockson

2k *Paul David; *b* 1963; *m* 1990 *Kathryn Cuddihy

3k *Gregory James; *b* 1965; *m* 1992 *Kristin Evans

4k *Martin John; *b* 1966; *m* 1993 *Helen Conlon

5k *Cameron Peter; *b* 1975

6k *Matthew Leighton; *b* 1978

7k *Regan Michael; *b* 1981

1k *Mylene Joanne; *b* 1969

2j *Maureen Anne; *b* 1948; *m* 1966 *Robin Bruce Lindsay, and has issue:

1k *Gene Bruce; *b* 1966; *m* 1994 *Sherry Gillard

2k *Shane Michael; *b* 1970

1k *Sharon Lee; *b* 1968; *m* 1989 *Kenneth Watkinson

2k *Tracey Sharleen; *b* 1972; *m* 1993 *Gregory James

3k *Kylie Maree; *b* 1983

3j *Karen Irene; *b* 1960; *m* 1982 *Warren Crawford and has:

1k *Holly Diane; *b* 1991

4j *Diane Marie (twin); *b* 1960; *m* 1982 *Paul Morony, and *d* 1982

3i *Peggy Agnes [Mrs Aubrey Hopson, 170 Tukapo St, New Plymouth, New Zealand]; *b* 1924; *m* 1944 *Aubrey Edgar Hopson, and has issue:

1j *Wayne Leighton John; *b* 20 April 1946; *m* 1973 *Heather Henderson, and has issue:

1k *Candy Leighton; *b* 1977

2j *Brian James; *b* 7 Jan 1948; *m* 1972 *Elizabeth Lawson, and has issue:

1k *Gareth Brian; *b* 1982

2k *Bryce James; *b* 1985

3k *Kieran Paul; *b* 1989

1j *Valerie Margaret; *b* 20 Jan 1952; *m* 1975 *Graeme McEldowney, and has issue:

1k *Steven Craig; *b* 1977

2k *Dale Andrew; *b* 1979

3k *Aaron John; *b* 1980

2j *Barbara Irene; *b* 15 June 1953; *m* 1973 *Lindsay Gault, and has issue:

1k *Shane David; *b* 1978

1k *Karen Marie; *b* 1974

2k *Julie Heather; *b* 1976

4i *Barbara Winifred [Mrs Barbara Gosling, 70 Dundebar Rd, Wannaroo, Perth, W Australia 6065]; *b* 1933; *m* 1954 (*divorce* 1978) David Walter Gosling, and has issue:

1j *Ronald David [Ronald Gosling Esq, 25 Celestine St, Wanneroo, Perth, W Australia 6065]; *b* 1955; *m* 1978 *Julie Dawn Bailey, and has issue:

1k *Vicky Rachel; *b* 1983

2k *Donna Colette; *b* 1987

2j *Ian Peter [Ian Gosling Esq, 70 Dundebar Rd, Wannaroo, Perth, W Australia 6065]; *b* 1957; *m* 1980 *Clare Lucy Knights, and has issue:

1k *Thomas Iain; *b* 1980

2k *Matt Luke; *b* 1981

3k *James Patrick; *b* 1985

4k *Daniel Shane; *b* 1986

1k *Jessica Barbara; *b* 1983

2k *Rebecca Clare; *b* 1989

1j *Clare Annette [Mrs Dale Jenkins, 300 South Hospital Drive, Apt 805, Jacksonville, Arkansas, USA]; *b* 1963; *m* 1st 1980 (*divorce* 1983) Michael Currer; *m* 2nd 1984 (*divorce* 1990) George Lubert, of Arkansas; *m* 3rd 1993 *Dale Jenkins, and has issue by 2nd husb:

1kj *Gary Paul; *b* 1980

1k *Melissa Dawn; *b* 1986

2k *Tiffany Nicole; *b* 1987

4h George Arnold; *b* 1901; *m* 1945 Peggy Patricia Greener (*d* 1991) of Wanganui, NZ, and *d* 1980, leaving:

1i +Wayne Arnold [Wayne Montgomerie Esq, 4 Stanley Ave, Palmerston North 5301, New Zealand]; *b* 1947; *m* 8 May 1971 *Christine Mary, dau of Bernard Colin Williams, and has issue:

1j *Darien Mary; *b* 1975

2j *Loren Patricia; *b* 1978

2i +Peter John [Peter Montgomerie Esq, 73 Whiterock Rd, Whiterock, NSW 2795, Australia]; *b* 1951; *m* 1977 *Jennifer Joan, dau of Hugh Carter Milroy, and has issue:

1j +Shane Peter; *b* 1983

1j *Fiona Jenny; *b* 1982

5h Alexander Edward; *b* 1905; WW II with NZEF (POW); *d* unm 1 Nov 1960

1h Mary Elizabeth; *b* 1895; *m* 1924 Jack Staite, and had issue

2h Kathleen Minna; *b* 1897; *m* 1925 Rex Cameron Bailey, of Manuwatu, NZ, and had issue

2g Roger Arnulph; *b* 20 Oct 1866; *m* 27 April 1893 Annie (*d* 1958), dau of Archibald Mason of Wanganui, NZ, and *d* 26 Oct 1936, leaving issue:

1h Roger Oswald; *b* 13 Oct 1896; WW I as Lt RFC and RAF; *m* 1940 *Beryl Victoria, QSM [Mrs Roger Montgomerie QSM, 13 Laurence St, Tauranga, New Zealand], yst dau of Guy Carlton Clark, of Melbourne, Australia, and *d* 4 Dec 1965, leaving issue:

1i +John Clark [John Montgomerie Esq, 11 Gardiner Place, Havelock North, New Zealand]; *b* 23 Aug 1943; *m* 1972 *Glenis Erina, dau of Norman Cameron, of Masterton, NZ, and has issue:

1j +Richard John; *b* 1974

1j *Meredith Jane; *b* 1977

2i +Roger Clark [Roger Montgomerie Esq, 36 Aiken Rd, Wanganui, New Zealand]; *b* 16 Oct 1945; *m* 1971 *Patricia Clare, dau of Vincent Donnelly of Paevoa, NZ, and has issue:

1j +Hayden James; *b* 1979

1i *Beverley Joan; *b* 28 Feb 1941; *m* 1963 *Edward William Gudopp, and has issue:

1j *David Charles; *b* 10 Oct 1967

1j *Deborah Jane; *b* 30 Dec 1965

2i *Helen Victoria; *b* 20 Oct 1959

2h Hew Seton, JP (NZ 1930); *b* 23 June 1898; WW I as Lt Sherwood Foresters and RAF, WW II as Lt NZ Temp Staff and F/O RNZAF (despatches); *m* 1938 Violet Muriel (*d* 1976), dau of Donald Harry Rait, MRCVS, and *d* 12 Aug 1969, leaving:

1i *Susana Seton; *b* 20 April 1940

2i *Egidia Seton [Mrs Jerome DesRoches, PO Box 24, Mangonui, Northland, Kerikeri, New Zealand]; *b* 24 July 1942; *m* 1980 *Jerome Robert DesRoches

1h (Annie Hylda) Winifred; *b* 24 May 1894; *d* unm 21 Feb 1970

2h *Sybil Alexandra [Mrs David Jackson, 5 Tulloch St, St John's Hill, Wanganui, New Zealand]; *b* 29 Oct 1902; *m* 5 Aug 1925 David Rayney Jackson (*d* 21 Nov 1968), only son of Edward Rayney Jackson, of Wanganui, and has:

1i *David Rayney Montgomerie; *b* 11 June 1929; *m* 1959 *Diana Georgina, yr dau of Frank Gailbraith Hyde, of Central Otago, NZ, and has issue:

1j *Edward Hyde Rayney; *b* 1963

1j *Sarah Jane Rayney; *b* 1960

2j *Belinda Elizabeth; *b* 1962

1i *Priscilla Rayney; *b* 16 May 1926; *educ* Dunedin U (BA 1947)

3g Hew Winton; *b* 1872; *m* 25 Sept 1906 Mary Laura, yst dau of Charles J de Greenlaw, of Sydney, NSW, and *d* 1920, leaving:

1h +Ian Hew; *m* 1st (*divorce* 1948) Elizabeth Isabella Gregg, est dau of George Rowland Stratford of Auckland, NZ, and has issue:

1i +Hew Winton Rowland [Hew Montgomerie Esq, 51 Rawhiti Rd, Onehunga, Auckland, New Zealand]; *b* 30 Aug 1941; *m* 1st 21 Jan 1967 Carol Leonie, yst dau of Stanley Rollingston Cromwell, Headmaster, of Kawerau, and has:

1j +Stuart Seton; *b* 1974

1j *Rachel Leonie; *b* 1970

1i (cont.) Hew Montgomerie *m* 2nd 1984 *Joanna Tinisivo, dau of Autiko Quna, of Fiji, and has issue:

2j +Ian Hew Mocewai; *b* 1992

1h (cont.) Ian Montgomerie *m* 2nd 1948 *Marjorie Thelma, dau of Albert Eugene Brookes, of Auckland, NZ, and by her has:

1i *Lynetta Eugene; *b* 14 Jan 1952; *m* 1971 *Albert John Bainbridge, and has issue:

1j *Brent Albert; *b* 1976

1j *Tanya Lyn; *b* 1973

2j *Sacha Lee; *b* 1975

1h *Barbara; *m* 1942 *Ernest Clement Dawson, twin son of Ernest Dawson of Rotorua, NZ, and has issue:

1i *Ernest John Linnaeus [Ernest Dawson Esq, 19 Kimberley St, Christchurch, New Zealand]; *b* 2 June 1945

2i *Bernard Stanley Winton; *b* 18 July 1953

1i *Ann Michelle de Greenlaw; *b* 29 July 1943

2i *Linda Egidia Montgomerie; *b* 28 Nov 1949

4g Archibald William Eglinton; *b* 1874; *m* 1901 Elizabeth Grace (*d* 1956), dau of Duncan Blair, of Rapanui, NZ, and *d* 5 Dec 1951, having had issue:

1h Winton Archie; *b* 1907; *d* unm 19 Dec 1938

1h *Nancy Edith [Miss Nancy Montgomerie, 54 Durie St, Durie Hill, Wanganui, New Zealand]; *b* 1903

2h *Betty Sybil; *m* 26 Sept 1936 *Frank Barnard Wingfield, son of Rev Albert Wingfield, of Wellington, NZ, and has Wingfield, issue:

1i *Blair Winton; *b* 5 Nov 1941

1i *Elisabeth Jane; *b* 19 Sept 1938; *m* 16 March 1963 *Francis Brian Charles Bolt, son of Dr F Bolt, and has:

1j *Francis Charles Wingfield; *b* 29 Nov 1966

1j *Elizabeth Sarah; *b* 19 May 1965

5g John Eglinton; *b* 1878; Capt NZ Forces Boer War; *m* 1st 1910 Edith Lilian (*d* 24 May 1921), dau of Hon George Young, MLC, of Melbourne; *m* 2nd Dec 1928 Sarah (*m* 2nd George Crowe), dau of — Mitchell, of Arbroath, Scotland, and *d* June 1930, having by his 1st w had:

1h *Sheila Elizabeth [Mrs Francis Triggs, 5–89a Royal Rd, Massey, Auckland, New Zealand]; *b* 7 Aug 1911; *m* 26 June 1940 Francis Churtain Triggs (*d* 1977), est s of Francis William Triggs, of Napier, NZ, and has issue:

1i *Michael Francis; *b* 28 July 1942; *m* 1972 *Susan Marlene, dau of James Lincoln Todd, of Auckland, NZ

1i *Mary Seton; *b* 4 Sept 1946; *m* 1964 *Stafford John Reed, and has issue:

1j *Darren Stafford; *b* 3 Aug 1965

2j *Mark; *b* 6 May 1967

2h *Edith Mary Seton; *m* 1938 Samuel Allan Smith, and has issue

3h *Bettie Winton [Mrs Thomas Howden, 2/119 Lumsden Rd, Hastings, New Zealand]; *m* 1940 *Thomas Charles Howden, and has issue

1g Betty; *m* 1879 William Donald Anderson and *d* his widow 25 May 1930, leaving issue

2g Margaret; *b* 1862; *m* 1880 James Winthrop Anderson (*d* Dec 1927), of Wanganui, NZ, and *d* 1940, leaving issue

3g Minna; *m* 1887 Harry Yates Lethbridge, and *d* May 1931, leaving issue

4g Mary Seton; *m* 1885 Joseph Henry Richard Tripe (*d* 1932) and *d* 18 July 1960, leaving issue

5g Hilda; *m* 1897 George Yates Lethbridge (*d* 1929), and *d* 7 April 1944, leaving issue

6g Sybil Susannah; *b* 23 Sept 1879; *m* 25 April 1905 William Arthur Izard (*d* 1939), and *d* 1963, leaving issue

2f John Eglinton, CB, JP, DL (Ayrshire); *b* 23 Dec 1825; Adml, Naval ADC to HM QUEEN VICTORIA; *d* unm 10 Sept 1902

3f Rodger, JP, DL; *b* 22 Oct 1828; advocate, MP N Ayrshire 1874–80, Dep Clerk Register; *d* unm 25 Oct 1880

4f Thomas George; *b* 23 April 1830; Col RE, FRS; *m* 11 Feb 1865 Jane (*d* 20 July 1916), dau of Maj-Gen John James Farrington, Bengal Artillery, and *d* 31 Jan 1878, leaving issue:

1g Hastings Seton, TD; *b* 6 Jan 1872; MA Oxon; Maj 9th Bn Middx Regt; *d* unm Nov 1949

1g Egidia Oswald; *d* unm 24 Dec 1952

2g Beatrice Laura; *d* unm 2 Sept 1943

5f Archibald William; *b* 14 Oct 1838; *d* unm 26 Dec 1877

1f Susannah; *m* 7 Feb 1861 Sir John Tilley, KCB, Sec GPO, and *d* 4 March 1880, leaving issue

2f Elizabeth; *d* unm 20 Feb 1924

3f Mary; *m* 8 Aug 1872 John Thomas Anderson, QC (Canada) (*dsp* 2 April 1894), and *d* 1914

2e Alexander; *b* 30 July 1790; R-Adml; *d* unm 26 Dec 1863

3e Hugh; *b* 10 May 1792; Madras CS; *m* Jane, dau of Lt-Gen Rumley, HEICS, and *d* 1864

1e Elizabeth; *m* Rt Hon David Boyle and *d* 14 April 1822

2e Hamilla; *m* Alexander W Hamilton, of Pinmore, Ayrshire, and *d* his widow 10 March 1852

3d Archibald; *b* 3 June 1751; HEICS; *m* Marie Chantrey, and *d* 5 Jan 1831, having had:

1e Edmund; HEICS; *m* 1829 Isabella Anne (*d* 8 June 1878), dau of Gen Sullivan, and *dsp* 19 Aug 1861

4d James; *b* 26 Feb 1755; Lt-Gen; *m* 1810 Harriet Elizabeth, dau of Thomas Jackson, of Westbury, Glos, and *dsp* 13 April 1829

1d Lillias; *m* 1762 John Hamilton, of Sundrum, and *d* 3 July 1827, having had issue

4a Robert; Maj-Gen of Horse Battle of Worcester, Gentleman of the Bedchamber after the Restoration; *m* (contract 4 Sept 1662) Hon Elizabeth Livingston (*m* 2nd Capt George Douglas, 5th s of Hon Sir William Douglas of Kelhead; *see* QUEENSBERRY, M), dau of James, 1st Viscount Kilsyth, and *d* 1684, having had two sons (*dsp*)

1a Margaret; *m* 1st 1642, as his 2nd w, 1st Earl of Tweeddale (*see* TWEEDDALE, M); *m* 2nd, as his 2nd w, 9th Earl of Glencairn (*see* CUNINGHAME, Bt)

(4) Thomas (Sir), of Over Olwestob; *m* Agnes, dau of Thomas Drummond of Corskeply, and *dspm*

(5) John (Sir), of St Germains, Haddington; *m* 1620 Margaret, dau of William Kellie, WS, and had issue (male line now extinct)

(1) Isabel; *b* 30 Nov 1593; *m* 1st 1st Earl of Perth (*qv*); *m* 2nd Francis Stewart, est s of Francis, the attainted Earl of Bothwell (*see* MORAY, E), and had issue by both hubs

2 Agnes; *m* 4th Lord Sempill (*qv*)

The 11th EARL's cousin,

HUGH MONTGOMERIE, **12th Earl of Eglinto(u)n**, KT (1812); *b* 5 Nov 1739; served army 1756 on (fought War American Independence), Lt-Govr Edinburgh Castle, MP (Whig) Ayrshire 1780–81, 1784–89 and June-Oct 1796, rep S peer 1798–1806, *cr* 15 Feb 1806 BARON ARDROSSAN, of Ardrossan, Co Ayr (UK), Ld-Lt Ayrshire 1796–1819, rebuilt Eglinton Castle, constructed Ardrossan Harbour and the Paisley Canal; *m c* 3 June 1772 Eleanora (*d* Feb 1817), yst dau and coheir of Robert Hamilton of Bourtree Hill, Ayrshire, and *d* 14 Dec 1819, having had issue:

1 Archibald, *Lord Montgomerie*; *b* 30 July 1773; Maj-Gen; *m* 29 March 1803 Mary (*m* 2nd 30 Jan 1815 Sir Charles Lamb, Bt (*d* 21 March 1860), and *d* 12 June 1848), er dau and eventual heiress of **11th Earl of Eglinto(u)n**, and *d* Alicante 4 Jan 1814, leaving issue:

(1) ARCHIBALD, **13th Earl**

2 Roger; RN; *d* Port Royal June 1799

1 Jane; *m* 1828 Archibald Hamilton (*d* 1848), Capt HEICS, of Rozelle, Ayrshire, and *dsp* 23 Feb 1860

2 Lilias; *m* 1st, 1796 R D Macqueen of Braxfield; *m* 2nd, 1817 R A Oswald (*d* 1841), and *d* 10 Sept 1845

The 12th EARL's gs,

ARCHIBALD WILLIAM MONTGOMERIE, **13th Earl of Eglinto(u)n** and **1st Earl of Winton** (UK), so *cr* 17 June 1859, KT (1853), PC (1852); *b* 29 Sept 1812; *educ* Eton; DCL and LLD; served heir male gen in Scotland of 4th EARL OF WINTON (of the 1660 *cr*) 22 Dec 1840, Ld Lt and Sheriff Principal Ayrshire 1842–61, Ld Lt Ireland 27 Feb 1852-Jan 1853 and 1858–59; organised the Eglinton Tournament 1839 which cost some 20 times its estimated budget of £2,000 (*i.e.* nearly £1.5m in late–1990s terms) and in which rain persistently stopped play; *m* 1st 17 Feb 1841 Theresa Newcomen (*d* 16 Dec 1853), widow of Capt Richard Howe-Cockerell, RN, and one of the eight illegitimate children of Thomas Gleadowe-Newcomen, 2nd and last Viscount Newcomen, by Harriet Holland, and had issue:

1 ARCHIBALD WILLIAM MONTGOMERIE, **14th Earl of Eglinto(u)n** and **2nd Earl of Winton**, DL (Lanarks and Ayrshire); *b* 3 Dec 1841; *m* 6 Dec 1862 Lady Sophia Adelaide Theodosia Pelham (*d* 21 Sept 1886), only dau of 2nd Earl of Yarborough (*qv*), and *d* 30 Aug 1892, having had issue:

(1) Sophia Constance; *b* 28 Nov 1863; *m* 15 Jan 1885 Capt Samuel Hynman ALLENBY later ALLENBY-MONTGOMERIE (roy licence 1893), DL (*d* 15 June 1915), and *d* 7 March 1942, leaving issue

(2) Theresa; *b* 17 July 1866; *m* 15 July 1866 John Cross (*d* 6 June 1936), of Melton Mowbray, and *d* 5 March 1953, leaving issue

(3) Gertrude; *b* 26 July 1867; *m* 7 Feb 1893 Ernest Bruce Acland Lawford, 2nd s of Thomas Acland Lawford, and *d* Sept 1936, leaving issue

(4) Diana; *b* 19 March 1870; *m* 1st 14 Dec 1889 (*divorce* 1894) Sir Claud Alexander, 2nd Bt (*d* 18 March 1945), and had issue (*see* HAGART-ALEXANDER, Bt); *m* 2nd 30 Aug 1894 Harold Kenneth Allison, 3rd s of William Henry Allison of Lockerbie, and *d* 27 Oct 1914, leaving further issue

2 Seton Montolieu; *b* 15 May 1846; Lt Scots Fus Gds; *m* 11 June 1870 Nina Janet Bronwen (*d* 9 April 1939), dau of Lt-Col Peers Williams, MP, of Berkshire, and *d* 26 Nov 1883, having had issue:

(1) May Egidia; *b* 4 April *d* 2 Dec 1874

(2) Alswen Dorothy Rose; *d* unm 23 Dec 1943

(3) Viva Seton; *d* unm 14 April 1959

3 GEORGE ARNULPH, **15th/3rd Earl**

1 Egidia; *m* 4 July 1861 5th Baron Rendlesham (*qv*) and *d* 13 Jan 1880, leaving issue

The **13th/1st Earl** *m* 2nd 3 Nov 1858 Lady Adela Capell (*d* 31 Dec 1860), only dau of 6th Earl of Essex (*qv*), and *d* 4 Oct 1861, having by her had further issue:

2 Sybil Amelia Adela; *d* unm 3 Feb 1932

3 Hilda Rose; *m* 23 Feb 1881 1st and last Baron Anslow (*d* 20 Aug 1933) and *d* 18 June 1928, leaving issue (*see* RAVENSDALE, B)

The 14th/2nd EARL's bro,

GEORGE ARNULPH MONTGOMERIE, **15th Earl of Eglinto(u)n** and **3rd Earl of Winton**; *b* 23 Feb 1848; Lt Gren Gds, Ld Lt Ayrshire; *m* 13 Nov 1873 Janet Lucretia, DBE (1920), LLD Glasgow (*d* 6 Oct 1923), dau of Boyd Alexander Cuninghame, yr son of John Cuninghame, of Renfrewshire, and *d* 10 Aug 1919, having had issue:

1 ARCHIBALD SETON, **16th/4th Earl**

2 William Alexander; *b* 29 Oct 1881; Lt 2nd Dragoons (Scots Greys); *d* unm 9 May 1903

3 Francis Cuninghame; *b* 25 Jan 1887; Capt Life Gds, formerly Capt 4th Bn KOSB; *m* 4 Aug 1910 Alice Dudley (*d* car crash 24 Nov 1951), only dau of Thomas Glen Arthur, JP, bro of 1st Baron Glenarthur (*qv*), and *d* 16 March 1950, having had issue:

(1) Henry Hugh Arnulph; *b* 11 June 1911; Lt Coldstream Gds; *d* in an accident 16 May 1947

(2) Thomas; *b* 14 March 1914; Capt Black Watch WW II; *ka* N Africa 18 Aug 1942

1 Georgiana Theresa; *m* 25 April 1895 Lt-Col William Mure, JP, DL (*d* 14 June 1912), of Caldwell, Ayrshire, and *d* 21 Aug 1983, leaving issue

2 Edith Mary; *m* 22 July 1901 Col Algernon Richard Trotter, DSO, MVO, JP, DL (*d* 23 Dec 1945), 12th of Mortonhall, Midlothian (*see* TWEEDDALE, M), and 3rd of Charterhall, Berwickshire, and *d* 8 Sept 1947, leaving issue

The 15th/3rd EARL's est son,

ARCHIBALD SETON MONTGOMERIE, **16th Earl of Eglinto(u)n** and **4th Earl of Winton**, DL (Ayrshire); *b* 23 June 1880; Maj Gds MG Regt, Lt 2nd Life Gds and Maj Ayrshire Yeo WW I (despatches); *m* 1st 1 June 1908 (*divorce* 1922) Lady Beatrice Susan Dalrymple (*d* 10 May 1962), er dau of 11th Earl of Stair (*qv*), and had:

1 ARCHIBALD WILLIAM ALEXANDER, **17th/5th Earl**

2 George Seton; *b* 29 Sept 1919; *d* 14 Aug 1934

1 Barbara Susan; *b* 23 Aug 1909; *m* 4 Feb 1930 Christopher Gerald Gore (*see* TEMPLE OF STOWE, E)

2 *Janet Egidia [The Lady Robert Crichton-Stuart, Wards Cottage, Gartocharn, Dunbartonshire]; *b* 3 May 1911; *m* 18 April 1934 Lord Robert Crichton-Stuart (*d* 26 June 1976), 2nd son of 4th Marquess of Bute (*qv*), and has issue

3 Betty Mary Seton; *b* 8 May 1912; *m* 25 Feb 1933 George Vane Hay-Drummond (*see* KINNOULL, E), and *d* 15 Oct 1996, leaving issue

The **16th/4th Earl** *m* 2nd 16 Aug 1922 Marjorie (*d* 7 Dec 1963), dau of Thomas Walker McIntyre and widow of Guy Vernon (*see* LYVEDEN, B), and *d* 22 April 1945, having by her had further issue:

3 +Roger Hugh, DFC (1944) [The Hon Roger Montgomerie DFC, Lanehead, Dunscore, Dumfries]; *b* 1 July 1923; *educ* Eton and New Coll Oxford (MA 1949); F/Lt RAF WW II

4 Anne; *m* 8 Dec 1942 (*divorce* 1951) Maj Gordon Alexander Smith, 12th Roy Lancers, s of Alexander Smith, of Arbroath, and had issue

The 16th/4th EARL's est son,

ARCHIBALD WILLIAM ALEXANDER MONTGOMERIE, **17th Earl of Eglinto(u)n** and **5th Earl of Winton**; *b* 16 Oct 1914; *educ* Eton and New Coll Oxford (BA 1936); Maj Ayrshire Yeo (TA) and Lt Scots Gds (SR) WW II; V-Lt Ayrshire 1953– (DL 1948–53), memb Roy Coy of Archers, Chm Ayrshire TA 1957, Grand Master Mason Scotland 1957; *m* 10 Nov 1938 Ursula Joan (*d* 1987), er dau of Hon Ronald Bannatyne Watson, 6th s of 1st and last Baron Watson (*see* 1899 edn), and had issue:

1 ARCHIBALD GEORGE MONTGOMERIE, **18th and present Earl of Eglinto(u)n and 6th and present Earl of Winton**

1 *Susanna [The Lady Susanna Crawford, Newington House, Cupar, Fife KY15 4NW]; *b* 19 Oct 1941; *m* 25 May 1963 *Capt David Dundas Crawford, late RSG, only s of Brig Alastair Wardrop Ewing Crawford, JP, DL, of Stirlingshire, by Helena Beatrice, 2nd dau of Adml Sir Charles Hope Dundas of Dundas, KCMG, and has:

(1) *Alexander William Ewing; *b* 21 March 1967; *educ* Eton

(2) *Daniel Dundas Ewing; *b* 21 March 1967

(1) *Arabella Sara; *b* 18 May 1965; *m* 20 Dec 1995 *Ewan Christian, s of Lt-Col John Christian, of West Woodhay, Berks

2 *Elizabeth Beatrice [The Lady Elizabeth Barne, Culeaze, Wareham, Dorset]; *b* 29 Aug 1945; *m* 27 May 1976 *Maj Christopher Miles Barne, Blues and Royals, only child of Lt-Col Anthony Miles Barne, OBE, Roy Dragoons, of Dorset, and has issue:

(1) *Charles Miles; *b* 1978

3 Egidia Seton; *b* 29 Aug 1945; *d* 30 Jan 1957

Lineage (of Seton): ALEXANDER de SETON; witnessed a charter granted by DAVID I *c* 1150; probably f of:

PHILIP de SETON; had a charter of confirmation from WILLIAM THE LION *c* 1185 of the lands of Seton, Winton and Winchburgh, Lothian, which had belonged to his f; had:

ALEXANDER de SETON; had a charter of the same lands *c* 1195; probable ancestor of:

Sir ALEXANDER de SETON, Govr Berwick 1328–33, had numerous grants of land, including the territorial Baronies of Seton and Winchburgh; *m* Christian Cheyne, dau of the Laird of Straloch, and *dspms c* 1348; gf of:

MARGARET de Seton; *m c* 1347 Alan de WYNTOUN, said to have been her kinsman, and had, with a dau (Christian, *m* 9th Earl of Dunbar/March; *see* DUNBAR, Bt, of Mochrum):

Sir WILLIAM de SETON; feudal Ld of Seton, from which he took his name; granted the lands of Wester Fansyde to his esquire John de Fansyde *c* 1367, a grant confirmed by ROBERT II 20 June 1371; *m* Janet, dau of Sir David Fleming, and *d c* March 1409/10, having had issue:

1 JOHN (Sir)

2 Alexander; doubtfully *cr c* 1437 a Ld of Parl as Lord Gordon according to some sources; *m* between 27 March 1407/8 and 20 July 1408 Elizabeth, dau and heir of Sir Adam Gordon of Gordon and Huntly (*see* HUNTLY, M), who brought him those lands (confirmed to them 20 July 1408), and *d* between 31 Aug 1440 and 3 April 1441, having had issue (*see* also SETON, Bt, of Abercorn, and SETON, Bt, of Pitmedden)

1 Janet; *m c* 3 March 1413/4 George Dunbar, s of George, 10th and last Earl of Dunbar/March (*see* DUNBAR, Bt, of Mochrum)

2 Anna, *m* as his 2nd w Sir John Hamilton of Fingaltoun (*see* STIRLING-HAMILTON, Bt)

The er son,

Sir JOHN SETON of Seton; had a charter of confirmation of the territorial Baronies of Seton and Tranent and the lands of Winchburgh 24 March 1410/1; hostage for JAMES I 1424; *m* Katherine (living 28 March 1450, when she had confirmation of a charter), dau of Sir William Sinclair of Hermanstoun, and *d c* 1434, leaving with a dau (Christian), *m* Sir Norman Leslie of Rothes; *see* ROTHES, E:

Sir WILLIAM SETON; *m* Janet (*m* 2nd Sir Adam Johnstone of that Ilk (*see* ANNANDALE AND HARTFELL, E), allegedly dau of 10th Earl of Dunbar, and *dvp, ka* Battle of Verneuil 17 Aug 1424 during the Hundred Years War fighting with the French against the English, leaving (with a dau, Catherine, *m* 1st Sir Alan Stuart of Darnley (*see* MORAY, E); *m* 2nd 1st Lord Maxwell *see* MAXWELL, Bt):

GEORGE SETON, 1st LORD SETON, so *cr* just after 22 March 1450/1, PC (S 1458); ktd *c* late summer 1439, went as envoy to France 1448 and England 1472; *m* 1st by 8 Jan 1436/7 Margaret, dau and heir of John Stewart, Earl of Buchan, Constable of France (*see* MORAY, E), 2nd s of Robert, Duke of Albany, and by her had issue:

1 John, *Master of Seton*; *m* (dispensation 20 Jan 1458/59) Christian (*m* 2nd 1476 Robert Cunningham, s and heir of 1st Earl of Glencairn (*see* CUNINGHAME, Bt), and *d* 1496), dau of 1st Lord Lindsay of the Byres (*see* LINDSAY, E), and *dvp*, leaving:

(1) GEORGE, 2nd LORD

(2) John; living 1491

(3) Alexander; living 1501

(1) Margaret; *m* 2nd Lord Lyle and *dsp*

The 1st LORD *m* 2nd by 8 Jan 1460/1 Christian, dau of Sir William Murray of Tullibardine (*see* ATHOLL, D), and *d* just after 15 July 1478, having by her had:

1 Christian; *m* Hugh Douglas of Borg

The 1st LORD SETON's gs,

GEORGE SETON, 2nd LORD SETON, PC (S 1496); fndr Collegiate Church of Seton 1493; *m c* 14 Sept 1469 Lady Margaret Campbell, dau of 1st Earl of Argyll (*see* ARGYLL, D), and *d* between 11 June 1507 and 6 April 1508, leaving, with other issue (including a dau Martha, *m* William Maitland of Lethington and Thirlestane; *see* LAUDERDALE, E):

GEORGE SETON, 3rd LORD SETON; *m* by 25 Jan 1506/7 Lady Janet Hepburn, est dau of 1st Earl of Bothwell (title forfeited 1567), and was *k* Battle of Flodden 9 Sept 1513, having had, with at least two daus (Mariot, *m* 1st William, Master of Borthwick (*see* BORTHWICK, L), 2nd **2nd Earl of Eglinto(u)n** (*see* above), 3rd Alexander Graham, of Wallastoun; Margaret, *m* David Hamilton of Langton and Olivestob; *see* STIRLING-HAMILTON, Bt):

GEORGE SETON, 4th LORD SETON, PC (S March 1542/3); Extra Ld of Session 1533; *m* 1st *c* 15 June 1527 Elizabeth, dau of 3rd Lord Hay of Yester (*see* TWEEDDALE, M), and had, with other issue:

1 GEORGE, 5th Lord

2 John; *m* Isabel Balfour, with whom he acquired the lands of Carraldstane in Fife, of which he and his w had a charter 9 Oct 1553; ancestor of the SETONs of Cariston

1 Marion; *m* 1st 1548 4th Earl of Menteith (*see* MONTROSE, D); *m* 2nd 11th Earl of Sutherland (*qv*) and *d* 23 June 1567, leaving issue

2 Margaret; *m* Sir Robert Logan of Restalrig

3 Eleanor; *m* 7th Lord Somerville (*d* 1597; *see* 1870 edn) and had issue

4 Beatrix; *m* Sir George Ogilvy of Dunlugus

The 4th LORD *m* 2nd *c* Feb 1538/9 Marie (who was in the retinue of MARY OF LORRAINE, mother of MARY QUEEN OF SCOTS), dau of — Pyerres or Pierre, of Le Plessir Baudoin, and *d* 17 July 1549, having by her had, with other issue:

5 Mary; one of the 'four Marys' who accompanied MARY QUEEN OF SCOTS to France 1548 and returned with her to Scotland as Maid of Honour 1561

The est son,

GEORGE SETON, 5th LORD SETON, PC (1573); *b* 1531; *educ* in France; Provost Edinburgh 1557–59, one of the Commrs apptd by Parl 17 Dec 1557 to attend the marriage of MARY QUEEN OF SCOTS with the DAUPHIN of France, Master Household 1563 on MARY's return from France, accommodated her and Bothwell at Seton for some days after Lord Darnley's murder, during which time the contract of marriage between them was signed, was one of those who waited for MARY on the banks of Lochleven when she made her escape May 1568, conducted her via his castle of Niddry to Hamilton and joined the Association on her behalf, fled to the Low Countries after her defeat at Battle of Langside 1568 and remained there in exile for two years where he earned his living as a waggoner (a picture of him in the role was in the long gallery at Seton); returned to Scotland and worked on behalf of MARY April 1570; sent to the Low Countries to invoke the Duke of Alva's help on her behalf, Amb to France 1583; *m* (contract 2 Aug 1550) Isabel (*d* 13 Nov 1604), dau of Sir William Hamilton of Sorn and Sanquhar, and *d* 8 Jan 1585/6, having had:

1 George, *Master of Seton*; *d* March 1562

2 ROBERT, 6th LORD

3 John (Sir), of Barns; Kt Order of St Iago, Master Household, Gentleman of Bedchamber to PHILIP II of Spain, recalled to Scotland by JAMES VI and made Extra Ld of Session instead of his bro Alexander 17 Feb 1587; *m* 8 Sept 1588 Anne, yst dau of 7th Lord Forbes (*qv*), and *d* by 11 June 1594; ancestor of the SETONs of Barns

4 ALEXANDER SETON, 1st EARL OF DUNFERMLINE (S), so *cr* 4 March 1604/5, as also earlier 4 March 1597/8 LORD FYVIE (both S), with in the latter case remainder, failing male heirs of his body, to his next er bro John in like manner, PC (S 1585, E 1609)); *b* 1555; *educ* Jesuits' Coll Rome but turned Protestant on going back to Scotland; Prior Pluscarden 1565–77 and again 1581; a Ld of Session Extrdy 1585/6–87/8 and Ordinary as Lord Urquhart 1588–93, Ld Pres Court of Session 1593–1605, Ld Provost Edinburgh 1598–1608, Ld Chllr Scotland 1605–22; *m* 1st *c* 1590 but by 1 July 1592 Lilias (*dspm* 8 May 1601, having had by him three daus: Anne, *m* Alexander Viscount Fentoun (*see* MAR and KELLIE, E); Isabel, *m* 1st Earl of Lauderdale, *qv*; Margaret, *m* 1st Earl of Seaforth; *see* CROMARTIE, E), 2nd dau of 3rd Lord Drummond (*see* PERTH, E); *m* 2nd *c* 27 Oct 1601 Grizel, half-sis of John Earl of Rothes (*qv*); *m* 3rd 1607 Margaret, sis of 1st Earl of Tweeddale (*see* TWEEDDALE, M), and *d* 16 June 1622, leaving by her:

(1) CHARLES SETON, 2nd EARL OF DUNFERMLINE, PC (S 1640–48 and 1660/1); *b* late Nov 1615; a leading Covenanter but later turned royalist, High Commr Gen Assembly Ch Scotland 1642, Extrdy Ld Session 1669–72, Privy Seal Scotland 1671–72; *m c* between spring and autumn 1632 Mary, 3rd dau of 7th Earl of Morton (*qv*), and *d c* 11 May 1672, having had, with a dau (Henrietta, *m* 1st 5th Earl of Wigton, *m* 2nd 2nd Earl of Lindsay (*qv*) and 18th Earl of Crawford; *see* CRAWFORD and BALCARRES, E):

1a ALEXANDER SETON, 3rd EARL OF DUNFERMLINE; *b* 12 June 1642; *dsp c* Sept 1677

2a JAMES SETON, 4th EARL OF DUNFERMLINE; outlawed and his title forfeited 1690 for taking the deposed JAMES II's part in the Battle of Killiecrankie 27 July 1689; *m c* 6 July 1682 Lady Jean Gordon, dau of 3rd Marquess of Huntly (*qv*), and *dsp* St Germains 26 Dec 1694, when his titles either expired or became dormant

4 (cont.) By one of his ws the 1st EARL also had:

(1) Jean; *m* 1624, as his 1st w, 1st Earl of Tweeddale (*see* TWEEDDALE, M)

5 William (Sir), of Kyllismore; PMG Scotland 1620; *m* Agnes Stirling and *d* July 1635, leaving:

(1) William (Sir), of Grange, PMG Scotland; *d* unm 1662

1 Margaret; *m* 1 Aug 1574 1st Lord Paisley and had issue (*see* ABERCORN, D)

The 5th LORD's est surv son,

ROBERT SETON, 6th LORD SETON and 1st EARL OF WINTON, so *cr* 16 Nov 1600, PC (S *c* March 1584/5); *b c* 1552; *m c* 19 May 1583 Lady Margaret Montgomerie (*d* 9 April 1624), est dau of **3rd Earl of Eglinto(u)n** (*see* above), and *d* 22 March 1603, leaving issue

EGMONT

Arms: Arg. on a chief indented gu. three crosses-patée of the field. **Crest:** A thistle erect leaved ppr. **Supporters:** Dexter, an antelope arg., attired and unguled or, ducally gorged and chained of the last; sinister, a stag sa., attired and unguled or, ducally gorged and chained of the last; each holding in the mouth a thistle ppr.
Motto: *Sub cruce candida* ('Under the white cross').
Creations: Bt. (I) 9 Sept 1661; B. (I) 21 April 1715 (Perceval of Burton), (GB) 7 May 1762 (Lovel and Holland), (I) 23 May 1770 (Arden of Lohort Castle); V. (I) 25 Feb 1722/3 (Perceval of Kanturk); E. (I) 6 Nov 1733.

THE 11TH EARL OF EGMONT, Co Cork, **Viscount Perceval of Kanturk**, Co Cork, **Baron Perceval of Burton**, Co Cork, **Lord Lovel and Holland, Baron Lovel and Holland of Enmore**, Co Somerset, and a **Baronet** (Sir Frederick George Moore Perceval, Bt) [The Rt Hon The Earl of Egmont, Two-Dot Ranch, Nanton, Alberta, Canada]; *b* 14 April 1914; *s* f (*de jure* 10th Earl only) 1932 but did not establish claim until 1939; *m* 31 Aug 1932 *Ann Geraldine, dau of Douglas Gerald Moodie, of Calgary, Alberta, and has had issue:

1 +THOMAS FREDERICK GERALD, *Viscount Perceval; b* Aug 1934

2 Patrick; *b* 3 Dec 1936; *d* 22 Feb 1937

3 Gordon Joseph; *b* 6 Aug 1945; *d* 1949

1 *Geraldine Elizabeth Ursula; *b* 31 Jan 1939

Lineage: DAVID PERCEVAL, Lord of Tykenham, Rolleston, etc, Somerset; *m* Alice, dau of Thomas Bythemore, of Overwere, and *d* 1534, leaving issue:

1 James; *dsp* 1548

2 GEORGE, of whom presently.

3 Thomas, ancestor of the PERCEVALs of Royton, Lancs

The 2nd son,

GEORGE PERCEVAL, Lord of Tykenham, etc; *m* Elizabeth, dau of Sir Edward Bampfylde, of Poltimore (*see* POLTIMORE, B), Devon, and *d c* 1599, leaving, with a dau (Elizabeth, *m* Richard Gilbert):

RICHARD PERCEVAL; *b* 1550; *educ* St Paul's; confidential agent to Lord Burghley (*see* EXETER, M), and deciphered for him 1586 the secret letters which gave ELIZABETH I the first intelligence of the Spanish Armada; Sec Court of Wards, Registrar Court of Wards Ireland 1616, acquired large estates there; *m* 1st Joan, dau of Henry Young, of Buckorn Weston, Dorset, and had three sons and two daus; *m* 2nd Alice, dau of John Sherman, of Ottery St Mary, Devon, and *d* 1620, leaving by her:

Sir PHILIP PERCEVAL; acquired some 100,000 acres of forfeited lands in Ireland; *m* 1626 Catherine, gdau of Sir William Usher, Clerk PC, and dau of Arthur Usher by Judith, dau of Sir Robert Newcomen, of Mosstown, Co Longford, and had issue:

1 JOHN (Sir), **1st Bt**

2 George, Registrar Prerogative Court, Dublin; *b* 15 Sept 1635; *m* Mary (*m* 2nd 30 April 1677 Richard Aldworth and *d* 15 Oct 1705), dau and heir of William Crofton, of Temple House, Co Sligo, and was drowned off Holyhead 25 March 1675, having had, with other issue:

(1) William (Very Rev), Archdeacon Cashel and Dean of Emly; *b* 14 Dec 1671; *m* 5 April 1708 Catherine (*d* 3 Dec 1730), dau of Henry Prittie (*see* DUNALLEY, B), of Silvermines, Co Tipperary, and *d* 29 Aug 1734, leaving a 2nd s:

1a William, barrister; *b* 24 June 1711; *m* 1st 1738 Elizabeth (*dsp* June 1739), dau of John Croker, of Dublin; *m* 2nd 30 June 1748 Elizabeth (*d* 30 Nov 1770), dau of Robert Ward, and *d* 2 Aug 1784, having had a middle s:

1b William, Capt 104th Regt; *b* 9 Sept 1754; *m* 15 Oct 1784, Jane, 2nd dau of John Brereton, of Rathgilbert, and *d* 10 Sept 1793, leaving, with other issue:

1c William John, JP Queen's Co, Capt 9th Regt; *b* 2 July 1789; *m* 2 April 1818 Mary (*d* 15 Feb 1869), dau of Arthur Brereton, of Limerick, and *d* 2 Nov 1848, leaving three sons and three daus; the 2nd s:

1d Arthur (Rev), Rector Wakerley, Stamford; *b* 7 Nov 1821; *educ* Trin Coll Dublin (BA); *m* 4 Aug 1848 Emile Caroline (*d* 1908), dau of George Bevill Granville Grenfell, of Penzance, and *d* 26 Nov 1905, leaving issue:

1e Arthur William Bernard, VD; *b* 23 Oct 1859; *educ* Queen's Coll Oxford; 31st Regt (E Surrey), Capt Australian Cwlth Forces, Ch Staff Offr Hobart, cmded S District Scouts Natal, served Boer War 1899–1902 (medal, three clasps); *m* 15 Oct 1935 Dorothy Margaret (*d* 27 Mar 1961), 2nd dau of Rev Thomas Grenfell Vyvyan, MA (*see* VYVYAN, Bt), and *d* 22 April 1952

2e Francis John; *b* 1 Jan 1864; *d* unm Jan 1946

3e Cyril Ambrose, MA; *b* 27 Nov 1866; *m* 10 Sept 1889 Charlotte Persis (*d* 16 Jan 1947), 3rd dau of Rev Enoch Trees, of Ossington, Notts, and *d* 16 Feb 1951, leaving issue:

1f Francis Cyril Grenfell; *b* 15 Sept 1892

2f William Vincent St Leger; *b* 20 July 1896; *d* 15 April 1937

3f John Cecil Riversdale; *b* 21 June 1898; *d* unm 29 Jan 1969

1f Elsie Marguerite, JP, Chm Radnorshire Fedn WIs 1953–56, memb: House Laity Church Assembly 1935–45 for Diocese of Southwark, Presteigne UDC from 1946 (Chm 1950–51, 1955–56 and 1961–62), Radnorshire Health Ctee from 1945, Radnorshire Exec Cncl from 1948, Radnorshire Educn Ctee and sub-Cttees from 1946, Wales Gas Consultative Council 1948–62; Chm Govrs Presteigne GS from 1962; *m* 14 April 1913 William Henry Howse, MBE, FSA (*d* 15 Feb 1966), s of William Henry Howse, of Leamington Spa, and left issue:

1g *Marguerite Elisabeth; *b* 21 April 1915; *m* 17 March 1943 John Allen Dowman (*d* 20 Nov 1957), s of Paul Dowman, of Black Rock, Co Cork, and has:

1h *John Patrick Allen; *b* 27 May 1945; *m* 7 May 1966 *Jeanette Patricia Stanley and has:

1i *Emma Katherine; *b* 15 Oct 1966

1h *Lynn Marguerite; *b* 24 Oct 1943; *m* 23 June 1962 *Thomas Frank Mayfield, AMINucE, son of Lt-Cdr Thomas Noel Mayfield, RN, and has issue:

1i *Johnathan Paul Dowman; *b* 16 April 1963

2i *Benedict Charles Grenfell; *b* 4 March 1966

1i *Claudia Elisabeth Louise; *b* 29 April 1969

2h *Alison Frances; *b* 26 Sept 1949

3h *Joanna Mary Granville; *b* 20 Sept 1955

2g *Veronica Mary [Mrs Guy Harland, The Coach House, 5 The Crescent, Colwall, Worcs WR13 6QW]; *b* 29 March 1918; *m* 11 Sept 1948 *(Robert) Guy Aufrere Harland, ARCO, LRAM, s of Rev Claude Harland, Canon Emeritus St Paul's, of Herne, Kent, and has issue:

1h *Rosamund Claire; *b* 29 Aug 1949; *m* 19– *Peter Ditchfield, and has:

1i *Emily Louise; *b* 1979

2h *Anthea Mary Jane Grenfell; *b* 30 Aug 1952; *m* 19– *Nicholas Nakorn and has:

1i *Adam; *b* 1990

2f Winifred Helen; *d* 7 March 1959

1e Jane Russell; *d* unm in Australia

2e Milicent Mary Grenfell; nun; *d* 1947

3e Alice Emilie

4e Emma Lucia Theodora

5e Ida Eleanor Clarice; *b* 19 April 1873; *d* unm 19 Oct 1966

Sir PHILIP *d* 10 Nov 1647; his er son,

Sir John Perceval, 1st Bt (I), so *cr* 9 Sept 1661; *b* 7 Sept 1629; *m* 14 Feb 1655 Catherine (*d* 17 Aug 1679), dau of Robert Southwell, of Kinsale, Co Cork, and *d* 5 Nov 1655, having had:

1 **Sir Philip Perceval, 2nd Bt**; *b* 12 Jan 1656; *d* unm 11 Sept 1680

2 Robert, *b* 18 Feb 1657; *d* unm 5 June 1677, murdered in the Strand

3 **Sir John Perceval, 3rd Bt**; *m* Feb 1680 Catherine (*m* 2nd 1690 Col — Butler and *d* 1691), dau of Sir Edward Dering, 2nd Bt (*see* 1956 edn), and *d* 29 April 1686, having had issue:

(1) **Sir Edward Perceval, 4th Bt**; *b* 30 July 1682; *d* unm 9 Nov 1691

(2) **Sir John Perceval, 5th Bt**, and **1st Earl of Egmont**, Co Cork, so *cr* 6 Nov 1733, as also earlier 21 April 1715 BARON PERCEVAL OF BURTON, Co Cork, with remainder to the heirs male of his f's body, and 25 Feb 1722/3 VISCOUNT PERCEVAL OF KANTURK, Co Cork (all I), PC (1704); *b* 22 July 1683; FRS, MP (Whig) Co Cork 1703–15 and Harwich 1722–34, first Pres Georgia 1732; *m* 10 June 1710 Catherine (*d* 22 Aug 1749), est dau of Sir Philip Parker, 2nd Bt, of Erwarton, Suffolk, and had surv issue:

1a JOHN, **2nd Earl**

1a Catharine; *m* 14 April 1733 Thomas Hanmer, of The Fenns, Co Flint (*see* HANMER, Bt)

1a Helena; *m* 10 Nov 1741 John Rawdon, 1st Earl of Moira (*see* LOUDOUN, E), and *d* 11 June 1746

4 Charles

1 Catharine; *m* 1st Sir William Moore, of Roscarbery; *m* 2nd, as his 2nd w, Maj John Montgomery; *m* 3rd Brig-Gen — Freke

2 Helena; *m* Col Daniel Dering

The 1st EARL *d* 1 May 1748; his son,

JOHN PERCEVAL, **2nd Earl of Egmont**, PC; *b* 24 Feb 1710/1; *cr* 7 May 1762 LORD LOVEL AND HOLLAND, BARON LOVEL AND HOLLAND OF ENMORE, Co Somerset (GB); *m* 1st 15 Feb 1736/7 Catherine (*d* 16 Aug 1752), 2nd dau of 5th Earl of Salisbury (*see* SALISBURY, M), and *d* 4 Dec 1770, leaving:

1 JOHN JAMES PERCEVAL, **3rd Earl of Egmont**; *b* 23 Jan 1738; *m* 4 June 1765 Isabella (*d* 8 Sept 1821), only dau and heir of Lord Nassau Powlett, 3rd s of 2nd Duke of Bolton (*see* WINCHESTER, M), and *d* 25 Feb 1822, leaving issue:

(1) JOHN PERCEVAL, **4th Earl of Egmont**; *b* 13 Aug 1767; *m* 10 March 1792 Bridget (*d* 24 Jan 1826), only dau of Lt-Col Glynn Wynn, bro of 1st Baron Newborough (*qv*), and *d* 31 Dec 1835, having had issue:

1a HENRY FREDERICK JOHN JAMES PERCEVAL, **5th Earl of Egmont**; *b* 3 Jan 1796; *educ* Trin Coll Cambridge (MA); MP (Tory) E Looe 1826; *m* Dec 1828 Louisa Maria, yst dau of Count d'Orselet, and *dsp* 23 Dec 1841

2 Cecil Parker; *b* 19 Oct 1739; *d* 4 March 1753

3 Philip Tufton; *b* 10 March 1741; *d* 21 April 1795

4 Edward; *b* 21 April 1744; *m* 1775 Sarah (*d* 1808), dau of John Howarth, and *d* 1829, leaving issue:

(1) Margaret Cecil; *d* unm 22 Jan 1950

(2) Mary; *d* unm 4 Jan 1847

(3) Isabella

5 Frederick Augustus; *b* 11 Feb 1749; *d* 21 Jan 1757

1 Catherine; *m* 15 Sept 1766 1st Baron Newborough (*qv*) and *d* June 1782

The **2nd Earl** *m* 2nd 26 Jan 1756 Catherine (*cr* 23 May 1770 **Baroness Arden of Lohort Castle**, Co Cork (I), with remainder to the heirs male of her body; *d* 17 June 1784), 3rd dau of Hon Charles Compton (*see* NORTHAMPTON, M), and by her had issue:

6 CHARLES GEORGE, **2nd Baron Arden of Lohort Castle**, MP Launceston 1780–90, Warwick 1790–96 and Totnes 1796–1802, a Ld of Admlty, Registrar Admlty Court; *b* 1 Oct 1756; *cr* 20 July 1802 BARON ARDEN, of Arden, Co Warwick (UK); *m* 1 March 1787 Margaret Elizabeth (*d* 20 May 1851), est dau of Gen Sir Thomas Spencer Wilson, 6th Bt (*see* 1956 edn), and *d* 5 July 1840, having had, with other issue:

(1) John; *b* 13 April 1793; *m* 20 Aug 1816 Elizabeth Anne (*m* 2nd 16 March 1824 7th Viscount Midleton of Midleton (*qv*)), and *d* 24 Nov 1824), dau of 6th Earl of Cardigan (*see* AILESBURY, M), and *dvp* 15 March 1818, leaving issue:

1a Elizabeth Helena; *d* young 14 Nov 1823

(2) GEORGE JAMES PERCEVAL **6th Earl of Egmont** (as which *s* cousin 23 Dec 1841) and **3rd Baron Arden of Lohort Castle** and 2nd BARON ARDEN (as which *s f* 5 July 1840); *b* 14 March 1794; joined RN 1805, was at Trafalgar, served Egypt, cmded fleet Battle of Algiers, R-Adml 1851, V-Adml 1857, Adml 1863, MP (C) W Surrey 1837–40, Pres Roy Ag Soc 1847; *m* 24 July 1819 Jane (*d* 14 Oct 1870), est dau of John Hornby, of The Hook, Hants, and *dsp* 2 Aug 1874

(3) Edward; *b* 30 July 1795; *m* 20 March 1821 his cousin Jane (*d* 13 Jan 1824), est dau of Rt Hon Spencer Perceval (*see* below), and *dsp* 10 March 1840

(4) Charles George (Rev), Rector Calverton, Bucks; *b* 25 Dec 1796; *m* 1st 21 April 1829 Mary (*d* 6 Nov 1832), only dau of Rev Primatt Knapp, Rector Shenley Mansell, and had, with a s (*d* young):

1a Mary; granted rank of earl's dau; *m* 12 Oct 1865 Rev Richard Norris Russell, Rector Beachampton, and *d* 25 April 1891, leaving issue

(4) (cont.) The Rev Charles Perceval *m* 2nd 13 Sept 1842 Frances Agnes (*d* 16 Oct 1873), 2nd dau of Ven George Trevelyan, Archdeacon Taunton (*see* TREVELYAN, Bt, of Nettlecombe), and *d* 26 July 1858, having by her had:

1a CHARLES GEORGE PERCEVAL, **7th Earl of Egmont**, DL Surrey; MP Midhurst 1874–75, Capt Bucks Yeo Cav; *b* 15 June 1845; *m* 4 May 1869 Lucy (*m* 2nd 12 Dec 1898 Alfred Brisco (*d* 14 Dec 1927), 6th s of Sir Robert Brisco, 3rd Bt (*qv*), and *d* 1 June 1932), dau of Henry King, and *dsp* 5 Sept 1897

(5) Arthur Philip (Rev), BCL Oxon, Rector E Horsley, Surrey, Chaplain to HM QUEEN VICTORIA; *b* 22 Nov 1799; *m* 15 Dec 1825 Charlotte Anne (*d* 21 June 1856), est dau of Rev Hon Augustus George Legge (*see* DARTMOUTH, E), and *d* 11 June 1853, having had, with other issue:

1a Augustus George; *b* 2 May 1829; *m* 1st 12 Aug 1852 Emma (*d* 27 March 1873), 2nd dau of John Matthews; *m* 2nd 6 Feb 1875 Margaret Amelia Frances (*d* 14 Feb 1911), dau of William John Clemow, Capt 41st Foot, and *dsps* 19 Aug 1896

2a Charles John; *b* 19 May 1831; *m* 1st 19 May 1852 Eleanor (*d* 11 June 1865), yst dau of John Matthews, and had issue:

1b AUGUSTUS ARTHUR PERCEVAL, **8th Earl of Egmont**; *b* 4 June 1856; *m* 1881 Kate (*d* 6 Nov 1926), dau of Warwick Howell, of S Carolina, USA, and *dsp* 11 Aug 1910

2b CHARLES JOHN PERCEVAL, **9th Earl of Egmont**; Natal CS; *b* 29 June 1858; *m* 15 Jan 1890 Florence (*d* 31 Dec 1954), dau of George Gibson, MD, and *dsp* 10 Jan 1929, when the Barony of Arden expired and the Earldom of Egmont and the other titles became dormant

2a (cont.) Charles Perceval *m* 2nd 19 June 1869 Maria (*dsp* 5 Aug 1876), widow of Alfred Julius Sickler and dau of John Summers, MD; *m* 3rd 19 Nov 1877 Elizabeth (*d* 24 March 1928), dau of William Wyer, of Ripplingale, Lincs, and *d* 14 Oct 1894

3a Spencer Arthur; *b* 27 June 1832; *m* 2 June 1857 (*divorce* 1900) Marianne, est dau of Rev George Dunnage, of Papanui, NZ, and *d* 4 Feb 1910, having had issue:

1b Arthur Philip Charles; *b* 2 April 1858; *m* 1879 Elizabeth Sarah (*d* 1888), dau of John Searle, and *dsp* 11 May 1893

2b Henry Godfrey; *b* 20 Aug 1861; *m* 27 Dec 1882 Mary Cornelia, dau of Rev George C Tanner, and was murdered with his w and dau in Nebraska 29 Sept 1884, having had:

1c Ellen Mary

1b Mary Henrietta; *m* 1st 20 Nov 1883 her cousin Rev Gilbert Vyvyan Heathcote, Rector W Deeping, Lincs, 3rd s of Sir William Heathcote, 5th Bt, of Hursley (*qv*), and had issue; *m* 2nd 25 Feb 1897 Henry Gourlay, JP, of Kempshott Park, Hants, and *d* 22 Nov 1937, leaving issue. He *d* 1915

2b Lousia Charlotte; *d* unm 31 March 1892

1a Frances Charlotte; *m* 20 Aug 1846 Rev H S Cerjat, Rector W Horsley, Surrey, and *d* 3 Sept 1846. He *d* 1894

2a Caroline Adelaide; *m* 14 Feb 1865 Rev Edward Henry Landon, MA, and *d* 23 May 1930, leaving issue. He *d* 1877

3a Charlotte Isabella; *m* 25 Jan 1865 Rev James Stanley Percival, Vicar St Mark's, Peterborough, yr s of Stanley O Percival, of Bridgefoot House, Barnet, and *d* 15 Aug 1877, leaving issue. He *d* 22 Dec 1873

(1) Helena; *m* 9 Jan 1816 Rev Frederic Steuart Trench, est s of Very Rev T Trench, DD, Dean Kildare and n of 1st Baron Ashtown (*qv*), and *d* 17 March 1881, leaving issue

(2) Caroline Frances; *m* 8 Nov 1825 Sir W Heathcote, 5th Bt, of Hursley (*qv*), and *d* 3 March 1835, leaving issue

7 Spencer, PC, MP; *b* 4 Nov 1762; *educ* Harrow; barrister, slr, Attorney-Gen, Chllr Exchequer 1807, PM and Chllr; *m* 10 Aug 1790 Jane (*m* 2nd 12 Jan 1815 Lt-Col Sir Henry Carr, KCB, and *d* 26 Jan 1844), 2nd dau of Lt-Gen Sir Thomas Spencer Wilson, 6th Bt (*qv*), and was assassinated 11 May 1812 in the lobby of the House of Commons by John Bellingham, having had, with other issue:

(1) Spencer, of Elm Grove, Ealing, MP; *b* 11 Sept 1795; *m* 3 July 1821 Anna Eliza (*d* 2 Oct 1889), yst dau of Gen Norman Macleod of Macleod, and *d* 16 Sept 1859, having had issue, with five daus (*d* unm):

1a Spencer, barrister; *b* 20 Sept 1828; *d* 2 Jan 1890

2a John Spencer, Lt 1st Waikatoo Roy Victorian Vols; *b* 3 Feb 1833; *k* 23 Oct 1863 in a skirmish with Maoris on the Mauka River

3a Norman Spencer, Capt RA; *b* 31 Oct 1838; *m* 2 Feb 1859 Elizabeth (*d* 4 Dec 1910), dau of James Patmore, and *dsp* 1 Oct 1902

1a Maria Anne; *m* 12 Aug 1884 Major-Gen Arthur Stevens and *dsp* 2 June 1895

2a Eleanor Irving; *m* 17 April 1860 Sir Alexander Matheson, 1st Bt, MP (*qv*), and *d* 6 Dec 1879, leaving issue. He *d* 26 July 1886

3a Jane; *m* 25 Aug 1870 Howard Marsh, ScD, FRCS, MA, Master Downing Coll and Prof of Surgery Cambridge, and *d* 24 Sept 1896 leaving issue. He *d* 24 June 1915

(2) Frederick James; *b* 6 Oct 1797; *m* 1st 25 July 1827 Mary (*d* 24 April 1843), est dau of William Barker, of Burn House, Derbys, and had issue:

1a Spencer Frederick John; *b* 24 Nov 1829; *m* 30 March 1867 Ellen Anne (*d* 10 Oct 1889), 2nd dau of Owens Norton, of Edgbaston, Warwicks, and *d* 21 May 1887, leaving issue:

1b Frances Emma Maryon; *m* 28 Jan 1890 Roderick Macdonald, MD, FRCSE, MP Cromarty, and *d c* 1900

1a Frederica Mary Jane; *m* 18 April 1860 William Waterhouse, of W Kensington, and *d* 14 Feb 1903, leaving issue. He *d* 24 Jan 1890

(2) (cont.) Frederick Perceval *m* 2nd 6 April 1844 Emma (*d* 23 Dec 1870), 2nd dau of Ralph Gilbert, and *d* 22 July 1861, having by her had issue:

2a George Drummond Ince; *b* 7 March 1847; *m* 4 Oct 1870 Marianne, dau of Edward Baxter, and *d* 19 Jan 1920, leaving issue:

1b FREDERICK JOSEPH TREVELYAN, *de jure* 10th EARL OF EGMONT; *b* 27 April 1873; *m* 13 June 1911 Cecilia (*d* 12 Dec 1916), dau of James Burns Moore, of Montreal, Canada, and *d* 16 May 1932, leaving issue:

1c FREDERICK GEORGE MOORE, **11th and present Earl of Egmont**

2b George Ernest Spencer; *b* 18 July 1874; *m* 21 Sept 1910 Margaret (*d* April 1946) dau of Peter Eadington, of Liverpool, and *d* Calgary 10 Dec 1965

3a Charles Augustus Trevelyan; *b* 19 July 1848; *m* 2 April 1890 Annie (*d* 5 April 1932), 3rd dau of Thomas Evison, of Hornsey, and *d* 5 Jan 1898, leaving issue:

1b Gordon Lawrence; *b* 19 Dec 1891; *m* 15 June 1914 Constance Mary Victoria, est dau of Samuel Ernest Yelland, of Hove

4a Montagu William Cairns, MRCP; *b* 25 Jan 1850; *m* 1st 27 June 1871 Elizabeth Anne (*d* 1871), dau of William Middleton, of Oakley Wood Farm, Warwicks, and had issue:

1b Emma; *b* 1872; *d* unm Jan 1956

2b Clara Elizabeth; *b* 1873 *m* 1899 Rev Edward George Higgin, Vicar W Tamworth, NSW, and *d* 9 Aug 1970, leaving issue. He *d* 1934

4a (cont.) Montagu Perceval *m* 2nd 21 Aug 1879 Jane Teresa Louisa (*d* 193–), widow of K J A Kendrick and er dau of Bond Coxe, barrister, and *d* 1923

5a James Wilde Godfrey; *b* 20 March 1854; *m* 2 March 1882 Jane Milne (*d* 20 March 1940), dau of James Louttit, MD, of Blackheath, and *d* 14 Jan 1905, having had issue:

1b Spencer Ralph; *b* 7 Sept 1889; *m* 23 March 1918 Mabel, dau of Alfred Annerley Newbold

1b Emma Johanna; *b* 26 April 1884; *m* 23 Dec 1918 Edward Vere Monday, s of Edward Goddard Monday, and *d* 11 June 1965. He *d* 18 Sept 1953

2b Christina Jane; *b* 25 Dec 1885; *m* 4 Sept 1923 William Francis Fowke, of Brocton, Staffs, and *d* 11 Feb 1960. He *d* 2 May 1936

(3) Henry (Rev), Rector Elmley Lovett, Worcs; *b* 2 Aug 1799; *m* 27 March 1826 his cousin Catherine Isabella (*d* 12 Feb 1870), dau of Andrew Berkeley Drummond, of Cadland, (*see* PERTH, E), and *d* April 1885, leaving:

1a Henry Spencer; *b* 8 Jan 1827; *m* 11 June 1853 Fanny (*d* 27 Aug 1874), est dau of Rev Thomas Tayler, and *d* 21 Jan 1876, having had issue:

1b Ascelin Spencer (Rev), BA Oxon; Headmaster Malvern Ho Sch, Derby, Vicar Mackworth; *b* 13 Feb 1855; *d* unm 24 April 1910

1b Amy; *d* unm 16 Oct 1948

2b Lilian; *d* unm 13 March 1942

1a Catherine Mary; *d* 9 April 1923 aged 94

(4) Dudley Montagu; *b* 22 Oct 1800; *m* 24 July 1827 Mary Jane (*d* 21 May 1888), dau of Gen Sir Richard Bourke, KCB, Govr NSW, and *d* 2 Sept 1856, leaving issue:

1a Charles Spencer, barrister, LLD, FSA, Sec to Commrs of Lunacy; *b* 11 Feb 1829; *m* 2 Jan 1868 Mary Elinor Vere (*d* 19 June 1924), est dau of Hon Robert O'Brien and n of 13th Baron Inchiquin (*qv*), and *d* 29 Jan 1889, leaving, with other issue:

1b Dudley; *b* 9 Aug 1874; *m* 6 July 1914 Hon Mary Elizabeth Massey (*d* 16 Dec 1960), er dau of 5th Baron Clarina (*see* 1949 edn), and *d* 31 Jan 1956, leaving issue:

1c Philip Edward; *b* 26 March 1915; *educ* St John's Coll Cambridge (BA 1936, MA 1940, MB, BCh 1940, MD 1950); served WW II; *m* 20 Nov 1945 Joan Margaret (*d* 1993), only dau of Lt-Col Alfred Hacking, DSO, MC, of Sussex, and *d* 23 May 1996, leaving:

1d *Elizabeth Margaret [Miss Elizabeth Perceval, 11 Condover Park, Condover, Salop SY5 7DU]; *b* 14 July 1947

1c *Mary Leonora [Miss Mary Perceval, Armadale, Aston St, Aston Tirrold, Oxon OX11 9DJ]; *b* 17 Oct 1916

2b Edward, Lt KRRC; *b* 29 Jan 1877; *ka* Boer War 18 Feb 1900

1b Margaret; *b* 3 June 1870; *d* unm 1943

1a Isabel Jane; *m* 30 April 1851 Arthur Armitage, of Ross, Herefs, and *d* 27 Dec 1921 aged 91, leaving issue. He *d* 1892

(5) John Thomas, Capt 1st Foot Gds; *b* 14 Feb 1803; *m* 31 March 1834 Anna (*d* 23 Jan 1883), dau of Thomas Gardner, and *d* 28 Feb 1876, having had issue, with two other daus (*d* unm):

1a Alice Frederica; *b* 1836; *d* unm 10 June 1941

2a Selina Maria; *m* 23 June 1870 Sir Horatio George Walpole, KCB, and *d* 5 Nov 1925, leaving issue (*see* WALPOLE, B)

(6) Ernest Augustus, of Seven House, Henbury, Glos, and Longwitton Hall, Morpeth, Northumberland; Capt 15th Hus; *b* 17 May 1807; *m* 13 May 1830 his cousin Beatrice (*d* 19 March 1898), 4th dau of Sir John Trevelyan, 5th Bt, of Nettlecombe (*qv*), and *d* 19 Jan 1896, having had, with two other sons and six daus:

1a Ernest Augustus, of Longwitton Hall; Capt 88th Foot Crimea (medal with clasp for Sebastopol, Turkish medal, 5th Cl Medjidie) and Indian Mutiny (medal with clasp); *b* 28 March 1835; *d* 14 March 1924

2a Spencer George; *b* 8 July 1838; *educ* Trin Hall Cambridge (BA); *d* 7 March 1922

3a Alfred Spencer; *b* 14 July 1843; *m* 8 Sept 1881 Agnes Laura (*d* 1 Nov 1921), 3rd dau of Rev Augustus James Tharp, Rector Snailwell with Chippenham, and gdau of John Tharp, of Chippenham Park, Cambs, and *d* 11 March 1935

4a Cecil Henry Spencer; *b* 8 May 1849; *m* 24 Jan 1895 Henrietta Mary Murray (*d* 11 April 1936), 2nd dau of Rev Jermyn Pratt, of Ryston Hall, Norfolk, and *d* 8 May 1920

(1) Jane; *m* 20 March 1821 her cousin Hon Edward Perceval (*see* above) and *dsp* 13 Jan 1824

(2) Isabella; *m* Rt Hon Spencer Horatio Walpole (*see* WALPOLE, B) and *d* 16 July 1886

2 Mary; *m* 2 April 1781 Andrew Berkeley Drummond, of Cadland, Hants (*see* PERTH, E) and *d* 18 Sept 1839, leaving issue

3 Frances; *m* 6 June 1803 1st Baron Redesdale (*qv*) and *d* 22 Aug 1817 leaving issue

4 Margaret; *m* 1 Dec 1803 Thomas Walpole, Amb Bavaria (*see* WALPOLE, B) and *d* 12 Dec 1854

EGREMONT, LECONFIELD and

Arms: Azure a chevron between three lion's heads erased or within a bordure wavy of the last. **Crest:** A lion's head erased or within a fetterlock, the lock gold, and the bow counter-company or and azure, the head charged with a saltire wavy gules. **Supporters:** Dexter, a winged lion azure, wings inverted and plain collared or; sinister, a griffin argent guttée de sang, plain collared gules. **Motto:** *Au bon, droit* ('To what is just and what is right'). **Creations:** B. (UK) 14 April 1859 (Leconfield of Leconfield) and 27 Nov 1963 (Egremont).

THE 2ND BARON EGREMONT, of Petworth, Co Sussex, and **7th Baron Leconfield of Leconfield**, in the East Riding of Co York ((John) Max Henry Scawen Wyndham, DL (W Sussex)) [The Rt Hon The Lord Egremont DL, Petworth House, West Sussex GU28 0AE]; *b* 21 April 1948; *s* f 1972; *educ* Eton and Ch Ch Coll Oxford; Tstee Wallace Collection 1988– and Br Museum 1990–, memb Roy Commn Historical MSS. 1989–, Chm: Friends Nat Libraries 1985 and Sussex Branch CPRE, author (as Max Egremont): *The Cousins* (1977), *Balfour* (1980), *The Ladies' Man* (1983), *Dear Shadows* (1986), *Painted Lives* (1989), *Second Spring* (1993) and *Under Two Flags: The Life of Major General Sir Edward Spears* (1997); *m* 1978 *(Audrey) Caroline, er dau of Alexander Ronan Nelson, of Muckairn, Taynuilt, Argyll, and Hon Lady Musker (*see* 1949 edn QUEENBOROUGH, B), and has issue:

1 +GEORGE RONAN VALENTINE; *b* 31 July 1983

1 *Jessica Mary; *b* 1979

2 *Constance Rose; *b* 1980

3 *Mary Christian; *b* 1985

Lineage (of Windham/Wyndham): Sir JOHN WINDHAM, of Orchard Windham, Somerset, and Felbrigg, Norfolk; *b c* 1559; *d* 1 April 1645, leaving, with eight yr sons:

JOHN WINDHAM, of Orchard Windham; *m* Catharine, sis of 1st and last Baron Hopton of Stratton (the celebrated royalist cdr in the West Counry during the Civil War) and dau of Robert Hopton, of Witham, Somerset, and *d* by May 1649, leaving:

Sir WILLIAM WINDHAM, 1st Bt (E), so *cr* 9 Dec 1661 (having been earlier *cr* a Bt by OLIVER CROMWELL 28 Aug 1658 but this being revoked after the Restoration); *b c* 1633; *educ* Lincoln's Inn; MP Somerset 1656–58 and Taunton 1660, 1660–61 and 1661–79, ktd in or after April 1600 but before April 1661; *m c* 21 April 1656 Frances, dau of Anthony Hungerford, of Farley Castle, Wilts (*see* SAINT DAVIDS, V), and *d* 29 Oct 1683, leaving an only surv s:

Sir EDWARD WYNDHAM, 2nd Bt; *b c* 1667; MP Ilchester 1685–87, 1689–90 and 1690–95; *m* 16 May or possibly in June 1687 Catharine, sis of Sir William Leveson-Gower, 4th Bt (*see* SUTHERLAND, D) and was *bur* 29 June 1695, leaving an only s:

Sir WILLIAM WYNDHAM, 3rd Bt, PC (1713); *b c* 1688; *educ* Ch Ch Oxford; MP (Tory) Somerset 1710–40, Master Buckhounds 1719, Sec at War 1712–13, Chllr Exchequer 1713–14; imprisoned Tower of London as a Jacobite 1715 but let out on bail July 1716 and never tried due to intercession by his f-in-law 6th Duke of Somerset (*see* below); *m* 1st 15 July 1708 Lady Catharine Seymour (*d* 9 April 1731), sis of 7th Duke of Somerset (*qv*), who was *cr* 1749 EARL OF EGREMONT (GB), with remainder to his nephew (*see* **Lineage (of Seymour)** below); *m* 2nd 1 June 1734 Maria Catherina, dau of Peter de Jonge, of Utrecht, and widow of William Godolphin, Marquess of Blandford (*see* MARLBOROUGH, D), and *d* 17 July 1740, leaving:

1 Sir CHARLES WYNDHAM, 4th Bt, and 2nd EARL OF EGREMONT, PC (1761); *b* 19 Aug 1710; *educ* Westminster and Ch Ch Oxford; MP (Tory) Bridgewater 1735–41, Appleby (Tory to 1743, Whig thereafter) 1741–47 and Taunton 1747–50; Sec of State Southern Dept 1761–63, Ld Lt Cumberland 1751–59 and Sussex 1762–63, custos rotulorum Cumberland 1751–63, V-Adml Cumberland 1755–63; *m* 12 March 1750/1 Hon Alicia Maria Carpenter (*m* 2nd 6 June 1767 Hans Moritz, Count von Brühl, Saxon Amb, and *d* 1 June 1794; *see* also POLWARTH, L), dau of 2nd Baron Carpenter of Killaghy and sis of 1st Earl of Tyrconnel, and *d* 21 Aug 1763, having had issue:

(1) Sir GEORGE O'BRIEN WYNDHAM, 5th Bt, and 3rd and last EARL OF EGREMONT; *b* 18 Dec 1751; *educ* Westminster, Eton and Ch Ch Oxford; owned 110,000 acres in W of England, Cumberland, Yorkshire, Ireland and W Sussex; a leader in ag improvement; Col Sussex Yeo 1794; Ld Lt and custos rotulorum Sussex 1819–35, V-Adml Sussex 1820–31, FRS 1797, FSA 1800; *m* 16 July 1801 Elizabeth (*d* 30 Dec 1822), dau of Rev — Iliffe, of Westminster Sch, and *dspml* 11 Nov 1837, having had by her within wedlock a dau (Elizabeth, *d* an infant 1803) and by her born before their marriage:

1a GEORGE, **1st Baron**

2a Henry (Sir), KCB; *b* 12 May 1790; inherited the Cockermouth and Egremont estates in Cumberland; Ensign 1st Foot Gds 1806, ADC to 1st Duke of Wellington (*qv*) in Portugal (Battles of Rolica and Vimiero) 1808, Sir John Moore's Staff (Retreat to Corunna) 1809, Capt 10th Hus and Maj 8th Portuguese Cav 1811, Maj 60th Regt 1813, Capt Coldstream Gds, fought Waterloo 1815, Lt-Gen; MP; *m* Elizabeth (*d* 1827), est dau of Lord Charles Somerset (*see* BEAUFORT, D), and *dsp* 3 Aug 1860

3a Charles, of Rogate, Sussex; *b* 1796; Cornet 7th Hus 1811, Col; *m* Hon Elizabeth Anne (*d* 21 Aug 1873), 3rd dau of 6th Lord Polwarth (*qv*), and *d* 18 Feb 1866, leaving issue

1a Frances; *m* 4 July 1808 Sir Charles Merrik Burrell, 3rd Bt (*qv*), and *d* 28 Sept 1848

2a Mary; *m* 18 Oct 1819 1st Earl of Munster (*qv*), and *d* 3 Dec 1842

3a Charlotte; *m* July 1823 John James King, of Coates Castle, Sussex

(1) (cont.) It has been suggested that the 3rd Earl was f of 2nd Viscount Melbourne of Kilmore, PM 1834 and 1835–41; Melbourne's mother was certainly at one time his mistress

(2) Percy Charles; *b* 3 Sept 1757; *d* unm 5 Aug 1823

(3) Charles William; *b* 8 Oct 1760; *dsp* 8 July 1828

(4) William Frederick; *b* 6 April 1763; *m* 21 July 1784 Frances Mary Harford, illegitimate dau of Frederick Calvert, 6th and last Baron Baltimore (*dspl* 4 Sept 1771), and *d* 11 Feb 1828, having had issue:

1a Sir GEORGE WYNDHAM, 6th and last Bt, and 4th and last EARL OF EGREMONT; *b* 30 Aug 1786; RN: joined 1799, Capt 1812; *m* 14 Nov 1820 Jane, dau of Rev William Roberts, V-Provost Eton, and *dsp* 2 April 1845, when his titles expired

1a Frances; *m* 1st George Miller; *m* 2nd Vicomte de Valmer

2a Laura; *m* Rev Charles Boultbee

3a Julia; *d* unm 1811

(1) Elizabeth; *m* 1st Earl of Carnarvon (*qv*)

(2) Frances; *m* 1st Earl of Romney (*qv*)

The 3rd EARL's est illegitimate son,

GEORGE WYNDHAM, **1st Baron Leconfield of Leconfield**, in the East Riding of Co York (UK), so *cr* 14 April 1859; *b* 5 June 1787; midshipman HMS *Amelia* 1799, Cornet 5th Dragoon Gds 1802, Lt 3rd Dragoon Gds 1803, Capt 72nd Highrs and ADC to Sir Eyre Coote (Lt-Govr Jamaica) 1805, DAAG to 1st Earl Cathcart (*qv*) (bombardment of Copenhagen) 1807, Lt and Capt 1st Foot Gds (Walcheren Expdn) 1809, Maj 78th Regt and 12th Light Dragoons 1811, Lt-Col 20th Light Dragoons (Siege of Ciudad Rodrigo) 1812; *m* 25 April 1815 Mary Fanny (*d* 23 May 1863), only dau of Rev William Blunt, of Crabbett, Sussex, and *d* 18 March 1869, leaving, with other issue:

1 HENRY, **2nd Baron**

2 Percy Scawen, of Clouds, Wilts, JP and DL (Sussex, Wilts and Cumberland); *b* 30 Jan 1835; Capt Coldstream Gds; MP W Cumberland 1860–85, High Sheriff

Wilts 1896; *m* 16 Oct 1860 Madeline Caroline Frances Eden (*d* 8 March 1920), 6th dau of Maj-Gen Sir Guy Campbell, 1st Bt, and *d* 13 March 1911, leaving:

(1) George, of Clouds, PC, JP Cheshire; *b* 29 Aug 1863; Coldstream Gds, Suakin Expdn 1885, Lt-Col Cheshire Yeo; DCL Oxford and LLD Glasgow, Hon LLD Edinburgh; MP (C) Dover 1889–1913, U-Sec War 1898–1900, Ch Sec Ireland 1900–05; Ld Rector Glasgow U 1902 and Edinburgh U 1908; *m* 7 Feb 1887 Sibell Mary (*d* 4 Feb 1929), dau of 9th Earl of Scarbrough (*qv*) and widow of Earl Grosvenor (*see* WESTMINSTER, D), and *d* 8 June 1913, leaving:

1a Percy Lyulph, of Clouds; *b* 5 Dec 1887; Lt Coldstream Gds WW I; *m* 17 April 1913 Hon Diana Lister (*m* 2nd 1918 Capt Arthur Edward Capel, CBE, Legn Hon (*d* 22 Dec 1919), s of Arthur Capel; *m* 3rd 7 June 1923 14th Earl of Westmorland (*qv*)), yst dau of 4th Baron Ribblesdale (*see* 1924 edn), and was *ka sp* 12 Sept 1914

(2) Guy Percy, CB (1913), MVO (1908); *b* 19 Jan 1865; Col 16th Lancers S African War 1899–1902 (two medals with seven clasps, despatches three times, brevet), Mil Attaché St Petersburg 1906–11 (Order St Anne Russia 2nd Cl), AAG War Office 1913–1918; *m* 1st 14 May 1892 Edwina Virginia Joanna (*d* 4 Oct 1919), dau of Rev Frederick Fitzpatrick, Rector Cloone, Co Leitrim, and widow of John Monck Brooke, and had issue:

1a George Heremon; *b* 25 Oct 1893; WW I as Lt 3rd Bn Devonshire Regt; *ka* unm 24 March 1915

2a Guy Richard Charles, MC; *b* 29 Aug 1896; *educ* Wellington; Capt KRRC WW I (wounded), WW II as Maj 56th Searchlight Regt (TA), Coronation Medal 1937; *m* 1st 20 Oct 1920 (*divorce* 1925) Iris Winifred Youell, only dau of Andrew Percy Bennett, CMG, Br Min Panama and Costa Rica, of 5 Devonshire Place, London W, and had issue:

1b *Joan Olivia; *b* 11 Oct 1921; *m* 1st 5 Dec 1947 (*divorce* 1952) Maurice Stansbury Rowdon, s of William James Rowdon, of Wandsworth, and has:

1c *Clare Viola; *b* 1947; *m* 19– *J Soares

1b (cont.) Mrs Joan Rowdon *m* 2nd 1952 *Alexander (Shura) Shivarg, and by him has:

2c *Camilla Gabrielle [Ms Camilla Shivarg, 34 Edith Grove, London SW10]; *b* 1953

2a (cont.) Maj Guy Wyndham *m* 2nd (*divorce* 1963) Grethe, dau of G Wulfsberg, of Bergen, Norway, and was *k* Palestine 19 May 1948, leaving by her:

2b *Ingrid Olivia Georgia; *m* 1st 25 July 1951 (*divorce* 1963) 3rd Baron Moyne; (*qv*) and has issue; *m* 2nd 7 Aug 1963 *Baron Kelvedon (*qv*), and has further issue

1a Olivia Madeline Grace Mary; *m* 23 April 1930 (*divorce* 1931) Howland Spencer, of New York

(2) (cont.) Col Guy Wyndham *m* 2nd 11 June 1923 Violet Lutetia, dau of Ernest Leverson, of Mayfair, and *d* 15 April 1941, leaving by her:

3a +Francis Guy Percy [Francis Wyndham Esq, 530A Harrow Rd, London W9 3QF]; *b* 2 July 1924; *educ* Eton and Ch Ch Oxford

4a +Hugh Guy Osbert [Hugh Wyndham Esq, 64 Osborne St, Swindon, Wilts]; *b* 24 Feb 1926; *educ* Eton and Corpus Christi Coll, Oxford; Lt Coldstream Gds; *m* 8 June 1961 (*divorce* 1966) (Edith) Elizabeth Creswick, er dau of John Watson, FRIBA, of Old Mains, Giffnock, Glasgow, and has:

1b *Rachel Olivia Violet Wyndham; *b* 1 April 1963

(1) Mary Constance; *m* 9 Aug 1883 11th Earl of Wemyss (*qv*) and *d* 29 April 1937, having had issue

(2) Madeline Constance Blanche, CBE (1937), JP Cambs; CA Cambs; *m* 23 July 1888 Charles Adeane, CB (*d* 11 Feb 1943), of Babraham, Cambs, and *d* 31 July 1941, having had issue

(3) Pamela Adelaide Genevieve; *m* 1st 11 July 1895 1st Baron Glenconner (*qv*) and had issue; *m* 2nd 4 June 1922 1st Viscount Grey of Fallodon (*see* GREY, E) and *d* 18 Nov 1928

1 Fanny Charlotte; *m* 12 Oct 1842 Alfred Montgomery, s of Sir Henry Conyngham Montgomery, 1st Bt, and *d* 27 Jan 1893 aged 72

2 Blanche Julia, CIA, VA; *m* 31 Oct 1838 6th Earl of Mayo (*qv*) and *d* 31 Jan 1918, leaving issue

3 Caroline Sophia; *m* 13 March 1851 Sir Robert Nigel Fitzhardinge Kingscote, GCVO, KCB, MP W Gloucester (*d* 22 Sept 1908), and *dsp* 19 March 1852

4 Constance Elizabeth; *m* 28 April 1859 Lt-Col William Mure (*d* 9 Nov 1880), of Caldwell, Ayrshire, Scots Fus Gds, MP, and *d* 21 Jan 1920 leaving issue

The 1st BARON's er s,

HENRY WYNDHAM, **2nd Baron Leconfield of Leconfield**, JP, DL Sussex; *b* 31 July 1830; Capt 1st Life Gds; V-Chm and Alderman W Sussex CC, MP (C) W Sussex 1854–69; *m* 15 July 1867 Lady Constance Evelyn Primrose (*d* 1939), 2nd dau of Archibald Primrose, Lord Dalmeny, est s of 4th Earl of Rosebery (*qv*), and *d* 6 Jan 1901, having had:

1 George O'Brien; *b* 17 Nov 1868; Lt Gren Gds; *d* unm 13 Jan 1895

2 CHARLES HENRY WYNDHAM, **3rd Baron Leconfield of Leconfield**, GCVO (1935), JP (Sussex and Cumberland); *b* 17 Feb 1872; *educ* Winchester; Lt 1st Life Gds; CA West Sussex (formerly Chm CC), Ld Lt and custos rotulorum Sussex 1917–49, Pres Sussex TAA, Master Lord Leconfield's Foxhounds 1901–42; *m* 8 Nov 1911 Beatrice Violet (*d* 22 May 1956), er dau of Col Richard Hamilton Rawson JP, DL, MP, of Gravenhurst, Sussex, by Lady Beatrice Anson, dau of 2nd Earl of Lichfield (*qv*), and *dsp* 17 April 1952

3 William Reginald; *b* 16 March 1876; 1st Life Gds, formerly Lt 17th Lancers; *ka* unm 6 Nov 1914

4 HUGH ARCHIBALD WYNDHAM, **4th Baron Leconfield of Leconfield**; *b* 4 Oct 1877; *educ* Eton and New Coll Oxford (BA); FSA, FRHistS; WW I in S African Forces (despatches), Order Star of Italian Solidarity 2nd Cl; *m* 25 Feb 1908 Hon Maud Mary Lyttelton (*d* 22 June 1953), est dau of 8th Viscount Cobham (*qv*), and *dsp* 6 July 1963

5 EDWARD SCAWEN, **5th Baron**

6 Everard Humphrey, MC (1919); *b* 4 Dec 1888; *educ* Eton; WW I (despatches); Col cmdg Life Gds, AAG Northern Cmd 1937–40, Brig Gen Staff War Off 1940, ret 1942, ADC to HM GEORGE VI 1938–42; *m* 14 April 1920 Ruth Constance (*d* 1984), only dau of Hubert Delaval Astley (*see* HASTINGS, B), and *d* 1970, having had issue:

(1) David Francis; *b* 13 Dec 1922; *educ* Eton; WW II, Lt KRRC; *ka* Normandy 16 Aug 1944

(2) +Michael Patrick [Michael Wyndham Esq, Quarry House, Ampney Crucis, Glos GL7 5RP]; *b* 10 June 1929; *educ* Eton; Capt Life Gds; *m* 1st 20 June 1957 Shelagh Anne (*d* 1967), dau of Dr Sydenham Frederick Moore, OBE, of Cairo, and formerly w of H Michael Barker, and has:

1a *Samantha Madeline; *b* 3 Jan 1962

2a *Georgina Maria; *b* 9 July 1963; *m* 1990 *Jimmy G Penfold, s of Graham Penfold, and has:

1b *Alexander Michael James; *b* 1989

1b *Jessica Lara Anastasia; *b* 1992

(2) (cont.) Michael Wyndham *m* 2nd 1967 Mrs Laura Prudence Rosamund Murray (*d* 1983), dau of Mervyn Stutchbury and formerly w of Christopher Mark Henry Murray (*see* 1935 edn JERNINGHAM Bt); *m* 3rd 1985 *Alison, dau of Sir Reay Geddes, KBE, and formerly w of Martin Dean

(1) *Mary Constance; *b* 12 Feb 1921; *m* 1st 20 June 1945 (*divorce* 1966) Ralph Hamilton Cobbold (*d* 1987), only s of Col Ralph Patteson Cobbold-Sawle, DSO, of Penrice, St Austell, Cornwall, and has:

1a *David Anthony [David Cobbold Esq, 13 Blvd des Frères Voisin, Paris 75015, France]; *b* 5 Oct 1946; *educ* Eton; *m* 1972 (*divorce* 1982) Christine Elisabeth Pearcey and has:

1b *Melissa Eve; *b* 1975

1a *Charlotte Ruth [Ms Charlotte Cobbold, 1 York Villas, Springfield Rd, Uplands, Stroud, Glos GL5 1TP]; *b* 20 Aug 1949; *m* 1st 1979 (*divorce* 1984) George Michael Maguire and has:

1b *Leo George; *b* 1981

1a (cont.) Mrs Charlotte Maguire *m* 2nd 1993 *David Thomas Williams and has by him, though keeping her maiden name:

2b *Rafe Thomas; *b* 1993

(1) (cont.) *Mrs Mary Cobbold *m* 2nd 27 July 1966 *Baron Peyton of Yeovil (LP, *qv*)

1 Mary Caroline; *b* 17 Nov 1870; *m* 18 Dec 1899 Gen Sir Frederick Ivor Maxse, KCB, CVO, DSO, and *d* 21 Jan 1944, leaving issue (*see* BERKELEY, B)

2 Maud Evelyn; *b* 1 Sept 1874; *m* 24 Aug 1899 Vincent Wodehouse Yorke and *d* 23 July 1963, leaving issue (*see* HARDWICKE E)

3 Margaret Blanche; *b* 9 Oct 1879; Woman Bedchamber to HM QUEEN MARY 1938–51, Extra Woman Bedchamber 1951–53; *d* unm 26 Feb 1965

The 4th BARON's surv bro,

EDWARD SCAWEN WYNDHAM, **5th Baron Leconfield of Leconfield**, DSO (1914), JP; *b* 30 April 1883; Col Life Gds WW I (wounded, despatches, brevet), served WW II; *m* 14 Oct 1907 Gladys Mary , only dau of Fitzroy James Wilberforce Farquhar (*see* FARQUHAR, Bt), and *d* 1967, having had:

1 Henry Scawen; *b* 3 Nov 1915; *educ* Eton; Lt 9th Lancers WW II; *ka* unm El Alamein 29 Oct 1942

2 JOHN EDWARD REGINALD, **6th/1st Baron**

3 +Mark Hugh, OBE, MC [The Hon Mark Wyndham OBE MC, Newmans Cottage, Froxfield Green, Petersfield, Hants]; *b* 7 Aug 1921; *educ* Eton; Capt 12th Roy Lancers WW II Middle East, Italy 1943–45 and Palestine 1946 (twice wounded); Chm C of E Children's Soc 1967–82; *m* 1st 21 Jan 1947 (*divorce* 1982) Anne, yst dau of Hon Reginald Henry Winn (*see* SAINT OSWALD, B), and has:

(1) +Henry Mark [Henry Wyndham Esq, The Old Rectory, Southease, Lewes, E Sussex]; *b* 19 Aug 1953; *educ* Eton and Sorbonne, chm Sotheby's 1994–97, Sotheby's Europe 1997–; *m* 1978 *Rachel Sarah, yst dau of Leslie Gordon Francis Pritchard, MBE, TD (*see* WHELER, Bt), and has issue:

1a +Edward (Ned) Francis Reginald; *b* 1983

2a +Leo David; *b* 1985

3a +William Henry; *b* 1988

(1) *Elizabeth Jane; *b* 17 Jan 1948; *m* 1970 *Lord Charles George William Colin Spencer-Churchill (*see* MARLBOROUGH, D)

(2) *Melissa Anne; *b* 18 March 1949

3 (cont.) The Hon Mark Wyndham *m* 2nd 1986 *Patricia, yr dau of Lt-Col Esmond Charles Baring, OBE (*see* ASHBURTON B), and formerly w of Maj Henry Claude Lyon Garnett, CBE

1 Ursula Constance; *b* 20 Sept 1913; *d* unm 1995

The 5th BARON's er surv s,

JOHN EDWARD REGINALD WYNDHAM, **1st Baron Egremont**, of Petworth, Co Sussex (UK), so *cr* 27 Nov 1963, and **6th Baron Leconfield of Leconfield**, MBE; *b* 5 June 1920; unpaid Priv Sec to PM 1957–63; *m* 1947 *Pamela [The Rt Hon The Dowager Lady Egremont, Cockermouth Castle, Cockermouth, Cumbria], yst dau of Capt Hon Valentine Wyndham-Quinn, RN (*see* DUNRAVEN AND MOUNT-EARL, E), and *d* 1973, leaving:

1 (JOHN) MAX HENRY SCAWEN WYNDHAM, **2nd and present Baron Egremont (and 7th and present Baron Leconfield)**

2 +Harry Hugh Patrick; *b* 28 Sept 1957; *educ* Eton; *m* 1985 *Susan Fiona McLean, est dau of Bruce Woodall, of Kensington, and has:

(1) +Alexander; *b* 1986

(2) +Richard; *b* 1990

1 *Caroline Elizabeth; *b* 23 December 1951; *m* 1976 *Colin Chisholm, son of Archibald Hugh Tennent Chisholm, CBE, and has issue:

(1) *Hugh Archibald John; *b* 1976

(2) *Mark Colin; *b* 1980

(1) *Laura Carlyn; *b* 1978

Lineage (of Percy/Seymour): ELIZABETH Percy (*see* NORTHUMBERLAND, D); *b* 26 Jan 1666/7; *m* 3rd 20 May 1682, as his 1st w, Charles SEYMOUR, 6th Duke of Somerset (*qv*), and *d* 23 Nov 1722, having had by him (with three other sons and another dau):

1 ALGERNON SEYMOUR, 1st EARL OF EGREMONT, so *cr* 3 Oct 1749, as also BARON COCKERMOUTH, both Co Cumberland (and both GB), with a special

remainder, failing heirs male of his body, to his nephew Sir CHARLES WYNDHAM, 4th Bt (*see* above), and the latter's issue male, failing whom to his other nephew Percy Wyndham later O'Brien, Earl of Thomond, they being sons of his sis, Lady Katharine; Lord Egremont was also 7th Duke of Somerset and 1st Earl of Northumberland; *b* 11 Nov 1684; *m* Frances, dau of Hon Henry Thynne (*see* BATH, M), and *dspms* 7 Feb 1749/50

1 Elizabeth; *m* 4 June 1707 8th and last Earl of Thomond (*see* INCHIQUIN, B) and *dsp* 2 April 1734

2 Katharine; *m* Sir WILLIAM WYNDHAM, 3rd Bt (*see* above), and had:

(1) CHARLES (Sir), 4th Bt, and 2nd EARL

(2) PERCY WYNDHAM later WYNDHAM-O'BRIEN (under terms of will of his unc the last Earl of Thomond), 1st and last EARL OF THOMOND, so *cr* 11 Dec 1756, as also BARON IBRACKAN (both I), PC (1757); *b c* 1723; *educ* St Mary Hall Oxford; MP (Tory) Taunton 1745–47, Minehead 1747–54 and 1761–68, Cockermouth 1754–61 and Winchelsea 1768–74, a Ld Treasury 1755–56, Treasurer Household 1757–61, Cofferer Household 1761–65, Ld Lt Somerset 1764–73; *d* unm 21 July 1774, when his titles expired

(1) Elizabeth; *m* Rt Hon George Grenville, 2nd s of Countess Temple (*see* TEMPLE OF STOWE, E) in her own right

Seat: Petworth House, Petworth, W Sussex. Though closely associated with the 3rd Earl of Egremont, who was J W Turner's patron, and to honour whom his protégé painted the celebrated views of the house and grounds, Petworth was a Percy property to begin with. All that remains visible of the early structure is a medieval chapel (though a medieval spiral staircase was discovered during renovation work in early 1998), the present building dating almost entirely from the short reigns of JAMES II and his elder daughter MARY, when the 6th Duke of Somerset (*see* above) commissioned a complete new building from an architect or architects unknown. Appropriately, since JAMES eventually settled in France and MARY married a Dutchman, the sole internal feature to date from then, the marble hall, is a medley of French and Dutch ornamental features attributed to a Huguenot, Daniel Marot. Another hall, from which the staircase rises, has Laguerre murals, while the Grinling Gibbons room is a masterpiece of wood-carving by that craftsman. It is the paintings, chiefly the Van Dycks in the square dining-room decorated in the 3rd Earl of Egremont's time and the Beauty Room, with its Kneller and Dahl portraits of belles of Queen Anne's day, that are the most celebrated feature of Petworth. Nevertheless the collection of sculptures from antiquity that Lord Egremont built up was in his own day just as famous.

ELDON

Arms: Arg. an anchor erect sa. between three lion's heads erased gu.; on a chief wavy az. a portcullis with chains or. **Crest:** A lion's head erased gu., gorged with a chain and therefrom a portcullis pendant or. **Supporters:** On either side a lion guardant ppr., gorged with a double chain, a portcullis attached thereto, from which is suspended a shield arg., charged with a civic wreath vert. **Motto:** *Sit sine labe decus* ('Let honour be without stain'). **Creation:** E. and V. (UK) 7 July 1821, B. (GB) 18 July 1799.

THE 5TH EARL OF ELDON, Co Durham, **Viscount Encombe**, of Encombe, Co Dorset, and **Baron Eldon**, of Eldon, Co Durham (John Joseph Nicholas Scott) [The Rt Hon The Earl of Eldon, House of Lords, London SW1A 0PW]; *b* 24 April 1937; *s f* 1976; *educ* Ampleforth and Trin Coll Oxford; late 2nd Lt Scots Gds, Lt Army Emergency Reserve; *m* 1 July 1961 *Countess Claudine Maria Olga Columba Fidelis, yst dau of Count Franz von Montjoye-Vaufrey et de la Roche, of Hasenauerstrasse 45, Vienna 18 (France *cr* 1736), and has issue:

1 +JOHN FRANCIS THOMAS MARIE JOSEPH COLUMBA FIDELIS, *Viscount Encombe*; *b* 9 July 1962; *educ* Ampleforth

1 *Tatiana Maria Laura Rose Columba Fidelis; *b* 26 June 1967; *m* 1989 *Anthony C Wilson, est s of Jeffery Graham Wilson, of Northwood, Middx

2 *Victoria Laura Maria Magdalene; *b* 9 Sept 1968

Lineage: WILLIAM SCOTT, of Newcastle-upon-Tyne, broker between coal- and shipowners; *m* Jane (*d* 1800 aged 92), dau of Henry Atkinson and gdau of John Lawson, of Longhirst, Northumberland, and *d* 1776, leaving, with another dau (*d* unm):

1 WILLIAM SCOTT, 1st and last BARON STOWELL OF STOWELL PARK, Co Gloucester (UK), so *cr* 17 July 1821, PC (1798); *b* 17 Oct 1745; *educ* Roy GS Newcastle and Corpus Christi Coll Oxford; Fell Univ Coll 1765 and Tutor 1765–76, Camden Reader Ancient History 1773–85, DCL 1779; barrister Middle Temple 1780, Bencher 1794, Reader 1799, Treas 1807, Admlty Advocate 1782–88, Registrar Court Faculties 1783, King's Advocate-Gen 1788–98, ktd 1788, Judge Consistory Court London and Vicar-Gen Province Canterbury 1788–1821, MP (Tory) Downton 1790–1801 and Oxford U 1801–21, Judge High Court Admlty 1798–1828, Memb BOT 1798–1836; *m* 1st 1782 Anna Maria, est dau and coheir of John Bagnall, of Erleigh Court, Berks; *m* 2nd 1813 Louisa Catherine, widow of 1st Marquess of Sligo (*qv*), and *d* 28 Jan 1836, leaving issue by his 1st w (with a son, *d* unm):

(1) Marianne; *m* 1st 1809 Thomas Townshend, of Honington, Warwicks; *m* 2nd 1823 1st Viscount Sidmouth (*qv*) and *dsp* April 1842

2 Henry; *s* to his f's business; *m* Mary, dau of John Cook, of Togston, and *d* 1779, leaving issue:

(1) Mary; *m* 1794 Joseph Forster, of Seaton Burn

3 JOHN, **1st Earl**

1 Jane; *m* Sir Thomas Burdon and *d* 1822

The 3rd son,

JOHN SCOTT, **1st Earl of Eldon**, Co Durham, so *cr* 7 July 1821, as also VISCOUNT ENCOMBE, of Encombe, Co Dorset (both UK), and earlier 18 July 1799 BARON ELDON, of Eldon, Co Durham (GB), PC (1799), KC (1783); *b* 4 June 1751; *educ* Roy GS Newcastle and Univ Coll Oxford (Fell 1767, BA 1770, MA 1773, DCL 1801, High Steward 1801–38); barrister Middle Temple 1776, MP ((High) Tory) Weobley 1783–96 and Boroughbridge 1796–99, Slr-Gen 1788, ktd 1788, Attorney-Gen 1793–99, Ld Ch Justice Court Common Pleas 1799, Ld Chllr 1801–06 and 1807–27, FRS 1793, FSA 1792; *m* 19 Nov 1772 Elizabeth (*d* 28 June 1831), est dau of Aubone Surtees, banker, of Newcastle-upon-Tyne, and Hedley, and *d* 13 Jan 1838, having had, with other issue:

1 John; *b* 8 March 1774; *m* 22 Aug 1804 Henrietta Elizabeth (*m* 2nd James William Farrer, of Ingleborough, Yorks, Master in Chancery), only dau of Sir Matthew White-Ridley, 2nd Bt (*see* RIDLEY, V), and *dvp* 24 Dec 1805, leaving:

(1) JOHN, **2nd Earl**

1 Elizabeth; *m* 27 Nov 1817 George Stanley Repton, architect and landscape gardener, 4th s of Humphrey Repton, the celebrated landscape gardener, also an architect, of Hove, and Aylsham, Norfolk, and *d* 16 April 1862, having had issue. He *d* 29 June 1858

2 Frances Jane; *m* 6 April 1820 Rev Edward Bankes, of Soughton Hall, Flint, and *d* 6 Aug 1838, leaving issue. He *d* 24 May 1867

The 1st EARL's gs,

JOHN SCOTT, **2nd Earl of Eldon**; *b* 10 Dec 1805; *educ* Winchester and New Coll Oxford; MP (Tory) Truro 1829–32, DCL 1834; ajudged insane 1853; *m* 1 Oct 1831 Hon Louisa Duncombe (*d* 18 Nov 1852), dau of 1st Baron Feversham (*qv*), and had issue:

1 JOHN, **3rd Earl**

1 Charlotte Elizabeth; *m* 9 Oct 1856 her cousin Preb Eldon Surtees Bankes and *d* 22 Feb 1864, leaving issue. He *d* 1 Feb 1915

2 Augusta Henrietta; *m* 9 Sept 1859 2nd Baron Cottesloe (*qv*) and *d* 4 Nov 1906, leaving issue

3 Katherine Frances; *m* 2 Sept 1858 8th Viscount Boyne (*qv*), and *d* 30 Dec 1907, leaving issue

4 Gertrude Louisa; *m* 18 Sept 1860 Lord Eustace Brownlow Henry Cecil, 3rd s of 2nd Marquess of Salisbury (*qv*), and *d* 30 April 1919, leaving issue

5 Selina Jane; *m* 10 Nov 1864 Nathaniel Bond, of Creech Grange, Dorset, and *d* 17 Dec 1891, leaving issue. He *d* 21 Aug 1910

6 Rachel Adela; *d* 11 Dec 1869

The 2nd EARL *d* 18 Sept 1854; his son,

JOHN SCOTT, **3rd Earl of Eldon**, JP Dorset, Glos; CA Glos, Hon Col 1st Dorset Roy Vols; *b* 8 Nov 1845; *m* 1 July 1869 Henrietta Minna (*d* 30 Aug 1921), est dau of Capt Henry Turnor (*see* MACDONALD, B), and had issue:

1 John, *Viscount Encombe*, BA Oxon; *b* 8 May 1870; *m* 25 May 1898 Hon Mary Laura Fraser (*d* 3 Dec 1946), dau of 13th Lord (Fraser of) Lovat (*qv*), and *d* 18 Aug 1900, leaving issue:

(1) JOHN, **4th Earl**

(2) Michael Simon, 2nd Lt Scots Gds (SR); *b* 1 April 1900; *educ* Ampleforth and New Coll Oxford; *m* 31 Dec 1928 Ruth (*d* 1972, having *m* 2nd 6 June 1944 Lt-Cdr Adams Batcheller, Jr, who *d* 20 Feb 1951), 2nd dau of James Cox Brady, of Hamilton Farm, NJ, and *d* 4 Feb 1938, leaving issue:

1a +John; *b* 2 Oct 1929

2a Michael Richard; *b* 20 Aug 1937; *m* 25 Jan 1964 *Pamela Hanford [Mrs Marshall Jeanes, Long Lane, Far Hills, NJ 07931, USA] (*m* 2nd 19– Marshall Jeanes), dau of William Wellington Vandeveer, of Bernardsville, NJ, and *d* 1981, leaving issue:

1b +Michael Simon; *b* 6 May 1966

2b +Andrew Fraser; *b* 1973

1b *Wendy Vandeveer; *b* 15 April 1967

2b *Katherine Brady; *b* 1970

1a *Sheila Mary [Mrs Philip Smith, Box 176, Far Hills, NJ 07931, USA]; *b* 7 May 1932; *m* 26 June 1952 *Philip Webster Smith, Jr, s of Philip Webster Smith, of Far Hills, and has issue:

1b *Philip Webster III [Philip Smith III, Box 944, Far Hills, NJ 07931, USA]; *b* 1955; *m* 1983 *Hillary, dau of Vincent R Bailey, and has:

1c *Philip Webster IV; *b* 1988

1c *Courtney Converse; *b* 1986

2b *Michael Simon [Michael Smith, Box 56, Far Hills, NJ 07931, USA]; *b* 1959; *m* 1987 *Anne Marie, dau of Cornelius Murray, and has issue:

1c *Katherine Fraser; *b* 1989

2c *Elizabeth Clarke; *b* 1992

1b *Elizabeth Brady [Mrs Wayne Lawrence, 144 Larch Row, Wenham, Mass 01984, USA]; *b* 1954; *m* 1979 *Wayne Barry Lawrence, and has:

1c *Andrew Brady; *b* 1986

1c *Alexandra Webster; *b* 1984

2 Ernest Stowell (Sir), KCMG (1931), MVO (1905), JP Dorset; Envoy Extrdy and Min Plen Uruguay 1925–30; *b* 1 Nov 1872; *educ* Winchester; *m* 8 Dec 1941 Winifred Kathleen Brodrick (*d* 1990), and *d* 6 Nov 1953, leaving issue:

(1) *Anna [Mrs Thomas Pope, Stratton Mill, Stratton, Dorset]; *b* 1942; *m* 29 June 1963 *Thomas Cecil Rolph Pope, yr s of A C R Pope, of Wrackleford House, Dorchester

(2) *Margaret Rachel [Mrs Margaret Tennant, 19 Lambourn Rd, London SW4]; *b* 23 Nov 1943; *m* 3 Dec 1964 (*divorce* 1973) David Edward Wyndham Tennant (*see* GLENCONNER, B)

3 Osmund; WW I 1916–18 in RASC (MT), Dist Head Rotherfield Div Soldiers' and Sailors' Help Soc; *b* 24 March 1876; *educ* Winchester; *m* 12 Sept 1906 Mary Cecilia (*d* 20 Nov 1941), dau of Cdr Dudley Charles Stuart, RN (*see* BUTE, M), and *d* 9 Sept 1948, having had issue:

(1) Harold Eldon, JP (Dorset 1955), DL (1962); CC 1955 Dorset, Lt-Col QO Roy W Kent Regt WW II; *b* 4 Sept 1907; *educ* Winchester and RMC Sandhurst; *m* 7 April 1938 Daphne Josephine (*d* 1985), er dau of Col FitzHardinge Hancock, of Congham Hall, King's Lynn, Norfolk, *d* 30 Jan 1997, leaving:

1a +David Eldon [David Scott Esq, East Wing, Encombe House, Corfe Castle, Dorset BH20 5LQ]; *b* 25 July 1939; *educ* Winchester and RAC Cirencester; *m* 12 March 1966 *Clover, dau of His Honour Judge Sidney Henry Noakes, JP, and has:

1b +Rupert Eldon; *b* 1967

2b +Henry Eldon; *b* 1969

1a *Verena Mary; *b* 23 Nov 1942; *m* 15 June 1963 *Simon Norman Philips (*see* DUCIE, E) and has issue:

1b *Lucy Jane; *b* 1964

2b *Sophie Ann; *b* 1966

2a *Angela Lindsay [Countess Orssich, Mayfield, W Grafton, Wilts SN8 3BY]; *b* 30 March 1949; *m* 1st 1978 (*divorce* 1987) Daniel Sicardi and has:

1b *Rebecca Tania; *b* 1983

2a (cont.) Mrs Angela Sicardi *m* 2nd 1987 *Count Christopher Levin Orssich (*see* FARINGDON, B), and has issue:

1b *Nicholas Robert; *b* 1988

3a *Suzanne [Mrs Suzanne Wolozynska, 14 Brunswick St, Bath BA1 6PQ]; *b* 19 April 1952; *m* 1977 (*divorce* 1994) Peter Wolozynski, s of A Wolosynski, and has issue:

1b *Harry Maximilian Andrew; *b* 1982

1b *Emily; *b* 1980

(2) Osmund Stuart, WW II in Roy Signals; *b* 14 May 1909; *educ* Bradfield and Oxford; *d* 1985

(3) Alan Dudley, ARIBA, AA Dipl, Capt RE WW II; *b* 26 Sept 1910; *m* 5 Sept 1936 Dorothy Dulany (Thea) (*d* 1988, having *m* 2nd 8 Dec 1953 Major Alexander Soldatenkov, who *d* 14 April 1954), only dau of Lt-Col Sefton Dulany Brancker, and *d* 29 April 1951, leaving issue:

1a +Dudley John Eldon [Dudley Scott Esq, Patrijsstraat 49, 6971 VP Brummen, The Netherlands]; *b* 7 Jan 1939; *educ* Down House, Northiam; *m* 1st 25 March 1961 Irene Florence, only dau of Frederick James Smith; *m* 2nd 1982 *Annelies, dau of Jacobus Leonardus Arnoldus Hotz, and by his 1st w has issue:

1b +Alan James; *b* 1964

1b *Marion Lynn; *b* 1963

1a *Caroline Edith Mary [Mrs Anthony Garrett, 4 Castilian Mews, Ramleaze Drive, Shaw, Wilts SN5 9PR]; *b* 8 June 1946; *m* 1st 1969 (*divorce* 1984) Michael John Theobald; *m* 2nd 1992 *Anthony Terence Garrett and by her 1st husb has issue:

1b *Emma Caroline Mary; *b* 1975

2b *Amelia Margaret Jennifer; *b* 1978

2a *Jennifer Dorothy Dulany; *b* 6 Sept 1948

(4) +Eric Surtees, MBE (1945) [Lt-Col Eric Scott MBE, Pound House, Wareham, Dorset BH20 4LQ]; Lt-Col The Buffs WW II; *b* 20 May 1912; *educ* Bradfield and RMC Sandhurst; *m* 26 Sept 1938 *Rose Anne, only dau of Col Charles Edward Stewart, RA, and has issue:

1a +Michael Ian Eldon, CB (1997), CBE (1987), DSO (1982); CO 2nd Bn Scots Gds, Equerry to HRH THE DUKE OF GLOUCESTER 1965–66, Adj 2nd Bn Scots Gds 1966–68, ADC to Maj-Gen Earl Cathcart 1968–69, served S Atlantic Campaign 1982, cmded 8th Inf Bde NI 1984–86, RCDS 1987, Dep Mil Sec 1988, GOC Scotland and Govr Edinburgh Castle 1993–95, Mil Sec 1995–97; *b* 3 March 1941; *educ* Bradfield and RMA Sandhurst; *m* 22 March 1968 *Veronica Mary, yr dau of Capt J H Daniell and Mrs J A Hilton, of Chelsea, and has issue:

1b +Charles Daniell Eldon; *b* 25 April 1970

1b *Louisa Claire; *b* 1971

1a *Veronica Susan [Mrs Michael Phayre-Mudge, Wadmill Farm, Stour Row, Shaftesbury, Dorset]; *b* 6 Oct 1944; *m* 19 June 1965 Michael Conway Phayre-Mudge (*d* 1983), s of Col Albert Edward Phayre-Mudge, OBE, of Norfolk, and has issue:

1b *Marcus Andrew; *b* 14 April 1968

1b *Zoë Catherine; *b* 27 May 1970; *m* 16 Aug 1997 *Giles John Palmer

(5) Kenneth Bertram, MC; Maj Roy W Kent Regt SR WW II; *b* 17 Aug 1915; *m* 21 Oct 1939 Denise Primrose Garnet (Kim) (*m* 2nd 19 Oct 1952 Alun Blackwell and *d* 11 Sept 1968), 2nd dau of Garnet Leslie Clark, of Tadworth, Surrey, and was *ka* Sicily 9 Aug 1943, leaving issue:

1a +John Kenneth Eldon; *b* 8 Oct 1940; *educ* privately and Ruskin Sch of Art Oxford

(1) Margaret Mary; *b* 30 Sept 1919; *d* 4 Sept 1920

(2) Rachel Amy; *b* 20 Aug 1921; *d* 14 Sept 1923

4 Denys; Capt RA (TA) and Roy Tank Corps, served Boer War, WW I and WW II (HG); *b* 1 June 1877; *educ* Winchester; *m* 19 June 1907 Lillias Amy (*d* 1970), 3rd dau of Cdr Dudley Charles Stewart, RN (*see* BUTE, M), and *d* 1962, having had issue:

(1) +John Ernest Dudley [John Scott Esq, Ridgeway, Eastacombe, nr Barnstaple, N Devon EX31 3NT]; AFRAeS, S/Ldr RAFO; *b* 10 May 1908; *m* 1st 26 July 1934 (*divorce* 1937) Joan Gwendolyn, dau of R Clayton-Cooper, and has issue:

1a +Peter Denys John, QC (1978) [Peter Scott Esq QC, 4 Eldon Rd, London W8 5PU]; barrister Middle Temple 1960, chm Bar Cncl 1987 (v-chm 1985–86), 2nd Lt RHA; *b* 19 April 1935; *educ* Monroe High Sch, Rochester, NY, and Balliol Coll Oxford (BA)

(1) (cont.) John Scott *m* 2nd 12 June 1937 Ethel Daphne Smith (*d* 15 Nov 1956), and by her has issue:

2a +Roger John Stuart; *b* 18 July 1939; *educ* Uppingham and RAF Technical Coll Henlow, S/Ldr RAF; *m* 1st 15 July 1967 (*divorce* 1991) Mary Alexandra, est dau of Alexander Lynch, of Limerick; *m* 2nd 1991 *Sally Constance, dau of Donald Golege-Steel, of Hurley Cottage, Berks, and by his 1st w has issue:

1b +Alexander John Stuart; *b* 3 Dec 1968

1b *Louise Katherine; *b* 1973

1a (Daphne) Charmian; *b* 22 May 1942; *m* 18 Jan 1964 *Jeremy David Pickett-Heaps, s of Harold S Pickett-Heaps, of Sydney, NSW, and was *k* in a flying accident 5 June 1971, leaving issue:

1b *David Angus; *b* 1967

1b *Rebecca; *b* 1969

2a *Georgina Rosemary [Mrs Peter Machin, 30 Frankley Bldgs, Camden Rd, Bath]; *b* 31 Dec 1944; *m* 8 Nov 1969 *Peter Machin

(1) (cont.) John Scott *m* 3rd 25 May 1957 Margaret Lila (*d* 1973), MRCS, LRCP, dau of Bertram John Monro; *m* 4th 1975 Barbara Anne Veit (*d* 1990)

(2) Frederick Denys; 2nd Lt DCLI (SR); *b* 2 Dec 1909; *d* 1996

(3) +Eustace Ian [Eustace Scott Esq, Lower Uppacott Farm, Upper Tawstock, Barnstaple, N Devon], Capt RA WW II; *b* 18 April 1911; *educ* Harrow; *m* 22 June 1950 *Daphne Ann, yst dau of Lt-Col Arthur O'Brien ffrench Blake, of Canterbury

(4) Anthony James; *b* 18 Jan 1921; *k* by enemy action Oct 1940

(1) Sybil Maud; *b* 26 April 1914; *d* 4 Aug 1919

5 Michael, OBE (1919), served WW I, Order Black Star France and Aviz Portugal; *b* 31 Aug 1878; *educ* Winchester; *m* 1st 6 March 1907 (*divorce* 1919) Cecilia, dau of William Bruton, of Sydney, NSW, and had:

(1) Heather Alice Cecily; *b* 16 June 1908; *d unm c* 1965

5 (cont.) Michael Scott *m* 2nd 8 June 1940 Marie Madelaine Martinella (*d* 22 Aug 1956); *m* 3rd 12 Aug 1958 *Dorothie Primrose (*m* 3rd 21 June 1969 Surgn V-Adml Sir Edward Greeson, KBE, CB (*d* 10 June 1979)), widow of Eric Hoy Stuart (*see* BUTE, M) and dau of Major C Murray-Stewart, and *d* 9 Jan 1959

1 Louisa Katherine; *b* 22 May 1871; *m* 26 May 1898 John Augustine Longley, only s of Sir Henry Longley, KCB, and *d* 5 Aug 1940

2 Margaret Rachel; *b* 5 April 1874; *m* 27 April 1897 Hon Frederick Hamilton-Russell, s of 8th Viscount Boyne (*qv*), and *d* 27 Jan 1938

The 3rd EARL *d* 1926; his grandson,

JOHN SCOTT, **4th Earl of Eldon**, GCVO (1963, KCVO 1952), DL (Devon 1957–66), JP (Hants 1938); *b* 29 March 1899; *educ* Ampleforth and Magdalen Coll Oxford; Ld-in-Waiting to TM GEORGE VI 1937–52 and THE QUEEN 1952–68; Lt Scots Gds (SR), F/Lt No 930 (Hants) Sqdn AAF, served WWs I and II, Grand Offr Legion of Honour 1960; *m* 10 April 1934 Hon Magdalen Mary Charlotte Fraser, OBE (1953), OStJ (*d* 27 Sept 1969), est dau of 16th Lord Lovat (*qv*), and *d* 20 Oct 1976, leaving issue:

1 JOHN JOSEPH NICHOLAS SCOTT, **5th and present Earl of Eldon**

2 +Simon Peter [The Hon Simon Scott, Frogden, Kelso, Roxburghshire TD5 8AB], Page of Honour to HM THE QUEEN 1953–56, Lt Scots Gds (AER); *b* 13 Sept 1939; *educ* Ampleforth, Sorbonne, Us of Salamanca and Madrid; *m* 28 Oct 1966 *Isabel, 2nd dau of Andrew Ramon Dalzell de Bertodano (*see* MEXBOROUGH, E), and has:

(1) +Sebastian Andrew; *b* 1967

(2) +Bendedict Simon; *b* 1971

(3) +James Joseph Michael; *b* 24 June 1974

(1) *Maria Sylvia Rose; *b* 13 Sept 1968

3 A son; *b* and *d* 6 Sept 1955

ELGIN and KINCARDINE

Arms: Or a saltire and chief gules, on a canton argent a lion rampant azure, armed and langued of the second. **Crest:** A lion statant azure, armed and langued gules. **Supporters:** Two savages proper, wreathed about the temples and loins with laurel vert. **Motto:** *Fuimus* ('We have been'). **Creations:** L. (S) 21 June 1633 (Bruce of Kinloss) and 26 Dec 1647 (Bruce of Torry), E. (S) 21 June 1633 (Elgin) and 26 Dec 1647 (Kincardine), B. (UK) 13 Nov 1849.

THE 11TH EARL OF ELGIN and 15TH EARL OF KINCARDINE, Lord Bruce of Kinloss, Lord Bruce of Torry, Baron Elgin, of Elgin (Sir Andrew Douglas Alexander Thomas Bruce, KT (1981), CD (1981), JP (Fife 1951)) [The Rt Hon The Earl of Elgin and Kincardine KT CD JP, Broomhall, Dunfermline, Fife KY11 3DU]; *b* 17 Feb 1924; *s f* 1968; *educ* Eton and Balliol Coll Oxford (BA 1949, MA 1959); Lt Scots Gds WW II (wounded), Ld High Commr Gen Assembly Ch Scotland 1980–81, Ld Lt Fife 1987– (DL 1955–87); Lt-Col Fife Bn ACF, Hon Lt-Col and County Cmdt ACF Fife 1951–65; Grand Master Mason Scotland 1961–65, Pres Boys Bde and Roy Caledonian Curling Club, memb Roy Co Archers, Pres Roy Scottish Automobile Club 1961, dir Dominion Insur, Wine Traders Consortium (Scotland) Ltd and Scottish Local Bd United Dominions Tst, Pres Scottish Amicable Life Assur 1971– and Arthritis and Rheumatism Cncl Scotland 1975–; *m* 27 April 1959 *Victoria Mary, only dau of Maj Dudley George Usher, MBE, TD, Scottish Horse, of Larach Bhan, Kilchrenan, Ayrshire, by Antonia Mary, er dau of Maj-Gen Sir Percival Spearman Wilkinson, KCMG, CB, of Rosebery House, Gorebridge, Midlothian, and has issue:

1 +CHARLES EDWARD, *Lord Bruce* [Lord Bruce, 11 Muschamp Rd, London SE15 4EG; Blackhall Farm, Grange Road, Dunfermline KY11 3DY]; *b* 19 Oct 1961; *educ* Eton and St Andrews (MA); Page of Honour to HM QUEEN ELIZABETH THE QUEEN MOTHER 1975–77; *m* 1990 *Amanda Leigh, yr dau of James Movius, of Fairbanks, Alaska, USA, and has issue:

(1) +James Andrew Charles Robert, *Master of Bruce*; *b* 16 Nov 1991

(2) +George Benjamin Thomas; *b* 1993

(1) *Antonia Jean; *b* 1990

2 +Adam Robert [The Hon Adam Bruce, 8 Montgomery St, Edinburgh EH7 5JS]; *b* 18 Jan 1968; *educ* Trin Coll Glenalmond, Balliol Coll Oxford (MA, Pres Oxford Union 1989) and Edinburgh U (LLB); C Parly candidate NE Fife 1997 gen election

3 +Alexander Victor; *b* 31 March 1971; *educ* Trin Coll Glenalmond

1 *Georgiana Mary; *b* 4 June 1960

2 *Antonia Katherine; *b* 30 Aug 1964; *m* 1989 *Marcel Ballot, son of Jacques-Henri Ballot, of Paris

Lineage: THOMAS BRUCE, a near relative of the Bruce Kings of Scotland, organised, along with Robert, the 7th High Steward (afterwards ROBERT II), a rising in Kyle against English rule 1334, in reward for which he was granted part of the Crown demesnes of Clackmannan; *m* Marjorie Charteris, and had, with other issue:

ROBERT BRUCE; had charters of Clackmannan (Gartlet) and Rate 1359, 1364 and 1367/8; *m* Isabel, dau of Sir Robert Stewart, of Durisdeer, Fife, and had, with two yr sons (Sir Edward, allegedly ancestor of the BRUCEs of Airth (*see* BRUCE, Bt, of Stenhouse); James, Chllr Scotland and Bp Dunkeld):

Sir ROBERT BRUCE; had charters of Rate 1393 and Clackmannan and others 1394; *m* — Scrymgeour, alleged dau of Sir John Scrymgeour of Dudhope (*see* DUNDEE, E), and had, with an illegitimate son (Thomas, of Wester Kennet, whose line ended with Margaret, *m* Archibald Bruce, son of David Bruce of Green, yr s of Sir David Bruce of Clackmannan):

Sir DAVID BRUCE of Clackmannan; *m* Jean, dau of Sir John Stewart of Lorn and Innermeath, and had, with a yr s (Parick):

JOHN BRUCE of Clackmannan; *m* Elizabeth, dau of David Stewart, of Rossyth, and had, with a yr s (Robert, ancestor of the BRUCEs of Cultmalindie):

Sir DAVID BRUCE of Clackmannan; ktd by JAMES IV; *m* 1st Janet, dau of Sir William Stirling of Keir (*see* 1970 edn STIRLING-MAXWELL, Bt), and had issue:

1 Robert; had a charter of Rate 1484 (confirmed 1488); had issue:

(1) David; resigned his right to Clackmannan to his unc David Bruce (*see* below) 1 Feb 1506/7; his descendants towards the end of the 16th century were the BRUCEs of Fingask

Sir DAVID *m* 2nd Mariot, dau of Robert Herries of Terregles (*see* HERRIES OF TERREGLES, L) and widow of David Stewart of Rosyth, by whom he had:

2 DAVID (Sir)

1 Christian; *m* Sir James Shaw of Sauchie

The 2nd son,

Sir DAVID BRUCE; Clackmannan settled on him by his f 1497; *m* Janet, dau of Sir Patrick Blackadder of Tulliallan, and had issue:

1 John; *dvp*, leaving:

(1) Robert (Sir), of Clackmannan; the last male heir in the direct line Henry, of Clackmannan, *dsp* 1772; his only surv sis was w of Dr William Bruce, of Newton and Cowden; her ggdau and rep, Margaret Bruce, of Cowden *m* 1838 8th Earl of Airlie (*qv*) and was mother of Hon William Henry Bruce Ogilvy (*dsp* 20 April 1912), heir of line of the BRUCEs of Clackmannan

2 EDWARD

3 Robert, of Lynmiln; had:

(1) Robert; *dsp*

(1) Marjory; *m* Ronald Masterson of that Ilk

4 David, of Green, near Clackmannan; had:

(1) Archibald; *m* Margaret Bruce, heiress of Easter Kennet, and was ancestor of the BRUCEs of Kennet (*see* BALFOUR OF BURLEIGH, L)

5 Patrick, of Valleyfield

1 Elizabeth; *m* 1st Alexander Dundas of Fingask; *m* 2nd Robert Collace of Balnamoon

2 Mariot; *m* 1st Sir Robert Bruce of Airth; *m* 2nd Marcus Sinclair of Carberry

3 Agnes; *m* Sir James Cunninghame of Polmaise (*see* CUNINGHAME, Bt)

4 Alison; *m* Sir James Colville of Easter Wemyss (*see* COLVILLE OF CULROSS, V)

The 2nd son,

EDWARD BRUCE of Blairhall, which he bought 1541; *b* 1505; had letters of protection from JAMES V 1533, a charter of Easter Kennet 1537 (confirmed 1539) and a charter of Bergandy and two-thirds of Shirresmiln from William, commendator of Culross 1540 (confirmed 1542/3); *m* Alison, dau of John Reid of Aikenhead and sis of Robert Reid, Bp of Orkney, Pres Court of Session, and *d* 1565, leaving issue:

1 Robert, of Blairhall; *m* 1593 Margaret (*d* 1614), dau of John Hamilton, Archbp of St Andrews; their only son Robert, of Blairhall, *m* Katherine, dau of Sir John Preston of Valleyfield, and had issue:

(1) Thomas, of Blairhall; *m* Jean, dau of Sir John Henderson of Fordel, and had issue:

1a John, of Blairhall; *m* Jean, dau of James Leslie, 2nd Lord Lindores, and widow of John Stewart, of Innernytie, and had a dau and heir:

1b Mary; *m* Dugald Stuart, bro of 1st Earl of Bute (*see* BUTE, M), a Ld of Session, whose issue inherited Blairhall

2a Alexander; *m* Katherine, dau of Robert Stewart of Irry, and *dsp*

1a Margaret; *m* John Aytoun of Kinnaldy

2a Catherine; *m* 4 April 1685, as his 2nd w, 8th Earl of Menteith (title dormant 1694) and *dsp* 1693

(2) Sir WILLIAM BRUCE, 1st Bt (NS), so *cr* 21 Oct 1668, of Balcaskie, which he bought 1663 from John Moncrieff and sold to Sir Robert Anstruther 1698; designed Holyrood House for CHARLES II; subsequently acquired the territorial Barony of Kinross from the Earl of Morton and built Kinross House; *m* 1st Mary, dau of Sir James Halket of Pitfirrane, Bt, and had:

1a Sir JOHN BRUCE, 2nd and last Bt; *m* Christian (*dsp*), Dowager Marchioness of Montrose (*see* MONTROSE, D), and *dspm* shortly after his f 19 March 1710, when the title expired

1a Anne; *m* 1st Sir Thomas Hope of Craighall, 4th Bt (*qv*), and had issue; *m* 2nd Sir John Carstairs of Kilconquhar; her issue by the two marriages successively inherited Kinross

(2) (cont.) Sir WILLIAM *m* 2nd Magdalene Scot (*dsp* 21 April 1710) and *d* 1 Jan 1710

(1) Christian; *m* **4th Earl of Kincardine** (*see* below)

2 Sir EDWARD BRUCE, 1st LORD KINLOSS (S), so *cr* 2 Feb 1601/2, with remainder to heirs and assigns, and 8 July 1604 BARON BRUCE OF KINLOSSE [*sic*](S), with remainder to the heirs male of his body, whom failing, to his heirs male whatsoever (the reason for this near-duplication of title being a doubt as to the legality of erecting former Church property into temporal honours, Sir EDWARD having been Commendator (lay proprietor) of the Cistercian Abbey of Kinloss, Elgin, from 1593 till he surrendered it and received back the title of Lord of Parliament of Feb 1601/2 with the title of Free Baron), also 3 May 1608 LORD BRUCE OF KINLOSS (S), with remainder to the heirs male of his body, whom failing to his heirs and assigns, PC (1603); *b* 1548; advocate, Ld of Session 1597–1604, Amb England 1598 and 1601, where he was instrumental in smoothing the way for the peaceful accession of JAMES I; he accompanied JAMES to London 1603, when the Manor of Whorlton and part of the possessions of Jervaulx Abbey were conferred on him; naturalized an English subject and apptd Master of the Rolls, built Cubors Abbey House 1608 but sold it to 1st Earl of Dundonald (*qv*), from whose descendants it was acquired by Sir Robert Preston, of Valleyfield (who rebuilt it 1830) and willed it to Hon Robert Preston Bruce (*see* below); *m* Magdalene (*m* 2nd 9 April 1616 Sir James Fullerton), dau of Alexander Clerk, of Balbirnie, Fife, and *d* 14 Jan 1610/11, having by her had issue:

(1) Robert; *dsp* & *vp*

(2) EDWARD BRUCE, 2nd LORD KINLOSS, 2nd BARON BRUCE OF KINLOSSE and 2nd LORD BRUCE OF KINLOSS, KB (1610); Gentleman Bedchamber; *k* unm Holland Aug 1613 in a duel with 4th Earl of Dorset (*see* SACKVILLE, B)

(3) THOMAS BRUCE, **1st Earl of Elgin**, so *cr* 21 June 1633, as also LORD BRUCE OF KINLOSS (both S), with remainder to his heirs male forever bearing the name of Bruce, in addition *cr* 29 July 1641 BARON BRUCE OF

WHORLTON, Co York (UK), to him and the heirs male of his body; also 3rd LORD KINLOSS, 3rd BARON BRUCE OF KINLOSSE and 3rd LORD BRUCE OF KINLOSS; *b* 2 Dec 1599; MA (Oxford) 1636; ktd 1638; *m* 1st 4 July 1622 Anne (*d* 20 March 1627), dau of Sir Robert Chichester, of Raleigh, Devon (*see* CHICHESTER, Bt), and had:

1a ROBERT BRUCE, **2nd Earl of Elgin** and 1st EARL OF AILESBURY, Bucks, so *cr* 18 March 1663/4, as also VISCOUNT BRUCE OF AMPTHILL, Beds, and BARON BRUCE OF SKELTON, Co York (all E), PC (1678); *b* by 1638; Ld Lt: Beds (Jt 1660, sole 1667), Hunts 1681 and Cambs and Hunts 1685; MP Beds 1661–63, Gentleman Bedchamber, Commr for the office of Earl Marshal, Ld Chamberlain 1685; *m* 16 Feb 1645/6 Lady Diana Grey (*d* 1690), dau of 1st Earl of Stamford (*see* 1970 edn), and *d* 20 Oct 1685, having had with other issue:

1b THOMAS BRUCE, **3rd Earl of Elgin** and 2nd EARL OF AILESBURY; *b* 1656; MP Marlborough 1679–81, Wilts 1685, Groom Bedchamber 1685–88, remained faithful to JAMES II at the Glorious Revolution of 1688 and begged him to return after fleeing London, subsequently attending him to Rochester after he had returned but was denied access to Whitehall; later took the oath to the new regime but was imprisoned in the Tower of London Feb 1695/6 on suspicion of plotting to bring back JAMES; afterwards allowed to emigrate; *m* 1st 31 Aug or 30 Oct 1676 Elizabeth (*d* 12 Jan 1697), sis of 3rd Duke of Somerset (*qv*), from whom she inherited the Tottenham and Savernake Forest, Wilts, estates, and *d* Brussels Nov 1741, having had issue:

1c Robert, *Lord Bruce*; *b* 6 Aug 1679; *dsp* & *vp*

2c CHARLES BRUCE, **4th Earl of Elgin** and 3rd and last EARL OF AILESBURY; *b* 29 May 1682; MP Gt Bedwyn 1705–08 and Marlborough 1710–11, called up to Ho Lds 29 Dec 1711 *vp* in f's Barony of Bruce of Whorlton, *cr* 17 April 1746 BARON BRUCE OF TOTTENHAM, Wilts (GB), with remainder, failing heirs male of his body, to his n Thomas Bruce Brudenell (*see* AILESBURY, M); *m* 1st 7 Feb 1705/6 Lady Anne Saville (*d* 18 July 1717), dau and coheir of 2nd Marquess of Halifax (*see* HALIFAX, E, preliminary remarks), and had issue:

1d George; *d* young

2d Robert; MP Gt Bedwyn; *m* 8 Feb 1729 Frances, dau of Sir William Blackett, 1st Bt (*qv*), of Wallington, Northumberland, and *dsp* 30 Aug 1738

1d Mary; *m* 21 Dec 1728 2nd Duke of Chandos (*see* TEMPLE OF STOWE, E) and *d* 1738, leaving issue (*see* KINLOSS, L)

2d Elizabeth; *m* 26 Nov 1732 Hon Benjamin Bathurst (*dvp* 23 Jan 1767), est s of 1st Earl Bathurst (*qv*), and *dsp* 12 Nov 1771

2c (cont.) The **4th Earl of Elgin** *m* 2nd 2 Feb 1719/20 Lady Juliana Boyle (*dsp* 26 March 1739), dau of 3rd Earl of Cork (*see* CORK and ORRERY, E) and 3rd Earl of Burlington; *m* 3rd 18 June 1739 Caroline (*m* 2nd 19 Dec 1747 FM Henry Seymour Conway, PC (*see* HERTFORD, M), and *d* 17 Jan 1803), dau of 4th Duke of Argyll (*qv*), and *dspm* 10 Feb 1747, when the Earldom of Ailesbury, Viscountcy of Bruce of Ampthill and Barony of Bruce of Skelton expired, the Barony of Bruce of Tottenham passed to his n and right to the Scottish Lordships of Kinloss and Bruce of Kinloss (of the 1608 *cr*) passed to the 2nd Duke of Chandos, while right to the Scottish titles of Baron Bruce of Kinlosse (of the 1604 *cr*) and the actual Earldom of Elgin and Lordship of Bruce of Kinloss (of the 1633 *cr*) passed to his heir male (*see* below), although that heir male did not assume the 1604 title, which would thus appear to have become dormant, having by her had a dau:

3d Mary; *m* 1 April 1757 3rd Duke of Richmond and Lennox (*see* RICHMOND and GORDON, D) and *dsp* 5th Nov 1796

1c Elizabeth; *m* 15 May 1707 3rd Earl of Cardigan and *d* Dec 1745, leaving issue (*see* AILESBURY, M)

1b (cont.) The **3rd Earl of Elgin** *m* 2nd 27 April 1700 Charlotte d'Argenteau, Countess d'Esneux and Baroness de Melsbroeck, Flanders (*d* 23 July 1710), and had further issue:

2c Maria Teresa Charlotte; *b* 19/30 Sept 1704; *m* 1722 Maximilian Emanuel, Prince de Hornes; their gdau *m* Prince Charles Edward Stuart

1b Diana; *m* 1st Sir Seymour Shirley, 5th Bt (*see* FERRERS, E); *m* 2nd 1st Duke of Rutland (*qv*) and *d* 15 July 1672

2b Anne; *m* Sir William Rich, Bt, of Sunning, Berks (*see* 1970 edn)

3b Christian; *m* 1st John Rolle, son of Sir John Rolle, KB, of Stevenston, Devon; *m* 2nd Sir Robert Gayer, KB, of Stoke Poges, Bucks, and *d* 5 April 1720

4b Mary; *m* Sir William Walters, Bt, of Saresden

5b Annie Charlotte; *m* Nicholas Bagenal, of Newry

(3) (cont.) The **1st Earl of Elgin** *m* 2nd Diana (*d* 26 Feb 1658), dau and coheir of 2nd Earl of Exeter (*see* EXETER, M) and widow of 18th Earl of Oxford (*see* SAINT ALBANS, D), and *d* 21 Dec 1663, having had no issue by her

(1) Christian; *m* 10 April 1608 2nd Earl of Devonshire (*see* DEVONSHIRE, D), and *d* 16 June 1674

3 George (Sir), of Carnock, Fife, which he bought from Sir A Lindsay, and Werty Gellett (renamed Broomhall), Fife, bought from John Pitcairn of that Ilk *c* 1600; MP Culross, where he established extensive submarine coal mines (the first in Scotland to be machine-drained) and salt works; built Culross Palace 1597; ktd by JAMES VI, memb ctee to negotiate union with England 1604; *m* Margaret, dau of Archibald Primrose of Burnbrae, and *d* 6 May 1625, leaving:

(1) George, of Carnock; *m* Mary, dau of Sir John Preston, of Valleyfield, Bt, and had issue:

1a EDWARD BRUCE, **1st Earl of Kincardine**, so *cr* 26 Dec 1647, as also LORD BRUCE OF TORRY (both S), with remainder to heirs male; MP Stirling 1644; *d* unm 1662

2a ALEXANDER BRUCE, **2nd Earl of Kincardine**, PC (S Feb 1660/1, E 1674–76); *b c* 1629; Jt Commr Treasury Scotland 1666–74, Extrdy Ld Session 1667–80; *m c* 16 June 1659 Veronica (*d* 28 April 1701), dau of Corneille van Arsen van Sommelsdyck, Lord of Sommelsdyck and Spyck, Holland, and *d* 9 July 1680, leaving issue:

1b Charles, *Lord Bruce*; *dvp* unm 1680

2b ALEXANDER BRUCE, **3rd Earl of Kincardine**; *bapt* 5 June 1666; sold territorial Barony of Carnock and bulk of estate 1700 to Col Hon John Erskine (*see* BUCHAN, E); *d* unm 10 Nov 1705

1b Mary; based a claim to the Earldom on a resignation in her favour by her late bro; the Crown had the power to validate this, it was maintained, and had it done so it would have been good, even though the late Earl's sanity was in doubt; but the Crown did not, and after the Act of Union 1707 it was held that the Crown's power to validate such grants had expired; nevertheless Lady Mary registered protests at the elections of rep S peers in 1708 and 1710; *m* 19 April 1681 William Cochrane of Ochiltree and had:

1c 8th EARL OF DUNDONALD (*qv*)

2b Anne; *m* 16 April 1684 Sir David Murray of Stanhope, Bt

3b Elizabeth; *m* 24 March 1704 James Boswell, 7th of Auchinleck (*d* 21 April 1749), and had issue

1a Margaret; *m* Sir John Lumsden of Innergelly

2a Magdalene; *m* Sir John Arnot of Fernie

3a Mary; *m* 1655 David Erskine, Lord Cardross (*see* BUCHAN, E)

(2) Alexander, of Alva; *dsp* 1638

(3) Robert, of Broomhall; advocate, Ld of Session as Lord Broomhall 1649; *m* Helen, dau of Sir James Skene of Curriehill, and *d* 25 June 1652, leaving, with two daus (Janet, *m* Sir Thomas Burnet of Crimond; Helen, *m* Sir William Weir of Blackwood):

1a ALEXANDER BRUCE, **4th Earl of Kincardine**, of Broomhall; MP Culross 1661–63, 1669–74, 1678 and 1685–86 and Sanquhar 1692, Jt Receiver-Gen Supply and Excise 1693–95, ktd by 1670*4*; *m* his cousin Christian, dau of Robert Bruce of Blairhall (*see* above), and *d* 10 Oct 1706, leaving, with other issue:

1b ROBERT BRUCE, **5th Earl of Kincardine**; *d* unm 1718

2b ALEXANDER BRUCE, **6th Earl of Kincardine**; *b* 19 Jan 1662; WS; *m* Jean (Nisbet?) and *dspm* 1721, leaving:

1c Jane; *m* John Napier of Kilmahew

3b THOMAS BRUCE, **7th Earl of Kincardine**; *b* 19 March 1663; Jacobite, advsr to Prince Charles Edward Stuart; *m* 1699 Rachel (*d* 17 March 1753), dau of Robert Pauncefort, of Herefs, and *d* 23 March 1739/40, leaving, with other issue:

1c WILLIAM BRUCE, **8th Earl of Kincardine**; *m* 14 Feb 1726 Janet (*d* 29 March 1772), dau of James Roberton, Pncpl Clerk Session (s of Archibald Roberton, of Bedlay, Lanarks), and *d* 8 Sept 1740, having had issue:

1d CHARLES BRUCE, **9th Earl of Kincardine** and **5th Earl of Elgin** (as which s cousin Feb 1746/7); *b* 15 July 1732; *educ* Rugby; *m* 1 June 1759 Martha (Governess to PRINCESS CHARLOTTE OF WALES; *d* 21 June 1810), only child of Thomas Whyte, London banker, and *d* 14 May 1771, having had issue:

1e WILLIAM ROBERT BRUCE, **6th Earl of Elgin** and **10th Earl of Kincardine**; *b* 28 Jan 1764; *d* 15 July 1771

2e THOMAS, **7th/11th Earl**

3e Charles Andrew; *b* 18 Jan 1768; Govr Prince of Wales's Island; *m* 1st 20 May 1796 Anne Maria (*dsp* 19 Sept 1798), 8th dau of Sir Charles William Blunt, 3rd Bt (*qv*); *m* 2nd Charlotte Sophia (*m* 2nd 1813 James Alexander, of Somerhill), est dau of Thomas Dashwood (*see* DASHWOOD, Bt, of Kirtlington Park), and *d* 27 Dec 1810, having by her had issue:

1f Charles Dashwood; *b* 1802; *m* 18 Sept 1841 Hon Harriet Elizabeth Pitt (*d* 18 July 1876) Maid of Honour to HM QUEEN VICTORIA, 2nd dau of 3rd Baron Rivers (*see* 1880 edn), and *dsp* 25 Aug 1864

2f Brudenell; *b* 1804; Lt 3rd (Scots) Gds; *d* Poros 8 Oct 1828

1f Louisa; *m* 14 July 1835 Sir William Richard Powlet-Geary, Bt, and *d* 9 Aug 1870

4e James; *b* 23 March 1769; MP Marlborough; drowned crossing the Don, Barnbydown, Yorks, 10 July 1798

1e Charlotte; *m* 1799 Adml Sir Philip Charles Durham, GCB, and *d* 1816

2d Thomas; Lt-Gen, MP Marlborough 1796 and Gt Bedwyn 1796; *d* Exeter 12 Dec 1797

1d Christian; *m* 28 April 1762 James Erskine of Cardross (*see* BUCHAN, E) and *d* 28 May 1810

1c Rachel; *m* James Drummond of Lundin, self-styled 10th Earl of Perth (*qv*)

1d Veronica; *m* Duncan Campbell of Kames

(1) Anne; *m* 1641 Sir James Arnot of Fernie

(2) Magdalene; *m* Sir John Erskine of Balgony

(3) Christian; *m* Lawrence Mercer of Aldie

(4) Nicholas; *m* 1st Sir John Morrison of Dairsie; *m* 2nd John Dick of Braid

(5) Margaret; *m* Francis Nicholls, of Middle Temple, and *d* 1652, leaving issue

4 William; priest Kinloss Abbey; *d* 1609

The 6th/10th EARL's bro,

THOMAS BRUCE, **7th Earl of Elgin** and **11th Earl of Kincardine**, PC (1799); *b* 20 July 1766; *educ* Harrow and Westminster and St Andrews and Paris Us; commnd Foot Gds 1785, Gen 1837, Ld Lt Fife 1807, rep S peer 1790–1807 and 1820–41, Amb Constantinople 1799–1803; while *en poste* he acquired the sculptures on the Parthenon known as The Elgin Marbles and transported them to the UK at an alleged total cost of £74,000 (over £2.8m in late 1990s terms), selling them to the nation for deposit in the Br Museum, of which he was an Elgin Tstee 1816–41, for under half that; given the controversy that has engulfed the marbles in the late 20th century it is worth bearing in mind that their removal caused a furore at the time; Elgin's fellow-old Harrovian and fellow-peer Byron wrote one of his worse couplets on the subject, rather caddishly linking the collapse of Elgin's marriage with the man's temerity in wrenching Greek antiques from their original setting; to the historian of the peerage the point of interest is why they fail to commemorate Lord Elgin's other main title, in that logically they should be called the 'Elgin and Kincardine Marbles'; *m* 1st 11 March 1799 (*divorce* 1808) Mary (*m* 2nd Robert Ferguson, of Raith, and *d* 9 July 1855), only child of William Hamilton Nisbet, of Dirleton and Belhaven, Haddington, and had issue:

1 George Charles Constantine, *Lord Bruce*; *b* 5 April 1800; *dvp* unm 1840

1 Mary; *m* 28 Jan 1828 Robert Adam DUNDAS later CHRISTOPHER later still NISBET-HAMILTON, PC, JP, MP (*d* 9 June 1877), Chllr Duchy of Lancaster 1852, of Bloxholm Hall, Lincs, and *d* 21 Dec 1883, leaving issue (*see* OGILVY, Bt)

2 Matilda Harriet; *m* 14 Oct 1839 Sir John Maxwell, 8th Bt, of Pollock (*dsp* 6 June 1865) (*see* STIRLING-MAXWELL, Bt), and *d* 31 Aug 1857

3 Lucy; *m* 14 March 1828 as his 2nd w John Grant, JP, DL (*d* 20 Jan 1873), of Kilgraston and Pitkeathly, Perths, and *d* 4 Sept 1881, leaving issue

The **7th/11th Earl** *m* 2nd 21 Sept 1810 Elizabeth (*d* Paris 1 April 1860), yst dau of J T Oswald, MP, of Dunnikeir, Fife, and *d* 14 Nov 1841, having by her had further issue:

2 JAMES, **8th/12th Earl**

3 Robert; *b* 15 March 1813; Maj-Gen, Govr to HM EDWARD VII when PRINCE OF WALES; *m* 2 May 1848 Katherine Mary (VA 4th Cl, Bedchamber Woman-in-Ordinary to HM QUEEN VICTORIA 1866; *d* 3 Dec 1889), 2nd dau of Sir Michael Shaw-Stewart, 6th Bt (*qv*), and *dsp* 27 June 1862

4 Frederick William Adolphus (Sir), GCB; *b* 14 April 1814; barrister Lincoln's Inn, diplomat, Agent and Consul-Gen Egypt, Envoy China, Min USA 1865; *d* unm Sept 1867

5 Thomas Charles, DL (Banffshire); *b* 15 Feb 1825; barrister, MP Portsmouth 1874–85; *m* 19 Nov 1863 Sarah Caroline (*d* 22 July 1913), sis of Sir Thomas Thornhill, 1st Bt, and *d* 23 Nov 1890, having had issue:

(1) Charles Thomas; *b* 21 Feb 1865; memb Roy Co of Archers; *m* 1st 8 July 1897 Edith Mary (*d* 13 May 1912), dau of Samuel Sandbach Parker, of Aigburth, and had issue:

1a Robert Charles, MC; *b* 16 May 1898; Lt Gren Gds WW I; *m* 15 July 1919 Hon Kate Mary Maugham (*d* 30 Oct 1961), dau of 1st Viscount Maugham (*see* 1970 edn), and *d* 31 Aug 1953, having had issue:

1b David; *b* 5 June 1920; *educ* Eton; Capt Welsh Gds WW II (wounded twice); *m* 11 Oct 1949 (*divorce* 1958) Elizabeth Joan, yr dau of Maj-Gen Philip Saxon Gregson-Ellis, CB, OBE, of The Constable's Tower, Dover, and *d* 1978, leaving issue:

1c *(Cynthia) Penelope Helen [Mrs Charles Pumphrey, 23 Trinity Cres, London SW17 7AG]; *b* 28 Oct 1951

2b Charles John; *b* 26 May 1921; Lt Gren Gds WW II; *ka* NW Europe April 1945

1b *Katherine Mary [Mrs Francis Wilson, Garth House, Llangammarch, Wells, Breconshire]; *b* 16 May 1928; *m* 1st 19 June 1948 (*divorce* 1960) Capt John James Scott, late Argyll and Sutherland Highrs, s of Lt-Col John Creagh Scott, DSO, OBE, of Killadysert, Co Clare, and has issue:

1c *Caroline Judith; *b* 8 Jan 1950; *m* 1970 *Michael David Sykes

2c *Katherine Dinah (twin); *b* 8 Jan 1950; *m* 1971 *John Hunter Pemberton

1b (cont.) Mrs Katherine Scott *m* 2nd 1 March 1968 *Francis Amcotts Wilson (*see* WILSON, Bt, of Eshton Hall)

(1) (cont.) Charles Bruce *m* 2nd 7 July 1914 Gwendolen Mary (*d* 2 Dec 1934), est dau of Robert Thomas Napier Speir, of Culdees, Perthshire, and *d* from illness contracted on service in Flanders 23 Oct 1915

(2) Robert Arthur; *b* 3 April 1875; *d* 16 Aug 1896

(1) Elizabeth Marjorie; *m* 17 July 1895 Col Algernon George Arnold Durand, CB, CIE, and *d* 29 April 1929, leaving issue (*see* DURAND, Bt)

(2) Augusta Mary

4 Charlotte Christian; *m* 2 July 1850 Frederick LOCKER later LOCKER-LAMPSON (*m* 2nd 6 July 1874 Hannah Jane, only dau of Sir Curtis Miranda Lampson, 1st Bt (*see* KILLEARN, B), and *d* 30 May 1895), s of Edward Hawke Locker, Commr Greenwich Hosp, and *d* 26 April 1872

5 Augusta Frederica Elizabeth; Ldy-in-Waiting to DUCHESS OF KENT, Resident Bedchamber Woman to HM QUEEN VICTORIA; *m* 16 Dec 1863 Very Rev Arthur Penrhyn Stanley, DD, FRS, Dean Westminster (*see* STANLEY OF ALDERLEY, SHEFFIELD and, B), and *d* 1 March 1876

6 Frances Anne; Ldy-in-Waiting to HRH THE DUCHESS OF EDINBURGH; *m* 15 Feb 1855 Evan Peter Montagu Baillie (*dvp* 9 Nov 1874), Sec Legation Stuttgart, son of Evan Baillie of Dochfour, and *d* 16 Aug 1894, leaving issue (*see* BURTON, B)

The 7th/11th EARL's est surv son,

JAMES BRUCE, **8th Earl of Elgin** and **12th Earl of Kincardine**, KT (1847), GCB (1858), PC (1857); *b* 20 July 1811; *educ* Eton and Ch Ch Oxford; MP (Ind) Southampton July-Dec 1841, Elgin Tstee Br Museum 1841–63, Govr-Gen Jamaica 1842–46 and Canada 1846–54, Ld Lt Fife 1854–63, Plen China 1857–59 and 1860–61, *cr* 13 Nov 1849 BARON ELGIN, of Elgin (UK), PMG 1859–60, Viceroy India 21 Jan 1862–20 Nov 1863; *m* 1st 22 April 1841 Elizabeth Mary (*d* 7 July 1843), only child of Charles Lennox Cumming-Bruce, of Dunphail and Roseisle, Stirling, MP Elgin and Nairn, and had issue, with another dau:

1 Elma; *m* 18 Oct 1864 5th Baron Thurlow (*qv*) and *d* 27 Nov 1923, leaving issue

The **8th/12th Earl** *m* 2nd 7 Nov 1846 Lady Mary Louisa Lambton, CI (*d* 9 March 1898), er surv dau of 1st Earl of Durham (*qv*), and *d* Dhurmsala, India, 20 Nov 1863, having by her had, with another s and dau:

1 VICTOR ALEXANDER, **9th/13th Earl**

2 Robert Preston, DL (Fife); *b* 4 Dec 1851; MA; Capt Fife Artillery Militia, MP Fife 1880–85 and W Fife 1885–89; *d* unm 8 Dec 1893

3 Frederick John; *b* 16 Sept 1854; Page-of-Honour to HM QUEEN VICTORIA; *m* 3 June 1879 Katherine (*d* 28 Feb 1917), dau of E W Fernie, of Gt Berkhamsted, Herts, and widow of Logan W Raeburn, of Charlesfield, Midlothian, and *d* 26 Jan 1920, leaving issue:

(1) Lewis; *b* 12 March 1880; *m* 11 Jan 1911 Anne Margaret Macdonald (*d* 8 Dec 1961), 2nd dau of Robert Burt Ranken, WS, of Edinburgh, and *d* 23 March 1961, having had issue:

1a +John Frederick Lambton [John Bruce Esq, Lambda Cottage, Wick Hill, Finchampstead, Berks]; *b* 20 Oct 1912; *m* 11 Jan 1941 his cousin *Marjory Katherine Fernie, est dau of Charles Bruce, of Liskeard, Cornwall (*see* below), and has issue:

1b *Penelope Margaret; *b* 26 Sept 1943

2b *Juliet Louisa; *b* 11 March 1950

3b *Janet Marion; *b* 3 Jan 1956

2a +Robert Richard Fernie, DFC (1944), and bar (1945) [Robert Bruce Esq DFC and bar, 1 Orchard Close, Hardwicke, Glos GL2 4SZ]; *b* 17 Aug 1915; *educ* Rugby and Edinburgh U (MusB 1938); WW II as F/Lt RAFVR; *m* 6 July 1941 *Beatrice, dau of Vincenzo Antonio Gregorio Tombolini, of Pontypool, and has issue:

1b +Richard Stephen Witherington [Richard Bruce Esq, 347 Crawford Rd, Inglewood, W Australia 6052]; *b* 14 Aug 1942; *educ* Rugby and Middx Hosp Med Sch (MB, BS, FFARCS); *m* 1st 17 July 1965 (*divorce* 1969) Frances Mary, er dau of Kenneth George Morgan, MRCVS, of Chepstow, Mon; *m* 2nd 1969 (*divorce* 1984) Katherine Jane, dau of Mrs J A Hunter of W Australia, and has issue by his 1st w:

1c *Katharine Blanche Mary; *b* 1 Dec 1966

2b +Anthony James Lewis [Anthony Bruce Esq, Sportsmanstraat 10, 2341JG, Oegstgeest, The Netherlands]; *b* 25 June 1948; *educ* Rugby; BSc; *m* 1st 1972 (*divorce* 1991) Glenys Vaughan, dau of J Jones, of Caernarvon; *m* 2nd 1994 *Veronica Ellen, dau of A Seccombe, of Mansfield, and has by his 1st w:

1c +Elgan Lewis; *b* 1977

1c *Lowri Ann; *b* 1975

2c *Catrin Ellen; *b* 1981

1b *Katharine Anne Russell [Mrs John Clements, 7A Rua Calçada da Frandina, 7100 Estremoz, Portugal]; *b* 9 March 1945; MCSP; *m* 1968 *John Mervyn Henry Clements, s of Henry Clements, of Co Antrim, and has:

1c *Timothy Robert Henry; *b* 13 Sept 1968

2c *Charles Richard; *b* 1971

1c *Victoria Penelope Louise; *b* 1972

3a James Alexander; *b* 14 Feb 1919; *m* 1952 *Joan Beryl Marion Elizabeth, dau of Granville Alexander Silby and widow of G/Capt Walter Donald Butler, RAF, and *d* 1989, leaving issue:

1b +Nigel Charles; *b* 9 Nov 1954

1b *Miranda Veronica; *b* May 1953

1a Mary Witherington; *b* 21 Oct 1911; *m* 15 March 1951 *Japh Alexander Oxenford, and *d* 2 Sept 1958, leaving:

1b *Rosalind Clare; *b* 19–; *m* 19– *Henry Dodsworth (*see* below)

2a *Katharine Anne Doughty [Mrs Sidney Doe, Coriander Cottage, Deer Park View, Odiham, Hook, Hants RG29 1JY]; *b* 12 May 1921; ARCM 1949; *m* 1971 Sidney John Doe (*d* 1993)

(2) Charles; *b* 23 Feb 1883; Capt Scottish Horse TAR; *m* 30 Aug 1918 *Joan [Mrs Charles Bruce, Rubec Cottage, Wick Hill, Finchampstead, Berks], dau of Isaac Newton Woodiwiss, of Trusthorpe Hall, Lincs, and *d* 18 Sept 1958, having had issue:

1a David Charles Richard; *b* 12 Nov 1928; Lt RN; *m* 4 April 1950 *Georgina Poppy (*m* 2nd 19 April 1968 Peter Joseph Bruce-Souster, s of Arthur William Souster, of Kettering), er dau of George Edward Keay, of Bexleyheath, Kent, and *d* 10 March 1957, leaving issue:

1b +Roland Christopher; *b* 23 May 1956

1b *Clarissa Jane Fernie; *b* 4 Jan 1952

2b *Fiona Geraldine; *b* 1 Oct 1953

3b *Miranda Jacqueline; *b* 3 March 1955

1a *Marjory Katharine Fernie; *b* 4 Aug 1919; *m* 11 Jan 1941 her cousin *John Frederick Lambton Bruce (*see* above) and has issue

2a *Isobel Seton [Mrs Joseph Clift, 5 Lemin Parc, Reawla Lane, Gwinear, Hayle, Cornwall TR27 5HJ]; *b* 14 Feb 1921; *m* 4 July 1956 Joseph Henry Clift (*d* 1986), son of Ernest Albert Clift, of Redruth, Cornwall, and has issue:

1b *Michael Charles David; *b* 21 Aug 1957

2b *Simon Paul; *b* 8 Oct 1963

3a *Zenobie Margaret; *b* 10 Jan 1922; *m* 30 July 1942 *Walter Bevan Coulson Tregarthen, son of William Neil Craze, of Hayle, Cornwall, and had:

1b *Bruce Coulson Tregarthen; *b* 31 July 1943; *educ* Clifton

4a *Jill Rosalind [Mrs Bryan Dodsworth, The Old Rectory, East Bridgford, Nottingham]; *b* 7 July 1927; BA (Oxon) 1949; *m* 1st 10 Dec 1949 (*divorce* 1968) James Mayo Alastair Gunn, MA (Oxon), Col S Notts Hus Yeo (TA), yst son of Henry Somerville Gunn, of Badminton, Glos; *m* 2nd 1977 *Bryan L Dodsworth, and has issue by her 1st husb:

1b *Henry Alastair Bruce; *b* 25 March 1951; *educ* Radley; *m* 19– *Rosalind Oxenford (*see* above)

2b *David James Paul; *b* 19 Nov 1956; *educ* Radley

1b *Nicola Fernie; *b* 4 Oct 1952

2b *Ann Veronica; *b* 4 Aug 1954

(3) James; *b* 2 Dec 1887; *ka* 1917

(4) Richard Frederick David; *b* 1 March 1894; Capt 4th/5th Bn Black Watch; *m* 1919 Mary Elizabeth Neville-Dahm (*d* 1953), and *d* 3 Jan 1928

(1) Margaret; *b* 23 Aug 1881; *m* 15 April 1913 Rev Cuthbert Creighton, of King's Sch, Worcester, son of Rt Rev Mandel Creighton, Bp London, and *d* 2 Feb 1923, leaving issue

(2) Marion; *b* 9 Sept 1884; *m* 1920 Maj Thomas Ranken, 8th Roy Scots (*d* 27 April 1950), er son of Robert Burt Ranken, WS, and *d* 25 March 1966, leaving issue

(3) Katherine; *b* 24 Dec 1885; *m* as his 2nd w 2 July 1918 Thomas Augustus Hardcastle, MA (*d* 21 June 1941), est s of Thomas Hardcastle, of Bradshaw Hall, Lancs, and *d* 23 Nov 1967, leaving issue

(4) Janet Elizabeth; *b* 7 July 1890; *d* unm 19 Nov 1966

The 8th/12th EARL's est son,

VICTOR ALEXANDER BRUCE, **9th Earl of Elgin** and **13th Earl of Kincardine**, KG (1899), PC (1886), GCSI, GCIE; *b* 16 May 1849; *educ* Trin Coll Glenalmond, Eton and Balliol Coll Oxford; MA Oxford; Treas Household, First Commr Works 1886, Viceroy India 1894–99, Sec State Colonies 1905–08, Ld Lt Fife, Pres Fife TFA, Capt Roy Co Archers, Hon Col 1st Fife RGA Vols; Hon DCL Oxon, Hon LLD St Andrews, Aberdeen, Edinburgh, Glasgow and Cambridge; *m* 1st 9 Nov 1876 Lady Constance Mary Carnegie, CI (*d* 24 Sept 1909), 2nd dau of 9th Earl of Southesk (*see* FIFE, D), and *d* 18 Jan 1917, leaving issue:

1 EDWARD JAMES, **10th/14th Earl**

2 Robert, CBE (1956), JP (Morayshire), DL; *b* 18 Nov 1882; Maj 11th Hus, Adj and Quartermaster Cav School 1909–12, Capt 11th Hus 1911–12, Cmdt Cav Cadet School 1916, Brevet Maj 1917, Dis Remount Officer 1920; *m* 30 June 1910 Mary Katharine (*d* 1982), only child of Maj-Gen Hon John Edward Lindley, s of Baron Lindley (*see* 1921 edn), and *d* 31 Oct 1959, having had issue:

(1) Robert; *b* 4 April 1915; F/O RAFVR, WW II; *ka* May 1941

(1) *Veronica Mary; *b* 15 May 1911; dancer and choreographer, ballerina with ENSA and CEMA WW II; Dir Cygnet Ballet, Forres, and Intimate Ballet Theatre, Glenerney

(2) *Ursula Isabel [Miss Ursula Bruce, 114 Watchfield Court, Sutton Court Rd, London W1 4ND]; *b* 23 June 1920; WW II in WRNS

3 Alexander; *b* 29 July 1884; *educ* Balliol Coll Oxford (BA); DC Br E Africa; *d* in E Africa Oct 1917

4 David; DL Sutherland; *b* 11 June 1888; *educ* Eton; Col Seaforth Highrs WW I (wounded, despatches, brevet, Croix de Guerre Belgium); *m* 23 May 1919 Jennet, OBE (*d* 7 March 1982), dau of Rt Rev Atherton Gwillym Rawstorne, Bp of Whalley, of Balderstone Grange, Blackburn, Lancs, and *d* 26 Aug 1964, leaving issue:

(1) Peter Alexander; *b* 21 June 1925; *educ* Eton and Trin Coll Oxford (BA 1947); barrister Inner Temple 1948; *m* 29 March 1967 *Margaret Ann, ARCM, dau of Edward Matthew Phillips, of Vancouver, BC, Canada, and *d c* 1982

(1) *Rachel Mary [Mrs Bryan Durant, The Old House, Bighton, nr Alresford, Hants]; *b* 12 Aug 1922; WW II in Coastguard; *m* 6 Oct 1967 R-Adml Bryan Cecil Durant, CB, DSO, DSC, only s of Francis Durant

5 John Bernard, DL (Sutherland 1959, Hants 1962); *b* 9 April 1892; Capt RN, WWs I and II; High Sheriff Hants 1955; *m* 2 June 1923 Helen Rachel (*d* 4 Nov 1983) dau of Henry Feilden Rawstorne, of Fareham, Hants, and *d* 3 Aug 1971, having had issue:

(1) +Henry Victor, JP, DL (Hants 1984) [Lt-Cdr Henry Bruce of Salloch JP DL, Barley Down House, Ovington Down, Alresford, Hants]; *b* 3 April 1924; *educ* Eton and RAC Cirencester; Lt-Cdr RN WW II; RDC Winchester 1963, Chm Hants Scout Cncl 1964–, Gen Commr Income Tax 1967–; recognised in the name of Bruce of Salloch by Lord Lyon 1985; *m* 17 May 1951 *(Helen) Vernon Wallop, 2nd dau of V-Adml Sir Peveril Barton Reibey Wallop William Powlett, KCB, KCMG, CBE, DSO (*see* PORTSMOUTH, E), and has had issue:

1a +Peveril John [Peveril Bruce Esq, Hampage House, Ovington, Hants SO24 0HY]; *b* 6 Oct 1953, *educ* Eton; ACA 1976, FCA 1981, farmer; *m* 1986 *Rosamond Cornelia McLay (Minna), yr dau of Neil McLay Mills, and has:

1b +Otto Feilden; *b* 14 April 1989

2b +Finn Cardigan; *b* 26 May 1992

3b +Todd Heron; *b* 12 June 1996

2a +Alastair Andrew Bernard Reibey [Alastair Bruce of Crionaich, 22 Comeragh Rd, London W14 9HP; Tigh na Feidh, Inverie, Knoydart, Inverness-shire]; *b* 25 June 1960; *educ* Milton Abbey and RMA Sandhurst; Lt Scots Gds, S Atlantic Campaign 1982, Maj TA; recognised in the name of Bruce of Crionaich by Lord Lyon 1984; CStJ; Assist V-Pres Merrill Lynch 1983–89; author, TV documentary maker and commentator, Govr Milton Abbey; Fitzalan Pursuivant of Arms Extraordinary 1998, memb Roy Co Archers

1a *Robina Helen; *b* 27 May 1952; SRN, memb Nightingale Fund Cncl; *m* 16 April 1977 *Nigel Edward Charles Talbot-Ponsonby, and has issue (*see* SHREWSBURY and WATERFORD, E)

2a *Lucinda Jane; *b* 1 Jan 1956; *m* 22 Aug 1981 *Laurence Keith Scott, of Martyr Worthy, Hants, and has issue:

1b *Henry Edward Osborne; *b* 9 Aug 1982

2b *Toby Alexander Peveril; *b* 5 March 1984

3b *Oliver Charles Somerville; *b* 16 Feb 1987

4b *Barnaby Richard Laurence; *b* 6 March 1989

5b *Harvey Michael Lucknam; *b* 29 Aug 1991

(2) John Rawstorne; *b* 29 July 1925; *d* 16 Aug 1935

(3) +Francis Bernard (Rev) [The Rev Francis Bruce, 6 Gloucester St, Cirencester, Glos GL7 2DG]; *b* 22 Feb 1930; *educ* Eton and Trin Coll Oxford (BA 1952, MA 1956); Deacon 1954, Assist Curate St Mary the Virgin, Bury, Lancs 1954–58 and Sherborne Abbey, Curate i/c St Paul's Sherborne 1958–61, Rector Croston 1961–86; Vicar Bibury with Winson and Rector Barnsley, Glos, 1986–95; Chaplain to High Sheriff Glos 1997–98; *m* 30 April 1957 *Fiona Jane Beryl, only dau of Capt John Robert Sutherland Haines, CBE, RN, of Droxford, Hants, and has issue:

1a +Simon Jock; *b* 4 Feb 1959; *m* 1988 *Emma Félise, only dau of Sir Martin Wakefield Jacomb, and has issue:

1b +Patrick Francis Martin; *b* 1991

2b +Dominic Simon Mark; *b* 1993

1b *Zoe Fiona Evelyn; *b* 1995

2a +Jonathan Francis; *b* 25 March 1967

1a *Emma Cecilia Rachel; *b* 20 Nov 1960

(4) +Victor Robert [Dr Victor Bruce, 8 Claremont Rd, Marlow, Bucks]; MB; *b* 7 Feb 1932; *educ* Eton and London Hosp (MB, DRCOG); late Surgn-Lt RN; *m* 12 May 1956 *Dorothy May, yst dau of Rev Arthur Eli Pavey, of Hamble, Hants, and has issue:

1a +Angus Robert John; *b* 13 April 1960; *m* 1985 *Jill Moughlin and has:

1b +John Yardley; *b* 1989

2b +Ben River; *b* 1995

1b *Hannah May; *b* 1991

2a +Hamish Charles Victor; *b* 30 July 1962; *educ* Eton; *m* 1990 *Susan Mary Landreth and has:

1b +David Alexander; *b* 1993

2b +Jonathan Peter; *b* 1996

(5) +Alexander Rawstorne [Alexander Bruce Esq, 9 Av de Foestraets, 1180 Brussels]; *b* 26 Aug 1936; *educ* Eton and Trin Coll Oxford; *m* 30 June 1962 *Beatrice Germaine, dau of Jacques-Etienne Rossier, of Champbaband, Veytaux, Vaud, Switzerland

(1) *Constance Madeleine; *b* 7 July 1927; *m* 9 April 1949 *Lt-Cdr Godfrey Joseph Hines, RN (ret), yst s of P E Hines, of Trentham, Staffs, and has issue:

1a *Catherine Angela; *b* 27 July 1950; *m* 9 Sept 1972 *Clive Ward, s of W Ward, of Hayesford Park, Bromley, Kent

2a *Fiona Madeleine Hines; *b* 5 Nov 1952

(2) *Mabel Cecilia Helen (Celia) [Mrs Mackintosh of Mackintosh, Moy Hall, Tomatin, Inverness IV13 7YQ]; *b* 25 Jan 1939; *m* 10 Feb 1962 Lt-Cdr The Mackintosh of Mackintosh, OBE, JP, DL, FSA (Scot), RN (*d* 26 Dec 1995), Ld Lt Inverness, Cllr Highland Regn Cncl 1974–95, only s of V-Adml Mackintosh of Mackintosh, CB, DSO, DSC, and has:

1a *John Lachlan [The Mackintosh of Mackintosh, Moy Hall, Tomatin, Inverness IV13 7YQ]; *b* 2 Oct 1969

1a *Louisa Celia; *b* 1 Nov 1962; *m* 11 April 1987 *Stuart Cross

2a Anne Helen; *b* 28 April 1964; *d* 15 Nov 1971

3a *Bridget Margaret [Mrs Paul Dickson, 48 Pentland Drive, Comiston, Edinburgh EH10 6PX]; *b* 3 June 1966; *m* 30 Jan 1993 *Paul W Dickson and has:

1b *Calum William Duncan; *b* 30 Jan 1996

1b *Heather Mackintosh; *b* 24 March 1994

5 (cont.) Capt The Hon John and Mrs Bruce also adopted:

*Timothy Robertson [Timothy Bruce Esq, The Old Rectory, Combs, Stowmarket, Suffolk IP14 2JS]; *b* April 1942; *educ* Radley; *m* 1st 20 May 1972 (*divorce* 1983) (Diana) Olivia, dau of Raymond Tibbitt; *m* 2nd 1988 *Mrs Susan Mary Nicholson, dau of John Fraser Carnegie, DFC (*see* FIFE, D), and has issue by his 1st w:

1a *Tanya Romayne; *b* July 1973

1a *Diana Iona; *b* 1975

6 Victor Alexander; *b* 13 Feb 1897; Lt 11th Hus (SR) WW I; *m* 27 April 1929 Maud Rudolff (*m* 2nd 1934 John Navarino Fellowes Edwards and *d* 5 Nov 1961), dau of H Rudolff Sneddon, of Riga, and *d* 19 Dec 1930

1 Elisabeth Mary; *b* 11 Sept 1877; *m* 22 Sept 1898 Sir Henry Babington Smith, GBE, CH, KCB, CSI (*d* 29 Sept 1923), and *d* 13 May 1944, leaving issue

2 Christian Augusta; *b* 25 Jan 1879; *m* 15 Dec 1904 Sir Herbert Kinnaird Ogilvy, 12th Bt (*qv*), and *d* 12 Sept 1940

3 (Constance) Veronica, MBE (1920); *b* 24 Feb 1880; *d* unm 7 July 1969

4 Marjorie; *b* 12 Dec 1885; *d* 23 May 1901

5 Rachel Catherine; *b* 23 Feb 1890; *m* 7 Dec 1911 Lt-Col Sir Harry Calvert Williams Verney, 4th Bt (*qv*), and *d* 17 Dec 1964, leaving issue

The **9th/13th Earl** *m* 2nd 19 Nov 1913 Gertrude Lilian (whose issue are all in remainder to the Barony of Le Despenser (*see* FALMOUTH, B); *m* 3rd 30 Aug 1923 Lt-Col John Alexander Stirling (*d* 28 Nov 1957), DSO, MC of Kippendavie, Perthshire, and *d* 13 Feb 1971), dau of Cdr William Sherbrooke, of Oxton Hall, Notts (*see* WESTMORLAND, E), and widow of Capt Frederick Charles Ashley Ogilvy (*see* OGILVY, Bt), and by her had:

7 +Bernard, MC (1943); *b* 12 June 1917; *educ* Eton and New Coll Oxford (BA 1938); Capt (hon Maj) Scots Gds, SR, P/O RAFR WW II (despatches); *m* 1st 19 March 1958 (*divorce* 1968) Mary Coxe, dau of Philippus Miller, of Philadelphia, USA, and former w of Humphrey Humphreys; *m* 2nd 5 Dec 1970 (*divorce* 1976) Georgina Julia Susan, yr dau of Philip Pandely Argenti, CVO, MBE, of Rome; *m* 3rd 2 July 1976 *Mary Patricia [The Hon Mrs Bernard Bruce, Culross Abbey House, Culross, Dunfermline, Fife KY12 8JB], dau of Maj Donald Ramsay Macdonald, DSO, MC, of Hollymouth, Co Carlow, and former w of Gerald R Annesley, and *d* 1983

The 9th/13th EARL's est son,

EDWARD JAMES BRUCE, **10th Earl of Elgin** and **14th Earl of Kincardine**, KT (1933), CMG (1919), TD, CD, JP (Fife); *b* 8 June 1881; *educ* Eton and Balliol Coll Oxford; Hon LLD Glasgow and St Andrews; Col TR, Hon Col City of Edinburgh (Fortress) RE, Hon Col Elgin Regt perm Militia of Canada 1928–68, Capt Forfar and Kincardine RGA Militia, Lt-Col Highland (Fife) RGA, Hon Col 71st AA Regt RA (TA) 1939–47, Hon Col Elgin Regt and 357 (M) Regt RA (TA) and 471 (M) HAA Regt RA (Forth) TA, Hon A/Cdre 948 Sqdn RAF 1940; Ld Lt Fife, Pres Fife TAA 1935–65, WW I (despatches twice); Roy Co Archers, Assist Priv Sec to Sec State Colonies 1905–08, Assist Dir Labour and T/Col 1918–19, Grand Master Mason of Scotland 1921–24, Chm Carnegie UK Trust 1923–46, Ld High Commr to Gen Assembly Church of Scotland 1925 and 1926, Chm: Forth Conservancy Board 1926–41, Educn Endowments Commn (Scotland) 1929–37, Scottish Nat Council for Juvenile Employment 1929–46, Fife CC 1930–38, re-elected 1946 and V-Convener, Pres: Scottish Devpt Cncl 1931–46, Edinburgh and E Scotland Coll of Ag 1933–40, Chm Govrs Newbattle Abbey Coll 1935–68, Memb BBC Advsy Cncl 1937–48 and 1952, Pres Empire Exhibition (Scotland) 1938, V-Pres Nat Tst Scotland, Pres Roy Highland Ag Soc 1949, Provost Roy Burgh of Culross 1954–63, Chm Tstees Nat Centl Library, Pres Dunfermline Bldg Soc, V-Pres Bldg Soc Assoc, Extrdy Dir Roy Bank Scotland; Grand Cross Polonia Restituta; *m* 5 Jan 1921 Hon Katherine Elizabeth Cochrane, DBE (*d* 1989), dau of 1st Baron Cochrane of Cults (*qv*), and *d* 27 Nov 1968, leaving:

1 ANDREW DOUGLAS ALEXANDER THOMAS BRUCE, **11th and present Earl of Elgin and 15th and present Earl of Kincardine**

2 +James Michael Edward, CBE (1992), JP (Perthshire 1962) [The Hon James Bruce CBE, Dron House, Balmanno, by Perth PH2 9HG]; *b* 26 Aug 1927; *educ* Eton, RMC Sandhurst and RAC Cirencester (Dipl 1950); late Lt Scots Gds; FRSA, FinstD; Chm Scottish Woodland Owners Assoc (Commercial) Ltd, memb Home Grown Timber Advsy Ctee, Chm SWOAC Holdings Ltd 1967–1993, Hon Fell Scottish CDI 1993, Hon Fell Game Conservancy 1993; *m*

1st 29 July 1950 (*divorce* 1974) Hon (Margaret) Jean Dagbjørt Coats, only dau of 2nd Baron Glentanar (*see* 1970 edn), and has issue:

(1) Robert James Thomas; *b* 24 June 1953; *educ* Eton; *d* unm 14 July 1979

(2) +John Edward [John Bruce Esq, Balmanno Castle, by Perth, PH2 9HG]; *b* 13 Nov 1958

(3) +Michael Andrew [Michael Bruce Esq, Glen Tanar House, Aboyne, Aberdeenshire AB34 5EU]; *b* 29 May 1961; *m* 1988 *Claire, est dau of James Mattocks, of Brussels, Belgium, and has:

1a +Alasdair James Thomas; *b* 1991

2a +Angus William Robert; *b* 1996

1a *Eleanor Marie Jean; *b* 1993

(1) *(Janet) Clare [Mrs John Carson, Congalton, N Berwick, E Lothian EH39 5JL]; *b* 15 Dec 1954; *m* 1979 *John Seton Burrell Carson, er son of Alan Carson of Drumbain, Dunure, Ayrshire, and has issue:

1a *David; *b* 1986

1a *Iona Jane; *b* 1981

2a *Rachel Anne; *b* 1983

3a *Alice Mary; *b* 1989

4a *Rosanna Jean; *b* (triplet) 1989

5a *Sophie Katherine; *b* (triplet) 1989

2 (cont.) The Hon James Bruce *m* 2nd 26 April 1975 *Morven-Anne, dau of Alistair Macdonald, of Dalguise, Perthshire, and by her has further issue:

(4) +Alexander James; *b* 1977

(5) +Simon Alistair; *b* 1979

(2) *Katherine Anne; *b* 1980

(3) *Emma Victoria; *b* 1987

3 +(Edward) David [The Hon David Bruce, Blair Hill, Rumbling Bridge, Kinross]; *b* 29 Feb 1936; *educ* Eton and Balliol Coll Oxford (BA 1960); late Lt Intell Corps; chm Bruce Stevenson Ltd, Chm Youth Clubs Scotland; *m* 30 April 1960 *Sarah Elizabeth Wallop, yr dau of Capt Newton James Wallop William-Powlett, DSC, RN (*see* PORTSMOUTH, E), and has:

(1) +Newton Edward John; *b* 27 Aug 1964

(1) *Anna Catherine; *b* 1 Oct 1962; *m* 1988 *Edward H Hocknell, er s of Peter Hocknell, of Willaston, Cheshire, and has issue:

1a *Henrietta Jean Wallop; *b* 1992

2a *Catherine; *b* 19–

3a *Grizel Patience; *b* 30 Jan 1998

1 *Martha Veronica, OBE (1958), TD, JP (Fife 1951) [The Lady Martha Bruce, Gardener's Cottage, The Old Orchard, Limekilns, Dunfermline KY11 3HS]; *b* 7 Nov 1921; Lt-Col WRAC (TA) 1961, WW II; Ldy-in-Waiting to HRH THE PRINCESS ROYAL 1965, Govr Greenock Prison 1970–75 and Cornton Vale Instn Stirling 1975–83

2 *Jean Christian; *b* 12 Jan 1923; *m* 21 July 1945 *David Wemyss of that Ilk (*see* WEMYSS and MARCH, E) and has issue

3 *Alison Margaret [The Lady Alison Stewart-Patterson, Drishane Farm, 251 Senneville Rd, Senneville, PQ, Canada]; *b* 17 Oct 1931; LRAM 1951; *m* 6 July 1957 *Cleveland Stewart-Patterson, s of Donald Stewart-Patterson, of Montreal, and Mrs H Markey, and has:

(1) *David Henry Cleveland; *b* 20 June 1958

(2) *Donald Iain Edward; *b* 15 May 1960

(1) *Christian Mary Lorraine; *b* 18 July 1962

ELIBANK

Arms: Quarterly, 1st and 4th, or a fetterlock azure, on a chief of the second three stars argent (for MURRAY of Blackbarony); 2nd and 3rd, azure, three stars within a double tressure flory counter-flory argent, and in the centre a martlet or (for SETON). **Crest:** A lion rampant gules holding a battleaxe proper. **Supporters:** Two horses argent, bridled gules. **Motto:** *Virtute fideque* ('By virtue and faith').
Creations: Bt. (NS) 16 May 1628, L. (S) 18 March 1643.

THE 14TH LORD ELIBANK, of Ettrick Forest, Co Selkirk, and a **Baronet** (also titular Earl of Westminster, *cr* by James III of 12 Aug 1759) (Sir Alan D'Ardis Erskine-Murray, Bt) [The Rt Hon The Lord Elibank, House of Lords, London SW1A 0PW]; *b* 31 Dec 1923; *s* cousin 1973; *educ* Bedford Sch and Peterhouse Coll Cambridge (BA 1949, MA 1953); RE 1942–47, barrister Middle Temple 1949 (practising 1949–55), with Shell Internat Petroleum 1955–80, personnel consultant: Deminex UK Oil and Gas 1981–86; *m* 1 Sept 1962 Valerie Sylvia (*d* 13 Jan 1997), only dau of Herbert William Dennis, of St Margaret's, Twickenham, and has issue:

1 +ROBERT FRANCIS, *Master of Elibank* [The Master of Elibank, 50 Reporton Rd, Fulham, London SW6 7JR]; *b* 10 Oct 1964; *educ* Harrow and Reading U (BA 1987); *m* 20 Jan 1996 *Antonia, dau of Roger Carrington, of Hants, and has:

(1) *Isabella Valerie Elibank; *b* 31 March 1997

2 +Tim(othy) Alexander Elibank; *b* 6 May 1967; *educ* Eton and Exeter U

Lineage: ANDREW MURRAY of Blackbarony (*see* MURRAY, Bt, of Blackbarony); *d* 1 Sept 1572, leaving a 3rd s:

Sir GIDEON MURRAY, PC (S 1610); acquired Elibank or Eliburne, Selkirkshire, by charter under the Great Seal 15 March 1594/5; ktd 1605, Commr for the Borders 1605–17, one of the New Octavians (ctee of eight persons) controlling Scottish Treasury business 1611, Ld of the Articles for the small Barons 1612, Treasurer Depute 1612, a Ld of Session as Lord Elibank 1613–21; *m* Margaret, dau of Dionis Pentland, and *d* 28 June 1621 leaving, with at least one dau (Agnes, *m* Sir William Scott of Harden and had issue; *see* POLWARTH, L) an est s:

Sir Patrick Murray, 1st Bt (BS), so *cr* 16 May 1628, and **1st Lord Elibank** (S), so *cr* 18 March 1643, with remainder to heirs male whatsoever, of Ettrick Forest, Selkirkshire; *b* before his parents' marriage but with other of their children *b* before 4 June 1601 legitimated by Edinburgh Commissaries then; *educ* Oxford (MA 1605) and Gray's Inn; Keeper Caerlaverock Castle 1611, one of the six peers who opposed the handing over of CHARLES I to the E Parl Jan 1646/7; *m* 1st (contract 21 Aug 1610) Margaret, dau of Sir Alexander Hamilton of Innerwick, and had, with a s (*d* young):

1 Christian; *m* 1631 George Douglas of Bonjedburgh, and had issue

The **1st Lord** *m* 2nd (contract 24 Jan 1616/7) Elizabeth, dau of Sir James Dundas of Arniston, and by her had further issue:

1 PATRICK, **2nd Lord**

2 William, of Spot, of which he had a charter 31 March 1674; *m* 1st Isobel Douglas; *m* 2nd Margaret Baillie and *d* 17 Aug 1684, having had issue by both

2 Elizabeth; *m* 1637 Archibald Stirling, est s of Sir Archibald Stirling of Garden

3 Agnes; *m* 1643 George Auchinleck, est s of Sir William Auchinleck of Balmanno

4 Jean; *m* 1644 Sir William Murray, 2nd Bt, of Dunerne (*qv*), and had issue

5 Isobel; *m* 25 April 1644 Sir James Murray of Cavens, and had issue

The **1st Lord** *m* 3rd 16 Jan 1627/8 Helen, dau of Bernard Lindsay of Lockhill, and by her had further issue:

3 Walter, of Ravilly, Co Carlow; *m* Jane Butler, sis of 1st Viscount of Galmoye (*see* ORMONDE, M), and *d* 1695, having had issue:

(1) William, of Ravilly; *m* Mary, dau of Oliver Grace, of Gracefield, but *dsp* 1696

(2) Richard, of Ravilly; *d* 1761, leaving:

1a Oliver

4 George, of Pittencreiff, Fife; Lt-Col Horse Gds; *m* 1st 1667 Margaret, dau of Sir John Moncreiffe, Bt (*see* ERROLL, E); *m* 2nd 13 Feb 1670 Elizabeth, dau of Sir John Erskine and widow of James Clerk, of Pittencrieff, and Id *c* 1702, leaving issue

5 Helen; *m* 1st 1648 Sir Alexander Auchmutie of Gosford; *m* 2nd Capt William Carstairs, s of Sir John Carstairs of Kilconquhar

The **1st Lord** *m* 4th 11 Dec 1636 Agnes (*d* 16 Nov 1637), dau of Thomas Nicolson, and by her had issue:

5 Thomas; *b* 12 Nov 1637; *d c* 15 Feb 1659

The **1st Lord** *m* 5th (contract 24 March 1637/8) Katherine (*d* by 16 Oct 1655), dau of Cornelius Weir, of Edinburgh, and widow of Sir James Murray of Kilbaberton, and *d* 12 Nov 1649

His est surv s,

PATRICK MURRAY, **2nd Lord Elibank**; joined royalists under Montrose Civil War and was fined 20,000 marks (£13, 333 6s 8d); *m* 9 April 1643 Lady Elizabeth Stewart, dau of 1st Earl of Traquair (*see* MORAY, E), and *d* 13 Feb 1661, having had, with five daus:

1 PATRICK, **3rd Lord**

2 William; Offr Gds

3 John; *bapt* 20 Dec 1649; Capt in the Army; *ka* Battle of Antrim

The 2nd LORD's est s,

PATRICK MURRAY, **3rd Lord Elibank**, PC (S 1685–86; removed for opposing repeal of Penal Laws); cmded militia troop of Roxburgh and Selkirk; *m* Anna, dau of Alexander Burnet, Archbp St Andrews, and widow of 7th Lord Elphinstone (*qv*), and *d* 1686, leaving surv issue:

1 ALEXANDER, **4th Lord**

1 Mary; *m* 25 April 1701 2nd Earl of Cromarty (*see* CROMARTIE, E) and had issue

2 Helen; *m* 13 Aug 1703, as his 2nd w, Sir John MacKenzie, 3rd Bt, of Coul (*qv*)

The 3rd LORD's only s,

ALEXANDER MURRAY, **4th Lord Elibank**; *b* 9 March 1676/7; a fndr Soc of Improvers in the knowledge of Ag in Scotland 1723; *m* 24 Feb 1697/8 Elizabeth (*d* 11 Nov 1756), dau of George Stirling, surgn, of Edinburgh, MP Edinburgh, and *d* 6 Feb 1735/6, having had, with other issue:

1 PATRICK MURRAY, **5th Lord Elibank**; *b* 27 Feb 1702/3; advocate 1723, Lt-Col (1739) cmdg Wynyard's Marines Cartagena Expdn 1741; *m* 1735 Maria Margaretta (*d* 6 June 1762), dau of Cornelius de Jonge d'Ellemeet, Receiver-Gen United Provinces, and widow of William, 6th Baron North (*see* 1970 edn) and 2nd Baron Grey of Rolleston, and *dsp* 3 Aug 1778

2 GEORGE MURRAY, **6th Lord Elibank**; *b* 14 May 1706; R-Adml 1756; accompanied Lord Anson (*see* LICHFIELD, E) in his circumnavigation; *m* 8 Jan 1760 Isabella (*d* 28 Dec 1801), dau of 3rd Earl of Cromarty (*see* CROMARTIE, E), and *d* 12 Nov 1785, having had:

(1) Maria Murray later Murray-Mackenzie (added on inheriting the Cromarty estates); *m* 3 May 1790 Edward Hay, of New Hall, bro of 7th Marquess of Tweeddale (*qv*), and *d* 8 Oct 1858

(2) Isabella Murray later Murray-Mackenzie (added on inheriting the Cromarty estates)

3 Gideon (Rev); DD; Preb Durham, Chaplain to 43rd (later 42nd) Highrs 1745, Chaplain-Gen Army 1749; *m* 30 June 1746 Elizabeth (*d* 21 Nov 1796), only dau of Gen David Montolieu, Baron de St Hypolite (HRE *cr*, a Huguenot), and *d* 21 June 1776, leaving:

(1) ALEXANDER, **7th Lord**

(2) David; *b* 10 May 1748; MP Peebles 1785 and New Radnor 1790; *m* 8 Oct 1783 Elizabeth (*d* 9 July 1824), 4th dau and coheir of Rt Hon Thomas Harley, bro of 4th Earl of Oxford and Mortimer (*see* OXFORD AND ASQUITH, E, preliminary remarks), and *d* 8 May 1794, leaving issue:

1a David Rodney (Rev); *b* 12 April 1791; Rector Brampton Brian, Herefs; *m* 4 Dec 1828 Frances (*d* 1892), dau of John Portal, of Freefolk, Hants (*see* PORTAL, Bt), and *d* 4 Nov 1878, leaving, with other issue:

1b David Mortimer; *b* 11 May 1832; Maj 64th Regt; *m* 3 Jan 1861 Ida (*d* 24 Nov 1869), dau of Capt Lewis Fenton, of Underbanks, Yorkshire, MP Huddersfield, and *dsp* 24 Jan 1881

2b Elibank Harley; *b* 26 Sept 1833; V-Adml; *d* unm 27 Sept 1901

3b Alexander William; *b* 29 Jan 1836; HEICS; *k* Indian Mutiny 14 Sept 1857

4b Francis Rodney; *b* 9 March 1838; *m* 1 June 1865 Jane Celestria (*d* 1914), dau of Gerald Noel Hoare, and *d* 3 March 1919, having had issue:

1c Rodney Montolieu; *b* 22 June 1869; *dsp* 19 Jan 1900

1c Frances Jane; *m* 14 Sept 1892 Col Harry Shuldham Shuldham-Legh, MVO (*d* 25 March 1930), and *d* 10 Sept 1930, leaving issue

2c Mary Celestria; *m* 17 Jan 1893 Capt Conyers Lang, RN (*d* 5 Sept 1917), s of Maj Frederick Lang, of Parkstone, Dorset, and *d* 13 June 1945, leaving issue

1b Elizabeth Clara; *m* 10 Aug 1853 Robert John Hopkins (*d* 26 April 1899) and *d* 1 May 1903, leaving issue

2b Louisa Sophia; *m* 3 May 1860 Rev Reginald Whitehall Margesson, and *d* 2 Jan 1893, leaving issue

3b Agnes Adeliza; *m* 5 June 1879 Charles Francis Burgmann, and had issue

1a Elizabeth; *m* 1810 R-Adml William H Shirreff

2a Maria Clara; Maid of Honour to HM QUEEN VICTORIA; *m* 1819 Sir Edmund Hungerford Lechmere, 2nd Bt (*qv*), and *d* 29 Jan 1865, leaving issue

3a Louisa; *m* 6 Jan 1814 Sir John Chandos Reade, 7th Bt (*qv*), of Shipton Court, Oxon, and *d* 6 Feb 1821, leaving issue

4 Alexander, 1st titular Earl of Westminster (E), so *cr* by the titular James III 12 Aug 1759, with remainder, failing heirs male of his body, to his bros by primogeniture; *b* 9 Dec 1712; Ensign 26th Foot 1737; Jacobite; committed to Newgate Prison Feb-June 1751 after opposing the govt at the Westminster election 1750; later lived in France; probable fomentor of the Elibank Plot of 1752–53, in which an elite force of Jacobites aimed to take St James's Palace, mount an attack on the Tower of London and kidnap or slaughter the Royal Family; returned to GB *c* 1765 and his exile formally terminated under the Privy Seal April 1771; *d* unm 27 Feb 1778

5 James; Gen, cmded left wing of Wolfe's Army taking of Quebec 1759, Govr Quebec 1759, first Br Govr Canada 1763; *m* 1st the dau and coheir (Idsp 26 June 1779) of John Collier, of Hastings; *m* 2nd 14 March 1780 Anne (*d* 2 Aug 1824), dau of Abraham Whitham, of Minorca, and *d* 18 June 1794, having by her had issue:

(1) James Patrick, CB; *b* 21 Jan 1782; Maj-Gen; *m* 31 Jan 1803 Elizabeth (*d* 15 Nov 1865), dau of Edward Rushworth, of Freshwater House, IoW, by Hon Catherine Holmes, dau of Leonard, last Baron Holmes (*d* 1804), and *d* 5 Dec 1834, leaving, with other issue:

1a James Edward Ferguson; *b* 19 April 1806; Lt RN; *m* 15 Dec 1830 Katherine Jane (*d* 22 July 1836), dau of John Slaughter, and *dvp* 17 July 1834, leaving issue:

1b James Pulteney; *b* 8 June 1833; Capt RMLI; *m* 11 Sept 1862 Henrietta Victoria (*d* 14 Feb 1918), only dau of Arthur Browne Blakiston, and *d* 21 Aug 1874, having had issue:

1c James Arthur (Rev); *b* 16 Oct 1865; MA, BD Dublin; *d* unm

2c William Harry Elibank; *b* 5 Dec 1866; BOT medal for saving life at sea; *m* 14 Dec 1892 Bertha Delamore (*d* Feb 1959), dau of Patrick Brougham, and *d* 28 Sept 1937, leaving issue:

1d Douglas Elibank; *b* Nov 1898; WW I 1915–18 Australian Light Horse (Palestine), and WW II 1939–43; *m* 1st 24 April 1935 (*divorce* 1944) Rewa, dau of Joseph Patrick O'Hara, of Fiji; *m* 2nd 12 July 1947 *Ngaio Milva Barnott (*d* 1976), and *d* 1989, having had issue by his 1st w:

1e +William Eion Elibank [William Murray Esq, Lot 8, Burraga Rd, Rockley, NSW 2795, Australia]; *b* 8 April 1938; *m* 1970 *Sheila Marion, dau of Walter Robert Pont, of E Maitland, NSW, and has:

1f +James Douglas Elibank; *b* 1970

1f *Alexandra Naomi; *b* 1974

1e *Pamela Anna Elibank [Mrs C McKenna, 78 Fairfield Rd, Hamilton, NZ]; *b* 6 June 1940; *m* Feb 1967 *C T McKenna

2e *Rita Gail Elibank [Mrs Graham Burns, PO Box 213, Lindfield, NSW]; *b* 25 Feb 1942; *m* 1974 *Graham John Horrigan Burns

1d Rita Lindsey; *m* 1917 John Frederick Wyly (*d* 21 Dec 1960)

2d Mabel de Vaux; *d* unm Nov 1939

3c Edward Rushworth Blakiston; *b* 7 Dec 1868; Col IA WW I, Afghan War 1919, NWF India 1919–20, Hon Brig-Gen 1921, Order St Stanislas Russia; *m* 15 Aug 1905 Hilda Dorothea (*d* as a result of enemy action 1942), est dau of Reginald Paul, and *d* as the result of enemy action 1942, leaving issue:

1d James Patrick, CMG (1958); *b* 10 Oct 1906; *educ* St Edward's Sch Oxford and Ch Ch Oxford (BA 1928); Commr N Rhodesia in UK, Sr Provincial Commr N Rhodesia; *m* 21 May 1934 Margaret Ruth [Mrs James Murray, Trewen, Shaftesbury Road, Woking, Surrey, GU22 7DU], dau of Rev Alfred Edward Buchanan, of Blandford Ave, Oxford, and *d* 8 Jan 1993, having had issue:

1e +(James) Alex(ander) Gideon [Alex Murray Esq, Selhurst, Selhurst Common, Surrey GU5 0LS]; *b* 18 Sept 1936; *educ* Trin Coll, Glenalmond; FCA; chm Standard Commercial Corp; *m* 11 Sept 1965 *Gillian Mary, dau of H Gordon Adcock, of St Albans, Herts, and has issue:

1f +(James) Richard [Richard Murray Esq, Cottage on the Green, Meysey Hampton, Glos]; *b* 20 May 1967; *educ* Bradfield and Durham U (MA); schoolmaster

2f +Andrew Thomas [Andrew Murray Esq, 22 Ambrose Rd, Bristol]; *b* 6 Nov 1968; *educ* Bradfield and Exeter U (BSc); assistant producer BBC

2e +Patrick Edward [Patrick Murray Esq, 1 Chelsea Dve, Durban 4051, Natal]; *b* 11 Aug 1939; *educ* Trin Coll Glenalmond; *m* 1963 *Marie-Danielle, dau of Henri C du Cladier de Curac, of Lusaka, Zambia, and has issue:

1f +Charles Patrick; *b* 1971; *educ* Hilton Coll Natal and Cape Town U

1f *Danielle Jeanne; *b* 10 Feb 1964; *m* 19– *Terence Maritz, of Johannesburg and has issue

2f *Diana Ruth; *b* 23 Nov 1965

3e +Thomas Walter [Thomas Murray Esq, The White House, Pembroke Rd, Woking, Surrey GU22 7EB]; *b* 17 Jan 1942; *educ* Trin Coll Glenalmond; slr; *m* 1975 *Annette Timms, dau of Clifford Tapper of Solihull, Staffs, and has:

1f +David Thomas; *b* 18 Nov 1976; *educ* St George's Weybridge and Durham U

2d Thomas Edward Elibank (Rev); *b* 31 July 1908; *educ* St Edward's Sch Oxford; WW II as Capt Gordon Highrs; Rector Holy Trinity Church, Monifieth; *m* 20 May 1932 Hester Doreen (*d* as the result of enemy action 1942), dau of Capt C A C Bentley, Roy Warwickshire Regt, and *d* 27 May 1979

1d *Elizabeth [Miss Elizabeth Murray, 2 Churchill, Morningside, Edinburgh]; *b* 29 Sept 1911

1c Georgina Maria; *d* unm 15 Aug 1939

2c Henrietta; *d* unm 28 Jan 1959

1b Georgina Maria; *m* 15 Jan 1854 Lt Young, RA, and *dsp* 16 Dec 1855

2b Katherine Elizabeth; *m* 30 Aug 1855 Lt-Col Thomas Mahon, RA (*d* 22 Aug 1897), and *d* 20 March 1893

2a Pulteney; *b* 9 July 1807; Capt 36th Regt; *m* 23 May 1848 Jane (*d* 19 Oct 1851), dau of J Mackenny, and *d* 20 Sept 1875, leaving:

1b Pulteney Henry; *b* 17 Nov 1849; Col cmdg N Lancs Bde, 2nd Bn King's Shropshire LI and 4th Regtl Dist; *m* 20 Jan 1876 Mary Leaycraft (*d* 1922), dau of Hon S S Ingham, of Bermuda, and *d* 15 Nov 1912, having had issue:

1c Pulteney Charles Rushworth; *b* 1 April 1877; *d* 3 May 1882

2c Bertie Elibank, DSO (1916); *b* 10 May 1881; Col (ret) 1st Bn KSLI, Somaliland 1908–10 (medal with clasp), WW I (despatches five times, Brevet Lt-Col), Cdr 158th (Roy Welch) Inf Bde (TA) 1930–33, WW II cmdg 38th Divl Sch 1939–40, 6th Bn Hereford HG 1940–45; *m* 30 June 1927 Agnes Laetitia (*d* 22 Nov 1964), widow of Capt Barrington Blomfield Dickson, Northants Regt, of Grovesbrook, Fleet, Hants, and *dsp* 14 Sept 1960

3c Percy James Alexander; *b* 30 May 1884; Lt Dorsetshire Regt; *d* Australia 1920

4c Gerald Graham MURRAY later MURRAY-MOORE (roy licence 15 July 1931), MC; *b* 17 Sept 1888; Capt York and Lancs Regt WW I (despatches); *m* 13 March 1922 Lilian Julietta (*d* 7 Nov 1953), dau of Henry John Simonds and widow of Randall Kingsmill Moore, DL, of Barne Park, Co Tipperary, and *d* 8 July 1949

1c Catherine Gladys; *b* 18 Jan 1886; *m* 4 Aug 1914 Capt Maurice Fiennes Fitzgerald Wilson, DSO, RN (ret) (*d* 16 Feb 1975), er s of Maurice Fitzgerald Wilson, of London SW, and *d* 12 April 1958, leaving issue

3a Charles; *b* 30 Dec 1814; Capt 76th Foot; *m* 12 Oct 1844 Anne Mitchell, est dau of Robert Scott, and *dsp* 6 April 1848

4a Douglas Alexander; *b* 2 Jan 1824; *m* 1st Mary Ann Murphy (*dsp* 10 May 1851); *m* 2nd 8 March 1855 Mary, widow of John Simms, and *d* 19 July 1866, leaving issue:

1b James Patrick; *b* 1856

1b Catherine Beltzhoore

2b Elizabeth Rushworth

3b Susan Douglas

1a Catherine Anne; *m* 1826 Gen Sir Charles Routledge O'Donnell (*d* 18 Nov 1870), and *d* 26 Feb 1895

2a Harriet Elizabeth; *m* 14 July 1834 Rev Henry Hodges (*d* Sept 1870), Rector Alphamstone, Essex, and *d* 29 June 1872

3a Mary Johanna; *m* 1st 10 July 1834 A Newton, MD (*dec*); *m* 2nd 1849 William Francis Harvey (*d* 23 April 1893), of Purbrook Heath House, Hants

4a Cordelia Maria; *m* 30 March 1864 Gen Sir Charles Trollope, KCB (*d* 5 July 1888), and *d* 3 Dec 1909, leaving issue (*see* TROLLOPE, Bt)

(1) Cordelia; *m* 1803 Rev Henry Hodges (*d* 1 July 1837), and had issue

(2) Wilhelmina; *m* 18 May 1813 James, 4th and last Baron Douglas of Douglas (*see* HAMILTON and BRANDON, D), and *dsp* 25 Feb 1866

(3) Anne Harriet; *d* 1850

1 Barbara; *m* 1 Sept 1719 Sir James Johnstone, 3rd Bt, of Westerhall (*qv*), and *d* 15 March 1773, leaving issue

2 Anne; *m* 3 Feb 1733 James Ferguson, Ld of Session as Lord Pitfour, and *d* 2 Jan 1793

3 Janet; *m* 22 June 1750 Sir Robert Murray, 6th Bt, of Dunerne (*qv*), and *d* 9 Aug 1759, leaving issue

4 Helen; *m* 12 Sept 1716 Sir John Stewart, Bt, of Grandtully, and *dsp* 28 Dec 1809

The 6th LORD's nephew,

ALEXANDER MURRAY, **7th Lord Elibank**; *b* 24 April 1747; Lt 3rd Foot Gds 1763–70, Ld Lt Peeblesshire 1794–1820, Pres Roy Co Archers 1816–20; *m* 1st 20 May 1776 his cousin Mary Clara Montolieu (*d* 19 Jan 1802), dau of Lewis Charles, Baron de St Hypolite, and had, with other issue:

1 ALEXANDER MURRAY, **8th Lord Elibank**; *b* 26 Feb 1780; Offr Coldstream Gds; *m* 8 March 1803 Janet (*d* 9 June 1836), dau and heir of John Oliphant, of Bachilton, Perthshire, self-styled Lord Oliphant, and *d* 9 April 1830, having had, with other issue:

(1) ALEXANDER OLIPHANT MURRAY, **9th Lord Elibank**; *b* 23 May 1804; HEICS; *m* 6 Aug 1838 Emily Maria (*d* 3 June 1879), only dau of Archibald Montgomery and niece of Sir James Montgomery, 2nd Bt, of Stanhope (*qv*), and *d* 31 May 1871, having had, with other issue:

1a MONTOLIEU FOX OLIPHANT MURRAY, **10th Lord** and 1st VISCOUNT ELIBANK OF ELIBANK, Co Selkirk (UK), so *cr* 3 July 1911, JP (Selkirkshire), DL (Peeblesshire); *b* 27 April 1840; Cdr RN, China Expdn 1860 (medal), cmded naval detachment suppression of negro rising Morant Bay Jamaica 1865; Ld Lt Peeblesshire 1896–1908; *m* 2 May 1868 Blanche Alice (*d* 22 Oct 1936), est dau of Edward John Scott, of Portland Lodge, Southsea, Hants, and *d* 20 Feb 1927, having had, with other issue:

1b ALEXANDER WILLIAM CHARLES OLIPHANT, PC (1911), 1st and last BARON MURRAY OF ELIBANK, so *cr* 13 Aug 1912; *b* 12 April 1870; Comptroller Household 1905–09, Parly U-Sec India 1909–10, Lib Ch Whip 1910–12; *m* 1 Aug 1894 Hilda Louisa Janey Wolfe (*d* 27 Sept 1929), yr dau of James Wolfe Murray, of Cringletie, Peeblesshire (*see* MURRAY, Bt, of Blackbarony), and *dsp* & *vp* 13 Sept 1920, when the Barony expired

2b Edward Oliphant; *b* 22 Oct 1871; Capt QO Cameron Highrs, S African War 1901 (Adj Lovat Scouts); *m* 9 Jan 1900 Mary Millard (*d* 6 Sept 1943), dau of Henry Christian Allhusen, and was *ka* Quaggafontein, Orange River, 20 Sept 1901, leaving issue:

1c Mary Alice Oliphant; *m* 1 June 1921 Capt Hon Harry Nugent Morgan-Grenville, OBE (*see* KINLOSS, L), and had issue

3b (CHARLES) GIDEON MURRAY, **11th Lord Elibank** and 2nd VISCOUNT ELIBANK OF ELIBANK; *b* 7 Aug 1877; S African War (Queen's Medal); Assist Priv Sec Lt-Govr Br New Guinea 1898, RM W Div Br New Guinea 1900, A/Cmdt Native Constab 1901, Priv Sec Commr Native Affairs 1901, Assist Native Commr Transvaal 1902, Assist Priv Sec PUS Colonies 1907, Administrator of St Vincent 1909–14 (A/Gov Windward Islands 1912) and St Lucia 1914–18, Food Commr W Scotland 1917–18, MP St Rollox Div Glasgow 1918–22; Ld Lt Peeblesshire 1934–45, Memb Roy Coy Archers, Hon Col 8th Bn Roy Scots 1939–45, Past Pres Fedn Chambers Commerce Br Empire; *m* 23 Jan 1908 Ermine Mary Katherine, JP, DJStJ, Order of Mercy, Silver Jubilee and Coronation Medals (*d* 22 March 1955), dau of Henry Robert Madocks, of Glanywern, Denbighs, and Llay Hall, Gresford, by Hon Anne Amelia, dau of 1st Baron Napier of Magdala (*qv*) and widow of Lt-Col James Henry Aspinwall, 5th and 3rd Dragoon Gds, and *dsp* 11 March 1951

4b ARTHUR CECIL MURRAY, **12th Lord Elibank** and 3rd and last VISCOUNT ELIBANK OF ELIBANK, CMG (1918), DSO (1916); *b* 27 March 1879; Lt-Col 2nd King Edward's Horse (SR), Capt KOSB, ADC to: Lt-Govr Bengal 1900, GOC 1st Inf Div Delhi Manoeuvres 1902, Lt-Govr Bengal (Delhi Durbar) 1902; China Expdn 1900 (medal), cmded Mounted Inf Co protecting Sinho-Shanhaikwan Rlwy 1901–02, NWF India and Chitral with 5th Gurkja Rifles 1903–07; MP Kincardineshire 1908–23, Quebec Tercentenary Celebrations 1908 (guest of Canadian Govt) as rep Gen Hon James Murray 1st Br Govr Canada, PPS to Parly U-Sec India 1909 and For Sec 1910–14, passed Bill through H of C to ameliorate conditions of worn-out horse traffic 1914, helped raise 2nd King Edward's Horse 1914 in which served with 1st Canadian Inf Div Belgium and France 1915–16 (despatches), Assist Mil Attaché Washington 1917–18, Memb Roy Coy of Archers, dir LNER 1923–48, Wembley Stadium Ltd 1927–60, author: *Memorials of Sir Gideon Murray of Elibank and His Times 1560–1621*, *The Five Sons of 'Bare Betty'* (1936), *A Modern Marvel* (1938), *Master and Brother* (1945), *British Foreign Policy 1918–39* (1946), *At Close Quarters* (1947), *Decisive Battles in History in a Nutshell* (1947), *The Whirlpool of Corrievreckan* (1949) and *An Episode in the Spanish War, 1739–1744* (1952); *m* 3 July 1931 Faith Celli (actress: played title role *Peter Pan* 1918; *d* 16 Dec 1942), dau of Francis H Standing, and *dsp* 5 Dec 1962, when the Viscountcy expired

1b Emily Blanche; *b* 20 Dec 1872; DGStJ, medal of Queen Elisabeth of Belgium; *m* 29 April 1893 Sir Robert Grenville Harvey, 2nd Bt (*d* 4 April 1931), and *d* 21 Oct 1935, leaving issue

2b Alice Florence Murray later Oliphant-Murray (deed poll 22 Nov 1956); *b* 12 Dec 1873; fndr and Hon organiser King Albert's Civilian Hospital Fund 1915, medal of Queen Elisabeth of Belgium; *m* 1st 15 July 1902 (*annulled* 1909) Sir Stephen Leech, KCMG (*d* 12 May 1925); *m* 2nd 24 July 1919 David Fell, JP, MLA NSW (*d* 6 Jan 1956), s of Capt T W Fell, of Langside, Scotland, and *dsp* 25 Feb 1966

3b Nina Charlotte; *b* 7 April 1875; *m* 18 Feb 1896 Hylton Philipson (*d* 4 Dec 1935), 3rd s of H Philipson, of 77 Lancaster Gate, London W, and *d* 1 June 1966, leaving issue

4b Clara Isabel; *b* 24 Oct 1880; *m* 6 Aug 1902 (*divorce* 1934) 2nd Baron Doverdale (*d* 23 March 1935; *see* 1949 edn), and *d* 22 Dec 1945, leaving issue

5b Evelyn Izme, JP (IoW); *b* 13 Feb 1886; *m* 1st 18 Oct 1906 Capt George Crosfield Norris Nicholson (*ka* 11 March 1916) and had issue (*see* NICHOLSON, Bt); *m* 2nd 31 July 1917 1st Baron Mottistone (*qv*) and *d* 11 Aug 1976, leaving issue by both husbs

2a Dudley Oliphant; *b* 20 Nov 1846; barrister 1870, memb Bar Queensland 1880; *d* 19 Dec 1928

1a Florence Emily; *m* 23 June 1888 Hon Edward Grenville Gore-Langton (*d* 16 March 1936), bro of 4th Earl Temple of Stowe (*qv*), and *d* 24 Dec 1902, leaving issue

2a Blanche Emmeline; *m* 20 July 1884 Baron von Keudell (*d* 26 July 1888), and *d* 8 June 1921, leaving issue

(2) John Oliphant; *b* 3 July 1808; Chamberlain to HM THE KING OF BAVARIA, Kt Grand Cross Order St Michael of Merit; *d* Dresden 11 Dec 1865

(3) Patrick Oliphant; *b* 3 Nov 1819; Capt Madras MS; *m* 28 Oct 1852 Harriet Philips (*d* 22 Nov 1898), dau of James Collom, of Plymouth, and *d* 22 Feb 1877, leaving issue:

1a Alexander William Oliphant (Rev); *b* 16 Oct 1853; *educ* Worcester Coll Oxford (MA); Rector Chignal Smealy, Essex; *d* 9 Nov 1935

1a Janet Oliphant; *m* 12 Aug 1886 Capt Thomas Leonard Leader, 79th Highrs (*d* 1891), of The Maples, Maple Cross, Rickmansworth, and *d* 1931, having had issue

(1) Janet Oliphant; *m* 5 April 1829 John Steuart, of Dalguise, Perthshire, Master Supreme Court Cape of Good Hope, and *d* 9 Aug 1871, leaving issue (*see* RICKETTS, Bt)

(2) Charlotte; *m* 9 Oct 1849 William Henry Oliphant and *d* 5 Nov 1883 aged 74

(3) Jane Ferguson; *m* 5 Feb 1839 Lt-Col John Money Carter, 1st Royals (*d* 28 Nov 1888), and *d* 24 Dec 1904, leaving issue

(4) Marianne Oliphant; *m* 11 April 1848 Peter Hay Paterson, of Carpow, Perthshire, and *d* 6 Sept 1873

1 Elizabeth; *m* 14 Sept 1803 William Buchanan of Ardroch, and *d* 17 May 1846

2 Mary; *m* 12 July 1830 Augustus Frederick Lindley and *d* 23 Oct 1854

The **7th Lord** *m* 2nd 1804 Catherine, dau of James Steuart, and *d* 24 Sept 1820, having by her had issue:

2 James; *b* 4 May 1810; advocate; *m* 3 May 1882 Isabella (*d* 11 March 1875), only child of James Erskine of Aberdona (*see* ROSSLYN, E), and *d* 17 Feb 1844 (*k* in Borneo), leaving issue:

(1) Alexander Erskine MURRAY later ERSKINE-MURRAY, of Edinburgh; *b* 9 Dec 1832; *m* 26 April 1866 Helen (*d* 3 Aug 1916), dau of Robert Pringle, WS, of Symington, and *d* 17 Dec 1907, leaving issue:

1a James Robert; *b* 24 Oct 1868; DSc, FRSE; Maj RAF; *m* 1898 Alleine Frederica Florinda (*d* 2 July 1941), dau of Maj-Gen G F Gildea, CB, and *d* 12 Feb 1927, leaving issue:

1b JAMES ALASTAIR FREDERICK CAMPBELL ERSKINE-MURRAY, **13th Lord Elibank**; *b* 23 June 1902; *educ* Harrow, RMC Sandhurst,and Glasgow U (MA); Maj HLI, comded HLI 1922, Turkey, Egypt India and WW II; Scottish HQ Commr Rover Scouts 1951–63, Hon Advsr RT to Scottish Scout HQ 1963–69, FSA Scot, FZS Scot; *d* unm 2 June 1973

2a Walter Pringle; *b* 18 April 1872; Lt BSA Mounted Police; *d* unm 25 July 1906

3a Robert Alan, OBE (1919); *b* 24 Oct 1874; AMICE; T/Maj RE WW I (despatches); *m* 16 Jan 1922 Eileen Mary (*d* 7 May 1970), dau of John Percy MacManus, of Piersfield House, Co Westmeath, and *d* 21 Aug 1939, having had:

1b ALAN D'ARDIS ERSKINE-MURRAY, **14th and present Lord Elibank**

2b +Patrick Elibank [Patrick Erskine-Murray Esq, 3 Park View, Bakewell, Derbys]; *b* 2 June 1927; *educ* Bedford Sch and Pembroke Coll Cambridge (BA 1951, MA 1953); FICE (1968); *m* 28 Sept 1957 *Jenny Mary Margaret, dau of John Brown, of Bowbank, Middleton-in-Teesdale, Co Durham, and has had issue:

1c *Vivien Mary; *b* 10 Sept 1958; *m* 1992 *John David Jarvis and has:

1d *William Tom; *b* 17 July 1996

2c *Clare Ruth; *b* 5 June 1960

3c Hilary Margaret; *b* 20 Oct 1965; *d* 1976

1b Dawn; *b* 25, *d* 26 Feb 1926

2b *Helen Veronica [Mrs Neil MacDonald, 22 Old Broadway, Manchester M20 3DF]; *b* 11 July 1931; MB, BS (Lond) 1955; *m* 13 Sept 1958 *Neil MacDonald, FRCS, yr s of Dr Malcolm Angus MacDonald, MC, of Lowestoft, Suffolk, and has issue:

1c *Sally; *b* 18 June 1959

2c *Fiona; *b* 18 April 1961

3c *Juliet; *b* 25 July 1964

4a Arthur, CBE (1943), DSO (1916), DL (Warwicks); *b* 9 Oct 1877; Lt-Col RA, S Africa 1901–02 and WW I (despatches), AQMG 1916, WW II in HG, Assist Co Army Welfare Offr Warwicks, Order Crown of Italy, Mil Medal for Merit 1st Cl Czechoslovakia; *m* 1906 Ena Nelson (*d* 22 June 1942), dau of Henry Ernest Trestrail, FRCS, MRCP, and *d* 1 Jan 1948, leaving issue:

1b +(Arthur) Sydney Elibank [Sydney Erskine-Murray Esq, Myrtle Bank, Gt Amwell, Ware, Herts SG12 9SN]; *b* 1909; *educ* Bedford Sch and Birmingham U (BSc), MICE, MBIM; dir Eric White and Partners Ltd and Heinemann Training Services Ltd, formerly dir Inbucon Ltd, Assoc Industrial Consultants Ltd, Learning Systems Ltd and John Sturgeon Ltd; *m* 29 June 1940 *Florence Duncan, dau of William Duncan Robertson, and has issue:

1c *Ann [Mrs Anthony Bartleet, Bucklers Farm, Great Tey, Coggeshall, Essex CO6 1SB]; *b* 29 Aug 1942; BA; *m* 4 Sept 1965 *Anthony Peter Bartleet, s of E A Bartleet, of Broad Eaves, Broxbourne, Herts, and has:

1d *James Murray; *b* 1967

2d *Thomas Anthony ; *b* 1969

3d *William Arthur; *b* 1971

2c *Susan [Mrs Godfrey Shocket, 7 Genoa Ave, London SW15]; *b* 24 Jan 1945; *m* 1975 *Godfrey S Shocket

1a Elizabeth Macfarlane; *m* 26 Sept 1916 John W Lewis, Lt RNVR (*d* 1951), and *d* 28 Feb 1960

(2) James St Hypolite Erskine; *b* 16 July 1835; *d* 14 Aug 1853

(1) Jane Isabella Erskine; *d* 20 Oct 1864 accidentally from burns

(2) Edith Catherine; *m* 17 April 1865 Joseph Bell, MD

ELIOTT

Arms: Gules on a bend or a baton azure. **Crest:** A hand couped at the wrist in armour holding a cutlass in bend proper. **Supporters:** Dexter, a ram; sinister, a goat; both proper and gorged with a laurel branch vert, horned and hooved or. **Mottoes:** 1 (above crest) *Fortiter et recte* ('Boldly and rightly'), 2 (below arms) *Soyez sage* ('Be wise'). **Creation:** Bt. (NS) 3 Dec 1666.

SIR CHARLES JOSEPH ALEXANDER ELIOTT, 12TH BT, of Stobs [Sir Charles Eliott Bt, 27 Cohoe Street, Toowoomba, Queensland 4350, Australia]; *b* 9 Jan 1937; *s* kinsman 1989; *educ* St Joseph's Christian Brothers' Coll, Rockhampton, nr Brisbane; *m* 1959 *Wendy Judith, dau of Henry John Bailey, of Toowoomba, Qld, and has issue:

1 +RODNEY GILBERT CHARLES; *b* 1966; *m* 88 *Andrea Therese Saunders, and has issue:
(1) +Steven Charles; *b* 1990
(1) *Cassandra Jane; *b* 1989
1 *Elizabeth; *b* May 1960; *m* — Armanasco, and has issue:
(1) *Daniel Charles
(1) *Lindsay Clare
(2) *Kimberley Jane; *b* 1991
2 *Jenny; *b*1962; *m* — Land
3 *Josephine Mary Anne; *b* 1963; *m* — Grofski and has:
(1) *Ethan Joseph; *b* 1990
(1) *Brigitte Kate; *b* 1992
4 *Clare Melinda; *b* 1973

Lineage: ROBERT ELWALD of the Redheugh, so designated *c* 1476; *d c* 3 May 1497, having had:

ROBERT ELWALD of the Hermitage; *dvp c* Nov 1491, having had issue:

ROBERT ELWALD of the Redheugh; *d* by 1526, having had, with an est s (allegedly K Battle of Flodden):

1 ROBERT
2 William of Larriston; living 29 Jan 1515/6
3 Archibald of Falnash; ancestor of the ELLIOTs of Falnash, SCOTT-ELLIOTs of Arkelton and ELLIOTs of Thorlieshope
4 Martin of Braidley; led the Clan after death of his nephew, Robert Elliot of Redheugh; ancestor of the ELLIOTs of Phillop and ELLIOTs of Harwood (*see* 1970 edn) and Clifton Park

The est son,

ROBERT ELWALD of Redheugh; Capt of Hermitage Castle; *d c* Jan 1562/3, having had:

ROBERT ELWALD or ELLOT of the Redheugh; Capt Hermitage Castle June 1563; *m* Jean Scot (*m* 2nd Gavin Ellot, who bought Stobs from the Gladstones 1580, yr s of Gavin Ellot of Horsliehill, and had a further three daus), and *d c* 1566, leaving issue:

1 Robert of Redheugh, whose line is extinct
2 William of Hartsgarth, called 'Robyns Will', whose line is extinct
3 GILBERT of Stobs
4 Archibald
5 Gavin of the Brugh; *m* Margaret Chisholm and *d c* 20 Oct 1631; ancestor of the ELLIOTs of Brugh and of Wells

The 3rd son,

GILBERT ELLOT of Stobs, Kirkton and Horsliehill; bought Stobs 1607 from the heirs of his stepfather Gavin Elliot of Stobs; *m* Margaret, dau of Walter Scott of Harden (*see* POLWARTH, L), and *d* 24 June 1634, having had issue:

1 WILLIAM, of Stobs
2 Gilbert of Craigend; *m* (contract 16 March 1638) Alison Kerr, and *dsp* Feb 1690
3 Archibald of Middlestead; *m* Elizabeth, dau of Sir John Leirmont, of Birkhill
4 Gavin of Grange and Midlem; ancestor of the Earls of Minto (*qv*)
5 John; advocate; *m* Marion, dau of David McCullo of Goodtrees, and had an only child:
(1) Margaret
6 James; *m* 1657 Margaret, dau and heiress of Robert Elliot of Redheugh and Larriston by Lady Jean Stewart, dau of Francis Stewart, Earl of Bothwell, and *d c* 19 July 1661; ancestor of the extinct ELLIOTs of Larriston
1 Elizabeth; *m* John Turnbull of Minto
2 Margaret; *m* 1624 Andrew Scott of Faulsyde
3 Ann; *m* 1636 Andrew Bell, yr of Colcross
4 Esther; *m* 1634 Andrew, gs of Andrew Ker of Yair
5 Jean; *m* 1624 Robert Pringle of Blindlie

The est s,

WILLIAM ELIOTT of Stobs, MP Roxburgh 1640–51; *m* (contract 28 Nov 1621) Elizabeth, dau of William Douglas, of Cavers, and *d* July 1654, having had issue:

1 GILBERT (Sir), **1st Bt**
2 Archibald of Craigend and Deanfoot, heir of his uncle, Gilbert Eliott; *d c* 1683, having had:
(1) Gilbert of Craigend and Deanfoot; sold the lands to Earl of Tarras (LP) and *d c* 1696
(2) John; *m* April 1696 Agnes, dau of Robert M Dougall, of Crichen
3 Gavin; *m* 1st *c* 1683 Barbara, dau of John Crichton of Craufurdstone; *m* 2nd *c* 1688 Jean, dau and heir of Sir James Nicholson of Cockburnspeth, and *d c* 23 Feb 1694, leaving:
(1) Gavin
4 William of Grange and of Mordington
5 John
6 Richard of Reperlaw; had issue:
(1) Gilbert
(2) William
1 Margaret; *m* 1641 William Bennet, Rector of Ancrum
2 Anna; *m* 1641 John Maxwell, Yr. of Cowhill
3 Mary; *m* John Young of Gulyhill
4 Isobel; *m* Francis Scott of Arkelton
5 Elspeth

The est son,

Sir Gilbert Eliott of Stobs, 1st Bt (NS), so *cr* 3 Dec 1666; ktd 1651; *m* 1st *c* 1649 Isabella, yst dau of James Master of Cranstoun, and had issue:

1 WILLIAM (Sir), **2nd Bt**
2 John of Lymiecleugh
3 James

Sir Gilbert *m* 2nd (contract 19 April 1661) Magdalen, dau of Sir John Nicholson of Lasswade, and *d* Sept 1677, having had further issue:

4 Thomas; *d c* 1671
5 Gilbert of Stonedge, whose line is extinct
6 William; apprenticed 1691 to Patrick Johnston, merchant, served heir to his sister Janet 3 July 1694, and had:
(1) Gilbert; Ch Clerk War Off, Agent at Gravesend
(2) George; Exciseman at Gravesend; *m* Mary, dau and heiress of — Fortrey, of Woomwell Hall, Gravesend, and *d* by 28 March 1770, having had issue:
1a Eliott, of Woomwell Hall; Capt; *m* and *d c* 1795, leaving:
1b A dau; *m* 20 Nov 1795 William Wilson, of Upper Tooting
1a Mary; *m* 22 Aug 1768 Rev — Currey, of Dartford, Kent
1 Janet; *d* unm 1694
2 Magdalen; *m* (contract 19 July 1688) Sir John Pringle, 2nd Baronet (*qv*)

The 1st Bt's est son,

Sir William Eliott of Stobs, 2nd Bt; MP Roxburgh 1689–1693; *m* 1st Elizabeth, dau of Sir John Scott of Ancrum; *m* 2nd 3 Feb 1680 Margaret, dau of Charles Murray, of Hadden, and *d* 19 Feb 1699, having by her had issue:

1 GILBERT (Sir), **3rd Bt**
2 William; apprenticed to Edinburgh merchant 19 June 1700
1 Elizabeth; *m* William, est son of James Scott of Bonnington
2 Magdaline; *m* 12 Feb 1711 Alexander Scott of Sinton

The 2nd Bt's er son,

Sir Gilbert Eliott of Stobs, 3rd Bt; *m* (contract 14 April 1702) Eleanor, est dau of William Elliot of Wells, and *d* 27 May 1764, having had issue, with two sons who *d* young:

1 JOHN (Sir), **4th Bt**
2 William; *b* 29 Aug 1706; merchant of London; *dsp* (will proved 12 May 1779)
3 Gilbert; *b* Edinburgh 3 Aug 1707; HEICNS; *dsp* East Indies *c* 1756
4 Charles; *b* 21 Oct 1709; Attorney-Gen N Carolina; *dsp* Newbern, NC, 2 Oct 1756
5 Archibald; *b* Stobs 16 Oct 1710; London merchant, Sec Ramsgate Harbour; *m* 1 Dec 1737 — Seer, and *d* Aug 1759, having had an only son, Vernon Elliot Eliott, alive May 1775
6 Elliot Eliott; *b* Stobs 19 Feb 1712; Capt RN; *d* at sea unm 26 June 1745
7 Gavin; *b* 12 June 1713; Capt, HEICNS; *dsp* East Indies *c* 1756
8 GEORGE AUGUSTUS ELIOTT, 1st BARON HEATHFIELD OF GIBRALTAR, of Heathfield, Sussex (GB), so *cr* 14 June 1787 with thanks of Parl; *b* 14 Dec 1717; Lt-Gen, defended Gibraltar against French June 1779–1783; *m* 10 June 1748 Anne Pollexfen, dau of Sir Francis Drake, Bt, of Buckland, Devon, and *d* 6 July 1790, leaving an only surv son:
(1) FRANCIS AUGUSTUS ELIOTT, 2nd and last BARON HEATHFIELD OF GIBRALTAR; *b* 31 Dec 1750; Lt-Gen; *d* unm 26 Jan 1813, when the Barony expired

The 3rd Bt's est son,

Sir John Eliott of Stobs, 4th Bt; *b* 27 July 1705; *m* Mary Andrews, and *d* 31 Dec 1767, having had, with a dau (Ann, *d* unm):

Sir Francis Eliott of Stobs, 5th Bt; *m* 10 Oct 1767 Euphan Dickson, and *d* 20 June 1791, having had, with a yr s (John, Capt 29th Regt Dragoons, *d* unm 11 Aug 1795):

Sir William Eliott of Stobs, 6th Bt; *m* 14 April 1790 Mary (*d* 6 June 1850), dau of John Russell, of Roseburne, near Edinburgh, and sister of Sir William Russell, 1st Bt, HEICS, and *d* 14 May 1812, having had, with other issue:

1 WILLIAM FRANCIS (Sir), **7th Bt**

2 John; Maj 8th Hus; *d* unm 1838

3 Gilbert; Speaker Legislative Ho of Assembly, Brisbane, Queensland; *m* 21 April 1830 Isabella Lucy (*d* 1871), dau of Rev Robert Elliot, Vicar of Askham, Yorks, and *d* 30 June 1871, leaving issue:

(1) Gilbert William; *b* 24 Jan 1831; *m* 1854 Jane Penelope (*d* 1919), dau of Thomas Thomson, and *d* 23 March 1893, leaving issue:

1a Gilbert Francis, CE; *b* 18 May 1859; *m* 12 July 1887 Emily Kate (*d* 22 Aug 1936), dau of W H Palmer, of Gippsland, Victoria, and *d* 24 Dec 1943, having had:

1b Keith Archer; *b* 2 Jan 1890; *m* 16 Aug 1919 Beatrice, dau of Alfred Markey, of Co Meath, and *dsp* 21 May 1937

1b Joan Mary; *b* 29 Aug 1897; *m* 1925 Otto Sadler Hirschfeld (*d* 1957), Chllr Queensland U, and had issue

2b Emily Innes; *b* 17 July 1901; *m* 1928 Eric S Newman

2a Harry; *b* 24 March 1866; *m* 16 April 1900 Beatrice Annie, dau of Charles F L Tooth, and *d* 27 Jan 1937, having had a dau (*d* young)

1a Kate Eliza; *m* 12 Dec 1878 William A Steedman (*d* 1904), and *d* 1 Aug 1939, leaving issue

2a Helen Ada; *m* 12 Dec 1878 Alfred P Mackenzie (*d* 28 April 1924), and *d* 28 April 1924

3a Maud Celia; *m* 12 Feb 1887 Charles Edward Loveday (*d* 1920), and *d* 14 Nov 1951

4a Constance May; *m* 1894 Frederick Tooth

(2) Francis Willoughby; *b* 1 June 1832; *m* 2 Dec 1854 Sara Jane (*d* 11 Aug 1903), dau of Capt W Richards, of Winterbourne, New England, and *d* 27 June 1882, leaving issue:

1a Francis Willoughby Charles; *b* 12 Nov 1855; *d* 26 Sept 1920

2a Gilbert William Henry; *b* 2 Dec 1857; *m* 1886 Emily (*d* 1925), dau of Capt C F Chatfield, RN, of Sydney, and *d* 1947, having had issue:

1b Charles Francis, MC; *b* 24 Jan 1889; Capt Australian Inf, WW I (twice wounded, 1914–15 Star, two medals, despatches); *d* Aug 1931

2b Gilbert William, JP; *b* 21 July 1894; Australian Forces; *m* 1921 Lilian Mary (*d* 1968), dau of William Towle, and widow of Neville Dalley, and *d* 10 Jan 1961, leaving issue:

1c +Gilbert Rowley Roxburgh [Gilbert Eliott Esq, 53 Epping Rd, Epping, NSW, Australia]; *b* Nov 1923; *educ* Sydney U (BDS 1952); F/Lt RAAF; *m* 1944 *Helen Ross, yr dau of A H Martin, MA, PhD, of Sydney, NSW, and has:

1d *Gilbert William Heathfield; *b* 27 Aug 1961

1d *Christine; *b* 1945; *educ* New England U, NSW (BSc), and Sydney U (Dip Educn)

2d *Virginia Ruth; *b* 1947

3b Francis Ferguson; *b* 13 June 1898; WW I with Australian Art; *d* July 1934

1b Jane Isabella; *b* 21 June 1887; *m* 1st 27 April 1918 Robert Walter Stewart (*d* 1922); *m* 2nd 1943 Arthur A Bateman, and *d* 17 Oct 1954

2b Emily Alice; *b* 20 Aug 1890; *m* 16 Dec 1918 Henry Campbell Kerr Oakes

3b Eleanor Lilian; *b* 15 Dec 1892

3a Edward Percy; *b* 22 Feb 1860; *m* 1890 Annie (*d* 28 Dec 1944), dau of John Conolly, of Queensland, and *d* 1931, leaving issue:

1b Gilbert; *b* 31 Aug 1891; *m* 6 Feb 1929 Barbara, yst dau of Charles Saddlier, of Gayndah, Queensland, and *d* 9 April 1962

1b Marjorie; *b* 12 Nov 1892; *m* 16 Aug 1938 Robert Livingston Boyd

4a William Russell; *b* 15 Jan 1862; *m* 1893 Margaret Irwin, and *d* 23 April 1916

5a Clifton Hazlewood; *b* 21 Nov 1872; *m* 3 May 1905 Mary Isabel (*d* 6 Aug 1960), est dau of Rev R W Wilson, Vicar of Walcha, New England, and *d* 1938, leaving issue:

1b Francis Heathfield; *b* 4 Aug 1908; *m* 1939 *Florence Nell [Mrs Francis Eliott, Congi, Woolbrook, NSW, Australia], dau of O B Briggs, and had issue:

1c +Graham Francis Heathfield [Graham Eliott Esq, 26 Kerferd St, Watson, ACT 2602, Australia]; *b* 6 March 1941; *m* 1970 *Karen Joyce, er dau of Robert John Taylor of Mt Druitt, NSW, and has issue:

1d *Miles Francis Heathfield; *b* 1977

2d *Martin Graham Heathfield; *b* 1979

3d *Tristan Robert Heathfield; *b* 1984

1d *Louise Karen Florence; *b* 1986

2c +Geoffrey Osmer Heathfield [Geoffrey Eliott Esq, Congi, Woolbrook, NSW, Australia]; *b* 22 Sept 1942; *m* 1974 *Sally Green, of Moorabindi, Taroom, Qld, and has issue:

1d +Mitchell Francis Heathfield; *b* 1978

2d +Lachlan Edward Heathfield; *b* 1980

2b +Roger Clifton Heathfield [Roger Eliott Esq, 85 Oak St, Tamworth, NSW 2340, Australia]; *b* 17 Dec 1909; Australian Imp Forces; *m* 1st 1942 (*divorce* 1947) Winifred Maud, only dau of Rev H E West, Vicar of Tenterfield, NSW; *m* 2nd 1948 *Betty Muriel, dau of H Williams, of Landsbrough, Queensland, and by her has issue:

1c +Roger John [Roger Eliott Esq, Bective Station, Tamworth, NSW 2340, Australia]; *b* 15 April 1955; *m* 1980 *Dianne Jennifer, yr dau of William Henry Waugh, of Northbridge, NSW, and has issue:

1d *Anika; *b* 1982

1c *Robyn Jeanette; *b* 16 Sept 1949; *m* 1st 1974 (*divorce* 1979) Jeffrey Alan Anderson, and has issue:

1d *Kris; *b* 1975

1c (cont.) Mrs Robyn Anderson *m* 2nd 1986 *Bruce Raymond Melville, and has further issue:

1d *James Raymond; *b* 1988

2d *Catherine Elizabeth; *b* 1990

2c *Wendy Sue; *b* 8 Jan 1954; *m* 1973 *Alan John Hillier, and has issue:

1d *Damien John; *b* 1976

2d *Brendan; *b* 1978

3b +Lyndsay Raine Heathfield [Lyndsay Eliott Esq, Greenwells, Walcha, New England, NSW, Australia]; *b* 24 Dec 1919; Australian Imp Forces; *m* 1949 *Rosemary Margaret, yr dau of Gordon W Phillips, of Walcha, New England, NSW, and has issue:

1c +Andrew Clifton Heathfield; *b* 15 Oct 1954; *m* 1983 *Melissa Helen, only dau of R A Lee, of Armidale, NSW, and has issue:

1d +Dougal Heathfield; *b* 1987

2d +Stuart Heathfield; *b* 1988

1c *Gaeling Heathfield; *b* 3 Feb 1950

2c *Ruth Heathfield; *b* 3 March 1952

3c *Rosemary Anne Heathfield; *b* 11 April 1956

1b Isabel Heathfield; *b* 15 Feb 1906; *m* 1st 1950 Donald Finlay, and had issue:

1c *Patricia Mary; *b* 21 April 1932

2c *Anne; *b* 8 Feb 1935

2b Madge Heathfield; *b* 22 July 1907; *m* 1943, Alex Euston Gidley King, AIF, and had issue:

1c *Robert Gidley; *b* 24 June 1946

1c *Sally; *b* 7 Dec 1950

3b *Dorothy Mary Heathfield [Mrs D Kilpatrick, Dickinson Court, Dickinson St, Charlestown, NSW 2290, Australia]; *b* 2 Dec 1911; *m* 3 May 1933 (*divorce* 1957) Archibald John Kilpatrick, and has issue:

1c *John Eliott; *b* 13 Nov 1936; *m* 10 Sept 1960 *Janice Ellen Stidolph, and has issue:

1d *Andrew John; *b* 1966

2d *Peter Gordon; *b* 1972

1d *Leanne Jane; *b* 1962

2d *Donna Louise; *b* 1963

2c *Owen Heathfield; *b* 13 May 1942; *m* 25 March 1963 *Marie Maynard, and has issue:

1d *Russell Owen; *b* 1964

1d *Alison Lyn; *b* 1966; *m* 1988 *James Sidney Chappell

1c *Jillian Mary [Mrs John Stuart, 26 Ker St, Charlestown, NSW 2290, Australia]; *b* 31 July 1934; *m* 8 Sept 1955 John Stuart (*d* 1984), and has issue:

1d Paul Andrew; *b* 1960; *d* 1983

2d *Michael John; *b* 1961

3d *David Allan; *b* 1963

4d *Anthony Mark; *b* 1970

4b Marcie Isseh Heathfield; *b* 14 Oct 1917; *m* 1939 Archer John Croft (*d* 1971), yst s of Sir Hugh Matthew Fiennes Croft, 12th Bt, of Croft Castle (*qv*), and *d* 1976, leaving issue

1a Lucy Isabella; *m* 1884 Percy Hall Ross

2a Elinor Mary Harriet; *m* 1887 Henry Hall Ross

4 Daniel (Sir), KCSI; *b* 3 March 1798; HEICS; *m* 19 Dec 1818 Georgina (*d* 16 Feb 1874), dau of Gen George Russell, and *d* 30 Oct 1872, having had, with other issue:

(1) William Russell; *b* 1 July 1820; Maj-Gen; *m* 1st 5 May 1860 Jessie (*d* 16 Feb 1873), dau of Robert McIntosh, and had issue:

1a Claud Daniel Russell; *b* 3 April 1865; *d* 10 March 1866

2a Hugh Russell; *b* 10 Feb 1873; Capt Worcs Regt; *m* 26 July 1913 Constance Mary, dau of A O Sedgwick, of Watford, and was *ka sp* 12 Oct 1914

1a Georgina Jessie; *d* unm 31 Aug 1939

2a Emma Frances; *d* unm 6 Nov 1933

3a Constance Maud; *d* 22 March 1869

(1) (cont.) William Russell *m* 2nd 22 April 1876 Frances Helen (*d* 1884), dau of P L Cloete, and widow of Capt Aubrey J F Gordon, Madras SC, and *d* 1893

(2) Henry Manning; *b* 9 May 1827; Maj-Gen; *m* 13 Nov 1860 Jessie (*d* 22 Nov 1927), dau of Rev Alfred Fennell, and *dsp* 1894

(3) Edward Frederick; *b* 6 June 1834; *m* 7 Aug 1856 Rykie Sophia (*d* 1891), dau of P L Cloete, and *d* 27 Oct 1873, leaving issue:

1a Lawrence Edward; *b* 3 Sept 1859; Maj IA; *m* 4 July 1898 Emily Charlotte Eliott (*d* Aug 1954), dau of Capt J J Wood (*see* below), and *dsp* 25 Oct 1902

2a Francis Hardinge, CSI (1915); *b* 1 April 1862; Lt-Col IA, Commr Irrawaddy Div, Burma 1911–17, Burmese Expdn 1888–89 (medal with clasp); *m* 1900 Mary Agnes (*d* June 1954), dau of Robert Wardrop, and *d* 26 Dec 1928

1a Hester Sullivan; *m* 1884 Lt-Col H H Aspinall, IA, and *d* 1925, leaving issue

(1) Georgina Mary; *m* 16 April 1864 John Hutcheson Fergusson

(2) Caroline; *m* 1849 Col Charles Colville Young, CB, RA (*d* 1856), and *d* 1895, leaving issue

(3) Emma; *m* 11 March 1847 Richard Stuart Palmer (*d* 18 Oct 1862), and *d* 22 Aug 1856, leaving issue

(4) Mary Bethia; *m* 3 Feb 1848 Maj-Gen W C Russell, RA, and *d* 26 Oct 1854, leaving issue

(5) Cecilia Wheatley; *m* 1 July 1856 Maj-Gen Eustace Hill, and *d* 1916, leaving issue

(6) Claudine Frances Leonora; *m* Dec 1869 Rev T D Gray, Chaplain, Bengal Army, and *d* 20 Feb 1877, leaving issue

5 George Augustus; *b* 24 May 1799; Adml; *m* 1st 6 May 1837 Alice Anne (*d* 19 May 1864), dau of Hon Thomas Jeffrey, of Halifax, Nova Scotia; *m* 2nd 22 Dec 1868 Harriett Sophia, est dau of Adml of the Fleet Sir John West, GCB, and *d* 13 May 1872, having had issue by 1st w:

(1) George Augustus; *b* 12 Aug 1838; Maj Roy Scots (1st Foot); *m* 1st Helen Jane (*d* 30 April 1876), dau of W Jardine Gallen; *m* 2nd 1877 Mary Anna, dau of J Crampton, and *d* 1884, having had, with other issue, by 1st w:

1a Francis Augustus Heathfield, DSO (1907), JP (Natal); *b* 3 July 1867; Lt-Col 3rd Regt S African Mounted Riflemen, Matabele War 1893, Bechuanaland campaign 1896–97 (medal and clasp), S African War 1899–1902 (despatches twice, two medals and four clasps), Kalahari Desert, Cape Colony 1904–07 (German SW African medal, DSO, 2nd cl Order Roy Crown of Prussia with swords), WW I, comded 3rd SAMR in German SW Africa, and 4th S African Horse in German E Africa (despatches twice); *m* 9 Oct 1896 Evelyn Georgina Stirling (*d* 24 April 1937), dau of Richard William Macdermott, of Dublin, and *d* 29 July 1937, leaving issue:

1b Heathfield George Henry; *b* 15 Aug 1897; African Def Force, PF, WW I with SA Artillery (star two medals); *m* 6 March 1922 Rhoda Isadora, dau of Frederick William Augustus Daly, and had issue:

1c +Ian Cecil Heathfield [Ian Eliott Esq, PO Box 41, Sunninghill 2157, Republic of S Africa]; *b* 13 June 1923; *m* *Berenice Washington, and has issue:

1d +Anthony John; *b* 1949; *m* 1974 *Sheila Kirkness

2d +Christopher Thomas; *b* 1953

2c +Ivor Keith Heathfield [Ivor Eliott Esq, 300 Lister Rd, Rembrandt Park, Johannesburg, S Africa]; *b* 24 Feb 1926; WW II; *m* 1 Sept 1962 *Edythe Gloria, dau of John Marshall Harrison, of Cape Town, and has issue:

1d +Graeme Allan; *b* 7 Dec 1964

2d +Kevin John; *b* 1973

1d *Lynette Anne; *b* 28 Aug 1963

2d *Louise; *b* 1967

2b Herbert Hugh Heathfield, OBE (1946), TD; *b* 27 Feb 1903; *educ* Eastbourne Coll and RMC Sandhurst; Lt-Col Roy Fus, WW II (despatches), Ch Instructor Sch of Infantry 1943, Assist Cmdt ME Sch of Infantry 1945; Dir and Gen Manager Sure Form Plastics Ltd and Mould Form Tools Ltd (Cos within Birmid Qualcast Group); *m* 6 Jan 1927 Barbara (*d* 1983), dau of John Cullen Marsh, of Penge, Kent, and had issue:

1c *Ann Georgina Heathfield [Mrs William Bullock, the Mill Farm, Guarlford Rd, Malvern, Worcs WR14 3QP]; *b* 31 Jan 1929; *m* 20 Nov 1954 *William John Bullock, and has issue:

1d *Anthony John; *b* 1 June 1957; *m* 1985 *Catherine Sally Greville Fox, and has issue:

1e *James William Basil; *b* 1989

2e *Edward Adam Hugh; *b* 1993

2d *Nigel Timothy; *b* 10 March 1960; *m* 1989 *Susan Lindsay, dau of Kenneth Ellis, of Tal-y-Bont, Gwynedd, N Wales and has:

1e *Georgina Lindsay; *b* 17 May 1997

1b Evelyn Heather; *b* 1898; *m* 1923 Horace Wellesley Burgess, Lt Dragoon Gds, and *d* 1996, leaving:

1c *John Francis Wellesley [John Burgess Esq, Braces Leigh, Newland, Malvern, Worcs]; *b* 10 Oct 1929; *m* 1 Aug 1953 *Heather Mildren, and has issue:

1d *Jonathan Nigel; *b* 19 Nov 1955

1d *Grace Clare; *b* 24 Oct 1958

1c *Margaret Jean [Mrs Richard Andrews, 53 Middlebrook Rd, High Wycombe, Bucks]; *b* 19 Nov 1924; *m* 12 May 1951 *Richard Henry Andrews, son of H W Andrews, of Highcliffe, Hants, and has issue:

1d *Christopher John; *b* 4 Aug 1952

2d *Peter Richard; *b* 1 July 1957

2c *Jennifer Evelyn; *b* 29 June 1938

2b Marie Ida; *b* 1900; *m* 31 Aug 1923 William Joseph Merrifield, son of William John Geach Merrifield, of Twickenham, and had issue:

1c *Daphne Joan; *b* 5 Jan 1925; *m* 5 June 1954 Lt-Col John Neil Reeve, RA

3b Dymphna Helen Cynthia; *b* 1906; *m* 1930 John Richard Vernon, Nigerian CS (ret) (*d* 1984), and had issue:

1c *Joanne Georgina Dymphna; *b* 17 Sept 1933; *m* March 1953 (*divorce* 1963), Jorgen Lagoni, son of Capt Otto Lagoni, Roy Danish Navy, of Copenhagen, and has issue:

1d *Steen Frederick Christian; *b* 22 Sept 1955

1d *Jane Inge; *b* 25 Jan 1954

2d *Jacqueline Anne; *b* 28 Sept 1958

2a Gerald Otho Rousski, OBE (1919); *b* 28 March 1874; Cdr RNR, Boer War, WW I as Naval Tport Offr; Gen Supt Canadian Pacific Steamships Ltd, Port Convoy Offr, Halifax and Quebec, Canada; *m* 10 June 1908 Lydia Edith (*d* 16 Feb 1941), dau of Thomas Aspden, of Manchester, and *dsp* 5 Sept 1955

(2) Francis John Jeffrey; *b* 31 Jan 1844; Capt RN; *m* 1874 Hortense Caroline, dau of Leon Schmidt, and *d* 8 Dec 1903, leaving issue:

1a Mabel Alicia Georgina; *m* 1915, Fletcher Leon Gresty, and *d* 1954

6 Russell; *b* 26 March 1802; Adml; *m* 1st 2 Feb 1830 Bethia (*d* 22 Aug 1843), dau of Sir William Russell, 1st Bt, and had surv issue, two sons and two daus; *m* 2nd 24 Feb 1852 Henrietta (*d* 15 Oct 1878), dau of Sir John Kaye, 1st Bt, of Denby Grange, Yorks, and widow of John Ward, and *d* 28 Dec 1881

1 Euphemia Elizabeth Anne; *m* 7 Oct 1859 Very Rev Daniel Bagot, DD, Dean Dromore, Vicar-Gen Newry and Mourne (*d* 1892), and *d* 21 Dec 1899

The 6th Bt's est son,

Sir William Francis Eliott of Stobs, 7th Bt; *b* 1792; *s* 1818 his cousin Rt Hon William Eliott, MP, in the estate of Wells, Roxburghshire; *m* 22 March 1826 Theresa (*d* 1836), est dau of Sir Alexander Boswell, 1st Bt, and *d* 3 Sept 1864, having had, with other issue:

1 **Sir William Francis Augustus Eliott of Stobs, 8th Bt**, JP and DL (Roxburghshire) *b* 2 Feb 1827; 93rd Highrs, FRS; *m* 1st 1 Dec 1846 Charlotte Maria (*d* 29 Nov 1878), dau of Robert Wood, and had issue:

(1) Grace Theresa Blanche; *b* March 1851; *d* unm 24 July 1932

1 (cont.) **Sir William** *m* 2nd 22 April 1879 Hannah Grissell (*d* 23 Aug 1927), dau of H T Birkett, of Foxbury, Surrey, and widow of Henry Kensall, and *dspm* 6 April 1910

2 Alexander Boswell, RN; *b* 10 July 1830; *m* 1st 1855 Katherine, dau of William Craigie, and had issue:

(1) **Sir Arthur Augustus Boswell Eliott of Stobs, 9th Bt**; *b* 13 July 1856; *educ* Haileybury; *m* 1884 Lilia (*d* 24 Nov 1945), only child of John Burbank, of Boston, USA, and *d* 15 Jan 1926, having had issue:

1a **Sir Gilbert Alexander Boswell Eliott of Stobs, 10th Bt**; *b* 5 May 1885; memb Roy Co Archers, Lt RA, previously with Canadian Forces; *m* 10 Oct 1912 Dora Flournoy (*d* 28 May 1978) only dau of Alexander Stephens Hopkins, of Atlanta, Georgia, and *d* 26 July 1958, having had issue:

1b **Sir Arthur Francis Augustus Boswell Eliott of Stobs, 11th Bt**; *b* 2 Jan 1915; *educ* Harrow and King's Coll Cambridge (MA 1950); 2nd Lt KOSB 1939, Maj 1944, E Africa and Burma 1941–45, KAR, memb Roy Co Archers; author: *The Elliots, The Story of a Border Clan* (1974); *m* 23 Aug 1947 *Frances Aileen [Frances Lady Eliott, Redheugh, Newcastleton, Roxburghshire], er dau of Lt-Col Sir Francis Kennedy McClean, AFC, and formerly w of Richard Victor Charles Westmacott, and *d* 1989, leaving:

1c *Margaret Frances Boswell [Mrs Margaret Eliott, Redheugh, Newcastleton, Roxburghshire]; *b* 13 Nov 1948; resumed maiden name and is chief of the Border ELIOTTs; *m* 1st 1974 Anthony E B Vaughan-Arbuckle (*d* 1986), yr s of K H Vaughan-Arbuckle, of Devon; *m* 2nd Christopher Powell Wilkins and has by her 1st husb:

1d *Benjamin; *b* 1978

1d *Kate; *b* 1981

2b John Livingston Hopkins Boswell; *b* 24 Jan 1916; *educ* Trin Coll Cambridge (BA); F/Lt RCAF WW II; *ka* over Germany May 1942

1b *Charlotte Elgitha Veronica Boswell; *b* 9 Aug 1913; *m* 1st 29 Oct 1936 (*divorce* 1942) Landon Ketchum Thorne, er s of L K Thorne, of Long Island, USA; *m* 2nd May 1946 Stanley Herbert Maxted (*d* 10 May 1963); *m* 3rd 6 Nov 1964 Thomas Talfourd Mosby, son of T T Mosby, of Washington, DC

2b *Jean Cecilia Constance; *b* 8 June 1920; *m* 1st 3 Feb 1940 Maj Alfred Nigel Parker, QO, Cameron Highrs (*ka* Holland 23 Oct 1944), yr son of Alwyn Parker, CB, CMG, of Godalming, Surrey, and has issue:

1c *Alwyn Colin John; *b* 13 Nov 1940; *educ* Harrow; *m* 3 Sept 1966 *Sarah Ann, dau of Henry Hays, of Cumberland, and has issue:

1d *Nigel Henry; *b* 25 Dec 1968

1c *Veronica Gillean; *b* 25 May 1942

2b (cont.) Mrs Alfred Parker *m* 2nd 8 Jan 1953 Maj Alan Edward Seton Jackson, MBE, MC, KOSB (*d* 10 Dec 1964), only son of Lt-Col Edward Darby Jackson, DSO, OBE, of Mossrig, Lilliesleaf, Roxburghshire, and by him has:

2c *Andrew Conway; *b* 30 Aug 1954; *educ* Harrow

3c *Roderick Edward; *b* 7 July 1956

1a Marie Vera Margaret Emily Boswell; *m* 1st 4 June 1912 Edward Boies Cowles, of New York, s of David Smith Cowles, and had issue; *m* 2nd 14 Dec 1921 John Francis Barry (*d* Dec 1954), and *d* Aug 1955

2a Beatrice Maud Boswell; *m* 19 Jan 1925 Frank V Burton (*d* 18 March 1953), and *d* Feb 1975, leaving issue

1b *Leila Eliott; *b* 22 Sept 1926; *m* 1st 2 March 1944 (*divorce* 1946) Arthur Twining Hadley II, and has issue:

1c *Arthur Twining III; *b* 24 Feb 1945

1b (cont.) Mrs Leila Hadley *m* 2nd 24 Jan 1953 *Yvor Hyatt Smitter, and has further issue:

2c *Matthew Boswell Eliott Burton; *b* 7 July 1955

1c *Victoria C Van Duzer; *b* 21 Nov 1953

2c *Caroline Allison Faith; *b* 6 March 1959

2 (cont.) Alexander Boswell *m* 2nd 29 Nov 1858 Annabella, dau of Neil Carmichael, and *d* 2 March 1882, having by her had issue:

(2) Alexander Boswell Vassal; *b* 9 Jan 1867; *m* 30 Dec 1891 Hannah Josephine (*d* 1943), dau of Thomas M C Kavanagh, and *d* 12 April 1924, leaving issue:

1a Charles Rawdon Heathfield; *b* 16 Nov 1901; *m* 29 June 1927 Emma Elizabeth Harris and *d* 18 Aug 1972, leaving issue:

1b Sir CHARLES JOSEPH ALEXANDER ELIOTT OF STOBS, **12th and present Bt**

2b Clive John; *b* 5 July 1940; *m* 1961 *Estelle Maude Kelland, and *d* 1971, leaving issue:

1c +Bradley John; *b* 1962

2c +Anthony Charles; *b* 1966

3c +Dale Thomas; *b* 1969

3b +Keith Robert Vincent [Keith Eliott Esq, 65 Bunya Street, Grunslopes, Brisbane, Queensland 4120, Australia]; *b* 5 Oct 1942; *m* 4 Jan 1965 *Annette May 2nd dau of William George Nielsen-Kyirgaard, of Rockhampton, and has:

+Brett Robert Vincent; *b* 5 Feb 1966

4b +Raymond Francis; *b* 20 May 1945

1b *Dulcie Josephine; *b* 20 Dec 1928; *m* 29 Sept 1949 Joseph Heather, and has issue:

2b *Irene Gertrude [Mrs Peter Brown, Box 4, Yeppon, Queensland, Australia]; *b* 15 May 1930; *m* 26 April 1950 *Peter Brown

3b *Myrtle Doris Trease; *b* 29 Sept 1935

4b *Belle Loraine; *b* 15 Nov 1939

1a Gertrude May; *b* 29 Jan 1893; *m* 1929 Henry Wilson Mercer

2a Constantine Elizabeth; *b* 17 July 1894; *m* Clarence Quinn

3a Annabella Carmichael; *b* 20 March 1897; *m* 1927 James Bryson

(3) Rawdon Popham Vassall; *b* 1869; *m* Nellie Thompson, of Victoria, BC, and *dsp* 7 Nov 1925

(4) Charles James; *b* 1875; *dsp* 1953

3 George Augustus Leslie; *b* 20 Dec 1833; *m* 1853 Mary, dau of James Rattray, and *d* 21 March 1854, leaving:

(1) George Augustus Cuming; *b* 14 Jan 1854; *m* 29 April 1886 Edith Maude, dau of R Fisher Hamilton, of Dublin, and *dsp* 1892

1 Jessie Blanche Adelaide; *m* 30 Dec 1868 Capt James John Wood, formerly 45th Regt, of Hyde Park, and *d* 26 Jan 1898, leaving issue

2 Frances Elizabeth; *m* 1 Aug 1855 Edmond Forrest (*d* 1896), of Forrest Lodge, Berks, and *d* 21 Aug 1869, having had issue

ELIS-THOMAS

Creation: B. (LP, UK) 1992

THE BARON ELIS-THOMAS, of Nant Conwy in the County of Gwynedd (Dafydd Elis THOMAS later ELIS-THOMAS (deed poll 1992)) [The Rt Hon The Lord Elis-Thomas, Preswylfa, Y Glogwyn, Caernarfon, Gwynedd LL55 1HY]; *b* 18 Oct 1946; *educ* Ysgol Dyffryn Conwy and U Coll N Wales; research worker Bd Celtic Studies 1970, Tutor Welsh Studies Coleg Harlech 1971, Lecturer English Dept U Coll N Wales 1974, MP (Plaid Cymru) Merioneth Feb 1974–83, Merionydd Nant Conwy 1983–92, Pres Plaid Cymru 1984–91, Chm Welsh Language Bd 1993–; *m* 1st 1970 (*divorce*) Elen M Williams and has three sons and two daus; *m* 2nd 1993 *Mair Parry Jones

ELLENBOROUGH

Arms: Erm. on a bend engrailed between two cocks gu. three mullets pierced or. **Crest:** A cock gu., chained round the neck and charged on the breast with a mitre or. **Supporters:** Two eagles, wings elevated sa., the dexter chained round the neck and pendant therefrom on the breast a mitre or; the sinister with a like chain and pendant therefrom a covered cup of the second. **Motto:** *Compositum jus fasque animi* ('Law and equity combined').

Creation: B. (UK) 19 April 1802.

THE 8TH BARON ELLENBOROUGH, of Ellenborough, Co Cumberland (Richard Edward Cecil Law) [The Rt Hon The Lord Ellenborough, Withypool House, Observatory Close, Church Rd, Crowborough, Sussex TN6 1BN]; *b* 14 Jan 1926; *s* f 1945; *educ* Eton and Magdalene Coll Cambridge; late ptnr McNally Montgomery, stockbrokers, and Towry Law, pres Nat Union Ratepayers' Assocs 1960–90; *m* 1st 9 Oct 1953 Rachel Mary (*d* 1986), only dau of Maj Ivor Mathews Hedley, 17th Lancers, and Mrs James Hamilton, of 147 Gloucester Rd, London SW7; *m* 2nd 1994 *Mrs Frances Kimberley and by his 1st w has issue:

1 +RUPERT EDWARD HENRY; *b* 28 March 1955; *educ* Eton and RMA Sandhurst; Maj Coldstream Gds (ret), with Coutts & Co 1988–, *m* 20 June 1981 *Hon Grania Janet Gray, only dau of Baron Boardman (LP, *qv*), and has:

(1) +James Rupert Thomas; *b* 8 March 1983

(2) +Frederick George Towry Gray; *b* 1990

(1) *Georgina Poppy; *b* 1984

2 +Edmund Ivor Cecil; *b* 21 Dec 1956; *educ* Eton and Peterhouse Cambridge (MA); *m* 1982 *Susan Claire, er dau of Derek Baker, of Cambridge, and has:

(1) +David Christopher; *b* 1984

(2) +John Christian; *b* 1986

3 +Charles Adrian Christian Towry; *b* 7 Nov 1960; *educ* Eton and York U (BA)

Lineage: According to Paley (the friend and biographer of Edmund Law, Bp Carlisle (*see* below)) the LAWs originated in Askham, Westmorland

EDMOND LAW owned Cordale, nr Haweswater, parish of Bampton (sold 1837 under the will of his ggs, Rev Edmund Law, Vicar of Whittingham); *m* Elizabeth Wright (*d* March 1685), of Colby, and *d* Dec 1689, leaving a yst son:

Rev EDMUND LAW; Curate Staveley, Lancs, 1693–1741; *b* 1673; *m* 29 Nov 1701 Patience (*d* 1733), dau of Christopher Langbaine, of Kendal, by Elizabeth Edmundson, and *d* March 1741, leaving issue:

Rt Rev EDMUND LAW; Bp Carlisle 1768; *educ* St John's Coll Cambridge (BA 1723), MA Christ's Coll 1727, DD 1754, Archdeacon Carlisle 1743, Master Peterhouse Cambridge 1756, author of religious and scientific works; *b* 1703; *m* 20 April 1740 Mary (*d* 1762), dau of John Christian, of Ewanrigg, Cumberland, by Bridget, dau of Humphrey Senhouse, of Ellenborough, and had, with other issue:

1 John (Rt Rev); Archdeacon Carlisle 1777, Chaplain to Ld Lt Ireland 1782, Bp Clonfert 1782, Killala 1787 and Elphin 1795; *b* 1745; *educ* Christ's Coll Cambridge (BA 1766, MA 1769, DD 1782, 2nd Wrangler and Sr Class Medallist); *m* 17 Jan 1782 Anne (*d* 13 March 1813), dau of Rev William Plaskett and widow of John Tomlinson, of Carlisle, and *dsp* 19 March 1810

2 Ewan, MP; memb Commn Naval Inquiry 1802–05; *m* 28 June 1784 Henrietta Sarah (*d* 15 Aug 1844), est dau of William Markham, Archbp York, and *d* 24 April 1829, leaving issue

3 EDWARD, of whom presently

4 Thomas; HEICS; *b* 1756; *m* Eliza, est dau of John Parke Custis, stepson of Gen GEORGE WASHINGTON, 1st Pres of the USA (*see* Section Washington AMERICAN PRESIDENTIAL FAMILIES, 1994, Morris Genealogical Books SA), and *d* July 1834, leaving a dau

5 George Henry (Rt Rev); Bp Chester 1812 and Bath and Wells 1824; *b* 12 Sept 1761; *educ* Queens' Coll Cambridge (BA, 2nd Wrangler and Sr Class Medallist 1781, MA 1784, DD 1804); *m* 13 July 1784 Jane (*d* 27 Sept 1826), est dau of Gen James Whorwood Adeane, MP Cambs, and *d* 22 Sept 1845, leaving issue (*see* WILLIAMS, Bt, of Tregullow)

1 Mary; *m* 5 April 1764 Rev James Stephen Lushington, Preb Carlisle, and *d* 24 July 1768, leaving issue

2 Joanna; *m* 2 May 1772 Sir Thomas Rumbold, 1st Bt (*qv*), and *d* 4 Jan 1823, leaving issue

The Bp *d* 14 Aug 1787; his 3rd son,

EDWARD LAW, **1st Baron Ellenborough**, of Ellenborough, Co Cumberland (UK), so *cr* 19 April 1802, PC (1802); *b* 16 Nov 1750; *educ* Charterhouse and Peterhouse Cambridge (BA, Fell 1771, MA 1774); barrister Lincoln's Inn 1780, KC 1887, Attorney-Gen 1801, MP Newtown IoW 1801–02, Ld Ch Justice King's Bench 1802–18, memb 'All Talents' Cabinet 1806–07, ktd 22 Feb 1801, FSA 1798; *m* 17 Oct 1789 Anne (*d* 16 Aug 1843), dau of Capt George Philip Towry, RN, of Shipley, Northumberland, and *d* 13 Dec 1818, having had, with other issue:

1 EDWARD LAW, **2nd Baron Ellenborough** and 1st and last EARL OF ELLENBOROUGH, Co Cumberland, so *cr* 22 Oct 1844, as also VISCOUNT SOUTHAM, of Southam, Co Gloucester (both UK), GCB (1844), PC (1828); *b* 8 Sept 1790; *educ* Eton and St John's Coll Cambridge (MA); MP (Tory) St Michael's 1813–18, Ld Privy Seal 1828, Pres Bd Control 1828–30, 1834–35, 1841 and 1858, Govr-Gen India 1841–44, First Ld Admlty 1846; *m* 1st 11 Dec 1813 Octavia Catherine (*dsp* 5 March 1819), yst dau of 1st Marquess of Londonderry (*qv*); *m* 2nd 15 Oct 1824 (*divorce* 1830 owing to her adultery with Prince von Schwarzenberg) Jane Elizabeth (*d* 11 Aug 1881), only dau of Adml Sir Henry Digby (*see* DIGBY, B), and *d* 22 Dec 1871, when the Earldom and Viscountcy expired, having had:

(1) Arthur Dudley; *b* 1828; *d* 1830

2 Charles Ewan, QC; Recorder London, MP Cambridge U 1835–50; *b* 14 June 1792; *educ* St John's Coll Cambridge (MA, LLD); *m* 22 May 1811 Elizabeth Sophia (*d* 25 June 1864), dau of Sir Edward Nightingale, 10th Bt (*qv*), and *d* 13 Aug 1850, having had, with other issue:

(1) CHARLES EDMUND LAW later TOWRY-LAW, **3rd Baron Ellenborough**; Col; *b* 17 Nov 1820; *m* 1st 23 Nov 1840 Eleanor Cecil (*d* 15 June 1852), est dau of 4th Earl of Wicklow (*see* 1970 edn); *m* 2nd 28 June 1855 Anna Elizbeth (*d* 29 Feb 1860), dau of Rev John Fitzgerald Day, of Beaufort House, Killarney, and by her had issue:

1a CHARLES TOWRY HAMILTON LAW later TOWRY-LAW **4th Baron Ellenborough**; *b* 21 April 1856; *d* unm 26 June 1902

(1) (cont.) The **3rd Baron** *m* 3rd 26 Aug 1863 Isabella (*d* 22 April 1874), only child of Alexander Ogilby, of Pellipar, Co Londonderry, and by her had issue:

1a Gertrude Edith; *b* 4 Jan 1869; *d* 19 March 1895

2a Emily Julia; *b* 9 Dec 1872; *d* unm 21 Nov 1926

(1) (cont.) The **3rd Baron** *m* 4th 1 Dec 1874 Beatrice Joanna (*d* 17 May 1932), yst dau of Sir Joseph Knatchbull, 10th Bt (*see* BRABOURNE, B), and *d* 9 Oct 1890

(1) Mary; *m* 3 Sept 1839 3rd Baron Kilmaine (*qv*) and *d* 23 April 1888, leaving issue

(2) Elizabeth Sophia; nun, First Abbess and Foundress Franciscan Order at Drumshambo, Co Leitrim; *d* 5 Dec 1888 aged 70

(3) Frederica; *m* 1st 17 May 1848 Edmund Law (*d* 26 March 1867); *m* 2nd 1870 Henri Grève and *d* 15 Nov 1889, leaving issue

3 Henry Spencer, DL Kent; MA Cantab, barrister, 1st Life Gds and 28th Regt, Priv Sec to First Ld Admlty 1846 and Pres Bd Control 1858; *b* 10 May 1802; *m* 16 May 1839 Dorothea Anne (*d* 25 Nov 1871), est dau of Col John Staunton Rochfort, of Clogrenane, Co Carlow, and niece of Ulysses, last Baron Downes, and *d* 15 July 1885, having had, with other issue:

(1) EDWARD DOWNES TOWRY-LAW, **5th Baron Ellenborough**; Cdr RN, served Baltic 1855 (medal), China War 1857–61 (medal with clasp) and Gold Coast Ashanti War 1873–74 (medal); *b* 9 May 1841; *m* 19 Dec 1906 Hermione (*d* 26 Aug 1942), dau of E W H Schenley, Rifle Bde, of Little Warsash, Hants, and *dsp* 9 Dec 1915

(2) CECIL HENRY, **6th Baron**

(1) Louisa Isabella; *m* 26 Oct 1889 Augustus George Crowder and *d* 14 Oct 1899, leaving issue

(2) Ethel Beatrice; granted rank of baron's dau 1902; Sister Community of Bethany Lloyd's Square, WC1; *d* 13 Nov 1937

4 William Towry; *b* 16 June 1809; *educ* Peterhouse Cambridge; served 51st KOYLI and Gen Gds 1825–30, Vicar E Brent and Harborne, Staffs, Chllr Diocese Bath and Wells (resigned on becoming RC); *m* 1st 15 March 1831 Augusta (*d* 16 Oct 1844), 4th dau of 2nd Baron Graves (*qv*), and had, with other issue:

(1) Augustus Henry (Rev); SJ, formerly RN; *b* 21 Oct 1833; *d* S Africa 25 Nov 1880

(2) Francis Towry Adeane, CB; Maj-Gen RA, served Crimea, Indian Mutiny, China War, Galeka Campaign in S Africa and Zulu War, Roy Humane Soc medal; *b* 9 Jan 1835; *d* unm 27 March 1901

(3) Thomas Graves; Hon LLD Edin, Librarian Signet Library Edin; *b* 4 Dec 1836; *m* 15 April 1880 Wilhelmina Frederica (*d* 20 April 1931), yst dau of Capt John James Allen, RN, of Errol Park, Perth, by Lady Henrietta, dau of 1st Earl of Camperdown (*see* HAMILTON-DALRYMPLE, Bt), and *d* 12 March 1904, leaving, with other issue:

1a Henry Duncan Graves, CIE (1927); ICS, Political Agent Baluchistan 1927, Consul-Gen Meshed 1929–30, Min Info 1940–45; *b* 13 Aug 1883; *educ* Westminster, Edinburgh U (MA 1904) and Trin Coll Cambridge; *m* 1st 10 April 1909 Jean (*d* 5 March 1956), dau of Peter Graham, RA, of St Andrews, *m* 2nd 28 May 1958 Nancy Olive Legge (*d* 13 May 1977) yr dau of Sir Henry Frederick Oswald Norbury, and *d* 28 Jan 1964, leaving by his 1st w:

1b +Richard Graham [Richard Law Esq, High Trees, Ramsay Wood, Gatehouse-of-Fleet DG7 2HJ]; FRCOG 1961; *b* 12 Sept 1918; *educ* Tonbridge and Peterhouse Cambridge (BA 1940, MA, MB 1947, MD 1952); *m* 27 April 1944 *Barbara, MB, BS, DPH, dau of Horace Wright, and has :

1c +Nigel Graham; *b* 5 Jan 1949; *m* 1st 1973 Sandra Rush; *m* 2nd 1992 *Caroline Southwood and by his 1st w has:

1d *Tamsin Barbara; *b* 1976

2d *Emily Penelope; *b* 1977

2c +David Jocelyn Wright; *b* 4 Aug 1950; *m* 1976 *Michelle Davis, and has issue:

1d +Alexander Tasman; *b* 1987

1d *Katherine Hazel; *b* 1983

1c *Penelope Jane; *b* 3 June 1955; *m* 1995 *James Muir and has:

1d *Duncan Russell; *b* 1995

2d *Alastair James; *b* 1997

2b +Christopher [Christopher Law Esq, Appleyard, Little Chart, Kent TN27 0PY]; ARIBA (1966); *b* 3 March 1921; *educ* Tonbridge and Peterhouse Cambridge; *m* 1954 *Alison Mitchell and has:

1c +Jonathan; *b* 26 Nov 1958; *m* 1987 *Diane Joyce French

2c +Ian Graham; *b* 24 Feb 1961; ARICS; *m* 1990 *Fiona Mary McIntyre, and has issue:

1d +Duncan Graham; *b* 1989

2d +Thomas Henry; *b* 1993

1d *Katrina Mary; *b* 1988

1c *Fiona Jean; *b* 18 June 1955

3b +Michael Haldane [Michael Law Esq, 90A Upper Tollington Park, London N4 4NB]; *b* 17 April 1925; *educ* Tonbridge and Peterhouse Cambridge; lecturer Leeds U; *m* 1954 *Dorothea von Schön-Kreuzenau and has:

1c +Richard Anthony; *b* 1955

2c +Peter Andrew; *b* 28 Sept, 1958 m1979 *Carol Rattee and has:

1d *Naomi Kirsten; b 1986

2d *Gemma Nicole; b 1991

3c +John Martin; *b* 3 May 1961; has by *Melanie Ruth Day:

1d *Holly Katrina Day LAW

4c +Stephen Francis; *b* 3 Sept 1966

1a Frida Margaret Graves; *m* 11 April 1908 Charles Paul Taylor, and *d* 1953, leaving issue. He *d* 1952

2a Frances Augusta Laura; *m* 6 June 1902 John Ayling, and had issue. He *d* 15 June 1935

3a Augusta Isobel Amelia; *m* 4 Jan 1910 Roden Horace Powlett Orde, OBE, BA, 3rd s of Capt Henry Powlett Shafto Orde, and had issue. He *d* 24 May 1941

4a Louisa Georgina Wilfrid; *m* 30 June 1920 Frederick Charles Ellis and *d* 10 Aug 1958, leaving issue

(4) Frederick Charles, Cdr RN, Sec to Lt-Govrs Ontario 20 years, served Baltic and Black Sea Crimean War; *b* 27 March 1841; *m* 28 May 1874 Charlotte Margaret (*d* 1 Oct 1914), est dau of Hon John Willoughby Crawford, Lt-Govr Ontario, and *d* 13 Dec 1922, leaving issue:

1a John Crawford, Capt Roy Canadian Regt Inf, Assist Coll E African Protectorate; *b* 9 May 1876; *m* 8 Jan 1917 Eleanor Agnes Laetitia, 3rd dau of Rupert E Kingsford, of Toronto, and *d* 28 May 1919, leaving issue:

1b *Margaret Augusta Eleanor; *b* 1918; *m* 1st 1940 Capt Denys Symons, RTR; *m* 2nd 1966 Oliver Bosshardt Bennett, CBE (*d* 1983), s of G E Bennett, and by her 1st husb has:

1c *Ivor James; *b* 1944

1c *Dianna Venetia; *b* 1940

2a William Victor; Capt 123rd Canadian Inf Res of Offrs, branch manager Bank of Montreal, Toronto, Canada, served Boer War 1901–02 and WW I; *b* 2 April 1880; *m* 27 Jan 1912 Helen Violet (*d* 1971), dau of Henry Morris Watson, and *d* 7 May 1967, leaving issue:

1b Frederick Henry; *b* 27 Nov 1912; Lt RCNVR; *m* 1937 *Ruth, dau of George H Dill, of Toronto, and *d* 1986, leaving issue:

1c +Stephen Frederick [Stephen Law Esq, 1657 Truscott Dr, Mississauga, Ont, Canada L5J 1Z5]; *b* 2 April 1943; *m* 1966 *Julika Fietus-Winkler, and has issue:

1d +Adrian Crawford; *b* 1979

1d *Alexandra Juliane Erika; *b* 1977

1c *Sharron Constance [Mrs James Brazier, 106 Hawthorne Avenue, Stouffville, Ont L4A 7Z8, Canada]; *b* 3 Oct 1937; *m* 15 Jan 1955 *James Wilfred Brazier, and has issue:

1d *Frederick James; *b* 10 Sept, 1955; *m* 1980 *Mary Maresa, dau of Giovanni Battista Garlatti, and has issue:

1e *Ryan Garlatti; *b* 1982

2e *Jeremy Frederick; *b* 1984

1e *Nadine Constance; *b* 1988

2d *Danny Allen [Danny Brazier Esq, 316 Lori Ave, Stouffville, ON L4A 6C2, Canada]; *b* 16 April 1957; *m* 1990 *Deborah Jane, dau of Frank Clifford Carr

3d *Timothy Stewart [Timothy Brazier Esq, 300 West 49th St, Apt 314, NY 10019, USA]; *b* 1 Dec 1960

1b *Charlotte Mary [Mrs John Horne, Apt 227, Cedarwood Gdns, 121 Colbornn St, S Simcoe, Ont N3Y 4H4, Canada]; *b* 1917; *m* 1st 1939 Capt W Marshall Cleland, Govr-Gen of Canada's Horse Gds, Canadian Army (*d* 5 Nov 1958); *m* 2nd 1960 John Franklin Horne (*d* 1974) and by her 1st husb has issue:

1c *William Marshal [William Cleland Esq, 30 Wellington St E, Toronto, ON M5E 1S3, Canada]; *b* 1944; *educ* Waterloo U (BA 1967); *m* 1st Aug 1967 Sheila, dau of Jack M Reid, of Kingston, Ontario; *m* 2nd 1979 *Lois, dau of Robert Charles Pettigrew

2c *Donald Law [Donald Cleland Esq, RRI, Vittoria, Ontario, Canada]; *b* 1947; *m* 1974 *Kathryn, dau of Ward E Kitchen, and has issue:

1d *Eric William; *b* 1978

1d *Kimberley Dawn; *b* 1982

3c *Calder Bruce [Calder Cleland Esq, 685 Sarah St, Gravenhurst, Ontario, Canada]; *b* 1949; *m* 1st 1969 Sandra, dau of Louis Melnyke, of Brantford, Ontario; *m* 2nd 1978 *Wendy, dau of Henry Collens, of Port Carling, Ontario, and by her has:

1d *Jeremy Marshal; *b* 1978

2d *Calder Daniel; *b* 1981

4c *Peter Andrew [Peter Cleland Esq, 260 Hwy 54, RR7, Brantford, Ontario N3T 5L9, Canada]; *b* 1957; *m* 1st 1981 (*divorce* 1994) Vicky, dau of Stephen Kochany, of Simcoe; *m* 2nd 17 June 1995 *Ellen Catherine, dau of David Frederick Watson, of Kearney, Ontario, and has by his 1st w:

1d *Kristin Michele; *b* 1984

2d *Amanda Lindsay; *b* 1986

3a Frederick Wilfred; Cdr RN WW I; *b* 5 Sept 1882; *d* 25 Sept 1932

4a Augustus Leonard Paget; Trooper 4th Canadian Mounted Rifles, served WW I 1916 (severely wounded); *b* 1883; *m* 1919 Maud Mary, dau of George Sherwood Crawford, and *dsp* 21 Nov 1960

5a Adrian Aloysius Sherwood; Maj RCRI WW I; *b* 1885; *m* 1914 Maud (*d* 1960), dau of Hon Louis Arthur Audette, Puisne Judge Exchequer Court Canada, and *d* 12 May 1945, leaving issue:

1b (Charles) Anthony Francis, DSC, CD, served WW II (despatches twice), painter, artist in residence St Mary's U, Halifax, Nova Scotia 1967–80, Hon D Litt St Mary's U, Halifax, 1981, memb Bd Govrs Nova Scotia Coll of Art and Design; *b* 15 Oct 1916; *m* 1942 *Jane Brumm Shaw [Mrs Anthony Law, 8 Halls Rd, Boulderwood, Halifax, NS B3P 1P3, Canada], dau of Milton Maurice Shaw, and *d* 15 Oct 1996

2b Adrian Augustus Stuart, F/Lt RCAF WW II; *b* 1918; *m* 1st 1942 (*divorce* 1951) Wilhelmina Nobel Angus; *m* 2nd May 1952 *Muriel Beverley [Mrs Adrian Law, 2582 MacDonald Drive West, Queenswood, Victoria, BC V8N IX8, Canada], dau of Brooke Vaio, and *d* 24 March 1968, leaving by his 1st w:

1c John Stuart; *b* 1 Aug 1946; *d* 30 March 1972

1c *Moira Jean [Miss Moira Law, 1 Luton Court, Broadstairs, Kent CT10 2DE]; *b* 25 Nov 1943; SRN

1a Mary Helen Augusta; *m* 24 June 1911 James Aloysius Stewart, of Easton, Maryland, USA, and *d* 1926

(5) Victor Edward, Maj-Gen IA , Madras Cav, IPD, Kt Order St Gregory; *b* 24 Nov 1842; *m* 1st 14 May 1867 Mary Elizabeth (*d* 19 Dec 1870), 5th dau of Henry Bowen, and had issue:

1a Mary Augusta Catherine; nun; *d* 1928

(5) (cont.) Victor Law *m* 2nd 7 June 1875 Helen Florence (*d* 16 Feb 1932), 3rd dau of Hon John Willoughby Crawford, Lt-Govr Ontario, and *d* 15 April 1910, having by her had issue:

1a A son; *d* in infancy

(1) Augusta Caroline Louisa; *b* 1844; *m* 15 Sept 1862 Capt Windsor Charles Cary Elwes, Scots Gds, and *d* 18 July 1920, leaving issue. He *d* 11 April 1916

4 (cont.) William Law *m* 2nd 25 Jan 1846 Matilda (*d* 17 June 1894), 2nd dau of Sir Henry Montgomery, 1st Bt, and *d* 31 Oct 1886, having by her had, with other issue:

(6) Ernest Philip Alphonso, CB (1920), CVO (1926); barrister Inner Temple, FSA; *b* 26 Aug 1854; *educ* Lond U (BA); *m* 21 May 1890 Katherine Helen Campbell (*d* 12 March 1954 aged 99), widow of Capt Rupert Lonsdale, CMG, and dau of John Russell, of Newforge, Co Antrim, and *d* 25 Feb 1930

(7) (William) Algernon (Sir), KCMG (1916), CB (1908); Controller Commercial and Consular Affrs FO 1912, Assist Under-Sec FO 1914–16; *b* 7 Aug 1856; *m* 1st 22 Dec 1885 Constance Mary (*d* 11 Feb 1909), dau of Rev Charles William Bagot, Chllr Bath and Wells (*see* BAGOT, B); *m* 2nd 5 March 1912 Hon Catherine Hozier (*d* 31 July 1930), 2nd dau of 1st Baron Newlands (*see* 1970 edn SPENCER-CHURCHILL, B), and *d* 27 Oct 1943, leaving by his 1st w:

1a Nigel Walter; 1st Sec Dip Serv, Min Ec Warfare, Min Info and FO WW II; *b* 26 March 1890; *educ* Eton and Trin Coll Cambridge (BA 1912); *m* 16 May 1929 Anastasia, CBE, DGStJ (*d* April 1976), formerly w of Sir Milne Cheetham and dau of Nicholas Muravieff, Imp Russian Amb Rome, and *dsp* 17 April 1967

(2) Geraldine Isabella Cecilia; *b* 22 Nov 1848; *d* unm 18 Sept 1940

1 Mary Frederica; *m* 10 July 1827 Lt-Gen Thomas Dyneley, CB, RA, and *d* 16 Sept 1851. He *d* 21 June 1860

2 Elizabeth Susan; *m* 3 Feb 1836 2nd Baron Colchester (*see* 1917 edn), and *d* 31 March 1883, leaving issue. He *d* 18 Oct 1867

3 Anne; *m* 15 Oct 1841 9th Baron Colville (*see* COLVILLE OF CULROSS, V) and *d* 30 May 1852

4 Frederick Selina; *m* 8 Aug 1829 Capt Henry James Ramsden, 3rd s of Sir John Ramsden, 4th Bt (*qv*), and *d* 16 April 1879, having had issue

5 Frances Henrietta; *m* 1st 8 March 1832 Charles Des Voeux, est s of Sir Charles Des Voeux, 2nd Bt (*see* 1940 edn); *m* 2nd 29 Sept 1841 Sir Robert Charles Dallas, 2nd Bt (*see* 1902 edn), and *d* 2 March 1894 aged 82, leaving issue

The 5th BARON's brother,

CECIL HENRY TOWRY-LAW, **6th Baron Ellenborough**, CB (1900), JP, DL Dorset; Col Dorset Regt, served Afghan War 1878–79 (medal) and Boer War 1899–1902 (despatches, brevet, two medals with seven clasps); *b* 25 Nov 1849; *m* 22 July 1884 Alice Caroline (*d* 3 Nov 1916), dau of John Harvey Astell, DL, MP, of Woodbury Hall, Beds, and *d* 22 Jan 1931, leaving issue:

HENRY ASTELL TOWRY LAW, **7th Baron Ellenborough**, MC, JP, DL Dorset; Maj 1st Bn KOYLI, memb Gentlemen-at-Arms 1934, chm CPRSE Dorset, served WW I (despatches); *b* 11 July 1889; *m* 31 Jan 1923 *(Helen) Dorothy, DStJ [The Rt Hon The Dowager Lady Ellenborough, Shockerwick House, Shockerwick, Bath BA1 7LL], only dau of Harry William Lovatt, and *d* 19 March 1945, leaving issue:

1 RICHARD EDWARD CECIL LAW, **8th and present Baron Ellenborough**

2 +Cecil Towry Henry [The Hon Cecil Law, 6 Sussex Square, London W2 2SJ]; late Lt 1st King's Dragoon Gds (Reserve), Lloyd's insur broker 1952, chm Towry Law 1958–; *b* 17 Oct 1931; *educ* Eton; *m* 22 Feb 1957 *Daphne Mary Jean, 2nd dau of Hon Laurence Paul Methuen (*see* METHUEN, B), and has:

(1) +Edward Henry Towry; *b* 1971; *educ* Eton and Exeter U (BA)

(1) *Cecilia Diana; *b* 6 Aug 1958; *m* 1985 *James E Chamberlain, s of E J R Chamberlain, of Box, Glos, and has:

1a *Jasper Edward; *b* 1992

1a *Natasha Diana; *b* 1990

(2) *Marianne Jean; *b* 23 July 1960; *educ* St Hilda's Coll Oxford (MA); *m* 1986 *George Alexander Wheeler-Carmichael and has issue (*see* GIBSON-CRAIG-CARMICHAEL, Bt)

(3) *Catherine Rose; *b* 6 March 1962; *educ* Edinburgh U (MA); *m* 1985 *Dr Anthony Charles Murray Ayles, 2nd s of Dr William Ayles, of Moray Place, Edinburgh, and has issue:

1a *William Anthony Carrington; *b* 1992

1a *Charlotte Catherine Mary; *b* 1988

2a *Emily Flora Isobel; *b* 1990

ELLES

Creation: B. (LP, UK) 1972.

THE BARONESS ELLES, of the City of Westminster (Diana Louie Newcombe) [The Rt Hon The Baroness Elles, 75 Ashley Gdns, London SW1B 1HE; Villa Fontana, Ponte del Giglio, Lucca, Italy]; *b* 19 July 1921; *educ* London U (BA); Flight Offr WAAF (Intelligence, Air Ministry) WW II; barrister Lincoln's Inn 1956 (Hon Bencher 1993); care ctee worker S London 1956–72; memb: Outside Organisation Sub-Ctee C Women's Nat Advsy Ctee 1960–72 and Women's Nat Advsy Ctee 1961–62 and 1969–71 (Chm Sub-Ctee on One Parent Families 1970); UK Del UN Gen Assembly 1972, Memb UN Sub Commn Prevention Discrimination and Protection Minorities 1973 and 1974; Chm C Party Internat Office 1973–78, Internat Chm European Union of Women 1973–79, Memb UK Delegn European Parl 1973–75, Oppn Spokesman For Affrs Ho Lds 1975–79, MEP Thames Valley 1979–89, V-Pres European Parl 1982–87, Chm Legal Affrs Ctee European Parl 1987–89; author: *The Housewife and the Common Market* (1971, pamphlet) and *Human Rights of Aliens* (1980); *m* 1945 *Neil Moncrieff Elles, barrister, and has issue:

1 *James Edmund Moncrieff [The Hon James Elles MEP, 14 Ave Maurice, 1050 Brussels, Belgium]; *b* 1949; *educ* Eton and Edinburgh U; *m* 1977 *Françoise, dau of François Le Bail, and has issue:

(1) *Nicholas; *b* 1982

(1) *Victoria; *b* 1980

1 *(Elizabeth) Rosamund [The Hon Mrs Rosamund Lockhart-Mummery, 26 Sheffield Terrace, London W8 7NA]; *b* 1947; *educ* St Andrews U (MA) and Courtauld Inst, (MA); *m* 1971 (*divorce* 1992) Christopher John Lockhart-Mummery, QC, s of Sir Hugh Evelyn Lockhart-Mummery, KCVO, and has issue (*see* DACRE, B)

Lineage: Col STEWART FRANCIS NEWCOMBE, DSO; *m* Elisabeth Chaki and had issue:

DIANA LOUIE, *cr* a **Baroness**

ELLIOTT

Arms: Arg. on a chevron sa. between three bunches of grapes ppr. as many bezants. **Crest:** A garb purpure charged with a fleur-de-lys or.
Motto: *Cum aliis pro aliis* ('With others, for others').
Creation: Bt. (UK) 21 June 1917.

SIR CLIVE CHRISTOPHER HUGH ELLIOTT, 4TH BT, of Limpsfield, Surrey [Sir Clive Elliott Bt, FAO/AGPP, Via delle terme di Caracalla, 00100 Rome, Italy]; *b* 12 Aug 1945; *s* f 1989; *educ* Bryanston, Univ Coll Oxford (BA) and Cape Town U (DPhil); research offr Cape Town U FitzPatrick Inst of Ornithology 1968–71, 1st offr in charge Nat Unit Bird-ringing Admin 1972–75, FAO: UN project manager Chad 1975–78, Tanzania 1975–86 and Kenya 1986–89, Ag Ops Div Rome 1989–95, Sr Offr Migratory Pests Plant Protection Serv 1995–, memb S African Ornithological Soc, Field Staff Assoc FAO (chm 1992), author: *Quelea Quelea: Africa's Bird Pest* (1989); *m* 1975 *Marie Thérèse, dau of H R Rüttimann, of Hohenrain, Switzerland, and has issue:

1 +IVO ANTONY MORITZ; *b* 9 May 1978

2 +Nicholas Johann Clive; *b* 1980

Lineage: HENRY ELLIOTT, of Stroud, Glos; *b* 9 Oct 1800; *m* 25 Dec 1825 Caroline Tripland and *d* 22 Oct 1853, leaving issue:

THOMAS HENRY ELLIOTT, of Paris; *b* 23 Oct 1826; *m* 1 Oct 1853 Mary Ann (*d* 9 Nov 1892), dau of William Worton, of Oswestry, and *d* 11 Dec 1893, leaving issue:

1 THOMAS HENRY (Sir), **1st Bt**

1 Mary Ann; *m* 27 Sept 1884 Henri Auguste Compagnon, s of Henri Antoine Compagnon, of France, and *d* 1936, having had issue

THOMAS ELLIOTT's only son,

Sir Thomas Henry Elliott, 1st Bt (UK), so *cr* 21 June 1917, KCB (1902, CB 1897); joined Inland Revenue 1872, Pncpl Clerk 1887, Priv Sec to Pres Local Govt Bd 1889–92, Sec to Bds Ag and Fisheries 1892–1913, UK Del Internat Ag Conf Rome 1905, Dep-Master and Comptroller Roy Mint 1913–17, Public Works Loan Commr 1914–19, UK Del Internat Inst Ag and Counsellor Rome Embassy 1919; *b* 7 Sept 1854; *m* 30 June 1880 Ellen (*d* 17 Oct 1942), 3rd dau of James Rowe, and had:

1 IVO D'OYLY (Sir), **2nd Bt**

1 Beatrice Marguerite; *b* 13 April 1881; *d* unm 11 Nov 1938

Sir THOMAS *d* 4 June 1926; his only son,

Sir Ivo D'Oyly Elliott, 2nd Bt; *b* 7 March 1882; *educ* Harrow and Balliol Coll Oxford (MA); joined ICS 1906, U-Sec Dept Commerce and Industry India 1916–19, Magistrate and Collector UP 1922, Sec to Govt UP 1926, ret 1932; Fin Commr Mauritius 1931; Franchise Officer Kashmir State 1933–34; Order Sacred Treasure Japan; *m* 31 Oct 1911 Margery Helen (*d* 19 Dec 1968), dau of Francis Carey, of Burgess Hill, Sussex, and had:

1 HUGH FRANCIS IVO (Sir), **3rd Bt**

2 Thomas Anthony Keith, CMG (1968); Capt KSLI, For Serv 1947–76: 2nd Sec Belgrade 1949, 1st Sec Peking 1957–59 and Athens 1960–61, FO 1961–65, Political Advsr Hong Kong Govt 1965–68, Counsellor Washington 1968–70 (Min and Head Chancery 1970–72), Amb: Helsinki 1972–74 and Israel 1974–76; *b* 27 May 1921; *educ* Eton and Balliol Coll Oxford (BA 1945, MA 1950); *m* 6 Oct 1951 *Alethea [Mrs Thomas Elliott, 1 Windrush, nr Burford, Oxon], er dau of Maj Alistair B H Richardson (*see* HOTHAM, B), and *d* 1976, leaving:

(1) +Thomas Anthony William; *b* 1 Aug 1959; *educ* Eton and Balliol Coll Oxford; *m* 1986 *Carolyn Smith and has issue:

1a +Anthony William Felix; *b* 1991

1a *Evelyn Alethea; *b* 1993

(1) *Victoria Carey; *b* 25 Aug 1952; *m* 1983 *Frederick Dolan and has:

1a *Caitlin Emily; *b* 1987

2a *Alethea Cecilia; *b* 1990

(2) *Catherine (Katie) Frances; *b* 13 June 1954; *m* 1982 *George Cardona and has:

1a *Anthony; *b* 1985

2a *Alexander; *b* 1988

1a *Natalie; *b* 1987

(3) *Anne Louisa; *b* 8 Dec 1956; *m* 1981 *Jurek Bielecki and has:
1a *Anton Andrej; *b* 1984
2a *Kazimir; *b* 1986
3a *Lukas; *b* 1989
4a *Roman; *b* 1990
5a *Darius; *b* 1993
1 *Anne Carey [Mrs John Thomson, The Knoll, Fulbrook, Burford, Oxon]; *b* 28 Aug 1914; *educ* LMH Oxford (BA 1938); *m* 18 Feb 1939 *John Thomson, and has:
(1) *Robert Hugh Gordon; *b* 14 June1947; *educ* Sedbergh and Exeter Coll Oxford (BA 1968); *m* 1976 *Rosalie Zoë Twitchin and has issue:
1a *Alix Rebecca; *b* 1978
2a *Camilla Rachel; *b* 1981
(2) *Andrew John; *b* 27 Feb 1949; *educ* Sedberghand Keble Coll Oxford; *m* 1976 *Alison Monica Berkley and has issue:
1a *Anna Marie; *b* 1977
2a *Pauline Clare; *b* 1979
(1) *Janet Carey [Mrs Keith Robbins, Rhyd y Fran, Cribyn, Lampeter, Dyfed SA48 7HW]; *b* 14 June 1941; *educ* LMH Oxford (BA 1962); *m* 24 Aug 1963 *Keith Gilbert Robbins, MA, DPhil, DLitt, FRS, ES, and has issue:
1a *Paul John Gilbert; *b* 1965
2a *Daniel Henry Keith; *b* 1967
3a *Adam Edward Ivo; *b* 1972
1a *Lucy Helen; *b* 1970
2 *Pauline Margery [Miss Pauline Elliott, 46 Witney St, Burford, Oxon]; *b* 27 Feb 1917; ARCM 1939, Hon Fell 1972
Sir IVO *d* 18 Sept 1961; his er s,

Sir Hugh Francis Ivo Elliott, 3rd Bt, OBE (1953); *b* 10 March 1913; *educ* Eastbourne Coll and Univ Coll Oxford (BA 1936, MA 1947); Tanganyika Admin Service 1937–61, Dist Offr and Magistrate 1939, Assist Sec Secretariat, 1947, seconded as Administrator of Tristan da Cunha 1950–52, Dist Commr Tanganyika 1953–54, Pncpl Assist Sec 1954–58, Perm Sec to Min of Natural Resources Dar es Salaam 1958, ret 1961, Liaison Offr London 1961, Actg Sec-Gen 1962, and Substantive Sec-Gen 1964–66 Internat Conservation of Nature, Morges, Switzerland, i/c Union's Ecology Commn Office London 1966–70, Sec British Ornithologists' Union 1962–66 (Pres 1975–79), Tstee Br Museum 1971–81; *m* 12 Dec 1939 *Elizabeth Margaret, er dau of Adolphus George Phillipson, of N Finchley, and *d* 1989, leaving:
1 Sir CLIVE CHRISTOPHER HUGH ELLIOTT, **4th and present Bt**
1 *Susan Elspeth [Mrs James Tedder, c/o Westminster Bank, 96 Terminus Rd, Eastbourne, Sussex]; *b* 4 Nov 1940; *m* 20 Dec 1969 *Lt-Col (Timothy) James Tedder, Gren Gds, s of Col H J Tedder, and has:
(1) *Zara Elizabeth; *b* 1971
(2) *Laura; *b* 1974
2 *Judith Margery; *b* 16 Sept 1942; *educ* Edinburgh U (MA 1963); *m* 13 July 1968 *Erik Geissler, MA, DPhil, yr s of William H Geissler, of Edinburgh, and has:
(1) *Stephen Francis; *b* 1975
(1) *Beatrice Alison; *b* 1974
(2) *Leonie Elizabeth Pauline; *b* 1978

ELLIOTT OF MORPETH

Arms: Gules on a bend or, cotised dancetty argent bendwise, in chief a tripletowered castle gules, masoned argent, the portal azure with portcullis down gold. **Crest:** Upon a mount vert in front of an oak tree proper, fructed or, a fountain ensigned by a crown flory azure. **Supporters:** Dexter, a stag proper, attired and unguled gold; sinister, a seahorse erect argent, scaled gold, the compartment comprising three grassy mounts proper with, between that in the centre and those on either side, water barry wavy of four argent and azure. **Motto:** *Imprimis honor* ('Honour above all').
Creation: B. (LP, UK) 1985.

THE BARON ELLIOTT OF MORPETH, in the County of Northumberland and of the City of Newcastle-upon-Tyne (Sir (Robert) William Elliott, DL (Northumberland 1985)) [The Rt Hon The Lord Elliott of Morpeth DL, Hindley Hall, Stocksfield, Northumberland NE43 9RY]; *b* 11 Dec 1920; *educ* Morpeth GS; farmer 1939–; MP (C) Newcastle upon Tyne North 1957-83; PPS to: Jt Parly Secs Min Tport & Civil Aviation 1958–59, Parly U-Sec Home Office 1959–60, Min State Home Office 1960–61, Sec Technical Co-opn 1961–63, Assist Govt Whip 1963–64, Oppn Whip 1964–70, Comptroller Household 1970, V-Chm C Party 1970–74, Chm Select Ctee Ag, Fisheries and Food 1980–83, ktd 1974; *m* 1956 *Jane, dau of John Burton Morpeth, of Newcastle, and has issue:
1 *Richard John, *b* 1959; *educ* Sedburgh, Edinburgh U (BA) and RMA Sandhurst; *m* 1988 *Susu, yr dau of Lionel Robertson, of Abbey Lodge, Park Rd, London, and has issue:
(1) *Romy; *b* 1990
(2) *Laura; *b* 1992
1 *Alison Mary, *b* 1957; *educ* Oxenford Castle Sch; *m* 1985 *Hugh A Campbell Adamson, yr s of Lt-Col William John Campbell Adamson, TD, JP, of Careston Castle, Brechin, Angus, and has issue:
(1) *James William; *b* 1989
(1) *Rosemary Jane; *b* 1987
(2) *Catherine Grace; *b* 1991
2 *Catherine Victoria; *b* 1962; *educ* St Mary's Convent Berwick-upon-Tweed and Durham U (BA); *m* 1988 *Alexander Julian Taylor, est s of J A Taylor, of Rumer Hall, Welford-on-Avon, Warwicks, and has issue:
(1) *Alexander William John; *b* 1990
(2) *George Arthur James; *b* 1992
(1) *Milly; *b* 4 Sept 1996
2 *Sarah Ann, *b* 1962 (twin); *educ* New Hall Sch Essex and Edinburgh U (BA); *m* 1986 *George Evelyn Atkinson-Clark and has issue (*see* SUFFIELD, B)
4 *Louise Jane, *b* 1967; *educ* St Anne's Windermere and Durham U (BA)

Lineage: RICHARD ELLIOTT, of Morpeth, Northumberland; *m* Mary Elizabeth, dau of William Fulthorpe, of Morpeth, and had issue:
ROBERT WILLIAM, *cr* a **Baron**

ELPHINSTONE, Lord

Arms: Quarterly, 1st and 4th, argent a chevron sable between three boar's heads erased gules, armed of the field and langued azure (for ELPHINSTONE); 2nd grand quarter, counterquartered, 1st, gules a chevron within a double tressure flory counterflory argent (for FLEMING); 2nd, azure three frases argent (for FRASER); 3rd, argent on a chief gules three pallets or (for KEITH); 4th, or three bars wavy gules (for DRUMMOND); 3rd grand quarter, argent a chevron between three otter's heads erased gules within a bordure of the last (for FULLERTON); 4th grand quarter, sable on a cross argent, square-pierced of the field, four eagles displayed of the first, in the dexter canton an arm embowed proper issuing out of a naval crown, the hand holding a trident or (for BULLER). **Crest:** A lady from the waist upwards, richly habited in red, her arms extended, the right hand supporting a tower, the left holding a branch of laurel, all proper. **Supporters:** Two wild men, wreathed about the temples and loins with laurel, and each carrying on his exterior shoulder a club, all proper. **Motto:** *Cause causit* ('Cause caused it').
Creations: L. (S) 14 Jan 1509/10, B. (UK) 30 Dec 1885.

THE 19TH LORD ELPHINSTONE, of Elphinstone, Stirlingshire, and **Baron Elphinstone**, of Elphinstone, Co Haddington (Alexander Mountstuart Elphinstone) [The Rt Hon The Lord Elphinstone, Whitberry House, Tyninghame, Dunbar, E Lothian EH42 1XL]; *b* 15 April 1980; *s f* 1994

Lineage: ALEXANDER ELPHINSTONE; *d c* 1290, leaving, with two yr sons (Alan; Duncan):

Sir JOHN ELPHINSTONE of that Ilk; held the lands of Elphinstone, Lothian, from Sir Alexander Seton of that Ilk (*see* EGLINTON and WINTON, E); *m* Margaret, dau of Sir Christopher Seton of that Ilk, and *d c* 1338, leaving:

ALEXANDER ELPHINSTONE of that Ilk; *m* Agnes/Marjory Airth, through whom he acquired the Airth lands in Stirlingshire, and *d* by 1399, having had, with three yr sons (Alexander; Norman; James):

Sir WILLIAM ELPHINSTONE of that Ilk; granted 1399 a charter of lands he held from Sir William Lindsay of the Byres (*see* LINDSAY, E) made out to himself and his male issue with remainder to his bros; had:

1 Alexander, of that Ilk; ktd 1436 following the Scottish victory over the English of Piperden; had:

(1) Agnes; inherited the Elphinstone lands in Lothian; *m* Sir Gilbert Johnston, only s of Sir Adam Johnston of that Ilk by his 2nd w

2 Henry (Sir), of Pittendriech; inherited the Stirlingshire lands; *d* by 1496, having had:

1a James, Yr. of Pittendriech; had:

1b JOHN, for whom *see* further below

2b Alexander

2a Laurence, of Selmys; ancestor of the Elphinstone Bts of Logie (*qv*)

3 William; had:

(1) William; Bp Aberdeen, Chllr Scotland 1488, fndr King's Coll Aberdeen; *d* 25 Oct 1514

Sir HENRY ELPHINSTONE of Pittendreich's gs,

JOHN ELPHINSTONE of that Ilk and of Pittendriech; granted charters of his Stirlingshire lands 1496 and 1497 but resigned them to his overlord Patrick, 4th Lord Lindsay of the Byres (*see* LINDSAY, E), to be held direct from the Crown and erected into the territorial Barony of Elphinstone; *d* a short while after July 1508, leaving:

ALEXANDER ELPHINSTONE, **1st Lord Elphinstone** (S), so *cr* 14 Jan 1509/10; granted certain lands in the Earldom of Mar (*qv*; at this stage an earldom in Scotland was virtually conceived of as a territorial entity, hence the wording here) which were gathered together in the territorial Barony of Innernochty and later amalgamated with Kildrummy (of the castle of which he was Govr) to create the territory of the Lordship of Elphinstone, though Kildrummy was regranted 1513 to him and his w; *m* by 1507 Elizabeth Barlow/Berlay (*m* 2nd 1515, as his 2nd w, 6th Lord Forbes, *qv*, and *d* 1518), an Englishwoman in the Household of QUEEN MARGARET (w of JAMES IV of Scotland and sis of HENRY VIII of England), and was *ka* Battle of Flodden 9 Sept 1513, leaving, with three daus (Isabel, *m* 1st David Lindsay of Dunrod and 2nd Robert Maxwell of Calderwood; Eupheme, *m* John Bruce of Cutmalindie but also had an illegitimate s by James V KING OF SCOTS who was *cr* 28 Oct 1581 Earl of Orkney and Lord Zetland; Elizabeth, *m* Sir David Somerville of Plain):

ALEXANDER ELPHINSTONE, **2nd Lord Elphinstone**; *b* 22 May 1510; *m* Katherine, dau of 4th Lord Erskine (*see* MAR and KELLIE, E), and was *ka* Battle of Pinkie 10 Sept 1547, having had:

1 ROBERT, **3rd Lord**

2 John; Parson of Innernochty

3 James; *m* by 10 June 1589, as her 3rd husb, Janet (*d* 17 Dec 1591), dau of 4th Earl of Rothes (*qv*), and *d* in or after 1599

4 Michael (Sir); Master Household to JAMES VI and I

3 William; ancestor of the ELPHINSTONEs of Calderhall and Hatton

1 Margaret; *b* 14 Feb 1528/9; *m* by 8 May 1552 John Livingstone of Dunipace and had issue

2 Isabel; *m* James Hamilton of Haggs and had issue

3 Marjory; *m* Sir Robert Drummond of Carnock

4 Janet; *m* Robert Leslie, s of 4th Earl of Rothes (*qv*)

The 2nd LORD's est son,

ROBERT ELPHINSTONE, **3rd Lord Elphinstone**; *b* 9 Sept 1530; *m* 1546 Margaret, dau and coheir of Sir John Drummond of Innerpeffray (*see* PERTH, E) by Lady Margaret Stewart, legitimated dau of JAMES IV, and had:

1 ALEXANDER, **4th Lord**

2 George; Rector Scottish Coll Rome

3 JAMES ELPHINSTONE, 1st LORD BALMERINOCH (S) (the lands of the Abbey of Balmerinoch having been erected for him into the territorial Barony of Balmerinoch 1603/4), so *cr* 11 July 1606, of Innernochty and Barnton, PC (E 1603); Ld of Session 1586 as Lord Innernochtie and Pres Court of Session 1605, one of the 'Octavians' (eight-strong panel of Commrs of Scottish Treasury) 1595, Sec State 1598; convicted of treason and attainted 10 March 1608/9 for fabricating a bogus letter from JAMES VI and I to POPE CLEMENT VIII; *m* 1st 21 March 1588 Sarah (living 14 Dec 1592), dau of Sir John Menteith of Carse, and had:

(1) JOHN ELPHINSTONE, 2nd LORD BALMERINOCH (restored 4 Aug 1613); leading Covenanter; his trial and conviction in connection with the 'supplication' (a list of grievances to CHARLES I) of 1633, though followed by a pardon, did the monarchy great harm in Scotland; *m* 1613 Anne, sis of Robert Ker, 1st and last Earl of Somerset of the 1613 *cr* (*see* LOTHIAN, M), and had:

1a JOHN ELPHINSTONE, 3rd LORD BALMERINOCH and 2nd LORD COUPAR (as which *s* unc; *see* below); *b* 18 Feb 1623; obliged to sell nearly all his estates to pay off his f's debts; *m* 30 Oct 1649 Lady Margaret Campbell (*d* 1665), dau of 1st Earl of Loudoun (*qv*), and had:

1b JOHN ELPHINSTONE, 4th LORD BALMERINOCH and 3rd LORD COUPAR, PC (S 1687); *b* 26 Dec 1652; Govr Mint, Sheriff Co Edinburgh; *m* 1st 16 Feb 1672 Lady Christian Montgomerie, dau of 7th Earl of Eglinto(u)n (*see* EGLINTON and WINTON, E), and had, with two er sons (*dvp*):

1c JAMES ELPHINSTONE, 5th LORD BALMERINOCH and 4th LORD COUPAR; *b* 24 Nov 1675; Ld of Session as Lord Coupar 1714; *m* 1718 Lady Elizabeth Carnegie, dau of 4th Earl of Northesk (*qv*), and *dsp* 5 Jan 1746

1c Margaret; *m* Sir John Preston of Prestonhall and had a s and dau

2c Jean; *m* 1700, as his 2nd w, 7th Earl of Moray (*qv*) and *d* 13 May 1739

1b (cont.) The 4th LORD BALMERINOCH and 3rd LORD COUPAR *m* 2nd Ann (*d* 1712), dau of Arthur Ross, Archbp St Andrews, and *d* 13 May 1736, having by her had:

2c ARTHUR ELPHINSTONE, 6th LORD BALMERINOCH and 5th LORD COUPAR; *b* 1688; Jacobite 1715 and 1745 Uprisings (Col 2nd Horse Gds); *m* Margaret (*d* a pauper aged *c* 56 24 Aug 1765), dau of Capt Chalmers, was captured Battle of Culloden 1746, attainted and beheaded *sp* 18 Aug 1746

3 (cont.) The 1st LORD BALMERINOCH *m* 2nd by 23 Dec 1597 Marjory, dau of Hugh Maxwell of Tealing, and *d* 21 June 1612, having by her had:

(2) JAMES ELPHINSTONE, 1st LORD COUPAR (S), so *cr* 20 Dec 1607 (the lands of the Abbey of Coupar, Fife, having been erected into a temporal territoriality in favour of himself and his issue male, whom failing his f and heirs male and of entail); *b c* 1587; Extrdy Ld of Session 1649; resigned his estates and title in favour of his w and her heir but this nullified by the Court of Session on the objection of his half-nephew the 3rd LORD BALMERINOCH (*see* above), who was ajudged heir to both estates and title 1671; *m* 1st Margaret, dau of Sir James Halyburton of Pitcur; *m* 2nd 1667 Marion (*m* 2nd 3rd Lord Lindores; *see* ROTHES, E), dau of 2nd Earl of Airlie (*qv*), and *dsp* 1639

(1) Margaret; *m* 1618 2nd Lord Fraser (*see* SALTOUN, L)

1 Jean; *m* as his 1st w Walter Barclay of Towie (*k* 1587 by William Meldrum of Montcoffer)

2 Agnes; *b* 3 Oct 1559; *m* as his 1st w 1st Lord Ogilvy of Deskford (*see* SEAFIELD, E)

3 Elizabeth; *m* 1 Oct 1582 Robert Innes, 19th of that Ilk (*see* ROXBURGHE, D) and *d* 26 Feb 1613

4 Margaret; *m* John Cunninghame of Drumquhassel

The 3rd LORD *d* 18 May 1602; his son,

ALEXANDER ELPHINSTONE, **4th Lord Elphinstone**; *b* 28 May 1552; Extrdy Ld of Session 1599–1610, Ld High Treasurer Scotland 1599–1601; following litigation John, Earl of Mar (*qv*), in 1626 took back Kildrummy and other Aberdeenshire estates on the grounds that they had not been JAMES IV's to grant when he did so to the **1st Lord Elphinstone**; *m c* 10 Aug 1579 Jean, dau of 6th Lord Livingstone, and *d* 11 Jan 1638, having had, with other issue:

1 ALEXANDER ELPHINSTONE, **5th Lord Elphinstone**; *m c* 5 July 1608 Elizabeth, dau of 3rd Lord Drummond (*see* PERTH, E), and *d* 1649, leaving:

(1) Lilias; *m* her cousin **6th Lord Elphinstone** (*see* below)

2 James, of Barns; *m* Margaret, dau of John Forbes of Brux (*see* FORBES, Bt, of Craigievar), and had:

(1) ALEXANDER, **6th Lord**

1 Agnes; *m* 1 Feb 1600 12th Earl of Sutherland (*qv*)

2 Jean; *m* 1 Feb 1600 9th Lord Forbes (*qv*)

3 Margaret; *m* 1601 Sir John Bruce of Airth

4 Helen; *m* 1st Sir William Cockburn of Langton; *m* 2nd Henry Rollo of Woodside

The 5th LORD's n,

ALEXANDER ELPHINSTONE, **6th Lord Elphinstone**; royalist Civil War, hence fined £1,000 1654; *m* his cousin Lilias (*d* Nov 1675; *see* above) and *d* 26 Oct 1654, having had, with a dau (Anne, *m* 1671 6th Lord Torphichen; *qv*):

1 ALEXANDER ELPHINSTONE, **7th Lord Elphinstone**; f's fine of 1654 reduced by two-thirds 1655 because of the family's impoverishment; *m* 10 Sept 1667 Anne (*m* 2nd 3rd Lord Elibank; *qv*), dau of Alexander Burnet, Archbp St Andrews, and *dsp* May 1669

2 JOHN ELPHINSTONE, **8th Lord Elphinstone**; *m* 23 April 1670 Isabel (*d* Oct 1706), dau of 3rd Earl of Lauderdale (*qv*), and *d c* March 1717/8, having had:

(1) CHARLES, **9th Lord**

(2) William; *ka* Battle of Preston 1715

(1) Elizabeth; *m* Hon John Campbell, of Mamore

(2) Margaret; *m* 1st 1706 George, Count Leslie of Balquhain; *m* 2nd Sir James Gordon, Bt, of Park

(3) Mary; *m* Thomas Buchan of Cairnbulg

The 8th LORD's surv son,

CHARLES ELPHINSTONE, **9th Lord Elphinstone**; *b* Dec 1676; *m* Elizabeth (*d* 18 Feb 1738), dau of Sir William Primrose, 2nd Bt (*see* ROSEBERY, E), and *d* 20 Feb 1757, having had, with other issue:

1 John; *m* Margery (*d* 1784), dau of Sir Archibald Fleming, Bt, of Ferme, Lanarks, but *dsp* & *vp* 1753

2 CHARLES, **10th Lord**

3 Archibald; Army Offr; *d* Siege of Cartagena 1741

1 Primrose; *m* 1757 9th Earl of Home (*qv*) and *d* 1759

The 9th LORD's 2nd son,

CHARLES ELPHINSTONE, **10th Lord Elphinstone**; *m* 1735 Clementina (*d* 1 Jan 1799), dau and eventual sole heir of 6th Earl of Wigtoun by Lady Mary Keith, dau of 9th Earl Marischal (*see* KINTORE, E), and *d* 2 April 1781, having had, with another s and two other daus:

1 JOHN ELPHINSTONE, **11th Lord Elphinstone**; *b* Jan 1737; rep S peer 1784–94, Lt-Govr Edinburgh Castle; *m* 1762 Anne (*d* 28 Oct 1801), dau of 3rd Lord Ruthven of Freeland (*see* CARLISLE, E), and *d* 19 Aug 1794, having had, with other surv issue:

(1) JOHN ELPHINSTONE, **12th Lord Elphinstone**; *b* 1764; Lt-Gen, Col 26th Foot, Ld Lt Dunbartonshire, rep S peer 1803–07; *m* 31 July 1806 Janet Hyndford (*d* 23 Aug 1825), yst dau of Cornelius Elliot of Woolflee, Roxburghshire, and widow of Sir John Gibson-Carmichael, 6th Bt (*see* 1926 edn), and *d* 2 May 1813, leaving:

1a JOHN ELPHINSTONE, **13th Lord Elphinstone**, GCB (1859), GCH (1836), PC (1836); *b* 23 June 1807; Capt RHG (Blues), rep S peer 1832–34 and 1847–59, Govr Madras and Bombay during Indian Mutiny 1857, for which *cr* 21 May 1859 BARON ELPHINSTONE, of Elphinstone, Co Stirling (UK); *d* unm 19 July 1860 when the UK barony expired

(2) Charles ELPHINSTONE later ELPHINSTONE-FLEEMING (added on inheriting estates of Earls of Wigton); *b* 1774; MP Stirlingshire, Adml, Govr Greenwich Hosp; *m* June 1816 Catalina Paulina Alessandro, of Spain (*m* 2nd Capt James Edward Katon, RN), and *d* 30 Oct 1840, leaving issue:

1a JOHN ELPHINSTONE-FLEEMING, **14th Lord Elphinstone**; *b* 11 Dec 1819; Lt-Col; *d* unm 13 Jan 1861

1a Clementina; *m* 24 March 1845 4th Viscount Hawarden (*qv*) and *d* 19 Jan 1865, leaving issue

2a Mary Keith; *m* 1st 20 April 1843 (*divorce* 1847) Alexander Macalister of Torriedale; *m* 2nd 1848 Morgan Lloyd (*d* 5 Sept 1893), QC, MP, and *d* 11 March 1859, leaving issue

3a Anne Elizabeth; granted by roy licence 12 Oct 1860 rank of Ld of Parl's dau; *m* 12 June 1851 William Cunninghame Bontine of Ardoch, est son of R C Cunninghame Graham of Gartmore and Finlayston (*d* 6 Sept 1883), and *d* 27 March 1925, leaving issue

(3) Mountstuart; *b* 1779; DCL, ICS, Commr in India, Govr Bombay; *d* 29 Nov 1859

2 William ELPHINSTONE later FULLERTON-ELPHINSTONE; Dir HEIC and previously Cdr of an Indiaman; *m* 24 June 1774 Elizabeth (*d* 3 May 1834), est dau of William Fullerton, of Carstairs, Lanarks, and heir to her unc John Fullerton, of Carberry, and had, with other issue:

(1) Charles; *b* 1784; RN; lost in the *Blenheim*

(2) William George Keith, CB; Maj-Gen; *d* 24 April 1842

(3) James Drummond FULLERTON-ELPHINSTONE later BULLER-FULLERTON-ELPHINSTONE; *b* 1788; Lt-Col; *m* 1st 30 Sept 1820 Diana Maria (*dsp* 24 Dec 1821), only dau of Charles John Clavering; *m* 2nd 25 Feb 1824 Anna Maria (*d* 16 Feb 1845), only child of Adml Sir Edward Buller, Bt, MP, of Trenant Park, Cornwall, and *d* 8 March 1857, having had issue:

1a WILLIAM, **15th Lord**

2a Edward Charles, of Inveresk Lodge, Musselburgh; *b* 17 Nov 1832; granted with siblings 5 Oct 1861 rank of Ld of Parl's dau/yr s, Capt 92nd Highrs; *m* 5 May 1859 Elizabeth Harriette (*d* 13 Nov 1909), yst dau of Rt Hon Sir George Clerk, 6th Bt, of Penicuik (*qv*), and *d* 29 June 1915, having had:

1b Charles James; *b* 14 Aug 1860; *d* 15 Jan 1868

2b George Keith (Sir), KBE (1920); *b* 11 May 1865; *m* 1st 25 April 1899 Katherine Amy (*d* 4 May 1925), dau of Col Alfred James Wake, RA, of Blackheath, and had issue:

1c Rosemary; *b* 13 Dec 1900; *m* 2 Feb 1927 Rev Edward Frank Circuit, Rector Little Glenham, Woodbridge, Suffolk, and *d* 1945, leaving issue

2b (cont.) Sir George Buller-Fullerton-Elphinstone *m* 2nd 16 Feb 1926 Isobel Penrose (*d* 8 Jan 1953), 4th dau of Sir Theodore Fry, 1st Bt, and *d* 6 July 1941

1b Lilias Mary; *b* 22 Sept 1861; *d* unm 3 Oct 1909

2b Elizabeth Margaret; *b* 26 April 1874; *m* 19 Nov 1902 Col Montagu James Grant-Peterkin, OBE (*d* 27 March 1954), of Grange Hall, Forres, Morayshire, er son of James Grant-Peterkin, and *d* 30 Jan 1945, leaving issue

3a John Frederick; *b* 21 April 1837; Lt-Col Scots Fus Gds; *dsp* 22 Nov 1874

4a George James; *b* 7 Jan 1841; *m* 23 July 1868 Annie (*m* 2nd 1884 Rev Hugh McLachlan (*d* 1903)), dau of Rev John MacIntyre, LLD, and *d* 1 March 1879

1a Gertrude; *m* 16 April 1850 James Hope and *d* 29 March 1894, leaving issue (*see* HOPE, Bt)

2a Clementina Fleming; *m* 8 April 1858 Lt-Col Douglas Jones (*d* 1879) and *dsp* 2 Sept 1916

3a Anna Maria; *m* 4 March 1857 Thomas Henry Montgomery and *d* 20 March 1914, leaving issue (*see* MONTGOMERY, Bt)

4a Elizabeth Mary; *m* 17 Jan 1860 Very Rev James Francis Montgomery, DD (*d* 21 Sept 1897), Dean Edinburgh, and *dsp* 24 Sept 1902

(1) Clementina; *m* 18 Jan 1809 V-Adml Sir Pulteney Malcolm, GCB, and *dsp* 19 Nov 1830

3 GEORGE KEITH ELPHINSTONE, 1st and last VISCOUNT KEITH (UK), so *cr* 1 June 1814, as also earlier 16 March 1797 BARON KEITH OF STONEHAVEN MARISCHAL (I), with special remainder, failing heirs male of his body, to his dau Margaret, also 15 Dec 1801 BARON KEITH OF STONEHAVEN MARISCHAL, Co Kincardine (UK), and 17 Sept 1803 BARON KEITH OF BANHEATH, Co Dunbarton (also UK), with remainder, failing heirs male of his body, to his dau Margaret, GCB (1815, KB 1794); *b* 7 Jan 1745/6; RN: joined 1761, R-Adml 1794, V-Adml 1795, took Cape Town 1795, Cdr Sheerness at the time of the Mutiny at The Nore, which he helped put down, C-in-C Mediterranean 1799–1802, participating in mil ops at Aboukir Bay and taking of Alexandria, Adml the Blue 1801, White 1805 and Red 1810, C-in-C: Plymouth 1803, N Sea and E Channel 1803–07 and Channel Fleet 1812; MP (Whig) Dunbartonshire 1781–90 and Stirlingshire 1796–1801; Kt of the Crescent Ottoman Empire, Kt Grand Cross SS. Maurice and Lazarus Sardinia; *m* 1st 10 April 1787 Jane (*d* 12 Dec 1789), dau and coheir of William Mercer (gs of 2nd Lord Nairne; *see* MERSEY, V), of Aldin, Perthshire, and had issue:

(1) MARGARET MERCER Keith, BARONESS KEITH OF STONEHAVEN MARISCHAL and BARONESS KEITH OF BANHEATH, as which *s* f 1823 according to the special remainders in those titles, and LADY NAIRNE, as which *s* cousin 7 Dec 1837, all in her own right; *b* 12 June 1788; *m* 20 June 1817 Auguste Charles Joseph, COUNT De FLAHAULT De La BILLARDRIE (*d* 2 Sept 1870), s of Mme de Souza by (it is widely accepted) Charles Maurice, Marquis de Talleyrand-Périgord, Prince of Benevento (the diplomatist Talleyrand), and *d* 11 Nov 1867, when her Baronies expired but the S Ldship passed to her est dau (*see* MERSEY, V)

3 (cont.) The 1st and last VISCOUNT *m* 2nd 10 Jan 1808 Hester Maria (*d* 31 March 1857), dau and coheir of Henry Thrale, and *d* 10 March 1823, when the Viscountcy and Barony *cr* 1801 expired, leaving by her:

(2) Georgiana Auguste Henrietta; *m* 1st 20 Sept 1831 Hon Augustus John Villiers (*see* JERSEY, E); *m* 2nd 10 May 1870 Lord William Godolphine Osborne (*d* 28 Dec 1888), bro of 8th Duke of Leeds (*see* 1963 edn), and *dsp* 21 Sept 1892

1 Eleanor; *m* 1777 Rt Hon William Adam of Blair Adam, Kinross-shire, and Woodston, Kincardineshire, Baron Exchequer Scotland, Ld Ch Commr of the Scottish Jury Court, and *d* Feb 1808

2 Clementina; *m* 31 March 1785 1st and last Lord Perth, Baron Drummond (*see* PERTH, E) and *d* 31 Aug 1822, leaving issue

The 14th LORD's cousin,

WILLIAM BULLER FULLERTON-ELPHINSTONE, **15th Lord Elphinstone**, DL; *b* 18 Nov 1828; Capt RN, Kt Medjidie, rep S peer 1867–85, Ld-in-Waiting 1874–80 and 1886–92; *cr* 30 Dec 1885 BARON ELPHINSTONE, of Elphinstone, Co Haddington (UK); *m* 16 June 1864 Constance Euphemia Woronzow (*d* 16 March 1922), dau of 6th Earl of Dunmore (*qv*), and *d* 18 Jan 1893, having had:

1 James Drummond, *Master of Elphinstone*; *b* 15 April 1865; Lt 3rd Bn Gordon Highrs; *d* 9 Nov 1890

2 SIDNEY HERBERT, **16th Lord**

3 Mountstuart William; *b* 5 March 1871; Priv Sec to Mil Sec War Office WW I; FRPS, Assoc Inst Br Photographers; *d* unm 7 April 1957

1 Lilian; *b* 11 Feb 1867; *d* unm 23 Aug 1956

2 Constance Lothian; *b* 5 Oct 1873; *d* 18 March 1895

The 15th LORD's est son,

SIDNEY HERBERT ELPHINSTONE, **16th Lord Elphinstone**, KT (1927); *b* 27 July 1869; LLD Aberdeen U, Capt Gen Roy Co Archers, Ld High Commr Gen Assembly Ch Scotland 1923–24, Ld Clerk Registry Scotland and Keeper Signet 1944–55, Chllr Order Thistle 1949–55; *m* 14 July 1910 Lady Mary Frances Bowes-Lyon, DCVO (1939) (*d* 8 Feb 1961), 2nd dau of 14th Earl of Strathmore and Kinghorne (*qv*), and *d* 28 Nov 1955, leaving issue:

1 JOHN ALEXANDER ELPHINSTONE, **17th Lord Elphinstone**, DL (Angus 1955); *b* 22 March 1914; *educ* Eton and Ch Ch Oxford; Capt Black Watch (SR) WW II (POW), Lt Roy Co Archers, Pres Scottish Assoc Boys' Clubs, Chm Cncl Scottish Branch BRCS, Pres Roy Zoological Soc Scotland, dir Bank of Scotland and Scottish Provident Inst; *d* unm 15 Nov 1975

2 Andrew Charles Victor (Rev); *b* 10 Nov 1918; *educ* Eton and New Coll Oxford; T/Capt 4th Bn Cameron Highrs (TA), ADC to Viceroy India 1941–43, Rector Worplesdon 1953–62; *m* 29 May 1946 *Jean Frances, CVO, Extra Woman of the Bedchamber to HM THE QUEEN (*m* 3rd 14 April 1980 Lt Col John William Richard Woodroffe), dau of Angus Valdimar Hambro, of Milton Abbas, Dorset, and widow of Capt Hon Vicary Paul Gibbs, Gren Gds (*see* ALDENHAM and HUNSDON OF HUNSDON, B), and *d* 19 March 1975, leaving issue:

(1) JAMES ALEXANDER, **18th Lord**

(1) *Rosemary Elizabeth; *b* 13 Aug 1947 (HM THE QUEEN stood sponsor); *m* 14 Jan 1967 *James Ronald Pigé Leschallas (*see* ROMNEY, E) and has:

1a *Andrew James; *b* 7 Oct 1970

2a *Alexander Charles; *b* 1978

1a *Sophie Elizabeth; *b* 16 May 1968; *m* 1993 *James Digby Charles Gaselee, Life Gds, son of Nicholas Auriol Digby Charles Gaselee, of Saxon Cottage, Lambourn, Berks

1 (Mary) Elizabeth; *b* 2 July 1911; *d* unm

2 *Jean Constance MVO (1983) [The Hon Mrs Wills MVO, Allanbay Park, Binfield, Berks]; *b* 3 April 1915; Extra Ldy-in-Waiting to HRH PRINCESS MARGARET, COUNTESS OF SNOWDON, 1970; *m* 25 July 1936 *Maj John Lycett Wills (*see* WILLS, Bt, of Hazlewood) and has issue

3 *Margaret [The Hon Mrs Rhodes, The Garden House, Great Windsor Park, Windsor, Berks SL4 2HP]; *b* 9 June 1925; a bridesmaid to HRH PRINCESS ELIZABETH 20 Nov 1947, Ldy-in-Waiting to HM QUEEN ELIZABETH THE QUEEN MOTHER 1991–; *m* 31 July 1950 *Denys Gravenor Rhodes, er son of Maj Arthur Tahu Gravenor Rhodes, Gren Gds, of Mount Offham, W Malling, Kent, by Hon Helen Cecil Olive, est dau of 5th Baron Plunket (*qv*), and has:

(1) *Simon John Gravenor; *b* 22 Feb 1957; *educ* Harrow; Page of Honour to HM THE QUEEN 1971–73; *m* 1983 *Susan, est dau of Eden Simon, of Tara Farm, Bindura, Zimbabwe

(2) *Michael Andrew Gravenor; *b* 8 June 1960

(1) *Annabel Margaret; *b* 21 Feb 1952; *m* 1st 1978 Christopher J Strickland-Skailes, twin s of Frank Strickland-Skailes, of Lea Hall, Hatfield Heath, Essex; *m* 2nd 1986 *G V (Charles) Cope, 2nd s of Herbert Vallack Cope, of Rose Hill, Bideford, Devon, and has by her 1st husb:

1a *Andrew James Downing; *b* 1980

(2) *Victoria Ann; *b* 27 Sept 1953 (HM THE QUEEN stood sponsor); *m* 1974 Nicholas Deans (*d* 1991)

The 17th LORD's n,

JAMES ALEXANDER ELPHINSTONE, **18th Lord Elphinstone**; *b* 22 April 1953; *educ* Eton and RAC Cirencester; ARICS 1979; *m* 22 April 1978 *Willa Mary Gabriel, 4th dau of Maj (George) David Chetwode, MBE (*see* CHETWODE, B), and *d* 19 Dec 1994, leaving:

1 ALEXANDER MOUNTSTUART ELPHINSTONE, **19th and present Lord Elphinstone**

2 +ANGUS JOHN; *b* 1982; heir presumptive

3 +Fergus David; *b* 1985

1 *Clementina Rose; *b* 1989

ELPHINSTONE, Bt, of Logie

Arms: Argent on a chevron sable between three boar's heads erased gules, armed and langued azure, an episcopal mitre of the first.
Crest: A dexter hand proper holding a garb or.
Motto: *Non vi sed virtute* ('Not by strength but by valour').
Creation: Bt. (NS) 2 Dec 1701.

SIR JOHN ELPHINSTONE OF GLACK, 11th Bt, of Logie Elphinstone, Co Aberdeen and Nova Scotia [Sir John Elphinstone Bt, Pilgrims, Churchfields, Sandiway, Cheshire CW8 2JS]; *b* 12 Aug 1924; *s* uncle 1970; *educ* Repton and Emmanuel Coll Cambridge (BA 1950); Lt RM 1942–48, ARICS, QALAS, chartered surveyor, land agent with ICI 1956–83, consultant Gandy & Son Northwich 1983–88, past Pres Cheshire Ag Valuers' Assoc, past Chm Land Agency & Ag Div Lancs, Cheshire & IOM branch RICS, memb Lancs River Authority 1970–74; *m* 23 May 1953 *Margaret Doreen, dau of Edric Tasker, of Cheltenham, and has:

1 +ALEXANDER (with his two yst bros, but not the 2nd prefers his surname ELPHINSTON) [Alexander Elphinston Esq, High Banks, Sandy Lane, Brampford Speke, Devon EX5 5HW]; *b* 6 June 1955; *educ* Repton and St John's Coll Durham; slr; *m* 1986 *Ruth Mary, er dau of Rev Robert Curtis Dunnett, of Edgbaston, Warwicks, and has issue:

(1) +Daniel John; *b* 24 Sept 1989

(2) +David Robert; *b* 8 Oct 1997

(1) *Sarah Elizabeth; *b* 21 Sept 1992

2 +Charles [Charles Elphinstone Esq, West Water House, Edzell, Brechin, Angus]; *b* 11 April 1958; *educ* Repton; *m* 1981 *Lucy, dau of Maj M D Reynolds, Malton, N Yorks, and has issue:

(1) +William James; *b* 3 July 1986

(2) +Thomas George; *b* 18 Aug 1988

(1) *Mary Abigail; *b* 24 June 1984

(2) *Charis Clare; 1 June 1992

3 +Andrew James [Andrew Elphinston Esq, 27 Effingham Rd, Reigate, Surrey RH2 7JN]; *b* 22 Aug 1961

4 +William Robert [William Elphinston Esq, Pilgrims, Churchfields, Sandiway, Cheshire CW8 2JS]; *b* 3 July 1963

Lineage: Sir HENRY ELPHINSTONE of Pittendriech, of which he had a charter 1477, had:

1 James; ancestor of Lord Elphinstone (*qv*)

2 LAURENCE, for whom *see* below

3 John; Baillie Glasgow; *m* Elizabeth Douglas and had issue

Sir HENRY's 2nd son,

LAURENCE ELPHINSTONE of Selmys; *m* Margaret Hamilton and had, with an er s (Andrew, of Selmys, *m* Isabel Keith and had issue which died out in the 2nd generation):

NICHOLAS ELPHINSTONE of Glack, of which he had a charter from his cousin William Elphinstone, Bp of Aberdeen, Chllr of Scotland, who acquired that estate from Nicholas's bro Andrew by surrender 13 Nov 1499; *m* Elizabeth Abercrombie, of Pitmeddow, and had:

WILLIAM ELPHINSTONE of Glack; *m* Elizabeth Cromme and *d c* 1586, leaving:

JAMES ELPHINSTONE of Glack; *m* 1559 Marjorie, 4th dau of Alexander Leslie, 4th territorial Baron of Pitcaple, and *d c* 1595, leaving an est s:

ALEXANDER; *dvp*, leaving:

JAMES ELPHINSTONE of Glack; *m* Elizabeth Wood, of Bonnytoun, and had:

1 James, of Glack; *s f c* 2 June 1670 and recorded his arms in the Lyon Office *c* 1672; Commissary for Inverurie Scottish Parl, Hon Burgess Inverurie 1671; *m* 1641 Janet Leslie and had:

(1) John, of Glack, to which he *s c* 15 Aug 1676; Hon Burgess Inverurie 1671; *m* Anna Irvine (*d* 1703), dau of James Irvine of Artamford, and had:

1a JOHN, of Glack *de jure* 5th Bt

2 William, of Ressiviot, in Milntoun of Durnoch, which he bought 27 May 1653; *m* Margaret Forbes and *d c* 16 Dec 1664, leaving, with other issue:

(1) **Sir James Elphinstone, 1st Bt** (NS), so *cr* 2 Dec 1701, with remainder to his heirs male whatsoever; *b* 1642; WS 1671; bought the lands of Logie Durnoch 1676; MP (S Parl) Aberdeenshire 1693–1702, Judge Commissary Court Edinburgh 1696; *m* 2 Sept 1673 Cecilia (*d* 10 Nov 1706), dau of John Denholme of Muirhouse and W Shield, and *d* 10 March 1722, leaving an est s:

1a **Sir John Elphinstone, 2nd Bt**; *b* 1675; advocate 15 Feb 1699, Sheriff Aberdeenshire; *m* 23 Aug 1703 Mary (*d* 18 May 1767), dau of Sir Gilbert Elliot, 1st Bt (*see* MINTO, E), and *d* 14 March 1732, having had:

1b **Sir James Elphinstone, 3rd Bt**; *b c* 1710; advocate 23 Jan 1728; *m* 4 Oct 1733 Jean (*m* 2nd 2 April 1747 Lt-Col George Mure and *d* 25 Sept 1765), 2nd dau of Rt Rev Thomas Rattray, 20th Laird of Craighall-Rattray, DD, Primus of Scotland, and *dspm* April 1739, leaving at least one dau (Mary, *m* Robert Dalrymple-Horn-Elphinstone; *see* STAIR, E)

2b Gilbert; *b* 9 Feb 1713; *d* young

3b **Sir John Elphinstone, 4th Bt**; *b* 11 Jan 1717; *d* unm Jan 1743, when the Btcy became dormant until 1927

4b Hugh; *b* 1 March 1720

The 4th Bt's kinsman,

JOHN ELPHINSTONE, of Glack, *de jure* 5th Bt;Hon Burgess Aberdeen 1731; served heir to his f in Glack 15 Jan 1735; *m* 1st 1691 Margaret (*d* 1730), dau of Alexander Forbes of Foveran, and had four daus; *m* 2nd 1734 Jean (*d* 1794), dau of Alexander Achyndachy of that Ilk, Chamberlain of Fyvie, and *d* Sept 1758 in his 93rd year, leaving by her:

ALEXANDER ELPHINSTONE of Glack, *de jure* 6th Bt; infeft 8 Aug 1751 on an entail executed by his f; advocate 1766, Sheriff Depute Aberdeenshire 1777; *m* 25 Oct 1766 Jean, 2nd dau of Colin Mackenzie of Kilcoy, and *d* 26 Nov 1795; his est s:

JOHN ELPHINSTONE, *de jure* 7th Bt; *b* 15 May 1771; HEICS, memb Cncl of Bombay; *m* 19 March 1799 Maria Prudence, dau of James Robertson, of London, and *d* 16 April 1835; his only s:

ALEXANDER ELPHINSTONE, *de jure* 8th Bt; *b* 3 April 1801; Bombay CS, memb Cncl of Bombay; *m* 1st 28 June 1831 Charlotte Hunter and *d* 28 Nov 1888, having had, with other issue:

1 JOHN, *de jure* 9th Bt

2 Alexander; *b* 24 Nov 1840; *m* Louisa Pillans, and *dsp* 9 Aug 1881

3 Thomas Phillips; *b* 14 March 1842; *d* unm 23 May 1893

The *de jure* 8th Bt *m* 2nd 19 April 1868 Margaret Rachel Roberts and by her had, with other issue:

4 Robert Gray; *b* 6 May 1872; *m* 1st 19 April 1910 Marion Stewart (*d* 5 Nov 1919), dau of Thomas Stewart, of BC, Canada; *m* 2nd 23 June 1937 Eleanor Sarah (*d* 17 Feb 1968), dau of George Gladstone McTurk, of Ryland Hill, South Care, Yorks, and *dsp* 26 Feb 1947

5 Alexis; *b* 4 Dec 1873; Lt-Col Argyll & Sutherland Highrs; *m* 12 July 1905 Ethel Margaret (*d* 20 Nov 1946), dau of Louis M Cantlon, barrister, and *d* 20 Feb 1958, leaving:

(1) +Colin Anthony John; *b* 27 June 1906; *m* 25 Oct 1952 Margaret Douglas Fisher (*d* 1971), dau of Frederick Ramsay Palmer

The *de jure* 8th Bt's est son,

JOHN ELPHINSTONE, *de jure* 9th Bt; *b* 16 Dec 1834; Bombay CS; *m* 20 March 1875 Emma Eliza (*d* 20 March 1936), 2nd dau of G R Betham, and *d* 30 June 1893, leaving:

1 **Sir Alexander Logie Elphinstone, 10th Bt**; *b* 8 March 1880; joined Army 1899, Capt 1906, Maj 1915, on Staff 1900–02 and 1917–21 (Vth Corps BEF, War Off), Boer War (Queen's medal and six clasps, King's medal and two clasps), WW I (1914–15 star, two medals), WW II with BRC; Freeman City London, Liveryman and Freeman Needlemakers' Co; established claim to btcy 30 Nov 1927; *m* 1st 18 July 1911 Agnes Gertrude Blanche Durell (*d* 29 April 1961), er dau of Capt T E Charles King, W Yorks Regt; *m* 2nd 18 Oct 1962 Muriel Eileen (*d* 5 Oct 1977), 2nd dau of John MacComish, of Belfast, and widow of James Patterson Sayles, and *d* 16 Dec 1970

2 Thomas George, JP (Kent); *b* 7 Aug 1882; *educ* Repton and Emmanuel Coll Cambridge (BA 1904); barrister Middle Temple 1913, memb Church Assembly 1935–48, Public Prosecutor Province of Sind 1918–29, Chm Wingham (Kent) Session Court, Dep Chm E Kent QS; *m* 18 June 1913 Gladys Mary, er dau of Col Ernest Charles Lambert Congdon, RMLI, and *d* 25 Dec 1967, having had issue:

(1) Sir JOHN ELPHINSTONE OF GLACK, **11th and present Bt**

(1) *Marjorie Mary; *b* 2 June 1915; *m* 1 Sept 1939 Maj-Gen Reginald Carteret de Mussenden Leathes, CB, MVO, OBE, RM (*d* 1987), s of Carteret de Mussenden Leathes, of Herringfleet, Suffolk, and has:

1a *Rupert de Mussenden [Rupert Leathes Esq, The Annexe, West Barn, West St, Abbotsbury, Dorset DT3 4JT]; *b* 6 Oct 1941; *educ* Sherborne, Emmanuel Coll Cambridge (MA 1966) and London U (MA 1981, MSc 1983); lecturer Business Sch Bournemouth; *m* 29 March 1967 *Nicole Jeanne Anne, er dau of Marius Alexandre Foucaud, of Communay, Rhone, France, and has issue:

1b *Thomas Joanny de Mussenden; *b* 17 Oct 1970

1b *Isabelle Annette de Mussenden; *b* 27 Nov 1973

2b *Francine Charlotte de Mussenden; *b* 19 Feb 1976

2a *Simon William de Mussenden; *b* 14 Feb 1948; *educ* Sherborne and Emmanuel Coll Cambridge (BA 1969); *m* 1971 *Belinda Haire and has:

1b *Timothy de Mussenden; *b* 1978

1b *Annabel de Mussenden; *b* 1976

3a *David Burlton de Mussenden (Rev); *b* 22 Sept 1949; *educ* Sherborne and RAC Cirencester; *m* 1975 *Mary Cross and has:

1b *Benjamin John de Mussenden; *b* 1979

1b *Miriam Frances de Mussenden; *b* 1982

1a Rosemary Sarah de Mussenden; *b* 25 July 1944; *m* 1976 *Arthur Horsley and *d* 14 Jan 1996

(2) Althea; *b* 24 Jan 1919; *d* 28 March 1921

3 John William Robert; *b* 28 June 1884; *m* 1st 1912 (*divorce* 1924) Vera Mary, dau of Lloyd Griffith, of Folkestone; *m* 2nd 1924 (*divorce* 1931) Bettine Ariana

(*d* 1969), 3rd dau of Sir William Michael Curtis, 4th Bt (*qv*); *m* 3rd 1938 *Edna M Nethersole and *d* 14 March 1949, leaving by her:

(1) John Philip; *b* 18 Jan 1940; *m* 1967 *Beverley Madge Fischer and *d* 198–, leaving:

1a +Colin Edward; *b* 1967

1a *Angela; *b* 1974

4 William Graham, MC; *b* 5 June 1886; Col-in-C Poona Horse (IA), WW I in France and Egypt (MC), and WW II in MI, GHQ Middle East; *m* 17 April 1934 Ethel Rosemary, er dau of John F Burstall, of Quebec, and *d* 20 Nov 1952

5 Colin; *b* 29 July 1888; *educ* Repton; *m* 8 June 1922 *Marjorie, MBE, yr dau of Llewellyn Eddison Buckley, CSI, late ICS, and *dsp* 6 Aug 1968

1 Laura Charlotte Gertrude; *m* 14 July 1917 Col Rowley Philip Arthur Helps, OBE, MC, DL, Roy Signals, s of T H P Helps, 53rd KSLI, of Cheshire, and *d* 8 April 1965, leaving a dau

2 Marjorie Rose; *b* 16 Aug 1891; *m* 20 Jan 1916 Lt-Col Charles Hector Congdon, RM (*d* 11 Jan 1958), son of Col Ernest Charles Lambert Congdon, RMLI, and had issue

ELPHINSTONE, Bt, of Sowerby

Arms: Arg. guttée de sang, on a chevron embattled sa. between three boar's heads erased gu, two swords ppr, pommels and hilts or. **Crest:** Out of a mural crown gu. a demi-woman affrontée, habited, in her dexter hand a sword erect ppr, pommel and hilt or, in the sinister an olive branch vert. **Motto:** *Semper paratus* ('Always ready'). **Creation:** Bt (UK) 25 May 1816.

SIR JOHN HOWARD MAIN ELPHINSTONE, 6TH BT, of Sowerby, Cumberland [Sir John Elphinstone Bt, Garden Cottage, 6 Amherst Rd, Sevenoaks, Kent TN13 3LS]; *b* 25 Feb 1949; *s f* 1995; *educ* Loretto; food hygiene and quality system manager Enviroguard (UK) Ltd 1988–; Diploma Quality Assur 1984, memb Soc Food Hygiene Technology 1986–, Advanced Food Hygiene Cert 1996; *m* 20 Oct 1990 *Diane Barbara Quilliam, dau of Dr Brian Quilliam Callow, of Johannesburg

Lineage: RENE (or RAINY) ELPHINSTONE, with whom the registered pedigree in the Lyon Office begins, was probably son of Peter (or Patrick) Elphinstone and Magdeleine de Lespine, he being son of Michael Elphinstone, son of Jock Elphinstone, memb Scots Gd in France 1494, and Catherine le Noble. Jock in turn was 2nd son of John Elphinstone, Baillie Glasgow 1485. RENE ELPHINSTONE settled in Scotland from France along with Lord Robert Stewart, Earl of Orkney, and was granted lands in Orkney. He *m* Janet Halcro and *d* 1587, having had:

1 Harry; *k* in battle in Germany

2 Robert, of Hammegar; Page to PRINCE HENRY, s of JAMES VI of Scotland and I of England; *m* Elizabeth Smyth and *d* 1628, leaving issue:

(1) John, of Walls and Lopness; *m* Joanna Cock, heiress of Lopness, and had, with other issue:

1a Robert, of Lopness; Steward Justiciary, High Adml and Chamberlain of the Isles of Orkney and Zetland

2a John; *m* Elizabeth Moore and had issue:

1b John, RN; *m* Anne Williams and had:

1c John; Capt RN, Adml in Russian service, cmdg CATHERINE THE GREAT's fleet at the Battle of Cheshme or Tchesme 1770, when the Turkish fleet was destroyed; *b* 1722; *m* 23 Oct 1750 Amelia (*d* Feb 1786), dau of John Warburton, Somerset Herald, and *d* 28 Feb 1785, leaving, with three other sons:

1d Samuel William; Capt Russian Navy; *m* Catherine, dau of Adml — Krewse, and *d* 1789, leaving:

1e Alexander Francis, of Livonia, Devon; *b* 6 Feb 1789; allegedly of noble rank in the Russian province of Livonia; Capt RN; *m* 5 May 1819 Amelia Anne (*d* 14 Feb 1874), dau of A Lobach, of Kumenov, nr Riga, and *d* 24 Sept 1865, leaving:

1f John; *b c* 1824; Maj-Gen HEICS; *dspms* 15 Sept 1877

2f (Sir) (self-styled) Nicholai William Elphinstone; Lt-Col (served Army 1845–65), Dep Commr Punjab, Chev Legn Hon; assumed the Elphinstone btcy (NS) of the 20 June 1628 *cr*, which had been dormant since 1645, on his er bro's death; *b* 16 Dec 1825; *m* 19 Dec 1860 Georgiana Henrietta (*d* 1 Aug 1913), dau of Lt-Gen Rt Hon Sir George Arthur, 1st Bt (*qv*), and *d* 3 Feb 1907, leaving three daus

3f Percy Augustus, Col; had:

1g (Sir) (self-styled) Arthur Percy Archibald; Lt-Col, CO 22nd Bn Northumberland Fus, late IA; *b* 22 July 1863; *m* 31 Oct 1891 Augustine Pauline Ludovine (*d* 28 Aug 1918), eld dau of Antoine Cheappe, of Paris, and was *ka* 1 July 1916, leaving issue

4f Howard Craufurd (Sir), VC, KCB; *b c* 1830; Maj-Gen, served Crimean War; *dspm* 8 March 1890, drowned off Tenerife

2d Thomas; Post-Capt RN; *m* Isabella Jones and *d* 1821, leaving two daus

3d HOWARD (Sir), **1st Bt**

1 Anne Charlotte Maria; *m* Sir Francis John Hartwell, 1st Bt (*qv*), and *d* 6 June 1809

2 Jane Alice Amelia; *m* Rev John Dymoke.

3 Catherine Sarah; *m* Rev Thomas Roe, of Kirkby-upon-Bane, Lincs

The 6th son,

Sir Howard Elphinstone, 1st Bt (UK), so *cr* 25 May 1816, CB; Maj-Gen, Col-Cmdt RE, assisted in capture Cape of Good Hope, also served Egypt and Peninsular War; *b* 4 March 1773; *m* 14 Feb 1803 Frances (*d* 24 Aug 1858), est dau of John Warburton, and had issue:

1 HOWARD (Sir), **2nd Bt**

1 Frances; *m* 6 Sept 1836 William Masters Smith, of Camer, MP W Kent, and *dsp* 31 Oct 1905. He *d* 24 Dec 1861

2 Harriet; *m* 25 April 1849 Rev William Twiss Turner, MA, Rector Ore, Sussex, and *d* 13 Feb 1892, leaving issue. He *d* 1884

3 Louisa; *m* 1st 1 Oct 1832 Lt-Col Robert Anstruther (*see* ANSTRUTHER, Bt); *m* 2nd 15 Aug 1861 Andrew Bonar, of Hamilton House, Leamington, and *dsp* 1903. He *d* 15 Feb 1874

Sir HOWARD *d* 28 April 1846; his only son,

Sir Howard Elphinstone, 2nd Bt; MA, DCL, barrister, MP Hastings 1835–37 and Lewes 1841–47; *b* 9 June 1804; *m* 30 Sept 1829 Elizabeth Julia (*d* 14 Jan 1891), dau of E J Curteis, MP, of Windmill Hill, and had issue:

1 HOWARD WARBURTON (Sir), **3rd Bt**

1 Julia; *m* 23 April 1855 Gen Walter Douglas Patton Bethune, Col 2nd Bn HLI, of Clayton Priory, Sussex, and *d* 20 Oct 1909, leaving issue. He *d* 28 Jan 1901

Sir HOWARD *d* 16 March 1893; his only son,

Sir Howard Warburton Elphinstone, 3rd Bt, JP Sussex; *b* 26 July 1830; *educ* Trin Coll Cam (MA); barrister; *m* 4 Aug 1860 Constance Mary Alexander (*d* 13 March 1936), 3rd dau of John Alexander Hankey, of Balcombe Place, Sussex, and *d* 3 Jan 1917, having had issue:

1 Howard John, Lt HLI; *b* 30 May 1862; *m* 22 Oct 1889 Katherine (*d* 23 May 1896), 4th dau of Herbert Mascall Curteis, of Windmill Hill Place, Sussex, and *dvp* 2 Feb 1895, leaving issue:

(1) Katherine Elizabeth; *b* 24 June 1892; *m* 20 April 1921 Sir William Wigham Richardson, 2nd Bt, MBE (*see* 1970 edn), and *dsp* 10 July 1945. He *d* 15 Nov 1973

2 Graham Warburton, Indian CS; *b* 17 Oct 1886; *m* 13 Oct 1896 Susan Sophy (*d* 1 Oct 1962, having *m* 2nd 3 July 1909 (*divorce*) George Middleton, son of Capt R W E Middleton, RN), dau of Henry Casper Raper Harley, of Madanapalle, India, and *dvp* 21 Feb 1903, leaving issue:

(1) **Sir Howard Graham Elphinstone, 4th Bt**; *b* 28 Dec 1898; *educ* Sedbergh, served WW I from 1917; Kenya CS from 1921; *m* 14 July 1924 Alice Mary Emerton (Mollie), er dau of Philip John Emerton Brown, of Ealing, and *d* 18 May 1975, leaving issue:

1a *Elizabeth Mary [Mrs Giles Poole, 16 The Mowbrays, Framlingham, Suffolk IP13 9DL]; *b* 29 Aug 1926; *m* 4 July 1952 *Cdr Giles Antony St George Poole, RN, only s of Capt Anthony James Poole, of The Glebe, Coates, Glos, and has:

1b *Philip Anthony Howard; *b* 19 Feb 1955

2b *Timothy Giles Elphinstone; *b* 24 Aug 1956

1b *Rosalind Kate Elizabeth; *b* 1961

2a *Rosalind Constance; *b* 25 March 1930; *m* 1950 *Robert William Atherstone, and has issue:

1b *Howard Ian Damant; *b* 1954

1b *Anne Margaret Herschel; *b* 1950

2b *Rosemary Jane Herschel; *b* 1956

3b *Katherine Sarah Damant; *b* 1961

4b *Patricia Damant; *b* 1961

(1) Lucy Constance; *b* 13 Aug 1897

3 Douglas Bonar, Lt RE; *b* 9 Jan 1871; *d* unm 28 Dec 1892

4 Maurice Curteis (Rev); Canon Emeritus Wakefield Cathedral; *b* 27 Jan 1874; *educ* Eton and Trin Coll Cambridge (BA 1895, MA 1899); *m* 30 July 1908 Christiana Georgiana (*d* 5 Jan 1975), est dau of Dr Hely Hutchinson Almond, Headmaster Loretto, and *d* 14 May 1969, having had issue:

(1) **Sir (Maurice) Douglas Warburton Elphinstone, 5th Bt**; TD (1946); *b* 13 April 1909; *educ* Loretto and Jesus Coll Cambridge (BA 1931, MA 1949); Maj London Scottish and Sierra Leone Regt RWAFF WW II, memb Stock Exchange 1957–74, FFA; *m* 30 June 1943 *(Helen) Barbara [Barbara Lady Elphinstone, 11 Scotby Green, Steading, Cumbria CA4 8EH], dau of George Ramsay Main, of Houghton, Kilmacolm, and *d* 5 Dec 1995, leaving:

1a Sir JOHN HOWARD MAIN ELPHINSTONE, **6th and present Bt**

1a *Janet Christian Helen; *b* 11 Oct 1953; *educ* Manchester U (BA); *m* 1983 *Kevin Grant and has:

1b *Ruari Jack Elphinstone; *b* 1991

(2) Harold George Almond; Maj RE WW II; *b* 9 April 1910; *educ* Jesus Coll Cambridge (BA); *ka* 5 June 1944

(3) Kenneth John Tristram (Rev); Vicar South Stoke, Somerset, barrister Inner Temple 1934 and Lincoln's Inn 1938, QC 1977, Capt Rifle Bde WW II 1939–42 (POW), Chllr Diocese of Chester 1950 and Hereford 1953, Priest 1964, Vicar S Stoke 1966–80; Dean of the Arches, Auditor of Chancery Court of York 1977–80; *b* 29 Nov 1911; *educ* Loretto and Jesus Coll Cambridge (BA 1933, MA 1950); *m* 29 Sept 1938 *Felicity [Mrs Eric Back, 46 St Ann Place, Salisbury, Wilts SP1 2SU] (*m* 2nd 22 July 1982 *Cdr Eric F S Back, DSC, RN), 4th dau of His Honour Judge Sir Gerald Berkeley Hurst, QC, and *d* 1980, leaving:

1a Tristram Gerald; *b* 28 Dec 1940; *d* unm 12 Nov 1962

1a *Margaret Norah [Ms Margaret Elphinstone, 1 Old Blanefield Cottages, Kirkoswald, Maybole, Ayrshire KA19 8HH]; *b* 23 Sept 1948; BA Dunelm; *m* 30 Aug 1969 (*divorce* 1985, resumed maiden name) John David Button, BA, MPhil, s of David Button and has:

1b *Rosalind Margaret ELPHINSTONE; *b* 10 April 1972

2b *Catherine (Katy) Joanna ELPHINSTONE; *b* 6 Jan 1974

(4) Rowland Henry; Surgn-Lt RNVR WW II; *b* 9 Feb 1915; *educ* Loretto and Jesus Coll Cambridge (BA 1936, MA, MB, BChir); *m* 8 July 1954 *Hester Frances MA, [Mrs Rowland Elphinstone, 8 Haytor Drive, Newton Abbot, Devon], er dau of Rev Charles Ravenscroft Bull, of The Vicarage, Milton Abbas, Dorset, and *d* Oct 1997, leaving:

1a +HENRY CHARLES; *b* 7 July 1958; heir presumptive

1a *Mary Georgiana, MBE (Civil 1982); *b* 9 Aug 1955; *educ* London U (MB, BS, BSc)

2a *Constance Hester; *b* 19 Jan 1957; has:

1b *Ruth; *b* 19–

(1) *Norah Christine [Mrs William Browne, 97 Rennies Mill Rd, St Johns, Newfoundland A1B 2PI, Canada], MB, BS, MRCS, LRCP, DCH, CRCPSC, FRCP (C); Hon LLD Newfoundland U 1987; *b* 27 Oct 1917; *educ* King's Coll London and King's Coll Hosp; *m* 1st July 1968 George Rex Renouf (*d* 1971), s of Charles Hugh Renouf, of St Johns, Newfoundland; *m* 2nd 1973 William Joseph Browne, PC, QC (*d* 1989)

5 Kenneth Vaughan, Resident N Nigeria; *b* 11 Jan 1878; *educ* Wellington and Trin Coll Cambridge (BA 1902, MA 1905); *d* unm 10 Feb 1965

6 Lancelot Henry (Sir); ktd 1931, Ch Justice, FMS 1929–32, KC Ceylon 1925, barrister, Maj Inns of Court OTC, Chm Pensions Appeals Tbnl 1944–54; *b* 2 Sept 1879; *educ* Eton and Trin Coll Cambridge (BA 1902, MA 1905); *m* 7 Feb 1913 Jane Edith (*d* 8 Oct 1959), yr dau of Robert Jarvie Jamieson, of 33 Buckingham Terrace, Edinburgh, and *dsp* 11 Oct 1965

1 Constance Julia; *b* 13 April 1864; *m* 10 Oct 1889 Capt John Russell Compton Domvile, 7th Bombay Cav, and *d* 19 Sept 1958, having had issue. He *d* 1 July 1893

2 Frances Mary; *b* 14 Aug 1865; *m* 10 Feb 1891 Edward Alfred Chandler, of Culmer Hill, Wormley, Surrey, and *d* 1946, having had issue

3 Isabel Harriet; *b* 31 Dec 1868; *m* 12 Nov 1912 Rev Gordon Kenmure Roberts, Rector Bloxworth, Dorset, and *d* May 1942, leaving issue. He *d* 19 Jan 1937

4 Selina Beatrice; *b* 26 Aug 1875; *m* 26 Dec 1902 Lt-Col Sir Charles Richard Mackey O'Brien, KCMG, yr s of Sir Terence O'Brien, KCMG, and *d* 11 Dec 1965, leaving issue. He *d* 29 Nov 1935

5 Gladys Christine; *b* 1 July 1884; *m* 18 July 1913 Rev Harold Frederic Edward Wigram and had issue (*see* WIGRAM, Bt)

ELTON, Baron

Arms: Paly or. and gu. a bend and on a chief sa. three pierced mullets or. **Crest:** Out of a wreath of laurel fructed or a dexter arm embowed in mail ppr., tied about the elbow a cord or, the gauntlet grasping a scimitar ppr., hilt and pommel or. **Supporters:** Dexter, a knight in mail and white surcoat supporting with the exterior hand a sword point downwards ppr., hilt and pommel or; sinister, a viking habited ppr., mantled az., supporting with the exterior hand a battleaxe head downwards and outwards ppr.
Motto: *Fide quam fortuna* ('By faith rather than fortune').
Creation: B. (UK) 16 Jan 1934.

THE 2ND BARON ELTON, of Headington, Co Oxford (Rodney Elton, TD (1970)) [The Rt Hon The Lord Elton TD, House of Lords, London SW1A 0PW]; *b* 2 March 1930; *s* f 1973; *educ* Eton and New Coll Oxford (MA); Ld of Manor of Adderbury, late Capt The Queen's Own Warwicks and Worcs Yeo (TA), Maj Leics and Derbys Yeo, assist master Loughborough GS 1962–67 and Fairham Comprehensive Nottingham 1967–69, lecturer Bp Lonsdale Coll of Educn 1969–72 v-chm Harborough C Assoc 1964–66, dir Pom Stacey Ltd publishers, publisher Yendor Books, dep chm Andry Montgomery Ltd 1978–79 and 1986–, C Whip Ho Lds 1974–76, Oppn Spokesman 1976–79, Parly U-Sec: NI 1979–81, DHSS 1981–82 and Home Office 1982–84, Min State Home Office 1984–85 and Environment 1985–86, memb Ho Lds Delegated Powers Scrutiny Ctee 1993–96, and Exec Ctee Assoc of C Peers 1986–93 and 1994–97 (Dep Chm 1990–93), Chm FIMBRA 1989–90, memb Panel on Takeovers and Mergers 1989–90, Chm: Enquiry into Discipline in Schs in England and Wales 1988–89 (Report 1989), Intermediate Treatment Fund 1990–93 and Divert Tst 1993–, Dep Sec Ctee on Internat Affrs of C of E 1976–78, V-Pres Inst Trading Standards Admin 1990–; *m* 1st 18 Sept 1958 (*divorce* 1979) Anne Frances, est dau of Brig Robert Adolphus George Tilney, CBE, DSO, TD, DL (*see* 1936 edn PAGET, Bt, of Sutton Bonnington), of The Hall, Sutton Bonnington, Leics; *m* 2nd 1979 *(Susan) Richenda, CVO (1998), Ldy-in-Waiting to HM THE QUEEN 1987–, yst dau of Sir Hugh Gurney, KCMG, MVO (*see* FIFE, D), and by his 1st w has:

1 +EDWARD PAGET; *b* 28 May 1966; *educ* Harrow

1 *Annabel; *b* 24 Oct 1960; *m* 1986 *Donald M Peebles, est s of Dr Robert Anthony Peebles, of Hampton Court, Surrey, and has issue:

(1) *Emma Richenda; *b* 1988

(2) *Rosalie; *b* 1990

2 *Jane; *b* 15 Jan 1962; *m* 1989 *James A J Cronin, s of Vincent Archibald Patrick Cronin, of Hyde Park Sq, London W2, and Le Manoir de Brion, Dragey Par 50530, Sartilly, Normandy

3 *Lucy; *b* 19 Dec 1963; *m* 1993 *Hon Andrew Godfrey Diarmid Stuart Campell-Gray, Master of Gray, s of 22nd Lord Gray (*qv*), and has issue

Lineage: RICHARD ELTON, of Newent; *b c* 1630; *m* Anne — and *d* 1695, leaving, with two yr sons and a dau:

SAMUEL ELTON, of Twisling, Hope Mansel, Herefs; *m* Mary Meek (*d* 1746) and had:

JOHN ELTON, of The Priory and later Walford Court; *m* 1736 Mary Thomas (*d* 1784), sister of Rev Theophilus Thomas, of Llangattock, Rector Brynwyn, and had, with an an est s (John, *bapt* 1737, *dsp* 1798):

WILLIAM ELTON, of Bristol and Clifton Wood; *b* Sept 1740; *m* Margaret (*d* Aug 1837), dau of Thomas Mitchell, of Sheerness, Surveyor RN, and had an est s:

JOHN ELTON, of Weston-super-Mare, Somerset; *b* 5 July 1784; *m* 5 June 1810 Sarah, dau of Samuel Whitchurch, of Frome Selwood, and *d* 1856, leaving a 2nd s:

Rev EDWARD ELTON; Rector Sherington, Bucks; *b* 1816; *m* 1st 6 Oct 1842 Harriet Vashon, dau of R-Adml Volant Vashon Ballard, CB, and had two daus; *m* 2nd 1859 —, 2nd dau of Rev Fiennes Samuel Trotman, of Dallington Park, Northants, and by her had, with a yr s:

EDWARD FIENNES ELTON, of Burleigh Court, Glos, and Ovington Park, Hants; *b* Nov 1860; *m* Dec 1887 Violet Hylda (*d* 15 Feb 1933), dau of Rev C J H Fletcher, Rector Carfax, Oxford, and had issue:

1 GODFREY, **1st Baron**

2 Hubert; *b* 11 Aug 1902; *d* 4 Nov 1937

1 Angela; *m* 28 Sept 1922 (*divorce* 1938) Christopher Benjamin Henry Lefroy, est s of Christopher Benjamin Langlois Lefroy, and had issue:

(1) *Christopher John Elton (Rev); Vicar Christ Church, Highbury; *b* 15 Feb 1925; *educ* Wellington and Clare Coll Cambridge (BA 1946, MA 1949); *m* 14 May 1957 *Sarah Ursula, yr dau of William Henry Randoll Blacking, FRIBA, FSA, of Salisbury, and has issue:

1a *Jeremy John Elton; *b* 30 May 1959

2a *David Christopher; *b* 25 May 1961

3a *Matthew William; *b* 8 Dec 1962

1a *Elizabeth Sarah; *b* 9 Dec 1964

(1) *Jennifer; *b* 8 July 1927; *m* 2 Jan 1954 *Cyril Alfred Reginald Ashdown, est s of Harry Ashdown, and had:

1a *Jonathan Giles Benjamin; *b* 8 July 1958

1a *Dedi Angela; *b* 7 Nov 1955

2a *Caroline Sarah; *b* 3 June 1960

3a *Susanna Jane (twin); *b* 3 June 1960

EDWARD ELTON *d* 10 Nov 1925; his est s,

GODFREY ELTON, **1st Baron Elton**, of Headington, Co Oxford (UK), so *cr* 16 Jan 1934 (UK); *b* 29 March 1892; *educ* Rugby and Balliol Coll Oxford (BA 1919, MA 1920); WW I as Capt 4th Hants Regt, at Siege of Kut-el-Amara 1915–16 (wounded), POW Turkey 1916–18, Fell Queen's Coll Oxford 1919–39, Supernumerary Fell 1939–73, lecturer modern history 1931–39, Dean 1921–23, Tutor 1926–34, expelled from Lab Party for supporting Ramsay MacDonald 1931, Hon Pol Sec Nat Labour Ctee 1932 and ed its news letter, sec Rhodes Tst 1939–49, chm exec ctee Road Accidents Emergency Cncl 1936 and Cwlth Youth Sunday, pres Christian Service Union and Metropolitan Assoc Bldg Socs, Nuffield Medical Tstee, broadcaster, author: *Schoolboys and Exiles* and *Years Of Peace* (verse), *The Revolutionary Idea of France, Years of Peace, England Arise, St George or the Dragon, Imperial Commonwealth, The Unarmed Invasion* (historical and gen), *Simon Peter* (religious), a biography of his friend Ramsay MacDonald, *Among Others* (autobiography), *The Testament of Dominic Burleigh, Against the Sun, The Stranger* (novels); *m* 17 Aug 1921 Dedi (*d* 15 March 1977), dau of Gustav Hartmann, of Oslo, and *d* 18 April 1973, leaving:

1 RODNEY ELTON, **2nd and present Baron Elton**

1 *Audrey [The Hon Mrs Goodrich, Hill House, Enford, Pewsey, Wilts]; *b* 22 June 1922; *m* 1 May 1948 Rev Brian William Frere Goodrich (*d* 1977), Assist Commr Singapore Police, est s of Albert Frere Goodrich, and has:

(1) *John; *b* 1 Nov 1952; *educ* Marlborough

(2) *Peter; *b* 13 Sept 1954; *educ* Marlborough

(3) *Simon; *b* 18 Aug 1957

(4) *Justin; *b* 6 April 1962

(5) *Alexander; *b* 19 Jan 1968

(1) *Sarah (Sasha); *b* 22 Jan 1949

(2) *Rosemary [The Hon Mrs Attlee, Brockley House, Leintwardine, Craven Arms, Salop]; *b* 22 Jan 1925; *m* 1st 14 Sept 1946 (*divorce* 1955) Capt William Yates, Queen's Bays, er s of William Yates, of Appleby, Westmorland, and has:

1a *William; *b* 7 Oct 1951; *educ* Gordonstoun

1a *Elizabeth Anne [Mrs Oliver Greene, Holton Hall, Holton St Mary, Colchester, Essex]; *b* 30 June 1948; *m* 12 Sept 1975 *Oliver Raymond Greene, only s of Dr Raymond Greene, and has had issue:

1b *William Charles Raymond; *b* 1979

2b *Nicholas Graham Raymond; *b* 1981

1b Charlotte Eleanor; *b* and *d* 1983

2b *Annabel Lucy Raymond; *b* 1985

2a *Angela Faith; *b* 7 April 1950; *m* 1st 1972 (*divorce* 1980) Denis Delahunt, and has issue:

1b *Christopher William; *b* 1974

2b *Thomas James; *b* 1977

2a (cont.) Mrs Angela Delahunt *m* 2nd 1983 *G Stafford and by him has:

3b *David Charles; *b* 1986

(2) (cont.) Mrs Rosemary Yates *m* 2nd 10 Dec 1955 *David Charles Attlee (*see* ATTLEE, E) and by him has:

2a *James Tristram; *b* 28 July 1956; *m* 1986 *Charlotte de Courcy and has:

1b *Joseph; *b* 1990

1b *Grace; *b* 1988

3a *Helena Rosemary [Mrs Alexander Ramsay, Bryncalled, Bucknell, Craven Arms, Salop]; *b* 13 June 1958; *m* 1986 *Alexander Ronald Dalhousie Ramsay, FRGS, er s of Patrick George Alexander Ramsay, FRSA, of Abcott Manor, Abcott, Clungunford, nr Ludlow, Salop

ELTON, Bt

Creation: Bt (GB) 31 Oct 1717.

SIR CHARLES ABRAHAM GRIERSON ELTON, 11TH BT, of Bristol [Sir Charles Elton Bt, Clevedon Court, Somerset BS21 6QU; 24 Maida Ave, London W2 1ST]; *b* 23 May 1953; *s f* 1973; *educ* Eton and Reading U (BA 1976); *m* 2 March 1990 *Lucy Lauris, dau of Lukas Heller and Mrs Caroline Garnham, and has:

1 +ABRAHAM WILLIAM; *b* 1995

1 *Lotte Caroline; *b* 1993

Lineage: THOMAS ELTON, physician, *b* Ledbury 1573 (yr s of Antony Elton, of the Hazle, Herefs/Glos borders, where the family had lived some generations); settled parish of St Philip's, Barton Regis, nr Bristol, by 24 Feb 1608; *m* Jane, dau of Sir Edward Aston, of Tixall, and *d* Bath 1618, leaving a 2nd s:

RICHARD ELTON; *bapt* 29 April 1610; Col London Trained Bands, Dep Govr Hull, Parliamentarian Civil War, author: *The Compleat Body of the Art Military* (1659)

A memb of the same family,

ISAAC ELTON, of St Philip's parish, Barton Regis, citizen and freeholder of Bristol; *m* Elizabeth — (*bur* 28 Nov 1677) and was *bur* 31 March 1695, leaving:

Sir Abraham Elton, 1st Bt (GB), so *cr* 31 Oct 1717, of Clevedon Court, Winford, and Whitestaunton Manors, Somerset; *bapt* 3 July 1654; Master Merchant Venturers Bristol 1708, Mayor Bristol 1710, Sheriff Glos 1716, MP Bristol 1722–27, helped suppress Jacobites 1715; *m* 11 Sept 1676 Mary (*d* 25 April 1728), dau of Robert Jefferies, of Pilegreen, Glos, and had issue:

1 ABRAHAM (Sir), **2nd Bt**

2 Isaac, merchant; *d* Oct 1714, having had two daus

3 Jacob, Mayor Bristol 1733; *m* 1st — Small, of Gloucester; *m* 2nd 2 April 1739 Elizabeth, widow of George Bridges, and *d* 15 June 1765, having by her had:

(1) Abraham, Mayor Bristol 1753; *m* Mary Thrubshaw and *d* 14 Aug 1762, leaving issue:

1a Mary

(2) Isaac, Mayor Bristol 1761; *m* Mary, dau of Edward Mortimer, of Trowbridge, and *d* 6 June 1776, having had, with other issue:

1a Isaac, of Stapleton House, Sheriff Bristol 1765 and 1770; *b* 1739; *m* 1st 21 Feb 1763 Sarah (*d* 15 Dec 1763), dau of Samuel Peach, of Bristol, and had a s (*d* young); *m* 2nd 20 Oct 1768 Ann (*d* 15 Aug 1816), dau of James Tierney, of Crutched Friars, London, and *d* 31 March 1790, having by her had, with other issue:

1b Isaac, of Stapleton House, Glos; *b* 1771; *m* 5 June 1794 Catherine (*d* 1853), 2nd dau of Robert Bayard, of Stubbington House, Hants, and *d* 19 April 1837, leaving, with other issue:

1c Robert James, of Whitestaunton, Somerset; *b* 1800; *m* 19 July 1855 Hon Mary Henrietta (*d* 30 Nov 1866), dau of 6th Viscount Chetwynd (*qv*), and *dsp* 28 Feb 1869

2c William Tierney (Rev), Rector Whitestaunton; *m* 2 Jan 1828 Lucy Caroline (*d* 1888), dau of **Sir Charles Abraham Elton, 6th Bt** (*see* below), and *d* 30 Aug 1874, leaving, with other issue:

1d Frederick Cockayne, VC, Lt-Col 21st Fus; *m* 10 June 1863 Maria Jane, dau of Robert Fleetwood Rynd, of Ryndville, Co Meath, and *dsp*

2d William Hallam, Cdr RN; *b* 1837; *m* 1st 27 July 1865 Eliza Sophia (*d* 22 May 1874), dau of Capt James Charles Baird, 15th Hus, and had, with other issue:

1e Maurice Arthur; *b* 17 May 1868; *m* 1898 Ellen Mary (*d* 2 Jan 1929), dau of William Henry Laxton, of Dudley, Worcs, and *d* 17 Dec 1943, leaving issue:

1f *Violet Mary Agnes; *b* 29 Feb 1907; *m* 1931 Francis Martin Shirey, of Virginia, USA, and has issue:

1g *Richard Francis Elton [Richard Shirey, 544 Crosby Road, Virginia Beach, VA 23452, USA]; *b* 24 March 1933; *educ* William and Mary Coll Va. (BA 1959); *m* June 1958 *Sandra Andrews, dau of Lennart H Berg, of Virginia, and has issue:

1h *Frederick Elton; *b* 3 April 1962

1h *Mary Melissa; *b* 1 May 1960

1e Mary Alice; *m* 1910 Rev Henry Rolph, Vicar Ryarsh, Kent, and *d* 23 Oct 1960

2e Margaret Ada; *m* 18 Jan 1888 Rev John Vicars Foote, and *d* 23 Jan 1952, leaving issue

2d (cont.) Cdr William Elton *m* 2nd 5 Oct 1875 Phoebe (*d* 4 June 1899), dau of Frederick Feacham, and *d* 25 Nov 1910, having by her had issue:

2e Richard Algernon; *b* 17 Dec 1876; *m* 1899 (*divorce* 1924) Annie Keartland Jones (*d* 19 Aug 1939), and *d* 26 March 1931, having had:

1f Violet Hallam; *b* 19 March 1904; *m* 4 July 1934 Maj Walter Kendal Bushe, s of Lt-Col Charles Kendal Bushe, RA, and *d* 9 Oct 1966, leaving issue

2f Rosalie Mary Hallam; *b* 25 Nov 1913; *d* 27 Sept 1932

3f Lucy Charlotte; *d* unm

4f Rosalie Isabel

3d Henry Strachan; Maj-Gen IA, Hon Col 76th Punjabis; *b* 30 Dec 1841; *m* 7 Jan 1882 Maria Georgina (*d* 24 June 1931), dau of William Helder, and *d* 25 Aug 1934, leaving issue:

1e Violet Helen Strachan; *d* unm 4 March 1969

4d Charles Tierney, CE; *b* 1852; *m* 7 March 1881 Mary (*d* 14 March 1937), dau of James Higgs, JP, of Holsworthy, N Devon, and *d* 11 May 1919, leaving issue:

1e Henry Brown, OBE (1919); BA, MB, BCh, served WW I (1914 star, two medals); *b* 1882; *m* 30 Jan 1917 Mary Constance (*d* 16 Jan 1961), yr dau of J Percy Maule, and *d* 17 July 1962

1d Frances Matilda; *m* 18 Sept 1861 Rev Charles John Young, of Court Hall, Sidbury, Devon, and *d* May 1908, leaving issue

2d Louisa; *dsp*

3d Lucy Octavia; *m* 20 June 1882 Rev José Fortescue Lawrence Gueritz, Rector St Mary, Montrose, and had issue

4d Henrietta Sophia; *m* 19 Nov 1874 Rev Henry Antrobus Cartwright, Rector Whitestaunton, and *d* 10 Dec 1922, leaving issue. He *d* 1915

3c Frederick Bayard; *b* Aug 1811; *m* 1st Mary Elizabeth (*d* 26 Sept 1840), dau of **Sir Charles Abraham Elton, 6th Bt** (*see* below), and had:

1d Charles Isaac, of Manor House, Whitestaunton, JP, QC; FSA, Fell Queen's College Oxford, MP W Somerset 1884–85 and Wellington 1886–92, Ld of Manor and Patron Living Whitestaunton; *b* 6 Dec 1839; *m* 6 Aug 1863 Mary Augusta (*d* 2 Feb 1914), dau of Richard Strachey, of Ashwick Grove, Oakhill, Bath (*see* STRACHEY, Bt), and *dsp* 23 April 1900

3c (cont.) Frederick Elton *m* 2nd 1843 Caroline Elizabeth, Baroness d'Alberdyhill, and *d* 4 Oct 1877, having by her had:

2d Frederick, of Whitestaunton Manor; Ld of Manor and Patron Living there, Cdr RN, S African War medal 1879 and medal for saving life at sea; *b* 3 May 1854; *m* 29 July 1893 Ernestine (*d* 9 Jan 1951), dau of Ernest White, JP, of Beaudesert Estates, Logan River, Queensland, and *d* 2 Nov 1922, having had issue:

1e Frederick Ernest Bayard; Lt 3rd Bn Welsh Regt (SR); *b* 30 Jan 1895; *educ* Radley; *m* 1st 16 June 1914 (*divorce* 1925) Dorothy, dau of Adml Thomas Young Greet, and had issue:

1f *Daphne; *b* 18 April 1917; *m* 14 Nov 1936 Derek Maxwell Sanderson (*d* 1983), yr s of Sir Frank Bernard Sanderson, 1st Bt (*qv*), and has issue

2f *Stephanie; *b* 28 Sept 1920; *m* 1947 *Eden James Hungerford Morgan, of Ivybridge, Devon, and has issue

1e (cont.) Frederick Elton *m* 2nd 1925 (*divorce* 1932) Vera Ida (*d* 1956), dau of Hugh Goldie, of Osborne Grange, Bournemouth; *m* 3rd 1939 *Katherine Mary, dau of Arthur Hamilton Hackett, and *d* 1976, leaving by her:

1f +John Arthur Bayard; *b* 30 July 1940; *educ* Hardye's, Dorchester; *m* 1971 *Jennifer Elizabeth, est dau of William George Thomson, and has issue:

1g +James Edmund Bayard; *b* 24 Oct 1972

1g *Katherine Elizabeth; *b* 1975

2g *Juliet; *b* 1977

2e Eric d'Alberdyhill; *d* an inf

3e +(Cedric) Edward Baynard; *b* 4 Sept 1904; Capt Roy Fusiliers; *m* 1928 *Barbara May, dau of William Parrott, and has issue:

1f +Nicholas Edward Bayard; Royal Signals 1948–50; *b* 2 Jan 1930; *m* 1960 *Eileen Dorothy, dau of Arthur Preece, of Linden House, Ross-on-Wye, and has issue:

1g +Patrick Edward Bayard; *b* 31 Oct 1966

1g *Nicola Jane; *b* 1 July 1961

1e Muriel Agnes; *m* 1st 20 Oct 1921 (*divorce* 1934) Lt-Col Edwin Darling, MC, RA, s of Robert Alexander Darling, of Berwick-on-Tweed, and has issue:

1f *Fiona Muriel Ruth; *b* 1928; *m* 1948 Richard Byron Caws, FRICS, s of Maxwell Caws, and has had issue

1g *Eian Richard Edwin; *b* 22 April 1950

2g Andrew Maxwell Byron; *b* 10 Jan, *d* 14 May 1952

1g *Genevra Fiona Penelope Victoria; *b* 21 Feb 1949

2g *Alexandra Mary Darling; *b* 27 July 1953

1e (cont.) Mrs Muriel Darling *m* 2nd 8 Jan 1935 G/Capt Charles Lennox Gilbert, RAF (*d* Oct 1944), s of John Mark Gilbert, and had further issue:

2f *Deirdre Anne Elton [Mrs Michael Page, Windrush, Highfield Close, Northwood, Middx HA6 1EX]; *b* 6 Sept 1935; *m* 19 July 1958 *Michael James Page, s of Reginald James Page, JP, and has:

1g *Anthea Deirdre Rosemary; *b* 11 June 1960; *m* 11 June 1983 (*divorce* 1997) Bruce Ian Howard

2g *Caroline Sheila Page; *b* 19 April 1962; *m* 28 April 1990 *Stephen Wilson and has:

1h *Victoria Kate; *b* 5 May 1992

2h *Philippa May; *b* 16 May 1995

3g *Kathleen Elizabeth; *b* 9 Nov 1964; *m* 8 July 1989 *Gary Frederick Walter and has:

1h *James Frederick; *b* 12 Oct 1997

1h *Natalie Charlotte; *b* 25 Nov 1993

2h *Georgina Katherine; *b* 26 Feb 1995

2e *Cynthia Ernestine; *m* 12 April 1933 Mr Justice Cecil Harry Andrew Bennett, CBE, QC (*d* 19 Sept 1967), est s of H G Dudley Bennett, and has issue:

2f *(Timothy) Elton Dudley; actor; *b* 18 Oct 1935

3f *Paul Oliver Andrew; *b* 3 Sept 1939

1f *Felicia Marjorie [Mrs David Williams, 82 Lofting Road, London N1 1JB]; *b* 5 Feb 1938; *m* 28 April 1962 *David Malcolm Younger Williams, s of W/Cdr N Alun Williams, and has issue:

1g *Hugo Andrew Younger; *b* 18 March 1965

2g *Charles Andrew Younger; *b* 8 Oct 1967

3g *Edward David Younger; *b* 15 April 1978

3d Arthur Bayard, Maj Yorks Regt; *b* 6 Nov 1857; *m* 22 July 1905 Rosina (*d* 13 Nov 1932), widow of John Moore, and *d* 11 Jan 1916

1d Caroline Julia

2d Katherine Pauline; *m* 1884 Charles Blomefield Douglas, and had issue

3d Charlotte Louis; *m* 8 Feb 1876 Gerard Noel Douglas, of California, and had issue

4d Isabel Mary

1c Katherine; *m* 1st Richard Elwes; *m* 2nd Auguste Charles Joseph de Janti

2c Charlotte; *m* 17 July 1824 John Payne Elwes, MP, of Stoke

3c Matilda; *m* Sir J Strachan

3b Jacob, of Bristol and Dedham, Essex; Lt 11th Foot, taken prisoner and held at Forte de Scaope, Ostend, for two years from May 1798; *m* 1st 13 May 1799 Charlotte, dau of James Young, Adml the White, and had:

1c James Frederick, of Nailsworth, Glos; Capt 40th Foot; *b* 1810; *m* 9 July 1835 Charlotte, 2nd dau of James Young, R-Adml the Blue, and *d* 30 Oct 1844, leaving issue:

1d Frederick Coulthurst, CB; Col RA; *b* 15 July 1837; *m* 9 May 1866 Olivia Georgiana (*d* 29 May 1929), dau of Maj John Power, 29th Foot, of Belle Vue, Co Kilkenny, by Emilia Magdalen Louisa, dau of Sir George Sinclair, 2nd Bt (*qv*), and *d* 25 Dec 1919, leaving:

1e Frederick Algernon George Young, of Preston Lodge, Horsham, Sussex; Brig-Gen RA; *b* 5 April 1867; *m* 14 Oct 1902 Katherine Elizabeth (*d* 23 Dec 1956), dau of Rev Nesfield Andrews, Vicar Southwater, Sussex, and *d* 3 Aug 1921, leaving issue:

1f (Mary Katherine) Gloria; Assist Co Dir BRCS Herts, Order Mercy 1938, Fell Roy Philatelic Soc; *b* 10 May 1904; *m* 4 Sept 1926 Maj Stanley George Reeves BARRATT later ELTON BARRATT (roy licence 1970), OStJ (*d* 28 July 1973), 16th/15th Lancers (Res), of Blackwell Hall, nr Chesham, Bucks, only surv s of Sir Albert Barratt, JP, of Totteridge Park, Herts, and *d* 1 April 1996, leaving:

1g *John Charles Stanley [John Elton Barratt Esq, Millfield Cottage, Millfield Lane, Little Hadham, Herts SG11 2ED]; 12th Roy Lancers; *b* 17 Feb 1930; *educ* Harrow; *m* 23 July 1957 *Olivia Golding Milward, only dau of Lt-Col Charles William Milward Rogers, TD, RE, and has had issue:

1h Thomas George Sinclair; *b* 30 Jan 1964; *d* 1983

1h *Katharine Joanna Milward [Mrs John Singer, The Star, Furneux Pelham, Herts SG9 0LN]; *b* 5 Jan 1961; BSc; *m* 1986 *John Geoffrey Singer, s of Dr Geoffrey Singer BSc, Dip Eng, and has:

1i *George Thomas; *b* 1993

1i *Rebecca Golding; *b* 1990

2g *Frederick James Young; late RHG (The Blues); *b* 1 Feb 1934; *educ* Millfield

1g *Gloria Anne Rosemary [Mrs Charles Skrine, Ballyrankin House, Bunclody, Co Wexford]; Jt MFH Shillelagh 1960–62; *b* 22 July 1928; *m* 7 Sept 1960 Cdr Charles John Skrine, RN (*d* 12 Nov 1966), est s of Walter Clarmont Skrine, of Ballyrankin, Ferns, Co Wexford, and has issue:

1h *David Charles Sinclair; *b* 11 June 1961; *m* 1988 *Elizabeth Mary, dau of James Kavanagh, of Kiltilly, Co Wexford, and has issue:

1i *Tara Rosemary Kathleen; *b* 1993

1h *Susan Nesta Rosemary; *b* 27 April 1963; *m* 1986 *Stephen Geoffrey Clapham, est s of Col Derek Clapham, of Blue House Farm, Mattingley, Hants, and has:

1i *Christopher Derek Charles; *b* 1987

2i *Nicholas Walter Geoffey; *b* 1991

2f Monica Sinclair; *b* 22 Aug 1907; *m* 1st 20 Aug 1932 (*divorce* 1966) Lt-Col Malcolm Edward Durant Cumming, CB, OBE, 60th Rifles Res of Offrs, only s of Charles Malcolm Cumming, and had a dau; *m* 2nd 15 Dec 1966 *Maj Claude Robert Leetham, Bucks Yeo, s of Alfred Leetham, of Ganton, Yorks, and *d* 21 Jan 1969

2c Robarts William; HEICS; *m* 1st 19 Nov 1831 Ashley (*d* 17 Dec 1855), est dau of Henry Edward Holder, MD, of Barbados, and had a 2nd s:

1d James Frederick; Capt Bengal Army, later in French Army, Br Consul Portuguese Africa 1875; *b* 3 Aug 1840; *d* 19 Dec 1877

2c (cont.) Robarts Elton *m* 2nd 10 March 1857 Sarah, widow of H C Haynes, and *d* 12 March 1861

3b Jacob Elton; *m* 2nd Maria Bayfield

2a Jacob; *m* Elizabeth Matthews (*m* 2nd Rev John Casberd, DD, and *d* 1802) and *d* 1762

3a Edward, of Winford Manor, Bristol; High Sheriff Somerset 1780; *b* 21 Oct 1742; *m* 1772 Frances (*d* Nov 1780), dau and coheir of James Marwood, of Widworthy, Devon, and *d* 20 Sept 1811, having had, with other issue:

1b James Marwood, of Widworthy; High Sheriff Devon 1813; *b* 1776; *m* 1799 Anne (*d* 17 Feb 1811), dau of Edward Storey, and *d* 4 Dec 1827, leaving, with other issue:

1c Sir EDWARD ELTON later MARWOOD-ELTON (roy licence 1 Aug 1831), 1st and last Bt (UK), so *cr* 1 Aug 1838, of Widworthy, Devon, QC, DL, High Sheriff Devon 1858; *b* 19 May 1800; *d* unm 18 April 1884, when the btcy expired

2b Henry, of Winford; *b* 1778; *m* Anne (*d* 1858), dau of Thomas Wedlake, of Hornchurch, Essex, and *d* 16 Feb 1829, having had, with another s:

1c Henry Edward, of Winford; *b* 15 Feb 1808; *m* 28 April 1829 his cousin, Sarah Frances (*m* 2nd 28 Sept 1842 Thomas Davis Bayley and *d* 10 June 1867), dau of Rev James Lewis Clutterbuck, of Newark Park, Glos, and *d* 15 Feb 1842, having had, with four other sons and two daus:

1d Alfred ELTON later MARWOOD-ELTON (roy licence 1885 under terms of will of his cousin Sir Edward Marwood-Elton, 1st and last Bt) (Rev), JP (Devon), of Widworthy Court, Honiton, Devon; Ld of Manor and Patron Living there; BA Oxon; *b* 1836; *m* 1865 Jane Frances (*d* 2 May 1919), dau of Rev Augustus Bernard Handley, Rector Fisherton, Wilts, and *dsp* 20 April 1911

2c James Stevens; *b* 1811; *m* 1846 Elizabeth Anne, 2nd dau of Charles Wade, of Bitton, Glos, and *dsp* 1849

3c William Warry, of Avishays, Somerset; *b* 27 Nov 1813; *m* 7 April 1859 Mary (*d* 27 April 1904), er dau and coheir of James Thomas Benedictus Notley, of Combe Sydenham Hall, Somerset, and *d* 4 Jan 1906, leaving issue:

1d William ELTON later MARWOOD-ELTON (deed poll 11 June 1910 under terms of will of his cousin, Sir Edward Marwood-Elton, 1st and last Bt), JP, DL Somerset, of Widworthy Court, Lord of Manor and Patron Livings Widworthy and Whitestaunton, Col Cmdt Cadets Somerset, Lt-Col cmdg 3rd Bn Welsh Regt, Boer War 1899–1902 (two medals with five clasps), WW I (despatches); *b* 31 March 1865; *m* Aug 1909 Juliet (*d* 23 Feb 1964), only child of Robert Spelman Marriott, of Pencraig Court, Ross, and *d* 14 Oct 1931, leaving:

1e +Nigel William David, DFC; G/Capt RAF WW II (despatches twice, POW); *b* 22 Aug 1911; *m* 22 Dec 1952 *Daphne, formerly w of — Lee and er dau of Gordon Richards, of Kintbury, Berks, and Chiltern Court, London NW3

2e Mervyn Edward Philip, Merchant Navy; *b* 1 May 1923; *d* car crash S Africa 5 Feb 1946

1e Beryl; *b* 21 Aug 1910; *m* 19 Nov 1930 Hallam Edmund Arthur Elton, only s of Edmund Hallam Elton, and *d* 17 Jan 1966, leaving issue (*see* below). He *d* 13 May 1963

1d Mary; *m* 1st 1900 George Notley Murray Harding, of Edgarley Lodge, Glastonbury. He *d* Dec 1905. She *m* 2nd 12 Aug 1908 Whyting Roach, MA, and *d* 23 July 1924

4c Thomas Marwood; *b* 1815; *m* 1838 Charlotte Maria (*d* 20 April 1902), widow of Henry Tapscott and dau of Thomas May and *d* 19 Sept 1863, leaving, with other issue:

1d Mary Anne; *m* 2 Nov 1869 Surgn-Maj Henry Nathanial Elton, IMS, and *d* Feb 1913, leaving issue. He *d* 29 Oct 1907

2d Charlotte; *m* C B Fosbroke and *d* 21 Feb 1919, leaving issue. He *d* 21 Aug 1917

3d Annie Elizabeth; *m* 8 June 1870 Thomas Walter Paterson, and *d* 24 June 1921, leaving issue. He *d* 18 March 1914

1a Sarah; *b* 1773; *m* Rev John Amyatt Chaundy and *d* 1824, leaving issue. He *d* 1820

2a Frances; *b* 1774; *m* Rev James Lewis Clutterbuck and *d* 1836, leaving:

1b Sarah Frances; *m* her cousin, Henry Edward Elton (*see* above)

3a Mary Anne; *b* 1780; *m* Robert Norris, and *dsp* 1856. He *d* 1863

1a Mary; *b* 1747; *m* Michael Miller, and *d* 4 July 1773

1 Elizabeth; *m* Peter Day, of Bristol

Sir ABRAHAM *d* 9 Feb 1727/8; his est son,

Sir Abraham Elton, 2nd Bt; Sheriff Bristol 1710, Master Merchant Venturers, Mayor Bristol 1719, MP Taunton 1724–27 and Bristol 1727–42; *bapt* 30 June 1679; *m* 14 May 1702 Abigail, dau of Zachary Bayly, of Charicot House, Westbury, Wilts, and Northwood Park, Glastonbury, Somerset, and *d* 20 Oct 1742, having had:

1 **Sir Abraham Elton, 3rd Bt**; Sheriff Bristol 1728, Mayor 1742; *b* 1703; *d* unm 29 Nov 1761

2 Jacob; Capt RN; *m* Caroline (*m* 2nd John Aspinal), dau and coheir of Charles Yate, and *dsp*, *ka* in a sea battle with the French 29 March 1745

3 ABRAHAM ISAAC (Sir), **4th Bt**

1 Mary; *m* James Heywood, of Maristow

2 Elizabeth; *m* Capt Forster

The 3rd Bt's brother,

Sir Abraham Isaac Elton, 4th Bt; barrister, Town Clerk Bristol, Master Merchant Venturers 1767, Chm Somerset QS; *b* 1717; *m* 26 Dec 1747 Elizabeth, dau of James Read, of Bristol, and *d* 5 Feb 179, having had, with two daus (Mary, *m* Oldfield Bowles, of North Aston, Oxon, and had issue; Sarah, *m* Rev Hector Munro, and had issue):

Rev Sir Abraham Elton, 5th Bt; *b* 23 March 1755; *educ* Christ's Coll Cambridge (MA), Chm Somerset QS; *m* 1st 7 Nov 1776 Elizabeth (*d* 29 March 1822), est dau of Sir John Durbin, of Walton Manor House, Somerset, Bristol merchant, and had:

1 CHARLES ABRAHAM (Sir), **6th Bt**

2 William, Lt-Col Dragoon Gds' *b* 6 Jan 1785; *d* unm 1 June 1847

3 Henry; Capt RN; *b* 16 July 1786; *m* 20 July 1816 Mary (*d* 12 May 1872), widow of Peter Touchet and dau of Sir Francis Ford, Bt (*see* ST CLAIR-FORD, Bt), and *d* 10 Nov 1858, having had two daus (*d* unm)

1 Julia Maria; *m* Jan 1807 Henry Hallam, historian, and *d* 28 April 1840, leaving issue. He *d* 21 Jan 1859

Sir Abraham *m* 2nd 29 March 1823 Mary (*dsp* 6 Dec 1849), est dau of William Stewart, of Castle Stewart, Wigtownshire, and *d* 23 Feb 1842

His est son,

Sir Charles Abraham Elton, 6th Bt; Offr 48th Regt, Lt-Col Somerset Militia, translator of Hesiod, author: *Specimens of the Classic Poets, The Brothers, a Monody*, and other poems; *b* 31 Oct 1778; *m* 27 Feb 1804 Sarah (*d* 14 March 1830), dau of Joseph Smith, of Bristol, and *d* 1 June 1853, having had issue:

1 Abraham

2 Charles; both drowned 20 Sept 1819

3 **Sir Arthur Hallam Elton, 7th Bt**, DL; High Sheriff Somerset 1857, served 14th Regt 1836–41, MP Bath 1857–59; *b* 19 April 1818; *m* 1st 10 June 1841 Rhoda Susan (*d* 1 Nov 1873), widow of Capt James Charles Baird, 15th Hus, and dau of James Willis, of Atherfield and Freshwater House, IoW, and had issue:

(1) Laura Beatrice; *m* 3 Jan 1864 George Louis Monck Gibbs, of Belmont, Somerset, and *d* 30 Aug 1911, leaving issue (*see* ALDENHAM and HUNSDON OF HUNSDON, B)

(2) Octavia Maria, twin with Beatrice; *d* an infant

(3) Mary Agnes; *m* 7 July 1868 her cousin **Sir Edmund Harry Elton, 8th Bt**, and *d* 28 Feb 1925, leaving issue

3 (cont.) **Sir Arthur** *m* 2nd 20 Nov 1876 Eliza (*d* 5 Jan 1884), widow of Rev William Mathias, Incumbent of Burtle, Somerset, and dau of Edward Anstice Stradling, and *d* 14 Oct 1883

4 Edmond William, of Florence; painter; *b* 14 Dec 1822; *m* 1st June 1845 Lucy Maria (*d* 16 May 1846), dau of Rev John Morgan Rice, and had issue:

(1) EDMOND HARRY (Sir), **8th Bt**

4 (cont.) Edmond Elton *m* 2nd 1850 Clementina Sandryk, of Florence, and *d* 2 Dec 1859, having by her had:

(1) Minna Antonetta Beatrice; *m* 17 April 1873 Robert Frederick Boyle (*see* CORK and ORRERY, E), and *d* 21 June 1876

(2) Elma Marion; Sister All Saints' Hospital, Eastbourne; *d* 7 Jan 1923

5 Henry George Tierney (Rev); Vicar W Hatch, Somerset; *b* 6 May 1825; *m* 6 May 1856 Georgina Flora (*d* 5 Nov 1900), dau of Capt W A Willis, RN, of Greenwich Hospital, and *d* 12 Oct 1905, leaving issue:

(1) Charles Henry; *b* 12 Feb 1857; *m* 1st 18 Oct 1879 Emily Grace, est dau of Thomas Christmas, 8th Hus, and had issue:

1a Flora Grace

2a Maud Marian

3a Vera May; *m* 1916 Geoffrey Lionel Jobling, of Ottawa, Canada, and had issue

4a Rhoda Madeline; *m* 1914 Kenneth Jobling, of Livingstone, N Rhodesia. He *d* 1917

5a Evangeline Alice; *m* 1916 William F H Gann, of Surrey, and had issue

(1) (cont.) Charles Elton *m* 2nd 1 Jan 1897 (*divorce* 1927) Edith May, dau of J F Ward, of Port Elizabeth, S Africa, and *d* 13 June 1929, having by her had issue:

1a Charles Tierney; *b* 1898; *m* 1924 Helen (*d* 1963), dau of Capt Frederick Patrick Waud, Merchantile Marine, and had:

1b *Heather Agnes Campbell; *b* 1928

2a Arthur Hallam; *b* 1901; *m* 1926 Georgina (*d* 1963), dau of A W Hemming, and had:

1b +Anthony Charles Hallam; *b* 1942

1b *Rosemary Patricia Hallam; *b* 3 April 1930; *m* 8 March 1952 *Colin Walmsley Glazebrook and has issue:

1c *Jennifer Rosemary; *b* 3 May 1960

2c *Belinda Colleen; *b* 4 June 1962

3c *Nicholette Moya; *b* 19 Oct 1964

1b (cont.) Mr and Mrs C W Glazebrook also adopted:

*David Martin; *b* 4 April 1957

*Lesley Robyn; *b* 17 May 1955

2b *June Margaret Hallam; *b* 14 Oct 1933; *m* 12 Feb 1955 *Pieter Greeff and has:

1c *Garth John; *b* 9 Jan 1958

2c *Wayne Michael; *b* 24 July 1960

1c *Celeste Rose; *b* 17 Dec 1956

2c *Amanda Sue; *b* 27 Aug 1964

6a *Kathleen Patricia Hallam [Kathleen Elton, 58 Hurd Street, Newton Park, Port Elizabeth, S Africa]; *b* 1908; *m* 1940 (*divorce* 1947, resumed maiden name) Frank Baker

(2) Edmund Hallam; *b* 16 March 1860; *m* 1887 Ada Constance, dau of J H Webb, of Cape Town, and *d* 30 June 1925, leaving issue:

1a Hallam Edmund Arthur; *b* 1898; *m* 19 Nov 1930 Beryl (*d* 17 Jan 1966), only dau of Col William Marwood-Elton, JP, DL, and *d* 13 May 1963, having had issue:

1b Simon Hallam; *b* 26 Feb 1932; *k* flying accident 1 Nov 1955

2b Timothy Hallam; *b* 22 June 1933; *m* 11 Jan 1964 *Linda Susan [Mrs Timonthy Elton, Thaba' Nchu, PO Box 1, Cashel, Zimbabwe], er dau of Major George Richard Paton Pollitt, of Makalanga, Mazoe, Zimbabwe, by Linda Rosemary, only dau of Col Rupert Edward Holmes à Court, DSO (*see* HEYTESBURY, B), and *d* 1978, leaving issue:

1c +Simon Marwood Hallam; *b* 5 Jan 1965

2c +Anthony Hallam; *b* 5 April 1966

1c *Sarah Katharine; *b* 1970

1a May Constance Hallam; *b* 1887; *m* 23 April 1908 Col Bertram Christopher Judd, OBE, S African Artillery, 2nd s of Bertram Scott Judd, of Rickling, Essex, and *d* 20 March 1961, leaving issue. He *d* 21 March 1962

2a Iris Georgina Hallam; *b* 1889; *m* 4 Feb 1911 William Francis Lucius Austen-Holcroft, MB, BCh, and *d* 18 Feb 1945 leaving issue. He *d* 23 Aug 1932

3a Lillian Avice Hallam; *b* 1896; *m* 1st 1934 (*divorce* 1946) L J Lake; *m* 2nd 23 Jan 1968 Henry Adrian Harington (*d* 1969)

(3) Arthur Tierney; *b* 25 July 1863

(1) May Flora; *m* 22 Jan 1880 Rev Frederick Granville Christmas, incumbent of Duncan, Vancouver Is, BC, and had issue. He *d* 13 Oct 1931

1 Julia Elizabeth; *m* 6 Jan 1836 Thomas Clements Parr, of Clifton, barrister, and *d* 27 April 1881, leaving issue. He *d* 1 Dec 1863

2 Caroline Lucy; *m* 25 April 1844 Thomas Onesiphorus Tyndall, of The Fort, Bristol, and *d* 16 April 1882, leaving issue. He *d* 14 Sept 1869

3 Lucy Caroline; *m* 2 Jan 1828 Rev W Tierney Elton and *d* 1888, leaving issue (*see* above)

4 Laura Mary; *m* 10 Nov 1840 Charles Samuel Grey and *d* 24 March 1848, leaving issue (*see* GREY, Bt)

5 Katherine Maria; *m* 24 Aug 1841 Rev Edward Douglas Tinling, MA, Canon Gloucester, Inspr Training Colleges, and *d* 3 July 1876, leaving issue. He *d* 2 Dec 1897

6 Maria Katherine; *m* 28 May 1833 Major George Robbins, 17th Lancers, of Forest Lodge, Southampton, and *dsp* 24 Dec 1899. He *d* 29 Nov 1873

7 Mary Elizabeth; *m* Frederick Elton and *d* 26 Sept 1840, leaving issue (*see* above)

8 Jane Octavia; *m* 17 Nov 1841 Rev Canon W B H Brookfield, MA, Rector Somerby, Lincs, and Chaplain-in-Ordinary to HM QUEEN VICTORIA, and *d* 27 Nov 1896, leaving issue. He *d* 12 July 1874

The 7th Bt's nephew,

Sir Edmund Harry Elton, 8th Bt, JP, VD; CC Somerset, High Sheriff 1895, Maj and Hon Lt-Col 1st Vol Bn Gloucester Artillery, Ld of Manor and Patron Living St John's, Clevedon; *b* 3 May 1846; *educ* Bradfield and Jesus Coll Cambridge; *m* 7 July 1868 his cousin Mary Agnes (*d* 28 Feb 1925), dau and coheir of **Sir A H Elton, 7th Bt** (*see* above), and had issue:

1 AMBROSE (Sir), **9th Bt**

2 Bernard Arthur; Lt Somerset Vol Regt; *b* 21 June 1874; *educ* Jesus Coll Cambridge (BA); *d* 9 July 1938

1 Kathleen Agnes Rhoda; *m* 30 July 1903, Maj Guy Molesworth Kindersley, OBE, JP (*see* KINDERSLEY, B), and *d* 10 May 1950, leaving issue

2 Winifred Lucy; *m* 30 Aug 1898 Maj Arthur Herbert Platt, Dorset Regt, and *d* 1951, leaving issue

3 Angela Mary; *d* unm 6 April 1950

Sir EDMUND *d* 17 July 1920; his er son,

Sir Ambrose Elton, 9th Bt, JP; *b* 23 May 1869; *educ* Jesus Coll Cambridge (BA); barrister Middle Temple 1896; *m* 18 April 1901 Dorothy Wynne (*d* 28 May 1957), only dau and heir of Arthur Robert Wiggin, of Oddington Estate, Ceylon, and had issue:

1 ARTHUR HALLAM RICE (Sir), **10th Bt**

2 Ralph Ambrose, documentary film unit 1936, WW II as film correspondent to Min Info; *b* 22 March 1914; *educ* Lancing and St Catharine's Coll Cambridge; *m* 29 April 1950 Patricia Elmore, widow of Gerald Francis O'Bryen and est dau of Elmore Wright Brewerton, FRCS, and *dsp* 13 Sept 1968

Sir AMBROSE *d* 11 July 1951; his er son,

Sir Arthur Hallam Rice Elton, 10th Bt; *b* 10 Feb 1906; *educ* Marlborough and Jesus Coll Cambridge (BA 1927); film consultant Empire Mktg Bd and GPO Film Unit, supervisor film production Min Info 1940–44, chm Scientific Film Assoc 1943–46, 1952–55 and 1963, film advsr Danish Govt 1946, Info Servs Control Germany 1947–48, Shell Ltd, dir Film Centre (Int) Ltd 1938–57 (chm 1963), govr BFI 1949–50, memb Cncl Nat Film Archive 1956, dir Nat Film Inst Canada 1956, gen manager publicity AEI 1960–63, chm Friends of Nat Film Archive 1962, pres Br Nat Film Catalogue 1963, memb BBC Advsy Cncl 1964–67, chm N Somerset *Mercury* 1966, chm Br Industrial and Scientific Film Assoc 1967; *m* 10 Jan 1948 Margaret Ann, FSA, BA (*d* 16 May 1995), dau of Prof Olafur Bjornson, MD, CM, FRCS, of Winnipeg, Canada, and *d* 1 Jan 1973, leaving issue:

1 Sir CHARLES ABRAHAM GRIERSON ELTON, **11th and present Bt**

1 *Julia Margaret Hallam; *b* 24 May 1949

2 *Rebecca Wiggin; *b* 6 June 1951; *m* 1984 *L Neal FitzSimons, of Kensington, Md., USA, s of T L FitzSimons and Mrs Wells N Thompson

ELY

Arms: Sable a chevron engrailed ermine between three trefoils slipped argent. **Crest:** A boar's head erased and erect argent. **Supporters:** Two eagles, wings inverted argent, beaked and legged or, each charged on the breast with a trefoil slipped vert. **Mottoes:** 1 (under arms) *Prends moi tel que je suis* ('Take me as I am') 2 (over the crest) *Loyal à mort* ('Loyal unto death'). **Creations:** Bt (I) 18 Dec 1780, *b* (I) (Loftus of Loftus Hall) 28 June 1785 and (UK) (Loftus of Long Loftus) 19 Jan 1801, V. (I) 28 Dec 1789, E. (I) 2 March 1794 and *m* (I) 1 Jan 1801.

THE 8TH MARQUESS OF ELY (Sir Charles John Tottenham, Bt), **Earl of Ely, Viscount Loftus of Ely, Baron Loftus of Loftus Hall**, Co Wexford, **Baron Loftus of Long Loftus**, Co York, and a **Baronet** [The Most Hon The Marquess of Ely, Trinity College School, Port Hope, Ont L1A 3W2, Canada]; *b* 30 May 1913; *s* cousin 1969; *educ* Collège de Genève, Internat Sch Geneva and Queen's U Kingston, Ontario (BA); Pncpl Boulden Ho, Trin Coll Sch, Port Hope, Ontario 1937–81, instructor in French RMC Canada 1936–37; *m* 1st 23 June 1938 Katherine Elizabeth (*d* 27 Jan 1975), dau of Lt-Col W H Craig, of Kingston, Ontario, and has issue:

1 +(CHARLES) JOHN, *Viscount Loftus* [Viscount Loftus, 23 Springfield Park, SE, Calgary Alberta T2X 2Z2, Canada]; head French dept Strathcona-Tweedsmuir Sch, Calgary, Canada; *b* 12 Feb 1943; *educ* Trin Sch, Port Hope, Internat Sch Geneva and Toronto U (BA, MA 1967); *m* 27 Dec 1969 *Judith Marvelle, dau of Dr John Jacob Porter, FRS, of Calgary, Alberta, and adopted:

*Andrew John; *b* 26 Feb 1973

*Jennifer Katherine; *b* 29 June 1975

2 +Timothy Craig [The Lord Timothy Tottenham, 22 Shortt St, Port Hope, Ontario L1A 3S7, Canada]; *b* 17 Jan 1948; *educ* Trin Coll Sch, Port Hope, and Ontario Teachers' Coll; *m* 16 June 1973 *Jane Elizabeth, dau of Grant McAllister, of Ottawa, and has issue:

(1) +Scott Craig; *b* 14 April 1977

(2) +John Douglas; *b* 25 April 1981

3 +Richard Ivor [The Lord Richard Tottenham, 819 Grace St, Newmarket, Ontario L3Y 2L6, Canada]; *b* 27 Jan 1954; *educ* Trin Coll Sch, Port Hope, and U of W Ontario (BA 1976); sales compliance offr Investment Dealers Assoc of Canada, Toronto; *m* 29 April 1978 *Virginia Murney, dau of William Murney Morris, of Toronto, and has issue:

(1) *Elizabeth Murney; *b* 11 Jan 1983

(2) *Katherine Ann; *b* 9 Sept 1985

1 *Ann Elizabeth; *b* 21 July 1940; *educ* Toronto U (BA, STB, STM, BEd) and Union Seminary, New York (MTB); headmistress Bishop Strachan Sch, Toronto 1981–95, Suffragan Bp Toronto

The 8th MARQUESS *m* 2nd 28 Dec 1978 Elspeth Ann (*d* 1 Nov 1996), only dau of P T Hay, of Highgate, London

Earlier peerage creations involving Ely: All these, together with the present Marquessate and Viscountcy, appear to refer to a place name in Ireland rather than the cathedral town in Cambridgeshire. The area Ely O'Carroll covers the westernmost parts of the modern Cos Laois (formerly Queen's Co) and Offaly (formerly King's Co) and extends into north Co Tipperary.

Teige or Thady O'Carroll, whose father Ferganayn had been Chief of Ely O'Carroll, was created Baron of Ely in the Irish peerage by EDWARD VI in 1552. He died without legitimate issue in 1554, but his brother William Odhar O'Carroll was promised a peerage of the rank of barony for life by ELIZABETH I, though the pledge was never made good. He was, however, appointed Captain of Ely O'Carroll (a post also held by his brother) by the English authorities. This seems likely to have been in some sense a formal recognition by the English of the O'CARROLLs' status as Irish chiefs.

Lineage: EDWARD LOFTUS, of Swineshead, Yorks; had:

1 ROBERT; had, with an er s:

(1) ADAM LOFTUS, 1st VISCOUNT LOFTUS OF ELY, King's Co (I), so *cr* 10 May 1622, PC (I 1608); *b* 1568; Archdeacon Glendalough, Co Wicklow, 1594–1643, ktd 1604, MP King's Co 1613–15, Ld Chllr Ireland 1619–38; *m* 1597 Sarah, dau of — Bathow and widow of Richard Meredyth, Bp Leighlin, and *d* 1643, having had:

1a Robert (Sir); ktd 1619; *m* Aug 1621 Elinor, dau of Sir Francis Ru(i)she; *dspms* & *vp* 11 Oct 1640, leaving:

1b Henry; *d* Nov 1640

1b Anne; *m* Richard LENNARD later BARRETT (*see* DACRE, B)

2a EDWARD LOFTUS, 2nd VISCOUNT LOFTUS OF ELY; *b c* 1598; ktd Jan 1622/3; *m* 28 Feb 1635 Jane, dau of Arthur Lindley, of Middleham Castle, Yorks, and *d* 11 April 1680, leaving issue:

1b ARTHUR LOFTUS, 3rd VISCOUNT LOFTUS OF ELY; *bapt* 18 June 1644; *m* 1st *c* 23 Dec 1675 Douglas [*sic*] (*dsp* 1677), dau of William Savage, of Castle Rheban, Co Kildare; *m* 2nd *c* 12 Dec 1676 Anne (*d* March 1701/2), dau of William Hawkins, of Dublin, and widow of (a) Capt Oldfield and (b) Sir Andrew Owens; *m* 3rd 2 April 1706 Letitia (*m* 2nd 1st Viscount Loftus of Ely of the 1756 *cr* and *dsp* 1765), dau of Sir John Rowley, of Castle Roe, Co Derry (*see* LANGFORD, B), and *dspms* 6 Nov 1725, when the Viscountcy expired, while his Monasterevan estate passed to his only dau Jane's s (by Charles, Lord Moore), 4th Earl of Drogheda (*qv*)

2 Adam; Private Chaplain to Ld Deputy Ireland; Archbp Armagh Jan 1562/3 and Dublin 1567, Ld Keeper Gt Seal 1573, Ld Chllr Ireland 1578, a fndr Trin Coll Dublin and its first Provost to 1594; *m* Jane, est dau of Adam Purdon, of Lurgan Race, Co Louth, and had, with 15 other children:

(1) DUDLEY (Sir)

(2) Thomas (Sir); Constable Wicklow Castle, granted estates of Kilyan and Clonard; *m* Ellen, widow of Francis Cosby, of Stradbally Hall, and dau of Robert Hartpole, of Shrule, Queen's Co, and was ancestor of the LOFTUSes, of Kilbride, Co Wicklow

(1) Anne; *m* 1st Sir Henry Colley (*see* WELLINGTON, D) and had issue; *m* 2nd Capt George Blount, of Dundass, Co Clare; *m* 3rd 1st Baron Blayney and had issue by all husbs

(2) Alice; *m* Sir Henry Warren, of Warrenstown, King's Co

(3) Martha; *m* as his 1st w Sir Thomas Colclough and *d* 19 March 1609, leaving issue

The Archbp *d* 5 April 1605 aged 72; his est s,

Sir DUDLEY LOFTUS, of Rathfarnham; *b* 1561; *m* Anne, dau of Sir Nicholas Bagenal, of Newry, and had, with other issue, including a 3rd and 4th s (Edward, of Ballnyebarney, Co Wicklow, *m* Anne, dau of G Hartpole, of Shrule, and had several children; Samuel, *m* Mary, dau of N Bagenal, and had issue):

1 Adam (Sir); *m* Jane, dau of Walter Vaughan, of Golden Grove, and had:

(1) Arthur (Sir), of Rathfarnham; MP Wexford; *m* 1624 Lady Dorothy Boyle, dau of 1st Earl of Cork (*see* CORK and ORRERY, E), and had, with three daus:

1a ADAM LOFTUS, 1st VISCOUNT LISBURNE, so *cr* 29 Jan 1685/6, as also BARON OF RATHFARNHAM, Co Dublin (both I); *m* Lucy, dau and coheir of 6th Baron Chandos of Sudeley, and *das spm*(s?) 15 Sept 1691 while cmdg a regt for WILLIAM III at the Siege of Limerick, when his titles expired, leaving:

1b Lucy (*d* 1717); *m* 1st Marquess of Wharton (*see* WHARTON, B)

2 Nicholas, of Fethard; *b* 1592; Jt-Clerk Pells and Treasury Ireland; *m* 1623 Margaret, dau and heir of Thomas Chetham, of Nuthurst, Lancs, and Hacketstown, Co Dublin, and *d* 1666, leaving an est surv s:

(1) Nicholas (Sir), of Fethard; *b* 1635; *m* 1st Susan, dau of Thomas Adderley, of Innishannon, Co Cork, and had a surv dau (Margaret, *m* Thomas Mildmay, of Lisburn); *m* 2nd Eleanor, 3rd dau of Sir Edmund Butler, Bt, of Garryhundon, Co Carlow, and had further issue (all the sons *dspm*)

(2) Henry, of Loftus Hall; *b* 1636; *m* 1st Amy, dau of John Gorges, of Coleraine, and had a s (*d* young) and three daus (including Jane, *m* Maj Thomas Cosby (*d* 15 May 1735), 3rd s of Alexander Cosby, of Stradbally Hall, and *d* 3 March 1734, leaving issue; Margaret, *m* Highhate Boyd, of Rosslare, and had a dau; *see* WIGRAM, Bt); *m* 2nd Anne, dau and heir of Henry Crewkern, of Exeter, and widow of Oliver Keating, of Ballynury, and *d* 1716, having by her had, with a yr s (Henry, *d* unm):

1a NICHOLAS LOFTUS, 1st VISCOUNT LOFTUS OF ELY, so *cr* 19 July 1756, as also earlier 5 Oct 1751 BARON LOFTUS OF LOFTUS HALL, Co Wexford (both I), PC (I 1753); *b c* 1687; MP Fethard 1710–13, Clonmines 1713–15 and Co Wexford 1711, Govr Co Wexford; *m* 1st after April 1706 Anne, 2nd dau of 1st Viscount Duncannon (*see* BESSBOROUGH, E); *m* 2nd Letitia (*see above*), widow of his cousin, 3rd and last Viscount Loftus of Ely, and *d* 31 Dec 1763, having by his 1st w had issue:

1b NICHOLAS LOFTUS later HUME-LOFTUS, 1st EARL OF ELY, Co Wicklow, so *cr* 23 Oct 1766 (I), PC (I 1764); *m* 18 Aug 1736 Mary (*d* Oct 1740), est dau and heir of Sir Gustavus Hume, 3rd Bt, of Co Fermanagh, and *d* 31 Oct 1766, leaving:

1c NICHOLAS LOFTUS later HUME-LOFTUS, 2nd EARL OF ELY, Govr Co Fermanagh 1767; *b* 11 Sept 1738; *d* unm 12 Nov 1769, when the Earldom expired

2b HENRY LOFTUS, 1st EARL OF ELY, Co Wicklow (I), of the 2 Dec 1771 *cr*, also 4th VISCOUNT LOFTUS OF ELY etc, KP (1783), PC (I 1771); *b* 18 Nov 1709, High Sheriff Co Wexford 1744, MP Bannow 1747–68 and Co Wexford 1768–69; *m* 1st 1745 Frances (*d* Aug 1774), dau of Henry Monroe, of Rose Hall, Co Down; *m* 2nd 1775 Anne (*d* 14 Aug 1821), dau of Capt Hugh Bonfoy, RN, and *dsp* 8 May 1783, when all his titles expired, his estates passing to his sis Elizabeth's s

1b Mary; *m* May 1734 William Alcock, of Wilton, Co Wexford (*d* 1779), and had issue

2b Anne; *m* Charles Tottenham, Surveyor-Gen Leinster, MP New Ross, yr bro of **Sir John Tottenham, 1st Bt** (*see* below), and *d* 10 Nov 1768, leaving issue. He *d* 10 Nov 1795

3b Elizabeth; *m* 31 Dec 1736 **Sir John Tottenham, 1st Bt**, so *cr* 18 Dec 1780 (*d* 29 Dec 1786), MP Tottenham Green, est s of Charles Tottenham, of Tottenham Green, Co Wexford, MP, and *d* June 1747, leaving:

1c CHARLES, **1st Marquess**

1c Anne; *m* 8 Dec 1756 Joseph Rogers, of New Ross, and had issue

2c Ellinor; *m* 29 May 1766 Rev John Orr and had issue

3c Mary; *m* 5 Dec 1766 Richard Annesley, of New Ross (*d* 5 June 1798), and had issue

The 1st and last EARL OF ELY (of the 1771 *cr*)'s n,

Sir CHARLES TOTTENHAM later LOFTUS (roy licence 1783), **2nd Bt**, and **1st Marquess of Ely**, so *cr* 1 Jan 1801, as also previously 28 June 1785 BARON LOFTUS OF LOFTUS HALL, Co Wexford, 28 Dec 1789 VISCOUNT LOFTUS OF ELY and 2 March 1794 EARL OF ELY(all I), and subsequently 19 Jan 1801 BARON LOFTUS OF LONG LOFTUS, Co York (UK), PC; *b* 23 Jan 1738; MP New Ross 1761–68, Bannow 1768–76, Fethard 1776–83 and Co Wexford 1783–85, *m* 23 June 1766 Jane (*d* 21 Feb 1807), est dau and coheir (with her sister Hannah, w of Sir Hercules Langrishe, 1st Bt; *qv*), of Robert Myhill, of Killarney, Co Kilkenny, and *d* 22 March 1806, having had:

1 JOHN TOTTENHAM later LOFTUS, **2nd Marquess of Ely**, KP (1807), PC (1800); *b* 15 Feb 1770; *m* 1810 Anna Maria (*d* 6 Sep 1857), dau of Sir Henry Watkin Dashwood, 3rd Bt, of Kirklington Park (*qv*), and *d* 26 Sept 1845, having had, with other issue:

(1) JOHN HENRY TOTTENHAM, **3rd Marquess of Ely**; *b* 19 Jan 1814; *m* 29 Oct 1844 Jane (*d* 11 June 1890), memb Roy Order VA 3rd Cl, Ldy Bedchamber to HM QUEEN VICTORIA, dau of James Joseph Hope-Vere (*see* LINLITHGOW, M), and *d* 15 July 1857, leaving:

1a JOHN HENRY WELLINGTON GRAHAM LOFTUS, **4th Marquess of Ely**; *b* 22 Nov 1849; *m* 9 Dec 1875 Caroline Anne (*d* 27 May 1917), dau of George Caithness, and *dsp* 3 April 1889

1a Marion Jane; *m* 1st 6 June 1867 (*divorce* 1875) George Osborn Springfield, 5th Dragoon Gds, and had issue; *m* 2nd 29 Dec 1875 Col Sir James Dyson Bourne, 2nd Bt, 5th Dragoon Gds (*dsp* 11 Nov 1883); *m* 3rd 6 Dec 1884 Lt-Col James John Neil Buchanan, 5th Dragoon Gds, and had further issue. He *d* 26 Nov 1893. She *m* 4th 24 Oct 1894 Rev James Weller, of Amersham, and *d* 28 Oct 1933. He *d* 16 June 1928

(2) George William; Gren Gds; *b* 11 May 1815; *m* 21 June 1846 Martha (*d* 6 Apr 1858), est dau of J Fuller, of Norwich, and *dsp* 19 Jan 1877

(3) Adam (Rev); Rector Magheraculmoney, Co Fermanagh; *b* 13 May 1816; *m* 11 June 1846 Margaret (*d* 3 May 1902), 4th dau of Robert Fannin, of Leeson St, Dublin, and *d* 25 Dec 1866, having had issue:

1a JOHN HENRY LOFTUS, **5th Marquess of Ely**; *b* 6 March 1851; *m* 21 Nov 1895 Margaret Emma (*d* 1 Aug 1931), yst dau of F A Clark, of Lynton Court, Sussex, and Gracefiel Park, Bucks, and *dsp* 18 Dec 1925

2a Adam Robert Charles; *b* 31 March 1853; *d* 18 Jan 1866

3a GEORGE HERBERT LOFTUS, **6th Marquess of Ely**; *b* 19 April 1854; granted rank of marquess's yr s 12 May 1896; *m* 1st 29 April 1848 Emily Harriet (*d* 27 Nov 1886), yr dau of Maj Arthur Vandeleur, RA, of Rathlahine, Co Clare, and had:

1b Adam John St George; Lt Roy Inniskilling Fus; *b* 30 Jan 1885; *d* unm 27 May 1909

1b Anna Mary Kathleen; *b* 6 Aug 1886; *m* 16 Sept 1913 (*divorce* 1937) Thomas Leslie Craven, yr s of Thomas Craven, DL, of Kirklington Hall, Notts, and *d* 23 Sept 1961, leaving issue

3a (cont.) The **6th Marquess** *m* 2nd 7 June 1902 Ethel Beatrice Lempriere (*d* 23 Oct 1927), dau of Nigel John Davies Gresley, JP, of Hobart, Tasmania, and *d* 10 April 1935, leaving by her:

2b GEORGE HENRY WELLINGTON LOFTUS, **7th Marquess of Ely**; High Sheriff Co Fermanagh, Maj NI Horse WW II; *b* 3 Sept 1903; *educ* Lancing; *m* 5 Sept 1928 *Thea Margaret Gordon [The Most Hon Thea Marchioness of Ely, Bernards Gate, 22 Lavant Rd, Chichester, W Sussex], dau of Lars Gronvold, of Hove and Norway, by Amy Maria Gordon, 2nd dau of Huntly Gordon Murray of Craigie, and *d* 31 May 1969, having had issue:

1c Ann; *b* and *d* 10 July 1933

1a Marianne; *m* 12 Feb 1874 as his 1st w Robert O'Brien Studdert, JP, DL, of Cullane, Co Clare, and *d* Aug 1879, leaving issue. He *d* 31 Jan 1936

(4) Augustus William Frederick Spencer, GCB, PC; Govr NSW 1879–85, Amb Berlin and St Petersburg; *b* 4 Oct 1817; *m* 9 Aug 1845 Emma Maria (*d* 1 Jan 1902), est dau of Adml Henry Francis Greville, CB (*see* WARWICK, BROOKE and, E), and *d* 7 March 1904, having had issue:

1a Henry John, DL Middx; Page-of-Honour to HM QUEEN VICTORIA, 3rd Sec Dip Serv 1870–78; *b* 8 Nov 1849; *m* 22 Sept 1880 S Josephine (*d* 16 Aug 1921), dau of William Leech, of Philadelphia, and *d* 1924

2a Augustus Pelham Brooke; ADC to Govr NSW; *b* 6 July 1851; *m* 1887 Ethel (*d* 1939), dau of P S Labertouche, of Melbourne, Australia, and *d* 25 March 1924, leaving:

1b Guy Alvo Greville; 2nd Lt Gren Gds WW I; *b* 26 Aug 1899; *m* 7 July 1930 Renee Clementine Eleanor Favin and *dsp* 7 Aug 1965

3a Montagu Egerton, MVO 4th Cl (1908); Consular Serv; *b* 22 Jan 1860; *educ* Eton; *m* 1st 2 Sept 1897 Margaret Julia Agnes Fairfax (*dsp* 3 June 1900), dau of John Harvey Astell, of Woodbury Hall, Beds; *m* 2nd 19 Oct 1904 Colina Marion (*d* 13 Nov 1940), yst dau of Charles Hames Hale Monro, JP, of Ingsdon Manor, Newton Abbot, S Devon, and *d* 27 Nov 1934

1a Evelyn Ann Frances; *d* unm 28 Sept 1861

2a Emma Anne Caroline Bloomfield; *m* 1st 15 Dec 1873 (*divorce* 1882) Col Hon Frederick Arthur Wellesley, yst s of 1st Earl Cowley (*qv*); *m* 2nd 14 Feb 1903 Leberecht Kurt von Koller

(5) Henry Yorke Astley; *b* 9 April 1822; *m* 5 July 1864 Louisa, Dowager Countess of Seafield (*d* 2 Sept 1884 aged 66; *qv*), dau of R G Maunsell, and *dsp* 28 Feb 1880

(1) Charlotte Elizabeth; *m* 18 Dec 1830 1st Baron Egerton of Tatton and *d* 11 Sept 1878, leaving issue (*see* 1956 edn). He *d* 21 Feb 1883

(2) Catherine Henrietta Mary; *m* 8 Jan 1863 Capt Arthur John Loftus, Keeper Jewels Tower London, 18th Hus, only s of Capt Arthur Loftus, RN, and *d* 22 Feb 1908, leaving issue. He *d* 3 Sept 1891

2 Robert Ponsonby TOTTENHAM (Rt Rev); Bp Clogher; *b* 5 Sept 1773; *m* 28 May 1807 Hon Alicia Maude (*d* 21 Dec 1866), 6th dau of 1st Viscount Hawarden (*qv*), and *d* 26 April 1850, having had, with other issue:

(1) Charles John, of Woodstock, Co Wicklow, and Berwyn House, Denbighshire, JP, DL; Capt 2nd Life Gds, Hon Col Denbighshire Yeo Cav; *b* 27 June 1808; *m* 11 Sept 1839 Hon Isabella Maude (*d* 11 July 1892), est dau of 3rd Viscount Hawarden (*qv*), and *d* 17 Dec 1878, leaving:

1a Charles Robert Worsley, JP, DL Merioneths, JP Denbighshire and Co Wicklow, of Woodstock and Plas Berwyn; Maj 3rd Bn Roy Welch Fus; High Sheriff Co Wicklow 1888; *b* 21 Feb 1845; *educ* Ch Ch Oxford (MA); *m* 1st 5 Nov 1874 Dorothea Anne (*d* 8 Jan 1903), dau of Leonard Cornwall, of Brownstown House, Co Meath, and had:

1b Charles Loftus Watkin, of Woodstock and Plas Berwyn, JP Denbighs and Merioneths; High Sheriff 1930; *b* 28 Nov 1876; *educ* Exeter Coll Oxford (MA); *m* 1st 28 April 1906 Ethel Frances (*d* 29 June 1937), dau of H A Cowper, of Trudder, Co Wicklow; *m* 2nd 13 Oct 1941 Alice Mary (*d* 24 Aug 1951), widow of W de Vins Wade, of Dunmow, Essex, and dau of Frederick Woodman, MD, of Deal, Kent, and *dsp* 4 Oct 1943

2b George Leonard; *b* 20 April 1879; *m* 1 Aug 1912 Cécile Elizabeth, 3rd dau of James Salkeld Burra, JP, of Bockhanger, Kennington, Kent, and *d* 9 June 1928, leaving:

1c CHARLES JOHN TOTTENHAM, **8th and present Marquess of Ely**

2c George Robert, CD, RD (1969); Cdr RCN (ret), Lt-Cdr RNR WW II, head modern languages Roy Masonic Sch, Rickmansworth; *b* 22 July 1914; *educ* Queen's U Kingston, Ontario (BA), granted with sis rank of marquess's dau/yr s 1973; *m* 7 Oct 1944 *Jane Elizabeth [The Lady George Tottenham, Trullwell, Box, Glos GL6 9HD], dau of Arthur Martin, of Windsor, Ontario, and *d* 5 Aug 1975, leaving:

1d Michael George; *b* 6 Dec 1949; *d* 22 Feb 1958

2d Martin; *b* 14, *d* 15 Sept 1951

3d Terence Peter; *b* 22 June 1955; *d* 4 Dec 1960

1d *Jane Elizabeth [Mrs Mark Robinson, Trullwell, Box, nr Stroud, Glos GL6 9HD]; *b* 29 Nov 1945; *m* 31 July 1971 *Capt Mark G Robinson, late RA, er s of W A Robinson, and has:

1e *Nano Sophie Tottenham; *b* 1973

1c *Dora Elizabeth, JP (Inner London 1968) [The Lady Dora Pink JP, 24 The Gateways, London SW3]; Lt WRCNS WW II; *b* 9 Nov 1919; *educ* Queen's U Ontario (BA); *m* 1st 1946 Lt (E) Bernard Edgar Hall, RN (*d* 25 March 1947), s of Capt E E Hall, of Bearsted, Kent; *m* 2nd 17 June 1950 Sir Ivor Thomas Montague Pink, KCMG (*d* 28 Jan 1966), Amb Hungary 1963–65, er s of Leonard Montague Pink, and by him has:

1d *Celia Elizabeth; *b* 5 Sept 1952

1b Sophia (Lai) Dora Elizabeth; *m* 1st 30 April 1902 Maj Peter La Touche, of Bellevue, Co Wicklow (*dsp* 13 March 1904); *m* 2nd 17 Jan 1907 Joseph Frederick Cowper, of Trudder, Co Wicklow, and *d* 16 Jan 1973 aged 95, leaving issue. He *d* 1947

2b Amy Maude; *m* 12 May 1920 Maj Lambert John Dopping Hepenstall, OBE, JP, DL, RE, of Derrycassan, Granard, Co Longford, 1 Albany Road, Bedford, and 73 Harcourt St, Dublin, and *d* 24 May 1968, leaving issue. He *d* 5 Dec 1928

1a (cont.) Maj Charles Tottenham *m* 2nd 11 July 1905 Eleanor Cockburne (*d* 1964), dau of Maj Alexander J Lindsay, RA, and *d* 31 Oct 1923

1a Adelaide Alicia; *m* 10 Aug 1875 Col Edward Richard Bayly, JP, DL, and *d* 24 Nov 1930, leaving issue (*see* ANGLESEY, M)

2a Emily Anna; *m* 1st 11 Nov 1880 Lt-Col Latham Coddington Brownrigg, 60th Rifles. He *d* 20 Oct 1882. She *m* 2nd 12 April 1887 Henry Barker and *d* 23 April 1902

3a Florence Isabella Maude; *m* 27 Oct 1896 Rev Mordaunt Elrington-Bisset, Rector Bangor, Wrexham, and *d* 30 Sept 1909. He *d* 23 Oct 1927

(2) Robert Loftus (Rev); Chaplain UK Legn Florence; *b* 27 Sep 1809; *m* 10 Dec 1833 Anne Dorothea (*d* 16 Oct 1891), est dau of William Anketel, of Anketel Grove, Co Monaghan, and *d* 5 Feb 1893, leaving:

1a Robert, Maj RA; *b* 2 Oct 1834; *m* 9 Nov 1864 Mary Ann Kate (*d* 10 Jan 1925), 2nd dau of H W Harvey, Lt RN, of Walmer, Kent, and *d* 12 Aug 1872, having had:

1b Robert Loftus; Lt-Col IA; *b* 29 Oct 1865; *m* 14 Feb 1899 Hilda May (*d* 24 May 1961), dau of F G Brook Fox, CE, and *d* 24 Jan 1925, leaving:

1c Mavis; *m* 1st 18 Sept 1919 (*divorce* 1944) Capt Charles Finch Farley, MC, 4th Dragoon Gds, s of Reuben Farley, of Sandy, Beds, and had issue. He *d* 8 Sept 1969. She *m* 2nd 24 Feb 1944 Philip Harman Stewart Brown, RM, er s of Ronald Stewart Brown (*see* BROWN, Bt)

2c Merle; *b* 22 Jan 1901; *d* unm 18 July 1958

3c Lynda Lucie; *m* 1st 28 June 1927 Maurice Bernhard Baron, gs of Bernhard Baron, and had issue; *m* 2nd Sept 1939 Lt James Hamilton Martin, RNVR, only s of Hugo Hamilton Martin. He *das* 29 June 1940; *m* 3rd 2 Oct 1947 Capt Christopher Simpson, DSC, RN, s of Rev Arthur Hume Simpson

2a Frederick William; 27th Foot; *b* 4 April 1839; *d* 19 July 1863

3a Adam, of Kalgoorlie, W Australia; *b* 30 July 1840; *d* unm 25 Sept 1920

4a Francis Cornwallis; *b* 23 Oct 1843; *d* 9 Aug 1894

5a Alfred Oliver; Lt RN; *b* 28 July 1845; *d* unm

1a Anna Maria Sarah; *m* 17 Oct 1854 Charles Uniacke Townsend, of Myross, Co Cork, and *d* 8 April 1873, leaving issue. He *d* 21 Jun 1907

2a Caroline Isabel; *m* 10 Dec 1863 Douglas Arthur Onslow and *d* 20 Feb 1928, leaving issue (*see* ONSLOW, Bt)

3a Alicia Georgina Frances; *m* 21 Dec 1889 Edward David Stuart Ogilvie, of Yilgibar, NSW, and *dsp* 24 July 1922. He *d* 1896

4a Lucy Matilda; *m* 4 Feb 1868 William Walter Bagot, of Pipe Hayes, Warwicks, and *d* 1895, leaving issue (*see* BAGOT, B)

5a Madeline Emma; *m* 4 Feb 1878 Sir Alexander Campbell Onslow, Ch Justice W Australia, and *d* 5 Oct 1926 leaving issue (*see* ONSLOW, E)

(3) Ashley; Capt 4th Madras Cav; *b* 24 Sep 1813; *kas* Seonee, nr Jubbulpore, 10 Nov 1857

(4) Henry (Rev); BD, Rector Donacavey; *b* 17 Sep 1814; *d* unm 6 Jan 1875

(5) John Francis, JP Co Leitrim; Cdr RN; *b* 28 July 1822; *m* 3 Sep 1851 Laura Ellen Dodd (*d* 18 Jul 1912), 2nd dau of Edward Taylor Janverin, of the Great Salterns, and *d* 18 May 1906, having had:

1a Francis Edward Janverin; Lt RN; *b* 26 April 1855; *d* 30 Sept 1889

2a Henry Loftus, CB (1914); Adml, ADC to HM EDWARD VII 1908–10, Supt Malta Dockyard 1914, cmded 7th Cruiser Sqdn 1915, served Egypt War 1882 and against King of Nimbi and Chiefs of Brass 1895; *b* 7 Aug 1860; *m* 9 Nov 1897 Florence Elizabeth (*d* 25 March 1950), dau of Thomas Coles, of Titchmarsh, Northants, and *d* 24 Feb 1950, leaving:

1b Henry Thomas Lloyd Loftus; Capt RE, publicity manager Middle East and USA Chase Organics (GB), Spanish translator; *b* 22 June 1900; *educ* RNCs Osborne and Dartmouth, Cheltenham and RMA Woolwich, *d* unm 27 Aug 1970

3a William Frederick Loftus; Imp Forest Serv, Order White Elephant Siam; *b* 12 Aug 1866; *m* 22 July 1909 Clementina Isabel Maude (*d* 15 Aug 1961), er dau of Capt Hon Cornwallis Maude (*see* HAWARDEN, V), and *d* 29 May 1936

4a Ponsonby Julian John Loftus; *b* 27 June 1869; *d* 6 Jan 1879

5a Alexander Robert Loftus (Sir); CIE (1925); ktd 1931; ICS (ret), memb Centl Bd Revenue India and Jt Sec Finance Dept 1923, Administrator Pudukkottai State 1934; *b* 31 July 1873; *educ* Clifton and Queen's Coll Oxford (MA); *d* unm 13 Nov 1946

1a Alicia Catherine Loftus; *m* 21 Feb 1882 R-Adml Richard Carter and *d* 10 July 1934, leaving issue. He *d* 1887

2a Emily Isabella Loftus; *m* 1892 Edward Lloyd Edwards, of Trevor Hall, Trevor, nr Wrexham, and *d* 25 Oct 1946, leaving issue

3a Laura Ellen Loftus; *m* 6 June 1895 James Coster Edwards, of Bryn Howel, Trevor, nr Wrexham, and *d* Aug 1942, having had issue. He *d* 21 Jan 1934

4a Martha Georgiana Loftus; *d* unm 12 Aug 1953

5a Maude Loftus; *d* unm 26 June 1944

6a Caroline Anna Loftus; *d* unm 9 Jan 1937

7a Anne Georgina Susan Loftus; *b* 11 Sept 1871; *d* unm 2 Feb 1972

(6) George (Very Rev); Canon St Patrick's, Dublin, MA Cantab, Rector Innismacsaint, Dean Clogher; *b* 20 Oct 1825; *m* 27 Jan 1858 Emily Frances (*d* 23 April 1903), 2nd dau of Rev William Maclean, Preb Tynan, and *d* 19 Oct 1911, having had:

1a Ponsonby John Loftus; Maj S Staffs Regt Boer War (Queen's medal with three clasps) and Draft Conducting Offr WW I (1914 star, two medals); *b* 17 Nov 1858; *d* 12 Oct 1927

2a William Henry Loftus; *b* 21 Dec 1859; *d* 25 Aug 1873

3a Cornwallis George Loftus; *b* 13 Jan 1864; *m* 7 Sept 1904 Isabel Sinclair (*d* 2 April 1947), 4th dau of Dr David Thomas, of Valparaiso, and *d* 15 March 1945

4a Edward Loftus; CS (Inland Revenue), Imp Yeo Boer War (Queen's medal and five clasps); *b* 1 Nov 1867; *m* 1899 Jessie Hilda (*d* 20 Oct 1938), dau of John Honey Trace, and *d* 1 Jan 1949, having had:

1b +George William Loftus [George Tottenham Esq, Blaney, Enniskillen, Co Fermanagh]; *b* 18 June 1911; *m* 23 Nov 1949 *Margaret Mary Hamilton (Pearl), dau of Thomas Valentine Powell, and has:

1c +Robert Ashley Christopher; *b* 30 Nov 1953; *m* 1st 1978 Philippa Jane (*d* 1981), er dau of Maj P F Stevens, of Cornmongers, Runwick, Farnham, Surrey *m* 2nd 1983 *Gabriele Maria, dau of Anton Schüle, of Rötenbach, Wolfegg, W Germany, and by his 1st w has:

1d +Joe; *b* 1980

1c *Alison Margaret; *b* 9 Jan 1951; *m* 1976 *Roger Jones and has issue

1b Dorothy Lilian; *m* 25 Aug 1927 Walter L Townshend, son of C L Townshend, of Reigate, and *d* 2 June 1928

2b *Emily Frances [Mrs Henry Sansom, 15 Old Rossopy Park, Enniskillen, Co Fermanagh]; *m* 6 June 1931 *Henry Gordon Sansom and has:

1c *Frank Edward; *b* 25 Feb 1934; *m* 28 Oct 1955 *Mary Doreen, dau of Edward Hassard, of Drumrainey, Co Fermanagh

2c *Anthony Gordon; *b* 13 Aug 1936; *m* 13 Dec 1958 *Ruth Martha, dau of George Riley, of Liverpool, and has:

1d *Christopher Gordon; *b* 9 Oct 1961

2d *Andrew Fraser; *b* 5 June 1964

1d *Julie Caroline; *b* 6 May 1960

1c *Ann Hilda; *b* 10 Sept 1938; *m* 25 Nov 1961 *Samuel James Wright, s of Richard Apsley Wright, of Magheramorne, Co Antrim, and has:

1d *James Michael; *b* 9 Sept 1966

2d *Jonathan Peter; *b* 29 Dec 1967

2c *Sheila Eileen; *b* 14 Nov 1939; *m* 25 March 1961 *Anthony Charles Ford, s of L J Ford, of Bridgwater, Somerset, and has:

1d *Anthony Michael; *b* 16 Dec 1962

3b Georgina Alice Christine; *m* 24 Oct 1930 Eric Lowthian Bell and *d* Jan 1947

1a Alicia Jane; *d* unm 10 April 1945

2a Georgina Isabella; *d* 19 April 1923

3a Emily Millicent; *d* unm 13 Sept 1930

(1) Isabella; *m* 23 July 1844 Col Robert George Archibald Hamilton Gun Cuninghame, of Mount Kennedy, Co Wicklow, and *d* 5 Aug 1904, leaving issue. He *d* 12 May 1880

ELYSTAN-MORGAN

Creation: B. (LP, UK) 1981.

THE BARON ELYSTAN-MORGAN, of Aberteifi, Co Dyfed ((Dafydd) Elystan Elystan-Morgan) [The Rt Hon The Lord Elystan-Morgan, Carreg Afon, Dolau, Bow Street, Ceredigion, Dyfed SY24 5AE]; *b* 7 Dec 1932; *educ* Ardwyn GS Aberystwyth and U Coll Wales Aberystwyth (LLB Hons 1953); slr 1957; MP (Lab) Cards 1966–74, Chm Welsh Parly Lab Party 1967–68 and 1971–74, Pres Welsh Local Authorities Assoc 1967–73, Parly U-Sec Home Office 1968–70, Spokesman Welsh Affrs 1972–74, Ho Lds Spokesman Legal and Home Affrs 1981–85; barrister Gray's Inn 1971, Recorder 1983, Circuit Judge 1987–; *m* 1959 *Alwen, dau of William E Roberts, and has issue:

1 *Owain; *b* 1962; *m* 1994 *Deborah, dau of Hugh Jones, of Llanbadarn, Aberystwyth

1 *Eleri; *b* 1960; LLB: *m* 1989 *Peter Gerard Hurt, 2nd s of Rudolph Hurt, of Hathern, Loughborough, Leics

Lineage: DEWI MORGAN; *m* Olwen — and had issue:

(DAFYDD) ELYSTAN later ELYSTAN-MORGAN, *cr* a **Baron**

EMERTON

Creation: B. (LP, UK) 1 Jan 1997.

THE BARONESS EMERTON, of Tunbridge Wells, in the County of Kent, and of Clerkenwell in the London Borough of Islington (Dame Audrey Caroline Emerton, DBE (1989), DL (Kent 1992)) [The Rt Hon The Baroness Emerton DBE DL, House of Lords, London SW1A 0PW]; *b* 10 Sept 1935; *educ* Tunbridge Wells GS; nurse, Co Commr St John Ambulance Kent 1985–88, Ch Nursing Offr St John Ambulance 1988–96, Hon V-Pres RCN 1994–, Tstee Kent Community Housing Tst 1993–, Ch Offr Care in the Community St John Ambulance 1996–, Chm Brighton Health Care NFS Tst 1994–

Lineage: GEORGE MERTON; *m* Lily Squirrell and had:

AUDREY CAROLINE, *cr* a **Baroness**

EMSLIE

Creation: B. (LP, UK) 1979.

THE BARON EMSLIE, of Potterton, in the District of Gordon (George Carlyle Emslie, MBE (1946), PC (1972)) [The Rt Hon The Lord Emslie MBE PC, 47 Heriot Row, Edinburgh EH3 6EX]; *b* 6 Dec 1919; *educ* The High Sch Glasgow and Glasgow U (MA, LLB, Hon LLD); WW II N Africa, Italy, Greece and Austria (despatches), Bde Maj 1944-46, advocate Scotland 1948, QC (S) 1957, Advocate Depute Sheriff Courts 1955–57, Jr Assessor Edinburgh 1955–57, memb Scottish Ctee Cncl on Tbnls 1962–70, chm Scottish Ag Wages Bd 1968, Sheriff Perth and Angus 1963–66, Dean Faculty Advocates 1965–70, Sr Assessor Edinburgh 1965–70, Ld of Session as Lord Emslie 1970, Ld Justice Gen Scotland and Ld Pres Court Session 1972–89, V-Chm Bd Tstees Nat Library Scotland 1975–, Hon Bencher Inner Temple 1974, FRSE 1987; *m* 1942 *Lilias Ann Mailer, dau of Robert Hannington, of Glasgow, and has:

1 *(George) Nigel Hannington, QC (S 1986) [The Hon Nigel Emslie QC, 20 Inverleith Place, Edinburgh EH3 5QB]; *b* 1947; *educ* Edinburgh Acad, Trin Coll Glenalmond, Gonville and Caius Coll Cambridge (BA) and Edinburgh U (LLB); advocate 1972, Standing Jr Counsel: Forestry Cmmn Scotland and Dept Ag and Fisheries Scotland 1981–82 and Inland Revenue Scotland 1982–86, pt-time chm Medical Appeal Tbnls 1988–, Dean Faculty of Advocates 1997–; *m* 1973 *Heather Ann, dau of Arthur Frank Davis, of Bristol, and has a s and two daus

2 *Derek Robert Alexander, QC (S 1987) [The Hon Lord Kingarth, 35 Ann St, Edinburgh EH4 lPL]; *b* 1949; ed Edinburgh Acad, Trinity Coll Glenalmond, Gonville and Caius Coll Cambridge (BA)and Edinburgh U (LLB); advocate 1974, Standing Jr Counsel DHSS 1979–87, Advocate Depute 1985–88, pt-time chm Pension Appeal Tbnl Scotland 1988–, Medical Appeal Tbnl Scotland 1990–, Ld of Session as Lord Kingnorth 1997–; *m* 1974 *Elizabeth Jane Cameron, dau of Andrew McLaren Carstairs, of Newport-on-Tay, and has a s and two daus

3 *Richard Hannington [The Hon Richard Emslie, PO Box 1212, Hilton, Kwa Zulu Natal, 3245, S Africa]; *b* 1957; *educ* Edinburgh Acad, Trinity Coll Glenalmond and Gonville and Caius Coll Cambridge (MA); scientific and projects offr Rhino Specialist Gp

Lineage: ALEXANDER EMSLIE; *m* Jessie Blair and had:

GEORGE CARLYLE, *cr* a **Baron**

ENNISKILLEN

Arms: Arg. a bull passant sa., armed and unguled or, within a bordure of the second charged with eight bezants; on a canton sinister per pale gu. and az. a harp or, stringed of the field.
Crest: A demi-dragon, wings elevated vert, langued gu., holding in the dexter claw a dart or, headed and feathered arg., and in the sinister an escutcheon charged as the canton.
Supporters: Two dragons regardant vert, each holding a dart or.
Motto: *Deum cole, regem serva* ('Worship God; honour the King').
Creations: E. (I) 18 Aug 1789, V. (I) 20 July 1776, B. (I) 8 Sept 1760 and (UK) (Grinstead) 11 Aug 1815.

THE 7TH EARL OF ENNISKILLEN, Viscount Enniskillen, Co Fermanagh, **Baron Mountflorence of Florence Court**, Co Fermanagh, **Baron Grinstead**, of Grinstead, Co Wilts (Andrew John Galbraith Cole) [The Rt Hon The Earl of Enniskillen, House of Lords, London SW1A 0PW]; *b* 28 April 1942; *s f* 1989; *educ* Eton; Capt Irish Gds 1965, md Kenya Airways 1979–81; *m* 3 Oct 1964 *Sarah Francis Caroline, only dau of Maj-Gen John Keith-Edwards, CBE, DSO, MC, of Nairobi, and has:

1 *Amanda Mary; *b* 4 May 1966
2 *Emma Frances; *b* 14 Feb 1969
3 *Lucy Caroline; *b* 8 Dec 1970

Lineage: Sir WILLIAM COLE settled in Ireland in Co Fermanagh early in the reign of JAMES 1; was granted 1611 1,000 acres of escheated lands there and 1612 320 acres, of which 80 were assigned for charter, consisting of a provost and twelve burgesses, Sir William Cole being the first Provost; raised and cmded a regt successfully against the Confedn of Kilkenny 1643; *m* Susannah, widow of Stephen Segar, Lt Dublin Castle, and dau and heir of John Croft, of Lancs, and *d* 1653, leaving issue:

1 MICHAEL
2 Sir JOHN COLE, 1st Bt (I), so *cr* 1660, of Newland, Co Dublin; MP Fermanagh; *m* Elizabeth, dau of John Chichester (*see* DONEGALL, M), by Mary, sis of 2nd Viscount Ranelagh of the 1628 *cr*, and had an est s:
(1) Sir ARTHUR COLE, 2nd Bt, and 1st BARON RANELAGH, of Ranelagh, Co Wicklow (I), so *cr* 18 April 1715; *b c* 1669; *m* 1st 8 Sept 1692 Catherine (*d* 19 Nov 1746), dau of 3rd Baron Byron (*qv*); *m* 2nd 26 June 1748 Selina, dau of Peter Bathurst, and *dsp* 5 Oct 1754, when the peerage expired. His widow *m* 2nd 12 Nov 1755 Sir John Elwill, Bt (*dsp* 9 Feb 1781)
(1) Elizabeth; *m* her cousin Sir Michael Cole (*see* below)
1 Mary
2 Margaret

The er son,

MICHAEL COLE; *m* 7 July 1640 Catherine, dau of Sir Laurence Parsons (*see* ROSSE, E), and *dvp c* 1663, leaving an only surv child:

1 Michael (Sir); MP Enniskillen; *m* 1st Alice (dsp 24 Aug 1671), dau of Chidley Coote (*see* COOTE, Bt); *m* 2nd 20 Feb 1672 his cousin Elizabeth (*d* 19 Aug 1733), dau of Sir JOHN COLE, 1st Bt, and *d* 11 Feb 1710, leaving:
(1) John, of Florence Court; MP Enniskillen; *bapt* 12 April 1680; *m* 1st 10 July 1707 Florence, only dau of Sir Bourchier Wrey, 4th Bt and had, with other issue:
1a JOHN, **1st Baron**
2a Henry (Rev), had issue
1a Letitia; *m* 1st Maj Burton Johnson; *m* 2nd Thomas Dancer Eyre, of Eyreville, s of Samuel Eyre, and had issue. He *d* 1779
(1) (cont.) John Cole *m* 2nd Jane (*dsp*), dau of Robert Saunderson, and *d* July 1726

The er s,

JOHN COLE, **1st Baron Mountflorence of Florence Court** (I), so *cr* 8 Sept 1760; MP Enniskillen; *b* 13 Oct 1709; *m* Oct 1728 Elizabeth (*d* April 1771), dau of Hugh Willoughby Montgomery, of Carrow, Co Fermanagh, and had, with several daus (of whom Flora Caroline *m* 10 Dec 1755 Col William Irvine, of Castle Irvine (*d* May 1814), and *d* 20 Oct 1757, leaving issue, and Catherine, *m* Richard Browne):

1 WILLIAM, **1st Earl**
2 Arthur COLE later COLE-HAMILTON, of Skea, Co Fermanagh; High Sheriff 1778, MP; *b* 8 Aug 1750; *m* 1780 Letitia (*d* 7 Feb 1823), dau of Claud Hamilton, of Beltrim, 4th in descent from Sir Claude Hamilton, bro of 1st Earl of Abercorn (*see* ABERCORN, D), and *d* 1810, leaving:
(1) Claud William; High Sheriff Co Tyrone 1811; *b* 7 July 1781; *m* 10 Oct 1805 Nichola Sophia (*m* 2nd 1826 Joseph Pratt, of Cabra), dau of Richard Chaloner, of Kingsfort, Co Meath, and *d* 25 April 1822, leaving:
1a Arthur Willoughby, of Beltrim, Co Tyrone, JP Cos Tyrone and Londonderry, DL Co Tyrone; High Sheriff 1830, Maj Roy Tyrone Fus Militia; *b* 23 Nov 1806; *m* 16 Dec 1831 Emilia Katherine (*d* 19 Nov 1869), dau of Rev Charles Cobbe Beresford (*see* WATERFORD, M), and *d* 16 Dec 1891, having had, with other issue:
1b William Claud; RM, Capt 88th Regt; *b* 8 Aug 1833; *m* 10 June 1858 Caroline Elizabeth Josephine (*d* 23 Jan 1930), 7th dau of Hon Andrew Godfrey Stuart (*see* CASTLESTEWART, E), and *dvp* 26 Nov 1882, having had, with other issue:
1c Arthur Richard, of Beltrim, Gortin, Newtownstewart, Co Tyrone, and Caddagh, Wilkinstown, Co Meath, JP, DL Co Tyrone; Lt-Col cmdg 6th Service Bn E Lancs Regt, Lt-Col and Hon Col 6th Bn Roy Irish Rifles, Capt 7th Hus and Roy Scots Fus, Egypt 1882, Sudan 1885–86 (medal with clasp, bronze star), WW I (despatches); *b* 29 April 1859; *m* 1st 2 Jan 1882 Jeannette (*d* 7 April 1883), est dau of Samuel Moore, of Moorlands, Lancs, and had:
1d William Moore, of Beltrim; Maj RASC, Lt KRRC, Boer War 1901–02 (medal with five clasps), WW I; *b* 3 April 1883; *m* 1903 Ada Beatrice (*d* 5 April 1954), yst dau of William Peter Huddle, of Dover, and *d* 6 July 1948, having had:
1e William Arthur Richard; *b* 11 Dec 1906; *m* 1 June 1932 Barbara (*d* 15 March 1946), yst dau of Edward J Deane, of Grassendale Park, Liverpool, and *d* 30 April 1936, leaving issue:
1f Margaret Alice; *b* 21 June 1934; *d* 13 Jan 1938
1f *Nora Kathleen; *m* 1st 15 April 1926 (*divorce* 1944), Carl Rudolf Baltzar von Braun, MRCS, LRCP, Capt RAMC, er s of Carl Gustaf Johan von Braun (*d* 29 Nov 1968); *m* 2nd 12 Sept 1944 John Matthew Shufflebotham, s of John Plant Shufflebotham, of Three Elms, Hereford
1c (cont.) Col Arthur Cole-Hamilton *m* 2nd 18 Feb 1884 Florence Alice (*d* 22 Oct 1930), dau of James Duke Hughes, of Burntwood, Surrey, and was *ka* Dardanelles 10 Aug 1915
2c William Andrew Thomas; Capt 4th Bn Roy Irish Fus Boer War 1901; *b* 6 July 1864; *m* 3 Oct 1891 Lizzie Alexander (*d* 13 April 1951), widow of Capt Ashton Rendle and dau of Christopher S Penny, of York House, Bideford, and *d* 25 May 1903, leaving:
1d Con William Eric; Capt Roy Scots and RFC; *b* 7 March 1894; *k* in a flying accident, 2 July 1917
1d Clodagh Madeline Janie; *b* 13 Nov 1897
3c Claud George, CMG (1917), DSO (1902) and bar (1919); Ch Constable Breconshire 1912–47, KStJ, KPM, JP, DL, Lt-Col Roy Irish Rifles, Boer War 1901–02 (despatches, DSO, medal with five clasps) WW I (despatches four times, wounded, gassed, POW); *b* 27 Jan 1869; *m* 4 April 1893 Lucy Charlewood (*d* 14 Nov 1941), dau of Reginald Henry Thorold (*see* THOROLD, Bt), and *d* 6 Jan 1957, leaving:
1d Isabel Katherine
2d Lucy Alice
3d Norah Elizabeth; *m* 8 Aug 1926 James Gordon Mitchell, only surv s of Andrew Alexander Mitchell, JP, of Woodfield, Stevenage, Herts, and had issue
1c Isabel Mary; *m* 15 Dec 1885 Francis Richard Pease, JP, DL, of Hesslewood, Yorks, and *d* 21 Dec 1942, leaving issue. He *d* 18 Jan 1913
2b Claud COLE-HAMILTON later CHALONER (roy licence April 1886), of Kingsfort, Meath, JP Cos Cavan and Meath; *b* 20 Nov 1838; *m* 2 June 1875 Henrietta Ann (*d* 18 April 1927), est dau of Alexander Montgomery, of Kilmer, Co Meath, and *d* 21 June 1917, having had, with other issue:
1c Richard Alexander; Lt Royal Inniskilling Fus; *b* 2 June 1879; *d* unm 22 April 1902, of wounds recd at Rooival, Transvaal
2c Claudius Willoughby; Maj 3rd Bn Roy Inniskilling Fus Assist Colonial Sec Gold Coast, Boer War 1901–02 (medal, five bars), WW I; *b* 22 Jan 1882; *m* 17 Oct 1918 Adelaide Winifred (*d* 9 June 1969), dau of Col Alexander Sinclair Grove, DSO, MC, and *d* 18 Jan 1963, leaving:
1d +Desmond Willoughby Richard [Desmond Chaloner Esq, High Bank, Chearsley, Aylesbury, Bucks]; late Lt Roy Inniskilling Fus, WW II with KAR; *b* 8 Jan 1920; *educ* Shrewsbury and Trin Coll Dublin (BA 1943)
1d *Nancy Winifred [Mrs John Pringle, Beechtrees, Rathmore, Naas, Co Kildare, Ireland]; *b* 10 Aug 1921; *m* 1st 12 June 1945 Francis Gabriel CORNWALL formerly LEWIS-CROSBY (*d* 17 Oct 1949, having changed name Jan 1944 on inheriting Rathmore under will of his uncle, Francis Victor Cornwall), 3rd s of Very Rev Ernest Henry Lewis-Crosby, Dean Christchurch Cathedral Dublin and has:
1e *Francis David Willoughby; *b* 26 Oct 1947; *educ* Harrow and Trin Coll Dublin
1e *Ann Patricia [Mrs Robert Woods, Beechmount, Orwell Rd, Dublin 14]; *b* 1 Feb 1950; *m* 1973 *Robert Tristram Rowan Woods and has:
1f *Robert Seton Rowan; *b* 1986
2f *John Francis Cornwall; *b* 1986
1f *Nicola Clare; *b* 1982
2f *Lucinda Ann; *b* 1983
1d (cont.) Mrs Francis Cornwall *m* 2nd 31 July 1959 Prof John Seton Pringle, FRCS, s of James Alexander Pringle, KC, of Cranmore Park, Belfast. He *d* 1975
3c John; Lt RASC; *b* 28 May 1889; *educ* Trin Coll Dublin (MA, BAg); *m* 14 Feb 1922 Monica Katherine (*d* 1975), dau of Rev William Ralph

Westropp Roberts, DD, of Kelston, Stillorgan, Dublin, and *d* 4 Jan 1940, leaving issue:

1d *Charity Patricia [Mrs Charity FitzGibbon, Anna Liffey House, Lucan, Co Dublin, Ireland]; *b* 17 March 1923; *m* 21 Nov 1949 (*divorce* 1973) Henry FitzGibbon, MD, MAO (Dublin), FACOG (*d* 1989), 2nd s of Gibbon FitzGibbon, MD, FRCPI, FRCOG, of 9 St James's Terrace, Clonskeagh, and has issue:

1e *John [John FitzGibbon Esq, 638 Monterey Ave, Victoria, BC V85 4T9, Canada]; *b* 20 May 1951; *m* 1976 *Paula Gammell and has:

1f *Fletcher; *b* 1987

1f *Gamelle; *b* 1984

2e *Thomas; *b* 10 June 1953

1e *Frances; *b* 8 Sept 1954; *m* 1993 *—

2e *Pamela Anne; *b* 16 July 1959; *m* 1994 *Wayne Clayton

2e *Mary Frances Jonet; *b* 16 Dec 1925; *m* 29 April 1950 *Richard John Shackleton, s of John Wigham Shackleton, of Beech Park, Clonsilla, Co Dublin, and has issue:

1e *Richard Chaloner; *b* 13 Oct 1953; *educ* Portora Royal Sch; *m* 1988 *Sarah Caroline Benton, and has issue:

1f *Christopher Mark; *b* 1989

2f *James Richard; *b* 1991

1f *Deborah Mary; *b* 1993

2e *Michael Beattie; *b* 22 Jan 1959

1e *Christine Mary; *b* 10 May 1951; *m* 1988 *Samir Habouch

2e *Jonet Rhoda [Mrs Thomas Egan, White Lodge, Kennedy Rd, Dunboyne, Co Meath, Ireland]; *b* 2 Aug 1956; *m* 1984 *Thomas Mary Egan, and has issue:

1f *Eoin Shackleton; *b* 1987

2f *Peter John; *b* 19 July 1994

3d *Henrietta Sophia [Mrs Robert Twigg, 38 Meadow Grove, Churchtown, Co Dublin, Ireland]; *b* 29 Dec 1930; *m* 1959 *Robert Frederick Twigg, and has issue:

1e *Robert Chaloner [Robert Twigg Esq, Amber Hill, Kilmeaden, Co Waterford, Ireland]; *b* 1960; *m* 1985 *Janet Beck, and has issue:

1f *Nathan Robert; *b* 1988

1f *Kate Beck; *b* 1986

2f *Lucy Astrid; *b* 1989

1e *Nicola; *b* 1962; *m* 1993 *Christopher Woods

2e *Fiona [Mrs Frank O'Reilly, Granite Lodge, Enniskerry, Co Wicklow, Ireland]; *b* 1963; *m* 1987 *Frank O'Reilly and has:

1f *Stephen Peter; *b* 1988

2f *Alan Robert; *b* 1990

1f *Karen Sophie Anne; *b* 1993

3e *Sarah; *b* 1970

1c Sophia Elizabeth; *b* 22 Feb 1877; *m* 5 Aug 1914 Arthur Stuart Harman, yst s of William Harman, of Crossdrum, Oldcastle, Co Meath, and *d* 22 Aug 1964, leaving issue. He *d* 14 March 1956

2c Emily; *b* 11 May 1878; *m* June 1914 Rev Robert Francis Shirley, Rector Rathconnell, Killucan, Co Westmeath, and had issue. He *d* 21 Oct 1948

3c Henrietta Frances; *b* 2 Jan 1881; *m* 18 Jan 1911 Trevor Broughton Bomford, 6th s of John Francis Bomford, JP, of Oakley Park, Co Meath, and *d* 27 March 1970, having had issue. He *d* 3 Oct 1963

3b Charles Richard COLE-HAMILTON; Cdr RN; *b* 6 Dec 1842; *d* unm 13 Oct 1911

4b Arthur Henry COLE-HAMILTON (Rev); Rector Castle Ashby, Northants; *b* 17 April 1846; *m* 17 April 1873 Harriet Elizabeth (*d* 20 May 1913), dau of John Tisdall, of Charlesfort, Co Meath, and *d* 15 Dec 1889, leaving:

1c Henry Arthur; Capt Res of Offrs, Hon Capt 3rd Imp Yeo, JP for District of Heilbron, Boer War 1900–02 (despatches twice, two medals and five clasps); *b* 30 April 1874; *m* 7 June 1916 Johanna Louise (*d* 22 Feb 1941), yst dau of Hon Rudolph Philip Botha, of Bloemhof, Cape Province, and *d* 27 April 1919

2c George William, JP Herts; Basutoland Mounted Police; *b* 12 Sept 1875; *educ* Selwyn Coll Cambridge (BA); *m* 25 April 1908 Katherine Edith (*d* 9 Oct 1960), yr dau of William Clinton-Baker, of Bayfordbury, Herts, and *d* 28 May 1946, leaving:

1d Katherine Letitia; *b* 21 April 1909; *m* 15 Jan 1930 Maj Bernard Alleyne Murray, MC, TD, RA (*d* 1984), s of Rev John D Munro Murray, and *d* 17 Nov 1996, leaving:

1e *Katherine Elizabeth [Mrs Robert Shirley, 2307-23rd St, Vernon, V1T 4J4, Canada]; *b* 7 May 1932; *m* 1962 *Robert Hugh Shirley, and has issue:

1f *Michael Bruce; *b* 1 Nov 1964

1f *Katherine Judith; *b* 25 Dec 1966

2e *Mary Bridget [Mrs John Edwards, 32 Ormond Ave, Hampton, Middx]; *b* 24 Nov 1935; BM, BCh, DCH 1962; *m* 1st 1964 (*divorce* 1974) Randall Clive Smith; *m* 2nd 1975 *John Robin Edwards

2d Anne, Cmdt JWO BRCS and OStJ WW II; *b* 30 Dec 1910; *m* 1st 2 July 1938 her cousin Lt David Edmund Cole-Hamilton, DSC and Bar, RN (*see below*); *m* 2nd 24 July 1959 Oswald Graham Noel Turnbull, MC, (*d* 1970), 3rd s of Reginald March Turnbull, of Whitby, and Highgate, by Frances Clitheroe Kesterson, of St Kilda, Melbourne, Australia, and *d* 19–

3d *Mary, TD [Mrs Donald Girling, Highworth Farm, Charlwood, Surrey], served as Chief Cmdt ATS 1939–46; *b* 2 Feb 1913; *m* 1st 25 April 1936 (*divorce* 1952) Lt-Col John Carew-Jones, TD, RA, er s of Osman Carew-Jones; *m* 2nd 12 Dec 1952 John Locke Lovibond, TD, MD, FRCP, s of Maj JL Lovibond, TD, of Underwood, Hexham, Northumberland (*d* 4 May 1954); *m* 3rd 6 Oct 1956 Col Donald Barry Girling, MC, TD, RA (TA) (*d* 1986), er s of AW Girling, of Southwold, Suffolk

4d *Elizabeth Peace [Mrs Geoffrey Armstrong, Axmas Cottage, Rusper, Sussex]; MFH Surrey Union; *b* 11 Nov 1918; *m* 1st 15 April 1939 Lt-Cdr Rodney Athelstan Price, RN (*ka* April 1943), yr s of Athelstan Elder Price, of Culverwood House, nr Hertford, and has:

1e *David George [David Price Esq, Woodcock, Thirsk, Yorks]; 2nd Lt Black Watch (TA); *b* 22 March 1940; *educ* Wellington and Emmanuel Coll Cambridge (BA 1963 MA 1967); *m* 14 March 1970 *Diana Catherine Symington, dau of Thomas Alastair Symington Davie, of Grangehill, Beith, Ayrshire, and has:

1f *Toby Charles Rodney; *b* 1972

2f *Simon James Esward; *b* 1974

4d (cont.) Mrs Rodney Price *m* 2nd 16 Nov 1945 Col Geoffrey Russell Armstrong, DSO, MC, TD, HAC, est s of William Robinson Armstrong, of Banstead, Surrey, and has further issue:

2e *Johny [Johny Armstrong Esq, Woodlands House, Woodlands Lane, Colgate, Horsham, W Sussex]; *b* 16 Oct 1946; *educ* Wellington and Emmanuel Coll Cambridge (BA 1968); *m* 1976 *Elsie Borodale, dau of Frederick S Peters, of Englewood, NJ, and has:

1f *Geoffrey Read; *b* 1980

2f *Graham Whitney; *b* 1983

1e *Ruth Margaret [Mrs Harry Calvert, Holmbush, Faygate, W Sussex RH12 4SE]; *b* 24 Jan 1949; *m* 1976 *Henry (Harry) Clifton Calvert (*see* BROWN, Bt) and has:

1f *Piers Henry; *b* 20 Oct 1977; *educ* Harrow and Edinburgh U

1f *Henrietta Amelia; *b* 2 Dec 1980; *educ* Benenden

3c Richard Mervyn (Ven); Hon CF, Rector Llangattock, Breconshire 1913–48, T/CF 1915–16, Canon Brecon 1941, Archdeacon Brecon 1947–55; *b* 14 Dec 1877; *educ* Haileybury and Worcester Coll Oxford (BA 1901, MA 1903); *m* 1st 12 Oct 1911 Margaret, JP (*d* 29 July 1954), dau of Edmund Grove Bennett, of The Close, Salisbury, and had:

1d Richard Arthur; Maj Cameronians (TA), Second Master Fettes; *b* 24 Oct 1912; *educ* Marlborough and Worcester Coll Oxford (BA 1935); *m* 9 Aug 1947 *(Ruth) Kathleen Betty [Mrs Richard Cole-Hamilton, Hawthorn Villa, 386 Ferry Rd, Edinburgh EH5 3QG], only dau of Sir William Lorenzo Parker, 3rd Bt of Shenstone (*qv*) and *d* 1992, leaving:

1e +Robin [Robin Cole-Hamilton Esq, 39 Fawnbrake Ave, London SE24 OBE]; *b* 24 Dec 1948; *educ* Trin Coll Glenalmond; *m* 1982 *Helen, dau of Rev Canon Gerald Archer Luckett, of Meonstoke, Hants, and has:

1f +Jonathan Archer; *b* 1986

1f *Katharine Faith; *b* 1983

2e +(Richard) Simon [Simon Cole-Hamilton Esq, Elm Cottage, 54 Culcabock Ave, Inverness IV2 3RQ]; *b* 4 May 1951; *educ* Trin Coll Glenalmond; *m* 1982 *Anni, dau of J G M Watt, of Edinburgh, and has:

1f *Joanna Ruth; *b* 1983

2f *Sarah Constance; *b* 1985

3e +William Mervyn John [William Cole-Hamilton Esq, Lethenty Cottage, Fyvie, Aberdeenshire AB53 8NE]; *b* 17 Oct 1954; *educ* Trin Coll Glenalmond; *m* 1978 *Jill, yst dau of Dr J C Johnston, and has:

1f +Richard James; *b* 1983

1f *Emma Judith; *b* 1985

2d David Edmund, DSC (1941) and bar (1942); Lt RN WW II (despatches); *b* 6 April 1914; *m* 2 July 1938 *Anne (*m* 2nd 24 July 1959 Oswald Graham Noel Turnbull (*d* 1970), 3rd s of Reginald March Turnbull, of Whitby and Highgate), 2nd dau of George William Cole-Hamilton, JP (*see above*), and was *kas* in the Mediterranean, June 1942, leaving:

1e +Michael Anthony [Lt Michael Cole-Hamilton RN, 355 Park Ave, Newmarket, Ont L3Y 1V4, Canada; The Ridge, RR2 Lyndhurst, Ont KOE 1NO]; Lt RN; *b* 16 July 1940; *educ* Bradfield; *m* 25 May 1963 *Jane Elizabeth Mary, er dau of Arthur Maurice Stewart-Wallace, MD, FRCP, of The Moot House, Ditchling, Sussex, and has:

1f +William Michael David; *b* 28 Nov 1967; *educ* Queen's U Kingston, Ont

1f *(Ellen) Susannah; *b* 21 Dec 1965; *educ* McGill (BA); *m* 1993 *Graham Lunt, er s of Ronald Lunt, of Boscheok Farm, Duiwelskoof, S Africa

2f *Alexandra Jane; *b* 21 March 1971

3d +Anthony Mervyn [Lt-Cdr Anthony Cole-Hamilton RN, Marine Cottage, Alleyn's Rd, Stevenage, Herts]; RN WW II (despatches); *b* 25 Nov 1919; *m* 1st 25 Nov 1944 Monica Mary, 3rd Offr WRNS (*d* as the result of an accident 8 Sept 1954), dau of Lt-Col John Rogers Cartwright, DSO, of Seafield House, Seaton, Devon, and had:

1e +David John; lecturer inorganic chemistry Liverpool U, Irvine Prof Chemistry St Andrews; *b* 22 May 1948; *educ* Haileybury; *m* 1973 *Elizabeth Ann; dau of Bruce Lloyd Brown, of Victoria, BC, Canada, and has issue:

1f +Alexander Geoffrey; *b* 1977

2f +Nicholas Anthony Michael; *b* 1986

1f *Rose Monica Elizabeth; *b* 1979

2f *Sian Fiona Non; *b* 1986

1e *Susan Joan; *b* 19 Aug 1945; *m* 1st 1969 (*divorce* 1978) Andrew Wallace; *m* 2nd 1978 *Gerard Garra

2e *Isobel Margaret; *b* 7 Jan 1950

3e *Patricia Anne; *b* 6 Nov 1952; *m* 1982 *F Tomlin and has:

1f *Lucy Sarah Patricia; *b* 1980

2f *Alison Kirsty; *b* 1982

3d (cont.) Lt-Cdr Anthony Cole-Hamilton *m* 2nd 7 April 1956 *Angela Elizabeth, formerly w of Michael AG Hanschell and dau of Joshua Isidore Baeza, FRCS, DPH, of Barbados

1d Joan Margaret, MBE; with FO; *b* 15 Oct 1917; *kas* in an air crash 17 July 1945

3c (cont.) The Ven Richard Cole-Hamilton *m* 2nd 12 July 1955 Elsie Irene (*d* 28 June 1975), widow of Richard Gladstone Warner, of Condover, Shrewsbury, and dau of William Henry Pendlebury, of Shrewsbury, and *d* 5 Sept 1959

4c John Claud; Cdr RN WWs I and II; *b* 24 March 1879; *m* 23 Nov 1915 Evelyn (*d* 30 June 1968, aged 91), yr dau of Christopher Wolston, MD, of Bayswater, and *d* 23 May 1951

5c Charles (Rev), MC (1919); Rector Fawley, Hants, 1934, CF 4th Cl, TA R O RAMC 1914, T/CF WW I; *b* 15 Jan 1885; *d* unm 19 April 1940

5c John Isaac; *b* 12 July 1851; *m* 21 Feb 1884 Elinor Bourne (*d* 20 Dec 1952 in her 96th year), dau of Henry Royds, of Elm House, Wavertree, and *d* 1 May 1936, leaving:

1c Hugh Arthur Willoughby, DSO (1919); Lt-Col 2nd Bn Yorks and Lancs Regt, WW I 1914–18 (despatches three times, wounded and a POW 1918), WW II (invalided); *b* 10 Oct 1887; *m* 27 Sept 1932 *Eileen Mary, only child of Rev Precentor Charles Vereker Chester Atkinson, Rector Kilpeacon, Co Limerick, and *dsp* 7 July 1947

2c John Beresford, CB (1943), CBE (1941); AVM RAF, RN, WW I (despatches, twice), WW II; *b* 1 Dec 1894; *m* 12 June 1928 Hilda Violet Leslie (*d* 22 April 1945), yr dau of Charles Leslie Fox, of Rumwell Hall, Taunton, and *d* 22 Aug 1945, leaving:

1d *Diana Patricia Selina [Mrs Diana Ford, The Old Vicarage, Greywell, Basingstoke, Hants]; *b* 31 Aug 1932; *educ* Girton Coll Cambridge (BArch 1953); *m* 2 Nov 1957 (*divorce* 1968) Stephen Wilbraham Ford, s of Maj John Meredith Randle Ford, OBE, MC, of Bowhay, Iwerne Minster, Dorset, and has:

1e *Jonathan Hugo; *b* 8 Sept 1960

1e *Joanna Margaret Randle; *b* 13 Nov 1958

1c Margaret Selina; Assist Administrator WRNS and WRAF, WW I in FANY, Croix Civique, Medaille de la Reine Elisabeth (Belgium) and Medaille de la Reconnaissance (France); *b* 18 Nov 1884; *d* unm 11 June 1974

1b Emily Harriet; *m* 29 April 1858 John Gordon Bowen, of Burt House, Co Donegal, and *d* 28 Sept 1885, leaving issue

2b Selina; *m* 31 Dec 1870 Capt Robert George Gaussen, Gren Gds, of Brookmans Park, Herts, and *d* 21 Jan 1915, leaving issue. He *d* 10 Jan 1906

3b Letitia Grace; *m* 17 Aug 1869 Hon Sir Henry George Louis Crichton, KCB (*see* ERNE, E) and *d* 13 Jan 1888, leaving issue

2a Richard COLE-HAMILTON later CHALONER (deed poll 1932), of Kingsfort, Co Meath, JP; High Sheriff 1842, Lt 12th Lancers; *b* 25 April 1810; *m* Feb 1835 Henrietta (*d* 22 Nov 1890), 2nd dau of Charles Arthur Tisdall, of Charlesfort, Kells, Co Meath, and *dsp* 29 Nov 1879

(1) Letitia; *m* Aug 1815 Major Randall Stafford, of Tully, Co Cavan, and *d* 1853

(2) Elizabeth Ann; *m* 1820 Henry Slade, and *d* 1849

(3) Isabella; *m* James Hamilton, and *d* 1827

The 1st BARON *d* 30 Nov 1767; his er s,

WILLIAM WILLOUGHBY COLE, **1st Earl of Enniskillen**, so *cr* 18 Aug 1789, also earlier 20 July 1776 VISCOUNT ENNISKILLEN, Co Fermanagh (both I); *m* 3 Nov 1763 Anne (*d* Sept 1802) sis of 1st Earl Belmore (*qv*), and had, with two other sons and another dau:

1 JOHN WILLOUGHBY, **2nd Earl**

2 Galbraith Lowry (Sir), GCB; Gen, Col 27th Foot, Govr Gravesend and Tilbury, Mauritius and Cape of Good Hope, thanks of Parl for services Peninsular War; *b* 1 May 1772; *m* 15 June 1815 Lady Frances Harris (*d* 1 Nov 1847), 2nd dau of 1st Earl of Malmesbury (*qv*), and *d* 4 Oct 1842, having had, with other issue:

(1) Arthur Lowry, CB; Col 17th Regt, Kt Medjidie; *b* 24 Aug 1817; *m* 29 Nov 1854 Elizabeth Frances (*d* 22 May 1889), dau of V-Adml Villiers Francis Hatton, and *d* 30 March 1885, leaving, with other issue:

1a Arthur Willoughby George Lowry, CB, DSO; Col, T/Brig-Gen, Roy Welch Fus, Cmdt N Nigeria Regt 1904–07, Burma 1885–87, W Africa 1900, Boer War 1901, W Africa 1906 and WW I; *b* 29 Nov 1860; *m* 28 Feb 1908 Mary Gertrude (*d* 26 Dec 1941), widow of Lt-Col Charles Cecil Hayford Thorold (*see* THOROLD, Bt), and dau of Thomas Browning, of Sale, Cheshire, and *dsp* of wounds recd in action 9 May 1915

1a Florence Kate Lowry; *m* 17 April 1888 Rev Frank Henry Payne-Gallwey (*see* FRANKLAND-PAYNE-GALLWEY, Bt), and *d* 10 Dec 1927, leaving issue

2a Mabel Henrietta Lowry; *d* unm Sept 1952

3 William Montgomery (Very Rev); Dean Waterford; *d* 1804

1 Sarah; *m* 1790 Owen Wynne, MP; and *d* 14 March 1833

2 Elizabeth Anne; *m* 1788 Col Richard Magennis and *d* 1807, leaving issue. He *d* 6 March 1831

3 Florence; *m* 1797 Blaney Townley Balfour, of Townley Hall, Co Louth, and *d* 1 March 1862, aged 83. He *d* 22 Dec 1856

4 Henrietta Frances; *m* 1805 5th Baron Lucas of Crudwell (*qv*) and *d* 2 July 1848

The 1st EARL *d* 22 May 1803; his s,

JOHN WILLOUGHBY COLE, **2nd Earl of Enniskillen**, KP; rep I peer; *b* 23 March 1768; *cr* BARON GRINSTEAD, of Grinstead, Co Wilts, 11 Aug 1815 (UK), Ld Lt and custos rotulorum Co Fermanagh; *m* 15 Oct 1805 Charlotte (*d* Jan 1817), 4th dau of 1st Earl of Uxbridge (*see* ANGLESEY, M), and had:

1 WILLIAM WILLOUGHBY, **3rd Earl**

2 Henry Arthur; MP Enniskillen 1844–51 and Fermanagh 1855–80, Lt-Col 7th Hus and 12th Foot; *b* 14 Feb 1809; *d* unm 2 July 1890

3 John Lowry; MP Enniskillen; *b* 8 June 1813; *d* unm 28 Nov 1882

4 Lowry Balfour; *b* 1815; *d* 1818

1 Jane Anne Louisa Florence; *d* 1891

The 2nd EARL *d* 31 March 1840; his est s,

WILLIAM WILLOUGBY COLE, **3rd Earl of Enniskillen**; DCL, FRS FGS, LLD, Hon Col 3rd Bn Royal Inniskilling Fus; *b* 25 Jan 1807; *m* 1st 16 Jan 1844 Jane (*d* 13 May 1855), est dau of James A Casamaijor, and had:

1 John Willoughby Michael, *Viscount Cole*; *b* 16 Dec 1844; *d* 15 April 1850

2 LOWRY EGERTON, **4th Earl**

3 Arthur Edward Casamaijor, JP Norfolk and Co Fermanagh; Lt Rifle Bde; *b* 9 March 1851; *m* 24 April 1877 Adelaide (*d* 20 March 1938), yst dau of James Blackwood, of Melbourne, Australia, and *d* 17 Aug 1908, leaving:

(1) Lowry Arthur Casamaijor, MBE (1919); T/Lt RASC, and Staff Lt 1918, Order Black Star; *b* 10 April 1878; *m* 12 April 1910 Adelaide Grizel (*d* 17 Dec 1965), only dau of Frederick Pratt Barlow by Rachel Maria, dau of Capt Catesby Paget (*see* ANGLESEY, M), and *d* 25 Sept 1955, leaving:

1a +Arthur Lowry Frederick (Rev); CF Assist Chaplain RMA Sandhurst 1952–54, Sr Chaplain Cyrenaica District, MELF 1950–52, Vicar Wroxham 1954–59, Assist Priest St Paul's Knightsbridge 1959–60, Diocesan Chaplain, Coventry Diocese 1960–64, Assist Priest All Saints' Margaret Street, London W1, 1964; *b* 26 Feb 1911; *educ* Eton

1a Rachel Adelaide; *b* 21 Sept 1912; *m* 1st 25 Oct 1939 (*divorce* 1948) Antony John Cecil Prickett, s of R-Adml Cecil Burnaby Prickett, of Loch Eye House, Fearn, Ross-shire, and had:

1b *Jonathan Willoughby; *b* 3 Aug 1941; *educ* King's Canterbury; *m* 10 Aug 1962 *Christina Mary, dau of Noel James de Mille, of Dunbreck, Glasgow, and has:

1c *David Burnaby; *b* 26 Sept 1964

1c *Katharine Christina; *b* April 1966

2c *Clare Harriet; *b* July 1968

1a (cont.) Mrs Rachel Prickett *m* 2nd 7 Dec 1963 *Lt-Cdr Harry Brian Baker RN (ret), s of George Percival Baker, of Sevenoaks, Kent

2a *Elizabeth Joan; *b* 2 Nov 1919

3a Florence Margaret; *b* 9 Jan 1923; *m* 1st 7 Jan 1948 (*divorce* 1959) John Walter, er s of John Walter, of Bear Wood, Berks, and has:

1b *John; *b* 23 Feb 1953; *educ* Eton

3a (cont.) Mrs Florence Walter *m* 2nd 30 April 1959 Vladimir Georgieff Daskaloff

1 Charlotte Jane; *m* 1 Dec 1874 James Hugh Smith-Barry, bro of 1st and last Baron Barrymore, and *d* 3 Sept 1933, leaving issue. He *d* 30 July 1927

2 Florence Mary; *m* 28 Dec 1870 4th Earl Erne (*qv*) of Crom Castle and *d* 23 March 1924, leaving issue

3 Alice Elizabeth; *m* 30 June 1891 Rt Hon Evelyn Ashley (*see* SHAFTESBURY, E) and *d* 25 Aug 1931, leaving issue

4 Jane Evelyn; *d* unm 19 March 1941

The **3rd Earl** *m* 2nd 5 Sept 1865 Hon Mary Emma Brodrick (*d* 25 May 1896), est dau and coheir of 6th Viscount Midleton (*qv*), and *d* 12 Nov 1886

His est surv son,

LOWRY EGERTON COLE, **4th Earl of Enniskillen**, KP, JP, DL Co Fermanagh; High Sheriff 1870, MP Enniskillen 1880–85, Hon Col 4th Royal Inniskilling Fus, formerly Lt Rifle Bde; *b* 21 Dec 1845; *m* 12 July 1869 Charlotte Marion (*d* 30 Jan 1937), dau and coheir of Douglas Baird (*see* KINTORE, E), and *d* 28 April 1924, having had:

1 William Willoughby; *b* 26, *d* 28 June 1870

2 JOHN HENRY MICHAEL COLE, **5th Earl of Enniskillen**, CMG (1916); *b* 10 Sept 1876; *educ* Eton; Lt-Col NI Horse, formerly Lt 7th Hus, ADC to Ld Lt Ireland 1918, Boer War and WW I (despatches); *m* 1st 11 April 1907 (*divorce* 1931) Irene Frances (*d* 15 Aug 1937), 2nd dau of Alfred Edward Miller Mundy, DL, of Shipley Hall, Derbys; *m* 2nd 4 May 1932 Mary Cicely (*d* 18 July 1963), widow of Maj Thomas Syers, RA, and dau of Hugh Neville, and *d* 19 Feb 1963, having by his 1st w had:

(1) Michael Galbraith Lowry, *Viscount Cole*; Lt Irish Gds WW II; *b* 25 Nov 1921; *educ* Eton; *d* unm 26 Aug 1956

(1) Ann Florence; *b* 12 Dec 1910; *m* 5 July 1935 (*divorce* 1950) Sir Jack James, KCVO, CB (formerly known as John Hastings James, CB), s of Clement Fletcher James, and had:

1a *Michael John Frederick Lowry; *b* 1941; *m* 28 April 1965 *Raye V, dau of P V W Donaldson

(2) *Frances Jane [The Lady Frances Hanmer, 1 Church Way, Grendon, Northampton]; Subaltern (Hon Jr Cdr) ATS WW II; *b* 16 Dec 1914; *m* 10 July 1954 as his 2nd w, G/Capt Henry Ivan Hanmer, DFC, RAF and bar (*see* HANMER, Bt), and has issue

(3) Kathleen Irene; *b* 17 May 1919; *m* 1st 3 July 1940 (*divorce* 1948) Capt Desmond Ralph Lloyd Verney, yst s of Sir Harry Lloyd Verney, GCVO (*see* VERNEY, of Claydon House, Bt); *m* 2nd 21 July 1948 Tadeusz Borkowski, s of Romuald Borkowski, JP, of Warsaw, Poland, and *d* 2 July 1976

3 Galbraith Lowry Egerton; Lt 10th Hus Boer War; *b* 8 March 1881; *m* 7 Dec 1917 Lady Eleanor Balfour, dau of 2nd Earl of Balfour (*qv*), and *d* 6 Oct 1929, leaving:

(1) DAVID LOWRY, **6th Earl**

(2) +ARTHUR GERALD [Arthur Cole Esq, 2 Orchard Brae, Edinburgh EH4 1NY]; Capt Irish Gds; *b* 15 Nov 1920; *educ* Eton; heir presumptive; *m* 5 Feb 1949 *Prudence Tobina, only dau of Algernon Richard Aubrey Cartwright (*see* BUXTON, Bt) and has:

1a +Berkeley Arthur [Berkeley Cole Esq, 151 Battersea Rise, London SW11 1HP]; *b* 17 Dec 1949; *educ* Milton Abbey; *m* 14 Oct 1978 *Hon Cecilia Ridley, est dau of 4th Viscount Ridley (*qv*) and has:

1b +Joshua Berkeley; *b* 1986

2b +Richard David; *b* 1991

2a +Hugh Galbraith; *b* 4 June 1954; *educ* Milton Abbey

3a +Richard Lowry; *b* 2 June 1956; *educ* Eton; *m* 1st 1977 (*divorce* 1988) Susan Elizabeth, dau of David Allen, of Nairobi; *m* 2nd 1988 (*divorce* 19–) Karen, dau of Ernest Robert Victor Ingram, of Chippenham, Wilts, and has by his 1st w:

1b +Arthur Berkeley David; *b* 1983
1a *Marian Rose [Mrs Bruce Hobson, Rosslyn Est, Box 63707, Nairobi, Kenya]; *b* 24 March 1951; *m* 1979 *Bruce Hobson and has:
1b *Amelia Rose; *b* 1986
4 Reginald Berkeley; MLA Kenya Colony, Lt 9th Lancers Boer War 1900; *b* 26 Nov 1882; *d* 27 April 1925
1 Charlotte Jane Christian; *b* 5 March 1872; *d* 27 April 1892
2 Kathleen Mary; *b* 25 Nov 1873; *m* 1 Aug 1903 Lt-Col Charles Walter Villiers, CBE, DSO and *d* 17 June 1956, leaving issue (*see* CLARENDON, E)
3 Marion; *b* 22, *d* 30 Dec 1874
4 Florence Ame; *b* 3 Feb 1878; *m* 11 July 1899 3rd Baron Delamere (*qv*) and *d* 17 May 1914, leaving issue
5 Muriel Augusta Mary; *b* 28 Aug 1879; *d* 21 April 1880

The 5th EARL's n,
DAVID LOWRY COLE, **6th Earl of Enniskillen**, MBE; *b* 10 Sept 1918; *educ* Eton and Trin Coll Cambridge (BA Ag); Capt Irish Gds WW II, 1953–55 Kenya Emergency as Prov Cmdt Kenya Police Reserve, MLC Kenya 1961–63, formerly memb Kenya Meat Commn, Executive Kenya NFU, Kenya Bd Ag and Land and Ag Bank Kenya, dir Solio Ranch Ltd, memb Fermanagh CC 1963–69, DL 1963–78, JP 1972–78 Co Fermanagh, Capt UDR 1971–73; *m* 1st 31 July 1940 (*divorce* 1955) Sonia Mary (*d* 1982), dau of Major Thomas Syers, RA, and the Countess of Enniskillen (*see* above), and had:
1 ANDREW JOHN GALBRAITH COLE, **7th and present Earl of Enniskillen**
1 *Linda Mary [The Lady Linda Muir, Park House, Blair Drummond, Stirling, Perths]; *b* 26 March 1944; *m* 29 Aug 1975, as his 2nd w, Sir Richard James Kay Muir, 4th Bt (*qv*) and has issue

The **6th Earl** *m* 2nd 7 May 1955 Nancy Henderson (*d* 24 Feb 1998), former Washington and UN correspondent *New York Times*, former assist attaché and V-Consul US Foreign Serv, author: *Florence Court, My Irish Home* (1972) and *Amulree and its Church* (1990), dau of Dr John Alexander MacLennan, of Bridgeport, Conn., and *d* 30 May 1989

ERNE

Arms: Arg. a lion rampant az. **Crest:** A dragon's head couped vert, emitting fire from the mouth and ears ppr. **Supporters:** Two lions az., each crowned with an earl's coronet ppr. **Motto:** God send grace. **Creations:** B. (I) 15 July 1768 and (UK) (Fermanagh of Lisnaskea) 13 Jan 1876, V. (I) 6 Jan 1781, E. (I) 19 Aug 1789.

THE 6TH EARL ERNE OF CROM CASTLE, Co Fermanagh, **Viscount Erne of Crom Castle, Baron Erne of Crom Castle**, Co Fermanagh, and **Baron Fermanagh of Lisnaskea**, Co Fermanagh (Henry George Victor John Crichton, JP (Co Fermanagh)) [The Rt Hon The Earl Erne JP, Crom Castle, Newtown Butler, Co Fermanagh BT92 8AP]; *b* 9 July 1937 (HM GEORGE VI stood sponsor); *s* f 1940; *educ* Eton; Lt NI Horse 1960–68, Page of Honour to HM THE QUEEN Aug 1952–Jan 1954, memb Roy Ulster Ag Soc and Roy Forestry Soc; Ld Lt Co Fermanagh; *m* 1st 5 Nov 1958 (*divorce* 1980) Camilla Marguerite, er dau of W/Cdr Owen George Endicott Roberts, RAF, and gdau of Capt Marshall Owen Roberts, Scots Gds (*see* ATHOLL, D); *m* 2nd 21 June 1980 *Anna Karin, formerly w of — Hitchcock and dau of Sven Andres Bjorck, of Gavle, Sweden, and by his 1st w has issue:
1 +JOHN HENRY MICHAEL NINIAN, *Viscount Crichton* [Viscount Crichton, Flat 4, 40 Harcourt Terrace, London SW10 9JR]; *b* 19 June 1971; *educ* Sunningdale Prep Sch, Shiplake Coll, L'Institut de Touraine, Tours
1 *Cleone Lucinda; *b* 27 Aug 1959; *m* 1989 *Richard F Versen and has:
(1) *Frederick James; *b* 1992
2 *Davina Jane [The Lady Davina Scarr, Lee Park Lodge, Lee, Hants SO51 9ZD]; *b* 25 June 1961; *m* 1990 *Nicholas J R Scarr, er s of Peter R R Scarr, and has issue:
(1) *Oliver Peter Renforth; *b* 1992
(1) *Sabrina Katherine Renforth; *b* 1993
3 *Katherine Patricia [The Lady Katherine Townsend-Rose, Maxton Westend, Maxton, St Boswells, Roxburghshire TD6 0RL]; *b* 4 Nov 1962; *m* 1989 *Jonathan C Townsend-Rose, s of Colin Townsend-Rose, and has:
(1) *Rory Dixon Crichton; *b* 1993
(1) *Alexandra Lucy Flora; *b* 1992
4 *Tara Guinevere; *b* 9 May 1967; *m* 1993 *James William Loyd, yr s of Christopher Lewis Loyd, MC, of Lockinge, Wantage, Berks, and Mrs Simon Burne, of Charlton, Malmesbury, Wilts

Lineage: THURSTANUS de CRICHTON witnessed the foundation charter of the Abbacy of Holyrood House 1128

WILLIAM de CRICHTON; feudal Ld of Crichton 1240; had:

THOMAS de CRICHTON; one of the great Scottish barons (magnates rather than peers of Parl) who swore fealty to EDWARD I of England 1296; *m* Eda — and *d* *c* 1300, leaving:
1 NICHOLAS, of whom presently
2 William, ancestor of the Marquesses of Bute (*qv*)
3 Thomas, Burgess of Berwick, had a s (William, Rector Crichton)

The est s,
NICHOLAS de CRICHTON; *fl temp* ROBERT I (THE BRUCE) (1306–31); had:
Sir JOHN de CRICHTON; feudal Ld of Crichton *c* 1340; *d* *c* 1358, leaving, with a yr s (John, of Hounam and Crailing, Roxburghshire, 1367):

Sir WILLIAM de CRICHTON; was granted lands of W Burnstoun, Pennycuik (confirmed by charter 29 March 1373); *m* Margaret — (who had a charter 20 July 1410 of the lands of Gilbertown (afterwards called Brunston), Co Edinburgh) and had:
1 John (Sir), of Crichton; *m* Christian — and had:
(1) Sir WILLIAM CRICHTON of Crichton, 1st LORD CRICHTON (S), so *cr* between 1443 and 1447; Ld Chllr Scotland 1437; ancestor of the 1st and last Viscount of Frendraught and Lord Crichton (*see* OXFUIRD, V); had:
1a Agnes; *m* 1st just prior to 17 Feb 1449/50 2nd Lord Glamis (*see* STRATMORE AND KINGHORNE, E); *m* 2nd 20 Oct 1487 Walter Ker of Cessford (*see* LOTHIAN, M)
2 Stephen, of Carnis; f of:
(1) GEORGE CRICHTON, 1st and last EARL OF CAITHNESS of the 1452 *cr*, Ld High Adml Scotland
3 Thomas; living 1373
4 Edward, of Burnstown/Brunston and Gilbertown; *fl* 1419 and 1425; *d* 1447, leaving:
(1) Thomas, of Brunston; living 27 April 1450; *d* 1456, leaving:
1a George, of Brunston; in holy orders; *d* 19 Oct 1461
2a John, of Brunston and Daltonwick; *d* 24 March 1487, leaving:
1b EDWARD, his heir
2b John of Newbigging; *d* on or after 18 Jan 1504/5

JOHN CRICHTON's er s,
EDWARD CRICHTON of Brunston; *m* Agnes Cockburn, dau of the Laird of Ormiston, and *d* 1506, leaving an est surv s:

JOHN CRICHTON of Brunston; *m* Janet, dau of Sir Alexander Hamilton of Innerwick, E Lothian, and *d* May 1536, having had issue:

ALEXANDER CRICHTON of Brunston; Protestant, originally supported, later opposed Cardinal Beaton; diplomat; attainted 14 Dec 1548 (attainder reversed 5 Dec 1558); *m* by 1530 Janet, dau of John Pennycuik of that Ilk, and *d* by 26 Jan 1554, having had issue:

JOHN CRICHTON of Brunston and Stanyhil; sold his estates 8 Nov 1597; *m* Margaret Adamson, dau of the Laird of Graycrook, near Edinburgh, and *d* by 30 May 1604, having had, with two other sons:
1 James; settled at Aghalane Castle, Co Fermanagh, by 17 Aug 1616; *m* *c* 20 May 1565 Jane, dau of Robert Fairlie, Laird of Braid, and had issue
2 Abraham, of Dromboory, on Lough Erne, settled in Ireland by 17 Aug 1616; *m* Nichola — and *d* by 1631, leaving:
(1) ABRAHAM
(1) Jane; *m* by 1656 Marmaduke Greene, of Druminisklin, Co Fermanagh (*d* 24 June1681), and had issue
(2) Elizabeth; *m* 9 May 1670 Hugh Hamill, of Lifford, Co Donegal

The only son,
ABRAHAM CR(E)ICHTON/CREIGHTOUN, of Dromboory and later, through marriage, Crom Castle on Lough Erne (previously granted 1624 to Bp Spottiswoode); Co Fermanagh: High Sheriff 1673 and MP 1692, MP Enniskillen 1695, defended Crom against JAMES II's Army 22 March 1689 and again 28 July following; cmded a Williamite regt Battle of Aughrim, Co Galway, 12 July 1691 (Jacobite defeat); *m* 1655 Mary, widow of Thomas Perkins, of Lifford, and dau of James Spottiswoode, Bp Clogher, by his 2nd w Elizabeth Staunton, and *d* March 1705, having had, with other issue:
1 James; Capt in f's regt Aughrim; *m* 26 Oct 1686 Hester, est dau of Sir John Hume, 2nd Bt, of Castle Hume, Co Fermanagh, by Sidney, dau and coheir of James Hamilton, of Manor Hamilton, and *dvp* 1702, having had:
(1) John, of Crom Castle; High Sheriff 1715; *dsp* between 14 Nov 1715 and 19 March 1715/6
(1) Mary; *m* Oliver Moore, of Salestown, Co Meath (*d* Dec 1756), and *d* between 17 July 1770 and 1771, leaving issue
(2) Sidney; *m* Gilbert Eccles, s of Gilbert Eccles, of Shanoke, Co Fermanagh
2 Abraham; *m* 9 Aug 1680 Mary, only surv child of Thomas Golborne, of Spring Town, Co Tyrone, by Elizabeth, dau of James Spottiswoode, Bp of Clogher, and *dsp* 1684
3 DAVID
1 Jane; *m* John Hamilton, of Brown Hall, Co Donegal, and had issue
2 Marianna; *m* Hugh Willoughby, of Callow, and had issue

The yst s,
DAVID CR(E)ICHTON, of Crom Castle; Maj-Gen; *s* his nephew 1716; helped defend Crom Castle 1689; Master and Govr Roy Hosp, MP Agher, Co Tyrone, 1695 and Lifford 1695–1728, Hon LLD Trin Coll Dublin; *m* by 1695 Katherine (*d* March 1759) sis of 1st Baron Southwell of Castle Mattress (*see* SOUTHWELL, V), and *d* 1 June 1728, having had, with other issue:
1 ABRAHAM, **1st Baron**

1 Meliora; *bapt* 24 Sept 1706; *m* March 1742 Nicholas Ward, of Knockballymore, Co Fermanagh, and *d* 1792, having had issue. He *d* 1751

The only surv son,

ABRAHAM CR(E)ICHTON, **1st Baron Erne of Crom Castle**, Co Fermanagh (I), so *cr* 15 July 1768; MP Lifford 1727–68; *b c* 1700; Govr Co Fermanagh; *m* 1st 31 July 1729 Elizabeth (*d* 6 Aug 1761), est dau of John Rogerson, Ld Ch Justice King's Bench, and had, with other issue:

1 JOHN, **1st Earl**

2 Abraham; Registrar of Forfeitures, High Sheriff Co Fermanagh 1774, MP Lifford; *m* 5 Nov 1793 Mary, widow of — Ashenhurst, and *d* 29 Aug 1810, leaving:

(1) Elizabeth Charlotte; *m* Aug 1815 Loftus Anthony Tottenham, of Glenade, and *d* 29 Sept 1819, leaving issue

1 Charlotte; *bapt* 15 April 1738; *m* 1st 21 May 1766 Edward Madden, of Roslea Manor, Springrove (*d* 1790); *m* 2nd March 1793 Edward King, MP, and *dsp* 24 March 1819

The **1st Baron** *m* 2nd 7 Sep 1763 Jane (*d* by 8 March 1800), widow of Arthur Acheson (*see* GOSFORD, E) and only dau of John King, of Charlestown, Co Roscommon, and *d* 10 June 1772

His er surv s,

JOHN CRICHTON, **1st Earl Erne of Crom Castle**, so *cr* 19 Aug 1789, as also earlier 6 Jan 1781 VISCOUNT ERNE OF CROM CASTLE, Co Fermanagh (both I), PC (I 1804), MP Lifford 1761–72; *b* 1731; *m* 1st 25 Feb 1761 Catherine (*d* 15 June 1775), 2nd dau of Rt Rev Robert Howard, DD, Bp Elphin, and sis of 1st Viscount Wicklow (*see* 1970 edn WICKLOW, E), and *d* 15 Sept 1828, leaving, with three other daus:

1 ABRAHAM CRICHTON, **2nd Earl Erne of Crom Castle**; MP Lifford 1790–97; *b* 10 May 1765; *d* unm 10 June 1842

2 John; Lt-Col, Govr Hurst Castle; *b* 28 June 1772; *m* 9 Dec 1797 Jane (*bur* 30 Nov 1849), 2nd dau of Walter Weldon, and *d* 10 May 1833, leaving, with other issue:

(1) JOHN, **3rd Earl**

(2) Henry; granted with surv siblings rank of earl's dau/yr s Aug 1842; Maj 6th Dragoons; *b* 1 Oct 1804; *m* 24 July 1849 Elizabeth (*d* 30 Oct 1860), yst dau of Lt-Col Hawkshaw, of Divernagh, Co Armagh, and *dsp* 23 Feb 1864

1b Jane Anne; *b* 19 Oct 1798; *m* 20 Aug 1820 Robert Fowler, of Rahinston, Co Meath, est s of Rt Rev Robert Fowler, DD, Bp Ossory, and *d* 19 May 1828, leaving issue. He *d* 6 Feb 1863

(2) Catherine; *b* 5 Feb 1800; *m* 31 May 1825 Rev Francis Saunderson, RD and Rector Kildallon, and *d* 14 Oct 1860. He *dsp* 22 Dec 1873

(3) Mary; *b* 22 Nov 1808; *m* 17 Jan 1856 Rev John H King (*see* KING, Bt) and *d* 7 Nov 1898

1 Elizabeth; *b* 20 June 1762; *m* 19 May 1783 James King and *d* 28 Jan 1794, leaving issue (*see* KING, Bt)

The **1st Earl** *m* 2nd 22 Feb 1776 Lady Mary Caroline Hervey (*d* 10 Jan 1842), est dau of 4th Earl of Bristol (*see* BRISTOL, M), and by her had:

2 Caroline Elizabeth Mary; *m* 30 March 1799 1st Baron Wharncliffe (*see* WHARNCLIFFE, E) and *d* 23 April 1856, leaving issue

The 2nd EARL's nephew,

JOHN CRICHTON, **3rd Earl Erne of Crom Castle**, KP (1868); rep I peer (C), Lt and custos rotulorum Co Fermanagh, High Sheriff 1827, *cr* 13 Jan 1876 BARON FERMANAGH OF LISNASKEA, Co Fermanagh (UK); *b* 30 July 1802; *m* 6 July 1837 Selina Griselda (*d* 6 Sep 1884 aged 80), 2nd dau of Rev Charles Cobbe Beresford (*see* WATERFORD, M), and had issue:

1 JOHN HENRY, **4th Earl**

2 Charles Frederick, of Mullaboden, Co Kildare, JP, DL; Col Gren Guards, BA Oxford; *b* Nov 1841; *m* 2 Jan 1873 Lady Madeline Taylour (*d* 27 Jan 1876), est dau of 3rd Marquess of Headfort (*qv*), and *d* 20 Aug 1918, leaving issue:

(1) Hubert Francis; Maj Irish Guards, Nile Expdn 1898, Imp Yeo Boer War 1902 and BEF 1914; *b* 17 Dec 1874; *m* 14 July 1903 Esther Eliza (*m* 2nd 16 Sept 1920 Maj-Gen Spencer Edmund Hollond, CB, CMG, DSO, Rifle Bde (*d* 5 Feb 1950), and *d* 10 Nov 1965), 3rd dau of Llewellyn Traherne Bassett Saunderson, of Kingstown, Dublin, JP (*see* 1935 edn CLONMELL, E), and was *ka* 1 Sept 1914, leaving issue:

1a Doris Madeline; *b* 30 May 1904; *m* 11 Dec 1925 Maj Philip Ivan Pease (*d* 7 Nov 1964), of Underley Grange, Kirkby Lonsdale, Carnforth, Lancs, er s of Reginald Pease, of Sledwich, Barnard Castle, and *d* 1993, leaving:

1b *Nigel Crichton [Nigel Pease Esq, Sledwich, Barnard Castle, Durham DL12 8UU]; *b* 1934; *educ* Eton; *m* 1963 *Ailsa Smith-Maxwell and has:

1c *Karen; *b* 1970

2b *Simon Philip [Simon Pease Esq, Underley Grange, Kirby Lonsdale, Lancs]; *b* 1945; *educ* Eton; *m* 1979 *Mrs Clementine Hebeler and has:

1c *Philip John Simon; *b* 1981

1b *Bridget [Mrs David Wentworth-Stanley, Gt Munden House, nr Ware, Herts]; *b* 1926; *m* 1951 *(Geoffrey) David Wentworth-Stanley and has:

1c *(David) Michael; *b* 1952; *educ* Eton; *m* 1975 *Jane, est dau of Lt-Col Thomas Armitage Hall, OBE (*see* DUFFERIN AND CLANEBOYE, B), and has:

1d *Laura Clare; *b* 1978

2d *Emma Jane; *b* 1981

3d *Harriet Sarah; *b* 1985

2c *Nicholas Philip; *b* 1954; *educ* Eton; *m* 1985 (*divorce* 1997) Clare H, yst dau of Anthony N Steel, of Rock House Farm, Lower Froyle, Hants, and has:

1d *James Nicholas; *b* 1985

2d *Harry David; *b* 1989

1d *Louisa Clare; *b* 1993

3c *Christopher James; *b* 1962; *educ* Eton

4c *Adrian Charles; *b* 1965; *educ* Eton; *m* 1992 *Ann N, dau of Capt M L Moorberg, USAF, and Mrs Robert DeBord, of Branford, Conn. and has:

1d *Charles Edward; *b* 1995

1d *Olivia Ann; *b* 1997

2b *Alison Beatrix [Mrs Christopher Weatherby, Whaddon House, Whaddon, Bucks]; *b* 1928; *m* 1954 *Christopher Nicholas Weatherby and has:

1c *Andrew Christopher; *b* 1955

2c *Jonathan Roger; *b* 1959; *m* 1993 *Sophie, dau of Roger Cliffe-Jones

3c *Roger Nicholas; *b* 1962

1c *Clare Alison; *b* 1957; *m* 1982 *Hon Peter Gilbert Greenall and has issue (*see* DARESBURY, B)

3b *Carol Esther [Mrs William Fox, Rudham House, East Rudham, King's Lynn, Norfolk]; *b* 1932; *m* 1959 *William E A Fox and has:

1c *William Philip; *b* 1960

2c *Robert James Ayscough; *b* 1970

1c *Annabel Carol; *b* 1962

2c *Jane Cordelia; *b* 1965

2a Enid Irene Adelaide; *b* 27 Feb 1907; *m* 24 July 1930 Leslie Ashurst Judd, er s of Walter Albert Judd, of Holly Hill, Stoke Poges, Bucks, and *d* 5 April 1974, leaving issue. He *d* 25 March 1967

(1) Amelia Madeline Louisa; *b* 20 Jan 1876; *m* 1st 6 Dec 1900 Sir John Peniston Milbanke, 10th Bt, VC (*ka* 21 Aug 1915; *see* 1956 edn); *m* 2nd 1920 Sir Bryan Thomas Mahon, KCB, KCVO, DSO, PC, and *d* 6 Dec 1927. He *d* 24 Sept 1930

3 Henry George Louis (Sir), KCB (1911), JP Hants; V-Lt, CC Hants, Lt-Col 10th and 21st Hus, Chm Hants TFA, Hon Col Hants Yeo and 5th Bn Hants Regt, T/Lt-Col and Co Cmdt Hants Vol Regt, ADC to HM EDWARD VII; *b* 7 April 1844; *m* 1st 17 Aug 1869 Letitia Grace (*d* 13 Jan 1888), dau of Maj Arthur Willoughby Cole-Hamilton, JP, DL (*see* ENNISKILLEN, E), and had:

(1) Charles William Harry, DSO (1915); Col 10th Hus, Boer War 1899–1900 and WW I 1914 (wounded, despatches); *b* 7 July 1872; *m* 7 Nov 1912 Dorothy Maud (*d* 16 April 1959), er dau of Hon Eustace Henry Dawnay (*see* DOWNE, V), and *d* 8 Nov 1958, leaving:

1a +Ronald Henry [Ronald Crichton Esq, Flat 2 Clarence House, 8 Granville Rd, Eastbourne, Sussex BN20 7EG]; Capt Rifle Bde, with Br Cncl 1946–67 Greece, Belgium, W Germany and London, assist music critic *Financial Times* 1967; *b* 28 Dec 1913; *educ* Radley and Ch Ch Oxford

2a +Brian John, OBE (1977) [Brian Crichton Esq OBE, Plas Trefor, Llansadwrn, Menai Bridge, Anglesey]; High Sheriff Anglesey 1967, chartered land agent; *b* 27 Jan 1918; *educ* Radley and Trin Coll Camb; *m* 23 May 1953 *Anne Radclyffe, DL (Gwynedd 1989), yr dau of Lt-Col Thomas Hassard Montgomery, DSO, JP, of Cadogan House, Shrewsbury, and has had:

1b Susan Jane; *b* 10 Oct 1955; *m* 1977 *Michael Patrick York, of Boulder, Colorado, and *d* 1991, leaving:

1c *Adam Patrick Crichton; *b* 1980

2c *Nicholas Brian; *b* 1990

2b *Diana Mary [Mrs Richard MacMullen, The Verderers, Bradenham, Norfolk]; *b* 9 Dec 1957; *m* 1984 *Richard John Charlton MacMullen, 2nd s of James MacMullen, MC, of Laxey, IoM, and has issue:

1c *Patrick James Montgomery; *b* 1989

3b *Judith Anne Crichton [Mrs Michael Preece, Shalaka, Middle Rd, Llandegfan, Anglesey LL59 5TH]; *b* 31 July 1959; *m* 1st 1983 Anthony Wall (*d* 1989), of Ghorst Farm, Leysters, Herefs, est s of Lt-Col E Wall, RE; *m* 2nd June 1996 *Michael Preece

(2) Reginald Louis; Capt RN WW I; *b* 23 Dec 1874; *m* 21 Oct 1902 Hester Beatrix (*d* 30 Oct 1961), only dau of Rev Richard Allen White, Rector Wing, Rutland, and *d* 2 Aug 1929, having had issue:

1a Marcus Henry Reginald, of Fernbank, Banchory, Kincardineshire; Cdr RN WW II, Inspr Coastguard E Scotland 1952; *b* 17 Aug 1904; *m* 4 May 1935 *Elizabeth Frances, only dau of Col Francis Holland Dorling, DSO, The Manchester Regt, of The Crouch, Seaford, and *d* 1985, leaving issue:

1b *Catherine Elizabeth [Mrs Christopher Bates, 10 Station Road, Harston, Cambridge]; *b* 15 Aug 1937; *m* 12 Sep 1968 *Christopher John Bates, PhD, only s of J G Bates, of Seven Kings, Ilford, Essex, and has:

1c *Gemma Clare Irene; *b* 1974

2b *Frances Margaret; *b* 13 April 1942; *m* 3 Aug 1962 *Maj Patrick Lloyd Ker Thompson, s of Canon William Grainger Thompson, of Foches Corner, Crediton, Devon, and has issue:

1c *James Marcus Crichton; *b* 24 March 1966

1c *Bridget Clare; *b* 21 March 1964

3b *Madelaine Louise [Mrs Peter Dodds, Meadow Ridge, Stockton, NJ 08559, USA]; *b* 19 Nov 1944; *m* 2 Sept 1967 *Peter G R Dodds, only s of George Ridley Dodds, MB, BS, of Masham, Yorks, by Ann Renea, dau of Capt Guy Dalrymple Fanshawe, RN (*see* below), and has issue:

1c *George Alexander Crichton; *b* 1970

1c *Lucy; *b* 1972

2a (Francis) Michael; served Yangtse River 1937–39 and WW II Atlantic, Mediterranean, Burma and Pacific, life fell Roy Cwlth Soc, Roy Sailing Master 1948–51, Priv Sec and Sr ADC to Govr-Gen Fedn Rhodesia and Nyasaland 1958; *b* 19 Oct 1909; *d* 17 Dec 1996

3a John Richard, of Ellens, Woolton, Bekesbourne, nr Canterbury, Kent; WW II as T/Lt RNVR; *b* 22 Feb 1912; *educ* Radley; *d* 19–

1a Doreen Grace; *b* 18 Jan 1906; *d* 20 June 1908

2a *Elisabeth Hester [Mrs Francis Lepper, Trewollack House, St Wenn, Bodmin, Cornwall]; *b* 30 Oct 1914; *m* 16 Sept 1939 *Francis Alfred Lepper, MA, FSA, Sr Tutor and Fell (now Emeritus) of Corpus Christi Coll Oxford, only s of Alfred William Lepper, of Marche Manor, nr Shrewsbury, and has:

1b *Patrick Francis Dalway [Patrick Lepper Esq, Falkland House, 21 Kings Rd, Berkhamsted, Herts]; *b* 17 March 1941; *educ* Marlborough and New Coll Oxford; *m* 21 June 1966 *Anthea Eve, er dau of Walter Douglas Campbell Scott, of 1 Holly Place, London NW3, and has issue:

1c *Edward Patrick Robert; *b* 1971

1c *Francesca Eugenie; *b* 17 Dec 1967

1b *Jane Helen Veronica [Mrs Roger Willoughby, 35 Defoe Avenue, Kew, Richmond, Surrey TW9 4DS]; *b* 30 Dec 1942; *m* 1970 *Roger James Willoughby

3a *Patricia Jane [Lady Mount, Woolton Farm, Bekesbourne, Canterbury, Kent]; WRNS WW II; *b* 1 July 1920; *m* 1st 30 May 1946 John Herbert Mount (*d* 1973), only surv s of Herbert Mount, of Littlebourne Court, nr Canterbury, and has issue:

1b *John Richard Herbert Crichton; *b* 7 Sept 1953; *educ* Gordonstoun; *m* 1977 *Martha, only dau of Prof Emeteus, of Cambridge

2b *Mark Donald Crichton; *b* 4 Jan 1957; *educ* King's Canterbury

1b *Virginia Jane; *b* 9 Aug 1947; *m* 4 Oct 1968 *Richard Henry Ringrose Latham, yr s of Lt-Col Edward Latham, MC RHA, Queen's Messenger, of Oak Knoll, Sunningdale, Berks (*see* JELLICOE, E), and has issue

2b *(Selina) Clare; *b* 9 April 1950; *m* 1st 1974 (*divorce* 1978) Alexander Brunton Badenoch; *m* 2nd 1978 *Andrew Pirie Stuart Robinson

3a (cont.) Mrs John Mount *m* 2nd 1975 *Sir James Williams Spencer Mount, CBE

(3) Frederick Marcus (Rev); MA Oxford, Curate St Barnabas Bethnal Green 1905–09 and Godalming 1910–14; *b* 10 Aug 1877; *d* unm 22 May 1917

(4) Richard Edward, OBE (1944), JP, DL Hants; Col KRRC, Mounted Inf Boer War 1901–02 (severely wounded, despatches, medal with three clasps), WW I (despatches four times, brevet, Croce di Guerra and Order SS. Maurice and Lazarus Italy) and WW II (cmdg Nat Defence Cos and 8th Bn Hampshire Regt 1939–40 and Portsmouth Group HG and Meon Valley Sector HG 1942–45); *b* 21 June 1879; *educ* Radley; *m* 24 Jan 1915 Cecil Nona (*d* 28 Dec 1960), yst dau of Adml Lord Frederic Herbert Kerr (*see* LOTHIAN, M), and *d* 24 Nov 1962

(5) John Arthur; T/Maj 5th Bn Hampshire Regt; *b* 19 Aug 1883; *das* 6 Feb 1917

(1) Emily Florence; *b* 25 Oct 1870; *m* 9 July 1895 1st Baron Mottistone (*qv*) and *d* 9 Aug 1913, leaving issue

(2) Louisa Charlotte; *b* 14 Aug 1881; *m* 16 Aug 1910 Capt Guy Dalrymple Fanshawe, RN, s of Adml of the Fleet Sir Arthur Fanshawe, GCB, GCVO, and *d* 6 Sept 1948, leaving issue. He *d* 19 June 1962

3 (cont.) Sir Henry Crichton *m* 2nd 29 Jan 1890 Lady Emma Baring, CI, CBE (*d* 17 Jan 1936), only dau of 1st Earl of Northbrook (*qv*), and *d* 10 May 1922

1 Louisa Anne Catherine; *b* 27 May 1838; *d* unm 29 Aug 1866

The 3rd EARL *d* 3 Oct 1885; his est s,

JOHN HENRY CRICHTON, **4th Earl Erne of Crom Castle**, KP (1889), PC; Co Fermanagh: Lt and custos rotulorum 1885–1914, High Sheriff 1864 (and Co Donegal 1867); MP (C) Enniskillen 1868–80 and Co Fermanagh 1880–85, Chm Fermanagh CC 1899, 1905 and 1908, Ld of Treas (C whip) 1876–80, MA Oxford; *b* 16 Oct 1839; *m* 28 Dec 1870 Lady Florence Mary Cole (*d* 23 March 1924), dau of 3rd Earl of Enniskillen (*qv*), and had issue:

1 Henry William, *Viscount Crichton*, MVO 4th Cl (1906), DSO (1900); Maj and Brevet Lt-Col RHG, ADC to HM GEORGE V when DUKE OF CORNWALL during his Colonial tour 1901, Equerry to HM GEORGE V when PRINCE OF WALES 1901–09 and Extra Equerry 1909–10, Extra Equerry to HM GEORGE V 1910–14, served Boer War 1899–1900 (despatches, Queen's medal with five clasps) and WW I 1914 (despatches), 4th Cl Legn Honour; *b* 30 Sept 1872; *m* 10 June 1903 Lady Mary Cavendish Grosvenor (*d* 14 Jan 1959, having *m* 2nd April 1918 Col Hon Algernon Francis Stanley, DSO (*d* 10 Feb 1962), 7th s of 16th Earl of Derby (*qv*)), 5th dau of 1st Duke of Westminster (*qv*), and was *ka* 31 Oct 1914, having had:

(1) George David Hugh; *b* 12, *d* 18 May 1904

(2) JOHN HENRY GEORGE, **5th Earl**

(1) (Mary) Kathleen, DCVO (1969); granted rank of earl's dau 29 Sept 1920, Mistress Robes to HM QUEEN ELIZABETH THE QUEEN MOTHER 1964–90; *b* 8 July 1905 (HM QUEEN MARY stood sponsor); *m* 9 Feb 1928 4th Duke of Abercorn (*qv*) and *d* 1990, leaving issue

2 George Arthur Charles (Hon Sir), GCVO (1933), DL (Berks); Comptroller Ld Chamberlain's Dept 1920–36, Extra Equerry to TM GEORGE V 1935–36, EDWARD VIII 1936 and GEORGE VI 1936–52, Registrar and Sec Centl Chancery Orders Kthood, Col Coldstream Gds, Boer War 1900–02 (wounded) and WW I; *b* 6 Sept 1874; *m* 11 June 1913 Lady Mary Augusta Dawson (*d* 23 July 1961), yr dau of 2nd Earl of Dartrey (*see* 1933 edn), and *d* 5 March 1952, leaving:

(1) David George, LVO (1968, MVO 4th Cl); *b* 31 July 1914; *educ* Eton; jnlst with *Daily Telegraph*, *Daily Sketch* and *Manchester Guardian*; Maj Derbys Yeo (TA) WW II (despatches), FO: served Belgrade, Alexandria, La Paz, Santiago and Miami, Consul-Gen Nice 1970–74 and HM's Rep Monaco; *m* 1st 9 Aug 1941 Joan ('Susie') Fenella (*d* in a car crash 1992), dau of Lt-Col Douglas Whyte Cleaver, DSO, of Park Palace, Monte Carlo, and had issue:

1a +Charles David Blayney; *b* 31 Oct 1953; *educ* Eton; *m* 1st 1977 Nicola Sian, yr dau of W/Cdr Peter E Berry, DFC, RAF, of Loxley Cottage, Little Bookham, Surrey; *m* 2nd 1988 *Harriet E, yr dau of Martin Monier-Williams, of Burrell House, Chiddingfold, Surrey, and by her has:

1b *Jessica Eloise; *b* 1991

1b *Flora Susie; *b* 1993

1a *Fenella Jane; *b* 9 Jan 1948; *m* 1st 1969 (*divorce* 1974) Hon Anthony Henry Amherst Cecil (*see* AMHERST OF HACKNEY, B); *m* 2nd 1978 *John Ernest and by him has:

1b *Charlotte Maria; *b* 1986

(1) (cont.) Maj David Crichton *m* 2nd 1994 *Betty, dau of Col M G Lee, of Christchurch, NZ, and widow of Andrew George Hughes-Onslow (*see* ONSLOW, E), and *d* 22 Jan 1997

(2) +Richard John Vesey, CVO (1986), MC [Col Richard Crichton CVO MC, Derment House, Hartley Wintney, Hants RG27 8RE]; Col cmdg Coldstream Gds WW II (despatches, twice wounded), memb Gentlemen-at-Arms 1966 (Lt 1981–); *b* 2 Nov 1916; *educ* Eton; *m* 15 July 1948 *Yvonne Avril Catherine, formerly w of Kenneth Lindsay Oliver and yst dau of Dr Harry Edward Worthington, of Birchington, Kent, and has:

1a +Vesey George [Vesey Crichton Esq, 4 Morley Rd, Twickenham, Middx TW1 2HF]; *b* 3 Oct 1949; *educ* Eton and UEA; *m* 5 April 1987 *Emma Joy Louise, dau of Barnaby Hannam, of W Sevington Farm, Yatton Keynell, Wilts

2a +Adrian David [Adrian Crichton Esq, 2 Kersley St, London SW11 4PT]; *b* 16 May 1952; *educ* Eton, Bristol U and INSEAD; *m* 11 July 1974 *Janie, yr dau of Duncan Wauchope, of Pinns Farm, Wellow, Romsey, Hants, and has:

1b *Sophie Alexandra Mary; *b* 8 June 1981

2b *Henrietta Catherine Louise; *b* 4 Oct 1983

3b *Laura Julia Caroline; *b* 2 July 1985

3a +Simon Patrick [Simon Crichton Esq, Shute End Farm House, Alderbury, Salisbury, Wilts]; *b* 28 Aug 1956; *m* 1983 *Fiona Jane, dau of Colin Midwood, JP, of Grange Cottage, Funtington, W Sussex, and has issue:

1b +Edward William Richard; *b* 1989

2b +Charles Patrick Vesey; *b* 1992

1b *Georgina Caroline Nicola; *b* 1986

(3) +Patrick Henry Douglas, OBE (1991) [Maj Patrick Crichton OBE, West Field Cottage, Upton Grey, Hants RG25 1LG]; Page of Honour to HM GEORGE V 1932–36, Maj Berks Yeo (TA) WW II (despatches), dep chm Foreign & Colonial Investment Tst 1974–; *b* 16 Aug 1919; *educ* Eton and Oxford; *m* 1 Oct 1948 *Gillian Moyra, yst dau of Sir Alexander Cadogan, OM, GCMG, KCB, PC (*see* CADOGAN, E), and has:

1a +Hugh Patrick George; *b* 9 Aug 1949; *m* 1984 *Kerry, er dau of L M Kyle-Little, of Brisbane, Australia, and has issue:

1b *Georgina Jane; *b* 1988

2b *Laura Juliette; *b* 1988

2a +Desmond Cadogan [Desmond Crichton Esq, 6 Rumbold St, London SW6 2JA]; *b* 10 March 1953; *educ* Eton; *m* 1990 *Emma Jane, er dau of Maj (Walter Brian) Julian Crawshay, of Tasburgh Grange, Norwich, and has:

1b +A son; *b* 1992

2b +A son; *b* 16 Feb 1995

1b *A dau; *b* 1994

1a *Jane Elizabeth [Mrs Bevil Granville, Ibworth, Basingstoke, Hants]; *b* 9 Aug 1949; *m* 1977 *Bevil Charles Fitz Ives Granville, yr s of Maj Richard St Leger Granville, and has issue:

1b *Harry Court Crichton; *b* 1979

1b *Camilla Jane; *b* 1982

(1) Barbara Mary Cynthia; *b* 19 July 1922; *m* 14 June 1947 *Lt-Col Alastair Malcolm Nicholson, TD, Berks Yeo, of Tundry House, Dogmersfield, nr Basingstoke, Hants, 2nd s of Lt-Col Malcolm Nicholson, OBE, of Springhill, Mortimer West End, nr Reading, Berks, and *d* 1992 in the same car crash as her sis-in-law Mrs David Crichton (*see* above), leaving:

1a *Michael Alistair George; *b* 27 Nov 1951; *educ* Eton

1a *Jennifer Mary; *b* 23 May 1949

2a *Sara Kathleen; *b* 14 Apr 1957

(2) *Mary Bridget Anne [Mrs John Cole, The Little Barn, West Woodhay, Newbury, Berks RG20 0BJ]; *b* 13 April 1927 (HM QUEEN MARY stood sponsor); *m* 30 June 1951 *Maj John William Burke Cole, JP, DL, Coldstream Guards, est s of Lt-Col John James Burke Cole, OBE, MC (*see* LONGFORD, E), and has issue:

1a *James William John [James Cole Esq, The Malt House, West Woodhay, Newbury, Berks RG15 OBD]; *b* 12 July 1952; *educ* Eton; *m* 1989 *Yvonne, dau of R Hawkins, of Hitchin, Herts, and has issue:

1b *Robert William James; *b* 1990

1b *Annabel Charlotte Mary; *b* 1992

2b *Emma Sophie Elizabeth; *b* 1994

2a *Michael George; *b* 5 April 1955; *educ* Radley

1a *Elizabeth Anne [Mrs Simon Hayes, The Barn, West Woodhay, Berks RG20 0BJ]; *b* 19 July 1961; *m* 1984 *Simon Leigh Hayes, er s of Roger Hayes, of Seaford, Sussex, and has:

1b *Johnnie Kinloch de Vere; *b* 15 Jan 1997

3 Arthur Owen, Lt 3rd Bn Gordon Highrs, Hon Capt, Boer War 1901–02 and WW I (despatches twice, 1914 star), Order Crown Belgium; *b* 15 Aug 1876; *educ* Eton and Ch Ch Oxford; *m* 13 June 1906 Katherine Helen Elizabeth (*d* 12 April 1964), 3rd dau of Col Hon Walker Rodolph Trefusis, CB (*see* CLINTON, B), and *d* 11 July 1970, leaving:

(1) Michael Henry, OBE (1944); Lt-Col RHG WW II, High Sheriff Co Fermanagh 1950; *b* 18 April 1907; *educ* Eton; *m* 1 July 1942 *Alice Elizabeth, dau of R Sims, of Wabash, Indiana, and *dsp* 16 April 1970

(1) *Jean Trefusis [Mrs Montague Lowry-Corry, Clover Farm, Shalden, Alton, Hants]; *b* 15 May 1912; *m* 1st 15 May 1933 Lt-Col Eion James Henry Merry, MC (*d* 23 Sept 1966), RHG, s of Archibald William Merry, of Belladrum, Beauly, and 18 Hill Street, London W1, by Hon Ida Helen Lizzie, sis of 8th Viscount Chetwynd (*qv*), and has issue:

1a *Davinia Jean [Lady Gibbs, Patney Rectory, Devizes, Wilts SN10 3QZ]; *b* 1934; *m* 27 Oct 1955 *FM Sir Roland Christopher Gibbs, CBE, DSO, MC, 60th Rifles (*see* ALDENHAM and HUNSDON OF HUNSDON, B), and has issue

2a Diane; *b* 1937; *d* 1980

(1) (cont.) Mrs Eion Merry *m* 2nd 30 Sept 1969 Capt Montague W Lowry-Corry (*see* BELMORE, E)

4 James Archibald, DSO (1918); Capt Rifle Bde, GSO3 1916, Bde Maj 1917, Boer War 1901–02 and WW I (wounded, despatches 1914 star), Croix de Guerre; *b* 8 Dec 1877; *d* unm 3 Aug 1956

1 Evelyn Louisa Selina; *b* 21 July 1879; *m* 7 Nov 1899 Hon Gerald Ernest Francis Ward, MVO, yst s of 1st Earl of Dudley (*qv*), and *d* 4 May 1955

2 Mabel Florence Mary, MBE (1919); *b* 31 March 1882; *m* 1st 21 April 1906 Capt Lord Hugh William Grosvenor, 8th s of 1st Duke of Westminster (*qv*), and had issue; *m* 2nd 29 Sept 1920 Maj Robert Hamilton Stubber, DSO, of Marston Hill, Fairford, Glos, and *d* 15 Aug 1944, leaving further issue. He *d* 27 Jan 1963

The 4th EARL *d* 2 Dec 1914; his gs,

JOHN HENRY GEORGE CRICHTON, **5th Earl Erne of Crom Castle**, JP, DL Co Fermanagh; Ld-in-Waiting to HM GEORGE VI, Page of Honour to HM GEORGE V 1921–24, Lt Res of Offrs RHG, Maj NI Horse, WW II; *b* 22 Nov 1907 (HM GEORGE

V stood sponsor); *m* 15 July 1931 Lady Davidema (Davina) Katherine Cynthia Mary Millicent Bulwer Lytton (*m* 2nd 28 Aug 1945 4th Baron Terrington (*qv*) and *d* 10 Sept 1995), yr dau of 2nd Earl of Lytton (*qv*), and *das* 23 May 1940, leaving:

1 HENRY GEORGE VICTOR JOHN CRICHTON, **6th and present Earl Erne of Crom Castle**

1*Rosanagh Mary [The Lady Rosanagh Raben-Levetzau, 23 Stack House, Cundy St, London SW1]; *b* 12 Aug 1932; *m* 27 June 1956 Baron Michael Paul Raben-Levetzau (*d* 1990), yr s of Count Siegfried Victor Raben-Levetzau, of Denmark, and has had issue:

(1) *Matthew Siegfried John [Matthew Raben Esq, 35 Fontenoy Rd, London SW12 9LX]; *b* 20 Oct 1962; *educ* Eton; *m* 1987 *Sarah Jane L, dau of Vernon Gordon-Lennox Stratton, of St Helens Station, IOW, and has issue:

1a *Frederick Michael James; *b* 1990

2a *Timothy Peter William; *b* 1995

1a *Sophie Eleanor Rose; *b* 1993

(2) *Alexander Peter Vincent; *b* 20 Oct 1964

(3) *Christopher Victor Patrick; *b* 24 Sept 1968

(4) *Seamus Julian Henry; *b* 15 March 1971

(1) Mary Rosanagh; *b* 14 Sept, *d* 25 Sept 1961

2 *Antonia Pamela Mary [The Lady Antonia Beckwith, The Dower House, Kirklington, nr Bedale, N Yorks DL8 2LX]; *b* 18 April 1934; *m* 1st 25 July 1953 Timothy William Wardell, 2nd s of Brig John Michael Stewart Wardell, MBE (*see* CROSSLEY, Bt); *m* 2nd 1981 *Charles William Beckwith and by her 1st husb has issue:

(1) *Michael John William; *b* 19 July 1956; *educ* Eton and Australian Nat U; *m* 1980 (*divorce* 1991) Elizabeth O'Neil and has issue:

1a *Francesca Mary Louise; *b* 1984

2a *Sophie Helen Mary; *b* 1986

(2) *Antony Henry Constantine; *b* 9 Jan 1959; *m* 7 Oct 1989 *Nichola M L, dau of Thomas Wright, of Maudlin Farmhouse, Steyning, Sussex, and has:

1a *Thomas William; *b* 1993

1a *A dau; *b* 1991

(3) *David Stewart Timothy; *b* 26 Feb 1963

(1) *Sabrina Mary Louise; *b* 18 Dec 1954; *m* 1974 *Michael L F Smith, s of Leonard Smith, of Wellington, NZ

(2) *Henrietta Pamela Mary; *b* 25 Aug 1967

Seat: Crom Castle. The present structure was erected in neo-Tudor style 1829 to designs by Edward Blore. It replaced a genuine castle dating from the Plantation period (1611) which burnt down in 1764.

ERRINGTON, Bt

Arms: Or an open book clasped, on a chief az. a spur rowel upwards between two portcullises chained or. **Crest:** A liver bird supporting with the dexter claw an oak sapling ppr. **Motto:** *Petit ardua virtus* ('Virtue seeks out hardship'). **Creation:** Bt. (UK) 26 June 1963.

SIR GEOFFREY FREDERICK ERRINGTON, 2ND BT, of Ness, in the Co Palatine of Chester [Col Sir Geoffrey Errington Bt, Stone Hill Farm, Sellindge, Kent TN25 6AJ; 203a Gloucester Place, London NW1 6BU]; *b* 15 Feb 1926; *s f* 1973; *educ* Rugby and New Coll Oxford; Regular Army Offr The King's Regt 1945–75 (Col); chm: managing ctee King's and Manchester Regt's Assoc 1973–86, dir: Personnel Services, Br Shipbuilders 1977–78, Shipbuilding ITB 1977–78, chm Exec Appointments Ltd 1982–90, Harefield Hosp NHS Trust 1991–97, memb: Kent Consumers Consultative Ctee, Southern Water Authority 1984–89, V-chm Assoc for Prevention of Addiction 1991–94, chm 1994–, chm FRSA 1994, Liveryman, Broderers' and Coachmakers' and Coach Harness Maker's Co and Freeman City London 1980; *m* 24 Sept 1955 *Diana Kathleen Forbes, dau of Edward Barry Davenport, of Edgbaston, and has:

1 +ROBIN DAVENPORT [Robin Errington Esq, 68 Orbain Rd, London SW6 7JY]; *b* 1 July 1957; *educ* Eton; FRSA 1994

2 +John Davenport [John Errington Esq, 10 Dighton Rd, London SW18]; *b* 23 July 1959; *educ* Eton; *m* 1989 *Prue, dau of Brig Michael Lee, OBE, of Fulham, and has issue:

(1) *Isabel Jane Davenport; *b* 1993

3 +Andrew Davenport [Andrew Errington Esq, 14 Nottingham Rd, London SW17 7EA]; *b* 23 July 1959; *educ* Eton; Offr Welsh Gds 1978–82; *m* 1983 (*divorce* 1989) Georgina Sophie, yr dau of Lt-Gen Sir Derek Boorman, KCB, of Goodnestone, Kent

Lineage: Sir Eric Errington, 1st Bt (UK), so *cr* 26 June 1963, of Ness, in the Co Palatine of Chester, JP Liverpool; *b* 17 March 1900; *educ* Oxford (MA 1923); 2nd Lt Gordon Highrs 1918, barrister Inner Temple 1923; WW II: P/O AAF 1939, W/Cdr 1944; MP (C) Bootle 1935–45 and Aldershot 1954–70, chm Nat Executive Ctee C and U Assocs 1952–57, Pres Nat Fedn Property Owners 1956–60, pres: Wessex Area Nat Union C and U Assocs 1963–64 and Hire Purchase Trade Assoc 1965, ktd 1952; *m* 12 Sept 1924 Marjorie (*d* 27 Nov 1973), dau of Aida Grant Bennett, and *d* 3 June 1973, leaving:

1 Sir GEOFFREY FREDERICK ERRINGTON, **2nd and present Bt**

2 +Stuart Grant, CBE (1994), JP (Berks 1970) [Stuart Errington Esq CBE JP, Earleywood Lodge, Ascot, Berks SL5 9JP]; *b* 23 June 1929; *educ* Rugby and Trin Coll Oxford (MA), 2nd Lt RA 1947–49, with Ellerman Lines 1952–59 and Astley Ind Tst 1959–70, chm Mercantile Credit 1985 (md 1977, exec dir 1970), chm and ch exec Mercantile Gp 1988–89, chm Equipment Leasing Assoc 1976–78, European Fedn of Leasing Assocs 1978–80, Finance Houses Assoc 1982–84, Nat Assoc of Citizens Advice Bureaux 1989–94, dir Barclays Merchant Bank, Barclays Bank UK 1979–86, Kleinwort Overseas Investment Tst 1982–, Municipal Mutual Insur 1989–, Northern Electric 1989–96, Nationwide Building Soc 1989–97, memb Cncl RHBNC 1989– (v-chm 1995); *m* 19 June 1954 *Anne, yr dau of Alfred Eric Baedeker, of Edgbaston, Birmingham, and has issue:

(1) +David Grant [David Errington Esq, 47 Southdean Gdns, London SW19]; *b* 16 Aug 1957; *educ* Rugby; *m* 1982 *Catherine Ann, yr dau of Kenneth Neville, of Sydney, Australia, and has issue:

1a +Timothy Grant; *b* 1983

2a +Nicholas David; *b* 1985

3a +Frederick Charles; *b* 1988

(2) +Charles Stuart; *b* 18 April 1961; *educ* Rugby; *m* 1992 *Nicole Cauverien, and has:

1a *Molly Wilhelmina; *b* 1997

(1) *Elizabeth Anne [Mrs Jaimie Corke, Burltons, Donhead St Mary, Wilts]; *b* 22 Oct 1958; *m* 1983 *Jaimie Coltart Corke, s of David Corke, of Lyndhurst, Hants, and has issue:

1a *Milo Jaimie; *b* 1991

1a *Daisy Elizabeth; *b* 1985

2a *Imogen Sally; *b* 1986

3a *Ella Clementine; *b* 1994

1 *(Anne) Jacqueline [Miss Jacqueline Errington, 2 Willow Tree Close, Wickham Market, Suffolk IP13 0TB]; *b* 12 Sept 1935; *educ* Wycombe Abbey; community rels offr RAF Bentwaters 1964–85

ERROLL

Arms: Argent three inescutcheons gules; over the shield, suspended from an ox yoke proper, bows gules, in front two batons argent tipped or in saltire, and Earl's coronet, thereon a helmet, the mantling gules doubled ermine. **Crest:** Issuing out of a coronet a falcon volant proper, armed, jessed and belled or. **Supporters:** Two savages wreathed about the middle with laurel, each bearing on his shoulder an ox-yoke proper, bows gules. **Motto:** *Serva jugum* ('Maintain the yoke'). The HAY arms are as born by the Norman family of La Haye, Seigneurs of Le Mesnil-Geldouin (later Le Guislain), La-Haye-Hue (alias La Haye-Comtesse or La Haye-Bellefond), La Haye-Belouze, Villebaudon and Beaucoudray, whose fiefs bordered on that of Soules near St Lo. **Creations:** L. (S) by March 1429/30, E. (S) 12 June 1452, Bt. (NS) 1685.

THE 24TH EARL OF ERROLL, Lord Hay, Lord Slains and a **Baronet** (Sir Merlin Sereld Victor Gilbert Hay, Bt) [The Rt Hon The Earl of Erroll, Woodbury Hall, Sandy, Beds SG19 2HR]; *b* 20 April 1948; *s* mother in peerages and as 28th Hereditary Lord High Constable of Scotland (is as such the first subject in Scotland after the Blood Royal; also presides (though usually by deputy) over the

Court of the Verge, or Constabulary Court, his jurisdiction being supreme in all matters of assault and riot within four miles of the Sovereign's person when in Scotland), Sr Great Offr of the Roy Household in Scotland and 33rd Chief of the Hays (Celtic title *MacGaraidh Mor*) 1978; is also with the Earl of Angus (*see* HAMILTON and BRANDON, D) a Hereditary Ld Assessor Court of Lord Lyon King of Arms and as Earl of Erroll retains a private officer-of-arms (Slains Pursuivant); *s f* as 12th Bt 1985; *educ* Eton and Trin Coll Cambridge; Rifleman Queen's Roy Rifles (parachutist) 1966; Page to Lord Lyon King of Arms 1956, memb Court Fishmongers' Co 1988– and Roy Co Archers, Lt Atholl Highrs, Hon Col RMPTA 1992–97, OStJ 1977; *m* 8 May 1982 *Isabelle Jacqueline Laline, only dau of Thomas Sidney Astell Hohler, MC (*see* GORT, V), and has:

1 +HARRY THOMAS WILLIAM, *Lord Hay*; *b* 8 August 1984

2 +Richard Merlin Ian; *b* 1990

1 +Amelia Diana Jacqueline; *b* 1986

2 +Laline Lucy Clementine; *b* 1987

Lineage (of Hay): Although settled in Scotland since 1160, the chiefs of the Hay clan derive their name (Latinised as *Haia*, in Gaelic *Garadh*) from a 'hale' or stockade on the castle motte-hill at La Haye, Cotentin Peninsula, Normandy.

WILLIAM de la HAYE, 1st Ch; Butler of Scotland *c* 1153–1214 (nephew of Ranulf de Soules, feudal Ld of Liddesdale and also Butler of Scotland, in whose family that post was hereditary till forfeited for their plotting to seize the throne during the early 14th-century Wars of Independence); a hostage for the Treaty of Falaise 1174, Envoy to England 1199; granted charter of the feudal Barony of Erroll in the Tay Estuary, Perthshire, *c* 1178–82; *m* Eva, Celtic heiress of Pitmilly and (possibly) of other lands near the Tay Estuary, and *d c* 1201, having had, with other issue:

1 DAVID

2 William; ancestor of the HAYs of Aithmuir

3 John, of Naughton; Sheriff Perth 1226; *m* Joanna/Juliana de Lascelles and was ancestor of the HAYs of Naughton

4 Robert; probable ancestor of the Marquesses of Tweeddale (*qv*)

The est son,

DAVID de la HAYE, 2nd feudal Baron of Erroll, of which had a charter *vp* 17 Sept 1195, Sheriff Forfar 1214; *m* 1st Ethna, dau of Gilbert, Earl of Strathearn, and *d c* 27 April 1241, leaving, with other issue, including a yr s (William, of Leys, Amb England 1258, ancestor of the HAYs of Leys (*see* NEAVE, Bt) and of Megginch, Sir James Hay (*see* CARLISLE, E, preliminary remarks) and the Earls of Kinnoull, *qv*):

GILBERT de la HAYE, 3rd feudal Baron of Erroll; a Regent of Scotland 1255 and 1258, Sheriff of Perth; *m* Lady Idoine Comyn, dau of William, Earl of Buchan (*see* BUCHAN, E, preliminary remarks), and had:

NICHOLAS de la HAYE, 4th feudal Baron of Erroll; Sheriff Perth; forced to swear fealty 1296 to EDWARD I, who summoned him as a Baron to Parl at St Andrews 5 March 1303/4; *m* Joan — and *d c* Sept 1306, leaving:

Sir GILBERT de la HAYE, 5th feudal Baron of Erroll; supported ROBERT I (THE BRUCE), to whom Constable cmdg his bodyguard; fought Battle of Methven against the English, Amb to England to negotiate truce after Bannockburn 1314; ROBERT I granted him the lands of Slains, Aberdeenshire, and 1309 (made hereditary by charter 12 Nov 1314) the post of Gt Constable of Scotland (both previously forfeited by his cousin Sir Gilbert Comyn); *d* April 1333, leaving:

NICHOLAS de la HAYE; allegedly *ka* & *vp* Battle of Dupplin against KING EDWARD BALLIOL 1332, leaving:

Sir DAVID de la HAYE, 6th feudal Baron of Erroll; *m* 1st —, dau and heiress of Sir John Keith of Innerpeffer, and was *ka* Battle of Neville's Cross against the English 17 Oct 1346, leaving by her:

Sir THOMAS de la HAYE, 7th feudal Baron of Erroll; hostage in England for DAVID II's ransom 1354; styled Lord the Hay 1405, but probably as a magnate who was Ch of his Name; *m c* 7 Nov 1372 ELIZABETH, dau of ROBERT II, and *d* July 1406, having had, with other issue, including a yr s (Sir Gilbert, of Dronlaw, ktd 1408, among the Scots kts with Joan of Arc at coronation of CHARLES VII OF FRANCE 1429; ancestor of the HAYs of Delgaty and Hays, Bt, of Park, *qv*) and at least two daus (Elizabeth, *m* Sir George Leslie of Rothes (*see* ROTHES, E); Alice (alleged dau), *m* as his 2nd w Sir William Hay of Locherwort and Yester; *see* TWEEDDALE, M):

Sir WILLIAM of the HAYE, **1st Lord Hay** (S), so *cr* by March 1429/30 following an Act of 1428 drawing a distinction between Lds of Parl and ordinary lairds in the Scots baronage; a Commr 1423 to treat for ransom of JAMES I, Jt Ld Warden Marches 1430; *m* Margaret, dau of Sir Patrick Gray of Broxmouth (*see* GRAY, L), and *d* 1437, having had an est son:

GILBERT of the HAYE; hostage in England for JAMES I's ransom 1424; *m* his cousin Alice, dau of Sir William Hay of Yester (*see* TWEEDDALE, M), and *dvp* 7 Sept 1436, leaving, with other issue, including a yr s (Gilbert, ancestor of the HAYs of Urie, *m* Beatrix, dau and heiress of Sir John Dunbar of Crimond, a barony in Buchan, and *d c* 12 Sept 1487):

Sir WILLIAM HAY, **1st Earl of Erroll** (s), so *cr* 12 June 1452, also granted territorial Earldom of Erroll and Lordship of Slains by charter 31 July 1452; Commr to conclude treaty with England 1457; *m c* 17 March 1449/50 Beatrix, dau of James, 7th Earl of Douglas, and *d* 1462, leaving:

1 NICHOLAS HAY, **2nd Earl of Erroll**; *m* 1461 Elizabeth (*m* 2nd 2nd Lord Kennedy; *see* AILSA, M), dau of 1st Earl of Huntly (*see* HUNTLY, M), and *dsp* 1470

2 WILLIAM HAY, **3rd Earl of Erroll**, PC; *m* 1st Isabel, dau of 2nd Earl of Huntly (*d* HUNTLY, M), and had, with other issue:

(1) WILLIAM HAY, **4th Earl of Erroll**; Hereditary Sheriff Aberdeen 10 Feb 1510/1; *m* 1st *c* 24 April 1492 Christian Lyon, dau of 3rd Lord Glamis (*see* STRATHMORE AND KINGHORNE, E), and had, with other issue (including a dau Elizabeth, *m* 5th Lord Saltoun (*qv*) of Abernethy):

1a WILLIAM HAY, **5th Earl of Erroll**, PC; Envoy France 1515 and England 1516; *m* Elizabeth (*m* 2nd 2nd Lord Ross of Halkhead), dau of 1st Lord Ruthven (*see* CARLISLE, E), and *d* 28 July 1522, leaving:

1b WILLIAM HAY, **6th Earl of Erroll**; *m* Lady Helen Stuart, dau of 12th Earl of Lennox (*see* MORAY, E), and *d* 11 April 1541, having had:

1c Jean; *b c* 1540; *m c* 16 June 1552 her cousin **8th Earl of Erroll** (*see* below)

(1) (cont.) The **4th Earl** *m* 2nd *c* 17 May 1509 Margaret, dau of Andrew Kerr of Cessford (*see* LOTHIAN, M, and ROXBURGHE, D) and widow of Sir James Sandilands of Calder (*see* TORPHICHEN, L), and was *ka* Battle of Flodden 9 Sept 1513

(2) Thomas; *m* Margaret, dau of Lyon Logie of that Ilk (*see* KILMARNOCK, B) and heiress of the feudal Barony of Logie Almond, Perthshire, and was *ka* Battle of Flodden 1513, leaving:

1a GEORGE, **7th Earl**

2 (cont.) The **3rd Earl** *m* 2nd Lady Elizabeth Leslie, dau of 1st Earl of Rothes (*qv*), and *d* 14 Jan 1506/07 having by her had, with other issue:

(1) Elizabeth; *m* 8th Earl of Crawford (*see* CRAWFORD and BALCARRES, E)

1 Margaret; *m* 1st Alexander Fraser, 4th of Philorth (*see* SALTOUN, L); *m* 2nd Sir Gilbert Keith of Inverugie; *m* 3rd Jan 1499/1500, as his 2nd w, Sir Robert Douglas of Lochleven (*see* MORTON, E)

The 6th EARL's cousin,

GEORGE HAY, **7th Earl of Erroll**, PC; Ld Lt Centl Scotland 1559; supported MARY QUEEN OF SCOTS after her enforced abdication and, refusing to officiate as Ld High Constable at JAMES VI's coronation 1567, resigned the post to the Master of Erroll *c* 1570; *m* 1st *c* 12 Nov 1528 Margaret, dau of Alexander Robertson of Struan, 5th Ch Clan Donnachaidh, and had, with other issue:

1 ANDREW, **8th Earl**

2 John, of Muchalls; *m* Elizabeth, dau of John Butter of Gormock, and *d* May 1579, leaving issue

3 Laurence; imprisoned his bro the **8th Earl** in Slains Castle 1576

4 George, of Ardlethen; helped Laurence seize Slains; *m* Marjorie Keith and had, with other issue:

(1) Francis; *k* Gordon of Gight's bro and was beheaded by the Gordons Dec 1615, the resulting feud lasting till 1617, when JAMES VI personally ordered the two Chiefs to make it up

1 Elizabeth; *m* William, Lord Keith, est son of 4th Earl Marischal, and had issue (*see* KINTORE, E)

2 Margaret; *m* 4th Lord Oliphant

3 Beatrix; *m* William Hay of Delgaty and had issue

The **7th Earl** *m* 2nd *c* 12 June 1561 Helen, dau of Walter Bruce/Bryson of Pitcullen, and *d* 30 Jan 1573/74, having had further issue

His est son,

ANDREW HAY, **8th Earl of Erroll**; *m* 1st his cousin Lady Jean Hay (*d* Aug 1570), only child of **6th Earl of Erroll**, and had issue:

1 Alexander, *Master of Erroll*; deaf mute, hence set aside by Parl on his f's death from the Earldom and Constabulary; insane by 1596

2 FRANCIS HAY, **9th Earl of Erroll**; Catholic who with Spanish arms and money rose in rebellion, defeating 7,000 govt troops at Glenlivet 3 Oct 1594; subsequently refused to fight against JAMES VI, who marched north in person and blew up Slains Castle; pardoned 1597 following some years' exile; Commr to negotiate Union with England 1604; *m* 1st *c* 1584 Margaret (*dsp*), dau of 1st Earl of Moray (*qv*); *m* 2nd *c* Jan 1586/7 Mary (*dsp*), dau of 4th Earl of Atholl (*see* ATHOLL, D); *m* 3rd 1590 Elizabeth, dau of 6th Earl of Morton (*qv*), and *d* 16 July 1631, having by her had, with other issue:

(1) WILLIAM HAY, **10th Earl of Erroll**, PC; *m* 1618 Lady Anne Lyon (*d* 8 Feb 1637), dau of 1st Earl of Kinghorne (*see* STRATHMORE AND KINGHORNE, E), and *d* 7 Dec 1636, soon after which the Perthshire lands were sold to pay his debts, thus fulfilling an old prophecy allegedly foretelling that when an ancient oak at Erroll (around which the Hays performed an annual family ritual at Hallowe'en) fell, so too would the fortunes of the house, leaving:

1a GILBERT HAY, **11th Earl of Erroll**, PC; royalist Civil War, Col of Horse in an attempt to rescue CHARLES I 1648; later raised a regt for CHARLES II; obtained a regrant of his honours with power to nominate his heirs 1666, choosing 1674 his cousin Sir John Hay of Keillour and the latter's heirs male, whom failing Sir John's heirs female, whom failing certain Tweeddale Hays ; *m* Lady Katherine Carnegie, dau of 2nd Earl of Southesk (*see* FIFE, D), and *dsp* March 1674

1a Margaret; *m* 1st 4 Feb 1638 Harry, Lord Ker, est s of 1st Earl of Roxburghe (*see* ROXBURGHE, D); *m* 2nd *c* 1644 6th Earl of Cassillis (*see* AILSA, M) and *d* April 1695

(1) Anne; *m* 1609 3rd Earl of Winton (*see* EGLINTON and WINTON, E)

(2) Jean; *m* 1620 19th/3rd Earl of Mar (*qv*)

(3) Mary; *m c* 1616 1st Earl of Buccleuch (*see* BUCCLEUCH and QUEENSBERRY, D)

(4) Elizabeth; *m* 1st *c* 1620 5th Lord Sempill (*qv*); *m* 2nd by 20 May 1643 1st Lord Mordington (*see* HAMILTON and BRANDON, D)

(5) Sophia; *m* 1626 1st and last Viscount of Melgum and Lord Aboyne (*see* HUNTLY, M)

(6) Margaret; *m* 1642 Sir John Seton of Barns

3 Thomas; apparently also a deaf mute; insane by 1596; living 1610

1 Helen; *m c* Jan 1583/4 1st Earl of Linlithgow (*see* LINLITHGOW, M, preliminary remarks) and had issue

The **8th Earl** *m* 2nd *c* 20 Sept 1581 Agnes (*m* 2nd Alexander Gordon of Strathdon, bro of 1st Marquess of Huntly, *qv*), dau of 4th Earl of Caithness (*qv*) (this marriage led the HAYs to fear he might disinherit his 1st w's children, so that in 1576 two of his bros (*see* above) invaded Slains Castle and imprisoned him with menaces, JAMES VI later entrusting his fief to Alexander Hay, Ld Clerk Register, on the children's behalf), and *d* 8 Oct 1585, having by her had:

4 George, of Keillour; *m* Isabel, dau of Patrick Cheyne of Essilmont and widow of Patrick Hay of Megginch (*see* KINNOULL, E), and had, with other issue:

(1) Andrew (Sir), of Keillour; *m* Margaret, sis of 1st Lord Kinnaird (*see* 1970 edn), and *d c* 1672 leaving, with other issue:

1a JOHN, **12th Earl**

5 William, of Fetterletter; *m* 1st Lilias, dau of Sir George Gordon of Gight; *m* 2nd, as her 3rd husb, Marie, sis of Sir Robert Innes, 1st Bt, of that Ilk (*see* ROXBURGHE, D)

The 11th EARL's second cousin of the half blood,

JOHN HAY, **12th Earl of Erroll**; Sheriff Aberdeen 1685, Chllr King's Coll Aberdeen 1700–04; *m c* 1 Oct 1674 Lady Anne Drummond (who made Slains the principal landing-place for Jacobite secret agents from France), dau of 3rd Earl of Perth (*qv*), and *d* 30 Dec 1704, having had, with other issue:

1 CHARLES HAY, **13th Earl of Erroll**, titular KT (conferred by James III); Chllr King's Coll Aberdeen 1705–16; took part in abortive Jacobite invasion of 1708, following which was imprisoned in Edinburgh Castle; *d* unm 13 Oct 1717

1 MARY Hay, **Countess of Erroll** in her own right; Jacobite 1745; *m c* Aug 1722 Alexander FALCONER later HAY of Delgaty (*d* July 1745), bro of 5th Lord Falconer (*see* KINTORE, E), and *dsp* 19 Aug 1758

2 Margaret; *m c* 1707 5th Earl of Linlithgow (*see* LINLITHGOW, M, preliminary remarks) and had:

(1) James Livingston, *Lord Livingston*; *dvp* 30 April 1715

(1) Anne Livingston; Jacobite who detained General Hawley at dinner to ensure the victory at Falkirk 1746; *m* 15 June 1724 4th Earl of Kilmarnock (*see* KILMARNOCK, B) and *d* 14 Sept 1747, leaving, with other issue:

1a JAMES BOYD later HAY, **15th Earl of Erroll**; *b* 20 Dec 1726; rep S peer 1770–74; *m* 1st 15 Sept 1749 Rebecca (*d* 2 May 1761), dau of Alexander Lockhart, Ld of Session as Lord Covington, and had issue:

1b Mary; *m* General John Scott of Balcomie

1a (cont.) The **15th Earl** *m* 2nd 1762 Isabella (*d* 3 Nov 1808), dau of Sir William Carr, Bt, of Etal, Northumberland, and *d* 3 July 1778, having had by her, with other issue:

1b GEORGE HAY, **16th Earl of Erroll**; *b* 13 May 1767; Lt-Col 1st Gds, served Walcheren Expdn, rep S peer 1796; *m* 25 Jan 1790 Elizabeth Jermina (*m* 2nd 12 Sept 1816 John Hookham Frere, PC, of Roydon Hall, Norfolk (*d* 7 Jan 1846), and *d* 17 Jan 1831), dau of Joseph Blake, of Ardfry, Co Galway (*see* 1917 edn WALLSCOURT, B), and having inadvertently disclosed a secret entrusted to him by the PM, Pitt the Younger, committed suicide on a point of honour 14 June 1789

2b WILLIAM, **17th Earl**

2b Augusta; *m* 4th Earl of Glasgow (*qv*) and *d* 1822

The 16th EARL's bro,

WILLIAM HAY later CARR (roy licence 28 March 1795, though he forfeited his maternal gf's bequest of Etal on succeeding to the Earldom), **17th Earl of Erroll**; *b* 12 March 1772; Kt Marischal Scotland 1805, rep S peer 1806, Ld High Commr Ch Scotland; *m* 1st 9 Jan 1792 Jane (*d* 14 April 1793), dau of Matthew Bell, and had issue:

1 Dulcibella Jane; *m* 1821 Ven Charles Nourse Wodehouse (*see* KIMBERLEY, E) and *d* 10 Jan 1885, leaving issue

The **17th Earl** *m* 2nd 3 Aug 1796 Alicia (*d* 24 April 1812), yst dau of Samuel Eliot, of Antigua, and by her had issue:

1 James, *Lord Hay*; Ensign 1st Gds; *ka* Quatre Bras 16 June 1815

2 WILLIAM GEORGE, **18th Earl**

3 Samuel; *b* Jan 1807; Army Capt; *m* 2 April 1832 Louisa (*d* 18 April 1898), only dau of V-Adml Hon Duncombe Pleydell-Bouverie (*see* RADNOR, E), and *d* 25 Nov 1847

2 Isabella; *m* 14 April 1820 Lt-Gen William Wemyss (*d* 30 Nov 1852; *see* WEMYSS, E), and *d* 28 July 1868, leaving issue

3 Harriet Jemima; *m* 12 Dec 1822 Daniel Gurney (*d* 14 June 1880), of North Runcton, Norfolk, and *d* 8 Feb 1837, leaving issue

4 Caroline Augusta; *m* 18 Sept 1823 John Morant (*d* 5 May 1857), of Brockenhurst, Hants, and *d* 19 Aug 1877, having had issue

5 Emma; *m* 8 Aug 1826 R-Adml James Wemyss of Wemyss (*d* 3 April 1854), RN, MP, and *d* 17 July 1841, leaving issue (*see* WEMYSS, E)

The **17th Earl** *m* 3rd 14 Oct 1816 Harriet (*d* 28 Jan 1864), sis of 16th Lord Somerville, and *d* 26 Jan 1819, having by her had:

4 Somerville (Rev); *b* 20 July 1817; *m* 6 June 1843 Alicia Diana (*m* 2nd 5 Jan 1858 Capt James Young (*d* 1877) and *d* 31 Oct 1891), dau of 12th Earl of Buchan (*qv*), and *d* 25 Sept 1853, leaving issue:

(1) Somerville; *b* 19 Nov 1853

6 Fanny; *m* 2 Aug 1848 Rev Stephen Ralph Cartwright (*d* 9 Aug 1862), Rector Aynhoe, Northants, and *d* 28 Aug 1853, leaving a dau

7 Margaret Julia; *b* posthumously; *m* 23 Sept 1846 Frederick Astell Lushington (*see* LUSHINGTON, Bt), and *d* 31 Oct 1891, leaving issue

The 17th EARL's est surv son,

WILLIAM GEORGE HAY later CARR, **18th Earl of Erroll**, KT, GCH; *b* 21 Feb 1801; rep S peer 1823–31, Ld Steward Household, Master Buckhounds, Kt Marischal Scotland, Ld Lt Aberdeenshire; *cr* 17 June 1831 BARON KILMARNOCK, of Kilmarnock, Ayrshire (UK (*qv*)); *m* 4 Dec 1820 Elizabeth FitzClarence (*d* 16 Jan 1856), sis of 1st Earl of Munster (*qv*), and natural dau of King William IV by Mrs Jordan, the actress, and *d* 19 April 1846, having had issue:

1 WILLIAM HARRY, **19th Earl**

1 Ida Harriet Augusta; bridesmaid to HM QUEEN VICTORIA; *m* 1 Nov 1841 2nd Earl of Gainsborough (*qv*) and *d* 22 Oct 1867, leaving issue

2 Agnes Georgiana Elizabeth; *m* 16 March 1846 5th Earl of Fife (*see* FIFE, D) and *d* 18 Dec 1869, leaving issue

3 Alice Mary Emily; *m* 16 May 1874 Charles Edward Allen, self-styled Col Count Charles Edward d'Albanie (*d* 24 Dec 1880), only son of Charles Allen, self-styled Charles Edward Stuart, Count d'Albanie, by Anna, dau of Hon John de la Poer Beresford, bro of 1st Marquess of Waterford (*qv*), and *d* 7 June 1881

The 18th EARL's only son,

WILLIAM HARRY HAY, **19th Earl of Erroll**; *b* 3 May 1823; Maj Rifle Bde, wounded at the Alma Crimean War, fndr Port Erroll; *m* 20 Sept 1848 Eliza Amelia (*d* 11 March 1916), VA 3rd Cl, Ldy-in-Waiting to HM QUEEN VICTORIA, est dau of Gen Hon Sir Charles Gore, GCB, KH (*see* ARRAN, E), and *d* 3 Dec 1891, having had issue:

1 Charles Gore, *Lord Kilmarnock*; *b* 12 Oct 1850

2 CHARLES GORE, **20th Earl**

3 Arthur, CVO (1926); *b* 16 Sept 1855; Maj 2nd Bn QO Cameron Highrs, Capt Scots Gds, served Egypt 1882, Tel-el-Kebir (medal with clasp and bronze star), Burma as Cmdt Lower Burma Mil Police 1887–93 (medal and clasp), Maj and Adj Gds Res Regt 1900–01, Gentlemen Usher to TM QUEEN VICTORIA 1896–1901, EDWARD VII 1901–10 and GEORGE V 1910–25, Extra Gentleman Usher 1925; *d* unm 11 May 1932

4 Francis; *b* 14 Aug 1864; Page of Honour to HM QUEEN VICTORIA; committed suicide Queensland 24 Sept 1898

1 Florence; *d* an infant 15 May 1859

2 Cecilia Leila; *b* 4 March 1860; *m* 31 Oct 1883 Capt George Allan Webbe (*d* 19 Feb 1925), 15th Hus, of Errollston, Ascot, and *d* 7 Jan 1935

3 Florence Agnes Adelaide; *b* 31 May 1872; *m* 9 May 1895 Maj Henry Wolrige-Gordon (*d* 9 Oct 1923), 79th Cameron Highrs, and *dsp* 16 Oct 1935

The 19th EARL's est son,

CHARLES GORE HAY, **20th Earl of Erroll**, KT, CB, JP (Cumberland), DL (Aberdeenshire); *b* 7 Feb 1852; Ld-in-Waiting to HM EDWARD VII 1903–05, Hon Maj-Gen, Lt-Col cmdg RHG, served Boer War and WW I; *m* 11 Aug 1875 Mary Caroline (*d* 12 Oct 1934), dau of Edmund L'Estrange by Lady Henrietta Susan Beresford Lumley (*see* SCARBROUGH, E), and *d* 8 July 1927, having had issue:

1 VICTOR ALEXANDER SERELD, **21st Earl**

2 Sereld Mordaunt Alan Josslyn, OBE (1919); *b* Nov 1877; Cdr RN, Cdr-Instr RNVR, S African Div 1913 and WW I, Assist NTO Cape Town 1914–15 (ret 1917); *m* 26 April 1915 Violet, 2nd dau of Lt-Col Duncan Chisholm Oliver Spiller, of Chelsea, and *dsp* 12 Nov 1939

3 Ivan Josslyn Lumley, MBE (1932); *b* 31 Oct 1884; Page of Honour to TM QUEEN VICTORIA and EDWARD VII, Capt Res 5th Lancers WW I; *m* 8 Nov 1921 Pamela (*d* 23 Nov 1977), dau of Francis George Burroughes, of Blakeney Holt, Norfolk, and *d* 6 Sept 1936, leaving issue:

(1) Alexandra Cecilia Mary; *b* 26 Sept 1922 (HM QUEEN ALEXANDRA stood sponsor); *d* 29 April 1991

(2) +Elizabeth Anne [Mrs Elizabeth Gurney, 22 Lennox Gdns, London SW1]; *b* 3 Feb 1925; WW II in WRNS; *m* 20 Oct 1945 (*divorce* 1970) Lt Jeremy Christopher Gurney, RN, yr son of Christopher Gurney, and has issue:

1a +Michael Jeremy; *b* 3 Nov 1946; *educ* Eton; *m* 14 Feb 1981 (*divorce* 1997) Hon Miranda Cumming-Bruce, dau of 8th Baron Thurlow (*qv*), and has issue

2a +William Ivan; *b* 25 March 1948; *educ* Eton and Bristol U; *m* 10 Aug 1973 *Anne Marie, dau of Robert Deutsch, and has issue

(3) +Penelope Constance [Mrs George Dare, 9 Launceston Pl, London W8 5RL]; *b* 26 March 1930; *m* 25 May 1957 *George Harold Armine Dare, son of Harold Dare, MC, and Mrs William Edridge Yockney (*see* MORRIS, Bt), and has:

1a +Henry James; *b* 3 March 1959; *educ* Stowe and Keele U

1a +Amelia Alexandra Elizabeth; *b* 27 Nov 1961

The 20th EARL's est son,

VICTOR ALEXANDER SERELD HAY, **21st Earl of Erroll**, KCMG; *b* 17 Oct 1876 (HM QUEEN VICTORIA stood sponsor); Min Dip Serv, HC Inter-Allied Rhineland Commn with local rank of Amb 1921–28; *m* 22 May 1900 Mary Lucy Victoria (*d* 18 Jan 1957), only dau of Sir Allan Russell Mackenzie, 2nd Bt, of Glen Muick (*qv*), and *d* 20 Feb 1928, having had issue:

1 JOSSLYN VICTOR, **22nd Earl**

2 GILBERT ALLAN ROWLAND, 6th BARON KILMARNOCK (*qv*)

1 Rosemary Constance Ferelith; *b* 15 May 1904; *m* 1st 29 May 1924 (*divorce* 1935) Lt-Col Rupert Sumner Ryan, CMG, DSO, RA (*d* Aug 1952), only son of Maj-Gen Sir Charles Ryan, KBE, CB, CMG, and had issue:

(1) Patrick Victor Charles; *b* 1925; *m* 1949 *Rosemary Elizabeth [Mrs Patrick Ryan, 76 Park St, S Yarra, Victoria 3141, Australia], only child of Francis Rupert Chesterman, of Orford, Tasmania, and *d* 1989, leaving issue:

1a +Dominic Rupert Charles [Dominic Ryan Esq, 43 Otter St, Collingwood, Victoria 3066, Australia]; *b* 21 May 1956

1a +Siobhan Ferelith Ryan [Mrs Mark Douglass, 356 Glen Eira Rd, Elsternwick, Victoria 3185, Australia]; *b* 1959; *m* 1994 *Mark Douglass and has:

1b +Hunter; *b* 1990

1 (cont.) Lady Rosemary Ryan *m* 2nd 27 June 1935 Maj James Frank Gresham (*d* 1983), late Welsh Gds, er son of Frank Gresham, and *d* 19 May 1944

The 21st EARL's er son,

JOSSLYN VICTOR HAY, **22nd Earl of Erroll**; *b* 11 May 1901; Hon Attaché and Priv Sec to Amb Berlin 1920–22, MLC Kenya 1938–41, Capt Kenya Regt 1939, Eritrean Campaign 1940 (despatches), Dep Dir Man-Power and Mil Sec E Africa Cmd 1940–41; *m* 1st 22 Sept 1923 (*divorce* 1930) Lady Idina Sackville (*d* 5 Nov 1955), dau of 8th Earl De La Warr (*qv*), and had issue; *m* 2nd 8 Feb 1930 Mrs Edith Mildred Mary Agnes Ramsay-Hill (*d* 13 Oct 1939), dau of Richard Watson Maude, of Cleveland, Knaresborough, Yorks, and was murdered nr Nairobi 24 Jan 1941, leaving by his 1st w:

DIANA DENYSE Hay, **Countess of Erroll** in her own right; *b* 5 Jan 1926; OStJ, Hon Pres 45 Assoc, DStJ; *m* 1st 19 Dec 1946 (*divorce* 1964) **Sir (Rupert) Iain Kay Moncreiffe of that Ilk, 11th Bt**, CVO, Capt Scots Gds, Albany Herald, and had:

1 MERLIN SERELD VICTOR GILBERT HAY, **24th and present Earl of Erroll**

2 +Peregrine David Euan Malcolm MONCREIFFE OF MONCREIFFE, feudal Baron of Easter Moncreiffe and fiar of the feudal Barony of Moncreiffe [The Hon Peregrine Moncreiffe of Moncreiffe, Easter Moncreiffe, Bridge of Earn, Perthshire PH2 8QA]; *b* 16 Feb 1951; *educ* Eton and Ch Ch Oxford; banker, Slains Pursuivant 1970, Lt Atholl Highrs 1978, investment banker: White Weld & Co/Credit Suisse First Boston Ltd 1972–82, Lehman Brothers Kuhn Loeb/Shearson Lehman 1982–86, E F Hutton & Co 1986–88, exec dir Buchanan Ptnrs 1990–; Roy Commn Ancient and Historical Monuments Scotland 1989–94, Chm Scottish Ballet 1988–90, Tstee Save the Rhino; memb Roy Co Archers, Freeman City London, Liveryman Fishmongers's Co; *m* 1988 *Miranda Mary, yr dau of Capt (Edward Arthur) Mervyn Fox-Pitt (*see* DUNDEE, E), and has issue:

(1) +Ossian Peregrine T G; *b* 1991

(1) +Idina May; *b* 1992
(2) +A dau; *b* 2 Feb 1995
(3) +A dau; *b* 19 Nov 1996

1 +Alexandra Victoria Caroline Anne [The Lady Alexandra Connell, 65 Sterndale Rd, London W14 OHU]; *b* 30 July 1955; has issue by Michael Wigan (*see* WIGAN, Bt):

(1) *Ivor Francis Grey de Miremont WIGAN; *b* 1979

1 (cont.) Lady Alexandra *m* 1989 *Jolyon (John) Christopher Neill Connell, late dep ed *Sunday Telegraph*, ed *The Week*, est son of James Christopher Ferrier Connell, of Pitlochry, Perthshire, and by him has issue:

(1) +Flora Diana Catharine Cecilia; *b* 1990

The **Countess of Erroll** *m* 2nd 27 Nov 1964 *Maj Raymond Alexander Carnegie (*see* FIFE, D) and *d* 17 May 1978, leaving by him:

3 +Jocelyn Jacek Alexander Bannerman [The Hon Jocelyn Carnegie, Craggish, Comrie, Perthshire PH6 2JT]; *b* 21 Nov 1966; *educ* Trin Coll Glenalmond; *m* 1990 *Susie Mhairi, dau of Thomas Mitchell Hastie Butler, of Eastmillhill, Crimond, and has had issue:

(1) +Merlin Thomas Alexander Bannerman; *b* 1991
(2) +Maximilian Archibald Josslyn; *b* 21 Dec 1995
(1) Cecilia Diana Catriona Pearl; *b* 1993; *d* 1994

Lineage (of Moncreiffe): The name derives from a feudal Barony of Moncreiff, Perthshire, itself derived from the Gaelic *Monadh Craoibhe*, 'the Hill of the Sacred Bough' (presumably oak, immemorially the family plant-badge). The feudal Barony has been in the family's possession since before surnames were first adopted in Scotland. They are the oldest family in Perthshire to have retained their original lands in the male line. On the summit of Moncreiffe Hill the ancient Kings of the Picts had their principal stronghold, apparently called *Dun Monaidh*.

The Moncreiffe arms suggest they are a branch of the house of Maldred (*see* O'NEILL, B, also ABERGAVENNY, M), Regent of the Cumbrians and brother of KING DUNCAN, killed by MACBETH 1040—possibly the same line as Dundas.

The names of the early Lairds are only traditional: Ramer, Gaspar, Gerard and Roger, Frankish names that may derive from an important local marriage of an heiress of the house of Maldred to a powerful baron of the great Norman house of Mowbray. Accordingly,

Sir MATHEW OF MONCREIFFE, the first to be recorded in a Roy Charter, is now counted as 1st Laird of Moncreiffe; had a charter 1 Feb 1248 confirming him in the lands of Moncreiffe; also held Balgony near Abernethy in the Clan Macduff country and the Atholl lands of Culdares and Duneaves in the mouth of Glenlyon; *m* Marjorie, sister of John of Dundemor, lord of Dundemor in Fife, co-Regent of Scotland during the minority of ALEXANDER III, and acquired through her the lands of Dunbarrow near Strathmiglo, Fife; had:

Sir JOHN MONCREIFFE OF THAT ILK, 2nd Laird; forced to do homage to EDWARD I 1296; made over Easter Moncreiffe 1312 to a yr s Mathew, ancestor of the first line of MONCREIFFEs of Easter Moncreiffe; his est s:

WILLIAM MONCREIFFE OF THAT ILK, 3rd Laird; had:

DUNCAN MONCREIFFE OF THAT ILK, 4th Laird; *d* 1357; his successor (and presumably son):

JOHN MONCREIFFE OF THAT ILK, 5th Laird; *d* 1410, leaving:

MALCOLM MONCREIFFE OF THAT ILK, 6th Laird; memb of JAMES II's Cncl of Lds Auditors (effective govt); received a new charter incorporating his Highland and Lowland estates into a free Barony of Moncreiffe 1 Dec 1455; *m* Elna (*d* 1458), dau of Sir David Murray of Tullibardine (*see* ATHOLL, D), and *d* 1464/5, leaving:

JOHN MONCREIFFE OF THAT ILK, 7th Laird; Chamberlain and Esquire to JAMES III 1464; *m* Beatrix, dau of James Dundas of that Ilk by Cristina Stewart (*see* MORAY, E), and *d* between 1466 and 1475, having had, with other issue:

1 JOHN, 8th Laird

2 George, of Tippermaloch, granted him by JAMES III 1473, in whose Household he was Squire in charge of the royal armour; *m* Mettey, a Danish Ldy-in-Waiting to JAMES III's QUEEN MARGARET, also from Denmark; ancestor of the MONCREIFFs of Tippermaloch, one of whom helped kill MARY QUEEN OF SCOTS' secretary Rizzio

3 Andrew; murdered by Ramsay of Kilgour 1494

4 Thomas; mutilated by John Watson 1511

The est son,

JOHN MONCREIFFE OF THAT ILK, 8th Laird; convicted of misappropriating the lands of Kinmonth 1484; feuded with the John Ramsay of Kilgour who killed his brother; *m* 1st Margaret, dau of Sir Robert Levingston of Drumry, Laird of Easter Wemyss, and had, with other issue:

1 John (Sir), 9th Laird; *m* Beatrix, niece of Andrew Forman, Archbp St Andrews, and was *k* Scots defeat by English of Flodden 9 Sept 1513, leaving, with other issue:

(1) William, 10th Laird; captured by the English at their victory of Solway Moss 1542; *m* 1526 Margaret, dau of Sir Andrew Murray of Balvaird (*see* MANSFIELD and MANSFIELD, E), and *d* 15 Dec 1579, having had, with other issue:

1a William; *b c* 1526; hostage in England for his father's ransom 1543; released (the ransom never paid) to take part in Lennox's rebellion 1544 (*see* above); entered the French Service 1552; raised and cmded Moncreiffe's Regt of Scottish mercenaries in the Swedish service; joined a plot to reinstate the mad ERIC XIV OF SWEDEN by killing KING JOHN during an exhibition sword dance but the plot failing he was arrested April 1574 and never heard of again; *m* 1550 Jean, dau of Laurence, 3rd Lord Oliphant, and had, with four daus:

1b William, 11th Laird; last to have the hereditary right to sit in Parl as a feudal Baron before the statute providing for the election of Commissioners to represent the barons; Gentleman of the King's Chamber 1580; sold Highland lands of Culdares and Duneaves to buy the Fife barony of Carnbee 1599; *m* 1586 Anne, dau of Robert Murray of Abercairny, and *d* 27 Sept 1624, leaving issue (*see* MONCREIFF, B)

2b Archibald; hereditary Prior of Elcho 1600, a dignity he exchanged for the old Moncreiffe estate of Balgony 1610; Min of Abermethy 1586–1633; *m* Margaret, sister of Sir George Auchinleck of Balmanno, Lord Balmanno, and *d* 1633; ancestor of the Barons Moncreiff (*qv*)

3b John (Sir); for whom in 1592 Easter Moncreiffe was erected into a free Barony, giving its lairds the same powers of life and death as those already held by the Lairds of Moncreiffe; advocate and Sheriff Depute Perthshire; *m* Jean, dau of John Spens of Condie, Ld Advocate, and *d* after Nov 1635, leaving issue:

1c John; drowned himself in the Earn 1616, leaving descendants who held Easter Moncreiffe and Kinmouth till 1674

2c Gerard; *d* of plague 1608

3c Robert; *d* of plague 1608

4c Andrew Moncreiffe of Boghall; *s f* as Sheriff Depute Perthshire

4b Andrew; Commendator of Elcho, Min of Crail; *m* Jonet, dau of David Moncreiffe, Apparent of Tippermaloch, and *d* 8 Aug 1596, leaving issue

5b Hew, of the Cotes of Elcho; wounded trying to save his host in the Gowrie House Affair 1600 (*see* CARLISLE, E); later pardoned by JAMES VI personally; *m* 1st Helen Dundas, of Fingask (*see* ZETLAND, M), and had issue; *m* 2nd Agnes, dau of Thomas Dischington of Ardross, and *d* after 6 Nov 1635, having by her had further issue

2a James, of Barnhill; *m* Margaret Balnavis/Piper (*d* 22 Oct 1613), dau of James Balnavis, and *d* by 29 Nov 1596, leaving issue

3a John; Vicar of Dunbarny, murdered by the Master of Oliphant Dec 1579

4a Alexander; *m* Euphame Crichton of Strathurd and *d* 8 Dec 1610, leaving issue; ancestor of the MONCREIFFs of Culfargie and Bandirran, the MONCRIEFFs of Kinmouth and in the female line the SCOTT-MONCREIFFs

1a Euphamie; *m c* 1542 John Leslie of Parkhill and Cleish, 2nd son of 3rd Earl of Rothes (*qv*)

2a Elisabeth; *m* Alexander Ruthven of Freeland, yst son of 2nd Lord Ruthven (*see* CARLISLE, E)

3a Isobel; *m* George Rollo of Duncrub (*see* ROLLO, L)

(2) John; Prior Blantyre 1535–47; had an illegitimate son:

1a Gillbert; legitimated by JAMES VI 1585; dr to royal household; ancestor of the MONCREIFFs of Myreside

(3) Alexander

2 Hew, 1st of Easter Rhynd; also held Pitgorno and Mundy; Gentleman Household 1503–13; *m* 3rd 1524 his cousin Elisabeth, dau of Sir John Dischington of Ardross, a Fife baron, and had, with other issue:

(1) David, 2nd of Easter Rhynd; *k* Scots defeat by English of Pinkie 1547

(2) Peter, 3rd of Easter Rhynd, which he made over to his bro James 14 Nov 1548 due to physical incapacity

(3) James, 4th of Easter Rhynd; took part with the Laird of Moncreiffe in the unsuccessful rebellion of Lennox (*see* MORAY, E) and Glencairn (*see* CUNINGHAME, Bt) against the Regent Arran 1544; *m* 1st (*divorce* due to consanguinity 1550) Eupheme, sister of Archibald Dundas of Fingask (*see* ZETLAND, M), and had issue; *m* 2nd Margaret Tyrie of Drumkilbo and *d* 1587, leaving by her a 4th son:

1a David; *m* Isabel, dau of William Robertson of Struan, 6th Chief of Clan Donnachaidh, and *d c* 1625, having had, with other issue:

1b Thomas; merchant in Kirkwall; *m* 1620 Elspeth (*d* 26 March 1689), dau of Thomas Baikie and sister of James Baikie, 1st of Tankerness, and had, with other issue:

1c **Sir Thomas Moncreiffe of that Ilk, 1st Bt** (NS), so *cr* 30 Nov 1685, with remainder to heirs male whatsoever, also 14th Laird; *b* 1626; Baronies of Moncreiffe and Easter Moncreiffe united in his favour 1674; original memb Roy Co Archers; Clerk Exchequer and Treasurer Scotland; *m* 1st Bethia (*d* 1703), dau of Alexander Hamilton of Hill, Ld Justice Clerk during the Protectorate; *m* 2nd Mary (*d* Nov 1723), dau of Sir Thomas Hope of Kerse, Ld Justice Gen, and widow of Sir John Young of Leny, and *dsp* 15 Jan 1715

2c Harie; Bailie Kirkwall 1703; sea captain; *m* 10 Oct 1676 Barbara, dau of Harry Erbury/Herbert, and had an est son:

1d THOMAS (Sir), **2nd Bt**

1c Elspeth; *m* 5 July 1665 Arthur Baikie, 2nd of Tankerness

1 Margaret; *m* 1st Sir Duncan Campbell of Glenorchy, Mac Chailein mac Dhonnachaidh (*k* Flodden 1513), and had issue (*see* 1970 edn BREADALBANE AND HOLLAND, E); *m* 2nd Sir William Menteith of Kerse and Alva (*d* 18 Feb 1523) and *d* Nov 1554

JOHN MONCREIFFE OF THAT ILK, 8th Laird, *m* 2nd Janet Strathauchin/Strachan, sister of Gilbert Strathauchin, Canon of Aberdeen and Prothonotary Apostolic, and *d c* 1496

The 1st Bt's n,

Sir Thomas Moncreiffe of that Ilk, 2nd Bt, 15th Laird; *bapt* 3 Oct 1678; *educ* St Andrews; memb Roy Co Archers; *m* (contract 22 Dec 1701) Margaret, dau of Patrick Smythe, of Methven, and had issue:

1 THOMAS (Sir), **3rd Bt**

2 David MONCREIFFE later STEUART MONCREIFFE (5 Dec 1768 as heir of William Steuart, King's Remembrancer in the Exchequer) of Moredun; *b* 1710; Baron of the Exchequer, Exchequer Judge 1781; *d* 17 April 1790

1 Margaret; *b* 1707; *m* 1740 Maj-Gen Alexander Gordon of Auchintoul, Russian Imp Serv, Jacobite leader, and *d* 19 Sept 1788

2 Jean; *b* 1712; *d* unm

3 Janet; *b* 1715; *m* 11 Feb 1768 Hon Charles Maitland, 2nd son of 6th Earl of Lauderdale (*qv*), and *dsp* 6 Nov 1799

Sir THOMAS *d* Oct 1738; his er son,

Sir Thomas Moncreiffe of that Ilk, 3rd Bt, 16th Laird; *b* 31 Dec 1704; *educ* Edinburgh U; memb Roy Co Archers; *m* (an elopement) 2 June 1730 Katharine (*d* 24 June 1735), dau of the Jacobite Sir William Murray of Ochtertyre, 3rd Bt, and *d* 3 May 1739, having had, with other issue:

Sir William Moncreiffe of that Ilk, 4th Bt, 17th Laird; *b* 11 Feb 1732; *educ* Glasgow U and Holland; *m* Clara (*d* 31 March 1785), dau of Robert Guthrie, brother of James Guthrie, 1st of Craigie, and *d* 28 Sept 1784, leaving, with a dau (Jean, *m* Andrew Cunningham of Bonnington):

Sir Thomas Moncreiffe of that Ilk, 5th Bt, 18th Laird; *b* 7 Jan 1758; *educ* St Andrews; Ensign 36th Foot 1774, Cornet 10th Dragoons 1776; feeble-minded, hence the estate placed in the care of guardians 1791; *m* 13 Aug 1786 Lady Elisabeth Ramsay (*d* 3 June 1848 when her night-cap took fire from a candle), dau of 8th Earl of Dalhousie (*qv*), and *d* 26 March 1818, having had, with a dau (Georgina Elisabeth, *b* 20 Aug 1790, *m* 5 March 1818, as his 1st w, 2nd Earl of Bradford (*qv*) and *d* 12 Oct 1842, leaving issue):

Sir David Moncreiffe of that Ilk, 6th Bt, 19th Laird, DL (Perthshire); *b* 31 Dec 1788; *educ* Eton; Maj 3rd King's Own Light Dragoons 1814; memb Roy Co Archers, Capt Roy and Ancient Golf Club St Andrews, Pres Roy Caledonian Hunt; *m* 21 Jan 1819 (as the result of a successful wager) Helen (*m* 2nd 30 Oct 1849 her sis-in-law's widower 2nd Earl of Bradford (*qv*) and *d* 25 April 1869), dau of Capt Æneas Mackay of Scotstoun (*see* REAY, L), and had, with two daus:

1 THOMAS (Sir), **7th Bt**

2 William Æneas; *b* 19 Jan 1825; Offr 92nd Highrs, exchanged as Maj into the 72nd after a row with his colonel; went to Australia; *d* unm 5 Jan 1906

Sir DAVID *d* 20 Nov 1830 (winning as a result a bet with Whyte Melville, who was obliged to give the famous Silver Putter, bearing both their Arms, to the Roy and Ancient Golf Club at St Andrews for not dying first); his er son,

Sir Thomas Moncreiffe of that Ilk, 7th Bt, 20th Laird; *b* 9 Jan 1822; *educ* Harrow; Lt Gren Gds 1839–43; Capt Atholl Highrs, V-Lt Perthshire, Hon Col Roy Perthshire Rifles, memb (aged 15) Roy Co Archers, Capt Roy and Ancient Golf Club St Andrews, Chm Perthshire C Assoc; *m* 2 May 1843 Lady Louisa Hay (*d* 4 Sept 1898), est dau of 11th Earl of Kinnoull (*qv*), and *d* 15 Aug 1879, having had:

1 David Maule; *b* 12 Dec 1854; *d* 25 April 1857

2 **Sir Robert Drummond Moncreiffe of that Ilk, 8th Bt**, 21st Laird, CB, CMG (1915), VD, TD, DL (Perthshire); *b* 3 Nov 1856; *educ* Harrow; Lt Scots Gds 1876–81, ADC to HM GEORGE V, Hon Col 6th (Perthshire) Bn Black Watch, Capt Atholl Highrs, WW I: cmded Perthshire Bn Black Watch (despatches twice) 1915, cmded at Edinburgh Castle 1918; *m* 6 April 1880 his cousin Evelyn Elisabeth Vane (*d* 16 Jan 1938), est dau of Col Hon Charles Rowley Hay Drummond of Cromlix (*see* KINNOULL, E), and *dsp* 8 June 1931

3 (Thomas George) Harry; *b* 9 Oct 1861; *educ* Harrow; planter in India; *m* 31 Aug 1883 Elisabeth (*d* 20 Feb 1947), dau of Sir John Muir, of Deanston, 1st Bt, Ld Provost Glasgow, and *d* of fever at Calcutta 26 March 1887, leaving issue:

(1) **Sir (John Robert) Guy Moncreiffe of that Ilk, 9th Bt**, 22nd Laird; *b* 30 June 1884; *educ* HMS *Britannia*; Cdr RN, served blockade of Venezuela (bombardment of Puerto Cabello) 1902–03, Roy Yacht *Victoria and Albert*, WW I as a Submarine Cdr, Lt Atholl Highrs; *m* 29 April 1919 Mary, Offr Order Orange-Nassau Netherlands, dau of John Balli, of London and Paris, and *d* 7 Sept 1934, leaving:

1a **Sir David Gerald Moncreiffe of that Ilk, 10th Bt**, MC (1944), 23rd Laird; *b* 29 July 1922; *educ* Eton and Edinburgh U; Capt Scots Gds WW II (wounded), Capt Atholl Highrs; memb Roy Co Archers; *d* unm in a fire which destroyed his family seat 17 Nov 1957

1a (Katherine) Elisabeth, 24th of Moncreiffe; *b* 23 May 1920; WW II in WRNS; *d* 29 May 1997

(2) (Thomas) Gerald Auckland; *b* 13 Sept 1886; *educ* HMS *Britannia*; Lt-Cdr RN WW I (wounded); *m* 17 June 1918 Hilda (*m* 2nd 7 April 1923 Capt Geoffrey Lionel Smith, of Kenya, yst s of Sir William Smith; *m* 3rd 1931 Charles Arthur Gordon McMinn, of Nanyuki, Kenya, and *d* 14 Jan 1960), dau of Count François de Miremont, and *d* 3 June 1922, leaving issue:

1a **Sir (Rupert) Iain Kay Moncreiffe of that Ilk, 11th Bt**, DL (Perthshire 1961), CVO (1980), DL (Perthshire), QC (Scotland 1980); *b* 9 April 1919; *educ* Switzerland, Stowe, Heidelberg, Ch Ch Oxford (MA 1945) and Edinburgh U (LLB 1950, PhD 1958); Capt Scots Gds WW II (wounded), ADC to Gen Sir Andrew Thorne 1944–45, Mil Liaison Offr Norway to Adml Sir William Whitworth 1945, Priv Sec to Amb and Attaché Moscow 1946, advocate Scottish Bar 1950, underwriting memb Lloyd's 1952–85, Maj cmdg Strathearn Dist Perthshire HG 1954–57, memb Advsy Ctee Scottish Nat Portrait Gallery 1957–85, Hon Sheriff Substitute Perth and Angus 1958–85, Albany Herald 1961–85, Capt Atholl Highrs, memb Roy Co Archers, Pres Duodecimal Soc GB, Hon Pres Scottish Genealogy Soc, Pres Assoc Genealogists and Record Agents 1980–85; Hon Pres Dorened Soc GB 1966–85; Patron Scottish Tartans Soc, fndr memb Scottish Plebiscite Soc and Puffin's Club (Edin) 1962, chm Debrett's Peerage Ltd 1976–82, author: *Simple Heraldry* (with D Pottinger, 1953), *Simple Custom* (1954), *Blood Royal* (1956), *Map of Scotland of Old* (1960), *The Highland Clans* (with David Hicks, 1967), *Royal Highness* (1982), *Royal Scotland* (with Jean Goodman, 1983), FSA, FZS, FSA Scot, Fell American Soc Genealogists, KStJ, Cross With Sword Grand Offr of Merit SMO Malta 1982, Gold Medal Sacred and Constantinian Order of St George 1982; *m* 1st 19 Dec 1946 (*divorce* 1964) Diana Denyse, **Countess of Erroll** in her own right (*see* above), and had issue; *m* 2nd 1 May 1966 *Hermione Patricia [Lady Moncreiffe of that Ilk, 24 Gordon Place, London W8 4JE], dau of Lt-Col Walter Douglas Faulkner, MC (*see* BUCCLEUCH and QUEENSBERRY, D), and *d* 1985, leaving issue

4 William; *b* 19 Jan 1863; *educ* Harrow and Trin Coll Cambridge; rancher Wyoming 1888–1923; served Roosevelt's Rough-Riders Spanish-American War 1898; *m* 9 March 1909 Edith Mary (*d* 21 Dec 1957), dau of Hugh Conyngham Boyd, of Ash Grove, Newry, Co Down, and *dsp* 31 May 1944

5 Ronald; *b* 3 May 1864; *educ* Harrow; Capt Worcs Imp Yeo, served Matabele War 1896, Boer War (on Baden Powell's staff throughout Siege of Mafeking when not in close arrest) 1900–02, took part in the Jameson Raid; *m* 8 Oct 1906 Edith Evelyn Kathleen (*m* 2nd Guy Hylton Gardiner), only dau of Arthur Arthington Worsley, and *dsp* 6 Aug 1909

6 Malcolm; *b* 29 Oct 1866; *educ* Harrow; rancher Wyoming; *m* 23 April 1901 Amy Morehead (*d* 22 Sept 1954), sis of Countess of Portsmouth, dau of Samuel Walker, of Frankfort, Ky., and gdau of Samuel Morehead, Govr Kentucky American Civil War, and *dsp* 15 June 1948

7 Claude; *b* 21 June 1869; *d* an infant

8 John Alexander, MC, DCM; *b* 2 Aug 1871; *educ* Harrow; Maj Oxfordshire Hus Boer War (severely wounded), Lt Younghusband's Horse ops Cape Colony 1902, WW I: cmded Cav Machine Gun Sqdns (wounded, despatches, Croix de Guerre with palm); *m* 4 Oct 1910 Lady Beatrice Constance Grosvenor (*d* 12 Jan 1911), 2nd dau of 1st Duke of Westminster (*qv*) and widow of 3rd Baron Chesham (*qv*), and *dsp* 21 June 1933

1 Louisa; *b* 11 June 1844; *m* 29 Oct 1863 7th Duke of Atholl (*qv*) and *d* 8 July 1902, leaving issue

2 Helen; *b* 18 July 1845; *m* 5 April 1864 Sir Charles John Forbes, 4th Bt, of Newe (*qv*), and *d* 12 Nov 1913, leaving issue

3 Georgina Elisabeth, RRC, DJStJ; *b* 9 Aug 1846; served BRCS Boer War and WW I; *m* 21 Nov 1865 1st Earl of Dudley (*qv*) and *d* 2 Feb 1929, leaving issue

4 Harriet Sarah; *b* 7 Feb 1848; *m* 7 Dec 1866 (*divorce* 1875) Sir Charles Mordaunt, 10th Bt (*qv*), and *d* 9 May 1906, leaving issue

5 Blanche; *b* 2 June 1849; *m* 11 June 1878 Charles Archibald Murray, of Taymount (*see* MANSFIELD and MANSFIELD, E), and *d* 4 July 1926, leaving issue (*see* MACGREGOR OF MACGREGOR, Bt)

6 Frances Rose; *b* 22 Sept 1850; *m* 21 Feb 1871 Sir Alexander Muir-Mackenzie of Delvine, 3rd Bt (*qv*), and *dsp* 7 July 1923

7 Selina; *b* 4 Oct 1851; *m* 20 July 1869, as his 2nd w, Maj-Gen William Arbuthnot, CB, 14th Hus, and *d* 26 Nov 1877, leaving issue (*see* ARBUTHNOT, Bt, of Edinburgh)

8 Mary Katherine; *b* 3 Dec 1859; interior decorator; *m* 26 Oct 1880 (*divorce* 1905) Sir Basil Templer Graham Montgomery, 5th Bt (*qv*), and *d* 30 July 1910, having had issue

ERROLL OF HALE

Arms: Per bend az. and gu., on a bend embellished of six electric flashes or a fleur-de-lys and two lozenges sa. **Crest:** A chevronel round embattled sa. **Supporters:** Dexter, an elephant guardant sa.; sinister, a bear regardant arg., muzzled az., cord sa., ringed or and reflexed over the back. **Motto:** It will come out all right.

Creation: B. (UK) 19 Dec 1964.

THE 1ST BARON ERROLL OF HALE, of Kilmun, Co Argyll (Frederick James Erroll,TD, PC (1960)) [The Rt Hon The Lord Erroll of Hale TD PC, House of Lords, London SW1A 0PW]; *b* 27 May 1914; *educ* Oundle and Trin Coll Cambridge (BA 1935, MA 1938); CEng, FIEE, MIMechE, Tech Adj 4th Co London Yeo (Sharpshooters) (TA) and Tank Div Min of Supply WW II, Col 1945, MP (C) Altrincham and Sale 1945–64, Parly Sec Min Supply, Ec Sec Treasury 1958–59, BOT: Parly Sec 1956–58, Min State 1959–61, Pres 1961–63, Min Power 1963–64, pres London Chamber Commerce 1966–69, Dep Chm Decimal Currency Bd 1966–71; *m* 19 Dec 1950 *Elizabeth, dau of Richard Sowton Barrow, of Foxholes, Exmouth, Devon

Lineage: JACOBUS BERGMANS, of Rotterdam; *b* 11 Dec 1812; *m* 29 Dec 1830 Maria van Campen and *d* 26 July 1883, having had issue:

THEODOR JOHN BERGMANS, of Rotterdam, merchant and broker London; *b* 27 April1841; *educ* privately; *m* 10 June 1869 Margaret (*d* 7 April 1924), dau of James Murison, of 7 Buckingham Terrace, Hillhead, Glasgow, and *dvp* 19 July 1879, leaving issue:

1 Theodor James BERGMANS later ERROLL (deed poll 1914), stockbroker; *b* 29 April 1871; *educ* privately; *d* unm 28 April 1924

2 GEORGE MURISON, of whom presently

1 Mary Josephine; *b* 13 April 1873; *m* 2 June 1909 Harry Petty Coulson, of Finnartmore, Kilmun, Argyllshire, and *d* 23 March 1964, leaving issue. He *d* 6 Nov 1930

The yr son,

GEORGE MURISON BERGMANS later ERROLL (deed poll 1914), of 3 Milnthorpe Road, Eastbourne; mechanical engr, Lt RFC WW I; *b* 10 May 1874; *educ* privately and King's Coll London; *m* 29 April 1913 Kathleen Donavon (*d* 29 Aug 1952), dau of George Brodrick Edington, of Hillhead, Glasgow, and *d* 20 Nov 1926, leaving:

FREDERICK JAMES, **Baron Erroll of Hale**, of Kilmun, Co Argyll (UK), so *cr* 19 Dec 1964

ERSKINE, Bt

Arms: Quarterly, 1st and 4th, gu. an imperial crown within a double tressure flory counter-flory or (for KELLIE); 2nd and 3rd, arg. a pale sa. (for ERSKINE) the whole within a bordure wavy erm. **Crest:** On a garb fesswise or, banded az., a cock, wings elevated ppr., charged with a bendlet wavy sinister of the second. **Motto:** *Veillant et vaillant* ('Vigilant and valorous'). **Creation:** Bt. (UK) 27 Aug 1821.

SIR (THOMAS) DAVID ERSKINE, 5TH BT, of Cambo, Fife, JP (Fife 1951) [Sir David Erskine Bt JP, West Newhall, Kingsbarns, St Andrews, Fife KY16 8QD]; *b* 31 July 1912; *s f* 1944; *educ* Eton and Magdalene Coll Cambridge (BA); with Butterfield and Swire 1934–41; V-Ld Lt Fife 1981–87 (DL 1955–81), Convener Fife CC 1970–73, Maj IA Engrs WW II; *m* 4 Oct 1947 *Ann, dau of Lt-Col Neil Fraser Tytler, DSO, MC, TD, of Aldourie Castle, Inverness, and has issue:

1 +(THOMAS) PETER NEIL [Peter Erskine Esq, Cambo House, Kingsbarns, Fife KY16 8QD]; *b* 28 March 1950; *educ* Eton, Birmingham U and Edinburgh U; photographer; *m* 1972 *Catherine Jean Killoy, 2nd dau of Col G H K Hewlett, of Willow Cottages, Cocklake, Wedmore, Somerset, and has:

(1) +(Thomas) Struan; *b* 6 Feb 1977

(2) +James Dunbar; *b* 1979

(1) *Gillian Christian; *b* 1983

(2) *Mary Caroline; *b* 1986

2 +William [Dr William Erskine, c/o ICARDA, PO Box 5466, Aleppo, Syria]; *b* 6 July 1952; *educ* Eton; PhD; *m* 1st 29 Sept 1973 Sarah Jane McElroy, est dau of Dr Charles William McElroy Pratt, MA, MD, of Orwell Grange, Orwell, Cambs; *m* 2nd 1982 *Mireille, dau of Georges Abdelnour, of Aleppo, Syria, and has:

(1) +Thomas Georges; *b* 1989

(2) +Philip Neil; *b* 1991

1 Caroline Sarah; *b* 19 Sept 1948; *m* 22 March 1974 *(Edmund) Christopher Hope Sharpe, er s of Edmund Sharpe, of Haverbrack House, nr Milnthorpe, Westmorland, and *d* 5 Jan 1976, leaving:

(1) *Titus [Titus Sharpe Esq, Cambo House, Kingsbarns, nr St Andrews, Fife KY16 8QD]; *b* 3 Sept 1974; *educ* Loretto and Nottingham U (BSc 1997)

Lineage: Sir David Erskine, 1st Bt (UK), so *cr* 27 Aug 1821, of Cambo (illegitimate gs of 9th Earl of Kellie; *see* MAR and KELLIE, E); *b* Sweden 6 Feb 1792; *m* 27 Aug 1821 Jane Silence (*d* 9 March 1886), dau and heir of Rev Hugh Williams, of Conway, and had issue:

1 THOMAS (Sir), **2nd Bt**

2 David Holland, Capt 92nd Regt, UK Consul Maderia; *b* 4 Sept 1828; *m* 23 Dec 1856 Augusta Jane (*d* 1896), dau of George Stoddart, his predecessor as Consul, and *d* 20 June 1869, having had issue:

(1) George Holland; *b* 19 Dec 1858; *d* unm

(2) James Malcolm Monteith (Sir), JP Sussex; MP St George's Westminster 1921–29; *b* 18 July 1863; *m* 7 Sept 1898 Cicely Grace (*d* 2 Aug 1969 aged 95), dau of Rev Charles Penrose Quicke, Rector Ashbrittie Somerset, and *d* 5 Nov 1944, leaving:

1a Denys Malcolm; *b* 5 Sept 1903; *educ* Radley; *m* 7 June 1923 Aleda Julia (*d* 1971), dau of E C Brownfield, of Saskatchewan, and *d* 30 Oct 1966, leaving:

1b Denise Elizabeth Grace; *b* 7 March 1924; *m* 1st 30 April 1949 (*divorce* 1965) Richard Pigott, est s of Richard Mountford Pigott, MC, JP, FRIBA, and adopted:

*Richard Christopher Erskine; *b* 18 Nov 1950; *educ* Charterhouse

*Stephen Robert Erskine; *b* 29 Feb 1952; *educ* Millfield

1b (cont.) Mrs Denise Pigott *m* 2nd 9 Feb 1966 *John James Delaney, MC, only s of John Delaney, of Co Durham, and *d* 19–

2b *(Margaret) Lucile [Mrs Kenneth Warner, 44 Rosedale Ct, Newcastle-on-Tyne]; *b* 27 June 1927; *m* 1st 26 Nov 1960 Anthony Colin Radclyffe, only son of Percy Frederick Radclyffe. He *d* 25 Oct 1976. She *m* 2nd 1978 *Kenneth Warner

2a Derek Quicke (Sir); ktd 1964, MLC Kenya 1948–51 and 1961–63, Maj Res Offrs King's Dragoon Gds, Ch Whip Kenya African Nat Union Parl Gp 1961–64, DAQMG E African Command, pres Kenyan Amateur Athletic Assoc; *b* 12 Feb 1905; *educ* Eton and RMC Sandhurst; *m* 21 June 1927 *Elizabeth Mary Stretton [Lady Erskine, Riverside Paddocks, PO Box 14968, Nairobi, Kenya], yr dau of Major Reginald Stretton Spurrier, King's Dragoon Gds, and *d* 1977, leaving issue:

1b +Francis David Monteith, MC [Francis Erskine Esq MC, Sanctuary Farm, PO Box 244, Naivasha, Kenya]; Capt The Kenya Regt; *b* 7 Sept 1929; *m* 7 Nov 1958 (*divorce* 1963) Marie Claude Irène, dau of Roland M A Mange, of Paris, and has issue:

1c +Clive Patrick Monteith; *b* 28 May 1959; *m* 1985 *Patrizia Pandora, dau of Michele Koris, of Canino, Viterbo, Italy, and has issue:

1d *Charlotte Irene; *b* 1987

2c +Guy Francis; *b* 23 Feb 1961; *m* 1988 *Juliet, dau of John Dallas Amos, of Edinburgh, and has issue:

1d +James Francis; *b* 1989

2b +Charles Malcolm; *b* 11 Oct 1949

1b *Jane Petal [Mrs David Allen, PO Box 14712, Nairobi, Kenya]; *b* 24 March 1928; *m* 1st 10 June 1950 (*divorce* 1963) William Lee Harragin, er s of Sir Walter Harragin, CMG, QC, and has issue:

1c *Mark Savill Austin; *b* 19 March 1956; *m* 1990 *Patricia Walker, and has issue:

1d *Daniel; *b* 1992

1d *Corinne Florence; *b* 1994

1c *Vanessa Jane; *b* 1951; *m* 1977 *Kirby McCaffrey and has issue:

1d *James Flynn Cassius; *b* 1980

2c *Robyn Elizabeth; *b* 1953; *m* 1986 *Peter Boone Hussey, and has issue:

1d *Mary Victoria; *b* 1988

2d *Serwen; *b* 1991

3c *Georgia Frances; *b* 1954

4c *Serena Claire; *b* 16 Sept 1959

1b (cont.) Mrs Jane Harragin *m* 2nd 28 June 1963 (*divorce* 1972) Robert William Young, er s of Robert William Young; *m* 3rd 1973 *David Wanric Allen

3a Keith David; slr, RA WW II (despatches twice); *b* 11 June 1907; *educ* Westminster; *m* 1st 21 Oct 1936 (*divorce* 1940) Kathleen Diana, yr dau of Charles William Kayser, JP, of Eaton Hall, Retford; *m* 2nd 23 Nov 1944 *Audrey Rosemary [Mrs Keith Erskine, Beech Hurst, Waterhurst Lane, Kingswood, Surrey], 2nd Offr WRNS, dau of John Skinner, and *d* 1974, leaving by her:

1b +Simon David; *b* 22 Feb 1953

1b *Sarah Gay; *b* 21 Oct 1946; *m* 1967 *Alex Ryan and has:

1c *Robert Keith; *b* 1973

2c *Audrey Mary; *b* 1970

2b *Aleda Grace Elizabeth; *b* 7 April 1948

3b *Fiona Margaret; *b* 11 Aug 1949; *m* 1971 *Richard Mottram

4b *Deborah Mary [Mrs David Holt, Pixie, Sandy Lane, Kingswood, Surrey]; *b* 10 March 1951; *m* 1974 *David Langford Holt and has issue:

1c *Benjamin; *b* 1976

2c *James; *b* 1976

1c *Sara Maria; *b* 1978

5b *Kathrina Jane; *b* 16 Aug 1957

4a James Monteith; *b* 11 June 1907; *educ* Charterhouse; Gren Gds WW II; *m* 17 Nov 1931 *Kathleen, BA [Mrs James Erskine, 2 Francis Ct, Cranes Park Ave, Surbiton, Surrey], dau of William Charles Brookes, of Edinburgh, and *d* 25 Sept 1965, leaving issue:

1b +David Monteith; slr 1960; *b* 14 June 1933; *educ* Oundle and Trin Hall Cambridge (MA); *m* 17 Sept 1960 *Tessa Victoria, dau of Dr James Anthony Vernon, MRCS, LRCP, and has issue:

1c +Dominic James; *b* 3 Feb 1962

2c +Malcolm David Vernon; *b* 1 Oct 1963

1c *Susan Eileen; *b* 1970

1b *Shirley Monteith [Mrs Barry Clarke, The Long House, Woodgreen, Hants]; *b* 14 June 1933; *educ* The Mount, York, and Newnham Coll Cambridge (BA); *m* 3 July 1954 *Barry Michael Clarke, s of Dr Humphrey Clarke, and has issue:

1c *Thomas James Woodchurch; *b* 23 Dec 1958

1c *Eleanor Margaret; *b* 6 Feb 1962

1a Janet Monteith; Offr QMAAC 1918; *b* 17 June 1899; *m* 21 April 1921 John Wardrop-Moore, of Greenhall, Lanarks, s of Col — Wardrop-Moore, and *d* 26 Feb 1967, leaving two daus. He *d* 10 June 1965

(3) David Wingfield; *b* 5 Dec 1868; *m* 10 July 1899 Emily Margarette (*d* 29 Jan 1904), dau of John Burden Blandy, and *d* 4 Nov 1931, leaving issue:

1a Winifred; *b* 19 Jan 1901; *m* 18 Oct 1923 Col Charles Maxwell Orr Sawers, OBE (*d* 22 Aug 1967), 9th Royal Deccan Horse, only s of Charles Dundas Sawers, and had issue:

1b *David Maxwell ERSKINE later JEREMY CONWAY; dir Theatrical Agency, Personal Management Ltd; *b* 16 Jan 1939; *educ* Radley and Guildhall Sch of Music and Drama

1b *Julia Anna [Mrs Martin Welford, Little Orchard, Stock, Essex]; *b* 18 Jan 1928; *m* 30 April 1949 Martin Erskine Welford, s of Hylton Welford, and has issue:

1c *Christopher Charles; *b* 23 Nov 1951

2c *Stephen Maxwell; *b* 16 Jan 1956

2c *Joanna Valerie; *b* 28 Jan 1953

2a Violet; *b* 9 Jan 1904; *m* 1 July 1926 Capt Charles Albert Cairns, Roy Deccan Horse, 2nd surv s of Rev John Edgar Cairns, and *d* 21 April 1966, leaving a dau. He *d* 4 April 1931 as the result of polo accident

(1) Alice Augustua; *m* 1 Jan 1891 Wilfred Leigh Pemberton (*see* KINGSDOWN, B), and *d* 20 Feb 1949, having had issue

(2) Mary Silence; *m* 19 June 1889 John Milberne Leacock, s of Thomas Slapp Leacock, of Madeira, and *d* 6 Nov 1945, leaving issue. He *d* 19 May 1915

(3) Annie May; *d* unm 28 Aug 1954 aged 93

(4) Blanche Anstruther; *m* 1892 Col John Hart, Leinster Regt, and *d* 21 Feb 1929, leaving issue. He *d* 1909

(5) Gwenydd; *m* 21 Dec 1893 George Edward Wilson Cruttwell, MInstCE, s of Wilson Clement Cruttwell, and *d* 11 Jan 1949, leaving issue. He *d* 10 Nov 1933

(6) Caroline Carew; *d* unm 31 Jan 1963

3 Hugh Henry; *b* 1839; *m* 2 Jan 1866 Gwenydd Frances (*d* 8 June 1892), widow of Capt Hamilton Sandford Pakenham (*see* LONGFORD, E) and dau of Hon Richard Thomas Rowley (*see* LANGFORD, B), and *d* 4 Jan 1907, leaving issue:

(1) Francis Conwy; *b* 1867; *d* 5 Jan 1931

(2) Henry Vere; *b* 1868

1 Jane Silence; *d* 1826

2 Harriett; *d* 10 Jan 1860

3 Mary; *d* 1853

4 Caroline; *d* unm 16 Jan 1893

Sir DAVID *d* 1841; his est son,

Sir Thomas Erskine, 2nd Bt, JP Co Wexford, JP, DL Denbighshire, Caernarvonshire and Fife; Lt 71st Foot, Capt Denbigh Rifle Militia, Lt-Col 1st Fife Rifle Vol; *b* 23 July 1824; *m* 15 July 1847 Zaida Maria (*d* 1 Dec 1897), only dau of John Ffolliot, MP, of Hollybrook, Co Sligo, and had issue:

1 FFOLLIOTT WILLIAMS (Sir), **3rd Bt**

2 Thomas Harry; JP and DL Fife; Lt-Col cmdg Fife and Forfar Yeo, Hon Col Armoured Car Cos 1922, France WW I; *b* 12 May 1860; *m* 5 April 1913 Kathleen Matilda, JP (*d* 1945), est dau of James Crosbie, DL, of Ballyheigue Castle, Co Kerry, and *d* 6 May 1924

1 Zaida Mary; *m* 12 Jan 1875 Lt-Col Philip Robert Anstruther and *d* 18 April 1922, leaving issue (*see* ANSTRUTHER, Bt)

2 Elythia Ruth; *m* 9 Dec 1882 Maj-Gen Andrew Gilbert Wauchope, CB, CMG, and *dsp* 1833. He *d* 11 Dec 1899

3 Harriet Caroline; *m* 10 April 1890 John Campbell Shairp, advocate, of Houstoun, Uphall, Linlithgow, and *d* Feb 1949, leaving issue. He *d* 31 Dec 1913

4 Jane Holland Gwenydd; *b* 28 July 1869; *d* unm 1959

5 Mary Lucy; *b* 28 July 1869; *d* unm 3 Feb 1955

Sir THOMAS *d* 27 Sept 1902; his er son,

Sir Ffolliott Williams Erskine, 3rd Bt, DL Fife; Lt-Col Scots Gds; *b* 28 Oct 1850; *m* 2 July 1879 Grace (*d* 1937), est dau of Thomas Hargreaves, of Arborfield Hall, Berks, and had issue:

1 THOMAS WILFRED HARGREAVES JOHN (Sir), **4th Bt**

1 Zaida Grace; *m* 17 Dec 1913; Frederick Lewis Scrymgeour Wedderburn and *d* 27 Feb 1943, leaving issue (*see* DUNDEE, E)

Sir FFOLLIOT *d* 9 Jan 1912; his only son,

Sir Thomas Wilfred Hargreaves John Erskine, 4th Bt, DSO (1916), DL, Lt-Col Cameron Highrs WW I (despatches); *b* 27 May 1880; *m* 14 Aug 1911 Magdalen Janet (*d* 15 Feb 1953), 2nd dau of Sir Ralph William Anstruther, 6th Bt (*qv*), and *d* 29 April 1944, leaving:

1 Sir THOMAS DAVID ERSKINE, **5th and present Bt**

2 Ralph John, Lt RN; *b* 17 Sept 1914; *d* 1 Dec 1937

1 Mary Ruth; *b* 18 Aug 1913; *d* unm 23 Oct 1968

2 *Diana Mildred [Mrs David Buxton, Rectory Cottage, Simpling, Norfolk]; *b* 12 Nov 1915; *m* 1st 21 Aug 1941 T/Maj Nigel Robert Robert Mackie Skene, DSC, RM (*ka* in HMS *Avenger* Nov 1942), s of Rev Robert Erskine Skene; *m* 2nd 3 Jan 1945 *Maj David Grant Buxton, Middx Regt, only s of Frank Grant Buxton, of Highgate, and by him has issue:

(1) *Andrew Ralph; *b* 19 Sept 1947; *educ* Tonbridge; *m* 1979 (*divorce* 19–) Sally Higginbottom and has:

1a *A dau; *b* 19–

(1) *Lucinda Deirdre; *b* Oct 1945; *m* 1973 *Tudor Venn and has two sons and a dau

3 *Victoria Margaret [Miss Victoria Erskine, 41 Thurleigh Court, London SW12]; 2nd Offr WRNS WW II; *b* 22 Feb 1919

4 Penelope Anne; 3rd Offr WRNS WW II; *b* 19 Feb 1920; *educ* St Andrews (BSc 1940); *m* 15 Oct 1941 Lt-Cdr Peter Goldthorpe Sugden, DSC, RN (*d* in an accident May 1943), est s of Brig-Gen Richard Edgar Sugden, CB, CMG, DSO, TD, and *d* 1988, leaving:

(1) *Paul Ralph [Paul Sugden Esq, Cooks Mill Cottage, Fordham Heath, Essex]; Capt Black Watch; *b* 12 Sept 1942; *educ* Marlborough; *m* 13 Aug 1966 *Janet Mary, dau of S/Ldr J M Rumsey, RAF, of Beaminster, Dorset, and has:

1a *Thomas Ralph; *b* 29 Sept 1969

2a *Christopher; *b* 1975

1a *Caroline Anne; *b* 2 March 1968

5 *Constance Gertrude [Mrs Oliver Patch, Conduit, Barkers Hill, Semley, Shaftesbury, Dorset]; *b* 21 April 1921; *m* 13 June 1942 Maj Oliver Patch, DSO, DSC, RM (*d* 1991), 2nd s of James Patch, and has issue:

(1) *Janet Mary [Mrs Janet Patch, 58 Shelgate Rd, London SW11 1BG]; *b* 25 Feb 1945; *m* 1976 (*divorce* 1986) Simon Scott

(2) *Olivia Cynthia [Mrs James Sholto Douglas, 43 Cadogan Sq, London SW1]; *b* 28 July 1946; *m* 1st 1972 Dimitri Tiomkin (*d* 1979); *m* 2nd 1988 *James Alastair Sholto Douglas, s of Maj Henry James Sholto Douglas, Scots Gds, of Hemingford Abbots, Huntingdon (*see* DONEGALL, M)

(3) *Emily Dorothea; *b* 14 Oct 1949; *m* 1st 1980 (*divorce* 19–) Kenneth Page and has issue:

1a *Harriet Constance Zenia; *b* 1980

(3) (cont.) Mrs Emily Page *m* 2nd 19– *Gavin Scott and has further issue:

1a *Tobias Oliver; *b* 1986

(4) *Diana Elizabeth [Mrs Diana McDowall, Undercliffe, Donhead St Mary, Wilts]; *b* 25 Dec 1953; *m* 1974 (*divorce* 1981) Stephen Sullivan; *m* 2nd 1995 *Terence Patrick McDowall

(5) *Penelope Margaret Christian [Mrs Gerald Olson, Orchard View, Eastling, Kent]; *b* 16 Aug 1957; *m* 1983 *Gerald Olson and has:

1a *Nicholas Oliver; *b* 1984

1a *Natalie; *b* 1986

2a *Hannah; *b* 1988

6 *Harriet Katherine Lucinda [Mrs Hugh Doheny, 95 Moulton Hill, RR1, Lennoxville, Quebec Prov, J1M 2A2, Canada]; *b* 12 May 1924; *m* 8 June 1945 *Lt-Cdr Hugh Doheny, RCNVR, est s of Hugh Doheny, of Montreal, and has:

(1) *Hugh Erskine; *b* 7 April 1946; *m* 1987 *Margaret Collins

(1) *Penelope Anne; *b* 17 Sept 1949; *m* 1st 1972 (*divorce* 1982) Ronald Carter; *m* 2nd 1986 *Mario Bousquet, of Mount Orford, Quebec

(2) *Kathleen Janet; *b* 31 March 1951; *m* 1972 *Brian Hanna, of Grandmere, Quebec

(3) *Mary Harriet; *b* 21 July 1952

(4) *Lucinda Margaret Ruth; *b* 28 Aug 1956; has:

1a *Mira Harriet Kathleen; *b* 1992

(5) *Victoria Diana; *b* 18 March 1960; *m* 1982 *Brian Herring, of Lennoxville, and has issue:

1a *Charles Thomas; *b* 1983

1a *Margaret Lucinda; *b* 1985

2a *Mary Grace; *b* 1988

ERSKINE-HILL

Arms: Quarterly, 1st grand quarter, azure a hill argent charged with two pens, points downwards in saltire, quills or, feathers sable, in chief the sun in his splendour (for HILL); 2nd grand quarter, counterquartered, 1st and 4th, argent on a pale sable a cross-crosslet fitchée or (for ERSKINE of Shielfield); 2nd, azure a bend between two cross-crosslets fitchées or (for MAR); 3rd, or on a bend azure three mascles of the field, and in the sinister chief a round buckle of the second (for HALIBURTON); all within a bordure per pale azure and sable, a canton or charged with a fleur-de-lys of the second for difference; 3rd grand quarter, counterquartered, 1st, argent on a mount in base a lion rampant vert, on a chief of the second a crescent between two mullets or (for HALCRO); 2nd, or a fess chequy azure and argent, a border gules charged with eight round buckles of the first (for STEWART of Barscube); 3rd, or on a bend gules three buckles of the first (for BONKYLL of that Ilk); 4th, argent a heart purpure ensigned with an imperial crown proper, on a chief gules three pallets or (for KEITH of Galston); 4th grand quarter, argent a lion rampant azure, armed and langued gules, on a chief of the second an elephant's head cabossed of the first, tusked or, accompanied by two lymphads of the first under full sail proper (for GALLOWAY). **Crests:** 1 A stag's head couped proper, attired sable; 2 A dexter arm from the elbow, couped proper, the hand grasping a cross-crosslet fitchée or. **Mottoes:** 1 Think well and prevail, 2 Think well. **Creation:** Bt. (UK) 22 June 1945.

SIR (ALEXANDER) ROGER ERSKINE-HILL, 3RD BT, of Quothquhan, Co Lanark [Sir Roger Erskine-Hill Bt, c/o Salestrack, 3 Manor Court, Dix's Field, Exeter, Devon EX 1ST]; *b* 15 Aug 1949; *s f* 1989; *educ* Eton and Aberdeen U (LLB); dir: Salestrac 1985–, Map Marketing 1988–, The Offer Shop 1990–; *m* 1984 (*divorce* 1994) Sarah Anne, er dau of Dr Richard John Sydenham Clarke, and has issue:

1 +ROBERT BENJAMIN; *b* 6 Aug 1986

1 *Kirsty Rose; *b* 1985

Lineage: ROBERT ALEXANDER HILL, of Coney Hill House, Bridge of Allan, Stirlingshire; *b* 17 June 1870; *educ* Edinburgh U; slr and broker; *m* 1890 Marion Clark (*d* 25 Dec 1962), dau of John Galloway, of Kilmeny, Ardossan, Ayrshire, and *d* May 1931, leaving issue:

1 ALEXANDER GALLOWAY (Sir), **1st Bt**

2 Ian Cameron Miller, OBE

1 Margaret Halcro Erskine; *b* 30 Dec 1892; *m* 23 June 1913 Rev Roland Audley Smith, JP, DL (*d* 2 Dec 1946), of Hertingfordbury Park, Herts, and *d* 29 Jan 1965, leaving issue

ROBERT HILL's er s,

Sir ALEXANDER GALLOWAY ERSKINE HILL later ERSKINE-HILL (additional surname and arms of ERSKINE recognised by Ld Lyon 1943), **1st Bt** (UK), so *cr* 22 June 1945, KC (1935), DL (Edinburgh); *b* 3 April 1894; *educ* Rugby and Trin Coll Cambridge (BA 1915, MA and LLB 1919); barrister Inner Temple 1920, dir LNER and Clydesdale Bank, Capt Cameronians and Cameron Highrs WW I, Hon Col 1940, Scottish advocate 1920, Standing Jr Counsel Dept Ag Scotland 1932, Advocate Depute 1932–35, Parly Sec to Ld Advocate 1939, Chm C Membs Ctee 1940–44, MP Edinburgh N 1935–45; *m* 3 Dec 1915 Christian, MBE (1944) (*d* 13 Sept 1947), only dau of John Colville, MP (*see* CLYDESMUIR, B), and *d* 6 June 1947, having had:

1 **Sir Robert Erskine-Hill, 2nd Bt**, of Quothquhan; *b* 6 Feb 1917; *educ* Eton and Trin Coll Cambridge (BA 1938); chartered accountant, memb Roy Co Archers, Lt RNVR WW II 1939–42, chm Life Assoc of Scotland and Assoc of Investment Tst Cos; *m* 7 Aug 1942 *Christine Alison [Christine Lady Erskine-Hill, Harelea House, Libberton, Carnwarth, Lanarks ML11 8LX], only dau of Capt Henry James Johnstone of Alva, RN (*see* JOHNSTONE, Bt), and *d* 1989, having had, with a dau (*d* at birth):

(1) Sir ALEXANDER ROGER ERSKINE-HILL, **3rd and present Bt**

(2) +Henry James; *b* 16 Feb 1953; *educ* Eton; *m* 1979 *Gwen Carolyne, dau of Ian Russell Chalmers

(1) *Carola Marion [Mrs Robin Stormonth Darling, Balvarran, Enochdu, Blairgowrie, Perthshire PH10 7PA]; *b* 6 June 1943; *m* 19 Nov 1963 (*divorce* 1978) (Richard) David Christopher Brooke (*see* BROOKE, Bt, of Norton Priory); *m* 2nd 1981, as his 3rd w, *Robin Andrew Stormonth Darling and has issue by her 1st husb

(2) *Alison [Mrs John North Lewis, Walwick Hall, Humshaugh, Hexham, Northumberland NE46 4BJ]; *b* 9 July 1945; *m* 2 July 1966 *John Selby North Lewis, only s of John Clifford North Lewis and Mrs Philip Coad, and has issue:

1a *Selby James [Selby North Lewis Esq, Edge House, Barrasford, Hexham, Northumberland]; *b* 13 Dec 1968; *m* 1995 *Emma Clare, dau of Richard Gaisford, and has:

1b *Jack Selby; *b* 29 Sept 1996

1a *Harriet Alison; *b* 1970

2a *Rebecca Elspeth; *b* 1975

3a *Hannah Margaret; *b* 1979

2 John Colville, DSC, VRD; *b* 23 March 1921; *educ* Eton and Trin Coll Cambridge; Lt RNVR (despatches) WW II, ADC to Govr Bombay 1945–46, dir Guthrie & Co (UK); *m* 12 Dec 1959 *Myra Elizabeth [Mrs John Erskine-Hill, South Lodge, Forest Row, Sussex], only dau of Cdr Richard Homewood, RN, and *d* 1984, leaving:

(1) +Mark Colville [Mark Erskine-Hill Esq, The White House, Walking Bottom, Peaslake, nr Guildford, Surrey]; *b* 29 Sept 1960; *m* 1992 *Lucy Diana Elspeth, dau of D B Hulme, of Reigate, Surrey, and has issue:

1a +David; *b* 15 Feb 1996

1a *Alice; *b* 1993

(2) +David John; *b* 4 June 1962

1 Elspeth Christian; *b* 9 Oct 1918; *d* unm 29 June 1950

2 *Jean Halcro [Mrs George Smith-Wright, 34 Moore Street, London SW3 2QW]; *b* 23 Jan 1928; *m* 1st 16 Sept 1950 Derek John Seth-Smith (*d* 24 June 1964), yr s of Keith Seth-Smith, and has issue:

(1) *Frederick Alexander [Frederick Seth-Smith Esq, 88 Navigation Rd, Altrincham, Cheshire]; *b* 28 June 1963; *m* 1992 *Kathryn, est dau of Cmdt Barry O'Sullivan, of Naas, Co Kildare, and has issue:

1a *Jack Alexander; *b* 1994

1a *Ellen Gemilla; *b* 1996

(1) *Kay Christian [Mrs Charles King, 12 Hambalt Rd, London SW4]; *b* 17 June 1951; *m* 1981 *Charles W King, yr s of Col C W King, and has issue:

1a *Henry Charles James; *b* 1983

1a *Laura Christian; *b* 1983

2a *Alice Jane; *b* 1987

(2) *Rosemary Jean [Mrs Peter Gwatkin, Hall Farm House, Moat House Lane, Shustoke, Warwicks]; *b* 22 May 1954; *m* 1977 *Maj Peter F S Gwatkin, Welsh Gds, s of John Stapleton Gwatkin, and has issue:

1a *Frederick John Stapleton; *b* 1983

1a *Amy Jean Stapleton; *b* 1980

2a *Martha Elspeth; *b* 1986

3a *Hannah Rosemary Theophila Stapleton; *b* 1990

(3) *(Mary) Jane; *b* 16 Nov 1957; *m* 1984 *William Lee Rothery, s of George W Rothery, and has issue:

1a *Charles Alexander; *b* 1987

2a *Arthur George; *b* 1992

1a *Rosemary Anne; *b* 1985

2 (cont.) Mrs Derek Seth-Smith *m* 2nd 23 Sept 1972 *George Henry Smith-Wright

ESHER

Arms: Quarterly; 1st and 4th, gu, within an orle of crosses botonnée fitchée or, a lion rampant of the last, holding in the dexter fore-paw a fasces erect ppr.; 2nd, per pale or and gu. three leopard's faces counterchanged; 3rd, az., three bear's heads couped arg., muzzled gu. **Crest:** A lion passant gu., charged on the shoulder with a cross botonnée fitchée or and holding in the dexter fore-paw a fasces ppr. **Supporters:** Dexter, a boar; sinister, a lion, both sa. and each charged on the shoulder with a cross botonnée fitchée or, and holding between the paws a fasces erect ppr. **Motto:** *Vicimus* ('We have conquered'). **Creations:** B. (UK) 24 July1885, V. (UK) 11 Nov 1897.

THE 4TH VISCOUNT ESHER, of Esher, and **Baron Esher**, of Esher, Surrey (Lionel Gordon Baliol Brett, CBE (1970)) [The Rt Hon The Viscount Esher CBE, Snowball Hill, Russell's Water, Henley-on-Thames, Oxon RG9 6EU]; *b* 18 July 1913; *s* f 1963; *educ* Eton and New Coll Oxford (BA 1936, MA 1946); DIsTP, Hon DLitt Strathclyde, Hon DUniv York, Hon DSc Edinburgh, Hon Fell American Inst of Architects, architect and town planner, PRIBA 1965–67, memb Roy Fine Arts Commn 1951–69 and Arts Cncl 1972–77, Tstee London Museum 1964— (Govr 1970–77), Rector and V-Provost RCA 1971–78, Pres Chiltern Soc, Maj RA, WW II (despatches), author: *Houses* (1947), *The World of Architecture* (1963), *Landscape in Distress* (1965), *York: A Study in Conservation* (1969), *Parameters and Images* (1970), *Shell Guide to N Wales* (1971), *A Broken Wave* (1981), *The Continuing Heritage* (1982), *Ourselves Unknown* (1985), *The Glory of the English House* (1991); *m* 22 Oct 1935 *Helena Christian Olive, est dau of Col Ebenezer John Lecky Pike, CBE, MC, of Dale Park, Arundel, Sussex, and has:

1 +CHRISTOPHER LIONEL BALIOL [The Hon Christopher Brett, Watlington Park, Oxon]; *b* 23 Dec 1936; *educ* Eton and Magdalen Coll Oxford; *m* 1st 28 Feb 1962 (*divorce* 1970) Camilla Charlotte, yst dau of Sir (Horace) Anthony Claude Rumbold, 10th Bt, CB, CMG (*qv*), and has issue:

(1) +Matthew Christopher Anthony [Matthew Brett Esq, Hill House, Kingston Blount, Oxon OX9 4SJ]; *b* 2 Jan 1963; *educ* Eton and Exeter Coll Oxford; barrister; *m* 1992 *Hon Emma Charlotte Denison-Pender, er dau of 3rd Baron Pender (*qv*), and has issue:

1a +Jack Alexander Baliol; *b* 14 June 1996

1a *Eleanor Rose; *b* 11 June 1994

(1) *Miranda Jane; *b* 16 March 1964; *m* 1990 *Martin Nicholas Caleb Thomas, yr s of Prof (Antony) Charles Thomas, CBE, DL, of Lambessow, St Clement, Truro, Cornwall, and has issue:

1a *Joseph Achilles Caleb; *b* 1990

2a *Frederick Jacob Theseus; *b* 1992

(2) *Rebecca Catherine; *b* 10 Oct 1966

1 (cont.) The Hon CHRISTOPHER BRETT *m* 2nd 4 Feb 1971 *Valerie, yst dau of Maxwell Maurice Harrington, and has further issue:

(2) +Oliver Maxwell; *b* 1972

(3) +William Falkland; *b* 1982

(2) *Susannah Mary; *b* 1973

(3) *Clare Christian; *b* 1973

2 +Michael Jeremy Baliol; *b* 26 April 1939; *educ* Eton and Architectural Assoc Sch of Architecture, ARIBA; *m* 1971 *Sarah Calloway, of Shelbyville, Ky.

3 +Guy Anthony Baliol; *b* 18 Oct 1942; *educ* Eton; sometime art critic *The Times*; *m* 1975 *Alexandra Altamirano, of Santiago, Chile, and has issue:

(1) *Luciana; *b* 1976

4 +(Maurice) Sebastian Baliol; *b* 16 May 1944; *educ* Eton and Trin Coll Oxford; *m* 1st 1968 (*divorce* 1971) Pauline R, dau of Lt-Cdr Paul Murray-Jones, RN, of Cordwainers, Titchfield, Hants; *m* 2nd 1971 (*divorce* 1980) Mary Maddox, and has:

(1) +Judd; *b* 1972

4 (cont.) The Hon Sebastian Brett *m* 3rd 1980 *Leticia Garrido and by her has:

(1) *Claudia; *b* 1985

5 +Stephen Patrick Baliol; *b* 26 Aug 1952; *educ* Bryanston

1 *Olivia Clare Teresa; *b* 29 Nov 1947; *m* 1970 (*divorce* 1985) Anthony Grey Gascoigne (*see* WIGAN, Bt) and has:

(1) *Fenn; *b* 1977
(2) *May; *b* 1979

Lineage: JOSEPH GEORGE BRETT, of Grove House, Old Brompton; *b* 1760; *m* 1st Isabella Maria Christiana Forbes (*d* July 1802), dau and heiress of George Forbes, of Edinglassie and Auchnerrach, Aberdeenshire, by Isabel Steuart of Drummin, and had, with other issue:

1 JOSEPH GEORGE (Rev)

1 Margaret; *m* Fairfax Best, of the Gren Gds and of Wierton Park, Staplehurst, Kent, and left four daus

2 Amelia; *m* John Davidson, MD, of the Bengal Army, and left three daus.

3 Sophia; *m* her cousin Harry Brett, and left issue. He *d* 1855

4 Harriet; *m* Col George R Jervis, of the Bombay Engineers, and *d* 29 May 1869, leaving issue

5 Caroline; *b* 1800; *m* Frederick A Clarke and *d* 1869, leaving two sons and five daus

JOSEPH BRETT *m* 2nd Elizabeth Templeton and *d* 17 June 1845, leaving by her:

2 James Brett; Maj-Gen Madras Cav; *m* I Cleveland, dau of Gen Cleveland, and left issue

3 Harry Augustus, Madras CS; *m* Jane Roberts, and left issue

6 Anna; *m* Christopher P Lochner, of Doctors' Commons, and had a s

The est son,

Rev JOSEPH GEORGE BRETT, of Ranelagh, Chelsea; Vicar Lenham, Kent, incumbent Hanover Chapel, Regent Street; *b* 1790; *educ* Jesus Coll Cambridge (LLB); *m* Dorothy, dau of George Best, of Chilston Park, Kent, MP, by Caroline, dau of Edward Scott, of Scott's Hall, Kent, and *d* May 1852, leaving:

1 Wilford George, of Esher, Surrey, JP; barrister Middle Temple, Ch Sec to Master of the Rolls; *educ* Magdalene Coll Cambridge (MA); *dsp*

2 WILLIAM BALIOL, **1st Viscount**

3 Reginald Best; Major RA; *m* Charlotte Drummond and *dsp* India

4 Wilford (Sir), KCMG; Col 76th Foot, Mil Sec to Govr Malta 1864; *b* 1824; *m* 1859 Isabel (*d* Jan 1892), dau of Thomas Stephen, and *dsp* 30 Oct 1901

5 Richard Rich Wilford; 2nd Bombay Cav; *m* Emily Elliot and *d* in Indian Mutiny, leaving:

(1) Ernest

(2) Cecil Michael Wilford (Sir), CSI, JP Surrey; barrister Middle Temple 1884, Bengal CS 1872–1913, Judge High Court Bengal 1900–13; *b* Aug 1852; *m* 1885 Margaret Ellen (*d* 25 May 1938), 3rd dau of Henry Davies, and *d* 12 Nov 1939, having had issue

6 Francis Augustus; Madras NI; *m* — Matthews and had:

(1) Pera

1 Isabella Maria Christiana; *m* Col Arthur Prescott, 2nd Bombay Cav, and had three daus

2 Anna Dora; *m* 31 May 1849 James P Currie, a Dir Bank of England, and *d* 14 May 1858, leaving issue. He *d* 18 June 1908

The 2nd son,

WILLIAM BALIOL BRETT, **1st Viscount Esher** of Esher, Surrey, so *cr* 11 Nov 1897, as also previously 24 July 1885 BARON ESHER, of Esher, Surrey (both UK), PC (1876), QC (1860); *b* 13 Aug 1815; *educ* Westminster and Caius Coll Cambridge (MA 1840); barrister 1846; Slr-Gen 1868, MP Helston 1866–68, Judge Court Common Pleas 1868, Ld Justice of Appeal 1876, Master Rolls 1882–97; *m* 3 April 1850 Eugenie (*d* 4 June 1904), dau of Louis Mayer and step-dau of Col Gurwood, CB, and had issue:

1 REGINALD BALIOL, **2nd Viscount**

2 Eugene Leopold Selwyn; Lt Scots Gds; *b* 3 March 1855; *d* 8 Dec 1882

1 Eugenie Violet Adele; *m* 24 Oct 1876 William Humble Dudley Ward and *d* 13 March 1938, leaving issue (*see* DUDLEY, E)

The 1st VISCOUNT *d* 24 May 1899; his son,

REGINALD BALIOL BRETT, **2nd Viscount Esher**, KCB (1902, CB 1897), GCVO (1905, KCVO 1901), PC (1922), DL Berks; *b* 30 June 1852; *educ* Eton and Trin Coll Cambridge (MA), Hon LLD Cambridge and St Andrews; MP (Lib) Falmouth and Penryn 1880–85, Pres TAA London 1912–21, Dep Govr and Constable Windsor Castle 1901–28, Govr and Constable 1928–30, Tstee Br Museum, London Museum and Wallace Collection, Keeper Roy Archives, perm memb Ctee Imp Def 1905–18, Sec to Office of Works 1895–1902, Hon Col: 5th Bn Roy Fus and 63rd London Bde, RFA, KJStJ, Cdr Legn Hon and Spanish Order Merit, memb Commn of Enquiry Boer War, chm War Office Reconstitution Ctee; govr Imp Coll of Science and Technology, Cmmr 1851 Exhibition and Chm Bd of Managers, ed *The Girlhood of Queen Victoria* (letters, 1912); *m* 24 Sept 1879 Eleanor Frances Weston, RRC (*d* 7 Feb 1940), DJStJ, 3rd dau of Sylvain Van de Weyer, Belgian Min to UK, and had:

1 OLIVER SYLVAIN BALIOL, **3rd Viscount**

2 Maurice Vyner Baliol, OBE (1918), MVO (5th Class 1902); Lt-Col 6th Bn The Black Watch, formerly Capt Coldstream Gds, Offr Legn Hon, ADC to FM Viscount French 1904–12 and Lt-Gen Sir J S Ewart 1914, DAAG 1916, Dep Keeper and Librarian London Museum 1919, served WW I (despatches four times); *b* 24 April 1882; *m* 23 Jan 1911 Florence Hariette Zena (Zena Dare the actress; *d* 11 March 1975 aged 88), est dau of Arthur Albert Dones, Clerk Divorce Court, of Maida Vale, and *d* 18 Aug 1934, leaving:

(1) Antony Reginald Forbes Baliol, MBE (1945); Maj Black Watch (RHR) WW II, Steward St Bartholomew's Hosp 1948–77; *b* 18 June 1913; *educ* Stowe and Trin Coll Cambridge; *m* 2 Oct 1939 Bay Helen (*d* 1989), dau of Charles Neville Brownell, of Birkenhead and Calcutta, and *d* 1981, leaving:

1a +Simon Baliol [Simon Brett Esq, 12 Blowhorn St, Marlborough, Wilts SN8 1BT]; *b* 27 May 1943; *educ* Ampleforth and St Martin's Sch of Art; *m* 31 Aug 1974 *Juliet Wood, dau of Dr Paul Hamilton Wood, OBE, MD, Melb, FRCP, of The National Heart, Hammersmith and Brompton hospitals, and formerly w of Richard Shirley-Smith, and has:

1b *Emily Agnes; *b* 4 Nov 1977

1a *Vanessa Baliol; *b* 22 April 1947; *m* 1977 *William Northrop Parker, s of G F Parker, of Repton, Derbys, and has:

1b *Guy Hugo; *b* 1987

1b *Rebecca Brett; *b* 1980

(1) *Angela Mariel Baliol [Mrs Kenneth Thornton, Woodside Cottage, Windsor Forest, Berks LS4 2DP]; *b* Oct 1911; *m* 24 April 1934 Maj Kenneth Marcus Thornton, yr son of T B Thornton, and has:

1a *Timothy Kenneth [Timothy Thornton Esq, Juthware Hall, Halstock, nr Yeovil, Somerset BA22 9SG]; late Lt Coldstream Gds; *b* 7 March 1935; *educ* Eton; *m* 17 May 1966 *Mrs Jacqueline Green, yr dau of David Hillman, of 3 Stanhope Gate, London W1, and formerly w of John Green, of Malmesbury, Wilts, and has:

1b *Daniel Timothy; *b* 7 April 1968; *educ* Eton and Trin Coll Cambridge (MA 1992); slr 1993

1b *Katharine; *b* 5 Oct 1970; *educ* Durham U (BA 1992)

2a *Brian Maurice [Brian Thornton Esq, Priors Mense, Aylburton, Lydney, Glos GL15 6DX]; *b* 26 Feb 1937; *educ* Eton; *m* 25 April 1959 *Verity, 2nd dau of Guy Gordon Lawrence, of Little Easton Manor, Dunmow, Essex, and has:

1b *Guy Dominic; *b* 20 Feb 1960; *educ* Gordonstoun; *m* 1st 24 Oct 1983 (*divorce* 1990) Hon Diana Cara Broughton, er dau of 3rd Baron Fairhaven (*qv*); *m* 2nd 21 Sept 1996 *Samantha Nancy Diana, er dau of Frederick Grant Barker, and by his 1st w has:

1c *Thomas George Cranbrook; *b* 1986

2b *Benjamin Douglas; *b* 7 June 1965; *educ* Eton and Edinburgh U (BSc) and Cranfield U (MBA); *m* 26 July 1996 *Emma Janet, er dau of John Walys Moss

3b *Giles Marcus; *b* 8 July 1966; *educ* Gordonstoun

4b *Jolyon Kenneth; *b* 14 April 1970; *educ* Harrow and Warwick U (BA); *m* 26 Oct 1996 *Sarah Louise Elizabeth, er dau of Patrick Arthur Wyndham Nicholls

5b *Sam Fergus; *b* 1976; *educ* Harrow and Edinburgh U

1b *Kim Marie [Mrs Geoffrey Wheating, The Limes, Rectory Lane, Meonstoke, Hants SO32 3NF]; *b* 28 July 1961; *m* 1986 *Geoffrey Stuart Wheating and has:

1c *Tara Nel; *b* 1988

2c *Matilda Rose; *b* 1990

(2) *Marie Louise [Mrs Archibald Cheyne, Spring Hill, Burleigh Road, Ascot, Berks SL5 8ER]; *b* 22 March 1916; *m* 29 Sept 1938 Cdr Archibald Rider Cheyne, RN (accidentally *k* at Setubal, nr Lisbon, 20 Oct 1950), est son of Col Reginald Edmonstone Cheyne, IA, of Ditchingham, Norfolk, and has:

1a *Mark Rider [Mark Cheyne Esq, 38D Whistlers Ave, London SW11 3TS]; *b* 15 Sept 1941; *educ* Rugby; FCA

1a *Angela Zena Dorothy [Ms Angela Cheyne, 65 Portland Rd, London W11 4LQ]; *b* 15 May 1947

1 Dorothy Eugenie; artist; *b* 10 Nov 1883; *d* unm 27 Aug 1977

2 Sylvia Leonora; *b* 25 Feb 1885; *m* 21 Feb 1911 HH Sir Charles Vyner de Windt Brooke, GCMG, Rajah of Sarawak 1917–46, est son of HH The Rajah of Sarawak (Sir Charles Anthony Johnson Brooke, GCMG), and had issue. He *d* 9 May 1963

The 2nd VISCOUNT d 22 Jan 1930; his er son,

OLIVER SYLVAIN BALIOL BRETT, **3rd Viscount Esher**, GBE (1955, MBE 1918); *b* 23 March 1881; *educ* Eton; FRIBA (hon), FRSL, Capt 16th Bn Co of London Regt (Westminster Rifles), attd Mil Intell Branch War Office, Priv Sec to Sec State India 1905–10, Tstee London Museum and Nat Theatre, chm London Theatre Cncl, pres SPAB, chm Victorian Soc, govr Old Vic, memb gen purposes ctee Nat Tst, pres Br Drama League and London Soc; *m* 1 Oct 1912 Antoinette (*d* 22 July 1965), only dau of August Heckscher, of New York, and *d* 8 Oct 1963, leaving:

1 LIONEL GORDON BALIOL BRETT, **4th and present Viscount Esher**

1 Virginia Anne Charlotte; *b* 18 June 1916; *d* 1990

2 *Nancy Mildred Gladys [The Hon Lady Shuckburgh, High Wood House, Watlington, Oxon]; *b* 28 Sept 1918; *m* 25 Sept 1937 Sir (Charles Arthur) Evelyn Shuckburgh, KCMG, CB (*d* 12 Dec 1994), est son of Sir John Evelyn Shuckburgh, KCMG, CB, and has issue:

(1) *Julian John Evelyn [Julian Shuckburgh Esq, 22 Ellingham Rd, London W12 9PR]; *b* 1940; *m* 1st 1963 (*divorce* 1970) Faith Beatrice, dau of Sir Paul Herve Giraud Wright, and has:

1a *Benjamin Evelyn [Benjamin Shuckburgh Esq, 41 Artesian Rd, London W2 5DB]; *b* 1966; *m* 1991 *Emma M, yr dau of Sir Bernard Albert Ashley, and has:

1b *Samuel; *b* 1995

1b *Rose; *b* 1997

1a *Matilda Ann; *b* 1964; *m* 1st 1983 (*divorce* 1988) Scott Ziegler, s of Douglas Ziegler, of Hermosa Beach, Calif. USA; *m* 2nd 1993 *Lyle McCormick, s of Thomas J McCormick, of Petaluma, Calif., USA, and by her 1st husb has:

1b *Emma Dorothy; *b* 1985

(1) (cont.) Julian Shuckburgh *m* 2nd 1975 (*divorce* 1992) Sarah Elizabeth, dau of Sir David (Valentine) Willcocks, CBE, MC, and by her has:

2a *Alexander William; *b* 1982

2a *Amy Catherine Lorna; *b* 1977

3a *Hannah Jane Elizabeth; *b* 1979

(2) *Robin Anthony [Robin Shuckburgh Esq, Holton Place House, Holton, Oxon]; *b* 1948; *m* 1972 *Philippa Mary, dau of Nicholas Spargo, of Maidengrove, Henley-on-Thames, and has:

1a *Jacob Nicholas Anthony; *b* 1978

1a *Laura Mary; *b* 1983

(1) *Catherine; *b* 1939; *m* 1961 (*divorce* 1970, resumed maiden name) (John) David Caute, author and playwright, and has:

1a *Edward Peter; *b* 1963

2a *Daniel Alexander; *b* 1965

3 *Priscilla Léonie Helen [The Hon Lady Beckett, 3 St Alban's Grove, London W8]; *b* 31 May 1921; *m* 22 Feb 1941 *Capt Sir Martyn Gervase Beckett, 2nd Bt (*qv*), and has issue

ESMONDE

Arms: Erm. on a chief gu. three mullets arg. **Crest:** Out of a mural crown a Saracen's head ppr. **Mottoes:** 1 (over the crest) Jerusalem, 2 (below the arms) *Malo mori quam foedari* ('I prefer death to dishonour'). **Creation:** Bt (I) 28 Jan 1628/9.

SIR THOMAS FRANCIS GRATTAN ESMONDE, 17TH BT, of Ballynastragh, Co Wexford [Sir Thomas Esmonde Bt, 6 Nutley Ave, Donnybrook, Dublin 4, Ireland]; *b* 14 Oct 1960; *s* f 1987; *educ* Sandford Park Sch, Ranelagh, Dublin, and Trin Coll Dublin; MB, BCh, BAO 1984, MRCPI, MRCP (UK), jr house offr Whiteabbey Hosp 1984–85, sr ho offr Roy Victoria, Musgrave Park and Whiteabbey Hosps 1985–87, Altnaglevin Hosp Londonderry 1987–88, Med Registrar Roy Gwent Hosp Newport 1988–89, Registrar in Neurology U Hosp Wales 1989–90, Clinical Res Fell Dept of Neuroscience Western Gen Hosp Edinburgh 1990–92, Sr Registrar Neurology Roy Victoria Hosp Belfast 1992–96, Consultant Neurologist Roy Victoria Hosp Belfast 1996–; *m* 26 April 1986 *Pauline Loretto, 2nd dau of James Vincent Kearns, and has:

1 +SEAN VINCENT GRATTAN; *b* 8 Jan 1989

1 *Aisling Margaret Pamela Grattan; *b* 1991

2 *Niamh Pauline Grattan; *b* 1996

Lineage: JAMES ESMONDE, of Johnstown, Co Wexford; *m* Isabel, dau of Thomas Rosseter, of Rathmacknee Castle, and had:

LAURENCE ESMONDE, of Johnstown; *m* Eleanor, dau of Walter Walsh, of The Mountains, and had, with a yr s:

WALTER or WILLIAM ESMOND(E); *m* Margaret, dau of Michael Furlong, of Horetown, and had, with seven daus:

1 Robert; living 1618; had, with two daus:

(1) William, of Johnstown; MP Wexford 1634; had:

1a Laurence, of Johnstown; executor to Lord Esmonde (*see* below); *d* 1652

1a Mary; *m* Anthony Colclough, of Rathglin

2a Ellinor; *m* Walter Talbot, of Ballnamory, and had issue

(2) Richard, served under his unc Lord Esmonde (*see* below) in Fort Duncannon; granted admon of Lord Esmond's estate 1646

2 LAURENCE

3 James; had a dau

4 Patrick; Sheriff Carlow 1627; *m* Katherine, dau of Sir Edward Gough by Ellice, dau of Walter Butler and afterwards w of Lord Esmonde (*see* below), and had six daus

The 2nd son,

Sir LAURENCE ESMOND, 1st and last LORD ESMOND, BARON OF LIMERICK, Co Wexford (where his seat of Limerick was — that, rather than the city in SW Ireland, being the place commemorated) (I), so *cr* 20 May 1622; V-Constable Blackwater (River) 1594, served in Connaught and cmded 1601–02 a troop of 150 foot and horse in ELIZABETH I's service, ktd 1603, Constable Fort Duncannon, Co Wexford, 1606–45, Sheriff Co Waterford 1607, MP Wicklow 1613–15, Maj-Gen of all JAMES I's forces in Ireland 1622; sided with Parl Civil War 1644, handing over Duncannon but subsequently being besieged there by forces representing the Confederacy of Kilkenny, to whom he surrendered March 1644/5; *d* 26 May 1645, having allegedly *m* as his 1st w a sister of — O'Flaherty, Dynast of Iar Connacht, and (?)had issue(?):

1 Sir THOMAS ESMOND(E), **1st Bt**

There is a story that the first(?) Lady Esmonde, a devout Roman Catholic, feared her child would be brought up a Protestant, hence spirited it away to her family in Connaught. This may have suited Lord Esmond, who *m* (2nd?) by Dec 1628 Elizabeth or Ellice (*d* 16 Jan 1644/5), widow of (a) John Shirlock and (b) Sir Edward Gough, and dau of Walter Butler, 4th son of 9th Earl of Ormond and Ossory (*see* MOUNTGARRET, V), but it has been argued that the fact of administration of the deceased Lord Esmond's state being granted April 1646 to his n Richard by a bro of the full blood makes the story implausible.

The 1st and last LORD ESMOND, BARON OF LIMERICK's putative (illegitimate?) son,

Sir Thomas Esmonde, 1st Bt (I) so *cr* 28 Jan 1628/9; ktd 1628; MP Enniscorthy, Co Wexford, 1641–42, royalist Gen of Horse during period of Civil War; *m* 1st *c* 19 March 1629 Ellice (*d* 16 Jan 1644), widow of 2nd Baron Caher of the 1583 *cr* and dau of Sir John FitzGerald or Fitzgerald, of Dromana, Co Waterford (of the line of Desmond), and *d* 1674, leaving by her, with other issue:

1 **Sir Laurence Esmonde, 2nd Bt**, of Huntington Castle, nr Clonegall, Co Carlow (built by his gf(?) Lord Esmonde 1625 and called after the ancient seat of his ancestors at Huntington, Lincs); *b* 1634; *m* 1st Lucia (*d* 17 April 1685), est dau of Col Hon Richard Butler, of Kilcash, Co Tipperary (bro to 1st Duke of Ormonde; *see* MOUNTGARRET, V); *m* 2nd Lucy (*m* 2nd *c* 1691 Col Hon Richard Butler, of Galmoy), dau of Charles Cavanagh, of Carrickduff, Co Carlow, 2nd son of Sir Morgan Cavanagh, of Clonmullen, and *d* by 22 Oct 1688, having had by his 1st w, with two other daus:

(1) **Sir Laurence Esmonde, 3rd Bt**, PC; served French Army; *m* 1703 Jane Lucy, er dau of Matthew Forde, of Coolgreany, and *d* 1720, leaving:

1a **Sir Laurence Esmonde, 4th Bt**; *d* unm 20 Feb 1739

2a Richard, of Ballyconlore, Co Wexford; Capt; *m* his cousin Helen (*m* 2nd Richard Butler, of Westcourt), 3rd dau of Thomas Butler, of Kilcash, by Lady Margaret de Burgh, dau of 7th Earl of Clanricarde and *dsp* 1738 after accidentally shooting himself with his fowling-piece in the hall of Huntington Castle

3a **Sir John Esmonde, 5th Bt**; Capt Spanish Army 1735; *m c* 22 Oct 1742 Helen, dau of William Galway, of Lota, Co Cork, by Mary, dau of Col John Butler (*see* MOUNTGARRET, V), and *d* 30 June 1758, having had, with two other daus:

1b Helen; *m* 1764 Richard Durdin, of Shanagarry, Co Cork; they founded the town of Huntington, Pa., and had:

1c Alexander; *dsp*

4a **Sir Walter Esmonde, 6th Bt**; *m* Joanna, widow of James Butler, of Caherbane, Co Clare, and 2nd dau of 5th Baron Caher, and *d c* 1 Feb 1767, leaving:

1b Frances; *m* 11 Feb 1750 Stanislaus MacMahon, of Clare, Chief of his name, and had issue

2b Lucy

3b Elizabeth; *d* unm 7 April 1791

1a Frances; *m* Morgan Kavanagh, of Borris

2a Lucy; *m* Robert Devereux, of Carrigmenan

2 James, of Ballynastragh; *m* Barbara, sis of Alderman John Vincent, of Limerick, and had, with other issue:

(1) Laurence, of Ballynastragh; *d* aged 90 falling from his horse while hunting; *m* 1st 10 May 1700 Elizabeth (*d* 7 Aug 1713), dau of Henry Brownrigg, of Wingfield, Co Wexford; *m* 2nd Mary, dau of Thomas Masterson, of Moneyseed, Co Wexford, and widow of Francis Wyse, of the Manor of St John; *m* 3rd — Bagg but had issue only by his 1st w (together with another dau):

1a JAMES (Sir), **7th Bt**

1a Frances; *b* 23 Aug 1707; *m* 1735, Howard Kyan, of Mount Howard, Co Wexford, and Ballymurtagh, Co Wicklow, and *d* 1785, leaving issue. He *d* 1766

2a Mary; *b* 16 Dec 1708; *m* Francis Magan, of Emoe, Co Westmeath, and had with other issue:

1b Thomas, of Emoe

3a Elizabeth; *b* 23 March1710; *m* Richard Doyle and had issue

4a Jane; *m* Terence Dunne, of Ard, Queen's Co, son of John Dunne, and had issue. He *d* 17 July 1774

(2) Marcus, of Wexford; *m* Elizabeth, dau of Philip Hay, of Ballinkeele, and had two daus

(3) Patrick; called the Chevalier d'Esmonde; Col Austrian serv, when captured by Turks; had a son, Maurice, in the Austrian serv (*d* unm) and an only dau and heir, who *m* Charles, Count Kavanagh (of the family of Borris), Gen of Cav in the Imp Army

(4) Patrick; Spanish Army; *d* unm in Spain

(1) Mary, *m* — Plunkett, of Dunshaughlin

Sir Thomas *m* 2nd Joane, widow of (a) George Bagenal, of Dunleckney, and (b) Theobald Purcell, of Loughmoe, Co Tipperary, and 5th dau of 11th Earl of Ormonde (*see* MOUNTGARRET, V), by whom he had no issue

The 1st Bt's ggs,

Sir James Esmonde, 7th Bt; *b* 23 April 1701; Offr in French serv; *m* Ellice, only dau and heir of Thomas White, of Pembrokestown, Co Waterford, and *d* 1767, leaving:

1 **Sir Thomas Esmonde, 8th Bt**; *b* 1758; *m* 1st March 1776 Mary, dau and sole heir of Myles Dowdale, of Cloon, Co Meath; *m* 2nd *c* 18 Aug 1802 Letitia Hill Devereux (*dsp* 13 Nov 1851), niece and heir of Nicholas Devereux, of Ringville, Co Kilkenny, and *dsp* 22 Nov 1803

2 John; MD; *m* Helen (*m* 2nd Col Hervé de Montmorency and *d* 1854), dau and coheir of Bartholomew O'Callan, of Osberstown, Co Kildare, and was *k* 13 June 1798 in the uprising of that year, leaving:

(1) **Sir Thomas Esmonde, 9th Bt**, PC; *b* 10 Dec 1786; *m* 1st 1812 Mary (*d* 7 March 1840), only dau of E Payne; *m* 2nd 16 April 1856 Sophia Maria (*d* 22 Nov 1867), widow of Hamilton Knox Grogan Morgan, of Johnstown Castle, and dau of Ebenezer Radford Rowe, of Ballyharty, Co Wexford, and *dsp* 31 Dec 1868

(2) Bartholomew (Rev); SJ; *b* 12 Dec 1789; *d* 15 Dec 1862

(3) James; Cdr RN; *b c* 1791; *m* 16 Sept 1824 Anna Maria (*d* 25 June 1869), dau of James Murphy, of Ringmahon Castle, Co Cork, and n of Most Rev Dr Murphy, RC Bp Cork, and *d* 4 Oct 1842, leaving:

1a **Sir John Esmonde, 10th Bt**, JP, DL Co Wexford; MP Waterford 1852–76, Jr Ld Treasury 1874, Lt-Col Waterford Artillery Militia; *b* 16 May 1826; *m* 12 April 1861 Louisa (*d* 31 Jan 1880), 4th dau and coheir of Henry Grattan, MP, of Tinnehinch, Co Wicklow, s of Rt Hon Henry Grattan, and *d* 9 Dec 1876, having had:

1b **Sir Thomas Henry Grattan Esmonde, 11th Bt**, DL; sometime Chm Co Wexford CC, MP S Co Dublin 1885–92, W Kerry 1892–1900 and N Wexford 1900–18, Senator Irish Free State 1922, Chamberlain Vatican Household 1898, Grand Offr Order Holy Sepulchre and rep the Order for Ireland; *b* at Pau 21 Sept 1862; *m* 1st 21 July 1891 Alice Barbara (*d* 5 Dec 1922), dau of Patrick Donovan, JP, of Frogmore, Co Kerry, and n of Sir

Henry Donovan; *m* 2nd 15 Sept 1924 Anna Frances (*d* 15 July 1941), dau of Peter Levins, of Mount Hope, NY, and *d* 15 Sept 1935, having by his 1st w had:

1c **Sir Osmond Thomas Grattan Esmonde, 12th Bt**; MA Oxford, TD Wexford Dáil Eireann 1923–36; *b* 4 April 1896; *d* unm 22 July 1936

2c John Henry Grattan; Midshipman RN; *b* 8 May 1899; *ka* Jutland 31 May 1916

1c Patricia Alison Louisa Grattan; Ldy Order Holy Sepulchre; *b* 28 Aug 1894; *m* 18 Nov 1927 R-Adml John Baptist Heffernan, USN, Sec Naval Historical Fndn, Washington, s of William Heffernan, of Washington, Ind., and had:

1d *Henry Grattan (Rev); SJ; *b* 5 Nov 1930

1d *Patricia Grattan; *b* 1 Jan 1929

2d *Eithne Mary Grattan; *b* 1 April 1933; *m* 17 May 1958 *Thomas Michael Hartnett, s of Joseph L Hartnett, of Johnstown, Pa., and has:

1e *Thomas Michael; *b* 10 Feb 1960

2e *John Joseph; *b* 23 Feb 1963

1e *Kathleen Francis; *b* 17 Feb 1959

2e *Elizabeth Ann; *b* 25 May 1961

3e *Eithne Grace; *b* 9 Oct 1964

4e *Patricia Grattan; *b* 14 Aug 1967

3d *Kathleen Barbara Grattan [Mrs Raymond Wach, 3810, Garfield Street NW, Washington, DC 20007, USA]; *b* 20 April 1937; *m* 5 Nov 1960 *Raymond Joseph Wach, son of Edward P Wach, of Dayton, Ohio, and has:

1e *Raymond Penafort Edward; *b* 6 Sept 1961; *m* 13 July 1986 *Constancia Miralles Macawile and has:

1f *Raymond Vivencio; *b* 14 Sept 1989

2f *Edward Ignacio; *b* 24 April 1991

3f *Joseph Christopher; *b* 30 June 1992

2e *Damian Aquinas; *b* 14 March 1963; *m* 15 Dec 1995 *Naoko Grace Horie and has:

1f *Chie Kathleen Horie; *b* 19 Dec 1996

3e *Gregory Joseph Grattan; *b* 1 Sept 1972

1e *Kathleen Terese; *b* 4 Dec 1964; *m* 13 April 1991 *Joseph Peter Ellsworth and has:

1f *Martin Hakeem; *b* 10 Jan 1991

2f *John Xavier; *b* 27 Dec 1992

3f *Patrick Joseph; *b* 12 June 1994

2e *Marie Olukemi; *b* 22 Aug 1967; Capt US Air Force; *m* 2 Feb 1991 *Scott Thomas Kokotajlo and has:

1f *Daniel Bendisi; *b* 30 Aug 1992

2f *Timothy Culver; *b* 10 March 1995

1f *Bethany Malisa; *b* 28 Oct 1996

3e *Margaret Marie; *b* 16 May 1968; has:

1f *Siobhán Keelan; *b* 30 Oct 1992

2c *Alngelda Barbara Mary Grattan

3c Eithne Moira Grattan; *m* 9 June 1927 **Sir Anthony Charles Esmonde, 15th Bt**, and had issue (*see* below)

2b **Sir Laurence Grattan Esmonde, 13th Bt**; barrister King's Inns, Dublin; Lt-Col Waterford RFA, Special Res, Boer War 1899–1902 with RA, Cmdt S African Constabulary, WW I as Lt-Col cmdg 27th Northumberland Fus (4th Bn Tyneside Irish Bde), subsequently raised and cmded 10th and 11th Bns Roy Dublin Fus (despatches); *b* 3 Nov 1863; *m* 1st 12 Dec 1906 Sarah May (*d* 11 Oct 1911), dau of Alexander John Spittall, of Ballaughton, IoM; *m* 2nd 18 June 1928 Pauline (*d* 1 June 1941), 7th dau of Joshua James McEvoy Netterville by Hon Mary, 2nd dau of 7th Viscount Netterville, and *dsp* 1 Feb 1943

3b Walter George Grattan; Capt S African Constabulary; *b* 27 March 1875; *d* unm 21 Dec 1908

4b John Geoffrey Grattan; *b* 22 July 1873; *d* 6 Jan 1913

1b Henrietta Pia; *b* 9 Jan 1865; *d* 23 Jan 1874

2b Louisa Ellice Benedicta Grattan; *b* 1 Sept 1871; *m* 28 June 1896 Col Henry Lionel Pilkington, CB, 21st Hus, of Tore, Co Westmeath, and *d* 24 Aug 1936, leaving issue. He *d* 4 March 1914

3b Annetta Frances Grattan; *b* 7 May 1875; *m* 7 April 1904, Walter Sutherland Wilkinson, CBE, of 50 South Eaton Place, London SW1, est s of Walter L Wilkinson, of London, and *d* 18 Oct 1925, leaving issue. He *d* 8 July 1943

2a James, of Drominagh, Co Tipperary, JP, DL; *b* 17 Sept 1827; *m* 20 Oct 1859, Caroline (*d* 7 Sept 1908), dau of John Sugrue, JP, and *d* 1 Sept 1894, leaving:

1b James, of Drominagh; *b* 16 Sept 1860; *d* unm 17 Oct 1899

2b John Joseph, of Drominagh; LRCSI, MP N Tipperary 1910–15, T/Capt RAMC 1915; *b* 27 Jan 1862; *m* 1st 7 May 1888 Rose (*d* 6 Aug 1901), er dau of John Magennis, of London, and had:

1c **Sir John Lymbrick Esmonde, 14th Bt**; barrister King's Inns, Dublin, Sr Counsel 1942, Bencher 1948, MP N Tipperary 1915–18, served WW I Leinster Regt, Capt Roy Dublin Fus, Intell Corps, TD Co Wexford Dáil Eireann 1937–43 and 1948–51; *b* 15 Dec 1893; *m* 1922 Eleanor, dau of Laurence Fitzharris, of Dublin and Monread, Co Kildare, and *dsp* 6 July 1958

2c Geoffrey; Lt 4th Tyneside Irish Bn Northumberland Fus; *b* 1897; *ka* 9 Oct 1916

3c **Sir Anthony Charles Esmonde, 15th Bt**; LRCS, LRCP, Kt SMO Malta (1957), Surgn-Lt RN 1921–25, TD Co Wexford Dáil Eireann 1951, memb Consultative Assembly Cncl of Europe 1954 and Irish Nat Health Cncl 1956, chm ctee on Ag Cncl of Europe; *b* 18 Jan 1899; *m* 9 June 1927 Eithne Moira Grattan, 3rd dau of **Sir Thomas Henry Grattan Esmonde, 11th Bt** (*see* above), and *d* 1981, leaving:

1d **Sir John Henry Grattan Esmonde, 16th Bt**; TD, Circuit Court Judge Western Circuit, barrister King's Inns, Dublin, 1950, memb Leinster Bar, Sr Counsel 1971; *b* 28 June 1928; *educ* Nat U of Ireland (BCom 1950); *m* 23 April 1957 *Pamela Mary [Pamela Lady Esmonde, 6 Nutley Ave, Donnybrook, Dublin 4, Ireland], er dau of Dr Francis Stephen Bourke, FRCPI, MRIA, and *d* 1987, leaving:

1e Sir THOMAS FRANCIS GRATTAN ESMONDE, **17th and present Bt**

2e +Harold William Grattan; *b* 4 Nov 1964; *educ* Sandford Park Sch and Trin Coll Dublin

3e +Richard Anthony Grattan; *b* 1969; *educ* Sandford Park Sch and Trin Coll Dublin

1e *Karen Maria Grattan; *b* 15 Dec 1965

2e *Lisa Marion Grattan; *b* 1968; *educ* Nat U Dublin

2d +Bartholomew Thomas Grattan [Bartholomew Esmonde Esq, Ballynastragh, Gorey, Co Wexford, Ireland]; *b* 17 Jan 1937; *educ* Glenstal Abbey

3d +Anthony James Grattan [Anthony Esmonde Esq, St Oliver's, Coolbawn, Co Tipperary, Ireland]; *b* 14 Oct 1943; *educ* Glenstal and U Coll Dublin

1d *Alice Mary Grattan [Miss Alice Esmonde, 8 Palmerston Park, Dublin 6, Ireland]; *b* 6 Oct 1929; *educ* Nat U of Ireland (BSc 1951)

2d *Eithne Marion Grattan [Miss Eithne Esmonde, Ballynastragh, Gorey, Co Wexford]; *b* 28 Nov 1931; LRAM 1958

3d *Anne Caroline Grattan; *b* 9 April 1940

1c Rose Mary

2c Caroline; *b* 29 March1900; *d* unm 18 Jan 1929

3c *Frances; *m* 18 April 1934 Edward Smithers, s of Richard Smithers, of Dublin, and has issue. He *d* 2 Sept 1950

2b (cont.) John Esmonde *m* 2nd 24 July 1904 Eily (*d* Dec 1957), dau of Dr D A O'Sullivan, of Kensington, and *d* 17 April 1915, leaving by her:

4c Owen James; Offr Australian Dept External Affrs; *b* 15 May 1905; *educ* Downside; *m* 19 Feb 1938 *Eira Margaret Antonia [Mrs Owen Esmonde, Cloneen, Glendalough, Co Wicklow, Ireland], dau of George Henry Louis Mackenzie (*see* MACKENZIE, Bt, of Coul), and *d* 1993, leaving:

1d +Eugene Patrick Mackenzie; Capt Royal Australian Artillery, ADC to GOC Northern Cmd 1968, served S Vietnam; *b* 22 Aug 1942; *educ* Blackrock Coll Dublin, Christian Brothers ACT, RMC Duntroon ACT and Queensland U (BEcon); Lt-Col RAA (ret 1981), md Sharpe Gp 1982–; *m* 1972 *Jennifer Ann, dau of Sir Frank Victor Sharpe, CMG, OBE, of Brisbane, and has:

1e +Godfrey Christian; *b* 1980

2e +Eugene James; *b* 1983

1e *Grania Adelaide; *b* 1986

1d *Deborah Anne Barbara; *b* 9 Jan 1939; *m* 1968 *Peter John Fraser Coutts, BEE, MA, MSc, PLD

2d *Gillian Mary Antonia; *b* 9 Dec 1940; *m* 1963 *Colin Leslie Rosewarne, of Hardigreen Park, Mittagone, NSW, Australia, and has:

1e *Andrew John; *b* 5 March 1964

2e *Liam Patrick; *b* 1974

1e *Allison Mary; *b* 8 Jan 1966

2e *Maria Patricia; *b* 11 May 1969

3d *Vivienne Mary Patricia [Mrs Charles Creswell, Cilwych Farm, Bwlch, Powys]; *b* 22 March 1945; *m* 1970 *Charles Timothy Creswell and has:

1e *Dominic Sydney; *b* 1975

1e *Laragh Veronica Storm; *b* 1973

4d *Rosemary Carolyn [Mrs Robert 275A Nelson Rd, Mount Nelson, Hobart, Tasmania 7007, Australia]; *b* 4 Sept 1946; *m* 1966 *Maj Robert Keith Peterswald, RAR, and has:

1e *Charlotte Antonia; *b* 11 Sept 1968

2e *Georgina Ann; *b* 1972

5c +Donal (Rev); *b* 27 June 1906; *educ* Downside

6c John Witham, OBE (1943), DSC; Capt (E) RN, WW II; *b* 13 Aug 1907; *m* 29 Oct 1940 *Aileen Mary [Mrs John Esmonde, Ballyellis, Buttevant, Co Cork, Ireland], dau of Harold Philip Harold-Barry, of Ballyvonare, Co Cork, and *d* 1983, leaving:

1d +Peter Witham; *b* 4 Aug 1945

2d +Kevin Harold; *b* 28 May 1948

1d *Helen Mary Karin; *b* 29 July 1950; *m* 1st 1976 Paul Douglas Clark, of Toronto; *m* 2nd 1985 *Lt-Col Robert Charles Couldrey, 7th DEO Gurkha Rifles, only s of C J Couldrey, of Limpsfield Common, Oxted, Surrey, and by him has:

1e *David Witham James; *b* 1988

1e *Annabel Mary; *b* 1986

7c Eugene, VC (posthumous, 1942), DSO; F/Lt RAFO, Lt-Cdr (A) RN, WW II; *b* 1 March 1909; *ka* Channel Straits 12 Feb 1942

8c James Bartholomew; MIMM; *b* 1 March 1909; *d* unm 9 May 1970

9c +Patrick, MC [Maj Patrick Esmonde MC, Ocklynge Manor, Mill Rd, Eastbourne, Sussex BN21 2PG]; LRCP and LRCS Ireland, Maj RAMC WW II, Colonial Medical Service 1946–62; *b* 12 Dec 1914; *m* 3 April 1943 *Norah Marcia, dau of William Cooper, of Seven Acres, Malton, Yorks, and has:

1d *Margaret Shane [Mrs Peter Henderson, Court Farm, Corsley, Wilts BA12 7PA]; *b* 25 March 1944; *m* 30 April 1966 *Col Peter Alexander Henderson, 22nd Cheshire Regt, and has:

1e *Dominic Patrick Alexander; *b* 31 Jan 1968

2e *Oliver Thomas Alexander; *b* 1971

2d *Grania Mary [Mrs Loudon Greenlees, Haymakers Farm, Back Lane, Waldron, E Sussex TN21 0NH]; *b* 29 Oct 1947; *m* 1st 7 March 1970 (*divorce* 1974) Denis Edward Chambers, yr son of J C Chambers, and has issue:

1e *Laragh Victoria; *b* 26 May 1971

2d (cont.) Mrs Grania Chambers *m* 2nd 1975 *(Ian Hugo) Loudon Greenlees and has further issue:

1e *Rupert Hugo Loudon; *b* 2 Feb 1976

2e Thomas Ian Esmonde; *b* 8 Oct 1985; *d* 2 Dec 1985

2e *Camilla Shane; *b* 3 Nov 1978

3e *Daisy Thomasina; *b* 7 June 1987

4c *Mary Carmel; *b* 13 March 1912; *m* 1935 *Dermot St John Gogarty, F/O RAFVR, of Nairobi, and has:

1d *Michael Dermot St John; *b* 1936

3b Charles Francis; *b* 31 March 1863; *d* 6 Feb 1898

1b Ellen Mary; *b* 22 June 1865; *d* unm 23 June 1938

3a Thomas, VC (1855); Lt-Col 18th Royal Irish Regt, Dep-Insp-Gen Constabulary Ireland, at Siege of Sebastopol; *b* 25 Aug 1831; *m* 24 Nov 1859 Matilda Marie, dau of Peter de Pentheny O'Kelly, of Barrettstown, Co Kildare, and *d* 14 Jan 1872, leaving:

1b Thomas Louis; *b* 14 Dec 1864; *m* 1913 Mary Alice Philomena, dau of George Mansfield, JP, DL, of Morristown Lattin, Naas, Co Kildare, and *d* lost at sea 10 Oct 1918

1b Eva Mary; *b* 3 Nov 1860; *m* 7 Sept 1892 James Charles Comerford and *d* 5 Sept 1949, leaving issue

2b Matilda Mary; *b* 23 June 1862; *d* unm 14 Sept 1937

3b Frances Josephine; *b* 9 March 1864; *m* 1896 Arthur Westropp Dawson and *d* 17 May 1955

4b Georgina Helen Mary; *b* 4 May 1867; *d* unm 2 May 1924

(4) Laurence; called the Chevalier d'Esmonde; Col Grens of Gd in French serv, Chev Legn Hon; *b* 26 Dec 1793; *m* July 1853 Marie Louise, dau of Marquis de Montendre, and *d* Dec 1883, leaving:

1a Helena; *b* 13 June 1854; *m* 1880 Charles Marie Meinrad, Marquis d'Amedor de Mollans, and *d* 1938, leaving issue. He *d* 22 Feb 1933

2a Marie Caroline; *b* 25 June 1855; *m* 1882 Count de Masson d'Autume and *dsp* 12 Feb 1944

(5) John; Capt RN, served under Lord Cochrane (*see* DUNDONALD, E) in Chilean service; *k* in an engagement with a Spanish frigate

(1) Margaret; Hon Canoness Order St Anne of Bavaria; *m* 1st 3 Jan 1831 Peter Warren Locke, of Athgoe Park, Co Dublin. He *dsp* 7 Dec 1833. She *m* 2nd 15 Nov 1843 John Harold Barry and *dsp* 25 Dec 1875. He *d* 30 July 1867

3 James, of Sallins, Co Kildare; *m* Anne, dau of John Fitzgerald, of Yeomanstown, and had issue

1 Elizabeth; *m* — Doyle

2 Katherine; *m* 21 July 1789 John Dogherty, of Middleton, Co Dublin

3 Frances; *m* 1st 1785 Richard Durdin, of Huntington, Pa., and had issue; *m* 2nd — Lewis

4 Mary; *m* 1st by licence 12 March 1773 Matthew White, of Scarnagh, Co Wexford, and had issue. He *d c* 3 Dec 1791. She *m* 2nd by licence 2 Aug 1794 John Nash, of Ballymagooly

Esplen

Arms: Sa. on a pile between two mascles or a lymphad of the field. **Crest:** In front of a demi-eagle displayed sa, charged on each wing with a mascle as in the arms, an anchor fesswise or. **Motto:** Be faithful. **Creation:** Bt (UK) 14 July 1921.

John Graham Esplen [John Esplen Esq, Lauriston, Weycombe Rd, Haslemere, Surrey GU27 1EL]; *b* 4 Aug 1932; *s f* 1989 but does not use title; *educ* Harrow and St Catharine's Coll Cambridge (BA 1955); late Lt King's Dragoon Gds and Northumberland Hus; *m* 6 Oct 1956 (*divorce* 19–) Valerie Joan, yr dau of Maj-Gen Albert Percy Lambooy, CB, OBE, of Chelsea, and has:

1 +WILLIAM JOHN HARRY; *b* 24 Feb 1967

1 *Wendy Anne; *b* 5 April 1959

2 *Fiona Mary; *b* 31 Dec 1960

3 *Mary Caroline; *b* 30 Nov 1962

Lineage: Sir John Esplen, 1st Bt (UK), so *cr* 14 July 1921, of Hordress Court, Canterbury, Kent, KBE (1918); sr dir Esplen, Sons & Swainstone, consulting engrs and naval architects, ch technical advsr Min Shipping WW I; *b* 7 April 1863; (s of William Esplen, of Blundellsands); *m* 26 Jan 1898 Laura Louise (*d* 28 July 1936), dau of John Dickenson, of Sutherland, and had issue:

1 WILLIAM GRAHAM (Sir), **2nd Bt**

1 Laura Ray; *m* 10 July 1929 Sir Peter William Hoare, 7th Bt, of Barn Elms (*qv*), and *d* 1992, leaving issue

Sir JOHN *d* 7 Feb 1930; his son,

Sir William Graham Esplen, 2nd Bt; *b* 29 Dec 1899; *educ* Harrow; *m* 11 Oct 1928 (*divorce* 1951) Aline Octavia, yst dau of A Octavius Hedley, and had:

1 Sir JOHN GRAHAM ESPLEN, **3rd and present Bt**

Essex

Arms: Gu. a lion rampant between three cross-crosslets fitchée or. **Crest:** A demi-lion rampant or, holding in the dexter paw a cross-crosslet fitchée gu. **Supporters:** Two lions or, ducally crowned gu. **Motto:** *Fide et fortitudine* ('By fidelity and fortitude'). Allusion was made to the coat of arms by a Cavalier poet in 1665 when he wrote of the fervently royalist 1st Baron Capell of Hadham (*see* below) that during the Civil War 'Our lyonlike Capel undaunted stood/Beset with crosses in a field of blood'. **Creations:** B. (E) 5 Aug 1641, E. and V. (E) 20 April 1661.

THE 10TH EARL OF ESSEX, Viscount Malden, Co Essex, and **Baron Capell of Hadham**, Co Hertford (Robert Edward de Vere Capell) [The Rt Hon The Earl of Essex, 2 Novak Place, Torrisholme, Morecambe, Lancs LA4 6PG]; *b* 13 Jan 1920; *s* 3rd cousin once-removed 1981; F/Sgt RAF WW II; *m* 3 Jan 1942 *Doris Margaret, dau of George Frederick Tomlinson, of Morecambe, and has:

1 +(FREDERICK) PAUL DE VERE, *Viscount Malden* [Viscount Malden, 35 Pinewood Avenue, Brookhouse, Lancaster LA2 9NU]; *b* 29 May 1944; *educ* Skerton Boys Sch, Lancaster Roy GS, Didsbury Coll of Educn and Northern Sch of Music; ACP, LLCM (TD), FRSA; Dep Head and Act Head Marsh County Primary Sch 1966–78, Headteacher Cockerham Parochial C of E Sch 1979–80, teacher, Dep Head and Act Head Skerton County Primary Sch 1981–95

Earldom of Essex: Geoffrey de Mandeville, who like his fellow (the 2nd) Earl of Essex of the present creation was Constable of the Tower of London, was created Earl of Essex in 1140 by KING STEPHEN. He already held numerous manors in Berks, Bucks, Essex, Herts and Middx, which had belonged to his grandfather, another Geoffrey, at the time of the Domesday Survey in 1086. The family originated in Normandy, but precisely where is unclear, since there are several place names there akin to Mandeville (which seems originally to have been in Latin *Magna Villa* or 'Great Town'). De Mandeville later sided with the EMPRESS MAUD, who granted him a more generously framed charter, including a clause making the post of Constable of the Tower hereditary. Later still de Mandeville again sided with STEPHEN but subsequently rebelled yet again. His son was recreated Earl of Essex by MAUD in Jan 1155/6, the rebellious habits of the father and perhaps also the appointive nature of earldoms at the time (*see* NORTHUMBERLAND, D, and RUTLAND, D, for a discussion of early earldoms) requiring a regrant.

After the death of the 3rd de Mandeville Earl, right to the title passed through a female branch but these descendants of the original de Mandevilles took the old family name and were recognised as Earls of Essex in the time of KINGs JOHN and HENRY III. The male line failed again in 1230 and for the next 150 years the title was born along with the Earldom of Hereford by the de Bohuns. The elder daughter of the last of the de Bohuns married Thomas of Woodstock, EDWARD III's seventh and youngest son, who was known as Earl of Buckingham and Essex from 1377 before being created Duke of Gloucester in 1385. He too died without male issue and one of his grandsons, Henry Bourchier, by Anne, his only daughter who had children, was created Earl of Essex in 1461. On the death of Bourchier's grandson the 2nd Earl in March 1539/40 the earldom of 1461 became extinct. A month later Thomas Cromwell, HENRY VIII's chief minister, was created Earl of Essex but enjoyed the title only 10 weeks before falling from favour and being attainted.

Three years later William Parr, brother of HENRY VIII's Queen KATHERINE and son-in-law of the last Bourchier Earl of Essex, was created Earl of that county. With his attainder in 1553 the Earldom once more expired. In 1572 another connection of the Bourchiers was created Earl of Essex when Walter Devereux, great-grandson of Cicely, sister of the last Earl of Essex of the 1461 creation, was granted a peerage under that title. Walter's wife Lettice, daughter of Sir Francis Knollys and a niece of ANNE BOLEYN, is mentioned in Shakespeare's *A Mid-*

summer Night's Dream. It was their son Robert, 2nd Earl of Essex, who was the spoiled favourite of ELIZABETH I and rebelled against her in the early part of the year 1600/1.

Lineage: Sir WILLIAM CAPELL; Alderman of London and Ld Mayor 1503–04 and 1509–10 (2nd son of John Capell, of Stoke-by-Nayland, Suffolk); fined £1,600 (just under £600,000 in late-1990s terms) by Empson and Dudley, HENRY VII's notoriously extortionate ministers, objected to a second fine of £2,000 (say £750,000) on a trumped up charge of failing to prosecute a coiner when in office as Ld Mayor and was imprisoned in the Tower of London till HENRY's death 1509; *m* Margaret, dau of Sir Thomas Arundell, of Lanherne, Cornwall, and *d* 1515, leaving (with two daus, Elizabeth, who *m* 1st Marquess of Winchester (*qv*), and Dorothy, who *m* 8th Lord (Baron) Zouche (of Haryngworth) (*qv*)):

Sir GILES CAPELL, of Raines or Rayne Hall, Essex; ktd for bravery at Sieges of Thérouanne and Tournai and Battle of Spurs 1513, present Field of Cloth of Gold 1520; Sheriff Herts and Essex *c* 1529; *m* twice and left issue by his 2nd w Isabel, dau and heir of Sir Thomas Newton:

1 Henry (Sir), of Raines Hall

2 Edward (Sir), of Raines Hall; *m* Anne, dau of Sir William Pelham, and had an er s:

(1) Henry (Sir); Sheriff Essex and Herts; *m* Lady Catherine Manners, dau of 1st Earl of Rutland (*see* RUTLAND, D), and had, with a dau Mary (*m* Humphrey Mildmay, of Danbury (*see* ST JOHN MILDMAY, Bt), and *d* 12 Oct 1633):

1a Arthur (Sir); Sheriff Herts 1592; *m* Margaret, dau of Lord John Grey, of Pirgo, and had, with ten other sons and nine daus:

1b Henry (Sir); *m* Theodosia, sis of 1st Baron Montagu of Boughton (*see* MANCHESTER, D), and had issue:

1c ARTHUR CAPELL, **1st Baron Capell of Hadham** (E), so *cr* 6 Aug 1641, PC (March 1644/5); MP Herts Short Parl April–May 1640 and Long Parl 1640–41; royalist in Civil War and accordingly beheaded 9 March 1648/9; *m* 28 Nov 1627 Elizabeth, dau and sole heir of Sir Charles Morrison, Bt, of Cassiobury, Herts, and had issue:

1d ARTHUR, **1st Earl**

2d HENRY CAPELL, 1st and last BARON CAPELL OF TEWKESBURY, Co Gloucester (E), so *cr* 1692, KB; Lt of Ireland; *dsp* 1696 when the title expired

1d Mary; *m* 1st 28 June 1648 Henry Seymour, Lord Beauchamp (*see* SOMERSET, D); *m* 2nd 17 Aug 1657 1st Duke of Beaufort (*qv*) and *d* 7 Jan 1714/5, leaving issue

2d Elizabeth; *m* 1653 3rd Baron Dormer (*qv*) of Wyng and *d* 30 July 1678, having had issue

3d Theodosia; *m* by 26 Jan 1660/1 2nd Earl of Clarendon of the 1661 *cr* (*see* CLARENDON, E, preliminary remarks), and *d* 22 March 1661/2, leaving issue

4d Anne; *m* John Strangways, of Melbury Sandford, Dorset

The 1st BARON's er son,

ARTHUR CAPELL, **1st Earl of Essex**, so *cr* 20 April 1611, as also VISCOUNT MALDEN, Co Essex (both E), with remainder to heirs male of the body of his f (in gratitude to whose faithfulness CHARLES II granted the titles), PC (1672–Jan 1680/1); *bapt* 28 Jan 1631/2; Ld Lt Herts 1660–81 and Wilts 1668–72, Ld Lt Ireland 1672–77, 1st Ld Treasury March–Nov 1679, accused of taking part in the Rye House Plot to assassinate CHARLES II and place his illegitimate but Protestant son the Duke of Monmouth (*see* BUCCLEUCH and QUEENSBERRY, D) on the throne instead of the Catholic Duke of York (JAMES II) and imprisoned June 1683 in Tower of London; cut his own throat there 13 July 1683; *m* 19 May 1653 Lady Elizabeth Percy (*d* 5 Feb 1717/8), dau of 4th Earl of Northumberland (*see* NORTHUMBERLAND, D), and had (with five er sons, all of whom *d* young):

1 ALGERNON CAPELL, **2nd Earl of Essex**, PC (1708); *b* 28 Dec 1670; Gent Bedchamber to WILLIAM III 1691–1702, Ld Lt Herts 1692–1710, Constable Tower London 1706–10, Col 4th Dragoons 1693–1710, Brig Gen 1701/2, Maj-Gen 1704, Lt Gen 1708; *m* 28 Feb 1691/2 Mary (*m* 2nd 1714 Conyers d'Arcy (*see* DARCY DE KNAYTH, B) and *d* 20 Aug 1726), dau of 1st Earl of Portland (*qv*), and had:

(1) WILLIAM, **3rd Earl**

(1) Elizabeth; *m* 1st Samuel Molyneux (*d* 1728); *m* 2nd Nathaniel St André

(2) Mary; *m* 7 May 1729 2nd Viscount Midleton (*qv*) and *d* 12 Nov 1762, leaving issue

1 Anne; *m* 3rd Earl of Carlisle (*qv*)

The 2nd EARL *d* 10 Jan 1709/10; his only s,

WILLIAM CAPELL, **3rd Earl of Essex**, KG (Feb 1737/8), KT (1724/5–38), PC (?Feb 1734/5); *b* 1697; *m* 1st 27 Nov 1718 Lady Jane Hyde (*d* Jan 1723/4), est surv dau of 4th Earl of Clarendon of the 1661 *cr*, and had, with two other daus:

1 Charlotte; *m* 30 March 1752 1st Earl of Clarendon of the 1776 and current *cr* (*qv*; so *cr* as a consequence of this marriage) and *d* 3 Sept 1790, leaving issue

2 Mary; *m* 25 Aug 1758 Adml Hon John Forbes, s of 3rd Earl of Granard (*qv*), and *d* April 1782, leaving issue

The **3rd Earl** *m* 2nd 3 Feb 1726 Elizabeth (*d* 8 June 1784), dau of 2nd Duke of Bedford (*qv*), and by her had further issue, with an er s (*d* young) and two daus, who lived to maturity

He *d* 8 Jan 1743; his only surv s by his 2nd w,

WILLIAM ANNE HOLLES CAPELL later CAPEL, **4th Earl of Essex**; *b* 7 Oct 1732; *m* 1st 1 Aug 1754 Frances (*d* 19 July 1759), dau and coheir of Sir Charles Hanbury-Williams, KB, and gdau maternally of Thomas, Earl of Coningsby, and had:

1 GEORGE CAPEL later CAPEL-CONINGSBY, **5th Earl of Essex**; *b* 13 Nov 1757; DCL, FSA, Ld Lt Herefs 1802–17, Recorder and High Steward Leominster, assumed the surname and arms of CONINGSBY on inheriting the estates of his great-aunt, the Countess of Coningsby; *m* 1st 6 June 1786 Sarah (*d* 16 Jan 1838), widow of Edward Stephenson and dau of Henry Bazett, of St Helena; *m* 2nd 14 April 1838 Catherine (*d* 22 Feb 1882, aged 87), dau of Edward Stephens, of Leadwell, Oxon, and *dspl* 23 April 1839, leaving an illegitimate dau (Harriet, *b c* 1806, *m* 1824 Richard Ford (*see* BERNERS, B) and *d* 14 May 1837)

1 Elizabeth; *m* 13 July 1777 3rd Baron Monson (*qv*) and *d* his widow 23 Feb 1834, leaving issue

The **4th Earl** *m* 2nd 3 March 1767 Harriet (*d* 12 March 1821), dau of Col — Bladen, and *d* 5 March 1799, having by her had, with other issue:

2 John Thomas; *b* 2 March 1769; *m* 2 April 1792 Caroline, est dau of 1st Earl of Uxbridge (*see* ANGLESEY, M), and *d* 5 March 1819, leaving issue:

(1) ARTHUR ALGERNON CAPEL later CAPELL (roy licence 23 July 1880), **6th Earl of Essex**; *b* 27 Jan 1803; *m* 1st 14 July 1825 Lady Caroline Janetta Beauclerk (*d* 22 Aug 1862), dau of 8th Duke of Saint Albans (*qv*), and had, with other issue:

1a Arthur de Vere, *Viscount Malden*; Lt-Col Herts Yeo Cav, Lt RHG; *b* 22 July 1826; *m* 23 Jan 1853 Emma Mary (*d* 22 Nov 1905), 3rd dau of Sir Henry Meux, 1st Bt, and *dvp* 10 March 1879, leaving, with other issue:

1b GEORGE DEVEREUX DE VERE CAPELL, **7th Earl of Essex**, JP, DL; V-Lt Herts, Gren Gds, Col TF, ADC to HM KING EDWARD VII; served Imp Yeo Boer War 1900–01; *b* 24 Oct 1857; *m* 1st 12 July 1882 Ellenor Harriet Maria (*d* 31 Dec 1885), dau of William Henry Hartford, of Oldtown, Glos, and had:

1c ALGERNON GEORGE DE VERE CAPELL, **8th Earl of Essex**; *b* 21 Feb 1884; *educ* Eton; Lt 7th Hus and Herts Imp Yeo, T/Capt Remount Service; *m* 1st 28 Sept 1905 (*divorce* 1926) Mary Eveline Stewart (*d* 30 Oct 1955), est dau of William Russell Stewart Freeman, JP, DL, of The Manor House, Wingrave, Bucks, and had:

1d REGINALD GEORGE DE VERE CAPELL, **9th Earl of Essex**, TD; *b* 9 Oct 1906; *educ* Eton and Magdalene Coll Cambridge (BA 1928); Hon Col 47 Signals Regt Middx Yeo TA, Lt-Col 1947, cmded 16th Airborne Div Signals Regt (TA) 1948; *m* 1st 2 March 1937 (*divorce* 1957) Mary Reeve, widow of Col George Ashton Strutt, of Brailsford, Derbys, formerly w of William Rodney Winterbottom and only dau of F Gibson Ward, of Rosemount, Bermuda; *m* 2nd 14 Nov 1957 Nona Isobel (*d* Jan 1997),widow of Francis Sydney Smythe, of Yew Tree Cottage, Colgate, Sussex, and dau of David Wilson Miller, of Christchurch, NZ, and *dsp* 18 May 1981

1c (cont.) The **8th Earl** *m* 2nd 10 Feb 1926 (*divorce* 1950) Alys Montgomery (*d* 19 March 1977), formerly w of Ernest Scott-Brown and dau of Robert Hayes Falkiner; *m* 3rd 10 Dec 1950 (*divorce* 1956) Mildred Carlson, formerly of the US Consular Staff, Melbourne; *m* 4th 1957 Christine Mary (*d* 1985), dau of George Frederick Davis, of Handsworth Wood, Warwicks, and *d* 8 Dec 1966

1b (cont.) The **7th Earl** *m* 2nd 14 Dec 1893 Adela (*d* 28 July 1922), est dau of Beach Grant, of New York, and *d* 25 Sept 1916, leaving by her:

1c Iris Mary Athenais de Vere; *b* 8 June 1895; *educ* Oxford; *d* unm 4 Oct 1977

2c Joan Rachel de Vere; *b* 28 Feb 1899; *educ* Oxford; *m* 19 June 1922 1st Viscount Ingleby (*qv*) and *d* 1979, leaving issue

1b Evelyn de Vere; granted with her sis rank of earl's dau 6 Jan 1893; *m* 5 Sept 1883 Hon Eustace Henry Dawnay, s of 7th Viscount Downe (*qv*), and *d* 13 Nov 1939, leaving issue

2b Sybil de Vere; *m* 18 Sept 1890 1st Earl Brassey and *d* 20 Feb 1934, leaving issue (*see* BRASSEY OF APETHORPE, B)

2a Reginald Algernon CAPEL, JP Herts; *b* 3 Oct 1830; *m* 24 April 1858 Mary Eliza (*d* 19 June 1911), dau of John Nicholas Fazakerley, of Burwood Park, Surrey, and niece of Lord Rokeby, and *dsp* 31 July 1906

1a Adela Caroline Harriet; *b* 4 March1828; *m* 3 Nov 1858 13th Earl of Eglinton and (1st Earl of) Winton (*qv*), and *d* 13 Dec 1860, leaving issue

(1) (cont.) The **6th Earl** *m* 2nd 3 June 1863 Louisa Caroline Elizabeth (*d* 5 May 1876), er dau of Charles, Viscount Dungarvan, and gdau of 8th Earl of Cork (*see* CORK and ORRERY, E), and by her had issue:

3a Arthur Algernon; barrister; *b* 27 July 1864; *m* 23 Dec 1890 Isabel Anne (*d* 19 Feb 1939), dau of Col Townshend Wilson, Coldstream Gds, and *d* 18 Feb 1940, leaving issue:

1b Constance Audrey; *b* 21 Oct 1891; *m* 9 Oct 1917 Capt Sir Harold Lister Farquhar, KCMG, MC (*see* FARQUHAR, Bt), and *d* 28 Oct 1963, leaving issue

2b Rachel Julia; *b* 4 April 1894; *d* unm 20 Nov 1949

2a Beatrice Mary; *b* 7 Dec 1870; *m* 16 Oct 1913 Edmund Banbury and *d* 22 Jan 1954, leaving issue (*see* BANBURY, of Southam, Bt)

(1) (cont.) The **6th Earl** *m* 3rd 25 April 1881 Louisa Elizabeth (*d* 25 Jan 1914), widow of Gen Lord George Paget, yst son of 1st Marquess of Anglesey (*qv*), and yr dau of Charles Fieschi Heneage, and *d* 11 Sept 1892

(2) Algernon Henry Champagne; granted with surv siblings rank of Earl's dau/yr s May 1839; Capt RN; *b* 23 Oct 1807; *m* 10 Dec 1832 Caroline (*d* 11 June 1880) 2nd dau of Adml Hon Sir Charles Paget, KCB (*see* ANGLESEY, M), and *d* 21 Nov 1886, leaving, with other issue:

1a Reginald Randolph Algernon; Indian Navy; settled in Australia; *b* 31 May 1841; *m* 1875 Marion (*d* 1937), dau of John Struthers, of Madras, and had, with eight other children:

1b Caroline; *b* 1880; *m* 1899 Thomas Alexander Clapperton and had issue

2b Millicent Florence; *b* 1892; *m* 1913 Henry Knox Paul and had issue

2a Charles Horatio Algernon; *b* 5 Aug 1845; *m* 28 June 1868 Alice Peel (*d* 18 Jan 1936), dau of Frederick Bellairs, of The Downes, Bideford, Devon, and *d* 14 Oct 1924, leaving:

1b Arthur Algernon de Vere; *b* 6 April 1869; *educ* Deal Coll and Oxford; *m* 1st 1890 Alice Ann (*d* 1913), dau of William Yewett Pine, and had:

1c Arthur Algernon de Vere; *b* 1891; *m* Jan 1940 *Alice M Reynolds and *d* 1950

1c Elfreda Beatrice de Vere; *b* 1892; *m* 1915 Rudolph Henry Weston and had a dau

2c Alice Maud de Vere; *b* 1896; *m* 1920 Thomas James Garpham (*d* 1963) and had two sons and a dau

3c Lilly; *d* unm

1b (cont.) Arthur Capell *m* 2nd 1916 Alice Mabel (*d* June 1951), dau of James Currie, of Wimbledon, and *d* 14 April 1924, leaving by her:

2c ROBERT EDWARD DE VERE CAPELL, **10th and present Earl of Essex**

4c *Elsie Elfreda [Mrs Ernest Walls, Flat 28 Raglan Lodge, 23 North Lodge Rd, Parkstone, Dorset]; *b* 1922; *m* 1943 Ernest Walls (*d* 1968) and has:

1d *Derek Arthur; *b* 1950

1d *Jennifer Dawn; *b* 1948

1b Gertrude Blanche Constance; *d* unm

2b Beatrice Alice Georgina; *m* 1st 21 April 1914 Tudor George Trevor, er s of Rev George Trevor, DD, Canon York and Rector Beeford, E R Yorks. He *d* 3 Aug 1921. She *m* 2nd 23 April 1924 Charles Bonneau and *d* 6 June 1939

3b Edith Florence Caroline; *d* unm 16 Dec 1960

4b Evelyn Maud Mary; *m* 1908 George Ernest Richards, BSc, s of Charles Richards and *d* 17 Nov 1943

5b Mabel Lillian Violet; *d* unm 23 Aug 1974

1a Millicent Florence Evelyn; *m* April 1870 Richard Cole and *d* 27 July 1932

(3) Adolphus Frederick Charles Molyneux; *b* 28 June 1813; *m* 15 Dec 1834 Charlotte Mary (*d* 27 June 1871), est dau of 3rd and last Viscount Maynard, and *d* 13 Aug 1899, leaving:

1a Arthur Algernon Adolphus Frederick Pierce de Capell; *b* 11 June 1837; *m* 21 May 1867 Elizabeth (*d* 7 June 1882), yst dau of Owen Owen, of Gadlys and Llangfigad, Anglesea, and *dspl* 5 May 1870

2a Horatio Bladen (Rev); Rector Gt Easton, Dunmow, 1877–1918; *b* 10 Oct 1839; *m* 1st 16 Aug 1866 Ada Augusta (*d* 18 Aug 1916), 2nd surv dau of Theophilus Hawkins, of Newton Abbot, and had, with other issue:

1b Horace Charles George Arthur; *b* 6 July 1868; *m* 18 Oct 1896 Clara Isabel (*d* 25 Feb 1939), formerly w of Charles Molonieux Nevil Reade, and dau of Ozro Jackson, of Nebraska, and *d* 8 Feb 1953, leaving:

1c Bladen Ozro; farmer and cattleman; *b* 10 July 1897; *m* 1st 14 June 1920 (*divorce* 1929) Madge Elizabeth (*d* 1956), dau of Ruel Crawford, of Parris, Idaho; *m* 2nd 19– Hazel Kruse and *d* 27 Aug 1959, leaving by his 1st w:

1d Bladen Horace; merchant; *b* 26 Aug 1922; *m* 12 Feb 1945 *Mae Elizabeth [Mrs Bladen Capell, 873 Copper Avenue, Yuba City, CA, USA], dau of William J Walley, of Hannibal, Mo., and *d* 1978, leaving:

1e +William Jennings [William Capell, 2462 Eckhart Road, Yuba City, CA 95991, USA]; *b* 9 Aug 1952; *m* 1971 *Sandra Elaine, dau of Chester M Matson, and has:

1f *Jennifer Elaine; *b* 1974

1e *Dorita Mae; *b* 17 Oct 1948; *m* 1971 *Robert Cooper and has:

1f *Michael Keith; *b* 1974

2f *Bobby Ryan; *b* 1977

2e *Raylene Dee; *b* 25 April 1958; *m* 1976 *Theodore Schwartz

1d *Ada [Mrs Kay Boren, North 4904, Elm St, Spokane, Washington, USA]; *b* 1 June 1924; *m* 28 Feb 1941 *Kay Boren, s of Jesse Reed Boren, of Pocatello, Idaho, and has:

1e *Denis Kay; *b* 3 Nov 1941

2e *Larry Dean; *b* 26 March 1943

3e *Jeffery Lee; *b* 7 March 1957

1e *Toni Carol; *b* 28 Aug 1946

2d *Helen Lucille [Mrs Leonard Sampson, 2711, N Nelson Street, Spokane, Washington, USA]; *b* 13 Aug 1926; *m* 31 Oct 1945 Leonard A Sampson, s of Henry Andrew Sampson, of Oslo, and has:

1e *David Andrew; *b* 16 Nov 1947

2e *Danny Jay; *b* 29 Nov 1957

1e *Barbara Jean; *b* 6 July 1956

1c Mary Daisy; *b* 14 Feb 1899; *m* 1st 26 Oct 1922 (*divorce* 1937) William Edward Park, s of William Park, of Carlisle, Cumberland, and had issue; *m* 2nd 1944 Edward William Beltz, of Vancouver Island, BC, and *d* 1 Jan 1962

2c *Ada Lorena; *b* 27 March 1901; *m* 14 July 1923 Arthur Foster Dagnall, s of William Samuel Dagnall of S Vancouver

2b Algernon Essex, CBE (1924), DSO (1900); Col 2nd Rhodesia Regt, Commr Police and Comdt-Gen S Rhodesia, Insp S African Constabulary, Ch Police Grenada, WI; Boer War 1899–1901 (despatches, two medals, six clasps) and Br E Africa WW I, Croix de Guerre; *b* 1 Nov 1869; *m* 3 March 1903 Lois Ethel (*d* 22 April 1944), dau of William Slatter, of Stratton, Glos, and *d* 23 Feb 1952, leaving:

1c Algernon Arthur; Paymaster Native Affairs Dept S Rhodesia; *b* 7 Dec 1903; *m* 8 Jan 1933 Violet Mary (*d* 1987), dau of Andrew Boyd, of Dumfries, and *d* 13 Aug 1950, leaving:

1d Colin Algernon Andrew; *b* 3 Dec 1935; *m* 5 Oct 1957 *Cecily Ann [Mrs Colin Capell, PO Box 1, Haenertsburg 0730, S Africa], yr dau of Arend Smith, of Salisbury, Rhodesia, and *das* 1977, leaving:

1e +Clint Andrew Devereux; *b* 15 Aug 1960; *m* 1981 *Jeanne, dau of Robert Bolton, of Sinoia, Zimbabwe, and has:

1f *Joanne Victoria; *b* 1981

2e +Craig Robert Lawrence [Craig Capell Esq, PO Box 3418, Pietersburg 0700, S Africa]; *b* 7 July 1962; *m* 1985 *Janet Elizabeth, dau of David Sloman, of Johannesburg, and has:

1f +Dylan Colin David; *b* 1987

1f *Sherilyn May Ann; *b* 1993

2d +Robert Devereux Boyd [Robert Capell Esq, 961 Montcalm Drive, Kelowna, BC V1Y 3M8, Canada]; *b* 20 Oct 1942; *educ* U Coll Rhodesia and Nyasaland (BA, PCE (Lond)); *m* 19 Aug 1967 *Elin Rosemary, dau of Alan Lesley Earle, of Bulawayo, Rhodesia, and has:

1e *Jennifer Rosemary; *b* 4 April 1975

1d *Rosemary Susan Lois [Mrs Cyril Hughes, PO Box 33, Plumtree, Zimbabwe]; *b* 21 Feb 1934; *m* 3 May 1958 *Cyril Bryan St Clair Hughes, er s of Cyril V Hughes, of Wem, Salop, and Mrs Tuckey, of Marazion, Cornwall, and has:

1e *Barry William Vaughan; *b* 23 May 1961

2e *Kevin Bryan Vaughan; *b* 1 Dec 1962; *m* 1992 *Catherine Ann, dau of Derek Verinals, and has:

1f *Genevieve Ayn; *b* 29 June 1995

2f *Natasha Clare; *b* 14 May 1997

3e *Ross Anthony Vaughan; *b* 24 May 1967; *m* 1996 *Maria Magdalena, dau of Benjamin Steyn

1e *Susan Anne Lois Vaughan; *b* 15 Jan 1969

2c Robert Devereux [Robert Capell Esq, 19 Magazine Road, Pietermaritzburg, Natal, S Africa]; *b* 11 Jan 1909; *m* 1931 *Audrie Clare (*m* 2nd 1937 Rodger Ferguson), dau of Charles Stratton Lightening, of Selukwe, S Rhodesia, and *d* 23 Sept 1936, leaving issue:

1d Allan Robert Devereux; Civil Engineer; *b* 8 Feb 1932; *educ* Natal U (BSc (Eng) 1958); *m* 2 Jan 1960 Lorna Anne, dau of Col James Valentine McNally, RAMC, of Natal, and was *k* with his w in an air disaster 4 March 1962, leaving:

1e Anne Caroline; *b* 3 Feb 1961; *k* with her parents 4 March 1962

2d Owen Maynard; *b* 21 May 1935; *d* unm 15 Jan 1956

1c Joan Lois; *b* 22 July 1905; *m* 1930 Walter James Evans and *d* 1986, leaving:

1d *Walter Robin; *b* 2 Jan 1931; *m* *Jennifer Huntley, dau of Huntley Shaw, of Salisbury, Rhodesia, and has:

1e *David Huntley; *b* 1963

1e *Susan Mary; *b* 1958

2e *Bronwyn Gay; *b* 1959

2d *David Anthony; ARIBA, ptnr M N Clinton & D A Evans, Chartered Architects, of Salisbury, Rhodesia, and Blantyre, Malawi; *b* 25 July 1932; *educ* Cape Town U (B Arch); *m* 1st (*divorce*) Phyllis Anne, dau of Dr Desmond Drew, of Mbabane, Swaziland; *m* 2nd 13 Feb 1967 *Monica Frances Winson, and has:

1e *Richard Warwick; *b* 6 Dec 1968

1d Carol Ann; *b* 4 Jan 1938; *m* 19 Jan 1959 *Millar Rankin, and *d* 1988, leaving:

1e *Bruce Ian; *b* 4 Jan 1961

1e *Lynette Gayle; *b* 24 Nov 1964

3b Henry Addison Devereux; T/Lt HLI; *b* 12 June 1873; *educ* Felsted; *m* 1 Aug 1901 Olive Mary (*d* 1937), dau of William Richardson-Bunbury (*see* RICHARDSON-BUNBURY, Bt), and *d* 19 Feb 1925, leaving:

1c +Robert; *b* 1903

1b Mary Kathleen; *m* 1st 1894 Francis George West, s of Rev George West, of Horeham Hall, Essex, and has issue. He *d* in S Africa 1900. She *m* 2nd June 1900 (*divorce* 1906) Edward Aubrey Courtauld Lowe, of Cantfield, Takeley, Essex; *m* 3rd 1914 Capt William Frederick Ullathorne Cosens, 13th Hus, and had further issue

2a (cont.) The Rev Horatio Capell *m* 2nd 1916 Violet Annie (*d* 1960), dau of Robert Frost, of Snape, Suffolk, and *d* 17 April 1933, leaving by her:

2b *Beatrix Violet De Vere [Mrs Edward Tranter, Essex House, Great Easton, Dunmow, Essex CM6 2HG]; *b* 1919; *m* 1st 1939 (*divorce* 1950) Raymond Smith and has:

1c Anthony Capel; *b* 5 Aug 1940; *m* 1968 (*divorce* 1980) Evelyn Hamilton Bentink Martin, adopted dau of Charles Penryn Ackers and formerly w of Michael Charles Butler Johnson, and *d* 1993, leaving:

1d *Matilda Amelia CAPEL-MAUROO; *b* 1967; *m* 1995 *Kevin Stuart Mauroo

2d *Emily Jane; *b* 1969

2b (cont.) Mrs Beatrix Smith *m* 2nd 1950 *Edward Reginald Tranter

3a George Marie (Rev); BA Oxford, Rector Passenham, Northants, Domestic Chaplain to Earl of Essex; *b* 11 Jan 1845; *m* 4 Jan 1870 Annie (*d* 26 Nov 1928), dau of Peter Stanley Lowe, of Whitehall, Churchstow, Devon, and *d* 28 Jan 1915, leaving:

1b Arthur George Coningsby; Capt 2nd Bn Northants Regt, Boer War 1902 (Queen's medal, two clasps), WW I (despatches); *b* 28 June 1879; *m* 20 Oct 1914 Phyllis (*m* 2nd 17 June 1919 Edward Davenport Broster (*d* 8 Oct 1953), s of Arthur Erdswick Broster, of Wirksworth, Derbys), dau of Maurice Deacon, of Chase Cliffe, Whatstandwell, Derbys, and was *ka* at Neuve Chapelle 14 March 1915

1b Dora Amy Isabel; *d* unm 16 March 1949

2b Marie Kathleen; *m* 1st 21 Jan 1897 (*divorce* 1915) D'Arcy Mackinnon Dawes, 3rd s of Sir Edwin Sandys Dawes, KCMG, of Mount Ephraim, Faversham, Kent. He *d* 9 Jan 1930. She *m* 2nd 5 June 1943 Capt Rudolph Keane Franks, MBE only s of Edward Franks, India Office, and *d* 4 June 1970 aged 98. He *d* 29 Dec 1970 aged 92

3b Leonie Annie; *d* unm 3 Aug 1958

4b Hilda Amalie Violet; *d* unm 15 May 1960

5b Bertha Sybil; *d* 13 Oct 1969 aged 91

1a Harriet Mary; *m* 1st 24 Oct 1855 Viscount Forth (*d* 8 Oct 1861); *m* 2nd 29 Oct 1861 E C Dering and *dsp* 30 April 1868

2a Florence Louisa Amelia; *m* 1st 6 Oct 1859 Francis Nevil Reade, 21st Fus, and had issue. He *d* 9 Nov 1882. She *m* 2nd 1 Dec 1883 Francis Maurice Drummond Drummond (*see* PERTH E) and *d* 9 Nov 1924

(1) Harriett Jane; *m* 26 Dec 1817 as his 2nd w David Okeden Parry-Okeden, of Moor Critchell, and *d* 24 June 1819, leaving issue. He *d* 28 Oct 1833

(2) Georgiana; *m* 1st 16 Aug 1821 Ralph Smyth, of Gaybrook; *m* 2nd 18 June 1831 Pierce O'Brien Butler, of Dunboyne Castle, Meath, and *d* 19 Oct 1835

(3) Maria; *m* 13 Dec 1821 Marquis Marius d'Espinassy de Fontenelle and *d* 30 Dec 1856, leaving issue

(4) Louisa Anne; *m* Nov 1827 Count Auguste d'Espinassy de Fontenelle and *d* 28 July 1842

(5) Horatia; *m* 16 Oct 1851 Col Count de Septeuil and *d* in a fire at Cassiobury 22 May 1864

(6) Jane; *m* Nov 1833 D Macloughlin, MD, and *d* 2 Nov 1849

(7) Amelia; *m* 25 April 1857 Hon Henry Stevenson Blackwood (*see* DUFFERIN AND CLANEBOYE, B) and *d* 29 May 1892

3 William Robert (Rev); MA, Chaplain to HM QUEEN VICTORIA, Rector Raine, Essex, Vicar Watford, Herts; *b* 28 April 1775; *m* 7 June 1802 Sarah (*d* 19 April 1874), only dau of Samuel Salter, of Rickmansworth, Herts, and *d* 3 Dec 1854, having had, with other issue:

(1) William; *b* 21 April 1804; *m* 14 April 1831 Jane Anne, dau of Thomas Clutterbuck, of Micklefield, Herts, and *d* 18 Feb 1876

(2) Edward Samuel; Lt-Col Bengal Army; *b* 16 Jan 1811; *m* 5 June 1838 Elizabeth (*d* 19 Nov 1851), est dau of James Binnie, and *d* 28 May 1896, having had, with other issue:

1a Arthur William; Lt-Col Bengal Cavalry; had:

1b Terence; Capt RFC; *b* 1891; *m* 1919 Florence Penelope (*d* 1963), dau of William Whitham; and *d* 1962, leaving:

1c +William Terence; *b* 1921; late Capt 11th Hus; *m* 1963 *Petronella, dau of Maj Peter Beale Lewis, MC, Roy Ulster Rifles, and has:

1d *Georgina Penelope; *b* 1964

2d *Rosalind Elizabeth Maud; *b* 1968

1a Ada; *m* 18 June 1874 Adml Sir John Reginald Thomas Fullerton, GCVO, CB, s of Rev Weston Fullerton, Rector Thrybergh, Yorks, and *d* 17 Aug 1922, leaving issue. He *d* 29 June 1918

(1) Jane Selina; *m* 9 May 1826 T T Clarke, of Swakeleys, Middx, and had issue. He *d* 5 April 1890

(2) Louisa; *m* 21 March 1831 Rev J C Clutterbuck, Vicar Long Wittenham, Bucks, and *d* 1 Oct 1908 aged 100, leaving issue. He *d* 8 May 1885

(3) Georgiana; *m* 27 Sept 1829 Rev Nathaniel F Wodehouse and *d* 1892, leaving issue (*see* KIMBERLEY, E)

(4) Isabelle; *m* 10 May 1854 Rev A Hawkes, MA

4 Thomas Bladen (Sir), KCB; V-Adml the Blue; *b* 25 Aug 1776; *m* 10 May 1816 Harriet Catherine (*d* 30 July 1866), dau of Francis George Smyth, and *dsp* 4 March 1853

EVANS

Arms: Gyronny of eight gu. and or, overall a lion passant between two fleurs-de-lys in pale sa. **Crest:** In front of a wall embattled and masoned ppr., a lion as in the arms. **Motto:** *Fide et virtute* ('With faith and virtue'). **Creation:** Bt (UK) 31 Jan 1920.

SIR ANTHONY ADNEY EVANS, 2ND BT, of Wightwick Hall, Wolverhampton, Co Stafford [Sir Anthony Evans Bt, Almer Manor, Blandford, Dorset BT11 9EN]; *b* 5 Aug 1922; *s f* 1954; *educ* Shrewsbury and Merton Coll Oxford; *m* 1st 1 May 1948 (*divorce* 1957) Rita Beatrice, formerly w of Larry Rupert Kirsch and dau of Alfred David Kettle, of Whitton, Middx, and Souldern, Oxon; *m* 2nd 1958 *Sylvia Jean — and by his 1st w has:

1 +A son; *b* 19—

2 +A son; *b* 19—

1 *A dau; *b* 19—

Lineage: JOHN EVANS, of West Bromwich, Staffs; *b* 1782; *d* 25 July 1866, leaving:

JOSEPH EVANS, of Culwell House, Staffs; *b* 1809; *d* 16 Oct 1868, leaving:

JOSEPH EVANS, of The Lindens, Wolverhampton, JP Staffs; *b* 3 Feb 1843; *m* 23 July 1869 Christina, 4th dau of James Shelley, of Trysull, Staffs, and *d* 31 Jan 1908, leaving:

1 Joseph Osmond; *b* 4 May 1870; *d* 22 May 1960

2 WALTER HARRY (Sir), **1st Bt**

3 George Herbert; *b* 19 May 1874; *m* 30 April 1908 Mary (May) (*d* 16 Nov 1951), dau of A Felix Stevens, MD, of St Malo, Seaford, and *d* 1 Nov 1922, leaving:

(1) *George Joseph Armstron; *b* 16 July 1909

(2) *John William, Dr; *b* 27 Nov 1910

The 2nd son,

Sir Walter Harry Evans, 1st Bt (UK), so *cr* 31 Jan 1920; CC Staffs; *b* 19 May 1872; *m* 16 Dec 1907 Margaret Mary (*d* 2 March 1969), yr dau of Thomas Adney Dickens, of Ellerdine, Salop, and *d* 7 Nov 1954, having had:

1 Walter Terence; *b* 18 Sept 1911; *educ* Harrow and U Coll Oxford; *d* unm 4 April 1932 following an accident whilst fishing on a lake in Connemara

2 Sir ANTHONY ADNEY EVANS, **2nd and present Bt**

1 Eileen Margaret; *b* 1 Oct 1908; *m* 24 June 1933 (*divorce* 1943) Rev Charles Everard Cradock Royds, er s of Rev Canon Charles Cradock Twemlow Royds, Rector Heysham, Lancs, and *d* 28 June 1957, leaving issue

2 *Diana Gillian Mary; *b* 13 March 1926; *m* 1st 18 Sept 1948 (*divorce* 1954) Capt John Richard Pugh, RA, er s of Sydney John Pugh, of Boston Manor, London, and has:

(1) *Vanessa Gillian Webber (adopted by her stepfather 13 March 1960); *b* 15 Sept 1950

2 (cont.) Mrs Diana Pugh *m* 2nd 28 Nov 1959 Maj Alan Joseph Webber, TARO (*d* 19–), 2nd s of Charles Webber, of Beckenham, Kent, and by him has:

(1) *Daryl Adney; *b* 29 Nov 1960

EVANS OF PARKSIDE

Creation: B. (LP, UK) 19 April 1997.

THE BARON EVANS OF PARKSIDE, of St Helens, Co of Merseyside (John Evans) [the Rt Hon The Lord Evans of Parkside, 6 Kirkby road, Culcheth, warrington, Cheshire WA3 4BS]; *b* 19 Oct 1930; *educ* Jarrow Central Sch; apprentice marine fitter 1946–49, 1950–52; RE 1949–50; engr Merchant Navy 1952–55, generally 1955–65, 1968–74; worked in engineering etc; memb: Heburn UDC 1962 (Leader 1969, chm 1972); secretary and Agent Jarrow Lab Pty 1965–68; MP (Lab) Newton 1974–83, St Helens North 1983–97, assist Govt Whip 1978–79, Oppn Whip 1979–80, PPS to Leader of Oppn 1980–83, Oppn Spokesman Employment 1983–87, MEP 1976–78, memb Lab Party NEC 1982–96, Chm Lab Party 1991–92, Political secretary Nat Union Lab and Socialist Clubs; *m* 1959 *Joan Slater and has two sons and a dau

Lineage: JAMES EVANS; *m* Margaret Robson and had:

JOHN, *cr* a **Baron**

EVANS-BEVAN

Arms: Arg. three boar's heads couped sable, on a chief gules a demi-lion rampant erased or between two castles of the field. **Crest:** Issuing from the battlements of a tower argent a demi-lion rampant or gorged with a collar gules holding between the paws a boar's head as in the arms. **Creation:** Bt (UK) 9 July 1958.

SIR MARTYN EVAN EVANS-BEVAN, 2ND BT, of Cadoxton-juxta-Neath, Co Glamorgan [Sir Martyn Evans-Bevan Bt, Felinnewydd, Llandefalle, Brecon, Powys LD3 0NE]; *b* 1 April 1932; *s f* 1973; *educ* Uppingham; High Sheriff Breconshire 1967–68, Freeman City London, Liveryman Farmers' Co; *m* 12 Oct 1957 *Jennifer Jane Marion, yr dau of Robert Hugh Stevens, of Lady Arbour, Eardisley, Herefs, and has:

1 +DAVID GAWAIN; *b* 16 Sept 1961; *m* 1987 *Philippa Alice, yst dau of Patrick Sweeney, of E Moors, Helmsley, N Yorks, and has:

(1) +Patrick David; *b* 9 Feb 1994

(1) *Alice Laura; *b* 1989

2 +Richard Martyn; *b* 20 Feb 1963

3 +Thomas Rhydian; *b* 6 Feb 1966

4 +Huw Evan; *b* 2 Aug 1971

Lineage: DAVID BEVAN; *b* 1825; *m* 20 Nov 1846 Mary (*d* 28 May 1889), dau of Evan Evans, of Crinallt, nr Neath, Glam, and *d* 9 July 1888, leaving:

EVAN EVANS BEVAN, of Cadoxton House, Neath; colliery and brewery owner, High Sheriff Breconshire 1913; *b* 28 June 1855; *m* 24 Jan 1895 Caroline (*d* 15 June 1923), dau of Richard Thomas, of Abernant, Glynnallt, and *d* 1 Oct 1929, leaving:

1 DAVID MARTIN (Sir), **1st Bt**

1 Mary Caroline; *b* 18 July 1898; *m* 23 April 1928 Edward Richard Whittington-Moe (*d* 7 Nov 1965), s of John Edward Moe, of Wasa, Finland, and had:

(1) *Caroline Mary [Mrs William Bagnell, East Worldham House, Alton, Hants]; *b* 20 Aug 1930; *m* 16 May 1962 *Capt William David Armstrong Bagnell, RHG (ret), er s of Capt Robert Armstrong Bagnell, of Longdown Chase, Hindhead, Surrey, and has:

1a *William Edward Henry; *b* 2 March 1966

1a *Sophia Mary; *b* 3 Dec 1963

The only s,

Sir David Martyn Evans-Bevan, 1st Bt (UK), so *cr* 9 July 1958, JP (Glam 1932), DL (1935); *b* 4 March 1902; *educ* Uppingham; High Sheriff Breconshire 1929, DL (1953), JP (1932) Glamorgan, High Sheriff Glam 1951, a Devpt Commr 1936–5, dir: Barclays Bank, Phoenix Assur, pres Brecon Hunts, KStJ; *m* 1 Oct 1929 *Eira Winifred [Eira Lady Evans-Bevan, Spring Valley, St Ouen, Jersey, CI], est dau of Sidney Archibald Lloyd Glanley, 2nd s of Rev David Lloyd Glanley, and *d* 9 Sept 1973, leaving:

1 Sir MARTYN EVAN EVANS-BEVAN, **2nd and present Bt**

1 *Marigold Evans [The Rt Hon The Countess of Rothes, Tanglewood, W Tytherley, Salisbury, Wilts SP5 1LX]; *b* 3 Nov 1934; *m* 8 July 1955 *21st Earl of Rothes (*qv*)

EVANS-TIPPING

Creation: Bt (UK) 17 June 1913.

David Gwynne Evans-Tipping; *b* 25 Nov 1943; *s f* 1993 but does not use title; *educ* Trin Coll Dublin (BAgS); E Midlands consulting offr Low Cost Prodn Servs, Milk Mktg Bd 1973

Lineage: EVAN EVANS, of Wain, Cards; *m* 17 Dec 1841 Mary, widow of Charles Gwynne Pryse, of Gogerddan, Cards, and dau of William Evans, of St Johns's, Brecon, and *d* 19 July 1855, leaving:

Sir WILLIAM EVANS later GWYNNE-EVANS (roy licence 1913), **1st Bt**, so *cr* 17 June 1913 (UK); *b* 3 Feb 1845; *m* 1st 1 Aug 1866 Mary Anna (*d* 16 Oct 1902), dau of Evan Williams, of Berthllyd, Carmarths, and had issue:

1 EVAN GWYNNE (Sir), **2nd Bt**

1 Edith Mary; *b* 3 Aug 1867; *d* 12 Jan 1874

2 Beatrice Alice; *b* 13 Aug 1869; *m* Oct 1899 William Page May DSc, Fell and Lecturer UCL, and *d* 16 Nov 1963, having had a dau. He *d* 19 Jan 1910

3 Jean Anne; *b* 11 March 1871; *m* 11 Dec 1894 Guy Estelle Morley, of Highgate, and *dsp* 26 April 1938. He *d* 13 Aug 1952

4 Elizabeth Wynne Gertrude; *b* 25 Aug 1875; *d* unm 26 Feb 1966

5 Ethel Irene Penelope; *b* 24 June 1884; *m* 5 Jan 1912 Edward Wallace Hadingham, son of S Wallace Hadingham, of The Old House, Newnham, and *d* 28 Dec 1936, leaving issue

Sir WILLIAM *m* 2nd 12 Oct 1909 Blanche Sophia (*d* 20 Jan 1963), dau of Rev John Charles Eldridge Besant, Vicar of Lydney, Glos, and by her had issue:

2 +John [John Gwynne-Evans Esq, c/o Barclays Bank, DCO, PO Box 1004, Johannesburg, S Africa]; *b* 11 Oct 1910

6 Bettina May; *b* 8 Feb 1912; *m* 20 Dec 1944 (*divorce* 1950, resumed maiden name) Josef H Przysiezny, Cross of Valour, Polish Navy, s of Jan Przysiezny, and had issue:

(1) *Richard William GWYNNE-EVANS (deed poll); *b* 20 Sept 1945

The 1st Bt *d* 23 Jan 1927; his s,

Sir Evan Gwynne Gwynne-Evans, 2nd Bt; Lt RASC, BA Oxford, High Sheriff Glos, 1943; *b* 4 May 1877; *m* 13 March 1908 Ada Jane, OStJ (*d* 24 Dec 1977 aged 93), dau of Walter Scott Andrews, of New York, and *d* 2 Feb 1959 leaving:

1 **Sir Ian William Gwynne-Evans, 3rd Bt**; dep chm Real Estate Corp S Africa 1973–79 (md and chm 1950–73), dir Grootvlei (Pty) Mines (retired 1982), Lt RN; *educ* RNC Dartmouth; Cadet RN 1922, WW II; *b* 21 Feb 1909; *m* 1st 11 July 1935 (*divorce* 1946) Cornelia Elspeth Grianaig, only dau of Sir Godfrey Pattison Collins, KBE, CMG, PC, MP, and had:

(1) *Sylvia Ada [Mrs Duncan Smith, 1 Almond Way, Annaty Bank, Tokai, Cape Town, S Africa]; *b* 22 Jan 1938; *m* 1967 *Duncan Godfrey Stableford Smith, yst s of Clifford Edgar Smith, of Lynedoch, Cape Province, and has:

1a *Andrew Duncan; *b* 1973

1a *Philippa Silvia; *b* 1976

(2) *Gwenllyan Mary Hope [Mrs Robert Neill, 10 Cecil Avenue, Melrose, Johannesburg, S Africa]; *b* 24 Oct 1939; *m* 1963 *Robert Chumley Bruce Neill, er s of R C Neill, of Durban, and has:

1a *Robert Ian Grant; *b* 1965

1a *Angela Elspeth; *b* 1970

2a *Belinda Gwen; *b* 1973

1 (cont.) **Sir Ian** *m* 2nd 8 July 1946 *Monica [Monica Lady Gwynne-Evans, 57 Eastwood Rd, Dunkeld, Johannesburg, S Africa], formerly w of — Dalrymple and dau of Douglas Clinch, of Durban, and *d* 1985

2 Sir FRANCIS LORING GWYNNE-EVANS later GWYNNE EVAN-TIPPING (deed poll 1943) later still GWYNNE-EVANS, **4th Bt** (deed poll 1958); professional singer as 'Francis Loring'; *b* 22 Feb 1914; *m* 1st 9 Oct 1937 (*divorce* 1958) Elisabeth Fforde, dau of J Fforde-Tipping, of Bellurgan Park, Dundalk, Ireland, and had:

(1) DAVID GWYNNE EVANS-TIPPING, **5th and present Bt**

2 +CHRISTOPHER EVAN [Christopher Evans-Tipping Esq, Symonds Farmhouse, Childrey, Oxon OX12 9UA]; *b* 27 Feb 1946; heir presumptive; *m* 3 Aug 1974 *Fenella Catherine, dau of Cdr Edwin Allen Morrison, OBE, DL, of The Bury House, Odiham, Hants, and has:

1a +Guy Edward Francis; *b* 10 May 1978

1a *Amy Clare; *b* 10 Aug 1976

(1) *Carolyn Eve Loring; *b* 23 Nov 1947; *m* 1984 *Eamon Peter Toner and has:

1a *Edward Evan; *b* 1987

1a *Evelyn Frances; *b* 1985

2 (cont.) Sir FRANCIS *m* 2nd 1958 *Gloria Marie [Lady Gwynne-Evans, Casa Rosada, c/Los Jazmines 329, El Rosario 29600, Marbella, Spain], dau of Thomas Reynolds, and *d* 29 Dec 1993, leaving by her:

(3) +Francis Tristan Gwynne-Evans; *b* 30 Jan 1960

(2) *Melody Louise Bernadette Gwynne-Evans; *b* 24 Sept 1958

(3) *Clelia Marie Gwynne-Evans; *b* 1965

(4) *Soraya Charlotte Gwynne-Evans; *b* 1967

2 (cont.) Sir FRANCIS and Lady GWYNNE-EVANS also adopted:

*Teo Leslie Gwynne-Evans; *b* 1962

EVERARD

Arms: Arg. a fess wavy between three estoiles gu. **Crest:** A pelican in her piety ppr. **Motto:** *Virtus in actione consistit* ('Virtue consists in action'). **Creation:** Bt. (UK) 30 June 1911.

SIR ROBIN CHARLES EVERARD, 4TH BT, of Randlestown, Co Meath [Sir Robin Everard Bt, Church Farm, Shelton, Long Stratton, Norfolk NR15 2SB]; *b* 5 Oct 1939; *s f* 1984; *educ* Harrow and Sandhurst; Duke of Wellington's Regt 1958–61, md P Murray-Jones 1962–76 (consultant 1976–91), management consultant 1976–, money broker; *m* 28 Sept 1963 *Ariel Ingrid, est dau of Col Peter Cleasby-Thompson, MBE, MC, of Blackhill House, The Arms, Little Cressingham, Thetford, Norfolk, and has:

1 +HENRY PETER CHARLES; *b* 6 Aug 1970; *educ* Gresham's

1 *Catherine Mary; *b* 1964

2 *Victoria Frances; *b* 1966

Lineage: The estate of Randlestown, originally Randulphstown, was acquired by this family by marriage with the heiress of Randolph or Randulph, its owners.

PATRICK EVERARD, of Randlestown, Co Meath; *m* Margaret, dau of James Bath by Maryon Scurlock, and had:

1 RICHARD

1 Margaret; *m* Thomas Barbey

2 Anne; *m* James Caddell

His s,

RICHARD EVERARD, of Randlestown; *m* and had issue:

PATRICK EVERARD, of Randlestown; living 1518; *m* Catherine, dau of Sir Alexander Plunket, of Rathmore (Ld Chllr I 1492), and had:

1 JAMES

2 Patrick, of Newtown; *m* Catherine, dau of Thomas FitzJohn, of Fyanstown

The er s,

JAMES EVERARD, of Randlestown; High Sheriff Co Meath 1542; *m* 1st Margaret, dau of Sir John Plunket (*d* 1501), of Bewley; *m* 2nd Elenor Bellew, widow of Nicholas Plunket, and *d* 20 March 1564/5, leaving by his 1st w:

RICHARD EVERARD, of Randlestown; *m* Jane, dau of Patrick Ganand or Gernon, of The Water, Co Louth, and *d* 11 Dec 1575, having had:

JAMES EVERARD, of Randlestown; *b* 1551; *m* Catherine, dau of Sir Patrick Barnewall (living 1578), of Crickstown, Co Meath, and *d* 1611, having had:

1 JOHN

2 Patrick; built the Chapel of St Anna de Randalstowne

The er s,

JOHN EVERARD, of Randlestown; *m* Elizabeth, dau of Christopher Darditz, of Darditrath, Co Louth, and had:

RICHARD EVERARD, of Randlestown; *m* Maud, dau of Capt Thomas Netterville, of Blackcastle, Co Meath, 7th s of 1st Viscount Netterville, and *d* 1640, leaving:

1 THOMAS

2 Patrick; MP Kells in JAMES II's 1689 Irish Parl; *m* Catherine, dau of Alexander Plunkett, of Gibbstown, and *d* 1720 having been attainted and his estates forfeited 1697, leaving issue

The er s,

THOMAS EVERARD, of Randlestown; *m* Anne, dau of Thomas Barnewall, of Stackallen, Co Meath: his estate was confiscated during the Interregnum but partly restored 1662; *d* on or after 22 May 1687, leaving with three daus:

1 Mathias; Lt-Col in JAMES II's Army, but benefitted from Treaty of Limerick and kept some of his family estates in Co Meath; *d* 14 March 1714

2 CHRISTOPHER EVERARD; *m* 1st 1715 Teresa, dau of Mark Baggott, of Co Kildare, and had two daus; *m* 2nd Teresa (*m* 2nd 2 Jan 1732 John Dillon, of Killymynen, Co Westmeath), dau of Capt Thomas Plunkett bro of 10th Baron of Dunsany (*qv*), and by her had:

(1) JOHN

(2) Thomas; Capt of Cav; *ka* Bohemia June 1757 while serving under the Duke of Cumberland

(3) Francis; Lt-Col Neapolitan Regt of Gds

(1) Catherine

CHRISTOPHER EVERARD *d* 1731; his est s,

JOHN EVERARD; *b* 1722; *m* Margaret, dau of Hugh O'Reilly (*see* NUGENT, Bt, of Ballinlough) and *d* 1764, leaving:

THOMAS EVERARD, of Randlestown; High Sheriff Co Meath 1795; raised and cmded Kilberry Yeo in the 1798 Uprising; *m* (settlement 21 May 1777) his cousin Barbara (*bur* 24 March 1806), dau of James O'Reilly (*see* NUGENT, Bt, of Ballinlough), and had, with two other daus:

1 John, of Randlestown; Col; *m* his cousin Barbara, dau of Sir Hugh O'Reilly Nugent, 1st Bt, of Ballinlough (*qv*), and *dsp*

2 Thomas; Capt RN; lost his right arm in the affair of 'Wasps'; *d* unm of yellow fever in the West Indies

3 Matthias, of Randlestown, CB, KH; led the failed mil action at Montevideo 1807, fought at Corunna and Siege of Flushing 1809, cmded flank Bn at storming of Bhurtpore 1825, Maj-Gen; *d* unm 1857

4 William; Lt RN; *d* unm of yellow fever in the West Indies

5 James; Lt 46th Foot; *d* unm of yellow fever in the West Indies

6 George (Rev), of Randlestown; Rector Donaghpatrick; *d* unm 1863

7 RICHARD

1 Margaret; *m* 1817 Joseph Barnewall, of Bloomsbury, Co Meath, and *d* Nov 1841. He *d* July 1852, leaving issue

THOMAS EVERARD was *bur* 9 March 1830; his yst s,

RICHARD NUGENT EVERARD, of Randlestown; Capt Rifle Bde; *m* 17 June 1843 Arabella Matilde, dau of George Alexis, Marquis d'Amboise, and *d* 18 Feb 1863, having had:

1 NUGENT TALBOT (Sir), **1st Bt**

2 Arundel (Rev); *m* Louisa (*d* 17 Oct 1938), dau of Hon Thomas McCombie, of Melbourne, Australia, and *d* Nov 1935, having had issue

1 Mathilda Barbara Ellen; *m* 2 July 1864 John Richards Roberts, of Dormstown Castle, and had issue

2 Grace; *m* George W Dixon and *d* 1898

3 Rosabel; *m* Frederick Hoyle Newbury and *d* 1890

4 Katherine; *m* 30 April 1879 Edward Hamilton Woods, DL, of Milverton Hall, Co Dublin, and *d* 16 March 1894, leaving issue

5 Amy; *d* unm

The est s,

Sir Nugent Talbot Everard, 1st Bt (UK), so *cr* 30 June 1911, JP Co Meath; Lt and custos rotulorum Co Meath, High Sheriff 1883; *b* 24 Oct 1849; *educ* Trin Coll Camb (MA), Lt-Col and Hon Col cmdg 5th Bn Leinster Regt, Senator Irish Free State; *m* 6 Nov 1873 Sylvia Priscilla (*d* 9 Oct 1935), dau of William Humphreys, DL, of Ballyhaise, Co Cavan, and *d* 11 July 1929, leaving:

Sir Richard William Everard, 2nd Bt; Capt and Hon Major 5th Bn Leinster Regt; *b* 9 Sept 1874; *m* 23 March 1904 Louise Charlotte Cole (*d* 31 March 1930), 2nd dau of Robert Henry Metge, MP, of Athlumney, Co Meath, and had:

1 NUGENT HENRY (Sir) **3rd Bt**

2 Matthias Richard; Lt Loyal Regt; *b* 4 Oct 1906; *educ* Harrow; *m* 20 July 1938 Maighréad Mary (*d* 1973), dau of Michael Joseph Macardle, of Miltown Grange, Castlebellingham, and *d* 23 Dec 1949, leaving:

(1) +Patrick Michael [Patrick Everard Esq, White Mills Castlebellingham, Co Louth, Ireland]; *b* 28 May 1943; *educ* Harrow; *m* 25 June 1968 *Felicity Anne Brigid, only dau of Brig Ralph Nevill Thicknesse, of The Old Farmhouse, Standen Manor, Hungerford, Berks, and has:

1a +Anthony Matthias; *b* 1980

2a +Michael Ralph; *b* 1988

1a *Patricia Karen; *b* 1973

2a *Katherine Sophie; *b* 1 Nov 1982

The 1st Bt *d* 22 July 1929; his er s,

Sir Nugent Henry Everard, 3rd Bt; *b* 28 Feb 1905; *educ* Harrow; Lt-Col Duke of Wellington's Regt (ret 1958), WW II; *m* 19 May 1933 Frances Audrey (*d* 1975), yst dau of John Charles Jesson, of Kew, and *d* 1984, leaving:

1 Sir ROBIN CHARLES EVERARD, **4th and present Bt**

1 *Susan Louise [Mrs Henry Dormer, Downside, Shortheath Rd, Farnham, Surrey]; *b* 9 Nov 1935; *m* 24 Aug 1957 *Lt-Col Henry George Dormer, RA , only s of H J Dormer, of Chilton Court, Sudbury, Suffolk, and has:

(1) *Sara Louise; *b* 6 July 1958

(2) *Charlotte Rose; *b* 7 June 1962

EVERY

Arms: Erm. two chevronels az. between two others gu.
Crest: A demi-unicorn arg, gutté de-sang and crined or.
Motto: *Suum cuique* ('Every man to his own').
Creation: Bt (E) 26 May 1641.

SIR HENRY JOHN MICHAEL EVERY, 13TH BT, of Egginton, Co Derby [Sir Henry Every Bt, Cothay, 26 Fishpond Lane, Egginton, Derbys DE65 6HJ]; *b* 6 April 1947; *s* f 1988; *educ* Malvern; FCA, ptnr Deloitte and Touche chartered accountants, Pres Birmingham and W Midlands Dist Soc of Chartered Accountants 1995–96 (Chm Dist Trng Bd 1991–93), Tstee Nat Memorial Arboretum 1996–, ctee memb Lunar Soc 1991–, FRSA 1996; *m* 1 June 1974 *Susan Mary, er dau of Kenneth Beaton, JP, of Eastshotte, Hartford, Cambs, and has:

1 +EDMUND JAMES HENRY; *b* 3 July 1975

2 +Jonathan Charles Hugo; *b* 1977

3 +Nicholas John Simon; *b* 1981

Lineage: JOHN EVERY, of Chattcombe and Chardstock, Somerset; Gent Serjeant-at-Arms to ELIZABETH I; *m* Magdalen — and *d* 1584, leaving, with a yr s (Thomas, *d* in or after 1618 leaving two daus) and five daus:

JOHN EVERY, of Chattcombe and Chardstock; MA and Fell Magdalen Coll Oxford; *m* Elizabeth, sis of William Lambert, of Oxford and Buckingham, and *d* 1623, leaving:

Sir Simon Every, 1st Bt (E), so *cr* 26 May 1641; *b* 1602; *educ* Wadham Coll Oxford; MP Leicester 1640; royalist Civil War; *m* Anne (*m* 2nd June 1653 Lawrence Squibb, of Winterbourne Whitchurch, Dorset, and *d* 1673), est dau and coheir of Sir Henry Leigh, of Egginton, and *d c* 1647, leaving:

1 **Sir Henry Every, 2nd Bt**; *bapt* 15 Nov 1629; *m* Vere (*bur* 26 Feb 1706/7), dau of Sir Henry Herbert, Master of the Revels to CHARLES I, and *d* 29 Sept 1700, leaving an est s:

(1) **Sir Henry Every, 3rd Bt**; *b* 1649; *m* 1st by licence 30 April 1685 Mary (*bur sp* 16 March 1692), dau of 3rd Viscount Tracy; *m* 2nd Anne (*m* 3rd Sir John Guise, 3rd Bt (*qv*) and *d* 22 Feb 1734/5), widow of Richard Lygon, of Madresfield Court, Worcs (*see* 1970 edn BEAUCHAMP, E), and dau and coheir of Sir Francis Russell, 2nd Bt, of Strensham, and *dsp* Sept 1709

(2) **Sir John Every, 4t Bt**; Capt RN; *m* 1st 28 April 1704 Martha (*d* 9 Feb 1715), dau of 1st Lord Haversham; *m* 2nd Dorothy (*d* 1749), dau of Godfrey Meynell, of Bradley, Derbys, and *dsps* 1 July 1729

(3) **Rev Sir Simon Every, 5th Bt**; Rector Nauntby, Lincs, MA Cambridge; *m* Mary (*d* 10 Aug 1723), est dau of Rev Joshua Clark, Rector of Somerby, Lincs, and Preb Lincoln, and *d* 12 Jan 1753, leaving an est s:

1a **Sir Henry Every, 6th Bt**; *b* 25 Aug 1708; *m* 1 July 1741 Frances (*d* 21 Sept 1754), dau of James Ibbetson, and *dsp* 31 May 1755

2a **Rev Sir John Every, 7th Bt**; MA Cambridge, Rector Waddington, Lincs; *b* 17 Oct 1709; *m* 1 Dec 1767 Dorothy Pakeman (*bur* 29 Aug 1769) and *dsp* 29 June 1779

2 Francis, of Castle Donington, Leics; *d* Sept 1708, leaving:

(1) John, of Castle Donington and All Saints, Derbys; *d* 4 April 1746 aged 74, leaving:

1a Henry, of St Peter's, Derby; *bapt* 3 April 1701; *bur* 15 March 1775, leaving an est s:

1b John, of Derby; *bapt* 20 Jan 1724/5; *m* Mary Lunn and was *bur* April 1767, leaving an only s:

1c **Sir Edward Every, 8th Bt**; *bapt* 15 Aug 1754; *m* 4 Sept 1776 Mary (*m* 4th 10 March 1790 Ashton Nicholas Mosley (*see* RAVENSDALE, B) and *d* 9 March 1826), dau of Edward Morley, of Horsley, Derbys, and widow of (a) William Elliot and (b) Joseph Bird, and had:

1d HENRY (Sir), **9th Bt**

2d John; *m* 1813 Charlotte (*d* his widow 2 Jan 1860), only dau and heir of William Osborne, MD, of Old Park, Kent

3d Edward; Midshipman; lost at sea 1801

1d Sophia Annie; *m* 31 Jan 1804 Sir Oswald Mosley, 2nd Bt (*see* RAVENSDALE, B), and *d* 8 June 1859, leaving issue

2d Frances; *m* Maj William Miller and *d* 1824, leaving issue

Sir EDWARD was *bur* 4 Jan 1786; his s,

Sir Henry Every, 9th Bt; *b* 4 June 1777; *m* 22 Dec 1798 Penelope (*d* 30 Aug 1812), dau of Sir John Parker Mosley, 1st Bt (*see* RAVENSDALE, B), and had:

1 Henry; Offr 1st Life Gds 1823–31; *b* 16 Nov 1799; *m* 1st 16 May 1826 Maria Charlotte (*dsp* 26 Aug 1827), dau of Very Rev Charles Talbot (*see* SHREWSBURY and WATERFORD, E); *m* 2nd 26 March 1829 Caroline (*d* 17 April 1840), dau of 4th Viscount Ashbrook (*qv*), and by her had:

(1) HENRY FLOWER (Sir), **10th Bt**

(2) Edward; *b* 21 Jan 1834; *k* storming of the Redan Crimean War 1855

(3) Oswald William; Capt 75th Foot, Govr Dartmoor Prison 1880–92; *b* 26 June 1835; *m* 1st 3 June 1862 Cecilia Charlotte (*d* 1882), est dau of Henry Charles Burney, LLD, and had:

1a Edward; *b* 28 Aug 1865; *m* 27 Aug 1902 Adaline (*d* 9 Dec 1948), dau of Ranson Smith, and had:

1b +Edward Malcolm; *b* 22 July 1903; *m* 5 April 1934 *Clarice Mildred, dau of Elmer Doane, and has:

1c +Thomas Owen; *b* 20 Sept 1938

1c *Barbara Ann; *b* 7 Feb 1942

2b +Roderick Desmond; *b* 9 Oct 1904; *m* 1 Sept 1935 *Carolyn Norma, dau of Paul Tyler, and has:

1c *Roderick Douglas; *b* 8 Dec 1936

1c *Lynn Gertrude; *b* 20 April 1943

3b +Donovan Richmond [Donovan Every, Evansville, Wisconsin, USA]; *b* 2 Jan 1911; *m* 19– *Evelyn, dau of Fred Rodd, and has:

1c +Donovan Rodd; *b* 25 July 1941

2a Oswald, JP Salop; T/Capt 7th Bn Dorsetshire Regt, formerly Lt West India Regt, served suppression rising Sierra Leone 1898–99 (medal and clasp) and WW I; *b* 25 May 1872; *m* 11 Feb 1902 Edith (*d* 18 April 1944), dau of James Whitaker, JP, of Hampton Hall, Salop, and *d* 9 March 1951

3a Arthur; *b* 27 March 1879; *d* young

1a Florence; *m* 1886 Rev Alexander de Gex, Rector Meshaw and Creacombe, Devon, and *d* 1908, leaving issue

2a Beatrice; *b* 1864; *m* 13 Dec 1887 Thomas Husband Gill, of Devonport, and *d* 5 Dec 1893

3a Cissy Vere; *b* 1878; *d* 1930

4a Mabel; *b* 1880; *d* unm 1977

(3) (cont.) Oswald Every *m* 2nd 22 Sept 1885 Florence Amy, dau of William Sherwin, of Fawsley, Devon, and *d* 26 Jan 1892, leaving by her:

4a Victor George; *b* 1886; MInstLocEng; *m* 14 June 1938 (*divorce* 1947) Edith Maud, dau of George Francis Silverwood, of Keighley, Yorks, and *d* 17 July 1973

5a John; Capt RASC (Res); *b* 1888; *m* 11 July 1922 Kathleen Mary Agnes (*d* 16 Oct 1962), dau of P R Cripps, JP, of Winford Manor, Somerset, and *dsp* 20 April 1968

6a Francis William John Flower; *b* 20 Nov 1890; *m* 9 Nov 1912 Mary Louisa (*d* 29 May 1965), est dau of William John Murton, and *d* 20 June 1979, leaving:

1b +Christy Oswald [Christy Every Esq, 24 St Georges Ave, Axminster, Devon EX13 5ER]; *b* 3 July 1920; *m* 20 Nov 1948 *Winifred Jessie, 2nd dau of Luke Richards, and has:

1c +Geoffrey Francis [Geoffrey Every Esq, 16 Coleridge Rd, Nether Stomery, Bridgwater, Somerset TA5 1NJ]; *b* 7 June 1949; *m* 21 Aug 1971 (*divorce* 1992) Rosemarie, dau of Otto Plec, of Borham Wood, and adopted:

*Darren Every; *b* 8 Nov 1972

2c +Stephen Victor [Stephen Every Esq, 5 Loretto Rd, Axminster, Devon]; *b* 30 July 1950; *m* 1975 *Valerie Ena, dau of Peter Arthur Guest, of Axminster, and has:

1d *Caroline Amanda; *b* 1 March 1980

2d *Joanne Louise; *b* 2 Jan 1982

3d *Kathryn Frances; *b* 26 Aug 1984

1c *Virginia Dawn [Mrs Alan Fry, 2 Moor Fields, Colyton, Devon]; *b* 23 Dec 1953; *m* 1972 *Alan George Fry

2c *Katrinia Mary [Mrs Michael Neale, 35 Clive Rd, London SW19 2JA]; *b* 9 Oct 1957; *m* 29 Oct 1977 *Michael John Neale and has:

1d *David Michael Ian; *b* 14 Nov 1980

1d *Laura Jane Alana; *b* 2 Dec 1982

(1) Caroline Penelope; *m* 29 April 1852 Sir George Ebenezer Wilson Couper, 2nd Bt, KCSI, CB, CIE (*qv*), and *d* 28 Nov 1910, leaving issue

(2) Jane Charlotte Rose; *m* 23 Nov 1858 Rev Rowland Mosley and *d* 5 July 1874, leaving issue (*see* RAVENSDALE, B)

(3) Maria Georgina; *b* Feb 1836; *m* 21 Oct 1863 Rev William Mills Parry Pym (*see* PYM, B) and *d* 7 Nov 1915, leaving issue

(4) Eliza Sophia; *m* 29 Aug 1857 Francis Grant Hartwell, only s of Francis Hartwell, of Eccleston Square, London SW, and *d* 29 Nov 1906. He *d* 1895

1 (cont.) Henry Every *m* 3rd 20 Feb 1844 Jane (*d* 31 Aug 1860), widow of George Powney and dau of Rev Sir John Robinson, Bt, and *dvp* 27 Feb 1853

2 Edward EVERY later EVERY-CLAYTON (roy licence 1835), JP, DL, of Rowley, Lancs; Lt-Col 1st Lancs Militia, Capt 80th Regt; *b* 28 May 1801; *m* 1st 10 Feb 1835 Elizabeth (*d* 28 Sept 1853), only child of Col Thomas Clayton, of Carr Hall, Lancs, and had:

(1) Thomas Edward, of Carr Hall, Nelson, Lancs; Army Capt; *b* 1841; *m* 29 July 1862 Eliza Henrietta (*d* 1908), only dau of James Whitaker, of Broadclough, Lancs, and *d* 26 June 1886, leaving:

1a Edward; *b* 28 July 1867; *m* 1st 22 Sept 1892 Mary Featherstonhaugh (*d* 1 Oct 1905), dau of Alexander Heylin, and had:

1b Edward Arthur, of Hardwicks, Egginton; purser merchant service, WW I (two medals, Torpedo Badge); *b* 11 Sept 1899; *m* 24 June 1926 Elsie, dau of A Ritchie Reid, of Waynflete, New Barnet, Herts

1b Dorothy Mary; *b* 16 Feb 1895

2b Edith Margaret; *b* 30 April 1897

3b *Ruth Featherstonhaugh; *b* 11 Sept 1905

1a (cont.) Edward Every-Clayton *m* 2nd 29 July 1907 Emily May (*d* 1958), only dau of Arthur Edward Tooze, barrister, and *d* 12 June 1936, having by her had:

2b Frederick Oswald; *b* 1 June 1912; *d* unm 30 March 1936

2a Leopold Ernest Valentine, of Liss, Hants; MD, London, FRCS, LPCP, T/Capt RAMC; *b* 1869; *m* 1898 Dorothy Anne Elizabeth (*d* 23 Oct 1954), dau of Edward Bennett, MRCS, of Marsden Hall, Lancs, and *d* 18 Nov 1954, leaving:

1b Cecil Edward EVERY-CLAYTON later EVERY (deed poll 1930); *b* 1901; *educ* Winchester and Trin Coll Cambridge (BA 1923, MA 1929); *m* 3 Sept 1927 Viola (*d* 16 Oct 1966), yr dau of Edward Ledger, of Hampstead, and *d* 4 April 1974, leaving:

1c +Simon Flower [Simon Every Esq, The White House, Crawley, Winchester, Hants]; *b* 20 Nov 1929; *m* 3 April 1956 *Diana Mary Jennifer, dau of Cdr Lionel John Francis Howard-Mercer, RN (ret), and has:

1d +James Edward [James Every Esq, 8 The Glade, Woodside Rd, Sevenoaks, Kent TN13 3HD]; *b* 7 May 1961; *m* 1988 *Caroline Anne, dau of John Frederick Mallett, and has:

1e +Henry John Edward; *b* 2 Nov 1996

1e *Elizabeth Joanna; *b* 18 Nov 1993

2e *Alexandra Margaret; *b* 18 Nov 1993

1d *Jennifer Ann; *b* 5 Oct 1958; *m* 1995 *Philip John Hopkins and has:

1e *Rachel Ann; *b* 1 Aug 1996

2d *Frances Elizabeth; *b* 29 June 1964 *m* 1990 *William Thomas Pattisson and has:

1e *Frederick James; *b* 1992

1e *Mary Mia Charlotte; *b* 1 April 1995

2e *Louisa Bridget; *b* 11 Feb 1997

1c *Ann; speech therapist BBC World Service Overseas News Bulletins 1977; *b* 1 Aug 1933

1b Marion; *b* 1905; *d* 16 Nov 1984

3a George Frederick William; *b* 1871; *m* 1st 1892 Sarah (*d* 1912), dau of William Whittaker, and had:

1b Herbert Edward; *b* 1892; *m* 1913 Gwendolin Cox (*d* 1931) and *d* 1961, leaving:

1c +Herbert Newbery; *b* 1917

1c *Andrita Valentine; *b* 14 Feb 1919; *m* 30 June 1938 *William Kenneth Franklin and has:

1d *Daniel William; *b* 11 July 1941; *m* 27 March 1965 *Frances Yohradsky and has:

1e *William; *b* 19–

1d *Christine Louise; *b* 18 Nov 1939; *m* 22 July 1961 *Robert Toutant and has:

1e *Dianne Michelle; *b* 27 Dec 1962

2e *Jacqueline Marie; *b* 3 Aug 1964

2b George Ernest William; 72nd Seaforth Highrs Canada, WW I; *b* 1897; *ka* Vimy Ridge 1917

3b John Oswald, DSC; Master Mariner, WWs I (torpedoed) and II as Lt Canadian Navy Reserve and Capt Merchant Navy (1939–45 War Medal, Canadian Vol Medal, Africa Star, Italy Star, Atlantic Star, 1939–45 Star); *b* 1898; *educ* U Sch Victoria BC; *m* 1925 *Marie, dau of William Lloyd, of Liverpool, and *d* 1979, leaving:

1c +George William; *b* 1929; *educ* Canadian Public Schs and BC U; *m* May 1950 *Margot Isabel, dau of William Forrest, of Victoria, BC, and has:

1d +Stephen Douglas; *b* 13 Nov 1954

2d +Michael Bruce; *b* 13 Dec 1957

1d *Kathleen Patricia; *b* 24 Dec 1952

2d *Margaret Anne; *b* 17 Aug 1960

4b Thomas Edgar; *b* 1899; *m* 1943 *Ellen May Hill and *d* 1986, leaving:

1c +Wayne Thomas; *b* 1944; *m* 1974 *Mary Hall and has:

1d *Patricia Mary; *b* 1975

5b Reginald Whittaker; Fraternal Order of Eagles; *b* 1904

6b +Frederick Harris; *b* 1906; *m* 1937 *Ann Brown Morrison and has:

1c *Barbara Ann Gail; *b* 1939; *m* 19– *Donald Anderson, of Campbell River, BC, and has:

1d *Nancy Janet; *b* 1959

2d *Cindy Donna; *b* 1962

7b +Arthur Eric Francis; *b* 1910; *m* 1948 *Edna Beatrice Longley

1b Beatrice Mary; *b* 1895; *m* 1932 David Erfyl Evans and has issue

2b Marion Ethel; *b* 1901

3b *Penelope Maud Valentine; *b* 1903; *m* 1934 George Anderson Churchill-Emery (*d* 1941) and has:

1c *Elizabeth Joy; *b* 4 April 1937; *m* 4 June 1955 (*divorce* 1978) Arthur Frederick Thompson, s of Arthur G Thompson, of Heriot Bay, BC, and has:

1d *Anthony Gordon; *b* 13 Jan 1958; *m* 1984 *Kelly Charlton and has:

1e *Justin Joseph; *b* 1985

2d *Michael Arthur George; *b* 24 May 1959; *m* 1988 *Monica Rambie and has:

1e *Mack Ramsey; *b* 1989

1e *Farleigh Taylor; *b* 1976

4b *Edith Minnie; *b* 1912; *m* 1943 Norton Hopkins (*d* 21 Oct 1961)

3a (cont.) George Every-Clayton *m* 2nd 1913 Evelyn May Yeates (*d* 25 May 1961), and *d* 1928

4a Reginald Arthur Eric; FRICS; *b* 17 March1874; *m* 21 Aug 1902 Fanny (*d* 27 Jan 1958), 3rd dau of William Wilding, of Bolton, and *d* 4 March 1965, leaving:

1b John Arthur; *b* 2 June 1903; *m* 1937 Martha Parker (*d* 1988), of Danville, Indiana, and *d* 1969, leaving issue

1c *Margaret Lois; *b* 5 June 1940; *m* 1st 28 Aug 1959 (*divorce* 1976) Terry Lee Williams, attorney for Bank of America; *m* 2nd 1976 *William Smutz

2b William Wilding; *b* 19 Feb 1905; *m* 1940 *Joan Adelaide [Mrs William Every-Clayton, 51 Church Hill, Honiton, Devon], dau of Ronald John Bennett, of Exeter, and *d* 1992, leaving:

1c +(Henry) John [John Every-Clayton Esq, 3 Chestnut Way, Melton Mowbray, Leics LE13 0EB]; *b* 1941; *m* Oct 1963 *Frances Anne, BA Exeter, dau of Henry William Sangster, and has:

1d *Catherine; *b* 14 Jan 1967

2d *Tessa; *b* 24 March 1969

2c +Alan William [Alan Every-Clayton Esq, Beacon Down Cottage, Holcombe Burnell, Longdown, Devon]; *b* 1945; *m* 1968 *Myra Winn, dau of Robert Arthur, of Axminster, Devon, and has:

1d +Richard William; *b* 1971

1d *Anita Caroline; *b* 1973

3c +Robert Edward [Robert Every-Clayton Esq, Ashton House, St Mary Church, Cowbridge, S Glam]; *b* 1948; BA, FCA; *m* 1973 *Karen Elizabeth Paine, BSc, of Sidbury, Devon, and has:

1d +Andrew John; *b* 1979

1d *Katherine Lucy; *b* 1982

2d *Elizabeth Clare; *b* 1984

4c +David Stuart; *b* 6 Sept 1955; *m* 1979 *Angela Dauber, of Broadhambury, Devon, and has:

1d +Christopher James; *b* 1985

1d *Helen Louise; *b* 1987

1c *Pamela Nora Anne (twin); *b* 6 Sept 1955; *m* 1981 (*divorce* 1989) Jeremy Peter Leeds

3b Thomas Edward; *b* 28 March 1906; *m* 1938 Irmgard Adele (*d* 1982), dau of Arthur Jaekel, of Finland, and *d* 1991, leaving:

1c +Glenn Thomas [Glenn Every-Clayton Esq, Seminario Congregacional, Rua Arealva 19, Tejipió, 50930-190 Recife PE, Brazil]; *b* 30 Aug 1941; *educ* Kingston GS and Christ's Coll Cambridge (BA 1963), BD; ALBC; *m* 1971 *Joyce Elizabeth Winifred, er dau of Hugh McKee, of Randalstown, Co Antrim

2c +Clive William [Clive Every-Clayton Esq, 14A E Aubinaustraat, 1932 St Stevens-Woluwe, Belgium]; *b* 22 Dec 1942; *educ* Kingston GS and London Bible Coll (BD, ALBC 1965); *m* 1970 *Dorothy, dau of Archibald M O Dobbie, of Dalry, Ayrshire, and has:

1d +Mark Brian; *b* 1975

2d +Paul David Christian; *b* 1979

1d *Grace Esther Josette; *b* 1973

2d *Joy Claire Joanna; *b* 1977

4b George Herbert; *b* 29 June 1907; *educ* Rutgers U (BSc); *m* 1931 Jane Cecelia Welsh (*d* 1981), of NJ, and *d* 1993, leaving:

1c +Donald George [Donald Every-Clayton, Paseo de los Halcones 202, Mayorazgos de los Gigantes, Antizapan de Zaragoza, Edo de Mexico, Mexico]; *b* 1935; *m* 1957 *Celia Yolanda, dau of — Garcia, of Mexico City, and has:

1d +Geoffrey; *b* 1961; *m* 1988 *Andrea Garcia Puente, of Mexico City

1d *Lisa; *b* 1959; *m* 1983 *Angelo Ceciarelli, of Mexico City

2d *Jennifer; *b* 1963; *m* 1979 *Eduardo Ezquerro, of Mexico City, and has:

1e *Pamela; *b* 1980

2e *Priscilla; *b* 1985

3d *Noreen; *b* 1969

2c +Jon Arthur [Jon Every-Clayton, 438 Old Trail, Baltimore, MD 21212, USA]; Lt Inf US Army, 101st Airborne Div Vietnam 1966–67 and 1970–71, Bronze Star for Valour and Purple Heart for Wounds; *b* 15 Dec 1938; *m* 1968 (*divorce* 1982) Janet Theresa Sabo, of Lakewood, NJ, and has:

1d +Jon Ernest; *b* 1970; Private US Army Res

1d *Janina Theresa; *b* 1973

2d *Malinda Jane; *b* 1978

1c *June Moonyeen [Mrs Daniel Young, 419 Dumbarton Rd, Baltimore, MD 21212, USA]; *b* 1940; *m* 1969 *Daniel Herbert Young III and has:

1d *Jonathan Herbert; *b* 1970

1d *Heather Jane; *b* 1972

1a Constance Isabel; *m* 1898 Lt-Col Luigi Sabbatini, of Turin, and *d* 10 July 1937

2a Florence Penelope Ethel; LRAM; *d* unm; 25 Sept 1941

3a Beatrice Maud Mary; *m* 19 Sept 1891 Harry Besford Marsden Wyatt Granger, and *d* 22 Oct 1955, leaving issue. He *d* 28 March 1923

(2) Henry; *b* 1851

2 (cont.) Edward Every-Clayton *m* 2nd 10 Oct 1854 Eliza Halsted (*d* 1889), dau of Robert Holgate, of Burnley, and *d* 11 Oct 1885, having by her had:

(3) Charles Edward EVERY-CLAYTON later EVERY-HALSTED (roy licence 1886), of Hill House, Bath, JP Lancs; *b* 1857; Maj 3rd Bn Roy Lancaster Regt; *m* 18 March 1892 Lucy Clara (*m* 2nd 17 Dec 1936 Thomas FitzRoy Phillipps Fenwick, of Thirlestaine House, Glos, who *d* 1 Sept 1938, and *d* 14 Nov 1955), dau of Lt-Col George Frederick Dallas, and *d* 14 Oct 1935, leaving:

1a Evelyn Stella; *b* 14 April 1893; *m* 19 May 1915 Lt-Col Arthur George Pardoe, RE (TF), s of Arthur John Pardoe, of Purslow Hall, Salop, and had two sons and two daus. He *d* 26 March 1951

2a Mary Ruth; *b* 7 May 1898; *m* 1st 23 April 1918 (*divorce* 1941) Capt Gerald Hargreaves Mawson, MC, RE (TF), and had four sons and a dau; *m* 2nd 26 Dec 1951 Rev Henry William John Lancelot Reed Haywood (*d* 1957), s of Joseph Haywood, of Heene Terrace, Worthing, Sussex, and by her 1st husb had:

1b *John Arthur Hargreave; *b* 1923

2b *Charles Edward Hargreave; *b* 1926

(1) Penelope; *m* 2 Dec 1856 Count Vincenzo Sabatini Bonafede, Maj-Gen Italian Army, and *d* 1913. He *d* 1896

(2) Elizabeth; *m* 3 March 1863 James Whitaker, of Hampton Hall, Salop, and *d* 26 Dec 1900, leaving issue. He *d* 18 June 1913

(3) Caroline; *m* 1858, Alfred Powles and *d* 2 July 1928, leaving issue

(4) Frances; *d* 1924

(5) Edith; *m* 1875 M Watson, of Woodside, Nelson, Lancs, and *d* 31 Jan 1918

(6) Harriot Anne; *m* 1885 Rev John Todd Atkinson, Rector Asheldham, Essex, and *d* 4 March 1920, leaving issue

(7) Ellen Vere; *m* 13 Oct 1881 Edward James Artindale and had issue. He *d* 1934

(8) Amelia Jane Eliza; *m* 1886 Maj Thomas Henry Bairnsfather, ISC, and had issue. He *d* 1945

3 John; *b* 5 Sept 1802; *d* Sept 1830

4 Frederick Simon, of New Zealand; *b* 5 June 1804; *m* 3 June 1834 Mary (*d* 11 Feb 1878), dau of W Brutton, of The Warren House, Dawlish, Devon, and *d* 24 April 1888, having had, with other issue:

(1) Frederick; *b* 9 April 1836; *m* 22 May 1872 Henrietta, dau of Rev Charles Jeffreys, and *dsp* 3 Nov 1892

(1) Mary Eliza; *m* 1 May 1858; John Borton, of New Zealand and *d* 1880.

(2) Penelope Caroline; *m* 1 May 1853 W H Valpy, of New Zealand. He *d* 1924

1 Penelope; *d* 25 July 1892 aged 85

The 9th Bt *d* 28 Dec 1855; his gs,

Sir Henry Flower Every, 10th Bt, DL Derbys; High Sheriff 1863; *b* 23 Dec 1830; *m* 1st 8 Feb 1855 Gertrude (*d* 26 Feb 1858), dau of Rev Hon Baptist Wriothesley Noel (*see* GAINSBOROUGH, E), and had:

1 Florence Gertrude; *b* 8 May 1858.

Sir Henry *m* 2nd 12 Oct 1859 Mary Isabella (*d* 9 Oct 1935), est dau of Rev Edmund Holland, of Benhall Lodge, Saxmundham, and by her had:

1 Henry Edmund; Capt S Wales Borderers; *b* 9 Oct 1860; *m* 18 Nov 1884 Leila Frances Hartford (*d* 4 Feb 1890), dau of Rev Henry Adderley Box, and *dvp* 1 Dec 1892, having had:

(1) EDWARD OSWALD (Sir), **11th Bt**

(2) Ronald Gaisford Leigh; *b* 3 Sept 1888; *d* an infant

2 Edward Francis (Rt Rev), CBE (1936); Hon DD, Assist Bp Derby, Rector Egginton 1937, Bp in Argentina 1910–37, Bp Falkland Islands; *b* 3 April 1862; *educ* Trin Coll Cambridge (MA); *d* unm 16 Jan 1941

3 Ernest Holland; *b* 10 July 1870; *m* 20 Dec 1902 Beatrice May (*d* 21 March 1949), est dau of Harvey Young, of Colorado Springs, and *d* leaving:

(1) +Ernest Henry; *b* 14 Feb 1906; *m* 1949 *Virginia Kelly

(1) *Patricia; *b* 26 March 1904; *m* 1st 1937 Friedrich Schiller and has issue. He *d* 1947. She *m* 2nd 1952 (*divorce* 1956) Valentin Benedict

1 Alice Vere; *d* unm 18 Dec 1956

2 Eleanor Maude; *d* unm 7 Dec 1935

3 Constance Margaret; *d* 3 March 1919

4 Clara Helen; *m* 11 Oct 1899 Rev Edward Digby Stopford Ram, of Clonattin, Co Wexford, Rector Oxted, Surrey, and *d* 14 June 1935, leaving issue. He *d* 24 July 1917

5 Agnes Mabel; *d* unm 21 Feb 1938

The 10th Bt *d* 26 Feb 1893; his gs,

Sir Edward Oswald Every, 11th Bt; *b* 14 Jan 1886; *educ* Harrow and Trin Coll Cambridge (BA), Maj Norfolk Yeo; *m* 17 Aug 1909 Ivy Linton (*d* 27 June 1976 aged 86), yr dau of Major Alfred Meller, JP, of The Limes, Rushmere, Ipswich, and had:

1 JOHN SIMON (Sir), **12th Bt**

2 +Charles Henry Sherard [Charles Every Esq, Casa Das Primas, Carvoeiro, Lagoa 8400, Algarve, Portugal]; *b* 20 Jan 1916; *educ* Harrow; *m* 11 Feb 1950 (*divorce* 1953) Deirdre Veronica, yst dau of Dr T A du Toit, of Johannesburg, S Africa, and has:

(1) *Vanessa Leila [Mrs Terence de Beer, 17A Milton Rd, Westville, N 3630, Natal, S Africa]; *b* 1950; *m* 1974 *Terence William de Beer, and has:

1a *Ryan Jeffrey; *b* 1979

1a *Kelly Gillian; *b* 1981

1 *Leila Penelope [Mrs Vivian Ward, Long Meadow House, Little Cornard, Sudbury, Suffolk]; *b* 20 April 1911; *m* 15 Feb 1935 *Maj Vivian Horrocks Ward, TD, 5th Bn Sherwood Foresters (TA), er s of Percy Harold Ward, MRCS, LRCP, Dir Medical Services, Rhodesia, and has:

(1) *Peter Every [Peter Ward Esq, Pinfold, Pin Mill Lane, Chelmondiston, nr Ipswich, Suffolk]; *b* 9 July 1938; *m* 26 May 1962 *Rosalind Brereton, yr dau of Giffard Page, of King's Lynn, Norfolk, and has:

1a *Rupert; *b* 1969

2a *Edward; *b* 1970

(2) *Simon Charles Vivian [Simon Ward Esq, The Dower House, Bulmer, Sudbury, Suffolk CQ10 7EN]; memb London Stock Exchange; *b* 23 March1942; *educ* Shrewsbury and Trin Coll Cambridge (MA); memb Securities Inst; *m* 18 Sept 1965 *Myrtle Jillian Eileen, BA Trin Coll Dublin, only dau of Thomas Roycroft East, of Rathfarnham, Dublin, and has:

1a *Victoria Penelope Jane; *b* 3 July 1969; *m* 15 July 1995 *Matthew William Monteith Doull

2a *Antonia Lisa; *b* 1971

3a *Lucinda Fiona; *b* 1971

The 11th Bt *d* 11 Nov 1959; his er s,

Sir John Simon Every, 12th Bt; *b* 24 April 1914; *educ* Harrow; Lt Sherwood Foresters WW II, Co dir 1945–60; *m* 1st 14 Sept 1938 (*divorce* 1940) Annette Constance, only child of Maj Francis William Massy Drew, DSO, Prince of Wales's Vol (S Lancs Regt), of Drewscourt, Co Cork; *m* 2nd 1943 *Janet Marion, est dau of John Page, ARIBA, of Blakeney, Norfolk, and *d* 1988, leaving by her:

1 HENRY JOHN MICHAEL EVERY, **13th and present Bt**

1 *Celia Jane; *b* 22 Feb 1944; *m* 1st 1 May 1965 Nicholas Charles Harcourt Stephens (*d* 1984), only s of Cdr Robert John Hilary Stephens, of San Pawl, Tat-Targa, Malta; *m* 2nd 19– *Robin Christopher Moore and by her 1st husb has:

(1) *Jasper Roland Every; *b* 1972

(2) *Toby Oliver Every; *b* 1974

(1) *Candida Imogen Every; *b* 20 June 1969

2 *Juliet Frances [Mrs John McCullagh, Bramleys, Alleyns Lane, Cookham Dean, Berks]; *b* 13 June 1945; *m* 16 May 1964 *John Coltman McCullagh, only s of John Andrew McCullagh, of Oxted, Surrey, and has:

(1) *Andrew John; *b* 31 March 1968

(1) *Diana Mary; *b* 15 Oct 1965

EWART

Arms: Or three swords, two in saltire and one in fess, between a cross-crosslet fitchée in chief and a dexter hand couped in base gu. **Crest:** A hand erect, gauntleted ppr., holding a cross-crosslet fitchée gu. **Motto:** *In cruce spero* ('In the cross I place my hope'). **Creation:** Bt (UK) 13 Sept 1887.

SIR (WILLIAM) MICHAEL EWART, 7TH BT, of Glenmachan, Co Down [Sir Michael Ewart Bt, Hill House, Hillsbrough, Co Down BT26 6AE]; *b* 10 June 1953; *s f* 1995; *educ* Radley

Lineage: WILLIAM EWART, of Glenbank, nr Belfast (s of William Ewart, of Belfast, formerly of Annahilt, Co Down; *b* Sept 1759; *d* 24 Nov 1851); Alderman Belfast; *b* 30 March 1789; *m* 1st April 1810 Mary Anne (*d* 4 May 1856), dau of John Rossman, of Coote Hill, Co Cavan; *m* 2nd 17 April 1857 Maria (*dsp* 7 May 1884), widow of John Wilcocks Eves, of Armagh, and *d* 22 Sept 1873, having had, with other issue:

1 WILLIAM (Sir), **1st Bt**

1 Sarah Jane; *m* 21 Jan 1847 Very Rev Edward Maguire, MA, Dean Down, Chllr and Rector Bangor, Co Down, and *d* 14 May 1856

2 Eliza; *m* 2 Dec 1853 Rev John Thomas Barter, MA, incumbent Glenties, Co Donegal, and *d* 11 Dec 1867, leaving issue

WILLIAM EWART's est s,

Sir William Ewart, 1st Bt (UK), so *cr* 13 Sept 1887, of Glenmachan, Co Down, JP, MP (C) Belfast 1878–89, Mayor Belfast 1859–60, head William Ewart & Son, Pres Irish Linen Tde and Flax Supply Assocs; rep NI linen trade negotiating French Treaty 1864; *b* 22 Nov 1817; *m* 10 Dec 1840 Isabella Kelso (*d* 8 Jan 1905), dau of Lavens Mathewson, of Newtown Stewart, Co Tyrone, and *d* 1 Aug 1889 having had, with other issue:

1 **Sir William Quartus Ewart, 2nd Bt,** of Glenmachan, JP Co Down, DL Belfast; High Sheriff Co Antrim 1897, KGStJ; *b* 14 June 1844; *educ* Trin Coll Dublin (MA); head William Ewart & Son; *m* 23 Nov 1876 Mary Warren (*d* 26 Feb 1929), est dau of Robert Heard, JP, of Kinsale and Pallastown, Co Cork, and *d* 17 Oct 1919 having had, with other issue:

(1) **Sir Robert Heard Ewart, 3rd Bt;** *b* 5 Nov 1879; *educ* Trin Coll Dublin (BA); dir William Ewart & Son; *d* unm 12 Aug 1939

(2) Charles Gordon, CStJ; *b* 21 June 1885; *educ* Trin Coll Dublin (MA); *m* 14 Dec 1915 Mary Elizabeth, only dau of Joseph Malcomson Greeves, of Benagh, Strandtown, Belfast, and *d* 4 Aug 1936

(1) Charlotte Hope; *m* 9 Nov 1911 Col George Harding, DSO, RASC, of Tulach Nore, Borris-in-Ossory, Co Laois, and *d* 20 June 1934, leaving issue

(2) Isabella Kelso; *d* unm 2 Feb 1966

(3) Mary Gundreda; *m* 15 June 1927 Col John Vincent Forrest, CB, CMG, AMS, *s* of William Forrest, of Champions Hall, Woodham Ferrers, Essex, and had issue. He *d* 10 Oct 1953

2 Lavens Mathewson, of Glenbank, JP; *b* 1 Nov 1845; *m* 22 Feb 1873 Mary Elizabeth (*d* 9 Dec 1908), est dau of Frederick Villiers Clarendon, of Dublin, and *d* 13 Dec 1898, having had, with other issue:

(1) **Sir Lavens Mathewson Algernon Ewart, 4th Bt;** *b* 6 Sept 1885; *d* unm 21 Sept 1939

(1) Isabel Margaret; *m* James Frederick Dawson and *d* 22 Dec 1919, leaving a dau

(2) Violet Villers; *m* 1904 Gerald Leslie Mace Lutwyche and *d* 1944, leaving issue

3 Richard Hooker; *b* 24 July 1848; *m* 29 April 18– or 19– Fanny Melbourne (*d* 6 Nov 1913), dau of Charles P Talbot, of Lowell, Mass. and *d* 18 Oct 1918, leaving:

(1) **Sir Talbot Ewart, 5th Bt;** *b* 2 Nov 1878; *educ* Harvard (BA); *m* 29 April 1913 Sydney Stuart (*d* 11 April 1958), 2nd dau of Louis P Henop, of New York, and *dsp* 23 Oct 1959

4 James Mathewson, of New York; *b* 28 Sept 1854; *m* 2 June 1884 Katharina Kingsley, yst dau of John Walpole Talbot, of Centerville, Mich., and *dsp* 7 Aug 1898

5 George Herbert, of Firmount, Belfast; *b* 27 Feb 1857; *educ* Trin Coll Dublin (MA); *m* 20 Oct 1886 Alice Flora (*d* 18 Aug 1945), dau of Richard Tipping Hamilton, of Little Clandeboye, Newtownards, and *d* 26 March 1924, leaving issue:

(1) Grace Hamilton; *d* unm 4 Aug 1958

(2) Alice Rosalind; Superintending Inspr Factories; *d* unm 23 Feb 1971

(3) Anna Kathleen; *m* 17 Dec 1925 James Ogilvie Duncan, only s of A J Duncan, of Dundee, and had issue. He *d* 1954

(4) Frances Madeleine; *b* 1896; *m* 13 Sept 1917 Paymaster-Lt-Cdr Philip Smiles, RN, s of William Holmes Smiles, of Belfast, and had issue:

1a *Alan; *b* 1924

2a *Roger Philip; *b* 1927

1a *Honor Madeleine; *b* 19–

2a *Margaret; *b* 19–

(5) Helen Flora; *b* 1898; *m* 3 Nov 1920 Lt-Col Louis Sydney Henshall, DSO, TD (*d* 1957), S Lancashire Regt, s of Louis Henshall, of Stockton Heath, Cheshire, and had:

1a *Herbert Ewart; *b* 1923

2a *James Arthur; *b* 1926

1a *Enid; *b* 1921

6 Frederick William; BA Oxon; barrister, DL; *b* 14 Oct 1858; *m* 14 June 1883 Mary Anne Elizabeth (*d* 31 Dec 1922), 3rd dau of Thomas Valentine, of The Moat, Strandtown, and *d* 7 March 1934, having had:

(1) Gerald Valentine, OBE (1919), DL; Maj RASC; *b* 8 April 1884; *educ* Trin Coll Dublin (BA); *m* 6 Sept 1911 Annie Ruth (Pearl), dau of Rev T R S Collins, BD, Chaplain to Archbp Dublin, and *d* 20 April 1936, leaving:

1a *Eileen Geraldine [Mrs George Cotton, Clontagh House, Crossgar, Co Down]; *m* 30 Sept 1939 Lt-Cdr George Lennox Cotton, DSC, RNVR, and has:

1b *Caroline Mourne Lennox; *b* 1942

2b *Elizabeth Grania Lennox; *b* 1944

3b *Kathleen Anne Lennox; *b* 1945

(2) Cecil Frederick Kelso; Capt 11th Bn Roy Irish Rifles; *b* 1887; *ka* 1 July 1916

(3) William Basil; Maj 15th Bn Roy Irish Rifles; *b* 1890; *m* 31 July 1917 Rébé Annette (*d* 3 Nov 1939), er dau of George Annesley Grindle, and *d* 13 Feb 1920, leaving:

1a **Sir (William) Ivan Cecil Ewart, 6th Bt,** DSC (1945); High Sheriff Co Antrim 1976; *b* 18 July 1919; *educ* Radley, Lt RNVR Coastal Forces WW II (POW), chm: William Ewart & Son 1968–73, Ewart Northern Ltd, Belfast, 1973–77, NI del Duke of Edinburgh's Study Conf Oxford 1956, chm: Belfast Youth Advsy Serv 1951–57 and Flax Spinners' Assoc 1961–66, Belfast Harbour Commr 1968–77 and NI Chamber Commerce 1974, E Africa Rep Roy Cwlth Soc for Blind Uganda, Kenya and Tanzania 1977–84; *m* 21 July 1948 Pauline Chevallier (*d* 5 Sept 1964), est dau of W/Cdr Raphael Chevallier Preston, OBE, AFC, JP, of Derry Hill, Ballydugan, Downpatrick, Co Down, and *d* 20 Nov 1995, leaving:

1b Sir (WILLIAM) MICHAEL EWART, **7th and present Bt**

1b *Susan Eveleen [Mrs Colin Cunningham, 61 Ballymorran Rd, Tullycone, Killinchy, Co Down BT23 6UA]; *b* 1 Feb 1950; *m* 6 Oct 1973 *Colin R Cunningham, s of H Cunningham, of The Cottage, Newtownards, and has:

1c *Katherine (Katie) Pauline; *b* 25 Feb 1976

1c *Jennifer (Jenny) Alicia; *b* 11 May 1978

2b *Patricia Rébé [Mrs Jeremy Browne, Claim Farm House, Manley, Frodsham, Cheshire WA6 6HT]; *b* 30 Dec 1951; *m* 1971 *Jeremy J C Browne and has issue:

1c *Gordon Cawood Ivan; *b* 15 Jan 1977

1c *Anita Zaidee; *b* 16 Jan 1973

(1) Ethel Elizabeth Isabella; *m* 1st 23 Oct 1924 Isaac Whitla Corkey, MC, FRCS (*d* 7 March 1927), only s of Isaac Corkey, of Warrenpoint, Co Down, and had:

1a *Patrick William Isaac; *b* 13 March 1926; *educ* Pembroke Coll Cambridge (MA); *m* 4 Feb 1967 *Elizabeth Phyllis Mary, dau of Rev Chancellor Richard James Williamson, of Clones, Co Monaghan, and has issue:

1b *Jonathan Whitla Glover; *b* 10 Sept 1968

(1) (cont.) Mrs Isaac Corkey *m* 2nd 19 June 1934 Rev William John Parr, Rector Lambeg, Lisburn, Co Antrim, s of William Parr, of Lambeg. He *d* 7 Oct 1954. She replaced by deed poll 26 Sept 1935 the name PARR with CORKEY

1 Marianne; *m* 19 April 1870 Rev Edward McConkey McCready, MA, MB (Trin Coll Dublin), Vicar Magheradroll, Ballynahinch, Co Down, and *d* 22 March 1931, leaving issue. He *d* 1896

2 Lavinia; *m* 22 April 1879 Rev Thomas William Clarendon, BA, BD (Dublin), Dean Dromore, Rector Maralin, Co Down, and *d* 25 May 1913, leaving issue

EWING OF KIRKFORD

Creation: B. (LP, UK) 1992.

THE BARON EWING OF KIRKFORD, of Cowdenbeath, District of Dunfermline (Harry Ewing, DL (Fife 1995)) [The Rt Hon The Lord Ewing of Kirkford DL, Gowanbank, 45 Glenlyon Rd, Leven, Fife KY8 4AA]; *b* 20 Jan 1931; *educ* Beath HS Cowdenbeath; with Union of Post Office Workers 1962–71, Sec Scottish Lab Gp 1972–74, Parly Under-Sec Scottish Office 1974–79, Sr V-Chm Tde Union Gp Lab MPs 1979–, Memb Cncl Europe and WEU 1987–, MP (Lab) Stirling and Falkirk 1971–74, Stirling, Falkirk and Grangemouth 1974–83 and Falkirk E 1983–92, on Lab Front Bench Ho Lds to Nov 1996, Jt Chm Scottish Constitutional Convention 1990–, Hon Pres Girls' Bde Scotland 1993–; *m* 1954 *Margaret, dau of John Greenhill, of Leven, and has:

1 *Alan William John; *b* 1961; *m* 1986 *June, da of William Adamson, of Kirkcaldy, Fife, and has a s and a dau

1 *Alison Margaret; *b* 1966; *m* 1991 *Ian Binnie, s of Sydney Binnie, of Arbroath, and has a son

Lineage: WILLIAM EWING, of Cowdenbeath, Dunfermline; had:

HARRY, *cr* a **Baron**

EXETER

Arms: Barry of ten arg. and az., over all six escutcheons, three, two and one sa., each charged with a lion rampant of the first. **Crest:** On a chapeau gu. doubled erm. a garb or, supported by two lions rampant, the dexter arg., the sinister az. **Supporters:** Two lions erm. **Motto:** *Cor unum via una* ('One heart, one way'). **Creations:** B. (E) 25 Feb 1570/1, E. (E) 4 May 1605, M. (UK) 4 Feb 1801.

THE 8TH MARQUESS OF EXETER, Earl of Exeter and **Baron of Burghley**, Co Northampton ((William) Michael Anthony Cecil) [The Most Hon The Marquess of Exeter, RR3 Kelsey Site C 21, Sechelt, BC V0N 3A0, Canada; The Courtyard, Mickleton, Glos GL55 6SF]; *b* 1 Sept 1935; *s f* 1988; *educ* Eton; rancher, Hereditary Grand Almoner, Ld Paramount of the Soke of Peterborough, author: *Spirit of Sunrise* (coauthor, 1979), *The Long View* (1985), *The Rising Tide of Change* (1986) and *Living at the Heart of Creation* (1990); *m* 3 May 1967 (*divorce* 1992) Nancy Rose, dau of Lloyd Arthur Meeker, of Loveland, Colorado, and has:

1 +ANTHONY JOHN (does not use courtesy title); *b* 9 Aug 1970; *educ* Eton and Oxford; *m* 1996 *Holly Stewart

1 *Angela Kathleen; *b* 19 May 1975

Exeter, marquessate and dukedoms of: Previous creations exclusively under this title were almost all of dukedoms, although the de Reviers Earls of Devon were often known as Earls of Exeter and in 1525 the Courtenay Earl of Devon (*qv*) of the day was promoted Marquess of Exeter. A century and a half earlier John de Holand, great-great-grandson of HENRY III through his mother Joan, the Fair Maid of Kent (whose 2nd husband was Thomas de Holand, Earl of Kent; *see* ZOUCHE, B), had been created Duke of Exeter. The day of his promotion (he had previously been created Earl of Huntingdon) was 29 Sept 1397, when his half-brother RICHARD II created five dukedoms in a single day (another of the beneficiaries being John's nephew) — an act of extravagance without parallel in English peerage history. After HENRY IV's usurpation John was degraded from his dukedom and executed.

The next creation was in favour of Thomas Beaufort, an illegitimate son of John of Gaunt (himself son of EDWARD III) by Katherine Swynford. Beaufort was legitimated in 1306 and made Duke of Exeter in 1416. He had been left in charge of Harfleur after its capture by HENRY V at the start of the Agincourt campaign the year before. On his death without surviving issue in 1426 the dukedom expired. The title was revived for a son of the original Holand grantee in January 1443/4 but became extinct on the death of the 2nd Duke, son of the latest grantee, in 1475.

Lineage: ADAM Ap SEISYLL TURBERVILLE (the family name also occurs as SITSILLT, later mutating to CYCILL or CYSSELL); *m* —, dau of Robert Cecil, of Bewpyr (probably identical with Beaupré, Glam), and had:

ROBERT; had:

THOMAS SEISYLL, of Alltyrynys, Walterstone, Ewias, Herefs; *m* Margaret, dau of Gilbert Wynston, yr s of John Wynston, of Tre-wyn, Cwmyoy, Mon, and had:

PHILIP; *m* Margaret, dau of John Philips, and had:

RICHARD; *m* 1st Alison, dau of Philip Barry, of Ewias, Herefs; *m* 2nd Margaret, dau of William Vaughan, Constable Aberystwyth, Cards, yr s of Philip Fychan, of Tyle-glas, Felindre, Brecon, and by her had:

1 Philip; continued the sr line at Alltyrynys; gf of:

(1) Matthew CECIL; bequeathed Alltyrynys to his cousin **1st Baron of Burghley** (*see* below)

2 John

3 DAVID

4 James/Jenkin

1 Margaret

The 3rd s,

DAVID CECIL; Water Bailiff Wittlesea Mere 1511/2; Serjeant-at-Arms 1513/4; Steward Ldship of Collyweston 1523/4; Sheriff Northants 1531/2 (references occur to him as 'David Cyssel'); *m* 1st Alice, dau of Sir John Dickons; *m* 2nd Joan Roos and *d* 1536, leaving by his 1st w:

RICHARD CECIL, of Burghley, Lincs; Page of Crown to HENRY VII; Yeoman of the Robes; Sheriff Rutland 1539 (references occur to him as 'Richard Cycill'); *m* Jane (*b c* 1501; *d* 10 March 1587/8), dau of William Heckington, of Bourne, Lincs, and *d* 19 March 1552/3, leaving, with three daus (Margaret, *m* Roger Cave (*see* CAVE-BROWN-CAVE, Bt); Elizabeth, *m* 1st Robert Wingfield, of Upton, and 2nd Hugh Alington; Anne, *m* Thomas White, of Tuxford, Notts; *see* WHITE, Bt, of Wallingwells):

WILLIAM CECIL, **1st Baron of Burghley**, Co Northampton (E), so *cr* 25 Feb 1570/1, KG (1572), PC (1550–53 and again from 1558); *b* Bourne 13 Sept 1521; *educ* Grantham Sch (thus becoming the first of two products of that town's educational system to sway England's destiny as the sovereign's chief minister), Stamford Sch, St John's Coll Cambridge (U Chllr 1559–98) and Gray's Inn; MP Stamford 1547–52, Lincs 1555 and 1559 and Northants 1562–67, Master Requests 1547–49, Sec of State 1550–53 and 1558–72, ktd 1551, Chllr Order of Garter 1552–53, Ld High Treasurer 1572–98; *m* 1st 8 Aug 1541 Mary (*d* 22 Feb 1543/4), sis of Sir John Cheke, the humanist tutor to EDWARD VI, and had:

1 THOMAS, **1st Earl of Exeter**

The **1st Baron** *m* 2nd 21 Dec 1545 Mildred, dau of Sir Anthony Coke, of Gidea Hall, Essex, by Anne, 2nd dau of Sir William FitzWilliam or Fitzwilliam (*see* 1970 edn, FITZWILLIAM, E), and by her had surv issue:

2 ROBERT, 1st EARL OF SALISBURY (*see* SALISBURY, M)

1 Anne; *m* 19 Dec 1571 17th Earl of Oxford (*see* SAINT ALBANS, D)

2 Elizabeth; *m* William, est s of 2nd Lord (Baron) Wentworth (*see* LYTTON, E)

The 1st BARON *d* 4 Aug 1598; his er s,

THOMAS CECIL, **1st Earl of Exeter** (E),so *cr* 4 May 1605, KG (1601); *b* 5 May 1542; MP Stamford 1563–67, 1571 and 1572–83, Lincs 1584–87 and Northants 1592–93, ktd 1575, Ld Lt Yorks 1599–1603, Ld Pres Cncl of the North 1599–1603; *m* 1st 27 Nov 1564 Dorothy (*d* 23 March 1608), dau and coheir of John Nevill(e), 3rd Lord (Baron) Latymer (*qv*), and had, with another s and three other daus:

1 WILLIAM, **2nd Earl**

2 Richard (Sir), of Wakerley, Northants; MP; *b* 1570; *m* Elizabeth, dau of Sir Anthony Cope, Bt, of Hanwell, Oxon (*see* 1970 edn), and had:

(1) DAVID, **3rd Earl**

(1) Elizabeth; *m* J Havers, of Stockerston, Leics

3 EDWARD CECIL (Sir); *b* 1571; mil cdr, *cr* VISCOUNT WIMBLEDON but *dspm* 1638, when the title expired (*see*, however, LIMERICK, E)

4 Thomas; *b* 1578; *m* Anne dau of Sir R Lee, Ld Mayor London

1 Lucy; *m* 28 Feb 1586/7 4th Marquess of Winchester (*qv*) and *d* Oct 1614, having had issue

2 Mildred; *m* 1st Sir Thomas Read; *m* 2nd Sir Edmund Trafford (*see* DE TRAFFORD, Bt)

3 Elizabeth; *m* 1st Sir William Hatton; *m* 2nd Sir Edward Coke (*see* LEICESTER, E)

4 Dorothy; *m* Sir Giles Alington, of Horseheath

5 Frances; *m* 1st Earl of Thanet and had issue (*see* DE CLIFFORD, B)

The **1st Earl** *m* 2nd 1610 Frances (*d* 1663), dau of 4th Baron Chandos of Sudeley and widow of Sir Thomas Smith, Master of Requests to JAMES I, by whom he had an only dau

The 1st EARL *d* 8 Feb 1622/3; his est s,

WILLIAM CECIL, **2nd Earl of Exeter**, KG (1630), PC (1626); *b* Jan 1565/6; turned RC by 1585/6, MP Stamford 1586–87 and 1588–89, ktd 1603, Ld Lt Northants 1623–40; *m* 1st Jan 1588/9 Elizabeth, BARONESS (De) ROS in her own right (*d* 19 May 1591; *see* DE ROS, B), only dau and heir of 3rd Earl of Rutland (*see* RUTLAND, D), and had:

1 WILLIAM CECIL, 17th LORD (Baron) (De) ROS in right of his mother; *m* Elizabeth, dau of Sir Thomas Lake, of Cannons, Middx, and *dsp* & *vp* 1618

The **2nd Earl** *m* 2nd Elizabeth (*d* 26 Feb 1654), dau of Sir William Drury, of Hawsted, Suffolk, and by her had:

1 Elizabeth; *m* 1st Earl of Berkshire (*see* SUFFOLK and BERKSHIRE, E) and had issue

2 Diana; *m* 1st 18th Earl of Oxford (*see* SAINT ALBANS, D); *m* 2nd 1st Earl of Elgin (*see* ELGIN and KINCARDINE, E) and *dsp*

3 Anne; *m* 1st Earl of Stamford and had issue (*see* 1970 edn)

The 2nd EARL *d* 6 July 1640; his n,

DAVID CECIL, **3rd Earl of Exeter**; *m* Lady Elizabeth Egerton, dau of 1st Earl of Bridgwater (*see* GREY EGERTON, Bt), and *d* 18 April 1643, having had:

1 JOHN, **4th Earl**
2 Thomas; *bur* 20 May 1641
1 Frances; *m* 15 April 1650 1st Earl of Shaftesbury (*qv*) and *d* 1654

The er s,

JOHN CECIL, **4th Earl of Exeter**; *b* 1628; *m* 1st 8 Dec 1646 Lady Frances Manners, dau of 8th Earl of Rutland (*see* RUTLAND, D); *m* 2nd 24 Jan 1669/70 Mary Fane (*d* 16 Oct 1681), widow of Francis Palmes and dau of 2nd Earl of Westmorland (*qv*), and *d* 18 March 1677/8, leaving by his 1st w:

1 JOHN CECIL, **5th Earl of Exeter**; *m* (licence 4 May 1670) Anne Cavendish, widow of Charles, Lord Rich (*dsp* & vp 16 May 1664), only s and heir of 4th Earl of Warwick (*see* WARWICK, E, preliminary remarks), and only dau of 2nd Earl of Devonshire (*see* DEVONSHIRE, D), and had, with three other sons and four daus, the majority of whom *d* unm:

(1) JOHN, **6th Earl**
(1) Elizabeth; *m* 4th Earl of Orrery (*see* CORK and ORRERY, E)

The 5th EARL *d* 29 Aug 1700; his s,

JOHN CECIL, **6th Earl of Exeter**; Ld Lt Rutland; *b* 15 May 1674; *m* 1st 9 Feb 1697 Annabella (*d* Aug 1698), sis of 1st Earl of Tankerville (*qv*), by whom he had no issue; *m* 2nd Sept 1699 Elizabeth (*d* 28 Nov 1723), dau and coheir of Sir John Brownlow, Bt (*see* BROWNLOW, B), and *d* 24 Dec 1721, leaving:

1 JOHN CECIL, **7th Earl of Exeter**; *d* unm 9 April 1722
2 BROWNLOW, **8th Earl**
1 Elizabeth; *m* William Aislabie, of Studley, Yorks

The 7th EARL's yr bro,

BROWNLOW CECIL, **8th Earl of Exeter**; *m* 18 July 1724 Hannah Sophia (*d* 30 April 1765), dau and heir of Thomas Chambers, of Derby, and *d* 3 Nov 1754, leaving (with other issue, who *dsp*):

1 BROWNLOW CECIL, **9th Earl of Exeter**; Ld Lt Rutland, Recorder Stamford; *b* 21 Sept 1725; *m* 1st 24 July 1749 Letitia, dau and heir of Hon Horatio Townshend (*see* TOWNSHEND, M); *m* 2nd 23 April 1770 Anne Maria, dau of Job Cheatham, of Sodor Hall, and *dsp* 26 Dec 1793

2 Thomas Chambers; *m* 20 Feb 1751, Charlotte Garnier and *d* 14 Aug 1773, leaving:

(1) HENRY, **1st Marquess**
1 Elizabeth; *m* 24 Nov 1757 John Chaplin, of Blankney, Lincs (*d* 1764), and had issue (*see* CHAPLIN, V)

The 9th EARL's n,

HENRY CECIL, **1st Marquess of Exeter**, so *cr* 4 Feb 1801 (UK); *b* 14 March 1754; *m* 1st 23 May 1776 Emma (*d* 1791), only dau and heir of Thomas Vernon, of Hanbury, Worcs, and had no surv issue; *m* 2nd 3 Oct 1791 Sarah ('the peasant Countess'; *d* 18 Jan 1797), dau of Thomas Hoggins, of Bolas, Salop, and by her had:

1 BROWNLOW, **2nd Marquess**
2 Thomas; *b* 1 Jan 1797; Col; *m* 8 Aug 1838 Lady Sophia Lennox (*d* 17 Jan 1902), dau of 4th Duke of Richmond (*see* RICHMOND and GORDON, D), and *dsp* 29 Nov 1873
1 Sophia; *m* 1818 Rt Hon Henry Manvers Pierrepont and *d* 1823

The **1st Marquess** *m* 3rd 19 Aug 1800 Elizabeth (*d* 31 Jan 1837), dau of Peter Burrell, of Langley Park, Kent, and widow of 8th Duke of Hamilton (*see* HAMILTON and BRANDON, D)

The 1st MARQUESS *d* 1 May 1804; his er s,

BROWNLOW CECIL, **2nd Marquess of Exeter**; KG, *b* 2 July 1795; Ld Steward Household 1858–59, Ld Lt Rutland 1826–27 and Northants 1842–67; *m* 12 May 1824 Isabella (*d* 6 March1879), yst dau of William Stephen Poyntz, of Midgham, Berks, and Cowdray House, Sussex, and had:

1 WILLIAM ALLEYNE, **3rd Marquess**
2 Brownlow Thomas Montagu, Col 3rd and 4th Bns Northants Regt, Capt Scots Gds; *b* 27 Feb 1827; *m* 1st 27 Aug 1854 Charlotte Alexandrina Mabell (*dsp* 17 Oct 1888), only dau of Edward Thompson Curry, UK Consul Ostend; *m* 2nd 11 May 1896 Stella (*d* 6 Feb 1944), dau of Rev William Randall, DD, and *dsp* 22 May 1905
1 Mary Frances; *m* 3 Oct 1861 3rd Earl of Harrowby (*qv*), and *d* 27 July 1917
2 Victoria; *b* 6 Nov 1843 (HRH THE PRINCE CONSORT stood sponsor); *m* 15 Dec 1866 8th Baron Carbery (*qv*) and *d* 22 Feb 1932, leaving issue

The 2nd MARQUESS *d* 16 Jan 1867; his est s,

WILLIAM ALLEYNE CECIL, **3rd Marquess of Exeter**, PC; Capt Gentlemen-at-Arms, Treasurer Household 1866, MP (C) S Lincs 1847–57 and N Northants 1857–67, Hon Col 3rd and 4th Bns Northants Regt, ADC to HM QUEEN VICTORIA, custos rotulorum Soke of Peterborough; *b* 30 April 1825; *m* 17 Oct 1848 Lady Georgina Sophia Pakenham (*d* 26 March 1909), 2nd dau of 2nd Earl of Longford (*qv*), and had, with other issue:

1 BROWNLOW HENRY GEORGE, **4th Marquess**
2 Francis Horace Pierrepont; Lt RN; *b* 5 July 1851; *m* 14 Oct 1874 Edith (*m* 2nd 26 April 1892 Adml Philip Francis Tillard (*d* 23 Feb 1933) and *d* 9 May 1923), dau of Sir William Cunliffe Brooks, 1st Bt, and *d* 23 June 1889, leaving:

(1) Ean Francis; Lt Lincolnshire Regt, Boer War 1900; *b* 8 June 1880; *educ* Eton; *m* 1st 12 Dec 1901 Hilda Mary Daubeny (*d* 13 July 1939), yr dau of Col Francis Charteris Wemyss, memb Gentlemen-at-Arms, and had:

1a Aileen Hilda Frances; *b* 16 April 1903; *m* 30 April 1932 *Major Hon Gavin George Carew, MBE, TD, 2nd s of 5th Baron Carew (*qv*), and *d* 1974, leaving issue

(1) (cont.) Ean Cecil *m* 2nd 24 Sept 1941 *Minnie, yr dau of William Reekie, of Perth, and *d* 22 Feb 1942

(2) Richard William Francis; Capt Gen List and Lt 4th Bn Lincs Regt; *b* 7 Aug 1882; *m* 21 Oct 1901 *Jessie, 2nd dau of John Hardy Bain, JP, of Ardilea, Green Island, Co Antrim, and *d* 6 Sept 1933, having had:

1a Richard Francis Bain; Lt RN, F/O RAF; *b* 31 Jan 1902; *m* 28 Sept 1926 *Marjorie Joan (*m* 2nd 1939 B Grosvenor Harris, of Monxton Manor, Andover, Hants), est dau of William Lloyd-Evans, of Postlip Hall, Glos, and *d* 6 Feb 1929 following a plane crash, leaving:

1b *Jean Frances [Mrs Henry Jennings, Eastwell, Upper Lansdown Mews, Bath]; *b* posthumously 20 May 1929; *m* 6 Sept 1952 *Cdr (L) Henry Walton Jennings, RN, yr s of Lt-Col Walton Jennings, DSO, of Broomholm, Bacton, Norwich, and has:

1c *Dirmuid Brian Cecil [Dirmuid Jennings Esq, Studley Cottage, Haw Lane, Bledlow Ridge, Bucks]; *b* 27 Sept 1957; late RN; *m* 1983 *Angela, er dau of W Wilson, of Aughton, Lancs
2c *Stephen Francis; *b* 13 Jan 1960

(1) Ethel Frances Sophia; *m* 1st 13 April 1899 Maj Edward Crichton HAWKSHAW later PARRY HAWKSHAW (deed poll 17 July 1924), RA, of Oakbank, Tuffley, Glos, and had issue. He *d* 23 Oct 1928. She *m* 2nd 28 Nov 1928 Sir James Stanhope Cockburn, 10th Bt (*qv*), and *d* 20 May 1953

(2) Violet Dorothea; *m* 1st 5 Sept 1901 Lt-Col Oswald Henry Ames, 2nd Life Gds, of Dunsfold Hall, Dunsfold, Surrey, s of Lt-Col Lionel Ames, of The Hyde, Bedford, and had issue. He *d* 6 Nov 1927. She *m* 2nd 1 Sept 1942 Sir Maurice Bromley-Wilson, 7th Bt (*see* BROMLEY, Bt), and *d* 2 Feb 1953

(3) Edith Celandine; *m* 1st 24 Aug 1905 (*divorce* 1922) 5th Baron Sudeley (*qv*); *m* 2nd 26 Sept 1922 Eric Henri Kennington, RA (*d* 13 April 1960), and *d* 1975, leaving by him:

1a *Christopher John; *b* 26 March 1925; *educ* Leighton Pk and Trin Coll Cambridge (MA 1953); *m* 14 March 1953 *Elisabeth June dau of Frank Percy Restall, of Edinburgh, and has:

1b *David John; *b* 18 April 1954; *educ* Bradfield
2b *Eric Alasdair; *b* 7 July 1956
3b *Benjamin Bruce James; *b* 16 April 1964

1a *Catherine Diana; MAOT, SROT; *b* 22 Feb 1927

3 William, CVO (1909); Capt Gren Gds, Lt-Col and Hon Col 4th Bn Lincs Regt, Groom-in-Waiting to HM QUEEN VICTORIA 1892–1901, Extra Gentleman Usher to TM GEORGE V 1924–36, EDWARD VIII 1936 and GEORGE VI 1937, GCStJ; *b* 2 Nov 1854; *m* 1st 2 Sept 1885 Mary Rothes Margaret, Baroness Amherst of Hackney (*qv*), and had issue; *m* 2nd 14 Aug 1924 Violet Maud, DGStJ (*d* 9 Jan 1957), formerly w of Herbert Oswald Collyer and dau of Percy Freer, and *d* 16 April 1943

4 John Pakenham CECIL later JOICEY-CECIL (roy licence 1898), JP Soke of Peterborough; Lt-Col and Hon Col cmdg 4th Bn Lincolnshire Regt, formerly Lt Gren Gds, Lt-Col cmdg 8th Bn Wilts Regt, 1st Bn Roy Berks Regt and Roy Def Corps WW I, MP Stamford 1906–10; *b* 3 March 1867; *m* 15 Sept 1896 Isabella Maud (*d* 18 Nov 1949), dau of Col John Joicey, MP, of Newton Hall, Northumberland, and *d* 25 June 1942, having had:

(1) John Francis James; Lt Gren Gds; *b* 18 Sept 1897; *ka* 25 Sept 1916
(2) Edward Wilfrid George; *b* 14 Jan 1912; *educ* Eton; *m* 28 April 1945 Rosemary Lusia, VAD (*d* 18 Jan 1989, only dau of Capt Hon Fergus Bowes-Lyon (*see* STRATHMORE AND KINGHORN, E), and *d* 6 Oct 1985, leaving:

1a +James David Edward [James Joicey-Cecil Esq, 49 Clapham Common South Side, London SW4 9BX]; *b* 24 Sept 1946; *educ* Eton; *m* 5 April 1975 *Jane Susanna Brydon, yr dau of Capt P W B Adeley, of Delcombe Manor, Milton Abbas, Dorset, and has:

1b *Katherine Mary; *b* 7 June 1978
2b *Susanna Maud; *b* 25 March 1981

1a *(Elizabeth) Anne [Mrs Alastair Malcolm, Hart Hill Farm, Woodfalls, Wilts SP5 2LJ]; *b* 8 Feb 1950; *m* 16 March 1971 *Alastair Richard Malcolm QC and has:

1b *Colin Andrew Fergus; *b* 6 June 1973; *educ* Eton and St Catherine's Coll Oxford
2b *William James Ronald; *b* 10 Oct 1975; *educ* Eton and St Hugh's Coll Oxford

(1) Isabella Rosamond Georgiana; *b* 22 Aug 1901; *m* 21 Sept 1926 Maj-Gen Sir John Noble Kennedy, GCMG, KCVO, KBE, CB, MC, est s of Rev James Kennedy, of Port Patrick, and *d* 22 Sept 1941, leaving issue (*see* SAINT LEVAN, B)

(2) Maud Lettice Mary; *b* 24 Oct 1906; *m* 23 Dec 1930 Maj-Gen Robert Hallam Studdert, CB, DSO, MC, RA (*d* 2 Oct 1968), est s of George Hallam Studdert, JP, of Hazelwood, Quin, Co Clare, and has:

1a*Hallam John Cecil [Hallam Studdert Esq, 69 Collingswood Avenue, London N10]; BA, LLB; *b* 17 Sept 1931; *m* 1 Sept 1961 *Lilian Joan, only dau of William John Brown, of Springfield, Frenchay, Bristol

1a *Moira Winifred [Mrs Peter Hope, 82 Etheldene Avenue, London N10]; MA 1958, LLB 1955; *b* 9 May 1933; *m* 25 May 1957 *Peter Hope, MusB, only s of Henry Hope, of Edgeley, Stockport, Cheshire, and has:

1b *Roderick Jonathan; *b* 10 Feb 1966
1b *Louisa Dionysia; *b* 26 Sept 1961

1 Isabella Georgiana Katherine; *m* 7 Aug 1884 William Henry Battie-Wrightson, of Cusworth Park and Warnsworth Hall, Yorks, and *d* 29 Oct 1917, leaving issue. He *d* 28 April 1903
2 Mary Louisa Wellesley; *m* 24 May 1880 2nd Baron Newlands (*see* 1970 edn SPENCER-CHURCHILL, B) and *d* 12 Aug 1930. He *dsp* 5 Sept 1929
3 Catherine Sarah; *m* 28 June 1881 9th Baron Barnard (*qv*) and *d* 14 March 1918, leaving issue
4 Frances Emily; *d* unm 23 Dec 1951
5 Louisa Alexandrina; *d* unm 28 July 1950

The 3rd MARQUESS *d* 14 July 1895; his est s,

BROWNLOW HENRY GEORGE CECIL, **4th Marquess of Exeter**, PC, DL Lincs; custos rotulorum Soke of Peterborough; MP (C) N Northants 1877–95, Col 3rd and 4th Bns Northampton Regt, Capt Gren Gds, V-Chamberlain to HM QUEEN VICTORIA 1891–92; *b* 20 Dec 1849; *m* 7 Sept 1875 Isabella (*d* 12 July 1917), only child of Sir Thomas Whichcote, 7th Bt, and *d* 9 April 1898, leaving:

1 WILLIAM THOMAS BROWNLOW CECIL, **5th Marquess of Exeter**, KG (1937), CMG (1919), TD, JP (Lincs Kesteven, Peterborough, Rutland, and Northants); Hereditary Grand Almoner; Ld Lt Northants 1922–51, Col RA (TA) 1918–33 (ret); *b* 27 Oct 1876; *educ* Eton and Magdalene Coll Cambridge; Pres Northants TAA to 1951, ADC to HM GEORGE V 1920–31, Capt 3rd Bn Northamptonshire Regt, custos rotulorum Soke of Peterborough, Chm: Soke of Peterborough CC 1910–40, Stamford Bd Gdns from 1898, Govrs Stamford

Endowed Schs; Mayor Stamford 1909–10, Pres: Land Union 1932 and County Councils Assoc 1943; Hon Freeman Peterborough, KStJ; *m* 16 April 1901 Hon Myra Rowena Sibell Orde-Powlett, CStJ, only dau of 4th Baron Bolton (*qv*), and *d* 6 Aug 1956, leaving:

(1) DAVID GEORGE BROWNLOW CECIL, **6th Marquess of Exeter**, KCMG (1943), JP (Soke of Peterborough 1958), DL (Northants 1937–46 and Huntingdon and Peterborough 1965), Hereditary Grand Almoner, Hereditary Lord Paramount Soke of Peterborough, LLD St Andrews (1950), Rector St Andrews U 1950–52, Mayor Stamford 1961, Lt-Col Res of Offrs Gren Gds, Hon Col 5th Bn Northamptonshire Regt 1938–48, MP Peterborough 1931–45, winner of one Olympic, three Br Empire and eight Br athletics championships, chm Br Olympic Cncl 1936–66, doyen Internat Olympic Ctee 1954–66, pres AAA and Internat Amateur Athletic Fedn, PPS to 1st Viscount Hailsham World Conf 1932 and Min Supply 1939, chm Jr Imp League 1933–37 (pres 1939), chm: Propaganda Ctee Nat Advsy Cncl Physical Trng and Recreation 1939, Priory Ctee's Economy Sub-Ctee on Timber, Tin Plate, Paper and Packaging 1940–43, Assist Dir Tank Supply 1941–42, Controller Repair and Storage, Aircraft and Overseas Supplies, 1942–43, Govr and C-in-C Bermuda 1943–45, Hon Col Bermuda Militia 1943–45, Pres Fedns Chambers Commerce Br Empire 1952–54, pres Radio Industries Cncl 1952–54, MFH: own pack 1935–39, E Sussex 1939–53 and Burghley 1957–66, Jt MFH Old Berks 1953–57, pres: Br Horse Soc 1963, BTA 1966–69 and Clay Pigeon Shooting Assoc, chm Birmid/Qualcast to1975, dir Nat West Bank, Leader UK Industl Missions Pakistan 1950 and Burma 1954, memb Exec Ctee King George VI Nat Memorial Fund, KStJ; *b* 9 Feb 1905; *educ* Eton and Magdalene Coll Cambridge (MA 1926); *m* 1st 10 Jan 1929 (*divorce* 1946) Lady Mary Theresa Montagu-Douglas-Scott, 4th dau of 7th Duke of Buccleuch and (9th Duke of) Queensbury (*qv*), and had:

1a John William Edward; *b* 1 June 1933; *d* 6 July 1934

1a *Davina Mary DStJ [The Lady Davina Barnard, The Yews, Barningham, Richmond, N Yorks DL11 7DU]; *b* 29 June 1931; *m* 8 Oct 1952 (*divorce* 1992) 11th Baron Barnard (*qv*) and has issue

2a *Gillian Moyra Katherine [The Lady Gillian Kertesz, Holly House, Northchapel,W Sussex GU28 9HJ]; *b* 8 March 1935; *m* 1st 23 Nov 1954 (*divorce* 1978) Sir Giles Henry Charles Floyd, 7th Bt (*qv*), and has issue; *m* 2nd *George Michael Kertesz, s of Zultan Kertesz, of Budapest, and has issue (*see* FLOYD, Bt)

3a *Angela Mary Rose, LVO (1993) [The Lady Angela Oswald LVO, Flitcham Hall, King's Lynn, Norfolk PE31 6BY]; Woman Bedchamber to HM QUEEN ELIZABETH THE QUEEN MOTHER 1981–; *b* 21 May 1938; *m* 21 April 1958 *(William Richard) Michael Oswald, CVO, DSC, MA, KORR, Capt RF, Manager Roy Studs 1970–97 and dir 1997–, er s of Lt-Col William Alexander Hugh Oswald, ERD, of Little Orchard, St George's Hill, Weybridge, Surrey, and has:

1b *William Alexander Michael; *b* 26 May 1962; *educ* Harrow and RMA Sandhurst; Page of Honour to HM THE QUEEN 1976–77, Capt Life Gds 1985–86; *m* 1994 *Arabella, dau of Nicholas Sydney Cobbold, and has issue

1b *Katherine Davina Mary; *b* 19 March 1959; *m* 1983 *Lt-Col Alexander Fergus Matheson the Younger, of Matheson, Coldstream Gds, yr s of Sir Fergus John Matheson of Matheson, 7th Bt (*qv*), and has issue

(1) (cont.) The **6th Marquess** *m* 2nd 12 Dec 1946 Diana Mary (*d* 6 June 1982), widow of Lt-Col David Walter Arthur William Forbes, MC, Coldstream Gds, and er dau of Hon Arnold Henderson, OBE (*see* FARINGDON, B), and *d* 21 Oct 1981, leaving by her:

4a *Victoria Diana, DL (Cambs 1993) [The Lady Victoria Leatham DL, Burghley House, Stamford, Lincs PE9 3JY; Flat 18, Chelsea House, 24 Lowndes St, London SW1]; *b* 28 June 1947; dir: Burghley House Preservn Tst and Sotheby's, memb: Samuel Courtauld Tst and Finance and Planning Ctee HHA, runs Ancestral Collections (mail order firm) 1995–, Hon Col 158 (Roy Anglian) Regt RLC (Volunteer), Tstee Stoneleigh Abbey Preservn Tst; *m* 25 April 1967 *Simon Patrick Leatham, est s of Maj Patrick Magor Leatham, 10th Roy Hus, and has issue:

1b *Richard David; *b* 5 April 1971; *m* 4 Oct 1996 *Georgina Susan, dau of Simon Mounsey of Barnes House, Piltdown, E Sussex

1b *Miranda Rosemary; *b* 19 Oct 1969; *m* 1997 *Orlando William Adam Rock, s of Timothy Rock

(2) (WILLIAM) MARTIN ALLEYNE CECIL, **7th Marquess of Exeter**; Sub-Lt RN (ret); *b* 27 April 1909; *educ* RNC Dartmouth; author: *Being Where You Are* (1974), *On Eagles' Wings* (1977) and *Beyond Belief* (1986); *m* 1st 17 Jan 1934 Edith Lilian (*d* 29 March 1954), only dau of Aurel Csanady de Telegd, of Budapest, Hungary, and had issue:

1a WILLIAM MICHAEL ANTHONY CECIL, **8th and present Marquess of Exeter**

(2) The **7th Marquess** *m* 2nd 3 Sept 1954 *Lillian Jane [The Most Hon the Dowager Marchioness of Exeter, 100 Mile House, PO Box 2054, BC VOK 2EO, Canada], est dau of Roy Peter Kopf Johnson, of Milwaukee, Wisconsin, and *d* 1988, having by her had issue:

1a *Marina June [The Lady Marina Castonguay, 100 Mile House, PO Box 2170, BC VOK 2EO, Canada]; *b* 16 June 1956; *m* 1980 *Peter Jules Workman Castonguay, s of Nelson Castonguay, of Ottawa, and has:

1b *Dylan Martin Nelson; *b* 1984

1b *Majessa Lillian; *b* 1983

2a Janine Dawn; *b* 12 Jan, *d* 3 May 1958

(1) (Letitia Sibell) Winifred; Ldy-in-Waiting to HRH THE DUCHESS OF GLOUCESTER 1935–37; *b* 20 Nov 1903; *m* 16 Dec 1937 7th Baron Hotham (*qv*) and *d* 1992, leaving issue

(2) *Romayne Elizabeth Algitha, OBE (1986) [The Lady Romayne Brassey, Pond House, Barnack, Stamford, Lincs PE9 3DN]; VAD WW II, attd RN ARRC 1943; *b* 22 March 1915; *m* 12 Dec 1944 *Lt-Col Hon Peter Esmé Brassey, yst s of 1st Baron Brassey of Apethorpe (*qv*), and has issue

Seat: Burghley House, Stamford, Lincs. Although no longer occupied by the head of the family, Burghley still counts as a true Cecil property inasmuch as it is presided over by Lady Victoria Leatham, the only child of the **6th Marquess** by his second wife. There was a religious house on the site of the present structure as early as the 12th century and it was the dissolution of the monasteries in the 1530s that gave the 1st Lord Burghley's father the opportunity to build up an estate. But it was Burghley himself who erected the actual mansion, seemingly even trying his hand as his own architect. He completed the house that is named after him almost ten years before his death but it was the **5th Earl** who is responsible for much of the interior now on display, in particular the baroque painted ceilings and walls by Verrio. Outside the house much of the present landscaping is by 'Capability' Brown, whom the **9th Earl** employed.

EXMOUTH

Arms: Gu. a lion passant guardant, in chief two chaplets of laurel or, on a chief of augmentation wavy arg. a representation of Algiers, with a British man-of-war before it flying the flag of an Admiral of the Blue, all ppr. **Crest:** Upon waves of the sea the wreck of the *Dutton*, East Indiaman, upon a rocky shore off Plymouth garrison, all ppr. **Supporters:** Dexter, a lion guardant or, navally crowned az., resting the sinister hind paw upon an increscent arg.; sinister, a male figure, representing slavery, trousers arg., striped az., the upper part of the body naked, holding in the sinister hand broken chains ppr., the dexter arm elevated and holding a cross or. **Mottoes:** 1 (over the crest) *Deo adjuvante* ('God being my helper'), 2 (under the shield) Algiers. **Creations:** Bt (GB) 18 March 1796; B. (UK) 1 June 1814; V. (UK) 10 Dec 1816.

THE 10TH VISCOUNT EXMOUTH , **Baron Exmouth of Canonteign**, Co Devon, and a **Baronet** (Sir Paul Edward Pellew, Bt) [The Rt Hon The Viscount Exmouth, Canonteign, nr Exeter, Devon]; *b* 8 Oct 1940; *s f* 1970; *educ* Downside; *m* 1st 10 Dec 1964 (*divorce* 1974) Maria Krystina, only dau of Don Recaredo de Garay y Garay, of Madrid, and has issue:

1 *Patricia Sofia [The Hon Patricia Pellew, Paseo de Rosales 3Z, Madrid, Spain]; *b* 14 April 1966

The 10th VISCOUNT *m* 2nd 1975 *Rosemary Frances, only dau of Francis Harold Scoones, MRCS, LRP, JP, of 83 Abbotsbury Rd, London W14, and formerly w of 14th Duke of Saint Albans (*qv*), and by her has:

1 +EDWARD FRANCIS; *b* 30 Oct 1978

2 +Alexander Paul; *b* 30 Oct 1978

Lineage: HUMPHRY PELLEW, of Flushing, near Falmouth, Cornwall, *m* Judith Sparnon (*d* 1753) and was *bur* 9 Feb 1722, leaving a 6th s:

SAMUEL PELLEW; *b* 1712; *m* Constantia, dau of Edward Langford, of Trungle, Cornwall, and had:

1 Samuel Humphrey; *m* Jane Bawden and *d* 18 Feb 1843, leaving:

(1) Samuel

(1) Jane

2 EDWARD

3 Israel (Sir), KCB; Adml RN, cmded the *Conqueror* at Battle of Trafalgar; *m* Mary, dau of George Gilmore, and had:

(1) Edward; Capt Life Gds; *k* in a duel Paris 6 Oct 1819 by Lt Theophilus Walsh, of the same regt

4 John; Ensign; *k* Battle of Saratoga, N America

1 Catherine; *m* Charles Louis, Count Jejerskjold, V-Adml Sweden

2 Jane; *m* Lt — Spriddle, RN

The 2nd son,

Sir Edward Pellew 1st Bt, and 1st Viscount Exmouth, Co Devon, so *cr* 18 March 1796 (for saving troops and crew of the transport *Dutton*) and 10 Dec 1816 (for destroying the fleet and arsenal of Algiers 27 Aug that year) respectively, as also earlier 1 June 1814 BARON EXMOUTH OF CANONTEIGN, Co Devon (both UK), of Treverry, Cornwall, GCB (1816, KCB 1815); *b* 19 April 1757; RN: joined 1770, Cdr 1780, Post Capt 1782, ktd 1793 for capturing the French frigate *Cleopatra*; Col Marines 1801–04, MP (Tory) Barnstaple 1802–04, R-Adml 1804, V-Adml 1808, Adml the Blue 1814, V-Adml UK 1832–33, C-in-C E Indies 1804–09, N Sea 1810, Mediterranean 1811–16 and Plymouth 1817–21; Kt Grand Cross: Order Charles III Spain, St Ferdinand and Merit Naples, Wilhelm of the Netherlands, SS. Maurice and Lazarus Savoy, Kt Annunciation Savoy, Er Bro Trin House

1823–33, High Steward Yarmouth 1832–33; *m* 28 May 1783 Susannah (*d* 29 Oct 1837), 2nd dau of James Frowde, of Knoyle, Wilts, and *d* 23 Jan 1833, having had issue:

1 POWNOLL BASTARD PELLEW, **2nd Viscount Exmouth**; *b* 1 July 1786; Capt RN; *m* 1st 1 Oct 1808 (*divorce* 1820) Eliza Harriet, est dau of Sir George Hilaro Barlow, 1st Bt, of Fort William, Bengal (*qv*), and had:

(1) EDWARD PELLEW, **3rd Viscount Exmouth**; *b* 14 Feb 1811; *m* 1850 Madame Madeline Honorine Dobrowolska (*d* 22 Jan 1870), and *d* 11 Feb 1876

(2) Percy Taylor; Offr Madras Cav; *b* 15 April 1814; *m* May 1836 Anne Amelia (*d* 7 June 1905), 3rd dau of Francis Lascelles, and *d* 31 Dec 1848, leaving:

1a Gertrude; *m* 8 May 1861 Capt Granville Lewin, IA, est s of Sir G A Lewin, QC, and *d* 9 June 1867

(1) Juliana Sarah; *m* 1836 Thomas Veale Lane, of Coffleet, Devon, and *d* 31 Aug 1891, leaving issue. He *d* 25 Nov 1888

1 (cont.) The **2nd Viscount** *m* 2nd 2 April 1822 Georgina Janet (*d* 15 Feb 1870), est dau of Mungo Dick, and *d* 2 Dec 1833, having by her had, with another s and a dau:

(3) Fleetwood John; *b* 6 Nov 1830; *m* 28 April 1860 Emily Sarah (*m* 2nd 5 Sept 1871 Octavius Bradshaw, DL, of Powderham Castle, and *d* 30 May 1913), yst dau of Thomas Ferguson, of Greenville, Co Down, and Ryde, IoW, and *d* 2 Aug 1866, having had, with another s:

1a EDWARD FLEETWOOD JOHN PELLEW, **4th Viscount Exmouth**, JP, DL Devon; Capt 5th Vol Bn Devon Regt, Lt Roy 1st Devon Yeo Cav; *b* 24 June 1861; *m* 3 June 1884 Edith (*d* 26 Aug 1914), dau of Thomas Hargreaves, of Arborfield Hall, Berks, and *d* 31 Oct 1899, leaving:

1b EDWARD ADDINGTON HARGREAVES, **5th Viscount Exmouth**; Lt 7th Service Bn Roy Berks Regt and RAF; *b* 12 Nov 1890; *d* unm 16 Aug 1922

1b Georgina Cicely; *b* 18 Dec 1885; *d* unm 17 May 1930

(4) Barrington Reynolds; Maj Rifle Bde, ADC to Gen Sir C Van Straubenzee, KCB; *b* 18 April 1833; served Kaffir War, Siege of Sebastopol Crimean War, the storming of Canton and capture of Lucknow, where *dsp* 6 Dec 1858

2 Fleetwood Broughton Reynolds (Sir), CB, KCH, Adml the Blue; *b* 13 Dec 1789; *m* 1st 5 June 1816 Harriet (*d* 7 Aug 1849), only dau of Sir Godfrey Webster, 4th Bt, of Battle Abbey, Sussex, by Elizabeth Vassall, Lady Holland, and had issue:

(1) Harriet Bettina Frances; *m* 11 Nov 1841 4th Earl of Orford (*see* WALPOLE, B) and *d* 9 Nov 1886, leaving issue

2 (cont.) Sir Fleetwood Pellew *m* 2nd 22 Feb 1851 (*divorce* 1859) Cecile (*d* 1 Nov 1914), dau of Count Edward de Melfort Drummond (*see* PERTH, E), and *d* Marseilles 28 July 1861

3 George (Very Rev); DD, Dean Norwich, Preb York and Rector Chart, Kent; *b* 3 April 1793; *m* 20 June 1820 Frances (*d* 27 Feb 1870), 2nd dau of 1st Viscount Sidmouth (*qv*), and *d* 13 Oct 1866, having had:

(1) HENRY EDWARD PELLEW, **6th Viscount Exmouth**; *b* 26 April 1828; *educ* Trin Coll Cambridge; *m* 1st 5 Oct 1858 Eliza (*d* 22 Dec 1869), dau of Judge William Jay, of New York; *m* 2nd 14 May 1873 his deceased w's sis Augusta (*d* 24 Jan 1917) and *d* 4 Feb 1923, leaving by her an only dau (Marion, *b* 13 July 1878) and by his 1st w, with an er s (William Henry Edward George, *b* 1859, *d* unm) and a dau (Violet Lisa Mary, *d* an infant 7 Oct 1870):

1a CHARLES ERNEST PELLEW, **7th Viscount Exmouth**; *b* 11 March 1863; Capt Signal Corps US Vols Spanish-America War, Fell Chemical Soc, memb American Fedn of Artillery; *m* 1st 1886 Margaret (*d* 3 May 1922), dau of Prof C F Chandler, of New York; *m* 2nd 12 May 1923 Mabel (*d* 28 March 1948), dau of Richard Gray, of Queen's Co, Ireland, and San Francisco, was readmitted to UK nationality 1931 and *d* 7 June 1945, having had by his 1st w a dau (Anne, *b* 13 April 1889, *d* unm Jan 1928)

(1) Frances Ursula; *d* 1840

(2) Georgiana Susan; *m* 29 Sept 1848 3rd Viscount Sidmouth (*qv*) and *d* 2 Jan 1896, leaving issue

(3) Charlotte Augusta; *m* 12 Oct 1852 Louis C H Tonge, Cdr RN, and *d* 21 May 1866, leaving issue

(4) Henrietta Agneta; *m* 18 June 1856 Rev James Ambrose Ogle and *d* 17 Dec 1920, leaving issue. He *d* 20 Feb 1900

(5) Marian Hilary Adelaide; *m* 24 April 1862 Rev Godfrey Harry Arkwright, of Sutton Scarsdale, and *d* 22 Dec 1901, leaving issue. He *d* 17 Dec 1866

4 Edward (Rev); *b* 3 Nov 1799; *m* 10 April 1826 Marianne (*d* 6 March 1867), dau of Stephen Winthrop, MD, and *d* 29 Aug 1869, leaving, with other issue:

(1) Pownoll William; Cdr RN; *b* 27 Jan 1837; *m* 20 June 1867 Mary Elizabeth, dau of Rev John Armstrong Bagnel, and *d* 12 March 1872, leaving:

1a EDWARD IRVING POWNOLL, **8th Viscount**

(2) Fleetwood Hugo; Commr Dacca; *b* 13 Dec 1838; *m* 3 July 1869 Dorothy Mary (*d* 1926), dau of Rev Philip Anderson, and *d* 24 May 1906, having had, with other issue:

1a Fleetwood Hugo; Maj W Yorks Regt; *b* 23 Dec 1871; *m* 25 May 1909, Violet Annie (*d* 3 Aug 1964), yr dau of James Du Pre, and *d* 28 March 1961, leaving:

1b +(Fleetwood) Hugo [Lt-Col Hugo Pellew, Waye Farm, Lustleigh, Devon TQ13 9SQ]; Lt-Col Roy Signals (ret), ADC to Govr and C-in-C Nigeria 1935–38; *b* 20 Feb 1910; *educ* Malvern and RMA Woolwich; *m* 14 Jan 1939 *Geraldine Mildred, dau of Maj William Gerald Hole, of Parke, Bovey Tracey, S Devon, and has:

1c *Pamela Geraldine; *b* 2 March 1946; *m* 1979 *Brian E Jones and has issue

2b Anthony Pownoll; Cdr RN, WW II; *b* 16 Feb 1911; *m* 1st 4 Oct 1941 (*divorce* 1953) Margaret Julia, dau of Clive Cookson, of Nether Warden, Hexham, Northumberland, and had:

1c +Mark Edward, LVO (1980) [Mark Pellew Esq LVO, 4/51 St George's Sq, London SW1V 3QN]; Dip Serv 1965–; *b* 28 Aug 1942; *educ* Winchester and Trin Coll Oxford (BA 1965); Amb to Holy See 1998–; *m* 11 Dec 1965 *Jill Hosford, dau of Prof Frank Thistlethwaite, CBE, late V-Chllr UEA, of St John's Coll Cambridge, and has:

1d +Adam Lee; *b* 30 Dec 1966; *educ* Eton, Bristol U (BSc) and Imperial Coll (MSc); MICE

2d +Dominic Stephen; *b* 6 Aug 1968; *educ* Winchester and Merton Coll Oxford; slr

2c +Robert (Robin) Anthony; *b* 27 Sept 1945; *educ* Marlborough and Edin U; Dir World Wildlife Fund; *m* 1975 *Pamela, yst dau of Dr P D MacLellan, of Beckenham, Kent, and has:

1d +Toby James Pownoll; *b* 1982

1d *Sophie Harriet; *b* 25 July 1979

1c *Phoebe Sarah; *b* 15 Nov 1947; *educ* London U; *m* 1974 *Faisal Hamzah Ghoth, of Medina, Saudi Arabia, and has:

1d *Arabi Faisal; *b* 1974

2d *Ibrahim; *b* 1976

2b (cont.) Cdr Anthony Pellew *m* 2nd 7 Sept 1957 *Hilary Frances [Mrs Anthony Pellew, 3 Glencairn House, 70 Ridgway, London SW19], dau of Capt Alfred Garbett Pape, of Edinburgh, and *d* 1992, leaving by her:

3c +Nicholas Charles; *b* 22 Feb 1959; *educ* Wellington, Exeter U and Cambridge; *m* 1989 *Doone Philippa, dau of Robert Selbie, of Hurstbourne Priors, Hants, and has:

1d +Christopher Anthony Lloyd; *b* 1992

4c +Philip Esmond; *b* 7 March 1962

3b +Myles Addington [Myles Pellew Esq, 2 Little Chesters, Beech Lane, Walton-on-the-Hill, Surrey KT20 7SH]; *b* 18 May 1919; *educ* Malvern; *m* 26 Oct 1957 *Jill Twentyman Primrose Twentyman, yst dau of Capt Alfred Maurice Davis, OBE, of Chelsea, and has:

1c +Simon Du Pre; *b* 28 Jan 1959; *educ* Charterhouse, Bristol U and Imperial Coll; *m* 17 Oct 1988 *Shunu Arnetha, dau of Gopal Chowdroy, of Chittagong, and has:

1d *Sarah Chowdhroy; *b* 9 April 1994

1c *Alexandra Twentyman; *b* 20 March 1961; *m* 1987 (*divorce* 1996) Jeffrey G Fowler, s of J T G Fowler, of Lambeth; *m* 2nd 25 Jan 1997 *Adam Pappworth, s of Sidney Pappworth, FRCS, and by her 1st husb has:

1d *James Vernon; *b* 1988

1d *Olivia Lucinda; *b* 1990

2c *Miranda Frances; *b* 23 Jan 1964; *m* 1996 *Peter John Seymour, s of Maurice Seymour

4b +Timothy Winthrop [Timothy Pellew Esq, 31 Churchill Avenue, Willowdale, Ontario, Canada]; *b* 4 Feb 1921; *educ* Cambridge U (MA 1947); MICE; Hon Capt late REME; *m* 15 April 1950 *Margaret Richmond, dau of Edmund George Hamilton Mewburn, of Richmond, Surrey, and has:

1c +Fleetwood Timothy; *b* 26 May 1952

2c +Adrian Harold; *b* 16 Jan 1954; *m* 1991 *Leanne Eileen, dau of Edmund C Randell, of Mississauga, Ontario, and has:

1d *Mallory Anne; *b* 1993

3c +Owen Simon; *b* 10 May 1958

4c +Colin David; *b* 7 May 1961

1c *Mabel Audrey; *b* 9 June 1955; *m* 1983 *Milenko Milicev, of Toronto

1b *Anne [Mrs Denis Burns, Clumps End, Lower Bourne, Farnham, Surrey GU10 3HF]; *b* 1915; *m* 1st 3 May 1941 (*divorce* 1947) Capt John Pearce Gould, RASC, s of Hugh Pearce Gould; *m* 2nd 8 Feb 1947 *Denis Owen Burns, s of Samuel Burns, of Aughnahoe, Lisburn, Co Antrim

1a Dorothy; *d* unm 1960

2a Margaret Alma; *m* 15 Aug 1907 Frank Moss Bennett, 2nd s of Henry Mellor Bennet, of Croydon, and *d* 26 Feb 1955, leaving issue. He *d* 23 Feb 1952

3a Anna Helen; *m* 4 Jan 1910 Edward Francis Wells, artist, s of William Howley Wells, of Evershot, Dorset, and *d* 19 May 1924, leaving issue

4a Caroline; *d* unm 11 April 1963

5d Constantia Langford Frances; *m* 10 Oct 1914 H Camville Layard, 2nd s of Lt-Col Layard, of Deep Cove, Vancouver, BC, and had issue

(1) Elizabeth Julia; *m* 1847 Rev J R Anderson and *d* 16 July 1890, leaving issue. He *d* 1872

(2) Mary Anne; *m* 11 March 1852 Robert Hill Pinhey and had issue. He *d* 21 Aug 1896

(3) Emma Susan; *m* 25 July 1856 William D'Oyly, Bombay CS, and *d* 6 Sept 1909, leaving issue

(4) Frances Helen; *m* 19 Aug 1858 Rt Hon Sir Louis Mallet, CB, and *d* 7 May 1917, having had issue. He *d* 16 Feb 1890

(5) Georgina Caroline; *m* 24 April 1877 Frederick Howard and *d* 23 April 1940. He *d* 13 July 1904

1 Emma Mary; *m* Dec 1803 Adml Sir Lawrence William Halsted, GCB, and *d* March1835, leaving issue

2 Julia; *m* 11 Jan 1810 Capt Richard Harward, RN, and *d* 26 Dec 1831. He *d* May 1854

The 7th VISCOUNT's 2nd cousin

EDWARD IRVING POWNOLL PELLEW, **8th Viscount Exmouth**, OBE; *b* 3 May 1868; *educ* Trin Coll Cambridge (BA); MRCS, LRCP, T/Capt RAMC 1914–18, memb Roy Ag Soc, Chev de Mérite Agricole France; *m* 1902 Frances (*d* 1963), dau of Alfred Wells Edwards, and had:

1 POWNOLL IRVING EDWARD, **9th Viscount**

1 Rose Mary; *b* 25 Sept 1903; *m* 25 Sept 1942 (*divorce* 1949, resumed maiden name) Maurice Louis Odilon Van de Goor, s of Cdr Maurice Van de Goor, of Antwerp, Belgium, and had issue

The 8th VISCOUNT *d* 19 Aug 1951; his only s,

POWNELL IRVING EDWARD PELLEW, **9th Viscount Exmouth**; *b* 28 May 1908; *educ* Oundle; *m* 2 Jan 1938 Maria Luisa (Marquesa de Olias in Spain (*cr* 1652) by Philip IV, *s* 1940; *d* 28 Dec 1994), widow of Don Gonzalo Alvarez-Builla y Alvera and dau of Luis de Urquijo, Marqués de Amurrio and the Marquesa de Zarreal, of Madrid, and *d* 2 Dec 1970, leaving:

1 PAUL EDWARD PELLEW, **10th and present Viscount Exmouth**

2 +Peter Irving; *b* 20 Oct 1942; *educ* Downside and Madrid U

1 *Mary Rose; *b* 2 Oct 1938; *m* 1974 *Don Roman Llanso

2 *(Mary) Elizabeth Josephine [The Hon Mrs d'Erlanger, Manor Farm House, Compton Valence, Dorset]; *b* 16 March 1947; *m* 4 Jan 1969 *Robin Gerard d'Erlanger, ACA, only s of Sir Gerard d'Erlanger, CBE, of Mayfair, and has:

(1) *Gerard Pownoll; *b* 11 Dec 1970

(2) *Hugh Robin; *b* 6 Aug 1976

(1) *Josephine Louise; *b* 1972

(2) *Marietta Elizabeth; *bapt* 3 Aug 1974

(3) *Emilia Mary Florence; *b* 1982

EZRA

Creation: B. (LP, UK) 1983.

THE BARON EZRA, of Horsham, Co West Sussex (Derek Ezra, MBE (1945)) [The Rt Hon The Lord Ezra MBE, House of Lords, London SW1A 0PW]; *b* 23 Feb 1919; *educ* Monmouth Sch and Magdalene Coll Cambridge (MA, Hon Fell 1977); Army WW II, joined NCB 1947, regnl sales manager 1958–60, dir-gen mktg 1960–65, dir 1965–67, dep-chm 1967–71, chm 1971–82, ktd 1974, V-Pres BIM 1978 (Chm 1976–78), chm Assoc Heat Servs plc 1966–, Sheffield Heat and Power 1985–, Assoc Gas Supplies 1987–95 and Energy and Tech Servs Gp 1990–, Pres: Ec Research Cncl 1985– and Combustion Engrg Assoc, memb Internat Advsy Bd Banca Nazionale del Lavoro 1984–, author: *Coal and Energy* (1978), *The Energy Debate* (1983); *m* 1950 *Julia Elizabeth, da of Thomas Wilkins, of Portsmouth, Hants

Lineage: DAVID EZRA; *m* Lillie — and had:

DEREK, *cr* a **Baron**

FAGGE

Arms: Gules two bends vair. **Crest:** An ostrich, wings expanded argent, beaked, legged and ducally gorged or, holding in the beak a horseshoe proper. **Motto:** *Tutus si rectus* ('Safe if upright').

Creation: Bt. (E) 11 Dec 1660.

SIR JOHN WILLIAM FREDERICK FAGGE, 11TH BT, of Wiston, Sussex, and Mystole, Kent [Sir John Fagge Bt, 11 Forbes Road, Faversham, Kent ME13 8QF]; *b* 28 Sept 1910; *s* unc 1940; *m* 11 May 1940 Ivy Gertrude (*d* 1992), dau of William Edward Frier, of Newington, Kent, and has issue:

1 +JOHN CHRISTOPHER; *b* 30 April 1942; *m* 1974 *Evelyn Joy Golding

1 *Pauline Joy; *b* 25 Aug 1943

Lineage: JOHN FAGGE, of Brensett, Kent; *m* Adryn, dau and heir of Clement Cobb, of Canterbury, and had issue:

JOHN FAGGE, of Rye, Sussex; *m* Elizabeth Hudson and had issue:

Sir John Fagge, 1st Bt (E), *so cr* 11 Dec 1660, of Wiston, Sussex, and Mystole, Kent; MP Rye 1645–53, Sussex 1654–59 and 1681–85 and Steyning 1660–81 and 1685–1701, Col Parly Army, memb Cncl of State 1659; *m* 1st 19 March 1645 Mary (*d* 20 Nov 1687), dau of Robert Morley, of Glynde, Sussex; *m* 2nd Anne Henshaw (*d* 11 May 1694), dau of Philip Weston, and *d* 18 Jan 1700/1, having had by his 1st w, with 11 other children (*d* unm):

1 **Sir Robert Fagge, 2nd Bt**; MP Shoreham 1679–81 and Steyning 1690–95 and 1701–02; *m* 21 Sept 1671 Elizabeth, dau of Benjamin Culpepper, of Lindfield, Sussex, and *d* 26 Aug 1715, leaving:

(1) **Sir Robert Fagge, 3rd Bt**; *m* Christian (*d* 30 Aug 1765), dau of Sir Cecil Bishopp, 4th Bt (*see* ZOUCHE, B), and *d* 22 June 1736, having had, with two other daus (*d* unm):

1a **Sir Robert Fagge, 4th Bt**; *bapt* 20 Sept 1704; MP Steyning 1734–40; *m* 1729 Sarah (*m* 2nd 1753 Roger Talbot, of Woodend), dau of William Ward, MD, and *dsps* 14 Sept 1740, having willed his estates in Kent and Sussex to his sis Elizabeth, although the baronetcy passed to his 2nd cousin

1a Elizabeth; *m* 20 April 1743, as his 2nd w, Sir Charles Matthew Goring, 5th Bt (*qv*), and *d* 23 Feb 1784, leaving issue

2a Margaret; *m* 1723 Gawen Harris Nash, of Petworth, Sussex

2 Charles, of Mystole; *bapt* 1 Jan 1661; *m* Mary Hyland and *d* 10 March 1714, having had:

(1) Charles, of Mystole; *m* Feb 1728 Elizabeth, dau of William Turner, of Whitefriars, Canterbury, and *d* 8 April 1739, having had, with other issue:

1a WILLIAM (Sir), **5th Bt**

1a Sarah; *m* as his 1st w Sir William Young, 1st Bt of Dominica (*qv*), and *dsp*

3 Thomas; *m* Elizabeth, widow of John Meres, and had a s (John, *m* and left issue)

1 Elizabeth; *m* Sir Philip Gell, 3rd and last Bt (*dsp* 14 July 1719)

2 Mary; *m* John Spence

The 4th Bt's 2nd cousin,

Sir William Fagge, 5th Bt; *m* Elizabeth (*d* 27 Feb 1785), dau of Abraham Le Grand, of Canterbury, and *d* 14 Nov 1791, having had issue:

1 JOHN (Rev Sir), **6th Bt**

1 Helen Ward; *m* Rev Philip Williams, Preb Winchester, and *d* 1833

2 Sarah; *m* 2 Feb 1777 Edwyn Humphrey Sandys and *d* 1782

The 5th Bt's est s,

Rev Sir John Fagge, 6th Bt; *educ* Cambridge (MA); Rector Chartham, Kent; *m* 27 Aug 1789 Anne (*d* 16 June 1857), only dau and heir of Daniel Newman, barrister, and *d* 23 Sept 1822, having had, with three other daus:

1 **Sir John Fagge, 7th Bt**; *b* 8 Sept 1798; *d* unm 16 April 1873

2 John William Thomas; *m* 24 July 1824 Frances (*d* Nov 1859), yst dau of William Carter, MD, of Canterbury, and *d* 1 Oct 1840, leaving, with two other sons and two other daus:

(1) JOHN WILLIAM CHARLES (Sir), **8th Bt**

(1) Jane Mary Georgiana; *m* 10 June 1858 Eldred Harry Littlehales and *d* 30 April 1877, having had issue

(2) Julia Augusta Lee; *m* 8 April 1875 David Charles Poole (*d* 1881), barrister, and *d* 20 Sept 1906

(3) Amelia Elizabeth; *m* 8 Sept 1870 Capt William Lithgow (*d* 1905), Indian Navy, and *d* 15 March 1907

3 Rev John Frederick; *b* 5 Oct 1814; Vicar Aston Cantlow, Warwicks; *m* 1st 3 Sept 1844 Rose Emily Ward (*d* 29 May 1859), 4th dau of George Baker and gdau of Very Rev Dr Andrews, Dean Canterbury, and had, with two other sons and four other daus:

(1) Edmund Lancelot; *b* 20 Nov 1858; *m* 1888 Amelia Hellyar (*d* 1947), dau of Charles Ross Foord, JP, of Rochester, and *d* 6 May 1925, leaving issue:

1a Sybil Winifrid Ross; *b* 10 June 1889; *d* unm 12 Feb 1966

2a Dorothy Beatrice Rose; *b* 31 May 1890; *d* unm 21 April 1961

3a Cicely Millicent Ruth; *b* 26 Feb 1903

(1) Alice Geraldine; *m* 1 June 1876 Rev William Cater Randolph (*d* 1898) and *d* Nov 1923

(2) Gertrude Jane Fielding; *m* 1889 Franz Frauenberger (*d* 1908), of Vienna, and *d* 1 Nov 1927

3 (cont.) The Rev John Fagge *m* 2nd 17 July 1861 Jessie (*d* 2 April 1921), dau of William Clark, and *d* 30 March 1884, having by her had, with three other sons:

(2) Eustace; *b* 10 April 1876; *m* 8 May 1922 Nancy (*d* 11 Feb 1954), 2nd dau of Emanuel Gold, of Cardiff, and *d* 8 April 1936, having had issue:

1a Patricia; *b* 19 Jan 1927; *d* unm

(3) Bertha Lillian; *d* unm 30 Jan 1939

(4) Jessie Kathleen; *d* unm

(5) Sarah Elizabeth; *m* 1889 George Goldie (*d* 1904), JP Manitoba, Canada, and *d* 1 Feb 1946, leaving issue:

1a Ethelreda Marie Teresa; *b* 1899; *m* 1936 Lawrence Henry Shattock, FRIBA, Kt of St Gregory

(6) Madeline Augusta; *d* unm 17 Oct 1948

(7) Agnes; *d* unm 7 May 1949

1 Augusta; *m* 6 Dec 1827 Rev Henry Feilding and had issue (*see* DENBIGH and DESMOND, E)

2 Jemima; *m* 1 Feb 1844 her bro-in-law Rev Allen Feilding (*see* DENBIGH and DESMOND, E) and *dsp* 19 Feb 1894

The 7th Bt's n,

Sir John William Charles Fagge, 8th Bt; *b* 10 Oct 1830; Lt 21st Regt; *m* 1st 1 Sept 1864 Anne Elizabeth (*d* 17 Dec 1877), only dau of Thomas Holttum, of Sturry, Kent; *m* 2nd 6 Nov 1901 Catherine Mary, 2nd dau of Isaac Goodwin, of Wickhambreaux, Kent, and gdau of Young Waterman, of High Halden, and *d* 13 April 1909, having by his 1st w had, with another s (*d* young):

1 **Sir John Charles Fagge, 9th Bt**; *b* 6 April 1866; *d* unm 17 Jan 1930

2 **Sir John Harry Lee Fagge, 10th Bt**; *b* 25 Sept 1868; *m* 1st 1912 Jennie Isabelle (*d* 1917), dau of Stephen Taylor, of Massachusetts; *m* 2nd 15 Oct 1930 Florence, dau of W H Goss, of Stoke-on-Trent, and widow of Albert Murdoch, of Boston, and *d* 18 March 1940, leaving issue by his 1st w:

(1) *Lucy Harriet Gertrude; *b* 1913

3 William Archibald Theodore; *b* 31 May 1875; *m* 6 Nov 1909 Nellie (*d* 23 June 1924), 2nd dau of H T D Wise, of Faversham, and *d* 17 July 1924, leaving:

(1) Sir JOHN WILLIAM FREDERICK FAGGE, **11th and present Bt**

(1) *Gwendoline Beatrice May; *b* 23 Oct 1914

2 Eveline Frances Anne; *b* 3 July 1867

FAIRBAIRN

Arms: Argent on a chevron between three boar's heads couped gules three bezants. **Crest:** The sun in splendour or. **Motto:** *Semper eadem* ('Always the same'). **Creation:** Bt. (UK) 2 Nov 1869.

SIR (JAMES) BROOKE FAIRBAIRN, 6TH BT, of Ardwick, Lancashire [Sir Brooke Fairbairn Bt, Barkway House, Bury Road, Newmarket, Suffolk CB8 7BT]; *b* 10 Dec 1930; *s* f 1972; *educ* Stowe; owns J Brooke Fairbairn & Co textile converters and furnishing fabric wholesalers, Upper Bailiff Weavers' Co; *m* 1st 5 Nov 1960 Mary Russell (*d* 1992), only dau of William Russell Scott, MB, ChB, FFARCS, of Weymouth, Dorset, and has issue:

1 +ROBERT WILLIAM; *b* 10 April 1965; *educ* King's Sch Ely and Durham U (BA); investment manager with GT Management; *m* 1990 *Sarah Frances Colleypriest, er dau of Roger Griffin, of Malmesbury, Wilts, and has issue:

(1) *Imogen Mary Colleypriest; *b* 1993

2 +George Edward; *b* 5 July 1969; *m* 5 Oct 1996 Lena Maria, dau of Adolf Gstöttner, of Hamburg

1 *Fiona Mary; *b* 3 Jan 1967; *m* 3 Aug 1996 *Lt-Col James Gordon, only s of Graeme Gordon, of New Galloway, Kirkcudbrightshire

Sir BROOKE *m* 2nd 22 Feb 1997 *Mrs Victoria Washbourn

Lineage: JOHN FAIRBAIRN; *b* Nenthorn, Roxburghshire, 1714; *m* Helen Anderson, of Crailing, and *d* Galashiels 1796, having had, with other surv issue:

1 Andrew; *b* 10 Feb 1758 Smailholme, Roxburghshire; agricultural labourer and skilled ploughman, conscript War American Independence, later tenant farmer of 300 acres; *m* 12 Dec 1783 Margaret Henderson (*d* 21 Jan 1820), of Jedburgh, and *d* 14 Jan 1844, having had

(1) WILLIAM (Sir), **1st Bt**

(2) Thomas; drowned at sea nr Archangel 1812

(3) Peter (Sir); *b* 11 Sept 1799; engr and inventor, especially of machines for spinning silk waste and rope yarn, Mayor Leeds 1857–58 and 1858–59 (town cncllr 1836–42, Alderman 1854), ktd 1858 on occasion of HM QUEEN VICTORIA's visit; *m* 1st Margaret (*d* 13 Aug 1843), dau of Robert Kennedy, of Glasgow, and had issue:

1a Andrew (Sir), JP (Leeds and W R Yorks), DL (W R Yorks), of Askham Hall, nr York; *b* 5 March 1828; *educ* Geneva, Glasgow and Peterhouse Coll Cambridge (MA, 37th Wrangler); barrister Inner Temple 1852, Mayor Leeds 1866 and 1867–68, Capt Yorks Hus Yeo 1875–77, Maj 7th York Roy Vols, ktd 1868, MP (Lib) E Div W R Yorks 1880–85 and Otley 1885–86 (fought Leeds 1868, Knaresborough 1874 and Pudsey 1895), High Sheriff Yorks 1892, chm: Fairbairn, Lawson, Combe, Barbour Ltd, machine-makers, and Leeds Sch Bd 1870–78, KGStJ, Hon DSc; *m* 6 Nov 1862 Clara Frederica, LGStJ (*d* 2 March 1922), yst dau of Sir John Lambton Loraine, 10th Bt (*see* 1963 edn), of Kirk Harle, Northumberland, and *dsp* 31 May 1901

1a Elizabeth Yorstoun; *m* 17 Feb 1859 William Wailes, of Bath, and *d* 4 Aug 1917, leaving:

1b William Fairbairn WAILES later WAILES-FAIRBAIRN (roy licence 10 March 1902), DL, of Askham Grange, Yorks

2a Robina Fairbairn; *m* Dec 1868 Frederick Wordsworth Haydon and *d* 9 Jan 1873, leaving issue

(3) (cont.) Sir Peter *m* 2nd Rachel Anne (*d* 25 June 1886), 4th dau of Robert William Brandling, of Low Gosforth, Northumberland, and widow of Capt Charles Bell, RN, of Woolsington, and *d* 4 Jan 1861

2 Peter; Sec to Govr Barbados and Berbice; *d* West Indies 1823

ANDREW FAIRBAIRN's est s,

Sir William Fairbairn, 1st Bt (UK), so *cr* 20 Nov 1869 for scientific eminence, of The Polygon, Ardwick, Manchester; *b* 19 Feb 1789; apprentice in colliery nr Newcastle 1803–04, millwright March–Dec 1811; manufactured sausage-machines, nail-machines and cotton-mill machinery and built bridges 1811 on, ptnr in Fairbairn & Lillie 1817–*c* 1835; friend of George Stephenson (who consulted him when designing the Menai Bridge between Anglesey and the Wesh mainland); MICE 1830; from *c* 1830 pioneered the construction of iron canal boats, riveting machines and devices to prevent boilers exploding; a judge London Exhibitions 1851 and 1862 and Paris Exhibition 1855, Legn Hon 1855; corresponding memb Inst of France, Roy Soc gold medal 1860, PBA 1861, Hon LLD Edinburgh 1860 and Cantab 1862, Pres: Inst Mechanical Engrs 1854 and Manchester Lit and Philosophical Soc 1855–60, FRS; *m* 16 June 1816 Dorothy (*d* 11 Jan 1882 aged 93), dau of John Mar, burgess of Kelso, and *d* 18 Aug 1874, having had, with two other sons and another dau:

1 THOMAS (Sir), **2nd Bt**

2 William Andrew; *b* 22 Dec 1824; *m* 1st 12 Sept 1849 Marianne (*d* 29 March 1859), 2nd dau of William Murray, MP Newcastle-under-Lyme, and had issue:

(1) William Murray (Rev); *b* 21 Nov 1850; BA Cantab, Rector Loxbeare, Devon; *m* 24 July 1879 Frances Elizabeth (*d* 14 June 1929), est dau of John Bury, of Ayton Lodge, Yorks, and *d* 16 May 1929, leaving issue:

1a Bernard William Murray, CBE (1934, OBE 1919); *b* 18 April 1880; *educ* HMS *Britannia*; RN: Lt 1901, Cdr 1914, Capt 1919, R-Adml 1931, V-Adml 1936, Pres Ordinance Ctee 1934–36 (V-Pres 1932–34), Cdre Convoys 1939–42 WW II, Flag Offr cmdg Milford Haven 1942–45, US Legn Merit; *m* 29 April 1905 Alice Mary (*d* 16 Nov 1970), only dau of William Phillipps, of Plymouth, and *d* 5 April 1960, having had, with other issue:

1b +Alan Bernard Murray, MBE (1973); *b* 20 Feb 1906; *educ* Sherborne; served WW II (despatches); *m* 18 Dec 1943 *Adeline Hilda, only dau of Lt-Col Edward Herbert Sweet, CMG, DSO, of Crowthorne, Berks, and has issue:

1c +John Alan (Rev); *b* 2 Jan 1946; *educ* Wellington and Trin Coll Cambridge (MA); *m* 1982 *Susan Patricia, dau of Dr Charles Sergel, of Milford-on-Sea, and has issue:

1d +Timothy John Charles; *b* 1983

1d *Katherine Mary; *b* 1985

2b +David Patrick [Lt-Cdr David Fairbairn RN (ret), The Firs, Ryhall, Stamford, Lincs PE9 4HF]; *b* 30 March 1919; *educ* Sherborne; CEng, MIMechE, FIMarE; *m* 2 Sept 1950 *Margaret Winifred Ferrers, late 2nd Offr WRNS, er dau of Ronald Ernest Ferrers Courage, of Kings Brompton, Dulverton, and Mrs Courage, JP, of Hartshsorn House, Syresham, Brackley, Northants, and has issue:

1c +William David Murray [Cdr William Fairbairn RN, Woodland View, Upton Noble, Shepton Mallet, Somerset BA4 6BB]; *b* 17 Oct 1953; *educ* Radley and Magdalene Coll Cambridge (MA); Cdr RN; *m* 1983 *Rowena Katherine, dau of Walter Angus Murray, of West Hill Court, Ottery St Mary, Devon, and has issue:

1d +Oliver James Murray; *b* 1987

1d *Fiona Nina Katherine; *b* 1992

1c *Anne Mary [Mrs Harry Fox, 49 Walsingham, St John's Wood Park, London NW8 6RJ]; *b* 17 June 1951; formerly Sister of the Soc of St Margaret, St Saviour's Priory, Haggerston; *m* 1993 *Harry Fox

1b Betty Rosemary Alice; *b* 24 Aug 1913; *m* 17 Aug 1937 (*divorce* 1948) Lt Col Colin Gordon Irving-Bell (*d* 4 Dec 1970), Roy Norfolk Regt, s of H Irving-Bell, of Hove, and had:

1c *Raymond Gordon; *b* 21 June 1944; *educ* St Edward's Sch Oxford; RN 1962–64, assist manager Jokai (Assam) Tea Co from 1964

1c *Angela Rosemary; *b* 23 May 1940; *m* 15 Aug 1964 *Capt Colin John Bruce Campbell, CFS, RM, s of Richard Galbraith Campbell, of Arduaine, Argyll, and has issue:

1d *Shuna Catherine Islay; *b* 20 Jan 1965

2d *Fiona Jane Alison; *b* 27 Feb 1967

2b Patricia; *b* 18 March 1921; WRNS WW II; *m* 17 July 1943 Col Robert Windham O'Neale Collis, RM, and *d* 13 March 1966, leaving two sons and a dau

2a Aubrey John Murray; *b* 6 March 1888; Lt KAR (despatches) WW I; *m* 23 Oct 1920 Florence Adela Augusta Jane, yst dau of Col Thomas Andrews Rawlins, of Berrow, Somerset, and *d* 1 July 1961, leaving issue:

1b +Ian Aubrey; *b* 30 July 1927

1a Guendolen Elizabeth Marianne; *b* 11 Nov 1885; *m* 1932 Maurice Allen (*d* 1937), of Upton St Leonards, Glos, and *d* 26 April 1937

(1) Emily Jane; *b* 11 Feb 1853; *m* 8 May 1873 Samuel Dickinson (*d* 13 Sept 1908), barrister, 2nd s of William Dickinson, of New Park, Hants, and *d* 9 Feb 1935

(2) Edith Marianne; *b* 26 July 1854; *m* 2 Dec 1886 Francis Alvey Rhodes Darwin (*d* 31 May 1937), of Stainley House, South Stainley, Harrogate, and *d* 13 Jan 1928, leaving issue

(3) Ada Maria; *b* 25 Feb 1856; *m* 18 July 1877 her cousin **Sir Thomas Gordon Fairbairn, 4th Bt** (*see* below), and *d* 2 Sept 1893, leaving issue

2 (cont.) William Fairbairn *m* 2nd 26 May 1864 Helen (*d* 15 Feb 1928), dau of Richard Birley, of Manchester, and *d* 26 Jan 1910, having by her had issue:

(1) Francis Richard (Rev); *b* 13 April 1865; Vicar Alderminster, Stratford-on-Avon; *m* 19 Dec 1895 Sophie Ernle (*d c* 1946), dau of Maj-Gen Robert Cotton Money, and *dsp* 31 May 1945

(2) Edward Percy; *b* 7 June 1866; *m* 1st 23 May 1894 Mary (*d* 3 June 1903), only dau of John Sholto Douglas, of Tilquhillie, Kincardineshire, and had:

1a William Douglas; *b* 24 Feb 1895; Lt-Cdr RN; *d* 6 May 1932

1a Vanda Marr; *b* 3 Oct 1896; *m* 1st 2 June 1919 Flag-Lt F C Bottomley, RN (*d* 1921); *m* 2nd 1 March 1924 Cdr F J Wylie, RN, and *d* 4 May 1934, leaving issue

(2) (cont.) Edward Fairbairn *m* 2nd 22 Oct 1908 Constance, er dau of William Gaven Eden (*see* HENLEY, B), and *d* 15 Sept 1931, leaving by her:

1a +George William [George Fairbairn Esq, Flat 17, Hamilton Ct, Saltern Rd, Exmouth, Devon]; *b* 5 Aug 1911; ARIBA 1939, Lt 4th Bn Devon Regt (TAR), 4th Lincoln Regt 1939, RE 1942; *m* 3 Feb 1940 Katharine Elizabeth (*d* 1991), dau of Dr William Deane, of Waddington, Lincs, and has:

1b *Jacqueline Elizabeth; *b* 8 Aug 1948; *m* 1978 *Luis Filipe Espadinha Fialho, of Casa Charna, Algarve, Portugal, s of Pedro Manuel Fialho and Maria B Espadinha, of Estoril, and has:

1c *Miguel Filipe; *b* 1980

2c *Andre Simon; *b* 1984

2a +Patrick Yelverton [Patrick Fairbairn Esq, Applegarth, Bradfield, Berks RG7 6AS]; *b* 5 Oct 1913; *educ* Charterhouse; Capt 2nd/15th Punjab Regt IA

WW II; *m* 25 June 1940 Dorothy Mary (*d* 1986), yr dau of Lewis Henshaw, OBE, of Madras, and has issue:

1b +Edward James [Edward Fairbairn Esq, Applegarth, Bradfield, Berks RG7 6AS]; *b* 11 Aug 1950; *educ* Charterhouse and W Surrey Coll of Art and Design (DipAD); *m* 1974 *Fiona Catherine, dau of Maj M C Gray, and has issue:

1c *Miranda Sarah; *b* 1976

2c *Rosalind Nesta; *b* 1979

1b *Judith Constance [Mrs Keith Hornby, 11 St Ann's Villas, London W11]; *b* 30 Sept 1946; *m* 1970 *Keith Anthony Delgado Hornby, barrister, and has issue:

1c *Jamie Alexander Fairbairn; *b* 1976

2c *Nicholas Thomas Fairbairn; *b* 1980

1c *Katya Eugenie; *b* 1973

(3) George; *b* 22 Dec 1869; *das* S Africa 12 March 1901

3 Peter; *b* 13 Oct 1828; *m* Dec 1854 Maria Christiana (*m* 2nd 6 Aug 1867 Edward Halford), est dau of Col — Cleather, and *d* 18 Aug 1859, having had issue

4 George; *b* 24 March 1830; *m* 11 July 1855 Bessie Anne (*d* 11 Nov 1918), dau of Rev Charles Frederic Bagshawe, MA, and *dsp* 5 Dec 1868

5 Adam Henderson (Rev); *b* 16 Oct 1836; Rector Fawley, Bucks; *m* 7 Feb 1864 Anna Gertrude (*d* 16 May 1929), est dau of Thomas Fuller-Maitland, of Wargrave, Berks, and *d* 21 July 1888, leaving issue:

(1) Adam Maitland; *b* 24 Nov 1866; *m* 14 June 1906 Grace Henfield, er dau of George Henry Bagshawe, of Whalley Range, Manchester, and *d* 15 May 1921

(2) William; *b* 26 April 1869; *m* 20 April 1907 Mary Louisa Henrietta (*d* 28 Aug 1935), yr dau of William F Swindell, of Melyniog Hall, Salop, and *d* 22 June 1930, leaving issue:

1a William Alan Thomas, TD (1951); *b* 13 July 1908; *educ* Uppingham and Trin Coll Cambridge; Roy Hants Regt and 9th Bn Mobile Def Corps (both TA), Maj WW II (despatches), Freedom Aalst Belgium 1945, sr master Stonar Sch, Atworth; *m* 4 July 1944 *Marian Ruth, yr dau of Capt William T Wyllie, of Tower House, Old Portsmouth, and *d* 1992, leaving issue:

1b +Stephen Alan [Stephen Fairbairn Esq, Borgarholtsbraut 57, Kopavogur, Iceland]; *b* 2 Dec 1947; *educ* Radley and Bath Acad of Art (DipAD); *m* 28 Nov 1970 *Margaret Joelsdottir, and has issue:

1c *Hilda; *b* 29 March 1973

2c *Sandra; *b* 1979

1b *Susan Mary [Mrs Richard Sommerin, Wainsford Farm, Wainsford Rd, Pennington, Hants]; *b* 14 April 1953; *educ* Stonar; *m* 1974 *Richard Ivor Sommerin and has issue:

1c *James Adrian; *b* 1974

(3) Thomas Archibald; *b* 24 April 1870; *m* 15 Sept 1909 Edith Georgette, dau of Rev G G MacLean, of Wadhurst, Sussex, and *dsp* Oct 1944

(4) Hugh; *b* 2 Nov 1874; *d* unm Dec 1944

(5) Alan John FAIRBAIRN later FAIRBAIRN WYNNE-EYTON (deed poll 4 April 1929); *b* 4 Jan 1878; *educ* Haileybury and Roy Sch of Mines; mining engr, High Sheriff Flintshire 1938; *m* 12 Dec 1928 Violet Hope, JP (1930), only child of Maj John Hope Wynne-Eyton, of Leeswood Hall, Mold, and *dsp* 14 Nov 1960

(6) David Alexander, OBE (1919); *b* 3 Sept 1882; Maj Duke of Wellington's (W R) Regt; *m* 10 April 1920 Emmeline Mary (*d* 1964), dau of Alfred Coxon, of Surbiton, and widow of Capt T A Abbot, RFA, and *d* 30 Nov 1950, leaving:

1a +Norman David Nigel; *b* 3 March 1921; *educ* Wellington and Cape Town U (BA); ARIBA, MIA, served Union Def Force (S African Artillery) 1939–45 and RA 1943–44 and 17th/21st Lancers 1944–45; *m* 20 Oct 1951 *Mary Josephine, dau of Hector Hillaby, barrister, of Chelsea, and has issue:

1b +Jonathan David; *b* 14 Oct 1952

2b +Mark Benson Hector; *b* 25 Oct 1960; *m* 1990 *Fiona, er dau of Cdr Graham P Stock, of Thornford, Dorset

1b *Carol Evangeline Mary; *b* 1 May 1954

2b *Alexandra Josephine Margaret; *b* 5 Sept 1957

(1) Frances Gertrude; *m* 4 Oct 1898 Rev Canon Phillip Cunningham (*d* 9 Feb 1942), Rector Compton, Hants, and *d* 1951, leaving issue

(2) Hilda Margaret; *d* unm 21 Oct 1917

(3) Rosamond; *d* unm Aug 1948

(4) Helen Dorothy; *d* unm 1 Feb 1914

(5) Ida Mary; *m* 6 April 1907 Sidney Herbert NATHAN later FAIRBAIRN, MD (deed poll 8 April 1921; *d* July 1940), of S Kensington, and had issue

1 Anne; *b* 30 March 1817; *m* 1 Sept 1841 John Frederic La Trobe-Bateman, FRS (*d* June 1889), of Moor Park, Surrey, and *d* 26 May 1894, leaving issue

Sir WILLIAM's 3rd s,

Sir Thomas Fairbairn, 2nd Bt, DL; *b* 18 Jan 1823; *m* 23 March 1848 Allison (*d* 8 Feb 1907), dau of Thomas Callaway, of Chislehurst, Kent, and *d* 12 Aug 1891, having had, with other issue:

1 **Sir Arthur Henderson Fairbairn, 3rd Bt**; *b* 11 April 1852; Hon Treas Roy Assoc in Aid of the Deaf and Dumb; *m* 5 July 1882 Florence Frideswyde (*d* 22 March 1941), dau of Richard Penruddocke Long, MP (*see* LONG, V), and *dsp* 2 June 1915

2 THOMAS GORDON (Sir), **4th Bt**

3 Reginald; *b* 18 Jan 1856; *educ* Trin Coll Cambridge (BA, LLB); barrister Lincoln's Inn; *m* 7 Jan 1880 May Elizabeth, only dau of J F Holt, and *d* 1921, leaving issue:

(1) Ada; *b* 30 March 1882

4 James Brooke; *b* 6 Sept 1863; Capt Durham LI

1 Mary Allison Dorothy; *b* 9 Aug 1860; *m* 1st 16 Dec 1880 (*divorce* 1903) Sir Archibald Lennox Napier, 10th Bt of Merchistoun (*qv*), and had issue; *m* 2nd 1 June 1904 G Graham Kirklinton, JP, DL (*d* 1 Aug 1927), of Kirklinton Hall, nr Carlisle, and *d* 7 Nov 1936

The 3rd Bt's bro,

Sir Thomas Gordon Fairbairn, 4th Bt; *b* 26 May 1854; *educ* Jesus Coll Cambridge (BA); *m* 1st 18 July 1877 Ada Maria (*d* 2 Sept 1893), yst dau of William Andrew Fairbairn (*see* above), and had issue:

1 Roderic Gordon; *b* 11 March 1881; *d* unm 24 July 1909

1 Ada Florence; *b* 21 July 1878; *d* 9 April 1926

2 Violet Edith; *b* 6 Oct 1883

3 Ina Muriel; *d* an infant 1889

Sir Thomas *m* 2nd 12 April 1899 Jennie Cora, dau of Albert Davies, of Allston, Mass., and *d* 19 Dec 1931, leaving further issue:

2 **Sir William Albert Fairbairn, 5th Bt**, of Ardwick, Manchester; *b* 6 April 1902; *educ* privately; *m* 2 Dec 1925 *Christine Renée Cotton [Lady Fairbairn, 45 Williams Way, Radlett, Herts], yst dau of Rev Canon Robert William Croft, Vicar Kelvedon, Essex, and *d* 18 Dec 1972, having had issue:

(1) Sir (JAMES) BROOKE FAIRBAIN, **6th and present Bt**

(2) +(William) Andrew [Andrew Fairbairn Esq, Midway Cottage, Norton, W Sussex PO20 6NJ]; *b* 28 Aug 1934; *educ* Stowe; FCA, MSI; *m* 6 May 1961 *Elspeth Alison, only dau of Robert Hally, of Brookfield, Barnham, Sussex, and has issue:

1a +James Andrew; *b* 20 Oct 1967; *m* 1994 *Samantha Jane, only dau of David Harwicke, of The Paddocks, Hurst, Berks, and has:

1b *Maddie Louise; *b* 24 Jan 1998

1a *Nicola Christine [Mrs Peter Gist, 16 Oakwood Rd, London NW11 6QY]; *b* 31 May 1962; *m* 1986 *Dr Peter Gist, s of F E Gist, of Honiton, Devon, and has issue:

1b *Duncan Edward; *b* 1989

1b *Rosemary Eleanor; *b* 1988

2b *Philippa Helen; *b* 1992

2a *Katharine Alison; *b* 22 Feb 1964

(1) Patricia Doreen; *b* 2 July 1927; *d* 9 April 1941

(2) Angela Christine; *b* 24 Jan 1940; *m* 11 Sept 1965 *Brooke Elliot Mackelcan Johns, ACA, er s of Jack Elliot Mackelcan Johns, and *d* 198–, leaving:

1a *Jeremy Elliot Mackelcan; *b* 14 June 1967

1 *Mildred Dorothy; *b* 26 March 1903

2 Rosalind Gordon; *b* 21 April 1905; *d* unm

3 *Constance Matilda; *b* 19 June 1908

FAIRFAX OF CAMERON

Arms: Or three bars gemels gules surmounted by a lion rampant sable. **Crest:** A lion passant-guardant sable. **Supporters:** Dexter, a lion guardant sable; sinister, a bay horse proper. **Motto:** *Fare, fac* ('Speak and act'). **Creation:** L. (S) 18 Oct 1627.

THE 14TH LORD FAIRFAX OF CAMERON (Nicholas John Albert Fairfax) [The Rt Hon The Lord Fairfax of Cameron, 10 Orlando Rd, London SW4 0LF]; *b* 4 Jan 1956; *s* f 1964; *educ* Eton and Downing Coll Cambridge (LLB 1981); barrister Gray's Inn 1977; *m* 17 April 1982 *Annabel Ruth, er dau of Henry Lester Louis Morriss (*see* JACKSON, Bt, of The Manor House, Birkenhead), and has:

1 +EDWARD NICHOLAS THOMAS; *b* 20 Sept 1984

2 +John Frederick Anthony; *b* 1986

3 +Rory Henry Francis; *b* 1991

Lineage: HENRY FAIRFAX; gf of:

RICHARD FAIRFAX, of Askham, Yorks; living 1205; ancestor of:

RICHARD FAIRFAX, of Walton, Yorks; living *temp* HENRY VI; *m* Anastatia (*m* 2nd Thomas Ridley), dau and heir of John Carthorpe, and had, with other issue:

1 William, of Walton; *m* Catherine, dau of Sir Humphrey Nevill(e), of Thornton Bridge (*see* ABERGAVENNY, M), and had:

(1) Thomas (Sir); *m* Anne, dau of Sir William Gascoigne, of Gawthorpe, Yorks, by Lady Margaret Percy, dau of 3rd Earl of Northumberland (*see* NORTHUMBERLAND, D), and had an est s:

1a Nicholas (Sir), of Walton and Gilling Castle, Yorks; Sheriff Yorks; *m* 1st Alice, dau of Sir John Harrington, but had no issue by her; *m* 2nd Jane, dau of Guy Palmes, of Lindley, Yorks, and *d* 1570, having had a yr s:

1b William (Sir); Sheriff Yorks 1540; *m* 1st Agnes, est dau of George, 1st Baron Darcy (of the 1548 *cr* or restoration of the attainted *cr* of 1529; there is some doubt as to which date his Barony was created), but had no issue by her; *m* 2nd Jane, dau of Bryan Stapleton, of Burton Joyce, Notts, and *d* 1 Nov 1597, having by her had an only s:

1c Sir THOMAS FAIRFAX, 1st VISCOUNT FAIRFAX OF EMMELEY, Co Tipperary (I), so *cr* 10 Feb 1628/9; *b* 1574; MP Boroughbridge 1601 and Hedon 1620–22 and 1624–26; ktd 1603, Sheriff Yorks 1627–28; *m* 1st *c* 1594 Katherine, sis of 1st Viscount Dunbar and dau of Henry Constable, of Burton Constable, Yorks; *m* 2nd *c* 1 Jan 1626/7 Mary, widow of Sir William Bamburgh, Bt, and dau of Robert Ford, of Butley, Suffolk, and *d* 23 Dec 1636, leaving by his 1st w, with other issue:

1d THOMAS FAIRFAX, 2nd VISCOUNT FAIRFAX OF EMMELEY; *b* *c* 1599; *m* Alathea, dau of Sir Philip Howard, of Naworth, Cumberland, s of Lord William Howard, s of 4th Duke of Norfolk (*qv*), and *d* 24 Sept 1641, leaving, with other issue:

1e WILLIAM FAIRFAX, 3rd VISCOUNT FAIRFAX OF EMMELEY; *b* 6 June 1620; *m* Elizabeth, dau of Alexander Smith, of Stutton, Suffolk, and *d* 1648, leaving, with a yr s (*d* young):

1f THOMAS FAIRFAX, 4th VISCOUNT FAIRFAX OF EMMELEY; *d* young and unm by 25 Feb 1650/1

1f Catherine; *b* *c* 1648; *m* 17th Lord (Baron) FitzWalter (*qv*) and *d* 20 March 1724/5, leaving issue

2e CHARLES FAIRFAX, 5th VISCOUNT FAIRFAX OF EMMELEY; *m* by 18 March 1664 Abigail, dau of Sir John Yate, 2nd Bt, of Buckland, Berks, and *dspm* 6 July 1771, leaving an only child:

1f Alathea; *m* 3rd Baron Widdrington

3e John; *m* Mary, dau of Col Thomas Hungate, s of Sir Philip Hungate, Bt, of Saxton

4e Nicholas; *m* Elizabeth, 4th dau of Sir Thomas Davison, of Blakiston, Co Durham, and widow of John Chaytor, of Croft, and had an est s:

1f Nicholas; *m* Mary, dau of William Weld, of Lulworth, Dorset, and *d* 26 Feb 1702/3, having had, with a dau (Mary; *m* as his 2nd w her cousin 9th and last VISCOUNT FAIRFAX OF EMMELEY, *see* below):

1g CHARLES FAIRFAX, 6th VISCOUNT FAIRFAX OF EMMELEY; *d* young and unm 23 Oct 1715

2f CHARLES FAIRFAX, 7th VISCOUNT FAIRFAX OF EMMELEY; *bapt* 25 April 1665; *d* unm 6 Jan 1718/9

2d Henry; *m* Frances, dau of Henry Baker, of Hurst, Berks, and had, with other issue:

1e Henry; *m* Frances, dau of Sir Thomas Browne, the author of *Religio Medici* and *Urn Burial*, and had:

1f Frances; *m* 1697, as his 1st w, 9th Earl of Buchan (*qv*) and *d* 31 July 1719, having had issue

3d William, of Lythe, Yorks; *m* Mary, dau of Marmaduke Cholmeley, of Brandsby, Yorks, and had, with an er s:

1e WILLIAM FAIRFAX, 8th VISCOUNT FAIRFAX OF EMMELEY; *m* Elizabeth, dau of Capt — Gerard, and was *bur* 5 Nov 1738, leaving:

1f CHARLES GREGORY FAIRFAX, 9th and last VISCOUNT FAIRFAX OF EMMELEY, of Gilling Castle; Ld of Manors of Walton, Gilling and others; *m* 1st 17 Nov 1719 Elizabeth (*dsp* 23 April 1721), est dau of 2nd Baron Clifford of Chudleigh (*qv*) and widow of William Constable, 4th Viscount Dunbar; *m* 2nd his cousin Mary (*see* above), sis of 6th VISCOUNT, and *dspms* 20 Jan 1772, when the Viscountcy expired, having had, with eight other children (*d* young):

1g Anne; inherited her f's estates; *d* unm 8 May 1793

1f Alathea; *m* Ralph Pigott and had:

1g Nathaniel; had:

1h Charles Gregory PIGOTT later FAIRFAX; inherited his cousin Anne's estates

1d Margaret; *m* 1st Watkinson Payler; *m* 2nd, as his 2nd or 3rd w, Sir John Hotham (*see* HOTHAM, B), but had no issue by him

1b Edward; *m* Ursula, dau of 2nd Lord (Baron) Mordaunt (*see* MORDAUNT, Bt)

2 Brian

3 Guy (Sir), of Steeton Castle, Yorks; Judge King's Bench 1477; *m* Isabel, dau of Sir Robert Ryther, of Ryther, and *d* 1495, leaving an er s:

(1) William, of Steeton and Bolton Percy; Judge Common Pleas 1509; *m* Elizabeth, est dau of Sir Robert Manners, ancestor of Duke of Rutland (*qv*), and *d* 1535, leaving an only s:

1a William (Sir); High Sheriff Yorks 1525 and 1540; *m* 1514 Isabella, dau and heir of Thomas Thwaites, of Denton Castle, Askwith, Yorks, and *d* 31 Oct 1557, leaving:

1b Thomas (Sir), of Denton and Nun Appleton, Yorks; *b* 1521; High Sheriff Yorks 1571, MP Yorks 1586–87; *m* Dorothy (*d* 20 Jan 1595/6), dau of George Gale, of Acomb Grange, goldsmith and Ld Mayor York 1534 and 1539, and widow of John Rokesby, and *d* 28 Jan 1599/1600, having had, with two daus:

1c THOMAS, **1st Lord**

2c Charles (Sir); Col; *ka* Siege of Ostend

3c Edward, of Newhall; poet and translator of Tasso

2b Gabriel; inherited Steeton; had:

1c Mary; *m* Thomas Gower, of Stittenham, Yorks, and had issue (*see* SUTHERLAND, D)

The est s,

Sir THOMAS FAIRFAX, **1st Lord Fairfax of Cameron** (S), so *cr* 18 Oct 1627; *b* 1560; cmded a regt in Low Countries, MP Lincoln 1586–87, Aldborough 1588–89 and Yorks 1601 and 1625, ktd 1591, envoy to JAMES VI of Scots before his accession as JAMES I of England, memb Cncl North; *m* 1582 Ellen (*d* 23 Aug 1620), dau of Robert Aske, of Aughton, Yorks, and *d* 2 May 1640, having had, with other issue:

1 FERDINANDO FAIRFAX, **2nd Lord Fairfax of Cameron**; *b* 29 March 1584; ktd Jan 1607/8, MP Boroughbridge 1614, 1620–22, 1624–26, 1628–29 and 1640 and Yorks 1640–48; Parly Gen (of forces in north) Civil War, won Marston Moor 1644 with his s, Govr York 1644–48; *m* 1st 1607 Lady Mary Sheffield (*bur* 4 June 1619), dau of 1st Earl of Mulgrave (*see* NORMANBY, M, preliminary remarks), and had, with other issue:

(1) THOMAS FAIRFAX, **3rd Lord Fairfax of Cameron**; *b* 17 Jan 1611/2; ktd Jan 1640/1, Parly Gen of Horse 1642, participated in victory of Marston Moor 1644 with f, C-in-C Parly Army Jan 1644/5–50, winning victories over royalists at Naseby 14 June 1645 and Langport 10 July 1645, then capturing Bridgwater, Bristol, Dartmouth, Exeter and Oxford; Constable Tower London 1647–50; MP Cirencester 1648/9–53, W R Yorks 1654–55 and Yorks 1659 and 1660; memb Cncl State 1649–51 and 1659–60; Ld IoM 1652–60; supported Restoration; *m* 20 June 1637 Anne (*d* 16 Oct 1665), dau and coheir of 1st Baron Vere of Tilbury (*see* SAINT ALBANS, D), and *d* 12 Nov 1671, having had issue:

1a Mary; *m* 15 Sept 1657 2nd Duke of Buckingham (*see* JERSEY, E) and *dsp* 20 Oct 1704

2a Elizabeth; *d* an infant 1642

(2) Charles; *b* 22 March 1614/15; *ka* Marston Moor 7 July 1644

(1) Ellen; *m* Sir William Selby, and *d* 17 March 1671

(2) Frances; *m* Sir Thomas Widdrington and *d* 4 May 1649, leaving issue

(3) Elizabeth; *m* 1st 30 March 1646 Sir William Craven (*d* 1655) and had issue; *m* 2nd Capt Thomas Prior (*d* 1690), of Essex and Rathdowney, Queen's Co

(4) Mary; *m* 24 May 1638 Henry Arthington, and *d* Dec 1678, leaving issue

(5) Dorothy; *m* Richard Hutton and *d* 7 June 1687, leaving issue

1 (cont.) The **2nd Lord** *m* 2nd 16 Oct 1646 Rhoda (*bur* 11 Oct 1686), dau and heir of Thomas Chapman and widow of Thomas Hussey, and *d* 14 March 1647/8, having had further issue:

(6) Ursula; *m* 1669 William Cartwright, of Aynho, and *d* 25 July 1702, leaving issue

2 Henry (Rev), of Oglethorpe, Yorks; Rector Bolton Percy; *m* 1st 27 Sept 1623 Katherine (*d* 24 Dec 1623), dau of Richard Dukenfield, of Dukenfield, Cheshire, and widow of John Tempest, of Tong; *m* 2nd 4 Feb 1626/7 Mary (*d* 8 Jan 1650), dau of Sir Henry Cholmeley, of Roxby, Yorks, and *d* 6 April 1665, having by her had issue:

(1) Thomas; *b* 7 March 1627/8; *d* unm 28 April 1640

(2) HENRY, **4th Lord**

(3) Bryan; *b* 6 Oct 1633; LLD Cambridge; *m* 22 April 1675 Charlotte (*d* 14 Nov 1709), dau and heir of Sir Edmund Cary, and *d* 20 Sept 1711, leaving issue

3 Charles, of Minsington, Yorks; *b* 5 March 1597; barrister, Col, Govr Hull; *m* Mary (*d* Oct 1657), dau and heir of John Breary, of Scow Hall, Minsington, and *d* 22 Dec 1673, leaving issue

1 Dorothy; *m* 15 Feb 1608 Sir William Constable, Bt (*dsp* 15 June 1655), and *d* 9 March 1655/6

2 Anne; *m* George Wentworth, of Wolley, Yorks, and *d* 19 Aug 1624

The 3rd LORD's cousin,

HENRY FAIRFAX, **4th Lord Fairfax of Cameron**; *b* 20 Dec 1631; MP (Tory) Yorks 16798–81; *m* Frances (*d* 14 Feb 1683/4), dau and heir of Sir Robert Barwick, of Toulston, Yorks, and *d* 9 April 1688, having had, with other issue:

1 THOMAS FAIRFAX, **5th Lord Fairfax of Cameron**; *b* 16 April 1657; MP (Tory) Malton 1685–87 and Yorks 1689–1702 and Jan-Aug 1707, Lt-Col 3rd Horse Gds 1689, Brig-Gen 1701/2; *m* *c* 1685 Catherine (*d* 1719), dau and heir of 2nd Baron Colepeper of Thoresway, Govr Virginia 1675–82, and heiress of 300,000 acres in the Shenandoah Valley there as well as Leeds Castle, Kent, and *d* 6 Jan 1709/10, having had, with another s and two other daus:

(1) THOMAS FAIRFAX, **6th Lord Fairfax of Cameron**; *bapt* 31 Oct 1692; settled in Virginia 1749, Lt Frederick Co there; *d* unm at his plantation of Greenway Court, nr Winchester, Va., which he had built himself, 9 Dec 1789

(2) ROBERT FAIRFAX, **7th Lord Fairfax of Cameron**; *b* 1707; Maj 1st Life Gds; MP Maidstone 1740–41 and 1747–54 and Kent 1754–68; *m* 1st 25 April 1741 Martha, dau and heir of Anthony Collins, of Baddow, Essex; *m* 2nd 15 July 1749 Dorothy (*d* 21 May 1750), dau of Mawditsly Best, of Boxley, Kent, and *dsps* 15 July 1793

(1) Margaret; *m* 15 Nov 1725 Rev David Wilkins, DD, and *dsp* 30 March 1755

(2) Frances; *m* Denny Martin (*see* Introduction, AMERICAN PRESIDENTIAL FAMILIES, 1994, Morris Genealogical Books SA) and *d* 13 Dec 1791, leaving issue, who inherited the Leeds Castle estate

2 Henry, of Toulston; *b* 20 April 1659; High Sheriff Yorks 1691; *m* 17 Sept 1684 Anne, dau and coheir of Richard Harison, and *d* 1708, leaving, with other issue:

(1) William, of Belvoir, Va.; *bapt* 30 Oct 1691; Govr Bahamas, agent Fairfax estates Virginia; *m* 1st 27 March 1717 Sarah (*d* 18 Jan 1731), dau of Maj Thomas Walker, Ch Justice Bahamas, and had issue:

1a George William, of Toulston and Bath, Somerset; *b* 1724; *m* 17 Dec 1748 Sarah (*d* 2 Nov 1811), dau of Col Wilson Cary, of Ceelys, Virginia, and *dsp* 3 April 1787

2a Thomas; Midshipman RN; *ka* unm 26 June 1746

1a Anne; *b* 1728; *m* 1st 19 July 1743 Lawrence Washington (*d* 22 July 1752), half-bro of Gen GEORGE WASHINGTON, 1st Pres USA (*see* section Washington, AMERICAN PRESIDENTIAL FAMILIES, 1994, Morris Genealogical Books SA); *m* 2nd 16 Dec 1752 Col George Lee, of Virginia (*see* Ibid.), and *d* 14 March 1761, leaving:

2a Sarah; *m* Maj John Carlyle, of Alexandria, Va., and had:

1b Sarah; *m* William Herbert and had:

1c Margaret; *m* as his 3rd w her cousin *de jure* 9th LORD FAIRFAX OF CAMERON (*see* below)

(1) (cont) William Fairfax *m* 2nd 28 Oct 1731 Deborah, dau of Francis Clarke, of Salem, Mass., and *d* 3 Sept 1757, having by her had further issue:

3a BRYAN, **8th Lord**

4a William Henry; Offr 28th Regt; *ka* unm Gen Wolfe's capture of Quebec 1759

3a Hannah; *m* Warner Washington, cousin to Gen GEORGE WASHINGTON (*see* op. cit.), and had issue
(1) Dorothy; *m* 1731 Henry Chapman, and had issue
1 Dorothy; *m* 1st Robert Stapleton; *m* 2nd Bennet Sherard and *d* 1744, leaving issue
2 Frances; *m* 26 Oct 1686 Rev Nicholas Rymer and *d* 1723
3 Anne; *m* 2 Sept 1690 Ralph Carr and had issue

The 7th LORD's cousin,

Rev BRYAN FAIRFAX, **8th Lord Fairfax of Cameron**; *b* 1737; loyalist in War American Independence; ordained 1789, lived at Mount Eagle, nr Cameron, Va.; chief mourner at funeral of his kinsman GEORGE WASHINGTON; right to title confirmed by Ho Lds 6 May 1800; *m* 1st 1759 Elizabeth (*d* 1778), yst dau of Col Wilson Cary, of Ceelys, Va.; *m* 2nd Jane Dennison and *d* 7 Aug 1802, having by his 1st w had, with other issue:
1 THOMAS, *de jure* 9th LORD
2 Ferdinando; *b* 1766; *m* 1796 his cousin Elizabeth Blair (*d* 19 Jan 1822), dau of Col Wilson Miles Cary, of Ceelys, Virginia, and *d* 24 Sept 1820, leaving issue:
(1) George William; *b* 5 Nov 1797; *m* Nov 1815 Isabella, dau of Maj W Gibbs MacNeill, of New York, and had:
1a Donald MacNeill; *b* 1821; R-Adml USN, the only one of his family who sided with the North in the American Civ War; *m* 1st 1854 Virginia Cary (*d* 1878), dau of Thomas Ragland, and had issue:
1b William MacNeill; *b* 1858; *d* unm 1928
1a (cont.) R-Adml Donald Fairfax *m* 2nd 1879 Josephine, dau of R-Adml A H Foote, USN, and *d* 1894
(2) Wilson Miles Cary, of Washington, DC; *b* 1 Dec 1798; *m* 2 March 1824 his cousin Lucy Anna (*d* Jan 1861), dau of Rev David Griffith, of Virginia, and *d* 8 Aug 1860, leaving, with three other sons and two other daus:
1a Llewellyn; *b* 23 Sept 1826; *dsp* & *vp*, drowned in the Potomac
2a Frederick, of Alexandria, Va., and Washington, DC; *b* 26 Sept 1835; *m* 14 Jan 1868 Mary Allen (*d* 1909), dau of John Aquila Cooke, Lt-Col USN, and *d* 5 March 1904, having had issue:
1b Lilian Vere; *b* 1869; *d* unm 1938
2b Gwendolin Owner; *b* 1871; *m* 1916 Jacquelin Ambler Moncure, MD, of Washington, DC (*d* 1917), and *d* 2 July 1938
3b Evelyn Leopoldine; *d* unm 18 Sept 1896
1a Emily Cary; *b* 15 Dec 1824; *m* 15 May 1848 Rt Rev F Whittle, DD, LLD, Bp Virginia, and *d* 19 March 1894, leaving issue
2a Alice; *b* 28 Sept 1839; *m* L Lyne, banker, of Henderson, Kentucky, and *dsp* May 1866
(3) Ferdinando; *b* 9 Jan 1803; MD; *m* 1st 11 Jan 1831 Mary Anne (*d* 6 May 1848), dau of B Jett, and had issue:
1a Ferdinando; *b* 21 Sept 1832; *dsp*
2a William Henry; *b* 10 Dec 1834; MD; *m* 26 Feb 1866 Eleanor (*d* 1922), dau of E C Griffith, and *d* 3 April 1907, having had issue:
1b Frederick Griffith; *b* 25 Oct 1867; *m* 29 April 1903 his cousin Mary Fernando (*d* 18 Feb 1961), dau of Capt Edmund L Wharton, and *d* June 1948, leaving issue:
1c William Henry; *b* 27 Oct 1904; *m* 21 Nov 1936 *Grace Woodson, of Atlanta, Ga., and *d* 27 Aug 1969, leaving:
1d *Gloria Lucille [Mrs Bonnie Rowe, 5085 Evin Rd, Atlanta, GA 3031, USA]; *b* 8 Sept 1938; *m* 1st 5 Nov 1956 (*divorce* 1961) Burton A Greer and has:
1e *Susan Rebecca Greer; *b* 11 May 1958
1d (cont.) Mrs Gloria Greer *m* 2nd 17 Feb 1962 *Bonnie Gordon Rowe
2c Edmund Wharton; *b* 1914; US Army; *m* 1943 *Nancy [Mrs E W Fairfax, The Hague, VA 22469, USA], dau of James L King, of Pittsburg, and *d* 30 June 1966, leaving issue:
1d +Edmund Wharton [Edmund W Fairfax, The Hague, VA 22469, USA]; *b* 1944
2d +Bryan Griffith; *b* 13 Jan 1959
1d *Jean Anne [Mrs Charles W Fallin, PO Box 145, Hague, VA 22469, USA]; *b* 6 July 1951; *m* May 1969 *Charles W Fallin, and has issue:
1e *Mary Ann [Mrs John Maine, 4829 Southwind Dve, Kingsport, TN 37664, USA]; *b* 23 Dec 1969; *educ* Virginia Poly Inst and State U; industrial engr; *m* 25 June 1994 *John Tennison Maine, and has:
1f *Jacob Tennison; *b* 18 Feb 1997
2d *Barbara Jane; *b* 26 May 1953
3c +Frederick Griffith; *b* 1916; *m* 1st 1940 (*divorce* 1956) Dorothy Brooke, and has issue:
1d +Frederick Griffith [Frederick Fairfax, RRI Box 4, Hague, Virginia, USA]; *b* 1947
2d +William [William H Fairfax, RRI Box 4, Hague, Virginia, USA]; *b* 1950
1d *(Dorothy) Eleanor Griffith; *b* 1946; *m* 19– *— Demastus
2d *Ada Carter; *b* 1949; *m* 19– *— Wright
3d *Grace Kate [Mrs Grace Fairfax, RRI Box 4, Hague, Virginia, USA]; *b* 1952; retained maiden name; *m* twice and has issue by 2nd husb:
1e *Mary Lynette; *b* 1960; *m* 19– *— Roane
3c (cont.) Frederick Fairfax *m* 2nd 1957 *Annette Aiken, of Atlanta
1c *Edith Wharton; *b* 1 Dec 1906; *m* 1933 Harold Benjamin Lang (*d* 1962) and has:
1d *Ann Fairfax; *b* 1936; *m* 1958 *Virgil A Ponzoli, MD, and has:
1e *Linda Marie; *b* 1960
2e *Patricia; *b* 1961
3e *Susanne Joan; *b* 1963
4e *Amy Carolyn; *b* 1968
2c *Fernando Griffith; *b* 16 June 1908
3c *Annie Staunton [Mrs Edward Greco, 2314 Grove Avenue, Falls Church, Virginia, USA]; *b* 20 July 1911; *m* 1933 *Edward Greco and has:
1d *Edward Fairfax; *b* 1935; *m* 27 Aug 1966 *Barbara Ruth Gomez, of Rio Vista, Calif., and has:
1e *William Edward Fairfax; *b* 1972
1e *Michelle Anne; *b* 1968
2d *Frederick Dominic [Frederick Greco Esq, 6618 Ivy Hill Drive, McLean,VA 22101, USA]; *b* 1937; *m* 1962 *Carole Ann Drake, of Falling Waters, West Virginia, and has issue:
1e *William Scott; *b* 1969
2e *Michael Drake; *b* 1972
4c *Katherine Rambsey [Miss Katherine Fairfax, La Grange, The Hague, Virginia, USA]; *b* 1919
2b Colville Lee; *b* 17 Jan 1877
1a Emma; *m* 23 Dec 1870 James Chandler and had issue
2a Ella Louisa; *m* 1881 Capt Edmund L Wharton and had issue
(3) (cont.) Dr Ferdinando Fairfax *m* 2nd 28 Nov 1855 Mary Jane (*d* 15 July 1864), dau of James Jett, and *d* 30 Dec 1873, having by her had issue:
3a Ferdinand; *b* 3 Nov 1859; *dsp*
3a Evangeline May; *m* 23 Dec 1881 N W Boyd, of Portsmouth, Arkansas, and had issue
4a Mary Jett; *m* 30 May 1882 William Henderson Musser, of Danvers, Mass., and had issue
5a Ethel Blair; *b* 8 May 1861; *m* 13 Dec 1881 William C Van Hook (*d* 3 Oct 1946), and *d* 3 Dec 1934, leaving issue
6a Ada Susan; *m* 4 Oct 1892 Allan Monroe Chandler, of Montross, Westmoreland Co, Virginia, and had issue
(4) Archibald Blair; *b* 22 May 1809; Cdr USN, Confederate States Navy 1861–65; *m* 1st Nov 1832 Sarah Carlyle (*d* 23 Jan 1850), dau of Hon J C Herbert, and had issue:
1a Eugene; *b* 26 May 1838; Confederate States Army; *ka* Williamsburg 2 May 1862
2a Julian; *b* 14 Dec 1841; *educ* U of Virginia (MA); Midshipman Confederate States Navy 1861–65; *d* unm Jan 1877
3a Archibald Carlyle; *b* 24 Aug 1843; 17th Va Inf (Stonewall Bde) Confederate States Army 1861–65; *m* 30 April 1873 Virginia Caroline (*m* 2nd 29 Nov 1892 Henry Byrd Lewis (*d* 1917), of Cleve Manor, King George Co, and Fowkes, Port Conway, Va., and *d* 18 May 1922), dau of W H Redwood, and *d* 4 Aug 1879, leaving issue:
1b John Carlyle; *b* 22 Dec 1874; Lt-Col, Spanish War 1898 (medal), Philippine Insurrection 1901–02 (medal), Pulahan Campaign Philippines 1905–06, WW I France 1918–19 (three bronze stars); *m* 1909 Winifred Mary (*d* June 1960), dau of Lt-Col Otis Wheeler Pollock, US Army, and *d* 21 April 1944, leaving issue:
1c John Pollock; *b* 18 Feb 1911; *m* 22 Feb 1935 *Dorothy Elsa, dau of Reginald Charles Steeple, of California, and *d* 1983, leaving issue:
1d *Dorothy Anne [Mrs Jack Margolis, 1520 Middlefield Rd, Palo Alto, Calif. 94301, USA]; *b* 29 Aug 1936; *m* 1st 4 Aug 1956 (*divorce* 1961) Frederick W Timby, Jr, s of Frederick W Timby, of Palo Alto, and has issue:
1e *Jeffrey William Fairfax; *b* 24 Aug 1957
2e *Christopher Cory; *b* 16 Oct 1959
1d (cont) Mrs Dorothy Timby *m* 2nd 9 April 1961 (*divorce* 1973) Henry Mohr Hermann, of San Francisco, and has further issue:
1e *Susan Mohr; *b* 30 April 1963
1d (cont) *Mrs Dorothy Hermann *m* 3rd 1974 *Jack Margolis
2d *Jain Pollock [Mrs Michael Langston, 2790 South Reed St, Denver, CO 80227, USA]; *b* 2 Sept 1937; *m* 1st 14 Feb 1960 (*divorce* 1968) John Phillip De Angeles, s of John De Angeles, of Atherton, Calif., and has:
1e *Melissa Jain; *b* 7 Feb 1962
2e *Jenna Lynne; *b* 12 April 1963
2d (cont) Mrs Jain De Angeles *m* 2nd 9 Aug 1968 (*divorce*) Terry Ernest Jamison, of Charleston, SC; *m* 3rd 1983 *Michael Langston, of Denver
1c *Sallie Virginia; *b* 29 March 1912; *m* 11 Aug 1934 Paul Nyeland, s of Knud Nyeland, of San Mateo, Calif., and has:
1d *David Fairfax; *b* 27 Jan 1936; *m* 12 April 1962 *Beverly Louise, dau of Frederick Bachich, of Yellow Pine, Idaho
1d *Nancy Hoff; *b* 1 Dec 1938; *m* 1957 *Robert Harlow Leekley, and has issue
2b William Redwood; *b* 3 Dec 1876; *d* 29 March 1952
(4) (cont.) Cdr Archibald Fairfax *m* 2nd 2 March 1852 Eliza Mary, dau of Rev O Norris, and *d* 3 Jan 1867, having by her had further issue:
4a Edward Herbert; *b* 11 Dec 1852; *dsp* 1878
5a Llewellyn Cary; *b* 28 Aug 1855; *m* 1880 Priscilla Hall, dau of R Wright, MD
6a Arthur Percy; *b* 2 Feb 1857; *m* 1st 2 Feb 1882 Nancy Hunter (*dsp* 1919), dau of Judge John Blair Hoge, of Martinsburg, W Virginia; *m* 2nd 1919 Mary, dau of James C Alexander Hamilton Hyland, of Maryland, USA, and widow of Charles E Ways, and *dsp* Nov 1925
1 Elizabeth; *m* Rev David Griffith, and had issue

The 8th LORD's er son,

THOMAS FAIRFAX, *de jure* 9th LORD FAIRFAX OF CAMERON (never assumed the title or took steps to establish his right thereto), of Vaucluse, Fairfax Co, Va.; *b* 1762; *m* 1st Nov 1795 Mary Aylett (*dsp* 30 April 1796); *m* 2nd Feb 1798 Louisa (*dsp* 28 April 1798), dau of Warner Washington (*see* section Washington, op. cit.); *m* 3rd 31 Dec 1800 his cousin Margaret (*d* 7 March 1858), only dau of William Herbert, of Alexandria, Va., by Sarah, dau of Maj John Carlyle, also of Alexandria, by Sarah, dau of William Fairfax, of Belvoir (*see* above), and *d* 21 April 1846, having by her had issue:
1 Albert, of Vaucluse; *b* 15 April 1802; *m* 8 April 1828 Caroline Eliza (*m* 2nd William G Sanders and *d* 28 Dec 1899), dau of Richard Snowden, of Oakland, Md, and *dvp* 9 May 1835, leaving issue:

(1) CHARLES SNOWDEN FAIRFAX, *de jure* 10th LORD FAIRFAX OF CAMERON (never assumed title and took no steps to establish his right thereto); *b* 8 March 1829; migrated to California 1851, Speaker Ho Delegates California 1854, Clerk Supreme Court California 1857–62; *m* 10 Jan 1855 Ada (*d* 26 Sept 1888), 2nd dau of Joseph S Benham, lawyer, of Cincinnati, Ohio, and *dsp* Baltimore 4 April 1869
(2) JOHN CONTÉE, *de jure* 11th LORD
2 Henry, of Ashgrove; *b* 4 May 1804; *m* 1827 Anna Caroline, dau of Hon John C Herbert, of Alexandria, and *d* 14 Aug 1847, leaving issue:
(1) Raymond; civ engr; *b* 19 July 1829; *m* 7 Jan 1865 Anna, dau of Sylvester L Burford, of Virginia, and *d* 6 March 1907, having had issue:
1a Ronald Randolph; *b* 22 Aug 1870; *m* 1901 Annie Ridge (*d* 10 Oct 1964), dau of Charles Early, of Washington, DC, and *d* March 1961, having had:
1b Ronald Randolph; *b* 1902; *d* an inf
2a Guy Percy; *b* 21 Feb 1872; *m* 1900 Elgie Ida (*d* 10 July 1962), dau of James D Crook, of New York, and *d* 18 Nov 1943 leaving issue:
1b Alice Monimia; *b* 13 Dec 1908; BA; *m* 17 Oct 1931 Samuel Miller Stone, Jr, and *d* 28 Feb 1971, leaving two daus
3a Henry Reginald; *b* 2 Aug 1875; MD; *m* 1907 Nell Virginia (*d* 6 Dec 1956), dau of Marion O Randolph, of Williamson, W Virginia, and *d* Feb 1954, leaving issue:
1b +Reginald Randolph; *b* 25 Dec 1908; *m* June 1934 *Genevieve, dau of J W McKee, of Brookhaven, Miss.
2b +Ronald Cary; *b* 22 Feb 1915; *m* 9 Oct 1954 *Judith Victoria, dau of Jonathan Breckenridge Stovall, of Virginia
1b *Marion Avery; *b* 24 July 1918; *m* 1943 *Colin Freeman Baker, Jr, MD, and has issue
2b Edith Virginia; *b* 28 Aug 1927; *d* 31 May 1928
1a Isabell Christian; *m* John Winfree, of Lynchburg, Virginia
2a Ada Raymond; *m* 1921 Cleland Messerve, of Alderwood Manor, Washington State, and *d* 1950
3a Monimia; *m* William A Tanner, and *d* 1926
(2) Albert; *b* 4 June 1836; *d* unm
(3) Herbert Carlyle; *b* 29 April 1838; *m* 3 June 1861 Jane Davies, dau of Dr Frederick Baker, and had issue:
1a Eugenia Chalmers
2a Caroline Herbert
(4) Henry Malcolm; *b* 9 Oct 1849; *d* unm 1928
(1) Mary Isabel; *d* unm 9 July 1851
(2) Eugenia; *d* young
3 Orlando; *b* 1806; MD; *m* 21 May 1829 his cousin Mary Randolph, dau of Wilson Jefferson Cary, of Carysbrook, VA, and *d* 1882, leaving, with other issue:
(1) Monimia; *m* 1866 G Davis, and *d* July 1888
(2) Mary Edith; *m* 1877 Dr J J Moncure, and *dsp* 1916
4 Reginald; *b* 1822; Cdr USN; *d* unm July 1862
1 Eugenia; *m* 1st Edgar Mason; *m* 2nd Charles Keith Hyde, and had issue
2 Aurelia; *m* 1852 Col James W Irwin, of Washington, DC, and had issue
3 Monimia; *m* 15 Nov 1838 Archibald Cary, of Virginia (*d* 1854), and had issue

The 10th LORD's brother,

JOHN CONTÉE FAIRFAX, *de jure* 11th LORD FAIRFAX OF CAMERON (never assumed title or took steps to establish his right thereto); *b* 13 Sept 1830; MD, practising (as Dr Fairfax) at Northampton, Bladensburg, Md.; *m* 8 Oct 1857 Mary Brown (*d* 14 March 1912), dau of Col Edmund Kirby, US Army, and *d* 28 Sept 1900, having had:
1 ALBERT KIRBY, **12th Lord**
2 Charles Edmund; *b* 29 April 1876; *m* 19 Feb 1920 Lillian Newton, dau of William Lawrence Hobitzell, and *dsp* 1947
1 Caroline Snowden; *b* 20 Aug 1858; *d* 12 March 1924
2 Josephine; *m* 1892 Tunstall Smith, of Baltimore, Md. (*d* 8 May 1926), and *d* 1951, leaving issue
3 Mary Cecilia; *d* unm 28 Feb 1935
4 Frances Marvin; *m* 1st 1903 Edward Lowndes Rhett, of Brooklyn, NY (*d* 12 Dec 1913); *m* 2nd 18 June 1917 Clarence Meredith Roberts (*d* 1940), of Inglewood, Landover, Md., and *d* 1951

The 11th LORD's er son,

ALBERT KIRBY FAIRFAX, **12th Lord Fairfax of Cameron**; *b* 23 June 1870; naturalised UK citizen and established claim to title with Ho Lds 17 Nov 1908, rep S peer 1917, memb Fairfax & Co, of George Street, London EC, ptnr Bonbright & Co, George St; *m* 19 Jan 1922 Maud Wishart (*m* 2nd 22 Oct 1947 Maj Cecil Rookhurst Wigan, MC, Welsh Gds (*d* 23 Oct 1958), only s of Harold Wigan, of Belmont Park, Bedhampton; *m* 3rd 12 April 1962 Brig Felix Alexander Vincent Copland-Griffiths, DSO, MC, KStJ, Welsh Gds (*d* 10 April 1967), yst s of Arthur Edward Copland-Griffiths, of Meadow Bank Grange, Melksham, Wilts, and *d* 18 Sept 1973), dau of James McKelvie, of Duckyls Park, E Grinstead, and *d* 4 Oct 1939, having had issue:
1 THOMAS BRIAN McKELVIE, **13th Lord**
2 +Peregrine John Wishart [The Hon Peregrine Fairfax, Mindrum, Northumberland]; *b* 8 March 1925; *educ* Eton and Trin Coll Cambridge; late Lt 12th Roy Lancers; *m* 5 Oct 1965 *Virginia Alexandra de L'Etang, yr dau of Hon Philip Leyland Kindersley (*see* KINDERSLEY, B), and has issue:
(1) +Thomas Philip; *b* 10 May 1966; *educ* Eton
(1) *Doune Alexandra Wishart; *b* 31 May 1968

The 12th LORD's er son,

THOMAS BRIAN McKELVIE FAIRFAX, **13th Lord Fairfax of Cameron**; *b* 14 May 1923; *educ* Eton; Lt Gren Gds, rep S peer 1945–58, PPS to Ld Pres Cncl 1951, Assist Whip (C) Ho Lds 1947–54, Ld-in-Waiting 1954–57; *m* 17 April 1951 *Sonia Helen , JP (Berks 1957), T/Ldy Bedchamber to HM THE QUEEN 1967, yr dau of Capt Cecil Bernard Gunston, MC (*see* GUNSTON, Bt), and *d* 8 April 1964, having had issue:
1 NICHOLAS JOHN ALBERT FAIRFAX, **14th and present Lord Fairfax of Cameron**
2 +Hugh Nigel Thomas; *b* 29 March 1958; *educ* Eton; *m* 25 Feb 1984 *Victoria Janet, er dau of Digby John Sheffield Neave (*see* NEAVE, Bt) and has:
(1) +Alexander Thomas Digby; *b* 1986
(1) *Laura Jane Ulla; *b* 1987
(2) *Marina; *b* 1989
3 +Rupert Alexander James; *b* 21 Jan 1961; additional assist Priv Sec to HRH THE PRINCE OF WALES 1986–88
1 *Serena Frances; *b* 12 Dec 1952; *m* 17 July 1976 *(William) Robert Geoffrey Bell, est s of William Archibald Ottley Juxon Bell, of Cottisford House, Brackley, Northants, and has issue:
(1) *William Thomas D; *b* 1986
(1) *Francesca Rose; *b* 1982

FAIRHAVEN

Arms: Argent two bars and in the dexter chief point a saltire couped gules. **Crest:** In front of a bull's head erased sable, collared and chained or, three fleur-de-lys gold. **Supporters:** On either side a winged bull sable, each armed and gorged with a chain or, pendant therefrom an escutcheon charged with the arms of Broughton. **Motto:** *Si je puis* ('If I can'). **Creation:** B. (UK) 25 July 1961.

THE 3RD BARON FAIRHAVEN, of Anglesey Abbey, Cambridgeshire (Ailwyn Henry George Broughton, JP (Cambs 1975), DL (Cambs and Isle of Ely 1973)) [The Rt Hon The Lord Fairhaven JP DL, Anglesey Abbey, Cambridge, Cambs CB5 9EJ]; *b* 16 Nov 1936; *s f* 6 April 1973; *educ* Eton and RMA Sandhurst; RHG 1955–71 (ret as Maj), V-Ld Lt Cambs 1977–84, memb Jockey Club 1977 (Sr Steward 1985–89), Kt of White Rose of Finland 1970, CStJ 1983; *m* 23 Sept 1960 *Kathleen Patricia, er dau of Col James Henry Magill, OBE, Coldstream Gds, of Queen's House, Ousden, Newmarket, Suffolk, and has issue:
1 +JAMES HENRY AILWYN; *b* 25 May 1963; *educ* Harrow and RMA Sandhurst; late Maj Blues and Royals; *m* 1990 *Sarah Olivia, dau of Harold Digby Fitzgerald Creighton, of Upper Brook St, London W1, and has issue:
(1) +George Ailwyn James; *b* 1997
(1) *Sophie Rose; *b* 1992
(2) *Emily Patricia; *b* 1995
2 +Huttleston Rupert; *b* 16 May 1970; *educ* Eton
3 +Charles Leander; *b* 12 July 1973; *educ* Eton
4 +Henry Robert; *b* 2 Oct 1978
1 *Diana Cara; *b* 28 Aug 1961; *m* 1st 24 Oct 1983 (*divorce*) Guy Dominic Thornton (*see* ESHER, V) and has issue; *m* 2nd 1991, as his 3rd w, *Alan Brodie Henderson
2 *Melanie Frances; *b* 23 Aug; *m* 1st 1989 (*divorce* 1992) Matthew Eric Smith and has issue (*see* HILL-WOOD, Bt); *m* 2nd 19– *Andrew Edgar and by him has:
(1) *Archie; *b* 1997
(1) *Alice Isobel; *b* 1995

Lineage: BERIOGE BROUGHTON, of N Kilworth, Leics; *b c* 1545; *m* 3 May 1568 Agnes Focill (*d* Dec 1618) and *d* June 1619, leaving issue:

THOMAS BROUGHTON, of Thurnby, Leics; *bapt* 30 Nov 1578; *m* 1st 26 Sept 1613 Elizabeth French (*d* 15 March 1628) and had issue; *m* 2nd 16 Aug 1629 Agnes Penn, widow, and by her had issue, with an est s (*d* young) and two daus:

FRANCIS BROUGHTON, of Wigston Magna and later Husbands Bosworth, Leics; *bapt* 1 Dec 1633; *m* Elizabeth — and had, with other issue:

THOMAS BROUGHTON, of Gilmorton, Leics; *bapt* 2 July 1673; *m* 13 May 1695 Mary Loomes (*d* 1719) and *d* Dec 1714, having had, with other issue:

ROBERT BROUGHTON, of Gilmorton; *bapt* 2 Nov 1707; *m* 14 Oct 1732 Hannah Newton (*d* Aug 1786) and *d* July 1754, leaving, with other issue:

THOMAS BROUGHTON, of Gilmorton; *bapt* 23 March 1734; *m* 6 Nov 1763 Frances Wood (*d* Sept 1831) and *d* Dec 1815, leaving an est surv s:

THOMAS BROUGHTON, of Gilmorton; *bapt* 25 Aug 1765; *m* 11 Sept 1786 Ann Deacon (*d* Oct 1835) and *d* June 1848, having had, with other issue:

DANIEL BROUGHTON, of Leeds, Yorks; *b* 16 March 1788; *m* Ann Groocock and had, with other issue:

JOHN BROUGHTON, of Farnall Heath, Worcs; *b* 30 March 1831; rlwy manager; *m* 26 Sept 1854 Abigail Elizabeth (*d* 10 Jan 1919), dau of Edward O'Hanlon, of Belle Vue, Manningham, Yorks, and *d* 22 April 1920, having had, with two other sons and three daus:

1 URBAN HANLON

1 Jessie Radcliffe; *m* 3 Aug 1880 Rev Llewellyn Walter Lloyd (*d* 7 Dec 1921), Vicar Ticknall, Derbys, and *d* 2 June 1921, leaving issue

2 Beatrice Clara; *m* 6 Jan 1884 Charles James Fox (*d* 1937), of Ladbroke Gdns, London, and *d* 24 June 1918, leaving issue

3 Annie Lilian Gwendoline; *m* 8 Aug 1906 John Amherst Walter (*d* 17 March 1951), formerly of Groton House, Walmer, Kent, and *d* 17 March 1953, leaving issue

JOHN BROUGHTON's est s,

URBAN HANLON BROUGHTON, of Park St, London W1, and Park Close, Englefield Green, Surrey; *b* 12 April 1857; *educ* Grove Pk Sch Wrexham and London U; engrg apprentice with Low and Thomas, civil and mining engrs, 1875–78, involved in various rail, dock and drainage projects throughout UK 1878–87 and USA (pres and dir: Virginia Rlwy, Utah Consolidaed Mining Co and Shone Co; v-pres, dir and gen man Utd Metals Selling Co; v-pres Nat Copper Bank of New York) 1887–1912, Lt Vol Forces 1883–85, Br memb judges6 panel World's Columbian Exposition 1892, MP (C) Preston 1915–18, AMICE 1883 (Miller Prizeman 1877); *m* 12 Nov 1895 Cara Leland, Lady (Baroness) Fairhaven (*d* 18 March 1939), dau of Henry Huttleston Rogers, of New York, and *d* 30 Jan 1929 (before his intended elevation to the peerage, but by roy warrant 2 May 1929 his w was allowed the same style and title as if her husb had recd the title and dignity of Baron Fairhaven, though without the statutory rights and privileges of a peer's widow), leaving issue:

1 URBAN HUTTLESTON ROGERS BROUGHTON, **1st Baron Fairhaven**, of Anglesey Abbey, Cambridge, so *cr* 25 July 1961, with special remainder to his yr bro and the latter's heirs male, as also earlier 20 March 1929 BARON FAIRHAVEN, of Lode, Cambridge (both UK), with ordinary remainder to heirs male of his own body, JP, DL; *b* 31 Aug 1896; *educ* Harrow and RMC Sandhurst; Lt 1st Life Gds 1916–24, Liaison Commr Red Cross and St John War Organisation WW II, Hon MA Cantab 1950, KStJ, FSA; *d* unm 20 Aug 1966, when the 1929 Barony expired

2 HENRY ROGERS BROUGHTON, **2nd Baron Fairhaven**, of Anglesey Abbey, Cambridge; *b* 1 Jan 1900; *educ* Harrow and RMC Sandhurst; Maj RHG; granted rank 2 May 1929 of baron's yr s; *m* 1st 28 June 1932 Hon Diana Rosamond (*d* 12 May 1937), only dau of Capt Hon Coulson Churchill Fellowes, 1st Life Gds (*see* DE RAMSEY, B), and had issue:

(1) AILWYN HENRY GEORGE ROGERS BROUGHTON, **3rd and present Baron Fairhaven**

2 (cont.) The **2nd Baron** *m* 2nd 14 March 1953 Joyce Irene (*m* 3rd 19 May 1982 V-Adml Sir Geoffrey Thistleton-Smith, KBE, and *d* 1989), dau of Edward Arthur Miller and widow of Lt Gerald Henry Charles Dickens, RN, and *d* 6 April 1973

Seat: Anglesey Abbey, Lode, Cambs. This was originally an Augustinian priory, founded in 1135, though the oldest part of the building to be converted to domestic use following the Reformation seems to have dated from rather later, that is to say the early 13th century. In any case it was not till the very end of ELIZABETH I's reign that the core of the present building started to take its basic L shape. In 1627 the estate was bought by the prosperous Cambridge carrier Thomas Hobson, whose policy of obliging his customers to hire only the horse available according to strict rotation among his stable of animals gave rise to the expression 'Hobson's Choice'. Yet another owner whose name gave rise to a popular expression was Sir George Downing, 3rd Bt, whose grandfather, the 1st Bt, had spent his youth in Massachusetts (his uncle John Winthrop being Governor there) and so impressed the other settlers with his untrustworthiness that such a man was called 'an arrant George Downing'. (He also gave his name to Downing Street.) The Sir George Downing who owned Anglesey founded Downing College Cambridge.

In the mid-19th century the then owner the Rev John Hailstone undertook drastic remodelling, chiefly to the north side. The south is thought to remain relatively untouched from the time when larger windows were inserted into the mid-13th century facade around 1600.

The **1st Baron Fairhaven** added a wing to house the library, also an art gallery connected to the main structure by a bridge, filling the whole with his varied and sumptuous art collection. The chief architect of the 20th-century alterations to the main house was Sidney Parvin. Sir Albert Richardson is responsible for the art gallery.

FAIRLIE-CUNINGHAME

Arms: Quarterly, 1st and 4th, argent a shake-fork between a bugle in chief and two castles in base sable (for CUNINGHAME); 2nd and 3rd, or a lion rampant, in chief three stars gules (for FAIRLIE). **Crests:** 1 A unicorn's head proper, armed or (for CUNINGHAME), 2 A lion's head or (for FAIRLIE). **Supporters:** Two knights in complete armour, holding in their exterior hands a baton or. **Mottoes:** 1 (over the crests) *Fortitudine* ('By fortitude'), 2 *Paratus sum* ('I am prepared'), 3 (under the arms) 'Over fork over'. **Creation:** Bt. (NS) 25 Nov 1630.

SIR WILLIAM HENRY FAIRLIE-CUNINGHAME, 16TH BT, of Robertland, Co Ayr [Sir William Fairlie-Cuninghame Bt, 29a Orinoco Rd, Pymble, NSW 2073, Australia]; *b* 1 Oct 1930; *s* f 1981; *m* 1972 *Janet Menzies, dau of Roy Menzies Saddington, and has issue:

1 +WILLIAM ROBERT; *b* 19 July 1974

Lineage: The 1st EARL OF GLENCAIRN (*see* CUNINGHAME, Bt) had a 2nd s:

WILLIAM CUNINGHAM, 1st of Craigends, Renfrewshire, and Robertland, Ayrshire (charter of latter 10 July 1506, confirmed by JAMES IV 1510); *m* 2nd (contract 12 March 1497/8) Marion, dau of Sir John Auchinleck of Auckinleck and widow of George Campbell, Sheriff of Ayr, and *d* by 19 June 1520, leaving a yr s:

DAVID CUNINGHAM of Robertland, Stewarton, Ayrshire (acquired 1530); had a Charter of Bartonholm incorporated in the Charter of the Free Barony of Robertland confirmed by JAMES V 5 March 1539/40; *m c* 22 Jan 1540/1 Margaret, dau of William, 2nd Laird of Craigends, and widow of Sir John Colquhoun of Luss (*see* COLQUHOUN, Bt), and *d* by 16 Jan 1543/4, leaving, with a yr s (Patrick, of Lochrig, living 1597):

DAVID CUNINGHAM of Robertland; a minor 1544; *m* 1st Elizabeth, dau of William Cunningham of Glengarnock and widow of John Schaw of Greenock, and had issue; *m* 2nd March 1555/6 Grizel (*d* 16 Feb 1562/3), dau of James Hamilton of Stenhouse by Grizel, er dau of 3rd Lord Sempill (*qv*), and *d c* 1 Dec 1592, having by her had a dau (Jane, *m* John Hamilton in Glengarwell and had issue); his s by his 1st w:

Sir DAVID CUNINGHAM of Robertland; minor on succession; granted a charter of Hoilhouse, confirmed 30 April 1566; *m* Jean, dau of Alexander Cunningham of Aiker, and *d c* 18 Dec 1607, having had, with two daus:

1 David (Sir), of Robertland; retoured heir to his f and gf 1607; had charter of Glengarnock 1614; *m* Margaret, dau of Patrick Fleming of Barochan, Renfrewshire, and *d* April 1619, having had, with two other sons:

(1) **Sir David Cuningham, 1st Bt** (NS), so *cr* 25 Nov 1630, with remainder to heirs male whatsoever, of Robertland; served heir gen of his f 1619 and heir special in Robertland, Glengarnock, etc 1628; Master of the Horse to JAMES VI; *m* (licence 8 June 1637) Elizabeth, dau of Robert Joyce, Keeper of the Robes, and widow of James Heriot, and *d* after 8 Oct 1661 but before Nov 1671, leaving:

1a **Sir David Cuningham, 2nd Bt**; *m* Jean (*d* 8 May 1665), dau of 8th Lord Boyd (*see* KILMARNOCK, B) and *dsp c* 2 Nov 1671

(2) **Sir Alexander Cuningham, 3rd Bt**; served heir to his n 1672 and his bro 1692; sold Robertland to his cousin Sir David Cunynghame, 1st Bt, of Milncraig (*qv*); *m* his cousin Elizabeth, dau and coheir of John Cuninghame of Cambuskeith, 2nd s of 7th Earl of Glencairn (*see* CUNINGHAME, Bt), and *d c* 1696, having had issue:

1a **Sir David Cuningham, 4th Bt**; sold the rest of the family estates to pay debts 1696; accused of various frauds and conspiracy to parricide; *m* Elizabeth (*d* in or after 1679), 2nd dau and coheir of 2nd Duke of Hamilton (*see* HAMILTON and BRANDON, D) and widow of James Cunningham, Lord Kilmaurs (est surv s of 9th Earl of Glencairn; *see* CUNINGHAME, Bt), and *dspm* in or after Aug 1705, having had:

1b David; *dvp*

1b Diana; *m* Thomas Cochrane of Polkellie, Ayrshire, yr bro of 2nd Earl of Dundonald (*qv*)

1a Jean; *m* Sir Alexander Forrester, Sec to the Duke of Lauderdale (*see* LAUDERDALE, E)

(3) James (Sir); Gentleman of the Bedchamber to CHARLES I

(1) Euphemia; *m* (contract 10 Dec 1639) 1st Viscount Kilsyth (*d* 7 Sept 1661)

2 Frederick

3 William; *educ* Glasgow U

4 John; *educ* Glasgow U

5 Christierne; tutor (guardian) to his est bro's children 1619; *educ* Glasgow U; *m* Margaret, dau of Sir James Campbell of Gargunnock, and had issue:

(1) John, of Wattieston; *m* Elizabeth Campbell, and had:

1a William, of Auchinskeith, Parish of Riccarton; *m* — McIlvain, of Gremmet, Ayrshire, and *d* June 1727, leaving:

1b **Sir William Cuningham, 5th Bt**; served heir male of his gggf Sir David Cuningham of Robertland 3 Aug 1778; *m* 1741 Margaret (*d* 1811), dau and heir of William Fairlie of Fairlie, Ayrshire, and *d* 25 Oct 1781, having had issue:

1c Sir WILLIAM CUNIGHAM later CUNINGHAM-FAIRLIE, **6th Bt**; *m* Anne, dau of Robert Colquhoun, of St Christopher, WI (by Frances, dau of Matthew Mills), and sis of Frances, w of Sir John Shaw-Stewart, 4th Bt (*qv*), and *d* 15 Oct 1811, having had, with another dau:

1d **Sir William Cuningham-Fairlie, 7th Bt**; *m* 1st 21 May 1818 Anne, only dau of Robert Cooper, of Woodbridge, Suffolk; *m* 2nd Marianne, dau of Sir James Campbell, 3rd Bt, of Aberuchill (*qv*), and *dsp* 1 Feb 1837

2d **Sir John Cuningham-Fairlie, 8th Bt**; *b* 29 July 1779; *m* 8 Aug 1808 Janet Lucretia (*d* 25 June 1877), dau of John Wallace, of Kelly, Renfrewshire, and *dsp* 28 Feb 1852

3d **Sir Charles Cuningham-Fairlie, 9th Bt**; *b* 22 Sept 1780; *m* 10 June 1806 Fanny (*d* Pisa 12 May 1848), 3rd dau of Sir John Call, Bt, and *d* 1 June 1859, having had, with another s:

1e **Sir Arthur Percy Cuningham-Fairlie, 10th Bt**; *b* 22 Oct 1815; *m* 5 Feb 1839 Maria Antonia (*d* 9 Jan 1897), 6th dau of Hon William Bowman Felton, MP (Canadian Parl), and *d* 21 Sept 1881, having had issue:

1f Sir CHARLES ARTHUR CUNINGHAM-FAIRLIE later FAIRLIE-CUNINGHAME, **11th Bt**; *b* 2 Jan 1846; *m* 7 Nov 1867 Caroline Madelina (*d* 27 Nov 1902), yst dau of Capt William Fordyce Blair, RN, of Blair, Ayrshire, and *d* 27 Dec 1897, having had issue:

1g Edith Magdalen; *m* 1st 1894 Mathew Charles Edward Fortescue, DL (*dsp* 24 Aug 1914), of Stephenstown, Co Louth; *m* 2nd 25 March 1918 Rev Henry A PYKE later PYKE-FORTESCUE (*d* 24 Sept 1936), Chaplain AIF, of Sydney, NSW

2g Geraldine Mary Georgina; *m* 29 April 1905 Maj Corry Langrishe Connellan, The Buffs (*d* 5 May 1923), 2nd s of Peter Connellan, JP, DL, of Coolmore, and *d* 3 April 1940, leaving issue

3g Violet Antonia; *m* 17 Oct 1902 Maj Arthur Cochrane Hamilton, 6th Dragoon Gds, s of Capt Hamilton, RN, and had issue

2f **Sir Alfred Edward Fairlie-Cuninghame, 12th Bt**; *b* 2 April 1842; *m* 12 Nov 1885 Arabella Annie (*d* 19 April 1932), only dau of Frederick Church, RN, and *dsp* 14 Nov 1910

1f Rosa Matilda; *m* 1st 17 May 1873 Arthur Bryden (*d* 1897) and had issue; *m* 2nd 19 Feb 1898 Trevor Eardley-Wilmot and *d* 27 Oct 1945, leaving further issue (*see* EARDLEY-WILMOT, Bt)

2f Margaret Helen Gertrude; *m* 12 Aug 1876 Hans George Leslie Shand, yst s of James Shand, MD, of Hall Hills, Turriff, Aberdeenshire, and *d* 2 Nov 1931

1e Rosa; *m* 1843 her 1st cousin John (*d* 1855), 3rd s of John Cuningham of Craigends, and *d* 12 Nov 1888 aged 79

2e Florence Anna; *m* 1831 Charles Eugene Laffitte (*d* 1875), of Paris, and *d* 1901, leaving issue

1d Margaret; *m* 1st Capt Robert Maxwell of Pollok; *m* 2nd July 1800 John Cuninghame of Craigends and *d* 24 Jan 1862, having had issue

2d Anne; *m* June 1795 Sir William Bruce, 7th Bt, of Stenhouse (*qv*), and had issue

2c Alexander; Collector of Customs; *m* Sarah, dau of John Reid by Anna, dau of Robert Cuninghame of Auchenharvie, and had, with two daus:

1d William; *b* 4 April 1787; Maj HEICS; *m* 31 Dec 1816 Rebecca (*d* 19 April 1875), dau of William Armstrong, HEICS, Commr Nuddea, Bengal, and *d* 11 Aug 1838, having had, with other issue:

1e William Robert; *b* 14 July 1819; Maj-Gen HEICS; *d* unm 17 Sept 1899

2e Hastings; *b* 30 Aug 1825; *m* 29 Jan 1849 Agnes Henrietta, dau of Edward Micklewaite Curr, of St Helliers, Melbourne, and *d* 19 Sept 1908, having had, with other issue:

1f WILLIAM EDWARD (Sir), **13th Bt**

2f Herbert Norfolk; *b* 1858; *m* 1882 Charlotte, dau of Philip Francis Adams, Surveyor-Gen Sydney, NSW, and *d* 10 June 1900, leaving issue:

1g Hastings; *b* 1886; *d* unm 1907

1g Fairlie; *b* 1 Feb 1883

2g Phyllis; *m* 20 Feb 1912 Lachlan Macalister Henderson, Lt AIF (*das* 9 April 1915), 2nd s of John Cunningham Henderson, of Mahrigong, Queensland

3f Fairlie Percy; *m* 1898 Gertrude Constance, dau of Richard Randolph Machattie, and *d* 12 Dec 1936, leaving:

1g Herbert Alexander

1g Kathleen May

4f Charles Rawdon; *m* 14 March 1894 Harriet Maria (*d* 1953), dau of Edward Hardman Macartney (*see* MACARTNEY, Bt), and *d* 1909, having had, with other issue:

1g Eric de Burgh; *b* 1900; *m* 19 Dec 1934 *Betty Maurice [Mrs Michael Kirkpatrick, Closeburn, 197 Walker St, N Sydney, NSW 2060, Australia] (*m* 2nd 15 April 1952 Henry William Hardress Waller (*d* 28 Oct 1962); *m* 3rd 21 Feb 1969 Michael Alexander Addison Kirkpatrick, BA, LLB, late S/Ldr RAAF, who *d* 1991), dau of Mrs M Barton, of Roslyn, Leura, NSW, and *d* Sept 1946, leaving issue:

1h *Anthea; *b* 18 Aug 1936; *m* 3 Jan 1959 *Michael Havelock Marchbank, only s of Frank Havelock Marchbank, of Newton Hall, Stockfield-on-Tyne, Northumberland, and has:

1i *Jonathan Havelock; *b* 22 Dec 1964

1i *Joanna Cuningham; *b* 21 April 1960

2i *Katharine Jane; *b* 13 May 1962

2h *Rhonwen; *b* 10 March 1943; BA, Dip Soc Studies Sydney U 1967; *m* 1971 (*divorce* 1981, resumed maiden name) Jack Aylward Mooney, and has issue:

1i *Sean Aylward Michael; *b* 1972

2g +Alister Gordon [Alister Cunningham Esq, 8 Park Lane, Albury, NSW 2640, Australia]; *b* 1902; AIF WW II; *m* 10 Feb 1948 *Catherine Ida, dau of Hugh Rule, of Rockhampton, and has:

1h +Robert Gordon; *b* 25 Sept 1953; *m* 1983 *Christine Anne, dau of Dr William Goldwin Gray, of Ontario, and has:

1i *Emily Marguerite; *b* 1985

2i *Joanna Christine Mary; *b* 1986

3i *Jane Fairlie; *b* 1988

3g Archibald Loudoun; *b* 1905; AIF WW II; *m* 1936 Nancy Maurice (*d* 1994, having *m* 2nd 1946 Robin Ellison Cuningham (*see below*)), dau of Mrs M Barton, and was *ka* Malaya 1942, leaving:

1h *Nancy Robin [Mrs Peter Bell, 285a Durham St, Bathurst, NSW 2795, Australia]; *b* 12 Nov 1939; *m* 5 Dec 1964 *Peter Edwin Bell, yr s of Leonard Christian Charles Bell, of Chailey Green, Sussex, and has issue:

1i *Alastair Christian Loudon; *b* March 1967; *m* 1992 *Anastasia Louise Lord

1i *Belinda Jane; *b* 5 Dec 1965; *m* 1994 *Terence John Betts

2i *Fairlie Louise; *b* March 1972; *m* 1996 *Ronald Eugene Long

4g Robin Ellison; *b* 1905; WW II in AIF; *m* 1946 Nancy Maurice, widow of his bro Archibald Loudoun Cuningham (*see* above), and *d* 1984, having had issue:

1h *Georgine Ellison; *b* 14 Dec 1951; *m* 1975 *Robert Ranald Machay, of Tinagroo, Scone, NSW, and has issue:

1i *Robert Gordon; *b* 1983

1g Dulcie Eila Minnie; *m* 6 Nov 1930 Noel Travis Cox, 2nd s of John Claude Cox, of Clarendon, Tasmania, and had issue

1f Rebecca Harriet; *m* 1882 her cousin James William Cuningham (*see* below), and *d* 1922

2f Amye; *m* 1880 Herbert Hammill, of Melbourne, Victoria, and *d* 15 Feb 1924, leaving issue

3f Agnes; *d* Aug 1936

4f Edith; *m* 1896 Frederick Norris Lowther Crofton and *d* 1951, leaving issue (*see* CROFTON, B)

3e James Macnab, CSI; *b* 2 June 1829; MD, LLD, KHS; Surgn-Gen Indian Med Serv; *m* 1st 2 March 1854 Mary Falconer (*d* 1883), dau of Surgn James McRae, HEICS, and had, with other issue:

1f James William; *b* 15 July 1857; *m* 1882 his cousin Rebecca Harriet (*d* 1922), dau of Hastings Cuningham (*see* above), and *d* 1939

2f Arthur Mactier; *m* 1888 Agnes Murray and *d* 8 July 1940, leaving:

1g Mary Mactier

2g Phylis Fairlie; *m* 19 July 1918 Maj James Carstairs Kininmonth, DSO, and *d* 4 May 1927, leaving issue

3g Nora; *m* 1920 Leslie Albert Austin, Lt AIF, and had issue:

1h *Derek Leslie; *b* 1921

3f John Fairlie; *b* 22 June 1862; *m* 1894 Margaret Campbell, and *d* 1935, leaving, with other issue:

1g John Henry; *b* 1898; Lt RA WW I 1916–19; *m* 1924 Kathleen, MB, MS, FRCS, dau of Prof T E Clouston, DD, and *d* 1969, having had issue:

1h +James Boyd Fairlie; *b* 1932

2g +Donald McRae; *b* 16 June 1904; *m* 18 June 1929 *Rose Eleanor, dau of Samuel Wilde Witts, of Llanilo Station, Walgett, NSW, and has issue:

1h +John Fairlie; *b* 18 Dec 1943

1h *Florence Anne; *b* 21 Sept 1933; *m* May 1957 *David Jones, BVSc, Sydney U, and has issue

1g Mary Stewart

1f May Constance; *m* 1st 1885 Arthur Blackwood, of Melbourne; *m* 2nd 3 April 1905 Hon Assheton Edward Harbord, s of 5th Baron Suffield (*qv*), and *d* 7 Feb 1928

3e (cont.) James Cuningham *m* 2nd 11 April 1889 Georgina, dau of Robert Reid Macredie, and *d* 25 June 1905, having by her had issue:

4f Robert Macredie; *b* 9 April 1891; *d* 9 May 1939

4e Francis Goode; *b* 16 April 1836; *m* 1st June 1864 Anne Colquhoun (*d* 22 Sept 1877), dau of Boyd Alexander Cuninghame, and had issue:

1f Ida; *m* 1913 John Caldwell Uhthoff, MD, FRCS (*d* 19 Jan 1927), and *d* 22 Sept 1938

4e (cont.) Francis Cuningham *m* 2nd 16 Oct 1879 Jean Elizabeth (*d* 1939), dau of Col William Forbes Hutton, HEICS, and *d* 28 April 1911, having by her had further issue:

1f Francis George Glencairn CUNINGHAM later CUNINGHAME; *b* 9 Aug 1880; Lt-Col Argyll & Sutherland Highrs, Boer War 1899–1900 (wounded, Queen's medal, two clasps) and WW I (despatches); *m* 9 July 1912 Violet Jessie Phipps (*d* 28 June 1957), dau of Capt Geoffrey Stanley Phipps Hornby, Rifle Bde, and *d* 14 July 1956, leaving:

1g William Glencairn; *b* 17 June 1913; *m* Feb 1935 Doris, dau of John Bishop, of Swindon, and *d* 20 Dec 1959, leaving:

2h Anthony Glencairn; *b* 3 Sept 1935; *m* 21 Sept 1961 *Pamela [Mrs Anthony Cuninghame, Stones, Uffcott, Broad Hinton, Wilts SN4 9NB], dau of Robert Horton, of The Manor, Broad Hinton, and *d* 1982, leaving:

1i +Andrew Glencairn; *b* 22 Aug 1965

1i *Sally Helen; *b* 1 Dec 1962

2i *Clair Elizabeth; *b* 21 April 1964; *m* 1991 *Martin Brian Anstice, s of Malcolm Anstice, of Huish Episcopi, Somerset, and has:

1j *Henry James; *b* 13 Aug 1994

1j *Elizabeth Grace; *b* 23 April 1997

1g *Carol Jean [Mrs John Watney, The Lodge, N Cheriton, Wincanton BA8 0AL]; *b* 25 Dec 1915; *m* 6 May 1950 W/Cdr John Douglas Philip Watney, RAF (*d* 11 Aug 1976), er s of Col Charles Norman Watney, CIE, TD, of Bishops Caundle House, nr Sherborne, and has issue:

1h *Guy Charles Glencairn; *b* 5 Aug 1954; *m* 1st 1980 (*divorce* 1986) Mary Jane, er dau of S/Ldr John Sands, RAF; *m* 2nd 1990 Anne, dau of H McHugh, of Kansas City, and has issue by her

2f William Fairlie; *b* 17 Sept 1881; *d* unm 5 Dec 1947

3f John Loudoun; *b* 18 June 1887

2f Eleonora Rose; *d* 15 Nov 1919

3f Isabel Jean; *m* 13 Jan 1912 Sidney Hancock (*d* 13 Nov 1934), and *d* 24 Aug 1952, leaving issue

The 12th Bt's third cousin,

Sir WILLIAM EDWARD CUNINGHAM later FAIRLIE CUNINGHAME (deed poll 1912), **13th Bt**; *m* 1 June 1887 Georgiana Maud (*d* Feb 1951), dau of Edward Hardman Macartney (*see* MACARTNEY, Bt), and *d* 5 May 1929, leaving:

1 **Sir Hussey Burgh Fairlie-Cuninghame, 14th Bt**; *b* 22 Aug 1890; Lt Res Offrs Australian Artillery WW I 1916–18; *m* 31 March 1917 Alice Mona, er dau of Dr Robert Stewart, of Adelaide, S Australia, and *dspm* following an accident 7 Feb 1939, leaving:

(1) *Margaret Alice [Mrs Stanley Wood, 43 Honeyton St, Seaton, S Australia]; *m* 1946 Stanley G Wood (*d* 1971) and has:

1a *Harold Anthony; *b* 1948

1a *Norma Margaret [Mrs George Knight, 23 Fairfax Ave, Millswood, S Australia]; *b* 1947; *m* 1968 *George Miller Knight and has:

1b *Peter Stanley; *b* 1972

2b *Robert Reginald; *b* 1981

1b *Helen Margaret; *b* 1973

2b *Elizabeth Georgie; *b* 1983

2a *Janice Alice [Mrs Edward James, 17 Tereva Crescent, Mulgrave, Victoria, Australia]; *b* 1952; *m* 1970 *Edward James and has:

1b *Simon Stanley; *b* 1976

2b *David Matthew; *b* 1979

1b *Julie Alice; *b* 1971

2b *Karen Linda; *b* 1973

2a *Ann [Mrs Arlie Vout, 26 Cranbrook Ave, Cremorne, Sydney, NSW, Australia]; *m* Aug 1955 Arlie William Vout (*d* 1985)

(3) *Patricia; *m* April 1960 *Peter Goddard Sheldon and has:

1a *Robert Stewart; *b* 1961; *m* 1992 *Sharon Susan Armstrong

2a *Anthony Stewart; *b* 1966

1a *Jane Stewart; *b* 1963

2 WILLIAM ALAN (Sir), **15th Bt**

3 John Hastings; *b* 1899; *educ* Sydney U (BArch); Capt Australian Forces; *m* 1934 Margaret Ruth, dau of Charles Woodhill, of NSW, and *d* Sept 1997, leaving:

(1) +David Hastings [David Fairlie-Cuninghame Esq, 47 Cremorne Rd, Sydney, NSW 2090, Australia]; *b* June 1937; ACA; *m* 1963 *Susan Gai, dau of Henry White, of Coolah, NSW, and has issue:

1a +Charles Hastings; *b* 1966

1a *Annabel; *b* 1964

(2) +Peter Hastings [Peter Fairlie-Cuninghame Esq, 9 Austinmer St, Austinmer, NSW, Australia]; *b* April 1939; *m* 1972 (*divorce* 1992) Felicity Helen, dau of Douglas Service, of Sydney, and has issue:

1a +Samuel John; *b* 1976

1a *Georgina Mary; *b* 1979

(1) *Elizabeth; *b* July 1941; *m* 1st 22 Sept 1962 (*divorce* 1972) William Leslie Murray Robson; *m* 2nd 1974 Peter Thomas Glanville (*d* 1975) and has by her 1st husb:

1a *Andrew Fairlie Murray; *b* 7 Dec 1963

2a *Hamish Hastings Murray; *b* 1 March 1965

(2) *Georgiana Jane; *b* March 1947; *m* 1972 *Christopher Harold Martin, of Norfolk, Cassilis, NSW, and has issue:

1a *Jonathan Hastings; *b* 1977

2a *Toby; *b* 1980

1a *Amber; *b* 1979

4 Edward Hardman Macartney; *b* 1904; *m* 1943 Patricia June, dau of Dr Alexander H Rutherford, of Sydney, and *dsp* 1964

1 Georgiana Maud

2 Agnes Henrietta; *b* 9 Nov 1896; *m* 1 Sept 1920 Herbert Arnold St John Kent (*d* 5 April 1968), n of William Kent, Lt AIF, of Queensland, and had issue:

(1) *William Arnold; *b* 5 Feb 1927; *m* 25 June 1956 *Margaret Naomi Cameron, dau of John Waugh, of Queensland, and has issue:

1a *William St John; *b* 2 Oct 1957

2a *Lachlan Cameron; *b* 13 June 1962

1a *Robin Margaret Cameron; *b* 14 April 1960

(1) *Winifred Fairlie; *b* 28 May 1923; *m* 28 Feb 1953 *Dietrich Max Schmelzer, s of Max Gustav Schmelzer, of Posen, Germany, and has issue:

1a *Roland Dietrich Arnold; *b* 12 July 1957

2a *Andreas Jock; *b* 25 Nov 1968

1a *Barbara Sabine; *b* 13 May 1954

2a *Elisabeth Fairlie; *b* 10 April 1956

3a *Ingrid Bettina; *b* 26 Dec 1960

(2) *Elizabeth Audrey; *b* 30 Jan 1925

(3) *Virginia; *b* 28 Aug 1932; *m* 8 Aug 1961 *John Patrick McConnel Trier, s of Cdr Patrick Aster Trier, OBE, RN, of Southport, Queensland, and has:

1a *Alister John Kent; *b* 9 April 1963

1a *Susan Audrey; *b* 14 May 1968

(4) *Hastings Loraine; *b* 6 April 1935; *educ* Sydney Tech Coll; *m* 24 March 1956 *John Danvers Nott, s of F Nott, of Rannes, Qld, and has had:

1a *Christopher John; *b* 25 Oct 1959

2a *Gregory Kent Nigel; *b* 16 Jan 1963

1a Tempe Helen; *b* 23 Feb 1957; *d* 24 April 1959

3 *Amabel Marguerite [Mrs Alick Osborne, Minkara Nursing Home, Bayview, NSW 2104, Australia]; *b* 10 Oct 1901; *m* 11 Jan 1933 Alick Scott Osborne (*d* 14 Jan 1957), s of William Alexander Osborne, of Wollongong, and has issue:

(1) *William Fairlie Cuninghame; *b* 11 Nov 1934; *m* 10 Oct 1964 *Janet Stewart, er dau of Stewart Stevenson, of Mandurama, NSW, and has issue:

1a *Alick Stevenson; *b* 11 Sept 1968; *m* Feb 1993 *Kirsten, dau of Warren Porter, of Sydney, and has:

1b *William Henry Porter; *b* 24 Feb 1994

1b *Emily Nicole; *b* 5 July 1995

2b *Georgia Phoebe; *b* 18 Sept 1997

2a *Stewart William; *b* 1970

1a *Susan Margaret; *b* 22 Feb 1967

(2) *Andrew Hastings; *b* 11 Jan 1937; *m* 1st 12 March 1966 Barbara Constance (*d* 1973), dau of A C Heron, of Wahroonga, NSW; *m* 2nd 1974 *Judith Nancy Pope and has by his 1st w:

1a *Philip Scott; *b* 9 Jan 1967

1a*Eleanor Marguerite Loretta; *b* 17 March 1969

(1) *Mary MaCartney [Mrs John Laurie, 40 Kenthurst Rd, St Ives, NSW, Australia]; *b* 26 Sept 1933; *m* 21 Nov 1959 *John William Laurie and has:

1a *William Alick Osborne; *b* 5 April 1963

1a *Margaret Kathleen; *b* 7 March 1961

2a *Sarah Elisabeth (twin); *b* 5 April 1963

3a *Georgina Mary; *b* 27 June 1969

The 14th Bt's bro,

Sir William Alan Fairlie-Cuninghame, 15th Bt, MC (1919); *b* 31 Jan 1893; BEng Sydney U; Lt 5th Pioneer Bn AIF WW I; Research Offr Cwlth Sci Industl Research Orgn Meteorology Div 1943–58; *m* 2 July 1929 Irene Alice, dau of Henry Margrave Terry, and *d* 1981, leaving:

Sir WILLIAM HENRY FAIRLIE-CUNINGHAME, **16th and present Bt**

FALCONER OF THOROTON

Creation: B. (LP, UK) May 1997.

THE BARON FALCONER OF THOROTON, of Thoroton in the County of Nottinghamshire, QC (1991) (Charles Leslie Falconer) [The Rt Hon The Lord Falconer of Thoroton QC, House of Lords, London SW1A 0PW]; *b* 19 Nov 1951; *educ* Trin Coll Glenalmond and Queens' Coll Cambridge; barrister Inner Temple 1974 (Master Bench 1997), Slr-Gen 1997–98, Min State Cabinet Office 1998–; *m* 1985 *Marianna Catherine Thoroton, dau of Sir David Henry Thoroton Hildyard, KCMG, DFC, Amb Chile 1970–73 and UN Geneva 1973–76, and has:

1 *Hamish; *b c* 1986; child actor (roles include Seriozha in *Anna Karenina*)

2 *Rocco; *b c* 1989

3 *Johnnie; *b c* 1993

1 *Rosie; *b c* 1991

Lineage: JOHN LESLIE FALCONER; *m* Anne Mansel and had:

CHARLES LESLIE, *cr* a **Baron**

Falkender

Creation: B. (LP, UK) 1974.

THE BARONESS FALKENDER, of West Haddon, Co Northants (Marcia Matilda Field, CBE (1970)) [The Rt Hon The Baroness Falkender CBE, 3 Wyndham Mews, Upper Montagu St, London W1H 1RS]; *b* 1932; *educ* Queen Mary Coll London (BA); Sec to Gen Sec Labour Party 1955–56; Private Sec to PM 1964–70 and 1974–76; political columnist *Mail on Sunday* 1982–88, Lay Govr Queen Mary Coll 1988–, Pres UNIFEM UK, UN Devpt Fund for Women UK Ctee, dir Peckham Building Soc 1986–91, S London Investment & Mortgage Corp 1986–91; took by deed poll 1974 the surname Falkender; *m* 1955 (*divorce* 1960) George Edmund Charles Williams and has two sons

Lineage: HARRY FIELD; *m* — and had:

MARCIA MATILDA, *cr* a **Baroness**

Falkiner

Arms: Or, three falcons close proper, belled gules. **Crest:** A falcon's lure proper between two wings azure. **Motto:** *Fortuna favente* ('With Fortune's favour'). **Creation:** Bt. (I) 24 Aug 1778.

SIR BENJAMIN SIMON FALKINER, 10TH BT, of Anne Mount, Co Cork; *b* 16 Jan 1962; *s f* 1997; *educ* Queen Elizabeth's Barnet; shop manager; *m* 6 Feb 1998 *Linda Mason, and has:

1 +SAMUEL JAMES MATTHEW; *b* 30 Aug 1993

1 *Alice Katherine Sally; *b* 19 Oct 1996t

Lineage: JOHN FALKINER; had:

WILLIAM FALKINER, of Leeds, Yorks; *bapt* 9 March 1594/5; had:

MICHAEL FALKINER, of Brigart, Leeds; *bapt* 26 June 1622; settled Ireland *c* 1651; *m c* 6 Aug 1639 Susan, dau of Christopher Jackson, of Hunslet, Leeds, and had, with another s and two daus:

1 Michael; *b* 2 March 1640; *m* Mary, sis of Benjamin Waight, of Dublin, and *d* between 12 March 1711/2 and 12 March 1712/3, leaving, with other issue:

(1) Michael; *m* 1704 Elizabeth Pepper and *dsp*

(2) Daniel; *m* 21 Aug 1712 Jane Lord; *d* between 3 March 1726/7 and 28 March 1727, leaving issue

2 DANIEL

3 Richard; ancestor of the FALKINERs of Mount Falcon

MICHAEL FALKINER's 2nd s,

DANIEL FALKINER, of Dublin; *bapt* 16 Dec 1641; *m* 1694 Rebecca, dau of — Blackwell and widow of Henry Hamilton, of Bailieborough, Co Cavan, and *d* between 8 March and 8 April 1705, having had issue:

1 John, of Nangor, Co Dublin; High Sheriff Co Dublin 1721; *m c* 7 Oct 1700 Mary (*d* between 17 March 1745 and 20 Jan 1748), dau and heir of Joseph Budden, and *d* between 17 Oct 1742 and 20 Jan 1745/6, leaving, with two sons (*dsp*):

(1) Elizabeth; *m* 1722 Freeman Rogers, of Ballynaven, Co Tipperary, and had issue

(2) Rebecca; *m* William Gibton and had issue

(3) Sarah; *m* 1733 Thomas Taylor, Ld Mayor Dublin 1750, and had issue

2 Daniel; *b* 1698; MP (I Parl) Baltinglass, Co Wicklow, 1727–59, Ld Mayor Dublin 1735; *m* Sarah, dau of George Spence, of Dublin, and *d* 20 Jan 1759, leaving, with a dau Lucinda (*d* unm, *bur* 22 Feb 1742/3):

(1) Frederick, of Abbotstown, Co Dublin; *m* 3 Aug 1730 Elizabeth (*bur* 7 April 1768), er dau of James Hamilton, MP Carlow, and was *bur* 7 Feb 1782, leaving issue, with another s (*d* unm):

1a Daniel, of Abbotstown; *educ* Trin Coll Dublin (BA 1755); barrister 1759; *m c* 15 Jan 1761 Dorothy (*bur* 28 April 1796), dau of Henry Faure, of Egham, Surrey, and was *bur* 3 June 1798, leaving:

1b Sir FREDERICK JOHN FALKINER, 1st and last Bt (UK), so *cr* 21 Dec 1812; *b* 8 April 1768; *educ* Trin Coll Dublin (BA); MP: Athy, Carlow and Dublin, High Sheriff Co Dublin 1801, Col 100th Regt; *m* 23 Oct 1798 Anne Frances (*d* between 7 Aug 1852 and 26 April 1853), dau and coheir of Sackville Gardiner, of Dublin, and *dsp* Oct 1824, when the btcy expired

1b Elizabeth; *m c* 26 Nov 1795 William Arthur Crosbie (*d* March 1803), of Dublin, and *d* 7 March 1841, leaving issue

2b Maria Josepha; *m* 31 Dec 1799 Hon Robert Moore (*d* 17 Sept 1831), s of 5th Earl of Drogheda (*qv*), and *dsp* 23 Sept 1846

3b Dorothea; *m* 21 July 1808 Maj John Christopher Nuttall (*d* 7 Nov 1849), of Tittour, Co Wicklow, and *d* 24 March 1860, leaving issue

2a John (Rev); MA Dublin, DD Edinburgh, Rector Carlow, Chaplain to Duke of Leinster; *m* 11 May 1780 Mary (*bur* 28 Jan 1833), dau of Samuel Galbraith, of Old Derrig, Queen's Co (now Co Laois), and was *bur* 27 May 1821, having had, with other issue:

1b Frederick John; *b* 10 Dec 1784; *m* 21 May 1823 Helena Maria, dau of Harman FitzMaurice, and had two sons and four daus

1b Emily Olivia; *m* 21 Dec 1802 James Herring and had issue

2b Catherine; *m* Aug 1798 William Martin, Capt 9th Dragoons

1a Anne; *m c* 7 Sept 1750 Benjamin Geale, Ld Mayor Dublin, and *d* 1 April 1763, leaving issue

2a Frances; *m c* 2 July 1778 Maj James Wilson, RA

3 CALEB

1 Hannah; *m* Trial Trevors

DANIEL FALKINER's 3rd s,

CALEB FALKINER, of Cork; merchant; *m* 1st 1707 Ruth (*d* by 1727), dau of Edward Riggs, of Riggsdale, Co Cork, and had issue:

1 RIGGS FALKINER (Sir), **1st Bt**

1 Elizabeth; *m* 1728 Elis Herrick, of Shippool

CALEB FALKINER *m* 2nd Mary (*d* by 1766), dau of John Newport, and *d* Jan 1765, having by her had, with another dau:

1 Caroline; *m* 20 March 1755 John Minchin, of Annagh, only s of Charles Minchin, of Annagh, and had issue

CALEB FALKINER's only s,

Sir Riggs Falkiner, 1st Bt (I), so *cr* 24 Aug 1778, of Anne Mount, Co Cork; MP (I Parl) Clonakilty 1768–76 and Castlemartyr 1776–83; *m* 1st *c* 5 Jan 1737 Mary (*d* May 1762), sis of Samuel Barker, MP Co Waterford; *m* 2nd Oct 1764 Anne, only dau of Rev Gabriel James Maturin, DD, Dean St Patrick's Cathedral, Dublin, and *d* between 9 Aug 1796 and 3 Aug 1797, having had by his 1st w:

1 Caleb; *m* Lydia, dau of Rev Thomas Browne, Precentor Cork and s of Rt Rev Jemmett Browne, Archbp Tuam, and *dvp*, leaving issue:

(1) Isabella; *m* 29 May 1810 Justin McCartie, of Carrignavar, Co Cork

(2) Mary; *m* 20 Dec 1808 Capt Prescott, 5th Dragoon Gds, s of Gen Prescott

2 SAMUEL FALKINER (Sir), **2nd Bt**

1 Ruth; *m* 1761 Francis Chute, of Chute Hall, Co Kerry

2 Elizabeth; *m* Attiwell Wood, barrister

3 Mary; *m* Thomas Parsons, of Pembroke, Co Cork

4 Samia; *m* Rev George Warner

5 Sarah Anne; *m* 12 July 1784 2nd Baron Ventry (*qv*) and *dspm* Nov 1788

The 1st Bt's only surv s,

Sir Samuel Falkiner, 2nd Bt; *b* by(?) 1745; *m c* 1789 Sarah (*d c* 1847), dau of Charles Leslie, MD, and *d* 22 Dec 1825, having had issue:

1 **Sir Riggs Falkiner, 3rd Bt**; *b* 1789; *educ* Ch Ch Oxford (BA 1809); *d* unm 25 Jan 1850

2 **Sir Charles Leslie Falkiner, 4th Bt**; *b* 1790; joined RN 1803, Midshipman 1804, Lt 1810, headed the *Shannon*'s maindeck boarders at the memorable capture of the American ship *Chesapeake* in 1813 during the War of 1812, made Cdr in consequence, Capt; *d* unm 7 Feb 1858

3 SAMUEL EDMUND FALKINER (Sir), **5th Bt**

4 John Leslie

The 2nd Bt's 3rd s,

Sir Samuel Edmund Falkiner, 5th Bt; *b* 1791; *educ* Winchester; served Peninsula War (wounded thrice, present at Talavera, Busaco and Salamanca (medal with three clasps)), Lt-Col 31st Foot 1831; *m* 24 July 1834 Mary (*d* 19 Dec 1844), dau of James Bouwens, of Connaught Place, by Margery, dau of Sir Richard Nelson Rycroft, 1st Bt (*qv*), and *d* 30 Dec 1867, having had issue:

1 SAMUEL EDMUND (Sir), **6th Bt**

1 Edith Mary; *m* 29 April 1856 Joseph Wood, only s of Joseph Carter Wood, of Marden Pk, Surrey, and *d* 14 April 1881, leaving issue

2 Rose Frances; *m* 16 April 1859 Charles William Moore, Bengal CS, and *d* on the P&O Steamer *Nemesis* 22 May 1860

3 Emily Eliza; *m* 8 Jan 1867 William George Herbert (*see* CARNARVON, E) and *dsp* 30 May 1911

The 5th Bt's only s,

Sir Samuel Edmund Falkiner, 6th Bt; *b* 2 Feb 1843; *m* 21 Nov 1865 Blanche (*d* 14 May 1896), yst dau of Sir William Berkeley Call, 3rd Bt, and *d* 12 May 1893, leaving issue:

1 LESLIE EDMUND PERCY RIGGS (Sir), **7th Bt**

1 Mabel Rose; *b* 25 March 1868; *m* 21 Jan 1902 Capt Pennant Athelwold Iremonger Lloyd, RN (*d* 14 Sept 1916), of Pentrehobyn, Mold, N Wales, and *d* 26 Aug 1963, leaving issue

The 6th Bt's only s,

Sir Leslie Edmund Percy Riggs Falkiner, 7th Bt; *b* 2 Oct 1866; *m* 1st 16 Oct 1894 Elaine Maynard (*dsp* 28 Dec 1900), yr dau of William Mortimer Maynard Farmer, of London SW, and Maynardville, Cape of Good Hope; *m* 2nd 16 April 1902 Kathleen Mary (*d* 7 Jan 1948), er dau of Hon Henry Robert Orde-Powlett (*see* BOLTON, B), and *d* 19 Jan 1917, having by her had:

1 **Sir Terence Edmond Patrick Falkiner, 8th Bt**, of Anne Mount, Co Cork, DL (Herefs 1965); *b* 17 March 1903; *educ* Oratory Sch Birmingham; Lt-Col

Coldstream Gds WW II (wounded), Assist Mil Sec: E Command 1948–51 and S Command 1951–55, KStJ; *m* 29 Sept 1925 *Mildred Katherine, yst dau of Sir John Richard Geers Cotterell, 4th Bt (*qv*), and *d* 1987, leaving issue:

(1) **Sir Edmond Charles Falkiner, 9th Bt**; *b* 24 June 1938; *educ* Downside; probation offr 1969–97, hon chm Drugcare (St Albans) 1986–94; *m* 8 Oct 1960 (*divorce* 1997) Janet Iris, dau of Arthur Edward Bruce Darby, of The Park, Stoke Lacy, Herefs; *m* 2nd *Diana — [Diana Lady Falkiner, 111 Wood St, Barnet, Herts EN5 4BX] and was *k* in a car crash in Spain 20 Sept 1997, leaving by his 1st w:

1a Sir BENJAMIN SIMON FALKINER, **10th and present Bt**

2a +Matthew Terence; *b* 9 Jan 1964; *educ* Queen Elizabeth's Barnet; has:

1b +William; *b* 19 Oct 1996

2b +George; *b* 19 March 1997

(2) +Henry Leslie Basil [Henry Falkiner Esq, Dormer Cottage, Frensham, Surrey]; *b* 18 Sept 1940; *educ* Downside; *m* 14 Oct 1967 *(Dorothea) Angela, only dau of Peter Wolfe-Taylor (*see* GRANTCHESTER, B), and has:

1a +Tobias Peter Riggs; *b* 1972; *educ* Millfield

2a +Max Henry Wolfe; *b* 1974; *educ* Millfield

(1) *Elizabeth Anne Thérèse [Lady Hogg, 19 Woodlands Rd, London SW13 0JZ]; *b* 1929; *m* 1956 *Sir Michael David Hogg, 8th Bt (*qv*), and has issue

(2) *Mary Clare [Mrs Geoffrey Smith, 22 Penny Plock, Madley, Herefs]; *b* 8 June 1934; *m* 1st 25 Aug 1956 (*divorce* 1980) Noel John Taylor, s of Charles Taylor, of Wylow, Mordiford, Herefs; *m* 2nd 1991 *Geoffrey Smith and by her 1st husb has:

1a *Paul John; *b* 16 Feb 1957; *educ* Hereford Sch

2a *Mark Robert; *b* 5 April 1965; *educ* Hereford Sch; has:

1b *Robert; *b* 1990

1b *Emma; *b* 1992

3a *David James; *b* 7 March 1969; *educ* Hereford Sch; has issue:

1b *Ashley; *b* 1992

2b *Thomas; *b* 1993

1a *Jane Clare; *b* 20 Jan 1961

2a *Sarah Kate; *b* 1971; has:

1b *Lucy Jane; *b* 1988

(3) *Veronica Cicely [Mrs William Brown, The Old Manse, Fownhope, Herefs]; *b* 20 July 1935; *m* 19 May 1956 *William David Brown, only s of William Moir Brown, MB, ChB, FRCS, of Cantilupe Cottage, Marden, Herefs, and has issue:

1a *Adrian William; *b* 9 Feb 1958; *educ* Whitefriars Sch Cheltenham; *m* 25 May 1996 *Emily Maria, only dau of Peter James, of Enfield

2a *Edward David, MBE; *b* 22 Aug 1960; *educ* Whitefriars Sch; *m* 1993 *Ruth Mary, yr dau of John Sandy, of Millfield, Surrey, and has:

1b *Rosanna Honor Grace; *b* 7 Aug 1996

3a *Rupert Duncan; *b* 25 March 1963; *educ* Whitefriars Sch; *m* 29 Aug 1997 *Nina Karen, est dau of Peter Talbot-Ponsonby (*see* BESSBOROUGH, E)

4a *Dominic George Andrew; *b* 5 Feb 1966; *educ* Whitefriars Sch

2 Lucien Leslie; *b* 27 April 1907; Capt Oxon and Bucks LI WW II, Indian Gen Serv medal with clasp; *m* 10 May 1935 Hon Lucy Agnes Vera Verney-Cave, only dau of 6th Baron Braye (*qv*), and was *ka* nr Cassel *c* 30 May 1940

3 Gervase Leslie; *b* 24 Feb 1909; Maj Coldstream Gds WW II (wounded); *m* 28 July 1934 Rosemary (*d* 17 Feb 1990), er dau of Herbert Smith, of Tower, Mold, Flintshire, and *d* 5 Dec 1988, leaving:

(1) +Richard Gervase [Richard Falkiner Esq, Ledley House, Ebrington, Glos GL55 6NL]; *b* 10 March 1936; *educ* Ampleforth; *m* 15 May 1959 *Gabrielle Mary, only dau of Frank Woodgate, of Ledley House, Ebrington, and has:

1a +Sebastian Thomas; *b* 3 Dec 1963; *m* 2 Jan 1993 *Jan Marie, er dau of Trevor Boyle, of Wellington, NZ and has:

1b +Harry Augustus; *b* 25 April 1994

1b *Isabella Milly; *b* 11 Jan 1996

1a *Sophia Mary; *b* 27 Jan 1962; *m* 31 Aug 1985 (*divorce* 1995) Raymond Andrews, of Felixstowe, and has:

1b *Caleb Finbar; *b* 14 Sept 1988

2b *Storm Gregory; *b* 25 July 1991

1b *Vivienne Erica; *b* 11 June 1993

2b *Alexandra Ruth; *b* 6 Oct 1995

(2) +Michael George Patrick [Michael Falkiner Esq, Downclose Stud, North Perrott, Somerset TA18 7SH]; *b* 26 Feb 1940; *educ* Ampleforth; *m* 1 Aug 1970 *Joanna, est dau of (Walter) Peter Baxter (*see* HAWARDEN, V), and has:

1a *Caroline Helen; *b* 1972

2a *Emily Rosemary; *b* 1974

1 Naomi Elaine Mary; *b* 27 May 1905; nun; *d* 28 Jan 1986

FALKLAND

Arms: Quarterly, 1st and 4th, argent, on a bend sable three roses of the field, barbed and seeded proper (for CARY); 2nd, sable two bars nebuly ermine (for SPENCER of Spencercombe); 3rd, France and England quarterly, within a bordure compony argent and azure. **Crest:** A swan, wings elevated, proper. **Supporters:** Dexter, a unicorn argent, armed, maned, tufted and unguled, or; sinister, a lion guardant proper, ducally crowned and gorged with a plain collar or. **Motto:** *In utroque fidelis* ('Faithful in both'). **Creations:** V. and L. (S) 10 Nov 1620.

THE 15TH VISCOUNT (OF) FALKLAND, of Falkland, Co Fife and **Lord Carye** (Lucius Edward William Plantagenet Cary) [The Rt Hon The Viscount Falkland, House of Lords, London SW1A 0PW]; *b* 8 May 1935; *s f* 1984; premier Viscount in Scottish peerage; *educ* Wellington and Alliance Française Paris; 2nd Lt 8th King's Roy Irish Hus, late ch exec Bowring Tding, Bowmaker (Plant) Ltd and Bowring Steamship Co, now export mktg consultant, Dep Lib Dem Whip Ho Lds 1989–; *m* 1st 26 April 1962 (*divorce* 1990) Caroline Anne, only dau of Lt-Cdr George Gerald Augustin Francis Butler, DSC, RN, of Ashton House, Ashton Keynes, Wilts, and Mrs Patrick Parish, of Shotters Farm, Newton Valence, Hants, and has had:

1 +(LUCIUS) ALEXANDER PLANTAGENET, *Master of Falkland*; *b* 1 Feb 1963; *educ* Westminster, Loretto and RMA Sandhurst; Capt Scots Gds (ret); *m* 1993 *Linda, dau of Raymond Purl, of Colorado City, USA, and has issue:

(1) +A son; *b* 6 Feb 1995

1 Camilla Anne; *b* 3 Feb 1965; *d* 6 June 1972

2 *Samantha Camilla; *b* 30 March 1973

3 *Lucinda Mary; *b* 11 Dec 1974

The 15th VISCOUNT *m* 2nd 1990 *Nicole, dau of Milburn Mackey, and by her has:

2 +Charles Byron Milburn; *b* 1992

Lineage: ADAM de KARRY or CARY; feudal Ld of Castle Cary, Somerset, 1198; ancestor of:

Sir JOHN de CARY, of the Manor of Cary, in the parish of St Giles in the Heath, Devon; had:

Sir JOHN de CARY, of Upper Cary; Ld Ch Baron Exchequer 1386; one of five judges summoned by RICHARD II to Shrewsbury 20 Aug 1387; impeached 1388 and banished to Waterford; *m* 1376 Margaret, dau of Richard de Holeway, of Northlaw, Beaworth and Morton Devon, and *d* Waterford 1404, leaving issue:

Sir ROBERT CARY, of Cockington and Clovelly; *m* 1st Margaret, dau of Sir Philip Courtenay (*see* DEVON, E); *m* 2nd Mrs Jane Wadham (*d* 4 Dec 1449), dau of Sir William Hangesford, and *d* by 1435, having by his 1st w had:

Sir PHILIP CARY, of Cockington; MP Devon 1433; *m* Christiana (*m* 2nd Walter Portman; *see* PORTMAN, V), dau and heir of William Orchard, and *d* 1437, leaving:

Sir WILLIAM CARY, of Cockington; *b* 12 Aug 1437; *m* 1st Elizabeth, dau of Sir William Paulet, and had a s (Robert, of Cockington, ancestor of the CARYs of Torr Abbey, Devon); *m* 2nd Alice, dau of Sir Baldwin Fulford, of Fulford, and was beheaded 6 May 1471 after the Battle of Tewkesbury, having by her had issue, with a dau (Mary, *m* Sir John Delaval, of Seaton Delaval):

THOMAS CARY; *m* Margaret, er dau and coheir of Sir Robert Spencer by Alianor, dau and coheir of Edmund Beaufort, Duke of Somerset (*see* BEAUFORT, D), and *d c* 21 June 1536, having had, with other issue, including a yr son (William, *m* Mary Boleyn, sis of QUEEN ANNE BOLEYN, and was ancestor of the CAREYs, Lords Hunsdon (*see* ALDENHAM and HUNSDON OF HUNSDON, B) and Earls of Dover, and the CAREYs Earls of Monmouth):

Sir JOHN CARY, of Plashey, and Thremhall Priory, Essex; *b c*? 1495; *m* Joice (*d* between 10 Nov 1560 and 30 Jan 1560/1), sis of Sir Anthony Denny and widow of William Walsingham, and *d* 9 Sep 1552, having had issue:

1 Wymond (Sir), of Snettisham, Norfolk; *b* 6 March 1538; *m* by licence 9 May 1589 Catherine, dau of John Jernegan, of Somerleyton, Suffolk, and widow of Henry Crane, and *dsp* 13 April 1612

2 Edward (Sir), of Aldenham and Berkhamsted, Herts; *b c* 1540; Master of the Jewel Office to ELIZABETH I and JAMES I; *m* Catherine (*d* 30 Dec 1622), dau of Sir Henry Knyvett, of Buckenham, Norfolk, and widow of 2nd Baron Paget (*see* ANGLESEY, M), and *d* 18 July 1618, having had:

(1) HENRY, **1st Viscount**

(2) Adolphus, of Berkhamsted; *m* 9 Aug 1596 Anne (*d* 1601), dau and coheir of Sir Robert Corbet, of Moreton Corbet, Salop (*see* 1970 edn CORBET, Bt), and *dsp* 10 April 1609

(3) Philip, of Cardington, Beds, and Hunslet, Yorks; *m* Elizabeth (*d* 1623), dau and heir of Richard Bland, of Carleton, Yorks, and was *bur* 13 June 1631, leaving issue (*see* WILLOUGHBY DE ERESBY, B)

(1) Elizabeth; *m* 20 Nov 1586 Sir John Savile, afterwards Baron Savile, and had issue. He *d* 31 Aug 1630

(2) Frances; *m* 1st Ralph Baesh; *m* 2nd 3 March 1605 7th Earl of Rutland (*see* RUTLAND, D) and was living 1 April 1644

(3) Katherine; *m* 15 Jan 1597 Sir Henry Longueville, of Wolvercote, Bucks. He *d* 17 May 1621

(4) Muriel; *m* 23 Oct 1597 Sir Thomas Crumpton, of Skerne, Yorks, and Hounslow. He was assassinated Abbeville 16 May 1659/60

(5) Jane; *m* 17 Oct 1627 1st and last Lord Barret of Newburgh (*bur* 2 Jan 1644/5; *see* also DACRE, B), Chllr Exchequer, and was *bur* 2 Jan 1632/3

(6) Anne; *m* 16 Sept 1607 Sir Francis Leke, Earl of Scarsdale (*d* 9 April 1655), and *d* by 1660, leaving issue

Sir EDWARD's est s,

HENRY CARY, **1st Viscount of Falkland**, so *cr* 10 Nov 1620, also LORD CARYE (both S); *b c* 1576; MP Herts 1620–22, Ld Dep Ireland 1622–29, author: *The History of the most unfortunate Prince EDWARD II, with choice political observations on him and his unhappy favourites, Gaveston and Spencer* (printed 1680); *m* (contract 27 June 1602) Elizabeth (*d* Oct 1639), only dau and heir of Sir Laurence Tanfield, Ch Baron Exchequer, and was *bur* 25 Sept 1633, having had, with two other sons and six daus (four of whom became nuns in France):

1 LUCIUS CARY, **2nd Viscount of Falkland**, PC (Jan 1641/2); *b* 1610; *educ* Trinity Coll Dublin and St John's Coll Cambridge; MP Newport (IoW) 1640–42; at first supported Parl, but later joined the royalists; Sec of State to CHARLES I 1642–43; *m* Letitia (*bur* 27 Feb 1646/7), dau of Sir Richard Morison, of Tooley Park, Leics, and was *ka* Battle of Newbury 20 Sept 1643, having had, with two other sons:

(1) LUCIUS CARY, **3rd Viscount of Falkland**; *bapt* 5 July 1632; *d* unm Montpelier, France, 27 Sept 1649

(2) HENRY CARY, **4th Viscount of Falkland**, PC (I, 1662); *bapt* 21 Nov 1634; imprisoned in the Tower of London under the Commonwealth on suspicion of being involved in Sir George Booth's plot to restore CHARLES II 1659, MP Oxon 1659 and 1661–63, Oxford City 1660 and (I Parl) Fore 1662–63, Ld Lt Oxon, author: *The Marriage Night* (a comedy); *m* 14 April 1653 Rachel (*m* 2nd Sir James Hayes and *d* 24 Feb 1717/8), dau of Anthony Hungerford, of Blackbourton and Farleigh Castle, Somerset, and *d* 2 April 1663, leaving:

1a ANTHONY CARY, **5th Viscount of Falkland**; *b* 15 Feb 1656; MP (Tory) Oxon 1685–88, Gt Marlow 1689–90 and Gt Bedwyn 1690–94, Treasurer Navy 1681–89, Commr Admlty 1690/1–93, 1st Ld Admlty 1693–94; the H of C resolved 7 Jan 1693/4 that 'one of its members, Viscount Falkland, was guilty of a high misdemeanour and breach of trust by begging and receiving £2,000 [just under £100,000 in late-1990s terms] from His Majesty contrary of the ordinary method of issuing and bestowing the King's money, and that he be committed to the Tower'; *m* Rebecca (*d* 1709), dau of Sir Rowland Lytton (*see* LYTTON, E), and *d* 24 May 1694, having had an only child Harriott (*d* an infant 21 Oct 1683)

2 Lawrence; *bapt* 5 Oct 1613; *ka* suppressing the 1641 Uprising in Ireland at the English victory of Swords, Co Dublin, 1642

3 Patrick, of Dublin; *b* Ireland *c* 1623; admitted Lincoln's Inn 10 Feb 1651/2; *m* 1653 Susan (*d* 25 July 1658), dau of Francis Uvedale, and *d* 15 March 1657/8, having had (with a 2nd s and two other daus):

(1) Edward, of Caldecot; *bapt* 25 April 1656; *m* Anne (*m* 2nd Lord Archibald Hamilton; *see* HAMILTON and BRANDON, D), dau and coheir of 2nd Lord Lucas of Shenfield (*see* LUCAS OF CRUDWELL, B), and *d* by 24 Nov 1692), having had:

1a LUCIUS HENRY, **6th Viscount**

1a Frances; *m* Feb 1705/6 5th Viscount Grandison of Limerick (*see* JERSEY, E) and *d* 17 Feb 1768, leaving issue

(1) Catherine; *m* (contract 2 Aug 1622) 2nd Earl of Home (*qv*) and *dsp*

(2) Victoria; *m* 1st Sir William Uvedale, of Wickham (*bur* 3 Dec 1682); *m* 2nd 14 Aug 1653 Bartholmew Price, of Linlithgow

The 5th VISCOUNT's cousin,

LUCIUS HENRY CARY, **6th Viscount of Falkland**; *b* 27 Aug 1687; *cr* 13 Dec 1722 titular Earl of Falkland by the Old Pretender James III; *m* 1st 5 Oct 1704 Dorothy (*d* 26 Jun 1722), dau of Francis Molyneux, a woollen draper, and had, with other issue:

1 LUCIUS CHARLES, **7th Viscount**

2 George, of Leven Grove, and Southerskelfe, Yorks; Gen; *m* Isabella (*d* 12 April 1799), only dau and heir of Arthur Ingram, of Barrowby, Yorks, and *d* 11 April 1792, leaving issue:

(1) Elizabeth; *m* 26 March 1767 1st Baron Amherst (*see* AMHERST OF HACKNEY, B) and *dsp* 22 May 1830

(2) Catherine; *m* 25 Oct 1775 Sir John Russell, 8th Bt, and *d* 26 Dec 1782, leaving issue. He *d* 7 Aug 1783

The **6th Viscount** *m* 2nd Laura (*d* 12 July 1741), sis of 10th Viscount Dillon (*qv*) of Costello-Gallin, and *d* 31 Dec 1730, having by her had:

1 Lucy; *m* Lt-Gen Count de Rothe, Col Irish Regt of Rothe in French serv, and *d* 7 Feb 1804

The 6th VISCOUNT's est s,

LUCIUS CHARLES CARY, **7th Viscount of Falkland**; *m* 1st 16 April 1734 Jane (*d* 20 Dec 1751), dau and heir of Richard Butler, of London, and widow of James, Lord Villiers (*see* JERSEY, E), and *d* 27 Feb 1875, having had, with two other daus:

1 Lucius Ferdinand, *Master of Falkland*; C-in-C Br Forces Tobago; *m* March 1760 Anne dau of Col Alexander Leith (*see* LEITH- BUCHANAN, Bt), and *dvp* 20 Aug 1780, leaving issue:

(1) HENRY THOMAS CARY, **8th Viscount of Falkland**; *b* 27 Feb 1766; *d* unm 28 May 1796

(2) CHARLES JOHN, **9th Viscount**

(1) Charlotte-Maria; *m* Samuel Charters and had issue

(2) Lucia; *m* 10 Jan 1783 Lt-Col John Grattan, 100th Regt, Adj-Gen India

(3) Lavinia Matilda

(4) Almeria Augusta; *m* 20 Aug 1800 Rev William Digby and *d* 24 June 1811

(5) Emilia Sophia; granted 1834 rank of viscount's dau; *m* 24 April 1798 Maj Charles Thomas Grant of Grant (*see* STRATHSPEY, B)

1 Mary Elizabeth; *m* Rev John Law, DD, Archdeacon Rochester, and *d* 1 Oct 1783, leaving issue. He *d* 5 Feb 1827

2 Frances Dorothy; *m* 12 July 1760 William Plumer, of Gilston Park, Herts, MP Herts, and *d* 1761

3 Charlotte; *m* June 1779 Anthony Chapman

The **7th Viscount** *m* 2nd 10 Oct 1752 Sarah (*d* 27 May 1776), dau of Thomas Inwen, of Southwark, and widow of 10th Earl of Suffolk (*see* SUFFOLK and BERKSHIRE, E), and *d* 27 Feb 1785

The 8th VISCOUNT's bro,

CHARLES JOHN CARY, **9th Viscount of Falkland**; *b* Nov 1768; Capt RN; *m* 25 Aug 1802 Christiana Anton (*d* 25 July 1822) and *d* 28 Feb 1809 of wounds recd in a duel two days earlier with one Arthur Powell, leaving, with a dau (*d* unm):

1 LUCIUS BENTINCK CARY, **10th Viscount of Falkland**, PC, GCH; *b* 5 Nov 1803; rep S peer 1831–32, *cr* 15 May 1832 BARON HUNSDON OF SCUTTERSKELFE, Yorks (UK), Govr Bombay 1848–53; *m* 1st 27 Dec 1830 Amelia FitzClarence (*d* 2 July 1858), illegimate dau of WILLIAM IV and sis of 1st Earl of Munster (*qv*), and had issue:

(1) Lucius William Charles Augustus Frederick, *Master of Falkland*, DL (N R Yorks); *b* 24 Nov 1831; Army Capt; *m* 11 May 1858 Sarah Christiana (*m* 2nd 8 Feb 1876 Col Boyle Vandeleur, 5th Lancers (*d* 12th April 1898), 2nd s of Rev William Vandeleur, Vicar Julianstown, Co Meath, and *d* 4 Oct 1902), only dau of Maj Henry Peach Keighly, of Idlicote, JAG Madras Army, and *dsp* 6 Aug 1871

1 (cont.) The **10th Viscount** *m* 2nd 10 Nov 1859 Elizabeth Catherine, Dowager Duchess of Saint Albans (*qv*; *d* 2 Dec 1893), and *d* 12 March 1884, when the UK Barony expired

2 PLANTAGENET PIERREPOINT CARY, **11th Viscount of Falkland**; *b* 8 Sept 1806; Adml; *m* 27 April 1853 Mary Anne (*d* 2 Jan 1863), only child of John Francis Maubert, of Norwood, Surrey, and *dsp* 1 Feb 1886

3 Byron Charles Ferdinand Plantagenet; *b* 5 Oct 1808; Capt RN; *m* 19 Feb 1844 Selina Mary (*d* 10 Aug 1868), dau of Rev Francis Fox, of Fox Hall, Co Longford, and *d* 21 Feb 1874, having had, with other issue:

(1) BYRON PLANTAGENET, **12th Viscount**

(1) Emma Amelia; granted with her yr sisters 29 Sept 1886 rank of viscount's dau; *m* 8 March 1869 Thomas Benyon Ferguson, barrister, and *d* 2 Dec 1931, leaving issue. He *d* 12 Nov 1875

(2) Selina Catherine; *m* 27 Sept 1877 Charles Edward Fox, barrister, Master of Equity High Court Bombay, and *d* 28 Feb 1946 leaving issue. He *d* 6 Nov 1897

(3) Anne Christiana; *m* June 1898 Maj Servante Morland, of Hextle House, Tonbridge, Kent, s of Thomas Morland, of Montreal, and *d* 14 Jan 1923

The 11th VISCOUNT's n,

BYRON PLANTAGENET CARY, **12th Viscount of Falkland**, JP, DL (N R Yorks); *b* 3 April 1845; Lt-Col Roy Sussex Regt, cmded 4th Bn Yorkshire Regt; rep S peer 1894–1922; *m* 25 Sept 1879 Mary LGStJ (*d* 17 Nov 1920), dau of Robert Reade, of New York, and *d* 10 Jan 1922, having had issue:

1 LUCIUS PLANTAGENET, **13th Viscount**

2 Byron Plantagenet, DSO; *b* 25 Jan 1887; Lt-Cdr RN WW I (despatches); *k* at sea 16 Sept 1917

3 Philip Plantagenet; *b* 24 Sept 1895; *educ* Eton; Maj Gren Gds, served WWs I and II; Bluemantle Pursuivant at Arms 1919–23, York Herald 1923–32, FSA; *m* 20 March 1920 Esther Mildred, only dau of Sir George Edward Leon, 2nd Bt, and *d* 21 June 1968, leaving issue:

(1) *Mary Philippa; *b* 31 March 1922; WW II as 3rd Offr WRNS; *m* 23 April 1947 6th Baron Dunalley (*qv*) and has issue

1 Catherine Mary; *m* 3 June 1912 Lt-Col Sir Godfrey Dalrymple Dalrymple-White, 1st Bt (*qv*), and *d* 16 Oct 1972, leaving issue

2 Mary Selina; SSStJ; *d* unm 6 Nov 1960

3 Lettice Cary; *m* 1st 6 June 1918 Cdr Ralph Neville, RN (*see* BRAYBROOKE, B), and had issue; *m* 2nd 26 Jan 1937 Maj Philip John Sherwin Pearson-Gregory, MC (*d* 12 June 1955), only s of Thomas Sherwin Pearson-Gregory, of Harlaxton Manor, Grantham, and *d* 19 Dec 1963

The 12th VISCOUNT's est surv s,

LUCIUS PLANTAGENET CARY, **13th Viscount of Falkland**, OBE (1919); *b* 23 Sept 1880; *educ* Eton; Capt and Brevet Maj Gren Gds Boer War 1900–02, KAR 1903–05 and WW I, Dep Govr Wandsworth Prison 1910–14, Chev Legn Hon, rep S peer 1922–31; *m* 6 April 1904 Ella Louise (*d* 4 May 1954), er dau of Edward Walter Catford, of Twickenham, and *d* 24 July 1961, having had issue:

1 LUCIUS HENRY CHARLES PLANTAGENET, **14th Viscount**

2 Byron Godfrey Plantagenet; *b* 28 June 1908; *educ* Repton; 2nd Lt Gren Gds, F/O RAFVR WW II; *m* 22 June 1932 Daphne Helen (*d* 11 Jan 1997), er dau of Capt Edward Westcott King, RA, and Mrs J St Vincent Hand, and *d* 1971, having had issue:

(1) +Robert Byron; *b* 30 Nov 1944; *educ* Repton

(1) *(Rosemary) Sally [Mrs Neil Pugh, 118 High St, Wivenhoe, Essex]; *b* 18 June 1935; *m* 1980 *Neil Pugh

(2) *Susan Jane [Mrs Ronald Featherstone, 20 Clinton Rd, Lower Buckland, Lymington, Hants]; *b* 30 Jan 1938; *m* 1960 *Ronald Frederick Featherstone and has issue:

1a *Angus Frederick; *b* 1962
1a *Penelope Helen; *b* 1961; *m* 1985 *Mark Williams
2a *Louise; *b* 1964; *m* 1987 *Mark Snodgrass
3a *Greta Jane; *b* 1965
4a *Katy Ann Lorraine; *b* 1967
5a *Ingrid Laura; *b* 1980

3 +Richard Lorenzo Plantagenet; *b* 31 March 1915; *educ* Repton and Downing Coll Cambridge; *m* 31 July 1959 *Dorothy Denise, yst dau of Mrs Edith Lloyd, of Yorks

1 Rosemary Sylvia; *b* 22 Feb 1910; *m* 1st 17 Aug 1928 (*divorce* 1936) John de Perigault Gurney Mayhew, er s of Lt-Col Sir John Dixon Mayhew, TD, JP, DL, MP, of Newton Hall, Dunmow, Essex; *m* 2nd 6 Jan 1937 Maj Aubrey Esson-Scott, s of David Esson Scott, and had issue by her 1st husb

2 Sheila Cary; *b* 20 March 1912; *m* 8 April 1931 William Philip Neville Edwards, CBE, of Littlehampton, and *d* 20 March 1976, leaving issue

The 13th VISCOUNT's est s,

LUCIUS HENRY CHARLES PLANTAGANET CARY, **14th Viscount of Falkland**; *b* 25 Jan 1905; *educ* Eton; F/O RAFVR WW II 1941–45 (invalided); *m* 1st 14 Oct 1926 (*divorce* 1933) Joan Sylvia, only child of Capt Charles Bonham Southey, Rifle Bde, of Frinton-on-Sea, and had issue:

1 *Elizabeth-Ann Bevil; *b* 20 Aug 1927; *m* 21 Nov 1945 Maj Sir William Vernon Hope Nelson, 3rd Bt (*qv*), and has issue

2 *Jean Rosemary Vera [The Hon Mrs Winch, Castle Barn, Minffordd, Gwynedd]; *b* 29 Oct 1928; artist; *m* 14 Dec 1950 Capt Henry Herman Evelyn Montagu Winch (*d* 1987), only s of Henry Winch (*see* NEWBOROUGH, B)

The **14th Viscount** *m* 2nd 9 Aug 1933 (*divorce* 1958) Constance Mary (*d* 1995), dau of Capt Edward Berry, and by her had issue:

1 LUCIUS EDWARD WILLIAM PLANTAGENET CARY, **15th and present Viscount of Falkland**

The **14th Viscount** *m* 3rd 24 April 1958 (*divorce* 1974) Charlotte Anne, er dau of Bevil Granville, of Wellesbourne, Warwicks, and *d* 16 March 1984

FALMOUTH

Arms: Erm. a rose gu., barbed and seeded ppr. **Crest:** A falcon close ppr. **Supporters:** Two sea-lions erect on their tails arg., guttée de larmes. **Mottoes:** 1 *Patience passe science* ('Patience arrives at knowledge'); 2 *In caelo quies* ('There is peace in heaven'). **Creations:** B. (E) (le Despenser) 24 June 1295/29 July 1314, V. and B. (GB) 9 June 1720.

THE 9TH VISCOUNT FALMOUTH, Baron of Boscawen Rose, Co Cornwall, and **Lord** (Baron) **Le Despenser** (George Hugh Boscawen, JP (Kent 1958)) [The Rt Hon The Viscount Falmouth JP, Tregothnan, Truro, Cornwall TR2 4AW]; *b* 31 Oct 1919; *s* f 1962; *educ* Eton and Trin Coll Cambridge (MA 1947); Capt Coldstream Gds WW II (wounded, despatches), Ld Lt Cornwall 1977–94 (DL 1968–77); *m* 9 May 1953 *(Beryl) Elizabeth Price, er dau of Arthur Harold Browne, of Spring Field, W Peckham, Kent, and has:

1 +EVELYN ARTHUR HUGH; *b* 13 May 1955; *educ* Eton and RAC Cirencester; *m* 23 July 1977 (*divorce* 1995) Lucia Caroline (*m* 2nd 3 May 1997 David Borradaile), est dau of Ralph William Vivian-Neal, FRICS, of Poundisford Park, Taunton, Somerset, and has issue:

(1) +(Evelyn George) William; *b* 1 Oct 1979

(1) +Laura Frances (in remainder to Barony of le Despenser only, as are other female members of the family or issue of such females with a +); *b* 21 Nov 1982

1 (cont.) The Hon Evelyn Boscawen *m* 2nd 7 Oct 1995 *Katherine, est dau of Mark Maley, of Spring House, Alphamstone, Bures, Suffolk, and by her has:

(2) +Frederick Mark; *b* 4 Sept 1996

2 +Nicholas John [The Hon Nicholas Boscawen, Peckham Place, Peckham Bush, Kent TN12 5NA]; *b* 14 Jan 1957; *educ* Eton and RAC; *m* 1985 *Virginia Mary Rose, yr dau of Robin Beare, MB, BS, FRCS, of Scraggs Farm, Cowden, Kent, and has issue:

(1) +Louisa Emily Chiara; *b* 1990
(2) +Georgia Olivia Catharine; *b* 1992

3 +Charles Richard [The Hon Charles Boscawen, Dennington Lodge, Dennington, Suffolk]; *b* 10 Oct 1958; *educ* Eton and Trin Coll Cambridge (MA); *m* 1985 *Frances Diana, yst dau of Maj Hon George Nathaniel Rous (*see* STRADBROKE, E), and has:

(1) +Arthur George; *b* 1991
(2) +John Charles; *b* 1993
(1) +Rosanna Frances; *b* 1989

4 +Vere George [The Hon Vere Boscawen, Bullocks Horn Place, Charlton, Wilts]; *b* 18 Sept 1964; *educ* Eton and Exeter U; *m* 11 May 1991 *Catharine (Kate) Mary, dau of Christopher Halliday, of Whitton Hall, Westbury, Salop, and has issue:

(1) +Harry Christopher; *b* Nov 1992
(2) +Guy William; *b* 11 July 1997
(1) +Isabella Catharine; b 18 Nov 1994

Falmouth (previous creation): Charles Berkeley, a remote connection of the Berkeleys of Berkeley Castle (*see* BERKELEY, B), was created Earl of Falmouth in March 1663/4. The title became extinct a little over a year later on his death without surviving male issue in a naval encounter with the enemy during the Second Dutch War. George FitzRoy, the illegitimate son of CHARLES II who was created Earl of Northumberland in 1674 (*see* NORTHUMBERLAND, D, preliminary remarks), was granted also as a subsidiary title the Viscountcy of Falmouth. Both this and the Earldom of Northumberland became extinct on his death in 1716.

Barony of Le Despenser: The name le Despenser seems to derive from the post of dispenser (a post of second-rank importance in a noble or royal household — somewhere perhaps between under-butler and comptroller — with responsibility for allocating victuals). The Despensers who gave their name to the Barony that is still extant and currently held by the Viscounts Falmouth were originally dispensers to the Earls (or perhaps Constables) of Chester in the early 13th century. Lands could be held by the perfomance of such services to a feudal superior. Another family of dispensers served HENRY III himself and his successors, one of them even being called to Parliament by writ in 1387, though the summons was not repeated to any of his descendants. Nevertheless under later peerage law doctrine a right to the Barony deemed to have been created by the writ of summons of 1387 would have vested in descendants and ultimately passed, via the 2nd Earl of Lovelace (*qv*) and his elder brother, to the Earls of Lytton (*qv*).

The date of creation of the le Despenser Barony held by the Viscounts Falmouth is problematical. The award of the Barony of le Despenser to Lady (Mary) Fane (*see* ABERGAVENNY, M, and WESTMORLAND, E) in 1604 (as a consolation prize for her failure to make out her claim to the Barony of Bergavenny) was with precedence of 1264. But the assembly of 1264 to which the Sir Hugh le Despenser who lived from *c* 1223 to 1265 was summoned is not now considered a bona fide Parliament, and certainly not for the purpose of creating baronies by writs of summons, since it was convened by a rebel, Simon de Montfort, Earl of Leicester, and the writs issued by HENRY III's nominal authority were made out under duress and to a 'packed' body of designated 'Lords of Parliament'. (A similar judgement to the Despenser one — equally impossible to repeat in today's climate of informed opinion — was made over the DE ROS case (*qv*) in 1616.) On a strict interpretation of the 1604 judgement two baronies, created respectively in 1295 and 1338, each with identical wording as to title, and which were both revived in 1461 after early forefeitures had been reversed, were now vested in a single person and with a precedence earlier than either. It is a classic illustration of the amorphous nature of the doctrine of barony by writ of summons as it was developing then and has continued to develop since.

Lineage of Le Despenser: THOMAS le DESPENSER; had:

1 Thomas; feudal lord of Arnesby, Leics; *dsp c* Oct 1218

2 HUGH (Sir)

3 Geoffrey, of Martley; *m* Emma (living 1265), dau of Richard, Sire d'Harcourt, and widow of John de St John, of Stanton (*d* 1229), and *d* 1251, leaving issue:

(1) John; *m* Joan (*d* by 1266), dau of Robert le Lou, of Castle Carlton, and *dsp* 1275

1 Roese; *m* Stephen de Segrave (*d* 1241), of Segrave (*see* MOWBRAY, SEGRAVE and STOURTON, B)

THOMAS le DESPENSER's 2nd s,

Sir HUGH le DESPENSER; feudal Ld of Loughborough, Burton, Hugglescote, Freeby and Arnesby, Leics, Parlington and Hillam, Yorks, Sibsey and Aukborough, Lincs, and Ryhall and Belmesthorp, Rutland; *d* between 23 Feb and 30 May 1238, leaving issue:

1 Sir HUGH le DESPENSER, 1st LORD (Baron) DESPENSER of the putative 1264 *cr*; *b* by 1223; ktd *c* 1244, Constable Horston Castle 1255, one of twelve representatives selected by the barons at the Parl (a convention rather than full Parliament as recognised today) of Oxford June 1258 to press for action by HENRY III to right the wrongs done them and negotiate with the King's Cncl, nominated Justiciar of England by the barons and accordingly appointed to that post by HENRY 1260 but dismissed by him 1261, renominated 1263 by the barons and reappointed with HENRY's agreement, Constable: Tower of London 1263 and Devizes, Oxford, Orford and Nottingham Castles 1264; called to a form of Parl 24 Dec 1264 by writ (*see* preliminary remarks above) whereby according to peerage law doctrine as it stood at the time of the judgement of 1604 he may be reckoned to have been *cr* LORD (Baron) LE DESPENSER (E); *m* Aline or Aliva (*m* 2nd Roger le Bigod, Earl of Norfolk), dau of Sir Philip Basset, of Wycombe, Bucks, and was *k* Battle of Evesham 4 Aug 1265, fighting for Simon de Montfort, Earl of Leicester, against HENRY III, having had issue:

(1) HUGH, *de jure* 2nd LORD (Baron) DESPENSER of the 1264 *cr* and **1st Lord** (Baron) **le Despenser** of the 1295 *cr*

(1) Joan; *m* as his 1st w 1st Lord (Baron) Furnivall(e) (*see* PETRE, B)

1 Pernell; *m* Geoffrey le Sauvage (*d* 1230), of Hintes

HUGH le DESPENCER's s,

HUGH le DESPENSER ('THE ELDER DESPENSER'), **1st Lord** (Baron) **le Despenser** of the 1295 *cr* and 1st and last EARL OF WINCHESTER (E), so *cr* 10 May 1322; *b* 1 March 1260/1; called to Parl by writ 24 June 1295, thus being deemed to have been *cr* a baron (E); sole person of rank to take EDWARD II's part in the quarrel with his nobles over the notorious royal favourite Piers Gaveston, whom EDWARD was eventually induced to banish; later represented EDWARD in negotiating a treaty with his nobles at the time of Gaveston's murder by them in 1312; at Battle of Bannockburn 1314; banished from court by the machinations of his enemies Feb 1314/5; disinherited and exiled in perpetuity Aug 1321, together with his son the younger Despenser, for their alleged misgovernment through and malign influence over EDWARD; this judgement reversed Jan 1321/2 and May 1322; *m* by 1286 Isabel de Beauchamp (*d c* 30 May 1306), dau of William, Earl of Warwick (*see* WARWICK, BROOKE and, E), and widow of Sir Patrick de Chaurces or Chaworces, and after EDWARD had fled to Wales was convicted as a traitor and hanged 27 Oct 1326, when all his honours were forfeited, leaving issue:

HUGH le DESPENSER ('THE YOUNGER DESPENSER'), **1st Lord** (Baron) **le Despenser** of the 29 July 1314 *cr*, KB; associated with his f in the period of ascendancy over EDWARD II in the early 1320s but reckoned more deserving than his f of the hatred of the generality of the baronial class; *m* 1306 Lady Eleanor de Clare (*m* 2nd 1st Lord (Baron) Zouche (of Richard's Castle, Mortimer or Ashby) *see* ZOUCHE, B) and *d* 30 June 1337), dau of 6th Earl of Gloucester and Hertford by his 2nd w Joan (dau of EDWARD I); convicted as a traitor and hanged 29 Nov 1326, when all his honours were forfeited, leaving:

1 HUGH le DESPENSER, 1st and last LORD (Baron) DESPENSER of the 1338 *cr* and *de jure* 2nd/3rd LORD (Baron) LE DESPENSER; *b c* 1308; present Battles of Sluys 1340 and Crécy 1346 during early phase of Hundred Years War, called to Parl by writ 15 Nov 1338 thus becoming LORD (Baron) LE DESPENSER (E); *m* by 27 April 1341 Lady Elizabeth de Montagu (*m* 3rd Guy Lord (Baron) Briene and *d* 31 May 1359), widow of 2nd Lord (Baron) Badlesmere of the 1309 *cr* and dau of William, 1st Earl of Salisbury (*see* SALISBURY, M, preliminary remarks), and *dsp* 8 Feb 1348/9, when the Barony *cr* by writ 1338 expired

2 Edward (Sir), of Pelsthorpe; *m* 20 April 1335 Anne (*d* 8 Aug 1367), dau of Sir William de Ferrers, of Groby, Leics, and *dvp* 30 Sept 1342, leaving issue:

(1) EDWARD le DESPENSER, 1st LORD (Baron) LE DESPENSER (E), so *cr* by writ of summons to Parl 15 Dec 1357, KG (1361); *b* 24 March 1335/6; fought at Battle of Poitiers 1356, Constable English army in an unsuccessful invasion of France 1373–74; *m* by 2 Aug 1354 Elizabeth (*d* 26 July 1409), who by a later doctrine would have been reckoned Baroness Burghersh in her own right, dau and heiress of 4th Lord (Baron) Burghersh of the 1303 *cr*, and *d* 11 Nov 1375, having had issue, with two er sons (*d* young) and an er dau:

1a THOMAS le DESPENSER, **2nd Lord** (Baron) **Le Despenser** of both the 1295 and 1314 creations, also 2nd and last LORD (Baron) DESPENSER of the 1357 *cr* and 1st and last EARL OF GLOUCESTER (E), so *cr* in Parl 29 Sept 1397 (in which same Parl he got the forfeiture of his ggf and gggf (the Elder and Younger Despensers) lifted, thereby becoming rightful holder of their baronies — also presumably the Earldom of Winchester of the 1322 *cr*, though he seems not to have been referred to under such a title), KG (1399); *b* 22 Sept 1373; *m* between 16 April 1378 and 14 Jan 1383/4 Constance (*d* 28 Nov 1416), dau of Edmund, Duke of York, 5th s of EDWARD III, and was beheaded 13 Jan 1399/1400 (after an unsuccessful attempt to overthrow HENRY IV following the latter's usurpation of the throne from RICHARD II the previous year (when THOMAS was degraded from his Earldom), so that when Parl met in Jan 1400/1 all his remaining titles were declared forfeited inasmuch as he had been a traitor), having had issue:

1b Richard; *b* 30 Nov 1396; *dsp* 7 Oct 1414

1b Elizabeth; *d* young

2b Isabel; *b* 26 July 1400; *m* 1st Richard de Beauchamp, Earl of Worcester and Lord (Baron) Bergavenny or Beauchamp de Bergavenny (*see* ABERGAVENNY, M; he *dspm* March 1421/2), and had issue; *m* 2nd, as his 2nd w, Richard de Beauchamp, Earl of Warwick (*see* WARWICK, BROOK and, E; he *d* 30 April 1439), and *d* 27 Dec 1439, having had further issue

1a Anne; *m* 1st by 1 Nov 1376 Sir Hugh de Hastings (*see* HASTINGS, B) and had issue; *m* 2nd by Oct 1390, as his 2nd w, 4th Lord (Baron) Morley (*see* MORLEY, E, preliminary remarks), and *d* 30 or 31 Oct 1426, leaving no issue by him

2a Elizabeth; *m* 1st John d'Arundel and had issue (*see* NORFOLK, D); *m* 2nd, as his 2nd w, 3rd Lord (Baron) (La) Zouche (*qv*) (of Haryngworth)

1 Isabel; *m* as his 1st w 10th/3rd Earl of Arundel (*see* NORFOLK, D)

The forfeiture of the Barony(-ies?) of Le Despenser, both of the 1295 and 1314 creations, had been instituted when the House of Lancaster had newly come to power. It was lifted in 1461 during the brief ascendancy of the Yorkist King EDWARD IV, but by then right to it/them had fallen into abeyance. (For fuller particulars of its/their descent in the century and a half before the abeyance was terminated (25 May 1604), *see* ABERGAVENNY, M). The beneficiary of the determination of the abeyance was:

MARY Nevill(e), **Baroness le Despenser** in her own right; *b* 25 March 1554 (dau and heir of 4th Lord (Baron) Bergavenny, ggs of 1st Lord (Baron) Bergavenny by his 1st w Lady Elizabeth Beauchamp (only child of Richard, Earl of Worcester, by his w Isabel (*see above*), who was in her turn the only child to have issue of the **2nd Lord** (Baron) **le Despenser**); *m* 12 Dec 1574 Sir Thomas FANE, of Badsall, Kent, and *d* 28 June 1626, leaving issue:

FRANCIS FANE, **4th Lord** (Baron) **le Despenser** and 1st EARL OF WESTMORLAND, with whose descendants (*see* WESTMORLAND, E) the Barony remained until the death *sp* 26 Aug 1762 of the 7th EARL OF WESTMORLAND and **10th Lord** (Baron) **le Despenser**, when it fell into abeyance between Sir Francis Dashwood, 2nd Bt, of West Wycombe (*qv*; he was s of Sir Francis Dashwood, 1st Bt, by Mary, est surv dau of 4th Earl of Westmorland and **7th Lord** (Baron) **le Despenser**) and Sir Thomas Stapleton, 5th Bt (s of Sir William Stapleton, 4th Bt, by Catherine, dau of William Paul, of Braywick, Berks, by Catherine, 2nd surv dau of 4th Earl of Westmorland and **7th Lord** (Baron) **le Despenser**). The abeyance was terminated 19 April 1763 in favour of the former:

Sir FRANCIS DASHWOOD, 2nd Bt, and **11th Lord** (Baron) **le Despenser**; *b* Dec 1708; *m* 3 Dec 1745 Sarah (*d* 19 Jan 1769), dau and coheir of George Gould, of Iver, Bucks, and widow of Sir Richard Ellis, and *dsp* 11 Dec 1781, when the Barony again fell into abeyance until the death *sp* 16 May 1788 of his sis Rachel, widow of Sir Robert Austen, 3rd Bt, of Bexley, when it devolved on:

Sir THOMAS STAPLETON, 6th Bt, and **12th Lord** (Baron) **le Despenser** (s of Sir Thomas Stapleton, 5th Bt, above mentioned); *b* 10 Nov 1766; *m* 29 July 1791 Elizabeth (*d* 3 July 1848), dau of Samuel Eliot, of Antigua, and *d* 3 Oct 1831, having had, with two other daus (*d* unm):

1 THOMAS STAPLETON, of Greys Court, Henley-on-Thames, and Mereworth Castle, Kent; *b* 24 April 1792; *m* 2 Feb 1816 Maria Wynne (*d* 15 Oct 1823), yr dau of Henry Bankes, of Kingston Lacy, Dorset, and *dvp* 1 June 1829, leaving issue:

(1) MARY FRANCIS ELIZABETH Stapleton, **Baroness le Despenser** in her own right; *s* her gf 1831; *m* 29 July 1845 Evelyn BOSCAWEN, **6th Viscount Falmouth** (*d* 6 Nov 1889) and *d* 20 Nov 1891, leaving issue (*see* below)

2 William; Lt Bengal Native Inf; *b* 2 Dec 1797; *d* unm 26 Sept 1826

3 Miles John (Rev); *b* 21 March 1801; Rector Mereworth, Kent; *m* 29 Dec 1820 Anne Byam, dau of T N Kerby, of Antigua, and *dvp* 11 June 1830, leaving issue (with a yst dau, *d* unm):

(1) Adelaide; *m* 23 Oct 1851 Capt Catesby Paget (*see* ANGLESEY, M)

(2) Anne Byam; *m* 17 Aug 1858 Augustus Thomas Hotham (*see* HOTHAM, B)

(3) Jane Elizabeth; *m* 30 April 1862 Archibald Godley (*see* KILBRACKEN, B)

4 Sir FRANCIS STAPLETON, 7th Bt (*see* 1970 edn)

1 Maria Frances Catherine; *m* 9 Jan 1813 3rd Earl of Roden (*qv*)

2 Emma; *m* 5 May 1825 6th Viscount Midleton (*qv*) of Midleton

3 Emily; *m* Nov 1817 Lt-Gen Hon Sir Hercules Robert Pakenham (*see* LONGFORD, E)

4 Anna Frances Esther; *m* 3 Dec 1828 7th Baron Farnham (*qv*)

Lineage of Boscawen: The family name derives from the lordship of Boscawen Rose, Cornwall, a manor held by the Boscawens *temp* KING JOHN.

HENRY BOSCAWEN; had:

JOHN BOSCAWEN, of Boscawen Rose; *fl c* 1335; *m* Joan, dau and heir of John Tregothnan, of Tregothnan, Cornwall, and *d* 1357, leaving issue:

JOHN BOSCAWEN, of Boscawen and Tregothnan; *m* Joan, only dau and heir of Otho de Albalanda, and had issue:

JOHN BOSCAWEN; *m* Rose, dau of William Brett, and had:

HUGH BOSCAWEN; *m* Joan, only child of Ralph Trenouth by his 2nd w Maud, dau and heir of John Tregarick, and had issue:

RICHARD BOSCAWEN; *m* 1st Elizabeth, dau of Geoffrey St Aubin; *m* 2nd Maud, dau and heir of Lawrence Hallop, of Trewonwall, and had issue:

JOHN BOSCAWEN; *m* Elizabeth, dau of Nicholas Lower, and had, with an er s:

HUGH BOSCAWEN; *m* Philip, dau and coheir of Nicholas Carminow, and had:

NICHOLAS BOSCAWEN; *m* Alice (*bur* 18 Sept 1580), dau and heir of John Trevantin, and was *bur* 10 May 1626, leaving issue:

HUGH BOSCAWEN, of Tregothnan; *bapt* 28 April 1578; MP Cornwall, Recorder Truro; *m* 22 June 1622 Margaret (*bur* 19 Feb 1635), dau of Robert Rolle, of Heanton Satchville, Devon, and was *bur* 9 Jan 1641, leaving:

EDWARD BOSCAWEN; *bapt* 21 Nov 1628; MP Truro 1660–81; *m* 5 Jan 1665 Jael, dau of Sir Francis Godolphin, KB, and sis of 1st Earl of Godolphin, and *d* between 28 July 1685 and 3 May 1686, leaving issue:

HUGH BOSCAWEN, **1st Viscount Falmouth**, so *cr* 9 June 1720, as also BARON OF BOSCAWEN ROSE, both Co Cornwall (both GB); *b c* 1680; Capt St Mawes Castle 1696–1710 and 1714–34, Groom Bedchamber to DUKE OF GLOUCESTER (s of QUEEN ANNE) 1698–1700 and to PRINCE GEORGE OF DENMARK (ANNE's husb) 1702–08, MP (Whig) Tregony 1702–05, Cornwall 1705–10 and Penryn 1713–20, Warden Stannaries 1708–10 and 1714–34, Comptroller Household 1714–20, Jt V-Treas Ireland 1717–34; *m* 23 April 1700 Charlotte (Maid of Honour to QUEEN ANNE; *d* 22 March 1754), er dau and coheir of Col Charles Godfrey by Arabella Churchill, sis of 1st Duke of Marlborough (*qv*), and *d* 25 Oct 1734, leaving:

1 HUGH BOSCAWEN, **2nd Viscount Falmouth**, PC (1756); *b* 20 March 1706/7; MP (Whig) Truro 1727–34, Capt Yeomen Gd 1747–82, Maj-Gen 1755, Lt Gen 1759, Gen 1772, V-Adml Cornwall 1761–82; *m* 6 May 1736 Hannah Catherine Maria, dau of Thomas Smith, of Worplesdon, and widow of Richard Russel, and *dspl* 4 Feb 1782

2 Edward, PC; *b c* 1711; Adml the Blue, Gen Marines, a Ld of Admlty, recd 6 Dec 1758 the unanimous thanks of the H of C for his mil services in N America; *m* 1742 Frances (*d* 1805), dau of William Evelyn Glanville, of St Clair, Kent, and *d* 10 Jan 1761, leaving issue, with two er sons:

(1) GEORGE EVELYN, **3rd Viscount**

(1) Frances; *m* 5 July 1773 Adml Hon John Leveson-Gower (*see* SUTHERLAND, D)

(2) Elizabeth; *m* 2 Jan 1766 5th Duke of Beaufort (*qv*)

3 George; *b* 1 Dec 1712; Gen; *m* 3 Feb 1742/3 Anne (*d* 1783), dau of John Morley Trevor, of Trevalyn, Denbighs, and *d* 3 May 1775, leaving issue:

(1) George; *b* 4 Sept 1745; *m* Annabella, 2nd dau of Rev Sir William Bunbury, 5th Bt (*qv*)

(2) William; *b* 1752; *m* 1786 Charlotte (*d* 1804), 2nd dau of Rev James Ibbetson, DD, and *d* 1811, leaving:

1a Grace Trevor Charlotte; *m* 1st 1828 William Fleming, of Rayrigg Hall, Lancs; *m* 2nd 1838 Rev James Sydney Darvell and *d* 10 Jan 1871

2a Anne Arabella; *m* Rev C Parkins and *d* 1825, leaving issue

3a Catherine Emily; *m* 1st 1828 Henry Griffiths-Rowlands; *m* 2nd 1836 Rev Fletcher Fleming, of Rayrigg, Westmorland

4a Elizabeth Mary; *m* 17 June 1830 Thomas Griffith (*d* July 1856), of Panpompren, Cards, and *d* 30 Jan 1875, leaving issue

5a Julia; *d* unm 1832

(1) Anne; Maid of Honour to QUEEN CHARLOTTE; *d* 1831

(2) Charlotte; *d* 1829

4 John; *b* Jan 1714; Maj-Gen; *m* Dec 1748 Thomasine, dau of Robert Surman, of Vanentine House, Essex, and *d* 1767, leaving issue:

(1) William Augustus Spencer; *b* 7 Jan 1750; MP; Lt-Col Foot Gds; *d* 1828, leaving issue:

1a George; *b* 1802; Capt RE; *d* 1832

2a Evelyn Spencer; *b* 1803; Capt Army; *d* 1845
1a Mary; *m* 1st 1827 Capt W H Foy (*d* 1838), HEICS; *m* 2nd 1840 William Newnham
2a Elizabeth Spencer; *m* 1829 John Foy
(2) Hugh; Kt Marshal Roy Household; *d* 1795
5 Nicholas (Rev); DD; *b* 16 Aug 1720; Dean St Buryan, Cornwall; *m* Jane (*d* Jan 1797), yst dau of John Woodward, of Eton and Butler's Marston, Warwicks, and widow of Hon Edward Finch Hatton (*see* WINCHILSEA and NOTTINGHAM, E), and *d* 4 July 1793, having had issue:
(1) Nicholas; *b* 1756; army offr; *m* 1784 Mary Brown and *dsp*
1 Lucy; *m* 18 Aug 1746 Sir Charles Frederick, KB, and *d* 17 Jan 1784, leaving issue
2 Charlotte; *m* 11 Feb 1719/20 4th Earl of Drogheda (*qv*) and *dsp* 4 April 1735
3 Anne; *m* 1726 Sir Cecil Bisshopp, 6th Bt (*d* 15 June 1778; *see* ZOUCHE, B), and was *bur* 11 May 1749, leaving issue
4 Mary; *m* 17 Aug 1732 Sir John Evelyn, 2nd Bt, MP (*d* 11 June 1767), of Wotton, and *d* 19 Sept 1749, leaving issue

The 2nd VISCOUNT's n,
GEORGE EVELYN BOSCAWEN, **3rd Viscount Falmouth**, PC (1790); *b* 6 May 1758; *m* 26 June 1784 Elizabeth Anne (*d* 10 Aug 1793), dau and heir of John Crewe, of Bolesworth Castle, Cheshire, and *d* 8 Feb 1808, leaving issue:
1 EDWARD BOSCAWEN, **4th Viscount Falmouth** and 1st EARL OF FALMOUTH (UK), so *cr* 14 July 1821; *b* 10 May 1787; *m* 27 Aug 1810 Anne Frances (*d* 1 May 1864), est dau of Henry Bankes, of Kingston Lacy, Dorset, and *d* 29 Dec 1841, leaving issue:
(1) GEORGE HENRY BOSCAWEN, **5th Viscount Falmouth** and 2nd EARL OF FALMOUTH; *b* 8 July 1811; High Steward Wallingford 1845; *d* unm 29 Aug 1852, when the Earldom expired
2 John Evelyn (Rev); *b* 1790; Canon Canterbury, Rector Wotton, Vicar Ticehurst; *m* 1814 Catherine Elizabeth (*d* 30 July 1859), dau of Arthur Annesley (*see* VALENTIA, V), and *d* 12 April 1851, leaving, with other issue:
(1) EVELYN BOSCAWEN, **6th Viscount**
(2) John Townshend (Rev); MA; *b* 30 Oct 1820; Rector Lamorran, Cornwall; granted rank of viscount's yr s; *m* 13 Feb 1851 Mary (*d* 25 Nov 1895), dau of John Hearle Tremayne, of Heligan, Cornwall, and *d* 7 July 1889, having had:
1a John Hugh; *b* 2 Dec 1851; Lt RN (Ashanti War Medal); Lt-Col NZ Army; *m* 1st 1876 Katherine Isabel (*d* 1884), dau of Rev John W Conway Hughes, Vicar Nydd, nr Leeds, and had issue:
1b Hugh Townshend; *b* 1880; Capt NZ Inf; *m* Kathleen, dau of Richard Crowe, Sec Educn Bd, Auckland, and was *ka* 1917, leaving issue:
1c *Patricia; *b* 1910
1b Valentia Maud; *m* 29 Jan 1899 (*divorce*) Maj James Skitt Matthews, Canadian Inf, and had issue
2b Gwladys Evelyn; *m* 1911 Bruce Shearer Treliving Joll and had issue
1a (cont.) Lt John Boscawen *m* 2nd 15 Sept 1886 Ellen (*d* 21 Jan 1895), yst dau of Henry Parker, of Louth, Lincs, and had further issue:
2b Spencer; *b* 1887; Capt NZ Artillery WW I (despatches, Croix de Guerre); *m* 1919 Sydney Iris Kelly (*d* 1982) and *d* 1957, leaving issue:
1c +John Roger [John Boscawen Esq, Whitford Park Rd, Manurewa RD2, Auckland, NZ]; *b* Sept 1922; F/Lt RNZTAF WW II SW Pacific 1943–45 (Star, Pacific Star, two medals), with NZ Shipping Co and Seaport Operations Ltd, Auckland
2c +Owen Tremayne [Owen Boscawen Esq, 232 Whitford Park Rd, Whitford, Auckland, NZ]; *b* 1925; *educ* Otahuhu Coll and Royal NZ U (BSc, BA, DipEd); Pncpl Otahuhu Coll; WW II as LAC RNZAF; *m* 1st 1954 (*divorce* 1981) Beverly Rose, dau of — Wheeler, of Papatoetoe, NZ; *m* 2nd 1982 *Mrs Mary Joan Hilford and has had issue by his 1st w:
1d +John Spencer; *b* 1956
1d Leanne Kay; *b* 1960; *d* 1980
1c *Diana Margaret [Mrs Alan Arlington, PO Box 9, Whitford, Auckland, NZ]; *b* 1926; *m* 1950 *Alan Frederick Arlington
2c *Sydney Joy [Mrs Walter Flatz, 104 Rebout Rd, Manukau City, Auckland, NZ]; *b* 1931; *m* 1959 *Walter Flatz
3c *Vanda Vivian [Mrs Clement Harris, 172 Whitford Park Rd, Manurewa RD, Auckland, NZ]; *b* 1935; *m* 1958 *Clement Henry Harris
4b Dorothy Beryl; *b* 1890
1a (cont.) Lt John Boscawen *m* 3rd 1896 Teresa Catherine, BA (NZ U) (*d* 1949), 2nd dau of C Gerkens, of NZ, and *d* 20 April 1937, having by her had:
3b +Edward Aroha [Edward Boscawen Esq, 119 Victoria Street, Potts Point, Sydney, NSW, Australia]; *b* 1898; Lt NZ Mounted Rifles and Camel Corp WW I Palestine
2a George Henry; *b* 1859; *d* 3 April 1891
3a Arthur Townshend (Rev), JP; *b* 9 July 1862; Rector Ludgvan, Cornwall, Hon Canon Truro Cathedral, T/Chaplain 1st Bn Cornwall Vol Regt 1917; *m* 2 Sept 1902 Christian Chapell (*d* 13 Nov 1940), dau of Chapell Hodge, of Pounds, Plymouth, and *d* 17 July 1939, leaving issue:
1b *Violet Mary [Mrs Humphrey Tyringham, Little Wood, Buckland Monachorum, Devon]; *b* 12 June 1903; *m* 1st 7 Aug 1929 Lt-Cdr David Cameron Williams, RN (*d* 26 Sept 1931), est s of Rev Leonard Williams, and has issue (*see* WILLIAMS, Bt, of Tregullow); *m* 2nd 17 June 1946 Humphrey Douglas Tyringham (*d* 1986), 2nd s of Roger William Giffard Tyringham, JP, of Trevethoe, Cornwall, formerly of Tyringham, Bucks
2b *Karenza Margaret [Mrs Richard Weatherby, Nanceglos, Madron, Penzance, Cornwall]; *b* 11 Nov 1904; *m* 3 March 1943 Richard Copeland Weatherby (*d* 4 Oct 1953)
4a Townshend Evelyn; *b* 10 Dec 1864; *m* 3 July 1902 Mary Sophia (*d* 22 Dec 1948), est dau of Thomas Algernon Smith Dorrien-Smith, DL, of Tresco Abbey, Scilly Isles, and *d* 16 Sept 1936, leaving issue:
1b John Perceval Townshend, MBE (1945); *b* 14 Feb 1960; *educ* Eton; Maj Gren Gds WW II; *m* 21 April 1931 *Lady Mary Helen Alma Graham (*m* 2nd 15 Dec 1975 Brig Leslie C Dunn, TD, DL, who *d* 1990), er dau of 6th Duke of Montrose (*qv*), and *d* 9 Oct 1972, leaving issue:
1c James Townshend; *b* 8 May 1932; Lt Gren Gds; *m* 24 Feb 1955 *Deirdre Elsie Elizabeth [Lady Drinkwater, Boltachan House, Aberfeldy, Perthshire] (*m* 2nd 17 Jan 1998 Sir John Drinkwater, QC), yr dau of Frederick Henry (Derek) Curtis-Bennett, QC, and *d* 1992, leaving issue:
1d *Caroline Elizabeth; *b* 2 Nov 1959; *m* 12 June 1982 *Angus G Fleming, er s of Maj Richard Fleming, of Zimbabwe, and has issue:
1e *James; *b* 1991
2e *George; *b* 1994
1e *Lucy; *b* 16 June 1984
2d *Diana Mary *b* 14 July 1962; *m* 1991 *Nigel R Fielder, s of Geoffrey Fielder, of Wells, Somerset, and has:
1e *Edward Townshend Farrar; *b* 1994
1e *Georgina Louise; *b* 1992
2c +Simon John Evelyn [Simon Boscawen Esq, Jackson's Cottage, Rudgwick, Sussex]; *b* 10 Sept 1936; *educ* Eton; 2nd Lt Gren Gds; *m* 21 April 1961 *Judith Perdita Rosemary, only dau of Arthur Gregory George Marshall, JP, by Rosemary Wynford, 2nd dau of Marcus Southwell Dimsdale, MA (*see* 1956 edn Foreign Titles Section), and has:
1d +Alistair John Evelyn [Alistair Boscawen Esq, 18 Graham Rd, London SW19]; *b* 24 May 1963; *m* 1990 *Victoria A M, dau of William Porter, of Wimbledon
2d +David Simon Townshend; *b* 24 May 1965; *m* 1993 *Clare Victoria, est dau of John Edmund Kincaid Floyd (*see* FLOYD, Bt), and has:
1e *Megan; *b* 19–
2e *Flora Rose; *b* 19 March 1997
3d +John Michael Arthur; *b* 14 Feb 1969
1b *Edith Joan [Mrs Peter Cookson, Manor Farm, Upper Slaughter, Glos]; *b* 27 Sept 1909; *m* 18 Feb 1944 Capt Peter Henry Cookson, MC, 10th Roy Hus, yr s of Col Philip Blencowe Cookson, CMG, OBE, of Meldon Park, Northumberland, and has issue:
1c *Robert Edwin; *b* 27 Nov 1946
1c *Mary Anne; *b* 29 April 1952
5a Perceval Noel; *b* 25 Dec 1870; *d* unm 11 Oct 1905
1a Mary; *d* 2 Feb 1888 aged 34
2a Catherine Elizabeth; *d* 11 Sept 1875
3a Ethel; *d* unm 12 Jan 1942
4a Caroline; *d* 28 April 1870
5a Maud; *d* 17 March 1861
6a Blanche; *d* unm 26 Feb 1953
7a Margaret; *d* unm 31 March 1942
(1) Charlotte; granted with her sisters rank of viscount's dau; *m* 6 Aug 1838 Rev G B Moore, MA, Rector Tunstall, Kent, and *d* 28 Aug 1851, leaving issue
(2) Frances; *m* 12 Feb 1850 her cousin Arthur Edward Somerset and *d* 23 Oct 1882, leaving issue (*see* BEAUFORT, D)
(3) Catherine; *m* 13 June 1848 Rev Lewis Francis Bagot, MA (*d* 14 Aug 1870), Rector Leigh, and *d* 11 Aug 1891
(4) Anne; *m* 13 July 1854 Rev Leveson Cyril Randolph, MA (*d* 1 March 1876), Vicar St Luke's, W Norwood, and *d* 27 Feb 1899, leaving issue
(5) Lucy; *m* 26 July 1864 Col Bonar Millett Deane (*d* 28 Jan 1881), 2nd s of Rev George Deane, Rector Bighton, Hants, and *d* 25 March 1886, leaving issue
1 Elizabeth; *m* 23 June 1808 Lord Arthur John Henry Somerset (*d* 18 April 1816), 4th s of 5th Duke of Beaufort (*qv*), and *d* 3 March 1872, leaving issue
2 Anne Evelyn; *m* 3 Oct 1810 Sir George Warrender, 4th Bt (*see* BRUNTISFIELD, B), and *dsp* 5 March 1871

The 5th VISCOUNT's cousin,
EVELYN BOSCAWEN, **6th Viscount Falmouth**; *b* 18 March 1819; *m* 29 July 1845 Mary Frances Elizabeth (*d* 20 Nov 1891) **Baroness le Despenser** in her own right (*see* above) and *d* 6 Nov 1889, leaving:
1 EVELYN EDWARD THOMAS, **7th Viscount**
2 Hugh le Despenser, JP (Middx and Co Wicklow), DL (Co Wicklow); *b* 28 Feb 1849; Lt 1st Life Gds; *m* 23 May 1872 Lady Mary Fitzwilliam (*d* 1 July 1921), dau of 6th Earl Fitzwilliam (*see* 1970 edn), and *dsp* 8 April 1908
3 John Richard de Clare, JP (Kent and Cornwall), DL (Cornwall); *b* 19 Dec 1860; Capt and Hon Maj 4th Bn Oxfordshire LI; *m* 11 June 1890 Margaret Florence Lucy (*d* 6 March 1945), dau of 2nd Earl of Strafford (*qv*), and *d* 12 Dec 1915, leaving:
(1) Catherine Margaret, JP (Essex); *b* 29 May 1891; *m* 1st 28 June 1913 16th Baron Petre (*qv*) and had issue; *m* 2nd 21 July 1921 Sir Frederick Carne Rasch, 2nd Bt (*qv*)
1 Mary Elizabeth Frances Catherine; *m* 26 June 1894 Rev Arthur Murray Dale, Rector Ladbroke, Warwicks, and *d* 21 Jan 1916
2 Edith Maria; *d* unm 24 Sept 1906
3 Mabel Emma; *m* 18 April 1882 Maj Charles Henry Bennett Williams, 5th s of Sir Hugh Williams, 3rd Bt, of Bodelwyddan (*qv*), and *d* 26 Oct 1927, leaving issue

The 6th VISCOUNT's est s,
EVELYN EDWARD THOMAS BOSCAWEN, **7th Viscount Falmouth**, KCVO (1905, MVO 1897), CB (1885), JP (Kent), DL (Kent and Cornwall); *b* 24 July 1847; Dep Warden Stannaries 1911, Maj-Gen 1898, Col 1886 and Col cmdg 1893 Coldstream Gds (served Egypt 1882 and Nile Expdn 1884–85), Chm Cornwall TFA, Assist Mil Sec to C-in-C Ireland; *s* mother 1891 as **14th Lord** (Baron) **le Despenser**; *m* 19 Oct 1886 Hon Kathleen Douglas-Pennant (*d* 29 Dec 1953), dau of 2nd Baron Penrhyn (*qv*), and *d* 1 Oct 1918, having had:
1 EVELYN HUGH JOHN, **8th Viscount**
2 George Edward, DSO; *b* 6 Dec 1888; Brevet Maj RA, ADC to HRH DUKE OF CONNAUGHT when Govr-Gen Canada 1913, DAAG 1915, GSO2 1916; *d* 6 June 1918 of wounds recd in action
3 Vere Douglas; *b* 3 Aug 1890; Lt Coldstream Gds Special Res; *ka* nr Ypres 29 Oct 1914

4 Mildmay Thomas, DSO (1916), MC; *b* 5 Feb 1892; *educ* Eton and Trin Coll Cambridge (BA); Lt-Col Res of Offrs, Capt Rifle Bde, WW I (despatches); *d* unm 13 Nov 1958

1 Kathleen Pamela Mary Corona; *b* 29 April 1902; *m* 22 April 1937 Maj Henry Sherek (*d* 23 Sept 1967), Rifle Bde, s of Bernard Sherek, of Beaulieu, France, and *dsp* 25 June 1995

The 7th VISCOUNT's est s,

EVELYN HUGH JOHN BOSCAWEN, **8th Viscount Falmouth**; *b* 5 Aug 1887; *educ* Eton and Trin Coll Cambridge (BA 1908); Capt Coldstream Gds, Hon Capt RAF, WW I, CA, LCC 1931–37, chm govrs Imp Coll Science and Technology 1947 (Hon Fell 1944); *m* 17 March 1915 Mary Margaret Desiree, CBE (1946), OStJ, only dau of Hon Frederick George Lindley Meynell (*see* HALIFAX, E), and *d* 18 Feb 1962, having had issue:

1 Evelyn Frederick Vere; *b* 25 Aug 1916; *educ* Eton and Magdalene Coll Cambridge (BA); Lt Coldstream Gds WW II; *ka* 21 May 1940

2 GEORGE HUGH BOSCAWEN, **9th and present Viscount Falmouth**

3 +Henry Edward [The Hon Henry Boscawen, The Garden House, The High Beeches, Handcross, Sussex]; *b* 4 Oct 1921; *educ* Eton and Peterhouse, Cambridge; MICE, Lt RE WW II, High Sheriff W Sussex 1979–80; *m* 14 July 1951 *Anne Philippa, er dau of Col Sir Edward Courtenay Thomas Warner, 2nd Bt (*qv*), and has issue:

(1) +Thomas Edward; *b* 10 Feb 1964

(1) +Sarah Kathleen; *b* 13 March 1958; *m* 1986 *Jeremy M Bray, yr s of Christopher Bray, of Southwold, Suffolk, and has issue:

1a +Alice Frances; *b* 1988

2a +Emily Sarah; *b* 1991

3a +Susannah Nesta; *b* 1993

(2) +Jessica Frances; *b* 14 June 1960; *m* 1990 *Hubert Alastair Speare-Cole, s of Cdr M B Speare-Cole, and has:

1a +Antonia Margaret; *b* 1991

2a +Rebecca Anne; *b* 1993

4 +Robert Thomas, MC (1944), PC (1992) [The Rt Hon Robert Boscawen MC, PC, Ivythorn Manor, Street, Somerset BA16 0TZ]; *b* 17 March 1923; *educ* Eton and Trin Coll Cambridge; Capt Coldstream Gds WW II (wounded); MP (C) Wells 1970–83 and Somerton and Frome 1983–92, Assist Govt Whip 1979–81, Ld Commr Treasury 1981–83, V-Chamberlain Household (Govt Whip) 1983–86 and Comptroller 1986–88, memb London Exec Cncl NHS 1954–65, V-Chm C Parly Health and Social Security Ctee 1974, underwriting memb Lloyd's 1952–; *m* 19 Nov 1949 *Mary Alice, JP (London 1961), er dau of Col Sir Geoffrey Ronald Codrington, KCVO, CB, CMG, DSO, OBE, TD (*see* CODRINGTON, Bt, of Dodington Park (1721)), and has:

(1) +Hugh Geoffrey Robert; *b* 7 Feb 1954; *educ* Eton and Bristol U (BA); Lt-Col Coldstream Gds, Gulf War 1991, cmded 1st Bn Coldstream Gds 1994–96, (QGVS 1997); *m* 1981 *Alexandra Marie-Monique, dau of Anthony Eden, of Torberry House, W Harting, Sussex, and has:

1a +Veryan John Hugh; *b* 1987

2a +Aldwyn George Hugh; *b* 1989

(1) +Dozmary Carolyn Claire; *b* 24 June 1951; *m* 1984 *David B Keller, s of Col Blanton S Keller, and has:

1a +Nicholas Francis David; *b* 1988

(2) +Karenza Pamela Mary; *b* 8 Aug 1961

1 +Mary Kathleen, JP (Cornwall 1960) [The Hon Mrs Verney JP, Trevella, St Erme, Truro, Cornwall]; *b* 11 June 1926; WW II WRNS; *m* 17 Jan 1948 Lt-Cdr David Verney, RN (*d* 1992), yr s of Lt-Col Sir Ralph Verney, 1st Bt, of Eaton Square (*qv*), and has issue

FANSHAWE OF RICHMOND

Arms: Quarterly, 1st and 4th, per pale or and sable on a chevron per pale sable and or, between three fleurs-de-lys, as many leopard's heads counterchanged (for ROYLE); 2nd, or a chevron between three fleurs-de-lys sable (for FANSHAWE); 3rd, checky azure and argent, overall a cross gules (FANSHAWE augmentation 1649). **Crest:** On a chapeau sable, doubled erminois, a dragon's head erased or, breathing flames of fire proper. **Supporters:** Two dragons or, winged sable, each breathing flames of fire proper and gorged with a collar checky argent and azure rimmed gules. **Motto:** *Dux vitae ratio in cruce victoria* ('Leadership in life depends on victory in the Cross'). **Creation:** B. (LP, UK) 1983.

THE BARON FANSHAWE OF RICHMOND, of South Cerney, Co Glos (Sir Anthony Henry Fanshawe Royle, KCMG (1974)) [The Rt Hon The Baron Fanshawe of Richmond KCMG, 47 Cadogan Place, London SW1; The Chapter Manor, South Cerney, Glos]; *b* 27 March 1927; *educ* Harrow and RMA Sandhurst; Capt Life Gds 1945–48, 21st SAS Regt (TA) 1948–51; MP (C) Richmond 1959–83; PPS to: Parly U-Sec Colonies 1960, Sec for Air 1960–62, Min Aviation 1962–64; V-Chm C Parly For Affrs Ctee 1965–67, Memb Assembly Cncl Europe and WEU 1965–67, C Whip 1967–70, Parly U-Sec FCO 1970–74, V-Chm C Party Orgn 1979–84 (Chm Internat Offices 1979–84); chm: Wilkinson Sword Gp 1980–83, Sedgwick Gp 1993–97 (dir 1984–); dir Westland Gp 1985–94, Rank Xerox UK 1988–, TI Gp 1990–; Esteemed Family Order Brunei 1st Cl 1975; *m* 1957 *Shirley, dau of John Ramsay Worthington, and has:

1 *Susannah Caroline Fanshawe; *b* 1960; *m* 1992 *Guy C Lester, yr s of Gerald Lester

2 *Lucinda Katherine Fanshawe; *b* 1962

Lineage: Sir LANCELOT CARRINGTON ROYLE, KBE; had:

ANTHONY HENRY FANSHAWE, *cr* a **Baron**

FARINGDON

Arms: Or three piles issuant from the sinister vert, on a chief erm. three torteaux. **Crest:** A hand holding a torteau charged with a mullet of six points arg. **Supporters:** Dexter, a chevalier armed at all points holding in his dexter hand a lance with Lord Faringdon's pennon bearing the motto *'Sursum corda'* all ppr.; sinister, a centaur drawing his bow ppr. **Motto:** *Sola virtus nobilitat* ('Virtue alone ennobles'). **Creations:** Bt. (UK) 5 Aug 1902, B. (UK) 24 Jan 1916.

THE 3RD BARON FARINGDON, of Buscot Park, Co Berks, and a **Baronet** (Sir Charles Michael Henderson, Bt) [The Rt Hon The Lord Faringdon, Buscot Park, Faringdon, Oxon SN7 8BU]; *b* 3 July 1937; *s* unc 1977; *educ* Eton and Trin Coll Cambridge (BA 1961); dir Cazenove 1968–, chm: Witan Investment Co plc 1980–, Bd of Govrs Royal Marsden Hosp 1980–85, RCHM 1994–; Ld in Waiting 1998–; *m* 30 June 1959 *Sarah Caroline, only dau of Maj John Marjoribanks Eskdale Askew, CBE, DL (*see* SUTHERLAND, D), and has issue:

1 +JAMES HAROLD [The Hon James Henderson, Eaton Grange, nr Grantham, Lincs NG32 1ET]; *b* 14 July 1961; *educ* Eton and Pembroke Coll Cambridge; *m* 1986 *Lucinda Maria, yst dau of Desmond Hanson, of Knipton, Lincs, and has issue:

(1) +George Alexander; *b* 18 May 1992
(2) +Frederick Walter; *b* 16 July 1994
(1) *Annabel Rose; *b* 1989

2 +Thomas Alexander Gavin; *b* 9 Feb 1966; *educ* Eton; *m* 1997 *Eve Crame
3 +Angus George; *b* 30 Sept 1969; *m* 11 Oct 1997 *Alexia, only dau of Mrs Y M Hedley, of Westwood, Wilts, and K H Hedley, of Chagford, Devon
1 *Susannah Jane; *b* 10 May 1963; *m* 1986 *Aidan James Maitland-Robinson, only s of Joseph W C Maitland-Robinson, of Jersey, and has:

(1) *Joseph Charles; *b* 1989
(2) *Samuel; *b* 199–
(1) *Joanna Alice; *b* 1987
(2) *Sarah Florence; *b* 1990
(3) *Helena; *b* 1992

Lineage: JOHN HENDERSON; *m* Elizabeth, dau of John Haldane, MP Dumfries (S Parl) and Perth (GB Parl), and *d* 1752, leaving:

BERNARD HENDERSON; *b* 29 June 1750; *m* 20 April 1772 Christiana Robinson (*d* 19 Sept 1790) and *d* 13 June 1812, leaving:

GEORGE HENDERSON, of Langdon, Dumfriesshire, and Edinburgh; settled London 1805; *b* 15 April 1781; *m* 10 Aug 1813 Elizabeth Stalker (*d* April 1836), and *d* 17 July 1856, leaving:

GEORGE HENDERSON, of Langholm, Dumfriesshire; translated Gospel of St Matthew and the song of Solomon into Lowland Scottish, sub-ed *British Bee Journal*; *b* 11 Dec 1819; *m* 20 May 1845 Eliza (*d* 22 Nov 1918 aged 91), dau of George William Cockshott, of York, and *d* 21 Dec 1889, having had issue:

1 George; *b* 7 Aug 1846; *m* Elizabeth Wilson and *d* 1894, leaving issue:
(1) Bernard; *b* 186–; *m* 1898, Winifred Rix and *d* 1940, leaving issue:
1a Eric George; *b* 1899; *d* unm 1959
1a *Elvira; *b* 1903; *m* 1934 *John Humphreys and has issue:
1b *Peter John; *b* 1935; *m* 1959 *Janet Marshall
1b *Veronica Jane; *b* 1945
(2) Douglas; *b* 1870; *m* Caslott Price, and had issue:
1a Sylvia
(3) Duncan Ross; *b* 1873; *m* Margaretta Huxtable (*d* 1956) and *d* 1957, leaving:
1a William
1a Eda; *m* — and had issue
2a Violet; *m* — and had issue
(4) George Frederick; *b* 22 Sept 1876; *m* 15 March 1905 Elizabeth Mary Ann Goode and *d* 13 Oct 1953, leaving:
1a *Reginald Goode; *b* 30 Dec 1914; *m* 16 Sept 1956 *Margaret Elizabeth Sharp
1a *Marjory; *b* 8 Sept 1906; *m* 14 Sept 1935 *Walden John Rowland and has issue:
1b *Rosemary Jane; *b* 19 April 1939
(5) Sydney; *b* 1880; *d* 1901
(6) Howard; *b* 1881
(7) Harry Haldane; *b* 1882; *m* Edith Meadows, and was *k* with her by a bomb 1942, leaving issue:
1a Owen; *m* Sylvia — and had issue:
1b *Penelope; *b* 1945
2a *Donald; *b* 1923; *m* 19– *Monica Packer, and has issue:
1b *Mark; *b* 1954
1b *Christine; *b* 1948
1a Jessie; *b* 1913; *k* by a bomb 1942
(1) Mildred; *b* 20 Oct 1876; *m* 14 July 1900 Frank Barton (*das* 23 Aug 1915), and *d* 9 Feb 1963, leaving issue
(2) Jessie Louise; *b* Oct 1874
(3) Janie; *b* 29 May 1883

2 ALEXANDER, **1st Baron**
3 Bernard; *b* 11 Aug 1852; *d* unm 8 Feb 1906
4 Frank; *b* 7 March 1858; *m* Nov 1887 Agnes Augusta Nunn (*d* 1 Feb 1941), and *d* 21 June 1935, leaving:
(1) Kenneth; *b* 31 Oct 1889; *m* 1st 25 June 1915 (*divorce* 1923) Winifred Ellen Lester, and had issue:
1a *Kenneth Ian; *b* 13 April 1916; *m* 1947 *Mary Templeton Lawrence and has issue:
1b *Thomas Lawrence; *b* 26 Aug 1954
1b *Anna Francesia; *b* 8 Sept 1947
2a *Nigel Graeme; *b* 1 April 1917; *m* 25 Jan 1943 *Karin Judith Stephen and has issue:
1b *Edward Stephen; *b* 17 March 1954
2b *Stephen Nigel; *b* 13 Nov 1956
1b *Clement Drusilla; *b* 4 Aug 1944
2b *Justine; *b* 23 Feb 1946
1a *Fiona Susan; *b* 13 April 1918; *m* 14 March 1936 Alister George Douglas Watson and has issue:
1b *Sarah; *b* 18 Dec 1936
(1) Kenneth Henderson *m* 2nd 26 Nov 1925 Elsie Norah Christie and by her had issue:
3a *Malcolm Hugh; *b* 22 June 1927; *m* 26 Dec 1959 *Sylvia Cardemil and has issue:
1b *Kenneth Albert; *b* 26 Dec 1961
1b *Valcria Anne; *b* 7 Jan 1961
2a *Dorothy Annette; *b* 14 July 1930; *m* 8 March 1952 *John Alexander Kemp McCulloch and has issue:
1b *Ian Kemp; *b* 7 July 1960
1b *Helen Lynnette; *b* 20 Aug 1954
2b *Daphne; *b* 12 Jan 1956
(1) Dorothy; *b* 9 Oct 1888; *m* 21 June 1913 Col Douglas Lyall Grant and *d* 9 Nov 1920, leaving issue
(2) *Ines; *b* 11 Dec 1903; *m* 16 May 1931 *Ambrose Kennedy Cassells and has issue:
1a *Michael Kennedy; *b* 10 May 1933
2a *David Kennedy; *b* 3 July 1935
3a *Patrick Kennedy; *b* 21 July 1938
4a *Neil Andrew Kennedy; *b* 19 April 1943

5 Henry William, of West Woodhay House, Newbury, Berks; *b* 28 May 1862; *m* 14 June 1890 Elvira de Orihuela (Elvira Todd) (*d* 18 Dec 1901), and *d* 16 March 1931, leaving issue:
(1) Ronald Henry White; Maj; *b* 1 Dec 1893; *m* 1 Feb 1917 (*divorce* 1928) Marjorie May Garrard and *d* 12 Feb 1956, leaving issue:
1a *Hugh Chetwode; *b* 27 Nov 1918; *m* 1st 18 March 1943 (*divorce* 1960) Marion Alice, Mather; *m* 2nd 5 Nov 1963 *Pamela Violet, formerly w of Lt-Col Gerald Vigors de Courcy, The O'Grady, MC, and er dau of Col Thomas Anson Thornton, CVO, DL, of Brockhall, Northants, and by his 1st w has:
1b *Richard Ian [Richard Butler-Henderson Esq, 10 Arden House, Earls Court Road, London SW10]; *b* 2 Sept 1945; *educ* Eton; *m* 14 Oct 1972 *Anne Elizabeth Mary, 4th dau of M A Callender, of Chelsea, and Woodside Lodge, East Lulworth, Dorset, and has:
1c *Horatia; *b* 12 June 1977
1b *Virginia Anne [Miss Virginia Butler-Henderson, 11 Argyll Mansions, Beaufort Street, London SW3]; *b* 5 June 1944
2b *Lorraine Rosemary [Mrs John Grant, La Carlina, Noetinger, Cordoba, Argentina]; *b* 7 Sept 1946; *m* 19– John Alistair Grant, s of Malcolm R Grant
3b *Louise [Miss Louise Butler-Henderson, 26 Cheyne Walk, London SW3]; *b* 21 March 1952
2a *John Ronald MBE (1945), JP (Berks 1955); V-Ld Lt Berks 1979, High Sheriff 1962, Maj (ret) 12th Lancers, ADC to FM Viscount Montgomery of Alamein 1942–46; *b* 6 May 1920; *educ* Eton and Trin Coll Cambridge; *m* 1st 8 Nov 1949 Katherine Sarah (*d* 1972), yr dau of Maj-Gen Merton Beckwith-Smith, DSO, MC, of The Manor House, Stratton, Audley, Oxon, and Aberarder, Inverness-shire, and has issue:
1b *Nicholas John; racehorse trainer; *b* 10 Dec 1950; *educ* Eton; *m* 10 June 1978 *Diana, jockey, twin dau of John Thorne, of Chesterton Stud, Leamington Spa, Warwicks
2b *Henry Merton; *b* 25 April 1952; *educ* Eton
1b *Joanna Sarah; *b* 23 March 1955
1a Elvira; *b* 1 Dec 1923; *d* 16 Feb 1926

(1) Aline; *b* 12 April 1891; *m* 15 Feb 1911 Brig-Gen John Tyson Wigan, CB, CMG, DSO, TD, DL (*d* 23 Nov 1952), of Bolney Lodge, Sussex, and *d* 20 July 1973, leaving issue

(2) Elvira Maude; *b* 23 July 1892; *m* 16 July 1912 Edward Wynne Chapman (*das* 18 Nov 1914) and *d* 22 Jan 1958, leaving issue

(3) Violet, MBE (1919), Order of Mercy; *b* 23 Jan 1897; *m* 8 Nov 1919 Lt-Col Ughtred Elliott Carnegy Carnegy, 12th of Lour, DSO, MC, JP, DL (*d* 1 Feb 1973), of Lour, Forfar, Angus, and *d* 4 Oct 1965, having had, with a yr dau:

1a ELIZABETH PATRICIA CARNEGY OF LOUR, BARONESS CARNEGY OF LOUR (LP, *qv*)

6 Brodie Haldane (Sir), KCMG, CB, JP, DL Herts; High Sheriff 1924, Hon Brig-Gen RE; *b* 6 March 1869; *m* 18 Oct 1901 Charlotte Ella, JP (Herts 1939), dau of James Jones, JP, DL, of Lechlade Manor, Glos, and *d* 28 Sept 1936, leaving:

(1) *Gerald Brodie; *b* 11 Oct 1902

(2) *Neil Brodie; *b* 11 March 1904; *m* 25 June 1929 *Conn, est dau of Sir Charles Edward Madden, 1st Bt (*qv*), and has issue:

1a *Ian Brodie; *b* 25 Oct 1930; *educ* Eton; *m* 28 June 1961 *Veronica, dau of Ralph Pain, of Rio de Janeiro, and has:

1b *Nicholas Brodie; *b* 3 May 1963; *educ* Eton

2b *James Brodie; *b* 30 Dec 1964; *educ* Haileybury

1b *Lavinia Brodie; *b* 9 May 1962

2a *Alan Brodie; *b* 30 July 1933; *educ* Eton; *m* 1st 25 April 1956 (*divorce*) Antonia, only dau of James McMullen, of Belgravia, and has:

1b *Bryan Brodie; *b* 2 June 1960

2b *Gavin Brodie; *b* 13 Jan 1963

1b *Karena Brodie; *b* 11 March 1958

2a Alan Henderson *m* 2nd 9 June 1969 *Fiona Douglas, Lady-in-Waiting to HRH THE DUCHESS OF KENT, er dau of Thomas Douglas Pilkington, JP, and by her has issue:

3b *David Brodie; *b* 16 Nov 1970 (HRH THE DUCHESS OF KENT stood sponsor)

4b *A son; *b* 3 March 1976

1a *Jean Brodie; *b* 18 Nov 1940; *m* 12 April 1961 Hon William Southwell Russell, yr s of 26th Baron de Clifford (*qv*), and has issue

(3) *Andrew Brodie; *b* 30 Nov 1913; *m* 1st 31 March 1944 (*divorce* 1956) Stella Marion Evelyn Matson; *m* 2nd 16 Nov 1956 *Irene Bebis and by his 1st w has issue:

1a *Christopher Brodie Andrew; *b* 17 Aug 1948

1a *Sandra Marion Brodie; *b* 28 Feb 1947

(1) *Joan Ella Brodie; *b* 21 July 1916; *m* 7 Aug 1941 *Sir Fiennes William Strang Steel, 2nd BtP (*qv*), and has issue

1 Eliza Cockshott; *b* 16 Feb 1854; *m* 30 April 1892 Walter Crossland (*d* 2 Oct 1943) and *d* 17 Feb 1947, leaving issue

2 Caroline; *b* 8 March 1856; *d* unm 9 Feb 1927

3 Louisa; *b* 7 March 1858

The est son,

Sir Alexander Henderson, 1st Bt, and **1st Baron Faringdon**, of Buscot Park, Co Berks (both UK), so *cr* 5 Aug 1902 and 24 Jan 1916 respectively, CH (1917), JP Berks; High Sheriff 1912, MP (Lib U) W Staffs 1898–1906 and St George's Hanover Sq 1913–15, dep chm LNER to 1934, Govr Br Trade Corp, chm GC Rlwy and v-chm Shipping Control Ctee, KGStJ; *b* 28 Sept 1850; *m* 2 Sept 1874 Jane Ellen, V-Pres League Order of Mercy (*d* 3 May 1920), dau of Edward William Davis, of Ealing, and *d* 17 March 1934, having had issue:

1 Harold Greenwood, CVO (1919), JP Berks; MP N Berks 1910–16, Lt-Col Berks Yeo, Parly Sec to Dir Recruiting 1915–16, Mil Sec to Govr-Gen Canada 1916–20, Capt and Adj 1st Life Gds WW I, 2nd Cl Order Rising Sun Japan; *b* 29 Oct 1875; *educ* Eton; *m* 19 Feb 1901 Lady Violet Charlotte Dalzell (*d* 1 Oct 1956), yr dau of 14th Earl of Carnwath (*see* 1940 edn), and *d* 1 Nov 1922, leaving:

(1) ALEXANDER GAVIN HENDERSON, **2nd Baron Faringdon**; *b* 20 March 1902; *educ* Eton McGill and Ch Ch Oxford (BA 1924); LLC 1958–61, Alderman 1961, Column Offr NFS 1940–48; memb Exec Ctee Fabian Society 1943–66 (chm 1960–61), memb: Colonial Social Welfare Advsy Ctee, Colonial Ec and Devpt Cncl Colonial Office and Centl Housing Advsy Ctee Min Local Govt and Housing, Tstee Wallace Collection 1946–53 and 1965–73, memb Lab Pty Parly Ctee 1957–60, pres Br Fire Servs Assoc 1960, Assist Plumbers' Co 1960–65, memb Historic Building Cncl Min Public Building and Works 1964, chm Theatres Advsy Cncl, Cdr de l'ordre du Saint Sepulchre Orthodoxe; *m* 2 June 1927 (*annulled* 1931) Hon Honor Chedworth Phillipps (*k* car crash nr Madrid 18 July 1961), yst dau of 1st and last Baron Kylsant (*see* SAINT DAVIDS, V), and *dsp* 29 Jan 1977

(2) Michael Thomas; Lt-Col 16th/5th Lancers (Res); *b* 2 Jan 1906; *educ* Harrow and RMC Sandhurst; granted 24 Dec 1934 with siblings rank of baron's dau/yr s; *m* 1st 14 Jan 1929 (*divorce* 1948) Oonagh Evelyn HENDERSON (reverted to her former married name from MOTION by deed poll 12 Sept 1961), er dau of Lt-Col Harold Ernest Brassey, RHG (*see* BRASSEY OF APETHORPE, B); *m* 2nd 9 June 1948 *Esther Isabelle, formerly w of Harold Seymour Glendinning and er dau of Alfred Edward Coleman, and *d* 19 Nov 1953, having by his 1st w had:

1a Alexander Harold James; *b* 27 Nov 1932; *educ* Eton; *d* following a motor-cycle crash 19 Nov 1951

2a CHARLES MICHAEL HENDERSON, **3rd and present Baron Faringdon**

(3) +Roderic Harold Dalzell; *b* 3 March 1909; *educ* Eton and Pembroke Coll Cambridge (BA); dir Ellis Memorial Boston, Mass., Hon Attaché Stockholm 1932–33 and Uruguay, Civil Attaché and Priv Sec Buenos Aires 1943–46, Rome 1946, Stockholm 1947

(1) Margaret Violet (Peggy); *b* 3 Feb 1904; *m* 10 May 1932 Henry Charles Minshull Stockdale and *d* 25 Sept 1976, leaving issue (*see* STOCKDALE, Bt)

2 Alec Puleston; Hon Maj TAR Berks Yeo; *b* 23 Oct 1876; *educ* Eton and Hertford Coll Oxford; *m* 1st 11 Feb 1905 Henrietta Emily Cecil (*dsp* 7 June 1913), 3rd dau of Capt Frederick Arthur Bertie (*see* LINDSEY and ABINGDON, E); *m* 2nd 23 Jan 1915 Gladys Rhoda (*d* 28 Jan 1953) (*m* 2nd 5 Nov 1934 Sir Murrough John Wilson, KBE (*d* 30 April 1946)), only child of Maj Donald Maclean, of Clewer, Windsor, and *d* 2 Nov 1931, leaving by her:

(1) Ian Alexander, Capt RHG WW II; *b* 5 Oct 1918; *educ* Eton; *m* 1st 16 Feb 1945 (*divorce* 1955) Patience, only dau of Lt-Col John Charles Brand, DSO, MC (*see* HAMPDEN, V), and had:

1a *Veronica; *b* 29 July 1946; *m* 23 Sept 1967 *Oliver Alexander Guy Baring (*see* ASHBURTON, B), and has issue

(1) (cont.) Ian Henderson *m* 2nd 21 Dec 1955 *Sarah Veronica [Mrs Ian Henderson, Westmeads, Butlers Marston, Warwicks], est dau of Maj Cosmo Stafford Crawley, of The Manor House, Lower Woodford, Wilts, by Rosemary, 2nd dau of Sydney Richardson Christie-Miller, JP, of Clarendon Park, Salisbury, and Craigentinny, Edinburgh, and *d* 31 Dec 1968, having by her had:

1a Alexander Cosmo; *b* 12 Oct, *d* 15 Oct 1956

2a +Shamus Alec; *b* 24 Feb 1958; *m* 1986 *Camilla Carolyn, dau of Robert Ashton Adams, and has issue:

1b +James Archie; *b* 1988

1b *Laura Natasha; *b* 1990

(2) Adrian Donald; RAF WW II; *b* 29 Nov 1922; *educ* Eton; *m* 1st 29 Jan 1944 (*divorce* 1958) Marieluz (Muffet), er dau of Capt Robert Peel Dennistoun-Webster, DSC, RN, of Hurst Grange, nr Twyford, and *d* 1994, leaving:

1a Gavin Adrian Alexander; *b* 5 Nov 1944; *educ* Eton; *m* 1984 *Juliet Victoria, yr dau of Sir Mark Baring, KCVO (*see* CROMER, E), and *d* 1991, leaving:

1b *Violet Gweneth; *b* 1985

2a +Mark Alistair; *b* 29 Sept 1946; *educ* The Oratory Sch, Reading

(2) (cont.) Adrian Henderson *m* 2nd 12 Jan 1959 Angela Mary Oriana (*d* 1990), formerly w of Sir John Michael Hungerford Pollen, 7th Bt (*qv*), and er dau of Maj Felix John Russi, MC, 5th Roy Inniskilling Dragoons, of Radcot House, Clanfield, Oxon, and by her has issue:

3a +Alexander Jonathan; *b* 9 Jan 1962; *m* 1987 *Fiona Mary, yr dau of David McLeod, of Park House, Old Hunstanton, Norfolk

1a *Victoria Angela [Mrs John Underwood, 39 Herondale Ave, London SW18 3JN]; *b* 30 Dec 1956; *m* 1979 *John Jeremy Campbell Underwood and has:

1b *James Michael Campbell; *b* 1981

2b *Toby George Campbell; *b* 1984

2a *Fiona Mary; *b* 9 Jan 1962; *m* 1988 *Antony William Dodd-Noble (*see* CORK and ORRERY, E)

(1) *Susan Violet [Mrs Charles Pretzlik, Millers House, Isington, Hants] *b* 30 Dec 1915; *m* 1st 25 Feb 1936 Mark Leslie Pilkington MC (*ka* Middle East 18 Nov 1942), Capt Life Gds (SR), est s of Hubert Carlisle Pilkington, of Little Offley, Herts, and has:

1a *Simon Mark [Simon Pilkington Esq, Chalmer's Lodge, 29 Ballantre Drive, Ayr KA7 2RG, Scotland]; *b* 1938; *m* 1963 *Angela Mary Monica, dau of Lord Patrick Crichton-Stuart (*see* BUTE, M), and has issue:

1b *Rupert Charles; *b* 1964

2b *Mark Patrick; *b* 1965

1b *Jane Susan; *b* 1966

2b *Kate Sophie; *b* 1970

(1) (cont.) Mrs Mark Pilkington *m* 2nd 30 April 1943 F/Lt *Charles Pretzlik, RAFVR, and by him has:

1a *Nicholas Charles [Nicholas Pretzlik Esq, 44 Honiton Street, London W9]; *b* 30 July 1945; *educ* Eton; *m* 21 May 1970 *Ursula Scheuring and has:

1b *Charles Oliver; *b* 1971

2b *Luke Nicholas; *b* 1972

1a *Jacqueline Susan [Mrs Peter Maine, 57 Chesilton Road, London SW6]; *b* 18 March 1944; *m* 22 Aug 1970 *Peter Maine and has:

1b *Simon Patrick Wallace; *b* 1973

2b *Nancy Susan Wallace; *b* 1971

(2) *Rosemary Gladys; *b* 9 Jan 1917; *m* 17 May 1941 *Count Robert Philip Orssich, s of Count Paul Levin Robert Orssich de Slavetich by his 1st w Ethel Nicholson, and has:

1a *Paul Alexander; *b* 1 May 1942; *educ* Malvern

2a *Christopher Levine; *b* 3 Feb 1948; *educ* Stanbridge Earls

1a *Susan Rosemary; *b* 18 Dec 1943; *m* 1st 11 Dec 1963 (*divorce*) Richard Lionel Terry, only s of Maj William Lionel Terry, and has issue:

1b *Simon Richard Brett; *b* 13 May 1964

2b *Jonathan Paul Brandon; *b* 25 March 1966

3b *Nicholas Damian Blaine; *b* 8 April 1967

3 Frank; Lt 7th Hus; *b* 11 Oct 1877; *educ* Eton; *d* unm 20 Jan 1924

4 Philip; Maj 2nd Co London Yeo, T/Lt-Col Tank Corps, MICE, MIME; *b* 16 March 1881; *educ* Eton; *m* 20 July 1908 Rachel Madeleine Mary (*d* 28 Oct 1953), dau of James Charles Hope-Vere (*see* LINLITHGOW, M), and *d* 21 March 1939, having had:

(1) Philip Anthony; *b* 26 Dec 1910; *d* 9 Feb 1919

(2) David Hope Achie; *b* 14 March 1912; *educ* Eton; *m* 1st 10 Oct 1935 (*divorce* 1938) Alice Reed Rawle, yr dau of Anthony Geyelin, of Philadelphia; *m* 2nd 12 March 1944 *Eleanora Anderson [Mrs David Henderson, Achie Farm, New Galloway, Kirkcudbrightshire], dau of Maj David Anderson Spence, VD, Black Watch, of Dunninald Mains, Montrose, and *d* 1977, leaving by her:

1a +Philip David Hope [Philip Henderson Esq, 21 Bowerdean St, London SW6]; *b* 17 Feb 1947; *educ* Eton and RAC Cirencester; FRICS

2a +Ian Ramsey Hope [Ian Henderson Esq, 20 Westbourne Park Rd, London W2 5PH]; *b* 6 Jan 1949; *educ* Eton and Edinburgh U (MA, LLB); FCA; *m* 1978 *Virginia Theresa, yr dau of Lt-Col John Edward Broke Freeman (*see* NORFOLK, D), and has issue:

1b +Alexander Storm David Hope; *b* 1982

2b +Charles John Bernard Hope; *b* 1984

3b +George Ian Henry Hope; *b* 1987

(3) Alistair Philip; Lt Black Watch WW II; *b* 6 Feb 1919

(4) +Ralph Alexander [Ralph Henderson Esq, Rua Santa Clara 47 Apt 1201, Copacabana, Rio de Janeiro, Brazil]; 3rd Sec Br Embassy Lisbon 1945–46; *b* 15 March 1923; *educ* Eton and Trin Coll Cambridge; *m* 21 June 1950 Myriam (*d* 1987), dau of Adml A C de Souza e Silva, Brazilian Navy, and has issue:

1a +Ralph Peter; *b* 12 March 1951; *m* 1977 *Maria Elisa, dau of Luiz Pessoa de Luna, of Rio de Janeiro

2a +Charles James; *b* 12 March 1951; *m* 1983 (*divorce* 1989) Alice, dau of Herly Sampaio Vitor

1a *Lavinia Magdeliene Marie; *b* 28 Aug 1954; *m* 1975 *Pedro Rabello Cotrim, and has issue:

1b *Nelson; *b* 1977

1b *Cecilia; *b* 1978

5 Arnold OBE (1919), TD, Capt Wilts Yeo; *b* 1 July 1883; *m* 17 Feb 1908 Helen Madeline (*d* 2 May 1961), dau of Gen Evans Gordon, and *d* 12 March 1933, leaving:

(1) Roger Arnold; WW II as F/Lt RAFVR; *b* 22 June 1909; *educ* Radley; *m* 4 April 1934 *Judith Violet Christine (*m* 2nd 12 Jan 1946 Robert Edward Manifold, of Australia, and *d* 1966, leaving further issue), yr dau of Edmund Thornley, of Australia, and was *kas* 23 Nov 1941, leaving issue:

1a +David Arnold Thorney [David Henderson Esq, Koorrnang, Tarcutta, NSW 2652, Australia]; *b* 9 Jan 1937; *educ* Geelong GS; *m* 8 Feb 1962 *Sophie Jacqueline Fern, dau of Nicholas Welsh, of SYarra, and has:

1b +Roger David; *b* 27 Feb 1963

2b +Nicholas John Welsh; *b* 13 Aug 1964

1b *Anna Jacqueline Judith; *b* 20 Feb 1966

1a *Darrina Christine; *b* 15 Nov 1935; *m* 1st 25 Feb 1961 (*divorce* 1974) Dr Peter Kaye Bryan; *m* 2nd 1974 *Richard Lawrence Baillieu and by her 1st husb has issue:

1b *Roger Jon; *b* 31 Dec 1961

2b *Christopher Peter; *b* 12 March 1968

1b *Rebecca [Mrs Nigel Trinca, 341 Auburn Rd, Hawthorn, Vic 3122, Australia]; *b* 7 July 1963; *m* 1990 *Nigel Richard Drake Trinca and has:

1c *Lucy Elizabeth Davina; *b* 1993

(2) John Alexander Arnold; Capt Welsh Gds WW II; *b* 24 March 1913; *educ* Eton; *m* 20 Aug 1938 *Anne Marie (*m* 2nd 24 April 1947 Michael Colefax, of Grange Farm, Shaw, nr Newbury, Berks, yr s of Sir Arthur Colefax, KBE, KC), dau of Waldemar Paul Sorrensen, of Berlin, and was *ka* Belgium 11 Sept 1944

(1) Diana Mary; *b* 10 Jan 1911; *m* 1st 2 July 1931 Lt-Col David Walter Arthur William Forbes, MC, Coldstream Gds (*d* of wounds recd in action 13 Nov 1943), and had issue; *m* 2nd 12 Dec 1946 6th Marquess of Exeter (*qv*) and *d* 6 June 1982, leaving further issue

(2) Rachel Daphne; *b* 12 April 1916; *m* 21 April 1939 Dr Dan Goedhuis, Civil Air Attaché Netherlands Embassy, and had:

1a *Michael Arnold Johannes; *b* 18 May 1941; *educ* Eton

2a *Jonathan Daniel; *b* 24 March 1949; *educ* Milton Abbey

1a *Diana Adeline; *b* 6 May 1946

6 Eric Brand HENDERSON later BUTLER-HENDERSON (deed poll 21 Dec 1910), Capt Berks Yeo, High Sheriff Northants 1929, CStJ; *b* 26 Sept 1884; *educ* Eton; *m* 10 Dec 1910 Hon Sophia (Zoe) Isabelle Butler Massy (*d* 1977), 2nd dau of 5th Baron Clarina (*see* 1949 edn), and *d* 18 Dec 1953, leaving issue:

(1) Lionel, TD, Maj RA (TA) WW II; *b* 8 Nov 1911; *educ* Eton; *m* 25 Nov 1936 Una (*d* 1992), dau of Guy Fenwick, and *d* 1 July 1961, leaving issue:

1a +Guy [Guy Butler-Henderson Esq, Beckfield House, Sandon, Herts]; *b* 23 April 1948; *m* 1st 6 July 1968 (*divorce* 1975) Glynis, er dau of Kenneth Bladon, and has issue:

1b +Timothy; *b* 1971

1b *Gemma; *b* 1975

1a (cont.) Guy Butler-Henderson *m* 2nd 1977 *Valerie, er dau of Thomas Taylor, of Cheshire, and formerly w of John Arthur Handforth, and by her has:

2b +Charles Guy; *b* 1978

1a *Jane [Mrs Albert Etheridge, Watermill Farm, Middleton, Suffolk IP17 3LW]; *b* 18 Dec 1938; *m* 1st 10 June 1957 (*divorce* 1967) John Guy Mercer, twin s of Lt-Col G H J Mercer, and has issue:

1b *Christopher John; *b* 4 June 1960

1b *Belinda; *b* 21 May 1958

1a (cont.) Mrs Jane Mercer *m* 2nd d 24 Feb 1968 (*divorce* 19–) George Fred Hewitt, RHG, and by him has:

2b *Anthony George; *b* 1970

1a (cont.) Mrs Jane Hewitt *m* 3rd 1979 *Albert George Etheridge and by him has:

2b *Susan; *b* 1980

(2) Patrick; WW II as A/Lt RAFVR; *b* 8 March 1913; *educ* Eton; *m* 1st 2 June 1943 (*divorce* 1963) Kathleen Rebe Curtis (Section Offr WAAF), er dau of Lt-Col Herman Curtis Clarke, CBE, DSO; *m* 2nd 21 Oct 1968 *Pamela Livingston Gilks [Mrs Patrick Butler-Henderson, Apple Tree Cottage, Quenington, Glos GL7 5BW], formerly w of John Godrich, of Ludlow, Salop, and *d* 16 June 1979, leaving by his 1st w:

1a +Eric Alexander [Eric Butler-Henderson Esq, The Old Thatch, Stanway, Glos]; *b* 16 Oct 1946; *educ* Tabley House Sch; *m* 1st Aug 1970 Leslie Hallingan; *m* 2nd 1993 *Pauline Anne Lowe and by his 1st w has:

1b +Chad Stuart; *b* 1976

1b *Kerryn; *b* 1975

1a *Christine; *b* 25 March 1944; *m* 1st 1971 Maj Neil James Cameron Sutherland, QO Highrs, s of Col G D McK Sutherland, and has issue:

1b *Alasdair Patrick Cameron; *b* 1972

1b *Rachael Bridget; *b* 18 May 1974

1a (cont.) Mrs Sutherland *m* 2nd 1981 *Julian Russell Sturgis and has further issue (*see* BORTHWICK, Bt)

2a *Amalia Zoe [Mrs Simon Taylor, Ardgilzean House, Elgin, Morayshire IV30 3XT]; *b* 20 Sept 1945; *m* 29 April 1970 *Capt Simon Brian Taylor and has issue (*see* SMITH-DODSWORTH, Bt)

(3) +Edward [Edward Butler-Henderson Esq, Flat 11, 3 West Halkin St, London SW1X 8JJ]; *b* 9 June 1916; *educ* Eton; Lt-Col 99th (Roy Bucks Yeo) Field Regt, RA (TA), WW II, chm Waydale Servs Ltd; *m* 15 Sept 1939 Elizabeth Marjorie Dacres (*d* 1988), only dau of Henry George Dacres Dixon (*see* YARBOROUGH, E), and has:

1a +Alan [Alan Butler-Henderson Esq, The Ridings, Lot 1772 DD 221, Sha Ha Rd, Sai Kung, Hong Kong]; *b* 3 April 1943; *educ* Eton; *m* 1st 29 Jan 1964 (*divorce* 1975) Maria Cassy Ugena, est dau of Jebub Cassy Diaz, of Madrid, and has issue:

1b +David James; *b* 5 Jan 1967

1b *Elizabeth Cassy; *b* 13 Dec 1965

1a (cont.) Alan Butler-Henderson; *m* 2nd 1975 *Jacqueline Wright and by her has:

2b +Benjamin; *b* 25 Sept 1976

3b +Jason; *b* 1982

1a *Penelope [Mrs Ian Pilkington, Warennes Wood, Mortimer, Berks]; *b* 19 Nov 1940; *m* 1 May 1962 *Ian Alan Douglas Pilkington, er s of Maj Thomas Douglas Pilkington, JP, of Hyde Mill, Stow-on-the-Wold, Glos, and has issue:

1b *Rory Ian Douglas; *b* 6 May 1968

1b *Camilla Douglas; *b* 8 May 1966; *m* 1990 *Angus Charles Gordon Lennox and has issue (*see* RICHMOND and GORDON, D)

2b *Sarah Douglas; *b* 1973

(4) +Kenneth [Kenneth Butler-Henderson Esq, 11 Egerton Place, London SW3 2EF]; dir Gonite Gp 1975; *b* 19 May 1929; *educ* Eton; *m* 26 April 1952 *Phyllis Daphne, only dau of Lt-Col Alfred Cartmel, CIE, MM, IA, and has:

1a +Julian; *b* 5 Nov 1956; *m* 1980 (*divorce* 1988) Bridget Anne, dau of James Robert Patrick Sullivan; *m* 2nd 1990 *Adina, dau of Peter Smallwood, of Witney, Oxon, and by his 1st w has issue:

1b +Oliver Stephen; *b* 21 Sept 1982

1a *Serena Anne; *b* 12 May 1953; *m* 1990 *Arthur Eugene Burland, late Queen's Roy Irish Hus, and has issue:

1b *Heloise Alice; *b* 1991

2a *Clare; *b* 8 April 1954

(1) Mary; *b* 20 Jan 1915; *m* 9 Dec 1939 Maj Algernon Desmond Wigan (*d* 1989), MC, TD, 23rd Hus, and *d* 17 Oct 1994, leaving:

1a *Desmond [Desmond Wigan Esq, Waresley Cottage, Waresley, Sandy, Beds]; *b* 15 June 1941; *m* 1969 *Anne Louise, dau of Prof A N Black, and has:

1b *Desmond Patrick Neil; *b* 17 Sept 1970

1b *Zoe Margaret; *b* 1972

2a *Peter [Peter Wigan Esq, Witches Cottage, Fletching, E Sussex TN22 3YD]; *b* 5 Aug 1943; *educ* Eton; *m* 1973 *Victoria Mary Riddle and has:

1b *Patrick Claude; *b* 1974

1b *Jane Lucy; *b* 1976

3a *Christopher [Christopher Wigan Esq, 42 Halsey St, London SW3 2PT]; *b* 2 Jan 1947; *educ* Eton; *m* 1st 17 Feb 1970 (*divorce* 1986) Hon Caroline Kinnaird, est dau of 13th Lord Kinnaird (*see* 1970 edn); *m* 2nd 1988 *Christina Mary Lechte, of Melbourne, Australia, and by his 1st w has had:

1b George Rowan; *b* 1977; *d* unm 5 Feb 1998

1b *Leila Willow; *b* 1974; *m* 13 Sept 1997 *Henry P Hope-Frost, s of Tim Hope-Frost and Mrs Linda Hope-Frost

1a *Susan [Mrs David Lyons, Girt Cottage, Combe Martin, N Devon]; *b* 26 Jan 1945; *m* 1985 *David Lyons, and has issue:

1b *Iella; *b* 1980

(2) *Doreen [Mrs William Blackwood, The Old Post House, Mawley Rd, Quenington, Glos GL7 5BH]; *b* 2 Jan 1920; *m* 1st 25 April 1939 (*divorce* 1961) Lt-Col John Gordon Wordsworth, OBE, Suffolk Regt (*d* 1995), er s of Rev Christopher William Wordsworth, MA; *m* 2nd 29 June 1962 G/Capt William Digby Blackwood (*d* 1993), OBE, DFC, RAF, and by her 1st husb has issue:

1a *Antony Christopher Curwen [Antony Wordsworth Esq, Little Brockholds Farm, Radwinter, Saffron Walden, Essex CB10 2TF]; *b* 24 April 1940; *m* 3 Nov 1962 *Rosamond Anne, est dau of Maj John David Summers, JP, and has issue:

1b *Mark Edward Curwen [Mark Wordsworth Esq, 20 Redan St, London W14 0AB]; *b* 1965; *m* 1991 *Eleanor Margaret, only dau of Ian Mapherson, of Broughton, nr Romsey, Hants, and has issue

1b *(Katherine) Lucy; *b* 1968; *m* 1993 *Nicholas A K Brown, er s of Michael Brown, and has issue

2b *Evelyn Mary; *b* 1972

2a *Michael [Michael Wordsworth Esq, Marsh Court, Eldersfield, Glos GL19 4PN]; *b* 22 Oct 1942; *m* 1966 *Christine Stella Lear, and has issue:

1b *Giles Patrick John; *b* 1969

1b *Zara Caroline; *b* 1972

3a *Charles William; *b* 7 May 1946; *m* 1968 *Maria Reyes Garscia Contillo and has:

1b *Alexander Carlos; *b* 1978

1b *Cristina; *b* 26 Feb 1970

2b *Veronica; *b* 1975

4a *Peter John [Peter Wordsworth Esq, The Old Post House, Mawley Rd, Quenington, Glos GL7 5BN]; *b* 28 May 1949; *m* 1979 *Joan, dau of T W Hannigan and has:

1b *Caroline Louise; *b* 1980

2b *Emma Harriet; *b* 1984

1 Margaret; *b* 6 April 1879; *m* 10 Nov 1900 Capt Charles Shuldham Schreiber (*see* MARLESFORD, B) and *d* 11 July 1946, leaving issue

FARNHAM

Arms: Quarterly, 1st and 4th, arg. a saltire sa., on a chief of the first three pallets of the second (for MAXWELL); 2nd and 3rd, barry of six arg. and gu (for BARRY). **Crest:** A buck's head, erased ppr. **Supporters:** Two bucks ppr. **Motto:** *Je suis prêt* ('I am ready'). **Creations:** Bt. (NS) 18 or 28 March 1627; B. (I) 6 May 1756.

THE 12TH BARON FARNHAM, of Farnham, Co Cavan, and a **Baronet** (Sir Barry Owen Somerset Maxwell, Bt) [The Rt Hon The Lord Farnham, 11 Earls Court Gdns, London SW5 OTD; Farnham, Co Cavan, Ireland]; *b* 7 July 1931; *s* gf 1957; *educ* Eton and Harvard; Lt RHG 1950–51, chm: Brown Shipley, merchant bankers, 1984–91 (dir 1959–91), Brown Shipley Hldgs 1976–91, Avon Rubber plc 1978–97 (dir 1966–97), Provident Mutual Life Assur Assoc 1989– (dir 1967–), Pro Grand Master Utd Grand Lodge England 1991–, pres Tree Cncl 1992–; *m* 19 Jan 1959 *(Diana) Marion, CVO (1998), JP, Ldy Bedchamber to HM THE QUEEN 1987–, er dau of Nigel Eric Murray Gunnis (*see* MARGADALE, B), and adopted:

*Harriet Virginia; *b* 23 July 1964; *m* 1990 *James David Huntly Naylor, est s of David Naylor, of Oakridge Lynch, Glos, and has:

1a *Henry James Huntly; *b* 5 Oct 1995

1a *Araminta Sheelin Huntly; *b* 1 Oct 1993

*Sophia Mary; *b* 14 Feb 1967

Lineage: Sir ROBERT MAXWELL of Calderwood, Lanarks (2nd s of Sir John Maxwell, of Pollok; *see* MAXWELL, Bt, and for a more immediate lineage 1970 edn STIRLING-MAXWELL, Bt); entailed the family estates in concert with his bro Sir John Maxwell 18 Dec 1400; *m* 1st 1402 Elizabeth, dau of Sir Robert Denniston of Denniston, and had issue:

Sir JOHN MAXWELL of Calderwood; *fl* 1424–29; *m* by 4 Dec 1450 Margaret, dau of 1st Lord Borthwick (*qv*), and *d* 1476, having had, with a yr s (George, ancestor of the MAXWELLs of Newark):

Sir JOHN MAXWELL of Calderwood; *m* Janet/Marion, dau of Sir Thomas Boyd, 5th of Kilmarnock (*see* KILMARNOCK, B), and *d* 1490, leaving, with a dau (Janet/Mariota, *m* 1st Lord Boyd; *see* KILMARNOCK, B):

Sir GAVIN MAXWELL of Calderwood; had a charter from his f of all his lands in Lanarks 14 Feb 1486; *m* Elizabeth — and *d* 1492, having had, with a yr s (William, ancestor of Maxwell, Bt, of Cardoness)

Sir ROBERT MAXWELL of Calderwood; *m* Sibella, dau of Sir Walter Carmichael of Hyndford, and *d* 1531, having had, with an er s (Robert, *d* 1568) and a dau (*m* 1st Lord Boyd; *see* KILMARNOCK, B):

Sir JOHN MAXWELL of Calderwood; *m* 1st Elizabeth, dau of Sir James Hamilton of Finart; *m* 2nd Elizabeth, dau of Sir Robert Stewart of Minto, and *d* 1571, having by his 1st w had:

1 James (Sir), of Calderwood; *m* 1st Helen (*d* 1573), dau of John Porterfield of Porterfield, Renfrewshire, and had two daus; *m* 2nd *c* 12 Feb 1579 Isabel, dau of Sir Alexander Hamilton of Innerwick, and by her had, with two other sons and six daus:

(1) **Sir James Maxwell, 1st Bt** (NS), of Calderwood, so *cr* 28 March 1627, with remainder to his heirs male whatsover; *m* 1st Jean, dau of Sir James Hamilton of Evandale by Margaret, dau of 6th Earl of Glencairn (*see* CUNINGHAME, Bt), and had an only dau; *m* 2nd *c* 1 July 1637 Mary, dau of James Coattes, of Edinburgh, and *d c* 1670, having by her had:

(1) **Sir William Maxwell, 2nd Bt**, of Calderwood; *b c* 1640; *m* by 9 Nov 1666 Jean, dau and coheir of his paternal uncle, Sir Alexander Maxwell of Saughton, by Janet, dau of Thomas Moodie, of Saughton, but *dsps* 30 April 1703

(1) (cont.) **Sir James** *m* 3rd 8 Sept 1610 Margaret (*d c* 1622), widow of Sir James Hamilton of Evandale and dau of 6th Earl of Glencairn, and *d* 1622, having by her had, with two sons and four daus:

2a John; Col; *m* Elizabeth, dau of Sir James Elphinstone of Blythswood, and was *k* Battle of Dunbar 1650, leaving issue:

1b William, *de jure* 3rd Bt, of Calderwood; did not assume the title; *m* Margaret, dau of Capt — Wood, of Culter, and *d* by 23 March 1716, leaving:

1c **Sir William Maxwell, 4th Bt**, of Calderwood; *m* Christian, dau of Alexander Stewart of Torrance, and *d* 1750, having had issue:

1d **Sir William Maxwell, 5th Bt**, of Calderwood; *m c* 1747 Grizel, dau of James Peadie, of Roughill, and *d* 2 Jan 1789, leaving issue:

1e **Sir William Maxwell, 6th Bt**, of Calderwood; *b* 7 Jan 1748; *m* 5 May 1807 Hannah Leonora (*d* 19 July 1857), dau of Robert Pasley, of Mount Annan, Dumfries, and *dsp* 12 Aug 1829

2d John; Col; *dsp*

3d Alexander, of Leith; *m* Mary, dau of Hugh Clerk, of Edinburgh, and had issue:

1e **Sir William Maxwell, 7th Bt**, of Calderwood; Gen American War of Independence; *b* 4 Dec 1754; *m* 2 July 1792 Isabella (*d* 1 Oct 1829), dau and heir of Henry Wilson, of Newbottle, Co Durham, and *d* 16 March 1837, having had issue:

1f **Sir William Alexander Maxwell, 8th Bt**, of Calderwood; Col 1st Dragoons; *b* 30 April 1793; *m* 15 June 1847 Catherine Cameron (*d* 13 Oct 1866), dau of Walter Logan, of Fingaton, Lanarks, and widow of Capt Paget Gill, 50th Foot, and *dsp* 4 April 1865

2f Robert Wilson; HEICS; *d* unm 31 Jan 1851

3f Henry, of Leith; *d* unm 29 Jan 1853

4f **Sir Hugh Bates Maxwell, 9th Bt**, of Calderwood; advocate; *b* 14 Feb 1797; *m* 1 May 1827 Mary Anne Barbara (*d* 18 July 1875), dau of John Hunter, of Lisburn, Co Antrim, and *d* 9 Feb 1870, leaving issue:

1g **Sir William Maxwell, 10th Bt**, of Calderwood; *b* 11 Aug 1828; *m* 20 April 1880 Jane (*m* 2nd 1887 George Leader Owen, DL, of Withybush (*dsp* 9 Feb 1905), and *d* 24 May 1942), dau of Frank Baird, and *dsp* 4 Dec 1885

2 Robert (Very Rev); migrated to Ireland near the end ELIZABETH I's reign; Dean Armagh; *m* 1st Susan Armstrong and had issue:

(1) ROBERT

(2) Henry, of Finnebrogue, Co Down; *m* Jane (*m* 2nd Ven William Fullerton, Archdeacon Armagh), 3rd dau of Rt Rev Robert Echlin (*see* ECHLIN, Bt), and had:

1a Jane; *m* her cousin James Maxwell (*see* below) and had issue

(3) James; of Mullatinny (Elm Park), Co Armagh; *m* Jane Norris and had, with a yr s:

1a Henry; *m* his cousin Margaret, dau of Dr Robert Maxwell, Bp Kilmore (*see* below), and had, with an er dau:

1b Margaret; *m* 1st Sir Robert Maxwell, of Orchardtown; *m* 2nd Capt James Butler, of Bromlestown, Co Kildare, and had issue:

1c Catherine; *m* Rev Samuel Close

(1) Elizabeth; *m* Robert Berkeley, DD, Dean Clogher

(2) Phoebe

2 (cont.) The Very Rev Robert Maxwell *m* 2nd Isabel, dau of — Seton of Lathrisk

His est s by his 1st w,

Rt Rev ROBERT MAXWELL; *educ* Trin Coll Dublin (DD); Rector Tynan, Diocese of Armagh, and Archdeacon Down by 1641, Bp Kilmore 1643 and Ardagh 1661; held manors of Farnham and Fellows Hall; *m* Margaret, est dau of Rt Rev Robert Echlin (*see* ECHLIN, Bt), and *d* 1672, having had, with four other daus:

1 John, of Farnham, Co Cavan; *dsp* 1713

2 James, of Fellows Hall, Co Armagh; *m* his cousin Jane, dau of Henry Maxwell, of Finnebrogue (*see* above), and had, with three daus:

(1) Robert (Rev); *dsp* 1737

3 Henry (Rev), of College Hall, Co Armagh; Rector Derrynoose, Diocese of Armagh, Preb Tynan; *m* Anne, dau of Col George Stewart, of Culmore, Co Londonderry, only son of Sir Robert Stewart, MP, Capt Culmore Castle, and had:

(1) JOHN, **1st Baron**

(2) Robert, of Fellows Hall; Capt of Horse; *m* Grace, est dau of Rev John Leavens, and had, with three sons (*dsp*):

1a Mary; *m* Maxwell Close, of Elm Park

2a Isabella; *m* Hector Graham, of Rutland Sq, Dublin, and had issue:

1b Grace; *m* 2 June 1778 1st Earl of Norbury (*qv*)

3a Anne; *m* Robert Bowyer

4a Margaret; *m* Alderman John Tew, of Dublin (*see* STRONGE, Bt)

(1) Jane; *m* her cousin Rt Hon H Maxwell, of Finnebrogue

4 William, of Falkland, Co Monaghan; High Sheriff 1691, ancestor of the MAXWELLs of Falkland

1 Jane; *m* Rev Simon Chichester, Vicar Belfast and Templepatrick, s of Henry Chichester, of Marwood, Devon

2 Margaret; *m* her cousin Henry Maxwell (*see* above)

The Rev HENRY MAXWELL's est s,

JOHN MAXWELL, **1st Baron Farnham**, of Farnham, Co Cavan (I), so *cr* 6 May 1756; MP Co Cavan 1727–56; *m* June 1719 Judith (*d* 5 April 1771), dau and heir of James Barry, of Newton Barry, Co Wexford, and Dublin, and *d* 6 Aug 1759, having had issue:

1 ROBERT MAXWELL, **2nd Baron Farnham** and 1st and last EARL OF FARNHAM, of Co Cavan, so *cr* 13 May 1763, also 10 Sept 1760 VISCOUNT FARNHAM, Co Cavan (both I); *m* 1st 11 Oct 1759 Henrietta, sole dau and heir of Philip Cantillon, a Paris banker, and widow of 3rd Earl of Stafford (*see* STAFFORD, B), and had issue:

(1) John, *Viscount Maxwell*; *d* a minor 7 Aug 1778

(1) Henrietta; *m* 1780 Rt Hon Denis Daly, of Dunsandle, Co Galway, and *d* 6 March 1852, leaving issue. He *d* 10 Oct 1792

1 (cont.) The **2nd Baron** *m* 2nd 1 Dec 1771 Sarah, widow of Rt Hon Arthur Upton (*see* DONEGALL, M) and only dau of Pole Cosby, of Stradbally Hall, Queen's Co, and *dspm* 16 Nov 1779, when the Viscountcy and Earldom expired

2 BARRY MAXWELL, **3rd Baron Farnham** and 1st EARL OF FARNHAM, so *cr* 22 June 1785, as also 10 Jan 1781 VISCOUNT FARNHAM, Co Cavan (both I); *m* 1st 15 Jan 1757 Margaret (*d* 4 Dec 1766), 2nd dau and coheir of Robert King, of Drewstown, Co Meath, and had issue:

(1) JOHN JAMES MAXWELL, **4th Baron Farnham** and 2nd and last EARL OF FARNHAM; *b* 5 Feb 1759; *m c* 30 Dec 1783 Grace (*d* 10 Feb 1856), only dau of Thomas Cuffe, of Grange, Co Kilkenny, and *dsp* 23 July 1823, when the Viscounty and Earldom expired

(1) Anne; *m c* 15 Dec 1787 Richard Fox, of Fox Hall, Co Longford, and had issue

(2) Judith; *d* unm 1818

2 (cont.) The **3rd Baron** *m* 2nd 5 Aug 1771 Grace (*d* 8 March 1816), yst dau of Arthur Burdett, of Ballymaney, Co Kildare, and *d* 7 Oct 1800, leaving by her:

(3) Grace; *m* 22 May 1802 Sir Ralph St George Gore, 7th Bt (*qv*), and *d* 19 June 1866, leaving issue

(4) Elizabeth; *d* unm Jan 1782

3 Henry (Rt Rev); DD, Bp Dromore 10 March 1765 and Meath 15 April 1766; *m* 1759 Margaret, sis of John, Lord Oriel (*see* MASSEREENE and FERRARD, V), and *d* 7 Oct 1798, leaving surv issue:

(1) JOHN MAXWELL BARRY MAXWELL, **5th Baron Farnham**, PC; Col Cavan Militia, rep I peer; *b* 18 Jan 1767; *m* 4 July 1789 Juliana Lucy (*d* 10 Oct 1833), dau of Arthur, Earl of Mountnorris (*see* VALENTIA, V), and *dsp* 20 Sept 1838

(2) Rev HENRY MAXWELL, **6th Baron Farnham**; *m* 5 Sept 1789 Lady Anne Butler (*d* 29 May 1831), est dau of 2nd Earl of Carrick (*qv*), and *d* 19 Oct 1838, having had, with five other sons and another dau:

1a HENRY MAXWELL, **7th Baron Farnham**, KP (1845); rep I peer 1839–68; *b* 9 Aug 1799; *educ* Trin Coll Dublin; MP (Tory) Co Cavan 1824–38, genealogist specialising in roy descents and armorial quarterings numbering 16 and more; *m* 3 Dec 1828 Anna Frances Esther, yst dau of Sir Thomas Stapleton, 6th Bt, 12th Lord (Baron) le Despenser (*see* FALMOUTH, V), and *dsp* 20 Aug 1868 together with his w in a fire caused by a railway accident on the L&NWR line nr Abergele, N Wales

2a SOMERSET RICHARD, **8th Baron Farnham; MP (Tory) Co Cavan 1839–40**; *b* 18 Oct 1803; *m* 1st 30 May 1839 Dorothea (*d* 30 Nov 1861), yst dau of Richard Pennefather, a Baron Exchequer Ireland; *m* 2nd 31 May 1864 Mary Anne (*d* 1 Nov 1873), yr dau of Samuel Francis Delap, of Monellan, Co Donegal, and *dsp* 4 June 1884

3a **Sir James Pierce Maxwell, 11th Bt** (as which *s* 6th cousin twice-removed 1885), and **9th Baron Farnham**; Lt-Col 97th Foot; *b* 1813; Kt Medjidie; severely wounded Crimean War, MP (C) Co Cavan 1843–65; *d* unm 26 Oct 1896

4a Richard Thomas, of Fortland, Co Cavan; *b* 19 Feb 1815; *m* 7 March 1848 Charlotte Anne (*d* 1 March 1910), 2nd dau of Rev Henry Preston Elrington, DD, Rector Templeshambo and Precentor Ferns, Co Wexford, and *d* 22 Jan 1874, leaving issue:

1b SOMERSET HENRY, **10th Baron**

2b Henry Edward, DSO (1900), of Arley, Mountnugent, Co Cavan, JP, DL; High Sheriff 1910, Col cmdg Black Watch (Roy Highrs) Boer War 1899–1902 (wounded Paardeberg); *b* 27 Nov 1857; granted with sisters 14 May 1897 rank of baron's dau/yr s; *m* 10 Aug 1887 Edith Augusta Emily (*d* 3 Feb 1944), dau of Col Robert Godolphin Cosby, of Stradbally Hall, Queen's Co, and *d* 2 March 1919, leaving issue:

1c Richard Sydney Somerset; Capt Black Watch WW I (severely wounded); *b* 29 May 1893; *educ* Harrow; *d* unm 12 July 1967

1c Ismay Alice; *b* 19 May 1888; *d* unm 3 March 1955

1b Isabella Sarah; *m* 11 April 1894 James Hugh Moore Garrett, of Corrie Wood, Castlewellan, Co Down, and *d* 15 May 1902

2b Harriet Elizabeth; *b* 19 Nov 1875

3b Anne Frances; *m* 15 April 1885 Thomas Cosby Burrowes, of Lismore, Crossdoney, Co Cavan, and *d* 5 April 1937, leaving issue. He *d* 20 Feb 1925

1a Sarah Juliana; *m* 18 March 1828 Alexander Saunderson, of Castle Saunderson, Co Cavan, MP, Col Co Cavan Militia, and *d* 17 Dec 1870

2a Harriet Margaret; *m* 1st 1826 3rd Viscount Bangor (*qv*); *m* 2nd 1841 Maj Andrew Nugent, 36th Regt, and *d* 4 July 1880

3a Anne; *m* 17 Oct 1836 W M Bayly, of Annamult, Co Kilkenny, and *d* Dec 1857. He *d* 1840

The 9th BARON's nephew,

SOMERSET HENRY MAXWELL, **10th Baron Farnham**; Capt and Hon Maj 4th Bn Princess Victoria's Roy Irish Fus, Lt 98th Regt, Ld Lt Co Cavan, rep I peer; *b* 7 March 1849; *m* 5 Aug 1875 Lady Florence Jane Taylour (*d* 16 Aug 1907), 5th dau of 3rd Marquess of Headfort (*qv*), and had issue:

1 Barry Somerset; *b* 6 Aug 1876; *d* 20 Sept 1897

2 ARTHUR KENLIS, **11th Baron**

3 Edward Saunderson John; *b* 20 Nov 1889; *d* unm 6 Sept 1907

4 Denis Crichton (Hon Sir), KCB (1952, CB 1948), CBE (1945); *b* 26 Sept 1892; *educ* RNCs Osborne, Dartmouth, Keyham and Greenwich; FIMechE, FRSA, V-Adml, ADC to HM GEORGE VI 1945–46, Engr-in-Ch the Fleet 1950–53; *m* 11 July 1923 Theodora Mary (*d* 1986), dau of Arthur Hickling, of The Old Hall, Wing, Rutland, and *d* 16 Jan 1970, leaving issue:

(1) *Elizabeth Crichton; *b* 5 Aug 1926; *m* 5 Feb 1953 (*divorce* 19–) Ivor Mabberley, of Victoria, BC, s of Ivor Mabberley, of Wanborough, Wilts

1 Zoe Emma; *b* 29 July 1881; *d* unm 24 Nov 1968

2 Stella Frances; *b* 19 Sept 1866; *d* unm 11 Dec 1966

The 10th BARON *d* 22 Nov 1900; his est surv s,

ARTHUR KENLIS MAXWELL, **11th Baron Farnham**, DSO (1918), DL Co Cavan; *b* 2 Oct 1879; rep I peer, Lt-Col NI Horse Yeo, Actg Lt-Col cmdg Service Bn Roy Inniskilling Fus, Lt 10th Hus, Boer War 1901–02 and WW I (despatches); *m* 8 Oct 1903 Aileen Selina (*d* 1 Feb 1964), 2nd dau of Charles Purdon Coote (*see* COOTE, Bt), and *d* 5 Feb 1957, having had:

1 Somerset Arthur; MP King's Lynn 1935–42, Lt-Col Middx Yeo (Roy Signals) WW II; *b* 20 Jan 1905; *m* 15 Oct 1930 (Angela) Susan (*k* plane crash Jamaica 10 April 1953, having *m* 2nd 20 Oct 1944 Lt-Cdr Henry Harrison Proctor, LLD, USNR (accidentally drowned 6 July 1948), only s of Charles A Proctor, of Boston, Mass., and 3rd 7 Dec 1950 Lt-Col Edward Remington-Hobbs, DSO, OBE, Argyll and Sutherland Highrs, and had further issue), only dau of Capt Marsall Owen Roberts, of Mayfair, and *d* of wounds recd in action El Alamein Dec 1942, leaving:

(1) BARRY OWEN SOMERSET MAXWELL, **12th and present Baron Farnham**

(2) +SIMON KENLIS [The Hon Simon Maxwell, The Dower House, Westcote, Kingham, Oxon]; *b* 12 Dec 1933; heir presumptive; *educ* Eton; granted with sis rank of baron's dau/yr s 1959; Lt 10th Roy Hus; *m* 5 May 1964 *Karol Anne, er dau of Maj-Gen George Erroll Prior-Palmer, CB, DSO, of Appleshaw House, Andover, Hants, and has issue:

1a +Robin Somerset; *b* 15 Sept 1965; *m* 1993 *Tessa M, dau of David Shepherd, of Stansted, Essex

2a +Mark Erroll; *b* 30 Jan 1968

1a *Lorna Suzanna Katherine; *b* 30 Jan 1968

(1) *Sheelin Virginia [The Rt Hon The Viscountess Knollys, The Bailiff's House, Bramerton Hall Farm, Norwich NR14 7DN]; *b* 5 Dec 1937; *m* 1 Oct 1959 *3rd Viscount Knollys (*qv*) and has issue

2 Barry Charles William; *b* 16 July 1909; *d* 22 April 1916

3 Arthur Edward; *b* 18 Oct 1913; *d* 13 April 1916

1 Marjory Florence; *b* 24 April 1906; *m* 10 July 1929 Col Lancelot Merivale Gibbs, CVO, DSO, MC, and *d* 5 May 1939, leaving issue (*see* ALDENHAM and HUNSDON OF HUNSDON, B)

2 Verena Aileen; *b* 4 Aug 1907; *m* 1st 3 Feb 1934 Charles Lambart Crawley, yst s of Kenneth Crawley, of Quarry Hill, Brancepeth, Co Durham, and had issue. He *d* 24 July 1935. She *m* 2nd 12 Feb 1938 Maj Sir Mark Vane Milbank, 4th Bt (*qv*), and *d* 1995, having had further issue

Seat: Farnham, Co Cavan, Ireland. JAMES I granted Sir Richard Waldron lands in Co Cavan on which the present house was later built. Sir Richard's descendant Henry Waldron, of Dromellan Castle, who was attainted by JAMES II 1689 and had the estate confiscated (though he got it back in 1690 from WILLIAM III), renamed the place after his wife's maiden name of Farnham. In 1697 he sold it to Robert Maxwell, Bishop of Kilmore. John, the Bishop's son, put up a new structure in 1700 and the **3rd Baron Farnham** altered it *c* 1780, in particular by employing James Wyatt to add a library. The **4th Baron** employed an only slightly less distinguished architect, Francis Johnston, to remodel the house from 1802 on, though he is considered to have carried out a somewhat unexciting job. At least he did not destroy Wyatt's work entirely, but instead incorporated the library. The **7th Baron** extended the house further in the late 1830s, obliterating still more of Wyatt's work. This addition was demolished from c 1960 by the **12th Baron**, who tried to give Wyatt's surviving features more prominence. The landscape around the house is particularly admired.

FARQUHAR

Arms: Arg. a lion rampant sa., armed and langued gu., between two sinister hands couped and apaumée in chief of the last, a crescent in base az. **Crest:** An eagle rising ppr. **Motto:** *Mente manuque* ('By mind and hand'). **Creation:** Bt (GB) 1 March 1796.

SIR MICHAEL FitzROY HENRY FARQUHAR, 7TH BT [Sir Michael Farquhar Bt, Manor Farm, West Kington, Wilts SN14 7JG]; *b* 29 June 1938; *s f* 1986; *educ* Eton and RAC Cirencester; *m* 29 June 1963 *Veronica Geraldine, er dau of Patrick Rowan Hornidge, Falmouth, Cornwall, and has:

1 +CHARLES WALTER FitzROY; *b* 21 Feb 1964; *educ* Stowe

2 +Edward Peter Henry FitzRoy [Edward Farquhar Esq, 109 Harbord St, London SW6 6PS]; *b* 6 Dec 1966; *educ* Stowe and RMA Sandhurst; *m* 9 Sept 1995 *Nicola, only dau of Michael Stone, of Ozleworth Park, Wotton-under-Edge

Lineage: Sir ROBERT FARQUHAR of M(o)unie; a cadet of the FARQUHARs of Gilmilnscroft, Ayrshire; Dep Receiver Scotland 1644, royalist Provost Aberdeen 1646; *dsp* 1676

His nephew or great nephew,

JAMES FARQUHAR, of Lenturk, Aberdeenshire; *m* — Reid, of Houghton, and *d* 1711, leaving issue:

JOHN FARQUHAR, of Lenturk; *m* Margaret (*d* 1723), dau of — Forbes of Newe (*see* FORBES, Bt, of Newe), and *d* 1744, leaving an est son:

Rev ROBERT FARQUHAR, of Lenturk; Min Chapel of Garioch, Aberdeenshire, 1738–87; *b* 1699; *m* 1729 Katherine (*d* 7 Nov 1798), dau of Rev Walter Turing (*see* TURING, Bt), and *d* 4 Feb 1787, leaving:

Sir Walter Farquhar, 1st Bt (GB), so *cr* 1 March 1796; Physician to PRINCE OF WALES (later GEORGE IV), MA, MD Aberdeen, FCP (Edin), FLCP (Lond); *b* Oct 1738; *m* 1771 Anne (*d* 23 Sept 1793), widow of Dr Harvie and 4th dau of Thomas Stevenson, and had, with other issue:

1 THOMAS HARVIE (Sir), **2nd Bt**

2 Sir ROBERT FARQUHAR later TOWNSEND-FARQUHAR (roy licence 19 July 1824), 1st Bt (UK), so *cr* 21 Aug 1821; *b* 14 Oct 1776; Dip Serv, Govr Penang, Prince Edward Island and Mauritius, Govr HEICS, MP Hythe; *m* 10 Jan 1809 Maria Frances Geslip (*m* 2nd 15 Feb 1834 Capt Thomas Hamilton (*see* STIRLING-HAMILTON, Bt), and *d* 27 Aug 1875), 4th dau and coheir of Joseph François Louis de Latour, of Hexton House, Herts, and *d* 16 March 1830, leaving:

(1) Sir WALTER MINTO TOWNSEND-FARQUHAR, 2nd Bt; Dip Serv; *b* 26 Oct 1809; *m* 25 Aug 1835 Erica Catherine Mackay (*d* 21 Jan 1899), illegitimate dau of 7th Lord Reay (*qv*), and *d* 18 June 1866, leaving:

1a Sir ERIC ROBERT TOWNSEND-FARQUHAR, 3rd Bt; *b* 14 July 1836; Dip Serv, Sec Legn Peking; *d* there unm June 1867

2a Sir MINTO WALTER TOWNSEND-FARQUHAR, 4th Bt; *b* 18 Dec 1837; *dsp* 8 June 1872

3a Sir JOHN HENRY TOWNSEND-FARQUHAR, 5th Bt; *b* 2 Aug 1839; Capt 20th Hus, served Indian Mutiny (when defended Lucknow), 7th Light Bengal Cavalry; *d* unm 14 Aug 1877

4a Sir ROBERT TOWNSEND-FARQUHAR, 6th and last Bt; *b* 26 Sept 1841; Lt RA; *d* unm 30 June 1924, when the btcy expired

5a Sir HORACE BRAND TOWNSEND-FARQUHAR later FARQUHAR, 1st and last Bt (UK), and 1st and last EARL FARQUHAR, so *cr* 25 Oct 1892 and 30 Nov 1922 respectively, as also between whiles 20 Jan 1898 BARON FARQUHAR OF ST MARYLEBONE and 21 June 1917 VISCOUNT FARQUHAR (all UK), GCB (1922), GCVO (1902, KCVO 1901), PC (1907), JP and DL (Middx); *b* 19 May 1844; Govt clerk, subsequently with Sir Charles Forbes & Co, India merchants; a cavalier financier and conduit for subscriptions to party political funds (both C and (Lloyd George) Lib) by aspirants to titles; as the full extent of his irregular business dealings became apparent after his death he was considered lucky to have escaped prosecution for fraud while alive; MP W Marylebone 1895–98, memb E Marylebone LCC 1899–1901, pres London Municipal Soc 1894–1901, Master Household 1901–07, Extra Ld in Waiting to TM EDWARD VII 1907–10 and GEORGE V 1910–15, Ld Steward Household 1915; *m* 5 Jan 1895 Emilie (who brought him a fortune and *d* 6 April 1922), widow of Sir Edward Henry Scott, 5th Bt (whose banking house Farquhar had previously joined), of Sundridge Park (*see* SCOTT, Bt, of Lytchet Minister), and yst dau of Lt-Col Henry Packe, Gren Gds, of Twyford Hall, Norfolk, and *dsp* 30 Aug 1923 (leaving an estate whose net value was zero despite munificent bequests to the Royal Family and other friends), when all his titles expired

3 Walter; *m* 9 March 1805 Maynard Eliza, est dau of Sir John Hadley D'Oyly, 6th Bt (*qv*), and *dsp* 9 Feb 1813. She *m* 2nd Rev Thomas Snow and *d* 21 June 1866, leaving issue

1 Anne; *m* 17 June 1797 Rev James Hook, DCL, FSA, Dean Worcester, and *d* 10 Sept 1844, having had issue. He *d* 5 Feb 1828

2 Charity Greeme; *m* 13 July 1807 Rev Anthony Hamilton, and *d* 9 Nov 1869, leaving issue (*see* BELHAVEN AND STENTON, L)

Sir WALTER *d* 21 March 1819; his son,

Sir Thomas Harvie Farquhar, 2nd Bt; *b* 27 June 1775; *m* 11 July 1809 Sybella Martha (*d* 20 April 1869), only dau and heir of Rev Morton Rockcliffe, of Woodford, Essex, and *d* 12 Jan 1836, having had, with other issue:

1 WALTER ROCKCLIFFE (Sir), **3rd Bt**

2 Harvie Morton; *b* 7 Nov 1816; *m* 25 Sept 1849 Hon Louisa Harriet Ridley Colborne (*d* 22 Aug 1870), dau and coheir of 1st and last Baron Colborne (*see* RIDLEY, V), and *d* 11 Nov 1887, having had, with another s and dau:

(1) Ernest; *b* 8 Nov 1853; *m* 22 May 1890 Maria Theresa (*d* 1 June 1950), est dau of Sir Thomas Villiers Lister, KCMG, and *d* 2 Sept 1930, leaving issue:

1a Harold Lister (Sir), KCMG (1950, CMG 1945), MC (1919); Amb Stockholm 1948–51, Envoy Abyssinia 1946–48, Maj Res Offrs Coldstream Gds, formerly 2nd Life Gds, WW I (wounded); *b* 15 April 1894; *m* 9 Oct 1917 Constance Audrey (*d* 28 Oct 1963), dau of Hon Arthur Algernon Capell (*see* ESSEX, E), and *d* 31 Jan 1953, leaving issue:

1b +Ian Rupert [Maj Ian Farquhar, Hamlyns House, Chudleigh, S Devon]; Maj Gren Gds WW II; *b* 5 Nov 1918; *m* 18 March 1944 Margaret Eugenie (*d* 1977), yr dau of Francis John Gordon Borthwick (*see* BORTHWICK, L), and has:

1c +Francis Rupert; *b* 29 Dec 1953; *educ* Eton

2b Adrian Capell; Capt KRRC WW II 1943–46; *b* 18 Aug 1924; *m* 27 July 1955 *Ann Elizabeth [Mrs Adrian Farquhar, Redlynch House, Salisbury, Wilts], dau of Edward John Johnston-Noad, of Paris, and *d* 27 Oct 1982, leaving issue:

1c *Annabel Cristina [Mrs Christopher Yates, 31 Lilyville Rd, London SW6 5DP]; *b* 7 Jan 1958; *m* 1983 *Christopher Mark Yates, s of T Gordon Yates, of Covers, Lynchmere, W Sussex, and has issue:

1d *Eden Mark Farquhar; *b* 1988

2d *Kieran Alexander Francis; *b* 1990

2a Rupert, MC; Lt Gren Gds WW I (despatches); *b* 7 July 1897; *d* 17 Sept 1917 of wounds recd in action

(1) Florence; *m* 14 Oct 1875 John Henry Ponsonby and *d* 30 April 1922, leaving issue (*see* BESSBOROUGH, E)

(2) Helen Laura; *d* unm Nov 1952

1 Caroline Eliza, VA; Woman Bedchamber to HM QUEEN VICTORIA; *m* 26 July 1836 Lt-Gen Hon Charles Grey, s of 2nd Earl Grey (*qv*), and *d* 4 Nov 1890, leaving issue

2 Ann Sybella Martha; *m* 2 May 1835 George Clive, MP, of Perrystone Court, Herefs, and *d* 16 Feb 1907, leaving issue. He *d* 7 June 1880

3 Barbarina Sophia; *m* 24 March 1845 Mark William Vane Milbank (*see* MILBANK, Bt) and *d* 30 Oct 1850, leaving issue

4 Maria; *m* 24 May 1860 William Halliday, of Glenthorne, Devon, and Bilsington, Kent, and *d* 27 Dec 1889, leaving issue. He *d* 11 May 1898

The 2nd Bt's est son,

Sir Walter Rockcliffe Farquhar, 3rd Bt, of Cadogan House, Middx, JP Middx, JP, DL Surrey; High Sheriff 1859; *b* 4 June 1810; *m* 28 Nov 1837 Mary Octavia (*d* 7 Sept 1906), dau of 6th Duke of Beaufort (*qv*), and *d* 15 July 1900, leaving:

1 **Sir Henry Thomas Farquhar, 4th Bt**, JP, DL Ayrshire; *b* 13 Sept 1838; inherited the Gilmilnscroft estate from his distant cousin Miss Jane Farquhar; *m* 8 July 1862 Hon Alice Brand (*d* 20 March 1925), est dau of 1st Viscount Hampden (*qv*), and *dspms* 15 Jan 1916, having had issue:

(1) Trevor, Lt Seaforth Highrs; *b* 27 Dec 1865; *das* Black Mountains Expdn 23 Oct 1888

(2) Francis Douglas, DSO; Maj Coldstream Gds, on staff Boer War 1899–1900 (despatches, medal with five clasps), Somaliland 1903–04 (medal with clasp) and WW I 1915, cmded Princess Patricia's Canadian LI, Legn Hon; *b* 17 Sept 1874; *m* 27 April 1905 Lady Evelyn Hely Hutchinson (Ldy-in-Waiting to HRH PRINCESS ARTHUR OF CONNAUGHT; *d* 18 Sept 1962, having *m* 2nd 3 May 1923 Sir Dougal Orme Malcolm, KCMG (*d* 30 Aug 1955), 2nd son of William Rolle Malcolm, of Walton Manor, Epsom), est dau of 5th Earl of Donoughmore (*qv*), and was *ka* 20 March 1915, leaving issue:

1a Norah Frances Sapphire; *b* 19 May 1906; *m* 1st 28 Jan 1925 (*divorce* 1948) Mark OLIVER later FARQUHAR-OLIVER (1931), RSG, son of Frederick Scott Oliver, of Edgerston, Roxburghshire, and had issue:

1b *Robin Mark; *b* 2 Dec 1925; *educ* Eton; *m* 16 Nov 1968 *Penelope Anne Keddie

1b *Catriona Mary; *b* 2 July 1928; *m* 1952 (*divorce* 1966) Theobald Matthew John Smyth

2b *Norah Elizabeth [The Rt Hon The Countess of Lindsey and Abingdon, 3 Westgate Terrace, London SW10; Gilmilnscroft, Sorn, Mauchline, Ayrshire]; *b* 26 July 1932; *m* 5 Jan 1957 *14th Earl of Lindsey and (9th Earl) of Abingdon (*qv*) and has issue

1a (cont.) Mrs Norah Farquhar-Oliver *m* 2nd 26 Jan 1948 John Roland Preece, son of John Preece, of Ivy House, Hanley Castle, Worcs. He *d* 1974

2a *Sybil Barbara; *b* 18 Feb 1909; *m* 1st 4 Nov 1930 (*divorce* 1946) Lt-Cdr Anthony Boyce Combe, RN, est son of Maj Boyce Combe, of Great Hall, Dockenfield, Surrey, and has issue; *m* 2nd 28 March 1946 Charles Robert Archibald Grant, only son of Gen Sir Charles John Cecil Grant, KCB, KCVO, DSO. He *d* 1972

(1) Gertrude; *b* 6 June 1863; *d* unm 14 June 1914

(2) Katherine; *b* 7 Jan 1865; *m* 30 July 1887 Sir Almeric William FitzRoy, KCB, KCVO, and *d* 24 Nov 1933, leaving issue (*see* GRAFTON, D)

2 Walter Randolph; *b* 6 Jan 1842; *m* 29 May 1877 Hon Kathleen Mary (*d* 20 July 1935), dau of 1st Baron Deramore (*qv*), and *d* 27 Aug 1901, leaving issue:

(1) WALTER RANDOLPH FitzROY (Sir), **5th Bt**

3 Arthur; Col Egyptian Army, Ch Staff to Hicks Pasha, Capt Coldstream Gds; *b* 26 March 1843; *k* Sudan 1883

4 Granville Frederick Richard; *b* 12 June 1849; *m* 8 Jan 1896 Helen Margaretta (*d* 13 June 1929), dau of Edward Louis Livingston, of New York, and *d* 14 Dec 1934, having had, with another s (*ka* 1917):

(1) Guy William John, Lt Coldstream Gds WW I; *b* 27 Jan 1899; *educ* Eton and Ch Ch Oxford; *m* 1st 11 July 1928 (*divorce* 1947) Daphne, 2nd dau of Col Vivian Henry, CB (*see* MILBANK, Bt); *m* 2nd 22 Sept 1961 *Vera Kathleen, formerly w of Capt Francis Richard Heywood Sutton, MC (*see* SUTTON, Bt), and dau of John Waldock, and *d* 1 April 1962, leaving by his 1st w:

1a Edward Vivian; Capt 11th Hus, dir Mann Crossman and Paulin Ltd, chm Watney Mann 1972; *b* 4 June 1929; *educ* Eton; *m* 1st 8 Sept 1956 (*divorce* 1983) Polly, yr dau of Adml of the Fleet Sir Philip Louis Vian, GCB, KBE, DSO, of Pit House Farm, Ashford Hill, nr Newbury, Berks; *m* 2nd 1985 *Careena [Mrs Edward Farquhar, 3 Ormond Ave, Richmond, Surrey TW10 6TN], only dau of William Thomas, of Hebron, Dyfed, and *d* 4 Dec 1995, leaving by his 1st w:

1b +Peter Christopher Edward; *b* 3 Aug 1959; *educ* Eton; *m* 1st 1986 Susan Jane, only dau of Michael Williams, of Fairfield House, Pedmore, Worcs; *m* 2nd 1992 *Victoria Susannah, er dau of Brig Peter Collins, of Camberley, Surrey, and has:

1c +Edward Peter Grattan; *b* 30 May 1997

2b +Alastair Vian; *b* 5 Feb 1966; *educ* Harrow

1b *Diana Susan; *b* 27 Sept 1961; *m* 1988 *Nicholas David Morant, yst s of Maj G C H Morant, of Pigeon House Farm, Hatherden, Hants, and has:

1c *Maximilian George Vian; *b* 1991

2c *Jack Edward Chearnley; *b* 1993

2a +Peter Guy Powlett [Peter Farquhar Esq, 17 Netheravon Rd, London W4 2NA]; *b* 13 Feb 1936; *educ* Eton; *m* 1st 3 June 1961 (*divorce* 1973) Rosemary Anne Eaton, only dau of Charles Allix Eaton Hammond, of Hill House, Wroxham, Norfolk, and has issue:

1b +Richard Charles; *b* 7 April 1962; *educ* Eton; *m* 1988 *Emma de Hoghton, er dau of Jonathan Reeves (*see* CHELMSFORD, V), and has:

1c *Araminta Claire; *b* 17 Oct 1991

2c *Lydia Rose; *b* 17 Dec 1994

2b +James Edward; *b* 6 Dec 1963; *educ* Eton; *m* 1991 *Victoria Josephine, 2nd dau of Michael Dennis Arthur Clinton, of Sedgehill, nr Shaftesbury, Dorset, and has:

1c +Michael Edward; *b* 25 April 1992

2c +Jonathan Peter Clinton; *b* 30 July 1994

2a (cont.) Peter Farquhar *m* 2nd June 1974 *Carolyn, er dau of David Graham Robertson, of Sydney, NSW, and has:

3b +George Peter; *b* 29 Feb 1980; *educ* Eton
4b +Hugh Graham; *b* 7 June 1984; *educ* Harrow
1b Jane Elizabeth; *b* 12 Dec 1982; *d* 10 Feb 1983
2b *Alice Rose Jane; *b* 17 Nov 1987
1a *Antonia Daphne Diana [Mrs Antony Leaf, Cleeve House, Ampney St Peter, Glos]; *b* 31 July 1932; *m* 1 Aug 1956 *Antony Noel Gordon Leaf, late 15th/19th King's Roy Hus, yr s of Maj James Gordon Leaf, 15th/19th King's Roy Hus, of Copse Hull, Osmaston, Derbys, and has:
1b *Guy Edmond James; *b* 3 Oct 1962; *educ* Harrow, Hertford Coll Oxford and RMA Sandhurst; Capt 15th/19th Hussars, *m* 1st 11 Dec 1993 (*divorce* 1997) Noelle Browning, of California; *m* 2nd 31 Jan 1998 *Sally Ann, formerly w of Ian Rawlinson and dau of Lt-Col Michael Scott, Scots Gds
1b *Anna Georgina; *b* 26 Aug 1958; *m* 1988 *George Francis Windsor-Clive and has issue (*see* PLYMOUTH, E)
(1) Diana Mary; *b* 19 July 1901; *m* 12 Nov 1919 5th Earl of Durham (*qv*) and *d* 28 Aug 1924, leaving issue
5 FitzRoy James Wilberforce, OBE; Lt 13th Hus Boer War 1900–02 (two medals, six clasps) and WW I (despatches three times); *b* 6 Nov 1858; *m* 24 April 1884 Ada Mary (*d* 24 June 1944), dau of Sir John William Cradock-Hartopp, 4th Bt (*qv*), and *d* 23 Feb 1941, leaving issue:
(1) Arthur Ronald, DSC (1918); Cdr 1924 and Capt RN (ret), WWs I (despatches, Croix de Guerre) and II; *b* 20 April 1888; *d* unm 30 Aug 1978
(1) Gladys Mary; *m* 14 Oct 1907 5th Baron Leconfield and *d* 10 July 1971, leaving issue (*see* EGREMONT, LECONFIELD and, B)
1 Mary Blanche; *m* 11 Oct 1871 2nd Baron Raglan (*qv*) and *d* 15 June 1916, having had issue
2 Sybella Charlotte; *m* 28 July 1866 Rt Hon Evelyn Ashley, and *d* 31 Aug 1886, leaving issue (*see* SHAFTESBURY, E)
3 Charlotte Louisa; *d* 26 Jan 1923
4 Harriet Blanche Elizabeth; *m* 13 Oct 1885 Lt-Col Hon George Aubrey Vere Bertie, 4th son of 6th Earl of Abingdon (*see* LINDSEY and ABINGDON, E), and *d* 30 Jan 1923, leaving issue
5 Caroline Emily Horatia; *d* 23 March 1938

The 4th Bt's nephew,

Sir Walter Randolph FitzRoy Farquhar, 5th Bt; Hon Attaché St Petersburg 1898, ADC to Lord Lamington in Australia, T/Capt ASC and RFA, ADC to Brig-Gen A Cator 58th Div, WW I Gallipoli, Egypt and France; *b* 31 May 1878; *m* 17 Dec 1903 Violet Maud (*d* 6 Jan 1959), est dau of Col Charles Seymour Corkran, Gren Gds, and was *ka* 1918, leaving issue:
1 PETER WALTER (Sir), **6th Bt**
2 Charles Richard, MC and bar, DL (Staffs 1962); Hon Col Staffs Yeo WW II; *b* 14 May 1906; *educ* Eton; *m* 7 Oct 1939 (Dorothy) Nancy (*d* 14 June 1997), 2nd dau of Maj James Gerald Thewlis Johnson, DSO, of Foston, Derbys, and *d* 1980, leaving issue:
(1) *Daphne Violet [Mrs Terence Pardoe, North Hazelrigg, Chatton, Alnwick, Northumberland]; *b* 31 Dec 1945; *m* 1973 *Terence John Pardoe, yr s of Maj Robert Hugh Pardoe, FLAS, of Carnforth, Lancs, and has issue:
1a *Robert Charles; *b* 1977
1a *Amanda Susan; *b* 1975
(2) *Angela Dorothy; *b* 11 Jan 1948; *m* 1977 *Richard John Hassan Meade, OBE, and has issue:
1a *James Richard; *b* 1981
2a *Harry Michael; *b* 1983
1a *Lucy Margaret; *b* 1985
3 Reginald Arthur, P/O RAFO, 2nd Lt 16th/5th Lancers; *b* 7 Sept 1908; *m* 6 Feb 1933 *Betty Isobel [Mrs Reginald Farquhar, Ardsallagh, Fethard, Co Tipperary, Ireland], widow of Hon Gilbert Greenall (*see* DARESBURY, B) and dau of John Shields Crawford, and *d* 15 Feb 1937
1*Ruth Violet Mary [The Rt Hon Ruth Lady Dulverton, Barnbrook Cottage, Milton Lilbourne, Pewsey, Wilts SN9 5LQ; Fassfern, Fort William, Inverness-shire]; *b* 1 Feb 1910; *m* 1st 14 Dec 1932 (*divorce* 1961) Maj Richard Gennys Fanshawe (*d* 1988), 16th/5th Lancers, yst son of Lt-Gen Sir Edward Arthur Fanshawe, KCB; *m* 2nd 28 April 1962 2nd Baron Dulverton (*d* 1992) and by her 1st husb has:
(1) *David Valentine Fanshawe [Col David Fanshawe, Ash House, St Mary Bowne, Hants SP11 6BG]; *b* 1933; Col Gren Gds; *m* 1963 *Sheila Christine, er dau of Maj-Gen John Malcolm McNeill, CB, CBE, and has:
1a *Angus Edward; *b* 1965; *m* 1995 *Marianna, yst dau of Peter Anninos, of Cadogan Sq, London SW1
2a *Robert Leighton; *b* 1967; Capt Gren Gds; *m* 1992 *Charlotte, yr dau of Hon Mr Justice (Sir Anthony Howell Meurig) Evans, RD, of Bucklers Hard, Hants
3a *William David; *b* 1971
(2) *Brian Edward [Brian Fanshawe Esq, Manor Barn House, Nether Westcote, Oxon OX7 6SD]; *b* 1936; Capt 9th/12th Roy Lancers; *m* 1960 *Elizabeth, dau of Geoffrey Pugh, of Temple Guiting House, Glos, and has issue:
1a *James Robert [James Fanshawe Esq, Pegasus Stables, Snailwell Rd, Newmarket, Suffolk CB8 7DJ]; *b* 1961; *m* 1990 *Jacqueline Mary Joan, dau of Geoffrey Cherry-Downes, and has:
1b *Tom Anthony Frederick; *b* 19 April 1997
2a *Antony Geoffrey; *b* 1964
1a *Sarah Rose; *b* 1967

Sir WALTER was *ka* 15 Oct 1918; his est son,

Sir Peter Walter Farquhar, 6th Bt, DSO (1942) and bar (1944), JP (Dorset 1955); *b* 8 Oct 1904; *educ* Eton; Lt-Col 16th/5th Lancers WW II (twice wounded), cmded 3rd Hus 1942–44, MFH Meynell 1931–34, Jt MFH Whaddon Chase 1934–38 and Portman 1947–59, chm: Dorset Assoc Boys' Clubs 1947–62 and Nat Assoc Boys' Clubs Devpt Ctee 1964; *m* 23 June 1937 Elizabeth Evelyn (Betty) (*d* 30 Oct 1983), formerly w of Andrew Knowles and dau of Lt-Col Francis Cecil Albert Hurt, JP, of Alderwasley, Derbys, and *d* 1986, leaving:
1 Sir MICHAEL FitzROY HENRY FARQUHAR, **7th and present Bt**
2 +Anthony Charles [Anthony Farquhar Esq, St Gennys House, St Gennys, Cornwall EX23 0NW]; *b* 10 March 1942; *educ* Eton; *m* 25 Oct 1969 *(Elizabeth) Jane, dau of Col Timothy M Braithwaite, of Honey Cottage, Limpley Stoke, Bath, and has:
(1) *Alexandra Elizabeth; *b* 4 Aug 1971
(2) *Annabelle Jean; *b* 9 June 1973
(3) *Antonia Katharine; *b* 9 Sept 1977
3 +Ian Walter, LVO (1972); *b* 11 Dec 1945; *educ* Eton and RMA Sandhurst; Capt Queen's Own Hussars, MFH Bicester and Warden Hill 1973, Jt MFH Beaufort 1985; *m* 18 Nov 1972 Pamela Jane, 2nd dau of Charles L Chafer, of Elleron Lodge, Pickering, Yorks, and has issue:
(1) *Emma Elizabeth; *b* 1977
(2) *Victoria Rose; *b* 1979
(3) *Rosanne Catherine; *b* 1983

FARRINGTON

Arms: Erm. on a chevron gu. between three leopard's faces sa. as many bombs or, fired ppr. **Crest:** A dragon, wings elevated, tail nowed vert bezanty, gorged with a mural crown arg., and a chain reflexed over the back or, charged on the body with two caltraps fesswise of the last. **Motto:** *Le bon temps viendra* ('Good times will come'). **Creation:** Bt. (UK) 2 December 1818.

SIR HENRY FRANCIS COLDEN FARRINGTON, 7TH BT [Sir Henry Farrington Bt, Higher Ford, Wivelscombe, Somerset TA4 2RL]; *b* 25 April 1914; *s f* 1944; *educ* Haileybury; Maj RA, ret 1960 (now Hon Col), served WW II; *m* 22 March 1947 *Anne, est dau of Maj William Albert Gillam, DSO, of Exmouth, Devon, and has issue:
1 +HENRY WILLIAM [Henry Farrington Esq, Castle, Wiveliscombe, Somerset TA4 2TJ]; *b* 27 March 1951; *educ* Haileybury and RAC Cirencester; ARICS; *m* 8 Sept 1979 *Diana Donne, ALI, yr dau of Geoffrey Albert Broughton, of Impens, N Petherton, Somerset, and has issue:
(1) +Henry John Albert; *b* 4 Jan 1985
(2) +Charles George Donne; *b* 23 April 1988
1 *Susan Maria [Miss Susan Farrington, Tipnoller Cottage, Wiveliscombe, Somerset TA4 2RL]; *b* 10 May 1949

Lineage: Gen Sir Anthony Farrington, 1st Bt (UK), so *cr* 2 Dec 1818; Gen, CO 1st Bn RA and Field Train, Hon DCL Oxford; *b* 6 Feb 1741/2 (s of Col Charles Farrington, RA); *m* 9 March 1766 Elizabeth (*d* 12 April 1824), dau of Alexander Colden, Lt-Govr New York, and *d* 3 Nov 1823, having had:
1 Charles Colden; Capt 33rd Foot; *b* 1 June 1770; *m* 23 Dec 1793 Caroline, dau of Philip Boland, of Cork, and *dvp* 2 March 1796, leaving issue:
(1) **Sir Charles Henry Farrington, 2nd Bt**; Capt 31st Regt, fought Battles of Talavera and Waterloo; *b* 26 Sept 1794; *d* unm India 26 March 1828
2 HENRY MATURIN (Sir) **3rd Bt**
1 Elizabeth Anne; *m* 19 Dec 1798 Capt James Gilbert, RA
2 Harriet; *m* 1 Feb 1794 Lt-Gen Walter Cliffe and *d* 24 June 1838
3 Mary Sophia; *m* 1824 Maj-Gen Loftus Owen and *d* 3 Feb 1860

Sir CHARLES's uncle,

Sir Henry Maturin Farrington, 3rd Bt; Lt-Col; *b* 31 March 1778; *m* 1st 6 Sept 1802 Clarissa Claringbould (*dsp* 28 May 1803); *m* 2nd 5 Oct 1805 Laura Maria (*d* 15 Dec 1808), dau of Charles Bromley, of Madras, and had:
1 Laura Elizabeth; *m* 22 Feb 1832 Rev Thomas Edward Allen (*d* 28 March 1841) and *d* 3 Jan 1894, leaving issue

Sir Henry *m* 3rd 18 July 1810 Jane (*d* 8 Oct 1828), dau of Roger Curry, and by her had issue:
1 HENRY ANTHONY (Sir), **4th Bt**
2 Edward Holmes (Rev), Rector Landcross, Devon; *b* 28 Oct 1812; *m* 1st 8 Sept 1840 Rosabella Maria (*d* 2 May 1845), and had two sons (*d* young); *m* 2nd 1849 Sophia Elizabeth, dau of Robert Walker, of Alphington, Devon, and *d* 1894, having by her had issue:
(1) George Walker; *b* 5 March 1850; *m* 1894 Constance May (*d* 14 Nov 1922), dau of Francis Newton Lowe, and *d* 22 March 1928, leaving:

1a Maude Mary; *m* 1930 Josiah Samuel Gist Billett (*d* 1954) and *d* 21 Dec 1987
2a *Winifred Frances; *m* 22 April 1920 Edward Gordon Stone (*d* 1930)
(2) Francis John, of Bideford; *b* 27 Oct 1854; *m* 1880 Marion Elizabeth, dau of Michael Webb Marshall, of Exeter, and *d* 31 May 1945, leaving issue:
1a George Edward Marshall; *b* 2 Feb 1882; *m* 1911 Nellie, only dau of William B Fraser, of Griqualand, East S Africa, and *d* 1 April 1960, leaving issue:
1b Marshall Francis William; *b* 1912; *m* 1939 Christine (Crystal) Joanna (*d* 1992), dau of William John MacSeveney, of Nsoko, Swaziland, and *d* 30 March 1986, leaving issue:
1c +Alastair Edward; *b* 27 Aug 1946; *m* 1964 *Nesta Eureka Minnie and has:
1d +Craig Grant; *b* 6 March 1965
2d +Alastair Ian; *b* 5 July 1965; *m* 1990 *Julie Rene van Lingen and has:
1e *Kirsty; *b* 22 Oct 1991
2d (cont.) Mr and Mrs Alastair Farrington also adopted:
*Kennedy; *b* 7 Feb 1982
*Slade Alastair; *b* 28 Aug 1984
*Jaydee; *b* 7 April 1987
*Shaylee; *b* 7 April 1987
1d *Charlene Debra; *b* 16 June 1966; *m* 1992 *Mark Philip Schroder and has:
1e *Alexander Mark; *b* 1992
2d *Desiré Marshall; *b* 1968
2c +Graham William; *b* 30 June 1947; *m* 1970 (*divorce* 1978) Persis Eleanor Tozer
3c +Ian Fraser; *b* 28 Dec 1948; *m* 1972 *Daphne Grace Colling and has:
1d +Bradley Graham; *b* 29 June 1974
2d +Wayne Lewis; *b* 1 Jan 1977
1c Jacqueline Valerie; *b* 10 Nov 1941; *m* 1962 *Leopold William Kenneth Ferreira, and *d* 2 Aug 1981
1b *Lorna; *b* 2 Jan 1918; *m* 1945 Bernard Christoffel Pretorius and has issue
1a Dorothy Maria; *b* 26 June 1885; *m* 25 July 1906 her cousin **Sir Henry Anthony Farrington, 6th Bt**; and *d* 14 June 1969, leaving issue (*see* below)
(3) Loftus Henry; *b* 9 Sept 1863; *m* 23 Sept 1908 Jessie de Prado, dau of Eben MacMillan, of Glasgow and Lisbon, and *d* 1935
(1) Ellen; *b* 25 March 1857; *d* unm 30 Oct 1942
(2) Mary Elizabeth; *b* 10 Dec 1860; *d* unm 11 March 1932
3 Charles Loftus; *d* an infant
4 Loftus; *d* an infant
5 Charles James; 45th Regt Madras Native Inf; *d* 17 Aug 1854
2 Jane Mary; *b* 8 March 1814; *m* 20 June 1838 Rev John Warren, BA, Rector Bawdrip, Somerset, and *d* 1887, leaving issue. He *d* 1886
3 Mary Sophia; *b* 10 Aug 1815; *m* 27 March 1835 Col John Cumberlege, 41st Bengal Native Inf, and *d* 14 March 1895 in her 80th year, leaving issue. He *d* 1852
4 Margaret Anne; *b* 20 Dec 1816; *m* 10 April 1840 Edmund Boult, Bengal Medical Service, and *d* 27 June 1904, leaving issue. He *d* 24 Jan 1863
5 Elizabeth; *d* unm 10 Nov 1849
6 Maria Harriet; *b* 5 Nov 1820; *m* 1 Jan 1840 Rev George H Evans, MA, Rector Woodchester, Glos, and *d* 6 June 1901, leaving issue. He *d* 13 Jan 1878

Sir Henry *m* 4th 6 Feb 1834 Susanna (*m* 2nd 12 June 1838 Maj F E Manning, Bengal Army) dau of Robert Kekewich, and *d* 4 Oct 1834

The 3rd Bt's est son,

Sir Henry Anthony Farrington 4th Bt; *b* 6 May 1811; *m* 16 May 1833 Frances Elizabeth (*d* Jan 1843), est dau of Rev J Warren, DD, of Port View, Devon, and had, with other issue:
1 WILLIAM HICKS (Sir), **5th Bt**
2 Anthony Charles; LRCP Edin, MRCS; *b* 7 Aug 1842; *m* 1 Nov 1870 Catherine Harriet (*d* 1896), yst dau of Rev William Smythies Beevor, MA, of Bury St Edmunds, and *d* 15 Oct 1920, leaving issue:
(1) Charles Anthony Beevor; *b* 18 April 1873; *m* 7 July 1908 Mabel (*d* 18 Aug 1970), dau of George Hastings Rust D'Eye, and *d* 8 Jan 1939, leaving issue:
1a Berners Charles D'Eye; engr; *b* 1 April 1909; *d* unm 19 Nov 1963
1a *Marjorie Joan Cicely [Miss Majorie Farrington, 8 Naish Rd, Barton-on-Sea, Hants BH25 7PU]; *b* 12 Oct 1910
(1) Evelyn Catherine; *b* 5 Aug 1871; *d* unm 13 June 1944
1 Mary Jane Warren; *b* 25 Sept 1839; *m* 5 July 1866 Rev Charles Rogers Covey, LLB, Rector Alderton, Cheltenham, 1875–1915, and *d* 13 Dec 1916 leaving issue. He *d* 22 Nov 1918

Sir HENRY *d* 19 Sept 1888; his est s,

Sir William Hicks Farrington 5th Bt; MD, MRCSE, LSA; *b* 26 Jan 1838; *m* 7 Dec 1870 Amy Florence (*d* 15 July 1925), yst dau of Alexander Glendining, of Redleaf, Penshurst, and had issue:
1 HENRY ANTHONY (Sir), **6th Bt**
2 Alexander; *b* 5 Dec 1872; *educ* Haileybury and Peterhouse Cambridge; *m* 7 March 1905 Ellen Katherine (*d* 18 July 1965), yst dau of Rev William Wilberforce Howard, of Stanmore, Northam, N Devon, Sr Insp Schs, and *d* 13 Jan 1958, leaving issue:
(1) William Howard; Cdr RN; *b* 2 May 1907; *m* 21 April 1934 Barbara (*d* 4 May 1975), dau of Herbert Smale, and *d* 14 March 1988, leaving:
1a +Andrew James [Andrew Farrington Esq, Bay Cottage, Wembury, Devon PL9 0HR]; *b* 8 Nov 1942; *educ* Marlborough and Birmingham U (BSc); *m* 24 July 1965 *Susan Kathleen, BSc, dau of Dr Ronald Hugh Wylsher Britton, MRCS, LRCO, and has issue:
1b +William James; *b* 16 Sept 1967
1b *Eleanor Kathleen; *b* 4 April 1970; *m* 16 Sept 1995 *Simon Merchant
2b *Alice Joanna; *b* 9 May 1973
1a *Susan [Mrs Susan Farrington, 3 Cedar Close, Wokingham, Berks RG11 1EA]; *b* 10 Jan 1937; *m* 1980 (*divorce* 1987, resumed maiden name) Ieuan Davies Williams
2a *Jenifer [Mrs Martin Sheldon, The Old Vicarage, New Town, Salop SY4 5NU]; *b* 9 Oct 1938; *m* 31 July 1965 *Maj Martin Rothery Sheldon, RSG, s of Lt-Col C D Sheldon, DSO, and has issue:
1b *Bryony Claire; *b* 9 Oct 1966
2b *Camilla Frances; *b* 16 April 1968
3b *Holly Samantha; *b* 1973
3a *Angela [Mrs Andrew Rose, Drimbuie, Kilchrenan, Taynuilt, Argyll PA35 1HF]; *b* 28 July 1941; *m* 8 Jan 1966 *Andrew Arthur Rose, s of Charles Anderson Rose, of Edinburgh, and has issue:
1b *David Andrew; *b* 12 Jan 1967
1b *Susannah Angela; *b* 5 Dec 1968
2b *Elizabeth Iona; *b* 1972
(2) Anthony Herbert James; *b* 26 July 1911; *d* unm 30 March 1948
(1) Aurea Elizabeth; *b* 17 March 1906; *d* unm 11 April 1964
3 John Marsden; *b* 2 Sept 1874; *educ* Eastbourne Coll; *m* 23 Dec 1917 Lynda May (*d* 28 March 1981), dau of George T Simmonds, and *d* 12 Dec 1965, leaving:
(1) +John Anthony; F/Lt RAF; *b* 18 Jan 1934; *educ* Eastbourne Coll; *m* 10 May 1958 *Patricia Rose, dau of John William Fowler, of Norwich, and has had:
1a +Charles Henry; *b* 22 Feb 1963; *educ* Shrewsbury; *m* 11 Aug 1990 *Claire, er dau of Francis Derek Rowland, and has:
1b *Holly; *b* 24 Dec 1992
2a +Richard John; *b* 7 May 1964; *educ* Shrewsbury; *m* 28 Aug 1993 *Jasmine, dau of Bill Pereira
1a Lesley Patricia; *b* 1959; *d* 18 Sept 1962
(1) Mary Joyce; *b* 16 Dec 1918; *m* 1st 11 April 1942 Maj Thomas Southall Porter (*ka* 18 July 1943), Carleton and York Regt, Canadian Forces, s of Horace A Porter, KC, of Rothesay, NB; *m* 2nd 21 Sept 1946 Vincent Allison White (*d* April 1950), of Ottawa, s of Garfield A White, of Sussex and St John, NB, Canada; *m* 3rd 1955 *Philip Challis [Philip Challis Esq, 97 Alinora Crescent, Goring-by-Sea, Sussex] and *d* 9 Oct 1983
1 Aurea; *b* 21 Feb 1878; *m* 10 Dec 1907 Maj Herbert Edgington and *d* 27 April 1967. He *d* 1948

Sir WILLIAM *d* 5 Jan 1901; his eldest son,

Sir Henry Anthony Farrington, 6th Bt; *b* 1 Oct 1871; *educ* Haileybury and Cooper's Hill; Ch Conservator Forests CP India 1922–26; *m* 25 July 1906 his cousin Dorothy Maria (*d* 14 June 1969), only dau of Francis John Farrington, of Bideford, Devon (*see* above), and *d* 6 Sept 1944, leaving:
1 Sir HENRY FRANCIS COLDEN FARRINGTON, **7th and present Bt**
1 Margaret; *b* 4 Feb 1913; *m* 1st 25 July 1933 (*divorce* 1959) Edward Hugh Lee Rowcliffe, TD, Maj R A (TA), only s of Edward Lee Rowcliffe, of Hall Place, Cranleigh, Surrey, and has issue (*see* NEWALL, B); *m* 2nd 11 Nov 1959 *Arthur Wilfrid Nicholson [Arthur Nicholson Esq, Rhyll Manor, Dulverton, Somerset] (*see* NICHOLSON OF WINTERBOURNE, B) and *d* 19 Oct 1992

FARRINGTON OF RIBBLETON

Creation: B. (LP, UK) 20 Aug 1994.

THE BARONESS FARRINGTON OF RIBBLETON, of Fulwood, Co Lancaster [The Rt Hon The Baroness Farrington of Ribbleton, 114 Victoria Rd, Fulwood, Lancs PR2 4NN]; *b* 29 June 1940; Lancs CC: memb 1977, Chm Educn Ctee 1981–91, Chm 1992; ACC: Chm Policy Ctee 1993–94, Leader Lab Gp 1987–94, V-Chm 1990–94, Chm 1994–96; memb Consultative Cncl for Local Govt Fin 1987–, UK Rep Ctee of Regns 1994– (Chm Educn and Trg Ctee 1994–), Pres Cncl of Europe Ctee for Culture, Educn and Media 1989–94), Govt Whip 1997–, UK European Woman of the Year 1994; *m* 1960 *Michael James Farrington and has three sons

FAYRER

Arms: Arg. on a bend invected sa. between in chief an eastern crown gu. and in base the staff of Aesculapius ppr., enfiled with a like crown, three horse-shoes or. **Crest:** In front of a sword erect ppr., pommel and hilt gold, a horse-shoe or between two wings gu. **Motto:** *Ne tentes aut perfice* ('Either do not attempt or else accomplish'). **Creation:** Bt. (UK) 7 Feb 1896.

SIR JOHN LANG MACPHERSON FAYRER, 4TH BT, of Devonshire Street, St Marylebone [Sir John Fayrer Bt, Overhailes, Haddington, E Lothian, EH41 3SB; 9 Westfield St, Edinburgh]; *b* 18 Oct 1944; s f 1976; *educ* Edinburgh Acad and Scottish Hotel Sch U of Strathclyde; assoc memb Roy Soc for Promotion of Health 1968, catering manager Castle Hotel Taunton 1968–

Lineage: JOSEPH FAYRER, of Harmony Hill, Milnthorpe, Westmorland; *bapt* 17 July 1743; *m* 7 April 1777 Bridget (*d* 14 March 1807), dau of John Dickinson, and *d* 11 Jan 1801, having had with other issue:

1 Joseph (Rev), Vicar St Teath, Cornwall; *b* 21 Jan 1786; *m* Sarah, dau of George Clay, and *d* 10 May 1838, having had issue

2 ROBERT JOHN

1 Hannah; *m* 18 Jan 1815 Rev Joseph Coates, Vicar Huddersfield, and *d* 31 Dec 1817, leaving issue

2 Nancy; *m* Jan 1824 Rev John Kirkby, MA Cantab, and *d* 29 March 1837, leaving issue

The 2nd son,

ROBERT JOHN FAYRER, of Milnthorp; Cdr RN; *b* 11 March 1788; *m* 12 Aug 1817 Agnes (*d* 1861), dau of Richard Wilkinson, of Westmorland, and *d* 20 April 1869, having had a 2nd s:

Sir Joseph Fayrer, 1st Bt (UK), so *cr* 7 Feb 1896, KCSI; FRS, MD, LLD, FRCP, FRCS, Surgn-Gen Army, Pres Medical Bd India Office, Hon Physician to HM QUEEN VICTORIA, Hon Physician (Mil) and Physician Extrdy to HM EDWARD VII, Govr Wellington Coll; *b* 6 Dec 1824; *m* 4 Oct 1855 Bethia Mary (*d* 12 May 1916), est dau of Maj-Gen Andrew Spens, Bengal Army, and had issue:

1 Robert Andrew; Sec to Indian Midland Rlwy Co; *b* 27 June 1856; *d* unm 28 Dec 1904

2 Joseph Henry Spens; *b* 9; *d* 11 Dec 1857

3 JOSEPH (Sir), **2nd Bt**

4 James Outram Spens; Lt-Col 5th Gurkha Rifle Regt, IA; *b* 20 Feb 1861; *m* 31 Aug 1892 Katharine (*d* 11 Sept 1959 aged 89), dau of Frederick Steward, and *d* 15 Oct 1918, leaving issue:

(1) Joseph Steward; 2nd/37th Dogras IA; *b* 30 April 1897; *ka* 21 Jan 1916

(1) Evelyn Bethia; *m* 1st 22 June 1926 (*divorce* 1955) Capt Reginald Hamilton Fyers Turner, s of Lt-Col H H F Turner, 2nd Lancers; *m* 2nd 4 May 1957 *Frederick Righton

(2) Wynifred Georgiana Joscelyn; *m* 1928 Joseph Pearson Evans (*d* 13 April 1959), and had issue:

1a *Pamela; *m* 27 Dec 1961 *Clifford Leeb, s of Johann Leeb, of Vienna, and has issue:

1b *Gavin Joseph Ignatius; *b* 11 Oct 1962

1b *Kira Hermione; *b* 17 March 1964

5 Henry Wadham Spens; Lt 3rd Bn KO Royal Lancaster Regt; *b* 12 Aug 1862; *d* 25 March 1922

6 Frederick Durand Stirling; Lt-Col IMS, MRCS, LRCP, memb Medical Bd India Office 1917–19, DADMS Indian Contingent Peace Celebrations 1918–19, served WW I (1914–15 star, two medals); *b* 28 Oct 1869; *educ* Trin Coll Cambridge (MA); *m* 3 Feb 1898 Amy Gertrude (*d* 18 Aug 1969 aged 100), 5th dau of Thomas Wilkinson Tetley, of Claughton, Cheshire, and *d* 2 Dec 1938, having had issue:

(1) Frederick Wilkinson Spens; *b* 26 Oct 1903; *d* 14 June 1930

(2) Colin Robert; *b* 28 Feb 1907; *educ* Malvern; *m* 24 Aug 1946 *Evelyn Elinor May [Mrs Colin Fayrer, 20 The Manor, Churchdown, Glos], dau of Judge R Thomas Carey, of Ceylon, and *d* 1983, leaving issue:

1a *Anne Patricia [Mrs Roderick McKellar, 66 Lower Sloane St, London SW1]; *b* 17 Sept 1947; *m* 1991 *Roderick John McKellar

2a *Wendy Elizabeth [Mrs David Allworthy, Forest House, 99 Blean Common, Blean, Kent]; *b* 5 Aug 1949; *m* 1974 *David L Allworthy and has:

1b *James Jonathan Fayrer; *b* 1977

2b *Anna Elizabeth; *b* 1979

(1) Bethia Maud; *b* 17 March 1900; *m* 4 Oct 1924 (*divorce* 1943) Brig Sir Eric Alexander Ogilvy Hutchison, 2nd Bt, RA (*see* 1970 edn), and *d* 19 Feb 1971, leaving issue

1 Diana Agnes; *m* 19 April 1888 Rev Richard Arnold Edgell, Rector Beckley, E Sussex, and *d* Oct 1941 leaving issue. He *d* Feb 1940

2 Bethia Marion; *m* 15 April 1891 William Dobrée Young-Herries, DL, of Spottes, Kirkcudbrightshire, and *d* 26 March 1892, leaving issue

Sir JOSEPH *d* 21 May 1907; his est surv son,

Sir Joseph Fayrer, 2nd Bt, CBE; RHG, Lt-Col 2nd Scottish Gen Hosp RAMC WW I, MA Cambridge, FRCSE, MD, CM St Andrews, LRCS, LRCP, LFPS Edin and Glasgow, Fell Medical Soc; *b* 8 March 1859; *m* 30 Dec 1890 Ella (*d* 1 April 1952), dau of Col William Augustin John Mayhew, Bengal Army, and had issue:

1 JOSEPH HERBERT SPENS (Sir), **3rd Bt**

1 Phyllis Bethia Josephine; *b* 24 Aug 1898; *m* 22 June 1921 Capt Andrew Keith Tod and *d* 1973, leaving issue:

(1) *Andrew Leonard Fayrer Keith; Capt RA WWII; *b* 2 April 1924; *educ* Gordonstoun; *m* 13 Jan 1951 *Eileen Jane, dau of Rev Edward Labouchere Ruthven Thornton, ICS, and has:

1a *Christopher Edward Keith; *b* 2 April 1954; *educ* Gordonstoun

1a *Eileen Bridget; *b* 17 Feb 1952

2a *Jennifer Phyllis; *b* 2 April 1954

(1) *Priscilla Anne Josephine; *b* 4 Feb 1928; *m* 5 Jan 1952 *Col Alan Patrick Smith, OBE, BA, MICE, MIMechE, RE, only s of Alan Kenyon Smith, ICS (*see* BOUGHEY, Bt), and has issue:

1a *Alan Simon Nicholas; *b* 16 May 1954; *educ* Uppingham

2a *Richard Michael Patrick; *b* 20 Oct 1956

1a *Ann Elizabeth Phyllis; *b* 12 Jan 1962

2a *Lucy Jane Mary; *b* 2 Sept 1964

(2) *Elizabeth Rosemary Phyllis; *b* 19 Feb 1930; *m* 1 Sept 1967 *Graham Johnson, RAF (ret), and has issue

2 Eileen Margaret; *b* 21 Sept 1901; *d* unm 12 Nov 1956

Sir JOSEPH *d* 13 April 1937; his son,

Sir Joseph Herbert Spens Fayrer, 3rd Bt, DSC (1941); *b* 20 Oct 1899; *educ* Wellington; Lt KOSB WW I, Lt-Cdr RNVR WW II; *m* 1st 2 Nov 1926 (*divorce* Scottish courts 1936) Elizabeth, dau of Capt William Claude Frederick Vaudrey-Barker-Mill, of Mottisfont Abbey, Hants, by Hon Mary Brenda Nepenthe, dau of 1st and last Baron Collins (*see* 1911 edn), and had issue:

1 Nathaniel MacPherson; *b* 3 Dec, *d* 6 Dec 1928

Sir Joseph *m* 2nd 5 Aug 1939 Helen Diane Scott (*d* 14 Oct 1961), only dau of Capt John Lang, of Edinburgh, and by her had issue:

2 Sir JOHN LANG MACPHERSON FAYRER, **4th and present Bt**

1 Eleanor Jean Spens; *b* 6 May 1945; *m* 21 March 1967 *Michael Ronald Henbrey and had:

(1) *Samantha; *b* 29 Jan 1968

Sir Joseph *m* 3rd 5 Nov 1964 *Noreen [Noreen Lady Fayrer, Overhailes, Haddington, E Lothian EH41 3SB], formerly w of Lt Cdr John Killick Wright, RN, and only dau of Rev John Yuill Walker, of Innerleithen, and *d* 1976

FEILDEN

Arms: Arg. on a fess cotised az., between two martlets in chief and a rose in base gu., barbed and seeded ppr., three lozenges or. **Crest:** A nuthatch perched upon a hazel branch fructed ppr., holding in its beak a rose gu., slipped ppr. **Mottoes:** *Virtutis præmium honor* ('Honour is the reward of virtue'), *Crescit sub pondere virtus* ('Virtue grows under pressure') **Creation:** Bt. (UK) 21 July 1846

SIR HENRY WEMYSS FEILDEN, 6TH BT, of Feniscowles, Co Lancaster [Sir Henry Feilden Bt, Littledene, Heathfield Rd, Burwash, E Sussex TN19 7HN]; *b* 1 December 1916; *s* cousin 1976; *educ* Canford and King's Coll London; RE WW II, ret civ serv; *m* 25 Aug 1943 *Ethel May, dau of John Atkinson, of Annfield Plain, Co Durham, and has issue:

1 +HENRY RUDYARD [Henry Feilden Esq, 16 Surrey Close, W Totton, Hants SO40 2QQ]; *b* 26 Sept 1951; *educ* Kent Coll Canterbury and Bristol U (BVSc); MRCVS, vet with Tuckett, Gray & Ptnrs (Aylesbury, Bucks) 1976–78; Fraser, Smith (Binfield, Berks) 1978–83, L A Gould (Rossendale, Lancs) 1983–4, advsr Solvay-Duphar Veterinary Ltd (Southampton) 1984–96, Riverside Veterinary Surgery, Bishopstoke, Hants, 1996–; *m* 1982 (*divorce* 1997) Anne, dau of William Frank Bonner Shepperd, and has issue:

(1) +William Henry; *b* 5 April 1983

1 *Jennifer May [Mrs Graham Donald, 45D Seabird Lane, Discovery Bay, Lantau Island, Hong Kong]; *b* 1944; *m* 1st 1972 (*divorce* 1981) Philip Andrew Cooper; *m* 2nd 1981 *Graham Alexander Donald and by her 1st husb has issue:

(1) *Harry Edward; *b* 1975

(2) *Paul Andrew; *b* 1978

2 *Anne Margaret [Mrs William Stokoe, Chantry Down, Echopit Rd, Guildford, Surrey GU1 3TN]; *b* 1947; *m* 1970 *William Hugh Stokoe and has issue:

(1) *Rupert William; *b* 1980

(1) *Joanna Mary; *b* 1976

Lineage: Sir William Feilden, 1st Bt (UK), so *cr* 21 July 1846, of Feniscowles, Lancs; *b* 13 March 1772 (3rd s of Joseph Feilden, of Witton, by Margaret, dau and coheiress of William Leyland, and brother of John Feilden, of Mollington Hall); MP Blackburn 1832–1847, High Sheriff Cheshire 1833; *m* 30 March 1797 Mary Haughton (*d* 9 Jan 1867), dau of Edmund Jackson, memb Jamaican Ho of Assembly, and had issue:

1 WILLIAM HENRY (Sir), **2nd Bt**

2 Montague Joseph, JP, DL Lancs, of The Chain, Preston, Lancs; *b* 8 May 1816; Lt-Col 3rd Bn Loyal N Lancs Regt, MP Blackburn 1853–1857; *m* 1st 8 Jan 1846 Mary Anne (*dsp* 21 Sept 1859), only dau and heir of William Valentine, of Samlesbury, Lancs; *m* 2nd 26 Oct 1865 Alice (*d* 31 Aug 1899), 2nd dau of James Thoume, of Bon Air, Guernsey, and *d* 17 Oct 1898, leaving issue:

(1) Montague Leyland; *b* 11 March 1867; *m* 1891 A Woodland and *dsp* 13 Feb 1900

3 John Leyland; Lt 3rd Loyal N Lancs Regt; *b* 29 Sept 1821; m 1st 8 Oct 1851 Eliza Whigham (*d* 1888), dau of James Kennedy, of Ancoats; *m* 2nd 31 Oct 1894 Charlotte Isabella (*d* 5 May 1928), 4th dau of Peter Collin, of Maryport, Cumberland, and *d* 12 March 1915

1 Mary Haughton; *m* 20 June 1825 Rev J W Whittaker (*d* 3 Aug 1854) and *d* 30 Nov 1871, leaving issue

2 Catherine Margaret; *m* 11 May 1824 James Hozier, of Mauldslie Castle, Lanark, and *d* 27 April 1870, leaving issue. He *d* 13 Jan 1878

3 Georgiana Amelia; *m* 20 June 1831 Daniel Willis, of Halsnead Hall, Lancs (*d* 15 April 1873)

4 Frances Eliza; *m* 1st 2 April 1842 Andrew Hamilton (*d* 1853); *m* 2nd 14 Jan 1868 John Ranking and *d* 17 Nov d 1889 aged 90. He *dsp* 24 Feb 1870

5 Maria Leyland; *m* 22 June 1830 Rev Robert Hornby, MA, and *d* 23 July 1856

6 Caroline Reid; *d* 1835

The 1st Bt *d* 1850; his est s,

Sir William Henry Feilden, 2nd Bt; JP, DL; Capt 17th Lancers, Maj Duke of Lancaster's Own Militia; *b* 15 Nov 1812; *m* 15 Jan 1835 Mary Elizabeth (*d* 23 June 1890), dau of Col James Balfour Wemyss, of Wemyss Hall, Fife, and had issue:

1 WILLIAM LEYLAND (Sir), **3rd Bt**

2 Henry Wemyss, CB, JP Norfolk; *b* 6 Oct 1838; Col and Ch Paymaster Army Pay Dept, 42nd and 44th Regts, Indian Mutiny 1857, China 1860, Polar Expdn 1875–76, Transvaal 1881 and Boer War 1900–01; *m* 27 Oct 1864 Julia (*d* 12 June 1920), dau of David McCord, of S Carolina, and *d* 18 June 1921

3 Haughton Montague James; Lt-Col RA; *b* 20 April 1842; *m* 1881 Bessie, dau of L J Cohen, of Catford Bridge, and *dsp* ; 4 July 1903

4 Arthur Edward Cecil McDuff; *b* 1849; *m* 30 Jan 1873 Helen Pauline, 2nd dau of N P Krohn, of Grahamstown, S Africa, and *dsp* 26 Oct 1885

1 Mary Elizabeth; *m* 1st 23 Oct 1860 Capt Richard Newsham Pedder, 7th and 10th Hus, est s of Edward Pedder (*d* 1863), of Ashton Park, Lancs, and had issue; *m* 2nd 27 June 1867 Sir Musgrave Horton Brisco, 4th Bt (*qv*), and *d* 31 July 1922, leaving further issue

2 Frances Maria Caroline; *m* 19 March 1863 Rev Edmund Juxton Wemyss Whittaker, Chaplain St Mary Magdalen, Bath, s of Rev J W Whittaker, Vicar Blackburn, and *d* 12 Jan 1918, leaving issue

3 Blanche Harriet Juaneta Georgina; *m* 27 April 1871 Sir William Ridley Charles Cooke, 9th Bt (*qv*), and *d* 24 Feb 1930, having had issue

The 2nd Bt *d* 12 Jan 1879; his est s,

Sir William Leyland Feilden, 3rd Bt, JP Lancs; Lt 5th Light Dragoons and Bde-Major Lancs Rifle Vols; *b* 5 Nov 1835; *m* 16 Feb 1860 Catherine Jane (*d* 15 July 1913), est dau of Edward Pedder, JP, DL, of Ashton Park, Lancs, and *d* 9 June 1912, having had issue:

1 **Sir William Henry Feilden, 4th Bt**, JP Staffs 1903; Maj 2nd/1st Derbys Yeo TFR, 3rd Bn Roy Lancaster Regt, Boer War 1900, APM Lond Dist 1916 and W Cmd 1916–19; *b* 8 March 1866; *m* 22 April 1891 Evelyn Mary (*d* 11 Feb 1946), est dau of Sir Morton Manningham-Buller, 2nd Bt (*see* DILHORNE, V), and *d* 23 Feb 1946, leaving issue:

(1) **Sir William Morton Buller Feilden, 5th Bt**, MC; Capt Derbyshire Yeo, Dist Remount Officer Western Cmd 1919, served WWs I (wounded, despatches twice, Italian silver medal for valour) and II, Cdr No 6 Gp Midland Area, Roy Observer Corps 1938–45; *b* 20 May 1893; *m* 1st 8 Nov 1922 Margery Hannah (*d* 26 Nov 1925), only dau of Robert Knowles, of Ednaston Lodge, Derbys; *m* 2nd 28 Feb 1927 Reva Sarah Mary (*d* 9 Oct 1971), widow of Maj Guy Winterbottom and dau of Martin Morrison, of Faceby Manor, Yorks, and *dsp* 22 June 1976

(1) Beatrice Ida; *m* 1st 6 May 1916 (*divorce* 1936) Col Henry Fergusson Brace, DSO, MC, 15th Hus (*d* 26 Nov 1948), and had issue; *m* 2nd 28 Sept 1936 (*divorce* 1948) Maj James Haggas, 15th/19th Hus, est s of Sir James Haggas, of Woodville, Keighley, Yorks, and *d* 15 April 1973. He *d* 1 May 1956

(2) *Cynthia Evelyn; *m* 9 June 1937 Maj Geoffrey Charles Barn Charlesworth, TD, Yorks Hus Yeo, est s of Col William Gryce Charlesworth, TD, JP, DL, of Chestnut Grove Hall, Boston Spa, Yorks, and has issue:

1a *William Brian; *b* 1 Sept 1947; *educ* Eton and RAC Cirencester

2 Edward Leyland Cooke, OBE (1919); Maj, Capt HLI, served Crete massacres 1898 and WW I; *b* 19 June 1868; *m* 5 Feb 1907 Hon Marjorie Graham-Murray (*d* 24 Dec 1967), yst dau of 1st Viscount Dunedin (*see* 1940 edn), and *d* 31 Jan 1921, leaving issue:

(1) Iris Blanche Julie Edith; *b* 2 Sept 1909; *d* 1965

(2) *Esmé Mary Graham [Mrs George Shaw, Crossbank Hill, Hurworth-on-Tees, Co Durham] *b* 3 Oct 1913; *m* 1935 George Richard Shaw (*d* 1983), 5th s of William Shaw, of Saltburn, Yorks, and has issue:

1a *(John George) Graham [Graham Shaw Esq, Westbank, Duchal Rd, Kilmacolm, Renfrewshire PA13 4AY]; *b* 23 April 1948; *m* 1972 *Patricia Alexandra, dau of William Veitch, and has issue:

1b *William Graham; *b* 1981

1b *Katharine Alexandra; *b* 1976

2b *Philippa Jane; *b* 1978

1a *Angela Mary Graham; *b* 5 Feb 1936; *m* 3 Sept 1955 (*divorce* 1990) A/Cdre Anthony Walkinshaw Fraser, RAF, and has issue:

1b *Robert Anthony Walkinshaw; *b* 1963; *m* 1986 (*divorce* 1994) Kyoko — and has:

1c *Mami; *b* 1986

1b *Amanda Evelyn; *b* 1956; *m* 1st 1978 (*divorce* 1992) Mark Chaytor Dickinson and has issue (*see* CHAYTOR, Bt); *m* 2nd 1994 *Hon Timothy Leland Buxton (*see* BUXTON OF ALSA, B)

2b *Antonia Mary; *b* 1959; *m* 1983 *Richard Heard and has:

1c *William James; *b* 1991

1c *Samantha Mary; *b* 1986

2c *Rosie Anne; *b* 1988

3b *Alexandra Esmé; *b* 1960; *m* 1986 *Simon James Reid-Kay and has:

1c *Hamish George Strathern; *b* 1989

2c *Robert Simon; *b* 1991

3c *Angus Drummond; *b* 1994

2a *Fiona Esmé Gildroy [Mrs Fane Gaffney, Crossbank Hill, Hurworth, Co Durham DL2 2JB]; *b* 24 March 1942; *m* 10 June 1962 *Maj (Edward) Fane Travers Gaffney, late Welsh Gds, and has issue:

1b *Edward William Bay [Edward Gaffney Esq, 2A Wyfold Rd, London SW6 2SJ]; *b* 1962; *m* 1988 *Helen, dau of Henry Ernest Tugwell, and has issue:

1e *Frederick Henry; *b* 1992

2e *Jack Erik; *b* 1995

2b *Richard Desmond; *b* 1963

3b *Adrian Toby George Hannaford; *b* 1972

1b *Miranda Mary [Mrs Christopher Legard, Grizzlefield House, Thirsk]; *b* 1967; *m* 1986 *Christoper John Charles Legard, er s of Sir Charles Thomas Legard, 15th Bt (*qv*), and has issue

3a *Gelda Susan Marjorie Feilden [Mrs Robert Churton, Greenside House, Greenside, Tyne & Wear NE40 4AA]; *b* 28 Jan 1947; *m* 7 Sept 1968 *Capt Robert Harding Churton, 15th/19th KRH, yst s of T R H Churton, of Skewsby House, Skewsby, York, and has issue:

1b *Thomas Edward Harding; *b* 1972

2b *David Richard Harding; *b* 1975

3 Wemyss Gawne Cunningham, CMG (1917); Col and Ch Paymaster RAPC, Lancs Fus, Boer War 1899–1902 (King's and Queen's medals with four clasps); *b* 9 Aug 1870; *educ* Marlborough and RMC Sandhurst; *m* 20 Dec 1915 Winifred (*d* 1980), dau of Rev William Reyner Cosens, DD, and *d* 21 June 1943, leaving:

(1) Sir HENRY WEMYSS FEILDEN, **6th and present Bt**

(2) +Randle Richard [Randle Feilden Esq, Chartridge, West St, Mayfield, E Sussex TN20 6DS]; barrister Lincoln's Inn 1949, Assist Curate: St Andrew's, Moulsecomb, Brighton, 1955–57, and Steyning, Sussex, 1957–58, Tutor-Organiser WEA NE Lancs 1958–63, resigned Holy Orders 1959, Schs Inspr 1963–66, assist ed *Keesing's Contemporary Archives* 1967–81, memb Gen Synod C of E 1970–80; *b* 12 Jan 1923; *educ* Marlborough, Corpus Christi Coll Camb (BA 1944, MA 1948) and Cuddesdon Theological Coll; *m* 1st 6 July 1957 Leonora Mary (*d* 1991), er dau of John Lawrence Marshall, of Leicester; *m* 2nd 12 Dec 1992 *Mrs Eileen Hilda Braid

4 Randle Montague, CBE (1918); Lt-Col Egyptian Army, formerly Oxon LI, Civil Administrator during construction Port Sudan, Red Sea, 1905–08, Govr Bahr-el-Ghazal Province and OC Bahr-el-Ghazal Dist 1910–17, Civ Sec Sudan Govt 1917–21, Pasha 1920 (ret 1921), Mohmand Field Force 1897 (medal with clasp), Tirah Expdn 1897–98 (clasp), Boer War 1901–02 (despatches, medal with four clasps) and Sudan 1904–05 (medal with clasp), cmded Agaakir Dinkas Patrol 1913 (3rd Cl Medjidie), Nyma Patrol 1917–18 (medal with clasp), Roy Humane Soc's medal 1895, 4th Cl Medjidie 1905, 4th Cl Osmanieh 1910, 3rd Cl Order Nile 1915 and 2nd Cl 1921; *b* 17 July 1871; *educ* Charterhouse and RMC Sandhurst; *m* 5 June 1924 Rachel Mary Gordon (*d* 22 May 1933), only dau of Horace Gordon Lowe, and *d* 23 March 1965, leaving:

(1) +John Randle; *b* 17 Nov 1931; *educ* Eton

(1) *Fay Adah Rachel [Mrs John Hodson, The Sail Loft, Mulberry Quay, Falmouth, Cornwall TR11 3HD]; *b* 1925; *educ* UCL (BA Psy 1961); PhD Lond, DipPsych, lecturer and research worker London U 1962–82, Emeritus Reader Clinical Psychology London, fndr/dir Centre for Personal Construct Psychology 1982–; *m* 1st 14 July 1948 (*divorce* 1958) Anthony John Fransella, RAF, only s of Denis John Fransella, of White House, Epsom, Surrey; *m* 2nd 11 March 1968 *John Royden Cole Hodson, sometime regions ed *Financial Times*, s of Harry Ward Hodson, of Birkenhead

5 Rodolph; Capt and RTO Alnwick 1918–19, Capt Durham LI, Boer War 1900–01 (Queen's medal with three clasps) and WW I; *b* 7 March 1876; *educ* Radley; *m* 16 May 1903 Rose Christina (*d* 24 July 1960), dau of Col H C Ryder, of Minden House, Richmond, Yorks, and *dsp* 21 July 1955

1 Edith Haughton Wemyss, of Feniscowles House and Feniscowles, Scarborough; *d* 1 May 1922

2 Blanche Amelia Mary; *d* an infant

3 Adah Isabel; *m* 24 Feb 1903 Darcy Philip Assheton Gray, Capt TAR, s of Col William Gray, of Farley Hill Place, Berks, and *d* 22 Oct 1949. He *d* 13 Nov 1944

FELDMAN

Arms: Per chevron argent guttee de sang and gules guttee d'eau, in chief two apple trees eradicated and fructed proper in base a phoenix rising from flames also proper. **Crest:** A mount issuant therefrom between two sprigs of basil both flowered a dexter cubit arm the hand grasping a wreath of laurel all proper. **Supporters:** Dexter, A lion reguardant or holding in the dexter paw a copper handbell and in the mouth a sprig of pink camelia both proper; sinister, a hind reguardant or gorged with a portcullis attached to a chain sable and holding in the mouth a sprig of basil flowered proper. **Motto:** *Melius quo citius* ('The sooner the better'). **Creation:** B. (LP, UK) November 1995.

THE BARON FELDMAN, of Frognal, London Borough of Camden (Sir Basil Feldman) [The Rt Hon the Lord Feldman, House of Lords, London SW1A 0PW]; *b* 23 Sept 1926; *educ* Grocers' Sch; Dep Chm Gtr London Nat Union C and U Assocs 1975–78, Chm 1978–81, Pres 1981–85, V-Pres 1985–; V-Pres Gtr London YCs 1975–77; fought GLC election Richmond 1973; Chm Nat Union C Party 1985–86, V-Chm 1982–85, V-Pres 1986, Treas 1996–; chm: Martlet Servs Gp 1973–81, Solport Ltd 1981–85, The Quality Mark 1987–92, Better Business Opportunities 1990–, Watchpost Ltd 1983–; underwriting memb Lloyd's 1979–96; Govr Sports Aid Fndn 1990–; ktd 1982, FRSA 1987; *m* 1952 *Gita Julius and has two sons and a dau

Lineage: PHILIP FELDMAN; *m* Tilly — and had:

1 BASIL (Sir), *cr* a **Baron**

1 *Fenella Marion [Miss Fenella Fielding, c/o CCA Management, 4 Court Lodge, 48 Sloane Sq, London SW1W 8AT]; *b* 17 Nov 1934; *educ* N London Collegiate Sch; actress as Fenella Fielding

FERGUSON DAVIE

Arms: Quarterly, 1st and 4th, argent a chevron sable between three mullets pierced gules; 2nd and 3rd, azure three cinquefoils two and one or, upon a chief of the last a lion passant gules. **Crests:** 1 A pascal lamb regardant gules, 2 A halcyon, wings elevated proper, holding in the beak a branch of olive vert fructed or. **Motto:** *Auspice Christo* ('Under the auspices of Christ'). The halcyon, or kingfisher, is the royal crest of Portugal. The John Davy who was Mayor of Exeter in 1584 received during his term of office the pretender to the throne of Portugal, Dom Antonio, who had briefly proclaimed himself King of that country in 1580, despite being illegitimate, but who had gone into exile on Portugal's annexation by Spain. In gratitude Dom Antonio allowed Davy and his decendants to bear the device on his coat of arms. The lion passant gules on a chief is a feature of the BARDOLPHs, from whom John Davy descended through his mother. (The Davys did not, however, represent the family of Bardolph.) **Creation:** Bt. (UK) 9 Jan 1847.

SIR JOHN FERGUSON DAVIE, 7TH BT, of Creedy, Co Devon [Sir John Ferguson Davie Bt, 63 Hillgate Place, London SW12 9ES]; *b* 1 May 1906; *s* cousin 1997; *educ* Winchester; *m* 4 April 1942 Joan Zoë Charlotte (*d* 1987), dau of Raymond Hoole, of Vancouver, BC, and has:

1 +MICHAEL [Michael Ferguson Davie Esq, 63 Hillgate Pl, London SW12 9ES]; *b* 10 Jan 1944; *educ* St Edward's Sch Oxford; *m* 13 July 1968 (*divorce* 1993) (Margaret) Jean, only dau of Douglas John Macbeth, of Bowdon, Cheshire, and has had issue:

(1) James Michael; *b* 28 May 1970; *d* 1988

2 +Julian Anthony [Julian Ferguson Davie Esq, Rue Aux Fleurs 26, 1380 Ohain, Belgium]; *b* 6 July 1950; *educ* Uppingham; *m* 1976 *Louise, dau of John Marsden, of Huttons Ambo, Yorks, and has issue:

(1) +Charles John; *b* 10 Oct 1978

(2) +John Robert; *b* 1981

(3) +William Edward; *b* 1986

Lineage: WILLIAM de la WEY/de WY, of Wey (now Way), nr Torrington, Devon, *temp* HENRY II; had, with an est s (Walter, of Wey, *d* by 1242, leaving Elizabeth, *m* Walter Pollard, whose descendants inherited Wey) and a yst s (Henry, of Barlington, nr Torrington):

WILLIAM de VIE, of Ebberleigh, nr Torrington, had:

1 Richard de la WEYE/de WY/de VIE, of Ebberleigh, held land at Langley 1248; *d* 1277, leaving:

(1) William de WY/de VIE, of Ebberleigh; *dsp*

2 David de WY; moved to Cornwall, where he held Trewithinek of the king in chief; had:

(1) Thomas; held Trewithinek of the king in chief and by kt's serv lands at Tregeminion of Thomas de Pridias, lands at Boswoer and Penwodys of Serlo de Nansladron and land at Tregollas of John de Trelagu, and *d* 1299, having had:

1a David de WY/de VYE, of Trewithenek and Ebberleigh; *b* 1289; did fealty to the king for Trewithenek May 1305; *m* —, dau and heir of Gilbert Upcot, of Upcot, and had issue:

1b Robert, of Ebberleigh; *m* Letticia, dau and heiress of Thomas de Owlacombe, and had issue:

1c Roger DAVY, of Ebberleigh; *m* Thomazin, dau and heiress of John Fitzwalter, and *d* 1423, leaving issue:

1d William, of Ebberleigh, MP Melcombe Dorset 1425; *m* Alice, dau of Richard Reyney, of Eggesford, Devon, and left issue:

1e William, of Ebberleigh, MP Barnstaple 1446; had:

1f Richard, of Ebberleigh; had:

1g William, of Ebberleigh; *m* — Barry, of Winscot, and had:

1h John, of Ebberleigh; *m* Isott (*bur* 27 Jan 1560), dau and coheir of John Blinsam, of Blinsam, and was *bur* 1 July 1565, having had three sons and two daus. The est son inherited Ebberleigh, the second Upcot, the third Owlacombe, where their descendants survived for several generations. (Henry Davy, of Upcot, *b* 1592, *m* Margaret, dau of John Gay, of Gouldsworthy, is referred to by a contemporary as an antiquary'. Hugh Davy, of Owlacombe, last of this line, *d* 1763)

2h ROBERT

The younger son,

ROBERT DAVY; moved to Crediton, where he flourished in the cloth trade; *m* 1st — and had:

1 John, of Crediton; *m* 1st Margaret, dau and heir of — Brasier; *m* 2nd Elizabeth —, who survived him, and *d* by 30 Oct 1576, leaving by his 1st w, with other issue:

(1) John, of Crediton; *m* Anna, dau of Emmanuel Drewe, of Kenn, and had:

1a Emmanuel, of Ruxford; *m* 1st 16 June 1601 Katherine (*bur* 5 May 1620), dau of John Northcote (*see* IDDESLEIGH, E); *m* 2nd Abigail — (*bur* 12 Nov 1639); *m* 3rd 20 June 1640 Anne Clevelshly and was *bur* 4 May 1641, leaving, with other issue:

1b John, of Ruxford; *m* 1st Rebeckah (*bur* 12 Feb 1643), dau of Sir Symon Leech, and had three sons and five daus; *m* 2nd Elizabeth, gdau of Dr Cotton, Bp Exeter, by whom he had four sons, and was *bur* 8 Aug 1647; his est s:

1c John, of Ruxford; *bapt* 12 April 1635; *m* Dorothy — (*bur* 27 Jan 1706) and was *bur* 28 May 1680, having had, with other issue:

1d John; *bapt* 10 Dec 1667; *bur* 17 April 1679

1d Dorothy; *bapt* 3 Nov 1663; *m* 1689 3rd Baron Altham (*see* VALENTIA, V) and *d* by 1718, having had issue

2d Lucy; *bapt* 4 Nov 1674; *m* Rev Hon Leopold Finch (*see* WINCHILSEA and NOTTINGHAM, E)

2 Gilbert, of Canonteign (which his f bought 1542); *m* Mary (*d* 1591), dau of John Geere, of Heavitree, and *d* by 8 Nov 1585, having had, with other issue:

(1) Robert, of Canonteign; *bapt* 1564; *m* Anne, dau of John Northcote (*see* IDDESLEIGH, E), and had, with other issue:

1a Gilbert, of Canonteign; *m* Gertrude, dau of Sir Hugh Pollard, and had:

1b Anne; *b* 1617; *m* John Parker (*see* MORLEY, E)

2a Robert; *m* Rachel, dau of Sir Robert Lee, Ld Mayor London, and had issue

3a Edmund, MD; *b* 1630; *d* 1692

3 Lawrence, of Medland; *m* Johanna, dau of Simon Westlake, of Exbourne, and *d* by 6 Feb 1601, having had, with other issue:

(1) John, of Medland; *m* Elizabeth, dau of John Trobridge, of Trobridge, and had, with other issue:

1a John, of Medland; *b* 1610; *m* Mary, dau and heir of Andrew Elworthy, of Thellbridge, and had, with other issue:

1b John, of Medland; *m* Mary (*d* 11 Sept 1693), dau of — Every, and *dsp* 10 Feb 1695

2b Andrew, of Medland and Foldhay; *b* 1640; *m* Susanna (*d* 27 Feb 1672/3), dau of Francis Drew, of Killerton and Grange, and *dsp* 2 Oct 1669

3b Lawrence, of Medland; *m* Joan (*d* 18 April 1680), dau of — Atwill, and *d* 1686, leaving issue:

1c Andrew, of Medland, last of this line; *dsp* 1722

4 Ellis; *m* and moved to London; had a s Thomas

ROBERT DAVY *m* 2nd —, dau and heir of John Thomas or Bardolph, of Titchfield, Hants, by —, dau and heir of William Bardolph, and *d* of plague by 8 June 1570, leaving by her, with two daus (Thomazin, *m* Robert Alford; Johanna, *m* — Avery and had issue):

5 John, of Creedy; *b* 1541/2; Mayor Exeter 1584, 1594, 1604; *m* 1st 7 May 1570 Willmott Peter (*d* by 1588); *m* 2nd Margaret (*d* by 20 Jan 1614), dau of George Southcote, of Caverley, by Frances, dau and coheir of William Robins, of London, and *d* by 28 May 1612, leaving, with a dau (Margaret, *m* by 14 March 1610 Gideon Haydon, of Farwood, Epford and Cadhay, and *d* after 23 May 1662):

(1) Sir JOHN DAVY/DAVIE, 1st Bt (E), so *cr* 9 Sept 1641, of Creedy, MP Tiverton 1621, High Sheriff Devon 1629; *b* 1589; *m* 1st Juliana (*d* 1627), dau of Sir William Strode, of Newenham, and sis of William Strode, MP (one of the Five Members CHARLES I tried to impeach 1642), and had issue:

1a Sir JOHN DAVIE, 2nd Bt; High Sheriff Devon 1671, MP Tavistock 1661; *bapt* 6 Dec 1612; *m* 1st Eleanor (*dsp*), dau of Sir John Acland, 1st Bt of Columb John (*qv*); *m* 2nd Triphoena (*bur* 1 Feb 1658/9), dau and coheir of Richard Reynell, of Lower Creedy, through whom he acquired that estate, and by her had an only s (John, *dsp* unm, *bur* 11 Jan 1667/8); *m* 3rd Mary, dau of Edmund Parker, of North Molton; *m* 4th Amy (*bur sp* 25 April 1670), widow of — Hele and dau of Edmund Parker (*see* MORLEY, E), and *dsps*, being *bur* 31 July 1678

2a Emmanuel; *b* and *d* 1613

3a William, of Dira; Counsellor at Law Inner Temple 1639–40; *bapt* 13 Nov 1614; *m* 3 Oct 1648 Margaret (*bur* 4 July 1702), dau of Christopher Clarke, Mayor Exeter, and sis of Sir Francis Clarke, and was *bur* 28 Nov 1663, having had, with other issue:

1b Sir JOHN DAVIE; 3rd Bt; High Sheriff Devon 1691, MP Saltash; *b* 1660; *d* unm 30 Sept 1692

2b Sir WILLIAM DAVIE, 4th Bt; High Sheriff Devon 1693 and 1694; *bapt* 1 July 1662; *m* 1st Mary Stedman (*bur* 4 March 1690/1) and had issue:

1c Mary; *m* after 1708 Nicholas Hooper, of Raleigh, s of Sir Nicholas Hooper

2b (cont.) Sir WILLIAM *m* 2nd Abigail (*bur* 14 April 1725), dau of John Pollexfen, and *dspm*, *bur* 24 March 1706/7, having by her had, with other issue:

2c Margaret; *m* Stephen Northleigh, of Peamore

3c Frances; *m* Sir George Chudleigh, 4th Bt

1b Frances; *bapt* 9 May 1655; *m* 13 April 1680 Sir John Tremayne (*d* 1694), of Heligan, Memb Inner Temple, Serjeant at Arms, MP Tregony, and *d* 1683, leaving issue

2b Mary; *bapt* 4 Dec 1656; *m* Christopher Spicer and *d* 24 Aug 1728, leaving:

1c William; Master Chancery

4a Robert; *b* and *d* 1617

5a Robert; *bapt* 15 April 16–; *d* by 1677, leaving issue

6a Humphrey; London merchant, later of Boston, Mass., and Hartford, Conn.; *bapt* 24 Aug 1625; Puritan, migrated to New England 1662, as Commr Mass. organised Devon County 1664, memb Ancient and Honorable Artillery Co, Freeman Boston 1665, Dep Gen Court representing Billerica and Woburn 1666–79, Capt Boston Militia 1675, Assist Gen Court and ex-officio Overseer Harvard Coll 1679–86, Justice First Court Sessions Hartford 1687; *m* 1st by 25 May 1655 Mary (*d* 30 Dec 1681), dau of Edmund White, London haberdasher, and had, with other issue:

1b Edmund; *educ* Harvard; MD of Padua; *d* by 1688

2b JOHN (Sir), 5th Bt

3b Rowland; *b* and *d* 1664

4b Humphrey; *b* 10 June 1673; *bapt* 22 June 1673, *dsp* by 1684/5

1b Elizabeth; *m* Daniel Taylor, of Saybrook, Conn.

2b Margaret; *b* 19 Feb 1666; *bapt* 24 Feb 1666; *m* 22 Dec 1702 Henry Franklin, vintner (*d* 1713)

6a (cont.) Humphrey Davy *m* 2nd 14 Dec 1683 Sarah (*m* 3rd 30 May 1706 Col Jonathan Tyng, of Dunstable and Woburn, Mass.; *d* 8 Feb 1714 aged 68), widow of James Richards (*see* MILVERTON, B), and dau of William Gibbons, and *d* 18 Feb 1688/9, having by her had:

5b Humphrey; brazier; *b* 1684/5; granted 400 acres by Gen Assembly Conn. 1714; *m* 22 April 1714 Margaret (*d* 1729), dau of William Gedney, of Salem, Mass., and *d* 1718, leaving:

1c Elizabeth; *b* 6 March 1715/6; *m* 17 May 1739 James Butler, goldsmith, Capt Militia, s of James Butler, of Boston, and *d* 15 Feb 1740, leaving issue:

1d James; *b* 15 Feb 1740; *d* 1776

6b William; Boston merchant; *b* 27 June 1686; *educ* Harvard; *d* unm

1a Mary; *bapt* 25 March 1611; *bur* 22 June 1615

2a Mary; *bapt* 3 Nov 1615; *m* 1 Jan 1635 John Willoughby, of Payhembury, s of John Willoughby, of Payhembury, and *d* 1650

3a Elizabeth; *bapt* 24 Sept 1618; *m* 9 April 1642 Arthur Coplestone, of Bowden, s and heir of Henry Coplestone, and was living 1677

4a Juliana; *bapt* 1 Jan 1622/3; *m* 5 July 1648 Thomas Beare, of Huntsham

5a Margaret; *bapt* 20 May 1627; *m* 25 Feb 1649 Richard Beavis, of Old Clist House, and was living 1672

(1) (cont.) Sir JOHN *m* 2nd 1629 Isabel Hele (*bur* 29 Oct 1656), of Gnaton, and was *bur* 13 Oct 1656, leaving by her:

6a Isabel; *bapt* 9 Oct 1631; *m* 30 March 1639/40 Sir Walter Yonge, 1st Bt (*d* 21 Nov 1670), of Culliton

The 4th Bt's cousin,

Sir JOHN DAVIE, 5th Bt, *educ* Harvard 1681; Rate Collector Poquonock (later incorporated as Groton), New London 1695, Selectman 1696, first Town Clerk Groton 1707, High Sheriff Devon 1715; *m* by 1691 his step-sis Elizabeth (*bur* 3 Dec 1713), dau of James Richards (*see* MILVERTON, B), and had, with other issue:

1 JOHN (Sir), 6th Bt

2 Humphrey; *b* 12 April 1702; *d* unm, *bur* 28 May 1749

3 William; *b* 22 March 1705/6; *m* 28 May 1728 Ellen (*bur* 25 Jan 1776), dau of Nicholas Jackson, of Bristol; *d* 14 Nov, *bur* 17 Nov 1757

1 Mary; *b* 30 June 1693; *m* Rev Thomas Bishop, of Barnstaple

2 Sarah; *b* 21 Oct 1695; *m* Christopher Savery, of Shilston

3 Elizabeth; *b* 17 March 1697/8; *m* Ebenezer Mussell, of London

Sir JOHN was *bur* 29 Dec 1727; his est son,

Sir JOHN DAVIE, 6th Bt; *b* 27 July 1700; *m c* 1 March 1725 Elizabeth (*bur* 25 March 1738), sis of Sir Hugh Acland, Bt, of Killerton (*see* ACLAND, Bt, of Columb John), and had, with other issue:

1 JOHN (Sir), 7th Bt

2 William (Rev); Rector Exminster, Preb Exeter; *bapt* 10 Dec 1734; *educ* BNC Oxford (MA 1760); *m* Bridget, dau of John Bertie, Rector Kenn, Preb Exeter, and *d* 1778, having had issue:

(1) John; *ka* aboard HMS *Nymph* in the capture of the *Cleopatra* 1793

(2) Thomas; *d* yellow fever WI 1787

(1) Frances; *m* William Henry Beauchamp and had issue (*see* PROCTOR-BEAUCHAMP, Bt)

(2) Bridget; *m* Thomas Beaumont, of Buckland (*see* BEAUMONT, Bt)

1 Anne; *b* 1726; *m* Rev Thomas Hurrell (*d* 21 Feb 1781), of Drewsteignton, and *d* 1804

Sir JOHN was *bur* 3 Sept 1737; his est surv s,

Sir JOHN DAVIE, 7th Bt; *bapt* 4 Aug 1731; *educ* Magdalen Coll Oxford (MA 1754), High Sheriff Devon 1761; *m* 7 July 1763 Catherine (*bur* 24 Dec 1776), dau of John Stokes, of Rill, Glos, and *d* 18 Sept 1792, having had, with other issue:

1 Sir JOHN DAVIE, 8th Bt; High Sheriff Devon 1802; *b* 3 Jan 1772; *educ* Magdalen Coll Oxford; *m* 6 Sept 1796 Anne (*d* 7 Dec 1812 aged 39), dau of Sir William Lemon, Bt, of Carclew, and *d* 8 May 1803, having had, with other issue:

(1) Sir JOHN DAVIE, 9th Bt; *b* 8 March 1798; High Sheriff Devon 1821; *d* unm 18 Sept 1824

(2) William; *b* 8 March 1798; *d* following a hunting accident at Stover 1 June 1822

(1) FRANCES JULIANA, of whom presently

2 Sir HUMPHREY PHINEAS DAVIE, 10th and last Bt; *b* 12 Jan 1775; *educ* Eton and Ch Ch Oxford; Ensign 111th Regt, Lt 106th Regt, Maj 1795; served 1799 Walcheren Expdn, Gibraltar 1800; Brevet Lt-Col 1801, Lt-Col 5th Regt 1805, in Germany 1806, attack on Buenos Aires 1807, sold Lt Colonelcy 1808, Inspr Excise and Customs 1811, High Sheriff Devon 1829; *d* unm 12 Jan 1846, when the btcy expired, being *s* in his estates by his n FRANCES (*see* above and below)

1 Catherine; *b* 7 Jan *bapt* 2 June 1765; *m* 9 April 1795 Joseph Hunt (*d* 10 Jan 1816) and *d* 1882, having had issue

The 10th and last Bt's n,

FRANCES JULIANA Davie; *b* 4 Aug 1802; *m* 22 March 1823 Sir HENRY ROBERT FERGUSON later FERGUSON DAVIE (roy licence 9 Feb 1846; *d* 30 Nov 1885), **1st Bt** (UK), so *cr* 9 June 1847 (illegitimate s of Robert Ferguson, of Raith; (*see* 1934 edn NOVAR, V)), Capt 9th Lancers, Lt-Col 1st Bn Gren Gds, Hon Col 73rd Highrs, Gen, MP Haddington Boroughs 1847–77, Freeman Haddington, Jedburgh and N Berwick, and *d* 12 April 1882, having had:

1 Henry Davie; Lt Rifle Bde; *b* 1825; *d* 1850

2 **Sir John Davie Ferguson Davie, 2nd Bt**, JP, DL (Devon and Carmarths), JP (Somerset), High Sheriff Carmarths 1873; *b* 27 Oct 1830; Lt-Col 1st Devon Militia, Capt Gren Gds Crimea 1855–56, MP Barnstaple 1859–65; *m* 17 March 1857 Edwina Augusta (*d* 15 Aug 1889), est dau of Sir James Hamlyn Williams, 3rd Bt, of Edwinsford and Clovelly, and *d* 16 June 1907, having had issue:

(1) Mary Fanny; *b* Oct 1857; *d* in infancy

3 WILLIAM AUGUSTUS (Sir), **3rd Bt**

4 Charles Robert (Rev); MA Cantab; Rector Yelverton, Norfolk; *b* 20 June 1836; *m* 2 Aug 1866 Anne Clarissa (*d* 18 Sept 1889), only child of Biggs Andrews, QC, of Heavitree House, Devon, and gdau of Sir James Gibson-Craig, 1st Bt (*see* GIBSON-CRAIG-CARMICHAEL, Bt), and *d* 6 April 1887, leaving issue:

(1) Francis Andrews; Capt Black Watch, Hon Maj Canadian Militia, Boer War (two medals, four clasps); *b* 15 July 1867; *m* 1st 9 March 1891 (*divorce* 1895) Amanda, dau of John von Juch de Fabris, and had issue:

1a William Francis Washington; *b* 22 Feb 1892; *dspm* 3 June 1929

(1) (cont.) Maj Francis Ferguson-Davie *m* 2nd 1917 Alice Moore, dau of William Moore West, CE, of Hastings, Ontario, and *d* 14 Aug 1917

(2) Henry Herrick; *b* 26 June 1869; *m* 1891 Eleanora Inloes (*d* 19 March 1913), dau of William Schultz, of Philadelphia, and *d* 16 Feb 1913, leaving issue:

1a Henry Herrick; Lt Scottish Rifles; *b* 7 Jan 1894; *m* 1919 Julia Victoria, dau of John Stokes, of London, and *d* 28 Oct 1952, having had issue:

1b +Henry Herrick [Henry Ferguson Davie III, 1420 Washington Ave, Severn, Baltimore, Md., USA]; Tech Sgt US Marine Corps WW II; *b* 26 March 1920; *m* 1st 20 June 1941 (*divorce* 1943) Joyce Marilyn, dau of Clarence Sanders, of Brooklyn, Baltimore, and has:

1c +Henry Herrick IV; *b* 194–

1b (cont.) Henry Ferguson Davie III *m* 2nd 2 Sept 1951 *Anna Marie, dau of Bender Clarke, of Gambrillo, Md., and by her has issue:

1c *Anna Louise; *b* 27 May 1952

2a Charles Francis; Lt Northants Regt and Chinese Labour Corps WW I; *b* 2 Jan 1898; *m* 30 Dec 1924 Alice Clarke (*k* plane crash Windhoek 20 April 1968 aged 81), est dau of Henry Newman, of Potterne, Wilts, and *d* 22 March 1967, leaving issue:

1b *Muriel Frances; *b* 23 June 1926; *m* 1st 27 March 1948 (*divorce* 1952) Basil Anthony King, s of Rev Percy King, of Johannesburg; *m* 2nd 29 Nov 1952 *Bernard William Pearce, s of Cecil Roland Pearce, of Malvern, and has issue:

1c *Michael Stephen; *b* 5 Oct 1953; *m* 1st 1975 (*divorce* 1977) Judith Melanie McClelland; *m* 2nd 1979 *Carol Ann Ebelthite and has issue:

1d *Clinton Noel; *b* 1990

1d *Megan Bernardine; *m* 1980

2d *Mandy; *b* 1985

3d *Tamsin; *b* 1988

2c *Geoffrey Mark; *b* 19 July 1956; *m* 1981 *Belinda Ryall, of Natal, and has issue:

1d *Raymond; *b* 1984

2d *Bronwyn Muriel; *b* 1983

3c *Robert Andrew; *b* 21 April 1959; *m* 1st 1980 (*divorce* 1988) Odette Jean-Jacques, and has issue:

1d *Dylan Bradley; *b* 1983

2d *Lloyd; *b* 1985

3c (cont.) Robert Pearce *m* 2nd 1992 *Beverley Ann Smith

3a William Carey; Capt Res Offrs Green Howards; *b* 25 March 1900; *m* 25 March 1922 Katherine (*d* 1986), dau of William Robertson Kay, of Sutton, Dublin, and *d* 1974, leaving issue:

1b William George Michael; CEng, FICE; *b* 5 Dec 1923; *educ* Trin Coll Dublin (BA, BAI); *m* 11 Dec 1953 *Margaret Mary, dau of Capt William J Fowler, and *d* 1973, having had issue:

1c +Christopher Mark; *b* 19 Sept 1956; *m* 1st 1976 (*divorce* 1982) Wendy K, dau of John McGillivray, of Castlegar, BC, Canada; *m* 2nd 1984 *Joanne Elma, dau of David James Thomas, QC

1c *Deidre Ann; *b* 18 Jan 1955; *m* 1977 (*divorce* 1988) Herbert J Markgraf, of Kelowna, BC, Canada

2c *Jean Elizabeth; *b* 27 June 1961; *m* 1986 *Gordon Richard Boothe, of Summerland, BC

1b *Jean Anne [Mrs George Hellyer-Crawford, 31 Seabank Ct, Sandycove, Co Dublin, Ireland]; *b* 26 April 1932; *m* 1958 *George Hellyer-Crawford, s of Samuel Hellyer Crawford, BA, of Dublin, and has issue:

1c *Anne Katherine; *b* 15 April 1959; *m* 1984 *Thomas P O'Reilly, of Tullamore, Co Offaly, and has issue:

1d *Nanci Jean; *b* 1994

2c *Alison Jane; *b* 5 June 1963

(3) Charles James (Rt Rev); MA, DD Cantab, Warden Anglican Hostel, Fort Hane Coll 1933–44, Bp Singapore 1909–27; *b* 16 March 1872; *m* 1st 3 Nov 1902 Charlotte Elizabeth, OBE (1927), MD (*d* 24 March 1943), dau of Prof Edward Hull, FRS, LLD; *m* 2nd 24 Jan 1948 Marie Antoinette Jacobine (*d* 25 Feb 1963), widow of Gilbert Randles, barrister, and dau of J A Hax, of Caterham Valley, Surrey, and *d* 11 Sept 1963, leaving an adopted dau:

*Dorothea Clare (formerly Fraser) [Mrs Denis Butler, 6 Edinburgh St, Umkomaas 4170, Natal, S Africa; c/o Kingswood College, Grahamstown B140, E Cape Province, S Africa]; *b* 24 Feb 1920; *educ* Rhodes U Coll (BA); *m* 5 July 1943 *Denis Ryall Butler, s of Harold Challacombe Butler, of Kuruman, S Africa, and has issue:

1b *Anthony Ryall; *b* 22 Nov 1946

2b *Julian Harold Charles; *b* 23 Feb 1950

1b *Rosemary Elizabeth; *b* 8 Jan 1948

2b *Angela Clare; *b* 9 Dec 1952

(1) Anne Helen; *m* 1st 12 Oct 1908 William Robert Pickett (*d* 22 Feb 1914); *m* 2nd 8 Feb 1918 Robert Patrick Thomson (*d* 29 March 1926) and *dsp* 9 Dec 1945

1 Harriet Anne; *b* 23 June 1824; *m* 1851 Gen Hon Sir Robert Rollo, KCB (*see* ROLLO, L)

2 Caroline; *b* 16 Aug 1827; *m* Chevalier Charles de Santi and had issue

3 Fanny Julia; *b* 1 Aug 1829; *m* 1857 Col Sir Robert Thomas White-Thomson, KCB (*d* 13 March 1918), of Broomford, and *d* 28 April 1923, having had issue

The 2nd Bt's bro,

Sir William Augustus Ferguson Davie, 3rd Bt, CB, JP Devon; MA Cantab; Pncpl Clerk Public Bill Off H of C; *b* 13 April 1833; *m* 4 Sept 1862 Frances Harriet (*d* 18 June 1923), 5th dau of Sir William Miles, 1st Bt (*qv*), and *d* 18 Jan 1915, having had issue:

1 **Sir William John Ferguson Davie, 4th Bt**; Maj Border Regt; *b* 17 June 1863; *m* 2 April 1891 Phina (*d* 7 Oct 1939), dau of Thomas Nelson, of Friars Carse, Dumfriesshire, and *dsp* 12 July 1947

2 Henry Augustus (Sir), CB; Pncpl Clerk Public Bill Off H of C; *b* 22 Aug 1865; *m* 4 Aug 1897 Adeline (*d* 23 March 1951), dau of Thomas Holdsworth Newman (*see* NEWMAN, Bt, of Mamhead), and *d* 31 Jan 1946, leaving two daus (*d* unm)

3 Arthur Francis, CIE, DSO; *b* 11 July 1867; Lt-Col 51st Sikhs IA: Waziristan Expdn 1894–95, Chitrai 1895, Tirah 1897–98, Waziristan 1901–02, NW Frontier India 1902 and 1908 and WW I; *m* 2 Aug 1906 Eleanor Blanche Daphne (*m* 2nd 9 July 1918 Maj John Horace Wyndham Knight-Bruce (*d* 31 Aug 1951), Roy Warwicks Regt, est s of Rt Rev G W H Knight-Bruce, DD, Bp Mashonaland, and *d* 8 Nov 1964), er dau of Charles Topham Naylor, of Dean House, Alresford, Hants, and *d* 11 April 1916 of wounds recd in action, leaving issue:

(1) William Anthony; Lt RA; *b* 8 May 1907; *d* 2 May 1934

(2) **Rev Sir (Arthur) Patrick Ferguson Davie, 5th Bt**, TD; *b* 17 March 1909; *educ* Wellington, Lincoln Coll Oxford (BA 1939, MA 1945) and Ely Theological Coll; Deacon 1934, Priest 1935, Curate Littleham-cum-Exmouth 1934–37 and St Augustine's Kilburn 1938–39, CF (TA) 1937, 4th Bn Devonshire Regt 1939–40, 130 Inf Bde 1940, Gibraltar 1940–43, BNAF 1943–44, CMF 1944–45, Hon CF 1945, Vicar St John's Torquay 1945–48, Hon Chaplain to Bp Exeter 1949, RD Cadbury 1966–68, Ld Manors of Creedy, Carswell, Combe Lancelles, Ruxford and Upton Hellions; *m* 8 Dec 1949 Iris Dawn Cable-Buller (*d* 1992), only dau of Michael Francis Buller, of Downes, Crediton, Devon, by Hon Dawn Weston, est dau of 1st and last Baron Cable (*see* 1927 edn), and *d* 1988, leaving issue:

(1) **Sir Antony Francis Ferguson Davie, 6th Bt**; *b* 23 March 1952 (HH PRINCESS MARIE LOUISE stood sponsor); *educ* Stanbridge Earls and Birkbeck Coll London (BA); *d* unm 19 May 1997

4 Edward Cruger; *b* 19 Nov 1868; *m* 29 June 1905 Blanche Evelyn (*d* 23 Feb 1959), 3rd dau of William Wyndham Hasler, of Aldingbourne, and *d* 12 Oct 1948, leaving issue:

(1) Sir JOHN FERGUSON DAVIE, **7th and present Bt**

5 Herbert George; T/Lt RM; *b* 27 March 1873; *m* 1st 4 July 1902 Gwendolen Ursula (*dsp* 17 Dec 1902), 3rd dau of Arthur Lloyd, of Leaton Knolls, Salop; *m* 2nd 10 June 1911 Ethel Marion (*d* 2 Jan 1959), est dau of Col Alfred Luther Lane, of Timsbury, Bath, and was *ka* Dardanelles 1 May 1915

6 Walter Christie; *b* 26 July 1875; *d* 24 Feb 1878

1 Eleanor Harriott; *m* 27 Dec 1894 Brig-Gen George Northcote Colvile (*d* 21 May 1940), DSO, of Njoro, Kenya Colony, 43rd Oxon LI, er s of Lt-Gen Sir Fiennes Middleton Colvile, KCB, and *dsp* 24 Nov 1948

2 Mary Frances; *m* 29 Dec 1900 William Arthur Knight (*d* 25 Aug 1954), MA, DSc, assist master Marlborough, and *d* 14 Nov 1949, leaving issue

FERGUSSON

Arms: Az. a buckle arg. between three boar's heads couped or, in a dexter canton arg. a saltire az., surmounted of an inescutcheon or charged with a lion rampant within a double tressure flory counter-flory gu. **Crest:** A bee on a thistle ppr. **Supporters:** Two gryphons or, armed and beaked gu. (granted 1753 in recognition of the 2nd Bt's legal prowess.) **Mottoes:** 1 (over crest) *Dulcius ex asperis* ('All the sweeter for having undergone bitterness'), 2 (on compartment) *Ut prosim aliis* ('May I profit others'). **Creation:** Bt. (NS) 30 Nov 1703.

SIR CHARLES FERGUSSON, 9TH BT, of Kilkerran [Sir Charles Fergusson Bt, Kilkerran, Maybole, Ayrshire KA19 7SJ]; *b* 10 May 1931; *s f* 1973; *educ* Eton, Edinburgh and E Scotland Coll of Ag (Scottish Dip Ag); *m* 15 July 1961 *Hon Amanda Mary Noel-Paton, est dau of Baron Ferrier, ED (LP, *see* 1970 edn), and has:

1 +ADAM; *b* 29 Dec 1962; Maj Army Air Corps; *m* 2 Sept 1989 *Jenifer Kirsty, yr dau of Adam Thomson, of Ormiston, E Lothian, and has issue:

(1) +James; *b* 2 April 1996

(1) *Samantha Kirsty; *b* 24 Jan 1992

(2) *Lucy Alice; *b* 8 Nov 1993

2 +Joseph Victor; *b* 9 Jan 1965; *m* 15 Sept 1990 *Emma Sarah Louise, yr dau of (William) Martin Cracknell, of Freuchie, Fife, and has issue:

(1) +Oliver William; *b* 20 Sept 1993

(1) *Flora Lucy; *b* 19 Dec 1995

(2) *Louisa Katherine; *b* 23 April 1998

Lineage: The loss about the 17th century of all the FERGUSSON muniments has left their origin obscure. They probably claimed descent from Fergus, Celtic Ld of Galloway (*d* 1161), whose s Gilbert (*d* 1 Jan 1185) was f of Duncan (*d* 1250), 1st Earl of Carrick of the *cr* made by 1196.

The territorial Barony of Kilkerran was held 1434 by Duncan, son of Colin, who was probably f of:

JOHN FERGUSSON of Kilkerran; living 1464; named as heir of tailzie to John Kennedy of Blairquhan 1479; *d c* 10 Oct 1483, leaving:

FERGUS FERGUSSON of Kilkerran; had a charter of lands from JAMES II 1466; *m* Jonet, dau of John Kennedy of Blairquhan, and *d c* 28 July 1512, leaving, with two yr sons (John, living 1498; Thomas, living 1513):

DUNCAN FERGUSSON of Kilkerran; *b c* 1473; *m c* 1508 Jonet Campbell, probably of the CAMPBELLs of Torrinzean, and *d c* 1553, leaving, with two yr sons (Gilbert, in Balcamie, living 1574, had two daus, Marion and Margaret; Thomas, in Balquhirn, living 1554, f of Hector; probably ancestor of the FERGUSSONs of Dalduff):

WILLIAM FERGUSSON; *k* Battle of Pinkie 10 Sept 1547, leaving, with four yr sons (David; Gilbert; Thomas; Finlay) and a dau (Marion):

BERNARD FERGUSSON of Kilkerran; he and many of his family supported the KENNEDYs of Cassillis (*see* AILSA, M) in contemporary feuds; *m* 1st Isobel Adair (*d* 1568), apparently a dau of William Adair of Kinhilt, Wigtownshire, and had:

1 Simon; served heir-gen to his mother 1580; *m* 1589 Christian (*m* 2nd Gilbert Ross, Provost Collegiate Church of Maybole, and had further issue), er dau and coheir of Robert Forrester of Boquhan, Provost Stirling, and *dvp* Aug 1591, leaving issue:

(1) JOHN, for whom *see* below

(2) Thomas; *b* posthumously

BERNARD FERGUSSON *m* 2nd Agnes Schaw (*d* 1576) and *d c* 1600, leaving by her:

2 William

3 James; *m* Margaret Chalmer and was probably f of:

(1) James (Rev); *b* 1620; Minister Kilwinning; *m* Jean Inglis (*d* 1687) and *d* 1667, having had issue

BERNARD FERGUSSON's gs,

Sir JOHN FERGUSSON of Kilkerran, which he encumbered with debts through his royalism in the Civil War; ktd 1641; *m c* 1612 Helen, dau of Sir Thomas Kennedy of Culzean (2nd s of 3rd Earl of Cassillis; *see* AILSA, M) and widow of James Mure, Yr. of Auchindrane, and *d* abroad July 1647, leaving issue:

1 Alexander, of Kilkerran; *m c* 1643 Margaret, dau of Thomas Sydserf, Bp Galloway, and *d* July 1685, leaving:

(1) Alexander, of Kilkerran, which he sold 1700 to **Sir John Fergusson, 1st Bt** (*see* below); *m* 1667 Katharine, dau of Sir William Weir of Stanebyres, and had:

1a John, of Underwood; *m* 1st Margaret, dau of David Crauford of Kerse, and had issue; *m* 2nd Elizabeth, dau and heiress of William Boswell of Knockroon, and *d* 1719, having by her had:

1b Margaret

2a William; *m* Agnes, est dau and coheir of John Kennedy of Auchinblain, and *d c* 1746, leaving issue:

1b Alexander; *b* 1690; Minister Kilwinning; *m* 1725 Katherine (*d* 1766), est dau of William Watson, writer (legal practitioner) in Edinburgh, and *d* 1770, having had:

1c William; *b* 1729; *d* unm 1757

2b John; *m* Margaret Cockburn and *d* Jamaica 1730, having had, with other issue:

1c David; *b* 22 June 1727; Provost Ayr 1765–90; *m* Mary, er dau of John Mure of Blairstoun, and *d* 3 March 1791, having had issue

3a Alexander; Capt; *d* at the Scottish settlement of Darien

(2) James (Rev); C of E clergyman

2 James; royalist Capt Civil War; *d* unm

3 John; royalist Capt Civil War; *m* Jean McDowell and *d* May 1697, leaving issue

4 Simon, of Auchinwyne; *m* Jean Crauford and had, with other issue:

(1) JOHN, **1st Bt**

1 Jonet; *m* Thomas Fergusson of Threave, and had issue

ALEXANDER FERGUSSON (last of his branch of the family of Kilkerran)'s 1st cousin,

Sir John Fergusson, 1st Bt (NS), so *cr* 30 Nov 1703; *b* 1656; advocate 1681; bought the Barclanachan estate next to Kilkerran; the latter, which he had by now bought from his cousin, was erected into a free (territorial) Barony by charter 7 Feb 1701; granted 1719 undifferenced arms as Ch of the name of Fergusson; moved the family seat from the old house of Kilkerran, now a ruin, to Barclanachan or Balmaclanachan, formerly a Kennedy property; *m* 1684 Jean (*d* 1740), dau of James Whitefoord of Dunduff by Isobel, dau of Sir Bryce Blair of Blair and sis of Sir Adam Whitefoord of Blairquhan, 1st and last Bt, and *d* 14 Feb 1729, leaving, with other issue, including a dau (Jean, *m* Alexander Macdowall of Garthland and had issue):

Sir James Fergusson, 2nd Bt; *b* 1688; *educ* Edinburgh and Leyden Us; advocate 1711, MP Sutherland 1734–35, Ld of Session 1735 as Lord Kilkerran, Ld of Justiciary 1749; his compilation of Court of Session decisions 1738–53 published 'by his son' (probably George, *see* below) 1775; *m* 8 Sept 1726 Jean (*d* 29 March 1766), only child of James, Viscount Maitland (*see* LAUDERDALE, E), and *d* 20 Jan 1759, having had, with other issue:

1 John; *b* 1727; Ensign Lord Halifax's Regt of Foot 1745/6, Cornet Cobham's (later Mordaunt's) Dragoons 1747; *dvp* unm 1750

2 **Sir Adam Fergusson, 3rd Bt**; *b* 7 May 1733; advocate 1755 (LLD), MP Ayrshire 1774–80, 1781–84 and 1790–96 and Edinburgh 1784–89, Commr Trade and Plantations 1781; unsuccessfully claimed Earldom of Glencairn (*see* CUNINGHAME, Bt); *dsp* 25 Sept 1813

3 Charles; London vintner; *b* 26 Jan 1740; *m* 21 Dec 1764 his cousin Anne (*d* 1782), 2nd dau of Thomas Fordyce of Ayton, and *d* 9 Dec 1804, having had, with other issue:

(1) JAMES (Sir), **4th Bt**

(1) Jean; *b* 12 Oct 1766; *m* 25 Oct 1785 Capt John Hamilton Dempster, half-bro of George Dempster of Dunnichen, MP, and *d* 5 May 1798, leaving issue

(2) Catherine; *m* Rev Leslie Moodie, DD (*d* 1840), Minister Inveresk, and *d* 27 July 1841

4 George; *b* 25 Aug 1743; advocate 1765, a Ld of Session 1799–1826 and of Justiciary 1808–26 as Lord Hermand; *m* 23 Dec 1793 his cousin Graeme, dau of William Macdowall, of Castle Semple, and *dsp* 9 Aug 1827

1 Helen; *b* 16 May 1741; *m* 20 March 1770 Sir David Dalrymple, 3rd Bt, Lord Hailes (*see* STAIR, E), and *d* 10 Nov 1810, having had:

(1) Jean; *m* as his 1st w her cousin **Sir James Fergusson, 4th Bt** (*see* below)

The 3rd Bt's nephew,

Sir James Fergusson, 4th Bt; *b* 20 Oct 1765; fndr Ayrshire Ag Assoc; *m* 1st 8 Nov 1799 Jean (*d* 6 May 1803), 2nd dau of Sir David Dalrymple, 3rd Bt, Lord Hailes (*see* above), and had, with two daus (*d* unm):

1 CHARLES (Sir), **5th Bt**

Sir James *m* 2nd 5 Dec 1804 Henrietta (*d* 14 May 1850), 2nd dau of Adml 1st Viscount Duncan of Camperdown (*see* 1933 edn CAMPERDOWN, E), and *d* 14 April 1838, having by her had further issue:

2 George Hermand; *b* 22 Aug 1810; *m* 1st 1841 Jane (*dsp* 26 Dec 1844), dau of Walter Little Gilmour of CraigmiLlar (*see* GILMOUR OF CRAIGMILLAR, B) and widow of Maj Robert Gordon of Halhead; *m* 2nd 28 July 1857 Georgina Grace (*d* 4 May 1862), dau of Archibald Buchanan of Auchentorlie, and *d* 27 April 1870, leaving issue:

(1) George James FERGUSSON later FERGUSSON-BUCHANAN (1890) of Auchentorlie, Dunbartonshire, JP, DL; *b* 27 April 1862; Hon Lt-Col Roy Scots Fus, memb Roy Co Archers, served Boer War (medal and three clasps) and WW I; ADC to Govr Bombay 1882–85; *m* 8 Dec 1886 Grace (*d* 21 Nov 1935), dau of Claud Hamilton of Barns, Dunbartonshire, and *d* 30 Nov 1928, leaving:

1a Noel Grace; *m* 21 June 1914 Maj Colin Charles Forbes Mackenzie (*d* 1943), of Portmore, and *dsp* 1 Sept 1960

2a Avril Nora; *m* 18 Oct 1921 Cdr Mervyn Boyd Alexander-Sinclair, RN, of Dorchester, er s of Adml Sir Edwyn Sinclair Alexander-Sinclair, GCB, MVO, and had issue

(1) Mary; *m* 19 Dec 1878 Capt James Creagh Richard Scott, RMLI, of Crevagh, Co Clare, and *d* 9 April 1914, having had issue

3 James Alexander Duncan; *b* 30 July 1812; Lt-Col 6th Bengal Light Cav, served Punjab Campaign 1848; *m* 15 Nov 1844 Margaret (*d* 9 Dec 1896), dau of James Hope, WS, and *d* 8 Nov 1864, leaving issue:

(1) Alice Jane; *m* 29 Aug 1872 Maj-Gen Andrew Smythe Montagu Browne, JP, DL (*d* 1916), of St John's Point, Killough, Co Down, and *d* 30 Nov 1928, leaving issue

4 Robert Duncan; *b* 16 Sept 1813; Maj Roy Ayrshire and Wigton Rifles, Offr Rifle Bde; *m* 1st 30 Jan 1852 Helen (*d* 21 July 1863), 2nd dau of John Blackburn, of Killearn, Stirling; *m* 2nd 21 May 1866 Margaret Eliza (*d* 21 Jan 1888), dau of William Fairlie and widow of John Stuart Hay-Newton of Newton (*see* TWEEDDALE, M), and *d* 15 Feb 1878, leaving by his 1st w issue:

(1) Harry James; *b* 18 Dec 1852; Maj Rifle Bde, Mil Sec and ADC to Gen Sir J Ross, GCB, cmded Canadian troops; *m* 1897 Frances, dau of Col — Brandling, and *d* 9 Feb 1902

(2) John Blackburn, JP (Ayrshire); *b* 2 Dec 1855; *educ* Trin Coll Cambridge (LLB); barrister Inner Temple; *m* 27 July 1880 Effie Mary Ramsey, only dau of Andrew Blackburn, and *d* 29 March 1930, leaving issue:

1a Robert Duncan; *b* 21 Aug 1881; *m* 14 Jan 1913 Edith Katherine, dau of W D Russell, of Maulside, Ayrshire, and *d* 4 April 1923

(1) Lucy Jane; Extra Lady-in-Waiting to HRH PRINCESS BEATRICE 1909; *m* 1st 9 Nov 1877 Hon Arthur Hay David Fraser (*see* SALTOUN, L) and had issue; *m* 2nd 25 April 1887 Francis John Stuart Hay-Newton, MVO (*see* TWEEDDALE, M), and *d* 10 March 1939

5 Henry Duncan, WS Edinburgh; *b* 30 Sept 1814; *m* 16 June 1846 Anna (*d* 31 Aug 1910), dau of Robert Nasmyth, FRCS Edinburgh, and *d* 22 Oct 1866, leaving, with other issue:

(1) Robert Henry Duncan; *b* 17 Dec 1849; *m* 27 Sept 1877 Mabel Frances (*d* 25 Jan 1930), dau of Robert Balfour Wardlaw-Ramsay of Whitehill and Tillicoultry, and *d* 14 Sept 1904, leaving:

1a Robert Arthur George; *b* 9 Aug 1878; *m* 16 July 1912 Laura Gwendolen (*d* 1962), dau of Arthur William English, of Wisbech, Cambs, and *d* 13 Nov 1939, leaving issue:

1b +Irwine Arthur; *b* 19 Oct 1913; *educ* Fettes; *m* 21 Oct 1939 *Pamela Vera, est dau of Col P R Ayers, MC, of Newton Abbot, Devon, and has:

1c +Peter John Charles [Peter Fergusson Esq, Little Barn, 161 Oatlands Drive, Weybridge, Surrey]; *b* 23 April 1943; *m* 1st 1966 Angela Starr, dau of Capt W H Behenna, of Bitterne, Hants; *m* 2nd 1981 *Anne Marie Ghislaine, yr dau of Maj Tom Brown, OBE, MC, and by his 1st w has:

1d +Sean James; *b* 1973

1d *Fiona Starr; *b* 1978

2c +Christopher Simon Arthur [Christopher Fergusson Esq, 215 London Rd E, Batheaston, Bath, Avon]; *b* 23 Feb 1949; *m* 1970 *Susan Ann, yst dau of A Probert, of Knowle, Bristol, and has issue:

1d *Charlotte; *b* 1972

2d *Harriette; *b* 1974

1c *Valerie Ann; *b* 21 Aug 1941

2c *Sheena; *b* 28 March 1958

2b +Donald Andrew; *b* Aug 1920; *educ* Fettes; *m* 1958 *Patricia Dorothy, dau of D K Orton, of Entebbe, Uganda, and has issue:

1c +Colin Ivan Paul; *b* 1960

2c +Martin Arthur; *b* 1963

1c *Heather Dorothy; *b* 1963

3b +Michael Ramsey [Michael Fergusson Esq, Box 959, Mutare, Zimbabwe]; *b* 17 Aug 1922; *educ* Fettes and Rhodes U Grahamstown S Africa (BA 1948); *m* 12 Aug 1961 *Joanna Rosalind, dau of H Stratton, of Stert, Devizes, Wilts, and has issue:

1c +Richard Anthony; *b* 1963

1c Irene Hilda; *m* Douglas Langhorne, and had issue

(1) Georgina Frederika; *b* 2 Nov 1852; *m* 30 Sept 1879 Charles N Orbell, of Timaru, NZ, and *d* 12 Sept 1933, leaving issue

6 Hew Dalrymple Hamilton, JP Ayrshire; *b* 6 Dec 1817; HEICS; *m* 11 Sept 1838 Louisa (*d* 10 May 1904), dau of Gen C Godby, CB, ADC, and *d* 19 Aug 1911, leaving issue:

(1) James; *b* 18 Sept 1840; Offr 73rd Regt; *m* 9 Nov 1887 Annie Gillespie (*d* 2 May 1912), dau of William Gillespie Mitchel, of Carwood, Lanarks, and *dsp* 19 July 1917

(2) Charles Robert Kenneth; *b* 25 Sept 1842; Offr 79th Highrs; *m* 1st 5 Dec 1872 Eleanora Dalrymple (*d* 19 April 1905), dau of Duncan Davidson of Tulloch by Eleanora, dau of **Sir James Fergusson, 4th Bt** (*see* below); *m* 2nd 6 April 1907 Alice Eliza (*d* 15 June 1946), 2nd dau of Adml Henry Duncan Grant, CB, and *d* 24 Oct 1926, leaving by his 1st w:

1a Muriel Catherine; *m* 6 Feb 1907 her cousin Alan Walter John Fergusson, yst son of **Sir James Fergusson, 6th Bt** (*see* below), and both *dsp* 6 Aug 1909

2a Sybil Henrietta; *m* 1st 6 Dec 1906 Capt Malcolm Cosmo Bonsor (*ka* 1918), est s of Sir Henry Orme Cosmo Bonsor, 1st Bt (*qv*); *m* 2nd 12 May 1920 Mervyn Adrian Touchet Ridley, MC (*d* 21 Dec 1951), and *d* 7 Feb 1966, leaving issue (*see* RIDLEY, V)

7 Robert Dundas Octavius; *b* 23 Sept 1819; *m* 10 Dec 1842 Amelia, dau of Capt George Macdonald, of Morar, and *d* 1882, having had, with other issue:

(1) George Adam Duncan Camperdown; *b* 12 July 1847; *m* 16 Jan 1883 Marianne McDonald (*d* 1914), dau of Henry Paul, of Topsham, Devon, and widow of Alfred Stephens, of Bridport

(2) Robert Dundas Arthur Graham; *b* 13 July 1851; *m* 17 Jan 1877 Mary Rachel Katherine (*d* 19 June 1923), dau of Maj Francis Whitworth Russell (*see* RUSSELL, Bt, of Swallowfield), and *d* 1896, having had, with other issue:

1a Alice Mary Adelaide Gordon; *b* 17 Oct 1877

(1) Henrietta Sarah; *m* 5 Nov 1868 Rev Joseph Richards, MA (*d* 1895), Rector Shelley, and *d* 2 Oct 1926, leaving issue

(2) Julia; *m* 27 June 1876 George James MacDonald (*d* 1890)

(3) Jane Roberta Bruce

(4) Edith Jemima Mary Amelia; *m* 1905 J Myrddin Rees, of Llanelly

8 Frederick William Brown Gustave; *b* 30 March 1826; Maj Ayrshire Militia; *m* 17 Oct 1871 Alice Wilhelmina Mary (*d* 1896), 2nd dau of John Stuart Hay-Newton of Newton (*see* TWEEDDALE, M), and *dsp* 20 July 1903

1 Jane Dalrymple Hamilton; *m* 22 April 1848 Robert Bruce Kennet (*d* 13 Aug 1864), of Clackmannanshire, and had issue (*see* BALFOUR OF BURLEIGH, L)

2 Catherine; *m* 17 Jan 1838 Henry Ritchie, of Busbie, Craigton and Cloncaird (*d* 6 Nov 1843)

3 Eleanora Dalrymple; *m* 1841 Duncan Davidson, of Tulloch, Ross-shire, and *d* 26 Dec 1845, leaving issue (*see* above)

4 Mary Jemima Dundas Adamina; *m* 20 Nov 1845 Andrew Buchanan of Auchentorlie (*d* 1886) and *d* 1902

Sir JAMES's est son,

Sir CHARLES FERGUSSON later DALRYMPLE-FERGUSSON (on inheriting the Newhailes estate 1838 from his aunt Christian Dalrymple), **5th Bt**; *b* 26 Aug 1800; added the Drummellan estate to Kilkerran; *m* 1 June 1829 Helen (*d* 26 June 1869), dau of Rt Hon David Boyle (*see* GLASGOW, E), and *d* 18 March 1849, having had, with other issue:

1 JAMES (Sir), **6th Bt**

2 Sir CHARLES DALRYMPLE, 1st Bt, of Newhailes, so *cr* 1887 (*see* STAIR, E)

3 John Adam; *b* 7 May 1845; Col Rifle Bde; Prof Tactics, Mil Law and Admin RMC Sandhurst, cmded Prov Bn Rifle Bde 1901–02; *m* 13 July 1871 Sarah (*d* 25 May 1936), 2nd dau of Joseph Gilbert, of Pewsey Vale, S Australia, and *d* 5 Dec 1920, having had issue:

(1) Gilbert Charles Dalrymple; *b* 15 Aug 1874; Lt Rifle Bde; *ka* Boer War 11 Dec 1899

(2) William Alexander; *b* 1 April 1877; *d* 8 April 1879

(1) Catherine Helen Dalrymple; *b* 1873; *d* 23 March 1909

(2) Anna Mary; *b* 1875; HM Insp of Schools; *d* unm 29 March 1963

(3) Edith Nora; *b* 1879; *educ* London U (BA 1899); *d* unm 3 May 1968

(4) Jean Dalrymple, LRAM (1904); *b* 1881; *d* unm 30 Dec 1960

(5) Olive; *b* 1884; *d* unm 5 Aug 1973

(6) Margaret Agnes; *b* 1886; *d* unm 6 May 1971

(7) Sarah Faith; *b* 1889; *d* unm 14 April 1982

1 Henrietta Duncan; *m* 5 Dec 1882 Rt Rev George Wyndham Kennion, DD (*d* 19 May 1922), Bp Bath and Wells 1894–1921, and *d* 12 Dec 1937

2 Mary Dalrymple; *m* 28 Dec 1866 Walter Severn (*d* 22 Sept 1904), and *d* 3 Jan 1916, leaving issue

3 Eleanor Charlotte Dalrymple; *m* 31 Aug 1871 Rev David Robertson, MA (*d* 11 April 1916), Rector Hartlebury 1880–1911, yst s of Hon Lord Benholme, and *d* 23 Sept 1929, leaving issue

Sir CHARLES's est son,

Sir James Fergusson, 6th Bt, GCSI, KCMG, CIE, PC, JP, DL Ayrshire; *b* 18 March 1832; Capt Roy Co Archers, served Gren Gds Crimea 1854–55 (wounded, two medals, three clasps); MP Ayrshire 1854–57 and 1859–68 and NE Manchester 1885–1906, Parly U-Sec: India 1866–67, Home Dept 1867–68 and For Affrs 1886–91, PMG 1891–92; Govr and C-in-C: S Australia 1868–73, NZ 1873–75 and Bombay 1880–85; LLD; *m* 1st 9 Aug 1859 Lady Edith Christian Ramsay (*d* 28 Oct 1871), yr dau of 1st Marquess of Dalhousie (*see* DALHOUSIE, E), and had issue:

1 CHARLES (Sir), **7th Bt**

2 James Andrew (Sir), KCB, KCMG; *b* 16 April 1871; Adml, ADC to HM GEORGE V 1916–17, Ld Admlty and Dep-Ch Naval Staff 1919–20, R-Adml cmdg 1st Light Cruiser Sqdn 1920–22, C-in-C N America and W Indies Station 1924–26, Adml 1926 (ret 1928), served Boer War (despatches, promotion, Queen's medal, 4 clasps) and WW I (despatches), Legn Hon, Orders Rising Sun Japan and St Anne of Russia; *m* 6 Nov 1901 Enid Githa (*d* 11 Jan 1964), yst dau of Thomas C Williams, of Wellington, NZ, and *d* 13 April 1942, leaving:

(1) *Margaret Edith [Mrs Ralph Schofield, Flat 8, 52 Onslow Gdns, London SW7]; *b* 5 Jan 1903; *m* 9 Sept 1961 Ralph Beckett Schofield (*d* 1976), of Howden, Yorks

(2) *Augusta Susan [Mrs A Marx, Longwood, Bishops Waltham, Hants]; *b* 22 June 1904; *m* 2 June 1932 Capt George Francis Locke Marx, OBE, RN (*d* 2 Oct 1965), s of Adml John Locke Marx, CB, MVO, DSO, of Andover, Hants, and had issue:

1a *Andrew John Locke; *b* 20 March 1933; Cdr RN; *m* 1963 (*divorce* 1982) Rosemary Evangeline, dau of Christopher William Edward Collins, of Bury St Edmunds, Suffolk, and has:

1b *John William Francis; *b* 1973

1b *Caroline Elizabeth; *b* 3 Sept 1964

2b *Annabelle Mary; *b* 8 Dec 1967

2a *David George Locke; *b* 28 Jan 1936; *educ* Marlborough; md John Rigby and Sons

(3) Jean Anne; *b* 7 Feb 1908; *m* 15 July 1930 Edward Lindsay Orr Ewing, MC (*see* ORR EWING, Bt)

(4) *Anne Mary [Miss Anne Fergusson, 24 Napier Ct, London SW6]; *b* 2 Jan 1919

1 Susan Georgina; *m* 10 Nov 1880 John George Alexander Baird (*d* 6 April 1917), MP Glasgow, and *d* in an accident 13 July 1951, leaving issue

2 Edith; *d* unm 14 April 1900

Sir James *m* 2nd 11 March 1873 Olive Cl (*d* 8 Jan 1882), yst dau of John Henry Richman, of Warnbunga, S Australia, and by her had, with other issue:

3 Alan Walter John; *b* 16 Aug 1878; *m* 6 Feb 1907 Muriel Catherine, est dau of Charles Robert Kenneth Fergusson, 79th Highrs (*see* above), and both *dsp* 6 Aug 1909

Sir James *m* 3rd 5 April 1893 Isabella Elizabeth (*d* 10 Feb 1910), dau of Rev Thomas Twysden, Rector Charlton, Devon (*see* 1970 edn TWYSDEN, Bt), and widow of Charles Hugh Hoare, of Morden, Surrey, and was *k* in an earthquake in Jamaica 14 Jan 1907

His est son,

Sir Charles Fergusson, 7th Bt, GCB (1932, KCB 1915, CB 1911), GCMG (1924, KCMG 1918), DSO (1898), MVO (4th Cl 1906), JP; *b* 7 Jan 1865; *educ* Eton and RMC Sandhurst; joined Gren Gds 1883, attd Egyptian Army 1895–1903, Brevet-Col 1900, cmded 3rd Bn Gren Gds 1904–97, Col 1907, Maj-Gen 1908, Lt-Gen 1914, Gen 1921, Brig-Gen Gen Staff, Irish Cmd 1907–08, Inspr Inf 1909–12, GOC 5th Div Irish Cmd 1913–14, 5th Div BEF 1914, 2nd Army Corps 1915–16, 17th Army Corps 1916–18, Mil Govr Occupied German Territory 1918–19 (ret 1922); Govr-Gen and C-in-C NZ 1924–30, chm W Indies Closer Union Commn 1932–33, Dongola Expdn 1896 (despatches, medal, two clasps), Nile Expdn 1897–99 (wounded, despatches four times, two brevets, six clasps), served WW I (despatches seven times), Grand Offr Legion of Honour, Crown of Belgium, Croix de Guerre France and Belgium, Medijidie 2nd Cl; Ld Lt Ayrshire 1937–50, Pres TAA; *m* 18 July 1901 Lady Alice Mary Boyle (*d* 1 Jan 1958), 2nd dau of 7th Earl of Glasgow (*qv*), and *d* 20 Feb 1951, having had issue:

1 JAMES (Sir), **8th Bt**

2 Simon Charles David (Rev); *b* 5 June 1907; *educ* Eton and RMC Sandhurst; Lt-Col Argyll & Sutherland Highrs WW II; ordained 1957, Minister Barr Ayrshire 1957; *m* 22 Feb 1945 *Auriole Kathleen [Mrs Simon Fergusson, Alton Albany, Barr, Girvan, Ayrshire KA26 9TJ], est dau of Cdr Sir Geoffrey Henry Hughes-Onslow, KBE, DSC, RN (*see* ONSLOW, E), and *d* 1982, having had:

(1) +Alexander Charles Onslow [Alexander Fergusson Esq, Alton Albany, Barr, Girvan, Ayrshire KA26 9TJ]; *b* 8 April 1949; *educ* Eton; *m* 1974 *Jane Merryn, est dau of G/Capt Bertram Barthold, of Langarth, St Merryn, N Cornwall, and has issue:

1a +Iain Alexander Onslow; *b* 1975

2a +Dougal George Onslow; *b* 1977

3a +Christopher David Onslow; *b* 1986

(2) +John Geoffrey Onslow [John Fergusson Esq, Old Nisthouse, Harray, Orkney Isles KW17 2LQ]; *b* 7 Sept 1954; *educ* Trin Coll Glenalmond; *m* 1979 *Ann Caroline, yst dau of G/Capt Bertram Barthold, OBE, RAF, and has:

1a *Catherine Alice; *b* 1982

2a *Joannah Ruth; *b* 1989

(1) Charity Alice Onslow; *b* 24 Nov 1945; *d* 5 Aug 1950

(2) *Henrietta Charity Onslow; *b* 8 Jan 1952

3 BERNARD EDWARD FERGUSSON, BARON BALLANTRAE, of Auchaime, Co Ayr, and Bay of Islands, NZ (LP, UK), so *cr* July 1972, KT (1974), GCMG (1962), GCVO (1963), DSO (1943), OBE (1950); *b* 6 May 1911; *educ* Eton and RMC Sandhurst; Brig Black Watch (ret 1958, Col 1969, served WW II); Govr-Gen and C-in-C NZ 1962–67, KStJ; Hon DCL Canterbury U NZ 1966, Hon DU U of Waikato NZ 1957, FRGS, FRSL, author; *m* 22 Nov 1950 Laura Margaret (*d* 1979), dau of Lt-Col Arthur Morton Grenfell, DSO, TD (*see* GRENFELL, B), and *d* 1980, leaving:

(1) +George Duncan [George Fergusson Esq, Ladyburn Lodge, Kilkerran, Maybole, Ayrshire; 32 Wilkinson St, London SW8] (does not use courtesy title); *b* 30 Sept 1955; *educ* Eton and Magdalen Coll Oxford; *m* 1981 *Margaret Sheila, er dau of Michael John Wookey, of Camberley, Surrey, and has:

1a +Alexander Bernard Raukawa; *b* 1984

1a *Laura Margaret Huia; *b* 15 Nov 1982

2a *Alice Mary Marama; *b* 1986

3a *Elizabeth; *b* 1991

4 Charles; *b* 16 Jan, *d* 22 Jan 1917

1 Helen Dorothea; *b* 15 Oct 1902; *m* 20 Oct 1925 Maj Leonard Proby Haviland, 6th Lancers, IA, of Godalming, Surrey, yst s of Rev Arthur Coles Haviland, and had issue:

(1) *Julian Arthur Charles; *b* 8 June 1930; *educ* Eton and Magdalene Coll Cambridge; political corresp ITN; *m* Sept 1959 *Caroline Victoria, yst dau of George Freeland Barbour (*see* POLWARTH, L), and has issue:

1a *Peter Leonard; *b* 31 Dec 1961

2a *Charles Freeland; *b* 28 Jan 1964

3a *Richard Francis; *b* 5 Oct 1967

(2) *Simon Knyvett; *b* 29 March 1935; *educ* Eton and Magdalene Coll Cambridge

(1) *Dorothea Margaret; *b* 4 Aug 1926; *m* 1 May 1948 *Edgar David Stogdon, of Welwyn, Herts, only s of Rev Edgar Stogdon, and has issue

Sir CHARLES'S est son,

Sir James Fergusson, 8th Bt, JP; *b* 18 Sept 1904; *educ* Eton and Balliol Coll Oxford, LLD Glasgow, FRSE; Ld Lt Ayrshire 1969–73, memb Roy Co Archers; bookseller and publisher, memb Roy Commn Historical MSS., Tstee Nat Library Scotland, talks producer BBC Edinburgh 1934–40, BBC Overseas Serv 1940–44, jnlst *Glasgow Herald*, Keeper Records Scotland 1949–69, Tstee Nat Galleries Scotland, author: *The Curragh Incident* (1969), *The Man Behind Macbeth* (1969), *The Declaration of Arbroath* (1970); *m* 17 July 1930 Louise Frances Balfour Stratford (*d* 1988), only dau of Edgar Trevelyan Stratford Dugdale (*see* DUGDALE, Bt), and *d* 25 Oct 1973, having had issue:

1 Sir CHARLES FERGUSSON, **9th and present Bt**

2 +Adam Dugdale [Adam Fergusson Esq, 15 Warwick Gdns, London W14 8PH]; *b* 10 July 1932; *educ* Eton and Trin Coll Cambridge; politician, jnlst and author; MEP W Strathclyde 1979–84; Special Advsr FCO 1985–89; *m* 11 Dec 1965 *(Elizabeth Catherine) Penelope, est dau of (Thomas) Peter Hughes, of Furneaux Pelham Hall, Herts, and has issue:

(1) +James; *b* 2 Nov 1966; *educ* Eton and BNC Oxford

(2) +Marcus Francis; *b* 6 Jan 1972; *educ* Eton and Worcester Coll Oxford

(1) *Petra Christian; *b* 6 March 1968; *educ* Wycombe Abbey, Bristol U and London U; *m* 17 Oct 1997 *Patrick Randal Gordon Cramsie, yr s of James Arthur Cramsie, of Lambourn, Berks

(2) *Lucy Josephine; *b* 14 Jan 1970; *educ* Wycombe Abbey and St Peter's Coll Oxford

1 *Alice Blanche Helen [The Rt Hon The Lady Renton of Mount Harry, Mount Harry House, Offham, Lewes, Sussex]; *b* 15 Sept 1934; *m* 2 April 1960 *Baron Renton of Mount Harry (*qv*) and has issue

2 Christian Frances; *b* 6 March 1940; *d* in a car crash 3 April 1954

FERMOY

Arms: Gu. three roaches naiant in pale arg., a canton of the last. **Crest:** Standing on a rock ppr. an osprey, or sea-eagle, with wings displayed arg., collared gemelle az., membererd or, holding a roach in its claw. **Supporters:** Dexter, a lion erm., gorged with a collar sa., therefrom pendant an escutcheon gu., charged with three roaches naiant in pale arg.; sinister, a greyhound pean, gorged with a collar or, therefrom pendant an escutcheon per pale of the second and gu., charged with three lions passant guardant in pale counter-charged. **Motto:** *Mon Dieu est ma roche* ('My God is my rock'). **Creation:** B. (UK) 10 Sept 1856.

THE 6TH BARON FERMOY, of Co Cork ((Patrick) Maurice Burke Roche) [The Rt Hon The Lord Fermoy, Nethercote House, Nethercote, Warwicks CV23 8AS; 21 Paultons Ho, Paultons Sq, London SW3 5DV]; *b* 11 Oct 1967; *s* f 1984; *educ* Eton; Page of Honour to HM QUEEN ELIZABETH THE QUEEN MOTHER 1982–84, served Blues and Royals 1987–95, assist manager *The Windsor Castle* pub Campden Hill, London W8; *m* 26 March 1998 *Mrs Tessa Ledger

Barony of Fermoy: In 1489 HENRY VII recognised various Irish peerages as already existing although there was no real indication of just when they had been created. Such peerages are accordingly called creations by prescription. One of them was a Barony of Roche of Fermoy, which is first known of around 1461, during EDWARD IV's first reign. But from its position in the roll of Irish peers it may have been much older. It was also occasionally ranked among the viscountcies, despite there being no evidence for its creation as a viscountcy. Accordingly its high position in the relative table of precedence is no very conclusive argument as to how old it was. The family who held the barony as Lords Roche of Fermoy were called Roche also, though allied with the MacCARTY MOOREs, the FitzGerald Earls of Desmond and the BUTLERs of Dunboyne among other representatives of the 'native' Irish and 'Old English' Irish. The title is thought to have become extinct or dormant in 1733. No known connection exists between the Roches who held it and those who became Lords Fermoy in the mid-19th century.

Lineage: EDWARD ROCHE FitzMAURICE FitzEDMUND; *d* 1626, leaving, with two yr sons (Edward; Maurice):

FRANCIS ROCHE; High Sheriff Co Cork 1641, entertained Sir Warham St Leger, Pres Munster, at his seat Trabolgan (rebuilt in the 18th century to take advantage of the site overlooking the sea; sold 1880); *m* Jane Coppinger and *d* 1669, leaving, with a yr s (Edmond):

EDWARD ROCHE, of Trabolgan; *m* 1672 Catherine, dau of James Lavallin, of Walterstown, Co Cork, and *d* 1696, leaving issue, with an er s:

EDMUND ROCHE; *m* 1739 Barbara, dau of James Hennessy (*see* WINDLESHAM, B), and *d* 1750, leaving, with another s:

1 EDMUND

2 Francis, of Rochemount, Co Cork; *m* 1796 Esther, only dau of John Webb, and *d* 1826, leaving issue

3 Edward, of Trabolgan; Col Imokilly Horse; *m* 1781 Susanna, dau of Sir George Wombwell, 1st Bt (*qv*), and *dsps* 1828

The est son,

EDMUND ROCHE, of Kildinan; *m* 1768 Frances, only dau and heir of George Coghlan, of Ardoe, Co Waterford, and *d* 1823, leaving, with two daus (Frances, *m* Richard Power; Georgina, *d* unm 1813):

EDWARD ROCHE, of Trabolgan and Kildinan; *b* 13 July 1771; *m* 1805 Margaret Honoria, only child and heir of William Curtain and a near relation of the statesman and political philosopher Edmund Burke, and *d* March 1855, leaving issue:

1 EDMUND BURKE, **1st Baron**

1 Frances Maria; *m* 6 May 1834 James Michael Kelly, of Cahircon, Co Clare, and Ballybricken Castle, Co Limerick, MP Limerick, and had issue. He *d* 18 May 1875

His only son,

EDMUND BURKE ROCHE, **1st Baron Fermoy**, of Co Cork (I), *cr* 10 Sept 1856; *b* Aug 1815; Ld Lt and Custos Rotulorum Co Cork 1856–74, MP (Lib) Co Cork

1837–55 and Marylebone 1855–69; *m* 22 Aug 1848 Eliza Caroline (*d* 26 April 1897), est dau of James Brownell Boothby, of Twyford Abbey, Middx (*see* 1970 edn BOOTHBY, B), and *d* 17 Sept 1874, leaving issue:

1 EDMUND FitzEDMUND BURKE ROCHE, **2nd Baron Fermoy**, JP, DL Co Cork, (High Sheriff 1873), JP Co Limerick; *b* 23 May 1850; *m* 28 May 1877 Hon Cecilia O'Grady (*d* 17 Sept 1919), only surv child of 3rd Viscount Guillamore (*see* 1956 edn), and had issue:

(1) Ada Sybil; *b* 29 June 1879; *m* 14 Oct 1908 Godfrey Nigel Everard Baring and *d* 15 May 1944, leaving issue (*see* NORTHBROOK, B)

2 JAMES BOOTHBY BURKE, **3rd Baron**

3 Alexis Charles Burke; Gentleman-in-Waiting to Ld Lt Ireland; *b* 30 June 1853; *m* 24 April 1889 Hon Lucy Maude Goschen (*d* 16 March 1909), est dau of 1st Viscount Goschen (*qv*), and *d* 17 Dec 1914, leaving issue:

(1) George Denis Burke, MC (1919); UK V-Consul Comodoro Rivadavia, Argentina, 1925–27, Capt Army WW I 1917–19 (despatches); *b* 24 April 1893; *m* 7 July 1921 Aletta S (*d* 1982), dau of M M Venter, of Comodoro Rivadavia and Cape Province, and *d* Nov 1954, having had issue:

1a +Alexis Martinus Burke [Alexis Roche Esq, Rosales 2571, Olivos, Buenos Aires, Argentina]; *b* 25 March 1922; Capt RE; *m* 1st 1945 (*divorce* 1974) Leonora Alice Hudson (*d* 1985) and has issue:

1b *Rosalie Anne Burke; *b* 1945

2b *Caroline Jean Burke; *b* 1950

3b *Christine Lorna Burke; *b* 1956

1a (cont.) Alexis Burke Roche *m* 2nd 1974 *Vera Haydee, dau of Luis Uffenheimer, and has issue:

1b *Peter Martin Burke; *b* 1974

4b *Vanessa Caroline Burke; *b* 1976

2a Reginald Rupert Burke; 2nd Lt RUR, attd Roy Inniskilling Fus, WW II; *b* 8 June 1923; *ka* Italy June 1944

(2) Edmund Burke; *b* 23 Dec 1897; *m* 8 Feb 1944 *Vivien Eustace, er dau of Lt-Col William Kenneth Eustace Jameson, DSO, DL, RHA, of Heritage House, Warley, Essex, and *dsp* 30 April 1962

(1) Moira Burke; *b* 24 Oct 1891; *m* 6 March 1918 Brig Desmond Henry Sykes Somerville, CBE, MC, S Wales Borderers, est s of Aylmer Coghill Somerville, and *d* 21 Aug 1976, leaving issue. He *d* 18 March 1976

1a *Christopher; Capt RA WW II; *b* 11 July 1921; *educ* Winchester and New Coll Oxford; *m* 6 Aug 1949 *Celia Penelope, er dau of Maj Leonard Maurice Edward Dent, DSO, of Hillfields, Burghfield Common, nr Reading, Berks, and has issue:

1b *Thomas Clinton; *b* 22 Dec 1952

2b *John Henry; *b* 22 March 1956

1b *Harriet Elizabeth; *b* 28 Oct 1950

2a *John Nicholas; Lt-Col S Wales Borderers WW II 1942–45; *b* 16 Jan 1924; *educ* Winchester; *m* 6 Aug 1951 *Jennifer Dorothea, dau of Capt Walter Macdonald Nash, RN, and has issue:

1b *Robin Nicholas; *b* 8 Aug 1959

1b *Philippa Wren; *b* 15 Oct 1953

2b *Penelope; *b* 10 Nov 1954

(2) Sheila Margaret Burke; *b* 6 Aug 1894; *m* 28 Jan 1922 Maj Alfred Geoffrey Horace Mayhew, MC, RE, s of William French Mayhew, of London, and *d* 12 March 1959, having had, with another s or other sons who *d* relatively young:

1a *PATRICK BARNABAS BURKE MAYHEW, *cr* BARON MAYHEW OF TWYSDEN (LP) 1997 (*qv*)

4 Ulick de Rupe Burke, CB (1900); Lt-Col cmdg 11th Bn Roy Welsh Fus, S Wales Borderers, served Burma and S Africa; *b* 16 Jan 1856; *m* 1st 23 Sept 1882 Agnes Blair (*dsp* 25 Jan 1905), est dau of Gen Jasper Otway Mayne, RE; *m* 2nd 15 Feb 1906 Dorothea Blanche (*d* 7 April 1963, having *m* 2nd 5 Dec 1931 Percy William Allday, of Coniston, Solihull, Warwicks, who *d* 7 April 1937), 5th dau of John Jones, DL, of Ynysfor, Merioneths, and *d* 23 April 1919, leaving issue:

(1) Ulick Edmund Burke; Maj S Wales Borderers WW II, ret 1947; *b* 26 Sept 1906; *educ* Repton and RMC Sandhurst; *m* 27 Oct 1949 *Primrose Eda [Mrs Ulick Burke Roche, Ynysfor, Penrhyndeudraeth, Gwynedd], only dau of Sir John Karslake Thomas Buchan-Hepburn, 5th Bt (*qv*), and *d* 1990, leaving:

1a *Rosemary Evelyn Sybil Burke; *b* 2 Oct 1951; *m* 1982 (*divorce* 1989) Michael Menelaou and has issue:

1b *Alexander Demitri Burke; *b* 1983

2b *Nicholas Edmund Burke; *b* 1986

5 Edmund Burke; *b* 29 Sept 1859; *m* 1912 Elizabeth Blanche, dau of John Greaves Clapham, of Quebec, and *dsp* 21 June 1948

1 Eleanor Charlotte Burke; *m* 21 June 1881 William Nicholas Leader, of Dromagh Castle, Co Cork, and *d* 16 April 1938

2 Eliza Caroline Burke; *m* 24 Jan 1905 Friedrich Maximilian, Count Hochberg, s of HSH THE PRINCE OF PLESS, re-admitted to Br nationality 28 Sept 1925 and *d* 8 Nov 1940. He *d* 16 Sept 1921

3 Ethel Kathleen Burke; *m* 20 Aug 1891 Norman McLean, s of Hon J D McLean, MLA, of Westbrook, Darling Downs, Queensland, and Guirding, Sydney, NSW, and *d* 10 Dec 1935. He *d* 15 Nov 1928

The 2nd BARON *d* 1 Sept 1920; his brother,

JAMES BOOTHBY BURKE ROCHE, **3rd Baron Fermoy**; *b* 28 July 1851; *educ* Trin Coll Cambridge (MA); MP E Kerry 1896–1900; *m* 22 Sept 1880 (*divorce* 1891) Frances (*d* Jan 1947), est dau of F Work, of New York, and had issue:

1 EDMUND MAURICE, **4th Baron**

2 Francis George; *b* 15 May 1885; *d* unm Oct 1958

1 Eileen Burke; *b* and *d* 1882

2 Cynthia Burke; *b* 10 April 1884; *m* 1st 10 June 1906 Arthur Scot Burden (*d* June 1921); *m* 2nd Aug 1922 Guy Fairfax Cary, s of Clarence Cary, and *d* 8 Dec 1966, leaving issue. He *d* 1950

The 3rd BARON *d* 30 Oct 1920; his er son,

EDMUND MAURICE BURKE ROCHE, **4th Baron Fermoy**; *b* 15 May 1885; BA Harvard; F/Lt RAF, MP King's Lynn 1924–35 and 1943–45, Mayor King's Lynn 1931; *m* 17 Sept 1931 Ruth Sylvia, DCVO (1966), OBE (1952), JP (Norfolk 1944), Hon Freeman King's Lynn 1962, Woman Bedchamber to HM QUEEN ELIZABETH THE QUEEN MOTHER March 1960, Extra Woman of the Bedchamber June 1956–March 1960, musician, Hon RAM 1968, Hon MusD UEA 1975 (*d* 1993), yst dau of Col William Smith Gill, CB, VD, of Dalhebiy, Bildside, Aberdeenshire, and had issue:

1 EDMUND JAMES BURKE, **5th Baron**

1 *Mary Cynthia Burke [The Hon Mrs Mary Burke Roche, 12M Warwick Square, London SW1V 2AA]; *b* 19 Aug 1934; *m* 1st 25 Nov 1954 (*divorce* 1966) Hon Sir Anthony George Berry (assassinated Brighton bombing 1984), yst s of 1st Viscount Kemsley (*qv*), and has issue; *m* 2nd July 1973 (*divorce* 1980) Denis Roche Geoghegan; *m* 3rd 1981 (*divorce* 1989) Michael Robert Fearon Gunningham and resumed maiden name 1987

2 *Frances Ruth Burke [The Hon Mrs Frances Shand Kydd, Callanish, Isle of Seil, Oban, Argyll PA134 4TN]; *b* 20 Jan 1936; tstee Colmcille Tst, counsellor with CRUSE 1996–, patron Highland and Islands Music and Dance Festival, Oban, 1985–; *m* 1st 1 June 1954 (*divorce* 1969) 8th Earl Spencer (*qv*) and has issue; *m* 2nd 2 May 1969 (*divorce* 1990) Peter Shand Kydd

The 4th BARON *d* 8 July 1955; his only son,

EDMUND JAMES BURKE ROCHE, **5th Baron Fermoy**; *b* 20 March 1939; *educ* Eton, RMA Sandhurst and RAC Cirencester; Capt RHG, memb Newbury DC 1976–79, chm Eddington Bindery Ltd, dir Kennet Estates, memb Pheasant Tst; *m* 22 June 1964 *Lavinia Frances Elizabeth (*m* 2nd Sept 1995 Nigel Corbally Stourton (*see* MOWBRAY, SEGRAVE and STOURTON, B)), only dau of Capt John Pitman, 3rd Hus, of Foxley House, Malmesbury, Wilts, and *d* by his own hand 19 Aug 1984, leaving issue:

1 PATRICK MAURICE BURKE ROCHE, **6th and present Baron Fermoy**

2 +EDMUND HUGH BURKE; *b* 5 Feb 1972; heir presumptive

1 *Frances Caroline Burke [The Hon Mrs Stanley, New England Stud, Newmarket, Suffolk]; *b* 31 March 1965; *m* 1990 *Peter Hugh Charles Stanley (*see* DERBY, E)

2 Elizabeth; *b* 27 March, *d* 2 April 1966

FERRERS

Arms: Paly of six or and az. a quarter ermine. **Crest:** A Saracen's head in profile, couped ppr., wreathed about the temples or and az. **Supporters:** Dexter, a talbot erm., eared gu. and ducally gorged or; sinister, a reindeer gu., billettée and charged on the shoulder with a horse-shoe arg., attired and ducally gorged or. **Motto:** *Honor virtutis premium* ('Honour is the reward of virtue'). **Creation:** Bt. (E) 22 May 1611; V. and E. (GB) 3 Sept 1711.

THE 13TH EARL FERRERS, Viscount Tamworth, of Co Stafford, and a **Baronet** (Sir Robert Washington Shirley Bt, PC (1982), DL (Norfolk 1983)) [The Rt Hon The Earl Ferrers PC DL, Ditchingham Hall, Bungay, Suffolk NR35 2LE]; *b* 8 June 1929; *s* f 1954; *educ* Winchester (Fell 1988) and Magdalene Coll Cambridge (MA 1953); Lt Coldstream Gds Malaya 1949, Ld-in-Waiting (Govt Whip) Ho Lds 1962–64 and 1971–74, Parly Sec MAFF Jan–March 1974, Jt Dep Ldr Oppn Ho Lds 1976–79, Min State MAFF 1979–83, Dep Ldr Ho Lds 1979–83 and 1988–97, Min State: Home Office 1988–94, DTI 1994–95, Environment 1995–97, High Steward Norwich Cathedral 1979–, chm Roy Comm Historical Monuments 1984–88, tstee Savings Bank of E England 1975–79, dir: Norwich Union Insur Gp 1975–79, TSB Trustcard Ltd 1978–79, Central Tstee Savings Bank Ltd 1978–79, Chatham Historic Dockyard Tst 1984–88 and Economic Forestry Group PLC 1985–88; *m* 21 July 1951 *Annabel Mary, only dau of Brig-William Greenwood Carr, CVO, DSO, of Ditchingham Hall, and has:

1 +ROBERT WILLIAM SASWALO, *Viscount Tamworth* [Viscount Tamworth, The Old Vicarage, Shirley, Derbys DE6 3AZ]; *b* 29 Dec 1952; *educ* Ampleforth; FCA, chartered accountant, gp auditor and sr treasury analyst BICC plc 1986–88, fin controller Viking Property Gp 1987–92 (dir 1987), dir: Norseman Hldgs 1987–92, Ruffer Investment Management 1994–; *m* 21 June 1980 *Susannah Mary, yst dau of Charles Edward William Sheepshanks, of Arthington Hall, Otley, W Yorks, and has issue:

(1) +William Robert Charles; *b* 10 Dec 1984

(2) +Frederick James Walter; *b* 1990

(1) *Hermione Mary Annabel; *b* 11 Dec 1982

2 +Andrew John Carr Sewallis [The Hon Andrew Shirley, Collycroft House, Clifton, Derbys DE6 2GN]; *b* 24 June 1965; *educ* Ampleforth; ARICS, Regional Land Agent CLA 1996–; *m* 3 Oct 1992 *Tamara, dau of Donald Halfpenny, of Sutton in Ashfield, Notts, and has:

(1) +Henry Benedict John; *b* 6 April 1997

1 *Angela Mary [The Lady Angela Ellis, The Old Rectory, Thurning, Norfolk NR20 5QX]; *b* 16 June 1954; *m* 19 July 1975 *Jonathan Felix Hugh Ellis, ACA, s of Maj Timothy Basil Ellis, of Mendham Mill, Harleston, Norfolk, and ggs of 1st and last Baron Hirst (*see* 1940 edn), and has issue:

(1) *Charles William Donald *b* 29 April 1979

(1) *Louise Mary; *b* 18 Oct 1977

(2) *Georgina Hermione; *b* 1981

2 *Sallyanne Margaret; *b* 22 March 1957

3 *Selina Clare; *b* 1 July 1958; *m* 1989 *Antoine Bertrand Robert Chenevière, yr s of Bertrand Chenevière, of Geneva, and has issue:

(1) *Alexandre Bertrand; *b* 24 Aug 1995

(1) *Francesca Mary; *b* 1990

(2) *Tatiana Annabel Haritina; *b* 1992

Title of Ferrers: A Sir John Ferrers, of Chartley (whence his subsequent Barony of Ferrers sometimes being referred to, mistakenly, as 'of Chartley' in full rather than in parenthesis), in Staffordshire, and manors in Huntingdonshire and Northamptonshire, was son and heir of the last Ferrers Earl of Derby of the 1138 creation (*see* DERBY, E, preliminary remarks), who had lost or been deprived of his lands and without them was deemed by contemporary doctrine incapable of sustaining an earl's position, so that his title ceased probably before his death in 1279 and certainly with it.

Sir John tried unsuccessfully to recover his father's lands, for which he incurred EDWARD I's displeasure. Nevertheless he was called to Parliament by writ of summons in 1299 and according to later doctrine thereby became 1st Lord Ferrers. The Barony thus created passed down through his descendants till the 7th Lord (Baron) died without male issue in 1450. The latter's daughter married Sir Walter Devereux, who was made Lord Ferrers in February 1461/2 (*see* below, also HEREFORD, V).

Whether this should be seen as a fresh creation or a recognition of a right to the old Barony through his wife is a moot point. The view of baronies was changing at the time and the era was one of confusion where peerage creations were concerned. (When the abeyance of this Barony was terminated in 1677 it was assigned a precedence of 1299, which certainly suggests that the latter view prevailed by then.)

The Devereuxes were promoted to the Viscountcy of Hereford in the mid-16th century, a title which has survived, and to the Earldom of Essex (*see* below) in 1572, a title which has not (at any rate as held by them). With the evolving doctrine in the 17th century of the heritability through the female line of baronies in the English peerage created by writ of summons, that of Ferrers survived the death of the 3rd and last Earl of Essex of the 1572 creation and passed to the **1st Earl Ferrers** (*see* below for kinship with the Earls of Essex).

After the **1st Earl Ferrers**'s death the Barony accordingly passed not to his male heir but to his heir general, a granddaughter, thence to her surviving daughter, and thence to the surviving daughter's son, the 3rd Marquess Townshend (*qv*). When Lord Townshend's son the 4th Marquess died childless in 1855 the Ferrers Barony fell again into abeyance between his two sisters or their issue.

A younger brother of the Robert Ferrers created 1st Lord (Baron) Ferrers in 1299, one Sir William, held among other manors that of Groby, in Leicestershire. His son, another Sir William, was called to Parliament by writ of summons in 1299, thereby becoming Lord Ferrers also. As has been remarked elsewhere in this work, the absurdity of two peers of Parliament with the same title sitting at the same time is a strong argument for doubting that these early writs of summons were intended to create hereditary titles of honour. Nevertheless this other notional Barony of Ferrers (of Groby) was deemed by later doctrine to have been created in 1299 and descended to the 6th Lord (Baron), who died in 1455. The latter's granddaughter married Sir Edward Grey, who received writs addressed to Lord Ferrers of Groby in the 1440s and 1450s. Their grandson in the male line was recognised as Lord Ferrers of Groby before being promoted Earl of Huntingdon (*qv*; preliminary remarks) and Marquess of Dorset. His grandson was in turn promoted Duke of Suffolk but was attainted in February 1553/4 (after his attempt to put his daughter Lady Jane Grey on the throne), when all his titles were forfeited.

Lineage: SEWALLIS; held lands at Etendon (Ettington), Warwicks; Ticemerse (Tichmarsh), Northants; Witence, Lincs; and Hoga (Hoon), Hatun (Hatton) and Etewelle (Etwall), Derbys, 1086; *d c* 1086, leaving:

1 Henry; monk; *d* after 1148

2 FULCHER

3 Hugh; *d* in or after 1138, leaving:

(1) William de Etwall, of Etwall; *dsp* after 1186

(1) Emma; *m* Thomas de Cuckney

4 Sewallis; living 1125

5 Ralph, of Chippenham; living 1141; had:

(1) Hugh de Monjoye, of Yeldersley; living 1162; had:

1a William de Monjoye; held Winster under Robert fitz Col; *dsp*

(2) Ralph de Monjoye, of Yeldersley; living 1190; had:

1a Serlo de Monjoyed, of Yeldersley; *m* Avice, dau of Henry de Shirley (*see* below), and had:

1b Serlo de Monjoyed; *dsp* & *vp*

2b Sewallis de Monjoye, of Yeldersley; *m* Joan (*m* 2nd Philip de Ulecotes, 3rd Oliver de Albini, 4th Walter de Godarvill and *d* 1226), dau of Robert de Meynell, and *dsp* 1200

3b Ralph de Monjoye, of Yeldersley and Winster; had:

1c Serlo de Monjoye, of Yeldersley; *m* Illaria — and *d* 1254, leaving:

1d Ralph de Monjoye (Sir), of Yeldersley; High Sheriff Lancs; in 1302 held half a fee in Yeldersley and half one in Locke; *m* 1st Elizabeth — and had:

1e Serlo de Monjoye, of Yeldersley; *m* Margaret — and *dsp* by 1317

1d (cont.) Sir Ralph *m* 2nd Isolda — and had:

1e Isolda; *m* Robert de Ireland, of Yeldersley

2d Robert de Monjoye, of Winster; living 1302; had:

1e Thomas de Monjoye, of Winster; living 1331; had:

1f Roger de Monjoye, of Winster; living 1352

2e Robert de Monjoye, of Twyford

4b William de Monjoye, of Shelston and Cubley; living 1190; had:

1c William de Monjoye, of Shelston and Cubley; living 1272

2c Hugh de Monjoye

(3) William de Monjoye, of Yeldersley; held one third of a lead mine from William de Ferrers by 1191

The 2nd s,

FULCHER fitz SEWALLIS, of Ettington, Shirley etc; living 1141; had:

1 Jordan de Ible, of Ible; living 1139; *dspl*, leaving illegitimately:

(1) Simon de Ible; living 1166; had:

1a Jordan de Snitterton, of Snitterton; *d* 1248, leaving three daus (Sarah, *m* 1240 Robert de Markham, of Markham, Notts (*d* 1289), and had issue; Adelicia, *m* Sir Gerard de Sutton, of Sutton-in-Ashfield, Notts, and had issue; Agnes, *m* 1st Robert fitz Harvey and 2nd her cousin William fitz Ranulph de Ible, of Aldwark (*see* below))

(2) Ranulph de Ible; living 1190; had, with an er s (Ranulph de Ible, *dsp* 1230):

1a John de Ible, of Aldwark; living 1210; had:

1b Ranulph de Ible, of Snitterton; living 1304; had:

1c Ranulph de Snitterton, of Snitterton; living 1317; had, with two yr sons (Thomas, living 1304; John, living 1357):

1d Ranulph de Snitterton, of Snitterton; living 1327; *m* Cecilia (*m* 2nd Thomas de Ferrers, of Tamworth, Staffs) — and had:

1e Ranulph de Snitterton, of Snitterton; living 1345

2b William; *m* his cousin Agnes (*see* above) and had:

1c Nicholas, of Aldwark; had:

1d Robert fitz Nicholas de Ible, of Aldwark; living 1304

2 Henry de Ireton, of Ireton Parva, parish of Kedleston; living 1176; had:

(1) Fulcher de Ireton, of Ireton; living 1210; *m* Matilda, dau of Sampson de Dune, of Breadstall, and had, with an est s (John, *dsp*) and a yst s (Henry), a second s:

1a Fulcher (Sir); ktd by 1236; contested advowson of Edensor with Richard de Edensor 1225; *m* Geva — and *d c* 1257, leaving, with three yr sons (William, of Derby; *m* Philippa, dau of Sir Henry Chandos, of Radburne, and had a s, Fulcher of Weston Underwood, living 1300, who had a s William, of Weston Underwood, living 1326; Richard, of Weston Underwood, living 1326; Fulcher):

1b Henry (Sir); *m* Clementia — and was *ka* Battle of Chesterfield 1264 in the Barons' War between HENRY III and his opponents among the nobility (*see* LEICESTER, E, preliminary remarks), leaving, with an er s (Flucher, *dsp* & *vp*):

1c Henry, of Ireton Parva; living 1313; ancestor of the Cromwellian General Henry Ireton, whose male line died out 1724

(2) Nicholas; had:

1a John de Weston; living 1261/2; probably identical with the John de Ireton who was Coroner of Whitby and *d* 1265

(3) Robert; had:

1a Stephen, of Hatton; living 1262; had a dau (Joanna)

3 Sewallis de Shirley, of Shirley, Derbys; *m* 1st Alice — (*dsp*); *m* 2nd Matilda Ridel and by her had, with four other sons (*dsp*):

(1) HENRY

(2) Hugh; Chaplain at Longford *c* 1200

4 Fulcher de Edensor, of Edensor; living 1155; *m* 1st Margaret, dau of Thomas de Boylestone, and had two daus; *m* 2nd Agnes — and *d c* 190, leaving by her:

(1) Adam, of Edensor; *m* Sarra [*sic*], sis of Hugh fitz Ralph, and *d* by 1205, leaving, with a yr s (William, of Yoxall, Staffs):

1a Richard, of Edensor; *m* Isolda de Grendon and *d* 1230, leaving:

1b Adam (Sir), of Edensor; living 1242; had a dau (Philippa, living 1281, *m* Robert de Bozon or de Edensor, which he held in right of his w to the extent of one (kt's?) fee, and had issue)

2b Thomas (Sir); *m* Lucia, dau and coheir of Geoffrey le Savage, who held half Tissington, and *d* 1245, leaving a s (Thomas, of Tissington, Stangrave (Hartington), King's Weston, Paveley, Baginton and Baddesley, Warwicks, *dsp* 1285) and three daus (Amicia, *m* 1st Andrew de Darley, of Darley (Dale), and 2nd Walter de Meriden, of Meriden, Warwicks; Philippa, *d* unm; Joan, *m* Sir Richard de Harthill, of Harthill)

3b Richard (Sir), of Longstone, Brushfield and Pilsley; living 1240; *m* Avice, sis and heiress of Richard de Sandiacre, and had, with a yr s (William, clerk (*i.e.* in holy orders)) and a dau (Loscia, *m* Ralph fitz Waltheof and had issue)

(2) Thomas; *m* 1st Lucy —; *m* 2nd Margaret —; *m* 3rd Mabel de Curzon and by her had three sons (Robert, of Yoxall; Thomas; Adam)

(3) Ralph; living 1200; had, with two er sons (Robert, *dsp*; Thomas):

1a Michael, of Holywell, Chesterfield; living 1190; *m* Lenca — and had two sons (Robert; Thomas, f of Peter de Dronfield)

1 Emma; *m* Roger de Grendon

2 A dau

SEWALLIS de SHIRLEY's 2nd s,

HENRY de SHIRLEY, of Shirley; living (of age by ?) 1195; *m* 1205 Joanna, dau of John de Clinton, of Essex, and had, with a yr s (Ralph) and a dau (Avice, *m* her cousin Serlo de Monjoye (*see* above) and had issue:

SEWALLIS de SHIRLEY, of Shirley; living 1167; *m* Isabel (*m* 2nd Joscelin de Nevill and 3rd Ralph Musard, of Staveley), dau of Robert de Meynell, of Meynell Langley, and d in or after 1228, leaving, with a dau (Elizabeth):

HENRY de SHIRLEY, of Shirley; had:

SEWALLIS de SHIRLEY; Coroner Derby 1242, as which is recorded as being *insufficiens* (*i.e.* Not up to the job (?) or perhaps overworked with too many cases); had:

Sir JAMES de SHIRLEY; *m* 1st well before 1280 Agnes — and had a dau (Isabella, *m c* 1296 William de Yeaveley); *m* 2nd by 1280 Isabella, widow of John de Brunston, and *d* in or after 1296, leaving by her:

Sir RALPH de SHIRLEY, JP 1298 [this seems too early; other sources refer to him as JP Warwicks *c* 1310]; Constable Shrewsbury Castle *c* 1300; *m* Margaret, dau of Walter de Waldeshef [*sic*], of Fairfield, Oxon, and *d* 1327, leaving:

Sir THOMAS SHIRLEY; MP Warwicks *c* 1321; fought Hundred Years War; *m* Isabel, (illegitimate?, half?-)sis and eventual heir of Ralph Basset, 3rd Lord (Baron) Basset of Drayton (*dsp* 10 May 1390, since when that Barony has been abeyant or dormant), and *d* 1362, leaving:

Sir HUGH SHIRLEY; inherited Basset estates; Grand Falconer to HENRY IV 1400; *k* 1403 Battle of Shrewsbury, being one of those who were dressed as the King and mistaken for him by the enemy; *m* Beatrix, sis and heir of John de Braose, of West Neston, Sussex, and had:

Sir RALPH SHIRLEY; a cdr under HENRY V Battle of Agincourt 1415; *m* Joan, dau and heir of Thomas Basset, of Brailsford, Derbys, and had an only s:

RALPH SHIRLEY; Constable Melbourne Castle and the Castle of the Peak, both Derbys; *m* 1st Margaret, dau and sole heir of John de Staunton, of Staunton Harold, Leics, and had a s; *m* 2nd Elizabeth, dau of Sir John Blount, by whom he had a s (Ralph, Esq of the body to HENRY VII; *m* Joan, dau of Thomas Bellingham, of Lymster [*sic*], Sussex, and *d* 1510, leaving two sons, Sir Richard, of Whiston, whose line continued till at least 1678, and Thomas, of W Grinstead, whose line died out 1606); *m* 3rd Lucia, dau of Sir John Aston, of Atherton, widow of Sir John Byron and Sir Bertine Entwissel; his s by his 1st w:

JOHN SHIRLEY; *m* Eleanor, dau of Sir Hugh Willoughby, of Wollaton, Notts, and *d* 1485, leaving:

Sir RALPH SHIRLEY, KB; fought Battle of Stoke 16 June 1487; *m* 1st —; *m* 2nd Elizabeth, dau and coheir of Thomas Walsh, of Wanlip, Leics, and had a dau (Anne, *m* Sir Thomas Pulteney, of Misterton, Leics); *m* 3rd Jane, dau of Sir Robert Sheffield, and had a s; *m* 4th — and *d* 1517; his only s:

FRANCIS SHIRLEY, of Staunton Harold and Brailsford; Sheriff Warwicks and Leics *c* 1557; *m* Dorothea, widow of John Congreve, of Congreve, and dau of Sir John Giffard, 12th of Chillington, Staffs, and *d* 27 July 1571, having had:

JOHN SHIRLEY; *m* Jane, only dau and heir of Thomas Lovett (Lovell?), of Astwell, Northants, and *dvp* 12 Sept 1570, leaving:

Sir George Shirley, 1st Bt (E), so *cr* 22 May 1611, of Staunton Harold; *m* 1st *c* 21 Feb 1586/7 Frances (*d* 29 Dec 1595), dau of 7th Lord (Baron) Berkeley (*qv*), and had, with other issue, two sons (the yr being Thomas, antiquary); *m* 2nd Dorothy, widow of Sir Henry Unton, of Faringdon, Berks, and dau of Sir Thomas Wroughton, of Wilcot, Wilts, and *d* 27 April 1622, having by her had no issue; his er s:

Sir Henry Shirley, 2nd Bt; *m* 1 Aug 1616 Dorothy (*m* 2nd 1634 William Stafford, of Blatherwick, and *d* 30 March 1636), yst dau of 3rd Viscount Hereford (*qv*), and *d* 8 Feb 1632/3, leaving:

1 **Sir Charles Shirley, 3rd Bt**; *b* 9 Sept 1623; *d* unm 7 June 1646

2 **Sir Robert Shirley, 4th Bt**; royalist, committed by CROMWELL to the Tower, where he *d* 6 Nov 1656, possibly from poison; *m* Catherine (*d* 18 Oct 1672), dau of Humphrey Okeover, of Okeover, Staffs, and had:

(1) **Sir Seymour Shirley, 5th Bt**; *b* 23 Jan 1646/7; *m* 29 Jan 1666 Diana (*m* 2nd 10 Nov 1671 1st Duke of Rutland (*qv*) and *dsps* 15 July 1672), dau of 2nd Earl of Elgin (*see* ELGIN and KINCARDINE, E), and *d* 16 July 1667, leaving:

1a **Sir Robert Shirley, 6th Bt**; *b* postumously Jan 1667/8; *bur* 11 March 1708/9

(2) ROBERT, **1st Earl**

(1) Dorothy; *m* as his 2nd w George Vernon, of Sudbury (*see* VERNON, B)

1 Lettice; *m* as his 1st w 7th Earl of Clanricarde (see SLIGO, M)

The 6th Bt's unc,

Sir Robert Shirley, 7th Bt, and **1st Earl Ferrers**, so *cr* 3 Sept 1711, as also VISCOUNT TAMWORTH, of Co Stafford (both GB); became 7th LORD (Baron) FERRERS with precedence of 1299 on termination of abeyance of that title in his favour 14 Dec 1677, PC (1699–1714); *bapt* 20 Oct 1650; *educ* Ch Ch Oxford; *m* 1st 28 Dec 1671 Elizabeth (*d* 2 Oct 1693), dau and heir of Laurence Washington, of Garsden, Wilts (*see* AMERICAN PRESIDENTIAL FAMILIES, 1994, Morris Genealogical Books, SA) and had, with other issue:

1 Robert; *b* 4 Sept 1673; *m* 1st Catherine (*d* 27 Sept 1697), dau of Peter Venables; *m* 2nd 27 Sept 1688 Anne, dau of Sir Humphrey Ferrers, of Tamworth Castle, and *d* 25 Feb 1698, leaving, with two daus:

(1) Robert, *Viscount Tamworth*; *d* unm 5 July 1714

(1) Elizabeth; *m* 3 March 1715/6 5th Earl of Northampton and *d* 13 March 1740/1, leaving issue (*see* NORTHAMPTON, M)

2 WASHINGTON SHIRLEY, **2nd Earl Ferrers**; *b* 22 June 1677; *m* Mary, dau of Sir Richard Levinge, 1st Bt (*qv*), and *dspm* 14 April 1729, leaving issue:

(1) Elizabeth; *m* 24 June 1725 Joseph Gascoigne Nightingale, of Enfield, Middx, and had issue

(2) Selina; *m* 3 June 1728 7th Earl of Huntingdon (*qv*) and *d* 17 June 1791, leaving issue

(3) Mary; *m* 20 June 1730 9th Viscount Kilmorey (*see* KILMOREY, E) and *dsp* 12 Aug

3 HENRY SHIRLEY, **3rd Earl Ferrers**; *b* 14 April 1691; *d* unm and insane 6 Aug 1745

4 Laurence, of Staunton Harold; *b* 26 Sept 1693; *m* Anne (*d* 27 May 1782), 4th dau of Sir Walter Clarges, 1st Bt, and *d* 27 April 1743, leaving issue:

(1) LAURENCE SHIRLEY, **4th Earl Ferrers**; *b* 18 Aug 1720; *educ* Ch Ch Oxford; *m* 16 Sept 1752 (she procured a separation due to his cruelty 20 June 1758) Mary (*m* 2nd Lord Frederick Campbell, bro of 4th Duke of Argyll (*qv*)), sis of Sir William Meredith, 3rd Bt, of Henbury, Cheshire; though never committed, Lord Ferrers was prone to such rages as in the eyes of observers approached insanity; in one of these rages he shot dead in Jan 1760 his steward, an aged man called Johnson, for which he was tried by his peers 16 and 17 April 1760, unanimously found guilty 18 April 1760 and hanged at Tyburn 5 May 1760 (with a silken cord rather than a common hempen rope, as was his privilege as a peer); *dspl*, leaving illegitimately by Margaret, dau of Richard Clifford, of Beedon, Leics (his agent);

1a Margaret; *b* 13 Aug 1744; *m* Philip Godkin, of Melbourne, and had issue

2a Anna Maria; *b* 16 March 1745; *m* John Louis Pasteur (*d* 2 Aug 1782) and *d* 26 Jan 1816, being with him grandparent of John Louis Pasteur (1802–22 May 1819)

3a Elizabeth; *b* 4 April 1748; *m* Samuel Leech, draper, of Cheapside

4a Mary; *b* 8 Sept 1749; *d* unm Aug 1823

(2) WASHINGTON SHIRLEY, **5th Earl Ferrers**; V-Adml the Blue; *b* 26 May 1722; *m* Anne, dau of John Elliot, of Plymouth, and *dsp* 11 Oct 1778

(3) ROBERT SHIRLEY, **6th Earl Ferrers**; *b* 18 July 1723; *m* 26 Dec 1754 Catherine (*d* 16 March 1786), dau of Rowland Cotton, of Etwall, Derbys, and *d* 17 April 1787, having had:

1a ROBERT SHIRLEY, **7th Earl Ferrers**; FSA; *b* 21 Sept 1756; *m* 1st 13 March 1778 Elizabeth (*d* 14 Sept 1799), dau of John Prentise, and had:

1b Robert Sewallis, *Viscount Tamworth*; *b* 9 Nov 1778; *m* 5 Aug 1800 Sophia Caroline (*d* 3 Feb 1849), only dau of 2nd Baron Scarsdale (*see* SCARSDALE, V), and *dsp* 6 June 1824

1a (cont.) The **7th Earl** *m* 2nd 28 Sept 1799 Elizabeth (*dsp* 22 Feb 1827), yst dau of Wrightson Mundy, of Markeaton, Derbys, and *dspmsl* (an illegitimate dau *m* Hylton Jolliffe, MP; *see* HYLTON, B) 2 May 1827

2a WASHINGTON SHIRLEY, **8th Earl Ferrers**; *b* 13 Nov 1760; *m* 1st 24 July 1781 Frances (*d* 4 March 1812), n of 1st Viscount Dudley and Ward (*see* DUDLEY, E), and had, with two daus:

1b Robert William, *Viscount Tamworth*; *b* 24 Aug 1783; *m* 12 Dec 1821 Anne (*d* 7 Oct 1839), dau of Richard Weston, and *d* 3 Feb 1830, leaving:

1c WASHINGTON SEWALLIS SHIRLEY, **9th Earl Ferrers**; *b* 3 Jan 1822; *m* 23 July 1844 Augusta Annabella (*m* 2nd 15 June 1864 Frederick Henry Walsh, Capt 78th Regt, and *d* 9 Oct 1914), dau of 4th Marquess of Donegall (*qv*), and *d* 13 March 1859, having had, with another s and dau (both *d* young):

1d SEWALLIS EDWARD SHIRLEY, **10th Earl Ferrers**, JP Derbys; MA Cantab, KStJ, Prov Grand Master Freemasons Leics and Rutland; *b* 24 Jan 1847; *m* 24 Oct 1885 Lady Ina Maude White (*d* 8 June 1907), dau of 3rd Earl of Bantry (*see* 1891 edn), and *dsp* 26 July 1912

1d Augusta Amelia; *m* 19 Aug 1873 Sir Archdale Robert Palmer, 4th Bt, of Wanlip Hall (*qv*), and *d* 10 Feb 1933

2c Robert William Devereux; Lt 87th Regt; *b* 14 Dec 1825; *dsp* 4 June 1849

1c Rosamond Ann Myrtle; *m* 19 June 1841 Henry Hanbury-Tracy (*see* SUDELEY, B)

2a (cont.) The **8th Earl** *m* 2nd 29 Sept 1829 Sarah (*d* 30 June 1835), dau of William Davy, and *d* 2 Oct 1842

(4) Walter (Rev); *b* 28 Sept 1726; *educ* Univ Coll Oxford (BA); Rector Loughrea, Co Galway; *m* 27 Aug 1766 Henrietta Maria (*d* 15 Dec 1792), sister of Lt-Col Molesworth Phillips, of Belcotton, Co Louth (who accompanied Capt Cook on his last voyage and shot the native who killed him), and dau of John Phillips, of Swords, Co Dublin, by Henrietta (dau of John Eccleston, of Termonfeckin, Co Louth, s of William Eccleston, of Drumshallon, by Rose, dau of Capt James Brabazon (*see* MEATH, E)), and *d* 7 April 1786, having had:

1a Walter (Rev), of Westpoint, Co Mayo; Rector Brailsford, Derbys; *b* 1768; *m* 1796 Alice, dau of Sir Edward Newenham, s of William Newenham, of Coolmore, Co Cork, and had:

1b Walter Augustus (Rt Rev), DD; *educ* New Coll Oxford (MA, DD 1846); Preb Lichfield, Archdeacon Derby 1841–46, Bp Sodor and Man 10 Jan 1847; *b* 30 May 1797; *m* 4 Sept 1827 Maria (*d* 10 Jan 1859), dau of William Waddington, of St Rémy, Normandy, and *d* 21 April 1847, leaving issue:

1c Walter Waddington (Rev); DD Oxford; Canon Ch Ch, Regius Prof Ecclesiastical History Oxford; *b* 24 July 1928; *m* 4 July 1855 Philippa Frances Emilia (*d* 2 Feb 1902), only child of Samuel Knight, of Impington Hall, Cambs, and *d* 20 Nov 1866, having had, with another s (*d* young) and two daus (*d* unm):

1d WALTER KNIGHT, **11th Earl**

2d Ralph; granted rank of earl's yr s 1913; *b* 30 Dec 1865; *educ* New Coll Oxford (BA); *m* 1st 28 July 1903 Florence Beatrice (*d* 10 Oct 1926), dau of H Wright, of Didcot, Oxon; *m* 2nd 24 July 1935 Lilian Octavia Fortescue (*d* 30 April 1957), widow of Maj Venour Davidson and dau of Matthew Lisle Ingram, of Feckenham, Worcs, and *dsp* 29 Dec 1946

1d Alice; *m* 26 Jan 1887 Rev William Richardson Linton, Vicar Shirley, Derbys, and *d* 18 Jan 1911, leaving issue. He *d* 4 Jan 1908

1c Alicia Maria; *m* 7 Oct 1856 Capt C R W F Harris, 8th Madras Light Cav, and *d* 14 Nov 1857, leaving issue. He *d* 9 March 1862

1a Frances Anne; *b* 1770; *m* Rev John Going, Rector Mealiffe, Co Tipperary, and *d* 1838, leaving issue. He was murdered 1829 aged 60

2a Henrietta Eleanora; *b* 1772; *m* 1790 Rev H Bunbury and *d* 1841

3a Anna Augusta; *b* 1775; *m* 1798 G Maturin (*d* 1840)

(5) Thomas, of Horkston, Lincs; Adml RN; *b* 6 April 1733; *m* 1st 30 March 1773 Mary (*dsp* 1808), widow of Sir Stephen Anderson, 3rd Bt, and dau of W Elsgood; *m* 2nd 6 Nov 1809 Anne (*m* 2nd Col John Tufnell, of Horkston, Lincs), dau of Thomas Hele, and *dsp* 7 April 1814

The **1st Earl** *m* 2nd Aug 1699 Selina (*d* 20 March 1762), dau of George Finch, of London, and *d* 25 Dec 1717, having by her had, with three other sons and three other daus (of whom two *d* unm):

5 George, of Ettington; *b* 23 Oct 1705; *m* 28 Dec 1749 Mary (*d* 22 Oct 1787), dau of Humphrey Sturt, and *d* 22 Oct 1787 leaving issue:

(1) Evelyn, of Ettington; *b* 17 Dec 1756; *m* 3 July 1781 Phillis Byam (*d* 22 June 1836), dau of Charlton Wollaston, MD, FRS, and *d* 1 May 1810, leaving, with other issue:

1a Evelyn John, of Ettington and Lough Fea, Co Monaghan; DCL, MP Co Monaghan and S Warwicks; *b* 26 April 1788; *m* 16 Aug 1810 Eliza (*d* 30 April 1859), only dau of Arthur Stanhope, and *d* 31 Dec 1856, leaving:

1b Evelyn Philip, of Ettington and Lough Fea, DL; LLD, MP Co Monaghan and S Warwicks; *b* 22 Jan 1812; *m* 4 Aug 1842 Mary Clara Elizabeth (*d* 25 Aug 1894), dau of Sir Edmund Hungerford Lechmere, 2nd Bt (*qv*), and *d* 19 Sept 1882, having had, with another dau (*d* unm):

1c Sewallis Evelyn, of Ettington and Lough Fea, JP Warwicks, DL; High Sheriff 1884, MP Co Monaghan 1868–80; *b* 15 July 1844; *m* 23 Sept 1884 Emily Jean (*d* 12 July 1918), est dau of Col William Macdonald, of St Martin's Abbey, Perthshire, by Clara Anne Jane, dau of 1st Baron Lurgan (*see* 1970 edn), and *d* 7 March 1904, leaving, with other issue:

1d Evelyn Charles, of Lough Fea and Ettington Park, JP, DL Co Monaghan; Lt-Col Gen Staff and Maj Warwickshire Yeo, High Sheriff Co Monaghan 1914; *b* 27 Feb 1889; *m* 12 April 1921 Kathleen Mary Phyllis (*d* 23 March 1977), only dau of Lt-Col George Ambrose Cardew, CMG, DSO, of W Kensington, and *d* 9 Aug 1956, leaving:

1e +John Evelyn [Maj John Shirley, Ormly Hall, Ramsey, IoM]; Maj KRRC (ret 1955), served WW II 1941–45; *b* 11 Nov 1922; *educ* Eton; *m* 17 Jan 1952 *Judith Margaret, yr dau of Sir William Francis Stratford Dugdale, 1st Bt (*qv*), and has:

1f +Philip Evelyn; *b* 29 Sept 1955; *educ* Eton; *m* 1989 *Augusta, er dau of Hugo Southern, of Wilts, and has:

1g +Evelyn Robert; *b* 1990

2g +Horatio John; *b* 1993

3g +Nathaniel Guy; *b* 14 July 1995

1g *Perdita Rose; *b* 27 June 1997

2f +Hugh Sewallis; *b* 3 Oct 1961

1f *Emily Margaret [The Hon Mrs Robert Grimston, Elm Farm, Sibford Ferris, Banbury, Oxon OX15 5AA]; *b* 3 Nov 1957; *m* 1984 *Hon Robert John Sylvester Grimston, er s of 2nd Baron Grimston of Westbury (*qv*), and has issue

1e *Mary Louisa Phyllis; *b* 1931

1d Emily Phyllis; *m* 3 June 1916 Capt Wilfrid Herbert Cecil Brownlow, Northumberland Fus, s of Col Cecil Barry Brownlow, IA, of Forest Row. He was *ka* 28 May 1918

2d *Winifred Mary Frances; *m* 21 Oct 1929 Lt-Col Julius Francis Chenevix Trench, DSO, OBE, DL (*see* ASHTOWN, B)

1c Mary Clara; *m* 2 May 1872 Rev William Kyle Westwood Chafy, DD, of Rouse Lench Court, Worcs, and *d* 16 June 1929, leaving issue. He *d* 1916

2c Katherine; *m* 14 Nov 1899 her cousin Capt Arthur Horatio Shirley, RN (*see* below), and *dsp* 25 April 1945

2b Arthur, Maj-Gen; *b* 8 Feb 1813; *m* 4 July 1840 Christine, dau of James Wardrop, MD, and *dsp* 27 Jan 1877

3b Walter Devereux; Maj Monaghan Militia; *b* 20 July 1829; *m* 26 July 1856 Hannah Knox (*d* 5 April 1913), only dau of William Knox Faucette, and *d* 23 April 1908, leaving:

1c Louisa; *m* 17 March 1887 Frank Thorwaldsen Liebich, s of Immanuel Liebich, barrister, of Breslau. He *d* 16 Jan 1922

1b Selina; *m* 18 May 1841 Sir William Heathcote, 5th Bt, of Hursley (*qv*), and *d* 17 July 1901, having had issue

2b Louisa; *m* 2 Sept 1843, as his 2nd wife, Neil Malcolm of Poltalloch, and *d* 5 Oct 1887. He *d* 2 Oct 1857

2a Henry Robert, Lt RN; *b* 1789; *das* at sea May 1808

3a Charles, Gen Coldstream Gds, served Peninsular War; *b* 15 Nov 1792; *m* 7 Dec 1819 Anne Charlotte (*d* 9 Feb 1858), dau of Rev Hon George Bridgeman (*see* BRADFORD, E), and *dsp* 12 Dec 1855

4a William; Maj 7th Light Dragoons, fought Quatre Bras and Waterloo 1815

5a James (Rev), Rector Frettenham; *b* 15 Jan 1802; *m* 29 Dec 1831 Catherine Louisa (*d* 20 Oct 1867), dau of Rev John Dolphin, and *d* 7 Jan 1870, leaving three sons and four daus (all *d* unm)

6a Horatio (Sir), KCB; Chev Legn Hon, Gen Col 88th Foot at the Alma, Inkermann and Sebastopol; *b* 3 Dec 1805; *dsp* 11 April 1879

7a Arthur George Sewallis (Rev), MA, Vicar Stinsford, Dorset; *b* 20 July 1810; *m* 1st 24 Aug 1841 Georgina Emily (*d* 8 July 1852), dau of Rev William Cookson, and had, with two other sons and a dau (*d* unm):

1b Sewallis; *b* 18 June 1843; *m* 28 March 1878 Christiana (*d* 14 Feb 1932), dau of Rev Henry Blackstone Williams, MA, and *dsp* 27 Nov 1898

7a (cont.) The Rev Arthur Shirley *m* 2nd 3 Sept 1853 Mary Beadon (*d* 3 April 1877), widow of Francis Jackson and dau of Edward Turner, and by her had, with other issue:

2b Arthur Horatio, JP Devon; *b* 25 June 1854; Capt RN; *m* 14 Nov 1899 his cousin Katherine (*d* 25 April 1945), yr dau of Evelyn Philip Shirley (*see* above), and *dsp* 30 Nov 1933

3b William (Rev), MA Keble Coll Oxford, Rector Bursledon Hants 1908–20; *b* 23 Aug 1856; *m* 22 April 1884 Alice Louisa (*d* 8 Sept 1929), dau of Rev Frederick Bell Pryor, and *d* 1 March 1949, leaving issue:

1c Sewallis Robert, MC; psc, Col IA, T/Brig India 1935–37, Home Office and CID 1938–39, Regnl Offr CD 1940–41, Admiralty Small Vessels Pool 1942–44, RN Minewatching Serve 1951; served Mohmand Expdn 1908 (despatches), WW I (despatches twice) and NWF India 1930; *b* 31 Jan 1885; *educ* Winchester and RMC Sandhurst; *m* 1st 10 March 1917 (*divorce*) Hilda Grace, dau of Harry Gavin Young, Indian Police, and had:

1d *Eileen Diana [Mrs Malcolm Young, Whyr Farm, Winterbourne Bassett, Swindon, Wilts]; *b* 11 Sept 1922; *m* 27 April 1946 *Malcolm Rhondda Young and has issue:

1e *Peter Malcolm Gavin [Peter Young Esq, 22 Belmont Rd, Mosman, NSW 2088, Australia]; *b* 5 Aug 1947; *educ* Winchester and Cambridge; *m* 1989 *Anne Elizabeth Sadleir

2e *Richard William Shirley [Richard Young Esq, 6 Nassau Rd, London SW13 9QE]; *b* 21 March 1949; *educ* Wellington and Essex U; *m* 1973 *Deborah Anne Greene French and has:

1f *James Malcolm Sewallis; *b* 1985

1f *Juliet Anne Verity; *b* 1978

2f *Stefanie Clare Elizabeth; *b* 1980

1c (cont.) Brig Sewallis Shirley *m* 2nd 31 July 1940 *Edna Blodwen [Mrs Sewallis Shirley, 7 Minster House, Abbey Park Rd, Beckenham, Kent], dau of Albert William Laking, and *d* 8 Nov 1969, leaving by her:

2d *Anne Devereux [Mrs Richard Notley, Cheviot, Cricketer's Row, Herongate, nr Brentwood, Essex]; *b* 21 Aug 1943; *m* 22 Dec 1962 *Capt Richard Norman Notley, Roy Hants Regt (ret), and has issue:

1e *John Norman Devereux; *b* 19 March 1964

1e *Diana Phillida; *b* 30 March 1966

2c Geoffry Stanhope; Conservator Indian Forest Serv Burma; *b* 19 July 1888; *d* unm 12 March 1960

3c Ralph Devereux; architect, T/Lt Rifle Bde; *b* 19 Aug 1889; *m* 1926 Marie Louise Josephine (*d* 1936), dau of M Jouve, of Calais

1b Phyllis; *b* 30 Dec 1858; *m* 15 July 1886 Lt-Gen Sir Henry Richard Legge Newdigate, KCB, and *d* 19 March 1906, having had issue. He *d* 17 Jan 1908

2b Emily Gertrude; *b* 4 July 1861; *m* 1905 George William Floyer, of Stafford, Dorchester, and *d* 1915. He *d* 25 Dec 1927

3b Louisa; *b* 25 Oct 1863; *m* 1895 Lt-Col George Ambrose Cardew, CMG, DSO, RFA, s of Capt Christopher Baldock Cardew, and *d* 6 April 1949, leaving issue. He *d* 2 Feb 1941

7a (cont.) The Rev Arthur Shirley *m* 3rd 1878 Francesca Vincenzia Edith, widow of John Symons, of Tremayne, and dau of Capt John Ernle Money, and *d* 8 Oct 1891

1a Mary; *m* 19 April 1813 George Morant and *d* 17 Feb 1838, leaving issue. He *d* 11 Dec 1875

2a Emily Harriet; *m* 12 Sept 1826 3rd Baron Suffield (*qv*) and *d* 3 Jan 1881, leaving issue

6 Sewallis; Comptroller Household to QUEEN CHARLOTTE; *m* 25 May 1751 Margaret, Baroness Clinton (*qv*) in her own right and Dowager Countess of Orford (*see* WALPOLE, B) and *dsp* 25 Oct 1765

1 Anne; *m* 15 May 1729, as his 3rd wife, Sir Robert Furnese, 2nd Bt, and *d* 25 Feb 1779

2 Selina; *m* Peter Bathurst, of Clarendon Park, Wilts, and had issue (*see* MALCOLM, Bt, and SUDELEY, B)

The Rev WALTER SHIRLEY's est surv s,

WALTER KNIGHT SHIRLEY, **11th Earl Ferrers**; architect; *educ* New Coll Oxford (BA); *b* 5 June 1864; *m* 9 July 1890 Mary Jane (*d* 10 Jan 1944), dau of Robert Moon (*see* MOON, Bt, of Copsewood), and had:

1 ROBERT WALTER, **12th Earl**

2 Andrew; Assist Keeper Fine Art Dept Ashmolean Museum Oxford 1925–29, manager Times Book Club 1939–50; *b* 29 Dec 1900; *educ* Winchester and New Coll Oxford (BA 1922, MA 1926); *m* 30 April 1927 Ethel Muriel, dau of John Henry David Ellis Lewis, and *d* 20 June 1958, leaving issue:

(1) Mary Teresa; *b* 2 Dec 1927

1 Margery Joan; *b* 25 Nov 1891; *m* 22 Sept 1920 Lancelot Sackville Fletcher, barrister, and *d* 1 June 1952

2 Elizabeth Mary; *b* 30 Dec 1892; *d* 9 Nov 1893

3 Phillida; nun; *b* 4 Nov 1896

The 11th EARL *d* 2 Feb 1937; his est son,

ROBERT WALTER SHIRLEY, **12th Earl Ferrers**; *b* 7 July 1894; *m* 28 Feb 1922 Hermione Justice, JP (Leics 1949; *d* 16 July 1969), dau of A Noel Morley, of Lychwood, Worplesdon, Surrey, and *d* 11 Oct 1954, leaving issue:

1 ROBERT WASHINGTON SHIRLEY, **13th and present Earl Ferrers**

1 Elizabeth Hermione; WW II 1942–45 in WRNS, dir Wichester Branch Princess Roy Tst for Carers 1995–97; *m* 24 Oct 1959 John Fownes Luttrell (*d* 1985), Hon Capt Intelligence Corps, yr s of Hugh Courtenay Fownes Luttrell, of Ward House, Bere Alston, Devon (*see* OGILVY-WEDDERBURN, Bt), and *d* 7 Oct 1997, leaving:

(1) *Robert Hugh Courtenay Fownes; *b* 20 June 1961; *m* 1991 *Pauline Margaret Cecilia, dau of John Roddy, of Sydney, Australia, and has issue:

1a *Madeline Louise Fownes; *b* 26 Sept 1992

2a *Lucinda Marie; *b* 12 June 1996

2 *(Jane) Penelope Justice [The Lady Penelope Robson, Bristow's Close, Southrop, Glos GL7 3QA]; *m* 17 May 1944 Rev Canon John Maurice Robson (*d* 1989), TD, MA, Canon Emeritus Derby (Hon Canon 1975), Vicar Shirley, Rector Brailsford, RD Ashbourne, yst s of Rev James Robson, Vicar W Harton, Co Durham, and has issue:

(1) *David Edward Shirley [David Robson Esq, Slip of Wood, Cranleigh, Surrey GU6 7BE]; *b* 2 Jan 1947; *educ* Repton; *m* 1st 16 June 1973 (*divorce* 1976) Carol Diana, yr dau of Wilfrid Durose, of Ireton Wood Hall, Derbys; *m* 2nd 1980 *Josephine Ann Charlotte, dau of Richard Manwaring-White, and by her has:

1a *Oliver Charles Richard; *b* 1986

2a *Jonathan Hugo David; *b* 1990

(1) *Julia Phillida Shirley [Mrs James Jermain, 7 Park Rd, Winchester, Hants SO22 6AA]; *b* 23 March 1953; *m* 4 Nov 1972 *James Douglas Jermain, est s of Cdre D Jermain, DSC, RN, of Petersfield, Hants and has:

1a *Katharine Hermione; *b* 1975

2a *Abigail Marion; *b* 1976

3a *Eleanor Shirley; *b* 1980

FEVERSHAM

Arms: Quarterly, 1st and 4th, per chevron engrailed gules and argent three talbot's heads erased counterchanged (for DUNCOMBE); 2nd and 3rd, argent or chevron sable between three crosses flory of the second (for ANDERSON). **Crests:** 1 Out of a ducal coronet or a horse's hind leg sable, the shoe argent (for DUNCOMBE); 2 A water spaniel passant or (for ANDERSON). **Supporters:** Dexter, a horse of a dark iron-grey colour guttée-d'or, ducally gorged of the last; sinister, a lion argent, powdered with fleurs-de-lys sable, his head adorned with a plume of six feathers argent and azure, issuing out of a ducal coronet or. **Motto:** *Deo regi patria* ('For God, king and country'). **Creation:** B. (UK) 14 July 1826.

THE 6TH BARON FEVERSHAM OF DUNCOMBE PARK, Yorkshire ((Charles Anthony) Peter Duncombe) [The Rt Hon The Lord Feversham, Duncombe Park, Helmsley, Yorks YO6 5EB]; *b* 3 Jan 1945; *s* 4th cousin (3rd Earl of Feversham, on whose death the earldom expired) in Barony only 1963; *educ* Eton and Inner Temple, chm: Yorks Arts Assoc 1969–80 (and Pres 1987–91), Standing Conf Regnl Arts Assocs 1969–76, Tstees Yorks Sculpture Pk 1981–, Govr Leeds Poly 1969–76, Pres: Soc of Yorkshiremen in London 1974, Yorks and Cleveland Local Councils Assoc 1977, Yorkshire Local Cncls Assoc 1986– and Nat Assoc Local Cncls 1992–, Co-Pres (with Ted Hughes, Poet Laureate) Arvon Fndn 1976–86, author: *A Wolf in Tooth* (novel, 1967) and *Great Yachts* (1970); *m* 1st 12 Sept 1966 Shannon (*d* 13 Aug 1976), yst dau of Sir Thomas Arthur Wyness Foy, CSI, CIE, and Mrs Arthur MacDonald, of Levisham, Pickering, Yorks, and has issue:

1 +JASPER ORLANDO SLINGSBY; *b* 14 March 1968

2 +Jake Barnaby; *b* 17 March 1972

1 *Melissa Rose; *b* 1973

The 6th BARON *m* 2nd 6 Oct 1979 *Pauline M, dau of John Aldridge, of Newark, Notts, and by her has:

3 +Patrick Charles Kildare; *b* 1981

Feversham, previous creations: George Sondes, whose family seat of Lees Court was near Feversham (modern Faversham), Kent, was created Earl of Feversham in 1676, with remainder to his son-in-law Louis de Duras. The grantee's own sons had all died young, one of them murdered by another, who was hanged for it. The son-in-law, who inherited the title in 1677, was of noble French stock, being nephew of the celebrated Marshal Turenne and grandson through his mother of the Duke of Bouillon, while his elder brother held the male-line family Dukedom of Duras and Lorge. Louis was naturalised an Englishman in 1665 and became Keeper of the Privy Purse to the Duke of York (later JAMES II) two years afterwards, beginning at the same time a one-year tour of duty as English Ambassador to his former homeland of France. He remained faithful to JAMES II for a great deal longer than most of the noblemen whose families had been English for centuries and was one of four peers who tried to bring the King back to London after he had fled the capital in late 1688. His wife's sister was ancestress of the Earls Sondes who died out in 1996 (*see* MONSON, B).

An Earldom of Feversham was one of the subsidiary titles conferred on Ermengarde von der Schulenburg when she was made Duchess of Kendal for life in 1719. She was regarded by contemporaries (and indeed subsequent commentators) as the most important of GEORGE I's mistresses. Certainly her sole possible rival for this accolade, Sophie-Charlotte Countess von Kielmansegge, was made only a Countess in her own right in the British peerage. One of the Duchess of Kendal/Countess of Feversham's daughters by the King married the 4th Earl of Chesterfield (*see* 1967 edn CHESTERFIELD and STANHOPE, E). It was the letters of this Lord Chesterfield to his son that were famously apostrophised by Dr Johnson (who was doubtless well aware of the parentage of Lady Chesterfield) as teaching the morals of a strumpet.

Lineage: The DUNCOMBEs seem for nearly three hundred years to have been established in Buckinghamshire; among their places of residence were Bulbec Castle, Ivinghoe, and Barley End.

One WILLIAM DUNCOMBE is mentioned in Court Rolls of the manor of Ivinghoe. But the Heralds' Visitation of Buckinghamshire begins the Duncombe pedigree only with:

THOMAS DUNCOMBE, of Barley End, Okelays and Buttelers, all in Bucks, who bought land in Little Tring, Wylstone and Aldbury; *m* Joane (*d* 1539) and *d* 7 Aug 1531, having had, with four other sons and four daus:

1 JOHN

2 William, of Ivinghoe; bought 1550 the manor of Great Brickhill, Bucks, and was ancestor of the Duncombe Bts, of Tangley Park, Surrey (title *cr* 4 Feb 1661/2, expired July 1706), and of the devisor of the Gt Brickhill estate to Sir Philip Pauncefort-Duncombe, 1st Bt (*qv*)

THOMAS DUNCOMBE's est s,

JOHN DUNCOMBE, of Barley End; *b* 1504; *m* Alice, dau of — Egleston, of Edlesborough, Bucks, and *d* 29 Dec 1594, leaving an est s:

WILLIAM DUNCOMBE, of Barley End; *m* 21 Nov 1580 Faith, dau of Thomas Clarke, of Hitchendon, Bucks, and *d* 25 April 1630, having had, with an est s (Thomas, of Barley End, *bapt* 1582, *m* 1st Ann (*d* 21 Jan 1611), dau of Robert Barber, of Kensworth, Herts, *m* 2nd Amy, dau of Joseph Lake, of Bucklands, Bucks, and *d* Oct 1659, having had seven sons and two daus) and a yst one (Robert, of Stocks-in-Aldbury, Herts, had issue):

WILLIAM DUNCOMBE, of Drayton, Bucks; *b* 1585; *m* 1 Feb 1607 Margaret, dau of John Theed, and had issue:

1 Francis (Rev); Vicar Ivinghoe; his male issue died out 1741

2 Alexander, of Drayton; *bapt* 13 May 1619; probably steward to Sir William Tiringham or Tyringham, of Tiringham, Bucks; *m* 15 May 1645 Mary (*bur* 7 Nov 1716 aged 97), dau of Richard Paulye, Ld Manor of Whitchurch, Bucks, and had issue:

(1) Charles (Sir); *bapt* 16 Nov 1648; goldsmith and banker, a Clerk in Chancery 1682–83, MP: Hedon, Yorks, 1685–87, Yarmouth (IoW) 1690–95, Downton, Wilts, 1695–98 and 1702–11 (expelled from Parl for supposedly self-confessed fraud 1698), stood unsuccessfully for Parl in the City of London 1700–01, 1701 and 1702, Receiver Customs *temp* CHARLES II and JAMES II; bought the Helmsley estate, N R Yorks, for almost £90,000 (a little under £3,800,000 in late-1990s terms), at that time the largest sum expended on such an acquisition by a subject in English history, also that of Barford, Downton, Wilts; ktd 1699, City of London: Alderman Broad St Ward 1683–86 and Bridge Ward 1700, Sheriff 1699 (in which capacity he showed leniency to those imprisoned for debt), Treasurer Artillery Co April 1703–29 Feb 1703/4, Ld Mayor 1708–09; *d* unm and intestate 9 April 1711

(2) Anthony; *m* Jane, est dau and coheir of Frederick Cornwallis, 2nd s of 1st Baron Cornwallis (*qv*), and had:

1a ANTHONY DUNCOMBE, 1st and last LORD FEVERSHAM, BARON OF DOWNTON, Co Wilts (GB), so *cr* 23 June 1747; *b c* 1695; inherited half his unc Sir Charles Duncombe's immense wealth, MP (Whig) Salisbury 1721–34 and Downton 1734–47; *m* 1st 1 Jan 1715/6 Margaret Verney (*d* 9 Oct 1755), only dau of 12th Lord (Baron) Willoughby de Broke (*qv*), and had three sons and a dau (all *d* young); *m* 2nd Nov 1756 Frances (*d* 21 Nov 1757), dau of Peter Bathurst, of Clarendon Park, Wilts, by Selina, dau of 1st Earl Ferrers (*qv*), and had:

1b Frances, of Old Dalby Hall, Leics; *b* 12 Nov 1757; *m* 1778 John Bowater (*d* 1810), est s of Edward Bowater, of Woolwich, and *dsp* 29 July 1827

1a (cont.) LORD FEVERSHAM *m* 3rd 10 July 1758 Anne (*m* 2nd 22 July 1765, as his 3rd w, 1st Earl of Radnor (*qv*) and *d* 18 June 1795), 3rd dau of Sir Thomas Hales, 3rd Bt, by Mary, sis of 1st Baron (of) Romney (*see* ROMNEY, E), and *d* 18 June 1763, when the Barony expired, leaving by her:

2b Anne; *m* 24 Jan 1777 her mother's stepson 2nd Earl of Radnor (*qv*) and *d* 14 Oct 1829, leaving issue

(1) Ursula; inherited the other half of her bro Sir Charles Duncombe's fortune; *m* 1678 John or Thomas BROWN later DUNCOMBE, of the City of London, Receiver-Gen of Excise, who built the house of Duncombe Park in 1718 and formed the park there, and had:

1a THOMAS

1a Mary; acted as Ldy Mayoress during her unc Sir Charles's term of office; *m* 30 Dec 1701, as his 1st w, 2nd Duke of Argyll (*qv*) and *dsp*, as well as separated from her husb, 16 Jan 1716/7 aged 35

ALEXANDER DUNCOMBE's gs through his dau Ursula,

THOMAS DUNCOMBE, of Duncombe Park; High Sheriff Yorks 1728; *m* Mary, dau of Sir Thomas Slingsby, 4th Bt, and *d* 1746, having had, with another s and two daus:

1 Thomas, of Duncombe Park; *m* 1st 1740 Lady Diana Howard (*d* 6 March 1770), dau of 4th Earl of Carlisle (*qv*), and had, with another dau:

(1) Anne; *m* Robert Shafto, MP, of Whitworth, Co Durham, and had three sons

1 (cont.) Thomas Duncombe *m* 2nd a dau of Sir Philip Jennings Clerke, 1st and last Bt, and had:

(2) Frances; *m* Sir George Henry Rose, GCH, PC, DL (Hants) (*b* 1771; MP Southampton 1794–1813 and Christchurch 1818–44, Clerk of Parl and Envoy Extrdy Munich and Berlin; *d* 1855), s of Rt Hon George Rose (*b* 1744; MP Launceston 1784–88 and Christchurch 1788–1818, V-Pres BOT 1804–06 and 1807–12, Jt Paymaster-Gen 1804–06 and Treasurer Navy 1807–12 and 1812–18; *d* 1818), who in turn was formally s of David Rose, a Scottish clergyman who refused to swear loyalty to WILLIAM III after the Glorious Revolution of 1688, holding that his oath to the deposed JAMES II was inviolable, but whom contemporaries held to be an illegitimate s of the 3rd and last Earl of Marchmont (the *Dictionary of National Biography* rejects this, but Lord Marchmont certainly bequeathed Rose a substantial legacy as well as appointing him his executor); Lady Rose *d* 12 Oct 1761, having had, with four daus and another s:

1a William (Sir), KCB; Clerk Parl; *d* 1885

2a Sir HUGH HENRY ROSE, 1st and last BARON STRATHNAIRN OF STRATHNAIRN, Co Nairn, and OF JHANSI, in the East Indies (*i.e.*, India) (UK), so *cr* 31 July 1866, GCB (1858, KCB 1855, CB 1842), GCSI 1866 (KCSI 1861), PC (Indian, 1865) JP; *b* Berlin 6 April 1801 and *educ* there; commissioned as Ensign 93rd Foot (Sutherland Highrs) 8 June 1820 but did not enter that regt, joining 19th Foot 6 July 1820 instead (Lt 1821, Capt 1824, unattached Maj 1826), Maj 92nd Highrs 1829, Equerry to HRH THE DUKE OF CAMBRIDGE 1830, Lt-Col 1839, served on a special mission in Syria 1840–41 (despatches, Order of Nishan Iftihar from Sultan of Turkey picked out in diamonds, sabre of honour), commanded Br detachments Syria with local rank of Col 1841, Consul-Gen Syria 1841, gold war medal (Ottoman Empire) and Order of St John (Prussia), Sec of Embassy Constantinople 1851 and Chargé d'Affaires 1852, Brevet-Col 1851, Queen's Commr HQ French forces Crimean War 1854 with local rank of Brig-Gen, Maj-Gen 1854, local rank of Lt-Gen 1856, Cdr Legion of Honour (France) 1856, served in suppression of Indian Mutiny 1857–58 as Cdr Centl India Field Force, in particular in capture 1858 of rebel strongholds of Jhansi (whence its featuring in his title) and Gwalior, Col 45th Foot 1858, substantive Lt-Gen 1860, C-in-C Bombay Army 1860, C-in-C India with local rank of Gen 1860, DCL Oxford 1865, one of HM's Commrs for Ltcy of City of London, Cdr Forces Ireland 1865–70, Col 92nd Foot 1866, Pres Army Transport Ctee 1866, Col RHG 1869, Hon LLD Dublin 1870, FM 1877; *d* unm Paris 16 Oct 1885, when the Barony expired

1 (cont.) Thomas Duncombe *m* 3rd Charlotte (*m* 2nd, as his 2nd w, 2nd Earl of Onslow, *qv*), dau of William Hale, of King's Walden, and *dspm* 1799

2 CHARLES SLINGSBY

1 Barbara; *m* Christopher Crowe (*dsp* 1776), of Kiplin, Yorks, s and heir of Christopher Crowe, of Woodford, Essex, by Lady Charlotte Lee, est dau of 1st Earl of Lichfield of the 1674 *cr* (*see* LICHFIELD, E, preliminary remarks, also JERSEY, E, and Introduction, AMERICAN PRESIDENTIAL FAMILIES, 1994, Morris Genealogical Books SA)

THOMAS DUNCOMBE's next bro,

CHARLES SLINGSBY DUNCOMBE, of Duncombe Park; *m* Isabel, dau of Robert Soulby, and *d* 11 Sept 1803, having had, with several daus:

1 CHARLES, **1st Baron**

2 Thomas, of Copgrove, nr Boroughbridge, W R Yorks; *b* 1769; *m* 1795 Emma (*d* 1840), est dau of Rt Rev Dr John Hinchcliffe, Bp Peterborough, by Elizabeth Crewe, sis of 1st Baron Crewe of Crewe, and *d* 7 Dec 1847, leaving, with other issue, including or possibly comprising exclusively yr sons:

(1) Thomas Slingsby; *b* 1796; *educ* Harrow; Ensign Coldstream Gds 1811, ADC to Gen Ferguson Holland campaign 1813–14, Lt 1815, ret 1819, Whig Parly candidate Pontefract 1820 and Hertford 1823, MP (Whig, later leaning towards Radicals; he was said to be the best-dressed man in the House of Commons) Hertford 1826–32 and Finsbury 1834–61 (presented Chartists' petition to Parl 1842), memb cncl Friends of Italy (Mazzinian nationalist body) 1851; *d* 13 Nov 1861

(1) Frances Barbara; *m* 24 April 1830, as his 1st w, Rev Hon John Venables-Vernon (*see* VERNON, B) and *d* 7 Dec 1848

3 Slingsby, of Winthorpe Hall; *b* Nov 1779; Capt 1st Foot Gds; *m* 23 June 1812 Martha (*d* 24 March 1871), dau of Henry Elvy, and *d* 12 Oct 1851, leaving, with another s and several daus:

(1) George Thomas DUNCOMBE later DUNCOMBE PEIRSE (roy licence 1887), of Winthorpe Hall; *b* 14 June 1825; Capt: 11th Hus and Coldstream Gds; *m* 27 July 1853 Arabella Georgiana (*d* 9 Oct 1920), only child of Richard William Peirse, of Northallerton, N Riding Yorks, formerly Capt 3rd Dragoon Gds, and *d* 5 Feb 1910, having had three sons and six daus

CHARLES SLINGSBY DUNCOMBE's est s,

CHARLES DUNCOMBE, **1st Baron Feversham of Duncombe Park**, Co York (UK), so *cr* 14 July 1826; *b* 5 Dec 1764; High Sheriff Yorks 1790, MP (Tory) Shaftesbury 1790–96, Aldborough 1796–1806, Heytesbury 1812–18 and Newport (IoW) 1812–26; *m* 24 Sept 1795 Lady Charlotte Legge (*d* 5 Nov 1848), only dau of 2nd Earl of Dartmouth (*qv*), and *d* 16 July 1841, having had, with a yst s and another dau:

1 Charles; *b* c 1795; *educ* Eton; *d* unm at Rome 1819

2 WILLIAM DUNCOMBE, **2nd Baron Feversham of Duncombe Park**; *b* 14 Jan 1798; *educ* Eton and Ch Ch Oxford (BA 1820, MA 1823); MP (Tory) Grimsby 1820–26, Yorks 1826–31 and N R Yorks 1832–41, Pres Roy Ag Soc 1864; *m* 18 Dec 1823 Lady Louisa Stewart (*d* 5 March 1889), dau of 8th Earl of Galloway (*qv*), and *d* 11 Feb 1867, having had, with other issue:

(1) Albert; *b* 11 Feb 1826; *educ* Eton; *d* unm 14 Sept 1846

(2) WILLIAM ERNEST DUNCOMBE, **3rd Baron Feversham of Duncombe Park** and 1st EARL OF FEVERSHAM OF RYEDALE, North Riding of Co Yorks, so *cr* 25 July 1868, as also VISCOUNT HELMSLEY, of Helmsley in the N Riding of Co Yorks (both UK), VD, JP, DL; *b* 28 Jan 1829; *educ* St John's Coll Oxford; CC N R Yorks, Hon Col 5th Bn Yorks Regt and Capt Yorks Yeo Hus, MP (C) E Retford 1852–57 and N R Yorks 1859–67, MFH Sinnington, Pres Roy Ag Soc 1892; *m* 7 Aug 1851 Mabel Violet (*d* 28 Aug 1915), 2nd dau of Sir James Graham, 2nd Bt, of Netherby (*qv*), and *d* 13 Jan 1915, having had:

1a William Reginald, *Viscount Helmsley*; *b* 1 Aug 1852; *educ* Eton; Lt Yorks Hus and 1st Life Gds, MP (C) N R Yorks 1874–81; *m* 23 Dec 1876 Lady Muriel Frances Louisa Talbot (*m* 2nd 6 June 1885 Hugh Darby Annesley Owen (*d* 12 March 1908), of Bettws Hall, Montgomeryshire, and *d* 2 March 1925), yst dau of 19th Earl of Shrewsbury and Waterford (*qv*), and *d* 24 Dec 1881, leaving:

1b CHARLES WILLIAM REGINALD DUNCOMBE, **4th Baron Feversham of Duncombe Park** and 2nd EARL OF FEVERSHAM OF RYEDALE, DL (N R Yorks); *b* 8 May 1879; *educ* Eton and Ch Ch Oxford (BA 1901, MA); MP (C) Thirsk and Malton 1906–15, Assist Priv Sec to First Ld Admlty 1902–05, MFH Sinnington to 1916, Lt-Col Yorks Hus then 21st Service Bn KRRC WW I; *m* 19 Jan 1904 Lady Marjorie Blanche Eva Greville (*m* 2nd 1 Nov 1917, as his 2nd w, Hon Sir (William) Gervase Beckett, 1st Bt (*qv*), and *d* 25 July 1964), dau of 5th Earl of Warwick (*see* WARWICK, BROOKE and, E), and was *ka* 15 Sept 1916, leaving:

1c CHARLES ('SIM') WILLIAM SLINGSBY DUNCOMBE, **5th Baron Feversham of Duncombe Park** and 3rd and last EARL OF FEVERSHAM OF RYEDALE, DSO (1946), TD, JP, DL (N R Yorks); *b* 2 Nov 1906; *educ* Eton; Col: Yorks Hus Yeo and 13th/18th Roy Hus WW II, OStJ, Ld-in-Waiting to TM GEORGE V 1934–36 and EDWARD VIII 1936, Parly Sec Min Ag and Fish 1936–39, MFH Sinnington 1946–63, dir: Midland Bank and Clydesdale and N of Scotland Bank, pres Nat Assoc Probation Offrs 1929, chm Nat Assoc for Mental Health from 1946; *m* 9 May 1936 Lady Anne Dorothy Wood, OBE (1980, MBE 1950), JP (Ryedale, N R Yorks, 1958), MFH Sinnington (*d* 25 March 1995), only dau of 1st Earl of Halifax (*qv*), and *dspm* 4 Sept 1963, when the Earldom and Viscountcy expired, leaving:

1d *Clarissa [The Lady Clarissa Collin, Wytherstone House, Pockley, York YO6 5TE]; *b* 11 Oct 1938 (HRH PRINCESS MARINA DUCHESS OF KENT stood sponsor); *educ* Heathfield and in Paris; High Sheriff N Yorks 1998–99; *m* 14 Dec 1966 *Maj Nicholas Spencer Compton Collin, late Coldstream Gds, s of Maj Francis Spencer Collin, of Belgravia and W Sussex, and has issue:

1e *Frederick Slingsby; *b* 30 Oct 1967

1e *Laura Anne; *b* 25 Aug 1969

2c David William Ernest; *b* 8 Feb 1910; *d* 8 Sept 1927 following a car crash

1c (Mary) Diana; *b* 19 March 1905; *m* 31 May 1927 Lt William Greville Worthington, RNVR (*d* following an accident 19 March 1942), er s of William Worthington Worthington, JP (*see* AYLESFORD, E), and *d* Oct 1943, leaving issue (*see* NORMAN, Bt)

1b Mabel Theresa; *b* 16 Oct 1877; *m* 12 Feb 1896 Capt Hon Sir (William) Gervase Beckett, 1st Bt (*qv*), and *d* 2 April 1913, leaving issue

2a James Henry; *b* 20 Oct 1853; Scots Gds; *d* unm 10 Jan 1886

3a Hubert Ernest Valentine, DSO; *b* 14 Feb 1862; MP W Cumberland 1895–1900, Hon Lt-Col, Maj 2nd Vol Bn Yorks Regt and Col cmdg 14th Bn Imp Yeo Boer War; *d* unm 21 Oct 1918

1a Hermione Wilhelmina; *m* 17 Jan 1884 5th Duke of Leinster (*qv*) and *d* 19 March 1895, leaving issue

2a Helen Venetia; *m* 24 Sept 1890 1st and last Viscount d'Abernon, GCB, GCMG, PC (*d* 1 Nov 1941; *see* 1940 edn) and *dsp* 16 May 1954

3a Mabel Cynthia; *m* 27 June 1889, as his 2nd w, Sir Richard James Graham, 4th Bt, of Netherby (*qv*), and *d* 25 April 1926, leaving issue

4a Ulrica; *m* 15 Sept 1904 Brig-Gen Hon Everard Baring, CVO, CBE, s of 1st Baron Revelstoke (*qv*), and *d* 27 April 1935, leaving issue

(3) Cecil, JP, DL, of the Grange, Nawton, Yorks; *b* 27 May 1832; Capt 1st Life Gds, CC Yorks; *m* 26 Oct 1859 Eleanor Jane Mills (*d* 24 May 1904), sis of 1st Baron Hillingdon (*see* 1970 edn), and *d* 20 May 1902, leaving issue:

1a (Charles) William Ernest, CBE (1918), TD, JP (N R Yorks), DL; *b* 15 March 1862; Imp Yeo Boer War 1900–01, KGStJ, Lt-Col and Hon Col cmdg Yorks Hus Yeo 1908–12, ed *Ryedale* (1935); *m* 1st 8 Feb 1890 Lilian Bertha (*dsp* 14 Feb 1904), step-dau of Archibald Stuart-Wortley; *m* 2nd 26 July 1910 Frances Adelaide (*d* 30 July 1934), est dau of Rev Henry Montagu Villiers (*see* CLARENDON, E) and widow of Arthur Francis Walrond, and *dsp* 8 May 1945

1a Eleanor Rachel; *b* 15 Sept 1860; *d* unm June 1903

2a Violet Helen; *m* 22 July 1885 William Herbert St Quintin, JP, DL (*d* 21 Jan 1933), of Scampston Hall and Lowthorpe Lodge, Yorks, and *d* 26 Nov 1943, leaving issue

3a Emily Katharine Louisa, MBE; *b* 3 Feb 1866; *d* unm 14 June 1959

(1) Jane; *m* 11 April 1849, as his 2nd w, Hon Lawrence Parsons, 3rd s of 2nd Earl of Rosse (*qv*), and *d* 3 April 1901, leaving issue

(2) Gertrude; *m* 27 Nov 1849 Francis Horatio FitzRoy (*see* GRAFTON, D) and *d* 24 Feb 1916, leaving issue

(3) Helen; *m* 18 July 1855 William Beckett-Denison, MP (Notts), of Meanwood Park, Leeds, yr bro of 1st Baron Grimthorpe (*qv*), and *d* 24 Nov 1896, leaving issue

3 Henry (Rev); *b* 25 Aug 1800; *m* 27 Sept 1827 Lucy Elizabeth (*m* 2nd 5 Jan 1837 Rev Charles Hotham (*d* 11 Feb 1866) and *d* 10 Dec 1877), dau of Rev Christopher Sykes, and *dsp* 1 Oct 1832

4 Arthur, of Kilnwick Percy, Pocklington, Yorks; *b* 24 March 1806; Adml, Groom-in-Waiting to HM QUEEN VICTORIA 1841–46, MP E R Yorks 1851–68, a Ld Admlty 1852; *m* 1st 14 July 1836 Delia (*d* 5 May 1873), yst dau and coheir of John Wilmer Field, of Heaton Hall, Yorks, and had issue:

(1) Charles Wilmer, JP (E R Yorks), of Kilnwick Percy; *b* 19 Sept 1838; Maj-Gen, Col 1st Life Gds; *m* 23 July 1906 Blanche Marie, dau of Ambroise Rivière, Col Engrs French Army, and *dsp* 19 Dec 1911

(2) Arthur DUNCOMBE later GREY (roy licence 9 Oct 1905), JP, DL (N and E R Yorks), of Bradgate House, Leics, and Sutton Hall, Easingwold; *b* 11 Feb 1840; *educ* Oxford (MA); Yorks: CA N R, Chm QS E R, MP E R 1885–92, barrister; *m* 12 June 1869 Katherine Henrietta Venezia (*d* 31 Oct 1926), er dau of Henry John Milbank (*see* MILBANK, Bt), and *d* 12 July 1911, leaving:

1a Alice Louisa; *b* 1 March 1874; *m* 28 July 1898 Lt-Col Roland d'Arcy Fife, CMG, DSO (*d* 17 Nov 1946), of Nunnington Hall, York, 19th Regt, and *d* 1 Aug 1898

2a Cecily; *b* 30 March 1877; *m* 1st 1 June 1897 15th Viscount Mountgarret (*qv*); *m* 2nd 12 July 1919 Lt-Col Charles Hervey GREY formerly HOARE, DSO (*d* 24 July 1955), and *d* 8 April 1961

3a Muriel Katherine; *b* 15 March 1880; *m* 12 Dec 1900 4th Baron Deramore (*qv*) and *d* 22 March 1960, leaving issue

(3) Frederick William; *b* 28 Jan 1842; Capt Gren Gds; *m* 28 July 1868 Lady Katherine Acheson (*d* 5 March 1898), yst dau of 3rd Earl of Gosford (*qv*), and *d* 6 Feb 1878, having had issue:

1a Basil Archibald Charles; *b* 12 Jan 1870; heir to his unc Maj-Gen Charles Duncombe; *m* 12 Jan 1896 Ida (*d* 17 Aug 1935), dau of Alfred Hope Doeg, and *d* 22 Sept 1930, leaving issue:

1b Hubert Basil Elliot; *b* 21 May 1901; *d* 25 Oct 1931

1b Phyllis Gertrude; *m* 1st 1917 (*divorce* 1930) Capt Cecil Francis Cureton Taylor, York and Lancaster Regt, yr s of Francis Walter Taylor; *m* 2nd 31 July 1936 (*divorce* 1947, resumed maiden name) John Creyghton Ainsworth-Davis, MA, MD, FRCS, late W/Cdr RAFVR, s of Prof James Richard Ainsworth-Davis; *m* 3rd 13 April 1950 Leslie George Whalan (*d* 30 March 1969)

2b Katherine; *m* 1919 Lt-Col Hugh Ferguson James Williamson, MBE, RA, and *d* 14 June 1963, leaving issue

2a Wilfred Arthur DUNCOMBE later DUNCOMBE-ANDERSON (roy licence June 1905), OBE (1919), JP (Hants); *b* 30 Sept 1871; *educ*

Sherborne; Capt: TFR and Cheshire Yeo and Lt 6th Dragoon Gds Boer War 1900 and WW I (despatches twice); *m* 7 June 1905 Margaret Louise (*d* 21 Feb 1952), est dau and coheir of Francis Foljambe Anderson, of Lea Hall, Lincs (*dvp* 15 Sept 1881), 2nd s of Sir Charles Henry John Anderson, 9th and last Bt, of Lea Hall, and *d* 13 Oct 1952, having had issue:

1b Antony John, TD; *b* 4 Feb 1907; *educ* Hertford Coll Oxford (MA); Col W Yorks Regt WW II (despatches), Sr Control Offr Control Commn for Germany; *m* 9 Oct 1931 *Gloranna Georgina Valerie [Mrs Anthony Duncombe, Knipe's Hill, Helmsley, Yorks] (who on behalf of herself and her two children dropped by deed poll 12 March 1954 the ANDERSON), er dau of Maj C E Irvine McNalty, of King's Worthy Court, Winchester, and *d* 20 Nov 1949, leaving issue:

1c (CHARLES ANTHONY) PETER DUNCOMBE, **6th and present Baron Feversham of Duncombe Park**

1c *Juliet Priscilla Mary; *b* 11 June 1937; *m* Dec 1960 *Wilfred Trevor Woodley, pianist, and has issue:

1d *Karin Lee; *b* 1961

2b Roland Frederick; *b* 18 April 1908; Maj 1st Bn E Surrey Regt WW II; *m* 31 Aug 1935 *Elizabeth Frances [Mrs Howard Greene, Glebe Cottage, Bishopstron, Warminster, Wilts], er dau of Algernon F A Mawson, of Norman Court, Upper Clatford, Andover (she *m* 2nd 19 June 1952 Brig Howard Greene, CBE, DSO, MC, s of George Percy Greene, Madras Survey), and was *ka* Belgium May 1940, leaving issue:

1c +Alastair Guy [Alastair Duncombe-Anderson Esq, 91 Gloucester Rd, Thornbury, Glos]; *b* 4 Oct 1938; *educ* Sherborne; *m* 11 April 1961 *Judith Anne, only dau of F E Abbot, of Painswick, Glos, and has issue:

1d +Alastair Mark; *b* 1962

2d +Nicholas; *b* 1963

3d +Timothy Guy; *b* 1965

1d *Rebecca Elizabeth; *b* 1966

2d *Justine Anne; *b* 1971

3b Wilfred George; *b* 6 Feb 1911; *educ* Sherborne and Worcester Coll Oxford; Maj Roy Signals (TA) WW II; *m* 1st 30 April 1942 Valerie (*d* 3 Aug 1969), dau of Capt S M Pemberton, of Washington, W Sussex, and had:

1c +David Martin [David Duncombe-Anderson Esq, Brookside, Milton Mills, Milton Abbas, Dorset DT11 0BQ]; *b* 7 Aug 1944; *educ* Sherborne; *m* 1st 28 Oct 1967 Marlene Kathleen, dau of Herbert Edwin Peet and widow of Lt-Cdr Earle Peter Weavind, and has issue:

1d *Rachel Katherine Louise; *b* 1972

1c (cont.) David Duncombe-Anderson *m* 2nd 1991 *Brenda Janet Goddard

1c *Jane Louise Valerie [Mrs Peter Clementson, Rose Cottage, Acre St, West Wittering, W Sussex]; *b* 28 June 1946; *m* 1st 3 Sept 1969 (*divorce* 19–) Charles Tatton Sykes, s of R T Sykes, of S Kensington, and has:

1d *Oliver Tatton; *b* 1974

2d *Nicholas Tatton; *b* 1977

1c (cont.) Mrs Jane Sykes *m* 2nd 1989 *Peter Clementson, FRICS

3b (cont.) Maj Wilfred Duncombe-Anderson *m* 2nd 22 April 1972 *Enid Mary Gabrielle (Gay), dau of Rev Charles Anthony van Charraute and widow of — Nicholl, and *d* 1982

1a Ethel Coralie; *b* 6 Nov 1872; *m* 11 July 1900 John Quayle, of Andover

(4) Sir GEORGE AUGUSTUS DUNCOMBE, 1st and last Bt (UK), so *cr* 16 May 1919, JP, DL (E R Yorks); *b* 25 May 1848; *educ* Harrow; Hon Col 3rd Bn E Yorks Regt; *m* 15 July 1890 Hester, yst dau of Col John McDermid Allardice, and had a s (*d* young); *dsps* 22 Nov 1933, when the btcy expired

(1) Charlotte; *m* 1st 12 May 1859 J A Sykes (*d* 1 Sept 1865), of Raywell, Yorks, and had issue; *m* 2nd 29 April 1889 Rev William Rowe Jolley, MA, Rector Huggate, Yorks, and *d* 30 Nov 1904

(2) Mary Louise Duncombe; *m* 1st 21 Feb 1871 Hon Ashley Carr Glyn (*see* WOLVERTON, B); *m* 2nd 1886 Rt Rev Isaac Hellmuth, DD, DCL, Bp of Huron (*d* 28 May 1901), and *d* 20 May 1919

(3) Edith Frances; *m* 22 April 1873 R-Adml Charles Francis Walker, s of Sir James Walker, 1st Bt of Sand Hutton (*qv*), and *d* 9 Oct 1906, leaving issue

4 (cont.) Arthur Duncombe *m* 2nd 13 March 1877 Jane Maria (*d* 23 Aug 1917), dau of Sir James Walker, 1st Bt of Sand Hutton (*qv*), and *d* 6 Feb 1889

5 Augustus (Very Rev); *b* 2 Nov 1814; DD, Dean York; *m* 13 May 1841 Lady Harriet Christian Douglas (*d* 26 July 1902), dau of 5th Marquess of Queensberry (*qv*), and *d* 26 Jan 1880, having had, with other issue:

(1) Alfred Charles, JP (Staffs and Derbys), of Calwich Abbey; *b* 5 June 1843; High Sheriff Staffs 1883 and CC, Capt 1st Life Gds and Maj Staffs Yeo Cavalry; *m* 5 Dec 1876 Lady Anne Florence Adelaide Montagu (*d* 16 Jan 1940), yst dau of 7th Earl of Sandwich (*qv*), and *dsp* 22 Feb 1925

(2) Adolphus Montagu, JP (W R Yorks); *b* 6 June 1852; Maj Yorks Hus; *m* 7 Dec 1881 Beatrice Dorothy Mary (*d* 8 July 1936), dau of Rev William Bridgeman-Simpson (*see* BRADFORD, E), and *dsp* 3 April 1904

(5) Octavius, of Waresley Park, Beds; *b* 8 April 1817; Lt 1st Life Gds, MP N R Yorks; *m* 31 March 1842 Lady Emily Caroline Campbell (*d* 22 May 1911), er dau of 1st Earl Cawdor (*qv*), and *d* 3 Dec 1879, having had, with other issue:

1a Walter Henry Octavius, of Waresley Park and Westerdale Hall, Grosmont, Yorks; *b* 21 May 1846; Capt 1st Life Gds and Hon Col 4th Bn Suffolk Regt, High Sheriff Cambs and Hunts 1899, CA Hunts; *d* unm 6 Jan 1917

1a Maud Augusta Louisa; *m* 22 July 1869 6th Baron Calthorpe (*see* 1970 edn) and *d* 9 March 1925, leaving issue

1 Frances; *m* 31 May 1832 Sir Thomas Digby Legard, 8th Bt (*qv*), of Ganton, Yorks, and *d* 15 June 1881

2 Louisa; *m* 1 Oct 1831 2nd Earl of Eldon (*qv*) and *d* 18 Nov 1852, leaving issue

FFOLKES

Arms: Quarterly, 1st, per pale vert and gu. a fleur-de-lys erm. (for FFOLKES); 2nd, sa. a crescent or (for HOVELL); 3rd, arg. a wolf rampant sa. (for FORD); 4th, arg. a fess erm. between three roses gu. (for LILLY). **Crest:** A dexter arm embowed, habited and parted as the field, the cuff doubled erm., the hand holding a javelin ppr.
Mottoes: 1 (over crest) *Qui sera sera* ('What will be, will be'), 2 (under arms) *Principiis obsta* ('Stand on your principles').
Creation: Bt. (GB) 26 May 1774.

SIR ROBERT FRANCIS ALEXANDER FFOLKES, 7TH BT, of Hillington, Norfolk, OBE (1990) [Sir Robert Ffolkes Bt OBE, Coast Guard House, Morston, Holt, Norfolk NR25 7BH]; *b* 2 Dec 1943; *s f* 1960; *educ* Stowe and Ch Ch Oxford

Lineage: SIMON FFOLKYS, of Westley Waterless, Cambs; *m* Margaret — and *d* 1508, leaving, with other issue:

MARTIN FFOLKYS; *d* 1569; probably f of:

MARTIN FOLKES, of Westerley Waterless; held lands in Westley, Burgh and Newmarket; *d* 1571/2, having had, with two yr sons (John, of the Nunrie, Swaffham Bulbeck, Cambs; Thomas, of Newmarket) and two daus (Joan, *m* 1st Stephen Hovell, of High Hall, Horningsea, Cambs, ancestor by her of the HOVELLs of Elstree, *m* 2nd Thomas Willowes/Willys, ancestor by her of the WILLYs Bts; Pernel, *m* — Clarke):

WILLIAM FOLKES, of Westley Waterless; *m* Agnes — and *d* 1594, leaving, with other issue, including an er s (Simon, of Westley and Burgh):

MARTIN FOLKES, of Rushbrook, Suffolk; *b* Nov 1579; *m* 1st 15 Oct 1617 Elizabeth (*d* Nov 1621), dau of Thomas Canham, of Lowestoft, and had issue; *m* 2nd Margaret Canham, of Rowdham, Norfolk (*d* Dec 1635), and by her had further issue; his s by his 1st w:

MARTIN FOLKES, of Rushbrook; *b* 14 Feb 1618/9; *m* Elizabeth Bourne (*d* 4 May 1687) and *d* 27 July 1671, having had an est s:

MARTIN FOLKES, of Hillington, Norfolk; lawyer; *b* 28 Aug 1640; *educ* Gray's Inn; barrister 1669–70, Bencher 1689–90, Slr-Gen 1695, Attorney-Gen 1697 to CATHERINE, widow of CHARLES II; *m* 2nd *c* 1683 Dorothy (*d* 22 Oct 1724), 2nd dau and coheir of Sir William Hovell, of Hillington, and *d* 17 Feb 1705, leaving:

1 Martin, of Hillington and Queen Sq, London; Pres Royal Soc; *b* 29 Oct 1690; *m* 18 Oct 1715 Lucy Bradshaw and *d* 28 June 1754, having had issue

2 WILLIAM

3 Henry, of Marylebone; *b* 17 Dec 1703; Mary — and *d* 1773, leaving issue:

(1) Elizabeth; *b* 23 Aug 1694; *m* 30 July 1715 Thomas Payne, of Hough, Lincs, and left issue

The 2nd son,

WILLIAM FOLKES, of Hillington, barrister Inner Temple; *b* 5 July 1700; *m* 1st Ursula, dau of Samuel Taylor, of King's Lynn, and had issue:

1 Ursula; *m* Adml John Macbride

2 Dorothy; *m* Edmund Rolfe, of Heacham, Norfolk, and had issue

3 Mary; *m* J B West

4 Elizabeth; *m* M Western

WILLIAM FOLKES *m* 2nd 1747 — (*d* 8 April 1773), dau and heir of Sir William Browne, MD, of King's Lynn, Pres Royal Coll of Physicians, and *d* 10 April 1773, having by her had:

(1) **Sir Martin Browne Ffolkes, 1st Bt** (GB), so *cr* 26 May 1774; FRS; *b* May 1740; *m* 28 Dec 1777 Fanny (*d* 30 Nov 1813), dau and coheir of Sir John Turner, Bt, of Warham, Norfolk, and had, with other issue:

1a WILLIAM JOHN HENRY BROWNE (Sir), **2nd Bt**

1a Fanny Mary; *b* 1778; *m* Gilbert Harvey West, and *d* 1813

2a Lucretia Georgiana; *m* 26 Aug 1822 Sir Edward West, Recorder of Bombay, and *d* 15 Oct 1828

Sir MARTIN *d* 11 Dec 1821; his only surv son,

Sir William John Henry Browne Ffolkes, 2nd Bt; FRS; *b* 30 Aug 1786; *m* 21 April 1818 Charlotte Philippa (*d* 23 Dec 1882), sis of 1st Baron Oranmore and Browne (*qv*), and *d* 24 March 1860, having had, with other issue:

1 Martin William Browne, of Congham Lodge, Norfolk; *b* 16 Jan 1819; *m* 30 March 1843 Henrietta Bridget (*d* 14 Nov 1855), 2nd dau of Gen Sir Charles Wale, KCB, of Little Shelford, Cambs, and *dvp* 12 July 1849, having had:

(1) **Sir William Hovell Browne Ffolkes, 3rd Bt**, KCVO, JP, DL Norfolk; Hon Maj 2nd Bde Eastern Div RA, High Sheriff Norfolk 1876, Chm and Alderman Norfolk CC, MP King's Lynn, 1880–85; *b* 21 Nov 1847; *educ* Harrow and Trin Coll Cambridge (MA); *m* 6 April 1875 Emily Charlotte (*d* 30 Sept 1915), 3rd dau of Robert Elwes, JP, DL, of Congham House, Norfolk, and *d* 9 May 1912, leaving:

1a Dorothy; *b* 21 June 1876; *m* 24 July 1902 9th Viscount Downe (*qv*) and *d* 26 March 1957, leaving issue

(2) Martin William Browne; CE; *b* 19 July 1849; *m* 28 Jan 1882 Wilhelmine Mary Emily (*d* 1 Nov 1943), dau of Lt-Col John Davy Brett, 17th Lancers, and *d* 3 Nov 1901, leaving issue:

1a Audrey; *m* 1st 14 Nov 1912 Rev Alfred Edward Alston (*d* 13 May 1927), Rector Framingham Earl Norfolk, and had issue; *m* 2nd 25 Aug 1932 W Lincolne Sutton, FIC (*d* 1959), and *d* 1 July 1966

2a Barbara, DBE (1923); *b* 2 April 1884; *m* 1st 23 Feb 1911 Capt Francis Joseph Cresswell (*ka* 23 Aug 1914), Norfolk Regt, and had issue; *m* 2nd 17 July 1918 Gen Sir Edward Peter Strickland, KCB, KBE, CMG, DSO, DL (*d* 23 June 1951), of The Old Hall, Snettisham, Norfolk, and *d* 20 March 1977, leaving issue

3a Cynthia Mary; *m* 1st 1 Nov 1913 (*divorce* 1918) Philip Francis Hamilton Bedingfeld (*d* 17 March 1955), of Madul Kelle, Ceylon; *m* 2nd 19 April 1920 Charles Augustus Hare, of Heacham, King's Lynn, Norfolk, and *d* 28 April 1967

(1) Etheldreda Isabella; *m* 26 Sept 1871 Henry Birkbeck (*d* 1 Feb 1895), of Stoke Holy Cross, Norwich, and *d* 16 Nov 1939, leaving issue

2 Henry Edward Browne (Rev); Rector Hillington, RD Lynn, Norfolk; *b* 20 Dec 1823; *educ* Univ Coll Oxford (MA); *m* 24 April 1860 Sophia Louisa (*d* 23 March 1916), 2nd dau of Rev Edward Browne Everard, Rector Burnham Thorpe, Norfolk, and *d* 24 March 1912, having had, with other issue:

(1) **Sir William Everard Browne Ffolkes, 4th Bt**, JP Norfolk; Lt 4th Bn Suffolk Regt, Hon Capt 3rd Vol Bn Norfolk Regt; *b* 15 Feb 1861; *m* 21 April 1896 Sybil Compton (*d* 8 April 1947), dau of Rev Richard Compton Maul, Rector Rickinghall, Suffolk, and *d* 15 Dec 1930, having had:

1a William Rupert Compton; Lt KRRC; *b* 7 Aug 1898; *ka* 30 Dec 1917

(2) Edward George Everard, of Toronto; *b* 24 Jan 1862; *m* 1891 Agnes, er dau of John Strachan, of Goderio, Canada, Judge, and gdau of Rt Rev John Strachan, 1st Bp Toronto, and *dsp* accidentally drowned Toronto 1 April 1916

(3) FRANCIS ARTHUR STANLEY (Sir), **5th Bt**

(4) Robert Walling Everard; *b* 1 Feb 1865; *m* 1884 Ada (*d* 1906), dau of Col — Brierley, and *d* 27 April 1931, leaving issue:

1a Mary Emily Margaret; *b* 1885; *m* 1910 Douglas Lancaster Jemmett (*d* 21 June 1937), of Ottawa, and *d* 19 Nov 1968, leaving issue

2a Evelyn Maud; *b* 1889

3a Muriel Everard; *b* 1891; *m* 1916 Maj Alan Clarkson McCaul, Canadian Army, and had issue

(5) Geoffrey Charles Hovell; *b* 3 Aug 1867; *m* 27 Jan 1897 Edith Louise Pollen (*d* 28 Oct 1921), widow of Rev Charles E Cumings and dau of Frederick Haworth, and *dsp* 6 March 1943

(6) Harold Lewis Henry; *b* 20 Aug 1873; drowned Oxford 12 Feb 1892

(1) Margaret Louisa Everard; *m* 1st 4 May 1888 Rev John Erasmus Philipps, MA (*d* 3 May 1923), Vicar Staindrop, Darlington, Rector Cockfield, Durham, Domestic Chaplain to Lord Barnard, and had issue; *m* 2nd 15 June 1926 17th Viscount Dillion (*qv*) of Costello-Gallin and *d* 12 July 1954

(2) Helen Sophia Everard; *d* unm 24 Jan 1961

(3) Charlotte Philippa Marian Everard; *m* 25 Oct 1894 Sir Augustus Vere Foster, 4th Bt (*d* 7 Nov 1947), and *d* 29 Sept 1938, having had issue

(4) Mabel Olive Emily; *d* unm

1 Margaret, Charlotte; *m* 8 July 1847 Francis Hay Gurney (*d* 1 Dec 1890), of N Runcton, Norfolk, and *d* 23 May 1899 leaving issue

The 4th Bt's bro,

Rev Sir Francis Arthur Stanley Ffolkes, 5th Bt, MVO (1908), JP; Rector Hillington, Norfolk, and Chaplain-in-Ordinary to TM EDWARD VII, GEORGE V 1910–36, EDWARD VIII 1936 and GEORGE VI 1937, Chaplain KO Norfolk Yeo, Hon Chaplain to TM QUEEN VICTORIA 1900–01 and EDWARD VII 1901–03, SCF to 74th Div Egyptian Expdny Force WW I (despatches); *b* 8 Dec 1863; *m* 27 Sept 1893 Isabel Laura Newbery (*d* 16 April 1941), 7th dau of John Newbery Boschetti, of Eccles, Lancs, and *d* 19 Oct 1938, leaving:

1 **Sir (Edward John) Patrick (Boschetti) Ffolkes, 6th Bt**; *b* 16 Jan 1899; *educ* Gresham's and RMC Sandhurst; IA WW II and E African Forces; *m* 15 Dec 1939 Geraldine (Gill) (*d* 10 Feb 1978), dau of William Thomas Roffey, of Writtle, Essex, and *d* 27 March 1960, leaving:

(1) Sir ROBERT FRANCIS ALEXANDER FFOLKES, **7th and present Bt**

(1) *Sara Elizabeth [Mrs Jocelyn Wingfield, 18 Chiddingstone St, London SW6 3TG]; *b* 4 Dec 1946; *m* 25 May 1968 *Maj Jocelyn James Rhys Wingfield (*see* POWERSCOURT, V) and has issue

1 Philippa Frances Boschetti; *b* 12 June 1896; *d* unm 3 July 1968

ffRENCH

Arms: Erm. a chevron sa. **Crest:** A dolphin embowed ppr. **Supporters:** Dexter, a falcon gu., armed, membered, belled and wings inverted or; sinister, a unicorn gu., armed, unguled, crined and tufted or, holding in the mouth a rose branch with two red roses thereon. **Motto:** *Malo mori quam foedari* ('I had rather die than be dishonoured') or *Mors potius macula* ('Death before dishonour'). **Creations:** Bt. (I) 17 Aug 1779, B. (I) 12 March 1798.

THE 8TH BARON ffRENCH OF CASTLE ffRENCH, Co Galway, and a **Baronet** (Sir Robuck John Peter Charles Mario ffrench, Bt) [The Rt Hon The Lord ffrench, Clonbrock, Ahascragh, Co Galway, Ireland]; *b* 14 March 1956; *s* f 1986; *educ* Ampleforth and Blackrock Co Dublin; *m* 1987 *Dörthe Marie-Louise, dau of Capt Wilhelm Schauer, of Zürich, and has:

1 *Tara Elise Sofia Eleonora; *b* 1993

Lineage: The common ancestor of the BARONS ffRENCH and DE FREYNE was WALTER ffRENCH, of Wexford and subsequently Galway 1425; Ch Magistrate Galway 1444–45; ancestor of:

JOHN ffRENCH; Mayor Galway 1538–39; *d* 1545, leaving, with an er s (Dominick):

ROBUCK ffRENCH; Mayor Galway 1582–83; *d* 27 Jan 1598, leaving, with a yr s (Walter):

EDMUND ffRENCH; Mayor Galway 1606–07; *d c* 1618, leaving, with an er s (Dominick):

JOHN ffRENCH; bought by 1636 the castle and lands of Clogher (now Castle ffrench) in the Baronies of Kilconnell and Killyan, Co Galway, and *d* 1642, leaving:

JASPER ffRENCH, of Clogher; deprived of his estate 1655 by the Cromwellian Commissions but bought it back again 1671 (confirmed 1677); rebuilt the castle 1683; had, with an er s (Patrick, *m* 1 April 1676 Barbara, 2nd dau of Anthony ffrench, of Calla, and *dsp* & *vp*):

MARTIN ffRENCH, of Clogher; *m* —, dau of — Lynch, of Levally, and had issue:

THOMAS ffRENCH, of Clogher; *m* 3 June 1717 Clara, dau of Charles Hamilton, of Fairfield, Co Galway, and *d* 21 July 1755, leaving, with other issue:

1 Martin; Dominican friar; *bur* Athenry Abbey after 1783

2 CHARLES (Sir), **1st Bt**

1 Anne; *m* Patrick Lynch (Fitzmark), of Galway, merchant, and had issue

The 2nd son,

Sir Charles ffrench, 1st Bt (I), so *cr* 17 Aug 1779, of Castle ffrench (otherwise Clogher), Co Galway, Mayor Galway 1773–74; *m* 25 June 1761 Rose (*d* 8 Dec 1805), *cr* 12 March 1798 **Baroness ffrench of Castle ffrench**, Co Galway (I), with remainder to her issue by her late husband (peerage conferred in recognition of services rendered by their only son Sir Thomas Hamilton ffrench, a leading memb of the Catholic Ctee in the 1790s; GEORGE III's objection to promoting Catholics entailed ennobling the mother (nominally Protestant) rather than son (a strict Catholic)), est dau of Patrick Dillon, of Roscommon, and *d* between 11 Jan 1783 and 20 Oct 1784, leaving, with other issue:

1 THOMAS HAMILTON, **2nd Baron**

1 Catherine; *m* 1st *c* 3 Dec 1787 Anthony Brabazon, of Birch Grove, Co Galway, and had issue (*see below*); *m* 2nd 1804 Edmund Whitehead and *d* 10 Jan 1833, having had further issue

2 Jane; *m* 18 July 1787 Sir Gonville Bromhead, 1st Bt (*qv*), and *d* 2 Sept 1837, having had issue

BARONESS ffRENCH's only son,

Sir Thomas ffrench, 2nd Bt, and **2nd Baron ffrench of Castle ffrench**; *m* 1785 Margaret (*d* 7 Dec 1849), est dau of Thomas Redington, of Kilcornan, Co Galway, and had, with other issue:

1 CHARLES AUSTIN, **3rd Baron**

2 Martin; *b* April 1793; *m* 1 Dec 1825 Margaret (*d* 25 Sept 1882), 2nd dau of Maj Thomas Bodkin, of Rahoon, Co Galway, and *d* 27 Nov 1871, having had, with other issue:

(1) Thomas; *b* Jan 1833; *m* March 1859 Victoria (*m* 2nd Maj-Gen Andrew Browne, CB (*d* 8 April 1883), and had issue), dau of Maurice Blake, of Ballinafad, Co Mayo, and *dsp* 30 May 1859

(1) Josephine; *m* 1872 Walter Eakins, of Richmond Spa, Well Road, Wexford, and had issue

(2) Anne; *m* 10 July 1865 Michael Joseph Chevers, of Killyan, Co Galway, and *d* 3 Oct 1898. He *d* 10 April 1889

3 Nicholas; RC priest; *b* Feb 1796; *d* 1 July 1838

4 Gonville, of Clarmont, Co Roscommon; *b* May 1797; *m* 16 July 1823 Clare (*d* 12 Oct 1864), yst dau of William Kennedy, of Kilclogher, Co Galway, and *dsp* 29 April 1866

1 Sarah; *m* 14 Oct 1810 Edward J Beytagh, of Cappagh, Co Galway. He *d* 19 March 1832

2 Rose; *m* 14 Oct 1810 Francis Blake Foster, of Ashfield, Co Galway, and *d* 13 Dec 1857

The 2nd BARON *d* 9 Dec 1814; his est son,

CHARLES AUSTIN ffRENCH, **3rd Baron ffrench of Castle ffrench**; *b* 9 April 1786; *m* 26 Sept 1809 Maria (*d* June 1827), est dau of John Browne, of Moyne, Co Galway, and *d* 25 Sept 1860, having had, with other issue:

1 THOMAS ffRENCH, **4th Baron ffrench of Castle ffrench**, DL; *b* 13 Sept 1810; *m* 18 Oct 1851 Mary Anne (*d* 3 June 1906), only dau and heiress of Richard Thompson, of Stansty Hall, Denbighshire, and *d* 20 Jan 1892, leaving a dau

2 John; RC priest; *b* 5 Aug 1812; *d* 31 May 1873

3 MARTIN JOSEPH, **5th Baron**

1 Margaret; *m* 7 Jan 1836 Valentine O'Connor Blake, of Tower Hill, Co Mayo, and *d* 16 July 1869. He *d* 9 Aug 1879

The 4th BARON's bro,

MARTIN JOSEPH ffRENCH, **5th Baron ffrench of Castle ffrench**, JP; barrister, RM Co Tipperary 1846–82; *b* 1 Oct 1813; *m* 2 July 1862 his cousin Catherine Mary Anne (*d* 6 March 1908), only dau of John O'Shaughnessy, of Birchgrove, Galway, by Ellen, dau of Anthony Brabazon, of Birchgrove, and Catherine (dau of **Sir Charles ffrench, 1st Bt**; *see* above), and *d* 2 Nov 1893, having had issue:

1 CHARLES AUSTIN THOMAS ROBERT JOSEPH ffRENCH, **6th Baron ffrench of Castle ffrench**; *b* 20 June 1868; *m* 1st 1 Sept 1892 Margaret (*d* 27 May 1944), dau of Matthew James Corbally, DL, of Rathbeale Hall, Co Dublin, and had issue:

(1) Martin Joseph Mathew; *b* 26 July 1893; *d* 26 Jan 1894

1 (cont.) The **6th Baron** *m* 2nd 8 June 1951 Catherine Elizabeth (*d* 25 July 1960), yst dau of Sir Christopher John Nixon, 1st Bt (*qv*), and *dspms* 4 March 1955

2 John Martin Valentine Joseph; Capt 7th (Service) Bn Leinster Regt, Kt SMO 1932; *b* 19 July 1872; *m* 27 March 1915 Sophia, yst dau of Giovanni Brambila, of Villa Sucota, Como, Italy, and *d* 7 May 1946, leaving issue:

(1) PETER MARTIN JOSEPH CHARLES JOHN ffRENCH, **7th Baron ffrench of Castle ffrench**; *b* 2 May 1926; *m* 5 Aug 1954 *Katherine Sonia, 2nd dau of Digby Coddington Cayley, JP, of Rougham Chantry, Bury St Edmunds (*see* CAYLEY, Bt), and *d* 1986, leaving:

1a ROBUCK JOHN PETER CHARLES MARIO ffRENCH, **8th and present Baron ffrench of Castle ffrench**

1a *Rose Sofia Iris Mary; *b* 27 Jan 1957; *m* 1989 *Dr Albert Alois Fuchs, only s of Albert Alois Fuchs, of Pocking, Bavaria, and has issue:

1b *Julia Katherina Sonia Mariele; *b* 1992

2a *Clare Katharine Grace Mary; *b* 18 July 1958; *m* 1989 *Alexander Timothy Joynson and has issue:

1b *Peter William; *b* 1994

(2) +JOHN CHARLES MARY JOSEPH FRANCIS [John ffrench Esq, PO Box 323, 11 Main St, Stockbridge, MA 01262, USA]; *b* 5 Oct 1928; heir presumptive; *m* 1963 *Sara-Primm, dau of James A Turner, of Stockbridge, and has:

1a *Johanna Felicitas; *b* 1964

2a *Teodora Crispina; *b* 1965

3a *Dorcas Sofia; *b* 1967

(1) *Frieda Dora Katherine Mary Josephine [Mrs Hans Vajda, 16 Wakefield Rd, London N15]; *b* 24 March 1916; *m* 30 Nov 1946 *Hans Vajda, of Budapest, and has issue

(2) *Katherine Mary Margaret Frances Josephine; *b* 25 June 1917; *m* 17 Dec 1935 *Lt Christopher Valerio Edward Paul Banon, RN, est s of Christopher Banon, of Broughall Castle, Kilcormack, Co Offaly, and has had:

1a *Christopher Benedict Edward Patrick Fitzsimon [Christopher Banon Esq, Carrig, Mount William Rd, Lancefield 3435, Victoria, Australia]; *b* 1943; *m* 1969 *—

1a Susan Anne Katherine; *b* 1940; *m* 1970 *Ronald Senior and *d* 1980 leaving:

1b *Jaqueline; *b* 4 Aug 1974

2a *Camilla Mary Rose [Miss Camilla Banon, Carrig, Mount William Rd, Lancefield 3435, Victoria, Australia]; *b* 1947

3a *Clemency Mary Katherine [Mrs John Simpson, 25 Packenham St, Blackburn 3130, Victoria, Australia]; *b* 24 Nov 1956; *m* 1981 *John Robert Simpson and has:

1b *Robert Keith Christopher; *b* 24 Nov 1990

(3) *Ellen Frances Anna-Maria Josephine [Mrs Thomas Agnew, Cregmore, Ardrahan, Co Galway, Ireland]; *b* 1 Dec 1918; *m* 14 Dec 1946 *Thomas Anderson Courtney Agnew

1 Ellen Mary Anne Josephine; nun; *d* 29 Sept 1918

2 Maria Anne Josephine Catherine; nun; *d* 1928

3 Frances Catherine Mary Anne Josephine; *d* unm 28 Aug 1940

4 Margaret Elizabeth Mary Anne Josephine; *d* unm 18 Sept 1945

1a *Nicholas John Mary; *b* 1950

1a *Catherine Mary; *b* 1948

2a Lucillla Veronica Maria Sophia; *b* 1952; *d* 1974

FIFE

Arms: Quarterly, 1st grandquarterly, or a lion rampant gu., armed and langued az. (for DUKEDOM OF FIFE); 2nd grandquarter, counter-quartered, 1st and 4th, gu. three lions passant guardant in pale or (for ENGLAND), 2nd, or a lion rampant within a double tressure flory counter-flory gu. (for SCOTLAND), 3rd, az. a harp or, stringed arg. (for IRELAND); differenced by a label of five points arg., the points charged with two thistles between three crosses of St George gu. (for HRH THE PRINCESS ROYAL, DUCHESS OF FIFE); 3rd grandquarter, counter-quartered, 1st and 4th, vert a fess dancettée erm. between a hart's head cabossed in chief and two escallops in base or (for DUFF of Braco); 2nd and 3rd, gu. three skeans paleways argent, hafted and pommelled or, surmounted of as many wolf heads couped of the third (for SKENE of that Ilk); 4th grandquarter, gu. a banner displayed arg. charged wih a canton az., a saltire of the second (for BANNERMAN of Elsick); over all an inescutcheon ensigned of an earl's coronet arg., an eagle displayed az., armed, beaked and membered gu., on its breast an antique covered cup or (for CARNEGIE). **Crests:** 1 (centre) a thunderbolt ppr., winged or (for CARNEGIE), 2 (dexter) a knight (denoting the ancient MacDuff) armed at all points on a horse at full speed, in his dexter hand a sword erect, all ppr., his jupon arg., on his sinister arm a shield or charged with a lion rampant gu., the visor of his helmet shut, over which, on a wreath of his liveries with a long mantling flowing therefrom behind him and ending in a tassel of the fourth, doubling of the third, is set a lion rampant issuing out of the wreath of the third and fourth, the caparisons of the horse gu., fimbriated or, and thereon six shields of the last, each charged with a lion rampant of the fourth (for DUKEDOM OF FIFE), 3 (sinister) a man in armour, issuing from the loins and wearing a tabard emblazoned of the arms arg. on a fess between three boar's heads erased gu. three mascles or, sustaining with his dexter hand a banner developed arg. having a canton az. charged with a saltire of the first (for ETHEL BANNERMAN, COUNTESS OF SOUTHESK). **Supporters:** Dexter, a lion rampant guardant gu., armed and langued az., charged with a label of five points arg., the points charged with two thistles between three crosses of St George gu.; sinister, a talbot arg., collared gu., the collar charged with a label of three points arg. **Mottoes:** 1 (over the shield) *Deo juvante* ('God helping'), 2 Dred God, 3 *Pro patria* ('For my country'), 4 (under the shield) *Virtute et opera* ('By virtue and through work'). **Creations:** L. (S) 14 April 1616 (Carnegie of Kinnaird), E. and L. (Carnegie of Kinnaird and Leuchars) (S) 22 June 1633, Bt. (NS) 20 Feb 1663, B. (UK) 7 Dec 1869, D. and E. (Macduff) (UK) 24 April 1900.

THE 3RD DUKE OF FIFE, **Earl of Southesk**, **Earl of Macduff**, **Lord Carnegie of Kinnaird**, **Lord Carnegie of Kinnaird and Leuchars**, **Baron Balinhard of Farnell**, Co Forfar, and a **Baronet** (Sir James George Alexander Bannerman Carnegie, Bt) [His Grace The Duke of Fife, Kinnaird Castle, Brechin, Angus DD9 6TZ; Elsick House, Stonehaven, Kincardineshire AB39 3NT]; *b* 23 Sept 1929 (HM GEORGE V stood sponsor); *s* aunt as 3rd Duke 1959, *s* f as 12th Earl of Southesk and 9th Bt 1992; *educ* Gordonstoun and RAC Cirencester; Malaya 1948–50 with Scots Gds; Freeman City London 1954, Liveryman Clothworkers' Co 1954, Pres ABA 1959 (V-Pres 1969–76), Life Memb Br Olympic Assoc, Dep Pres W Ham Boys Club, V-Patron Braemar Highland Soc, Ship's Pres HMS *Fife* 1967–87; *m* 11 Sept 1956 (*divorce* 1966) Hon Caroline Cicely Dewar (*m* 2nd 7 Nov 1980, as his 2nd w, Gen Sir Richard (Edward) Worsley, GCB, OBE), er dau of 3rd Baron Forteviot (*qv*), and has issue:

1 +DAVID CHARLES, *Earl of Southesk* [Earl of Southesk, Kinnaird Castle, Brechin, Angus DD9 6TZ]; *b* 3 March 1961; *educ* Eton, Pembroke Coll Cambridge (BA 1982, MA 1986), RAC Cirencester and Edinburgh U (MBA 1990); with Cazenove 1982–85, Bell Lawrie and Co 1988–89; Chartered Accountant

with Reeves and Neylan 1992–96; *m* 1987 *Caroline, only dau of Martin Bunting, MBE, of Odiham, Hants, and has:

(1) +Charles Duff, *Lord Carnegie*; *b* 1 July 1989

(2) +George William; *b* 23 March 1992

(3) +Hugh Alexander; *b* 10 June 1993

1 *Alexandra Clare; *b* 20 June 1959 (HM THE KING OF NORWAY and HRH PRINCESS ALICE DUCHESS OF GLOUCESTER stood sponsors); memb Roy Geographical Soc

Fife, previous creations: Fife constituted one of the Mormaerships (*see* BUCHAN, E, for further details) into which much of pre-1st Millennium Scotland was divided. By the beginning of the 12th century the former Mormaer of Fife was beginning to be called Earl of Fife. The first of the new designation seems to have been Beth, who as either Earl of Fife or of Moray (more probably the former) is recorded as having been active in 1115. (The historic figure Macbeth was son of a Mormaer of Moray, and since *Mac* means 'son of' there may be a connection.) However, another figure referred to as Earl of Fife about the same time, that is to say during the reign of DAVID I (reigned 1124–53), is a shadowy personage called in contemporary documents either 'Ed' or 'Head' and identified by leading authorities with Edelread, son of MALCOLM III (reigned 1058–93). Yet a third Earl of Fife appears to have existed in the person of Constantine, who died in the late 1120s. (It is possible that 'Ed'/'Head' was really Earl of Forthreve.)

The first person to hold the Earldom of Fife on a hereditary basis may well have been Gillemicel Macduff, who died about the mid-1130s. Certainly the title remained in his family, passing almost always from father to son, till 1353, when the 8th Earl's only child, Elizabeth or Isabel, became Countess of Fife. She married four times, each of her husbands being known as Earl of Fife in right of his wife. She died without issue, having made over the Earldom to her second husband's brother Robert Stewart, Earl of Menteith, her 2nd husband and he being second and third sons respectively of ROBERT II. For further details of the Earldom of Fife thereafter, *see* MORAY, E.

Lineage (of Duff): The lands of Muldavit, Banffshire, were granted 1404 by ROBERT III to David Duff and his wife Agnes Chalmer, dau of Maud of Muldavate, but were sold by John Duff of Muldavit to the INNESEes 1481, though bought back by his gs Andrew Duff 1504.

JOHN DUFF; had charter of Muldavit 1550; *m* 1st — and had a s (John, sold Muldavit 1626); *m* 2nd Margaret Gordon (*m* 2nd Walter Ogilvie of Milton), of the Cairnbarrow family, and *d c* 1598, having by her had, with ten other sons and at least one dau (Margaret Ogilvie, *m* by 1666 John Stewart of Ardbreck):

ADAM DUFF, in Ardrone and later in Clunybeg; royalist Civil War; *d c* 1674, leaving an est s:

ALEXANDER DUFF of Keithmore; bought much land in Banffshire and Aberdeenshire just prior to the Union of S and E Parls 1707, a time when many of the old lairds were greatly impoverished; *m* Helen (*d* 1694), heiress dau of Archibald Grant of Ballentomb (see GRANT, Bt, of Monymusk), and *d c* 1700, having had:

1 Alexander, of Braco, Banffshire; *b* 1650; added greatly to the estates acquired by his father, which by now included Aberlour, Keith, Grange and Mortlach, the latter including Balveny; MP Banffshire *c* 1707, WS; *m* Margaret, dau of Sir William Gordon, Bt, of Lesmore (*see* 1834 edn), and had, with three daus:

(1) William, of Braco; *m* 1706 Helen Taylor and *dspms* 1718

2 WILLIAM

3 Patrick, of Craigston; *m* Anne Innes (*see* INNES, Bt, of Balvenie, Bt); ancestor of the DUFFs of Hatton and DUFFs of Fetteresso

The 2nd son,

WILLIAM DUFF, of Dipple, Banffshire, which he bought with Pluscardine and other estates in Morayshire; *m* 1st Helen, dau of Sir George Gordon of Edinglassie, and had issue; *m* 2nd Jean, dau of Sir William Dunbar, Bt, of Durn (*qv*), and by her had issue; *d* 1722, leaving his estates (whose annual rental of £6,500 (almost £400,000 in late-1990s terms) then represented the largest fortune in the north of Scotland) to his only s by his 1st w:

WILLIAM DUFF, 1st EARL FIFE, so *cr* 29 April 1759, as also VISCOUNT MACDUFF and earlier BARON BRACO OF KILBRYDE, Co Cavan (all I), of Braco and Dipple; *b* 1697; MP (Whig) Banffshire 1727–34; bought large estates in Aberdeenshire, Banffshire and Morayshire; built the new castle or house of Balvenie *c* 1724, also (for £70,000 (over £4m in late-1990s terms)) Duff House 1740–45; supported Govt 1745 Uprising; *m* 1st 1719 Janet (*dsp* 1721), dau of 1st Earl of Seafield (*qv*) and widow of Hugh Forbes, Yr. of Craigievar (*see* FORBES, Bt, of Craigievar); *m* 2nd 1723 Jean (*d* 16 Jan 1788 aged 82), 2nd dau of Sir James Grant or Colquhoun, Bt (*see* COLQUHOUN, Bt), and *d* 30 Sept 1763, having had by her, with other issue:

1 JAMES DUFF, 2nd EARL FIFE; *b* 28 Sept 1729; MP (Whig to 1783, Pittite thereafter) Banffshire 1754–84 and Morayshire 1784–90; nearly doubled the family acreage by astute purchases; renamed the town of Doune Macduff and got it made into a burgh 1783; *cr* 5 July 1790 BARON OF FIFE, Co Fife (GB); Ld Lt Banffshire 1795–1809; *m* 4 June 1759 Lady Dorothea Sinclair, only child of 9th Earl of Caithness (*qv*), and *dsp* 24 Jan 1809, when the GB Barony expired

2 ALEXANDER, 3rd Earl

3 George; *m* 7 April 1757 Frances, dau of Gibson Dalziel and gdau of Gen Robert Dalziel by Ann Maria, dau of Sir John Gibson (*see* GIBSON-CRAIG-CARMICHAEL, Bt), and *d* 23 Nov 1818, leaving:

(1) George

4 Ludovic; Capt 8th Regt; *m* Deborah, dau of Griffith Davis, and *dsp* 14 Oct 1811

5 Arthur, of Orton; advocate; MP Elginshire 1774–79; *d* unm 20 April 1805

1 Janet; *m* 1st Sir William Gordon, Bt, of Park (attainted and *d* Douai 1751); *m* 2nd George Hay of Montblary and *d* 3 March 1758

2 Jane; *m* 25 Oct 1753 Keith Urquhart of Meldrum, Sheriff Banffshire

3 Helen; *m* 1764 her cousin Robert Duff of Logie and Fetteresso (*d* 6 June 1787), V-Adml the Red, and *d* 20 Sept 1778, leaving issue

4 Sophia Henrietta; *m* 13 July 1774 Thomas Wharton, Commr Excise Scotland, and had issue

5 Margaret; *m* 6 March 1768 James Brodie of Brodie (*d* 17 Jan 1824) and *d* in a fire 24 April 1786, leaving issue

The 2nd EARL's bro,

ALEXANDER DUFF, 3rd EARL FIFE; *b* 1731; *m* 17 Aug 1775 Mary, dau of George Skene of Skene, Aberdeenshire, and *d* 17 April 1811, having had issue:

1 JAMES DUFF, 4th EARL FIFE, KT (1827), GCH (1823); *b* 6 Oct 1776; *educ* Westminster and Oxford; Maj-Gen Spanish army Peninsular War (wounded Battle of Talavera 1809 and capture of Fort Matagorda, near Cadiz, 1810 (Kt of San Fernando Spain and Sword of Sweden)); inherited through his mother the Skene and Cariston estates 1827; a great collector of paintings; Ld Lt Banffshire 1813–56, MP (Tory) Banffshire 1818–27, a Ld Bedchamber 1819–21 and 1827–35, *cr* 27 April 1827 BARON FIFE, Co Fife (UK); *m* 9 Sept 1799 Mary Caroline (*d* 20 Dec 1805), 2nd dau of John Manners by Louisa, Countess of Dysart (*qv*) in her own right, and *dsp* 9 March 1857, when the UK Barony expired

2 Alexander (Sir), GCH, of Delgaty Castle, Aberdeenshire; Gen, Col 37th Foot; Lt and Sheriff-Pncpl Elgin; *m* 16 March 1812 Anne (*d* 14 Feb 1859), yst dau of James Stein, of Kilbogie, and *d* 21 March 1851, leaving issue:

(1) JAMES, 5th Earl

(2) George Skene; *b* 13 Sept 1816; MP Elgin 1847–57, Ld Lt Morayshire; granted with sisters 2 June 1857 rank of earl's dau/yr s; *d* 15 March 1889

(1) Catherine; *m* 11 Aug 1841 John Lewis Ricardo, DL, MP (*d* 20 Aug 1862), and *d* 6 Dec 1869, leaving issue

(2) Louisa; *m* 12 Dec 1848 Sir Richard Brooke, 7th Bt (*qv*), of Norton Priory, and *d* 23 Sept 1864, leaving issue

1 Jane; *m* 2 Dec 1802 Maj Alexander Francis Tayler, 21st Foot, and *d* 22 May 1850

2 Anne; *m* 16 Oct 1809 Richard Wharton Duff, of Orton, and *d* 24 Jan 1829

3 Sarah; *m* 20 June 1807 Daniel Collyer, of Gray's Inn, and *d* 1811

4 Mary; *d* young

The 4th EARL's nephew,

JAMES DUFF, 5th EARL FIFE, KT (1860); *b* 6 July 1814; MP (Lib) Banffshire 1837–57, Ld Lt Elgin 1851–56 and Banffshire 1856–79, *cr* 1 Oct 1857 BARON SKENE, of Skene, Co Aberdeen (UK); *m* 16 March 1846 Lady Agnes Georgiana Elizabeth Hay (*d* 18 Dec 1869), dau of 17th Earl of Erroll (*qv*), and had issue:

1 ALEXANDER WILLIAM GEORGE, **1st Duke**

1 Anne Elizabeth Clementina; *m* 17 Oct 1865 5th Marquess Townshend (*qv*), and *d* 31 Dec 1925, leaving issue

2 Ida Louisa Alice; *m* 1st 3 June 1867 (*divorce*) Adrian Elias Hope and had issue; *m* 2nd 20 Sept 1880 William Wilson (*d* 16 Feb 1905), of Hill Street, Mayfair, and *d* 29 May 1918

3 Alexina; *m* 2 July 1870 Henry Aubrey Coventry (*see* COVENTRY, E) and *dsp* 30 April 1882

4 Agnes Cecil Emmeline; *m* 1st 4 Oct 1871 (*divorce* 1876) Viscount Dupplin (*see* KINNOULL, E); *m* 2nd 5 Aug 1876 Herbert Flower (*d* 30 Dec 1880); *m* 3rd 4 July 1882 Sir Alfred Cooper, FRCS, and *d* 11 Jan 1925, leaving issue (*see* NORWICH, V)

The 5th EARL *d* 7 Aug 1879; his only son,

ALEXANDER WILLIAM GEORGE DUFF, **1st Duke of Fife**, so *cr* 24 April 1900, as also EARL OF MACDUFF, Co Banff, with special remainder, in default of male issue, to his first and other daus by his then w, and their male issue, also earlier 13 July 1885 EARL OF FIFE and 29 July 1889 MARQUESS OF MACDUFF, Co Fife, and DUKE OF FIFE (all UK), with remainder to the heirs male of his body, KG (1911), KT (1881), GCVO (1901), VD , PC (1880), DL (Cos Aberdeen and Banff); *b* 10 Nov 1849; *educ* Eton; MP (Lib) Elgin and Nairn 1874–79, Ld Lt Elgin 1871–1902, Capt Gentlemen-at-Arms 1880–81, Hon Col Banffshire Artillery Vols 1884–1908, Ld Lt and Custos Rotulorum London 1900–12, Pres TFA Co London 1908–12, ptnr Sir Samuel Scott & Co, bankers; fndr Chartered Co S Africa; Memb Cncl Duchy Lancaster, Ld High Constable Coronations 1902 and 1911, Roy Victorian Chain; *m* in the chapel at Buckingham Palace 27 July 1889 HRH PRINCESS LOUISE VICTORIA ALEXANDRA DAGMAR, THE PRINCESS ROYAL, VA, CI, Col-in-Ch 4th/7th Dragoon Gds (*d* 4 Jan 1931), est dau of HM EDWARD VII, and *dspm* 29 Jan 1912, when all his titles expired bar those *cr* 1900, leaving:

1 HH PRINCESS ALEXANDRA VICTORIA ALBERTA EDWINA LOUISE, **Duchess of Fife** in her own right; *b* 17 May 1891; Counsellor of State during Sovereign's absence abroad 1939, 1943 and 1944, Col-in-Chief RAPC 1939, GCStJ, RRC; *m* 15 Oct 1913 HRH PRINCE ARTHUR FREDERICK OF CONNAUGHT, KG, KT, GCMG, GCVO (*d* 12 Sept 1938), only s of HRH THE DUKE OF CONNAUGHT, and *d* 26 Feb 1959, having had:

(1) ALASTAIR ARTHUR, 2nd DUKE OF CONNAUGHT AND STRATHEARN (as which *s* gf 1942); *b* 9 Aug 1914; Lt Roy Scots Greys WW II; *d* unm 26 April 1943

2 HH PRINCESS MAUD ALEXANDRA VICTORIA GEORGINA BERTHA; *b* 3 April 1893; granted 9 Nov 1905 title of Princess with qualification HH and rank immediately after members of the Royal Family bearing the style HRH; *m* 12 Nov 1923, as his 1st w, **11th Earl of Southesk** (*see* **Lineage (of Southesk)** below), and *d* 14 Dec 1945, leaving issue:

(1) JAMES GEORGE ALEXANDER BANNERMAN CARNEGIE, **3rd and present Duke of Fife**

Lineage (of Carnegie): GOCELYNUS de BALINHARD; living 1204–35; possibly kin to:

JOHN de BALINHARD, nr Arbroath, Angus; *d c* 1275; ggf of:

JOHN de BALINHARD later de CARNEGIE, Forfarshire, of which lands and territorial Barony got a grant from Walter de Maule 1358; *d* 1370, leaving, with an est s (John, of that Ilk, line ended *c* 1530) a 2nd s or n:

DUTHAC de CARNEGIE; acquired part of the lands of Kinnaird, Forfarshire, 1401 and a charter of confirmation 1409; *k* Battle of Harlaw 1411, leaving:

WALTER de CARNEGIE of Kinnaird; fought with the royalist troops against the Earl of Crawford (*see* CRAWFORD and BALCARRES, E) Battle of Brechin 18 May 1452, following which his house of Kinnaird was burnt by Crawford in retaliation; *d* 1479, leaving:

JOHN de CARNEGIE of Kinnaird; granted 4 Nov 1480 by his cousin, 5th Earl of Crawford (*see* CRAWFORD and BALCARRES, E), life-rent of the lands of Glenesk; *m* — Waus and *d* 1508, leaving:

JOHN de CARNEGIE of Kinnaird; *m* Eupheme Strachan and was *k* Battle of Flodden 9 Sept 1513, leaving, with a dau (Janet, *m* William Maule of Boath):

Sir ROBERT CARNEGIE of Kinnaird; Ld of Session 1547, Envoy to England 1548 to negotiate ransom of Chllr of Scotland; captured at Scots defeat by English of Pinkie 1547, ktd on returning to Scotland, Envoy France 1550 and 1559, commr to treat with the English 1555 and 1557; *m* Margaret, dau of Guthrie of Lunan, and *d* 5 Jan 1565, having had issue:

1 John (Sir), of Kinnaird; granted charters of the lands of Erlisfield, Aberdeenshire, 3 Dec 1546, and Balbardy, Fife, and Sunderthercs, Forfarshire, 4 Oct 1548 and Feb 1549/50; *m* 1st Agnes, dau of David Wood of Craig, Comptroller Scotland, and had:

(1) Margaret; *m* Patrick Kinnaird of Kinnaird, Perthshire

1 (cont.) Sir John *m* 2nd Margaret Keith (*dsp*) and *dspm* 1595

2 DAVID

3 John; had a charter of the territorial Barony of Many, Aberdeen, from his f-in-law 22 Jan 1556/7; *m* Margaret, dau of John Waus of Many

4 Robert; head of the Maison Dieu (presumably a religious foundation) of Brechin; *d* April 1597

5 James; ancestor of the CARNEGIEs of Balmachie

6 Hercules, of Cookstoun; ancestor of the CARNEGIEs of Craigs

7 William; ancestor of the CARNEGIEs of Leuchland

8 George; *d* by 2 Nov 1580, leaving a dau

1 Helen; *m* 1st William Lundie of Benholm; *m* 2nd Robert Turing of Foveran (*see* TURING, Bt); *m* 3rd John Gordon of Glenbucket

2 Elizabeth; *m* Andrew Arbuthnott of that Ilk (*see* ARBUTHNOTT, V)

3 Catharine; *m* David Ramsay of Balmain (*see* RAMSAY, Bt, of Balmain) and had issue

4 Isabel; *m* Gordon of Glenbucket

5 Jean; *m* Gilbert Reid of Colliestoun

6 Mary; *m* Strachan of Carmyle

7 Christian

8 Margaret; *m* Sir James Scrymgeour of Dudhope (*see* DUNDEE, E) and had issue

Sir Robert CARNEGIE's 2nd son,

DAVID CARNEGIE of Kinnaird, PC (S); an Octavian (one of eight Commrs Treasury) 1595; *m* 1st Elizabeth, dau of Henry Ramsay of Colluthie, Fife, who brought him Colluthie and the lands of Leuchars and Broadlands, Fife, and had two daus (Elizabeth, *m* 15 Nov 1579 John Inglis of Tarvit and had issue; Margaret, *m c* 10 Jan 1582/3 William Dundas of Fingask but *dsp* 4 Sept 1589); *m* 2nd (contract 4 Oct 1568) Eupheme, dau of Sir John Wemyss of Wemyss (*see* WEMYSS, E), and *d* 19 April 1598, having by her had issue:

1 DAVID, **1st Earl**

2 JOHN CARNEGIE, 1st EARL OF NORTHESK (*qv*)

3 Robert (Sir), of Dunnichen; *m* (contract 30 July 1623) Isabel, dau of 6th Lord Gray (*qv*), and *dsp* Dec 1632

4 Alexander; ancestor of the CARNEGIEs of Balnamoon

3 Jean; *m* (contract 25 April 1590) James Carmichael of Bamedie

4 Katherine; *m* (contract 25 April 1590) John Aytoun of Kinnaldie

5 Agnes; *m* 26 Dec 1594 Sir Alexander Falconer of Halkertoun (*see* KINTORE, E) and had issue

6 Eupheme; *m* (contract 20 Oct 1599) Robert Graham of Morphie

The est son,

DAVID CARNEGIE, **1st Earl of Southesk**, so *cr* 22 June 1633, as also LORD CARNEGIE OF KINNAIRD AND LEUCHARS (S), with remainder to his heirs male for ever, and earlier 14 April 1616 LORD CARNEGIE OF KINNAIRD (all S), PC (S Jan 1616/7); *b* 1575; ktd 1603, a Ld of Session 1616–25/6 and Extrdy Ld of Session Feb 1625/6–28, T/Pres Scottish Cncl April-May 1625, signed the Covenant 1638, Sheriff Forfarshire 1646; *m* (contract 8 Oct 1595) Margaret (*d* 9 July 1614), dau of Sir David Lindsay of Edzell (*see* CRAWFORD and BALCARRES, E), and *d* Feb 165/8, having had issue:

1 David, *Lord Carnegie*; *m* (contract 14 Sept 1613) Lady Margaret Hamilton (*m* 2nd 31 Jan 1647, as his 3rd w, 1st Earl of Hartfell (*see* ANNANDALE AND HARTFELL, E)), 3rd dau of 1st Earl of Haddington (*qv*), and *dvp* 25 Oct 1633, having had issue:

(1) Margaret; *m* 21 July 1637 2nd Earl of Carnwath (*see* 1940 edn)

(2) Magdalen; *m* 1st Sir Gideon Baillie of Lochend (*d* 30 Aug 1640); *m* 2nd Sir John Crawfurd, 1st Bt of Kilbirnie and by him had issue (*see* SHAW-STEWART, Bt)

2 JAMES CARNEGIE, **2nd Earl of Southesk**, PC (S Feb 1660/1); ktd by 29 Jan 1627/8; Covenanter but later royalist; captured by English Parliamentarians after Battle of Preston 1648 but escaped by late June 1649; a Commr chosen for Scotland to sit in the Parl of England Aug 1652; killed the Master of Gray (*see* GRAY, L) by accident while engaged in what was claimed was a friendly fencing bout (at Biggleswade, Beds, Aug 1660) but which may well have been a duel and in any case took place after what contemporary sources call a 'convivial' meeting, suggesting alcohol played a part; *m* 1st (contract 21 Feb 1629) Lady Isabel Ker (*d* at Leuchars April 1650), yst dau of 1st Earl of Roxburghe (*see* ROXBURGHE, D) and widow of Sir James Haliburton of Pitcur, and had issue:

(1) ROBERT CARNEGIE, **3rd Earl of Southesk**, PC (S Jan 1681/2); Capt of a company of Scots Gds France 1659, Col Forfarshire Militia, Jt Sheriff Forfar 1660–69 and 1682–Feb 1687/8, sole Sheriff 1669–82; *m c* 1660 (separated by 1671) Lady Anne Hamilton (*d* Oct 1695), est dau of 2nd Duke of Hamilton (*see* HAMILTON and BRANDON, D), and *d* 19 Feb 1687/8, having had issue:

1a CHARLES CARNEGIE, **4th Earl of Southesk**, PC (S 1688); *b* 7 April 1661; *m* (contract 15 July 1691) Lady Mary Maitland, 2nd dau of 3rd Earl of Lauderdale (*qv*), and *d* 9 Aug 1699, leaving an only son:

1b JAMES CARNEGIE, **5th Earl of Southesk**; *b* 4 April 1692; Jacobite 1715, hence attainted 1716 and his honours forfeited; lived on the Continent from 1716; *m* 1713 Lady Margaret Stewart (*m* 2nd 16 Aug 1733 John, Master of Sinclair (*see* SINCLAIR, L), and *d* 2 Nov 1750), est dau of 5th Earl of Galloway (*qv*), and *d* in France 10 Feb 1730, having had a s and dau (both *d* young)

2a William; *k* in a duel at Paris 1681 by William Talmash, 3rd s of Elizabeth, Countess of Dysart (*qv*)

(1) Jean; *m* 1st (contract 26 June 1647) James Murray, 2nd Earl of Annandale of the 1st *cr* (*see* ANNANDALE AND HARTFELL, E); *m* 2nd 9 Aug 1659 4th Viscount of Stormont (*see* MANSFIELD and MANSFIELD, E), and had issue

(2) Katherine; *m* 7 Jan 1658 11th Earl of Erroll (*qv*) and *d* 1693

2 (cont.) The **2nd Earl** *m* 2nd by 9 April 1681 Janet Adamson (*dsp* June 1683) and *d* Jan 1668/9

3 John (Sir), of Craig; *m* (contract 27 Oct 1632) Jane, dau of Sir John Scrymgeour of Dudhope (*see* DUNDEE, E), and *d* 22 Nov 1654, leaving issue:

(1) David, of Craig; *m* 28 Dec 1654 Lady Catherine Wemyss (*m* 2nd 16 Aug 1864 Sir Andrew Ker of Greenland and *dsp* 24 Feb 1668), dau of 1st Earl of Wemyss (*see* WEMYSS, E), and *dsp* 1663

4 Alexander (Sir), of Pittarrow; *m* Margaret (*d* 1701), sister of 1st Viscount of Arbuthnott (*qv*), and *d* March 1682, having had, with six yr sons and three daus:

(1) **Sir David Carnegie, 1st Bt** (NS), so *cr vp* 20 Feb 1663; *m* 1st (contract 29 Oct 1663) Catherine, sister of 1st Earl of Rosebery (*qv*), and had, with five daus:

1a JOHN (Sir), **2nd Bt**

(1) (cont.) **Sir David** *m* 2nd (contract 29 Oct 1684) Catherine (*bur* 4 Nov 1692), dau of Robert Gordon of Pitlurg and widow of 2nd Viscount of Arbuthnott (*qv*), and by her had a s (*d* young); *m* 3rd *c* 1696 Jean (*bur* 15 May 1740), dau of James Burnet of Monboddo, and *d* Nov 1708, having by her had three sons (*dsp*) and five daus

1 Margaret; *m* (contract 3 Oct 1617) 1st Earl of Dalhousie (*qv*) and *d* 1661, having had issue

2 Agnes; *m* (contract 8 Aug 1620) James Sandilands, f of 1st Lord Abercrombie (*see* also TORPHICHEN, L), and had issue

3 Catherine; *m* (contract 14 Sept 1620) 1st Earl of Traquair (*see* MORAY, E) and had issue

4 Marjory; *m* 1st (contract 31 Oct 1622) William Haliburton of Pitcur; *m* 2nd 1639 1st Viscount of Arbuthnott (*qv*) and *d* 22 Dec 1651, having had issue

5 Elizabeth; *m* 1628 Andrew, Lord Balvaird (*see* MANSFIELD and MANSFIELD, E), and had issue

6 Magdalen; *m* 10 Nov 1629 1st Marquess of Montrose (*see* MONTROSE, D), and *d* Nov 1645, having had issue

The 1st Bt's only surv s,

Sir John Carnegie, 2nd Bt, of Pittarrow; *bapt* 27 Jan 1673; *m* 2 Oct 1712 Mary (*d* 5 June 1754), dau of Sir Thomas Burnett, 3rd Bt, of Leys (*see* 1970 edn), and had, with four other sons (*dsp*) and five daus:

1 JAMES (Sir), **3rd Bt**

2 George; *b* 18 Nov 1726; Jacobite, memb Prince Charles Edward's Body Guard, escaped to Sweden after the Battle of Culloden 1746 and became a merchant at Gothenburg; on his return to Scotland bought the Pittarrow estate from his brother the **2nd Bt** 1767; *m* 1 March 1769 Susan (*d* 14 April 1821), dau of David Scott, of Benholm, Kincardineshire, and *d* 12 April 1799, leaving, with three other sons and three daus:

(1) John CARNEGIE later FULLERTON-CARNEGIE; *b* 5 Jan 1771; *m* 23 April 1796 Mary Strachan Fullerton (*d* 6 July 1806) and *d* 25 Dec 1805, leaving:

1a George; *b* 1 Dec 1799; *m* April 1823 Madeline, dau of Sir John Connell, and *d* Oct 1851, leaving issue, with another s and a dau (*d* unm):

1b George; *b* 13 Feb 1826; Maj-Gen Bengal SC; *m* 4 Dec 1852 Maria Priscilla (*d* 22 April 1880), dau of Lt-Col J H Wakefield, and *d* 1898, leaving, with another s and dau (*d* unm):

1c Howard James; *b* 26 Dec 1861; Capt Prussian Army; *m* 1896 Baroness von der Goltz, dau of FM Baron von der Goltz, and *dsp* 1900

2c Edward Hugo Wakefield, OBE (1920), of Aytoun Hill, Newburgh-on-Tay, Fife; *b* 5 Aug 1870; *m* 1893 Emilie (*d* 3 Sept 1942), dau of Anton Prage, of Uruguay, and *d* 2 March 1955, leaving issue:

1d George David Howard, MC; *b* 12 July 1894; 1st Sec Dip Serv, 1st/7th Roy Highrs and Intell Corps WW I (despatches, wounded twice); *m* April 1920 Margery (*m* 2nd 20 Nov 1946 Staffan John Söderblom, Swedish Amb China, s of Archbp Söderblom, of Uppsala), dau of Rev R L Lacey, of Castle Pk, Exmouth, and *d* 23 Dec 1937, leaving issue:

1e +George Travers [Maj George Fullerton-Carnegie, Stronvar, Balquhidder, Perthshire; Aytounhill, Newburgh-on-Tay, Fifeshire]; *b* 14 March 1921; *educ* Winchester and Ch Ch Oxford; Maj Scots Gds WW II; *m* 3 Jan 1945 *Frances May dau of Lt-Col Alexander Sydney Duggan, MBE, and has issue:

1f +George Christopher Howard; *b* 18 June 1946; *educ* Applegarth, La Cleirlere, Switzerland, and Lausanne U

2e +David Howard; *b* 26 April 1926

1e Diana Mary; *b* 3 Aug 1923; *m* 1st 1 Dec 1942 Lt Philip Le Roy Shephard, Gren Gds (*ka* 27 April 1943), s of J W Shephard, of Glovers, Charlwood, Surrey; *m* 2nd 11 Aug 1945 (*divorce* 1955) Capt Anthony Greville-Bell and *d* following an accident 23 July 1961, leaving issue

2d James Edward; *b* 9 Jan 1899; Lt Black Watch; *d* unm 27 June 1942

1c Madeline Lila; *m* 1st 25 June 1881 Baron Henri Denaint, of Paris (*d* 1886), and had issue; *m* 2nd 1889 Baron Marcel Denaint and *d* 1908, having had further issue

(2) David, of Gothenburg; *b* 8 Feb 1772; *m* 1801; *d* 1837, leaving issue:

1a Susan Mary Anne; *m* Nov 1845 her cousin David Carnegie (*see below*)

(3) James; *b* 8 Jan 1773; Capt HEIC Naval Serv; *m* Dec 1801 Margaret (*d* 25 Feb 1828), dau of John Gillespie, of Kirkton, and *d* 18 Dec 1851, having had further issue (with five daus *d* unm):

1a James; *b* 26 Oct 1806; *m* 1829 Charlotte (*m* 2nd 19 Aug 1845 Rev John Hodgson and *d* 13 Nov 1878), dau of Neil Benjamin Edmonstone, Dir HEIC, and *dsp* 26 March 1831

2a David, of Stronvar, Perths, JP (Perths and Herts), DL (Perths); *b* 3 May 1813; went to Gothenburg 1830 and became a partner in the firm of his uncle David Carnegie; bought the Stronvar estate 1849 and the Eastbury one (later sold) 1857; High Sheriff Herts 1877; *m* 1st 16 May 1839 Julie (*d* 22 Feb 1841), dau of Etatsraad Zeuthen, of Tollose, Denmark, Judge Supreme Court Copenhagen, and had a dau (*d* in infancy); *m* 2nd Nov 1845 his cousin Susan Mary Ann (*d* 22 April 1859) and *d* 15 Feb 1890, having by her had, with another s (*d* young):

1b James, of Stronvar and Carphin, Fife, JP, DL (Fife), JP (Perths); *b* 9 Sept 1846; *m* 13 Oct 1872 Mary Bethune (*d* 11 Oct 1938), dau of David Gillespie, of Mountquhanie, Fife, and *d* 31 May 1925

1b Julie Isabella; *b* 10 July 1850; *m* 4 Oct 1881 Capt Charles Hope, 60th Rifles (*see* LINLITHGOW, M), and *d* 1 Nov 1930

Sir JOHN *d* 3 April 1729; his est son,

Sir James Carnegie, 3rd Bt, of Pittarrow; *b* c 1715; Capt Battles of Fontenoy 1745 and Culloden 1746; MP Kincardineshire 1741–65; *m* 5 July 1752 Christian (*d* 4 Nov 1820), est dau of David Doig, of Cookstoun, by Magdalen Symmer, heiress of Balyordie, and had, with another s (*d* young) and two daus (*d* unm):

1 DAVID (Sir), **4th Bt**

2 John; *b* 12 Aug 1757; Offr 11th Dragoons; *m* Oct 1791 Catherine, only dau of Rev Preb Tireman, Sub-Dean Chichester, and *d* 1823, having had issue:

(1) James (Rev); Vicar Seaford, Sussex; *dsp* 8 Feb 1864

3 George; *b* 2 Jan 1759; advocate 1782; *d* unm 19 May 1786

Sir JAMES *d* 30 April 1765; his est son,

Sir David Carnegie 4th Bt, of Southesk; *b* 22 Nov 1753; MP Montrose Burghs 1784 and Forfarshire 1796–1805; *m* (contract 29 April 1783) Agnes Murray (*d* 9 June 1860 aged 96), dau of Andrew Elliot, of Greenwells, Lt-Govr New York and unc of 1st Earl of Minto (*qv*), and had, with four daus (*d* unm):

1 JAMES (Sir), **5th Bt**

2 John CARNEGIE later RENNIE-STRACHAN-CARNEGIE, of Tarrie, Forfarshire; *b* 9 June 1802; *m* 7 Sept 1848 Elizabeth Susan (*d* 15 June 1878), dau of Col John Grey, of Backworth, and *d* 22 Feb 1879, having had issue:

(1) Claud Cathcart, of Tarrie, JP (Devon, Forfarshire); *b* 9 Dec 1849; Maj 5th Bde Scottish Div RA; *m* 16 April 1874 Mary Madeline (*d* 20 Oct 1936), dau of William Breakenridge, of Kingston, Ont, and *d* 19 Aug 1930, leaving:

1a Alan Bruce Strachan; *b* 27 Jan 1875; *educ* Charterhouse and Trin Coll Cambridge (BA 1896); Capt N Scottish RGA and Forfar and Kincardine Militia, advocate 1902; *d* 6 Aug 1948

1a Dorothy Olivia Strachan; *b* 27 March 1877; *m* 9 Jan 1907 David Horndon, JP (*d* 11 July 1938), s of David William Hicks John Horndon, DL, of Pencrebar, Callington, Cornwall, and *d* 9 June 1954

1 Elizabeth (twin); *d* unm 3 July 1884 aged 100 years and 5 weeks

2 Anne; *m* 17 April 1822 R-Adml Robert Wauchope (*d* June 1852) and *d* 23 April 1879, having had issue

3 Eleanor; *m* (contract 9 June 1828) James Evans, of Norwood, and *dsp* 27 Sept 1855

4 Mary; *m* 6 March 1829 Thomas Henry Graham, of Edmond Castle, Cumberland, and *dsp* 22 Nov 1877

5 Emma; *m* (contract 6 Sept 1820) James Douglas, of Cavers, Roxburghshire (*d* 1861), and *d* 25 Sept 1882 aged 88, leaving issue

6 Magdalene; *m* 11 June 1816 Sir Andrew Agnew of Lochnaw, 7th Bt (*qv*), and *d* 21 Jan 1858, leaving issue

Sir DAVID *d* 25 May 1805; his er son,

Sir James Carnegie, 5th Bt; *b* 28 Sept 1799; *m* 14 Nov 1825 Charlotte (*d* 10 April 1848), dau of Rev Daniel Lysons, MA, FSA, of Hempstead Court, Glos, and had, with a dau (*d* young):

1 JAMES, **9th Earl**

2 John; *b* 14 Oct 1829; Capt RN; *d* unm 5 July 1883

3 Charles, JP, DL (Forfarshire); *b* 14 May 1822; MP Forfarshire 1860–72, Lt 27th Regt, Inspr Constabulary Scotland 1872–84; *d* unm 12 Sept 1906

1 Charlotte; *m* 1st 16 June 1860 Thomas Frederick Scrymsoure of Fothringham and Powrie, Forfarshire Fothringham (*d* 7 March 1864), and had issue; *m* 2nd 8 Dec 1868 Sir Frederick Boileau Elliot, KCB (*see* MINTO, E), and *d* 15 Jan 1880, leaving issue

Sir JAMES *d* 30 Jan 1849; his est son,

Sir James Carnegie, 6th Bt, and **9th Earl of Southesk**, as which restored 1855, KT (1869), DL (Forfarshire); *b* 16 Nov 1827; *educ* RMC Sandhurst; LLD; Lt Gren Gds, Ld Lt Kincardineshire 1849–56; *cr* 7 Dec 1869 BARON BALINHARD, of Farnell, Forfar (UK); *m* 1st 19 June 1849 Lady Catherine Hamilton Noel (*d* 9 March 1855), 2nd dau of 1st Earl of Gainsborough (*qv*), and had issue:

1 CHARLES NOEL, **10th Earl**

1 Arabella Charlotte; *m* 7 Feb 1878 Samuel Henry Romilly, DL (*d* 14 March 1940), of Huntington Park, Herefs, and *d* 14 Feb 1907, leaving issue

2 Constance Mary, CI; *m* 9 Nov 1876 9th Earl of Elgin and (13th Earl of) Kincardine (*qv*) and *d* 24 Sept 1909, leaving issue

3 Beatrice Cecilia Diana; *m* 28 July 1874 Rev Henry Holmes Stewart, MA (*d* 20 March 1937), Rector Michaelston-le-Pit, s of James Stewart, of Cairnsmore, Newton Stewart, Wigtownshire, and *d* 11 Nov 1934, leaving issue

The **9th Earl** *m* 2nd 29 Nov 1860 Susan Catherine Mary (*d* 27 April 1915), dau of 6th Earl of Dunmore (*qv*), and by her had, with another dau (*d* unm):

2 Lancelot Douglas (Sir), GCVO (1917), KCMG (1916), PC (1924); *b* 26 Dec 1861; Counsellor Paris 1908–13 (Min Plen 1911–13), Envoy Extrdy and Min Plen Lisbon 1913 (Amb Extrdy and Plen 1924–28, Grand Cross Order Christ, Order S Tiago da Espanda); *m* 2 Jan 1890 Marion Alice de Gournay (*d* 23 Aug 1961 aged 93), yst dau of Henry Ford Barclay, JP, DL, of Monkhams, Essex, and *d* 15 Oct 1933, leaving issue:

(1) James Murray; *b* 29 Jan 1909; *educ* Eton and Ch Ch Oxford; Capt RA (TA) WW II; *m* 25 April 1939 *Diana Winifred Mary [Mrs James Carnegie, Polefields, Cowden, Kent], dau of Henry Arthur Renshaw (*see* RENSHAW, Bt), and *d* 1985, having had issue:

1a Carolyn Mary; *b* 25 June, *d* 27 Dec 1940

2a *Susan Diana [Miss Susan Carnegie, Polefields, Cowden, Kent]; *b* 27 June 1943

3a Sarah Elisabeth; *b* 10 July *d* 3 Oct 1948

4a *Charlotte Marion; *b* 2 April 1954

5a *Sophie Winifred (twin); *b* 2 April 1954

(1) *Mariota Susan; *b* 18 Dec 1892; *m* 3 July 1911 Sir Hugh Gurney, KCMG, MVO (*d* 7 March 1968), 3rd s of John Gurney, of Sprowston Hall, Norfolk, JP, and had issue

(2) Dorothea Helena; *b* 6 Aug 1906; *m* 19 July 1928 7th Earl of Mansfield and Mansfield (*qv*), and had issue (*see* ELTON, B)

3 Robert Francis; *b* 6 May 1869; *educ* Eton; Capt and Brevet Maj 2nd Bn Gordon Highrs Boer War 1899–1901 (wounded twice, despatches twice, brevet, medal four clasps), Br E Africa Protectorate Forces 1914–15; *m* 26 Nov 1913 Violet Mabel, yr dau of Philip Affleck Fraser, of Reelig, Inverness-shire, and *d* 13 May 1947, leaving issue:

(1) David James; *b* 4 July 1915; *educ* Lancing; Lt KAR WW II (despatches); *m* 29 April 1949 *Stella Therese (Wendy), only dau of James John Cleveland, of Blackheath, and widow of F/Sgt James Peter Mosley Leigh, RAF, and *d* 7 Feb 1994

(2) Robert Murray; *b* 3 July 1917; *educ* Wellington; WW II in E African Army Service Corps, E African Electrical and Mech Engrs, Lt KAR; *m* 2 Feb 1949 Pauline Frances (*d* 9 Dec 1954), dau of Capt Francis Farmer, of Fairseat, Kent, and *d* from injuries received in an aeroplane accident 18 Dec 1954, leaving issue:

1a +Ian Francis; *b* 30 Oct 1949; *educ* Wellington

2a +Alastair Robert; *b* 15 July 1951; *educ* Wellington

3a Keith Hamilton Peter; *b* 22 Oct 1954; *d* following a car crash 3 March 1961

(3) +John Fraser, DFC [John Carnegie Esq DFC, O Cabeço, Estrada da Serra, 7300 Portalegre, Portugal]; *b* 4 Sept 1922; *educ* Prince of Wales's Sch Nairobi; F/Lt RAF WW II; *m* 30 April 1955 *Gunhild Aline Avalon, only dau of Cdr The Mackinnon of Mackinnon, OBE, RN, of The Oast House, Hollingbourne, Kent, and has had:

1a James Robert; *b* 24 June 1956; *educ* Trin Coll Glenalmond; *d* 1976

1a *Susan Mary; *b* 24 Dec 1957; *m* 1st 1980 (*divorce* 1987) Mark Julian Lloyd Nicholson, s of George Raymond Tibbitt and Mrs Hugo Romer Nicholson, of Topps Farm, Braemore, Hants (*see* AGNEW, Bt, of Great Stanhope Street), and has issue:

1b *Rosalie Sheonagh; *b* 1983

1a (cont.) Mrs Susan Nicholson *m* 2nd 1988, as his 2nd w, *Timothy Robertson Bruce, of the Old Rectory, Combs, Stowmarket, Suffolk, adopted s of Capt Hon John Bernard Bruce (*see* ELGIN and KINCARDINE, E)

4 David Wynford; *b* 23 March 1871; Assist Resident N Nigeria, explorer in Australian desert; *d* unm 27 Nov 1900

4 Dora Susan; *m* 27 June 1894 Maj Ernest De RODAKOWSKI later De RODAKOWSKI-RIVERS, ASC (*d* 9 Jan 1944), 1st Regt Australian Lancers, s of Josef de Rodakowski by Ottilia, *née* Countess Wrangel, and *d* 29 May 1952, leaving issue

5 Helena Mariota; *b* 13 Oct 1865; *d* unm 24 Jan 1943

6 Katharine Agnes Blanche; *m* 5 Aug 1890 1st Viscount Tredegar and *d* 4 Oct 1949, having had issue (*see* 1963 edn)

The 9th EARL *d* 21 Feb 1905; his est son,

CHARLES NOEL CARNEGIE, **10th Earl of Southesk**, JP, DL (Angus and Aberdeen), DL (Kincardineshire); *b* 20 March 1854; Lt-Col and Hon Col Forfar and Kincardine Artillery; Hon LLD St Andrews; *m* 1 Aug 1891 Ethel Mary Elizabeth (*d* 10 Dec 1947), only child of Sir Alexander Bannerman, 9th Bt (*qv*), and had:

1 CHARLES ALEXANDER, **11th Earl**

2 Alexander Bannerman; *b* 22 Dec 1894; Cdr RN; *m* 1st 23 May 1919 his cousin Susan Ottilia (*d* 18 Jan 1968), dau of Maj Ernest de Rodakowski-Rivers (*see* above), and had issue:

(1) +Raymond Alexander [Maj Raymond Carnegie, Crimonmogate, Lonmay, Aberdeenshire]; *b* 9 July 1920; *educ* Eton; Maj Scots Gds WW II (wounded three times, despatches); *m* 1st 17 April 1943 (*divorce* 1953) Patricia Elinor Trevor, yst dau of Sir Hugh Trevor Dawson, 2nd Bt (*qv*), and has:

1a *Alexandra Susan Anne [Mrs John Sherman, 97 Barkston Gdns, London SW5 0EU]; *b* 4 Feb 1944; *m* 26 March 1969 John Sherman, only s of Hoyt Sherman, of Florida, and has issue:

1b *Charles Alexander Hoyt; *b* 17 Feb 1970

2b *Ian Andrew Henry; *b* 15 July 1972

3b *Peter Anthony Carnegie Sherman; *b* 2 June 1978

2a *Susan Katharine Maud [Mrs Edward Harding-Newman, Arabella House, Tain, Ross-shire IV19 1QJ]; *b* 22 Jan 1946; *m* 1st Jan 1968 Lt Dudley Gordon de Chair, 5th Roy Inskilling Dragoon Gds, yr s of Cdr Henry Graham Dudley de Chair, DSC, RN, and has issue:

1b *Oliver Dudley Raikes; *b* 17 April 1970

1b *Natasha Alexandra; *b* 29 June 1971

2a (cont.) Mrs Susan de Chair *m* 2nd 11 Dec 1974 *Maj (Rupert) Edward Harding-Newman, 4th/7th Dragoon Gds and has by him:

2b *Rupert Alexander; *b* 6 Oct 1976

2b *Sophia Katharine Louise; *b* 15 April 1979

(1) (cont.) Maj Raymond Carnegie *m* 2nd 27 Nov 1964 *Diana Denyse, Countess of Erroll (*qv*), and by her had further issue

2 (cont.) Cdr The Hon Alexander Carnegie *m* 2nd 5 Aug 1969 *Cynthia Averil, est dau of Brig Harold Vincent Spencer Charrington, DSO, MC, of Winchfield House, Hants, and formerly w of Capt Alexander Hugh Gurney, TD, KRRC

3 (James) Duthac, TD (1945), JP (Perths 1954); *b* 26 Sept 1910; *educ* Eton and Trin Coll Cambridge (BA); Maj 4th/5th Bn The Black Watch (TA); *m* 26 Feb

1935 *Claudia Katharine Angela, yst dau of Hon Lord Blackburn (Ld of Session) (*see* STRATHMORE AND KINGHORNE, E), and *d* 14 Jan 1996, leaving:

(1) +Robin Andrew Duthac [Robin Carnegie Esq, 31 Hasker St, London SW3 2LE]; *b* 24 March 1937; *educ* Eton; late Capt 1st The Queen's Dragoon Gds; V-chm Ware Carnegie Gp 1973; *m* 1st 1 June 1962 (*divorce* 1969) Hon (Selina) Polly Dawson Eccles, only dau of 1st Viscount Eccles (*qv*), and has:

1a +Andrew James; *b* 6 Feb 1963

(1) (cont.) Robin Carnegie *m* 2nd 3 April 1970 (*divorce* 1979) Jennifer Louise, yr dau of G H Robins, CBE, of Bermuda, and formerly w of Patrick Michael Puxley, and by her has:

2a +Simon Duthac; *b* 8 April 1971

1a *Tessa Lucinda; *b* 5 Oct 1972

(1) (cont.) Robin Carnegie m 3rd 1980 *Avice Rosemary, dau of Dr Richard Montagu Littledale, of Kent

1 Katherine Ethel; *b* 12 June 1892; *m* 18 June 1917 (*divorce* 1940) Maj Arthur Rivers Bosanquet, MC, KO Roy Lancaster Regt (*d* 30 Sept 1971), er s of Richard Arthur Bosanquet, and had issue (David, Annette and Mariota)

2 Mary Elisabeth; *b* 4 March 1899; *m* 28 Dec 1932 V-Adml Sir (Edward Michael) Conolly Abel Smith, GCVO, CB (*d* 1985), 2nd s of Eustace Abel Smith, of Longhills, Lincs, and *d* 23 June 1996, leaving:

(1) *Michael James [Michael Abel Smith Esq, The Old Rectory, Daylesford, Glos GL56 0YQ]; *b* 12 July 1939; *educ* Eton and Trin Coll Cambridge; *m* 1972 *Karen Moireach Aileen, yr dau of Ian Donald Malcolmson, TD, of Icomb Place, Stow-on-the-Wold, Glos, and has issue:

1a *Jessica Karen Abel; *b* 1977

(1) *Rosemary Jane [Mrs Robert Wolrige Gordon of Esslemont, Ellon, Aberdeenshire AB 41 8PA]; *b* 1 March 1936; *m* 11 July 1956 Capt Robert Wolrige Gordon of Hallhead and Esslemont, Gren Gds (*d* 13 Jan 1995), and has had:

1a *Charles Iain Robert; *b* 19 June 1961; *m* 1988 *Angela Clare, twin dau of Simon Rollo Frisby, of Bramley Grange, Bramley, Hants, and has issue:

1b *Henry Conolly Robert; *b* 1990

2b *Charles Rollo; *b* 1994

1b *Flora Louisa; *b* 1991

1a Henrietta Anne; *b* 10 April 1959; *k* in a motor accident 1983

The 10th EARL *d* 10 Nov 1941; his est son,

CHARLES ALEXANDER CARNEGIE, **11th Earl of Southesk**, KCVO (1926), DL (Kincardineshire 1930 and Angus 1947); *b* 23 Sept 1893; *educ* Eton and RMC Sandhurst; Maj Res Offrs Scots Gds, ADC to Viceroy India 1917–19, re-employed WW II; *m* 1st 12 Nov 1923 HH PRINCESS MAUD ALEXANDRA VICTORIA GEORGINA BERTHA of Fife, WVS 1939–45 (*d* 14 Dec 1945), yr dau of **1st Duke of Fife** (*see* above), and had:

1 JAMES GEORGE ALEXANDER BANNERMAN, **12th and present Earl of Southesk and 3rd and present Duke of Fife**

The **11th Earl** *m* 2nd 16 May 1952 Evelyn Julia (*d* 30 Aug 1992), er dau of Lt-Col Arthur Peere Williams-Freeman, DSO, OBE, late DCLI, and widow of Maj Ion Edward FitzGerald, DCLI (*see* CAMPBELL, Bt), and *d* 16 Feb 1992

FINLAY

Arms: Arg. on a chevron az., between in chief two roses gu. barbed and seeded ppr. and in base an estoile of eight points gu. within two wings conjoined and erect az., an ancient coronet or. **Crest:** In front of an oak tree fructed a whippet sejant ppr. gorged with an ancient coronet, pendant therefrom by the chains a portcullis az. **Motto:** Be just. **Creation:** Bt. (UK) 31 Dec 1964.

SIR DAVID RONALD JAMES BELL FINLAY, 2ND BT, of Epping, Co Essex [Sir David Finlay Bt, c/o Greig Middleton, 30 Lombard St, London EC3V 9EN]; *b* 16 Nov 1963; *s f* 1987; *educ* Marlborough, Grenoble U and Bristol U (BSc); Freeman City London 1991, with Peat Marwick McLintock 1986–91, Hill Samuel Financial Servs 1992–94, Gerrard Vivian Gray 1994–97, Greig Middleton 1997–

Lineage: WILLIAM FINLAY; seised of lands in Knock, Parish of Torphichen, Linlithgowshire; *m* Helen Nymo and *d* June 1630, leaving, with five daus:

JOHN FINLAY, of Knock; *m* Isobel Aitken (*d* Dec 1685) and *d* 1690, leaving issue:

JAMES FINLAY or FFINLAW, of Knock, *m* 29 Dec 1691 Jean Finlay or Ffinlaw and *d* by 27 Feb 1718, having had, with a yr s:

WILLIAM FINLAY or FFINLAY; as well as his paternal inheritance seised of lands at Starlaw and *s* to John Finlay of Burnhead 6 July 1750; *b* 8 March 1703; *m* 29 March 1741 Janet Waddel, of Whitburn, and *d* by 5 June 1778, leaving, with six yr sons and three daus:

JAMES FINLAY; as well as his paternal inheritance *s* his mother in lands at Falside 21 Dec 1792; *m* Elizabeth Chalmers and *d* 17 Jan 1817, leaving, with an er s and two daus:

ALEXANDER FINLAY; dominie (schoolmaster) at Torphichen and Bathgate over 50 years; *b* 1795; *m* 1837 Jean Finnie (*b* Torphichen 1817) and *d* 5 Oct 1866, leaving, with five yr sons and two daus:

JAMES FINLAY; admitted to Bar S Dakota, USA; Attorney and Counsellor-at-Law Washington State Bar 1904; *b* 4 Sept 1839; *m* 9 June 1869 Elizabeth, dau of Robert Pettigrew, of Roxhill, Calderbank, Lanarks, by Mary Bell, and sis of Prof James Bell Pettigrew, MD, LLD, FRS, FRCP, Chandos Prof Medicine St Andrews U, and *d* Odessa, Washington State, 1917, leaving, with two yr sons and three daus:

JAMES BELL PETTIGREW FINLAY, of Portskewett House, nr Chepstow, Mon; co-fndr Finlay Engrg Co, of Newport; *b* 16 April 1860; *educ* Airdrie Academy; *m* 30 July 1903 Margaret Helena (*d* 26 Dec 1961), dau of John Euston Davies, JP, of Dunmarklyn, Newport, Mon, and *d* 30 Dec 1936, leaving issue:

1 *John Euston Bell, CB (1959), OBE (1946), TD (1947); *b* 11 Sept 1908; *educ* Marlborough and Geneva U; slr 1932, Jr Legal Assist Bd Customs 1933, Sr Legal Assist 1945, Pncpl 1948, Assist Sec 1949, Commr and Dir Establishments (U-Sec) 1954–65, i/c Internat and Tariff Divs 1965–68, Chm Fin Ctee Customs Co-opn Cncl Brussels 1967–68, ret 1968, Govr St Dunstan's Educnl Fndn 1963, part-time consultant Unilever and Tate & Lyle, 2nd Lt 1st (Rifle) Bn Monmouthshire Regt (TA) 1934, WW II with 38 Div and W Cmmd (ADC to GOC-in-C and GSO(2) Ops), psc 1942, seconded Special Airborne Force AIF WW II New Guinea, Moluccas, Phillippines and Borneo as GSO(2) and GSO(1) (special ops), FRGS 1958; *m* 2 May 1942 *Zoe Josephine, dau of Brig Edward Frederick William Lees, DSO (*see* THURLOW, B), and has:

(1) *George Edward Bell; *b* 14 April 1948; *educ* Harrow and Ch Ch Oxford; stockbroker; *m* 1980 *Rose Alexandra Walker and has:

1a *John Jocelyn Bell; *b* 19–

1a *Alexandra Margaret Bell; *b* 19–

(1) *Robina Bell, *b* 31 Aug 1944, *educ* Tudor Hall Sch

2 GRAEME BELL (Sir), **1st Bt**

3 Robert James Bell, OBE (1952, MBE 1946); Cadet RN 1937, Midshipman 1938, WW II, Lt-Cdr 1950, Korean War, Sec Flag Offr Germany 1957–58, *b* 26 Feb 1920; *educ* Marlborough; *m* 18 Sept 1965 *Frances Elizabeth, yr dau of Charles Congreve Butt, of Wellington, NZ, and St John's Wood

1 Frieda Bell; *b* 3 June 1904; *m* 23 April 1931 Richard Ridley Wilson, s of Thomas Bishop Ridley Wilson, slr, and had a s and two daus

2 Margaret Morris Bell; *b* 31 Oct 1913; *m* 25 July 1936 Gwyn Rocyn-Jones, MA, MD, DPH, OStJ, of Woodcote House, Caerwent, Mon, s of Sir David Rocyn-Jones, CBE, JP, DL, MB, MS, DPH, and *d* 6 Oct 1966, leaving two daus

The er s,

Sir Graeme Bell Finlay, 1st Bt (UK), so *cr* 31 Dec 1964, ERD (1962); *b* 29 Oct 1917; *educ* Marlborough and UCL; barrister Gray's Inn 1946, MP (C) Epping 1951–64, PPS Min Health 1952–55, Assist Govt Whip 1957–59, Ld Cmmr Treasury 1959–60, V-Chamberlain Household 1960–64, Dep Judge County Courts 1967, 2nd Lt S Wales Borderers (24th Regt) (SR) 1939, 5th Roy Gurkha Rifles (Frontier Force) 1942–45, Martial Law Offr Upper Sind Force 1943, Actg/Maj and Offg DAAG NW Army 1945, Hon Capt Roy Regt Wales (24th/41st Foot); *m* 22 May 1953 *June Evangeline [Lady Finlay, 45 Artesian Rd, London W2 5DB], yr dau of Col Francis Collingwood Drake, OBE, MC, DL, 10th Roy Hus, of Mill Hurst, Harlow, Essex, and *d* 1987, leaving:

1 Sir DAVID RONALD JAMES BELL FINLAY, **2nd and present Bt**

1 *Fiona Daphne Margaret Bell [Miss Fiona Finlay, 18 Callcott Rd, London NW6 7EA]; *b* 7 Feb 1956

2 *Catrina Mary Bell [Mrs Robin Knight Bruce, The Sanctuary, Shobrooke, Crediton, Devon EX17 1BG]; *b* 16 Nov 1959; *m* 1984 *Robin Nigel Cleave Knight Bruce, er s of Nigel Knight Bruce, of Crediton, Devon, and has:

(1) *Robert Evelyn Cleave; *b* 1993

(1) *Siena-Rose; *b* 1990

(2) *Vita June; *b* 1992

FISHER

Arms: Arg., in chief two demi-lions rampant erased gu. and in base the stern of an ancient battleship showing three lanterns ppr. **Crest:** A dexter hand in armour, couped at the wrist, grasping the head of a trident erect, all ppr. **Supporters:** On either side a sailor of the Royal Navy supporting in the exterior hand an anchor cabled, that to the dexter in bend sinister and that to the sinister in bend dexter, all ppr. **Motto:** Fear God and dread nought.
Creation: B. (UK) 7 Dec 1909.

THE 3RD BARON FISHER, of Kilverstone, Thetford, Co Norfolk (John Vavasseur Fisher, DSC (1944), JP (Norfolk 1970)) [The Rt Hon The Lord Fisher DSC JP, Marklye, Rushlake Green, E Sussex TN12 9PN]; *b* 24 July 1921; *s* f 1955; *educ* Stowe and Trin Coll Cambrige (BA 1948); Lt RNVSR WW II, DL Norfolk 1968–72, dir Kilverstone Latin-American Zoo and Wild Life Park 1973–91, memb: E Gas Bd 1962–71 and E Anglia Ec Planning Cncl 1971–77; *m* 1st 25 July 1949 (*divorce* 1969) Elizabeth Anne Penelope, yr dau of Maj Herbert P Holt, MC, of Nassau, Bahamas, and has issue:

1 +PATRICK VAVASSEUR [The Hon Patrick Fisher, Kilverstone Hall, Thetford, Norfolk IP24 2RL]; *b* 14 June 1953; *m* 5 Nov 1977 *Lady Karen (Kay) Jean Carnegie, er dau of 13th Earl of Northesk (*qv*), and has issue:

(1) +John Carnegie Vavasseur; *b* 1979
(2) +Benjamin Carnegie Vavasseur; *b* 1986
(3) +Robin Carnegie Vavasseur; *b* 28 March 1996
(1) *Juliet Elizabeth; *b* 1978
(2) *Penelope Mary-Jean; *b* 1981
(3) *Suzannah Jane; *b* 1984
(4) *Liberty Jean; *b* 28 March 1996

2 +Benjamin Vavasseur [The Hon Benjamin Fisher, Overway House, Nowton, Bury St Edmunds, Suffolk]; *b* 21 Sept 1958; *m* 1985 *Pamela Margaret, only dau of A Cooper, of Tolcarne, Rough Close, Staffs, and has issue:

(1) +Peter Vavasseur; *b* 1986
(1) *Rose Kathleen; *b* 1988

1*Frances Alice [The Hon Mrs White, Cooks Farm, Nuthurst, W Sussex]; *b* 1 March 1951; *m* 1981 *Angus J White, s of Dr R A White, of Mile Ash, Tower Hill, Horsham, Sussex, and has issue:

(1) *Thomas Holt; *b* 1983
(1) *Sally; *b* 1985

2 *Bridget Anne [The Hon Mrs Montgomery, Chandlers Farm, Dippenhall St, Crondall, Hants GU10 5NX]; *b* 24 Dec 1956; *m* 21 Aug 1982 *Bruce Stewart Irlam Montgomery, s of Dr S R Montgomery, of Telegraph Cottage, Blackdown, Surrey, and has:

(1) *Patrick Christopherson Ross; *b* 1987
(1) *Caroline Jean; *b* 1984
(2) *Katherine Frances; *b* 1985

The 3rd BARON *m* 2nd 1970 *Hon Rosamund Ann Clifford, dau of 12th Baron Clifford of Chudleigh (*qv*) and formerly w of Geoffrey Forrester Fairbairn

Lineage: CLEMENT FISHER, of Eastcote, Barston, Warwicks; *b c* 1435; *m* Agnes — and had issue:

THOMAS FISHER, of Eastcote and Fulbroke Park, Warwicks (granted a life tenancy by HENRY VII, to whom he was Yeoman of the Cellar); *m* Cecily, dau of John Goddard, of Poulton, Berks, and had issue:

THOMAS FISHER, of Eastcote and Balsall End, Barston; *m* 1st Agnes — (*d* 1558); *m* 2nd Joan — (*d* 1605) and was *bur* 12 Jan 1577, leaving by her, with other issue:

WILLIAM FISHER, of Eastcote; *b c* 1577; *m* Susanna — and *d* 1651, leaving:

1 JOHN
2 Clement, of Eastcote Hall; *dspm*
3 Humphrey (Rev); *b* 1630; Vicar Choral Hereford 1664–1700, Vicar Pipe 27 June 1684; *m* 16 June 1670 Margaret Phillpotts, of Hereford (*d* 16 June 1721), and *d* 19 Jan 1700, leaving issue:

(1) Abraham; *bapt* 28 Aug 1673; *d* unm 22 Nov 1721
(2) Humphrey (Rev); Vicar Wistour Leics 1715 and Melton Mowbray 1730; *educ* Corpus Christi Coll Oxford (BA 1702); had:

1a John; *educ* Clare Coll Cambridge 1728 and Pembroke Coll Oxford

WILLIAM FISHER's est s,

JOHN FISHER, of Hereford; *bapt* 21 July 1628; *m* Anne — and *d* 8 May 1712, leaving issue:

WILLIAM FISHER, of St John the Baptist's, Hereford; *bapt* 12 March 1677; *m* Mary (*d* 1722), dau of Matthew Williams, of Hereford, and *d* 1746, leaving, with other issue:

Rev Canon JOHN FISHER, of Bodmin, Cornwall; *bapt* 27 Jan 1709; *educ* Wadham and Trin Colls Oxford (BA 1731); *m* 22 July 1734 Elizabeth, dau of Robert Bradford, and *d* 19 Sept 1776, leaving issue:

Rev JOHN FISHER, Preb Exeter; *b* 1741; *educ* Exeter Coll Oxford (BA 1763); *m* Catherine, dau of James Hosken, and *d* 26 Feb 1801, leaving issue (with a yr s, Capt William Fisher, 40th Regt, *k* Waterloo):

Rev JOHN FISHER; *b* 13 April 1774; *educ* Pembroke Coll Oxford (BA 1797, MA 1824); Rector Wavendon, Bucks, 1805–46; *m* Caroline Lucas, of Newport Pagnell, Bucks, and *d* 25 Dec 1846, leaving, with other issue (including an er s, Rev John Fisher, DD, Fell Magdalen Coll Oxford):

WILLIAM FISHER; *b* 2 Feb 1811; Capt 78th Highrs, ADC to GOC Ceylon and Govr Ceylon; *m* Sophia (*d* 27 Jan 1895), dau of Alfred Lambe, of Mayfair, by Anne Philpot, n of Alderman John Boydell, Ld Mayor London, and had, with other issue:

JOHN (JACKIE) ARBUTHNOT FISHER, **1st Baron Fisher**, of Kilverstone, Thetford, Co Norfolk (UK), so *cr* 7 Dec 1909, GCB (1902, KCB 1894, CB 1882), OM (1905), GCVO (1908); *b* 25 Jan 1841; memb CID, Hon Col 1st Roy Naval Bde 1914, Capt RN 1874, R-Adml 1890, V-Adml 1896, Adml 1901 and Adml of the Fleet 1905 (ret 1911), served Crimean War 1854 (medal), China War 1860 (medal with two clasps), Bombardment Alexandria 1881 (3rd Cl Osmanieh, medal), Dir Naval Ordnance 1886–90, ADC to HM QUEEN VICTORIA 1887–90, Adml-Supt Portsmouth Dockyard 1891–92, a Ld Admlty and Controller Navy 1892–97, C-in-C N America 1897–99, Mediterranean 1899–1902 and Portsmouth 1903–04, Br Del Peace Conference The Hague 1899, 2nd Sea Ld 1902, 1st Sea Ld and 1st and Pncpl Naval ADC to HM EDWARD VII 1904–10, 1st Sea Ld 1914–15, chm Inventions Bd 1915, Grand Cross Charles III of Spain, Order St Alexander Nevsky Russia, Grand Cordon Osmanieh, Legion of Honour and Order of Rising Sun with Paulownia, LLD Cambridge; *m* 4 April 1866 Frances Katharine Josephia (Order Chefekat 1st Cl) (*d* 18 July 1918), only dau of Rev Thomas Delves Broughton (*see* BROUGHTON, Bt), and *d* 10 July 1920, leaving:

1 CECIL VAVASSEUR, **2nd Baron**
1 Beatrix Alice; *b* 7 Jan 1867; *m* 28 Jan 1896 R-Adml Reginald Rundell Neeld (*d* 1 Aug 1939), 4th s of Sir John Neeld, 1st Bt, and *d* 28 June 1930
2 Dorothy Sibyl; Order Chefekat 2nd Cl; *m* 28 Dec 1908 Adml Sir Eric John Arthur Fullerton, KCB, DSO (*d* 9 Nov 1962), s of Adml Sir John Fullerton, GCVO, and *d* 18 Jan 1962, leaving issue
3 Pamela Mary, Order Chefekat 2nd Cl; *m* 14 July 1906 Adml Henry Blackett, CBE (*d* 1 Dec 1952), and *d* 22 Nov 1949, leaving issue (*see* BLACKETT, Bt)

The 1st BARON's s,

CECIL FISHER later VAVASSEUR FISHER (roy licence 8 July 1909), **2nd Baron Fisher**; *b* 18 July 1868; *educ* Magdalen Coll Oxford (MA); Bengal CS; *m* 22 Nov 1910 Jane (*d* 28 Jan 1955), dau of Randal Morgan, of Chestnut Hill, Philadelphia, USA, and *d* 11 May 1955, leaving issue:

1 JOHN VAVASSEUR FISHER, **3rd and present Baron Fisher**
1 Anna; *b* 27 July 1916; *m* 10 Aug 1936 Thomas Williams Clark, s of Percy Hamilton Clark, of Pennsylvania, and had:

(1) *Frederic William; *b* 6 May 1939
(2) *Hugh Roberts; *b* Jan 1948
(1) *Jane Morgan; *b* May 1940
(2) *Elizabeth; *b* 6 June 1946

2 *Katharine [The Rt Hon Katharine Lady Clifford of Chudleigh, Flat c, The Care House, Les Blancs Bois, Rue Cohu, Guernsey, CI GY5 7SY]; *b* 3 Nov 1919; *m* 29 Jan 1945 13th Baron Clifford of Chudleigh (*qv*) and has issue
3 *Barbara [The Hon Mrs Buswell, Le Petit Feugerel, St John, Jersey, CI JE3 4FX]; *b* 1 Oct 1925; *m* 21 July 1961 *Leslie Charles Croft Buswell, only s of Charles Gerald Buswell, of Aylesbury and Johannesburg, and has issue:

(1) *Gerald John Croft; *b* 6 Sept 1965
(1) *Pamela Gwendolyn; *b* 10 July 1968

FISHER OF REDNAL

Creation: B. (LP, UK) 1974.

THE BARONESS FISHER OF REDNAL, of Rednal, Birmingham (Doris Mary Gertrude Satchwell, JP (Birmingham)) [The Rt Hon The Baroness Fisher of Rednal JP, 60 Jacoby Place, Priory Rd, Birmingham B5 7UW]; *b* 13 Sept 1919; *educ* Tinker's Farm Girls' Sch, Fircroft Coll and Bournville Day Continuation Coll; City Cncllr Birmingham 1952–74; memb: Lab Party 1945–, UNESCO study gp, Warrington New Town Devpt Corp 1975– and New Towns Staff Commn 1976–; Crown Rep GMC 1975–; Nat Pres Co-op Women's Guild 1961–62; Pres Birmingham Roy Inst for the Blind 1980– and Br Fluoridation Soc 1994–; Guardian Birmingham Assay Office 1982–89; Memb: Hallmarking Cncl 1989; MP (Lab) Ladywood 1970–74, MEP 1975–81; Chm Govrs Baskerville Special Sch 1981–87; Govr Hunter's Hill Special Sch 1988–94; *m* 1939 *Joseph Fisher and has:

1 *Pauline Mary [The Hon Mrs Platt, Little Acre, Ridings Way, Cublington, Beds]; *b* 1940; *m* 1961 *Michael James Platt
2 *Veronica Mary [The Hon Mrs Pickering, 8 Marlborough Ave, Bromsgrove, Worcs]; *b* 1945; *m* 1968 *John Adrian Pickering and has issue

Lineage: FREDERICK JAMES SATCHWELL, BEM; had:

DORIS MARY GERTRUDE, *cr* a **Baroness**

FISON

Arms: Per fess az. and erm., in chief three battle-axes erect arg., the staves or, and in base an heraldic tiger passant of the last. **Crest:** A demi heraldic tiger rampant or, collared gules, holding between the paws an escutcheon argent charged with a battle-axe sable. **Motto:** *Deo confide* ('Trust in God'). **Creation:** Bt. (UK) 27 July 1905.

SIR (RICHARD) GUY FISON, 4TH BT, of Greenholme, Burley-in-Wharfedale, West Riding of Yorkshire, DSC (1944) [Sir Guy Fison Bt DSC, Medwins, Buryfields, Hants RG29 1NE]; *b* 9 Jan 1917; *s* f 1964; *educ* Eton and New Coll Oxford; RNVR WW II, wine merchant, Master of Wine 1954, dir: Charles Kinloch & Co, Saccone and Speed 1952–82, Percy Fox & Co 1982–83, Wine Devpt Bd 1982–83 and Fine Vintage Wines plc 1985–, pres Wine and Spirit Assoc 1977–78, Vintners' Co: Hon Freeman 1976, Renter Warden 1981–82, Upper Warden 1982–83, Master 1983–84; *m* 28 Feb 1952 Elyn (*d* 1987), only dau of Mogens Hartmann, of Bordeaux, and Fru Peterson, of Oslo, and formerly w of Count Renaud Doria, and has:

1 +CHARLES WILLIAM [Charles Fison Esq, 114 Dalling Rd, London W6]; *b* 6 Feb 1954; *educ* Eton

2 *Isabelle Frances; *b* 6 May 1957

Lineage: ROBERT FISON, of Langham, Suffolk; *m* Dorothy — and *d* 1748, leaving, with two er sons:

JAMES FISON, of The White House, Barningham, Suffolk; *b* 1734; *m* 25 Nov 1757 Anne Cornell (*d* 12 Dec 1773), of Elmswell, Suffolk, and *d* 9 Nov 1806, leaving:

JAMES FISON, of Barningham; *b* 1761; *m* 21 Dec 1784 Sarah (*d* 26 Jan 1838), dau of John Sparham, of Sapiston, Suffolk, and *d* 18 Jan 1817, leaving issue:

THOMAS FISON, of Barningham; *b* 25 Oct 1790; *m* 28 Nov 1811 Mary Mathew (*d* 27 June 1823), dau of John Gostling, of Cotton, Suffolk, and *d* 11 Jan 1861, leaving issue:

WILLIAM FISON, of Greenholme, Yorks, JP; *b* 19 Feb 1820; *m* 15 July 1846 Fanny (*d* 18 Aug 1892), dau of Jonas Whitaker, JP, of Greenholme, and *d* 6 April 1900, leaving issue:

Sir Frederick William Fison, 1st Bt (UK), so *cr* 27 July 1905, JP, DL; *b* 4 Dec 1847; *educ* Rugby and Ch Ch Oxford (MA 1847); MP (C) Doncaster 1895–1906; *m* 23 April 1872 Isabella (*d* 1 May 1932), 2nd dau of Joseph Crossley, of Broomfield, Halifax, and Belsfield, Bowness, Westmorland, and n of Sir Francis Crossley, 1st Bt, MP (*see* SOMERLEYTON, B), and *d* 20 Dec 1907, having had:

1 **Sir Francis Geoffrey Fison, 2nd Bt**, MC, JP (W R Yorks); *b* 12 March 1873; *educ* Harrow and Ch Ch Oxford (BA 1896); Capt KRRC WW I (wounded); *d* unm 19 Jan 1948

2 Hugh Valentine; *b* 3 May 1875; *educ* Harrow; 2nd Lt Northumberland Fus; *d* unm of enteric contracted at Battle of Omdurman 5 Oct 1898

3 WILLIAM GUY (Sir), **3rd Bt**

1 Edith; *m* 20 July 1910 Rev John Henry Hodgson (*d* 23 Dec 1939), Rector Dogmersfield, Hants, and *d* 30 March 1943, having had issue

2 Dorothy; a Sister of Bethany; *d* 30 July 1962

Sir FRANCIS's yr bro,

Sir William Guy Fison, 3rd Bt, MC; *b* 25 Oct 1890; *educ* Eton and New Coll Oxford (BA 1912); Capt RFA (TF) WW I (despatches); *m* 3 Feb 1914 Gwladys Rees (*d* 14 March 1963), only dau of John Robert Davies, CBE, of Treborth, Bangor, N Wales, and *d* 6 Dec 1964, leaving issue:

1 Sir (RICHARD) GUY FISON, **4th and present Bt**

2 +John Michael [John Fison Esq, 9 de Walden St, London W1]; *b* 7 July 1920; *educ* Eton; RA WW II (wounded)

1 Elizabeth Rees; *b* 2 July 1915; *m* 22 May 1946 Maj-Gen William Richard Beddington, CBE (*d* 1975), est s of Gerald Beddington, CBE, of The Court, Crondall, Hants, and had issue:

(1) Rupert Gerald; *b* 16 March 1947; *educ* Eton; *d* 1 Aug 1965

(2) *Guy Francis [Guy Beddington Esq, 55 Ladbroke Rd, London W11 3PD]; *b* 22 July 1949; *educ* Eton

FITT

Creation: B. (LP, UK) 1983.

THE BARON FITT, of Bell's Hill, Co Down (Gerard Fitt) [The Rt Hon The Baron Fitt, House of Lords, London SW1A 0PW]; *b* 9 April 1926; *educ* Christian Brothers' Sch Belfast; Merchant Navy 1941–53; Cnclr Belfast Corp 1958–81 (Alderman); MP NI Parl (Eire Lab) Dock Div Belfast 1962–72, (Republican Lab) W Belfast 1966–83, (Ind Socialist)1979–83; co-fndr and Leader SDLP 1970–79; Memb: (SDLP) NI Assembly N Belfast 1973–75, NI Constitutional Convention 1975–76; Dep Ch Exec NI Exec 1974; *m* 1947 Susan Gertrude Doherty (*d* 23 Jan 1996 and has had, with another dau (*d* young):

1 *Joan; *m* Vincent —

2 *Eileen; *m* Paul —

3 *Patsy; *m* Stephen —

4 *Betty

5 *Geraldine

Lineage: GEORGE PATRICK FITT; *m* Mary Ann — and had:

GERARD, *cr* a **Baron**

FitzGERALD of Geraldine Place

Arms: Erm. on a saltire gu., two arrows in saltire points downward arg., on a chief enarched of the second a galley, sails furled, between two towers of the third. **Crest:** On a mount in front of a hurst a knight in complete armour on horseback, all ppr., his shield gu., charged with a civic crown or. **Motto:** *Muir na' crann* ('A sea of trees'). **Creation:** Bt. (UK) 10 Oct 1903.

Rev Daniel Patrick FitzGerald; *b* 28 June 1916; *s* bro 1988 but does not use title; RC priest

Lineage : DONAL FitzGERALD, of Crossmahon, S Kilmurray, Cork; *b* 1760; *m* 1790 Julia Murphy (*d* 1838 aged 72), of Teraleen, Kilmichael, Co Cork, and *d* 1836, having had, with three yr sons and two daus:

DANIEL FitzGERALD, of Gurtsmourane, Iveleary, Co Cork; *b* 1801; *m* 1827 Elizabeth (*d* 27 March 1893 aged 84), dau of John Corcoran, of Clashbradane, Kilmichael, and *d* Oct 1876, leaving, with three er sons and five daus:

Sir Edward FitzGerald, 1st Bt (UK), so *cr* 10 Oct 1903; Ld Mayor Cork 1901, 1902 and 1903, Order Sacred Treasure Japan; *b* 24 Nov 1846; *m* 31 Jan 1872 Johanna Anne, dau of John O'Donoghue, and had issue:

1 Daniel Michael; *b* 1 Oct 1873; *d* 17 Feb 1888

2 JOHN JOSEPH (Sir), **2nd Bt**

3 Edward (Rev Canon); *b* 17 Aug 1883

4 Andrew; *b* 3 Dec 1885; *m* 1916 Elizabeth Barry-Murphy (*d* 1952) and *d* 1969, leaving:

(1) +JOHN FINNBARR [John FitzGerald Esq, Meadowlands, Wilton Rd, Cork, Ireland]; *b* 1918; heir presumptive; *m* 1949 *Margaret Hogg and has:

1a +Andrew Peter; *b* 1950

1a *Geraldine; *b* 1953

(2) +Andrew Joseph [Andrew FitzGerald Esq, 60 Glenbrook Park, Rathfarnham, Dublin 14, Ireland]; *b* 1922; *m* 1953 *Patricia Clark and has issue:

1a +Paul Andrew; *b* 1966

1a *Anne; *b* 1955

2a *Helen; *b* 1959

(1) *Margaret Mary; *b* 1920

(2) *Katherine; *b* 1925

5 William; *b* 2 June 1892
1 Elizabeth; *b* 31 July 1878
2 Ellen (Helena); *b* 11 Jan 1881
3 Mary; *b* 14 Oct 1887; *d* 17 Jan 1889
4 Anne Maria; *b* 20 July 1890
5 Julia Monica; *b* 4 July 1894

Sir EDWARD *d* 22 June 1927; his est surv son,

Sir John Joseph FitzGerald, 2nd Bt; *b* 20 Feb 1876; *m* 26 April 1911 Mary Thomasine, dau of John Burke, of Bandon, Co Cork, and *d* 1957, leaving issue:

1 **Rev Sir Edward Thomas FitzGerald, 3rd Bt**, of Cork; RC priest; *b* 7 March 1912; *d* 1988
2 John Joseph; *b* 5 Dec 1914; *d* 1957
3 Rev (Sir) DANIEL PATRICK FitzGERALD, **4th and present Bt**
1 Johannah; *b* 23 April 1913; *d* 13 Sept 1914

FitzGERALD of Valencia

Arms: Erm. a saltire gu., charged with a cross formée arg. **Crest:** An armed knight on horseback, all ppr. **Motto:** *Mullachar à buadh* ('My presence is victory') **Creation:** Bt. (UK) 8 July 1880.

SIR GEORGE PETER MAURICE FitzGERALD, 5TH BT, of Valencia, Co Kerry, **The 23rd Knight of Kerry**, MC (1944) [Maj The Knight of Kerry Bt MC, Colin's Farm House, 55 High St, Durrington, Salisbury, Wilts SP4 8AQ]; *b* 27 Feb 1917; *s f* 1967; *educ* Harrow and RMC Sandhurst; Maj (ret 1948) Irish Gds, served Palestine 1939 (despatches) and WW II; *m* 29 Aug 1939 *Angela Dora, dau of Capt James Rankin Mitchell, of 2 Mansfield St, London W1, and has issue:

1 +ADRIAN JAMES ANDREW DENIS [Adrian FitzGerald Esq, 16 Clareville St, London SW7 5AW]; *b* 24 June 1940; *educ* Harrow; ed *Monday World* (organ of The Monday Club) 1967–74, Cncllr Kensington and Chelsea 1974, Mayor 1984–85, chm Educn and Libraries Ctee 1995–, dep ldr London Fire and Civil Def Authority 1989–90, chm Anglo-Polish Soc 1989–92, V-Chm London Chapter Irish Georgian Soc 1990–; Kt of Hon and Devotion SMO Malta 1995

1 *Rosanna [Countess Richard Gurowski, North End House, Damerham, Fordingbridge, Hants SP6 3EU]; *b* 5 Feb 1945; *m* 2 Sept 1964 *Count Richard Melchior Beaumont Gurowski (*cr* Prussia 1787), only s of Capt Count Richard Dudley Melchior Gurowski, Scots Gds, and has issue:

(1) *Iona; *b* 22 July 1967; *m* 15 June 1996 *Oliver Forge, s of John Forge
(2) *Anya; *b* 9 July 1970

Lineage: THOMAS Fitz MAURICE (*see* LEINSTER, D, and PLYMOUTH, E); acquired Shanid and the feudal Ldship of Connello, Co Limerick; *m* Sabina/Sadhbh (*m* 2nd Nicholas Fitz Leon) and *d* 1213 or 1214, leaving, with a yr s (Maurice Fitz Thomas; *see* LANSDOWNE, M):

JOHN Fitz THOMAS; feudal Ld of Connello and in right of his w of Decies and Desmond; *m* 1st Margery, dau and coheir of Thomas Fitz Anthony, feudal Lord of Decies and Desmond, and was *k* at Callan, Kerry, 23 July 1261 in an encounter with the MacCARTHYs of Carbery, leaving:

1 Maurice Fitz John; *m* Maud de Barry and was *k* with his f, leaving issue:

(1) Thomas Fitz Maurice, *A nAppagh* ('The Monkey-nurtured', from a legend that he was cared for by an ape during a time of trouble; *see* also LEINSTER, D, for an almost identical legend) also 'The Crooked Heir'; *b c* April 1261; Justiciar Ireland 1295; feudal Ld of Decies and Desmond; *m* by 7 Feb 1283/4 Margaret (*m* 2nd Reynald Rosel/Russel), dau of 1st Lord (Baron) Berkeley (*qv*), and *d* 4 June 1298, leaving issue:

1a Thomas Fitz Thomas; *b c* 2 April 1290; *dsp* by 2 April 1309
2a MAURICE Fitz THOMAS, 1st EARL OF DESMOND, so *cr* 27 Aug 1329 (*see* DENBIGH and DESMOND, E, preliminary remarks)
3a John Fitz Thomas; *m* — and *d* 1324, leaving issue:

1b Thomas Fitz John (Sir), ancestor of the McTHOMAS GERALDINEs of Pallas, nr Bruree, Co Limerick, and Stradbally and Woodhouse, Co Waterford; also the FitzGERALDs of Knockmoan

JOHN Fitz THOMAS *m* 2nd Honora, dau either of Hugh, The O'Connor Kerry, or of Phelim MacHugh, The O'Connor Don, of Connaught, and was *k* at Callan in Glennaraghta by the McCARTHYs 23 July 1261, being *bur* in the Dominican Abbey in Tralee, Co Kerry, which he had founded that year. Tradition says he had four (possibly five) illegitimate sons by four different mothers, three of whom he made knights by virtue of his royal status as a Count Palatine, though other sources say they were knighted by EDWARD III at the Battle of Halidon Hill 19 July 1333. The knighthoods probably became hereditary by long usage because the heads of these junior branches of the Geraldine family were almost always so created on an individual basis. Whatever the actual facts, the descendants of the three Knights have been styled as such by Acts of Parliament, patents under the Great Seal and in legal proceedings for many centuries (though not, curiously and rather Irishly, actually referred to as 'Sir Desmond FitzGerald' (or whoever) in speech or writing). The first authentic record of the use of the title White Knight is in 1401, of Knight of Glin (the Black Knight) in 1424 and of Knight of Kerry (the Green Knight) in 1468, though this does not necessarily mean the titles were not in use earlier. The surname now in use, FitzGerald, seems to have been adopted at some point in the 16th century. JOHN Fitz THOMAS's sons were:

1 Sir Gilbert Fitz JOHN, traditionally by the w of O'Cuinnin; was ancestor of the FitzGIBBONs, the White Knights, extinct or dormant since 1612
2 Sir John Fitz JOHN, traditionally by the wife of O'Coileáin; was ancestor of the FitzGERALD Knights of Glin, the Black Knights
3 Sir MAURICE BUIDHE Fitz JOHN, **1st Knight of Kerry**, of whom presently
4 Thomas Fitz JOHN, traditionally by the wife of O'Connor Kerry; was ancestor of the FitzGERALDs of Ardengragh, Co Kerry, and of the septs called Sleoght Edmond and Sleoght Morris Duff, Co Kerry

JOHN Fitz THOMAS also had another son, probably illegitimate:

5 Philip; may be the true ancestor of the FitzGERALDs of Co Limerick whom the traditional accounts derive from his brother Sir JOHN; in any event had issue (with other sons):

(1) Sir Maurice Fitz PHILIP; *d* a prisoner in Dublin 1346

The 3rd son,

Sir MAURICE BUIDHE Fitz JOHN, **1st Knight of Kerry**, also called Sir MAURICE BUIDHE O'CINNEIDIGH since his mother was traditionally the wife of O'Cinneidigh; *m* and had issue:

1 RICHARD, **2nd Knight**
2 Robert Fitz MAURICE; living 1345

The er son,

Sir RICHARD Fitz MAURICE, **2nd Knight of Kerry**; ktd between 1330 and 1345, a follower of his cousin Maurice, 1st Earl of Desmond, Keeper of the Peace in Fermoy, Co Cork, 1347 and 1356; *m* and had issue:

Sir MAURICE Fitz RICHARD, **3rd Knight of Kerry**; *m* by 1382 Margaret or Margery (brought her husband the manors of Ballycrenan, Rathcourcy and Killeagh, Co Cork), dau and coheir of Sir Nicholas FitzJohn de Courc(e)y, and had:

1 EDMOND, **4th Knight of Kerry**; said to have been expelled from his lands by his brother Nicholas; ancestor of the FitzGERALDs of Ballycrenan, Co Cork
2 NICHOLAS, **5th Knight**
3 John, of Cahirmona, Co Cork; by 1600 his sept were dispossessed of their Cork lands
4 Gerald; Canon Limerick and Cloyne 1394; *d* by March 1406
5 David; living 1402

Sir MAURICE Fitz RICHARD also had an illegitimate son:

6 Richard Fitz MAURICE; living 1442; ancestor of the FitzGERALDs, Seneschals of Imokilly, and other Co Cork families

The 2nd son,

NICHOLAS Fitz MAURICE, **5th Knight of Kerry**; made Bp Ardfert *c* 1408 by the Avignon POPE GREGORY XII; ordered deprived of his bishopric 25 Oct 1409 by POPE ALEXANDER V; restored 26 Jan 1410/1 by the anti-POPE JOHN XXIII; had issue:

1 James; one of the Munster magnates who joined in 1468 to restore James, Earl of Desmond, to his inheritance; *dsp*
2 JOHN CAOCH, **6th Knight of Kerry** by 1479, when he is mentioned with his wife and six sons as among the many nobles of Kerry who kept Philip, Bp Ardfert, out of his see; granted the site for the Friary of Glanworth, Co Cork, by 1475; *m* Helena — and had issue:

(1) MAURICE, **7th Knight**
(2) Nicholas; living 1479
(3) Richard; living 1479
(4) Edmond; living 1479
(5) Gerald; living, 1479
(6) James; living 1479
(7) Patrick; killed 1489 by Tadhg MacCarthy Móre

The est son,

MAURICE, **7th Knight of Kerry**, pardoned 1496 for his part in the attempted usurpation of Perkin Warbeck; *m* by 1479 Joan — and had issue:

JOHN or SHANE, **8th Knight of Kerry**; Canon Ardfert, Bp Ardfert 20 Nov 1495; is said in a source writing *c* 1580 to have fathered on a dau of More, O'Connor Kerry, who was w of 'Shane de Moor of Culemoyly in the Co of Kerry, Steward to the Earl of Desmond', with two yr sons and two daughters (one of whom *m* Thomas FitzGerrot Og ('The Younger'), of Kilmacowe, Co Waterford, a grandson of Thomas, Earl of Desmond):

WILLIAM, **9th Knight of Kerry**; *m* Una, dau of 9th Baron of Kerry and Lixnaw (*see* LANSDOWNE, M) and by his 1st w, and had:

1 JOHN, **10th Knight**
2 Richard; *m* — Hussey, of Co Kerry, and had three sons
3 William McRudderie; rose against the English 1582; pardoned as William FitzGerald, alias FitzKnight, of Ballyheighne, Co Kerry, 1601; *m* — Ferriter, of Co Kerry, and had, with a yst s:

(1) John

(2) Maurice McWilliam; pardoned with his f 1601
4 Gibbon or Gilbert; priest; f of:
(1) William
5 Oliverus; *m* — FitzGerald, of Co Kerry, and had issue:
(1) Maurice McOliverus; *m* — Moriarty, of Co Kerry
(2) John McOliverus, of Garran, Co Kerry; pardoned for rebellion 1601 and 1604; *m* — McCrehon
1 A dau; *m* James FitzJohn FitzGerald, of Strancally, Co Waterford, n of Thomas McGerrot Og mentioned above

The est son,

JOHN FitzGERALD, **10th Knight of Kerry**; rose against the English in 1579/80; *m* Shile, dau of Donal O'Sullivan More, and *d* 7 Sept 1595, leaving:
1 WILLIAM, **11th Knight**
2 Maurice McRuddery; pardoned 1601 as 'Maurice FitzJohn Gerald, alias FitzKnight' and again, as of Inismore, in 1603; *m* — dau of Thomas Og FitzGerald, of Ardnegraph, Co Kerry, and *d* and was *bur* in Flanders
3 Patrick; pardoned 1601
4 Gerald, of Inismore; pardoned 1603
1 Una; *d* 1599
2 Helen; *m* 1st Connor O'Maheny Fionn, of Ardintenant, Co Cork, Chief of his name (*d* 1592); *m* 2nd Teig McConnor O'Driscall
3 Elinor; *m* by 1582, as his 2nd w, Sir John FitzEdmond FitzGerald, of Cloyne, Co Cork

The est son,

WILLIAM FitzGERALD, **11th Knight of Kerry**; pardoned at Rathanan 1603 and 1604; *m* 1st Margaret (*d* by 1582), widow of (a) Morrogh Balbh MacSheehy and previously (b) Nicholas Power (an illegitimate son of 1st Baron Power) and dau of Thomas Tobin, of Killaghy, Co Tipperary; *m* 2nd by 1603 Mary, widow of Edward Hussey, of Mulhussey, Co Kildare, and dau of Calvagh O'Connor, of Derrymullen, King's Co, and *d* 6 Nov 1640, having by her had issue:
1 JOHN, **12th Knight**
2 William
3 Patrick; admitted as a Kt of Santiago Spain 1645
4 Maurice; *dsp*
1 Ellen; *d* unm

The est son,

JOHN FitzGERALD, **12th Knight of Kerry**; *m* Katherine, dau of 17th Baron of Kerry and Lixnaw (*see* LANSDOWNE, M), and had:
1 Thomas; *m* Jane Everard and *dvp*, leaving issue:
(1) Amy
2 JOHN, **13th Knight**
3 Edmond; *d* unm by 6 May 1676
4 Patrick, of Gallerus, Co Kerry; living 1676; *m* Thomasine, dau of Edward Spring, and had issue:
(1) John
(1) Katherine; *m* James Conway, of Cloghan, and had issue:
(2) Anne; *m* 1700 Thomas Conway
(3) Lucy; *m* Richard Ferriter, of Dingle, Co Kerry
1 Elinor; living 1676; *m* Florence McCarthy More, of Pallas, Co Kerry

The 2nd son,

JOHN FitzGERALD, **13th Knight of Kerry**; *m* Honora O'Brien, dau of 2nd Viscount Clare, and had issue:
1 MAURICE, **14th Knight**
2 John; *d* unm
3 Daniel, of Ballinruddery, later of Killacrim; *m* Elinor, dau of Darby Long, of Monollig and Clashafadda, Co Cork, and had issue:
(1) Maurice; Offr in Lord Clare's Regt; *d* unm France 1767
(2) John; *m* Anne, dau of Henry Parr, of Dingle, Co Kerry, and *dsp*
(3) William
(1) Honora; *m* Francis Griffin, of Glaunalappa
(2) Elinor; *m* Richard Griffin, of Glaunalappa
4 Thomas, of Ardglass
1 Katherine; *m* The MacElligott and had three sons
2 Elinor; *m* 1703 Richard O'Donovan, 3rd s of The O'Donovan
3 Honora

The est son,

MAURICE FitzGERALD, **14th Knight of Kerry**; *m* 30 June 1703 Elizabeth, 2nd dau of David Crosbie, of Ardfert (by Jane, yr dau and coheir of William Hamilton), and sis of 1st Baron Branden (*see* 1832 edn), and *d* 9 Dec 1729, leaving with other issue (*d* young or unm):
1 JOHN FitzGERALD, **15th Knight of Kerry**; *m* 12 April 1732 Margaret, dau of Rt Hon Joseph Deane, Ld Ch Baron Exchequer, and *d* 1741, leaving issue:
(1) MAURICE FitzGERALD, **16th Knight of Kerry**; *m* 10 June 1764 Lady Anne FitzMaurice, only dau of 2nd Earl of Kerry (*see* LANSDOWNE, M), and *dsp* 1780
(1) Elizabeth; *m* Richard Townsend, of Castle Townsend, Co Cork
2 ROBERT, **17th Knight**
1 Jane; *m* George Herbert
2 Honora; *m* Richard Meredith, of Dicksgrove
3 Bridget; *m* 1st Thomas Sandes, of Sallow Glen; *m* 2nd Stephen Creagh, of Reens
4 Anne; *m* John Stack
5 Lucy; *b* 1715; *m* Rev John Day
6 Margaret; *m* John Hewson
7 Marion; *m* William Meredith, of Dicksgrove
8 Mary; *m* 1st Robert Collis; *m* 2nd Thomas Rice, of Mount Trenchard (*see* MONTEAGLE OF BRANDON, B)
9 Barbara; *m* Bastable Herbert

The 16th KNIGHT's unc,

ROBERT FitzGERALD, **17th Knight of Kerry**; *b* 1716; LLB, Judge Admlty Court, MP Dingle; *m* 1st Lucy, dau of John Leslie, of Tarbert, Co Kerry; *m* 2nd 1752 Catherine, widow of Thomas Freke Crosbie and only dau of Thomas FitzGerald, Knight of Glin; *m* 3rd Katherine, dau of Launcelot Sandes, of Kilcaven, and *d* 5 Dec 1781, leaving issue only by his 3rd w (with a yr s Robert, *k* 1799 Siege of Seringapatam leading Grenadiers of 33rd Regt and a dau, Mary, *d* 1800):

MAURICE FitzGERALD, **18th Knight of Kerry**, PC (1801), JP, DL; MP Co Kerry (I) 1794–1801 and (UK) 1801–31, Commr Customs 1799–1801, Ld Treasury 1827 and Admlty 1834, V-Treasurer Ireland 1830; *b* 29 Dec 1772; *m* 1st 5 Nov 1801 Maria (*d* 1829), dau of Rt Hon David Digges La Touche, of Marlay, Co Dublin, and had:
1 Robert; *d* in infancy
2 Maurice; *b* 1803; *d* unm Koblenz 1836
3 David; *b* 1804; *d* Sligo of famine fever 1848
4 Robert; *b* 1805; *m* Ellen, est dau of Peter Bodkin Hussey, of Farrinakilla House, Co Kerry, and *d* 1835, leaving:
(1) Maria; *m* Maj John William Percy, 9th Regt
5 Brinsley; *b* 1806; *d* unm India 1832
6 PETER GEORGE (Sir), **1st Bt**
7 Stephen Edward; *b* 1816; *m* Margaret, dau of Rev R Story, of Rosneath, Scotland
1 Elizabeth Emily; *b* 1807; *m* 11 Nov 1835 Crofton Thomas Croasdaile Vandeleur, of Wardenstown, Co Westmeath, and *d* 10 April 1860, leaving issue. He *d* 13 Aug 1876
2 Maria; *b* 1810; *d* unm
3 Gertrude; *b* 1812; *d* Dublin 1827
4 Catharine; *m* 20 June 1835 Edward Symes Bayly, of Ballyarthur, Co Wicklow, DL, Lt-Col Wicklow Militia, and *d* 1898, leaving issue (*see* ANGLESEY, M)

The **18th Knight of Kerry** *m* 2nd Cecilia Maria (*d* 15 Oct 1859), widow of George Knight, and *d* 6 March 1849

His sixth son,

Sir Peter George FitzGerald, 1st Bt (UK), so *cr* 8 July 1880, of Valencia (modern Valentia), Co Kerry, **19th Knight of Kerry**, JP, DL, High Sheriff Co Kerry 1849 and Co Carlow 1875; *b* 15 Sept 1808; *m* 11 Aug 1838 his sis-in-law Julia (*d* 5 Nov 1896), dau of Peter Bodkin Hussey, and had:
1 MAURICE (Sir), **2nd Bt**
2 Robert John, JP, DL Co Kerry; High Sheriff 1910; *b* 12 Jan 1852; *m* 1st 1878 Marion, CBE (1920) (*d* 11 Feb 1928), dau of Mahony Harte, barrister, of Batterfield House, Co Kerry, and had issue:
(1) (Peter) Francis, DSO (1917); Lt-Col King's Salop LI Boer War 1899–1901 (despatches, wounded, medal with seven clasps) and WW I (wounded, despatches four times, brevet), Order Crown Belgium; *b* 22 Sept 1879; *m* 14 April 1909 Baroness Adrienne de Geer (*d* 12 Dec 1973 aged 95), only child of Baron Gustave de Geer, of Zeist, Holland, and *d* 28 Jan 1968, having had:
1a +(Peter) Desmond [Desmond FitzGerald Esq, Querns House, Cirencester, Glos]; Capt RTR WW II, Kt SMO Malta; *b* 22 May 1910; *educ* Lancing; *m* 27 June 1945 *Elizabeth Janet Cameron, dau of Donald Norman and Mrs Albert Croad, of S Kensington, and has had issue:
1b +Anthony Desmond; *b* 24 Dec 1953; *educ* Ampleforth; Sloane Fell London Business Sch; *m* 1986 *Janine Heather, est dau of A R Miller, of Godalming, Surrey, and has issue:
1c +Peter Desmond Orlando; *b* 1989
1b *Caroline Rosemary [Mrs Philip Statham, 10 Wyatts Dve, Thorpe Bay, Southend-on-Sea, Essex]; *b* 4 July 1946; *m* 7 Nov 1970 *Maj Philip Statham, RA, and has issue:
1c *Charles Reginald; *b* 1971
2c *Christopher Desmond; *b* 1977
2b *Olivia Margaret [Ms Olivia Graham, 37 Cromwell Rd, London SW7]; *b* 16 March 1948; has issue:
1c *Alexandra Clare; *b* 1974
3b *Louise Elizabeth [Mrs Richard Burden, 54 Emlyn Rd, London W12 9TD]; *b* 15 Jan 1951; *m* 1982 *Richard John Burden, and has issue:
1c *Jonathon Max Robert; *b* 1986
1c *Georgina Ann; *b* 1983
4b Georgina Mary Penelope; *b* 10 March 1960; *d* 4 Aug 1962
2a +Mervyn Robert Gustaaf [Mervyn FitzGerald Esq, Penn Mill Cottage, Penselwood, Wincanton, Somerset]; *b* 8 Sept 1911; *educ* Lancing; *m* 17 Aug 1940 *Hilary, yr dau of Percy Houghton Brown, LLD, and has issue:
1b +Alastair Mervyn Malcolm [Alastair FitzGerald Esq, Red House Farm, Swallowcliffe, Wilts SP3 5PJ]; *b* 5 Oct 1941; *educ* Milton Abbey; *m* 11 July 1964 *Penelope Jane, er dau of Lt-Col John Stewart Eyre, of Southfield House, Whatley, Somerset, and has issue:
1c +Colin John; *b* 1970
1c *Fiona Margaret; *b* 7 Oct 1965; *m* 1996 *Andrea Tiana
2c *Katherine Lucy; *b* 20 Feb 1967; *m* 31 Aug 1991 *Richard Longbourne
2b +Peter Robin [Peter FitzGerald Esq, Pen Mill Farm, Penselwood, Wincanton, Somerset]; *b* 23 July 1943; *educ* Canford and Trin Coll Oxford; *m* 1976 *Sarah P, only dau of John Christopher Dykes, of Kensington and Corhampton Down, Hants, and has issue:
1c *Alanna Clare Juliet; *b* 1978
2c *Miranda Jessica; *b* 1980
3c *Harriet Sarah Isabel; *b* 1986
1b *Elizabeth Ann [Mrs Francis Dineley, Aubrey House, Aubrey Walk, London W8; Woodlands, Berwick St John, Shaftesbury, Dorset]; *b* 20 Aug 1945; *m* 1969 *Francis Mark Dineley and has issue:
1c *Alexander Perin; *b* 1973
1c *Maria Frances; *b* 1971
3a Adrian John; Maj RE WW II; *b* 17 May 1914; *kas* 13 April 1942

(2) Robert Brinsley, MC; Capt Gen List WW I (despatches three times), Legn Hon, Crown Italy, Order Leopold Belgium, Croix de Guerre; *b* 9 March 1884; *m* 2 Oct 1920 Helen Margaret (*d* 19 June 1974), widow of Capt Rupert Cholmeley Yea Dering, KOSB (*see* 1970 edn DERING, Bt), and dau of James FitzGerald, of Dublin, and *dsp* 23 May 1952

2 (cont.) Robert FitzGerald *m* 2nd 18 June 1930 *Mrs Isabel Parker, dau of William Mure Steel, and *d* 5 Aug 1934

3 Peter David, JP Cos Cork and Limerick; *b* 29 Dec 1855; *m* 1st 1890 Helen Mary (*d* 6 Jan 1904), widow of Capt Leslie Martin, 12th Lancers, and dau of Maj William Francis Percy, 9th Regt; *m* 2nd 2 Oct 1906 Charlotte Honor (*d* 23 Dec 1929), er dau of Lt-Col Thomas S MacAdam, of Blackwater, Co Clare, and *d* 31 Aug 1935, having by his 1st w had issue:

(1) James Brinsley Peter, JP Bucks; Capt 4th (RI) Dragoon Gds WW I (despatches); *b* 25 Jan 1894; *educ* Dean Close Sch Cheltenham; *m* 3 June 1924 Lady Moyra Marjorie Dawson-Damer (*d* following a car crash 17 April 1962), yst dau of 5th Earl of Portarlington (*qv*), and *d* in the same crash as his w, leaving:

1a +Michael George Maurice [Michael FitzGerald Esq, Gawcombe, Church Westcote, Oxon]; *b* 7 June 1925; *educ* Stowe and Trin Coll Cambridge; *m* 19 July 1959 *Frances Ruth, only dau of Maj Philip Alexander Francis Spence, Black Watch, of Deddington Manor, Oxon, by his 2nd w Sybil, er dau of Sir John Latta, 1st Bt (*see* 1940 edn), and has issue:

1b +Peter Desmond Philip; *b* 10 Jan 1961

1b *Sarah Moyra; *b* 4 June 1962

2b *Ann Rachel; *b* 4 June 1962; *m* 1989 *Maj Timothy David Edward Morris, 7th Gurkha Rifles, and has:

1c *Christopher; *b* 1991

2c *Guy; *b* 1993

(2) Maurice Robert; Lt Irish Gds; *b* 1895; *d* 19 April 1918 of wounds recd in action

(3) Peter John; Cdr RN, served WWs I and II; *b* 1900; *m* 11 April 1927 *Penelope, only dau of Lt-Col Leonard Markham Crofts, DSO, of Stewards, Hertford, and *d* Oct 1985

(1) Joan Mary; *b* 1892; *d* unm 14 Jan 1944

(2) Julia Gertrude; *b* 1897; *d* 1927

4 Brinsley John Hamilton, CB (1916), Lt-Col 2nd County of London Yeo, ADC to Viscount French Boer War and as Priv Sec on personal staff of C-in-C WW I, Croix de Guerre, Order Leopold Belgium, Legn Hon; *b* 25 Sept 1859; *m* 5 Jan 1918 Margarita Armstong Drexel, dau of John A Armstrong, and *d* 9 Feb 1931

1 Mary Emily Frances; *m* 15 Jan 1863 Sir Capel Molyneux, 7th Bt, of Castle Dillon (*see* 1940 edn), and *d* 26 Jan 1917, leaving issue. He *d* 24 Jan 1879

2 Emily; *d* unm 20 Sept 1932

3 Frances Caroline; *d* unm 30 Sept 1921

4 Katherine; *m* 17 April 1873 Rev Henry Bell, Vicar Muncaster, Cumberland, and Hon Canon Carlisle, and *d* 7 Nov 1927, leaving issue. He *d* 1919

5 Elizabeth Ann; *m* 28 Sept 1882 4th Baron Monteagle of Brandon (*qv*) and *d* 11 Dec 1922, leaving issue

6 Julia Emma Isabella; *m* 1st 12 Jan 1888 Stephen Edward Spring Rice, CB, and had issue (*see* MONTEAGLE OF BRANDON, B); *m* 2nd 11 Sept 1935 her 1st husb's 1st cousin (who was also her dead er sis's husb) 4th Baron Monteagle of Brandon (*qv*) and *d* 9 May 1936

7 Eileen Gertrude; *m* 30 Nov 1886 Brig-Gen Edward Kaye Daubeney, CBE, DSO, S Staffs Regt, est s of Rev Robert Thomas Daubeney, Vicar Ampney, Glos, and had issue. He *d* 3 Nov 1932

Sir PETER *d* 6 Aug 1880, less than a month after being *cr* a Bt; his est son,

Sir Maurice FitzGerald, 2nd Bt, and **20th Knight of Kerry**, CVO, JP, DL Cos Kerry and Carlow, also Suffolk and Cambs; Equerry to HRH THE DUKE OF CONNAUGHT, Capt Rifle Bde, ADC to Sir Archibald Alison in Ashanti War (mentioned in despatches, medal and clasp); *b* 5 Feb 1844; *m* 4 Oct 1882 Amelia Catherine (*d* 12 Nov 1947), dau of Henri Louis Bischoffsheim, of Bute House, S Audley St, Mayfair, and *d* 22 Oct 1916, having had issue:

1 Arthur Maurice; *b* 5 June 1883 (HRH THE DUKE OF CONNAUGHT stood sponsor); *d* 21 June 1883

2 **Sir John Peter Gerald FitzGerald, 3rd Bt**, and **21st Knight of Kerry**, MC; *b* 4 May 1884; Maj RHG, Staff Capt 1916–18 WW I (despatches); *m* 14 Oct 1919 Lady Mildred (*d* 7 June 1969), widow of Brig-Gen Gilbert Burrell Spencer Follett, DSO, MVO, and dau of 7th Earl of Dunmore (*qv*), and *dsp* 19 Feb 1957

3 **Sir Arthur Henry Brinsley FitzGerald, 4th Bt**, and **22nd Knight of Kerry**; *b* 6 July 1885 (HRH THE DUKE OF CONNAUGHT stood sponsor); *educ* Harrow; Capt Irish Gds as ADC to FM Viscount Ypres 1917 WW I, ADC and Camp Cmdt to Gen Sir Adrian Carton de Wiart, VC, 61 Division 1939–40, ADC to FM Viscount Gort, VC, 1940 and to Sir Roger Lumley, Govr Bombay 1940–41, WW II; *m* 19 Feb 1914 Mary Eleanor (*d* 7 Sept 1967), est dau of Capt Francis William Forester (*see* FORESTER, B), and *d* 30 Nov 1967, having had issue:

(1) John Brinsley; Capt Irish Gds WW II; *b* 25 Dec 1914; *m* 1941 *Mrs Barbara Thomas (*m* 3rd 1946 Desmond Molins, of 54 Eaton Sq, London SW1) and was *ka* 27 April 1943

(2) Sir GEORGE PETER MAURICE FitzGERALD, **5th and present Bt and 23rd and present Knight of Kerry**

(1) Mary Finola; *b* 5 Aug 1919; *m* 1st 1 Feb 1940 (*divorce* 1949) Lt-Col Henry Steuart Phillpotts, MC, Irish Gds, of Russelstown Park, Co Carlow, s of Brig-Gen Louis Murray Phillpotts, CMG, DSO, and had issue; *m* 2nd 25 May 1949 Maj Richard Rashleigh Shelley, CVO (*d* 22 Feb 1971), Manager HM THE QUEEN's Thoroughbred Studs, est s of Dr L W Shelley, MC, of Sevenoaks, and *d* 11 Sept 1977, having had further issue

1 Louise Nesta Pamela; *b* 8 Jan 1889; *m* 1st 30 April 1908 Lord Richard Wellesley (*ka* 29 Oct 1914), Capt Gren Gds, 2nd s of 4th Duke of Wellington (*qv*), and had issue; *m* 2nd New York 12 March 1917 her bro-in-law Lord George Wellesley and *d* 21 Feb 1946, leaving further issue

FitzHERBERT

Arms: Gu. three lions rampant or. **Crest:** A cubit arm in armour erect, the hand appearing clenched within the gauntlet, all ppr. **Motto:** *Ung je serviray* ('I will serve but one master'). **Creation:** Bt. (GB) 22 Jan 1784.

SIR RICHARD RANULPH FitzHERBERT, 9TH BT, of Tissington Hall, Co Derby [Sir Richard FitzHerbert Bt, Tissington Hall, Ashbourne, Derbys DE6 1RA]; *b* 2 November 1963; *s* unc 1989; *educ* Eton; *m* 1993 *Caroline Louise, dau of Maj Patrick Shuter, of Grangefield House, Tetbury, Glos, and has:

1 +FREDERICK DAVID; *b* 23 March 1995

1 *Francesca Norah; *b* 21 April 1998

Lineage: Sir WILLIAM FitzHERBERT, of Norbury, Derbys; living *temp* HENRY III (*see* STAFFORD, B); had:

WILLIAM FitzHERBERT; had:

THOMAS FitzHERBERT, of Somersal Herbert, Derbys, 1268; ancestor of:

JOHN FitzHERBERT, of Somersal Herbert; *d* in or after 1439, leaving, with an est s (John, ancestor of the FitzHERBERTs of Somersal Herbert) and yst s (William), a 2nd s:

NICHOLAS FitzHERBERT, of Upton and Tissington, Derbys; *b* 1400; *m* between 1459 and 1466 Margaret, dau of Robert Franceys, gdau and coheir of Sir Thomas Clinton (2nd s of 3rd Lord (Baron) Clinton, *qv*) and ggdau and coheir of Ralph Meynell, of Langley Meynell, and *d* 1473, leaving:

ROBERT FitzHERBERT, of Tissington; *m* Grace Eyre, of Holme Hall, Bakewell, and *d* 1535, having had:

GEORGE FitzHERBERT; *m* Agnes, dau of Humphrey Beresford, of Newton Grange, Derbys, and *dvp* 1515, leaving, with another s (Humphrey, *dsp*):

ROBERT FitzHERBERT, of Tissington; living 1589; *m* 1st Elizabeth, dau of John Cotes, of Woodcote, Salop, and had;

1 FRANCIS ROBERT FitzHERBERT; *m* 2nd Jane, dau of Thomas Bassett, of Hints, Staffs and *d* 7 July 1595, leaving by her:

2 John; *b* 1557; *dsp* & *vp* c 1590

3 Ralph, of Hints; *m* Griselda, dau of Erasmus Wolseley (*see* WOLSELEY, Bt, of Wolsley), and had:

(1) Robert, of Hints; *b* 1597; *m* Elizabeth, dau of Robert Wassing, of Oversley, Warwicks, and *d* in or after 1663, having had:

1a Ralph; Capt royalist forces Civil War; *ka vp* unm at Ashby, Leics, 1644

1a Elizabeth

2a Dorothy; *m* William Kempson, of Arden's Grafton, Warwicks

3a Anne; *m* — Cronkshanke

(2) John; *m* Anne, dau of William Price

(3) Thomas; soldier in Germany (probably during Thirty Years War)

1 Dorothy; *m* John Hill, of Little Pype, Staffs

ROBERT FitzHERBERT's only s by his 1st w,

FRANCIS FitzHERBERT, of Tissington; *b* 1539; High Sheriff Derbys 1598–99 and 1602; *m* 1st Jane, dau of Hugh Armstrong, of Wissall, Notts; *m* 2nd 26 Jan 1595 Elizabeth, dau of John Bullock, of Darley Abbey, Derbys, and *d* 13 Jan 1619, having by her had, with other issue:

Sir JOHN FitzHERBERT, of Tissington; High Sheriff Derbys 1624, ktd 1624; *b* 1599; *m* his distant cousin Elizabeth (*d* 17 Feb 1630), dau of Anthony FitzHerbert, of Norbury, and sis and coheir of Sir John FitzHerbert, of Norbury (*see* STAFFORD, B), and *d* 2 Aug 1641, having had:

1 William, of Tissington; *b* 1629; *m* 1st Mary (*d* 8 April 1676), dau of Thomas Cromwell, Earl of Ardglass (*see* CROMWELL, B, preliminary remarks), and had issue; *m* 2nd Anne, widow of John Parker, of London, and dau of Richard Breton, of Elmsthorpe, Leics, and *dspm* 24 June 1697

2 John, of Derby; barrister; had:

(1) William, of Tissington; Recorder Derby; *b* 1671; *m* 1709 Rachel (*d* 1762), dau and eventual heir of Thomas Bagshaw, of Bakewell and Ridge, Derbys, and *d* 6 Nov 1739, having had, with other issue:

1a WILLIAM
1a Catherine; *m* 11 June 1755 Richard Bateman (*bur* 14 July 1762), of Hartington Hall, Derbys, and *d* 19 Feb 1776, leaving issue

The est son,

WILLIAM FitzHERBERT, of Tissington; MP Derbys, a Ld of Trade and Plantations; *b* 1712; *m* Mary (*d* 28 Feb 1753), dau of Littleton Poyntz Meynell, of Bradley, Derbys, and had, with other issue:

1 WILLIAM (Sir), **1st Bt**
2 ALLEYNE FitzHERBERT, 1st and last BARON SAINT HELENS, of St Helens, Co Southampton (UK), so *cr* 31 July 1801, as also earlier 26 Jan 1791 BARON SAINT HELENS (I), PC (GB 1787, I 1787); *b* 1 March 1753; *educ* Derby GS, Eton and St John's Coll Cambridge; Min Resident Brussels 1777–82, Min Plen: Brussels and Paris 1782–83, Envoy Extrdy and Min Plen: St Petersburg 1783–87 and Madrid 1790–94, Amb The Hague 1794–95 and St Petersburg 1801–02, Ch Sec Ireland 1787–89; *d* unm 19 Feb 1839, when his titles expired
1 Selina; *m* Henry Gally Knight, of Langold, Notts, and *d* 2 Jan 1823, leaving issue

WILLIAM FitzHERBERT *d* 2 Jan 1772; his er son,

Sir William FitzHerbert, 1st Bt (GB), so *cr* 22 Jan 1784, of Tissington Hall; Gentleman Usher to GEORGE III, barrister, Recorder Derby; *b* 27 May 1748; *m* 14 Oct 1777 Sarah (*d* 1795), only dau of William Perrin, of Jamaica, and *d* 30 July 1791, having had, with other issue:

1 **Sir Anthony Perrin FitzHerbert, 2nd Bt**; *b* 21 July 1779; *d* unm 2 April 1798
2 HENRY (Sir), **3rd Bt**

The 2nd Bt's bro,

Sir Henry FitzHerbert, 3rd Bt; *b* 4 Aug 1783; *m* 27 Dec 1805 Agnes (*d* 25 Nov 1863), 2nd dau of Rev William Beresford, and had, with two other daus (*d* unm):

1 WILLIAM (Sir), **4th Bt**
2 Richard Henry, of Somersal Herbert; Maj Rifle Bde, Lt-Col Br-Italian Legion; *b* 29 Oct 1809; *m* 1st 8 Oct 1841 Ellen Margaret (*d* 21 May 1845), er dau of James Hepburn, of Tovil Place, Kent, and had, with other issue:
(1) Walter Hepburn Melitas, of Somersal Herbert; Maj Rifle Bde; *b* 18 Nov 1842; *m* 1886 Mary Joanna Sophia (*d* 11 Feb 1937), dau of Rev Thomas William Carr, Rector Barming, Maidstone, and *d* 3 June 1930, having had, with other issue:
1a Nicholas Hepburn, Jt Headmaster Stancliffe Hall 1925–33; *b* 24 Oct 1888; *educ* Repton and Pembroke Coll Cambridge (BA 1910)
1a Harriet Majorie; *b* 1891
(1) Adeline Francis Henrietta; *b* 1843; *m* 20 June 1862 Francis Beresford Wright, JP (*d* 16 Dec 1911), of Wootton Court, Warwicks, and *d* 5 May 1924, leaving issue
(2) Ellen Margaret Hepburn; *b* 1845; *m* 3 May 1870 Col Charles Bill, MP (*d* 9 Dec 1915), of Farley, Staffs, and *d* 14 April 1926, leaving issue
2 (cont.) Maj Richard FitzHerbert *m* 2nd 14 Sept 1848 Susan (*d* 2 May 1894), dau of Michael Hinton Castle, of Stapleton Grove, Bristol, and *d* 2 Sept 1885, having by her had issue:
(2) Reginald Henry Castle (Rev); Rector Somersal Herbert; *b* 18 Aug 1849; *educ* St John's Coll Cambridge (BA); *d* unm 8 April 1946
(3) Arthur Richard, of Somersal Marton, NZ; Trooper NZ Expdny Force WW I; *b* 9 Nov 1853; *m* 1881 Mary Lucy (*d* 1942), dau of Maj — Marshall, 65th Rgt, and *d* 29 March 1917 of wounds recd in action, leaving issue:
1a Arthur Geoffrey Marshall; NZ contingent Boer War 1901–02, NZ Expdny Force WW I; *b* 1882; *m* 1908 Hilda Eunice (*d* 1966), dau of W Gray, of Marton, NZ, and *d* 1974, leaving issue:
1b +Arthur William; RNZAF, P/O RAF WW II 1942–45; *b* 2 Sept 1922; *m* 1952 *Noeline Coral, dau of Richard Charles Kerkham, of Suva, Fiji, and has:
1c +Arthur Gray; *b* 5 Aug 1954
1c *Madeline Grace; *b* 17 June 1953; *m* 1971 (*divorce* 1987) Barry Edward Fairburn, of Wanganui, NZ, and has:
1d *Aaron Karl; *b* 1972
2d *Daniel Craig; *b* 1974
1d *Lisa Marie; *b* 1975
1b *Eileen Mildred [Mrs John Shere, Kahuterawa Rd, Palmerston North, New Zealand]; *b* 13 Aug 1919; *m* 30 June 1956 *John Charles Shere, s of Mervyn Shere, of Palmerston North, and adopted:
*Ian Geoffrey; *b* 30 March 1961; *m* 1984 *Christine Gae Murcott and has:
1d *Caleb Charles David; *b* 1992
1d *Katie Elisabeth; *b* 1985
2d *Kelly Rose; *b* 1989
2a Beresford Close; *b* 1884; *m* 1918 Gladys Ruby (*d* 1985), dau of John Owens, of Auckland, and *d* 15 July 1969, leaving issue:
1b *Adeline Beryl [Mrs Adeline Moore, 1/6 Speight Rd, Kohimarama, Auckland, New Zealand]; *m* 1946 (*divorce* 1961) F/O Maxwell Robert Moore (*d* 1967), RNZAF, and has issue:
1c *Jennifer Beryl; *b* 11 June 1947; *m* 1973 *John Charles Mortland, of Te Awanutu, NZ, and has issue:
1d *Nicholas John; *b* 1975
2d *Hamish Alexander Maxwell; *b* 1980
1d *Katie Beryl; *b* 1978
2c *Alison Anne [Mrs Philip Allen, 21 Lammermore Drive, St Heliers Bay, Auckland, New Zealand]; *b* 22 July 1951; *m* 1973 *Philip Royce Allen, and has issue:
1d *Scott Philip; *b* 1978
1d *Ainsley Alison; *b* 1981
3c *Beverley Robin [Mrs Barry West, 2 Seascape Rd, Renuera, Auckland, New Zealand]; *b* 4 Sept 1955; *m* 1978 *Barry James Anthony West, and has issue:
1d *Cameron James; *b* 1988
1d *Hannah Claire; *b* 1984
2d *Georgia Beryl; *b* 1991
2b *Dorothy Grace; *m* 1945 *Robert William Smith, F/O RNZAF, and has:
1c *Robert Phillip Beresford; *b* 19 July 1951
1c *Dorothy Christine; *b* 28 March 1946
2c *Pauline Beresford; *b* 21 Aug 1947
3c *Barbara Anne; *b* 28 Aug 1954
3b *Ngaire Beresford; *m* 1950 (*divorce* 1972) F/O John McRobert Calder, RNZAF, and has issue:
1c *John Beresford [John Calder Esq, 232 Cook Drive, Whitianga, New Zealand]; *b* 6 Feb 1953; *m* 1975 *Christine Doreen Orange and has:
1d *Jude Anthony; *b* 1976
1d *Casey Beresford; *b* 1988
1d *Philippa Chrystal; *b* 1981
2c *Peter McRobert [Peter Calder Esq, 64A Vale Rd, St Heliers, Auckland, New Zealand]; *b* 10 June 1955; *m* 1st 1980 (*divorce* 1991) Rosalind Mary Webb; *m* 2nd *Sandra Joy Welsh
3a Hugo Blois; *b* 1885; *m* 1st 1926 Phyllis (*d* 1927), dau of James Wilson, of Marton, NZ; *m* 2nd 1942 *(Margaret) Winifred [Mrs Hugo FitzHerbert, Waireka, 139 Glasgow Street, Wanganin, NZ], dau of Percy Wotton, of Wanganui, NZ
1a Mildred Mary
(4) Norman CMG (1917), CBE (1919); Lt-Col NZ Expdny Force Boer War 1900–01 and WW I; *b* 3 Jan 1858; *m* 28 April 1908 Esther Beresford, widow of Neville Sinclair, MD, and 2nd dau of Henry Sproule, of Ennis, Co Clare, and *dsp* 21 Feb 1943
(5) Anthony Francis; *b* 29 March 1863; *m* 1893 Catherine Anne (*d* 1954), only child of Charles Bull, of Fielding, NZ, and *d* 17 March 1925, leaving issue:
1a Dulce; *b* 1894; *d* unm 4 April 1960
2a *Cicely Beresford; *b* 1900; *m* 11 Aug 1931 Henry William Petre (*see* PETRE, B)
3a *Nellie; *b* 1905; *m* 19 Jan 1927 Strachan Agnew Goldingham (*d* 1980), S/Ldr RNZAF, 2nd s of Francis Strachan Goldingham, of Palmerston North, and has had issue:
1b Heather Linda; *b* 23 Sept 1929; *m* 1st 10 Jan 1953 (*divorce* 1964) Lt-Cdr Michael Clinton Danby, RN; *m* 2nd 4 Nov 1964 *(Lionel) Peter Winterton Twiss, OBE, DSC and bar, of Titchfield, Hants, 2nd s of Lt-Col D C Twiss, MC, and *d* 1988, leaving by her 1st husb:
1c *Edward Strachan Clinton; *b* 27 Sept 1960
1c *Brigette Anne Rosemary; *b* 21 Sept 1956; *m* 1984 *Robin Buchanan, and has issue:
1d *Angus Edward; *b* 1985
1d *Violet Victoria; *b* 1987
2d *A dau; *b* 1993
(3) Florence Kate; *b* 1851; *m* 4 Jan 1871 3rd Baron Moncreiff (*qv*) and *d* 23 Nov 1926, leaving issue
(4) Mildred; *b* 1852; *m* 29 Oct 1880 Hon Francis Jeffrey Moncreiff, 5th s of 1st Baron Moncreiff (*qv*), and *d* 24 Jan 1943, leaving issue
(5) Augusta Rose; *b* 1856; *m* 30 Oct 1884 Col Frederick William Peacock, CB, TD, DL (*d* 8 May 1924), and *d* 17 April 1938
(6) Agnes Beresford; *b* 1861; *m* 9 Aug 1894 Rev Reginald Harvey (*d* 20 Sept 1895) and *d* 9 Feb 1940
(7) Cicely Frances; *b* 1865; *m* 11 Dec 1889 Alfred Ernest Dickinson (*d* 11 Oct 1926), of Avening, Glos, and *d* 15 May 1935, leaving issue
(8) Hilda Mary; *b* 1867; *d* unm 17 May 1950
3 Alleyne (Rev); Rector Warsop, Notts; *b* 9 May 1815; *m* 5 May 1841 Angelina (*d* 10 Aug 1896), 3rd dau of James Haffenden, of Langford Hall, Notts, and *d* 15 April 1860, leaving, with other issue:
(1) Herbert Haffenden, of NZ; *b* 25 March 1842; *m* 1st 8 Dec 1861 Anne Farmer (*d* 1867) and had, with other issue:
1a Egbert; *b* 20 Oct 1863; *m* 1st Dec 1891 Florence Grace (*d* 3 April 1905), dau of Edward Gregory, of Feilding, NZ; *m* 2nd 28 Aug 1912 Margaret, widow of Charles Joseph Little, of Kensington, and dau of Benjamin John Holloway, of Thame, Oxon, and *d* 1944, having by his 1st w had issue:
1b John Alleyne, MC; WW I with 1st Australian Tunnelling Co (despatches); *b* 27 Dec 1896
2b +Herbert Haffenden [Herbert FitzHerbert Esq, 101 Messines Rd, Karori, Wellington, New Zealand]; *b* 21 March 1905; *m* Aug 1934 *Stella Marguerite, dau of W F Seymour, of Auckland, NZ
1b Margaret Eunice; *b* 22 June 1893; *m* 1921 Robert Hugh Oakley Caldwell, and had issue
2a Horace; *b* 5 Jan 1865; *m* Elizabeth Drury and *d* 1931, leaving issue:
1b Herbert; *b* 1887; *m* 27 Jan 1915 Winifred (*d* 1932), dau of William Walpole, and *d* 29 Dec 1958, leaving:
1c William Michael; with 2 NZEF 1941–45; *b* 12 Nov 1915; *m* 29 March 1947 *Elsie Lillian, dau of Charles Ogle, of Haweram, NZ, and *d* 1994, leaving issue:
1d +William Anthony [William FitzHerbert Esq, RD3, Hunterville, New Zealand]; *b* 4 July 1950; *m* 1980 *Gaylene Patricia, dau of Philip John Dawson, of Marton, and has issue:
1e +Timothy William; *b* 1982
1e +Peter; *b* 1985
1d *Annette Margaret [Mrs Raymond Moss, RD7, Feilding, New Zealand]; *b* 28 April 1948; *m* 1968 *Raymond Ernest Moss and has:
1e *Helen Jane; *b* 1970
2e *Jo Ann; *b* 1972
3e *Nicola Ann; *b* 1978
2d *Jennifer Ann; *b* 25 March 1953; *m* 1st 19– (*divorce* 19–) Gordon Bason and has:
1e *Andrew Gordon; *b* 1975
1e *Anna Elise; *b* 1970

2d (cont.) Mrs Jennifer Bason *m* 2nd 19– *Nigel Basin and by him has:

2e *Patrick; *b* 1991

2e *Elizabeth Frances; *b* 1985

3e *Emma; *b* 1991 (triplet)

4e *Katie; *b* 1991

1c *Mary Winifred [Mrs Raymond Windelborn, 19 Wilson St, Pahiatua, New Zealand]; *b* 3 Oct 1917; *m* 20 March 1941 *Raymond George Edge Windelborn, s of Louis Charles Windelborn, of Crofton, NZ, and has issue

2c *Eleanor Margaret [Miss Eleanor FitzHerbert, 66 Brunswick St, Lower Hutt, New Zealand]; *b* 18 Feb 1919

2b Norman, JP; *b* March 1889; *m* 11 Oct 1919 Evelyn (*d* 30 Aug 1992), dau of Robert M Pemberton, CE, of Waikare, NZ, and *d* 9 Dec 1961, leaving issue:

1c +John Anthony [John FitzHerbert Esq, 31 Russell Terrace, Putaruru, New Zealand]; *b* 24 Sept 1920; *m* 1st 23 Sept 1942 Martha Betty (*d* 26 Jan 1967), dau of William George Hope; *m* 2nd 31 March 1968 *Gaynor Hudson, widow of John Gordon Martin, of Hastings, NZ, and dau of Frederick Robertson Martin, of Cornwall, and by his 1st w has:

1d +David Anthony [David FitzHerbert Esq, 10 Kurahaupo St, Orakei, Auckland, New Zealand]; *b* 23 May 1945; ACA; *m* 26 April 1969 *Leith Alix Margaret, dau of Clive Allister Morton, of Remuera, NZ, and has:

1e +Nicholas Anthony; *b* 1975

2e +Jochen Richard; *b* 1978

3e +Matthew David; *b* 1981

2d +Timothy John [Timothy FitzHerbert Esq, Martins Bay, RD 2, Warkworth, New Zealand]; *b* 23 Jan 1951; *m* 1974 *Prudence Mary, dau of T W Bush, of Auckland, NZ, and has issue:

1e +Stephen John; *b* 1983

1e *Anna Elizabeth; *b* 1979

2e *Jane Prudence; *b* 1981

1d *Catherine Mary [Mrs Gary Sigley, 12 Bannockburn Place, Auckland 5, New Zealand]; *b* 20 Oct 1947; *m* 7 June 1969 *Gary Victor Sigley, and has issue:

1e *Michael Ainsley; *b* 1974

1e *Christina Evelyn; *b* 1971

2e *Haidee Margaret; *b* 1979

2d *Margaret Alison [Mrs Robert Wickman, 35 Western St, Matamata, New Zealand]; *b* 2 Nov 1952; *m* 1973 *Robert Stephen Wickman, and has issue:

1e *John Stephen; *b* 1983

1e *Chloe Jennifer; *b* 1986

2c +Richard Gurden [Richard FitzHerbert Esq, 4 Anderson St, Putaruru, New Zealand]; *b* 11 Jan 1922

(1) (cont.) Herbert FitzHerbert *m* 2nd 27 April 1868 Janet Maclean, dau of Dr Frederick John Knox, of Johnsonville, Wellington, NZ, and *d* 30 Oct 1873, having by her had issue:

3a Augustus; *b* 27 Jan 1872; *m* 1902 Ellen, dau of John Curd, and *d* 1908, leaving issue:

1b Donald

2b +James Bruce; *b* 1908; *m* 1940 *Eileen Olson, of New Plymouth, NZ

1b *Janet Ruth; *b* 1904; *m* 1939 *Robert Steele Martin, MBE, JP, engr, and has:

1c *Luke Steele, JP [Luke Martin Esq JP, PO Box 878, Rotorua, New Zealand]

2b *Maude Mount Cashel; *b* 1906

1a Rowena; *m* 1891 Robert John Knox and had issue

2a Ethel; *m* 1894 James Thompson Wilson Hogg (*d* 17 Sept 1919) and *d* 1930, leaving issue

(2) James (Rev); MA Cantab, Vicar Tissington; *b* 11 Sept 1843; *m* 20 July 1875 Cecil Mary Lefroy (*d* 1882), est dau of Rev William Maule, MA, Vicar Privett, Hants, and *d* 24 Sept 1915, having had, with other issue:

1a Humphrey Beresford; Lt RAF; *b* 27 March 1879; *m* 1907 Kathleen (*d* 1941), dau of Charles Alexander, of Liverpool; *m* 2nd 1941 Winifred Ivy Bing (*d* 1962) and *d* 1951, having by her had:

1b +Humphrey Bing Vivian [Humphrey FitzHerbert Esq, 36 Westover Rd, Broadstairs, Kent]; *b* 1942; *m* 1971 *Pamela Joan, dau of James Sidney Pitt, of Westgate-on-Sea, Kent

1b *Susan Eirene Angelina [Mrs Robert Jensen, 6 Balliol Rd, Broadstairs, Kent]; *b* 1945; *m* 1964 *Robert Viggo Jensen and has:

1c *Jetta Elva; *b* 1965

2a Douglas Cecil; Capt Merchantile Marine (BT Co); *b* 24 Sept 1882; *m* 24 July 1924 Daphne (*d* 9 Jan 1979), er dau of Henry Joseph Wigram (*see* WIGRAM, Bt), and *d* 25 April 1933, leaving issue:

1b +(Alleyne) John; *b* 23 Nov 1931; *educ* Denstone Coll; Capt Sherwood Rangers Yeo (TA) (ret); *m* 27 Nov 1959 *Judith Mary, dau of Ernest T Walker, of Barleythorpe Hall, Rutland, and has:

1c *Amanda Sara; *b* 20 Nov 1964; *educ* Oakham and Swansea U (BSc)

1a Dorothy Maule; *b* 4 Dec 1876; *m* 22 Nov 1909 William Evan Tibbs, MC, Lt RFA (TA), and *d* 3 Nov 1959, leaving issue

(3) Henry Ralph; *b* 29 Nov 1852; *m* 19 Oct 1881 Martha (*d* 1909), dau of W F Kennedy, of Wellington, NZ, and *d* 1917, leaving issue:

1a Claude Kennedy; *b* 1884; *m* 1910 Averil Alexandra (*d* 1962), dau of Rev William Alexander Woodward, Rector Flax Bourton, nr Bristol

1a Maisie Harriet

(4) Charles; *b* 5 May 1856; *m* 1889 Katherine, dau of Thomas U Mackenzie, of Rangitikei, NZ, and *d* 1927, leaving issue:

1a Reynold Hall; *b* 1890; *d* 23 June 1938

(5) Alleyne (Rev); Rector Manby, Louth, Lincs; *b* 6 Feb 1860; *educ* St John's Coll Cambridge (MA); *m* 3 Feb 1887 Frances Elizabeth (*d* 7 July 1922), dau of Rev Henry Smith, of Clarendon House, Redcar, Vicar Easton Maudit, Northants, and *dsp* 25 Feb 1949

(1) Mary Cecilia; *m* 1 June 1869 Rev William Alexander Woodward (*d* 1912), Rector Flax Bourton, and had issue

(2) Harriet Cecilia; *m* 16 Jan 1872 Rev Arthur Alfred Wilmot (*d* 11 May 1876), 4th s of Sir Henry Sacheverell Wilmot, 4th Bt (*qv*), and 25 Oct 1921, leaving issue

(3) Grace; *m* 9 Sept 1879 Edward Evelyn Harcourt-Vernon (*see* VERNON, B) and *dsps* 9 March 1881

(4) Selina; *m* 19 May 1886 Benjamin Newton (*d* 1926), of The Lindens, Stockton-on-Tees, and had issue

4 Anthony, of West Farleigh, Kent; *b* 10 May 1818; *m* 24 June 1852 Elizabeth Martha (*d* 8 Oct 1905), only dau of Rev William Horne, MA, of Epping House, Herts, Rector Barming, Kent, by Elizabeth, est dau of Jacob Hans Burke, JP, of Theobalds Park and Ponsbourne Park, Herts, and *d* 11 May 1855, leaving issue:

(1) Gerard Horne, of Overton House, Hants; *b* 17 March 1853; *m* 1875 Emma (*d* 23 Dec 1937), dau of Thomas Fantam, and *d* 1899, leaving, with other issue:

1a Henry Gerard; *b* 1876; *m* — and *dsp* 1948

2a Arthur Lionel; *b* 1877; *m* — and *d* 1934, leaving issue

3a William Horne; *b* 1880; *d* 1960

4a Leonard; *b* 1886; *m* — and *d* 19–

1a Lilian Maud; *m* — and *dsp* 1933

2a Eva May; *m* — and *d* 1916

3a Kathleen; *m* — and *d* 1954, leaving issue

4a *Rhoda; *m* 1938 Thomas A MacMaster (*d* 1960)

(2) Francis, of Ratclyffe, Devon; *b* 18 Dec 1854; *m* 24 June 1902 Edith (*d* 8 June 1935), yst dau of John Knight FitzHerbert (*see* below), and *d* 4 May 1929, leaving issue:

1a +Geoffrey Francis; *b* 29 April 1903; *educ* Sherborne; *m* 1st 16 Nov 1929 (*divorce* 1938) Violet Wrench, yst dau of James Watts Wyncoll, of Colchester; *m* 2nd 25 Jan 1939 *Elizabeth, dau of Hugh O'Neill, of Belfast

1a *Elizabeth; *b* 30 March 1905; *m* 7 Sept 1937 Tom Bokenham Reddick and has issue

5 John Knight; MA; *b* 27 March 1820; *m* 9 Aug 1859 Arabella Penelope (*d* 1896), 3rd dau of William White, of Shrubs, Co Dublin, and *d* 29 July 1894, leaving issue:

(1) Henry; Capt Berks Regt; *b* 3 June 1862; *m* 1895 Mary Oliphant, dau of Hon Eugene M Wilson, of Minneapolis, and *d* S Africa 12 Jan 1901

(2) Godfrey White; *b* 16 June 1864; *m* 25 June 1900 Anna Rachel (*d* 12 June 1961), est dau of Henry Alleyne Pile (*see* ALLEYNE, Bt), and *d* 8 Aug 1939, leaving:

1a Henry; *b* 30 Aug 1908; *m* 30 Nov 1940 *Betty (*m* 2nd 19– Robert Fulton), dau of Arthur W Barnley, of Kenya, and *d* 28 June 1960, leaving:

1b +Henry Nicholas [Henry FitzHerbert Esq, 4 Swallow St, Flamingo Vlei, Cape Town 7405, S Africa]; *b* 30 March 1952; *m* 1st 1975 (*divorce* 1982) Karin Schweiger; *m* 2nd 198– — and by his 1st w has:

1c +Stuart; *b* 198–

1c *Liesel Tanya FitzHerbert; *b* 1979

2b +Simon John; *b* 14 April 1953

1a Joan; MRCS, LRCP, DPM; *b* March 1902; *m* 3 April 1923 Lt-Cdr John Hugh Lhoyd Lhoyd-Owen RN, and had issue

2a Cecily; *b* Aug 1904; *d* unm 9 Jan 1970

3a Margaret, OBE; FRCOG, MRCS, LRCP; *d* unm Addis Abba 29 Oct 1971 aged 67

4a *Judith Agnes [Miss Judith FitzHerbert, c/o Emmanuel Grammar School, Derwen Fawr Rd, Swansea]; *b* July 1914

(1) Isabel; *m* 1884 James Lowndes Randall (*d* 1932), and *d* 12 Nov 1933, leaving issue

(2) Maude; *d* unm 8 Nov 1949

(3) Rachel Helen; *d* unm 13 Feb 1939

(4) Edith; *m* 24 June 1902 her cousin Francis FitzHerbert, son of Anthony FitzHerbert (*see* above), and *d* 8 June 1935, leaving issue

1 Selina; *m* 12 Aug 1830 Francis Wright, JP, DL (*d* 21 Feb 1873), of Osmaston Manor, Derbys, and *d* 30 Dec 1888, leaving issue

2 Frances Rafela; *m* 13 Nov 1844 Rev Godfrey H Arkwright (*d* 17 Dec 1866), 3rd s of Robert Arkwright, of Sutton Hall, and *d* 9 July 1849, leaving issue

3 Augusta Isabella; *m* 11 March 1851 Sir John Gay Newton Alleyne, 3rd Bt (*qv*), and *d* 9 Sept 1910, leaving issue

Sir HENRY *d* 1 June 1858; his est son,

Sir William FitzHerbert, 4th Bt, DL Derbys, High Sheriff 1866; *b* 2 June 1808; *m* 20 Feb 1836 Annie (*d* 14 Dec 1864), 2nd dau of Sir Reynold Abel Alleyne, 2nd Bt (*qv*), and had, with other issue:

1 RICHARD (Sir), **5th Bt**

1 Ages Rebekah; *m* 16 Oct 1867 Maj-Gen William Reid Martin (*d* 1892), Indian Staff Corps, and *d* 4 Jan 1921

2 Annie Ida; *m* 30 Jan 1890 Charles Edward Fletcher, and *dsp* 25 Nov 1890

3 Frances Theresa; *m* 22 Aug 1883 Edward Evelyn Harcourt-Vernon and *d* 20 Feb 1937, leaving issue (*see* VERNON, B)

Sir WILLIAM *d* 12 Oct 1896; his only surv son,

Rev Sir Richard FitzHerbert, 5th Bt; MA Cantab, Rector Warsop; *b* 12 April 1846; *m* 10 Oct 1871 Mary Anne (*d* 17 Jan 1949), yst dau of Edward Arkwright, of Hatton, and *d* 4 Jan 1906, leaving:

1 **Sir Hugo Meynell FitzHerbert, 6th Bt**; *b* 3 July 1872; *educ* Trin Hall Cambridge (BA); High Sheriff Notts 1909, Lt 8th Hus; *m* 1st 15 June 1920 (*divorce* 1930) Diana Isobel, 2nd dau of Thomas Erskine (*see* BUCHAN, E); *m* 2nd 5 Jan 1931 Muriel (*d* 5 Feb 1959), dau of J A Dorey, of Alresford, Hants, and *dsp* 12 Sept 1934

2 **Sir William FitzHerbert, 7th Bt**; JP Worcs 1909–37, Derbys 1939–63; *b* 21 Sept 1874; *educ* Charterhouse and Trin Hall Cambridge (BA 1896, MA 1938); High Sheriff Derbys 1940; *m* 24 Oct 1899 Lady Nora Maitland (*d* 19 April 1948), dau of 13th Earl of Lauderdale (*qv*), and *dsp* 8 Oct 1963

3 Richard Arkwright; Lt 4th Bn Sherwood Foresters; *b* 16 April 1876; *d* unm 20 June 1957

4 Henry Edward (Ven); Rector Seale Staffs 1930–38, RD Repton 1932–38, Hon Canon Derby 1936, Archdeacon Derby 1943–52, Rector Weston-on-Trent 1940–47, Hon Chaplain to TM GEORGE VI 1940–52 and THE QUEEN 1952–54; *b* 29 Dec 1882; *educ* Trin Hall Cambridge (MA); *m* 4 April 1907 Hon Margaret Elinor Holmes A'Court (*d* 3 March 1957), only dau of 3rd Baron Heytesbury (*qv*), and *d* 3 April 1958, leaving issue:

(1) **Sir John Richard Frederick FitzHerbert, 8th Bt**, TD ; *b* 15 Sept 1913; *educ* Charterhouse and RAC Cirencester; FLAS, Lt 8th Bn Sherwood Foresters (TA) WW II 1939–41 (POW); *m* 30 Aug 1957 (Kathleen) Anne (*d* 9 Feb 1993), formerly w of Henry Thornton Astell and yst dau of HT Rees, and *d* 1 March 1989

(2) David Henry (Rev), MC; *b* 9 Sept 1918; *educ* Charterhouse; 7th Queen's Own Hus WW II; *m* 4 Oct 1962 *Charmian Hyacinthe [Mrs David FitzHerbert, Sycamore House, Tissington, Derbys], yr dau of Samuel Ranulph Allsopp, CBE, DL (*see* HINDLIP, B), and *d* 1976, leaving:

1a Sir RICHARD RANULPH FitzHERBERT, **9th and present Bt**

1a *Selina Helen; *b* 20 March 1965

2a *(Juliet) Sarah [Mrs Anthony Clay, Broome Hall, Chatwall, Salop]; *b* 20 March 1965; *m* 1992 *Anthony (Anto) J Clay and has:

1b *Henry Hastings; *b* 1 Aug 1996

1b *Posy; *b* 11 Feb 1995

3a *Lucy Hyacinthe; *b* May 1967

(3) +Alec Benjamin; *b* 15 March 1923; *educ* Charterhouse

(1) Mary Ida; *b* 20 Aug 1908

(2) Sybil Helen; *b* 23 Nov 1909

(3) Elinor Ruth; *b* 12 Nov 1911; *m* 1st 26 Nov 1936 Raymond Johnson German (*ka* 11 Sept 1944), yst s of Lt-Col George German, of Highfields, Ashby-de-la-Zouch; *m* 2nd 6 Sept 1947 John Puxley White Jamie, MC, TD, DL, son of Robert Wyatt Jamie, MA, MB, CM, DPH, and had issue:

1a *John Robert FitzHerbert; *b* 8 Oct 1948; *educ* Uppingham

(4) *Ann [Miss Ann FitzHerbert, The Old Rectory, Thorpe, Derbys DE6 2AW]; *b* 22 Nov 1916

1 Avril; *b* 27 April 1873

2 May; *b* 27, *d* 30 April 1873

3 Violet Annie; *m* 16 Sept 1913 James Frederic Cartmell (*d* 3 March 1926) and *d* 26 March 1943, leaving issue

FitzWALTER

Arms: Arg. a chevron between two mullets pierced in chief and an annulet in base sa., a crescent sa. for difference. **Crest:** A phoenix or out of flames ppr. **Badge:** An estoile or. **Motto:** *Je garderay* ('I will guard'). **Creation:** B. (E) 24 June 1295.

THE 21ST LORD (Baron) FitzWALTER ((FitzWalter) Brook Plumptre, JP (Kent 1949)) [The Rt Hon The Lord FitzWalter JP, Goodnestone Park, Canterbury, Kent CT3 1PL]; *b* 15 Jan 1914; *s* unc on termination of abeyance 1953; *educ* Diocesan Coll Cape Town and Jesus Coll Cambridge (BA 1937); Capt The Buffs WW II NW Europe and India, Govr King's Canterbury; *m* 29 Sept 1951 *Margaret Melesina, 3rd dau of Herbert William Deedes (*see* DEEDES, B), and has:

1 +JULIAN BROOK; *b* 18 Oct 1952; *educ* Radley and Wye Coll London U; *m* 1988 *(Alison) Sally, only dau of I M T Quiney, and has issue:

(1) +Edward Brook; *b* 26 April 1989

(2) +Tom Alexander; *b* 1991

(3) +Max Ian; *b* 1993

2 +Henry Bridges; *b* 18 Feb 1954; *educ* Radley; *m* 1981 *Susie, only dau of F T Payne, of Waverley Station, NSW, and has issue:

(1) +Sam Anthony Bridges; *b* 1982

(1) +Camilla; *b* 1984

3 +(Wyndham) George [The Hon George Plumptre, Rowling House, Goodnestone, Canterbury, Kent CT3 1QB]; *b* 24 April 1956; *educ* Radley and Jesus Coll Cambridge (BA 1978); Sotheby's rep Kent 1991–97, dir Sotheby's S Africa 1997, jnlst, author: *Royal Gardens* (1981), *Collins Book of British Gardens* (1985), *The Fast Set* (1985), *Barclays World of Cricket* (ed, 1986), *Back Page Cricket* (ed, 1987), *Homes of Cricket* (1988), *The Latest Country Gardens* (1988), *Cricket Caricatures and Cartoons* (1989), *Garden Ornament* (1989), *Back Page Racing* (ed, 1989), *The Golden Age of Cricket* (1990), *Private Gardens*; *m* 1984 *Alexandra Elizabeth, dau of Prince Michael Cantacuzene, Count Speransky (*see* section Grant AMERICAN PRESIDENTIAL FAMILIES, 1994, Morris Genealogical Books SA), and has:

(1) +Wyndham James Alexander; *b* 1986

(2) +Piers Harry Constantine; *b* 1987

(1) +Hermione Amy Katherina; *b* 1991

4 +William Edward; *b* 23 July 1959; *educ* Milton Abbey; *m* 1991 *Joanna, yr dau of William Dargue, of Los Gigantes, Tenerife, and has issue:

(1) +Jeremy William; *b* 1992

5 +Francis Charles; *b* 30 May 1963; *educ* St Edmund's Sch Canterbury

Lineage: RICHARD I(?), DUKE OF NORMANDY; had an illegitimate s:

GODFREY, COUNT OF BRIONNE; had:

GILBERT, COUNT OF BRIONNE; benefactor of the Abbey of Bec in Normandy; had:

RICHARD Fitz GILBERT, also known as de BIENFAITE (from the quantity of his fiefs), de CLARE or de TONBRIDGE (from actual fiefs); *b* by 1035; went with his cousin WILLIAM I THE CONQUEROR to England and was granted 176 Lordships, 95 of them associated with the Honour (feudal unit of administration) of Clare, Suffolk, and others with Tonbridge, Kent; *m* Rohese, dau of Walter Giffard the er, and *d c* 1090, having had, with older issue (*see* HERTFORD, M, and PEMBROKE and MONTGOMERY, E, preliminary remarks):

ROBERT Fitz RICHARD; *m* Maud de Senlis (*d* 1140), dau of Simon de St Liz, Earl of Northampton, and *d* 1134 or 1136, leaving:

WALTER Fitz ROBERT; feudal Ld of Woodham Walter, Essex; *m* 1st Maud, dau and heir of Richard de Lucy, of Diss, Norfolk, and *d* 1198, leaving:

ROBERT Fitz WALTER; feudal Ld of Woodham Walter; foremost of the 25 Barons (magnates rather than peers of Parl) enforcing Magna Carta; *k* siege of Damietta, Egypt, 9 Dec 1235, leaving by Rohesa, his 2nd w:

Sir WALTER Fitz ROBERT, of Woodham Walter; *m* Ida, dau of William Longespee, Earl of Salisbury (*see* SALISBURY, M, preliminary remarks), and *d* by 10 April 1258, leaving:

ROBERT Fitz WALTER, **1st Lord** (Baron) **FitzWalter** (E), so *cr* according to later doctrine by writ of summons to Parl 24 June 1295; *b* 1247; ktd 1274; served in wars against Welsh 1277 and 1282 and in France 1286, Gascony 1296–97 and Scotland (present Battle of Falkirk 22 July 1298 and Siege of Caerlaverock July 1300); *m* 1st Devorguille (*d* 1284), est dau and coheir of Sir John de Burgh, of Wakerley, Northants, and had:

1 Walter; *b* 1275; *m* 1286 Joan (*m* 2nd Sir Adam de Welle, of Well, Lincs, and *d* 1 June 1315), dau of Sir John Engaine, of Laxton, Northants, and *d* 1293, having had:

(1) Robert; *b* 1291; *d* an infant

The **1st Lord** *m* 2nd 1289 Alianore, dau of Sir Robert de Ferrers, of Chartley, Staffs, sometime Earl of Derby (*see* preliminary remarks to DERBY, E, FERRERS, E, and HEREFORD, V), and by her had issue:

2 ROBERT, **2nd Lord**

The **1st Lord** *m* 3rd *c* 10 May 1308 Alice, widow of Sir Warin del Isle, of Campton, Beds, Nedging, Suffolk, Rampton, Cambs, and various other manors, and *d* 18 Jan 1325/6

The son by the 2nd w,

ROBERT FitzWALTER, **2nd Lord** (Baron) **Fitzwalter**; *b* by 1300; *m* Joan de Multon (*d* 16 June 1363), est dau of Thomas, Lord (Baron) Multon, and *d* 6 May 1328, having had:

JOHN FitzWALTER, **3rd Lord** (Baron) **FitzWalter**; *b* by 1315; campaigned in France during Hudnred Years War 1346 on; *m* Alianore, dau of Henry, Lord Percy (*see* NORTHUMBERLAND, D), and *d* 18 Oct 1361, leaving, with at least one dau (Alice, *m* 10th Earl of Oxford; *see* SAINT ALBANS, D):

WALTER FitzWALTER, **4th Lord** (Baron) **FitzWalter**; *b* 31 May 1345; campaigned in France during Hundred Years War 1370, about which time he was taken by the French and held to ransom; a commander of the fleet in the abortive attack on the Spanish fleet at Sluys Nov 1377; Marshal of the Army in invasion of Brittany 1380–81, took part in Siege of Nantes; *m* 1st *c* 23 June 1362 Alianore, dau and heir of Thomas, Lord (Baron) Dagworth, and had issue; *m* 2nd by 27 June 1385 Philippa (*m* 2nd by 13 Nov 1389 Sir John Golafre (*d* 18 Nov 1396); *m* 3rd by 24 Oct 1404 EDWARD, DUKE OF YORK (gs of EDWARD III), and *d* 17 July 1431), 2nd dau and coheir of John, Lord (Baron) Mohun, and *d* near Oronse, Galicia, Spain 26 Sept 1386; his son by his 1st w:

WALTER FitzWALTER, **5th Lord** (Baron) **FitzWalter**; *b* 5 Sept 1368; *m* Joan (*m* 2nd Hugh, Lord (Baron) Burnell, and *d* May 1409), only dau of John, Lord (Baron) Devereux, and *d* at Venice 16 May 1406, having had, with a dau:

1 HUMPHREY FitzWALTER, **6th Lord** (Baron) **FitzWalter**; *b* 18 Oct 1398; *d* unm 1 Sept 1415

2 WALTER FitzWALTER, **7th Lord** (Baron) **FitzWalter**; *bapt* 22 June 1400 or 1401; Master of the King's Harthounds 1420, ktd by Jan 1420/1, cdr Hundred Years War, participating in Siege of Melun July-Nov 1420 and Battle of Beaugé 22 March 1420/1, where captured by French, but later continuing mil service in France till at least 1431; *m* Elizabeth (*m* 3rd by 5 Nov 1438 Sir Thomas Cobham, of Sterborough, Surrey, and *d* 14 June 1464), widow of William Massy, King's Esquire, and dau of Sir John Chidiok, of Chideock, Dorset, and *dspm* 25 Nov 1431, having had:

(1) ELIZABETH FitzWalter, **Baroness FitzWalter** in her own right according to later doctrine; *b* 28 July 1430; *m* 1st by 27 Oct 1444 John RADCLIFFE (*k* fighting for the Yorkists at Ferrybridge (a skirmish just prior to Towton) 28

March 1461), of Attleborough, Norfolk, son and heir of Sir John Radcliffe, KG (*see also* RADCLIFFE, Bt); *m* 2nd *c* 15 March 1466/7, as his 1st w, John, Lord (Baron) Dinham, and *d* by 22 Aug 1485; her son by her 1st husb:

1a JOHN RADCLIFFE, **9th Lord** (Baron) **FitzWalter**; *b* 1 Jan 1451/2; Steward Household by 19 Oct 1485, Jt Warden and Ch Justice King's Forests S of Trent 14 Jan 1485/6 and all King's Forests 25 Feb 1485/6; allegedly *m* 1st Anne, sis of Richard Whetehill, of Calais; *m* (?)2nd(?) *c* 6 July 1475 Margaret — (possibly it was she who was dau of Robert Whetehill) and by her had issue; implicated in conspiracy of Perkin Warbeck and attainted of high treason soon after 14 Oct 1495, when his lands and honours became forfeited; imprisoned at Guines, nr Calais, and after an abortive jail break was beheaded at Calais *c* 24 Nov 1496; his s by his (?)2nd(?) w:

1b ROBERT RADCLIFFE/RATCLYFFE, **10th Lord** (Baron) **FitzWalter** (attainder reversed 3 Nov 1505) and 1st EARL OF SUSSEX, so *cr* 8 Dec 1529, as also earlier 18 June 1525 VISCOUNT FitzWALTER (both E), KG (1524), KB (1509), PC (by 5 Feb 1525/6); *b c* 1483; campaigned in France 1512–13 and 1522, Chamberlain Exchequer 1532–42, Gt Chamberlain 1540–42; *m* 1st Lady Elizabeth Stafford, dau of 2nd Duke of Buckingham (*see* STAFFORD, B), and had issue:

1c HENRY RADCLIFFE/RATCLYFFE, **11th Lord** (Baron) **FitzWalter** and 2nd EARL OF SUSSEX, KG (1554), KB (1533), PC (1553); *b c* 1507; in suite of Wolsey on latter's Embassy to France 1527; campaigned in France 1544, Jt Ld Lt Norfolk 1551, 1552 and 1553 and Ld Lt Norfolk and Suffolk 1556–Feb 1556/7; *m* 1st by 21 May 1524 Lady Elizabeth Howard (*d* 18 Sept 1537), 5th dau of 2nd Duke of Norfolk (*qv*), and had, with other issue:

1d THOMAS RADCLIFFE/RATCLYFFE, **12th Lord** (Baron) **FitzWalter** and 3rd EARL OF SUSSEX, KG (1557), PC (1570); *b c* 1525; campaigned in France, where present Siege Boulogne (ktd 30 Sept 1544 following its capitulation) and in Scotland (present Battle of Pinkie 10 Sept 1547); MP Norfolk 1553, Capt Gentlemen Pensioners 1553–83, sent as Commr to Spain 1554 to arrange marriage of QUEEN MARY and PHILIP II, Ld Dep Ireland 1556–60 and Ld Lt Ireland 1560–65, Ld-Pres Cncl of the North 1568–72, Ld Lt of the North 1569–70, Ld Chamberlain 1572–83; *m* 1st by 1 Nov 1545 Lady Elizabeth Wriothesley (*d* Jan 1554/5), dau of 1st Earl of Southampton (*see* SOUTHAMPTON, B, preliminary remarks); *m* 2nd by 29 April 1555 Frances (*d* 9 March 1558/9, fndr with a legacy of £5,000 (over £800,000 in late-1990s terms) of Sydney Sussex Coll Cambridge), dau of Sir William Sydney, of Penshurst Co Kent (*see* DE L'ISLE V), and *dsp* 9 June 1583

2d HENRY RADCLIFFE/RATCLYFFE, **13th Lord** (Baron) **FitzWalter** and 4th EARL OF SUSSEX, KG (1589), PC (I by late Feb 1556/7); *b c* 1532; ktd 1553, MP Maldon 1555, Hants 1571 and Portsmouth 1572–83, also (I Parl) Carlingford 1559, Lt Queen's and King's Cos Ireland 1557–64, Govr of Portsmouth 1571 and Jt Ld Lt Hants 1585–93; *m c* 6 Feb 1548/9 Honor, dau and coheir of Anthony Pound, of Hants, and *d* 14 Dec 1593, leaving:

1e ROBERT RADCLIFFE/RATCLYFFE, **14th Lord** (Baron) **FitzWalter** and 5th EARL OF SUSSEX, KG (1599); *b* 12 June 1573; Col of a foot regt Cadiz Expdn, where ktd, 1596, Earl Marshal Oct-Dec 1597 and Oct-Dec 1601, briefly placed under house arrest Feb 1600/1 for alleged complicity in Essex's Rebellion, Ld Lt Essex 1603–25 and 1626–29; *m* 1st by 1592 Bridget (*bur* 11 Dec 1623, having had four children by him, all *d* young), dau of Sir Charles Morrison, of Cashiobury, Herts; *m* 2nd Dec 1623 Frances, widow of Edward Shute and dau of Hercules Meautys, of West Ham, Essex, and *dspl* 22 Sept 1629, leaving by his 2nd w (but *b* before their marriage):

1f Jane; *b c* 1610; inherited with her 1st husb the Attleborough estate from her f; *m* 1st 7 June 1623 Sir Anthony Radcliffe, KB, of Ordsall; *m* 2nd Dr Lewes and *d* in or after 1674

1c The **11th Lord** *m* 2nd by 21 Nov 1538 (*divorce* by 13 Nov 1555) Anne, dau of Sir Philip Calthorp, and *d* 17 Feb 1556/7, leaving by her:

3d Egremont; took part in the failed rebellion of the Northern Earls (*see* ABERGAVENNY, M, and NORTHUMBERLAND, D), fled the country and was put to death at Namur by order of Don John of Austria

1d FRANCES Radcliffe/Ratclyffe; *m* Sir Thomas MILDMAY (*d* 1608), of Moulsham, Essex (*see* ST JOHN-MILDMAY, Bt), and had:

1e Thomas (Sir), of Moulsham; *dsp* 1625

2e Sir HENRY MILDMAY, of Moulsham, *de jure* 15th LORD (Baron) FitzWALTER, for which title he unsuccessfully petitioned Parl 9 Aug 1641 and 17 June 1645; *b c* 1585; *m* Elizabeth, 2nd dau and coheir of Thomas Darcy, of Tolleshunt Darcy, Essex, and *d* 1654, having had, with other issue:

1f Robert, of Overstone, Northants; *m* Mary, 3rd dau and coheir of Sir Thomas Edmonds, of Overstone, and *dvp* 1646, leaving:

1g HENRY MILDMAY, *de jure* 16th LORD (Baron) FitzWALTER, for recognition as which he petitioned Ho of Lords Aug 1660; *d* unm and was *bur* 24 March 1661/2

2g BENJAMIN MILDMAY, **17th Lord** (Baron) **Fitzwalter**; petitioned Ho Lds for recognition Feb 1667 but not summoned to Parl till 10 Feb 1669/70, with ultimate precedence as the last Baron *cr* in EDWARD I's reign; *m* 6 Dec 1669 Catherine (*d* 20 March 1724/5), only dau of 3rd Viscount Fairfax of Emmeley (*see* FAIRFAX OF CAMERON, L), and *d* 1 June 1679, leaving:

1h CHARLES MILDMAY, **18th Lord** (Baron) **FitzWalter**; *b* 31 Aug 1670; *m* 8 June 1693 Elizabeth (*d* 20 Dec 1738), dau of Hon Charles Bertie (*see* LINDSEY and ABINGDON, E), and *dsps* 16 Feb 1727/8

2h BENJAMIN MILDMAY, **19th Lord** (Baron) **FitzWalter** and 1st and last EARL FitzWALTER, so *cr* 16 May 1735, as also VISCOUNT HARWICH, Co Essex (both GB), PC (1735); *bapt* 27 Dec 1672; Commr of Excise 1720–28, 1st Ld Trade 1735–37, Treasurer Household 1737–55, Ld Lt Essex 1741–56; *m* 18 June 1724 Frederica (*d* 7 Aug 1751), widow of Robert Darcy, Earl of Holderness (*see* DARCY DE KNAYTH, B), and dau and coheir of 3rd Duke of Schomberg and 1st Duke of Leinster, and *dsps* 29 Feb 1756 (when the Earldom and Viscountcy expired but the Barony of Fitzwalter fell into abeyance), bequeathing the Moulsham and Burnham-on-Crouch estates to his kinsman, Sir William Mildmay, Bt (*see* ST JOHN-MILDMAY, Bt)

1g MARY, for whom *see* below

2c Humphrey (Sir), of Elstow, Beds; *m* Isabel, dau and heir of Edmond Harvey, of Elstow, and *d* 1566, having had issue:

1d EDWARD RADCLIFFE, 6th and last EARL OF SUSSEX; *b* by 10 Nov 1559; MP Petersfield 1586–87, Beds 1588–89, 1601 and 1604–11 and Portsmouth 1593 and 1594; ktd by 30 May 1594; High Sheriff Beds 1598–99; *m* 1st on or after 28 Feb 1581/2 but before 16 Aug 1583 Elizabeth, half-sis of 1st Baron Petre (*qv*) and widow of John Gostwicke; *m* 2nd 30 May 1594 Jane, widow of (a) John Catesby and (b) William West and dau of Sir Francis Hynde, of Madingley, Cambs; *m* 3rd 22 May 1634 Eleanor (*m* 3rd 30 March 1646 Robert Rich, 2nd Earl of Warwick (*see* WARWICK, BROOKE and, E, preliminary remarks); *m* 4th *c* 1659, as the 4th of five ws, 2nd Earl of Manchester (*see* MANCHESTER, D) and *d* 20 Jan 1666/7), widow of Sir Henry Lee, 1st Bt, and dau of Sir Richard Wortley, of Wortley, Yorks, and *dsp* July Aug 1643, when his honours expired

1b (cont.) The **10th Lord** *m* 2nd Lady Margaret Stanley, only dau of 2nd Earl of Derby (*qv*), and by her had:

1c Anne; *m* 1547 2nd Baron Wharton (*qv*) and had issue

2c Jane; *m* 1st Viscount Montagu and had issue

1b (cont.) The **10th Lord** *m* 3rd 14 Jan 1536/7 Mary (*m* 2nd 19 Dec 1545 19th/12th Earl of Arundel (*see* NORFOLK, D) and *d* 21 Oct 1557), yr dau of Sir John Arundell, of Lanherne, Cornwall, and *d* 27 Nov 1542, leaving by her:

3c John (Sir); *dsp*

The sis of the 16th and 17th LORDs FitzWALTER,

MARY Mildmay; *b* 1637; *m* Henry MILDMAY (*d* 13 Dec 1692), of Graces, Little Baddow, Essex, and *d* 15 April 1715, having had, with four sons and two other daus (*d* infants):

1 Mary; *m* Charles Goodwin, of Rowvant, Sussex (*d* 9 June 1731), and *dsp* 17 Jan 1723/4

2 Lucy; *m* Thomas Gardiner, of Tollesbury, Essex, and had issue

3 Elizabeth; *m* 17 Sept 1696 Edmund Waterson and *dsp* 19 July 1746

4 FRANCES

5 Catherine; *m* 1697 Lt-Col Thomas Townshend and *d* April 1708, leaving:

(1) Thomas Townshend; Capt; *dsp* 1731

Mrs MILDMAY's 4th dau,

FRANCES Mildmay; *b* 28 March 1666; *m* 29 Oct 1689 Christopher FOWLER, of London, and *d* 1705, leaving:

1 EDMUND FOWLER, of Graces; *b* 1701; *m* 5 Oct 1744 Elizabeth Pateshall, of Worcester, and *d* 1751, leaving:

(1) FANNY Fowler; *b* 5 Dec 1746; *m* 11 June 1765 Sir Brook BRIDGES, 3rd Bt (*b* 17 Sept 1733; *d* 4 Sept 1791; *see also* ROMNEY, E), and *d* 16 March 1825, having had, with other issue:

1a Sir BROOK WILLIAM BRIDGES, 4th Bt; Cdr RN; *b* 22 June 1767; *m* 1st 14 Aug 1800 Eleanor (*d* 29 Jan 1806), er dau and eventual coheir of John Foote, banker, of Lombard St, London, and had issue:

1b Sir BROOK WILLIAM BRIDGES, 5th Bt, and 1st and last BARON FitzWALTER OF WOODHAM WALTER, Co Essex (UK), so *cr* 17 April 1868; *b* 2 June 1801; *educ* Winchester and Oriel Coll Oxford; MP (V) E Kent Feb-July 1852 and 1857–68; claimed Barony of Fitzwalter 1841; *m* 4 July 1834 Fanny, dau of Lewis Cage of Milgate, Kent, and *dsp* 6 Sept 1875

2b Rev Sir BROOK GEORGE BRIDGES, 6th Bt, Rector Orlingbury, Northants 1827–53, and Blankney, Lincs, 1858–78; *b* 12 Oct 1802; *m* 15 Nov 1832 Louisa (*d* 21 Jan 1884), 4th dau of Charles Chaplin, MP, of Blankney (*see* 1970 edn CHAPLIN,V), and *dsp* 1 April 1890

1b ELEANOR, for whom *see* below

1a (cont.) The 4th Bt *m* 2nd 15 Dec 1809 Dorothy Elizabeth (*d* 17 May 1826), er dau of Sir Henry Hawley, 1st Bt (*qv*), and *d* 21 April 1829

His only dau,

ELEANOR Bridges; *b* 13 Nov 1805; *m* 10 April 1828 Rev Henry Western PLUMPTRE, MA, Rector Eastwood, Notts (*d* 23 April 1863), and *d* 24 Jan 1892, having had an est s:

JOHN BRIDGES PLUMPTRE, JP; Maj Kent Rifle Vols; *b* 30 Sept 1832; *m* 31 May 1859 Elizabeth (*d* 2 April 1909), 2nd dau of Francis Wright, DL, JP, of Osmaston Manor, Derbys, and *d* 10 Nov 1888, having had:

1 HENRY FitzWALTER PLUMPTRE, **20th Lord** (Baron) **FitzWalter**, as which summoned to Parl by writ 30 Sept 1924 on termination of abeyance in his favour, JP, CA Kent; *b* 12 Dec 1860; *m* 1st 26 April 1892 Maude Dora Gertrude (*d* 4 May 1893), dau of Capt Thomas Carpendale Baird, of Flatfield, Ayrshire; *m* 2nd 1 Feb 1908 his dead w's sis Emily Harriet Jemina (*d* 15 Jan 1951), er dau of Capt Thomas Carpendale Baird, and *dsp* 12 Sept 1932, when the Barony became dormant until his nephew was summoned to Parl by writ 28 May 1953

2 John Bridges (Rev); Rector Danbury, Essex; *educ* Oriel Coll Oxford (MA); *d* 18 Nov 1930

3 Francis Fitzherbert; *b* 23 March 1864; *d* unm 3 Nov 1943

4 George Beresford; Lt E Kent Yeo Boer War (two medals, five clasps); *b* 21 March 1869; *m* 18 Feb 1908 his cousin Mary Augusta (*d* 3 Feb 1953), 2nd dau of Rev Henry Western Plumptre, of Eastwood, Notts, and *d* 23 April 1934, leaving:

(1) (FitzWALTER) BROOK PLUMPTRE, **21st and present Lord (Baron) FitzWalter**

(2) Peter Bridges, MBE (1944); Maj The Buffs WW II (POW, wounded); *b* 25 March 1916; *educ* Diocesan Coll Cape Town and King's Sch Canterbury; *m*

1944 *Maude Helen, dau of Geoffrey Henry Baird, of Goodnestone, nr Canterbury, and *d* 3 Jan 1995, leaving:

1a +Timothy George; *b* 29 April 1945; *m* 1975 *Christine Hamilton and has:

1b +Peter Hamilton; *b* 1980

1b +Tamsin Mary; *b* 1978

2a +Jeremy Peter; *b* 20 Oct 1947; *m* 1985 *Carmen Nozal Gonzalez

3a +Michael John; *b* 10 March 1955

1a +Rosalin Helen [Mrs David Bowler, Beechwood, Heathfield, Tavistock, Devon]; *b* 2 July 1952; *m* 1970 *David Alan Bowler and has:

1b +Nathan Plumptre; *b* 1972

1b +Lucy Plumptre; *b* 1971

(1) Margaretta

(2) +Judith Patricia [Miss Judith Plumptre, Flat 1, The Old Mitre, Lower Acreman St, Sherborne, Dorset DT9 3EX]; *b* 1910

(3) +Elizabeth Mary [Mrs Philip Pennant, 2 Manor Close, Bradford Abbas, Sherborne, Dorset DT9 6RN]; *b* 31 March 1912; *m* 11 Jan 1941 *Rev Philip Vivian Rogers Pennant, TD, MA, Capt RWF, yst son of David Falconer Pennant, DL, JP, of Nantlys, Flintshire, and has issue:

1a +Thomas George Edmund; *b* 11 Nov 1947; *educ* Wrekin Coll and Trin Coll Cambridge (BA); *m* 1979 *Eva Gertrud Elisabeth, er dau of Dr Heinz Esser, of D5093 Burscheid am Jungholzkamp, Germany, and has issue:

1b +Christina Agnes Katharina; *b* 1981

2a +Philip Pearson; *b* 18 Nov 1952

3a +Stephen Owen Falconer [Stephen Plumptre Esq, 19 Fossil Rd, London SE13 7DE]; *b* 18 Feb 1956; *m* 1985 *Jean Madeline, dau of Rev Rene Tassell, of Upton-upon-Severn, Worcs, and has issue:

1b +Douglas Hunter; *b* 1987

1b +Elizabeth Madeline; *b* 1985

2b +Florence Maria; *b* 1991

1a +Philippa Berain Elizabeth [Mrs Bryan Farr, Worksop Manor, Worksop, Notts S80 3DG]; *b* 11 Nov 1942; *m* 30 June 1962 *Bryan Henry Farr, JP, yst s of Capt John Farr, of Worksop Manor, and has issue:

1b +Henry John Philip; *b* 15 July 1966

1b +Rosalinde Mary [Mrs Paul Gray, 23 Baskerville Rd, London]; *b* 23 June 1963; *m* 19– *Paul Douglas Gray and has:

1c +John Henry Douglas; *b* 1 June 1995

1c +Willa Jane Elizabeth; *b* 23 Feb 1994

2b +Susannah Margaret; *b* 2 Feb 1965

2a +Sarah Fariana Mary Agnes [Mrs Michael Girdlestone, The Wharf House, Cropredy, Oxon OX17 1PQ]; *b* 3 Sept 1944; *m* 1st 22 Oct 1966 (*divorce* 1984) Robert Iain Bescoby Jenkins; *m* 2nd 1984 *Maj Michael Owen Girdlestone, RA, and by her 1st husb has issue:

1b +Robert Brook Pennant; *b* 1970

2b +Philip David Alexander; *b* 1971

1b +Katie Serena Margaret; *b* 1977

3a +Helen Michèle [Mrs Jay Brewer, Pedlars Cottage, Worthing Rd, Rustington, W Sussex BN16 3PS]; *b* 29 Sept 1949; *m* 1986 *Jay Hilton Brewer and has:

1b +Rosie Margaretta; *b* 1988

(4) Frederica Anne; *b* 1919; *m* 15 Aug 1942 Anthony Durnford Gaymer (*d* 1985), FRIBA, Maj RA, and *d* 1995, leaving:

1a +Nigel Anthony; *b* 17 Nov 1944; FCA; *m* 1969 *Kathryn Helen Adams and has:

1b +Adam Timothy; *b* 1973

1b +Kirsten Anne; *b* 1976

1a +Felicity Anne [Mrs John Parker, 4590 Sumner Place, Victoria, BC V8N 3V7, Canada]; *b* 25 April 1950; *m* 1972 *John Edward Parker and has:

1b +Geoffrey James; *b* 1973

2b +Anthony William; *b* 1974

3b +Jonathan George; *b* 1982

1b +Olivia Felicity Anne; *b* 1976

2b +Victoria Rose; *b* 1980

1 Margaretta Agnes; *m* 20 May 1892 Albert Leslie Wright, JP (*d* 4 Sept 1938), of Butterley Hall, Derbyshire, and *d* 21 Sept 1907, leaving:

(1) Edward FitzWalter; *b* 1902; *m* 1927 Jane Fairie Wilson (*d* 1989), dau of Thomas Chalmers McGuffie, and *d* 1957, leaving issue:

1a +John Leslie FitzWalter [John Wright Esq, Kirby House, Kirby Bedon, Norfolk NR14 7DZ]; *b* 1934; *educ* Winchester and Ch Ch Oxford; late 2nd Lt Sherwood Foresters; *m* 1974 *Susan Annette, dau of Maj-Gen Allan Elton Younger, DSO, OBE, of The Manor House, Twyford, Hants, and has:

1b +Francis Gideon FitzWalter; *b* 1975

2b +David Nathanael Beresford; *b* 1979

3b +James Emanuel Shakespeare; *b* 1981

4b +John Joseph Camplyon; *b* 1981

1b +Jemimah Alianore; *b* 1977

1a Margaretta Jane; *b* 1928; *m* 1949 (*divorce* 1965) Cdr Robert Ian Langlands PEARSE, RN, took name LANGLANDS 1977 and *d* 1984, leaving issue:

1b +Robert Simon Hugh [Robert Langlands, c/o Bank of Scotland, 14–16 Cockspur St, London SW1]; *b* 1950; *m* 1975 *Jane Isobel, dau of Raymond Timothy Porter, of Te Awamatu, NZ, and has issue:

1c +Timothy George; *b* 1977

2c +Rupert Hugh Chalmers; *b* 1988

1c +Joanna Jane Margaretta; *b* 1980

2b +Adam Philip; *b* 1955

3b +Dominic Walter; *b* 1959; *m* 1986 Frances Symons (*d* 1989)

2a Jennifer Marion; *b* 1930; *m* 1952 *Lt-Cdr Sir John Muir Drinkwater, RN, QC, and *d* 1990, leaving issue:

1b +Jonathan Dominick St Clair; *b* 1956; *m* 1984 *Philippa Anne, dau of Anthony van Beugen Bik, of Busbridge Farmhouse, Godalming, Surrey, and has issue:

1c +Charles Alexander John; *b* 1991

2c +Harriet Frances Jessanda; *b* 1989

1b +Jane Fairrie; *b* 1954; *m* 1977 *Timothy John Comyn, of Hardington Mandeville, Somerset, and has issue:

1c +James Edward Daniel; *b* 1982

2c +Edward John FitzWalter; *b* 1989

1c +Cressida Rose Katherine; *b* 1985

2b Joanna Elizabeth; *b* 1958; *d* 1995

3b +Juliet Caroline Leslie; *b* 1961; *m* 1992 *Jeffrey George Puckett and has:

1c +Melissa Jennifer Lilian; *b* 1994

2c +Augusta Joanna Caroline; *b* 1996

4b +Jessanda Katherine Jemima [Mrs Richard Farrant, Rose Cottage Farm, Leigh Rd, Norwood Hill, Surrey]; *b* 1964; *m* 1991 *Richard Granville Farrant

3a +Caroline Leslie; *b* 1932 [Miss Caroline Wright, Hilltop Cottage, Shutford, Oxon OX15 6PL]

(1) Marion; *m* 1920 7th Viscount Hawarden (*qv*) and *d* 1984, leaving issue

(2) Margaretta; *m* 1918 Arthur Philip Coote and *d* 1977, leaving issue (*see* COOTE, Bt)

2 Selina Fanny; *m* 26 Feb 1897 Lionel Sherbrooke Osmaston, JP (*d* 29 March 1969), Dep-Surveyor New Forest, and *d* 14 June 1949, leaving:

(1) Robert Lionel; *b* 1903, MB, BCh; *educ* Cambridge U (BA 1924, MB, Bch 1932); MRCS England and LRCP London 1927; *m* 1945 *Dorothy [Mrs Robert Osmaston, 11 Lower Stoke, Limpley Stoke, nr Bath, Avon BA3 6HT], dau of Albert Edward Ward, and *d* 10 July 1994, leaving:

1a +Margaret Elizabeth [Mrs William McIvor, 42 Belsay, Toothill, Wilts SN5 8HB]; *b* 1946; *m* 1st 1968 (*divorce* 1985) John Richard Bradley, BDS, LDS, RCS; *m* 2nd 1987 *William Birkmyre Sutherland McIvor and by her 1st husb has:

1b +Robert John; *b* 1979

2b +Nicholas James; *b* 1982

2a +Dorothy June; *b* 1947

(1) Gwendolen Selina; *b* 1905; *m* 1935 Thomas Gerald Elwin Nash (*d* 1963) and *d* 1989, leaving:

1a +Stephen Thomas [Stephen Nash Esq, The Cottage, Goodnestone, nr Canterbury, Kent]; *b* 1942; *m* 1st 1967 Rose-Marie Birgitta Bornstrand and has:

1b +Maurice; *b* 1971

1a (cont.) Stephen Nash *m* 2nd 1977 *Boonying Permkasikan and by her has:

2b +Joseph Thomas Elwin; *b* 1997

1b +Tanya Selina; *b* 1977

2b +Linda Helen; *b* 1985

(2) +Marion Margaretta [Mrs Frank Williams, 63 Beech Way, Twickenham, Middx]; *b* 1915; *m* 1st 1941 Capt David Harold Archer, MC (*ka* Tunisia 1943), Roy W Kent Regt; *m* 2nd 1953 Lt-Cdr Frank Williams, RN (*d* 1978), and by him has:

1a +Sally Elizabeth; *b* 1954

3 Elizabeth Eleanor; *m* 12 Nov 1902 Maurice Beresford Wright, OBE (*d* 1951), MD, and *d* 28 June 1953, leaving:

(1) Nigel; *b* 1908; *m* 1948 *Patricia Kidd [Mrs Nigel Wright, 16 Heatherwood, Petersfield Rd, Midhurst, Sussex] and *d* 1989, leaving:

1a +Andrew Firman [Dr Andrew Wright, Ashleigh, 14 Ashfield Drive, Macclesfield, Cheshire SK10 3DQ]; *b* 1953; MIBiol, PhD; *m* 1977 *Susan Bowlas and has:

1b +Alan Nigel; *b* 1986

1b +Joanna; *b* 1983

1a +Susan Jane [Mrs Robert Allison, Mill House, Nutbourne, Pulborough, W Sussex]; *b* 1951; *m* 1974 *Robert Andrew Allison and has:

1b +Elizabeth Sarah; *b* 1980

2b +Caroline Jane; *b* 1983

(1) +Marjorie Prunella [Mrs Charlie Grunsell, Greenloaves, Mead Lane, Sandford, nr Bristol BS19 5RG]; *b* 1912; *m* 1939 *Charlie Stuart Grunsell, CBE, FRCVS, and has issue:

1a +Robin Nigel Stuart [Robin Grunsell Esq, 17 Lowman Rd, London N7]; *b* 1946; *m* 1968 *Angela Boulton and has:

1b +Jonah Charles; *b* 1977

1b +Leila; *b* 1973

1a +Elspeth Ann Grant [Mrs Edward Cantrell, Waterside Cottage, Walhampton, Hants SO41 5SD]; *b* 1940; *m* 1965 *Edward Godfrey Cantrell, MB, MRCP, and has:

1b +Matthew Ross; *b* 1968; *m* 1997 *Korinne Simmons

1b +Tamsin [Mrs Danny Byrne, 24 Solent Close, Lymington, Hants]; *b* 1970; *m* 1992 *Danny Byrne and has:

1c +Thomas Edward; *b* 1994

1c +Emily May; *b* 1992

2a +Susanna; *b* 1943

FLATHER

Creation: B. (LP, UK) 1990.

THE BARONESS FLATHER, of Windsor and Maidenhead, Co Berks (Shreela Rai, JP (Maidenhead 1971), DL (Berks 1994) [The Rt Hon The Baroness Flather JP DL, House of Lords, London SW1A 0PW]; *b* 19–; *educ* UCL (LLB, Fell 1992); barrister Inner Temple 1962, infant teacher ILEA 1965–67, taught English as 2nd lang 1968–78, memb: Ctee Inquiry Educn Children Ethnic Minority Gps 1979–85, CRE 1980–86, Police Complaints Bd 1982–85, Ld Chllr's Legal Aid Ctee 1985–88, Ho Lds Select Ctee Medical Ethics 1993–, Cncl Winston Churchill Meml Tst 1993–, Cncl Atlantic Coll 1993–, C Women's Nat Ctee 1978–89, Exec Ctee Anglo-Asian C Soc 1979–83, NEC C Pty 1989–90, LWT Programme Advsy Bd 1990–94, Servite Houses Ctee Management 1987– and Carnegie Inquiry Third Age 1991–, UK Del Ec and Social Ctee EC 1987–90, UK Rep ECC Enquiry Racism and Xenophobia 1994–95, Pres: Cambs, Chilterns and Thames Rent Assessment Panel 1983–, League Friends Broadmoor Hosp 1991– and Community Cncl Berks 1991–, V-Pres: Assoc DCs 1990–, Cwlth Countries League 1990–, Assoc Met Authorities 1991–,V-Chm Refugee Cncl (Chm UK Policy Gp) 1991–, dir Meridian Bdcstg 1991– , Star FM 1992– and Thames Valley Enterprise 1990–, Tstee Hillingdon Hosp Tst 1990–, Councillor Windsor and Maidenhead 1976–91, Dep-Mayor 1985–86, Mayor 1986–87, Sec Windsor and Maidenhead C Gp, Govr Cwlth Inst 1993–, chm Parly Race and Community Gp April–July 1995; *m* 19– *Gary Denis Flather, QC, s of Denis and Joan Flather, and has:

1 *Paul; *b* 1954
2 *Marcus; *b* 1957

Lineage: RAI BAHADUR AFTAB RAI, of New Delhi; had:

SHREELA, *cr* a **Baroness**

FLOWERS

Creation: B. (LP, UK) 1979.

THE BARON FLOWERS, of Queen's Gate, in the City of Westminster (Brian Hilton Flowers) [The Rt Hon The Lord Flowers, 53 Athenaeum Rd, London N20 9AL]; *b* 13 Sept 1924; *educ* Bishop Gore GS, Gonville and Caius Coll Cambridge (MA, Hon Fell 1974) and Birmingham U (DSc); physicist, Head Theoretical Physics Div Atomic Energy Research Establishment Harwell 1952–58, Manchester U: Prof Theoretical Physics 1958–61, Langworthy Prof Physics 1961–72 and Chllr 1994–, Pres: Inst Physics 1972–74, European Science Fndn 1974–80, Chm: SRC 1967–73, Roy Commn Environmental Pollution 1973–76, Standing Commn Energy and Environment 1978–81, London U Working Party Future of Medical and Dental Teaching Resources 1979–80, Ctee V-Chllrs and Pncpls 1983–85, Ho Lds Select Ctee Sci and Technology 1989–93, London Sch Hygiene and Tropical Medicine 1994– (memb bd management 1992–) and Nuffield Fndn 1987– (Managing Tstee 1982–), Rector Imp Coll Sci and Technology 1973–85, V-Chllr London U 1985–90, Fndr Memb: SDP 1981– and Exec Cncl Academia Europaea 1988, V-Chm Cncl Roy Postgrad Medical Sch 1991– (memb Cncl 1990–), FinstP 1961, Hon FCGI 1975, Hon MRIA 1976, Hon FIEE 1975, Offr Legn Hon 1981, Sr Fell RCA 1983, Hon DSc: Sussex 1968, Wales 1972, Manchester 1973, Leicester 1973, Liverpool 1974, Bristol 1982, Oxford 1985, NUI 1990, Hon DEng Nova Scotia 1983, MA Oxon, Hon DSc Oxon, Hon ScD Dublin 1984, FRS 1961 (Rutherford Medal and Prize 1963), IPPS Glazebrook Medal and Prize 1987, Chalmers Medal Chalmers U of Tech Sweden 1980, ktd 1969, author: *Properties of Matter* (1970, with E Mendoza), *An Introduction to Numerical Methods in C++* (1995); *m* 1951 *Mary Frances, er dau of Sir Leonard Frederick Behrens, CBE

Lineage: Rev HAROLD J FLOWERS, of Swansea; had:

BRIAN HILTON FLOWERS, *cr* a **Baron**

FLOYD

Arms: Sa. a lion rampant-regardant arg., on a chief embattled or a sword erect ppr., pommel and hilt gold, enfiled with an Eastern crown gu., between two tiger's faces also ppr. **Crest:** A lion rampant-regardant arg., murally crowned gu., bearing a flag representing the standard of Tippoo Sultan flowing to the sinister ppr. **Motto:** *Patiens pulveris atque solis* ('Putting up with the dust and the sun'). **Creation:** Bt. (UK) 30 March 1816.

SIR GILES HENRY CHARLES FLOYD, 7TH BT [Sir Giles Floyd Bt, Tinwell Manor, Stamford, Lincs PE9 3UD]; *b* 27 Feb 1932; *s* f 1975; *educ* Eton; High Sheriff Rutland 1968, chm Burghley Estate Farms; *m* 1st 23 Nov 1954 (*divorce* 1978) Lady Gillian Moyra Katherine Cecil, 2nd dau of 6th Marquess of Exeter (*qv*); *m* 2nd 1985 *Judy Sophia, er dau of William Leonard Tregoning, CBE, of Launceston, Cornwall, and formerly w of Thomas Ernest Lane, of Tickencote Hall, Stamford, and by his 1st w has:

1 +DAVID HENRY CECIL; *b* 2 April 1956; *educ* Eton and RMA Sandhurst; late 15th/19th Hussars, ACA 1983, FCA 1993, merchant banker; *m* 20 June 1981 *Caroline Ann, dau of John Henry Beckly, of Manor Farm, Bowerchalke, Wilts, and has:
(1) *Suzanna Mary Caroline; *b* 1983
(2) *Claire; *b* 1986
2 +Henry (Harry) Edward Cecil; *b* 3 Aug 1958; *educ* Stanbridge Earls and New Mexico Inst Mining and Technology; *m* 13 April 1994 *Leonor, dau of Sergio Castillo, of Santiago de Chile, and has:
(1) +Henry William; *b* 18 Nov 1994
(1) *Daniela Sophia; *b* 24 Oct 1996

Lineage: The FLOYDs, of Welsh descent, at one point lived at Beeston Castle (destroyed 1645 at the time of the Civil War), also Prestbury, Cheshire, and Shrewsbury. They included:

HUGO FLOYD, of Calais *temp* HENRY VIII; gf of:

JOHN FLOYD, of Calais and Batrichosey, Surrey, Assist Comptroller Exchequer 1623

Also,

DAVID FLOYD, of Foss-y-Bleidied; served at sea Dutch Wars, Capt 1685 in the Earl of Oxford's Regt (Horse Gds Blues), Groom Bedchamber to JAMES II, whom he followed into exile and on whose behalf he carried despatches between the Jacobite court in exile at St Germains and England; had:

DAVID FLOYD; had:

STAINBANK FLOYD, of Shrewsbury; Jacobite 1745; *d* 24 Feb 1788, leaving, with an er dau:

ISABELLA; *m* 17 July 1810 Sir George Duckett, 2nd Bt, of Hartlam House, Wilts (*d* 15 June 1856; *see* 1850 edn), and had issue

Also,

JOHN FLOYD; Capt 1st Dragoon Gds, of Prestbury and St Chad's, Shrewsbury; *b* 1707; served Seven Years War, fought Battle of Minden 1759; *m* 28 Oct 1746 Mary (*b* 1713; *d* 8 Nov 1782), dau of Rev Richard Bate, of Chilham, Kent, and *d* of wounds 12 Sept 1759, having had issue:

1 JOHN (Sir), **1st Bt**
2 Thomas; Lt RN, served Arctic Expdn 1773; *b* 1751; *d* unm aboard HMS *Conqueror* off Sandy Hook 16 Oct 1778
1 Elizabeth Powys; *b* 1752; *d* unm 11 April 1830
2 Caroline; *m* John Christopher Ridout, of Baughurst House, Hants, and *d* 7 March 1821, leaving issue. He *d* 21 Oct 1817

Capt FLOYD's est son,

Sir John Floyd, 1st Bt (UK), so *cr* 30 March 1816; *b* 22 Feb 1748; Cornet Eliot's Light Horse (15th Hus) 1760, fought Battle of Emsdorf 1760, Col 19th Light Dragoons, cmded cavalry Mysore campaigns India 1790–99, 2ic capture of Seringapatam 1799, Gen, Col 8th Light Dragoons, Govr Gravesend and Tilbury Fort; *m* 1st 29 Jan 1791 Rebecca Juliana (*d* 3 Feb 1802), dau of Charles Darke, Madras merchant, and had issue:

1 HENRY (Sir), **2nd Bt**

1 Miranda; *m* 18 Nov 1815 Lt-Gen Sir Joseph Fuller, GCH, Col 75th Regt, and *d* 23 Sept 1869, leaving issue. He *d* 1841

2 Julia; *m* 8 June 1820 Sir Robert Peel, 2nd Bt, MP, PM (*see* PEEL, E), and *d* 27 Oct 1859

3 Flavia; *d* 1 Feb 1802

Sir John *m* 2nd 29 July 1805 Anna (*d* 4 Dec 1844), widow of Sir Barry Denny, 2nd Bt, of Castle Moyle (*qv*), and dau of Crosbie Morgell, of Mount Morgell, Co Limerick, and *d* 10 Jan 1818

His only son,

Sir Henry Floyd, 2nd Bt; Maj-Gen, ADC to Gen William Clinton Sicily and Spain, Capt 10th Roy Hus Waterloo campaign; *b* 2 Sept 1793; *m* 30 Aug 1821 Mary (*d* 27 Oct 1879), est dau and coheir of William Murray, of Latium, Jamaica, and Bryanston Sq, London, and *d* 4 March 1868, having had issue:

1 **Sir John Floyd, 3rd Bt**; Maj 2nd Roy Lanarks Militia, Capt 3rd Buffs, served Crimea; *b* 31 July 1823; *m* 10 June 1851 Thomasine Harriot (*d* 16 Feb 1856), dau of Sir Frederick Shaw, 3rd Bt (*qv*), and *dsp* 12 May 1909

2 William Murray; *b* 20 March 1826; *m* 10 May 1887 Lucy Anne, 2nd dau of Robert Fausset, JP, of Willesborough, Co Sligo, and *dsp* 22 July 1898

3 Robert Peel; Capt Roy Cheshire Militia and 85th Regt; *b* 24 March 1828; *m* 1st 4 Dec 1852 Mary Jane (*dsp* 11 Oct 1853), only dau of Henry Carew, of Ayshford, Sidmouth; *m* 2nd 10 Jan 1855 Jane Caroline (*d* 24 July 1885), widow of Charles William Montgomery (*see* MONTGOMERY, Bt) and dau of Richard Rennards, of York; *m* 3rd 1896 Caroline Augusta (*d* 18 Dec 1928), dau of Henry Coore, of Scruton Hall, Yorks, and *d* 3 May 1899, having by his 2nd w had issue:

(1) HENRY ROBERT PEEL (Sir), **4th Bt**

(1) Sarah Beatrice; *b* 28 May 1857; *d* unm 4 Jan 1952

(2) Constance Caroline Montgomery; *b* 2 March 1861; *m* 25 Oct 1882 Henry Carew Cox and *d* Aug 1937, leaving issue. He *d* 1929

4 Charles Greenwood (Rev); Rector Runcton Holme, Norfolk; *b* 14 June 1830; *educ* Ch Ch Oxford (MA); *m* 14 April 1880 Edith Ellen (*d* 10 April 1929), est dau of Lt-Col John Marcon, of Wallington Hall, Norfolk, and *d* 26 Feb 1903, having had issue:

(1) John Marcon, RAF; *b* 25 March 1882; *d* unm 22 Feb 1919

(2) Arthur Bowen, DSO (1919), OBE (1945); Lt-Col Roy Norfolk Regt WW I (despatches) and WW II (despatches); *b* 21 Jan 1888; *educ* Wellington; *m* 27 July 1922 Iris Clare (*d* 26 Aug 1975), widow of Capt A Stewart Ritchie, MC, Black Watch, and dau of D Turner Belding, of E Dereham, Norfolk, and *d* 28 May 1965, leaving:

1a Jo(hn) Anthony; *b* 12 May 1923; *educ* Eton; KRRC 1941–46; chm Christie's 1974–85 (dep chm 1973–74, ptnr 1954) and Christie's Internat 1976–88 (dir to 1992); *m* 5 Oct 1948 *Margaret Louise [Mrs John Floyd, Ecchinswell House, Newbury, Berks RG20 4UA], only dau of Maj Hugo Rosselli, of Worlington Old Hall, Bury St Edmunds, Suffolk, by Maud Heath, yr dau of Oswald Harrison, and *d* 20 Feb 1998, leaving:

1b *Elizabeth Joanna; *b* 8 Feb 1951

2b *Caroline Philippa; *b* 18 July 1953; *m* 14 June 1984 *Charles Henry Curzon Coaker, s of Maj-Gen Ronald Coaker, CB, CBE, MC, of Daleacre House, Lockington, Derbys, and has issue:

1c *Henry John Curzon; *b* 8 Jan 1986

2c *Thomas James Curzon; *b* 12 Feb 1987

1c *Molly Harriet; *b* 13 March 1990

(1) Helena Margaret; *b* 3 March 1881; *m* 11 July 1906 Cecil James Shuttleworth Holden, est s of Rev James Shuttleworth Holden, Rector Lackford, and *d* 24 March 1929, leaving issue. He *d* 15 March 1920

5 Henry Ridout; Maj 25th Regt; *b* 16 April 1835; *d* unm 20 June 1895

6 Charles Ashburnham; 9th Lancers; *b* 10 June 1838; *m* 25 Sept 1867 Mary (*d* 4 July 1907), dau of George Pomeroy, of Exeter, and *d* 7 Aug 1920, having had:

(1) Harry; *b* 30 April 1861; *m* 10 Dec 1903 Adele Lina Dorina (*d* 5 April 1937), dau of Baron S de Neufville, of Paris, and *d* 24 Feb 1933, leaving:

1a Ashburnham Henry Alex; *b* 24 Sept 1904; *m* 14 Nov 1935 *Mary Lethbridge Newberry, of S Africa and Australia

2a Roderick Pierre; *b* 24 Sept 1904

1a Griselda Mary Adeline; *m* 6 Dec 1928 Edward Kingsley Milbourne, est s of Lt-Col Kinsley Milbourne, of Les Fougeres, Guernsey, and had issue

2a Dorina Marjorie Gertrude; *m* 1934 Cdr Percy Frank Pilkington Wood, RN

(2) Arthur; *b* 16 Aug 1865

(1) Julia Miranda Laura; *m* 22 June 1926 Col John Spottiswoode Purvis, CBE, RE. He *d* 15 April 1927

(2) Gertrude Frederica Mary Ashburnham

7 Walter Combermere Lee, of Kelston Knoll, nr Bath; MICE, Dep Consulting Engr Rlwys Govt India; *b* 24 Feb 1841; *m* 1st 4 May 1869 Elizabeth Jane (*d* 27 Aug 1870), er dau of Richard Dunning, of Devon, and had:

(1) Walter; *b* and *d* 19 Aug 1870

7 (cont.) Walter Floyd *m* 2nd Cecilia Mary Louisa (*d* 24 Dec 1928), dau of James Findlay, of Easterhill, Lanarks, and *d* 31 March 1917, having by her had:

(2) James Francis Murray; naturalist and artist, Demonstrator Zoology Dept Glasgow U, Hon Capt MGC WW I, Lt RA HAA WW II; *b* 5 March 1889; *educ* Queen's Coll Oxford (MA); *d* unm 2 Nov 1954

(3) Sandford; Trooper Wellington Mounted Rifles NZ Expdny Force WW I, Private Dorsetshire Regt WW II; *b* 2 Aug 1893; *d* unm 19 Feb 1965

(1) Mary Eleanor; CD WW II, memb Bath CC 1947–57; *b* 18 Jan 1886; *m* 18 April 1918 Rev Ernest Walter Poynton (*d* 20 April 1943), Rector Kelston, Somerset, s of Rev Francis John Poynton, and *d* 6 Nov 1963

(2) Cecila Margaret; *b* 13 Aug 1891; *m* 27 Aug 1930 Claude George Coventry Mallet, s of Sir Claude Coventry Mallet, CMG. He *d* 10 June 1966

8 Arthur Wellesley; RN; *b* 9 Aug 1845; *d* Gibraltar 29 Nov 1859

1 Elizabeth Anna; *m* 10 June 1843 Edward W Bonham, CB, Consul-Gen Tabriz, Persia, and *d* 30 Nov 1844, leaving issue. He *d* 1886

2 Mary Caroline; *d* unm 13 June 1870

3 Florence; *m* 3 June 1872 Benjamin Were Kennet Dawson, yst s of Richard Kennet Dawson, of Frickley Hall, Yorks, and *d* 21 Sept 1906, leaving issue. He *d* 22 July 1904

Sir JOHN's nephew,

Sir Henry Robert Peel Floyd, 4th Bt; Capt RN, served E Africa 1890 (despatches) and Boer War 1899–1900; *b* 1 Nov 1855; *m* 16 Oct 1895 Edith Anne (*d* 2 Feb 1955), yst dau of Maj John Kincaid-Smith, of Polmont House, Stirlingshire, and *d* 25 May 1915, having had issue:

1 **Sir Henry Robert Kincaid Floyd, 5th Bt**, CB (1945), CBE (1944); *b* 7 May 1899; *educ* Eton and RMC Sandhurst; Ld Lt Bucks 1961–68 (DL 1959), KStJ, Brig (ret 1945), Col 15th/19th Hus 1947–57, WW I 1918 and WW II, Ch Staff 8th Army Italy 1944–45, Actg Maj-Gen 1945, ADC to High Commr Egypt and Sudan 1925–26, Equerry to HRH THE DUKE OF GLOUCESTER 1927–28, memb Gentlemen-at-Arms 1949–67 (Standard Bearer 1953, Adj 1957, Clerk of the Cheque 1957, Lt 1966), chm Roy Nat Orthopaedic Hosp 1954, Cdr US Legn Merit; *m* 9 April 1929 Hon Kathleen Fanny Gretton (*d* 3 May 1976), er dau of 1st Baron Gretton (*qv*), and *d* following a riding accident 5 Nov 1968, leaving:

(1) Bridget Mary; *b* 3 Oct 1930; *m* 11 March 1953 Maj Edward Henry Lancelot Aubrey-Fletcher, yst s of Maj Sir Henry Lancelot Aubrey-Fletcher, 6th Bt (*qv*), and *d* 6 Jan 1977, leaving issue

(2) Julia Maud; *b* 6 June 1934; *m* 19 Jan 1955 (*divorce* 1972) Richard Jervoise Scott, TD, yst s of Col Sir Jerviose Bolitho Scott, 1st Bt of Rotherfield Park (*qv*), and *d* 1974, leaving issue

2 JOHN DUCKETT (Sir), **6th Bt**

3 Charles Murray, OBE (1945); *b* 12 Sept 1905; *educ* Eton and Trin Coll Cambridge (BA 1927, MA 1961); High Sheriff Wilts 1962, memb Wilts CC 1965, Fell Linnean Soc 1965, Lt-Col RE, chm Avon India Rubber and George Spencer Moulton Ltd 1955–68, FRICS, FLAS, served WW II (despatches), Pres Roy Forestry Soc England and Wales 1954–55, memb: Nat Ctee (England) Forestry Commn, Roy Commn Common Land 1955–58, Nature Conservancy 1958–67; *m* 1st 15 Dec 1945 (*annulled* 1947) Diana, dau of Capt Grenville Fortescue, Rifle Bde (*see* FORTESCUE, E); *m* 2nd 7 Feb 1948 *Mary Elizabeth, OBE, JP, DL [Mrs Charles Floyd, Broughton House, Broughton Gifford, Wilts], widow of Lt-Col Patrick John Salvin Boyle (*see* GLASGOW, E) and only child of Robert Fleetwood Fuller (*see* FULLER, Bt), and *d* 27 June 1971, leaving issue:

(1) +Robert Charles [Robert Floyd Esq, DL, Great Chalfield Manor, Melksham, Wilts SN12 8NJ]; *b* 6 Jan 1949; *educ* Eton, Keble Coll Oxford and Wharton Sch Philadelphia; *m* 1977 *Patricia Jan, yst dau of W/Cdr Timothy Ashmead Vigors, DFC, RAF, of Coolmore, Fethard, Co Tipperary, and has issue:

1a +Charles Oliver; *b* 1978

2a +James Robert; *b* 1981

3a +Alexander Edward; *b* 1987

(2) +Thomas Henry [Thomas Floyd Esq, Withey Place, Shalden, Hants]; *b* 6 July 1951; *educ* Eton and Univ Coll Oxford; *m* 22 Jan 1977 *(Penelope) Sarah, er dau of Sir James Clemison, MC, DL, of Loddon Hall, Norfolk, and has:

1a +Henry James; *b* 1979

2a +John Edward; *b* 1981

(3) +William Duckett [William Floyd Esq, Bosveldveg 63, 1180 Brussels, Belgium]; *b* 5 March 1956; *educ* Eton and New Coll Oxford; *m* 1989 *Princess Donna Vittoria Valeria, er dau of Prince Raimondo Alliata di Villafranca, of Palermo, and has issue:

1a +Antony; *b* 1996

1a *Priscilla; *b* 1992

1 (Elizabeth) Anne; *b* 22 May 1897; *m* 9 Oct 1929 Lt-Col (John) Humphrey Nicholson, MC (*see* NICHOLSON OF WINTERBOURNE, B), and *d* 26 Aug 1982

Sir HENRY's bro,

Sir John Duckett Floyd, 6th Bt, TD; *b* 1 Nov 1903; *educ* Eton and Trin Coll Cambridge (BA); slr 1928, Lt-Col TA WW II; *m* 11 Feb 1929 Jocelin Evadne (*d* 17 Jan 1976), er dau of Sir Edmund Charles Wyldbore-Smith (*see* SMITH-MARRIOTT, Bt), and *d* 1 April 1975, having had issue:

1 David John Wyldbore; 2nd Lt 15th/19th King's Roy Hus; *b* 12 Nov 1929; *educ* Eton; accidentally *k* on service Germany 9 Dec 1949

2 Sir GILES HENRY CHARLES FLOYD, **7th and present Bt**

3 +John Edmund Kincaid [John Floyd Esq, Turkdean Manor, Northleach, Glos]; Capt 15th/19th King's Roy Hus 1955–61, Capt RARO, fndr and chm Floyd Oil Participations plc 1979–88; *b* 8 Sept 1936; *educ* Canford; *m* 1st 27 Jan 1965 (*divorce* 1978) Victoria Jane (*m* subsequently Bryan Norman), er dau of Richard Neville Cannon, OBE, of Coombe Place, Lewes, Sussex; *m* 2nd 1978 *Jocelyn Ishabel Ann, 2nd dau of Sir John MacLeod, TD (*see* DULVERTON, B), and widow of David Algernon Fleming (*see* BORTHWICK, Bt), and by his 1st w has:

(1) *Clare Victoria; *b* 13 Oct 1966; *m* 1993 *David Simon Townshend Boscawen (*see* FALMOUTH, V) and has issue

(2) *Nicola Anne; *b* 29 Dec 1967; *m* 1 June 1996 *Henry Pettifer, yr s of David Pettifer

(3) *Marina Jocelin; *b* 14 April 1971

FOLEY

Arms: Arg. a fess engrailed between three cinquefoils sa., all within a bordure of the last. **Crest:** A lion rampant arg., holding between the forepaws an escutcheon charged with the arms.
Supporters: Two lions arg., semée of cinquefoils sa.
Motto: *Ut prosim* ('Let me be useful').
Creation: B. (GB) 20 May 1776.

THE 8TH BARON FOLEY OF KIDDERMINSTER, Co Worcester (Adrian Gerald Foley) [The Rt Hon The Lord Foley, c/o Marbella Club, Marbella, Malaga, Spain]; *b* 9 Aug 1923; *s f* 1927; composer and pianist; *m* 1st 23 Dec 1958 (*divorce* 1971) Patricia, dau of Joseph Zoelner III, of Pasadena, California, and formerly w of Minor de Uribe Meek; *m* 2nd 1972 *Ghislaine, only dau of Cornelius William Dresselhuys, of The Hague, by Edith, Viscountess Kemsley (*qv*), and formerly w of (a) 6th Earl of Caledon (*qv*) and (b) 4th Baron Ashcombe (*qv*), and by his 1st w has:

1 +THOMAS HENRY; *b* 1 April 1961

1 *Alexandra Mary [The Hon Alexandra Foley, Apt 7A, 225 East 63rd St, New York, NY 10021, USA]; *b* 3 April 1960; *m* 1st 1987 (*divorce* 1989) (Somerset) Carlo de Chair, 3rd surv s of Somerset Struben de Chair (*see* 1970 edn FITZWILLIAM, E); *m* 2nd 1991 (*divorce* 1994) Janos Klamar; resumed her maiden name 1989 and again 1994

Lineage: RICHARD FOLEY, of Dudley, Worcs; *m* Anne — and *d* by 4 March 1600, leaving:

1 RICHARD
2 John; *b* by 1600; *d* between 8 Aug 1641 and Oct 1648, leaving issue
3 Edward; *bapt* 13 Dec 1584; living 1600; had a s (Richard)
1 Katherine; *m* 9 Oct 1594 Thomas Mason or Robinson

The est son,

RICHARD FOLEY, of Stourbridge, Worcs; Mayor Dudley 1616, prosperous ironmaster; *b* 1580; *m* 1st — and had, with two daus:

1 Richard, of Longton Hall, Staffs; *bapt* 27 March 1608; *m* three times but *dspms*

RICHARD FOLEY *m* 2nd Alice (*bur* 28 May 1663), dau of William Brindley, of Willenhall, and sis of George Brindley, of the Hyde, Kinver, Staffs, and *d* 6 July 1657, having had, with other issue:

2 THOMAS
3 Robert, of Stourbridge, High Sheriff Worcs 1671; *bapt* 19 Sept 1624; *m* 1st 8 Feb 1645 Anne Blurton; *m* 2nd Elizabeth (*m* 2nd in or after 1681, as his 3rd w Capel Hanbury (*see* SUDELEY, B), n of Brian Duppa, Bp Winchester and was *bur* 1 Dec 1676, leaving issue, now extinct
4 Samuel, of Clonmel and Dublin; *m* Elizabeth (*d* 1695), sis of Col Solomon Richards, 17th Regt, of Solsboro', Co Wexford, and had issue (settled in Ireland)
1 Anne; *bapt* 21 Sept 1611; *m* 28 May 1632 William Normansell, of Wolverhampton
2 Priscilla; *bapt* 17 Dec 1615; *m* 1st 23 Nov 1635 Ezekiel Wallis, of Bristol; *m* 2nd 1665 Henry Glover, of Stourbridge, and was *bur* 6 April 1687

RICHARD FOLEY's est s here mentioned by his 2nd w,

THOMAS FOLEY, of Witley Court, Worcs; MP 1659–60; *b* 3 Dec 1617; *m* Anne, dau and heir of John Browne, of Spelmonden, Kent, and had issue:

1 Thomas, of Witley Court; MP Worcs and Droitwich; *m* Elizabeth, dau of Edward Ashe, of Heytesbury, Wilts, and *d* 1 Feb 1700/1, having had, with other issue:

(1) THOMAS FOLEY, 1st BARON FOLEY OF KIDDERMINSTER, Worcs (GB), so *cr* 1 Jan 1711/2; MP (Tory) Stafford 1694–1712, FRS 1696; *m* Mary (*d* Oct 1735), dau and heir of Thomas Strode, Serjeant-at-law, and *d* 22 Jan 1732/3, having had issue:

1a THOMAS FOLEY, 2nd and last BARON FOLEY OF KIDDERMINSTER; *b* c 1705; *educ* Ch Ch Oxford (DCL); *d* unm 8 Jan 1766, when the Barony expired but the estates passed to his cousin Thomas, **1st Baron Foley of Kidderminster** of the 1776 *cr* (*see* below)

(1) Elizabeth; *m* 12 May 1685 the statesman Robert Harley, 1st Earl of Oxford and Mortimer, and had issue
(2) Sarah; *m* Edward Harley, MP, bro of 1st Earl of Oxford and Mortimer
(3) Mary; *m* Sir Blundel Charlton, 3rd Bt, of Ludford, Herefs
(4) Anne; *m* 1690 Salwey Winnington (*see* WINNINGTON, Bt)

2 PAUL
3 Philip, of Prestwood, Staffs, MP; *m* Penelope, dau of 5th Baron Paget (*see* ANGLESEY, M), and had:

(1) Paul, of Prestwood; MP Aldborough 1713–15 and Weobley 1715; *m* Elizabeth, dau of William Turton, of Alrewas, and *d* 27 Nov 1739, leaving issue:

1a William; *m* and had an only dau:
1b Elizabeth; *m* John Hodgetts, of Prestwood, and had an only dau:
1c Anna Maria, *m* 21 March 1790 Hon Edward Foley, of Stoke Edith and Prestwood (*see* below)

(2) Robert; *m* Mary, dau of Rev Ralph Markland, and had issue:

1a Thomas; Capt RN; *m* Mary, dau of Adml — St Lou, and *d* 1770, leaving issue
2a Philip (Rev); Rector Shelsley, Worcs; *m* Anne, only dau of John Titmarsh, of Barrington, Cambs, and had, with other issue:
1b Richard; Maj-Gen; *m* 1801 Dorothy (*d* Jan 1862), dau of John Lodwick, and *d* Feb 1824, having had issue:
1c Henry, of Wistow, Hunts, and Ersham House, Canterbury, JP Hunts, DL Berks, Capt 6th Regt; *b* 12 May 1804; *m* 2 June 1831 Elizabeth, dau of Edward Curteis, of Glenburne, and had seven daus and a s (*dsp*)
2c Edward; Capt RN; *b* 29 Oct 1807; *m* 21 May 1850 Elizabeth Fanny (*d* 5 June 1903), only surv child of John Cuming, barrister, and *d* 28 Sept 1894, leaving issue:
1d Ernest Edward; Capt Middx Regt; *b* 18 Jan 1854; *m* 30 Nov 1879 Olivia Ann, dau of Rev John William Finlay, of Corkagh, Co Dublin, and *d* 31 Oct 1906, having had issue
2d Arthur Paul; *b* 2 April 1860; *educ* New Coll Oxford (BA); *d* 1 Nov 1949
3d George Loftus; *b* 10 Nov 1861; *d* 11 Oct 1932
4d Frank Wigram, CB (1919), DSO (1901), JP Surrey; Chm Camberley Petty Sessions, Col Roy Berks Regt, Boer War and WW I (severley wounded); *b* 24 June 1865; *m* 5 Aug 1903 Eva Mary FitzHardinge, Baroness Berkeley (*qv*) in her own right, and *d* 7 Oct 1949, leaving issue
1d Fanny Isabella; *d* unm 2 April 1926
2d Elizabeth Bligh; *m* Nov 1884 John Henry Knight, of Farnham, Surrey, s of John Knight, of Weybourne House, Surrey, and *d* April 1940. He *d* 12 Sept 1917
3d Katherine Amelia; *m* 6 Jan 1903 John Thackeray, 3rd s of Rev Richard Thackeray, Vicar Hunsdon, Herts, and *d c* 1935
4d Theodosia Sophia; *d* unm 1943
5d Margaret Alice; *d* unm 9 Jan 1955
1c Rosa; *m* her cousin Philip Foley and *dsp*
2c Marianne
3c Helen; *m* — Musgrave and had issue
3a Edward; *d* unm
4a Sir ROBERT RALPH FOLEY, 1st and last Bt (GB), so *cr* 1 July 1767, of Thorpe Lee, Surrey; *m* 1770 Dorothy (*d* 19 Jan 1809), only dau of Thomas Hinchcliffe, of Hinchcliffe, Yorks, and *dsp* 7 March 1782, when the btcy expired
5a Harry Thomas (Rev); Rector Holt, Worcs
1a Penelope; *m* Rev Henry Whitmore

1 Martha; *m* William Jolife, of London
2 Sarah; *m* 1st Essex Knightley, of Fawsley; *m* 2nd John Hampden, of Great Hampden

The 2nd son,

PAUL FOLEY, of Stoke Edith, Herefs; Speaker H of C 14 March 1694/5; *m* 1668 Mary, dau of John Lane, Alderman City of London, and *d* 1699, leaving an er s:

THOMAS FOLEY, of Stoke Edith; MP Hereford 1700–22 and Stafford 1722–27 and 1734–37; *m* his cousin Anne, dau and heir of Essex Knightley, of Fawsley, and *d* 10 Dec 1737, having had, with two daus (Anne, *m* Anthony Lechmere, of Hanley Castle; Mary, *m* Rev N Wickens):

THOMAS FOLEY, of Stoke Edith; MP Herefs 1734–47; *m* 1st Hester, dau and heir of Thomas Andrews by Elizabeth, dau and heir of Edward Young, of Thorpe, and had issue:

1 THOMAS, **1st Baron**
2 Martin Andrew; *dsp*

THOMAS FOLEY *m* 2nd Mary, dau of John Warter, of Barbados, and by her had:

3 Robert (Very Rev), DD, Dean Worcester; *m* Ann, dau of Rev W Dowdeswell, and *dsp* 1783
1 Sarah; *m* Boulter Tomlinson, of Cheltenham

THOMAS FOLEY *m* 3rd Elizabeth, dau of Henry Wolstenholme and by her had:

4 Paul Jermyn; *dsp*

THOMAS FOLEY *m* 4th Elizabeth, dau and coheir of Robert Unett, of Birchend; *m* 5th Catherine, dau of Francis Gwyn, of Ford Abbey, Devon, but by her had no issue

His est son,

THOMAS FOLEY, **1st Baron Foley of Kidderminster**, Co Worcester (GB), so *cr* 20 May 1776; *b* 8 Aug 1716; *m* 28 March 1740 Grace Granville (*d* 1 Nov 1769), dau and coheir of George, 1st and last Baron Lansdowne of Bideford, by Mary Villiers, dau of 1st Earl of Jersey (*qv*), and had issue:

1 THOMAS, **2nd Baron**
2 Edward, of Stoke Edith and Prestwood; MP 1768–1806; *b* 16 March 1747; *m* 1st 20 Oct 1778 (*divorce* 1787) Lady Anne Coventry, dau of 6th Earl of Coventry (*qv*); *m* 2nd 21 March 1790 his cousin Eliza Maria Foley (*d* 9 July 1805), dau

and heir of John Hodgetts, of Prestwood (*see* above), and *d* 22 June 1808, having by her had:

(1) Edward Thomas, of Stoke Edith; MP 1826–41, DCL; *b* 21 Dec 1791; *m* 16 Aug 1832 Lady Emily Graham (*d* 1 Jan 1900), 4th dau of 3rd Duke of Montrose (*qv*), and *dsp* 30 March 1846

(2) John Hodgetts FOLEY later HODGETTS-FOLEY (roy licence 4 April 1821), of Prestwood, JP, DL, MP E Worcs; *b* 17 July 1797; *m* 20 Oct 1825 Charlotte (*d* 9 Sept 1855), dau of John Gage (*see* GAGE, V), and *d* 13 Nov 1861, leaving:

1a Henry John Wentworth, of Prestwood, DL; MP S Staffs 1857–68, Capt Worcs Militia; *b* 9 Dec 1828; *m* 12 Dec 1845 Jane Frances Anne (*d* 2 Dec 1860), dau of 1st Baron Vivian (*qv*), and *d* 23 April 1894, leaving issue:

1b Paul Henry, of Prestwood and Stoke Edith, JP, DL Herefs and Staffs; High Sheriff 1906, barrister; *b* 19 March 1857; *m* 9 Feb 1904 Dora (*d* 2 Nov 1959), only child of Hamilton William Langley, of Bedstone Court, Bucknell, Salop, and *d* 21 Jan 1928, leaving issue:

1c Henry Thomas Hamilton, MBE (1944), JP, of Stoke Edith Park; High Sheriff Herefs 1947, Maj Rifle Bde; *b* 25 April 1905; *educ* Eton and BNC Oxford (BA); *m* 24 June 1936 Helen Constance Margaret, OStJ (*d* 1985), er dau of Sir Robert Barclay Pearson, of Johnston Lodge, Laurencekirk, Kincardineshire, and *d* 13 Dec 1959, leaving:

1d +Andrew Thomas [Andrew Foley Esq, Stoke Edith Park, Herefs]; late Capt Rifle Bde; *b* 30 June 1937; *educ* Eton; *m* 1st 26 March 1968 *Gillian, only dau of William Carleton Brown, of Hares Chase, Over Alderley, Cheshire, and has issue:

1e +Rupert Thomas; *b* 16 March 1970

2e +Ian Richard; *b* 24 July 1973

1d (cont.) Andrew Foley *m* 2nd 19–*Melanie Jacqueline Westall-Reece and by her has:

1e *Emily Charlotte Esme; *b* 19 April 1995

2d +John Paul (Sir), KCB (1994, CB 1991), OBE (1979), MC (1976) [Maj-Gen Sir John Foley KCB OBE MC, Ministry of Defence, Whitehall, London SW1A 2EU]; *b* 22 April 1939; *educ* Bradfield, Grenoble and Madrid Us, Mons OCS; Lt Roy Green Jackets 1959, RMCS and Army Staff Coll 1970–71, Ch Staff 51 Inf Bde Hong Kong 1974–76, Instructor Army Staff Coll 1976–78, CO 3rd Bn RGJ 1978–80, Commandant Jr Div Staff Coll 1981–82, Arms Dir MOD 1983–85, RCDS 1986, ACDS MOD 1989–92, Cdr Br Forces Hong Kong and Maj-Gen Bde Gurkhas 1992–94, Col Comdt 1st Bn Roy Green Jackets 1991–94, The Light Div 1994–, Memb Ct Skinner's Co 1996–; *m* 3 June 1972 *Ann Rosamund, only dau of John William Humphries, of Coval Court, Sunningdale, Berks, and has:

1e *Annabel Frances Helen; *b* 11 July 1973

2e *Joanna Beatrice; *b* 8 May 1976

1d *Anne Victoria Helen [Mrs Hugh Henshaw, 3 Fernshaw Close, London SW10 0TA]; *b* 12 June 1943; *m* 1980 *Hugh Nigel Henshaw, s of Harold Henshaw, of Rottingdean, Sussex, and has issue:

1e *Thomas Spencer Edward; *b* 1983

1e *Katharine Louise Emily; *b* 1981

2c Paul Robert, OBE (1945); G/Capt AAF WW II; *b* 30 April 1910; *educ* Eton and Ch Ch Oxford (BSc 1932); *m* 1st 1939 (*divorce* 1952) Cecilia Margaret Anne Yolande, only dau of Frank Seddon, of Severn House, Hampstead; *m* 2nd 7 Dec 1954 *Oriel Leonie, formerly w of Brig Guy Patrick Gregson, CBE, DSO, MC, and yr dau of Col Edward Lucas-Scudamore, of Kentchurch Court, Herefs

(1) Elizabeth Maria; *m* 8 March 1813 4th Viscount Gage (*qv*) and *d* 13 June 1857, leaving issue

(2) Anna Maria; *m* 7 May 1821 Sir Henry John Lambert, Bt (*qv*), and *d* 5 March 1857, leaving issue

3 Andrew; MP Droitwich 1774–1818; *m* 7 May 1773 Elizabeth (*d* 22 July 1811), dau and heir of Boulter Tomlinson, and *d* 28 July 1816, leaving, with other issue:

(1) Harriet Mary; *m* 7 July 1801 Ven Archdeacon Richard Francis Onslow (*see* ONSLOW, E) and *d* 4 May 1860

(2) Anna Maria; *m* 24 Feb 1823 Cdr John Lechmere, RN, of Hill House, Oxon, and Ludford Park, Herefs, and *d* 21 Jan 1878. He *dsp* 7 Dec 1866

1 Grace; *m* 21 May 1774 2nd and last Earl of Clanbrassill and *d* 9 Jan 1813, leaving issue. He *d* 6 Feb 1798

2 Mary; *m* Richard Clerk, of Kingston, Oxon, and *d* Dec 1844

3 Elizabeth; *d* unm 13 Oct 1776

4 Anne; *m* 12 Sept 1776 Sir Edward Winnington, 2nd Bt (*qv*), and *d* 9 Dec 1794, leaving issue

The 1st BARON *d* 18 Nov 1777; his est s,

THOMAS FOLEY, **2nd Baron Foley of Kidderminster**; MP Herefs 1767–74 and Droitwich 1774–77; *b* 24 June 1742; *m* 20 March 1776 Henrietta (*d* 2 Jan 1781), 4th dau of 2nd Earl of Harrington (*qv*), and *d* 2 July 1793, having had, with a dau (Harriet, *m* 16 Aug 1796 Christopher Bethell Codrington (*see* CODRINGTON, Bt, of Dodington (1876)), and *d* 1 Jan 1843):

THOMAS FOLEY, **3rd Baron Foley of Kidderminster**, PC; Ld Lt Worcs; *b* 22 Dec 1780; *m* 18 Aug 1806 Cecilia Olivia (*d* 27 July 1863), dau of 2nd Duke of Leinster (*qv*), and *d* 16 April 1833, having had issue:

1 THOMAS HENRY FOLEY, **4th Baron Foley of Kidderminster**, PC; Capt Gentlemen-at-Arms; *b* 11 Dec 1808; *m* 16 July 1849 Mary Charlotte (*d* 8 April 1897), est dau of 13th Duke of Norfolk (*qv*), and *d* 20 Nov 1869, leaving:

(1) HENRY THOMAS FOLEY, **5th Baron Foley of Kidderminster**, JP, DL Surrey and London; *b* 4 Dec 1850; *m* 25 Oct 1899 Evelyne Vaughan, ARRC (*d* 21 Jan 1968 aged 92), only dau of Arthur Radford, JP, of Smalley, Derbys, and Bradfield Hall, Berks, and *dsp* 17 Dec 1905

(2) FitzALAN CHARLES JOHN FOLEY, **6th Baron Foley of Kidderminster**, DL Surrey; Capt and Hon Maj 3rd Bn Sherwood Foresters; *b* 27 Sept 1852; *d* unm 14 Feb 1918

2 Augustus Frederick; Col Gren Gds; *b* 9 Dec 1810; *d* unm 9 Oct 1881

3 St George Gerald (Sir), KCB; Gen, Hon Col 2nd Bn Staffs Regt (38th), Cdr Legn Hon, Kt Medjidie, Govr Guernsey; *b* 10 July 1814; *m* 6 July 1865 Augusta Selina (*d* 21 Feb 1901), dau of Henry Charles Sturt, of Crichel House, Dorset, and sis of 1st Baron Alington (*see* 1940 edn), and *d* 24 Jan 1897, leaving:

(1) Henry St George; Priv Sec to For Sec; *b* 3 June 1866; *m* 14 July 1894 Lady Mary Adelaide Agar (*d* 7 June 1921), yst dau of 3rd Earl of Normanton (*qv*), and *d* 13 April 1903, leaving issue:

1a GERALD HENRY, **7th Baron**

1a Mildred Caroline; granted rank of baron's dau 1920; *b* 18 May 1895; *d* unm 10 Feb 1977

(2) Cyril Pelham; Lt-Col RAF; *b* 1 Nov 1868; *b* 9 March 1936

4 FitzGerald Algernon Charles, JP Hants; *b* 5 Sept 1823; Adml; *m* 1st 27 Aug 1850 Frances (*d* 23 Feb 1867), yst dau of Sir George Campbell (*see* STRATHEDEN and CAMPBELL, B), and had issue:

(1) Cecil FitzGerald; Cdr RN Ashanti War 1873 (medal); *b* 1 Sept 1851; *d* 1922

(2) Algernon Campbell, Lt-Col and Brevet-Col RE, served Afghan War, Sudan and Boer War; *b* 17 Jan 1853; *m* 1901 Mabel Molyneux Seel, dau of Vincent Eustace McDonagh, of Dublin, and *d* 14 March 1926

(3) Francis John; V-Adml; *b* 3 Dec 1855; *m* 19 June 1883 Frances Jane (*d* 26 Jan 1931), dau of Delabere Pritchett Blayne, and *d* 5 March 1911, leaving:

1a Thomas Algernon FitzGerald; Lt Norfolk Regt; *b* 29 Dec 1889; *ka* 25 Oct 1914

1a Geraldine; *m* 29 Jan 1913 Gen Sir Ivo Lucius Beresford Vesey, KCB, KBE, CMG, DSO (*see* DE VESCI, V), and *d* 16 Sept 1963, leaving issue

2a Mildred Adelaide Charlotte; *d* unm 6 July 1965

(4) Reginald Edward; Capt 45th Sikhs IA; *b* 5 Sept 1864; *m* 12 Sept 1893 Margaret Emily (*d* 27 Nov 1957), est dau of Laurence Peel, of Avonside, Hants, and *d* 7 Feb 1900, leaving:

1a Lawrence FitzGerald; Cdr RN; *b* 31 July 1894; *m* 1st 8 July 1924 (*divorce* 1933) Vera Mable, only dau of Col C R Johnson, 5th Gurkhas; *m* 2nd 7 Feb 1942 *Beatrice Monica, widow of F/Lt M Noblston, RAF, and dau of F A Lloyd, of Wrexham

2a Guy Francis, CMG (1945), OBE (1942), MC; Maj RA, WW I (wounded) and WW II (despatches), Dir Stores and Ordnance Sudan 1936–43, Controller-Gen War Supply and Dir Economics and Tde 1943–46, Bursar Wellington Coll 1946–57, Order Nile 4th Cl; *b* 27 Oct 1896; *educ* Wellington; *m* 12 Sept 1928 *Helen Frances, 2nd dau of Maj Spencer Charles Ferguson, OBE, of Red Roof, Brockenhurst, and *dsp* 13 Oct 1970

(1) Adelaide Mary Philippa; *m* 1 June 1893 Lt-Col Charles Bulkeley Godman, JP, DL, of Woldringfold, Horsham, 7th s of Joseph Godman, JP, of Park Hatch, Surrey, and Merston, Sussex, and *d* 24 Dec 1896, leaving issue. He *d* 18 Jan 1941

(2) Frances; *m* 6 Aug 1891, as his 2nd w, Sir Edward Robert Pearce-Edgcumbe, JP, DL, LLD, and *d* 1 Jan 1953, leaving issue. He *d* 29 Sept 1929

(3) Edith; *d* an infant, 1 March 1867

4 (cont.) Adml FitzGerald Foley *m* 2nd 21 July 1874 Renira Anna (*d* 16 Oct 1926), widow of Capt Edward Henry Gage Lambert, RN (*see* LAMBERT, Bt), and dau of Rev Richard Fortescue Purvis, and *d* 26 July 1903

1 Cecilia Olivia; *m* 5 Aug 1834 Sir Charles Rushout, 2nd Bt, of Sezincote, Glos (*see* 1931 edn), and *d* 3 March 1863. He *d* 19 Sept 1869

2 Geraldine Augusta; *m* 10 Dec 1844 her cousin Philippe Ferdinand Augustus de Rohan Chabot, Count de Jarnac, Fr Amb to UK, s of Maj-Gen Vicomte de Chabot by Lady Isabella Charlotte, dau of 2nd Duke of Leinster (*qv*), and *d* 23 March 1887. He *d* 22 March 1875

3 Georgina Louisa; *m* 27 Feb 1844 Thomas Molineux Montgomerie, of Garboldisham Hall, Norfolk, and *d* 21 Nov 1864. He *d* 28 Feb 1855

4 Adelaide Georgiana Frederica; *m* 8 Feb 1860 Lt-Gen Hon Thomas Ashburnham, CB (*see* 1924 edn ASHBURNHAM, E), and *d* 19 Jan 1861. He *dsp* 3 March 1872

The 6th BARON's cousin,

GERALD HENRY FOLEY, **7th Baron Foley of Kidderminster**, F/Lt RAF; *b* 15 April 1898; *m* 24 May 1922 Minoru (*d* 18 April 1968), dau of Harry Greenstone, of Johannesburg, and *d* 3 April 1927, leaving:

1 ADRIAN GERALD FOLEY, **8th and present Baron Foley of Kidderminster**

FOOKES

Arms: Sable four towers in cross their bases conjoined argent between four fuschias in saltire stamens outwards or. **Supporters:** On either side a cat statant erect sable gorged with a naval crown, attached thereto a chain reflexed over the back or. **Motto:** *Armaturam Dei induite* ('Put on the whole armour of God'). **Creation:** B. (LP, UK) 1997.

THE BARONESS FOOKES, of Plymouth, Co Devon (Dame Janet Fookes, DBE (1989)) [The Rt Hon The Baroness Fookes DBE, House of Lords, London SW1A 0PW]; *b* 21 Feb 1936; *educ* Hastings and St Leonard's Ladies' Coll, Hastings High Sch for Girls and Roy Holloway Coll London U; teacher 1958–70; memb: Hastings Cncl 1960–61 and 1963–70 (Chm Educn Ctee 1967–70), MP (C) Merton and Morden 1970–74, Plymouth Drake 1974–97, Sec C Parly Educn Ctee 1971–75, memb: Unopposed Bills Ctee 1973–75, Servs Ctee 1974–76, Speaker's Panel 1976–97, Select Ctee Home Affairs 1984–92, Dep Speaker H of C 1992–97, Chm: Educn, Arts and Home Affairs Sub Ctee Expenditure Ctee 1975–79, C West Country Membs Ctee 1976–77 (V-Chm 1977), Parly Gp Animal Welfare 1985–92 (Sec 1974–82); memb: Cncl RSPCA 1975–92 (Chm 1979–81), Nat Art Collections Fund, Cncl SSAFA 1980–, Cncl Stonham Housing Assoc 1980–92, Cncl Management U Coll of St Mark and St John 1989–, Cwlth War Graves Commn 1987–97, RHS, Nat Tst

Lineage: LEWIS AYLMER FOOKES; *m* Evelyn Margery Holmes and had:

JANET, *cr* a **Baroness**

FOOT

Arms: Or on a chevron engrailed sable, between three lion's gambs erect and erased gules, three wheels or. **Crest:** Perching on a tower sable, supported by two lion's gambs erect gules, a Cornish chough proper. **Supporters:** Dexter, a buck; sinister, a Dartmoor pony, each gorged with a wreath of yew proper, and supporting between the legs a sword erect sheathed or, the whole upon a compartment of rock, in the middle thereof a pit proper. **Motto:** *Pro lege et libertate* ('For freedom and the rule of law'). **Creation:** B. (LP, UK) 1967.

THE BARON FOOT, of Buckland Monachorum, Co Devon (John Mackintosh Foot) [The Rt Hon The Lord Foot, Yew Tree, Crapstone, Devon PL20 7 PJ]; *b* 17 Feb 1909; *educ* Bembridge and Balliol Coll Oxford (BA 1931); slr 1934; WWII: RASC (GSO(3) 43rd Div, GSO(2) 12th Corps, despatches), Hon Maj; memb Dartmoor Nat Park Ctee 1963–74, Commn on the Constitution 1969–73; Chm: UK Immigrants Advsy Service 1970–78 (Pres 1978–84), Cncl Justice 1984–89; Pres: Dartmoor Preservation Assoc 1976–1994, Commons Open Space and Footpaths Preservation Soc 1976–82; *m* 1936 *Anne Bailey, dau of Clifford Bailey Farr, MD, of Bryn Mawr, Pa., and has:

1 *John Winslow [The Hon John Foot, Knaven Hill Farrn, Alderminster, Stratford upon Avon, Warwicks CV37 8PQ]; *b* 1939; *educ* Sidcot Sch and Philadelphia Coll of Art

1 *Katherine Elliott [The Hon Mrs Illingworth, 36 Albert Park Place, Montpelier, Bristol]; *b* 1937; *m* 1st 1955 David Stavely Gordon; *m* 2nd 19– David Illingworth (*d* 1976) and has issue by both husbs

Lineage: JAMES FOOT, of Horrabridge, Devon; had:

ISAAC FOOT, of Ladywell, Plymouth, Devon; *b* 21 Feb 1842; *m* 1869 Eliza Ryder (*d* 1922) and *d* 1926, leaving, with four other sons and two daus:

ISAAC FOOT, PC (1937), JP (Cornwall 1943), of Pencrebar, Callington, Cornwall; *b* 23 Feb 1880; *educ* Plymouth Public Sch and Hoe GS; slr 1902, sr ptnr Foot & Bowden, Plymouth, Hon LLD Exeter 1960, MP (Lib) Bodmin 1922–24 and 1929–35, Sec for Mines 1931–32, Dep Mayor Plymouth 1920–21, Ld Mayor 1945–46, memb: Round Table Conf India 1930 and Jt Select Ctee India, FRSL, V-Pres Methodist Conf 1937–38, Hon Treas Temperance Cncl Christian Churches, Pres: Nat Commercial Temperance League, Brotherhood Movement 1936–37, Nat Sunday Sch Union 1938–39, Lib Party 1947, Nat Educn Assoc; dir UK Provident Inst, Dep Chm Cornwall QS, author: *Oliver Cromwell and Abraham Lincoln, a Comparison* (1944) and *Michael Verrar and Thomas Carlyle* (1946); *m* 1st 22 Sept 1904 Eva, JP (Cornwall 1930, *d* 17 May 1946), dau of Angus Mackintosh, MD, of Fincastle, Perthshire, by Sarah, dau of William Dingle, JP, of Callington, Cornwall, and had:

1 Dingle Mackintosh (Sir), QC (1954); *b* 24 Aug 1905; *educ* Bembridge Sch and Balliol Coll Oxford (BA 1928, Pres Union 1928); barrister Gray's Inn 1930 (Bencher 1952), MP (Lab) Dundee 1931–45 and Ipswich 1957–70, Parly Sec Min Ec Warfare 1940–45, Chm Observer Tst 1953–55, Slr-Gen 1964–67, ktd 1964; *m* 7 Jan 1933 Dorothy Mary, er dau of Maj William Rowley Elliston, OBE, TD, of Ipswich, and *d* 197–

2 HUGH MACKINTOSH FOOT, BARON CARADON, of St Cleer, Co Cornwall (LP, UK), so *cr* 27 Oct 1964, GCMG (1957, KCMG 1951, CMG 1946), KCVO (1953), OBE (1939), PC (1968); *b* 8 Oct 1907; *educ* Leighton Park and St John's Coll Cambridge (BA 1929, Hon Fell 1960, Pres Union 1929); Admin Offr Palestine Govt 1929–37, attd Colonial Off 1938–39, Assist Br Resident Transjordan 1939–42, Br Mil Admin Cyrenaica 1943, Colonial Sec Cyprus 1943–45, Actg Govr: Cyprus 1944 and Jamaica 1945–46; Ch Sec Nigeria 1947–51, Capt-Gen and Govr-in-Ch Jamaica 1951–57, Govr and C-in-C Cyprus 1957–60, Amb and Advsr UK Mission UN and Perm UK Rep UN Tsteeship Cncl 1961–62, Min State For Affrs and Perm UK Rep UN 1964, author: *A Start in Freedom* (1964), KStJ; *m* 26 March 1936 *Florence Sylvia, CStJ, er dau of Arthur White Milar Tod, OBE, of Lasswade, Midlothian, and had:

(1) *Paul Mackintosh [Paul Foot, Private Eye, 6 Carlisle St, London W1V 5RG]; *b* 8 Nov 1937; *educ* Shrewsbury and Univ Coll Oxford (BA 1961, Pres Union 1961); fndr ed *Private Eye* (on edtl staff again 1993–), ed *Socialist Worker* 1974–75, jnlst *Daily Mirror* 1979–93, author: *Immigration and Race in British Politics* (1965), *The Politics of Harold Wilson* (1968), *The Rise of Enoch Powell* (1969), *Who Killed Hanratty?* (1971), *Why You Should Be a Socialist* (1977), *Red Shelley* (1981), *The Helen Smith Story* (1983), *Murder at the Farm: who killed Carl Bridgewater?* (1986), *Who Framed Colin Wallace?* (1989), *Words as Weapons* (1990); *m* 1st 23 June 1962 (*divorce* 1970) Monica, dau of Dr Robert Percy Beckinsale, of UCL, and has:

1a *John Mackintosh; *b* 8 Nov 1964; *educ* Hampstead Sch

2a *Matthew Isaac; *b* 18 Aug 1966; *educ* Hampstead Sch

(1) (cont.) Paul Foot *m* 2nd 27 July 1971 *Roseann, dau of Robert Harty, of Elm Close, Kingston Bagpuize, Berks, and by her has, with a dau:

3a *Tom; *b* 1979

(2) *Oliver Isaac; *b* 19 Sept 1946; *educ* Leighton Park, RAC Cirencester and Goddard Coll, Vt.; late head Orbis (flying eye hosp), now with Air Jamaica; *m* 7 March 1970 (*divorce* 1975) Nancy, dau of Robert Bruce, of Locust Valley, NY, and has:

1a *Jessa Isaac; *b* 10 Oct 1972

2a *Mary Rachel; *b* 8 June 1971

(3) *Benjamin Arthur; *b* 19 Aug 1949; *educ* Leighton Park and U Coll Swansea; *m* 18 April 1981 *Sally Jane, only dau of Maj Mark Francis Swain Rudkin, MC, of Shoreham Beach, W Sussex, and has:

1a *Alexander Mark Isaac; *b* 1986

1a *Joanna Dingle; *b* 1983

(1) *Sarah Dingle; *b* 24 Sept 1939; *m* 13 May 1961 *Maj Timothy Nicholas Percival Winter Burbury, RHG, s of Surgn-Col Dermot Roland Winter Burbury, of Honiton, Devon, and has:

1a *Charles Alexander Winter; *b* 15 Jan 1964; *educ* Tavistock and Callington Coll

1a *Camilla Jane Winter; *b* 30 June 1962; *m* 1988 *Mark Lindfield, s of Dr Robert Lindfield

3 JOHN MACKINTOSH, *cr* a **Baron**

4 *Michael Mackintosh, PC (1974) [The Rt Hon Michael Foot, 308 Gray's Inn Rd, London WC1X 8DY]; *b* 23 July 1913; *educ* Leighton Park and Wadham Coll Oxford (BA 1936, Pres Union 1936, Hon Fell 1969); MP (Lab) Devonport 1945–55 and Ebbw Vale 1960–83 and Blaenau Gwent 1983–92, Ld Pres Cncl and Leader H of C 1976–79, Leader Lab Pty 1980–83 (Dep Leader 1976–80), memb Lab NEC 1971–83; assist ed *Tribune* 1937–38, Actg Ed *Evening Standard* 1942, md *Tribune* 1945–74 (ed 1948–52 and 1955–60); author: *Armistice 1918–39* (1940), *Trial of Mussolini* (1943), *Brendan and Beverley* (1944), *Still at Large* (1950), *Full Speed Ahead* (1950), *Guilty Men* (with Mervyn Jones, 1957), *The Pen and the Sword* (1957), *Parliament in Danger* (1957) and *Aneurin Bevan*, vol 1 (1962), vol 2 (1973), *Debts of Honour* (1980), *Another Heart and*

Other Pulses (1984), *Loyalists and Loners* (1986), *The Politics of Paradise* (1988), *H.G.: the history of Mr Wells* (1995); *m* 21 Oct 1949 *Jill Craigie, formerly w of Jeffery Dell

5 *Christopher Isaac [Christopher Foot Esq, Weekhayne Farm, South Leigh, nr Colyton, Devon]; *b* 4 July 1917; *educ* Leighton Park, Wadham Coll Oxford (BA 1939) and Grenoble U; WW II as Maj RASC, Field Security Police Intell Corps, slr 1950

1 Margaret Elizabeth (Sally); *b* 8 Jan 1911; *educ* Lausanne; *d* unm 22 March 1965

2 Jennifer Mackintosh; *b* 13 Jan 1916; *educ* Grenoble, Freiburg and Perugia Us; *m* 16 Aug 1944 James Cochrane Highet, s of David Highet, of Ayr, and had issue

ISAAC FOOT *m* 2nd 11 Aug 1951 Catherine Elizabeth (*d* 1969–), dau of Frederick Dawe, of Liskeard, Cornwall, and former w of — Taylor, and *d* 13 Dec 1960

FORBES

Arms: Azure three bear's heads couped argent, muzzled gules.
Crest: A stag's head attired with ten tynes proper.
Supporters: Two bloodhounds argent, collared gules.
Motto: *Grace me guide* ('Thankfulness is my watchword').
Creation: L. (S) Oct 1444–July 1445.

THE 23RD LORD FORBES (Sir Nigel Ivan Forbes, KBE (1960), JP (1955), DL (Aberdeenshire, 1958)) [The Rt Hon The Lord Forbes KBE JP DL, Castle Forbes, Keig, Aberdeenshire; Balforbes, Alford, Aberdeenshire AB33 8DR]; *b* 19 Feb 1918; *s* f 1953; premier Lord of Parl in Scottish peerage; *educ* Harrow and RMC Sandhurst; Maj Gren Gds (RARO), served WW II (wounded), Adj Gren Gds 1941–43, Staff Coll 1945–46, MA High Commr Palestine 1947–48; rep S peer 1955–63, Min State Scottish Off 1958–59, Dist Cncllr 1955, pres Roy Highland and Ag Soc Scotland 1958–59, chm Nat Playing Fields Assoc (Scottish Branch) 1965–80, memb Sports Cncl Scotland 1966–71, chm River Don District Bd 1962–73, dep chm Tenant Caledonian Breweries 1964–74, memb: Nature Conservancy Scottish Ctee 1961–66, Inter-Parly Union Delegn Denmark 1956, Cwlth Parly Assoc Delegation Canada 1961, Inter-Parly Union Delegn Hungary 1965, Cwlth Parly Delegn Pakistan 1962, dir Grampian TV 1960–88; *m* 23 May 1942 *Hon Rosemary Katharine Hamilton-Russell, only dau of 9th Viscount Boyne (*qv*), and has:

1 +MALCOLM NIGEL, *Master of Forbes*, DL (Aberdeenshire 1996) [The Master of Forbes DL, Castle Forbes, Alford, Aberdeenshire AB33 8BL]; *b* 6 May 1946 (HRH THE PRINCESS ROYAL stood sponsor); *educ* Eton and Aberdeen U; chm Impulse Publications, Aberdeen, and Castle Forbes Collection Ltd 1996–, jnlst *Scottish Daily Express*, dir Instock Disposables 1974–; *m* 1st 30 Jan 1969 (*divorce* 1982) Carole Jennifer Andrée, dau of Norman Stanley Whitehead, of Aberdeen, and has issue:

(1) +Neil Malcolm Ross; *b* 10 March 1970

(1) *Joanne Carole; *b* 1972

1 (cont.) The *Master of Forbes* *m* 2nd 1988 *Mrs Jennifer Mary Gribbon, dau of Ian Peter Whittington, of Tunbridge Wells

2 +Jonathan Andrew [The Hon Jonathan Forbes, East Cevidley, Alford, Aberdeenshire AB33 8BH]; *b* 20 Aug 1947; *educ* Eton and RAC Cirencester; Capt Gren Guards (ret 1977), dir Profile Security Servs 1980–; *m* 1981 *Hon Nicola Frances Hawke, dau of 10th Baron Hawke (*qv*), and has:

(1) +James Frederick Nicholas; *b* 1987

(1) *Camilla Rose; *b* 1983

(2) *Annabella Jane; *b* 1985

1 *Gillian Rosemary [The Hon Mrs Foster, Church Farm House, Blakesley, Northants NN12 8RA]; *b* 3 April 1949; *educ* St Mary's Wantage; *m* 26 March 1969 *Alexander Neil Foster (*see* PERTH, E), and has:

(1) *Michael Alexander; *b* 1973

(1) *Lucia Katharine; *b* 1970

Lineage: The lands of Forbes, Aberdeenshire, described as the duthus or tribe-land of the chief of the Forbeses, were originally held independently of any feudal tenancy system and traditionally by 'first occupation', or in effect a superior kind of squatting (and on a vast scale). They seem to have been incorporated into a feudal system of tenure 1271/2. At that time DUNCAN, feudal Ld of Forbes had a charter of the lands of Forbes and Kern as a baronial fief from ALEXANDER III in 1272. His s:

JOHN de FORBES; paid homage to EDWARD I 12 March 1295/6 but seems later to have supported ROBERT I (THE BRUCE); Govr Urquhart Castle; by tradition fell in battle 1305, leaving by his w (possibly a dau of John del Ard), a posthumous s:

JOHN de FORBES of that Ilk; witnessed two charters of the Earl of Mar (*qv*) 1359; *d* by 1362, leaving issue:

Sir ALEXANDER de FORBES of that Ilk; *d* by 3 July 1364, leaving issue:

JOHN de FORBES of that Ilk; had charter from 9th Earl of Mar (*qv*) of the lands of Edinbanchory and Craiglogy, which was confirmed by DAVID II 3 July 1364 and 15 Nov 1374; Sheriff Aberdeen 1374; had granted to him and his w Margaret by Bp of Moray 18 July 1378 the lands of Findrassie; had:

Sir JOHN FORBES of that Ilk; *s* f by 20 Aug 1387, by 6 April 1391; *m* Elizabeth/Margaret Kennedy, of Dunure, and *d* between May and Nov 1406, having had:

1 ALEXANDER

2 William (Sir), of Kinaldie; *m* Agnes, dau of Sir William Fraser, 2nd of Philorth (*see* SALTOUN, L) and had issue (*see* FORBES, Bt, of Newe)

3 John (Sir); got Tolquhon by marriage with Marjory, dau and coheir of Sir Henry Preston of Formartin, and was ancestor of the FORBESes of Tolquhon, Foveran, Waterton and Culloden

4 Alaster Cam; got Brux by marriage with Katherine, dau and heir of Sir Ewen Cameron, and was ancestor of the FORBESes of Brux

Sir JOHN's est s,

ALEXANDER FORBES, **1st Lord Forbes** (S), so *cr* between Oct 1444 and July 1445; *b c* 1380; among Scots contingent in French army at victory over English of Beaugé during Hundred Years War 1421; had a charter of the lands and (territorial) barony of Forbes 16 Oct 1423; *m* 6–16 Oct 1423 Elizabeth (*m* 2nd Sir David Hay of Yester; *see* TWEEDDALE, M), only dau of 1st Earl of Angus of the 1389 *cr* (*see* HAMILTON and BRANDON, D) and gdau of ROBERT III, and *d* 1448, having had issue:

1 JAMES, **2nd Lord**

2 William; Provost St Giles, Edinburgh

1 Annabella; *m* 1445 Patrick, Master of Gray

2 Margaret; *m* — Meldrum of Fyvie

3 Elizabeth; *m* Alexander Irvine of Drum

The 1st LORD's s,

JAMES FORBES, **2nd Lord Forbes**; licensed 1456 to fortify his castle of Druminnor, commonly called Forbes, then the chief seat of the family (the name Castle Forbes was later transferred to Putachie); *m* Egidia/Gille, dau of 1st Earl Marischal (*see* KINTORE, E), and *d* between 20 Sept 1460 and 30 July 1462, having had, with another s:

1 WILLIAM, **3rd Lord**

2 Duncan; *m* Christian, dau of — Mercer, of Balliol, and widow of Gilbert Skene of that Ilk, and was ancestor of the FORBESes of Corsindae and Monymusk (*see* STUART-FORBES, Bt)

3 Patrick, of Corse; ancestor of the FORBESes of Craigievar and the Earls of Granard (*qv*)

1 Egidia; *m* Malcolm Forbes of Tolquhon

The 2nd LORD's est s,

WILLIAM FORBES, **3rd Lord Forbes**, called 'Gray Willie'; *m c* 8 July 1468 Lady Christian Gordon, dau of 1st Earl of Huntly (*see* HUNTLY, M), and *d* between 9 July 1477 and 5 July 1483, having had issue:

1 ALEXANDER FORBES, **4th Lord Forbes**; *m* Margaret (*m* 2nd by 9 Aug 1509 1st Earl of Cassillis, *see* AILSA, M), only dau of 1st and last Earl of Arran of the 1467 *cr* (*see* KILMARNOCK, B), and *dsp* between Aug 1488 and 6 May 1491

2 ARTHUR FORBES, **5th Lord Forbes**; *m* Agnes, dau of 3rd Lord Glamis (*see* STRATHMORE AND KINGHORNE, E), and *dsp* 1493

3 JOHN FORBES, **6th Lord Forbes**; *m* 1st Catherine, dau of 1st Earl of Atholl of the 1457 *cr* (*see* MORAY, E), and had a s (James, *d* young) and a dau (Elizabeth, *m* John Grant of Freuchie; *see* STRATHSPEY, B); *m* 2nd by 26 Feb 1509/10 Christian, dau of John Lundin of that Ilk, and by her had:

(1) John, *Master of Forbes*; *m* as her 1st husb Elizabeth, dau of 6th Lord Glamis (*see* STRATHMORE AND KINGHORNE, E); *dsp*, executed 17 July 1537 for conspiracy to murder JAMES V

(2) WILLIAM, **7th Lord**

(2) Margaret; *m* Andrew Fraser of Muchalls

(3) Elizabeth; *m* 1st Gilbert Keith of Troup; *m* 2nd Alexander Innes, 14th of that Ilk (*see* ROXBURGHE, D); *m* 3rd Alexander Dunbar of Conzie (*see* DUNBAR, Bt, of Mochrum)

(4) Marjory; *m* Alexander Forbes of Brux

3 (cont.) The **6th Lord** *m* 3rd by 29 July 1515 Elizabeth, widow of 1st Lord Elphinstone (*qv*) and dau of — Barlow/Berlay, and *d* 1547, leaving:

(3) Arthur, of Putachie; *m* as her 2nd husb Elizabeth, dau of Alexander Innes, 13th of that Ilk (*see* ROXBURGHE, D); *k* Battle of Tillieangus Oct 1571

(5) Janet; *m* 1st 3rd Earl of Atholl of the 1457 *cr* (*see* MORAY, E); *m* 2nd Alexander Hay of Delgaty; *m* 3rd William Leslie of Balquhain (*see* LESLIE, Bt)

1 Christian; *m* 1st Lord Ruthven and had issue (*see* CARLISLE, E)

The 6th LORD's yr s,

WILLIAM FORBES, **7th Lord Forbes**; Gentleman of the Bedchamber 1539; *m* 19 Dec 1538 Elizabeth, dau and coheir of Sir William Keith of Inneruggie, and *d* 1593, having had, with two other sons (*d* young):

1 JOHN, **8th Lord**

2 William, of Fodderbirse; *b* 2 March 1543/4; had issue

3 Arthur, of Logie; *b* 3 April 1550; *k* 1574

4 James, of Lethenty; *b* 16 July 1551; *m* Margaret, er dau and coheir of William Forbes of Pitsligo (*see* FORBES, Bt, of Newe), and had issue

5 Robert, Commendator Monymusk; *b* 1 Jan 1555/6; *m* Agnes, dau of William Forbes of Corse, and had issue
6 Abraham, of Blacktown
1 Jean; *m* James, Lord Ogilvy of Airlie (*see* AIRLIE, E)
2 Elizabeth; *m* as his 2nd w 5th Lord Sinclair (*qv*)
3 Christian; *m* George Johnston of that Ilk and Caskieben and had issue (*see* JOHNSON, Bt)
4 Isabel; *m* John Gordon of Pitlurg
5 Catherine; *m* — Barclay of Gartly
6 Margaret; *m* George Sinclair of Mey
7 Barbara; *m* 1st Robert Allardyce of Allardyce; *m* 2nd Alexander Hay of Delgaty; *m* 3rd Sir Archibald Douglas of Keillor (*see* MORTON, E)
8 Anne; *m* 1st Sir John Seton of Barns; *m* 2nd John Hamilton

The 7th LORD's s,

JOHN FORBES, **8th Lord Forbes**, PC (S Jan 1593/4); *b* 3 July 1542; supported JAMES VI against the Catholic Lords 1594/5; *m* 1st Nov 1558 Margaret (*divorce* 1574), est dau of 4th Earl of Huntly (*see* HUNTLY, M), and had:
1 William; *b* 1562; Capucin monk Ghent from 13 Feb 1588/9; *dsp* 21 March 1591/2
2 JOHN FORBES, **9th Lord Forbes**; *b* 1570; Capucin monk Tournai from 2 Aug 1593; *d* unm 11 Aug 1606
1 Jean; *m* William Comyn of Earnside
2 Isobel; *d* unm
3 Margaret; *m* 1st 1600 George Sinclair of Dunbeath; *m* 2nd 1628 Claud Hamilton

The **8th Lord** *m* 2nd 1580 Janet (*d* 2 Feb 1616), dau of William Seton of Touch and widow of Sir John Bellenden, and *d* 29 June 1606 after obtaining 28 Dec 1598 a charter purporting to resettle the Lordship and (territorial) Barony of Forbes on his male issue by her, having further had, with another s (*d* young):
3 ARTHUR, **10th Lord**
4 Katherine; *m* William Gordon, of Rothiemay

The 8th LORD's only surv s by his 2nd w,

ARTHUR FORBES, **10th Lord Forbes**; *b* 25 April 1581; *m* 5 Feb 1600 Jean, dau of 4th Lord Elphinstone (*qv*), and had, with four other sons:
1 ALEXANDER, **11th Lord**
2 John; *b* 2 Nov 1608; bore a letter of recommendation from CHARLES I to The Shah of Persia 1635; *d* unm
1 Barbara; *m* 2nd Earl of Seaforth (*see* CROMARTIE, E)
2 Anne; *m* Arthur Forbes of Echt
3 Elizabeth; *m* James Skene of Skene

The 10th LORD's est s,

ALEXANDER FORBES, **11th Lord Forbes**; Lt-Gen Thirty Years War under KING GUSTAVUS ADOLPHUS OF SWEDEN, cmded Scottish Army Ireland 1643; *m* 1st his distant cousin Anne, sis of 1st Lord Forbes of Pitsligo (*see* FORBES, Bt, of Newe), and had, with three other sons and a dau:
1 WILLIAM FORBES, **12th Lord Forbes**; *m* 1st 1648 Jean (*d* 10 Dec 1660), er dau and coheir of John Campbell of Cawdor (*see* CAWDOR, E); *m* 2nd *c* 26 March 1668 Anna (*dsp*), sis of 2nd Earl of Kellie (*see* MAR and KELLIE, E); *m* 3rd *c* 11 Dec 1682 Barbara (*dsp*), dau of — Forbes of Asloun, and *d* 1697, leaving by his 1st w:
(1) WILLIAM, **13th Lord**
(2) Arthur, of Auchintoul and Breda; *m* Elizabeth Forbes, of Echt, and had a s (Alexander)
(3) Archibald, of Putachie; *m* Margaret Forbes, of Leslie, and was *bur* 29 Nov 1723, having had three daus and a s David
(1) Margaret; *m* 1st Alexander, Lord Duffus; *m* 2nd Sir Robert Gordon, Bt, of Gordonstoun, and *d* April 1677
(2) Elizabeth; *m* John Leith of Whitehaugh

The **11th Lord** *m* 2nd Elizabeth, dau of Robert Forbes of Rires, Fifeshire, and *d* Stockholm 20 April 1672, having by her had, with eight other sons and eight other daus:
1 Marie; *b* 26 July 1651; *m* 1st (contract 30 Jan 1679), as his 2nd w, Hugh Rose, 14th of Kilravock (*d* 1687), and had issue; *m* 2nd Alexander Kinnaird of Culbin

The 12th LORD's son,

WILLIAM FORBES, **13th Lord Forbes**, PC; *b c* 1656; supported the Union of Scottish and English Parls 1707, Ld Lt Aberdeenshire and Banffshire 1715–16 specifically to suppress the Jacobite Rising; *m* 1680 Anne, dau of James Brodie of Brodie, and *d* July 1716, having had, with another s:
1 WILLIAM FORBES, **14th Lord Forbes**; *m* (contract 3 Sept 1720) Dorothy, dau of William Dale, of Covent Gdn, London, who brought him a fortune of £20,000 (over £1m in late-1990s terms) which he lost in the South Sea Bubble 1720 and other injudicious speculations, and *d* 26 June 1730, having had, with two other daus (*d* young):
(1) FRANCIS FORBES, **15th Lord Forbes**; *b* 19 Dec 1721; *d* 8 Aug 1734
(1) Jean; *m* 22 April 1748 James Dundas of Dundas and *d* 28 July 1774
(2) Elizabeth; *m* 1752 Prof John Gregory, MD, and *d* 1761
2 JAMES, **16th Lord**
1 Mary; *m* John Ogilvy of Balbegno

The 15th LORD's unc,

JAMES FORBES, **16th Lord Forbes**; *b* 1689; *m* 1st 1715 his distant cousin Mary, dau of 3rd Lord Forbes of Pitsligo (*see* FORBES, Bt, of Newe), and had:
1 JAMES FORBES, **17th Lord Forbes**; *b c* 1725; Dep Govr Fort William 1764; *m* Jan 1760 Catherine (*d* 16 April 1805), only dau of Sir Robert Innes, 6th Bt, of Balvenie (*qv*), and *d* 29 July 1804, having had, with three other sons:
(1) JAMES OCHONCAR, **18th Lord**
(1) Margery; *m* 1st 4 June 1786 John, Lord Macleod, eldest s of the attainted 3rd Earl of Cromarty (*see* CROMARTIE, E); *m* 2nd 11 March 1794 4th Duke of Atholl (*qv*) and *d* 4 Oct 1842, leaving issue
(2) Mary Elizabeth; *m* 9 July 1785 Sir John Hay, Bt, of Smithfield and Hayston, and *d* 2 Nov 1803, leaving issue (*see* LOVAT, L)
1 Sophia; *m* Charles Cumine of Kininmont, and *d* 13 March 1790
2 Mary; *m* James Gordon of Cobairdy, and *d* 21 June 1793, leaving issue
3 Anne; *m* 20 Nov 1746 Thomas Erskine of Pittodrie and *d* 30 Oct 1750, leaving issue

The **16th Lord Forbes** *m* 2nd 1741 Elizabeth (*dsp* 12 June 1792), dau of Sir James Gordon, Bt, of Park, and *d* 20 Feb 1761

The 17th LORD's est s,

JAMES OCHONCAR FORBES, **18th Lord Forbes**; *b* 7 March 1765; Kt Roy Sicilian Order St Januarius; Gen, Col 21st Scots Fus, rep S peer 1806–43, High Commr to Gen Assembly Ch of Scotland 1826; *m* 2 June 1792 Elizabeth (*d* 11 Oct 1830), est dau of Walter Hunter of Polmood, Peeblesshire (*see* CROMARTIE, E), and *d* 4 May 1843, having had, with four other sons and another dau:
1 WALTER, **19th Lord**
2 Robert; *b* 1 June 1808; HEIC's CS Bengal; *m* 26 March 1828 Frances Dorothy (*d* 3 June 1895), 2nd dau of Thomas Law Hodges, MP, of Hemel Hempstead, and *d* 2 June 1883, leaving issue:
(1) Robert Ochoncar Hawkins; *b* 17 Feb 1829; Col RSC; *m* 1858 Jessie Smith and *d* 20 Nov 1882, leaving issue:
1a Robert Ochoncar; *b* 7 Sept 1859; *m* 9 Sept 1898 Juliana Olga (*d* 23 Feb 1954), dau of Maj John Nevinson, 4th Hus, and *d* 3 Nov 1913, leaving issue:
1b *Rosalie Jessie Olga; *b* 1904; *m* 19 Sept 1938 Thomas Percival Durant Beighton (*d* 1971), est s of Thomas Durant Beighton, ICS
2a James Smith; *b* 1861
1a Jessie Frances Hodges
(2) Frederick Murray Hay; *b* 30 March 1830; Maj Bengal Staff Corps; *m* 5 Jan 1858 Honoria Matilda, dau of Rev William Knox Marshall, Preb Hereford, and *d* 3 Dec 1870, leaving, with two other daus (Florence and Alice, *d* unm):
1a Malcolm (Rev); *b* 3 March 1860; *m* 24 Nov 1888 Ella Constance Josephine Brenton (*d* 9 Dec 1937), dau of Rev Adolphus Carey, Vicar Brixham, Devon, and *d* 12 July 1941, leaving issue:
1b Malcolm Hay Ochoncar; *b* 22 Aug 1891; Maj 3rd Bn Gordon Highrs WW I and II as Instructor (Seamanship) RANVR; *m* 1st 19 Dec 1921 Edith Maud (*d* 20 Feb 1962), only dau of G A McMillan, and *d* 1973, leaving:
1c *Helen Mary Hay; *m* 9 April 1945 *Terence Dudley Thompson, F/Lt RAAF, and has issue:
1d *Ian Forbes; *b* 18 Feb 1951
1d *Pamela Forbes; *b* 25 Feb 1947
2d *Jane Forbes; *b* 21 Dec 1948
3d *Georgina Helen Forbes; *b* 26 Aug 1968
1b (cont.) Maj Malcolm Forbes *m* 2nd 1966 Helen Roslyn (*d* 1970), dau of A C Graham and widow of Alexander Dickson
1b Helen Stuart Angus; *b* 10 Sept 1889
2a Norman Hay, JP Kent; *b* 1 March 1863; FRCS Edin, FRS Edin, Order of Mercy; *m* 12 Jan 1897 Ellen (*d* 28 May 1927), widow of Charles W Robinson and dau of Jason Wilshin, of Hayes, Middx, and *d* 27 June 1916, leaving:
1b Eilidh McLeod Hay, *b* 9 Oct 1897; *d* unm 25 Aug 1970
3a Lindsay Anstruther; *b* 21 Oct 1865; Maj IA, Consul Basra; *m* 1911 Gertrude B (*d* 1960), dau of G F Lambert, of Basingstoke, and *dsp* 5 April 1953
4a Atholl Murray Hay, DSO (1917); *b* 22 July 1870; Lt-Col 1st Bn Roy Scots Fus, NW Frontier India 1897–98 (medal with two clasps) and WW I (wounded, despatches twice); *m* 16 Feb 1915 Alice Rose (*d* 17 Feb 1968 aged 97), dau of N C Tuely, FLS, and widow of Maj George Alfred Keef, Roy Scots Fus, and *dsp* 10 April 1942
1a Edith Russell; *m* 8 March 1893 Lt-Col Daniel Edward Mocatta (*d* 28 Nov 1936), IA, and *dsp* 15 Nov 1950
2a Katherine Hamilton; *m* 22 July 1896 Archibald William Forbes Russell, MA, MB, IMS, and *d* 3 June 1934, having had issue. He *d* 21 June 1898
(3) Henry Twisden; *b* 27 May 1832; Col Bengal Staff Corps; *m* 7 Nov 1856 Emily Jane (*d* 1892), 2nd dau of Maj John Inglis, and *d* 1895, leaving issue:
1a Robert Inglis; *b* 10 Oct 1860; Maj Hants Regt, Govr Aberdeen Prison, Burmese War 1885–87 (despatches, medal and clasp); *m* 1892 Helena Eleanor (*d* 1944), dau of Edward Townsend, of Co Galway, and *d* 1945, leaving:
1b William Robert Townsend; *b* 1893; Capt Black Watch WW I (wounded); *m* 26 Aug 1925 Evelyn (*d* 1989), only dau of Very Rev Preb H Erskine-Hill, DD, and *d* 1967, leaving:
1c +Ian Robert Patrick [Ian Forbes Esq, 93 Steyne Rd, Southbourne, Hants]; *b* 24 Oct 1926; *m* 26 Sept 1953 (*divorce* 1971) Patricia, only dau of D Heginbotham, of Hove, Sussex
2c +William Michael [Lt-Cdr William Forbes RN (ret), 21 Rosenau Crescent, London SW11]; *b* 13 Nov 1934; *m* 21 Sep 1957 (*divorce* 19–) Wendy Ann, dau of Stanley Thomas Birch, and has issue:
1d +David Charles; *b* 1 Jan 1959
2d +Simon Robert; *b* 6 April 1964
3d +Jeremy Andrew; *b* 26 Oct 1966
1d *Anne Lesley; *b* 25 June 1960; *educ* Bristol U (MD)
3c +Patrick [The Rev Patrick Forbes, 14 East St, Lilley, Beds LU2 8LP]; *b* 21 Nov 1938; *educ* Westminster and Lincoln Theological Coll; broadcasting offr C of E; *m* 16 June 1962 *Annette Margaret, only child of Robert Rew Miller, of Upper Norwood, and has issue:
1d +Stephen Robert; *b* 10 Sep 1967
1c Elizabeth Anne; *b* 25 Sept 1933; *m* 1st 1953 (*annulled* 1955) Tom Richard Denning, yr s of T H Denning; *m* 2nd 30 June 1956 *William Lathrop Bauhan, of NH, USA, er s of Col R W Bauhan, and had issue:
1d *Patrick Lathrop; *b* 7 March 1957
1d *Sarah Forbes; *b* 8 Sept 1959
2b Kenneth Herbert; *b* 1899; JP Karachi 1945–47; *m* 1st 29 Nov 1929 (*divorce* 1938) Zara Muriel, only dau of Walter Currie, of South Africa, and had issue:

1c *Susan; *b* 6 July 1933; *m* 14 June 1958 *Iain Stuart Bain, s of James Bain, MC, of Kirkcudbright, and has:

1d *Christina Mary; *b* 28 Oct 1961; *m* 1993 *Alasdair Anderson

2d *Catriona Frances, *b* 29 March 1964

2b (cont.) Kenneth Forbes *m* 2nd 10 Sept 1947 *Dorothy Joan [Mrs Kenneth Forbes, Orchard Cottage, Coopers Hill Lane, Englefield Green, Surrey], only dau of Alfred Percival Folkard, and *d* 1981, leaving by her:

1c +Colin Kenneth [Colin Forbes Esq, 46B Addison Gdns, London W14 0DP]; *b* 12 March 1956

2a Herbert Russell; *b* 1863; *m* 30 March 1896 Amy Ella (*d* 15 Jan 1935), dau of W D Scott, and *d* 17 April 1920, leaving issue:

1b Marjorie Alice; *b* 1900; *m* 21 July 1920 John Taylor Porritt (*d* 1976), s of Edward Porritt, and had issue:

1c *Joan April; *b* 1921; *m* 19– — Yates

2c *Gillian [Mrs Lindsey-Renton, PO Box 747, Olifantsfontein 1665, S Africa]; *b* 1927; *m* 19– — Lindsey-Renton and has two daus

3a Charles Twisden; *b* 1864; *m* 28 Aug 1895 Alice Park (*d* 1940), dau of Surgn-Col A H Hilson, CIE, and *d* 14 Dec 1913, leaving issue:

1b Archibald Herbert d'Esterre, MC; *b* 1889; 2nd Lt Service Bn Roy W Surrey Regt; *m* 7 Aug 1924 Emily Flora (*d* 1991), yst dau of S K Keyes, and *d* 31 Oct 1956, leaving issue:

1c *Isla Hamilton [Mrs Philip Brownless, The Hornpipe, Oak Meadow, Birdham, Chichester, W Sussex]; *b* 31 Oct 1926; BA 1948; *m* 6 July 1948 *Rev Philip Paul Stanley Brownless, MA, est s of Rev William Stanley Brownless, of Somerset, and has had:

1d Andrew Hamilton; *b* 3 Feb 1952; *d* 19–

2d *Benjamin Stanley; *b* 15 Oct 1956

1d *Alison Kilworth; *b* 24 May 1950; *educ* Bristol U; *m* 1973 *Alan Geoffrey Browne, MICE, and has issue:

1e *Radley Alan Forbes; *b* 1978

1e *Carola Jody Merchant; *b* 1981

2c *Rona Kilworth [Mrs Raymond Hunter, RRI, Lawrencetown, Annapolis Co, Nova Scotia, Canada]; *b* 1 Nov 1928; MA 1951; *m* 17 May 1952 *Raymond Frank Abraham Hunter, MC, Dist Offr Benin City, Nigeria, s of Rev Walter Frederick William Hunter, of Birmingham, and has had:

1d Robert William Forbes; *b* 10 June, *d* 19 Aug 1954

2d *Charles William Forbes; *b* 2 Nov 1955; *m* 1976 * (Mairi) Christine Parker and has issue:

1e *Robyn Beatrice; *b* 1981

2e *(Mairi) Chantal; *b* 1984

3d *Jolyon Nigel Forbes; *b* 9 Oct 1958; *m* 1983 *Maura Cameron and has issue:

1e *Matthew Archibald Cameron; *b* 1988

2e *(Raymond) Alexander Cameron; *b* 1991

3e *Charles Robert Forbes; *b* Aug 1995

1e *Sarah Lindsey; *b* 1986

2e *Emily Jean; *b* 1993

4d *Mark Raymond Forbes; *b* 23 Sep 1960; *m* 1985 *Pauline Irvin and has issue:

1e *Abby Catherine Irvin; *b* 1990

5d *William John Forbes; *b* 25 Nov 1965; *m* 1988 *Rebecca Houtsma and has issue:

1e *(William) Piers; *b* May 1996

1e *Tegan Anneke; *b* 1992

2e *(Rona) Katherine; *b* 1994

1b Alison Park; *b* 1902; *m* Hugh Charteris Duncan (*d* 1953), of Kuttal, Cachar, and *d* 7 Nov 1927, leaving:

1c *Alistair Charteris; *b* 1927

4a Arthur Trevor; *b* 1866; ICS; *m* 1st 15 Jan 1890 Caroline Eliza (*d* 4 July 1915), dau of Richard Vicary Gorham, of Suffolk, and had issue:

1b Trevor Courtenay; *b* 9 Nov 1898; Lt 7th Bn Suffolk Regt

1b Edith Marjorie; *m* 10 Sep 1934 Lt-Col Graham Brunel Ingle Nokes, RIASC, er s of G A Nokes, and has issue:

1c *Daphne Veronica; *b* 16 May 1942

4a (cont.) Arthur Forbes *m* 2nd 25 Dec 1916 Cornelia (*d* 1956), dau of Rev Thomas Robert Matthews, Rector Moviddy, Crookstown, Co Cork, and *d* 28 March 1933

5a Percy Bowie Barrington; *b* 1872; *m* 1909 Helen Ardamine Georgette, dau of Rev John Galloway Garrett, of Kandy, Ceylon, and *dsp* 15 Jun 1947

6a Alec Inglis; *b* 1874; *m* 13 Dec 1899 Katherine Macpherson (*m* 2nd 15 Oct 1913 Maj William Bucknell Coney, Sherwood Foresters, Derbyshire Regt, and *d* 1951), dau of Ernest Gray, of Hoon Hay, NZ, and *dsp* 29 July 1910

7a Cyril D'Esterre; *b* 1878; *m* June 1914 Sara Moore (*d* Sept 1924), dau of James Carr, of Saskatchewan, Canada

1a Constance Louisa Sandys; *d* unm 20 Nov 1940

2a Edith Frances; *m* 23 July 1931 Rev Acton Warburton, MA, er s of Rev Thomas Acton Warburton, DCL

3a Alice Gertrude; *m* 1899 Matthew Young, ICS, of Guildford, Surrey, and had issue

(4) Walter Ernest; *b* 23 May 1840; Col Bengal Staff Corps; *m* 12 Sept 1860 Louisa Charlotte (*d* 18 July 1916), est dau of James Colquhoun, and *d* 1895, having had, with other issue:

1a Francis Sutherland Courtenay; *b* 1867; *m* 1896 Adrienne Eva Blanche, dau of Col Charles Cecil Rookes, of Auckland, NZ, and had issue:

1b Haydon Marriott Sutherland, DSC; *b* 1897; Lt-Cdr RN; *m* Cicely, dau of Capt Armitage, RN, and was *k* on flying duty 9 June 1927, leaving:

1c *Pamela Patricia, *b* 1925

2a Ernest Colebrook; *b* 1868; *m* 1891 Anne Maud (*d* 14 Feb 1942), dau of John Cashel, of Onehunga, Auckland, NZ, and *d* 1912, leaving issue:

1b Atholl Courtenay; *b* 1892; *m* 1924 Veronica Elizabeth (*m* 2nd 1939 L A C Houston and *d* 7 Jan 1966), dau of Arthur George Willis, of Gisborne, NZ, and *d* 3 May 1952, leaving issue:

1c *Pamela Jane; *b* 1929; late Sister Tutor QARNNS; *m* 20 Sep 1958 *Richard Bostock, BA, FCA, AIMTA, s of Edward Bostock, and has:

1d *John Edward; *b* 25 Feb 1960; *m* 1986 *Katherine Helen Dandy

2d *David Forbes; *b* 5 Jan 1962; *m* 1990 *Yujin Chung and has issue:

1e *Richard Daejin; *b* 1990

1d *Julia Elizabeth; *b* 4 Jan 1965; *m* 1993 *Kevin David Kinsella

2b Ernest Twisden; *b* 1902; *m* 1932 Mavis Amy (*d* 1973), of Norfolk Island, S Pacific, dau of Edward Ingham, of Melbourne, Australia, and *d* Jan 1966, leaving issue:

1c *Barbara Beatrice; *b* 1934; *m* 1963 *Hubert Andrew Thebo, BS, and has issue:

1d *Christine Forbes; *b* 16 March 1967

1a Margaret Louisa; *m* 19 April 1902 Capt Robert James Longden, Yorks and Lancs Regt, of Vancouver, and had issue

(5) John Charles Marriott; *b* 18 April 1842; *m* 1870 Ellen Frances, dau of Pierre Augier, and *d* 22 May 1888, leaving:

1a Charlotte Emily

2a Mabel Fanny Russell; *m* 22 Oct 1904 Lt-Col Edwin Harold Brown, MD, MRCP, IMS

3a Ida Caroline

(6) Edward Millet; *b* 6 Oct 1843; Lt-Col ISC; *m* 1st 1871 Eva Rebecca, dau of John Taylor, and had issue:

1a Edward Ernest, DSO (1919); *b* 16 Jan 1875; Lt-Col IA; *d* 26 March 1922

1a Fanny Louisa

2a Lilian Julia

3a Eva Maria; *d* unm 8 April 1953

(6) (cont.) Col Edward Forbes *m* 2nd 5 June 1901 Juliet Amy, dau of Herbert John Reynolds, CSI, and *d* 25 Sept 1905

(7) Arthur St Quintin; *b* 16 March 1846; *m* 15 Aug 1876 Alice Margaret, dau of Rev J M Whitelaw, LLD, of Athelstances, Drem, NB, and had issue:

1a Bertie St John Ochoncar; *b* 1882; *m* 1902 Margaret Smith (*d* 1946) and *d* 1953, leaving issue:

1b +Bertie St John Ochoncar; *b* 1918; Maj IA and Roy Scots WW II; *m* 1942 *Anne More Crozer and has issue:

1c +Graham Richard; *b* 1946; *m* 1971 *Anne Catherine Haigh, of Edinburgh, and has issue:

1d +Callum Richard; *b* 1972

1c *Gillian Margaret; *b* 1951

1a Alice Margaret Whitelaw; *b* 1906; *m* 1929 Robert Gray Pottinger (*d* 1933) and has issue:

1b *Ronald Forbes; *b* 1933; MB and ChB Edinburgh 1959; *m* 1960 *Marija Ozanic and has issue:

1c *David Forbes; *b* 1964

(8) William Law Hodges; *b* 28 March 1848; *m* 30 Nov 1874 Ella Martha, dau of Sylvanus Gaylord, and had issue:

1a David Law Hodges; *b* 27 Jan 1881; mining engr (ret 1954); *educ* Toronto U (MED Eng); *m* 17 Sept 1913 Helen Winifred Downey and *dsp*

1a Frances Emily; *b* 20 Sep 1876; *d* unm 13 Aug 1959

(1) Fanny Caroline; *m* 16 Nov 1854 Alexander Elliott Russell, Bengal CS, and *d* 1 May 1879, leaving issue

(2) Helen Isabella; *m* 16 Nov 1854 George Louis Martin

1 Caroline Elizabeth; *m* 16 Nov 1818 George Fairholme and *d* 14 April 1865, leaving issue. He *d* 19 Nov 1846

2 Charlotte Elizabeth; *m* 15 Sep 1825 Sir John Forbes, 6th Bt, of Craigievar (*qv*), and *d* 5 Nov 1883 aged 82

3 Mary Stuart; *m* 28 Aug 1839 Charles Benjamin Lee Mainwaring, of The Abbey, Knaresborough, and *d* 2 Feb 1897, leaving issue. He *d* 10 Jan 1874

4 Isabella Drummond; *m* 28 Aug 1839 Baron Ernest de Poeinitz and *d* 9 Jan 1897, leaving issue

The 18th LORD's est surv s,

WALTER FORBES, **19th Lord Forbes**; *b* 29 May 1798; served Coldstream Gds Waterloo; *m* 1st 31 Jan 1825 Horatia (*d* 24 Dec 1862), 7th dau of Sir John Gregory Shaw, 5th Bt, of Eltham, and *d* 2 May 1868, having had, with other issue:

1 HORACE COURTENAY GAMMELL FORBES, **20th Lord Forbes**, DL Aberdeenshire; *b* 24 Feb 1823; *educ* Oriel Coll Oxford (BA 1849, MA 1851); rep S peer 1874–1906; *d* unm 23 June 1914

2 Charles Murray Hay, of Brux, Aberdeenshire; *b* 13 March 1830; Offr 95th Foot; *m* 17 July 1860 Caroline Louisa Elizabeth (*d* 30 March 1901), 3rd dau of Lt-Col Hon George Spencer (*see* CHURCHILL, V), and *dsp* 17 May 1874

3 ATHOLL MONSON, **21st Lord**

The **19th Lord Forbes** *m* 2nd 4 April 1864 Louisa (*d* 26 Jan 1921), 2nd dau of James Ormond, and by her had:

4 Walter Robert Drummond, JP Aberdeenshire; *b* 14 May 1865; Capt Gordon Highrs, GSO(3) 1914; *m* 13 Feb 1888 Eveline Louisa Michell (*d* 18 April 1924), only dau of Frederick Farwell, and *d* 25 March 1929, leaving issue:

(1) (Victor) Courtenay Walter (Sir), KCMG (1945); *b* 29 Jan 1889; Envoy Extrdy and Min Plen Peru and Ecuador 1933–44, Amb Extrdy and Plen Peru 1944–45, ret Dec 1945; *m* 1st 22 July 1916 (*divorce* 1949) Luisa, dau of Hon Sir Henry Hubert Juta, and had issue:

1a *Sara Elizabeth Ninita; *b* 4 May 1917; *m* 1938 Hugh Gyle-Thompson (*d* 1972) and has issue:

1b *David Courtenay Gladstone; *b* 25 Sept 1943; *educ* Charterhouse and Ch Ch Oxford (BA); *m* 9 May 1970 *Penelope Fearnly, of Devizes, and has issue:

1c *Camilla Kate; *b* 1974

1b *Donita Helen Elizabeth; *b* 15 Sept 1939; SRN; *m* 16 Oct 1965 *George Oliver Papps, of NJ, USA, and has:

1c *Gillian Sara; *b* 11 Jan 1967
2c *Luisa Elizabeth; *b* 1970
2b *Sara Anne Robina; *b* 3 July 1941; BSc; *m* 1969 *Christopher Watson and has issue:
1c *Timothy Hugh James; *b* 1970
2c *Angus Christopher Hugo; *b* 1972
(1) (cont.) Sir Courtenay Forbes *m* 2nd 16 March 1950 *Mary Lloyd, dau of Francis George Olivieri and widow of Walter Carter Bizley, and *d* 26 Jan 1958
5 Montagu Ormond; *b* 5 May 1866; *m* 21 April 1894 Helen (*d* 12 Jan 1937), dau of William Henry Campbell, and *d* 9 Oct 1938, leaving issue:
(1) (Courtenay) Fergus Ochoncar Grey; *b* 7 Oct 1898; Col Coldstream Gds WW I, N Russia and Mesopotamia 1919–21, WW II as Dep Provost Marshal London District 1944–46; *m* 1st 7 July 1924 (*divorce* 1929) Gundrede Mary, yr dau of Capt Graham Owen Robert Wynne (*see* KILLANIN, B), and had:
1a +(Fergus) Patrick; *b* 7 July 1925; *m* 1st 6 Feb 1950 (*divorce*) Margaret Elizabeth, dau of John Percy Wayte, of Bloxham, Oxon, and has issue:
1b +Christopher Michael Fergus; *b* 24 Dec 1955
1b *Grania Helen; *b* 5 Aug 1950
2b *(Moira) Isobel; *b* 29 Jan 1957; *m* 19– *William Underhill, s of His Hon Judge (Michael) Underhill and Mrs William Beaumont, of Richmond, Surrey, and has two daus (*b* 1992 and 1994)
1a (cont.) Patrick Forbes *m* 2nd 1967 *Jeannette, dau of Jeanette Fendryk, of Baltimore, Md., and by her has a s (*b* 1974)
(1) (cont.) (Courtenay) Fergus Forbes *m* 2nd 21 Oct 1929 Mary Shelagh (*d* 15 Feb 1932), dau of Col Arthur Llewllyn, Somerset LI, of Wribbenhall, Worcs; *m* 3rd 31 Dec 1932 (*divorce* 1954) Dorothea Garnier, 2nd dau of His Hon Henry Staveley-Hill, TD, JP, DL, of Oulton House, Norbury, Staffs, and by her had:
2a +(John) Alistair Ponsonby [Alistair Forbes Esq, All Saint's House, nr Axminster, Devon EX13 7LR]; *b* 22 April 1937; *educ* Eton; Capt Royal Wilts Yeo and Wessex Yeo, late Coldstream Gds; *m* 2 April 1965 *Mary Dorothea, only dau of Sir William Macnamara Goodenough, 1st Bt (*qv*), and has:
1b +James William Courtenay; *b* 1970
1b *Sophie Louise Dorothea; *b* 16 Jan 1968
(1) (cont.) (Courtenay) Fergus Forbes *m* 4th 12 Nov 1954 *Emilie Frances, dau of Mrs Edward Brooks (*d* 1981), of New York, and widow of 5th Baron Monteagle of Brandon (*qv*), and *d* 1971

The 20th LORD's bro,
ATHOLL MONSON FORBES, **21st Lord Forbes**, JP, DL Aberdeenshire; *b* 15 Feb 1841; *m* 19 Sept 1876 Margaret Alice (*d* 6 Feb 1943), yst dau of Sir William Dick-Cunyngham, 8th Bt (*see* 1940 edn), and *d* 31 Jan 1916, having had:
1 ATHOLL LAURENCE CUNYNGHAM, **22nd Lord**
2 Ivan Courtenay; *b* 11 Dec 1883; *d* unm 21 June 1907
1 Marjory Winifred; *b* 18 Oct 1879; *m* 24 June 1913 Capt Hugh Edward Walker (*see* WALKER, Bt, of Sand Hutton), and *d* 14 Sept 1945, leaving issue

The 21st LORD's only surv s,
ATHOLL LAURENCE CUNYNGHAM FORBES, **22nd Lord Forbes**, JP, DL Aberdeenshire; *b* 14 Sept 1882; memb Aberdeenshire TAA, Maj Gren Gds WW I, DAAG 1916, rep S peer 1917–24; *m* 12 Oct 1914 Lady Mabel Anson (*d* 21 March 1972), 2nd dau of 3rd Earl of Lichfield (*qv*), and *d* 26 Nov 1953, having had:
1 NIGEL IVAN FORBES, **23rd and present Lord Forbes**
2 Malcolm Atholl; *b* 9 Dec 1928; *d* 6 March 1929

FORBES, Bt, of Craigievar

Arms: Azure a cross patée fitchée or between three bear's heads couped argent, muzzled gules. **Crest:** A cock proper. **Supporters:** Dexter, a knight in armour of the 15th century, armed at all points, leaving the beaver of his helmet up and leaning on a shield or, charged with a lion rampant gules, armed and langued azure, within a double tressure flory counterflory with fleurs-de-lys of the second; sinister, a bear argent, muzzled gules. **Motto:** Watch. **Creation:** Bt. (NS) 20 April 1630.

SIR JOHN ALEXANDER CUMNOCK FORBES, 12TH BT, of Craigievar, JP (Wigtown 1978) [Sir John Forbes Bt JP, Benevean, Keudoon Dalry, Kirkcudbrightshire DG7 3UB]; *b* 29 Aug 1927; *s* kinsman 1991; *educ* Stowe and RMC Sandhurst; Capt Seaforth Highrs 1945–49; dir Garrick Theatre 1951–65, The Cinema Newton Stewart 1966–94, ACE Centre of Equitation Ltd 1972–94, equestrian photo-jnlst, Baillie Newton Stewart Town Cncl 1965–76, Fndr-Convenor Cree Valley Community Cncl 1976, chm PR and Promotions (Scottish Branch) BSJA; *m* 1st 1956 (*divorce* 1963) Penelope Margaret Anne, only dau of Arthur Gordon Grey-Pennington; *m* 2nd 1966 *Jane Carolyn, only dau of Charles Gordon Evans, of Portpatrick, Wigtownshire

Lineage: The 2nd LORD FORBES (*qv*) had a 3rd s:

PATRICK FORBES of Corse; Armour-Bearer to JAMES III, had a feu-charter from the Crown of Coull, Kincraigie and Corse 1482; his s:

DAVID FORBES of Forthirbirss; had the same lands confirmed to him 1506 bar Coull (which he had resigned); they were erected into the (territorial) Barony of Oneil 1511; *m* Elizabeth Panter and had:

PATRICK FORBES of Corse; *m* Marjory, dau of Lumsden of Cushny, and had:

WILLIAM FORBES of Corse; *m* Elizabeth, dau of Strachan of Thornton, and *d* 1596, having had, with other issue:
1 Patrick, of Corse; *b* 1564; Bp Aberdeen 1618–35; *m* Lucretia, dau of Spens of Warmiston, and had, with other issue:
(1) John; Prof Theology Aberdeen U (expelled from his chair by the Covenanters); had:
1a George, of Corse, whose male line failed
2 WILLIAM
3 John; Minister Alford, deprived for Presbyterianism; settled Delft, Holland; *m* Christian, dau of Barclay of Mathers, and had issue:
(1) Arthur
(2) Patrick; Bp Caithness 1662–80
4 Sir ARTHURD FORBES, 1st Bt (NS); f of 1st EARL OF GRANARD (*qv*)

The 2nd son,
WILLIAM FORBES of Menie, also Craigievar, which he bought from John Mortimer 1610 and of which he completed the construction started by Mortimer, having made a fortune in trade overseas when younger; *m* Margaret, dau of Nicol Udward, Provost of Edinburgh, and *d* Dec 1627, having had issue:
1 WILLIAM (Sir), **1st Bt**
2 Robert (Sir), of Newton; *m* Margaret Lindsay
3 John; Minister Kincardine
4 James; *m* a dau of Burnet of Cowcardie

The est son,
Sir William Forbes, 1st Bt (NS), so *cr* 20 April 1630, with remainder to heirs and assigns whatsoever, of Craigievar; MP (S Parl) Aberdeenshire 1639–41, 1644 and 1645–46, cmded a troop of Parly Horse Civil War; *m c* 1636 Bethia, dau of Sir Archibald Murray, 1st Bt, of Blackbarony (*qv*), and had:

Sir John Forbes, 2nd Bt ('The Red Sir John'); *b* 1636; M (S Parl) Aberdeenshire 1689 and 1689–1702; *m c* 1659 Margaret, dau of Young of Auldbar, and had:
1 WILLIAM (Sir), **3rd Bt**
2 Patrick, of Balfour and Tillyfour; *b* 1661; *m* 1683 Margaret, dau and heiress of Col James Forbes of Foulis, gs of 7th Lord Forbes (*qv*), and had issue
3 Robert (Sir), of Learnie; *b* 1667; *m* a dau of Sir James Elphinstone, 1st Bt of Logie (*qv*), and had issue
4 Arthur, of Schivas; *b* 1669; *m* and had issue
5 Francis; *b* 1673; Capt Swedish Army, Sheriff Depute Aberdeen 1719; had issue
6 John, of Kincardine; *b* 1675; *m* Elizabeth, dau of Farquharson of Inverey
7 Alexander; *b* 1679
8 Charles; *b* 1683
1 Bethia; *m* 1686 Alexander Garden of Troup
2 Mary; *m* 1st Ramsay of Leathers; *m* 2nd James Buchan of Auchmacoy and had issue by both husbs
3 Margaret; *m* 1st David Lumsden of Cushnie; *m* 2nd Thomas Forbes of Echt

Sir JOHN *d* 1703; his est son,
Sir William Forbes, 3rd Bt; *b* 1660; *m* 16 Oct 1684 Margaret, dau of Hugh Rose of Kilravock, and had, with other sons (*d* young or *dsp*):
1 Hugh; *b* 1695; *m* 1716 Lady Janet Ogilvie (*m* 2nd 1719 1st Earl of Fife; *see* FIFE, D), dau of 1st Earl of Seafield (*qv*), and *dsp*
2 ARTHUR (Sir), **4th Bt**
3 Alexander; Maj; *d* unm in serv abroad 1746
1 Elizabeth; *m* 1709 James Burnett of Monboddo

Sir WILLIAM *d c* 1730; his er surv son,
Sir Arthur Forbes, 4th Bt; *b* 1709; MP Aberdeenshire 1732–47; *m* 1st 1729 Christian, est dau of Ross of Arnage, and had:
1 Jean; *b* 1730; *m* 1749 Forbes of Culloden and had issue
2 Elizabeth; *b* 1731; *m* Leith of Overhall and had issue

Sir Arthur *m* 2nd 1750 Margaret, dau of Strachan of Balgall and widow of John Burnett of Elrick, Aberdeenshire, and by her had, with two other sons (*d* young) and two other daus:
1 WILLIAM (Sir), **5th Bt**
2 Duncan FORBES later FORBES-MITCHELL, of Thainstone; *b* 26 March 1757; *m* 27 March 1777 Katherine Ann (*d* 27 Dec 1836), dau of William Fraser of Fraserfield, and *d* 6 Oct 1796, leaving, with two daus (*dsp*):
(1) Arthur Andrew, of Thainstone; *b* 1779; *d* unm 3 May 1801
(2) William, of Thainstone; *b* 3 Aug 1782; RN; *d* unm 11 May 1808
(3) Duncan, of Thainstone; *b* 1784; *d* 7 March 1812
(4) John, of Thainstone; *b* 21 March 1786; *m* 8 Feb 1809 Ann (*d* Sept 1861), dau of Lt-Col George Powell, HEICS, and *d* 9 July 1822, having had, with another s (*d* young):

1a Duncan, of Thainstone, JP, DL; *b* 30 Oct 1812; *m* 18 Feb 1834 Maria (*d* 1892), er dau of Robert Anthony Bromley, Lt-Col HEICS, and *d* 13 Aug 1870, having had, with a dau (*d* unm):

1b John, of Thainstone, JP, DL; *b* 25 June 1843; *m* 28 July 1870 Jane Maria (*d* 13 Oct 1919), er dau of Thomas James Rawson, MD, of Barrowville, Co Carlow, and *dsp* 25 April 1882

1b Maria; *m* 20 July 1878 John Alexander Stuart, of the Admlty and War Office

2b Elizabeth Erksine; *m* 20 Sept 1870 Lt-Col John Nathaniel Gower, 78th Regt (*d* 1905), and *d* 17 May 1928, leaving issue

2a John George; *b* 4 March 1814; Maj HEICS; *m* 17 June 1837 Eliza Maria (*d* 10 July 1857), dau of John Leckie, and *d* 29 April 1860, leaving issue:

1b Charles Pulteney; *b* 29 Nov 1840; Maj-Gen POW's Leinster Regt; *m* 13 Jan 1864 Hannah (*d* 28 Feb 1931), dau of John Sims, and *d* 12 April 1919

2b William Erskine; *b* 14 Aug 1847; *d* unm 14 June 1877

3a Arthur Andrew Charles; *b* 29 March 1815; *dsp*

4a David Erskine; *b* 7 April 1816; *m* Aug 1848 Margaret, 5th dau of Alexander Low, and *dsp* 1882

5a Frederick; *b* 21 June 1818; *m* 29 Oct 1840 Rachel (*dsp*), 4th dau of Alexander Forbes, and *d* 1883

6a Alexander Kinloch; *b* 7 July 1821; High Court Judge Bombay; *m* 25 March 1846 Margaret Moir (*d* 1 Nov 1904), dau of Henry David Forbes of Balgownie (*see below*), and *d* 31 Aug 1865, having had issue:

1b John Fraser (Rev); *b* 17 June 1847; MA Oxon; Chaplain Bombay; *m* 13 June 1878 Edith Palin (*d* 4 Dec 1914), dau of Henry Wenden, and *d* 1887, having had issue:

1c Alister Esmé Buchan, OBE (1919); *b* 4 Aug 1881; Maj IA Res of Offrs, Mech Engr Indian State Rlwys; *m* 1920 Ena Catherine Elizabeth, dau of Capt George James Campbell, of Cessnock and Treesbank, Ayrshire, and widow of Dr T W Quinn

1c Agnes Dorothy Mary

2c Emmeline Brita Cahusac

3c Edith Margaret Lyndhurst; *m* 1919 Capt Hugh Percival Cotton, RN (*d* 9 April 1956)

2b Henry David Erskine; *b* 19 April 1849; Bombay Revenue Dept; *m* 1884 Alice Georgina (*d* 19 July 1932), dau of Henry Ingle, and *d* 7 Aug 1920

3b Alexander Abernethie; *b* 30 June 1851; *dsp*

4b Edward Esmé (Rev); *b* 1 Sept 1855; Vicar Roffey Sussex 1909–13, formerly Maj Indian SC; *m* 1st 10 July 1880 Frederica Maud, dau of Col G F de Berry; *m* 2nd 8 April 1902 Florence Emily Louise (*d* 18 Sept 1833), yst dau of Capt W Pemberton Hesketh, 42nd Roy Highrs and 18th Hus, and *d* 8 Nov 1920

1b Margaret Theodora Lawrence; *d* unm 7 Aug 1939

2b Emmeline Maria Elizabeth; *m* 1st 1899 Charles Scott Chisholme; *m* 2nd 10 June 1908 Frederick Anthony Glyn, s of Thomas Anthony Glyn, of Yealmton, Devon, and *d* 29 Aug 1932

(5) Alexander; *b* 13 Oct 1788; *m* 11 Sept 1811 Janet (*d* 15 Feb 1846), dau of Sir William Forbes, 5th Bt, of Craigievar (*see below*), and *d* 3 Feb 1843, leaving:

1a Duncan, of Ernan Lodge, Aberdeenshire, JP; *b* 7 Nov 1815; *m* 14 April 1852 Hon Sarah Forbes (*d* 6 Oct 1891), dau of Sir John Forbes, 7th Bt, of Craigievar (*see* SEMPILL, L), and *d* 1894, leaving issue

2a William; *b* 29 May 1820; Maj-Gen Bengal Army; *m* 1st Sophia Adams Fell and had:

1b John; *b* 1853; *dsp*

2a (cont.) Maj-Gen William Forbes *m* 2nd Frances Helen (*d* 1896), dau of Capt Richard S M Spry, HEICS, and *d* 6 May 1877, leaving by her, with another dau (*d* unm):

2b William Alexander; *b* 9 March 1861; *m* 20 Aug 1902 Katherine Fanny, dau of Rev E Royds, of Brereton, and *d* 2 April 1928

3b Duncan James; *b* 21 Feb 1864

1b (Henrietta) Janet; *d* unm

2b Rachel Helen; *d* unm

1a Sarah; *m* 20 Feb 1844 Alexander Gordon (*d* 8 Aug 1868), of Newton, and *d* 4 April 1851, leaving issue

2a Katherine Anne; *m* 1 Dec 1840 John Angus (*d* 6 Nov 1878) and *d* 2 Aug 1903, leaving issue

3a Rachel; *m* 29 Oct 1840 Frederick Forbes (*see above*) and *dsp*

4a Janet Sempill; *m* 1st 2 July 1850 John Newton (*dsp* 22 Oct 1859), of Bagenalston House, Co Carlow; *m* 2nd 10 Nov 1863 Thomas Rawson, MD

5a Margaret; *m* 30 July 1840 M F Anderson and *dsp* 10 Dec 1843

(6) Henry David, of Balgownie, JP, DL; *b* 12 Nov 1790; *m* 27 May 1816 Margaret (*d* 19 Aug 1839), est dau of Alexander Fraser and heiress of Fraserfield (*see* SALTOUN, L), and *d* 24 July 1869, leaving, with two other daus (*d* unm):

1a Duncan, of Balgownie, JP; *b* 7 Oct 1817; *m* 23 March 1847 Janet Dyce (*d* 11 July 1899), only dau of Robert Forbes, of Castleton, Kincardineshire, and *dsp* 2 July 1893

2a Alexander; *b* 9 Nov 1818; *d* young

3a Henry Erskine, of Kinmundy, Aberdeenshire, JP; *b* 14 July 1821; Lt-Col, Maj 21st Hus; *m* 12 April 1855 Letitia Angelina (*d* 29 Oct 1857), est surv dau of Gen Sir George St Patrick Lawrence, KCSI, CB, and *d* 1891, leaving:

1b Margaret Isabella; *d* unm 25 Oct 1927

2b Louisa Letitia; *m* 7 Oct 1879 Capt Christian Ernst Arp von During, Prussian Army, and *d* 1936, leaving issue

1a Margaret Moir; *m* 25 March 1846 Alexander Kinloch Forbes, Bombay CS (*d* 30 Aug 1865), and *d* 1 Nov 1904, leaving issue (*see above*)

2a Rachel Louisa; *m* 1848 Maj-Gen Francis Gregory Urquhart, CB, Roy Regt of Foot, and had issue

3a Emmeline; *m* 29 April 1851 Rev John Gabriel Ryde (*d* 7 Dec 1868) and *d* 4 April 1881, having had 10 children

4a Georgiana Mary Agnew; *m* 24 Dec 1857 Robert Spottiswood Farquhar Spottiswood (*d* 2 April 1872), of Muiresk, Aberdeenshire, and *d* 2 May 1905, having had issue

(7) Mansfield; *dsp*

3 Arthur; *b* Sept 1760; Lt-Col 32nd Regt, ADC to Sir Ralph Abercromby; *m* 1 Jan 1805 Isabella (*d* 1856), dau of Roderick Macleod, of King's Coll Aberdeen, and *d* Dec 1850, leaving (with two daus *d* unm):

(1) Arthur FORBES later FORBES-GORDON (on inheriting 1857 the Rayne estate from his cousin John Gordon of Avochie and Rayne, of Rayne, Aberdeenshire), JP, DL; *b* 2 June 1806; *m* 20 April 1843 Charlotte (*d* 1890), est dau of Col William Balfour, 82nd Regt, and *d* 21 Aug 1873, having had issue:

1a Arthur Newton, of Rayne, JP, DL Aberdeenshire, JP Co Carlow; *b* 22 Jan 1844; Capt and Adj 79th Highrs, Commr Supply Aberdeenshire; *m* 1st 22 Oct 1872 Christian (*d* 25 Oct 1873), 2nd dau of James Dalrymple, of Langlee, Roxburghs, and Green Knowe, Berwicks, and had:

1b Arthur Dalrymple, of Langlee and Greenknowe; *b* 29 Sept 1873; WW I as Maj 6th Cameron Highrs, formerly 2nd Lt 20th Hus; memb Roy Co Archers; *m* 1 Jan 1902 Dorothy Ione Helen (*d* 23 Jan 1964), dau of Frederick Morton Eden (*see* EDEN OF WINTON, B), and *d* 16 May 1931, leaving:

1c Arthur Ewan FORBES-GORDON later FORBES-DALRYMPLE of Greenknowe (on inheriting the Greenknowe estate 1931); *b* 22 Oct 1912; F/Lt WW II; *m* 3 Nov 1955 *Aimée Stephanie Ilona Antonia [Mrs Arthur Forbes-Dalrymple of Greenknowe, 32 Tite St, London SW3; Villa Bellavista, Roquebrune, AM, France], dau of Count Friedrich Colloredo-Mels and widow of Denis Irwin-Clark, DFC, and *dsp* Corsica 29 May 1970

1c *Christian Dorothy [Mrs Christian Royle, Alfoxton Park Hotel, Halford, Bridgwater, Somerset]; *b* 9 May 1910; *m* 1st 24 July 1935 (*divorce* 1938) Maj Frederick George Margaritus Grey, Highland LI, only s of C W Grey; *m* 2nd 1939 Maj John Popplewell Royle, Glider Pilot Regt (*ka* Arnhem Sept 1944), and by him has:

1d *Mark John Forbes Royle; *b* 1941; *m* and has three children

1c (cont.) Mrs John Royle *m* 3rd 31 Aug 1950 (*divorce* 1959, resumed 2nd husb's name 1959) Lt-Cdr John Charles Grattan, DSC, RN, yr s of Lt-Col John Grattan, IA

2c *Catherine Helen; *b* 26 Sept 1915; *m* 1st 6 April 1938 (*divorce* 1939) Lt Robert Sinclair Scott, Highland LI, er s of Cedric Scott, of Stroove, Skelmorlie, Ayrshire; *m* 2nd Aug 1941 (*divorce* 1954) Charles Albert Andres, of Brussels

1a (cont.) Arthur Forbes-Gordon *m* 2nd 17 April 1876 Adeline Sarah (*d* 21 Feb 1879), dau of Philip Jocelyn Newton, JP, DL, of Dunleckney Manor, Co Carlow, and by her had issue:

2b Alistair Hugh FORBES-GORDON later FORBES; *b* 8 Feb 1877; *m* 9 June 1903 Evelyn Harriet Margaret (*d* 21 Nov 1955), dau of Rev Elliott Henry Stapleton (*see* STAPLETON, Bt), and *d* 11 July 1961, having had:

1c A son; *b* 9 and *d* 10 March 1904

1b Adeline Winifred; *b* 3 Feb 1879

1a (cont.) Arthur Forbes-Gordon *m* 3rd April 1881 Penelope (*d* 1 Oct 1938), dau of Maj Napier T Christie, 11th Foot, and *d* 7 March 1930, leaving by her:

2b Amesbury Frances Mary; *b* 29 Sept 1882

3b Alice Ida Kathleen; *b* 17 March 1884; *m* 1st 29 July 1909 (*annulled* 1912) Robert Heywood Haslam; *m* 2nd 11 Feb 1924 Francis Ellis and *d* 3 Aug 1965

4b Helen Charlotte; *b* 26 May 1891; *educ* Cheltenham Ladies' Coll and RAM (LRAM)

2a William Balfour FORBES-GORDON later FORBES; *b* 10 Dec 1845; Capt RN, Straits of Malacca 1874 (Peral medal and clasp) and WW I (despatches, promotion), Albert Medal 2nd Cl; *m* 25 Nov 1889 Helen Arabella (*d* 6 Oct 1958), dau of Capt Walter Blakeney Persse, 90th LI, and *d* 9 May 1928, having had issue:

1b Arthur Walter, DSO (1917); *b* 5 May 1892; Lt RN; *m* 5 Sept 1917 Eveline Betty (*m* 2nd 31 Oct 1919 Cdr John Gordon Aitchison, OBE, RN (*see* AITCHISON, Bt), and *d* 16 July 1961), yr dau of William Tudor Sutherland and gdau of Evan Charles Sutherland, of Skibo Castle, and was lost at sea on active service March 1918, leaving issue:

1c +Arthur Michael Gerald Sutherland [Maj Arthur Forbes, 11 Coxwell Ct, Cirencester, Glos GL7 2BQ]; *b* posthumously 26 June 1918; *educ* Sherborne and RMC Sandhurst; Maj KOSB (ret), NW Frontier India, WW II and Korea 1951; exec Shell; *m* 8 March 1947 Phoebe Mabel (*d* 1989), dau of Lt-Col Cyril Charles Johnson Barrett, CSI, CIE, and has issue:

1d *Christine Helen [Miss Christine Forbes, 1 Walton Place, London SW3]; *b* 24 April 1949

2d *Lorna Betty May [Mrs Guy Knights, Jenners Cottage, Poulton, Glos GL2 5JO]; *b* 22 June 1952; *m* 1974 *(Martin John) Guy Knights, MA, MB, BS, MRCGP, DA, and has issue:

1e *Lucy Mary; *b* 1980

2e *Amelia May; *b* 1981

3e *Daisy Stella; *b* 1987

2b William Persse; *b* 1906; *m* 1936 Dorothy Hirsberg, of Pittsburg

1b Helen Violet; *m* 1st 9 June 1919 (*divorce* 1940) Maj Champion Andrew Branfill, MC, Derbys Yeo (*d* 4 Sept 1973), formerly of Upminster Hall, Essex; *m* 2nd 1940 Maj Ian Alastair Ewing and *d* 26 Oct 1972

3a John Whetham; *b* 11 Aug 1849; *d* 22 April 1928

1a Charlotte Susan; *m* 11 July 1877 John Alexander Burnett, JP, of Kemnay, Aberdeenshire, and *d* 5 Dec 1925, leaving issue

(1) Isabella; *m* 1st Beauchamp B Newton, JP, of Rathwade, Co Carlow; *m* 2nd 1853 James Kearney Aylward-Kearney, JP, DL (*d* 1 Feb 1884), of Shankill Castle, Co Kilkenny, and *d* Aug 1881

3 Margaret; *b* 1752; *m* Peter Scott of Rossie

4 Mitchell; *m* — Shaw and *dsp*

Sir ARTHUR *d* 1 Jan 1773; his est surv son,

Sir William Forbes, 5th Bt; *b* 1755; *m* 4 June 1780 Hon Sarah Sempill (*d* 8 Dec 1799), est dau of 13th Lord Sempill (*qv*), and *d* 15 Feb 1816, having had issue:

1 **Sir Arthur Forbes, 6th Bt**; *b* 1784; offr 7th Hus; *d* unm 1823
2 JOHN (Sir), **7th Bt**
3 William; Offr, RN; *d* unm
4 Hugh; *b* 1799; *m* 1834 Agnes (*d* 3 Jan 1864), dau of James Gordon Morgan, MD, and *d* 1856, leaving issue:
(1) William James; *b* 1835; *m* Letitia Duviver and *d* 1889, leaving:
1a Edgar; *b* 1868
(2) Arthur St George, of Auckland, NZ; *b* 23 April 1841; *m* 1872 Anne Laurence (*d* 20 May 1894), dau of Thomas Ryan, of Templemore, Co Tipperary, and *d* 16 March 1910, having had, with other issue:
1a Mary Agnes
2a Jessie Helen Winifred; *m* 27 Aug 1906 Thomas James Mathew (*d* 17 April 1932), and *d* 8 Sept 1963, leaving a s and two daus
(1) Janet Anne; *m* 1868 L G Cleroy and had issue
(2) Agnes; *m* 1873 Victor Mornington Camus and had issue
1 Janet; *m* 11 Sept 1811 her cousin Alex Forbes (*d* 3 Feb 1843) and *d* 15 Feb 1846, having had issue (*see* above)
2 Margaret; *m* Robert Wallace, of Kelly, MP
3 Sarah; *m* Rev S Roberts, DD, and *d* 3 July 1872, having had issue
4 Elizabeth; *m* Rev Christopher Capel (*d* 8 Oct 1846), of Prestbury House, and *d* 13 June 1872, leaving two sons
5 Catherine; *m* 8 June 1812 John Gordon, of Cairnbulg, Aberdeenshire, and had issue
6 Maria; *m* — Ward, and had issue
7 Jane; *m* Rev Dr Carpenter and had two sons

The 6th Bt's brother,

Sir John Forbes, 7th Bt, JP, DL Aberdeenshire; *b* 2 July 1785; Judge HEICS; *m* 15 Sept 1825 Charlotte Elizabeth (*d* 5 Nov 1883), dau of 18th Lord Forbes (*qv*), and *d* 16 Feb 1846, having had (with three other daus *d* young or unm):
1 WILLIAM (Sir), **8th Bt** and 17th LORD SEMPILL
2 James Ochoncar, of Corse, Lumphanan, JP Aberdeenshire; *b* 6 Nov 1837; granted with siblings 14 April 1887 rank of ld of Parl's dau/yr s; *m* 4 Aug 1863 Harriet (*d* 1 March 1894), 3rd dau of Sir Charles Hall, V-Chllr, and *d* 5 May 1900, having had issue:
(1) John Walter, of Corse; *b* 20 June 1865; *d* unm 6 July 1912
(2) James Ochoncar, of Corse, JP, DL; *b* 21 Jan 1867; Lt-Col Gordon Highrs; *m* 21 Dec 1912 Norah Maude (*d* 17 Oct 1958), er dau of Douglas Charles Abercromby (*see* ABERCROMBY, Bt), and *d* 26 July 1945, leaving:
1a Patrick Walter, of Corse, OBE (1959), DL (1963); *b* 11 May 1914; *educ* Stowe and RMC Sandhurst; Lt-Col Gordon Highrs (ret 1960), cmded 1st Bn 1956–59, Offr i/c RHQ Gordon Highrs 1960–68; *m* 16 Dec 1939 *Margaret Hawthorne, dau of Charles Hawthorne Lydall, of Brightling, Sussex, and *d* 1979, leaving:
1b +ANDREW IAIN OCHONCAR [Maj Andrew Forbes, 12 Denham Green Place, Edinburgh EH5 3PB]; *b* 28 Nov 1945; heir presumptive; *educ* Trin Coll Glenalmond, RMA Sandhurst and St Catherine's Coll Oxford (BA 1969); Maj Gordon Highrs (ret)
1b *Mhairi Margaret; *b* 26 June 1942; with World Organisation for Intellectual Property UN
2b *Shelagh Ann [Miss Shelagh Forbes, 1 Rosay Gdns, London SW7]; *b* 20 Feb 1948; with J & H Internat
2a +David Ochoncar [David Forbes Esq, Mains of Corse, Lumphanan, Aberdeen]; *b* 2 Jan 1917
1 Elizabeth; *m* 25 July 1854 Robert Grant and *d* 29 Dec 1890, leaving issue (*see* SEMPILL, L)
2 Sarah; *m* 14 April 1852 her cousin Duncan Forbes, JP (*see* above), and *d* 6 Oct 1891, leaving issue (*see* SEMPILL, L)
3 Caroline Ann; *m* 11 June 1862 Rev Frederick Walter Robberds and *d* 19 March 1896, leaving issue (*see* SEMPILL, L)

The 7th Bt's er son,

Sir WILLIAM FORBES later FORBES-SEMPILL, **8th Bt** and 17th LORD SEMPILL, VD, JP, DL (Aberdeenshire); *b* 20 May 1836; *educ* Eton; Ensign Coldstream Gds 1854–57 Crimea, Capt, later Hon Col 9th Aberdeenshire Rifle Vols 1859–61; *m* 1st 23 June 1858 (*divorce* 1861) Caroline Louisa (*d* 11 Dec 1872), only dau of Sir Charles Forbes, 3rd Bt, of Newe (*qv*), and had:
1 Katherine Charlotte Elizabeth Stewart, MBE; *m* 5 Dec 1907 George Muirhead, LLD, of Speybank, Fochabers (*d* 29 Jan 1928), and *d* 22 March 1938

Sir WILLIAM *m* 2nd 18 Nov 1862 Frances Emily (*d* 13 May 1887), yst dau of Sir Robert Abercromby, 5th Bt (*qv*), and by her had:
1 **Sir John Forbes-Sempill, 9th Bt** and 18th LORD SEMPILL, JP and V-Lt Aberdeenshire; *b* 21 Aug 1863; *educ* Eton; Cameron Highrs: Sudan 1886, Lovat Scouts Boer War 1901–02 (wounded, medal, five clasps), cmded 8th Black Watch WW I (severely wounded, despatches, three medals); rep S peer, Chm TAA Aberdeenshire, ADC to HM GEORGE V, Hon Col 5th Bn Gordon Highrs; *m* 22 June 1892 Gwendolen Emily Mary (*d* 2 March 1944), er dau of Herbert Prodgers, of Kington St Michael, Wilts, and *d* 28 Feb 1934, having had:
(1) **Sir William Francis Forbes-Sempill, 10th Bt** and 19th LORD SEMPILL, AFC; *b* 24 Sept 1893; *educ* Eton; WW I: W/Cdr RN and Col RAF, Capt IJN; special tech manager USA 1918, cmded Br Aviation Mission to organise, equip and train Imp Japanese Naval Air Serv 1921, reported on reorganisation Greek Naval Air Serv 1926, rep S peer 1935–65; FRAeS, FRSA, Chm Roy Aero Soc 1926–28 (Pres 1928–30), Pres Inst Production Engrs 1935–37, Pres Inst Motor Industry 1946–48, V-Pres London Chamber Commerce 1945–65, memb Court Foreign Bondholders, Chm Br Cncl Rehabilitation, memb Exec Ctee Navy League, RNLI and Air League Br Empire, Dep Chm Roy Empire Soc, Pres Design and Industry Assoc, memb Roy Soc Arts, memb Jr Inst Engrs (Pres 1941), V-Pres Japan Soc, memb Standing Ctee Civil Aviation Section London Chamber Commerce 1934–35, Pres Br Gliding Assoc 1935, Chm Cncl London Chamber of Commerce Internat Commn Study Motorless Flight, memb Advsy Ctee Science Museum and Advsy Ctee Aeronautics Hull U, Rep Air Min Advsy Ctee for Aeronautics Civ Air Transport, Br Engrg Standards Ctee and Timber Ctee Scientific Socs, 2nd Cl Order Sacred Treasure Japan, 3rd Cl Order Rising Sun Japan, Order Crown Italy, 2nd Cl Order Pole Star Sweden, Kt Cdr Order St Gregory the Great; *m* 1st 20 Feb 1919 Eileen Marion (*d* 18 July 1935), only dau of Sir John Lavery, RA, and formerly wife of James Dickinson, KC, and had issue (*see* SEMPILL, L); *m* 2nd 1 Feb 1941 Cecilia Alice (*d* 1984), er dau of Bertram Edward Dunbar-Kilburn, of Ledwell, Sandford St Martin, Oxon, and *d* 30 Dec 1965, when the Ldship passed to his est dau and the btcy to his bro, leaving by her further issue (*see* SEMPILL, L):
(2) **Sir Ewan Forbes, 11th Bt**, of Craigievar; *b* 6 Sept 1912; *educ* Munich and Aberdeen Us (MB, ChB 1944); matriculated arms at Lyon Court 15 May 1965; *m* 10 Oct 1952 *Isabella, dau of Alexander Mitchell, of Glenrinnes, Banffshire, and *dsp* 1991
(1) Gwendolen Janet; *b* 26 Dec 1897; *d* 10 March 1910
(2) Margaret, JP (Aberdeenshire); *b* 30 Aug 1905; WW II as W/O WAAF (despatches twice, US Bronze Star); *k* in a motor accident 28 Oct 1966
2 Douglas, DSO; *b* 19 Jan 1865; Maj Seaforth Highrs; *d* unm 21 Feb 1908, *ka* Indian Frontier
3 William; *b* 27 June 1866; *d* 6 Nov 1867
4 Robert Abercromby; *b* 21 March 1870; Lt 5th Bn Gordon Highrs; *d* 2 June 1915 of wounds received in action
5 Arthur Lionel Ochoncar; *b* 24 Sept 1877; R-Adml (ret 1923), China 1900, WW I (despatches, promotion, Russian Order St Stanislas 2nd Cl with swords), cmdg Nore area 1922, WW II as Lt-Col HG; *m* 1st 25 Nov 1903 (*divorce* 1914) Muriel Emily (*d* 24 June 1954 having *m* 2nd as his 2nd w 1st and last Baron Mount Temple; *see* SHAFTESBURY, E), est dau of Rev Walter Spencer, of Fownhope Court, Herefs; *m* 2nd 27 Nov 1919 Helen Mabel (*d* 18 June 1921), yr dau of Maj John Allen, of Brackley House, Brackley, Northants, and by her had issue:
(1) *Janet [Mrs Norman Forbes-Walker, The Post House, Midlem, Selkirk PD7 4QB]; *b* 16 Oct 1920; WW II in ATS; *m* 9 Sept 1958 Norman Forbes-Walker (*d* 1994), s of Harry Walker, of Moseley, Warwicks, and has issue:
1a *Ian; *b* 11 Jan 1960
5 (cont.) R-Adml The Hon Arthur Forbes-Sempill *m* 3rd 28 Aug 1926 Mary Cutting Holland (*d* 5 Sept 1940), only dau of Arthur J Cummock, of 521 Park Avenue, New York, and *d* 9 May 1962, leaving by her:
(1) Sir JOHN ALEXANDER CUMNOCK FORBES, **12th and present Bt**
2 Evelyn Courtenay; *b* 4 Oct 1868; *m* 7 June 1894 Lt-Col Duncan Vernon Pirie, OBE, JP, DL, formerly Capt 3rd Hus (*d* 11 Jan 1931), est s of Gordon Pirie, of Waterton, Aberdeenshire, and *d* 1 March 1934, leaving issue (*see* SEMPILL, L)
3 Gertrude Emily; *b* 22 Nov 1872; *d* unm 28 April 1958

Sir WILLIAM *m* 3rd 30 April 1890 Mary Beresford (*d* 18 Dec 1930), yst dau of Henry SHERBROOKE formerly LOWE, of Oxton, Notts, and *d* 21 July 1905

FORBES, Bt, of Newe

Arms: Quarterly, 1st and 4th, az. three bear's heads couped arg., muzzled gu. (for FORBES); 2nd and 3rd, az. three cinquefoils arg. (for FRASER). **Crest:** A falcon rising ppr. **Supporters:** Two bears arg., muzzled gu. **Motto:** *Altius ibunt, qui ad summa nituntur* ('They will end higher who climb to the top').
Creation: Bt (UK) 4 Nov 1823.

SIR HAMISH STEWART FORBES, 7TH BT, MBE (1945), MC (1945), of Newe, Co Aberdeen [Maj Sir Hamish Forbes Bt MBE MC, Newe, Strathdon, Aberdeenshire AB36 8TY]; *b* 15 Feb 1916; *s* kinsman 1984; *educ* Eton, Lawrenceville USA and SOAS London; Maj Welsh Gds WW II 1939–40 (POW, captured Dunkirk); KStJ 1984; *m* 1st 2 June 1945 (*divorce* 1981) Jacynthe Elizabeth Mary, only dau of Eric Gordon Underwood; *m* 2nd 1981 *Mary Christine, MBE, dau of Ernest William Rigby, and by his 1st w has issue:
1 +JAMES THOMAS STEWART [James Forbes Esq, The Cottage, Hambleden, Oxon RG9 6RT]; *b* 28 May 1957; *educ* Eton and Bristol U (BA); proprietor Spats Catering, Forbes Mt Veeder Vineyards; *m* 1986 *Kerry, only dau of Rev Lee Toms, of Sacramento, Calif., and has issue:
(1) *Theodora Christine; *b* 1989
(2) *Katherine Elizabeth; *b* 1990

1 *(Caroline) Serena; *b* 21 July 1947; *m* 1984 *E Nicholas D Herbert, only s of Ivor Herbert, of Bradenham, Bucks

2 *Jane Henrietta Mary; *b* 8 April 1950; *m* 3 July 1976 *Tarka Richard Bourke Leslie-King (*see* LESLIE, Bt) and has issue

3 *Christian Clare; *b* 17 Nov 1961; *m* 1988 *Benjamin Victor Sheddon Scrimgeour and has issue (*see* HUNTINGDON, E)

Lineage: Sir WILLIAM FORBES of Kinaldie; next yr bro of 1st Lord Forbes (*qv*); *m* 24 July 1423 Agnes, dau of Sir William Fraser, 2nd of Philorth (*see* SALTOUN, L), who brought him the Pitsligo estate, and *d* 1445/6, leaving:

ALEXANDER FORBES of Pitsligo, Aberdeenshire; *d* 1477, having had:

WILLIAM FORBES; *dvp c* 1470, leaving:

ALEXANDER FORBES of Pitsligo and Kinaldie; *d c* 1496, leaving:

1 John, of Pitsligo; *m* by 1523, as her 2nd husb, Elizabeth est dau of Sir James de Innes, 12th of that Ilk (*see* ROXBURGHE, D); *d* 1556, leaving:

(1) Alexander, of Pitsligo; *m* Beatrix, dau of 4th Lord Saltoun (*qv*) of Abernethy, and *d* 1562, leaving a 2nd s:

1a Alexander, of Pitsligo; *m* as her 2nd husb Margaret (*m* 3rd Alexander Gordon of Abergeldie), dau of William Mackintosh of Mackintosh and widow of Duncan Grant, Yr. of Freuchie (*see* STRATHSPEY, B), and *d c* 1586, leaving:

1b John, of Pitsligo; *m* Christian, est dau of 1st Lord Ogilvy of Deskford (*see* SEAFIELD, E), and *d* Sept 1625, leaving an only s:

1c ALEXANDER FORBES, 1st LORD FORBES OF PITSLIGO (usually known, along with his successors in the title, as LORD PITSLIGO) (S), so *cr* 24 June 1633, with remainder to heir male of his body or their heirs, whom failing to his heirs male whatsoever of the name of Forbes; the ambiguity in the wording of the remainder makes it unclear whether, on the extinction of the direct male descendants of the grantee (to say nothing of the attainder of 1746), the title would vest in the heirs general or heirs male; it was claimed by Sir John Stuart Hepburn-Forbes, 8th Bt, of Monymusk (ggs of Hon Mary Forbes by Sir William Forbes, 4th Bt, of Monymusk; *see* below); since Sir John *dspm*, right to the title, if it passes to heirs male, vests with the Forbes Bts of Newe here treated; *m* Lady Jean Keith, 2nd dau of 6th Earl Marischal (*see* KINTORE, E), and *d* 26 Oct 1636, leaving an only s:

1d ALEXANDER FORBES, 2nd LORD (FORBES OF) PITSLIGO; of age *c* 1649; *m* Lady Mary Erskine, dau of 6th Earl of Buchan (*qv*), and *d* between 7 June and 1 Nov 1690, leaving an only s:

1e ALEXANDER FORBES, 3rd LORD (FORBES OF) PITSLIGO; *b c* 1655; *m* 1676 Lady Sophia Erskine, dau of 4th Earl of Mar (*see* MAR and KELLIE, E), and *d* Dec 1690, leaving:

1f ALEXANDER FORBES, 4th LORD (FORBES OF) PITSLIGO; *b* 24 May 1678; opposed Union of E and S Parls; Jacobite 1715 and 1745 Uprisings, accordingly attainted 1746, when his title and lands were forfeited; *m* 1st by 1713 Rebecca, dau of John Norton, a London merchant, and had issue; *m* 2nd *c* 26 Sept 1731 Elizabeth Allen (*dsp* 1759) and *d* 21 Dec 1762, leaving by his 1st w an only s:

1g John, *Master of Pitsligo*; *b c* 1713; *m* 2 Aug 1750 Rebecca, dau of James Ogilvy of Auchiries, and *dsp* 30 Aug 1781

1f Mary; *m* 1st Sir William Forbes, 4th Bt, of Monymusk, and had issue (*see* STUART-FORBES, Bt); *m* 2nd 16th Lord Forbes (*qv*)

2 WILLIAM FORBES of Dauch and Newe; ancestor of:

WILLIAM FORBES, 5th guideman (*i.e*, 5th goodman, or yeoman occupier of land, in succession, *e.g*, father to son) of Newe; had, with two er sons:

GEORGE FORBES of Bellabeg; *b* 10 Jan 1668; *m* 1st Isabel, dau of William Meldrum, of Hatton; *m* 2nd Isabel, dau of William Forbes of Asloun, and *d* June 1745, leaving issue:

JOHN FORBES, of Bellabeg; *b* 1707; *m* Christian, dau of Rev John Shepherd, of Logie Coldstone, and had:

Rev GEORGE FORBES, of Lochell; *b* 24 June 1738; *m* 28 Nov 1767 Katherine (*d* 3 Nov 1808), only dau of Gordon Stewart of Drumin, and *d* 30 Aug 1799, leaving, with other issue, including a yr s (George (Rev), DD, of Blelach, *m* 16 April 1809 Mary Ann (*d* 19 April 1848), dau of Capt Alexander Forbes, 97th Regt, of Inverernan, Aberdeenshire, and *d* 15 Feb 1834, leaving issue):

Sir Charles Forbes, 1st Bt (UK), so *cr* 4 Nov 1823; *b* 3 April 1773; Bombay merchant; declared heir to 3rd LORD PITSLIGO 1833 and allowed the Pitsligo arms and supporters by the Lyon Office; *m* 28 Feb 1800 Elizabeth, widow of William Ashburner (*d* 14 April 1861) and dau of John Cotgrave, Maj HEICS, and *d* 20 Nov 1849, having had, with other issue:

1 John, MP; *b* 15 Dec 1801; *m* 10 Dec 1828 Mary Jane (*d* 24 Feb 1869), est dau of Henry Lannoy Hunter, of Beach Hill, Berks, and *dvp* 20 Dec 1840, leaving, with five daus:

(1) **Sir Charles Forbes, 2nd Bt**; *b* 15 July 1832; *d* unm 23 May 1852

2 CHARLES (Sir), **3rd Bt**

3 George, of Bereleigh, Hants, JP, DL; *b* 13 Sept 1805; *m* 16 March 1843 Johanna Agnes, dau of John Hopton Forbes, of Westwood, Hants, and *dsp* 22 Jan 1863

The 2nd Bt's uncle,

Sir Charles Forbes, 3rd Bt; Capt 17th Lancers; *b* 21 Sept 1803; *m* 21 Aug 1830 Caroline (*d* 6 Sept 1877), 2nd dau of George Battye, of Campden Hill, and *d* 2 Nov 1877, having had issue:

1 **Sir Charles John Forbes, 4th Bt**, DL Aberdeenshire; memb Roy Co Archers; *b* 24 March 1843; *m* 5 April 1864 Helen (*d* 12 Nov 1913), 2nd dau of Sir Thomas Moncreiffe of that Ilk, 7th Bt (*see* ERROLL, E), and *d* 24 July 1884, leaving:

(1) **Sir Charles Stewart Forbes, 5th Bt**; Capt 4th Vol Bn Gordon Highrs; *b* 19 Jan 1867; *m* 2 July 1888 Emma Theodora (*d* 14 Nov 1953), yst dau of Robert Maxwell, and *d* 12 Dec 1927, having had issue:

1a **Sir John Stewart Forbes, 6th Bt**, DSO (1940), JP (Aberdeenshire 1954); V-Lt Aberdeenshire 1973–84 (DL 1953); *b* 8 Jan 1901; *educ* Wellington and RMA Woolwich; Col RE, WW II (despatches twice), Hon Col 51st (H) Divl Engrs 1960–67; *m* 10 Oct 1933 Agnes Jessie (*d* 1988), er dau of Lt-Col David Lorraine Wilson-Farquharson, DSO, Black Watch, of Allargue, Corgarff, Aberdeenshire, and *d* 1984, having had issue:

1b *Bridget Rosemary Zilla, JP, DL (Aberdeenshire 1996) [Mrs Francis Tuck JP, DL, Allargue, Corgarff, Strathdon, Aberdeenshire]; *b* 17 May 1935; *m* 17 Aug 1962 *Col Francis Mitchell Kent Tuck, RE, yst s of Maj-Gen George Newsam Tuck, CB, OBE, RE, of Hartlands, Foyle Hill, Dorset, and has:

1c *Rosemary Jean Winter [Mrs Adrian Walker, Upland House, Saxham St, Stowupland, Suffolk]; *b* 10 July 1963; *m* 1985 *Adrian Jeremy Walker, er s of Sir Patrick Jeremy Walker, KCB, and has:

1d *Thomas George Farquharson; *b* 1987

2d *Harry Charles Cosby; *b* 16 March 1995

1d *Imogen Frances Katharine; *b* 1989

2d *Cecily Mary Elspeth; *b* 1993

2c *Caroline Frances Stewart [Mrs Charles Ross Stewart, 4 Turret Grove, London SW4 0EU]; *b* 7 Dec 1964; *m* 1993 *Charles Denholm Ross Stewart, yr s of David Ross Stewart, of Blackett Place, Edinburgh, and has:

1d *Kirsty Ellen; *b* 199–

3c *Ellen Alexandra Farquharson; *b* 27 June 1968

2b *Elspeth Ann [Mrs George Hardie, House of Newe, Strathdon, Aberdeenshire AB3 8TJ]; *b* 10 March 1937; *educ* Aberdeen U (MA 1958); *m* 29 Oct 1960 *George Mcintosh Hardie, DA, s of John Hardie, and has had:

1c David John; *b* 10 April 1965; *d* 15 Feb 1966

2c *Jonathan Forbes; *b* 14 March 1967

1c *Katharine Ann; *b* 24 May 1961

2c *Ruth Mary; *b* 28 Jan 1964

3b *Veronica Jean [Mrs Edward Lancaster, 31 MacLeod Rd, Balloch, Inverness-shire IV1 2JW]; *b* 12 Sept 1938; *m* 4 April 1958 *Edward Donald Lancaster, ARIBA, only s of William Edward Lancaster, of Aberdeen, and has:

1c *Alan Stewart; *b* 22 Jan 1961; *m* 1984 (*divorce* 1988) Sabine Wolniczak and has issue:

1d *Jonathan; *b* 1984

1d *Franziska; *b* 1987

2c *Kevin Edward; *b* 23 Sept 1965; *m* 1991 *Iona McGillivray and has:

1d *Hector John; *b* 1996

1d *Megan Janet; *b* 1994

1c *Fiona Margaret; *b* 5 Oct 1958; *m* 1980 *Robert Seymour and has:

1d *Duncan Robert; *b* 1991

2d *Hannah Frances; *b* 1987

4b *Margaret Xanthe Patricia [Mrs James Petrie, 126 Desswood Place, Aberdeen AB15 4DQ]; *b* 25 March 1940; *educ* Aberdeen U (MB, ChB); *m* 16 July 1964 *Prof James Colquhoun Petrie, CBE, MB, ChB, FRCP (Lond, Edin and Ireland), FFPM, prof Clinical Pharmacology and Head Dept Medicine and Therapeutics Aberdeen U, er s of Dr James Beattie Petrie, of Aberdeen, and has issue:

1c *John Ross; *b* 17 Dec 1965; MB, ChB, BSc (Hons), PhD, MRCP; *m* 1995 *Dr Rosaleen Ciara Cecilia Kelly, MB, ChB, MRCP Psych, and has:

1d *Celia May; *b* Aug 1997

2c *Mark Colquhoun; *b* 20 May 1969; MB, ChB, BSc (Hons), MRCP; *m* 1993 *Dr Ciara McColgan, MB, ChB, BSc, MRCP

1c *Rachel Xanthe Ann, *b* 17 June 1967; MB, ChB, BSc (Hons), MRCP Psych

2c *Paula Jane; *b* 1970; MB, ChB, MRCP; *m* Aug 1997 *Dr James D'Arcy McKinney, BSc, PhD

5b *Alison Stewart [Mrs Alison Ouchterlony, Kinghorne St, Arbroath, Angus DD11 2LZ]; *b* 15 Sept 1946; *m* 20 April 1968 (*divorce* 1981) Thomas Angus Ouchterlony, yr s of Cdr Thomas Charles Alexander Heathcote Ouchterlony, RN, of The Guynd, by Arbroath, Angus, and has issue:

1c *Peter Anthony Heathcote; *b* 19 April 1971

2c *James Angus Heathcote; *b* 9 Aug 1973

1c *Teresa Mary; *b* 22 June 1969

2a Charles Harry Grenfell; *b* 18 March 1906; *d* 13 June 1913

1a Theodora Cecille; *b* 21 Jan 1889; *d* in infancy

2a Evelyn Marjorie; *b* 12 Nov 1892; *m* 9 March 1918 Francis Edward Foster, Lt RNVR, 5th s of John Foster, JP, DL, of Coombe Park, Pangbourne, and *d* 9 April 1953, leaving issue. He *d* 25 Feb 1953

3a Dorothy Helene Mabel; *b* 3 Jan, *d* 23 Feb 1895

4a Katherine Manuela Bettine; *b* 10 April 1897; *d* unm 1 April 1962

5a Bridget Roberta; *b* 10 Nov 1899; *d* unm 20 Aug 1924

6a Katharine Stewart; *b* 5 April 1903; *d* 5 March 1995

7a Mary Veronica; *b* 4 Sept 1904; *m* 22 Oct 1929 Edward Collins, er s of Charles Millington Collins, JP, of Kelvindale, Lanarks, Baronchan, Renfrewshire, and Rowardennan, Stirlingshire. He *d* 5 March 1948

(1) Evelyn Elizabeth, CBE (1922); DGStJ; *m* 1st 5 March 1889 William Dodge James, CVO, of West Dean Park, Chichester, and had issue (*see* NORFOLK, D, and RADNOR, E). He *d* 22 March 1912. She *m* 2nd 30 Aug 1913 (*divorce* 1927) Lt-Col John Chaytor Brinton, CVO, DSO, Life Gds, and *d* 13 May 1929. He *d* 6 April 1956

(2) Helen Blanche; *m* 16 Jan 1901, as his 2nd w, John Blundell Leigh, DL, of Manor House, Stratton Audley, and Harley St, London W1, and *d* 7 June 1934. He *d* 27 July 1931

(3) Mabel Susan; *m* 10 Oct 1892 2nd Baron St Oswald (*qv*) and *d* 14 Feb 1919, leaving issue

2 George Stewart, of Aslown, NB; *b* 26 Oct 1844; *m* 14 June 1869 Henrietta Maria (*d* 30 March 1935), yr dau of Hon Humble Dudley Ward (*see* DUDLEY, E), and *d* 8 July 1894, leaving issue:

(1) James Stewart, of Aslown, Aberdeenshire; Hon Lt-Col 9th Lancers, Boer War as Cmdt 2nd Bn Imp Yeo and WW I Res Regt of Lancers; *b* 6 Feb 1872; *m* 1st 27 April 1896 (*divorce* 1907) Lady Angela Selina Bianca St Clair-Erskine (*d* 22 Oct 1950), dau of 4th Earl of Rosslyn (*qv*), and had issue:

1a Marigold; *b* 26 Aug 1897; *m* 18 May 1918 1st Viscount Thurso (*qv*) and *d* 1975, leaving issue

2a Flavia; *b* 18 Dec 1902; *m* 1st 9 April 1923 (*divorce* 1928) Sir Lionel Frederick Heald, QC, MP, yr s of James Heald, and had issue; *m* 2nd 27 July 1933 (*divorce* 1938) Lt-Col Lionel Herbert de Pinto (*d* 30 May 1953), of Kineton, Warwicks; *m* 3rd 17 June 1939 (*divorce* 1958) Sir Alexander Hay Seton, 10th Bt of Abercorn (*qv*), and *d* 13 Oct 1959

(1) (cont.) Col James Forbes *m* 2nd 8 Dec 1910 Feridah (*d* 5 Jan 1953), dau of Hugh Lewis Taylor, and *d* 29 Sept 1957, having by her had issue:

1a George Stewart; MRCVS, fndr Veterinary Bloodstock Agency; *b* 3 Sept 1911; *educ* Eton and Dublin Vet Coll; *m* 1st 4 March 1938 (*divorce* 1949) Violet Mabel, formerly w of William Patterson Doyle and dau of Kenward Stuart Barker, of Watchbury, Barford, Warwicks; *m* 2nd 8 April 1949 *Joan [Mrs George Forbes, Brindledown, Upper Lambourn, Berks RG17 8QT], yr dau of Frederick James Turvey, of Elim, Cottingham, Yorks, and *d* 13 Nov 1969, leaving by her:

1b *Fiona Hay Lavens [Mrs Christian Marner, Kingwood Stud, Lambourn, Berks]; *b* 4 June 1950; *m* 1st 1970 (*divorce* 1992) Nicholas Ashmead Cliffe Vigors; *m* 2nd Dec 1995 *Christian Marner and by her 1st husb has:

1c *Charles Stewart Cliffe; *b* 1973

2c *Sarah Louise Rosemary; *b* 1974

2b Alison Feridah; *b* 25 Feb 1952; *m* 1973 *John Albert King, of Wheatlands Cottage, Finchampstead, Berks, and *d* 1983, leaving issue:

1c *James Stewart; *b* 1976

1c *Georgina Louise; *b* 1979

3b *Teresa Frances Ida; *b* 18 Nov 1953; *m* 1978 *Martin Gerard Byrne, of Mudgee, Australia, and has issue:

1c *Simon Thomas; *b* 1988

1c *Clare Joan; *b* 1986

4b *Joanna Grace; *b* 20 July 1955; *m* 1983 *Alan Gerard Clarke, of Sydney, Australia, and has issue:

1c *Owen Taylor Stewart; *b* 1987

1c *Mevagh Alison; *b* 19–

5b *Sarah Georgina; *b* 22 Oct 1967

6b *Nicola Jane Stewart; *b* 2 Nov 1969

2a Sir HAMISH STEWART FORBES, **7th and present Bt**

3a Ian Dudley Stewart, DSC; Cdr RN, Yr Bro Trin House, served WW II 1939–42 (POW); *b* 10 Sept 1919; *m* 1st 19 June 1950 (*divorce* 1960) Lady Penelope Anne Rous, yr dau of 4th Earl of Stradbroke (*qv*); *m* 2nd 19 May 1961 *Gunilla, dau of Maj Fritz Ryman, Swedish Army, and *d* 1992, leaving by his 1st w:

1b +Charles Stewart; *b* 23 Jan 1956; *educ* Westminster and Trin Coll Oxford (MA, MSc); *m* 1989 *Alison, dau of Maj E R Payne

1b *Catriona [Mrs Michael Bradley, 17 Worfield St, London SW11 4RB]; *b* 1 Aug 1951; *m* 1981 *Michael Neville Charles Bradley, s of Malcolm Bradley, of Lymington, Hants, and has issue:

1c *Edward Benjamin Michael; *b* 1982

1c *Belinda Daisy; *b* 1984

2c *Henrietta; *b* 1989

2b *Caroline Ianthe [Mrs Caroline Forbes, 53 St Dunstans Rd, London SW6]; *b* 23 Nov 1952; *educ* York U (BA); photographer; *m* 1977 (*divorce* 1982) Katsuhisa Sakai and has issue:

1c *Tyler Christopher Forbes; *b* 1978; *educ* Latymer Upper Sch

3a *Mevagh [Mrs Julius Horton, The Garage, 10A Edith Grove, London SW10]; *b* 23 April 1914; *m* 2 April 1948 Julius Joseph Alfred Horton, s of Francis Horton. He *d* 17 Jan 1963

4a *Juanita Ann Stewart [Mrs Richard Stickney, 3 Eyot Green, London W4 2PT]; *b* 25 Jan 1929; *m* 1st 26 July 1949 (*divorce* 1954) Capt Anthony Maitland Steel, Parachute Regt, actor, er s of Maj E G Steel, MC; *m* 2nd 25 Jan 1961 *Richard Currier Stickney and by him has issue:

1b *Francis Robin Christopher; *b* 25 Jan 1962; *m* 1990 *Lucy Anne, dau of Leonard H R Byng (*see* MORAY, E)

(1) Ida Agnes Eleanor; *m* 30 Nov 1895 Sir Archibald Edmonstone, 5th Bt (*qv*), and *d* 21 Dec 1946, leaving issue

1 Caroline Louisa; *m* 1st 23 June 1858 17th Lord Sempill (*qv*) and had issue; *m* 2nd 19 June 1862 Septimus E Carlisle and *d* 11 Dec 1872

FORBES-LEITH

Arms: Quarterly of four, 1st grand quarter, or a cross-crosslet fitchée sa. between three crescents in chief and as many fusils in base gu. (for LEITH); 2nd grand quarter, quarterly 1st and 4th, az. on a chevron between three bear's heads couped arg., muzzled gu., a man's heart ppr. between two skenes of the first, pommelled or (for FORBES of Balfing); 2nd, az. a fess chequy arg. and of the first between three boar's heads erased or, within a bordure indented of the second (for GORDON); 3rd, arg. a fir tree growing out of a mount in base vert, surmounted of a sword in bend supporting on its point an imperial crown ppr., in sinister chief and dexter base a lion's head erased az., armed and langued gu. (for GREGORY); 3rd grand quarter, parted per fess az. and arg., in chief three bear's heads couped of the second, muzzled gu., and in base as many unicorn's heads erased sa. (for FORBES of Ballogie); 4th grand quarter, arg. on a bend gu. between two mullets in chief and in base a hunting horn sa., stringed of the second, three buckles or (for BURN). **Crests:** 1 (centre) A cross-crosslet fitchée sa. (for LEITH), 2 (dexter) A bear's head and neck couped arg., muzzled az. (for FORBES), 3 (sinister) A dexter cubit arm in armour bendways, the hand naked ppr., holding a cross-crosslet fitchée in pale gu. (for BURN). **Mottoes:** 1 Trustie to the end; 2 *Spe expecto* ('I wait in hope'); 3 *Deo juvante* ('With God assisting'). **Creation:** Bt. (UK) 7 March 1923.

SIR ANDREW GEORGE FORBES-LEITH OF FYVIE, 3RD BT, of Jessfield, nr Edinburgh, Co Midlothian [Sir Andrew Forbes-Leith of Fyvie Bt, Dunachton, Kingussie, Inverness-shire PH21 1LY]; *b* 20 Oct 1929; *s* f 1973; *educ* Eton and Millfield; RA 1948–49; *m* 17 July 1962 Jane Kate (*d* 17 June 1969), only dau of David McCall-McCowan, of Dalwhat, Moniaive, Dumfriesshire, and has:

1 +GEORGE IAN DAVID; *b* 26 May 1967; *m* 19– *Milly — and has:

(1) *India Rose; *b* 27 July 1997

2 +John Charles; *b* 9 June 1969

1 *Miranda Jane; *b* 5 July 1963; *m* 1990 *Julian N W McHardy, s of Col W G McHardy, CVO MBE, MC, of Woodend House, Banchory, Kincardineshire, and has issue:

(1) *Andrew William Jock; *b* 1992

(1) *Iona Jane; *b* 1994

2 *Louisa Mary; *b* 4 April 1965; *m* 1991 *Thomas William Leader, yr s of Henry William Leader, of W Kensington, and Mrs G H Maingot, of Sugar House, Tobago, and has:

(1) *Frederick Henry; *b* 4 July 1996

(2) *Ruaraidh William Percy; *b* 30 March 1998

(1) *Josephine; *b* 199–

Lineage (of Leith): WILLIAM LEITH of Barnis, Aberdeenshire; *fl temp* DAVID BRUCE; allegedly male rep of the LEITHs of Edingariock; Provost Aberdeen 1350; held the lands of Caprinton, Aberdeenshire; *d temp* ROBERT II, leaving, with a yr s (John, Amb England 1412):

LAURENCE LEITH of Barnis; Provost Aberdeen 1401, 1403 and 1411; *d temp* JAMES II, leaving:

NORMAN LEITH; *m* Elizabeth, dau of 4th (territorial) Baron of Balquhain by Agnes, dau of Irvine of Drum, and *d temp* JAMES III, leaving, with other issue, incuding a yr s (John, ancestor of the LEITHs of Overhall):

HENRY LEITH; living 1430; *m* Mariette Stewart and had:

WILLIAM LEITH; living 1469; had:

HENRY LEITH of Barnis; *m* Elizabeth Gordon and *d* by 1479, leaving:

1 George; held other lands besides Barnis; *d c* 1505, leaving, with two daus:

(1) John; served heir to his father 1506; *d* unm

(2) William; served heir to his bro 1508; *d* unm

2 WILLIAM

3 Patrick; ancestor of the LEITHs of Harthill

The 2nd s,

WILLIAM LEITH of Edingariock, which he acquired by charter 31 Jan 1499 from George Leslie of Leslie; *m* a dau of Gordon of Strathdon, and had, with an er s (Patrick, of Edingariock, *dsp* after 10 March 1515):

WILLIAM LEITH of Edingariock; served heir to his unc George Leith of Barnis 1550; *d c* 1598, leaving an est s:

PATRICK LEITH of Likliehead; *m* Jean, 2nd dau of 7th (territorial) Baron of Balquhain by Elizabeth, dau of Sir Walter Ogilvie of Boyne, and *d c* 1625, leaving, with other issue, including an er s (Patrick, sold Edingariock and Likliehead to John Forbes of Leslie, *dsp*):

LAURENCE LEITH of Kirkton de Rain; *m* 1st Agnes (*dsp*), 3rd dau of Alexander, 3rd of Wardes, by Margaret, dau of Alexander Forbes of Towie; *m* 2nd Bessie, dau of George Gordon of Cocklarochie, and had:

JOHN LEITH; sold Kirkton de Rain and bought the New Leslie, Peill, Lyde and Arnbog lands; *m* Margery, dau of Arthur Forbes, 4th s of 6th Lord Pitsligo (*see* FORBES, L), and had with a yr s (Alexander, called 'Hard Head', ancestor of the LEITHs of Bucharne Blair) and two daus:

JAMES LEITH of New Leslie; *m* Margaret, dau of Alexander Strachan of Glenkindie, and had, with other issue, including a yr s (Alexander, ancestor of the LEITHs of Glenkindie and Freefield; *see* BURGH, B):

JOHN LEITH of Leith Hall; bought the estate of Leslie in the Garloch and regained Edingariock; *m* Janet Ogilvie, dau of George, 2nd Lord Banff, by his w Agnes Falconer, dau of 1st Lord Halkerton, and *d* 1727, having had, with other issue:

JOHN LEITH of Leith Hall; *m* Mary, dau of Charles Hay of Rannes, and *d* 1736, leaving, with a dau:

JOHN LEITH of Leith Hall; added the lands of Lair and Adlair to his estates; *m* Harriot, dau and heiress of Alexander Steuart of Auchluncart, and *d* 1763, leaving:

1 John, of Leith Hall; *dsp* 1778

2 ALEXANDER

3 James (Sir), GCB; Lt-Gen, Grand Cordon Order Merit France, Govr Barbados, Cdr Forces Windward and Leeward Islands; *d* 16 Oct 1816

The 2nd s,

ALEXANDER LEITH later LEITH-HAY (on inheriting the Rannes estate from Andrew Hay); Gen 73rd Regt; *b* 1758; *m* 1784 Mary (*d* 1824), est dau and coheir of Charles Forbes of Ballogie (a cadet of the FORBESes of Tolquhon; *see* FORBES, L), and *d* 16 May 1838, having had, with two other daus:

1 Andrew (Sir), of Rannes and Leith Hall, JP, DL; Lt-Col, MP Elgin 1833–38 and 1841–47, Govr Bermuda 1838–41; *b* 17 Feb 1785; *m* 1816 Mary Margaret (*d* 1859), dau of William Clark, of Buckland Ho, Devon, and *d* 13 Oct 1862, having had issue

2 John James; *b* 22 Oct 1788; R-Adml; *m* 27 June 1843 Margaret, only surv child of ALEXANDER FORBES of Blackford (*see* below), and *d* 25 Oct 1854, leaving:

(1) ALEXANDER JOHN FORBES-LEITH, 1st and last BARON LEITH OF FYVIE, of Fyvie, Co Aberdeen (UK), so *cr* 18 Dec 1905, JP, DL; *b* 6 Aug 1847; RN 1860–72 (ret as Lt); *m* 19 Oct 1871 Marie Louise (*d* 9 June 1930), dau of Derick Algernon January, of St Louis, Mo., and *dspms* 14 Nov 1925, when the Barony expired, having had:

1a Percy; 2nd Lt Roy Dragoons; *b* 13 March 1881; *das* Boer War 31 Dec 1900

1a Ethel Louise, OBE; *b* 10 Aug 1872; LGStJ, Cmdt and Matron Stoodley Knowle Aux Hosp, Torquay (despatches twice, two medals); *m* 22 July 1891 Col Sir Charles Rosdew BURN later FORBES-LEITH OF FYVIE, **1st Bt**, OBE, yst s of Gen Robert Burn, Col Cmdt RA (*d* 1878), and *d* 1 Jan 1930, leaving issue

(2) Albert Howe FORBES-LEITH later LEITH; *b* 1 June 1851; *m* June 1902 Margaret Shaw, and *dsp* 15 June 1903

(1) Margaret Mary; *m* Sept 1876 Patrick Stirling of Kippendavie (Perthshire), DL (*d* 9 Dec 1899), and *d* 19 Nov 1907, having had issue

(2) Elizabeth Alexandrina; *m* 16 Nov 1880 Maj Duncan Forbes Gordon, MVO, 92nd Highrs (*d* 30 Sept 1920), s of Alexander Gordon, of Newton, and *d* 29 Nov 1913, leaving issue

1 Harriet Christian; *m* Sir Harry Niven Lumsden, Bt, and *dsp* 1820

2 Elizabeth; *m* as his 2nd w her bro's f-in-law ALEXANDER FORBES of Blackford (*see* below) and *dsp*

The 1st and last BARON LEITH OF FYVIE's s-in-law,

Sir Charles Rosdew BURN later FORBES-LEITH OF FYVIE (roy licence 1925), **1st Bt** (UK), so *cr* 7 March 1923, OBE; *b* 20 Feb 1859; memb Gentlemen-at-Arms and Roy Co Archers, ADC to HM GEORGE V 1910–26, MP Torquay 1910–23, Col TA, Hon Col 22nd (Co of London) Armoured Car Co, Lt-Col and Hon Col Imp Yeo, Lt-Col Roy Dragoons, served Hazara Expdn 1888 (despatches, medal and clasp), Boer War 1900 (medal with three clasps) and WW I (despatches twice, Offr Legn Hon and Crown Belgium, 1914 star, two medals); *m* 22 July 1891 Hon Ethel Louise Forbes-Leith (*see* above) and had issue:

1 Arthur Herbert Rosdew, 2nd Lt Roy Dragoons; *b* 30 June 1892; *ka* 30 Oct 1914

2 (ROBERT) IAN ALGERNON (Sir), **2nd Bt**

1 Lorna Marsalie; *m* 1st 4 Nov 1916 (*divorce* 1933) Capt Conyers Frederick Woodroffe Lang, Devon Regt; *m* 2nd 9 June 1933 Lt-Col George Edward Redvers Prior, DSO, MC, Devon Regt (*d* 12 June 1956), s of Maj-Gen J E H Prior, and by her 1st husb had issue:

(1) *Charles Douglas Conyers, MC (1944); *b* 26 Sept 1918; *educ* Eton; WW II as Capt Devon Regt

(2) *Robin Arthur [Robin Lang Esq, 46 Avenue Lakanal, 33 Le Bouscat, France]; *b* 19 Nov 1928; *m* 14 Nov 1964 *Pierrette Bertrand, of Bordeaux, and has:

1a *Claire; *b* 2 Nov 1965

2a *Dominique; *b* 10 June 1967

Sir CHARLES *d* 2 Nov 1930; his only surv son,

Sir (Robert) Ian Algernon Forbes-Leith of Fyvie, 2nd Bt, MBE (1946), JP (1945), DL (Aberdeenshire 1946, Co of City of Aberdeen 1964); *b* 27 Dec 1902; *educ* Eton; Aberdeen: CC 1938, V-Convenor 1950, Convenor 1955–58, V-Lt 1953, Ld Lt 1959–73, Govr N of Scotland Coll of Ag 1953–73 and Rowett Research Inst, P/O AAF, Lt 14th Bn London Regt (London Scottish), WW II as Maj RA (despatches), Hon A/Cdre 612 (Co of Aberdeen) Sqdn AAF 1946–55, Memb Roy Co Archers, ktd 1972, Hon LLD Aberdeen; *m* 23 Feb 1927 Ruth Avis (*d* 11 May 1973), dau of Edward George Barnett, of Northumberland, and *d* 17 March 1973, having had:

1 John Alexander; *b* 31 Aug 1928; *educ* Eton; 2nd Lt Scots Gds (despatches); *kas* Malaya 25 Sept 1949

2 Sir ANDREW GEORGE FORBES-LEITH OF FYVIE, **3rd and present Bt**

1 *Anne Rosdew [Mrs Angus Pelham Burn, Knappach, Banchory, Kincardineshire]; *b* 10 April 1932; *m* 19 Dec 1959 *Angus Maitland Pelham Burn, only s of Brig-Gen Henry Pelham Burn, CMG, DSO, of Biallaid, Newtonmore, Inverness-shire, and has issue:

(1) *Amanda Mary; *b* 4 March 1961

(2) *Lucy Rosdew; *b* 7 May 1963

(3) *Emily Louise; *b* 21 Nov 1964

(4) *Kate Ruth; *b* 11 Oct 1966

2 *Mary Elizabeth [Mrs James Gresley-McGowan, Benridge Hall, Ponteland, Northumberland]; *b* 14 Sept 1934; *m* 5 April 1961 *Maj James Gresley-McGowan, 15th/19th King's Roy Hus (ret), only s of Capt William McGowan, and has issue:

(1) *Charles Gresley [Charles Gresley-McGowan Esq, Southlands Farm, Gunnerton, Hexham, Northumberland NE48 4EA]; *b* 20 March 1962; *m* 1989 *Deborah Ann, dau of Dr Joseph Edward Gordon, of Newcastle, and has:

1a *Hector Joseph Gresley; *b* 1991

1a *Rosanna Mary; *b* 1994

(2) *Hugo John; *b* 20 Feb 1964

(1) *Lorna; *b* 13 Aug 1967

Lineage (of Forbes): The 2nd LORD FORBES (*qv*); had a 2nd s:

DUNCAN FORBES of Corsindae; *m* Christian Mercer and was ancestor of the FORBESes of Monymusk, Corsindae and Leslie; his descendant:

JOHN FORBES of Leslie; *m* Margaret, dau of Skene of Skene, and had a 2nd s:

ALEXANDER FORBES of Auquorthies, Aberdeenshire; had a s:

ALEXANDER FORBES of Auquorthies; *m* Anna, dau of William Seton of Minnes, and had, with other issue, including an er s (John, of Auquorthies and Lethenty, Aberdeenshire, *b* 1653, *m* Barbara Skene (*d* 1709) and *d* 1726, leaving a dau Margaret, who *m* Alexander Skene of Dyce and had issue):

ALEXANDER FORBES, of Blackford, Aberdeenshire; *b* 1657; *m* 1702 Helen, only dau of Alexander Gellie of Blackford, and *d* 1712, leaving:

ALEXANDER FORBES of Blackford; *m* 16 Aug 1727 Elizabeth, dau of John Aksew, and had:

ALEXANDER FORBES of Blackford; *m* 16 April 1754 Catherine, dau and coheir of William Gordon of Badenscoth, and had, with an er s (Alexander, of Blackford, *b* 22 Jan 1755, *d* unm 1784):

JOHN FORBES of Blackford; *b* 19 Sept 1758; *m* 9 Sept 1784 Anna Margaretta, dau of John Gregory, MD, by Elizabeth (*d* 1825), sis and heiress of 15th Lord Forbes (*qv*), and had, with other issue:

1 ALEXANDER

2 James Keith; *b* 1790; *m* 1817 Marian, dau of James Brown, and *d* 1842, leaving:

(1) John Gregory, of London; *m* 1844 Harriet Elizabeth, dau of William Macyntyre, MD, and had issue

3 William Nairne; Maj-Gen Bengal Engrs; *b* 1796; *m* 1836 Sarah, dau of Charles Bartlett Greenlaw, and had issue

4 Jonathan FORBES later LESLIE (on inheriting Rothie Norman, Aberdeenshire, from his cousin Robert Leslie), JP, DL; *b* 1798; Lt-Col 78th Highrs; *m* 1825 Margaret (*d* 1882), dau of John Urquhart, of Craigston Castle, and *d* 1877, leaving issue

1 Mary Elizabeth; *m* 1797 William Moir of Park and *d* 1843, leaving issue

JOHN FORBES *d* 1 May 1840; his est son,

ALEXANDER FORBES of Blackford; *b* 1786; *m* 1st Margaret (*d* 1825), dau of Charles Bannerman; *m* 2nd Elizabeth (*dsp*), dau of Gen Alexander Leith-Hay, of Rannes and Leith Hall (*see* above), and *d* 28 Oct 1851, having by his 1st w had, with other issue:

MARGARET Forbes, of Blackford, which she sold 1858; *m* 27 June 1843 R-Adml John James LEITH (*d* 25 Oct 1854) leaving issue (*see* above)

FORBES ADAM

Arms: Arg. a mullet pierced between three cross crosslets fitchée gu., a chief of the last thereon a pale or charged with a rose of the second, barbed and seeded ppr. **Crest:** A cubit arm arg., holding in the hand a cross crosslet fitchée in bend sinister and charged on the wrist with a rose, both as in the arms. **Motto:** *Crux mihi grata quies* ('The cross is to me a welcome rest').
Creation: Bt. (UK) 15 Feb 1917.

SIR CHRISTOPHER ERIC FORBES ADAM, 3rd Bt [Sir Christopher Forbes Adam Bt, 46 Rawlings St, London SW3 2LS]; *b* 12 Feb 1920, *s* unc 1982, *educ* Abinger Hill Sch, Surrey, and privately; jnlst *Yorkshire Post*; *m* 17 Sept 1957 *Patricia Anne, yr dau of John Neville Wreford Brown, of Maltings, Abberton, Colchester, Essex, and has adopted:

*Sarah Anne, *b* 18 Oct 1960; *m* 1986 *Andrew J (ALLEN formerly EDEN, deed poll 1964), s of Prof Alec Eden, and has issue:

(1) *Edward Christopher, *b* 1989

(1) *Alicia Elizabeth, *b* 1991

Lineage: JAMES GRAHAM ADAM, of Denovan House, Dunipace, Stirlingshire, *b* 30 July 1800, s of Francis Adam, of Glasgow (*d* 1844); *m* 4 Dec 1835 Jane Brown (*d* 19 March, 1891), dau of Charles McIndoe, of Carbeth, Strathblane, by Janet Buchanan, and *d* 24 Feb 1860, leaving issue:

Sir Frank Forbes Adam, 1st Bt (UK, so *cr* 15 Feb 1917, CB (1919), CIE (1888), JP and DL Lancs; Hon LLD Manchester U 1908, Chm of Council 1904, Pres of Bombay Chamber of Commerce 1884–89, Tstee Port of Bombay 1884–90, MLC Bombay 1884–90, Pres Bank of Bombay, Pres of Manchester Chamber of Commerce 1894–99 and 1903–05, Chm Manchester and County Bank 1914; *b* 17 June 1846, ktd 1890; *m* 31 Aug 1883 Rose Frances (*d* 3 April 1944), dau of Charles Gurdon Kemball, Judge High Court Bombay, and *d* 22 Dec 1926, having had:

1 **Sir Ronald Forbes Adam, 2nd Bt**, GCB (1946, KCB 1941, CB 1939), DSO (1918), OBE (1919), of Hankelow Court, Gen, entered RA 1905, GSO (1), Staff Coll 1932–35 and War Office, 1935; T/Brig and Dep Director of Military Operations 1936, Cmdr RA, 1st Div 1936–37, T/Maj-Gen and Cmdt Staff Coll Camberley, 1937, Maj-Gen 1937; Dep CIGS from 1938 with local rank of Lt-Gen; Gen 1942; served WW I France and Italy (Despatches) and WW II 1939–41 (despatches), Cmded 3rd Corps France, 1939–40; GOC-in-C Northern Cmd 1940, Adj-Gen Forces, 1941; Col-Cmdt RA and Army Educn Corps 1940; ret 1946; Chm Br Cncl 1946–54, Pres MCC 1946–47; Pres British Inst of Adult Edcn 1948–64, Chm Nat Inst Industrial Psychology 1947–52, Chm Executive Board, UNESCO 1952–54; Chm U of London, Inst of Educn 1946–67; Chm Exec Ctee UNA 1956–61; Pres UNA 1961, *b* 30 Oct 1885; *m* 7 Jan 1915 Anna Dorothy (*d* 2 May, 1972), 2nd dau of Frederic Islay Pitman, of Searlets, Twyford, Berks, and *d* 26 Dec 1982, having had issue:

(1) *Barbara [Lady Proctor, 102 High St, Lewes, E Sussex], *b* 11 June 1917, *m* 29 Aug 1953 Sir Philip Dennis Proctor, KCB (*d* 1983), s of Sir Philip Bridger Proctor, KBE, of Thursley House, Mayfield, Sussex, and adopted:

*David, *b* 21 March, 1958

*Jonathan, *b* 21 June, 1959

*Ruth, *b* 28 June, 1962

(2) Margot Forbes; *b* 14 Oct 1918; *d* unm 10 Oct 1937

(3) *Bridget Islay MBE (1960) [Col Bridget Forbes Adam MBE, Ardmore, Netherhampton, Wilts SP2 8PU], Col WRAC; *b* 17 Dec 1927

(4) *Isobel [Miss Isobel Forbes Adam, 4 Alderville Rd, London SW6 3RJ], *b* 17 Dec 1927 (twin)

2 Eric Graham, CMG (1923), First Sec FO, *b* 3 Oct 1888, *educ* Eton and King's Coll Camb (BA), *m* 23 Nov 1918 Agatha Perrin (*d* 10 Sept 1956), widow of Sidney Spooner, and eldest dau of Reginald Walter Macan, DLitt, Master of Univ Coll Oxford, and *d* 7 July, 1925, leaving issue:

(1) Sir CHRISTOPHER ERIC FORBES ADAM, **3rd and present Bt**

3 Colin Gurdon, CSI (1924), DL (1958–66), JP (1936) ER Yorks, entered ICS 1912, Assist-Collector and Magistrate 1913–18, Under-Sec to Govt Bombay 1919, Priv Sec to Govr Bombay 1920–24, T/Lt WW I; *b* 18 Dec 1889; *educ* Eton and King's Coll Cambridge; *m* 3 Dec 1920 Hon Irene Lawley (*d* 1976), dau of 3rd Baron Wenlock (*see* 1932 edn), and *d* 1982, having had issue:

(1) +(STEPHEN) TIMOTHY BEILBY (Rev) [The Rev Timothy Forbes Adam, Woodhouse Farm, Escrick, York YO4 6HT]; *b* 19 Nov 1923; heir presumptive; *educ* Eton, RADA and Chichester Theological Coll; T/Capt Rifle Bde 1942–47, ordained 1962, Rector Barton-in-Fabis with Thrumpton 1964–70, priest in charge Southstoke 1974–84; *m* 28 Sept 1954 *Penelope, dau of George Campbell Munday, MC, of Leverington Hall, Wisbech, Cambs, and has issue:

1a *Anna Victoria, *b* 14 July 1955

2a *Catherine Mary, *b* 8 Nov 1956; *m* 1991 *Kristan David Stone, 2nd s of Staley Stone

3a *(Teresa) Lucy, *b* 5 Oct 1960

4a *Sonia Clare, *b* 28 Nov 1966

(2) Desmond Francis; *b* 27 Jan 1926; *educ* Eton and King's Coll Cambridge; *m* 15 Jan 1949 *Hon Vivien Elizabeth [The Hon Mrs Forbes Adam, 11 Mulberry Walk, London SW3], only dau of Sir Oswald Mosley, 6th Bt (*see* RAVENSDALE, B), and *d* as the result of an accident 3 Jan 1958, leaving:

1a +Rupert Colin [Rupert Forbes Adam Esq, Richardsons, Skipwith, nr Selby, N Yorks], *b* 11 Aug 1957; *m* 1981 *Mrs Anya B Hillman, dau of Richard Cadbury Butler

2a *Cynthia Rebecca [Mrs Clive Chaddock, The Manse, Harray, Orkney], *b* 2 Feb 1950; *m* 1978 *H Clive Chaddock, only s of H Chaddock, and has:

1b *Jack Colin, *b* 1981

2b *Harry Desmond, *b* 1984

3b *Benjamin Gabriel, *b* 1987

3a *Arabella Irene, *b* 17 May 1952; has issue:

1b *Archie Desmond Hugh, *b* 1980

2b *Wilfrid Peter Jamie, *b* 1983

3b *Alfy Sholto, *b* 1988

(3) +Nigel Colin, JP, DL (1991) [Nigel Forbes Adam Esq JP DL, Skipwith Hall, Selby, N YorksYO8 7SQ]; late Capt Yorks Hus (TA), High Sheriff N Yorks 1976; *b* 7 Dec 1930; *educ* Eton and King's Coll Cambridge; *m* 1st 7 May 1954 *Teresa Hermione Idena, dau of Cdr David Lambert Robertson, RN (ret), and has:

1a +Charles David [Charles Forbes Adam Esq, Charity Farm, Skipwith, N Yorks YO8 7SL]; *b* 8 Oct 1957; *m* 1987 *Rosalind Cecilia, dau of Geoffrey Colvile, and has issue:

1b +(Crispin) Beilby; *b* 1987

2b +Hal; *b* 1989

3b *Charlotte India; *b* 1992

2a +Titus Desmond; *b* 24 Jan 1960

3a +Julian Nigel Peregrine; *b* 3 Feb 1961; *m* 1986 *Christina Maria, dau of Colin Woodiwiss, and has issue:

1b +Luke George Nigel; *b* 1987

4a +Harry Crispin; *b* 18 Aug 1962

(3) Nigel Adam; *m* 2nd 1987 *(Mildred) Malise Hare, formerly w of David Ropner (*see* ROPNER, Bt) and dau of Col George Armitage

(1) *Virginia Mary; *b* 9 April 1922; *m* 24 April 1948 Capt Hugo Charteris (*d* 1970; *see* WEMYSS and MARCH, E) and has issue

1 Hetty Reay Clifford Forbes, MBE (1943)

FORD

Arms: Vert a chevron between a dexter and a sinster wing in chief and in base a pyramid, all or. **Crest:** A sphinx, wings elevated, its head ensigned with a plume, and supporting between its forepaws a papyrus stalk, flowered and leaved or. **Motto:** *Fortuna fortior fortitudo* ('Fortitude rises above good or bad fortune').
Creation: Bt. (UK) 27 July 1929.

SIR ANDREW RUSSELL FORD, 3RD BT, of Westerdunes, Co of East Lothian [Sir Andrew Ford Bt, 20 Coniston Rd, Chippenham, Wilts SN14 0PX]; *b* 29 June 1943; *s f* 1989; *educ* Winchester, New Coll Oxford, Loughborough Coll of Educn (DLC 1967), London U (External BA) and Birmingham U (External MA); lecturer Chippenham Coll 1974–, formerly schmaster; *m* 8 Aug 1968 *Penelope Anne, only dau of Harold Edmund Relph, of West Kirby, Wirral, and has:

1 +TOBY RUSSELL; *b* 11 Jan 1973
2 +David Andrew; *b* 1984
1 *Julia Mary; *b* 1970

Lineage: WILLIAM FORD, of Leith; merchant; *d* 2 Feb 1876, having had issue:

JAMES FORD, of Edinburgh; *b* 25 Sept 1820; *m* 5 May 1875 Agnes Campbell Cassels (*d* 26 Jan 1922), dau of Alexander Cassels, WS, and *d* 7 March 1905, having had, with a dau (Agnes Cassels, *m* 8 Aug 1899 Henry Vivian Phillips, barrister, of Tonbridge, Kent):

Sir Patrick Johnston Ford, 1st Bt (UK), so *cr* 27 July 1929; *b* 5 March 1880; *educ* Edinburgh Acad and New Coll Oxford (MA 1904); LLB Edinburgh 1907; advocate 1907, Lt 4th Bn Cameron Highrs and on Special Duty WW I, Hon Sec Scottish War Savings Assoc 1915, MP (U) N Edinburgh 1920–23 and 1924–35, Hon Treasurer Imp Soc Kts Bachelor (ret 1935), Hon Col 4th Heavy Bde RA (T) (ret 1935), Hon memb Roy Scottish Acad, memb Roy Co Archers, Jr Ld Treasury 1922–23, Hon Sec and Pres Scottish U Assoc; ktd 1926; *m* 19 Dec 1905 Jessie Hamilton (*d* 15 Sept 1962), er dau of Henry Field, WS, of Moreland, Kinross-shire, and Middleluff, Manitoba, and *d* 28 Sept 1945, leaving:

1 HENRY RUSSELL FORD (Sir), **2nd Bt**

2 Harold Frank; *b* 17 May 1915; *educ* Winchester and Univ Coll Oxford (BA 1937); LLB Edinburgh 1945; Lt Lothians and Border Yeo 1939, served WW II (POW), Capt 1945, advocate 1945, Sheriff-Substitute Perth and Angus 1951; *m* 29 July 1948 *Lucy Mary, dau of John Rudolph Wardlaw Burnet, KC, BA, LLB, Sheriff Fife, Kinross and Edinburgh, and *d* 19 June 1994, leaving:

(1) +Patrick John [Patrick Ford Esq, Tigerton, Menmuir, Angus DD9 7RL]; *b* 14 Sept 1952; *educ* Ampleforth and Magdalene Coll Cambridge (MA) and Edinburgh U (LLB); slr, WS

(1) *Claire Lucy; *b* 3 Aug 1949; *m* 1975 *John W Blair, of Clint House, Stenton, E Lothian, and has issue:

1a *Charles; *b* 1980
1a *Zepherine; *b* 1978
2a *Molly; *b* 1985

(2) *Harriet Mary; *b* 20 May 1955; *m* 1992 *Mark James Cazalet and has:

1a *Felix James; *b* 1994

(3) *Katharine Anne; *b* 5 Aug 1958; *m* 1989 *Timothy Paul Cullinan, MRCP, MSc, MD, and has

1a *Finbar; *b* 1989
2a *Mungo; *b* 1991
3a *Bruno; *b* 1994

1 Joan Cassels; *m* 18 April 1938 John Calthrop, s of Donald Calthorp, and had issue

2 *Marjorie Elaine [Mrs Alan Murray, Apt 84, 1 Seabeach Ave, Mona Vale NSW 2103, Australia]; *b* 1913; *m* 29 March 1941 Alan Murray (*d* 1975), s of John Murray, of Australia, and has issue:

(1) *Peter Johnston [Peter Murray Esq, 5 Tobruk Ave, Balmain, NSW 2041, Australia]; *b* 1943; *educ* Scotts Coll Sydney and NSW U (BA Architecture); Master Town and Country Planning, Sydney U; *m* 1967 (*divorce* 1987) Jennifer Lee, dau of Harold Ambrose Terrey, of Lane Cove, NSW

(1) *Gillian Elaine [Mrs Gillian Murray, 150 Green Point Drive, Green Point, via Forster, NSW 2428, Australia]; *b* 1946; *m* 1967 (*divorce* 1978, resumed maiden name) Gary Richardson and has issue:

1a *Damien; *b* 1971
2a *Nathan; *b* 1974
3a *Heath; *b* 1977
1a *Kelly Ann; *b* 1969

Sir PATRICK's est s,

Sir Henry Russell Ford, 2nd Bt, JP (E Lothian 1951), TD (1960); *b* 30 April 1911; *educ* Winchester and New Coll Oxford (MA); Lt-Col RA, WW II (despatches); chm E Lothian U Assoc 1948–51 and 1958–60; *m* 8 Aug 1936 Mary ('Molly') Elizabeth (*d* 28 March 1997), yst dau of Godfrey Fitzherbert Wright, JP, of Whiddon, Bovey Tracey, and *d* 1989, leaving issue:

1 Sir ANDREW RUSSELL FORD, **3rd and present Bt**

1 *Jill Dorothy [Miss Jill Ford, Seaforth, Gullane, E Lothian]; *b* 10 Aug 1937

2 *Alison Patricia; *b* 27 July 1946; *m* 1970 *Robert M Cowe, of Fountain Hall, Pencaitland, E Lothian, and has issue:

(1) *Peter Henry McNab; *b* 1972
(2) *Ian Duncan McNab; *b* 1974
(1) *Anne Louise; *b* 1978

3 *Belinda Christine; *b* 19 Feb 1951; *m* 1974 *Graeme P C McWilliam, of Bridge End Cottage, Ulpha, Broughton-in-Furness, Cumbria, and has issue:

(1) *Ralph Andrew Campbell; *b* 1984
(2) *Alastair James; *b* 1992
(1) *Amelia Mary; *b* 1976
(2) *Louise Sarah; *b* 1979
(3) *Dorothy Helen; *b* 1987

FORESTER

Arms: Quarterly, 1st and 4th, quarterly per fess indented arg. and sa., in the 1st and 4th quarters a bugle-horn of the last, garnished or (for FORESTER); 2nd and 3rd, az. a fess nebuly between three crescents, two and one erm., a cross crosslet fitchée for difference (for WELD). **Crests:** 1 A talbot passant arg., collared sa., line reflexed or (for FORESTER), 2 A wyvern sa. guttée, collared, wings elevated, line reflexed over the back or, on the wing an escallop of the first (for WELD). **Supporters:** On either side a talbot arg., collared sa., therefrom pendant a bugle-horn, as in the arms, line reflexed over the back or. **Motto:** *Semper eadem* ('Always the same'). **Creation:** B. (UK) 17 July 1821.

THE 8TH BARON FORESTER OF WILLEY PARK, Co Salop ((George Cecil) Brooke Weld-Forester, DL (Salop) 1995) [The Rt Hon The Lord Forester DL, Willey Park, Broseley, Salop TF12 5JJ]; *b* 20 Feb 1938; *s* f 1977; *educ* Eton, and RAC Cirencester (MRAC); dir: Pett Hammett 1970, Linley Farms 1974–, Sipolilo Estates 1977–, Bridgnorth Home Care Co-op 1992, Broseley Hosp Tst 1994 and Calkilo 1996, past Chm Shropshire CLA, Shropshire Tree Cncl and Regnl Advsy Ctee Forestry Commn, Pres The Greenwood Tst 1990– and Shropshire FWAG 1991–96, memb: W Midland Cncl for Sport and Recreation 1991–95, Exec Ctee CLA 1990–95, CLA Cncl 1987–95, Minerals Working Party CLA 1980–97 and Marches SB co-ordinating ctee 1992; *m* 14 Jan 1967 *Hon (Elizabeth) Catherine Lyttelton (High Sheriff Salop 1997–98), 2nd dau of 10th Viscount Cobham (*qv*), and has issue:

1 +CHARLES RICHARD GEORGE; *b* 8 July 1975

1 *Selina Lucy; *b* 7 Feb 1968; *m* 11 July 1998 *Ian W Graham, s of Michael Graham, of Raffingora, Zimbabwe

2 *Alice Sophie; *b* 2 June 1969

3 *Alexandra Elizabeth; *b* 17 May 1973

Lineage: The FORESTERs were orginally of Watling Street, Salop, and were indeed foresters, having the custody in fee of Wellington Hay, a portion of the Wrekin Forest, and holding half a virgate of land in Wellington by serjeantry (performance of a service).

HUGH FORESTER; living 1187–97; possibly kin to:

ROBERT de WELLINGTON; forester; living 1227; had:

ROBERT FORESTER, of Wellington; *d* 1278, leaving:

ROGER Fitz ROBERT, of Wellington; *b c* 1253; *d* by 1283, leaving:

ROGER Fitz ROGER, of Wellington; one of the six Royal Foresters summoned to assist at the Perambulation of Shropshire Foresters 1300; had, with other sons (John Fitz Roger le Forester, *bapt* 20 July 1314, *d* 10 Sept 1349; William le Forester, *d* 29 Sept 1394, leaving a s Roger Fitz William Forseter (*b c* 1379; *d* by 3 Nov 1397)):

ROGER FORESTER; *d* 21 July 1403, leaving:

ROGER FORESTER, of Wellington; *b c* 1377; *d* 15 June 1443, leaving:

JOHN FORESTER; *b c* 1422; *d* Feb 1466, leaving:

EDWARD FORESTER, of Watling Street or Wellington; *b c* 1430; had:

JOHN FORESTER, of Watling Street; *m* Anna, dau of Thomas Banester, of Hadnell, and had, with another s (Richard, *dsp*):

JOHN FORESTER, of Watling Street; living 1506; *m* 1st Alice, dau of Thomas Charlton, of Apley Castle; *m* 2nd Isabel, dau of William Lyster, of Rowton, and by her had, with a yr s (Richard):

JOHN FORESTER, of Watling Street; *m* Joyce, dau and heiress of Philip Upton, of Upton; *d* 13 March 1591, having had:

WILLIAM FORESTER; *m* Margaret, dau and heir of John Weaver, of Stranford, Herefs, and *dvp* 4 May 1590, leaving:

FRANCIS FORESTER, of Watling Street; *m* Cicely, dau of Andrew Charlton, of Apley Castle, and *d* 6 May 1637, leaving an est surv s:

FRANCIS FORESTER, of Watling Street; *b* 1599; *m* Dorothy, dau of James Skrimsher, of Norbury, Staffs, and *d* Jan 1664/5, leaving:

FRANCIS FORESTER, of Dothill Park, Wellington; High Sheriff Salop 1652; *b* 1623; *m* Mary, dau of 1st Baron Newport of High Ercall (*see* BRADFORD, E), and had:

Sir WILLIAM FORESTER, KB, of Dothill; MP Wenlock 1678–81 and 1688–1718; *b* 10 Dec 1655; *m* Lady Mary Cecil, dau of 3rd Earl of Salisbury (*see* SALISBURY, M), and *d* Feb 1717/8, leaving:

WILLIAM FORESTER, of Dothill; MP Wenlock 1714, 1734 and 1754; *b* 1690; *m* Catherine (*d* 27 Aug 1755), dau and heiress of William Brooke, of St John's Sq, Clerkenwell, and *d* 12 Nov 1758, leaving, with other issue:

1 Brooke, of Dothill; MP Wenlock 1739–68; *b* 7 Feb 1716/7; *m* 1st 4 May 1734 Elizabeth (*bur* 28 May 1753), only dau and heir of George Weld, of Willey Park, Salop; *m* 2nd Elizabeth (*d* 1 Nov 1795), dau of Robert Barniston, of Chester, and *d* 8 July 1774, having by her had a dau and by his 1st w had, with other issue (*d* unm):

(1) George, of Dothill and Willey Park; MP Wenlock; *b* 21 Dec 1735; *d* unm 13 July 1811, leaving the Willey estate to the **1st Baron**

2 CECIL

1 Mary; *m* 1st 2 May 1738 Sir Brian Broughton-Delves, 4th Bt, and had issue (*see* BROUGHTON, Bt); *m* 2nd Jan 1764 Humphrey Mackworth Praed, MP Trevethoe, and was *bur* 27 Sept 1779, leaving further issue. He *d* 6 March 1803

The 2nd son,

CECIL FORESTER, of Rossall, nr Shrewsbury; Lt-Col, MP Wenlock 1761–68; *m* Anne (*d* 24 May 1825), dau and coheir of Robert Townshend, and *d* 22 Aug 1774, leaving with other issue:

1 CECIL WELD, **1st Baron**

2 George Towshend FORESTER later TOWNSHEND-FORESTER (12 Aug 1791); Recorder Wenlock; *b* 9 April 1768; *m* Ann, dau of J Jones, of Chirk, Denbighs, and *dsps* 29 May 1845

3 Townshend (Rev); DD, Preb Worcester, Rector Broseley; *b* 5 April 1772; *m* 5 Jan 1786 Anna Maria (*d* 21 Feb 1842), dau of Maj — Byne, and *d* 4 Oct 1841, leaving issue

4 Francis; Maj RHG, MP Wenlock 1820–26; *b* 19 Aug 1774; *m* 29 July 1813 Lady Louisa Catherine Barbara Vane (*d* 8 Jan 1821), dau of 1st Duke of Cleveland (*see* BARNARD, B), and *d* 21 Oct 1861, leaving:

(1) William Henry, of Somerby, Leics; *b* 1819; *educ* Westminster; *m* 1 Feb 1858 Hon Eleanor Alexandrina (*d* 12 May 1914), sis of 17th Lord Saltoun (*qv*) of Abernethy, and *d* 7 Jan 1891, leaving, with a dau:

1a Francis William, of Somerby; Capt 3rd Hus, Lt-Col W Somerset Yeo 1895–1900; *b* 1860; *educ* Eton; *m* 10 April 1894 Aline Laura, est dau of Sir Powlett Charles John Milbank, 2nd Bt (*qv*), and *d* 20 Sept 1942, leaving:

1b Henry William; 17th/21st Lancers 1918–29, WW II as Maj Norfolk Yeo (A/T Regt) RA (despatches), Sec to Min Resident ME 1943–44; *b* 1899; *m* 1930 *Helen, dau of Eugene Noble Foss, of Boston, Mass., and had:

1c *Barbara Laura; *b* 1934; *m* 1st 1957 Gordon Scott Vinson (*d* 1964); *m* 2nd B F Austin

1b Mary Eleanor; *b* 1895; *m* 19 Feb 1914 Sir Arthur FitzGerald, 4th Bt, of Valentia (*qv*), and *d* 7 Sept 1967, leaving issue

2b *Aline (Margaret); *b* 1904; *m* 24 Oct 1934 Capt John Bailward, s of Thomas Henry Methuen Bailward, of Horsington Manor, Templecombe, Somerset. He *dsp* 8 Dec 1946

3b Catherine Augusta; *m* 22 Jan 1931 Maj George Henry William Baird (*see* BAIRD, Bt, of Newbyth) and *d* 1986, leaving issue

The est son,

CECIL FORESTER later WELD FORESTER (roy licence 15 Aug 1811), **1st Baron Forester of Willey Park**, Co Salop (UK), so *cr* 17 July 1821; *bapt* 7 April 1767; *m* 16 June 1800 Lady Katherine Mary Manners (*d* 1 May 1829), 2nd dau of 4th Duke of Rutland (*qv*), and *d* 28 May 1828, having had, with other issue:

1 JOHN GEORGE WELD FORESTER, **2nd Baron Forester of Willey Park**, PC; MP Wenlock 1826–28; *b* 9 Aug 1801; *m* 10 June 1856 Countess Alexandrina Julia Theresa Whilhelmina Sophia (*d* 7 July 1894), widow of 3rd Viscount Melbourne and dau of Joachim Charles Louis Mortimer, Count von Maltzan, and *dsp* 10 Oct 1874

2 GEORGE CECIL WELD FORESTER, **3rd Baron Forester of Willey Park**; Gen, MP Wenlock 1828–74, Comptroller Household 1852 and 1858–59; *b* 10 May 1807; *m* 8 Nov 1862 Hon Mary Anne (*d* 7 March 1893), widow of Col David Ochterlony Dyce Sombre and only surv dau of 2nd Viscount Saint Vincent (*qv*), and *dsp* 14 Feb 1886

3 Charles Robert Weld; Maj 12th Lancers and Assist Mil Sec Ireland; *b* 28 Dec 1811; *m* 11 June 1848 Lady Maria Jocelyn (*d* 17 March 1894), yst dau of 3rd Earl of Roden (*qv*), and *dsp* 16 Sept 1852

4 ORLANDO WATKIN WELD, **4th Baron**

1 Anne Elizabeth; *m* 30 Nov 1830 6th Earl of Chesterfield (*see* 1967 edn CHESTERFIELD and STANHOPE) and *d* 27 July 1885, leaving issue

2 Elizabeth Katherine; *m* 17 June 1822 2nd Baron Carrington (*qv*) and *d* 22 July 1832, leaving issue

3 Isabella Elizabeth Annabella; *m* 30 Nov 1830 Gen Hon George Anson and *d* 29 Dec 1858 leaving issue (*see* LICHFIELD E)

4 Henrietta Maria; *m* 6 July 1833 1st Baron Londesborough (*qv*) and *d* 22 April 1841

5 Selina Louisa; *m* 30 April 1844 3rd Earl of Bradford (*qv*) and *d* 25 Nov 1894, leaving issue

The 3rd BARON's bro,

Rev ORLANDO WATKIN WELD FORESTER, **4th Baron Forester of Willey Park**; *b* 18 April 1813; MA Cantab; Canon York, Preb Langtoft, Rector Gedling 1867–87, Chllr York 1874–79; *m* 1st 14 July 1840 Sophia Elizabeth (*d* 2 April 1872), dau of Richard Norman, and had issue:

1 CECIL THEODORE, **5th Baron**

The **4th Baron** *m* 2nd 5 Oct 1875 Emma Maria (*d* 24 June 1898), est dau of William Tollemache (*see* DYSART, E), and by her had issue:

2 Orlando St Maur (Rev); *b* 13 Oct 1877; *educ* Trin Coll Cambridge (MA); Missionary Diocese of W China 1909–14, CF 1914–15, Missionary Yokohama 1916–24, Rector Cheadle Staffs 1927–36, Vicar Battersea 1936–42, Rector Trowbridge 1942–44; *m* 15 Jan 1913 Dorothy Salome Wynne (*d* 4 Sept 1963), dau of Rev William Wynne Wilson, and *d* 30 Oct 1944, leaving issue:

(1) John Orlando; *b* 21 Nov 1913; *educ* Trin Coll Cambridge (MA); joined Colonial Educn Serv 1938, Assist Dir African Educn N Rhodesia 1959–61, Assist Sec to Min Educn Lusaka 1961–64, Lt 2nd N Rhodesian Regt; *m* 23 July 1938 *Lydia Gertrude [Mrs John Weld-Forester, 25 Toms Close, Chard, Somerset TA20 2HD], yr dau of Rev Stephen Harold Wingfield Digby, Canon Salisbury, Wilts, and Mombasa, Kenya, and *d* 23 Feb 1995, leaving issue:

1a *Priscilla Mary [Mrs Neville Vereker, 6 Curzon Ave, Beaconsfield, Bucks]; *b* 20 Sept 1939; *m* 1974 *Neville Henry Prendergast Vereker (*see* GORT, V) and has issue

2a *Elizabeth; *b* 3 Nov 1941; *m* 11 Aug 1962 *John Jeremy Inskip Hawkins, er s of Arthur John Inskip Hawkins, OBE, of Rhodesia, and has issue:

1b *John Edward Inskip (Rev) [The Rev John Hawkins, St Nicholas Church Vicarage, Dee St, London E14 0DT]; *b* June 1963; *m* 1986 Rev Emma Woodhead (*d* 1990)

2b *Bruce James Orlando; *b* 16 April 1965; *m* 1993 *Fabienne Tamborini and has:

1c *Jade Marie; *b* 1994

1b *Veronica Caroline; *b* 13 Nov 1967

2b *Sarah Elizabeth [Mrs Jonathan Levesley, 67 Walsingham Close, Hatfield, Herts]; *b* 1969; *m* 1991 *Jonathan Mark Levesley

3a *Dorothy Katherine [Mrs John Simson, The Old Rectory, Mottistone, Newport, IoW]; *b* 24 Dec 1944; *m* 4 Sept 1967 *John Wyndham Simson, only s of John Adhemar Simson, DSC, and has issue:

1b *Christopher Adhemar; *b* 8 June 1969

1b *Henrietta Katharine; *b* 1971

2b *Penelope Anne; *b* 1974

3b *Philippa Lydia Rosamond; *b* 1977

4a *Caroline Lydia [Mrs Frank Wakefield, Rothley, Kingsgate Rd, Winchester, Hants]; *b* 28 July 1948; *m* 1970 *Frank John Montague Wakefield, and has:

1b *Nicholas John Alexander; *b* 1978

1b *Anna Charlotte; *b* 9 June 1972

2b *Holly Christina; *b* 1974

5a *Rosamund Eleanor; *b* 17 March 1950; *m* 1971 (*divorce* 1978) Raymond James Edmonds

(1) *Katherine Dorothy; *b* 20 Jan 1916; *m* 11 Feb 1956 *Sydney Herbert Brenan

The 4th BARON *d* 22 June 1894; his er son,

CECIL THEODORE WELD FORESTER, **5th Baron Forester of Willey Park** JP, DL Salop, JP Wenlock; MP Wenlock 1874–85, CC Salop, Mayor 1898, 1899 and 1909; *b* 3 Aug 1842; *m* 18 Dec 1866 Emma Georgina (*d* 21 Oct 1922), dau and coheir of Sir Willoughby Wolstan Dixie, 8th Bt (*see* 1970 edn), and had, with other issue:

1 GEORGE CECIL BEAUMONT, **6th Baron**

2 Charles Cecil Orlando; Lt Salop Imp Yeo; *b* 27 Oct 1869; *m* 1st 23 Nov 1898 (*divorce* 1912) Elspeth Lascelles (*d* 29 July 1931), dau of Alexander Mackenzie, Madras LC; *m* 2nd 1 April 1913 Marian Elizabeth (*d* 1 Dec 1945), yr dau of Capt Walter Montiford Westropp-Dawson, DL, of Charlesfort, Co Wexford, by Laura Felicia Susan, dau of Sir William Clay, 1st Bt (*qv*), and *d* 23 Nov 1937, leaving by his 1st w:

(1) Wolstan Beaumont Charles, CBE (1957); Lt-Cdr RN, V-Consul: Tangier 1930–34, Durazzo Albania 1934–38 (local rank 2nd Sec Dip Serv) and Munich 1938–39 (Actg Consul-Gen June-Sept), Consul: Basra 1940–43 and Suez 1943–44, Actg Consul-Gen Damascus 1944–46, 1st Sec Addis Ababa 1946, Chargé d'Affaires 1947–48, Consul-Gen Salonika 1949–52, Oporto 1952–55 and Nice 1955–57 (ret 1957), served WWI; *b* 27 Aug 1899; *m* 27 Sept 1932 Anne Grace Christian (*d* 1987), er dau of Capt William Augustus Stirling Home Drummond Moray, JP, DL, 20th of Abercairny Perthshire, and *d* 26 Oct 1961, leaving issue:

1a +Wolstan William; *b* 19 March 1941

1a *(Beatrice) Nicola Grace [Nicola Marchioness of Bute, Tylers Barn, Wood Norton Rd, Stibbard, Norfolk NR21 0EX]; *b* 19 Nov 1933; *m* 19 April 1955 (*divorce* 1977) 6th Marquess of Bute (*qv*) and has issue

(2) Raymond Cecil; *b* 11 Aug 1900; *d* unm 6 March 1957

3 Francis Henry Cecil, JP Salop; Lt-Col 3rd Bn Salop LI, High Sheriff Salop; *b* 2 Feb 1871; *m* 1st 31 Oct 1901 Alexina Josephine Arbuthnott (*d* 31 March 1934), dau of Maj Frederick Wollaston, DL, of Shenton Hall, Leics; *m* 2nd 26 Jan 1937 Grace (*d* 12 July 1973 aged 95), formerly w of Joseph Wingfield Henry and dau of Archibald Peel, JP, DL (*see* PEEL, E) and *d* 12 March 1952, leaving by his 1st w:

(1) Katherine Georgina Josephine; *b* 31 July 1902; *m* 9 Oct 1924 V-Adml Cecil Dacre Staveley Raikes, CBE (*d* 15 Feb 1947), 3rd s of Henry Cecil Raikes, PC, JP, DL, MP Llwynegrin, and *d* 6 May 1983, leaving issue:

1a *Dacre Francis Arthur; md The Borneo Co (Thailand) Ltd, chm Br Chamber of Commerce Bangkok, 2nd V-Pres Bd of Trade Thailand, pres Bangkok Music Gp, WW II in RN 1943–46; *b* 20 Dec 1925; *educ* Radley

1a *Cecila Heather; *b* 1 July 1927; *m* 1st 26 March 1949 (*divorce* 1955) James Fleming, Black Watch; *m* 2nd Jan 1956 *John Power George and has issue

4 Edgar Cecil Wolstan; *b* 2 Feb 1871; *m* 9 Oct 1943 Margaret Ida Isabel (*d* 24 July 1960), 2nd dau of Rev Canon Macbeth, LLD, Precentor Ferns Cathedral, and *dsp* 20 Nov 1948

5 Arthur Orlando Wolstan Cecil, MVO; Maj Gren Gds, ADC to Viceroy India; *b* 13 July 1877; *d* 1 Nov 1914 of wounds recd Ypres

6 Edric Alfred Cecil, CVO (1950); JP (Oxon 1920, Glos 1937), DL (Glos 1953); *b* 26 Feb 1880; Clerk Cheque and Adj Yeomen Gd 1945, served Boer War 1900 and WW I (severely wounded), Maj Rifle Bde GSO(2) 1916; *m* 10 April 1916 Lady Victoria Alexandrina (*d* 28 March 1966), widow of Nigel Walter Legge-

Bourke (*see* DARTMOUTH, E) and dau of 1st and last Marquess of Lincolnshire (*see* CARRINGTON, B), and *d* 24 Sept 1963, leaving issue:

(1) Charles Robert Cecil; Capt Rifle Bde WW II 1939–40 (POW, despatches twice); *b* 8 Jan 1919; *educ* Stowe; *m* 30 April 1940 (*divorce* 1948) Lady Moyra Rosamond Butler (*d* 26 May 1959), only dau of 5th Marquess of Ormonde (*see* MOUNTGARRETT, V), and had issue:

1a Piers Edric; *b* 23 April 1946; *educ* Harrow; *m* 6 June 1973 Georgina, model (*d* Paris air crash 3 March 1974), dau of Chaplain-Gen Ven John R Youens, of W Byfleet, Surrey, and *d* 30 Oct 1977

(1) (cont.) Charles Weld-Forester *m* 2nd 15 April 1948 (*divorce* 1962) Venetia de Winton, er dau of Lt-Col Sir (Ernest) Edward de Winton Wills, 4th Bt, of Hazlewood (*qv*) and by her had:

2a +Anthony Edward [Anthony Weld-Forester Esq, Old Manse, Gartmore, by Stirling FK8 3RP]; Lt Scots Gds; *b* 24 Oct 1954; *educ* Harrow; *m* 1979 *Joanna Mary, yst dau of Eric Cyprian Perry Whiteley, TD, and has issue:

1b +Henry James; *b* 1981

2b +Alfred Charles; *b* 1983

1b *Jocelyn Victoria; *b* 1986

2b *Clementine Ruth Katey; *b* 1989

1a *Mary Sylvia [Mrs Mary Boyd, 1179 N W Rockwood Lane, Bend, OR 97701, USA]; *b* 6 May 1957; *m* 1986 (*divorce* 1996) Bradley Steven Boyd, s of Robert Boyd, of California, and has issue:

1b *Alexandra Marisa; *b* 1987

2b *Jennifer Louise; *b* 1991

(1) (cont.) Charles Weld-Forester *m* 3rd 17 May 1963 Delia (*d* 1992), formerly w of Robert Alan Keith and yr dau of Lt-Col Guy Andrew Heineky Buxton, and *d* 1988

(1) *Mary Cecilia Georgina; *b* 22 Jan 1917; *m* 4 May 1939 *Maj Hon (William) Nicholas Somers Lawrence Hyde Villiers, yr s of 6th Earl of Clarendon (*qv*), and has issue

(2) *Elizabeth Rosalind [Mrs Francis Hunt, Inholmes Holt, Woodlands St Mary, Berks RG16 7SX]; *b* 25 May 1923; *m* 14 Nov 1942 *Maj Francis Holdsworth Hunt, ERD, late Coldstream Gds, and has issue:

1a *Charles Edric Holdsworth [Charles Hunt Esq, Haworth House, Kintbury, Berks RG15 0TP]; Capt Coldstream Gds; *b* 25 Dec 1943; *educ* Eton; *m* 10 Oct 1968 *Sarah Mary, er dau of Anthony Peter Howorth Greenly, of Everington House, Newbury (*see* 1970 edn GIBSON, Bt, of Great Warley), and has:

1b *Guy Eric Holdsworth; *b* 1970

2b *Edward Charles Holdsworth; *b* 1972

1b *Sacha Victoria Holdsworth; *b* 1975

1a *Elizabeth; *b* 20 April 1947; *m* 1st 10 July 1969 (*divorce* 1980) Maj Conway John Edward Seymour (*see* HERTFORD M); *m* 2nd 1980 *Maj A F Gradidge, late 17th/21st Lancers

1 Mary Isabella Sophia Louisa; *b* 8 March 1873; *m* 31 Oct 1905 Maj James Whitaker, JP, 20th Hus, of Winsley, Salop, and *d* 2 May 1950, leaving issue. He *d* 18 March 1946

The 5th BARON *d* 20 Nov 1917; his est son,

GEORGE CECIL BEAUMONT WELD FORESTER, **6th Baron Forester of Willey Park**, JP, DL Salop; *b* 9 Sept 1867; *educ* Harrow and Trin Coll Cambridge; Lt-Col Salop Yeo, Capt RHG, CC Salop, Mayor Wenlock 1920–22, KJStJ; *m* 8 Feb 1896 Christine Isabel, DJStJ (*d* 1 April 1948), dau of Duncan Henry Caithness Reay Davidson, of Tulloch, and *d* 10 Oct 1932, having had, with two yr sons (Willoughby George Orlando, *b* 18 April, *d* 6 Aug 1901; John George, *b* and *d* 3 March 1903):

CECIL GEORGE WILFRED WELD FORESTER, **7th Baron Forester of Willey Park**; JP (1936), DL (Salop 1947); CA Salop 1960, Col RHG, Lt MG Regt, WW I and WW II (despatches), Hon Col 48 Inf Div RAOC (TA); ADC to Govr Gen and C-in-C Union S Africa 1924–26, Mayor Wenlock 1936 and 1961, Alderman Wenlock 1943–77, KStJ; *b* 12 July 1899; *m* 2 June 1931 Marie Louise Priscilla (*d* 1988), DGStJ, er dau of Col Sir Herbert Charles Perrott, 6th and last Bt, CH, CB (*see* 1922 edn), and *d* 4 Jan 1977, leaving issue:

1 (GEORGE CECIL) BROOKE WELD FORESTER, **8th and present Baron Forester of Willey Park**

1 *Christine Helena [The Hon Mrs Miles, Hinton Hall, Lea Cross, Salop SY5 8JA]; *b* 20 March 1932; *m* 1st 31 July 1951 (*divorce* 1981) 7th Baron Bolton (*qv*) and has issue; *m* 2nd 1985 *Philip David Miles (*see* GREENWELL, Bt)

2 Juliet Mary; *b* 1 Aug 1934; *m* 5 Oct 1957 *(Arthur) Robin Ian Hill (*see* DOWNSHIRE, M) and *d* April 1986, leaving issue

3 (Kythe) Priscilla; *b* 18 June 1941; *d* July 1992

4 *(Mary Angela) Fiona [The Hon Lady Barttelot, Stopham Park, Pulborough, W Sussex RH20 1EB]; *b* 26 Feb 1944; OStJ 1992; *m* 20 Nov 1969 *Col Sir Brian Walter de Stopham Barttelot, 5th Bt (*qv*), and has issue

FORESTIER-WALKER

Arms: Erminois, on a pile embattled azure a mural crown charged with the word 'Badajoz' between two caltraps in pale or. **Crest:** On a mural crown or, encircled by a wreath of laurel vert, an ostrich proper, resting the dexter foot on a shell exploding proper. **Supporters:** Dexter, a lion regardant proper, gorged with a riband gules, fimbriated azure, therefrom pendant a representation of the medal and clasps presented to Sir George Walker, 1st Bt, for his services in the Pennisular War; in the mouth a broken flagstaff reversed, with the eagle and French tricolour flag also proper, the latter inscribed with the word 'Orthes'; sinister, an ostrich supporting the colours of the 50th Regt, thereon an escroll gules inscribed with the word 'Vimiera' in letters of gold. **Motto:** *Nil desperandum* ('Never give in'). The 50th Regt was that commanded by Sir George Walker, 1st Bt, at the victory of Vimiera over the French in the Peninsular War 1808. It was at Orthes that Sir George in Feb 1814 was wounded while commanding a brigade in one of the last victories over the French before NAPOLEON's first abdication. **Creation:** Bt. (UK) 28 March 1835.

SIR MICHAEL LEOLIN FORESTIER-WALKER, 6TH BT, of Castleton, Monmouth [Sir Michael Forestier-Walker Bt, Bibury, 116 Hogshill Lane, Cobham, Surrey KT11 2AW]; *b* 24 April 1949; *s* kinsman 1983; *educ* Wellington and Roy Holloway Coll London U (BA, CertEd); master Feltonfleet Sch Cobham; *m* 1988 *Elizabeth, dau of Joseph Hedley, of Bellingham, Northumberland, and has:

1 +JOSEPH ALAN; *b* 2 May 1992

1 *Chloë; *b* 1990

Lineage: — WALKER, of Staffs; had:

1 John; *b* 1588; *educ* Oriel Coll, Oxford, living 1615

2 Walter (Sir), of Bushey Hall, Herts, and Stretham, Isle of Ely; *b* 1600 at Barton-under-Needwood, Staffs; *educ* Oriel Coll Oxford and Christ's Coll Cambridge; LLD, ktd 1661, advocate to CATHERINE OF BRAGANZA, CHARLES II's w; *m* Mary, dau of George Lynne, of Southwick Hall, Northants, and *d* 1674, leaving issue:

(1) Sir GEORGE WALKER, 1st Bt, so *cr* 18 Jan 1679 (E), of Bushey Hall, Hertford, ktd 1676; *m* 1677 Susannah, dau and coheir with her sis, Frances, Lady Pelham, of John Bine or Byne, of Rowdell (Rodmell?), Sussex, and had (with two daus, of whom one, Bine or Byne *m* John Spence, of S Malling, Sussex, and Ledbury Manor, Herts):

1a Sir WALTER WALKER, 2nd and last Bt, DCL; *dspm*, when the btcy expired

(2) William; *m* but was living without issue 1692

3(?) Thomas, of Henley-on-Thames, Oxon; wheelwright; had:

(1) Joseph (he seems definitely to have been a kinsman of the Sir WALTER who lived 1600–74, being probably his n), of St James's, Westminster, described in his gs Nathaniel's will as cousin of Sir George Baker, 1st Bt; *m* 18 June 1698 Mary Price and *d* in or after 1714, leaving issue:

1a Nathaniel, of St James's; *b* 29 Oct 1700; builder; *m* Elizabeth Jane, dau of Peter Pytot, surgeon, and *d* 23 May 1753, having had, with other issue (*d* young):

1b Nathaniel, of Bedford St, Bloomsbury; *b* 26 April 1740; agent to Huntingdon Milita, Maj Roy American Rangers in War of Independence; *m* 5 May 1763 Henrietta (*d* May 1829), only dau and heir of Capt John Bagster, RN, of W Cowes, IOW, and Abergavenny, by Dorothy, dau of Daniel Hall, of Richmond, and *d* Jamaica Dec 1780, leaving:

1c GEORGE TOWNSHEND (Sir), **1st Bt**

2c Frederick Nathaniel, KCH, of the Manor Ho, Bushey, Herts; Gen RA; *m* 1809 Annabelle (*d* May 1827), yst dau of Maj Edward Cane, of Donnybrook, Dublin, and *d* 3 Feb 1857, leaving issue:

1d Edward Walter Forestier (Sir), KCB, of the Manor Ho, Bushey; *b* 1812; Gen cmdg Scots Fus Gds 1858; *m* 20 July 1843 Lady Jane

Ogilvie Grant (*d* 16 Sept 1861), only dau of 6th Earl of Seafield (*qv*), and *d* 27 July 1881, leaving:

1e Frederick William Edward Forestier (Sir), GCMG (1900), KCB (1894); *b* 1844; C-in-C Egypt 1891–95, Govr Gibralter 1905–10, Gen Col KOSB, KGStJ; *m* 1887 Mabel Louisa (*m* 2nd 1911 Capt Norman Ernest Playfair (*d* 1914)), yst dau of Col Ernest Ross, Northumberland Fus, and *d* 30 Aug 1910, leaving issue:

1f Ian Frederick Walter; *b* 1888; Lt Scots Gds

3c Charles Montagu Hudleston; *b* 1779; Capt RN; *m* 5 Oct 1811 Anna Maria (*d* 22 Feb 1859), dau and heir of Walter Riddell, of Glenriddell, and *d* 9 July 1833, having had issue

1c Mary; *m* Stawell Chudleigh, of Furze Place Farm, Hants, and *d* 4 Jan 1843

2c Harriet Louisa; *m* James Grierson

Maj NATHANIEL WALKER's est s,

Sir George Townshend Walker, 1st Bt (UK), so *cr* 28 March 1835, GCB (1817, KCB 1815); *b* 25 May 1764; Ensign 95th Foot1782, Lt 1783, tfd 71st Foot 1783, tfd 36th Foot 1784 (served Poligar Campaign India), exchanged into 35th Foot 1787, ADC to Gen Bruce in Ireland 1788, Capt-Lt 14th Foot 1789, Capt 60th Foot 1791 (served Flanders Campaign 1793–94), Maj 1796, ADC to Gen Simon Fraser and Prince of Waldeck in Portugal 1797, Lt-Col 50th Foot 1798 (served Portugal, Malta, Ireland, Copenhagen expedn), served Peninsula War 1808–14 (*see* also note under the blazon), Col 1808, Brig-Gen 1810, Maj-Gen 1811, wounded at storming of Badajoz 1812 (where his bde played a crucial part, also present Orthes; *see* note under blazon), Kt Cdr Portuguese Order Tower and Sword, Lt-Gen 1821,C-in-C Madras 1825–31, Lt-Govr Roy Hosp Chelsea 1837, Gen 1838, Col 50th Regt 1839, Groom of Chamber to DUKE OF SUSSEX; *m* 1st Anna (*d* 15 Feb 1814), dau of Richard Allen, of Bury, Lancs, and had two daus (*d* unm); *m* 2nd 15 Aug 1820 Helen (*d* 23 Aug 1859), yst dau and coheir of Alexander Caldcleugh, of Broad Green, Croydon, and *d* 14 Nov 1842, leaving by her, with another dau (*d* unm):

1 GEORGE FERDINAND RADZIVILL (Sir), **2nd Bt**

2 George Frederick Arthur; *b* 12 Jan 1827; 43rd Regt; *d* 25 May 1845

3 George Edmund Lushington; *b* 16 Oct 1828; Maj-Gen; *m* 24 Feb 1852 Camilla Georgina (*d* 1876), only dau of Maj-Gen J Patrick Calder, RE, and *d* 6 May 1893, leaving, with three other daus (*d* unm):

(1) Edmond Somerville Forestier; *b* 10 May 1860; Lt-Col RA; *m* 1887 Ellen Mary Camilla (*d* 15 Dec 1939), dau of Maj F A Fenton, Madras SC, and *d* 29 Nov 1922, leaving, with a dau (*d* young):

1a Edmond Alec WALKER later FORESTIER-WALKER (deed poll 1909); *b* 4 Sept 1888; *educ* Wellington; Col RTC, Capt Cheshire Regt WW I (despatches), Cdr of a Sub-Area WW II; *m* 7 July 1921 Eileen de Renzy (*d* 11 Sept 1977), 4th dau of Col Osborne Henry Channer, IMS, of Fordingbridge, Hants, and *d* 9 Oct 1952, leaving issue:

1b +Edmond Annesley [Maj Edmond Forestier-Walker, Broombank, Aldeburgh, Suffolk IP15 5PQ]; *b* 27 May 1922; *educ* Felsted; Maj RA WW II N Africa and Italy with 12th HAC Regt RHA (despatches), admin manager Touche Ross 1969–83; *m* 1st 12 Aug 1944 Bridget (*d* 22 Dec 1961), 3rd dau of Cdr Sir Geoffrey Henry Hughes-Onslow, KBE, DSC, JP, RN (*see* ONSLOW, E), and has issue:

1c +(George) Clive; *b* 17 April 1946; *educ* Wellington and RMA Sandhurst; Maj Coldstream Gds; *m* 8 April 1970 *(Ruth) Christian, yst dau of John Gurney, JP, of Walsingham Abbey, Norfolk (*see* OGILVY, Bt), and has:

1d *Camilla Christian; *b* 1973; *m* 27 Aug 1994 *Robert Byk, yst s of Peter Byk, of Swanley, Kent

2d *Susanna Charlotte; *b* 1976

3d *Liza Bridget; *b* 1980

4d *Mary Sarah; *b* 1983

1c *Sally Eileen; *b* 30 Nov 1948; *m* 1972 *Mark Andrew Muspratt-Williams, only s of Lt-Col M J Muspratt-Williams, and has:

1d *Alexander Mark; *b* 3 March 1977

1d *Catriona Louise; *b* 1975

1b (cont.) Maj Edmond Forestier-Walker *m* 2nd 25 April 1966 *Dreenagh Denise, dau of Kenneth G Chavasse, of London, and by her has:

2c +David Anthony; *b* 8 Sept 1972

2c *Annabel Dreenagh; *b* 28 June 1974

2b +Claude Osborne [Claude Forestier-Walker Esq, Babbacombe, Snape Bridge, Saxmundham, Suffolk IP17 1ST]; *b* 15 March 1924; *educ* Felsted; *m* 30 Sept 1950 *Gillian Mary, only dau of Maj Guy Richard Pedder, of Park Ho, Hoxne, Norfolk, and has issue:

1c +Hugh Anthony Claude [Hugh Forestier-Walker Esq, Kencot Hill Farmhouse, Filkins, Glos GL7 3QY]; *b* 12 March 1954; *educ* Abbotsholme; co dir; *m* 1976 *(Elizabeth) Jane, yr dau of Rev Christopher Halhed Lovett Birdwood (*see* BIRDWOOD, B), and has issue:

1d +Edward; *b* 6 Oct 1982

1d *Caroline Louise; *b* 24 Aug 1978

2d *Rebecca Jane; *b* 1980

1c *Melanie Diana; *b* 3 April 1956

2c *Katherine Susan; MA Cantab; jnlst; *b* 4 April 1960; *m* 1988 *Zhang Zeming, of Hong Kong, and has issue:

1d *Lydia Yishi; *b* 1990

2d *Laura Yiya; *b* 1992

2a Claude Frederick, CBE (1945, OBE 194–), MC (1916) and bar (1917); *b* 1 Oct 1896; *educ* Bedford Sch; Brig 11th Hus, RA, WWs I (despatches twice) and II (despatches twice); *m* 1st 1 Dec 1926 (*divorce* 1930) Agnes Nivison, only dau of Sir William Dingwall Mitchell-Cotts, 1st Bt, KBE; *m* 2nd 25 March 1933 *Simone, yr dau of Lt-Col Mark Le Gallais, of Jersey

(2) Frederick Howard Forestier; *b* 10 March 1862; Lt E Kent Regt; *k* Tokar, Egypt, 4 Feb 1884

(3) George Townshend Forestier (Sir), KCB (1919, CB 1915); *b* 2 Aug 1866; *educ* Rugby and RMA Woolwich; Maj-Gen, T/Lt-Col, Chf Staff Offr and AQMG Somaliland 1903–04, AQMGS Cmd 1910–12, Brig-Gen Staff I Cmd 1912–14, Brig-Gen Gen Staff 1914–15, cmded 21st and 27th Div 1915–19, Col Cmdt RA 1931–36, ADC to HM GEORGE V 1907–15, Boer War 1899–1900 (despatches, Queen's medal with four clasps), E Africa 1902–04 (despatches twice, wounded, brevet, medal with two clasps) and WW I (despatches nine times), Grand Cross Order Redeemer Greece 2nd Cl, Cdr Legn Hon; *m* 17 Nov 1892 Lady Mary Liddell (*d* 24 April 1958), er dau of 2nd Earl of Ravensworth (*see* RAVENSWORTH, B), and *d* 23 Jan 1939, having had issue:

1a George Forestier; *b* and *d* 31 May 1898

2a Cortlandt Simon Michael Forestier; *b* 20 Nov 1902; *d* 29 Aug 1903

1a Lilian Diana Forestier; *b* 12 Jan 1894; *d* 5 Aug 1922

2a Helen Mary Cecilia Forestier; *b* 17 April 1895

(4) Claude Edward Forestier; *b* 19 Feb 1868; DSO (1917); Lt-Col RA WW I (despatches, wounded); *m* 29 June 1897 Ethel (*d* 4 Oct 1932), dau of Capt Allix Wilkinson, 15th Regt, and *d* 29 Dec 1932, leaving issue:

1a Claudine Doris; *b* 6 April 1898; *m* 23 July 1932 Cdr Robert Maxwell Grenfell Knight, RN, yr s of Edward Joseph Knight, of Pencoed, Glamorgan

2a Aura Camilla Desmond; *b* 25 May 1905; *m* 4 Oct 1930 Lt-Col Ian James Kilgour, 5th Fus, of Blackthorn Cottage, Bampton, Oxford, s of Col Henry Kilgour, 5th Fus, and had issue:

1b *Joanna Camilla Walker; *m* 30 May 1953 *Sir Mark Annesley Norman, 3rd Bt (*qv*), and has issue

(1) Eva Catherine Forestier; *m* 17 Feb 1887 Sir Courtenay Bourchier Vyvyan, 10th Bt (*qv*), and *d* 3 Jan 1928, having had issue

(2) Camilla Sophia Forestier; *d* unm 19 Feb 1953

(3) Vera Helen Forestier; *m* 16 Oct 1907 William Douglas Braithwaite (*d* 25 June 1944), er s of Rev Canon P R P Braithwaite, Res Canon Winchester, and *d* 26 April 1956, leaving issue

4 George Albert Augustus; *b* 28 Jan 1834; Capt RHA; *d* 1881

1 Anna Matilda Catherine; *m* 1st 24 Sept 1851 Maj Henry William Paget (*see* ANGLESEY, M); *m* 2nd 8 June 1880 Maj-Gen Sir William Scrase Dickens, KCB (*d* 29 June 1914), 3rd s of Charles Scrase Dickins, DL, of Coolhurst, and *d* 23 June 1901, leaving issue

Sir GEORGE's est s,

Sir GEORGE FERDINAND RADZIVILL WALKER later FORESTIER-WALKER (deed poll 1893), **2nd Bt**, JP, DL; *b* 24 May 1825; Capt Coldstream Gds; *m* 9 Oct 1854 Hon Fanny Henrietta Morgan (*d* 2 Sept 1887), 3rd dau of 1st Baron Tredegar (*see* 1932 edn), and *d* 1 Aug 1896, leaving, with another s (*d* an infant):

1 **Sir George Ferdinand Forestier-Walker, 3rd Bt**, JP, DL Mon; *b* 7 July 1855; Maj Roy Welsh Fus; *m* 26 Aug 1897 Georgina (*d* 26 Sept 1910), yst dau of Robert Deane Chamberlain, 31st Regt, and *d* 18 July 1933, leaving:

(1) **Sir George Ferdinand Forestier-Walker, 4th Bt**, of Castleton, Mon; *b* 20 May 1899; *educ* Wellington and RMC Sandhurst; Maj Coldstream Gds; *d* unm 1 Oct 1976

(2) Godfrey George; *b* 3 Sept 1901; *d* 15 Oct 1906

(1) Nesta; *b* 8 June 1900; *m* 25 April 1931 Capt Robert Orlando Rodolph Kenyon-Slaney (*see* KENYON, B) and *d* 22 Feb 1947, having had issue

2 Radzivill Frederick; *b* 13 July 1856; *m* 9 Oct 1894 (*divorce* 1905) Eva Laura (*d* 4 March 1947), 2nd dau of Col Francis Justice, of Craig-yr-Hall, Cardiff, and *d* 2 July 1934, leaving issue:

(1) Radzivill Clive; *b* 23 July 1895; Lt RE; *m* 11 June 1921 Kathleen Rose (*d* 1975), dau of William George Tinkler, of King's Lynn, Norfolk, and *d* 1973, leaving issue:

1a **Sir Clive Radzivill Forestier-Walker, 5th Bt**; *b* 30 April 1922; *m* 1st 22 Sept 1948 (*divorce* 1976) Pamela Mercy, dau of Clifford Leach, of Chiswick, and *dspm* 14 March 1983, leaving issue:

1b *Lesley Jane [Mrs John Wheaton, 23 Grove Rd, Rayleigh, Essex SS6 8PU]; *b* 15 Jan 1951; *m* 1968 *John Wheaton and has issue:

1c *Joanna Lesley; *b* 1970

2c *Jacqueline; *b* 1971

2b *Heather [Mrs John Gray, 28 Grove Rd, Rayleigh, Essex SS6 8PU]; *b* 24 June 1954; *m* 1972 *John Gray and has issue:

1c *Steven John; *b* 1977

2c *Adam James; *b* 1981

3b *Elizabeth [Mrs David King, 21 Juniper Rd, Leigh-on-Sea, Essex SS9 4BQ]; *b* 23 Feb 1958; *m* 1974 *David King and has issue:

1c *Daniel David; *b* 1975

1c *Kerryann; *b* 1976

1a *June Vivienne; *b* 1 Dec 1923; *m* 22 March 1954 *Leonard Raymond Hayes, s of James Roberts Hayes

3 Clarence Francis; *b* 8 Aug 1857; *m* 15 Oct 1891 Blanche Lancaster (*d* 21 Feb 1933), dau of George Thomas Clark, DL, of Tal-y-Garn, Glamorgan, and *dsp* 28 March 1907

4 Ivor Augustus; *b* 14 Oct 1860; *m* 1st 23 Sept 1891 Georgina (*dsp* 18 May 1910), dau of John Osborne, QC; *m* 2nd 30 July 1912 Agnes Maud (*d* 4 Feb 1949), er dau of Rev Caleb Baskett Mayhew, of Arran, St Albans, and *d* 31 Aug 1928, leaving issue:

(1) Alan Ivor, MBE (1950); *b* 1 Dec 1913; *educ* Newton Coll, Newton Abbot, and RMA Sandhurst; Lt-Col 7th Gurkha Rifles, Lt Welch Regt, WW II (POW), tfd to RA 1947 and Gurkhas 1948, Malaya 1948–51 (despatches), GSO(2) War Office; *m* 24 Sept 1945 Margaret Joan, only dau of Maj Henry Bennett Marcoolyn, MBE, IA, and was *ka* Malaya 2 Feb 1954, leaving issue:

1a Sir MICHAEL LEOLIN FORESTIER-WALKER, **6th and present Bt**

1a *Michelle [Mrs Christopher Metz, North Brook End House, Steeple Morden, Herts SG8 0PJ]; *b* 21 July 1946; *m* 1970 *Christopher Metz and has:

1b *Camilla; *b* 28 July 1977

2b *Rosamond; *b* 1979

3b *Marguerite; *b* 1984

(2) Urbain Evelyn; *b* 16 Jan 1915; *educ* Newton Coll, Newton Abbot, and Jesus Coll Cambridge; WW II in RAFVR; *m* 6 Sept 1941 Aileen (*d* 1976), MCSP, dau of Thomas Morrissey, and *d* 1974, leaving issue:

1a +Alan David; *b* 29 Aug 1944; *educ* Prior Park Coll Bath and RMA Sandhurst; Lt 1st Bn 7th Duke of Edinburgh's Own Gurkha Rifles; *m* 7 Nov 1969 *Adela Judith, dau of Simon Philip Davis, of Hampstead, and has:

1b +Robin Peter; *b* 1978

1b *Clare Elaine; *b* 1971

2b *Louise Anne; *b* 1972

1a *Anne Patricia; *b* 9 Aug 1942

5 Devereux Philip; *b* 25 July 1864; Capt Queen's Own (Roy W Kent Regt); *m* 2 Jan 1896 Isabella Constance (*d* 18 March 1949), dau of Frederick Gonnerman Dalgety, of Lockerley Hall, Hants, and widow of Capt Charles William Selwyn, RHG, and *d* 10 Sept 1936, leaving issue:

(1) *Freda Gladys; *b* 10 April 1897; *m* 17 May 1921 William Henry Cartwright (*d* 4 Jan 1962), Coldstream Gds, s of E C Cartwright, and has:

1a +Julian William Devereux [Julian Cartwright Esq, 400 Trail St, Kimberley, BC, Canada]; *b* 10 Oct 1923; late RCAF; *m* 18 April 1949 *Margaret Elaine, dau of E Ewing, and has issue:

1b *Elena Marr; *b* 22 May 1950; *m* 1976 *Donald John Rouse

2b *Lorena Joanne; *b* 13 Nov 1951; *m* 1972 *Jacobus Antonius Ferdinand Remak and has issue:

1c *Jason William Johannes; *b* 1976

3b *Shelley Rae; *b* 5 Feb 1953; *m* 1973 *Terrance Glenn Pruden

4b *Tracy Dell; *b* 22 April 1961

1a *Barbara Mary; *b* 8 March 1922; *m* 27 Jan 1954 *John Bannatyne McLeod, s of Earl Rohra Baugh McLeod, of Calgary, Canada

(2) Honor Dorothy; *b* 4 Jan 1899; *m* 8 Feb 1934 Capt Thomas Willington Lane (*d* 1977), RA, s of Frederick Robbins Lane, of Woodborough Manor, nr Marlborough, and had issue:

1a *Patrick Anthony Willington [Patrick Lane Esq, 28 High St, Manton, Marlborough, Wilts SN8 4HH]; *b* 14 April 1938; *educ* Millfield; *m* 1978 *Dinah, dau of B W Righton, of Town Farm, Ebrington, Glos, and has issue:

1b *Martin Nicholas; *b* 1980

1b *Sarah Ann; *b* 1979

1a *Gillian; *b* 17 Feb 1935

6 Sir (CHARLES) LEOLIN WALKER later FORESTIER-WALKER, 1st and last Bt (UK), so *cr* 27 June 1929, KBE (1925), JP, DL Mon; *b* 6 May 1866; chm Mon CC 1923–24, Welsh Church Commr, MP Monmouth 1918–34, Parly Forestry Commr 1920–29, KGStJ; *m* 26 June 1894 Alice (*d* 13 Nov 1950), est dau of Col John Blandy-Jenkins, JP, DL, of Llanharan, Glamorgan, and *dspm* 13 May 1934, when the btcy expired, leaving:

(1) Rosemary; *b* 27 Aug 1898; *m* 16 July 1925 John David Griffiths, est s of William Griffiths, of Merthyr, and *d* 23 March 1958, leaving issue

(2) Daphne; *b* 3 Dec 1902; *m* 25 April 1922 (*divorce* 1947) Maj Gavin David Young, Welsh Gds, only s of George Young, of Bude, Cornwall, and had issue

7 Roland Stuart, DSO (1916); *b* 30 Oct 1871; Lt-Col and Brevet-Col Roy Mon RE Mil (Hon Col 1936), Boer War 1900–01 and WW I (despatches twice); *m* 1st 14 April 1904 (*divorce* 1918) Olive (*d* 4 July 1926), yr dau of Ralph Thurstan Basset, of Crossways, Glam; *m* 2nd 18 Jan 1921 Norah Jacintha (*d* 22 Feb 1935), 2nd dau of Charles Nicholas Paul Phipps, of Calcot, Wilts, and widow of Sir John Michael Fleetwood Fuller, 1st Bt, KCMG, and *d* 20 Feb 1938

8 Charles Evelyn, JP Glam; *b* 14 April 1875; *m* 27 April 1905 Ada Llewelyn (*d* 17 Sept 1960), yst dau of Col Robert Henry Mansel, JP, DL, of Abergavenny and Caerleon, Mon, and *d* 7 June 1931, leaving issue:

(1) Evelyn Rodney; *b* 20 March 1906; *educ* Wellington; *m* 29 June 1935 Mollie Dora, LGSM, portrait painter, er dau of John Clifford Wing, of Abbot's Leigh, Somerset, and *d* 10 Oct 1959

(2) Charles Jocelyn; *b* 18 July 1912; *educ* Wellington; WW II in RE; FRMetS; *m* 25 July 1942 *Joy, er dau of Lt-Cdr John Robert Gill, RNR, of Christchurch, Newport, Mon, and *d* 1992, leaving issue:

1a +Charles Robert Piers [Charles Forestier-Walker Esq, Bron Garnedd, Llanfrothen, Penrhyndeudraeth, N Wales]; *b* 14 April 1950; *educ* Wellington; *m* 1974 (*divorce* 1979) Phillippa Jean White, step-dau of Dr C Bondy, and has issue:

1b +Rowan; *b* 1977

1a *Elenith Camilla [Mrs James Allen, 46 Hertford St, Cambridge CB4 3AG]; *b* 28 Sept 1947; *m* 1st 20 Feb 1968 (*divorce* 1982) Malcolm Anthony Luker, s of Malcolm Gilbert Luker, of Poole, Dorset, and has issue:

1b *James Robert; *b* 16 March 1971

2b *Benjamin Gavin; *b* 1975

1a (cont.) Mrs Elenith Luker *m* 2nd 1983 *James Stephen Allen and by him has:

3b *Richard Arthur Llewellyn; *b* 1983

4b *Charles Alexander Titus; *b* 1988

1b *Camilla Imogen Maud; *b* 1984

(3) (Robert Jestyn) Gwent; *b* 2 Oct 1919; *educ* Wellington; FRIBA, F/Lt RAFVR WW II (despatches); *m* 3 Aug 1956 *(Elizabeth) Ann [Mrs Gwent Forestier-Walker, Barberry Ho, Clifford, Herefs HR3 5HF], er dau of Brig John Harte Harris Willans, RA, and *d* 28 Sept 1994, leaving:

1a +(Charles) Aidan Gwent; *b* 11 Feb 1966

1a *(Evelyn) Rosamond; *b* 7 Aug 1961; *m* 1987 (*divorce* 1990) Hon Hugh Francis Kindersley (*d* 1991), 2nd s of 3rd Baron Kindersley (*qv*)

2a *Vivien Serena Charlotte; *b* 10 March 1963; *m* 19– *G Nicholas Tucker, s of Maj K O Tucker, and has:

1b *Harry Albert; *b* 1994

3a *(Daphne) Miranda Clare; *b* 11 Nov 1964

FORRES

Arms: Arg. a saltire wavy between a mullet in chief and another in base, and as many boar's heads couped in the flanks sa., armed and langued gu. **Crest:** A garb or. **Supporters:** Two condors ppr. **Motto:** *Modice augetur modicum* ('Little is made larger by little'). **Creation:** Bt. (UK) 29 July 1909, B. (UK) 19 June 1922.

THE 4TH BARON FORRES, of Glenogil, Co Forfar, and a **Baronet** (Sir Alastair Stephen Grant Williamson, Bt) [The Rt Hon The Lord Forres, 4 Arthur St, Edgecliffe, NSW 2027, Australia]; *b* 16 May 1946; *s* f 1978; *educ* Eton; chm Agriscot Pty, dir Jaga Trading Pty, Australian Rep Tattersalls; *m* 2 May 1969 *Margaret Ann, dau of George John Mallam, of Mullumbimby, NSW, and has:

1 +GEORGE ARCHIBLAD MALLAM; *b* 16 Aug 1972

2 +Guthrie John; *b* 14 April 1975

Lineage: ARCHIBALD WILLIAMSON, of Anstruther, Fife; *b* 25 Jan 1787; *d* 7 Sept 1847, leaving:

STEPHEN WILLIAMSON, of Copley, Thornton Hough, Cheshire, and Glenogil, Forfarshire; MP St Andrews 1880–85 and Kilmarnock 1886–95; *b* 28 June 1827; *m* 27 April 1859 Annie (*d* 15 Nov 1922), dau of Rev Thomas Guthrie, DD, of Edinburgh and *d* 17 June 1903, leaving issue:

1 ARCHIBALD, **1st Baron**

2 Thomas Guthrie; *b* 11 April 1863; *m* 6 Jan 1894 Vera (*m* 2nd 8 March 1919 John Alfred Turner, who *d* 23 July 1924), dau of Francis Caesar Braun, and *d* 14 Nov 1917, leaving issue:

(1) Dorothea Guthrie; *m* 19 Nov 1914 Harold Molyneux Fletcher, yst s of Alfred Fletcher, JP, DL, of Allerton, Lancs, and had issue. He *d* 23 Sept 1944

3 Alexander Balfour; *b* 20 June 1865; *m* 24 April 1901 Louisa Clifton (*d* 18 Nov 1956), est dau of James Clifton Brown (*see* BROWN Bt), and *d* 27 Oct 1930

4 Stephen Anstruther, of Valparaiso, Chile; *b* 1 Jan 1867; *m* 25 Jan 1900 Elena (*d* 2 July 1967 aged 92), er dau of William Macqueen, of Valparaiso, and *d* 23 Dec 1919, leaving issue:

(1) Stephen Guthrie; *b* 1900; had issue

(2) William Henry; *b* 1908; had issue

(3) Cyril Edgar; *b* 1907; *m* 1941 Elizabeth, dau of Henry Timewell Down, of Westfield, NJ, and had:

1a *Peter Anstruther; *b* 1949

1a *Jane; *b* 1947

(1) Evelyn Mary; *b* 1904

(2) *Louisa Clementine; *b* 10 Sept 1911; *m* 14 Sept 1938 Bernard Vaughan, s of Patrick William Vaughan, of Essex. He *dsp* 11 Oct 1959

(3) Sylvia Anne; *b* 1902; *m* 1928 Arthur S Armstrong and *d* 1945, having had issue. He *d* 31 Dec 1957

(4) Julia Helen; *b* 1909; *m* 1st Geoffrey Francis Friend and had two daus; *m* 2nd Edward Jesser-Coope and had a dau; *m* 3rd Ronald Edward Welton and *d* 1958. He *d* 1964

5 Charles James; *b* 15 May 1871; *m* 30 June 1897 Quenelda Mary (*m* 2nd 20 April 1922 1st Baron Royden, CH (*d* 6 Nov 1950; *see* 1949 edn), and *d* 17 Feb 1969), est dau of Harry Clegg, DL, of Plas Llanfair, Anglesey, and *d* 15 Jan 1921, leaving:

(1) Marjorie Guthrie; *b* 1898; *m* 26 May 1920 Maj Sir (Arthur) Harold Bibby, 1st Bt (*qv*), and *d* 1985, leaving issue

(2) Quenelda Anne; *m* 1st 30 March 1922 (*divorce* 1930) Thomas Humphrey Naylor, of The Grange, Ashton, Cheshire, 2nd s of John Naylor, JP, of Leighton Hall, Welshpool, Montgomeryshire, and had issue; *m* 2nd — Stedman and *d* 1941

6 Norman Welsh; *b* 14 Dec 1874; *m* 14 Nov 1901 Constance Marion (*d* 23 Sept 1959), 2nd dau of A Marmaduke Tulk-Hart, of Vicarage Park, Woolwich, and *d* 1 Jan 1954

7 Henry Cecil Roxburgh; *b* 5 March 1879; *m* 17 Nov 1909 Muriel de la Praed Stewart (*d* 5 Sept 1960), ward of Rt Hon Charles Stuart Parker, of Fairlie, Ayrshire, and had:

(1) *Archibald

1 Anita Guthrie; *b* 1 Dec 1868; *m* 7 June 1897 Ernest Freshfield Dent, of Broughton House, Stockbridge, Hants, est s of Rev Joseph Jonathan Dent, Vicar Hunsingore, Wetherby, and *d* 31 Jan 1948, leaving issue. He *d* 27 March 1959

The est s,

Sir Archibald Williamson, 1st Bt, and **1st Baron Forres**, of Glenogil, Co Forfar (both UK), so *cr* 29 July 1909 and 19 June 1922 respectively, PC (1918); MP (Lib) Elgin and Nairn 1906–18 and Moray and Nairn 1918–22, chm Centl Argentine Rlwy and Lobitos Oilfields, ptnr Balfour, Williamson & Co, merchants, Fin Sec War Office, Memb Army Cncl 1919–21; *b* 13 Sept 1860; *m* 1st 7 June 1887 Caroline Maria (*d* 3 June 1911), est dau of James Charles Hyne, of S Kensington, and had:

1 STEPHEN KENNETH GUTHRIE, **2nd Baron**

2 Gerald Hayne Guthrie; Capt TAR; chm Balfour, Williamson & Co; *b* 14 Jan 1893; *educ* Eton; *m* 5 May 1917 Christian Alice Hersey (*d* 26 Jan 1958), er dau of Edmund Batten Forbes (*see* STUART-FORBES, Bt), and *d* 9 June 1966, leaving:

(1) (Alexander) Fergus Forbes; Lt RNVR WW II; *b* 12 March 1919; *educ* Eton; *m* 22 Dec 1943 *Sabrina Ann [Mrs Fergus Williamson, Tigh-na-Coille, Kincraig, by Kingussie, Inverness-shire], late WRNS, only dau of Col Sir Dermot McMorrough Kavanagh, GCVO, and *d* 1987, leaving issue:

1a +James David Alexander [James Williamson Esq, Alvie, Kincraig, by Kingussie, Inverness-shire]; *b* 1 July 1947; *educ* Gordonstoun, U of New Brunswick and Aberdeen U (BSc, PhD); *m* 1976 *Lynette Robyn, only dau of James Stewart, of New Feilding, NZ, and has issue:

1b +Ruaraidh James Stewart; *b* 1976

1b *Joanna Mary; *b* 1980

2b *Catherine Ngaire; *b* 1985

2a +Dermot Fergus; *b* 15 Sept 1950; *educ* Eton and Dundee U; *m* 1987 *Yu Yu Su, of Beijing, and has:

1b *Paula Jiao-Jiao; *b* 1988

2b *Emma Tian-Tian; *b* 1989

1a *Caroline Ann [Mrs Colin MacGregor, The Dairy House, Corton Denham, Dorset DT9 4LX]; *b* 13 Nov 1945; *m* 26 Oct 1968 *Capt Colin Laird MacGregor, RN, yr s of Lt-Col Raymond Guy MacGregor, of Burley, Hants, and has:

1b *James Patrick; *b* 1972

1b *Katherine Helen; *b* 20 Feb 1970

2a *Rolline Charlotte [Mrs Robert Frewen, Park Hall, Healaugh, Richmond, N Yorks DL11 6UL]; *b* 31 Aug 1956; *m* 1989 *Robert Edward Jerome Frewen and has issue (*see* SELBY, V)

(2) David Archibald Forbes, MC, Capt 11th Hus WW II; *b* 30 Oct 1922; *educ* Eton; *m* 31 Jan 1953 *Elizabeth Wilbur [Mrs David Williamson, 33 Fifth Avenue, San Francisco, CA, USA], dau of Roy Case, of Seattle, and *d* 1980, leaving:

1a Bruce; *b* and *d* 21 Jan 1957

2a +(David) Stephen Charles; *b* 10 Aug 1958; *m* 1st 19– Susan; *m* 2nd 1994 *Alexandra Bomes and has by her:

1b *Daisy Case; *b* 1995

3a +Alexander Fergus Case; *b* 21 Nov 1960; *m* 1997 *Amy Baker

1a *Charlotte Mary; *b* 12 Aug 1955

(1) *Hersey Caroline Ann [Mrs Hersey Robertson, Barr, Minard, by Inveraray, Argyll PA32 8YB]; Jr Cdr ATS M East 1942–44 (despatches) and Italy 1944–45 (despatches); *b* 14 Aug 1920; *m* 1st 9 Feb 1943 Lt Oliver Breakwell, Coldstream Gds (*ka* N Africa March 1943), s of E R Breakwell, of Kilburn; *m* 2nd 5 May 1945 (*divorce* 1973) Maj Donald Struan Robertson (*d* 1991), Scots Gds, only surv s of Sir Malcolm Arnold Robertson, GCMG, KBE, PC, and by him has had:

1a Melville Alexander Struan; *b* 24 June 1946; *educ* Eton; *d* unm 2 March 1969

1a *Christian Sarah Hersey [Mrs Pierre Daviron, 92 Greenhaver Rd, Rye, NY 10580, USA]; *b* 27 May 1948; *m* 1984 *Pierre Henri René Daviron and has issue:

1b *Olivier Melville Raoul; *b* 1985

1b *Juliette Isabelle Christian; *b* 1987

2a *Alexandra Charlotte [Mrs James Blair, Marvins Farmhouse, Kingston Deverill, Wilts BA12 7HG]; *b* 16 June 1952; *m* 1980 *James Chandos Blair and has issue:

1b *Hamish Chandos; *b* 1982

1b *Charlotte Rose; *b* 1985

3a *Lucinda Margaret Ann [Mrs Stephen Mahony, Broadclose House, Babcary, Somerset TA11 7ED]; *b* 23 July 1960; *m* 1983 *Stephen Dominic Patrick Mahony and has issue:

1b *Dermot Edward Struan; *b* 1988

1b *Caroline Mary Hersey; *b* 1987

(2) *Jane Christian Forbes [Miss Jane Williamson, Balnespick, Kincraig, by Kingussie, Inverness-shire PH21 1NX]; *b* 11 March 1931

1 Winifred Elspeth Guthrie; *b* 12 June 1891; *m* 1st 12 June 1912 (*divorce* 1941) John Murray Naylor, JP, of Upham, Hants, and Chelsea, late of Leighton Hall, Montgomeryshire, and had issue. He *d* 25 Oct 1969. She *m* 2nd 5 July 1941 Capt Theobald John Claud Purcell-Buret, CBE, DSO, Cdre Royal Mail Fleet 1939–42, s of John Claud Buret, of London, by Alice Maria, est dau of John Purcell, of Kilkenny, and *d* 30 April 1965

The **1st Baron** *m* 2nd 27 Nov 1912 Hon Agnes Freda Herschell, OBE (1920), DGStJ (*d* 5 May 1942), dau of 1st Baron Herschell (*qv*), and *d* 29 Oct 1931

His er s,

STEPHEN KENNETH GUTHRIE WILLIAMSON, **2nd Baron Forres**; *b* 20 March 1888; *educ* Eton and Trin Coll Cambridge (BA); Maj Westminster Dragoons TA WW I (despatches), dir Balfour, Williamson & Co, chm Lobitos Oilfields, Dir-Gen Office Machinery BOT 1942–45; *m* 26 Sept 1918 Jessica (*d* 4 July 1972), er dau of William Alfred Harford, JP, of Petty France, Badminton, and had:

1 JOHN ARCHIBALD HARFORD, **3rd Baron**

2 Angus Stephen; *b* 19 Dec 1929

1 *Jean Mary [The Hon Mrs Longmore, Cross Lane Cottage, Bishops Waltham, Hants SO3 1FL]; *b* 17 June 1919; *m* 28 April 1941 W/Cdr William James Maitland Longmore, CBE, RAF (*d* 1988; *see* MAITLAND, Bt), 2nd s of ACM Sir Arthur Longmore, GCB, DSO, and has:

(1) *Virginia Marjorie; *b* 17 Jan 1945; *m* 28 Nov 1973 *Henry D N B Candy, s of Derrick Warren John Candy, of Kingston Warren, Berks, and has issue:

1a *Emma Juliet; *b* 1974

2a *Sophie Bridget; *b* 1978

(2) *Carolyn Mary [Mrs Michael Poland, Lower Preshaw House, Upham, Hants SO32 1HP]; *b* 26 Aug 1946; *m* 1st 6 June 1966 (*divorce* 1976) Michael Edward Denison, CA, yr s of Brig Edward Wolseley Denison, of Chobham, Surrey; *m* 2nd 1981 *Michael Desmond Poland (*see* STAFFORD, B) and by her 1st husb has:

1a *James Edward; *b* 22 June 1968; *m* 1994 *Sara Jane Evans, of Arreton, IoW

1a *Lucinda Mary; *b* 1971

(3) *Jennifer Maitland [Mrs Patrick Snowball, The Old Rectory, Longham, Norfolk NR19 2RG]; *b* 29 Jan 1953; *m* 27 Sept 1975 *Capt Patrick J R Snowball, 4/7th R Dragoon Gds, er s of Brig E J D Snowball, of Ballochneck, Thornhill, Stirling, and has issue:

1a *Robert Joseph Arthur; *b* 1981

2a *Thomas Edward James; *b* 1984

3a *Edward William George; *b* 1990

The 2nd BARON *d* 26 June 1954; his er s,

JOHN ARCHIBALD HARFORD WILLIAMSON, **3rd Baron Forres**; *b* 30 Oct 1922; *educ* Eton and Trin Coll Cambridge; Capt Black Watch WW II (despatches); *m* 1st 21 Aug 1945 (*divorce* 1967) Gillian Ann MacLean (*m* 2nd 1968 Miles Herman de Zoete (*d* 1987)), er dau of Maj John McLean Grant, RA, and had:

1 ALASTAIR STEPHEN GRANT WILLIAMSON, **4th and present Baron Forres**

1 *Juliet Anne [The Hon Mrs Bankes, Home Farm House, Williamscott, Oxon]; *b* 29 Aug 1949; *m* March 1972 *Nigel John Eldon Bankes, er s of John Wynne Bankes, of St John's Wood, and has:

(1) *William Nigel Wynne; *b* 1974

(1) *Louisa Juliet; *b* 1977

(2) *Fiona Gillian; *b* 1981

2 *Astrid Signe; *b* 20 Dec 1951; *m* 21 Aug 1976 *Peter Karl Dobrée Bell, er s of G/Capt P M Dobrée Bell, and has:

(1) *Hugh John; *b* 1982

(1) *Lucy Claire; *b* 1984

The **3rd Baron Forres** *m* 2nd 22 Sept 1969 (*divorce* 1974) (Cecily) Josephine (*m* 3rd 1982 3rd Earl Lloyd George of Dwyfor (*qv*)), widow of 2nd Earl of Woolton (*qv*) and er dau of Maj Sir Alexander Penrose Gordon Cumming, 5th Bt (*qv*), and *d* 22 Sept 1978

FORTE

Arms: Argent four pallets gules, over all a bend argent fimbriated azure and on a chief azure three mullets of six points gyronny of twelve or and argent. **Crest:** Out of the battlements of a tower azure a bunch of grapes between two ears of corn proper.
Supporters: Dexter, a pheasant proper; sinister, a salmon proper.
Motto: *Fortis ut jus* ('Strong like justice').
Creation: B. (LP, UK) 1982.

THE BARON FORTE, of Ripley, Co Surrey (Sir Charles Forte) [The Rt Hon The Lord Forte, House of Lords, London SW1A 0PW]; *b* 26 Nov 1908; *educ* Alloa Academy, Dumfries Coll and Mamiani Rome; Fell and Memb Exec Ctee Catering Inst 1949–; Memb: Small Consultative Advsy Ctee Min Food 1946, Cncl BTA, London Tourist Bd; Pres Forte plc 1992–96 (chm 1982–92, exec chm 1978–81, dep chm 1970–78, ch exec 1971–78); ktd 1970, Hon Consul Gen Republic San Marino; FIMgt (FBIM 1971), FRSA, Hon DU Strathclyde 1992, Grand Offr Order Merit Italy, Kt Grand Coss Italy, Kt of Labour Italy; *m* Jan 1943 *Irene Mary, da of Giovanni Chierico, of Venice, and has issue:

1 *Rocco John Vincent (Sir) [The Hon Sir Rocco Forte, Savannah House, 11 Charles II St, London SW1]; *b* 1945; *educ* Downside and Pembroke Coll Oxford (MA); ch exec THF plc, dir BTA, Treas CPS 1998–, ktd 1995; FMICA, ACA; *m* 1986 *Aliai, yr dau of Prof Giovanni Ricci, of Rome, and has:

(1) *Charles; *b* 1991

(1) *Lydia Irene; *b* 1987

(2) *Irene; *b* 1988

1 *Olga, CBE (1990) [The Hon Mrs William Shawcross CBE, 3 Clarendon Close, London W2]; *b* 1947; *m* 1st 1966 Marchese Alessandro Polizzi di Sorrentino (*k* car crash 1980) and has issue:

(1) *Alexandra; *b* 1971; *educ* Oxford; manager Criterion Restaurant Piccadilly Circus

(2) *Charlotte; *b* 1974

1 (cont.) The Hon Mrs Polizzi *m* 2nd 1993, as his 3rd w, *Hon William Hartley Hume Shawcross, er s of Baron Shawcross (*qv*)

2 *Marie Louise [The Hon Mrs Burness, 4 Clarendon Close, London W2]; *b* 1950; *m* 1975 *Robert Alexander Burness, restaurateur, and has issue:

(1) *Georgina Gerda; *b* 1976; *educ* UCL; *m* 24 Jan 1988 *Kenneth Closs

(2) *Julia Irene; *b* 1978

3 *Irene [The Hon Mrs Danilovich, 37 Carlyle Sq, London SW3]; *b* 1956; *m* 1977 *John J Danilovich and has issue:

(1) *John Charles Amadeus; *b* 1981

(2) *Alexander Gregory; *b* 1993

(1) *Alice Irene Angelica; *b* 1985

4 *Giancarla [The Hon Mrs Alen-Buckley, 4 Lansdowne Rd, London W11]; *b* 1959; *m* 1981 *Michael Ulic Anthony Alen-Buckley and has:

(1) *Luke Charles Ulic Locke; *b* 1987

(1) *Portia; *b* 1991

5 *Portia; *b* 1964

Lineage: ROCCO GIOVANNI FORTE, of Casalattico, Italy; had:

CHARLES, *cr* a **Baron**

FORTESCUE

Arms: Az. a bend engrailed arg., plain cotised or. **Crest:** An heraldic tiger statant arg., armed, maned and tufted or. **Supporters:** Two greyhounds arg., ducally gorged and lined gu. **Motto:** *Forte scutum salus ducum* ('A strong shield is the salvation of leaders'). The French Fortescues (*see* below) bore argent three bends azure and in another case azure three bends argent. At one period the senior English line of Preston bore azure a bend argent (*i.e.*, with the bend unengrailed). The engraving and reduction of two of the bends to cotises would be a natural development of early differencing.

Creations: B. (GB) 5 July 1746, V. and E. (GB) 1 Sept 1789.

THE 8TH EARL FORTESCUE, Viscount Ebrington, Co Gloucester, and **Baron Fortescue of Castle Hill,** Co Devon (Charles Hugh Richard Fortescue) [The Rt Hon The Earl Fortescue, Ebrington Manor, Ebrington, Glos GL55 6NG]; *b* 10 May 1951; *s f* 1993; *educ* Eton; *m* 12 Dec 1974 *Julia B, er dau of A/Cdre John Adam Sowrey, of Aldgate, Keiton, Rutland, and Knightsbridge, and has:

1 *Alice Penelope; *b* 1978

2 *Kate Eleanor; *b* 1979

3 *Lucy Beatrice; *b* 1983

Lineage: It is held that the English FORTESCUEs were a cadet branch of those in Normandy, who were Seigneurs de St Evremont-sur-l'Ozanne and Mesnil-Angot.

RADULFUS FORTESCU; held land in Modbury parish, Devon; made gifts to Modbury Priory; seems to have been a youth in 1066; had:

RICHARD FORTESCU; also held land in Modbury parish; had:

RICHARD FORTESCU; *m* Ysemeine —; *fl* 1190–1200; f or gf of:

JOHN FORTESCUE of Wymondston, Modbury, which he was granted or confirmed as holding 1209; f(?) of:

Sir RICHARD FORTESCUE; granted his lands of Stoliford to Walter Faber of Modbury.

A certain ADAM FORTESCUE held Wymondston of the Honour of Tremeton by one knight's fee 1302; f of:

ADAM FORTESCUE, of Wympstone; granted lands there 1304; f(?) of:

ADAM FORTESCUE; *m* Anne, dau and coheir of William Delaport, and *d* by 1342, leaving issue:

WILLIAM de FORTESCU, of Wymondston; inherited his mother's estate of Oldport; *m* Alice, dau of Walter Strechleigh and *d* by 1375, leaving issue:

WILLIAM FORTESCU, of Wymondston; *d* after 1394, leaving issue:

WILLIAM FORTESCU, of Wymondston; *m* by 1394 Elisabeth, dau and eventual coheir of Sir John Beauchamp, of Ryme, and widow of Richard Branscombe, and had issue:

1 William, of Wimstone (Wymondston); ancestor of the FORTESCUEs of Wimston, Preston and Spridleston and the FORTESCUE Bts of Wood

2 John (Sir); Govr Meaux *temp* HENRY V; *m* Eleanor, dau and heir of William Norreis, and had, with other issue:

(1) Henry; Ld Ch Justice Common Pleas Ireland

(2) John (Sir); Ld Ch Justice England 25 Jan 1442, allegedly made Ld Chllr by HENRY VI after his deposition 1461; author: *De Laudibus Legum Anglice*; *m* Isabella, dau of John Jamys, and *d* Ebrington, Glos, aged 90, having had:

1a Martin; *m* 10 Sept 1454 Elizabeth (*m* 2nd Sir Richard Pomeroy), dau and heir of Richard Deynsell, of Filleigh and Wear Gifford, Devon, and *dvp* 12 Nov 1472, leaving issue:

1b JOHN

2b William, of Buckland Filleigh, Devon; ancestor of the FORTESCUEs of Buckland Filleigh, the FORTESCUEs of Dromisken and Ravensdale and the FORTESCUEs who were Barons 1770–1829, Viscounts 1776–1929 and Earls of Clermont 1777–1829

MARTIN FORTESCUE's er s,

JOHN FORTESCUE, of Filleigh and Wear Gifford; *b* 1460; *m* 1480 Jacquet, dau of Ralph St Leger, of Annery, and *d* 2 June 1503, leaving issue:

BARTHOLOMEW, of Filleigh and Wear Gifford; *m* Ellen, dau of Maurice Moore, of Moore Hays, and had:

RICHARD FORTESCUE, of Filleigh; *m* Joan Moreton and *d* 1570, leaving issue:

HUGH FORTESCUE; *m* Elizabeth, sis of Sir Arthur Chichester (*see* CHICHESTER, Bt), and had:

JOHN FORTESCUE; *m* Mary, dau of Humphry Speccot, and *d* 1605, leaving:

HUGH FORTESCUE; *m* 1612 Mary, dau of Robert Rolle, of Heanton Sackville, and *d* 1661, leaving, with other issue:

ARTHUR FORTESCUE, of Penwarne, Cornwall; *b* 6 Dec 1622; *m* Barbara, dau of John Elford, and *d* 1694, leaving an est s:

HUGH FORTESCUE, of Filleigh and Wear Gifford; MP; *m* 1st his cousin Bridget (*d* 1708), only dau and heir of Hugh Boscawen (*see* CLINTON, B and LINCOLN, E) and had:

1 HUGH FORTESCUE, **1st Baron Fortescue of Castle Hill**, Co Devon (GB), so *cr* 5 July 1749, with special remainder to his half-bro, as also 1st and last EARL CLINTON (both GB), with ordinary remainder to the heirs male of his body, KB (1725); *b* 1696; called to Parl 15 March 1720/1 as 14th LORD (Baron) CLINTON (*qv*), a title he inherited from his maternal grandmother; Ld Lt Devon 1721–23; *dsp* 3 May 1751, when the Earldom expired and the Barony of Clinton fell into abeyance

1 Margaret; *d unm* 14 March 1760

HUGH FORTESCUE; *m* 2nd Lucy (*d* 18 Feb 1767), dau of 1st Baron Aylmer (*qv*), and *d* 25 Nov 1710, leaving by her:

2 MATTHEW, **2nd Baron**

2 Lucy; *m* 15 June 1742 1st Baron Lyttelton (*see* COBHAM, V) and *d* 19 Jan 1746

The 1st BARON's half-bro,

MATTHEW FORTESCUE, **2nd Baron Fortescue of Castle Hill;** *b* 31 March 1719; *m* 8 July 1752 Anne (*d* 26 May 1812), 2nd dau of John Campbell (*see* CAWDOR, E), and had:

1 HUGH, **1st Earl**

2 Matthew; Capt RN; *b* 12 April 1754; *m* 1st 1 Nov 1778 Henrietta, dau of Col — Archer, and had issue:

(1) Matthew, of Belvedere, Dublin; *b* 1786; *m* 12 Oct 1811 Erskine (*d* 28 Oct 1868), 4th dau of James Christie, of Durie, Fife, and *d* 14 Aug 1852, leaving, with other issue:

1a Matthew Charles Maitland; *b* 14 Aug 1812; *m* 1849 Maria Jane (*d* 22 July 1884), dau of T K Bower, of Hereford, and *d* 11 Aug 1857

1a Mary Turner Erskine; *m* 23 June 1846 Capt Frederick J Isacke, 5th Fus, and had issue. He *d* 8 June 1885

2a Harriet Boswell Erskine; *m* 1 June 1852 Capt James Stirling Crawford Stirling-Stuart, of Castlemilk and Milton, King's Dragoon Gds, and *d* 5 April 1917, leaving issue. He *d* 8 June 1887

3a Margaret Lucy; *m* 22 Jan 1846 Martin de Winton Corry, of Yately Hall, Hants, and had issue. He *d* Feb 1885

(2) William (Rev); LLB, Rector Wear Gifford and George Nympton; *b* 1788; *m* 1st 6 Feb 1819 Isobel Barclay (*d* 11 Oct 1826), 2nd dau of James Christie, of Durie, Fife, and had issue:

1a Archer FORTESCUE later IRVINE-FORTESCUE (added 1875 under terms of will of his w's unc, John Irvine-Boswell), of Kingcausie, Kincardineshire, and Swanbister, Isle of Orkney, JP, DL Kincardineshire and Orkney; *b* 12 Dec 1819; *m* 31 Aug 1848 Anne Irvine (*d* 28 Aug 1909), dau of Patrick Syme, RSA, of Dollar (and gdau of Claud Irvine-Boswell, 12th of Balmuto, Fife, a Ld of Session as Lord Balmuto, and Anne Irvine, 10th of Kingcausie), and *d* 7 Feb 1907, having had, with other issue:

1b William Archer, JP Orkney, of Kingcausie and Swanbister; MB, CM, Aberdeen; *b* 5 April 1851; *m* 18 April 1877 Edith Virginia (*d* 16 March

1946), dau of John Robert Duguid, of Gibraltar, and *d* 10 March 1941, leaving:

1c Archer, of Kingcausie and Swanbister, DSO (1919), JP, DL Kincardineshire; Col RAMC WW I (despatches four times, 1914–15 star, two medals), Waziristan 1922–23 (despatches, medal and clasp) and Kurdistan 1927 (medal), memb Anglo-Persian Mil Commn 1919–21 (Actg Lt-Col), Inspr Medical Servs Iraq 1926–29, DDMS Scottish Command Edinburgh Sept 1939, ADMS No 4 Mil Mission 1940, ADMS Br Advsy Staff HQ Polish Resettlement Corps 1946, 2nd Cl Orders of Lion and Sun Persia and St Stanislas of Russia with Swords, Polish Distinction of Odznaka Sluszby Zdrovia, Jubilee Medal 1935 and Coronation medal 1937; *b* 6 July 1880; *educ* Aberdeen GS, Aberdeen U (MB, ChB) and Edin U (BCom); *m* 5 Feb 1916 Ruth Olive (*d* 25 April 1971), dau of Henry Boddington, JP, of Pownall Hall, Wilmslow, Cheshire, and *d* 10 March 1959, having had issue:

1d +James William, of Kingcausie (Swanbister sold 1965), JP, DL (Kincardineshire 1957) [Maj James Irvine-Fortescue JP DL, Kingcausie, Maryculter, Aberdeen AB12 5FR]; chartered accountant 1948, CC Kincardineshire 1952–58 and 1964–73, Maj and Staff Paymaster RAPC WW II 1940–46, FSA Scot 1981; *b* 7 June 1917; *educ* Edin Acad and Aberdeen U (MA 1937); *m* 16 May 1953 *Margaret Guise, dau of Lt-Col George Dougal Yates, of Todhill-wood, Canonbie, Dumfriesshire, and has issue:

1e +Grenville Archer; *b* 4 Nov 1954; *educ* Fettes; Maj Gordon Highrs; *m* 1985 *Virginia, dau of Patrick William Townsend, of The Dower House, Gisburn, nr Clitheroe, Lancs, and has issue:

1f +Alexander Thomas; *b* 8 May 1987

2f +Simon Archer; *b* 15 Dec 1988

3f +Edmund William; *b* 2 May 1995

1f *Juliet; *b* 3 Aug 1991

2e +Henry Boswell [Henry Irvine-Fortescue Esq, The Old Coach House, Kingcausie, Maryculter AB12 5FR]; *b* 19 June 1958; *educ* St Andrews (MA 1982); *m* 1989 *Hazel J, 2nd dau of Ernest Wood

3e +James Robert [James Irvine-Fortescue Esq, Fagertunveien, Bekkestua, Norway]; *b* 10 Sept 1960; *educ* Aberdeen U and Imp Coll London (BSc); *m* 1990 *Wendy Jayne, dau of S A W Milne, of King's Gate, Aberdeen, and has:

1f *Camilla; *b* 18 Oct 1994

1e *Rachel Sarah; *b* 13 Sept 1956

2d David Alexander; *b* 18 May 1920; *d* 28 May 1930

1d *(Agnes) Virginia [Miss Virginia Fortescue, Village au Brun, N Dame de Cenilly, 50210 France]; MusB Cape Town U 1957, LRAM 1941; *b* 20 May 1922; *m* 1st 29 Dec 1944 Donald Spencer Nuttall, Lt RA (*ka* Burma 14 March 1945), s of Maj Ellis Nuttall, of Hazelgrove, Sparkford, Yeovil, Somerset; *m* 2nd 27 Aug 1949 (*divorce* 1964) Jerzy Wladyslaw (George) Jaholkowski, only s of Wladyslaw Jaholkowski, of Hawrylkowicze, Poland; *m* 3rd 1973 (*divorce* 1986, resumed maiden name) Eric Lee Attwell

2c John Faithfull (Rev); Minister Caldwell, Lt RASC WW I 1915–16; *b* 6 June 1883; *educ* Aberdeen U; *m* 17 April 1917 Anne (*d* 1976), dau of Joseph Brockhurst Souter, of Newhaven, and *d* 6 Sept 1957, having had issue:

1d Francis John; *b* 10 Oct 1926; *d* 15 Jan 1929

2d +Hugh William [Hugh Irvine-Fortescue Esq, Fernlea, 3 Broom Pk, Kelso, Roxburghs TD5 7SN]; CEng, MIEE 1968, Lt and Paymaster RAPC BAOR 1954–56; *b* 14 Sept 1930; *educ* Glasgow Acad and U (BSc 1961); *m* 18 March 1967 *Patricia Anne Elizabeth, dau of Francis John Dudgeon, of Edinburgh, and has issue:

1e +John Hugh [John Irvine-Fortescue Esq, 7 Katherine's Ct, Ampthill, Beds]; *b* 18 June 1968; *educ* George Watson's Coll Edinburgh; matriculated arms Lyon Office 15 Aug 1974

1e *Caroline Ann Patricia [Dr Caroline Fortescue, 14b Bayham St, London NW1]; *b* 20 Feb 1971; *educ* Dame Alice Harpur Sch Bedford, London U (BSc 1992) and Roy Free Hosp Sch of Medicine London; MB, BS (1995)

2e *Katherine Helen Isobel; *b* 26 Nov 1974; *educ* Dame Alice Harpur Sch Bedford and UEA (BA 1996); *m* 25 Oct 1997 *Benjamin James Whitlock

1d *Edith Caroline [Miss Edith Irvine-Fortescue, 5 Seton Place, Edinburgh 9]; *b* 28 May 1921; *educ* Glasgow U (MA 1942)

3c William Grenville, MC (1916) and bar (1919), Lt-Col RE WWI 1915–18, served WW II; *b* 26 May 1897; *m* 1st 9 Aug 1921 (*divorce* 1929) Joan Evelyn Mary, yr dau of Henry Sydney Powell, and had:

1d +Henry [Maj Henry Irvine-Fortescue, Credit Andorra, S Julia de Loria, Andorra]; Maj 5th RTR, WW II in Poona Horse, Korea 1953, Malaya 1955 and Cyprus 1957, ret 1959, Dip Mktg, MIM&SM 1966; *b* 11 July 1922; *educ* Cheltenham; *m* 1st 5 May 1951 Bridget Unity (*d* 1981), only dau of Col Edmund Portman Awdry, MC, TD, DL, of Coters, Chippenham, Wilts; *m* 2nd 1983 (*divorce* 1987) Anne van Gruisen and by his 1st w has issue:

1e +Alexander Ramsay [Alexander Irvine-Fortescue Esq, Chernocke House, St Cross Rd, Winchester, Hants SO23 9PQ], matriculated arms Lyon Office 25 Oct 1966; *b* 13 Dec 1952; *educ* Wellington, King's Coll London (BScEng) and U of Cape Town (MBA); *m* 1980 *Kathryn, dau of Paul Randles, of Natal, and has:

1f +Mark Paul; *b* 7 Dec 1980

2f +Nicholas Alexander; *b* 1983

3f +James Ramsay; *b* 1987

2e +Ian Henry; *b* 26 June 1954; *educ* Wellington and Keele U (BSc); *m* 1986 *Vanessa Louise Mary Marion Lloyd, dau of John Grey Haswell, of Johannesburg, and has had issue:

1f Logan McWatt; *b* 1988; *d* 1990

2f +Drummond McLeod; *b* 1990

1f *Brittany Avalon; *b* 1991

2f *Romney Foy; *b* 1993

1e *Victoria Awdry [Mrs Graham Tibbot, 7 Delph Lane, Delph, Saddleworth, Lancs OL3 5HX]; *b* 15 Jan 1957; *m* 1982 *Graham Herbert Tibbot and has:

1f *Graham Henry; *b* 1985

1f *Bridget Elizabeth; *b* 1986

2f *Sarah Hannah; *b* 1990

3f *Martha Victoria; *b* 1993

1d *Valerie Faith [Miss Valerie Irvine-Fortescue, 54c Ashgrove Rd, Aberdeen AB25 3AD]; WRNS WW II; *b* 28 May 1925

3c (cont.) Col William Irvine-Fortescue *m* 2nd 28 Aug 1941 Kathleen Sheila (*d* 1985), dau of William James Bennett-Jones, MD, of Liverpool, and *d* 1980, leaving by her:

2d +William Archer [William Irvine-Fortescue Esq, Wingham House, Canterbury Rd, Wingham, Kent CT3 1BH]; matriculated arms Lyon Office 29 July 1966; *b* 10 Nov 1945; *educ* Wellington, Wadham Coll Oxford and Queen's U Kingston, Ontario (MA 1968); *m* 1979 *Clare, er dau of Bernard Ungerson, CBE

2d *Margaret Ann [Mrs Richard Jacob, 2 Christchurch Rd, Norwich NR2 2AD]; *b* 20 July 1944; *educ* Aberdeen U (MA 1966) and St Anne's Coll Oxford; *m* 31 March 1979 *Richard John Jacob and has issue:

1e *Mark Robert; *b* 1980

2e *Peter Richard; *b* 1984

2b Archer Irvine Boswell; *b* 2 Oct 1852; *d* March 1853

3b Thomas Dyke Acland; *b* 30 Aug 1856; *d* 31 Oct 1935

1b Isobel Barclay; *m* 12 April 1883 Peter Duguid, of Auchlunies, Kincardineshire, and Bourtie, Aberdeenshire, and *d* 28 Aug 1952, leaving issue. He *d* 12 April 1898

2b Margaret Anne; *m* 6 July 1892 Lt-Col Francis Newell Innes and *d* 15 Oct 1923, leaving issue (*see* INNES, Bt, of Balvenie)

3b Eleanor Balfour; *d* unm 29 Aug 1944

4b Jessy Thomson; *d* unm 16 April 1936

(2) (cont.) The Rev W Fortescue *m* 2nd 18 Feb 1832 Elizabeth, est dau of Rev Robert Freke Gould, and *d* 13 Sept 1856

2 (cont.) Capt The Hon Matthew Fortescue *m* 2nd 6 June 1795 Henrietta Anne (*d* 5 Sept 1841), widow of Sir Thomas Acland, 9th Bt, of Columb John (*qv*), and dau of Sir Richard Hoare, 1st Bt, of Luscombe (*qv*), and *d* 19 Nov 1842, leaving:

(3) Henry, of The Old Manor, Beckenham, Kent; Cdr RN; *b* 10 Aug 1796; *m* 2 Nov 1824 Caroline (*d* 6 March 1869), dau of Sir Henry Russell, 1st Bt of Swallowfield (*qv*), and *d* 6 Dec 1875, leaving:

1a Francis, DL; Capt Scots Fus Gds; *b* 19 Aug 1826; *m* 16 June 1855 Katherine Frederica (*d* 13 April 1884), 2nd dau of Capt Alexander Ellice, RN, and *d* 15 Nov 1897, leaving issue:

1b Henry, Brevet-Col, JP Cambs and Suffolk; Col King Edward's Horse, Lt-Col cmdg 17th Lancers, DAQMG E Cmmd 1914, Mil Sec Intell Dept 1917, Cdr Order of Crown of Italy; *b* 15 May 1856; *m* 26 May 1885 Maud Elizabeth (*d* June 1940), 2nd dau of William Holden, of Palace House, Lancs, and *dsp* June 1940

2b Francis Alexander, CB (1911), CMG (1918); Hon Brig-Gen, cmdg 4th Bn KRRC, Col Gen Staff S Africa 1908–09, cmdg Devon and Cornwall TA Bde 1911–12, cmdg Rifle Depot 1912–14, T/Brig-Gen cmdg 41st Inf Bde 1914–15, Gen Staff MEF 1915–16, T/Brig-Gen cmdg 208th Bde 1916–18, Advsr Safety Servs Min Munitions 1918–22, served Afghan War 1880 (bronze star medal, two clasps), Transvaal 1881, Egypt 1883–88 (3rd Cl Osmanieh), S Africa 1896 (medal) and 1899–1900 (despatches twice, Queen's medal, three clasps) and WW I (despatches twice, 1914–15 star, two medals); *b* 10 April 1858; *m* 25 June 1885 Mary Teresa (*d* 26 Feb 1935), dau of Henry T J Jenkinson, of Alveston, Warwicks, and *d* 12 Oct 1942, leaving issue:

1c Katherine May Frederica; *m* 20 Nov 1923 Col Arthur George Bayley, CBE, DSO, 3rd s of Kennett Bayley, of Inchicore, Co Dublin, and *d* 31 Aug 1952, leaving issue (*see* LAURIE, Bt)

3b Hugh Charles; Maj and Hon Lt-Col 4th Bn Oxford LI, T/Maj 1916; *b* 7 July 1860; *m* 1892 Minnie Anne (*dsp* 1908), dau of Peter Duncan, of Leith, and *d* 12 Oct 1937

The 2nd BARON *d* 10 July 1785; his er s,

HUGH FORTESCUE, **1st Earl Fortescue**, so *cr* 1 Sept 1789, as also VISCOUNT EBRINGTON, Co Gloucester (both GB); *b* 12 March 1753; *educ* Eton and Univ Coll Oxford; FSA, DCL, MP (Pittite) Beaumaris 1784–85, Ld Lt and V-Adml Devon 1788–1839; *m* 10 May 1782 Hester (*d* 13 Nov 1847), dau of Rt Hon George Grenville (*see* KINLOSS, L), and had issue:

1 HUGH, **2nd Earl**

2 George Matthew, of Boconnoc, Cornwall, and Dropmore, Burnham, Bucks; MP Hindon 1826–31, Capt 25th Regt; *b* 21 May 1791; *m* 19 Feb 1833 Louisa Elizabeth (*d* 9 Jan 1899), 5th dau of 1st Earl of Harrowby (*qv*), and *d* 24 Jan 1877, having had, with other issue:

(1) John Bevill, of Boconnoc, and Dropmore, JP, DL Cornwall; High Sheriff 1894, barrister; *b* 1 Nov 1850; *m* 26 Aug 1891 Dorothy Augusta (*d* 7 March 1941), dau of Adml Sir William Legge George Hoste, 2nd Bt (*see* 1902 edn), and *d* 27 May 1838, leaving issue:

1a George Grenville; Sheriff Cornwall 1943; *b* 24 Dec 1892; *educ* Eton; *m* 15 Dec 1927 Olive Joan (*d* 11 March 1976), dau of Bertram Frankland Frankland-Russell-Astley (*see* HASTINGS, B), and *dsp* 1 Dec 1967

2a John Grenville; Lt Res of Offrs Coldstream Gds WW I (wounded); *b* 3 May 1896; *educ* Eton; *m* 7 June 1917 Daphne Marjorie (*d* 22 May 1962), only child of Hon Algernon Henry Bourke (*see* MAYO, E), and *d* 30 Sept 1969, leaving issue:

1b +(John) Desmond Grenville, JP (1963), DL (Cornwall 1964) [Desmond Fortescue Esq JP DL, The Stewardry, Boconnoc, Cornwall]; High Sheriff 1966–67, Capt Coldstream Gds Res of Offrs WW II; *b* 24 March 1919; *educ* Eton; *m* 21 Sept 1942 Nina (*d* 13 March 1976), dau of Ernest Kendall-Lane, of Saskatchewan; *m* 2nd 1988 *Angela Dorothy, widow of T C Keigwin, and by his 1st w has issue:

1c +Anthony Desmond Grenville [Anthony Fortescue Esq, Penvose, Boconnoc, Cornwall PL22 0RG]; *b* 7 Feb 1946; *educ* Eton; Freeman City of London, memb Furniture Makers Co; *m* 1977 *Elizabeth Ann Evered, dau of Maj Campbell Evered Poole, of Bank Farm House, W Malvern, Worcs, and has issue:

1d *Clare Elizabeth; *b* 4 Sept 1981

2d *Sarah Alexandra; *b* 10 Feb 1984

1c *Anne Desnia (Lulu); *b* 24 Aug 1948; *m* 10 Dec 1970 *Capt Iain Anthony Mackie, 15th/19th Hus, s of W/Cdr J A Mackie, and has issue:

1d *Hamish Anthony; *b* 1974

2d *Alastair Desmond; *b* 13 Aug 1977

3d *Archibald Iain; *b* 1979

1b *Rosemary Sylvia [Mrs Douglas White, The Manor, Berwick Bassett, Wilts]; *b* 1920; *m* 28 Oct 1944 *Douglas Frederick Thomas White, s of Frederick Thomas White, of Overtown Manor, and has:

1c *John Frederick Fortescue [John White Esq, Overtown Manor, Wroughton, Wilts]; *b* 12 April 1946; *educ* Milton Abbey and RAC Cirencester; *m* 1972 *Rosemary Kathleen, dau of Maj Edward Palmer, of Northam, N Devon, and has issue:

1d *Douglas John; *b* 1985

1d *Nancy Ruth; *b* 1976

2d *Jessica Rosemary; *b* 1979

2c *David Grenville [David White Esq, The Old Farmhouse, Berwick Bassett, Wilts]; *b* 12 Feb 1948; *educ* Milton Abbey and RAC Cirencester; *m* 3 Oct 1970 *Diana Penelope, yr dau of Peter Werden Wilson, of The Manor, Clyffe Pypard, Wilts, and has issue:

1d *Edward John Grenville; *b* 1973

1d *Lucia Genevieve Rosemary; *b* 1977

2d *Anastasia Sophie; *b* 1985

1c *April Rosemary; *b* 1 April 1950; *m* 1971 *Robert Edward Simpson, yr s of E Simpson, of Edinburgh, and has issue:

1d *Charles Robert; *b* 1980

1d *Nichola Rosemary; *b* 1971

2d *Rachel Elizabeth; *b* 1974

3d *Emma Louise; *b* 1976

2b *June Diana [Mrs Derek Bigham, Chalkestone House, Broad Hinton, Wilts]; *m* 23 Aug 1952 *Derek Alastair Bigham, only s of Capt Robert Alexander Bigham, and has issue:

1c *Diana Susan; *b* 17 May 1954; *m* 1985 *William Brandon Grundy and has issue:

1d *David Matthew; *b* 1988

2c *Julie Rosemary; *b* 30 April 1959; *m* 1988 *Anthony Peregrine Dudley Berendt (*see* HARROWBY, E)

(1) Louisa Susan Anne; *m* 25 June 1863 William Westby Moore, 2nd s of Richard Moore, Judge Queen's Bench Ireland, and *d* 30 March 1864, leaving issue

(2) Harriet Eleanor; *m* 29 March 1864 Adml Sir Augustus Phillimore, KCB, and *d* 4 Sept 1924, leaving issue (*see* PHILLIMORE, B)

(3) Mary; *m* 22 July 1884 Rev Vernon Harcourt Aldham, Rector Boconnoc and Braddock, Cornwall, 1874–1916, Hon Canon Truro 1889–1916, and *d* 9 Feb 1925. He *d* 11 Jan 1929

3 John (Rev); MA, Canon Worcester, Rector Poltimore, Devon; *b* 5 May 1796; *m* 13 April 1842 Sophia (*d* 29 Dec 1868), dau of Rev Henry William Nevile, Rector Cottesmore, Rutland, of Walcot and Wellingore, and *d* 3 Jan 1869, having had, with other issue:

(1) Hester Emily; *m* 14 Oct 1873 Ven Albert Eden Seymour, and *d* 17 July 1913, leaving issue (*see* CULME-SEYMOUR, Bt)

(2) Sophia Elizabeth; *m* 9 Jan 1877 Rev Leigh Thomas Rendell, MA, Rector Timsbury, Bath, and *d* 8 Oct 1911

1 Hester; *m* 1804 7th Lord King, Baron of Ockham (*see* LOVELACE, E), and *d* 1873

2 Catherine; *m* 24 June 1820, as his 2nd w, 4th Earl of Portsmouth (*qv*) and *d* his widow 17 April 1854

3 Anne; *m* 3 Sept 1814 George Wilbraham, of Delamere House, Cheshire, and *d* 28 Feb 1864, leaving issue. He *d* 24 Jan 1852

4 Mary; *m* 15 Feb 1823 Sir James Hamlyn Williams, 3rd Bt, and *d* 12 Aug 1874. He *d* 10 May 1866

5 Eleanor; *d* unm 1847

6 Elizabeth; *m* 27 Dec 1830 11th Earl of Devon (*qv*) and *d* 27 Jan 1867

The 1st EARL *d* 16 June 1841; his est s,

HUGH FORTESCUE, **2nd Earl Fortescue**, KG (1856), PC (1839); *b* 13 Feb 1783; *educ* Eton and BNC Oxford; MP (Whig) Barnstaple 1804–07, St Mawes 1807–09, Buckingham 1812–17, Devon 1818–20 and 1830–32, Tavistock 1820–30 and N Devon 1832–39, called up to Ho of Lds *vp* 28 Feb 1839 in f's Barony, FRS 1817, Ld Lt: Ireland 1839–41 and Devon 1832–39, Ld Steward Household 1846–50; *m* 1st 4 July 1817 Lady Susan Ryder (*d* 30 July 1827), dau of 1st Earl of Harrowby (*qv*), and had issue:

1 HUGH, **3rd Earl**

2 John William; Lt-Col E Devon Militia, MP; *b* 14 July 1819; *d* unm 25 Sept 1859

3 Dudley Francis; DL Devon and Co Waterford, MA Cantab, a Commr in Lunacy, High Sheriff Co Waterford 1870, MP Andover 1857–74; *b* 4 Aug 1820; *m* 8 June 1852 his cousin Camilla Eleanor (*d* 5 Aug 1920), dau of 4th Earl of Portsmouth, and *dsp* 2 March 1909

The **2nd Earl** *m* 2nd 26 July 1841 Elizabeth (*d* 4 May 1896), widow of Sir Marcus Somerville, 3rd Bt, and est dau of Piers Geale, and *d* 14 Sept 1861

His est s,

HUGH FORTESCUE, **3rd Earl Fortescue**, JP, DL Devon, JP S Molton; MP Plymouth 1841–52 and Marylebone 1854–59, a Ld Treasury 1846–47, Sec Poor Law Bd 1847–51; *b* 4 April 1818; called up to Ho of Lds *vp* 5 Dec 1859 in f's Barony; *m* 11 March 1847 Georgiana Augusta Charlotte Caroline (*d* 8 Dec 1866), est dau of Rt Hon George Lionel Dawson-Damer (*see* PORTARLINGTON, E), and had, with other issue:

1 HUGH, **4th Earl**

2 Seymour John (Sir), GCVO, CMG; Capt RN, Equerry-in-Waiting to HM EDWARD VII 1893–1910, Groom-in-Waiting, Gentleman Usher and Extra Equerry to HM GEORGE V 1910–36, Extra Equerry to TM EDWARD VIII 1936 and GEORGE VI 1937–42, Serjeant-at-Arms Ho Lds 1910–36, served Egypt 1882 and Suakin 1885, Naval ADC to Lord Roberts S Africa 1900, Kt Cdr Order St Benedict of Aviz Portugal and Order St Olaf Norway, Cdr Orders St Maurice, Dannebrog and Legn Hon; *b* 10 Feb 1856; *d* unm 20 March 1942

3 Lionel Henry Dudley; Maj 17th Lancers; *b* 19 Nov 1857; *m* 5 July 1895 Emily Elizabeth (*m* 2nd 3 Sept 1912 Walter B Ferrie, of Vancouver, and *d* 3 Feb 1932), 2nd dau of Rt Hon William Patrick Adam, CIE, of Blair Adam, Scotland, Govr Madras, and was *ka* Boer War 11 June 1900

4 Arthur Grenville; Capt Coldstream Gds; *b* 24 Dec 1858; *m* 12 Jan 1886 Lilla Gertrude Ellen (*d* 30 Oct 1913), 3rd dau of Rev Frederick Fane, of Moyles Court, Hants, and *d* 3 Oct 1895, having had issue:

(1) Grenville; Capt 11th Service Bn Rifle Bde, Lt Rifle Bde; *b* 15 March 1887; *m* 27 Nov 1912 Adelaide (*d* 1977, having *m* 2nd 10 March 1930 Brig Robin Leslie Hutchins, MC, Gren Gds (*d* 1973), s of Lt-Col Francis Hutchins, 4th Hus), est dau of Henry Lorenzo Jephson, and was *ka* 4 Sept 1915, leaving:

1a +Arthur Henry Grenville, MBE (1946), MC; Brig Coldstream Gds WW II (wounded, despatches); *b* 6 Sept 1913; *educ* Winchester and Ch Ch Oxford (BA); *m* 30 April 1946 *Rosita Anne (WRNS), dau of Maj-Gen John Charles Campbell, VC, DSO and bar, MC, and has issue:

1b Mark Charles Grenville (Billy); *b* 6 March 1947; *educ* Eton; *m* 10 Sept 1971 *Virginia Rose [Mrs Mark Fortescue, Church House, Steeple Ashton, nr Trowbridge, Wilts], formerly w of Richard Wilfrid Beavoir Berens and yst dau of Anthony William Fabio Caccia-Birch, MC, of Guernsey Lodge, Marton, NZ (*see* 1970 edn CACCIA, B), and *d* 1982, leaving issue:

1c *Sabina Thérèse; *b* 1973

2c *Clarissa Rose Frances; *b* 1975

2b +Nicolas Cecil John [Nicholas Fortescue Esq, 80 Langthorne St, London SW6]; *b* 3 April 1953; *m* 1985 *Tessa Jane, yr dau of Sir (Thomas) David Ainsworth, 4th Bt (*qv*), and has issue:

1c *Rosie Olivia; *b* 1990

2c *Lily Sarah; *b* 1990

1a *Diana [Mrs Diana Fortescue, Mill Meadow, Burley, Hants]; *b* 2 Jan 1915; *m* 15 Dec 1945 (*divorce* 1947, resumed maiden name) Lt-Col Charles Murray Floyd, OBE, RE, 3rd s of Sir Henry Floyd, 4th Bt (*qv*)

(1) Joyce Margaret; *b* 13 March 1892; *m* 10 April 1919 Col Peter Fitzwilliam Carew (*see* CAREW, Bt), and *d* 19 Aug 1974, leaving issue

5 John William (Sir), KCVO; LLD, LittD, FRHS, historian of the British Army, Librarian Windsor Castle 1905–26, Maj Roy N Devon Yeo Cav, Hon LLD Edin, Ford Lecturer Oxford 1911, Creighton Lecturer London 1915, Lees-Knowles Lecturer Cambridge 1913 and 1916, LittD Oxford 1925, Romanes Lecturer Oxford 1929; *b* 28 Dec 1859; *educ* Trin Coll Cambridge (BA, Hon Fell); *m* 30 April 1914 Winifred, authoress (*d* 9 April 1951), er dau of Rev Howard Beech, MA, Rector Barlavington and Burton-with-Coates, Sussex, and *dsp* 22 Oct 1933

6 Charles Granville, CB (1911), CMG (1899), DSO (1901); Col and Hon Brig-Gen Rifle Bde, Burma 1888–89, W Africa 1897–98, Boer War 1899–1902 and WW I, Order White Eagle Serbia 1st Cl with swords; *b* 30 Oct 1861; *m* 29 Dec 1906 Ethel Rosa (*d* 2 April 1967 aged 98), widow of Capt Ernest George Campbell, Rifle Bde, and dau of Gen Sir Charles Mansfield Clarke, 3rd Bt (*see* CLARKE, Bt, of Dunham), and *d* 1 Feb 1951, leaving:

(1) Anne Mary; *b* 17 July 1910; *m* 17 Oct 1929 Henry Reginald Aked Garnett (*d* 16 June 1944), est s of John W Garnett, of Apperley Bridge, Yorks, and had issue, and *d* 19–

(2) Lilah Rose; TD; ATS WW II; *b* 15 Oct 1912; *d* 19–

1 Mary Eleanor; *m* 26 Nov 1896 George Arthur Bridgeman Bridgeman (*see* BRADFORD, E) and *d* 12 Oct 1938

2 Lucy Catherine; *m* 3 Sept 1874 1st Earl Saint Aldwyn (*qv*) and *d* 19 March 1940, having had issue

3 Georgiana Seymour; *m* 26 Sept 1877 Lord Ernest Seymour, 3rd s of 5th Marquess of Hertford (*qv*), and *d* 24 Dec 1915, leaving issue

4 Frances Blanche; *m* 18 April 1894 Archibald Hay Gordon-Duff, of The Red House, Overbury, Tewkesbury, 2nd s of Lachlan Gordon-Duff, of Drummuir Castle, Banffshire, and *d* 24 Oct 1950 leaving issue. He *d* 19 May 1938

The 3rd EARL *d* 10 Oct 1905; his est s,

HUGH FORTESCUE, **4th Earl Fortescue**, KCB (1911), TD, JP S Molton; *b* 16 April 1854; *educ* Harrow and Trin Coll Cambridge; MP (Lib) Tiverton 1881–85 and W Devon 1885–92 (Lib to 1886, Lib U thereafter), High Steward 1908, Ld Lt Devon 1904–28, ADC to TM EDWARD VII 1903–10 and GEORGE V 1910–21, memb Cncl Duchy Cornwall 1918, Hon Col Roy N Devon Yeo; *m* 15 July 1886 Hon Emily Ormsby-Gore, CBE (*d* 12 July 1929), Extra Ldy Bedchamber to HM QUEEN MARY, dau of 2nd Baron Harlech (*qv*), and *d* 29 Oct 1932, having had:

1 HUGH WILLIAM FORTESCUE, **5th Earl Fortescue**, KG (1951), CB (1946), OBE (1942), MC (1917), PC (1952), JP (Devon); *b* 14 June 1888; Hon LLD Exeter 1956, Col Gen Staff 1939–43, Lt-Col Res of Offrs Roy Scots Greys (2nd Dragoons), Col Cmdt HAC 1935–41, Capt Gentlemen-at-Arms April-July 1945 and 1951–58, Ld Lt Devon 1936–58, memb Cncl Duchy Cornwall 1923, Ld-in-Waiting 1937–45, served WW I (despatches, wounded twice), Legn Hon, KStJ; *m* 8 Feb 1917 Hon Margaret Helen Beaumont, CBE (1957), JP Devon (*d* 10 June 1958), est dau of 1st Viscount Allendale (*qv*), and *d* 14 June 1958, having had:

(1) Hugh Peter, *Viscount Ebrington*; Lt Roy Scots Greys (2nd Dragoons) WW II 1939–42; *b* 9 Dec 1920; *educ* Eton and RMC Sandhurst; *ka* El Alamein 17 July 1942

(1) Diana Margaret; *b* 17 May 1919; *d* 6 April 1920

(2) *Margaret [The Lady Margaret Fortescue, The Garden House, Filleigh, Barnstaple, N Devon]; *b* 13 Dec 1923, *m* 30 July 1948 (*divorce* 1968) Bernard van Cutsem (*d* 8 Dec 1975), s of Henry Harcourt van Cutsem, of 3 Seymour Place, London W1, resumed her maiden name 1966 and has issue:

1a *Eleanor; *b* 28 May 1949; *m* 1974 *9th Earl of Arran (*qv*)

2a *Rosamund Isabelle; *b* 22 May 1952; *m* 1975 *Thomas William Fellowes (*see* HAMPDEN, V)

(3) *Elizabeth Joan [The Lady Elizabeth Baxendale, Hailwell House, Framfield, E Sussex]; *b* 1 Oct 1926; *m* 9 July 1946 Maj William Lloyd (John) Baxendale, JP, DL, Coldstream Gds (*d* 1982), only surv s of Capt Guy Vernon Baxendale, of Framfield Place, and has:

1a *David Hugh; *b* 1952; *m* 1977 *Jacqueline Loveday, dau of John William Hext, of Trelaske, Lewannick, Cornwall, and has issue:

1b *Guy Jonathan; *b* 1980

2b *Thomas Lloyd; *b* 1983

2a *Peter Anthony; *b* 1955

1a *Lucinda Margaret; *b* 1958; *m* 1st 1983 (*divorce* 1986) Jonathan Edward McCalmont Harington (*see* HARINGTON, Bt); *m* 2nd 1992 *Nicholas James Goland Crosthwaite, yr s of Maj Ivor Crosthwaite, DSO, and Mrs John Vincent Sheffield, and by him has:

1b *Rose Elizabeth Frances; *b* 1992

2 Geoffrey Faithfull; *b* 24 Jan 1891; *d* 16 Oct 1900

3 DENZIL GEORGE FORTESCUE, **6th Earl Fortescue**, MC, TD; *b* 13 June 1893; *educ* Eton and New Coll Oxford; Lt-Col 96th (Roy Devon Yeo) Regt RA WW I, cmded Roy Devon Yeo 1935–41 and 1st Heavy Regt RA 1942–44 WW II; *m* 1st 10 June 1920 (*divorce* 1941) Marjorie Ellinor, OBE (*d* 9 July 1964), only dau of Col Charles William Trotter, CB, TD, JP, of Barton Hartsorne Manor, nr Buckingham, and had:

(1) RICHARD ARCHIBALD FORTESCUE, **7th Earl Fortescue**, JP (Oxon 1964); *b* 14 April 1922; *educ* Eton and Ch Ch Oxford; Capt Coldstream Gds (Reserve); *m* 1st 24 Oct 1949 Penelope Jane (*d* 28 May 1959), yr dau of Robert Evelyn Henderson, and had issue:

1a CHARLES HUGH RICHARD FORTESCUE, **8th and present Earl Fortescue**

1a *Celia Ann [The Lady Celia Adams, Spilsbury Farm, Tisbury, Wilts SP3 6RU]; *b* 30 Dec 1957; *m* 1988 David Alastair Adams, furniture designer, yst s of Dr Michael Shirley Adams, of Alton House, Seaview, IoW, and has:

1b *Charles Michael Richard; *b* 1992

1b *Georgina Penelope Anne; *b* 1990

(1) (cont.) The **7th Earl** *m* 2nd 3 March 1961 (*divorce* 1987) Margaret Anne (*m* 2nd 28 Jan 1988, as his 3rd w, Jocelyn Hambro; *see* HAMBRO, B), dau of Charles Michael Stratton, of The Cottage, Mote Park, Maidstone, Kent, and Mrs James Windsor Lewis (*see* PERTH, E, and DUNMORE, E); *m* 3rd 1989 *Carolyn Mary [The Rt Hon Carolyn Countess Fortescue, The Old Rectory, Bradoc, Lostwithiel, Cornwall PL22 0RN], dau of Maj Clement Walter Rowland Hill (*see* HILL, V) and formerly w of Edward Lockwood, and *d* 7 March 1993, having by his 2nd w had issue:

2a *Laura Margaret, *b* 1 May 1962; *m* 1 July 1995 *Simon Jamieson (*see* NORFOLK, D) and has issue

3a *Sarah Jane; *b* 16 Aug 1963; *m* 19 Dec 1995 *Francis D S Chapman, est s of Michael Chapman, of Stoke-by-Nayland, Suffolk

(2) +MARTIN DENZIL [The Hon Martin Fortescue, Wincombe Park, Shaftesbury, Dorset]; *b* 5 Jan 1924; heir presumptive; *educ* Eton; Lt RN (ret); *m* 1st 23 April 1954 Prudence Louisa (*d* 1992), yr dau of Col Sir Charles Samuel Rowley, 6th Bt (*qv*), and has:

1a +John Andrew Francis [John Fortescue Esq, 12 Ursula St, London SW11]; *b* 27 March 1955; *educ* Eton; *m* 1990 *Phoebe Anne Cecilia, dau of Rev John Eustace Burridge, of Ham Vicarage, Surrey, and has issue:

1b +Thomas (Tom) Edmund Horatio; *b* 1993

2b +Hugh Augustus Francis; *b* 9 Nov 1995

2a +Anthony William [Anthony Fortescue Esq, Ryall's Lodge, Gussage St Michael, Wimborne, Dorset]; *b* 10 April 1962; *educ* Eton; *m* 1992 *Emma Davinia, dau of Peter Lambert, of Holly Tree Farm, Fearby, N Yorks, and has:

1b +William George; *b* 30 June 1994

1a *Katharine; *b* 30 Dec 1956; *m* 9 Sept 1995 *Robert Whitaker, only s of Evald Mattievich Whitaker

2a *Georgina Elizabeth; *b* 9 Nov 1958; *m* 31 July 1982 *Nicholas Hilary Stuart Armour, FCO, er s of Brig William Stanley Gibson Armour, of Brandsby, Yorks, and has issue:

1b *Emily Frances; *b* 1985

2b *Sophie Elizabeth; *b* 1987

(2) (cont.) The Hon MARTIN FORTESCUE *m* 2nd 18 Nov 1994 *Ms Caroline Loftie, of Bowerbank House, Pooley Bridge

(1) *Bridget Ellinor [The Lady Bridget Sinclair, Fairwood House, Great Durnford, Wilts SP4 6BD]; *b* 17 Oct 1927; *m* 25 Nov 1952 *W/Cdr Gordon Leonard Sinclair, OBE, DFC, RAF, s of Capt William Francis Sinclair, Palestine Police, and has issue:

1a *Alan Gordon William [Alan Sinclair Esq, The White House, Adstock, Bucks]; *b* 11 Sept 1956; *educ* Eton; Capt Coldstream Gds; *m* 1983 *Fiona B, er dau of Maj A M MacEwan, of Urless Farm, Corscombe, Dorset, and has issue:

1b *Thomas; *b* 1985

2b *Archie; *b* 1988

3b *Geordie; *b* 1993

2a *Robert Alistair; *b* 2 Feb 1965; *educ* Eton

1a *(Caroline) Fiona [Mrs Julian Smith, Balcombe House, W Sussex RH17 6PB]; *b* 5 Nov 1958; *m* 1982 *Julian Raymond Eric Smith and has issue (*see* BURRELL, Bt)

2a *Joanna Rosalind [Mrs Mark Rimell, 11 Louvaine Rd, London SW11 2AQ]; *b* 19 July 1963; *m* 1992 *Mark P R Rimell, er s of Philip Rimell, of London SW1, and has issue:

1b *Benjamin Charles Philip; *b* 1994

1b *Amelia Sophie; *b* 1996

3 (cont.) The **6th Earl** *m* 2nd 8 Aug 1941 *Hon Sybil Mary, OStJ, formerly wife of 4th Baron Penrhyn (*qv*) and yr dau of 3rd Viscount Hardinge (*qv*), and *d* 1 June 1977, leaving by her:

(3) +Seymour Henry [The Hon Seymour Fortescue, 22 Clarendon St, London SW1V 4RF]; *b* 28 May 1942; *educ* Eton, Trin Coll Cambridge (MA) and London Graduate Sch of Business Studies (MSc); Finance and Fund-Raising Dir Imp Cancer Research 1991–; *m* 1st 25 July 1966 (*divorce* 1990) Julia, only child of Sir John Arthur Pilcher, GCMG, Amb Japan, and has issue:

1a +James Adrian; *b* 1978; *educ* Stowe

1a *Marissa Clare; *b* 20 Oct 1973; *educ* Westminster and Worcester Coll Oxford

(3) (cont.) The Hon Seymour Fortescue *m* 2nd 1990 *Jennifer Ann, dau of Frank Simon, of Wrexham, and has:

2a *Alexandra Kate; *b* 1991

FORTEVIOT

Arms: Or on a pale vert the crozier of Saint Fillan ppr., on a chief engrailed gu. a holy lamb passant regardant, staff and cross arg., with the banner of St Andrew ppr. between two stalks of barley, slipped, also ppr. **Crest:** A cock ppr. **Supporters:** Dexter, the figure of St Fillan holding in his exterior hand his crozier; sinister, an eagle, wings elevated, all ppr. **Motto:** *Pro rege, lege et grege* ('For King, law and people'). **Creations:** Bt. (UK) 24 July 1907, B. (UK) 4 Jan 1917.

THE 4TH BARON FORTEVIOT, of Dupplin, Co Perth, and a **Baronet** (Sir John James Evelyn Dewar, Bt) [The Rt Hon The Lord Forteviot, Aberdalgie House, Perthshire PH2 0QD]; *b* 5 April 1938; *s f* 1993; *educ* Eton; ADC to Govr Gen NZ 1962–63, dir John Dewar 1977– and Buchanan-Dewar, memb Roy Co Archers; *m* 17 Oct 1963 *Elisabeth Jeronima, 3rd dau of 12th Earl Waldegrave (*qv*), and has:

1 +ALEXANDER JOHN EDWARD; *b* 4 March 1971; *educ* Eton and Newcastle U; *m* 5 April 1997 *Donryn, dau of Graham Clement and Mrs Mieke Clement, of Cape, S Africa

1 *Mary Emma Jeronima; *b* 1 June 1965; *m* 1988 *Hon Adam Humphrey Drummond, est s of Baroness Strange (*qv*), and has issue

2 *Miranda Phoebe; *b* 1 March 1968

3 *Henrietta Cynthia; *b* 27 Jan 1970

Lineage: JOHN DEWAR, of Shenavail, Dull, Aberfeldy, Perthshire; farmer; *m* Janet Scott and had issue:

JOHN DEWAR, of Perth, and Pittendynie, Moneydie, Perthshire; *b* 6 Jan 1805; fndr of the firm John Dewar and Son Ltd; *m* 24 June 1845 Jane (*d* 23 Aug 1900), dau of John Gow, of Pittendynie, and *d* 22 Jan 1880, leaving with two other sons and two daus:

1 James Gow, JP (Glos); *b* 9 Aug 1852; *m* 16 Sept 1898 Helen Mowat, dau of George Wilson, of Craigard, Perthshire, and *d* 12 May 1922, leaving issue:

(1) Violet Gow; *b* 2 July 1899; *m* 1st 1923 Neville Wakefield and had a s and two daus; *m* 2nd 1932 Thomas Houssemayne du Boulay and *d* 1992, leaving by him two daus

2 JOHN ALEXANDER, **1st Baron**

3 Charles, JP Norfolk; *b* 28 April 1858; CC Norfolk; *m* 21 June 1888 Jane Greig (*d* 6 June 1952), dau of David Smart, of Rockbank, Kinnoull, Perths, and *d* 12 Sept 1933, leaving:

(1) John Arthur; chm John Dewar & Sons, served WW I, Patron and Pres Gordon Hosp, Vauxhall Bridge Rd; *b* 3 Aug 1891; *educ* Aldenham; *m* 1932 Kathleen (*d* 5 July 1966), formerly w of Ronald Fitzroy Rous McNeill and dau of Charles Beart, of Johannesburg, and *dsp* 15 Aug 1954

(1) Margaret Morrison; *b* 28 Feb 1890; *m* 27 May 1915 Robert Shuckburgh Copeman, JP, FLAS, of Roydon Hall, Diss, Norfolk, est s of Thomas Copeman, of Old Hall, Aylsham, Norfolk, and *d* 16 Aug 1947, leaving issue. He *d* 16 July 1964

(2) Jean Gow; *d* unm 28 March 1953

(3) Mona Isobel; *b* 16 April 1896; *m* 1st C J W Crichton and had issue; *m* 2nd Sidney Field and had further issue

4 Arthur, KC 1903; MA Edin, advocate Edin 1885, Slr-Gen Scotland 1909–10, Ld of Session as Lord Dewar 1910–17, MP S Edinburgh 1899–1900 and 1906–10; *b* 14 March 1860; *m* 2 Aug 1892 Letitia Dalrymple (*d* 7 July 1955), dau of Robert Bell, of Clifton Hall, Midlothian, and *d* 14 June 1917, leaving issue

5 Sir THOMAS ROBERT DEWAR, 1st and last Bt, and 1st and last BARON DEWAR, of Homestall, Co Sussex (both UK), so *cr* 23 June 1917 and 20 May 1919 respectively, JP (Kent); Lt City London, High Sheriff 1897–98, memb LCC W Marylebone 1892–95, MP (C) Tower Hamlets St George's 1900–06, md John Dewar & Son, dir Distillers and Licences and Gen Insur; *b* 9 Jan 1864; ktd 18 Dec 1902; *d* unm 11 April 1930, when both titles expired

1 Jane; *b* 25 Aug 1862; *m* 2 Nov 1897 Ewan Cameron, of Rutherford, Peeblesshire, and had issue

JOHN DEWAR *d* 22 Jan 1880; his 4th son (but 2nd here mentioned),

Sir John Alexander Dewar, 1st Bt, and **1st Baron Forteviot**, of Dupplin, Co Perth (both UK), so *cr* 24 July 1907 and 4 Jan 1917 respectively, JP, DL; Ld Provost Perth 1893–99, MP (Lib) Inverness-shire 1900–17, chm John Dewar & Sons, Perth, Chm Perth TFA 1914–19; *b* 6 June 1856; *m* 1st 24 June 1884 Johann (*d* 15 Feb 1899), dau of William Tod, of Gospetry, Kinross-shire, and had issue:

1 JOHN DEWAR, **2nd Baron Forteviot**, OBE (1925), MC, TD, DL (Perthshire); Col 6th/7th Bn Black Watch, Res of Offrs (TA), Ld Provost Perth 1922–25, Brig Roy Co Archers; *b* 17 March 1885; *educ* Rugby and New Coll Oxford; chm Distillers Co, served Scottish Horse WW I; *m* 1st Nov 1919 Marjory Winton Isabel, ARRC (*d* 6 Sept 1945), 2nd dau of Lt-Col Sir Charles Henry Brabazon Heaton-Ellis, CBE, of Wyddiall Hall, Buntingford; *m* 2nd 20 Aug 1946 his sis-in-law *Muriel Cecil Harriette, widow of Maj Alwyn Cavendish (*see* DEVONSHIRE, D) and est dau of Lt-Col Sir Charles Heaton-Ellis, and *dsp* 24 Oct 1947

1 Agnes Roger; *b* 6 June 1888; *m* 24 Feb 1914 John James Strutt and *d* 30 March 1919, leaving issue (*see* RAYLEIGH, B)

2 Jane Gow; *b* 12 May 1890; *m* 9 June 1920 Capt Basil Hamilton Piercy, RN, s of G J Piercy, of Bournemouth, and *d* 6 June 1969, leaving issue. He *d* 4 June 1957

3 Margaret Dorothy; *b* 7 July 1891; *m* 24 Mar 1917 Lt-Col Arthur Laurence Cecil Neame, OBE, RE, er s of Arthur Neame, and *d* 11 Oct 1967, leaving issue. He *d* 23 April 1948

4 Elsie Joan Tod; *b* 24 Nov 1892; *d* unm 23 Feb 1917

5 Janet Bertha; *m* 20 April 1918 Sir John Armitage Stainton, KCB, KBE, QC, Parly Counsel Treasury 1929–46 (*d* 6 Sept 1957), s of J P Stainton, and had:

(1) *John David Adam; *b* 1 March 1921; *educ* Winchester and Ch Ch Oxford

(2) *Andrew Thomas; *b* 4 Aug 1925; *educ* Winchester and Ch Ch Oxford; *m* 2 Nov 1956 *Mikaela, dau of Constantine Lykiardopulos, of Athens, and has:

1a *John Andrew; *b* 9 Aug 1968

1a *Deborah Leila; *b* 16 Nov 1957

2a *Joanna Natalie; *b* 13 July 1959

3a *Antigone Maria; *b* 13 May 1962

(1) *Agnes Pauline [The Hon Mrs Richard Henniker-Major, 13 Market Cross Place, Aldeburgh, Suffolk]; *b* 10 July 1919; *m* 22 June 1946 *Hon Richard Arthur Otway Henniker-Major, yr s of 7th Baron Henniker (*qv*), and has issue

(2) *Sheila Catherine; *b* 11 Aug 1929

The **1st Baron** *m* 2nd 22 March 1905 Margaret Elizabeth (*d* 22 March 1940), dau of Henry Holland and Mrs James Wason, of Camberley, and *d* 23 Nov 1929, having by her had issue:

2 (HENRY) EVELYN ALEXANDER, **3rd Baron**

6 Irene Margaretta; *b* 21 July 1908; *m* 10 Jan 1934 Lt-Col Hugh Littleton Dewhurst, RA, yr s of Capt Gerard Powys Dewhurst, of Bodidris, Llandegla, N Wales, and had issue (*see* NAIRN, Bt, and RANKIN, Bt)

The 2nd BARON's half-brother,

(HENRY) EVELYN ALEXANDER DEWAR, **3rd Baron Forteviot**, MBE (1943), TD, JP (Perthshire 1957), DL (1961); *b* 23 Feb 1906; *educ* Eton and St John's Coll Oxford (BA 1929); chm John Dewar & Sons 1954–76, dir Distillers' Co 1956–76, Buchanan-Dewar and Roy Exchange Assur (Dundee branch), T/Maj Black Watch WW II (despatches); *m* 25 April 1933 Cynthia Monica (*d* 1986), est dau of Piers Cecil Le Gendre Starkie (*see* DE HOGHTON, Bt), and *d* 25 March 1993, leaving:

1 JOHN JAMES EVELYN DEWAR, **4th and present Baron Forteviot**

2 +Simon Thomas [The Hon Simon Dewar, Terling Park, Moree, NSW 2400, Australia]; *b* 11 Feb 1941; *educ* Bradfield; *m* 1st 3 Aug 1970 (*divorce* 1974) Helen Elizabeth, dau of W N Bassett, of Karoola Park, Roma, Queensland; *m* 2nd 4 Sept 1979 *Jennifer Alexandra, dau of John Edward St John Hedge, of Avoca Beach, NSW, and by her has:

(1) *Fiona Mary; *b* 20 Nov 1980

(2) *Alexandra Jean; *b* 1982

(3) *Mary Caroline; *b* 1984

1 *Caroline Cicely; *b* 12 Feb 1934; *m* 1st 11 Sept 1956 (*divorce* 1966) 3rd Duke of Fife (*qv*) and has issue; *m* 2nd 7 Nov 1980 *Gen Sir Richard Edward Worsley, KCB, OBE, s of Herbert Henry Knight Worsley, of Grey Abbey, Co Down, and by her 1st husb has issue

2 *Penelope Cynthia [The Hon Mrs Penelope Butler, 73 Duchess Drive, Newmarket, Suffolk]; *b* 29 April 1935; *m* 14 Dec 1959 (*divorce* 1977) Norman Frank Paul Butler, est s of Paul Butler, of Hinsdale, Ill., and has had:

(1) Paul; *b* 13 June 1960; *educ* Glenstal Abbey, Co Limerick; *d* 1988

(2) *Sean; *b* 25 Sept 1963; *educ* Glenstal Abbey, Co Limerick

(1) *Tracey Penelope; *b* 6 Nov 1961

FORWOOD

Arms: Per fess or and az., in chief a cormorant sa., beaked and legged gu., between two fleurs-de-lys of the second, in base an ancient ship with three masts of the first, sail arg., colours flying of the fourth. **Crest:** Between two wings arg. the battlements of a tower, thereon in front of a stag's head two hatchets in saltire, all ppr. **Motto:** *Fide virtute et labore* ('By faith, virtue and labour'). **Creation:** Bt. (UK) 5 Sept 1895.

SIR DUDLEY RICHARD FORWOOD, 3RD BT [Sir Dudley Forwood Bt, 43 Addison Rd, London W14; Uppacott, Bagnum, Hants BH24 3BZ]; *b* 6 June 1912; *s* f 1961; *educ* Stowe; late T/Maj Scots Gds Res of Offrs, Equerry to HRH THE DUKE OF WINDSOR 1937–39, Hon Attaché Vienna 1934–37, Master New Forest Buck Hounds 1957–65, underwriting memb Lloyd's, Hon Dir Roy Ag Show 1972–77 (V-Pres 1983–), Official Verderer New Forest 1974–82, Chm: New Forest Consultative Panel 1971–82, New Forest Ag Soc 1964–82 (Pres 1983), Crufts 1973–89, Tstee Kennel Club; *m* 27 May 1952 *Mary Gwendoline, formerly w of (a) 2nd Marquess of Willingdon (*see* 1970 edn), (b) Frederick Robert Cullingford and (c) Brig Donald Croft-Wilcock and est dau of Basil Samuel Foster, of Worcs, and has adopted his stepson:

*Rodney Simon Dudley [Rodney Forwood Esq, The Hermitage, St Catherine, Bath, Somerset]; took name FORWOOD by deed poll, late Capt Irish Gds, ADC to GOC Br Sector Berlin 1965–68; *b* 24 Sept 1940; *educ* Malvern; *m* 9 Dec 1964 *Jennifer Jane, er dau of Maj-Gen Sir John Nelson, KCVO, CB, DSO, OBE, MC (*see* GRAFTON, D), and has:

(1) *Patrick John Dudley; *b* 23 April 1967

(2) *James; *b* 16 March 1969

Lineage: THOMAS FORWOOD; Lt RM; *b* 8 Dec 1734 (s of Christopher Forwood); *m* 11 Sept 1758 Faith Friend (*b* 23 Sept 1739) and *d* 11 May 1781, having had, with another s and two daus:

GEORGE FORWOOD, of Liverpool; *b* 9 Nov 1776; *m* 12 Dec 1802 Mary Peploe, of Moreton Say, Salop (*d* 5 April 1819), and *d* 21 March 1835, having had a 2nd s:

THOMAS FRIEND BRITTAIN PEPLOE FORWOOD, of Thornton Manor, Thornton Hough, JP Cheshire; *b* 13 Jan 1811; *m* 2 July 1835 Charlotte (*d* 1 Aug 1861), est dau of William Bower, of Liverpool, and *d* 18 Dec 1884, having had, with other issue:

Sir Arthur Bower Forwood, 1st Bt (UK), so *cr* 5 Sept 1895, PC, JP Liverpool; MP (C) Ormskirk 1885–98, Alderman and Mayor Liverpool 1878–79, Parly Sec Admlty 1886–92; *b* 23 June 1836; *m* 1st 26 Oct 1858 Lucy (*d* 4 Nov 1873), dau of Simon Crosfield, of Liverpool, and had:

1 Emily Crosfield; *b* 16 July 1861; *m* 26 Sept 1893 Henry Grey Kellock (*d* 1926) and *d* 25 Jan 1955, leaving issue

2 Ethel Charlotte; *b* 8 May 1863; *m* 17 Aug 1901 Hugh Cunninghame Kelly and *d* 28 Dec 1937

3 Mildred Lucy; *b* 5 Feb 1870; *d* unm 9 July 1967

Sir Arthur *m* 2nd 1 Sept 1874 Mary Anne Eliza (*d* 24 March 1928), 2nd dau of Thomas Baines, FRS, and by her had:

1 DUDLEY BAINES (Sir), **2nd Bt**

2 Talbot Brittain; Lt-Col Duke of Lancaster's Own Yeo Boer War 1901–02 (medal with five clasps) and WW I (wounded, despatches, Croix de Guerre); *b* 13 April 1879; *educ* Harrow; *m* 12 April 1923 Geraldine (*d* 16 May 1963), dau of G W Mumford, of Oakfield, Gateacre, and *d* 26 July 1940

3 Arthur Noel; Lt Roy Fus WW I 1915–17; *b* 28 March 1881; *educ* Harrow; *m* 1st 3 June 1903 (*divorce* 1923) Evelyn Agnes Heathcote, only dau of W Forrester Addie, JP, of Powis Castle Park, Welshpool; *m* 2nd 1923 Hyacinth, (*d* 18 Nov 1972), dau of Henry Pollard, of Chester, and *d* 3 June 1959, leaving by her:

(1) +PETER NOEL [Peter Forwood Esq, Newhouse Farm, Shillinglee, Chiddingfold, Surrey]; *b* 15 Oct 1925; heir presumptive; *educ* Radley; Welsh Gds WW II 1945; *m* 1950 *Roy, dau of James Murphy, MBE, FRCS, LRCP, of Horsham, Sussex, and has:

1a *Susan Noel; *b* 21 July 1951

2a *Diana Geraldine; *b* 11 Sept 1953; *m* 1980 *Capt Edward Joshua Cooper, Irish Gds (ret), er s of Lt-Cdr Edward Francis Patrick Cooper, RN, of Markree Castle, Co Sligo (*see* CASTLEMAINE, B)

3a *Jane; *b* 11 Aug 1954

4a *Joanna Baines; *b* 15 April 1956

5a *Caragh Vivien; *b* 8 Nov 1958

6a *Amanda Elizabeth; *b* 30 April 1963

(1) *Enid; *b* 1924; *m* 1950 *Herbert J Wale, of Glebe Farm, W Haddon, Northants, and has issue:

1a *Robert Noel Cattell; *b* 1957

2a *Gerald Richard; *b* 1959

1a *Angela Mary; *b* 1954

(2) *Wendy Baines; *b* 1931

4 Eric Baines; Lt RFA WW I; *b* 26 June 1884; *educ* Harrow; *m* 19 July 1911 Mary Katharine (*d* 25 March 1965), yr dau of John Herbert, of Kenilworth, and *d* 8 Jan 1949, leaving issue:

(1) *Judith; *b* 17 Aug 1912

4 Ida Baines; *b* 11 July 1877; *m* 6 April 1904 Charles Nicholas Theodore Jeffreys, MBE, slr, s of Walter Powell Jeffreys, JP, DL, of Llandovery, and *d* 12 Oct 1959. He *d* 1957

Sir ARTHUR *d* 27 Sept 1898; his est son,

Sir Dudley Baines Forwood, 2nd Bt, CMG (1919); *b* 31 May 1875; *educ* Harrow; Lt-Col RFA, Gen Res Offrs, Maj and Hon Lt-Col 2nd Lancs RFA WW I (despatches), Master New Forest Buckhounds 1950–57; *m* 24 July 1901 Norah Isabella (*d* 18 Jan 1962), er dau of Richard Robertson Lockett, of Liverpool, and *d* 22 Dec 1961, having had:

1 Arthur Dudley; *b* 10 Feb, *d* 14 May 1908

2 Sir DUDLEY RICHARD FORWOOD, **3rd and present Bt**

FOSTER

Creation: Bt. (UK) 5 Feb 1930.

SIR JOHN GREGORY FOSTER, 3RD BT, of Bloomsbury, London [Sir John Foster Bt, 7 Caledon St, PO Box 1325, George 6530, Cape Province, S Africa]; *b* 26 Feb 1927; *s* f 1957; *educ* Michaelhouse Coll Natal, Witwatersrand U (MB, BCh 1951) and Roy Coll Physicians Edinburgh (MRCPE 1955, FRCPE 1981), S African Artillery WW II 1944–46, Dip Nat Health 1962, Consultant Physician, Hon Physician George Oudshoorn and Mossel Bay Hosps; *m* 24 Nov 1956 *Jean Millicent, est dau of Elwin Watts, FRCSE, of Germiston, and has:

1 +SAXBY GREGORY; *b* 3 Sept 1957; *m* 1 July 1989 *Rowen Audrey, dau of Reginald Archibald Ford, of Durban, and has:

(1) +Thomas James Gregory; *b* 1 May 1991

(2) +Robert John Gregory; *b* 10 Dec 1992

1 *Deborah Jean Gregory [Mrs Steffen Zoutendijk, 125 Wavecrest Ave, Venice, CA, USA]; *b* 2 April 1959; *m* 21 April 1986 *Steffen Zoutendijk and has issue:

(1) *Peter Gaelan Foster; *b* 26 March 1989

2 *Carolyn Gregory; *b* 17 Jan 1962

3 *Rosemary Gregory; *b* 22 Sept 1963

Lineage: Rev THOMAS FOSTER, of The Rectory, Fetcham, Surrey; MA Cantab; *d* 1 May 1836 aged 83, leaving:

THOMAS GREGORY FOSTER, of Cavendish House, Clapham; *b* Dec 1815; barrister Lincoln's Inn; *m* Aug 1858 Sophie (*d* 11 Jul 1911), dau of John Farquhar Allday, of Birmingham, and *d* 21 Dec 1903, leaving, with other issue:

1 THOMAS GREGORY (Sir), **1st Bt**

2 William Arthur John; *b* 1 Jan 1870; *m* 6 Oct 1897 Helen Sowerby, dau of Richard Stephen Wallis, MRCS, and *d* 25 July 1947, leaving issue:

(1) Richard Arthur Denys; *b* 9 Oct 1906; *educ* Harrow; *m* 6 Sept 1930 Helen Mary Foster, er dau of John George Burnett, of Powis House, Aberdeen, and has:

1a *(Ronald William) John; *b* 3 Feb 1934; *educ* Harrow; Capt RM

2a *David Malcolm; *b* 8 Nov 1935

1a *Rosemary Alison; *b* 16 June 1931; *m* 8 Oct 1955 Robert Tasker Paice, s of Charles Tasker Paice, of Glebe House, Whitsbury, Wilts, and has issue:

1b *William Tasker; *b* 2 April 1959

2b *Edward Charles Richard; *b* 13 April 1962

1b *Helen Amanda Catherine; *b* 11 July 1957

3 Alfred Edye Manning; *b* 1 Dec 1874; FRSL; *m* 1st 23 Oct 1901 Eleanor Margaret Elizabeth (*d* 23 Feb 1906), dau of Thomas Franks, JP, of Carrig Park, Mallow, Co Cork; *m* 2nd 29 Dec 1928 Olga Bijou Dina, 2nd dau of Brig-Gen William Frederick de Hubbenent Curtis, RA (*see* CURTIS, Bt), and *d* 25 Aug 1939, leaving by his 1st w:

(1) *Patrick Franks Manning; *b* 10 Feb 1906

1 Edith Jennett; *m* 1 June 1909 Rev Edward Frederick Hoernle, Canon and Chllr St Mary's Cathedral, Edinburgh (*d* 1916), s of Rev J Hoernle, missionary in India, and *d* 21 June 1932

2 Annie Mary Graeme; *b* 1 May 1868; *m* Oct 1905 Rev Joseph Depledge Crabtree and *d* 2 Nov 1911

3 Lilian Margaret; *b* 20 Nov 1872; *m* 1st 28 Dec 1898 Rev William Roger (*d* 8 Jan 1914) and had issue; *m* 2nd 3 July 1915 John Cumming, MD, FRCP, FRCS, of Strathearn Lodge, Strathearn Place, Edinburgh, and *d* Nov 1960

THOMAS FOSTER's est s,

Sir Thomas Gregory Foster, 1st Bt (UK), so *cr* 5 Feb 1930; *b* 10 June 1866; PhD, Fell UCL and Provost 1904–29, V-Chllr London U 1928–30, ktd 1917; *m* 1st 15 Aug 1894 Fanny Maude (*d* 8 Dec 1928), dau of James Sledge, of Hove; *m* 2nd 3 March 1931 Elise Johanna Emma (*d* 3 Oct 1931), dau of George Peter William Augener, and *d* 24 Sept 1931, leaving by his 1st w:

1 THOMAS SAXBY GREGORY (Sir), **2nd Bt**

2 Lewis Marshall Gregory; *b* 3 Feb 1904; F/Lt RAF WW II; *m* 6 June 1931 *Margaret Amy, dau of Max O Tillard, of Modderfontein, Johannesburg, and *d* 1970, leaving issue:

(1) +Richard Tillard [Richard Foster Esq, PO Box 86, Southbroom, Natal, S Africa]; *b* 7 March 1935; late F/Lt RAF; *m* 1964 (*divorce* 1973) Carola Margaret, dau of Rev George Henry Edward Talbot Roe, Rector Wheathampstead, Herts; *m* 2nd 1975 *Winifred Moira Cameron, dau of — Walker, and has by his 1st w:

1a *Polly Tillard; *b* 21 Dec 1965

2a *Candy Tillard; *b* 1970

(1) *Eve Tillard [Mrs Donald Croudace, Woodcote Granary, Rouncil Lane, Kenilworth, Warwicks]; *b* 23 Feb 1932; *m* 27 Feb 1954 *Donald Miller Croudace, s of F R Croudace, of Newcastle, and has issue:

1a *Brigid Lucy; *b* 7 Jan 1959

2a *Charlotte Polly; *b* 1 June 1962

3 Margaret Gregory; *m* 5 Feb 1924 Arthur Loraine Lawford, of CP, S Africa, and *d* 21 Nov 1934, leaving issue

4 Helen Morley Gregory, MRCS, LRCP; *m* 10 Oct 1935 her bro-in-law Arthur Loraine Lawford and had:

(1) *David Loraine; *b* 9 Feb 1940

(1) *Margaret Loraine; *b* 20 July 1937; *m* 9 May 1964 *Carl Richard Mackay Anderson, s of Carl Anderson, of Johannesburg

Sir THOMAS's est s,

Sir Thomas Saxby Gregory Foster, 2nd Bt; *b* 1 Feb 1899; *educ* Marlborough; Lt RFA WW I 1917–19, Lt-Col S African Artillery WW II; *m* 17 June 1925 Beryl, yst dau of Alfred Ireland, MD, of Cradock, CP, S Africa and *d* 17 May 1957, leaving:

1 Sir JOHN GREGORY FOSTER, **3rd and present Bt**

1 Barbara Maude Gregory; *b* 22 May 1929; *m* 1st 20 Nov 1954 (*divorce* 19–) Derek Norman Spurgeon, s of Norman C A Spurgeon, of Manor House Hotel, Leamington Spa, Warwicks, and had issue:

(1) *Susan Ann; *b* 26 July 1956; *m* 19– *Tjeert Boonen, of Holland, and has:

1a *Marc

2a *James

1 (cont.) Mrs Barbara Spurgeon *m* 2nd 19– *Ronald Gordon and *d* 2 April 1991, leaving by him:

(1) *Andrew

(2) *Kirsten Louise

FOULIS

Arms: Arg. three bay-leaves slipped vert. **Crest:** A dexter hand couped, holding a sword in pale, sustaining a wreath of laurel all ppr. **Mottoes:** 1 (over crest) *Mente manuque præsto* ('I am prepared mentally and manually'), 2 (under arms) *Non jure deficit* 'He does not transgress against what is right'). **Creation:** Bt. (NS) 7 June 1634.

SIR IAN PRIMROSE LISTON FOULIS, 13TH BT, of Colinton, Edinburgh [Sir Ian Foulis Bt, Aptdo de Correos 7, Portal 5–2–C, San Agustin de Guadalix, 28750 Madrid, Spain]; *b* 9 Aug 1937; *s* cousin 1961, dropped LISTON as surname 1988; *educ* Stonyhurst and Cannington Farm Inst Somerset (Dip Ag); served Argyll & Sutherland Highrs 1957–59; landowner 1961, language tutor Madrid 1959–61 (Dip Spanish Madrid), trainee exec Bank of London and S America 1962 and Bank of London and Montreal Nassau 1963, Guatemala 1963–64, Managua 1964–65, Toronto (Sales) 1965–66, life memb Nat Tst for Scotland, memb Spanish Soc of Friends of Castles, Friends of the St James Way, pilgrimage Somport to Santiago 1971 on foot

Lineage: A family history in the present Bt's possession asserts that the FOULISes are of Norman origin and that the name is a corruption of (de) *feuilles* or 'leaves', the device on their coat of arms. It is further claimed that the family produced at least two Secretaries to Kings of Scots, one to MALCOLM II, the other to JAMES II. No detailed pedigree linking medieval FOULISes with 16th-century persons of that name appears to be available, however.

JAMES FOULIS; MP (S Parl); Judge 1526, Ld of Session 1532, Ld Clerk Register; bought Colinton; *m* Catherine Brown and had:

HENRY FOULIS of Colinton; Depute Marishal; *m* Margaret Haldane and had:

JAMES FOULIS of Colinton; *m* Agnes (*d* 5 Aug 1593), dau and heir of Robert Heriot of Lumphoy, and had:

1 James (Sir), of Colinton; MP Edinburgh 1612; *m* Mary, dau of Sir John Lauder of Hatton, and had, with a dau (Margaret, *m* Louis Dick):

(1) **Sir Alexander Foulis, 1st Bt** (NS), so *cr* 7 June 1634, with remainder to his heirs male whatsoever; *m* (settlement 30 March 1619) Elizabeth, dau and coheir of Robert Hepburn of Ford and widow of Sir John Stewart, Sheriff Bute, and *d c* 1672, leaving an only s:

1a **Sir James Foulis, 2nd Bt**; MP Edinburgh 1645–84; engaged in Scottish wars following the death of CHARLES I; Ld of Session 1661, Ld Justice Clerk 1684 as Lord Colinton; *m* 1st Barbara, dau of Andrew Ainslie, Edinburgh merchant, and had two sons; *m* 2nd (contract 1 June 1661) Margaret, dau and coheir of Sir George Erskine of Inverteil and widow of Sir John Mackenzie, 1st Bt, of Tarbat (*see* CROMARTIE, E), and *d* 19 Jan 1688, leaving an est s:

1b **Sir James Foulis, 3rd Bt**, PC 1702; Ld of Session as Lord Redford 1674, MP Co Edinburgh 1686–93, opposed Union of E and S Parls; *m* 4 Sept 1670 Margaret, dau and heir of John Boyd, Dean of Guild of Edinburgh, and *d* 1711, leaving, with a 2nd s:

1c **Sir James Foulis, 4th Bt**, MP Edinburgh 1704–7; *d* unm July 1742

3c Henry; *m* Jean, dau of Adam Foulis, Edinburgh merchant, and had:

1d **Sir James Foulis, 5th Bt**; *m* Mary, dau of Archibald Wightman, and *d* 3 Jan 1791, leaving an only surv s:

1e **Sir James Foulis, 6th Bt**; sold Colinton; *m* 1st —, of Spain; *m* 2nd 17 June 1791 Margaret, dau of William Dallas, and *dsp* 1825

2 George, of Ravelston; merchant, Baillie Edinburgh, Master Mint; *m* 1603 Janet, only child of George Bannatine, and *d* 28 May 1633, leaving:

(1) George, of Ravelston; *b* 6 April 1606; Master Mint; *m* Jean, dau of Sir John Sinclair of Stevenson, and had:

1 a Sir JOHN FOULIS, 1st Bt (NS), so *cr* 15 Oct 1661, of Ravelston, also of Woodhall, Juniper Green, which he bought 1701; *b* 20 Feb 1638; *m* 1st 5 Sept 1661 Margaret (*d* 15 April 1690), est dau of Sir Archibald Primrose, 1st Bt (*see* ROSEBERY, E), who brought him Dunipace; *m* 2nd 28 Aug 1690 Agnes (*d* 16 Jan 1696), est dau of Walter Dundas, 20th of Dundas; *m* 3rd 29 March 1697 Mary (*d* 27 Dec 1702), dau of John Murray of Polmaise and widow of John Cunninghame of Enterkin; *m* 4th 7 Sept 1705 Agnes (*bur* 26 June 1720), dau of — Scot and widow of Andrew Bruce, of Edinburgh, and *d* 5 Aug 1707, having had, with other issue:

1b George FOULIS later PRIMROSE of Dunipace; *b* 10 May 1667; *m* 3 April 1691 Janet (*d* 29 Dec 1758), dau of Sir William Cunningham of Caprington, Bt (*see* 1850 edn), and *dvp* 1707, having had, with other issue:

1c Sir ARCHIBALD PRIMROSE, 2nd Bt; *b c* 1692; sold Ravelston; *m* 1st Lady Margaret Fleming (*dsp*), dau of 6th Earl of Wigtoun; *m* 2nd 19 Nov 1724 Mary (*d* 17 Dec 1746), dau of 1st Earl of Rosebery (*qv*), and was hanged at Carlisle 15 Nov 1746 for his part in the 1745 Uprising, his title and estate being forfeited, leaving, with surv daus (on whom a pension of £200 was later granted) an only surv s (Archibald, *d* unm 28 Jan 1747)

2b William, of Woodhall; *b* 20 May 1674; advocate; *m* Janet Cuningham and *d* June 1737, leaving:

1c John, of Woodhall; *b* 25 Feb 1709; *d* Dec 1732, leaving an only s:

1d William, of Woodhall; *b* 6 Nov 1732; *m* the dau of — Campbell, of Carsebank, and *d* June 1796, leaving:

1e JAMES (Sir), **7th Bt**

1b Jean; *m* 4 July 1685 John Hay, Yr. of Linplum (*see* TWEEDDALE, M)

3 Sir DAVID FOULIS, 1st Bt (E), so *cr* 6 Feb 1619/20 (*see* 1877 edn)

4 John, of Leadhills; gf of Anne (heir of Leadhills, *m* Sir James Hope of Hopetoun, *see* LINLITHGOW, M)

The 6th Bt's sixth cousin,

Sir James Foulis, 7th Bt, of Woodhall; *b* 9 Sept 1770; *m* 29 Aug 1810 Agnes, est dau of John Grieve, of Edinburgh, and *d* 2 May 1842, having had issue:

1 WILLIAM (Sir), **8th Bt**

2 John, MD; *b* 1816; Dr in Sydney, NSW; *m* 1st 1842 Mary Buchanan, dau of William Blair, of Greenwich; *m* 2nd 25 June 1844 Jane Selina (*d* 1871), dau of Isaac Nathan, of Byron Lodge, Sydney, and *d* 1870, leaving issue:

(1) James, MD, FRCPE; *b* 18 Feb 1846; *m* 19 Sept 1878 Henrietta Baird (*d* 8 May 1930), dau of William N Fraser, of Findrack, Aberdeenshire, and *d* 4 Oct 1901, leaving issue:

1a Wilfrid Venour; *b* 19 June 1884; Governing Dir LAMDA; *m* 1st 27 Nov 1909 (*divorce* 1923) Clara Millington, dau of Alfred Dow, and had issue:

1b Michael Venour Primrose, DFC and bar; *b* 11 April 1915; Actg /S/Ldr RAFVR WW II; *ka* April 1944

1a (cont.) Wilfrid Foulis *m* 2nd 7 June 1924 Ida, dau of Rev Joshua Brookes, Canon Lahore Cathedral, and *d* 28 Dec 1951, having by her had:

1b *Ursula Patricia Carey Sibella; *b* 10 March 1926; *m* 14 March 1947 (*divorce* 1970) William Joseph Kiernan, of Sevenoaks, Kent

1a Lilian Carey; *d* unm 10 Jan 1956

2a Henrietta; *d* 1 March 1951

(2) William; *b* 4 Oct 1848; *m* 6 Jan 1874 Louisa May (*d* 22 June 1939), dau of John Bell, of Sydney, NSW, and *d* 22 July 1912, having had, with other issue:

1a William Bell; *b* 10 May 1877; *m* 23 June 1923 Martha Elizabeth Child and *dsp* 5 Sept 1944

2a John Everard; *b* 14 June 1878; *m* 27 Nov 1908 Ada Florence, dau of Capt Woodward, and *dsp* 13 Sept 1916

3a James Foulis; *b* 30 Nov 1880; *d* unm 17 Jan 1915

4a Harold Liston; *b* 5 April 1884; *d* May 1885

1a Louisa May; *b* 23 June 1885

(1) Florence Jane; *m* 23 June 1885 Alexander Henry Clarke, of Earls Court, London, and *d* 1930

1 Thomasina Agnes; *m* 2 July 1844 Col William Low, HEIMS, and *d* 6 March 1870

2 Jane; *m* 2 July 1844 William Logan White, of Kellerstain, Edinburgh

The 7th Bt's er son,

Sir WILLIAM FOULIS later LISTON FOULIS (added on marriage), **8th Bt**; *b* 27 July 1812; *m* 1st 20 June 1843 Henrietta Ramage Liston, of Millburn Tower, Co Edinburgh (*d* 1850), er surv dau of Capt Ramage Liston, RN, and great-niece and heiress of Sir Robert Liston, GCB, Amb Constantinople; *m* 2nd 7 April 1852 Mary Anne (*d* 5 Feb 1905), est dau of Robert Cadell, of Ratho, Midlothian, and *d* 22 Feb 1858, having had, with other issue, including a dau (Janet Agnes Harriet, *m* 29 Nov 1865 Maj Irvine Low (*d* 1881), Bengal Cav, yst s of Gen Sir John Low, KCB, of Clatto, Fife, and *d* 14 Oct 1914):

Sir James Liston Foulis, 9th Bt; *b* 3 July 1847; *m* 8 Dec 1868 Sarah Helen (*d* 11 April 1918), est dau of Sir Charles Metcalfe Ochterlony, 2nd Bt, of Ochterlony (*see* 1956 edn), and *d* 29 Dec 1895, having had, with other issue:

1 **Sir William Liston Foulis, 10th Bt**; *b* 27 Oct 1869; *d* unm 16 April 1918

2 **Sir Charles James Liston Foulis, 11th Bt**; *b* 4 Jan 1873; Paymaster German E Africa 1916–19, T/Capt 1917–19; *m* 1902 Maria (*d* 17 June 1949), dau of Richard Moore, and *d* 18 Jan 1936, having had issue:

(1) **Sir Archibald Charles Liston Foulis, 12th Bt**; *b* 5 Aug 1903; *d* unm 9 Oct 1961

(1) Dorothy Helen; *d* an infant 8 Jan 1909

(2) *Gwynneth Beryl; *b* 10 Oct 1912; *m* 1940 *John Carl Pietersen, of Bulawayo, and adopted:

*Louise Marie; *b* 4 Sept 1946

3 Archibald Primrose; *b* 28 Aug 1874; Maj RM Artillery, Actg Lt-Col RGA; *m* 31 Oct 1907 Agnàse Eudora (*m* 2nd 15 July 1922 Lt-Col Neil Inglefield Eastman, RM), er dau of Capt George M Wingate, RA, of Craigengelt, Dunbar, and *das* 30 Nov 1917, leaving issue:

(1) James Alastair; *b* 31 July 1908; Lt-Col RA WW II; *m* 6 March 1934 Kathleen (*d* 5 Jan 1991), dau of Lt-Col John Moran, IA and Countess Olga De La Hogue, dau of Marquis De La Hogue, of Mauritius, and *das* 30 April 1942, leaving issue:

1a Sir IAN PRIMROSE LISTON FOULIS, **13th and present Bt**

1a *Simone Primrose [Mrs Geoffrey Hall, Flat 3, 10 Barton Terrace, Dawlish, Devon EX7 9QH]; *b* 20 Dec 1934; *m* 1973 *Geoffrey Richard Hall

2a *Susan Thérèsa Olga [Sra de José Larraz, Calle Mayor 3, Berdun, Huesca, Spain]; *b* 11 July 1941; *m* 1st 14 July 1962 Peter John Lely, of Godalming, Surrey, and has issue:

1b *Edward James Mounteney; *b* 23 May 1965

1b *Josephine Anne; *b* 22 April 1963

2a (cont.) Susan Thérèsa Olga *m* 2nd 1976 *José Luis Larraz (Casasus) and by him has:

2b *Mark; *b* 1977

3b *James; *b* 1978

2b *Sophie Anne; *b* 1986

(1) *Avril Primrose [Mrs Desmond Allhusen, Court Cott, 62 High West St, Dorchester, Dorset DT1 1UY]; *b* 5 April 1915; *m* 22 Nov 1946 Maj Desmond Allhusen (*d* 25 March 1977), KRRC, of Beaminster, Dorset

4 George Herbert, JP Edinburgh; *b* 14 Dec 1879; *educ* Edinburgh Acad; Lt Serv Bn Seaforth Highrs WW I, Archangel Expdn 1918–19; manager Edinburgh RBS; *m* 9 Oct 1919 Grace Marguerite, only child of Frederick Walter Carter, and *dsp* 10 June 1957

1 Ethel Charlotte; *b* 22 July 1878; *d* unm 29 July 1956

FOWKE

Arms: Vert, a fleur-de-lys argent. **Crests:** 1 A dexter arm embowed, vested vert cuffed argent, the hand proper grasping an arrow in bend sinister or, barbed and flighted silver, 2 An Indian goat's head erased vert, horns and beard argent. **Motto:** *Arma tuenter pacem* ('Weapons preserve peace'). **Creation:** Bt. (UK) 7 Feb 1814.

SIR DAVID FREDERICK GUSTAVUS FOWKE, 5TH BT, of Lowesby, Co Leicester [Sir David Fowke Bt, 1 Willyama Ave, Medindie, S Australia 5081, Australia]; *b* 28 Aug 1950; *s* unc 1987; *educ* Cranbrook Sch Sydney and Sydney U (BA)

Lineage: JOHN FOWKE, of Gunston, Staffs (s of William Fowke, of Brewood); *m* Agnes, dau and heir of John Newman, of Gunston, and had issue:

ROGER FOWKE, of Gunston; *m* Cassandra, dau of William Humfreston, of Humphrinston, and had issue:

JOHN FOWKE, of Gunston; *m* Anne, dau of John Bradshaw, of Windley, Derbys, and had issue:

FRANCIS FOWKE, of Gunston and Enborne, Berks; *m* 1st Joan, dau of John Raynsford, of Tew, Oxon; *m* 2nd Elizabeth, dau of John Conyers, and *d* 1575, having by his 1st w had issue:

JOHN FOWKE, of Gunston; *m* Dorothy, dau of John Cupper, of Glimpston, Oxon, and *d* between 7 May 1638 and 7 Oct 1642, having had:

ROGER FOWKE, of Gunston; admitted Inner Temple 3 Feb 1605/6; *m* Mary, dau of Sir William Bailey, and *d* by 30 Nov 1649, having had:

JOHN FOWKE, of Gunston; admitted Inner Temple 12 May 1632; *m* Joyce, sis of Sir George Marche, of Limehouse, Stepney and Tower of London; *d* Tower of London and was *bur* 15 March 1669/70, leaving issue:

1 Roger, of Gunston; *bapt* 15 May 1645; *dsp* between 2 Dec 1673 and 9 July 1698

2 Richard (Rev); Vicar Stanmore, Middx, Rector Greystoke, Cumberland; *educ* Trin Coll Cambridge (MA); *m* Elizabeth, dau of Sir Humphrey Sydenham, of Chilworthy, Somerset, and was *bur* 19 Feb 1692/3, having had issue

3 John; admitted Inner Temple 8 Feb 1683/4; *dsp* 1713

4 THOMAS

5 George, of St James's, Westminster; *m* Mary — and d on or after 8 March 1728/9, leaving issue

JOHN FOWKE's 4th s,

THOMAS FOWKE; Capt in Col Nicholas Lepell's Regt of Foot; *m* 1st *c* 21 Sept 1677 Anne, dau of Sir James Austin, of Southwark, and widow of Sir Anthony Vincent, 4th Bt, of Stoke D'Abernon, Surrey, and had issue; *m* 2nd — and *d* 1708, leaving by her:

1 THOMAS

2 Edmund Thorpe, of Newbury, Berks; *b* 3 Dec 1704; R-Adml RN; *m* Margaret Simonds (*d* 17 Jan 1783) and *d* 14 March 1784, leaving issue

1 Martha; *m* Arnold Sansom, barrister, and had issue

2 Mary; *m* Henry Villiers, of Chelsea, Middx

Capt THOMAS FOWKE's er s (by his 2nd w),

THOMAS FOWKE; Govr Gibraltar 1754–55, Ensign Lepell's Regt, Capt 1707, Col 2nd Queen's Regt, Lt-Gen and AG Ireland 1761; *m* 1st Elizabeth (*dsp*), dau of Sir William Ingoldsby, 2nd Bt; *m* 2nd Dorothy (*d* 1 Dec 1788), dau of Edward Randall, of Salisbury, Wilts, and *d* 17 March 1765, having had, with a dau (Theophila, *d* 21 July 1751):

Sir THOMAS FOWKE, of Lowesby, Leics, JP, DL; *b c* 1744; Lt-Gen, Groom Bedchamber to DUKE OF CUMBERLAND, ktd 1779; *m* 12 Aug 1772 — (*d* 25 Nov 1803), 2nd dau and coheir of Sir Isaac Woollaston, 2nd Bt, of Lowesby, and *d* 30 Nov 1786, having had issue:

Sir Frederick Gustavus Fowke, 1st Bt (UK), so *cr* 7 Feb 1814; *b* Jan 1782; *m* Oct 1815 Mary Anne (*d* 8 Sept 1863), dau and heir of Anthony Henderson, MP, and *d* 1856, leaving issue:

1 FREDERICK THOMAS (Sir), **2nd Bt**

1 Mary Sophia; *m* 25 Oct 1843 Rev William Lancelot Rolleston (*d* 4 June 1890), Vicar Gt Dalby and Scraptoft, Leics, er s of Rev John Rolleston, of Burton Joyce, Notts, and *d* 16 Sept 1889, leaving issue

2 Anne Elizabeth; *m* 6 Oct 1864 Charles Sherard Burnaby (*d* 1891), of Evington, Leics, and *d* 18 Oct 1900

Sir FREDERICK's s,

Sir Frederick Thomas Fowke, 2nd Bt, JP, DL; *b* 29 June 1816; barrister Middle Temple, Col 3rd Bn Leicester Regt, Chm Leics QS, Constable Leicester Castle; *m* 10 May 1849 Sarah Mary (*d* 11 Dec 1902), dau and coheir of Henry Leigh Spencer, of Banstead Park, Surrey, and *d* 12 May 1897, having had issue:

1 Frederick Gustavus, JP (Leics); *b* 10 Oct 1853; Maj 3rd Bn Leics Regt; *m* 7 Sep 1878 Cecilia Eva (*d* 28 March 1933), 6th dau of Edward Nathaniel Conant (*see* CONANT, Bt), and *dvp* 16 Feb 1893, leaving:

(1) FREDERICK FERRERS CONANT (Sir), **3rd Bt**

(2) Gustavus Henry Spencer; *b* 14 Oct 1880; Maj Gordon Highrs Res Offrs, Boer War 1900–02 and WW I (wounded); *m* 8 June 1912 Kathleen Nora (*d* 12 Aug 1958), 5th dau of Sir George Hector Leith-Buchanan, 4th Bt (*qv*), and widow of Capt James Marshall McLaren, Gordon Highrs, and *dsp* 24 June 1946

(3) Laurence Archdale; *b* 1883; Lt Leics Regt (wounded, despatches) WW I; *d* unm 14 Jan 1958

(1) Eva Mirabelle; *d* unm 14 Nov 1942

(2) Isabel Margaret; *m* 12 Feb 1923 Rev Percy Lane Hooson, MA, Rector All Saints, Tinwell, Stamford, and had issue

2 Henry Spencer; *b* 23 Nov 1856; Lt 3rd Bn Leics Regt; *d* unm 13 Sept 1880

3 Charles Rowland (Rev); *b* 28 Oct 1859; MA Cambridge, Vicar Priory Church of St Giles, Little Malvern, and Billesdon, Leics, Capt 3rd Bn Leics Regt; *m* 10 Feb 1892 Ela (*d* 13 March 1941), dau of Rt Rev Hon Arthur Gascoigne Douglas (*see* MORTON, E), and *d* 12 Aug 1920, having had issue:

(1) Charles Arthur Freer, MBE (1947), MC; *b* 9 Jan 1893; Capt 3rd Bn Oxon and Bucks LI WW I (wounded twice); *educ* Charterhouse; *m* 22 Aug 1942 Violet (*d* 23 Dec 1948), only dau of Brig-Gen Frederick William Lumsden, VC, CB, DSO, and widow of Maj Albert Kenlis North, and *dsp* 16 Dec 1969

(2) Rowland Douglas; *b* 21 Sept 1897; *d* 6 Nov 1898

1 Mary Elizabeth Audrey; *d* young 18 April 1860

2 Mirabell Frances; *d* unm 5 April 1928

3 Fanny Isabella; *d* young 19 Oct 1855

4 Kathleen Sarah; *d* young 2 July 1858

5 Margaret Woolaston; *m* 30 Sept 1896 Maj Norman Pochin, Roy Fus (*d* 23 March 1936), of Barkby Lodge, Barkby, Leics, and *d* 1942

Sir FREDERICK's gs,

Sir Frederick Ferrers Conant Fowke, 3rd Bt; *b* 13 May 1879; Maj Leicester Yeo TF, Lt Prince Albert's Own Leicester Inf Yeo, Hon Lt Army; *m* 1 Feb 1910 Edith Frances Daubeney (*d* 3 Oct 1958), dau of Rev Canon James Hamer Rawdon, and *d* 22 May 1948, leaving issue:

1 **Sir Frederick Woollaston Rawdon Fowke, 4th Bt**; *b* 14 Dec 1910; *educ* Uppingham; Capt Derbys Yeo WW II 1939–43 (wounded); *m* 25 June 1948 Barbara Ethel (*d* 1982), yr dau of Louis Percival Townsend, of Chard, Somerset, and *d* 1987, leaving issue:

(1) *Sarah Elizabeth [Mrs Jon Robinson, 54 Orchard Ave, Chichester, Sussex]; *b* 1 Aug 1949; *m* 1989 *Jon Robinson and has issue:

1a *Oliver; *b* 1980

1a *Kate; *b* 1981

2a *Alice; *b* 1990

(2) *Belinda Barbara [Mrs Richard Laban, 53 Arcot Park, Sidmouth, Devon]; *b* 12 Oct 1955; *m* 1983 *Richard Laban and has issue:

1a *Sam; *b* 1983

2a *Joe; *b* 1985

3a *Lily; *b* 1986

2 Gerrard George; *b* 20 March 1915; Lt-Col Welsh Gds WW II (despatches, Croix de Guerre); *m* 7 Aug 1946 Daphne [Mrs Gerrard Fowke, 4 Queen's Pk Rd, Bondi Junction, NSW 2022, Australia], dau of Aristos Monasterioti, of Corfu, and *d* 11 Oct 1969, leaving issue:

(1) Sir DAVID FREDERICK GUSTAVUS FOWKE, **5th and present Bt**

(1) *(Louise) Caroline Daphne; *b* 20 March 1948; *m* 1970 (*divorce* 1994) Bruce Theodore Davies

3 Michael Gustavus; *b* 17 April 1919; Cdr RN WW II (despatches twice); *m* 15 Feb 1943 Esme Muriel, yst dau of Philip John FitzGibbon, of Crohana, Stonyford, Co Kilkenny, and formerly w of R-Adml Clarence Dinsmore Howard-Johnston, and *d* 8 April 1977

1 *Betty Mirabelle; *b* 30 March 1912; *m* 12 June 1934 *Maj Charles Chichester, Roy Devon Yeo, of Hall, Barnstaple, s of Maj Charles Hamlyn Chichester, and has issue:

(1) *Penelope Anne; *b* 1935; *m* 1959 Col Martin Frederick William Maxse (*see* BERKELEY, B)

(2) *Diana Margaret; *b* 1939; *m* 1967 *(Edmond) Jerome ('Min') Mahony, of Holly Park, Craughwell, Co Galway, and has issue:

1a *Edmond (Eddie); *b* 30 Aug 1972

1a *Maria Lucia Mirabelle; *b* 1969

2a *Melissa; *b* 28 Dec 1970

(3) *Helena Elizabeth; *b* 1940

FRANK

Creation: Bt. (UK) 19 June 1920.

SIR (ROBERT) ANDREW FRANK 4TH BT, of Withyham, Sussex [Sir Andrew Frank Bt, Periac, Forest Rd, Binfield, Berks RG12 5HD]; *b* 1964; *s* f 1987; *educ* Eton; dramatic producer; *m* 1990 *Zoe Alia, er dau of S A Hasan, of Windsor, Berks

Lineage: FREDERICK FRANK, of Blackhurst, Tunbridge Wells, Kent; *d* Nov 1915, leaving issue:

Sir Howard George Frank, 1st Bt (UK), so *cr* 19 June 1920, GBE (1924), KCB (1918); *b* 10 Nov 1871; sr ptnr Knight, Frank and Rutley, FICS, dir Norwich Union Fire Insur Soc, pres Estate Agents' Inst 1910–12, govr Roy Ag Soc, Dir-Gen Lands War Office, Min Munitions and Air Min 1917–22, memb Roy Commns: Oxford and Cambridge U Estates 1919–21 and Police Powers and Procedure 1928–29, chm Ctees: on Crown and Govt Lands 1921–22 and Govt Properties 1930, Govr Star and Garter Home Richmond, V-Chm Cheyne Hosp Chelsea, ktd 1914; *m* 1st 11 Sept 1896 Mabel Helen (*d* 5 Dec 1920), yst dau of Joseph Arnold, of Tunbridge Wells, and had:

1 Mary Doreen; *m* 1st 1 Dec 1922 (*divorce* 1936) Lt Kenneth Norman Mackenzie Macrae, RN (*d* 2 July 1958), s of Alexander William Macrae, and had issue; *m* 2nd D Green

Sir Howard *m* 2nd 12 Jan 1922 Annie Muriel, OBE (*m* 2nd 11 July 1932 A/M Sir Arthur Coningham, KCB, KBE, DSO, MC, DFC, AFC, RAF, *k* in a flying accident in the Atlantic 30 Jan 1948), dau of John Brooks, and *d* 10 Jan 1932, leaving by her:

1 **Sir Howard Frederick Frank, 2nd Bt**; *b* 5 April 1923; Lt Gren Gds WW II; *ka* Belgium Sept 1944

2 **Sir Robert John Frank, 3rd Bt**; *b* 16 March 1925; *educ* Harrow; F/O RAFVR WW II, dir Ashdale Land and Property, FRICS, FAI; *m* 1st 10 June 1950 (*divorce* 1959) Angela Elizabeth, est dau of Sir Kenelm Henry Ernest Cayley, 10th Bt (*qv*), and had issue:

(1) *Maria Elizabeth Jane [Mrs Vivian Bairstow, Englewick, Englefield Green, Surrey]; *b* 26 Jan 1952; *m* 13 Sept 1975 *Vivian Murray Bairstow, 2nd s of Alan Murray Bairstow, of Egham, Surrey, and has issue:

1a *George Robert; *b* 1987

1a *Katharine Selina; *b* 1982

(2) *Katharine Lucy; *b* 22 Oct 1954; *m* 1976 *Ian Forbes McCredie, OBE, est s of J H McCredie, of Farthingales, Maidenhead, Berks, and has issue:

1a *James Howard; *b* 1981

1a *Alexandra Elizabeth; *b* 1983

2 (cont.) **Sir Robert** *m* 2nd 26 Jan 1960 *(Margaret) Joyce [Joyce Lady Frank, Ruscombe End, Waltham St Lawrence, Berks], only dau of Herbert Victor Truesdale, of Heswall, Cheshire, and *d* 1987, having by her had:

(1) Charles Frederick Edward; *b* 25, *d* 28 March 1961

(2) Sir (ROBERT) ANDREW FRANK, **4th and present Bt**

FRANKLAND-PAYNE-GALLWEY

Arms: Quarterly, 1st and 4th, per fess or and gu., in chief an eagle displayed with two heads of the last, in base a bridge of three arches doubled, towered, arg. (for GALLWEY); 2nd, gu. a fess between two lions passant arg. (for PAYNE); 3rd, az. a dolphin naiant or, on a chief of the last two saltires couped gu. (for FRANKLAND). **Crests:** 1 A cat-a-mountain passant guardant ppr., gorged with a collar gemelle and charged on the body with a cross patée or (for GALLWEY), 2 A lion's gamb erased erect arg., holding the lower part of a tilting-lance in bend sinster gu. (for PAYNE), 3 An anchor erect az., stock or, the shank entwined by a dolphin hauriant arg. (for FRANKLAND). **Motto:** *Malo mori quam fœdari* ('I prefer death to dishonour'). **Creation:** Bt. (UK) 8 Dec 1812.

SIR PHILIP FRANKLAND-PAYNE-GALLWEY, 6TH BT [Sir Philip Frankland-Payne-Gallwey Bt, The Little House, Boxford, Newbury, Berks; 29 Cadogan St, London SW3 2PP]; *b* 15 March 1935; *s* cousin 1964; *educ* Eton and RMA Sandhurst; Lt 11th Hus 1957, dir Br Bloodstock Agency Ltd 1968–

Lineage: RALPH PAYNE; royalist Civil War, fought Battle of Worcester 1651; had:

1 ABRAHAM

2 Sir CHARLES PAYNE, 1st Bt (GB), so *cr* 31 Oct 1737; *m* Janet, dau and coheir of Maj John MacArthur, Pres Cncl St Kitts, and *d* 1738, leaving an only surv s:

(1) Sir GILLIES PAYNE, 2nd and last Bt; *b* 14 Dec 1720; *m* 1771 Maria (*d* 18 May 1802), dau of John Keeling, and *dsps* 31 Jan 1801, when the btcy expired

3 Nathaniel; had an only dau (*m* William Woodley, Govr Leeward Islands)

The est son,

ABRAHAM PAYNE; *m* Anne, dau of Ralph Willett, and had issue:

RALPH PAYNE; Ch Judge St Christopher, WI; *m* 1st Alice, dau and heir of Francis Carlisle or Carlile, of Antigua, and had:

1 RALPH PAYNE, 1st and last BARON LAVINGTON OF LAVINGTON (I), so *cr* 1 Oct 1795, KB (1771), PC (1799); *b* 19 March 1739; MP Shaftesbury 1768–71, Camelford 1776–80, Plympton 1780–84, Fowey 1790–91 and Woodstock 1795–99, Govr Leeward Islands 1771–75 and 1799–1807, last Clerk Bd Green Cloth (1777–82) before that sinecure's abolition; *m* 1 Sept 1767 Frances, dau of Henry, Baron Kolbel of the HRE and Gen in Imperial Serv, and *dsp* 1 Aug 1807, when the barony expired

1 Elizabeth

RALPH PAYNE *m* 2nd Margaret Gallwey, of St Kitts, West Indies, by whom he had, with two daus:

2 STEPHEN PAYNE later PAYNE-GALLWEY (roy licence 21 March 1762), of Tofts Hall, Norfolk; *m* Phila, dau of Stephen de Lancy, Govr-Gen New York, and *d* 1803, leaving:

(1) Charlotte; *m* 1797 John Moseley, of Glenham House, Suffolk, and had issue

3 John Willett; R-Adml the Red, Sec to GEORGE IV as PRINCE REGENT, Govr Greenwich Hosp, Chllr Duchy Cornwall, MP Huntingdon 1785; *b* 1752; *d* unm 17 Nov 1803

4 Sir WILLIAM PAYNE later PAYNE-GALLWEY (roy licence 7 March 1814 under terms of will of Tobias Wall Gallwey, of St Christopher), **1st Bt** (UK), so *cr* 8 Dec 1812; *b* 1759; Lt-Gen, 2nd in command Spain; *m* 19 Nov 1804 Harriet (*d* 13 Dec 1845), only dau of 1st Earl of Dunraven and Mountearl (*qv*), and *d* 16 April 1831, having had, with other issue:

(1) **Sir William Payne-Gallwey, 2nd Bt**; Maj 7th Fus, MP Thirsk 1851–81; *b* 1807; *m* 10 Nov 1847 Emily Anne (took by roy licence 2 Oct 1882 name and arms of PAYNE-FRANKLAND in lieu of PAYNE-GALLWEY; *d* 13 Sept 1913), 3rd dau and coheir of Sir Robert Frankland-Russell, 7th Bt (*see* ZOUCHE, B), and *d* 19 Dec 1881, having had, with three daus (*d* unm):

1a Sir RALPH WILLIAM PAYNE-GALLWEY later FRANKLAND-PAYNE-GALLWEY (roy licence 4 April 1914), **3rd Bt**, of Thirkleby Park, Yorks, JP N Riding Yorks; *b* 19 Aug 1848; *educ* Eton; Lt Rifle Bde; *m* 25 April 1887 Edith Alice (*d* 12 Nov 1953 aged 98), yst dau of Thomas Masters Usborne, JP, of Blackrock, Co Cork, and *d* 24 Nov 1916, having had issue:

1b William Thomas, MVO (5th Cl 1908); Capt Gren Gds; Coronation Medal 1911, Boer War 1901–02 (Queen's medal with two clasps) and WW I 1914; *b* 25 March 1881; *ka* 14 Sept 1914

1b Margaret Emily; *d* unm 15 Sept 1946

2b Winifred; *m* 11 April 1905 Walter Donne and *d* 27 Dec 1922, leaving issue

3b Dorothy; Personnel Offr Metal Box Co, Hull, 1930–50; *b* 9 Oct 1886; *d* unm 13 April 1983

4b Geraldine; *d* unm 12 Nov 1956

2a Edwin John; Capt RN; *b* 31 Jan 1850; *m* 31 Jan 1889 Susan Isabel, yst dau of Maj Francis Gresley, and *d* 18 April 1906, leaving:

1b Sir JOHN PAYNE-GALLWEY later FRANKLAND-PAYNE-GALLWEY (roy licence 25 Oct 1919), **4th Bt**, Brevet Lt-Col RE, served WW I 1914 and WW II, JP Yorks (N Riding); *b* 23 Dec 1889; *m* 19 Sept 1915 Evelyn Florence, yr dau of James Lee, of Northampton, and *dsp* 13 Feb 1955

2b Lionel; *b* 19 May 1894; *m* 1924 Gladys Grace, dau of H P Reynolds, Indian Police, and *dsp* 5 Aug 1928

3a Lionel Philip; *b* 7 July 1851; *m* 2 Nov 1881 Caroline Lucille (*d* 1946 having *m* 2nd F E Taylor, of Highfield, Spanish Town, Jamaica), dau of E B Lynch, and *d* 1891, leaving issue:

1b Maurice Hylton Frankland; Lt Gren Gds; *b* 1889; *ka* 25 Sept 1916

1b Kathleen Lucille; *m* 3 May 1905 Richard Francis Malachy Pearson, CE, est s of Richard Pearson, and *d* 10 Aug 1920, leaving issue

2b Evelyn Mary; *m* 5 Aug 1913 Lt-Col William Douglas Baynes Conran, DSO, RE, and *d* 29 Feb 1960, leaving issue. He *d* 24 April 1951

3b Sybil Norah; *m* June 1911 John Louis Granville Sharpe, s of Col John Sharpe, of Queen's Sq, Bath, and had issue. He *d* 10 March 1940

4b Cecily Olive; *m* 10 April 1915 Capt Harold Moffat Swire Haughton, RE (SR), yr s of Roger Swire Haughton, of Jamaica. He *d* 13 Aug 1954

4a Wyndham Harry; *b* 11 June 1855; *m* 10 Nov 1887 Edith Millicent (*d* 16 Aug 1939), 2nd dau of Wainwright Crowe, of Cahircalla, Ennis, Co Clare, and *d* 2 Dec 1916, leaving issue:

1b **Sir Reginald Frankland Payne-Gallwey, 5th Bt**; Companion IEE, WW I in London Electrical Engs; *b* 15 April 1889; *educ* Lancing and St Edmund Hall Oxford; *m* 1st 17 June 1912 (*divorce* 1956) Rosetta Mabel (*d* 29 April 1977 aged 96), dau of Henry Durdle, of Reading, and had:

1c Joan Flower; *b* 29 Jan 1914; *m* 17 Aug 1940 *(Robert) Vincent Steven [Vincent Steven Esq, 227 Route de St Maurice, 1814 La Tour de Peilz, Vaud, Switzerland], est s of Thomas Cowan Steven, and *d* 8 July 1997, leaving:

1d *Patricia Susan; *b* 9 Aug 1942; *m* 1968 *Timothy John Charsley, BSc, and has issue:

1e *Jonathan Robert; *b* 1973

2e *Andrew Vincent; *b* 1976

2d *Margaret Sheila; *b* 25 Jan 1945; *m* 1st 1969 (*divorce* 1986) Michael John Wigginton; *m* 2nd 1988 Henry Michael Cunard Allen, RD (*d* 1993), and has issue:

1e *Alexander Steven; *b* 1974

1e *Julia Caroline; *b* 1972

1b (cont.) The **5th Bt** *m* 2nd 28 March 1956 Dorothy Gertrude (*d* 16 March 1971), widow of Stanley Bathurst and dau of Bertram Henry Madge, of London, and *d* 12 Jan 1964

(2) Philip; Capt 90th Foot; *b* 1812; *m* 26 May 1854 Frances (*d* 10 Sept 1917), dau of Ven Archdeacon Warburton, and *d* 23 Feb 1894, leaving, with other issue:

1a Stephen Philip; *b* 4 Aug 1857; *m* 1909 Linda Vera (*d* 15 Feb 1936), dau of Henry Steiner, of Lausanne, Switzerland, and *d* 26 April 1938

2a Arthur Wyndham; Memb FMS Cncl; *b* 8 Oct 1858; *m* 1888 Grace Stanley (*d* 1933), dau of William Pardy, of San Francisco, and *d* 1 April 1939, leaving:

1b Frances Pardy; *m* 11 Oct 1911 Gordon Megaw, s of Matthew George Megaw, of Greycroft, Newbury, and had issue

3a Francis Henry (Rev); Rector Sessay, Thirsk, 1912–28; *b* 31 Dec 1859; *educ* Trin Coll Cambridge (MA); *m* 1888 Florence Kate (*d* 10 Dec 1927), 2nd dau of Col Arthur Lowry Cole (*see* ENNISKILLEN, E), and *d* 30 Oct 1934, leaving:

1b Lowry Philip, OBE (1933), MC (1919); Lt-Col 7th Hus, T/Maj KAR 1930, served WWs I and II; *b* 10 June 1891; *educ* Trin Coll Cambridge (BA); *m* 27 July 1933 Janet (*d* 6 June 1996), dau of Albert Philip Payne-Gallwey (*see* below), and *d* 25 March 1958, leaving issue:

1c Sir PHILIP PAYNE-GALLWEY later FRANKLAND-PAYNE-GALLWEY (roy licence 18 July 1967), **6th and present Bt**

2b Philip Francis; Lt 21st Lancers; *b* 7 March 1893; *ka* 31 Oct 1914

1b Florence Mary; *m* 5 Aug 1915 Maj-Gen John Edward Utterson Kelso, CB, DSO, OBE, MC, Roy Scots Fus, son of Capt W E Utterson Kelso, and *d* 19 Feb 1955, leaving issue

2b Beatrice; *b* 10 June 1881; *m* 24 Sept 1918 Lt-Col Ernest John Nixon, DSO, MC, RA, 2nd s of Maj-Gen Nixon, and *d* 5 June 1959, leaving issue. He *d* 14 May 1969 aged 84

3b Helen Isabel; *m* 23 June 1925 Capt Robert Douglas Leigh-Pemberton, MBE, MC (*see* KINGSDOWN, B) and had issue

4a Sackville Alick; *b* 16 Oct 1861; *m* 15 Oct 1898 Norma Anne (*d* 31 Dec 1924), dau of John Edward Arthur Dick-Lauder (*see* DICK-LAUDER, Bt), and *d* 3 Oct 1923, leaving issue:

1b Violet Zella; *m* 1st 1926 Edward Gordon Reeve (*d* 6 Oct 1938); *m* 2nd 1939 C W Volz, of Scarsdale, NY, and *d* 16 Feb 1967

5a Herbert Philip, JP W Yorks; *b* 24 April 1864; *d* unm 6 June 1943

6a Frederick; Lt RN; *b* 24 June 1867; *d* 24 March 1930

7a Albert Philip, JP Derbys and Lincs; *b* 13 Dec 1871; *m* 17 Oct 1900 Katherine Mary (*d* 8 March 1962 aged 91), 2nd dau of Maj Vaughan Hanning Vaughan-Lee, JP, DL, MP, of Dillington Park, Somerset, and *d* 7 July 1931, leaving:

1b Peter, DSO and two bars (1941 and 1943); Hon Col 11th Hus, WW II (despatches); *b* 27 July 1906; *educ* Eton; *m* 27 Aug 1953 Ann Josephine (*d* 1988), 2nd dau of Roger John Kinloch Barber-Starkey (*see* LEGARD, Bt), and *d* 1971, leaving issue:

1c *Nicola [Mrs Henry Fetherstonhaugh, Plas Llewellyn, Dolwen, Abergele, Clwyd]; *b* 19 June 1955; *m* 1978 *Henry George Fetherstonhaugh and has issue (*see* GALWAY, V)

1b Janet; *m* 27 July 1933 her cousin Lt-Col Lowry Philip Payne-Gallwey (*see* above)

1a Lilian Fanny; *d* unm 1 April 1945

2a Edith Caroline; *d* unm 3 Nov 1946

(1) Caroline; *m* Count Lionel de Bonneval and *d* 12 Aug 1858

FRASER

Arms: Azure three cinquefoils argent, on a chief of the last three bear's heads couped of the field, muzzled of the second. **Crest:** A buck's head erased proper. **Motto:** *Furtachd is foir* ('Deliverance and help'). **Creation:** Bt. (UK) 12 July 1943.

SIR IAIN MICHAEL FRASER, 3RD BT, of Tain, Co Ross [Sir Iain Fraser Bt, 30/7 Elbe St, Edinburgh EH6 7HW]; *b* 27 June 1951; *s* f 1997; *educ* Trin Coll Glenalmond; *m* 1982 (*divorce* 1991) Sherylle Ann, dau of Keith Gillespie, of Wellington, NZ, and has issue:

1 +BENJAMIN; *b* 1986

1 *Joanna Karen; *b* 1983

Lineage: JOHN FRASER, of Easter Rarichie Farm, Ross-shire; *d* Dec 1903, leaving:

JAMES FRASER, of Easter Rarichie Farm; *b* 1859; *educ* Tain Roy Acad; *m* 1884 Margaret Boyack (*d* Aug 1914), yst dau of Alexander Mackay, of Hilton Farm, Tain, and *d* 1885, leaving issue:

Sir John Fraser, 1st Bt (UK), so *cr* 12 July 1943, KCVO (1937), MC, DL; *b* 23 March 1885; *educ* Tain Roy Acad and Edinburgh U (MB, ChB 1907, ChM 1910, MD 1912); memb Roy Co of Archers, FRCS Edinburgh 1910, Hon FRACS; served RAMC WW I, Assist Surgn Roy Hosp for Sick Children Edinburgh 1912–20 and Surgeon 1920–25, Consulting Surgn to Scottish Cmd 1925–44, Regius Prof Clinical Surgery Edinburgh U 1925–45, Pncpl and V-Chllr Edinburgh U 1944, FRSE, Hon FACS, Hon LLD Edinburgh 1944, Consulting Surgn RN Scotland, Consultant Surgery Dept Health Scotland, Hon Surgn Scotland to HM GEORGE V, Order Polonia Restituta 1945; *m* 12 Jan 1918 *Agnes Govane, dau of Rev William David Herald, MA, of The Manse, Duns, Berwickshire, and *d* 1 Dec 1947, leaving issue:

1 **Sir James David Fraser, 2nd Bt;** *b* 19 July 1924; *educ* Edinburgh Acad, Edinburgh U (MB, ChB 1948, ChM 1961) and Magdalen Coll Oxford (BA 1945); Maj RAMC (TA), Far East 1949–51, Sr Lecturer Dept Clinical Surgery Edinburgh U, Hon Consultant Surg Roy Infirmary Edinburgh 1951–70, Prof Clinical Surgery Southampton U 1970–80, Hon Consultant Surgeon Southampton Hosp Gp, Hon Sec Roy Coll Surgns Edinburgh, FRCSE 1953, FRCS 1973, FRCPE 1980, FRCSI 1984, FRACS 1984; *m* 16 Sept 1950 *Edith Maureen [Edith Lady Fraser, 2 Lennox St, Edinburgh EH4 1QA], F/O WAAF, dau of Rev John Reay, MC, BSc, of Bingham, Notts, and *d* Jan 1997, leaving:

(1) Sir IAIN MICHAEL FRASER, **3rd and present Bt**

(2) +Christopher John [Christopher Fraser Esq, 39 Devizes Rd, Salisbury, Wilts SP2 7AA]; *b* 22 March 1954; *educ* Trin Coll Glenalmond

1 Jean Margaret; *b* 1 April 1919; *educ* Edinburgh U; *m* 23 Feb 1944 Denis Johnston Cadzow, s of James Cadzow, of Duncrahill, and had issue:

(1) *Sally Jean; *b* 18 Oct 1945

(2) *Joan Margaret; *b* 3 Dec 1947

(3) *Nora Denise; *b* 12 March 1949

(4) Kirsteen Alice; *b* 4 Nov 1952; *d* 2 Aug 1957

FRASER OF CARMYLLIE

Creation: B. (LP, UK) 1989.

THE BARON FRASER OF CARMYLLIE, of Carmyllie in the District Angus (Peter Lovat Fraser, PC (1989), QC (1982)) [The Rt Hon The Lord Fraser of Carmyllie, Slade House, Carmyllie, by Arbroath, Angus DD11 2RE]; *b* 29 May 1945; *educ* Loretto, Gonville and Caius Coll Cambridge and Edinburgh U; advocate 1969, lecturer Constitutional Law Heriot-Watt U 1972–74, Standing Jr Counsel Scotland FCO 1979, MP (C) Angus S 1979—83 and Angus E 1983—87, PPS to Sec of State Scotland 1981–82, Slr-Gen Scotland 1982–89, Ld Advocate 1989–92, Min State: Scottish Off 1992–95 and DTI 1995–96, Min Energy 1996–97, chm JKX 1997–, Visiting Prof Law Dundee U 1986, Hon Bencher Lincoln's Inn 1989, Chm Scottish C Lawyers Law Reform Gp 1976; *m* 1969 *Fiona, dau of Hugh Murray Mair, of Lanark, and has:

1 *James Murray; *b* 1974
1 *Jane Helen Anne; *b* 1972
2 *Catriona Elizabeth; *b* 1981

Lineage: Rev GEORGE ROBSON FRASER, of Corrennie, Edinburgh; *m* Helen Jean Meiklejohn and had:

PETER LOVAT, *cr* a **Baron**

FREDERICK

Arms: Or, on a chief az. three doves arg. **Crest:** On a chapeau az., doubled erm., a dove as in the arms, holding in his beak an olive branch ppr. **Motto:** *Prudens simplicitas beat* ('Prudent simplicity is a blessing'). **Creation:** Bt. (GB) 10 June 1723.

SIR CHARLES BOSCAWEN FREDERICK, 10TH BT, of Burwood House, Surrey [Sir Charles Frederick Bt, Virginia Cottage, Stoke Trister, Wincanton, Somerset BA9 9PQ]; *b* 11 April 1919; *s f* 1956; *educ* Eton; WW II: 2nd Lt Gren Gds 1942, Capt 1945, Maj 1953 (despatches), Palestine 1946–47 (despatches), Malaya 1948–49 and Egypt 1952–53, memb London Stock Exchange 1954–62, memb Provincial Brokers' Stock Exchange 1962–75, Gen Commr Income Tax 1966, memb Council 1966, Chm: Stock Exchange Cncl 1973–75, Prov Unit 1973–75, JP (Bucks 1960–61); *m* 8 Oct 1949 *Rosemary, est dau of Lt-Col Robert John Halkett Baddeley, MC, of Home Close, Donhead St Mary, Dorset, and has issue:

1 +CHRISTOPHER ST JOHN [Christopher Frederick Esq, Home Farm, Batcombe, Somerset BA4 6HF]; *b* 28 June 1950; *educ* Eton; *m* 1990 *Camilla Elizabeth, only dau of Sir (Walter) Derek Gilbey, 3rd Bt (*qv*), and has:

(1) +Benjamin St John; *b* 29 Dec 1991
(1) *Amy Rose; *b* 11 July 1994

2 +James Boscawen; *b* 16 Sept 1963

1 *Anne Rosemary [Mrs Miles French, 77 rue du Moulin de Saquet, 94800 Villejuif, France]; *b* 1 Nov 1952; *m* 1st 1976 François Maurice and has issue:

(1) *Thomas James; *b* 1977
(2) *Nicholas Charles Roger; *b* 1979

1 (cont.) Mrs Maurice *m* 2nd 1991 *Miles Arthur Maitland French (*see* LAUDERDALE, E) and has by him:

(3) *Raphaël Maitland; *b* 1994
(1) *Naomi Hilda; *b* 1992

2 *Jill Elizabeth; *b* 30 June 1956; *m* 1986 *Stephen Douglas, of Los Angeles

Lineage: CHRISTOPHER FREDERICK, of London; Serjeant-Surgn to JAMES I; *d* Oct 1623, leaving a 4th s:

Sir JOHN FREDERICK; merchant, Sheriff City London 1655, Ld Mayor 1662; *b* 1601; pres Christ's Hospital (rebuilt the hall after the Fire of London at cost of £5,000 (*c* £350,000 in late-1990s terms), also helped found the mathematical school); *m* —, dau of Thomas Rouse, of London, and *d* March 1685, leaving issue:

THOMAS FREDERICK, of Westminster; *bapt* 7 July 1650; *m* 19 Feb 1674/5 Leonora (*d* 1730), dau and heir of Charles Marescoe, of London, and *d* 3 June 1720, leaving issue:

1 **Sir John Frederick, 1st Bt** (GB), so *cr* 10 June 1723, with eventual remainder to his bro Thomas; *b* 10 March 1677/8; *m* 15 July 1727 Barbara Kinnersley (*d* 11 Sept 1749) and *d* 3 Oct 1755, leaving issue:

(1) **Sir John Frederick, 2nd Bt**; *b* May 1728; *d* unm 24 March 1757

(2) **Sir Thomas Frederick, 3rd Bt**; *b* March 1730/1; *m* Elizabeth (*d* 11 Sept 1764), dau of Peter Bathurst, of Clarendon Park, Wilts, and *d* 16 Dec 1770, leaving issue:

1a Elizabeth; *m* 17 April 1778 Sir John Morshead, 1st Bt
2a Selina; *m* 1 Jan 1778 Robert Thistlewaite, of Southwick

2 Thomas (Sir); Govr Fort St David, E Indies; *bapt* 22 Jan 1680/1; *m* 11 Jan 1704/5 Mary Moncrieff (*m* 2nd 18 Jan 1734/5 William Poyntz, Consul-Gen Lisbon (*bur* 2 Oct 1748), and *d* 30 April 1767), and *d* 8 Feb 1730/1, leaving, with other issue (*see* YOUNG, Bt, of Bailieborough):

(1) **Sir John Frederick, 4th Bt**; MP Shoreham 1740–41, W Looe 1743–61; *b* 28 Nov 1708; *m* 22 Oct 1741 Susannah (*d* 29 Jan 1787), dau of Sir Roger Hudson, of Sunbury, and coheir of her bro Vansittart Hudson, and *d* 9 April 1783, having had, with another s (d young) and three daus:

1a **Sir John Frederick, 5th Bt**; MP Newport 1774–80, Christchurch 1781–90 and Surrey 1794–1807; *b* 18 March 1749; *m* 15 Oct 1778 Mary (*d* 18 Nov 1794), yst dau and coheir of Richard Garth, of Morden, and *d* 16 Jan 1825, having had, with four other sons and a dau:

1b **Sir Richard Frederick, 6th Bt**; Capt 9th Foot; *b* 30 Dec 1780; *d* unm 20 Sept 1873

2 Thomas Nathan; Lt RN; *b* 11 July 1783; *m* Charlotte, dau of Robert Burney, of Anningsley, Surrey, and *d* 1818, leaving a dau (*d* young)
1 Charlotte; *m* Rev R A St Leger, of Starcross, Devon, and *d* 1858
2 Mary; *m* James Chamness Fyler, of Twickenham, and *d* 2 April 1823
3 Frances; *m* Henry Fellowes, 2nd s of Robert Fellowes, of Shotsesham, Norfolk, and *d* 28 April 1874

(2) Charles (Sir), KB; Surveyor Ordnance, MP; *b* 21 Dec 1709; *m* 18 Aug 1746 Lucy Boscawen (*d* 17 Jan 1784), dau of 1st Viscount Falmouth (*qv*), and *d* 18 Dec 1785, leaving, with other issue:

1a Charles; Col HEICS; *b* 9 Oct 1748; *m* 20 March 1773 Martha, dau of Benjamin Rigden, of Faversham, and *d* 1791, leaving, with two other sons and a dau:

1b Charles; Capt 35th Regt; *b* 18 Oct 1778; *m* 1800 Lucinda Watkins, of Johnstown, Co Tipperary, and *d* 6 Aug 1809, leaving two sons (*d* unm)

2b Edward, CB; Gen; *b* 23 June 1784; *m* 1st 26 Oct 1826 Selina (*dsp* 7 Sept 1827), dau of George Grote; *m* 2nd 28 Oct 1841 Mary (*d* 22 July 1884), dau of Rev Edward St John, and *d* 5 Dec 1866, having by her had, with a dau (*d* unm):

1c CHARLES EDWARD (Sir), **7th Bt**

2c John St John; Capt Inniskilling Dragoons; *b* 6 Jan 1846; *m* 2 July 1890 Mary Theresa Caroline Alice, Baroness von Donop (*d* 22 Feb 1895), est dau of Baron de Reuter (*see* 1956 edn Foreign Titles Section), and *dsp* 10 Sept 1907

1b Martha; *m* Robert Steuart, 3rd son of Robert Steuart of Ballechin, and had issue
2b Augusta; *m* H Scott and had issue
3b Lucy; *m* Sir William Young, 1st Bt, of Bailieborough (*qv*), and had issue

2a Thomas Lennox; Adml; *b* 25 March 1750; *m* Annie Greigson and *d* 1797
3a Edward Boscawen; Col; *b* 1762; *m* 1835 Caroline Mowbray, dau of George Smith
1a Augusta; *m* Thomas Prescott, s of Sir G Prescott

(3) Marescoe; Maj-Gen; *b* 7 Dec 1725; *m* 1st 12 June 1760 Sarah (*d* 1774), dau of Robert Pickering, and had:

1a Thomas; Lt-Col; *b* 23 April 1764; *m* 10 June 1795 Anne Susannah (*d* 1829), dau of Rev John Glasse, Rector Pencombe, Herefs, and *d* 28 May 1844, having had, with other issue:

1b Arthur; *b* 12 June 1800; *m* 12 July 1825 Sophia Emily (*d* 1878), dau of Rev Thomas Watkins, of Pennoyre, Brecon, and *d* 7 Aug 1866, having had issue:

1c Arthur Thomas; *b* 13 Jan 1836; *m* 7 May 1859 Lydia Emily (*d* 10 Nov 1907), dau of Rev Andrew Nash, of Densworth, Sussex, and *d* 18 Sept 1927, having had issue:

1d Charles Arthur (Sir), GCVO, KCB; Lt-Col Coldstream Gds, Extra Equerry to TM EDWARD VII 1902–10, GEORGE V and QUEEN ALEXANDRA 1910–13, Dep-Master Household 1901–07, Actg Sec Bd Green Cloth 1903–07, Master Household to TM EDWARD VII 1907–10 and GEORGE V 1910–12; *b* 9 April 1861; *d* unm 21 Dec 1913

1d Olive Emily; *m* 27 June 1882 Sir Guy Thomas Saunders Sebright, 12th Bt (*qv*), and *d* 14 Dec 1951, having had issue

2c Marescoe Lloyd; RN; *b* 18 Aug 1837; *m* 16 April 1874 Maria Louisa (*m* 2nd 10 April 1905 Gladwin Cloves Cave, s of Thomas Saunders Cave, of Rossbrin Manor, Co Cork, and *d* 12 Oct 1907), dau of George White West, JP, barrister, of Ardenode, Co Kildare, and *d* 1886, leaving:

1d Elizabeth Emily Helza; *m* 22 March 1892 Robert Arden Lovett

1c Elizabeth; *m* 20 Dec 1853 Frederick Charles Ashworth, only son of Sir Charles Ashworth, KCB, KTS, and *d* 1865
2c Ellen; *m* 27 Nov 1851 George Atherley and had issue

2b George Septimus; *b* 22 April 1805; *m* 23 Sept 1851 Emily Caroline (*d* 30 Nov 1925 aged 92), dau of Robert Rising, of Horsey and *d* 1891, leaving, with other issue:

1c George Charles, CBE (1918); AICE, Capt RN, Naval Advsr BOT; *b* 2 Aug 1855; *m* 4 Jan 1881 Nellie (*d* 20 Oct 1942), dau of George Peter Martin, CB, JP, RN, of Highlands, Emsworth, Hants, and *d* 5 Jan 1951

2c Henry Penrice; *b* 19 Jan 1857; *m* 1st 12 Sept 1891 Margaret (*d* 17 July 1904), dau of Sir Thomas Beevor, 4th Bt (*qv*), and had, with another s (*d* young):

1d Thomas, MC; Capt (Actg Maj) 9th Bn Norfolk Reg WW I (despatches); *b* 7 March 1893; *das* 14 Dec 1917 of wounds recd nr Cambrai

2d Roger; Cdr RN, served WWs I and II (despatches); *b* 5 Sept 1900; *m* 1 Aug 1928 Nora Mary (Molly) (*d* 1977), dau of Col Herbert Mansfield Whitehead, OBE, of the Grange, Penkridge, Staffs, and *d* 1991, leaving:

1e +Roger Mansfield [Roger Frederick Esq, 16 Orchard Close, Yealmpton, Devon PL8 2JQ]; *b* 19 Jan 1930; *m* 31 Jan 1959 *Valerie Anne, dau of S A Watts, and has issue:

1f +Alan Marescoe; *b* 13 Jan 1960; *m* 1991 *Joanne Bennison and has issue:

1g +Benjamin John; *b* 1993

1g *Laura Anne; *b* 1992

2f +Jonathan Denley; *b* 12 June 1962

3f +Thomas Russell; *b* 15 March 1965; *m* 1988 *Rae Jervis and has:

1g *Annie Rae; *b* 1993

1f *Catherine Mary; *b* 1967

1e *Rowena Mary; *b* 18 Dec 1935; *m* 3 Aug 1957 *Lt-Col Ralph Plant, Roy Signals, yr s of N J Plant, of Thurnscoe, Yorks, and has:

1f *Naomi Elizabeth; *b* 24 Aug 1958; *m* 1982 *James Martin Ibbott

2f *Alison Mary; *b* 12 Dec 1959

3f *Stephanie Ann; *b* 20 April 1961

4f *Nicola Ruth; *b* 24 July 1964

5f *Vanessa Jane; *b* 17 Dec 1965

2e *Bryony Margaret [Mrs John Hamilton, 1 Kestrel Cottage, East Knoyle, Wilts SP3 6AD]; *b* 21 Dec 1941; *m* 5 Nov 1960 *G/Capt John Hamilton, RAF, son of J A Hamilton, of Belfast, and has issue:

1f *John Roger; *b* 25 April 1961

2f *David Nicholas; *b* 18 Jan 1963

1d Mary; *b* 6 Sept 1894; *m* 19 April 1922 Rt Rev George Ernest Ingle, MA, Bp Suffragan Willesden 1955–64 (*d* 10 June 1964), s of Rev George Henry Nathaniel Ingle, of Wells, Norfolk, and had issue:

1e *George Thomas David; *b* 17 April 1925, *m* 1st Sept 1953 (*divorce* 1961) Janet Moir, dau of Dr Campbell Andrews, of Harrow, Middx, and has issue:

1f *Jane Sarah; *b* 15 Sept 1955

1e (cont.) George Ingle *m* 2nd 30 Dec 1963 *Lydia, dau of — Rivera, of The Philippines, and by her has issue:

2f *Angela Nina Ann; *b* 28 Feb 1966

2e *Patrick Maynard; *b* 25 Feb 1929; *m* 1954 *Jean Mary, dau of — Brooks, of Bridgetown, Totnes, Devon, and has issue:

1f *Andrew Patrick George; *b* 22 Feb 1964

1f *Sarah Mary; *b* 23 April 1955

2f *Victoria Jane; *b* 14 Feb 1957

1e *Jean Mary [Mrs Christopher Penn, 19 Lanark Rd, London W9]; *b* 6 March 1923; *m* 22 Jan 1955 *Christopher Lawrence Penn and has:

1f *Caroline Jane; *b* 26 March 1957

2d *Sophy; *m* 23 March 1927 Ernest M A Feuerheerd (*d* 18 March 1948), s of H L Feuerheerd, of Oporto and London, and has issue:

1e *Thomas Frederick; *b* 5 Jan 1928

1e *Diana Patricia [Mrs Robert Troop, 24 Bennerley Rd, London SW11]; *b* 12 May 1929; *m* 29 April 1961 *Robert Livesey Troop, only s of Herbert Troop, of Lytham, Lancs, and has issue:

1f *Clarissa; *b* 26 Jan 1963

2e *Rosemary; *b* 11 June 1930; *m* 28 July 1957 *Stephen J Weiss, s of William Weiss, and has issue:

1f *Andrew William; *b* 12 Dec 1964

1f *Claudia Dahan; *b* 31 Jan 1960

2f *Alison Margaret; *b* 1 Jan 1962

2c (cont.) Henry Frederick *m* 2nd 25 April 1908 Diana (*d* 23 May 1940), 3rd dau of Sir William Foster, 2nd Bt, and *d* 23 Feb 1942

3c Ernest Prescott; MA Cantab; *b* 8 June 1858; *m* 1st 29 July 1890 Wilhelmina Lindsay (*d* 12 June 1901), yst dau of Rev William Lindsay Alexander, DD, LLD, and had issue:

1d Grace Emily Hannah; *m* 14 April 1920 Cdr Henry James Hartnoll, DSO, Croix de Guerre, RN, est s of Sir Henry Hartnoll, of The Old Glebe, Eggesford, N Devon, and *d* 19 Oct 1968, having had a s and three daus. He *das* 18 Nov 1940

2d Marjorie Pleasaunce Lindsay; *m* 26 Jan 1921 George Herbert Russell, CBE (*d* 30 April 1953), s of James Russell, of Auchenraith, Lanarks, and had issue:

1e James; Lt 3rd/15th Punjab Regt WW II; *b* 8 March 1923; *ka* 24 July 1944

1e *Marjorie Frederick; *b* 2 Aug 1926; *m* 25 Nov 1960 *Prof Thomas Egbert James, MA, BCL, PhD, 4th s of W Warwick James, FRCS, of London

3c (cont.) Ernest Frederick *m* 2nd 18 Dec 1919 Gladys Oliveria (*d* 4 July 1966), est dau of James Lindsay Travers, of Bredgar House, Kent, and *d* 22 March 1929, having by her had issue:

1d John Cromwell; Capt RN WW II; *b* 5 Dec 1920; *m* 1st 14 Aug 1942 (*divorce* 1965) Mary Oliveira, dau of Rev Wynyard Warner, MC; *m* 2nd 30 Oct 1965 *Margaret Lilian [Mrs John Frederick, Woodview, Meavy, Yelverton, Devon], dau of Maj Richard Henry Dalbiac (*see* SHERWOOD, B), and *d* 1974, leaving by his 1st w:

1e +John Peter Wynyard; *b* 6 Oct 1945; *educ* Monkton Combe Sch; *m* 1972 *Janie Mary, dau of Scott Gundersen, of NZ

1e *Sarah Ann; *b* 22 July 1943

4c Richard Rising, MA Cantab; *b* 12 April 1865; *m* 1st 7 Aug 1902 Mary Teresa (*d* 18 Nov 1943), widow of Maj Charles Wellesley Parish, RM, and dau of Col Thomas Robert Hay-Drummond-Hay, (*see* KINNOULL, E); *m* 2nd 15 Aug 1944 *Edith May, dau of Rev J W Parrington, and *d* 15 Feb 1952

5c Arthur Marescoe; *b* 23 June 1869; *m* 11 Aug 1900 Petrona Elena (*d* 25 Nov 1965), dau of C J F Davie, of Montevideo, and *d* 18 Feb 1963, leaving issue:

1d Arthur Roland; *b* 22 Aug 1901; *m* 19 July 1930 Maria Esther (*d* 1985), dau of Francisco Costa, of Montevideo, and *d* 1988, leaving:

1e +Richard Frank; *b* 20 June 1935; *m* 14 Nov 1960 *Gloria, dau of Carlos Garcia Arocena, and has issue:

1f +Ricardo; *b* 23 Dec 1963; *m* 1994 *Marina, dau of J Ferrari

1f *Odile Maria; *b* 8 Feb 1962; *m* 1983 (*divorce* 1991) H Pérez Noble

2f *Madelón Maria; *b* 19 June 1965; *m* 1992 *Alvaro Piñeirúa

1e *Lilian Susan; *b* 1932; *m* 15 Oct 1959 Hugo Sapelli Mendez (*d* 1988), son of Carlos Sapelli, of Montevideo

2d John Davie Geoffrey; *b* 4 April 1903; *m* 1st 19 Sept 192 Maria Mercedes (*d* 24 March 1950), dau of Luis Labadie, of Montevideo; *m* 2nd 14 July 1952 *Elisa, dau of Juan Lotero, of Montevideo, and *d* 1975, leaving by his 1st w:

1e +John [John Frederick Esq, Santa Rosa, Canelones, Uruguay, S America]; *b* 11 July 1930; *m* 1961 *Marta Rose, dau of Oscar Gulla, of Santa Rosa, Canelones, Urguay, and has issue:

1f +Carlos Alberto; *b* 1962; *m* 1985 *Rosa, dau of F Reggio, and has issue:

1g +Carlos Nicolás; *b* 1991

1g *Fabiana Lorena; *b* 1987

2g *Lourdes Mercedes; *b* 1993

2f +Rafael Daniel; *b* 1964; *m* 19– *Sonia, dau of E Baserga, and has issue:

1g +Daniel; *b* 1992

3f +Oscar Geoffrey; *b* 1966; *m* 19– *Melba, dau of J Olivera, and has issue:

1g *Luciana; *b* 1992

2e +Henry [Henry Frederick Esq, PO Box 18952, Montevideo, Uruguay, S America]; *b* 27 Sept 1933; *m* 1958 *Lia, dau of Julio Arocena Capurro, of Buenos Aires, and has issue:

1f +Henry Martin; *b* 1959; *m* 1992 *Aurora, dau of Dr Jaime Polto, and has issue:

1g +Henry José; *b* 1993

1g *Maria de los Milagros; *b* 1994

2f +Diego José; *b* 1962; *m* 1990 *Maria Claudia, dau of Claudino Miguez

3f +Jaime Luis; *b* 1966

1f *Mercedes Inés; *b* 1961; *m* 1985 *Marcelo Pittamiglio

1d *Louisa Carmen [Mrs W Van Wijngaarden, c/o H Frederick Esq, PO Box 18952, Montevideo, 11500 Uruguay]; *b* 1905; *m* 12 Nov 1934 W J H Van Wijngaarden. He *d* 1964

6c Edward Gurdon; MRCS, LRCP; *b* 13 April 1872; *m* 7 June 1899 Annie Margaret Balfour (*d* 27 Oct 1960), est dau of Thomas Shaw Vance, and *d* 28 April 1926, leaving:

1d Edward Vincent; MRCS, LRCP; *b* 4 Feb 1902; *m* 26 Sept 1946 *Joan Olive [Mrs Edward Frederick, 80 Rodmell Ave, Saltdean, Sussex BN2 8PJ], dau of Albert Dunford, of Brighton, and *d* 8 March 1969, leaving issue:

1e +Christopher Hugh [Christopher Frederick Esq, 80 Rodmell Ave, Saltdean, Sussex BN2 8PJ; *b* 20 May 1948, *educ* Embley Park, Romsey, Hants; *m* 1982 (*divorce* 1993) Mrs Diana Lesley Spiers, est dau of Leslie Kingham, of Coventry

1e *Helen Mary [Mrs Brent Heath, 441 Diehl Ave, San Leandro, CA 94577, USA]; *b* 15 April 1947; *m* 1987 *Brent Edwin Heath, s of Edwin C Heath, of Phoenix, Arizona

2e *Auriol Rosalind [Miss Auriol Frederick, 59B Camberwell Rd, London SE5 0EZ]; *b* 30 April 1952

1d Kathleen Patricia; *m* 21 Feb 1934 Deri Stephens, MRCS, LRCP, and *d* 31 Aug 1960, leaving a s and dau

7c Herbert; *b* 11 June 1874; *m* 2 June 1900 Alice Louise (*d* 23 Nov 1943), yst dau of W H Priest, and *d* 19 May 1949, leaving issue:

1d *Edith Nora [Miss Edith Frederick, 40 Rousham Road, Eastville, Bristol BS5 6XJ]

1c Susan Frances; *d* unm 21 Nov 1944

2c Ellen Betha; *d* unm 25 March 1954

1b Amelia; *m* 26 April 1836 Freeman Thomas, of Ratton, and had issue (*see* 1970 edn WILLINGDON, M)

2b Caroline; *m* 18 June 1829 Henry Cory and *d* 1903. He *d* 1876

2a Robert; Lt-Col; *b* 6 May 1774; *m* 1st 9 Feb 1796 Jemima, dau of Robert Thompson, of Dover, and had four daus; *m* 2nd Sarah, dau of William Tinker, of Cannock, and *d* 4 June 1844

(3) (cont.) Marescoe Frederick *m* 2nd Oct 1777 Sarah Davis (*dsp*)

(1) Mary; *m* 1733 Alexander Hume

(2) Henrietta; *m* 4 Sept 1746 Luke Spence, of West Malling

(3) Hannah; *m* 8 Oct 1746 Sir Abraham Hume, Bt

1 Jean; *m* 1st James Lannoy, of Hammersmith; *m* 2nd 1 April 1726 2nd Duke of Atholl (*qv*) and *d* 13 June 1748, leaving issue

The 6th Bt's cousin,

Sir Charles Edward Frederick, 7th Bt, JP Hants; High Sheriff 1889, Lt-Col 10th Hus 1861–73 and 21st Hus 1873–82; *b* 2 May 1843; *m* 4 Aug 1875 Emma Agnes (*d* 17 May 1925), 3rd dau of Thomas Taylor, Bengal CS, of Leinster Gdns, Lancaster Gate, and *dsp* 21 Oct 1938, leaving issue:

1 **Sir Charles Edward St John Frederick, 8th Bt**, OBE (1919), JP Northants, High Sheriff 1934, Capt Northampton Yeo WW I (despatches); *b* 11 Sept 1876; *m* 5 Dec 1911 Ada Louisa (*d* 24 Jan 1948), widow of Lt-Col George Seymour Charles Jenkinson, DSO (*see* JENKINSON, Bt), and only dau of Caesar Czarnikow, of Effingham Hill, Surrey

2 EDWARD BOSCAWEN (Sir), **9th Bt**

1 Florence Emma Ada; *m* 15 Feb 1905 George Nicholas Dickin, 4th son of Capt Thomas Archerley Massy Dickin, of Loppington House, Wem, Salop, and *d* 1963. He *d* 9 Feb 1954

Sir CHARLES's brother,

Sir Edward Boscawen Frederick, 9th Bt, CVO (1944); Lt-Col Roy Fus, Boer War 1899–1902 and WWs I (severely wounded) and II HG, Exon Yeomen Gd 1925–37, Ensign 1937–50; *b* 29 June 1880; *m* 22 July 1913 Edith Katherine (Kathleen) Cortlandt (*d* 23 Nov 1970), dau of Col William Hutchinson Mulloy, RE, of Hughestown, Co Roscommon, and *d* 26 Oct 1956, having had issue:

1 Sir CHARLES BOSCAWEN FREDERICK, **10th and present Bt**

2 John Christopher, Lt Gren Gds WW II; *b* 25 July 1921; *ka* Tunisia 20 April 1943

1 Kathleen Patricia; *m* 5 March 1935 George Edward Shiffner and *d* 1978, leaving issue (*see* SHIFFNER, Bt)

FREEMAN, Baron

Creation: B. (LP, UK) 2 Aug 1997

THE BARON FREEMAN, of Dingley, Co Northants (Roger Norman Freeman PC (1993)) [The Rt Hon The Lord Freeman PC, House of Lords, London SW1A 0PW]; *b* 27 May 1942; *educ* Whitgift Sch Croydon and Balliol Coll Oxford; chartered accountant 1969, Binder Hamlyn and Co 1964–69, general ptnr Lehman Bros 1969–86; MP (C) Kettering 1983–97, Parly U-Sec: Armed Forces 1986–88, DHSS 1988–90, Min State: Tport 1990–94, MOD 1994–95, Chllr Duchy Lancaster 1995–97, V-Chm C Party 1997–, FCA 1979, ptnr Coopers and Lybrand Corporate Finance 1997–; author: *Professional Practice* (1968), *Fair Deal for Water* (1985); *m* 1969 *Jennifer Margaret Watson and has a s and a dau

Lineage: NORMAN FREEMAN; *m* Marjorie — and had:

ROGER NORMAN, *cr* a Baron

FREEMAN, Bt

Arms: Per fess azure and vair ancient three fusils in chief and a crescent in base or, a bordure engrailed gules. **Crest:** A fusil or between two wings displayed azure. **Motto:** *E labore libertas* ('From labour comes liberty'). **Creation:** Bt. (UK) 4 July 1945.

SIR JAMES ROBIN FREEMAN, 3RD BT, of Murtle, Co Aberdeen [Sir James Freeman Bt, c/o Midland Bank, 192 Hoe St, Walthamstow, Essex E17 3AN]; *b* 21 July 1955; *s* f 1981

Lineage: WILLIAM RHODES FREEMAN, of Bayswater had, with an est s:

1 Max, OBE; *educ* Charterhouse and Lincoln Coll Oxford; Lt-Col, memb London Stock Exchange, sr ptnr Borthwick & Co; *m* *Eileen, dau of E M Harley, and *d* 20 May 1959, leaving issue:

(1) *Christopher Scott Max; *b* 14 Aug 1946; *educ* Charterhouse; 3rd Roy Green Jackets (Rifle Bde), ADC to Cdr Br Army Staff Washington, DC, 1965–66, with Howard Rotovator Co

(1) *Flora Mary; *m* 15 Sept 1962 *John David Octavius Wallace, s of John Wallace and Mrs Low, of California

(2) *Annabel H; *m* 19 March 1971 *K Christopher Knocker, s of W/Cdr K D Knocker and Mrs P A G Buckeridge

2 Sir WILFRED RHODES, **1st Bt**

1 A dau; *m* J H Walker; *d* 1961

2 A dau; *m* S L Furse

WILLIAM FREEMAN's 3rd s,

Sir Wilfred Rhodes Freeman, 1st Bt (UK), so *cr* 4 July 1945, GCB (1942, KCB 1937, CB 1932), DSO (1916), MC; *b* 18 July 1888; *educ* Rugby and RMC Sandhurst; Capt and Brevet-Maj Manchester Regt, WW I (despatches, Legn Hon), Dep Dir Ops and Intelligence Air Ministry 1927, cmdg RAF Trg Base Leuchars 1928, CSO Iraq Command 1930, cmdg HQ Transjordan and Palestine 1930–33, cmdt RAF Staff Coll 1934–36, air memb R&D Air Cncl 1936 (also for Production 1938–40), CAS 1940–42 (ret 1942), ch exec Min Aircraft Prodn 1942–45; *m* 1st 5 June 1915 (*divorce* 1935) Gladys, 3rd dau of John Mews, of Bayswater, and had issue:

1 **Sir John Keith Noel Freeman, 2nd Bt**; *b* 28 July 1923; *educ* Rugby and Ch Ch Oxford; F/Lt RAF WW II, dir LRC Internat 1968, md Monsanto Textiles Europe 1963–67, commercial dir Viyella Internat 1962, regnl dir Internat Wool Secretariat 1967, dir Assoc Leisure 1973–75; *m* 21 Dec 1946 *Patricia Denison [Patricia Lady Freeman, c/o Royal Bank of Scotland, 32 St Giles, Oxford OX1 3ND], yr dau of Charles W Thomas, of Sandown, IoW, and *d* 1981, having had:

(1) A son; *b* and *d* 18 Sept 1954

(2) Sir JAMES ROBIN FREEMAN, **3rd and present Bt**

(1) *Katharine Noel; *b* 17 Feb 1950; *m* 19 July 1972 *(John) Richard A Naylor, s of J A Naylor, of Westwood, Bridgnorth, Salop

2 *Bridget Anne Elizabeth [Mrs Godfrey Beese, Church House, East Grafton, Wilts]; *b* 6 March 1920; *m* 1st 8 Aug 1942 (*divorce* 1953) John Vernon Rob, Scots Gds, yr s of Dr Joseph W Rob, of Oatlands Park, Weybridge, Surrey, and has issue:

(1) *Joanna Elizabeth; *b* 1943

2 (cont.) Mrs Bridget Rob *m* 2nd 30 Jan 1954 *Godfrey Henry Beese, s of Geoffrey Gilbert Beese, of Westminster, and by him has:

(1) *Christopher David; *b* 1955

(2) *Thomas Jolyon; *b* 1957

(1) *Deborah Helen; *b* 1956

(2) *Philippa Lucy; *b* 1960

3 (cont.) **Sir Wilfred** *m* 2nd 17 April 1935 Elizabeth, MBE (1945), yr dau of Ernest Tatham Richmond, FRIBA, of Jerusalem, and *d* 15 May 1953, leaving:

3 *Joan Margaret [Mrs John Morgan-Grenville, Upperton House, Petworth, Sussex]; *b* 3 Aug 1936; *m* 7 July 1955 John Richard Bine Morgan-Grenville (*see* KINLOSS, L) and has issue

4 *Susan Hilary Philippa [Mrs Robin Malcolm, Duntrune Castle, Kilmartin, Argyll PA31 8QQ]; *b* 17 March 1939; *m* 27 Jan 1962 *Robin Neil Lochmell Malcolm, only s of Lt-Col George Ian Malcolm of Poltalloch, JP, DL, and has issue:

(1) *Ian Rory; *b* 1963

(2) *Andrew Neill; *b* 1965

(1) *Kirsty Elizabeth; *b* 1964

(2) *Josephine Clare; *b* 1969

FREYBERG

Arms: Or on a chief sable four mullets of the field. **Crest:** A demi-lion gules holding between the paws an eagle displayed sable. **Supporters:** On either side a salamander proper. **Motto:** New zeal and honour. **Creation:** B. (UK) 19 Oct 1951.

THE 3RD BARON FREYBERG, of Wellington, New Zealand, and of Munstead, Co Surrey (Valerian Bernard Freyberg) [The Rt Hon The Lord Freyberg, Munstead House, Godalming, Surrey GU8 4AR]; *b* 15 Dec 1970; *s* f 1993; *educ* Eton and Camberwell Coll Art

Lineage: JAMES FREYBERG, of Wellington, NZ; *b* 1828; *m* Julia Hamilton (*d* 1934), of Argyllshire, and *d* 1912, leaving, with other issue:

Sir BERNARD CYRIL FREYBERG, **1st Baron Freyberg**, of Wellington, NZ, and of Munstead, Co Surrey (UK), so *cr* 19 Oct 1951, VC (1916), GCMG (1946, CMG 1919), KCB (1942, CB 1936), KBE (1942), DSO (1915) and three bars (1918 twice and 1945); *b* 21 March 1889; *educ* Wellington Coll NZ; Govr-Gen NZ 1946–52, Dep Constable and Lt-Govr Windsor Castle 1953–63, RND WW I (wounded nine times, despatches six times) to 1917, cmded Inf Bde 1917–18, with Gren Gds 1918–29, cmded The 1st Bn Manchester Regt 1930–31, AQMGS Cmd 1931–33,

GSO1 War Office 1933–34, Maj-Gen 1934, ret 1937 recalled and served WW II as GOC Salisbury Plain Area Sept 1939, C-in-C NZ Forces 1939–45, C-in-C Allied Forces Crete 1941, Greece and Crete 1941, W Desert 1941–42, Tunisia 1943, Italy 1943–45, Pres Shaftesbury Homes and Arethusa Trg Ship 1953, Hon LLD St Andrews 1922, Hon DCL Oxford 1945, Hon DL NZ 1952; *m* 14 June 1922 Barbara GBE (1953), DStJ (*d* 24 Sept 1973), welfare worker Cairo 1941 (despatches), dau of Col Sir Herbert Jekyll, KCMG, of Munstead House, Godalming, Surrey, and widow of Hon Francis Walter Stafford McLaren (*see* ABERCONWAY, B), and *d* 4 July 1963, leaving issue:

PAUL RICHARD FREYBERG, **2nd Baron Freyberg**, OBE (1965), MC (1943); *b* 27 May 1923; *educ* Eton; Lt-Col Gren Gds, NZ Div Greece 1941, Long Range Desert Gp W Desert 1941–42, Gren Gds Tunisia and Italy 1942–45, BAOR 1950–51, Canal Zone 1954, Cyprus 1956–57 and 1958, Br Cameroons 1961, cmded HAC Inf Bn 1965–68, Def Policy Staff MOD 1968, Army Judge JS 19 Jan 1976, psc 1952, jssc 1959; *m* 23 July 1960 *Ivry Perronelle Katharine [The Rt Hon The Lady Freyberg, Munstead House, Godalming, Surrey, GU8 4AR], only dau of Cyril Harrower Guild, of Aspall Hall, nr Debenham, Stowmarket, Suffolk, and *d* 26 May 1993, leaving:

1 VALERIAN BERNARD FREYBERG, **3rd and present Baron Freyberg**

1 *Annabel Pauline; *b* 16 Aug 1961

2 *Venetia Rose [The Hon Mrs Phillips, 103 Richmond Ave, London N1 0LT]; *b* 28 May 1963; *m* 1991 *Robert Phillips, s of John Phillips, and has:

(1) *Gabriel Joseph; *b* 8 April 1995

(2) *Gideon Dylan; *b* 20 March 1997

3 *Christina Marie-Gabriel; *b* 24 Aug 1967

FULLER

Arms: Per pale nebuly azure and ermine two bars counterchanged, over all six martlets, two, two and two or. **Crest:** Issuant from a coronet flory or a lion's head per pale azure and ermine. **Supporters:** Dexter, a lion regardant proper; sinister, a wolf reguardant argent, each gorged with a collar or pendent therefrom an escutcheon per pale nebuly azure and or, charged with six martlets counterchanged. **Motto:** *Deo duce confido* ('I trust in God as my leader'). **Creation:** Bt. (UK) 7 July 1910.

SIR JAMES HENRY FLEETWOOD FULLER, 4TH BT; *b* 1 Nov 1970; *s* f 1998

Lineage: JOHN FULLER, of Neston Park, JP Wilts; High Sheriff 1823; *s* Jan 1796 to estates in Sussex of GERARD DUTTON FLEETWOOD (descendant of Sir Gerard Fleetwood, unc of the Gen Charles Fleetwood who *m* 1652 Bridget, est dau of OLIVER CROMWELL and widow of Gen Ireton); *m* 1789 Dinah (*d* 13 Jan 1856), dau of Jacob Jeans, and *d* 30 March 1839, leaving issue:

1 JOHN BIRD, of Neston Park

2 Neston Joseph; *b* Nov 1802; *m* 1 March 1826 Anne Margaret (*d* 24 March 1876), est dau of Col Hon John Browne (*see* KILMAINE, B), and *d* 16 July 1872

1 Georgiana; *m* 12 Sept 1816 Rev Thomas Heathcote and *d* 15 Jun 1881, having had issue (*see* HEATHCOTE, Bt, of Hursley)

2 Louisa Mary; *m* 25 June 1822 Rev John Andrew Methuen (*d* 19 June 1869), bro of 1st Baron Methuen (*qv*), and *dsps* 18 May 1871

JOHN FULLER's est s,

JOHN BIRD FULLER, of Neston Park, JP, DL; *b* 6 March 1801; High Sheriff 1852; *m* 22 June 1829 Sophia Harriet (*d* 16 April 1883), 2nd dau of William Hanning, of Dillington House, Somerset, and *d* 27 May 1872, having had, with other issue,

1 John Augustus; *b* 17 Sept 1831; *d* 28 Sept 1859

2 GEORGE PARGITER

1 Caroline Sophia; *b* 17 Oct 1839; *m* 19 May 1869 Rev Benjamin Speke (*d* 24 Feb 1881), Rector Dowlish Wake, Somerset, and *d* 23 Feb 1881, having had issue

2 Harriet Georgina; *b* 29 April 1842; *m* 5 Aug 1873 Maj Henry Nangle (*d* 6 May 1892) and had issue

JOHN FULLER's 2nd s,

GEORGE PARGITER FULLER, of Neston Park, JP Wilts; *b* 8 Jan 1833; High Sheriff 1878, MP W or Westbury Div Wilts 1885–95, Capt Wilts Yeo 1862–88; *m* 28 Jan 1864 Emily Georgina Jane (*d* 30 Dec 1930), 2nd dau of Sir Michael Hicks-Beach, 8th Bt (*see* SAINT ALDWYN, E), and *d* 2 April 1927, having had issue:

1 JOHN MICHAEL FLEETWOOD (Sir), **1st Bt**

2 William Fleetwood, DSO (1918), TD, JP (Wilts and Dorset); *b* 17 Sept 1865; Lt-Col Roy Wilts Yeo, CC Wilts, MFH VWH (Cricklade), served WW I (despatches); *d* unm 19 Aug 1947

3 Henry Fleetwood, JP (Oxon); *b* 7 Feb 1870; *m* 6 Feb 1894 Gwenllian Jane (*d* 21 May 1937), 2nd dau of John Cole Nicholl, of Methyr Mawr, Bridgend, and *d* 14 May 1956, leaving issue:

(1) Dillwyn Henry Fleetwood; *b* 3 July 1896; Capt Rifle Bde (Prince Consort's Own); *m* 20 Aug 1918 Dorothy Catherine (*d* 28 Feb 1959), only dau of Maj Edward Durourne Pickard-Cambridge, JP, and *d* 1 Oct 1971, leaving issue:

1a *Pamela Jane Fleetwood [Miss Pamela Fuller, 10 Sandpits Road, Petersham, Richmond, Surrey]; *b* 31 July 1919; WAAF WW II

2a *Mary Priscilla Jocelyn Fleetwood; *b* 15 April 1921; WRNS WW II; *m* 16 June 1946 Robert Brodie Leslie Inverarity, only s of Frederick Inverarity, and has issue:

1b *Robert Dillwyn; *b* 20 April 1947

2b *Geoffrey Fuller; *b* 23 Nov 1951

3a *Angela Dorothea [Miss Angela Fuller, 10 Sandpits Rd, Petersham, Surrey]; *b* 23 Aug 1922; MB, BChir

(1) Mary Gwenllian Fleetwood; *b* 5 Nov 1894; *m* Capt Tom Edmund Allen-Stevens and *d* 10 June 1960, leaving issue

(2) Joyce Fleetwood; *b* 7 Feb 1902; *m* Philip Stirling Eliot and had issue

4 Robert Fleetwood, JP, DL (Wilts); *b* 6 Nov 1875; Maj Roy Wilts Imp Yeo, High Sheriff 1926; *m* 1911 Mabel, OBE (1918) (*d* 5 Jan 1968), 2nd dau of T P Chappell, of Weir Bank, Teddington, and *d* 9 Sept 1955, leaving issue:

(1) Mary Elizabeth Fleetwood; *b* 8 Aug 1916; *m* 1st 11 June 1938 Lt-Col Patrick John Salvin Boyle (*see* GLASGOW, E) and had issue; *m* 2nd 7 Feb 1948 Lt-Col Charles Murray Floyd, OBE (*d* 27 June 1971), yst s of Sir Henry Floyd, 4th Bt (*qv*) and had further issue

5 Edward Fleetwood; *b* 7 Feb 1878; Lt Roy Wilts Yeo; *m* 8 Sept 1901 Margaret Olive (*d* 14 Oct 1944), dau of Edward Argles, and *d* 8 Oct 1914, leaving issue:

(1) *Edward Hamilton Fleetwood; *b* 27 July 1902; *educ* Winchester and Trin Coll Cambridge (BA); *m* 30 Jan 1959 *Pauline Elizabeth Lydia, dau of Guy Francis Johnson, CBE, of 29 Morpeth Mansions, London SW1, and has issue:

1a *Richard Hamilton Fleetwood; *b* 28 Jan 1960

1a *Julia Fleetwood; *b* 2 Oct 1961

(2) George Michael Fleetwood; Cdr RN; *b* 29 July 1903

1 Georgina Fleetwood; *b* 28 Jan 1867; *m* 24 April 1890 Sir Charles Edward Henry Hobhouse, 4th Bt (*qv*), and *d* 17 Dec 1927

GEORGE FULLER's est s,

Sir John Michael Fleetwood Fuller, 1st Bt (UK), so *cr* 7 July 1910, KCMG, JP (Wilts); *b* 21 Oct 1864 ; *educ* Ch Ch Oxford (MA); Maj Roy Wilts Imp Yeo, Hon Col 19th Australian Light Horse, ADC to Viceroy India 1894–95, CA Wilts, MP (Lib) Westbury 1900–11, Jr Ld Treasury 1906–07, V-Chamberlain Household 1907–11, Govr Victoria 1911–14; *m* 5 July 1898 Norah Jacintha (*m* 2nd 18 Jan 1921 Col Richard Forestier-Walker, DSO (*see* FORESTIER-WALKER, Bt), and *d* 22 Feb 1935), 2nd dau of Charles Nicholas Paul Phipps, MP, of Chalcot, Wilts, and *d* 4 Sept 1915, having had issue:

1 **Sir John Gerard Henry Fleetwood Fuller, 2nd Bt**, of Neston Park, JP (1946); *b* 8 July 1906; CC 1947, CA 1961 Wilts, Maj Life Gds, WW II (despatches), Jt MFH Avon Vale 1947–61 and 1962–64; *m* 1st 20 July 1931 (*divorce* 1944) Lady Fiona Pratt, yr dau of 4th Marquess Camden (*qv*); *m* 2nd 8 March 1945 Kathleen Elizabeth, MBE, DGStJ (Co Supt for Wilts from 1952) (*d* 8 April 1964), dau of Sir George Herbert Farrar, 1st and last Bt, DSO (*see* 1915 edn); *m* 3rd 21 Oct 1966 *(Katherine) Mary [Mary Lady Fuller, Bay Tree Cottage, Chapel Lane, Neston, Wilts SN13 9TD], est dau of Douglas Leigh Spence, MB, BCh, MRCS, of Melksham, Wilts, and formerly w of H Leventon, and *d* 1981, leaving by his 1st w:

(1) **Sir John William Fleetwood Fuller, 3rd Bt**; *b* 18 Dec 1936; *educ* Bradfield; Maj Life Gds; *m* 9 Jan 1968 *Lorna Marian [Lady Fuller, Neston Park, Corsham, Wilts SN13 9TG], only dau of F Richard Kemp-Potter, of Hillside, Findon, Sussex, and *d* 3 April 1998, leaving:

1a Sir JAMES HENRY FLEETWOOD FULLER, **4th and present Bt**

2a +ANDREW WILLIAM FLEETWOOD; *b* 1 Dec 1972; heir presumptive

3a +Edward Richard Fleetwood; *b* 1977

(2) +Anthony Gerard Fleetwood, CBE (1990) [Anthony Fuller Esq CBE, Little Chalfield Manor, Melksham, Wilts SN12 8NN]; *b* 4 June 1940; *educ* Eton; Lt Life Gds 1959–62, dir Fuller Smith & Turner plc 1967– (chm 1982–); *m* 19 Nov 1964 *Julia Mary, er dau of Lt-Col Eric Astley Cooper-Key, MBE, of Belgravia and has:

1a +William Gerard Fleetwood; *b* 13 July 1968

1a *Camilla Fleetwood; *b* 16 Feb 1966; *m* 9 Sept 1995 *Allan Christensen, 2nd s of Finn Christensen, of Denmark

2 Christopher Herbert Fleetwood TD (1943); *b* 3 June 1908; *educ* Winchester and Magdalen Coll Oxford; High Sheriff Wilts 1956, Lt-Col Roy Wilts Yeo (TA), served WW II, dir Jaggards, Corsham; *m* 12 Sept 1939 (Beatrice) Susan (*d* 1977), dau of Maj-Gen Sir Percival Otway Hambro, KBE, CB, CMG (*see* HAMBRO, B), and *d* 31 March 1976, leaving:

(1) +Charles Christopher Fleetwood; *b* 24 June 1945; *educ* Winchester; 5th Roy Inniskilling Dragoon Gds

(1) *Penelope Susanne Fleetwood; *b* 27 Aug 1942; *m* 29 Oct 1966 *Maj (George) Oliver Worsley, 2nd s of Col Sir William Arthington Worsley, 4th Bt (*qv*), and has issue

(2) *Victoria Henrietta Fleetwood; *b* 1 May 1944; *m* 10 Jan 1966 *Sir John Philip Starkey, 3rd Bt (*qv*), and has issue

(3) *Georgina Jacintha Fleetwood [Mrs Reuben Harford, Ashcroft House, Kingscote, Tetbury, Glos]; *b* 5 Feb 1951; *m* 1978 *Reuben Charles Harford, only s of Lt-Col Charles Evelyn Harford, and has issue:

1a *Hugh Scandrett; *b* 1980

2a *Christopher Evelyn; *b* 1985

1a *Beatrice Louise; *b* 1982
2a *Henrietta Mary; *b* 1987
1 Bridget Fleetwood; *m* 15 Nov 1927 John Percy Ernest Walker, 2nd s of Sir James Heron Walker, 3rd Bt, of Sand Hutton (*qv*), and *d* 28 April 1955, leaving issue
2 Patience Irene Fleetwood; *b* 31 May 1902; *m* 15 Oct 1924 Col Mark Edward Makgill Crichton Maitland, CVO, DSO, DL and *d* 23 April 1974, leaving issue (*see* LAUDERDALE, E)
3 Maude Fleetwood; *d* unm 7 Nov 1966
4 Victoria Jacintha Fleetwood, JP (Devon 1958); *m* 17 Nov 1936 Col Sir Michael Picton Ansell, CBE, DSO, 5th Roy Inskilling Dragoon Gds, only s of Lt-Col George Kirkpatrick Ansell, 5th Dragoon Gds, and *d* 13 Oct 1969, leaving:
(1) *Nicholas George Picton; *b* 17 Aug 1937; *educ* Wellington and Magdalene Coll Cambridge (BA); Maj 5th Roy Inskilling Dragoon Gds; *m* 17 June 1961 *Vivien, est dau of Lt-Col Anthony Donnithorne Taylor, DSO, MC, of North Aston Manor, Oxford, and has issue:
1a *Mark Picton; *b* 2 Jan 1963
2a *Julian Threepwood; *b* 8 March 1964
1a *Clare Victoria; *b* 26 Aug 1968
(2) *Antony Michael (Rev); *b* 6 March 1940; *educ* Wellington; late 9th/12th Roy Lancers, ADC to Govr S Australia 1961–64, dir Fuller Smith & Turner, Griffin Brewery, London W4, 1967; *m* 31 Oct 1964 *Mary Susan, er dau of Maj Charles Henry Liddell, MC, JP (*see* RAVENSWORTH, B), and has issue
(1) *Sarah Jennifer [Mrs Stephen Evans, 13 Cheyne Gardens, London SW3]; *b* 23 Jan 1945; *m* 23 Nov 1968 *Stephen Alexander Evans, yst s of Maj-Gen Roger Evans, CB, MC, of Stocklinch, Ilminster, Somerset

FURNESS

Arms: Per saltire argent and or a talbot sejant sable, on a chief wavy gules three plates. **Crest:** Issuant from a wreath of cinquefoils vert a bear's paw erect argent charged with a torteau and grasping a javelin in bend sinister sable, pendant therefrom by the straps proper two spurs or. **Motto:** I'll defend. **Creation:** Bt. (UK) 18 June 1913.

SIR STEPHEN ROBERTS FURNESS, 3RD BT, of Tunstall Grange, W Hartlepool, Co Durham [Sir Stephen Furness Bt, Stanhow Farm, Gt Langton, N Yorks DL7 0TJ]; *b* 10 Oct 1933; *s f* 1974; *educ* Charterhouse; Lt RN (ret); farmer, sporting and landscape artist as Robin Furness, memb: Armed Forces Art Soc and Darlington Art Soc, Jt MFH Bedale 1979–87; *m* 6 April 1961 *Mary, er dau of Jack Fitzroy Cann, of Newland, Cullompton, Devon, and has:

1 +MICHAEL FITZROY ROBERTS [Michael Furness Esq, Glebe Farm, S Otterington, Northallerton, N Yorks]; *b* 12 Oct 1962; *educ* Sedburgh and Askham Bryan Coll of Ag and Horticulture (HND); farmer
2 *Serena Mary; *b* 30 Dec 1964; *m* 1991 *Lt Mark F C Searight, RM, yst s of Maj M P C Searight, of E Witton, N Yorks and has issue:
(1) *Tristan Patrick Chamney; *b* 1995
(1) *Kate Isabella; *b* 1992

Lineage: JOHN FURNESS, of W Hartlepool, Co Durham; *m* 5 Feb 1835 Averill Eastor (*d* 5 Oct 1890), dau of John Wilson, of Naisbet Hall, Co Durham, and *d* 23 Dec 1885, having had, with other issue (*see* 1970 edn, FURNESS, V):

STEPHEN FURNESS, of The Manor House, Berwick St James, Wilts; *b* 28 May 1848; *m* 4 July 1870 Mary Anne (*d* 17 Oct 1898), dau of Dixon T Sharper, of W Hartlepool, and *d* 19 June 1911, leaving, with other issue:

Sir Stephen Wilson Furness, 1st Bt (UK), so *cr* 18 June 1913, of Tunstall Grange, W Hartlepool, JP; MP Hartlepools 1910–14; *b* 26 May 1872; chm Furness Withy & Co; *m* 5 Sept 1899 Eleanor (*d* 13 Nov 1936), dau of Matthew Forster, JP, CE, of Mount Brown, S Australia , and *d* 6 Sept 1914, leaving issue:

1 CHRISTOPHER (Sir), **2nd Bt**
2 Stephen Noel, JP (NR Yorks); MP Sunderland 1935–45; *b* 18 Dec 1902; *educ* Charterhouse and Oriel Coll Oxford (MA); barrister Middle Temple 1927, Maj London Irish Rifles, Assist Govt Whip 1937, Jr Ld Treasury 1938–40, chm Furness Shipbuilding Co, dir Economic Insur Co, Co Commr NR Yorks Boy Scouts 1946–61; *d* unm 14 April 1974
3 Frank Wilson, MBE (1967), JP (NR Yorks 1944); *b* 10 April 1906; *educ* Charterhouse and Pembroke Coll Cambridge (MA); High Sheriff N Yorks 1977, MFH Hurworth 1947–55; *m* 28 April 1949 *Georgeana Anne [Mrs Frank Furness, Knowle House, Kirby Knowle, Thirsk, N Yorks YO7 2JB], only dau of Col Victor Alexander Henry Daly, OBE, MC, of Pond Cottage, Darby Green, Blackwater, Camberley, Surrey, and widow of F/O Alan Guthrie, RAF, and *d* 1993, leaving issue:
(1) +John Wilson; *b* 7 Oct 1952; *educ* Wellington and RAC Cirencester; *m* 1983 *Grania Patricia, est dau of John Brabazon Booth, of Darver Castle, Dundalk, Co Louth (*see* GUINNESS, Bt), and has issue:
1a +Christopher; *b* 1990
1a *Virginia; *b* 1987
1 Eleanor Mary; *b* 29 Aug 1904; MFH Hurworth; *d* 19–

Sir STEPHEN's est s,

Sir Christopher Furness, 2nd Bt, of Tunstall Grange; *b* 18 Oct 1900; *educ* Charterhouse and Pembroke Coll Cambridge; Lt RNVR WW II 1940–45; *m* 8 Jan 1930 (Violet) Flower Chipchase, dau of Lt-Col Gerard Chipchase Roberts, of Hollingside, Co Durham, and *d* 21 June 1974, leaving issue:

1 Sir STEPHEN ROBERTS FURNESS, **3rd and present Bt**
2 +Simon John [Lt-Col Simon Furness, The Garden House, Netherbyres, Eyemouth, Berwicks TD14 5SE]; *b* 18 Aug 1936; *educ* Charterhouse and RMA Sandhurst; Lt Col, Hon Col 1993 LI, cmdg 5th Bn LI (ret 1978), Deputy Col Durham LI 1989–93, V-Ld Lt Berwicks 1990 (DL 1983)
3 +Colin Gerard [Colin Furness Esq, Cockerdale Farm, Coxwold, Yorks]; *b* 10 May 1939; *educ* Charterhouse; *m* 1958 *Margaret Grace, only dau of Alfred J Haddock, of St Paul's Cray, Kent, and has issue:
(1) +Francis Christopher; *b* 10 April 1963; *educ* Repton and Sidney Sussex Coll Cambridge
(1) *Fiona Elizabeth; *b* 23 April 1959; *m* 1987 *Peter Alan Cloke, only s of Roland Cloke, and has issue:
1a *Andrew Philip; *b* 1994
(2) *Julia Margaret; *b* 29 July 1960
(3) *Nicola Jane; *b* 6 Dec 1964
1 *Patricia Flower [Mrs Paul Payne, Whitehall, Old Cleeve, Minehead, Somerset TA24 6HU]; *b* 14 July 1931; *m* 9 Oct 1960 *Maj Paul Ian Craven Payne, The Roy Scots (the Roy Regt; despatches), only s of A Wyndham Payne, of The Hermitage, Sidmouth, and has issue:
(1) *Brian Wyndham; *b* 27 July 1961; *educ* Winchester and Bristol U (BSc, DipL); Capt The King's Troop RHA 1988–91, barrister Inner Temple 1993; *m* 1992 *Sally Jane, dau of Garnet Thomas, of Ferwig, Dyfed
(2) *Paul Frederick Craven; *b* 25 Oct 1964; *educ* Millfield, BA; ceramist; *m* 1989 (*divorce* 1994) Jennifer Anne, yst dau of James Donald Douglas, of Tenerife

GAGE

Arms: Quarterly, 1st and 4th, per saltire arg and az. a saltire gu. (for GAGE); 2nd and 3rd, az, the sun in splendor or (for ST CLERE). **Crest:** A ram statant arg., armed and unguled or. **Supporters:** Two greyhounds tenné ppr., each gorged with a coronet composed of fleurs-de-lis or. **Motto:** *Courage sans peur* ('Courage without fear'). **Creation:** Bt (E) 26 March 1622, V and B (Gage of Castlebar) (I) 14 Sept 1720, B (GB) 1 Nov 1790.

THE 8TH VISCOUNT GAGE OF CASTLE ISLAND, Co Kerry, **Baron Gage of Castlebar,** Co Mayo, **Baron Gage of High Meadow,** Co Gloucester, and a **Baronet** (Sir (Henry) Nicolas Gage, Bt, DL (E Sussex 1998)) [The Rt Hon The Viscount Gage DL, Firle Place, Lewes, East Sussex BN8 6LP]; *b* 9 April 1934; *s* bro 1993; *educ* Eton and Ch Ch Oxford; late 2nd Lt Coldstream Gds; *m* 1974 *Lady Diana Adrienne Beatty, er dau of 2nd Earl Beatty (*qv*), and has issue:

1 +HENRY WILLIAM; *b* 25 June 1975
2 +Richard David Benedict; *b* 21 Feb 1977

Lineage: JOHN GAGE, of Cirencester; had an only s:

JOHN GAGE; *m* Joan, dau and coheir of John Sudgrove, of Sudgrove-in-Miserder, Glos, and *d* c 1440, leaving:

Sir JOHN GAGE, of Burstow, Surrey, who acquired that seat and Penshurst, Kent, together with large estates in Sussex and Bucks by marriage with Eleanor, dau and coheir of Thomas St Clere (only son of Sir Philip St Clere, of Ightham, Kent, by Margaret, sole heir of Sir Nicholas de Lovayne, of Burstow, and gs of Sir Philip St Clere, MP Sussex 1377); *d* 30 Sept 1486, leaving (with a yr s John, ancestor of the GAGEs of Rushton, Northants):

WILLIAM GAGE; inherited Burstow and Penshurst, but sold the latter (*see* DE L'ISLE, V) and built a house at West Firle, Sussex, in the Manor of Heighton St Clere, which had come to his mother's family by the marriage of John de St Clere (*d* 1327) with Isolda, sole heir of Thomas de Aldham, of Ightham and Aldham, Kent; *m* Agnes, dau of Benjamin Bol(e)ney, of Bolney, Sussex, and sis of John Bol(e)ney, MP Sussex 1459, and *d* 1496, leaving an only son:

Sir JOHN GAGE, KG (1532), KB (1543), PC (*c* 1522–*c* 1548 and 1549), JP (Sussex 1510–22), of Firle; *b* 1479; participated in HENRY VIII's French campaign of 1513, Govr Guisnes 1522 and later Oye, Comptroller Calais 1522, V-Chamberlain to HENRY VIII 1528–40, MP Sussex 1529, granted various monastic lands (including Kelagh Priory 1540) despite being so pious he at one point contemplated becoming a Carthusian; Constable Tower London 1540–53 and 1553 on, Comptroller Household 1540–*c* 1548 and Chllr Duchy Lancaster 1540, cmded English army English victory over Scots of Solway Moss 1542, Ld Chamberlain 1553; *m* Philippa, dau of Sir Richard Guilford or Guldeford, KG (either gf or cousin of Jane, w of John Dudley, Duke of Northumberland), and *d* 18 April 1556, having had (with four daus, one of whom, Alice, *m* Sir Anthony Brown, KG, and another of whom, Anne, *m* John Thatcher, of Priestshaws, Sussex):

1 EDWARD (Sir)

2 John, of Bentley, Sussex; had:

(1) John, of Wormley, Herts; *m* Eleanor, widow of Sir Thomas Baskerville and dau of Richard Habingdon, and was ancestor of:

1a John Gage, of Bentley Park, Sussex; *m* 1701 Lucy, dau and heir of John Mayo, and had, with three sons (*dsp*):

1b Lucy; *m* William Herrick, of Beaumanoir, Leics

3 Robert, of Haling, Surrey; MP Lewes 1534; had:

(1) Robert; beheaded for supporting MARY QUEEN OF SCOTS

(2) John, of Haling; had:

1a Henry (Sir); royalist Govr Oxford Civil War; twice relieved Basing House but was *ka* Cullum Bridge 7 Jan 1644

4 William; *dsp*

Sir JOHN's est son,

Sir EDWARD GAGE, KB, of Firle; *m* Elizabeth, dau of John Parker, of Willingdon, Sussex, and *d* 1568, having had (with a 2nd and 4th s):

1 John; MP Lewes 1557; *dsp* 1595

3 Thomas; *b* 1541; *m* his cousin Elizabeth, dau of Sir Thomas Guilford or Guldeford, of Hemstead, Kent, and *d* 1590, leaving, with six other sons:

(1) JOHN (Sir), **1st Bt**

(1) Mary; *m* Sir Thomas Pordage

(2) Elizabeth; *m* Cressacre More, ggs of Sir and St Thomas More

5 Edward; *m* Margaret, 3rd dau of John Shelley, of Michel Grove, and had:

(1) Elizabeth; *m* Sir John Stradling, 1st Bt, and had issue

1 Agnes; *m* 1566 Sir Edward Stradling, of St Donat's Castle, Glam

2 Philippa; *m* Edward Saunder

3 Mary; *m* 1569 James Thatcher

4 Margery; *m* Anthony Kemp

5 Lucy

6 Margaret; *m* Henry Darell

Sir EDWARD's 2nd son,

Sir John Gage, 1st Bt (E), so *cr* 26 March 1622, of Firle; *m c* 28 June 1611 Penelope (*m* 3rd 1642 Sir William Hervey (*see* BRISTOL, M), and *d* 1661), widow of Sir George Trenchard, of Wolverton, Dorset, and dau and coheir of Thomas DArcy, 1st Earl Rivers of the 1626 *cr*, by Mary, dau and coheir of Sir Thomas Kitson, of Hargrave or Hengrave, Suffolk, and *d* 3 Oct 1633, having had issue:

1 THOMAS (Sir), **2nd Bt**

2 John; *dsp*

3 Sir EDWARD GAGE, 1st Bt (E), so *cr* 15 July 1662; *b c* 1626; *m* 1675 Frances, dau of 1st Earl of Desmond (*see* DENBIGH and DESMOND, E); inherited the Hengrave estate from his mother, and was ancestor of the GAGEs, later ROKEWODE-GAGEs, Bts, of Hengrave and Coldham Hall, Suffolk

4 Henry; *m* Henrietta, dau of Sir Thomas Jermyn, KB, of Rushbroke, Suffolk, and sis of 1st Baron Jermyn of St Edmundsbury, and had issue:

(1) John Gage, of Princethorpe, Norfolk

(1) Mary; nun

1 Frances; *m* 1st Sir William Tresham, Bt; *m* 2nd her cousin George Gage

2 Penelope; *m* Henry Merry, of Barton, Derbys

3 Elizabeth; *m* Sir Thomas Petre, of Cranham, Essex

4 Anne; *m* Henry Petre

Sir JOHN's est son,

Sir Thomas Gage, 2nd Bt, of Firle; *m* 1635 Mary (*m* 2nd May 1661 Sir Henry Goring, 2nd Bt of the 1622 *cr* (*see* GORING, Bt), and *d* 1694), est dau and coheir of John Chamberlain, of Sherborne Castle, Oxon, and *d* 2 July 1654, having had issue:

1 **Sir Thomas Gage, 3rd Bt**; *d* unm 22 Nov 1660

2 **Sir John Gage, 4th Bt**; Sheriff Sussex 1687–88; *m* 1st Mary (*d* 28 July 1686), dau and sole heir of Robert Middlemore, of Edgbaston, Warwicks, by Henrietta Maria, dau of Sir Maurice Drummond, and had issue:

(1) Mary; *m* 1st *c* 1690 Sir John Shelley, 3rd Bt (*qv*), and had issue; *m* 2nd George Mathew, of Thurles, Co Tipperary, and *d* by 1722

(2) Bridget; *m* July 1698 3rd Viscount Fauconberg of Henknowle and *d* 18 Nov 1732, leaving issue. He *d* 26 Nov 1718

2 (cont.) **Sir John** *m* 2nd Mary, dau of Sir William Stanley, 1st Bt, of Hooton, and *d* 27 May 1699, leaving further issue:

(1) **Sir John Gage, 5th Bt**; *b* 1692; *d* Jan 1700

(2) **Sir Thomas Gage, 6th Bt**; *d* abroad Oct 1713

(3) **Sir William Gage 7th Bt**; *b* 1695, KB (1725); conformed to C of E (the Gages previously having been recusants), MP Seaford 1727–44; *d* unm 23 April 1744

(3) Mary; *m* 22 Jan 1715/6 8th Baron Teynham (*qv*); *bur* 10 Jan 1716/7

3 Henry; *dsp*

4 Joseph, SJ; entered English Coll Rome 1670; *m* Elizabeth (*d* 5 Dec 1693), dau and eventual heir of Sir George Penruddock, of Hale, by Ursula, dau and heir of Sir E Lawley, of Wenlock, and widow of Sir R Bertie, KB (*see* LINDSEY and ABINGDON, E), and had issue:

(1) THOMAS, **1st Viscount**

(2) Joseph (Edward), Count (de) Gage(s); *b* 1678?; made and lost a fortune speculating on the French market in land in the Mississippi region of N America (stock in which he allegedly held *c* 1719 to the value of £13,000,000, or well over £885,000,000 in late-1990s terms); at the peak of his financial success offered £3,000,000 (well over £204,000,000 in late-1990s terms) for the Crown of Poland (this offer refused by KING AUGUSTUS), also offered to buy Sardinia from its king (offer again refused), later moved to Spain and involved in gold mining in the Asturias (unprofitable), later wreck salvage in Spanish and Spanish Indies (*i.e.*, probably Caribbean) coastal waters (moderately profitable); given a silver mine (very profitable) by PHILIP V OF SPAIN 1741 and made a Spanish Grandee of the 3rd Class; C-in-C Spanish forces Italy 1742–46, his mission being to put into effect the grand strategy of PHILIP's imperious 2nd w QUEEN ISABEL (she at one point ordered Gage to attack the enemy in three days or be relieved of his post), the strategy in question being to make her younger son Don Felipe King of Lombardy in the teeth of Austrian opposition; ably but in the long run unsuccessfully carried out his instructions, at one point giving a ball in Bologna to distract the local people while he prepared a surprise attack on the Austrians (it being winter, both armies had nominally suspended operations, as was customary then); the ensuing Battle of Camp Santo (4 Feb 1743) indecisive but treated in Spain as a victory, Gage being advanced to the rank of Grandee of the 1st Class; also held Order of St Januarius; (?)*m* 1st(?) Catherine, dau of John Caryll, of West Harting; *m* (2nd?) Lady Mary Herbert, dau of 2nd Marquess and 2nd titular Duke of Powis (*see* POWIS, E), and *d* 31 Jan 1753

(1) Elizabeth; *m* John Weston, of Sutton

(2) Anne; *m* Richard Arundell Bealing, of Lanherne, Cornwall

1 Frances; *m* Sir Charles Yate, 3rd Bt (*d* 1680), and had issue

2 Mary; *m* Anthony Kempe

3 Catherine; *m* after 1680, as his 2nd w, 3rd Lord Aston of Forfar and *dsp* 2 April 1720

The 7th Bt's cousin,

Sir Thomas Gage, 8th Bt, and **1st Viscount Gage of Castle Island**, Co Kerry, so *cr* 14 Sept 1720, as also BARON GAGE OF CASTLEBAR, Co Mayo (both I); *b* RC, later conformed to C of E but returned to RC Church by his death; FRS 1728, MP (Whig) Minehead April-May 1717 and Tewkesbury 1721–54; *m* 1st 1717 Benedicta/Beata Maria Theresa (*d* 25 July 1749), only dau and heir of Benedict Hall, of High Meadow, Glos, and had issue:

1 WILLIAM HALL GAGE, **2nd Viscount Gage of Castle Island**; MP Seaford 1744–47 and 1754–80; *b* 1 Jan 1718; *cr* 17 Oct 1780 BARON GAGE OF FIRLE, Co Sussex (GB) and 1 Nov 1790 BARON GAGE OF HIGH MEADOW, Co Gloucester (GB), with in the second case remainder failing heirs male of his body to his n Henry since by now he was without male issue; *m* 3 Feb 1757 Elizabeth Gideon (*d* 1 July 1783), sis of Sampson Eardley, *né* Gideon, 1st and last Baron Eardley of Spalding, and had an only son (*d* in infancy); *dsps* 11 Oct 1791, when the Barony of Gage of Firle expired

2 Thomas; *b* 1721; Lt 1741, Capt 62nd Foot 1745, Maj 55th Foot 1748, ADC to Earl of Albemarle (*qv*) Flanders 1747–48, Lt-Col 44th Foot 1751, campaigned under Braddock N America 1754 and subsequently there and Canada (Brig-Gen by 1759) till 1772 (Govr Montreal *c* 1760, Maj-Gen 1761, C-in-C N America 1763–72, Col 60th Royal American Regt, Col 22nd Foot, Lt-Gen 1770), Govr in Chief and Capt Gen Massachusetts Bay Province 1774 with HQ at Boston, C-in-C Forces N America 1775–76 during the early stages of the War of Independence, Col 17th Dragoons and later 11th Dragoons, Gen 1782; *m* 8 Dec 1758 Margaret (*d* 9 Feb 1824), dau of Hon Peter Kembal/Kemble, Pres Cncl of New Jersey, by Gertrude, dau of Samuel Bayard and Margaret, dau of Rt Hon Stephen Van Cortlandt, and *d* 2 April 1787, leaving issue:

(1) HENRY, **3rd Viscount**

(2) John, of Rogate, Hants; *b* 23 Dec 1767; *m* 20 May 1793 Mary (*d* 9 Nov 1846), only dau and heir of John Milbanke by Lady Mary Watson-Wentworth, sis and coheir of 2nd and last Marquess of Rockingham, KG, and *d* 24 Dec 1846, leaving, with other issue:

1a Thomas Wentworth (Rev); Vicar Higham Ferrers, Northants; *m* 17 Feb 1831 Mary Elizabeth (*d* 16 May 1888), dau and coheir of 5th Marquess of Queensberry (*qv*), and *d* 19 March 1837, leaving, with other issue:

1b Charles Wentworth; *b* 28 Feb 1832; *m* June 1862 Georgina, dau of C Toker, of Montreal, and *d* 17 May 1868, leaving issue:

1c Charles Wentworth; *b* 1 June 1868

1c Mary Clarissa

2a John William; *m* 4 Aug 1832 Mary Elizabeth, est dau of William Lushington, and *dsp* 10 Jan 1849

1a Mary; *m* 28 April 1820 Henry Peter Delme, of Cams Hall, Hants, and *d* 17 June 1870. He *d* 29 Jan 1883

2a Charlotte Margaret; *m* 20 Oct 1825 John Hodgetts Hodgetts-Foley (*see* FOLEY, B), and *d* 9 Sept 1851, leaving issue

3a Louisa Henrietta; *m* 16 Nov 1847 Ernest Rodolph, Baron Bertouch, of Denmark. He *d* 8 July 1869

(3) William Hall (Sir), GCB, GCH; a Ld Admlty, Adml of the Fleet 1862; *b* 2 Oct 1777; *dsp* 5 Jan 1864

(1) Maria Theresa; *m* 2 March 1792 Sir James Gregan-Craufurd, 2nd Bt (*see* CRAUFURD, Bt), and *d* 21 April 1832, leaving issue
(2) Louisa Elizabeth; *m* 13 Feb 1794 Sir James Henry Blake, 3rd Bt, of Langham (*see* 1970 edn), and *d* 21 Jan 1832, leaving issue. He *d* 21 April 1832
(3) Harriet; *d* unm 1835
(4) Charlotte Margaret; *m* 22 April 1802 Adml Sir Charles Ogle, 2nd Bt, and *d* Sept 1814, leaving issue. He *d* 16 June 1858
(5) Emily; *m* 27 Aug 1807 5th Earl of Abingdon (*see* LINDSEY and ABINGDON, E) and *d* 28 Aug 1838, leaving issue
1 Theresa; *m* George Tasburgh, of Bodney, Norfolk, and *dsp* 1775

The **1st Viscount** *m* 2nd 26 Dec 1750 Jane (*née* Godfrey; *d* 8 Oct 1757), widow of Henry Jermyn Bond, of Bury St Edmunds, and *d* 21 Dec 1754

The 2nd VISCOUNT's n,

HENRY GAGE, **3rd Viscount Gage of Castle Island**; Maj-Gen 1850; *b* 4 March 1761; *m* 12 Jan 1789 his cousin Susanna Maria (*d* 9 April 1821), only dau and heir of Lt-Gen William Skinner by Susan, dau and coheir of Adml Sir Peter Warren, KB, of Westbury, Hants, MP Westminster, and had, with other issue:
1 HENRY HALL, **4th Viscount**
2 Thomas William, of Westbury; *b* 4 Aug 1796; *m* 12 June 1824 Arabella Cecil (*d* 25 Feb 1840), dau of T W St Quintin, of Scampston Hall, Yorks, and *d* 26 Jan 1855, having had issue:
(1) William; *b* 26 Oct 1828; *d* unm 22 Aug 1846
(1) Arabella Elizabeth; *m* 17 Jan 1856 Gen Hon Edward Thomas Gage, CB, and *d* 8 Nov 1860, leaving issue (*see* below)

The 3rd VISCOUNT *d* 29 Jan 1808; his er son,

HENRY HALL GAGE, **4th Viscount Gage of Castle Island**; *b* 14 Dec 1791; *m* 8 March 1813 Elizabeth Maria (*d* 13 June 1857), est dau of Hon Edward Foley (*see* FOLEY, B), and had:
1 Henry Edward Hall; Lt-Col Roy Sussex Militia; *b* 9 Jan 1814; *m* 31 Aug 1840 Sophia Selina (*d* 4 May 1886), only dau of Sir Charles Knightley, 2nd Bt, and sister and in her issue heir of 1st and last Baron Knightley of Fawsley (*see* 1895 edn), and *dvp* 8 Sept 1875, having had, with other issue (*d* young):
(1) HENRY CHARLES, **5th Viscount**
(1) Selina Elizabeth; *m* 1st 22 July 1862 (*divorce* 1872) Henry Cavendish, of Chyknell, Salop; *m* 2nd 1873 J White, of Westbank, Fifeshire
2 Edward Thomas, CB; Lt-Gen, Col cmdg RHA, Kt Medjidie; *b* 28 Dec 1825; *m* 1st 17 Jan 1856 Arabella Elizabeth (*d* 8 Nov 1860), dau of Hon Thomas William Gage (*see* above), and had issue:
(1) William Henry St Quintin; *b* 12 Feb 1858; *educ* Exeter Coll Oxford; *d* unm 31 Dec 1939
(2) Francis Edward; Immigration Offr at a Tyne Port; *b* 13 Oct 1860; *educ* Wellington; *m* 1918 Alys Maude, dau of Mark Simpson, of Daglingworth, Glos, and *d* 10 June 1936
(1) Mary Cecil Elizabeth Wilhelmina; *b* 12 Sept 1856; *m* 28 Dec 1882 Rev Henry Steuart Gladstone, MA, of Hazelwood, King's Langley, Herts, Vicar Honingham, Norwich, and *d* 22 Jan 1929, leaving issue. He *d* 14 Jan 1929
(2) Georgiana Elizabeth; *b* 5 July 1859; *d* unm 28 Jan 1931
2 (cont.) Lt-Gen Edward Gage *m* 2nd 18 Nov 1862 Ella Henrietta (*d* 7 June 1916), dau of James and Lady Caroline Maxse (*see* BERKELEY, B), and *d* 21 May 1889, having by her had issue:
(3) Ælla Molyneux Berkeley, of Sludge Hall, Billesdon, Leics; Maj TFR, T/Lt-Col whilst Inspr of War Camps Egypt 1916, formerly Capt 14th Hus, Boer War 1899–1900 (Queen's medal with three clasps); *b* 29 Sept 1863; *m* 30 Oct 1888 Ethel Marion (*d* 27 Oct 1949), dau of John Lysaght, of Springfort, Glos, and *d* 25 Aug 1937, leaving issue:
1a John Fitzhardinge Berkeley; Lt-Cdr RNVR, Lt 4th Hus; *b* 3 June 1901; *educ* Eton; *m* 1st 29 Dec 1923 (*divorce* 1927) Olivia Beth (*d* 1948), adopted dau of Brig-Gen R G MacLachlan, Rifle Bde, of Rookley House, King's Somborne, Hants; *m* 2nd 31 Oct 1931 (*divorce* 1937) Griselda Margaret (*d* 1992), yr dau of R-Adml Sir Godfrey Marshall Paine, KCB, MVO, of Portsmouth; *m* 3rd 19– Jenny Elvira (*d* 1993), dau of —, and *d* 1967, having by his 2nd w had:
1b John Grenville Berkeley; *b* 28 Sept 1933; *educ* Eton; *m* 1961 *Pauline [Mrs John Gage, 45 Kew Rd, Richmond, Surrey], dau of Antony Paul Pape, and *d* 1983, leaving issue:
1c +Ælla Rupert Fitzhardinge Berkeley; *b* 1966
1c Cassandra Griselda Louise; *b* 1961; *d* 1992
2c *Emma Leonora Falaise; *b* 1963
2b +Thomas Ælla Godfrey [Thomas Gage Esq, Withypool, Somerset]; *b* 5 April 1935; *educ* Eton; *m* 1st 1960 (*divorce* 1982) Dorothy Isobel Margaret (*m* 2nd — Burton), dau of John Baxter Wylie; *m* 2nd 19 Oct 1983 *Ina Merete, dau of Johan Frederik Utke Meincke, of Denmark, and by his 1st w has:
1c +Andrew Thomas Berkeley; *b* 11 July 1961
2c +John Duncan Godfrey; *b* 22 Oct 1962
1c *Caroline Margaret; *b* 28 March 1966
2c *Amber Camilla; *b* 23 March 1969; *m* 6 Sept 1997 *George Dennis Bampfylde Stucley, er s and heir of Sir Hugh Stucley 6th Bt (*qv*)
3b +Malcolm Edward Fitzhardinge [Malcolm Gage Esq, c/o Barclays Bank, 1 Cockspur St, London SW1]; *b* 16 July 1936; *educ* Eton, late RHG; *m* 1971 Vanessa Smith (*d* 1984)
1b *Dawn Falaise [Mrs John Loughman, Creek Cottage, Saltern's Lane, Hayling Island, Hants]; *b* 22 Aug 1932; *m* 1st 11 Oct 1952 (*divorce* 1963) John Kershaw Sanders, only son of John Hearne Sanders, ICS; *m* 2nd 1963 *Capt John Pym Loughman, RN, and by her 1st husb has:
1c *John James Godfrey; *b* 1953
2c *Guy Dominic Robson; *b* 1955
3c *Hugo Thomas Kershaw; *b* 1957
(4) Roger Fitzhardinge; Consul Rouen and Cherbourg, Lt 4th Bn Liverpool Regt; *b* 5 March 1868; *d* unm 17 July 1904
(5) James Seton Drummond; Lt 5th Dragoon Gds, Capt Hampshire Yeo 1914, Dongola Expdn 1896 (two medals with two clasps), Boer War, including defence of Ladysmith (two medals, four clasps) and WW I (two medals); *b* 28 June 1870; *m* 20 Aug 1927 Beatrice Eleanor Genevieve (*d* 27 Jan 1953), only dau of John Reginald Grahame White, of Faygate House, Faygate, Sussex, and *dsp* 25 May 1952
(6) Moreton Foley, DSO, DL (Northants); Lt-Col 5th Dragoon Gds, GSO BEF 1914–16, Bde Cdr 1916–19, Hon Brig-Gen 1919, Mil Attaché Washington, DC, 1912–14, served Uganda 1898–99 (despatches, medal), Boer War 1899–1902 (despatches, Queen's medal with five clasps, King's medal with two clasps) and WW I (despatches, twice, brevet); *b* 12 Jan 1873; *m* 1st 8 Oct 1902 Anne Massie (*d* 12 April 1915), est dau of William Everard Strong, of New York, and had issue:
1a Berkeley Everard Foley (Sir), KCMG (1955, CMG 1949); Special Envoy UK Delegn Dumbarton Oaks and San Francisco Confs 1944 and 1945, Counsellor The Hague 1947–50 (Chargé d'Affaires 1947 and 1948), Consul Gen Chicago 1950–54, Amb Siam 1954–57 and Peru 1958–63, Chm Ctee Exports to Latin America, memb Br Nat Export Cncl, memb Cncl Vols Overseas 1964–66, Grand Cross Peruvian Order Sun; *b* 27 Feb 1904; *educ* Eton and Trin Coll Cambridge (BA 1925); *m* 1st 15 Jan 1931 (*divorce* 1954) Hedwig Maria Gertrud Eva, dau of Carl von Chappuis, of Liegnitz, Silesia; *m* 2nd 4 Oct 1954 *Lillian [Lady Gage, 24 Ovington Gardens, London SW3 1LE], formerly w of — Riggs-Miller and dau of Vladimir Vukmirovich, formerly Yugoslav Consul-Gen Chicago, and *d* 3 March 1994, having by his 1st w had:
1b Anthony St Clere Berkeley; *b* 9 Nov 1931; *educ* Gordonstoun and U of Chicago; *m* 1 May 1965 *Virginia Mary, dau of Denis Henry Ferens, of Orley House, Ipplepen, S Devon, and *d* 1984, leaving issue:
1c +Benjamin Francis; *b* 3 May 1969
2c +Gregory Bernard; *b* 5 May 1971
3c +Oliver; *b* 7 April 1973
2b +Ulick Charles Christopher [Ulick Gage Esq, 19 Bruce St, Stanmore, NSW 2048, Australia]; 2nd Lt 12th Lancers Cyprus 1959, architect 1969, ARIBA, ARIAA; *b* 7 Jan 1938; *educ* Eton and St John's Coll Cambridge (BA 1963, MA 1966); *m* 12 Dec 1964 *Helen Mary Janet, 2nd dau of AVM Evelyn Michael Thomas Howell, CBE, of Letchworth, Herts, and has:
1c +Marius Berkeley; *b* 21 Sept 1966
1c *Ulicia Mary; *b* 23 May 1965
2a +Edward Fitzhardinge Peyton [Maj Edward Gage, Château de Combecave, 82109 Bourg de Visa, Tarn et Garonne, France]; High Sheriff Salop 1963, Maj Coldstream Gds WW II; *b* 3 July 1906; *educ* Eton and Ch Ch Oxford (BA); *m* 21 Jan 1931 Thalia Westcott (*d* 8 June 1994), est dau of Stephen Caldwell Millett, of New York, and has:
1b +Robert ('Robin') Westcott Moreton [Robin Gage Esq, Strelley House, Lowdhare, Notts NG14 7BJ]; Lt Life Gds 1952–54; *b* 19 April 1934; *educ* Eton and Ch Ch Oxford (MA 1957); *m* 1st 4 April 1964 (*divorce* 1978) Maria Teresa Francisca, yr dau of Don Emilio Díaz-Caneja, of Santander, Spain; *m* 2nd 1990 *Elisabeth Nicola Maria, dau of Benjamin Hubert Dowson, and by his 1st w has had:
1c Henry St Clere Rokewood; *b* 12 June 1966; *d* 31 May 1996
1c *Dolores Isabella; *b* 2 March 1965
1b *Ann Caroline Thalia; *b* 25 Nov 1931; *educ* St Hilda's Coll Oxford (BA 1953); *m* 25 Feb 1960 *Hon Robin Alexander Baring, yr son of 6th Baron Ashburton (*qv*), and has issue
2b *Elizabeth Estling [Miss Elizabeth Gage, 20 Albemarle St, London SW1]; *b* 31 Dec 1937; *m* 1st 5 Dec 1957 (*divorce* 1964) David Vernon Russell, son of Brig Hugh Edward Russell, DSO; *m* 2nd 21 March 1970 David Bruce Douglas Lowe, s of *d* G A Lowe; *m* 3rd 1974 (*divorce* 1983) Richard Perkins
(6) Brig-Gen Moreton Gage *m* 2nd 30 Sept 1916 Frances (*d* 14 June 1955), yr dau of Senator Henry F Lippitt, of Rhode Island, and *d* 6 July 1953, having by her had issue:
3a +Quentin Henry Moreton [Maj Quentin Gage, Pelham Cottage, Church Lane, Hellingly, E Sussex BN27 4HA]; Maj Gren Gds WW II (wounded); *b* 22 Aug 1920; *educ* Eton and Ch Ch Oxford; *m* 16 April 1949 *Hazel Swinton, er dau of Col George Archibald Swinton Home, DSO, OBE, 5th Dragoon Gds, of Kenya, and has issue:
1b +Jonathan Moreton; Lt RARO; *b* 31 March 1954; *educ* Eton and RMA Sandhurst; *m* 1994 *Anna Hobson and has issue:
1c +Edward Moreton Quentin; *b* 4 Jan 1996
1b *Deborah Pamela; *b* 26 March 1950
1a *Dorothy Louise [Mrs Anthony Akers-Douglas, 23 Mytten Close, Cuckfield, W Sussex RH17 5LN]; *b* 29 Sept 1917; *m* 9 Aug 1941 Maj Anthony George Akers-Douglas and has issue (*see* CHILSTON, V)
(3) Mabel Maria; *b* 10 June 1866; *m* 27 April 1899 Gen Sir William Eliot Peyton, KCB, KCVO, DSO, 15th Hus, 3rd son of Col J Peyton, 7th Dragoon Gds, and *d* 12 May 1901, leaving issue. He *d* 14 Nov 1931
1 Caroline Harriet; *b* 23 July 1823; *m* 4 May 1847 4th Viscount Gort (*qv*) and *d* 8 May 1888, leaving issue
2 Fanny Charlotte; *b* 8 Nov 1830; *m* 15 Feb 1853 Capt William Tomline, 10th Hus, and *dsp* 23 Jan 1883. He *d* 18 May 1883

The 4th VISCOUNT *d* 20 Jan 1877; his grandson,

HENRY CHARLES GAGE, **5th Viscount Gage of Castle Island**, DL Sussex; *b* 2 April 1854; *m* 23 July 1894 Leila Georgina (*d* 17 March 1916), 2nd dau of Rev Frederick Peel (*see* PEEL, Bt), and *d* 18 April 1912, leaving issue:
1 HENRY RAINALD, **6th Viscount**
1 Irene Adelaide; *b* 9 Feb 1898; *m* 1st 30 Aug 1923 (*annulled* 1928) Capt Murray Shuldham Shuldham-Legh, Queen's Roy Regt, only son of Col H Shuldham-Legh, MVO, Roy Irish Regt; *m* 2nd 1 Oct 1928 (*divorce* 1942) Brig Frederick Cecil Bull, DSO, RA (*d* 14 April 1960), s of Col J F Bull, of Willets, Tillington, Sussex, and had issue; *m* 3rd 15 Feb 1950 Ernest William Dalrymple Tennant (*see* GLENCONNER, B)
2 Vera Benedicta; *b* 29 April 1899; *m* 10 Oct 1919 Lt-Cdr Francis Lyall Birch, CMG, OBE, RNVR, FRHS, son of John Arden Birch, of Rickmansworth Park, and Charlotte Viscountess Barrington (*see* 1970 edn). He *d* 14 Feb 1956

3 Yvonne Rosamund; *b* 20 July 1902; *m* 17 Dec 1938 Adrian Maximilian van der Horst and *dsp* 3 Feb 1960. He *d* 20 Aug 1955

The 5th VISCOUNT *d* 1912; his est s,

HENRY RAINALD GAGE, **6th Viscount Gage of Castle Island**, KCVO (1939), JP; CA E Sussex, V-Lt 1957–70 (DL 1927), Chm CC 1955–58, Pres Nat Fedn Housing Socs, Ld-in-Waiting 1924–29 and 1931–36, 1936 and 1937–39, PPS (unpaid) to Sec State India 1924–29, Pres Sussex Rural Community Cncl to 1973, author: *Memories of Firle*; *b* 30 Dec 1895; *educ* Eton and Ch Ch Oxford (BA 1919, MA 1970), Capt Res of Offrs Coldstream Gds, formerly 5th Bn Roy Sussex Regt, served WW I (wounded) and WW II; *m* 1st 26 Feb 1931 Hon Alexandra Imogen Clair Grenfell (*d* 3 Jan 1969), yr dau of 1st and last Baron Desborough (*see* GRENFELL, B), and had issue:

1 GEORGE JOHN ST CLERE GAGE, **7th Viscount Gage of Castle Island**; *b* 8 July 1932; *educ* Eton; *m* 1st 22 June 1971 (*divorce* 1975) Valerie Ann, yr dau of J E Dutch, of Horam, Sussex; *m* 2nd 1990 *Deirdre Melina Jane [The Rt Hon Deirdre Viscountess Gage, Firle Place, Lewes, E Sussex BN8 6LP], dau of Thomas James Simmons, and *dsp* 30 Nov 1993

2 (HENRY) NICOLAS GAGE, **8th and present Viscout Gage of Castle Island**

1 *Camilla Jane [The Hon Lady Cazalet, Shaw Farm, Plumpton Green, Sussex BN7 3DG]; dir Lumley Cazalet 1967–, memb Glyndebourne Arts Tst 1978–, memb Roy Nat Theatre Bd 1991–91, Cncl of Friends of Covent Gdn 1977– (Bd & Management 1995–); *b* 12 July 1937; *educ* Benenden; *m* 24 April 1965 *Hon Mr Justice (Edward Stephen) Cazalet, DL, er s of Peter Victor Ferdinand Cazalet, of Fairlawne, Tonbridge, Kent, and has issue:

(1) *David Benedict; *b* 24 June 1967; *educ* Eton
(2) *Henry Pelham; *b* 16 Sept 1969
(1) *Lara Imogen Leonora; *b* 25 May 1973

The **6th Viscount** *m* 2nd 14 Jan 1971 Diana (*d* 1992), widow of Lt Col Hon Ian Campbell-Gray (*see* GRAY, L) and 4th dau of Col Rt Hon Richard Frederick Cavendish (*see* DEVONSHIRE, D), and *d* 27 Feb 1982

Seat: Firle Place, Lewes, E Sussex. The original house was built by the Sir John Gage who served HENRY VIII and QUEEN MARY in various court and military posts. Although this was never actually pulled down, the alterations and extensions carried out 1713–54 all but obliterated the Tudor structure. The gable and dual courtyard on the south of the house seem to date from Sir John's time, however. The former Tudor great hall, into which the 18th-century front door opens directly, was later divided into two chambers: a staircase hall in the Palladian style and an entrance hall. The drawing room is also Palladian. The long gallery, which dates from the beginning of the 40-year period in which the major alterations were carried out, has a splendid view of the Sussex Downs.

GAINFORD

Arms: Per fess azure and gules a fess nebuly ermine between two lambs passant in chief argent, and in base upon a mount proper a dove rising argent, holding in the beak a pea stalk, the blossoms and pods also proper. **Crest:** Upon the capital of an Ionic column a dove rising, holding in the beak a pea stalk as in the arms. **Supporters:** On either side a barbary wild sheep ram guardant or. **Motto:** *Pax et spes* ('Peace and hope'). **Creation:** B. (UK) 3 Jan 1917.

THE 3RD BARON GAINFORD, of Headlam in the Co of Durham (Joseph Edward Pease) [The Rt Hon The Lord Gainford, Swallowfield, 1 Dedmere Court, Marlow, Bucks SL7 1PL]; *b* 25 Dec 1921; *s f* 1971; *educ* Eton and Gordonstoun; Sgt RAFVR WW II, with Hunting Aerosurveys 1947–49, Directorate Colonial Surveys 1951–53 and Soil Mech Ltd 1953–58, LCC 1958–65 and GLC 1965–78, memb Soc of Surveying Technicians, UK Del to UN 1973, memb Plaisterers' Co 1976, FRGS 1956; *m* 21 March 1953 *Margaret Theophila Radcliffe, dau of Henry Edmund Guide Tyndale, of Winchester College, by Ruth Isabel Walcott, 2nd dau of Alexander Nelson Radcliffe, of Bag Park, S Devon, and has:

1 *Joanna Ruth Miriam; *b* 22 Aug 1959

2 *Virginia Clare Margaret; *b* 13 Oct 1960

Lineage: Sir JOSEPH WHITWELL PEASE, 1st Bt, of Hutton Lowcross (*qv*) and Pinchinthorpe, Yorks, had a 2nd s:

JOSEPH ALBERT PEASE, **1st Baron Gainford** ,of Headlam in the Co of Durham (UK), so *cr* 3 Jan 1917, PC (1908), JP, DL (Co Durham), JP (N R Yorks); *b* 17 Jan 1860; *educ* Trin Coll Cambridge (MA), Mayor Darlington 1889–90, MP Tyneside 1892–1900, N Essex 1901–10 and Rotherham 1910–16, Jr Ld Treasury 1905–08, Parly Sec Treasury 1908–10, Chllr Duchy Lancaster 1910–11, Pres Bd Educn 1911–16 and PMG 1916, Pres Fedn Br Industs 1927–28, Chm BBC 1922–26, V-Chm 1926–32, Pres Nat Confedn Employers' Assocs 1932 and Radio Mfrs Assoc 1935, memb Claims Commn France and Italy WW I; *m* 18 Oct 1886 Ethel, OStJ (*d* 22 Oct 1941), dau of Lt-Gen Sir Henry Marsham Havelock-Allan, 1st Bt (*qv*), and *d* 15 Feb 1943, having had issue:

1 JOSEPH, **2nd Baron**

1 Miriam Blanche; *b* 22 Aug 1887; Inspr Factories Home Office 1916–38, Superintending Inspr W Midland Div 1938–42, Town Cncllr N Berwick 1954–58; *d* 30 Jan 1965

2 Faith Muriel; *b* 4 June 1902; *m* 29 Feb 1924 Maj Michael Wentworth Beaumont (*see* ALLENDALE, V) and *d* 16 Feb 1935, leaving issue

The 1st BARON's only s,

JOSEPH PEASE, **2nd Baron Gainford**; *b* 8 March 1889; *educ* Eton; Maj Lovat Scouts WW I (despatches) and RE WW II 1940–42; *m* 3 Feb 1921 Veronica Margaret (*d* 5 Nov 1995), only child of Sir George John William Noble, 2nd Bt, of Ardmore and Ardardan Noble (*qv*), and *d* 23 Sept 1971, leaving:

1 JOSEPH EDWARD PEASE, **3rd and present Baron Gainford**

2 +GEORGE [The Hon George Pease, Naemoor Gdns, Rumbling Bridge, Kinross KY13 7PY]; *b* 20 April 1926; heir presumptive; *educ* Eton; DipArch, DipTP, ARIBA, AMTPI, RNVR 1944–45, County Planning Offr Ross and Cromarty; *m* 18 Jan 1958 *Flora Daphne, 2nd dau of Dr Neville Alexander Dyce-Sharp, of Edinburgh, and has:

(1) +Adrian Christopher; *b* 1 Feb 1960; *educ* Dartington Hall
(2) +Matthew Edward; *b* 19 Nov 1962; *educ* Dollar Acad; *m* 1991 *Barbara, yr dau of E R John Griffiths, of Aachen, Germany, and has issue:
1a +Felix George; *b* 1992
(1) *Olivia Daphne; *b* 4 Dec 1958; *m* 1984 *Stephen Langford, er s of Roy Langford, of St Peter Port, Guernsey, and has issue:
1a *Rachel Veronica; *b* 1988
2a *Esther Rebecca; *b* 1992
(2) *Samantha Rachel; *b* 3 May 1965

3 +John Michael [The Hon John Pease, The Old Croft House, Roy Bridge, Inverness-shire PH31 4AH]; *b* 22 Sept 1930; *educ* Gordonstoun; *m* 1 June 1962 *Catherine Margaret, yst dau of Duncan F Shaw, of Turbiskie, Tayvallich, Argyll, and has issue:

(1) +David Michael; *b* 3 July 1964
(2) +Andrew Joseph; *b* 17 July 1967

GAINSBOROUGH

Arms: Or fretty gu., a canton erm. **Crest:** A buck at gaze arg., attired or. **Supporters:** On either side a bull arg., armed and unguled ppr., gorged with a naval crown az., therefrom a chain reflexed over the back gold, pendant from the crown an escutcheon, also az., charged with an anchor erect, encircled by a wreath of laurel or. **Motto:** *Tout bien ou rien* ('All well or nothing'). **Creations:** Bt. (GB) 22 Oct 1781; B. (Barham) (UK) 1 May 1805; B., V. and E. (UK) 16 Aug 1841.

THE 5TH EARL OF GAINSBOROUGH, Co Lincoln,**Viscount Campden of Campden**, Co Gloucester, **Baron Barham** of Barham Court and Teston, Kent, **Baron Noel of Ridlington, Rutland** and a **Baronet** (Sir Anthony Gerard Edward Noel, Bt, JP (Rutland 1957–74, Leics 1974)) [The Rt Hon The Earl of Gainsborough JP, Horn House, Exton, Leics LE15 7QU]; *b* 24 Oct 1923; *s f* 1927; *educ* Worth Abbey and Georgetown, MD USA; chm Oakham RDC 1952–67, v-chm CC 1958–, Pres RDCs Assoc England and Wales 1965, dep-chm Rutland Bench 1965, Master Gardeners' Co 1967, Bailiff Grand Cross SMO Malta (Pres Br Assoc 1968–74), chm Rutland CC 1970–73, KStJ 1970, Hon FICE; *m* 23 July 1947 *Mary, er dau of Hon John Joseph Stourton (*see* MOWBRAY, SEGRAVE and STOURTON, B), and has:

1 +ANTHONY BAPTIST, *Viscount Campden* [Viscount Campden, 105 Earls Court Road, London W8 6QH; Exton Park, Oakham, Rutland LE15 8AN]; *b* 17

Jan 1950; *educ* Ampleforth and RAC Cirencester; *m* 23 May 1972 *Sarah Rose, LVO (1996), Ldy-in-Waiting to late DIANA PRINCESS OF WALES, er dau of Col Thomas Foley Churchill Winnington (*see* WINNINGTON, Bt), and has:

(1) +Henry Robert Anthony; *b* 1 July 1977

2 +Gerard Edward Joseph; *b* 23 Jan 1955; *educ* Ampleforth and London U; *m* 1985 *Charlotte, yr dau of Sir William Stratford Dugdale, 2nd Bt (*qv*), and has:

(1) +Reginald; *b* 1987

(1) *Belinda Mary; *b* 1986

(2) *Lettice; *b* 1989

3 +Thomas [The Hon Thomas Noel, 24 Lennox Gdns, London SW1 0DQ]; *b* 9 March 1958; *educ* Ampleforth and RAC Cirencester

4 +Edward Andrew [The Hon Edward Noel, 16 Stratford Rd, London W8]; *b* 22 Oct 1960; *educ* Ampleforth and Br Inst Paris; *m* 1st 1990 (*divorce* 1994) Lavinia Jane, only dau of Cdr George Edward Bingham, of Grenville House, Droxford, Hants; *m* 2nd 19– *—

1 *Juliana Mary Alice; *b* 27 Jan 1949; *m* 29 Jan 1970 *5th Earl of Liverpool (*qv*) and has issue

2 *Maria [The Lady Maria Pridden, Fort Henry House, Exton, Leics]; *b* 3 Feb 1951; *m* 17 April 1971 *Robert Pridden, son of John Robert Pridden, of Bridge Way, Ickenham, Middx, and has issue:

(1) *Benedict John Anthony; *b* 23 Sept 1973

(1) *Lucy Charlotte Ivy; *b* 15 June 1975

3 Janet; *b* and *d* 23 Jan 1953

4 *Celestria Magdalen Mary [The Lady Celestria Hales, 8 Peel St, London W8 7PD]; *b* 27 Jan 1954; *educ* St Mary's Convent Ascot and St Hilda's Coll Oxford; social ed *Harpers & Queen* 1992–97; *m* 1990 *Timothy M Hales, son of S W M Hales, MC, and Mrs C G des Salles d'Epinoix, and has issue:

(1) *Catherine Rose Mary; *b* 1990

Lineage (of Noel): ROBERT Fitz NOEL; feudal Ld Ellenhall, granted *temp* HENRY I the major part of Granborough, Warwicks, by the Prior of Coventry; had:

1 Thomas (Sir); Sheriff Staffs seven years *temp* HENRY II, also 1189; *m* Margaret, dau of Guy Le Strange (*see* SAINT DAVIDS, V), and had:

(1) Alice; *m* Sir William de Harcourt (*see* VERNON, B) and had Ellenhall and other estates as her share of her father's property

(2) Jean; *m* William de Dunston and had for her share Raunton or Ronton, nr Ellenhall, the priory of which her gf had founded *temp* HENRY II

2 Philip; had Hilcote, Staffs, from his f; had:

(1) Robert; feudal Ld Hilcote; *m* Joan, dau of Sir John Acton; ancestor of:

1a James, of Hilcote, JP 1514; *m* —, dau of Richard Pole, of Langley, Derbys, and had, with four other sons:

1b Robert; continued the line at Hilcote

2b Andrew; granted Manor and preceptory of Dalby-upon-Wold, Leics, also Manor of Perrybarr, Staffs, at the dissolution of the monasteries, Sheriff Rutland *c* 1537 and *temp* EDWARD VI and MARY; bought 1548 Manor of Brook, Rutland; MP Rutland 1553; *m* 1st Elizabeth, dau and heir of John Hopton, of Hopton, Salop, and widow of Sir John Perient, and had, with other issue:

1c ANDREW

2b (cont.) Andrew Noel *m* 2nd Dorothy, widow of Roger Flower and dau of Richard Conyers, of Wakerley, Northants, and had:

2c John; ancestor of the extinct NOEL Bts, the extinct Viscounts Wentworth and the extant Earls of Lytton (*qv*)

ANDREW NOEL's est s,

Sir ANDREW NOEL, of Dalby, which he sold, thrice Sheriff Rutland, MP Rutland and *temp* ELIZABETH I; *m* Mabel, 6th dau Sir James Harrington, and sis and heir of John, Lord Harrington of Exton, and had, with other issue:

1 EDWARD (Sir)

2 Arthur

3 Alexander, of Whitwell; *m* and left issue

1 Theodosia; *m* Sir Edward Cecil, afterwards Viscount Wimbledon (*see* EXETER, M)

2 Elizabeth; *m* 1st Earl of Castlehaven (*see* 1970 edn AUDLEY, B)

Sir ANDREW *d* 9 Oct 1607; his est son,

Sir EDWARD NOEL, 1st Bt (E), so *cr* 29 June 1611, as also 23 March 1616/7 BARON NOEL OF RIDLINGTON, Co Rutland (E); *s* f-in-law as 2nd VISCOUNT CAMPDEN; MP Rutland 1601, ktd 1602, Sheriff Rutland 1608–09 and 1615–16; raised royalist troop on eve of Civil War; *m* 20 Dec 1605 Julian Hicks (*d* 25 Nov 1680), est dau and coheir of 1st Viscount Campden (*see* SAINT ALDWYN, E), so *cr* 5 May 1628 with remainder to his s-in-law, and *d* 8 March 1642/3, leaving:

1 BAPTIST, 3rd VISCOUNT

2 Henry; *m* Mary (*m* 2nd Sir William Fermor, *see* HESKETH, B), dau of Hugh Perry, of London, and *dsp* a prisoner of the Parliamentarians in the Civil War

1 Elizabeth; *m* 2nd Viscount Chaworth of Armagh and had issue

2 Mary; *m* Sir Erasmus de la Fontaine, of Kirby Ballers, Leics

3 Penelope; *d* unm

The 2nd VISCOUNT's er son,

BAPTIST NOEL, 3rd VISCOUNT CAMPDEN; *b* 1612; MP Rutland 1640–43, Col royalist horse regt, which he raised along with a corps of foot, consequently fined by Parl £9,000 (well over half a million pounds in late-1990s terms); in addition lost his house at Campden, nr Evesham, Glos, which a fellow Royalist, Lord Bard, burnt towards the close of the Civil War in 1645, nominally to prevent its capture by Parl but in fact quite uselessly according to the contemporary historian Lord Clarendon; *m* 1st 25 Dec 1632 Lady Anne Feilding (*dsps* 24 March 1636), dau of 1st Earl of Denbigh (*see* DENBIGH and DESMOND, E); *m* 2nd June 1636 Anne (*dsps* 25 Jan 1638/9), widow of Edward Bourchier, Earl of Bath, and dau of Sir Robert Lovet; *m* 3rd 21 Dec 1639 Hester, dau and coheir of 2nd Baron Wotton, by whom he had issue:

1 EDWARD NOEL, 4th VISCOUNT CAMPDEN and 1st EARL OF GAINSBOROUGH (E), Co Lincoln, so *cr* 1 Dec 1682, as also 3 Feb 1661 BARON NOEL OF TITCHFIELD, Co Southampton (E), with as regards both the fresh creations remainder, in default of male issue of his own, to his bros Baptist and John Noel; *bapt* 27 Jan 1640/1; MP Rutland 1661–78 and Hants Feb-July 1679, Ld Lt Hants 1678–87 and Rutland 1682–87, Govr Portsmouth 1682–87, Warden New Forest; *m* 1st May 1661, as her 2nd (?) husb (*see* PORTSMOUTH, E) Lady Elizabeth Wriothesley, dau and coheir of 4th Earl of Southampton, who brought him the feudal Lordship of Titchfield (hence its featuring in the title of his Barony), and had with other issue:

(1) WRIOTHESLEY BAPTIST NOEL, 2nd EARL OF GAINSBOROUGH; *b* by 1665; *educ* Winchester; MP (Tory) Hants 1684/5–86; *m* 30 Dec 1687 Catherine (*m* 2nd 12 March 1699, as his 2nd w 1st Duke of the County of Buckingham and of Normanby (*see* SHEFFIELD, Bt), and *d* 1704), est dau of 5th Baron Brooke (*see* WARWICK, BROOKE and, E), and *d* 21 Sept 1690, leaving:

1a Elizabeth; *m* 9 June 1704 1st Duke of Portland (*see* PORTLAND, E) and *d* 19 March 1737, leaving issue

2a Rachel; *m* 26 Feb 1705/6 2nd Duke of Beaufort (*qv*) and *d* 13 Sept 1709, leaving issue

(2) Frances; *m* 4th Baron Digby (*qv*) and *d* 29 Sept 1684, leaving issue

(1) Jane; *m* 22 May 1686 5th Baron Digby (*qv*) and *d* Sept 1733, leaving issue

1 (cont.) The 1st EARL *m* 2nd 23 April 1683 Mary (*d* 6 April 1693), widow of Sir Robert Worsley, 3rd Bt, of Appuldurcombe, IOW, and gdau of 4th Earl of Pembroke and (1st Earl of) Montgomery (*qv*), and *d* Jan 1688/9

2 Henry, of N Luffenham, Rutland; *m* Elizabeth, dau and heir of Sir William Wales, and had:

(1) Juliana; *m* 26 Jan 1687/8 2nd Earl of Burlington (*see* CORK and ORRERY, E), and *d* 17 Oct 1750, leaving issue

1 Mary; *m* 3rd Earl of Northampton (*see* NORTHAMPTON, M) and *d* 22 Aug 1719, leaving issue

2 Juliana; *m* 30 July 1664, as his 2nd w, 3rd Baron Alington and *d* 14 Sept 1667, leaving issue

3 Elizabeth; *m* 16 Aug 1677 10th Earl of Berkeley (*see* BERKELEY, B) and *d* 30 July 1719, leaving issue

The 3rd VISCOUNT *m* 4th 6 July 1655 Lady Elizabeth Bertie (*d* 20 July 1683), dau of 2nd Earl of Lindsey (*see* LINDSEY and ABINGDON, E), and *d* 29 Oct 1682, having by her had surv issue:

3 Baptist, of Luffenham; MP Rutland; *m* 1682 Susannah, dau and heir of Sir Thomas Fanshaw, and had issue:

(1) BAPTIST NOEL, 3rd EARL OF GAINSBOROUGH; *b* 1684; *m* by 13 Feb 1706/7 his cousin Lady Dorothy Manners (*d* 27 April 1734), dau of 1st Duke of Rutland (*qv*), and *d* 16 April 1714, having had, with other issue:

1a BAPTIST NOEL, 4th EARL OF GAINSBOROUGH; *b* May 1708; *educ* Eton and St John's Coll Cambridge; *m* 1728 Elizabeth (*m* 2nd Thomas Noel, gs of 3rd Viscount Campden; *d* 13 Dec 1771), dau of William Chapman, his gamekeeper, and *d* 21 March 1750/1, having had, with other issue:

1b BAPTIST NOEL, 5th EARL OF GAINSBOROUGH; *b* 8 June 1740; *educ* Eton; *d* 27 May 1759

2b HENRY NOEL, 6th and last EARL OF GAINSBOROUGH of the 1682 *cr*; *b* 1743; *educ* Eton and King's Coll Cambridge; *d* unm 8 April 1798, when all his titles expired

1b JANE Noel; *m* 8 Oct 1754 Gerard Anne EDWARDES, of Welham Grove, Leics (*bapt* 28 March 1734; *d* 29 Oct 1773), illegitimate s of Mary Edwardes (*d* 23 Aug 1743), dau and heir of Francis Edwardes, of Welham, by Lord Anne Hamilton (*see* HAMILTON and BRANDON, D), and *d* 1811, leaving issue:

1c GERARD NOEL (Sir), **2nd Bt**, for whom *see* further below

2b Juliana; *m* 3rd Baron Carbery (*qv*) and *d* 1760

3b Lucy; *m* Sir Horatio Mann, 2nd Bt

4b Sophia; *m* Christopher Nevile, of Wellingore, Lincs, and had issue

1a Susan; *m* 4th Earl of Shaftesbury (*qv*)

4 John; *m* 11 June 1696 Elizabeth (*d* 1 March 1746/7), widow of 2nd Viscount Irvine and dau of 2nd Baron Sherard, and *d* 26 Sept 1718, having had with other issue:

(1) Thomas, of Walcot, Northants; *m* Elizabeth (*d* 13 Dec 1771), dau of William Chapman and widow of 4TH EARL OF GAINSBOROUGH of the 1682 *cr* (*see* above), and *dsp* 18 June 1788

(1) Bridget; *m* 20 Nov 1724 David, Viscount Milsington, s and heir of 1st Earl of Portman and *d* 22 Aug 1729. He *dsp* & *vp* 10 March 1728/9

4 Catherine; *m* 8 Jan 1673/4 1st Duke of Rutland (*qv*) and *d* 24 Jan 1732/3, leaving issue

5 Martha Penelope; *m* — Dormer

The 6th EARL OF GAINSBOROUGH (of the 1682 *cr*)'s nephew,

Sir GERARD NOEL EDWARDES later NOEL (roy licence 5 May 1798 on inheriting estates of his unc the 6th and last EARL), **2nd Bt** (*s* his 1st f-in-law); *b* 17 July 1759; *m* 1st 20 Dec 1780 Diana, **Baroness Barham** in her own right (*see* **Lineage (of Middleton)** below); *m* 2nd 4 May 1823 Harriet (*dsp* 1826), dau of Rev J Gill, of Scraptoft, Leics; *m* 3rd 13 Aug 1831 Isabella (*dsp* 9 June 1867), widow of Raymond Evans, and *d* 25 Feb 1838, leaving by his 1st w, with other issue:

1 CHARLES, **1st Earl**

2 Gerard Thomas (Rev); MA, Canon Winchester; *b* 2 Dec 1782; *m* 1st Feb 1806 Charlotte Sophia (*d* 31 Aug 1838), dau of Sir Lucius O'Brien, 3rd Bt (*see* INCHIQUIN, B), and had, with two other daus:

(1) Anna Sophia; *m* 10 Oct 1832 Ven Philip Jacob, Archdeacon Winchester, and *d* 17 Feb 1857, leaving issue. He *d* 28 Dec 1884

(2) Charlotte Christiana; *m* 1832 Rev James Drummond Money and *d* 19 Dec 1848

(3) Emma; *m* 17 June 1830 Rev Charles Edward Kennaway (*see* KENNAWAY, Bt) and *dsp* 10 Oct 1843

(4) Elizabeth Welman; *m* 7 April 1853 Rev George Augustus Seymour, incumbent Holy Trinity, Winchester, and *d* 26 Sept 1868

2 (cont.) The Rev Gerard Noel *m* 2nd 1841 Susan (*d* 14 Feb 1890), dau of Sir John Kennaway, 1st Bt (*qv*), and *d* 1851, having by her had issue

3 William Middleton; MP Rutland 1838–40, Offr cmdg Rutland Militia 1839; *b* 2 May 1789; *m* 20 May 1817 Anne (*d* 6 Oct 1851), dau and sole heir of Joseph Yates, of Clanna Falls, Glos, and *dsp* 20 Jan 1859

4 Frederic; Capt RN; *b* 25 Feb 1790; *m* 7 Sept 1815 Mary (*m* 2nd 1838 Lt-Gen Sir Thomas Hawker, KCH; *d* 24 Jan 1867), est dau of William Woodley, and *d* 27 Dec 1833, leaving issue:

(1) Augustus William (Rev); Rector Stanhoe, Norfolk; *b* 30 July 1816; *m* 16 June 1841 Lucy Elizabeth (*d* 1874), dau of Capt Norris William Tonge, RN, of Alverston, and *d* 1884, having had issue:

1a Gerard Henry Uctred (Sir), GCB, KCMG, JP Norfolk; Adml the Fleet, a Ld Admlty 1893–98, ADC to HM QUEEN VICTORIA 1894–96, C-in-C China Station 1904–06 and the Nore 1906–08, served Ashanti and Crete; *b* 5 March 1845; *m* 11 Aug 1875 Charlotte Rachel Frederica (*d* 15 July 1927), est dau of Francis Joseph Cresswell by Hon Charlotte, dau of 4th Baron Calthorpe (*see* 1970 edn), and *d* 23 May 1918, leaving issue:

1b Francis Arthur Gerard, OBE (1919); Lt-Col RAF, Lt 4th S Midland Bde RFA, WW I with RFC and RAF; *b* 3 Dec 1880; *educ* Repton; *m* 24 July 1913 Evelyn (*d* 1988), 4th dau of Benjamin Bond-Cabbell, DL, of Cromer Hall, Norfolk, and *d* 7 July 1955, leaving issue:

1c Evelyn Diana; *b* 20 May 1914; *m* 1st 7 Nov 1936 Maj John Vivian Bailey, Roy Scots Fus (*ka* July 1943), only s of Brig-Gen Vivian Telford Bailey, CMG, DSO, of Tantallon Lodge, N Berwick, and had:

1d *Lucy [Mrs Thomas Farthing, Coombe Park, Lynton, N Devon]; *b* 1938; *m* 1962 *Thomas Harry Farthing and has issue:

1e *Harry Vivian Stuart; *b* 1964

1e *Isabella Jane; *b* 1968

1c (cont.) Mrs John Bailey *m* 2nd 13 April 1946 Sir Hector Wroth Lethbridge, 6th Bt (*qv*) and had issue; *m* 3rd 16 Jan 1979, as his 3rd w, David James Douglas Nugent, Baron Nugent (*d* 1988) (*see* WESTMEATH, E), and *d* 1996

2c *Susan Rachel; *b* 24 Nov 1917

1b Charlotte Ida Frederica, MBE (1919); *b* 11 March 1878; *m* 5 Jan 1929 Charles Alfred Edward Winnington, 2nd son of Sir Francis Salwey Winnington, 5th Bt (*qv*), and *dsp* 28 June 1961

2b Ida Constance Diana Mary; nun Soc Sacred Heart; *b* 21 June 1879; *d* 26 Feb 1953

(1) Fanny Louisa; *m* 28 June 1843 Henry Victor de Merindol Malan, MD, and *d* April 1901, leaving issue. He *d* 23 Jan 1879

5 Francis James (Rev); MA, Rector Teston and Nettlestead; *b* 4 May 1793; *m* 24 April 1822 Cecilia Penelope (*d* 27 June 1885 aged 87), sister of 1st Baron Methuen (*qv*), and *d* 30 July 1854, having had, with other issue:

(1) Edward Andrew, of Outwoods, Duffield, Derbys, formerly of Clanna Falls, Glos, JP, DL Glos, Notts and Derbys, memb Gentlemen-at-Arms, Capt 31st Foot, Col cmdg 1st Glos Roy Vols; *b* 2 Jan 1825; *m* 24 Aug 1848 Sarah Gay (*d* 15 June 1889), yst dau of William Brown Darwin, of Elston Hall, Notts, and *d* 18 Feb 1899, leaving issue:

1a William Frederick Noel, JP Glos and Mon; *b* 8 Aug 1849; Col RE; *m* 1st 4 Feb 1879 (*divorce* 1883) Josephine Annie (*d* 25 Feb 1904), dau of Joseph Watts Hallewell, of Stratford Park, Stroud, and had issue:

1b Edward William Middleton; Lt 2nd Bn Gloucester Regt; *b* 18 March 1880; *d* Bloemfontein, S Africa, 19 May 1900

2b Cecil Frederick Gerard, MC (1919); Capt Roy E Kent Yeo WW I 1915 (wounded); *b* 22 Dec 1880; *m* 25 March 1930 *Karen Dredge and *d* 13 Nov 1957

1a (cont.) Col William Noel *m* 2nd 21 Jan 1885 Beatrice Elizabeth (*d* 16 Oct 1889), dau of Rev Joseph Christopher Bradney, MA, and by her had issue:

3b Maurice Waldegrave, AFC; Lt-Col King's Regt, F/Lt RAFVR, served WW I 1914 (despatches) as Sqdn Cdr RFC; *b* 30 Dec 1888; *educ* Malvern; *m* June 1920 Elizabeth Christine Edith (*d* 1981), er dau of Charles Gairdner, of Tower of Lethendy, Perthshire, and *d* 19 Sept 1958, leaving issue:

1c Peter Maurice; AMIMechE, AFRGS, Lt (E) RN; *b* 17 Feb 1922; *educ* Malvern and London U (DIC); *m* 28 June 1946 *Patricia Margaret, yst dau of A C W Hill, of Mosman, Sydney, NSW, and *d* 1984, leaving:

1d *Diana Margaret; *b* 17 Nov 1947; *m* 1980 *Baron François Maurice Seymour Faverôt de Kerbrech and has issue:

1e *Chloë Elizabeth Noel; *b* 1980

2d *Susan Elizabeth Gay; *b* 28 Sept 1951

2c +Robert Gerard Charles [Robert Noel Esq, 68 Grove End Gdns, London NW8 9LN]; Lt RM (invalided), stockbroker, FIPR, MSI, OLJ; *b* 5 Feb 1928; *educ* Malvern; *m* Sept 1961 (*divorce* 1988) Gillian Margaret Halse, LRAM, ARCM

1b Sarah Dorothy Beatrice, JP; *b* 2 July 1886; *m* 27 Sept 1911 Col Malby Crofton, DSO (*see* CROFTON, Bt, of Longford), and *d* 9 Dec 1976, leaving issue

1a (cont.) Col William Noel *m* 3rd 2 Sept 1896 Laura Carolina (*d* 5 July 1897), dau of Charles Henry Beilby, and *d* 8 Oct 1923, leaving by her:

2b Audrey Beilby Noel; *b* 17 June 1897; *m* 15 Oct 1924 Richard Francis Orme Grafton, son of F F Grafton, of Clifford Manor, Newent, and had issue. He *d* 23 Jan 1968

2a Cecil Edward Berkeley; *d* 18 Jan 1869

3a Francis Charles Methuen; Adml, FRGS; *b* 5 June 1852; *m* 27 Oct 1886 Wilmot Juliana (*d* 10 Nov 1939), dau of Thomas Maitland Snow, of Cleve House, Exeter, and *d* 30 Dec 1925, leaving issue:

1b Francis Methuen; with Bank of England, A/Capt Devonshire Regt; *b* 28 Dec 1888; *ka* 26 Oct 1917

2b Montague Wriothesley; Cdr RN WW I Minelaying Flotilla (clasp, despatches) and Baltic (clasp), twice awarded medal for saving life at sea, ret 1936, Organising Fin Sec Lichfield Diocese 1935, served WW II 1939–41; *b* 12 Nov 1892; *m* 29 July 1926 Christabel Florence Arthur (*d* 29 Dec 1965), only child of Rev Henry Startin, Vicar Horrabridge, Devon, and *das* at sea in command of HMS *Torrent* 6 April 1941, leaving issue:

1c Henry Methuen; Lt KRRC, Capt Queen Victoria's Rifles (TAR); *b* 9 April 1927; *educ* Marlborough and New Coll Oxford (BA 1951, MA 1956), FCIS; *m* 14 Sept 1963 Helen Elizabeth Anne (*d* 1992), only dau of Sir William Oliphant Hutchinson, LLD, of Cholmondeley Lodge, Richmond, Surrey, and *d* 3 May 1998, leaving:

1d +Robert Montague; *b* 12 June 1964; BSc, ARICS; *m* 1992 *Sophie M J, dau of Jean-Marie Bourdaire, of Paris

2d +William Gerard; *b* 1 Aug 1965; PhD, MA(Cantab)

1d *Emma Margery; *b* 3 April 1969

2c +Gerard Lionel Gordon [Gerard Noel Esq, The Manor, Rockbeare, Exeter, Devon]; FRICS, FLAS 1958, ARICS 1956, Lt RE 1945–48; *b* 9 April 1927; *educ* Marlborough and Trin Hall Cambridge (BA 1950, MA 1955); *m* 28 June 1965 *Caroline Patricia, only child of Brig Eric Llewellyn Griffith Griffith-Williams, CBE, DSO, MC and bar, DL, RA, of Rockbeare Manor, Devon, by Delia, only dau of Lt-Col Henry Spencer Follett, CBE, of Rockbeare Manor, and only grandchild and heiress of William Champion, of Edale, Derbys, and Riddlesworth Hall, Norfolk, and has issue:

1d +Andrew Francis Methuen; *b* 26 April 1966; *educ* Eton and Reading U

2d +Thomas Charles Eric; *b* 26 May 1970; *educ* Eton and St Catharine's Coll Cambridge (MA, LLB)

1d *Delia Christabel Mary; *b* 12 Nov 1967; *educ* W Heath and St Andrews (MA)

2d *Matilda Theresa Caroline; *b* 5 Sept 1972; *educ* St Mary's Sch and Edinburgh U (MA)

3d *Amy Margaret; *b* 7 Jan 1979; *educ* Croft House Sch Dorset

3c +(Montague) Geoffrey Bickersteth [Geoffrey Noel Esq, Monastery House, Little Crawley, Bucks]; MRCS, LRCP 1956, FFRACS, Lt Roy Signals; *b* 18 Feb 1931; *educ* Marlborough and Trin Hall Cambridge (BA 1953); *m* 31 Jan 1958 *Audrey Mavis, dau of Alan Metcalf, of Wingerworth, Chesterfield, Derbys, and has issue:

1d +David Charles; *b* 25 Oct 1963

2d +Peter Richard; *b* 2 July 1966

3d +Michael John; *b* 2 July 1966

1d *Jennifer Anne; *b* 17 Dec 1958

1c *Celestria Wilmot Rosalie [Mrs David Bell, 6 Meadow Close, Tring, Herts HP23 5BT]; *b* 8 June 1935; *m* 16 Jan 1960 *David Jeffrey Bell, er s of Capt Alec Jeffrey Bell, OBE, of Medway House, Partridge Green, Sussex, and has:

1d *Charles Montague Jeffrey; *b* 27 Feb 1974

1d *Caroline Barbara Penelope; *b* 7 Dec 1960; *m* 1987 *Jeremy Wilfrid Duncombe and has:

1e *Jeffrey Charles William; *b* 1988

1e *Elizabeth Alice Rachael; *b* 1989

2d *Joanna Elizabeth Glencairn; *b* 21 May 1962; has:

1e *Alec Henry; *b* 1994

3d *Alice Cristabel Ann; *b* 8 Jan 1967; *m* 1993 *Stavros Stangos, of Athens, and has issue:

1e *Asteris; *b* 1993

2e *Ariadne; *b* 1995

4d *Christina Mary Noel; *b* 23 Dec 1968

1b Mary Penelope; *b* 10 Aug 1887; *m* 15 July 1916 Maj George Bryan Atkinson, 3rd Bn Northumberland Fus, s of Rev Thomas Atkinson, Rector Fakenham, Norfolk, and *d* 22 March 1969, having had a son. He *d* 28 Dec 1930

4a Robert Lascelles Gambier; Capt RN; *b* 27 June 1855; *m* 23 March 1887 Letitia Louisa Carmela (*d* 1940), dau of Rev S W Koelle, and *d* 7 Oct 1935, leaving issue:

1b Gambier Baptist Edward; T/Lt Sherwood Foresters WW I (wounded); *b* 24 June 1888; *m* 1st 10 Jan 1914 (*divorce* 1922) Beatrice Eva Tytler (*d* 1966), only child of R-Adml John Clarke Byng (*see* TORRINGTON, V); *m* 2nd 15 March 1924 (*divorce* 1931) Rosalie Sibyl, formerly w of Capt William Llewellyn Aplin Harrison, MC, and dau of Maj Stanley Smyth Flower, OBE, 5th Fus, of Tring, Herts, and *d* 1957, leaving by his 1st w:

1c Gambier John (Jack) Byng, CB (1969); R-Adml, served WW II (despatches (twice), Ch Staff (Tech) to C-in-C W Fleet; *b* 16 July 1914; *educ* RNC Dartmouth; *m* 3 March 1936 *Joan, dau of Percy Herbert Stevens, and *d* 9 Sept 1995, leaving issue:

1d *Caroline Byng; *b* 9 Oct 1936; *m* 1st 1973 Ivor Eagling (*d* 1979); *m* 2nd 1982 *William Cairns, MBE

2d *Penelope Byng; *b* 19 April 1939; *m* 1st 2 April 1960 (*divorce* 1967) Sir Anthony Henry John Rawlinson, 5th Bt (*qv*), and has issue; *m* 2nd 1967 (*divorce* 1984) Count Axel du Monceau de Bergendal

3d *Virginia Byng; *b* 25 Nov 1943; *m* 1967 *Prof Michael Stanley Tite and has:

1e *Sarah; *b* 1970

2e *Alice; *b* 1972

4d *Vanessa Jane [Mrs Vanessa McClure, 24 The Meadows, Guildford, Surrey GU2 5DT]; *b* 25 Nov 1943; *m* 17 Oct 1970 (*divorce* 1986) Colin Thomas McClure, est son of Thomas McClure, of Belfast

1c *Beatrice Louisa Frances [Mrs William Skelton, Boughton Cottage, Green Lane, Henley-on-Thames, Oxon RG9 1LR]; *b* 1915; Section Offr WAAF; *m* 14 May 1943 Cdr William Falcon Skelton, RN (*d* 4 Jan 1996), only s of Engr V-Adml Sir Reginald Skelton, KCB, CBE, DSO, of Aldingbourne, Sussex, and has issue:

1d *Peter William; *b* 3 June 1950; *educ* Wellington; DPhil

1d *Sally Ann [Mrs Marcel Wagner, 22 Wilson Ave, Henley-on-Thames, Oxon RG9 1ET]; *b* 7 March 1944; *m* 31 May 1969 *Marcel Wagner, son of E Wagner, of Pretoria, and has issue:

1e *Dameon; *b* 1972; MSc

1e *Cosima; *b* 1970; *m* 14 July 1993 *John Piggott and has:

1f *Suilven; *b* 17 Feb 1997

2d *Judith Victoria [Miss Judith Skelton, Boughton Cottage, Green Lane, Henley-on-Thames, Oxon]; *b* 23 Aug 1946; MA, BLitt (Oxon)

2b Norman Philpot Robert; Capt RFA WW I (despatches, wounded twice, Croix de Guerre); *b* 15 July 1891; *educ* Cheltenham; *m* 1 Oct 1927 *Jane Jones

3b John Andrew Vernatti; Capt RGA and RFC WWs I and II (Capt RA and CD); *b* 23 May 1893; *educ* Cheltenham; *m* 1 May 1923 Marion Shanks (*d* 31 Oct 1959), dau of John Shanks Wylie, of Edinburgh, and *d* 24 Jan 1966, having had issue:

1c Anthony Robert Alistair; FRHortS, lecturer Nottingham U 1949–54, Rhodes U, Grahamstown, S Africa, 1954–59 and U Coll Rhodesia and Nyasaland 1959; *b* 19 Jan 1927; *educ* Lond U (BSc 1948, PhD 1965); *m* 28 Feb 1958 *Marthina Cornelia [Mrs Anthony Noel, 4 The Park Gardens, Cape Town 8001, S Africa], dau of Dirk Johannes Rousseau, of Krugersdorp, and *d* 1984, leaving issue:

1d +Darwin John Robert; *b* 15 Sept 1958

2c John Edward Barham; Cpl RAF; *b* 22 Nov 1929; *m* 16 Aug 1952 *Grace Vera (*m* 2nd 11 March 1966 Anthony Maurice Thomas), yst dau of Arthur Paul, of Herne Hill, and *das* 1 Sept 1954, leaving issue:

1d *Jacqueline Susan [Mrs Jacqueline Hayton, 73 Andromeda Rd, Lordshill, Southampton, Hants]; *b* 1 June 1953; *m* 1972 (*divorce* 1983) Victor Clive Hayton and has had issue:

1e *Thor David Fewlass; *b* 1974

2e Jodi William; *b* 1976; *d* 1985

1c Eleanor Pamela Isabel; *b* 7 June 1925; *d* 29 Jan 1926

5a James Wriothesley; Lt Wilts Militia; *b* 3 Oct 1861; *m* 8 March 1890 Elizabeth Marion (*d* 11 March 1942), only surv child of Gen Frederic Arthur Willis, CB, and *d* 14 Jan 1932, leaving issue:

1b Darwin Edward; Capt RA WW I (despatches); *b* 30 March 1891; *d unm* 25 April 1972

1a Anne Noel; *m* 5 Aug 1873 Col Thomas Hamilton Forsyth, 62nd Regt, and *d* 10 Dec 1887, leaving issue

2a Matilda Catherine; *m* 19 Sept 1893 John Charles Griffith, JP, VD, of Deanwood House, Cheltenham, Col 2nd Vol Bn Gloucester Regt, and *d* 12 May 1923, leaving issue. He *d* 11 Nov 1934

3a Eleanor Agnes; *m* 31 Dec 1889 Francis Joseph Cade, MA, and *d* 21 Oct 1928. He *d* 23 Oct 1912

(2) Montague Henry (Rev); MA Oxon, Vicar St Barnabas, Oxford, 1869–99; *b* 18 Dec 1840; *d* 29 Oct 1929

(1) Matilda Catherine Emma; *m* 4 Aug 1849 Sir Edward Leigh Pemberton, KCB and *d* 5 Jan 1906, leaving issue (*see* KINGSDOWN, B)

(2) Millicent Mary; *m* 8 June 1852 her cousin Berkeley Noel, PC, of Moxhull Park, Warwicks, and *d* 18 Oct 1913, leaving issue (*see* below)

6 Berkeley Octavius; AM; *b* 3 Dec 1794; *m* 22 June 1820 Letitia Penelope (*d* 18 Jan 1860), widow of Andrew Hacket, of Moxhull Park, and only dau of Ralph Adderley, of Coton, Staffs, and *d* 28 March 1841, leaving issue:

(1) Berkeley Plantagenet Guilford Charles, JP, DL; *b* 29 July 1821; *m* 8 June 1852 Millicent Mary (*d* 18 Oct 1913), dau of Rev Hon Francis Noel (*see* above), and *d* 15 March 1906, leaving issue:

1a Charles Francis Adderley; 2nd Dragoon Gds; *b* 30 Aug 1854; *m* Frances Louise (*d* 5 Oct 1940), dau of Samuel Whipp, of Sydney, NSW, and *d* 18 Dec 1934

2a Edward Henry (Rev); Rector Frinsted, Kent, 1898–1906; *b* 12 Feb 1859; *educ* Ch Ch Oxford (MA); *m* June 1907 Caroline Ethel (*d* 30 May 1956), dau of James Crowley, and *d* 11 May 1941, leaving issue:

1b +Arthur Edward; RE; *b* 18 Oct 1908

3a James Harlington; *b* 17 Feb 1861; *m* 4 Jan 1923 Flora (*d* 19 Aug 1928), widow of Joseph M Vogel, of Alsace, and *d* 3 Jan 1950

1a Louisa Letitia Millicent; *d unm* 1912

7 Leland Noel (Rev); MA Cambridge, Hon Canon Peterborough, Vicar Exton; *b* 21 Aug 1797; *m* 30 Dec 1824 Mary Arabella (*d* 2 May 1859), dau of John Savile Foljambe (*see* LIVERPOOL, E), and *d* 10 Nov 1870, leaving, with other issue:

(1) Mary Penelope; *m* 24 April 1849 Rev Hon A G Stuart and *d* 24 Jan 1859, leaving issue. He *d* 16 Sept 1889

8 Baptist Wriothesley (Rev); MA; *b* 10 July 1799; *m* 17 Oct 1826 Jane (*d* 13 May 1889), est dau of Peter Baillie (*see* BURTON, B), and *d* 19 Jan 1873, having had issue:

(1) Wriothesley Baptist; barrister, Judge Insolvency, Land Tax Commr Melbourne; *b* 15 Aug 1827; *m* 1858 Margaret (*d* 6 June 1869), dau of John McKenzie, and *d* 19 May 1886, having had issue:

1a Guy; slr; *b* 28 Dec 1860; *m* 2 June 1883 Blanche Mabel Mayne (*d* Dec 1944), dau of James Hatch Gibbs, of Glenroy Park, Brighton, Victoria, barrister, and *d* 1942, leaving issue:

1b Beryl Vernon Lashbrooke; *b* 13 May 1884; *d* 18 Dec 1893

2b Eleanor Baillie; *b* 21 Aug 1885; *m* 1st 28 Nov 1910 (*divorce* 1939) Lt-Col George Nevile Wyatt, DSO, RFA, and had issue. He *d* 1956. She *m* 2nd 2 Nov 1939 F/O John Anthony Crosby Warren, RAFVR, and *d* 3 May 1961. He was *kas* 27 April 1944

3b Valerie Winifred Wriothesley; *b* 26 Oct 1888; *m* 24 April 1912 Charles John Brightman, OBE, of Upland Court, Northwood, Middx, est s of Charles E Brightman, of S Kensington, and *d* 19 Dec 1963, leaving issue. He *d* 10 Sept 1930

1a Eleanor; *b* 10 Nov 1858; *m* 1884 Alfred Cornish, of Melbourne, Australia

(2) Ernest, JP, DL Sussex, JP Norfolk; MP Dumfries Burghs 1874–86; *b* 18 Aug 1831; *m* 1st 24 June 1857 Louisa Hope (*dsp* 22 Aug 1870), only dau of Thomas Milne, of Warley House, Yorks; *m* 2nd 15 Oct 1873 Lady Augusta Keppel (*d* 31 Jan 1902), yst dau of 6th Earl of Albemarle (*qv*); *m* 3rd 30 Dec 1909 Sidney E G (*d* 12 Jan 1966 aged 86), dau of Rev W S Saunders, and *d* 20 May 1931

(3) Albert Leland; *b* 4 Nov 1835; *m* 21 June 1859 Ella (*d* 15 Aug 1915), 3rd dau of Rev Capel Molyneux (*see* MOLYNEUX, Bt), and *d* 27 Sept 1916, leaving, with other issue:

1a Barham Molyneux; *b* 8 Feb 1868; *m* 4 Dec 1895 Dorothy (*d* 12 May 1948), dau of Spencer Brunton, and *d* 15 July 1932, leaving issue:

1b Audrey Baillie; *b* 30 Dec 1896; *m* 25 Aug 1920 Maj-Gen François Henry Theron, CB, CBE, S African Envoy Extrdy and Min Plen Rome, Athens and Cairo (*d* 28 July 1967), s of S W Theron, of Harrismith, Orange Free State, and had issue:

1c Paul François Noel; *b* 10 Aug 1929; *d* Oct 1954

1c *Jacqueline Marie; *b* 20 Nov 1923; *m* 6 May 1947 (*divorce* 1967) Angus Christian Edward Malcolm, CMG, Dip Serv, yst s of Sir Ian Zachary Malcolm of Poltalloch, KCMG, JP, DL, and has issue:

1d *Caroline Jeanne; *b* 2 May 1948

2d *Christina Noel; *b* 14 Jan 1950

3d *Sophie Louisa; *b* 6 Oct 1954

4d *Anne Victoria Mary Christian; *b* 24 May 1957

1a Dorothy Manners; *m* 29 July 1914 Brig-Gen Capel Molyneux Brunker, CMG, DSO, JP, and *dsp* 1 Jan 1957. He *d* 17 March 1936

2a Ina Katharine; *d unm* 3 April 1949

(4) Eugene Frederick, JP Middx and Westminster; *b* 18 Sept 1839; *m* 1 Aug 1865 Ethel Maria (*d* 18 March 1904), only dau of Thomas Chapman, FRS, of Bryanston Sq, and *d* 12 April 1918, leaving issue:

1a Baptist Wriothesley Leland; *b* 9 Aug 1875; *d* 9 June 1891

2a Evan Baillie; *b* 23 Jan 1879; *educ* Trin Coll Cambridge (BA); *m* 6 June 1906 Marjorie (*d* 2 Sept 1955), er dau of R Deane Sweeting, MD, Sr Med Insp Local Govt Bd, and *d* 22 Dec 1928, leaving issue:

1b Gerard Baptist; BA Cambridge, Capt RA WW II; *b* 27 Nov 1915; *ka* 30 March 1943

1b Elizabeth Margaret; *b* 16 Nov 1907; *d* 30 March 1923

2b *Susan Diana Barham; *b* 8 June 1912; *m* 5 July 1940 Prof Geoffrey Frederic Powell (*d* 1982), DSO, S/Ldr RAF, slr, er s of George Frederic Charles Powell

1a Gwendolen Ethel; *d* 1892

2a Hilda Mary; *d* 25 Nov 1919

3a Margaret Eugenia; *m* 21 Oct 1911 Rev Arthur Hankey, Vicar St Stephen's Brighton, s of Herbert Hankey, of Hove, and *d* 20 Dec 1963, leaving issue. He *d* 1921

4a Cicely Jane; *m* 7 July 1925 Rev Preb Seymour Godwin Chance, er s of Thomas Godwin Chance, of Cambridge, and *d* 8 July 1975 aged 90, leaving a dau. He *d* 1962

5a Inula Edith; *d* 19 April 1916

(1) Mary Jane; *m* 23 April 1868 Thomas Anthony Denny, of Beeding Wood, Sussex, and *d* May 1887

(2) Emily Elizabeth; *m* 27 May 1852 her cousin Hon Henry Lewis Noel (*see* below) and *d* 3 Oct 1890, leaving issue

(3) Gertrude; *m* 8 Feb 1855 Sir Henry Flower Every, 10th Bt (*qv*), and *d* 26 Feb 1858, leaving issue

(4) Edith Louisa; *d unm* 30 Nov 1940

1 Louisa Elizabeth; *m* 10 Feb 1807 William Henry Hoare, of The Grove, Surrey, and *d* 6 April 1816, leaving issue. He *d* 18 Sept 1819

2 Emma; *m* 7 June 1808 Stafford O'Brien, of Blatherwycke Park, and *d* 19 Nov 1873, leaving issue. He *d* 3 March 1864

3 Charlotte Margaret; *m* 1st 1813 Thomas Welman, of Poundsford Park; *m* 2nd 1839 Thomas Thompson, of Vanbrugh House, and *d* 18 Aug 1869

4 Augusta Julia; *m* 1814 Thomas G Babington, of Rothley Temple, Leics, and *d* 1833. He *d* 19 Jan 1871

5 Juliana Hicks; *m* 1834 Rev Samuel Philips, and *d* 4 Jan 1855

The 2nd Bt's est son,

Sir CHARLES EDWARDES later NOEL (roy licence 5 May 1798), **3rd Bt**, in which he *s* his f 1838, **3rd Baron Barham**, in which he *s* his mother 1823 (*see* **Lineage (of Middleton)** below), and **1st Earl of Gainsborough**, Co Lincoln, so *cr* 16 Aug 1841, as also BARON NOEL OF RIDLINGTON, Co Rutland, and VISCOUNT CAMPDEN OF CAMPDEN, Co Gloucester (all UK); *b* 2 Oct 1781; MP (Whig) Rutland 1808–14; *m* 1st 1 July 1809 Elizabeth (*dsp* 1 Dec 1811), only dau of Thomas Welman, of Poundsford Park, Somerset; *m* 2nd 13 May 1817 Elizabeth (*d* 20 Sept 1818), dau of Hon Sir George Grey, 1st Bt (*qv*), and had by her:

1 CHARLES GEORGE, **2nd Earl**

The **1st Earl** *m* 3rd 29 June 1820 Arabella (*d* 4 Oct 1829), 2nd dau of Sir James Hamlyn William, Bt, of Clovelly, and by her had:

2 Gerard James, of Catmose, Oakham, PC, JP, DL, CA Rutland, MP Rutland 1847–83, Capt 11th Hus, Ld Treasury 1866–68, Parly Sec Treasury 1868, Ch Commr Works and Public Bldgs 1876–80; *b* 28 Aug 1823; *m* 30 June 1863 Lady Augusta Mary Lowther (*see* LONSDALE, E), and *d* 19 May 1911, leaving issue:

(1) Gerard Cecil, of Catmose; Capt 3rd Bn Northants Regt; *b* 4 Dec 1864; *m* 10 Feb 1897 Madeline Edith (*d* 21 Sept 1946), dau of Thomas Henry Clifton, of Lytham Hall, and *d* 28 June 1925, leaving issue:

1a Tom Cecil, MC and bar 1917; Lt KOSB and RAF WW I; *b* 12 Dec 1897; *ka* 22 Aug 1918

2a Charles Cecil; *b* 27 Nov 1904; *d unm* 15 Dec 1966

3a John Cecil; Capt RA (TA), F/O RAF WW II; *b* 28 July 1906; *m* 9 July 1936 *Nancy Margaret, dau of Col Edward Thesiger Frankland Hood, DSO, of Nettleham Hall, Lincs, and was *kas* 1942

(2) Henry Cecil; Capt 17th Lancers WW I; *b* 23 May 1868; *m* 1st 2 April 1902 (*divorce* 1926) Frances Mary (*d* 17 Aug 1944), yst dau of Frederick Pepys Cockerell, FRIBA; *m* 2nd 7 Aug 1926 Janet Muriel (*d* 15 July 1960), yr dau of William Baird, JP, DL, of Elie, Fife, and Cambusdoon, Ayrshire, and *d* 28 Aug 1931

3 Henry Lewis; Capt 68th Foot, High Sheriff Rutland 1863; *b* 30 Nov 1824; *m* 1st 27 May 1852 Emily Elizabeth (*d* 3 Oct 1890), dau of Rev Hon Baptist Wriothesley Noel (*see* above), and had issue:

(1) Gerard Thomas, JP Devon and Glos; Maj 3rd Bn Durham LI Boer War 1900–01; *b* 13 May 1856; *m* 19 Jan 1888 Edith Mary (*d* 24 May 1917), dau of Rev Hon William Byron (*see* BYRON, B), and *d* 9 Nov 1941, leaving issue:

1a John Byron, MC (1920); Maj KOYLI, attd 1st Vol Bn Karelian Regt WW I (POW), WW II; *b* 6 April 1891; *educ* Eton; *m* 20 Sept 1924 Rosamond (*d* 25 April 1971), only dau of Maj Charles Alers Hankey, and *dsp* 18 Oct 1969

2a William Henry Middleton; 2nd Lt Yorks Regt WW I, Capt 4th Armoured Car Regt S African Forces WW II; *b* 11 Sept 1898; *m* 12 Jan 1934 Jacqueline Naomi (*d* 1984), yr dau of R Bendall, of Ofcolaco, N Transvaal, and *d* 6 Aug 1954, leaving issue:

1b +Gerard Roland; *b* 16 July 1936; *m* 1975 *Lina, dau of E Micayabas, of Malaybalay, Philippines, and has issue:

1c +John William Bakun; *b* 1981

2b +Michael John; *b* 25 May 1944; *m* 1973 *Amanda Jane, only dau of W/Cdr A B Corfe, RAF, and has issue:

1c +William Gerard; *b* 1975

2c +Richard Roland; *b* 1979

3c +Andrew Corfe; *b* 1982

3b +Christopher William [Christopher Noel Esq, Wild Hawk Farm, PO Box 11, Ofcolaco 0854, NP, S Africa]; *b* 11 Sept 1947; *m* 1971 *Rhoda, only dau of H Allen, of Trichardt, E Transvaal, and has issue:

1c *Gillian Frances; *b* 1973

2c *Catherine Elizabeth; *b* 1976

4b +Wilfrid Byron [Wilfrid Noel Esq, Wild Hawk Farm, PO Box 13, Ofcolaco 0854, NP, S Africa]; *b* 22 Jan 1949; *m* 1975 *Patricia Maud, 2nd dau of W D J Van Niekerk, of Johannesburg, and has issue:

1c +Colin Byron; *b* 1980

2c +Gerard Vernon; *b* 1986

1c *Penelope Jacqueline; *b* 1976

2c *Susan Lianne; *b* 1977

1b *Margaret Celestria [Mrs Hugh Brown, Crake Valley Farm, PO Box 3025, Mutare, Zimbabwe]; *b* 9 Nov 1939; *m* 27 April 1963 *Hugh Boswell Brown, est s of Alan Boswell Brown, of Wateryeat, nr Ulverston, and has:

1c *Robert Jason; *b* 8 March 1969

1c *Catherine Ann; *b* 6 Feb 1964

2c *Joan Cécile; *b* 9 June 1965

3c *Nicola Noel; *b* 1971

1a Mary Cecily; *b* 15 Nov 1888; *m* 27 July 1921 Maj Alan Charles Grenville Luther, MC, Res Offrs KOYLI (*d* 23 June 1961), 2nd s of Fletcher Luther, of Brighton, and had issue (*see* STIRLING-HAMILTON, Bt)

2a Audrey; *b* 7 May 1894; *m* 14 Sept 1918 Lt-Col Thomas Bromhead Butt, KOYLI, est son of T B Butt, of Barkston Gdns, London, and *dsp* March 1966

(2) Hugh Middleton; *b* 3 April 1862; *m* 20 June 1901 Helen Winifred (*d* 1958), dau of Robert Gibbs, of Bedford, and *d* 1956, leaving:

1a Geoffrey Francis Middleton; *b* 1902; *d* unm Oct 1971

2a Leland Hugh Wriothesley; *b* 6 June 1906; landscape artist; *m* 1941 *Barbara Jean, dau of A H Meier, of Chico, California, and *d* 18 May 1996, leaving:

1b +William Hugh [William Noel Esq, 1414 Monroe St, Santa Rosa, Calif, USA]; *b* 1950

1b *Pamela Lee [Pamela Noel, 1724 Terrace Way, Santa Rosa, CA 95404, USA]; *b* 1948; *m* 1984 (*divorce* 1993) Lucas MacMath and has:

1c *Bryce Wolcott; *b* 1990

2c *Eston Meier; *b* 1990

3c *Talia Noel; *b* 1987

1a *Diana Catherine [Mrs Hollis Parker, 1526 Shoreline Drive, Santa Barbara, CA, USA]; *b* 9 Feb 1914; *m* 1942 Hollis H Parker, Sgt AA Art (*d* 1948), and has issue:

1b *Geoffrey Hollis; *b* 1944; US Coast Gd; *m* 1965 *Patricia Edwards and has:

1c *Geoffrey Hollis, Jr; *b* 1968

2c *Matthew Donovan; *b* 1976

1c *Michelle Diana; *b* 1969

2b *Stephen Hugh Anderson; *b* 1946; *educ* Hawaii U and Calif. State Coll, Long Beach

(3) Henry Hamlyn; *b* 8 June 1864; *m* 28 April 1897 Mary Jane Neame (*d* 1942), dau of John Lauer Oliver, and *d* 9 Sept 1941, leaving issue:

1a Edward Francis Hamlyn; MRCVS, Maj IA Waziristan 1921–23 (despatches) and WW II (invalided); *b* 4 Jan 1899; *educ* Cheltenham; *m* 2 Jan 1926 Doris Marie (*d* 20 Feb 1983), dau of Albert Claude Verriès, CIE, and *d* 12 May 1953, leaving issue:

1b +Gerard John Hamlyn [Gerard Noel Esq, Squirrels Hall, Stratford St Mary, Suffolk]; Capt RE (ret); *b* 8 Dec 1930; *educ* Wellington; *m* 7 Sept 1963 *Gillian Ralphia Barrand, only dau of Walter Terrance Barrand Head, of Meadow Brook, Frinton-on-Sea, Essex, and has issue:

1c +Richard Gerard Hamlyn; *b* 2 Feb 1965

1c *Victoria Gillian Emilia; *b* 27 Jan 1969

1b *Penelope Noel [Mrs Colin Jee, Ludgershall Rectory, Aylesbury, Bucks HP18 9PG]; *b* 11 Jan 1934; *educ* London U (BD); *m* 14 Sept 1962 *Rev Colin Scott Jee, MA, yr s of Col Ralph Jee, MC, Roy Signals, of Budleigh Salterton, Devon, and has:

1c *Jonathan Noel (Rev) [Rev Jonathan Jee, 7 Rosemary Way, Hinckley, Leics LE10 0LN]; *b* 27 July 1963; *m* 20 May 1989 *Juliet Elizabeth, est dau of Rev John Dudley Morris, of Rudgwick Vicarage, Horsham, W Sussex, and has:

1d *Thomas Peter; *b* 1991

2d *Daniel James; *b* 1993

3d *Timothy David; *b* 1996

1d *Rachel Clare; *b* 1993

1c *Mary Penelope [Mrs Andrew Rimmer, The Vicarage, 87 Perseus Place, Waterlooville, Hants PO7 8AW]; *b* 13 June 1965; *m* 8 July 1989 *Rev Andrew Malcolm Rimmer, and has:

1d *James Edward; *b* 1993

2d *Christopher David; *b* 1995

1d *Rebecca Mary; *b* 1991

2b *Lyn Noel [Mrs Lyn Kennedy, 1 Holmes Cottages, Back Lane, Letchmore Heath, Herts WD2 8EN]; *b* 30 Sept 1947; *m* 8 June 1965 (*divorce* 1991) Ian Thomas Kennedy, son of Dr Gordon Chester Kennedy, of Histon, Cambs, and has:

1c *Gordon Noel; *b* 27 May 1971

2c *James Edward; *b* 19 Aug 1972; *m* 27 Sept 1992 *Emma Alexandra Elizabeth, dau of Peter John Holmes, of Wellington Lodge, Maresfield Pk, E Sussex

1c *Emilia Jayne; *b* 2 March 1980

2a Gerard Hamlyn; *b* Feb 1900; *d* 23 June 1924

1a Mildred Mary Hamlyn; *b* 10 April 1904; *m* 18 Sept 1929, Lt-Col Norman Leslie Crozier Irwin, DSO and bar, 8th Gurkha Rifles, son of Rev Dt TJ Irwin, of Sutton, Co Dublin, and *d* 30 May 1988

(1) Evelyn Mary; *m* 10 Nov 1880 Herbert Robinson Arbuthnot, of Bayswater, 3rd s of George Arbuthnot, of Elderslie, Surrey, and *d* 23 March 1945, leaving issue. He *d* 18 Oct 1937

(2) Gertrude Arabella; *m* 3 Dec 1891 Thomas Cheney Garfit, JP, DL, of Kenwick Hall, Lincs, and *d* 15 Dec 1928, leaving issue

(3) Emilia Frances; *d* unm 19 March 1950

3 (cont.) The Hon Henry Noel *m* 2nd 31 Aug 1892 Anne Adelaide (*dsp* 30 April 1904), only child of Rev John Burnside, Rector Plumtree, Notts, and *d* 7 June 1898

1 Mary Arabella Louisa; *m* Aug 1846 Sir Andrew Agnew, 8th Bt, of Lochnaw (*qv*), and *d* 27 June 1883

2 Catherine Hamilton; *m* 19 June 1849 9th Earl of Southesk (*see* FIFE, D) and *d* 9 March 1855, leaving issue

The **1st Earl** *m* 4th 25 July 1833 Frances (*d* 12 May 1885), VA 2nd Cl, Ldy Bedchamber to HM QUEEN VICTORIA, dau of 3rd Earl of Roden (*qv*), and by her had issue:

4 Roden Berkeley Wriothesley; poet, Groom Privy Chamber 1867–71; *b* 27 Aug 1834; *educ* Trin Coll Cambridge (MA 1858); *m* 21 March 1863 Alice Maria Caroline (*m* 2nd 18 July 1895 Rev David MacAnally (*d* 1897); *d* 7 Nov 1919), dau of Paul de Broe, and *d* 26 May 1894, having had issue:

(1) Conrad Le Despencer Roden (Rev); Vicar Thaxted, Essex; *b* 12 July 1869, *m* 17 Sept 1895 Miriam (*d* 19 Aug 1961 aged 90), dau of James Greenwood, and *d* 22 July 1942, leaving issue:

1a *Barbara; *b* 7 Feb 1897; *m* 17 Sept 1921 *Rev John Cyril Putterill, s of John Harry Putterill, and has:

1b *Sylvia [Mrs Desmond Heath, 60 Esmond Rd, London W4]; *b* 1922; *m* 1952 *Desmond Butterworth Heath and has:

1c *Martin Christopher; *b* 1955

1c *Jenny Clare; *b* 1953

2c *Sally Christine; *b* 1959

2b *Cecilia Rosemary [Mrs Vernon Curtis, East Grove, Marsham Way, Gerrard's Cross, Bucks]; *b* 1929; *m* 1952 *Vernon John Curtis and has:

1c *Matthew John Stephen; *b* 1964

1c *Victoria Jane; *b* 1954

2c *Katherine Anne; *b* 1965

(2) Eric Charles Hampden; *b* 1 Nov 1871; *d* 10 Jan 1877

(1) Frances Gertrude Alice; *b* 5 Dec 1864; *d* unm

3 Victoria; *m* 12 June 1862 Sir Thomas Fowell Buxton, 3rd Bt (*qv*), and *d* 8 Aug 1916, leaving issue

The 1st EARL *d* 10 June 1866; his est son,

CHARLES GEORGE NOEL, **2nd Earl of Gainsborough**; Ld Lt Rutland; *b* 5 Sept 1818; MP (Lib) Rutland 1840–41, High Sheriff Rutland 1848; *m* 1 Nov 1841 Ida Harriet Augusta (*d* 22 Oct 1867), est dau of 18th Earl of Erroll (*qv*), and had:

1 CHARLES WILLIAM FRANCIS, **3rd Earl**

2 Edward; Lt-Col Rifle Bde Ashanti War 1873–74, Jowaki Expdn 1877–78 and Burmese War 1885–87; *b* 28 April 1852; *m* 7 Oct 1884 Ruth (*d* April 1926), 2nd dau of W H Lucas, of Treniffle, Cornwall, and *d* 9 Nov 1917, leaving issue:

(1) Edward William Charles, CIE (1918), DSO (1919); Lt-Col IA and Political Dept Govt of India, V-Consul Ahwaz 1915, special duty Caucasus 1918, served under HC Iraq 1918–20, Political Agent Kurram 1924, Consul Kerman and Persian Baluchistan 1929, Dep Commr Dehra Ismail Khan 1931, Dir Ag and Allied Depts NWFP 1933; *b* 14 April 1886; *educ* Oratory Sch Birmingham and RMA Woolwich; *m* 1st 6 April 1923 Katherine Florence (*d* 6 Feb 1952), er dau of Robert Leighton Ross; *m* 2nd 1954 Simone (*d* 27 Oct 1974), dau of Prof Jean Corbiau, of Louvain U, and *d* 10 Dec 1974, leaving by his 1st w:

1a Robert Anthony (Rev); ARCO 1943, rowed for Oxford 1948 Boat Race, RC Chaplain Southampton U 1959; *b* 26 Jan 1924; *educ* Oxford (MA 1949); *d* unm 15 Aug 1966

2a Denys Edward; *b* 23 Nov 1925; *m* 13 Dec 1947 *Petronelle Moore [Mrs Denys Noel, Weavers Cottage, Coombe St, Lyme Regis, Dorset], only dau of C Austin Bostock, of The Hermitage, Newnham, Cambridge, and Weybridge, Surrey, and *d* 1978, leaving issue:

1b +Julian Roden Bostock [Julian Noel Esq, La Bignette, La Bigne, 14260 Aunay-sur-Odon, France]; *b* 5 June 1949; *m* 1982 *Susanna Elisabeth, dau of Benjamin Bentley Dodd, of Eel Pie Island, Twickenham, Middx

1b *Laura Frances [Mrs Peter Coe, 33 Courthope Rd, London NW3]; *b* 6 Sept 1951; *m* 1979 *Peter Clement Coe and has:

1c *Toby Richard; *b* 1983

1c *Lucy Josephine; *b* 1985

2c *Jennifer Mary; *b* 1988

(2) Hubert Lewis Clifford; MRCS, LRCP, RAMC WW I; *b* 19 Oct 1888; *m* 25 Aug 1934 Mary Maxwell (*d* 1953), widow of Dr Francis Rutherford Russell, of Guildford, and dau of James Currie, of Edinburgh, and *dsp* 1954

(3) John Baptist Lucius, MC; FRSA, Maj Res Offrs E Yorks Regt WW I, WW II as Staff Offr Intell Corps, Assoc Roy Photographic Soc, hon life memb American Museum of Nat History, accompanied Mount Everest Expeditions 1922 and 1924 as official photographer, added forename John by deed poll 1908; *b* 26 Feb 1890; *m* 1st 1915 Sybil (*d* 1939), dau of J Graham; *m* 2nd 1941 Mary Sullivan (*d* 1984), and *d* 1989, leaving by her:

1a *Sandra Ruth Catherine [Miss Sandra Noel, 6 Barrow Hill Place, Ashford, Kent TN23 1NE]; *b* 15 April 1943

1 Blanche Elizabeth Mary Annunciata; *m* 6 March 1870 Thomas P Murphy and *d* 21 March 1881. He *d* 11 Oct 1890

2 Constance Julia Eleanor Georgiana; *m* 13 Jan 1874 Sir Alan Henry Bellingham, 4th Bt (*qv*), and *d* 8 April 1891, leaving issue

3 Edith Horatia Emma Frances; nun; *d* 22 Aug 1890

The 2nd EARL *d* 13 Aug 1881; his est son,

CHARLES WILLIAM FRANCIS NOEL, **3rd Earl of Gainsborough**, JP, DL Rutland, JP Worcs and Glos; Chm Rutland TFA, Lt 10th Hus; *b* 20 Oct 1850; *m* 1st 9 May 1876 Augusta Mary Catherine (*d* 5 Nov 1877), est dau of Robert Berkeley (*see* BERKELEY, B), and had issue:

1 Agnes Mary Catherine; *b* 9 Oct 1877; *d* unm 1 March 1915

The **3rd Earl** *m* 2nd 2 Feb 1880 Mary Elizabeth (*d* 17 Nov 1937), est dau of James Arthur Dease, of Turbotston, Co Westmeath, by Charlotte, ggdau of Sir William Jerningham, 6th Bt (*see* STAFFORD, B), and by her had issue:

1 ARTHUR EDWARD JOSEPH, **4th Earl**

2 Charles Hubert Francis, OBE 1919; Maj Coldstream Gds, T/Maj and DAQMG 1919, WW II 1939–42 as Capt and T/Maj RE; *b* 22 Oct 1885; *m* 31 Jan 1912 May (*d* 1 April 1964), est dau and heiress of Brig-Gen Archibald Campbell Douglas Dick, CB, CMG, of Pitkerro, Angus, and *d* 26 April 1947, leaving:

(1) Archibald Charles William, MC (1940); Col Welsh Gds WW II (POW) and Palestine 1945–46, cmded 1st Bn Welsh Gds 1952–55, Mil Attaché Pretoria 1962–66, 1st Mil Advsr Rep S Africa; *b* 5 Jan 1914; *educ* Oratory Sch and RMC Sandhurst; *m* 1st 30 Aug 1945 Bridget Mary (*d* 3 Sept 1976), only dau of Brig William Albany Fetherstonhaugh, CB, CBE, DSO, of Llanwenarth House, nr Abergavenny; *m* 2nd 22 Dec 1977 *Andrée Marie [Mrs Archibald Noel, 10 Felden St, London SW6 5AF], dau of Pierre Duchen, of Bayonne, France, and *d* 8 Feb 1997, having by his 1st w had:

1a +Charles William [Charles Noel Esq, 97 Harbord St, London SW6 6PN]; *b* 4 July 1948; *educ* Ampleforth and Trin Coll Cambridge (BA); *m* 1985 *Diane Margaret, only dau of Gerald A de Freitas, of S Kensington, and has:

1b +Alexander Charles Fitzwilliam; *b* 1989

1b *Elizabeth Bridget Maggie; *b* 1986

2a +Edward Albany [Edward Noel Esq, 26 King's Court, Hamlet Gdns, London W6]; *b* 28 Sept 1956; *educ* Stanbridge Earls

(2) David Francis Douglas; Lt-Col RARO Coldstream Gds WW II (wounded) and Malaya 1948–50 (despatches), Br Liaison Offr French Army Germany 1962–64, Mil Attaché Kabul 1965–67, ret 1969; *b* 18 May 1919; *educ* Oratory Sch; *d* unm 2 Jan 1974

(3) Andrew Mungo James; Br Vol Ambulance Corps 1940–44; *b* 27 July 1921; *educ* Oratory Sch; *m* 10 Jan 1950 *Edina Mary, 3rd dau of Col Charles Talbot Joseph Gerard Walmesley, DSO, MC, TD, of Pixes Cottage, Lustleigh, Devon, and *d* 21 Oct 1972

(4) +Douglas Robert George [Maj Douglas Noel, 25 Broomhouse Road, London SW6 3QU]; Maj Coldstream Gds WW II (wounded) Italy 1943–45 and Palestine 1945–48; *b* 1924; *educ* Oratory Sch; *m* 2 June 1949 *Eleanor Susan Jane, 2nd dau of Brig George Edward Younghusband, CBE, of The Neuadd, Crickhowell, S Wales, and has issue:

1a +James Douglas George [James Noel Esq, 74 Kingston Rd, Oxford]; *b* 14 Aug 1950; *educ* Downside, London U and Oxford U, BA, CertEd

2a +William Edward Douglas [William Noel Esq, BSc FRICS, Ipsden House, Ipsden, Oxon OX10 6AJ], late Lt Coldstream Gds; *b* 5 Aug 1953; *educ* Downside, RMA Sandhurst and Newcastle U (BSc), FRICS; *m* 1st 19 July 1975 (*divorce* 1984) his 4th cousin Victoria Mary, only dau of George Oswald Younghusband, of Bessborough House, Nenagh, Co Tipperary; *m* 2nd 1993 *Mrs Juliet Catherine Hayward, est dau of Col Arthur Harold Newmarch Reade, LVO, Queens Own Hussars, of Old Post House, Ipsden, and formerly w of Capt Henry Tristram Hayward, The Blues and Royals, and by his 1st w has:

1b *Arthur Douglas; *b* 6 Oct 1977; *educ* Downside

1b *Teresa Sybil; *b* 6 Feb 1976; *educ* St Mary's Shaftesbury and d'Overbroeck's Coll Oxford

1a *Caroline Mary Jane [Mrs Charles Wentzel, 81 Balham Park Rd, London SW12 8EB]; *b* 6 June 1956; *educ* St Mary's Convent Ascot and Bristol U; *m* 1987 *Charles Anthony Wentzel, son of John Brunette Wentzel, of Johannesburg, and has issue:

1b *Philippa Mary; *b* 1991

(1) Jane Isabelle Mary; *b* 21 Nov 1912; *m* 26 Sept 1942 Capt Guy Hunter Allgood, of Nunwick, Simonburn, Northumberland, and *d* 7 March 1952, leaving issue. He *d* 1 June 1970

(2) Carola Mary; *b* 3 June 1916; *m* 21 April 1936 Maj Thomas Steuart Fothringham, MC, TD, DL (*d* 9 Sept 1979) Black Watch, of Fothringham, Forfar, Angus, and *d* 12 March 1989 leaving issue

3 Robert Edmund Thomas More; Capt 6th Bn Roy Fus, attd Nigeria Regt; *b* 10 April 1888; *das* Massassi, German East Africa, 2 Feb 1918

2 Norah Ida Emily; *m* 8 Sept 1915 Count Robert Charles Bentinck and *d* 23 May 1939, leaving issue (*see* PORTLAND, E)

3 Clare Mary Charlotte; *m* 2 Oct 1907 Charles Mervyn King, Capt Coldstream Gds, only son of Mervyn Kersteman King, of Clifton, Bristol, by Agnes, er dau of Sir Charles Tilston Bright, and *d* 11 March 1962, having had issue. He *d* 25 Jan 1965

The 3rd EARL *d* 17 April 1926; his est son,

ARTHUR EDWARD JOSEPH NOEL, **4th Earl of Gainsborough**, OBE (1919), TD, JP Rutland; Maj TAR, Priv Chamberlain to HH THE POPE; Dip Serv 1908–14, WW I 1915 France; *b* 30 June 1884; *m* 10 Nov 1915 Alice Mary (*d* 11 June 1970), er dau of Edward Eyre, of Gloucester House, Mayfair, and *d* 27 Aug 1927, leaving:

1 ANTHONY GERARD EDWARD NOEL, **5th and present Earl of Gainsborough**

2 +Gerard Eyre Wriothesley [The Hon Gerard Noel, Westington Mill, Campden, Glos GL55 6EG]; barrister Inner Temple 1952, ed *Catholic Herald* 1971–81, (ed-in-ch 1981–), author: *Paul VI* (1963), *The Path from Rome* (1968), *Goldwater* (1964), *Harold Wilson* (1964), *Princess Alice* (1974), *The Great Lock-out of 1926* (1976), *Ena: Spain's English Queen* (1984) and various translations, Liveryman Stationers' & Newspapermakers' Co, Freeman City London; *b* 20 Nov 1926; *educ* Georgetown, and Exeter Coll Oxford; *m* 1 Feb 1958 *Adèle Julie Patricia, only dau of Maj Vivian Nicholas Bonville Were, of Carrington House, Mayfair, and has:

(1) +Philip Arthur Nicholas; *b* 26 May 1959; *educ* Ampleforth; memb's agent Lloyd's

(2) +Robert John Baptist [Robert Noel Esq, Bluemantle Pursuivant, College of Arms, Queen Victoria St, London EC4]; *b* 15 Oct 1962; Bluemantle Pursuivant Coll of Arms 1993–

(1) *Elizabeth (Lizzie) Mary Alice; *b* 24 Sept 1967; sometime memb psychological unit Wormwood Scrubs, Parly candidate (C) Sedgefield 1997 gen election; *m* 28 Sept 1996 *Henry John Pitman, Blues and Royals, s of Lt-Col Hugh Pitman and Mrs Andrew Parker Bowles (*see* MACCLESFIELD, E)

1*Maureen Thérèse Josephine [The Lady Maureen Fellowes, The Court, Chipping Campden, Glos GL55 6JQ]; *b* 7 March 1917; *m* 1st 18 Feb 1944 15th Baron Dormer (*qv*; *d* 27 Aug 1975) and has issue; *m* 2nd 1982, as his 2nd w, *Peregrine Edward Launcelot Fellowes

Lineage (of Middleton): ROBERT MIDDLETON, of Caldhame; *m* Helen, dau of John Strachan, and had issue:

1 JOHN MIDDLETON, 1st EARL MIDDLETON (*see* MIDDLETON, B, preliminary remarks)

2 Alexander; gf of:

(1) Robert; Collector Customs Bo'ness, Linlithgowshire; *m* Helen, dau of Charles Dundas of Arniston, Midlothian, and had issue:

1a **Sir Charles Middleton, 1st Bt** (GB), so *cr* 22 Oct 1781 with special remainder, failing male issue of his own, to his s-in-law Gerard Noel Edwardes, also **1st Baron Barham**, of Barham Court and Teston, Kent (UK), so *cr* 1 May 1805, with special remainder, in default of heirs male of his own, to his only dau and the heirs male of her body, PC (1805); *b* 14 Oct 1726; RN: Lt 1745, Post Capt 1758, cmded Frigate *Emerald* WI 1761, Comptroller Navy 1778–90, R-Adml 1787, V-Adml 1793, a Ld Admlty 1794–95, Adml the Blue 1795, 1st Commr for revising Navy's civil affrs and 1st Ld Admlty 1805–06, Adml the Red 1805, MP (Tory) Rochester 1784–90; *m* 21 Dec 1761 Margaret, a friend of Dr Johnson and Hannah More and an early opponent of slavery, dau of James Gambier, barrister and Warden Fleet prison, by Mary Mead, and *dspm* 17 June 1813, leaving issue:

1b DIANA, **Baroness Barham** in her own right; *b* 18 Sept 1762; *m* as his 1st w Gerard Noel EDWARDES later NOEL, later Sir GERARD NOEL, **2nd Bt** (*see* above), and *d* 12 April 1823, leaving issue (*see* above)

GALLACHER

Creation: B. (LP, UK) 1982.

THE BARON GALLACHER, of Enfield, in Greater London (John Gallacher) [The Rt Hon The Lord Gallacher, 27 Whitecliffs, The Leas, Folkestone, Kent CT20 2DT]; *b* 7 May 1920; *educ* St Patrick's High Sch Dumbarton and Co-op Coll Loughborough (Chartered Sec); Pres: Enfield Highway Co-op Soc 1954–68 and Inst of Meat 1983–86; Sec Co-op Union and dir Retail Consortium Ltd 1974–83, Pres, Ch Oppn Spokesman Ag and Food 1989–92; Cpl RAF Coastal Cmd and 2nd Tactical Air Force; *m* 1947 *Freda Vivian, dau of Alfred Chittenden, of Maidstone, Kent, and has:

1 *Robert John; *b* 1955; *educ* Broxbourne Sch, Herts

Lineage: WILLIAM GALLACHER, of Alexandria, Dunbartonshire; *m* Janet Stewart and had:

JOHN, *cr* a **Baron**

GALLOWAY

Arms: Or a fess chequy argent and azure, surmounted of a bend engrailed gules, within a double tressure flory counterflory of the last. **Crest:** A pelican in nest, vulning herself argent, winged or. **Supporters:** Dexter, a savage man, wreathed about the head and middle with laurel, and holding in the right hand a club resting on the shoulder, all proper; sinister, a lion gules. **Motto:** *Virescit vulnere virtus* ('Valour strengthens from a wound'). **Creations:** L. (S) 19 July 1607, E. (S) 19 Sept 1623, Bt. (NS) 18 April 1627 and 4 Nov 1687; B. (GB) 6 June 1796.

THE 13TH EARL OF GALLOWAY, Lord of Garlies, Baron Stewart of Garlies and a Baronet (Sir Randolph Keith Reginald Stewart, 12th Bt, of Corsewell, and 10th Bt, of Burray [The Rt Hon The Earl of Galloway, Senwick House, Brighouse Bay, Borgue, Kirkcudbrightshire DG6 4TP]; *b* 14 Oct 1928; *s f* 1978; *educ* Harrow; *m* 17 Oct 1975 *Lily May, yst dau of Andrew Miller, of Duns, Berwicks, and formerly wife of — Budge

Lineage: Sir JOHN STEWART (commonly called 'of Bonkyl'), yr son of Alexander, 4th Hereditary Ld High Steward of Scotland (*see* MORAY, E); *m* Margaret, dau and heir of Sir Alexander de Bonkyl, of Bonkyl, Berwicks, and was *k* Battle of Falkirk 22 July 1298, having had, with other issue:

1 Alan (Sir); granted the lands of Dreghorn, Ayr, for his services to ROBERT (THE) BRUCE; bought the lands of Crookston, including the (territorial) Ldship of Darnley 1330; *k* Battle of Halidon Hill 1333, leaving, with other issue:

(1) Alexander, of Darnley; *d c* 1372, leaving a 3rd s:

1a Alexander, of Darnley; *m* —, possibly sis of Sir John Turnbull of Minto, and *d c* 1404, leaving:

1b John (Sir), of Darnley; ktd *c* 1383; *k* at Orleans 1429; ancestor of the STEWART Earls and Dukes of Lennox and Lord Darnley, ancestor of the STUART sovereigns of England and Scotland; also possibly of Sir WILLIAM STEWART (*see* below)

2b(?) WILLIAM (Sir), for whom *see* further below

2 Walter (Sir), of Dalswinton; granted for his services to ROBERT (THE) BRUCE lands forfeited by the Comyns; granted also the Barony of Garlies (originally conferred by ALEXANDER III on Sir Walter's gf Alexander, 4th High Steward, for his part in defeating the Danes at the Battle of Largs 1263) by his nephew John Randolph, Earl of Moray, to whom it had come through his mother, Isabel (*see* below); Sir Walter's s:

(1) John (Sir), of Dalswinton; captured at Durham 1346; had, with other issue:

1a Walter (Sir), of Dalswinton; left an only child:

1b Marion, of Dalswinton; *m* 1396 Sir John Stewart, er s of Sir William Stewart (*see* below)

3 John (Sir), of Daldar; *k* with his bros at Halidon Hill 1333; according to one account *dsp* but acording to others was ancestor of:

1 William (Sir); gf or uncle of:

1a WILLIAM (Sir); *see* below

The putative gs of Sir John Stewart of Daldar or descendant of Sir John Stewart of Darnley; alternatively the putative (and thought most probable of the possibilities) yr s of Alexander (II) Stewart of Darnley,

Sir WILLIAM STEWART, Kt Banneret *c* 1385, referred to as 'of Jedworth', 'of Tevidale' and 'of Foresta' *i.e.*, of Selkirkshire; Clerk Royal Audit, Sheriff Teviotdale, Amb England, memb Gen and Special Cncls of Scotland, one of the councillors chosen to advise the Duke of Rothesay when appointed Lt or Regent for his f ROBERT III; among the Scottish leaders Battle of Otterburn 1388; granted the lands of Abercorn by the Earl of Douglas and those of Minto by Sir John Turnbull; *m* Isabel, dau of Sir Richard Oliver, and was put to death by Sir Henry ('Harry Hotspur') Percy (*see* NORTHUMBERLAND, D) when a prisoner of the English after the Battle of Homildon Hill 1402, leaving an er s:

Sir JOHN STEWART of Dalswinton and (in right of his w) Garlies, Wigtownshire; *m* (contract 17 Oct 1396) Marion (*m* 2nd *c* 1422 Sir John Forrester of Corstorphine; *see* VERULAM, E), only child and heiress of Sir Walter Stewart of Dalswinton (*see* above); captured with his f at Homildon Hill but escaped, joined the Scots Army sent to assist the Dauphin of France and was *k* fighting against the English 1419/20, leaving:

Sir WILLIAM STEWART, of Dalswinton and Garlies; *d* in or after 1479, leaving an est s:

Sir ALEXANDER STEWART of Garlies; Amb England 1485; fought on JAMES III's side at Battle of Sauchieburn 1487; *m* Elizabeth, dau of Sir Archibald Douglas of Cavers, and *d c* 1500, having had:

1 John, of Dalswinton; *m* Elizabeth, dau of Sir John Shaw of Haylie, and *dsp* & *vp*

2 ALEXANDER

3 Archibald

1 Agnes; *m* 4th Lord Maxwell (*see* MAXWELL, Bt)

2 Janet; *m* Sir John Dunbar of Mochrum (*see* DUNBAR, Bt of Mochrum) and had issue

The est surv son,

ALEXANDER STEWART of Garlies; *m* Elizabeth Kennedy (of Blairquhan?) and was *ka* Battle of Flodden 9 Sept 1513, leaving:

Sir ALEXANDER, of Garlies; *b c* 1507/8; captured Bttle of Solway Moss Nov 1542 by Matthew Stewart, Earl of Lennox, apparently a near relative; apparently released 1543 on handing over his s and heir as hostage; *m* 1st *c* 1521 Katherine, dau of Sir James Crichton; *m* 2nd Margaret (*d c* 1552), dau and heir of Sir Patrick Dunbar of Clugston, and by her had issue:

1 Alexander, Yr of Garlies; Commr for the Kirk of Nithsdale, memb Convention or Parl that met 1560, ktd 1565; *m* Catherine, dau of 3rd Lord Herries of Terregles (*qv*), and was *k vp* at the raid on Stirling 1571 by adherents of MARY QUEEN OF SCOTS in which the Regent Lennox was also killed, leaving:

(1) ALEXANDER

(1) Agnes; *m* 1577 Sir Andrew Agnew of Lochnaw (*see* AGNEW, Bt, of Lochnaw)

(2) Elizabeth; *m* 1st 1582 William Maxwell of Carnsalloch; *m* 2nd John Johnstone of Newbie; *m* 3rd Samuel Kirkpatrick

2 John; *d* 10 Aug 1592; ancestor of the STEWARTs of Physgill and Glasserton and the McTAGGART-STEWART Bts (*see* 1940 edn)

1 Margaret; *m* Patrick McKie of Lurg

Sir ALEXANDER *m* 3rd Katherine, dau of Walter Stewart of Barclye, and *d* Jan 1580/1, having by her had:

3 Anthony; *m* Barbara Gordon, heiress of Clary

4 Robert; *m* Mary Stewart, heiress of Cardonald

5 William, of Bargrennan

2 Helen; *m* William Gordon of Murefad and with his was ancestor of the GORDONs Viscounts of Kenmure and Lords Lochinvar

Sir ALEXANDER's est gs,

Sir ALEXANDER STEWART of Garlies; ktd 1590; *m* 1st Christian, dau of Sir James Douglas of Drumlanrig and had issue (including another dau, Barbara, *m* Sir Thomas Kirkpatrick of Closeburne; *see* KIRKPATRICK, Bt):

1 ALEXANDER (Sir), **1st Earl**

2 William, of Mains; *m* Barbara, dau and heir of James Stewart of Burray (*see* MORAY, E), and had, with other issue, a 4th but last surv son:

Sir Archibald Stewart, 1st Bt (NS), so *cr* 4 Nov 1687, with remainder to heirs male whatsoever, of (Mains and) Burray; memb royalist army that invaded England 1648 to rescue CHARLES I, later in Duke of Montrose's (*qv*) army, Offr at Battle of Worcester 1651, where captured; Lt-Col Orkney Militia 1683; *m* 1st Isabel (*d* 3 Aug 1683), dau of Sir William Murray of Abercairny, and had issue; *m* 2nd 16 Sept 1683 his maidservant Katherine (*dspm* in childbed 26 June 1684), dau of Patrick Rowsay, indweller at Stronsay, and *d* 13 May 1689, leaving an est s:

1a **Sir Archibald Stewart, 2nd Bt**; MP (S Parl) Orkney and Shetland 1702–07; *m* Margaret (*m* 2nd 5th Lord Lindores (*dsp* July 1719) and *d* Oct 1719), est dau of Hon Archibald Stuart, 4th son of 4th Earl of Moray (*qv*), and *d* 1704, leaving:

1b **Sir James Stewart, 3rd Bt**; *m* Anne, est dau of David Carmichael of Balmeady, and *dsp* 24 Aug 1756 in Southwark prison under suspicion of High Treason, when the btcy passed to the **6th Earl of Galloway** (*see* below)

1 Helen; *m* John Douglas of Stanhouse

2 Jane; *m* James Kennedy of Culzean and had:

(1) Egidia; *m* Sir John Grierson of Lag (*see* GRIERSON, Bt)

3 Nicola; *m* John Dunbar of Mochrum (*see* DUNBAR, Bt, of Mochrum)

Sir ALEXANDER *m* 2nd Elizabeth (*m* 3rd 1598 John Wallace of Craigie, and *d* 1637), dau of 7th Earl of Angus of the 1389 *cr* (*see* HAMILTON and BRANDON, D), and widow of 7th Lord Maxwell (*see* MAXWELL, Bt), and *d* 6 Oct 1596

His er son,

ALEXANDER STEWART (Sir), **1st Earl of Galloway**, so *cr* 19 Sept 1623, as also earlier 19 July 1607 LORD OF GARLIES (both S), further *cr* EARL OF GALLOWAY, with remainder to his heirs male bearing the name and arms of Stewart, PC; *m* 16 Oct 1600 Grisel, dau of Sir John Gordon of Lochinvar, and *d* 1649, having had:

1 Alexander, *Lord Garlies*; *m* 1st 29 Dec 1627 Anne, dau of 1st Earl of Nottingham of the 1597 *cr* (*see* EFFINGHAM, E); *m* 2nd 15 July 1633 Margaret (*m* 2nd 16th Earl of Crawford; *see* CRAWFORD and BALCARRES, E), dau of 7th Earl of Menteith (*see* MONTROSE, D), and *dvp* 1639, leaving by her:

(1) Alexander, *Lord Garlies*; predeceased his gf 1642

2 JAMES, **2nd Earl**

1 Anne; *m* Sir Andrew Agnew, 2nd Bt of Lochnaw (*qv*)

The 1st EARL's only surv son,

Sir James Stewart, 1st Bt (NS), of Corsewell, so *cr vp* 18 April 1627, and **2nd Earl of Galloway**; *b c* 1610; royalist Civil War, hence fined £4,000 in 1654; *m* 1642 Nicola, dau of Sir Robert Grierson of Lag, MP (*see* GRIERSON, Bt), and *d* June 1671, leaving, with a dau (*d* unm):

1 ALEXANDER, **3rd Earl**

2 Robert, of Ravenstone; *m* Elizabeth, dau of Sir David Dunbar of Baldoon, Bt, and had:

(1) Helennor; *m* Sir Thomas Kirkpatrick, 2nd Bt (*qv*), and *dsp*

(2) Elizabeth; *m* William Blair McGuffock, of Rusco Castle, and had issue

(3) Nicola; *m* John Gordon of Greenlaw

3 William, of Castlestewart; *m* Elizabeth, dau and heiress of John Gordon of Cardoness, and had:

(1) William; *m* 1st Isabel, dau of Sir William Maxwell, 1st Bt (*qv*); *m* 2nd Jean, dau of A Heron, of Kirrouchtrie, and had issue by each w

(1) Nicola; *m* Lt-Col William Maxwell and was ancestor of the MAXWELL Bts of Cardoness (*see* 1924 edn)

1 Grizel; *m* 5th Viscount Kenmure and had issue

The 2nd EARL's est son,

ALEXANDER STEWART, **3rd Earl of Galloway**; *m* Mary, dau of 2nd Earl of Queensberry (*see* QUEENSBERRY, M), and *d* Sept 1690, having had, with three other sons:

1 ALEXANDER STEWART, **4th Earl of Galloway**; *b* 8 Jan 1669/70; *d* unm 26 Sept 1690

2 JAMES, **5th Earl**

3 John, of Sorby; Brig-Gen; *d* unm at Sorby 1748

1 Margaret; *m* Sir John Clerk, Bt, of Penicuik (*qv*)

2 Henrietta; *m* 12th Earl of Glencairn and had issue (*see* CUNNINGHAME, Bt)

The 4th EARL's bro,

JAMES STEWART, **5th Earl of Galloway**, PC (S 1706); a Commr Treasury (S) 1705–06; *m c* 1694 Catherine (*d* Dec 1757), dau of 9th Earl of Eglinto(u)n (*see* EGLINTON and WINTON, E), and *d* 16 Feb 1746, having had, with other issue:

1 ALEXANDER, **6th Earl**

2 James; Lt-Gen and Col 37th Regt; MP Wigton burghs

3 William; Cav Offr; MP Wigton burghs

1 Margaret; *m* 1st 5th Earl of Southesk (*see* FIFE, D); *m* 2nd John, Master of Sinclair (see SINCLAIR, L), and *dsp*

2 Euphemia; *m* Alexander Murray of Broughton and had issue

The 5th EARL's est son,

Sir Alexander Stewart, 4th Bt, of Burray (as which *s* cousin 1756), and **6th Earl of Galloway**; *m* 1st 1718/9 Anne (*d* 1728), dau of 9th Earl Marischal (*see* KINTORE, E), and had an only surv child:

1 Mary; *m* 11 Sept 1741 Kenneth MacKenzie, Lord Fortrose (*d* 18 Oct 1761), est s of 5th Earl of Seaforth (attainted 1716; *see* CROMARTIE, E), and *d* 10 April 1751, leaving issue

The **6th Earl** *m* 2nd 1729 Lady Catherine Cochrane (*d* 15 March 1786), yst dau of 4th Earl of Dundonald (*qv*), and *d* 24 Sept 1773, having by her had, with another s and dau:

1 JOHN, **7th Earl**

2 Keith, of Glasserton; *b* 1739; Adml; *m* 13 May 1782 Georgiana Isabella (*m* 2nd 16 Feb 1797 Lt-Col Richard Fitzgerald, 2nd Life Gds, who was *ka* Waterloo 1815), dau of Simha D'Aguilar, and *d* 5 May 1795, leaving issue:

(1) James Alexander STEWART later STEWART-MACKENZIE (roy licence 1817); *b* 23 Sept 1784; Govr Ceylon, Ld High Commr Ionian Isles; *m* 21 May 1817 Hon Mary Elizabeth Frederica Humberston Stewart-Mackenzie (*d* 28 Nov 1862), est dau and coheir of 1st and last Baron Seaforth (*cr* 1797, *extinct* 1815), and widow of Sir Samuel Hood, 1st Bt (*extinct* 1790), and *d* 24 Sept 1843, leaving, with another s (*dsp*):

1a Keith William, of Seaforth, DL; *b* 6 May 1818; *m* 1st 17 May 1844 Hannah Charlotte (*d* 5 June 1868), est dau of James Joseph Hope-Vere (*see* LINLITHGOW, M), and had, with other issue:

1b JAMES ALEXANDER FRANCIS HUMBERSTON STEWART-MACKENZIE, 1st and last BARON SEAFORTH, of Brahan in Urray, Co Ross and Cromarty (UK), so *cr* 19 Jan 1921, JP; *b* 9 Oct 1847; *educ* Glenalmond, Harrow and RMC Sandhurst; 9th Lancers 1867, Afghan War 1878–80 (despatches twice, wounded), Brevet Maj, Mil Sec to Govr Madras 1886–88, Hon Col 4th/5th Bn Seaforth Highrs (Ross-shire Buffs), Lt-Col cmdg 9th Lancers 1891 (ret 1896); Convener Ross-shire CC, V-Lt Ross and Cromarty; *m* 18 July 1899 Mary Margaret, CBE, DGStJ (*d* 17 Feb 1933), only child of Edward Steinkopff, and *dsp* 3 March 1923, when the Barony expired

1b Susan Mary Elizabeth, DBE (1925, CBE 1923); *m* 1st 15 Aug 1871 Col Hon John Constantine Stanley, and had issue (*see* STANLEY OF ALDERLEY, SHEFFIELD and, B); *m* 2nd 17 Aug 1881 Francis Henry Jeune, 1st and last Baron St Helier, GCB, PC (*dsps* 9 April 1905; *see* 1906 edn), Pres Probate, Divorce and Admlty Div High Court, and *d* 25 Jan 1931

2b Julia Charlotte Sophia; *m* 1st 8 Oct 1873 9th Marquess of Tweeddale (*qv*); *m* 2nd 24 Jan 1887 Sir John Rose, 1st Bt, GCMG, PC (*d* 24 Aug 1888); *m* 3rd 2 Feb 1891 Maj Sir William Eden Evans Gordon (*d* 31 Oct 1913), MP Stepney, and *d* 17 May 1937

1a (cont.) Keith Stewart-Mackenzie *m* 2nd 2 June 1871 Alicia Almeira Seymour (*m* 2nd 28 Aug 1883 Col Walter Chidiock Nangle and *d* 21 Sept 1903), dau of R H Bell, of Bellbrook, Co Antrim, and *d* 18 June 1881, leaving by her:

3b Florence Meira Zelia; *m* 1897 Hugh St John Clarke, of Edinburgh, and had issue

2a George Augustus Frederick Wellington; *b* 21 Nov 1824; Army Offr; *m* 6 Nov 1850 Maria Louisa (*m* 2nd 5 Aug 1869 Capt E F N K Wasey, RN), yst dau of Lt-Gen Thomas Marriott, HEICS, and *dsp* 15 July 1852

1a Mary Frances; *m* 27 Aug 1838 Hon Philip Anstruther and *d* 31 Dec 1913, leaving issue (*see* ANSTRUTHER, Bt)

2a Caroline Susan; *m* 21 Dec 1844 John Berney Petre (*d* 9 Jan 1882), of Norfolk, and *d* 1867

3a Louisa Caroline; *m* 17 Nov 1858 2nd Baron Ashburton (*qv*) and *d* 2 Feb 1903, leaving issue

(2) Leveson Douglas; *b* 24 July 1786; *m* 16 Oct 1808 Elizabeth (*d* 18 April 1841), dau of Sir John Dalrymple Hay, 1st Bt (*qv*), and *d* 30 April 1819, leaving:

1a John; *b* 10 Jan 1813; *m* 11 March 1841 Elizabeth, only dau of Richard Thompson, of Nateby Hall, Lancs, and *d* 17 March 1867, leaving issue:

1b John Leveson Douglas, of Glenogil, Forfar; *b* 1 Aug 1842; *m* 15 July 1868 Margaret Anne (*d* 3 July 1921), dau of James Gibson Thomson, and *d* 1887, leaving, with other issue:

1c John, DSO (1919); *b* 21 May 1869; Lt-Col Black Watch, Boer War, WW I (despatches); *m* 1891 Valentia (*d* May 1947), dau of William Worship, and *d* 19 Feb 1931, leaving, with other issue:

1d Keith Ian Douglas, OBE (1945), JP; *b* 10 April 1904; *educ* Radley; Lt-Col (ret) RAPC, Capt Black Watch, WW II (despatches), memb Roy Co Archers, Priv Sec to Govr and C-in-C Windward Islands 1956–57; *m* 1st 11 Feb 1930 Helena Lucie (*k* by enemy action Oct 1940), yst dau of Edward Ashton St Hill, and had issue:

1e +John Edward Hamish Keith [John Stewart-Mackenzie Esq, 797 Te Atatu, Auckland, NZ]; *b* 23 Nov 1935

1e *Jennifer Mary Hamilton [Mrs David Livingstone, 4 Miller's Court, London W4 2PF]; *b* 20 Jan 1931; *m* 1st Aug 1951 (*divorce* 1962) John Innes Wood and has:

1f *James Keith; *b* 1956

2f *Jonathan Charles; *b* 1959

1f *Susan Deborah; *b* 1955

1e (cont.) Mrs Jennifer Wood *m* 2nd March 1963 (*divorce* 1976) Ian Bishop, FRCS, and by him has:

2f *Louise; *b* 1964

1e (cont.) Mrs Jennifer Bishop *m* 3rd 1977 Dennis Hart (*d* 1982); *m* 4th 1984 *David Livingstone, CBE

1d (cont.) Lt-Col Keith Stewart-Mackenzie *m* 2nd 1940 Philippa North (*d* 25 Feb 1966), est dau of Robert Nairn, FECS, of Hastings, NZ; *m* 3rd 1967 Frances Auckland Louise Bogue (*d* 1974), dau of Francis Joseph Hieronymus-Jones; *m* 4th 1977 *Joan Mary, dau of Alban J Francis, of Weston-super-Mare, and widow of Maj Philip Clarke, MC, Roy Worcs Regt, and *d* 1990

1d Amy Mary Hamilton; *m* 28 April 1920 Lt-Col Geoffrey Thornton Miller (*d* April 1967), s of Rev T Miller, of Ipswich, and *d* Nov 1966

1c Grace Hamilton; *m* 1894 Edwin Arthur Russell Benham and *d* 24 April 1966, having had issue

2a George; *b* 12 Sept 1814; *m* Sept 1843 Mary, dau of Thomas Corrie, and *d* 1893, leaving, with other issue:

1b Leveson Douglas; *b* 10 Dec 1844; *m* 10 Sept 1871 Kate (*d* 1915), dau of James Gillone, and *d* 28 March 1916, having had, with other issue:

1c Leveson Douglas; *b* 1873; *m* Elizabeth — and *d* 10 March 1905, leaving:

1d Elizabeth Leveson Douglas

2c Keith; *b* 25 March 1877; 48th Bn 3rd Canadian Pioneers; *m* 1919 Margaret, dau of Nicholas Fox, of Dublin, and had:

1d Ian Keith; *b* 1923

2d +Allan Galloway; *b* 18 March 1928; *m* 1st 1949 (*divorce* 1968) Vivian Waldon; *m* 2nd 1969 *Marie Marcelle Denise Morand and has by his 1st wife:

1e +Brian Keith; *b* 1952

1d *Jean; *b* 1919

2d *Barbara; *b* 1921

3d *Isobel Evelyn; *b* 8 Aug 1925

3c Thomas Corrie; *b* 27 Dec 1879; coal merchant

4c John; *b* 1882; 1st King's Liverpool Regt; *m* 1 Jan 1911 —, and had issue

1c Mary Frances

5c Randolph Douglas; *b* 23 Sept 1884; 7th King's Liverpool Regt; *m* 23 June 1916 Ellen Tullagher (*d* 1976), of Liverpool, and *d* 1961, leaving:

1d +Randolf Douglas Stewart [Randolph Stewart-Mackenzie Esq, 3 Forest Lawn, Liverpool L12 5JA]; *b* 1920; *m* 1947 *Mabel Thomson and has;

1e *Ann; *b* 1947; *m* 1969 *Michael Victor Guinney and has:

1f *Mark Stewart; *b* 1971

2f *Carl Stewart; *b* 1975

2e *Eileen [Mrs Peter Lawrence, 1 Gateacre Park Drive, Liverpool L25 1PA]; *b* 1950; *m* 1974 *Peter D Lawrence and has:

1f *Adam Harvey; *b* 1979

1f *Sarah Elizabeth; *b* 1976

2d Alexander; *b* 1924; *m* 1950 (*divorce* 1963) Marion G Baker and *d* 1994, leaving:

1e +Charles Anthony [Charles Stewart-Mackenzie Esq, 9 Chess St, Salisbury, 5109 S Australia]; *b* 1952; *m* 1973 (*divorce* 1984) Nonda Anne Route and has issue:

1f *Michelle Katrina; *b* 1974

2f *Kathrine Jane; *b* 1975

1e (cont.) Charles Stewart-Mackenzie has further issue by *Johann Christine:

3f *Stephanie Melissa; *b* 1987

1d *Catherine Emily [Mrs Albert Marrion, 74 Caesars Close, Castlefields, Runcorn, Cheshire]; *b* 1917; *m* 1939 *Albert Marrion and has:

1e *Norma; *b* 1940 [Mrs Gordon Tinsley, 11 Eskdale Cl, Beechwood West, Runcorn, Cheshire WA7 2QX]; *m* 1959 *Gordon Colin Tinsley, and has issue:

1f *Mark Stewart; *b* 1968

2e *Pauline [Mrs Anthony Wakefield, 21 Eskdale Cl, Runcorn, CheshireWA7 2QX]; *b* 1946; *m* 1967 *Anthony Joseph Wakefield and has issue:

1f *Andrew Anthony; *b* 1967
2f *Stewart Joseph; *b* 1971
2d *Lily [Mrs Richard Williamson, 28 Townfield View, Windmill Hill, Runcorn, Cheshire WA7 6QD]; *b* 1919; *m* 1943 *Richard E Williamson
3d Joan; *b* 1926; *m* 1946 *Charles Wright and *d* 1989, leaving two sons and a dau
4d *Jean [Mrs Stanley Davies, 104 Barons Hey, Cantrill Farm, Liverpool L28 0QE]; *b* 1934; *m* 1954 *Stanley R Davies and has issue:
1e *Julie [Mrs John Wishman, 4 Springfield Way, W Derby, Liverpool 12]; *b* 1959; *m* 1981 *John Wishman, and has:
1f *Michael John; *b* 1984
1f *Sarah Jean; *b* 1985
2b Thomas Corrie; *b* 22 June 1846; coffee planter Natal; *m* Maria, dau of William Cook, and *d* 7 April 1907, leaving issue:
1c George Henry; *b* 1873; *m* Agnes Robina Jessie (*d* 1949), dau of Lewis Storm of Scotland, and *d* 1931, leaving:
1d +Keith [Keith Stewart-Mackenzie Esq, Flat 105, Glendower Place, 99 Linksfield Rd, Edenvale 1610, S Africa]; *b* 1915; *m* 1st Kathleen Kruger (*d* 1975); *m* 2nd 1977 *Elsie, dau of Enos Ashworth and widow of Leslie George Smith, and has by his 1st w:
1e +Malcolm Keith [Malcolm Stewart-Mackenzie Esq, 15 Cole St, Kensington 2094, S Africa]; *b* 1948; *m* 1971 (*divorce* 1980) Joan Carrick and has issue:
1f +Craig; *b* 1972
2f +Neville Keith; *b* 1977
1f *Jacqueline; *b* 1974
1e *Audrey [Mrs Ernest Atkins, 7 Beaumont Rd, King Williamstown 5600, S Africa]; *b* 1951; *m* 1971 *Ernest Arthur and has:
1f *Chad; *b* 1976
1f *Natalie; *b* 1973
2c Leveson Douglas; *b* 1880; *m* Margaret Walker Wilson (*d* 1975) and *d* 1946, leaving:
1d +George Bruce; *b* 1923; *m* 1st 1950 Catherine Aspinall (*d* 1985); *m* 2nd 1986 *Shelagh Irene, dau of Albert Croft, and adopted:
*John Keith; *b* 1950
*Marie Lynne; *b* 1952
3c Cecil Francis; *b* 18–; *m* 19– Ethel Alexandria Marshall and *d* 1940, leaving:
1d +William Thomas
1d *Vera Alexandria
2d *Joan
3d *Dorothy; *b* 1923
3b Keith; *b* 31 Oct 1851; *m* 1908 Anne (*d* 24 March 1937), dau of Robert Brown, and *d* 11 Aug 1938
4b James Dalrymple Hay; *b* 31 July 1853; *m* 1887 Elizabeth Grace, dau of James Stewart (*see below*), and *d* 23 May 1914
1b Clementina Ross; *m* Lt-Col John Blair and *d* 1908, leaving issue
2b Isabella Lydia; *m* 15 Jan 1908 Ven George Bygrave Brooks (*d* 1914), Vicar Edlesborough, Bucks, Archdeacon Surrey, Jamaica, 1879–84
3a James; *b* 2 Oct 1816; *m* 20 Nov 1849 Sarah Georgina (*d* 9 Sept 1910), dau of Sir James Dalrymple Hay, 2nd Bt (*qv*), and *d* 1895, leaving, with other issue:
1b Leveson Douglas; *b* 22 Oct 1850; *m* 1881 Eleanora Georgina (*d* 21 Jan 1925), dau of Rev Thomas Blizzard Bell, and *d* 25 Sept 1930
2b James Dalrymple Hay, WS; *b* 12 Aug 1862; *educ* Edinburgh U (MA)
1b Anne
2b Elizabeth Grace; *m* 1887 James Dalrymple Hay Stewart (*see above*)
1a Susan; *m* 14 Dec 1854 Rev George Charles (*d* 4 Feb 1881), of Stranraer, and *d* 1897, leaving issue
2 Catherine; *m* 12 April 1751 James Murray (*d* 30 April 1799), of Broughton, MP
3 Susannah; *m* 23 May 1768 1st Marquess of Stafford (*see* SUTHERLAND, D) and *d* 15 Aug 1805, leaving issue
4 Margaret; *m* 22 April 1759 4th Earl of Aboyne (*see* HUNTLY, M) and *d* 12 Aug 1762, leaving issue
5 Harriet; *m* 25 May 1765 9th Duke of Hamilton and (6th Duke of) Brandon (*qv*) and *d* 26 Nov 1788, leaving issue
6 Charlotte; *m* 21 Feb 1759 4th Earl of Dunmore (*qv*) and *d* 11 Nov 1818, leaving issue

The 6th EARL's est son,

JOHN STEWART, **7th Earl of Galloway**, KT (1775); *b* 13 March 1736; rep S peer 1774–90, a Ld Bedchamber 1784–1806, *cr* 6 June 1795 BARON STEWART OF GARLIES, in the Stewartry of Kirkcudbright (GB); *m* 1st 14 Aug 1761 Lady Charlotte Mary Greville (*d* 31 May 1763), dau of 1st Earl of Warwick (*see* WARWICK, BROOKE and, E), and had a s (*d an inf*); *m* 2nd 13 June 1764 Anne (*d* 8 Jan 1830), 2nd dau of Sir James Dashwood, 2nd Bt (*qv*), of Kirtlington Park, and *d* 13 Nov 1806, having by her had, with two other sons and another dau:
1 GEORGE STEWART, **8th Earl**
2 William (Sir), GCB; *b* 10 Jan 1774; Lt-Gen; *m* 21 April 1804 Frances (*d* 6 Aug 1833), sis of 17th Earl of Morton (*qv*), and *d* 7 Jan 1827, leaving issue:
(1) Horatio; *b* 3 Aug 1806; Capt Rifle Bde; *m* 29 Nov 1833 Sophia (*d* 9 July 1888), dau of his unc Hon Montgomery Stewart, and *d* 20 Sept 1835, leaving:
1a Horatio Granville STEWART later MURRAY-STEWART (roy licence 7 May 1846), of Broughton, Wigtownshire, Cally and Rusko, Kirkcudbrightshire, and Killybegs, Co Donegal, JP, DL; *b* 25 Sept 1834; High Sheriff Co Donegal 1858, twice contested Kirkcudbright; *m* 9 Sept 1858 Anne Eliza (*d* 21 April 1919), 2nd dau of Rev John Digby Wingfield-Digby, Vicar Coleshill, Warwicks, and *dsp* 6 April 1904
(1) Louisa; *m* 29 Oct 1829 David Baillie and had issue
3 Charles James (Rt Rev); *b* 15 April 1775; DD; Bp Quebec; *d* unm 13 July 1837
4 Montgomery Granville John, of Castramont, NB; *b* 15 April 1780; *m* 22 Oct 1801 Catherine (*d* 16 Jan 1833), dau of Patrick Honyman, and *d* 10 Jan 1860, having had, with other issue:
(1) Alexander (Rev); *b* 12 April 1808; *m* 10 Dec 1833 Mary (*d* 22 Feb 1873), dau of Rev Marmaduke Lawson, of Yorks, and *d* 30 Oct 1837, leaving two daus (*d* unm)
(2) James (Rev); *b* 22 June 1819; MA; Rector Little Stukeley, Hunts; *m* 23 April 1861 Lucy (*d* 1910), 3rd dau of Rev Joseph Parker, Rector Wyton, and *d* 26 Sept 1895, having had issue:
1a Montgomery James; *b* 1803; *d* unm Malaya 1895
2a Frederick Granville; *b* 1865; *d* unm *c* 1930
3a Herbert Galloway; *b* 26 Sept 1866; *d* unm 16 Dec 1960
4a Douglas Campbell Murray; *b* 1869; *d* at sea *c* 1900
5a Percy Marlborough; *b* 28 Aug 1871; Maj Roy Fus; *m* 29 April 1901 Katharine (*d* 28 April 1939), dau of Jonathan Priestman, of Co Durham, and widow of Rev J A Bridges, and *d* 26 June 1962
6a Archibald Joseph Parker; *b* 1874; *d* unm *c* 1930
7a Horatio George Willoughby; *b* 21 Nov 1877; *m* 1929 Beatrice Maud (*d* 1984), dau of James Bedson, of Birmingham, and *d* 13 Nov 1943, leaving:
1b *Flora Margaret [Mrs Richard Revell, 16 Bellencroft Gdns, Merry Hill, Wolverhampton WV3 8DT]; *b* 11 April 1930; *m* 19 July 1951 Richard Arthur Revell, BA BSc (*d* 1986), and has issue:
1c *Nicholas Stewart [Nicholas Revell Esq, 7 Graspin Lane, Weston Favell Village, Northampton NN3 3BU]; *b* 7 Aug 1952; *m* 1981 *Rosemary Jean, yst dau of George Stephen Bradley, and has issue:
1d *Matthew James; *b* 1983
2d *Stewart George; *b* 1985
1d *Melanie Louise; *b* 1987
1c *Clare Victoria; *b* 29 Feb 1956; *m* 1982 *Stephen John Brown and has:
1d *Benjamin Jack; *b* 1993
2c *Jennifer Mary; *b* 13 Sept 1968
2b *Daphne Isabel [Mrs Neville Tasker, 85 Rickard Rd, Warrimoo, NSW 2775, Australia]; *b* 24 April 1932; *m* July 1956 Neville Tasker (*d* 1997), and has:
1c *Sheryl Anne; *b* 4 April 1959
2c *Melanie Jane; *b* 1 Jan 1963
8a Arthur Alexander Melville; *b* 16 Sept 1879; *d* unm 9 April 1967
9a Charles; *d an inf*
1a Flora Lucy; *b* 1864; *d* unm China 1 Aug 1895
2a Isabel Mary Josephine; *b* 1868; *m* 2 Aug 1900 Gordon Allen, AMICE (*d* 3 July 1940), of Cumloden, Perranporth, Cornwall, and *d* 20 Nov 1950
3a Eva Katharine Graham; *b* 1873; *m* 1917 Capt H Griffen, RFA, and *d* 17 April 1933, leaving one dau
4a Amy Grace Salome; *b* 1875; *d* 1877
5a Olivia Margaret Agneta; *b* 21 Nov 1877; *d* unm 8 Sept 1965
(1) Anne; *m* 17 Sept 1833 Rev S J I Lockhart, Vicar Hurstbourne, Hants, and *d* 22 Dec 1878, leaving issue
(2) Susan; *m* 12 Nov 1828 Rev E Willoughby Sewell and *d* 25 July 1839
(3) Sophia; *m* 29 Nov 1833 her cousin Capt Horatio Stewart (*d* 20 Sept 1835) and *d* 9 July 1888, leaving issue (*see above*)
(4) Catherine; *m* 21 Dec 1851 Capt Frederick Madan, HEIC (*d* 17 Nov 1863), and *d* 7 Feb 1899
(5) Caroline; *m* 7 Nov 1833 Sir John Heron-Maxwell, 6th Bt (*qv*), and *d* 22 Oct 1896
(6) Jane; *m* 9 Oct 1845 Rev James Lawson (*dsp* 19 March 1872), Vicar Buckminster, Leics, and *d* 15 Jan 1909
5 Edward Richard; *b* 5 May 1782; *m* Nov 1805 Katharine (*d* 8 Oct 1863), dau of Francis, Lord Elcho (*see* WEMYSS, E), and *d* 27 Aug 1851, having had, with other issue:
(1) Edward (Rev); *b* 9 Oct 1808; MA; Rector Lainston, Vicar Sparsholt, Hants; *m* 27 Feb 1838 Louisa Anne (*d* 14 May 1892), dau of C J Herbert, of Muckruss, Co Kerry, and *d* 21 March 1875, having had, with other issue:
1a Herbert (Sir), KCB; *b* 30 June 1843; Maj-Gen, ADC to HM QUEEN VICTORIA; *m* 19 Dec 1877 Georgina Janet (*d* 4 April 1910), dau of Adml Sir James Stirling and widow of Maj-Gen Sir Henry Tombs, VC, KCB, and was *ka* Egypt 16 Feb 1885, Battle of Metammeh, having had, with another son (*d* young):
1b Geoffrey; *b* 28 Oct 1878; Page of Honour to HM QUEEN VICTORIA, Capt Coldstream Gds; *m* 2 June 1908 Violet (*d* 8 June 1968, having *m* 2nd 1921 Rev Harold Omer Cavalier, MA, who *d* 12 Oct 1936), dau of William Clarence Watson, of Colworth, Beds, and was *ka* 22 Dec 1914, leaving:
1c +Malise Herbert, DFC; *b* 16 Feb 1911; F/Lt RAF (ret), late 2nd Lt Coldstream Gds, WW II
1c Jean Violet; *b* 25 March 1909; BA; *m* 1 June 1940 Maj-Gen Michael Whitworth Prynne, CB, CBE, MA, RE, s of Lt-Col Alan Harvey Lockyer Prynne, RM, of Bramley, Surrey, and was *k* in a car crash with her husb 27 Sept 1977, leaving:
1d *Andrew Geoffrey Lockyer; *b* 28 May 1953; *educ* Marlborough
1d *Bridget Mary; *b* 7 March 1941; *m* 8 May 1965 *Donald Ian Fleming Spence, er s of Brig Ian F M Spence, OBE, MC, TD, and has:
1e *Robert Ian James; *b* 14 June 1969
1e *Arabella Jean; *b* 16 Dec 1967
2d *Caroline Anne; *b* 29 June 1943; ARCM, GRSM; *m* 16 Oct 1965 *Terence Michael Kehoe, est son of Cdr (E) Terence Kehoe, DSC, RN, of Nunthorpe, Yorks, and has issue:
1e *Susanna Jane; *b* 18 March 1966
3d *Celia Jane; *b* 5 Sept 1947; BA; *m* 3 July 1971 *David Christopher Greenberg, yr s of Dr M J Greenberg, of Cambridge
2a William Anthony (Rev); *b* 19 May 1847; Vicar W Tisted; *m* 19 April 1881 Rose Elizabeth (*m* 3rd 8 Oct 1891 Maj-Gen Douglas M'Neil, CB, Madras Army (*d* 10 Jan 1904); *m* 4th 19 Sept 1907 Hon Lucius Murrough O'Brien,

2nd son of 13th Baron Inchiquin (*qv*), and *d* 30 July 1926), dau of Thomas Somers, of Mendip Lodge, Somerset, and widow of E M Williams, of Bibury Court, Glos, and *dsp* 31 July 1883

1a Winifred; *m* 5 Dec 1861 Sir John Blencowe Robinson, 8th Bt, of London (*qv*), and *d* 24 May 1919

2a Katharine Elizabeth; *m* 1 Aug 1865 Henry Herbert (*d* 18 Jan 1898), of Cahirnane, Killarney, and *d* 2 Aug 1912

3a Louisa Winifred; *m* 6 Dec 1866 Alexander Augustus Berens (*d* 31 May 1926) and *d* 21 March 1929, leaving issue

4a Augusta Francis Harriet; *m* 13 Oct 1875 Rev Henry Everett and had issue (*see* SMITH-MARRIOTT, Bt)

5a Jane; *m* 5 Nov 1873 Arthur Frederick Tyrwhitt-Drake, of Dogdean, Salisbury, and *d* 19 Sept 1908, leaving issue

(2) Algernon; *b* 7 March 1811; *m* Oct 1833 Charlotte (*d* 1861), dau of Col J Albeck Clement, RA, and *d* 4 Nov 1875, having had issue:

1a Charles Edward, CB, CMG, CIE; *b* 23 Feb 1836; Col Indian Staff Corps; *m* 23 Jan 1869 Annie Nairn (*d* 6 April 1931), dau of Philip Anstruther (*see* ANSTRUTHER, Bt), and *d* 26 Dec 1904, leaving, with other issue:

1b Algernon Bingham Anstruther, DSO; *b* 6 Dec 1869; Maj Seaforth Highrs, Chitral, S Africa, and WW I; *m* 8 Nov 1911 Edith Evelyn (*m* 2nd 19 June 1921 Henry de Grey Lennox (*see* RICHMOND and GORDON, D) and *d* 17 Feb 1932), dau of Sir Arthur Pendarves Vivian, KC (*see* SWANSEA, B), and was *ka* 23 May 1916, leaving:

1c *Sheila Anne; *b* 12 Feb 1915; *m* 11 Sept 1943 Maj Sir Charles Spencer Denman, 2nd Bt (*qv*), MC, and has issue

2c *Barbara Jean [Mrs George De Pree, 2 Fullerton Manor, Andover, Hants SP11 7LA]; *b* 12 Feb 1915; *m* 20 April 1939 Maj George De Pree (*d* 1992), 60th Rifles, er s of Gen Hugo De Pree, of Beckley, Sussex, and has:

1d *Andrew Hugo Stewart; *b* 17 Jan 1946; *m* 1972 *Victoria, only dau of David Neilson, of Catton Hall, Burton-on-Trent, and has:

1e *Emma; *b* 1975

2e *Alice; *b* 1978

3e *Olivia; *b* 1984

1d *Jane Mary [Mrs Giles Pitman, Auchmar, Drymen, Glasgow]; *b* 14 Nov 1940; *m* 20 July 1961 *Giles William Pitman, yr son of Maj John Pitman, 3rd Hus, of Malmesbury, Wilts, and has issue:

1e *George Eustace; *b* 22 Aug 1963

2e *John Struan; *b* 1 April 1969; *m* 1993 *Laura Louise Vincent

1e *Kate Jane; *b* 8 Jan 1965; *m* 1992 *Mark Christopher Dalton

2d *Rachel Ann; *b* 14 Feb 1950; *m* 1970 *James Edward Cory Liddell (*see* RAVENSWORTH, B)

2a Algernon Augustus; *b* 31 Jan 1839; Maj-Gen RA; *m* 25 Oct 1864 Sophia Anne Eleanor (*d* 20 Oct 1919), 4th dau of Very Rev Hon Henry Lewis Hobart (*see* BUCKINGHAMSHIRE, E), and *d* 23 July 1905, leaving:

1b Leopold Charles; *b* 21 Dec 1868; Coronation Medal 1902, RN Vols (medal); *m* 1921 Cecilia Letitia Gore (*m* 2nd 12 Nov 1930 Lt-Col Noel Percival Richard Preston, DSO, RA, who *d* 11 Nov 1937), dau of Capt Henry Unett, of Huntington Hall, Yorks, and *d* 19 Dec 1926

2b Philip George; *b* 3 May 1873; Lt 1st Bn Roy Scots Fus Punjab 1897–98 (medal with three clasps); *dsp* 5 Feb 1898

1b Charlotte Susan; *d* unm 1945

2b Eleanor Sophia Anne; *d* unm 1951

3b Albinia Frances Adelaide; *d* unm 15 Jan 1955

(3) Arthur; *b* 12 Dec 1813; *m* 29 July 1840 Mary (*d* 8 Nov 1872), yst dau of Rev Dr Spencer Madan, Rector Ibstock, Preb Peterborough, and *d* 30 June 1879, having had, with other issue:

1a Walter, CB; *b* 13 July 1841; R-Adml, ADC to HM QUEEN VICTORIA; *dsp* 26 Oct 1896

2a Alan; *b* 19 May 1844; BA Oxford; barrister; *m* 21 Jan 1875 Emily Louisa (*d* 3 May 1913), dau of John James Sawyer, of Halifax, Nova Scotia, and *d* 25 Dec 1924, having had issue:

1b Arthur Charles; *b* 18 Feb 1877; RBA; *m* 1st 15 July 1903 Geraldine Susan Louisa (*dsp* 20 Dec 1907), dau of Capt E W C Lloyd, 7th Roy Fus; *m* 2nd 1 Jan 1910 Sharon Watson, dau of W C Helsby, of Valparaiso, and *dsp* 10 June 1941

1b Catherine Frances; *b* 28 April 1878; *d* unm 27 May 1964

1a Sophia Louisa; *m* 26 Feb 1878 Maj-Gen George Fuller Walker (*d* 18 May 1907), and *d* 2 April 1929, leaving issue

2a Jessie Charteris; *m* 27 Oct 1875 Lt-Col John Rimington Sharp (*d* 16 Oct 1898), 2nd Bn KO Roy Lancaster Regt, and *d* 21 Sept 1903

3a Mary; *m* 26 April 1883 Col Henry Walter Philips, APD (*d* 31 July 1903), Capt W Kent (50th) Regt, and *d* 27 March 1942, leaving issue

(1) Jane Frances Clinton; *m* 11 Oct 1851 6th Duke of Marlborough (*qv*) and *d* 24 March 1897

6 James Henry Keith, CB; *b* 22 Oct 1783; Lt-Col; *m* 10 Aug 1819 Henrietta Anne (*d* 1829), dau of Rev Spencer Madan, DD, and *d* 18 July 1836, leaving, with other issue:

(1) Spencer; *b* 24 June 1820; Capt 4th Foot; *m* Jan 1846 Frances Olivia (*d* 1903), 3rd dau of Miles Sweeny, and *dsp* 19 May 1893

(2) Charles Patrick; *b* 27 May 1823; *m* 4 Aug 1859 Frances Anne (*d* 4 Jan 1910), dau of William Courtenay Cruttenden, of Mount Heaton, Lancs, and *d* 7 July 1882, leaving issue:

1a Alan Keith

2a Charles Nigel; *b* 19 Aug 1864; *m* 23 April 1895 Edith Mabel, dau of Julius Miller, MD, MRCS, and *d* 2 April 1915, leaving issue:

1b Herbert Nigel; *b* 1896; believed to have emigrated to USA

3a Arthur Courtenay, CBE (1919); *b* 1 May 1871; Capt RN, Naval Attaché Rome 1910–13, Cdr Crown Italy; *m* 18 Jan 1911 Gwendolyn Marion (*d* 1961), dau of Waldo Story, of Rome, and *d* 19 Feb 1958, leaving issue:

1b +Ivor Courtenay; *b* 29 July 1916; *educ* Cheltenham

1b *Fiametta Maud Courtenay; *b* 26 Oct 1911; *m* 5 Oct 1939 S/Ldr Gordon Addison Hope Kent, RAF, son of Rev Frank Kent, of Leeming, Northallerton, Yorks, and has issue

1a Alice Henrietta; *d* 9 May 1862

2a Charlotte Evelyn; *m* 24 Jan 1893 Rev Ernest George Beckwith (*d* 28 July 1950), and *d* 12 Sept 1953, leaving issue

3a Penelope Blanche; *d* 5 Jan 1948

1 Catherine; *m* 28 Sept 1781 Sir James Graham, 1st Bt, of Netherby (*qv*), and *d* 20 Sept 1836, leaving issue

2 Susan; *m* 15 Sept 1791 5th Duke of Marlborough (*qv*) and *d* 2 April 1841, leaving issue

3 Anne Harriet; *m* 8 Aug 1795 Lord Spencer Chichester (*see* DONEGALL, M) and *d* 30 Jan 1850

4 Elizabeth Euphemia; *m* 3 Jan 1798 William Philips Inge, of Thorpe Constantine, Staffs, and *d* 12 Nov 1855, leaving issue

5 Charlotte; *m* 12 Sept 1801 Hon Sir Edward Crofton, 3rd Bt (*d* 8 Jan 1816), and *d* May 1842, leaving issue (*see* CROFTON, B)

6 Caroline; *m* 1803 Rev Hon George Rushout (*d* Oct 1842), f of 3rd Baron Northwick (*see* 1887 edn), and *d* 1818

7 Sophia; *m* 21 July 1806 Hon William Bligh and *d* 1809, leaving issue (*see* DARNLEY, E)

The 7th EARL's est surv son,

GEORGE STEWART, **8th Earl of Galloway**, KT (1814); *b* 24 March 1768; Adml the Blue; *m* 18 April 1797 Jane (*d* 30 June 1842), 2nd dau of 1st Earl of Uxbridge (*see* ANGLESEY, M), and *d* 27 March 1834, leaving, with another dau:

1 RANDOLPH STEWART, **9th Earl**

2 Keith, CB; *b* 3 Jan 1814; Adml; *m* 9 Aug 1841 Mary Caroline (*d* 22 Nov 1895), only dau of Sir Charles FitzRoy, KCB (*see* GRAFTON, D), and *d* 15 Sept 1879, having had (with a s, *d* unm):

(1) Mary Jane; *m* 8 March 1864 Reginald Dykes Marshall, JP, DL (*d* 3 Oct 1913), of Castlerigg Manor, Cumberland, and *d* 30 Dec 1925, leaving issue

(2) Edith; *m* 19 April 1866 Edward St Aubyn and *d* 25 April 1875, leaving issue (*see* SAINT LEVAN, B)

(3) Blanche Caroline; *m* 11 Jan 1871 Adml Sir William Houston Shaw Stewart, GCB, and *d* 17 Sept 1927, leaving issue (*see* SHAW-STEWART, Bt)

(4) Louisa Wilhemina; *m* 26 Aug 1869 Kyrle Alfred Chapman (*dsp* 1891), of Roehampton, Surrey, and *d* 21 Aug 1938

(5) Ellinor Sydney; *m* 26 Aug 1869 Spencer Chapman (*d* 21 March 1918) and *d* 15 Dec 1901, leaving issue

(6) Rosa Frances; *m* 17 March 1873 Capt John Edmond Audley Harvey, DL (*d* 15 May 1937), 42nd Highrs, of Ickwell Bury, Beds, and *d* 12 July 1880, leaving issue

(7) Caroline Ethel Gertrude; *m* 14 July 1910 Capt Athol Augustus Chichester (*see* DONEGALL, M) and *d* 28 Aug 1947

(8) Mabel Augusta; *m* 12 Dec 1888 Capt Gilbert Gordon Blane, Scots Gds (*d* 25 Nov 1928), of Foliejon Park, Berks, and *d* 1 June 1946, leaving issue

(9) Hilda Eugenia; *m* 22 April 1901 (Arthur) Rhuvon Guest and *d* 15 April 1959, leaving issue (*see* WIMBORNE, V)

1 Jane; *m* 13 Jan 1819 6th Duke of Marlborough (*qv*) and *d* 12 Oct 1844, leaving issue

2 Louisa; *m* 18 Dec 1823 2nd Baron Feversham (*qv*) and *d* 5 March 1889, leaving issue

The 8th EARL's er son,

RANDOLPH STEWART, **9th Earl of Galloway**; *b* 16 Sept 1800; Ld Lt Kirkcudbrightshire 1828–45 and Wigtonshire 1828–51; *m* 9 Aug 1833 Harriet Blanche (*d* 25 May 1885), 7th dau of 6th Duke of Beaufort (*qv*), and *d* 2 Jan 1873, having had:

1 ALAN PLANTAGENENT STEWART, **10th Earl of Galloway**, KT (1887), JP, DL (Wigtonshire and Kirkcudbrightshire); *b* 21 Oct 1835; Hon Col 4th Bn Roy Scots Fus, formerly Capt RHG (The Blues); MP Wigtonshire 1868–73; Commr Gen Assembly Church of Scotland 1876–77; *m* 25 Jan 1871 Lady Mary Arabella Arthur Cecil (*d* 18 Aug 1903), 3rd dau of 2nd Marquess of Salisbury (*qv*), and *dsp* 7 Feb 1901

2 RANDOLPH HENRY, **11th Earl**

3 Alexander, DL (Cos Wigton and Kirkcudbright); *b* 8 Nov 1838; Maj-Gen RHA; *m* 12 June 1883 Adela Maria (*m* 2nd 25 April 1899 Col Basil Lloyd Anstruther (*see* ANSTRUTHER, Bt), Manchester Regt, and *d* 22 March 1915), dau of Sir Robert Loder, 1st Bt, MP (*qv*), and *d* 6 Jan 1896, having had, with other issue:

(1) Walter Robert, DSO (1918), MC; *b* 7 Feb 1888; Capt and Brevet Maj Rifle Bde; *m* 17 Jan 1914 Esmée Winifred Mary (*m* 2nd 20 Jan 1929 Maj Joseph Anthony Douglas Bell, RASC, who *d* 1 Aug 1956), er dau of Riversdale Francis John Grenfell, JP (*see* GRENFELL, B), and was *ka* 8 April 1918, leaving:

1a Alexander David, MBE (1945), TD; *b* 26 Dec 1914; *educ* Eton; Maj City London Yeo, WW II; *m* 1 June 1948 *Daphne Marion [Mrs Alexander Stewart, North Green, Kelsale, Suffolk], only dau of Sir Reginald Bonsor, 2nd Bt (*qv*), and widow of F/O Clyde Euan Miles Graham, RAF, and *d* 1985, leaving issue:

1b +ANDREW CLYDE [Andrew Stewart Esq, 9 Lennox Gdn Mews, London SW1]; *b* 13 March 1949; heir presumptive; *educ* Eton; *m* 5 March 1977 *Sara, only dau of Brig J P Pollock, of Upper Froyle, Hants, and has:

1c +Alexander Patrick; *b* 18 Nov 1980

1c *Tania Jane; *b* 5 Jan 1979

2c *Zoe Inez; *b* 23 Dec 1983

2b +(David) Mark [Mark Stewart Esq, The Old Hall, Reedham, Norwich, Norfolk NR13 3TZ]; *b* 28 Jan 1960; *educ* Stowe; *m* *Victoria Georgina, dau of Brig Thomas Geoffrey Henry Jackson (*see* JACKSON, Bt, of Birkenhead), and has issue:

1c +Samuel Mark; *b* 1990

2c +Harry Alexander; *b* 1992

1c *Chloe Rose; *b* 1994

1b *(Rosemary) Zara; *b* 5 March 1952; *m* 10 Sept 1977 *Geoffrey Ian Fleming, s of James Fleming, of Eyarth House, Ruthin, Clwyd, and has:

1c *Alistair James; *b* 18 Aug 1982

2a (Ian) Michael; *b* 1917; *educ* Eton; Capt Welsh Gds WW II; *m* 6 Sept 1941 (*divorce* 1952) Peggy Spencer (*d* 20 Oct 1957), twin dau of Spencer Ruthven Thornton, of Cranbourne Corner, nr Ascot, and *d* 1973, leaving issue:

1b +Alastair Grenfell [Alastair Stewart Esq, Highfield House, Nunnington, York]; *b* 22 Aug 1944; *educ* Eton; *m* 1973 *Sarah Monica Scott and has:

1c +James Henry; *b* 1975

1c *Victoria Rose; *b* 1977

1b Carolyn Mary; *b* 3 Aug 1942; *m* 19 Oct 1963 *Alec Charles Hinchliff Bond [Alec Bond Esq, Stud Farm House, Thenford, Oxon OX17 2BX], er s of Maj C F G Bond, and *d* 9 April 1996, leaving:

1c *William David Hinchcliff; *b* 1970

(1) Adiné Blanche; *m* 23 April 1914 Rev Canon Horace Ricardo Wilkinson, OBE, s of Horace Wilkinson, of Sevenoaks, Kent, and *d* 16 Aug 1952

4 FitzRoy Somerset Keith; *b* 19 Dec 1855; MA Oxford; *m* 17 July 1888 Elizabeth Louisa (*d* Feb 1935), dau of Rev Robert Green Rogers, of Yarlington, and widow of John Stanley Thompson, and *d* 21 July 1914, leaving issue:

(1) Lilian Blanche Mary; *b* 23 June 1889; *m* 16 Jan 1911 Ivor Andros De La Rue, 2nd son of Sir Thomas Andros De La Rue 1st Bt (*qv*) and *dsp* 19 Oct 1968

(2) Vera Jan Estelle; *b* 3 Feb 1893; *d* unm 25 Sept 1971

1 Helen Blanche; *m* 20 April 1896 Walter Clifford Mellow, s of Col Mellor, MP, and *d* 5 Jan 1903

2 Emma Georgiana; *m* 2 Dec 1858 2nd Baron Tollemache (*qv*) and *d* 24 Jan 1869, having had issue

3 Mary Louisa; *m* 13 Aug 1874 Charles Edward Stephen Cooke (*see* COOKE, Bt) and *d* 23 Feb 1929

4 Jane Charlotte; *m* 9 Feb 1881 Henry Anthony Spedding, JP, DL (*d* 21 Sept 1887), of Mirehouse, Cumberland, and *d* 24 Sept 1897, having had issue

5 Emily Octavia; *m* 4 Feb 1875 Capt Hon Francis Algernon James Chichester (*see* DONEGALL, M) and *d* 7 July 1929, leaving issue

6 Henrietta Caroline; *m* 3 Aug 1880 Algernon Turnor, CB (*d* 11 Dec 1921), and *d* 27 April 1930, leaving issue

7 Isabel Maud; *d* unm 28 Nov 1927

The 10th EARL's bro,

RANDOLPH HENRY STEWART, **11th Earl of Galloway**, JP (Wigtonshire); *b* 14 Oct 1836; Capt 42nd Roy Highrs, Crimea and Indian Mutiny; Provost Newton Stewart 1901–04; *m* 3 June 1891 Amy Mary Pauline (*d* 25 June 1942), only dau of Anthony John Cliffe, of Bellevue, Co Wexford, and *d* 7 Feb 1920, having had, with a yr s (Keith Anthony, *b* 8 Sept 1894, Lt Black Watch, *ka* 9 May 1915):

RANDOLPH ALGERNON RONALD STEWART, **12th Earl of Galloway**, JP; *b* 21 Nov 1892; *educ* Harrow and RMC Sandhurst; Capt Scots Gds WW I, Hon Attaché Legation Berne 1918, ADC to Mil Govr Cologne 1919; Lt-Col and Hon Col KOSB (TA), Chm Kirkcudbrightshire TAA 1933–47 (Pres 1932–78), Ld Lt Stewartry of Kirkcudbright 1932–75; Grand Master Mason Scotland 1945–49; *m* 14 Oct 1924 Philippa Fendall (*d* 22 Feb 1974), yr dau of Jacob Wendell, of New York, and *d* 13 June 1978, leaving:

1 RANDOLPH KEITH REGINALD STEWART, **13th and present Earl of Galloway**

1 *Antonia Marian Amy Isabel [The Lady Antonia Dalrymple, Newhailes, Musselburgh, Midlothian]; *b* 3 Dec 1925; *m* 5 April 1946 Sir (Charles) Mark Dalrymple, 3rd and last Bt (*dsp* 29 June 1971; *see* 1970 edn)

GALWAY

Arms: Quarterly, 1st and 4th, sa. six swallows, three, two and one, arg. (for ARUNDELL); 2nd and 3rd, sa. on a chevron, between three martlets or, as many mullets of the field (for MONCKTON). **Crests:** 1 On a chapeau az. doubled erm. a swallow arg. (for ARUNDELL), 2 A martlet or (for MONCKTON). **Supporters:** Two unicorns erm., crined, armed and unguled, each gorged with an Eastern diadem or. **Motto:** *Famam extendere factis* ('Extending my fame by deeds'). **Creation:** B. and V. (I) 17 July 1727, B. (UK) 4 July 1887.

THE 12TH VISCOUNT GALWAY, Co Galway, **Baron of Killard**, Co Clare, and **Baron Monckton of Serlby**, Co Nottingham (George Rupert Monckton, CD) [Lt-Cdr The Rt Hon The Viscount Galway CD RCN (ret), 787 Berkshire Drive, London, Ontario N6J 3S5, Canada]; *b* 13 Oct 1922; *s* cousin 1980; *m* 12 Oct 1944 *Fiona Margaret, dau of Capt Percival Walter de Putron Taylor, of Sooke, BC, Canada, and has issue:

1 +(JOHN) PHIL(IP) [The Hon Philip Monckton, 387 Castlefield Ave, Toronto, Ontario M5N 1L4, Canada]; *b* 8 April 1952; *educ* U of W Ontario (MA); gp product manager Scepter Corp, Toronto; *m* 1980 (*divorce* 1992) Deborah Kathleen, dau of A Bruce Holmes, of Ottawa, Canada; has by *Tracey Jean, dau of George Montegu [*sic*] Black III, of Toronto, with whom he contracted a common law marriage 1 Oct 1994 which is valid under Ontario law but would seem not to allow, the issue being ajudged in remainder to the peerages, and has by her:

(1) *Geoffrey Taylor Black; *b* 21 Sept 1996

1 *Sheelagh Margaret [The Hon Mrs Herd, 726 Galloway Crescent, London, Ontario, Canada N6J 2Y7]; *b* 14 July 1945; *m* 12 Aug 1967 *William Arthur Herd and has:

(1) *John David Fyfe Monckton; *b* 1981

(1) *Meghan Alexandra; *b* 10th April 1977

2 *(Fiona) Marilyn [The Hon Mrs Shank, 9770 SW Buckskin Terrace, Beaverton, OR 97005, USA]; *b* 21 Dec 1947; *m* 27 April 1974 *Robert Wilford Shank, BS, CPA, MSc Taxation, s of Wilford Eugene Shank, of Lexington, Mich. and has:

(1)*Kevin William; *b* 11 March 1976

(1)*Adriane Leigh; *b* 20 March 1978

3 *Rachel Jean [The Hon Mrs Rachel Monckton, 44A Bryon Ave East, London, Ontario N6C 1C5, Canada]; *b* 21 June 1957; *m* 22 Dec 1978 (*divorce* 1989, resumed maiden name) Ronald John Pressey, s of Thomas Pressey, of Sarnia, Ontario, and has:

(1) *Michael John; *b* 29 Jan 1980

(2) *Christopher Ellis; *b* 1981

Galway, other creations: There were two 17th-century Viscountcies of Galway, both Irish peerage dignities, and both held by the Bourke family, Earls of Clanricarde (*see* SLIGO, M). The first, created in 1628, was to the 4th Earl of Clanricarde, but with remainder to his father's heirs male in the event that his own failed. This actually occurred in 1657 with the death of the only son and heir of the 1st Viscount Galway of the 1628 creation, and even though the terms of the remainder meant that the Viscountcy could have been assumed by other living male issue of the 3rd Earl of Clanricarde, this did not happen, and the title was looked on as extinct, whereas the true position was that it became dormant.

The second 17th-century creation was in favour of the 4th son of the 7th Earl of Clanricarde, who (confusingly) could himself have assumed the 1628 Viscountcy. This later title had a short life, expiring with the death of its grantee fighting on behalf of JAMES II at the Battle of Aughrim in 1691 only four years after JAMES had conferred it on him.

By a quirk of history it was one of the Williamite officers in the same Battle of Aughrim who was the grantee of the next Galway peerage title. The Marquis de Ruvigny was a Huguenot who had settled in England after the Revocation of the Edict of Nantes. (His contemporary Jonathan Swift, however, reckoned he was without any religion at all.) Ruvigny was made Viscount Galway in 1692 and promoted Earl of Galway five years later. Both creations were in the Irish peerage, as was the Barony of Portarlington which was created simultaneously with the Viscountcy. The new Earl of Galway fought in Savoy and the Iberian Peninsula during the War of the Spanish Succession and was in command of the Allies when they were crushed at Almanza by the Duke of Berwick, nephew of the Great Duke of Marlborough (*qv*) and illegitimate son of JAMES II.

Lineage: THOMAS MONCKTON; Ld Manor of Cavil, Yorks, 1454; *m* Eleanor, est dau and coheir of William Mostyn, of Hunscot, Warwicks, and had issue:

1 ROBERT

2 John, ancestor of the MONCKTONs of Lincs and Warham Grange, Yorks

The er son,

ROBERT MONCKTON, of Cavil; *m* Janet, dau and heir of Robert Lucas, of Hornden, and had:

WILLIAM MONCKTON, of Cavil; living 1545; *m* Anne, dau of Sir Robert Aske by Elizabeth, dau of 9th Lord (Baron) Clifford (*see* DE CLIFFORD, B), and had:

1 CHRISTOPHER

2 Thomas; *m* Marjery St Quentin, of Courtead, and *d* 4 July 1584, having had issue

3 Robert

The est son,

CHRISTOPHER MONCKTON, of Cavil; MP Appleby; *m* Frances, dau of George Hussey, of Duffield, and had:

MARMADUKE MONCKTON, of Cavil; *m* 1571 Elizabeth, dau of Matthew Wentworth, of Bretton, Yorks, and had:

1 PHILIP (Sir)

2 John, of Garton and Burland, York; *m* Susanna, dau of William Berrie, of Lincoln, and *d* 1622, leaving:

(1) John Monckton, of Melton-super-Montem, Yorks; royalist Maj Civil War; *m* Mary, dau of Samuel Oldfield, of Oldfield, Yorks, and had issue:

1a Elizabeth; *m* 1666 John Fountaine, of Melton, and had issue:

1b Elizabeth; *m* Sir Richard Osbaldeston, of Hunmanby

2b Theodosia; *m* her cousin Robert Monckton (*see below*)

(2) Edmund (Sir); served Army; *m* Anne, dau of — Hammerton, of Hammerton, Yorks

(3) Marmaduke MONCKTON later BERRIE, of Hodroyd, Yorks; *m* Mary, dau and heir of Richard Berrie, MD, of Hodroyd Hall, and *dsp*

The er s,

Sir PHILIP MONCKTON, of Cavil; *b* 1574; ktd 1617; *m* Martha, dau and coheir of Francis Sutton, of Sutton, Cheshire, and *d* 1646, leaving:

Sir FRANCIS MONCKTON, ktd 1641; *m* Margaret, dau and coheir of Thomas Saville, of Northgatehead, Yorks, and had:

Sir PHILIP MONCKTON, of Cavil and Hodroyd; MP Scarborough, royalist Civil War, High Sheriff Yorks 1669; *m* 1658 Anne, est dau of Robert Eyre, of Highlow, Derbys, and had issue:

1 ROBERT

2 William; Lt RN; *k* 1706 Barcelona

1 Margaret

Sir PHILIP *d* Feb 1678; his est son,

ROBERT MONCKTON, of Cavil and Hodroyd; supported Glorious Revolution 1688, Commr Trade and Plantations, MP Pontefract and Aldborough; *m* Theodosia, yst dau and coheir of John Fountaine, of Melton-super-Montem (*see* above), and *d* 1722, leaving an only surv s:

JOHN MONCKTON, **1st Viscount Galway**, Co Galway, so *cr* 17 July 1727, as also BARON OF KILLARD, Co Clare (both I); *b* 1695; MP Clitheroe, Lancs, and Pontefract, Yorks, a Commr Revenue in Ireland May 1734, Surveyor-Gen Woods and Forests 1748 and 1749, Hon LLD Cambridge July 1749; *m* 1st Lady Elizabeth Manners (*d* 22 March 1730 aged 21), dau of 2nd Duke of Rutland (*qv*), and had:

1 WILLIAM, **2nd Viscount**

2 Robert; Lt-Gen, 2ic to Gen Wolfe at taking of Quebec, Govr and C-in-C New York, Govr Berwick and Holy Island

The **1st Viscount** *m* 2nd Nov 1734 Jane (*d* 1788), 4th dau of Henry Westenra, of Rathleagh, and *d* 26 May 1782, leaving issue:

3 John, of Fineshade Abbey, Northants; served Army; *b* 2 Aug 1739; *m* — Adams (*d* 20 Sept 1802) and *d* 3 Jan 1830, having had issue:

(1) Jane; *d* unm

(2) Eleanor; *m* 5th Earl of Harborough and *d* 1809

(3) Mary Anne; *m* Sir George Pigot, 3rd Bt (*qv*), and *d* 1833

4 Henry; Gen; *b* 13 July 1740; *k* War American Independence

5 Edward, of Somerford; *b* 3 Nov 1744; *m* 14 March 1776 Sophia (*d* 1 Jan 1834), illegitimate dau of Sir George Pigot, 1st Bt (*qv*), and *d* 21 July 1832, having had, with other issue:

(1) Henry, of Stretton Hall, Staffs; Gen; *b* 11 Dec 1780; *m* 23 Dec 1839 Anne (*d* 10 April 1878), only dau of John Groome Smythe, of Hilton, Salop, and *d* 29 June 1854, having had, with two other daus (*d* unm):

1a Francis, of Somerford Hall and Stretton Hall, Staffs, JP, DL; MP W Staffs 1871–85, High Sheriff 1895, Capt and Hon Maj QO Yeo Cav; *b* 7 March 1844; *m* 16 July 1889 Evelyn Mary (*d* 17 Nov 1941), dau of Algernon Charles Heber-Percy (*see* NORTHUMBERLAND, D), and *d* 30 Sept 1926, having had, with two other sons (*ka* WW I):

1b Reginald Francis Percy, TD, of Stretton Hall and Somerford Hall, DL 1927; V-Lt 1962–68, High Sheriff 1937, Maj (ret) Staffs Yeo (TA), Capt Montgomeryshire Yeo, WW I, Dep Mil Govr Jericho 1918–20, ADC and Priv Sec to HC Palestine 1920–25, WW II 1940–41 with PR Unit, memb House Laity Church Assembly, Ch Commr 1958–68, author: *Hunting Reflections* and *Key of Gold*; *b* 3 June 1896; *educ* Eton; *m* 15 April 1931 *Sheila, JP (1951) Staffs [Mrs Reginald Monckton, The White House, Stretton, Stafford], Jt MFH Goathland 1936–38, yst dau of Henry Gervas Stobart, of Thornton Hall, Thornton-le-Dale, Yorks, and *d* 30 Sept 1975, having had:

1c Reginald Peter; *b* 2 Feb 1932; *d* following an accident 9 Jan 1941

2c +Alan Stobart, DL (Staffs 1988) [Alan Monckton Esq DL, Stretton Hall, Stafford ST19 9LQ]; FLAS 1965, FRICS, High Sheriff Staffs 1975, Lt Queens' Bays, and Staff Yeo; *b* 5 Sept 1934; *educ* Eton; *m* 30 Sept 1961 *Joanna Mary, er dau of George Carlos Bird, of Appleton, Abingdon, Berks, and has had issue:

1d +Piers Alastair Carlos; *b* 23 Oct 1962; *m* 1988 *Georgiana Margaret Elizabeth, only dau of Julian Michael Byng (*see* STRAFFORD, E), and has had issue:

1e +Oliver George Carlos; *b* 1993

1e Isobel Mary Elizabeth; *b* 1989; *d* 1991

2e *Emily Louise; *b* 1991

2d Simon Francis Carlos; *b* 13 Nov 1967; *d* 12 April 1969

3d +Toby Philip Carlos; *b* 26 Feb 1970

1d *Davina Claire [Mrs Gerard Downes, Herrington House, Whiteparish, Wilts SP5 2RD]; *b* 21 May 1964; *m* 1987 *Gerard John Mytton Downes and has issue:

1e *Rupert John Mytton; *b* 1989

2e *Hugh William Charles; *b* 1991

2d *Sophie Louise; *b* 13 Nov 1967

1c *Daphne Alice Cavil [Mrs Nigel Estlick, Kent House, Amesbury, Wilts SP4 7AP]; *b* 28 June 1937; *m* 4 Jan 1958 *Col Nigel John Lincoln Estlick, RM, and has issue:

1d *Robin Monckton; *b* 25 Aug 1968

1d *Caroline Rosemary [Mrs Lajos Kalman, 5617 W 158th Terrace, Overland Park, KS 66223, USA]; *b* 22 Jan 1962; *m* 19– *Lajos Kalman

2d *Marian Heather [Mrs Rupert Boswall, 145 Salcott Rd, London SW11 6DG]; *b* 30 Nov 1965; *m* 19– *Rupert Boswall and has:

1e *Phoebe Delano Alice; *b* 1995

2c Rosemary Sheila; *b* 6 Nov 1945; *d* 11 June 1946

1b Evelyn Frances; *d* unm 5 March 1958

2b Constance Frances; *m* 1st 22 April 1915 Cyril Gwyer, Duke of Lancaster's Own Yeo and Gren Gds, 2nd s of Charles Gwyer, JP, of Eywood, Hereford, and had issue. He was *ka* 27 Aug 1918. She *m* 2nd 17 Aug 1920 Lt-Col Charles Fraser Kennedy, KOSB, est son of Col John Kennedy, of Brookside, Sandbach, Cheshire, and *d* 16 April 1968, leaving further issue. He *d* 27 July 1954

3b Violet Maude Frances, JP WR Yorks 1936–50; *m* 10 Feb 1925 Sidney James Farrer, JP, (*dsp* 26 Dec 1964) of Newby Cote, Clapham Yorks and *d* 1985

2a Arthur, of Normanston Hall, Oulton, Lowestoft, JP Worcs; *b* 20 July 1845; *m* 28 April 1896 Lady Gertrude Pleydell Bouverie (*d* 11 Jan 1940), dau of 4th Earl of Radnor (*qv*), and *d* 2 May 1917, having had, with another s (*ka* 1919):

1b Marmaduke; jnlst; *b* 29 July 1899; *educ* Eton and Balliol Coll Oxford; *d* 19–

1b Mary; 2nd Offr WRNS WW II; *b* 24 March 1897; *m* 10 Sept 1959 *Geoffrey Palgrave-Barker, er surv son of Rev Canon Rowland Vectis Barker, by Elizabeth, dau of Sir Inglis Palgrave, of Henstead Hall, Suffolk, and *d* 19–

2b Nora; *b* 7 July 1901; *d* 19–

1a Alice; *m* 30 April 1879, Rt Rev Watkin Herbert Williams, Bp Bangor 1899–1925, 2nd son of Sir Hugh Williams, 3rd Bt, of Bodelwyddan (*see* 1970 edn), and *d* 15 Jan 1937. He *dsp* 19 Nov 1944

(2) Philip; Judge Gorruckpoore, E Indies; *b* 3 March 1787; *m* 1811 Henrietta, dau of Michael Carter, and *d* 6 Jan 1820, leaving issue:

1a Edward Henry Cradock, of Fineshade Abbey; HEICS Bengal; *b* 12 Sept 1812; *m* 1st 1835 Caroline Rosa (*d* Sept 1838), yst dau of Charles Woodcock, and had issue:

1b Sophia Rosa; *m* 24 Jan 1872 Rev Cornelius Thompson and *d* 13 June 1910, leaving issue. He *d* 1884

1a (cont.) Edward Monckton *m* 2nd 7 Oct 1839 Maria Catherine (*d* 7 Oct 1896), yst dau of H W Tydd, and *d* 14 July 1878, having by her had issue:

1b Edward Philip, of Fineshade Abbey and Laundimer House, Oundle, Northants, JP Northants, Rutland and liberty of Peterborough; CC King's Cliffe Div Northants, High Sheriff Rutland 1883, barrister, Chm QS Peterborough, Recorder Northampton, Maj and Hon Lt-Col 3rd Bn Northampton Regt, MP N Northants 1895–1900, FSA; *b* 18 July 1840; *educ* Trin Coll Cambridge (MA); *m* 25 Sept 1866 Christabel (*d* 23 May 1899), 2nd dau of Rev C D Francis, Vicar Tysoe, Warwicks, and *d* 17 April 1916, leaving, with other issue:

1c George Edward; *b* 20 Nov 1868; *educ* Trin Coll Cambridge (MA) and Göttingen U (MA); *m* 21 April 1896 Marguerite Edith Evelyn Eleanor, yr dau of James Marigold, of Park House, Edgbaston, and *d* 27 Nov 1936, leaving issue:

1d Marguerite Ruby Marigold; *d* unm 1 Nov 1947

2d Doris Violet

3d *Cavil Grace Mary; *b* 1903; *m* 1925 Sydney Lipscomb Elborne MBE, (*d* 1986), JP, barrister, of Water Newton, Peterborough, Northants, and has:

1e *Robert Edward Monckton [Robert Elborne Esq, Seaton Old Rectory, Oakham, Leics LE15 9HU; 17 Bettridge Rd, London SW6 3QH]; *b* 1926; *educ* Eton and Trin Coll Cambridge, Lt Life Gds and Inns of Court Regt (TA), barrister Inner Temple 1950, slr 1958; *m* 1953 *Vivienne, yr dau of Lt-Gen Sir Ernest Wood, KBE, CB, CIE, MC, and has:

1f *Mark Edward Monckton [Mark Elborne Esq, Exeter House, Barrowden, Leics LE15 8ENB]; *b* 1958; *educ* Eton and Exeter U; *m* 1982 *Lucinda Alison, stepdau of Michael James Bower, of London SW18, and has:

1g *Simon Henry Monckton; *b* 1985

2g *Philip Timothy William; *b* 1986

3g *Timothy Oliver Rupert; *b* 1988

4g *Freddie George Monckton; *b* 1992

1g *Amelia Lucy Caroline; *b* 1983

2f *William Henry Alexander; *b* 1966; *educ* Eton

1f *Charlotte Julia Mary; *b* 1956; *m* 1978 *(Anthony) Julian Lyell Beare and has issue:

1g *James Oliver Lyell; *b* 1984

1g *Rosanna Sarah Cecil; *b* 1988

1e *Margaret; *b* 1934; *m* 1st 1955 (*divorce* 1966) Maj John Richard Montgomery Laird (*d* 19–), RA, and has issue:

1f *Duncan John Alexander; *b* 1958

1f *Caroline Margaret Ann; *b* 1956

1e (cont.) Mrs Margaret Laird *m* 2nd 1967 Edward William Ingram (*d* 1991) and has further issue:

2f *Claire Constance Cavil; *b* 1968

2c Philip Tunnard; Indian Police, Lt 3rd Bn Northants Regt; *b* 26 July 1870; *m* 16 March 1901 Agnes Carr (*d* 15 July 1956), dau of Maxwell Smith, and *d* 8 June 1928, leaving:

1d +Philip Anthony; *b* 1913; P/O RAFVR; *educ* Sherborne; *m* 19– *Ruth, only dau of Hugh Campbell McDonald, CMG, Provincial Commn Nyasaland, and has had issue:

1e Guy Hugh; *b* 24 Oct 1947

2d Guy Leonard; *b* 1915; *d* 8 Feb 1964

1d *Sybil Carr [Mrs George Lardner-Clarke, Parkholm, 97 Bainton Road, Oxford]; *b* Jan 1902; *m* 1st April 1927 (*divorce* 1949) Ronald Charles Keith-Smith; *m* 2nd 20 July 1955 Capt George Vincent Lardner-Clarke, King's Regt, s of Col J de W Lardner-Clarke, CBE. He *d* 15 July 1966

2d *Mary Philippa [Mrs Walter Smail, Calle Neptuno 14 Genova, Palma de Mallorca, Spain]; *b* 22 Sept 1912; *m* 1st July 1934 (*divorce* 1947) William Michael Gambier Sandwith, Supt Police Kenya, son of Rev William Fitzgerald Gambier Sandwith, of Littlestone, Kent; *m* 2nd Jan 1948 *Walter John Smail and by her 1st husb has issue:

1e *Caroline Ann; *b* 16 Aug 1938; *m* 5 Nov 1960 *Alan Pickering and has issue:

1f *Robert Alan; *b* 5 Feb 1964

1f *Tania Mary; *b* 28 March 1962

3c Noel; DC Br E African CS, Capt 3rd Bn Yorks Regt, Boer War 1899–1902; *b* 24 Dec 1871; *m* 1st 1895 Flora (*d* 19 May 1918), dau of Rev George Townsend Warner, of Newton Abbot; *m* 2nd 17 Aug 1920

Nora (*d* 24 Jan 1963), 3rd dau of Charles Parbury, of Knightsbridge, and *d* 19 Jan 1927, leaving by his 1st w:

1d Edward Philip Simon; Lt IA; *b* 28 Oct 1899; *d* 8 Sept 1936

1d Cecily Flora Noel; *b* 24 Sept 1896; *m* 23 Dec 1922 (*divorce* 1940, took name MONCKTON-HOW 1944) Cdr George Evelyn Paget How, RN, FSA Scot (*d* 13 Sept 1953), yst son of Maj John Herbert How, of Headley, Surrey and *d* 25 April 1950, leaving:

1e *Rachel [Mrs Peter Hutchinson, 21 rue de la Petite Chapelle, 85120 La Chapelle-aux-Lys, France]; author and jnlst; *b* 28 Aug 1928; *m* 9 Nov 1961 *Peter Hutchinson, MB, BS

4c Charles; *b* 26 Feb 1873; *m* 1 Feb 1905 Lilian Sewallis (*d* 17 Jan 1949), yst dau of R S Wayne, of Corwen, Clwyd, and *d* 8 March 1932

5c Christopher Cecil; *b* 8 March 1877; *m* 15 July 1913 Mabel Cordelia, dau of Rev C E Shirley Woolmer, Vicar of Sidcup, Kent, and *d* 8 March 1932

6c Thomas Anthony, OBE (1918); Cdr RNVR, Lt-Col RAF; *b* 22 Oct 1885; *educ* Trin Coll Cambridge (MA); *d* 16 Nov 1951

1c Frances Leonora; *b* 16 March 1882; *m* 15 July 1908 Walter John Marsham and *d* 16 Nov 1956, leaving issue (*see* ROMNEY, E)

2b Claud; CE; *b* 26 July 1844; *m* 1881 Eena Helena Theresa, dau of E A Hickey, and *dsp* 11 Oct 1897

3b William Parry, of Stone Court, Glos, JP; Lt-Col Hampshire Regt; *b* 7 April 1846; *educ* Gonville and Caius Coll Cambridge (BA); *m* 3 Sept 1891 Florence Georgina Sybella (*d* 15 April 1927), 2nd dau of James Sawrey-Cookson, JP, of Neasham Hall, Yorks, and Broughton Tower, Lancs, and *d* 17 Dec 1914, leaving issue:

1c Ivor Parry; Lt RASC; *b* 7 Sept 1892; *educ* Sherborne; *m* 1921 Olive Gertrude, dau of William Bassett, and *d* 1978 leaving issue:

1d +Dennahouse Parry [Maj Dennahouse Monckton, 10 Daniells Walk, Lymington, Hants SO41 3PN]; *b* 14 April 1930; *educ* Sherborne and RMA Sandhurst; Maj RCT, RWAFF and RASC; *m* 1966 *Mary Elizabeth Doreen, yst dau of James Carson, of Dromore, Co Down

1c Iris Florence Parry; *b* 5 July 1896; *d* unm 3 July 1966

4b Hugh; Governor's Commr, Stipendiary Magistrate Dist of Ba, Fiji (ret 1911); *b* 7 Aug 1847; *educ* Caius Coll Cambridge (MA); *m* 20 June 1878 Isabel Jane Gillis (*d* 22 March 1909), dau of John Chapman, and *d* 29 May 1925, having had issue:

1c Hugh Claud; Adviser Native Affrs, Fiji CS, MLC Fiji; *b* 20 Feb 1881; *educ* Bradfield; *m* 1st 1910 Emily Sophia Ray (*d* 15 Dec 1945), dau of E C Gibson; *m* 2nd 1946 Helen Atherton (*d* 1974), dau of P A Morris, of Sydney, NSW, and *d* 27 June 1970, having by his 1st w had:

1d +Basil Robert [Basil Monckton Esq, 11 Meadowview Drive, Palm Meadows, Gold Coast, Qld 4211, Australia]; *b* 24 July 1917; *educ* NZ U (BE), ME Adelaide (1964), BE (Hons) NZ (1939), MIC, MIEAust, Grad MNZIF, AMIEAust, civ engr Weapons Research Establishment, Elizabeth, S Australia, town engr Suva, Fiji, Dir Nasa Network Support Facility Overseas Property Bureau Dept For Affrs Canberra; *m* 1943 *Audrey Constance, dau of Arthur Charles Tribe, of Auckland, NZ, and has issue:

1e +Robert Parry [Dr Robert Monckton, Somerville, 38 Ashbarto Ave, Turramurra, Sydney NSW 2074, Australia]; *b* 17 Dec 1948; *educ* Flinders U Adelaide (BSc 1969) and Australian Nat U (BSc, Hons PhD 1970); sr research scientist Regnl Veterinary Laboratory Bendigo, Virus Research Manager Cynamid Websters; *m* 1975 *Joy Mary, dau of Frank Whitelam, of Leicester, and has issue:

1f +Christopher Parry; *b* 1977

2f +Timothy Alan; *b* 1980

2e +David Christopher [David Monckton Esq, 59 Longueval St, Moorooka, Qld 4105, Australia]; *b* 21 Sept 1951; *educ* Canberra Coll of Advanced Educn (BApplied Science) and Australian Nat U (BEc); *m* 1986 *Katrina Angela, dau of Mario Basile, of Brisbane, and has:

1f *Georgina Elizabeth; *b* 1987

2f *Harriette Susan; *b* 1994

3e +Peter Charles [Peter Monckton Esq, 77 Wood St, Manly, NSW 2095, Australia]; *b* 17 May 1955; *educ* Canberra Coll of Advanced Educn and Sydney U (BArch Hons 1982); AMIA; *m* 1983 *Diana (BA Des), dau of George Marsh, of Sydney

2d Hugh Noel Campbell, MICE, MNZIE, MRCI, MACI, ANZIA, consulting engr architect, BE (NZ) 1948; *b* 13 March 1923; *educ* NZ; *m* 31 Oct 1950 *Elizabeth Rubi Young [Mrs Hugh Monckton, 46 Woods Ave, Matua, Tauranga, NZ], dau of Arthur Boswell, of Takapuna, NZ, and *d* 1991, leaving issue:

1e +Hugh Geoffrey; *b* 15 Feb 1954; BE, BArch, ANZIA; *m* 1977 *Helen Eileen, dau of Leslie Dassler, and has issue:

1f *Catherine Jane; *b* 1990

2e +Roger John; *b* 7 July 1958; BE

1e *Elizabeth Anne; *b* 5 Jan 1953; BA

1d *Sybil Dorothy [Mrs Frederick Gearing, Unit 11/252 Mainroad, Regents Landing, Maroochydore, Qld 4558, Australia]; *b* 15 Feb 1916; *m* 1st 28 Dec 1940 P/O RAF Ernest Herbert Canard, RAF (*k* in a flying accident at George, S Africa, 4 Nov 1942); *m* 2nd 20 March 1957 (*divorce* 1962 resumed 1st husb's name by deed poll, 1964) Nils Ane Alexander Hilton Gyllenberg; *m* 3rd 1966 Frederick Alma Gearing (*d* 1991) and by her 1st husb has:

1e *Hugh Jason Paul [Hugh Canard Esq, Tata Beach, RD1 Takaka, New Zealand]; *b* 21 Sept 1942; *educ* Auckland and Canterbury Us; *m* 1968 *Elizabeth Frances, dau of G Wildridge, of Edinburgh, and has issue:

1f *Jamie Duncan; *b* 1971

2f *Dougal Stephen; *b* 1972; Dip Mus 1995

2c Eric Parry; *b* 1883; *m* 8 June 1917 Minna (*d* 1979), dau of H Erhard, of Sydney, NSW, and *d* 29 Aug 1953, leaving issue:

1d +James Hugh [James Monckton Esq, 121 Jenkins Rd, Carlingsford, NSW 2118, Australia]; *b* 29 Oct 1921; *m* 1981 *Edith Joan, dau of Albert Ernest Wearne, of Bingara, NSW

1d *Joan Harriette [Mrs Jack Stackpool, 14 Jackson Street, Balgowlah, Sydney, NSW, Australia]; *b* 17 May 1918; *m* 1940 Jack Anderson Stackpool (*d* 1971) and has issue:

1e *Michael John [Michael Stackpool Esq, 7 Oyama Ave, Manly, NSW 2095, Australia]; *b* 1946; ACIV, QRV, ARIE; *m* 1980 *Lyndall Rosemary, dau of Ian George Hudson, of Dural, and has issue:

1f *Miles Ian; *b* 1983

2f *Hugh Jack Monckton; *b* 1987

1f *Isobel Claire; *b* 1985

1e *Susan Jane [Mrs Susan Bowden, 73 Wydora Ave, Harbord, NSW 2096, Australia]; *b* 1947; *m* 1969 (*divorce* 1985) Stephen Bowden, and has issue:

1f *Peter Karl; *b* 1974; *m* 1993 *Candice Pippa Lawson

2f *Timothy Robert; *b* 1977

1c Gladys Viti; *b* 9 July 1888; *d* unm 1939

2b Harriet Leonora; *m* 10 Sept 1873 Rev H E Gedge, MA, of Wells, Somerset, and *d* 1933. He *d* 19 March 1913

3b Emily Jane; *m* 12 Dec 1877 Capt George A Harrisson, Cameron Highrs, and *d* 1917, having had issue. He *d* 1899

2a George Pakenham; *b* 5 Oct 1816; *m* 7 Dec 1843 Emily Mary (*d* 18 Dec 1911), dau of Sir Vansittart Stonhouse, 14th Bt (*qv*), and *dsp* 12 April 1894

3a John Edmonstone, Maj 2nd Madras Light Cav; *b* 1817; *m* 1st 13 Dec 1849 Julia (*d* 4 Aug 1851), dau of Col Henry Thornton, CB; *m* 2nd 27 Oct 1869 Lucy Harriet (*d* 21 May 1919), dau of Lt-Col John Smith, of Ellingham, and *d* 2 Aug 1891 leaving by his 1st w:

1b John Henry, of Meriden, Coventry; JP Warwicks; *b* 26 Sept 1850; Col 3rd Bn N Staffordshire Regt; *m* 9 Nov 1911 Flora Charlotte (*d* Mar 1941), dau of Lt-Col Arthur Reynell-Pack, CB, of Avisford, Sussex, and gdau of Sir Denis Pack, KBC, and *d* 17 Nov 1919

1a Charlotte Sophia; *m* 24 Feb 1842 Gen George Whichcote and *d* Nov 1880. He *d* 26 Aug 1891

2a Eliza Leonora; *m* 23 April 1844 Rev William George Leigh Wasey, Vicar Morvill, Salop, and *d* 29 July 1877. He *d* 9 June 1877

(3) William; *b* 19 April 1796; *m* 29 March 1825 Ellen (*d* 14 July 1883 aged 73), 4th dau of Col Goddard Richards, HEICS, and *d* 23 Jan 1874, having had, with other issue:

1a Henry; BCS; *b* 29 March 1827; *m* 3 March 1857 Elizabeth Charlotte (*d* 8 March 1870), 2nd dau of Rev Edward Judge, and *d* 13 Aug 1867, having had, with other issue:

1b Henry Grant; Cdr RN; *b* 28 Jan 1860; *m* 1890 Maud Lilian (*d* 13 Aug 1895), dau of Rev John W Hallowell, and *d* 26 Jan 1917, having had, with a s (*ka* 1915):

1c Frederick Hardy; MICE, Maj RE WW I, WW II; *b* 21 July 1892; *educ* Monkton Combe Sch and Downing Coll Cambridge (BA 1914); *m* 13 Sept 1941 Frances (*d* 14 Jan 1967), dau of Paul Ryan, of Dublin, and *d* 1981, leaving issue:

1d +Henry William [Henry Monckton Esq, 19 Queens Gate Drive, Birstall, Leics]; *b* 12 June 1945; *educ* Bedford Sch and Downing Coll Cambridge (BA 1967); MICE; *m* 1976 *Angela Mary, dau of Thomas Spencer, of Leek, Staffs

2d +Michael Frederick [Michael Monckton Esq, 30 Sedgebrook, Liden, Swindon, Wilts SN3 6EY]; *b* 11 April 1947; *educ* Bedford Sch and Manchester U (BSc); MICE

1c Maud Lilian Seaflower

2b William Gawler (Rev); *b* June 1866; *educ* Trin Coll Cambridge (MA); *m* 21 July 1902 Sophie Mary (*m* 2nd 1937 Robert John Millen, (*d* 1949) and *d* 8 Dec 1957), dau of Henry Oldham, of Napier, NZ, and *d* 8 Jan 1935, leaving issue:

1c Violet Arundell; *b* 7 July 1905; *m* 21 Sept 1933 Paul Jay, JP, of Coleshill House, Berkhamsted, Herts, s of William Clouston Jay, of Cambridge, NZ, and had issue:

1d *Christopher Laurence Monckton [Christopher Jay Esq, 34 Greenclose Road, Ilfracombe, Devon]; *b* 30 July 1942; *m* 20 Nov 1968 *Mary Margaret, dau of Ronald Holbrook, of Tring, Herts, and has issue

1d *Rosalind Mary Monckton; *b* 12 July 1934; *m* 1st 1955 (*divorce* 1963) Anthony David MAYES later MAYES-MONCKTON, (deed poll) s of Maj Guy Noel Mayes, Roy Suffolk Regt; *m* 2nd March 1965 Ronald William Inkpen

1b Alice Georgina; *d* unm 8 April 1943

2b Annie Blanche; *m* Thomas George Lloyd and *d* 20 April 1936

2a Frederick Edward, of Clevedon, Somerset; *b* 21 Aug 1829; *m* 24 Nov 1853 Winifred Penn (*d* 2 July 1927), dau of Capt Ray Boucaut, EICNS, and *d* 1881, leaving issue:

1b James Frederick (Rev); Vicar Sinnington, Yorks; *b* 15 Oct 1858; *m* 10 April 1885 Alice Australia (*d* 3 Oct 1931), dau of Neil Harper, and *d* 25 Oct 1946, leaving:

1c (James Frederick) Edward; Capt Northamptonshire Regt; *b* 1892; *educ* Gonville and Caius Coll Cambridge (MA 1927); *m* 20 Feb 1917 Dorothy Verrinder (*d* 1975), dau of George Wilson, of Upper Sydenham, and *d* 1985, having had issue:

1d Francis Edward; RAAF WW II; *b* 28 Feb 1921; *ka* 1942

1d *Georgiana Elspeth [Mrs Godfrey Thrift, Penn House, The Way, Reigate, Surrey RH2 0LB]; *b* 16 Nov 1917; *m* 1st 1938 Capt Peter Wilkinson Swift, Green Howards (*ka* 1942), and has:

1e *Patricia Elspeth; ARCM; *b* 23 Aug 1940; *m* 11 Aug 1962 *Robin William Langford Gritton, ARCM, ARCO, son of Eric William Gritton, FRCO, ARCM, of Reigate, Surrey, and has:

1f *Peter William; *b* 7 Dec 1963; *educ* Clare Coll Cambridge (MA); LRAM

1f *Susan Mary; *b* 31 Aug 1965; *educ* St Hilda's Coll Oxford (MA)
2f *Lucy Belinda; *b* 1970
1d (cont.) Mrs Peter Swift *m* 2nd 27 Aug 1946 *Godfrey Walter Thrift, Green Howards, and has further issue:
1e *Peter Walter Monckton; *b* 4 Feb 1949; Lloyd's underwriter
2d *Patricia Penn [Mrs Richard Ellis, Sinnington, 10 Cynthia Crescent, Armidale, NSW 2350, Australia]; *b* 29 Jan 1920; *m* 1942 *Lt Richard James Ellis, BE, RAN , and has issue:
1e *Peter Francis Monckton; *b* 11 Dec 1947; BSc Foresty, Dip Ed; *m* 1978 *Rosalie Turner and has issue:
1f *Martyn Giles; *b* 1979
1f *Jacinta Frances; *b* 1982
2e *Michael Richard Penn; *b* 26 May 1952; BSc Foresty, Dip Ed; *m* 1982 *Elizabeth Giles and has issue:
1f *Lucy; *b* 1982
2f *Emma; *b* 1984
3e *Timothy Willson; *b* 2 July 1961; *m* 1984 *Rebbeca Newland and has issue:
1f *Michael; *b* 1985
1e *Susan Patricia; *b* 20 Oct 1943; *m* 5 Sept 1970 *Geoffrey John Lawson, school master, and has issue:
1f *Patrick Geoffrey; *b* 1980
1f *Josephine Emily; *b* 1972
2e *Jennifer Ann [Mrs Richard Donaldson, Whitewood, Fosters Rd, Armidale, NSW 2350, Australia]; *b* 26 Feb 1949; jr sch matron; *m* 1978 *Richard Roderick Donaldson, farmer, and has issue:
1f *Warwick John; *b* 1979
2f *Christopher Richard; *b* 1980
1f *Rachel Patricia; *b* 1982
3e *Winifred Jill; *b* 21 Feb 1958; *m* 1979 *Laimonis Kavalieris, MA, PhD (Nat U of Canberra, ACT), of Dunedin, NZ
3d *Jean Mary [Mrs Edward18A Morella Avenue, Clifton Gardens, Mosman, NSW, Australia]; *b* 12 Sept 1927; *m* 1948 *Edward Richard Taylor, AM, BE, FIE Aust, and has issue:
1e *James Edward Monckton [James Taylor Esq, 5 Robert Ave, N Manly, NSW, Australia]; *b* 4 Sept 1950; BE, MIE Aust; *m* 1973 *Anne Alison, dau of Prof D G Stalley, of Manly, NSW, and has:
1f *Daniel James Monckton; *b* 1977
2f *Peter Edward Richard; *b* 1982
1f *Phillipa Alice; *b* 1980
2e *Richard; *b* 4 July 1955; *m* 1982 *Yasmin, dau of Steven Nagy
3e *David Matthew; *b* 4 July 1955
1e *Catherine Elizabeth Monckton; *b* 15 March 1949; *m* 19– (*divorce* 1983) Donald Ross Kennedy, BSc, and has issue:
1f *Rebecca Jean; *b* 1974
2f *Catriona Anne; *b* 1977
2c Gordon Cecil; Nigerian Admin Service, Lt-Col Northants Regt, Sr Control Offr, Control Commn for Germany and Br Resident in Germany 1947–51; *b* 1902; *educ* St Catharine's Coll Cambridge (MA 1932); *m* 1st 30 Aug 1928 (*divorce* 1948) Mary Catherine, est dau of Hugh MacCaffrey, of Clones, Co Monaghan, and had issue:
1d *Elizabeth Ann [Mrs Martin Rosoff, 15 Wellesley Ave, Yonkers, NY 10705, USA]; *b* 22 Dec 1930; *m* 1962 *Martin Rosoff, PhD, and has issue:
1e *David; *b* 1965
2c (cont.) Gordon Monckton *m* 2nd 1948 *Thérèse [Mrs Gordon Monckton, 47 Old Wokingham Rd, Crowthorne, Berks RG11 6SS], dau of Stephen Minarovic, of Austria, and *d* 1989, leaving:
1d +James Edward [James Monckton Esq, Poynings, Cookoo Corner, Urchfont, Wilts SN10 4RA]; *b* 1951; *educ* Trin Coll of Music (LTCL); *m* 28 Aug 1971 *Jacqueline Ann, only dau of Norman Conner, of Crowthorne, Berks, and has issue:
1e +Timothy Norman; *b* 1975
2e +Matthew Gordon; *b* 1976
1e *Jenna Florence Theresia; *b* 1979
2d *Evelyn Stephanie [Mrs David Penman, 14 Cornwall Rd, Dorchester, Dorset DT1 1RT]; *b* 1948; *m* 28 Jan 1972 *David John Penman, only son of Dennis James Penman, of Sutton, Surrey, and has:
1e *Philip David Spencer; *b* 1977
1e *Emma Charlotte; *b* 1980
3d *Valentine Penn [Mrs Robert Leach, PO Box 916, Wahroonga Hornsby, NSW 2076, Australia]; *b* 1950; *m* 1976 *Robert James Leach and has:
1e *Benjamin James; *b* 1983
1e *Emily Alice Penn; *b* 1986
4d *Helen Marina [Mrs Peter Engeler, 510 Bulga Rd, Wallaby Joe Flat, via Wingham, NSW 2429, Australia]; *b* 4 Nov 1953; *m* 1985 *Peter Engeler, and has issue:
1e *Rebekah Freda; *b* 1986
2e *Sarah Thérèse; *b* 1987
1c Winifred Penn; *b* 1891; *m* 5 Jan 1926 Charles Henry Richardson, of Clifton, Bristol (*d* 9 July 1931 following a cycle accident) and *d* 6 Jan 1971
2c Alice Elizabeth; *b* 1895; *educ* London U (BA 1922); *m* 1 Feb 1927 Thomas Evans Ryves, BM, BCh, Oxford, MRCS, er son of Mr Justice Ryves, of Allahabad, and had:
1d *Thomas Bruno; *b* 30 Sept 1930; *educ* Trin Coll Oxford (BA) and London U (BA); *m* 26 June 1954 *Ann Catherine, dau of J Bertram Roberts, of Kingston Hill, Surrey, and has:
1e *Alun Thomas McKellar; *b* 1 June 1958
2e *William Johnathan; *b* 21 Dec 1964
3e *David Bruno; *b* 26 Nov 1968
1e *Mary Ann McKellar; *b* 1 Aug 1962
1d *Margaret Elizabeth; *b* 30 Sept 1930; *educ* Newnham Coll Cambridge (MA)
2b Walter Hilary; *b* 16 March 1861; *m* 1888 Jean Bruce (*d* 1939), dau of Alexander Bruce Webster, of Aberdeen, and *d* 7 March 1924, leaving:
1c Hilary James; *b* 26 Sept 1889; *m* 30 Aug 1915 Ruby Rose (*d* 1982), dau of John Crisp, of Cooma, and *d* 1969, leaving:
1d +Walter John Bruce [Walter Monckton Esq, 1 Cromwell St, Cooma, NSW 2630, Australia]; *b* 19 Jan 1918; *m* 1st 15 Aug 1942 Betty Allen (*d* 1974), dau of C W Keele; *m* 2nd 1975 *Susan Jane, dau of Ian Antony Litchfield, of Cooma, NSW, and by his 1st w has:
1e *Robine Anne; *b* 27 Jan 1944; *m* 1969 *Martin Pitt, of Rose Bay, and has issue:
1f *Angus Andrew; *b* 1972
1f *Lucinda; *b* 1971
2e *Rosemary Joan; *b* 9 Jan 1946; *m* 1971 Geoffrey William James Stevens (*d* 1984), of Woollahra, NSW, and has issue:
1f *James Walter Monckton; *b* 1979
1f *Alexandra; *b* 1975
2f *Sophie; *b* 1977
3f *Jessica Clare; *b* 1981
3e *Frances Anne; *b* 1951; *m* 1980 *Nigel Geoffrey Howard Pilcher, of Edgecliff, NSW, and has issue:
1f *James Howard Monckton; *b* 1983
2f *Henry Nigel Monckton; *b* 1985
1d *Jean Winifred; *b* 30 May 1916; *m* 1940 Maj Charles Cuthbert Wolfe, Roy Australian Engrs (*d* 6 March 1969), and has had issue:
1e *Edwin Charles Monckton; *b* 27 Sept 1941; *m* 15 Feb 1968 *Sally Elaine dau of W G Cowley, of Armindale, NSW, and has issue:
1f *Matthew Charles; *b* 1974
2f *Benjamin James; *b* 1976
3f *Samuel Luke; *b* 1978
1f *Sarah Jane; *b* 9 June 1972
2e *Peter Hilary; *b* 20 June 1943
3e Stephen John; *b* 1 Aug 1950; *d* 27 Nov 1971 following an accident
1e *Elizabeth Jean; *b* 3 April 1955; *m* 1978 *Charles Ian Anthony Litchfield, of Cooma, and has:
1f *Stephen Charles Owen; *b* 1979
1f *Eleanor Jean; *b* 1981
2c Basil Bruce; *b* 16 Jan 1894; *m* 1st 11 June 1929 (*divorce* 1949) Edna, dau of E N R McMillan, of Rockdale, NSW; *m* 2nd 1949 *Violet Lillian [Mrs Basil Monckton, 8/822 Military Rd, Mosman, NSW, Australia], dau of P S O'Donnell, of Mosman, and *d* 1976, leaving by his 1st w:
1d *Margaret Heather [Mrs Keith Payne, 18C Kirkoswald Ave, Mosman, NSW, Australia]; *b* 2 Oct 1930; *m* 1952 *Keith Willoughby Payne, architect, and has issue:
1e *Geoffrey William; *b* 26 Sept 1953; *m* 1990 *Margaret Mary, dau of Geoffrey Hough, of Blakehurst, NSW
2e *David Bruce; *b* 15 Aug 1956; *m* 1987 *Clare Patricia, dau of Prof J E Morton, of Auckland, NZ, and has issue:
1f *Matthew John; *b* 1989
2f *Samuel David; *b* 1991
1e *Robyn Louise [Mrs Peter Smith, 19 Nash's Rd, Rutherglen, VIC, Australia]; *b* 27 May 1959; *m* 1984 *Peter Randolph Smith, and has issue:
1f *Timothy Ian; *b* 1990
1f *Karen Rose; *b* 1988
2f *Sheila Margaret; *b* 1993
3b Cecil Charles Fisk, MIEE, Fiji CS; *b* 8 May 1867; *m* 27 Nov 1902 Dorothy Tatham (*d* 1976), yr dau of Walter Tatham Hughes, ISO, of Bath, and *d* 6 May 1954, having had issue:
1c +Edward Walter, OBE (1944) [Lt-Cdr Edward Monckton OBE RN, 42 Ottoline Drive, Troon, Ayrshire, Scotland]; WW II; *b* 25 Sept 1903; *m* 8 Oct 1932 *Margaret Frances, yr dau of Brig-Gen Frederick Walter Radcliffe, CMG, CIE, CBE, of Weymouth, and has:
1d +Christopher John Edward [Christopher Monckton Esq, Craigower Lodge, Newtonmore, Inverness-shire, Scotland]; Midshipman RN; *b* 21 April 1942; *educ* Gordonstoun and RNC Dartmouth; *m* 1st 1965 (*divorce* 1976) Judith Benson, of Bournemouth, and has:
1e +Oliver Edward Walter; *b* 1974
1e *Emily Joanna; *b* 1966
2e *Heather Mary; *b* 1970
1d (cont.) Christopher Monckton *m* 2nd 19– *Anne Ide, of Guildford, Surrey, and has further issue:
2e +Lawrence Christopher Darwin; *b* 1977
2d +Hugh Francis [Hugh Monckton Esq, Tillytoghills House, Fettercairn, Kincardineshire, Scotland]; *b* 24 Sept 1948; *educ* Gordonstoun; Master Mariner, MNI, MRIN; *m* 19– *Nila Elizabeth, dau of John Snazell, of Taunton, Somerset, and has issue:
1e *Helen Margaret; *b* 1985
2c John Cecil; *b* 9 April 1908; *d* 3 Dec 1912
3c +Charles Tatham [Charles Monckton Esq, Dorville, Route Orange, St Brelade, Jersey, CI]; *b* 28 March 1913; WW II as Capt 4th/7th Dragoon Gds (wounded); *m* 27 March 1946 *Ruth Elizabeth, only dau of Richard Denis Blandy, CMG, OBE, of Adelaide, and has:

1d +Timothy James [Timothy Monckton Esq, Flat 7, John Forbes House, Pittville Crescent, Cheltenham, Glos GL52 2QZ]; *b* 23 Jan 1947; MRAC, GICM, CBiol, NJBiol; *m* 1971 (*divorce* 1989) Mary, dau of John McLeod, MIEE, of Blackburn, and has issue:

1e +Daniel James; *b* 1975; BA

2e +John Henry; *b* 1979

1e *Antonia Mary; *b* 1981

2d +Richard Charles BA [Richard Monckton Esq, 1/64 Benelong Rd, Cremorne 2090, NSW, Australia]; *b* 24 Nov 1960; *m* 10 Oct 1992 *Lesley Megan, dau of Bruce Fergus Graham, of Umina, NSW

1d *Felicity Ruth [Felicity Monckton Beydals, Gouden Regenhof 25, 3434 T J Nieuwegein, The Netherlands]; *b* 12 Oct 1949; *m* 1981 (*divorce* 19–) Robert Bastiaan Beydals and has:

1e *Alexander Herman; *b* 1986

2e *Sebastian Charles; *b* 1988

1b Ellen Winifred

2b Leonora Rose; *m* 1st 1880, George H Bayley (*d* 1889); *m* 2nd 1890 Lt-Col Horace Hutton Barnett, RE, and *d* 14 April 1902, leaving issue

3a Inglis George (Rev); Vicar Coven, BA; *b* 9 Feb 1832; *m* 2 Feb 1859 Elizabeth Esther (*d* 3 Aug 1875), dau of Francis Corser, and *d* 1 July 1899, leaving, with other issue:

1b Herbert Haden, of Birmingham; slr; *b* 28 July 1861; *educ* Wadham Coll Oxford (BA); *m* 8 Sept 1904 Dora May (*d* 29 Dec 1961), only dau of Alfred Henry Griffiths, JP, of Thornbury, Edgbaston, and *d* 4 Jan 1944, having had, with a dau (*d* an infant):

1c Elizabeth Joyce; *b* 22 Oct 1906; *d* unm 8 May 1960

2b William Leopold, OBE (1920); *b* 7 Sept 1865; *m* 1st 12 Aug 1905 Ethel Maud (*d* 5 Sept 1918), dau of Samuel Morton, of Llangollen; *m* 2nd 7 Oct 1919 *Myvanwy Doris, widow of Maj Percy Garrard, DSO, KAR, and *d* 16 April 1935

1b Georgiana Elizabeth; *b* 29 March 1860; *d* unm 14 Sept 1932

4a John Rivaz; *b* 13 May 1833; *m* 29 June 1854 Rose Catherine, 5th dau of Thomas Taylor, and was together with his wife and child murdered in the Indian Mutiny

5a Marmaduke Littlejohn; Lt-Col RA; *b* 27 May 1887; *m* 24 March 1874 Amelia Mary (*m* 2nd 1889 Dario Francesco Marchese Fornari, of Genoa, and *d* 1939), only child of Col H E Dyneley, and *d* 14 July 1882, leaving:

1b Mary Sophia; *m* 20 Dec 1900 Count Giulo Macchi di Cellere (*d* 29 May 1949), Lt-Col Genoa Dragoons, and had issue

1a Fanny Leonora; *m* 6 July 1871 Edward de Coetlogon Williams, EICS, and *d* 19 Sept 1878, leaving issue

2a Anna Maria; *m* 17 March 1874 Rev Henry Arthur Annesley and *d* 13 Dec 1927, leaving issue (*see* VALENTIA, V)

3a Charlotte Georgiana; *m* 10 Feb 1871 Francis Frederick Sunley Harral, and *d* 12 July 1916, leaving issue. He *d* 25 April 1906

1 Mary; *m* 1786 7th Earl of Cork and Orrery (*qv*) and *d* 1840

The 1st VISCOUNT *d* 15 July 1751; his est son,

WILLIAM MONCKTON later MONCKTON-ARUNDELL (roy licence 1769 under terms of will of his aunt Lady Frances Arundell, sister of 3rd Duke of Rutland and widow of Richard Arundell, only brother of John, Lord Arundell of Trerice), **2nd Viscount Galway**; Receiver-Gen Crown rents Yorks, Westmorland and Durham 1748, MP Pontefract and Thirsk; *m* 12 Aug 1747 Elizabeth (*d* 2 Jan 1792), dau of Joseph da Costa Villa-Real, and *d* 1772, leaving issue:

1 John; *d* unm 1769

2 HENRY WILLIAM MONCKTON later MONCKTON-ARUNDELL, **3rd Viscount Galway**; *b* 15 May 1749; *d* unm 2 March 1774

3 ROBERT, **4th Viscount**

1 Elizabeth; *m* 1st 1774 Sir Francis Sykes, 1st Bt, of Basildon (*qv*), and had issue; *m* 2nd Sir Drummond Smith, 1st Bt (*see* SPENCER-SMITH, Bt), and *d* 1835

2 Frances Charlotte; *m* 15 Feb 1785 Anthony Burlton Bennett and *d* 12 Sept 1825

The 3rd VISCOUNT's bro,

ROBERT MONCKTON-ARUNDELL, **4th Viscount Galway**, KB, PC; MP York and Pontefract; *b* 4 July 1758; *m* 1st 1 March 1779 Elizabeth (*d* 19 Nov 1801), dau of Daniel Mathew, of Felix Hall, Essex, and had, with other issue:

1 WILLIAM GEORGE, **5th Viscount**

1 Henrietta Maria; *m* 22 Aug 1808 Robert Pemberton Milnes, of Fryston Hall, Yorks, and *d* 1 May 1847, leaving issue

The **4th Viscount** *m* 2nd 24 May 1803 Bridget (*dsp* 15 Nov 1835), widow of Peter Auriol Hay-Drummond (*see* KINNOULL, E) and only child of Pemberton Milnes, of Wakefield, Yorks

He *d* 23 July 1810; his est son,

WILLIAM GEORGE MONCKTON-ARUNDELL later MONCKTON (roy licence 1826, but allowing his successors in the peerage to retain the MONCKTON-ARUNDELL while that of the yr children was to remain MONCKTON), **5th Viscount Galway**; *b* 28 March 1782; *m* 4 June 1804 Catherine Elizabeth (*d* 7 April 1862), only surv child of Capt George Handfield, of Serlby Hall, Notts, by Elizabeth, only dau of the Rev Sir William Smith, 6th Bt (*see* BOWYER-SMYTH, Bt), and *d* 2 Feb 1834, having had issue:

1 GEORGE EDWARD ARUNDELL MONCKTON-ARUNDELL, **6th Viscount Galway**; Ld-in-Waiting 1852; *b* 1 March 1805; MP E Retford 1847–76; *m* 25 April 1838 Henrietta Eliza (*d* 10 Sept 1891), only dau of Robert Pemberton Milnes and sister of 1st Baron Houghton (*see* 1940 edn CREWE, M), and 6 Feb 1876, leaving:

(1) GEORGE EDMUND MILNES MONCKTON-ARUNDELL, **7th Viscount Galway**, CB, JP DL Notts; MP N Notts, 1872–85; *educ* Ch Ch Oxford (MA); Hon Col Notts (Sherwood Rangers) Yeo (TD), Col cmdg 1882–1904, ADC to TM QUEEN VICTORIA 1897–1901, EDWARD VII 1901–10 and GEORGE V 1910–20, KJStJ, Ld High Steward E Retford; *b* 18 Nov 1844; *cr* 4 July 1887 BARON MONCKTON OF SERLBY, Co Nottingham (UK); *m* 24 July 1879 Vere, LJStJ (*d* 3 Jan 1921), only dau of Ellis Gosling, of Busbridge Hall, Surrey, and *d* 7 March 1931, leaving:

1a GEORGE VERE ARUNDEL MONCKTON-ARUNDELL, **8th Viscount Galway**, GCMG (1935), DSO, OBE, PC (1937), JP, DL Notts; *b* 24 March 1882; *educ* Ch Ch Oxford (MA); Col Life Gds, Hon Col 42nd (Foresters) AA Bn (TA), Col-Cmdt HAC 1933–35, Govr-Gen NZ 1935–41, KGStJ, WW I (despatches); *m* 24 June 1922 Hon Lucia Emily Margaret White (*d* 12 Jan 1983), yr dau of 3rd Baron Annaly (*qv*), and *d* 27 March 1943, leaving:

1b SIMON GEORGE ROBERT MONCKTON-ARUNDELL, **9th Viscount Galway**, DL (1963) Notts; *b* 11 Nov 1929; *educ* Eton; Hon Maj Life Gds; *m* 4 Nov 1953 Lady Teresa Jane Fox-Strangways (*m* 2nd Jan 1972 (Richard) Mark Walter Agnew (*see* AGNEW, Bt, of London), and *d* 1989), only dau of 7th Earl of Ilchester (*qv*), and *d* 1 Jan 1971, leaving:

1c *Charlotte Anne [The Hon Mrs Townshend, Melbury House, Dorchester, Dorset DT2 0LF]; *b* 16 April 1955 *m* 24 Sept 1983 (*divorce* 1987) Guy Martin James Morrison, art dealer, and has:

1d *Simon George Strangways; *b* 9 Aug 1984

1c (cont.) The Hon Mrs Charlotte Morrison *m* 2nd 24 June 1995 *James Townshend, s of H R Townshend (*see* ROWLEY, Bt), and by him has:

1d *Melissa Susan Charlotte; *b* 29 June 1996

1b *Mary Victoria [The Hon Mrs Chaworth-Musters, Felley Priory, Underwood, Notts NG16 5FL]; WW II in WRNS; *m* 1st 29 Aug 1947 (*divorce* 1972) David Henry Fetherstonhaugh, Coldstream Gds (*d* 1994), s of Lt-Col Timothy Fetherstonhaugh, DSO, FRGS, of Kirkoswald, Penrith; *m* 2nd 30 March 1974, as his 2nd w, Maj Robert Patricius Chaworth-Musters (*d* 1992), Coldstream Gds, and by her 1st husb has:

1c *Hugh Simon [Hugh Fetherstonhaugh Esq, Faenol Bach, Bodelwyddan, Clwyd]; *b* 25 Jan 1949; *educ* Eton; *m* 1971 *Louise, adopted dau of Hon (Richard) Hanning Philipps (*see* MILFORD, B), and has issue:

1d *Edward Dickon Hanning; *b* 1981

2d *Fergus Hugh; *b* 1990

1d *Sophie Lucia; *b* 1973

2d *Alice Maria; *b* 1975

2c *Henry George [Henry Fetherstonhaugh Esq, Plas Llewelyn, Dolwen, Clwyd]; *b* 16 Oct 1954; *educ* Eton; *m* 1st 1978 (*divorce* 1994) Nicola, only child of Lt-Col Peter Payne-Gallwey, DSO (*see* FRANKLAND-PAYNE-GALLWEY, Bt); *m* 2nd June 1996 *Davina, dau of Duncan Macleod, of Monkreaning House, Kilwinnink, Ayrshire, and by his 1st w has:

1d *Jack David James; *b* 1987

2d *Hector Albert Timothy; *b* 1990

1c *Victoria Bronwen; *b* 19 Jan 1951

2b Celia Ella Vere; *b* 1925; JP (Suffolk); Extra Ldy in Waiting to HRH PRINCESS ALEXANDRA, HON LADY OGILVY 1970; *m* 13 June 1959 Sir Joshua Francis Rowley, 7th Bt (*qv*), and *d* 13 Dec 1997, leaving issue

3b *Isabel Cynthia; *b* 1926; *m* 21 Sept 1970 *Baron King of Wartnaby (LP, *qv*)

1a Violet Frances; OStJ; *b* 14 May 1880; *m* 7 July 1904 Lt-Col Geoffrey Henry Julian SKEFFINGTON SMYTH later fitzPATRICK (deed poll 1938), DSO, yr s of Edward Randal Skeffington-Smyth, JP, DL, of Mount Henry, and *d* 24 Oct 1930, leaving issue. He *d* 11 March 1939

2 Charles Gustavus; Capt 88th Foot; *b* 11 May 1806; assassinated 9 Aug 1831 at Corfu

3 Augustus William; Cdr RN; *b* 8 April 1808; lost in *HMS Calypso* Feb 1833

4 Edmund Gambier; Col 1st Rifle Regt W Yorks Militia, Capt Rifle Bde; *b* 21 Dec 1809; *m* 10 June 1845 Arabella Martha (*d* 25 July 1880), dau of Rev John Robinson, Rector Widmerpool, Notts and *d* 7 Oct 1872, having had:

(1) William Henry, of the Manor House, Southwell; *b* 7 Aug 1846; *m* 11 Feb 1885 Rose Ethel (*d* 11 May 1939), dau of Henry Vatcher, of Rosemount, Jersey, and *d* 19 March 1900, leaving issue:

1a WILLIAM ARUNDELL MONCKTON-ARUNDELL, **10th Viscount Galway**; *b* 24 Sept 1894; *educ* Eton and Trin Coll Cambridge; *m* 1939 Joan (*d* 20 Sept 1973), only child of Maj G A Williams, S Staffs Regt, of Morelands, Purbrook, Hants, and *dsp* 15 Aug 1977

2a EDMUND SAVILE MONCKTON-ARUNDELL, **11th Viscount Galway**; slr 1930; *b* 11 Sept 1900; *educ* Charterhouse and Clare Coll Cambridge (BA 1922, MA 1944); *m* 20 April 1927 Kathleen Joyce (*d* 2 Feb 1975), yr dau of James Musgrave, MICE (*see* MUSGRAVE, Bt, of Tourin), and *dspm* 1980, leaving:

1b *Rose Wynsome; *b* 11 March 1937; occupational therapist

1a Ethel Mary; *b* 4 Jan 1888; *m* 29 Aug 1921 Lt-Col Claude Henry Maxwell Imbert-Terry, DSO (*see* IMBERT-TERRY, Bt), and *dsp* 16 Feb 1964

2a Joan Frances; *b* 29 Jan 1889; *m* 14 July 1914 Capt Frederick Thomas de Mallet Morgan, CBE, RN, s of Col Frederick Cyril Morgan, RA, and *d* 2 Jan 1959, leaving issue. He *d* 23 Aug 1959

3a Rosamond Vere; *b* 19 Jan 1892; *m* 2 May 1922 V-Adml Arthur Duncan Read, CB, son of Edward R Read, of Dublin, and *d* 6 Nov 1976, leaving issue. He *d* 30 Oct 1976

(2) Philip Edmund; Lt-Col RA, Mayor Christchurch; *b* 20 Dec 1850; *m* 22 July 1884 Bessie Gertrude (*dsp* 31 Dec 1885), dau of Henry Vatcher, of Rosemont, Jersey, and *d* 30 Dec 1911

(3) Marmaduke John; *b* 3 Nov 1853; *m* 14 July 1891 Kathleen Swan (*d* 13 Nov 1953), dau of Dep Surgn-Gen James Browne, MD, Bengal Medical Serv, and *d* 4 April 1922, leaving:

1a Philip Marmaduke; Lt Roy Welsh Fus, F/Lt RCAF; *b* 7 May 1892; *m* 19 Jan 1918 Lavender, dau of W J O'Hara, of St Albans, and *d* 4 Oct 1965, having had issue:

1b John Philip; F/O RCAF WW II; *b* 11 Oct 1919; *ka* 26 Feb 1943

2b GEORGE RUPERT MONCKTON, **12th and present Viscount Galway**

1b *Sylvia Margaret [Mrs Thomas Wilson, 1815 West 30th Avenue, Vancouver V6J 3A2, BC, Canada]; *b* 21 Jan 1921; *m* 12 April 1947 *Lt-Cdr Thomas Bruce Wilson, RCN, and has:

1c *Patrick John; *b* 16 July 1957
1c *Kathleen Elizabeth; *b* 15 April 1948; *m* 1st 1969 (*divorce* 1979) Roland R Stéphan; *m* 2nd 1985 *Henry Nichols Ervin II
2c *Rosemary Jean; *b* 20 Nov 1949; *m* 1st 1971 (*divorce* 1979) Niels Bols; *m* 2nd 1984 (*divorce* 1996) Edgar A Hendee
(4) Geoffrey Francis; *b* 30 April 1865; *d* 28 Dec 1927
(1) Caroline Emma; *d* unm 10 Feb 1919
(2) Alice Henrietta; *m* 27 Sept 1877 Frank Ricardo, of Bure Homage, Hants, and *d* 8 Jan 1930, leaving issue. He *d* 1897
(3) Rosamond Isobel; *m* 8 July 1886 Rev Canon James Raynold Morley Vatcher, RD, Vicar Clare, Suffolk, and *d* 19 March 1946, leaving issue. He *d* 5 Feb 1931
5 Frederick Smith (Rev); incumbent St Peter's Kingsland; *b* 31 May 1811; *d* 1861
6 Horace Manners; CO 3rd KO Hus; *b* 8 May 1824; *m* 1st 16 Oct 1856 Georgina (*d* 7 July 1879), dau of Sir Thomas Woolaston White, 2nd Bt (*see* WHITE, Bt, of Wallingwells), and had:
(1) Horace Woollaston; barrister; *b* 18 Aug 1857; *d* 14 Jan 1931
(2) Augustus George; Lt RMLI; *b* 31 Oct 1860; *d* unm 21 June 1886
(1) Catherine Elizabeth; *d* unm 17 Sept 1936
6 (cont.) Col Horace Monckton *m* 2nd 11 Nov 1885 Emily Sarah (*d* 28 Nov 1913), widow of W T Till, of Waingates, Surrey, and dau of James Cooper, and *d* 14 Jan 1904
1 Elizabeth Celia; *d* 20 May 1892
2 Caroline Isabella; *m* 25 March 1856 Rev T J Monson and *d* 9 April 1922, leaving issue (*see* MONSON, B)

GAMBLE

Arms: Or, on a pile gu., between two trefoils slipped in base vert, a fleur-de-lys of the first, a chief erm. **Crest:** On a mount between two trefoils slipped vert, a stork arg., holding in the beak a rose gu., stalked, leaved and slipped ppr. **Motto:** *Vix ea nostra voco* ('I scarce call these things ours'). **Creation:** Bt. (UK) 31 Aug 1897.

SIR DAVID HUGH NORMAN GAMBLE, 6TH BT, of Windlehurst, St Helens, Co Lancaster [Sir David Gamble Bt, Keinton House, Keinton Mandeville, Somerset TA11 4DX]; *b* 1 July 1966; *s* f 1984; *educ* Shiplake Coll Henley-on-Thames

Lineage: JOSIAS GAMBLE, of Lisbellaw, Co Fermanagh; migrated there from Scotland for 'conscience sake' (probably Presbyterianism) *temp* JAMES VI (later I of England); his est s:

DAVID GAMBLE, of Graan; *b* 1679; *m* Magdalen Hoapper and *d* 1763; his 2nd s:

DAVID GAMBLE, of Ratonagh, had a 4th s:

JOSIAS CHRISTOPHER GAMBLE; *b* Aug 1778; *educ* Glasgow U (MA 1797); *m* 16 Sept 1820 Hannah Gower (*d* 16 Dec 1852) and *d* 27 Jan 1848, leaving (with three daus, *d* young):

Sir David Gamble, 1st Bt (UK), so *cr* 31 Aug 1897, KCB, VD, of Windlehurst, St Helens, Lancs, JP Lancs Borough of St Helens; Mayor 1868–70, 1882–83, 1886–87, Hon Col 2nd Vol Bn (Prince of Wales's Vols) S Lancs Regt; *b* 2 Feb 1823; *m* 26 Jan 1847 Elizabeth (*d* 23 Oct 1899), dau of Thomas Haddock, of St Helens, and had:

1 JOSIAS CHRISTOPHER (Sir), **2nd Bt**
2 William, of Briars Hey, Rainhill, JP St Helens; CC Lancs; *b* 16 Aug 1852; *m* 26 April 1877 Eleanor Eliza (*d* 5 March 1942), est dau of Alan Ker, JP, of Claughton, Birkenhead, and *d* 15 Jan 1907, leaving issue:
(1) Dorothy Ethel; *b* 18 Jan 1879; *m* 8 Feb 1907 (*divorce* 1923) Percy Alexander Shaw
3 David, of Talardy, St Asaph, Flints; Capt and Hon Maj 2nd Vol Bn S Lancs Regt; *b* 9 June 1856; *m* 1st 13 Aug 1880, Josephine Henriette (*d* 24 June 1899), dau of Conrad von Dorner, and had, with other issue:
(1) Conrad Dorner; *b* 17 Aug 1881; *m* 2 Nov 1910 Edith Annie (*d* 19 Oct 1938), yst dau of Ven Percy Harris Bowers, Archdeacon Loughborough, Hon Canon Peterborough, and *d* 1 Feb 1931, leaving issue:
1a Robert Dorner; *b* 25 Sept 1911; *m* 1st 26 June 1937 (*divorce* 1946) Hester Vernon (*d* 1969), 3rd dau of William Vernon Judd, of Shrubbery, Sutton Scotney, Hants; *m* 2nd 1948 *Marjorie Maud [Mrs Robert Gamble, Claonoadh, 11 Big Sand, Gairloch, Ross-shire], dau of Jonathan Smithson, and *d* 1988, leaving by his 1st w issue:
1b Prudence Dorner; *b* 4 June 1941; *m* 1968 *James Edward Stanley [James Stanley Esq, Swallows, Owslebury, Hants SO21 1LU] and *d* 9 Sept 1996, having adopted:
*George Edward; *b* 22 Nov 1977
*Louise Melanie; *b* 2 June 1973
(2) Victor Felix, CIE (1923), CBE (1926); Capt 26th KGO Cavalry, IA, Priv Sec to Govr UP India 1918–23 and Govr Burma 1923–26, Hon Lt-Col HG WW II; *b* 7 Dec 1886; *m* 1st 11 Oct 1911 (*divorce* 1932), Myrta Vivienne, dau of Frederick Stubbs, of Liverpool, and had issue:
1a Victor Vivian David; *b* 23 Feb 1914; *m* 29 April 1938 (*divorce*) Hedy, er dau of Friedrich Lerner, of Vienna, and *dsp* 16 June 1961
(2) (cont.) Victor Gamble *m* 2nd 5 Feb 1936 Kathleen Anne (*d* 17 July 1968), formerly w of Arthur Myhill-Brewer and dau of Alfred Button, of Knowle, Warwicks, and *d* 3 March 1952
(3) Lorentz Harry; S/Ldr RAFVR; *b* 12 May 1893; *educ* Haileybury; *m* 16 Aug 1917 Annie Marian (*d* 1972), dau of T F Clarke, of Stony Stratford, and *d* 29 Aug 1968, leaving issue:
1a *Diana May [Miss Diana Gamble, Bramble's Place, 6 Abbey Sq, Turvey, Beds]; Jr Cdr ATS; *b* 6 Jan 1920
(1) Josephine Henrietta; *b* 7 Dec 1886; *m* 7 Sept 1912 Sutherland Jameson (*d* 27 April 1926)
(2) Elizabeth; *b* 10 July 1888; *m* 8 Jan 1918 John Wynne Paynter Reece (*d* 1956)
3 (cont.) David Gamble *m* 2nd 18 March 1901 Marion (*d* 1955), dau of Griffith Parsonage, of Australia, and *d* 3 Oct 1933, having by her had, with other issue:
(4) Graeme Neil; *b* 18 May 1904; *educ* Radley and Selwyn Coll Cambridge (BA); *m* 1936 *Mary George [Mrs Graeme Gamble, Coombe Cottage, Plainsfield, Over Stowey, Somerset] and *d* 1980, leaving:
1a *Sheila Ann [Mrs James Bateman, Lodmore Farm, East Harptree, Bristol]; *b* 1937; *m* 1959 *James Brindley Douglas Bateman, BSc, son of James Douglas Bateman, of Old Bridge House, Datchet, Bucks, and has:
1b *James Graeme Richard; *b* 1967
2b *William John Douglas; *b* 1974
3b *Angus Neil Cyril; *b* 1978
1b *Fiona Valerie; *b* 18 July 1964; *m* 1993 *Mark Rule
2b *Sylvia Mary; *b* 1966
3b *Rosalind Ann; *b* 1969
2a *Judith; *b* 1940; *m* 1962 *Hagen Voken Dietrich Stöckl and has issue:
1b *Alexander Duncan Dietrich; *b* 1963
1b *Natasha Judith; *b* 1964
3a *Jane Elizabeth; *b* 1943
4a *Tessa Marion [Mrs Malcolm Bennett, Summerstead House, Over Stowey, Somerset TA5 1HA]; *b* 1952; *m* 1976 *Malcolm Paul Bennett and has:
1b *Nicholas Paul; *b* 1984
2b *Jos Daniel Graeme; *b* 1986
1b *Fenella Heidi; *b* 1988
(5) +Alan Lionel [Alan Gamble Esq, 14 Lower Common South, London SW15]; *b* 19 Sept 1905
(6) Keith Desmond; *b* 16 Aug 1911
(3) Jean Marion; *b* 5 April 1908
4 George; *b* 10 Feb 1858; *m* 1 March 1884 Mary, dau of Rev James Percival Watts, and *d* 14 Feb 1911, leaving issue:
(1) Charles Lancelot; Lt RNVR; *b* 18 Aug 1885; *m* 1906 (*divorce* 1908) Zoe Armstrong; *m* 2nd 1909 and *d* 19–
(2) George Vivian; Lt 5th Bn Roy Sussex Regt; *b* 18 March 1894; *m* 20 April 1915 Gertrude Edith Bear
(1) Eileen May; *b* 10 Dec 1892; *m* 31 Oct 1922 F/Lt Ian Mackenzie Matheson, RAF, of Pollo, Ross-shire
5 Arthur (Rev); Vicar Bradbourne with Ballidon, Derbys; MA Cantab; *b* 28 June 1863; *m* 6 Aug 1891 Annie Isabel (*d* 9 Dec 1945), dau of Alan Ker, JP, of Claughton, Birkenhead, and *d* 14 Oct 1917, leaving issue:
(1) Arthur Christopher; *b* 17 Jan 1904; *educ* Charterhouse, and Lincoln Coll Oxford (BA 1926, MA 1927)
(2) Alan David; ARIBA; *b* 3 Feb 1907; *d* unm 20 Nov 1953
6 Henry; *b* 29 Aug 1868; *m* 23 Jan 1895 Ethel (*d* 9 June 1924) dau of Thomas Brewis, and *d* 20 July 1927, leaving, with other issue:
(1) +David Harry [David Gamble Esq, 14 First Cross Rd, Twickenham Green, Middx]; *b* 14 Feb 1911; *m* 14 Feb 1949 May (*d* 198–), widow of Henry L Daglish and only child of Oliver Swithenbank, JP, of Leeds
(1) Enid Kathleen; *b* 1896; *m* 1 Sept 1924 Archibald Todrick, MB, ChB, s of Robert Todrick, of Haddington, E Lothian. He *d* 1945
(2) *Winifred Kathleen [Mrs Fred Roberts, 14 First Cross Road, Twickenham Green, Middx]; *b* 1899; *m* 8 Aug 1927 Fred Russell Roberts (*d* 1953)
(3) Agnes Grace; *b* 23 Nov 1908; *m* 29 May 1930 (*divorce* 1945) Ronald Kerr, est son of G A Kerr, of Blackheath and Worthing, and has issue:
1a *Merry [Mrs John Woodeson, 4 Martindale Road, West Hounslow, Middx]; *b* 21 June 1934; *m* 24 Nov 1961 *John Woodeson and has issue:
1b *Ben Charles; *b* 27 Feb 1965
1 Ann Jane; *m* 9 July 1874 Charles Joseph Bishop, JP, of Edenhurst, Roby, nr Liverpool, and *d* 2 Oct 1932, leaving issue. He *d* 24 May 1923
2 Elizabeth; *m* 2 June 1887 Austin Cooper Carr, of St Helens and *d* 11 Jan 1942, leaving issue. He *d* 18 Nov 1918
3 Hannah; *b* 17 Sept 1861; *d* unm 12 Feb 1944
4 Alice; *m* 19 June 1906 Rt Rev Cyril Charles Bowman Bardsley, DD, Bp Leicester, and *d* 11 Feb 1932. He *d* 20 Dec 1940

5 Grace; *m* 11 Feb 1899 Martin J Hamill (*d* 10 April 1921) and *d* 11 Jan 1954

Sir DAVID *d* 4 Feb 1907; his est son,

Sir Josias Christopher Gamble, 2nd Bt, VD, JP Lancs and St Helens; Capt and Hon Maj 2nd Vol Bn S Lancashire Regt; *b* 7 Jan 1848; *m* 5 June 1873 Isabella (*d* 3 Feb 1937), dau of George S Sanderson, of Claughton, Birkenhead, and had issue:

1 DAVID (Sir), **3rd Bt**

2 Hugh; *b* 3 July 1877; *d* unm 23 Nov 1946

3 Josias Christopher Norman; *b* 15 Nov 1878; *d* unm 9 July 1963

4 John Arthur, JP Lancs; Memb Ho of Laity Ch Assembly, Private RASC; *b* 9 July 1883; *m* 21 July 1910 Lilian Jane Emily (*d* 24 Dec 1913), yst dau of Rev Arthur Raggett Cole, of Hurstbourne Priors, and *d* 12 March 1947, leaving:

(1) Robin Arthur Norman; Capt 61st (S Lancashire) Searchlight Regt RA (TA) WW II; *b* 6 Feb 1912; *educ* Uppingham; *m* 1st 7 Sept 1939 Cissie Emily Goddall (*d* 27 March 1944); *m* 2nd 26 April 1947 *Muriel Maud [Mrs Robin Gamble, Overcreek, St Just-in-Roseland, Cornwall], dau of John Hale, of Knowsley, Lancs, and *d* 1981, leaving by his 1st w:

1a *Elaine Lilian [Mrs Malcolm Gubbins, Heathside, Jackmans Lane, St John's, Woking, Surrey]; *b* 30 May 1941; *m* 1970 Malcolm Charles Gubbins (*d* 1987) and has issue:

1b *Fiona; *b* 1981

2a *Olga Evelyn; *b* 23 Jan 1944; *m* 1st 9 Dec 1965, as his 2nd w, her cousin **Sir David Arthur Josias Gamble, 4th Bt**; *m* 2nd 1989 *Anthony Poole, son of Frank Poole, of Leicester

Sir JOSIAS *d* 24 Sept 1908; his est son,

Sir David Gamble, 3rd Bt; Mayor St Helens 1913–14 and 1914–15; *b* 1 May 1876; *m* 23 April 1903 Eveline Frances Josephine (*d* 28 March 1952), 2nd dau of Rev Arthur R Cole, and had issue:

1 DAVID ARTHUR JOSIAS (Sir), **4th Bt**

2 Robert Meredith; Capt Wilts Regt; *b* 31 Jan 1909; *m* 1st 17 Oct 1931 (*divorce* 1940) Phyllis Mary, er dau of Charles E Bradbury; *m* 2nd 3 Feb 1940 Diana Burnaby (*d* 20 May 1977), only dau of Walter Francis Drayson, AMICE, of Bayswater, and *d* 1988, having had by her:

(1) Andrew Robert Christopher; *b* 30 May 1942; *d* 9 May 1945

(2) +HUGH ROBERT GEORGE [Hugh Gamble Esq, 34 Gallows Hill, Abbots Langley, Herts WD4 8LU]; *b* 3 March 1946; heir presumptive; *m* 1989 *Rebecca Jane, dau of Lt-Cdr David Odell, RN, of Havant, Hants, and has:

1a *Emily Jessica; *b* 1994

(1) *Catherine Frances Dorothy [Mrs Anthony Bertram, 20 Fraser Ave, Caversham, Berks RG4 6RT]; *b* 12 Dec 1940; *m* 1962 *Anthony David Weguelin Bertram, only son of Stephen Bertram, of Sonning Common, Berks, and has:

1a *Helen Diana Elizabeth; *b* 1965; *m* 1992 *Stephen Thurgood and has:

1b *Alison Siân; *b* 1994

2b *Claire Tanya; *b* 1997

2a *Isobel Catherine Joan; *b* 1966; *m* 1997 *Joseph John Paul Mrozowski

3a *Laura Margaret Louise; *b* 1970

4a *Victoria Susannah Mary; *b* 1974

(2) *Sylvia Helen Jean [Mrs John Goodale, Cairnmore, Crianlarich, Perth FK20 8QS]; *b* 22 April 1944; *m* 14 Oct 1967 *John Alan Goodale, only son of Gilbert A Goodale, of Norwich, and has issue:

1a *Benjamin John; *b* 1968; *m* 1995 *Linley French

2a *Thomas; *b* 1971

(3) *Rosemary Diana Margaret [Mrs Nicholas Rooker Roberts, Sheepwash Platt, Cooks Lane, Walderton, Sussex PO18 9EF]; *b* 26 July 1948; *m* 26 Aug 1967 *Nicholas Rooker Roberts, 2nd son of A E Rooker Roberts, of Moatfield, Southolt, Suffolk, and Hon Mrs Richard Robbins, of Highbury and has issue:

1a *Andrew Arthur Rooker; *b* 25 Aug 1970

1a *Eleanor Burnaby Rooker; *b* 30 Sept 1972

2a *Hannah Margaret Rooker; *b* 1 Aug 1976

3 John Christopher; *b* 25 Dec 1910; *educ* Shrewsbury and St John's Coll Cambridge; *m* 21 Oct 1939 (*divorce* 1963) Pamela Margaret Grace, dau of Maj Arthur Grayhurst Hewat (*see* AYLMER, Bt), and *d* 26 Aug 1989, leaving issue:

(1) *Antony (Tony) Aylmer; *b* 8 Feb 1941; *m* Sept 1961 *Julie Leslie and has:

1a +David Antony; *b* 1962; *m* 1982 *Louise Bott and has issue:

1b +Christopher David; *b* Jan 1984

2b +Dylan John; *b* 1992

1b *Holly Louis; *b* 1993

1a *Christine; *b* 1964

2a *Kathleen Doris; *b* 22 Aug 1967

3a *Jeanne; *b* 1971; *m* 1993 *Andrew Pennington

(1) *Ann; *b* 16 Nov 1943; *m* 22 Dec 1962 *David J F Bailey, RAN, of Tasmania

4 William; Lt RASC; *b* 21 April 1913; *educ* Shrewsbury and St John's Coll Cambridge (BA 1935, MA 1946); *m* 27 Nov 1948 Christine Mary (*d* 8 May 1967), only child of Robert Permain, of Camberley, and *d* 1993

Sir DAVID *d* 17 July 1943; his est son,

Sir David Arthur Josias Gamble, 4th Bt, JP; Chm Cirencester RDC 1958–59; *b* 9 Dec 1907; *educ* Shrewsbury and Wadham Coll Oxford (BA 1929, MA 1946), Political Serv N Provs Nigeria; *m* 1st 9 April 1932 Elinor Mary (*d* 23 March 1961), only dau of Henry Edward Cole, of Summers, Long Sutton, Hants, and had issue; *m* 2nd 9 Dec 1965 his cousin *Olga Evelyn [Mrs Anthony Poole, Wood End, Tregony, Truro, Cornwall] (*m* 2nd 1989 Anthony Poole), yr dau of Robin Arthur Norman Gamble, and *d* 1982, leaving by his 1st w:

Sir David Gamble 5th Bt; P/O RAFVR; *b* 5 June 1933; *educ* Shrewsbury; *m* 1956 *Dawn Adrienne [Lady Gamble, Keinton House, Keinton Mandeville, Somerset TA11 4DX], 2nd dau of P/O David Hugh Gittins, RAF, of The Manor House, West Hagley, Worcs, and Mrs J T Stuart, of The Old House, Bear Hill, Alvechurch, Warwicks, and *d* 1984, leaving issue:

1 Sir DAVID HUGH NORMAN GAMBLE, **6th and present Bt**

1 *Caroline; *b* 26 Sept 1957

2 *Elinor Josephine; *b* 25 Sept 1961

GARDNER OF PARKES

Arms: Per fess azure and vert, in chief a representation of the constellation of the Southern Cross argent, issuing in base a sun in splendour or, all within a bordure indented gold. **Supporters:** Dexter, a kangaroo or gorged with a crown palisado vert, grasping in the sinister forepaw a branch of Tudor roses slipped and leaved proper; sinister, a lion or gorged with a crown palisado vert, grasping in the dexter forepaw a branch of wattle slipped and leaved proper, the compartment comprising a grassy mount, growing therefrom two waratah flowers slipped and leaved proper. **Motto:** Keep going. **Creation:** B. (LP, UK) 1981.

THE BARONESS GARDNER OF PARKES, of Southgate, Greater London, and of Parkes, NSW ((Rachel) Trixie Anne McGirr, JP (N Westminster, Inner London 1971)) [The Right Hon The Baroness Gardner of Parkes JP, House of Lords, London SW1A 0PW]; *b* 17 July 1927; *educ* Monte Sant Angelo Coll and Sydney U; dentist, memb: Westminster City Cncl 1968–78 (Lady Mayoress 1987–88) and GLC (Havering 1970–73, Enfield Southgate 1977–86), Br Chm European Union of Women 1978–82, Nat Women's V-Chm C Party 1978–82, Industl Tbnl Panel London 1974–97, Govr Nat Heart Hosp 1974–90, UK Rep UN Status of Women Commn 1982–88, fought (C) Blackburn and N Cornwall gen elections 1970 and Feb 1974, dir LEB 1984–89 and Woolwich Bldg Soc 1988–93, V-Chm NE Thames RHA 1990–94, Chm: PLAN Int (UK) 1990–, Suzy Lamplugh Tst 1993– and Roy Free Hampstead NHS Tst 1994–; *m* 1956 *Kevin Anthony Gardner, Ld Mayor Westminster 1987–88, s of George Gardner, of Sydney, and has issue:

1 *Sarah Louise; *b* 1960; *m* 1991 *Timothy M Joiner, est s of Hugh Joiner, of Gustard Wood, Wheathampstead, Herts

2 *Rachel Trixie [The Hon Mrs Pope, Sakura, Camp Rd, Gerrards Cross, Bucks SL9 7PF]; *b* 1961; MB BS London 1984; *m* 1988 *Dr Alvan John Pope, s of Kenneth Pope, of the Old Rectory, Chastleton, Oxon, and has issue:

(1) *Christopher; *b* 1991

(2) *Philip; *b* 1997

(1) *Victoria; *b* 1993

(2) *Katherine; *b* 1995

3 *Joanna Mary; *b* 1964

Lineage: The Hon JOHN JOSEPH McGIRR; *m* Rachel —, OBE, and had an 8th child:

(RACHEL) TRIXIE ANNE, *cr* a **Baroness**

GAREL-JONES

Creation: B. (LP, UK) 2 Aug 1997.

THE BARON GAREL-JONES, of Watford, Co Herts ((William Armand Thomas)Tristan Garel-Jones, PC (1992)) [The Rt Hon The Lord Garel-Jones PC, House of Lords, London SW1A 0PW]; *b* 28 Feb 1941; *educ* King's Sch Canterbury; Pncpl Language Sch Madrid 1960–70; merchant banker 1970–74; Staff C Party 1974–79 (personal assist to Party Chm 1978–79), MP (C) Watford 1979–97, PPS to Min State CSD 1981, Assist Govt Whip 1982–83, Ld Commr Treasury 1983–86, Dep Govt Whip 1986–89, Dep Ch Whip 1989–90, Min State FCO 1990–93; *m* 1966 *Catalina Garrigues and has four sons and a dau

Lineage: BERNARD GAREL-JONES; *m* Meriel Williams and has:

(WILLIAM ARMAND THOMAS) TRISTAN, *cr* a **Baron**

GARTHWAITE

Arms: Az. a cross between, in 1st and 4th quarters, five ears of wheat banded, and 2nd and 3rd quarters a greyhound rampant, all or. **Crest:** In front of a capstan sa. garnished gold a fleur-de-lys also gold. **Motto:** *Cuique suum* ('To each his own'). **Creation:** Bt. (UK) 19 May 1919.

SIR (WILLIAM) MARK CHARLES GARTHWAITE, 3RD BT [Sir Mark Garthwaite Bt, 3 Hazlewell Rd, London SW15 6LU]; *b* 4 Nov 1946; *s* f 1993; *educ* Gordonstoun and U of Pennsylvania (BSc); md Seascope Insur Serv (Marine Insur Brokers) 1970–87 (md 1980–87), Brandram and Garthwaite Ltd 1987–88, dir Regis Low Lloyd's Brokers 1988–92, dir Steel Burrill Jones Ltd 1992–; *m* 1979 *Victoria Lisette, est dau of General Sir Harry Tuzo, GCB, OBE, MC, of Heath Farm House, Fakenham, Norfolk, and formerly w of Robert Henry Adolphus Hohler, and has issue:

1 +WILLIAM TUZO; *b* 14 May 1982

1 *Rosie Francesca; *b* 1981

2 *Jemima Victoria; *b* 31 Jan 1984

Lineage: WILLIAM GARTHWAITE, of Staindrop, Co Durham; had:

Sir William Garthwaite, 1st Bt (UK), so *cr* 19 May 1919, of Durham; shipowner and sugar planter, helped Admlty with shipping between Canada and France WWs I and II (voluntarily building a fleet of minesweepers abroad), memb Shipwrights' Co, Freeman City London, Chev Crown Belgium; *b* 11 July 1874; *m* 1st 1904 Francesca Margharita, dau of William Parfett, and had issue:

1 WILLIAM FRANCIS CUTHBERT (Sir), **2nd Bt**

Sir William *m* 2nd 25 Nov 1911 (*divorce* 1937) Janet, dau of Jose Carlos Rodrigues, LLB, of Rio de Janeiro, by Jane Sampson, dau of Henry Joseph Dale, of London, and by her had issue:

2 Anthony William; Scots Gds, Gen List and Leics Regt WW II (invalided 1942), V-Consul Kansas City 1942, Br Naval Liaison Office San Pedro 1944; *b* 10 Nov 1917; *educ* Harrow and New Coll Oxford (MA); *m* 1 Dec 1950 Hon Waveney Mancroft Samuel (*d* 1986), er dau of 1st Baron Mancroft (*qv*), and *d* 4 Oct 1972, leaving issue:

(1) +Nicholas Anthony William Mancroft; *b* 26 March 1952; *educ* Winchester; *m* 1982 *Caroline C, dau of Thomas Willbourne, of Thorney, Peterborough, and has issue:

1a +Oliver Julian; *b* 1986

2a +Felix Sebastian; *b* 1987

3a +Piers Marcus; *b* 1990

1 Josette; *b* 23 March 1913; *m* 7 Sept 1940 (*divorce* 1955) Robert Mouzillat, son of Gustave Mouzillat, of Paris, and *d* 27 Jan 1977, leaving issue

Sir William *m* 3rd 4 Feb 1937 Mrs Gladys Galie, dau of Daniel Montague Hardy, and by her had issue:

3 +Michael William Gladwyn [Michael Garthwaite Esq, c/o Barclays Bank Ltd, 160 Piccadilly, London W1]; *b* 21 July 1937; *educ* Trin Coll Sch Ontario

The 1st Bt *d* 21 June 1956; his est son,

Sir William Francis Cuthbert Garthwaite, 2nd Bt, DSC (1941) and bar (1942); Lt-Cdr Mediterranean Fleet WW II 1942 and RAF Fighter Command 1943 (despatches three times); *b* 3 Jan 1906; *educ* Bradfield and Hertford Coll Oxford; Lloyd's underwriter and insur broker 1926, farmer, fought (C) Hemsworth gen election 1931 and Isle of Ely 1935; *m* 1st 23 July 1931 (*divorce* 1937) Hon Dorothy (Dolly) Duveen, only dau of 1st and last Baron Duveen (*see* 1939 edn); *m* 2nd 27 June 1945 (*divorce* 1952) Patricia Beatrice Eden [Mrs Samuel Allen, The Old Rectory, Hawling, Glos GL54 5TA] (*m* 3rd 1953 *Samuel Carson Fitz William Allen), widow of Cdr Barry Warsop Cooper Leonard, RN, and er dau of Cdr Charles Eden Neate, RN, and had issue:

1 Sir (WILLIAM) MARK CHARLES GARTHWAITE, **3rd and present Bt**

Sir William *m* 3rd 4 April 1957 *Patricia Merriel, only dau of Sir Philip d'Ambrumenil, of St James's Court, Buckingham Gate, London SW1, and *d* 1993, having by her had:

2 +John William Philip [John Garthwaite Esq, Matfield Oast, Chestnut Lane, Matfield, Kent TN12 7JJ]; *b* 9 Jan 1958; *m* 7 May 1983 *Sarah Elizabeth, dau of Rev Charles Anthony Maclea March, of Brenchley, Kent, and has:

(1) *Joanna Rachel; *b* 1992

(2) *Rebecca Elizabeth; *b* 1994

3 +Andrew William David; *b* 1 April 1962

4 +Simon William James; *b* 1 April 1962 [Simon Garthwaite Esq, Ballingdon House, Gaddesdon Row, Herts HP2 6HX]; *m* 1989 *Caroline Sally, er dau of John Pigott, of Thrales End, Harpenden, Herts, and has issue:

(1) +James William John; *b* 1991

(2) +George William Angus; *b* 1993

1 Sarah Francesca Merriel; *b* 17 Aug 1960; *d* 24 June 1964

GARVAGH

Arms: Quarterly of six, 1st and 6th, arg. three Moor's heads in profile, two and one couped ppr., wreathed about the temples of the first and az. (for CANNING); 2nd, gu., three spear heads erect in fess arg. (for SALMON); 3rd, sa., a goat salient or (for MARSHALL); 4th, bendy arg. and az. within a bordure gu. (for NEWBURGH); 5th, per pale arg. and sa. a fess nebuly between three griffin's heads erased, within a bordure engrailed, all counterchanged (for SPENCER). **Crests:** 1 (centre) A demi-lion rampant arg., charged with three trefoils vert, holding in his dexter paw an arrow pointing downwards, pheoned and flighted ppr., shaft or, 2 (dexter) A demi-lion rampant arg., holding in his dexter paw a battle-axe ppr., 3 (sinister) A demi-griffin segreant sa., beaked and legged or. **Supporters:** Dexter, a griffin regardant, wings expanded az., guttée-d'or, beaked and legged of the last; sinister, an eagle regardant, wings expanded sa., beaked and legged or. **Motto:** *Ne cede malis sed contra* ('Yield not to misfortunes, but oppose them'). **Creation:** B. (I) 28 Oct 1818.

THE 5TH BARON GARVAGH, of Garvagh, Co Londonderry, Ireland ((Alexander Leopold Ivor) George Canning) [The Rt Hon The Lord Garvagh, 34 White St, Topsham, Devon EX3 0AA]; *b* 6 Oct 1920 (HM QUEEN ALEXANDRA stood sponsor); *s* f 1956; *educ* Eton and Ch Ch Oxford; Capt Guides Cavalry, Capt IA Burma WW II (despatches), late Associate Memb: American Inst Management and Br Inst Management Ctee, memb Irish Peers Assoc, chm and md Lord Garvagh and Assocs Ltd, consultants, London, and Ind Chartering Ltd, Camco Machinery Ltd, Intersal Commodities Ltd and Anglo-Brazilian Investments Ltd, dir C W Evans, de Redcliff Ltd and Campden Research and Sales Ltd, AODC (UK) Ltd, The Lord Garvagh & Partnrs Ltd, Stonehaven Tankers Ltd, Seaways (London) Ltd, Marwood Industrial & Commercial Developments Ltd, Camden Research and Sales Ltd, Careers Intervention Ltd, late Fell IOD, memb Inst of Exports, consultant ptnr Schtumel Towning WI & Ptnrs, Accredited Rep Trade Ind The Cayman Islands 1981, MBIM; *m* 12 July 1947 (*divorce* 1974) Edith Christine, yr dau of Jack H Cooper, of Little Bridley, Worplesdon, Surrey; *m* 2nd 10 June 1974 *Cynthia Valerie Mary, dau of Eric Ernest Falk Pretty, CMG, of Kingswood, Surrey, and by his 1st w has:

1 +SPENCER GEORGE STRATFORD DE REDCLIFFE [The Hon Spencer Canning, 1 Church Lane, Little Bedwyn, Wilts]; *b* 12 Feb 1953; *educ* Cranleigh and Centl London Poly (Surveying Dip 1977); *m* 14 July 1979 *Julia Margery Morrison, er dau of Col Francis Clifford Edward Bye, of Twickenham, Middx, and has issue:

(1) +Stratford George Edward de Redcliffe; *b* 7 Feb 1990

(1) *Cordelia Louise Morison; *b* 1985

(2) *Florence; *b* 1988

1 *(Christine) Alexandra; *b* 20 Sept 1949; *m* 4 Sept 1971 (*divorce* 1987) Louis David Lawrence, er s of Sir Guy Kempton Lawrence, DSO, OBE, DFC, of Ascot, Berks, and has:

(1) *Stafford Guy Spencer; *b* 30 Aug 1973

(2) *Lucas Mark Seymour; *b* 25 Feb 1976

2 *Louise Eleanor Alice [The Hon Mrs Lawrence, Croft House, All Cannings, Devizes, Wilts]; *b* 14 April 1951; *m* 22 March 1975 her sis's bro-in-law *Mark Lawrence, yr s of Sir Guy Lawrence and has:

(1) *Jack Canning; *b* 1982

(2) *Rufus Powell; *b* 1986

Lineage: The CANNINGs held the Manor of All Cannings, Wilts, till the sr line ended with coheiresses *temp* HENRY VII.

ROBERT CANYNGES, a yr s, settled in Bristol and founded a branch which prospered as merchants there in the 14th and 15th centuries; *fl* 1322; had:

WILLIAM CANYNGES; MP Bristol, six times Mayor; *d* on or after 2 Oct 1396, leaving, with other issue:

JOHN CANYNGE; twice Mayor Bristol, MP Bristol; *m* Joan Wotton and *d* 1405, leaving, with three daus:

1 John

2 THOMAS (Sir)

3 William; restored St Mary Redcliffe Church, mentioned in Chatterton's Rowley poems; twice MP Bristol, five times Mayor Bristol; lent money to EDWARD IV, who suggested he marry one of his (EDWARD's) illegitimate daus as a reward; took holy orders instead; Dean and fndr Coll of Westbury; *d* 1476

The 2nd s,

Sir THOMAS CANNINGE; Ld Mayor London 1456; *m* Agnes, est dau and coheir of John Salmon by Eustatia, dau and coheir of John le Marshall, thus acquiring the Foxcote estate, Warwicks, and had:

1 Richard, of Foxcote; *m* Mary, dau of Humphrey Compton, and had:

(1) THOMAS

(2) John, ancestor of the CANNINGs of Todenham, Glos

The er son,

THOMAS CANNINGE, of Foxcote; *m* Jane, dau of Richard Boughton, of Condecot, Glos, and had issue:

1 RICHARD CANNINGE, of Foxcote; *m* Elizabeth (*d* 4 Aug 1611), dau of Richard Petty, of Ilmington, Warwicks, and had issue:

(1) Richard; ancestor of the CANNINGs of Foxcote Hall, Warwicks

(2) Edward; ancestor of the CANNINGs of Euston, Oxon

(3) Isaac; Turkey merchant; *d* Constantinople

(4) Paul; Amb to the Mogul Emperor; *d* Agra

(5) William, of Basingshaw Blackwell Hall, London; Master Ironmongers' Co

(6) GEORGE

(1) Maria; *m* John Riland, of Queenton, Glos, and had issue

(2) Anne; *m* 11 Aug 1589 Thomas Rownie, of Darlingscot, Worcs

The yst son,

GEORGE CANNING, of Barton, Warwicks; migrated to Ireland *temp* ELIZABETH I; granted Manor of Garvagh, Co Londonerry; *m* Anne, dau of Gilbert Walker, of Walford, Worcs, and *d* 1646, having had issue:

1 Paul; built the church of Agivey

2 William; Col Londonderry Militia; *k* 1641 Uprising, leaving an only s:

(1) George; Williamite cdr of a company Siege of Derry; attainted by JAMES II; had:

1a George; *m* 1697 Abigail (*m* 2nd Maj Cudmore), dau of Robert Stratford and aunt of 1st Earl of Aldborough, and *d* 1711, leaving issue:

1b Stratford, of Garvagh; *b* 1703; *m* 1734 Letitia, dau and sole heiress of Obadiah Newburgh, of Ballyhaise, Co Cavan, and Kilbrahan, Co Kilkenny, and had issue:

1c George; barrister Middle Temple, poet; *m* May 1768 Mary Anne, actress (for which his f disinherited him), dau of Jordan Costello, of Connaught, and *dvp* 11 April 1771, leaving an only child:

1d George, PC (1800); *b* 11 April 1770; *educ* Eton and Ch Ch Oxford (MA, Hon DCL 1814); MP (Tory) Newtown IoW 1793–96, 1806–07 and 1826–27, Wendover 1796–1802, Tralee 1802–06, Hastings 1807–12, Liverpool 1812–23, Harwich 1823–26 and Seaford April-Aug 1827, U-Sec For Affrs 1796–99, Commr India 1799–1801, Jt Paymaster Forces 1800–01, Treasurer Navy 1804–06, For Sec 1807–09 and 1822–27, 1st Ld Treasury, PM and Chllr Exchequer April-Aug 1827; *m* 8 July 1800 JOAN (*b c* 1777; allegedly brought her husb a fortune of £100,000 (well over £2,500,000 in late-1990s terms); *cr* 22 Jan 1828 VISCOUNTESS CANNING OF KILBRAHAN, Co Kilkenny (UK); *d* 14 March 1837), dau and coheir of Maj-Gen John Scott, of Balconie, Co Fife, and *d* 8 Aug 1827, having had, with two er s (*d* young):

1e CHARLES JOHN CANNING, 2nd and last VISCOUNT CANNING OF KILBRAHAN and 1st and last EARL CANNING (UK), so *cr* 21 May 1859, KG (1862), GCB (1859), KSI (1861), PC (1846); *b* 14 Dec 1812; *educ* Eton and Ch Ch Oxford; MP (C) Warwick 1836–37, U-Sec For Affrs, Ch Commr Woods and Forests March–July 1846, PMG 1853–55, Govr-Gen India 1855–62; *m* 5 Sept 1835 Hon Charlotte Stuart (*dsp* 18 Nov 1861), est dau and coheir of 1st and last Baron Stuart de Rothsay (*see* BUTE, M), and *dsp* 17 June 1862, when his titles expired

1e Harriet; *b* 13 April 1804; *m* 4 April 1825 1st Marquess of Clanricarde (*see* SLIGO, M) and *d* 8 Jan 1876, leaving issue

2c PAUL

3c Stratford; merchant in London; *m* Mehitabel, dau of Robert Patrick, of Somerville, Co Dublin, and *d* May 1787, leaving:

1d Henry; Consul Gen Hamburg; *m* and had issue

2d William (Rev); Canon Windsor; *m* and *dsp* 24 Feb 1860

3d Charles Fox; ADC to Duke of Wellington; *k* Waterloo

4d STRATFORD CANNING, 1st and last VISCOUNT STRATFORD DE REDCLIFFE (UK), Co Somerset, so *cr* 24 April 1852, KG (1869), GCB (1829), PC (1820); *b* 4 Nov 1786; *educ* Eton and King's Coll Cambridge; FO from 1807 (2nd Sec Copenhagen Oct-Nov 1807, Sec Constantinople 1809–12, Min Plen Constantinople 1810–12, Envoy Extrdy and Min Plen Switzerland 1814–19 and 1847–48 also Washington 1820–23, Jt Plen negotiating with US Min London 1824, special mission St Petersburg 1824–25, Amb Constantinople 1825–29 also 1831–32 and 1841–58, Plen Greece 1828, Extrdy Mission Madrid 1832–33, Special Mission Athens, Berlin, Brussels, Dresden, Hanover, Munich and Vienna 1848), DCL, LLD, MP (Tory) Old Sarum 1828–30, Stockbridge 1831–32 and King's Lynn 1835–42, author of various poems and verse dramas, also religious pamphlets; *m* 1st 3 Aug 1816 Harriet (*dsp* 17 Feb 1817), dau of Thomas Raikes, Govr Bank of England; *m* 2nd 3 Sept 1825 Elizabeth Charlotte (*d* 25 Nov 1882), dau of James Alexander, of Somerhill, Kent, and *d* 14 Aug 1880, having had a s (*dvp* unm), when the Viscountcy expired

1d Elizabeth; *m* 1805 George Henry Barnett, JP, DL, of Glympton Park, Oxon, and *d* 1838, leaving issue. He *d* 26 April 1871

1c Mary; *m* Rev Henry Bernard, s of Rt Rev William Bernard, DD, Bp Derry

2c Jane Elizabeth; *m* 1st 14 Dec 1776 Westby Perceval, of Phillipstown; *m* 2nd Very Rev William Leigh, Dean Hereford, and had issue

3c Frances

STRATFORD CANNING *d* 30 Sept 1775; his 2nd son,

PAUL CANNING, of Garvagh, which he came into due to his er bro's being disinherited; Col Londonderry Militia; *m* 20 July 1776 Jane (*d* 24 Oct 1785), dau of Conway Spencer and sis and coheir (with Charlotte, Marchioness of Donegall (*qv*)) of Sir Brent Spencer, and *d* Nov 1784, leaving:

GEORGE CANNING, **1st Baron Garvagh**, of Garvagh, Co Londonderry (I), so *cr* 28 Oct 1818; Col Londonderry Militia, Lt Co Londonderry, MP (Tory) Sligo 1806–12 and Petersfield 1812–20, FRS, FSA; *b* 15 Nov 1778; *m* 1st 13 July 1803 Lady Georgiana Stewart (*dsp* 17 Nov 1804), 4th dau of 1st Marquess of Londonderry (*qv*); *m* 2nd 9 July 1824 Rosabelle Charlotte Isabella (*d* 23 Dec 1891), est dau of Henry Bonham, of Titness Park, Berks, MP, and had:

1 CHARLES HENRY SPENCER GEORGE, **2nd Baron**

2 Albert Stratford George, of the Lodge, Rostrevor, Co Down, JP Co Down, JP, DL Co Londonderry; *b* 24 Aug 1832; author; *d* unm 22 April 1916

1 Emmeline Rosabelle; *d* unm 9 Feb 1898

The1st BARON *d* 20 Aug 1840; his er son,

CHARLES HENRY SPENCER GEORGE CANNING, **2nd Baron Garvagh**, JP, DL; Capt 10th Hus; *b* 18 March 1826; *m* 10 June 1851 Cecilia Susannah (*d* 2 Jan 1898), sis of Col Sir Samuel Ruggles-Brise, KCB, JP, DL, of Spains Hall, Essex (*see* RUGGLES-BRISE, Bt), and had issue:

1 CHARLES JOHN SPENCER GEORGE, **3rd Baron**

2 Conway Stratford George; Maj 1st Bn KRRC; *b* 15 Dec 1854; *d* 19 Feb 1926

The 2nd BARON *d* 7 May 1871; his er son,

CHARLES JOHN SPENCER GEORGE CANNING, **3rd Baron Garvagh**, JP, DL Co Londonderry; *b* 2 June 1852; *educ* Ch Ch Oxford (BA 1874, MA 1877); *m* 9 Aug 1877 Florence Alice, MBE (1918) (*d* 17 May 1926), dau of Baron Joseph de Bretton, of Copenhagen, and *d* 7 Feb 1915, leaving issue:

LEOPOLD ERNEST STRATFORD GEORGE CANNING, **4th Baron Garvagh**, JP, DL Co Londonderry; Lt 4th Bn HLI and RFC; *b* 21 July 1878 (HRH PRINCE LEOPOLD DUKE OF ALBANY stood sponsor); *m* 1st 19 July 1904 (*annulled* 1909) Caroline Grace Elizabeth, only dau of Charles Ernest Rube, ptnr Wernher & Beit, of Belgrave Sq; *m* 2nd 1 Jan 1919 Dora (*d* 27 Jan 1982), widow of Lt-Col John Stephen Dimmer, VC, and dau of Bayley Parker, of Oaklands, Edgbaston, and *d* 16 July 1956, leaving issue:

1 (ALEXANDER LEOPOLD IVOR) GEORGE CANNING, **5th and present Baron**

2 Victor Stratford de Redcliffe, Lt Gren Gds WW II (despatches); *b* 7 Feb 1924; *ka* Italy 7 May 1944

1 *(Dora) Valerie Patricia [The Hon Mrs Sutcliffe, 28 Ashford Rd, Tenterden, Kent TN3 6QU]; *b* 31 Oct 1919; *m* 1st 13 Jan 1942 Lt Philip Anthony Wellesley-Colley, Lt RA (*ka* 6 June 1944), er s of Maj Wellesley-Colley, MC, of Lound Hill, Co Louth, and has:

(1) *Angela [Mrs David Anderson, 14 Lauriston Rd, London SW19 4TQ]; *b* 5 Dec 1942; *m* 25 Oct 1973 *David Campbell Anderson, only son of A F B Anderson, of Gerrards Cross, Bucks, and has issue:

1a *James; *b* 1978

(2) *Elizabeth Jane [Mrs Peter Wilson, Brook House, Charing, Kent], *b* posthumously 1 Jan 1945; *m* 16 July 1966 *Peter John Wilson, est son of S Wilson, of Aylesford, Kent, and has:

1a *Camilla Jane; *b* 4 March 1968

2a *Sarah Louise; *b* 9 Nov 1970

3a *Henrietta Mary; *b* 1973

4a *Claire Alexandra; *b* 1977

1 (cont.) The Hon Mrs Wellesley-Colley *m* 2nd 28 Aug 1950 Peter Stocks Sutcliffe (*d* 1991), only s of Ernest Sutcliffe, of Stewton House, Louth, Lincs, and has further issue:

(1) *James [James Sutcliffe Esq, Hemingby House, Hemingby, Lincs LN9 5QF]; *b* 9 March 1953; *educ* Stowe; *m* 1st 1980 (*divorce* 1984) Carol Leslie, only dau of Capt C P Pratt, of West End, Southampton, and Nigeria, and has:

1a *Hannah; *b* 1983

(1) (cont.) James Sutcliffe *m* 2nd 1988 *Susan Diana, dau of John Beaumont, of The Manor House, Mill Lane, Legbourne, Louth, and formerly w of Geoffrey Sharp, and has issue:

1a *William; *b* 1989

2 *Daphne Rose [The Hon Mrs Svenningson, Cavan Valley Farm, Bewdley RR#2, Ontario K0L 1E0, Canada]; *b* 16 Dec 1922; *m* 18 March 1950 *Bancroft Svenningson, yr son of Sven Svenningson, of Montreal, and has:

(1) *Victor Bancroft; *b* 31 March 1954

(1) *Jennifer Ann; *b* 24 Nov 1955

(2) *Andrea; *b* 27 Dec 1960

GEDDES

Arms: Az. three geds naiant or, on a chief engrailed of the last as many boar's heads couped sa., armed arg., langued gu. **Crest:** A demi-pike hauriant environed of the circlet of a Lord Baron's coronet, all ppr. **Supporters:** On a compartment semée of sea-pinks two geds ppr. **Motto:** *Capta majora* ('May the greater things be held to'). **Creation:** B. (UK) 28 Jan 1942.

THE 3RD BARON GEDDES, of Rolvenden, Co Kent (Euan Michael Ross Geddes) [The Rt Hon The Lord Geddes, Lime Tree House, Stradbroke, Suffolk IP21 5JX]; *b* 3 Sept 1937; *s f* 1975; *educ* Rugby, Gonville and Caius Coll Cambridge (BA 1961, MA 1965) and Harvard Business Sch USA (PMD 1969); Lt-Cdr RNR (ret), dir Hare Court Investment, Jenny Maclean & Co and Geddes & Co, former devpt manager P&O Bulk Shipping, dep manager P&O Asia (Hong Kong) 1975–; *m* 1st 7 May 1966 Gillian (*d* July 1995), yr dau of William Arthur Butler, of Stable House, Peppard Common, Oxon, and has issue:

1 +JAMES GEORGE NEIL; *b* 10 Sept 1969

1 *Margaret Clair; *b* 5 Oct 1967

The 3rd BARON *m* 2nd 7 Sept 1996 *Mrs Susan Margaret Hunter, yr dau of George Harold Hunter, of Kingswood, Surrey

Lineage: DAVID GEDDES, of Cromarty; *b c* 1665; *m* Marion, paternal gdau of George Graham, Bp Dunblane and Orkney 1615, and had:

GEORGE GADDES or GEDDES, of Stromness, Orkney; *b* 1717; sailor; *m* 1st Katherine, est dau of John Johnstone, of Stromness; *m* 2nd 14 Dec 1758 Anne Beaton and *d* 1791, leaving by his 1st w:

DAVID GEDDES; merchant, shipowner, agent Hudson Bay Co; Assist Dep Paymaster-Gen to Gen Burgoyne American War of Independence 1777 with rank of Col; *b* 1751; *m* Margaret, est dau of Andrew Cruikshank, and *d* Oct 1811, having had:

GEORGE GEDDES, of Geddes House, Stromness; merchant and Hudson Bay Co agent; *b* 28 Jan 1786; *m c* 1814 Elizabeth (*d* 1838), est dau of James Anderson, and *d* 1840, leaving:

ACLAND CAMPBELL GEDDES, of Edinburgh; civil engr India, designed Jumna Bridge and various rlwys; *b* 4 Feb 1831; *educ* Edinburgh Instn and Edinburgh U; *m* 1870 Christina Helen McLeod (*d* 24 June 1914), dau of Rev Dr Alexander Anderson, DD, LLD, of Chanonry, Old Aberdeen, and *d* 18 March 1908, having had:

1 Eric Campbell (Sir), GCB (1919), GBE (1917), PC (1917); ktd 1916, Hon LLD Sheffield U, MP Cambridge 1917–22, Lt-Col Engr and Rlwy Staff Corps RE (TF) 1913, Hon Maj-Gen 1916, Hon and T/V-Adml 1917; rlwy engr America, India and England, Dep Gen-Man NER, Dep Dir-Gen Munitions Supply 1915, Dir-Gen Mil Rlwys War Office 1916 and Tportn British Armies France, Inspr-Gen Transptn 1916–17, Navy Controller and Memb Bd Admlty 1917, 1st Ld Admlty 1917–18, Min Tport 1919–21, Pres Inst Tport 1919–20, Chm Ctee on Nat Expenditure 1921–22, V-Pres Jr Instn Engrs (Gustave Canet Medal) 1922, Pres FBI 1923 and 1924, Pres Assoc Trade Protection Socs 1923, Chm Imp Airways and Dunlop Rubber, Order Leopold Belgium and Croix de Guerre, Grand Offr Legn Hon; *b* 26 Sept 1875; *m* 2 Nov 1900 Ada Gwendolen (*d* 9 Oct 1945), dau of Rev Arthur Stokes, and *d* 22 June 1937, leaving:

(1) Acland Mackay; *b* 24 Aug 1907; *educ* Shrewsbury; *m* 1st 1938 (*divorce* 1944) Anne Markham; *m* 2nd 16 Feb 1945 (*divorce* 1952) Barbara, dau of John Leslie Sanford, and *d* 16 March 1974, leaving by her:

1a *Jobyna Mackay; *b* 30 Aug 1945; *m* 26 Feb 1965 (*divorce* 19–) Anthony Peter Scratchley, only s of Maj Peter John Scratchley, of Brooms Farm, Edenbridge, Kent

2a *Erica Mackay; *b* 2 May 1947

(2) Magnus Mackay; *b* 8 Aug 1908; *educ* Rugby and Gonville and Caius Coll Cambridge; *m* 23 Dec 1941 (*divorce*) Renée Angèle Rosalie, widow of Alfred Baldwin Raper, formerly MP E Islington, and dau of Hector Benoist, of Lille, France, and *dsp* 20 Feb 1953

(3) (Anthony) Reay (Mackay) (Sir), KBE (1968, OBE 1945); *b* 7 May 1912; *educ* Rugby and Magdalene Coll Cambridge, G/Capt RAF WW II, dir: Shell Tport and Trading 1968–82, Rank Orgn 1975–84, dep chm Midland Bank Ltd 1978–84 (dir 1967–84), part-time memb UKAEA 1960–65, memb NEDC 1962–65, chm: Shipbuilding Inquiry Ctee 1965–66, Dunlop Rubber 1968–78 (dir 1947), Br Nat Ctee Int Chamber Commerce 1974 (pres 1980), Charities Aid Fndn 1991–93 (chm 1985–90), Hon DSc Aston 1967, Hon LLD Leicester 1969, Hon DTech Loughborough 1970; *m* 14 April 1938 Imogen (*d* 14 Feb 1997), dau of Capt Hay Matthey, and *d* 19 Feb 1998, leaving:

1a *Duncan Mackay [Prof Duncan Geddes, 57 Addison Avenue, London W11 4QU]; *b* 6 Jan 1942; *educ* Eton and Magdalene Coll Cambridge (BA 1964, MA), Westminster Hosp Med Sch (MB, BS 1971, MD 1978); FRCP 1982, Consultant Physician Roy Brompton Hosp 1978–, Hon Consultant Roy London Hosp 1982–, Roy Marsden Hosp 1990–, dir Finsbury Worldwide Pharmaceutical Tst, author: *Practical Medicine* (1976), *Airways Obstruction* (1981), *Respiratory Medicine* (1990), *Cystic Fibrosis* (1995); *m* 15 April 1968 *Donatella, dau of Count Nardi dei Flaccomio, of Florence, and has:

1b *Gavin Reay MacKay; *b* 27 Feb 1971

2b *Acland Eric Anthony; *b* 31 March 1981

1b *Gaia Irene Olga; *b* 5 April 1973

2a *Piers Mackay [Piers Geddes Esq, 13 Wilton Crescent, London SW1]; *b* 6 March 1950; *educ* Eton

1a *Alison [Mrs Martin Dean, Arlington Lodge, Bibury, Glos]; *b* 22 June 1939; *m* 31 Aug 1962 *Capt (Edward) Martin Dean, Coldstream Gds, yr s of Lt-Col Frank Longueville Dean, TD, of Glen Usk, Caerleon, Mon, and has:

1b *Charles Daniel; *b* 19 May 1966

1b *Isabel Henrietta; *b* 19 June 1964

2a *Lindsay; *b* 2 July 1946; *m* 11 Sept 1971 *Douglas Blair Turnhaugh, son of Orville W Turnhaugh, of Bainbridge Island, USA

3a *Candida [Mrs Julian Hunt, 13 Wilton Crescent, London SW1]; *b* 17 April 1948; *m* 24 Oct 1974 *Julian Hunt, son of Robert Hunt, of Long Rake, Punchbowl Lane, Dorking, Surrey

2 AUCKLAND CAMPBELL, **1st Baron**

3 Irvine Campbell; Chm Anderson Green & Co and Orient Steam Navigation Co, dir Impl Airways and BOAC, Pres Chamber Shipping UK 1943, chm Gen Cncl Br Shipping 1944, Capt Scottish Rugby Union XV 1908; *b* 9 July 1882; *educ* George Watson's Coll Edin; *m* 1 Aug 1911 Dorothy Jefford (*d* 1 July 1976), dau of Sir George Jefford Fowler, and *d* 18 May 1962, leaving:

(1) *Ford Irvine, MBE (1943) [Ford Geddes Esq MBE, 8 Kensington Court Gardens, Kensington Court Place, London W8 5QE]; *b* 17 Jan 1913; *educ* Loretto and Gonville and Caius Coll Cambridge (BA); Maj RE WW II, dir: Bank of NSW (London Advsy Bd) 1950–81, Equitable Life Assur 1955–76 (pres 1963–71), Br United Turkeys 1962–69, 1976–78 (chm 1976–78), chm: P&O 1971–72 (dep chm 1968–71; dir 1960–72), Br Shipping Fndn 1965–68, pres Int Shipping Fndn 1967–69; *m* 8 Dec 1945 *Barbara Gertrude Vere, only dau of Charles Fitzmaurice Parry Okeden, JP, and has:

1a *David Ford; *b* 27 Sept 1959

1a *Jennian Ford [Mrs Nicholas Montagu, 13 Onslow Mews West, London SW7]; *b* 25 May 1947; *educ* Reading U (BA); *m* 8 Aug 1974 *Nicholas L J Montagu, CB, son of John Montagu, of 50 Fitzgeorge Ave, W14, and has:

1b *Clare Barbara; *b* 4 June 1976

2a *Merryn Ford; *b* 15 Sept 1948; *educ* Benenden and Harrow Sch of Art (Diploma); *m* 1 Aug 1969 *Michael Christopher Lloyd, er s of Martin Lloyd, Headmaster Uppingham, of The Abbey Farm, Gt Missenden, Bucks

3a *Fiona Ford; *b* 22 Nov 1950; *educ* Benenden; *m* 19– *Colin Goodwille, yst son of Dr George M Goodwille, of Attleborough, Norfolk, and has:

1b *Campbell Geddes; *b* 25 July 1983

1b *Janna Ford; *b* 8 Feb 1977

4a *Ailie Ford; *b* 24 Nov 1956

(2) Ian Irvine; Capt RA WW II; *b* 1 Jan 1915; *educ* Loretto and Gonville and Caius Coll Cambridge; *m* 30 Aug 1939 *Beverley Anketell, dau of Stanley Allen, of Melbourne, and *d* 4 July 1979, leaving issue:

1a *Roger Brian; *b* 23 Jan 1945

2a *Ian David; *b* 10 Dec 1946

1a *Merryn Campbell; *b* 17 April 1943

2a *Joan Catherine; *b* 10 March 1950

(3) Keith Irvine, DFC; S/Ldr RAF WW II, Capt Scottish Rugby XV 1945–46–47, Chm Alan Muntz Hldgs, dir Br United Turkeys, Economic Forestry Hldgs; *b* 25 Oct 1918; *educ* Loretto and Gonville and Caius Coll Cambridge (BA); *m* 1st 31 July 1946 (*divorce* 1966) Marion Olive, dau of Maj Sir John Stirling, KT, of Fairburn, Muir-of-Ord, Ross-shire, and had:

1a *Rorie Irvine [Rorie Geddes Esq, 10 Durraut Road, Parkstone, Poole, Dorset]; *b* 19 Dec 1948; *educ* Harrow

2a *Angus John [Angus Geddes Esq, Morlands Farm, Bledlow Ridge, High Wycombe, Bucks]; *b* 21 Sept 1954; *educ* Harrow

1a *Rona Marion [Mrs Julian Knight, 19a Claxton Grove, London W6]; *b* 24 May 1947; *m* 21 Sept 1974 *Julian C Knight, yst son of G M Knight, of Byfield House, S Godstone, Surrey, and has issue:

1b *A son; *b* 9 Aug 1983

1b *A dau; *b* 8 Jan 1977

2a *Shian Margaret; *b* 12 Oct 1951; *m* 28 April 1973 *William Carlow, er son of Charles Carlow, of Ardery, Troon, Ayrshire

(3) (cont.) Keith Geddes *m* 2nd 9 Jan 1968 *Anne Mary, dau of Cdr R H Pullen, RN (ret), of Poole, Dorset, and *d* 19–, leaving:

3a *Marcus; *b* 29 Aug 1975

3a *Katherine (Katie) Mary; *b* 29 Aug 1970; *m* 25 Oct 1997 *Count Jean de Pomereu d'Aligre, yr s of Marquis de Pomereu d'Aligre

4a *A dau; *b* 17 Aug 1973

1 Alexandra Mary Campbell, CBE 1917; MD; first Controller WAAC 1917–18 WW I, Physician Edinburgh Hosp for Women and Children; *b* 31 May 1872; *educ* St Leonard's Sch and St Andrews and Edin Us (MB, CM 1894, MD 1898); *m* 28 July 1898 Douglas Chalmers Watson, MD, FRCP (Edin), and *d* 7 Aug 1936, leaving issue. He *d* 6 April 1946

2 Helen Campbell; *b* 1 Dec 1876; *d* 12 Jan 1878

3 Margaret Campbell; Bailie 1939, Sr Magistrate 1941 Edinburgh; *b* 3 March 1878; *educ* St George's Sch Edinburgh; *d* unm 6 Feb 1956

4 Norah Campbell; *b* 29 Jan, *d* 18 Dec 1887

The 2nd son,

AUCKLAND CAMPBELL GEDDES, **1st Baron Geddes** (UK), of Rolvenden, Co Kent, so *cr* 28 Jan 1942, GCMG (1922), KCB (1917, CB 1917), MD, TD, PC (1917); *b* 21 June 1879; *educ* George Watson's Coll, Edinburgh U (MB and ChB 1903, MD and Gold Medallist 1908), Freiburg U, London Hosp, Paris, Berne and Vienna; FRS Edin 1909; Hon LLD McGill, Toronto, Yale, Princeton, Michigan, California, Lt 3rd HLI Boer War 1901–02 (Queen's Medal with 4 clasps) and WW I (despatches twice), Maj 17th Northumberland Fus 1914–15, staff GHQ France 1915–16 (Brevet Lt-Col), Dir Recruiting War Office 1916–17 (Brig-Gen), Assist Prof Anatomy Edin U 1906–09, Prof Anatomy: RCSI 1909–13 and McGill U, Montreal, 1913–14, MP Basingstoke 1917–20, Dir-Gen and Min Nat Service 1917–18, Pres Local Govt Bd 1918–19, Min Reconstruction Jan-May 1919, Pres BOT 1919–20, Amb USA 1920–24, Br Del Washington Conf Limitation Armaments 1921–22, Chm Roy Commn Food Prices 1924, Regnl Commr CD SE Regn 1939–41 and NW Regn 1941–42, chm Rio Tinto and Rhokana Corp 1924–47, Cdr Crown Belgium 1917; *m* 8 Sept 1906 Isabella Gamble (*d* 8 Jan 1962), 3rd dau of William Adolphus Ross, of Staten Island, New York, and had:

1 ROSS CAMPBELL, **2nd Baron**

2 Alexander Campbell, OBE (1945), MC (1940), TD; AIME, Lt-Col RA WW II, Mil Assist DCIGS 1942, consultg engr, dir Aero-Hydraulics; *b* 24 Sept 1910; *educ* Stowe, ICS Lond U (ARSM, BSc) and Ch Ch Oxford; *m* 1st 1 Aug 1934 (*divorce* 1964) Margaret Kathleen, 5th dau of Sir Charles Stewart Addis, KCMG, of Woodside, Frant, Sussex, and had:

(1) +Andrew Campbell (Sir) [The Hon Mr Justice Geddes, The Old Vicarage, Minster Lovell, Oxon OX8 5RR]; *b* 10 June 1943; *educ* Stowe and Ch Ch Oxford (BA 1965); barrister Inner Temple 1972, Recorder 1990, Circuit Judge Midland and Oxford Circuit 1994, High Court Judge 1995–, ktd 1995, author: *Product and Service Liability in the EEC* (1992), *Public Procurement* (1993), *The Rights of EU Citizens and their Protection in the National Courts* (1995); *m* 1st 1974 (*divorce* 1983) Jacqueline, 2nd dau of Emil Tan Bunzil by Isabelle Renaud, of Feistritz, Styria, and has issue:

1a +Nicholas Campbell; *b* 19 Nov 1975

2a +Dominic Oliver Campbell; *b* 1978

(1) (cont.) Sir Andrew *m* 2nd 1985 *Bridget Charlotte Helen, dau of Lt-Col Christopher White Bowring, of Whelprigg, Casterton, Cumbria, and formerly w of John Warren-Swetenham, and has by her:

3a *Leo Patrick; *b* 1981

1a *Katharine Arabella Campbell; *b* 1986

(2) +Alexander James Campbell [Alexander Geddes Esq, 29 Hugo Road, London N19]; jnlst *The Times*; *b* 3 Dec 1948; *educ* Harrow and Lincoln Coll Oxford; *m* 24 July 1971 *Vivien M, only dau of F H Salter, of Cardiff, and has:

1a +Christopher Edward Frederick; *b* 4 April 1983

1a *Emily Claire Kateryna; *b* 1984

(1) *Margaret Campbell [Mrs Peter Gross, 521, 6th Street, SE, Washington, DC, USA]; *b* 4 May 1937; *m* 28 June 1960 *Peter Watson Gross, s of Ernest Gross, attorney, of New York, and has:

1a *James Jonathan Geddes; *b* 26 Sept 1964

2a *Michael Carl; *b* 1968

3a *Daniel Paul Geddes; *b* 1970

4a *Adam John Geddes; *b* 1972

1a *Sarah Anne; *b* 1967

2a *Carla Elizabeth; *b* 1969

(2) *Christina Helen Campbell [Mrs Roy Horrell, 14 Linkoping Rd, Rondebosch 7700, Cape, S Africa]; *b* 17 May 1939; *educ* Edinburgh U (MB, ChB 1963, FFRadT); *m* 13 Nov 1965 *Roy Kenneth Horrell, MA Cantab, FRICS, AAI, s of Harry Horrell, of Launceston, and has issue:

1a *Jasper Mark Geddes; *b* 6 Sept 1968

2a *Hamish Harry Geddes; *b* 1970

1a *Eliza-Jane Geddes; *b* 19 Nov 1966

2a *Emma Clare Geddes; *b* 1972

(3) *Jenny Campbell [Mrs Christopher Verity, Boundary House, Brimpton Common, Berks RG7 4RT]; *b* 21 Dec 1940; *m* 26 Oct 1963 *Christopher Lubbock Verity, est s of Rev Ronald Meysey Verity, and has issue:

1a *Richard Christopher Geddes; *b* 4 Aug 1965

2a *Jonathan William Geddes; *b* 15 July 1967

(4) *Caroline Anne Campbell [Mrs David Kelly, 8 Crooms Hill, London SE10 8ER]; *b* 3 May 1947; *m* 1970 *David Kelly and has:

1a *Nathaniel David; *b* 1982

1a *Alexandra Mary; *b* 1972

2a *Tabitha May; *b* 1976

3a *Lucy Anna Margaret; *b* 1979

4a *Jemima Joanna; *b* 1985

(5) *Diana Elizabeth Campbell; *b* 6 May 1947; late jnlst *The Times*

2 (cont.) Col The Hon Alexander Geddes *m* 2nd 27 July 1964 *Altgräfin Marie-Ann Helene Emanuela zu Salm-Reifferscheidt Krautheim und Dyck (*m* 2nd 1978 Prof Otto Georg von Simson (*d* 1993), of Berlin), dau of HSH 6th Prince Franz-Joseph, Furst and Altgraf of Salm-Reifferscheidt Krautheim und Dyck, and *d* 22 Sept 1972, leaving by her:

(3) +Stephen George [Stephen Geddes Esq, 7 Queens Mansions, Brook Green, London W6 7EB]; *b* 28 June 1969

(6) *Camilla Joanna Isabella [Miss Camilla Geddes, 55 Chelsea Sq, London SW3 6LH]; *b* 10 Dec 1966

3 John Reay Campbell, TD; Capt Roy Gloster Hus (TA) WW II (wounded), PR Advsr S Pearson Ltd, memb Cncl Br Scientific Instrument Research Assoc; *b* 24 April 1915; *educ* Stowe and Edinburgh and Lond Us; *m* 3 May 1944 *Diana Elizabeth, JP [The Hon Mrs John Geddes, Carickeens, Moyard, Co Galway, Ireland], memb ILEA, est dau of Brig Charles Copley Swift, OBE, MC, RE, and Mrs William Maxwell Henning, and *d* 15 Dec 1978, leaving issue:

(1) +Hugh John Reay [Hugh Geddes Esq, 20 Gatcombe Rd, London N19]; *b* 6 April 1945; *educ* Eton, Magdalene Coll Cambridge (BA 1966, DipArch 1969) and U of Calif. at Berkeley (MLA 1981); *m* 27 Jan 1972 *Harriet Diana Christabel, theatrical costume designer, yr dau of S/Ldr Hon John Francis McLaren RAF (*see* ABERCONWAY, B), and has:

1a +Luke John McLaren; *b* 22 March 1974

2a +Sam Duncan McLaren; *b* 29 Aug 1975

4 David Campbell, TD; Capt Roy Hong Kong Def Force, Maj RA WW II, civil servant; *b* 11 March 1917; *educ* Stowe and Gonville and Caius Coll Cambridge (MA 1938); PhD London; *m* 31 Dec 1948 *Gerda, dau of Gerdt Meyer Bruun, of Bergen, Norway, and *d* 29 Nov 1995, leaving issue:

(1) *Jane [Mrs Peter Watt, Kirklands of Coull, Coull, Aboyne, Aberdeenshire AB34 4TS]; *b* 26 April 1950; *educ* Cambridge (BA) and London Us (PhD); *m* 1979 *Peter Watt and has:

1a *Henry George; *b* 1980

2a *David Peter; *b* 1983

(2) *Harriet [Mrs Hugh Devlin, 20 Windmill Rd, Saintfield, Co Down BT24 7DX]; *b* 18 March 1953; *educ* Cambridge (BA); AMA, MRSS; *m* 1st 1976 (*divorce* 1977) Jonathan Allen; *m* 2nd 1982 *Hugh Devlin and by him has issue:

1a *Thomas Halcro; *b* 1984

2a *James Alexander; *b* 1985

3a *Patrick David; *b* 1988

1 Margaret Campbell; *b* 18 March 1913; *m* 17 Nov 1937 HRH Prince Ludwig Hermann Alexander Chlodwig of Hesse und bei Rhein (*d* 30 May 1968), only surv s of HRH Ernest Ludwig Karl Albert Wilhelm, Grand Duke of Hesse, and *dsp* 26 Jan 1997

The 1st BARON *d* 8 Jan 1954; his est son,

ROSS CAMPBELL GEDDES, **2nd Baron Geddes**, KBE (1970), DL (Midlothian 1957); *b* 20 July 1907; *educ* Rugby and Gonville and Caius Coll Cambridge (BA 1929); dir P&O (ret 1972), chm Trident Tankers, Limmer Hldgs, Clerical Medical and Gen Life Assur, Monks Investment and BTA, dir Foseco Minsep, London Scottish Investment Tst, chm Westminster Medical Sch Cncl 1968, memb Governing Body Westminster Hosp, pres Inst Petroleum 1956–57 and Chamber Shipping UK 1968, Assist Dir Tanker Div Min War Tport 1940–42, Br Merchant Shipping Mission Washington 1942–44, Dep Dir Tanker Div Min War Tport 1944–45, Chm Min Tport Ctee Enquiry Carriers Licensing 1963–65; *m* 26 Jan 1931 *Enid Mary [The Rt Hon Enid Lady Geddes, c/o Lime Tree House, Stradbroke, Suffolk IP21 5JX], only child of Clarence Howell Butler, of Tenterden, Kent, and *d* 2 Feb 1975, having had:

1 Neil Ross; *b* 20 Sept, *d* 12 Oct 1932

2 EUAN MICHAEL ROSS GEDDES, **3rd and present Baron Geddes**

1 *Margaret Ross [The Hon Mrs van Koetsveld, Northacre, Shackleford, Surrey GU8 6AX], MAOT 1960; *b* 5 May 1934; *educ* Benenden; Memb Assoc Occupational Therapists; *m* 6 May 1961 *Ralph Emilius Quintus van Koetsveld, son of Johan Emilius van Koetsveld, of Rotterdam, and has issue:

(1) *Michael William; *b* 16 March 1963

(2) *Antony Guy Hans; *b* 30 July 1964

(3) *Christopher Dirk; *b* 11 Feb 1969

GERAINT

Creation: B. (LP, UK) 1992.

THE BARON GERAINT, of Ponterwyd, Cco Dyfed (Geraint Wyn Howells) [The Rt Hon The Lord Geraint, Glennydd, Ponterwyd, Dyfed SY23 3LB]; *b* 15 April 1925; *educ* Ardwyn GS Aberystwyth; farmer, CC Cards 1952–74; Chm Welsh Lib Pty 1972–74 (Pres 1974–78), MP (Lib) Cardigan Feb 1974–83 and (Lib 1983–88, Lib Dem 1988–92) Ceredigion and Pembroke N 1983–92, Dep Speaker Ho Lds 1994–; V-Chm Br Wool Mktg Bd 1971–83, Chm Wool Producers Wales 1977–87, Lib Spokesman Wales 1985–87, Alliance Spokesman Welsh Affrs 1987, Lib Spokesman Ag 1987–89, Lib Dem Spokesman Ag 1989–92, Memb Select Ctee H of C Servs, Sec Ponterwyd Eisteddfod; *m* 1957 *Mary Olwen Hughes, dau of Margaret Ann Griffiths, of Tregaron, Dyfed, and has:

1 *Gaenor Wyn; *b* 1960

2 *Mari Wyn; *b* 1964

Lineage: DAVID JOHN HOWELLS, of Brynglas, Ponterwyd, Cards; *m* Mary Blodwen — and had:

GERAINT WYN, *cr* a **Baron**

GERARD

Arms: Arg. a saltire gu. **Crest:** A lion rampant erm., ducally crowned or. **Supporters:** On either side a lion erm., ducally crowned or, gorged with a collar gemel gu. and supporting a tilting spear ppr. **Motto:** *En Dieu est mon esperance* ('In God is my hope'). **Creations:** Bt. (E) 22 May 1611, B. (UK) 18 Jan 1876.

THE 5TH BARON GERARD OF BRYN, Co Palatine of Lancaster, and **a Baronet** (Sir Anthony Robert Hugo Gerard, Bt) [The Rt Hon The Lord Gerard, House of Lords, London SW1A 0PW]; *b* 3 Dec 1949; *s* kinsman 1992; *educ* Harvard; *m* 1976 (*divorce* 1997) Kathleen, est dau of Dr Bernard Ryan, of New York, and has:

1 +RUPERT BERNARD CHARLES; *b* 17 Dec 1981

2 +John Frederick William; *b* 1986

Lineage: WILLIAM Fitz GERALD, of Carru Castle, Pembs, est s of Gerald FitzWalter, Constable Pembroke Castle *temp* HENRY I, and bro of Maurice Fitz-Gerald, Ld of Maynooth (*see* LEINSTER, D), went to Ireland with Strongbow in 1171 but *d* England 1173, leaving with other issue:

1 Otho; ancestor of the Barons Carew (*qv*)

2 WILLIAM

The yr s,

WILLIAM fitz WILLIAM Fitz GERALD; Justice in Eyre Chester; had:

WILLIAM; Ld of half of Kingsley, Cheshire, through his w Emma, 2nd dau and coheir of Richard de Kingsley, Ch Forester Delamere, and *d* by 1259/60, leaving:

WILLIAM GERRARD, of Kingsley; living 1309; *m* Margaret — and *d* by 1316, leaving:

WILLIAM GERRARD, of Kingsley and Catenhall; living 1330, *m* Matilda, dau of Henry de Glasshowse, of Kingsley, and *d* by 1352, leaving issue:

WILLIAM GERARD, of Kingsley and Catenhall; *b c* 1322; *m* Joan, dau and heir of Peter de Bryn, of Brynhill (Brindle), Lancs, and had issue:

Sir PETER GERARD, of Kingsley and Bryn, Lancs; *d* by 1380, leaving:

1 THOMAS

2 John; ancestor of the GERARDs of Ince, Lancs, and the GERARD Earls of Macclesfield

The er son,

Sir THOMAS GERARD, of Kingsley and Bryn; MP Lancs 1384–94, ktd 1393; *d* 27 March 1415/6, leaving:

JOHN GERARD, of Kingsley and Bryn; *m* Alice (*d c* 27 Feb 1442), dau of Sir John le Boteler, and *d* 10 April 1431, leaving:

Sir PETER GERARD, of Kingsley and Bryn; *m* Isobella Strangeways and *d* by 1446, having had issue:

Sir THOMAS GERARD, of Kingsley and Bryn; *b c* 1430; *m* Douce, est dau of Sir Thomas Assheton, of Ashton-under-Lyne (for whose early ancestry *see* CLITHEROE, B), and *d* by 1494, having had an er s:

PETER GERARD; *m c* 21 Aug 1481 Margaret, dau of Sir Thomas Stanley (*see* DERBY, E), and *dvp* 19 June 1485, leaving:

Sir THOMAS GERARD, of Kingsley and Bryn; *b c* 1488; *m* Margery, widow of (a) Nicholas Longford, of Longford, Derbys, and (b) Sir John Port, of Etwall, Derbys, and dau of Sir Edmund Trafford (*see* DE TRAFFORD, Bt), and was *k* in the Scottish wars 6 Nov 1523, having had an only s:

Sir THOMAS GERARD, of Kingsley and Bryn; MP Lancs 1562–67, High Sheriff 1548; *b c* 1512; *m* Jane (*divorce* 1550), dau of Sir Peter Legh, of Haydock, Lancs, and had issue:

Sir THOMAS GERARD, of Kingsley and Bryn; MP Lancs 1566–67, High Sheriff Lancs 1558, imprisoned Tower London for plotting on behalf of MARY QUEEN OF SCOTS, forced to make over his Bromley estate to his kinsman Sir Gilbert Gerard, Attorney Gen, and to mortgage his estates in Lancs, Leics, Derbys, Cheshire and Yorks (presumably to pay a fine); *m* Elizabeth, dau and coheir of Sir John Port, of Etwall, and *d* Sept 1601, leaving an est s:

Sir Thomas Gerard, 1st Bt (E), so *cr* 22 May 1611, of Bryn; *b* 1560; MP Liverpool 1597, Lancs 1614 and Wigan 1621, had returned to him the £1,000 fee he had paid for the btcy in consideration of the sufferings of his f Sir Thomas Gerard on behalf of MARY QUEEN OF SCOTS; *m* 1st 1580 Cecily, dau of Sir Walter Maney, and had:

1 THOMAS (Sir), **2nd Bt**

2 John; *dsp*

1 Frances; *m* Ralph Standish, of Standish, Lancs, and had issue

Sir Thomas *m* 2nd Mary, dau of Sir James Hawes, Ld Mayor London, and widow of (a) John Smythe, of London, and (b) Sir Robert Lee, Ld Mayor London, but by her had no issue; *m* 3rd Mary, widow of (a) Anthony Browne and (b) Sir Edward Uvedale and dau of Sir William Dormer (*see* DORMER, B), but by her had no issue, and was *bur* 16 Feb 1620/1

His only son,

Sir Thomas Gerard, 2nd Bt; MP Liverpool 1624; *m* Frances, dau of Sir Richard Molyneux, 1st Bt, of Sefton, and sis of 1st Viscount Molyneux (*see* 1970 edn SEFTON, E), and had, with four other sons (*d* unm) and a dau (Frances, a nun):

1 WILLIAM (Sir), **3rd Bt**

2 Richard, of Ince; *b* Oct 1612; soldier; *d* 5 Sept 1686; gf of:

(1) Richard, of Ince; f of:

1a William, of Ince; *dsp* 1743

1a Mary; *m* John Walmesley and *d* 13 Dec 1795, leaving issue

2a Elizabeth; *d* unm

3 Thomas (Dr); followed his brother Richard to Maryland; *m* Susannah, dau of Abel Snow, and *d* 1673, leaving issue

Sir THOMAS *d* 15 May 1630; his est son,

Sir William Gerard, 3rd Bt; royalist Civil War, gravely impoverishing himself thereby; *m* Elizabeth, dau of Sir Cuthbert Clifton, of Lytham and Westby, and had (with three other sons):

1 WILLIAM (Sir), **4th Bt**

1 Frances; *m* Francis Howard, of Corby (*see* NORFOLK, D)

Sir WILLIAM was *bur* 7 April 1681; his est son,

Sir William Gerard, 4th Bt; *m* 1st 1662 Anne, dau of Sir John Preston, 1st Bt, of Preston Patrick and Nether Levens, Westmorland, and the Manor and Abbey of Furness, Lancs, and had, with other issue (*d* unm):

1 WILLIAM (Sir), **5th Bt**

1 Anne; *m* Charles Waterton, of Walton, Yorks

Sir William *m* 2nd Mary, widow of James Poole, of Poole, Cheshire, and sis of Sir Edward Mostyn, 1st Bt (*qv*), but by her had no issue, and was *bur* 16 April 1702

His est son,

Sir William Gerard, 5th Bt; *bapt* 22 June 1662; *m* Mary (*bur* 18 July 1726), 2nd dau and eventually heir of John Cansfield, of Cansfield, and was *bur* 29 May 1721, leaving an est s:

Sir William Gerard, 6th Bt; *b* 27 Dec 1697; *m* 1720 Elizabeth, 4th dau of Thomas Clifton, of Lytham, Lancs, and *d* 9 Dec 1732, having had (with a dau, Mary):

1 **Sir William Gerard, 7th Bt**; *b* 4 Sept 1721; *d* unm 22 March 1740

2 **Sir Thomas Gerard, 8th Bt**; *m* Elizabeth Tasbrough and *dspm* 25 June 1780, having had two daus (the yr, Clare, *d* unm 5 April 1798)

3 **Sir Robert Cansfield Gerard, 9th Bt**; *m* 1770 Catherine (*d* 13 Jan 1821), dau of William Anderton, of Euxton, by Mary, dau of 5th Viscount Molyneux (*see* 1970 edn SEFTON, E) and widow of Thomas Clifton, of Lytham, and *d* 6 March 1784, having had (with three daus):

(1) **Sir Robert Gerard, 10th Bt**; *d* 26 Aug 1791

(2) **Sir William Gerard, 11th Bt**, *b* 2 July 1773; *m* 21 Dec 1795 Anna Maria (*d* 13 Sept 1808), 2nd dau of Miles Stapylton, of Richmond, Yorks, and *dsp* 2 Aug 1826

(3) John, of Windle Hall, Lancs; *m* 22 Feb 1803 Elizabeth (*m* 3rd William Gerard Walmsley), dau of Edward Ferrers, of Baddesley Clinton, Warwicks, and *d* 22 May 1822, having had, with other issue:

1a **Sir John Gerard, 12th Bt**; Col 3rd Regt Royal Lancs Militia; *b* 8 Dec 1804; *m* 3 Dec 1827 Monica (*d* 4 May 1865), dau of Thomas Strickland Standish, of Standish and Sizebergh, and *dsp* 21 Feb 1854

2a William; *b* 18 May 1806; *m* March 1829 Mary (*m* 2nd 19 Jan 1848 Hon Gilbert Stapleton (*d* 16 Dec 1856), bro of 8th Baron Beaumont (*see* NORFOLK, D), added the name BRETHERTON 16 June 1869 and was *cr* a Marchesa by HH THE POPE; *d* 22 Dec 1883), only dau of Bartholomew Bretherton, of Rainhill, Lancs, and *dsp* Oct 1844

3a ROBERT TOLVER, **1st Baron**

4a Frederic Sewallis, of Aspull House, Lancs, JP, DL; *b* 23 Dec 1811; *m* 2 Sept 1835 Mary Ann (*d* 28 March 1883), dau of Rev Thomas Wilkinson, Vicar Kirkallam, Derbys, and *d* 7 May 1884, leaving, with other issue:

1b Frederick, of Kinwarton, Alcester, JP Warwicks and Worcs; *b* 6 Aug 1839; Capt 23rd Fus; *m* 29 April 1869 Catherine (*d* 5 May 1906), yst dau of Charles Porter, of the Mythe, Tewkesbury, and *d* 23 Feb 1916, leaving:

1c Edith Mary Catherine; *m* 24 Sept 1896 Edward Charles Riddell, JP, of Hermeston Hall, Nottingham, and *d* 27 July 1948, leaving issue. He *d* 17 Sept 1940

1b Mary Anne; *m* 15 Oct 1856 Sir John Lawson, 2nd Bt (*see* HOWARD-LAWSON, Bt), and *d* 5 Nov 1868, leaving issue

2b Emma Eliza; *m* 1st 13 Sept 1859 3rd Baron Stafford (*qv*); *m* 2nd 24 Aug 1887 Basil Fitzherbert and *d* 11 Nov 1912 (*see* STAFFORD, B)

5a Thomas Alexander; *b* 11 July 1812; of the 29th Regt; *m* and *d* 3 April 1850, leaving issue

1a Eliza; *m* 20 April 1830 Henry Raymond Arundell and *d* 5 June 1872, leaving issue

The 12th Bt's yr bro,

Sir Robert Tolver Gerrard, 13th Bt and **1st Baron Gerard of Bryn**, Co Palatine of Lancaster (UK), so *cr* 18 Jan 1876; Col Lancs Hus Yeo Cav, ADC to HM QUEEN VICTORIA; *b* 12 May 1808; *m* 14 Feb 1849 Harriet (*d* 20 July 1888), dau of

Edward Clifton and bro of Thomas Clifton, of Lytham, and *d* 15 March 1887, leaving:

1 WILLIAM CANSFIELD GERARD, **2nd Baron Gerard of Bryn**, DSO; Hon Col Lancs Hus, Lt 2nd Life Gds; *b* 1 June 1851; *m* 7 Aug 1877 Mary Emmeline Laura (*d* 19 Feb 1918), est dau of Henry Beilby William Milner, of W Retford House, Notts (*see* MILNER, Bt), and *d* 30 July 1902, leaving:

(1) FREDERICK JOHN GERARD, **3rd Baron Gerard of Bryn**, MC (1918), JP, DL Lancs; Capt RHG, formerly Lancs Hus ImpYeo, served WW I (twice wounded, despatches); *b* 10 Nov 1883; *m* 17 Sept 1906 his cousin Mary Frances Emma (*d* 6 April 1954), dau of Sir Martin Le Marchant Hadsley Gosselin, GCVO, KCMG, CB, and *d* 12 Feb 1953, leaving:

1a ROBERT WILLIAM FREDERICK ALWYN GERARD, **4th Baron Gerard of Bryn**; *b* 23 May 1918; *educ* Ampleforth; RAF WW II; *d* 1992

1a (Violet) Ethel Mary, MBE (1954); Organiser Herts WVS; *b* 11 March 1908; *d* unm 16 April 1970

2a Patricia Clare Gabrielle (Mother Clare Emmanuel); nun Provincial Sisters of the Assumption; *b* 17 March 1909; *d* 27 Sept 1972

3a Heloise Katherine Marie; nun; *b* 21 June 1911

4a Mary Dorothy Fresia; *b* 9 Jan 1922; *m* 1947 Maj Eric George Davies and had:

1b *Mark; *b* 14 Nov 1947

(1) Ethel Catherine Hannah; *b* 16 May 1881; *m* 11 Feb 1904 Arnold Maurice, Count de Bendern (formerly Baron de Forest), Cncllr of State Principality of Liechtenstein, adopted s of Baron Hirsch, and *d* 27 Sept 1966, leaving issue. He *d* 6 Oct 1968

2 Robert Joseph GERARD later GERARD-DICCONSON (roy licence 1896), of Wrightington Hall, Lancs; Capt 3rd Bn KO Roy Lancaster Regt; *b* 8 Aug 1857; *m* 19 April 1888 Eleanor (*m* 2nd 12 Nov 1925 Mark Fenwick, of Abbotswood, Stow-on-the Wold (*d* 28 Jan 1945); *d* 3 March 1953), 2nd dau of William John BANKES formerly MURRAY, of Rosemount, Ross-shire, and *d* 16 Sept 1918, leaving:

(1) Charles Robert Tolver Michael Gerard, DSO (1918), OBE (1944), JP (Lancs 1924); Lt-Col Gren Gds, Brevet-Col 5th Bn Manchester Regt WW I (wounded), Dep Prov Marshal London WW II; *b* 28 Feb 1894; *educ* Eton; *m* 1st 19 Oct 1915 (*divorce* 1930) Aimee Gwendolyn, yr dau of Sir Rupert Havelock Clarke, 2nd Bt, of Rupertswood (*qv*); *m* 2nd 25 Sept 1930 Norma (*d* 15 April 1976), dau of Amos Frankford Rogers, MD, of Ottawa, and *d* 14 Jan 1971, leaving by his 1st w:

1a Rupert Charles Frederick, MBE (1946); Maj Gren Gds WW II; *b* 6 Oct 1916; *educ* Eton and Trin Coll Cambridge; *m* 29 March 1948 (*divorce* 1969) Huguette Reiss-Brian, dau of Hugo Reiss, of Brazil, and Mme Guy Brian, of Paris, and *d* 1 Dec 1978, leaving issue:

1b ANTHONY ROBERT HUGO GERARD, **5th and present Baron Gerard**

2b +Peter Charles Rupert [Peter Gerard Esq, 1824 Circle Rd, Baltimore, MD 21204, USA]; *b* 27 Sept 1951; *m* 16 June 1973 *Sophie Christine, est dau of Irénée du Pont May, of Wilmington, Delaware

2a (Robert) Guy Standish; Lt Gren Gds; *b* 16 Dec 1921; *educ* Eton; *m* 1st 16 Dec 1948 (*divorce* 1964) Barbara, dau of Leonard J Stone, of Merivale, Constant Spring, Jamaica; *m* 2nd 16 Nov 1964 Ursula (*d* 1993), formerly w of John Cogswell, of Panama, and dau of Andrew Mackenzie, of Vancouver, BC, and *d* 1980, leaving by his 1st w:

1b *Susan Roberta Caroline [Mrs Lucien Bowman, Ellman House, Glynde, Sussex]; *b* 21 Jan 1951; *m* 1st 11 Feb 1971 (*divorce* 1984) Andrew Nigel Wendover Beeson, s of Capt N W Beeson, Scots Gds, and Mrs Richard Hodges, and has issue:

1c *James Gerard; *b* 1976

1c *Susanna Caroline; *b* 27 June 1973

1b (cont.) Mrs Susan Beeson *m* 2nd 1984 *Lucien Lee Bowman and has by him:

2c *(Richard) Frederick Gerard; *b* 1988

2c *Lisa Ashley Annabel Helena; *b* 1985

2b *Diana Sarah [Mrs Michael Irwin, 2620 Monte Vista Ave, El Cerrito, CA 94530, USA]; *b* 31 May 1952; *m* 1991 *Michael Macfarlane Irwin

(1) Winifride Mary; *m* 1st 15 Oct 1908 Maj-Gen Sir Thomson Capper, KCMG, CB, DSO, s of William Copeland Capper, ICS. He *d* 27 Sept 1915 of wounds recd in action. She *m* 2nd 21 Jan 1920 Godfrey Newall Graburn, of Westridge House, Crowborough, Sussex, yr s of Newall Graburn, of Wepham House, Arundel, Sussex

(2) Evelyn; *m* 8 Oct 1910 Col John Edmond Hugh Balfour, CMG, DSO, DL, 11th Hus, of The Manor, Sidmouth, Devon, s of George Edmund Balfour, of Sidmouth Manor, Devon, and *d* 28 May 1973, leaving issue. He *d* 5 Oct 1952

1 Mary Monica; *m* 19 Nov 1878 Gen Sir Laurence James Oliphant, KCB, KCVO, Gren Gds, of Condie and Newton, Perthshire, and *d* 14 April 1926, leaving issue. He *d* 6 July 1914

2 Katherine Frances; *m* 10 Aug 1880 Sir Martin Le Marchant Hadsley Gosselin, GCVO, KCMG, CB, of Blakesware, Ware, Herts, Envoy Extrdy and Min Plen Lisbon, and *d* 19 April 1924, leaving issue. He *d* 26 Feb 1905

GETHIN

Arms: Vert a stag saliant arg., armed or. **Crest:** On a cap of dignity ppr. a stag's head erased arg., armed and ducally gorged or. **Motto:** Try. **Creation:** Bt. (I) 1 Aug 1665.

SIR RICHARD JOSEPH ST LAWRENCE GETHIN, 10TH BT, of Gethinsgrott, Co Cork [Sir Richard Gethin Bt, Trotts Ash, Sole St, Cobham, Kent DA12 3AY]; Maj RCT; *b* 29 Sept 1949; *s* f 1988; *educ* Oratory Sch, RMA Sandhurst, RMC Sci Shrivenham and Cranfield Inst Technology (BSc Civil Engrg, MSc); *m* 1974 *Jacqueline Torfrida, dau of Cdr David Cox, RN, of Forest Gate, Denmead, Hants, and has issue:

1 *Katherine Torfrida; *b* 1976

2 *Rosanna Clare; *b* 1979

3 *Belinda Jacqueline; *b* 1981

Lineage: Sir Richard Gethin, 1st Bt (I), so *cr* 1 Aug 1665, of Gethins Grot, Co Cork; MP Clonmel 1639–49 and Newtown Limavady 1661–66, granted at the Restoration land in Co Cork (part of which, Cariglemleary, was erected into a manor, called Gethinsgrot) on condition he established an English colony there; had issue:

1 RICHARD, of Ballyfenatur, Co Cork; *b* 1641; *m* Jane (*m* 2nd Dudley Thompson), dau of Anthony Stawell, and *dvp* between 6 Feb 1678/9 and 20 June 1679, leaving:

(1) RICHARD (Sir), **2nd Bt**

2 Percy; High Sheriff Co Sligo 1699; *m* Anne (*d* Feb 1714), widow of Sir Francis Gore (*see* GORE-BOOTH, Bt), and dau of Capt Robert Park, and *dsps* between 1714 and 1723

3 Randolph; *b* 1656; *m* 1691 Mary (*d* between 10 Oct 1745 and 1757), dau of John St Leger (*see* DONERAILE, V), and had:

(1) Arthur; had a dau, Mary

(2) Percy, of Firgrove; Co Cork; *m* 1732 Elizabeth Armstead

(1) Gertrude; *m* 1723 John Philpot

1 Gertrude; *m* Hon Francis Hawley

The 1st Bt's grandson,

Sir Richard Gethin, 2nd Bt; BA Dublin 1696; *b* 1674; *m* 1st *c* 15 Feb 1696/7 Grace (*dsp* 11 Oct 1697), dau of Sir George Norton, of Abbots Leigh, Somerset; *m* 2nd 1698 Sarah (*m* 2nd — Boyle), 3rd dau of Henry Farnham, of Nethet Hall, and *d* on or soon after 3 Aug 1709, leaving an est s:

Sir Richard Gethin, 3rd Bt; High Sheriff Co Sligo 1724; *b* 1698; *m* Margaret, dau of Col Eames (*d* between 15 Oct 1774 and 1778), and had (with a dau, Mrs Hyde, of Co Cork):

1 RICHARD (Sir), **4th Bt**

2 John, of Ballymoat, Co Sligo; *m* Victoria, dau of — Stone, and had issue:

(1) John; *m* Margaret, dau of David Jones, and had issue:

1a John; High Sheriff Co Sligo 1827; *b* Dec 1798; *m* Jan 1830 Ann Stuart, dau of Jones Taafe Irwin, and had:

1b John; Capt Sligo Rifle Regt; *b* 25 Jan 1831; *m* 1 June 1858 Emmeline (*m* 2nd 23 May 1867 Rev John Henry Hudleston; *d* 1910), dau of Thomas Horsfall, of Burley, Yorks, and *d* 1860, having had issue:

1c John Percy, JP W R Yorks; Brevet Col Manchester Regt; *b* 9 April 1859; *m* 19 Dec 1912 Emily Maria (*d* Feb 1944), 2nd dau of Gen Sir Robert Onesiphorus Bright, GCB, of Normandy Park, Guildford, and *d* 11 March 1934

2c Emmeline; *d* unm 5 May 1916

2b Richard Henry; *b* 20 Feb 1832; *d* unm

(2) Richard; *m* Catherine (*d* 1807), dau of Ormsby Jones, of Streida, Co Sligo, and *d* 9 Aug 1839, leaving:

1a Richard, of Earlesfield, Co Sligo; 13th Light Dragoons; *b* 3 Nov 1804; *m* 26 Jan 1836 Mary (*d* 1882), dau of Sir Alexander Crichton, of Sevenoaks, and *d* 1889, leaving, with other issue:

1b George, JP Co Sligo; High Sheriff 1893, Capt 20th Regt, served Indian Mutiny 1857–58 (medal and clasp for Lucknow); *b* 18 Oct 1836; *m* 5 Oct 1870 Mabel (*d* 5 April 1934), dau of Peter Connellan, DL, and *d* 14 Aug 1913, having had:

1c Randolph George, MBE (1919), JP Co Waterford; Capt and Hon Maj Special Res S Irish Horse, Capt 4th Bn Inniskilling Fus; *b* 28 June 1871; *m* 7 Nov 1911 Georgina Mary (*d* 21 Oct 1956), dau of Rev Canon George Beresford Power, of Kilfane Glebe, Thomastown, Co Kilkenny (*see* 1956 edn POWER, Bt, of Kilfane), and *d* 21 June 1945, having had:

1d John Percy Devayne DFC (1941); S/Ldr RAF WW II; *b* 1917; *d* of wounds recd in action June 1941

2d Desmond Richard le Poer; Maj Para Regt and Roy Irish Fus SR WW II (wounded); *b* 1919; *educ* Stowe; *m* 15 July 1950 *Susan (*m* 2nd 1988 Maj W P Mead), dau of Brig F Talbot Baines, of Molo, Kenya, and *d* 1984, leaving:

1e +Martin Anthony [Martin Gethin Esq, Cnwc y Morfol, Letterston, Dyfed SA6Z 5XE]; *b* 10 Sept 1952; *educ* St Columba's and Seale Hayne Coll; *m* 1978 *Christine Ann, dau of A F Bates, of Purley, Bognor Regis, Sussex, and has issue:

1f +Robert Lawrence; *b* 1984

2f +Jared Desmond; *b* 1986

1e *Deirdre Anne; *b* 21 April 1951

1d *Kathleen Beatrix [Miss Kathleen Gethin, Rincurran, Ardbrack, Kinsale, Co Cork, Ireland]; *b* 1912

2c Percy Francis; artist, 2nd Lt 3rd Bn Devonshire Regt; *b* 25 July 1874; *ka* 28 June 1916

3c Reginald Owen; *b* 1877; *d* Dec 1899 in Plumer's march to Relief Mafeking

2b Francis Reid; *b* 31 July 1848; *m* 9 Feb 1882 Harriet Georgina (*d* 20 Sept 1940), dau of Very Rev Arthur Moore, Dean Achonry, and *d* 23 March 1940, leaving issue:

1c Richard; Capt E African Corps, MP, Cmdt Italian POW Camp Kenya, Lt 3rd Bn N Staffs Regt and 3rd Bn KAR, served E Africa WW I and WW II; *b* 1886; *m* 1st 8 June 1927 (*divorce* 1953) Mary Hunter (*d* 1972), er dau of Willoughby James Bond, JP, DL, of Farragh, Co Longford; *m* 2nd 15 Oct 1953 *Winifred Louise [Mrs Richard Gethin, Registry Cottage, High Street, Limpsfield, Surrey], dau of Frank James Hall, of Sandon Lodge, Edgbaston, Birmingham, and *d* 1976, leaving by his 1st w:

1d +Richard Reid [Richard Gethin Esq, 6 Saxons Acre, Warminster, Wilts]; md Gethin & Dawson, Kisii, Kenya; *b* 15 July 1931; *educ* Portora Roy Sch; *m* 1980 (*divorce* 1994) Brenda Elizabeth, dau of Walter George Treadwell, of Sidcup, Kent

2d +Alexander Willoughby [Alexander Gethin Esq, Holly House, Orchehill Ave, Gerrards Cross, Bucks SL9 8PT]; Lt Res Royal Inniskilling Fus, geologist, late oil co manager; *b* 26 March 1935; *educ* Portora Royal Sch and Jesus Coll Cambridge (BA 1958, MA); *m* 11 June 1964 *Patricia, yr dau of Alfred Sweeney, of Fairfield, Gerrards Cross, and has issue:

1e *Alexandra Mary [Miss Alexandra Gethin, 2 Loris Rd, London W6 7QA]; *b* 14 March 1965; *educ* St Leonard's Mayfield and St John's Coll Cambridge (BA 1986, MA); ACA

2e *Frances Sheilagh [Mrs Quintus Travis, 78c Brook Green, London W6 7BE]; *b* 14 March 1965; *educ* St Leonard's Mayfield and Downing Coll Cambridge (BA 1986, MA); ACA; *m* 1991 *Quintus R C L Travis

3e *Elizabeth Alice [Miss Elizabeth Gethin, 1 Tasker Rd, London NW3 2Y]; *b* 17 April 1970; *educ* St Leonard's Mayfield

1c Harriet Gwendoline; *m* 1917 Rev William Frederick Crosthwait, MC, CF, and had issue. He *d* 28 Dec 1930

2c Mary Elizabeth Hilda; *d* unm 12 Dec 1968

1b Frances Katherine; *m* 22 May 1860 Frederick John Henry Fownes Hamilton, and *d* 10 Aug 1923, having had issue. He *d* 1893

1a Victoria; *m* George Dodwell, of Kelvinsfort, Co Sligo, and *d* 23 June 1843, having had issue

Sir RICHARD's er son,

Sir Richard Gethin, 4th Bt; *m* 15 Aug 1750 Mary (*d* 4 Aug 1787), only dau of 27th Baron of Howth, and *d c* 1778, leaving:

1 PERCY (Sir), **5th Bt**

1 Lucy

2 Mary

The only son,

Sir Percy Gethin, 5th Bt; High Sheriff Co Sligo 1780; *m* May 1786, Anne, dau of Thomas Nagle, of Mount Nagle, Co Cork, and aunt of Sir Richard Nagle Bt, and had with two sons (*d* unm):

1 Richard Capt 20th Regt, served Peninsular War, first through the wall at storming of Badajoz, with his Regt guarded NAPOLEON at St Helena 1815–21; *m* 17 Nov 1819 Jane (*d* 1831), 3rd dau of Lt-Col — South, 20th Regt, of Heavitree, nr Exeter, and *dvp* 5 Jan 1835, leaving issue:

(1) RICHARD (Sir), **6th Bt**

(2) William St Lawrence; *b* 29 Sept 1828; *m* 11 Dec 1857 Emily (*d* 1897), dau of William Fife, of Rothbury, Northumberland, and *d* 1910, having had:

1a Percy Addison Hayward, JP Bechuanaland, served Vryburg 1899, Relief Mafeking 1900, Intelligence Dept Boer War 1899–1902 (medals); *b* 1 Nov 1862; *m* 26 May 1888 Alberta (*d* 6 July 1948), dau of W Walpole, of Milgrove, Co Tipperary, and *d* 27 Feb 1907, leaving issue:

1b Percy St Lawrence, MBE (1941); Lt-Col 3rd KAR E Africa WW I and Middle East WW II, Mil Medal Hailie Selassie; *b* 2 Oct 1889; *m* 24 May 1913 Margery (*d* 1968), dau of James J Cleverly, RM, of Walvis Bay, Cape Colony, and *d* 1959, leaving issue:

1b +Patrick St Lawrence Cleverly [Maj Patrick Gethin, 4 Orchard Close, Berry Lane, East Hanney, Oxon OX12 OJD]; Maj Roy Inniskilling Fus WW II (wounded); *b* 22 Nov 1914; *educ* Cheltenham; *m* 12 Oct 1940 *Dagmar May, only child of N H J Daniell, of Race View, Coonoor, S India, and has issue:

1d *Rowene Margaret [Mrs Salvador Rodriguez-Perez, Namanga, Orchard Lane, E Hendred, Oxon OX12 8JW]; *b* 22 Feb 1944; *m* 1970 *Salvador Rodriguez-Perez and has:

1e *Marcus Lawrence; *b* 1974

2d *Elaine Patricia [Mrs Paul Marsh, 319 Beechgrove Drive, Scarborough, Ont, Canada M1E 4A2]; *b* 21 Oct 1946; *m* 22 June 1968 *Paul Disbury Marsh, yr s of R E Marsh, OBE, MA, of Clifton, Bristol and has:

1e *Jeremy Stephen; *b* 1973

1e *Nicola Clare; *b* 1970

1c *Sheelagh Grace [Mrs James Lindsay, 22 Wellington Drive, Kingston 6, Jamaica WI]; *b* 8 July 1923; *m* 24 May 1947 *James Wilson Lindsay, CBE, yr s of T K Lindsay, of Heathcote, Grangemouth, Stirlingshire, and has:

1d *Ian Gethin; *b* 15 Sept 1951; *m* 1978 *Ann Bettany, and has issue:

1e *Keri Francis Gethin; *b* 1986

1e *Emma Alexandra; *b* 1978

2a Henry Richard; Capt Marshall's Horse; *b* 24 Nov 1863; *m* Jan 1895 Clemence Mary, dau of Hon Alexander Wilmot, MLC, of Oatlands, Grahamstown, Cape Colony, and was *ka* S Africa 25 April 1900, leaving issue:

1b Richard Patrick Wilmot; 2nd Lt Roy Munster Fus; *b* 4 Jan 1896; *ka* 26 Sept 1915

1a Maria; *d* unm 18 Jan 1925

2a Emily Grace; *m* 16 Aug 1888 James Thomas Spencer Elliot, of Wolfelee, Roxburgh, and *d* 6 March 1912. He *dsp* 14 Dec 1982

(1) Mary Anne; *m* 1872 Walter Wilson and *d* 29 Jan 1903. He *d* 1884

(2) Maria; *m* 16 Feb 1855 J C Johnstone and had issue. He *d* 1892

Sir PERCY *d* 10 Oct 1837; his gs,

Sir Richard Gethin, 6th Bt; *b* 28 Dec 1823; Offr 20th Regt, 1st Dragoon Gds and 83rd Regt, Capt Turkish contingent Crimea 1856; *m* 25 June 1846 (*divorce* Jan 1862) Frances (*d* 27 Aug 1906), yst dau of George Weller Poley, of Boxted Hall, Suffolk, and had issue:

1a RICHARD CHARLES PERCY (Sir), **7th Bt**

2 Walter William St Lawrence; *b* 25 July 1850; *d* June 1870

Sir RICHARD *d* 1885; his only surv son,

Sir Richard Charles Percy Gethin, 7th Bt, JP Hants; barrister Inner Temple, Capt and Hon Maj 4th Bn Suffolk Regt Boer War 1900–02; *b* 30 Nov 1847; *m* 5 June 1876 Catherine (*d* 16 Dec 1932), est dau of Frederick Edward Burton Scott, of Claughton, Cheshire, and had issue:

1 RICHARD WALTER ST LAWRENCE (Sir), **8th Bt**

2 Frederic Durrant Scott; Maj and Brevet Lt-Col RA Boer War 1900–02 (Queen's medal with three clasps, King's medal with two clasps) and WW I; *b* 19 Oct 1879; *m* 12 June 1915 Margaret Cecilia (*d* 14 June 1955), only child of L R W Forrest, of Wimbledon, and *d* 20 Jan 1959, having had:

(1) John Amory Forrest; For Serv 1939–59; *b* 16 Feb 1916; *educ* Stowe and Ch Ch Oxford (BA 1938, MA 1948); *m* 12 May 1941 *Barbara Damarel Cicely [Mrs John Gethin, Brae View, Wester Galcantray, Cawdor by Nairn, Scotland], dau of Alan Robert Cecil Westlake, ICS, of Rowledge, Farnham, Surrey, and *d* 8 May 1965, leaving issue:

1a +Christopher John Forrest [Christopher Gethin Esq, Moorstone, Buckland-in-the-Moor, S Devon]; *b* 11 Dec 1945; *educ* Stowe, Magdalene Coll Cambridge (MA), U of Sydney (MTCP) and Sch of Homoeopathy (DipHom); *m* 1983 *Rebecca Mary, dau of Benjamin Thomas Gibbins, of San Remo, Italy, and has issue:

1b +Tobias John Forrest; *b* 1983

2a +Nicholas Geoffrey Forrest [Nicholas Gethin Esq, Shepherd's House, Chaldon Herring, Dorset]; *b* 30 Oct 1950; *educ* Stowe, Ch Ch Oxford (MA), RAM (LRAM) and Hochschule für Musik Vienna; *m* 1993 *Catherine, dau of John Nelson, of Cardiff

3a +Stephen Amory Forrest [Stephen Gethin Esq, Peyzac le Moustier, Les Eyzies de Tayac, France]; *b* 30 Oct 1950; *educ* Stowe and Magdalene Coll Cambridge (MA Vet MB); *m* 1992 *Christine, dau of Hervé Fondecave, of Toulouse, and has:

1b +Amory Lionel; *b* 13 March 1995

1a *Elizabeth Amoret [Mrs Nicholas du Cane Wilkinson, Birkwood Cottage, Croy, Inverness IV1 2PR]; *b* 3 June 1942; *m* 19 June 1965 *Lt-Cdr Nicholas John du Cane Wilkinson, RN, s of R du Cane Wilkinson, of Hampstead, and has:

1b *Piers Nicholas; *b* 1973

1b *Samantha Karen; *b* 12 June 1967; *m* 27 Aug 1994 *Matthew Godfrey-Faussett, yr s of Richard Godfrey-Faussett, of Badlesmere, Faversham

2b *Claire Felicity; *b* 15 Sept 1968; *m* 6 Sept 1997 *James Frank Lithgow, er s of Sir William James Lithgow

(2) Geoffrey Forrest, Capt RA WW II; *b* 14 June 1918; *ka* Italy 23 April 1944

(1) *Margaret Joan [Miss Margaret Gethin, 10 Bridge St, Saline, Dunfermline, Fife KY12 9TS]; *b* 22 July 1920

3 Percy Edward Lovell, OBE (1937), AFC (1918); Dir Surveys and Civil Aviation Tanganyika 1927–37, RAF Intell 1938, Maj RFC and RAF, Hon S/Ldr RAFR S Arabian Expdn 1909, WW I and WW II (despatches); *b* 11 Aug 1884; *educ* Radley; *m* 17 Jan 1918 Norah (*d* 29 April 1960), dau of James Norwood Stapledon, of Knapp, E Anstey, Devon, and *d* 8 July 1969, leaving:

(1) +(Robert) Hugh [Hugh Gethin Esq, 6 Montfort Fields, Kington, Herefs HR5 3AT]; Assist Dir Cwlth Bureau Animal Breeding and Genetics 1950–59, Br Cncl Science/Linguistics Offr Pakistan 1959–62, Intell Corps and 1st Airborne Div WW II; *b* 6 Dec 1918; *educ* Stowe and Corpus Christi Coll Cambridge (BA 1940, MA 1945); *m* April 1946 *Marjorie Gertrude, dau of B E Elliott, and has issue:

1a +Rupert Mark Lovell [Dr Rupert Gethin, 26 Morgan St, Bristol BS2 9LQ]; *b* 31 July 1957, *educ* Manchester U (BA, MA, PhD); *m* 1997 *Rita Elisabeth Maria, dau of Heinrich Langer, of Werne, Germany, and has:

1b *Leonard Alexander Hugh; *b* 1996

1a *Damaris Alicia Honor [Mrs José Albarrán, 11 Wolseley Ave, London SW19 8BG]; *b* 1 April 1952; *educ* UEA (BA) and Manchester U (MBA); *m* 1985 José Guillermo Albarrán (*d* 1988) and has:

1b *Isabel Grace; *b* 1987

(2) +(Percy) Amorey Beaufort [Amorey Gethin Esq, 60 Scotland Rd, Cambridge CB4 1QG]; served WW II 1943–44; *b* 28 Feb 1925; *educ* King's Sch Canterbury and London U (BA 1953); *m* 1st 16 Dec 1948 (*divorce* 1972) Sylva, dau of Bertil Olters, of Gothenburg, Sweden, *m* 2nd 1972 *Mieko, dau of Choji Suzuki, of Tokyo, and by his 1st w has:

1a +Terence Bertil Amorey [Terence Gethin Esq, 8 Elyne Rd, London N4 4RA]; *b* 22 Dec 1956; *educ* Imp Coll London (BSc)

Sir RICHARD *d* 17 June 1921; his est son,

Sir Richard Walter St Lawrence Gethin, 8th Bt, CMG (1919), DSO (1917); Col RA (ret), Offr i/c RA Record and Pay Office 1929–33, Boer War 1899–1901 (Queen's medal with five clasps) and WW I (despatches, Legn Hon), memb Inter-Allied Mil Mission Control Austria 1920 and Hungary 1921; *b* 16 Feb 1878; *m* 29 Dec 1906 Helen Frances Beatrice (*d* 27 Nov 1957), dau of Blundell Thornhill, of Castlebellingham, Co Louth, and had issue:

1 RICHARD PATRICK ST LAWRENCE (Sir), **9th Bt**

2 William Allan Tristram, MC [Lt-Col William Gethin MC, Carpenters, Chart Rd, Sutton Valence, Kent]; Lt-Col RA WW II Mauritius, France and Germany (despatches); *b* 13 Oct 1913; *educ* Oundle; *m* 17 Feb 1937 *Nancy Ruth, only child of Lt-Col H G MacGeorge, RE, of Paignton, and *d* 1995/6, leaving:

(1) +ANTHONY MICHAEL [Anthony Gethin Esq, Vale House, Loose, nr Maidstone, Kent]; *b* 10 Jan 1939; heir presumptive; *educ* Oundle and Magdalene Coll Cambridge (BA1962, MA); *m* 13 Feb 1965 *Vanse, yr dau of Col Cecil Disney Barlow, OBE, KSLI, and has issue:

1a +Nicholas Richard Tristram; *b* 15 Dec 1965

2a *William Anthony David St Lawrence; *b* 24 Nov 1970; *m* 1997 *Belinda Anthea, yst dau of Lt-Col Sir Blair Aubyn Stewart-Wilson, KCVO (*see* ORR EWING, Bt)

1a *Emma Kirstie; *b* 27 Feb 1968

(1) *Patricia Jane [Mrs Patricia Pringle, Rose Cottage, Loose, Maidstone, Kent]; *b* 14 Jan 1944; *m* 14 Oct 1967 (*divorce* 1981) Malcolm Pringle and has:

1a *Richard Malcolm Andrew; *b* 1974

1a *Caroline Georgina; *b* 1970

1 *Norah Helen Catharine [Mrs James Charles, 2 Atwater Court, Lenham, Maidstone, Kent]; *b* 23 Dec 1907; *m* 28 Sept 1938 James Andrew Paton Charles (*d* 1979), er son of Andrew Paton Charles, of Vale Copse, Tunbridge Wells, and has issue:

(1) *Michael James Paton [Michael Charles, 85 Wylde Rd, Morley, Perth, W Australia]; *b* 13 Oct 1939; *m* 1st 1964 (*divorce* 1969) Barbara Elizabeth, dau of A M Turner, of Strathfield, NSW; *m* 2nd 1969 *Maureen, dau of J Taylor, of Kiama, NSW, and by her has:

1a *Julian Andrew Paton; *b* 1973

2a *Dominic; *b* 1976

3a *Timothy; *b* 1979

(2) *Edward William; *b* 1944; BScAg and TropDip Trinidad, MPhil; *m* 1973 *Rosemarie, dau of K Kramer, of Winnipeg, Canada, and has issue:

1a *Daniel; *b* 1977

2a *Andrew; *b* 1980

3a *Simon; *b* 1984

1a *Elizabeth Helen; *b* 1975

(1)*Elizabeth Anne; *b* 29 April 1944; *m* 1975 (*divorce* 1985) Clive Cromarty Bloom

Sir RICHARD *d* 27 Aug 1946; his er son,

Sir Richard Patrick St Lawrence Gethin, 9th Bt; *b* 15 May 1911; *educ* Oundle; AMI MechE, Lt-Col REME WW II, OC No 11 Vehicle Depot Workshops to 1957, antique furniture restorer, Hon Research Fellow (Physics) Aston U Birmingham 1977; *m* 8 May 1946 *Fara Mary Zita [Dowager Lady Gethin, 68 Emanuel House, 18 Rochester Row, London SW1P 1BS], late 2nd Offr WRNS, yst dau of Joseph Henry Bartlett, and *d* 1988, leaving issue:

1 Sir RICHARD JOSEPH ST LAWRENCE GETHIN, **10th and present Bt**

1 *Helen Mary Elizabeth [Mrs David Strachan, 20 Pollock Esplanade, Woolgolga, NSW 2456, Australia]; *b* 22 Feb 1947; *m* 1975 *David Strachan and has:

(1) *Rachael Fara; *b* 1977

(2) *Roxanne Emma; *b* 1979

2 *Fara Mary Nicola; *b* 9 Feb 1948; *m* 1969 *Michael Smee, of Tolleshunt D'Arcy, Essex, and has issue:

(1) *Oliver Leo; *b* 1971

(2) *Milo Henry; *b* 1973

(3) *Leo Joseph; *b* 1976

3 *Georgina Jennifer Mary; *b* 1 Jan 1952; *m* 1979 *Daniel Meadows and has:

(1) *Harry Daniel; *b* 1980

(2) *Luke Roland; *b* 1982

(3) *Jack Richard; *b* 1987

4 *Mary Valentine Harriet; *b* 14 Feb 1954; *m* 1978 *Martin Philip Runnacles and has issue:

(1) *Elizabeth Jane Fara; *b* 1982

(2) *Sarah Caroline; *b* 1988

GIBBONS

Arms: Gu. a lion rampant or, debruised by a bend arg., charged with a torteau between two crosses patée fitchée sa. **Crest:** A lion's gamb erased and erect gu., charged with a bezant, holding a cross patée fitchée sa. **Motto:** *Gratior est a rege pio* ('It is more agreeable coming from a pious king'). **Creation:** Bt. (GB) 21 April 1752.

SIR WILLIAM EDWARD DORAN GIBBONS, 9TH BT, of Stanwell Place, Middlesex, JP (Portsmouth 1990–94, Westminster 1994) [Sir William Gibbons Bt JP, 5 Yarborough Rd, Southsea, Hants PO5 3DZ]; *b* 13 Jan 1948; s f 1982; *educ* Nautical Coll Pangbourne, RNC Dartmouth and Bristol U (BSc); DipBA, MCIT, Sealink UK: assist shipping and port manager Parkeston Quay 1979–82, serv manager (Anglo-Dutch) 1982–85, ferry line manager Harwich-Hook 1985–87, gen manager IoW servs 1987–90, Sealink Br Ferries tport and management consultant 1990–94, non-exec memb IoW Dock and Harbour Authority 1990–94; *m* 1972 *Patricia Geraldine Archer, LLB, barrister, only dau of Roland Archer Howse, of St Brelade, Jersey, and has issue:

1 +CHARLES WILLIAM EDWIN; *b* 28 Jan 1983

1 *Joan; *b* 1980

Lineage: Sir William Gibbons, 1st Bt (GB), so *cr* 21 April 1752; Speaker Ho Assembly Barbados; *m* Frances (*d* 1757), dau of Robert Hall, of Barbados, and *d* May 1760, leaving:

Sir John Gibbons, 2nd Bt, KB; MP Wallingford; *m* Martha, dau of Rev Dr Scawen Kenrick, DD, Rector Hambleden, Bucks, and had, with other issue:

1 WILLIAM (Sir), **3rd Bt**

2 John (Rev); Rector Brasted, Kent; *m* 1st Rebecca Ashley; *m* 2nd Margaret, widow of Rev William Peters, of Brasted Park, Kent, and dau and coheir of Rev John Kownsley, of Burton Fleming, Yorks, and *d* 1 May 1843 aged 82

3 Scawen Kenrick; *b* 18 Aug 1755; *m* 1783 Christian Skeele and *d* 1801, leaving issue

4 Robert; memb Cncl Barbados; *m* Margaret, dau of P Crookenden, of Barbados, and *d* 1805, leaving, with other issue:

(1) Frederick; Capt 56th Foot, Lt 7th Fus Peninsular War, severely wounded Albuera; *d* 1829

(2) Robert Kenrick; *b* 2 June 1797; *m* 11 July 1827 his cousin Louisa (*d* 27 April 1876), dau of **Sir John Gibbons, 4th Bt** (*see* below), and *d* 5 Aug 1880, having had, with other issue:

1a Robert (Rev); Vicar Handley, Dorset; *b* 24 Aug 1828; *m* 1st 28 Sept 1858 Sarah (*d* 25 July 1868), yst dau of John Nalder; *m* 2nd 21 Dec 1869 Catherine Tyrell (*d* 3 July 1923), widow of Capt F D Wyatt, 90th Regt, and dau of Tyrell Knapp, of Headington Hill, Oxford, and by his 1st w had:

1b Robert; *b* 15 June 1866; *m* 1893 Mildred Ethel (*d* 26 Jan 1956), dau of Gen Albert Henry Bamfield, JP Devon, IA, and *d* 17 July 1933, having had:

1c Robert Reginald, OBE (1919); Cdr RN WW I (wounded, three medals), Naval Control Serv WW II; *b* 11 May 1894; *m* 1st 5 Sept 1922 (*divorce* 1930) Mrs Olive Annie Judd, dau of William Blane, CBE; *m* 2nd 13 Sept 1930 (*divorce* 1939) Frances Ellery, dau of Maj-Gen Sir Charles Patrick Amyatt Hull, KCB; *m* 3rd 1939 Joan Winifred (*d* 1983), dau of F S Patterson, and *d* 21 Jan 1959, having by her had issue:

1d +Robert John [Robert Gibbons, The Poplars, 32 First Ave, Eastchurch, Kent ME12 4JN]; *b* 14 May 1944; *m* 1st 17 Sept 1966 (*divorce* 1971) Pauline Elizabeth, dau of Stanley Charles March; *m* 2nd 1973 (*divorce* 1980) Anne Marie, dau of Charles Lundberg; *m* 3rd 1986 *Elizabeth Jean, dau of W/Cdr Norman Henry Carrier, and by her has:

1e *Pippa Christine; *b* 1987

1d *Susan [Mrs Dennis Pollard, 27 School Lane, Ashurst Wood, Sussex RH19 3QW]; *b* 18 Nov 1941; *m* 26 March 1959 *Dennis Gordon Pollard and has issue:

1e *Peter Dennis; *b* 16 April 1964

1e *Lesley Susan [Mrs Edward Hart, 30 Stanmore Grove, Kirkstall, Leeds LS4 2RG]; *b* 25 Aug 1960; *m* 1978 *Edward John Hart and has issue:

1f *Jennifer Susan; *b* 1979
2e *Janet May [Mrs Andrew Brander, 5 Betchley Close, East Grinstead, W Sussex RH19 2DA]; *b* 1969; *m* 1989 *Andrew Paul Brander, s of Anthony Brander, and has issue:
1f *Christopher Iain; *b* 1993
1f *Emma Louise; *b* 1990
2c John; 2nd Lt Dorsetshire Regt; *b* 11 Nov 1897; *d* 6 June 1917 of wounds recd in action
3c Henry, MC; Lt-Col Devonshire Regt WW I Flanders and Russia (wounded, two medals), WW II Nigeria and India; *b* 11 Nov 1897
2a William (Sir), KCB; Pncpl Clerk H of C 1900–13; *b* 21 Jan 1841; *m* 20 Nov 1872 Sara Antoinetta (*d* 24 April 1930), 2nd dau of Stephen Cholmeley, and *d* 7 Jan 1930, having had, with other issue:
1b William Kenrick (Sir); CB (1938); Clerk H of C; ktd 1943, *b* 13 May 1876; *m* 13 July 1915 Aileen Margaret (*d* 1969), er dau of George James Elliot Trotter, JP, of the Deanery, Staindrop, Darlington, and *d* 26 March 1957, leaving issue:
1c *Diana Maynard [Miss Diana Gibbons, Bernedene, The Green, Letchmore Heath, Watford, Herts]; *b* 1916
2c *Priscilla Doreen; *b* 1918
3c *June Cecilia; *b* 1926
2b Edward Stephen, DSO; Maj Middx Regt, T/Lt-Col Highland LI, NW Frontier 1908 and WW I (despatches three times, seriously wounded); *b* 18 June 1883; *m* 2 Aug 1914 Annie Macgregor (*d* 22 March 1968), er dau of John Lyle; *ka* 19 Sept 1918, leaving issue:
1c John William; Lt-Cdr RN; *b* 13 Dec 1917; *m* 1st April 1940 (*divorce* 1947) Alix, dau of Bertram Lenox-Simpson, of Guernsey; *m* 2nd 1964 *Mrs Mary Lammin Stone [Mrs John Gibbons, Flat 4, Lions Hall, St Swithin St, Winchester, Hants], yst dau of G E Woof, and *d* 1993, leaving by his 1st w:
1d +Alan Clive [Alan Gibbons Esq, 4 Lions Hall, St Swithins St, Winchester, Hants]; *b* 1941
1c *Elisabeth Margaret [Mrs John Burstall, The Garden House, Orcheston, Wilts SP3 4RP]; *b* 12 Dec 1915; *m* 19 March 1936 Lt-Cdr John Edgar Burstall RN, (*d* 1979), er s of Capt John Burstall, and has issue:
1d *Mark Stephen; *b* 1945
1d *Elisabeth Ann; *b* 1937
2d *Gillian Margaret; *b* 1939
1b Sara Maud; *d* unm 1 Oct 1940
2b Eva Katherine; *d* unm 24 Feb 1947
3b Geraldine; *d* unm 4 Jan 1960
4b Dorothy Maynard; *m* 30 Sept 1908 Maj Edward Charles Talbot and *d* 29 Dec 1947, leaving issue (*see* SHREWSBURY and WATERFORD, E)
5b Margaret Helen; *m* 23 Oct 1912 Arthur Clement Knollys, MC, 3rd s of Sir Clement Courtenay Knollys, KCMG, and *d* 31 Oct 1957, leaving issue. He *d* 18 Jan 1944
(3) William Barton, JP Barbados; *b* 8 March 1802; Lt-Col; *m* 1st 24 Sept 1834 Mary Bishop (*d* 5 July 1834), dau of Hon John Braithwaite Skeete, Pres Barbados, and had, with other issue:
1a Frederick FitzRoy; Lt-Col cmdg 2nd Bn Devon Regt; *b* 12 Nov 1841; *m* 30 Oct 1867 Emma Ann Varley (*d* 1920), dau of John Hayton, and *d* 17 May 1914, having had, with other issue:
1b William Frederick; *b* 21 May 1870; *m* 31 Dec 1902 Ada (*d c* 1947), dau of Joseph James Foote, and *d* 16 May 1951
2b John Crookenden de Courcy; *b* 13 Aug 1874; *m* 1907 Gladys Russell Jones (*d* 1984), of Sydney, NSW, and *d* 1944, leaving issue:
1c John Hayton; *b* 1909; *m* 1945 *Phyllis [Mrs Donald Sheehan, 24 Springvale Rd, Killara, NSW, Australia] (*m* 2nd Donald Sheehan) and *d* 14 March 1963, leaving issue:
1d +John William; *b* 1954
1d *Victoria Hayton; *b* 1948
2d *Elizabeth; *b* 1951
2c Eric du Courcy; *b* 1913; *m* 1940 *Phyllis Mary — (*m* 2nd — Parker) and *d* 20 Aug 1962
1c *Marjorie Mary; *b* 1922; *m* 1944 *Clive Stanley Willey and has:
1d *Lyn Gladys; *b* 1947
2d *Rae Marjorie; *b* 1947
3d *Sue Phillis; *b* 1951
3b Charles Coulthurst; *b* 1884; *m* 1st (*divorce* 1923) Muriel Tidswell (*d* 1949) and had a dau; *m* 2nd 1924 Constance Winifred (*d* 1976), dau of David George Edward Wilkinson, and *d* 30 April 1926, leaving by her:
1c *Peta Jane Coulthurst [Mrs James Brown, Broadacres, 2 St John's Rise, Woking, Surrey]; *b* Nov 1926; *m* 1957 *James William Edward Brown
1b Mary Hayton; *d* unm 11 June 1939
2b Kathleen Tarifa; *m* 1st 20 Oct 1897 (*divorce* 1912) Sir Lionel Mabbot Woodward, Ch Judicial Commr FMS, and had issue. He *d* 5 Sept 1925; *m* 2nd 1912 Edward King, s of Appleby King, and *d* 30 Nov 1955, leaving further issue. He *d* 12 April 1955
1a Emily Craven; *m* 16 Sept 1857 Lt-Gen Sir William Bellairs, KCMG, CB (*d* 24 July 1913), s of Sir William Bellairs, of Mulbarton, Norfolk, and *d* 13 June 1866, leaving issue (*see* GLENCONNER)
(3) (cont.) Lt-Col William Gibbons *m* 2nd 3 April 1845 Ann Maxwell Hinds (*d* 20 Jan 1902), dau and coheir of John Abel Jackman and half sis of Sir Thomas Graham Briggs, Bt, and *d* 11 Aug 1872, leaving issue:
2a John Abel; *b* 31 Aug 1854; *m* 1884 Catherine Alice (*d* 14 Nov 1937), dau of Joseph S Salaman, and *d* 1894, leaving issue:
1b John Noel Graham, MC; Lt-Col RASC WW I (despatches twice), WW II (Assist Dir Supplies and Tport Br Troops NI and Scottish Cmd 1943–45); *b* 24 Dec 1889; *d* unm 17 Aug 1960
1b Dorothy Margaret Maxwell; *m* 1914 John Brook, of Ontario, and had:
1c John Burbridge; *b* 1914, chemical engr; *m* 1940 *Joanne Price, of Cleveland, Ohio, and had issue:
1d *David Jeremy; *b* 1947
2d *Calvin Price; *b* 1955
1d *Martha Lyn; *b* 1944
2c *Philip Roy, DFC; *b* 1918; F/Lt RCAF WW II, architect; *m* 1949 *Sonia Dixon, of Bournemouth, and has:
1d *Michael Brian; *b* 1951
2d *Gregory Laurence; *b* 1953
3d *Matthew Ian; *b* 1959
1d *Deborah Jane; *b* 1955
2d *Dinah Louise; *b* 1957
1c *June Rosemary [Mrs Charles Doty, 49 Huntly St, Toronto, Canada]; *b* 1920; *m* 1940 *Charles H Doty and has issue:
1d *Stephen Charles; *b* 1942
1d *Susan Jane; *b* 1944; *m* 19– *— Jacobsen, of Quebec
2d *Barbara Jane; *b* 1949
2b Marjorie Mabel; *m* 1916 James C Goff and *d* 24 June 19–, having had issue
3b Phyllis Crookenden; *d* as result of enemy action Oct 1940
3a Charles Kenrick; *b* 9 May 1856; *m* 21 Oct 1890 Emily Hinds (*d* 2 Dec 1958), dau of Charles Corbin, and *d* 15 April 1918, having had, with other issue:
1b Charles William Kenrick; *b* 30 Aug 1893; *m* 18 April Winifred Maud Ethel (*d* 29 Aug 1966), est dau of George Eccles, of Trinidad, and *d* 24 Jan 1969, leaving issue:
1c Colin Kenrick; Trooper RAC (Offr-Cadet) WW II; *b* 3 Aug 1923; *educ* Elizabeth Coll Guernsey and Dover Coll; *m* 22 Sept 1951 *Pamela June SRN, SCM, yr dau of W S Cousens, and *dsp* 7 Dec 1952
1c *Rose Margaret Emily [Miss Rose Gibbons, 80 Surbiton Hill Park, Surbiton, Surrey]; Lt QARANC; *b* 7 April 1926
2b Edward John Kenrick; slr 1929, Town Clerk Falmouth 1946–65, Roy Observer Corps WW II; *b* 11 Nov 1900; *educ* Dover Coll and Jesus Coll Cambridge (MA, LLB); *m* 19 April 1938 Marguerite Leslie (*d* 1977), yr dau of Nicolas Eyare Toke, MBE, of Folkestone, and *d* 1982, leaving:
1c *Carol Leslie Kenrick [Miss Carol Gibbons, Hillside, Harlequin Lane, Crowborough, E Sussex]; *b* 27 Jan 1939
1b Emily Hinds Graham
2b Rose Ethel Maxwell; *m* 28 Nov 1929 Charles La Coste Wilson (*d* 2 Feb 1964), s of George Wilson, of Trinidad, and had issue:
1c *(Charles) Richard Kenrick [Richard Wilson Esq, 43 Keswick Road, Great Bookham, Surrey KT23 4BG]; *b* 14 Sept 1936; *educ* St John's Leatherhead; CEng, MIMechE; *m* 1 Sept 1962 *Margrith Frieda, dau of Johann Baptist Barp, of Switzerland, and has issue:
1d *Juliette Nancy; *b* 18 July 1964; *m* 13 Feb 1994 *Henry Edmund Epsom, s of Dr Joseph Edward Epsom, of Bromley
2d *Tracey Petra; *b* 7 June 1966; *m* 19– *Philip John Lee Horne, s of Ronald Horne, of Essex, and has:
1e *Oliver John Kenrich; *b* 2 Sept 1993
1e *Sophie Ellen; *b* 19 June 1995
1c *Rose Elizabeth Graham [Mrs Colin Finucane, 47 Keswick Road, Great Bookham, Surrey KT23 4BG]; *b* 17 Aug 1934; *m* 1st 25 Sept 1965 George Ronald Brion (*d* 7 Dec 1978); *m* 2nd 19 Nov 1994 *Colin Michael Finucane
2a Marie Louise; *m* 1 Sept 1870 Ven Augustus Elder Smith, Archdeacon Trinidad, and had issue
3a Elizabeth Maxwell; *m* 9 June 1881 Maj Edward Chambers, est s of Sir George Henry Chambers, DL, and *d* 5 Aug 1923, leaving issue
(1) Martha; *m* Richard Tayler, of Charlton House, Middx
2 Emily; *m* 9 Nov 1820 Gerald FitzGerald, of Queen's Co (*d* 8 April 1845)

Sir JOHN *d* 9 July 1776; his son,

Sir William Gibbons, 3rd Bt; LLD; *b* 1751; *m* 3 Sept 1771 Rebecca (*d* 26 April 1811), dau of V-Adml Watson and sis of Sir Charles Watson, 1st Bt, and had, with four daus:
1 JOHN (Sir), **4th Bt**
2 William; Cdr RN; *d* 21 Oct 1860
3 George; Capt Army; *k* Albuera 16 May 1811
4 Edward; *m* Harriet Prescot and *d* 1835, leaving issue:
(1) Juliana; *m* 3 May 1859 James Haywood, of Dosthill House, Warwicks, and *d* 13 Dec 1898

Sir WILLIAM *d* 26 Nov 1814; his est son,

Sir John Gibbons, 4th Bt; *b* 8 Jan 1774; *m* 27 Oct 1795 Elizabeth (*d* 20 Oct 1835), dau of Richard Tayler, of Charlton House, Middx, and *d* 26 March 1844, having had, with other issue:
1 John; *b* 7 Oct 1801; *m* 1st 22 July 1824 his cousin Charlotte (*d* 28 Oct 1833), dau of Sir Charles Watson, 1st Bt, of Wratting Park, Cambridge, and had a dau (*d* unm); *m* 2nd 17 July 1838 Susannah (*d* 22 Feb 1890), est dau of Rev Alexander Cotton, Rector Girton, Cambridge, bro of Sir Charles Cotton, Bt, of Madingley, and *dvp* 31 Jan 1841, having by her had, with a dau (*d* unm):
(1) **Sir John Gibbons, 5th Bt**, JP, DL Middx; High Sheriff 1891, MA Oxon; *b* 30 Aug 1825; *d* unm 6 Jan 1893
(2) CHARLES (Sir), **6th Bt**
(3) Frederick; Capt Roy E Middx Militia; *b* 3 Jan 1832; *m* 6 Nov 1860 Hester (*d* 3 Sept 1924), yr dau of James Colquhoun Kemp, and *d* 15 Sept 1914, leaving:
1a Frederick Kenrick Colquhoun; Capt RN; *b* 14 June 1865; *m* 23 Sept 1895 Edith Kapiolani (*d* 2 March 1959 aged 88), dau of A T Atkinson, of Honolulu, and *d* 13 Sept 1954, leaving issue:
1b Marjorie Kapiolani; *b* 1896; *m* 28 Jan 1925 Lt-Col Pillans Scarth Whitehead, OBE, RA, yr s of C R Whitehead, of Canada, and had issue:
1c *Belinda Kapiolani; *b* 1929; *m* 1956 *Archibald Peter Brown and has:

1d *Archibald Steven; *b* 1958
2d *William Lambert; *b* 1964
1d *Isobel Clare; *b* 1960
2d *Judith Margaret; *b* 1964
2b *Nancy Alatau; *b* 1907; *m* 3 June 1939 *Hugo Wilhelm Runfelt, of Sweden, and has issue:
1c *Anne Marie; *b* 1941
2 Richard; Capt 60th Rifles; *b* 1807; *d* 26 April 1875
1 Eliza; *m* 13 March 1849 Rev Thomas Mann, of IoW, and *d* 21 Sept 1864
2 Louisa; *m* 11 July 1827 Robert Kenrick Gibbons and *d* 27 April 1876, leaving issue (*see* above)

The 5th Bt's bro,

Sir Charles Gibbons, 6th Bt, DL Middx; Capt RN; *b* 13 Jan 1828; *m* 5 April 1864 Lydia Martha (*d* 20 Feb 1924), 4th dau of Maj John Doran, 18th Regt, of Ely House, Co Wexford, and sister of Gen Sir John Doran, KCB, and had issue:
1 Charles John; *b* 17 Feb 1866; *d* unm 3 June 1892
2 ALEXANDER DORAN (Sir), **7th Bt**
3 Francis Robert; *b* 30 July 1875; *d* S Africa Feb 1901
1 Georgina Charlotte; *m* 2 Oct 1894 Maj Charles Mostyn Watkins, RE, s of Rev Charles Watkins, Vicar Hinton Charterhouse, and *d* May 1961, leaving issue. He *d* 13 July 1913
2 Adelaide Jeannette; *m* 1st 8 Aug 1889 Frank Terry, barrister, and had issue. He *d* 8 Feb 1929. She *m* 2nd 1930 Hugh Irvine and *d* 28 Dec 1953

Sir CHARLES *d* 5 Feb 1909; his est surv s,

Sir Alexander Doran Gibbons, 7th Bt; Maj 1st/5th Hants (Howitzer) Bde RFA, Capt 6th Bn Middx Regt, Boer War 1900–02 and WW I Mesopotomia and France; *b* 14 Dec 1873; *m* 12 July 1899 Gladys Constance Mostyn (*d* 15 April 1945), dau of Rev Charles Watkins, Vicar Hinton Charterhouse, and had:
1 George Francis Graham; *b* 5 June, *d* 19 Nov 1901
2 JOHN EDWARD (Sir), **8th Bt**
1 Dorothea Charlotte; *b* 11 April 1904; *m* 1st 12 Sept 1925 (*divorce* 1934) Ernest Gustav Byng, s of Gustav Byng, and had issue; *m* 2nd 1934 Conrad Ormond, of The Manor House, Chisledon, Wilts, and had further issue
2 Betty Lydia; *b* 25 May 1906; *m* 26 May 1931 Capt Alexander Hamilton Wheeler, MC, JP, DL, s of Charles Wheeler, of Philadelphia. He *d* 2 Nov 1942
3 *Vera Gladys, JP [Mrs Geoffrey Cumberlege JP, 7 Boxes Lane, Horsted Keynes, W Sussex RH17 7EJ]; *b* 18 Feb 1908; *m* 30 Nov 1927 Geoffrey Fenwick Jocelyn Cumberlege, DSO, MC (*d* 1979), yst s of Henry Morduant Cumberlege, of Walsted Place, Lindfield, Sussex, and has issue:
(1) *Geoffrey Mark; *b* 1930; *m* 1954 *Shirley Lancaster and has issue:
1a *Belinda; *b* 1956
2a *Elizabeth; *b* 1959
3a *Sarah; *b* 1960
4a *Patricia; *b* 1962
(2) *Patrick Francis Howard [Patrick Cumberlege Esq, Vuggles Farm, Newick, Lewes, Sussex]; *b* 1933; *m* 1961 *Baroness Cumberlege (LP, *qv*) and has issue
(3) *Francis Richard (Rev); *b* 1941; *m* 1983 *Christine Browne
(1) *Elizabeth Blanche; *b* 1925; *m* 1951 (*divorce* 1971) Patrick B Brown and has:
1a *Stephen; *b* 1952
2a *Nigel; *b* 1954
3a *Geoffrey; *b* 1959
1a *Caroline; *b* 1955
2a *Jennifer Catherine; *b* 1965
4 Joan Margaret, JP Somerset; *b* 15 May 1911; *d* unm 23 Sept 1972

Sir ALEXANDER *d* 30 Sept 1956; his only surv son,

Sir John Edward Gibbons, 8th Bt; Dorset Regt WW II Iran and Syria, Capt 1942, Assist Regl (Nottingham) Arts Cncl 1946–50; *b* 14 Nov 1914; *educ* Charterhouse and Peterhouse Cambridge; *m* 28 July 1937 (*divorce* 1951) Mersa Vivien Wentworth [Mersa Lady Gibbons, 30 Cornwallis Crescent, Clifton, Bristol 8], yst dau of Maj Edward Baynton Grove Foster, of Dorset, and *d* 1982, leaving issue:
1 Sir WILLIAM EDWARD DORAN GIBBONS, **9th and present Bt**
1 *Charlotte Anne Wentworth, JP Somerset [Mrs Hylton Bayntun-Coward, JP, Dunkerton Grange, nr Bath, Somerset]; *b* 1 Feb 1939; *m* 1 June 1963 *Hylton Henry Bayntun-Coward (High Sheriff Avon 1993), only s of Leslie L Bayntun-Coward, of Combe Royal, Bath, and has:
(1) *Edward William George; *b* 10 Jan 1966; *m* 19 – *Laura Catherine Banz
(2) *Jonathan Henry Alexander; *b* 29 July 1972
(1) *Emma Louise Wentworth; *b* 7 March 1964
(2) *Polly Jane Constance; *b* 1 June 1970
2 *Jane [Mrs Neville Grant, 13 Glenluce Rd, London SE3 7SD]; *b* 28 April 1942; *m* 3 Sept 1966 *Neville James Henry Grant, yst s of R D M Grant, of IoW, and has:
(1) *Thomas Paul Wentworth; *b* 1969
(2) *Alexander Hugh Wentworth; *b* 1973

GIBSON, Baron

Arms: Per pale azure and argent, three acorns slipped and leaved in fess between as many storks rising, all countercharged.
Crest: A stork rising argent between two acorns slipped and leaved and holding in the beak an acorn slipped, all proper.
Supporters: Two nightingales, each holding in the beak a scroll of music proper. **Motto:** *Per ardua ad alta* ('Through hardships to the heights'). **Creation:** B. (LP, UK) 1975.

THE BARON GIBSON, of Penn's Rocks, Co East Sussex ((Richard) Patrick Tallentyre Gibson) [The Rt Hon The Lord Gibson, Penn's Rocks, Groombridge, Kent TN3 9PA]; *b* 5 Feb 1916; *educ* Eton and Magdalen Coll Oxford (MA, Hon Fellow 1977); Maj Middx Yeo WW II N Africa 1940–41, POW 1941–43, SOE 1943–45, Political Intelligence FO 1945–46, chm: S Pearson & Son Ltd 1978–83, Pearson Longman Ltd 1967–78, Advsy Cncl V&A 1970–74, Arts Cncl 1972–77, Financial Times Ltd 1975–78, National Trust 1977–87, v-chm Westminster Press 1953–78, Pres S of England Ag Soc 1987, member board ROH 1977–87, Tstee Glyndebourne Festival Opera 1965–72 and 1977–86; *m* 1945 *(Elizabeth) Dione, dau of Hon (Bernard) Clive Pearson (*see* COWDRAY, V), and has issue

Lineage: THORNELY CARBUTT GIBSON; *m* Elizabeth Anne Augusta — and had:

(RICHARD) PATRICK TALLENTYRE, *cr* a **Baron**

GIBSON, Bt

Creation: Bt. (UK) 10 Aug 1931.

REV SIR CHRISTOPHER HERBERT GIBSON, 4TH BT, of Linconia in the Republic of Argentina, and Faccombe, Co Southampton, CP [The Rev Christopher Gibson, 5700 North Harlem Avenue, Chicago, IL 60631, USA]; *b* 17 July 1948; *s f* 1994; ordained 20 Dec 1975

Lineage: JOHN GIBSON, of Garnet Hill, Glasgow; mfr, merchant; *d* 9 March 1831, leaving a yst s:

THOMAS GIBSON, of Edinburgh and Argentina; *b* 28 Nov 1816; *m* 9 May 1854 Clementina (*d* 31 Aug 1886), dau of William Corbett, and *d* 2 Dec 1903, having had, with other issue:

Sir Herbert Gibson, 1st Bt (UK), so *cr* 10 Aug 1931, KBE (1919); *b* 8 July 1863; landowner, livestock-breeder, merchant in Argentina, Chm Br Chamber Commerce there, Inter-Allied Commn for purchase cereals Argentina and Uruguay 1917–19; *m* 6 July 1895 Madeleine Jessie (*d* 16 May 1953), dau of Rev W J Savell, of St Clement Dane's, and had (with a dau, Dorothy):
1 CHRISTOPHER HERBERT (Sir), **2nd Bt**
2 Clement Herbert; *b* 23 Aug 1900; *educ* Eton and Clare Coll Cambridge; *m* 24 June 1933 Marjorie Julia (*d* 1982), dau of Robert Anderson, of Buenos Aires, and *d* 1976, leaving:
(1) Geoffrey; *b* 11 June 1934; *educ* Eton; *m* 14 Nov 1964 *Anne-Marie [Mrs Geoffrey Gibson, Juncal 2174, ler piso 14, 1125 Buenos Aires, Argentina], dau of Martin de Selincourt, and *d* 1987, leaving:
1a +ROBERT HERBERT; *b* 1968; heir presumptive; *m* 1992 *Catherine Grace, dau of Ernest William Pugh, and has:
1b +William Barnaby Thomas; *b* 25 Oct 1997
1a +Alexander Herbert; *b* 1973
1a *Clemency Rose; *b* 8 Dec 1968
(2) +Clement Herbert; *b* 6 Aug 1936; *educ* Eton, Clare Coll Cambridge, U of Aix-en-Provence and Westcott House Cambridge; *m* 1966 *Mrs Barbara Peel
(3) +Thomas Herbert [Thomas Gibson Esq, Westwell Manor, Westwell, Burford, Oxon]; *b* 12 April 1943; *educ* Eton; *m* 18 June 1966 *Anthea Fiona Catherine, yr dau of Lt-Col A G Palmer, RE, and has:
1a +Miles Cosmo Archdale; *b* 17 Sept 1968

2a +Sebastian Thomas Maxmilian; *b* 1972
3a +Benjamin Hugh George; *b* 1973
3 Gerald Herbert; *b* 7 Sept 1902; *m* 14 May 1924 Ursula Marion Wilson, dau of William Greenwell Robson, and *d* 23 Feb 1951, leaving:
(1) +Roy Herbert; *b* 22 Oct 1933; *m* 1970 *Georgina Odette, dau of Santiago Even, and has:
1a *Valerie; *b* 1971
(1) *Diana Madeleine; *b* 17 Feb 1926
(2) June Catherine; *b* 22 June 1927; *d* 1967
4 Cosmo Livingstone Herbert; *b* 6 Sept 1904; *educ* Eton; *m* 14 Oct 1937 Josephine Austin, dau of James Austin Brown, and *d* 10 Feb 1964, leaving:
(1) +Herbert; *b* 26 Aug 1938; *educ* Radley; *m* 1964 *Margaret Jean, dau of John Bruce Donald, and has:
1a +James Bruce; *b* 1965
2a +Herbert Mark; *b* 1966
1a *Josephine Jean; *b* 1966
2a *Michel; *b* 1969
3a *Madeleine; *b* 1972
(2) +Cosmo David; *b* 16 Aug 1944
(3) +Noel Gerald; *b* 1954
(4) +David Hope; *b* 1956; *m* 1989 *Maria Pia Cullen and has:
1a +Michael; *b* 1992
1a *Jennifer; *b* 1990
(1) Josephine Madeleine Yvonne; *b* 16 Nov 1939; *m* 1962 Baron Gaston Carlos Perkins Peers de Niewburgh and had:
1a *Thomas Gaston; *b* 1964; *m* 1993 *Gianina, dau of Nestor Koaper, and has:
1b *Agustina; *b* 1994
1a *Enrique Gaston; *b* 1968; *m* 1989 *Soledad Bernal and has:
1b *Gaston Enrique; *b* 1990
1a *Yvonne Cecila; *b* 1967
(2) *Roxana; *b* 21 June 1943; *m* 1963 *Eduardo Francisco Pampillo and has:
1a *Francisco Severiano; *b* 1980
1a *Veronica Roxana; *b* 1963; *m* 1990 *Aaron Hodari and has:
1b *Juana; *b* 1991
2a *Edwina Alexandra; *b* 1965
3a *Victoria Patricia; *b* 1968; *m* 1988 *Pablo Barbieri and has:
1b *Martin; *b* 1989
1b *Agustina; *b* 1993
4a *Silvina Glora; *b* 1975

The 1st Bt *d* 28 Dec 1934; his est son,

Sir MEREDITH later CHRISTOPHER HERBERT GIBSON (replaced MEREDITH with CHRISTOPHER 5 June 1934), **2nd Bt**; *b* 12 Oct 1897; *educ* Eton and RMA Woolwich; Lt RHA, Memb Br Ornithologists Union, Br Soc Dowsers, author *Gran Chaco Calling* and *Enchanted Trails*; *m* 9 Sept 1919 Dorothy Edith Orme, dau of Maj W D Bruce, of Vancouver, BC, and *d* 20 July 1966, having had:

1 **Sir Christopher Herbert Gibson, 3rd Bt**; *b* 2 Feb 1921; *educ* St Cyprian's Eastbourne, St George's Coll Argentina; Lt 28th Canadian Armed Regt WW II (five medals), sales rep Nat Homes Ltd, manager Leach's Argentine Estates 1946–51, BC Canada manager Encyclopaedia Britannica 1952–55, design draughtsman Babcock and Wilcox USA 1956–57, tea plantation manager and poultry farmer; *m* 16 Aug 1941 *Lilian Lake, dau of Dr George Byron Young, and *d* 26 June 1994, leaving:
(1) Rev Sir CHRISTOPHER HERBERT GIBSON, **4th and present Bt**
(1) Penelope Lake; *b* 22 July 1946; *d* 8 Nov 1993
(2) *Pamela Dorothy Madeleine; *b* 14 April 1950; MD; *m* 17 Feb 1973 *Julio Caesar Muzio and has:
1a *Landon; *b* 4 April 1979
2a *Andreé; *b* 3 June 1981
3a *Alajandro; *b* 18 March 1983
1a *Paula; *b* 29 Oct 1976
(3) *Dawn [Mrs Daniel Carreras, Apt 3–1026 Commercial Drive, Vancouver, BC V5L 3W9, Canada]; *b* 14 June 1953; *m* 24 Dec 1972 *Daniel Carreras and has:
1a *Diego; *b* 26 July 1973
2a *Noël; *b* 10 Aug 1975
2a *Marie Noël; *b* 1975
2 Bruce Herbert; *b* 12 May 1923; *d* 2 April 1936
3 Ian Herbert; *b* 27 Feb 1927; memb Argentine Entomological Soc; *d* 17 Jan 1978

GIBSON-CRAIG-CARMICHAEL

Arms: Quarterly, 1st and 4th, ermine on a fess sable three crescents argent (for CRAIG); 2nd and 3rd, gules three keys fessways in pale, wards downwards or (for GIBSON). **Crest:** A knight on horseback in full armour, his right hand grasping a shattered tilting spear, all proper. **Supporters:** Dexter, a knight in full armour holding in his dexter hand a spear proper; sinister, a war horse argent, saddled and bridled proper. **Motto:** *Vive Deo et vives* ('Live by God, and you shall live truly'). **Creations:** Bt. (NS) 31 Dec 1702 and (UK) 30 Sept 1831.

SIR DAVID PETER WILLIAM GIBSON-CRAIG-CARMICHAEL, 15TH BT, of Keirhill, Co Edinburgh, and **8th Bt**, of Riccarton, Co Midlothian; *b* 21 July 1946; *s* f 1969; *educ* Queen's U Kingston, Ontarioa (BSc); *m* 1973 *Patricia, dau of Marcos Skarnic, of Santiago, Chile, and has issue:
1 +PETER WILLIAM; *b* 29 Dec 1975
1 *Margaret Anne; *b* 1977

Lineage (of Gibson of Keirhill): GEORGE GIBSON, of Goldingstones; Clerk of Session; *m* Elizabeth Airth and had:

Sir ALEXANDER GIBSON, of Durie, Fifeshire; Clerk of Session 1594, ktd 1594, Ld of Session as Lord Durie 1621, reapptd 1640, Pres Court of Session 1642; *m* 14 Jan 1696 Margaret, dau of Sir Thomas Craig of Riccarton, a feudal lawyer, and *d* 10 June 1644, leaving, with other issue:
1 Alexander (Sir), of Durie; ktd and made Ld Clerk Register 1641, Ld of Session as Lord Durie 1646, deprived of his offices 1649; *m* 1625 Cecilia, dau of Thomas Fotheringhame, of Powrie, Forfarshire, and *d* June 1656, having had four sons
2 JOHN (Sir)
3 George, of Balhouffie, Fifeshire; *d* 8 Sept 1669, having had:
(1) Margaret; *m* 1665 Andrew Bruce, Min of Carnbec later Pittenweem

The 2nd son,

Sir JOHN GIBSON, of Pentland and Addistone, Co Edinburgh; ktd 1647; *m* 1st Jean, dau and coheir of Alexander Hay, of Kennet, Clackmannanshire, and had:
1 Alexander (Sir), of Pentland; Pncpl Clerk of Session, ktd 1682; *m* Helen, dau of Sir James Fleming of Rathobyres, and *d* 1693, having had issue:
(1) John (Sir), of Pentland; ktd by 1700, Dep-Clerk Register 1696–1700; *m* 3 Nov 1687 Elizabeth, dau of Lewis Craig of Riccarton, and *d* 13 May 1704, having had issue:
1a **Sir Alexander Gibson, 3rd Bt**, of (Keirhill and) Pentland; *m* Margaret, dau of James Hamilton of Pencaitland, Haddington, Ld of Session, and *d* 15 April 1774, leaving:
1b Margaret; *m* William Murray of Touchadam and Polmaise and had issue
2b Anne; *m* as his 1st w George Seton of Mounie (*see* SETON, Bt, of Pitmedden)
2a John; merchant in London; had:
1b **Sir John Gibson, 4th Bt**, of (Keirhill and) Pentland; *m* 1775 Henrietta (*d* 8 March 1803), dau of James Watson, of Saughton, and *d* 29 March 1781, leaving:
1c Helen, of Pentland; *m* 1st Dewar Masterton (*dsp*); *m* 2nd Capt John Barr (*dsp*); *m* 3rd Maj-Gen David Anderson and had issue
2b **Sir Robert Gibson, 5th Bt** of Keirhill; *dsp* in America between 1796 and 1803
(2) Alexander, of Durie, which he bought from his brother; *m* 1st Elizabeth, dau of Sir John Foulis of Ravelston, and had:
1a John of Durie; *m* Helen Carmichael (*d* 2 June 1787), sis of 4th Earl of Hyndford and dau of Hon William Carmichael, of Skirling, Peeblesshire, by his 1st w Helen, only child of Thomas Craig of Riccarton, and *d* 18 Jan 1767, leaving issue:

1b Alexander, of Durie; *m* 19 Oct 1770 Margaret Bruce (*d* 22 Dec 1774), dau of Thomas Dundas of Fingask, and *d* 13 May 1785, leaving issue:

1c Sir JOHN GIBSON later GIBSON-CARMICHAEL (added on inheriting estates of Castle Craig and Skirling, Peeblesshire, and Hailes, Co Edinburgh, from his great-uncle 4th Earl of Hyndford), **6th Bt** of Keirhill; *b* 24 April 1773; *m* 15 Oct 1799 Janet Hyndford (*m* 2nd 31 July 1806 12th Lord Elphinstone (*qv*) and *d* 23 Aug 1825), dau of Cornelius Elliott, of Wolflee, and *d* 5 Nov 1803, leaving:

1d Eleanor Margaret; *m* 1828 Alexander Begbie (*d* 18 June 1860) and *dsp* 5 Dec 1883

2c **Sir Thomas Gibson-Carmichael, 7th Bt**, of (Keirhill and) Castle Craig; *b* 21 Dec 1774; Capt 58th Foot; *m* 1st 7 Feb 1806 Jane (*d* 7 June 1814), dau of Maj-Gen Thomas Dundas of Fingask and gdau of 9th Earl of Home (*qv*), and had issue:

1d **Sir Alexander Gibson Gibson-Carmichael, 8th Bt**, of (Keirhill and) Castle Craig; *b* 6 June 1812; *d* unm 8 May 1850

1d Eleanor Hyndford; *m* 5 June 1829 Sir David Kinloch, 9th Bt, of Gilmerton (*qv*), and *d* 15 Oct 1849, leaving issue

2d Margaret Anne; *d* unm 30 March 1842

3d Janet Maitland; *d* young 12 Jan 1818

2c (cont.) **Sir Thomas** *m* 2nd 8 June 1816 Hon Anne Napier (*d* 7 Dec 1862), dau of 8th Lord Napier (*see* NAPIER and ETTRICK, L), and *d* 13 Dec 1849, having by her had, with other issue:

2d **Sir Thomas Gibson-Carmichael, 9th Bt**, of (Keirhill and) Castle Craig; *b* 27 Oct 1817; Cdr RN; *m* 17 Oct 1849 Frances Marianne (*d* 1 Sept 1892), dau of Rev Joseph Story, of Bingfield, Co Cavan, and *dsp* 30 Dec 1855

3d **Rev Sir William Henry Gibson-Carmichael, 10th Bt**, of (Keirhill and) Castle Craig, DL; *b* 9 Oct 1827; *educ* St Peter's Coll Cambridge (BA 1850, MA 1853); *m* 12 May 1858 Eleanora Anne (*d* 6 Jan 1861), dau of David Anderson, of St Germains, and *d* 19 Dec 1891, leaving:

1e **Sir Thomas David Gibson-Carmichael, 11th Bt** (of Keirhill), and 1st and last BARON CARMICHAEL, of Skirling, Co Peebles (UK), so *cr* 7 Feb 1912, GCSI, GCIE, KCMG, JP, DL Co Edinburgh; *b* 18 March 1859; *educ* St John's Coll Cambridge (MA); Ld Lt Peeblesshire, Govr Victoria 1905–11, Madras 1911–12 and Bengal 1912–17; *m* 1 July 1886 Mary Helen Elizabeth, LGStJ (*d* 22 March 1947), est dau of Albert Llewellyn Nugent, and *dsp* 16 Jan 1926, when the Barony expired and the btcy passed to his cousin, **Sir Henry Thomas Gibson-Craig, 5th Bt** of Riccarton (*see below*)

2e George Henry, of Callands, West Linton, Scotland; *b* 24 Jan 1860; *d* unm 2 Sept 1903

3e John Murray; *b* 27 Dec 1860; Lt Roy Defence Force; *m* 1st 27 April 1892 Amy Katherine (*d* 9 March 1899), dau of Frederick Archdale, of Baldock, Herts, and had issue:

1f Alexander David; *b* 10 Feb 1895; Lt RN; *ka* in submarine action Sept 1916

1f Eleanora Fitzroy; *b* 13 Feb 1893; *m* 27 Nov 1916 Charles Irving Roddick (*d* 19 March 1966), son of George Roddick, of The Hook, Potters Bar, Herts, and *d* 23 March 1969, leaving issue

2f Violet Penelope; *b* 2 March 1899; *m* 27 April 1929 Dennis WHEELER later WHEELER-CARMICHAEL (deed poll 17 June 1929 and *d* 1980), er s of Montague Wheeler, and had:

1g Thomas Montague; *b* 23 Jan 1932; *m* 1 June 1957 *Jane [Mrs Thomas Wheeler-Carmichael, The Woodlands, The Street, Chilcompton, nr Bath BA3 4HB], est dau of Noël Cross, and *d* 1993, leaving:

1h *George Alexander; *b* 10 Sept 1959; *m* 1986 *Marianne Jean, 2nd dau of Hon Cecil Towry Henry Law (*see* ELLENBOROUGH, B), and has issue:

1i *James Henry; *b* 1990

2i *Guy; *b* 1992

2h *Charles Edward Thomas; *b* 16 Oct 1961

1g *Margaret Mary [Mrs Archibald Colville, 78 Lea Rd, Maidenhead, Berks]; *b* 5 July 1930; *m* 27 July 1949 *Archibald Colville (*d* 1970) and has issue (*see* CLYDESMUIR, B)

3e (cont.) John Murray Gibson-Carmichael *m* 2nd 21 May 1921 Beatrice Mary (*d* Oct 1964), dau of James Donoghue, of Co Westmeath, and *d* 6 May 1923

4d Maria Clavering; *m* 15 June 1852 Sir James Philip Lacaita, KCMG (*d* 4 Jan 1895), and *d* 20 April 1853, leaving issue

5d Sophia Caroline; *m* 2 May 1859 Francis Nevile Reid

1c Margaret; *b* 6 Oct 1771; *d* 8 March 1779

2b William; *m* Mary Cecilia, dau of James Balfour, of Pilrig, and *d* 6 May 1807, leaving issue:

1c John; merchant in Danzig; *b* 21 April 1763; *dsp*

2c Sir JAMES GIBSON later GIBSON-CRAIG (added with arms under terms of entail drawn up by Robert Craig of Riccarton 19 Aug 1818), **1st Bt** (UK), so *cr* 30 Sept 1831, of Riccarton, Midlothian; *b* 11 Oct 1765; Clerk of the Signet in Scotland; *m* 14 Sept 1796 Anne (*d* 24 May 1837), dau of J Thomson, of Edinburgh, and *d* 6 March 1850, having had, with seven daus (one of whom *m* Biggs Andrews, QC, and had issue; *see* FERGUSON DAVIE, Bt):

1d **Sir William Gibson-Craig, 2nd Bt**, of Riccarton, PC; *b* 2 Aug 1797; MP Midlothian 1837–41 and Edinburgh 1841–52, a Ld of the Treasury 1846–52, Ld Clerk Register and Keeper of the Signet for Scotland 1862–78; *m* 29 Aug 1840 Elizabeth Sarah (*d* 15 Feb 1895), dau of John Henry Vivian, MP Singleton, Glam, and sister of 1st Baron Swansea (*qv*), and *d* 12 March 1878, having had:

1e **Sir James Henry Gibson-Craig, 3rd Bt**, of Riccarton, JP, DL Midlothian; *b* 21 Sept 1841; *educ* Harrow and Trin Coll Cambridge (BA, Wrangler 1865, MA 1868); Commr of Supply, advocate, Brig Roy Co Archers; *m* 9 June 1870 Julia (*d* 4 Sept 1932), dau of Archibald Buchanan, of Curriehill, Midlothian, and *d* 28 Sept 1908, leaving:

1f William Buchanan; *b* 3 Oct 1878; *d* 17 Jan 1879

2f Robert James; *b* 5 June 1882; Lt 3rd Roy Scots; *d* Boer War 23 April 1900

3f **Sir Archibald Charles Gibson-Craig, 4th Bt**; *b* 24 Aug 1883; BA Cambridge; Lt Highland LI WW I (despatches); *ka* Battle of the Aisne 14 Sept 1914

4f Sir HENRY THOMAS GIBSON-CRAIG later GIBSON-CRAIG-CARMICHAEL (added on *s* his cousin Lord Carmichael 16 Jan 1920), **5th Bt** of Riccarton and **12th Bt** of Keirhill, JP; *b* 5 Jan 1885; Capt Res of Offrs, late 4th Highland LI, formerly Lt 3rd Bn Roy Scots, WW I in Egypt; *d* unm 5 Sept 1926

1f Henrietta Florence; *m* 10 Aug 1897 Adml Robert Stevenson Dalton Cuming, CBE, DSO, JP, DL (*d* 22 Feb 1940), of Turnpike House, Knightwick, Worcs, and *d* 30 April 1956, having had issue

2f Alice Gertrude; *m* 10 Aug 1904 Percy St George Kirke, MA, MICE, MIMechE (*d* 20 Feb 1966), 3rd son of Col St George Mervyn Kirke, RE, and *d* 17 June 1959, leaving issue

3f Grace Elizabeth; *m* 22 June 1909 Sholto James Douglas and *d* 27 March 1968 aged 90, leaving issue (*see* MORTON, E)

4f Mary Helen; *m* 29 Dec 1904 Henry Ralph Beaumont, JP (*d* 19 Aug 1948), of Whitley-Beaumont, nr Huddersfield, Yorks, and *d* 5 Dec 1963, leaving issue

5f Dulcie Eleanor; *d* unm 29 May 1941

2e William; *b* 22 Jan 1843; Lt Bengal Cav; *d* 17 March 1872

3e Henry Vivian, JP (Bucks); *b* 25 Sept 1847; *m* 27 June 1882 Emily Dulcibella (*d* 19 Dec 1943), dau of Montagu Wilmot, of Norton, Swansea, and sister of Sir Robert Wilmot, 6th Bt, of Osmaston, and *d* 19 May 1926, leaving issue:

1f EARDLEY CHARLES WILLIAM (Sir), **6th/13th Bt**

1f Dorothy Evelyn; *m* 1st 8 June 1905 (*divorce* 1926) Lt-Col James Gerald Lamb Searight, Roy Scots, and had issue; *m* 2nd 3 July 1926 Maj-Gen Geoffrey Francis Heremon Brooke, CB, DSO, MC, 16th/5th Lancers (*d* 26 June 1966), son of John Monk Brooke, of Elm Green, Co Dublin, and *d* 10 June 1955

2f Cecilia Dulcibella; *d* unm 21 May 1958

3f Marjorie Violet

1e Anne; *d* unm 11 Sept 1925

2e Henrietta Elizabeth; *m* 30 Sept 1869 Charles Howe Cuff Knox, Capt 8th Hus and Hon Col 3rd Bn Connaught Rangers (*d* Dec 1921), of Creagh, Ballinrobe, Co Mayo, and *d* 26 May 1942, leaving issue

3e Gertrude; *m* 28 Oct 1884 Rev William Henry Onslow Parson (*d* 1914), of Lynecombe Hill, Sandford, nr Bristol, Vicar of Lynchmere, Sussex

2d James Thomson; *b* 12 March 1799; Clerk Signet; *m* 23 Nov 1841 Jane (*d* 25 April 1863), 2nd dau of Sir John Grant and widow of Col Pennington, and *dsp* 18 July 1886

3c William; Master Attendant Point de Galle, Ceylon; *m* Margaret, dau of — Sharpe, of Madras, and had two daus

4c Alexander; merchant in Danzig; *dsp* 8 Jan 1836

5c Archibald, of Edinburgh, merchant; *dsp*

6c Lewis, of Ceylon; *b* 20 June 1773; *m* 20 Dec 1806 Caroline (*d* 4 Jan 1827), dau of Very Rev Charles Peter Layard, DD, Dean Bristol, and *d* 23 Aug 1845, leaving, with other issue:

1d William Charles, CMG; *b* 26 March 1812; Colonial Sec Ceylon, previously Auditor-Gen; *m* 15 Sept 1834 Louisa Sophia (*d* 17 Jan 1870), dau of Charles Edward Layard, Ceylon CS, and *d* 6 March 1892, having had issue, with three daus:

1e James Whitaker; *b* 10 Feb 1845; Ceylon CS; *m* 1882 Emily (*d* 3 Jan 1936), dau of Capt John Hammond, RN, and *d* 23 Nov 1906, having had issue:

1f William James Carmichael; *b* 21 Dec 1883; Capt Hampshire Regt and RAF WW I; *m* 6 Feb 1918 Maude, dau of Roger Buston, and *d* 1955, leaving issue:

1g +John Carmichael [John Gibson Esq, 10 Clanricarde Gdns, London W2]; *b* 9 Nov 1919

2f John Bruce; *b* 23 March 1887; Lt RMLI; *d* 18 Oct 1911

2e Thomas Maitland; *b* 31 Aug 1848; *educ* Trin Coll Oxford (MA); Ceylon CS, barrister; *m* 13 March 1879 Elizabeth Lucy (*d* 19 Aug 1934), dau of W Grant Allison, of Louth, Lincs, and *d* 16 Jan 1923, leaving issue:

1f William Maitland; *b* 16 April 1880; *educ* Trin Coll Oxford (MA); *m* 15 July 1919 Harriot Ada, dau of Maj Henry George Daniel, Roy Inniskilling Fus, and *dsp* 10 March 1955

2f Lewis Henry; *b* 19 May 1881; Lt Highland LI; *ka* S Africa 14 Aug 1900, unm

1f Helen Carmichael; *d* unm 14 Oct 1910

2f Margaret Louisa Carmichael; *d* unm 26 Sept 1915

7c Thomas; *d* 1803

8c Henry; HEICS

9c Andrew Mitchell; *b* 25 June 1784; Naval Serv HEICS; *m* 2 Dec 1818 Barbara (*d* 30 May 1830), dau of Capt Robert Thomson, and *d* 1 Feb 1852, leaving issue:

1d Robert Mitchell; had two sons and two daus

1d Mary; *m* 13 July 1852 William Rankine Fortune and had issue

1c Cecilia; *m* 1807 John Thomson

3b Thomas; Lt-Col 89th Foot

1b Margaret; *m* 1768 Alexander Gibson-Wright, of Cliftonhall, Edinburgh

2b Elizabeth; *m* 1770 David Hunter, of Blackness

2a Thomas; Principal Clerk of Session; *m* Jean, dau and heir of Col Thomas Dalzell, yst son of Sir John Dalzell, 1st Bt, of Glenae and *d* 1786, leaving an only surv child, Isabel (*d* unm *c* 1796)

3a Archibald; merchant in Danzig; *cr* Baron in Kingdom of Prussia; had:

1b Alexander Gibson; Br Consul Danzig; *d* 18 Oct 1811 aged 82

(2) (cont.) Alexander Gibson of Durie *m* 2nd Elizabeth Stewart, widow of Col Thomas Hamilton, of Little Preston and Fala, Haddingtonshire, and *d* 1 March 1729, having by her had a s and two daus

(3) Thomas; *m* — Wright, heiress of Cliftonhall, and had:

1a Alexander GIBSON-WRIGHT, of Cliftonhall and Kersie; *m* 29 Jan 1768 Margaret, dau of John Gibson of Durie and Helen Carmichael, and *d* 8 Nov 1819, leaving:

1b Helen; *m* 30 April 1785 Sir Alexander Charles Maitland, 2nd Bt (*qv*), and had issue

2b Anne; *m* 29 Aug 1800 Alexander Gibson Hunter, of Blackness

3b Margaret; *d* unm 16 March 1795

(4) James; *b* 1690; Adj-Gen to Gen Murray War of Spanish Succession 1704, Capt RHG (Blues) 1712, served Austrian Army as Chevalier Jacques de Gibson 1715, Adj to PRINCE EUGENE OF SAVOY 1717, Col Cmdt Fortress of Courtrai 1720, Maj-Gen 1733, Govr Courtrai 1740–44; *m* Catherine Minnaert, of Courtrai (*d* 4 Feb 1728), and *d* Vienna 9 May 1755, leaving with other issue:

1a Jean Alexander; *b* 1714; Lt-Col, Cmdt Fortress of Nieuport; *m* Jeanne, dau of Louis van de Walle, Sheriff of Nieuport, and *d* 1793, leaving, with another dau (*d* unm):

1b Henriette; *b* 1773; *d* 1855; *m* 30 April 1798 Louis Coppieters (*d* 1814), son of Charles Louis Coppieters, Seigneur de la Torre, Burgomaster of Nieuport, and had issue

2 George, of Auchmuty, Fife; *dsp*

3 John (Sir); Lt-Govr Portsmouth 1695, MP Portsmouth, ktd 6 Sept 1705; *d* 24 Oct 1717 aged 80, having had issue:

(1) Francis

(2) James

(1) Anna Maria; *m* Gen Robert Dalziel

(2) Susan; *d* unm 10 March 1758 in her 81st year

Sir JOHN *m* 2nd the widow of Sir James Fleming; *m* 3rd Elizabeth, dau of Sir Thomas Thomson, 1st Bt, of Duddingston, and by her had:

4 **Sir Thomas Gibson, 1st Bt** (NS), so *cr* 31 Dec 1702, with remainder to his heirs male for ever, of Keirhill, Co Edinburgh; bought the estate of King's Cramond, Co Edinburgh, 1694, but sold it 1697 and bought that of Keirhill; *m* 11 June 1701 Jean (*m* 2nd 22 June 1718 Rev George Arbuthnot and *d* 13 Feb 1724), dau of Edward Marjoribanks, of Hallyards, Co Edinburgh, and *d* 1713, leaving:

(1) **Sir Edward Gibson, 2nd Bt**, of Keirhill; bought Kinnaird, Fifeshire, 1726; *m* Barbara (*m* 2nd Helenus Halkerston, of Rathillet, and *d* 19 June 1782), dau of Hon Alexander Maitland, s of 3rd Earl of Lauderdale (*qv*), and was *bur* 2 June 1727, leaving:

1a Janet; *m* Capt James Bruce, 20th Regt, and *d* 4 Jan 1776, leaving issue

The 5th/12th Bt's cousin,

Sir EARDLEY CHARLES WILLIAM GIBSON-CRAIG later GIBSON-CRAIG-CARMICHAEL (added on *s* cousin), **13th Bt** of Keirhill and **6th Bt** of Riccarton; *b* 22 Nov 1887; *m* 2 Sept 1914 Emily Ellen, only dau of Henry Rummel, of Estancia Cerro Volean, San Julian, Argentine, and had issue:

1 ARCHIBALD WILLIAM (Sir), **14th/7th Bt**

1 *Emily Edith; *b* 1915

2 *Kathleen Joan; *b* 1919; *m* 6 July 1940 *Charles Taylor Darling, BA, of Universidad Nacional de Tucuman, Argentina, yr son of Prof C R Darling, formerly of RMA Woolwich, and has issue:

(1) *Anthony Robin; *b* 1941

(2) *Richard John; *b* 1944

(1) *Judith Ann; *b* 1946

Sir EARDLEY *d* 24 Feb 1939; his only son,

Sir Archibald Henry William Gibson-Craig-Carmichael, 14th Bt of Keirhill and **7th Bt** of Riccarton; *b* 28 March 1917; Capt 16th/5th Lancers WW II; *m* 12 Nov 1941 *Rosemary Anita, dau of George Duncan Crew, of Santiago, Chile, and *d* 1969, leaving:

1 Sir DAVID PETER WILLIAM GIBSON-CRAIG-CARMICHAEL, **15th and 8th (and present) Bt**

2 +Alasdair John; *b* 28 Feb 1948; *m* 1973 *Irene, dau of Bruno Haverbeck, of Santiago, Chile

3 +Andrew Charles; *b* 1952

1 *Susan Ann; *b* 18 April 1949; *m* 1970 *Richard John Darling and has:

(1) *Christopher John; *b* 1971

(2) *Nicholas Patrick; *b* 1973

GIBSON-WATT

Creation: B. (UK, LP) 1979

THE BARON GIBSON-WATT, of The Wye, in the District of Radnor ((James) David Gibson-Watt, MC (1943) and two bars (1944, 1945), PC (1974), JP (1946), DL (Radnorshire later Powys) [The Rt Hon The Lord Gibson-Watt MC and two bars PC JP DL, Doldowlod, Llandrindod Wells, Powys LD1 6HF]; *b* 1918; *educ* Eton and Trin Coll Cambridge (BA); Maj Welsh Gds WW II N Africa and Italy; MP (C) Hereford 1956–74, PPS to Parly U-Sec War Office 1957 and Chllr Exchequer 1962–64, Assist Govt Whip 1957–59, a Ld Commr Treasury 1959–61, Chm Livestock Export Council 1962–74, Cncl on Tbnls 1980–86 and Timber Growers UK 1987–, Min State Welsh Office 1970–74, a Forestry Commr 1976–85, FRAgS; *m* 1942 *Diana, dau of Sir Charles Hambro, KBE, MC, and has had:

1 Jamie; *b* 29 March 1943; *d* 24 Oct 1946

2 *David Julian, *b* 1946; *educ* Eton and Trin Coll Camb; *m* 1st 1970 (*divorce* 1978) Patricia Hope, est dau of Sir Lenox Hewitt, OBE, of Red Hill, Canberra, Australia; *m* 2nd 1983 *Marie-Therese, widow of Anton Wallich-Clifford and dau of Michael McQuade, of Newarthill, Lanarks

3 *Robin [The Hon Robin Gibson-Watt, Gelli-Garn, Llanyre, Llandindrod Wells, Powys]; *b* 1949; *educ* Eton; High Sheriff Powys 1981; *m* 1971 *Marcia Susan, est dau of Sir Roger Hugh Cary, 2nd Bt (*qv*), and has:

(1) *Anthony David; *b* 1975

(2) *Edward Ricardo; *b* 1978

(3) *Guy Charles; *b* 1982

(1) *Phoebe Charlotte; *b* 1980

1 *Claerwen [The Hon Mrs Green, Foxboro' Hall, Melton, Suffolk IP12 lND]; *b* 1952; *m* 1st 1970 (*divorce* 1979) Enrique Rene Ulvert, s of Marcel J Ulvert-Portocarrero, sometime Nicaraguan Amb UK, and has:

(1) *Marcel David Joaquin; *b* 1971

(2) *Charles Nicholas; *b* 1972

1 (cont.) The Hon Mrs Claerwen Ulvert Portocarrero *m* 2nd 1980 *(John) James Randal Green and has further issue (*see* BICESTER, B)

2 *Sian Diana; *b* 1962; *m* 1993 *5th Baron Biddulph (*qv*) and has further issue

Lineage: JAMES GIBSON, of an Ayrshirefamily; *m* Agnes, dau of James Miller, of Glasgow, by Margaret, dau of James Watt, the famous inventor, and *d* 1835, leaving, with two daus:

JAMES WATT GIBSON later GIBSON WATT (roy licence 1856 under terms of will of his great-uncle James Watt, of Doldowlod), JP, DL and High Sheriff Radnorshire; *b* 4 Aug 1831; *m* 17 Nov 1874 Emma, dau of Henry O'Reilly Hoey, and *d* 19 June 1891, leaving, with three daus:

JAMES MILLER GIBSON-WATT, JP, V-Lt and High Sheriff Radnorshire; *b* 6 Sept 1875; *educ* Eton; *m* 20 April 1911 Marjorie, MBE, JP, est dau of Lt-Col Henry Ricardo, of the same family as the celebrated economist, of Gatcombe Park, Glos, and *d* 4 Aug 1929, leaving, with two yr sons and two daus:

(JAMES) DAVID, *cr* a **Baron**

GIFFORD

Arms: Az. a chevron between three stirrups, leathers or, within a bordure engrailed arg., semée of pellets. **Crest:** A panther's head, couped at the neck and affrontée, between two branches of oak ppr. **Supporters:** Dexter, a bay horse ppr., charged on the shoulder with a portcullis or; sinister, a greyhound arg., charged on the body with three ermine spots in pale. **Motto:** *Non sine numine* ('Not without God's assistance'). **Creation:** B. (UK) 30 Jan 1824.

THE 6TH BARON GIFFORD OF ST LEONARD'S, Devon (Anthony Maurice Gifford, QC (1982)) [The Rt Hon The Lord Gifford QC, 8 King's Bench Walk, London EC4Y 7DU; 21 Church St, Kingston, Jamaica]; *b* 1 May 1940; *s* f 1961; *educ*

Winchester and King's Coll Cambridge (BA 1961); barrister Middle Temple 1962, chm: Ctee Freedom Mozambique Angola and Guiné 1968–75, S Kensington Lab Pty 1968–69, Mozambique Angola Ctee 1982–90, N Kensington Neighbourhood Law Centre 1974–77 (Hon Sec 1970–74), Legal Action Gp 1978–83, v-chm Defence and Aid Fund (UK) 1983–, Pres Ctee Human Rights Grenada 1987–, V-Pres Haldane Soc Socialist Lawyers 1986–, sr ptnr Gifford, Haughton and Thompson 1991–, author: *Where's the Justice?* (1986); *m* 1st 22 March 1965 (*divorce* 1988) Katherine Anne, dau of Dr Max Mundy, and has issue:

1 +THOMAS ADAM; *b* 1 Dec 1967

1 *Polly Anna; *b* 31 March 1969

The 6th BARON *m* 2nd 24 Sept 1988 *Elean Roslyn, dau of Bishop David Thomas, of Kingston, Jamaica, and has further issue:

2 *Sheba Chanel; *b* 1992

Lineage: ROBERT GIFFORD, of Exeter; grocer and linendraper; had:

ROBERT GIFFORD, **1st Baron Gifford of St Leonard's**, Devon (UK), so *cr* 30 Jan 1824, PC (1824); *b* 24 Feb 1779; MP (Tory) Eye 1817–24, ktd 1817, Slr-Gen 1817–19, Attorney-Gen 1819–24, Ld Ch Justice Common Pleas Jan-April 1824, Master Rolls April 1824–26, Dep Speaker Ho Lds, Recorder Bristol 1818–26; *m* 6 April 1816 Harriet Maria (*d* 26 May 1857), dau of Rev Edward Drewe, Rector Willand, and had, with three daus and another s:

1 ROBERT FRANCIS, **2nd Baron**

2 John (Rev); MA, Rector Siddington, Glos; *b* 27 Nov 1821; *m* 18 Sept 1851 Alice Fanny (*d* 6 March 1904), dau of Edward Simcoe Drewe, of The Grange, Devon, and *d* 2 Nov 1887 leaving, with other issue:

(1) Edward Herbert; Capt Roy 1st Devon Imp Yeo; *b* 7 Aug 1864; *m* 22 April 1926 Gwendolen (*d* 7 Jan 1947), yst dau of John Arthur Locke, and *d* 13 May 1933

(1) Alice Mildred; *m* 28 Jan 1875 Thomas Carew Daniel, 2nd Life Gds, of Stoodleigh Court, Devon, and *dsp* 1897

(2) Ethel Frances; *m* 4 Feb 1879 Rev C W H Kenrick, Vicar Holy Trinity, Reading, and *d* 30 Oct 1893

3 George Robert (Rev); MA, Rector Rackenford Devon; *b* 14 Nov 1826; *m* 1st 25 Oct 1853 Mary Ann Danet (*d* 23 Oct 1871), dau of Thomas Norbury, and had:

(1) George Henry (Rev); Rector Rackenford; *b* 10 Aug 1854; *d* 2 Feb 1917

(2) Robert; Capt 1st Bn Sherwood Foresters (Derbys Regt); *b* 23 June 1857; *d* unm Jan 1903

(3) (cont.) The Rev and Hon George Gifford *m* 2nd 1 June 1878 Louisa Mary (*d* 18 June 1907), est dau of Col Robert Webb, and *d* 25 Dec 1878

The 1st BARON *d* 4 Sept 1826; his est s,

ROBERT FRANCIS GIFFORD, **2nd Baron Gifford of St Leonard's**; *b* 19 March 1817; *m* 2 April 1845 Frederica Charlotte (*d* 25 Nov 1920), est dau of 1st Baron FitzHardinge (*see* BERKELEY, B), and *d* 13 May 1872, having had, with another s and dau:

1 EDRIC FREDERICK GIFFORD, **3rd Baron Gifford of St Leonard's**, VC; Maj 57th Regt Ashanti Expdn 1873–74 (medal with clasp) and Zulu War 1879 (medal with clasp); *b* 5 July 1849; *m* 22 April 1880 Sophie Catherine (*d* 14 Feb 1947; despatches, 1914 Star, two medals), dau of Gen John Alfred Street, CB, and *dsp* 5 June 1911

2 Edward Robert; Sub-Lt RN; *b* Nov 1853; drowned in the sinking of HMS *Eurydice* off IoW 24 March 1878

3 EDGAR BERKELEY GIFFORD, **4th Baron Gifford of St Leonard's**; Lt S Glos Militia; *b* 8 March 1857; *m* 1st 26 Nov 1879 Mary (*d* 15 Aug 1913), widow of Thomas Booth, of W Ashby Manor, Lincs, and dau of John Osborne, QC; *m* 2nd 5 June 1918 Anne Maud (*d* 24 Feb 1956), 2nd dau of Lt-Col William Aitchison, Scots Gds, of Drummore, Musselburgh, and *dspm* 29 Jan 1937, leaving:

(1) *Serena Mary [The Hon Mrs Danks, Loscombe, 39 High St, Sydling St Nicholas, Dorset DT2 9PD]; *b* 30 Sept 1919; *m* 1st 28 Sept 1940 (*divorce* 1945) Patrick de Gruchy Vignoles Crawshay Warren, yr s of Guy de Gruchy Warren, of Chelsea, by Evelyn Illtyd, yr dau of Francis Richard Crawshay, JP, of Treforest, S Wales, and has:

1a *Edgar Jeremy; *b* 19 July 1941; *educ* Tabley House; *m* 1962 (*divorce* 19–) Edith Mary, yst dau of Maurice Patrick Ind, of Minchinhampton, Glos, and has:

1b *Paul Frederick; *b* 2 March 1963

1b *Louisa Elizabeth; *b* 25 June 1964

(1) (cont.) The Hon Mrs Serena Warren *m* 2nd 17 Oct 1951 Capt Arthur Reginald Danks, MBE, TD, HAC (RHA) (*d* 29 Nov 1996), yr s of Arthur Benjamin Danks, of Kidderminster, and has by him:

2a *John Francis Reginald; *b* 9 July 1954; *educ* Winchester

1a *Fenella Christian Mary; *b* 4 Dec 1952; *m* 1981 *Hon John Philip Robert Best, only s of 8th Baron Wynford (*qv*)

4 Maurice Raymond, CMG; *b* 5 May 1859; *m* 21 Sept 1897 Marguerite (*m* 2nd 20 April 1920 George Hugh Rayner, Lt Roy Warwickshire Regt (*d* 19 Feb 1941); *d* 9 Jan 1958), only child of Capt Cecil Thorold (*see* THOROLD, Bt), and *d* 1 July 1910, leaving:

(1) CHARLES MAURICE ELTON, **5th Baron**

(1) Diana Frederica; *b* 22 Dec 1901; granted with her sis Joan rank of baron's dau 21 Sept 1937; *m* 27 Sept 1924 (*divorce* 1953) Leslie Frederick Talbot Price and *d* 1979, leaving issue (*see* PRICE, Bt)

(2) Joan; *b* 24 June 1903; *d* unm 11 Aug 1968

(3) Vera Mary; *b* 1 May 1906; *d* unm 5 Nov 1936

1 Eva; *m* 24 May 1866 Maj-Gen Sir Henry Trotter, GCVO, DL, Gren Gds, 11th of Mortonhall, Midlothian, and *d* 6 April 1915, leaving issue. He *d* 16 July 1905

2 Harriet Ella; *m* 5 Jan 1885 Lt-Col Hon Archibald Douglas-Pennant and *d* 12 Feb 1942, leaving issue (*see* PENRHYN, B)

3 Emily; *m* 2 June 1868 Robert Thomas Napier Speir, of Burnbraes, Renfrewshire, and *d* 28 June 1928, leaving issue (*see* SEAFIELD, E)

4 Evelyn Mary; *m* 31 Aug 1872 Thomas Arthur Fitzhardinge Kingscote, CVO, JP, 4th s of Col Thomas Henry Kingscote, JP, of Kingscote, Glos, and *d* 2 April 1947, leaving issue. He *d* 21 Sept 1935

5 Eleanore; *m* 5 Nov 1873 Lt-Col Edward Mashiter Dansey, OBE, 1st Life Gds, and *d* 8 Feb 1939, leaving issue. He *d* 13 Jan 1934

6 Elspeth FitzHardinge; *m* 30 Jan 1877 Lt-Col Francis John Paul Butler, 18th Hus (*d* 17 May 1936), of Wych Hall, Glos, and *d* 10 Dec 1913, leaving:

(1) Capt John FitzHardinge Paul Butler, VC, DSO; *d* 4 Sept 1916 of wounds recd in action

The 4th BARON's n,

CHARLES MAURICE ELTON GIFFORD, **5th Baron Gifford of St Leonard's**; Cdr RN, F/Lt RAF WW I and 1920–30, ADC to Govr NSW 1930–35, Organising Sec Roy Prince Alfred Hosp Sydney 1935–36, chm and md Theatre Tickets and Messengers Ltd, dir: Ashton and Mitchell's Roy Agy 1956–59, Challis and Benson and E Wood Ltd; *b* 4 March 1899; *m* 5 March 1939 Ellice Margaret (*d* 1990), 2nd dau of Arthur Wigram Allen, of NSW, and *d* 16 April 1961, leaving:

1 ANTHONY MAURICE GIFFORD, **6th and present Baron Gifford of St Leonard's**

GILBERT

Creation: B. (LP, UK) May 1997.

THE BARON GILBERT, of Dudley in the County of West Midlands (Dr John William Gilbert, PC (1978)) [The Rt Hon The Lord Gilbert PC, House of Lords, London SW1A 0PW]; *b* April 1927; *educ* Merchnat Taylors', St John's Coll Oxford and NY U (PhD Internat Economics); chartered accountant Canada, fought (Lab) Ludlow 1966 and Dudley March 1968, MP (Lab) Dudley 1970–74 and Dudley E Feb 1974–97, Fin Sec Treasury 1974–75, Min Tport DOE 1975–76, Min State (Def Procurement) MOD 1976–79 and 1997–; *m* 1st — and has two daus; *m* 2nd 1963 *Jean Olive Ross Skinner

GILBEY

Arms: Gules a fesse nebulée or, in chief a horse rampant between two estoiles and the like in base, all of the last. **Crest:** In front of a tower proper, issuant from the battlements a dragon's head gu., a fleur-de-lys or, the whole between two ostrich feathers arg. **Motto:** *Honore et virtute* ('By honour and virtue'). **Creation:** Bt. (UK) 4 Sept 1893.

SIR (WALTER) GAVIN GILBEY, 4TH BT, of Elsenham Hall, Essex [Sir Gavin Gilbey Bt, 8201 SW 115 St, Miami, FL 33156, USA]; *b* 14 April 1949; *s* f 1991; *educ* Eton; *m* 1st 1980 (*divorce* 1984) Mary Pacetti, dau of William E E Pacetti, of Florida, and Mrs Mary Greer; *m* 2nd 1984 (*divorce* 1997) Anna, dau of Edmund Prosser, of Birmingham

Lineage: NICHOLAS GILBEY, of Widdington, Essex; *m* Margaret — (*d* 1695) and *d* 1666, leaving issue:

NICHOLAS GILBEY, of Widdington; *m* Mary — (*d* 1711) and *d* 1719, leaving, with an er s (Nicholas, of Widdington; *b* 1692; *m* Elizabeth):

DANIEL GILBEY, of Ugley, Essex; labourer; *bapt* 15 March 1699; *m* 20 Oct 1724 Anne (*bur* 17 Aug 1773), dau of — Ricket, of Ugley, and was *bur* Aug 1750, having had:

1 John; *bapt* 6 March 1726

2 DANIEL, of whom presently

3 George; *bapt* 14 March 1730/1

4 William; *bapt* 20 April 1735; *bur* 26 Dec 1736

1 Anne; *bapt* 23, *bur* 25 Sept 1737

2 Anne; *bapt* 16 Oct 1737

The 2nd son,

DANIEL GILBEY, of Gt Hallingbury, Essex; forester Gt Hallingbury estate; *bapt* 23 Feb 1729; *m* Mary — (*d* June 1811) and *d* May 1785, having had, with a yr s John (*bapt* 8 Dec 1757, *bur* 20 June 1762) and two daus (Jane *bapt* 6 June 1754; Sarah *bapt* 25 April 1755):

DANIEL GILBEY, of The Old Bell, Stansted, Mountfichtet, Essex; *b* 1759; *m* Rebecca, dau of John Speed, of Bovinger Hall, Essex, and *d* Oct 1814, leaving, with other issue:

HENRY GILBEY, of Bishops Stortford, Herts; *b* 29 Jan 1789; *m* 1814 Elizabeth (*d* 12 Jan 1869), 2nd dau of William Bailey, of Stansted, by his 1st w Harriet Church, and *d* 29 Sept 1842, having had:

1 George; *b* 3 Jan *d* Feb 1817

2 Henry; *b* 17 March 1820; *d* March 1823

3 Henry Parry, of Stansted; *b* 24 March 1824; *m* Feb 1852 Catherine (*d* Dec 1893), dau of J Shepherd, of London, and *d* 12 Dec 1892, having had issue:

(1) Percy Shepherd; *b* 1853; *d* unm 1919

(2) Charles Herbert; *b* 1857; *dvp* 1876

(1) Laura; *b* 1860; *m* 1883 Henry Riviere and *d* 1931, leaving issue

(2) Ada Kate; *b* 1862; *m* 27 Oct 1887 Hon Richard Eustace-Bellew, yst s of 2nd Baron Bellew (*qv*), and *d* 20 March 1893, leaving issue

4 William James Church; *b* 30 April 1827; *d* 1847

5 WALTER (Sir), **1st Bt**

6 Alfred, of Wooburn House, Wooburn, Bucks, JP; *b* 23 Oct 1833; *m* 29 March 1858 Agnes (*d* 23 Aug 1920), dau of W Crosbie, of Winchester, and *d* 28 Nov 1879, leaving issue:

(1) Alfred, of Wooburn House, JP, VD; Lt-Col Bucks Vols 1900–06, raised and cmded Bucks Territorial Bn 1915–16, High Sheriff Bucks 1916; *b* 6 Jan 1859; *educ* Marlborough; *m* 1885 Beatrice Elizabeth (*d* 1926), dau of William J Holland, of Cadogan Gdns, and *d* 24 Oct 1927, leaving issue:

1a (Alfred) Ronald; *b* 23 April 1886; *educ* Eton; *m* 1st 28 April 1910 (*divorce* 1925) Florence Emily (*d* 17 April 1969), only dau of Sir Edwin Abercromby Dashwood, 8th Bt, of West Wycombe (*qv*); *m* 2nd 1934 Mrs Jane Elizabeth (Betty) Truran (*d* 24 Aug 1977), dau of — Scaife, and *d* 17 June 1954, leaving by his 1st w:

1b Ronald Dashwood, CBE; memb Westminster CC, parly candidate Greenwich 1950, memb LCC Holborn and St Pancras S 1952–58, memb St Pancas Borough Cncl 1959–62, GLC memb Haringey 1967–73, chm W & A Gilbey 1958–69, Nat Skating Assoc GB Licensees & Gen Insur, Pres St Pancras Chamber Commerce, London Centl Bd, memb Br Olympic Cncl; *b* 20 Feb 1911; *educ* Westminster; *m* 24 Jan 1947 *Anne, dau of Capt Gilbert Leslie-Smith, 24th Punjab Regt, IA, and *d* 31 July 1977, leaving:

1c *(Ronald) Nicholas Dashwood; *b* 30 June 1950; *m* 27 Aug 1976 *Mrs Shirley A Stone

1c *Thomasin Sarah; *b* 18 Nov 1947; *m* 19 July 1975 *Anthony James Nares, s of Lt J G A M Nares, RN, and Mrs David Buchanan-Dunlop, of Rome

1b *Susan; *b* 1919; *m* 1947 *Macleod Wallace, of W Wittering, Sussex, and has issue

2a Wilfrid Holland; *b* 1887; *educ* Eton; *m* 1924 Elsie, dau of — Wilson, of Dally, Qld, Australia, and *dsp* 1940

3a Geoffrey Holland, MC (1915); Capt Rifle Bde WW I; *b* 12 May 1889; *educ* Eton and Ch Ch Oxford; *m* 9 Dec 1919 (Violet Mary) Molly, dau of Dr S D Reid, of Kirkcudbright, and *d* 8 Oct 1969, leaving issue:

1b Rosemary Elizabeth; *b* 4 Nov 1921; *m* 1 July 1957 Simon Francis Carruthers, 3rd s of Lt-Col Francis John Carruthers, CB, Dormont, Dumfries, and *d* 2 May 1978, leaving:

1c *Elizabeth Jane; *b* 24 Jan 1959; theatre dir

2b *(Julia) Veronica Ann [Mrs Mick Webb, Pallington Farm, Tincleton, Dorset DT2 8QU]; *b* 18 Nov 1924; *m* 21 Oct 1952 *Brig (C) Mick F Webb, RA, and has:

1c *Charles Geoffrey Fane; *b* 1957; *educ* Wellington and Southampton U (BSc); FCMA; *m* 14 Sept 1985 *Rosaly Dorothy, dau of George Tuson, of Bournemouth, and has

1d *(Charles) Thomas Fane; *b* 19 June 1988

1d *Alexandra Victoria; *b* 6 June 1991

1c *Julia Anne Fane; *b* 1954; *educ* Whispers; *m* 25 Sept 1982 *Bryan Anthony ('Tin') McSwiney, Roy Scots Dragoon Gds, s of Bryan McSwiney, of Llandovery, and has:

1d *Oliver Charles Anthony; *b* 8 April 1986

2d *Giles Edward; *b* 12 Feb 1989

4a Oliver Holland; The Blues WW I; *b* 8 June 1894; *educ* Harrow; *m* 1926 Violet Elizabeth Gertrude (*d* 24 June 1972), dau of Thomas Burrows, of Esher, Surrey, and *d* 3 May 1971

5a Quintin Holland; Gren Gds, racing jnlist, author: autobiography and *Queen of the Turf*; *b* 9 June 1899; *educ* Eton and RMA Sandhurst; *m* 1st 1927 (*divorce* 1930) Elizabeth Thornton, only dau of Otho Ball, of Chicago, and had:

1b *Robin Alfred GILBEY later WELLESLEY (deed poll 1937); *b* 23 July 1928; *educ* Eton; *m* 7 March 1953 *Marianne, yr dau of John McDonald, of Chicago, and has issue:

1c *Gerald; *b* 26 Jan 1958

1c *Diana; *b* 9 Oct 1954

2c *Laura; *b* 24 July 1956

5a (cont.) Quintin Gilbey *m* 2nd 11 Feb 1933 (*divorce* 1942) Rosemary Marguerite, formerly w of Maj John Drury Boteler Drury-Lowe, Scots Gds, and yr dau of Lt-Col James Charles Hope-Vere, TD, JP, DL (*see* LINLITHGOW, M), and by her had:

2b *Anthony James [Anthony Gilbey Esq, White Lion House, Wangford, Suffolk NR34 8RL]; Lt (Res) Gren Gds, dir Craford & Gilbey, publishers; *b* 2 April 1933; *educ* Repton, Ecole des Roches and Ch Ch Oxford; *m* 1st 18 Oct 1958 Lenore (*d* 1983), only dau of W Joseph Shatton, of New York, and has:

1c *James Dennis; *b* 16 May 1959

2c *Paul Alfred; *b* 17 Aug 1964

1c *Emma Lenora; *b* 23 Jan 1961

2c *Mollie Keller; *b* 1967

2b (cont.) Anthony Gilbey *m* 2nd 19– —; *m* 3rd 1984, as her 3rd husb, *Penelope, dau of 4th Earl of Stradbroke (qv)

(2) William Crosbie, of The Lea, Denham, Bucks; *b* 1860; *m* 1886 Margerita, dau of Jose Carlos Gordon, of Jerez-de-la-Frontera, Spain, and *d* 1916, leaving:

1a William Gordon; *b* 1886; *m* 15 July 1911 Grace Mary Eleanor, Baroness Vaux of Harrowden (*qv*), and *d* 14 Feb 1965, leaving issue

2a Hugh Lionel; *b* 1891; *m* 1915 Phyllis Maud Byas (*d* 10 Dec 1973) and *d* 12 Nov 1970, leaving issue:

1b *Guy Hugh; *b* 1916; *m* 1944 *Joan Irene Warburton and has issue:

1c *Simon Byas; *b* 1945

2c *Paul Hugh; *b* 1947

1b *Pamela Maureen; *b* 1919; *m* 5 July 1939 her first cousin 10th Baron Vaux of Harrowden (*qv*)

2b *Jill Felicity; *b* 1929

3b *Jean Cynthia; *b* 1930; *m* 19– *Brian Reilly and has issue:

1c *Dominic

1c *Nicola

2c *Lesley

3c *Fiona

4c *A dau; *b* 25 Oct 1968

4b *Phyllis Anne; *b* 1933

3a Alban James; Lt Gren Gds WW I; *b* 1899; *educ* Oratory Sch; *m* 1924 Mercy Eleonore Adele, dau of Ernst Mark, and *dsp* 5 Feb 1968

1a Agnes; *b* 1888; *m* 1912 Kenneth Mackenzie

2a Maria Del Rosarie; *b* 1889

3a Mercedes Christina; *b* 1893; *m* 1923 Ricardo Gonzales (*d* 16 Nov 1944)

4a Winifred Hilda; *b* 1895; *m* 1928 Gabriel Gonzalez and *d* 11 July 1967

5a Marion Genevieve; *b* 1900

(3) Newman, JP Essex; *b* 2 March 1862; *educ* Forest Sch; *m* 14 Jan 1886 Maria Victorina (*d* 7 May 1937), dau of Enrique de Ysasi, of Jerez-de-la-Frontera, and *d* 12 June 1942, having had issue:

1a Henry Newman; *b* 15 Nov 1886; *educ* Beaumont and Stonyhurst; *m* 1st 12 Feb 1923 Myn Beatrice (*d* 19 Feb 1936), widow of Ernest Burleigh, and dau of Herbert Brunwin, of Colchester; *m* 2nd 17 Aug 1944 *Angela Everard, dau of Patrick Bushell, of Boyle, Co Roscommon, and *d* 17 Oct 1956, leaving by his 1st w:

1b Mark Newman; Capt Gren Gds WW II Italy 1943–45, Instr RMC Sandhurst 1946, chm Duncan, Gilbey and Matheson Ltd Lond, Duncan, Gilbey and Matheson SA Fribourg, Wellington Distilleries Sierra Leone, Gambia Distilleries, Duncan, Gilbey and Matheson (Zambia) and Duncan, Gilbey and Matheson (Malaysia), dir East African Distilleries Uganda and Duncan, Gilbey and Kennedy Ltd Jamaica, Hon Ecuadorian Consul Morocco 1967; *b* 21 Nov 1923; *educ* Beaumont and Trin Coll Cambridge; *d* 19–

2b *Simon Newman [Simon Gilbey, Chief's Farm, Great Bardfield, Essex]; *b* 12 March 1932; *educ* Oratory; *m* 16 June 1973 *Beverley M A, dau of Melville Crawford-Price, of Colchester, and has issue:

1c *William Henry Newman; *b* 20 Aug 1975

1c *Joan Carmen Simone; *b* 10 Nov 1977

1b Elizabeth Myn; *b* 15 Feb 1926; *d* unm 19 Sept 1968

2a John Newman; Capt Welch Regt; *b* 4 Feb 1888; *educ* Stonyhurst and RMC Sandhurst

3a Charles Newman; Capt Essex Yeo; *b* 5 Feb 1889; *educ* Beaumont and RMA Woolwich; *m* 22 June 1915 Lettice Charlotte (*d* 8 April 1968), dau of Ernest John Walker Watney, and *d* 17 Aug 1968, leaving issue:

1b *Nancy Veronica [Lady Agnew, Pinehurst, Friary Rd, S Ascot, Berks SL5 9HD]; *b* 17 July 1918; *m* 1st 22 Jan 1944 Adml Sir St John Reginald Joseph Tyrwhitt, 2nd Bt (*qv*; *d* 10 Oct 1961), and has issue; *m* 2nd 27 Sept 1965, as his 2nd w, Sir (William) Godfrey Agnew, KCVO (*d* 1995), only s of Lennox Edelsten Agnew

4a Francis Newman, OBE; Capt 15th Hus; *b* 1896; *educ* Beaumont; *m* 28 Sept 1920 Mary, dau of James Jump, and *d* 5 Feb 1973, leaving issue:

1b *James Newman; *b* 10 Sept 1921; *educ* Ampleforth; *m* 1 Sept 1949 *Celia, dau of Guy Sparrow, of Gillingham, Dorset, and has issue:

1c *Robert James Newman; *b* 30 Dec 1950; *m* 26 April 1984 *Amanda M, est dau of Alan Root, of Wendover, Bucks

2c *Guy Newman; *b* 23 Aug 1952

3c *Giles Newman; *b* 5 Nov 1956

2b *Ralph Newman; *b* 2 March 1925; *educ* Ampleforth and Trin Coll Cambridge; *m* 10 Oct 1949 *Barbara, dau of Francis Scott, of Hatfield Heath, Essex, and has issue:

1c *Thomas Newman; *b* 20 July 1951

2c *Francis Newman; *b* 12 May 1953

3c *James Newman; *b* 4 Oct 1956

1c *Helen; *b* 6 Dec 1959

5a Alfred Newman; ordained 1929, Priv secretary to Bp Brentwood 1929–32, RC Chaplain Cambridge U 1932–65, Domestic Prelate to HH THE POPE 1950, Hon Mgr 1950, Protonotary Apostolic 1963, Canon Brentwood, Grand Cross Conventual Chaplain *ad honorem* SMO Malta, author: *We Believe* (1979); *b* 13 July 1901; *educ* Beaumont, Trin Coll Cambridge and Beda Coll Rome; *d* 26 March 1998

1a Angeles (Lita); *b* 6 Dec 1892; *d* unm 22 April 1925

2a Carmen; *b* 2 June 1894

(4) Southard; *b* 1863; *m* 1892 Delia Prendergast and *dsp* 1941

(5) Henry; *b* 1865; *m* 1897 Dolores (*d* 1959), dau of Ricardo de la Quintana, and *d* 1951, leaving issue:

1a Henry Richard; *b* 1898; *m* 1929 Kathleen Mary, dau of Dr Maurice Hannigan

(6) Gilbert, of Overthorpe Hall, Banbury, Oxon; *b* 1874; *m* 24 April 1901 Edith Mary (*d* 7 June 1954), 2nd dau of Sir John Storey Barwick, 1st Bt (*see* 1970 edn), of Ashbrooke Grange, Sunderland, and *d* 24 Oct 1933, leaving:

1a John Gilbert; High Sheriff Berks 1972; *b* 1917; *educ* Eton and Ch Ch Oxford; *m* 21 Jan 1947 his first cousin *Angela Ruth, est dau of George Short Barwick, JP, and *d* 12 Dec 1982, leaving issue:

1b Christopher John Barwick; *b* 13 July 1949; *educ* Eton; *d* unm 7 Jan 1983

1b *Arabella Clare; *b* 14 July 1953; *m* 16 July 1977 *Thomas Charles Blackwell, only s of Thomas Francis Blackwell, of Langham Hall, Bury St Edmunds, Suffolk

1a Brenda; *b* 1903

2a Clare; *b* 1905; *d* unm 1942

3a *Margaret; *b* 1911; *m* 1938 Magin Coulter Hancock

(1) Agnes; *b* 1867; *m* 28 July 1891 Rt Rev Edward Domett Shaw, DD, Bp Buckingham, Archdeacon Oxford, 2nd s of Rev Edward Francis Shaw, Rector Pitchott, Bucks, and *d* 1944, having had four sons and six daus. He *d* 5 Nov 1937

(2) Mary; *b* 1869; *m* 20 April 1892 Charles Gold, JP, 3rd s of Sir Charles Gold, and *d* 6 Feb 1959, having had issue. He *d* 20 April 1950

(3) Elizabeth; *b* 1871; *m* 1892 Walter Gilbey Gold, 2nd s of Sir Charles Gold, and *d* 1917, leaving issue. He *d* 6 Oct 1954

(4) Kate; *b* 1872; *m* 1908 Rev Ernest Dalby Finch-Smith, Vicar Snodland, Kent, and *dsp* 22 Jan 1956. He *d* 10 Jan 1909

(5) Constance; *b* 1876; *d* unm

1 Caroline; *b* 9 Feb 1815; *m* Feb 1839 James Blyth and *d* 2 July 1894, leaving issue (*see* BLYTH, B)

2 Harriet; *b* 7 Jan 1818; *m* 29 Sept 1834 Arthur Nockolds, of Stansted, and *d* 1875

3 Emily; *b* 11 March 1822; *m* 31 Jan 1846 Jabez Thomas, of London, and *d* 1884

4 Julia Elizabeth; *b* 5 April 1829; *m* 11 March 1849 Alfred Ellis, of Bishop's Stortford, and *d* 5 June 1908, leaving issue

5 Charlotte Anne; *b* 12 May 1836; *m* 27 Dec 1858 Henry Gold, JP, of Cookham, Berks, 3rd s of Michael Gold, and *d* 16 Nov 1901, having had issue. He *d* 1 May 1900

6 Fanny Georgiana; *b* 24 July 1838; *m* 28 Dec 1859 Sir Charles Gold, JP, 4th s of Michael Gold, and *d* 1 May 1910, having had issue. He *d* 2 Nov 1924

The 5th son,

Sir Walter Gilbey, 1st Bt (UK), so *cr* 4 Sept 1893, of Elsenham Hall, Essex, JP, DL; *b* 2 May 1831; Pres Roy Ag Soc 1895, Smithfield Club, Hackney Horse Soc, Shire Horse Soc, Hunters' Improvement Soc, Pay Dept Crimean War, chm W & A Gilbey, wine merchants and distillers; *m* 3 Nov 1858 Ellen (*d* 16 Nov 1896), 4th dau of John Parish, and had issue:

1 HENRY WALTER (Sir), **2nd Bt**

2 Arthur Nockolds, JP Berks; High Sheriff Middx 1912; *b* 6 April 1861; *educ* Trin Coll Cambridge (MA); *m* 19 Aug 1885 Beatrice (*d* 19 June 1936), 2nd dau of Henry Gold, JP, DL, of Cookham, Berks, and *d* 8 Oct 1939, leaving issue:

(1) Sebastian Walter, Lt RASC WW I; *b* 6 May 1893; *educ* Harrow; *m* 22 July 1916 Jean Agnew (*d* 27 Aug 1970), only dau of George Milner, of Holland Park, London, and *d* 22 Sept 1971, having had issue:

1a Arthur Sebastian; Lt 4th Hus (SR) WW II (POW); *b* 18 Oct 1919; *educ* Harrow and BNC Oxford; *m* 20 Oct 1947 Jennifer Beryl (*d* 1991), formerly w of Jay Gould III and yr dau of William Nigel Ernie Bruce (*see* BRUCE, Bt, of Stenhouse), and *d* 25 May 1964, leaving issue:

1b +Christopher Sebastian Bruce [Christopher Gilbey Esq, Rosewood, Hanging Langford, Wilts]; *b* 20 Feb 1955; *educ* Harrow; *m* 1980 *Medina, dau of Sir Reginald Bennett, and has:

1c +Jasper Sebastian Christopher; *b* 1981

1c *Sophie; *b* 1983

1b *Patricia [Mrs Andrew Millar, Woodlands Cottages, Brixton Hill, Benson, Oxon]; *b* 22 Jan 1949; *m* 1973 *Andrew Michael Talbot Millar (*see* COCKBURN, Bt) and has issue:

1c *Alexander Derracot; *b* 9 July 1976

1c *Olivia Rosalind; *b* 1977

2b *Linda [The Hon Mrs Michael Gilbey, Pheasants Ridge, Hambleden, Oxon RG9 6SD]; *b* 14 Oct 1952; *m* 21 Aug 1971 *Hon Michael Christopher Gilbey, yst s of 10th Baron Vaux of Harrowden (*qv*), and has issue

2a Giles Milner, MC (1945); Capt 12th Roy Lancers WW II; *b* 12 Oct 1923; *m* 1 Oct 1962 *Mrs Diana Mary Ryerson [Mrs Giles Gilbey, Flat 11, 53 Rutland Gate, London SW7; Box 42, Colebrook, CT 06021, USA], only dau of W E Melville-Cook, of Parkstone, Dorset, and *d* 13 Dec 1983, leaving:

1b *Lisa Maria; *b* 16 April 1965

(2) Rupert Sydney; CC Wilts 1947; *b* 14 Dec 1900; *m* 20 July 1927 Anne Penelope (*d* 16 Feb 1970), only dau of Edgar S Prince, of Yew Tree House, Kemble, Glos, and *d* 14 Nov 1959, leaving issue:

1a +Simon Rupert; late Capt 8th KRI Hus; *b* 4 Aug 1929; *educ* Eton and RMA Sandhurst; *m* 1st 14 March 1953 (*divorce* 1966) Chloë Rio (*d* following a car crash 4 July 1966), er dau of Col Christopher Rawlinson Cadge, OBE, and has had issue:

1b A son; *b* and *d* 30 May 1954

2b +Rupert John; *b* 14 Jan 1960

1b *Juliet Rio; *b* 5 July 1955; *m* 1979 *John Michael Denison Bidwell and has:

1c *James Denison; *b* 1981

2c *Patrick Simon; *b* 1983

2b *Rachel Anne [Mrs Jonathan Dunn, Hackwood Farm, Robertsbridge, Sussex;] *b* 24 April 1957; *m* 1981 *Jonathan Dunn, er s of A Dunn, and has:

1c *Thomas Alan; *b* 1982

1c *Imogen Chloë; *b* 1985

2c *Jessica Rose; *b* 1988

1a (cont.) Simon Gilbey *m* 2nd 1 Aug 1966 *Sara Jane, formerly w of Christopher Evelyn Twiston Davies and 2nd dau of Capt Augustus Frederick Coryton, JP, DL, of Goleigh Farm House, Greatham, Hants, and by her has:

3b *Lisa; *b* 2 June 1967

1a *Sarah Anne [Mrs Patrick Bagshawe, Pond House, Meysey Hampton, Cirencester, Glos]; *b* 3 Aug 1933; *m* 11 April 1953 *Patrick Philip Bagshawe, yst s of Francis Ernest Gisborne Bagshawe, JP, of Snitterton Hall, Derbys, and has issue:

1b *Anthony William Newton; *b* 29 Feb 1956; *m* 1980 *Alison Katrina, dau of John Auld Macdonald

2b *Jasper Philip Adam; *b* 26 March 1960; *m* 1986 *Chloë Mary Johnson, and has:

1c *Samuel Oscar; *b* 1986

1c *Jessica Albinia; *b* 1988

1b *Charlotte Anne; *b* 14 March 1954; *m* 1st 1982 (*divorce* 1984) Stephen A Buckle, s of Lorne Buckle, of Quebec; *m* 2nd 1989 (*divorce* 1991) Robert Bringhurst

(1) Nina; *b* 25 Sept 1886; *m* 3 Oct 1906 Arthur Bayly Akroyd, er s of Bayly Nash Akroyd, and *d* 11 Oct 1969, leaving issue. He *d* 4 Aug 1945

(2) Sylvia; *b* 9 April 1889; *m* 15 March 1911 Edward Maurice Dowson, er s of Edward Dowson, and had issue. He *d* 22 July 1933

(3) Diana Beatrice; *b* 3 March 1909; *d* unm 6 Aug 1979

3 Tresham, of Whitehall, Bishop's Stortford, Herts, JP; fndr-ed *Baily's Hunting Directory*; *b* 6 Aug 1862; *m* 29 April 1886 Annie Sarah, JP (*d* 20 Sept 1941), only child of Sir John Barker, 1st and last Bt, of The Grange, Bishops Stortford, and *dsp* 16 Feb 1947

4 Sebastian; *b* 29 Nov 1863; *d* unm 31 Jan 1880

5 Guy, JP Essex; Capt Remount Service; *b* 9 March 1868; *m* 6 June 1902 Katherine Thurlow (*d* 23 May 1961), dau of Henry Merryweather, and *d* 14 June 1930

1 Maud Ellen; *b* 15 Feb 1865; *m* 20 July 1886 Daniel Thomas Hine and *d* 22 March 1951 leaving issue. He *d* 16 July 1933

2 Mabel Kate; *b* 13 July 1866; *m* 3 July 1889 Leonard Arthur Routledge and *d* 25 June 1945 leaving issue. He *d* 19 June 1935

3 Rose; *b* 24 June 1870; *m* 28 April 1891 Robert Stansfeld Barrow and *d* 20 Jan 1944 leaving issue. He *d* 26 March 1924

4 Emily Lucy; *b* 30 Sept 1872; *m* 21 Feb 1901 Herbert Stroyan, JP, yst s of Robert Stroyan, and *dsp* 2 Nov 1938. He *d* 3 Dec 1922

Sir WALTER *d* 12 Nov 1914; his est s,

Sir (Henry) Walter Gilbey, 2nd Bt, JP (Essex 1895); Pres London Cart Horse Parade Soc, Shire Horse Soc, Chm Roy Ag Hall Co, W & A Gilbey; *b* 1 Oct 1859; *m* 1st 26 Jan 1884 (*divorce* 1926) Isabella Mary (*d* 22 Sept 1940), dau of John Coutts Fowlie, and had issue:

1 Walter Ewart; Capt 16th Bn Lond Regt; *b* 30 June 1886; *m* 18 April 1912 (*divorce* 1933) Alice Dora (*d* 9 Feb 1961), only dau of Archibald Coysgarne Sim, and *dvp* 18 Nov 1941, leaving issue:

(1) **Sir (Walter) Derek Gilbey, 3rd Bt**; *b* 11 March 1913; *educ* Eton; Lt Black Watch WW II (POW); *m* 21 July 1948 *Elizabeth Mary [Elizabeth Lady Gilbey, Little Paddock, The Street, Bury, W Sussex RH20 1PA], dau of Col Keith Gordon Campbell, DSO, of Standen House, nr Newport, IoW, and Marjorie Syfret, and *d* 1991, leaving issue:

1a Sir (WALTER) GAVIN GILBEY, **4th and present Bt**

1a *Camilla Elizabeth; *b* 24 Nov 1953; *m* 21 July 1990 *Christopher St John Fredrick, er s of Maj Sir Charles Boscawen Frederick, 10th Bt (*qv*), and has issue

2 Eric; Lt 5th Bn Rifle Bde and Gren Gds; *b* 26 Dec 1888; *ka* 14 March 1915

Sir Walter *m* 2nd 9 Aug 1934 Marion, widow of Wilson Broadhead and dau of James Robert, of Farnley Tyas, and *d* 11 April 1945, having by her had issue:

3 +WALTER ANTHONY [Walter Gilbey Esq, Ballacallin Mooar, Crosby, Marown, IoM IM4 2HD]; *b* 26 Feb 1935; heir presumptive; *educ* Eton; fin dir Gilbeys Ltd 1962–72 and IDV to 1972, exec v-chm Duncan, Gilbey and Matheson, Memb Ho Keys, took by deed poll 1958 names Walter Anthony instead of Anthony Walter, with Kleinwort Benson 1954–62, chm: Mannin Tst Bank 1972–82, Mannin Industries 1972–, Mannin Int Ltd 1982–88, Manx Telecom, dir and chm Vannin Int Securities 1972–, dir: Gilbey Farms Ltd 1974–, Steam Packet Co Ltd 1976–, ptnr Gilbey Grianagh Horses 1978–, chm C Pty Candidate Ealing Southall 1971–74, Civil Service Cmmn and Whitley Cncl 1985–90, memb Dept Local Govt and Environment IoM 1987–90, chm Planning Ctee Dept Local Govt IoM 1987–90, memb Dept Highways Ports and Properties IoM 1990–, Berks CC 1966–74, Vintners' Co; *m* 20 April 1964 *Jenifer Mary, est dau of Capt James Timothy Noel Price, of Douglas, IoM (*see* O'BRIEN, Bt), and has:

(1) +Walter Anthony; *b* 20 Jan 1966

(1) *Caroline Anne; *b* 2 Oct 1967

3 (cont.) Mr & Mrs Walter Gilbey adopted:

*Sarah Elizabeth; *b* 3 Nov 1969

GILLETT

Arms: In front of a ship's helm ppr. an early 19th–century waistcoat az. semée de lys and purfled or, on a chief az. between two estoiles a balance ppr. **Crest:** A grey horse's head and neck erased ppr., gorged with a coronet composed of six fleur de lys affixed to a circlet chained or. **Motto:** *Vincit omnia veritas* ('Truth conquers all') **Creation:** Bt. (UK) 4 Dec 1959.

SIR ROBIN DANVERS PENROSE GILLETT, 2ND BT, of Bassishaw Ward, City of London, GBE (1976), RD (1965) [Sir Robin Gillett Bt GBE RD, 4 Fairholt St, London SW7 1EQ]; *b* 9 Nov 1925; *s* f 1976; *educ* Nautical Coll Pangbourne and Hill Crest Sch; Lt-Cdr RNR (ret), attd Sherborne House Marine Cadet Unit, Merchant Navy (Canadian Pacific Steamships) 1943–60, Master Mariner 1951, Staff Cdr 1957, underwriting memb Lloyd's, MinstOM, City London: Common Councilman Bassishaw Ward 1965, Alderman 1969, Sheriff 1973–74, Lt 1976, Ld Mayor 1976–77, Chm CD Ctee 1967–68, Pres CD Instrs Assoc, Exec and Finance Ctee City London Red Cross (V-Pres); memb Court Assists Master Mariners' Co (Sr Warden 1971–85, Master 1978–80), KStJ 1977, Er Bro Trin House, FInstAM 1973– (Pres 1980–84) Gold Medal 1982, (V-Pres 1985–94, Pres 1994–), FNI, FInstD, dir: Bevington Vaizey & Foster, Wigham Poland Home and Wigham Poland Management Servs 1965–86, St Katherine Haven 1979 (chm 1990–93), Pres Nat Waterways Tport Assoc 1979–83, Pres RLSS UK 1978–82, Dep Cwlth Pres 1982–96, Cwlth V-Pres, V-Chm PLA 1979–84, chm Lord Mayor's Flood Relief Fund and Princess Victoria's Distress Fund, V-Pres City Centre St John's Ambulance, Tstee Nat Maritime Museum and St Paul's Cathedral Tst, Lay V-Patron Missions to Seamen, Chm and Govr Pangbourne Coll 1978–92, Cncl RCM, FRCM 1991, V-Pres KGFS 1993–, Hon Cdr RNR, Gentleman Usher Purple Rod 1985–, Offr Order Leopard Zaire, Cdr Dannebrog, Johan Sedia Mahkota Malaysia, Grand Cross Municipal Order Merit Lima, Gold Medal Admin Management Soc USA, Hon DSc London 1976; *m* 22 Sept 1950 Elizabeth Marion Grace (*d* 12 May 1997), er dau of John Findlay, JP, of Busby House, Busby, Lanarks, and has:

1 +NICHOLAS DANVERS PENROSE [Nicholas Gillett Esq, 19 Woodland Ct, Bishop's Knoll, Sneyd Park, Bristol BS9 1NR]; *b* 24 Sept 1955; *educ* Durlston Ct Sch, Pangbourne Coll and Imp Coll London (BSc); ARCS, FBIS, Br Aerospace 1978–96, now Project Manager EG & Co Astrophysics, Liveryman Coachmakers' Co 1982–; *m* 3 Jan 1987 *Haylie, er dau of Dennis Brooks, of Abertawe, W Glam

2 +Chris(topher) John [Christopher Gillett Esq, 3 Wooley St, Bradford-on-Avon BA5 3HP]; *b* 16 May 1958; *educ* Durlston Ct Sch, Pangbourne Coll and King's Coll Cambridge (MA), RCM, Nat Opera Studio 1982–83; opera singer, Liveryman Musicians' Co 1981; *m* 1st 7 Jan 1984 (*divorce* 1996) Julia A, yr dau of W H Holmes, of Tunbridge Wells; *m* 2nd 27 July 1996 *Lucy, yst dau of H Schaufer, of Phoenix, Ariz., and by his 1st w has:

(1) +Adam Holmes; *b* 1989

(1) *Tessa Holmes; *b* 1987

Lineage: WILLIAM HENRY GILLETT; *b* Brize Norton, Oxon, 17 June 1831; *m* 8 April 1858 Emily Barton, of Lacock, Wilts, and *d* London 11 Dec 1870, leaving:

WILLIAM HENRY GILLETT, of Highgate; *b* 15 Jan 1859; *m* 16 Nov 1889 Amy Ford (*d* 29 April 1936 aged 79), dau of Edward Little, of Chippenham, Wilts, and *d* 22 Dec 1953, leaving:

1 **Sir (Sydney) Harold Gillett, 1st Bt** (UK), so *cr* 4 Dec 1959, MC (1916); *b* 27 Nov 1890; *educ* Marlborough; Lt City London, Common Councilman 1930–48, Alderman 1948–69, Sheriff 1952–53, Ld Mayor 1958–59, V-Pres London Chamber Commerce (Chm 1956–57), consultant Dixon, Wilson, Tubbs and Gillett, memb Gen Cncl Boy Scouts' Assoc, Govr: Nat Corp Care Old People, Grey Coat Hosp, Queen Anne's Sch and Utd Westminster Schs, Past Prime Warden Basketmakers' Co, Middx Regt WW I (TA) (despatches), 2A i/c 17 Bn Essex HG WW II, Hon Col 8th Essex (517 LAA) Cadet Regt, 2nd Cl Order Homayoun Iran, Gold Medal Madrid, KStJ; ktd 1953; *m* 19 June 1919 Audrey Isabel Penrose (*d* 30 July 1962), dau of Capt Edgar Penrose Mark-Wardlaw, and *d* 21 Sept 1976, leaving:

(1) Sir ROBIN DANVERS PENROSE GILLETT, **2nd and present Bt**

2 Herbert Edward; FRICS; *b* 29 July 1895; *m* 31 Aug 1921 Lilian Mary (*m* 2nd Thomas Nigel Baines), dau of Percival Martin Puckridge, and *d* 13 Oct 1953, leaving:

(1) +Alan Henry Puckridge; FRICS, FAI, late RE, ptnr Kemsley, Whiteley and Ferris, chartered surveyors; *b* 30 Oct 1930; *educ* Marlborough and Clare Coll Cambridge (MA); *m* 4 June 1955 *Patricia, dau of Dr John Talbot Gray, and has:

1a +Andrew Jonathan; *b* 2 April 1956

2a +Oliver James; *b* 25 Sept 1957

3a +Timothy Richard Puckridge; *b* 25 Jan 1961

1a *Sarah Lucy; *b* 22 Oct 1963

2a *Susannah Rachel; *b* 16 Oct 1968

(1) *Anne Rosemary [Mrs John Gould, 15 Upper Mall, London W6]; *b* 12 Feb 1923; *m* 2 Oct 1948 *John Pearce Gould, s of Hugh Pearce Gould, and has:

1a *Clare; *b* 9 April 1952

2a *Rosemary Enid; *b* 9 Sept 1955

(2) *Elizabeth Margaret [Mrs Charles Baines, De Montalt, Lyncombe Hill, Bath, Somerset]; *b* 17 June 1925; *m* 23 May 1953 *Charles Morris Baines, s of Thomas Nigel Baines, and has issue:

1a *Thomas Charles; *b* 6 Dec 1957

2a *Harry Edward; *b* 8 July 1960

3a *William Nigel; *b* 12 Sept 1963

1a *Georgina Mary; *b* 7 May 1955

(3) *Judith Mary; *b* 28 Feb 1927; *m* 5 June 1954 *Sir (John) Peter Crisp, 4th Bt (*qv*), and has issue

1 Frances Mary

GILLMORE OF THAMESFIELD

Creation: B. (LP, UK) 1 Jan 1996.

THE BARON GILLMORE OF THAMESFIELD, of Putney in the London Borough of Wandsworth (Sir David Howe Gillmore, GCMG (1994, KCMG 1990, CMG 1982) [The Rt Hon The Lord Gillmore of Thamesfield GCMG, House of Lords, London SW1A 0PW]; *b* 16 Aug 1934; *educ* Trent Coll and King's Coll Cambridge; with Reuters 1958–60, assist to dir-gen Polypapier SA Paris 1960–65, teacher with ILEA 1965–69, FCO 1970–94: 1st Sec Moscow 1972–75, Counsellor UK Delegn Vienna 1975–78, Head Def Dept FCO 1979–81, Assist Under-Sec 1981–83, HC Malaysia 1983–86, Dep Under-Sec 1986–90, PUS 1991–94, chm LAPADA 1995–, govr: Ditchley Fndn 1992– and Birkbeck Coll 1994–, novelist: *A Way From Exile* (1967); *m* 1964 *Lucile Morin and has two sons

Lineage: AVM A D GILLMORE, CB, CBE; had:

DAVID HOWE, *cr* a **Baron**

GILMOUR of Lundin and Montrave

Arms: Arg. on a chevron between three trefoils slipped vert as many hunting horns of the first. **Crest:** A dexter hand fessways couped at the wrist, holding a writing pen ppr. **Motto:** *Nil penna sed usus* ('Practicality not penmanship'). **Creation:** Bt. (UK) 1 Sept 1897.

SIR JOHN EDWARD GILMOUR, 3RD BT, DSO (1945), TD, JP (Fife 1957), of Lundin and Montrave, Co Fife [Col Sir John Gilmour Bt DSO TD JP, Montrave, Leven, Fife KY8 5NZ]; *b* 24 Oct 1912; *s* f 1940; *educ* Eton, Trin Hall Cambridge and Dundee Sch Economics; LLD 1952, MP (C) E Fife 1961–79, Lt-Col Fife and Forfar Yeo TA 1947–51 (Brevet-Col 1952), WW II NW Europe 1944–45 (wounded), Hon Col Highland Yeo RAC 1971–75, dep chm U Pty Scotland 1963, chm 1965–67, Capt Roy Co Archers, TAVR 1971–75, Ld Lt Fife 1980–87 (V-Lt 1979–80, DL 1953–79), Ld High Commr Gen Assembly Ch Scotland 1982–83; *m* 24 May 1941 *Ursula Mabyn, yr dau of Frank Oliver Wills, of Cote Lodge, Westbury-on-Trym, Bristol, and has issue:

1 +JOHN, DL (Fife 1988) [John Gilmour Esq DL, Balcormo Mains, Leven, Fife KY8 5QF]; *b* 15 July 1944; *educ* Eton and N of Scotland Coll Ag; Capt Fife and Forfar Yeo/Scottish Horse, memb Roy Co Archers, MFH Fife 1972; *m* 6 May 1967 *Valerie Jardine, yr dau of George Walker Russell and Mrs William Wilson, of Hilton House, Cupar, Fife, and has:

(1) +(John) Nicholas; *b* 1970; *m* 1996 *Aivin Thamrin, of Sulawesi, Indonesia

(2) +Patrick George William; *b* 1980

(1) *Corinna Valerie; *b* 1972

(2) *(Victoria) Juliet; *b* 1975

2 +Andrew Frank, JP (1984) [Andrew Gilmour Esq JP, Pratis House, Leven, Fife]; *b* 14 Sept 1947; *educ* Eton and W Scotland Coll Ag; memb Roy Co Archers and NE Fife DC 1984–; *m* 1971 *Mary Spiers, SSStJ, adopted dau of Sir Henry Campbell de la Poer Beresford-Peirse, 5th Bt (*qv*), and has issue:

(1) +Andrew Robert Campbell; *b* 1972

(2) +David Edward; *b* 1974

Lineage: JOHN GILMOUR, of S Walton, Renfrewshire; *m* Margaret Urie and had: ALLAN GILMOUR, of Lundin and Montave, Fife, South Walton, Quebec and Glasgow; *b* 29 Sept 1805; *m* 10 June 1839 Agnes (*d* 29 Nov 1849), 4th dau of John Strang, of St Andrews, New Brunswick, and *d* 18 Nov 1884, having had issue:

1 JOHN (Sir), **1st Bt**

2 Allen; *b* 19 Jan 1848; *d* unm 4 July 1870

1 Agnes; *b* 13 Feb, *d* 12 Nov 1840

2 Mary; *m* 1 Dec 1871 David Turnbull, WS, and *d* 4 Feb 1899, leaving issue

3 Margaret Agnes; *m* 19 Aug 1873 Andrew MacGeorge, of Glasgow (*d* 23 July 1894)

The er son,

Sir John Gilmour, 1st Bt (UK), so *cr* 1 Sept 1897, JP, DL Fife; Hon Col Fife and Forfar Yeo; *b* 24 July 1845; *m* 18 Sept 1873 Henrietta (*d* 2 Jan 1926), 2nd dau of David Gilmour, of Quebec, and had issue:

1 Allan; *b* 9 Aug 1874; *d* 11 Jan 1879

2 JOHN (Sir), **2nd Bt**

3 Harry, Capt 16th Lancers; *b* 15 Sept 1878; *d* 24 Dec 1925

4 Ronald Farquharson; *b* 1, *d* 23 Dec 1888

5 Douglas; 2nd Lt 7th Seaforth Highrs; *b* 13 Nov 1889; *m* 16 Dec 1910 Doris Hyacinth (*d* 1977), 2nd dau of Charles Paget Hooker, MD, of Cirencester, and *d* 16 Feb 1916 of wounds recd in action, leaving issue:

(1) *Doris Pamela Yvonne [Mrs Philip Marshall, Bowhayes, Chetnole, Dorset DT9 6PE], WAAF WW II; *b* 30 Jan 1914; *m* 9 Nov 1940 Maj Philip Donald Howitt Marshall, Middx Regt (DCO) (*d* 26 July 1996), est s of Harry Howitt Marshall, and has:

1a *Nicholas Charles Gilmour [Nicholas Marshall Esq, Glanhonddu House, Llandefaelog Fach, Brecon, Powys]; *b* 1950; *m* 1st 1974 (*divorce* 1983) Rosemary Anne, dau of Maj W J Kingdom, RA, and has issue:

1b *Emily Sarah; *b* 1978

2b *Harriet; *b* 1980

1a (cont.) Nicholas Marshall *m* 2nd 1988 *Fiona Anne, er dau of Christopher Anthony William Leng (*see* HERRIES, L), and has by her:

1b *Douglas James Gilmour; *b* 1990

3b *Scarlett Josephine; *b* 1992

1a *Sarah Gilmour [Mrs Christopher Legge, The Old House, Kingsclere, Hants RG20 5SP]; *b* 1948; *m* 1976 *Christopher David Legge and has issue:

1b *Louisa Rebecca; *b* 1977

2b *Octavia Christina; *b* 1980

3b *Henrietta Sarah; *b* 1984

2a *Teresa Gilmour [Mrs Michael Way, Upper Park House, Upper Park Rd, Kingston, Surrey KT2 5LD]; *b* 1953; *m* 1987 *Michael Denison Gale Way and has issue:

1b *Henry Charles; *b* 1990

2b *Giles William Philip; *b* 3 July 1994

(2) *Myrtle [Mrs Henry Bromilow, The Grange, Thornford, Dorset]; WAAF WW II; *b* 24 May 1915; *m* 1st 4 Jan 1937 Jack William Hathorn (*kas* flying accident Dec 1940); *m* 2nd 1 Aug 1945 (*divorce* 1949) Capt Cecil Horace Power Bellwood, Glos Regt; *m* 3rd 1949 (*divorce* 1952) Col Patrick Cussan Perfect, KOSB; *m* 4th 1991 *Lt-Col Henry Mesnard (Tim) Bromilow

1 Maud; *b* 2 Jan 1882; *m* 7 Feb 1906 2nd Viscount Younger of Leckie (*qv*) and *d* 28 Dec 1957, leaving issue

2 Henrietta Walton; *b* 8 April 1884; *m* 13 Dec 1904 Maj Robert Walter Purvis, of Gilmerton, Fife, yst s of John Purvis of Kinaldy, JP, and *d* 1 Dec 1962, leaving issue. He *d* 1957

Sir JOHN *d* 20 July 1920; his 2nd s,

Sir John Gilmour, 2nd Bt, GCVO (1935), DSO and bar (both 1918), TD, PC (1922), V-Lt Fife, Hon Capt, Hon LLD Glasgow, Edinburgh and St Andrews, Brig Roy Co Archers 1936, Rector Edinburgh U 1926–29, Freedom Edinburgh and Dundee 1928, Glasgow 1929, MP (C) E Renfrewshire 1910–18 and Pollok 1918–40, Jr Ld Treasury 1921–22, Sec State Scotland 1924, a Pncpl Sec State Scotland 1926–29, Min Ag and Fisheries 1931–32, Home Sec 1932–35, Min Shipping 1930–40, Ld High Commr Gen Assembly Ch Scotland 1938 and 1939, Lt-Col Fife and Forfar Yeo TA, Hon Col 1931, Boer War 1900–02 (despatches twice), WW I Gallipoli, Egypt and Palestine (wounded, despatches); *b* 27 May 1876; *m* 1st 9 April 1902 Mary Louise (*d* 2 Jan 1919), dau of Edward Tiley Lambert, of Telham Court, Sussex, and had:

1 Sir JOHN EDWARD GILMOUR, **3rd and present Bt**

1 *Anne Margaret (Dame), DBE (1957, CBE 1945) [Dame Anne Bryans DBE, 57 Elm Park House, Elm Park Gardens, London SW10 9QD]; dep commr BRC and St John's War Orgn Middle East 1943–45, Chm StJJ and BRCS Serv Hosps Welfare and VAD Ctee 1960–89, V-Chm Jt Ctee OStJ and BRCS 1976–81, BRCS WW II, memb ITA 1961–66, Bd Govrs Westminster Hosp 1961, Chm Govrs Roy Free Hosp 1968–74, memb: Area Health Authority Camden and Islington, Cncl for Professions Supplementary to Medicine 1973–79, Cncl Florence Nightingale Hosp, V-Pres RCN, DStJ, FRSM 1976, Hon FRSM 1994; *b* 29 Oct 1909; *m* 23 June 1932 Lt-Cdr John Reginald Bryans, FRGS, AFRAE, RN (*d* 1990), er s of Rev Reginald du Faure Bryans, MA, and has:

(1) *John Patrick Gilmour [Lt-Cdr John Bryans RN, Hatton House, Leven, Fife KY8 5QD]; *b* 1933; FRGS; *m* 1st 1959 (*divorce* 1970) Rosemary Ann, dau of Gp Capt H G Wheeler, RAF, and has issue:

1a *Anthony James Gilmour; *b* 1960

2a *Edward John Gilmour; *b* 1963

3a *Robert Henry Charles; *b* 1965

(1) (cont.) Lt-Cdr Bryans *m* 2nd 1972 *Patricia Mary, dau of W A MacPherson, and has by her:

1a *Lucy Anne; *b* 1977

Sir John *m* 2nd 17 April 1920 Violet Agnes, dau of Edward Tiley Lambert, JP, of Telham Court, Battle, Sussex, and *d* 30 March 1940, having by her had issue:

2 *Daphne Mary [Mrs Everett Baudoux, Shandaffa House, RR1, Merigomish, Nova Scotia B0K 1G0, Canada]; *b* 23 Jan 1922; *m* 8 March 1943 *G/Capt Everett Large Baudoux, DSO, DFC, CD, RCAF, 2nd s of A H Baudoux, and has had:

(1) *Michael Alfred; *b* 1951; *m* 1984 *Carol Anne Hingley and has:

1a *Katherine Anne; *b* 1986

(1) Patricia Mary; *b* 1944; *m* 1966 *Raymond Wayne Docker and *d* 1987, leaving:

1a *Thomas Everett; *b* 1970

2a *Philip Ian; *b* 1972

(2) *Sharon Jane; *b* 1948; *m* 1974 *J Lewis MacKay and has issue:

1a *James Jeffrey; *b* 1978

1a *Amy Kathleen; *b* 1976

GILMOUR OF CRAIGMILLAR

Arms: Quarterly, 1st and 4th, az. three writing pens palewise arg. (for GILMOUR); 2nd and 3rd, sa. on a saltire arg. a crescent gu. (for LITTLE). **Crest:** A dexter hand holding a scroll of paper within a garland of laurel ppr. **Motto:** *Nil penna sed usus* ('Practicality not penmanship'). **Creation:** Bt. (UK) 29 July 1926, B. (LP, UK) 1992.

THE BARON GILMOUR OF CRAIGMILLAR, of Craigmillar in the District of the City of Edinburgh, and a **Baronet** (Sir Ian Hedworth John Little Gilmour, Bt, PC (1973)) [The Rt Hon The Lord Gilmour PC, The Ferry House, Old Isleworth TW7 6BD]; *b* 8 July 1926; *s* f as Bt 1977; *educ* Eton and Balliol Coll Oxford; Lt Gren Gds, barrister 1952, ed: *Spectator* 1954–59 (owner to 1966), MP (C) Centl Norfolk 1962–74, Chesham and Amersham 1974–92, PPS to Quintin Hogg 1963–64, MOD: Parly Under-Sec 1970–71, Min State 1971–74, Sec State 1974, Chm CRD 1974–1975, Shadow: Home Sec 1975, Def Spokesman 1976, Ld Privy Seal 1979–81, Pres Medical Aid Palestine 1993–96, author: *The Body Politic* (1969), *Inside Right: a study of Conservatism* (1977), *Britain Can Work* (1983), *Riot, Risings and Revolution* (1992), *Dancing with Dogma* (1992) and *Whatever Happened to the Tories* (co-author, 1997); *m* 10 July 1951 *Lady Caroline Margaret Montagu-Douglas-Scott, yr dau of 8th Duke of Buccleuch and (10th Duke of) Queensberry (*qv*), and has issue:

1 +DAVID ROBERT [The Hon David Gilmour, 27 Ann St, Edinburgh EH4 1PL]; *b* 14 Nov 1952 (HRH PRINCESS MARGARET stood sponsor); *educ* Eton and Balliol Coll Oxford; author: *Lebanon: The Fractured Country*; *The Transformation of Spain from Franco to the Constitutional Monarchy*, *The Hungry Generations*, *Cities of Spain* and *The Last Leopard: A Life of Giuseppe di Lampedusa*; *m* 27 Sept 1975 *Sarah Anne, only dau of Michael Hilary George Bradstock (*see* HAWARDEN, V), and has issue:

(1) +Alexander Ian Michael; *b* 19 Feb 1980

(1) *Rachel Anne Caroline; *b* 21 Dec 1977

(2) *Katherine Victoria Mary; *b* 1984

(3) *Laura Elizabeth Rose; *b* 1985

2b +Oliver John; *b* 18 Dec 1953; *educ* Eton, Hertford Coll Oxford and Vienna Music Acad; *m* 1981 (*divorce* 1985) Hon Kathrine (Katya) Grenfell, 2nd dau of 2nd Baron Saint Just (*see* 1970 edn), and has issue:

(1) *Natalia Clare; *b* 1981

3 +Christopher Simon [The Hon Christopher Gilmour, 194 Queen's Gate, London SW7]; *b* 22 Sept 1956; *educ* Eton and UEA; *m* 1992 *Mardi, only dau of J L Haynes, of Louisa Beach, Qld, and has issue:

(1) *Leonora Rose Bonnie; *b* 1993

4 +Andrew James [The Hon Andrew Gilmour, 55 Pembridge Villas, London W11]; *b* 22 March 1964; *educ* Eton and Balliol Coll Oxford; *m* 1991 *Emma, only dau of Christopher Williams, and has issue:

(1) +Archie John Ludo; *b* 1993

(2) +Xan; *b* 20 Nov 1996

1 *Jane Victoria [The Hon Mrs Peter Pleydell-Bouverie, 38 Queensdale Rd, London W11 4SA; New Court Farmhouse, Downton, Wilts]; *b* 22 March 1959; *educ* St Paul's and St Hugh's Coll Oxford; *m* 1986 *Hon Peter John Pleydell-Bouverie, yr s of 8th Earl of Radnor (*qv*), and has issue

Lineage: JOHN GILMOUR; had charter 1580 of lands near Auchtermuchty, Perthshire; had:

JOHN GILMOUR; had charter of lands of Lochmalony, Fife; had:

Sir JOHN GILMOUR; bought property of (territorial) barony of Craigmillar 1660; *bapt* 1605; advocate 1628, ktd 1650/1, MP Co Edinburgh 1661–71, Pres Coll Justice 1661–70; *m* 3rd Margaret, est dau of Sir Alexander Murray, 2nd Bt, of Blackbarony (*qv*), and *d* 1671, having had, with 19 other children, an only surv s:

Sir ALEXANDER GILMOUR, 1st Bt (NS), so *cr* 1 Feb 1678; *bapt* 1657; MP Co Edinburgh 1698; *m* Grizel, est dau of 11th Lord Ross (of Halkhead; *see* GLASGOW, E) by Lady Grizel Cochrane, only dau of 1st Earl of Dundonald (*qv*), and *d* Oct 1731, having had, with nine other children:

1 Sir CHARLES GILMOUR, 2nd Bt, of Craigmillar, MP Edinburgh 1737–50, a Ld of Tde and Plantations; *m* 1733 Jean, 2nd dau of Sir Robert Sinclair, Bt, of Longformacus, by Christian, dau of Adam Cockburn of Ormiston, Ld Justice Clerk Scotland, and *d* 9 Aug 1750, having had, with other issue:

(1) Sir ALEXANDER GILMOUR, 3rd and last Bt, of Craigmillar; Offr 1st Gds, fought in France 1758, MP Co Edinburgh 1751–74; *d* unm 1792, when the btcy expired

1 Helen; *m* William Little, 7th of Liberton, and *d* 1737, leaving:

(1) Grizel; *m* July 1736 her cousin Walter Little (*d* 1758), s of Gabriel Ranken *alias* Little (which name he assumed, together with arms), of Orchardhead, 8th of Liberton (er bro of William Little aforesaid), by Sophia, dau of Sir John Clerk of Penicuik, and had:

1a WILLIAM CHARLES LITTLE later GILMOUR, 10th of Liberton and of Craigmillar; *m* 1763 Jean, dau of Robert Clerk, advocate, and bro of Sir John Clerk, 2nd Bt, of Penicuik (*qv*), and *d* 1797, having had, with five other sons and three daus:

1b Walter Little, of Liberton and Craigmillar; Lt 26th Regt; *b* 2 Feb 1764; *m* 6 July 1805 Anne Macdowell, heiress of Canonmills, and *d* 1 April 1807, leaving issue:

1c Walter James Little, of Liberton and Craigmillar, JP, DL Co Midlothian; *b* (posthumously) 24 April 1807; *d* 3 Sept 1887

1c JANE; *m* 1st 13 July 1825 Maj Robert GORDON (*d* 16 April 1838), 17th of Hallhead and 5th of Esslemont, and had issue; *m* 2nd 23 March 1841 George Hermand Fergusson, 3rd s of Sir James Fergusson 4th Bt (*qv*), and *d* 26 Dec 1844, leaving by her 1st husb an only surv child:

1d ANNE, heiress of Hallhead and Esslemont; *m* 27 May 1856 Henry Perkins WOLRIDGE (*d* 14 July 1906), only s of Col John Wolrige, RM, and took with him by deed poll 8 July 1864 the name GORDON-WOLRIGE and by another deed poll 17 March 1873 the name WOLRIGE-GORDON instead, and *d* 28 April 1874, having had, with other issue:

1e Sir ROBERT GORDON later GORDON-WOLRIDGE later still WOLRIGE-GORDON and finally GILMOUR (took last name on inheriting great-unc Walter James Little Gilmour's estates of Craigmillar and Liberton), **1st Bt** (UK), so *cr* 29 July 1926, CB (1902), CVO (1910, MVO 4th Cl 1905), DSO (1900), JP, DL Midlothian; Hon Brig-Gen Col cmdg Gren Gds, Capt Roy Co Archers, Zulu War 1879, Gordon Relief Expdn 1884–85, Boer War 1900–02 (despatches twice) and WW I (despatches twice, Croix de Guerre Belgium), Gentleman Usher Green Rod (Order Thistle) 1917, Grand Master Mason Scotland 1916–20, Pres Scottish U Assoc 1925–26; *b* 27 Feb 1857; *m* 19 Oct 1889 Lady Susan Lygon, DBE (*d* 28 Jan 1962 aged 91), 2nd dau of 6th Earl Beauchamp (*see* 1970 edn), and had issue:

1f JOHN LITTLE GILMOUR (Sir), **2nd Bt**

1f Mary; *m* 16 July 1912 Sir Hughe Montgomery Knatchbull-Hugessen, KCMG, and had issue (*see* BRABOURNE, B)

2f Margaret, JP Warwicks; *m* 5 Aug 1920 Sir William Francis Stratford Dugdale, 1st Bt (*qv*), and *d* 4 Oct 1965, leaving issue

3f Grizel; CStK, Kaisar-i-hind Gold Medal; *m* 2 June 1919 2nd Baron Rankeillour (*qv*) and *d* 6 May 1975, leaving issue

Sir ROBERT *d* 24 June 1939; his only s,

Sir John Little Gilmour, 2nd Bt; *b* 5 June 1899; *educ* Eton; Lt-Col Gren Gds, Order Crown Belgium with palm, Belgian Croix de Guerre with palm, dir Safeguard Industl Investments 1956–73; *m* 1st 22 July 1922 (*divorce* 1929) Hon Victoria Laura Cadogan, OBE, TD (*d* 1991), yst dau of Viscount Chelsea (*see* CADOGAN E), and had issue:

1 Sir IAN HEDWORTH JOHN LITTLE GILMOUR, **3rd and present Bt**, also *cr* a **Baron**

1 Diana; *b* 21 Oct 1923; *m* 1st 6 March 1943 (*divorce* 1949) Maj Alexander Gregory-Hood, MC (*see* HOOD, V) and had issue; *m* 2nd 9 June 1949 *Sir John Greville Stanley Beith, KCMG [Sir John Beith KCMG, Dean Farm Houses, Sparsholt, Hants], s of William M Beith, of Qld, and *d* 1987, having had by him:

(1) *Ian Mark; *b* 2 Dec 1950; *educ* Eton and Trin Coll Cambridge

(1) Laura; *b* 2 April, *d* 10 Aug 1954

(2) *Emma; *b* 27 April 1956

Sir John *m* 2nd 26 Nov 1930 Lady Mary Cecilia Rhodesia (*d* 1984), formerly w of Capt Robert Orlando Rodolph Kenyon-Slaney (*see* KENYON, B) and est dau of 3rd Duke of Abercorn (*qv*), and *d* 13 Feb 1977, having by her had issue:

2 +Alexander Clement, CVO (1990) [Alexander Gilmour Esq CVO, 1 Christopher Mews, Penzance St, London W11 4QZ]; dir Safeguard Industl Investments 1973, chm Nat Playing Fields Assoc 1976; *b* 23 Aug 1931; *educ* Eton; *m* 1st 2 Dec 1954 (*divorce* 1983) Barbara Marie-Louise Constance, est dau of Hon Denis Gomer Berry (*see* KEMSLEY, V); *m* 2nd 1983 *Susan Janet, er dau of Capt Voltelin James Howard Van der Byl, DSC, RN (ret), and formerly w of (a) Alwyn Richard Dudley Smith and (b) 2nd Baron Chetwode (*qv*), and by his 1st w has issue:

(1) +Rory Calvyn; *b* 26 June 1958

(2) +Christian Alexander; *b* 4 Oct 1970; *m* 1992 *Alexandra Ruth, yst dau of Rev C R Wolsey

(1) *Lucinda Roberte; *b* 26 March 1956; *m* 1st 1981 (*divorce* 1989) Robert Crofts Williams Llewellyn and has issue (*see* LLEWELLYN, Bt); *m* 2nd 1989 *Adrian G Burns and has by him:

1a *Jamie; *b* 1991

GISBOROUGH

Arms: Sa. a chevron between three cherubin or. **Crest:** A demi-seawolf or. **Supporters:** On either side a kneeling angel, wings elevated inverted and addorsed, each ensigned on the head with a cross, all or. **Motto:** Frugality is the left hand of fortune and diligence the right. The arms are allegedly those of the Sieur de Châlons, whom Trahaiarn ap Gwilym (*see* below) captured during one of the numerous medieval English military incursions into France, taking over his lands and the name of his fief. **Creation:** B. (UK) 23 June 1917.

THE 3RD BARON GISBOROUGH, of Cleveland, Co York (Thomas Richard John Long Chaloner JP (Langbaurgh East 1981), DL (N R Yorks 1973)) [The Rt Hon The Lord Gisborough JP DL, Gisborough House, Guisborough, Cleveland TS14 6PT; 37 Bury Walk, London SW3]; *b* 1 July 1927; *s* f 1951; *educ* Eton and RAC; KStJ 1981, CC N R Yorks 1964–74 and Cleveland 1974–77, Lt-Col cmdg Green Howards TAVR 1967–69, Capt Northumberland Hus 1955–61, Lt Welsh Gds 1946–48 and 16th/15th Lancers 1948–52, Hon Col Cleveland Cadet Force 1982–92, Ld Lt Cleveland 1981–96 (DL 1973); *m* 26 April 1960 *Shane, er dau of Sidney Arthur Newton (*see* NEWTON, Bt, of Beckenham), and has had (with two daus who *d* as infs):

1 +(THOMAS) PEREGRINE LONG [The Hon Peregrine Chaloner, PO Box 13 1015, Paradysk Loof, Stellenbosch 7600, S Africa]; *b* 17 Jan 1961; *educ* Eton; *m* 1992 *Karen, only dau of Alan Thomas and Mrs Wendy Ogiela, of Cape Town

2 +Robert Toby Long; *b* 13 July 1966; *educ* Gordonstoun

Lineage: MAELOG CRWM, of Arllechwedd Isaf, Caernarvs; *b c* 1130; had:

MADOG Ap MAELOG CRWM; had:

GWILYM Ap MADOG; had:

TRAHAEARN Ap GWILYM; according to tradition captured the Seigneur de Chalon(er)/s, in France, during the wars in that country, thereby acquiring his estates and coat of arms; the name Chaloner may alternatively derive from workers or sellers of cloth quilts called shalloons (from the French *chalon*, which, however, literally means a dragnet); had:

MADOG CRWM; possibly living 1291; *m* Joyce, dau of Maredudd Ddu, and had:

IORWETH CHALONER; *m* Leucu, dau of Ifor ap Gronwy, and had:

IORWETH FYCHAN; living *c* 1345; *m* Jonet, dau of John ap Richard Fychan, and had:

HYWEL CHALONER, of Denbigh; *m* Alice, dau of Richard ap Dafydd, of Wepre, Northop, Flints, and had:

DAVID CHALONER, of Denbigh; *m* Rose, illegitimate dau of Ithel Anwyl ab y Dai by Gwenllian (dau of Llywelyn ap Cynwrig), and had:

RHYS CHALONER; *m* Ursula, dau of Richard Peake, of Lleweni Green, Henllan, Denbighs, by Ursula, dau of Jenkin Don, of Utkington, Cheshire, and had, with an er s (David, of Denbighs, ancestor of Thomas Chaloner (*d* 1598), Dep Herald Cheshire and N Wales, also allegedly Ulster King of Arms; and Jacob Chaloner, heraldic painter and genealogist):

THOMAS CHALONER, of Beaumaris, Anglesey; *m* Agnes, dau of Ralph Thicknesse, of Betley, Staffs, and had:

ROGER CHALONER, of London; *m* Margaret, dau of Richard Middleton, of London, and *d* probably by 1550, having had:

1 THOMAS (Sir)
2 John; Sec State Ireland
3 Francis

The est son,

Sir THOMAS CHALONER, of Steeple Claydon, Bucks, and G(u)isborough, Yorks; *b c* 1521; Sec to Sir Henry Knyvett 1540, Head Clerk to PC, served wars in Scotland, ktd 1547, leased Guisborough Priory lands 1547 and bought them 1550, MP Knaresborough 1555, Envoy Spanish Netherlands 1559–60 and Spain 1561–64; *m* 1st Joanna (*bur* 11 Jan 1556), dau of William Cotton, possibly of Kent; *m* 2nd Ethelreda, dau of Edward Frodsham, of Elton, Cheshire, and *d* by 1579, having by her had:

Sir THOMAS CHALONER, of Steeple Claydon; *educ* Magdalen Hall Oxford (BA 1582, MA 1605) and Gray's Inn; MP St Mawes 1586–87 and Lostwithiel 1604–11, ktd 1591, Envoy Scotland, Govr HENRY PRINCE OF WALES 1603, Chamberlain 1610; *m* 1st Elizabeth (*d* 22 June 1603), dau of William Fleetwood, Serjeant-at-law and Recorder London, and had, with three daus:

1 Thomas; *d* young
2 Sir WILLIAM CHALONER, 1st and last Bt (E), so *cr* 20 July 1620, of Gisborough; *bapt* 24 March 1587/8; *educ* Magdalen Coll Oxford (BA); *dsp* Skanderoon, in the Ottoman Empire's domains, *c* 1641, when the btcy expired
3 EDWARD
4 Thomas, of Steeple Claydon; MP Richmond 1645–53 and Scarborough 1659, one of the judges who signed CHARLES I's death warrant 1648, excluded from pardon 1660; *m* — Southable and *dsp* Middleburg, Holland, 1661 (*bur* under name of George Saunders)
5 Henry; *d* young
6 Arthur; *d* young
7 James, of Steeple Claydon; *b c* 1602; MP Aldborough, Yorks, 1648–53, another of CHARLES I's judges 1648, Govr IoM 1658–60; *m* 28 Sept 1637 Ursula (*bur* 10 May 1650), dau of Sir William Fairfax, of Steeton, Co York, and *d* (probably as the result of imprisonment in Peel Castle) *c* 1660, leaving a yst dau Veriana (*m* Thomas Cobbe and had issue)

Sir THOMAS *m* 2nd 10 July 1604 Judith (*d* 30 June 1615), widow of John Gregory, of Hull, and dau of William Blount, of London, and by her had, with six other children:

1 Frances; *b* Feb 1612; *m c* 1630 Sir William Fairfax, of Steeton, and *d* 1692, having had issue. He *d* 18 Nov 1615

His 3rd son,

Rev EDWARD CHALONER, DD; *bapt* 25 July 1591; *educ* Magdalen Coll Oxford (BA 1607, MA 1610); Fell All Souls 1611, BD 1617, DD 1619, Pncpl Alban Hall Oxford 1624–25, Chaplain-in-Ordinary to JAMES I and CHARLES I; *m* 26 Nov 1622 Elizabeth (*m* 2nd Thomas Crompton, of Stone), dau of — Horendon, BD, Preb Canterbury, and *d* of the plague 25 July 1625, having by her had an only s:

EDWARD CHALONER; *m* —, dau of Sir Richard Ingleby, of Benborough, Bucks, had, with a yr s (Thomas) and two daus:

WILLIAM CHALONER, of Gisborough; *b* 1655; *m* 15 Aug 1682 Honora (*bur* 8 Oct 1715), dau of Sir David Foulis, 3rd Bt, of Ingleby Manor, Yorks, and was *bur* 18 Feb 1715, having by her had, with 13 other children (including William (Rev) *b* 17 May 1687, *educ* Queens' Coll Cambridge (MA) *m* 5 May 1724 Anne, dau of J Hodgson, of Bishop Auckland, Durham, and *d* 1754, having had issue; also a dau who *m* Richard, 2nd s of Sir Richard Graham, 1st Bt, of Norton Conyers, *qv*):

EDWARD CHALONER, of Gisborough; *b* 1683; *m* 11 June 1713 Anne, dau of Sir William Bowes, MP, of Streatlam Castle, Durham, and was *bur* 8 Oct 1737, leaving:

WILLIAM CHALONER, of Gisborough; *b* 1714; *m* Mary, dau and heir of James Finny, of Finny Lane, Staffs, and Durham, and *d* 1754, having had, with other issue:

1 WILLIAM
2 Edward James, of Lincoln; *bapt* 9 Feb 1749; *m* Theophania Burridge and had, with other issue:
(1) Theophania; *m* 12 Aug 1799 Thomas Lodington Fairfax, of Newton Kyme (*d* 1840), and *d* 1807 having had issue
1 Anne; *bapt* 20 Sept 1742; *m* 12 May 1761 1st Earl of Harewood (*qv*) and *d* 22 Feb 1805, leaving issue
2 Mary; *bapt* 16 Jan 1743; *m* 11 June 1763 Gen John Hale, of Plantation, nr Gisborough, Govr Londonderry, and *d* 27 Oct 1803, leaving issue. He *d* 20 March 1806
3 Jane; *bapt* 24 March 1751/2; *m* Sir Henry Wilson

WILLIAM CHALONER was *bur* 18 Feb 1754; his er son,

WILLIAM CHALONER, of Gisborough; *b* 14 Aug 1745; *m* 8 Aug 1771 Emma (*d* 1835), dau of William Harvey, of Chigwell, MP Essex, DCL Oxon, and sis of Adml Sir Eliab Harvey, GCB, and had, with other issue:

1 ROBERT
2 Henry (Rev); Vicar Alne, Yorks, 1820–50; *b* 22 Oct 1791; *educ* Trin Coll Cambridge (BA); *d* 26 Nov 1850, leaving issue
1 Anna Maria; *b* 22 Aug 1780; *m* John William Bethell and *d* 7 Dec 1861
2 Charlotte; *b* 12 April 1787; *m* 11 Jan 1825 Thomas Barton Bowen, barrister, and had issue
3 Caroline; *b* 2 Oct 1788; *m* 13 April 1819 Abraham Parry Cumberbatch. He *d* 10 Oct 1840
4 Williamina; *b* posthumously 6 Nov 1783; *m* 1 May 1817 Alexander Wynch

WILLIAM CHALONER *d* 8 May 1793; his er surv son,

ROBERT CHALONER, of Gisborough, JP, DL Yorks; MP York 1820; *b* 23 Sept 1776; *m* 24 Jan 1805 Frances Laura (*d* 27 Nov 1844), dau of 1st Baron Dundas (*see* ZETLAND, M), and *d* 7 Oct 1842, having had, with other issue:

1 William; *b* 19 Nov 1805; lost at sea en route to his regt at Halifax, Nova Scotia
2 Robert, of Gisborough; *b* 3 April 1813; *m* 29 Feb 1844 Laura Mary (*d* 16 April 1845), dau of Sir Thomas Butler, 8th Bt, of Cloughgrenan (*qv*), and *dsp* 15 May 1855
3 Thomas, CB, of Longhull, Gisborough, JP, DL Yorks; Adml, Lt-Col N R Vol Art; *b* 6 Feb 1815; *m* 1 Oct 1859 Amelia, dau of John Wylde, of London, and *dsps* 20 Oct 1884
1 MARGARET BRUCE; *b* 23 Dec 1806; *m* 8 June 1829 William Wentworth Fitzwilliam HUME later HUME-DICK (roy licence 17 June 1864; *d* 15 Sept 1892), of Humewood, Co Wicklow, PC, JP, DL, High Sheriff 1844, MP Wicklow 1852–80, and *d* 13 June 1837, having had, with other issue:
(1) CHARLOTTE ANNA; *m* 4 Oct 1853 Richard Penruddocke LONG, of Rood Ashton, Wilts, DL, MP (*d* 16 Feb 1875), and *d* 18 Dec 1899, having had, with other issue (*see* LONG, V), a 2nd s:
1a RICHARD GODOLPHIN WALMESLEY LONG later CHALONER (roy licence 14 Jan 1888), **1st Baron Gisborough**, of Cleveland, Co York (UK), so *cr* 23 June 1917, JP, DL, NR Yorks, JP Wilts; *b* 12 Oct 1856; *educ* Winchester; MP (C) W Wilts 1895–1900 and Liverpool Abercromby 1910–17, 2nd Lt 6th Dragoon Gds (Roy Carabiniers) 1878, Lt 1881, 3rd Hus 1882, Capt 1887 (ret 1893), Adj N Somerset Yeo 1888–93, cmded 1st Bn Imp Yeo 1900, Lt-Col and Hon Col cmdg 1st Wilts Rifle Vols 1900–03, T/Maj 4th Res Cav Regts 1914, Hon Lt-Col and Cmdt 1st Bn N R Vol Regt 1918, Afghan War 1879–80 (despatches, medal) and Boer War 1900 (medal with clasp); *m* 18 Nov 1882 Margaret Brocklesby (*d* 27 Aug 1941), est dau of Rev Weston Brocklesby Davis, Vicar Ramsbury, Wilts, and had:
1b Richard Godolphin Hume, JP N R Yorks; Capt 3rd Bn Wilts Regt, 16th Lancers; *b* 1883; *m* 9 July 1914 Evelyn Maud, JP (Cambridge 1947); granted 29 Sept 1917 rank of w of baron's est s; *m* 2nd 1 May 1918 Lt-Col John Clement Wolstan Francis, MBE, DL, 15th/19th Hus, only s of Wolstan Francis; *d* 1973), 2nd dau of Augustus William Benyon, of Ashe, Windsor, and was *kas* 3 April 1917, leaving:
1c *Diana Margaret Bruce; *m* 1 May 1948 Ian Melville Wright (*d* 1971), s of Rev Jabez H Wright
2b THOMAS WESTON PEEL LONG, **2nd Baron**
1b Margaret Bruce Esme; *d* unm 14 Sept 1958
2b Ursula Violet; Sectn Offr WAAF WW II
3b Cynthia Frances Charlotte; *m* 28 Sept 1921 Maj Herbert Ernest Pease, DSO, DLI, s of Alfred John Pease, of Rusthall, Kent, and *d* 6 Oct 1937, leaving issue
4b (Honora) Elizabeth (Bett) Dundas, JP (Salop 1951); Kaisar-i-Hind Silver Medal 1946; *m* 27 June 1929 Col Frank Drummond Shuttleworth Field, OBE, MC (*d* 27 March 1958), 5th/11th DCO Sikh Regt, s of Frank James Richard Field, and *d* 21 Jan 1997

The 1st BARON *d* 23 Jan 1938; his s,

THOMAS WESTON PEEL LONG CHALONER, **2nd Baron Gisborough**, TD, JP N R Yorks; *b* 6 May 1889; *educ* Trin Coll Cambridge (BA), Maj 4th Bn Green Howards, Hon Capt RAF, RFC WW I, F/Lt RAFVR WW II; *m* 7 Nov 1923 Esther Isabella Madeleine (*d* 1970), 2nd dau of Charles Oswin Hall, of Eddlethorpe Hall, Malton, Yorks, and *d* 11 Feb 1951, leaving issue:

1 THOMAS RICHARD JOHN LONG CHALONER, **3rd and present Baron Gisborough**
1 *(Angela) Mary [The Hon Mrs Mary Faure Walker, Geranium Cottage, Ditchling, Sussex]; *b* 5 April 1925; *m* 27 Nov 1946 (*divorce* 1973) Roderick Edward Faure Walker, Maj Coldstream Gds, yr s of Henry Faure Walker, of Highley Manor, Balcombe, Sussex, and has issue:
(1) *Rupert Roderick [Rupert Faure Walker Esq, Woodhill, Danbury, Essex CM3 4AN]; *b* 9 Sept 1947; *educ* Eton and Bristol U (BSc); *m* 1975 *Sally Anne Vivienne, MB, BCh, dau of Lt-Cdr Francis John Sidebotham, RN, of List House, Long Melford, Suffolk, and has issue:
1a *Nicholas Alexander; *b* 1978
1a *Julia Francis; *b* 1980
2a *Joanna Phoebe; *b* 1984
(2) *James Edward Bruce [James Faure Walker Esq, 88 Greenwood Rd, London E8 1NE]; *b* 6 Nov 1948; *educ* Eton, St Martin's Sch of Art (Dip AD) and RCA (MA, RCA); *m* 1st 1973 (*divorce* 1979) Caryn Lois, dau of Dr Robert Becker, of New York; *m* 2nd 1981 *Vivien Margaret, BA, dau of Donald Frank Knight, of Birmingham, and has:
1a *Edward James; *b* 1989
1a *Josephine Valerie Mary; *b* 1986
2a *Dulcie Mary; *b* 1991
(1) Camilla Mary; *b* 14 Oct 1953; *m* 1973 *Timothy J P Coghlan [Timothy Coghlan Esq, Weedon Lodge Cottage, Everdon, Northants NN11 6BZ], s of A F Coghlan, of Ludwell Grange, Horsted Keynes, Sussex, and *d* 1981, leaving issue:
1a *Christopher Austin; *b* 1980
1a *Alice Mary; *b* 1979

GLADSTONE

Arms: Arg. a savage's head affrontée, distilling drops of blood and wreathed about the temples with holly ppr., within an orle fleury gu., all within eight martlets in orle sa. **Crest:** Issuant from a wreath of holly ppr. a demi-griffin sa., supporting between the claws a sword, the blade enfiled by a wreath of oak also ppr. **Motto:** *Fide et virtute* ('By fidelity and valour'). **Creation:** Bt. (UK) 18 July 1846.

SIR (ERSKINE) WILLIAM GLADSTONE, 7TH BT, of Fasque and Balfour, Co Kincardine, JP (Flintshire 1982) [Sir William Gladstone Bt JP, Hawarden Castle, Clwyd CH5 3PB; Fasque, Laurencekirk, Kincardineshire]; *b* 29 Oct 1925; *s* f 1968; *educ* Eton and Ch Ch Oxford (MA); Sub-Lt RNVR 1943–46, assist master Shrewsbury 1949–50 and Eton 1951–61, head master Lancing 1961–69, CA Flintshire 1970–74, chm: Rep Body Ch in Wales 1977–92, cncl Trin Coll Glenalmond 1982–, Ch Scout UK and overseas branches 1972–82, memb World Scout Ctee (chm 1979–81), Ld Lt Clwyd 1985 (V-Lt 1984, DL 1974–84, DL Flints 1989–74); *m* 10 Sept 1962 *Rosamund Anne, yr dau of Maj Robert Alexander Hambro (*see* HAMBRO, B), and has:

1 +CHARLES ANGUS [Charles Gladstone Esq, Glen Dyne, nr Banchory, Kincardineshire]; *b* 11 April 1964; *educ* Eton and Worcester Coll Oxford; *m* 1988 *Caroline M, only dau of Sir Derek Morison David Thomas, KCMG, and has:

(1) +Jack William; *b* 28 July 1989

(1) *India Kate; *b* 1991

(2) *Tara Rosamund, *b* 1992

(3) *Xanthe; *b* 19–

(4) *Kinvara Rose; *b* 20 July 1997

2 +Rob(ert) Nicolas; *b* 18 Oct 1968; *m* 1993 *Nicola (Nicki), est dau of Forbes Playfair, of Bale, Norfolk, and has issue:

(1) +Tom Archie Playfair; b 17 Feb 1995

(1) *Rosie Lindsay; *b* 1993

(2) *Kate Isla; *b* 6 Nov 1996

1 *Victoria Frances; *b* 6 April 1967; *m* 1991 *Hugo C Merison, s of Paul Merison, of Chiddingly, Sussex, and has issue:

(1)*William Hugh; *b* 20 Oct 1995

(1) *Elinor Penelope; *b* 1994

Lineage: JOHN GLADSTONES, of Toft Combes, nr Biggar, Lanarks; *m* Janet Aitken and had:

THOMAS GLADSTONES, of Leith; *b* 3 June 1732; *m* 21 April 1762 Helen (*d* July 1806), dau of Walter Neilson, of Springfield, and *d* 12 May 1809, having had, with six other sons:

Sir JOHN GLADSTONES later GLADSTONE (roy licence 10 Feb 1835), **1st Bt** (UK), so *cr* 18 July 1846; *b* 11 Dec 1764; *m* 1st 1792 Jane (*dsp* 1798), dau of Joseph Hall, of Liverpool; *m* 2nd 20 April 1800 Anne (d 23 Sept 1835), dau of Andrew Robertson, Provost Dingwall and Sheriff-substitute Ross-shire, and *d* 7 Dec 1851, having by her had, with two daus (*d* unm):

1 **Sir Thomas Gladstone, 2nd Bt**; Ld Lt Kincardineshire, MA, DCL, MP (Lib) Queensborough, Portarlington, Leicester and Ipswich; *b* 25 July 1804; *m* 27 Aug 1835 Louisa (*d* 3 May 1901), 2nd dau of Robert Fellowes, of Shottesham Park, Norfolk, and *d* 20 March 1889, leaving, with six daus (*d* unm):

(1) **Sir John Robert Gladstone, 3rd Bt**, JP; Ld Lt Kincardineshire, Capt 1st Bn Coldstream Gds, Brig Roy Co Archers; *b* 26 April 1852; *d* unm 25 June 1926

2 Robertson, of Court Hey, Lancs, JP; *b* 15 Nov 1805; *m* 28 Jan 1836 Mary Ellen (*d* 23 Sept 1865), dau of Hugh Jones, of Larkhill, Liverpool and *d* 23 Sept 1875, having had, with six sons:

(1) Mary Ellen; *m* 16 Feb 1860 her 2nd cousin Robert Gladstone, s of Thomas Stewart Gladstone, JP, of Capenoch, and *d* 17 Sept 1895, leaving issue

(2) Anna Maria Heywood; *m* 14 Dec 1870 Edward John Thornwill, of Dove Cliff, Burton-on-Trent, and *d* 14 May 1901, leaving issue. He *d* 22 March 1901

3 John Neilson, of Bowden Park, Chippenham; Capt RN, MP Ipswich and Devizes; *b* 18 Jan 1807; *m* 7 Feb 1839 Elizabeth Honoria (*d* 11 Feb 1862), dau of Sir Robert Bateson, 1st Bt (*see* DERAMORE, B), and *d* 7 Feb 1863, having had, with other issue,

(1) **Sir John Evelyn Gladstone, 4th Bt**, JP, DL Wilts; High Sheriff 1897; *b* 23 Nov 1855; *educ* Eton and Ch Ch Oxford (MA 1888); Roy Wilts Yeo Cav; *m* 3 Jan 1888 Gertrude Theresa (*d* 14 March 1937), er dau of Sir Charles Hayes Miller, 7th Bt, of Chichester (*qv*), and *dspm* 12 Feb 1945, leaving:

1a Margaret Betty; *m* 5 Sept 1911 Hon Geoffrey Lawrence Parsons, 2nd s of 4th Earl of Rosse (*qv*), and *dsp* 16 May 1952

2a Olive Mary; *m* 18 March 1919 Maj Robert Lindsay Loyd, OBE, MC, Life Gds, KStJ (*d* 25 June 1977), 2nd s of Archie Kirkman Loyd, KC, JP, DL, of Downs House, Berks, and *d* 7 Aug 1977 leaving:

1b *Zelda Mary [Mrs Malcolm Dunlop, Ravenswood, Gregories Road, Beaconsfield, Bucks HP9 1HN]; *b* 10 Dec 1923; *m* 27 March 1954 *Malcolm Coit Dunlop, OBE, s of A Fergus Dunlop, and has:

1c *Lindsay Fergus; *b* 23 May 1958; *educ* Eton, Bristol U, and St Edmund Hall Oxford (MPhil); *m* 19 Aug 1995 *Miranda Grace, dau of Robert Elgin

1c *Teressa Mary; *b* 9 June 1956

2c *Celina Elizabeth; *b* 22 Sept 1960

3a Muriel Ivy; *m* 6 May 1929 2nd Baron Hollenden (*qv*) and *d* 6 June 1962

(1) Catherine; *m* 2 June 1881 Very Rev W C Lake, DD, Dean Durham, and *d* 25 Aug 1919. He *d* 8 Dec 1897

(2) Anne Elizabeth Honoria; *m* 22 Aug 1861 4th Earl Belmore (*qv*) and *d* 5 Oct 1919, leaving issue

(3) Edith Helen; *m* 27 Oct 1870 William Alexander Dumaresq, MA, and *d* 1 Sept 1941, leaving issue. He *d* 28 May 1880

(4) Constance (twin with Edith); *d* unm

4 William Ewart, PC; DCL, MA; *b* 29 Dec 1809; *educ* Eton and Ch Ch Oxford (Double First 1831); Sec State Colonies 1845, Chllr Exchequer 1852, 1859 and 1880–82, Ld HC Ionian Islands 1858, PM 1868–74, 1880–85, Feb-Aug 1886 and 1892–94, MP (Tory) Newark 1832–45, Oxford U (Lib) 1847–65, S Lancs 1865–68, Greenwich 1868–80 and Midlothian 1880–95; *m* 25 July 1839 Catherine (*d* 14 June 1900), est dau of Sir Stephen Richard Glynne, 8th Bt, and *d* 19 May 1898, having had, with other issue:

(1) William Henry, DL Flintshire; High Sheriff 1888, MP Chester 1865–68, Whitby 1868–80 and E Worcester 1880–85, a Ld Treasury 1869–74; *b* 3 June 1840; *m* 30 Sept 1875 Hon Gertrude Stuart (*d* 25 April 1935), dau of 12th and last Lord Blantyre (*see* 1900 edn), and *dvp* 4 July 1891, leaving:

1a William Glynne Charles, of Hawarden Castle, Flints; Assist Priv Sec to Ld Lt Ireland 1909, Hon Attaché Washington 1911, MP (Lib) Kilmarnock Burghs 1911–15, Ld Lt and Pres TFA Flintshire 1911–15, Lt 3rd Bn Roy Welch Fus 1914; *b* 14 July 1885; *educ* Eton and New Coll Oxford; *ka* 13 April 1915

1a Evelyn Catherine; *b* 2 Jan 1882; *d* unm 11 Dec 1958

2a Constance Gertrude; *b* 2 May 1883; *d* unm 11 March 1963

(2) Stephen Edward (Rev); Rector Hawarden 1872–1904 and Barrowby, Lincs 1904–11, RD Mold 1884–92; *b* 4 April 1844; *educ* Eton and Ch Ch Oxford (MA); *m* 29 Jan 1885 Annie Crosthwaite, JP (*d* 13 May 1931), dau of Charles Bowman Wilson, surgn, of Liverpool, and *d* 23 April 1920, leaving, with other issue:

1a **Sir Albert Charles Gladstone, 5th Bt**; MBE (1919), DL Flintshire; Lt City of Lond, High Sheriff Co London 1929; *b* 28 Oct 1886; *educ* Eton and Ch Ch Oxford (BA 1909, MA 1921); Capt 2nd/5th Gurkha Rifles IA Reserve WW I (despatches), Constable Flint Castle 1935–67; *d* unm 2 March 1967

2a CHARLES ANDREW (Sir), **6th Bt**

3a Stephen Deiniol, MC; dir Ogilvy, Gillanders & Co, Capt IA Res Offrs attd 9th Gurkha Rifles WW I (despatches); *b* 9 Dec 1891; *educ* Eton; *m* 31 July 1923 Mary St Claire (*d* 1976), dau of Lt-Col Charles Davidson, and *d* 21 Nov 1965, leaving issue:

1b +Stephen Charles [Stephen Gladstone Esq, Florance House, Groombridge, Tunbridge Wells, Kent]; Lt Welsh Gds WW II, ptnr Ogilvy, Gillanders & Co; *b* 20 May 1924; *educ* Eton; *m* 26 July 1952 *Susan Valerie, er dau of John Lindsay Guise, and has had issue:

1c Stephen James; *b* 6 Aug 1955; *educ* Eton; *d* 19-

1c *Clare Elizabeth; *b* 20 May 1953

2c *Catherine Mary; *b* 26 April 1959

3c *Juliet Anne [Miss Juliet Gladstone, Pinewood Hill, Wormley, Godalming, Surrey]; *b* 2 Dec 1960

4c *Victoria Jane; *b* 5 May 1963

2b +John Neville [John Gladstone Esq, Old Buckhurst, Mark Beech, Kent]; *b* 24 July 1932; *educ* Eton; *m* 12 Sept 1959 *Jane Gordon, only dau of Maj-Gen Robert Alexander Stephen, CB, CBE, MS, MD, ChM, FRCS, QHS, and has issue:

1c +David Gordon William; *b* 5 Oct 1960

2c +Peter Robert John; *b* 1963

1c *Claire Jane; *b* 8 March 1962

1b *Mary Felicity; *b* 24 March 1926

2b *Anne [Mrs Nigel Robson, Pinewood Hill, Wormley, Godalming, Surrey]; *b* 6 May 1928; *m* 28 Sept 1957 Nigel John Robson (*d* 1993), yr s of Col Hon Harold Burge Robson, TD, JP (*see* 1918 edn ROBSON, B), and has:

1c *Andrew Stephen; *b* 27 Nov 1958; *m* 1982 *Fiona, dau of Jeremy Veasey

2c *William Nigel; *b* 3 Jan 1960

3c *Hugo John; *b* 20 June 1962

1a Catherine; *d* unm 6 July 1947

2a Edith; *m* 12 July 1923 Thomas Henry Gilborn Stamper, CIE, MC and two bars, s of Salkeld Stamper, and had issue:

1b *Henry William Gilborn; Lt RN WW II; *b* 26 May 1926; *educ* Eton; *m* 1 April 1950 *Betty Eleanor, dau of Col Roy Morell, and has issue:

1c *Catherine Ione Eleanor; *b* 27 Dec 1951

2c *Elizabeth Julia; *b* 18 April 1954

3c *Anna Felicity; *b* 23 July 1959

2b Christopher Lincoln; Lt 8th Hus; *b* 15 April 1929; *educ* Eton; *m* 28 Dec 1957 *Jane Scott, dau of Arnold Scott Rose, of Pennsylvania, and *dsp* 18 March 1959

1b *Elizabeth Noel; *b* 23 Dec 1924; *m* 7 Jan 1950 *Walter Edward Ormerod, of The Old Rectory, Padworth, Berks, yr s of Prof Henry Ardene Ormerod, MC, and has:

1c *Henry; *b* 27 Jan 1951; *educ* Winchester

2c *William Patrick; *b* 17 March 1952; *educ* Eton

3c *Thomas Caton; *b* 25 March 1961

1c *Anne; *b* 10 April 1953

2c *Sarah; *b* 31 May 1954

3c *Eleanor; *b* 28 Aug 1955

4c *Philippa; *b* 28 May 1958

5c *Edith Mary; *b* 24 June 1959

(3) HENRY NEVILLE GLADSTONE, 1st and last BARON GLADSTONE OF HAWARDEN, of Hawarden, Co Flint (UK), so *cr* 22 June 1932; Ld Lt Flintshire, CA, Pres TAA, LLD, Fell King's Coll London, Treas Nat Library Wales, Priv Sec to PM, Ld Manor Hawarden, Constable Flint Castle; *b* 2 April 1852; *m* 30 Jan 1890 Hon Maud Ernestine Rendel, CBE, DGStJ (*d* 23 July 1941), 2nd dau of 1st and last Baron Rendel (*see* 1913 edn), and *dsp* 28 April 1935, when the Barony expired

(4) HERBERT JOHN GLADSTONE, 1st and last VISCOUNT GLADSTONE, of the Co of Lanark (UK), so *cr* 15 Feb 1910, GCB (1914), GCMG (1910), GBE (1917), PC (1894), JP Herts; *b* 7 Jan 1854; *educ* Eton and Univ Coll Oxford (MA); DCL Capetown 1911, Govr-Gen Union S Africa and HC 1910–14, Jr Ld Treasury 1881–85, Fin Sec War Office 1886, U-Sec Home Office 1892–94, Chm Commr Works and Public Bldgs 1894–95, Ch Lib Whip 1899–1905, Home Sec 1905–10, history lecturer Keble Coll Oxford 1877–80, MP (Lib) Leeds 1880–85 and W Leeds 1885–1910, Grand Offr Order Crown Belgium, KGStJ; *m* 2 Nov 1901 Dorothy Mary, DGStJ (*d* 20 June 1953), yst dau of Sir Richard Horner Paget, 1st Bt, of Cranmore Hall (*qv*), and *d* 6 March 1930, when the Viscountcy expired

(1) Agnes; *m* 27 Dec 1873 Very Rev Edward C Wickham, DD, Dean Lincoln, and *d* 9 May 1931, leaving issue. He *d* 18 Aug 1910

(2) Mary; *m* 2 Feb 1886 Rev Harry Drew, Rector Hawarden, Canon St Asaph, and *d* 1 Jan 1927, leaving issue. He *d* 31 March 1910

(3) Helen; Warden Women's U Settlement Blackfriars Rd, V-Pres Newnham Coll Cambridge; *d* unm 19 Aug 1925

The 5th Bt's bro,

(Sir) Charles Andrew Gladstone, 6th Bt, JP Flintshire; V-Lt 1948–68, High Sheriff 1951; *b* 28 Oct 1888; *educ* Eton and Ch Ch Oxford (BA 1911); master Eton 1912–46, attd RFC WW I (POW); proved claim to btcy but did not use title; *m* 3 Jan 1925 Isla Margaret (*d* 1987), dau of Sir Walter Erskine Crum, OBE, of Fyfield Manor, Abingdon, Berks, and *d* 28 April 1968, leaving issue:

1 Sir (ERSKINE) WILLIAM GLADSTONE, **7th and present Bt**

2 +Peter [Peter Gladstone Esq, Fasque, Fettercairn, Laurencekirk, Kincardineshire AB30 1DN]; master Shrewsbury, zoologist; *b* 26 Oct 1928; *educ* Eton and Ch Ch Oxford (MA); FIDE (Mech Elec Ch), FDEIS; *m* 1972 *Jean Loveday, dau of Allan Roy, and has:

(1) +Tom Xenophon; *b* 1973; *educ* Gordonstoun and St Edmund Hall Oxford (BA)

(2) +(Allan) Fergus (Fergie); *b* 1978; *educ* Gordonstoun and Loughborough U

(1) *Cleodie Selina; *b* 1975; *educ* Gordonstoun and York U (BA)

3 +James Francis [James Gladstone Esq, West End, Hawarden Castle, Clwyd]; *b* 20 June 1941; *educ* Eton and Ch Ch Oxford (BA); *m* 1st 28 Dec 1963 Janet Barbara (*d* 1970), est dau of Rudi F Schumacher, of Kenya, and has:

(1) *Melissa Janet; *b* 1970

3 (cont.) James Gladstone *m* 2nd 1972 *Hon Josephine Jones, dau of Baron Elwyn Jones (LP; *qv*), and has by her:

(1) +Andrew Elwyn; *b* 1974

4 Andrew Victor; *b* 14 Aug 1945; *educ* Eton; FRICS; *m* 1975 *Nicola Anne [Mrs Andrew Gladstone, Uphill House, Ponsworthy, Newton Abbot, Devon], dau of Lt-Col M L D Skewes-Cox, and *d* 30 Sept 1995, leaving:

(1) *Isla Sophie; *b* 1979

(2) *Clova Felicity; *b* 1982

1 *Penelope Anne; *b* 15 Dec 1930

2 *Sara Helen [Mrs Philip Young, East End Farm, Ringstead, Hunstanton, Norfolk]; *b* 18 Nov 1943; *m* 1970 *Philip John Young and has:

(1) *James Edward; *b* 1971

(2) *John Anthony; *b* 1974

GLADWIN OF CLEE

Creation: B. (LP, UK) 20 Aug 1994.

THE BARON GLADWIN OF CLEE, of Great Grimsby, Co Humberside (Derek Oliver Galdwin, CBE (1979, OBE, 1977), JP (Surrey 1969) [The Rt Hon The Lord Gladwin of Clee, 2 Friars Rse, Woking, Surrey GU22 7JL]; *b* 6 June 1930; *educ* Carr Lane Jr Sch Grimsby, Wintringham GS, Ruskin Coll Oxford (Chm Governing Cncl 1979–), LSE; with BR Grimsby Depot 1946–52, in fishing industry Grimsby 1952–56; GMWU: regnl offr 1956–63, nat industl offr 1963–70, Regnl Sec (S Regn) 1970–90; memb bd BR Aerospace 1977–91, Chm Lab Pty Conf Arrangements Ctee 1974–90, memb employment Appeal Tbnl 1992–; *m* 1956 *Ruth Ann Pinion and has a s

Lineage: ALBERT VICTOR GLADWIN; *m* Ethel Oliver and had:

DEREK OLIVER, *cr* a **Baron**

GLADWYN

Arms: Quarterly, vert and or, in the 1st quarter a falcon close arg. belled of the second; in the 4th, a lure of the third. **Crest:** A lure fesswise arg., thereon a falcon rising ppr., belled or. **Supporters:** Dexter, a brown bear ppr.; sinister, a unicorn arg., charged on the shoulder with a patriarchal cross bottony gu. **Motto:** *Spe et labore* ('By hope and work'). **Creation:** B. (UK) 12 April 1960.

THE 2ND BARON GLADWYN, of Bramfield, Co Suffolk (Miles Alvery Gladwyn Jebb) (The Rt Hon The Lord Gladwyn, E1 Albany, Piccadilly, London W1V 9RH; Bramfield Hall, Halesworth, Suffolk IP19 9HX]; *b* 3 March 1930; *s f* 1996; *educ* Eton and Magdalen Coll Oxford (BA 1953, MA 1959); Sr Management BOAC 1961–83, author: *The Thames Valley Heritage Walk* (1980), *A Guide to the South Downs Way* (1984), *Walkers* (1986), *A Guide to the Thames Path* (1988), *East Anglia* (1990), *A Guide to the Colleges of Oxford* (1992) and *Suffolk* (1995), ed *The Diaries of Cynthia Gladwyn* (1995)

Lineage: ALVERY JEBB; had:

SAMUEL JEBB; *b* 1664; *m* 1690 Elizabeth Gilliver, in right of descent from whom Canon John Jebb (*see* below) claimed to be heir-at-law of Jan de Witt, Grand Pensionary of Holland (1625–72), and had issue:

1 Richard; settled Drogheda; *m* — Stanley and had:

(1) John; *m* Alicia Forster and had:

1a Richard; Judge King's Bench Ireland, heir to his cousin, Sir RICHARD JEBB, 1st and last Bt (*see* below); *m* Louisa, dau of John Finlay, of Corkagh, Co Dublin, MP Co Dublin, and *d* 1834, leaving:

1b John (Rev); DD, Canon Hereford, Rector Peterstow, Herefs; *b* 21 Sept 1805; author: *The Choral Service* and *A New Translation of the Psalms*; *m* Sept 1831 Frances (*d* 15 Jan 1866), dau of Gen Sir Richard Bourke, GCB, of Thornfields, Co Limerick, and *d* 1886

2b Richard; barrister, Judge Ecclesiastical Courts IoM; *d* unm 8 Feb 1884

3b Robert; barrister; *m* Emily Harriet, dau of Heneage Horsley, Dean Brechin, and *d* 1885, leaving issue:

1c Richard Claverhouse (Sir), of Springfield, Newnham, Cambridge; OM, LittD, DCL, FBA, Hon LittD U of Wales, Hon LLD Dublin, Edin, Glasgow and Harvard, MP Cambridge U 1891–1905, Fell and Lecturer Trin Coll 1863, Public Orator 1896, Prof Greek Glasgow U 1875–89, Regius Prof Greek 1889–1905, Lecturer Johns Hopkins 1892, Memb Roy Commn Secdy Educn 1894, Fell London U 1897, Memb London U Commn 1898, Hon Prof Ancient History RA 1898, Memb: Roy Commn Irish U Educn 1901, Consultative Ctee Bd Educn 1900, ktd 1900, Tstee Br Museum 1903; *b* 27 Aug 1841; *educ* St Columba's Dublin, Charterhouse and Trin Coll Cambridge (MA); *m* 18 Aug 1874 Caroline Lane, widow of Gen A J Slemmer, US Army, and dau of Rev John Reynolds, DD, and *dsp* 9 Dec 1905

2c Heneage Horsley (Rev); Rector and RD Streatham; *educ* Lincoln Coll Oxford (MA); *m* 3 July 1879 Geraldine Croker, yst dau of Ven John Abraham Russell, Archdeacon Clogher, and *d* 1913, leaving issue:

1d Robert Russell Horsley, OBE; Colonial Civ Serv; *b* 12 Oct 1882; *educ* Keble Coll Oxford (BA); *d* unm 12 Sept 1954

1d Emily Frances; *d* unm 20 March 1961

2d Geraldine Emma May CBE (1952); Pncpl Bedford Coll 1930–51, Memb Senate London U, Lecturer Economics Armstrong Coll Newcastle 1919–29, Dir Studies and Lecturer Economics Newnham Coll Cambridge 1917–19; *educ* Newnham Coll Cambridge (MA); *d* unm 28 Dec 1959

3d Eglantyne Mary, CBE (1950); Assist English Tutor Somerville Coll Oxford 1913–19, Lecturer English Birmingham U 1919–31, Visiting Lecturer Wellesley 1928–29, Pncp Froebel Inst Roehampton 1931–35; *b* 22 Dec 1889; *educ* Streatham Coll for Girls, LMH Oxford (MA) and St Mary's Coll Lancaster Gate

3c Robert; *m* 27 Feb 1906 Marion Eugenia, 2nd dau of Arthur C Knight, of Tikao, NZ

1c Eglantyne Louisa; *m* April 1871 Arthur Jebb, JP, of the Lythe, Ellesmere, Salop, and had issue

2a John; DD, Bp Limerick; *b* 27 Sept 1775; *d* unm 9 Dec 1832
2 Samuel, of Nottingham and Stratford, Essex; *b* 1693; MD; *m* 1728 Jane, dau of William Lambe, of Stoke Poges, Bucks, and had issue:
(1) Sir RICHARD JEBB, 1st and last Bt, (GB), so *cr* 1778; MD, Physician Extrdy 1777 and Physician-in-Ordinary 1786 to GEORGE III and to PRINCE OF WALES 1780; *b* 1729; *d* unm 4 July 1787, when the title expired
(2) John; HEICS; *d* Black Hole of Calcutta 20 June 1756
(3) Avery; *dsp*
(4) Samuel; *dsp*
(5) Robert; *dsp*
3 Avery; *b* 1695
4 JOSHUA
5 John; DD, Dean Cashel; *m* Anne, dau of David Gansel, of Donnyland Hall, and had issue:
(1) John (Rev); MD, FRS; *educ* Cambridge (2nd Wrangler); *m* Anne, dau of Rev James Torkington, of Great Stukeley, Hunts, by Lady Dorothy Sherard, est dau of 2nd Earl of Harborough, and *dsp* 1787
(2) David; *m* Susan, dau of Francis Duggan, and had issue:
1a John; Capt RHG; *dsp*
2a Richard; Capt 10th Hus; *dsp*
3a David; Capt 3rd Light Dragoons; *m* — Thompson and had:
1b William; Lt RN; *m* Clarissa Marshall and had:
1c William Gansel
1 Hannah; *m* Robert Halifax and had two sons
2 Amelia; *m* James Oates and had issue

The 4th son,

JOSHUA JEBB; Alderman Chesterfield; *b* Jan 1698; *m* Mary, dau of John Woodhouse, of Crich, Derbys, and *d* 1797, having had issue:
1 Samuel; *b* 1720; *m* 1752 Anne, dau of William Harriot, of St Elizabeth, Jamaica, and *d* 1787, leaving:
(1) JOSHUA
2 Avery, of Tapton Grove, Derbys; *b* 1732; *m* Ann, dau of Richard Bower, of Gorse Hall, Derbys, and had:
(1) Richard; Judge India; *dsp*
(1) Marianne; *m* 14 June 1803 Godfrey Meynell, of Meynell Langley, Derbys, s of John Meynell, and *d* 1807, leaving issue. He *d* 14 June 1854

JOSHUA JEBB's gs,

JOSHUA JEBB; *b* Feb 1769; *m* Jan 1792 Dorothy, coheir of Maj-Gen — Gladwin, of Stubbing Court, Derbys, and *d* 1845, leaving issue:
1 JOSHUA
2 Samuel Henry, of Wide Bargate, Boston, Lincs; *b* April 1796; *m* Frances, dau of John Straw, of Skellingthorpe, Lincs, and *d* Feb 1875, having had, with other issue:
(1) Henry Gladwin (Rev), of Firbeck Hall, Yorks, which he inherited from his aunt, Mrs Miles (*see* below), JP W R Yorks; Rector Fontmell, Dorset, and Chetwynd, Salop; FSA; *b* 6 May 1826; *educ* St John's Coll Cambridge (BA 1851, MA 1872); *m* 29 Sept 1853 Emma Louisa (*d* 8 Oct 1901), dau of Robert Ramsden, of Carlton Hall, Notts, and *d* 19 April 1898, having had issue:
1a Eustace Henry Ramsden; *b* 25 Oct 1855; drowned 13 Jan 1871
2a Avery Frederick Richard; *b* 11 April 1860; drowned with his brother 13 Jan 1871
3a Henry Scrope Frescheville, JP W R Yorks; barrister Lincoln's Inn 1895, 3rd Hus; *b* 17 July 1867; *educ* Eton; *m* 1st 11 Aug 1888 Evelyn Lucy (*d* 2 March 1907), widow of Capt Francis Michael Goold-Adams, RA, and dau of Rev Edward Bristow Philips-Wynne, Rector Shoeburyness, and had:
1b Henry Cecil Edward, OBE (1934); WW I (despatches 1914), Order Nile 1st Cl, Dir Stores Ordnance and Supplies Sudanese Govt; *b* 14 July 1889; *m* 19– Marjorie Enid Clegg-Barklie, and *d* 19 April 1951, leaving:
1c *Henry Robert Gladwyn; S/Ldr RAF; *b* 17 Sept 1916
2c *Peter Cecil; Capt RASC; *b* 5 Feb 1925
3c *Timothy Edward; *b* 22 June 1927
2b Avery Richard Melville; *b* 26 June 1892; *d* 2 Oct 1901
3a (cont.) Henry Jebb *m* 2nd 23 April 1908, Winifred (*d* 27 Feb 1967), dau of Lt-Col Thomas Marriott-Dodington, JP, of Horsington House, and *d* 1 Nov 1939, having by her had issue:
3b Samuel Henry Dodington; Capt Royal Signals and RAPC; *b* 12 March 1909; *m* 23 April 1947 *Minette Colleen Helen, dau of Maj-Gen Walter Reginald Paul, CBE, and *d* 28 March 1960, leaving issue:
1c *John Henry Desmond; *b* 30 Jan 1948
2c *Henry Walter Gladwyn; *b* 10 July 1951
1c *Minette Caroline Mary; *b* 26 Sept 1949
1b *Winifred Mary Gladwin; *b* 14 Oct 1912; *m* 25 July 1946 *Capt John Anthony Garnett Thwaites, 3rd KOH, s of John Kenneth Thwaites, and has issue:
1c *Algernon Henry Daniel; *b* 8 March 1949
2c *Charles John Gladwyn; *b* 8 Aug 1950
1c *Sara Angela Mary; *b* 17 July 1952
1a Florence Emma Dorothy; *d* unm 27 June 1925
2a Edith Fanny Maud; *m* 25 April 1889 John Sidney Burton Borough, of Chetwynd Park, Salop, and *d* 8 Aug 1942, having had issue. He *d* 13 Sept 1924
(2) John Joshua; *b* Nov 1830; *m* 18– Georgina Hutton, dau of Rev Robert Evelyn Roy, DD, Rector Skirbeck, Lincs, and had:
1a George Samuel William; *bapt* 5 Oct 1861; *m* 29 Dec 1908 Georgina Martha, MBE (*d* 3 Sept 1942), dau of Charles Thomas Tunnard, JP, of Frampton House, Lincs
(3) Frederick William; Col, Adj-Gen Madras; *b* Nov 1835; *m* 1870 Mary, dau of Rev John de Chamfort Girardot, and *d* 20 Feb 1880
(4) Arthur; Lt-Col E Surrey Regt; *b* 1 July 1837; *d* 1 May 1915
(5) Avery; Lt 85th Regt; *b* April 1842; *m* 1872 Susan Clara, dau of Col A Boddam Whetham, of Kirklington Hall, Notts, and *d* 1917, leaving issue:
1a Avery Gladwin, DL; *m* 1903 Margery, dau of Edward Wilson, and had a s and dau
1a Agatha Frances Whetham Jebb; *d* 1879
(1) Susannah Gladwyn; *d* unm 10 Feb 1899
(2) Frances Dorothy; *m* 1856 Thomas Laurence Kington-Oliphant, JP, DL, MA, FSA, 11th of Gask, Perthshire, and *dsp* 11 Nov 1902. He *d* 8 July 1902
(3) Marianne; *d* 1 Dec 1916
3 John Beridge (Rev); *b* Dec 1808; *m* 1st Charlotte, dau of Richard Dunn, and had:
(1) John Beridge Gladwin; Lt 88th Regt; *b* Dec 1841; *m* 1st 1876 Bertha, dau of Hon James Macdougall, of Toronto, Canada, and had a dau; *m* 2nd Clara — and by her had issue:
1a Ralph Gladwyn
(1) (cont.) John Jebb *m* 2nd Mary, dau of Rev J Jenkinson, Rector Battersea, and *d* 1863, leaving a posthumous dau
4 Charles William; 60th Rifles; *b* Oct 1814; *m* 1840 Eliza, dau of John Yerbury, of Shirehampton, Bristol, and *d* 19 May 1905, leaving issue:
(1) John de Witt; Maj Scottish Rifles; *b* 1847; *m* 5 Dec 1885 Edith Victoria (*d* 1920), yst dau of William Murphy, of Mount Merrion, Co Dublin, and Kilbrew, Co Meath
(1) Francesca Romana Maria; *m* 31 May 1871 Robert Henry Ramsden, of Wigthorpe Hall, Worksop, Notts, est s of Robert Ramsden, of Carlton Hall, Notts, and *d* 3 Aug 1909, leaving issue. He *d* 19 May 1874
(2) Florence Emily; *m* W Cardbury
(3) Alice; *m* B Span
(4) Mary Edith; *m* Capt — Goodwin
(4) Amy Louise; *m* 11 Dec 1879 Andrew John Blackett Ord, of Whitfield Hall, Northumberland, and *d* 7 March 1941, having had issue. He *d* 20 March 1899
1 Frances Harriott; *m* 1829 William Miles (*d* 1844), of Clifton, Glos, and *dsp* Oct 1877, leaving for life Firbeck Hall with estates in Yorks and Notts to her n Henry Gladwyn Jebb (*see* above), with remainder to Joshua Gladwyn Jebb's est s (*see* below)
2 Marianne; *m* Rev Francis Sharpe and had issue

The est son,

Sir JOSHUA JEBB, KCB, Maj-Gen, Chm Dirs Convict Prisons, Inspr-Gen Mil Prisons, Surveyor-Gen Prisons; *b* May 1793; *m* 1st Mary Legh, dau of Wooton Thomas, of Highfield, Derbys; *m* 2nd 5 Sept 1854 Lady Amelia Rose Pelham (*d* 2 Jan 1884), dau of 2nd Earl of Chichester (*qv*), and *d* 26 June 1863, leaving by his 1st w:
1 JOSHUA GLADWYN
1 Mary; *m* Rev Henry Ellison, RD, Rector Haseley, Oxon, and *d* 1870, leaving issue
2 Emily Sarah; *m* 28 Jan 1860 Col Basil Charles Boothby and *d* 28 Nov 1890, leaving issue (*see* BOOTHBY, Bt)
3 Beatrice; *m* Rev Edmond Batty and had issue

The only son,

JOSHUA GLADWYN JEBB, of Barnby Moor House, Notts; Capt 54th Foot; *b* 16 March 1839; *m* 7 June 1867 Hon Alice Caroline (*d* 19 April 1924), dau of Rev Hon Charles Dundas (*see* MELVILLE, V), and *d* 22 June 1901, leaving issue:
1 SIDNEY GLADWYN
2 Joshua Henry Miles, DSO (1900), Col Manchester Regt, Adj 1899, Capt 1899, Boer War 1899–1902 (despatches twice, Queen's medal with 3 clasps, King's Medal with 2 clasps), WW I cmdg 4th Bn Manchester Regt (despatches twice); *b* 12 May 1875; *educ* Charterhouse; *m* 1923 Gwendolin Gladys, dau of W Yarnold, of Godmanchester, and *d* 27 May 1935, leaving issue:
(1) *Philip Nicholas Miles [Lt-Col Philip Jebb, The Tower, Scotney Castle, Lamberhurst, Kent]; Lt-Col RA; *b* 18 June 1924; *educ* Wellington; *m* 7 Aug 1956 *Susan Eve, only dau of Capt Thomas Francis Jeune Hanbury, MC, of Letcombe Bassett, Berks
(1) *Joanna; *b* 9 June 1930; *m* 2 Oct 1954 *George Bailiffe Fairbairn, only s of E E Fairbairn, and has issue
3 Gladwyn Dundas, CB (1930), CMG (1916), CBE (1919), DSO (1902); Boer War 1899–1902 (despatches twice, Queen's medal with three clasps, King's medal with two clasps), Capt 1902, Maj 1913, WW I Brig-Gen i/c Admin 1918, Dep Dir Recruiting and Orgn War Office 1925–27, Brig-Gen cmdg 126th E Lancs Inf Bde 1928–30, ret 1930, Chev Leopold Belgium; *b* 27 March 1877; *m* 2 Jan 1912 Norah May (*d* 3 Feb 1968), only dau of Lt-Gen Samuel Holt Lomax, CB, and *d* 19 Aug 1947, having had issue:
(1) *David Gladwyn, CBE (1965), DSO (1943); Brig (ret 1965), Cameronians WW II (despatches five times), cmded Bns Green Howards 1943, Malay Regt 1955–58 and Edinburgh Area 1962; *b* 18 Dec 1912; *educ* Charterhouse and RMC Sandhurst; *m* 19 May 1943 *Stephanie Dagmar, dau of William Ord Workman
(2) Michael, RAF; *b* 18 June 1918; *ka* 19 Sept 1940
1 Mary Mabel; *d* 4 July 1919
2 Dorothy Beatrice; *d* an inf

The est son,

SIDNEY GLADWYN JEBB, of The Manor House, Haslemere, Surrey, formerly Firbeck Hall, Rotherham, Yorks, JP W R Yorks 1900 T/Capt RGA, Capt Yorks Dragoons Imp Yeo; *b* 26 Feb 1871; *educ* Eton and RMA Woolwich; *m* 1st 18 April 1899 (*divorce* 1933) Rose Eleanor (*d* 18 Sept 1962), 3rd dau of Maj-Gen Hugh Chichester, RA; *m* 2nd 28 July 1943 *Bernice Cruwys, dau of Richard Henry Richards, and *d* 17 May 1950, having by his 1st w had:
1 (HUBERT MILES) GLADWYN JEBB, **1st Baron Gladwyn**, of Bramfield, Co Suffolk (UK), so *cr* 12 April 1960, GCMG (1954, KCMG 1949, CMG 1942), GCVO (1957), CB (1947); *b* 25 April 1900; *educ* Eton and Magdalen Coll Oxford (MA 1922, Beit U Prize Essay 1922, Hon Fell 1955, Hon DCL 1954); Hon Dr Essex and Syracuse, Ensign SR Coldstream Gds 1919, Dip Serv: joined 1924, Teheran 1924–27, FO 1927–31 and 1935–50, Rome 1931–35, FO: Priv Sec to: Parly Under Sec 1929–31 and PUS 1937–40, Head Ec and Reconstruction Dept

1942, Exec Sec Prep Commn UN 1945–46, Actg Sec-Gen UN Feb 1946, Dep to For Sec Cncl For Mins 1946, Assist U-Sec and UN Advsr 1946–49, UK Rep Perm Commn Brussels Treaty with rank Amb 1948, Dep U-Sec 1948–50, UK Rep UN 1950–54, Amb France 1954–60 (ret 1960); Min Ec Warfare: For Policy Advsr as T/Assist U-Sec 1940, seconded 1940–42; Dep Ldr Libs Ho Lds 1967–87, V-Chm Br Cncl Euro Movement, on Parly Delegn WEU and Cncl Europe Assemblies 1965–73, Lib Spokesman For Affrs and Def 1965–87, MEP 1972–76, Pres Campaign for Europe, V-Pres: European Movement, Atlantic Treaty Assocn, Atlantic Inst, UN Assoc, Memb ISS, Grand Cross Legn Honour, author: *Is Tension Necessary?* (1961), *The European Idea* (1965), *Half-way to 1984* (1966), *De Gaulle's Europe, or Why The General Says No* (1969), *Europe after De Gaulle, Memoirs of Lord Gladwyn* (1972); *m* 22 Jan 1929 Cynthia (*d* 1990), yr dau of Sir Saxton William Armstrong Noble, 3rd Bt, of Ardmore and Ardardan Noble (*qv*), and *d* 24 Oct 1996, leaving:

(1) MILES ALVERY GLADWYN JEBB, **2nd and present Baron Gladwyn**

(1) *Vanessa Mary [The Rt Hon The Lady Thomas of Swynnerton, 29 Ladbroke Grove, London W11]; *b* 17 Dec 1931; *educ* St Hugh's Coll Oxford (MA); *m* 5 May 1962 *Baron Thomas of Swynnerton (LP; *qv*) and has issue

(2) *Stella Candida [Baroness Joël de Rosnay, 146 Rue de l'Université, Paris VII, France]; *b* 7 Dec 1933; *m* 12 Dec 1959 *Baron Joël de Rosnay, Dir Cité des Sciences, Paris, scientific author, s of Baron Gaetan de Rosnay, of Paris and Mauritius, and has issue:

1a *Alexis Marc Louis Joël; *b* 26 April 1967; *m* 19– *—

1a *(Vanessa) Tatiana Louise; *b* 28 Sept 1961

2a *Cecilia Fiona Louise; *b* 28 Sept 1963; *m* 19– *— de Vaucleroy

1 Dorothy Mary; *b* 4 Dec 1901; *d* 4 Feb 1919

2 Marjorie Rose; *b* 15 March 1903; with her husb restored the castle-cum-hunting lodge of Il Trebbio, n of Florence, the only Medicean dwelling to be inhabited in the late 20th century as a private residence; *m* 19 Oct 1933 Enrico Scaretti (*d* 6 June 1961), banker, of Rome, and *d c* Sept 1982, leaving issue:

(1) *Lorenzo Giulio Oreste; *b* 21 July 1937; *educ* Nazareno Coll Rome, Oratory Sch Reading and Magdalene Coll Cambridge (BA 1959, MA 1961)

(1) *Virginia Rose Carlotta; *b* 29 April 1938; *m* 2 July 1957 *Don Francesco Borghese, yst s of Don Rodolfo Borghese, Prince of Nettuno

GLANUSK

Arms: Arg. between two bars three annulets in fess gu., all between as many martlets of the last. **Crest:** A griffin sejant arg., semée of annulets gu. **Supporters:** Dexter, a collier resting his exterior hand on the handle of a pick, all ppr; sinister, a master smith holding in his exterior hand a smith's hammer, all ppr. **Motto:** *Libertas* ('Liberty'). **Creations:** Bt. (UK) 5 July 1852, B. (UK) 26 Jan 1899.

THE 5TH BARON GLANUSK OF GLANUSK PARK, Co Brecon, and a **Baronet** (Sir Christopher Russell Bailey, Bt, TD (1977)) [The Rt Hon The Lord Glanusk TD, 51 Chertsey Rd, Chobham, Surrey GU24 8PD]; *b* 18 March 1942; *s* f 1997; *educ* Eton and Clare Coll Cambridge (BA Engrg 1964); TA 1959–83 (2nd Lt 7th Bn Cheshire Regt 1965–67, Lt Roy Berks 1967–69, Capt 94 Berks Yeo Signal Sqdn 1969–76, Capt 80 Cheshire Yeo Signal Sqdn 1976–79, Maj HQ 11 Signal Bde 1979–83; design engr English Electric Leo 1964–66 and Ferranti 1966–78, product mktg manager Bestobell Mobray 1978–83, sales engr STC Telecommunications 1984–86, gen manager Autocar Electricial Equipment 1986–97 and Wolfram Research Europe 1997–, memb Chobham PC 1987–, Tstee Chobham Poor Allotments 1990– and W C Lees Resthouses 1997–, Sec Valley End Inst 1989–; *m* 29 June 1974 *Frances Elizabeth, only dau of ACM Sir Douglas Charles Lowe, GCB, DFC, AFC, and has:

1 +CHARLES HENRY; *b* 12 Aug 1976; *educ* Eton and Balliol Coll Oxford (BA)

1 *Rosemary Elizabeth; *b* 16 May 1979; *educ* Wycombe Abbey

Lineage: JOHN BAILEY, of Wakefield, and Wenham, Suffolk; *b* 1747; (s of Joseph Bailey); *m* 7 July 1774 Susannah Crawshay (*d* 11 May 1812) and *d* 6 Oct 1813, leaving, with a yr s:

Sir Joseph Bailey, 1st Bt (UK), so *cr* 5 July 1852; MP Worcester and Breconshire, High Sheriff Mon 1826; *b* 21 Jan 1783; *m* 1st 10 Oct 1810 Maria (*d* 27 May 1827), dau of Joseph Latham, and had:

1 Joseph, of Easton Court, Herefs; MP Herefs 1841–50; *b* 9 Feb 1812; *m* 22 June 1839 Elizabeth Mary (*m* 2nd 4 July 1872 E O Partridge; *d* 23 Nov 1897), only child of William Congreve Russell, and *d* 31 Aug 1850, having had, with other issue:

(1) JOSEPH RUSSELL, **1st Baron**

(2) Henry James, of Rowden Abbey, Bromyard, JP, DL Herefs; MA Oxon; *b* 12 June 1844; *m* 19 April 1871 Edith Anne (*d* 14 May 1919), dau of Joseph Tarratt, and *d* 21 Aug 1922

(3) John Franklen, JP Merioneths; Capt 13th Foot; *b* 2 Dec 1845; *m* 25 Oct 1871 Ellen Isabella (*dsp* 1890), dau of Charles Prüst, and *d* 1 May 1905

(4) Richard Crawshay; BA Oxon; *b* 15 Jan 1849; *m* 1st 15 Feb 1881 Mabel Jane (*d* 16 Oct 1909), dau of Rev Charles Samuel Palmer (*see* PALMER, Bt, of Carlton); *m* 2nd 7 Nov 1911 Ellen (*d* 1941), dau of Henry Douglas, of Bromley, and *d* 19 July 1916, leaving by his 1st w:

1a Charles Henry (Rev Canon), MC; Rector Broadstairs, CF WW I (despatches), Hon Canon Canterbury 1946; *b* 16 April 1882; *educ* Haileybury and Univ Coll Oxford (BA 1905, MA 1923); *m* 24 Nov 1915 Ethel (*d* 21 Nov 1962), dau of George Milward, and *d* 29 March 1971, leaving issue:

1b *Mabel Anna [Mrs Ronald Ward, Ivall's Farm Cottage, Bentworth, Hants]; *b* 27 April 1920; *m* 31 May 1947 Maj Ronald Patrick Ward, MC, Border Regt (*d* 30 April 1996), s of H A Ward, and has issue:

1c *Charles Patrick; *b* 1949; *m* 1983 *Linda Brown and has issue:

1d *Rebecca Anne; *b* 1983

2d *Henrietta Elizabeth; *b* 1985

3d *Charlotte Deborah; *b* 1986

1c *Susan; *b* 1948; *m* 1970 *John Grosvenor Phillips and has issue:

1d *Charles Edward; *b* 1973

2d *George William; *b* 1976

2c *Deborah Rose; *b* 1957

2a Richard Fitzroy; BA Cantab, Head Master Quarry Bank Sch Liverpool; *b* 27 Nov 1883; *d* unm 1 March 1951

(1) Marian; *m* 19 April 1871 Fitzroy Paley Ashmore and *d* 14 March 1929, having had issue. He *d* 1883

2 Richard; *b* 19 Sept 1816; *d* 14 April 1853

3 John Crawshay; Capt RN; *b* 22 May 1818; *m* 4 Oct 1860 Maria Fowler (*d* 9 July 1916), yst dau of Charles Cooch, and *d* 28 Oct 1896, having had issue:

(1) John Arthur Crawshay; *b* 25 June 1861; *m* 20 Jan 1887 Josephine Mathilde (*d* 4 Aug 1927), dau of J H Grünewald, of Mainz, Germany, and *d* 13 April 1937, leaving issue:

1a John Henry; Gunner HAC WW I (gassed 1917); *b* 27 May 1889; *educ* Jesus Coll Cambridge; *m* 30 Aug 1913 Ruby (*d* 1972), only dau of Edward Giles, and *d* 3 Jan 1966, leaving issue:

1b *Margaret Elizabeth; *b* 2 July 1915; *m* 10 April 1939 Derrick Thomas Ashworth Douglas (*d* 1975), only s of Henry George Douglas, and has issue:

1c *Derrick John; *b* 28 Feb 1947; *m* 1st 1969 Penelope Elizabeth, dau of Rudi Krause, of Elmira, Ont; *m* 2nd 1978 *Marilyn — and by his 1st w has issue:

1d *Lee Christian; *b* 1971

2d *Todd Matthew; *b* 1973

2c *David Henry [David Douglas Esq, 6 Kersey Bay, Winnipeg, Manitoba, Canada]; *b* 28 Feb 1947; Sgt RCMP; *m* 1970 *Charlotte, dau of Stefan Johannson, of Gimli, Manitoba, and has issue:

1d *Stefan Nathan; *b* 1971

2d *Brendan Wyatt; *b* 1981

1d *Jill Elizabeth; *b* 1974

1c *Judy Ann; *b* 29 Oct 1941; *educ* Huron Coll U W Ontario (BA) and U of Toronto (BLSc); *m* 1971 *Herbert Flax and has:

1d *Timothy Aaron; *b* 1974

1d *Joanna Susan; *b* 1972

2b Josephine Lucy Anne; *b* 2 May 1924; *m* 1st 19 Dec 1943 Ronald Jenkins (*d* 27 Aug 1968), s of Rev Percy Jenkins, CMS, of Canton, China; *m* 2nd 1978 *John Gray and by her 1st husb had:

1c Susan Ann; *b* 25 Dec 1944; *m* 3 June 1967 *Graham Francis Holmes, s of Gilbert C Holmes, and had:

1d *Anthony Stephen; *b* 1973

2d *Jonathan Alistair; *b* 1976

3b *Barbara [Mrs Ernest Matthewson, Sa Fontansa, Bagur (Gerona), Spain]; *b* 15 Sept 1927; *m* 1 Sept 1945 *Capt Ernest Ronald Matthewson, s of Ernest James Frederick Matthewson, and has issue:

1c*Michael Derek [Michael Matthewson Esq, 18 Haynes Mead, Berkhamsted, Herts]; *b* 24 May 1946; *educ* St Edmund's Sch Canterbury, London U (BSc) and Salford U; *m* 1970 *Barbara Mary Saunders and has:

1d *Toby; *b* 7 Nov 1974

1d *Kirsty; *b* 24 Nov 1976

1a Josephine Nancy (Dolly); *m* 14 Sept 1909 Harold Henry Kelsey (*d* June 1933), only s of H G Kelsey, and *d* 11 Feb 1955, leaving issue

4 William Latham; *b* 14 Oct 1820; *m* 24 Aug 1848 Frances Byng (*d* 1892), yst dau of John McLean, of Campbelton, Argyllshire, and *d* 2 Jan 1875, leaving:

(1) William Joseph McLean; *b* 10 Aug 1850; *d* 16 Sept 1908

(2) John Lockhart; *b* 7 Oct 1853; *d* 5 Dec 1927

(3) Llewellyn Crawshay; *b* 25 April 1856; *d* 26 Feb 1933

(1) Mary Anne Margaret Frances Byng; *d* 25 Jan 1924

5 Henry, DL; *b* 31 Oct 1822; *m* 1st 28 May 1848 Mary Louisa (*d* 26 Oct 1865), yst dau of Sir Richard Puleston, 2nd Bt (*see* 1850 edn), of Emral Pk, Flints, and had issue:

(1) Henry, of Coates; Lt 29th Foot; *b* 11 June 1850; *d* 1896

(2) Crawshay Wellington BAILEY later PULESTON (roy licence 14 April 1904), of Emral Park, JP; *b* 18 June 1853; *m* 7 Nov 1891 Edith Elfrida, dau of Rev Thomas Bacon, and *d* 23 July 1935

(1) Elizabeth Maria; *m* 14 July 1881 George Francis Gregory (*dsp* 9 Sept 1902)
5 (cont.) Henry Bailey *m* 2nd 21 Sept 1881 Christina (*d* 1896), dau of Neale Thomson, of Camphill, Renfrewshire, and *d* 10 Aug 1889, leaving by her:
(3) Robert Neale Menteth; Clerk H of C, Lt E R Yorks Yeo WW I; *b* 21 Aug 1882; *d* 1 Dec 1917
(2) Helen Christina; *m* 1st 20 Oct 1904 George Crompton Lees-Milne and had issue (*see* GLENARTHUR, B); *m* 2nd 1 Oct 1953 *Henry T Horsfield, AFC, and *d* 15 May 1962
(3) Margaret Doreen; *m* 30 July 1912 William John Cunninghame, est s of Col William Cunninghame, 11th Hus, and *d* 5 March 1952. He *d* 19 March 1919
1 Maria Susan; *m* 25 Jan 1838 Ven Thomas Johnson Ormerod, JP, Archdeacon Suffolk, and *d* 26 Feb 1871, leaving issue. He *d* 2 Dec 1874
2 Margaret; *m* 22 June 1839 James Greenfield and *d* 15 July 1858, leaving issue. He *d* 16 May 1867
3 Jane; *m* 17 Dec 1846 Sir James Stuart-Menteth, 2nd Bt (*qv*), and *d* 14 Oct 1905
Sir Joseph *m* 2nd 19 Aug 1830 Mary Ann (*d* 26 June 1874), dau of John Thomas Hendry Hopper, of Witton Castle, Co Durham, and by her had a surv child:
4 Mary Anne Betha; *m* 31 May 1855 Alexander Young Spearman, est s of Sir Alexander Young Spearman, 1st Bt (*qv*), and *d* 14 Jan 1860, leaving issue
Sir JOSEPH *d* 20 Nov 1858; his gs,
Sir Joseph Russell Bailey, 2nd Bt, and **1st Baron Glanusk of Glanusk Park**, Co Brecon (UK), so *cr* 26 Jan 1899, VD, JP (Radnorshire and Herefs); *b* 7 April 1840; *educ* Harrow and Ch Ch Oxford; Breconshire: High Sheriff 1864, Ld Lt 1875–1905, MP Herefs 1865–85 and Hereford 1886–92, Hon Col 1st Vol Bn S Wales Borderers; *m* 9 April 1861 Mary Ann (*d* 18 April 1935), dau of Henry Lucas, MD, and *d* 6 Jan 1906, having had:
1 JOSEPH HENRY RUSSELL, **2nd Baron Glanusk of Glanusk Park**, CB (1911), CBE (1919), DSO (1900); *b* 26 Oct 1864; *educ* Eton and RMC Sandhurst; Ld Lt Breconshire 1905–28, Maj Gren Gds, Boer War 1900, Lt-Col Breconshire Bn S Wales Bdrs WW I; *m* 6 Aug 1890 Edith Elma, CBE (1920) (*d* 19 April 1938), dau of Maj Warden Sergison, DL, of Cuckfield Park, Sussex, by Emilia, yst dau of Sir William Gordon-Cumming, Bt (*qv*), and *d* 11 Jan 1928, leaving:
(1) WILFRID RUSSELL BAILEY, **3rd Baron Glanusk of Glanusk Park**, DSO (1916) and bar (1919); *b* 27 June 1891; Ld Ltd Breconshire, Pres Brecon TAA, Maj Gren Gds, Hon Col Brecknock Light AA Regt WW I (wounded twice, despatches, Croix de Guerre), Lt Col Welsh Gds and Col GHQ Home Forces WW II, OStJ; *m* 1st 27 Feb 1919 (*divorce* 1939) Victoria Mary Enid Ann (Vera), only dau of Lt-Col Frank Dugdale, CVO; *m* 2nd 17 March 1942 *Margaret Eldrydd, JP (1958) [The Rt Hon The Dowager Viscountess De L'Isle JP, Glanusk Park, Crickhowell, Powys NP8 1LP], CC Breconshire 1955–61, High Sheriff Powys 1977 (*m* 2nd 24 March 1966 1st Viscount de L'Isle, *qv*), dau of Maj-Gen Thomas Herbert Shoubridge, CB, CMG, DSO, and *d* Jan 1948, leaving:
1a *(Elizabeth) Shân Josephine, LVO (1988) [The Hon Mrs Legge-Bourke, LVO, Penmyarth, Glanusk Park, Crickhowell, Powys NP8 1LP]; *b* 10 Sept 1943; Ldy-in-Waiting to HRH THE PRINCESS ROYAL 1978–, High Sheriff Powys 1992; *m* 2 June 1964 *Capt William Nigel Henry Legge-Bourke, RHG and has issue (*see* DARTMOUTH, E)
(2) Gerald Sergison; Lt Gren Gds SR; *b* 22 Nov 1893; *ka* 10 Aug 1915
(3) Bernard Michael; Midshipman RN; *b* 17 Jan 1899; *ka* in naval action off Jutland 31 May 1916
(1) Dulsie Editha, OStJ; *b* 23 Nov 1896; *m* 12 Oct 1922, Alaistair Robertson Cooper, Capt RSG (*d* 26 Oct 1951), s of Sir George Alexander Cooper, 1st Bt, and *d* 16 April 1957, leaving issue
2 William, JP, DL Breconshire; Maj Welsh Horse Yeo, 11th Hus Res Offrs, India Frontier Expdn 1897 and WW I (despatches); *b* 28 Aug 1867; *d* unm 24 Dec 1942
3 Arthur; Capt E African Mtd Rifles, Boer War 1900–01, Br E Africa WW I; *b* 3 Dec 1868; *m* 1 July 1924 Ethel Sophia (*d* 25 Oct 1959), yst dau of James Ledger Hill, JP, of Bulford Manor, Wilts, and *d* 19 Jan 1929, leaving issue:
(1) Carola Mary; *b* 22 Sept 1925; *m* 1 June 1949 Capt Hugh Denman Way, MC (*d* 1971) RHA, est s of John Way, and *d* 26 Feb 1997, leaving:
1a *Nigel Arthur Denman [Nigel Way Esq, Fittleton House, Netheravon, Wilts]; *b* 11 March 1958
2a *Anthony Hugh Verelst; *b* 28 Oct 1961; *m* 1988 (*divorce* 1996) Andrea Elizabeth Dawson-Shephard
4 Herbert Crawshay, JP Middx; BA Oxon 1895, barrister Inner Temple 1897, Commr Bd Control 1924, Lt TA WW I; *b* 23 June 1871; *m* 23 April 1908 Kathleen Mary (*d* 2 May 1948), yr dau of Sir Shirley Harris Salt, 3rd Bt, of Saltaire (*qv*), and *d* 13 April 1936, leaving:
(1) DAVID RUSSELL BAILEY, **4th Baron Glanusk of Glanusk Park**; *b* 19 Nov 1917; *educ* Eton; Lt-Cdr RN WW II and after (invalided 1951), md Wandel and Goltermann 1966–82, chm: Hatfield Instruments and W & G Instruments 1982–87; *m* 25 Jan 1941 Lorna Dorothy (*d* 25 June 1997), only dau of Capt Ernest Courtenay Harold Norman Andrews, MBE, RA, and *d* 28 June 1997, leaving:
1a CHRISTOPHER RUSSELL BAILEY, **5th and present Baron Glanusk of Glanusk Park**
1a *Susan Mary [The Hon Mrs James, 104 Pottergate, Norwich, Norfolk]; *b* 22 Dec 1944; *m* 20 June 1970 *Peter Mansel Lloyd James, MB, BS, FRCS, s of John Richard Edwin James, and has:
1b *David Lloyd; *b* 14 Aug 1971
2b *Richard Lloyd; *b* 14 June 1976
3b *Caspar Lloyd; *b* 5 April 1980
1b *Victoria Mary; *b* 16 March 1974
(1) Deborah Mary; *b* 21 June 1910; *m* 26 Feb 1938 Cdr Anthony Vyvyan Thomas, OBE, JP, DL, RN (ret) (*d* 8 Aug 1981), only s of Vyvyan Hood Thomas, OBE, and *d* 18 Oct 1981, leaving:
1a *Deborah Willow Vyvyan; *b* 15 March 1940; *m* 1st 23 July 1960 Capt Peter Kenneth Cracroft, 4th/7th Roy Dragoon Gds, only s of Brig Hugh John Bernard Cracroft, DSO, RTR; *m* 2nd 1990 *David Hugh Meyer and by her 1st husb had:
1b Robert John; *b* and *d* Aug 1965
1b *Fenella Jane; *b* 20 Oct 1962; has:
1c *Bertram Thomas Cracroft MEYER; *b* 1993
1c *Polly Eleanor; *b* 1991
2b *Henrietta Louise; *b* 16 Dec 1966; *m* 1993 *Mark Charles Speirs and has:
1c *Charles Richard Cracroft; *b* 1995
3b *Miranda Susan; *b* 16 Dec 1966; *m* 1993 *Peter Granger and has:
1c *Joseph Richard Cracroft; *b* 1996
2a *Antonia Mary Vyvyan; *b* 5 Feb 1944; *m* 12 April 1969 *Robert Henry Stallybrass Hiscocks, er s of Henry Frederick Hiscocks, MB, BS, MRCS, LRCP, and has:
1b *Nicholas Robin Thomas; *b* 1975
1b *Sophie Jane Susannah; *b* 1972
(2) *Shirley Joan [The Hon Mrs Drayson, 27 Headbourne Worthy House, Winchester, Hants SO23 7JG]; *b* 28 April 1912; granted with her sis rank of baron's dau 1948; *m* 31 Jan 1946 George Dupin Drayson (*d* 1969), s of Charles Dupin Drayson, and has issue:
1a *Charles Dupin; *b* 12 Nov 1947; *educ* Marlborough; *m* 1974 *Rosemary Ann, dau of Capt D P Evans, RN, and has issue:
1b *Timothy William Dupin; *b* 1983
1b *Louise Claire; *b* 1978
2b *Caroline Gail; *b* 1980
(3) Rachel Kathleen; *b* 5 June 1914; *m* 30 April 1940 Brig Dimitry Dimitrievitch Zvegintzov, CBE, Border Regt, s of Col Dimitry Ivanovitch Zvegintzov, CMG, DSO, and *d* 13 April 1992, leaving:
1a *Ivan Dimitry; Capt Coldstream Gds; *b* 9 Nov 1943; *educ* Bloxham and Corpus Christi Coll Oxford; *m* 1 April 1967 *E L Caroline, dau of Lt-Col W Gordon Watt, and has:
1b *Piers Ivan Robin; *b* 20 Feb 1968
2b *Tania Arabella; *b* 1970; *m* 1992 *Thomas Addyman and has:
1c *Oscar Titus; *b* 1992
2c *Oliver Dimitri; *b* 1994
2a *Paul David; Lt 5th Royal Inniskilling Dragoon Gds; *b* 4 Oct 1945; *educ* Bloxham; *m* 28 Sept 1968 *Rose Maree, only dau of Maj James Thomas Paulton Mellor, MC, TD, DL, and has:
1b *Alexander Dimitri James; *b* 1972
2b *Nicholas Ivan; *b* 1976
1a *Elizavieta Mary; *b* 23 Aug 1942; *m* 16 Feb 1963 *Michael Anthony Robert Oakley, only s of Frederick George Oakley, DFC, and has issue:
1b *Mathew James; *b* 8 Dec 1967
1b *Frances Rachel; *b* 1971
(4) *Elspeth Lorraine [The Hon Lady Musson, Barn Cottage, Hurstbourne Tarrant, Hants SP11 0BD]; *b* 19 Dec 1915; *m* 28 Dec 1939 *Gen Sir Geoffrey Randolph Dixon Musson, GCB, CBE, DSO, late King's Shropshire LI, s of Robert Dixon Musson, and has had issue:
1a *Peter Geoffrey Dixon; *b* 27 March 1946; *educ* Wellington
1a Penelope Anne; *b* 1 April 1941; *m* 13 Jan 1962 *Capt William Richard Dudgeon, late Black Watch, er s of W/Cdr P W A Dudgeon, DFC, and *d* 1981, leaving issue:
1b *Angus Geoffrey Peter [Angus Dudgeon Esq, Lavender Cottage, Lower Pond St, Duddenhoe End, Essex CB11 4UP]; *b* 20 Aug 1963; *m* 1988 *Juliet Ann, dau of George Anthony Turnbull, and has issue:
1c *Charles William George; *b* 1992
1c *Kitty Penelope Ann; *b* 1991
1b *Deborah Elspeth; *b* 24 Nov 1968
5 John Lancelot; Capt S Wales Borderers WW I; *b* 2 Dec 1878; *m* 6 Aug 1903 Vivien Dora (*d* 25 Feb 1938), 2nd dau of Ferdinand Gaussen Carey, of Guernsey, and *d* 26 Oct 1918, leaving issue:
(1) Joseph Ferdinand Carey; *b* 16 April 1907; *m* 1st 12 Oct 1935 (*divorce* 1948) Alice Cecilia Anne, dau of Oswald Magniac, DL, and had issue:
1a +Lancelot Oswald; *b* 7 July 1936; *m* 1959 *Armelle Françoise, dau of Jean François Le Roux, of Candé, Maine-et-Loire, France, and has issue:
1b +Antoine Lancelot Gwenaël; *b* 1965
2a +Vernon Joseph Russell [Vernon Bailey Esq, 43 Prospect St, Montreal, Quebec, Canada H3Z 1W5]; *b* 9 June 1937; *m* 26 Oct 1968 *Melanie Frances, dau of Cecil Moore, and has issue:
1b +Julian Joseph Russell; *b* 1977
2b +Sebastian Philip Magniac; *b* 1979
1b *Rachel Marjorie; *b* 1969
2b *Priscilla Anne; *b* 1971
1a *Cynthia Mary; *b* 13 Feb 1940; *m* 1963 *Patrick Joseph Moran and has:
1b *Malachi Joseph; *b* 1965
2b *Roisin; *b* 1968
3b *Garett; *b* 1969
4b *Cormac
5b *Dairine
6b *Hugh
7b *Killian
1b *Fiona Mary; *b* 1964
(1) (cont.) Joseph Bailey *m* 2nd 10 July 1948 *Evelyn Marie, dau of Robert Phillips Brooks Blauveldt, UE, LLB, of Nova Scotia, and *d* 1984, leaving:
3a +Herbert van Courtland; *b* 18 April 1952; *m* 1989 *Kirsteen Susan, dau of Alexander Keith Boyle (*see* KENNAWAY, Bt), and has issue:
1b +Luke Alexander; *b* 1991
1b *Charlotte Evelyn; *b* 1990
2a *Josephine Blauveldt; *b* 18 May 1949; *m* 1977 *Teddy Dyer and has:
1b *Christopher Teddy; *b* 1979
2b *Patrick Nicholas Blauveldt; *b* 1982
3a *Deborah Evelyn Blauveldt; *b* 7 Oct 1950; *m* 1980 *Michael Collison and has issue:

1b *Andrew; *b* 1981
2b *Matthew; *b* 1983
3b *Daniel; *b* 1987
1b *Jessica; *b* 1992
(1) Jacqueline; *b* 18 Nov 1905; *d* 1975
(2) *Marjorie Vivienne [Mrs Oliver Lancaster, Daniel Zorrilla 5276, Colon Montevideo, Uruguay]; *b* 16 May 1910; *m* 23 Oct 1930 *Oliver Fowell Lancaster, 5th s of Rev Thomas Lancaster (*see* BUXTON, Bt)
1 Elizabeth Mabel, JP; *b* 16 March 1862; *d* unm 13 Oct 1952
2 Edith; *b* 18 Feb 1866; *m* 20 April 1892 Samuel Hood Cowper-Coles and *d* 22 Feb 1933. He *d* 20 Dec 1932
3 Cecile Mary; *b* 25 March, *d* 2 Nov 1870
4 Maragret Elinor; *b* 28 Oct 1873; *d* unm 22 May 1960
5 Gwladys Mary; *b* 29 March 1875; *d* unm 20 Jan 1960

GLASGOW

Arms: Quarterly, 1st and 4th, or an eagle with two heads displayed gules, armed and beaked azure (coat of augmentation for earldom); 2nd and 3rd, per bend embattled argent and gules (for BOYLE); over all an escutcheon or, charged with three stag's horns gules (for BOYLE of Kelburn). **Crest:** An eagle with two heads displayed per pale embattled gules and argent. **Supporters:** Dexter, a savage, wreathed about the loins and temples, holding in the dexter hand a branch of laurel, all proper; sinister, a lion per pale embattled argent and gules. **Motto:** *Dominus providebit* ('The Lord will provide').
Creations: L. (S) 31 Jan 1699, E., V. and L. (S) 12 April 1703, B. (UK) 23 July 1897.

THE 10TH EARL OF GLASGOW, Viscount of Kelburn, Lord Boyle of Kelburn, Stewartoun, Cumbrae, Finnick, Largs and Dalry, Lord Boyle of Stewartoun, Cumbraes, Fenwick, Largs and Dalry and **Baron Fairlie of Fairlie**, Co Ayr (Patrick Robin Archibald Boyle, DL (Ayrshire and Arran 1995)) [The Rt Hon The Earl of Glasgow DL, Kelburn, Fairlie, Ayrshire KA29 OBE]; *b* 30 July 1939; *s f* 8 June 1984; *educ* Eton and Sorbonne; Sub-Lt RNR 1960; TV documentary producer and dir, fndr Kelburn Country Centre 1977; *m* 30 Nov 1974 *Isabel Mary, adopted dau of George Douglas James, and has:
1 +DAVID MICHAEL DOUGLAS (does not use courtesy title); *b* 15 Oct 1978
1 *Alice Dorothy; *b* 10 June 1981

Lineage: Although documentary evidence is lacking it is probable that the ancestors of this family have held their lands at Kelburn since the 12th century.

ROBERT BOYLE, of Calburn (Kelburn), Ayrshire; living 1446; gf of:

WILLIAM BOYLE, of Kelburn; *d* in or after *c* 1477, leaving:

JOHN BOYLE, of Kelburn; granted 1536 a charter of South Ballochmartin, Island of Cumbray, and *d* 1555, leaving an est s:

PATRICK BOYLE, of Polruskane; *dvp c* 1547, leaving:

JOHN BOYLE, of Kelburn; *m* Agnes Fraser and *d* 1559, leaving:

JOHN BOYLE, of Kelburn; *m* Marion (*d* 1596), dau of Hugh Crawfurd of Kilbirnie, and *d* 1 Aug 1611; his est s:

JOHN BOYLE, of Kelburn; Rector Glasgow U 1630, Commissary Glasgow; *m* 9 March 1611 Agnes, dau and heir of Sir John Maxwell of Pollok, and *d* 1650, leaving an only child:

GRIZEL, of Kelburn; *m* 5 Aug 1635 her kinsman David BOYLE, est son of James Boyle of Halkishirst, s of David Boyle of Figgidock, s of John Boyle of Ballykewin, yr bro of Patrick Boyle of Polruskane (*see* above), and *d* 1672, leaving:

JOHN BOYLE, of Kelburn; MP Bute 1681; *m* 1st 22 March 1665 Marion, dau of Sir Walter Steuart of Allanton; *m* 2nd 28 April 1676 Jean, widow of Gavin Ralston, Yr. of that Ilk, and *d* 7 Oct 1685, having had by his 1st w:

DAVID BOYLE, **1st Earl of Glasgow**, so *cr* 12 April 1703, as also VISCOUNT KELBURN and LORD BOYLE OF STEWARTOUN, CUMBRAES, FENWICK, LARGS AND DALRY, and earlier 31 Jan 1699 LORD BOYLE OF KELBURN, STEWARTOUN, FINNICK, LARGS AND DALRY (all S), all with remainder to his heirs male whatsoever, PC (S, 1697); *b* 1666; *educ* Glasgow U; MP Bute 1689–99, rep S peer 1707–10, a Commr Union of E and S Parls 1707; *m* 1st 19 April 1687 Margaret (*d* 1695), sis of 1st Viscount Garnock (*see* LINDSAY, E), and had, with other issue:
1 JOHN, **2nd Earl**

The **1st Earl** *m* 2nd 16 June 1697 Jane (*d* 3 Sept 1724), widow of William Fairlie, Yr. of Bruntsfield, and *d* 31 Oct 1733, having by her had, with a s and three other daus:
1 Jane, heir of Rowallan; *m* 29 March 1720 Sir James Campbell, KB and *d* 13 Dec 1729 (*see* LOUDOUN, E)

His est surv son,

JOHN BOYLE, **2nd Earl of Glasgow**; *b* 1688; *m* (contract 11 Feb 1707) Helen (*d* 7 July 1770), dau of William Morison, of Prestongrange, Co Haddington, and *d* 22 May 1740, having had, with other issue:
1 JOHN BOYLE, **3rd Earl of Glasgow**; *b* 4 Nov 1714; Cornet Scots Greys Battle of Fontenoy (wounded), High Commr Gen Assembly Ch of Scotland 1754–1772; *m* 11 July 1755 Elizabeth (*d* 17 Oct 1791) eventual heir to her bro, 13th and last Lord Ross of Halkhead, and *d* 7 March 1775, having by her had, with two other daus, (*d* unm):
(1) GEORGE BOYLE later ROSS-LINDSAY-CRAWFURD-BOYLE, **4th Earl of Glasgow**, GCH (1830); *b* 26 March 1765; *educ* Eton; rep S peer 1790–1815; *cr* 11 Aug 1815 BARON ROSS OF HAWKHEAD, Co Renfrew (UK), FRS; *m* 1st 8 March 1788 Augusta (*d* 23 July 1822), dau of 14th Earl of Erroll (*qv*), and had, with other issue:
1a John, *Lord Boyle*; *b* 12 Aug 1789; naval offr; *d* unm 6 March 1818
2a JAMES BOYLE later CARR-BOYLE (roy licence 2 Aug 1823 on inheriting the Car estates through his mother), **5th Earl of Glasgow**; *b* 10 April 1792; Cdr RN, Ld Lt and Sheriff Principal Renfrewshire; *m* 4 Aug 1821 Georgina Ann (*d* 14 March 1895), dau of Edward Hay Mackenzie of New Hall and Cromarty (*see* CROMARTIE, E), and *d* 11 March 1869
1a Augusta; *m* 19 May 1821 Lt-Gen Lord Frederick FitzClarence (*see* MUNSTER, E) and *dsps* 28 July 1876
(1) (cont.) The **4th Earl** *m* 2nd 13 Nov 1824 Julia (*d* 19 Feb 1868), dau of Sir John Sinclair, Bt, of Ulbster (*see* THURSO, V), and *d* 3 July 1843, leaving by her:
3a GEORGE FREDERICK BOYLE, **6th Earl of Glasgow**, DL Renfrewshire and Fife; *b* 9 Oct 1825; Ld Clerk Register Scotland; *m* 29 April 1856 Montagu (*d* 22 April 1931), dau of 3rd Baron Abercromby (*see* 1924 edn), and *d* 23 April 1890, when the Barony of Ross of Hawkhead expired, leaving:
1b Gertrude Julia Georgina, OBE (1920); *b* 15 Nov 1861; *m* 2 Dec 1880 1st Baron Cochrane of Cults (*qv*) and *d* 12 Dec 1950, leaving issue
2b Muriel Louisa Diana; *b* 18 Nov 1872; *d* unm 3 April 1915
2a Diana; *m* 4 July 1849 2nd Baron Hampton (*qv*) and *dsp* 1 Jan 1877
1 Elizabeth; *m* 16 Oct 1786 Sir George Douglas, 2nd Bt (*d* 4 June 1821), and *d* 15 Feb 1801, leaving issue
2 Patrick (Rev), of Irvine, Ayrshire; *b* 7 Jan 1717; *m* 1st 14 Aug 1749 Agnes (*d* 27 May 1758), dau of William Mure of Caldwell, by whom he had no issue; *m* 2nd (contract 31 March 1763) Elizabeth (*d* 21 March 1832), dau of Alexander Dunlop, and *d* 26 Feb 1798, having by her had, with other issue, who *d* unm:
(1) David; *b* 26 July 1772; Ld Justice-Gen and Pres Court Session; *m* 1st 24 Dec 1804 Elizabeth (*d* 14 April 1822), est dau of Alexander Montgomerie (*see* EGLINTON and WINTON, E), and had, with other issue:
1a Patrick, of Shewalton, Ayrshire, DL; *b* 29 March 1806; *educ* Oxford (MA); *m* 17 Aug 1830 Mary Frances (*d* 15 Sept 1880), dau of Sir Robert Elphinstone, Bt, and *d* 4 Sept 1874, leaving surv issue:
1b DAVID, **7th Earl**
2b Robert Elphinstone; *b* 3 June 1837; Col IA; granted with siblings rank of earl's dau/yr s 1 Aug 1892; *d* 9 Aug 1924
3b Alexander James Grant; *b* 26 Feb 1842; 30th Foot; *m* 1st 20 July 1876 Maria Louise Jane (*dsp*), dau of William Hodgkinson; *m* 2nd 14 Nov 1892 Clare (*d* 23 June 1937), dau of John Banning and widow of William Sydney Jones, and *d* 29 Sept 1909, leaving issue:
1c Helen Graeme; *b* 14 Feb 1895; *d* 14 Jan 1899
4b Graeme; *b* 8 Feb 1848; *d* 28 Jan 1852
1b Elizabeth Magdalene Graeme; *d* unm 26 Aug 1925
2b Mary Helen; *d* unm 3 Jan 1919
3b Helen Jane; *d* unm 18 May 1928
2a Alexander; *b* 9 March 1810; V-Adml; *m* 2 July 1844 Agnes (*d* 16 April 1898), yst dau of James Walker, and *d* 8 June 1884, leaving issue:
1b Patrick David; *b* 24 Oct 1848; Col Gren Gds; *m* 3 Aug 1872 Kathleen Digby (*d* 17 June 1947), dau of John Henry Blagrave, of Calcot Park, Berks, and *d* 2 March 1932, leaving issue:
1c Godfrey Henry Patrick; *b* 4 Feb 1882; Maj Seaforth Highrs, Order Nile 4th Cl; *d* 16 Oct 1919
2c Cecil Alexander; CIE (1937), DSO (1921); *b* 28 March 1888; Col 5th (King Edward's Own) Probyn's Horse, IA, WW I, raised and cmded Arab and Turkish Levies Mesopotamia 1920–22, raised and cmded N Ayrshire HG 1940–41; *m* 27 June 1923 Gladys Mary (Dulcie) (*d* 1976), only dau of Lt-Col Robert Arthur Edward Benn, CIE, of Alassio, Italy, and *d* 1 July 1941, leaving issue:
1d *Mary Grizel [Mrs James Sackville Hamilton, Acklam Grange, Malton, Yorks YO17 9RG]; *b* 2 Nov 1924; *m* 10 Dec 1947 *Lt-Col James Berkeley Sackville Hamilton (*see* BOYNE, V) and has issue
2d *Patricia [Mrs Jonathan Alford, Le Moulin de Quatre Carres, 47150 Monflanquin, France]; *b* 11 Jan 1929; SRN; *m* 27 Aug 1955 (*divorce* 1980) Maj Jonathan Robert Alford, RE (*d* 1986), only son of John Bellenden Alford, by Betty, yst dau of Capt Francis Stewart Evelyn Boothby, OBE, DL (*see* BOOTHBY, Bt), and has:
1e *Michael Robert Patrick; *b* 15 Sept 1958
1e *Caroline Jane; *b* 22 Dec 1956
2e *Melissa Anne; *b* 24 Aug 1960
3e *Victoria Susan; *b* 26 March 1963

2b James, MVO (1904); *b* 27 Feb 1850; Consul Funchal, Madeira, 1907–19, earlier Galveston, Piraeus and Copenhagen, Capt Princess Victoria's Roy Irish Fus; *m* 30 April 1891 Blanche Eleanor Murray (*d* 5 Sept 1921), est dau of Rev Jermyn Pratt, of Downham, Norfolk, and *dsp* 23 Jan 1931

3b Alexander; *b* 24 Nov 1857; *m* 5 July 1883 Fanny, OBE (1918)(*d* 13 May 1930), dau of Michael Studholme (*see* STUDHOLME, Bt), and *d* 5 April 1923, leaving issue:

1c Alexander David; *b* 3 Nov 1887; Capt RN (ret), WW I (despatches, Croix de Guerre); *d* unm 31 Jan 1965

2c Alister Patrick; *b* 7 Jan 1905; *m* 1st 1932 Rosa Howard (*d* 26 Nov 1933), dau of Howard Tripp, of South Canterbury, NZ, and has issue:

1d *Jennifer Frances; *b* 21 July 1933

2c (cont.) Alister Boyle *m* 2nd 1936 *Lois Morton [Mrs Alister Boyle, 48 Cox St, Christchurch 8001, New Zealand], only dau of C M Ollivier, and *d* 1973, having by her had further issue:

2d *Mary Montgomerie [Mrs Laurence Holder, 9 Andover St, Christchurch 1, New Zealand]; *b* 8 April 1937; *m* 1964 Laurence George Holder (*d* 1974) and has issue

3d *Alexandra Montgomerie [Mrs Douglas Stephen, Canal House, 120 Lisson Grove, London NW8 8LB]; *b* 23 March 1943; *m* 1988 Douglas Cruden Stephen (*d* 1991)

1c Janet; *b* 22 Jan 1886; *m* 1907 Algar Temple Williams and had issue

2c Phyllis Montgomerie; *b* 9 Nov 1889; *d* unm 1 July 1961

1b Janet; *m* 16 Oct 1879 Maj William Henry Fife-Cookson (*d* 11 April 1912), 9th Lancers, of Co Durham and Yorks, and *d* 9 March 1916, having had issue

2b Elizabeth Helen; *d* unm 9 Jan 1926

3b Agnes Margaret; *m* 9 May 1876 Frank Pratt Barlow (*d* 1917), of Haslemere, Surrey, s of Francis Pratt Barlow, and *d* 18 April 1928, leaving issue

4b Henrietta Camilla; *m* 21 Jan 1880 Col John Sutton Rothwell (*d* 13 March 1893), RA, and *d* 28 May 1902, having had issue

5b Frances Montgomerie; *m* 16 July 1879 Charles Woodbine Parish (*d* 7 Sept 1922), FRGS, son of Sir Woodbine Parish, KCH, JP, FRS, FRGS, FGS, of St Leonard's-on-Sea, Sussex, and *d* 29 Jan 1889, leaving issue

3a John; *b* 9 Sept 1819; *educ* Balliol Coll Oxford (MA); barrister; *m* 6 Sept 1853 Jane (*d* 2 Feb 1911), 2nd dau of Theodore Walrond, of Calder Park, Lanarks, and *d* 22 March 1907, leaving issue:

1b Henry David; *b* 26 Dec 1856; *educ* Wellington; *m* 19 Sept 1882 Emma Chambres (*d* 6 Sept 1937), dau of Rev Hugh George Robinson, Hon Canon York, and *d* 15 Feb 1917, leaving issue:

1c David Hugh Montgomerie, CMG (1948); *b* 1 Sept 1883; *educ* Wellington and New Coll Oxford; 2nd Lt 4th Bn Argyll & Sutherland Highrs; Chinese Customs Service 1904, Political Offr, Ashanti 1912, attd FO 1919; *m* 27 April 1916 Laura Grant (*d* 1971), 3rd dau of James Tennant (*see* GLENCONNER, B), and *d* 1970, leaving:

1d +Alasdair David Forbes; *b* 28 Nov 1919; *educ* Wellington and RMC Sandhurst (psc); Maj Argyll & Sutherland Highrs WW II (wounded, despatches); Admin Dir Manchester Business Sch 1966–, Sec Manchester Business Sch Assoc 1967–, Sec and Dir Mancas Ltd 1968–, MBIM 1968; *m* 1st 28 April 1945 (*divorce* 1958) Elizabeth Winifred, only dau of Cdr Herbert Roderick Kelway-Bamber RN, and has:

1e +Roderick David Alasdair [Roderick Boyle Esq, Firs Cottage, College Grove, Malvern, Worcs WR14 3HP]; *b* 9 March 1951; *educ* Eton; *m* 1977 *Althea Victoria, yr dau of Maj Derek Leslie Lloyd, MC (*see* CHETWYND V), and has:

1f +Jamie Edward Rory; *b* 1978

1f *Harriet Elizabeth Victoria; *b* 1980

1e *Henrietta Elizabeth Flora; *b* 8 June 1948; *m* 14 Sept 1968 *Hon James Malcolm Rollo, yr s of 13th Lord Rollo (*qv*) of Duncrub

1d (cont.) Maj Alasdair Boyle *m* 2nd 26 March 1958 *Doris Louise, only dau of Victor Eaton Usherwood, of Tunbridge Wells, and formerly w of John Robert Clayton, and adopted:

*Camilla Josephine Brenda Louise; *b* Nigeria 30 Oct 1964

2d +Ranald Hugh Montgomerie, DSC (1944) [Ranald Boyle Esq DSC, The Wooden House, Fairlie, Ayrshire KA29 0DH; 906 Beatty House, Dolphin Sq, London SW1]; *b* 19 Aug 1921; *educ* Wellington and Exeter Coll Oxford; late Lt RNVR WW II (wounded), Dist Offr Sudan Political Service 1946–53, Dist Offr HMOCS Kenya 1956–64, 1st Sec Dip Serv 1964–70, Hambros Bank 1970–81, Arab Banking Corp 1981–83, Private Consultant 1983–96, memb Roy Co Archers; *m* 27 April 1957 *Norma, yst dau of Alexander Gray, of Calcutta and London, and has issue:

1e +Fergus David [Fergus Boyle Esq, Downcraig Fenny, Millport, Isle of Cumbrae]; *b* 20 April 1958; *educ* Wellington, St Andrews, Edinburgh Business Sch and Barony Coll Dumfries; late VSO Ghana, SCF Sudan

2e +Alexander Ranald [Alexander Boyle Esq, 25 Killyon Rd, London SW8]; *b* 13 Sept 1959; *educ* Wellington and Pembroke Coll Oxford

3e +Patrick Mungo [Patrick Boyle Esq, 56 Hutton Village, Shenfield, Essex]; *b* 6 Oct 1961; *educ* Wellington; *m* 24 May 1997 *Jane, yr dau of Percy Thomas Brierley, of Upminster Essex

4e +John Quentin; *b* 30 Dec 1964; *educ* Glenalmond, Bristol U and Strathclyde Business Sch; *m* 11 Oct 1997 *Diana, er dau of James Young, of Edinburgh

5e +Hamish William; *b* 20 Feb 1970; *educ* Glenalmond, Bournemouth U and Kellogg Coll Oxford

1e *Laura Grizel [Mrs Deane Pennick, 62 Denbigh St, Pimlico, London SW1]; *b* 12 Sept 1963; *educ* Downe House St Leonards; *m* 3 April 1993 *Deane C B Pennick, er s of Lt-Col Peter Pennick, of Villars, Switzerland, and has issue

2e *Beatrice Elizabeth [Mrs Richard Bath, Muiryhill, Thornhill, Dumfriesshire]; *b* 5 June 1966; *educ* St Leonards and UEA; *m* 3 Sept 1994 *Richard Bath, yr s of Alistair Bath, of Caversham, Berks and has issue

1d Iona Janet Flora; *b* 17 Aug 1933; *d* unm 19 March 1962

2b Montgomerie, TD (1919); *b* 20 March 1859; Maj 2nd SW Mtd Bde RASC, late Notts Yeo; *m* 7 April 1891 Constance Helen (*d* 21 Aug 1929), yst dau of Henry Abel Smith, DL, of Wilford House, Notts, and *d* 29 March 1919, leaving issue:

1c Marion Montgomerie; *b* 21 Aug 1892; *m* 2 Feb 1922 Rev Claude Beckwith, MA, Vicar E Meon, Hants 1924–31, yr son of Thomas Percival Beckwith, and *d* 20 July 1942, leaving issue

1b Jane Flora; *b* 8 Feb 1855; *d* unm 1943

4a William, CB; *b* 25 Jan 1821; Lt-Col 89th Regt; *m* 14 June 1853 Louisa Catherine (*d* 2 Feb 1873), est dau of Rev Henry Parsons, incumbent of Sandhurst, and *d* 14 Feb 1874, leaving:

1b William Henry David; *b* 11 Feb 1861, *educ* King's Coll Cambridge (MA); Treasury clerk; *m* 22 Sept 1888 Eleanor (*d* 15 Nov 1893), 3rd dau of Hon Henry Dugdale Curzon (*see* HOWE, E), and *d* 7 July 1879, leaving:

1c George Frederic; *b* 11 Oct 1893; Capt Roy Scots Fus; *m* 21 June 1920 (*divorce* 1929) Mary Jeffrey (*d* 13 May 1954), 2nd dau of Sir Peter Mackie, 1st and last Bt, and *d* in a plane crash 29 July 1929, leaving:

1d David Logan; *b* 15 Feb 1925; 2nd Lt Coldstream Gds WW II; *ka* Normandy Aug 1944

1d *Eleanor Mary [Mrs Derek Cardiff, Flat 1, 13 Embankment Gardens, London SW3 4LW]; *b* 25 June 1921; *m* 1st 23 June 1945 (*divorce* 1962) Capt Hon Arthur Cameron Corbett, Ayrshire Yeo, est s of 2nd Baron Rowallan (*qv*), and has issue; *m* 2nd 1963 *Col (Richard) Derek Cardiff, late Scots Gds, 2nd son of Col Richard Henry Wingfield Cardiff, JP, DLI, of Ludlow, Salop, and by him has:

1e *David Richard George; *b* 1 Aug 1964

1d Anna Louisa Alexandrina; *b* 4 Nov 1854; *d* 26 Feb 1938

1a Elizabeth; *m* 2 Dec 1828 James Hope and *d* 20 July 1880, leaving issue (*see* LINLITHGOW, M)

2a Helen; *m* 1 June 1829 Sir Charles Dalrymple Fergusson, 5th Bt (*qv*), and *d* 26 June 1869

(1) (cont.) David Boyle *m* 2nd 17 July 1827 Catherine Campbell (*d* 25 Dec 1880), est dau of David Smythe of Methven, a Ld of Session, and *d* 4 Feb 1853, having by her had, with other issue:

5a George David (Very Rev); *b* 17 May 1828; *educ* Oxford (MA); Dean Salisbury; *m* 7 Jan 1861 Mary Christiana (*d* 7 Jan 1907), est dau of William Robins, of Hagley, and *dsp* 21 March 1901

6a Robert; *b* 2 Dec 1830; Capt RA; *m* 9 July 1856 Frances Sydney Fremoult (*d* 14 Nov 1909), dau of Francis Fremoult Sankey, MD, and *d* 29 Aug 1869, leaving issue:

1b Charles Fremoult; *b* 5 July 1857; *m* 1st Sept 1883 (*divorce*) Martha Trotter; *m* 2nd Anna Graham and had by his 1st w:

1c Robert Fremoult; *b* 17 Feb 1887

1c Frances Minna Fremoult; *b* 4 July 1884; *d* an infant

2b Sydney Herbert; *b* 8 April 1863; *educ* Fettes and Keble Coll Oxford; Lt RP Regt Boer War 1900–02, E Africa campaign WW I; Transvaal Educn Dept 1902–05, Assist Master Jeppe High School Johannesburg 1920–25; *m* 13 May 1918 Amy, dau of Henry Black-Hawkins and widow of Arthur Carr, PWD Madras

3b Edward Louis Dalrymple, CMG (1917); *b* 19 Dec 1864; Cdr RN (emergency list), Egyptian War 1882, Sudan 1884, Naval Bde El Teb (Eygptian medal with two clasps and Khedive's star), WW I (despatches, Order Crown Italy); *m* 1st 14 Sept 1889 Theodosia Isabella (*d* 10 May 1910), 3rd dau of Edward David Stuart Ogilvie, of NSW, Australia, and had:

1c (Edward) Patrick Ogilvie, MVO (1927); *b* 22 July 1893; *educ* Wellington; Lt-Col Roy Scots Fus, Mil Kt Windsor 1956, Mil Sec to Govr-Gen NZ 1926–30, Staff HRH THE DUKE OF YORK's NZ Tour 1927; *m* 24 Jan 1934 *Audrey (*m* 2nd 18 Dec 1970 Maj Clarence Henny (*d* 1 June 1973)), only dau of Lt-Col Audley Lionel York Willis, of Newbury, Berks, and *d* 7 Dec 1966, leaving:

1d *Jennifer Mary [Miss Jennifer Boyle, 6 Stackhouse, Cundy St, London SW1W 9JS]; *b* 30 Dec 1934

1c Theodosia Frances; *b* 24 June 1890; *m* 1st 21 April 1914 Capt Douglas William Swire (*d* 8 April 1920), Shropshire Yeo, er s of William Swire, CBE, JP, DL, of Longden Manor, Shrewsbury, and had issue; *m* 2nd 22 Oct 1923 V-Adml Norman Atherton Wodehouse, CB, and *d* 6 July 1966, leaving further issue (*see* KIMBERLEY, E)

2c Irene Florinda Maude, OBE (1946); *b* 6 Jan 1895; FO and Peace Delegation, Paris, formerly Hon Attaché Br Emb Washington, (resigned 1950); *d* unm 29 April 1966

3b (cont) Capt Edward Boyle *m* 2nd 14 Sept 1912 Sybil Mary (*d* 22 April 1947), dau of Berkeley Paget, DL (*see* ANGLESEY, M), and *d* 15 Dec 1923

4b Cecil David; *b* 8 March 1869; Border Regt, Indian Tport Corps Tirah Campaign, Boer War, Commn Orange Colony Police, captured at De Wetsdorp 23 Nov 1900; *k* by Boers while prisoner Jan 1901

1b Catherine Minna; *b* 16 Sept 1859; *d* 14 June 1921

2b Constance Antonina; *b* 21 Dec 1865; Boer War (Hosp), WW I (Samaritan Order of Serbia, 4th cl); *d* unm 4 March 1943

(1) Helen; *m* 3 June 1791 Thomas Mure of Warriston (*d* 26 June 1806) and *d* 7 Aug 1805, leaving issue

(2) Elizabeth; *m* 10 Nov 1800 R-Adml John Rouett Smollett of Bonhill (*d* 1842) and *d* 6 Aug 1856, having had issue

The 6th EARL's cousin,

DAVID BOYLE, **7th Earl of Glasgow**, GCMG (1892), JP, DL Ayrshire; *b* 31 May 1833; Capt RN, Govr and C-in-C NZ 1892–97, Hon LLD Dublin and Glasgow, *cr* 23 July 1897 BARON FAIRLIE OF FAIRLIE, Co Ayr (UK); *m* 23 July 1873 Dorothea Elizabeth Thomasina (*d* 23 Jan 1923), est dau of Sir Edward Hunter Blair, 4th Bt (*qv*), and *d* 13 Dec 1915, leaving issue:

1 PATRICK JAMES, **8th Earl**
2 Edward George; *b* 16 June 1875; Lt Rifle Bde; *d* unm 23 Oct 1898
3 James; *b* 11 March 1880; Capt Roy Scots Fus, Boer War, WW I; *m* 15 Sept 1908 Katherine Isabel Salvin (*m* 2nd 17 July 1920 1st Viscount Trenchard (*qv*) and *d* 5 March 1960), dau of Edward Salvin Bowlby, of Herts and Knoydart, Invernesshire, and was *ka* 18 Oct 1914, leaving issue:
(1) Patrick John Salvin; *b* 21 April 1910; *educ* Eton and RMC Sandhurst; Lt-Col Roy Scots Fus, ADC to Govr-Gen Canada 1935–37; Adj 1st/6th Durham LI 1938 WW II; *m* 11 June 1938 Mary Elizabeth, OBE, JP (1950), DL (*m* 2nd 7 Feb 1948 Lt-Col Charles Murray Floyd, OBE (*d* 1971), 3rd s of Sir Henry Floyd, 4th Bt (*qv*) and *d* 26 Oct 1996), only child of Robert Fleetwood Fuller (*see* FULLER, Bt), and was *ka* nr Anzio 27 May 1944, leaving:
1a +Andrew Robert James [Andrew Boyle Esq, Fairhaven, North End, Bath]; *b* 20 March 1939; *educ* Eton and RMA Sandhurst; RSG 1959–64; *m* 1971 *Julia, dau of N W Gardener of Boxted Farm, Hemel Hempstead, Herts, and has:
1b +James William; *b* 1973
1b *Olivia Mary; *b* 1975
2a +Simon Hugh Patrick DL Gwent [Simon Boyle Esq DL, Penpergwm Lodge, Abergavenny, Gwent]; *b* 22 March 1941; *educ* Eton; High Sheriff Gwent 1993; *m* 1970 *Catriona, dau of W G Gordon, DFC, of Lude, Blair Atholl, Perths, and has:
1b *Alice Catriona Jane; *b* 1972
2b *Mary Helen Fenella; *b* 1974
3b *Susannah Elizabeth; *b* 1977
4b *Christian Laura Frances; *b* 1982
3a +David Thomas Alan JP [David Boyle Esq JP, Fairstead Hall, Terling, Essex CM3 2AT]; *b* 15 Jan 1943; *educ* Eton and Trin Coll Cambridge (BA 1964); *m* 28 Jan 1969 *Angela Rose, yst dau of George Frederick Pinney, CBE, of Haywards Heath, Sussex, and has issue:
1b +Robert John; *b* 1970; *educ* Eton and Bristol U (MB, ChB 1995)
2b +Edward George; *b* 1972; *educ* Eton and Edinburgh U (MA 1994)
3b +Patrick Thomas; *b* 1974; *educ* Eton and Trin Coll Cambridge (BA 1996)
1b *Katherine Griselda Eveline; *b* 1982
(2) Edward James; *b* 26 Feb 1912; Lt KOSB, F/O RAF 1936; *k* plane crash 16 Aug 1938
(1) *Belinda Margaret Graeme, OBE (1944), TD (1945); *b* 4 Dec 1913; Ch-Cmdt ATS, WW II; *m* 28 Feb 1947 Simon Fowell Buxton (*see* BUXTON, Bt) and has two adopted children
4 John David, CBE (1919) DSO (1917); *b* 8 July 1884; *educ* Winchester; A/Cdre RAF, Capt and Brevet Maj Rifle Bde, seconded RFC 1912, CASO, ADGB 1929, and cmded Fighting Area 1930–31 (ret 1932), memb Aerodrome Bd Air Min 1934–36, Cmdt RAF Vol Res Glasgow 1936–39, WW I (despatches twice, Order of St Maurice and St Lazarus of Italy), WW II; *m* 1st 9 Dec 1913 Ethel (*d* 12 July 1932), dau of Hon Sir Henry Edward Agincourt Hodges, High Court Judge, Melbourne, Australia; *m* 2nd 4 Oct 1934 Marie ('Bunny'), JP (1952), CC Wigtownshire (*d* 4 Oct 1997), dau of John Gibb, of Chillesford, Orford, Suffolk, and formerly w of George Chettle, and *d* 1974, leaving by his 1st w:
(1) Richard, MC; *b* 28 Oct 1914; *educ* Eton and RMC Sandhurst; Maj Black Watch (RHR) WW II, *ka* battle Rhine Crossings 28 March 1945
(2) Peter Norman; *b* 15 July 1922; *educ* Eton; S/Ldr RAF WW II (POW), memb Roy Co Archers, *k* 30 April 1960 cmdg Hull U Air Sqdn
5 Alan Reginald, AFC (1919); *b* 8 Oct 1886; *educ* Haileybury; Lt Roy Scots Fus and RAF WW I (despatches), WW II in HG, Naval Aux; AFRAeS, fndr Scottish Aeroplane Syndicate 1909, responsible for production of first British-built monoplane (Avis), Chm Aviation Cttee, Chm Scot Devpt Cncl 1932–45, Pres Scot Gliding Union 1934–45; *m* 5 Feb 1916 Isabel Julia (*d* 1977), yst dau of Edmund Charles Pendleton Hull, JP, of Richmond, Surrey, and *d* 10 Oct 1958, leaving:
(1) *Fenella Frances Dora; *b* 15 Feb 1918; F/O WAAF WW II; *m* 10 Sept 1954 *Robin Halliday Macartney, FRIBA, yst son of Sir George Macartney, KCIE
(2) *Jean Isabel; *b* 12 Nov 1919; *m* 17 June 1941 *Bartholomew Guy Ellison, son of Maj Guy Moreton Ellison, Lincs Regt, of Waddington, Lincs, and has:
1a *Caroline Anne Ellison; *b* 18 March 1942; *m* 19 Aug 1967 *John Anthony Hobbs, son of Dr Noel Hobbs, of Isleworth, Middx
2a *Joanne Fenella Ellison; *b* 3 Feb 1945
1 Augusta Helen Elizabeth; *b* 25 Aug 1876; *m* 1st 28 April 1898 Charles Lindsay Orr Ewing (*see* ORR EWING, Bt) and had issue; *m* 2nd 30 July 1914 1st Viscount Caldecote (*qv*) and *d* 12 May 1967, having had further issue
2 Alice Mary; *b* 18 Dec 1877; *m* 18 July 1901 Gen Sir Charles Fergusson, 7th Bt (*qv*), and *d* 1 Jan 1958, leaving issue
3 Dorothy Montagu, JP Suffolk; *b* 14 March 1879; CC E Suffolk; *m* 25 April 1899 3rd Earl of Cranbrook (*qv*) and *d* 17 March 1968, leaving issue

The 7th EARL's est son,

PATRICK JAMES BOYLE, **8th Earl of Glasgow**, DSO (1915); *b* 18 June 1874; *educ* HMS *Britannia*; Lt RN 1897, Cdr 1909, Capt (ret) 1919, WW I (despatches); Ayrshire: V-Lt 1942–63 (previously DL), Convener CC 1936–46; Lt Roy Co Archers; *m* 29 May 1906 Hyacinthe Mary, JP (Ayrshire 1935; *d* 1977), yst dau of William Abraham Bell, MA, MB, FRGS, of Pendell Court, Bletchingley, and *d* 14 Dec 1963, having had issue:
1 DAVID WILLIAM MAURICE, **9th Earl**
2 Patrick James; *b* 23 May 1917; *educ* Eton; Capt Scots Gds WW II, *das* Burma 4 May 1946 of internal illness
1 Grizel Mary; *b* 28 April 1913; *m* 23 April 1935 Maj Malcolm Victor Alexander Wolfe Murray (*see* MURRAY, Bt, of Blackbarony) and was lost at sea after enemy action 26 Sept 1942, leaving issue
2 *Hersey Margaret; *b* 11 July 1914; *m* 1st 29 June 1940 Cdr Hon John Montagu Granville Waldegrave, DSC, RN and had issue (*see* WALDEGRAVE, E); *m* 2nd 24 July 1947 *John Goring, TD, DL, and *d* 1993, having had further issue (*see* GORING, Bt)
3 *Margaret Dorothea [The Lady Margaret Stirling-Aird of Kippendavie, Kippendavie Lodge, Pisgah, Dunblane, Perthshire FK15 0HR; 9 Landsdowne Rd, London W11]; *b* 20 Nov 1920; *m* 1st 3 Feb 1944 (*divorce* 1963) Capt Oliver Payan Dawnay, CVO, Coldstream Gds (*see* DOWNE, V); *m* 2nd 1973 *Peter Douglas Miller Stirling-Aird of Kippendavie, TD, and has issue

The 8th EARL's only surv son,

DAVID WILLIAM MAURICE BOYLE, **9th Earl of Glasgow**, CB (1963), DSC (1941); *b* 24 July 1910 (HM QUEEN MARY stood sponsor); *educ* Eton; RN: Midshipman 1929, Lt 1934, Mediterranean and Far E 1930–36, WW II Atlantic, Arctic and E Indies (despatches), Dunkirk and sinking of *Bismarck*, Cdr 1945, cmded HMS *Actæon* S Atlantic Sqdn 1949–50, Capt 1952, Capt of the Fleet (Home Fleet) 1957–59, Cdre RN Barracks, Portsmouth 1959–61, R-Adml 1961, Flag Offr Malta 1961–63; memb Roy Co Archers, ADC to HM THE QUEEN 1961; *m* 1st 4 March 1937 (*divorce* 1962) Dorothea [Dorothea Viscountess Kelburn, Marwell House, Owlesbury, Hants; Albany Piccadilly, London W1], only dau of Sir Archibald Moir Park Lyle, 2nd Bt (*qv*), and had:
1 PATRICK ROBIN ARCHIBALD BOYLE, **10th and present Earl of Glasgow**
1 *Sarah Dorothea; *b* 3 June 1941; *m* 21 June 1962 *John Edward Baily, er son of Brig Michael Henry Hamilton Baily, DSO, and has issue:
(1) Michael; *b* 20 July 1963; *educ* Eton; *d* 1985
(2) *Peter; *b* 6 April 1967; *educ* Eton
(1) *Tanya Jane; *b* 23 July 1965
(2) *Polly Anne; *b* 6 Sept 1972
2 *Nichola Jane Eleanora (Minervina); *b* 21 Dec 1946; *m* 6 Dec 1976 *Thomas Garratt Carter, son of Harry Graham Carter, of Kingston Bagpuize, Oxon, and has issue:
(1) *John Matthew Garratt; *b* 13 Oct 1978
(1) *Ella Frances Lyle; *b* 1986

The **9th Earl** *m* 2nd 6 March 1962 Hon Ursula Vanda Maud (*d* 11 Nov 1984), yr dau of 4th Baron Vivian (*qv*) and formerly w of (a) Maj Philip Alexander Clement Bridgewater and (b) Sir William Fane Wrixon-Becher, 5th Bt (*qv*), and *d* 8 June 1984

GLENAMARA

Arms: Sable, four portcullises each dimidiating a covered cup two in chief one in base that in fesse between two bars gemel gold. **Crest:** Out of the top of a tower proper two trefoils vert volant therefrom a bee proper. **Supporters:** Dexter, a stag guardant proper the dexter foreleg supporting a board vert; sinister, a sea-horse proper. **Motto:** *Levavi oculos meos* ('I have lifted up mine eyes'). **Creation:** B. (LP, UK) 1977.

THE BARON GLENAMARA, of Glenridding in Co Cumbria (Edward (Ted) Watson Short, CH (1976), PC (1964)) [The Rt Hon The Lord Glenamara CH PC, 21 Priory Gdns, Corbridge, Northumberland NE45 5HZ]; *b* 17 Dec 1912; *educ* Bede Coll Durham (LLB); Capt DLI WW II, MP (Lab) Newcastle Centl 1951–76, Oppn Assist Whip 1955–61, Dep Ch Oppn Whip 1962–64, Parly Sec Treasury and Govt Ch Whip 1964–66, PMG 1966–68, Sec State DES 1968–70, Dep Leader Lab Party 1972–76, Ld Pres Cncl and Leader H of C 1974–76; chm Cable and Wireless 1976–80, Pres: Finchale Abbey Training Coll for Disabled 1985– and North East People to People 1989–, Chllr U of Northumbria 1993–, author: *The Story of The Durham Light Infantry* (1944), *The Infantry Instructor* (1946), *Education in a Changing World* (1971), *Birth to Five* (1974), *I Knew My Place* (1983) and *Whip to Wilson* (1989); *m* 1941 *Jennie, dau of Thomas Sewell, of Newcastle, and has:
1 *Michael Christian [The Hon Michael Short, Holly House, Whickharn, Tyne and Wear]; *b* 1943; *m* 1968 *Ann, dau of Joseph Gibbon, of Whickharn
1 *Jane Bronwen [The Hon Mrs Fraser, 62 Martis Av, Rarnsey, NJ 07446, USA]; *b* 1945; *m* 1970 *James Weir Fraser and has issue

Lineage: CHARLES SHORT, of Warcop, Westmorland; *m* Mary — and had:
EDWARD WATSON, *cr* a **Baron**

Glenarthur

Arms: Sa. an escarbuncle or within an orle of bezants. **Crest:** On a rock a pelican in her piety ppr. **Supporters:** Dexter, a bay horse ppr.; sinister, a lion rampant gu. **Motto:** *Fac et spera* ('Do and hope').
Creations: Bt. (UK) 10 Jan 1903, B. (UK) 27 June 1918.

THE 4TH BARON GLENARTHUR, of Carlung, Ayr, and a **Baronet** (Sir Simon Mark Arthur, Bt, DL (Aberdeenshire 1988)) [The Rt Hon The Lord Glenarthur DL, PO Box 11012, Banchory, Kincardineshire AB31 6ZJ]; *b* 7 Oct 1944; *s* f 1976; *educ* Eton; ADC to HC Aden 1964–65, 10th Roy Hussars (PWO): Capt 1970, Maj 1973, ret 1975, Roy Hus TA 1976–80, Brig Roy Co Archers, Capt BA Helicopters Ltd 1976–82, Ld in Waiting (Govt Whip) 1982–83, Parly U-Sec DHSS 1983–85, Home Office 1985–86, Min State: Scottish Office 1986–87, FCO 1987–89, dir Aberdeen and Texas Corporate Fin 1977–82, sr exec advsr Hanson plc and Imp Tobacco Gp plc, Hanson plc 1989–96, chm St Mary's NHS Tst 1991– and Br Helicopter Advsy Bd 1992, dir Lewis Gp 1993–, dep chm Hanson Pacific 1993–, dir Millenium Chemicals Inc 1996–, MCIT 1979, FRAeS 1992, Pres NCCP 1991–; *m* 12 Nov 1969 *Susan, yr dau of Cdr Hubert Wyndham Barry, RN (*see* BARRY, Bt), and has:

1 +EDWARD ALEXANDER; *b* 9 April 1973; *educ* Eton
1 +Emily Victoria; *b* 29 Oct 1975

Lineage: WILLIAM ARTHUR, of Paisley, s of Andrew Arthur, of Abbotsinch, Renfrew, and yr bro of Rev Archibald Arthur, Prof Moral Philosophy Glasgow U 1780–97; *m* Jean, dau of Matthew Robertson, and had, with other issue:

MATTHEW ARTHUR, of Foxbar, later Crofthead, Renfrewshire; *b* 16 June 1794; *m* 25 June 1814 Elizabeth (*d* 30 July 1871), dau of James Fraser and Cecilia Hamilton, and *d* 12 Feb 1861, leaving, with other issue:

JAMES ARTHUR, of Carlung, Ayrshire, and Barshaw, Renfrewshire, JP Renfrewshire, Ayrshire and Lanarks; *b* 6 March 1819; *m* 21 Dec 1847 Jane (*d* 25 May 1907), 2nd dau of Thomas Glen, of Thornhill, Renfrewshire, and had:

1 MATTHEW, **1st Baron**
2 Thomas Glen, JP Ayrshire, Chev Legn Hon; *b* 13 Dec 1857; *m* 26 Sept 1888 Elizabeth Winthrop (*d* 28 Jan 1923), est dau of Sir James Coats, 1st Bt (*qv*), and *d* 2 Feb 1907, leaving:

(1) James; Maj RAF, Lt Ayrshire Yeo; *b* 22 Oct 1889; *m* 21 May 1912 Eleanor Theresa (*d* Oct 1928), 2nd dau of Samuel Hynman Allenby-Montgomerie (*see* EGLINTON and WINTON, E), and was *ka* 7 June 1918
(1) Alice Dudley; *m* 4 Aug 1910 Capt Hon Francis Cuninghame Montgomerie (*see* EGLINTON and WINTON, E), and *d* following a car crash 24 Nov 1951, having had issue

3 James, of Montgomerie, Tarbolton, Ayrshire, JP; *b* 27 Oct 1860; *m* 27 April 1892 Olive Juana, MBE (*d* 6 June 1930), dau of James Stewart, of Blackhouse, and *d* 2 Aug 1935, leaving issue:

(1) Thomas Alan; Maj Ayrshire Yeo and Lt 2nd Life Gds WW I; *b* 16 Dec 1893; *d* 17 June 1935
(2) Evelyn Stewart, of Coilsfield, Tarbolton, Ayrshire, JP, DL, Lt 2nd Dragoons (RSG), Lt-Col TA, Chm TAA Ayrshire 1950–52, memb Roy Co Archers; *b* 1 Oct 1899; *m* 14 April 1926 Elizabeth, er dau of Gen Sir John Theodosius Burnett-Stuart of Dens and Crichie, GCB, KBE, CMG, DSO, and *d* 22 Aug 1963, having had issue:

1a *(John) Norman (Stewart), (Sir), KCB (1985), JP, Ld Lt Stewartry of Kirkcudbright 1996, (DL 1989–96) [Lt Gen Sir Norman Arthur KCB, JP Newbarns, Dalbeattie, Kirkcudbrightshire DG5 4PY]; Maj Roy Scots Greys, Col R Scots Dragoon Gds (Carabiniers and Greys) 1984–92, Brig Roy Co Archers, Govr Edinburgh Castle 1985–88; *b* 6 March 1931; *educ* Eton and RMA Sandhurst; *m* 1 Oct 1960 *Theresa Mary, yr dau of Francis Archibald Hopkinson (*see* COLYTON, B), and has had:

1b Ian Adrian Stewart; *b* 31 March; *d* 1 April 1964
1b *Camilla Jane; *b* 31 Aug 1962

1a (cont.) Sir Norman and Lady Arthur also adopted:
*Simon Francis Stuart; *b* 27 April 1967

2a Adrian James Burnett ARTHUR later ARTHUR-BURNETT-STUART OF DENS AND CRICHIE (added on death of gf Sir John Burnett-Stuart of Dens and Crichie 6 Oct 1958); Capt Rifle Bde; *b* 8 June 1932; *educ* Eton and RMA Sandhurst; *d* unm 9 Dec 1958

1a *Elizabeth Ann; *b* 3 April 1928; *m* 30 April 1954 Lt-Col Robert Hugh Garnett, MBE, KSLI (*d* 19–), er s of Walter Hugh Stewart Garnett, and has had:

1b *John Robert Stewart; *b* 10 April 1958
2b *Adrian Charles Hugh; *b* 14 July 1962
1b *Elizabeth Jane; *b* 20 May 1956
2b Lucy; *b* 10, *d* 11 April 1958
3b *Caroline Nina; *b* 6 July 1960; *m* 1983 *6th Baron Annaly (*qv*)

(1) Marjorie Olive; *m* 2 Aug 1922 Col Reginald Thompson, DSO (*see* THOMPSON, Bt, of Guiseley), and *d* 24 Oct 1929, leaving issue

4 Andrew, JP Ayrshire; Maj QO Roy Glasgow Imp Yeo; *b* 31 Dec 1862; *m* 24 April 1894 Elizabeth Frankland (*d* 19 Oct 1957), dau of William Connal, and *d* 23 Aug 1936, having had:

(1) Andrew Connal; *b* 21 Feb 1895; *d* 20 March 1917
(1) Jane, RRC; *m* 7 Aug 1923 Lt-Col Arthur Stuart Bellingham and had issue (*see* BELLINGHAM, Bt)

1 Jessie Fulton; *m* 1st 18 Nov 1874 John Moffat, CE, of Ardrossan, and had issue. He *d* 22 March 1882. She *m* 2nd 13 April 1886 Charles Edward Hay, 6th s of Sir John Hay, 7th Bt, of Park, (*qv*), and *d* 17 Nov 1931, having had further issue

JAMES ARTHUR *d* 17 June 1885; his est s,

Sir Matthew Arthur, 1st Bt, so *cr* 10 Jan 1903, as also 27 June 1918 **(1st) Baron Glenarthur**, of Carlung, Co Ayr (both UK), JP, DL Ayrshire and Glasgow; LLD Glasgow, memb Roy Co Archers; *b* 9 March 1852; *m* 8 July 1879 Janet Stevenson Bennett, OBE, JP Ayrshire, Hon Pres Ayrshire Branch BRCS (*d* 3 Oct 1946), yr dau of Alexander Bennett McGrigor, LLD, of Cairnoch, Stirling, and *d* 23 Sept 1928, leaving:

1 JAMES CECIL ARTHUR, **2nd Baron Glenarthur**; Capt Ayrshire Yeo and Lt 4th Bn Argyll and Sutherland Highrs; *b* 2 June 1883; *m* 5 Feb 1907 Evelyn (*d* 9 May 1959), er dau of Henry March-Phillipps, of Fairby, Tiverton, N Devon, and *d* 11 Dec 1942, leaving:

(1) MATTHEW ARTHUR, **3rd Baron Glenarthur**, OBE (1945, MBE 1943); T/Lt-Col (Staff) RSG WW II (despatches twice); *b* 12 May 1909; *m* 1st 9 April 1931 (*divorce* 1939) Audrey, only dau of George Crompton Lees-Milne (*see* GLANUSK, B), and had:

1a Prudence Armorel; *b* 13 Feb 1932; *m* 20 March 1953 Maj Edwin Rowland Winwood Robinson, MC (*d* 25 March 1997), only s of Capt Claude Robinson, MC, and *d* 31 Aug 1976, leaving:

1b *Henry Claude Winwood [Henry Robinson Esq, Moorwood, N Cerney, Cirencester, Glos]; *b* 28 Dec 1953; *educ* Winchester and Worcester Coll Oxford; *m* 23 June 1984 *Susan Tessa Faulkner and has:

1c *Alexander James Winwood; *b* 1 Nov 1985
1c *Lucinda Mary Winwood; *b* 23 Feb 1988
2c *Tessa Charlotte Winwood; *b* 4 Jan 1990

2b *Nicholas John Winwood [Nicholas Robinson Esq, Fox Farm, Wardour, Tisbury, Wilts]; *b* 18 Feb 1955; *educ* Winchester
3b *Richard Edwin Winwood [Richard Robinson Esq, The Mill, Windrush, Oxon]; *b* 2 Feb 1958; *educ* Winchester

(1) The **3rd Baron** *m* 2nd 1 Sept 1939 Margaret Risk (*d* 1993), only dau of Capt Henry James Howie, of Stairaird, Mauchline, and *d* 1976, leaving by her:

1a SIMON MARK ARTHUR, **4th and present Baron Glenarthur**
2a +Matthew Richard [The Hon Matthew Arthur, Bingfield East Quarter, Hallington, Newcastle NE19 2LH]; *b* 6 March 1948; *educ* Eton and RAC Cirencester; *m* 1974 *Veronica Rosemary, yr dau of Capt Michael Hall, RSG (*see* BASING, B), and has issue:

1b +Matthew Frederick Michael; *b* 1981
1b *Jessica Mary; *b* 1979

2a *Victoria; *b* 20 June 1946; *m* 1976 *Hugh Richard Mervyn Vernon (*see* LYVEDEN, B)

(1) Pamela Helen; *m* 1st 6 Oct 1927 (*divorce* 1944) Jack Drummond Rudd, only surv s of Percy Rudd, of Kimberley, S Africa, and had issue; *m* 2nd 19 Dec 1944 (*divorce* 1951) Lt-Cdr John Hamilton, RN, er s of Col Claud Lorn Campbell Hamilton, CMG, DSO, of Rozelle, Ayr, and had further issue; *m* 3rd 4 April 1951 William Hamilton Robertson-Aikman, er s of Lt-Col Thomas Stokes George Hugh Robertson-Aikman, CB, JP, DL (*d* 1981), of The Ross, Hamilton, and *d* 1977

1 Elizabeth Muriel; *m* 28 July 1904 Maj Ian Archibald Finlay, RSG and NI Horse, of Temple Hall, Coldingham, Berwick, late of Castle Toward, Argyll, and *d* Jan 1960, leaving issue. He *d* 9 Nov 1925

GLENCONNER

Arms: Arg. two crescents in fess sa., on a chief gu. a boar's head couped of the field, a bordure company of the second and first. **Crest:** A mast with a sail hoisted ppr. **Supporters:** Dexter, a stag ppr. gorged with a mural crown or; sinister, a tiger ppr. gorged with a crown palisado or, each charged on the shoulder with a thistle leaved and slipped gold. **Motto:** *Deus dabit vela* ('God will fill the sails'). **Creations:** Bt. (UK) 17 July 1885, B. (UK) 3 April 1911.

THE 3RD BARON GLENCONNER, of Glen, Co Peebles, and a **Baronet** (Sir Colin Christopher Paget Tennant Bt) [The Rt Hon The Lord Glenconner, Beau Estate, Soufrire, St Lucia, W Indies]; *b* 1 Dec 1926; *s* f 1983; *educ* Eton and New Coll Oxford; late Lt Irish Gds, dir C Tennant, Son & Co 1953 (dep chm 1960–67), Tennants Estates 1967–91, chm Mustique Co 1969–87; *m* 21 April 1956 *Lady Anne Veronica Coke, LVO, est dau of 5th Earl of Leicester (*qv*), and has had:

1 Charles (Charlie) Edward Pevensey; *b* 15 Feb 1957; *educ* Clifton and Frensham Heights Sch; *m* 1993, as her 2nd husb, *Sheilagh [The Hon Mrs Charles Tennant, 30 Fountainhall Rd, Edinburgh EH9 2LW], dau of Matthew Raymond Scott, of Peebles, and *d* 19 Oct 1996, leaving:

(1) +CODY CHARLES EDWARD; *b* 2 Feb 1994

2 Henry Lovell; *b* 21 Feb 1960; *m* 5 Jan 1983 *Teresa Mary [The Hon Mrs Henry Tennant, The Glen, Innerleithen, Peeblesshire], yr dau of John McRae Cormack (*see* DAVIES, B), and *d* 1990, leaving:

(1) Euan Lovell; *b* 1983

3 +Christopher Cary; *b* 25 April 1968; *educ* Stanbridge Earls; *m* 14 June 1996 *Anastasia, dau of Dimitrios Papadakos, of Athens, and has:

(1) *Bella; *b* Nov 1996

1 *(Flora) May Pamela; *b* 8 Nov 1970 (HRH PRINCESS MARGARET COUNTESS OF SNOWDON stood sponsor)

2 *Amy Jasmine Elizabeth; *b* 8 Nov 1970

Lineage: JOHN TENNANT, of Blairston Mill, Ayrshire; *b* 1635; *m* Jean Taggart (*d* 12 Feb 1723) and *d* 7 April 1728, leaving issue:

WILLIAM TENNANT, of Mains, Bridgend of Doon, Alloway; *b* 1695; *m* Agnes Reid (*d* 1746) and *d* 1744, leaving issue:

1 JOHN

2 Robert; Deacon and Convener Ayr

3 David, of Ayr; *b* 1734; *d* 1833, leaving:

(1) William, of Edinburgh; *b* 1765; *d* 1835, leaving:

1a William Dalrymple, of Edinburgh; *b* 1788; *d* 1862, leaving:

1b William; with Charles Tennant, Sons & Co, London; *b* 1836; *d* 1893, leaving:

1c William Augustus, of Orford House, Ugley, Essex; *b* 1861; *m* Agnes Gairdner and *d* 11 June 1941, leaving issue:

1d Ernest William Dalrymple, OBE (1919), of Orford House; Capt Intell Corps WW I; *b* 5 May 1887; *m* 1st 11 April 1912 (*divorce*) Eleonora (*d* 11 Sept 1963), dau of Brig-Gen Thomas Fiaschi, DSO, of Sydney, NSW, and had:

1e Julian William Fiaschi; *b* 1 Aug 1924; *educ* Eton; *m* 1 Dec 1954 *Miranda, dau of Sydney Fairbairn, of Steventon, Hants, and *d* 1995, leaving:

1f *Mungo William; *b* 30 Sept 1963; *educ* Eton

1f *Nell Angela; *b* 28 Sept 1958; *m* 19– *Jonathan Carey and has issue

2f *Angela Vanessa; *b* 28 May 1967

1e Vanessa; *b* 23 Aug 1919; *m* 9 Sept 1939 *Charles Brian Swann, s of Harold Swann, of Standon Lordship, Ware, Herts, and *d* 1995 leaving three daus

2e *June [Mrs Paul Bethell-Fox, The Limes Cottage, Smith's Green, Herts CM22 6NX]; *b* 11 Nov 1921; *m* May 1954 Paul Bethell-Fox (*d* 8 July 1968), s of Capt William Fox, of Stratford-on-Avon

3e *Camilla; *b* 22 Jan 1930; *m* 25 April 1957, as his 2nd w *William Yates, MP (C) Wrekin 1955–66, MP Holt, Victoria, Australia 1975–80 (*see* ELTON, B) and has four sons

1d (cont.) Ernest Tennant *m* 2nd 15 Feb 1950 Hon Irene (*d* 1989), formerly w of (a) Capt Murray Shuldham Shuldham-Leigh, Queen's Roy Regt, and (b) Lt-Col Cecil Frederick Bull, DSO, RA, and est dau of 5th Viscount Gage (*qv*), and *d* 31 July 1962

2d Alan; served WW I; *b* 7 Aug 1888; *ka* 9 May 1915

1d Margaret Edith; *m* 1st 4 Aug 1913 Maj Archibald Ariel Mercer (*d* 17 Nov 1914), 2nd Bn Dorset Regt, s of Charles Mercer, and had a dau; *m* 2nd 11 Aug 1922 Lt-Col James Leatham Birley, CBE, DM, FRCP, est s of Francis Hornby Birley, and had further issue. He *d* 6 March 1934

2d Agnes Dalrymple (Jancy)

2c John D; had:

1d William D

2d Charles G

1d Mona

2d Joan; *m* — Herdman

3c George F D; had:

1d Peter

2d David

1d Barbara (Peggy)

4c Hugh J; had:

1d Jim; *b* 1912

1d Betty; *b* 1912

1c Mary N R; *m* — Saunders and had a s and dau

2c Florence D; *m* — Baxter and had two sons

2a James (Sir), KCB (1852, CB 1849); Brig-Gen RA, served S Africa and India, Lt-Col 1837, cmded artillery Battles of Chilianwala and Gujerat, recd thanks of Parl; *b* 1789; *educ* Marlow Mil Sch; *d* 1854, leaving:

1b James Francis, CIE (1879); FRS, FRAS, joined RE 1847, Indian Mutiny 1858, Lt-Gen 1884, Govt Astronomer Madras 1859, PWD 1863, Master Mint Calcutta 1874–84; *b* 10 Jan 1829; *d* 6 March 1915

4 Alexander; *m* — McClymont

5 James; went to the West Indies

1 Jean

The est son,

JOHN TENNANT of Glenconner, Ochiltree; sometime factor Countess of Glencairn's estates; *b* 1725; *m* 1st Jean McClure and had:

1 William; *b* 1751; *d* an infant

2 James; *b* 1754; *m* Jean McClutchie and *d* 1835, leaving issue:

(1) James; *b* 1796; *m* and *d* 1872, leaving issue:

1a James; with Charles Tennant & Co Dundee, Carnoustie and St Rollox; *b* 1840; *d* 1930

1 Jean; *b* 1756; *m* W Mearns and *d* 1811

JOHN TENNANT *m* 2nd Margaret McClure (*d* 1784); *m* 3rd Jean McWilliam (*dsp*) and *d* 28 April 1810, having by his 2nd w had:

3 William (Rev); LLD, minister Forces India, author *Indian Recreations* (3 vols, 1803); *b* 1758; *d* unm 1813

4 John, of Auchenbay and Creoch; *b* 1760; *m* Margaret Colville and *d* 1853, leaving 11 children, of whom the yst s, David (1808–80, was ancestor of the Irish TENNANTs

5 David; Capt RN; *b* 1762; *m* Anne Green and *dsp* 1839

6 CHARLES

7 Alexander; emigrated to Cape Colony; *b* 1772; *m* Cornelia Sanderberg, of Cape Colony, and *d* 1814, leaving issue:

(1) Hercules; Civil Commr and RM Cape Colony; *m* Aletta Brand and had:

1a David (Hon Sir), KCMG (1892), JP Cape Town; ktd 1877, MLA Cape Colony 1866–96 and Speaker 1874–96, Agent-Gen London of Cape Colony 1896–1902, memb U Cncl Cape Good Hope, Chm Cncl S African Coll; *b* 10 Jan 1829; *m* 1st 1849 Josina (*d* 1877), dau of J du Toit, of Stellenbosch, Cape Colony, and had issue:

1b A son; *b* 3 March 1850; *m* 1874 Mary Cathcart, dau of Robert Graham, 14th of Fintry, and *d* 21 May 1925

2b David

1b Gertrude; *m* Maj — Copland and had a dau

1a (cont.) David Tennant *m* 2nd 1885 Amye Venour, dau of Lt-Gen Sir William Bellairs, KCMG, CB (*see* GIBBONS, Bt), and *d* 29 March 1905

8 Robert; settled NI; *b* 1774; *m* Mary Weir and *d* 1814

2 Agnes; *b* 1764; *m* George Reid and *d* 1787

3 Janet; *b* 1766; *m* Andrew Paterson and *d* 1813

4 Margaret; *b* 1770; *d* unm 1836

5 Elizabeth; *b* 1776; *m* — Haughton and *d* 1813

6 Katharine; *b* 1778; *d* unm 1848

7 Sarah; *b* 1780; *m* William Sloane and *d* 1864

8 Charlotte; *b* 1782; *d* unm 1869

The 6th son,

CHARLES TENNANT, of St Rollox, Lanarks; scientist, mfr; *b* 3 May 1768; *m* Margaret Wilson and *d* 1 Oct 1838, leaving issue:

1 JOHN

2 Charles James; *b* 1801; *d* 1870

1 Margaret; *m* James Dunlop and had eight children

2 Jean; *b* 1802

3 Charlotte; *b* 1803; *m* Dr John Couper and had three sons and three daus

4 Mary; *b* 1805; *m* W Couper, WS, and *d* 1871, leaving a s

5 Christina; *b* 1807; *m* Alexander Couper and had a dau

6 Catherine; *b* 1808; *m* Robert Wallace, WS, and had four sons and three daus

7 Elizabeth

The er son,

JOHN TENNANT, of St Rollox, Lanarks, JP, DL Lanarks; *b* 1796; *d* 1878, leaving:

1 John; had:

(1) John, of The Boltons, London SW; *b* 1847; *m* Margaret Galbraith and *d* 1931, having had issue:

1a William Galbraith; served WW I; *b* 1879; *m* 26 June 1907 Hon Winifred Chapple Norton (*d* 11 July 1914), 3rd dau of 5th Baron Grantley (*qv*), and was *ka* 1915, leaving issue:

1b David John Brinsley; *b* 1910

2a John Amherst; served WW I; *b* 1888; *ka* 1915

3a Hugh Vincent; *b* 1889; *d* 1927

1a Anne Fergusson; *b* 1876

2a Lilian Elizabeth; *b* 1883; *m* Felix John Watson Taylor and had a s and two daus

3a Margaret Groom; *b* 1885

(2) Charles; *m* Marion Hanson and *dsp*

(3) James; *b* 1852; *m* Henrietta Grant Fergusson and had issue:

1a Charles; served WW I; *ka* 1915

1a Ruth Janet Grant; *b* 1880; *m* T Leathart and had a dau

2a Sheena Lilian; *b* 1883; *m* Herbert Moorhouse Kendall and had a s

3a Laura Grant; *m* David Boyle and had two sons

4a Beatrice Grant; *m* G E Forman and had a s and three daus

5a Mary Eileen Grant; *m* M W Bailward and had two sons

2 **Sir Charles Tennant, 1st Bt** (UK), so *cr* 17 July 1885, of The Glen, Peeblesshire, and St Rollox, JP, DL; MP (Lib) Glasgow 1879–80 and Peebles and Selkirk 1880–86, Hon Col 4th Vol Bn Cameronians, Tstee Nat Gallery; *b* 4 Nov 1823; *m* 1st 2 Aug 1849 Emma (*d* 21 Jan 1895), dau of Richard Winsloe, of Taunton, and had issue (such of whom as are marked with a +, apart from the 1st Baron and his issue, are in remainder to the btcy only), with three other sons (*d* young) and another dau (*d* unm):

(1) EDWARD PRIAULX **1st Baron**

(2) Francis John, of Innes, Morayshire, and Bardowie, Stirling; *b* 20 Oct 1861; *m* 3 June 1886 Annie Geraldine (*d* 17 July 1956), dau of John Marriner Redmayne, JP, of S Dene, Co Durham, and *d* 4 Sept 1942, leaving issue:

1a John Edward, DSO (1918), MC, JP; Lt-Col Res Offrs Scots Gds WW I, cmdg RFC Mesopotamia 1916–18, Dir Aeronautics India 1918–19 (despatches, Legn Hon), G/Capt RAFVR WW II; *b* 12 Oct 1890; *m* 1st 22 May 1918 (*divorce* 1925) Georgina Helen, dau of Gen Sir George Macaulay Kirkpatrick, KCB, KCSI, and had issue:

1b +Iain Mark (Sir), KT (1986), JP (Morayshire 1961) [Sir Iain Tennant KT JP, Lochnabo House, Lhanbryde, Moray 1V30 3QY]; Ld-Lt Morayshire 1963–94 (DL 1954–63), Capt Scots Gds Supp Reserve Offrs WW II (POW), Lt Roy Co Archers, Chm: Govrs Gordonstoun 1956–72, Grampian TV 1967–89, dir Clydesdale Bank 1969–89, Crown Estates Commr 1970–90, FRSA 1971, Ld High Commr Gen Assembly Ch Scotland 1987 and 1988, Hon LLD Aberdeen 1990; *b* 11 March 1919; *educ* Eton and Magdalene Coll Cambridge; *m* 11 July 1946 *Lady Margaret Helen Isla Marion Ogilvy, 2nd dau of 9th Earl of Airlie (*qv*), and has issue:

1c +Mark Edward [Mark Tennant Esq, Innes House, Elgin, Moray, Scotland]; 2nd Lt Scots Gds; *b* 9 May 1947; *educ* Eton; *m* 1971 *Hermione Rosamond, dau of Lt-Col Maurice W Howe, OBE, and has issue:

1d +Edward Iain; *b* 1983

1d *Miranda Hermione Rosamond; *b* 1974

2d *Clementine Margaret Georgina; *b* 1977

2c +Christopher John; Page Honour to HM THE QUEEN 1964–66; *b* 16 June 1950; *educ* Eton; *m* 1994 *Mrs Andrea Lewis, yst dau of Donald Payne

1c *Emma Margaret; *b* 19 April 1954; *m* 1979 *Angus Geoffrey Bruce Ismay Cheape, late Scots Gds, 2nd s of (Hugh) Bruce Ismay Cheape, TD, and has issue:

1d *Henry Bruce Iain Ismay; *b* 1980

1a (cont.) Lt-Col John Tennant *m* 2nd 17 July 1926 Victoria Maud Veronica, MBE (1945) (*d* 5 July 1967), only dau of Sir Robert George Vivian Duff, 2nd Bt (*see* 1970 edn), and was *ka* 7 Aug 1941, leaving by her:

2b +Andrew Duff [Andrew Tennant Esq, Muiresk House, Turriff, Aberdeenshire]; Scots Gds 1945–48; *b* 17 June 1928; *educ* Eton; *m* 22 July 1953 (*divorce* 1967) Lucinda Evelyn, only dau of Maj Arthur Walter James (*see* NORTHBOURNE, B), and has issue:

1c *Ann Charlotte; *b* 4 June 1956

3b +Hugh Rinnes Duff [Hugh Tennant Esq, 4 Lecky St, London SW7]; *b* 1 Sept 1932; *educ* Eton; late Lt Scots Gds

1b Victoria Robina Duff; *b* 5 June 1927; *m* 23 Jan 1956 *Alberto Zancan, of Turin, only s of — Zancan, of Padua, and had issue:

1c *Michael Edward Guiseppe; *b* 9 Sept 1961

1c *Marina; *b* 20 March 1958

2b Laura Duff; *b* 11 July 1935; *m* 24 Sept 1955 *10th Baron Talbot of Malahide (*qv*) and *d* 1989, leaving issue

2a Mark; Capt 4th Seaforth Highrs, Lt Scots Gds and MGC; *b* 1892; *ka* 16 Sept 1916

3a Francis Michael, DSO (1918); Lt Scots Gds (SR) WW I (despatches); *b* 22 March 1899

1a Frances Lucy; *m* 23 July 1912 Hon Guy Lawrence Charteris (*see* WEMYSS, E), and *d* 5 Nov 1925, leaving issue

2a Geraldine Bryde (Dinah); *m* 10 Feb 1915 Sir Iain Colquhoun, 7th Bt (*qv*), and *d* 1974, leaving issue

3a Kathleen, JP; *m* 27 Jan 1916 9th Duke of Rutland (*qv*) and *d* 1989, leaving issue

(3) Harold John, PC (1914), JP Kent, DL Aberdeenshire; MP (Lib) Berwicks 1894–1918, Assist Priv Sec to Home Sec 1892–95, Parly Sec BOT 1909–11, Fin Sec War Office 1911–12, Parly U-Sec War 1912–16, Sec Scotland and V-Pres Ctee Cncl Educn 1916; *b* 18 Nov 1865; *educ* Trin Coll Cambridge (BA); *m* 1st 1 Oct 1889 Helen Elizabeth (*d* 9 May 1892), dau of Maj Gordon Duff, of Drummuir, Banffshire, and had a s (*d* young); *m* 2nd 8 July 1896 Margaret Edith, CH (1917), JP (*d* 11 July 1946), dau of George Whitley Abraham, of Rathgar, Co Dublin, and *d* 8 Nov 1935, having by her had, with another s (*ka* 1917):

(1) John, TD; Maj RA, Sub-Lt RN WW II (wounded, POW Tobruk), memb Roy Co Archers, KStJ; *b* 30 May 1899; *educ* RNCs Osborne and Dartmouth and Trin Coll Cambridge (BA 1920, MA 1965); *m* 1st 12 Feb 1929 (*divorce* 1939) Hon Antonia Mary Roby Benson, er dau of 1st Baron Charnwood (*see* 1956 edn), and had issue:

1a +Anthony John (Sir) [Sir Anthony Tennant, 18 Hamilton House, Vicarage Gate, London W8 4NL]; *b* 5 Nov 1930; *educ* Eton and Trin Coll Cambridge (BA); late Lt Scots Gds (Supp Res of Offrs), dir: Mather & Crowther 1959–66, mktg consultancy 1970, Watney Mann & Truman 1972–76, Morgan Stanley UK Gp 1993–, Exploration Co 1967–89, El Oro Mining and Exploration Co 1967–89, Grand Met 1977–87, Close Bro Gp 1980–90, GRE 1989–, Guardian Assur 1989–, BNP UK Hldgs 1990–, Argo Wiggins Appleton 1996–, Christie's Internat Plc 1993 (chm 1993–96), Forte Plc dep-chm 1992–96, md 1976–82 IDV (chm 1983–87), Guinness plc ceo 1987–89 (chm 1989–92), dep md Truman Ltd, Tstee RA Tst 1994–, chm Roy Acad Tst 1996–; ktd 1992; *m* 12 July 1954 *Rosemary Violet, er dau of Lt-Col Henry Charles Minshull Stockdale (*see* STOCKDALE, Bt), and has:

1b +Christopher Sebastian [Christopher Tennant Esq, 11 Lawrence St, London SW3 5NB]; *b* 5 Aug 1955; *educ* Eton and St Andrews (MA); *m* 1987 *Sally Jennifer, 3rd dau of Jack Berner, and has issue:

1c *Francesca Rose Antonia; *b* 1992

2c *Harriet Daisy; *b* 1993

2b +Patrick Charles [Patrick Tennant Esq, Hayward Holt, Hungerford, Berks RQ17 OQB]; *b* 24 Feb 1958; *educ* Eton, Trin Coll Cambridge (MA) and U of Pennsylvania (MBA, MA); *m* 1986 *Meredith Maye, er dau of Jerome Shively, and has issue:

1c +Oliver John; *b* 10 Aug 1994

2c +Barnaby Cyril; *b* 10 Aug 1994

1c *Jemima Jennifer; *b* 1990

2a +Mark Iain [Mark Tennant Esq, Royal Courts of Justice, Strand, London WC2A 2LL; Balfluig Castle, by Alford, Aberdeenshire AB33 8E]; *b* 4 Dec 1932; *educ* Eton and New Coll Oxford (BA 1956, MA 1959); territorial Scottish Baron of Balfluig, barrister Inner Temple 1958, Recorder 1987, Master Bench 1982, Master Supreme Court Queen's Bench 1988–, Lt Rifle Bde Supp Res Offrs; *m* 11 Dec 1965 *Lady Harriot Pleydell-Bouverie, yst dau of 7th Earl of Radnor (*qv*), and has issue:

1b +Lysander Philip Roby [Lysander Tennant Esq, 204 Iverson Rd, London NW6 2HL]; *b* 11 Nov 1968; *educ* Eton and New Coll Oxford (BA)

1b *Sophia Roby; *b* 1 May 1967; *educ* Magdalen Coll Oxford

(1) (cont.) Maj John Tennant *m* 2nd 3 May 1948 *Rosemary Irene [Mrs John Tennant, 3 Wittersham House, Wittersham, Kent TN30 7ED], yst dau of Senator Sir Alfred Theodore Hennessy, KBE, of Wynberg, S Africa, and *d* 11 June 1967, leaving by her:

3a +Ivo Simon [Ivo Tennant Esq, 70 Waterford Road, London SW6 2DR]; *b* 28 Nov 1955; *educ* Harrow; *m* 1985 *Carole V, dau of Maj C P Martel, of Richmond, N Yorks, and has issue:

1b +Thomas Simon Alfred; *b* 1991

1b *Camilla Rose; *b* 1987

1a *Aurea Mary Rose [Miss Aurea Tennant, 38 Franche Court Road, London SW17]; *b* 27 April 1949

(2) Archibald, barrister Lincoln's Inn 1933, memb Roy Co Archers, Lt-Col Scots Gds WW II; *b* 11 Oct 1907; *educ* Eton and Trin Coll Cambridge; *m* 16 Sept 1947 *Mrs Diana Primrose Gibbs [Mrs Archibald Tennant, 12 Victoria Square, London SW1], yst dau of Percy Cuthbert Quilter (*see* QUILTER, Bt), and *d* 31 May 1955, leaving issue:

1a *Veronica Clare [Mrs Julius Lister, 365 Wimbledon Park Rd, London SW19]; *b* 2 Aug 1950; *m* 1981 *Julius von Mengerhausen Lister and has:

1b *Marina Helen Clare von Mengerhausen; *b* 1982

2a *Pamela Mary Diana [Mrs Charles Sebag-Montefiore, 21 Hazlewell Rd, London SW15]; *b* 5 June 1953; *m* 1979 *Charles Adam Laurie Sebag-Montefiore and has issue (*see* MAGNUS, Bt)

(3) +Peter [Peter Tennant Esq, Laurel Bank, Ancaster Rd, Callander, Perths FK17 8EL]; *b* 27 April 1913; *educ* Eton, and Trin Coll Cambridge (BA 1934, MA 1951); *m* 23 April 1938 *Valerie, yst dau of John Sutton Nettlefold, JP, of The Manor House, Bampton, Oxon, and has issue:

1a *Alison Valerie [Mrs Roger Burnley, 23 Marchmont Crescent, Edinburgh EH9 1HQ]; *b* 24 Jan 1939; *m* 12 Oct 1962 *Roger Leon Burnley, only s of John Leon Burnley, of New York, and has issue:

1b *Julian Lee; *b* 23 June 1969

1b *Andrea Adwoa; *b* 15 Jan 1968

2a *Fiona [Mrs Neil Snow, Moor End, Invertrossachs, Callander, Perthshire]; *b* 3 June 1940; *m* 5 Sept 1964 *Neil Graham Douglas Snow, s of Herbert Douglas Snow, and has issue:

1b *Justin Douglas Tennant; *b* 28 Nov 1965

2b *Jonathan Peter; *b* 28 Feb 1968

1b *Catriona Louisa; *b* 24 Jan 1967

2b *Kirsten Fiona, *b* 1970

3a *Sheila [Mrs Edward Burnett, Rhynaclach, Port of Menteith, Kippen, Perthshire]; *b* 24 Jan 1946; *m* 1970 *Edward Findlay Burnett and has issue:

1b *Joseph Andrew; *b* 1976

1b *Helen Sheila; *b* 1978

(1) Alison Margaret; memb Westminster Cncl 1949–58 and 1963 on, LCC 1955–58 and 1961–65, Inner London Exec Cncl NHS 1964 on, V-Chm European Union Women 1955–63 (Chm Br Section 1956–65), Ch Cdr ATS WW II; *b* 29 Nov 1903

1 Pauline Emma; *b* 1855; *m* 2 Feb 1875 Thomas Duff Gordon-Duff, CBE, 9th of Drummuir, Keith and Park, Banffshire, and *d* 16 Nov 1888, leaving issue. He *d* 27 March 1923

2 Charlotte Monkton; *b* 1858; *m* 7 April 1877 4th and last Baron Ribblesdale, PC (*d* 21 Oct 1925), and *d* 2 May 1911, leaving issue

3 Katharine Lucy; *b* 1860; *m* 30 April 1879 Thomas Graham Smith and *d* 1942. He *dsp* 29 April 1908

4 Octavia Laura Mary; *b* 1862; *m* 21 May 1885 Hon Alfred Lyttelton, s of 4th Baron Lyttelton (*see* COBHAM, V), and *dsps* 24 April 1886

5 (Emma Alice) Margaret (Margot); *b* 1864; *m* 10 May 1894, as his 2nd w, 1st Earl of Oxford and Asquith (*qv*), and *d* 28 July 1945, leaving issue

6 Marion; *m* Rev R Wallace; *dsp*

Sir Charles *m* 2nd Nov 1898 Marguerite Agaranthe (*m* 2nd 13 Nov 1907 Maj Geoffrey Lubbock (*see* AVEBURY, B); *d* 26 May 1943), yst dau of Col Charles W Miles, and by her had, with a dau (*d* unm):

6 Margaret, DBE (1965); GCStJ, Hon LLD Queen's U Belfast 1957; *b* 4 Nov 1899; *m* 3 June 1920 2nd Baron Wakehurst (*qv*) and *d* 1994, leaving issue

7 KATHARINE Tennant, BARONESS ELLIOT OF HARWOOD (LP), of Rulewater, Co Roxburgh (UK), so *cr* 1958, DBE (1958, CBE 1946), JP Roxbughshire (1967); *b* 15 Jan 1903; *educ* Abbot's Hill Sch Hemel Hempstead; Hon LLD Glasgow 1959, Grand Silver Cross Austrian Order Merit 1961, UK Del UN 1954–56 and 1957, chm Nat Union C and Unionist Assocs 1957–58; *m* 4 April 1934, as his 2nd w, Walter ELLIOT, CH, MC, PC, MP, FRS (*d* 1958), s of William Elliot, of Muirglen, Lanarks, and *d* 1994, when the Barony expired

8 Nancy, OBE (1961); *b* 20 Aug 1904; *m* 16 Feb 1928 (*divorce* 1936) Sylvester Govett Gates, CBE, s of Walter George Gates, CB; *m* 2nd 22 Sept 1936 1st Baron Crathorne (*qv*) and *d* 17 May 1969, leaving issue

Sir CHARLES *d* 4 June 1906; his est surv son,

EDWARD PRIAULX TENNANT, **1st Baron Glenconner**, of Glen, Co Peebles (UK), so *cr* 3 April 1911, JP Wilts; Ld Lt Peeblesshire 1908–20, Ld High Commr Gen Assembly Ch Scotland 1911, 1912, 1913 and 1914, MP (Lib) Salisbury 1906–1910; *educ* Eton and Trin Coll Cambridge (MA 1885); *b* 31 May 1859; *m* 11 July 1895 Pamela Adelaide Genevieve (*m* 2nd 4 June 1922 1st Viscount Grey of Fallodon (*see* GREY, Bt); *d* 18 Nov 1928), yst dau of Hon Percy Scawen Wyndham (*see* EGREMONT, LECONFIELD and, B), and had:

1 Edward Wyndham, Lt Gren Gds SR; *b* 1 July 1897; *ka* 22 Sept 1916

2 CHRISTOPHER GREY, **2nd Baron**

3 David Pax; *b* 22 May 1902; *m* 1st 16 April 1928 (*divorce* 1937) Hermione Youlanda Ruby Clinton (the actress Hermione Baddeley; *d* 1986), dau of William Herman Clinton Baddeley, and had issue:

(1) +David Edward Wyndham [David Tennant Esq, Pyt Cottage, Tisbury, Wilts SP3 6NY]; late 2nd Lt Roy Irish Fus; *b* 10 May 1930; *educ* Eton; *m* 3 Dec 1964 (*divorce* 1973) Margaret Rachel, yr dau of Hon Sir Ernest Stowell Scott, KCMG, MVO, JP (*see* ELDON, E), and has:

1a +Aubone Christopher; *b* 7 May 1969; *educ* Eton and Durham U; Capt Scots Gds

2a +Ivan; *b* 1970; *educ* Stowe, St Pauls and UCL

1a *Laura Hermione; *b* 9 Feb 1967; *educ* St Paul's and Jesus Coll Cambridge; *m* 199– *Ian Irvine

(1) *Pauline Laetitia [Pauline Lady Rumbold, Hatch Cottage, Cokers Frome, Dorchester, Dorset]; *b* 6 Feb 1929; *m* 1st 17 Aug 1946 (*divorce* 1953) Capt Julian Alfred Lane-Fox Pitt-Rivers (*see* FORSTER, B); *m* 2nd 3 June 1954 (*divorce* 1970) Euan Douglas Graham (*see* MONTROSE, D); *m* 3rd 1974 Sir (Horace) Anthony (Claude) Rumbold, 10th Bt (*qv*)

3 (cont.) David Tennant *m* 2nd 23 Nov 1938 (*divorce* 1953) Virginia Penelope, dau of Alan Leonard Romaine Parsons by Viola, dau of Sir Herbert Beerbohm Tree; *m* 3rd 25 July 1963 *Shelagh Ann, dau of Maj Sean Rainey and Mrs Marion Wrottesley, and *d* 8 April 1968, leaving by his 2nd w:

(2) *Georgina Sky [Miss Georgina Tennant, Job's Mill, Warminster, Wilts]; *b* 4 Feb 1941; has by *Paul Stephen McNaney:

1a *Ella May; *b* 8 Feb 1984

(3) *Sabrina Viola (Josie); *b* 5 Dec 1943 (took by deed poll forename of Josie instead of Sabrina Viola and maiden surname TENNANT again); *m* 4 Oct 1963 (*divorce* 1977) Jonathan Gathorne Gathorne-Hardy (*see* CRANBROOK, E) and has issue

4 Stephen James Napier; *b* 21 April 1906; *d* 28 Feb 1987

1 Clarissa Madeline Georgiana Felicite; *b* 13 July 1896; *m* 1st 18 Aug 1915 (*divorce* 1918) Capt William Adrian Vincent Bethell (*d* 16 July 1941), 2nd Life Gds, only s of William Bethell, of Rise Park, near Hull, and had issue; *m* 2nd 27 March 1918 (*divorce* 1928) 3rd Baron Tennyson (*qv*) and had further issue; *m* 3rd 24 July 1928 (*divorce* 1939) James Montgomery Beck, s of Hon James Montgomery Beck, of Washington, reverted to name TENNYSON 1 Aug 1951 and *d* 3 Sept 1960, leaving further issue

2 Hester; *b* and *d* 1916

The 1st BARON *d* 21 Nov 1920; his 2nd son,

CHRISTOPHER GREY TENNANT, **2nd Baron Glenconner**; *b* 14 June 1899; *m* 1st 25 Sept 1925 (*divorce* 1935) Pamela Winefred (*d* 1989), 2nd dau of Sir Richard Arthur Surtees Paget, 2nd Bt, of Cranmore (*qv*), and *d* 4 Oct 1983, leaving:

1 COLIN CHRISTOPHER PAGET TENNANT, **3rd and present Baron Glenconner**

2 James Grey Herbert; FRGS, 2nd Lt RHG; *b* 5 March 1929; *educ* Eton and Trin Coll Cambridge (MA); *m* 1st 29 Oct 1955 (*divorce* 1962) Emily Fawaz, yr dau of George Licos, of Khartoum and Cairo; *m* 2nd 16 June 1962 *Elizabeth Marya [Mrs Philip Edwards, 37 Cadogan Place, London SW1] (*m* 3rd 1994 Philip Edwards), formerly w of Ian Romer, of Hawkley, Hants, and only dau of James Dales, of W Vancouver, and *d* 1992, leaving by his 1st w:

(1) +Alexander David Gabriel; *b* 17 Feb 1957

The **2nd Baron** *m* 2nd 25 March 1935 *Elizabeth [The Rt Hon Elizabeth Lady Glenconner, Rovinia, Liapades, Corfu, Greece], er dau of Lt-Col Evelyn George Harcourt Powell, Gren Gds, and by her has issue:

3 +Tobias William [The Hon Tobias Tennant, Shaws, Newcastleton, Roxburghshire]; *b* 1 June 1941; *educ* Eton and New Coll Oxford (Pres OU Boat Club); *m* 3 Sept 1963 *Lady Emma Cavendish, er dau of 11th Duke of Devonshire (*qv*), and has issue:

(1) +Edward Tobias; *b* 30 March 1967

(1) *Isobel; *b* 28 June 1964; *m* 9 Aug 1997 *Piers Hill, 2nd s of Simon Hill by Mrs Glen Joel

(3) *Stella; *b* 17 Dec 1970; model

1 *Emma Christina [Emma Tennant, c/o A D Peters & Co, 10 Buckingham St, London WC2]; *b* 20 Oct 1937; *educ* St Paul's; author: *The Colour of Rain* (as Catherine Aydy 1963), *The Time of the Crack* (1973), *The Last of the Country House Murders* (1975), *Hotel de Dream* (1976), *Bananas Anthology* (ed 1977), *Saturday Night Reader* (ed 1978), *The Bad Sister* (1978), *Wild Nights* (1979), *Alice Fell* (1980), *Queen of Stones* (1982), *Woman Beware Woman* (1983), *Black Marina* (1985), *Adventures of Robina By Herself, ed Emma Tennant* (1986), *Cycle of the Sun: The House of Hospitalities* (1987), *A Wedding of Cousins* (988), *The Magic Drum* (1989), *Two Women of London* (1989), *Sisters and Strangers* (1990), *Faustine* (1991), *Tess* (1993), *Pemberley* (1993), *An Unequal Marriage* (1994), *Strangers: A Family Romance* (1998), children's books: *The Boggart* (with Mary Rayner 1979), *The Search for Treasure Island* (1981), *The Ghost Child* (1984), fndr ed lit jnl *Bananas* 1975–78, FRSL 1982; *m* 1st 18 Nov 1957 (*divorce* 1962) Sebastian Yorke, only s of the Henry Vincent Yorke (the novelist Henry Green; *see* HARDWICKE, E), and has issue; *m* 2nd 3 April 1963 (*divorce* 1968) Christopher John Penrice Booker, jnlst, only s of John Michael Booker; *m* 3rd 13 Dec 1968 (*divorce* 1973) Alexander Claud Cockburn, est s of Claud Cockburn by Patricia Evangeline Anne, formerly w of Arthur Cecil Byron and yr dau of Maj John Bernard Arbuthnot (*see* ARBUTHNOT, Bt, of Edinburgh), and has by Michael Dempsey (deceased):

(1) *Daisy Alice; *b* 1969

(2) *Rose Hippolyta; *b* 1973

2 *Catherine Elizabeth [The Hon Lady Palmer, Mill Hill Farm, Sherborne, Northleach, Glos]; *b* 10 Nov 1947; astrologer *Daily Telegraph Magazine*, author: *The Lost Zodiac*; *m* 23 June 1976 *Sir (Charles) Mark Palmer, 5th Bt, of Grinkle Park (*qv*), and has issue

GLENDEVON

Arms: Azure on a chevron or between three bezants as many bay-leaves paleways vert. **Crest:** A broken sphere surmounted by a rainbow proper issuant from two bay-leaves slipped vert on either side of the sphere. **Supporters:** Two female figures denoting Hope, their hair dressed sable and braided vert, garnished or, richly vested argent, garnished of vert and sustaining bendways in their exterior hands light lifeboat anchors with long shafts azure garnished with chains or, and over their exterior shoulders garlands of white lilies proper. **Motto:** *Spes mea non fracta* ('My hope is unshattered').

Creation: B. (UK) 16 July 1964.

THE 2ND BARON GLENDEVON, of Midhope, Co Linlithgow (Julian John Somerset Hope) [The Rt Hon The Lord Glendevon, Mount Lodge, Mount Row, St Peter Port, Guernsey, CI]; *b* 6 March 1950; *s* f 1995; *educ* Eton and Ch Ch Coll Oxford; opera producer

Lineage: The 2nd MARQUESS OF LINLITHGOW (*qv*) had a yr twin s:

JOHN ADRIAN HOPE, **1st Baron Glendevon**, of Midhope, Co Linlithgow (UK), so *cr* 16 July 1964, ERD (1988), PC (1959); *b* 7 April 1912; *educ* Eton and Ch Ch Oxford (BA 1936); Lt-Col Scots Gds (Res) WW II (despatches), MP (C) N Midlothian and Peeblesshire July 1945–Feb 1950 and Edinburgh Pentlands Feb 1950–64, U-Sec For Affairs 1954–56, Parly U-Sec Cwlth Rels 1956–57, Jt Parly U-Sec Scotland 1957–59, Min Works 1959–62, dir Standard Telephones and Cables and Colonial Mutual Life Assur, dir and dep chm Ciba-Geigy 1971–78, Roy Cwlth Soc 1963–66, Fell Eton Coll 1956–67, FRSA 1962, author *Viceroy At Bay* (1971); *m* 21 July 1948 *Elizabeth (Liz) Mary, only dau of the writer William Somerset Maugham (*see* 1970 edn MAUGHAM, V) and formerly w of Vincent Paravicini (*see also* MACCLESFIELD, E), and *d* 18 Jan 1995, leaving:

1 JULIAN JOHN SOMERSET HOPE, **2nd and present Baron Glendevon**

2 +JONATHAN CHARLES HOPE; *b* 23 April 1952; heir presumptive; *educ* Eton

GLENDYNE

Arms: Per chevron or and azure, in chief two eagles displayed of the second and in base an eagle rising of the first. **Crest:** Upon the battlements of a tower proper a wolf passant sable, gorged with a collar and with line reflexed over the back or. **Supporters:** On either side a wolf sable, gorged with a collar with line reflexed over the back or, and charged on the shoulder with a saltire couped argent. **Motto:** *Exitus acta probat* ('The ends justify the means'). **Creation:** B. (UK) 23 Jan 1922; Bt. (UK) 21 July 1914.

THE 3RD BARON GLENDYNE, of Sanquhar, Co Dumfries, and a **Baronet** (Sir Robert Nivison, Bt) [The Rt Hon The Lord Glendyne, Craigeassie, by Forfar, Angus DD8 3SE]; *b* 27 Oct 1926; *s* f 1967; *educ* Harrow; late Lt Gren Gds, ptnr R Nivison & Co, chm Glenfriars Hldgs 1977–93; *m* 25 April 1953 *Elizabeth, yr dau of Sir (Stephen) Cecil Armitage, CBE, JP, DL, of Hawksworth Manor, Notts, and has issue:

1 +JOHN; *b* 18 Aug 1960; *educ* Harrow

1 *Linda [Countess Hartig, Henbergasse 9, A1170 Vienna, Austria]; *b* 23 Oct 1954; *m* 25 Sept 1976 *Dr Nikolaus Theodor Adolf Antonius Alexander, Count Hartig, only s of Wolfgang Franz, Count Hartig, of Vienna, and has issue:

(1) *Thomas; *b* 1982

(1) *Alexandra Sarah Elizabeth Andrea; *b* 1 May 1980

2 *Sarah Jane Moira [The Hon Mrs Dreverman, 2A Water St, Wahronga, NSW 2076, Australia]; *b* 1 May 1957; *m* 21 April 1979 *Ian Dreverman, est s of Arthur H Dreverman, of Gordon, NSW, and has:

(1) *James; *b* 29 April 1984

(2) *Jeremy; *b* 1 May 1988

(3) *Stephen; *b* 3 May 1990

(1) *Melissa; *b* 1 May 1982

Lineage: ROBERT NIVISON, of Sanquhar, Dumfriesshire, *d* 16 Dec 1862, leaving:

JOHN NIVISON, of Sanquhar; *b* 5 Aug 1824; *m* 23 Jan 1846 Janet, dau of James Hair, of Sanquhar, and *d* 14 Nov 1898, leaving issue:

1 ROBERT, **1st Baron**

2 James; *b* 2 July 1853; *d* 2 June 1917

3 William; *b* 9 April 1856; *m* 17 Oct 1893 Susan Mary (*d* 17 June 1923), dau of Hendrik Johannes Albertyn, and *d* 11 Sept 1938, leaving issue

4 John; *b* 28 Feb 1858; *m* 8 Oct 1885 Robina Scott (*d* 8 March 1926), dau of William Wilson, and *d* 9 May 1934, leaving issue

5 Samuel; *b* 17 July 1860; *m* Mary Louisa (*m* 2nd 8 Oct 1930 Ambrose Wootton Cross, CE (*d* 1936), of Wield Manor, Hants), only dau of Francis Robinson, of Essex Lodge, Loughborough, and *d* 17 Feb 1925

1 Agnes; *d* 20 March 1919

2 Annie; *d* 25 April 1925

JOHN NIVISON's est s,

Sir Robert Nivison, 1st Bt and **1st Baron Glendyne**, of Sanquhar, Co Dumfries (both UK), so *cr* 21 July 1914 and 23 Jan 1922 respectively, JP (Middx); *b* 3 July 1849; *m* 11 May 1877 Jane (*d* 25 Sept 1918), dau of John Wightman, of Sanquhar, and *d* 14 June 1930, having had issue:

1 JOHN, **2nd Baron**

2 Alexander Crighton; *b* 21 June 1883; *d* unm 17 Aug 1958

3 Robert Butler; *b* 7 June 1895; 2nd Lt KRRC; *ka* 15 Sept 1916

1 Helen Ingram Wightman; *m* 3 July 1909 Rev Roderick Macleod, DD (*d* 1950), s of William Macleod, of Beauly, and had issue

2 Jessie Hair; *m* 8 Feb 1908 Alfred Norman Rickett (*d* 16 Jan 1963), s of William Richard Rickett, of Hampstead, and *d* 6 Nov 1965, leaving issue

3 Alice Jane

4 Florence; *m* 19 Feb 1916 George Roger Mackay (*d* 23 June 1930), of Mayfair, and Bourne End, Bucks, yst s of Hugh James Mackay, and *d* 26 May 1954

5 Mabel Gertrude; *m* 5 Feb 1916 (*divorce* 1936) Arthur Ryder Bastard Owen, s of Rev Arthur Welsh Owen, of S Kensington

The 1st BARON's est s,

JOHN NIVISON, **2nd Baron Glendyne**; *b* 14 March 1878; *educ* Harrow; *m* 1920 Ivy May, dau of James Rose, of Bournemouth, and *d* 28 Jan 1967, leaving:

1 ROBERT NIVISON, **3rd and present Baron Glendyne**

1 Moira Jane; *d* 1976

2 Pamela Roxane; *m* 27 July 1955, as his 1st w, *Maj-Gen David John St Maur Tabor, CB, MC, RHG, yst s of Harry Ernest Tabor, of Beech House, Redcoats Green, Herts, and *d* 1987, leaving issue:

(1) *Patrick John; *b* 26 April 1957

(2) *Andrew James; *b* 2 April 1959

3 *Gillian Wightman [The Hon Mrs Leuchars, 5 Chelsea Square, London SW3 6LF]; *m* 10 June 1953 *Maj-Gen Peter Raymond Leuchars, CBE, BGCStJ, Welsh Gds, er s of Raymond Leuchars, of White Lodge, Alfriston, Sussex, and has issue:

(1) *Christopher John Raymond; *b* 24 Dec 1956

GLENTORAN

Arms: Or, on a chevron vair three billets of the field, on a chief crenellé, gules a tower proper between two fleurs-de-lys of the field. **Crest:** A demi-lion rampant azure charged on the shoulder with a cross patonce surrounded by a civic crown or. **Supporters:** Two war horses argent, unguled or, caparisoned proper, the shabraque sable, broidered of the second. **Motto:** *Fide et constantia* ('By faith and constancy'). **Creations:** B. (UK) 8 July 1939, Bt. (UK) 7 Oct 1903.

THE 3RD BARON GLENTORAN, of Ballyalloly, Co Down, and a **Baronet** (Sir (Thomas) Robin Valerian Dixon, Bt, of Ballymenoch, Co Antrim, CBE (1992, MBE 1969), DL (Co Antrim)) [The Rt Hon The Lord Glentoran CBE DL, Drumadarragh House, Ballyclare, Co Antrim BT39 0TA]; *b* 21 April 1935; *s* f 1995; *educ* Eton; Gren Guards: 2nd Lt 1954, Capt 1958, Maj 1966, Olympic Bobsleigh Gold Medallist 1964, md Redland NI 1972–; *m* 1st 12 Jan 1959 (*divorce* 1979) Rona, only child of Capt George Cecil Colville, CBE, RN (*see* COLVILLE OF CULROSS, V), and has:

1 +DANIEL GEORGE; *b* 26 July 1959; *educ* Gordonstoun; *m* 1983 *Lesley Hope, dau of Julian Hope Brooke, and has issue:

(1) +Anthony Thomas; *b* 1987

(2) +Marcus Hope; *b* 1989

2 +Andrew Wynne Valerian; *b* 22 Jan 1961; *educ* Dean Close Sch Cheltenham; 2nd Lt Gren Gds 1980; *m* 1991 *Karen Elizabeth, only dau of Hugh Charles Straker, of Gaucin, Spain

3 +Patrick Anthony [The Hon Patrick Dixon, 26 Tildarg Rd, Ballyclare, Co Antrim]; *b* 3 April 1963; *educ* Gordonstoun; *m* 1988 *Catharine M, yr dau of Theo Willy, of S Pethereton, Somerset

The 3rd BARON *m* 2nd 29 March 1979 (*divorce* 1988) Alwyn Gillian, dau of Hubert Arbuckle Mason, of Grove Lodge, Donaghadeg, Co Down; *m* 3rd 1990 *Margaret Ann, dau of William Rainey

Lineage: THOMAS DIXON, of Bun-na-Mairge, Ballycastle, Co Antrim; *b* 1770; *m* 1804 Mary McNeill (*d* 1827 aged 52) and *d* 1849, leaving:

THOMAS DIXON, of Larne, Co Antrim; *b* 1805; merchant and shipowner; *m* 24 Dec 1834 Sarah (*d* 4 Sept 1873), dau of Archibald McCambridge, of Mullarts, Cushendall, Co Antrim, and *d* 31 July 1868, leaving an est surv s:

Sir Daniel Dixon, 1st Bt (UK), so *cr* 7 Oct 1903, PC (I 1902), JP (Co Antrim), DL (Belfast and Co Down), of Ballymenoch, Holywood, Co Down, Ravensdale, Co Louth, and Glenville, Cushendall, Co Antrim; *b* 28 March 1844; *educ* Roy Academical Inst Belfast; sole ptnr Thos Dixon & Sons, shipowners and timber merchants, and Managers' Irish Shipowners' Co; Belfast: Mayor 1892 and Ld Mayor 1893, 1901, 1902, 1903, 1905 and 1906, chm Belfast Harbour Commrs, ktd 1892, High Sheriff Co Down 1896), MP (U) Belfast N 1905–07; *m* 1st 21 Aug 1867 Eliza (*d* 1868), dau of James Agnew, and had issue:

1 **Sir Thomas James Dixon, 2nd Bt**, PC (NI 25 Aug 1930), DL (Co Antrim); *b* 29 May 1868; High Sheriff Co Antrim 1912 and Co Down 1913, Senator NI, HM's Lt and custos rotulorum Co Belfast 1924–50; *m* 7 Feb 1906 Edith Stewart, DBE (1921) (*d* 20 Jan 1964 aged 92), yst dau of Stewart Clark (*see* STEWART-CLARK, Bt), and *dsp* 10 May 1950

Sir Daniel *m* 2nd 16 Aug 1870 Annie (*d* 2 June 1918), dau of James Shaw, of Belfast, and *d* 10 March 1907, having by her had issue:

2 Daniel; *b* 22 July 1875; Maj 12th Bn Roy Irish Rifles; *d* unm 25 April 1936

3 Frank; *b* 16 April 1877; Capt and Hon Maj 5th Bn Roy Irish Rifles; *d* unm 13 Aug 1949

4 HERBERT, **1st Baron**

5 Percy; *b* 8 Feb 1882; 2nd Lt 7th Roy Fus; *d* unm 26 Aug 1902

1 Kate; *m* 14 June 1902 Capt Charles Owen Slacke, Roy Irish Rifles (*ka* 1 July 1916), of Wheatfield, Belfast, and *d* 23 Dec 1921, leaving issue

2 Edith Sarah, OBE (1918); DGStJ; *m* 5 Oct 1899 Lt-Col Frank Augustus Douglas Stevens, CBE, DL, Ch Constable Beds (*d* 16 Oct 1939), est s of Col F E Stevens, of Clairmont, Bedford, and *d* 23 Sept 1934, leaving issue

3 Louise; *m* 9 Oct 1907 Col Harold Charles Webster Wortham, CMG, DSO (*d* 14 Sept 1939), Northampton Regt, and *d* 20 April 1970, leaving issue

4 Evelyn Annie; *m* 16 April 1918 Capt Herbert Bernard Ward (*see* BANGOR, V) and *d* 26 Nov 1925, leaving issue

5 Beatrice; *d* unm 8 March 1936

Sir THOMAS's half-bro,

Sir Herbert Dixon, 3rd Bt and **1st Baron Glentoran** (UK), of Ballyalloly, Co Down, so *cr* 8 July 1939, OBE (1919), PC (NI 28 Nov 1923), JP (Co Kildare), DL (Cos Down and Kildare); *b* 23 Jan 1880; *educ* Rugby and RMC Sandhurst; Capt Reserve of Offrs 6th Inniskilling Dragoons, Boer War 1901–02 (Queen's medal with five clasps) and WW I with Remount Serv (despatches), High Sheriff Co Kildare 1916, MP (NI) Belfast E 1921–29 and Belfast Bloomfield May 1929–50 (Parly Sec Min Finance NI 1921–42, Min Ag 1941–43 and Ch Whip from 1921), MP (U, UK Parl) Belfast Pottinger 1918–22 and Belfast E 1922–39, Hon Col 8th AA Regt RA (Supplementary Reserve of Offrs) 1939; *m* 25 Nov 1905 Hon Emily Ina Florence Bingham (*d* 25 April 1957), 2nd dau of 5th Baron Clanmorris (*qv*), and *d* 20 July 1950, having had issue:

1 DANIEL STEWART THOMAS BINGHAM, **2nd Baron**

1 *Angela Irene Evelyn [The Hon Mrs Horn, Luckington Court, Chippenham, Wilts]; *b* 1907; *m* 1st 10 Sept 1929 Lt-Cdr Peter Ross, RN (*ka* Mediterranean Oct 1940; *see* DE ROS, B) and has issue; *m* 2nd 12 Nov 1943 Lt-Col Trevor Langdale Horn, MC, 16th/5th Lancers (*d* 26 Dec 1966), s of W A Horn, and has by him:

(1) *June Victoria Langdale; *b* 5 May 1946

2 Daphne Maude; *m* 27 Sept 1930 Col Charles Edward Beckwith, 5th Northumberland Fus (*d* 23 March 1970), only s of Rev Ernest George Beckwith, MA, of Paignton, Devon, and *d* 6 April 1942, leaving issue

3 Anne Lavinia; *m* 24 Oct 1934 (*divorce* 1957, took name Morris-Bingham by deed poll 1965) Maj Miles Picton Morris, Roy Tank Regt, er s of Lt-Col Thomas Herbert Picton Morris, DSO, MC, Rifle Bde, and *d* 16 Sept 1971, leaving issue

4 *Patricia Clare [The Hon Mrs Mackinnon, 7c Chisbury Close, Forest Pk, Bracknell, Berks]; *b* 1919; *m* 1 June 1940 Lt-Cdr Adam McLeod Mackinnon, RN, only s of Adam Scott Mackinnon, of New York, and has issue:

(1) *Michael Bingham; *b* 29 May 1941; *educ* Wellington

(2) *Ian Dixon; *b* 24 Nov 1944; *educ* Wellington

(1) *Diana Patricia [Mrs Richard Lynes, Penn House, Bannerleigh, Bristol]; *b* 6 July 1950; *m* 1978 *Richard A B Lynes

(2) *Teresa Clare; *b* 21 Feb 1955; *m* 1993 *Raymond Crossen, s of J Crossen

(3) *Zara Lavinia; *b* 8 June 1959; *m* 19– *William Brogden

The 1st BARON's only s,

DANIEL (DANNY) STEWART THOMAS BINGHAM DIXON, **2nd Baron Glentoran**, KBE (1973), PC (NI 1953); *b* 19 Jan 1912; *educ* Eton and RMC Sandhurst; Gren Gds as ADC to GOC NI 1935–38, WW II (BEF N France 1939–40, liaison with US Armed Forces Washington DC, despatches Monte Cassino) and Palestine, ret as Lt-Col 1947, Ld Lt Co Down 1975, Hon Col 6th Bn (TA) Roy Ulster Rifles 1956–81, Ld Lt Belfast 1976–85 (HM's Lt Co Borough City of Belfast 1950–76), MP (NI) Belfast Bloomfield 1950–61: Parly Sec Min Commerce 1952–53, Min Commerce 1953–61, Min in NI Senate (also Leader) 1961–73, Speaker 1964–73, CStJ 1952; *m* 20 July 1933 Lady Diana Mary Wellesley (*d* 2 Jan 1984), er dau of 3rd Earl Cowley (*qv*), and *d* 22 July 1995, leaving:

1 (THOMAS) ROBIN VALERIAN DIXON, **3rd and present Baron Glentoran**

2 +Peter Herbert [The Hon Peter Dixon, The Old Rectory, Yattendon, Berks]; *b* 15 May 1948; *educ* Eton and Grenoble U; chartered accountant; *m* 2 Oct 1975 *Jane Blanche, dau of Eric Sturdee Cutler, of Grayshott Hall Farm, Grayshott, Hants, and has issue:

(1) *Louise Vyvyan Mary; *b* 16 March 1977

(2) *Rose Erika Clare; *b* 3 Feb 1980

1 *Clare Rosalind Dixon [The Hon Mrs Clare Agnew, 29 Felden St, London SW6 5AE]; *b* 15 Nov 1937; *m* 29 March 1965 (*divorce* 1980), as his 2nd w, Rudolph Ion Joseph FitzGerald Agnew, s of Rudolph John Agnew (*see* CAMPBELL, Bt, *cr* 1815), and has:

(1) *James Ion Daniel; *b* 23 April 1968; *m* 1992 *Sarah K, only dau of Peter Newman, of Frensham Surrey

(1) *Charlotte Diana Pamela Geraldine; *b* 17 Oct 1970

GLYN

Arms: Arg. an eagle displayed with two heads sa. guttée d'or, a crescent arg. for difference. **Crest:** An eagle's head erased sa. guttée d'or, holding in the beak an escallop arg. **Motto:** *Fidei tenax* ('Firm to my trust'). **Creations:** Bt. (GB) (Ewell) 25 Sept 1759 and (GB) (Gaunts) 22 Nov 1800.

SIR RICHARD LINDSAY GLYN, 10TH BT, of Ewell, Surrey, and **6th Bt**, of Gaunts, Dorset [Sir Richard Glyn Bt, Ashton Farmhouse, Stanbridge, Dorset BH21 4JD]; *b* 3 Aug 1943; *s* f 1980; *educ* Eton; late 2nd Lt 1st Bn Roy Hampshire Regt, photographer and antique dealer; *m* 26 Feb 1970 (*divorce* 1979) Caroline Anne, dau of Royal Frank Williams, of Pasadena, Calif., and has:

1 +RICHARD RUFUS FRANCIS; *b* 8 Jan 1971

1 *Eliza Jane Rose; *b* 1975

Lineage: WILLIAM GLYN, of Glyn Llyvon, Llandwrog, Caernarvs, living 1567; *m* Katherine, dau of Thomas Mostyn (*see* MOSTYN, B), and had (with an er s Thomas, ancestor of the GLYNNEs of Hawarden Castle, Flintshire):

Rev RICHARD GLYN; MA, Rector Llanvaethle and Chapelry of Llanvwrogin, Anglesey, 1587; *d* 1617, leaving, with an er s William:

THOMAS GLYN, of London; had:

Rev CHRISTOPHER GLYN; Vicar Burford; *b* 1596; *m* Margerie Needham and *d* 1663, leaving, with two yr sons and two daus:

Rev ROBERT GLYN; Rector Little Rissington, Glos; *b* 1623; *m* Mary Davies, of Shellingford, Oxon, and *d* 1702, leaving, with two er sons (including Edward, Rector Broughton Poggs, Oxon, had three sons and four daus) and a yst one:

ROBERT GLYN, of London; *b* 1673; *m* Ann Maynard, n of Sir William Lewen, of Ewell, and *d* 1746, leaving, with an er s (*d* young):

Sir Richard Glyn, 1st Bt (GB), so *cr* 25 Sept 1759; DCL Oxon, LLD, MP London 1758–68 and Coventry 1768–73, Sheriff London 1752, Ld Mayor 1758, banker, Pres Bridewell and Bethlem Hosps; *bapt* 13 June 1711; *m* 1st 8 June 1736 Susannah (*d* 4 Feb 1751), only child and heiress of George Lewen, of Ewell, and had, with two other sons (*d* unm):

1 **Sir George Glyn, 2nd Bt**; MA Oxon, barrister; *b* 1739; *m* 1st Jane (*d* 4 Sept 1790), yst dau of Rev Watkin Lewes, of Tredeval, Pembs, and had two sons (*d* unm); *m* 2nd 11 June 1796 Catherine (*d* 15 Dec 1844 aged 74), dau and coheir of Rev Gervas Powell, of Llanharen, Glam, and *d* 4 Sept 1814, leaving by her:

(1) **Sir Lewen Powell Glyn, 3rd Bt**; *b* 14 Aug 1801; *d* unm 28 July 1840

(2) **Rev Sir George Lewen Glyn, 4th Bt**; *b* 10 Sept 1804; *m* 1st 8 Sept 1838 Emily Jane (*d* 26 July 1854), er dau of Josiah Birch, of Lancs and St Petersburg, and *d* 7 Nov 1885, having had, with other issue:

1a **Sir George Turbervill Glyn, 5th Bt**; *b* 22 April 1841; *d* unm 19 May 1891

(2) (cont.) The **Rev Sir George** *m* 2nd 5 May 1859 his cousin Henrietta Amelia, est dau of Richard Carr Glyn (*see* below), and by her had:

2a **Sir Gervas Powell Glyn, 6th Bt**; FRGS, MA Oxfon; *b* 3 Oct 1862; *m* 19 April 1898 Dorothy (*d* 15 May 1947), dau of Edmund Charles Hislop, of Clapham Park, and *d* 17 July 1921

3a William Lewen; Lt 1st Bn Dorsetshire Regt; *b* 11 Dec 1867; *d* 13 Aug 1888

4a **Sir Arthur Robert Glyn, 7th Bt**, JP; *b* 5 Aug 1870; *educ* Pembroke Coll Cambridge (BA); *d* unm 4 Jan 1942

1a Anna Lydia; *d* unm 12 Dec 1895

2a Margaret Henrietta; *d* unm 3 June 1946

(1) Anna Margaret; *m* 1830 Joseph Hamilton MD, and *d* 29 March 1884

Sir Richard *m* 2nd 23 March 1754 Elizabeth (*d* 14 April 1814), dau and coheir of Robert Carr, of Hampton, Middx, and *d* 1 Jan 1773, having by her had issue:

2 **Sir Richard Carr Glyn, 1st Bt** (GB), so *cr* 22 Nov 1800, of London (Ld Mayor 1798); *b* 2 Feb 1755; banker, MP St Ives, 2nd Pres Bridewell and Bethlem Hosps; *m* 2 July 1785 Mary (*d* 2 Aug 1832), dau of John Plumptre, of Fredville, MP Nottingham, and *d* 27 April 1838, leaving:

(1) **Sir Richard Plumptre Glyn, 2nd Bt**; Gentleman Privy Chamber; *b* 13 June 1787; *d* unm 20 Dec 1863

(2) Robert Thomas John; *b* 5 Sept 1788; *m* 13 June 1829 Frederica Elizabeth, 3rd dau of Henry Harford, of Down Place, Berks, and *d* 27 March 1836, having had, with other issue:

1a RICHARD GEORGE (Sir), **3rd Bt**

1a Mary Frederica; *m* 22 Nov 1855 Thomas Leinster Goodlake and *d* May 1913. He *dsp* 3 June 1893

(3) Thomas Christopher; barrister; *b* 5 Oct 1789; *m* 24 March 1817 Grace Julia (*m* 2nd 1836 Henry Barne Sawbridge, of E Haddon Hall, Northants (*dsp* 1851); *d* 1872), dau of Thomas Charles Bigge, of Benton House, Northumberland (*see* 1970 edn SELBY-BIGGE, Bt), and *d* 19 Aug 1827, having had, with two other sons:

1a Charles Thomas (Rev); Rector Wycliffe, Yorks; *b* 1820; *m* 1847 Ann Hurst (*d* 15 Feb 1912) and *d* 17 June 1882, leaving, with other issue:

1b Charles Robert; *b* 1851; *m* 18 April 1873 Maria (*d* 18 March 1926), dau of Sir Theophilus John St George, 3rd Bt (*qv*), and *d* 29 April 1907, having had, with other issue:

1c Charles; *b* 1878; *m* 23 April 1912 Gwendolen (*d* 1982), dau of Charles T Mills, of Kenilworth, Cape Town, and *d* 1943, leaving:

1d +Ronald St George [Ronald Glyn Esq, 10 St Andrews Street, Melrose, Johannesburg, S Africa]; *b* 4 March 1913; *m* 1954 *Marion Mevagh, dau of Donald James Laing, of Johannesburg, and has issue:

1e +Donald Charles St George; *b* 1954

2e +Patrick St George; *b* 1956

1e *Rowena May; *b* 1960

2e *Virginia Aitchinson; *b* 1964

2d John St George; MB, ChB Cape Town U 1949, DMSA Edin 1961, Sr MO Fedn Rhodesia and Nyasaland; *b* 21 June 1916; *m* 1 Nov 1958 *Norma Baillie [Mrs John Glyn, Ballyrock, 81 Highway, Fish Hoek, Cape Town, S Africa], dau of Hugh Orlando Bean, of Zambia, and *d* 1985, leaving issue:

1e *Patricia Jane St George; *b* 10 Dec 1959; *educ* Capetown U (BA)

2e *Shirley Gwendoline St George; *b* 16 April 1962; *educ* Capetown U (BSc, LLB)

1d Patricia May; *b* 1917; *m* 1937 (*divorce*) John McDonald Hodgson, of Newcastle, and had issue

2d *Kathleen Philippa [Mrs Gordon Booth, 10 Roosevelt Road, Gillitts 3603, Natal, S Africa]; *b* 1920; *m* 1st Edward Charles Sawyer (*d* June 1957) and has issue; *m* 2nd 1962 *Gordon George Booth and by her 1st husb has:

1e *Charles Garth; *b* 1946

2e *Bruce Gavin; *b* 1948

1e *Amanda May; *b* 1953

2c Douglas John; *b* 1883; *m* 7 Aug 1926 Dorothy Margaret (*d* 1962), dau of Alexander Gordon, of Wynberg, and *d* 26 Nov 1952, leaving issue:

1d +William George Rutherford [William Glyn Esq, PO Box 2310, Somerset W 7130, CP, S Africa]; *b* 16 May 1927; *m* 9 Sept 1950 Lillamary (*d* 1988), dau of Isaac Willem Kretzen, of Beaufort West, CP, and has issue:

1e +Richard William Douglas; *b* 28 June 1951; *educ* Natal U (BCom, LLB) and Trin Hall Cambridge (LLB); *m* 1983 *Mary Elizabeth, dau of Robert Leonard Stanley

1e *Brenda Margaret; *b* 29 Nov 1954; *educ* Natal U (BSc); CA (SA)

3c Wilfrid Henry; *b* 1885; *m* 1933 Petronella (*d* 1975) dau of J P Strydom, and *d* 1967, leaving issue:

1d +Michael Robert Henry [Michael Glyn Esq, The 49 Steps, Gascoyne Street Observatory, Johannesburg, S Africa]; *b* 1933; *m* 1960 *Suzanne Ursula, dau of Thomas Patrick Lyons, and has issue:

1e +Alister Michael; *b* 15 June 1965

2e +Jeremy Charles; *b* 29 June 1969

1e *Caroline Frances; *b* 13 Aug 1963

1c Maria Gertrude Ann; *d* unm 1 May 1951

2c Florence Grace; *d* unm 26 Oct 1948

3c Kathleen Dorothy; *d* unm 22 Feb 1959

2b Thomas Richard; Incorporated Law Society's Prizeman 1878; *b* 11 July 1856; *m* 18 April 1901 Florence Ann (*d* 14 Oct 1928), 3rd dau of John Brownless, of Whorlton Grange, Co Durham, and *d* 12 Aug 1937, leaving:

1c *Cicely May; *b* 3 March 1906; *m* 9 Sept 1931 (*divorce* 1947) John William Murray, MD, and has issue:

1d *Caroline Glyn; *b* 1942

3b William Edward; *b* 1859; *m* 30 April 1900 Mary Rotch (*d* 22 March 1936), widow of Walter Langdon Kane and dau of Capt Charles Hunter, USN, of Newport, RI, and *dsp* 23 March 1939

4b Arthur Plumptre (Rev); Rector E Clandon Surrey 1900–46; *b* 1864; *educ* Marlborough and Ch Ch Oxford (BA 1888, MA 1894); *m* 1897 Alice Anne (*d* 20 April 1945), dau of Rev James Henry Coghlan, and *dsp* 7 March 1962

1b Julia Ann; *m* 11 May 1870 Rev Sir Hubert James Medlycott, 6th Bt (*qv*), and *d* 16 Nov leaving issue

(4) GEORGE CARR GLYN, *cr* BARON WOLVERTON (*qv*)

(5) Carr John (Rev); MA, Rector Witchampton and Little Hinton, Dorset; *b* 25 June 1799; *m* 1st 21 July 1831 Augusta (*d* 30 Jan 1837), dau of John Granville; *m* 2nd 25 April 1839 Anna (*dsp* 1887), 3rd dau of Capt W H Cleather, 1st Ceylon Regt, and *d* 1897, having by his 1st w had:

1a Carr Stuart, JP and CA, Capt 1st Roy Dragoons; *b* 25 Nov 1833; *educ* Univ Coll Oxford (BA); *m* 20 Oct 1864 Selina Catherine (*d* 2 Feb 1931), dau of R-Adml Sir Francis Augustus Collier, CB, KCH, and *d* 18 Dec 1923, having had, with another dau:

1b Augusta Julia Carr, OBE (1920); *d* unm 9 Jan 1944

2b Katherine Carr; *m* 18 Dec 1888 Rev John Henry Lonsdale, Rector Fontmell Magna, Dorset, and *d* Dec 1945, leaving issue. He *d* 16 Feb 1903

3b Frances Carr; *m* 19 April 1898 Mark John Paget and *d* 5 June 1941, leaving issue (*see* ANGLESEY, M)

2a John Plumptre Carr (Sir), KCB, JP Dorset; Lt-Gen, Col Cmdt Rifle Bde (Crimean medal and clasp, Ashanti Medal and clasp); *b* 11 Jan 1837; *m* 11 Sept 1866 Ellen (*d* 20 April 1928), est dau of James Robert Dalton Dewar, and *d* 28 March 1912, having had, with a s (*d* unm):

1b Nellie Georgiana Carr; *m* 11 June 1890 Sir George Henry Sutherland and *d* 18 April 1891, leaving issue. He *d* 11 May 1937

2b Ada Carr; *m* 24 Oct 1889 Lt-Col Dudley Granville Ryder (*see* HARROWBY, E) and *d* 1950

(1) Mary Elizabeth; *m* 14 Aug 1811 Edward Greathed and *d* 17 Jan 1864. He *d* Dec 1840

3 Thomas; Col Gren Gds; *b* 6 April 1756; *m* 6 Sept 1788 Henrietta Elizabeth Sackville (*d* 13 Jan 1845), dau and heiress of Ven Thomas Hollingberry, Archdeacon Chichester, and *d* 24 Aug 1813, having had, with other issue:

(1) Thomas Clayton (Rev), of Durrington House, Essex; *b* Nov 1789; *m* 20 July 1820, Jemima Julia (*d* 21 March 1847), dau of William Hammond, of St Albans Court, Kent, and *d* 17 June 1866, having had, with other issue:

1a Clayton William Feake, of Durrington House, Harlow, JP Essex; MA, barrister; *b* 13 Sept 1821; *m* 25 July 1855, Mary Jane (*d* 20 Nov 1888), dau of Thomas Perry, of Moor Hall, Essex, and *d* 30 Dec 1887, leaving:

1b Clayton Louis, of Durrington, JP Essex; MA Oxford, barrister; *b* 13 July 1857; *m* 27 April 1892 Elinor (*d* 23 Sept 1943), yr dau of Douglas Sutherland, of Toronto, and *d* 10 Nov 1915, leaving:

1c Margot Elinor, OBE (1920); *b* 7 June 1893; *m* 7 April 1921 Sir Edward Rae Davson, 1st Bt (*qv*), and *d* 9 Sept 1966, leaving issue

2c Juliette Evangeline, DBE (1937); DStJ, Govr BBC 1952–56, Chm Cwmbran New Town Development Corporation 1955–60, formerly Assist Sect Offr WAAF, authoress; *b* 17 Dec 1898; *m* 24 Feb 1921 Sir Rhys Rhys Williams, 1st Bt (*qv*), and *d* 18 Sept 1964, leaving issue

2b Egerton John, Capt Essex Regt; *b* 18 June 1863; *m* 1st 22 Oct 1889 Constance Helena (*d* 10 Sept 1927), dau of John Joliffe Tufnell, of Langley's Great Waltham; *m* 2nd 15 June 1929 Margaret (*d* 2 Dec 1940), 4th dau of Seth Taylor, and *d* 2 Feb 1936, having by his 1st w had:

1c John Murray Egerton; *b* 3 Nov 1894; *m* 9 March 1923 Iris Margaret, 2nd dau of John P Lawton, of San Gabriel, Los Angeles, and *d* 10 Sept 1936, leaving issue:

1d +John Murray Egerton; *b* 29 March 1926

1d *Margaret Helena; *b* 21 Aug 1931

1b Julia Mary; *m* 2 June 1891 William Griffith Richards, of S Kensington, and *d* 22 Sept 1923, leaving issue. He *d* 14 Oct 1933

2b Evelyn Margaret; *m* 7 March 1891 Col Henry Marsh Pratt, CB, IA, and *d* 20 July 1932, having had issue. He *d* 16 April 1919

3b Emily Georgiana; *d* 12 Sept 1924

2a Henry Thomas (Rev); Canon Salisbury, Rector Fontmell Magna, Dorset, RD, BA Oxon; *b* 21 April 1823; *m* 5 Oct 1848, Mary Frederica (*d* 3 Nov 1924), dau of Col James Alfred Schreiber, and *d* 22 Jan 1900, leaving, with other issue:

1b Charles Clayton; *b* 5 April 1850; *m* 22 April 1882 Jessie Hero Stephanie, dau of J D Deneulain, of Marseilles, and *d* 1940

2b Richard Montague; *b* 11 Nov 1854; *m* 1 Oct 1898 Hilda (*d* 21 Aug 1964 aged 97), dau of Alfred Wilson, JP, and *d* 13 Nov 1940, having had:

1c Henry Montague; *b* 14 April 1906; *d* unm 31 March 1926

1c Sylvia; *m* 1st 5 Feb 1921 (*divorce* 1934) Allan Hyde Johnson, RFA, and had issue; *m* 2nd 29 July 1934 John Frederick Dyson; *m* 3rd 26 Aug 1944 George Stuart Robertson (*d* 27 Jan 1951)

2c Veronica; *m* 17 Jan 1928 Rev Arthur William Watson Wallace, Hon CF, Rector Lutterworth, Leics, and had issue. He *d* 24 July 1939

3c Christobel; *m* 1 Nov 1938 James Binnie Morrison, BComm, CA, of Quillot Cottage, Meadway, Esher, Surrey, s of John Morrison, MB, of Bannockburn, Stirling, and had issue

3b Frederick Ware (Rev), JP; Rector Brancepeth, Co Durham, Priv Chaplain to Viscount Boyne, Hon Canon Durham; *b* 29 April 1857; *m* 31 Aug 1886 Eleanor Bayntun (*d* 3 Nov 1946), dau of John Bayntun Starky, of Spye Park, Wilts, and *d* 30 Oct 1918, leaving issue:

1c Edith Frances; M Litt, MA; *d* unm 24 Sept 1967

2c Eleanor Valentine; *b* 1 Feb 1896; *educ* Durham U (MA); *m* 23 Dec 1919 Maj John Lachian Forbes, DSO, MC, RA, s of Maj — Forbes, HEIC, 2nd Bengal Gren, of Culverhayes, Shillingstone, Dorset, and had issue. He *d* 27 April 1962

3c Angela Bayntun; *m* 21 July 1923 Lt-Col Rupert Lyne Hancock Nunn, RA, son of John Hancock Nunn, of Lealands, Hellingly, Sussex. He *d* 30 July 1962

3a Julius Richard (Sir), KCB; Gen, Col Rifle Bde, Kaffir War, Crimea and Indian Mutiny; *b* 15 April 1824; *m* 1st 9 May 1857 Adelaide (*d* 18 Feb 1879), dau of William Lea, of Areley House, Worcs; *m* 2nd 2 Oct 1890 Julia (*d* 12 Aug 1910), widow of Col Hamilton Maxwell, IA, and dau of Gen St George Showers, CB, and *d* 12 Aug 1910, having by his 1st w had:

1b Ada (Hilda); *d* unm 15 Dec 1945

2b Marion; *m* 30 July 1889 Col Wentworth Odiarne Cavenagh, JP, Bedfordshire Regt, and *d* 24 Feb 1950, leaving issue. He *d* 20 Feb 1935

3b Rachel; *m* 2 Sept 1896 Hugh Bertram Cox, CB, barrister (*d* 31 Dec 1930)

1c Henrietta Georgiana; *m* 9 Nov 1854 Gilbert John Ansley, of Green End, Hunts, and had issue. He *d* 1875

(2) Richard Carr; HEICS; *b* 5 Feb 1794; *m* 5 May 1828 Jane Florentia (*d* 23 July 1878), dau of Henry Creighton, and *d* 4 Dec 1875, leaving, with other issue:

1a Richard Thomas, CB, CMG; Lt-Gen, Col 24th Regt; *b* 23 Dec 1831; *m* 18 Nov 1856 Anne Penelope (*d* 28 March 1927), dau of Col — Clements, Canadian Rifles, and *d* 21 Nov 1900, leaving surv issue:

1b Annie Jane; *m* 7 Jan 1880 Lt-Col William Maxwell Brander, JP, 24th Regt, of Somerford Grange, Christchurch, Hants, and West Close, Wick, Bournemouth, and *d* 14 March 1943, leaving issue. He *d* 18 Sept 1927

2b Elizabeth Mary; *m* 18 June 1892 Charles Henry de Winton, of Maesderwen, Breconshire, and *d* 10 Feb 1956, leaving issue. He *d* 16 Nov 1936

3b Alice Farquhar; *d* unm 15 Dec 1935

1a Henrietta Amelia; *m* 5 May 1859 her cousin **Rev Sir George Lewen Glyn, 4th Bt**, and *d* 29 Nov 1903, leaving issue (*see* above)

The 2nd Bt (of Gaunts)'s n,

Sir Richard George Glyn, 3rd Bt, JP, DL; CC Dorset, High Sheriff 1869, Capt 1st Roy Dragoons Crimean War; *b* 22 Nov 1831; *m* 30 April 1868 Frances Geraldine (*d* 9 March 1924), yst dau of Maj H T G FitzGerald, of Maperton House, Somerset, and *d* 9 Aug 1918, leaving (with a dau Geraldine Mary, *m* 30 Nov 1898 Ralph Paget (*see* ANGLESEY, M, *d* 24 Dec 1960):

Sir Richard FitzGerald Glyn, 4th Bt, of Gaunts, as which *s* f 1918, and **8th Bt**, of Ewell, as which *s* cousin (*see* above) 1942, DSO (1916), JP, DL; High Sheriff Dorset 1927, Capt 1st Roy Dragoons, Boer War 1899–1902 (despatches, two medals with six clasps), WW I (wounded, despatches twice, Legn Hon); *b* 13 May 1875; *m* 12 Dec 1906 Edith Hilda (*d* 10 June 1957), er dau of Douglas George Hamilton Gordon (*see* ABERDEEN AND TEMAIR, M), and *d* 23 March 1960, having had:

1 **Sir Richard Hamilton Glyn, 5th Bt**, of Gaunts, and **9th Bt**, of Ewell, OBE (1955), TD (1945), JP (Dorset 1952), DL (1960); *b* 12 Oct 1907; *educ* Worcester Coll Oxford (BA1929); joined Dorset Yeo 1927, T/Maj 1940, T/Lt-Col 1944, WW II, cmdg QO Dorset Yeo 1944–45 and 1953–56, Col Dep Cdr 128 Inf Bde (TA) 1956–68, ADC (TA) to HM THE QUEEN 1958, Hon Col QOD and WJY 1961, barrister Lincoln's Inn 1935, Dep Chm Dorset QS 1952–57, MP (C) N Dorset 1957–70, PPS to Pres BOT 1958, Chm Cruft's 1963, Commr Cwlth War Graves 1965, memb Speaker's Conference Electoral Law 1966; *m* 2 Nov 1939 Lyndsay Mary (*d* 22 Oct 1971), only dau of Horace Baker; *m* 2nd 1970 Barbara (*d* 15 June 1998) dau of William Charles Ritchie Jardine and formerly w of Gp Capt Francis Henwood, and *d* 1980, leaving by his 1st w:

(1) Sir RICHARD LINDSAY GLYN, **6th and 10th (and present) Bt**

(2) +Jeremy George Trion [Jeremy Glyn Esq, 8 Guion Rd, London SW6]; *b* 5 March 1946; *educ* Eton

(1) *Amanda Jane [Mrs John Holroyd, Providence Cottage, Chute Cadley, Hants SP11 9EB]; *b* 24 Nov 1940; *m* 18 Jan 1969 *Lt-Col (Charles) John Holroyd (*see* CAIRNS, E), and has issue

2 Gerald Hugh; Capt QO Dorset Yeo and Force 133 WW II; *b* 20 Jan 1909; *educ* Radley; *m* 26 Oct 1954 *Philomena [Mrs Gerald Glyn, West Dene House, Beech, Alton, Hants], dau of Denis O'Leary, of Macroom, Co Cork, and *d* 1981, leaving:

(1) +Charles Gerald Hamilton; *b* 22 June 1959

(1) *Leslie Maye Patricia [Miss Leslie Glyn, 83 Lyric Rd, London SW13]; *b* 3 Oct 1955

3 Peter John; Lt Queen's Bays WW II; *b* 7 July 1919; *ka* Libya 25 Jan 1942

1 *Joanna May [Mrs James Browne, The Dormers, Tarrant Keynston, Blandford, Dorset]; *b* 14 Dec 1909; *m* 1st 20 May 1939 Maj John Willmore Hume James, RHA (*ka* Burma 4 May 1944), s of Lt-Col Edmund Henry Salt James, CIE, CBE, and has issue:

(1) *Charles John [Charles James Esq, Mask Cottage, E Garston, Berks RG17 7EU]; *b* 18 Aug 1940; *educ* Wellington and Clare Coll Cambridge (MA); *m* 10 Dec 1967 *(Rose) Virginia, yr dau of Maj John Dennistoun, and has issue:

1a *Edward Luke Daniel John; *b* 15 Nov 1969

2a *Andrew William; *b* 22 Feb 1974

1 (cont.) Mrs John James *m* 2nd 31 Dec 1946 *Lt-Col James Bernard Browne, late 16th/5th Lancers, s of Lt-Col Percival John Browne, CB, and by him has:

(2) *Peter James; *b* 30 March 1951; *educ* Eton and Wadham Coll Oxford

2 *Philippa Ann [Mrs Andrew Swan, The River House, Tarrant Rushton, Dorset]; MB, ChB Edin 1946; *b* 10 April 1915; *m* 24 Oct 1949 *Andrew Alexander Buchanan Swan, MB, ChB, BSc, MRCPE, s of John Swan, of Edinburgh, and has issue:

(1) *Jeremy Michael; *b* 19 Jan 1952; *educ* Bryanston

(1) *Jocelyn Ann; *b* 7 June 1956

GOFF OF CHIEVELEY

Creation: B. (LP, UK) 1986.

THE BARON GOFF OF CHIEVELEY, of Chieveley, Co Berks (Sir Robert Lionel Archibald Goff, PC (1982)) [The Rt HonThe Lord Goff of Chieveley PC, House of Lords, London SW1A 0PW]; *b* 12 Nov 1926; *educ* Eton and New Coll Oxford (MA 1953, DCL 1972); Scots Guards 1945–48; Fell and Tutor Lincoln Coll Oxford 1951–55; barrister Inner Temple 1951, QC 1967, Recorder 1974–75, Bencher 1975, ktd 1975, High Court Judge Queen's Bench 1975–82, Judge in charge Commercial List and Chm Commercial Court Ctee 1979–81, Ld Justice Appeal 1982–85, Ld Appeal in Ordinary 1986–98, Snr Law Lord 1996–; Chm: Cncl Legal Educn 1976–82 (V-Chm 1972–76, Chm Bd Studies 1970–76), Common Profnl Exam Bd 1976–78, Br Inst of Internat and Comparative Law 1986, Sub Ctee E (Law and Insts) Ho Lds Select Ctee EC 1986–88, Court London U 1986–91; Hon Prof Legal Ethics Birmingham 1980–81; Pres Chartered Inst Arbitrators 1986–91; Memb: Gen Cncl Bar 1971–74, Senate Inns of Court and Bar 1975–82 (Chm Law Reform and Procedure Ctee 1974–76); High Steward Oxford U 1990–; Hon Fell: Lincoln Coll Oxford 1985, New Coll Oxford 1986; FBA 1987, Hon DLitt City 1977, Reading 1990, Hon LLD Buckingham 1990, London 1990, Bristol 1996; author: *The Law of Restitution* (with Prof Gareth Jones, 1966); *m* 1953 *Sarah, er dau of Capt Gerald Roger Cousins, DSC, RN, of Child Okeford, Dorset, and has had, with another s (*d* young):

1 *(Robert) Thomas Alexander; *b* 1966 ; *m* 30 Nov 1996 *Catherine, only dau of Peter Cregeen, of Greatham, Hants, and Mrs Jennifer Cregeen, of Frensham, Surrey

1 *Katharine Isobel; *b* 1959

2 *Juliet Mary Constance; *b* 1961; *m* 1990 *Sean D Jackson, only s of David Jackson, of Armscote House, Stratford-upon-Avon, Warwicks, and has issue:

(1) *William David; *b* 1995

(1) *Anna Katharine, *b* 1992

Lineage: Lt-Col LIONEL TREVOR GOFF, RA, of Queen's House, Monk Sherborne, Hants; *m* Isobel Jane Denroche-Smith and had:

ROBERT LIONEL ARCHIBALD, *cr* a **Baron**

GOOCH of Benacre

Arms: Per pale arg. and sa. a chevron between three talbots statant, all counterchanged; on a chief gu. three leopard's faces or. **Crest:** A talbot statant per pale arg. and sa. **Motto:** *Fide et virtute* ('By fidelity and merit'). **Creation:** Bt. (GB) 4 Nov 1746.

SIR (RICHARD) JOHN SHERLOCK GOOCH, 12TH BT, of Benacre Hall, Suffolk , JP (Suffolk 1970) [Sir John Gooch Bt JP, Benacre Hall, Beccles, Suffolk NR34 7LJ]; *b* 22 March 1930; *s* f 1978; *educ* Eton; chm E Suffolk CC 1957–67, Capt Life Gds (ret 1963)

Lineage: PETER GOOCH, of St Margaret Ilketshall, E Suffolk (n (?) of Thomas Gooch, of Gt Peringland), owned land Suffolk, including at Rumborough; *bur* 7 Nov 1558, leaving, with other issue:

THOMAS GOOCH, of St Margaret Ilketshall; *bur* Sept 1570, leaving, with other issue:

ROBERT GOOCH; inherited land in Bungay, Ilketshall and Mettingham (all Suffolk) from his f; had, with nine yr sons and five daus:

WILLIAM GOOCH, of Mettingham, JP; *b* 1571; *m* Martha, dau of Christopher Layer, of Norwich, and had, with two yr sons (Thomas; Robert) and a dau (Barbara, *m* Sir Henry Bacon, 2nd Bt, *qv*):

WILLIAM GOOCH, JP; living Mettingham 1664; *m* Elizabeth, dau and heir of Richard Baspole, of Bungay St Mary, by Margaret, dau of — Flower, of Wissett, Suffolk, and widow of Francis Gooch, of St Margaret, Ilketshall, and *d* 1685, leaving, with two daus (Martha, *m* Richard Vinor, *d* 1700; Barbara, *m* Robert Rogerson):

1 William; *d* 1655

2 Richard, of Mettingham; *d* 1682, leaving issue

3 Thomas, Alderman Yarmouth; *m* Frances (*d* 25 July 1696), dau and heir of Thomas Lone, of Worlingham, Norfolk, and *d* 1688, having had:

(1) **Sir William Gooch, 1st Bt** (GB), so *cr* 4 Nov 1746, with remainder in default of male issue to his bro and the latter's issue male; *b* 12 Oct 1681; fought War of Spanish Succession, Lt-Govr Virginia 1727, Col of an American Regt 1740 (wounded Siege Cartagena), Brig-Gen; *m* Rebecca (*d* April 1775), dau of William Stanton, of Hampton, Middx, and *dsp* 1751

(2) **Rt Rev Sir Thomas Gooch, 2nd Bt**; DD, Pres 1716 and V-Chllr 1717 Caius Coll Camb, Bp: Bristol 1737, Norwich 1738 and Ely 1747; *m* 1st Mary, dau of William Sherlock, DD, Dean St Paul's Cathedral, and had:

1a THOMAS (Sir), **3rd Bt**

(2) (cont.) **Sir Thomas** *m* 2nd Hannah (*d* March 1746), dau of Sir John Miller, 2nd Bt, of Chichester (*qv*), and by her had:

2a John; DD, Rector Ditton-on-Wellingham, Cambs, Preb Ely; *b* Aug 1729; *m* 24 May 1751 Mary (*d* 1904), only child and heir of George Sayer, of Serle St, London, and *d* 1804, having had:

1b Mary; *m* 8 Jan 1793 Ven Houstoune Radcliffe, Archdeacon Canterbury, Vicar Gillingham, Kent

2b Rachel; *m* 19 Aug 1778 Richard Beadon, DD, Bp Gloucester and Bath and Wells, and *d* 3 Dec 1839

(2) **Sir Thomas** *m* 3rd Mary (*d* 19 April 1780), dau of Hatton Compton (*see* NORTHAMPTON, M), but by her had no issue

(1) Ann

(2) Elizabeth; *m* — Townshend and *dsp*

(3) Matilda; *m* Rev Matthew Postlethwaite, Archdeacon Norwich and Rector Denton, Norfolk

(4) Frances

The 2nd Bt *d* 14 Feb 1754; his er son,

Sir Thomas Gooch, 3rd Bt, of Benacre Hall, Suffolk; *b* 23 July 1720; *m* 1st 1743 Anne, dau and heir of John Atwood, of Yarmouth, and had, with another s and a dau:

1 THOMAS (Sir), **4th Bt**

2 William Thomas, of Edwinstow, Notts; *b* Aug 1749; *m* 13 May 1775 (*divorce* 1781) Elizabeth Sarah, dau of William Villa Real, of Edwinstow, and *d* 4 Jan 1833, having had, with another *s* (*dsp*):

(1) Henry Robert, of Southwold, Suffolk, Army Capt; *m* Nov 1822 Eliza (*m* 2nd George Frederick Souper, barrister Inner Temple), dau of Samuel Wayth, of Southwold, and *dsp* 30 Sept 1829

3 John (Ven); Archdeacon Sudbury, Rector Benacre; *b* 7 June 1752; *m* 24 Feb 1791 Barbara, dau of Walter Sneyd, MP Castle Rising, of Keele Hall, Staffs, and *d* 14 July 1823, having had,with two other sons (*d* unm):

(1) Henry Edward; Lt-Col Coldstream Gds; *b* 25 Dec 1793; *m* 23 Jan 1857 Frances, dau of Robert Knight, of Studley, Warwicks, and *dsp* 18 Jan 1867

(2) Frederick (Rev); DCL, Rector Bagington; *b* 10 April 1804; *m* 28 July 1853 Matilda Katherine (*d* 28 June 1861), dau of William Yates Peel (*see* PEEL, E), and *d* 29 Oct 1887, having had issue:

1a George Walter; *b* 29 June 1855

2a Henry Francis; Capt and Hon Maj 5th Bn Sherwood Foresters (Derbys Regt); *b* May 1860; *m* 1890 Annetta, widow of H Gerard and dau of Rev T Raby

(1) Caroline Barbara; *m* 28 July 1818 Rev Walter Davenport BROMLEY formerly DAVENPORT, of Ellaston, Staffs, and Capesthorne, Cheshire, and *d* 8 May 1827. He *d* 1 Dec 1862

1 Matilda; *m* 20 April 1776 Paul Cobbe Methuen and *d* 6 Dec 1826, leaving issue (*see* METHUEN, B)

Sir Thomas *m* 2nd Nov 1772 Phoebe (*d* 1 June 1793), dau of Isaac Norton, of London, and widow of Horatio Birttes, and *d* 10 Sept 1781, having by her had:

2 Georgiana; *m* Thomas Farr, of Beccles, Suffolk

His est son,

Sir Thomas Gooch, 4th Bt; *b* 1745; High Sheriff Suffolk 1785; *m* 23 Dec 1766 Anna Maria (*d* 28 Sept 1814), dau and heir of William Hayward, of Weybridge, Surrey, and had, with other issue (*d* young or unm):

1 THOMAS (Sir), **5th Bt**

2 William; Lt-Col; *b* 11 Dec 1769; *m* Dec 1797 Jane, dau and coheir of James Wilkinson, of Newcastle, and *d* 14 Oct 1851, leaving issue:

(1) William (Rev); Canon York, Rector Benacre, Vicar Stainton, Cleveland; *b* 18 Sept 1798; *m* 9 July 1822 Anne (*d* 1885), dau of Herbert Newton Jarrett, of Grove Place, Hants, and *d* 27 Feb 1876, having had:

1a George Cecil; Maj and Paymaster 18th Foot; *b* 30 April 1832; *m* 1st 7 March 1857 Julia Caroline (*dsp* 30 July 1860), est dau of Henry Van Straubenzee, JP, DL, of Spennithorne, Yorks; *m* 2nd 26 Oct 1861 Frederica Charlotte Agneta (*d* 8 Feb 1876), dau of William Gambier, of Sacombe Park, Herts; *m* 3rd 28 May 1877 Ellen Louisa (*d* 5 Jan 1903), widow of Capt Edmund Prideaux Chichester, 7th Dragoon Gds, and dau of John Fairlie, and *d* 1898, having by his 2nd w had:

1b Amy Maude; *b* 1886; *d* unm 1926

2b Anabel Mildred Annie; *b* 1870; *m* 1893 Beauchamp Urquhart Colclough, Staff-Paymaster RN, and *d* 11 May 1911, leaving issue

3b Eva Frederica; *b* 1873

2a Percy Fielding; Capt 92nd Highrs; *b* 10 Jan 1836; *m* 4 May 1872 Edith (*m* 3rd 15 June 1875 Col William Park), widow of Rev H Ewen and dau of Rev Stenning Johnson, and *d* 16 Sept 1874, leaving issue:

1b Percy William Jarrett; *b* 1 Dec 1873; *m* 1893 Clara Jane, dau of John Wigston, of Stratford-on-Avon, and *d* 1938, leaving issue:

1c Francis William; *b* 1902; *m* 1941 *Florence Ethel, dau of Frank Elston, of Victoria, BC

3a Edward George Tate, RN; *b* 20 Feb 1838; *m* 9 Nov 1877 Elizabeth Isabella, dau of William McKinney, and *d* 4 Aug 1915, leaving issue:

1b George Cecil William; *b* 1880

2b James Fletcher; *b* 1883

1b Annie Lillian Georgina; *b* 28 Sept 1878; *m* 1 Jan 1894 Francis William Bullen, of NZ, and had issue

4a Francis Harcourt (Rev), JP Suffolk; BA Oxon, Vicar Thursley, Surrey; *b* 20 May 1842; *m* 28 April 1868 Catherine (*d* 16 Sept 1925), only child of Richard Paine, and *d* 3 April 1931, leaving issue:

1b Richard Francis Knight, MC; ADC to Govr Ceylon, Capt Warwicks Yeo WW I (despatches), Order Nile; *b* 24 Sept 1872; *m* 31 July 1918 Gladys (*d* 14 Sept 1968), widow of Capt Bingham Alexander Turner, DSO, of Bourton Grange, Berks, and dau of John Swynfen St Vincent Jervis, and *d* 29 May 1938

1b Anne Elizabeth; *m* 26 April 1894 Rev Archdall Malden Hill, MA, Vicar and RD Hove 1914, and *d* 8 Dec 1923, leaving issue

2b Margaret Lily; *m* 18 Nov 1902 Rev Anthony Aylmer Astley, Rector Everleigh, Wilts, and *d* 20 April 1948, leaving issue (*see* 1970 edn ASTLEY, Bt)

3b Ethel; *d* unm

4b Dulcibella Amy; *m* 1897 John Edmond Henry Gray, s of Edmond Robert Henry Gray, and *dsp* 28 March 1949

1a Anna Maria; *m* 10 Aug 1852 Rev Charles George Torrington Barlow, Vicar Falmer, Lewes, and *d* 11 April 1907, leaving issue. He *d* 4 Jan 1891

2a Matilda Charlotte; *m* 10 Aug 1852 Rev James Allan Park and *d* 1891, having had issue. He *d* 4 Jan 1875

3a Mary Teresa; *m* 23 Feb 1854 Robert Calverley Bewicke, of Coulby Manor, Yorks, and *d* 2 Aug 1916, leaving issue. He *d* 31 Oct 1886

4a Louisa Edith; *m* 25 Jan 1876 Lt-Col John H Balmain and *d* 1918, having had issue. He *d* 1897

(1) Maria Jane (twin with William)

(2) Dulcibella; *m* 18 Nov 1841 Rev Henry L'Estrange Milles-Astley

(3) Matilda Mary; *m* 11 July 1814 Rev William Venables Vernon Harcourt and had issue (*see* VERNON, B)

3 Thomas; Lt-Col; *b* 25 April 1773; *m* Oct 1801 Hannah, widow of Philip Webb, of Milford House, Surrey, and dau of Sir Robert Barker, C-in-C E Indies, and *dsp* 14 March 1849

4 Richard (Rev); Rector N Cove-cum-Willingham, Suffolk; *b* 24 Dec 1781; *d* 22 March 1873

5 Paul (Rev); *b* 2 March 1786; *d* unm April 1867

1 Sophia; *m* 10 March 1818 Capt George William Manby, RN, FRS, of Gt Yarmouth, Norfolk, inventor of the life-boat

Sir THOMAS *d* 7 April 1826; his est son,

Sir Thomas Sherlock Gooch, 5th Bt; MP Suffolk; *b* 2 Nov 1767; *m* 12 May 1796 Marianne (*d* 9 April 1856), dau of Abraham Whittaker, of Lyston House, Herefs, sis of Charlotte Maria, Countess of Stradbroke (*qv*), and had:

1 EDWARD (Sir), **6th Bt**

2 Charles John (Rev); Rector S Cove, Suffolk, and Toppesfield, Essex; *b* 17 July 1803; *m* 17 July 1832 Agatha (*d* 18 Nov 1867), yst dau of Charles Hanbury, and *d* 25 June 1876, having had, with another dau (*d* unm):

(1) Philip Sherlock (Rev); Rector Benacre, BA Oxon; *b* 14 March 1839; *m* 28 June 1881 Mary Campbell (*d* 25 July 1927), dau of Rev Henry Jodrell, MA, n of Sir Richard Paul Jodrell, 2nd Bt (*see* 1929 edn), by Frances, Countess Cape St Vincent of Portugal, and *dsp* 29 April 1909

(1) Agatha; *m* 1st Aug 1864 William Henry Lawrence (*d* 1865), Capt 9th Lancers, and had issue; *m* 2nd 5 Sept 1876 Maj Robert Lawrence, 90th LI, and *d* 24 Jan 1895

3 Thomas Lewis; V-Adml; *b* 11 April 1807; *m* 28 Feb 1829 Anne Europa (*d* 8 Sept 1839), est dau of Gen Hon William Henry Gardner (*see* 1970 edn GARDNER, B), and *d* 13 June 1876, having had:

(1) Thomas Sherlock; Capt RN; *b* 17 Oct 1831; *m* 10 April 1861 Catherine Lydia Mackenzie (*d* 28 Dec 1914), dau of Capt John James, of Cambridge, 85th Regt, and *d* 16 Feb 1897, having had:

1a John Sherlock; Maj RGA; *b* 13 Dec 1865; *m* 1st 27 Dec 1894 Ella Cecilia Piercy (*d* 23 April 1907), dau of Ward Chipman Drury, of St John, New Brunswick; *m* 2nd 26 June 1912 Anne Dorothea (*d* 2 Sept 1950), dau of Cdr Mathew James Harrison, RN, and *d* 26 Aug 1929, having by his 1st w had a dau (*b* 30 Sept 1895, *d* 30 Sept 1896)

1a Anne Georgina Sherlock; *m* 1st 1886 Philip Edward Scholfield (*d* 1895), of Maltby Hall, Yorks; *m* 2nd 5 March 1903 Francis Edward James, s of Rev Henry James, Vicar Willingdon, Sussex, and *d* 24 Nov 1911

2a Katharine Marion Sherlock; *d* unm 17 Oct 1934

1 Marianne Anna Maria; *m* 1 Feb 1823 Andrew Lawson, of Aldborgh Manor, Yorks, and *d* 5 Nov 1855, leaving issue (*see* 1970 edn LAWSON, Bt, of Knavesmire)

2 Charlotte Matilda; *m* 17 June 1824 Rev Stephen Clissold, Rector Wrentham, Suffolk, and *d* 16 Aug 1852

3 Georgina Anne; *m* 30 May 1838 Rev Philip Scholfield, Vicar Coulceby, Lincs, and *d* 25 March 1878

Sir THOMAS *d* 18 Dec 1851; his est son,

Sir Edward Sherlock Gooch, 6th Bt; MP E Suffolk; *m* 1st 23 Jan 1828 Louisa Anna Maria (*d* 24 Feb 1837), 2nd dau of Sir George Beeston Prescott, 2nd Bt (*see* 1959 edn PRESCOTT, Bt, of Theobald's Park), and had, with another dau (*d* unm):

1 Florence Jane Charlotte Giva; *m* 23 Dec 1852 Rev Edward Mortimer Clissold, of Wrentham, Suffolk, and *d* his widow 6 Dec 1918, leaving issue

Sir Edward *m* 2nd 1 March 1839 Harriet (*m* 2nd 30 June 1858 Maj John St Leger; *d* 17 Oct 1883), 3rd dau of James Hope Vere, of Craigie, Linlithgow, and *d* 9 Nov 1856, having by her had, with a 2nd s (*d* young):

1 **Sir Edward Sherlock Gooch, 7th Bt**, JP, DL; *b* 16 May 1843; *m* 9 Oct 1866 Ellen Emily (*m* 2nd 28 July 1873 George Gream, MD; *d* 29 Nov 1921), est dau of Maj Robert Augustus Hankey Hirst, JP, DL, of Down Grange, Basingstoke, Hants, and *dsp* 27 May 1872

2 **Sir Francis Robert Sherlock Lambert Gooch, 8th Bt**, DL; Lt W Suffolk Militia; *b* 8 Sept 1850; *m* 16 July 1872 Sarah Annie (*d* 28 Oct 1879), dau of G A Sutherland, and *d* 13 Aug 1881, having had issue:

(1) Francis Sherlock; *b* 31 July; *d* 5 Dec 1873

3 **Sir Alfred Sherlock Gooch, 9th Bt**, DL Suffolk; High Sheriff 1885, Lt Roy Westminster Militia; *b* 25 Dec 1851; *m* 27 May 1880 Alice Elizabeth (*d* 27 Nov 1895), dau of Edward Williams (*see* WILLIAMS, Bt, of Tregullow), and had:

(1) THOMAS VERE SHERLOCK (Sir), **10th Bt**

2 Elizabeth; *m* 8 July 1874 William Charles Boden Elwell, MA Oxon, barrister Middle Temple, and had issue. He *d* 19 March 1901

3 Diana Anne; *m* 22 May 1866 Alfred Herbert Morse, JP, of Copdock House, Ipswich, Capt 96th and 73rd Regts, and *d* 1 March 1928, leaving issue. He *d* 23 April 1909

4 Harriet Sophia; *d* unm 9 Jan 1927

5 Charlotte Matilda; *m* 18 June 1873 Edward Annesley Owen, Recorder Walsall, and had issue. He *d* 1 Aug 1924

6 Isabel Edith; *m* 5 June 1875 Lascelles Wharton Ford, Capt 88th Connaught Rangers, est s of Col Burnet Ford, Madras Staff Corps, and *d* 23 Dec 1931, leaving issue. He *d* 1882

Sir ALFRED *d* 24 Feb 1899; his only son,

Sir Thomas Vere Sherlock Gooch, 10th Bt, JP; High Sheriff 1911; *b* 10 June 1881; *m* 10 July 1902 Florence Meta (*d* 16 Sept 1932), yst dau of James Finucane Draper, of Jersey, and had issue:

1 ROBERT ERIC SHERLOCK (Sir), **11th Bt**

2 Brian Sherlock, DSO (1946), TD, JP (Suffolk 1954), DL (1958); High Sheriff 1956, Brevet-Col cmdg Suffolk Yeo 1944–50, WW II (despatches), Dep Dir BRCS Suffolk 1955 (Dir 1957), Jt Master Norwich Staghounds 1946; *b* 1 Aug 1904; *m* 6 July 1935 Monica Mary (*d* 13 Oct 1975), only child of Nathaniel Arthur Heywood, of Glevering Park, Wickham Market, Suffolk, and *d* 15 April 1968, leaving:

(1) +Arthur Brian Sherlock Heywood [Brig Arthur Gooch, Manor Farmhouse, Chitterne, Wilts BA12 0LG]; *b* 1 June 1937; *educ* Eton and RMA Sandhurst; commissioned Life Gds 1956, Adj 1960–63, Assist Mil Attaché, Teheran 1973–75, cmded Life Gds 1978–81, Comdt J Div Staff Coll 1982–85, cmded Roy Armd Corps Centre 1987–89, Pres Regtl Commn Bd 1989–92, ADC 1989–92, Hon Col Kent and Sharpshooters Yeo 1992–; *m* 27 July 1963 *Sarah Diana Rowena Perceval Scott, JP, dau of Lt-Col John Francis George Perceval, of Templehouse, Co Sligo, and Mrs Diana Madeleine Scott, and has:

1a *Rowena Elizabeth; *b* 28 July 1965

2a *Katherine Sarah; *b* 22 Aug 1967; *m* 1992 *Edward J Hawkings s of Peter Hawkings

(2) +Thomas Sherlock Heywood [Thomas Gooch Esq, Chantry House, Greens Norton, Northants NN12 8BL]; *b* 12 Nov 1943; *educ* Eton; *m* 22 May 1970 *Elizabeth J C, dau of Brig Guy Arthur Eliot Peyton, OBE, of Bengal Manor, Greens Norton, and has issue:

1a +Robert Brian Sherlock; *b* 1976

1a *Caroline Elizabeth; *b* 28 Nov 1973

(1) *(Mary) Elise; *b* 20 March 1940; *m* 13 June 1964 *Sir Anthony Raymond Leopold Cuthbert Quilter, 4th Bt (*qv*), and has issue

(2) *Jennifer Isobel [Mrs John Chevallier Guild, Aspall Hall, Aspall, Stowmarket, Suffolk IP14 6PD]; *b* 7 May 1942; *m* 18 Dec 1965 *Lt-Cdr John Marjoribanks GUILD later CHEVALLIER GUILD (deed poll 1970), RN, er s of Cyril Harrower Guild, of Aspall Hall, Stowmarket, and has:

1a *John Barrington; *b* 2 May 1967; *m* 14 June 1997 *Dale Kerry, dau of David Hosking, of London

2a *Henry; *b* 20 Dec 1968

3 Richard Frank Sherlock, DSO (1945), MC (1940); *b* 8 Nov 1906; *educ* Harrow and Gonville and Caius Coll Cambridge (MA 1931); Coldstream Gds: Adj 2nd Bn 1934–37, WW II, cmded 2nd Bn 1946–49, psc 1942, AAG London Dist 1949–51, cmded 32 Gds Bde 1951, Brig (ret 1951); ADC to Viceroy India 1937–39; Marshal City London 1957, Sec to Ld Mayor 1957–62, Extra Gentleman Usher to HM THE QUEEN 1962–64, Gentleman Usher 1964–69, Extra Gentleman Usher 1969, Grand Sword Bearer Grand Lodge England 1954, Chev Crown Belgium with palm, Croix de Guerre with palm, Croix de Guerre Belgium with palm; *m* 18 April 1939 (Barbara) Susan (*d* 1981), yst dau of William Douro Hoare, CBE, and *d* 6 June 1973, leaving issue:

(1) +Richard Edward Sherlock; *b* 3 Jan 1942; *educ* Eton; *m* 1st 19 Aug 1967 Rosemary Irene, formerly w of — Hill; *m* 2nd 1981 *Linda Kathleen, dau of John Caradus, of Napier, NZ, and by his 1st w has issue:

1a +Tobias Douro Sherlock; *b* 31 Oct 1969

2a +Theodore Frank Sherlock; *b* 1972

(2) William David Sherlock; *b* 18 Dec 1944; *educ* Eton; *m* 1970 *Anna Nicholls and *d* 14 Dec 1978, *k* following a car crash, having had:

1a Samuel Guy Sherlock; *b* 14 Oct 1974; *d* 14 Dec 1978

1a *Elizabeth Anne; *b* 1971

1 Barbara Alexandra; *b* 27 June 1908; *m* 18 April 1936 Raymond John Steffe Crisp, JP, yr s of John Robert Crisp, JP, of Kirby Cane Hall, Norfolk, and had issue. He *d* 27 Nov 1966

2 Phyllis Elise, JP; *b* 7 Sept 1910

Sir THOMAS *d* 7 July 1946; his est son,

Sir Robert Eric Sherlock Gooch, 11th Bt, KCVO (1973), DSO (1941); High Sheriff Suffolk 1950, CC E Suffolk 1946 (V-Chm 1950–78), CA 1951; *b* 6 May 1903; *educ* Eton; WW II: cmded 1st Household Cav Regt Nov 1942–Dec 1944, Col cmdg Household Cav 1944–46 (ret 1946) (despatches twice), Hon Col: 4th Bn Suffolk Regt (TA) 1954–61, Suffolk and Cambs Regt (TA) 1961–68, memb Gentlemen-at-Arms 1950–1973 (Clerk Cheque and Adj 1963, Standard Bearer 1967, Lt 1968), Memb House Laity Ch Assembly 1948–55, Liaison Offr Min Ag 1952–62, memb Cncl Roy Ag Soc 1949 (Dep Pres 1960, V-Pres 1961, Pres 1961, Tstee 1964), Chm E Suffolk Ag Exec Ctee 1954–62, Pres Smithfield Club 1966; *m* 10 Nov 1926 Katharine Clervaux (*d* 1 March 1974), er dau of Maj-Gen Sir Edward Walter Clervaux Chaytor, KCMG, KCVO, CB (*see* CHAYTOR, Bt), and *d* 13 Nov 1978, having had:

1 Edward John Sherlock; *b* 28 Aug 1927; *d* 29 June 1928

2 Sir (RICHARD) JOHN SHERLOCK GOOCH, **12th and present Bt**

3 +TIMOTHY ROBERT SHERLOCK, MBE (1970) [Maj Timothy Gooch MBE, The Cedars, Covehithe, Wrentham, Suffolk NR34 7JW], Maj (ret) Life Gds; *b* 7 Dec 1934; *educ* Eton and RMA Sandhurst, Memb Gentlemen at Arms 1986–; *m* 17 Dec 1963 *Susan Barbara Christie, only dau of Maj-Gen Kenneth Christie Cooper, CB, DSO, OBE, and has issue:

(1) *Lucinda; *b* 13 July 1970

(2) *Victoria; *b* 15 March 1974

1 *Katharine Anne [Mrs Andrew Napier, Syleham Manor, Eye, Suffolk IP21 4LN]; *b* 29 March 1932; *m* 29 March 1967 Maj Andrew Patrick Forbes Napier, KStJ, DL, late Coldstream Gds, Memb Roy Co Archers (*d* 19–), yr s of Ian Patrick Robert Napier, MC, and Hon Mrs Mason, only dau of 1st Baron Essendon (*see* 1970 edn), and has:

(1) *James Frederick Brian; *b* 5 July 1968; *educ* Eton and RMA Sandhurst; late Capt Coldstream Gds

(1) *Katharine Louisa; *b* 1969

Seat: Benacre Hall, Benacre, Suffolk. The original structure is thought to have been the work of Matthew Brettingham. It was certainly constructed in the mid-1760s, more than a decade after the Baronet Bishop of Ely had bought the estate. Unfortunately it was badly damaged by fire in the mid-1920s. Now restored, it displays the Gooch crest of a talbot statant in the centre of the classical pediment.

GOOCH of Clewer

Arms: Per pale argent and sable, on a chevron between three talbots passant two escallops counterchanged, on a chief engrailed gules a wheel between two leopard's faces or. **Crest:** A talbot per pale sable and argent, gorged with a wreath of oak and resting the dexter foreleg on a wheel or. **Motto:** *Fide et virtute* ('By fidelity and valour'). **Creation:** Bt. (UK) 15 Nov 1866.

SIR TREVOR SHERLOCK GOOCH, 5TH BT, VRD [Sir Trevor Gooch Bt VRD, Jardin de la Rocque, Mont de la Rocque, St Brelade, Jersey, JE3 8BQ CI]; *b* 15 June 1915; *s* kinsman 1989; *educ* Charterhouse; F/Lt RAF 1939–46; *m* 1st 4 Dec 1956 Denys Anne (*d* 1976), only dau of Harold Victor Venables, of Palma de Mallorca, Balearic Islands, Spain; *m* 2nd 1978 *Jean, dau of John Joseph Wright, and has issue by his 1st w:

1 +MILES PETER; *b* 3 Feb 1963; *educ* Victoria Coll Jersey and Preston Poly Lancs (BEng)

1 *Beverly Jacqueline [Mrs Bernard Amy, 1 Le Clos de Debenaire, Richmond Rd, St Helier, Jersey, JE2 3GY CI]; *b* 24 June 1957; *m* 1st 1981 (*divorce* 1988) Laurence Andrew Wilde; *m* 2nd 1988 (*divorce* 1996) Bernard Charles Amy and has by her 1st husb:

(1) *Samantha Ria; *b* 28 Oct 1983 (legally adopted by stepfather 1991)

2 *Vanda Madeleine; *b* 2 Oct 1958; BSc; *m* 1997 *Dr Owen Innes Miller and has:

(1) *Hamish Charles Owen; *b* 3 Sept 1996

3 *Yvonne Daryl; *b* 5 Jan 1961

4 *Rowan Claire; *b* 1971

Lineage: JOHN GOOCH, of Beccles, Suffolk; *b* 11 Aug 1746; *m* Barbara (*d* 18 June 1818), dau of Michael Longridge, of Wallbottle, Northumberland, and *d* 24 Feb 1818, having had, with other issue:

JOHN GOOCH, of Bedlington, Northumberland; *b* 17 March 1783; *m* 23 Dec 1805 Anna (*d* 24 Nov 1863), dau of Thomas Longridge, of Newcastle, and *d* 28 Aug 1833, leaving issue:

1 Thomas Longridge, of Team Lodge, Saltwell, Gateshead-on-Tyne; *b* 1 Nov 1808; MICE; *m* 30 April 1836 Ruthanna (*d* 1 May 1895), 2nd dau of Robert Scaife, of Liverpool, and *d* 23 Nov 1882, having had issue

2 John Viret, of Cooper's Hill, Bracknell, Berks; *b* 29 June 1812; *m* 1st June 1840 Hannah Frances (*d* 1874), dau of Capt Elias Robinson Handcock, and had issue; *m* 2nd 16 March 1876 Emily Mary (*d* 16 Aug 1921), dau of Rev Charles Stonhouse (gs of Sir James Stonhouse, 7th and 10th Bt (*qv*)), and *d* 8 June 1900, having by her had issue

3 DANIEL (Sir), **1st Bt**

4 George Henry; *b* 16 Sept 1820; *m* 22 July 1862 Clara, 5th dau of John Fenwick, of North Shields, and widow of Thomas Wallis, and *d* 15 Jan 1900

5 William Frederick, of Wargrave, Newton-le-Willows, Lancashire, JP; *b* 19 April 1825; CE; *m* Dec 1852 Emma Brent, dau of Capt James E Biles, HEICS, and had issue

1 Anna Longridge; *m* 4 April 1852 Rev Thomas Henry FitzPatrick, CMG, and *d* 18 Feb 1863

2 Mary Ann; *m* 31 May 1853 Rev Alfred Cory Kingdom, Vicar Bunny St Mary, Notts, and *d* 29 Oct 1899, leaving issue

3 Frances; *m* 25 April 1865 Rev William Laing, Rector Langley, Staffs, and *d* 11 April 1889

JOHN GOOCH's 3rd s,

Sir Daniel Gooch, 1st Bt (UK), so *cr* 5 Nov 1866, DL; MP Cricklade 1865–85; *b* 24 Aug 1816; civil engr involved in laying the Atlantic cables of 1865 and 1866; *m* 1st 22 March 1838 Margaret (*d* 22 May 1868), dau of Henry Tanner, of Bishopswearmouth; *m* 2nd 17 Sept 1870 Emily (*d* 19 May 1901), yst dau of John Burder, of Norwood, Surrey, and *d* 15 Oct 1889, leaving by his 1st w:

1 **Sir Henry Daniel Gooch, 2nd Bt**; *b* 30 Dec 1841; *m* 23 Nov 1865 Mary Kelsall (*d* 11 March 1919), dau of Joseph Rodney Croskey, of Philadelphia, and *d* 24 June 1897, leaving issue:

(1) **Sir Daniel Fulthorpe Gooch, 3rd Bt**, JP (Berks); *b* 25 May 1869; *m* 23 June 1896 Mary Winifred (*d* 26 July 1921), only dau of Edward William Munro, of Clewer Hill, and *d* 22 Dec 1926, having had issue:

1a Lancelot Daniel Edward; *b* 18 Sept 1897; Midshipman RN; *das* 4 Oct 1915

2a **Sir Robert Douglas Gooch, 4th Bt**, of Clewer Park; *b* 19 Sept 1905; *educ* Brighton Coll; *m* 1st 5 Jan 1928 (*divorce* 1930) Moyra Katharine, only dau of Charles Howard Saunders, MB, BCh, of Southampton; *m* 2nd 18 Aug 1930 *Mary Eileen, dau of Colin George Barrett and widow of Maj H L Gifford, Roy Irish Rifles, and *d* 1989, leaving by her:

1b *Gillian Daphne; *b* 28 May 1931; *m* 1st 8 Aug 1953 (*divorce* 1973) Guy Stephen Foster Wilkin, MA only s of Stephen Foster Wilkin; *m* 2nd 1974 Kenneth George White (*d* 1988) and has by her 1st husb:

1c *Paul Guy Foster; *b* 20 Nov 1955; *m* 1978 *Carolyn Noakes and has:

1d *Mathew Paul Foster; *b* 1984

1d *Samantha Ann Foster; *b* 1982

2c *Mark Guy Foster; *b* 11 Nov 1957

1a *Phyllis Evelyn; *b* 30 March 1900; *m* 3 Aug 1920 (*divorce* 1940) Frank William Parrish, only s of William Parrish

2a Daphne; *b* 26 June 1910; *m* 1st 20 March 1934 (*divorce* 1944) James Pryce de Rees, only s of Maj J F de Rees, and had issue; *m* 2nd 3 Oct 1944 Howard Norman Clifford-Turner, s of Harry Clifford-Turner, and *d* 6 Oct 1954

(1) Algitha Maud; *m* 7 Feb 1906 Sir James Langrishe, 4th Bt (*qv*), and *d* 29 March 1922

2 Charles Fulthorpe, JP (Cardiff and Kent); *b* 31 Jan 1845; *m* 4 Jan 1876 Emma Susan (*d* 13 April 1929), 2nd dau of Joseph Hinson Astwood, of Bermuda, and *d* 12 April 1917, leaving, with a 3rd s (*d* unm *ka*):

(1) Eric Daniel Astwood; *b* 23 March 1886; Lt E African Mounted Rifles, Lt 5th Roy Irish Lancers; *m* 27 Sept 1910 Gwynedd (*d* Oct 1964), dau of Col George Brooke-Meares, Roy Fus, and *d* 19 Jan 1937, leaving issue:

1a *Pamela Vivian [Mrs Robert Smidt van Gelder, Rodlense House, Boldre, Hants]; *b* 7 July 1911; *m* 26 Feb 1934 *Robert Herbert Smidt van Gelder, Netherlands Diplomatic Consular Serv (ret), and has:

1b *Jacqueline; *b* 19 May 1935

2b *Pamela Gwynedd Marie [Mrs David Jamieson, Westerland Stud, Graffham, Sussex]; *b* 21 Oct 1946; *m* 15 May 1971 *David Lawrence Jamieson and has issue:

1c *Antonia Alexandra; *b* Dec 1972

2c *Melanie Pamela; *b* May 1976

3c *Emma Laura; *b* July 1988

3b *Margaret [Mrs Simon Parker, 15 Eccleston Sq, London SW1]; *b* 17 June 1950; *m* 30 June 1979 *Simon Charles Yarborough Parker and has:

1c *Robert George; *b* 9 Nov 1983

(2) Charles Trevor; *b* 24 Feb 1888; *educ* Charterhouse and Pembroke Coll Cambridge (BA); *m* 24 Sept 1914 Hester Stratford (*d* 14 Dec 1957), dau of Lt-Col Wright Sherlock, Roy Irish Regt, and *d* 1 April 1963, leaving:

1a Sir TREVOR SHERLOCK GOOCH, **5th and present Bt**

1a Hermione Ellen; *b* 22 Dec 1916; *m* 24 July 1948 (*divorce* 1962) Capt Victor Frederick Eoin Merrett, Roy Irish Fus (*d* 1966), and had issue:

1b *Gillian Sherlock; *b* 31 March 1950

(3) Geoffrey Fulthorpe; *b* 27 July 1892; Capt RGA; *ka* 1918

(4) Kenneth Thackeray, MC; *b* 10 March 1894; Capt RA Res of Offrs, served WW I and WW II (despatches); *d* 25 Jan 1948

3 Alfred William, CE; *b* 2 March 1846; *m* 1877 Frances Elizabeth (*d* 2 Jan 1899), dau of Stephen Jones, of Oxford and *d* 24 May 1887, leaving issue:

(1) Arthur Longridge; *b* 1878; *d* 1928

(2) George Daniel; *b* 1879; Capt RE; *educ* Cheltenham; *m* 31 Oct 1901 Rose Ellen (*d* 22 June 1946), dau of Sir Alfred Apperly, JP, of Rodborough Court, Glos, and *d* 13 April 1969, having had issue:

1a Alfred Daniel; *b* 16 Sept 1902; *educ* Cheltenham; *d* unm 13 Sept 1970

2a George Ernest, MBE (1945), TD; *b* 29 Jan 1905; Maj RA WW II (despatches twice), Offr Order Orange Nassau; *m* 26 April 1933 Jennifer Eve (*d* 1981), 2nd dau of Brig-Gen Philip Maud, CMG, CBE, RE (*see* 1970 edn REDCLIFFE-MAUD, B), and *d* 9 Feb 1958, leaving issue:

1b +John Daniel, VRD [Maj John Gooch VRD, The Schoolhouse, Oathlaw, Forfar, Angus DD8 3PQ]; *b* 9 Dec 1935; *educ* Cheltenham; Maj RM Force Vol Res; OStJ, FRICS; *m* 1972 *Ann Patricia, dau of David Miles Lubbock (*see* AVEBURY, B), and has issue:

1c *Katherine Janita; *b* 1974

2c *Diana Veronica; *b* 1976

2b +Peter Daniel [Peter Gooch Esq, 1111 Skeena Place, Victoria, BC, Canada]; *b* 22 Dec 1938 BSc; *educ* Cheltenham (MSc); *m* 8 May 1965 *Pamela Sarah, er dau of Robert Hartley, of Lancs, and has had issue:

1c +Adam Daniel; *b* 14 Feb 1969

2c +Thomas Daniel; *b* 1970

1c Fiona Louise; *b* 1972; *d* 1991

1b *Belinda [Mrs Harry Ash, 25 Essex Place, Newtown, PA, USA]; *b* 21 Oct 1944; ARCM, GRSH; *m* 1984 *Harry Merriman Ash and has:

1c *George Gooch; *b* 1985

1a Ethel Rose Eleanor; *b* 10 Oct 1907; *m* 24 April 1936 Capt André, Georges de Callataij, MBE, Belgian Army, s of Gen Georges de Callataij, of Brussels, and had issue

(1) Eleanor Emily; *b* 12 Jan 1883; *m* 31 March 1921 Charles Vernon Underhill Jay (*d* 15 Feb 1942), s of Robert Charles Jay, and *d* 14 Sept 1953, leaving issue

4 Frank; *b* 20 July 1847; Capt 4th Hus; *m* 30 March 1871 Teresa (*d* 13 Jan 1935), 3rd dau of Joseph Rodney Croskey, and *d* 29 Jan 1890, leaving with other issue:

(1) Herbert Daniel Cecil; *b* 29 Aug 1878; *d* unm 26 Nov 1943

(1) Mary Eveline Emily; *b* 19 Jan 1872; *m* 1st 23 Oct 1890 Andrew George Parker (*d* 1915); *m* 2nd 1917 Charles Richard Sillem (*d* 21 May 1931) and *d* 13 May 1953

(2) Margaret Frances; *b* 19 Oct 1874; *m* 11 July 1901 Ernest Edgar Morgan and *d* 5 Dec 1921

1 Anna Longridge; *m* 2 Aug 1859 Frederick Newton (*d* 1915), of Maida Hill, London, and *d* 24 March 1926, leaving issue

2 Emily Jane; *m* 19 Oct 1858 William Ponsford (*d* 1893) and *d* 17 March 1901, having had issue

GOODENOUGH

Arms: Or a chevron gu. between three guttes de sang.
Crest: A demi-wolf ppr. holding between his paws an escallop arg.
Motto: *Ad sanguinem* ('To the last drop of blood').
Creation: Bt. (UK) 19 Jan 1943.

SIR WILLIAM McLERNON GOODENOUGH, 3RD BT, of Broadwell and Filkins, Co Oxford [Sir William Goodenough Bt, The Old Rectory, Blickling, Norfolk NR11 6NF]; *b* 5 Aug 1954; *s f* 1996; *educ* Stanbridge Earls; *m* 1982 *Louise Elizabeth, dau of Capt Michael Ortmans, LVO, RN, and has:

(1) +SAMUEL WILLIAM HECTOR; *b* 11 June 1992

(1) *Sophie Julia; *b* 30 May 1986

(2) *Celia Isobel; *b* 8 Feb 1989

Lineage: RICHARD GOODYNOW, of Bradwell/Broadwell, Oxon, which until the 19th century included the parish of Filkins, owned land there (which remained in the family into the 20th century), also in the neighbouring parish of Langford; *d* between 1558 and 1560, leaving a 7th s:

WILLIAM GOODENOUGH, of Bradwell; *m* Emma — and *d* by 1617, leaving, with three yr sons and three daus:

EDMUND GOODENOUGH, of Bradwell; yeoman; *m* Mary and *d* by 10 April 1640, leaving, with three daus:

EDMUND GOODENOUGH, of Southwark; merchant taylor; *m* a dau of William Dyke, Master Taylor, and *d* by 15 Jan 1657, leaving:

WILLIAM GOODENOUGH; bought Broughton Hall, Broughton Poggs, Oxon; *b* 1645; *m* 1st Penelope Needham, of Bampton, Oxon, and had a dau (*d* an infant); *m* 2nd Annabella (*d* Sept 1718), dau of Sir Edward Bathurst, 1st Bt, of Lechlade, and *d* 16 March 1673, having by her had, with a dau (*d* age 7):

WILLIAM GOODENOUGH, of Broughton Poggs; *b* 21 April 1672; *m* Elizabeth, dau of John Southby, of Carswell, Berks, and *d* 10 June 1732, leaving, with four other sons and five daus (also Annabella, *b* 1704, *m* as his 1st w Sir John Honywood, 3rd Bt (*qv*), *d* 22 July 1737):

1 John; *b* 21 April 1706; Capt Richbell's Regt Battle of Culloden 1746

2 William (Rev); Vicar Kimpton, Hants, Rector Broughton Poggs; *b* 29 May 1707; *m* 4 March 1739 Elizabeth (*d* 11 Nov 1762), dau of Richard Serle, of Winchester, and *d* 11 Nov 1768, leaving, with three other sons:

(1) Samuel (Rev); DCL, Rector and Vicar Brize Norton, Vicar Broughton, Canon Windsor 1798, Dean Rochester 1802, Bp Carlisle 1808, fndr Linnean Soc; *b* 29 April 1743; *educ* Ch Ch Oxford; *m* 17 April 1770 Elizabeth (*d* 26 May 1827), dau of James Ford, MD, of Llangattock, Breconshire, Surgn Middx Hosp, and *d* 12 Aug 1827, leaving, with two er sons, a yst s and six daus:

3a Edmund (Rev); Preb York and Carlisle, Dean Wells 1831, Headmaster Westminster 1819–28; *b* 6 April 1785; *educ* Ch Ch Oxford; *m* 31 May 1821 Frances (*d* 1865), dau of Samuel Pepys Cockerell, and *d* 2 May 1845, leaving, with two other sons and four daus:

1b FREDERICK ADDINGTON

2b James Graham, CB, CMG; Cdre RN; *m* 31 May 1862 Victoria Henrietta (*d* 29 Jan 1917), sis of 10th Lord Belhaven and Stenton (*qv*), and was *k* 20 Aug 1875 by Maoris when cmdg the NZ station, leaving, with other issue:

1c William Edmund (Sir), GCB (1930), MVO 4th Cl (1912); Cdr light cruisers Heligoland Bight 1914 and Dogger Bank 1915, 2nd Light Cruiser Sqdn Jutland 1916, V-Adml 1920, Adml 1925, ADC to HM GEORGE V 1915–16, Pncpl Naval ADC 1919–20, C-in-C African Station 1920–22, the Nore 1924–27, Adml cmdg Reserve Fleet 1922–23, ret 1930, PRGS 1930–33, Croix de Guerre, Order St Vladimir Russia with swords, Rising Sun Japan; *b* 2 June 1867; *m* 12 June 1901 Hon Henrietta Margaret Stanley, OBE (1919) (*d* 21 Aug 1956), est dau of 4th

Baron Sheffield (*see* STANLEY OF ALDERLEY, SHEFFIELD and, B), and *d* 30 Jan 1945, leaving issue:

1d Katherine Margaret Anne; *b* 1902; *m* 1927 Cdr Alexander Dacre Lacy, RN; *d* 3 July 1969, leaving:

1e *Daphne Margaret [Mrs Ronald Cookson, Lested Lodge, Chart Sutton, Maidstone, Kent]; *b* 19 Oct 1928; *m* 30 Nov 1957 *Ronald Frederick Stephen Cookson and has issue:

1f *Stephen Alexander; *b* 27 Jan 1959

2f *William Simon; *b* 28 July 1961

3f *Richard Anthony; *b* 5 May 1963

2e *Elizabeth Anne Barbara; *b* 12 Feb 1931; *m* May 1962 *Rev Cornelius de Witt Hastie, of Boston, USA, and has:

1f *John Cornelius; *b* 19 Nov 1963

1f *Elizabeth de Witt; *b* 22 July 1969

3e *Monica Katherine; *b* 11 Oct 1938

2d Cecilia Phyllis Maisie; MA, STh, DD; *b* 9 Sept 1905; *educ* Rochester GS, Liverpool Coll Huyton, St Hugh's Coll Oxford; *d* 4 April 1998

3b William Howley (Sir), KCB; Lt-Gen RA, C-in-C Cape Town, Actg Adminr-Gen; *b* 5 April 1833; *m* 1 Sept 1874 Countess Anna Kinsky (*d* 11 Nov 1941), dau of Count Eugene Kinsky, of Moravia, and *d* 24 Oct 1898, leaving surv issue:

1c Eleanor; *m* 5 Feb 1898 Lt-Col George Algernon James Soltau-Symons, only s of George William Culme Soltau-Symons, JP, DL, and *d* 24 Feb 1967 aged 91, leaving a dau. He *d* 17 Jan 1947

2c Violet Isabel; *b* 21 Jan 1880; *d* unm 27 Feb 1971

The er son,

FREDERICK ADDINGTON GOODENOUGH, of London and Calcutta; E India merchant; *b* 6 July 1827; *m* 17 Oct 1861 Mary (*d* 9 Nov 1918), dau of Rev Anthony L Lambert, Rector Chilbolton, Hants, and *d* at sea 13 Sept 1869, leaving, with three daus:

1 Herbert Lane; Lt-Col IA; *b* 26 March 1865; *m* 25 Feb 1899 Muriel Grace Mitford (*d* 1 Dec 1955), dau of Charles Henry Ogbourne, JP, of Calcutta, and *d* 7 Feb 1937, leaving issue:

(1) Frederick Cockerell; Cdr RN WW II (despatches); *b* 10 March 1911; *educ* RNC Dartmouth; *d* following a flying accident 7 Oct 1951

(1) Ethel Mary, CBE; Dep Dir WRNS 1939; *b* 12 Jan 1900; *das* 10 Feb 1946

(2) Katharine Muriel; ATS and FANY WW II

2 Frederick Craufurd, of Filkins Hall; Ld Manor of Bradwell, Hon DCL Oxon, chm Barclays Bank, MLC India 1918–30; *b* 28 July 1866; *educ* Charterhouse; *m* 19 Feb 1898 Maeve (*d* 24 March 1953), dau of Nottidge Charles Macnamara, FRCS, and *d* 1 Sept 1934, leaving issue:

(1) WILLIAM MACNAMARA (Sir), **1st Bt**

(2) James Grenville; Cadet RAF WW I; *b* 19 Sept 1900; *educ* Wellington and Trin Coll Cambridge; *m* 1st 8 Dec 1926 (*divorce* 1954) Rosemary Dawn (*d* 16 Nov 1973), dau of Capt — Llewelyn, of Hackwood, Basingstoke; *m* 2nd 3 Nov 1955 *Harryet, dau of Clarence James Neal, of Wichita, Kansas, and *d* 8 Dec 1961, leaving by his 1st w:

(1) *Patrick James [Patrick Goodenough Esq, 11552, Hillpark Lane, Los Altos, CA 94022, USA]; *b* 6 July 1930; *m* 20 Sept 1952 *Judith, dau of Charles Weber, of Los Altos, and has issue:

1a *William; *b* 6 Sept 1955

2a *James; *b* 15 Nov 1957

3a *John; *b* 24 July 1959

(2) *Thomas Frederick; *b* 6 March 1936; *m* 26 Jan 1963 *Susan Mary, dau of Col John Hamilton Boag, OBE

(1) *Anne [Mrs William Moser, Menlo College, Menlo Park, CA, USA]; *b* 18 Oct 1927; *m* 9 June 1956 *William Moser, s of C J Moser, MD, of Grant's Pass, Oregon, and has issue:

1a *Margaret Anne; *b* 29 Oct 1959

2a *Nancy Jane; *b* 13 Oct 1961

3 Michael Grant, CBE (1946), DSO (1940); R-Adml 1954, served WW II, Cdr Orange-Nassau, US Bronze Star; *b* 18 June 1904; *educ* RNCs Osborne and Dartmouth; *m* 1934 *Nancy, dau of Sir (Alexander) Ransford Slater, GCMG, CBE, and *d* 31 Dec 1955, leaving issue:

(1) *Anthony Michael, CMG (1990), FCO: Assist U-Sec 1992–, 2nd Sec Athens 1967, Priv Sec to Parly U-Sec 1971 and Min State 1972, HC Ghana and Amb Togo 1989–92; *b* 5 July 1941; *educ* Wellington and New Coll Oxford (BA 1963, MA 1980); *m* 22 July 1967 *Veronica Mary, er dau of Lt-Col Peter Pender-Cudlipp, MVO, and has issue:

1a *A son; *b* 11 Dec 1970

1a *Eleanor Margaret; *b* 1 June 1968

(2) *Simon Ransford; *b* 5 Jan 1945; *educ* Wellington and Ch Ch Oxford

(1) *Susan Maeve; *b* 7 Sept 1936; *m* 15 Aug 1959 *George Christopher Band, only s of Rev Edward Band, and adopted:

*Nigel Edward; *b* 4 April 1964

*Rupert Alexander; *b* 22 Jan 1969

*Charlotte Louise; *b* 28 April 1966

1 Barbara Mary; *b* 29 Sept 1901; *m* 7 Dec 1928 Sir Julian Stanley Crossley, 2nd s of Charles Wheatley Crossley, JP, and had issue. He *d* 26 Jan 1971

2 Frances Maeve; *b* 1909; *d* 1929

The est son,

Sir William Macnamara Goodenough, 1st Bt (UK), so *cr* 19 Jan 1943, JP, DL Oxon; *b* 10 March 1899; *educ* Wellington and Ch Ch Oxford (MA 1922, Hon Student); CC Oxon (chm 1934–38), Dep Steward Oxford U 1939–51, memb Court Lond U 1945–51, chm: Barclays Bank 1947–51, Dominion Students Hall Tst, Export Guarantees Advsy Cncl, Exec Ctee Export Credits Guarantee Dept 1943, Nuffield Fndn, Hon Treas: Radcliffe Infirmary, Medical Research Cncl, memb Colonial Ec and Devpt Cncl 1946, chm VWH Cricklade Hunt Ctee; *m* May 15 1924 Dorothea Louisa, JP (Oxon 1942–51) (*d* 1987), WVS Centre Oraniser 1939–45, Co Commr Guides Oxon 1942–48, Co Organiser WVS 1953, er dau of Ven Hon Kenneth Francis Gibbs, s of 1st Baron Aldenham (*see* ALDENHAM and HUNSDON OF HUNSDON, B), and *d* 23 May 1951, leaving:

1 **Sir Richard Edmund Goodenough, 2nd Bt**; *b* 9 June 1925; *educ* Eton and Ch Ch Oxford; Coldstream Gds WW II (invalided); *m* 22 Dec 1951 *Jane Isobel [Jane Lady Gooch, 69 Oakwood Court, Abbotsbury Rd, London W14 8JF], only dau of Harry Stuart Parnell McLernon, of Gisborne, NZ, and *d* Dec 1996, leaving:

(1) Sir WILLIAM McLERNON GOOCH, **3rd and present Bt**

(1) *Rosemary Louise; *b* 23 Dec 1952; *m* 1st 1977 Frederick Charles le Roux; *m* 2nd 1993 *Patrick George MacGregor Masson, s of Dr George Aird Masson, MD, FRCPE, and by her 1st husb has:

1a *Amy Elizabeth; *b* 1978

2a *Nancy Jane; *b* 1983

(2) *Joanna Jane; *b* 2 May 1958

2 David William; *b* 19 Sept 1926; *d* 2 March 1927

3 +(Frederick) Roger, DL (Oxon 1989) [Roger Goodenough Esq DL, Broadwell Manor, Lechlade, Glos GL7 3QS]; FLS (Memb Cncl 1968, Treas 1970–75), High Sheriff Oxon 1987–88, Govr Shiplake Coll 1963–74 (chm 1965–70) and Wellington 1968–74, local dir Barclays Bank Oxford 1969–87, Barclays Bank DCO London Ctee 1966, dir Barclays Bank UK Management plc 1979–87, Barclays plc 1985–89, Barclays Bank plc 1979–89, Barclays Bank Intl 1977–87, advsy dir Barclays Bank Thames Valley Regn 1988–89, Curator Oxford U Chest 1974–93, Tstee Nuffield Med Tst and Nuffield Dominions Tst (Chm 1987–) 1968–, chm Nuffield Orthopaedic Tst 1981– and Oxford and Dist Hosps Improvment and Devpt Fund 1982–, Supernumerary Fell Wolfson Coll Oxford 1993–, Govr London Goodenough Tst for Overseas Graduates 1985–; *b* 21 Dec 1927; *educ* Eton, Magdalene Coll Cambridge (MA) and Oxford (MA); FRSA, FCIB 1968; RN 1946–78; *m* 15 May 1954 *Marguerite June, only dau of David Forbes Mackintosh, Headmaster Loretto, and has issue:

(1) +David Frederick; *b* 21 June 1955; *educ* Clifton and Grey Coll Durham (BSc); *m* 1988 *Nicola Dawn Foreman and has issue:

1a +Michael John Frederick; *b* 1989

2a +Mark William Anthonry; *b* 1991

(1) *Annabel Margaret; *b* 12 July 1957; *educ* LMH Oxford (BA); *m* 1980 *Col Paul Christopher Charles Molyneaux, RA, and has issue:

1a *Harriet Frances Rose; *b* 1986

2a *Emma Flora Louise; *b* 1989

(2) *Victoria Frances; *b* 10 Feb 1961; *educ* LMH Oxford (BA); *m* 1989 *David Richard Arden Bott, yr s of Dr Edward Bott, and has issue:

1a *Patrick Edward Arden; *b* 1991

2a *Archie Frederick Arden; *b* 1993

4 Samuel Kenneth Henry; FRICS, Govr Dominion Students Hall Tst 1961, ptnr Knight Frank and Rutley 1961; *b* 3 April 1930; *educ* Eton and Ch Ch Oxford (BA 1951, MA 1957); *m* 5 June 1979 *Mrs Patricia Nagle, er dau of Cedric Barnett, and *d* July 1983

1 *Mary Dorothea [Mrs Alistair Forbes, All Saints House, nr Axminster, Devon EX13 7LR]; *b* 19 Aug 1940; *m* 2 April 1965 *Capt (John) Alistair Ponsonby Forbes (*see* FORBES, L)

GOODHART, Baron

Creation: B. (LP, UK) 2 Aug 1997.

THE BARON GOODHART, of Youlbury, Co Oxon (Sir William Goodhart) [The Rt Hon The Lord Goodhart, 11 Clarence Terrace, London NW1 4RD; Youlbury House, Boars Hill, Oxford OX1 5HH]; *b* 18 Jan 1933; *educ* Eton, Trin Coll Cambridge and Harvard Law Sch; 2nd Lt Oxon and Bucks LI 1951–53; barrister Lincoln's Inn 1957, QC 1979, Bencher 1986, memb: Cncl Justice 1972– (Exec Ctee V-Chm 1978–88, Chm 1988–94), Cncl Legal Educn 1986–92, Conveyancing Standing Ctee Law Commn 1987–89, Lib Dem Policy Ctee 1988–, Tax Law Review Ctee 1994–, Internat Commn Jurists 1993–; Chm: SDP Cncl Arrangements Ctee 1982–88, Lib Dem Conf Ctee 1988–91, Lib Dem Lawyers' Assoc 1988–91, Cambridge U Court of Discipline 1993–; dir Bar Mutual Indemnity Fund Ltd 1988–; Tstee Campden Charities 1975–90, ktd 1989; author: *Specific Performance* (with Prof Gareth Jones, 1986), *Countdown to 1997* (jt author, 1992), *Human Rights in Kashmir* (jt author, 1995); *m* 1966 *The Hon Celia McClare Herbert, dau of 2nd Baron Hemingford (*qv*), and has issue

Lineage: Prof A L GOODHART, Hon KBE, QC, FBA; *m* Cecily Carter and had:

WILLIAM (Sir), *cr* a **Baron**

GOODHART, Bt

Arms: Gules a buck trippant argent, in chief two bees volant or, on a chief nebuly of the third a cross of Lorraine of the field between two eagles displayed sable. **Crest:** A beehive or between two bees, all within a rainbow terminating in clouds proper. **Motto:** *A Deo omnia* ('From God all things'). **Creation:** Bt. (UK) 1 July 1911.

SIR ROBERT ANTHONY GORDON GOODHART, 4TH BT, of St Marylebone and Holtye Place, Sussex [Sir Robert Goodhart Bt, Orchard Hill, Netherbury, Bridport, Dorset DT6 5NB]; *b* 15 Dec 1948; *s* f 1979; *educ* Rugby and Guy's (MB, BS); MRCS, LRCP 1972, MRCGP 1976, DObstRCOG, Dr Beaminster, Jr Medical Registrar Guy's 1974, GP Bromley 1976–80; *m* 1972 *Kathleen Ellen, er dau of Rev A D MacRae, MA, of Glenelg, Ross-shire, and has issue:

1 +MARTIN ANDREW; *b* 9 Sept 1974

2 +Iain Michael; *b* 1980

1 *Kim Elaine; *b* 1977

2 *Rachel Alice; *b* 1987

Lineage: JOHN HENRY GOODHART, of Borken, Hesse, Germany; *b* 1710; *m* Elizabeth (*d* Nov 1783), dau of Jacob Regenbogen, Chllr Borken, and *d* March 1783, leaving issue:

EMANUEL GOODHART, of Gt Ilford, Essex; settled England 1737, naturalised 30 July 1784; *m* 1st 1769 Charlotte Imson (*d* 3 Sept 1773), of Moringen, Westphalia, and had issue; *m* 2nd Maria — (*d* 2 April 1787) and by her had:

JOSEPH GOODHART, of The Grove, Hackney; *b* 12 July 1776; *m* Jan 1803 Charlotte Elizabeth (*d* 3 Dec 1844), er dau and coheir of Charles Gottfried Wolde, DD, DCL, and *d* 12 June 1819, leaving issue:

ALFRED HARRINGTON GOODHART, of Camden; *b* 3 Jan 1817; *m* 27 April 1843 Elizabeth Wilkinson (*d* 13 April 1904), dau of Alexander Goudge and Charlotte Wilkinson, of Hackney; *bur* 27 Aug 1852, having had:

1 Charles Alfred (Rev); *b* 19 April 1844; *educ* Corpus Christi Coll Cambridge (MA); Rector Lambourne, Essex 1893–1915; *m* 28 Nov 1878 Elizabeth Anne, dau of Charles Warner, and *d* 1918, leaving three sons and a dau

2 JAMES FREDERIC (Sir), **1st Bt**

3 Herbet Synnot; Ecclesiastical Commr; *b* 11 Jan 1847; *m* 5 Sept 1882 Katharine, dau of Alfred Goodman, and *d* 12 June 1936, leaving issue

4 Hugh Wilkinson; *b* 1 June 1848; *educ* Cambridge (MA); *d* unm 10 June 1901

5 Ernest; *d* young

1 Helen Maude; *d* unm 2 April 1943

ALFRED GOODHART's 2nd s,

Sir James Frederic Goodhart, 1st Bt (UK), so *cr* 1 July 1911, of Portland Place, St Marylebone, and Holtye, Sussex; *b* 24 Oct 1845; MD, CM Aberdeen U, FRCP London, Hon LLD Aberdeen; *m* 2 Sept 1879 Emma Sandford (*d* 8 Feb 1915), dau of William Bennett, JP, of Ashgrove, Marden, Herefs, and *d* 28 May 1916, leaving:

1 **Sir Ernest Frederic Goodhart, 2nd Bt**; *b* 12 Aug 1880; *educ* Westminster and Merton Coll Oxford (BA, 1902, MA 1935); barrister Inner Temple 1904; *m* 19 Dec 1906 Frances Evelyn (*d* 3 Jan 1953), dau of Montagu Fullerton Armstrong, 4th s of Sir Andrew Armstrong, 1st Bt, of Gallen (*qv*), and *d* 13 Jan 1961, having had issue:

(1) Frederic Charles Francis; *b* 29 Dec 1907; Lt Roy Sussex Regt; *d* 16 March 1937 of injuries recd while on patrol duty in Jerusalem

(1) Pamela Ernestine; *d* unm 22 Feb 1983

2 Gordon Wilkinson; *b* 24 July 1882; *educ* Trin Coll Cambridge (MA), MD, FRCP; Capt 2nd London Gen Hosp, RAMC (TF); *m* 15 April 1914 Alice Stransham, 4th dau of Lt-Gen William Puget La Touche, IA, and *d* 16 July 1948, leaving issue:

(1) JOHN GORDON (Sir), **3rd Bt**

(1) *(Dorothy) Joyce [Miss Joyce Goodhart, Bayfield, Copp Hill Lane, Budleigh Salterton, Devon EX9 6DT]; *b* 1921

(2) *Alice Mary [Miss Alice Goodhart, Bayfield, Copp Hill Lane, Budleigh Salterton, Devon EX9 6DT]; *b* 1926

Sir ERNEST's nephew,

Sir John Gordon Goodhart, 3rd Bt, of Portland Place; *b* 14 Dec 1916; LRCP 1941, Surgn-Lt WW II 1942–46; *m* 19 Feb 1944 *(Margaret Mary) Eileen, dau of Morgan Morgan, of Cray, Breconshire, and *d* 1979, leaving issue:

1 Sir ROBERT ANTHONY GORDON, **4th and present Bt**

1 *Anne Rosemary [Mrs John Soul, Trevenevow, Crapstone Road, Yelverton, Devon PL20 6BT]; *b* 4 April 1945; *m* 15 Feb 1969 *Surgn-Sub-Lt John Oliver Soul, RN, only s of Gordon Leslie Soul, of Guildford, and has:

(1) *Nicholas John; *b* 1971

(1) *Sarah Victoria; *b* 1974

GOODSON

Arms: Ermine on a chevron between three quatrefoils gules, leaved and slipped vert, as many garbs or. **Crest:** A wolf's head erased gules, collared and charged on the neck with a spur or. **Motto:** *Qui labor illi gaudia* ('Who labours rejoices'). **Creation:** Bt. (UK) 18 Jan 1922.

SIR MARK WESTON LASSAM GOODSON, 3RD BT, of Waddeton Court, Co Devon [Sir Mark Goodson Bt, Kilham, Mindrum, Northumberland TD12 4QS]; *b* 12 Dec 1925; *s* unc 1986; *educ* Radley and Jesus Coll Cambridge; *m* 4 May 1949 *Barbara Mary Constantine, dau of Surgn-Capt (D) Reginald Joseph McAuliffe Andrews, RN, of Crandel, Ferndown, Dorset, and has issue:

1 +ALAN REGINALD; *b* 15 May 1960; *educ* Ampleforth

1 *Phyllida Mary; *b* 25 March 1950; *m* 1973 *Dr Timothy Freeman White

2 *Hilary Frances; *b* 13 Oct 1953

3 *Christian Mary; *b* 20 Nov 1958; *m* 1983 *Christopher Collins

Lineage: Sir Alfred Lassam Goodson, 1st Bt (UK), so *cr* 18 Jan 1922, JP Cheshire and Devon; *b* 17 May 1867 (s of Alfred Goodson, of London, merchant); CC Cheshire 1904–07, High Sheriff Devon 1920, Pres OTC Selection Bd, Cdre Roy Dart Yacht Club; *m* 9 Sept 1892 Mary Ethel (*d* 6 April 1946), dau of Richard Baker, of Stretford, nr Manchester, and *d* 29 Nov 1940, leaving issue:

1 **Sir Alfred Lassam Goodson, 2nd Bt**, of Waddeton Court, Devon; *b* 26 Aug 1893; *educ* Radley; Lt-Col, Capt City London Yeo (despatches) WW I, cmded No 1 Bn Northumberland HG WW II, MFH Coll Valley 1924, Pres Br Percheron Horse Soc 1947–49, Pres Aberdeen Angus Cattle Soc 1949; *m* 1st 7 Oct 1920 Joan (*d* 16 Oct 1939), dau of Christopher John Leyland, of Haggerston Castle, Northumberland; *m* 2nd 24 June 1941 *Enid Clayton, 2nd dau of Col Robert Clayton Swan, and formerly w of (a) Capt J H Turner and (b) Capt Christopher Digby Leyland, and *dsp* 1986

2 Alan Richard Lassam; *b* 1 Jan 1896; Maj LRB; *m* 14 Aug 1923 Clarisse Mary Weston, dau of John Weston Adamson, of The Mount, Northallerton, Yorks, and *d* 11 Feb 1941, leaving issue:

(1) Sir MARK WESTON LASSAM GOODSON, **3rd and present Bt**

3 Hugh Lassam, OBE, JP (Devon 1938–52); *b* 9 July 1905; *educ* privately; High Sheriff 1954, Sub Lt RNVR 1942–44, memb: Cncl RYA 1934–46, MOI Advsy Cncl 1938–45, Management Ctee Br Seamen's Boys' Home 1941–63, Ford Park Sch, exec and finance Ctee Devon Queen Victoria and King Edward Comprehensive Fund, chm: Lib Nat Orgn SW Area 1940–43, Nat Assoc Boys' Clubs (Devon) 1948–51, RYS Syndicate taking Yacht *Sceptre* to USA 1958 for America's Cup, Sail Trg Assoc 1963–67 (Pres 1967), Cncl of St John (Devon) 1959–64, CstJ, Pres: Devon Arts Soc 1947, Boy Scouts Assoc No 6 Dist, chm RYS Sailing Ctee 1952, SSAFA S Devon Area, Fell IOD, R-Cdre Roy London Yacht Club 1935–39 and Roy Torbay Yacht Club 1935–46, Cdre Roy Dart Yacht Club 1949–58, dir Torbay Hotels Ltd and Devonshire Investment Estates; *m* 10 July 1945 *June Patricia, er dau of Maj Joseph Charles Hunter, CBE, MC, DL, of Crimple Brow, Pannal, Yorks, and *d* 1985, leaving:

(1) +Aldred Lassam; *b* 2 June 1946; *m* 1st 1970 Rosemary Anne Swales; *m* 2nd 1989 *Suzanne Harris and has by his 1st w:

1a +Barnaby; *b* 1972

2a +Alfred; *b* 1974

1a *Amy; *b* 1977

2a *Polly; *b* 1979

(2) +Hugh Anthony Lassam [Hugh Goodson Esq, Waddeton Court, Brixham, S Devon TQ5 0EN]; *b* 4 Sept 1955; chm Devonshire Investment Estates, R-Cdre Roy Torbay Yacht Club 1988; *m* 1977 *Jane Mary, dau of Brian Kirley, of Southside, Cobham, Surrey, and has issue:

1a +Hugo Matthew Lassam; *b* 1982

(1) *Sarah Jane; *b* 16 June 1947; *m* 3 June 1972 *Guy Arthur Louis Cruwys, only s of Geoffrey Edgar Cruwys, of Cruwys Morchard House, Tiverton, Devon, and has issue:

1a *Robert; *b* 1976

1a *Emily; *b* 1974

2a *Mary; *b* 1978

3a *Belinda; *b* 1982

(2) *Penelope Jane; *b* 13 June 1948; *m* 1975 *Capt Rhydian Peter Vaughan and has issue:

1a *Sholto; *b* 1977

2a *Orlando; *b* 1983

1a *Camilla; *b* 1980

1 *Kathleen May Lassam, JP (Devon 1941–53) [Mrs Roy Craig, The Old Parsonage, Wilmington, Honiton, Devon]; *b* 20 Dec 1901; *m* 28 June 1920 Roy Neville Craig, MD, LRCP, MFH, Lt-Col Army Cadet Force, est s of Eustace Craig, of Beaufort House, Ham Common, and has had issue:

(1) Ian Neville; *b* 19 Oct 1922; *ka* El Alamein Oct 1942

(2) *David Neville; *b* 18 Aug 1924

GOOLD

Arms: Azure on a fess or between five goldfinches, three in chief and two in base, proper, three mullets gules. **Crest:** A demi-lion rampant or. **Motto:** *Deus mihi providebit* ('God will provide for me'). **Creation:** Bt. (UK) 8 Aug 1801.

SIR GEORGE WILLIAM GOOLD, 8TH BT, of Old Court, Co Cork [Sir George Goold Bt, 180 Hargrave St, Paddington, NSW 2021, Australia]; *b* 25 March 1950; *s* f 1997; co dir; *m* 1973 *Julie Ann, dau of Leonard Crack, and has:

1 +GEORGE LEONARD POWELL; *b* 1 Dec 1975

2 +Jon; *b* 1977

Lineage: WILLIAM GOULD, Mayor Cork *temp* HENRY VII; ancestor of:

HENRY GOULD; *m* —, dau of George Hennessy (*see* WINDLESHAM, B), and had:

GEORGE GOOLD (changed spelling of surname), of Old Court, Co Cork; *m* Catherine May, dau of William Galwey, of Castletownsend, and *d* March 1789, having had, with other issue:

1 Henry Michael; *m* 27 May 1777 Catharine, dau of Donatt O'Callaghan, of Kilgory, Co Clare, and *d* 27 Oct 1786, leaving, with another dau (*d* unm):

(1) GEORGE (Sir), **2nd Bt**

(2) Henry, of Clonmore, Co Tipperary; *b* 22 Sept 1782; *m* 2 July 1801 Eleanor (*d* 1848), dau and coheir of Thomas Francis Hawkins, of Nash Court, Kent, and *d* 1835, leaving, with three other sons and three daus:

1a Henry Michael Francis; Capt 38th Regt HEICS; *b* 22 July 1803; *m* 1835 Matilda (*d* 1865), dau of Matthew O'Brien, of New Castle, Co Limerick, and *d* 1861, leaving, with other issue:

1b Francis; *b* 15 Oct 1839; Bengal Army; *m* 1861 Louisa, dau of Robert O'Dowd, of Calcutta, and had issue:

1c Denis; *b* 1 Oct 1862

2c Gerald; *b* 19 March 1863

2a Valentine Edmund; *b* 19 April 1813; *m* 9 March 1849 Charlotte (*d* 15 Oct 1902), dau of Robert Ritchie, and *d* 1892, leaving,with other issue:

1b Eleanor Hawkins; *m* 8 Oct 1879 Donald McArthur and *d* 29 Nov 1916, leaving issue

2b Anna Maria

1a Mary Catherine; *b* 29 June 1802; *m* 26 July 1834 Redmond Peter O'Carroll (*d* 8 Oct 1847), of Dublin, est s of John O'Carroll, of Ardagh, Co Galway, and *d* 5 June 1877, leaving issue

(1) Marcella; *m* Thomas Gillibrand, of Gillibrand Hall, Lancs

2 **Sir Francis Goold, 1st Bt** (UK), so *cr* 8 Aug 1801, with remainder in default of male issue to the heirs male of his f; *d* unm 20 Aug 1818

1 Anne; *m* John Donnellan, of Nutgrove

2 Margaret; *m* 1st O'Neill Segrave, of Cabra, Co Dublin; *m* 2nd John Agnew Connell

Sir FRANCIS's nephew,

Sir George Goold, 2nd Bt; *b* 29 March 1778; *m* 13 May 1802 Lady Charlotte Browne (*d* 1 Nov 1852), est dau of the Earl of Kenmare (*see* 1949 edn), and *d* 16 March 1870, having had, with two other sons (*d* unm) and five daus (*d* unm):

1 **Sir Henry Valentine Goold, 3rd Bt**; *b* 7 July 1803; *d* unm 18 June 1893

2 George Ignatius, JP (RM Waterford); *b* 7 Sept 1805; *m* 3 Nov 1840 Clara (*d* 9 March 1870), dau of Maj-Gen James Webber Smith, CB, and *d* 6 Nov 1879, having had, with four sons (*d* unm):

(1) JAMES STEPHEN (Sir), **4th Bt**

(2) Vere Thomas St Leger; *b* 2 Oct 1853; *m* 22 Aug 1891 Violet (*d* 1914), dau of Hippolyte Girodin, and *dsp* Sept 1909

(1) Frances Mary Anne

Sir HENRY's nephew,

Sir James Stephen Goold, 4th Bt; *b* 13 Oct 1848; *m* 8 Feb 1873 Bridget Mary (*d* 28 Jan 1898), dau of Patrick Jordan, of Adelaide, and *d* 8 Aug 1926, leaving issue:

1 GEORGE PATRICK (Sir), **5th Bt**

2 John Henry; *b* 24 July 1882; resident in S Australia

3 Joseph Ernest, of Salisbury, S Australia; *b* 24 May 1888

1 Mary Anne; *b* 1 May 1877; *m* 20 May 1896 John Hartman, s of John Hartman, of Samunda

2 Clara Agnes; *b* 29 May 1881

3 Catherine Anne; *b* 1 March 1892

Sir JAMES's est s,

Sir George Patrick Goold, 5th Bt (but his name never appeared on the official Roll of Baronets); *b* 9 July 1878; *m* 23 April 1902 Mary, dau of Nicholas Browne, and *d* Jan 1954, leaving issue:

1 GEORGE IGNATIUS (Sir), **6th Bt**

2 Leo Francis; *b* 18 Feb 1905; *d* 15 April 1968

1 Eileen Mary; *b* 15 March 1907; *m* 29 Oct 1932 George Langston

Sir GEORGE's est s,

Sir George Ignatius Goold, 6th Bt; *b* 29 April 1903; *m* *Rhoda, dau of Albert Benn, of Port Pirie, S Australia, and *d* 26 April 1967, having had issue:

1 **Sir George Leonard Goold, 7th Bt**; *b* 26 Aug 1923; *educ* St Mark's, Port Pirie, S Australia, and St John's Coll, Port Pirie; engr, memb Standing Cncl Btage; *m* 8 Dec 1945 *Joyce Cecelia [Joyce Lady Goold, 60 Canterbury Rd, Victor Harbour, S Australia 5211], dau of William Percival Cutler, of Melbourne, and *d* 31 Aug 1997, leaving:

(1) Sir GEORGE WILLIAM GOOLD, **8th and present Bt**

(1) *Dianne Joy [Mrs Gary Button, 28 Mary Penfold Dve, Rosslyn Park, Adelaide, S Australia 5072]; *b* 15 Sept 1946; *m* 31 Aug 1968 *Gary N Button and has:

1a *Darren Scott; *b* 1970; *m* 11 June 1994 *Penelope Kocent

1a *Kelly Lou; *b* 1972

(2) *Georgina Susan [Mrs Malcolm Sard, 12 First St, Napperby, S Australia]; *b* 2 Dec 1948; *m* 3 May 1969 *Malcolm Kennedy Sard and has:

1a *Stephen Kennedy; *b* 1970

2a *Michael Leonard; *b* 1974

(3) *Michelle Julie [Mrs John O'Dwyer, PO Box 771, Warragul, VIC 3820, Australia]; *b* 26 Aug 1956; *m* 1979 *John Joseph O'Dwyer and has:

1a *Stuart Goold; *b* 1981

1a *Rachel Louise; *b* 1985

2a *Sarah Kate; *b* 1988

3a *Hannah Charlotte; *b* 1990

(4) *Louise Mary; *b* 7 July 1962; *m* 1987 (but retains maiden name) *Paul James Christie

2 Douglas Harold; *b* 21 Aug 1927; *m* 4 Nov 1950 Beryl Ivy, dau of Vernon McKay, of Port Pirie, and *dsp*

GORDON

Arms: Azure a bezant between three boar's heads erased or, in dexter chief a canton of a Baronet of Nova Scotia. **Crest:** A dexter hand grasping a sabre, proper. **Motto:** *Dominus providebit* ('The Lord will provide'). **Creation:** Bt. (NS) 9 July 1706.

SIR ROBERT JAMES GORDON, 10TH BT, of Afton and Earlston, Kirkcudbrightshire [Sir Robert Gordon Bt, Earlstoun, Guyra, NSW 2365, Australia]; *b* 17 Aug 1932; *s* f 1982; probably next in remainder to Viscountcy of Kenmure and Lordship of Lochinvar (dormant since 1872); *educ* Barker Coll, Sydney, N Sydney Boys' Sch, Wagga Ag Coll (Dip Ag); farmer 1958–; *m* 1976 *Helen Julia Weston, dau of John Weston Perry, of Cammerary, NSW

Lineage: WILLIAM de GORDOUNE, 6th of Lochinvar; had a 2nd s:

ALEXANDER; ggf of:

JOHN GORDON of Earlston; *m* 1st 1582 Margaret, est dau of John Sinclair of Earlston, and *d* 1628, leaving a dau (Margaret, *m* 1st John McKnaught of Kilquhanidy, *m* 2nd Edward Maxwell of Balmangan and *dsp*); *m* 2nd 1585 Mary, 2nd dau of James Chalmers of Gaitgirth, and by her had, with two other sons (*dsp*):

1 ALEXANDER

2 William, of Carleton; had:

(1) James, 2nd of Carleton; *d* unm 1688, having settled Carleton on his cousin John

3 David, of Gordonstown in Galloway; had:

(1) Nathaniel, 4th of Carleton

The est son,

ALEXANDER GORDON, 2nd of Earlston; *b* 1587; royalist, MP (S Parl) Kirkcudbrightshire; offered a btcy but declined; *m* 4 Jan 1612 Elizabeth, dau of John Gordon 2nd of Pennynghame (gf of 5th Viscount Kenmure), and *d* Nov 1653, having had, with a s (*d* unm):

1 John, Yr. of Earlston; *b* 161–; *m* Jean, 3rd dau of David Boswell, and *dsp* & *vp* 29 Oct 1645

2 WILLIAM

1 Margaret; *m* 1638 Thomas Hay of Arieland

The 2nd son,

WILLIAM GORDON, 3rd of Earlston; *b* 1614; *m* 26 Nov 1648 Mary (*d* 1696), dau of Sir John Hope, Lord Craighall, and was *ka* Battle of Bothwell Bridge 22 June 1679, leaving:

1 ALEXANDER GORDON (Sir), **2nd Bt**

2 **Sir William Gordon, 1st Bt** (NS), so *cr* 9 July 1706, with remainder, failing heirs male of his body, to his bro Alexander and the heirs male of his body, of Afton; *b* 1654; joined army of Frederick, Duke of Brandenburg, 1670; participated in Duke of Monmouth's uprising 1685; later rejoined Prussian Army; subsequently memb WILLIAM III's entourage, landing with him Torbay 5 Nov 1688; fought Battle of Steenkirk July 1692, Lt-Col; Govr Fort William; *m* 26 Feb 1692 Mary (*dsp* 1733), dau of Sir George Campbell of Cessnock, and *dsp* Dec 1718

3 John, 3rd of Carleton

1 Margaret; *m* 1682 Sir James Holborn, of Menstrie

The 1st Bt's er bro,

Sir Alexander Gordon, 2nd Bt, of Earlston; *b* 1650; escaped to Holland after the Battle of Bothwell Bridge 1679; declared guilty of treason *in absentia*; sentenced to death and forfeiture of his estates 19 Feb 1681; captured at sea 21 Aug 1683 and ordered beheaded but pardoned and after 6 years' imprisonment Edinburgh Castle, on the Bass Rock and in Blackness Castle, was released 5 Jan 1689; *m* 1st 16 Nov 1676 Janet (*d* 26 Feb 1696), est dau of Sir Thomas Hamilton of Preston, and had, with other issue (*d* young):

1 THOMAS (Sir), **3rd Bt**

2 Robert; *b* 1688; *m* 1715 widow of Robert French, and *d* 1750, having had a dau Janet

3 Archibald; *b* 1691; Collector Excise; *m* 1721 Janet, dau of Sir Thomas Young of Rosebank, and *d* 1754, having had, with a dau (Margaret, *b* 1724, *d* unm 1779):

(1) Gilbert, of Halleaths; *b* 1722; *m* Margaret, dau of Capt Stewart, of the STEWARTs of Physgill, and *d* 1789, having had, with other issue (*d* unm):

1a Archibald, of Halleaths; *m* Anne Ponsonby and had, with two other sons (*d* unm):

1b Archibald; *d* 1847, leaving issue

1a Patricia Heron; *m* 1 Dec 1794, as his 1st w, 1st Baron Panmure of Brechin and Navar and *d* 11 May 1821, leaving issue (*see* DALHOUSIE, E)

1 Anne; *b* 1670; *m* 1697 John Neilson of Corsock (*d* 1708) and *d* 1761, having had issue

2 Mary; *b* 1681; *m* 1701 Edward Goldie of Craigmuie (*d* 1711) and *d* 1723, having had issue

3 Margaret; *b* 1687; *m* 1706 John McCartney, of Blacket (*d* 1723), and *d* 1715, having had issue

4 Janet; *b* 1692; *m* 1713 William Martin, of Kirkland, and *d* 1725, having had issue

The **2nd Bt** *m* 2nd 8 March 1698 Hon Marion Gordon (*d* 20 Oct 1748), dau of 5th Viscount Kenmure, and *d* 10 Nov 1726, having by her had further issue:

4 William, of Culvennan, formerly of Greenlaw; *b* 1706; *m* 1740 Isabel McCulloch Gordon (*d* Oct 1802), heiress of Culvennan, and upon her succession in 1750 assumed by virtue of the entail (confirmed by Act of Parl 1776) the sole name and designation of GORDON of Culvennan, and *d* Oct 1757, leaving, with another s (*d* unm):

(1) Alexander (Sir), of Culvennan; *b* 1748; advocate 1771; *m* 17 July 1769 Grace Dalrymple, only sis of Sir John Dalrymple Hay, Bt (*qv*), and *d* 21 Oct 1830, leaving:

1a David; *m* Agnes, dau of William Hyslop of Lochend, and had, with two other sons and two daus:

1b William, of Culvennan, JP; *b* 17 Aug 1800; *m* 17 Aug 1825 Agnes Marion (*d* 23 May 1853), dau of John Hyslop of Lochend, and *d* 27 Jan 1858, leaving issue:

1c David Alexander, of Culvennan, JP; *b* 29 Feb 1828; *m* 1 Jan 1855 Jane Lawrie (*d* 23 April 1927), only dau of Allan Bell, of Hillowtown, Kirkcudbrightshire, and *d* 28 Aug 1882, having had, with two other sons (*d* unm):

1d Lochinvar Alexander Charles, CB, CSI; *b* 26 May 1864; Maj-Gen RA WW I (despatches), Order White Eagle Serbia 3rd Cl with swords; *m* 30 April 1895 Maria (*d* 1945), dau of J T Withers, and *d* 7 Aug 1927, leaving:

1e Alexander William Kenmure, MC; *b* 19 Oct 1898; Lt-Col RA, WW I (severely wounded), WW II; *m* 4 Feb 1933 (*divorce* 1934) Kathleen Kerr, only dau of J C Dunfresne, of Vancouver

1e Jean Isobel Marion; *m* 16 Nov 1935 Godfrey Roydon Hughes (*d* 1957) and *d* 30 June 1968

2d Claude Augustus Rutherford; *b* 12 Aug 1867; *m* 1890 Alice Foster (*d* 28 March 1948), dau of Alfred Stretch, of Frodsham, Cheshire, and *d* 27 July 1936, leaving issue:

1e Margaret Isobel

1d Grace Marion; *m* 25 June 1879 Frederick Alexander Walker and *d* 23 July 1923, leaving issue

2d Beatrice Isobel Hilda; *m* 1 Nov 1898 Henry Adolphus Warre Slade and *d* 25 Sept 1940, leaving issue (*see* SLADE, Bt)

2c John Hyslop; *b* 6 Nov 1829; *m* 1 Feb 1859 Margaret (*d* 1878), dau of W Napier, and *d* 19 Oct 1869, leaving, with a s (*d* unm):

1d Mary Winifred; *m* 1896 René, Benoit Ritter, of Basle, and *d* 2 April 1921, leaving issue

3c James; *b* 1833; *m* 1863 Hannah Coleman Warwick Lisle (*d* 1921) and *d* 1864, leaving:

1d Agnes James

1c Agnes Marion; *m* 31 May 1860 Benjamin Hardwicke and had issue

(2) David, of Threavegrange; *b* 1750; joined 67th Regt of Foot, subsequently volunteered into the Russian serv and *d* unm Battle at Bucharest 24 Oct 1771

(1) Marion; *b* 1745; *m* 1st 1775 William Kirkpatrick of Raeberry (*d* 22 May 1778); *m* 2nd 31 March 1783 Alexander Herries Maxwell of Munshes (*see* HERRIES OF TERREGLES, L) and *dsp* 14 April 1839

(2) Isabella; *m* 1779 James Balmain

5 Grizell; *b* 1703; *m* 1721 Alexander Gordon, 5th of Carleton (*d* 1742), and *d* 1740, having had issue

The 2nd Bt's est son,

Sir Thomas Gordon, 3rd Bt; *b* 26 Oct 1685; *m* 1st 20 Jan 1710 Anne (*d* 8 April 1751), est dau of William Boick, and had, with other issue:

1 Thomas, Yr. of Earlston; *b* 1713; *m* 1737 Catharine, only child of Daniel Campbell of Shawfield, and *dvp* 1767, having had, with two sons (*d* unm):

(1) Catharine; *m* 1770 Maj-Gen Alexander Stewart of Afton (having acquired the Afton estate by *m*) and had issue

2 **Sir John Gordon, 4th Bt**; *b* 20 Dec 1720; Capt 70th Foot; *m* 18 April 1775 Anne (*d* 4 Nov 1822), dau of Thomas Mylne of Powderhall, and *dsp* 17 Oct 1795

3 Francis; *b* 1728; joined 60th Foot, twice made prisoner; massacred 1763

4 James, of Jamaica; *m* 1779 Christiana, dau of James Scarlett (*see* ABINGER, B), and *d* 1794, having had, with another s (*dsp*):

(1) **Sir John Gordon, 5th Bt**; *b* 4 Oct 1780; inherited the Carleton estate 1816 from John Gordon, 8th of Carleton; *m* 1st 10 April 1809 Juliana (*d* 13 Feb 1824), dau of Jervis Gallimore, of Greenfield; *m* 2nd 22 April 1825 Mary (*d* 8 March 1869), dau of William Irving, of Gribton, Dumfriesshire, and *d* 8 Jan 1843, having by her had, with two other sons and two other daus:

1a **Sir William Gordon, 6th Bt**, JP, DL Kirkcudbrightshire; *b* 20 Oct 1830; Lt-Col 17th Lancers, Crimea and India; *m* 1st 21 Sept 1857 Catherine (*d* 17 Jan 1864), 2nd dau of John Page, est s of Samuel Page, Surveyor-Gen Customs Ireland, and widow of P J Joyce, of Cultra Park, Co Galway, and had a

dau (*d* an infant); *m* 2nd 23 Aug 1866 Mary Grace (*d* 28 Feb 1923), est dau of Sir William Maxwell, 3rd Bt, of Cardoness, and *dsp* 12 May 1906
1a Mary Christian; *m* 3 May 1854 John Shand, MD, of Kirkcudbright, and *d* 21 Feb 1887, leaving issue
2a Julia; *m* 11 July 1872 Herbert James
3a John Anne; *m* 7 Aug 1861 Stevenson Forbes and had issue
(2) William; *m* Anne Carr Mowat (*d* 19 Feb 1849) and had issue:
1a John; *b* 18 March 1810; barrister, Official Assignee Calcutta; *m* Caroline, dau of Charles A Tulk, MP, and *d* 21 Feb 1849, having had issue:
1b CHARLES EDWARD (Sir), **7th Bt**
2b John Hart; *b* 22 Jan 1842; *m* 5 Sept 1879 Alice Letitia (*d* 21 Jan 1920), dau of George Miller, of Chippenham, and *d* 14 Jan 1918
1b Caroline Louisa; *m* 7 May 1857 Charles Harrison (*d* 1867), of Richmond, Surrey, and *d* 1920, leaving issue
2b Annie Picciola; *m* 1871 George Maxwell (*d* 21 March 1903), of Wellington, NZ, and *d* 9 Feb 1913, leaving issue
3b Sophia Susanna; *m* 3 March 1869 William Shepley Wilson (*d* 1873) and had issue
4b Eleanor Augusta; *m* 16 Sept 1878 Matthew Dando (*d* 1887) and had:
1c Anne Eliza; *m* 1st Samuel Barrett (*dsp*); *m* 2nd 1840 Martyn John Roberts, DL, of Pendarren House, Brecon, and had issue
(1) Annie; *m* 1st George Innes; *m* 2nd Jonathan Brown and had issue by him
1 Anna; *m* 1735 Alexander Copland, of Colliston, and had issue
The **3rd Bt** *m* 2nd — Gibson, of Whitehaven, and *d* 23 March 1769, having by her had no issue
The 6th Bt's cousin,
Sir Charles Edward Gordon, 7th Bt; *b* 14 April 1835; *m* 24 Sept 1857 Isabella Christina Campbell (*d* 18 Aug 1904) and *d* 2 July 1911, having had issue:
1 John Archibald; *b* 27 May 1860; *d* unm 25 Sept 1876
2 ROBERT CHARLES (Sir), **8th Bt**
1 Caroline Isabella; *m* 1888 Louis Leplastrier (*d* July 1932) and *d* July 1949, leaving issue
2 Amy Lucie; *d* unm 25 May 1942
The 7th Bt's only surv son,
Sir Robert Charles Gordon, 8th Bt; *b* 17 April 1862; *m* 28 Sept 1898 Elizabeth Ursula Maitland (*d* 17 Nov 1954), only dau of Rev John Maitland Ware, and *d* 30 Aug 1939, leaving:
Sir John Charles Gordon, 9th Bt, of Earlston, JP; *b* 4 Jan 1901; BEng Sydney U; Engr i/c NSW Govt Rlwys 1928–61; *m* 26 Sept 1928 Marion, 3rd dau of James B Wright, of Neutral Bay, N Sydney, and had issue:
1 Sir ROBERT JAMES GORDON, **10th and present Bt**
1 *Ann Gordon [Mrs Timothy Savill, 183 Raglan St, Balmoral Beach, NSW 2088, Australia]; *b* 8 July 1929; *m* 5 Sept 1953 Timothy Raymond Harry Savill (*d* 1992), er s of Lionel Savill, of E Grinstead, Sussex, and has issue:
(1) *Joanna Mary Gordon; *b* 24 Dec 1956; *m* 1988 *Giuliano Dambelli, s of Ilma Dambelli, of Brescia, and has issue
(2) *Lisbeth Jane Gordon; *b* 12 June 1958
(3) *Camilla Ann Gordon; *b* 15 Feb 1961; *m* 1990 *Bruce MacInnes, of Sydney, NSW, and has issue
(4) *Katherine Helen Gordon; *b* 15 Nov 1963; *m* 1996 *Gregory Johnson, of Sydney, NSW, and has issue

GORDON OF STRATHBLANE

Creation: B. (LP, UK) 2 Aug 1997.

THE BARON GORDON OF STRATHBLANE, of Deil's Craig, Stirling (James Stuart Gordon, CBE (1984)) [The Rt Hon The Lord Gordon of Strathblane CBE, Deil's Craig, Strathblane, Glasgow G63 9ET]; *b* 17 May 1936; *educ* St Aloysius' Coll Glasgow and Glasgow U; Political Ed STV 1965–73, md Radio Clyde 1973–96; memb: Scottish Devpt Agency 1981–90, Court Glasgow U 1984–, Ctee Inquiry Teachers' Pay and Conditions 1986, Scottish Advsy Bd BP 1990–, v-chm Melody Radio 1991 (dir 1990–); Chm Scottish Exhibition Centre 1983–89; ch exec Scottish Radio Hldgs 1991–96 (chm 1996–); dir Clydeport Holdings 1992–; DLitt Glasgow Caledonian 1994; *m* 1971 *Margaret Anne Stevenson and has two sons and a dau

Lineage: JAMES GORDON; *m* Elsie Riach and had:
JAMES STUART, *cr* a **Baron**

GORDON CUMMING

Arms: Quarterly, 1st and 4th, az. three garbs or; 2nd and 3rd, arg. three bendlets sa., each charged with as many roses of the field barbed or; over all, upon an escutcheon of pretence, the achievement of the arms of GORDON of Gordonstown (*viz.*, 1st and 4th, grand quarters counterquartered, 1st, az. three boar's heads couped or, armed and langued gu. (for GORDON); 2nd, or three lion's heads erased gu. (for BADENOCH); 3rd, or three crescents within the royal tressure (for SETON); 4th, az. three cinquefoils arg. (for FRASER); 2nd and 3rd grand quarters, gu. three stars or (for SUTHERLAND), all within a bordure of the last; Supporters: Dexter, a greyhound ppr., collared gu., charged with three buckles or; sinister, a savage ppr., wreathed about the head and waist with laurel vert, brandishing a club, also ppr; Motto: (above the crest) *Sans crainte* ('Without fear'); Crest: A cat sejant ppr.(for GORDON)). **Crest:** A lion rampant or, in the dexter paw a dagger ppr. (for CUMMING of Altyre). **Supporters:** Two horses argent. **Motto:** (over the crest) Courage. **Creation:** Bt. (UK) 21 May 1804.

SIR WILLIAM GORDON GORDON CUMMING, 6TH BT, of Altyre and Gordonstown, Co Moray [Sir William Gordon Cumming Bt, Altyre, nr Forres, Morayshire]; *b* 19 June 1928; *s* f 1939; *educ* Eton and RMC Sandhurst; Lt Roy Scots Greys (ret 1952), memb Conseil International de la Chasse; *m* 1st 15 July 1953 (*divorce* 1972) Elisabeth, est dau of Maj-Gen Sir (William) Robert Norris Hinde, KBE, CB, DSO, ADC, of Shrewton House, Salisbury, Wilts, by Evelyn Muriel, 3rd dau of Henry Fitzherbert Wright, JP, of Yeldersley Hall, Derbys; *m* 2nd 1972 (*divorce* 1976) Pauline Anne, sis of 13th Earl of Seafield (*qv*) and formerly w of James Henry Harcourt Illingworth; *m* 3rd 1989 *Sheila Bates and by his 1st w has:
1 +ALEXANDER ('ALASTAIR') PENROSE [Alastair Gordon Cumming Esq, Wardend House, Altyre, nr Forres, Morayshire]; *b* 15 April 1954; *m* 1991 *Louise, er dau of Edward Geoffrey Clifton-Brown (*see* BROWN, Bt), and has issue:
(1) +William; *b* 4 April 1993
1 *Sarah [Mrs Dominic Pearse, Holwell Downs Farm, Busford, Oxon]; *b* 4 Sept 1955; *m* 1990 *Dominic W Langlands Pearse, yst s of Cdr Ian Langlands Pearse, and has issue:
(1) *Ned; *b* 1993
2 *Charlotte; *b* 2 Feb 1958; *m* 1984 *Michael Edwards, s of John Edwards, of Darnaconnar, Barrhill, Girvan, Ayrshire
3 *Henrietta; *b* 23 June 1959; *m* 1988 *Donald Statham, s of D E S Statham

Lineage: ALEXANDER CUMMING, of Altyre, Elgin; *m* Grace Pearce, niece and sole heir of John Penrose, of Penrose, Cornwall, and had an est s:
Sir ALEXANDER PENROSE CUMMING later GORDON-CUMMING (under terms of will of Sir William Gordon, last Bt, of Gordonstown, whose heir and representative he was), **1st Bt** (UK), so *cr* 21 May 1804; joined 13th Regt, Lt-Col Strathspey Fencibles and suppressed a mutiny at Dumfries 1794, MP Inverness Burghs; *m* 9 Sept 1773 Helen (*d* Jan 1830), dau of Sir Ludovick Grant, 7th Bt (*see* SEAFIELD, E, and STRATHSPEY, B), and had, with five other sons and seven other daus:
1 WILLIAM (Sir), **2nd Bt**
2 Charles Lennox CUMMING later CUMMING-BRUCE, of Roseisle and Kinnaird; MP Inverness 1831–40 and Elgin and Nairn 1840–68; *b* 20 Feb 1790; *m* 20 June 1822 Mary Elizabeth (*d* 1874), only dau of James Bruce of Kinnaird, Stirlingshire, and *d* 1 Jan 1875, having had:
(1) Mary Elizabeth; *m* 22 April 1841 8th Earl of Elgin and (12th Earl of) Kincardine (*qv*) and *d* 7 July 1843, leaving issue
1 Margaret; *m* 8 Oct 1798 Maj Samuel Madden (*see* MADDEN, Bt) and had issue
2 Helen; *m* Sir Archibald Dunbar, 6th Bt, of Northfield (*qv*), and *d* 1819
3 Louisa; *m* John Hay Forbes, a Ld of Session as Lord Medwyn (*see* STUART-FORBES, Bt); *d* 1845

Sir ALEXANDER *d* 10 Feb 1806; his er s,

Sir William Gordon Gordon-Cumming, 2nd Bt; *b* 20 July 1787; MP Elgin and Banff; *m* 1st 11 Sept 1815 Eliza Maria (*d* 1842), est dau of John Campbell, Yr. of Shawfield and Islay (*see* ARGYLL, D), and had, with other issue:

1 ALEXANDER PENROSE (Sir), **3rd Bt**

2 Roualeyn George; Madras Cav, later Cape Mounted Rifles, African explorer; *b* 15 March 1820; *d* unm March 1866

3 Henry, of Pittyvaich, Dufftown; *b* 14 Nov 1822; *m* 14 Feb 1859 Elizabeth Newton (*d* 8 Jan 1905), dau of Maj Ludovick Stewart of Pittyvaich, 24th Regt, and *d* 12 Nov 1887, leaving issue:

(1) Henry William Grant; *b* 4 Dec 1859; *m* 3 Aug 1892 Evelyn Agnes (*d* 30 Oct 1948), dau of Hugh Barlow Lindsay (*see* CRAWFORD and BALCARRES, E), and *d* 1939, leaving issue:

1a Henry Ronald, OBE (1945); Cdr RN; *b* 26 May 1893; *m* 20 Sept 1927 Lorna Isabelle (*d* 1974), yr dau of Ernest W Morey, of Johannesburg, and *d* 25 Nov 1971, leaving issue:

1b +Henry Ian (Rev) [The Rev Henry Gordon Cumming, Bay Cottage, Brookside, Runcton, Chichester, Sussex PO20 6PX]; barrister Gray's Inn 1956, ordained 1957; *b* 10 Dec 1928; *m* Aug 1955 *Janet Elizabeth Latimer Cleave and has issue:

1c *Jane Evelyn; *b* 14 Jan 1957; *m* 1994 *Guy Hadland

2c *Joanna Mary *b* 15 Jan 1959; *m* 1988 *Christopher Morris and has:

1d *James; *b* 1993

1d *Julia; *b* 1990

3c *Lucille Clare; *b* 28 July 1962; *m* 1988 *Charles Thellusson and has:

1d *Amy Elizabeth; *b* 1993

4c *Deborah Diana; *b* 14 Oct 1965; *m* 1991 *Andrew Woodward

1a Evelyn Irene Katherine; *b* 13 July 1894; *d* unm 27 April 1962

2a Lettice Eliabeth; *b* 7 July 1897; *m* 1st 26 Feb 1920 (*divorce* 1939) Harold Claude Thwaits, S Rhodesian Civ Serv, of Harare, and had issue; *m* 2nd 1941 Philip Anthony Curtis, RINR (*d* 23 July 1967)

(2) Ludovic Seymour; Lt-Col Sherwood Foresters; *b* 24 Sept 1861; *m* 29 July 1895 Constance Mary (*d* 24 March 1906), only dau of Count de Morel, of Beaufort Gardens, and *d* 20 March 1924, leaving issue:

1a Katherine Marjorie

4 William Gordon, DL Banff; Lt-Col Bombay Staff Corps; *b* 2 June 1829; *m* 1st 18 June 1867 Alexa Angelica Harvey (*dsp* 8 Dec 1893), 5th dau of James Brand, of Balham; *m* 2nd 18 April 1895 Hon Lettice Hermione Violet Willoughby (*d* 9 Aug 1922), 4th dau of 8th Baron Middleton (*qv*), and *dsp* 28 April 1908

5 Francis Hastings Toone; Maj Bombay Staff Corps; *b* 28 March 1842; *m* 9 April 1863 Emma, dau of John Campbell, and *d* 1883, leaving:

(1) William; *b* 1864; *m* 1891 Rose (*d* 1934), dau of A White, of NZ, and *d* 1949, leaving issue:

1a Constance Alexa; *b* 1892; *m* 1925 Guy d'Eresby Goyder, of Victoria, Australia

2a Marjorie Alice Eleanora; *m* 1922 Alexander Donaldson and had issue

3a Mary Adela Rose; *b* 1895; *m* 1915 George Berners Knyvett and had:

1b *Henry Berners; *b* 1915

2b *Mark Alastair; *b* 1918; *m* 1941 *Ola B, dau of G F Peters, of Dannevirke, NZ

4a *Eila Campbell

5a *Ethel Fredereka; *b* 1899; *m* 1926 *Harold Sedcole Malcolm, of Wellington, NZ

(2) Charles Lennox; *b* 1865; *m* 1901 Mary Elizabeth, dau of W E Thomas, of Dallas, Texas, and *d* 27 Jan 1948, leaving:

1a Constance Alexa; *m* 1st 1922 Clarence Ray Herrington (*d* 5 Sept 1946), of Amarillo, Texas; *m* 2nd 31 Dec 1949 Q B Workman and by her 1st husb had:

1b *Phyllis Rae; *b* 7 April 1930; *m* 13 Feb 1954 John Snead Billups and has:

1c *Patti Jon; *b* 24 March 1956

2c *Molli Elizabeth; *b* 29 March 1958

2a *Marjorie Mary [Mrs Randle Culwell, 1121 Broadmoor, Amarillo, TX, USA]; *m* 11 June 1925 Randle James Culwell and has issue:

1b *Gordon James; *b* 26 Oct 1928; *m* 10 Sept 1948 *Grace Elaine, dau of Dr Bascom MacIntosh Puckett, and has:

1c *Michael James; *b* 8 May 1950

1c *Grace Victoria; *b* 30 May 1951

3a *Kathleen Elizabeth [Mrs Jerome Barker, 1306 West 6th St, Plainview, Texas, USA]; *b* 1909; *m* 29 Oct 1932 Jerome Maurice Barker

(3) George Roualeyn; *b* 1868

(4) Walter Penrose; *b* 1869

(1) Mary Ada; *m* 1st 9 Feb 1888 (*divorce* 1897) 4th Viscount Portman (*qv*); *m* 2nd 7 June 1899 Ralph Assheton Harbord and *d* 13 May 1900, leaving issue (*see* SUFFIELD, B)

1 Anne Seymour Conway; *m* 1 Aug 1843 Oswin Addison Baker Cresswell, s of Addison John Baker Cresswell, JP, DL, of Cresswell, Northumberland, and *d* 3 June 1858, leaving issue. He *d* 6 March 1856

2 Adelaide Eliza; *m* 4 June 1852 Capt William Gilfrid Cresswell and *d* 3 Aug 1870. He *d* 19 Sept 1854

3 Alice Henrietta; *m* 17 Nov 1852 John Henry Jenkinson and *d* 9 Dec 1859, leaving issue (*see* JENKINSON, Bt)

4 Eleanora; *m* 2 Oct 1855 Hon George Grant, yst s of 6th Earl of Seafield (*qv*), and *d* 5 April 1889, leaving issue

Sir William *m* 2nd 19 Dec 1846 Jane Eliza (*d* 6 Jan 1897), 2nd dau of William Mackintosh, of Geddes, Nairn, and by her had, with other issue:

5 Emilia; *m* 1st 8 Jan 1867 Maj Warden Sergison, DL, of Cuckfield Park, Sussex, and had issue. He *d* 16 July 1888. She *m* 2nd 12 Sept 1891 Rev William Seymore Edgell, Vicar Totteridge, Herts, and *d* 7 May 1917, leaving further issue

Sir WILLIAM *d* 25 Nov 1854; his est son,

Sir Alexander Penrose Gordon-Cumming, 3rd Bt; Lt-Col Elgin Vols, Capt 4th Light Dragoons and 71st LI; *b* 17 Aug 1816; *m* 28 Nov 1845 Anne Pitcairn (*d* 18 Aug 1888), only dau of Rev Augustus Campbell, Rector Liverpool, and had issue:

1 WILLIAM GORDON (Sir), **4th Bt**

2 Alastair (Alexander) Penrose; *b* 31 July 1853; *m* 25 April 1877 Frances Campbell (*d* 11 Dec 1936), only dau of Hon Charles Eames, formerly US Min Venezuela, and *d* 17 Jan 1913, having had issue:

(1) Margaret Campbell; *b* 3 April 1878; *d* 14 Sept 1897

3 Walter Frederick Campbell; Capt Bengal Native Inf, served Centl Africa 1894–98 (despatches, medals and clasp) and Boer War 1899–1902 (medals and clasps); *b* 16 July 1859; *educ* Eton; *d* 20 Feb 1913

1 Eliza Maria; *m* 5 Aug 1869 9th Baron Middleton (*qv*) and *d* 27 April 1922

Sir ALEXANDER *d* 2 Sept 1866; his est son,

Sir William Gordon Gordon-Cumming, 4th Bt; Lt-Col Scots Gds, served Zulu War 1879 (despatches, medal and clasp), Egypt 1882 (medal and clasp, Khedive's star) and Gds Camel Regt in Desert Column 1884–85 (two clasps); *b* 20 July 1848; *m* 10 June 1891 Florence Josephine (*d* 21 Sept 1922), dau of W Garner, Cdre NY Yacht Club, and had issue:

1 ALEXANDER PENROSE (Sir), **5th Bt**

2 Roualeyn Geoffrey; Lt Cdr RN; *b* 10 Sept 1895; *m* 26 June 1923 Mary Violet Katherine (*m* 2nd 22 Oct 1929 (*annulled* 1939) John S Newall, only s of J W Newall, of Ongar, Essex; *m* 3rd 23 Aug 1941 (*divorce* 1948) Geoffrey Hugh Wilkinson and *d* 1984), dau of Capt W M Marter, King's Dragoon Gds, and *d* 26 Feb 1928, leaving:

(1) +Alexander Roualeyn, CMG (1978) CVO (1969) [Gp Capt Alexander CMG CVO RAF (ret), Woodstock, West Way, Chichester, Sussex PO19 3PW]; *b* 10 Sept 1924; *educ* Eton; RAF: ret as G/Capt 1969, Assist Sec DTI, Dir Invest in Britain Bureau DTI 1979–84; *m* 1st 8 Dec 1965 Beryl Joyce MacNaughton (*d* 25 Jan 1973), yr dau of Naughton Dunn, LLD, MA, MB, ChB, of Edgbaston, Birmingham, and has issue:

1a *Ann Penrose; *b* 5 June 1968; *m* 1996 *Marcus Tarrant

(1) (cont.) G/Capt Alexander Gordon-Cumming *m* 2nd 1974 Elizabeth Patricia (*d* 1983), dau of Travers Roberty Blackley, CMG, CBE, of Gurrane, Fermoy, Co Cork, and has by her:

2a *Mary Elizabeth; *b* 1975

3 Michael Willoughby; Midshipman RN; *b* 24 Jan 1901; *educ* St Andrews (BSc); *m* 1st 25 June 1923 (*divorce* 1943) Rachael Jean (*d* 17 Sept 1968), 4th dau of Col John Anstruther-Thomson (*see* ANSTRUTHER, Bt); *m* 2nd 24 July 1943 (Shirley) Barbara (*d* 9 Dec 1996), yr dau of Torben Laub, of Rush Court, Wallingford, Berks, and *d* 1979, leaving by her:

(1) *Priscilla Jane [Mrs Edwin Osborn, 98 Southmoor Rd, Oxford]; *b* 6 Feb 1950; *m* 1991 *Edwin F Osborn, s of Rev Reginald Osborn, of Freeland, Oxford

(2) *Catherine (Katie) Rose [Mrs Desmond Fforde, High Croft, Church Place, Rodborough, Glos]; *b* 27 Sept 1952; *m* 1972 *Desmond Fforde

1 Elma; *b* 23 March 1892; *m* 1st 10 Jan 1912 (*divorce* 1923) Maurice Anthony Crutchley Gibbs and had issue (*see* ALDENHAM and HUNSDON OF HUNSDON, B); *m* 2nd 1923 Lennox Pelham Napier, MC, s of Sir Walter John Napier, and *d* 12 Nov 1973, having had further issue. He *d* 4 March 1940

2 Cecily; *b* 6 May 1904; *m* 1st 12 June 1931 (*divorce* 1946) Capt Christopher Arthur Vian, Coldstream Gds, yr s of Alsager Vian, of Chiddingstone, Kent. He *d* 22 Jan 1959. She *m* 2nd 16 Aug 1946 William Mure, CBE, er s of Lt-Col William Mure of Caldwell, JP, DL, and *dsp* 25 May 1970. He *d* 26 April 1977

Sir WILLIAM *d* 20 May 1930; his est son,

Sir Alexander Penrose Gordon Cumming, 5th Bt, MC, JP, DL, Morayshire; *b* 12 Sept 1893; *educ* Eton and Trin Coll Cambridge; Maj Cameron Highrs WW I (wounded, despatches), memb Roy Co Archers, memb Conseil International de la Chasse; *m* 9 Sept 1924 Elizabeth Topham (*m* 2nd 29 June 1961 5th Earl Cawdor (*qv*)), dau of John Topham Richardson, JP, of Harps Oak, Merstham, and *d* 23 Feb 1939, having had issue:

1 Sir WILLIAM GORDON GORDON CUMMING, **6th and present Bt**

1 *(Cecily) Josephine [The Rt Hon The Countess Lloyd George of Dwyfor, Glenogil, by Forfar, Angus; The Hall, Freshford, Bath; 47 Burton Ct, London SW3]; *b* 11 Dec 1925; *m* 1st 25 June 1957 2nd Earl of Woolton (*qv*) and has issue; *m* 2nd 22 Sept 1969 (*divorce* 1974) 3rd Baron Forres (*qv*); *m* 3rd 1982 *3rd Earl Lloyd George of Dwyfor (*qv*)

2 *Philippa [Mrs David Innes, Hensil House, Hawkhurst, Kent; Titsey Place, Oxted, Surrey]; *b* 29 Jan 1933; *m* 10 June 1955 *David Archibald Innes (*see* DOWNE, V) and has:

(1) *Guy Archibald; *b* 19 May 1956

(2) *John Hugh; *b* 31 May 1959; *m* 1988 *Deborah Jane, dau of Rev W A G Buxton, and has:

1a *Samuel David; *b* 1996

1a *Alice Louisa; *b* 1991

2a *Rose Elizabeth; *b* 1992

(1) *Davina Evelyn; *b* 25 Oct 1957; *m* 1989 *Wojciech Markiewicz and has:

1a *William David; *b* 1991

2a *James Josef; *b* 1994

GORE

Arms: Gu. a fess arg. between three cross-crosslets fitchée or.
Crest: A heraldic tiger rampant arg., collared gu.
Motto: *Sola salus servire Deo* ('Serving God is the sole salvation').
Creation: Bt. (I) 2 Feb 1621/2.

SIR NIGEL HUGH ST GEORGE GORE, 14TH BT, of Magherabegg, Co Donegal [Sir Nigel Gore Bt, Hillhaven, MS 852, Preston Rd, Hodgson Vale, Toowoomba, Qld 4352, Australia]; *b* 23 Dec 1922; *s* n 1993; *educ* C of E GS Brisbane and Gatton Ag Coll; AIF WW II; *m* 3 Sept 1952 Beth Allison (*d* 1976), yr dau of Richard Waverley Hooper, of Allawah, Tambo, Qld, and has issue:

1 *Seonaid Beth; *b* 25 March 1955

Lineage: GERARD GORE (*see* ARRAN, E); *d* 11 Dec 1607, leaving:

1 John (Sir); Ld Mayor London 1624; *see* TEMPLE OF STOWE, E

2 **Sir Paul Gore, 1st Bt** (I), so *cr* 2 Feb 1621/2, of Magherabegg, Co Donegal; Capt of Horse; settled in Ireland *temp* ELIZABETH I; granted much land, which he condensed into a manor, calling it Manor Gore; *m* Isabella, dau of Francis Wickliffe and n of Sir Thomas Wentworth, 1st and last Earl of Strafford of the Jan 1639/40 *cr* (*see* STRAFFORD, E, preliminary remarks), and *d* Sept 1629, having had, with five yr sons and seven daus (including Sidney, *m* Lewis Wingfield of Scurmore Co Sligo; *see* POWERSCOURT, V):

(1) RALPH (Sir), **2nd Bt**

(2) Sir ARTHUR GORE, 1st Bt (*see* ARRAN, E)

(3) Henry; Lt-Cdr; *m* Mary, dau and coheir of Robert Blayney, and *d* 2 Nov 1651, leaving:

1a Frances; *m* 1st Sir Robert King, 1st Bt (*see* KINGSTON, E); *m* 2nd Robert Choppyn, of Newcastle, Co Longford

(4) Francis (Sir), of Artaman, Co Sligo; *d* Sept 1629; *see* GORE BOOTH, Bt

Sir PAUL's est s,

Sir Ralph Gore, 2nd Bt; MP Donegal 1639–48; *m* 1640 Anne (*m* 2nd Sir Paul Harris; *m* 3rd Sir John Wroth), 2nd dau of 2nd Lord Caulfeild, Baron of Charlemont (*see* CHARLEMONT, V), and *d* by 1 Feb 1661/2, having had (with a dau Jane, *m* Chidley Cote, of Mt Coote, Co Limerick; *see* COOTE, Bt):

Sir William Gore, 3rd Bt, PC; custos rotulorum Co Leitrim, MP Banagher 1661–66; *m* Hannah (*d* 16 May 1733), n of 1st Viscount Boyne (*qv*), and had:

1 RALPH (Sir), **4th Bt**

2 William (Very Rev); Dean Down; *m* Honora (*d* 1767), dau of Henry Prittie (*see* DUNALLEY, B), and *d* 6 Jan 1731, leaving, with other issue:

(1) William (Right Rev); DD, Bp Limerick; *m* 1st Mary (*dsp*), widow of Guy Moore, of Abbey, Co Limerick, and dau of Chidley Coote, of Coote Hall; *m* 2nd Mary (*d* 25 March 1822), dau of William French, and *d* 25 Feb 1784, leaving:

1a William, of the Heath, Co Kildare; MP; *m* July 1788 Mary (*d* Nov 1848), dau of Michael Head, of Derry, Co Tipperary, and *d* 1 Sept 1832, having had, with other issue:

1b Nathaniel, of Clifton; *m* 1st 1 Jan 1836 Hannah (*d* March 1857), dau of Ven James Langrishe, Archdeacon Glendalough; *m* 2nd 18– Sarah, dau of Col — Graydon, RE; *m* 3rd 28 July 1863 Frances Louisa (*d* 6 May 1875), dau of Samuel Page, of Hadley House, Middx, and *d* 2 Dec 1876, having by her had issue:

1c Robert Clements, CB, CMG; Brevet Col Argyll and Sutherland Highrs, T/Brig-Gen and Bde Cdr 1916; *b* 3 Feb 1867; *m* 1899 Rachel Cecilia (*m* 2nd 2 Aug 1921 Capt Arthur Marsden, CBE, RN; *d* 16 June 1971), 3rd dau of Llewellyn Traherne Bassett Saunderson, and was *ka* 14 April 1918, leaving:

1d Adrian Clements, DSO (1943) and bar (1945); Brig Rifle Bde WW II; *b* 1900; *educ* Eton; *m* 4 Jan 1927 Enid Aimée (*d* 25 June 1997), yr dau of John Jameson Cairnes, and *d* 1990, leaving:

1e +Toby Clements [Toby Gore Esq, Monks Alley, Binfield, Bracknell, Berks; 94 Smith St, London SW3]; Maj Rifle Bde, High Sheriff Berks 1993; *b* 28 Dec 1927; *m* 28 July 1959 (Isolde) Marian (*d* 12 Nov 1996), yr dau of Edward H Macintosh, and has had issue:

1f *Fiona Marian; *b* 26 Sept 1960; *m* 1987 *Irvine J Maccabe, 2nd s of Jeffrey J Maccabe, of Dulwich Village

2f *Juliet Carolyn; *b* 18 April 1962

3f Tessa Jane; *b* 1967; *d* 1994

4f *Stephanie Serena; *b* 8 Aug 1969

1d *Dinah Priscilla; *b* 2 Feb 1930; *m* 21 Jan 1958 *Lt-Col (John) Richard Seymour Besly, Gren Gds, only s of Ernest Francis Withers John Besly, CMG, and has issue:

1e *Adrian Thomas; *b* 1963

2e *Michael John; *b* 1966

1e *Emma Belinda; *b* 1958; *m* 1984 *Keith Warner

2e *Lucinda Mary; *b* 1960

3e *Sara-Jane Beatrice; *b* 1964

2d *Belinda Beatrice; *b* 28 Oct 1940; *m* 1970 *Sir Anthony Frederick Milbank, 5th Bt (*qv*), and has issue

1c Frances Nora Prittie; *m* 1887 James Duncan Stuart Sim, CB, barrister, est s of James Duncan Sim, CSI, and had issue. He *d* 5 Sept 1912

2c Gertrude Rosabel Katherine; *m* 1 Nov 1893 Maj Gilbert McMicking, CMG, RA, and *d* 1920, having had issue. He *d* 15 Nov 1942

2b John (Rev); Rector Aghada, Co Cork; *m* Elizabeth (*m* 2nd — Kennedy), dau of Michael Harris, and *dsp* 19 March 1837

3b Frederick; *m* Mary, dau of John Parkinson, and had issue:

1c Mary; *m* 5 July 1865 John Pollard Micklethwaite, of Caerwent, Mon, and *d* 20 Oct 1921, leaving issue

1b Frances Arabella; *m* Rev John Walsh and had issue

2b Anne; *m* Rev Richard Nevile and had issue

(2) Henry; Capt Battleaxe Gds, MP; *m* 14 May 1749 Elizabeth (*d* 1774), widow of Albert Nesbitt and dau of Sir Nathaniel Gould, and *d* 1787

(3) Frederick; Provost Marshal-Gen Ireland, MP; *m* 1st 1751 Hon Mary Molesworth (*dsp* Sept 1761), only dau of 2nd Viscount Molesworth (*qv*); *m* 2nd 27 Oct 1762 Mary (*dsp*), dau of **Sir Ralph Gore, 4th Bt** (*see* below)

(1) Hannah; *m* 31 Jan 1729 Nathaniel Clements, PC, MP, and had issue (*see* 1953 edn LEITRIM, E)

Sir WILLIAM *d* between 1 March 1703 and 12 May 1705; his est son,

Sir Ralph Gore, 4th Bt, PC; MP Co Donegal, Chllr Exchequer and 1729 Speaker H of C Ireland; inherited Manor Hamilton estate through his mother; *m* 1st 1705 Elizabeth, dau of Sir Robert Colville, of Newtown, Co Leitrim, and had:

1 Hannah; *m* John Donellan

2 Rose; *m* Anthony Malone, PC

Sir Ralph *m* 2nd Elizabeth (*d* 7 Dec 1741), only dau of Rt Rev St George Ashe, DD, Bp Clogher, and *d* 23 Feb 1732/3, having by her had:

1 Sir ST GEORGE GORE later ST GEORGE (on inheriting his maternal unc Sir Richard St George's estates), **5th Bt**; MP Co Donegal; *m* 22 Sept 1743 Alice, only dau of Francis Burton, PC, of Buncraggy, and sis of 2nd Baron Conyngham of Mount Charles (*see* CONYNGHAM, M), and *dsp* 25 Sept 1746

2 **Sir Ralph Gore, 6th Bt**, 1st and last EARL OF ROSS, Co Fermanagh, so *cr* 4 Jan 1772, as also previously 30 June 1764 BARON GORE OF MANOR GORE, Co Donegal, and 25 Aug 1768 VISCOUNT BELLEISLE, of Belleisle, Co Fermanagh (all I); *b* 23 Nov 1725; *educ* Trin Coll Dublin; Lt 33rd Foot 1744, severely wounded Battle Fontenoy 1745, Capt his Bn Battle Lauffeld 1747, Lt-Col 92nd Foot 1760, Col 1772, Maj-Gen 1777, Col 32nd Foot 1781–1802, Lt-Gen 1782, Gen 1796, MP (I Parl) Co Donegal 1747–64, Sheriff Co Donegal 1755, Co Fermanagh 1760, C-in-C Ireland 1788; *m* 1st 23 Feb 1754 Catherine (*dsp* 4 May 1771), dau of Thomas Connolly, PC; *m* 2nd 22 Oct 1773 his cousin Alice, dau of Nathaniel Clements, PC, MP (*see* below), and *dsps* 1802, when his peerages expired, having by her had:

(1) Ralph, *Viscount Belleisle*; *b* 3 Oct 1774; *educ* Eton (?); *dsp* 1789

3 Richard, of Sandymount, Co Wicklow; *b* 16 Oct 1728; *m* 1 June 1766 Martha (*d* Oct 1773), dau of Rev Thomas Fiott, of Guernsey, and had, with two daus (Louisa, *m* St George Daly, PC, Judge King's Bench, *d* 1816; Elizabeth, *b* 1757):

(1) **Sir Ralph Gore, 7th Bt**; *m* 22 May 1802 Grace (*d* 19 June 1866), dau of 3rd Baron Farnham (*qv*), and *d* 20 March 1842, leaving:

1a **Sir St George Gore, 8th Bt**; *b* 1811; *d* unm 31 Dec 1878

1a Martha; *d* unm 25 Nov 1894 aged 88

2a Grace; *m* 2 June 1847 Frederick Dundas, MP (*see* ZETLAND, M), and *d* 15 Jan 1868

3a Elizabeth Esther; *d* 18 May 1904

(2) Anthony; *b* 5 Sept 1760; *m* 1780 Judith Dobrée and *d* 23 Sept 1836, leaving:

1a Martha; *m* Anthony Priaulx and *d* 1811. He *d* 12 Aug 1820

2a Harriet; *m* 6 Aug 1828 Col Thomas Fiott de Havilland, of Guernsey, and *d* 3 June 1857. He *d* 23 Feb 1866

(3) Thomas (Rev); Rector Mulrancan, Co Wexford; *b* 11 Nov 1767; *m* 22 Sept 1810 Elizabeth Margaret (*d* 1856), dau of Robert Corbet, of Corbet Hill, Co Wexford, and *d* 4 June 1834, leaving issue:

1a St George Richard, of Lyndhurst, Qld; *b* 22 March 1812; *m* 17 Aug 1840 Frances, dau of Edward Caldwell, of Lyndhurst, and *d* 16 Aug 1871, leaving:

1b **Sir (St George) Ralph Gore, 9th Bt**; *b* 21 Sept 1841; *m* 6 April 1876 Eugenia Marion (*m* 2nd 1893 Jairus Edwin Withers), only dau of Hon Eyles Irwin Caulfeild Browne, MLC Qld, and *d* 17 Oct 1887, having had:

1c **Sir Ralph St George Claude Gore, 10th Bt**; Maj Westminster Dragoons, Lt The Royals, V-Cdre Roy Yacht Sqdn 1944, Cdre 1947, Pres Roy Yachting Assoc 1945; *b* 12 May 1877; *m* 1st 19 Sept 1905 his sis's husb's sis Elsie Vaughan (*d* 6 April 1942), 2nd dau of Henry Tully Grigg, of Buenos Aires, and had issue:

1d **Sir (Ralph St George) Brian Gore, 11th Bt**; *b* 31 May 1908; *educ* Eton and RMC Sandhurst, Lt Col The Royals WW II; *m* 1st 15 March 1947 (*divorce* 1965) Phyllis Gabrielle, formerly w of Thomas Gilbert Brooke-Hitching and only dau of Maximilian von der Porten, of New York, and had issue:

1e *Maxine Marjorie St George [Mrs Timothy Eugster, Flat 1, 18 Hyde Park Gate, London SW7]; *b* 25 Oct 1947; *m* 16 Feb 1968 *Capt Timothy Basil Edward Eugster, Irish Gds, yr s of Lt-Gen Sir Basil Oscar Paul Eugster, KCVO, CB, CBE, DSO, MC and bar, Irish Gds, by Marcia Katherine Elaine, er dau of A/Cdre Sir (Henry) Percy Smyth-Osbourne, CMG, CBE, JP, DL, and has:

1f *Maximilian Brian Michael; *b* 23 Jan 1969

1f *Alexandra Marcia Gabrielle; *b* 27 April 1971

2f *Julia Clare Elizabeth; *b* 1974

1d (cont.) **Sir Brian** *m* 2nd Dec 1965 (*divorce* 1970) Mavis Pamela —; *m* 3rd 1971 *Irene Lamont (*m* 2nd 1975 James Biggar) [Mrs James Biggar, Old House, Willards Hill, Etchingham, Surrey], er dau of Albert James Marshall, and *d* 28 June 1973

1c (cont.) **Sir Ralph** *m* 2nd 3 July 1943 Beatrice Mildred, widow of Lt-Col Algernon Corbet Turnor, MC, RHG, and only dau of Cdr Hon Conyngham Albert Denison, RN (*see* LONDESBOROUGH, B), and *d* 27 March 1961

2c Irwin St John; Capt 4th Bn Glos Regt WW I (wounded); *b* 20 Jan 1880; *m* 29 July 1943 Beatrice (*d* 28 May 1953), widow of Rudolph Moritz, KC, and dau of — Turnbull, and *dsp* 19 Nov 1943

1c Hilda Grace; *m* 2 May 1905 (*divorce* 1929) Maj Ralph Stuart Grigg, 18th Hus, yst s of Henry Tully Grigg, of Buenos Aires, and *d* 26 July 1968, leaving issue. He *d* 14 Oct 1943

2c Leonie Gore; *m* 1 Jan 1914 Walter Owen Bentley, yst s of Alfred Bentley, of Regent's Park, London, and *d* 6 March 1919

2b Frederick Dundas Corbet; *b* 14 April 1853; *m* 23 June 1881 Margaretta Stenhouse (*d* 19 Dec 1943), dau of Donald Gunn, of Qld, and *d* 24 July 1921, leaving issue:

1c St George Richard; *b* 1883; *m* 6 July 1910 Loo Loo Ruth (*d* 9 Sept 1961), dau of E P Amesbury, of NSW, and *d* 28 Oct 1952, having had:

1d **Sir (St George) Ralph Gore, 12th Bt**; *b* 14 Dec 1914; *m* 25 Jan 1950 Shirley, 4th dau of Clement Tabor, of Wauchope, NSW, and *d* 1973, leaving:

1e **Sir Richard Ralph St George Gore, 13th Bt**; *b* 19 Nov 1954; *educ* King's Sch Parramatta, U of New England, Qld Coll Art; *d* 1993

1e *Annabel St George [Mrs Bruce Knowles, 18 Fairfax St, Red Hill, Qld 4059, Australia]; *b* 30 Jan 1951; *m* 1989 *Bruce Julian Knowles

2e *Elizabeth St George [Mrs Patrick Campbell, RSD 385, Devonport, Tasmania 7310, Australia]; *b* 1 Aug 1952; *m* 1981 *Patrick Hay Campbell and has issue:

1f *Georgina Louise Gore; *b* 1989

2f *Claudia Jane Gore; *b* 1991

3e *Juliet St George [Mrs David Butler, 31 Angus St, Goodwood 5034, S Australia]; *b* 13 Sept 1957; *m* 1982 *David Sheridan Butler

2d Sir NIGEL HUGH ST GEORGE GORE, **14th and present Bt**

1d *Phyllis Ruth St George [Miss Phyllis Gore, 5 Chelsea Court, Toowoomba, Qld 4350, Australia]; *b* 29 Sept 1912

2d Marjorie St George; *b* 9 June 1917; *d* 16 Feb 1919

3d *Margaretta Leonie St George [Mrs John Cory, PO Box 607, Goondiwindi, Qld 4390, Australia]; *b* 1 Jan 1921; *m* 12 June 1958 *John Henry Cory, est s of Fitzroy Bell Cory, of Warwick, Qld, and has issue:

1e *Alan Fitzroy; *b* 28 Jan 1961

1e *Janet Ruth [Mrs Anthony Gorring, Camiloroi, Pittsworth, Qld 4356, Australia]; *b* 25 April 1959; *m* 1995 *Anthony Peter Gorring, and has:

1f *Matthew John Thomas; *b* 1 Sept 1997

2c Frederick Dundas Corbet; Lt RFC (SR) 2nd Light Horse Regt AIF Egypt and Gallipoli and RFC WW I, Australian Army WW II; *b* 1 Dec 1885; *m* 17 May 1919 Ella Maud (*d* 17 July 1967), est dau of Charles Sydney-Jones, of Brisbane, and *d* 22 Oct 1964, leaving issue:

1d +DUNDAS CORBET [Dundas Gore Esq, 31 Ruskin Rowe, Avalon Beach, NSW 2107, Australia]; *b* 20 April 1921; heir presumptive; *educ* Sydney U (BEng); F/Lt RAAF WW II, 10 Sqdn Coastal Command; Hon FIE Aust; *m* 1956 *Jacqueline May Gilbert Dunston, of Perth, W Australia, and has adopted:

Anthony Corbet; *b* 1960; *d* 1976

*Victoria Ann; *b* 1962

*Bronwyn Jane; *b* 1966; *m* 1985 *Scott Andrew Beers and has issue

2d +Hugh Frederick Corbet [Hugh Gore Esq, 7 Romney Rd, St Ives, NSW, Australia]; *b* 31 Dec 1934; *m* 12 July 1963 *Jennifer Mary, est dau of Milton Gordon Copp, and has issue:

1e +Timothy Milton Corbet; *b* 1969

1e *Penelope Mary Corbet; *b* 10 Feb 1965

2e *Virginia Louise; *b* 22 May 1967

1d *Rosemary Ella Corbet [Mrs Nicholas Adams, 36 The Circle, Bilgola Plateau, Sydney, NSW 2107, Australia]; AIF WW II; *b* 2 April 1920; *m* 1957 *Nicholas George Knox Adams and adopted:

*David Alexander Ian; *b* 1963

2d *Barbara Corbet; *b* 6 March 1926; *m* 20 March 1954 *Robert Brian Irvine, s of Lionel Robert Herborn Irvine, and has issue:

1e *Robert Andrew; *b* 4 Jan 1955

1e *Jennifer Joan; *b* 6 March 1957

2e *Kate Dundas; *b* 23 Aug 1962

3c Ralph Thomas, CBE (1953); Judge Centl Court Papua; *b* 1888; *m* 12 July 1916 Mabel Frances Warner, dau of A H Warner Shand, and *d* 11 Aug 1968, having had issue:

1d Richard Ralph St George; Capt Papuan Native Inf WW II; *b* 8 May 1920; accidentally *k* 1950

1c Emily Margaretta St George; *d* 15 Feb 1989

3b William Francis; *b* 15 March 1857; *m* 3 Dec 1884 Ella Adele, dau of De Witt Clinton Barnes, of New York

1b Harriet; *d* unm 13 Nov 1915

2b Grace; *m* 23 June 1873 Francis Henry Needham (*see* KILMOREY, E) and *d* 1894

3b Louisa Isabel; *m* 1880 John Donald Macansh, of Qld, and *d* 1926, leaving issue

2a Robert Corbet; *b* 8 Nov 1813; *m* 17 March 1841 Mary Stewart, dau of Lt-Col Christopher Baldock, HEIC, and was lost at sea 11 March 1847 with his w and two sons, leaving an only dau:

1b Leonie Suvarov; *m* 18 May 1868 Jacques Blumenthal and *d* 14 Feb 1927. He *d* 14 Feb 1927

3a Ralph Thomas; *b* 27 Nov 1814; *m* 13 Oct 1853 Isabella Jane (*m* 2nd 17 June 1863 Osmond de Lancy Priaulx, of Guernsey; *d* 16 Feb 1874), dau of William Hopkins, of Frayne, Co Meath, and *d* 31 Oct 1860, having had:

1b St John Corbet (Sir), CB (1900), CVO (1925), CBE (1918); Lt-Col and Brevet Col 5th Dragoon Gds, cmdg Bde TF 1908, Lt Gentlemen-at-Arms 1926–38, Nile Expdn and Boer War; *b* 10 Dec 1859; *m* 22 June 1892 Isabella Charlotte (*d* 27 Dec 1937), dau of P G van der Byl, and *dsp* 5 Nov 1949

1b Lucinda Elizabeth Harriet; *m* 17 May 1877 Col Henry Tomkinson, 1st Roy Dragoons, and *d* 18 April 1925. He *d* 17 April 1915

4a St John Thomas; *b* 19 June 1816; *m* 17 June 1841 Elizabeth Martha (*d* 25 March 1906), dau of Col Thomas Fiott de Havilland, of Havilland Hall, Guernsey, and *dsp*

5a William Francis (Rev), of Feniton Court, Devon; *b* 9 Nov 1819; *m* 6 Feb 1844 Elizabeth Carey (*d* 1897), dau of Lt-Col Christopher Baldock, HEIC, and *d* 2 April 1885, leaving issue:

1b Francis Arthur; *b* 31 Jan 1847; *m* 1st 18 May 1870 Harriet Julia Louisa (*d* 25 May 1874), dau of R W Schneider, and had issue:

1c Francis William Baldock; *b* 5 April 1873; *m* 1920 Mary Isabel Kirsteen (*d* 1986), dau of Francis Corbet-Singleton, and *d* 28 Sept 1937, having had issue:

1d +(Francis) St John (Corbet), CBE (1986), FSA [St John Gore Esq CBE, Grove Farm, Stoke-by-Nayland, Suffolk CO6 4SL]; Capt Roy Northumberland Fus WW II, Tstee Wallace Collection 1975–89, Nat Gallery 1986–94; *b* 8 April 1921; *educ* Wellington; *m* 17 July 1951 (*divorce* 1975) Priscilla Margaret, only dau of Cecil Harmsworth King; *m* 2nd 1981 *Mary Sophia, yst dau of 3rd Earl of Selborne (*qv*) and widow of Maj Hon (Thomas) Anthony Edward Towneley Strachey (*see* O'HAGAN, B), and by his 1st w has issue:

1e +William Ralph St John [William Gore Esq, Pencarrow Farm, Advent, Cornwall PL32 9RZ]; *b* 31 Jan 1956; *m* 1984 *Mary Susan, yst dau of Edmund Arthur Collingridge, of Sydney, NSW, and has:

1f +Ralph St John Edmund; *b* 1985

1f *Alice Catharine Mary; *b* 1988

1e *Catharine Harriet Cecilia; *b* 4 July 1954; *m* 1977 *Richard Edward Geoffrey Gayner and has issue:

1f *John Robert Haydon; *b* 1983

2f *William Richard Francis; *b* 1986

2d Ralph Corbet; *b* 16 July, *d* 11 Nov 1922

3d +Alan Charles Corbet [Alan Gore Esq, Grandcourt Farm, East Winch, Norfolk]; *b* 27 Sept 1926; *educ* Wellington; *m* 1st 18 Sept 1949 (*annulled* 1951) Daphne Patricia, er dau of Lt-Gen Sir William Montgomerie Thomson, KCMG, CB, MC; *m* 2nd 12 June 1953 *Anne Sabine, er dau of William Dudley Keith Thellusson, and by her has:

1e +Francis Charles Storar; *b* 30 Sept 1957

2e +Thomas Corbet; *b* 5 July 1960; *m* 1989 (*divorce* 1996) Skye Gyngell and has:

1f *Holly; *b* 1989

1c Allys Mary; *b* 8 April 1874; *m* 1893 Michael Thomas Duggleby, of Davenport, Iowa, and *d* Dec 1918, having had issue

1b (cont.) Francis Gore *m* 2nd 2 Sept 1875 Emlyn Augusta (*d* 13 Jan 1933), dau of Lt-Col John Minshull Drake, 10th NI, and *d* 10 Jan 1904, having by her had issue:

2c Cyril Gerard; *b* 1876; *m* 11 Oct 1911 Gladys Maria Howard (*d* 1974), 2nd dau of Allan A Spowers, Surveyor-Gen Qld, and *d* 15 March 1954, leaving issue:

1d Francis Arthur; *b* 1921; *m* 1947 *Leonore, dau of Leonard Lee, of Qld, and *d* 1987, leaving issue:

1e +Simon Gerard; *b* 1955; *m* 1979 *Leonie Christine, dau of H Beck, of Qld, and has issue:

1f +Richard Anthony; *b* 1984

2f +Adam William; *b* 1986

3f +Francis Arthur Douglas; *b* 1991

1e *Leonie Christine; *b* 1948; *m* 1st 1972 James Cruden; *m* 2nd 1985 *Jean-Marie Alain Simart and by him has:

1f *Thomas Elliot; *b* 1987

1f *Clélia Aurélia; *b* 1990

2e *Amanda Leonore Gore; *b* 1954; *m* 1979 (*divorce* 1981) Robert John Lyttleton Turner, s of Roland Turner, of Tasmania

1d Nancy Emlyn; *b* 11 Dec 1912; *m* 1st 31 Oct 1937 Leslie Brierly Hirst, 10th Gurkhas; *m* 2nd 4 Feb 1942 Maj John Lytton Bellamy, 14th Punjab Regt, er s of Lt-Col R Bellamy, DSO, and has had twin sons and dau (*d* a few hours after birth); *m* 3rd 6 Oct 1948 Alastair Roderick Holmes-Tarn, yr s of Maj H Holmes-Tarn. He *d* 29 July 1967

2d *Leonie Frances; *b* 1918; *m* 1st 3 Sept 1938 Hugh John Walsh, er s of Hugh Lawrence Peregrine Walsh; *m* 2nd 1956 *Shane Page and by her 1st husb has issue:

1e *Joanna Leonie; *b* 1939; *m* 1959 *Mervyn Fitzhenry and has:

1f *William Hugh Shaun; *b* 1961

2f *Brendan Mervyn; *b* 1964

3f *Shamus Terence; *b* 1968

1f *Bridget Madeline; *b* 1963

2e *Emlyn Anna; *b* 1942; *m* 1960 *John Thompson and has issue:
1f *Simon Patrick; *b* 1963
1f *Leonie Helen; *b* 1961
2c Hessey Margaret; *b* 1878; *m* 1907 Daniel Douglas and *d* April 1963, leaving two sons and a dau. He *d* 29 Dec 1947
3c Leonie Lettice Marion; *m* 25 Feb 1903 Robert Lloyd Patterson, LRCP, of Moran, Assam, and *d* 3 June 1910, leaving issue
2b St George Corbet, CSI; Col RE, Surveyor-Gen India 1899–1904, served Afghanistan; *b* 24 Feb 1849; *m* 8 June 1876 Elizabeth Julia Mackinnon (*d* 23 Oct 1902), only child of Lt-Col Alexander Hervey Bruce (*see* BRUCE, Bt, of Downhill), and *d* 10 Nov 1913, leaving issue:
1c Paul Alexander; Lt Seaforth Highrs; *b* 24 April 1877; *ka* Atbara 8 April 1898
2c John; *b* 25 June, *d* 16 July 1878
1c Gladys Mabel; *m* 21 Feb 1905 Charles Turner Allen, CIE, s of Sir George Allen, KCIE, and had issue. He *d* 18 March 1958
3b Robert William; Lt RN; *b* 16 April 1851; *m* 1883 Ella (*d* 1949), dau of George Wyndham, and *d* 30 June 1895, leaving issue:
1c William Wyndham; *b* 1884; *m* 1906 Martha, dau of Walter Lord, of Todmorden, Yorks, and *d* 1957, leaving:
1d Thomas Gerard, DSO (1946), OBE (1944); Lt-Col RAOC WW II; *b* 15 Feb 1907; *educ* Wellington; *m* 1933 Mrs Barbara Young and *d* 5 Nov 1965, leaving issue:
1e +Gerard Anthony St George [Gerard Gore Esq, Private Bag X 20049, Empangeni 3880, S Africa]; Cyprus Police 1960, Lt 60th Rifles (KRCC) 1957–60, Capt S African Inf Res; *b* 16 Oct 1936; *educ* Radley; *m* 14 Dec 1957 (*divorce* 1973) Wendy Primrose, dau of E Jacomb, of Johannesburg, and Mrs E Rippon, of Natal; *m* 2nd 1975 (*divorce* 1985) Velma, dau of Capt — McKinnon and Baroness von Puttkamer; *m* 3rd 1986 *Felicity Ann, dau of Kathleen Ferreira, of Johannesburg, and by his 1st *w* has had:
1f +Sean Ralph St George; *b* 13 June 1961
1f Fiona Wendy; *b* 14 May 1959; *d* 15 July 1965
2f *Nicole Holly St George; *b* 3 June 1965
1d Margaret Wyndham, MBE (1944); Cdr ATA WW II; *b* 24 Jan 1913
2c St George Arthur; *b* 1886; *m* 1st 1914 Muriel Mary (*divorce* 1954), dau of John Broughton, Surveyor-Gen NSW; *m* 2nd 10 Dec 1954 Mildred Prudence (*d* 1979), dau of Charles James Vyner, MRCVS, of London, and *d* 1970, leaving by his 1st w:
1d +Thomas William St George; *b* 1915; *m* 19 Aug 1948 Jane Nichols (*d* 1968), widow of Lt Donald Stewart Fletcher, RAA, and only dau of Samuel Bennett, of W Australia, and has issue:
1e +Donald Stewart St George; *b* 4 Sept 1952
2d +Patrick St George; *b* 1921; *m* 9 Jan 1948 *Coralie May dau of Mark Ruben Venn, of Tasmania, and has:
1e +Robert Ralph St George; *b* 14 Nov 1949; *m* 1978 *Prudence, dau of Kenneth A McKercher Burnie, of Tasmania, and has issue:
1f +William Robert Kenneth St George; *b* 1978
2e +Jonothan Ian St George; *b* 7 March 1953
3e +Peter Simon St George; *b* 2 Aug 1955; *m* 1979 *Sylvia Joyce, dau of Cyril Gardiner, of Vittoria, NSW, and has issue:
1f +Stephen Gregory St George; *b* 1981
3c Thomas Richard Gerard; *b* 1891; *d* 13 May 1906
1c Maud Gwendolen; *m* 3 April 1911 Archibald Turnbull, of NSW, 3rd s of J D Turnbull, of Guy Fawkes, NSW, and had issue
4b Gerard Ralph; *b* 5 June 1855; *m* 2 Feb 1882 Christiana Mary (*d* 17 Jan 1938), dau of Lewis Adolphus Bernays, CMG, and *d* 13 April 1912, leaving:
1c Mary Elisabeth; *m* 29 April 1916 Ernest Arthur Target, s of C B Target, of Hobart, Tasmania, and *d* Oct 1958, leaving issue. He *d* 15 June 1947
2c Phyllis Emlyn; *m* 16 July 1906 John Elworthy Trude, of Qld, and *d* leaving a s and dau. He *d* 30 Aug 1952
5b Frederick St John; *b* 21 April 1857; *educ* Magdalen Coll Oxford (BA); *m* 25 Aug 1898 Georgiana Isabella Susan (*d* 19 March 1954), dau of Col James Gore-Booth (*see* GORE-BOOTH, Bt), and *dsp* 2 April 1903
1b Alice Margaret Grace; *m* 20 Nov 1867 Alexander Volkov Mouromtzov (A N Roussov, Russian painter), and *d* 1909, leaving issue
2b Katharine Mary; *m* 2 June 1881 Arthur Montague Bernard and *d* 9 Aug 1927, leaving issue. He *d* 22 Jan 1927
3b Beatrice Diana; *m* 14 June 1881 Baron Werner von Globig and had issue. He *d* 1889
4b Lilian; *m* 30 Aug 1902 Maj Alfred Capel Cure, RFA, 3rd s of Rev Lawrence George Capel Cure, JP, and *d* 11 June 1936. He *d* 10 June 1912
5b Gwendolen Maud; *m* 1895 Lt-Col John St Clair Macmillan, RFA, and *d* 12 Oct 1937, leaving issue
1a Louisa Susannah; *m* 3 March 1849 Francis Corbet Singleton and had issue. He *d* 10 May 1887
2a Isabel Elizabeth; *m* 27 Nov 1849 Gilbert John Elliot and *d* 20 Feb 1902, leaving issue (*see* MINTO, E)
3 Jane; *m* Charles Coote
4 Elizabeth; *m* Frederick Cary Hamilton, 2nd s of Henry Cary Hamilton, of Dungiven
5 Catharine; *m* as his 2nd w, James Daly, of Carrownakelly, and Dunsandle, Co Galway, and had issue
6 Mary; *m* 27 Oct 1762 Frederick Gore, MP, and *dsp* (*see* above)

GORE-BOOTH

Arms: Quarterly, 1st and 4th, arg. a chaplet of roses ppr. between three boar's heads, erect and erased pean (for BOOTH); 2nd and 3rd, gu. a fess between three cross crosslets fitchée or (for GORE). **Crests:** 1 A lion passant pean, the dexter forepaw resting on a chaplet as in the arms (for BOOTH); 2 A wolf rampant arg., ducally gorged or (for GORE). **Mottoes:** 1 *Genti aequus utrique* ('Just to either line'), 2 *Quod ero spero* ('I hope for what I shall be'), 3 *In hoc signo vinces* ('In this sign shalt thou conquer'). **Creation:** Bt. (I) 30 Aug 1760.

SIR JOSSLYN HENRY GORE-BOOTH, 9TH BT, of Lissadell, Co Sligo [Sir Josslyn Gore-Booth Bt, Selaby, Gainford, Co Durham DL2 3HF]; *b* 5 Oct 1950; *s* f 1996; *educ* Eton, Balliol Coll Oxford (BA) and INSEAD (MBA); *m* 1980 *Jane Mary, only dau of Rt Hon Sir Roualeyn Hovell-Thurlow-Cumming-Bruce (*see* THURLOW, B), and has issue:
1 *Mary Georgina; *b* 1985
2 *Caroline Sarah; *b* 1987

Lineage: Sir PAUL GORE, 1st Bt, of Manor Gore (*see* ARRAN, E), had a 4th s: Sir FRANCIS GORE, of Artarman, Co Sligo; *m* Anne (*m* 2nd Percy Gethin), dau and heiress of Robert Parke, of Newtown, Co Leitrim, and *d* Feb 1713, leaving an est s:

Sir ROBERT GORE, of Newtown; *m* Feb 1678 Frances (*d* 1 March 1735), est dau of Sir Thomas Newcomen, of Sutton, CoDublin, and *d* Dec 1705, having had, with six yr sons and four daus:

NATHANIEL GORE, of Artarman and Newtown Gore; *b* 1692; *m* 25 July 1711 Lettice, only dau and heiress of Humphry Booth, of Dublin, and had, with a yr s and three daus:

Sir Booth Gore, 1st Bt (I), so *cr* 30 Aug 1760, of Lissadell, Co Sligo; *m* 23 Dec 1743 Emily (*d* Nov 1778), dau of Brabazon Newcomen, of Co Carlow, and *d* 22 Aug 1773, having had, with a dau:
1 **Sir Booth Gore, 2nd Bt**, of Lissadell and Huntercombe House, Bucks; *d* unm 17 June 1804
2 Sir ROBERT NEWCOMEN BOOTH later GORE-BOOTH (roy licence 30 Aug 1804), **3rd Bt**; *m* 19 Nov 1804 Hannah, dau of Henry Irwin, of Streamstown, Co Sligo, by Anne Stewart, and had issue:
(1) ROBERT (Sir), **4th Bt**
(2) Henry; Scots Fus Guards; *b* 11 April 1809; *m* 8 May 1834 Isabella (*d* 23 June 1897), 2nd dau of James Smith, JP, FRS, of Jordanhill, Renfrewshire, and *d* 25 July 1881, having had, with other issue:
1a Robert Henry; *b* 16 Dec 1838; *d* 23 April 1916
2a James; Col RE; *b* 22 Sept 1840; *m* 20 July 1870 Louisa Charlotte (*d* 26 Oct 1926), dau of Henry Trench (*see* ASHTOWN, B), and *d* 15 Oct 1913, having had:
1b Douglas Bloomfield, Lt Dorset Regt; *b* 15 Nov 1875; *das* Natal 19 Jan 1900
1b Georgiana Isabella Susan; *b* 12 Jan 1873; *m* 25 Aug 1898 Frederick St John Gore (*see* GORE, Bt) and *d* 19 March 1954
2b Ethel Norah; *d* unm 13 March 1940
(1) Anne; *m* 7 Dec 1829 6th Earl of Kingston (*qv*) and *d* 14 June 1883
Sir ROBERT *d* 23 Oct 1814; his est s,
Sir Robert Gore-Booth, 4th Bt; MP and Ld Lt Co Sligo; *b* 25 Aug 1805; during Irish Famine of 1840s mortgaged the Lissadell estate to provide food for his tenants, refusing meanwhile to accept any rents; *m* 1st 23 March 1827 Hon Caroline King (*dsp* 13 Jan 1828), 2nd dau of 1st Viscount Lorton of Boyle (*see* KINGSTON, E); *m* 2nd 2 April 1830 Caroline Susan (*d* 16 Jan 1855), 2nd dau of Thomas Goold, of Dublin, a Master in Chancery, and *d* 21 Dec 1876, leaving:

Sir Henry William Gore-Booth, 5th Bt, of Lissadell, JP, DL Co Sligo; High Sheriff 1872; *b* 1 July 1843; Arctic explorer; *m* 29 April 1867 Georgina Mary (*d* 23 Jan 1927), only dau of Col Charles John Hill, of Tickhill Castle, Yorks, and n of 9th Earl of Scarbrough (*qv*), and had, with other issue:

1 JOSSLYN AUGUSTUS RICHARD (Sir), **6th Bt**

2 Mordaunt; *b* 5 Dec 1878; *educ* Balliol Coll Oxford (BA); *m* 31 Jan 1906 Evelyn Mary (*d* 20 Aug 1963), dau of Robert Stanley Scholfield, of Sandhall, Howden, E R Yorks, and *d* 20 Nov 1958, having had issue:

(1) PAUL HENRY, BARON GORE-BOOTH, of Maltby, W Riding, Co York (LP; UK), so *cr* 1969, GCMG (1965, KCMG 1957, CMG 1949), KCVO (1961); *b* 3 Feb 1909; *educ* Eton and Balliol Coll Oxford (BA 1931); Head European Recovery Dept, FO1948, Dir Gen Br Info Servs USA 1949–53, Amb Rangoon 1953–56, Dep U-Sec FO 1956–60, HC India 1960–65, PUS FO 1965–68, Head Dip Serv 1968–69, PUS FCO 1968–69, chm: Windsor Festival 1971–73, Sherlock Holmes Soc, Govrs SOAS 1970–79, Save the Children Fund 1970–76, Registrar Order St Michael and St George 1966–84, dir Nat & Grindlays Bank and UK Provident Instn; *m* 21 Sept 1940 *Patricia Mary [The Rt Hon The Lady Gore-Booth, 152 Rivermead Court, Ranelagh Gdns, London SW6 3SF], only dau of Montague Ellerton, of Yokohama, Japan, and *d* 1984, leaving:

1a +David Alwyn (Sir), KCMG (1997, CMG (1990)) [The Hon Sir David Alwyn Gore-Booth KCMG, c/o FCO, London SW1A 2AH]; *b* 15 May 1943; *educ* Eton and Ch Ch Oxford (MA); joined FO 1964, Counsellor Jedda 1980, Counsellor and Head Chancery UK mission UN 1983, Head Policy Planning Staff FCO 1987, Assist U-Sec Middle East FCO 1989, Amb Saudi Arabia 1993–96, HC India 1996–98; *m* 1st 27 June 1964 (*divorce* 1970) Jillian Sarah, yr dau of James Wyatt Valpy, of Vergelegen Estate, Somerset W, S Africa; *m* 2nd 7 Oct 1977 *Mrs Mary Elizabeth Janet Gambetta, only dau of Sir David Francis Muirhead, CMG, CVO (*see* HOLLENDEN, B), and has by his 1st w:

1b +(Paul Wyatt) Julian; *b* 29 July 1968

2a +Christopher Hugh; *b* 15 May 1943; *educ* Eton and Durham U (BA); *m* 1st 1979 (*divorce* 1988) Mrs Jolanta Maria Nicholls, only dau of Dr L S Bernacinski; *m* 2nd 1993 *Mrs Annette Sheila Melli, dau of Joseph Rose, and has by his 1st w:

1b +Oliver Lucian Ralph; *b* 1 Aug 1980

1a Celia Mary; *b* 6 Jan 1946; *educ* Downe House and LAMDA; *m* 1983 *Douglas George Gill [Douglas Gill Esq, 15a Pemberton Gdns, London N19 5RR] and *d* 7 Aug 1992, leaving issue:

1b *Fionn Paul; *b* 27 Oct 1984

2a *Joanna Rosamond Georgina; *b* 11 Feb 1954; *educ* Sherborne and New Hall Cambridge (MA); *m* 15 July 1978 *Paul Richard Teverson, only s of G E Teverson, of Beckenham, Kent, and has issue:

1b *Richard Hugh; *b* 29 May 1984

2b *Peter Henry; *b* 21 Oct 1991

1b *Cathryn Frances; *b* 18 Sept 1986

(2) Colum Robert; *b* 26 June 1913; *educ* Eton and Balliol Coll Oxford; *m* 1st 1 Aug 1939 (*divorce* 1947) Joan Yvonne Ballard, adopted dau of Rev Charles William Chastel de Boinville; *m* 2nd 16 Dec 1947 *Mary (*m* 2nd 1971 Michael William McLean Barker, who *d* 1982), er dau of Edward Paget Scholfield, of Sandhall, Howden, Yorks, and *d* 6 June 1959, leaving by her:

1a +Francis Peter; *b* 27 Sept 1948; *educ* Eton

2a +(Nicholas) Justin; *b* 13 April 1952; *educ* Berkhamsted; *m* 1982 *Patricia Roberts and has issue:

1b *Jane; *b* 1984

2b *Helen; *b* 1986

3b *Sarah; *b* 1988

1a *Susan Caroline; *b* 5 Dec 1950; *m* 1973 Ashley Casie-Chitty (*d* 1982)

(1) Angela Georgina; *b* 12 April 1911; *d* 1 Jan 1912

1 Con(stance) Georgine, Countess Markievicz; nationalist politician and participant in armed struggle for Irish independence, condemned to death for her part in the Easter Rising 1916 but reprieved and sentence commuted to penal servitude for life (released 1917), elected MP (Sinn Fein) to Imperial Parl, Westminster, for St Patrick's, Dublin, 1918–21 (the first woman so elected, but did not take her seat), elected rep Dublin City Provisional Dáil Ireland (also Min Labour) 1921–22 and as memb Irish Free State Dáil Eireann 1923–27; also a painter; *m* 29 Sept 1900 Casimir Dunin, Count Markievicz, of Zyvotovka, Staro Zyvotov, Poland, portraitist, and *d* 15 July 1927, leaving a dau. He *d* 2 Dec 1932

2 Eva Selina Laura; poetess: *Poems, Unseen Kings, The One and the Many, The Three Resurrections and the Triumph of Maeve, The Egyptian Pillar, The Sorrowful Princess, The Agate Lamp, The Perilous Light, The Death of Fionavar, The Sword of Justice* and *Broken Glory*; *b* 1870; *d* unm 30 June 1926

3 Mabel Olive; *m* 1 Dec 1900 Charles Percival Foster, 2nd Dragoons, s of John Foster, of Coombe Park, Whitchurch, and *d* 2 March 1955, leaving issue. He *d* 23 Feb 1946

Sir HENRY *d* 13 Jan 1900; his er s,

Sir Josslyn Augustus Richard Gore-Booth, 6th Bt, JP, DL; *b* 25 Feb 1869; *m* 12 June 1907 Mary Sibell (*d* 12 Feb 1968), dau of Rev Savile Richard William L'Estrange Malone, Rector Dalton Holme, Yorks, and *d* 14 March 1944, having had:

1 **Sir Michael Saville Gore-Booth, 7th Bt**; *b* 24 July 1908; *educ* Rugby and Trin Coll Cambridge; *d* unm 1987

2 Hugh; MA Oxon, QALAS, lecturer estate management Oxford, Lt Roy Irish Fus WW II (despatches); *b* 6 June 1910; *ka* Leros 12 Nov 1943

3 Brian; literary agent, Sub-Lt RN WW II; *b* 23 Dec 1912; *ka* while serving in HMS *Exmouth* 21 Jan 1940

4 **Sir Angus Josslyn Gore-Booth, 8th Bt**; *b* 25 June 1920; *educ* Radley and Worcester Coll Oxford (BA); Capt Irish Gds WW II; *m* 14 Aug 1948 (*divorce* 1954) Hon Rosemary Myra Vane, only dau of 10th Baron Barnard (*qv*), and *d* 26 Jan 1996, leaving:

(1) Sir JOSSLYN HENRY ROBERT GORE-BOOTH, **9th and present Bt**

(1) *(Georgina Clara Rosaleen) Eirenice [Mrs Eirenice Gore-Booth, Zetland House, 8 Westland Terrace, Staindrop, Darlington, Co Durham DL2 3JS]; *b* 13 May 1949; *m* 31 Oct 1970 (*divorce* 1981) Clive Abercromby Blomfield-Smith, only s of Col Denis Blomfield-Smith and Mrs R Abercromby, and has:

1a *Edward Abercromby; *b* 14 May 1973; *educ* Wellington

1a *Olivia Rosemary; *b* 8 Nov 1976; *educ* Wellington

1 Bridget Mary; *b* 20 July 1911

2 Rosaleen Rachel; *b* 13 Aug 1914

3 Aideen Joyce; *b* 7 July 1916

4 Gabrielle Maeve; *b* 29 Aug 1918; *d* unm 30 June 1973

Seat: Lissadell, Carney, Co Sligo. Lissadell is more famous for its pictorial and mythopoeic associations than its architecture. Pictorial inasmuch as its collection of portraits of the Gore-Booths and in some cases their retainers has attracted increasing attention since first executed. Artistic also in regard to the poetry written there by its resident versifier Eva or about the place by Yeats, a frequent house guest. Mythopoeic in the sense that it stoked both the smouldering peat fire of the Celtic Twilight and the more flagrant political committedness of Countess Markievicz which followed it.

Yet Lissadell is a distinguished piece of architecture in its own right. In a less lush setting it would seem stark, being neo-classical and lightly decorated externally, while inside some of the vaster rooms have a mildly depressing air about them. It was built by the London architect Francis Goodwin beween 1830 and 1835 for **Sir Robert**, the philanthropic **4th Baronet** who attempted his own progamme of famine relief and who had previously demolished an older structure closer to the sea. Even so, Lissadell's sea views are stunning. Yeats's lines ('The light of evening, Lissadell/Great windows open to the South') testify to the atmosphere of the place generally. Indeed he once claimed to have seen the house ghost.

GORELL

Arms: Azure two lions passant guardant ermine, each holding in the dexter paw a sprig of oak slipped or, between three annulets in pale argent. **Crest:** In front of a cubit arm in armour, the hand grasping a broken sword all proper, the wrist encircled by a wreath of oak or, five annulets interlaced and fesswise argent. **Supporters:** On either side a ram proper charged on the shoulder with two annulets interlaced azure. **Motto:** *Frangas non flectes* ('You may break, but you shall not bend me'). **Creation:** B. (UK) 16 Feb 1909.

THE 4TH BARON GORELL, of Brampton, Co Derby (Timothy John Radcliffe Barnes) [The Rt Hon The Lord Gorell, 4 Roehampton Gate, London SW15 5JS]; *b* 2 Aug 1927; *s f* 1963; *educ* Eton and New Coll Oxford; barrister Inner Temple 1951, Lt Rifle Bde, sr exec Roy Dutch-Shell Oil 1959–84; *m* 29 May 1954 *Joan Marion, yr dau of John Collins, of Moseley, Birmingham, and has adopted:

*Susan Elizabeth [Mrs Robin Clark, 33 Quintin Ave, London SW20]; *b* 26 Dec 1958; *m* *Robin H A Clark, er s of J A Clark, and has:

(1) *Kyle Hendrik Gorell; *b* 1988

*Jennifer [Mrs David Dally, 72 Grove Ave, London W7 3SE]; *b* 6 Oct 1960; *m* 1986 *David James Michael Dally, er s of B J M Dally, and has issue:

(1) *Thomas; *b* 1992 (triplet)

(2) *Samuel; *b* 1992 (triplet)

(1) *Megan Elizabeth; *b* 1991

(2) *Kate; *b* 1992 (triplet)

Lineage: EDMUND BARNES; *d* 1725, leaving:

JOHN BARNES, of Ashgate, Chesterfield, Derbys; *b* 1706; *m* Elizabeth (*d* 24 Sept 1787), dau of James Allison, of Brampton, Chesterfield, and *d* 18 Nov 1779, leaving, with other issue:

DAVID BARNES, of Ashgate; *b* 1741; *m* Eleanor (*d* 14 Nov 1822), dau of Edward Gorell, of Clapham, Yorks, and *d* 11 Oct 1805, leaving issue:

JOHN GORELL BARNES, of Ashgate; *b* 23 Dec 1777; *m* 1810 Elizabeth Taylor (*d* 10 Oct 1858), dau of John Clay, of N Wingfield, Derbys, and *d* 29 March 1858, having had, with other issue:

1 HENRY

2 Charles, of Mossley Hill, Lancs, JP; *b* 5 July 1818; *m* 29 Nov 1854 Marian (*d* 4 March, 1905), er dau of Rev William Peach, Vicar Old Brampton, Derbys, and *d* 7 June 1886, having had issue

3 Edmund, of Ashgate House; *b* 23 April 1820; *m* 6 April 1854 Sarah Anne, dau of Thomas Wilson, of Liverpool, and *d* 26 Jan 1870, leaving issue

4 Alfred, of Ashgate Lodge, JP, DL (Derbys); MP Chesterfield 1880–92; *b* 28 Sept 1823; *m* 6 April 1854 Charlotte, dau of Thomas Wilson, of Liverpool, and *d* 28 Nov 1901, having had issue

1 Emily; *b* 1 Nov 1815; *m* 29 July 1847 Rev Courtney Smith, Rector Pleasley, Derbys, and had issue

JOHN BARNES's est s,

HENRY BARNES, of Liverpool; *b* 21 Feb 1817; *m* 29 July 1847 Georgiana, dau of Rev Richard Smith, Rector Staveley, Derbys, and *d* 15 Feb 1865, leaving issue:

1 JOHN GORELL, **1st Baron**

2 Alan Sedgwick; *b* 9 Oct 1850; *m* Mary Elizabeth Welton (*d* 1910)

1 Charlotte Linda; *b* 22 Sept 1852; *m* 1882 Rev Henry Arthur Morgan, DD (*d* 3 Sept 1912), Master Jesus Coll Cambridge, and *d* 10 June 1929, leaving issue

2 Henrietta Georgiana; *b* 4 May 1855; *m* Augustus Frederick Warr, of Liverpool, MP, and *d* 16 July 1922, leaving issue

HENRY BARNES's est s,

JOHN GORELL BARNES, **1st Baron Gorell** (UK), of Brampton, Co Derby, so *cr* 16 Feb 1909, PC (1905); *b* 16 May 1848, MA Cantab, Hon LLD 1898, Hon Fell Peterhouse; barrister Inner Temple 1876, QC 1888, Bencher 1896, Judge High Court (Probate Divorce and Admlty Div) 1892, Pres 1905–09, ktd 1892; *m* 20 April 1881 Mary Humpston (*d* 28 Nov 1918), est dau of Thomas Mitchell, of West Arthurlie, and *d* 22 April 1913, leaving issue:

1 HENRY GORELL BARNES, **2nd Baron Gorell**, DSO; *b* 21 Jan 1882; *educ* Winchester, Trin Coll Oxford (MA 1908) and Harvard; barrister Inner Temple 1906, Maj 7th Lond Bde RGA WW I (despatches); *ka* 16 Jan 1917

2 RONALD GORELL, **3rd Baron**

1 Aura Ellida Gorell; *b* 31 Jan 1887; *d* unm 28 Feb 1945

The 1st BARON's 2nd s,

RONALD GORELL BARNES, **3rd Baron Gorell**, MC (1917), CBE (1919, OBE 1918); *b* 16 April 1884; *educ* Winchester, Harrow and Balliol Coll Oxford (MA); barrister Inner Temple 1909, Hon Fellow Roy Soc Teachers, Hon RWS; author, jnlst *The Times* 1911–15, Col Gen List, Capt and Adj Rifle Bde, Dep Dir Staff Duties (Educn) War Office 1918–20, initiated Roy Army Educnl Corps, memb Police Ctee 1919–20, Under-Sec Air 1921–22, chm: Miners Welfare Ctee 1921, Teachers Registration Cncl 1922–35, Soc of Authors 1928–35, King's Coll Hosp 1929–33, Art and Industry Ctee BOT 1931–32, Control of Private Flying Ctees 1933–34 and 1938–39, Roy Aero Club 1933–36 and 1943–45, PM's Ctee on Carlton House Terrace 1933–41 and Regent's Park Terraces 1946, Children's Refugee Movement 1939–49, Govrs Dulwich College and Alleyn's Sch 1949–58; Dep Pres Victoria League 1922–24, Pres Roy Soc Teachers 1929–35, ed *Cornhill Magazine* 1933–39, Upper Bailiff Weavers' Co 1944–46 and 1953–54, Pres Roy Lit Fund 1951–63, Company Cdr W Sussex HG 1940–45, Offr Order Leopold of Belgium, served WW I (despatches); *m* 10 Jan 1922 Maud Elizabeth Furse (*d* 26 April 1954), est dau of Alexander Nelson Radcliffe, of Bag Park, and *d* 2 May 1963, leaving issue:

1 TIMOTHY JOHN RADCLIFFE BARNES, **4th and present Baron Gorell**

2 +(RONALD ALEXANDER) HENRY GORELL [The Hon Henry Barnes, Fernbank, Mingoose, Mount Hawke, nr Truro, Cornwall TR4 8BX]; *b* 28 June 1931; heir presumptive; *educ* Harrow and New Coll Oxford; Lt Roy Fus; Capt 7th Bn RNF (TA), late PR offr P&O; *m* 17 Aug 1957 *Gillian Picton, yst dau of Picton Hughes-Jones, of Henstridge, Somerset, and has issue:

(1) +John Picton Gorell; *b* 29 July 1959; *educ* King's Sch Bruton and Cornwall Tech Coll Camborne

(1) *Elizabeth Gail; *b* 1 June 1961

1 Rosemary Eva; *b* 9 July 1925; *educ* Masters Sch, Dobbs Ferry, NY, USA, Froebel Inst and Bedford Coll London (BA); *m* 16 July 1961 *Peter Douglas Gill, only s of Charles Douglas Gill, CBE, of Loftus Hill, Ferrensby, Yorks, and had:

(1) *Nicholas Charles Ronald; *b* 20 Dec 1966

(1) *Katherine Elizabeth Louise; *b* 24 Oct 1962

(2) *Henrietta Patricia Mary; *b* 29 March 1964

GORING

Arms: Arg. a chevron between three annulets gu. **Crest:** A lion rampant-guardant sa. **Motto:** *Renascentur* ('May they rise again'). **Creation:** Bt (E) 18 May 1678 with precedency of 23 July 1627.

SIR WILLIAM BURTON NIGEL GORING, 13TH BT, of Highden, Sussex [Sir William Goring Bt, c/o Quilter & Co Ltd, St Helens, 1 Undershaft, London EC3A 8BB]; *b* 21 June 1933; *s* unc 1956; *educ* Wellington and RMA Sandhurst; late Lt Roy Sussex Regt; *m* 24 Sept 1960 (*divorce* 1993) Hon Caroline Elizabeth Thellusson, est dau of 8th Baron Rendlesham (*qv*); *m* 2nd 1993 Judith Rachel Walton (*d* 15 Dec 1995), dau of Rev Raymond John Walton Morris, OBE, of Shaftesbury, and formerly w of Thomas Richard Atkin Morison, QC

Lineage (of Goring): JOHN de GORING, Sussex; *fl temp* HENRY III; had:

JOHN de GORING; had:

ROBERT de GORING; had, with two yr sons (Thomas; Simon):

JOHN GORING; *fl temp* EDWARD III; had:

JOHN GORING, of Lancing, Sussex; had:

JOHN GORING, of Lancing; had:

JOHN GORING, of Lancing; MP Sussex 1467; *m* 1st Margaret, dau of Ralph Radmylde, by Margaret, dau and coheir of Sir Richard Camoys (*see* CAMOYS, B); *m* 2nd Joan, widow of Humphrey Hewster, of London, and *d* 1495, leaving by his 1st w an est s:

JOHN GORING, of Burton/Bodecton, W Sussex; *m* his stepmother's husb Humphrey Hewster's dau Joan and *d* shortly after his f, leaving (with Margery, *m* John Shirler, of Isfield):

JOHN GORING, of Burton; *m* Constance, dau and heir of Henry Dyke, and *d* 16 Oct 1520, leaving an er s:

Sir WILLIAM GORING, of Burton, Master Horse to HENRY VIII, Gentleman Privy Chamber to EDWARD VI, MP Sussex 1547, Sheriff Sussex and Surrey 1531, 1536 and 1550; *m* Elizabeth (*d* 16 Nov 1558), 2nd dau and coheir of John Covert, of Slaugham, Sussex, and *d* 2 March 1553, leaving:

1 HENRY

2 George, of Ovingdean and Danny Park, Sussex; Receiver Court Wards, Sheriff Sussex and Surrey 1578; *m* Mary, est dau and coheir of William Everard, of Alborne, Sussex, and *d* 7 Feb 1601, leaving:

(1) George; *m* Anne, dau of Henry Denny, of Waltham Abbey, Essex, and sis of Sir Edward Denny, Earl of Norwich (so *cr* 24 Oct 1626; *extinct* 27 Sept 1637), and had (with a dau, Mary, *m* John Hotham, *see* HOTHAM, B):

1a Sir GEORGE GORING, 1st EARL OF NORWICH, so *cr* 28 Nov 1644, as also previously 14 April 1628 BARON GORING OF HURSTPIERPOINT, Co Sussex (both E), PC (1639 and 1660); *b* 28 April 1585; *educ* Sidney Sussex Coll Cambridge; ktd 1608, Gentleman Privy Chamber to Prince of Wales 1610 and JAMES I 1611, Lt Gentlemen Pensioners 1614, MP Lewes 1620–22, 1624–26 and Feb-April 1628, Kt Marshal Household 1623, V-Chamberlain 1626–28 and Master Horse 1628–39 to QUEEN HENRIETTA MARIA, Wales: Sec, Clerk Signet and Clerk Cncl 1630, V-Chamberlain Household 1639–44, Amb France 1643–44, Gen royalist forces Essex and Kent 1648, captured by Parly forces and sentenced to death March 1648/9, though pardoned and freed May 1649, lived in exile 1650–60, Sec Cncl Wales 1661; *m* just before 1608 Mary, dau of 6th Lord (Baron) Bergavenny (*see* ABERGAVENNY, M), and *d* 6 Jan 1662/3, having had, with three daus:

1b George, *Lord Goring*; *b* 14 July 1608; Col regt mixed foot and horse Low Countries 1633, Govr Portsmouth Jan 1638/9–Sept 1642, MP Portsmouth 1640–42, Lt-Gen 1641, jt cdr royalist forces victories Boroughbridge Feb and (sole cdr) Seacroft Moor March 1642/3, beaten by Parly forces Wakefield May, imprisoned Tower London till March 1643/4, led one of the cav charges Marston Moor 1644, Lt-Gen royalist horse in the West Aug 1644, took St Austell 26 Aug 1644 but let Parly horse escape, in contravention of CHARLES I's orders, Lostwithiel 31 Aug 1644, Gen entire royalist horse under PRINCE RUPERT 4 Dec 1644 and Lt-Gen combined horse and foot Hants, Kent, Surrey, Sussex 21 Dec 1644, beaten

Langport, Somerset, by Parly forces under Fairfax (*see* FAIRFAX OF CAMERON, L) July 1645 following a futile and insubordinate siege of Taunton, having disobeyed PRINCE RUPERT's orders to relieve the royalists at Market Harborough, Leics, as also CHARLES I's orders to proceed to Newbury to draw Parly forces from investing Oxford; served Spanish armies against French 1647–48 and Spanish forces again 1652 in Siege Barcelona; *m* 25 July 1629 Lady Lettice Boyle, dau of 1st Earl of Cork (*see* CORK and ORRERY, E), but *dsvp* 25 July 1657

2b CHARLES GORING, 2nd and last EARL OF NORWICH; royalist Col Civil War (captured Marston Moor July 1644 but escaped or was freed and fought 2nd Battle Newbury Oct 1644), Clerk Cncl Wales 1661, Capt Yeomen Gd; *b c* 1615; *m* by 7 Jan 1658/9 Alice (*bur* 23 July 1680), widow of Thomas Baker, of Fressingfield, Suffolk, and dau and coheir of Robert Leman, of Brightwell Hall, Suffolk, and *dsp* 3 March 1670/1, when his titles expired

1b Catherine; reputedly PRINCE RUPERT's mistress; *m* Edward Scott, DCL, of Scots' Hall and Nettlestead Place, Kent, and had issue. He *d* 1665

(1) Dorothy; *m* 1st Sir Henry Bowyer (*dsp* 1606; *see* below: the 1st Bt of the 1678 and current *cr* was his 2nd cousin twice-removed), ggs of William Bowyer; *m* 2nd —

3 Robert; *m* Mary, dau of Thomas Olney and had:

(1) Elizabeth

4 Anne; *m* 1st Sir George Delalynde; *m* 2nd Francis Browne, bro of 1st Viscount Montagu

The est son,

Sir HENRY GORING, of Burton; ktd 1591, Sheriff Sussex and Surrey 1562 and Sussex 1569; *b* 1521; *m* Dorothy, 2nd dau and coheir of his yr bro George's w and dau of William Everard, and *d* 16 Dec 1594, leaving:

1 William, of Burton; *m* 1st 1563 Ann, dau and heiress of Robert Burbridge, of Hayes, Middx; *m* 2nd Margaret, dau of Thomas Chaloner, of Kenwards, Sussex, and widow of (a) William Courthope, of Hartfield, and (b) Richard Mill, of Greatham, both Sussex, and was f of George, ancestor of the GORINGs of Barcombe and Chailey, Sussex, extinct in the male line 1735. He *d* 1601, leaving issue (by his 1st w?):

(1) Henry (Sir), of Burton; *m* Eleanor, dau of Sir William Kingsmill, and *d* 16 July 1626, having had:

1a Sir WILLIAM GORING, 1st Bt (E), so *cr* 14 May 1622; *m* Eleanor/Bridget, dau and heir of Sir Edward Francis, and was *bur* 25 Feb 1657/8, leaving:

1b Sir HENRY GORING, 2nd Bt; *m* Mary, widow of Sir Thomas Gage, 2nd Bt (*see* GAGE, V), and *d* 8 June 1671, leaving:

1c Sir WILLIAM GORING, 3rd and last Bt; *m* Dorothy, widow of Philip Draycot and dau of Edmund Plowden (*see* PLOWDEN, B), and *dsp* 29 Feb 1723/4, when the btcy expired

1a Ann; *m* Richard Biddulph, of Biddulph Castle, Staffs and had issue (*see* CAMOYS, B)

2 EDWARD

1 Barbara; *m* Richard Ernley, of Ernley, Sussex

2 Elizabeth; *m* 1575 Thomas Selwin, of Friston, Sussex, and *d* 1625

3 Mary; *m* Sir Anthony Dering, of Surrenden Dering, Kent, and *dsp* (*see* 1970 edn DERING, Bt)

The 2nd son,

EDWARD GORING, of Wappingthorn, Steyning; Oakhurst, Billingshurst; and later Highden, Washington, all Sussex; Sheriff Sussex and Surrey 1613; *m* 1580 Elizabeth, dau and coheir of Thomas Wiseman, of Bulbridge, Wilts, and *d* 20 May 1617, leaving issue:

1 Henry, of Highden; MP Arundel 1640; *m* 18 Jan 1609/10 Mary, dau of Sir Thomas Eversfield, and *d* 26 Feb 1655 aged 72, having had, with another s (*d* young) and 10 daus:

(1) Henry (Sir), **2nd Bt**

2 Edward, of Cobden, Sussex; *m* 1618 Elizabeth, est dau of Sir Thomas Eversfield, of Denn, Horsham, Sussex, and *d* 1657, leaving issue, the male line seemingly failing *c* 1685

1 Maria; *m* 1600 Thomas Shelley, of Worminghurst, Sussex

2 Dorothea; *m* Nicholas Eversfield, of Hollington, Sussex

Lineage (of Bowyer): WILLIAM BOWYER; ggf (by another s to the gf of Sir Henry Bowyer mentioned above) of:

THOMAS BOWYER, of Leighthorne/Ley(gh)thorne, Sussex; *m* 2nd Jane, dau of John Birch, Baron Exchequer, and *d* 7 March 1594/5, leaving:

Sir THOMAS BOWYER, 1st Bt (E), so *cr* 23 July 1627; MP Midhurst 1614 and Bramber 1621–42, Sheriff Surrey and Sussex 1626–27; *b* 28 Nov 1586; *m* 1st by 1610 Anne, dau and coheir of Adrian Stoughton, of W Stoke, Surrey, Recorder Chichester, and had an est s:

1 Sir THOMAS BOWYER, 2nd Bt; *b c* 1610; *educ* Trin Coll Oxford; *m* 1st Katherine, dau and coheir of Richard Stany, of Elston, Sussex; *m* 2nd after 1648 Margaret — (*d* between 26 July 1687 and 22 Nov 1693) and *dspm* between 13 June and 21 Dec 1659

Sir THOMAS BOWYER, 1st Bt, *m* 2nd by 1634 Jane (*bur* 10 April 1640), dau and heir of Emery Cranley and widow of (a) Samuel Austen, of Stratford, and (b) Sir George Stoughton; *m* 3rd by 1642 Anne — (*bur* 11 Sept 1683, leaving issue) and was *bur* 28 Feb 1650, leaving 13 children in all, and by her:

2 **Sir James Bowyer**, 3rd and last Bt of the 1627 *cr* and **1st Bt** of the 1678 one; *b c* 1645; *educ* Winchester, New Coll Oxford (Fell 1663–65) and MiddleTemple; ruined himself and being childless procured a fresh grant of btcy 18 May 1678 (allegedly with precedence of the old btcy, on the patent of the latter being given up) with remainder, failing heirs of his own body, to his extremely distant relative Henry Goring and the heirs male of the latter's body, the arrangement being allegedly smoothed by a gift of money from Goring, the beneficiary; **Sir James** *dsp* and was bur 28 Feb 1679/80, when the 1627 btcy expired but that of 1678 devolved according to the highly unusual limitation on:

Lineage (of Goring, cont.): Sir Henry Goring, 2nd Bt, of Highden; *bapt* 22 May 1622; MP Sussex 1660 and 1685–87 and Steyning 1661–79; *m* 2 May 1642 Frances (*d* 14 Dec 1694), est dau of Sir Edward Bishopp, 2nd Bt, of Parham, Sussex, and *d* 3 April 1702, leaving an est s:

HENRY GORING, of Wappingthorn, Steyning; MP New Shoreham 1672, Bramber 1678–79 and Steyning 1685, Capt foot regt, Sheriff Sussex 1681–82; *b* 1646; *m* 1st *c* 3 Oct 1667 Elizabeth (*d* June 1673), dau and coheir of Anthony Morewood, of Alfreton, Derbys, and had, with other issue:

1 **Sir Charles Goring, 3rd Bt**; *b* 1668(?); *m* 16 Nov 1699 and again 12 May 1700 Elizabeth (*d* 27 March 1741), yst dau of Richard Bridger, of Combe Place, Sussex, and *dsp* 13 Jan 1712/3

Capt HENRY GORING *m* 2nd 2 Feb 1675 Mary (*m* 2nd Nicholas Best, of Horsham), yst dau and coheir of Sir John Covert, 1st Bt, of Slaugham, Sussex, and was killed *vp* 1687 by Sir Edward Dering, 3rd Bt (*see* 1970 edn), leaving, with other issue by her:

2 **Sir Harry Goring, 4th Bt**; Col 31st Foot, MP (Tory) Horsham 1707–08 and Jan-June 1715 and Steyning 1709–15, *cr* 2 Jan 1721/2 by the titular King James III Baron Bullinghel and Viscount Goring; *bapt* 16 Sept 1679; *m c* 25 Feb 1714 Elizabeth (*d* 28 July 1768 aged nearly 100), est dau and coheir of Adml Sir George Matthew, of Southwark and Twickenham, and *d* 12 Nov 1731, leaving an est s:

(1) **Sir Charles Matthew Goring, 5th Bt**; *b* 15 May 1706; *m* 1st 15 July 1731 Mary (*bur* 5 May 1739), yst dau of William Blackburn, of Morton Ash, Essex, and was *bur* 2 Sept 1769, having by her had, with a dau (*d* unm):

1a **Sir Harry Goring, 6th Bt**; *b* 26 April 1739; *educ* Magdalen Coll Oxford (MA); MP Shoreham 1790–96; *m* 1st 8 Sept 1767 John Anna (*d* 4 June 1774), only child of John Forster, Govr Fort William, Bengal, and had issue:

1b **Sir Charles Forster Goring, 7th Bt**; Sheriff Sussex 1827; *b* 11 July 1768; *m* 9 Nov 1799 Bridget (*d* 12 Jan 1816), dau of Henry Dent, of Canterbury, and *d* 26 March 1844, having had, with two daus (*d* unm):

1c **Sir Harry Dent Goring, 8th Bt**; *b* 30 Dec 1801; MA Oxon; MP Shoreham 1832–41; *m* 1st 2 Aug 1827 (*divorce* 21 June 1841) Augusta (*m* 2nd Edward John Trelawney), dau of John Harvey (*see* HARVEY OF TASBURGH, B), and had, with a dau (*d* unm):

1d **Sir Charles Goring, 9th Bt**; Lt 12th Lancers; *b* 2 June 1828; *m* 1st 11 Feb 1850 Margaret Anna (*d* 1856), dau of Jones Panton; *m* 2nd 21 April 1857 Eliza (*m* 2nd 22 Jan 1885 Col Robert Ashworth Godolphin Cosby, of Stradbally Hall, Queen's Co), 2nd dau of Rev Capel Molyneux, Vicar St Paul's, Onslow Sq, and *dsp* 3 Nov 1883

1c (cont.) **Sir Harry** *m* 2nd 11 May 1842 Mary Elizabeth (*d* 20 Oct 1871), widow of Jones Panton, of Plas Gwyn, Anglesey, and dau and heiress of John Griffith Lewis, of Llanddyfian, Anglesey, and *d* 19 April 1859, having by her had, with two more daus:

1d Margaret; *b* 31 Jan 1844; *m* 2 Oct 1873 Albert Edouard Fisher and *d* 4 Oct 1926. He *dsp* 1907

2d Diana; *b* 8 Feb 1848; *m* 1st 18 Aug 1870 Capt W Digby Lloyd (*d* 1883), 67th Regt, and had issue; *m* 2nd 22 Nov 1887 Anthony John Wright Biddulph and *d* 16 Feb 1931 (*see* CAMOYS, B)

2c Charles (Rev); Rector Twineham, Sussex; *b* 17 May 1805; *m* 2 Oct 1832 Maria Arabella (*d* 13 Jan 1890), dau of Hon Frederick St John (*see* BOLINGBROKE and SAINT JOHN, V), and *d* 4 Aug 1859, having had, with another s and three daus:

1d **Sir Craven Charles Goring, 10th Bt**; Capt 33rd Foot, Hon Col 3rd and 4th (Militia) Bns Roy Sussex Regt Abyssinian Expdn 1868 (medal); *b* 24 Oct 1841; *m* 14 Dec 1869 Agnes (*d* 16 Nov 1911), 2nd dau of Charles A Stewart, of The West Hall, High Leigh, Cheshire, and *d* 14 March 1897, leaving issue:

1e Agnes Venetia; *b* 21 Nov 1870; *m* 27 April 1896 Edwin Theobald Hohler and *d* 19 July 1933, leaving issue. He *d* 19 Aug 1921

3c George; Capt 64th Foot; *b* 29 Aug 1806; *d* unm 15 Sept 1838

4c Forster; Cornet 1st King's Dragoon Gds 1832–34, Clerk Exec Cncl NZ 1862–89; *b* 9 April 1810; *m* 19 July 1839 Hon Sydney Eloise Yelverton (*d* 13 March 1883), est dau of 3rd Viscount Avonmore (*see* 1910 edn), and *d* 8 Dec 1893, having had, with another s (*d* young):

1d **Sir Harry Yelverton Goring, 11th Bt**; Sgt-Maj 38th Regtl Dist 1881–86; *b* 19 July 1840; *m* 19 July 1875 Sarah Anne (*d* 20 Aug 1904), dau of John Hickin, of Lichfield, and *d* 20 Aug 1911, leaving:

1e **Sir Forster Gurney Goring, 12th Bt**; served ranks five years, 2nd Lt 1st Bn Roy Sussex Regt 1902, Boer War 1900–02 (Queen's medal and three clasps, King's medal and two clasps), Lt 1905 (ret 1912), Capt Invalids Roy Hosp Chelsea 1912; *b* 19 June 1876; *m* 1st 8 Sept 1917 Lenore Consuelo Marguerite (*d* 24 Jan 1941), only dau of Sir Walter Louis Rackham Currie, 4th Bt (*qv*); *m* 2nd 14 Aug 1943 Hilda Macmillan (*d* 11 June 1969), dau of Maj Robert Macmillan Dunlop, JP, and *dsp* 1 May 1956

2e Barry Heneage; *b* 26 June 1880; *d* unm 11 Feb 1931

3e Craven Charles; *b* 21 Oct 1881; *m* 15 Feb 1908 Mary Elizabeth (*d* 22 Nov 1959), dau of John Conlon, of Roscommon, and *d* 26 Jan 1952, leaving issue:

1f *Beryl Elizabeth [Mrs George Thawley, Castle Farm, Bridgwater Rd, Bristol, N Somerset BS13 8AF]; *b* 1909; *m* 25 Oct 1930 George Frederick Thawley (*d* 15 Aug 1958), s of Frank Thawley, and has issue:

1g *Peter Frederick [Peter Thawley, Castle Farm, Bridgwater Rd, Bristol, N Somerset BS13 8AF]; *b* 1940; *m* 1966 (*divorce* 1980) Christine Mary, dau of Charles Henry Jones Payne, and has issue:

1h *Nicholas; *b* 1971; *m* 4 Dec 1996 *Sarah, dau of Terence David Parker

1h *Lisa; *b* 1969

4e Harry George; *b* 9 Dec 1885; *d* 10 Nov 1888

5e Frederick Yelverton; Maj Roy Sussex Regt WW I (wounded three times); *b* 15 Oct 1893; *m* 8 April 1931 Freda Margaret (*d* 1993), only dau of Nigel Victor Ainsworth, MBE, JP, of Smithills Hall, Bolton, Lancs, and *d* 5 Nov 1938, leaving:

1f Sir WILLIAM BURTON NIGEL GORING, **13th and present Bt**

2f Edward Yelverton Combe; Lt-Cdr RN; *b* 20 June 1936; *educ* Wellington and RNC Dartmouth; *m* 1969 (*divorce* 1990) Daphne Christine Seller and *d* 1991, leaving issue:

1g *Elizabeth Christine; *b* 1970

2g *Joanna Margaret; *b* 1972

1e Sydney Eloise; *d* young 1890

2e Ida Augusta; *m* 16 July 1904 Frederick Charles Cooper and *d* 13 June 1942. He *d* 8 Aug 1959

3e Agnes Beryl; *m* 30 April 1919 John Martin, s of W J Martin, and had issue

2d Forster Yelverton; Lt-Col Roy NZ Artillery NZ War 1861–66 (medal); *b* 23 July 1846; *m* 26 June 1880 Bertha Virginia (*d* 12 June 1936), dau of Maj Herbert Dobie, Madras Army, and *d* 17 Feb 1923

3d Barry Yelverton; *b* 24 April 1851; *m* 1893 Marion Haslewood (*d* 1898), dau of Charles Pitt Pynsent, of Wellington, NZ, and *d* 29 Jan 1929, leaving issue:

1e Dorothy Edith

2e Barbara Yelverton; *m* 22 July 1922 Cdr Francis John Lambert, DSC, RN (*d* 29 April 1969), 3rd s of Col Joseph Alexander Lambert, JP, DL, of Brookhill, Co Mayo, and had issue:

1f Eloise Marion Grace Georgina; *b* 14 Nov 1926

1d Ida Julia; *m* 1st 23 Nov 1861 Capt T B Richards, 40th Regt; *m* 2nd 6 Feb 1878 A Chudleigh Wilmer, 85th Regt, and *d* 12 Dec 1931, leaving issue. He *d* 1882

2d Cecilia Augusta; *m* Feb 1868 Hon Walter Woods Johnston, MLC, of Wellington, NZ, and *d* 22 Dec 1922, leaving issue. He *d* 1907

3d Sydney Elizabeth; *m* 8 Aug 1866 Capt John Castell Robson, of Kelso, Scotland, and *d* 6 June 1936. He *d* 1880

4c William; *b* 5 Dec 1811; *m* 1st 1837 Louisa Smith (*d* 1839); *m* 2nd 6 April 1848 Catherine Barwell, only dau of Thomas Skryme, and *d* 9 May 1849, having by her had issue:

1d Emma Kathleen Ida; *b* 26 April, *d* 12 Aug 1849

1c Elizabeth; *b* 28 April 1808; *m* 19 May 1834 Joshua Robert Minnitt, of Anaghbeg, Co Tipperary, and *d* 1901, leaving issue. He *d* 1882

2c Ida; *b* 8 Aug 1814; *m* 13 Feb 1834 Aubrey William Beauclerk and *d* 23 April 1839 (*see* SAINT ALBANS, D)

1b Anna Maria; *b* 17 Sept 1769; *m* 11 April 1792 Thomas Lewis, of Gray's Inn, and *d* 24 July 1849

2b Frances; *b* 6 May 1774; *m* 1st 13 July 1799 Rev John Dring (*d* 1804), Vicar Poling, Sussex; *m* 2nd 5 July 1810 Rev John Rideout, Rector Woodmancote, Sussex, and *d* 3 Oct 1868

1a (cont.) **Sir Harry** *m* 2nd 23 Oct 1777 Elizabeth (*d* 10 July 1780), dau of Thomas Fisher, of Barbados, and *d* 1 Dec 1824, having by her had an only son (*d* unm)

1a Mary; *b* 1736; *m* 26 Nov 1767 Colvill Bridger, of Buckingham House, Sussex

(1) (cont.) **Sir Charles** *m* 2nd 20 April 1743 Elizabeth, sis of Sir Robert Fagge, 4th Bt (*qv*), and by her had:

2a Charles, of Wiston; *b* 1744; *m* 1st 20 April 1779 Sarah (*dsp* 6 Dec 1797), dau of Ralph Beard, of Hurstpierpoint; *m* 2nd 7 June 1798 Elizabeth (*d* 8 Aug 1811), dau of Edward Luxford, and by her had, with other issue:

1b Elizabeth; *b* 1799; *m* 25 Aug 1829 Rt Rev Walter John Trower, DD, Bp Glasgow later Gibraltar, and *d* 1876, leaving issue. He *d* 24 Oct 1877

2a (cont.) Charles Goring *m* 3rd 7 May 1812 Mary (*d* 18 Nov 1845), dau of Rev John Ballard, DD, Fell Winchester, Rector Gt Longford, Wilts, and *d* 3 Dec 1829, having by her had:

1b Charles, of Wiston; MP New Shoreham; *b* 14 July 1817; *m* 17 Sept 1849 Juliana Mary Caroline (*m* 2nd 1856 Henry Townsend Boultbee; *d* 1885), dau of Sir Willoughby Wolstan Dixie, 8th Bt (*see* 1970 edn), and *dsp* 19 Nov 1849

2b John (Rev), of Wiston, Sussex, JP; *b* 3 March 1824; *educ* Ch Ch Oxford (BA); *m* 24 Sept 1861 Isabella Mary (*d* 24 Aug 1885), dau of Freeman Thomas, of Ratton, Sussex (*see* 1970 edn WILLINGDON, M), and *d* 15 Jan 1905, having had, with other issue:

1c Charles, of Wiston, JP, DL; *b* 12 Sept 1862; *m* 26 July 1906 Gabrielle Beatrice Mary (*d* 20 Oct 1970), yst dau and coheir of Rev Arthur Osborne Alleyne, Rector St Edmund's, Exeter, and *d* 10 April 1924, leaving issue:

1d John, CBE (1964), TD, of Wiston and Findon, Sussex, DL (1948); Coldstream Gds and 98th Surrey and Sussex Yeo Field Bde RA, TA; *b* 27 June 1907; *educ* Eton; *m* 24 July 1947 Lady Hersey Margaret (*d* 1993), widow of Cdr Hon John Montague Granville Waldegrave, DSC, RN (*see* WALDEGRAVE, E), and 2nd dau of 8th Earl of Glasgow (*qv*), and *d* 1990, leaving issue:

1e +(RICHARD) HARRY, DL W Sussex 1994 [Harry Goring Esq DL, Findon Park House, Findon, W Sussex BN14 0RW]; *b* 10 Sept 1949; heir presumptive; *educ* Eton; High Sheriff W Sussex 1993; *m* 15 July 1972 *Penelope Ann, dau of John K Broadbent, of S Africa, and has issue:

1f +Richard John; *b* 25 May 1978

2f +Charles; *b* 18 March 1980

3f +Dominic James David; *b* 18 Nov 1989

1f *Eloise Isabella; *b* 11 March 1974

2f *Catherine Clare; *b* 3 Sept 1975

3f *Gabrielle Mary; *b* 7 Sept 1991

2e +John James [John Goring Esq, Upper Buncton, Wiston, Steyning, W Sussex]; *b* 25 Oct 1953; *educ* Eton; *m* 4 Dec 1982 *Maxine Jane, yr dau of ACM Sir David Evans, GCB, CBE, of Milton Ho, Little Milton, Oxon, and has:

1f +Jasper David George; *b* 1986

1f *India Catherine; *b* 1984

2f *Elizabeth Iona; *b* 1989

3f *Francesca Mary Hyacinth; *b* 1992

1e *Corinna Jane [Mrs Corinna Nicoll, 1st Floor, 2 Barclay Rd, London SW6 1EH]; *b* 8 June 1948; *m* 11 April 1969 (*divorce* March 1990) Nigel Edward Vere Nicoll, 2nd s of Raymond Guy Vere Nicoll, MC, and has issue (*see* MADDEN, Bt)

2e *Anne Elizabeth [Ms Anne Goring, 3 Linkylea Cottages, Gifford, E Lothian EH41 4PE]; *b* 15 April 1951

2d Christopher; Flight Cadet RAF; *b* 31 Dec 1911; *d* 5 Sept 1930 following an accident

1d Isabel; *b* 12 Nov 1909; *m* 7 June 1933 Maj Sir Thomas Calderwood Dundas, 7th Bt (*see* 1970 edn DUNDAS, Bt, of Arniston), MBE, Scots Gds (*d* 2 Dec 1970), and *d* 5 July 1997, leaving issue

2c Walter; Lt-Col and Brevet Col 3rd KOH Boer War 1899–1902 (Queen's medal with three clasps), WW I (despatches); *b* 21 Dec 1863; *m* 23 Aug 1905 Jane Margaret (*d* 1 May 1956), dau of John Frederick Starkey, JP, DL, and *d* 10 Dec 1951

3c Alan; Maj 20th Hus, Dep Assist Dir Remounts 1911, Dist Remount Offr Sussex 1919, Boer War 1901–02 (Queen's medal, four clasps); *b* 26 March 1873; *m* 21 Nov 1901 Violet Isobel (*d* 25 Dec 1945), dau of Col Gerald Charles Penrice Onslow, RE (*see* ONSLOW, Bt), and *d* 19 Dec 1945, leaving issue:

1d Harold; Lt-Col Baluch Regt, Lt Roy Sussex Regt; *b* 8 June 1903; *educ* Cheltenham; *m* 1st 29 June 1929 Mary Frances Eleanor (*d* 1 Feb 1975) (Kaisir-i-Hind medal), only dau of Capt Hamilton Augustus Woodruffe; *m* 2nd 1975 *(Joan) Henrietta Radcliffe, dau of Spencer Domett Secretan, and *d* 1990, leaving by his 1st w:

1e Brian Hamilton, MBE; Capt Roy Sussex Regt; *b* 24 Jan 1935; *educ* Cheltenham, Millfield and RMA Sandhurst; *m* 28 May 1958 *Prudence Mary [Mrs Brian Goring, Lowerwood House, New Lane, Billingshurst, W Sussex RH14 9DS], dau of George Baker, and *d* 1989, leaving:

1f *Alice Lucinda; *b* 30 Oct 1959; *m* 1984 *Dominique Bouilliez, of Lille, France, and has issue:

1g *Georges Brian Ferdinand Goring; *b* 1985

2g *William Philippe Xavier Goring; *b* 1987

1g *Esme Eleanor Joan Goring; *b* 1983

2f *Sya Charlotte [Mrs Marcus Elwes, Elder Farm, Grimston, Norfolk]; *b* 8 Jan 1964; *m* 1993 *Marcus Henry Robert Elwes, est s of Henry Arthur Elwes, of Congham, Norfolk, and has:

1g *Millicent Lettice Susan Mary Primrose; *b* 1994

3f *Lydia Mary; *b* 20 Sept 1965

2e +George [Maj George Goring, Holland House, Warnham, Horsham, W Sussex RH12 3RH]; Capt Middx Regt, Maj Queen's Regt (ret); *b* 2 Aug 1937; *educ* Cheltenham, Millfield and RMA Sandhurst; *m* 1969 (*divorce* 1987) Nicola Jean, dau of William Ian Gordon, of Rye, and has issue:

1f +Michael; *b* 1974

1f *Fiona Mary; *b* 1972

2d Arthur; Lt-Col Probyn's Horse, Indian Cav, Lt Roy Fus, NW Frontier 1936–39, WW II (despatches), Assist Commr-in-Chief St John Ambulance 1957, Order Cloud and Banner China, KStJ; *b* 25 Jan 1907; *educ* Cheltenham and RMC Sandhurst

4c Herbert; Capt 3rd Hus WW I (despatches); *b* 20 Aug 1880; *educ* Ch Ch Oxford (BA); *m* 27 July 1905 Marjorie Beatrice (*d* 22 Aug 1959), dau of Sir Archibald Smith, PC, Master Rolls, and *d* 14 May 1952

5c Francis; Capt Roy Sussex Regt TA WW I Egypt, Gallipoli, Flanders (star, two medals); *b* 2 April 1884; *d* unm 28 Oct 1953

1c Elisabeth; *b* 21 Dec 1863; *m* 13 Aug 1921 Capt George Frederick Glennie, RN, and *dsp* 4 July 1954. He *d* 25 April 1939

GORMANSTON

Arms: Or on a chief sa. three crescents or. **Crest:** On a chapeau gu., doubled erm., a fox passant ppr. **Supporters:** Dexter, a fox ppr.; sinister, a lion rampant or. **Motto:** *Sans tache* ('Without stain').
Creations: B. (I) *c* 1370, V. (I) 7 Aug 1478, B. (UK) (Gormanston of Whitewood) 8 Dec 1868.

THE 17TH VISCOUNT GORMANSTON, Lord (Preston of) Gormanston and **Baron Gormanston of Whitewood**, Co Meath ((Jenico) Nicholas Dudley Preston) [The Rt Hon The Viscount Gormanston, 8 Dalmeny House, 9 Thurloe Place, London SW7 2RY]; *b* 19 Nov 1939; *s* f 1940, premier viscount of Ireland; *educ* Downside; *m* 1st 1974 Eva Antonie (*d* 1984), dau of Felix Landzianowski, of Poland, and has:

1 +JENICO FRANCIS TARA; *b* 30 April 1974

2 +William Luke; *b* 3 May 1976

The 17th VISCOUNT *m* 2nd Nov 1997 *Lucy Arabella, dau of the actor Edward Fox and formerly w of David Grenfell

Lineage: PHILIP de PRESTON, of a merchant family from the Lancashire town of that name, some of whom had migrated to Ireland and built up property portfolios (mostly urban and comercial) there; gf of:

ROGER PRESTON; Judge Court King's Bench 1326 and Common Pleas (both Ireland) 1331–37 and 1342–46; *m* Maud, dau of Robert, s of Adam, of Preston, Lancs, and had:

Sir ROBERT PRESTON, **1st Lord (Preston of) Gormanston** (I), so *cr c* 1370 by being called to the I Parl, of Gormanston, Co Meath (a feudal ldship he bought from Amaury St Amand 1363, an ancestor of whose (another Amaury St Amand) had been granted it by HENRY III 1230, the original owner being Magorman or O'Gorman, a native Irishman), and through his w of Carbery, Co Kildare; ktd 1361, King's Serjeant, 2nd Justice Common Pleas 1342, Ch Justice 1358–78, Keeper Gt Seal 1388–89, Viceregent 1389–91, Ld Chllr 1391–92 (all Ireland); *m* 1st 1353 Margaret, dau and heir of Walter de Bermingham, of Kells, in Ossory, and Carbery; *m* 2nd Joan Hugeley and *d* 1396, leaving an only s:

CHRISTOPHER PRESTON, **2nd Lord (Preston of) Gormanston**; ktd 1397; *m* Elizabeth, dau and coheir of William Loundres, feudal Ld of the Barony of Naas, Co Kildare, and had an only s:

CHRISTOPHER PRESTON, **3rd Lord (Preston of) Gormanston**; *m* Jane, dau of Sir Jenico d'Artois, of Gascony, by Jane, dau of John Serjeant, of Castleknock, Co Dublin, and had an est s:

ROBERT PRESTON, **1st Viscount Gormanston** (I), so *cr* by patent 7 Aug 1478; Dep Chllr Ireland 1461, Kt St George (Ireland) 1472, Dep Ch Govr Ireland 1478 and 1493; *m* Janet, dau of Sir Richard Molyneux, of Sefton, Lancs (*see* 1970 edn SEFTON, E), and *d* 9 April 1503, leaving (with a dau Anne/Elizabeth, *m*(?) Christopher Nugent, *see* WESTMEATH, E) an est s:

WILLIAM PRESTON, **2nd Viscount Gormanston**; Dep Ch Govr Ireland 1493, Ch Govr 1515; *m* 1st Anne, dau of John Burnell, of Ballgriffin, Co Dublin; *m* 2nd Eleanor, widow of John Nangle, of Navan, and dau of Sir Henry/Thomas Dowdall, and *d* 21 Sept 1532, leaving by his 1st w an est s:

JENICO PRESTON, **3rd Viscount Gormanston**; *b c* 1502; *m* 1st Lady Catherine FitzGerald, dau of 9th Earl of Kildare (*see* LEINSTER, D); *m* 2nd Anne Luttrell (*d* his widow *sp* by him) and *d* 1560, leaving, with other issue:

1 CHRISTOPHER, **4th Viscount**

2 Nicholas

1 Elizabeth; *m* 1st Thomas Nangle, styled Baron of Navan; *m* 2nd 2nd Baron Delvin (*see* WESTMEATH, E)

1 Genet; *m* Henry Travers, of Monkstown Cooke, Co Dublin, and had issue

The er s,

CHRISTOPHER PRESTON, **4th Viscount Gormanston**; *b c* 1537; *m* 1st Catherine, dau of Sir William FitzWilliam, of Windsor Gt Park, Clerk Hanaper, but had no issue by her; *m* 2nd Catherine, dau of Sir Thomas FitzWilliam, of Meryon, Co Dublin, and *d* 24 Jan 1599/1600, leaving, with two intermediate sons and several daus:

1 JENICO, **5th Viscount**

4 THOMAS PRESTON, 1st VISCOUNT TARAGH, Co Meath (I), so *cr* 2 July 1650; *b c* 1585; *educ* Irish Coll Douai; served Spanish forces in Low Countries, Capt of an Irish Regt 1606 and Col of another 1635, Govr Genappe 1641, C-in-C Confedn Kilkenny forces Leinster 1642, Govr Galway 1651, served French forces 1653 on; *m* 1st by 1618 —, dau of Charles van der Eycken, of Brabant, Seigneur de St George; *m* 2nd by 1624 Marguerite de Namur and *d* by 21 Oct 1655, leaving by his 1st w:

(1) ANTHONY PRESTON, 2nd VISCOUNT TARAGH; *b* 20 June 1618; Col under his f Confedn of Kilkenny forces Co Kildare and Queen's and King's Cos 1641–42; *m* by 14 Feb 1642/3 his cousin Margaret, dau of Anthony Warren by Mary, dau of **4th Viscount Gormanston**, and *d* 24 April 1659, leaving, with two other daus, an only s:

1a THOMAS PRESTON, 3rd and last VISCOUNT TARAGH; *b c* 1653; *educ* Scots Coll Douai; *d* unm 6 July 1674 (when the viscountcy expired), almost certainly murdered by Sir Francis Blundel, Bt, of King's Co, and his bros William and Winwood, none of whom, however, was found guilty at their subsequent trial

1a Elizabeth; *m* her cousin Nicholas Preston and had issue (*see* below)

2a Thomasine; *m* Sir John Barnewall, Baron Exchequer (I), and had:

1b Mary; *m c* 28 April 1703 *soi-disant* 11th Baron Trimlestown (*qv*)

(2) Sir James/Don Diego; mil cdr with his f of Confedn of Kilkenny forces Ireland 1642; *d* unm(?) in or after 1656

(3) Thomas; *d* an infant(?)

(4) John George; *m* by 2 March 1646/7 and *d* in or after Sept 1663

5 William

The 4th VISCOUNT's est son,

JENICO PRESTON, **5th Viscount Gormanston**; *b c* 1585; *m* Margaret St Lawrence (*m* 2nd 1st Earl of Fingall (*see* 1970 edn; he *d* 16 Nov 1637), dau of 8th Lord (Baron) Howth, and *d* 14 March 1629/30, leaving (with a dau Mary; *m* 1st Sir Thomas Alen, Bt, of St Wolstan's; *m* 2nd Simon Luttrell, of Luttrelstown):

NICHOLAS PRESTON, **6th Viscount Gormanston**; *b c* 1608; Gen-in-Ch Confedn of Kilkenny forces 1641–42; *m* Mary Barnewall (*d* May 1642), dau of 1st Viscount Barnewall of Kingsland, and *d* 28 July 1643 (posthumously outlawed), leaving:

1 JENICO PRESTON, **7th Viscount Gormanston**, PC (1686 I), apptd Ld Lt Co Meath by JAMES II 1689 (still *de facto* King of Ireland even though he had abandoned the English throne in late 1688), subsequently indicted for high treason and posthumously outlawed (whereby his titles were deemed till 1800 to be under attainder) following Williamites' ascendancy over Jacobites 1691; *m* 1st Lady Frances Le(a)ke (*dsp* 29 July 1682), 5th dau of 1st Earl of Scarsdale (*see* SCARSDALE, V, preliminary remarks); *m* 2nd Nov 1683 Margaret (*m* 2nd 10 March 1692 James Butler, of Kilveagher, Co Tipperary), dau of 3rd Viscount Molyneux (*see* 1970 edn SEFTON, E), but *dspm* 17 March 1690/1 while defending Limerick on behalf of JAMES II, leaving an only dau:

(1) Mary; *m* 1700 her 1st cousin *de jure* 9th VISCOUNT GORMANSTON (*see* below)

2 Nicholas; *m* Elizabeth, dau of 2nd VISCOUNT TARAGH (*see* above), and had:

(1) JENICO PRESTON, *de jure* 8th VISCOUNT GORMANSTON; *m* Margaret — and *dsp* 1679

(2) ANTHONY PRESTON, *de jure* 9th VISCOUNT GORMANSTON; *m* 1700 his cousin Mary, only child of **7th Viscount**, and *d* 25 Sept 1716, leaving an only s:

1a JENICO PRESTON, *de jure* 10th VISCOUNT GORMANSTON; *b* 1707; *m* 9 Feb 1729/30 his cousin Thomasine Barnewall (*d* 10 Jan 1788), est dau of *soi-disant* 11th Baron Trimlestown (*qv*), and *d* 31 Oct 1757, having had, with other issue:

1b ANTHONY PRESTON, *de jure* 11th VISCOUNT GORMANSTON; *b* 1736; *m* 25Oct 1774 Henrietta (*m* 2nd 1794 Lt-Gen Christopher Jeaffreson, of Dullingham House, Cambs; *d* 6 Feb 1826), dau of Lt-Gen John Robinson, of Denston Hall, Suffolk, and *d* 8 Dec 1786, leaving an only s:

1c JENICO PRESTON, **12th Viscount Gormanston**, recognised as such Easter 1800 when the outlawing of the 6th and 7th Viscounts was pronounced void; *b* 3 Dec 1775; *m* 27 Dec 1794 Margaret (*d* 26 Jan 1820), est dau of 2nd Viscount Southwell (*qv*), and d 10 Feb 1860, having had, with other issue:

1d EDWARD ANTHONY JOHN, **13th Viscount**

2d Robert; Army Offr; *b* 23 Jan 1802; *d* 3 March 1869

3d Charles; Capt 24th Foot; *b* 28 April 1803; *m* 1853 Alicia Margaretta (*d* 11 Nov 1903), dau of William North, of Northbrook, Co Galway, and *d* 2 Feb 1888, leaving issue:

1e Jenico Edward, CB (1909), DSO (1887); Lt-Col IA Jowaki Expdn, Afghanistan and Burma; *b* 30 Nov 1855; *d* unm 27 Jan 1940

2e Charles Arthur; *b* 19 June 1857; *m* 3 Nov 1889 Miriam (*d* 1936), dau of Hon Charles Alleyne, and *d* 7 June 1924, leaving:

1f +Arthur; *b* 14 Oct 1902; *m* 14 April 1928 *Marion Blair, dau of John Dean, and has:

1g +Richard Dean; *b* 3 April 1929

2f +Hubert Philip; *b* 3 June 1905; *m* 26 Feb 1938 *Marie Hester, dau of Michael Joseph Aherne, QC, and has:

1g +Anthony Ernest Michael; *b* 17 Feb 1938

2g +Ronald Thomas Edward; *b* 20 Feb 1940

1g *Andrea Margaret; *b* 14 Aug 1941

2g *Michelle Joan Adrienne; *b* 21 Jan 1944

3g *Ruth Jocelyn Vickie; *b* 25 Feb 1945

4g *Louise Marie Isabel; *b* 27 May 1946

3f +Oswald; *b* 6 May 1907

1f Yvonne

2f Blanche; CStJ; *m* 1st 6 Sept 1916 Arthur Fitzpatrick (*d* 1938), only s of Sir Charles Fitzpatrick, GCMG, PC, and had issue; *m* 2nd 1941 George Blaikie (*d* 1948)

3f Mary; *m* 1922 Lt-Col Francis M Stanton, VD, RCA, and had:

1g John Preston; RCA WWII; *b* 19 Sept 1923; *ka* 26 Jan 1945

1g *Mary Frances [Mrs P Johnson, 22 Randolph Road, Toronto, Ont, Canada]; *b* 29 Dec 1937; *m* *P J Johnson and has:

1h *John Francis

2h *Paul Anthony

1h *Francesca Anne Margaret

2g *Elizabeth Anne; *b* 26 Oct 1937

4f Frances; *d* unm March 1937

4d Thomas, of Silverstream, Co Dublin, DL; Commr Nat Educn Ireland; *b* 3 May 1817; *m* 9 Aug 1843 Margaret (*d* 28 Dec 1891), 4th dau of John Hamilton, of Dundrum, Ayrshire, and *d* 29 Aug 1903, leaving, with four other daus:

1e Jenico John; Capt Rifle Bde; *b* 11 Feb 1846; *d* 30 April 1879

2e Thomas Edward, of Silverstream; *b* 16 May 1851; *d* unm 4 Feb 1919

3e Arthur James; *b* 19 June 1852; *m* 22 March 1887 Christina Maria Dundas (*d* 2 April 1914), only dau of Henry Spencer, and *d* 14 April 1896, having had:

1f Jenico Thomas; served WWs I and II; *b* 17 Feb 1891; *m* 1919 Violet Saunt and *dsp* 28 April 1962

2f Rudolph Arthur MC; RFC WW I; *b* 30 Aug 1893; *ka* 1916

1f Antoinette Eileen Maude; *b* 13 June 1888; *d* unm 18 June 1967

2f Ina Esme Hilda; *m* 7 June 1933 George Herbert Cuming Butler (*d* 1959)

3f Marguerite Irene; *b* 29 April 1892

4f Hermione Kathleen Mary; *d* unm 18 April 1960

4e Francis Edmund Alexander; *b* 28 March 1861; *d* unm 26 Sept 1942

1e Laura Mary; *d* unm 27 July 1941

2e Frances Harriette; *d* unm 13 Sept 1942

3e Mary Christina; *d* unm 11 Nov 1953

1d Matilda Margaret; *b* 1 Jan 1810; *m* 16 June 1842 Matthew Elias Corbally, MP, of Corbalton Hall, and *d* 22 Dec 1888 aged 78, having had issue. He *d* 1870

The 12th VISCOUNT's est son,

EDWARD ANTHONY JOHN PRESTON, **13th Viscount Gormanston**, also *cr* 8 Dec 1868 BARON GORMANSTON OF WHITEWOOD, Co Meath (UK); *b* 3 June 1796; Sheriff Co Meath 1831 and Co Dublin 1845; *m* 19 July 1836 Lucretia (*d* 5 Feb 1891), est dau of William Charles Jerningham (*see* STAFFORD, B), and had:

1 JENICO WILLIAM JOSEPH, **14th Viscount**

2 Edward Francis John, JP, DL; Co Meath, JP Dublin; Capt 9th Lancers, Lt Lancs Hus (Yeo), ADC to Ld Lt Ireland; *b* 3 March 1845; *m* 21 Jan 1891 Anne Genevieve (*d* 28 Jan 1929), dau of Samuel Grimshawe, of Errwood, Cheshire, and *dsp* 1 March 1901

1 Margaret Frances Agnes; *m* 27 April 1882 Vincent Anthony Eyre, of Lindley Hall, Leics, and *d* 14 June 1884. He *d* 22 March 1887

2 Lucretia Pauline Mary; *m* 19 July 1860 John Arthur Farrell, DL, of Moynalty, Co Meath, had issue and *d* 16 Feb 1916. He *d* 27 Nov 1904

3 Charlotte Agnes Mary; *m* 21 June 1870 Col Richard Donaldson, DL, of Hartlands, Co Meath, and *d* 18 April 1924. He *dsp* 27 May 1898

The 13th VISCOUNT *d* 28 Sept 1876; his er son,

JENICO WILLIAM JOSEPH PRESTON, **14th Viscount Gormanston**, GCMG (1897, KCMG 1887), JP, DL Cos Dublin, Cavan and Meath; High Sheriff Cos Dublin 1865 and Meath 1871, Lt 60th Rifles Indian Mutiny, Govr Leeward Islands 1885–87, Br Guiana 1887093 and Tasmania 1893–1900, Chamberlain to Ld Lt Ireland 1866–68, Commr Nat Educn Ireland 1875–85; *b* 1 June 1837; *m* 1st 8 Jan 1861 Hon Ismay Louisa Bellew (*dsp* 19 Aug 1875), 3rd dau of 1st Baron Bellew of Barmeath (*qv*); *m* 2nd 29 Oct 1878 Georgina Jane (*d* 9 April 1932), dau of Peter Connellan, of Coolmore, Co Kilkenny, and by her had issue:

1 JENICO EDWARD JOSEPH, **15th Viscount**

2 Richard Martin Peter, DSO (1917) and bar; Lt-Col TAR RA WW I (despatches), Pres Inst Metals 1940–42 (Platinum Medallist 1945); *b* 12 Aug 1884; *educ* Oratory Sch; *m* 1st 23 July 1908 Belle (*d* 29 Nov 1936), only dau of Frederick Harcourt Hamblin, and had issue:

(1) Jenico Richard Anthony; *b* 27 Jan 1910; *m* 21 Sept 1946 *Hannah Maria, widow of Col V Milkowski, Polish Army, and dau of Josef Krassowski by Jadwiga Baroness Golcz, and *dsp* 18 March 1973

(2) Christopher Edward Martin, OBE, DSC; Lt-Cdr RN WW II; *b* 13 Nov 1918; *m* 23 April 1949 Joy Celeste Agatha (*d* 1989), dau of Maj Hugh Davidson, IA, and *d* 1992, leaving issue:

1a +Philip Martin Jenico [Philip Preston Esq, Washbrook House, Aston-le-Walls, Daventry, Northants]; *b* 12 April 1950; *educ* Downside; *m* 1983 *Anita Caya-Speña and has issue:

1b +Edmund Philip Jenico; *b* 1984

2a +Stephen Richard Hugh; *b* 15 May 1952; *educ* Downside

3a Matthew Christopher Edward; *b* 30 Nov 1955; *d* 1993

4a +Anthony Thomas Patrick; *b* 2 March 1964

1a *Camilla Mary Lucy; *b* 18 Oct 1959

(1) *Ismay Elizabeth [Mrs Denzil Clarke, Puffins, 8 South Drive, Wokingham, Berks]; *b* 14 June 1912; *m* 24 Jan 1942 Lt-Col Denzil Robert Noble Clarke (*d* 1986), er s of Robert Thomas Clarke, and has issue:

1a *Michael Richard Neil; *b* 21 Aug 1946; *educ* Stonyhurst; *m* 1973 *Francine van Schepdael and has issue:

1b *Geraldine Anne Danielle; *b* 1973

2b *Muriel Louise Elizabeth; *b* 1978

1a *Jennifer Roberta Anne [Mrs Simon Aldridge, Great Bowsers, Little Walden, Saffron Walden, Essex]; *b* 30 Dec 1944; *m* 1968 *Simon Anthony Aldridge and has issue:

1b *Victoria Helmore Elizabeth; *b* 1 May 1969

2a *Francesca Elizabeth Anne [Mrs David Bull, 33 Alwyne Rd, London SW19 7AB]; *b* 12 Dec 1951; *m* 1976 *David Anselm Bull and has issue:

1b *Edward Anselm Anthony; *b* 1981

2b *James Frederick Simon; *b* 1983

1b *Alice Elizabeth; *b* 1978

2b *Georgina Victoria; *b* 1988

3b *Elizabeth Mary; *b* 1990

(2) *Diana Mary Bruce [Mrs John Golledge, Old Sun House, Riseley, Berks]; *b* 14 Aug 1914; *m* 28 Oct 1939, Lt-Col John Francis Colledge, RASC (*d* 27 Jan 1954), only s of Capt John Theodore Colledge, and has issue:

1a *Simon John [Simon Colledge Esq, The Well Cottage, Mattingley, Hants]; *b* 29 July 1940; *educ* Downside; *m* 2 Jan 1966 *Robina Elizabeth Anne, er dau of Harold L Light, and has:

1b *Thomas Andrew John; *b* 14 Feb 1967

2b *Patrick Richard; *b* 15 March 1968

3b *Henry Charles Valentine; *b* 1972

1b *Anna Elizabeth; *b* 1980

2a *Robert Patrick Francis; *b* 3 Jan 1950; *m* 1974 *Dena, dau of D Jones, of Southport, Lancs, and has issue:

1b *James Edward Daniel; *b* 1978

2b *Matthew William John; *b* 1981

1b *Kate Elizabeth Jane; *b* 1976

1a *Sarah Virginia Mary; *b* 7 April 1942

2a *Judith Cecilia Anne; *b* 28 Aug 1953; *m* 1974 *James Calderbank and has issue:

1b *William Michael; *b* 1975

1b *Rachel Claire Joanna; *b* 1978

(3) *Ursula Anne Marie [Mrs Charles Moseley, Kilmaloda House, Timoleague, Co Cork, Ireland]; *b* 12 May 1923; *m* 25 Aug 1952 Cdr Charles Sheridan Moseley, RN (*d* 1993), s of Dr John Grimson-Moseley, and has:

1a *Dominic Richard Sheridan; *b* 17 July 1955; *educ* Downside; *m* 1987 *Kathryn Fiona, dau of John McLean, and has:

1b *James William Sheridan; *b* 1988

2b *Edward John Wallace; *b* 1990

1b *Charlotte Elizabeth Anne; *b* 1992

2b *Emily Kathryn Louise; *b* 1994

2a *Christopher John Wallace; *b* 26 Feb 1957; *educ* Downside; *m* 1989 *Loretta Anna, dau of Alexander Millar-Brown, of Norwich and has:

1b *Isobel Mary Anne; *b* 1995

3a *Justin Robert Patrick; *b* 2 Feb 1962; *educ* Downside; *m* 1994 *Mary Teresa, dau of James Kavanagh, of Dublin, and has:

1b *Laura Anne; *b* 1996

1a *Virginia Clare Diana; *b* 22 July 1954; *m* 1987 *Anthony Cyril McGough, s of John McGough, of Manchester, and has:

1b *John Sheridan; *b* 1991

2b *Edmund Joseph; *b* 1994

3b *Dominic Peter; *b* 1996

1b *Lucy Margaret Anne; *b* 1988

2b *Francesca Mary; *b* 1989

2a *Lucy Elizabeth Anne [Sister Teresa of the Holy Child, Carmelite Convent, Notting Hill, London W10]; *b* 10 April 1960

2 (cont.) Lt-Col Richard Preston *m* 2nd 4 Sept 1943 Edith Sheilah (*d* 7 Jan 1951), widow of Lt-Cdr John Hay Forbes, DSO, RN (*see* STUART-FORBES, Bt), and er dau of Reginald de Crecy Steel, and *d* 20 May 1965, having by her had:

(3) Hubert Richard; *b* 13 Oct 1945; *d* 18 Nov 1964

3 Hubert Anthony John, MC; Capt 3rd Bn Roy Irish Regt (SR), Staff Capt 1918 WW I (wounded twice); *b* 20 Dec 1885; *m* 8 Jan 1917 Mary (*d* 1971), widow of Robert S Pringle, of Queen's Regt, and dau of William Kenny, Judge High Court Ireland, and *d* 12 July 1940, leaving issue:

(1) Penelope Sybil Mary; *b* 26 Oct 1917; *d* 5 May 1989

(2) *Georgina Ismay Mary [Mrs Alfred Head, Hardimans Cottage, High St, Queen Camel, Somerset BA22 7NE]; *b* 6 Dec 1919; *m* 16 July 1948 *Alfred Stanley Head, s of A J Head

1 Ismay Lucretia Mary; *b* 29 Oct 1882; *m* 1st 16 June 1906 Lord Ninian Edward Crichton-Stuart, MP (*ka* 2 Oct 1915), 2nd s of 3rd Marquess of Bute (*qv*), and had issue; *m* 2nd 30 April 1917 Capt Archibald Henry Maule Ramsay and *d* 16 Feb 1975, leaving further issue (*see* DALHOUSIE, E)

The 14th VISCOUNT *d* 29 Oct 1907; his est son,

JENICO EDWARD JOSEPH PRESTON, **15th Viscount Gormanston**, JP, DL Co Meath; T/Capt Roy Irish Fus, Lt 3rd Bn Manchester Regt, RTO 1916; *b* 16 July 1879; *m* 26 Oct 1911 Eileen (*m* 2nd 11 Aug 1934 John Black Atkins; *d* 28 March 1964), yr dau of Lt-Gen Sir William Butler, GCB, PC, by Elizabeth, *née* Thompson, the celebrated painter of military subjects known as Lady Butler, and *d* 7 Nov 1925, leaving:

1 JENICO WILLIAM RICHARD PRESTON, **16th Viscount Gormanston**; 2nd Lt (A/Capt) KOYLI WW II; *b* 7 Oct 1914; *m* 18 Feb 1939 Pamela (*m* 2nd 23 Dec 1943 Lt Maurice Bernard O'Connor, Irish Gds (*d* 9 Feb 1961); *d* 26 March 1975), dau of Capt Edward Dudley Hanly and Lady Marjorie Heath (*see* DENBIGH and DESMOND, E), and was *ka* France 9 June 1940, leaving issue:

(1) (JENICO) NICHOLAS DUDLEY PRESTON, **17th and present Viscount Gormanston**

2 Robert Francis Hubert PRESTON later SHAW-PRESTON (deed poll July 1947) later still PRESTON again; Capt 11th Hus WW II; *b* 7 Dec 1915; *educ* Downside; *m* 1st 8 Sept 1941 (*divorce* 1955) Jean, only child of Capt Charles Henry Shaw, 15th Hus, of Bourton Hall, Rugby; *m* 2nd 1970 Daphne Helen Anne (*d* 9 December 1992), formerly w of (a) Cdr Reginald Hughes-Onslow, RN (*see* ONSLOW, E), and (b) John Edward Mountague Bradish-Ellames and only child of Col Robert Hanbury Brudenell-Bruce, DSO (*see* AILESBURY, M), and *d* 7 Jan 1992, leaving by his 1st w:

(1) Josephine Ann; *b* 1 Feb; *d* 13 Feb 1944

(2) *Jennifer Anne [Mrs Istvan Siklóssy von Pernesz, 390 Ave de Tervuren, B-1150, Brussels, Belgium]; *b* 4 Jan 1946; *m* 5 March 1977 *Istvan Siklóssy von Pernesz, s of Joseph Siklóssy von Pernesz, of Vienna, and has issue:

1a *Georgina Isabella Maria; *b* 1977

2a *Stephanie Victoria Maria; *b* 1980

3 Stephen Edward Thomas; Lt Irish Gds WW II; *b* 10 July 1920; *ka* Anzio 29 Jan 1944

1 (Eileen) Antoinette Mary; *b* 16 Oct 1912; *m* 29 April 1939 *Peter Northcote Lunn, CMG, OBE, SIS to 1986, er s of Sir Arnold Lunn, the authority on skiing, by his 1st w Lady Mabel, sis of 3rd Earl of Iddesleigh (*qv*), and *d* 1976, leaving issue

GORT

Arms: Quarterly, 1st and 4th, az. on a chevron or a chaplet vert (for VEREKER); 2nd and 3rd, gu. a saltire vaire or and az. (for PRENDERGAST). **Crest:** Out of a mural crown gu. a stag's head ppr. **Supporters:** Dexter, a lion rampant ppr. gorged with a collar gu., fimbriated or, therefrom a chain passing through the forelegs and reflexed over the back of the last; sinister, a heraldic antelope erect ppr., tufted, attired and unguled or and gorged and chained as the dexter. **Motto:** *Vincit veritas* ('Truth triumphs').
Creations: B. (UK) 15 May 1810, V. (I) 16 Jan 1816.

THE 9TH VISCOUNT GORT, Co Galway, and **Baron Kiltarton of Gort**, Co Galway (Foley Robert Standish Prendergast) [The Rt Hon The Viscount Gort, The Coach House, Arbory St, Castletown, IoM IM9 1LJ]; *b* 24 Oct 1951; *s f* 1995; *educ* Harrow; *m* 15 Sept 1979 (*divorce*) 1987 Julie Denise, only dau of D W Jones, of Ballasalla, IoM; *m* 2nd 1991 *Sharon Lyn, dau of Arnold Quayle, and has issue:

1 +ROBERT FOLEY PRENDERGAST; *b* 5 April 1993

Lineage (of Prendergast): MAURICE, feudal Ld of Prendergast, Pembs, one of the Cambro-Norman kts who went with Strongbow, Earl of Pembroke (*see* PEMBROKE and MONTGOMERY, E, preliminary remarks), to Ireland 1169, acquiring much land there; gave Prendergast Castle in Wales to the Kts of St John of Jerusalem 1177 and eventually joined that order; Prior Kilmainham; *d* 1205, leaving (with a yst s Gerald, ancestor of the the PRENDERGASTs of Co Mayo) an est s:

PHILIP de PRENDERGAST; of age by 1206; *m* Maude, dau and heir of Robert de Quincy, through whom he acquired the town of Enniscorthy, Co Wexford, and the Constableship of Leinster, and *d* 1226, leaving, with an est s (Gerald, fndr Enniscorthy Abbey, *m* 1st Matilda, dau of Theobald le Botiller/Butler (*see* MOUNTGARRET, V), and had a dau Maria (*m* John de Cogan (*d* 1278), of Bampton, Devon), *m* 2nd Matilda, dau of Richard de Burgo/Burgh and sis of the Earl of Ulster, and *d* 1251, having by her had a dau Matilda (*m* Maurice de Rochfort)) and a yst s (David):

WILLIAM de PRENDERGAST; obtained feudal Barony/Ldship of Newcastle, Co Tipperary, from Geoffrey de Marisco (*alias* Marsh) *c* 1230 in exchange for other lands; *m* Alianore (coheir(?) of William de Bermingham) and had (with an er s (John, *dsp* 1275):

JEFFREY de PRENDERGAST; had an est s:

Sir PHILIP de PRENDERGAST; *d* 1303, leaving, with a yst s (Sir Philip, of Drangan, Co Tipperary):

1 Jeffrey; Sheriff Co Tipperary 1327; *m* Isolda Bermingham or Mac Phioris, dau of 3rd Lord Athenry

2 Maurice: had:

(1) John; blind; inherited feudal Barony of Newcastle; ancestor of:

1a James FitzThomas, of Newcastle; *m* Eleanor, dau of Sir John Grace, of Courtstown, and *d* 3 Feb 1575, leaving, with several yr sons:

1b Jeffrey, of Newcastle; *m* Joane, dau of 1st Baron Caher of the 1543 *cr* (and coheir to that Barony, assuming it became abeyant rather than expired when her half-bro the 2nd Baron *dsp* 1559) by his 2nd w Ellen, sis and heir of 12th Earl of Desmond (*see* DENBIGH and DESMOND, E, preliminary remarks), and *d* 12 March 1615, leaving, with three yr sons (James, *dsp*; Robert of Ballybeg; Richard):

1c Thomas; *m* 1st Eleanor, sis of 11th Earl of Ormonde (*see* MOUNTGARRET, V), and had issue; *m* 2nd Ellen, dau of Nicholas White, and *d* 1 March 1626, having by her had a dau Margaret; his sons by his 1st w:

1d James; *m* Catharine, dau of Sir John Fitzgerald, of the Decies, but *dsp*, *k* Cahir Castle, Co Tipperary, 12 Dec 1627 by his cousin 3rd/13th Baron (of) Dunboyne (*qv*) in a dispute over possession of the feudal Barony of Newcastle

2d Robert; *dsp*

3d Edmond; feudal Barony of Newcastle confirmed to him 1639 and 1641 but his estates later confiscated by OLIVER CROMWELL; *d c* 1658, leaving, with an er s (Jeffrey):

1e Thomas, of Croane, Co Limerick; *m* Eleanor, dau and coheir of David Condon, and *d* 1725, having had, with other issue (including Jeffrey, of Croane, *m* Margaret, dau of William Daniel, and *d* 1735, leaving issue):

1f Sir THOMAS PRENDERGAST, 1st Bt (I), so *cr* 15 July 1699(?), of Gort, Co Galway, an estate formerly belonging to but latterly forfeited by the O'Sha(u)ghnessys which he acquired by informing on fellow conspirators who had hatched a plot against WILLIAM III (in whose armies he served as a volunteer); MP (I Parl) Monaghan 1703–09, bought back the Mullough and Croane properties from the Commrs of forfeited estates; Brig-Gen War of Spanish Succession; *m c* 10 Aug 1697 Penelope (*d* 1746), sis of 1st Earl Cadogan (*qv*), and was *k* Battle of Malplaquet 11 Sept 1709, leaving:

1g Sir THOMAS PRENDERGAST, 2nd Bt, PC (I) 1733, of Gort; MP (I) Clonnel 1727–60 and (GB) Chichester 1733–39, PMG Ireland; *m* 1739 Anne, dau and heir of Sir Griffith Williams (*see* WILLIAMS-BULKELEY, Bt) and *dsp* 23 Sept 1760, when the Btcy expired

1g Juliana; *m* 13 Dec 1731 6th Earl of Meath (*qv*) and *d* 12 Dec 1758, leaving issue

2g Elizabeth; *m* 1st Sir John Dickson Hamon, 1st and last Bt (*dsp* 26 Jan 1727/8); *m* 2nd 21 Nov 1728 Charles Smyth, MP Limerick (*d* 18 Aug 1784), s of Thomas Smyth, Bp Limerick, and had, with two other sons and daus:

1h JOHN SMYTH later PRENDERGAST (changed name on the death 23 Sept 1760 of his unc the 2nd Bt, whose estates he inherited) later still PRENDERGAST-SMYTH (resumed SMYTH on *dsp* 14 Jan 1785 of his est bro Thomas Smyth), **1st Viscount Gort**, Co Galway, so *cr* 16 Jan 1816, as also previously 15 May 1810 BARON KILTARTON OF GORT, Co Galway (both I), both with remainder to his n Charles Vereker; *b* 1741, MP Carlow 1776–83 and Limerick 1785–97, Chamberlain Limerick, Govr Co Galway 1812–17; *d* unm 23 May 1817

1h Juliana; *m* 6 Aug 1759 Thomas Vereker, of Roxborough, Co Limerick (*see* below), and had:

1i CHARLES, **2nd Viscount**

2h Elizabeth; *m* 1757 Col William Newton, 86th Regt, Govr Senegal

3g Anne; *m* Samuel Hobson, of Muckridge

Lineage (of Vereker): JOHN VEREKER, of Brabant; soldier in CHARLES I's armies; was granted lands at Restoration in compensation for losses during Interregnum, settling at Grange, Co Cork; *m* Editha, sister of Henry Bennet, of Shandon, Co Cork, and *d* 1671, having had, with several daus (including Editha, *m* Martin Stokes) and a s John (*dsp*):

HENRY VEREKER, of Grange; *m* Mary (*m* 2nd 1692 William Chartres, Mayor Cork), dau and coheir of John Connell, of Barryscourt, Co Cork, and *d* 1691, having had (with a yr s Henry, of Ballyneet, and dau, Dorothy, *d* young):

CONNEL VEREKER, of Grange; settled at Roxborough; High Sheriff Co Limerick 1729; *m* Mary, dau of Amos Godsell, of Moorstown, and *d* 1733, leaving:

1 HENRY

2 Amos, of Leyden, MD; *m* 1743 Elizabeth, dau of James Langton, and *d* 1773, leaving:

(1) Elizabeth; *m* Moore Disney, of Churchtown, Co Waterford, and had:

1a Moore Disney (Sir), KCB; Gen

3 John; Mayor Limerick 1769; *d* 1783

The est son,

HENRY VEREKER, of Roxborough; *m* 15 Oct 1733 Anne, est dau, of Sir Nicholas Osborne, 6th Bt, of Newtown Anner, Co Tipperary (*qv*), and had:

THOMAS VEREKER, of Roxborough; *m* Juliana (*d* 13 July 1811), sis of **1st Viscount Gort** (*see* above), and *d* 16 Nov 1801, having had, with another s and four daus:

1 CHARLES VEREKER, **2nd Viscount Gort**, PC (I 1809, UK 1834); *b* 1768; MP Limerick 1794–1800 and 1802–17, defeated French forces under Gen Humbert at Killala Bay, Co Sligo, nr Coloony, 5 Sept 1798 (thanks of Parl, granted supporters and other honourable augmentations to arms), Ld Treasury 1807–12, Constable Limerick Castle 1809–42, Govr Co Galway 1814–31, rep I peer 1823–42; *m* 1st 7 Nov 1789 Jane (*d* 19 Feb 1798), widow of William Stamer, of Carnelly, Co Limerick, and dau of Ralph Westropp, of Attyflin, Co Limerick, and had, with other issue:

(1) JOHN PRENDERGAST, **3rd Viscount**

(1) Julia; *m* 31 Aug 1819 Col Thomas White, of Woodlands (bro of 1st Baron Annaly (*qv*)), and *d* 14 Feb 1866

(2) Georgina; *m* 2 Aug 1817 Col John Ferrier Hamilton, of Westport and Cairnhill, Scotland, and *d* 1847

1 (cont.) The **2nd Viscount** *m* 2nd 5 March 1810 Elizabeth (*d* 2 April 1858), est dau of John Palliser, of Derryluskan, Co Tipperary, and by her had, with other issue:

(2) Charles Smyth; Lt-Col cmdg 4th Bde S Irish Div RA; *b* 21 April 1818; *m* 10 May 1842 Kate (*d* 19 June 1905), yst dau of Robert Fannin, and *dsp* 12 May 1885

2 John; Maj Limerick Militia; *m* Elizabeth, dau of George Black, and *d* 7 May 1836, leaving, with other issue:

(1) Henry; *m* 1st 1 Nov 1858 Jane (*d* 1859), dau of Richard J Stackpoole, of Edenvale, Co Clare; *m* 2nd 5 July 1865 Martha Rogers, 3rd dau of Philip MacAdam, of Blackwater, Co Clare, and *d* 10 July 1871, leaving issue:

1a Julia; *m* Thomas Jervis, bro of Ch Justice Sir John Jervis, and *d* 14 May 1878

The 2nd VISCOUNT *d* 11 Nov 1842; his er son,

JOHN PRENDERGAST VEREKER, **3rd Viscount Gort**; *b* 1 July 1790; *educ* Harrow; MP (Tory) Limerick 1817–20, Mayor Limerick 1831–32, rep I peer June–Oct 1865; *m* 1st 15 Dec 1814 Maria (*d* 4 April 1854), est dau of 1st Viscount Guillamore (*see* 1956 edn), and had, with other issue:

1 STANDISH PRENDERGAST, **4th Viscount**

2 John Prendergast; MA, barrister, Ld Mayor Dublin 1863; *b* 1822; *m* 21 Dec 1858 Louisa (*d* 12 June 1906), only dau and heir of George Medlicott, of Rutland Sq, Dublin, by Emily, dau of Arthur Magan, MP, of Clonearl, and *d* Dec 1891, leaving:

(1) George Medlicott, JP Co Galway; Capt 3rd Bn Roy Dublin Fus; *b* 10 Jan 1860; *m* 13 Oct 1887 Frances Gore, MBE (*d* 21 Aug 1931), est dau of Robert Manders, of Dundrum, Co Dublin, and *d* 26 Sept 1924, leaving issue:

1a (George) Gordon (Medlicott) (Sir), KCMG (1948), MC; Capt Gren Gds (SR) WW I (despatches), Dip Serv: joined 1919, Actg Counsellor Moscow 1938–39, Envoy Extrdy and Min Plen Bolivia 1939, Min Finland 1940–41, Envoy Extrdy and Min Plen Uruquay 1943–49 (Amb 1944), ret 1949; *b* 11 Dec 1889; *educ* Eton and Trin Coll Camb; *m* 1st 27 March 1928 (*annulled* 1945) Marjorie Rosamond Seton Dower, dau of Col Herbert Hall Mulliner, of Clifton Court, Rugby; *m* 2nd 17 Feb 1945 Mrs Roxana Wentworth van Rensselaer (*d* 1968), only child of Clarence Winthrop Bowen, of New York and Woodstock, Conn., and *dsp* 14 March 1976

2a Robert Humphrey Medlicott; 2nd Lt Gren Gds; *b* 15 Oct 1892; *ka* 25 Aug 1914

1a Corinna Katherine; *b* 4 July 1891; *m* 1st 23 Feb 1911 (*divorce* 1925) her cousin **6th Viscount Gort** and had issue (*see* below); *m* 2nd 26 April 1930 Edgar Charles Blatt, s of Edgar Blatt, of San Francisco, and *d* 5 Oct 1940

(2) John Medlicott; Rlwy Tport Staff S Cmd, 4th Dragoon Gds, Nile Expdn 1884–85, Adj Imp Yeo Boer War 1900–01; *b* 14 Jan 1863; *m* 15 Nov 1892 (*divorce* 1914) Mary Agnes (*d* 15 May 1930), dau of Sir Charles William Cayzer, 1st Bt, of Gartmore, Perthshire (*qv*), and *d* 1 Nov 1940, having had:

1a John Cayzer Medlicott, MC; Lt-Col RASC, Capt Canadian Res Offrs WWs I and II; *b* 2 March 1895; *m* 2 March 1914 Dulcie Flores Elder (*d* 1973), only child of Alexander Randle Skene Radcliffe, of Nova Scotia, and *d* 12 Aug 1962, having had issue:

1b John Herbert Radcliffe Medlicott; Lt RN (FAA) WW II; *b* 3 Oct 1914; *m* 14 June 1939 Betty Eleanor Grace (*m* 2nd 1 May 1945 Capt Maurice Milton Jones, USAF, of Jackson, Miss.), only child of Charles Edward Shepherd, of Trerice Manor, Cornwall, and was *ka* 21 Dec 1940, leaving:

1c *Jocelyn [Mrs Ralph Johnston, Thorpes Gardens, St James, Barbados, W Indies]; *b* 25 Sept 1940; *m* 8 June 1963 *Ralph Lancelot Johnston, s of Stanley Everton Lancelot Johnson, and has:

1d *Amanda Louise; *b* 20 Dec 1964

2d *Tracy Kristina; *b* 1967

2b Derek Standish; Actg Maj 4th Gurkha Rifles WW II; *b* 13 July 1922; *ka* July 1944

3b Patrick Brian; Midshipman RN WW II; *b* 27 Dec 1923; *ka* in HMS *Neptune* 19 Dec 1941

1b *(Dulciebella) Joy [Mrs Buswell, Aldersnapp Cottage, Petersfield, Hants]; *b* 18 Sept 1918; took name BUSWELL by deed poll; *m* 1st 26 Oct 1935 (*divorce* 1946) Capt Hender Charles Molesworth St Aubyn (*d* 1986), 2nd s of Sir Hugh Molesworth St Aubyn, 13th Bt (*qv*), and has issue; *m* 2nd 21 June 1948 W/Cdr Harold Frederick Gurney Fry (*d* 1978), RAF, yr s of B E Fry, of Hampstead, and has further issue:

1c *Elizabeth Gurney; *b* 5 March 1950; *m* 1st 1969 (*divorce* 1974) Colin Maurice Sampson; *m* 2nd *Colin Roy Woolerton and by him has:

1d *George Peter Christopher; *b* 1975

2b *Shelagh Maureen [Mrs Shelagh Martin, Barton Cottage, Rosebery Rd, W Runton, Norfolk] WRNS WW II; *b* 18 April 1925; *m* 11 April 1947 (*divorce* 1971) Hugh Bellasis Martin, MBE, ICS, only surv s of Geoffrey Martin, and has issue:

1c *Clive Patrick; *b* 24 June 1955; *educ* Harrow and Wadham Coll Oxford (BA); *m* 1986 *Caroline Anne Freedman and has:

1d *Thomas Christopher; *b* 1987

2d *Luke Nicholas; *b* 1990

1c *Corinna Frances Avril; *b* 26 April 1948; *educ* St Margaret's Sch Bushey, Homerton Coll and Newnham Coll Cambridge (BEd); *m* 19– *Philip Charles Creasy, MA, and has issue:

1d *Matthew Henry; *b* 1974

1d *Stella Judith; *b* 1977

2a George Herbert Medlicott; Capt Machine Gun Section 1st Cav Bde, Res of Offrs 11th Hus; *b* 5 May 1896; *d* 4 July 1924

3a Stanley Lloyd Medlicott, OBE (1944); Capt RN WWs I and II; *b* 13 Sept 1899; *educ* RNCs Osborne and Dartmouth; *m* 16 April 1925 Elaine Irene (*d* 1982), dau of John Henry Edwards, and *d* 21 Nov 1967, leaving issue:

1b +(John) Stanley Herbert Medlicott [Stanley Vereker Esq, Mallam Waters, Fairfield, Glos; 118 Coleherne Court, London SW5]; *b* 6 July 1927; *educ* Rugby and Trin Hall Cambridge; *m* 1st 15 May 1954 (*divorce* 1976) Valerie Ann Virginia, 2nd dau of William James Threlfall, CIE; *m* 2nd 1980 *Mary St Joan Howard, yr dau of Bertram Eric Edmonds (*see* CARLISLE, E), widow of James Ewing Kennaway and formerly w of Brian C Kennaway Cummins, and by his 1st w has had:

1c Simon Lloyd William Medlicott; *b* 17 Dec 1955; *educ* Radley; *d* 15 Jan 1995

2c +Rupert David Peregrine Medlicott; *b* 31 July 1957; *educ* Radley; *m* 1986 *Philippa J, dau of J C Geoffrey Stocks, and has issue:

1d +Freddie; *b* 1990

2d +Jack; *b* 1992

3c +Hugo Dominic Charles Medlicott; *b* 4 Aug 1961; *m* 24 June 1983 (*divorce* 1990) Atalanta, dau of John Cowen and Mrs Gerald Cooper, of Balcombe, Sussex

2b +David William Leslie Medlicott [Lt-Cdr David Vereker RN, Holton House, Burwash, E Sussex TN19 7HX]; *b* 19 Oct 1930; *educ* Eton and Trin Hall Cambridge (MA); *m* 24 April 1964 *Jane Elizabeth, er dau of Alan Campbell Gairdner, FRCS, and has issue:

1c +William David Lloyd Medlicott; *b* 19 Dec 1966; *educ* Eton and Caius Cambridge

2c +Henry Alan Charles Medlicott; *b* 2 June 1969; *educ* Marlborough; *m* 1995 *Anna Lois, dau of R J Carr, of Flimwell, Sussex

4a Charles William (Bill) Medlicott; FICS, Cdr RN WW II, Harbour Master Simonstown S Africa 1946–48, V-Consul Kristiansand Norway 1948–51, Assist Ship's Manager 1951–55, legal exec Admlty Court 1957–78; *b* 21 Feb 1903; *m* 26 June 1937 Marjorie Hughes (*d* 1984), dau of William Hughes Whatley, and *d* 26 July 1995, leaving:

1b +Peter William Medlicott [Peter Vereker Esq, FCO, King Charles St, London SW1A 2AH]; RAFVR 1958–61, Dip Serv: 3rd and 2nd Sec Bangkok 1964, Consul Chiang Mai 1964–68, 1st Sec Canberra 1971, Consul-Gen Bangkok 1983, Dep Perm Rep UK Mission Geneva 1987, Ambass and UK Perm Rep OECD Paris 1995–; *b* 13 Oct 1939; *educ* Marlborough, Trin Coll Cambridge (MA) and Harvard 1961–62 (Henry Fellow 1962); *m* 1967 *Susan Elizabeth, only dau of Maj Gen Anthony John Dyball, CBE, MC, Ch Staff NI Cmd, and has issue:

1c +Connel Charles Medlicott; *b* 21 June 1971

2c +Toby John Medlicott; *b* 28 Dec 1973

3c +Rory James Medlicott; *b* 1981

2b +John Michael Medlicott , CB (1992) [John Vereker Esq CB, Dept of Internat Devpt, 94 Victoria St, London SW1E 5JL]; *b* 9 Aug 1944; *educ* Marlborough and Keele U (BA 1967); Min Overseas Devpt 1967, World Bank 1970–72, Priv Sec to Min Overseas Devpt 1976–78, PM's Office 1980–83, Pncpl Fin Offr ODA 1983–88, Dep Sec DES 1988–94, Perm Sec ODA (subsequently Dept Internat Devpt); *m* 1971 *Judith, dau of Hobart Rowen, of Washington, DC, and has:

1c +Andrew Shane Medlicott; *b* 24 March 1975

1c *Jennifer Gail; *b* 16 April 1973

1b *Corinna Mary [Mrs John Tadman, West End Mill, Donhead St Andrew, Dorset]; *b* 30 May 1938; *m* 8 April 1961 *Col John Tadman, Roy Anglian Regt, yr s of G R Tadman, and has issue:

1c *Miles William Vereker; *b* 1966

1c *Carey Joanna; *b* 1962

2c *Fenella Jane; *b* 1964

5a Denis Medlicott; *b* 1 Feb 1906; *educ* Harrow; *m* 1927 (*divorce* 1942) Marjory Mary, dau of Julius A Fryer, of Port Elizabeth, S Africa, and *d* 1976, leaving issue:

1b *Moyra Maureen; *b* 1928; *m* 1st 2 Feb 1962 (*divorce* 1971) Rodney Graham Smit, CA (SA), ACIS; *m* 1976 *Roy William Digby, MB, ChB

1a Eileen Mamie; *b* 16 Aug 1897; *m* 11 July 1918 Capt John Clark Heaton, s of F R Heaton, of Montreal

2a Norah Doreen Dods; *b* 3 Feb 1902; *m* 8 Sept 1923 Adml Sir Alan Kenneth Scott-Moncrieff, KCB, CBE, DSO and bar, DL, s of Robert Lawrence Scott-Moncrieff, and *d* 27 July 1973, leaving issue

3a Kathleen Sybil; *b* 19 July 1904; *m* 3 Nov 1931 Cdr Michael George Marriott, RN (*d* 1978), s of Charles Marriott, and has issue:

1b *Jeremy Edward Alan; late Lt RN, Shell rep; *b* 9 Feb 1937; *m* 26 Jan 1963 *Teresa Katherine, dau of Malcolm Francis Ogilvie Forbes, and has:

1c *Benedict Michael Andrew; *b* 26 Nov 1963

2c *Peter Malcolm; *b* 6 May 1966

1c *Felicity Anne; *b* 14 Jan 1969

1b *Bridget Mary; *b* 8 Jan 1934; *m* 1956 *Julius Horowitz, s of Robert Horowitz, of Johannesburg, and has issue:

1c *Adam Mark; *b* 1957

2c *Ivan Brandon; *b* 1961

3c *Seth William; *b* 1961

4c *Ben Robert; *b* 1964

1c *Robyn Esther; *b* 1956

2c *Yael Tayce; *b* 1959

(1) Maria Corinna; *b* 6 June 1861; *m* 28 Jan 1889 Francis Honorius Sisson Sitwell, and *d* 29 Aug 1890, leaving issue (*see* SITWELL, Bt)

(2) Emily Henrietta; *b* 15 April 1864; *m* 12 Feb 1890 (*divorce* 1914) Maj Henry Read Darley, DSO, OBE, 4th Dragoon Gds, s of T F Darley, and had issue. He *d* 25 April 1931

3 Henry Prendergast; BA, LLD, Consul Cherbourg; *b* 1824; *m* 10 Feb 1866 Louisa Elizabeth Mary (*d* 14 April 1920, dau of George Bagot Gosset, 4th Dragoon Gds, by Charlotte (*m* 2nd Marchese di Vinchiaturo), dau of James Douglas, of Belfast, and *d* 22 March 1904, leaving issue:

(1) Charles Granville; Maj and Brevet Lt-Col RA, attd Gen Staff 1914, Maj Instr Gunnery WW I; *b* 18 Sept 1869; *m* 1st 18 June 1895 Adeline Eleanor (*d* 1 Feb 1930), dau of Maj-Gen Thomas Porter Berthon, RA; *m* 2nd 4 Nov 1931 Leila Frances Helena (*m* 2nd 1973 Maj Robert Hugh Pardoe; *d* 1993), dau of Florian Gustavus Bosanquet, and *d* 17 Dec 1947, leaving by her:

1a +Neville Henry Prendergast [Neville Vereker Esq, Inglewood, 6 Curzon Ave, Beaconsfield, Bucks HP9 2NN]; FRICS; *b* 2 Aug 1934; *educ* Malvern; *m* 8 Aug 1974 *Priscilla Mary, dau of John Orlando Weld-Forester (*see* FORESTER, B), and has:

1b +John Charles Prendergast; *b* 11 Aug 1975; *educ* St John's Coll Durham (MSc)

2b +Richard Neville Forester; *b* 1977; *educ* Shiplake

1a *Louise Katherine [Mrs Louise Gotch, Flat N, 78/80 Holland Rd, London W14]; *b* 17 Feb 1933; *m* 28 Dec 1953 (*divorce* 1961) Geoffrey Whitaker Gotch, only s of Thomas Hepburn Gotch, and has issue:

1b *Peter Charles Thomas; *b* 18 March 1955; *educ* Birmingham (BSc) and Aston Us (DipSH); Inspr Factories HSE 1979–91, Health & Safety Advsr Babtie Gp 1991–; *m* 1982 *Deborah Jane Ward and has issue:

1c *Liam Paul; *b* 1984

1c *Gemma Jane; *b* 1982

(2) Henry Gosset; Cdr RN; *b* 6 April 1871; *m* 21 Dec 1903 Kate Beatrice (*d* 15 July 1915), er dau of Frank Herbert, and *d* 4 July 1916, leaving issue:

1a Charles Henry; *b* 29 March 1913; *educ* Lincoln Coll Oxford, MA (1942), DPhil (1951), Prof Political Theory and Institutions Durham 1966, Emeritus Prof 1973, Patron Buckingham U 1984, Hon DLitt 1985; *m* 6 Aug 1942 *Patricia, LLB Lond, JP (Co Durham 1969), only dau of Solomon Geshel Kastelian, MD, and *d* 22 July 1996, having had:

1b +Julian Charles Prendergast [Julian Vereker Esq, Tythe House, Odstock, Salisbury, Wilts]; *b* 7 May 1945; *educ* Bryanston; *m* 30 March 1968 *Elizabeth, dau of Cecil Glascott Wise, and has issue:

1c *Annabel Louise; *b* 1974

2b John Prendergast; *b* 10 Nov 1947; *d* 19 Sept 1951

1b *Katherine Elizabeth [Mrs Edward Gieve, 211 Highbury Quadrant, London N5]; *b* 26 June 1949; *m* 1972 *Edward John Watson Gieve and has issue:

1c *Daniel Vereker; *b* 1980

2c *Matthew Vereker; *b* 1982

2b *Deirdre Patricia; *b* 27 March 1954

(3) George Cadogan Smyth; *b* 11 Jan, *d* 7 Nov 1876

(1) Kathleen Louise; *b* 3 Jan 1867; *m* 1 Aug 1893 Walter Egerton John Green-Emmott, JP, of Emmott Hall, Lancs, and *d* 10 June 1939, having had issue. He *d* 11 March 1921

(2) Henriqua Elizabeth; *b* 26 Feb 1868; *m* 14 Nov 1903 Rodney Manners, yst s of Col Herbert Russell Manners, 51st KOYLI, and *d* 19–, leaving issue

(3) Alianore Maria Julia; *b* 23 Oct 1873; *d* unm 15 Jan 1899

4 Richard Prendergast; Capt KRRC; *b* 1829; *d* 30 April 1865

5 Adolphus Edward Prendergast; Capt 20th Foot; *b* 1833; *d* 12 Oct 1864

1 Maria Corinna; *m* 10 March 1852 Lt-Col Monteith Hamilton and *d* 20 July 1856, leaving issue. He *d* 10 Jan 1855

The **3rd Viscount** *m* 2nd 10 June 1861 Elizabeth Mary (*d* 11 Oct 1880), widow of George Tudor, MP Barnstaple, and dau and heir of John Jones, and *d* 20 Oct 1865

His est surv son,

STANDISH PRENDERGAST VEREKER, **4th Viscount Gort**, JP Co Galway; High Sheriff 1843, Hon Col 4th Bde S Irish Div RA; *b* 6 July 1819; *educ* Trin Coll Dublin (MA); *m* 4 May 1847 Caroline Harriet (*d* 8 May 1888), 3rd dau of 4th Viscount Gage (*qv*), and *d* 9 Jan 1900, having had:

1 JOHN GAGE PRENDERGAST VEREKER, **5th Viscount Gort**, JP Co Durham and IoW; Capt 4th Bde S Irish Div RA; *b* 28 Jan 1849; *m* 28 Jan 1885 Eleanor (*m* 2nd 27 June 1908 Col Starling Meux Benson, JP, 17th Lancers (*d* 27 Dec 1933)), dau and coheir of Robert Smith Surtees, of Hamsterley Hall, Co Durham, the sporting novelist, and *d* 15 Aug 1902, leaving:

(1) JOHN STANDISH SURTEES PRENDERGAST, **6th Viscount Gort** and 1st and last VISCOUNT GORT, of Hamsterley, Co Durham (UK), so *cr* 1946, VC (1918), GCB (1940, KCB 1938, CB 1937), CBE (1928), DSO (1917) and two bars (1917 and 1918), MVO (1910), MC (1915); *b* 10 July 1886; Gren Gds WW I (wounded three times, despatches eight times, brevet), Dir Mil Trg Army HQ India 1932–36, Cmdt Staff Coll Camberley 1936–37, Mil Sec to Sec State War and Sec Selectn Bd 1937, Gen 1937, CIGS and First Mil Memb Army Cncl 1937–39, C-in-C BEF France Sept 1939, C-in-C Br Field Forces 1939–40, Inspr-Gen Forces Trng 1940–41, Inspr-Gen HG, ADC Gen to HM GEORGE VI 1940–44, Govr and C-in-C: Gibraltar 1941–42, Malta 1942–44, FM 1943, HC and C-in-C Palestine, HC Transjordan 1944–45; *m* 23 Feb 1911 (*divorce* 1925) his cousin Corinna Katherine (*d* 5 Oct 1940), only dau of George Medlicott Vereker, JP (*see* above), and *d* 31 March 1946, when the UK Viscountcy expired, having had:

1a Charles Standish; *b* 23 Feb 1912; *educ* Trin Coll Cambridge (BA); *m* 21 April 1938 Yvonne Frances, dau of Maj Geoffrey Arthur Barnett, MBE, and *dsp* & *vp* 26 Feb 1941

2a Joscelyn Cecil Prendergast; *b* 27 July 1913; *d* 29 May 1915

1a Jacqueline Corinne Yvonne; Sr Cdr ATS WW II; *b* 20 Oct 1914; *m* 8 June 1940 1st Viscount De L'Isle (*qv*) and *d* 15 Nov 1962, leaving issue

(2) (STANDISH) ROBERT GAGE PRENDERGAST, **7th Viscount Gort**, MC; *b* 12 Feb 1888; *educ* Harrow and Trin Coll Camb; RHA (TF) WW I (wounded thrice, despatches), Hon Col 464 HAA Regt RA 1948–54, KStJ; *m* 11 June 1921 Bessy (*d* 14 April 1972), dau of Aubone Alfred Surtees, of Dinsdale Manor, Co Durham, and *dsp* 1975

2 Foley Charles Prendergast; Capt RN, FRGS, AICE, Naval Advsr Bd Tde; *b* 21 June 1850; *m* 25 March 1876 Ellen Amelia (*d* 18 Dec 1943), only dau of Rev Henry Michael Mydleton Wilshere, Rector Simonstown, Cape Good Hope, and *d* 24 Oct 1900, leaving issue:

(1) Standish Henry Prendergast, DCM; Colonial CS, Resident Nigeria, V-Consul Cherbourg 1901–04, Boer War 1900–01 (medal, despatches and medal for distinguished conduct in the field), IO attd Br Forces Cameroons and Mounted Inf WW I (three medals), CD WW II; *b* 12 Nov 1878; *m* 25 March 1908 Eleanor Elizabeth (*d* 28 July 1957), er dau of Henry Bott, OBE, MRCS, of Washenden Manor, Biddenden, Kent, and *d* 27 Jan 1953, leaving:

1a *Daphne Eleanor [Mrs Sydney Else, 139 Brook Gdns, Emsworth, Hants PO10 7LL]; *b* 2 Sept 1910; *m* 3 Aug 1933 Cdr Sydney Arthur Moorhouse Else, OBE, RN (*d* 1979), s of Capt — Else, and has issue:

1b *Patrick Arthur Henry [Patrick Else Esq, 39 Graemsdyke Ave, London SW14 7BH]; *b* 10 Nov 1934; *educ* Bradfield; *m* 24 July 1965 *Jane Ann, dau of Eric Smith Ickringill, of Keighley, Yorks, and has issue:

1c *Henry Patrick Arthur; *b* 14 May 1979; *educ* King's Coll Sch Wimbledon

1c *Sarah-Jane; *b* 25 July 1966

2c *Sophia Frances; *b* 1969; *m* 23 July 1994 *Andrew Hamilton and has:

1d *Holly Anna; *b* 6 Jan 1996

2b *Nigel Christopher John [Nigel Else Esq, 17 The Avenue, Hambrook, Sussex ME9 8LB]; *b* 18 March 1939; *educ* Monkton Combe; *m* 1972 *Sandra Whittaker and has issue:

1c *Lisa Catherine; *b* 1975

2c *Fiona Jane; *b* 1976

3b *Oliver Francis [Oliver Else Esq, The Hollies, Oad St, Borden, Kent ME9 8LB]; *b* 5 July 1948; *educ* Christ's Hosp (MB, BS); *m* 1972 *Elizabeth Holman and has issue:

1c *Timothy Stephen; *b* 1974

2c *Christopher John; *b* 1976

1b *Marion Elizabeth [Mrs Peter Gordon-Smith, Lower Farm, Up Marden, W Sussex PO18 9LA]; *b* 29 June 1940; *m* 1 Sept 1963 *Lt-Cdr Peter Russell Gordon-Smith, RN, only s of Lt-Cdr Russell Gordon-Smith, and has issue:

1c *Russell Guy Morris [Russell Gordon-Smith Esq, Waters Edge, The Gardens, W Ashling, nr Chichester, W Sussex]; *b* 1 Sept 1964; *m* 1989 *Fiona Rutland

2c *David Mark; *b* 10 Aug 1968

1c *Louise Anne [Mrs Michael Duffy, 1 More Place Cottages, Wonham Lane, Betchworth, Surrey RH13 7AD]; *b* 20 Dec 1965; *m* 1992 *Michael Craig Duffy and has issue:

1d *Matthew Peter Michael; *b* 1993

(2) Leopold George Prendergast, RD; *b* 26 Jan 1881 (HRH THE late DUKE OF ALBANY stood sponsor); Cdr RNR; *m* 18 Sept 1915 Helen Marjorie (*d* 11 March 1958), er dau of Colin Campbell, of Kenya, and *d* 16 Dec 1937, leaving:

1a COLIN (KIM) LEOPOLD PRENDERGAST VEREKER, **8th Viscount Gort**, JP (Castletown IoM 1962); *b* 21 June 1916; *educ* Sevenoaks; Lt Cdr RNVR WW II (despatches), memb House Keys IoM 1966–71, dir Roy Skandia IoM, Invesco Fund Managers IoM, Euronav IoM and Eurofish IoM; *m* 4 July 1946 *Bettine Mary Mackenzie, formerly w of Arthur Henry Jarand and only dau of Godfrey Green, of Douglas, IoM, and *d* 6 April 1995, leaving:

1b FOLEY VEREKER, **9th and present Viscount Gort**

2b +Nicholas Leopold Prendergast; *b* 6 Dec 1954; *educ* Harrow; *m* 1985 *Nicola F, yst dau of Michael W Pitt

1b *(E)Liz(abeth) Jane [The Hon Liz Vereker, Fruit Lawn House, Abbeyleix, Co Laois, Ireland; Green Hurst, Grove Mount, Ramsey, IoM]; *b* 25 Sept 1948; *m* 1988 (*divorce* 1994) Michael L Marshall, s of A E Marshall, of Baldrine, IoM; she has issue:

1c *Jason Coline Vereker; *b* 1974

1c *Sarah Jayne Vereker; *b* 1976

1a Eileen Ivy; *b* 9 March 1920; *m* 17 Jan 1942 William John Dean, RAF, and *d* 24 Aug 1982, leaving:

1b *Terence Anthony; *b* 13 Nov 1946; *m* 1st 5 Sept 1970 Mary Glenrose Porteous; *m* 2nd 18 Jan 1992 *Alison Riordan, of S Africa, and has:

1c *Tégan Eileen Isabelle; *b* 3 March 1993

1b *Anne Mary [Mrs Leonard Ruffell, 21 Abbotts Ann Rd, Harestock, Winchester SO22 6ND]; *b* 2 Feb 1943; *m* 14 March 1964 *Leonard Ernest Ruffell and has:

1c *Antonia Mary; *b* 30 Oct 1973; *m* 21 June 1997 *James Clennell Waring Daltrey

(3) Maurice Charles Prendergast, MC; Capt RHA WW I, HG WW II; *b* 21 Aug 1884; *educ* privately; *m* 15 Nov 1928 Winifred Joan (*d* 2 Dec 1982), est dau of Alberic Arthur Twisleton-Wykeham-Fiennes (*see* SAYE AND SELE, B), and *d* 26 July 1963, leaving issue:

1a +(Charles) John Prendergast, CBE (1995), JP (1965), DL (Warwicks 1993) [John Vereker Esq CBE JP DL, Lynn Cottage, Back Lane, Birdingbury, Warwicks CV23 8EN]; *b* 28 Dec 1935; *educ* Kelly Coll; CC Warwicks 1961–97 (Chm 1982–84, leader Conservative Gp 1984–87), Lt RA (TA), MIPD, MIMgt; *m* 1975 *Jennifer Lesley Ellaby and has:

1b +Richard John Prendergast; *b* 1978

2b +Nicholas Charles Prendergast; *b* 1982

1b *Elizabeth Margaret; *b* 1976

2a +Jeffrey Maurice Prendergast [Jeffrey Vereker Esq, The Post House, Bridge St, Fenny Compton, Warwicks]; *b* 24 Dec 1940, FRICS; *educ* Bloxham; *m* 1972 *Denzil Farnsworth, SRN, and has issue:

1b +Edward Foley Prendergast; *b* 1973

2b *Charlotte Louise; *b* 1974

1a *Margaret Joan; *b* 9 Dec 1929

2a *Brenda Rosemary [Mrs Harold Mills, Glebe House, Bentworth, Hants GU34 5RA], RSCN, SRN, HV; *b* 7 Sept 1931; *m* 24 April 1965 *Harold James Mills, BA, Hon Capt RA, s of Albert Mills, and has issue:

1b *Catherine Joanna; *b* 15 Oct 1967; BSc, ACA; *m* 1 Oct 1994 *James Paul Loweth, BA, RCA

(4) Foley Gerald Prendergast; Lt RN; *b* 12 April 1893; *m* 1st 17 Nov 1914 (*divorce* 1919) Annette Julia Richmond, only dau of William Scotland Dawson; *m* 2nd 27 March 1920 Muriel (*d* 28 July 1945), dau of Lindsay Horrocks, and *d* 14 Feb 1921, leaving issue:

1a Barbara Isma Prendergast; *b* posthumously 16 June 1921; *d* 16 Aug 1993

(1) Violet Eva; *b* 23 March 1882; *m* 12 Sept 1912 Rev Oswald James Hogarth, DD Oxon, Rector Severn Stoke Worcs 1932–44 and Kalk Bay, Cape Town, 1922–32, Archdeacon Cape 1928–32, ed *Church Chronicle* S Africa, only s of Prof O H Hogarth, and *d* 7 Feb 1953, leaving issue. He *d* 21 Aug 1961

(2) Lilian Isolda; *b* 1 May 1883; *m* 26 April 1911 Rev Lionel Smithett Lewis, Vicar Glastonbury (*d* 12 July 1953), 2nd s of Rev Gerrard Lewis, MA, Vicar Cliftonville, Margate and *d* 12 March 1977

(3) Muriel Agnes; BRCS WW I (two medals); *b* 19 Oct 1886; *d* unm 23 June 1943

(4) Ivy Mary; Anglo-Belge and No 47 Gen Hosp France WW I (two medals); *b* 21 Feb 1888; *m* 12 Oct 1915 Capt Edward George Gatacre, W R Regt, of Gatacre, Salop, and *d* 17 Jan 1973. He *d* 20 Feb 1916 of wounds recd in action

3 Standish William Prendergast; Lt Native Contingent; *b* 23 Feb 1854; *k* Zululand 22 Jan 1879

4 Jeffrey Edward Prendergast; Lt-Col RHA; *b* 27 March 1858; *m* 1902 Susan Harriet (*d* 20 March 1932), widow of Lt-Col James Shaw McClutchen, RAMC, and dau of Capt Edward Head, of Birr, Co Offaly, and *d* 2 Jan 1940, leaving:

(1) Lena Elizabeth; *m* 25 Oct 1924 Julian William Palmer, RA, s of William Clayton Palmer, and *d* 18 Sept 1941, leaving issue

1 Isolda Caroline; *m* 23 Nov 1870 Sir Charles William Frederick Crauford, 4th Bt (*qv*), and *d* 10 Sept 1927, leaving issue
2 Mabel Elizabeth; *d* unm 8 Feb 1930
3 Laline Maria; *d* unm 15 June 1929
4 Elizabeth Maria; Order Mercy; *m* 1st 7 Dec 1886 William Harvey Astell, DL (*d* 20 April 1896), of Woodbury Hall, Beds, and had, with other issue:
(1) Richard John Vereker; *m* 26 April 1922 Joan Evelyn Crichton-Stuart (*see* BUTE, M) and *d* 18 June 1969
(1) Laline Annette; *m* 1st 1910 Lt-Col Arthur Priston Hohler, DSO, Middx Regt and had a s (Thomas Sidney ASTELL formerly HOHLER, (*see* ERROLL, E); *m* 2nd 1927 Col Stanley Leonard Barry (*see* BARRY, Bt)
4 (cont.) The Hon Mrs Astell *m* 2nd 12 June 1902 3rd Baron de L'Isle and Dudley (*see* DE L'ISLE, V) and *d* 19 July 1958
5 Corinna Julia; *d* unm 25 Aug 1945

GOSCHEN, Viscount

Arms: Arg. a heart gu., flamant and transfixed by an arrow bendwise, point upwards ppr., two anchors erect in chief sa. **Crest:** Upon an arrow fesswise, the point to the dexter, a dove, wings addorsed, all ppr. **Supporters:** Dexter, a sailor of the Royal Navy, habited and accoutred; sinister, a private of the Royal Marines, habited, both ppr., each holding in his exterior hand a flag staff, also ppr., therefrom flowing a banner arg. charged with a pale gu., thereon an anchor cabled and erect or. **Motto:** *Pacem* ('For peace'). **Creation:** V. (UK) 18 Dec 1900.

THE 4TH VISCOUNT GOSCHEN, of Hawkhurst, Co Kent (Giles John Harry Goschen) [The Rt Hon The Viscount Goschen, Hilton House, Crowthorne, Berks RG11 6AH]; *b* 16 Nov 1965 *s f* 1977; *educ* Eton; Ld in Waiting (Govt Whip) 1992–94, Parly U-Sec Tport 1994–97, with Deutsche Morgan Grenfell 1998–; *m* 1991 *Sarah Penelope, dau of Alan G Horsnail, of Westbury-on-Trym, Bristol

Lineage: GEORGE JOACHIM GOSCHEN, of Leipzig, Hohenstedt and Grimma, Saxony; publisher; had:

WILLIAM HENRY GOSCHEN, of Templeton House, Roehampton, and Villa Goschen, Oberlosnitz, Saxony; fndr Fruhling & Goschen, London, 1815; *b* 3 July 1793; *m* 12 May 1829 Henrietta (*d* 14 March 1895), dau of William Alexander Ohmann, and *d* 28 July 1866, having had, with another s and three daus:
1 GEORGE JOACHIM, **1st Viscount**
2 Henry, of Heathfield, Addington, Surrey; Lt 2nd Punjab Irregular Cav; *b* 5 April 1837; *m* 10 Jan 1865 Augusta Eleanor (*d* 1 Nov 1921), dau of Geoffrey Joseph Shakerley (*see* SHAKERLEY, Bt), and *d* 14 Sept 1932, having had, with other issue:
(1) Sir HARRY (WILLIAM HENRY NEVILLE) GOSCHEN, 1st Bt (UK), so *cr* 1927, KBE (*see* 1940 edn)
(2) Arthur Alec, CB (1935), DSO (1901) and two bars (1916, 1918), DL (Glos 1953); ADC to HM GEORGE V 1932–34, Maj-Gen RA: Boer War and WW I (despatches, Croix de Guerre), Cmdt RMA 1934–38, re-employed 1939–41, Col-Cmdt RHA 1942–48; *b* 6 Jan 1880; *educ* Eton; *m* 2 April 1908 Marjorie Mary, dau of Maj William Blacker, of Castle Martin, Newbridge, Co Kildare, and *d* 28 June 1975, leaving issue:
1a Geoffrey William, DSO, MC and bar; Brig CRA 50th Inf Div (TA) 1958–62, RHA WW II; *b* 9 June 1911; *educ* Eton and RMA Woolwich; *m* 30 Sept 1946 *Mary Ernestine [Mrs Geoffrey Goschen, 2 Close Gdns, Tetbury, Glos GL8 8DU], yst dau of Lt-Col Ernest Fitzroy Morrison-Bell (*see* MORRISON-BELL, Bt), and *d* 1988, leaving issue:
1b *John Henry [John Goschen Esq, 2 Close Gdns, Tetbury, Glos GL8 8DU]; *b* 5 April 1949; *educ* privately
1b *Mary [Mrs David Moore, 10B Downfield Rd, Clifton, Bristol BS8 2JT]; *b* 18 Jan 1948; *m* 1973 David Robson Moore (*d* 1987), s of B G Moore, and has issue:
1c *Nathaniel James William; *b* 1974
1c *Roxanne Diana; *b* 17 Aug 1977
2a John Arthur, MC and bar; Capt RHA WW II; *b* 29 Aug 1918; *ka* Dec 1941
1a Grania; *b* 4 April 1909; *m* 7 July 1932 Lt-Col John Beaumont Hyde-Smith, yst s of Capt S Hyde-Smith, of Consall Hall, Staffs, and *d* 27 May 1990 leaving:
1b *Christopher John [Christopher Hyde-Smith Esq, 6 Heath Drive, Sutton, Surrey SM2 5RP]; Prof Flute RCM; *b* 11 March 1935; *educ* Eton and RCM; *m* 1st 6 May 1968 (*divorce* 19–) Marisa, harpist, est dau of D Cristobal Robles, of Madrid; *m* 2nd 1985 *Jane Dodd and by her has:
1c *Ellen Diana; *b* 8 Aug 1986
2c *Abigail Jane; *b* 14 March 1990
2b *Charles Sergison [Charles Hyde-Smith Esq, Kings Hay, East Leach, Glos]; Lt 15th–19th KRH; *b* 14 March 1947; *educ* Eton
2a Mary (Molly) Gwendolen, of Southrop Manor, Lechlade, Glos; *b* 13 Oct 1914; *educ* Westonbirt; Jt MFH VWH Cricklade; *m* 4 April 1941 Capt Alan Joseph Macdonald Richardson (*d* 11 Dec 1963), yr s of Joseph Richardson, DL, MP, of Potto Hall, Northallerton, Yorks, and *d* 17 Aug 1997, having had:
1b Donald Geoffrey; Roy Dragoons; *b* 23 April 1943; *d* following a car crash 14 July 1963
1b *Bridget Mary [Mrs Kenneth Combe, Ashlands Court, Malmesbury, Wilts SN16 9SP]; *b* 20 Jan 1942; *m* 1st 29 Oct 1963 (*divorce* 1972) William Peter Dwerryhouse, late Capt 10th Roy Hus, s of William Leslie Dwerryhouse, MRCVS, DVSM, and has:
1c *William Mark; *b* 29 Nov 1964
2c *Alan Damian; *b* 10 Nov 1966
1b (cont.) Mrs Bridget Dwerryhouse *m* 2nd 24 Oct 1972 *Kenneth Christian Combe, s of AVM Gerard Combe, CB, and has by him:
3c *James Gerard; *b* 19 March 1974
4c *Alexander Christian; *b* 8 May 1975
2b *Juliet Flora [Mrs John Gill, Chastleton Hill, Moreton-in-Marsh, Glos]; *b* 24 Jan 1946; *m* 3 June 1967 *Capt John Laurence Gill, late 17th/21st Lancers, er s of Henry Laurence Gill by Diana Mercy, only dau of Maj Henry Reginald Cholmondeley, DSO (*see* DELAMERE, B)
3b *Yda Hermione; *b* 26 April 1951
4b *Harriet Josephine; *b* 22 March 1953
3a *Diana Marjorie [Mrs K Mathews, 28 Ritchie Ct, 380 Banbury Rd, Oxford OX2 7PW]; *b* 18 Nov 1916; *educ* St Hugh's Coll Oxford (MA); *m* 19– *K Mathews
(1) Etheldreda Augusta; *m* 5 Sept 1901 Rev Alan Nigel Campbell, 2nd s of Col Walter Campbell, of Skipness Castle, Argyllshire, and *d* 19–. He *d* 7 July 1934
(2) Margaret; *b* 14 June 1869; *m* 5 June 1895 Henry Gerard Philip Hoare, JP, DL, of Stansted House, Godstone, Surrey, and *d* 10 May 1960, leaving issue. He *d* 16 Nov 1918
(3) Hilda Marion
(4) Kathleen Eleanor; *m* 12 March 1914 Lt Geoffrey Malcolm Gathorne-Hardy, MC (*see* CRANBROOK, E)
3 Charles Hermann; Lt City London, Dir Bank England, Chm Lloyd's, sr ptnr Fruhling & Goschen; *b* 21 Jan 1839; *m* 3 Feb 1864 Ann Helen Levick (*d* 28 Nov 1926) and *d* 22 March 1915, having had, with other issue:
(1) Charles Henry, of Woolley Grange, Bradford on Avon, Wilts; *b* 8 Nov 1879; *m* 11 Nov 1913 Amy Beatrice (*d* 9 Nov 1971 aged 83), dau of Sir (William) Cameron Gull, 2nd Bt (*qv*), and *d* 23 Aug 1939
(2) Kenneth; Lt City London; *b* 16 March 1882; *m* 4 July 1906 Violet (*d* 23 Oct 1945), dau of Leonard Micklem, and *d* 1 Oct 1939, leaving issue:
1a *Hugh Kenneth; MFH, chm Antony Gibbs & Sons, ret 1976; *b* 9 May 1907; *m* 1933 *Ethleen Mary Chapman and has had issue:
1b Timothy Sahne Kenneth; T/Maj 5th Roy Inniskilling Dragoon Gds, seconded to HC Fedn S Arabia 1965; *b* 27 Dec 1935; *educ* Eton; *k* air crash S Arabia 22 Nov 1966
2a *Donald Charles, MBE (1945); RA WW II (despatches); *m* 8 Jan 1953 *Sieglinde, dau of Emil Seidl, of Austria, and has issue:
1b *Charles Hermann; *b* 17 Aug 1958
2b *John Kenneth; *b* Sept 1967
1b *Caroline Jane; *b* 18 Dec 1956
1a *Marjorie Dora [Mrs Lawrence Rich, Springfield Cottage, Caldecote, Towcester, Northants]; *b* 28 Aug 1908; *m* 1st 11 Sept 1939 (*divorce*) Kenneth Edward Ling; *m* 2nd 28 Nov 1958 *Cdr Lawrence St George Rich, DSO, RN (ret), and by her 1st husb has:
1b *Christopher Kenneth; *b* 21 Dec 1931; *m* 22 Sept 1962 *Philippa Jane, dau of Norman Adams Jory, FRCS, and has issue:
1c *Edward Christopher Norman; *b* 11 Jan 1966
2c *Robert Charles; *b* 20 Jan 1968
1b *Doreen Jennifer [Mrs Timothy Bucknall, The Gables, Knayton, Thirsk, Yorks]; *b* 11 Sept 1930; *m* 12 Nov 1958 *Timothy Lowndes Bucknall, s of Capt Hugh Livingstone Bucknall, and has:
1c *Marcus Timothy; *b* 10 Oct 1959
2c *Richard Kenneth Lowndes; *b* 25 May 1961
2a *Nancy
(1) Florence Madeline; *d* unm 29 Nov 1957
(2) Mabel; *m* 11 Feb 1899 John Gerard Cobb and *d* March 1963
(3) Sybil; *m* 28 Jan 1896 John Reginald Head and *d* 15 July 1933, leaving issue. He *d* 15 May 1949
4 Alexander Heun; *b* 7 April 1844; *m* Oct 1869 Laura Sophia (*d* 13 Dec 1912), yr dau of Charles Whaley Spurgeon, and *d* 9 July 1928
5 WILLIAM EDWARD (Sir), 1st Bt, so *cr* 1916 (*qv*)
1 Henrietta Barbara; *m* 13 Jan 1877 Rev Charles Lyndhurst Vaughan, MA, and *dsp* 19 July 1906. He *d* 8 Aug 1895
2 Charlotte Ernestina; *m* 19 June 1861 Rev Robert Wood, MA, and *d* 14 July 1928, leaving issue
3 Emily Louisa; *m* 25 March 1863 Baron Gustav von Metzsch-Reichenbach and *d* 6 Jan 1877. He *d* 29 April 1931

The est son,

GEORGE JOACHIM GOSCHEN, **1st Viscount Goschen**, of Hawkhurst, Kent (UK), so *cr* 18 Dec 1900, PC (1865), JP, DL Kent, JP Sussex; *b* 10 Aug 1831; *educ* Rugby and Oriel Coll Oxford (BA 1853, MA 1875, Hon DCL 1881, Hon Fell 1882); ptnr Fruhling & Goschen 1857–65, Dir Bank England 1858–65, MP (Lib) City London 1863–80, Ripon 1880–85, Edinburgh E 1885–86 and St George's, Hanover Sq (Lib U to 1893, C thereafter) 1887–1900, V-Pres BOT 1865–86, Chllr Duchy Lancaster with Cabinet seat 1866, Pres Poor Law Bd 1868–71, 1st Ld Admlty 1871–74 and 1895–1900, Chllr Exchequer 1887–92, Special Amb Extrdy The Porte 1880–81, Lt City London, Ecclesiastical Commr 1882–85, Rector Aberdeen 1887 and Edin Us 1890, Chllr Oxford U 1903–07, Hon LLD: Aberdeen 1887, Cantab 1888, Edin 1890; *m* 22 Sept 1857 Lucy (*d* 21 Feb 1898), dau of John Dalley, and *d* 7 Feb 1907, having had:

1 GEORGE JOACHIM GOSCHEN, **2nd Viscount Goschen**, GCSI (1929), GCIE (1924), CBE (1918), VD (1905), PC (1930), JP (Sussex), DL (Kent); *b* 15 Oct 1866; *educ* Rugby and Balliol Coll Oxford; MP (C) E Grinstead 1895–1906, Hon Col 4th Bn E Kent Regt, Cmdt 2nd/5th Bn WW I, Priv Sec to Govr NSW 1890–92, Assist Priv Sec to 1st Ld Admlty 1895–1900, ADC to FM Earl Roberts 1900–02, Jt Parly Sec Bd Ag 1918, KGStJ, Govr Madras 1924–29, Viceroy and Actg Govr-Gen India 1929, Pres Guy's Hosp 1936, Cmdt Sussex Spec Constabulary 1940, dir Westminster, Ottoman and Br W Africa Banks, Memb House Laity Ch Assembly 1939; *m* 26 Jan 1893 Lady Margaret Evelyn Gathorne-Hardy, CI, LGStJ, Kaisar-i-Hind Gold Medal (*d* 11 July 1943), yst dau of 1st Earl of Cranbrook (*qv*), and *dspms* 24 July 1952, having had:

(1) George Joachim; Lt 5th Bn E Kent Regt; *b* 18 Nov 1893; *dvp* 16 Jan 1916 of wounds recd in action Kut-al-Amara

(1) Phyllis Evelyn; Ldy in Waiting to HRH THE PRINCESS ROYAL 1948–65; *b* 5 Aug 1895; *m* 31 Aug 1920 Lt-Col Francis Cecil Campbell Balfour (*see* BALFOUR, E) and *d* 7 May 1976, leaving issue

(2) Cicely Winifred; *b* 29 April 1899; *m* 27 Nov 1926 Maj Melville Edward Bertram Portal (*see* PORTAL, Bt) and *d* 1980, leaving issue

2 William Henry (Sir), KBE; ptnr Goschen & Cunliffe, Commr Public Works Loan Bd, Chm Lond Hosp and Jt Fin Ctee BRC and OStJ (Receiver-Gen, KGStJ); *b* 7 June 1870; *m* 25 July 1896 Geraldine Elizabeth (*d* 23 Nov 1918), dau of John William Mellor, PC, KC, and *d* 16 June 1943, leaving issue:

(1) William Henry; Brig Gren Gds WW II, ADC to Viceroy India 1936–38, OStJ; *b* 26 March 1900; *ka* Burma 6 May 1944

(2) JOHN ALEXANDER GOSCHEN, **3rd Viscount Goschen**, KBE (1972, OBE 1944); *b* 7 July 1906; *educ* Eton; Col Gren Gds WW II, Br Mil Mission Greece 1945–47, ADC to Govr Madras 1931, Capt Yeomen Gd and Assist Govt Ch Whip Ho Lords 1962–64 and 1970–71; *m* 1st 21 Nov 1934 (*divorce* 1949) Hilda Violet Ursula, yr dau of Col Hon St Leger Henry Jervis, DSO (*see* SAINT VINCENT, V); *m* 2nd 18 Aug 1955 *Alvin Moyanna Lesley [The Rt Hon Alvin Viscountess Goschen, Hilton House, Crowthorne, Berks RG11 6AH], yr dau of Harry England, of Durban, S Africa, and *d* 22 March 1977, leaving:

1a GILES JOHN HARRY GOSCHEN, **4th and present Viscount Goschen**

1a *Caroline Elizabeth; *b* 24 July 1963; *m* 1991 *William E J Grant, er s of Sir (Matthew) Alistair Grant, and has:

1b *John Alexander; *b* 1992

(1)Angela; granted with her sis rank of viscount's dau 23 May 1953; *b* 4 Sept 1897; *m* 7 June 1920 (*divorce* 1939) Lt-Col John Carne Hargreaves, Gren Gds, only s of John Reginald Hargreaves, of Drinkstone Park, Bury St Edmunds, and had issue

(2) Rosemary; *b* 19 April 1904; *m* 21 Nov 1929 Capt Ralph Eustace Lovett Tennyson-d'Eyncourt, MBE, Coldstream Gds, yst s of Edmund Charles Tennyson-d'Eyncourt, of Bayons Manor, Lincs, and *d* 6 Sept 1970, leaving issue. He *d* of wounds recd in action 20 Feb 1945

1 Lucy Maud; *b* 28 June 1858; *m* 24 April 1889 Hon Alexis Charles Burke Roche and *d* 16 March 1909, leaving issue (*see* FERMOY, B)

2 Alice; *b* 21 June 1868; *m* 12 June 1900 Ven Edward Hoare Hardcastle, MA, Canon Residentiary, Archdeacon Canterbury, and *d* 3 June 1941, leaving issue. He *d* 20 May 1945

3 Beatrice Mary, JP Berks; *b* 26 Sept 1872; *d* unm 11 March 1956

4 Fanny Evelyn; *b* 13 Nov 1875; *d* unm 27 Aug 1961

GOSCHEN, Bt

Arms: Arg. a heart gu. flamant and transfixed by an arrow bendwise, point upwards ppr. **Crest:** Upon an arrow fesswise, point to the dexter, a dove, wings addorsed, all ppr. **Motto:** *Pacem* ('For peace'). **Creation:** Bt. (UK) 17 Jan 1916.

SIR EDWARD CHRISTIAN GOSCHEN, 3RD BT, of Beacon Lodge, Southampton, DSO (1944) [Sir Edward Goschen Bt DSO, Lower Farmhouse, Hampstead Norreys, Berks RG16 OSG]; *b* 2 Sept 1913; *s* f 1933; *educ* Eton and Trin Coll Oxford; Capt and T/ Maj Tower Hamlets Rifles, Rifle Bde (TA), WW II (despatches), Dep Chm Stock Exchange Cncl 1963–71, High Sheriff Berks 1967, Cwlth War Graves Commr 1977–; *m* 6 Dec 1946 *Cynthia, JP (Berks 1957), 2nd dau of Sir Alexander George Montagu Cadogan (*see* CADOGAN, E), and has:

1 +(EDWARD) ALEXANDER [Alexander Goschen Esq, Pixton Stables, Dulverton, Somerset TA22 9HW]; *b* 13 March 1949; *educ* Eton; *m* 1976 *Louise Annette, only dau of Lt-Col Ronald Fulton Lucas Chance (*see* KINTORE, E), and has issue:

(1) *Charlotte Leila; *b* 2 Jan 1982

1 *Caroline Clare; *b* 26 Nov 1950; *m* 1989 *Jonathan Mendham

Lineage: The 1st VISCOUNT GOSCHEN (*qv*) had a yr bro:

Sir (William) Edward Goschen, 1st Bt (UK), so *cr* 17 Jan 1916, GCB (1911), GCMG (1909), GCVO (1905, KCVO 1904), PC (1905); *b* 18 July 1847; Attaché, 1869, Madrid 1870, 3rd Sec Buenos Aires 1873 and Paris 1875, 2nd Sec Rio 1877, special mission Constantinople 1880, 2nd Sec there 1881, Sec Legn Peking 1885, Copenhagen 1888, Lisbon 1890, Sec Embassy Washington 1893, St Petersburg 1894, Min Plen there 1897, Envoy Extrdy and Min Plen Belgrade 1898, Copenhagen 1900, Amb Vienna 1905, Berlin 1908–14, Gentleman Usher Sword State 1919–24, Grand Cross Dannebrog; *m* 24 Nov 1874 Harriet Hosta (*d* 15 Feb 1912), dau of Darius Clarke, of Boston, and had issue:

1 EDWARD HENRY (Sir), **2nd Bt**

2 George Gerard; Lt Gren Gds WW I (wounded), Hon Attaché, Berlin 1911–14; *b* 9 April 1887; *m* 23 July 1930 Vivienne (*d* 27 June 1957), dau of Bernard de Watteville, of Berne, by Florence Emily *née* Beddoes, and *d* 29 April 1953, leaving:

(1) David Bernard; *b* 19 Oct 1931; *educ* Bryanston; *m* 27 Feb 1954 *Angela [Mrs David Goschen, Oakwood Cottages, High Rougham, Suffolk], only dau of Lt-Col James Alexander MacNabb, TD, FCA, and *d* 1980, leaving:

1a +Sebastian Bernard; *b* 1 Jan 1959

2a Orlando Amadeus; *b* 7 Nov 1960; *d* unm 1981

1a *Chrysoula Angela; *b* 7 Dec 1955

2a *Mariora Vivienne [Miss Mariora Goschen, Oakwood Cottages, High Rougham, Suffolk]; *b* 11 Oct 1957

(1) *Tana Mary [Mrs John Fletcher, Dolphin Cottage, Altwood Rd, Maidenhead, Berks]; *b* 28 Nov 1932; *m* 26 May 1962 *John Alais Fletcher, s of Prof Basil Alais Fletcher, and has issue:

1a *Mark Alais; *b* 29 March 1963; *m* 1996 *Samantha, dau of Sir Mark Weinberg

1a *Miranda Clare; *b* 14 Aug 1964; *m* 1993 *Toby Hawkins and has:

1b *Gus; *b* 1996

1b *Fenella; *b* 1995

2a *Katherine Alice; *b* 22 April 1966; *m* 1996 *Sanjay Yadau

3a *Alexandra Sophia; *b* 10 May 1970; *m* 1997 *Vito Morawetz

The 1st Bt *d* 20 May 1924; his er son,

Sir Edward Henry Goschen, 2nd Bt; Controller Secretariat Egyptian Min Fin, Hon Attaché, St Petersburg 1897, Tangier 1901, Offr Order Crown Italy, 3rd Cl Medijidie, 3rd Cl Order Nile, S African War Medal; *b* 9 March 1876; *m* 31 July 1908 Countess Mary Danneskiold Samsöe (*d* 11 April 1964), 7th dau of Count Danneskiold Samsöe, of Denmark, and *d* 7 Aug 1933, having had:

1 Sir EDWARD CHRISTIAN GOSCHEN, **3rd and present Bt**

2 Alexander Gerard Lee, OBE (1954), MC and bar, Maj 60th Rifles WW II; *b* 17 Oct 1915; *educ* Eton; *m* 25 July 1960 *Suzette Alice, only dau of G N R Morgan, and *dsp* 10 Aug 1975

1 Dorothy Jean Hosta Henrietta; *m* 25 June 1936 Col Hugo Meynell, MC, JP,DL (*see* HALIFAX, E), and *d* 1993, leaving issue

2 Joyce Eileen Clara; *m* 10 Sept 1942 Lt-Cdr (S) Francis Charles Sackville Tufton (*see* HOTHFIELD, B), and *d* 1985, leaving issue

GOSFORD

Arms: Arg. an eagle displayed with two heads sa., beaked and membered or; on a chief vert two mullets or. **Crest:** A cock gu., standing upon a trumpet or. **Supporters:** Dexter, a leopard ppr.; sinister, another regardant, both collared and chained or. **Motto:** *Vigilantibus* ('To the watchful'). **Creations:** Bt. (NS) 1 Jan 1628, B. (I) 20 July 1776, V. (I) 20 June 1785, E. (I.) 1 Feb 1806, B. (UK) 13 June 1835 (Worlingham), B. (UK) 18 Sept 1847 (Acheson).

THE 7TH EARL OF GOSFORD, Viscount and **Baron Gosford of Market Hill**, Co Armagh, **Baron Worlingham of Beccles**, Co Suffolk, **Baron Acheson of Clancairney**, Co Armagh, and a **Baronet** (Sir Charles David Alexander John Sparrow Acheson Bt) [The Rt Hon The Earl of Gosford, House of Lords, London SW1A 0PW]; *b* 13 July 1942 (HM KING HAAKON VII OF NORWAY stood sponsor); *s f* 1966; *educ* Harrow, Byam Shaw Art Sch and RA Schs; *m* 1983 *Lynnette Redmond, of Sydney, NSW

Lineage: Capt PATRICK ACHESON, of Edinburgh, a cadet of the ACHESONs of E Lothian, had:

Sir Archibald Acheson, 1st Bt (NS), so *cr* 1 Jan 1628, of Gosford, Co Haddington; migrated to Ireland 1610 (made a denizen there 12 Feb 1618); granted 1611 lands in Co Armagh and 1612 in Co Cavan; bought more land from his bro Sir Henry Acheson, of Dromlech, Co Armagh; ktd 1620, Master Chancery I 1621–27, MP (S Parl) Haddington Constabulary 1625, Ld of Session 1627, Sec State Scotland; *m* 1st by 1610 Agnes Vernor, of Edinburgh, and had:

1 **Sir Patrick Acheson, 2nd Bt**; *m* 1634 Martha (*bur* 21 Feb 1674/5), only child of William Moore, Clerk Signet, and *dspm* 6 Oct 1638

1 Jane; *m* Sir Lewis Lauder, of Adiston, Edinburgh

2 Margaret; *m* Sir William Cockburn, Bt, of Langton (*see* 1880 edn), and had issue

Sir Archibald *m* 2nd *c* 20 July 1619 Margaret, only child of Sir John Hamilton, 2nd s of 1st Lord Paisley (*see* ABERCORN, D), and *d* 9 Sept 1634, leaving by her:

2 **Sir George Acheson, 3rd Bt**; High Sheriff Cos Armagh and Tyrone 1657; *bapt* 4 Aug 1629; *m* 1st 23 Jan 1654 Nichola, er dau and coheir of Sir Robert Hannay, 1st Bt (*see* 1834 edn), and had:

(1) NICHOLAS (Sir), **4th Bt**

2 (cont.) **Sir George** *m* 2nd 3 Nov 1659 Margaret, dau of 2nd Lord Caulfeild, Baron of Charlemont (*see* CHARLEMONT, V), and *d* between 10 March 1684 and 17 Nov 1685, having by her had further issue, including by one of his ws a dau Isabelle, who *m* Hector *Og* Maclean (*see* MACLEAN, Bt, of Dowart)

His est son,

Sir Nicholas Acheson, 4th Bt; MP Co Armagh 1695–99; *m* 1686 Anne, only dau of Thomas Taylor (*see* HEADFORT, M), and *d* between 8 Nov 1701 and 1702, leaving an est s:

Sir Arthur Acheson, 5th Bt; *b* 26 Jan 1688; *educ* Trin Coll Dublin (BA); MP Mullingar 1727–49; *m* 1715 Anne (*bur* 1 Nov 1737), only dau and heiress of Philip Savage, PC, Chllr Exchequer I, and had, with four intermediate sons:

1 ARCHIBALD, **1st Viscount**

6 Arthur; Capt Roy Irish Carabiniers; *m* 1753 Jane (*m* 2nd 1763 1st Baron Erne; *see* ERNE, E), dau of John King, of Charlestown, Co Roscommon, and *d* 1758

1 Anne; *m* 1742 Rt Rev Walter Cope, DD, Bp Ferns and Leighlin

2 Nicola; *m* 1746 Robert ffrench, of Monivea Castle, Co Galway, and had issue

Sir ARTHUR *d* 8 Feb 1748/9; his est son,

Sir Archibald Acheson, 6th Bt, and **1st Viscount Gosford of Market Hill**, Co Armagh, so *cr* 20 June 1785, as also previously 20 July 1776 BARON GOSFORD OF MARKET HILL, Co Armagh (both I), PC (I 1770); *b* 1 Sept 1718; *educ* Trin Coll Dublin; MP Dublin U 1741–60, Co Armagh 1761–76 (Dep Govr 1756–61), Enniskillen 1776; *m* 1740 Mary (*d* May 1792), yst dau of John Richardson, of Rich Hill, Co Armagh, and had, with other issue (*d* unm):

1 ARTHUR, **1st Earl**

1 Anna Maria; *m* 1st Alexander Boyd, of Ballycastle; *m* 2nd Rev Henry Maxwell, Rector Dromore, Co Down, 2nd s of Capt Robert Maxwell, of Fellows Hall, Co Armagh

2 Nichola; *m* Michael Obins, of Castle Obins, Armagh, and had issue

3 Julia Henrietta; *m* Alexander Macaulay and *d* 23 May 1829

4 Lucinda; *m* 1st Thomas St George; *m* 2nd Jeremiah ffrench (*d* 1819)

5 Mary; *m* 1778 Hugh Montgomery, of Castle Hume, Co Fermanagh, and *d* 10 April 1799, leaving issue. He *d* 1797

The 1st VISCOUNT *d* 5 Sept 1790; his est son,

ARTHUR ACHESON, **1st Earl of Gosford**, so *cr* 1 Feb 1806 (I), PC (I 1793); *b c* 1742; *educ* Trin Coll Dublin; MP Old Leighlin 1783–90; *m* 1774 Millicent (*d* 1 Nov 1825), dau of Lt-Gen Edward Pole (*see* POLE, Bt, of Wolverton, Hampshire), and had:

1 ARCHIBALD, **2nd Earl**

2 Edward, CB; Capt Coldstream Gds Waterloo; *d* unm 24 July 1828

1 Olivia; *m* 14 March 1797 Brig-Gen Robert Bernard Sparrow, of Brampton Park, Hunts, and Tanderagee Castle, Co Armagh, and *d* 12 Feb 1863, leaving issue. He *d* 1805

2 Mary; *m* 19 Feb 1803 Lt-Gen Lord William Bentinck (*see* PORTLAND, E) and *d* 1843

3 Millicent; *m* 12 Sept 1826 Rev J H Barber and *d* 13 Jan 1878

The 1st EARL *d* 14 Jan 1807; his er son,

ARCHIBALD ACHESON, **2nd Earl of Gosford**, GCB (1838), PC (1834); *b* 1 Aug 1776; *educ* Ch Ch Oxford; MP Co Armagh 1797–1807, Ld Lt Co Armagh 1831–49, rep I peer 1811–49, Ld in Waiting 1831–34, Capt Yeomen Gd July-Nov 1834 and April-June 1835, *cr* 13 June 1835 BARON WORLINGHAM OF BECCLES, Co Suffolk (UK), Govr Canada 1835–38, V-Adml Ulster; *m* 20 July 1805 Mary (*d* 30 June 1841), only dau of Robert Sparrow, of Worlingham Hall, Suffolk (*see* COLVILLE OF CULROSS, V, section **Seat**), and had, with other issue:

1 ARCHIBALD, **3rd Earl**

1 Mary; *m* 9 July 1835 4th Viscount Lifford (*qv*) and *d* 13 March 1850

2 Millicent; *m* 28 May 1842 Henry Bence-Jones, FRS, MD, DCL, of Brook St, Mayfair, and *d* 29 Aug 1887, having had issue. He *d* 20 April 1873

The 1st EARL *d* 27 March 1849; his only son,

ARCHIBALD ACHESON, **3rd Earl of Gosford**, KP (1855); *b* 20 Aug 1806; *educ* Ch Ch Oxford; MP (Lib) Co Armagh 1830–47, Ld Lt Co Armagh Feb-June 1864, Hon Col Armagh Militia, *cr* 18 Sept 1847 BARON ACHESON OF CLANCAIRNEY, Co Armagh (UK); *m* 22 June 1832 Lady Theodosia Brabazon (*d* 13 Feb 1876), only dau of 10th Earl of Meath (*qv*), and had, with other issue:

1 ARCHIBALD BRABAZON SPARROW, **4th Earl**

2 Edward Archibald Brabazon; Maj-Gen Coldstream Gds, Egypt 1882: Mahuta, Battle of Tel-el-Kebir (medal and clasp and bronze star); *b* 22 May 1844; *m* 1869 Clementina (*d* 30 April 1929), dau of Gen Sir John Gaspard Le Marchant, GCSI, KCB, and *d* 3 July 1921, leaving issue:

(1) Theodosia Margaret Hilda; *b* 5 Feb 1870; *m* 7 Dec 1898 Lancelot Squarey, s of Andrew Tucker Squarey, and *d* 14 May 1954, leaving issue. He *d* 18 Dec 1928

(2) Edith Maude; *b* 2 March 1871; *d* unm 1 Oct 1960

(3) Norah Sybelle; *b* 1874; *m* 7 Nov 1894 Frank Ramsden (*see* RAMSDEN, Bt) and *dsp* 24 Feb 1957

(4) Gladys; *b* 5 Dec 1875; *d* unm 13 July 1975

1 Gertrude Emily; *m* 20 Feb 1856 Francis John Salvile Foljambe, PC, of Osberton, Notts, and Aldwarke, Yorks, MP Notts, and *d* 17 Dec 1927, leaving issue. He *d* 5 Feb 1917

2 Mary; *m* 27 Feb 1862 Hon Leopold William Henry Fox-Powys, 2nd s of 3rd Baron Lilford (*qv*), and *d* 30 Jan 1892, leaving issue

3 Katharine; *m* 28 July 1868 Capt Frederick William Duncombe (*see* FEVERSHAM, B) and *d* 5 March 1898, leaving issue

The 3rd EARL *d* 15 June 1864; his er son,

ARCHIBALD BRABAZON SPARROW ACHESON, **4th Earl of Gosford**, KP (1869); *b* 19 Aug 1841; *educ* Harrow; Ld Lt Co Armagh 1882, V-Adml Ulster, Kt Grand Cross Dannebrog, Redeemer Greece, White Eagle Russia, Ld Bedchamber to HRH THE PRINCE OF WALES 1886–1901, V-Chamberlain to HM QUEEN ALEXANDRA 1901–22, Hon Col 3rd Bn Roy Irish Fus; *m* 10 Aug 1876 Lady Louisa Montagu, DBE (1920), DGStJ, Ldy Bedchamber to HM QUEEN ALEXANDRA (*d* 3 March 1944), 2nd dau of 7th Duke of Manchester (*qv*), and had issue:

1 ARCHIBALD CHARLES MONTAGU BRABAZON, **5th Earl**

2 Patrick George Edward Cavendish, DSO (1915), MVO (1904); Capt RN WW I, cmded Br Naval Flotilla Rhine 1919–21, Russian Order St Stanislaus 2nd Cl with swords, Croix de Guerre; *b* 30 June 1883; *m* 24 Dec 1915 Norah (*d* 18 Sept 1970), dau of Alfred Jones, of Halifax, Nova Scotia, and *d* 30 Aug 1957, having had:

(1) Nicholas Archibald Edward Patrick; Lt RN WW II; *b* 23 May 1917; *ka* Crete 29 May 1941

(2) Michael Ernest Brabazon; Sub-Lt RN (Fleet Air Arm) WW II; *b* 17 Dec 1923; *kas* in a flying accident 4 Oct 1944

(1) *(Blanche) Theodosia [Mrs Oliver Moore, Dash Hayes, Kington Magna, Dorset]; *b* 17 Dec 1923; *m* 28 Oct 1950 *Cdr Oliver Russell Moore, RN (ret), yst s of Arthur Montague Moore, of Holnest Park House, Holnest, Dorset, and has issue:

1a *Susan Theodosia; *b* 27 June 1952; *m* 1990 *Christopher Aston Maltin and has issue:

1b *Arthur Patrick Aston; *b* 1991

1b *Alice Mary Theodosia; *b* 1992

2a *Victoria Caroline; *b* 10 Nov 1954; *m* 1989 *Francis William Orlando Bridgeman-Sutton and has issue:

1b *Charles Frederick Orlando; *b* 1994

1b *Katharine Althea Acheson; *b* 1992

3a *Patricia Alexandra; *b* 19 July 1956; *m* 1985 *David Phillip Dowling Styles and has:
1b *Oliver Michael Dowling; *b* 1987
2b *Henry David Dowling; *b* 1989
1 Alexandra Louise Elizabeth (HM QUEEN ALEXANDRA stood sponsor); *m* 17 June 1905 Lt-Col Hon Frederick William Stanley, DSO, 10th Roy Hus, 8th s of 16th Earl of Derby (*qv*), and *d* 21 Jan 1958, leaving issue
2 Mary; *m* 24 July 1906 Hon Robert Arthur Ward, OBE, s of 1st Earl of Dudley (*qv*), and had issue
3 Theodosia Louisa Augusta; *m* 3 Aug 1912 Sir Alexander George Montagu Cadogan, OM, GCMG, KCB, PC, s of 5th Earl Cadogan (*qv*), and *d* 16 Oct 1977, leaving issue

The 4th EARL *d* 11 April 1922; his er son,

ARCHIBALD CHARLES MONTAGU BRABAZON ACHESON, **5th Earl of Gosford**, MC, DL (Co Armagh); Lt-Col Coldstream Gds, AAG War Office 1918, KGStJ, Boer War 1899–1901 (wounded Modder River, medal with five clasps), WW I (wounded twice, despatches, two brevets, Croix de Guerre); *b* 26 May 1877; *m* 1st 21 June 1910 (*divorce* 1928) Mildred (*d* 7 Sept 1965), only dau of John Ridgely Carter, US Minister Bucharest, and had issue:
1 ARCHIBALD ALEXANDER JOHN STANLEY, **6th Earl**
2 +PATRICK BERNARD VICTOR MONTAGU [The Hon Patrick Acheson, 207 Cornwall St N W, Leesburg, VA 22075, USA]; *b* 4 Feb 1915 (HRH PRINCESS VICTORIA stood sponsor); heir presumptive; *educ* Harrow, Trin Coll Cambridge (BA 1937) and Harvard (MBA 1939); *m* 21 Dec 1946 *Judith Bate, dau of Earle P Gillette, of Minneapolis, and Mrs F B Bate, of Waterford, Va., and has issue:
(1) +Nicholas Hope Carter; *b* 29 Oct 1947; *educ* Middlesex Sch, U of Virginia (BA 1969) and George Washington U (MBA 1971); *m* 1983 *Patricia, dau of James Beckford, of Jacksonville Beach, Fla., and has issue:
1a +Eric James Patrick; *b* 1988
1a *Kelly Lauren; *b* 1987
(2) +Christopher; *b* 23 Feb 1950; *educ* Milton Acad, U of Virginia (BA 1971) and Golden Gate U (MBA 1973); *m* 1977 *Sheryl, dau of Carl Benson, of Columbus, Ga., and has issue:
1a +Kendall Bate; *b* 1984
1a *Karen Erica; *b* 1982
(3) +John Alexander Simon; *b* 11 Sept 1957; *m* 1st 1982 (*divorce* 1985) Cara, dau of Ernest Kulik, of Purcellville, Va.; *m* 2nd 1988 *Lisa Kimberley Bickerstaff, dau of Carl Benson, of Columbus, Ga., and by her has:
1a *Katharine Genevieve; *b* 1988
2a *Emma Mary Camilla; *b* 1991
(1) *Alexandra Sarah Camilla; *b* 27 Feb 1962; *educ* Duke U NC (BA 1984); *m* 9 Nov 1991 *David England
(2) *Caroline Mary Patricia [Mrs David Seward, 2 Temperley Rd, London SW12 8QH]; *b* 27 Feb 1962; *educ* U of Virginia (BA 1984); *m* 6 Oct 1990 *David L'Estrange Seward, s of Peter L'Estrange Seward, and has:
1a *Camilla Nicola Elizabeth; *b* 11 April 1996
1 Patricia; *d* in infancy Aug 1913
2 Camilla Mildred Nicola; *m* 1st 25 Nov 1937 (*divorce* 1949) Freiherr Hans Christoph Schenk von Stauffenberg, s of Freiherr Schenk von Stauffenberg, and has:
(1) *John Sebastian Rudolph Hubertus Maria; *b* 10 June 1940
(2) *John Patrick Nicholas Frederic Hubertus Maria; *b* 3 Dec 1941
(3) *Damian Ignaz Carl; *b* 17 Feb 1944
2 (cont.) Freifrau Camilla Schenk von Stauffenberg *m* 2nd 20 June 1950 *Freiherr Axel von dem Bussche-Streithorst, and *d* 19–, leaving by him:
(1) *Nicola Georgina Mildred [Nicola Dietzsch-Doertenbach, Schlossstrasse 18, 7102 Lehrensteinsfeld, Germany]; *b* 21 March 1951; m 19– *— Dietzsch-Doertenbach
(2) *Jane Olivia; *b* 14 June 1955
3 Mary Virginia Shirley; *b* 1919; *m* 12 Dec 1941 Fernando Corcuera (*d* 1978), s of Pedro L Corcuera y Palomar, of Mexico City, and *d* 1996, leaving:
(1) *Juan Fernando Pedro; *b* 21 July 1948; *m* 1971 *Paloma Gonzalez and has:
1a *Fernando; *b* 1971
1a *Carmen; *b* 1974
2a *Camilla; *b* 1979
(2) *Jaime Marcos Pedro; *b* 12 Jan 1955; *m* 1983 *HI&RH ARCHDUCHESS MYRIAM ADELHAID HUGOLINE OMNES SANCTI MARCUS d'AVIANO MELCHIORA OF AUSTRIA, 3rd dau of HI&RH ARCHDUKE FELIX OF AUSTRIA, and has issue:
1a *Karl Sebastian; *b* 1984
2a *Pedro Johannes; *b* 1985
3a *Felipe; *b* 1987
4a *Andres; *b* 1988
1 Fernanda Mary; *b* 1 Oct 1942; *m* 1967 (*divorce* 1973) Manuel Valles and *d* 1992, leaving issue:
(1) *Fernanda; *b* 1967
2 *Monica Ana; *b* 16 June 1944; *m* 1970 *Harry Troop and has issue:
(1) *Ana Monica; *b* 1971
(2) *Isabel Gabriela; *b* 1972
(3) *Maria; *b* 1976
3 *Marisol Manuela; *b* 9 Aug 1946; *m* 1977 (*divorce* 1983) Luis Padilla and has:
(1) *Jimena; *b* 1977
(2) *Natalia; *b* 1979

The **5th Earl** *m* 2nd 1 Oct 1928 Beatrice (*d* 1967), formerly w of Robert P Breese, of New York, and dau of Arthur Clafin, of Southampton, NY, and *d* 20 March 1954

His er son,

ARCHIBALD ALEXANDER JOHN STANLEY ACHESON, **6th Earl of Gosford**; *b* 14 Jan 1911 (HM QUEEN ALEXANDRA stood sponsor); *educ* Harrow and Trin Coll Cambridge (BA, LLB 1932, MA 1946); G/Capt RAF WW II cmdg 613 Sqdn and 32 Wing, Assist Air Attaché, Paris 1938–40, Parly Sec MOD 1956–47, Parly U-Sec For Affs 1957–58, Ld in Waiting (Govt Whip) 1958–59, Memb Cncl Roy Br Olympic Assoc 1954, V-Pres RAF Assoc, Chm Br Rd Fedn, FRSA, Offr Legn Hon, Bronze Star USA; *m* 1st 14 Dec 1935 (*divorce* 1960) Francesca Augusta Maria, er dau of Francesco Cagiati, of Rome, and had issue:
1 CHARLES DAVID ALEXANDER JOHN SPARROW ACHESON, **7th and present Earl of Gosford**
1 (Francesca Georgina) Caroline; *b* 23 April 1940; *m* 15 Sept 1967 David Wallace Fleming (*d* Dec 1991), s of Wallace Fleming, of Santa Barbara, and *d* August 1991, leaving issue:
(1) *Alexander Montagu Acheson; *b* 5 Nov 1968
2 *Isabella Augusta [Mrs Tevita Maka, PO Box 1234, Nuku A'Lofa, Tonga, S Pacific]; *b* 17 Jan 1950; does not use courtesy title; *m* 1979 *Tevita T Maka and has:
(1) *Charles Nicholas; *b* 1980
(2) *Toby Manu; *b* 1985
(3) *James Alipate; *b* 1989

The **6th Earl** *m* 2nd 21 Sept 1960 *Cynthia Margaret [The Rt Hon The Dowager Countess of Gosford, Pine Cottage, Camberley, Surrey GU15 2DE], widow of Maj James Pringle Delius and dau of Capt Henry Cave West, MC, RHA, and *d* 17 Feb 1966

GOUGH

Arms: Quarterly, 1st and 4th, gu. on a mount vert a lion passant-guardant or, supporting with its dexter paw the Union flag flowing to the sinister ppr., and over the same in chief the words 'China', 'India', in letters of gold; 2nd and 3rd, az. on a fess arg. between three boar's heads couped or a lion passant gu.; in the centre chief point, pendant from a riband arg., fimbriated az., a representation of the badge of the Spanish Order of Charles III ppr., and on a chief a representation of the east wall of the fortress of Tarifa with a breach between two turrets, the dexter turret surmounted by the British flag flying, all ppr. **Crests:** 1 (centre) A boar's head, couped or, 2 (dexter) On a mural crown arg. a lion passant-guardant or, holding in the dexter paw two flag-staves in bend sinister ppr., one, the Union flag of Great Britain and Ireland, surmounting the other, the staff thereof broken, with a triangular banner flowing therefrom to represent a Chinese flag, having thereon a dragon, and in an escroll above the word 'China', 3 (sinister) A dexter arm embowed in facings of the 87th Regt (gu. faced vert), the hand grasping the colour of the said regiment displayed, and a representation of a French eagle, reversed and depressed, the staff broken ppr., in an escroll above the word 'Barossa'. **Supporters:** Dexter, a lion regardant or, gorged with an eastern crown gu., with chain reflexed over the back gold, the rim of the crown inscribed 'Punjab' in letters also gold; sinister, a Chinese dragon or, gorged with a mural crown sa., inscribed with the word 'China' and chained gold. **Mottoes:** Over the centre (family) crest '*Faugh a Ballagh*' ('Clear the way'); under the arms 'Goojerat'.
Creations: Bt. (UK) 23 Dec 1842, B. (UK) 25 April 1846, V. (UK) 15 June 1849.

THE 5TH VISCOUNT GOUGH OF GOOJERAT in the Punjab **AND OF** the city of **LIMERICK**, **Baron Gough of ChinKangFoo** in China **and of Maharajpore and the Sutlej** in the East Indies, and a **Baronet** (Sir Shane Hugh Maryon Gough, Bt) [The Rt Hon The Viscount Gough, Keppoch House, Strathpeffer, Ross-shire IV14 9AD; 17 Stanhope Gardens, London SW7 5RQ]; *b* 26 Aug 1941; *s* f 1951; *educ* Abberley Hall Worcs and Winchester; Lt Irish Gds, commissioned 1962, ret 1967, memb Roy Co Archers, memb Exec Ctee Standing Cncl Btage, local dir Centl London Bd Roy Insur, Tstee Gardner's Trust for the Blind and Schizophrenia Research, memb exec cncl RNIB and Scottish Lifeboat Cncl RNLI, FRGS

Lineage: JOHN GOUGH, of Cricklade later Stratford, Wilts; *d* between 20 May 1562 and 15 Jan 1563, leaving, with five other sons and a dau:

Rev HUGH GOUGH; Rector All Cannings, Wilts; MA Oxon; *m* Jane Clifford, of Clifford, and was *bur* 7 Aug 1625, having had:

1 Robert (Rev); chanter Limerick Cathedral, Archdeacon Ardfert; *b* 1584; *m* Sabina — and had issue

2 William, of Broomfield, Essex; *b* 1586; *m* Alicia, dau of Christopher Hanworth, and had issue

3 Michael, of All Cannings; had issue

4 Jeremy, of Benegar, Wilts; had issue

5 Francis, JP Co Limerick; MA Oxon; Bp Limerick; *b* 1594; *m* Elizabeth Greene and had issue

6 Edmund (Rev); Rector Gt Cheverell, Wilts, MA Oxon, Canon Salisbury; *b* 1595; *m* Margery, dau of Richard Freeman, of Henley, and had issue

7 HUGH

1 Judith; *m* John Bennett

2 Cicely; *m* Rev John Atkins and had issue

3 Katherine; *m* Rev Roger Flower

4 Elizabeth; *m* John Willis, MA

The 7th son,

Rev HUGH GOUGH, JP Co Limerick; MA Oxon, Preb and Chllr Limerick 1626, Rector Rathkeale, Co Limerick; *b* 1599; *m* Ellinor Bolton and *d* after 13 May 1682, leaving, with two daus (Frances, *m* Francis Livelis; Jane, *m* Rev Ezekiel Webb, Dean Limerick):

GEORGE GOUGH, of Rathkeale; *m* Jane, dau of James Roberts, of Ballymalan, Co Cork, and had, with another s (George, of Richmond, Surrey, *d* 1742) and dau (Anne, *m* Richard Lloyd, of Killodromin, Co Limerick):

Rev HUGH GOUGH; Rector Kilfinny; *educ* Trin Coll Dublin (MA 1688); *m* Dorothy Harrison and *d* between 17 Jan and 12 Aug 1730, leaving:

HUGH GOUGH; Cornet of Horse; *m* 1 Jan 1720 Alice, dau of John Miller, of Ballicasey, Co Clare, and had an est s:

GEORGE GOUGH, of Woodstown, Co Limerick; *b* 1720; *m* 1748 Elizabeth (*d* 17 Dec 1783), dau of Richard Waller, of Castle Waller, Co Tipperary, and *d* 19 Nov 1783, leaving an est s:

GEORGE GOUGH, of Woodstown; Lt-Col Limerick Militia; *b* 1750; *m* 20 Jan 1755 Letitia (*d* 1829), dau of Thomas Banbury, of Lisnevagh and Moyle, Co Carlow, and *d* March 1836, having had:

1 George; Maj 28th Regt; *b* 26 Dec 1775; *m* 1811 Sarah (*d* 14 Feb 1870), dau of Edward Croker, of Ballynagarde, and *d* 13 June 1841, leaving issue

2 Thomas Bunbury (Very Rev); Dean Derry; *b* 13 June 1777; *m* 19 March 1800 Charlotte (*d* 14 Feb 1862), 2nd dau of John Bloomfield and sister of 1st Baron Bloomfield of Oakhampton and Redwood, and *d* 8 May 1860, leaving issue

3 William; Maj 68th Regt Peninsular War Battles Salamanca and Vittoria (severely wounded); lost off Kinsale Head 1822

4 HUGH, **1st Viscount**

1 Jane; *m* Lt-Col R Lloyd and *d* Aug 1833. He was *k* Bayonne 1813

2 Elizabeth; *m* 22 March 1810 Benjamin Frend, of Boskell, Co Limerick, and had issue (*see* RANFURLY, E). He *d* Jan 1858

The 4th son,

Sir Hugh Gough, 1st Bt, of Synone and Drangan, Co Tipperary, so *cr* 23 Dec 1842, as also 15 June 1849 **1st Viscount Gough of Goojerat**, in the Punjab **and of** the city of **Limerick**, as also earlier 25 April 1846 BARON GOUGH OF CHINKANGFOO in China AND OF MAHARAJPORE AND THE SUTLEJ in the East Indies (all UK), KP (1857), GCSI (1866, KCSI 1861), KCB (1831, CB 1815), PC (1859); *b* 3 Nov 1779; Ensign 1794, Lt 78th Highrs 1795, Maj 87th Foot (then Prince of Wales's Irish Regt), cmdg at Talavera 1809 (severely wounded, Brevet Lt-Col), Barossa 5 March 1811, Tarifa (where defended against 10,000 French, winning him the honourable augmentation to his arms of a chief containing a representation of the breach; *see* above under **Arms**) 31 Oct 1811, Vittoria 21 June 1813 (severely wounded) and Nivelle 19 Nov 1813, ktd 1815, Col 1819, Maj-Gen 1830, Col 99th Foot 1839–41 and 87th Foot 1841–55, Lt-Gen 1841, as cdr China captured native forts defending Canton, also the city of Chin-keang-foo (hence wording of his Barony), C-in-C: Madras 1841–43, India 1843–49 (beat Mahrattas at Battles of Mahajpoor 29 Dec 1843, hence its featuring in wording of his Barony, and Sikhs (1st Sikh War) at Moodkee 18 Dec 1845, Ferozshahr 21–22 Dec 1845 and Sobraon 10 Feb 1846, also in 2nd Sikh War, following a draw at Chillianwallah 13 Jan 1849, at 21 Feb 1849 at Goojerat, hence its featuring in wording of his Viscountcy), Gen 1854, Col-in-Ch 60th Rifles 1854–69, Col RHG (Blues) 1855–69, FM 1862, Hon Col London Roy Irish Vols; *m* 3 June 1807 Frances Maria (*d* 15 March 1863), dau of Gen Edward Stephens, RA, and had, with another s (*d* young):

1 GEORGE STEPHENS, **2nd Viscount**

1 Letitia Mary; *m* 1836, Edward SUPPLE later COLLIS and *d* 25 Nov 1853, leaving issue

2 Gertrude Sophia; *m* 1837 Archibald Francis Arbuthnot, s of Sir William Arbuthnot, 1st Bt, of Edinburgh (*qv*), and *d* 21 Nov 1882, leaving issue

3 Jane Eliza Mona; *m* 1840 Lt-Col Gregory Haines, HEICS, and *d* 6 April 1898, leaving issue. He *d* 1874

4 Frances Maria; *m* 17 Sept 1844 FM Sir Patrick Grant, GCB, GCMG, and *d* 20 Jan 1892, leaving issue. He *d* March 1895

The 1st VISCOUNT *d* 2 March 1869; his only surv s,

GEORGE STEPHENS GOUGH, **2nd Viscount Gough of Goojerat and of Limerick**, DL Cos Galway and Tipperary; High Sheriff latter 1858; *b* 1815; FLS, FGS, Capt Gren Gds; *m* 1st 17 Oct 1840 Sarah Elizabeth (*dsp* Aug 1841), 3rd dau of Lt-Col Wray Bury Palliser, JP, of Derryluskan, Co Tipperary, and Comragh, Co Waterford; *m* 2nd 3 June 1846 Jane (*d* 3 Feb 1892), 2nd dau of George Arbuthnot, of Elderslie, Surrey, and by her had issue:

1 HUGH, **3rd Viscount**

2 George Hugh, CB; Col 14th Hus, Priv Sec to C-in-C Army 1897–98, Assist Mil Sec HQ DAAG Curragh 1887–89, BA Cantab; *b* 25 July 1852; *m* 13 March 1884 Hilda Eve (*d* 3 June 1947), yst dau of George Moffatt, MP, of Goodrich Court, Herefs, and *d* Norval's Pont S Africa 29 March 1900, leaving issue:

(1) Guy Vincent Hugh; Capt KRRC WW I; *b* 9 Dec 1887; *educ* Eton and RMC Sandhurst; *m* 8 Sept 1928 Lily Margaret, widow of Maj William Robert Gregory, MC, of Coole Park, Co Galway, and dau of G Graham Parry, of Cheltenham, and *dsp* 26 March 1959

(2) George Patrick; Capt Irish Gds WW I (wounded); *b* 29 March 1889; *d* unm 12 July 1936

(3) Harold Stewart; 2nd Lt KRRC WW I; *b* 5 Sept 1894; *ka* 16 June 1916

(4) Dermot Humphrey; Lt 10th Hus WW I; *b* 28 Dec 1896; *d* unm 7 Oct 1919

(1) Irene Frances Nora; *m* 2 Jan 1912 Col Henry Cecil Lloyd Howard, CB, CMG, DSO, DL, 16th Lancers, of Wigfair, Denbighshire, and *d* 21 Sept 1951. He *d* 24 Jan 1950

(2) Kathleen Mona; *m* 9 Aug 1921 Col Ivan Douglas Guthrie of Guthrie, MC, JP, DL, 10th Hus, and *d* 30 Dec 1963, leaving issue. He *d* 4 July 1964

(3) Hugh Rudolph; Lt Coldstream Gds; *b* 11 Jan 1856; *d* S Africa 19 April 1879

1 Frances Anne Mary; *d* 23 Jan 1855

2 Eleanor Laura Jane; *m* 29 July 1886 Robert Algernon Persse, JP, of Roxborough and Creg Clare, Co Galway, and *d* 21 Feb 1935, leaving issue. He *d* 25 May 1911

The 2nd VISCOUNT *d* 31 May 1895; his est s,

HUGH GOUGH, **3rd Viscount Gough of Goojerat and of Limerick**, KCVO (1904), DL Co Galway; *b* 27 Aug 1849; *educ* Eton and BNC Oxford (MA 1880); Dip Serv: Attaché, Rio 1873, 3rd Sec Madrid 1876, 2nd Sec Athens 1878 and St Petersburg 1885, Sec Legn: Rio 1887–88, Stockholm 1888–94, Sec Embassy: Washington 1894–96, Berlin 1896–1901, Min Res Dresden and Coburg 1901–07; *m* 5 Oct 1889 Lady Georgiana Pakenham (*d* 30 July 1943), er dau of 4th Earl of Longford (*qv*), and *d* 14 Oct 1919, having had:

1 HUGH WILLIAM GOUGH, **4th Viscount Gough of Goojerat and of Limerick**, MC, JP, DL Co Galway, DL Inverness-shire; *b* 22 Feb 1892; *educ* Eton and New Coll Oxford (BA 1913); Lt Irish Gds WW I (wounded, despatches twice, Brevet Maj), Lt-Col 1st Regt Iraq Cav 1922 and 1st Bn Irish Gds 1930–34, ret 1935, cmdg Training Bn Irish Gds and Inverness Burgh Bn HG WW II; *m* 12 Nov 1935 Margaretta Elizabeth (*d* 9 March 1977), only dau of Sir Spencer Maryon-Wilson, 11th Bt (*see* 1970 edn), and *d* 4 Dec 1951, leaving:

(1) SHANE HUGH MARYON GOUGH, **5th and present Viscount Gough of Goojerat and of Limerick**

1 Katharine Nora; *b* 6 Oct 1890; *m* 5 April 1910 Edward Vyse Sturdy, OBE, 3rd s of William Sturdy, of Paxhill, and *d* 21 April 1949, leaving issue. He *d* 18 Aug 1959

2 Hilda Frances; *d* an infant 5 May 1893

GOULD OF POTTERNEWTON

Creation: B. (LP, UK) 1993.

THE BARONESS GOULD OF POTTERNEWTON, of Leeds in West Yorkshire (Joyce Brenda Manson) [The Rt Hon The Baroness Gould of Potternewton, 1/5 Foulser Rd, London SW17 8UE]; *b* 29 Oct 1932; *educ* Roundhay High Sch for Girls and Bradford Tech Coll; dispensing chemist 1952–65; Lab Party: Assist Regnl Organiser 1969–75, Assist Nat Agent and Ch Women's Offr 1975–85, Dir Organisation 1985–93, Govt Whip Ho Lds 1997–; Sec: Nat Jt Ctee of Working Women's Organisations 1975–, Sec Yorks Nat Cncl of Civil Liberties; V-Pres Socialist International of Women 1978–86; Ctee Memb Campaign Against Racial Discrimination; Exec Memb Jt Ctee Against Racism; Memb Home Office Ctee on Electoral Matters; author: *Women and Health* (1979); *m* 1953 *Kevin Gould and has issue:

1 *Jeannette; *b* 1953

Lineage: SOLOMON JOSEPH MANSON; *m* Fanny — and had issue:

JOYCE BRENDA, *cr* a **Baroness**

GOULDING

Arms: Per bend or and arg. a gryphon segreant within an orle of martlets sa. **Crest:** A dexter hand apaumée and couped at the wrist, encircled with a chaplet of oak leaves bendwise and transfixed with an arrow bend sinisterwise, all ppr. **Motto:** *Virtute et valore* ('By strength and valour'). **Creation:** Bt. (UK) 22 Aug 1904.

SIR (WILLIAM) LINGARD WALTER GOULDING, 4TH BT, of Millicent, Co Kildare [Sir Lingard Goulding Bt, Dargle Cottage, Enniskerry, Co Wicklow, Ireland]; *b* 11 July 1940; *s* f 1982; *educ* Winchester and Trin Coll Dublin (BA, HDipEd); headmaster Headfort Prep Sch Co Meath 1977–

Lineage: WILLIAM GOULDING went to Ireland with Cromwell's Army; had, with two yr sons (Oliver, *k* Battle of the Boyne 1690; Richard, *k* Battle of Aughrim 1691):

WILLIAM GOULDING, of the Hollow Blades; *m* 1697 Mary Netterville and had, with a dau (Mary, *m* William Abbott, of Birr, King's Co):

WILLIAM GOULDING; *m* 1728 Sarah Abbott, of Birr, and had:

WILLIAM GOULDING; *m* 1757 Eleanor, dau of Humphrey Palmer, of Rathdowney, Queen's Co, and had an est s:

WILLIAM GOULDING; Lt Roscrea Corps Yeo Cav; *b* 3 April 1761; *m* 1st 14 Feb 1781 Frances, dau of Joshua Smith, of Shinrone, Co Tipperary, and had six sons and three daus (all *d* young or unm, as did the five yst sons); *m* 2nd Jane Carroll and had a child; *m* 3rd 1798 Susanna Franck and had a s (Thomas Frank, *dspm*) and *d* 21 Sept 1824; his est s by his 1st w:

JOSHUA GOULDING, of Birr; *b* 29 May 1788; *m* 1812 Sarah, dau of Humphreys Manders, and *d* 12 May 1826, leaving, with a yr s (Humphreys, *b* 1820, *m* Hannah Haughton and had an only surv dau):

WILLIAM GOULDING, of Summerhill House and Ballyrusheen, Co Cork, JP, DL Co Cork; MP Cork 1876–80; *b* 15 Nov 1817; *m* 1st Susan Smallman and had:

1 Mariane; *m* Alfred A Stokes and had issue

WILLIAM GOULDING *m* 2nd April 1855 Maria Heath (*d* 16 Sept 1892), dau of Edward Manders, of Dublin, by Ann, dau of Richard Manders, of Brackenstown, Swords, Co Dublin, and *d* 8 Dec 1884, having had, with other issue:

1 WILLIAM JOSHUA (Sir), **1st Bt**

2 Sir EDWARD ('PADDY') ALFRED GOULDING, 1st and last Bt, so *cr* 25 June 1915, as also 22 Nov 1922 BARON WARGRAVE, of Wargrave, Co Berks (both UK), PC (1918), JP London, Berks and Oxon, DL Co Cork; *b* 5 Nov 1862; *educ* St John's Coll Cambridge (MA); barrister Inner Temple 1887, memb LCC for Hammersmith 1895–1901, MP (C) E Wilts 1895–1906 and (U) Worcester 1908–22, chm Rolls-Royce Ltd; *dsp* 17 July 1936, when his titles expired

The er son,

Sir William Joshua Goulding, 1st Bt (UK), so *cr* 22 Aug 1904, PC (1917), JP, DL; chm W & H M Goulding, Property Losses (Ireland) and Gt S and W Rlwy of Ireland, dir National Bank, dep chm Fishguard Clearing House, memb Irish Convention 1917–18; *b* 7 March 1856; *m* 23 Feb 1881 Ada (*d* 6 March 1934), dau of Charles Lingard Stokes, of Pauntley, Worcs, and had issue:

1 WILLIAM LINGARD AMPHLETT (Sir), **2nd Bt**

1 Eileen; *m* 28 Sept 1904 Hugh Arthur Henry, JP, Maj Roy Dublin Fus, and *d* 24 May 1970 leaving issue He *d* 20 June 1947

2 Ada Gladys; *m* 9 Feb 1915 S/Ldr Kenneth Blair Harbord, s of Rev Harry Harbord, MA, of Colwood Park, Bolney, Sussex, and had a s and dau. He *d* 25 Oct 1959

3 Kathleen; *m* 21 Sept 1912 Capt Maurice Falkiner Dennis, Seaforth Highrs, s of Meade Caulfeild Dennis, of Fort Granite. He *d* 26 Dec 1960

4 Ida; *m* 9 Dec 1915 Col Thomas Wykeham Pragnell, DSO, 4th Hus, of Red House, Shiplake, Oxon, and *d* 20 Oct 1932, leaving a s and dau

The 1st Bt *d* 12 July 1925; his son,

Sir William Lingard Amphlett Goulding, 2nd Bt; *b* 4 Oct 1883; Capt 4th Bn Roy Irish Fus, Lt S Irish Horse, chm W & H M Goulding and GN Rlwy Co of Ireland, Govr Bank Ireland, dir E and J Burke Ltd, Imperial Smelting Corp and Metropolitan Vickers Electrical Co; *m* 20 June 1908 Nesta Violet (*m* 2nd 14 Feb 1939 Stanley John Adams; *d* 7 Dec 1968), 2nd dau of George Wright, Justice King's Bench Ireland, and gdau of Sir Croker Barrington, 4th Bt (*qv*), and had issue:

1 (WILLIAM) BASIL (Sir), **3rd Bt**

2 +Ossian; *b* 1 Jan 1913; *educ* Winchester and Ch Ch Oxford; *m* 1st 9 July 1936 (*divorce* 1943) Felice Martell, dau of — Darling, of Montreal, and has issue:

(1) *Lynn; *b* 31 March 1937; *m* 1st 6 Jan 1958 Lt Richard Edgeson Cathcart, RN, s of Percival John Cathcart; *m* 2nd 20 Jan 1966 *Ken Irwin

2 (cont.) Ossian Goulding *m* 2nd 19 Dec 1943 (*divorce* 1962) Yasuko Elisabeth Katherine, dau of Lennart Tham, of Husqvarna, Sweden; *m* 3rd 20 Aug 1962 Margaret Angela (*d* 1988), dau of Frank Chadwick, and by his 2nd w has:

(1) +George Michael Richard; *b* 24 Dec 1951; *m* 1979 *Hon Caroline Laurence Patricia Cavendish, er dau of 7th Baron Waterpark (*qv*), and has issue:

1a +William Roderick Ossian; *b* 12 Aug 1983

1a *Laura Yasuko Danielle; *b* 1986

(2) *Carola Nesta Katherine; *b* 16 Feb 1946

(3) *Sara Elizabeth Louise; *b* 1947

The 2nd Bt *d* 20 June 1935; his er s,

Sir William Basil Goulding, 3rd Bt; *b* 4 Nov 1909; W/Cdr RAFVR WW II, chm W & H M Goulding, dir: RTZ, Nat Bank Ireland, Bank Ireland, Hibernian Insur, Johnston Mooney & O'Brien; *m* 28 Aug 1939 *Valerie Hamilton Monckton [The Hon Lady Goulding, Dargle Cottage, Enniskerry, Co Wicklow, Ireland], only dau of 1st Viscount Monckton of Brenchley (*qv*), and *d* 1982, leaving:

1 Sir (WILLIAM) LINGARD WALTER GOULDING **4th and present Bt**

2 +TIMOTHY ADAM; *b* 15 May 1945; heir presumptive; *educ* Winchester; *m* 1971 *Patricia Moran, of Dublin

3 +Hamilton Paddy; *b* 23 June 1947; *educ* Winchester and Trin Coll Dublin; First Offr Aer Lingus; *m* 16 Dec 1970 *Yvonne Denise, er dau of S V Holmes Thompson, of Co Antrim

GOWRIE

Arms: Paly of six argent and gules. **Crest:** A ram's head couped sable, armed or. **Supporters:** Two goats sable, armed unguled and ducally gorged or, with chains also or reflexed over the back. **Motto:** *Deid schaw* ('Deeds show'). **Creations:** B. (UK) 28 Oct 1919 (Ruthven of Gowrie) and 20 Dec 1935 (Gowrie of Canberra), V. (UK) 8 Jan 1945, E. (UK) 8 Jan 1945.

THE 2ND EARL OF GOWRIE, Viscount Ruthven of Canberra, of Dirleton, E Lothian, **Baron Ruthven of Gowrie**, Perth, and **Baron Gowrie of Canberra**, Commonwealth of Australia and of Dirleton, E Lothian ((Alexander Patrick) Greysteil (Grey) Ruthven, PC (1983)) [The Rt Hon The Earl of Gowrie PC, 34 King St, Covent Gdn, London WC2]; *b* 26 Nov 1939; *s* gf in Earldom 1955 and great-uncle in Barony of Ruthven of Gowrie 1956; officially recognised in the Name of Ruthven by Lord Lyon King of Arms 1957; *educ* Eton, Balliol Coll Oxford and Harvard; Ld-in-Waiting (Govt Whip) 1972–74, Oppn Spokesman Ec Affrs 1974–79, Min State Employment 1979–81, NI 1981–83, Min Arts 1983–85, Chllr Duchy Lancaster 1984–85; Provost RCA 1985–, Chm: Sotheby's 1987–93, Devpt Securities Jan-Dec 1995 and by 1997 and Arts Cncl 1994–98, memb Bd Good Industrial Relations, author: *The Genius of British Painting*; *m* 1st 21 Dec 1962 (*divorce* 1974) Alexandra (*m* 2nd April 1978 Jeremy Hardie, son of Sir Charles Hardie), only dau of Col Robert Albert Glanville Bingley, CVO, DSO, OBE, of Higher Eggbeer, Exeter, Devon, by Mary Olivia, only dau of Lt-Col Hubert Maxwell Lennox-Conyngham, DSO, AVC, and has issue:

1 +(PATRICK LEO) BRER, *Viscount Ruthven of Canberra*; *b* 4 Feb 1964; ops dir Camphor Ltd; *m* 1990 *Julie Goldsmith and has issue:

(1) +Heathcote Patrick Cornelius Hore; *b* 28 May 1990

The 3rd EARL *m* 2nd 15 Nov 1974 *Countess Adelheid, yst dau of Gen Count Fritz-Dietlof von der Schulenburg, of Munich

Lineage: WALTER JAMES HORE later HORE-RUTHVEN (1853), **1st Baron Ruthven of Gowrie**, of Gowrie (UK), so *cr* 28 Oct 1919, and 9th LORD RUTHVEN OF FREELAND (*see* CARLISLE, E); had a 2nd s:

ALEXANDER GORE ARKWRIGHT HORE-RUTHVEN, **1st Earl of Gowrie**, so *cr* 8 Jan 1945, as also VISCOUNT RUTHVEN OF CANBERRA, as also earlier 20 Dec

1935 BARON GOWRIE, of Canberra, Australia, and of Dirleton, Co of East Lothian (all UK), VC (1898), GCMG (1935, KCMG 1928, CMG 1918), CB (1919), DSO (1916) and bar (1919), PC (1937); *b* 6 July 1872; *educ* Eton; served 3rd Bn HLI 1891, Egyptian Army, Sudan 1898 (despatches, medal with clasp, 4th Cl Osmanieh), White Nile 1899 (despatches, two clasps), Somaliland 1903–04 (medal, two clasps), Col and Hon Brig-Gen Welsh Gds WW I (severely wounded), Croix de Guerre France and Belgium, KGStJ, cmded 1st Gds Bde Aldershot 1925–28, Govr S Australia 1928–34 and NSW 1935–36, Govr-Gen Australia 1936–44, Col Welsh Gds, Lt-Govr and Dep Constable Windsor Castle 1945–52, Pres Empire Day Movements 1945–55, Pres MCC 1948, Hon DCL Oxford, Hon LLD Edin; *m* 1 June 1908 Zara Eileen, OStJ (*d* 19 July 1965), est dau of John Pollock, DL, of Lismany, Co Galway, and *d* 2 May 1955, having had issue:

1 (Alexander Hardinge) Patrick; *b* 30 Aug 1913; *educ* Magdalene Coll Cambridge (BA); T/Maj Rifle Bde (attd SAS) WW II 1939–42; *m* 5 Jan 1939 *Pamela Margaret, Extra Woman of the Bedchamber to HM QUEEN ELIZABETH THE QUEEN MOTHER 1948–51 (granted rank of w of earl's est son while widow June 1945; *m* 2nd 30 July 1952 Maj (George) Derek Cooper, OBE, MC, Life Gds, s of Capt George Stanley Cooper), 2nd dau of Rev Arthur Henry Fletcher, MA, of Chelsea, and *d* 24 Dec 1942 of wounds recd leading a commando raid Tripoli, leaving:

(1) (ALEXANDER PATRICK) GREY(STEIL) RUTHVEN, **2nd and present Earl of Gowrie**

(2) +Malise Walter Maitland Knox [The Hon Malise Ruthven, c/o Chatto and Windus, 30 Bedford Sq, London WC2]; *b* 14 May 1942; *educ* Eton and Trin Coll Cambridge; author: *Islam in the World* (1984), *The Divine Supermarket* (1989); *m* 1967 *Ianthe, dau of Cdr (Robert) Hugh Hodgkinson, and has:

1a *Chloe; *b* 1969

2a *Oonagh Orlanda; *b* 1970

2 Alistair Malise; *b* 2 Aug 1917; *d* an infant

GRAAFF

Arms: Argent, a paschal lamb proper, on a chief azure five stars of the first (representing the Southern Cross). **Crest:** A dexter arm embowed in armour, the hand holding a scimitar, in front of three spades, erect in pale, all proper. **Supporters:** Dexter, a Boer farmer supporting with the exterior hand a rifle; sinister, a miner supporting with the exterior hand a pick-axe, all proper. **Motto:** *Justis creator favet* ('A just creator favours [me]'). **Creation:** Bt. (UK) 6 Feb 1911.

SIR DE VILLIERS GRAAFF, 2ND BT, of Cape Town, in the Cape of Good Hope, Province of the Union of S Africa, MBE (1947) [Sir De Villiers Graaff Bt MBE, De Grendel, Private Bag GPO, Cape Town 8000, S Africa]; *b* 8 Dec 1913; *s f* 1931; *educ* Cape Town U (BA 1932) and Magdalen Coll Oxford (MA 1944, BCL 1936); SA Def Force (POW) WW II, barrister Inner Temple 1937, Advocate Supreme Court S Africa, MP Hottentots Holland in Union Parl 1948–58 and Rondebosch 1958–77, Ldr United Party 1956, Ldr Opposition 1957; *m* 20 April 1939 *Helena le Roux, er dau of Frederick Carol Marthinus Voight, Prov Sec Cape Province, and has issue:

1 +DAVID DE VILLIERS [David Graaff Esq, Box 1, Hex River, CP, S Africa]; *b* 3 May 1940; *educ* Diocesan Coll S Africa, Stellenbosch U (BSc Ag 1961), Grenoble U and Magdalen Coll Oxford (BA 1964); *m* 1969 *Sally, dau of Robin Williams, and has issue:

(1) +De Villiers; *b* 16 July 1970

(2) +Robert; *b* 1974

(3) +David John; *b* 1977

(1) *Leeza; *b* 1973

2 +Johann Frederick de Villiers; *b* 26 Aug 1946

1 *Genée de Villiers; *b* 28 Nov 1948

Lineage: JOHANNES JACOBUS GRAAFF, of Stellenbosch, Cape of Good Hope, S Africa; *bapt* 18 Aug 1790; *m* 21 March 1813 Johanna Catharina and *d* Dec 1822, leaving:

1 Dirk Johannes; *m* 4 May 1838 Elizabeth Maria Uys

2 Johannes Jacobus; *b* 18 Feb 1816

3 PETRUS NOVBERTUS

1 Elizabeth Maria

The 3rd s,

PETRUS NOVBERTUS GRAAFF, of Villiersdorp; *b* posthumously 15 July 1823; *m* 2 May 1846 Anna Elizabeth de Villiers (*d* 17 Dec 1900) and *d* 2 July 1875, leaving issue:

1 Johannes Jacobus Arnoldus, of Bloemhof, Beach Road, Sea Point, CP; *b* 26 April 1854; *m* 10 June 1879 Rosetta Harriott Grout; *dsp* 5 Feb 1921

2 DAVID PIETER DE VILLIERS (Sir), **1st Bt**

3 Jacobus Arnoldus Combrinck (Sir), KCMG, of Bordeaux, Beach Rd, Sea Point, CP; *b* 4 March 1863; MLC 1903–10, memb Senate Union S Africa 1910–27, Min without portfolio 1913, Min Public Works, Posts and Telegraphs 1920–21; *m* 22 May 1889 Susan Elsabie Maria (*d* 26 Aug 1952), dau of J W Hurten Theunisson, and *d* 5 April 1927, leaving issue:

(1) Johanna Catharina Elizabeth; *b* 13 Dec 1851; *m* 22 April 1897 Pieter Maritz Botha, of Oude Huis, Villiersdorp, CP, and *dsp* 28 July 1930

(2) Anna Elizabeth; *b* 16 Oct 1856; *m* 23 Jan 1882 Roelf Stephanus van der Merwe, of Merwela, Main Road, Sea Point, CP, and *d* 6 June 1926

PETRUS NOVBERTUS GRAAFF's 2nd s,

Sir David Pieter de Villiers Graaff, 1st Bt (UK), so *cr* 6 Feb 1911; *b* 30 March 1859; MLC Cape of Good Hope 1891–99 and 1907–10, Min without portfolio Cape Colony 1908–10, MP Union S Africa 1910–20, Min Public Works, Posts and Telegraphs 1910–12, Min without portfolio 1912–13, High Commr UK 1914, Min Finance 1915–16, Col Cape Garrison Artillery, Mayor Cape Town 1891–92; *m* 5 Feb 1913 Eileen (*d* 21 Oct 1950), dau of Rev J P Van Heerden, DD, LLD, of Cape Town, and *d* 13 April 1931, leaving issue:

1 Sir DE VILLIERS GRAAFF, **2nd and present Bt**

2 David Pieter de Villiers; *b* 7 July 1915; *educ* Cape Town U (BA 1936) and Magdalen Coll Oxford (MA 1938); *dsp*

3 +Johannes de Villiers [Johannes Graaff Esq, Morgenrood Rd, Kenilworth, CP, S Africa]; *b* 19 Feb 1928; *educ* Cape Town U (BA 1946) and Cambridge (PhD) 1950, Fell St John's Coll Cambridge 1951; *m* 30 June 1951 *Lillian Clare, er dau of Sir George Paget Thomson, Master Corpus Christi Coll, Cambridge, and has:

(1) +Pieter Johannes; *b* 4 Feb 1958

(1) *Janet Kathleen; *b* 12 Jan 1954

(2) *Anna Louise; *b* 18 Feb 1955

(3) *Teresa Clare; *b* 18 Feb 1955

(4) *Monica Suzanne; *b* 22 Oct 1960

(5) *Linda Elaine; *b* 15 Oct 1966

GRADE

Arms: Per chevron grady vert and or, in chief two pierced mullets or, and in base a bear's gamb erased sable armed gules. **Crest:** A sinister cubit arm erect, vested vert, cuffed argent, charged with a mask of comedy or, the hand proper holding a balalaika or sound box to the dexter. **Supporters:** Dexter, upon a lightning flash or, a lion proper gorged with a cord, pendant therefrom a representation of itself, all or; sinister, upon a lightning flash or, a horse sable, gorged with a cord, pendant therefrom a representation of itself, all or. **Motto:** *Quod promitto perficio* ('What I promise, I perform'). **Creation:** B. (LP, UK) 1976.

THE BARON GRADE, of Elstree, Co Herts (Sir Lew Grade) [The Rt Hon The Lord Grade, 34 Grosvenor St, London W1X 9FG]; *b* 25 Dec 1906; *educ* Rochelle St Sch London EC2; WW II in RA; chm and md ITC Entertainment 1958–82 (life chm 1995–), pres Associated Television Network Ltd, chm: Stoll Theatres Corp 1973–, Moss Empires 1973–, Bentray Investments Ltd, The Grade Co 1985–; chm and ch exec Associated Television Corp (Internat) 1973–82, Embassy Communications Internat 1982–85, dir Supervisory Bd Euro Disney SCA Paris 1988–; Govr Roy Shakespeare Theatre, ktd 1969, Fell BAFTA 1979, OStJ, KCSS; author: *Still Dancing* (1987); *m* 1942 *Kathleen Sheila, dau of John Moody, and adopted: *Paul Nicholas; *b* 1952; dir Ivy Restaurant, publisher; *m* 1st 19– (*divorce* 19–) Lisa Pearce; *m* 2nd 1986 *Beverly Hill and by his 1st w has:

1 *Daniel; *b* 1978

1 *Georgina Elizabeth Frances; *b* 1980

Lineage: ISAAC WINOGRADSKY, of Odessa; *m* Olga — (*d* 1981) and *d* 1936, leaving:

1 Leslie WINOGRADSKY later GRADE; *m* Winifred — and had:

(1) Michael Ian [Michael Grade Esq, First Leisure Corpn plc, 7 Soho St, London W1V 5FA]; *b* 8 March 1943; *educ* St Dunstan's Coll London; trainee jnlst *Daily Mirror* 1960, sports columnist 1964–66, theatrical agent Grade Orgn 1966, jt md London Management and Representation 1969–73, Dep Controller Programmes LWT 1973 and Dir Programmes 1977–81, Pres Embassy TV 1981–84, Controller BBC1 1984–86; Dir: Programmes BBC TV 1986–87, ITN 1989–93 and First Leisure 1991– (chm 1997–), Delfont Macintosh Theatres 1994–; chm VCI plc 1995–, ch exec Channel 4 1988–97; *m* 1st 1967 (*divorce* 1981) Penelope Jane Levinson and has a s and dau; *m* 2nd 1982 (*divorce* 1991) Hon Sarah Lawson, dau of 5th Baron Burnham (*qv*)

(1) Anita Penny [Mrs Brook Land, c/o Nabarro Nathanson, 50 Stratton St, London WIX 5FL]; *m* 7 Dec 1975 *(Harold) Brook Land, ptnr Nabarro Nathanson, slrs, s of David Land, impresario (co-producer *Evita* etc), and has:

1a *Daniel Edward; *b* 30 April 1983

1a *Lesley Olivia; *b* 19 Jan 1981

2 LEW WINOGRADSKY later GRADE, *cr* a **Baron**

3 BERNARD WINOGRADSKY later DELFONT, BARON DELFONT, of Stepney in Greater London (LP, UK), so *cr* 1976; *b* 5 Sept 1909; chm and ch exec EMI Film and Theatre Corp 1969–80, THF Leisure 1981–82, First Leisure Corp 1983–88 (chm 1988–92, Pres 1992–94); ktd 1974; *m* 1946 Helen Violet Carolyn (*d* 1986), the actress Carole Lynne, dau of Victor Cecil Haymen and formerly w of Derek Farr, actor, and *d* 28 July 1994, leaving:

(1) *David Stephen; *b* 1953; *educ* Millfield; *m* 1981 *Sarah, dau of Peter Edgington, and has:

1a *Joseph; *b* 1983

2a *Alexander; *b* 1985

(1) *Susan Jane; *b* 10 April 1947; *educ* Millfield; photographer (stills) for films and TV; *m* 1982 *Mark Derek Meddings, film special efects technician, and has a s and dau

(1) *Jennifer; *b* 1949; *m* 1974 *Andrew Morse and has two sons

GRAFTON

Arms: Quarterly, 1st and 4th, France and England quarterly; 2nd, Scotland; 3rd, Ireland; the whole debruised by a baton sinister compony of six pieces, arg. and az. (for CHARLES II with a difference for bastardy). **Crest:** On a chapeau gu., doubled erm., a lion statant guardant or, crowned with a ducal coronet az. and gorged with a collar, countercompony arg. and of the fourth. **Supporters:** Dexter, a lion guardant or, crowned with a ducal coronet az. and gorged with a collar countercompony arg. and of the second; sinister, a greyhound arg., gorged as the dexter. **Motto:** *Et decus et pretium recti* ('Both the grace and the prize of rectitude'). **Creations:** E., V. and B (all E) 16 Aug 1672; D. (E) 11 Sept 1675.

THE 11TH DUKE OF GRAFTON in the Co of Northampton, **Earl of Euston, Viscount Ipswich** and **Baron Sudbury of Sudbury** (Sir Hugh Denis Charles FitzRoy, KG (1976), DL (Suffolk 1973)) [His Grace The Duke of Grafton KG DL, Euston Hall, Thetford, Norfolk IP24 2QW]; *b* 3 April 1919; s f 1970; *educ* Oakham, Eton and Magdalene Coll Cambridge; Hereditary Ranger Whittlebury Forest, Northants, late Capt Gren Gds, ADC to Viceroy India 1943–47, V-Chm Tstees Nat Portrait Gallery 1967–92, Tstee: London Museum, Buildings at Risk Tst, Tradescant Tst and Sir John Soane's Museum (chm 1975–), Pres: Suffolk Preservn Soc 1957–, Internat Students House 1972–, E Anglia Tourist Bd 1973–93, memb: Cncl Nat Tst (chm E Anglia Ctee) and Properties Ctee 1981–94, Historic Buildings Cncl for England 1953–84, Historic Bldgs Advsy Ctee 1984–, English Heritage, Roy Fine Art Commn 1971–94, Cathedrals Advsy Ctee 1984–, Centl Cncl Care of Churches and formerly of Min Housing and Local Govt's Advsy Ctee, Chm: Exec Ctee Historic Churches Preservn Tst 1980–97, Architectural Heritage Fund 1976–94, Cathedrals Advsy Commn 1981–91, SPAB to 1989 (Pres thereafter) and Cncl Br Soc Master Glass Painters, Hon Air Cdre No 2623 (E Anglia) Training Sqdn RAAFR 1996–, Hon DCL UEA 1990, Hon FRIBA, FSA; *m* 12 Oct 1946 *(Ann) Fortune, GCVO (1980, DCVO 1970, CVO 1965), JP (London 1949, W Suffolk 1972–90), Ldy of Bedchamber to HM THE QUEEN 1953–66, Mistress Robes 1967–, only dau of Capt (Evan Cadogan) Eric Smith, of Lower Ashfold, Slaugham, Sussex, and has:

1 +JAMES OLIVER CHARLES, *Earl of Euston* [Earl of Euston, 6 Vicarage Gdns, London. W8; The Racing Stables, Euston, Thetford, Norfolk]; *b* 13 Dec 1947 (HM QUEEN ELIZABETH THE QUEEN MOTHER stood sponsor); *educ* Eton and Magdalene Coll Cambridge (BA 1969, MA 1973); Page of Honour to HM THE QUEEN 1962–63, FCA 1973, assist dir J Henry Schroder Wagg & Co 1973–82, exec dir Enskilda Securities 1982–87, dir: Jamestown Investments Ltd 1987, Central Capital Hldgs 1988 and Capel-Cure Myers Capital Management 1988; *m* 16 Sept 1972 *Lady Clare Amabel Margaret Kerr, 3rd dau of 12th Marquess of Lothian (*qv*), and has issue:

(1) +Henry Oliver Charles, *Viscount Ipswich*; *b* 6 April 1978

(1) *Louise Helen Mary; *b* 11 June 1973

(2) *Emily Clare; *b* 6 Dec 1974

(3) *Charlotte Rose; *b* 10 March 1983

2 +Charles Patrick Hugh, *b* 7 Jan 1957; *educ* Eton and Magdalene Coll Cambridge (BA 1978); dir Fine Art Courses Ltd, author: *Italy, a Grand Tour for the Modern Traveller* (1991); *m* 1988 *Diana M, dau of Hubert Miller-Stirling, of Cape Town, S Africa, and has issue:

(1) +Nicholas Augustus Charles; *b* 1991

(1) +George; *b* 1993

1 *Henrietta Fortune Doreen [The Lady Henrietta St George, 1 Chester Sq, London SW1W 9HH; PO Box F2666, Freeport, Grand Bahama, Bahamas]; *b* 14 Sept 1949; *m* 1 Dec 1979 *Edward Gerald Patrick St George, s of Marquis Barbaro St George (*see* 1956 edn Other Titled Nobility of the British Empire section), of Palazzo Armeria, Malta, and has issue:

(1) *Henry Edward Hugh; *b* 22 Sept 1983

(1) *Katherine Helen Cecilia; *b* 26 Nov 1984

2 *Virginia Mary Elizabeth; *b* 10 April 1954 (HM THE QUEEN stood sponsor); *m* 1st 6 Sept 1980 (*divorce* 1987) Lord Ralph William Francis Joseph Kerr, yr s of 12th Marquess of Lothian (*qv*); *m* 2nd 4 Aug 1995 *Roger Babington Hill, er s of Cdr Harold Babington Hill, of East Chiltington, Sussex

3 *(Olivia) Rose Mildred; *b* 1 Aug 1963; *m* 17 March 1995 *(John) Guy Monson (*see* MONSON, B)

Lineage: CHARLES II had a 2nd illegitimate s by Barbara, Duchess of Cleveland (*see* JERSEY, E):

HENRY FitzROY, **1st Duke of Grafton**, Co Northampton, so *cr* 11 Sept 1675, as also earlier 16 Aug 1672 following the first celebration of his marriage (when aged nine) BARON SUDBURY OF SUDBURY, VISCOUNT IPSWICH and EARL OF EUSTON, all Suffolk (all E), with special remainder, failing heirs male of his body to his yr bro (by CHARLES II out of Lady Castlemaine) the Duke of Northumberland, KG (1680); *b* 28 Sept 1663; *m* 1 Aug 1672 and again 6 Nov 1679 Lady Isabella Bennet (*m* 2nd by licence 14 Oct 1698 Sir Thomas Hanmer, 4th Bt (*dsp* 5 May 1746), and *d* 7 Feb 1722/3), only dau and sole heir of Henry Bennet, 1st Earl of Arlington, who was *cr* 14 March 1664/5 BARON ARLINGTON, of Arlington, Middlesex, with special remainder failing male issue to the heirs of his body (*i.e.*, so as to include females), and 22 April 1672 BARON ARLINGTON, of Arlington (modern Harlington), Middlesex, VISCOUNT THETFORD, Norfolk, and EARL OF ARLINGTON with similar special remainder, all of which titles his dau inherited at his death 28 July 1685; V-Adml England 1682–89, Govr IoW 1684–90, Ld High Constable England JAMES II's coronation, Ld Lt Suffolk 1685–89; helped put down the Duke of Monmouth's rising 1685; among the first to abandon his unc JAMES II for the Prince of Orange (WILLIAM III) 1688; distinguished himself at Battle of Beachy Head 1690, when an Anglo-Dutch fleet was defeated by a superior French one, being said by contemporaries to have saved the Dutch contingent, though modern historians emphasise how little and how feebly the English fought compared with the Dutch, and *d* 9 Oct 1690 from wounds sustained in the Siege of Cork during the war between WILLIAM III and JAMES II in Ireland, leaving issue:

CHARLES FitzROY, **2nd Duke of Grafton**, KG (1721), PC (1715); *b* 25 Oct 1683; *s* mother as 3rd EARL OF ARLINGTON etc 7 Feb 1722/3; Ld Lt Suffolk 1705–57, Ld of Bedchamber 1714–17, Ld Chamberlain 1724–57, LLD Cantab 1728, FRS 1749; *m* 30 April 1713 Henrietta (*d* 9 Aug 1726), gdau of 1st Duke of Beaufort (*qv*), and *d* 6 May 1757, having had:

1 Charles Henry, *Earl of Euston*; *b* 13 April 1714; *d* 1715

2 George, *Earl of Euston*; *b* 24 Aug 1715; *m* 23 Sept 1741 Dorothy, est dau of 3rd Earl of Burlington (*see* CORK and ORRERY, E), and *dsp* 7 July 1747

3 Augustus; *b* 16 Oct 1716; Capt RN, cmded the *Orford* Siege of Cartagena Feb 1740/1; *m* Elizabeth (*m* 2nd James Jeffreys and *d* 21 Dec 1788), dau of Col William Cosby, Govr New York (yr s of Alex Cosby, of Stradbally Hall, Queen's Co), and *d* 24 May 1741, leaving:

(1) AUGUSTUS HENRY, **3rd Duke**

(2) CHARLES FitzROY, 1st BARON SOUTHAMPTON (*qv*)

4 Charles; *b* 23 April 1718; *d* 20 July 1739

1 Caroline; *m* 2nd Earl of Harrington (*qv*)

2 Isabella; *m* 1st Marquess of Hertford (*qv*)

3 Harriet; *d* unm Aug 1735

The 2nd DUKE's gs,

AUGUSTUS HENRY FitzROY, **3rd Duke of Grafton**, KG (1769), PC (1765); *b* 28 Sept 1735; *educ* Westminster and Peterhouse Cambridge; MP (Whig) (Bury) St Edmunds 1756–57, Sec State Northern Dept 1765–66, 1st Ld Treasury and in effect PM 1766–70, Ld Privy Seal 1771–75 and 1782–83; *m* 1st 29 Jan 1756 (*divorce* 1769) Hon Anne Liddell (*m* 2nd 2nd Earl of Upper Ossory and *d* 1804), dau and sole heir of 1st and last Baron Ravensworth of the 1747 *cr* (*see* RAVENSWORTH, B), leaving issue:

1 GEORGE HENRY, **4th Duke**

2 Charles; *b* 14 July 1764; Gen; *m* 1st 20 June 1795 Frances (*d* 9 Aug 1797), er dau of Edward Miller-Mundy, of Shipley, Derbys, and had issue:

(1) Charles Augustus (Sir), KCB, KCH; *b* 10 June 1796; Lt-Col, Govr NSW; *m* 1st 11 March 1820 Lady Mary Lennox (*d* 7 Dec 1847), dau of 4th Duke of Richmond and Lennox (*see* RICHMOND and GORDON, D); *m* 2nd 11 Dec 1855 Margaret Gordon, widow of J J Hawkey, of Sydney, NSW, and *d* 16 Feb 1858, having by his 1st w had:

1a Augustus Charles Lennox; *b* 20 Sept 1821; Capt RA; *d* 11 Sept 1855 of wounds recd at Sebastopol

2a George Henry; *b* 13 Sept 1826; *m* 20 April 1865 Eugenia Susannah (*m* 2nd 25 Oct 1879 Col Edward St Aubyn (*see* SAINT LEVAN, B) and *d* 12 March 1886), 2nd dau of David Barclay Chapman, of Roehampton, and *d* 8 July 1868, having had two daus (*d* unm)

3a Arthur George; *b* 20 March 1827; Cdr RN; *d* 9 Jan 1861

1a Mary Caroline; *b* 20 Dec 1823; *m* 9 Aug 1841 Adml Hon Keith Stewart, CB (*d* 15 Sept 1859), and *d* 22 Nov 1895, leaving issue (*see* GALLOWAY, E)

2 (cont.) Gen Lord Charles FitzRoy *m* 2nd 10 March 1799 Lady Frances Anne Stewart (*d* 9 Feb 1810), est dau of 1st Marquess of Londonderry (*qv*), and *d* 20 Dec 1829, leaving by her:

(2) George, of Grafton Regis, Northants; *b* June 1800; Capt 1st Life Gds and Lt-Col Roy Bucks Militia; *m* 1st 6 July 1830 Louisa (*d* 6 Aug 1865), yst dau of John Harris, of Radford, Devon; *m* 2nd 8 Jan 1873 Charlotte Frances Bona (*d* 18 June 1919), dau of Lt-Col Hon George Augustus Spencer (*see* CHURCHILL, V), and *d* 4 Jan 1883, having by his 1st w had, with three daus:

1a George Robert; *b* 4 Oct 1831; Maj-Gen Coldstream Gds; *dsp* 8 Oct 1898

2a Francis; *b* 28 Oct 1832; barrister; *m* 26 June 1866 Mary Nesham (*d* 29 Jan 1933), est dau of Thomas Hillersden Bulteel, and *dsp* 26 Feb 1904

3a Charles Vane; *b* 1836; Capt Rifle Bde; *d* 1 May 1871

(3) Robert; *b* 5 July 1805;V-Adml RN, MP Durham 1841–43; *m* 1st Dec 1836 Mary Henrietta (*d* April 1852), 2nd dau of Maj-Gen Edward James O'Brien, and had, with three daus:

1a Robert O'Brien (Sir), KCB; *b* 2 April 1839; V-Adml, Naval ADC, Osmanieh 3rd Cl; *d* 7 May 1896

(3) (cont.) V-Adml Robert FitzRoy *m* 2nd 22 Feb 1854 his cousin Maria Isabella (*d* 29 Dec 1889), 3rd dau of John Henry Smyth, of Heath Hall, Yorks, and *d* 30 April 1865, leaving by her:

1a Laura Maria Elizabeth; *b* 24 Jan 1858; *d* unm 6 Dec 1943

(1) Frances; *m* 27 Nov 1824 4th Baron Dynevor (*qv*) and *d* 30 April 1878, leaving issue

1 Georgina; *m* 4 June 1778 Rt Hon John Smyth, of Heath, Yorks, and *d* 18 Jan 1799, leaving issue

The **3rd Duke** *m* 2nd 24 June 1769 Elizabeth (*d* 25 May 1822), dau of Rev Sir Richard Wrottesley, 7th Bt (*see* WROTTESLEY, B), and *d* 14 March 1811, having had, with other issue:

3 Henry (Rev); *b* 9 April 1770; Preb and Canon Westminster; *m* 10 Sept 1800 Caroline (*d* 1 Jan 1835), yst dau of Adml Hugh Pigot (*see* PIGOT, Bt), and *d* 7 June 1828, having had issue:

(1) Henry, of Salcey Lawn, Northants; *b* 22 Aug 1806; *m* 24 July 1830 Jane Elizabeth (*d* 15 July 1892), dau of C G Beauclerk (*see* SAINT ALBANS, D), and *d* 5 Dec 1877, having had, with other issue:

1a Algernon Henry, of Salcey Lawn; *b* March 1834; *d* 19 Feb 1927

2a Wriothesley Augustus; *b* 13 July 1837; 23rd Foot; *d* 23 Feb 1891

1a Cecilia Fanny; *m* 3 Dec 1857 Capt George F Sitwell, 2nd s of Sir George Sitwell, 2nd Bt (*qv*), and *d* 1 Nov 1873, leaving issue

2a Blanche Adeliza; *m* 1st 13 Oct 1860 Hon Charles Henry Maynard (*d* 2 Jan 1865), only s of last Viscount Maynard (*see* 1865 edn), and had issue; *m* 2nd 8 Nov 1866 4th Earl of Rosslyn (*qv*) and *d* 8 Dec 1933, leaving further issue

3a Evelyn Georgina Matilda; *m* 1st 1 Dec 1858 (*divorce* 1895) her cousin Aubrey de Vere Beauclerk and had issue (*see* SAINT ALBANS, D); *m* 2nd 16 Dec 1895 George S A Watson-Taylor, of Erlestoke Park, Wilts, and *d* 10 Jan 1931

(2) Hugh; *b* 14 May 1808; Lt-Col Gren Gds; *m* 1st 9 Aug 1831 Lucy Sarah (*d* 2 May 1855), dau of Sir Thomas Lethbridge, 2nd Bt (*qv*), and had, with other issue:

1a Almeric Hugh; *b* 10 Oct 1835; lost at sea aboard the *Camilla* 1860

1a Amy Emily Sarah; *m* 16 Sept 1858 Lt-Col Ralph Bradford Atkinson, Gren Gds, and had issue

(2) (cont.) Lt-Col Hugh FitzRoy *m* 2nd 4 Dec 1856 Emily Louisa (*d* 1897), dau of Reginald Macdonald, Chief of Clanranald, and widow of C Marsham, of Stratton Strawless, and *d* 27 Feb 1879, having had, with other issue:

2a Augusta Caroline; *b* 9 Feb 1859; *m* 25 Sept 1884 Robert William Rankine Wilson, barrister, and *d* 27 Dec 1888

(3) Augustus (Rev), JP; *b* 9 Dec 1809; Rector Gt Fakenham, Norfolk; *m* 1st 7 May 1833 Angelina Mary (*d* 29 April 1836), est dau of Stafford O'Brien, of Blatherwycke Park, Northants, and had issue:

1a Ernest James Augustus (Rev); *b* 9 June 1834; Vicar St Jude's, W Derby, Lancs 1879–95; *m* 17 Sept 1855 Elizabeth (*d* 13 May 1905), est dau of C Ellis, of Abbots Langley, Herts, and *d* 13 June 1916, leaving issue, with another s and two daus (all *d* unm):

1b Stafford Francis; *b* 1 July 1863; *m* 3 Aug 1893 Gertrude Ann, dau of Alfred Fortye, of Cheltenham, and *d* 9 Sept 1920

1b Lilias Evelyn Elizabeth; *m* 26 Nov 1902 Walter Thomas Fremlin (*d* 25 Feb 1925), of Milgate Park, Kent

(3) (cont.) The Rev Augustus FitzRoy *m* 2nd 23 Jan 1840 Emma (*d* 18 March 1885), 6th dau of Ebenezer Fuller Maitland, of Park Place, Henley-on-Thames, and *d* 12 Feb 1869, leaving by her:

2a Hugh Maitland; *b* 17 Aug 1843; Lt Rifle Bde and 3rd Buffs; *m* 4 Jan 1877 Bertha (*d* 16 March 1918), only child of Maj John Frederick Cecil Kearney, 15th Hus, and *d* 22 Aug 1903, leaving, with other issue:

1b Ronald Hugh; *b* 12 Feb 1878; Capt Scots Gds, Boer War 1901–02 and WW I; *d* unm 28 April 1960

2b Victor Robert Charles; *b* 4 July 1880; Capt Scots Gds, Boer War (4 clasps) and WW I; *d* 27 Oct 1946

(4) Francis Charles; *b* 15 March 1811; *m* 1st 10 July 1835 Caroline Octavia (*d* 2 Sept 1854), yst dau of Sir George Pigot, 3rd Bt (*qv*); *m* 2nd 1 Aug 1855 Harriet Anne (*d* 24 Jan 1883), dau of Christopher Musgrave, and *d* 21 Nov 1874, leaving by his 1st w:

1a Orlando Charles; *b* 9 May 1836; *m* 22 March 1860 Ella, adopted dau of Arthur Bedford, Proctor Doctors' Commons, and *d* 4 May 1880, having had a s and two daus (all *d* unm)

1a Lavinia; *m* 24 Oct 1882 Col Charles Clitherow Gore, MVO (*see* ARRAN, E), and *d* 16 May 1912

(1) Caroline; *m* 18 May 1839 Henry Wilson (*d* 1866), of Stowlangtoft Hall, Suffolk

4 William (Sir), KCB; *b* 1 June 1782; Adml RN, MP Thetford 1806–12; *m* 1816 Georgiana (*d* 2 Dec 1861), dau of Thomas Raikes, and *d* 13 May 1857, leaving:

(1) Francis Horatio, of Frogmore Park, Hants, JP, DL Hants; *b* 6 June 1823; *m* 27 Nov 1849 Hon Gertrude Duncombe (*d* 24 Feb 1916), 2nd dau of 2nd Baron Feversham (*qv*), and *d* 20 March 1900, leaving, with other issue:

1a Almeric William (Sir), KCB (1911), KCVO (1909); *b* 12 Nov 1851; Clerk to PC 1898–1923, BA Oxford, author *Memoirs*; *m* 30 July 1887 Katherine (*d* 24 Nov 1933), dau of Sir Henry Thomas Farquhar, 4th Bt (*qv*), and *d* 31 May 1935, leaving issue:

1b Nigel Horatio Trevor; *b* 4 July 1889; *m* 1st 30 Aug 1917 (*divorce* 1928) Constance (*d* 1974), only dau of Capt Robert Henry Paul, RN, of The Highlands, Banbury; *m* 2nd 14 Sept 1936 *Diana Frances [Mrs William FitzRoy-Yates, Upsend Stud Farm, Newmarket, Suffolk] (*m* 2nd 27 Nov 1958 William Edward Yates (*d* 10 Nov 1964), s of Maj S B Yates, of Broughton Grange, Banbury, Oxon), er dau of Brig Arthur Francis Gore Pery-Knox-Gore, DSO (*see* LIMERICK, E), and *d* 5 March 1953, leaving:

1c *Susanna Diana Georgina; *b* 18 June 1937; *m* 1st 22 Sept 1964 (*divorce* 1966) William Anthony Coleridge, yst s of Guy Coleridge; *m* 2nd 13 March 1967 *George Henry Peter-Hoblyn (*see* PHILIPSON-STOW, Bt) and by him has:

1d *John FitzRoy; *b* 23 Feb 1968; *m* 19– *Isabel — and has issue:

1e *Harry George FitzRoy; *b* 1994

1d *Emma Frances; *b* 15 July 1970

1b Yvonne Alice Gertrude; *b* 17 Oct 1891; with Scottish Women's Hosp Romania and Russia 1916–17, Orders St George and St Stanislaus Russia and Br and Allied War medals; *d* unm 20 March 1971

2a Cyril Duncombe; *b* 21 May 1861; Registrar RCA, Bd Educn; *m* 1st 9 July 1903 Leila Margaret (*d* 12 Oct 1904), dau of Robert Smith, of Goldings, Herts, and had issue:

1b Esmé Leila Gertrude; *b* 3 Oct 1904; *m* 19 Oct 1936 Lt-Col Reginald Henry Osgood Hanbury, MC, 15th/19th King's Roy Hus (*d* 9 Jan 1973), of Melgate, Slingsby, Yorks, er s of Col Lionel Henry Hanbury, CMG, VD, JP, of Hitcham House, Burnham, Bucks, and *d* 19– , leaving issue

2a (cont.) Cyril FitzRoy *m* 2nd 25 April 1908 Margaret (*d* 7 April 1948), only dau of Rev James Samuel William Durham, DD, Rector Ladbroke, Warwicks, and *d* 9 July 1939, leaving by her:

1b Charles Francis Mark, of N Lodge, Crimonmogate, Lonmay, Aberdeenshire; *b* 5 March 1909; *educ* Westminster; *m* 15 June 1936 *Baroness Irmgard von Dincklage, DipArch, est dau of Baron Rudolf von Dincklage, of Hanover, and *d* 1994, leaving issue:

1c +Felix Rudolf [Prof Felix FitzRoy, 26 Cairnhill Gdns, St Andrews, Fife KY16 8QX]; *b* 17 Aug 1938; *educ* UCL (BSc 1960), Aberdeen U (MSc 1961) and Heidelberg U (PhD 1968); *m* 1976 *Renate Brüninghaus and has:

1d +James Francis Stuart; *b* 1986

1d *Olga Henrietta; *b* 1982

1c *Christina Margaret [Mrs Ali Caba, Limanreis Mah, C. Resit Rey Sok. No 3, Navlidere, 35320 Izmir, Turkey]; *b* 20 June 1944; *educ* Edin U (BSc 1966); *m* 1974 *Ali Kemâl Caba, of Izmir, Turkey, and has:

1d *Elif Ina; *b* 1978

2d *Ozan Sinan; *b* 1981

2b Elizabeth Anne Horatia; *b* 21 Oct 1912; fndr Elizabeth FitzRoy Homes for the Handicapped Tst 1963 and Catholic Handicapped Children's Fellowship 1956; *d* 1982

1a Gertrude Louisa Georgiana; *m* 5 July 1871 Lt-Col Robert Hamilton Lloyd-Anstruther and *d* 17 July 1927, leaving issue (*see* ANSTRUTHER, Bt)

2a Helen Mary; *m* 14 Oct 1890 Charles Milnes Newton and *d* his widow 31 Oct 1935, leaving issue

3a Esmé; *m* 1st 19 Oct 1886 Col Hon Montagu Curzon and had issue (*see* HOWE, E); *m* 2nd 26 Oct 1909 Rev William Arthur King, MA, Vicar Woodhouse, Loughborough, and *d* 25 May 1939

(1) Harriet Elizabeth; *m* 8 May 1862 Col Michael Dawes, Bengal Artillery, and *d* his widow 14 July 1875

2 Elizabeth; *m* 4 July 1811 her cousin Lt-Gen Hon William FitzRoy (*see* SOUTHAMPTON, B) and *d* 30 March 1839

3 Augusta; *m* 19 Nov 1811 Rev G F Tavel (*d* 27 April 1829) and *d* 29 June 1839, leaving issue (*see* MURRAY, Bt, of Ochtertyre)

4 Frances; *m* 25 Nov 1800 1st Baron Churchill (*see* CHURCHILL, V) and *d* 7 Jan 1866, leaving issue

5 Isabella; *m* 11 Aug 1812 Barrington Pope Blachford, of Osborne, IoW, and *d* his widow 10 Dec 1866

The 3rd DUKE's est s,

GEORGE HENRY FitzROY, **4th Duke of Grafton**, KG (1834); *b* 14 Jan 1760; *educ* Harrow and Trin Coll Cambridge; MP (Whig) Thetford 1782–84 and Cambridge U 1784–1811, Ld Lt Suffolk 1790–1844; *m* 16 Nov 1784 Charlotte Maria (*d* 1 Feb 1808), dau of 2nd Earl Waldegrave (*qv*), and *d* 28 Sept 1844, having had, with other issue:

1 HENRY, **5th Duke**

2 Charles, PC; *b* 28 Feb 1791; MP and V-Chamberlain Household, Lt-Col Peninsula and Waterloo; *m* 25 Oct 1825 Lady Anne Cavendish (*d* 27 May 1871), dau

of 1st Earl of Burlington (*see* DEVONSHIRE, D), and *d* 17 June 1865, leaving issue:

(1) Cavendish Charles; *b* 21 June 1833; Maj 68th Light Inf (Alma, Inkerman and Sebastopol), ADC to Ld Lt Ireland; *m* 6 Dec 1859 Mary (*d* 10 Feb 1892), est dau of Thomas Lumsden Strange, and *d* 8 Jan 1894, leaving issue:

1a Harold Charles Cavendish; *b* 8 June 1870; Lt 3rd Bn DLI, WW I on Military Provost Staff Corps; *m* 5 May 1892 Eliza Mary (*d* 4 July 1924), est dau of Thomas Butt, of Priors Court, Worcs, and *d* 22 May 1939, having had, with a dau (*d* young):

1b Charles Cavendish; *b* 11 Aug 1900; *m* 1st 26 Jan 1926 Simone Andrée (*d* 1957), dau of Jules Hennebert; *m* 2nd 26 Oct 1957 *Nora Bardsley [Mrs Charles FitzRoy, 57 Harrow View, Harrow, Middx] and *d* 24 Feb 1960, leaving by his 1st w:

1c +Kenneth Cavendish [Kenneth FitzRoy Esq, Oaken Gates, Tompsets Bank, Forest Row, E Sussex RH18 5BG]; *b* 20 Sept 1928; *educ* Shrewsbury; airline pilot, late F/Lt RAF; *m* 1st 28 May 1952 (*divorce* 1970) Pamela Mary, dau of Leslie Dodson, of The Grange, Thorpe, Surrey; *m* 2nd 1980 Patricia Juliet (*d* 1989), dau of Hugo de Schanschieff; *m* 3rd 1992 *Sally Anne, dau of Malcolm Fullerton Laing, and has by his 1st w:

1d +Ian Charles Cavendish [Ian FitzRoy Esq, Scarletts, Furnace Lane, Cowden, Kent]; *b* 20 Feb 1954

1d *Susan Pamela [Mrs Philip Whall, Flat 3, Rutland Ct, London SE5 8EB]; *b* 17 Sept 1955; *m* 12 Oct 1997 *Philip Alan Whall

2d *Rosemary Alison [Ms Rosemary FitzRoy, 9 Tree View Court, Wray Common Rd, Reigate, Surrey]; *b* 7 Feb 1964

1b Mary Georgina Anne; *b* 29 Sept 1897; *d* 19–

1a Anne Isabella; *b* 14 June 1861; *m* 6 Feb 1894 Arthur Charles Hecht (*d* 31 March 1901) and *d* 10 Dec 1914, leaving issue

(1) Elizabeth Mary; *m* 4 Aug 1857 Henry Lee Steere (*d* 17 June 1899) and *d* 21 Aug 1906, leaving issue

1 Maria Anne; *m* 24 May 1810 Sir William Oglander, 6th Bt (*d* 17 Jan 1852; *see* 1874 edn), of Nunwell, and Parnham, and *d* 12 May 1855, leaving issue

2 Elizabeth Anne; *m* 1814 her cousin John Henry Smyth (*d* 1822), of The Heath, Yorks, and *d* 27 Oct 1867

3 Isabella Frances; *m* Joseph St John (*d* 1856) and *d* 27 Aug 1875 aged 83

The 4th DUKE's est s,

HENRY FitzROY, **5th Duke of Grafton**; *b* 10 Feb 1790; *educ* Harrow and Trin Coll Cambridge; MP (Whig) Bury St Edmunds 1818–20 and 1826–31 and Thetford 1834–42; *m* 20 June 1812 Mary Caroline (*d* 10 Sept 1873), 3rd dau of Adml Hon Sir George Cranfield Berkeley, GCB (*see* BERKELEY, B), and *d* 26 March 1863, leaving:

1 WILLIAM HENRY FitzROY, **6th Duke of Grafton**; *b* 5 Aug 1819; *educ* Harrow; MP (Lib) Thetford 1847–63; *m* 10 Feb 1858 Hon Marie Anne Louise Baring (*d* 8 April 1928), only dau of 3rd Baron Ashburton (*qv*), and *dsp* 21 May 1882

2 AUGUSTUS CHARLES LENNOX, **7th Duke**

3 Frederick John, JP (Northants and Sussex); *b* 4 April 1823; Col Gren Gds, sometime RN, MP Thetford 1863–65; *m* 27 Oct 1853 Catherine Sarah Wilhelmina (*d* 9 March 1914), dau of Rev William Wescomb, Rector Langford, and *d* Feb 1919, having had, with a s and two daus (*d* in infancy):

(1) Evelyn; *b* 23 Nov 1860; *d* 22 March 1924

(2) Anne Ethel; *b* 10 Nov 1859; *d* unm 9 Oct 1939

1 Mary Elizabeth Emily; *m* 7 Nov 1837 Rev Hon Augustus Frederick Phipps and *d* 22 Aug 1887, leaving issue (*see* NORMANBY, M)

2 Maria Louisa; *m* 26 Jan 1846 1st Baron Penrhyn (*qv*) and *d* 10 May 1912, leaving issue

The 6th DUKE's yr bro,

AUGUSTUS CHARLES LENNOX FitzROY, **7th Duke of Grafton**, KG (1883), CB (1873), JP Suffolk, Northants and Bucks, DL Suffolk; *b* 22 June 1821; *educ* Harrow; served Crimean War (severely wounded, medal three clasps, Turkish and Sardinian medals, 5th class Medjidie), Gen (ret 1881), Lt-Col Coldstream Gds, Equerry to HM QUEEN VICTORIA 1849–82, Hon Equerry 1882–1901, Hon Equerry to TM EDWARD VII 1901–10 and GEORGE V 1910–18; *m* 9 June 1847 Anna (*d* 23 Dec 1857), yst dau of James Balfour (*see* BALFOUR, E), and *d* 4 Dec 1918, having had issue:

1 Henry James, *Earl of Euston*, JP, DL Suffolk and Northants; *b* 28 Nov 1848; *educ* Harrow; Hon Col 4th Bn Northants Regt (VD), formerly ensign Rifle Bde, ADC to HM EDWARD VII 1901–02; *m* 29 May 1871 Kate (Kate Cooke of the Variety Theatre; *d* 24 Nov 1903), dau of John Walsh, and *dsp* 10 May 1912

2 ALFRED WILLIAM MAITLAND FitzROY, **8th Duke of Grafton**, JP, DL Northants and Suffolk; *b* 3 March 1850; Lt Coldstream Gds; *m* 1st 27 April 1875 Margaret Rose (*d* 10 March 1913), 3rd dau of Eric Carrington-Smith, DL, of Stonewick Sussex, and had:

(1) William Henry Alfred, *Viscount Ipswich*; *b* 24 July 1884; Lt 4th Bn Coldstream Gds and RAF WW I (wounded); *m* 27 Sept 1913 Auriol Margaretta (*m* 2nd 28 Oct 1929 Lt-Col Gavin Robert Vernon Hume-Gore, MC, Gordon Highrs, of The Castle House, Deddington, Oxon, est s of Capt George Robert Vernon Hume-Gore, Seaforth Highrs, and *d* 7 Feb 1938), only child of Maj James Brougham, 40th Regt, of Woodland Hall, Lancs, and Potterspury House, Northants, and was *k* in an aeroplane accident 23 April 1918, leaving:

1a JOHN CHARLES WILLIAM FitzROY, **9th Duke of Grafton**; *b* 1 Aug 1914; *educ* Trin Coll Cambridge (BA); *d* 4 Aug 1936, when the Earldom and Barony of Arlington fell into abeyance between his sisters Lady Jane Nelson and Lady Mary Rose Williams (the + against whose names and that of their living issue denotes being in remainder to these titles only)

1a +(Margaret) Jane; *b* 27 April 1916; granted with her sis rank of duke's dau 25 June 1931; *m* 10 Oct 1936 Maj Gen Sir (Eustace) John Blois Nelson, KCVO, CB, DSO, OBE, MC (*d* 1993), Gren Gds, yr s of Roland Hugh Nelson (*see* BLOIS, Bt), and has issue:

2b +Jennifer Jane [Mrs Rodney Forwood, Slade Bottom House, Stoke, Hants]; *b* 7 May 1939; *m* 8 Dec 1964 *Capt Rodney Simon Dudley Forwood, Irish Gds, and has issue:

1c +Patrick John Dudley; *b* 1967

2c +James Roland Nelson; *b* 1969

2b +Juliet Auriol Sally [Lady Cholmeley, Church Farm, Burton le Coggles, Grantham, Lincs]; *b* 4 Oct 1940; *m* 18 Oct 1960 *Capt Sir Montague John Cholmeley, 6th Bt (*qv*), and has issue

2a +Mary Rose [The Lady Mary Williams, The Green, Oddington, Moreton-in-Marsah, Glos]; *b* posthumously 7 Sept 1918; *m* 3 Nov 1945 (*divorce* 1952) Lt Francis Trelawny Williams, KRRC (*d* 1977), er s of Henry Harcourt Williams (*see* SALUSBURY-TRELAWNY, Bt), and has:

1b +Linda Jane Auriol; *b* 1 Feb 1947

(1) Lilian Rose; *b* 2 March 1876; *m* 20 July 1910 Charles Robertson (*d* 6 Jan 1968), of the Ministry of Educn, Egypt, s of John Robertson, and *dsp* 2 Jan 1960

(2) Mary Margaret; *b* 10 Dec 1877; *d* unm 5 Jan 1966

2 (cont.) The **8th Duke** *m* 2nd 8 Jan 1916 Susanna Mary (*d* 3 Oct 1961), DJStJ, Order of Mercy with bar, V-Patroness Roy Eastern Counties Inst, dau of Sir Mark John MacTaggart Stewart, 1st Bt, and widow of 20th Lord Borthwick (*qv*), and *d* 10 Jan 1930, having had by her:

(3) Elfrida Marie Susanna, *b* 15 March 1919; *d* 4 Jan 1920

(4) Cecilia Blanche Genevieve; *b* 13 May 1922; WAAF WW II; *m* 11 May 1949 Baron Howard of Henderskelfe (*see* CARLISLE, E) and *d* 1974, leaving issue

3 Charles Edward (Rev), JP W Suffolk; *b* 9 Dec 1857; MA Cantab; Rector Euston-with-Barnham, Norfolk, Chaplain in Ordinary to HM QUEEN VICTORIA 1890–1901, Hon Chaplain to TM EDWARD VII 1901–10 and GEORGE V 1910–11, CC W Suffolk; *m* 12 June 1883 Hon Ismay Mary Helen Augusta FitzRoy (*d* 22 April 1952), dau of 2nd Baron Southampton (*qv*), and *d* 27 Aug 1911, leaving:

(1) CHARLES ALFRED EUSTON, **10th Duke**

(2) Edward Henry; *b* 13 July 1893; Lt RN; *ka* at sea 23 Jan 1917

(3) John Percy Samuel; *b* 12 July 1899; granted with surv siblings rank of duke's dau/yr s 28 Oct 1936; *m* 9 May 1929 Kathleen Ruthar Mary (*m* 2nd Leonard Thomas Carr and *d* 1967), dau of Rev Arthur Willoughby Rokeby, of Clifton Manor, Shefford, Beds, and *d* 24 Sept 1945, leaving issue:

1a Henry Charles; *b* 3 April 1930; Lt RN; *k* flying Korea 25 Sept 1954

1a *Ismay Diana [Miss Ismay FitzRoy, Moat Cottage, Burnham Rd, Althorne, Essex]; *b* 14 Oct 1933

(1) Anna Ismay Ethel; *b* 9 April 1884; *m* 31 Jan 1921 10th Baron Byron (*qv*) and *dsp* 14 April 1966

(2) Victoria Alexandrina Mabel; *b* 26 Oct 1886; *m* 20 April 1911 Richard Sturgis Seymour and *d* 23 Nov 1969, leaving issue (*see* HERTFORD, M.)

(3) Violet Freddie; *b* 9 Nov 1888; *m* 3 Feb 1909 Maj-Gen Nigel Maitland Wilson, CB, DSO, OBE, IA, and *d* 30 June 1974, leaving issue (*see* WILSON, B)

1 Eleanor; *m* 1st 4 May 1872 Herbert FitzRoy Eaton, of Stetchworth Park, Cambs (*d* 8 April 1875); *m* 2nd 5 May 1875 (*divorce* 1900) Maj Hon Walter Harbord (*d* 28 Jan 1913), 5th s of 3rd Baron Suffield (*qv*), and had further issue; *m* 3rd 1904 Maj Herbert Richard Magniac, DSO, JP, DL (*dsp* 24 March 1909), and *d* 15 Sept 1905

The 9th DUKE's 1st cousin,

CHARLES ALFRED EUSTON FitzROY, **10th Duke of Grafton**, JP (1937), DL (Suffolk 1942); *b* 4 June 1892; *educ* Wellington and RMC Sandhurst; Maj Roy Welch Fus, ADC to Govr-Gen S Africa; *m* 1st 24 Jan 1918 Doreen Maria Josepha Sydney (*d* 28 July 1923), 2nd dau of 1st Earl Buxton (*see* BUXTON, Bt), and had:

1 HUGH DENIS CHARLES FitzROY, **11th and present Duke of Grafton**

2 Charles Oliver Edward; *b* 13 July 1923, *educ* Eton; Lt Gren Gds WW II; *ka* Normandy Aug 1944

1 *Anne Mildred Ismay [The Lady Anne Mackenzie, Farr, Inverness-shire; Bergh Apton Manor, Norwich, Norfolk]; *b* 7 Aug 1920; *m* 19 April 1947 *Maj Colin Dalzell Mackenzie, MBE, MC, V-Ld Lt Lochaber, Inverness and Badenoch and Strathsey 1986–, late Seaforth Highrs, er s of Lt-Col Douglas William Alexander Dalziel Mackenzie, CVO, DSO, JP, DL, of Farr, Inverness-shire, and has:

(1) *Philip Austin George [Philip Mackenzie Esq, Glenkyllachy, Tomatin, Inverness-shire IV13 7YA]; *b* 1949; *educ* Eton and Magdalen Coll Oxford (BA); FCA, MICFor; *m* 1976 *(Katherine) Emma, dau of Anthony Binney (*see* MUIR, Bt), and has issue,

1a *Lucy; *b* 1976

2a *Sabrina; *b* 1978

3a *Doune; *b* 1980

4a *Isla; *b* 1986

5a *Bettine; *b* 1991

(1) *Caroline Doreen; *b* 1952

(2) *Laura Patience Kathleen; *b* 1954; BA (Oxford); ALI; *m* 1980 *(Ian) Michael Osborne, 2nd s of Maj Gerald Michael Osborne, MC, TD, of Balmadies, Guthrie, Angus, and has issue:

1a *Julian; *b* 1982

2a *Oliver; *b* 1985

(3) *Harriet Anne; *b* 1958; *m* 1989 *Thomas St Andrew Warde-Aldam, yr s of Maj David Julian Warde-Aldam, of Healey Hall, Northumberland, and has:

1a *A dau; *b* 1992

The **10th Duke** *m* 2nd 6 Oct 1924 Lucy Eleanor (*d* 11 Sept 1943), dau of Sir George Stapylton Barnes, KCB, KCSI, of Foxholm, Cobham, Surrey; *m* 3rd 18 July 1944 Rita Emily (*d* 24 Aug 1970), dau of John Ralph Stockley Carr-Ellison and widow of Lt-Cdr John Thurburn Currie, RN, and *d* 11 Nov 1970, leaving by his 2nd w:

3 +Edward Anthony Charles, DL (Norfolk 1986) [The Lord Edward FitzRoy DL, Norton House, Norwich, Norfolk NR14 6RY]; *b* 26 Aug 1928; *educ* Eton and RMA Sandhurst; late Capt Coldstream Gds, High Sheriff Norfolk 1987, Chmn Govrs Wymondham Coll, Tstee Lloyds TSB Fndn England and Wales, dir: Ross Breeders Ltd, Nat Poultry Breeders (S Africa) Ltd, Ross Poultry NZ Ltd, dep chm Bd of Management of Eastern Region of TSB, Trustcard Ltd, chm Caledonian Cartridge Co Ltd, Norfolk Playing Fields Assoc, memb Cncl Norfolk Naturalists Tst, Cncl Roy Norfolk Ag Assoc; *m* 26 April 1956 *Veronica Mary, yr

dau of Maj Robert Francis Ruttledge, MC, of Cloonee, Ballinrobe, Co Mayo, and has:

(1) +Michael Robert Charles; *b* 2 Nov 1958; *m* 1987 *Cornelia A, yr dau of Peter Garnett, of Quakers' Orchard, Peaslake, Surrey, and has issue:

1a +Edwin; *b* 1992

1a *Olivia Lucy; *b* 1989

(1) *Joanna Lucy; *b* 18 April 1957; *m* 24 April 1982 *Martin J Kershaw, only s of R F Kershaw (*see* LINDSEY and ABINGDON, E), and has issue

(2) *Shauna Anne; *b* 17 June 1963; *m* 1989 *Adam L J Seccombe, yr s of J A (Alec) Seccombe, of Pique House, Stockcross, Berks, and has issue:

1a *Freddie; *b* 1992

2a *Dominick Jasper; *b* 1994

4 Michael Charles; *b* 18 March 1932; *educ* Eton; missing believed drowned Solomon Islands 15 July 1954

Seat: Euston Hall, Thetford, Norfolk. Euston was built for Lord Arlington, father-in-law of the **1st Duke**, but greatly altered by Matthew Brettingham in the **2nd Duke**'s time, though work seems to have continued after the latter's death in 1757. (The **2nd Duke** was also instrumental in getting Marylebone Road in London built.) Little remains of the 18th-century alterations inside. The loss of some ceilings by Verrio in a fire in 1900 is particularly sad. At the same time as the building was altered the grounds were landscaped by William Kent.

GRAHAM, Bt, of Dromore

Creation: Bt. (UK) 23 Jan 1964.

SIR JOHN MOODIE GRAHAM, 2ND BT, of Dromore, Co Down [Sir John Graham Bt, Les Bordes d'Arinsal, Andorra; 77 South Birch Rd 11D, Fort Lauderdale, FL 33316–1556, USA]; *b* 3 April 1938, *s* f 1966; *educ* Trin Coll Glenalmond and Queen's U Belfast (BSc 1960); Pres NI Leukaemia Research Fund; *m* 8 April 1970 (*divorce* 1982) Valerie Rosemary, dau of Frank Gill, of Belfast, and has:

1 *Suzanne Margaret; *b* 1971

2 *Alyson Rosemary; *b* 1974

3 *Lucy Christina; *b* 1978

Lineage: JOHN GRAHAM, JP, of Dromore House, Dromore, Co Down; *b* 1861; *m* Sarah Porter (*d* March 1919) and *d* 9 June 1924, leaving, with a dau (Essie, *d* unm):

1 James Porter, OBE (1948); *b* 5 Jan 1893; *educ* Banbridge Acad; *m* 4 Aug 1920 Violet Maude Laird, of Shantallow, Dromore, and *d* 23 March 1968, leaving:

(1) *James Edward Laird [James Graham Esq, Ardfoyle, Forthill, Lisburn, Co Antrim]; *b* 18 Dec 1936; *educ* Trin Coll Glenamond; *m* 24 April 1963 *Joyce Margaret, dau of Walter Connor, and has:

1a *Michael Edward James; *b* 5 Feb 1964

2a *Colin John; *b* 2 June 1966

3a *Robin Niall; *b* 8 Jan 1969

2 **Sir Clarence Johnston Graham, 1st Bt** (UK), so *cr* 23 Jan 1964; *b* 8 May 1900; *educ* Banbridge Acad and Queen's U Belfast (BSc 1919); MICE 1952, dir John Graham (Dromore) Ltd, engrg contractors, Chm Standing Ctee Ulster Unionist Cncl 1947–63 (V-Pres 1965), Pres Unionist Assoc S Down Centl, Iveagh Unionist Assoc, NI Leukaemia Research Fund, ktd 1952; *m* 14 Aug 1935 Margaret Christina (*d* 1 Jan 1954), dau of Robert Moodie, of Rubicon, Lisburn, and *d* 22 Dec 1966, leaving:

(1) Sir JOHN MOODIE GRAHAM, **2nd and present Bt**

GRAHAM, Bt, of Esk

Arms: Quarterly; 1st and 4th, or on a chief sa. three escallops of the field (for GRAHAM); 2nd and 3rd, or a fess chequy arg. and az., in chief a chevron gu. (for STUART). **Crest:** Two wings addorsed or. **Motto:** Reason contents me. **Creation:** Bt. (E) 29 March 1629.

SIR RALPH STUART GRAHAM, 14TH BT, of Esk, Cumberland [Sir Ralph Graham Bt, 7441 Highway 705, # 440, Nashville, TN 37221, USA]; *b* 5 Nov 1950; *s* f 1988; *educ* Hofstra U; *m* 1st 1972 Roxanne (*d* 1978), dau of Mrs Lovette Gurzan, of Elmont, Long Island; *m* 2nd 1979 *Denna, dau of William Robert Vandergrift, of Waukegan, Ill., and with her adopted:

*Gabriel Lawrence; *b* 1974

Lineage: FERGUS GRAHAM/GRAHME, of Plomp, Cumberland (for whom an imprecise link has been claimed with John Graham of Kilbride, yr s of 1st Earl of Menteith (*see* MONTROSE, D), and who may have been s of Matthew/Matthias Graham); *m* Sibill, dau of William Bell, of Godsbrigg, Scotland, and had, with an est and two yst sons:

Sir Richard Graham, 1st Bt (E), so *cr* 29 March 1629, of Esk(e) and Netherby (which he bought, together with the territorial Barony of Liddell, Cumberland), both Cumberland; MP Carlisle 1626 and 1628–29, Gentleman of the Horse to JAMES I; royalist Civil War (wounded Marston Moor 1644); *m* by 1624 Catherine (*d* 23 March 1649/50), dau and coheir of Thomas Musgrave, of Cumcatch, Cumberland, and *d* 28 Jan 1653/4, having had, with a yr s (Sir RICHARD GRAHAM, 1st Bt, of Norton Conyers; *qv*) and five daus:

Sir George Graham, 2nd Bt; *b c* 1624; *m* Lady Mary Johnstone (*m* 2nd Sir George Fletcher, 2nd Bt), dau of 1st Earl of Hartfell (*see* ANNANDALE AND HARTFELL, E), and *d* 19 March 1657/8, having had, with other issue:

1 **Sir Richard Graham, 3rd Bt**, and 1st VISCOUNT PRESTON, so *cr* 12 May 1681, as also LORD GRAHAM OF ESK (both S), and later 21 Jan 1688/9 titular Baron of Liddall, Co Cumberland, and Viscount Preston, of Amoundernesse, Co Lancaster (both E) by the self-exiled JAMES II at St Germain-en-Laye, France, the latter two creations being declared null by the Ho of Lds 12 Nov 1689 even though JAMES was not pronounced by Parl to have abdicated till at least a week after these last two creations had taken place, PC (1685); *b* 24 Sept 1648; *educ* Westminster and Ch Ch Oxford (MA); MP (Tory) Cockermouth 1675–81 and Cumberland 1685–87, Envoy Extrdy France 1682, Master Gt Wardrobe 1685, Ld Lt Cumberland and Westmorland 1687, Sec State 28 Oct 1688, imprisoned: for alleged treason 30 May-25 Oct 1689, for the misdemeanour of publishing his patent of creation as a peer by JAMES II 11–27 Nov 1689, and again for treason 1 Jan 1690/1, being sentenced to death 19 Jan 1690/1 but pardoned and freed 13 June 1691 (whereby it has been assumed ever since that the forfeiture of the E btcy brought about by the condemnation for treason was rescinded; the Scottish titles were never forfeited in the first place since the attainder of Jan 1690/1 did not apply to them), again imprisoned Aug 1691; *m* 2 Aug 1670 Lady Anne Howard, 2nd dau of 1st Earl of Carlisle (*qv*), and *d* 22 Dec 1695, having had, with two er sons (*d* young):

(1) **Sir Edward Graham, 4th Bt**, and 2nd VISCOUNT PRESTON; *b c* 1679–81; *educ* Univ Coll Oxford; had the forfeited estates restored Aug 1696; *m* 5 Jan 1702/3 Mary, dau and coheir of Sir Marmaduke Dalton, of Hawkswell, Yorks, and *d* 1710, leaving:

1a **Sir Charles Graham, 5th Bt**, and 3rd and last VISCOUNT PRESTON; *b* 25 March 1706; *m* Anne (*d* 11 Feb 1744/5), dau of Thomas Cox, a London wholesale grocer, and sis of Mary, w of 4th Earl of Peterborough (*see* MORDAUNT, Bt), and *dsp* 22 Feb 1738/9, when the Viscountcy and Lordship expired

(1) Catherine; *m c* July 1718, as his 2nd w, William Widdrington, who prior to his attainder Jan-Feb 1715/6 for participation in 1715 Jacobite Rising had been 4th Baron Widdrington of Blankney (*d* 19 April 1743), and *d* 11 Dec 1757, having willed the family estates in Cumberland (which she inherited 1738 from her n 3rd and last VISCOUNT PRESTON) to her cousin Rev Robert Graham (*see* GRAHAM, Bt, of Netherby)

(2) Mary Susan; *d* unm 1753

2 James, of Levens, Westmorland; MP Carlisle 1685–87, Appleton 1702–08 and Westmorland 1708–27, Col; *bapt* 3 April 1650; *m* 1st 23 Nov 1675 Dorothy, est dau of William Howard, s of 1st Earl of Berkshire (*see* SUFFOLK and BERKSHIRE, E); *m* 2nd 1702 Elizabeth (*d* 1709), widow of George Bromley and dau of Isaac Barton, and *d* 26 Jan 1729/30, leaving by his 1st w, with other issue:

(1) Henry; MP Westmorland; *m* 1705 Mary Tudor (*m* 3rd 26 Aug 1707 James Rooke; *d* 5 Nov 1726), widow of 2nd Earl of Derwentwater and illegitimate dau of CHARLES II by the actress/singer Mary Davies, and *dvp* & *sp* 7 Jan 1706/7

(1) Catherine; *m* 4th Earl of Berkshire (and 11th Earl) of Suffolk (*qv*) and *d* 14 Feb 1762, leaving issue

3 Fergus; *b* 1652, *dsp*

4 William (Very Rev); DD, Dean Carlisle and Wells, Clerk Closet and Chaplain to QUEEN ANNE; *m* 2nd Alicia — and *d* 9 Feb 1712/13, leaving:

(1) Charles (Rev); Rector S Church, Essex; *m* 6 Jan 1728/9 Priscilla (*m* 2nd Joseph Bezeley), dau of Case Billingley, of Tottenham, and was *bur* 12 April 1734, having had:

1a WILLIAM (Rev Sir), **6th Bt**

2a Thomas Fane Charles (Rev); *m* Anne, widow of Rev Francis Greenwood and dau of Joseph Harrington, of Clare, Suffolk

1a Bridget; *m* Thomas Elkington, of Coventry

(2) Robert (Rev), DD; inherited the Preston estates (*see* above and GRAHAM, Bt, of Netherby)

5 Reginald, of Pickhill, Yorks; *b* 1656; *m* Elizabeth — and had, with other issue:

(1) Metcalfe, of Pickhill; Col, Adj-Gen to Duke of Marlborough at Battle of Blenheim; *b* Aug 1680; *m* 1st Isabella Jacoba de Bons, of Breda (*bur* 25 May 1720); *m* 2nd 8 July 1721 Elizabeth Nevill and *d* 14 Jan 1758, leaving by his 1st w:

1a Jacoba Catherina; *m* 1st 5 June 1728 Sir Reginald Graham, 4th Bt, of Norton Conyers (*qv*), and had issue; *m* 2nd Col — Brown and was *bur* 1 Dec 1764

The 5th Bt's cousin,

Rev Sir William Graham, 6th Bt; *b* 1730; *m* 7 Nov 1761 Susannah (*d* 1788), widow of Richard French and dau of — Reeve, of Ashburnham, Sussex, and *d* 21 Sept 1774, leaving, with a yst s (William, *b* Aug 1771, *d* 1846) and three daus:

1 **Sir Charles Graham, 7th Bt**; *b* 11 Nov 1764; *d* unm 26 Nov 1795

2 **Sir Robert Graham, 8th Bt**; *b* 1 Oct 1769; *m* 25 April 1810 Elizabeth (*d* 16 Dec 1859), only dau of John Young, of Battle, Sussex, and had, with other issue:

(1) Richard John; Lt Bengal Native Inf; *b* 23 Nov 1817; *m* 1840 Anna Louisa (*m* 2nd 25 Dec 1850 William Martin Young; *d* 1897), dau of John Gibbs, and *d* 4 Aug 1844, leaving:

1a Ellen Louisa; *m* 1859 George Faithfull (*d* 1897)

2a Cecilia Elizabeth; *m* 23 July 1868 Edward Widdrington Joseph Temple and had issue

(2) EDWARD (Sir), **9th Bt**

(3) Stuart Frederick; Maj-Gen Bengal Staff Corps, Ch Commr Multan, India; *b* 12 Nov 1823; *m* 22 Feb 1849 Elizabeth Frances Bannatyne (*d* 16 May 1881), dau of William Bannatyne McLeod, CB, MD, and *d* 20 Sept 1878, leaving, with other issue:

1a Frederick; Lt-Col 1st Bn Middx Regt; *b* 5 Dec 1849; *m* 22 May 1877 Charlotte Barbara Roch (*d* 19 May 1940), only dau of Edward Joseph Thackwell, 3rd Hus, and *d* 19 Feb 1914, leaving:

1b Stuart Menteith; NW Mounted Police Canada, served WW I (wounded twice); *b* 26 March 1886; *m* 18 June 1919 Leonore Mollie, dau of Capt W Netherway-Morrish, Rifle Bde, and *d* 1957, leaving:

1c *Marjorie Barbara Stuart; *b* 28 Aug 1921; *m* 1963 *David Sherwin Walker

2b Fergus Stuart; Cdr RN, served WWs I and II; *b* 27 July 1893; *m* 1st 18 Dec 1924 Lily Beatrice, dau of Christopher Arnall, of Birmingham; *m* 2nd 11 Sept 1959 Audrey Eleanor Agnes, dau of Capt Horace Mann, Roy W Kent Regt

1b Gladys Eupheme Stuart; *b* 17 Sept 1884; *m* 1915 Henry F Hutteroth and had issue

2b Vera Patricia Stuart, Jr Cdr ATS; *b* 14 Aug 1888

2a William Bannatyne, Maj 2nd Bn Manchester Regt; *b* 28 May 1858; *m* 1884 Mary Beatrice (*d* 1941), dau of Rev E H Hansell, and *d* 1 Sept 1897, having had issue:

1b Edward William Harold; *b* 1888; with E Extension Telegraph Co, Cocos Keeling Islands; served WW I Italy; *d* 19–

2b Stuart Douglas, MC; Brig RA WW I (despatches twice), WW II (wounded), Jurat Roy Court Jersey; *b* 18 Feb 1890; *m* 11 July 1916 Marjorie Helen, er dau of George Harry le Maistre, India Public Works Dept, and had:

1c Pamela de Villeneuve; *b* 16 Dec 1921; *m* 24 April 1947 Patrick C Duff, Colonial Admin Serv, and *d* following an accident 2 Jan 1948

3b Roderic Arthur, MBE (1946); Lt-Col IA WW I (despatches), WW II; *b* 2 July 1891; *m* 1st 17 Jan 1927 Mrs Margaret Mary Wise, dau of James Brooks Close; *m* 2nd 1951 Blanche Gray Pyman and *d* 12 Oct 1964

1b Beatrice Muriel; *m* 2 March 1922 Frederick James Long, s of Robert George Williams Long, of Deal, Kent, and *d* July 1963

2b Marguerite Clarice; *m* 5 June 1912 Capt George Calthorpe Woodward, RN, yst s of V-Adml Robert Woodward, CB, of Hopton Court, Salop

3b Mary Dorothy; *educ* Lond U (BA 1915); *m* 6 Sept 1916 Wilfred Saunders, BSc, FIC, Imp Indian Educn Serv, and had issue

3a Henry Macleod; Col S Wales Bdrs, T/Maj-Gen and Brig-Gen 1915, Burma 1885–87; *b* 30 Nov 1860; *m* 10 Jan 1899 Mary Lucas, widow of David Shafto Hawks and dau of Vicomte de Satgé de St Jean, and *d* 11 Oct 1938

4a Walter Mayne; *b* 19 Feb 1864; *m* 1st 1890 Ethel Beatrice (*d* 19 July 1931), dau of William Aubrey Leake; *m* 2nd 5 Jan 1932 Evelyn Muriel, 3rd dau of Thomas Bowater Vernon, and *d* 23 Nov 1935, having y his 1st w had:

1b Florence Gertrude Morland; *b* 26 June 1892; *m* 1922 Claude Randolph Lawson Boxer and had issue. He *d* 13 Dec 1943

5a Stuart Bruce; Col IA, Sudan 1884–85, Burma 1885–87; *b* 7 June 1865; *m* 1st 1889 Lizzie (*d* 1933), dau of James Gordon; *m* 2nd 23 Nov 1935 Mary Winifred Fraser, er dau of Arthur Fraser Taylor, and by his 1st w had:

1b Eric Montrose; Lt S Wales Borderers (SR); *b* 1893; *d* 2 April 1915 of wounds recd in action

2b Ronald Macleod; Lt Essex Regt; *b* 2 Oct 1895; *ka* 12 or 13 March 1915

6a Sydney Munro; *b* 28 Jan 1868; *d* 22 April 1887

7a Norman Macleod; *b* 30 Nov 1870; *d* unm 13 Aug 1938

8a Malcolm Macleod; *b* 2 Sept 1872; *m* 4 Nov 1896 Leopoldina, dau of Mark Gallacher, of Rosario, Agentina, and had:

1b +Richard Walter Malcolm; *b* 7 Sept 1903

2b +Oswald Charles; *b* 6 June 1906

1b Agnes Beatrice; *b* 1897; *m* Jack Maclaughlin, of Buenos Aires

2b Ethel Amy; *b* 18 May 1901; *d* 19 July 1902

1a Alice Maud; *m* 1886 Lt-Col John Henry Leslie, DL, RA, and *d* 2 Oct 1924, leaving issue. He *d* 1943

(1) Elizabeth Susannah; *m* 15 Feb 1838 Lt-Col John Henry Simmonds, 55th Native Inf. He *d* 7 May 1869

(2) Euphemia Harriet; *m* 21 Sept 1842 Thomas George Vernon, of Tewkesbury, and *d* 13 Aug 1871, leaving issue. He *d* 13 March 1860

(3) Frances Anne; *m* 21 Jan 1842 Capt John Hoare Hatchell, 69th Bengal Native Inf, and *d* 12 Nov 1894. He *d* 12 Sept 1844

(4) Cecilia Jane Maria; *m* 21 June 1845 Col Edward Moody Ryan, 3rd s of Sir Edward Ryan, PC

Sir ROBERT *d* 27 Jan 1852; his est surv son,

Sir Edward Graham, 9th Bt; *b* 1 Jan 1820; *m* 1st 5 June 1841 Anne, widow of Charles Henderson; *m* 2nd 3 Aug 1844 Adelaide Elizabeth (*d* 12 March 1852), yst dau of James Dillon Tully, MD, Dep Inspr-Gen Hosps Jamaica, and by her had, with a dau:

1 **Sir Robert James Stuart Graham, 10th Bt**; *b* 2 Dec 1845; *m* 1 Aug 1874 Eliza Jane (*d* 3 July 1926), dau of Charles Burns, of Brooklyn, and *d* 11 May 1917, leaving:

(1) **Sir Montrose Stuart Graham, 11th Bt**; *b* 20 May 1875; *m* 5 Sept 1903 Helen Ursula (*d* 14 Sept 1968), 2nd dau of John Henderson, of Lerwick, Shetland, and *d* 15 Jan 1939, leaving:

1a **Sir Montrose Stuart Graham, 12th Bt**; *b* 4 Aug 1904; *m* 8 Oct 1932 *Elizabeth Ann, dau of John Gerken, of St Albans, Long Island, and had:

1b *Lynne Elizabeth [Mrs Robert Jager, 110 Elwood Ave, West Islip, Long Island, NY, USA]; *b* 21 June 1937; *m* 21 March 1959 *Robert H Jager, s of Henry T Jager Jr, and has:

1c *Marie Elizabeth; *b* 1 April 1960

2c *Cindy Kay; *b* 17 March 1961

2b *Dana Stuart [Mrs Robert Brust, 2501 Rutler St, Bellmore, Long Island, NY, USA]; *b* 27 Feb 1940; *m* 11 Feb 1961 *Robert G Brust, s of William E Brust, and has:

1c *Robert George; *b* 29 Dec 1961

2c *William Edward; *b* 26 Mar 1965

1c *Elizabeth Lynne; *b* 1971

2a John; *b* 17 Feb, *d* 24 April 1913

1a *Jessie Louise; *b* 1 Jan 1907; *m* 2 May 1936 Robert S Bolton and has had issue. He *d* 23 July 1944

2a Helen Elizabeth; *b* 18 Aug 1909; *d* 17 Feb 1912

(2) Percival Harris; *b* 17 Sept 1877; *m* 24 June 1901 Louise (*d* 24 Feb 1934), dau of John Wolfe, of Brooklyn, and *d* 1954, leaving:

1a RALPH WOLFE (Sir), **13th Bt**

(3) Robert Vernon; *b* 11 Aug 1883; *m* 15 Sept 1904 Charlotte (*d* 5 April 1937), dau of Gilbert Baldwin Smith, of Brooklyn, and *d* 22 June 1943, leaving:

1a James Robert Stuart; *b* 27 Dec 1907; *m* 5 Aug 1929 Agnes (*d* 1976), dau of Dennis Harvey, of New York, and *d* 24 March 1960, having had:

1b Robert James Stuart; *b* 28 June 1942; *d* 29 July 1946

1b *Roberta Naomi [Mrs James Munson, 226 Beach 119th Street, Rockaway Park, New York, USA]; *b* 12 June 1930; *m* 12 Oct 1957 *James Joseph Munson, s of James Joseph Munson, Sr, of New York, and has:

1c *James; *b* 28 June 1958

2c *John; *b* 1959

3c *Joseph; *b* 1964

1c *Marilyn; *b* 1963

2b *Joan Charlotte ; *b* 25 Sept 1933; *m* 8 Feb 1958 *Herbert John Nicol, s of Herbert John Nicol, Sr, of Brooklyn, and has:

1c *Robert; *b* 1959

2c *Stephen; *b* 1970

1c *Catherine; *b* 1962

2c *Linda; *b* 1967

3c *Susan; *b* 1972

2a Howard George William; *b* 8 June 1910; *m* 24 April 1938 Madelyn, dau of Joseph Fitzsimmons, of Archbald, Pa., and *d* 23 April 1957, leaving:

1b *Charlotte Elizabeth; *b* 13 Oct 1940; *m* April 1960 *Daniel Coradi and has:

1c *Robert; *b* 1961

2c *Kenneth; *b* 1963

3c *Andrew; *b* 1965

4c *Cregg; *b* 1973

3a Douglas Duncan; *b* 26 Oct 1912; *m* 1st 29 March 1937 (*divorce* 1948) Harriet, dau of Thomas Lloyd, and had:

1b *Harriet Mabel; *b* 23 Jan 1938

3a (cont.) Douglas Graham *m* 2nd 1948 *Sally [Mrs Douglas Graham, 1428 Bellmore Ave, Bellmore, NY, USA], dau of Thomas Gale, of Southampton, Long Island, and *d* 1984, leaving:

1b +James Robert; *b* 2 Jan 1952

2b +Roland Edward; *b* Sept 1954

2b *Brenda Gale; *b* 1949

4a Robert Donald; *b* 25 Jan; *d* 25 Dec 1928

1a Violet Beatrice; *m* 21 July 1929 Leonard S Higgs and had issue:

1b *Ralph; *b* 27 Feb 1932; *m* 19– *Megan Williams and has:

1c *Jeffrey; *b* 5 Feb 1957

1c *Janet; *b* 28 Aug 1960

1b *Phyllis; *b* 10 June 1938; *m* 19– *Edward Thomas and has:

1c *Edward; *b* 7 Dec 1958

2c *Laurie; *b* 25 Dec 1962

1c *Sharon; *b* 16 March 1960

2c *Lisa; *b* 6 June 1961

2a *Mildred Jane Elizabeth; *b* 29 April 1916; *m* 1st 1942 (*divorce* 1953) William E Young, RM; *m* 2nd 1965 F W Rementer (*d* 1994) and by her 1st husb has:

1b *William Ernest [William Young, Box 436, Millheim, PA 16854, USA]; *b* 4 June 1944; late USN, Dr; *m* 1976 *Marylou, dau of Charles Matz, of Ohio, and has:

1c *Jonathan; *b* 1984

1c *Gretchen; *b* 1983

(4) George Edward; *b* 19 Jan 1890; *m* 5 May 1912 Florence Ethel (*d* 1979), 2nd dau of George Alfred Milne, of Brooklyn, and *d* 1969, leaving:

1a +George Edward [Lt-Col George Graham USAF (ret), 329 Benton St, Orlando, Fla 32809, USA]; *b* Jan 1920; *m* 21 July 1945 *Jean Myra, dau of Rev J Allison MacRury, of Woodhaven, Long Island, and has:

1b +Stuart George; *b* 12 Jan 1949

1b *Leslie Jean; *b* 12 Aug 1951

1a *Dorothy; *b* Oct 1917; *m* 29 Oct 1938 *Ralph Alfred Hassler, s of R I Hassler, of Pittsburgh, and has:

1b *Donald Evan; *b* 1950

1b *Laura Jean; *b* 1948

2b *Judith Ann; *b* 1953

(2) Edward Charles; *b* 27 March 1850; *m* 1st 19 Nov 1879 Sarah Frances Swartz (*d* 31 July 1881) and had:

1a Ada Ellen; *b* 19 Sept 1880; *m* Dec 1901 Harry C Lester (*d* 1946)

(2) (cont.) Edward Graham *m* 2nd 4 May 1894 Ida Van Swearengen (*d* 1927) and *d* 17 March 1913, having by her had:

1a Carl Edward; *b* 8 Oct 1896; *m* 25 Nov 1937 his former sis-in-law *Pearl Marie and *d* 31 July 1965

2a Donald Bruce; MG/Sgt US Army WW I (wounded); *b* 20 May 1898; *m* 1st 20 Aug 1919 (*divorce* 1936) Pearl Marie Brownewell; *m* 2nd 29 March 1941 *Gertrude Lysle, dau of Thomas M Cowie, and *d* 19–, leaving by his 1st w:

1b Dorothy Pearl Graham; *b* 29 July 1920; *m* 24 Dec 1946 Dwight Robert Zink and had:

1c *David Graham; *b* 27 Dec 1961

Sir Edward *m* 3rd 20 Jan 1855 Amelia Ellen (*m* 2nd 1870 Thomas R Johnston; *d* April 1877), dau of William John Akers, and *d* 27 May 1864, having by her had, with two sons:

1 Ellen Elizabeth Sarah; *m* 1888 L F Gardner, of New York, and *d* Jan 1936, leaving issue

Sir MONTROSE *dspm* 1975; his cousin,

Sir Ralph Wolfe Graham, 13th Bt; *b* 14 July 1908; *m* 1st 16 June 1939 (*divorce* 1949) Gertrude Helen, dau of Charles Kaminski, of Brooklyn, NY; *m* 2nd 1949 *Geraldine, dau of Austin Velour, of Brooklyn, and *d* 1988, leaving by her:

1 Sir RALPH STUART GRAHAM, **14th and present Bt**

2 +ROBERT BRUCE; *b* 14 Nov 1953; heir presumptive; *m* 1974 *Denise, dau of T Juranich, of Floral Park, Long Island, and has:

(1) +Brian Robert; *b* 19 March 1979

(2) +Stephen Ralph; *b* 1981

GRAHAM, Bt, of Larbert

Arms: Or on a chief invected erm. three escallops of the field.
Crest: A falcon ppr., beaked and armed or, and killing a stork arg.
Motto: *Ne oublie* ('Forget not'). **Creation:** Bt. (UK) 4 Dec 1906.

SIR JOHN ALEXANDER NOBLE GRAHAM, 4th Bt, of Larbert, GCMG (1985, KCMG 1979, CMG 1972) [Sir John Graham Bt GCMG, Salisbury Place, Church St, Shipton under Wychwood, Oxon OX7 6BP]; *b* 15 July 1926; *s* f 1980; *educ* Eton and Trin Coll Cambridge; Lt Gren Gds 1946–47, Dip Serv 1950–86, Middle East Centre Arab Studies 1951, 3rd Sec Bahrain 1951, Kuwait 1952–53, Amman 1953–54, Assist Priv Sec to For Sec 1954–57, 2nd (later 1st) Sec Belgrade 1957–60, 1st Sec and Consul Benghazi 1960–61, FO 1961–66, Counsellor Kuwait 1966–69, Priv Sec to For Sec 1969–72, Head Chancery Washington 1972–74, Amb Iraq 1974–77, Dep U-Sec FCO 1977–78 and 1980–81, Amb Iran 1979–80, UK Perm Rep N Atlantic Cncl Brussels 1982–86; Dir Ditchley Fndn 1987–92, Registrar Order St Michael and St George 1987–; *m* 1st 7 Jan 1956 Marygold Ellinor Gabrielle (*d* 1991), 2nd dau of Lt-Col Clive Grantham Austin (*see* SCARBROUGH, E); *m* 2nd 1992 *Jane, widow of Christopher Howells, and by his 1st w has:

1 +ANDREW JOHN NOBLE, MBE (1993); *b* 21 Oct 1956; *educ* Eton and Trin Coll Cambridge; Col Argyll and Sutherland Highrs; *m* 1984 *Susan Mary Bridget, dau of R-Adml John Patrick Bruce O'Riordan, CBE, RN, and has:

(1) +James Patrick Noble; *b* 15 March 1990

(1) *Katharine Rose; *b* 1986

(2) *Louisa Christian; *b* 1988

(3) *Isabella Alice; *b* 1993

2 +George Reginald Clive; *b* 25 July 1958; *educ* Eton and Trin Coll Cambridge; jnlst; *m* 1988 *Carol, dau of Julian Madison, of Cleveland, Ohio, and has:

(1) +John Reginald Austin; *b* 1992

(2) +Julian Sequoyah Roger; *b* 1995

1 *Christian Rachel; *b* 6 March 1961; *m* 1985 *Dr Matthew Scott Dryden, er s of W S Dryden, and has:

(1) *Alexander William Scott; *b* 1988

(2) *Thomas Andrew; *b* 1992

(1) *Gabriella Josephine; *b* 1990

(2) *Iona Clare; *b* 1994

Lineage: This is a cadet branch of the GRAHAMs formerly of Auchencloich and Tamrawer.

JOHN GRAHAM, of Skelmorlie Castle, Ayrshire (6th s of William Graham, of Burntshields); *b* 17 March 1797; *m* 15 Jan 1836 Elizabeth (*d* 1 May 1889), dau of John Hatt Noble, JP, DL, of Leckhampstead and Mortimer, Berks, and *d* 4 Oct 1886, having had, with other issue:

Sir John Hatt Noble Graham, 1st Bt (UK), so *cr* 4 Dec 1906, JP Cos Stirling and Lanark and Glasgow; Capt 1st Lanarks Vol Rifles 1858–63; *b* 14 Aug 1837; with William Graham & Co, Glasgow merchants, and Graham's Co (London) E India Merchants; *m* 1st 2 Oct 1862 Jane Browne (*d* 1 June 1890), dau of James Graham Adam, and had:

1 JOHN FREDERICK NOBLE (Sir), **2nd Bt**

2 Cecil William Noble (Sir); Pres Bengal Chamber Commerce 1909–10 and 1911–12, chm exec ctee Victoria Meml Calcutta 1909–10 and 1911–12, MLC 1909–12, ktd 1912; *b* 19 Sept 1872; *d* unm 25 Feb 1945

1 Elinor Elisabeth; *m* 12 April 1888 Sir Edwin Bolton, 1st Bt, MBE, DL (*see* 1970 edn), and *d* 25 Feb 1944, leaving issue. He *d* 7 Oct 1931

2 Lilian Margaret; *m* 18 Dec 1895, Lt-Col George Staunton, of Monkton House, Ayr, s of Gen George Staunton, of Longbridge, and *d* 24 Feb 1931, leaving issue. He *d* 18 March 1942

3 Winifred Mary; *d* unm 21 Dec 1952

4 Constance Agnes; *m* 26 March 1912 Sir Edward Hugh Bray, CSI, est s of Judge Bray, and *d* 21 Dec 1957. He *d* 27 Nov 1950

5 Frances Jane; *m* 18 Jan 1917 Col Emanuel Constantine Apostolides, Calcutta Light Horse, Hon ADC to Viceroy India, s of Haralambos Apostolides, and *d* 22 Feb 1962, having had issue. He *d* 14 March 1942

Sir John *m* 2nd 3 Nov 1891 Frances Lucy (*d* 16 June 1925), est dau of Martin Cottingham Clodd, of Bury St Edmunds, and *d* 25 May 1926

His est son,

Sir (John) Frederick Noble Graham, 2nd Bt; Chm Glasgow Chamber Commerce 1910 and 1911; *b* 25 July 1864; *m* 9 June 1891 Irene Maud (*d* 12 March 1958), dau of William Campbell, 2nd s of James Campbell, of Tullichewan, and had issue:

1 JOHN REGINALD NOBLE (Sir), **3rd Bt**

2 Bevis Royal, CBE (1953, OBE 1949), Chm Karachi Chamber Commerce 1948–52, Pres Assoc Chambers Commerce Pakistan 1949–50 and 1951–52; *b* 26 June 1902; *educ* Eton; *m* 29 March 1934 Lena, dau of Mathew Alexander Murphy, CBE, and *dsp* 1986

3 Frederick Clarence Campbell, CB (1960), DSO (1945); Ld Lt Cntl Regn (Stirling and Falkirk Dists) 1975–79 (DL Perths 1966–75), Maj-Gen Argyll and Sutherland Highrs WW II (despatches three times), Cdr 61st (Lorried) Inf Bde 1951–53, Assist Cmdt RMA Sandhurst 1953–56, Dep-Cdr Land Forces Hong Kong 1956, GOC Highland Dist and 51st (Highland) Div (TA) 1959–62, Maj-Gen 1959 (ret 1962), Col Cmdt Scottish Div Jan-Nov 1968, Col Argyll and Sutherland Highrs 1958–88, Hon Col WRAC (TA) 1967–88, memb Roy Co Archers; *b* 14 Dec 1908; *educ* Eton and RMC Sandhurst; *m* 3 Oct 1936 Phyllis Mary (*d* 17 Oct 1997), dau of Maj-Gen Hugh Francis Edward MacMahon, CB, CSI, CBE, MC, and *d* 1988, leaving issue:

(1) +Colin Hugh Campbell [Colin Graham Esq, Mackeanston, Doune, Perthshire FK16 6AX]; Lt Argyll and Sutherland Highrs (TA) 1959–67, Capt 51st Highland Volunteers (TAVR) 1967–71, dir Grahams (Oporto) Ltd 1963–67, Grierson, Oldham and Adams Ltd rep Scotland 1967–70, export exec Macdonald and Muir Leith 1978 (dir 1988–91), memb Roy Co Archers 1983–; *b* 5 Nov 1940; *educ* Eton; *m* 10 Aug 1963 (*divorce* 1985) Kathleen Joanna, dau of David Chancellor, and has:

1a +William Frederick Chancellor; *b* 27 Dec 1963; *m* 1989 *Victoria, est dau of John Beasley, and has issue:

1b +Frederick Sebastian Chancellor; *b* 1994

1b *Alice Elizabeth; *b* 1991

2a +David Campbell; *b* 1969

1a *Suzanna Lucy; *b* 6 May 1967; *m* 1997 *Charles D'Oyly

(1) (cont.) Colin Graham *m* 2nd 1986 *Fiona Jacqueline Richmond, dau of John Michael Richmond Paton, of Hay Park, Stow, Borders, and by her has:

3a +Rory Michael Alexander; *b* 1988

4a +Neil Alasdair Richmond; *b* 1991

(2) Ewan Alastair MacMahon; Lt-Col Argyll and Sutherland Highrs, memb Roy Co Archers 1994–96; *b* 28 Sept 1944; *educ* Eton; *m* 1st 14 April 1967 (*divorce* 1982) Sara Diones, only child of Maj-Gen Reginald Geoffrey Stirling Hobbs, CB, DSO, OBE, of Lerags House, Oban, Argyll; *m* 2nd 1982 *Sarah Rose [Mrs Ewan Graham, The Stables, Duncrub Park, Dunning, Perthshire], dau of Cdr David Enderby Blunt, RN, and *d* 1996, leaving by his 1st w:

1a +Calum James MacMahon; *b* 13 Aug 1970

2a +Fergus Hugh Stirling; *b* 16 Aug 1973

(3) +(Kenneth) James [James Graham Esq, Home Idover Farm, Dauntsey, Wilts SN15 4JT]; 2nd Lt Argyll and Sutherland Highrs 1965–68, exec Digital Equipment Corp; *b* 30 June 1947; *educ* Eton and Northwestern U Chicago; *m* 5 May 1972 *Victoria Margaret Anne, yst dau of Maj Andrew Charles Stirling Home Drummond Moray, Scots Gds, of Easter Ross, Comrie, Perthshire, and has:

1a +Magnus James; *b* 1974

1a *Nina Louise; *b* 1976

2a *Georgina Carol Cecilia; *bapt* 28 Dec 1977

1 Glenda Victoria Maud, authoress, jnlst; *b* 5 Aug 1867; *m* 8 June 1934 Capt Hugh Spooner, 19th KGO Lancers, yst s of Maj W B Spooner, and *dsp* 1981, having adopted a dau. He was *k* in a flying accident 15 March 1935

Sir FREDERICK *d* 25 Nov 1936; his est son,

Sir (John) Reginald Noble Graham, 3rd Bt, VC (1917), OBE (1946); *b* 17 Sept 1892; *educ* Eton and Trin Coll Cambridge; Lt-Col Argyll and Sutherland Highrs TF, attd MGC, WW I, WW II Argyll and Sutherland Highrs, attd Staff Movement Control Scottish Cmnd (Lt-Col), S/Ldr Calcutta Light Horse, Cdr Bombay Light Patrol, Chm Karachi Chamber Commerce 1927–28 and 1931, manager Karachi and Bombay Graham's Trading Cos, Gen Sec Offrs' Assoc (Scottish Branch) and Earl Haig Fund (Scotland) 1946–64, Gentleman Usher Green Rod Order Thistle 1959, Haakon VII of Norway Liberty Cross; *m* 8 Nov 1920 Rachel Septima (*d*

1984), 5th dau of Col Sir Alexander Sprot, 1st Bt, CMG (*see* 1929 edn), and *d* 1980, leaving issue:

1 Sir JOHN ALEXANDER NOBLE GRAHAM, **4th and present Bt**

1 *Lesley [Mrs Jock Strang Steel, Haydean, Haddington, E Lothian EH41 4HN]; *b* 20 Aug 1921; *m* 14 Nov 1945 Jock Wykeham Strang Steel (*d* 1991), and has issue (*see* STEEL, Bt)

GRAHAM, Bt, of Netherby

Arms: Quarterly, 1st and 4th, or on a chief sa. three escallops of the field (for GRAHAM); 2nd and 3rd, or a fess chequy arg. and az., in chief a chevronel gu. (for STUART), in the centre of the quarters a crescent of the last, and all within a bordure engrailed of the third. **Crest:** Two wings addorsed or. **Motto:** Reason contents me. **Creation:** Bt. (GB) 15 Jan 1783.

SIR JAMES FERGUS SURTEES GRAHAM, 7TH BT, of Netherby, Cumberland [Sir James Graham Bt, The Tower, Kirkandrews-on-Esk, Cumbria CA6 5NF]; *b* 29 July 1946; *s* f 1997; *educ* Milton Abbey and RAC Cirencester; *m* 5 Feb 1975 *Serena Jane, 2nd dau of Ronald Frank Kershaw (*see* LINDSEY and ABINGDON, E) and has:

1 +ROBERT CHARLES THOMAS; *b* 19 July 1985

1 *Catherine Mary; *b* 16 Sept 1978

2 *Iona Susan Alice; *b* 1980

Lineage: Rev ROBERT GRAHAM, DD, of Netherby, Cumberland; Rector Arthuret (gs of Sir George Graham, 2nd Bt, of Esk, *qv*); *m* 1 June 1752 Frances (*d* 17 Feb 1801), dau of Sir Reginald Graham, 4th Bt, of Norton Conyers (*qv*), and had:

1 Charles; *m* 1781 Elizabeth (*m* 2nd 17 April 1784 Charles Henry Sheldon), dau of Richard Gorges, DCL, of Eye, Herefs, and *dvp* 15 Feb 1782, leaving an only dau

2 JAMES (Sir), **1st Bt**

3 Fergus (Rev); Rector Arthuret and Kirkandrews-on-Esk; *m* 1st 28 April 1792 Johanna, dau of Robert Gale, of Carlisle, and had:

(1) Fergus James; Consul Bayonne; *b* 1792; *m* 1st 1818 Alethea, only dau of William Evans James; *m* 2nd 1851 Frances, dau of William Ellis, and *d* 18 Jan 1881, leaving by his 1st w:

1a William Graham; *m* 1st Dora, dau of Richard Henry Holland; *m* 2nd 1873 Fanny Edith, dau of P Bright, of Brecon, and *d* 20 Feb 1908

3 (cont.) The Rev Fergus Graham *m* 2nd 21 Feb 1809 Jane (*d* 1826), dau of Ven William Paley, DD, Archdeacon Carlisle, and *d* 26 March 1829, having by her had, with other issue:

(2) William Paley (Rev); MA; *b* 12 April 1817; *m* Elizabeth (*d* 1849), dau of Rev James Bush, and *d* 29 April 1870, leaving issue:

1a Fergus; Maj Roy Irish Rifles; *b* 20 Aug 1846; *m* 13 April 1882 Caroline Mary (*d* 1896), dau of William Tinker, and *d* 27 March 1924, having had:

1b Fergus Reginald Winsford, DSO (1919), MC; Col Roy Ulster Rifles, WW I (wounded twice, despatches four times, brevet, Croix de Guerre), cmded Shanghai Vol Corps 1934–38, Gp Cmdt ROC WW II; *b* 26 Oct 1884; *m* 30 April 1915 Egeria Marion Spottiswood (*d* 1 April 1975), er dau of V-Adml Casper Joseph Baker, and *d* 3 Nov 1961, having had issue:

1c Malise James Fergus; *b* 23 Feb 1916; *d* 17 Aug 1926 following an accident

2c +Dominick Stuart, MC (1945) [Prof Dominick Graham MC, The Hollins, E Rounton, N Yorks DL6 2LG]; PhD, Maj RA (ret 1958) WW II (POW, wounded twice, despatches), Prof Emeritus History U of NB; *b* 24 July 1920; *m* 1st 18 Oct 1947 Valerie Mary, only dau of Farleigh H Greig, and has:

1d *Anita Caroline; *b* 14 Oct 1949

2d *Patricia Robin; *b* 19 July 1952

2c (cont.) Prof Dominick Graham *m* 2nd 1991 *Mary, dau of George Howson, MC, of The Hyde, Hambleden, Bucks, and widow of Sir Hugh Francis Bell, 4th Bt (*qv*)

1c *Caroline Egeria Malise [Mrs William Muir, Torquhan, Stow, Midlothian]; *b* 14 Aug 1929; *m* 30 Dec 1952 *Maj Thomas Wemyss Muir, Queen's Dragoon Gds, er s of Capt William Hugh Muir, MC, King's Dragoon Gds, and Mrs Jean Hargreaves Arkwright, and has:

1d *James Fergus Wemyss; *b* 12 April 1963

1d *Elizabeth Anne; *b* 24 July 1955; *m* 1979 *Lt-Col Sebastian John Lechmere Roberts, OBE, Irish Gds

2d *Sarah Jane; *b* 16 Sept 1957; *m* 1986 *Colin George Climie

3d *Alexandra Caroline; *b* 5 Sept 1959; *m* 1978 *Nicholas Leese

1a Charlotte; *d* unm 8 Dec 1927

2a Elizabeth Anne; *d* unm

(3) Robert Wilfrid; MICE; *b* 24 March 1923; *m* 21 Feb 1888 Anne Maria, widow of Gordon Mackenzie, and *d* 20 April 1917

The Rev ROBERT GRAHAM *d* 2 Feb 1782; his er surv son,

Sir James Graham, 1st Bt (GB), so *cr* 15 Jan 1783, of Netherby; *b* April 1761; *m* 28 Sept 1782 Lady Catherine Stewart (*d* 20 Sept 1836), dau of 7th Earl of Galloway (*qv*), and had, with other issue:

1 JAMES ROBERT GEORGE (Sir), **2nd Bt**

2 Charles, CB; R-Adml RN; *b* 1792; *d* unm 18 Nov 1858

3 George; Maj 1st Indian Regt, Registrar-Gen Births, Deaths and Marriages 1839–79; *b* 13 Sept 1801; *m* 12 April 1836 Maria (*d* Dec 1855), yst dau of Edward Hasell, and *d* 26 May 1888, having had:

(1) Alan; Capt 23rd Roy Welch Fus; *b* 30 April 1839; *d* unm 10 Dec 1874

(1) Emily; *b* 19 Feb 1837; *m* Dec 1867 Capt John William Herbert Cuninghame, 2nd Life Gds, and *d* 26 Jan 1887, leaving issue. He *d* 14 Nov 1915

(2) Florence Inger Maria; *b* 29 Sept 1850; *m* 6 May 1873 Graham Hutchison, DL, and *d* 25 Jan 1929, leaving issue

1 Elizabeth Anne; *m* 14 March 1816 Rev William Waddilove

2 Caroline; *m* 20 June 1821 Sir Wilfred Lawson, 1st Bt, of Brayton (*see* 1959 edn), and *d* 30 Oct 1870. He *d* 12 June 1867

3 Harriet Anne; *m* 10 July 1832 Capt Frederick Madan, EI Service, and had issue. He *d* 17 Nov 1863

4 Charlotte; *m* 26 June 1828 Sir George Musgrave, 10th Bt, of Hartley Castle (*qv*), and *d* 26 June 1873, leaving issue

Sir JAMES *d* 13 April 1824; his est son,

Sir James Robert George Graham, 2nd Bt, GCB (1854), PC (1830); LLD; *b* 1 June 1792; *educ* Westminster and Ch Ch Oxford; MP (Whig to 1835, more or less Tory 1835–45, Peelite 1845–52, Lib 1852–61) Hull 1818–20, St Ives 1820–21, Carlisle 1826–27 and 1852–61, Cumberland 1827–37, Pembroke 1838–41, Dorchester 1841–46 and Ripon 1847–52, 1st Ld Admlty 1830–34 and 1852–55, Home Sec 1841–46, Rector Glasgow U 1838; *m* 8 July 1819 Fanny (*d* 25 Oct 1857), yst dau of Col and Lady Elizabeth Callander, of Craigforth and Ardkinglass, and had, with other issue:

1 FREDERICK ULRIC (Sir), **3rd Bt**

2 Malise Reginald (Rev); MA, Rector Arthuret; *b* 15 Feb 1833; *m* 19 June 1862 his cousin Agnes (*d* 12 March 1901), 2nd dau of Sir George Musgrave, 10th Bt (*see* above), and *d* 18 Nov 1895, leaving:

(1) Arthur Malise; *b* 1865

(2) Reginald; *b* 1867; *m* 1897 Helen Dacia, dau of G S Herck, of St Petersburg, and *d* 15 Feb 1908, leaving:

1a Ernest Reginald *b* 1898

(3) Ivor Charles (Rev); Rector Arthuret; *b* 1868; *d* unm 18 Oct 1953

(1) Sophia Augusta, MBE (1919); *d* unm 1943

(2) Maud Agnes; *d* unm 7 March 1958

(1) Mabel Violet; *m* 7 Aug 1851 1st Earl of Feversham (*see* FEVERSHAM, B) and *d* 28 Aug 1915, leaving issue

2 Helen; *m* 25 Aug 1860 Lt-Gen Charles Baring and *d* 17 Jan 1914, leaving issue (*see* BARING, Bt)

Sir JAMES *d* 25 Oct 1861; his est son,

Sir Frederick Ulric Graham, 3rd Bt, DL; Attaché Vienna 1842, 1st Life Gds, High Sheriff Cumberland 1866; *b* 2 April 1820; *m* 26 Oct 1852 Jane Hermione (*d* 4 April 1909), est dau of 12th Duke of Somerset (*qv*), and had:

1 RICHARD JAMES (Sir), **4th Bt**

2 Hugh; *b* 11 Dec 1860; *m* 24 Nov 1888 Jessie (*d* 13 May 1934), yst dau of Andrew Low, of Savannah, Ga., and *d* 25 Nov 1921, having had:

(1) Ronald Andrew Hugh; *b* 1891; *d* 1899

(2) Alastair Hugh; Hon Attaché Athens 1927–29, Cairo 1929–33; *b* 27 June 1904; *educ* Wellington and BNC Oxford; the great friend in youth of Evelyn Waugh

(1) Sibyl Hattie Hermione; *b* 1893; *m* 12 June 1920 Lt-Col Lionel Henry Hickson, DSO, Roy W Kent Regt, and had issue. He *d* 1951

(2) Muriel Mary; *b* 1895; *d* 1918

3 James Reginald, of Scaurbank, Longtown, Cumberland; *b* 28 July 1864; *m* 16 Jan 1892 Florence Rose (*m* 3rd 1 Jan 1927 Sir Richard James Graham, 4th Bt, of Netherby (*qv*); *d* 7 Jan 1934), widow of Capt Cyprian Knollys and dau of J Carter Wood, and *d* 26 Sept 1910, leaving:

(1) Iris Enid Florence; *b* 14 Oct 1892; *m* 1st 20 Nov 1912 (*divorce* 1920) Noel van Raalte, s of Charles van Raalte, and had issue; *m* 2nd 31 Jan 1923 Louis Herve Coatalen and had further issue. He *d* 23 May 1962

1 Margaret Frances; *m* 1st 4 May 1875 Alexander Aeneas Mackintosh, 27th Chief of Mackintosh and 28th of Clan Chattan, JP, DL, and had issue. He *d* 17 Dec 1875. She *m* 2nd 30 April 1878 3rd Earl of Verulam (*qv*) and *d* 4 Oct 1927, leaving further issue

2 Violet Hermione, GBE; Hon LLD, DGStJ; *m* 24 July 1876 5th Duke of Montrose (*qv*) and *d* 21 Nov 1940, leaving issue

3 Helen; *d* young 11 Dec 1863

4 Sibyl Marcia; *m* 3 June 1880 1st and last Marquess of Crewe and *d* 19 Sept 1887, leaving issue (*see* 1940 edn). He *d* 20 June 1945

5 Hilda Georgiana; *m* 7 Oct 1895 1st Baron Wittenham and *d* 1 Feb 1946. He *dsp* 1 Feb 1931

Sir FREDERICK *d* 8 March 1888; his est son,

Sir Richard James Graham, 4th Bt, JP, DL, High Sheriff 1894, Lt Argyll and Sutherland Highrs; *b* 24 Feb 1859; *m* 1st 8 July 1886 Olivia (*dsp* 21 March 1887), dau of Lt-Gen Charles Baring (*see* NORTHBROOK, B); *m* 2nd 27 June 1889 Lady Mabel Cynthia Duncombe (*d* 25 April 1926), 3rd dau of 1st Earl of Feversham (*see* FEVERSHAM, B), and had issue:

1 FERGUS FREDERICK (Sir), **5th Bt**

2 +Richard Preston GRAHAM later GRAHAM-VIVIAN (roy licence 21 Aug 1929), MVO (1961), MC (1919); Lt KRRC WW I (wounded twice), Bluemantle Pursuivant 1933–46, Windsor Herald 1947–66, Norroy and Ulster King of Arms 1966, Earl Marshal's Sec 1954–61, FZS, OStJ; *b* 10 Aug 1896; *educ* Eton and Trin Coll Cambridge (BA 1919); *m* 7 Dec 1921 Audrey Emily, dau of Henry Wyndham Vivian (*see* SWANSEA, B), and *d* 30 Sept 1979, leaving:

(1) Henry Richard, TD (1955); High Sheriff Cornwall 1965, Capt DCLI (TA), Lt Coldream Gds WW II (severely wounded); *b* 13 April 1923; *educ* Eton and Ch Ch Oxford (BA 1949); *m* 9 Dec 1955 *Rosemary [Mrs Henry Graham, Bosahan, Manaccan, Helston, Cornwall], only dau of Col Giffard Loftus Tyringham, DL, and *d* 1993, leaving issue:

1a +Richard John; *b* 26 April 1957; *m* 1993 *Christine Trippear

1a *Lavinia; *b* 5 Feb 1959; *m* 1996 *Gregory Powlesland

(1) *Catherine Maude [Mrs Peter Thomson-Glover, Ludgates, Nutbourne, Pulborough, Sussex]; *b* 10 Nov 1926; *m* 24 June 1947 Lt-Col (John) Peter Thomson-Glover, MC, 9th/12th Roy Lancers (*d* 6 Oct 1968), er s of Col John William Thomson-Glover, CBE, IA, and has:

1a *Michael William [Michael Thomson-Glover Esq, 20 Crondace Rd, London SW6 4BS]; *b* 19 May 1948; *educ* Wellington and Trin Coll Cambridge (BA); *m* 1974 *Katherine, dau of John David Summers, and has issue:

1b *James Antony; *b* 1988

2b *Peter David; *b* 1988

1b *Sarah Emily; *b* 1977

2b *Rebecca Evelyn; *b* 1979

3b *Rachel Caroline; *b* 1981

2a *(Peter) James; *b* 1 Feb 1953; *educ* Wellington; FCA; *m* 1982 *Veronica Harrison and has:

1b *Edward; *b* 1984

1b *Rosie Catherine; *b* 1990

1a *Caroline Veronica; *b* 2 Sept 1950

1 *Daphne; W/O WAAF WW II; *b* 17 March 1903; *m* 12 Dec 1925 Sir Kenneth Ralph Barnes, s of Preb R H Barnes, and has had issue. He *d* 16 Oct 1957

Sir Richard *m* 3rd 1 Jan 1927 Florence Rose (*d* 7 Jan 1934), widow of James Reginald Graham and dau of J Carter Wood, and *d* 26 Aug 1932

His er son,

Sir (Frederick) Fergus Graham, 5th Bt, KBE (1956), TD, JP, DL; *b* 10 March 1893; *educ* Eton and Ch Ch Oxford (BA 1914, MA 1920); CA, Ld Lt Cumberland 1958–68, Hon Col (late Lt-Col) 4th Bn Border Regt (TA) 1951–56, Capt Irish Gds (SR), WW I (severely wounded, despatches), MP N Cumberland 1926–35 and Darlington Oct 1951–59, PPS Min Pensions 1933–35, PMG June 1935; *m* 1 Jan 1918 Mary Spencer Revell, CBE (1953), JP (Cumberland 1937) (*d* 1985), dau of Maj-Gen Raymond Northland Revell Reade, CB, CMG, and *d* 1 Aug 1978, having had:

1 **Sir Charles Spencer Richard Graham, 6th Bt**; *b* 16 July 1919; *educ* Eton; Maj Scots Gds WW II and Malaya 1949–50, Chm Cumberland River Authority 1954–64; Cumberland/Cumbria: High Sheriff 1955, DL 1971–83, Ld Lt 1983–94; V-Chm CLA 1965–69 and Pres 1971–73, memb Nat Water Cncl 1973–83 and Coop Fell Head Farmers 1976, Master Farmers' Co 1982–83, KStJ 1984; *m* 5 Feb 1944 *(Isabel) Susan Anne [Susan Lady Graham, Crofthead, Longtown, Cumbria CA6 5PA], only dau of Maj Robert Lambton Surtees, and *d* 11 July 1997, leaving:

(1) Sir JAMES FERGUS SURTEES GRAHAM, **7th and present Bt**

(2) +Malise Charles Richard [Malise Graham Esq, The Cottage, Sproxton, Leics LE14 4QS]; *b* 19 Sept 1948; *educ* Milton Abbey; *m* 27 April 1974 *Hon Pamela Winifred, yst dau of 1st Viscount Whitelaw (*qv*), and has:

1a *Arabella Mary Susan; *b* 19 May 1975

2a *Georgina Carol Cecilia; *b* 19 Sept 1977

3a *Laura Meliora Winifred; *b* 1981

4a *Victoria Malise Samantha; *b* 1985

(1) *Susanna Anne Mary; *b* 8 May 1951

1 Cynthia Mary; *b* 13 Nov 1923; *d* 13 Jan 1927

GRAHAM, Bt, of Norton Conyers

Arms: Quarterly, 1st and 4th, or on a chief sa. three escallops of the field (for GRAHAM); 2nd and 3rd, or a fess chequy arg. and az., in chief a chevronel gu. (for STUART); in the centre of the quarters a crescent of the last and all within a bordure engrailed of the third. **Crest:** Two wings addorsed or. **Motto:** Reason contents me. **Creation:** Bt. (E) 17 Nov 1662.

SIR JAMES BELLINGHAM GRAHAM, 11TH BT, of Norton Conyers, Co Yorks [Sir James Graham Bt, Norton Conyers Hall, Ripon, N Yorks HG4 5EH]; *b* 8 Oct 1940; *s f* 1982; *educ* Eton and Ch Ch Oxford (MA); *m* 1986 *Halina, yr dau of Maj Wiktor Grubert, of Putney

Lineage: Sir Richard Graham, 1st Bt (E), so *cr* 17 Nov 1662, of Norton Conyers, Yorks (2nd s of Sir Richard Graham, 1st Bt, of Esk, *qv*); *bapt* 11 March 1635/6; admitted Gray's Inn Feb 1651/2 and Inner Temple 1654; *m* by 1660 Elizabeth, dau of Col Sir Chichester Fortescue, of Dromiskin, Ireland, and was *bur* 21 Dec 1711, having had, with two est sons and a yst s (Richard, *m* a dau of William Chaloner, *see* GISBOROUGH, B) and two daus (Elizabeth, *m* Sir Robert Fenwick, Bt; Jane, *m* Rev James Musgrave; *see* MUSGRAVE, Bt, of Hartley Castle), a 3rd s:

Sir Reginald Graham, 2nd Bt; *bapt* 30 July 1670; Page Honour to JAMES II; *m* 1st by 1702 Frances, dau and heir of Henry Bellingham, of Whitwell, Yorks; *m* 2nd 9 April 1724 Anne, dau of Sir David Foulis, 3rd Bt, of Ingleby (*see* FOULIS, Bt), and *d* 20 May 1728, leaving by his 1st w, with a 3rd s (Richard):

1 **Sir Bellingham Graham, 3rd Bt**; *bapt* 20 Aug 1702; *d* unm 1 April 1730

2 **Sir Reginald Graham, 4th Bt**; *b* 16 May 1704; *m* 5 June 1727 Jacoba Catherina (*m* 2nd Col — Brown; *bur* 1 Dec 1764), dau of Col Metcalfe Graham, of Pickill, Yorks (*see* GRAHAM, Bt, of Esk), and *d* 29 Oct 1755, having had:

(1) BELLINGHAM (Sir), **5th Bt**

(2) Reginald, Capt RM; *m* a dau of Gen Jackman, RM

(3) Mitchell, Adml; *m* 1st a dau of Gen Jackman; *m* 2nd Maria Rebecca Bowater and *d* 8 March 1795, leaving:

1a John Bellingham, Capt RM

1a Maria

The 4th Bt's est son,

Sir Bellingham Graham, 5th Bt; *bapt* 14 June 1729; Sheriff Yorks 1770–71; *m* 24 June 1763 Elizabeth (*d* 1767), dau of Benjamin Hudson, of Bridlington, Yorks, and *d* 3 Oct 1790, having had, with two daus (Catherine, *m* Dec 1813 Henry Francis Fulke Greville (*see* WARWICK, BROOKE and, E); Elizabeth; *m* Maj-Gen John Smith):

Sir Bellingham Graham, 6th Bt; *b c* 1764; *m* 31 Oct 1785 Priscilla, sis of 1st and last Earl Whitworth (*see* RAVENSDALE, B), and *d* 13 April 1796, having had, with two daus (Priscilla Elizabeth, *m* 1st Lt-Col Simon George Newport, *m* 2nd Lt Col Bellingham John Smith, *d* 14 Dec 1874; Caroline, *m* Dec 1813 Algernon Greville (*see* WARWICK, BROOKE and, E), and had issue):

Sir Bellingham Reginald Graham, 7th Bt; *b* 3 Nov 1789; *m* 1st 10 Nov 1810 Harriet (*d* 9 Oct 1830), 3rd dau of George Clark, of W Hatch, Essex, and had, with three sons:

1 Harriot; *m* 1st 20 Oct 1833 Lt-Gen Sir Frederick Ashworth, KCB, Col 44th Regt (*d* 1 Aug 1858), and had issue; *m* 2nd 26 Feb 1862 3rd Marquess of Donegall (*qv*) and *d* 6 March 1884

Sir Bellingham *m* 2nd July 1831 Harriet (*d* 17 Jan 1903), 3rd dau of Rev Robert Cottam, MA, and by her had:

1 REGINALD HENRY (Sir), **8th Bt**

2 George Fergus; Maj-Gen IA; *b* 16 May 1836; *m* 12 Feb1871 Margaret Anne (*d* 20 Dec 1874), est dau of Thomas Jasper Atkinson, of Calcutta, and *d* 7 Sept 1930, having had issue:

(1) Fergus Bellingham *b* 24 Oct 1872; *d* 28 May 1873

(2) Fergus Bellingham Reginald; *b* 7 Dec 1874; *m* 25 Nov 1907 (*divorce* 1917) Blanche Josephine, only dau of John Swan

2 Augusta Clementina; *m* 21 Oct 1857 Maj Edmund de Feyl, Austrian Army, and *d* 11 June 1875. He *d* 1867

3 Charlotte Harriet; nun; *d* 12 Sept 1927

4 Gertrude Elizabeth Priscilla; *m* 1863 Count Arthur Dillon and *d* 4 Aug 1927, leaving issue. He *d* 1889

Sir BELLINGHAM *d* 15 June 1866; his son,

Sir Reginald Henry Graham, 8th Bt, JP, DL N R and W R Yorks and Liberty of Ripon; 14th Regt Crimea (Crimean and Turkish medals), Capt Rifle Bde 1856; *b* 22 April 1835; *m* 24 July 1876 Annie Mary (*d* 16 Dec 1917), 2nd dau of Thomas Shiffner (*see* SHIFFNER, Bt), and had:

1 REGINALD GUY (Sir), **9th Bt**

2 Nigel James Spencer; *b* 2 April 1880; *d* unm 26 March 1902

3 Malise, DSO (1918); Col 10th Hus, Maj and Brevet Lt-Col 16th/5th Lancers, GSO(1) 4th Cav Div 1917, 2nd Cav Div 1918–19, cmd'd 10th Hus 1923–27, 6th Cav Bde 1928–29, T/Brig and Asst Dir Remounts War Office 1929; *b* 12 Feb 1884; *m* 10 Aug 1915 Cecil Lorna (Dooney) (*m* 2nd 5 June 1935 3rd Baron Ailwyn (*d* 23 March 1976; *see* 1970 edn); *d* 12 July 1976), dau of Col Hugh Gurney Barclay, MVO, of Colney Hall, Norfolk, and *d* 14 Aug 1929, having had:

(1) Nigel; Lt RAC WW II; *b* 19 June 1919; *ka* Middle East Jan 1942

(1) June; *b* 25 June, *d* 2 Dec 1917

Sir REGINALD *d* 27 Dec 1920; his est son,

Sir Reginald Guy Graham, 9th Bt, DSO (1917), JP, DL N R Yorks; Lt 1st Bn Rifle Bde Boer War 1899–1902 (severely wounded), Maj 5th Bn York Regt, Assist Provost Marshal 37th Div 1915, 2nd Army Corps 1916 WW I (despatches, Croix de Guerre); *b* 28 May 1878; *m* 18 July 1911 Katherine Noel, JP (Liberty of Ripon 1941 and WR Yorks 1942), chm Yorkshire WLA 1939–46 (*d* 8 June 1966), only dau of Frank Stobart, DL, of Selaby, Co Durham, and had issue:

1 RICHARD BELLINGHAM (Sir), **10th Bt**

2 Alastair, MC; Maj Roy Dragoons WW II; *b* 16 June 1915; *educ* Eton; *m* 14 March 1942 *Gundreda Margaret [Mrs Alastair Graham, Middleton Quernhow, Ripon, Yorks HG4 5HY], only dau of John Laurence Graham-Jones, FRCS, of Bockhampton House, Dorchester, Dorset, and *d* 1975, leaving issue:

(1) +Patrick Martin; *b* 8 March 1948; *educ* Eton

(1) *Caroline Susan; *b* 8 Nov 1943; *m* 1990 *Robert H Richheimer, only s of Robert C Richheimer

(2) *Priscilla Ann; *b* 8 March 1948; *m* 3 Feb 1968 *Peter Norman Bingham Kennedy, TD, DL, est s of Maj Bruce Bingham Kennedy, TD, and has issue:

1a *Sara Margaret; *b* 15 July 1971

2a *Annabel Deborah; *b* 1973

3a *Caroline Anne; *b* 1980

4a *Rosanna Jane; *b* 1982

3 Patrick; Capt Yorks Dragoons Yeo WW II (despatches); *b* 4 Jan 1918; *d* of wounds N Africa April 1943

4 Jeremy Frank; *b* 8 July 1926; *m* Sept 1950 *Susan May [Mrs Jeremy Graham, Plaster Pitts, Ripon, N Yorks], 2nd dau of Lt Col Sir Thomas Eustace Smith, CBE, DL, of Barton Hall, Darlington, and *d* 1992, leaving:

(1) +Robin Guy; *b* 13 Oct 1953; *educ* Ampleforth; *m* 1979 *Annabel Mary Diana, er dau of Michael David Aykroyd (*see* AYKROYD, Bt, of Lightcliffe), and has issue:

1a +Andrew Guy Bellingham; *b* 1981

2a +Rory Michael; *b* 1984

(2) +Nigel Ronald; *b* 19 Aug 1957; *m* 1982 *Henrietta Jane Fane, dau of Maj Jerome De Salis (*see* MONK BRETTON, B), and adopted:

*Thomas Guy; *b* 8 Dec 1995

(1) *Jacoba Elizabeth [Mrs Christopher Oldham, 78 Paxton Rd, London W4 2QX]; *b* 28 Nov 1951; *m* 9 Jan 1971 *Christopher Russell Oldham, Roy Hus (ret), only s of Henry Russell Oldham and Mrs Keith Anderson, of Stone Court, Staplefield, Sussex, and has issue:

1a *Justin Russell; *b* 1974

2a *Mark Russell; *b* 1977

Sir REGINALD *d* 2 June 1940; his est son,

Sir Richard Bellingham, 10th Bt, OBE (1946), JP (N R Yorks 1953), DL (1961); High Sheriff Yorks 1961; *educ* Eton and Magdalene Coll Camb; W/Cdr RAFVR WW II (despatches), chm Yorkshire Insur 1964, Yorkshire TV 1968–82; *b* 17 May 1912; *m* 16 Sept 1939 Beatrice Mary (*d* 1992), only dau of Lt-Col Michael Seymour Spencer-Smith, DSO, MC (*see* SPENCER-SMITH Bt), and *d* 29 Jan 1982, leaving issue:

1 Sir JAMES BELLINGHAM GRAHAM, **11th and present Bt**

2 +WILLIAM REGINALD [William Graham Esq, Badger Bank, Norton Conyers, Melmberby, nr Ripon, Yorks]; *b* 7 July 1942; heir presumptive; *educ* Eton

3 +(Jeremy) Richard [Richard Graham Esq, Badger Bank, Norton Conyers, nr Ripon, Yorks]; *b* 23 Jan 1949; *educ* Eton; *m* 3 Jan 1976 *Judith, yr dau of Gerard McCann, of Castle House, Aldborough, Boroughbridge, Yorks, and has issue:

(1) +Samuel Reginald; *b* 1979

(2) +Edward Richard; *b* 1985

(1) *Sophia Harriet; *b* 1977

Seat: Norton Conyers, Ripon, N Yorks. The house dates from approximately a century before the present owners acquired it, that is to say the first part of the 16th century. The GRAHAMs are recorded as taking possession in 1624, so it was presumably the father of the **1st Bt** who bought the property. One of the chambers is called 'The James II Bedroom', though whether the King ever slept there is less certain. It is of course possible since the **2nd Bt** was that monarch's Page of Honour. In the 18th century the main elevation was embellished with a fresh facade. The garden still grows plants that were common in the Georgian age.

GRAHAM OF EDMONTON

Creation: B. (LP, UK) 1983.

THE BARON GRAHAM OF EDMONTON, of Edmonton in Greater London ((Thomas) Edward Graham) [The Rt Hon The Lord Graham of Edmonton, 2 Clerks Piece, Loughton, Essex IG10 1NR]; *b* 26 March 1925; *educ* WEA Co-op Coll and OU (BA 1976); Newcastle-upon-Tyne Co-op Soc 1939–52; organiser Br Fedn Young Co-ops 1952–53; Educn Sec Enfield Highway Co-op Soc 1953–62; Sec Co-op Union Southern Section 1962–67; Memb and Leader Enfield Cncl 1961–68; Nat Sec Co-op Party 1967–74; MP (Lab) Enfield Edmonton 1974–83, PPS to Min State Dept Prices and Consumer Protection 1974–76, Ld Commr Treasury 1976–79, Oppn Spokesman Environment 1980–83, Lab Ch Whip Ho Lds 1990–97; FIMgt: *m* 1950 *Margaret, dau of Frederick Golding, of Dagenham, Essex, and has issue:

1 *Martin Nicholas; *b* 1957

2 *Ian Stuart; *b* 1959

Lineage: THOMAS EDWARD GRAHAM, of Newcastle; had:

THOMAS EDWARD, *cr* a **Baron**

GRANARD

Arms: Az. three bear's heads couped arg., muzzled gu. **Crest:** A bear statant arg., guttée de sang, muzzled gu. **Supporters:** Dexter, a unicorn erminois, armed, maned, tufted and unguled or; sinister, a dragon, wings expanded, erm. **Motto:** *Fax mentis incendium gloriæ* ('The incitement to glory is the firebrand of the mind').

Creations: Bt. (NS) 29 Sept 1628, B. (Clanehugh) and V. (I) 22 Nov 1675, E. (I) 30 Dec 1684, B. (UK) 24 Feb 1806.

THE 10TH EARL OF GRANARD, Viscount of Granard and **Baron Clanehugh**, Co Longford, **Baron Granard of Castle Donington**, Co Leicester, and a **Baronet** (Sir Peter Arthur Edward Hastings Forbes 11th Bt) [The Rt Hon The Earl of Granard, Strathallen Cliff, Strathallen Rd, Onchan, Isle of Man]; *b* 15 March 1957; *s* unc 1992; *educ* Eton; *m* 1980 *Nora Ann (Noreen), dau of Robert Mitchell, of Upper Main St, Portarlington, Co Laois, Ireland, and has:

1 +Jonathan Peter Hastings, *Viscount Forbes*; *b* 24 Dec 1981

2 +David Robert Hastings; *b* 1984

1 *Lisa Ann; *b* 1986

Lineage: PATRICK FORBES, 3rd s of 2nd Lord Forbes (*qv*); armour-bearer to JAMES III KING OF SCOTS; had a charter of Cors(s)e, Aberdeenshire, 10 Oct 1482 and founded the line of FORBES of Corss; had:

DAVID FORBES of Cors(s)e, called 'Trail the Axe'; *d* by 1554, leaving:

PATRICK FORBES of Cors(s)e; *m* Majory Lumsden and had:

WILLIAM FORBES of Cors(s)e; *m* Elizabeth Straphan, dau of — Strachan of Thornton, and had, with five er sons (Patrick, Bp Aberdeen 1564–1635; William of Craigievar, ancestor of the FORBES Bts of Craigievar, *qv*; John, min at Delft, Holland; Alexander; James) and a yst s (Robert):

Sir Arthur Forbes, 1st Bt (NS), so *cr* 29 Sept 1628 with remainder to heirs male whatsoever, of Castle Forbes, Co Longford, Ireland, where he settled 1620 and became by patent 1 April 1622 a free denizen; granted land in Cos Leitrim and Longford which he erected into the manor of Castle Forbes; Col of a regt under KING GUSTAVUS ADOLPHUS OF SWEDEN in Thirty Years War; *m* between 1618 and 1623 Jane (defended Castle Forbes against the insurgents during the 1641 Uprising; was living 30 Sept 1642), widow of Sir Claud Hamilton, of Clonyn, Co Cavan, and dau of Robert Lauder, of the Bass, Scotland, and was *k* in a duel at Hamburg 14 April 1632, leaving an est s:

Sir Arthur Forbes, 2nd Bt, and **1st Earl of Granard**, so *cr* 30th Dec 1684, as also previously 22 Nov 1675 BARON CLANEHUGH and VISCOUNT OF GRANARD,

Co Longford (all I), PC (I 1670); *b c* 1623; royalist active in Scotland during Civil War; served under Duke of Montrose (*qv*), Commr Court Claims (I) 1661, MP (I Parl) Co Tyrone 1661–66, Marshal of Army (I) 1670–84, a Ld Justice (I) 1671, 1675–76 and 1684/5, Col 18th Roy Irish Foot 1684–86, Lt-Gen till resigned 1689, though he attended JAMES II's I Parl that year; *m c* 1655 Catharine (*d* 8 Dec 1714), widow of Sir Alexander Stewart, 2nd Bt of the 1623 *cr* (I; *see* 1949 edn), and dau of Sir Robert Newcomen, 4th Bt, of Moss Town, Co Longford, and *d* 1695, having had, with four other sons and a dau (Catherine, *m* 3rd Earl of Donegal; *see* DONEGALL, M):

ARTHUR FORBES, **2nd Earl of Granard**; Col 18th Foot 1686–88 but dismissed by WILLIAM III and imprisoned Tower London, served under Marshal Turenne, participated Battle Saspach, and helped the forces of the HRE capture Buda from the Turks 1686; *b c* 1656; *m* 1678 Mary (*d* 1 April 1724), est dau of Sir George Rawdon, 1st Bt, of Moira, Co Down (*see* LOUDOUN, E), and *d* 24 Aug 1734, having had, with two other sons and two daus (Jane, *m* Maj Josias Champagne, of Portarlington, *d* Oct 1760; Dorothy; *d* unm 17 May 1779):

GEORGE FORBES, **3rd Earl of Granard**, PC (I 1721); *b* 21 Oct 1685; called up to Ho Lords *vp* 27 Feb 1725/6 as Lord Forbes (although his f possessed no such title); RN: joined and held commission by 1706, R-Adml 1734, V-Adml 1735, MP (Whig) Queenborough, Kent, 1723–27 and Ayr Burghs 1741–47, C-in-C Caribbean Sept-Dec 1729, Plen Court of Muscovy 1733; *m* 1709 Mary (*d* 4 Oct 1765), widow of Phineas Preston, of Ardsallagh, Co Meath, and er dau of 1st Viscount Mountjoy, and *d* 29 Oct 1765, having had:

1 GEORGE FORBES, **4th Earl of Granard**; *b* 15 March 1710; Army: joined 1726 (though he fought in a naval battle against a Franco-Spanish fleet off Toulon 1743 alongside his bro the future Adml), Lt-Col Tangier Regt 1746, QMG 1754–57 (I), Col 76th Foot 1756–61 and 29th Foot 1761–69, Maj-Gen 1759, Lt-Gen 1765 with seniority from 1761; *m* 16 July 1736 his cousin Letitia (*d* 19 May 1778), dau of Arthur Davys, MP Carrickfergus, by Catherine Stewart, dau of 1st Viscount Mountjoy, and *d* 16 Oct 1769, leaving:

(1) GEORGE FORBES, **5th Earl of Granard**; *b* 2 April 1740; *m* 1st 1759 Dorothea (*d* 24 Feb 1764), 2nd dau of Sir Nicholas Bayly, Bt, and sister of 1st Earl of Uxbridge (*see* ANGLESEY, M), and had:

1a GEORGE, **6th Earl**

(1) The **5th Earl** *m* 2nd 20 April 1766 Georgiana Augusta (*m* 2nd after 1780 Rev Samuel Little, DD; *d* 24 Jan 1820), est dau of 4th Earl Berkeley (*see* BERKELEY, B), and *d* 16 April 1780, having by her had, with a dau (*d* unm):

2a Henry; *b* 6 Sept 1767; *m* 29 Dec 1794 Elizabeth, 2nd dau of John Preston

3a Frederick; *b* 7 Nov 1776; *m* 1796 (*divorce*) Mary, only dau of William Butler, and *d* 2 Feb 1817

1a Georgiana Anne; *m* 1796 Archibald McNeil of Colonsay

2a Augusta; *m* 14 Feb 1798 Lt-Gen Sir James Lieth, GCB

3a Louisa Georgiana; *m* 19 June 1806 Sir William Pratt Call, Bt (*see* 1903 edn), and *d* 25 Jan 1830

2 John; Adml of the Fleet, Gen RM; *m* 25 Aug 1758 Lady Mary Capell (*d* April 1782), 4th dau of 3rd Earl of Essex (*qv*), and *d* 10 March 1796, having had:

(1) Catherine Elizabeth; *m* 3rd Earl of Mornington (*see* WELLINGTON, D)

(2) Maria Eleanor; *m* 3rd Earl of Clarendon (*qv*)

1 Mary; *m* James Irvine, of Kingcaussie, and *d* his widow 22 Nov 1797

The 5th EARL's est s,

GEORGE FORBES, **6th Earl of Granard**, *cr* 24 Feb 1806 BARON GRANARD OF CASTLE DONNINGTON, Co Leicester (UK); *b* 14 June 1760; *m* 10 May 1779 Lady Selina Frances Rawdon (*d* 1827), 4th dau of 1st Earl of Moira (*see* LOUDOUN, E), and had, with other issue:

1 George John, *Viscount Forbes*; Maj-Gen, Ld Lt Co Longford; *b* 3 May 1785; *m* 4 Oct 1832 Frances Mary, VA, Extra Woman Bedchamber to HM QUEEN VICTORIA (*m* 2nd Thomas Nugent Vaughan (*d* 15 Sept 1947) and *d* 25 Dec 1877, leaving issue by him; *see* WIGRAM, Bt), dau and heiress of William Terrict, LLD, of Chilton Hall, Suffolk, and *dvp* 13 Nov 1836, leaving:

(1) GEORGE ARTHUR HASTINGS, **7th Earl**

(2) William Francis JP, DL Cos Leitrim and Longford; Special RM W Ireland, Capt Gren Gds, Hon Col 8th Bn The Prince Consort's Rifle Bde; *b* 15 Feb 1836; *m* 29 Oct 1863 Phyllis Gabriella (*d* 20 Feb 1904), 2nd dau of John Rowe, DL, of Ballycross, Co Wexford, and *d* 3 Feb 1899, leaving:

1a George Francis Reginald; Lt-Col Roy Irish Regt; *b* 6 Sept 1866; *m* 4 Aug 1904 Agnes Margaret (*d* 23 Sept 1944), er dau of Walter Ewing Crum, and *d* 17 March 1915 of wounds recd in action, leaving:

1b Walter Arthur Hastings; Lt-Col Cameronians, game warden Sudan; *b* 18 Dec 1905; *educ* Winchester; *m* 16 Dec 1946 *Joan Margaret [Mrs Walter Forbes, Brookfield, Silk Mill Lane, Winchcombe, Glos GL54 5HZ], formerly w of Maj Robert Malise Keith-Murray (*see* MURRAY, Bt, of Ochtertyre), and er dau of Maj Hugh Kettles-Roy, of Nairobi, and *d* 1987, leaving:

1c +Peter Patrick Spencer [Peter Forbes Esq, The Old Rectory, Farnham, Dorset DT11 8DE]; Lt 4th/7th Roy Dragoon Gds; *b* 6 Nov 1949; *educ* Milton Abbey, RMA Sandhurst and Manchester U; *m* 1981 *Victoria Anne, dau of Harry Tudor Bigge, and has:

1d +Arthur Edward Patrick; *b* 1987

2d +George Harry Hastings; *b* 1987

1d *Katherine Anne; *b* 1983

2d *Serena Victoria; *b* 1985

1c *Rolleen Anne [Mrs James Barclay, Rivers Hall, Waldringfield, Suffolk IP12 4QX]; *b* 25 Sept 1947; *m* 1974 *James Christopher Barclay and has:

1d *Robert James; *b* 1977

1d *Georgina Anne; *b* 1978

2a William Arthur Hastings; *b* 10 Oct 1867; *d* 10 Sept 1878

3a Ronald Ferdinande; Capt Roy Wilts Yeo Boer War 1900–02 and WW I (despatches); *b* 16 Jan 1879; *d* unm 23 June 1960

4a Raymond; *b* 26 June 1882; *m* 5 Nov 1913 Sybil Ada Florence, dau of Arthur Vesey Fitzherbert, of Ballintyre Hall, Dundrum, Co Dublin, and *dsp* 3 June 1961

1a Angela Ida Evelyn; *b* 30 June 1870; *m* 4 Feb 1903 John Whaley, of Bloomsbury, Kells, Co Meath, and *d* 22 Jan 1962, leaving issue

2a Flora Frances; *b* 11 April 1877; *d* unm 29 Nov 1954

3a Eva Adelaide; *b* 21 Oct 1880; *d* 13 Oct 1921

2 Francis Reginald; Min Plen Saxony 1858, Envoy Extrdy and Min Plen to Emperor Brazil (ret 1859); *b* 17 Sept 1791; *d* 5 Nov 1873

1 Elizabeth Maria Theresa; *m* 15 Oct 1807 2nd and last Baron Rancliffe (*see* 1850 edn) and *d* Feb 1852

The 6th EARL *d* 9 June 1837; his gs,

GEORGE ARTHUR HASTINGS FORBES, **7th Earl of Granard**, KP (1857); *b* 5 Aug 1833; *educ* Eton; V-Adml Connaught, Kt SMO Malta and Kt Grand Cross Order St Gregory the Gt, Lt-Col Cmdt and Hon Col 9th Bn Rifle Bde, Prince Consort's Own, memb Senate Roy U of Ireland; *m* 1st 2 June 1858 Jane Colclough (*d* 22 Jan 1872), yr dau and coheir of Hamilton Knox Grogan Morgan, MP, of Johnstown Castle, Co Wexford, and had, with two other daus (*d* young):

1 Adelaide Jane Frances; *m* 13 April 1880 Lord Maurice FitzGerald, 2nd s of 4th Duke of Leinster (*qv*), and *d* 18 Nov 1942, having had issue

2 Sophia Maria Elizabeth; *m* 11 Feb 1885 Sir Henry Christopher Grattan-Bellew, 3rd Bt (*qv*), and *d* 7 Nov 1942, having had issue

The **7th Earl** *m* 2nd 4 Sept 1873 Hon Frances Mary Petre (*d* 25 May 1920), est dau of 12th Baron Petre (*qv*), and by her had:

1 BERNARD ARTHUR WILLIAM PATRICK HASTINGS, **8th Earl**

2 Fergus Reginald George; *b* 20 Jan; *d* 18 Feb 1876

3 Reginald George Benedict; Capt Gordon Highrs attd Egyptian Army; *b* 25 June 1877; *d* unm 28 May 1908

4 Donald Alexander, DSO (1917), MVO (1911), JP Bucks; *b* 3 Sept 1880; Lt-Col RFA, Lt-Col and Brevet Col cmdg 99th Bucks and Berks Yeo Field Bde RA (TA), Mil Sec to Ld Lt Ireland 1911–14, Boer War 1901–02, WW I (despatches); *m* 25 April 1918 Mary Doreen (*d* 1987), dau of Andrew Sherlock Lawson, of Aldborough Manor, Yorks (*see* 1970 edn LAWSON, Bt, of Knavesmire), and *d* following a car crash 2 Aug 1938, leaving:

(1) Rosaleen Frances, Croix de Guerre; *b* 7 June 1919; *m* 9 April 1956 Anthony Rhodes, est s of Col George Ewart Rhodes, CBE, and *d* 22 Feb 1993

(2) *Penelope [Lady Sitwell, 4 Southwick Place, London W2 2TN; Renishaw Hall, Sheffield S31 9WB]; *b* 21 Oct 1923; *m* 31 Oct 1952 *Sir Reresby Sitwell, 7th Bt (*qv*), and has issue

5 Bertram Aloysius, CMG (1937), OBE (1919); Pasha, Brevet Lt-Col Roy Irish Rifles 1923, local Col Egypt 1932–37 (attd Egyptian army as Assist Inspr-Gen), WW I with Egyptian EF (despatches twice, medal and clasp), WW II 1941–42, MEF, Inspr POW Estabs, Grand Offr Order Nile; *b* 26 May 1882; *educ* Oratory Sch, *d* unm 5 Aug 1960

6 Fergus George Arthur; Capt Roy Irish Regt WW I (wounded); *b* 26 May 1882; *ka* 23 Aug 1914

3 Eva Mary Margaret; *d* unm 1968

4 Margaret Mary Theresa; *m* 22 Sept 1920 Capt Hon George Savile (*see* MEXBOROUGH, E), and *d* 19 May 1965

The 7th EARL *d* 25 Aug 1889; his est son,

BERNARD ARTHUR WILLIAM PATRICK HASTINGS FORBES, **8th Earl of Granard**, KP (1909), GCVO (1915), PC (1907, I 1918); *b* 17 Sept 1874; Ld Lt Co Longford, Dep Speaker Ho Lds, Senator Irish Free State 1922–34, memb Cncl State Ireland 1946, Ld-in-Waiting (Govt Whip) 1905–07, Master Horse 1907–15 and 1924–36, HM Comptroller Ascot 1936–45, Assist PMG 1906–09, Lt-Col Scots Gds, Lt-Col cmdg 8th City Lond Regt (PO Rifles), raised and commanded 5th Bn Roy Irish Regt 1914, Mil Sec Br Salonika Force 1916, chm Irish Food Control Ctee 1918, ADC to Ld Lt Ireland 1896–99 and to COC 1st Div Aldershot Cmd 1904–05, Boer War 1900–02 and WW I (despatches), G rand Cross Isobel La Catolica Spain, Charles III Spain, N Star Sweden, Dannebrog, SS Maurice and Lazarus Italy, Star Romania, Star Ethiopa, Christ Portugal, Companion Order Mil Merit Spain, Serbian White Eagle 4th Cl with swords, Grand Cross Order Ismail Egypt, Cdr Order Redeemer Greece, Grand Offr Legn Honour, Order of Pius; *m* 14 Jan 1909 Beatrice OBE (1920) (*d* 30 Jan 1972), dau of Ogden Mills, of NY State, USA, and *d* 10 Sept 1948, leaving:

1 ARTHUR PATRICK HASTINGS FORBES, **9th Earl of Granard**, AFC (1941); *b* 10 April 1915; *educ* Eton and Trin Coll Cambridge (BA 1937); V-Adml Connaught, dir Texaco 1972, Reckitt & Colman 1973, A/Cdre RAFVR WW II (despatches), Air Advsr Min State Middle East 1942, Legn Honour, Croix de Guerre with palm, US Legn Merit, Order George I Greece with crossed swords, Croix des Vaillants Poland; *m* 29 July 1949 Marie Madeleine Eugenie (*d* 1990), formerly w of Prince Humbert de Faucigny Lucinge and yst dau of Jean Maurel, of Millau, Aveyron, and *d* 1992, leaving:

(1) *Moira Beatrice [The Lady Moira Guerrico, 5 Avenue Princesse Alice, Monte Carlo, Monaco]; *b* 2 Feb 1951; *m* 2 Feb 1971 (*divorce* 1974) HH Prince Charles Antoine Marie Lamoral de Ligne de la Trémöille; *m* 2nd 1978 *José Guerrico and by him has:

1a *Killian Arthur; *b* 1987

1a *Shannon Moira Kiara Beatrice; *b* 1983

(2) *Georgina Anne [The Lady Georgina Forbes, 11 rue Louise de Savoie, Morges, Switzerland; Castle Forbes, Newtown Forbes, Co Longford, Ireland]; *b* 19 Sept 1952

2 John; F/Lt RAF; *b* 8 Oct 1920; *educ* Eton and Trin Coll Dublin (BA BAI 1947); *m* 23 Jan 1947 *Joan [The Hon Mrs John Forbes, Perigord II, 6 rue ses Lacets St Leon, Monte Carlo, Monaco], 3rd dau of A Edward Smith, of Sherlockstown House, Sallins, Co Kildare, and *d* 1982, leaving:

(1) PETER ARTHUR EDWARD HASTINGS FORBES, **10th and present Earl of Granard**

(1) *Susan; *b* 4 Jan 1948

(2) *Patricia Moira; *b* 19 Nov 1950

(3) *Caroline Mary [Mrs Robert Dillon-Mahon, Sainte Helene, Quartier Meaulx, 83830 Claviers, Callas, Var, France]; *b* 23 Sept 1954; *m* 1st 6 July 1975 (*divorce*) Dominick Charles Hamilton, 2nd s of Capt Paul Hamilton, of Moyne, Durrow, Co Laois (*see* also WILLIAMS-WYNN, Bt); *m* 2nd 1983 *Robert John George Dillon-Mahon and by him has issue (*see* MAHON, Bt)

1 *Moira Mary [The Lady Moira Forbes, 16 Chemin des Mouettes, 1007 Lausanne, Switzerland]; *b* 19 Feb 1910; *m* 1st 20 Dec 1934 (*divorce* 1936) Count Louis de Brantes, s of General le Marquis de Brantes, resumed maiden name; *m* 2nd 27 June 1942 (*divorce*) Count Rossi di Montelera, of Turin

2 Eileen Beatrice; *b* 1 July 1912; *m* 26 April 1932 5th Marquess of Bute (*qv*) and had issue

GRANT of Dalvey

Arms: Gules three antique crowns or within a bordure engrailed of the last. **Crest:** The trunk of an oak-tree sprouting out some leaves with the sun shining thereon, all proper. **Supporters:** Dexter, a highlander; sinister, a negro proper. **Motto:** *Te favente virebo* ('With you favouring me, I will flourish'). **Creation:** Bt (NS) 10 Aug 1688.

SIR PATRICK ALEXANDER BENEDICT GRANT, 14TH BT, of Dalvey [Sir Patrick Grant Bt, Tomintoul House, Flichity, Farr, Inverness-shire, IV1 2XD; Glen Dessany Estate, Spean Bridge, Inverness-shire PH34 4EL]; *b* 5 Feb 1953; *s f* 1961, also as Chieftain of Clan Donnachy (Donnachaidh); *educ* St Conleth's Coll Dublin, The Abbey Sch, Fort Augustus, Inverness-shire, and Glasgow U (LLB 1981); fndr and md Grants of Dalvey Ltd 1988– (Queen's Award for Export 1992, Highland Business of the Year 1994); *m* 1981 *Dr Carolyn Elizabeth Highet, MB, ChB, DRCOG, MRCGP, dau of Dr John Highet, of Glasgow, and has:

1 +DUNCAN ARCHIBALD LUDOVIC; *b* 19 April 1982; *educ* Eton

2 +Neil Patrick; *b* 1983; *educ* Eton

Lineage: JOHN MACONOCHIE GRANT; fndr of a branch of the GRANTs known as the Clan Donnachy; settled at Gartenbeg, parish of Duthil, late in the 15th century, and had:

DUNCAN GRANT of Gartenbeg; *m* twice and had issue:

1 John, of Gartenbeg; *m* Agnes Cumming and had issue:

(1) Sweton of Gartenbeg; *m* —, dau of Farquharson of Inveray, and had:

1a Duncan; *d* unm

2a **Sir James Grant, 1st Bt** (NS), so *cr* 10 Aug 1688, with remainder to his heirs male whatsoever, of Dalvey, parish of Cromdale, Elgin; advocate; Slr-Gen Scotland *temp* JAMES II; bought Dalvey from another branch of the Grant family; imprisoned in the Tolbooth Edinburgh 15 May 1689 for corresponding with the Jacobite Duke of Gordon; *m* (contract 8 April 1687) Agnes (*m* 2nd Dr William Rutherford), dau of Sir Gideon Scott (*see* POLWARTH, L), and *dsp* 1695

3a Sir LUDOVIC GRANT, *de jure* 2nd Bt; declared heir to his brother 14 May 1695 but did not assume the title, probably owing to the family's position as ruined Jacobites; *dspl* 4 Jan 1701

2 Donald of Kinveachy; had:

(1) Duncan of Kinveachy; had:

1a Sir SWETON GRANT, *de jure* 3rd Bt, of Gartenbeg; declared heir to his cousin's estate of Dalvey 24 Feb 1701, but sold it to his wife's bro later the same year; did not assume the btcy; *m* Margaret, dau of Donald Grant, of Inverlaidnan, and *dsp*

3 Sweton, of Inverlaidnan, Co Inverness; had:

(1) John, of Inverlaidnan; had:

1a John, of Inverlaidnan; had:

1b James, of Inverlaidnan; *m* Elspeth, dau of Robert Grant, of Glenbeg, and *d* 2 Jan 1667, having had:

1c Donald, of Inverlaidnan; *m* Mary, dau of Lt-Col Patrick Grant, s of Sir John Grant of Grant, and *d* 1735, leaving:

1d **Sir Patrick Grant, 4th Bt**; *b c* 1665; served heir male-gen to his cousin **Sir James Grant, 1st Bt**, 22 Aug 1752 and assumed the btcy; *m* Lydia, dau of William Mackintosh, of Borlum, and *d* 10 April 1755 in his 101st year, having had, with other issue:

1e **Sir Alexander Grant, 5th Bt**; made a fortune in the West Indies and bought in 1749 the estate of Grangehill and other lands in the parish of Dyke, both Elginshire, which he called Dalvey, also 1758 the estate of Kincarth in the parish of Dyke; in addition owned Bookham Grove, Leatherhead, Surrey; MP Inverness Burghs 1761–68; granted supporters to his arms by roy warrant 8 July 1761; *m* 1st Elizabeth, dau of Robert Coote, of Jamaica; *m* 2nd 1 Oct 1764 Margaret (*d* 30 July 1792), dau of Alexander Grant of Auchterblair, and *dsp* 1 Aug 1772

2e **Sir Ludovic Grant, 6th Bt**; *m* Margaret (*d* 12 March 1782), dau of Sir James Innes of Balveny, 5th Bt (*qv*), and *d* 17 Sept 1790, leaving:

1f ALEXANDER GRANT (Sir), **7th Bt**

2f Peter; *b* 1751; Serjeant-at-Arms Ho of Assembly Jamaica; *d* 25 Oct 1820, leaving two daus

3f James, of Vache Park, Chalfont St Giles, Bucks, later Goldington Grange, Watford, Herts, and later still 12 Welbeck St, London W1; HEICS; *m* 26 Dec 1790 Harriet Montagu (*d* 15 March 1823), illegitimate dau of 5th Earl of Sandwich (*qv*), and *d* 4 Feb 1816, having had, with two sons (*dsp*):

1g Margaret Anna; *m* 30 Aug 1824 Alfred William Begbie, HEICS, and *d* Aug 1827 leaving, with a yr dau:

1h Frances Charlotte; *b* 16 July 1825; *m* 14 Oct 1847 Maj-Gen John Peter William Campbell, BCS, 3rd s of Sir Duncan Campbell, 1st Bt, of Barcaldine (*qv*), and *d* 1 Jan 1874, leaving issue

1f Elizabeth; *m* 1st Maj William Grant of Ballindalloch; *m* 2nd John Burnett of Countesswells

2f Marjory; *m* 1772 Duncan Macdonnel of Glengarry

3f Margaret; *m* 1785 Sir Æneas Mackintosh, 1st and last Bt (*d* 21 Jan 1820), 23rd Chief of Mackintosh and 24th Chief of Clan Chattan, and *dsp*

The 6th Bt's est son,

Sir Alexander Grant, 7th Bt; *b c* 1750; sold the Dalvey estate; *m* 13 July 1775 Sarah (*d* 4 Feb 1803), dau and heir of Jeremiah Cray, of Ibsley, Hants, by Sarah (sis of Sir James and Sir George Colebrooke, Bts), and *d* 26 July 1825, having had:

1 **Sir Alexander Cray Grant, 8th Bt**; *b* 30 Nov 1782; *educ* St John's Coll Cambridge (BA 1803, MA 1806); MP Tregony 1812–18, Lostwithiel 1818–26, Aldborough 1826–30, Chm Ctees H of C 1826–32, MP Westbury 1830–31, memb Bd of Control India 1834–35, MP Cambridge Borough 1840 and 1841–43, Commr auditing Public Accounts 1843–54; *d* unm 29 Nov 1854

2 Ludovic James; *m* 1st 1838 Frances Povey (*d* 27 Dec 1857), dau of Sackville Hatch Lovett; *m* 2nd 30 March 1843 Anna Frances, n of Sir Thomas Neave, 2nd Bt (*qv*), and *dsp* 1851

3 **Sir Robert Innes Grant, 9th Bt**; *b* 8 April 1794; *m* 17 Dec 1825 Judith Towers (*d* 6 March 1884 aged 79), est dau of Cornelius Durant Battelle, of St Croix, West Indies, and *d* 1 Aug 1856, having had, with other issue:

(1) ALEXANDER GRANT (Sir), **10th Bt**

(2) Robert Innes; *b* 1833; Lt and Adj 1st Sikh Inf; *ka* Indian Mutiny

(1) Anna Frances; *m* 1 May 1851 William Marcus Westermann, of Copenhagen

The 9th Bt's est son,

Sir Alexander Grant, 10th Bt, DL; *b* 13 Sept 1826; *educ* Harrow and Balliol Coll Oxford (BA 1848, MA 1852), Fell Oriel Coll 1849–60 (Hon Fell 1882); Examiner ICS 1855, Examiner Classical Sch Oxford 1857, Inspr Schs Madras Presidency 1858, Prof History Elphinstone Coll 1860 (Prin 1862), V-Chllr Bombay U 1866, Dir Public Instr Bombay 1865, MLA Bombay 1868, Pncpl and V-Chllr Edinburgh U 1868–84, memb Bd Educn (S) 1872–78, Hon LLD Edinburgh 1865 and Glasgow 1869, Hon DCL Oxon 1880; *m* 2 June 1859 Susan (*d* 20 March 1895), 2nd dau of James Frederick Ferrier, Prof Moral Philosophy and Political Economy St Andrews, and *d* 30 Nov 1884, having had, with two sons (*d* in infancy):

1 **Sir Ludovic James Grant, 11th Bt**; *b* 4 Sept 1862; *educ* Balliol Coll Oxford (BA 1886); advocate 1887; Regius Prof Public Law Edinburgh 1890, Hon LLD Glasgow and Edinburgh; *m* 17 July 1890 Elizabeth Ethel Graham (*d* 9 Sept 1940), est dau of Henry Hill Lancaster, advocate, of Edinburgh, and *d* 11 Feb 1936, having had issue:

(1) Rosalind Margaret Innes; *b* 2 Dec 1893; *m* 21 Sept 1918 Capt Edward Coverley Kennedy, RN and *d* 1977, leaving issue (*see* AILSA, M)

2 Percy Frere; *b* 6 June 1869; *educ* Edinburgh U (MB, CM); Bechuanaland 1897 and Boer War 1899–1902; *m* Feb 1905 Theodora Gertrude (*d* 27 Sept 1938), dau of J H Goodrich, of Beaufort West, Cape Colony, and *d* 9 May 1909, leaving:

(1) *Winifred Anne St John [Mrs Gerard Thomson, 55 Kings Way, Warner Beach S Coast, Natal 4125, S Africa]; *b* Nov 1905; *educ* Cape Town U (BA 1928); *m* 1930 *Gerard Anthony Thomson, s of Gerard Morin Thomson, of The Residency, Rappen Island, CP, S Africa, and has issue:

1a *Anthony Grant; *b* 23 March 1931

2a *Christopher William Grant; *b* 3 Oct 1937

(2) *Susan Ursula [Mrs Christian Wahl, 10 Westerford Rd, Newlands, CP, S Africa]; *b* Nov 1907; *m* Jan 1930 Christian Arnold Wahl (*d* 20 Nov 1967) and has issue

3 (ALFRED) HAMILTON (Sir), **12th Bt**

1 Julia Mary; *b* 18 Feb 1864; *d* unm 28 March 1952

2 Sylvia; *b* 17 June 1867; *m* 17 July 1895 Alfred Douglas Farmer (*d* 8 Feb 1934), 3rd s of James Farmer, of Brownhills, St Andrews, and *d* 6 Sept 1935

3 Susan Ferrier; *b* 18 Aug 1873; *m* 12 Aug 1920 Aladar de Bajaz (*d* 30 Nov 1941), and *dsp* 26 May 1968

The 11th Bt's brother,

Sir (Alfred) Hamilton Grant, 12th Bt, KCSI (1922, CSI 1915), KCIE (1918, CIE 1908); *b* 12 June 1872; BA Oxford; ICS 1895–1922, Kabul Mission 1905–15, Waziristan 1919–20 (despatches), negotiated Peace Treaty with Afghanistan 1919, Order Rising Sun of Japan 2nd Cl; *m* 1st 28 Nov 1896 Mabel Bessie (*d* 5 Jan 1910), yr dau of Col Thomas Heaton Lovett, of Belmont, and had issue:

1 Alexander Lovett; *b* 22 April 1901; *m* 27 Nov 1926 Mary Angela (*m* 2nd 21 Dec 1936 (*divorce* 1955) Denis Francis Keegan, MBE, Capt IA (*d* Jan 1966), Imp Customs Serv and *d* 1 Nov 1987), 2nd dau of Rev Henry Arthur Mackenzie, DD, MusB, Vicar Shotley Bridge, Co Durham, and *dvp* 28 Sept 1935, leaving:

(1) DUNCAN ALEXANDER (Sir), **13th Bt**

(1) *Diana Mary [Mme Jean-Pierre Dalcher, Villa Fidelis, Chemin du Blessoney 18, 1092 Belmont-sur-Lausanne, Vaud, Switzerland]; *b* 28 June

1931; *educ* St Leonard's Sch and London U (BA 1954); *m* 9 Sept 1954 *Jean-Pierre Dalcher, only s of Albert Dalcher, of Lausanne, and has issue:

1a *Claude Francis; *b* 8 April 1957

2a *Derrick Albert Alexander; *b* 18 April 1959; *m* 1987 *Anne Parel and has:

1b *Samuel; *b* 19 Jan 1991

2b *Phillippe; *b* 30 April 1996

1b *Sarah; *b* 3 Aug 1988

2b *Rachel; *b* 2 March 1993

1a *Anne; *b* 1 April 1956; *m* 21 Oct 1995 *Daniel Venditti

1 Audrey Elizabeth Ferrier; *b* 1 Nov 1897; *m* 1 Nov 1920 Lt-Col Ogilvie David Bennett, IA, s of Col Bennett, IMS, and *d* 28 Feb 1938, leaving issue

Sir Hamilton *m* 2nd 12 March 1914 Margaret Lucia (*d* 6 April 1971), yst dau of Lt Alexander Cochran, RN, of Ashkirk, Selkirkshire, and *d* 23 Jan 1937, leaving by her:

2 +Patrick (Peter); *b* 22 Dec 1917; *educ* Canford and Balliol Coll Oxford (MA 1947); S/Ldr RAFVR WW II; *m* 5 April 1961 *Diana, dau of AG Sanderson, of Victoria, BC, Canada

2 *Esther; *b* 2 Feb 1915; *m* 1st 1936 Cecil Watt Paul Jones and has issue:

(1) *Luke [Luke Kitto Esq, 22 Church Rd, Newton Abbot, Devon]; *b* 22 Dec 1942; *m* 18 June 1966 *Mary, dau of Percy Wonnacott, of Hennock, S Devon, and has:

1a *Louise Victoria; *b* 10 April 1969

(1) *Julia; *b* 8 June 1938; *m* 1960 Nigel Keen and has issue

2 (cont.) Mrs Jones *m* 2nd 4 March 1944 F/Lt Francis Ernest Appleyard Kitto, RAFVR (*d* 28 Nov 1964, having adopted his stepson Luke, who took name KITTO 1945), er s of Brevet-Col WA Kitto, RE, of Bransgore, Hants, resumed her maiden name following her 2nd husb's death and has by him:

(2) *Alexander [Alexander Kitto Esq, Hamaugh Island, Shepperton, Middx]; *b* 15 Nov 1944; *m* 10 Feb 1968 *Susan Appleby

(3) *Crispin; *b* 27 May 1951

(2) *Belinda; *b* 14 May 1948

(3) *Grace; *b* 13 Feb 1955

3 Guinevere, DBE (1983), DL (Lancs 1971–74 and Co Merseyside 1974–76); *b* 8 Sept 1916; *educ* Westonbirt; WW II 2nd Offr WRNS; Priv Sec to Earl of Selborne 1949–54, Pres Nat Cncl Women of GB 1968–70, memb BBC Gen Advsy Cncl 1967–76, UK Rep UN Commn Status of Women 1970–73, Co-Chm Women Caring Tst 1972–75, Advsr to PM 1975–83; *m* 1st 19 Feb 1944 Capt K Lionel Hunter, Roy Canadian Dragoons (*d* 22 Nov 1947), s of A C Hunter, of Montreal, and had:

(1) *Tony Lionel HUNTER later HUNTER-TILNEY (deed poll Dec 1954); *b* 19 July 1947; *educ* Eton and Magdalen Coll Oxford; *m* 17 Dec 1970 *Juliet Mary, er dau of John Benson Faller, of Chelsea

3 (cont.) Mrs Lionel Hunter *m* 2nd 3 June 1954 Col Sir John Dudley Robert Tarleton Tilney, TD, JP, MP (*d* 1994), only surv s of Col R H Tilney, DSO, of Tattenhall, Cheshire, and *d* 4 April 1997, having had further issue:

(2) A son; *b* and *d* 16 June 1958

(1) Henrietta Daisy Margaret; *b* and *d* 7 Nov 1955

The 12th Bt's grandson,

Sir Duncan Alexander Grant, 13th Bt; *b* 16 Dec 1928; *educ* Gordonstoun and Newburgh Priory Coll; *m* 3 Aug 1949 Joan Penelope (*d* 1991), only dau of Sir Denzil Cope, 14th Bt (*see* 1949 edn), and *d* 25 March 1961, leaving:

1 Sir PATRICK ALEXANDER BENEDICT GRANT, **14th and present Bt**

2 +Denzil Mohun Bede [Denzil Grant Esq, Hubbards Corner, Gedding Rd, Bradfield St George, Suffolk]; *b* 19 April 1955; *educ* The Abbey Sch, Fort Augustus, Inverness-shire and West Dean Coll Chichester (BA); md Suffolk Fine Arts Ltd; *m* 1 Jan 1977 *Nicola, 2nd dau of A T Savill, of Godalming, and has:

(1) *Alexandra; *b* 1978

(2) *Diana; *b* 1983

(3) *Charlotte; *b* 1986

3 +Drostan John [Drostan Grant Esq, 34 Morehampton Rd, Dublin 4, Ireland]; *b* 27 Dec 1956; *educ* St Conlath's Coll Dublin, RCM Dublin, U Coll Dublin (BE), Trin Coll Dublin (MBA), Inst of Actuaries London; *m* 1986 *Celia Gabriella, er dau of Gerald Mattei, of Malta, and has:

(1) *Antonia Maria; *b* 1987

(2) *Christina Andrea; *b* 1989

1 *Fiona Mary Julia [Mrs Ian Craib, The Mill, Bulmer Rd, Sudbury, Suffolk CO10 7E2]; *b* 16 May 1950; *educ* Sacred Heart Convents Aberdeen and Dublin, Essex U (BA 1989), and Essex Sch of Occupational Therapy (DipCOT 1992); occupational therapist; *m* 1st 3 Sept 1966 (*divorce* 1989) Christopher Kanthack St John Bird, s of Christopher St John Bird, of Johannesburg, and has issue:

(1) *Christopher Kenelm Anthony; *b* 22 July 1967; *educ* Leys Sch Cambridge, Sussex U and LSE (MSc); jnlst; *m* 1992 *Rachel, dau of Rt Rev David Stancliffe, Bp Salisbury, and has:

1a *Alexander Kenelm; *b* 28 April 1991

2a *Matthew Caspar; *b* 30 July 1993

(2) *Theodore Denzil Drostan; *b* 15 June 1971; *educ* St Christopher's Sch, Letchworth, Herts, and Glasgow Sch of Art (BA 1993); industrial designer

(1) *Penelope Frances Julia; *b* 2 Nov 1968; *educ* St Christopher's Sch, Letchworth, Herts, and Welsh Horticultural Coll, Clwyd; *m* 1994 *Scott Pender

1 (cont.) Mrs Fiona Bird *m* 2nd 26 May 1990 *Dr Ian Craib, PhD, BA, AMLCP, of Essex U

2 *Maria-Teresa [Mrs Maria-Teresa Grant, 56 Alderney St, London SW1]; *b* 17 May 1951; *educ* Sacred Heart Convents Aberdeen and Dublin, Trin Coll Dublin; manager Setanta Gallery Dublin 1976–78, art historian, foreign exhibitions Fedn Br Artists London 1985–87, Admin Offr V&A 1989–95; Ladies' Irish Nat Fencing Champion 1967, 1971 and 1972; *m* 1 Feb 1969 (*divorce* 1995) Ramon Anthony Cooke, BE, CEng, MIEI, est s of Joseph Cooke, of Galway, resumed maiden name and has issue:

(1) *Jessica Fiona [Dr Jessica Cooke, 2 Woburn Court, Bernard St, London WC1N ILA]; *b* 22 Nov 1968; *educ* Mount Anville Sch, Dublin, Kilgraston Sch, Bridge of Earn, Perths, Trin Coll Dublin (BA Hons (AHA)1990) and Clare Hall Cambridge (PhD 1994); Lecturer W Suffolk Coll Bury St Edmunds 1995–; Soprano Gold Medal Perth Festival, Gold Medal LAMDA 1986; *m* 10 Sept 1994 *Dr Seán Faughnan, PhD, s of John Faughnan, of Dublin

GRANT of Monymusk and Cullen

Arms: Gu. three antique crowns or (for GRANT of that Ilk) within a bordure erm. **Crest:** A bible expanded ppr. **Supporters:** Two angels ppr., wings or. **Mottoes:** 1 (over crest) *Suum cuique* ('To each his own'), 2 (below shield) *Jehovah jireh* ('The Lord will regard it').
Creation: Bt. (NS) 7 Dec 1705.

SIR ARCHIBALD GRANT, 13TH BT, of Monymusk [Sir Archibald Grant of Monymusk Bt, House of Monymusk, Aberdeenshire AB51 7HL]; *b* 2 Sept 1954; *s* f 1966; *educ* Trin Coll Glenalmond and RAC Cirencester (Dip Farm Management); *m* 31 Dec 1982 *Barbara Elizabeth, est dau of Andrew Gordon Duff Forbes (*see* STUART-FORBES, Bt), and has:

1 *Christian Mariot; *b* 1986

2 *Catriona Elizabeth; *b* 1988

Lineage: JAMES GRANT, 3rd of Freuchie (*see* STRATHSPEY, B); had a yr s:

ARCHIBALD GRANT of Ballentomb, Morayshire; *m c* 1599 Isabella, dau of Cumming of Erneside, and had:

DUNCAN GRANT of Ballentomb; *m* Helen, dau of Alexander Gordon of Tulloch, and had:

ARCHIBALD GRANT; *m* Isabel, dau of Gordon of Lichistoune, and had:

ARCHIBALD GRANT of Ballentomb; *m* 1653 Christian, dau of Patrick Nairne of Cromdale, and *d* 1717, having had:

1 FRANCIS (Sir), **1st Bt**

2 Alexander; *s* to Ballentomb; *d* 1706, leaving:

(1) Archibald; *d* young

1 Helen; *m* William Grant of Lurg

The est son,

Sir Francis Grant, 1st Bt (NS), so *cr* 7 Dec 1705, with remainder to heirs male whatsoever, of Cullen, Buchan; *b* 1658; advocate 1691, Ld of Session 1709 as Lord Cullen; bought Monymusk 1713; *m* 1st 15 March 1694 Jean, dau of Rev William Meldrum of Meldrum; *m* 2nd 18 Oct 1708 Sarah (*dspm*), dau of Rev Alexander Fordyce of Ayton; *m* 3rd 18 July 1718 Agnes (*dsp*), dau of Henry Hay, and was *bur* 26 March 1726, leaving, with two yr daus (Anne, living 1750; Sarah):

1 ARCHIBALD (Sir), **2nd Bt**

2 William; advocate 1722, Ld Advocate 1746–54, MP Elgin burghs 1747, Ld of Session as Lord Prestongrange 1754; *m* Grizel, dau of Rev — Millar, and *d* 3 May 1764, leaving issue:

(1) Janet; *m* 16 Jan 1749 4th Earl of Hyndford and *dsp* 7 July 1818

(2) Agnes; *m* 7 June 1757 Sir George Suttie, 3rd Bt (*see* GRANT-SUTTIE, Bt), and had issue

(3) Jane; *m* 1756 Robert Dundas of Arniston and had issue (*see* DUNDAS, Bt, of Arniston)

1 Jean; *m* Alexander Garden of Troup, and had issue

2 Christian; *m* 7 April 1734 George Buchan and *d* 4 Aug 1784, leaving issue (*see* BUCHAN-HEPBURN, Bt)

3 Helen; *m* Andrew McDouall of Bankton, a Ld of Session

The er son,

Sir Archibald Grant, 2nd Bt; *b* 1696; advocate 1714, MP Aberdeen 1722–32; *m* 1st 17 April 1717 Anne, dau of James Hamilton of Pencaitland, and had two daus (*d* young); *m* 2nd 1731 Anne, dau of Charles Potts, of Castleton, Derbys; *m* 3rd 18 Aug 1751 Elizabeth Clark (*d* 30 April 1759), widow of Dr James Callander, of Jamaica, by whom he had no issue; *m* 4th 24 May 1770 Jane (*d* 25 Oct 1788), widow of Andrew Millar, of London, by whom he had no issue, and *d* 17 Sept 1778, leaving by his 2nd w an only s:

Sir Archibald Grant, 3rd Bt; *b* 17 Feb 1731; HEIC; raised a company of troops and went with them to India 1748; *m* 1st 27 May 1755 Mary (*d* 15 Feb 1787), dau and heir of Dr James Callender, of Jamaica, and had issue:

1 **Sir Archibald Grant, 4th Bt**; *b* 7 May 1760; *m* 1 Jan 1788 Mary (*d* 15 Nov 1852), only child of Maj John Forbes of Newe by Anne Duff, of Muirton, and *d* 17 April 1820, having had, with other issue:

(1) Archibald; *b* 1 Jan 1789; lost with the East Indiaman *Abergavenny* 6 Feb 1805

(2) **Sir James Grant, 5th Bt**; *b* 17 Feb 1791; *d* unm 30 Aug 1859

(3) **Sir Isaac Grant, 6th Bt**; *b* 5 July 1792; *d* unm 19 July 1863

(4) Robert, of Tillyfour; *b* 12 Feb 1797; Convener Aberdeenshire; *m* 14 March 1820 Charlotte (*d* 28 Nov 1847), sis of Sir William Walter Yea, 2nd Bt, of Pyrland, and *d* 15 March 1857, leaving, with other issue:

1a **Sir Archibald Grant, 7th Bt**; *b* 21 Sept 1823; Capt 4th Light Dragoons; *d* unm 5 Sept 1884

2a **Sir Francis William Grant, 8th Bt**; *b* 10 Feb 1828; Capt 16th Lancers; *m* 2 Dec 1886 Laura (*m* 2nd 9 June 1894 Lt-Col George Bentinck Macleod Cumberland, 42nd Highrs (*d* 1920), and *d* 6 Feb 1933), dau of John Fraser, of Bunchrew, and Netley Park, Surrey, and *dsp* 13 Dec 1887

1a Mary Jane Forbes; *m* 20 Oct 1853 John Gregson (*d* 27 Dec 1879), of Bramham House, Yorks, and *d* 16 April 1880, leaving issue

(1) Mary Ann; *m* 12 Sept 1812 John Farquharson, of Houghton, and *d* 20 Oct 1851

(2) Jessie; *m* 8 July 1817 Henry Iveson, of Blackbank, Yorks, and *d* his widow 9 May 1870

2 James Francis (Rev); Rector Merston, Sussex, and Wrabness, Essex; *m* Oct 1795 Anne, dau of Rev Arthur Oughterstone, and *d* 10 Nov 1837, having had, with other issue:

(1) Arthur, Cdr RN; *m* 13 April 1848 Eliza (*m* 2nd 19 June 1856 W S Gillet), dau of Thomas Coster, and *d* April 1850, leaving issue:

(1) ARTHUR HENRY (Sir), **9th Bt**

(1) Adela Annie Churchill; *m* 10 June 1885 Robert Gray Cobham (*dsp* 5 Feb 1905) and *d* 5 June 1934

1 Mary; *m* 19 Sept 1796 Rev Joseph Pickford Radcliffe (*d* 17 May 1804), 2nd s of Sir Joseph Radcliffe, 1st Bt (*qv*), and *d* 7 Nov 1834, leaving issue

Sir Archibald *m* 2nd 8 Aug 1794 Jessie (*dsp* 24 Oct 1836), dau of — McLeod of Colbecks, and *d* 30 Sept 1796

The 8th Bt's cousin,

Sir Arthur Henry Grant, 9th Bt; *b* 24 April 1849; *educ* Oriel Coll Oxford (MA); Hon Col Highland Div RE, Lt 27th Inniskillings, Maj Hants Yeo Cav; *m* 10 Oct 1878 Mary (*d* 20 Feb 1926), est dau of Capt Henry Sholto Douglas, 42nd Regt, and *d* 1 March 1917, having had issue:

1 ARTHUR (Sir), **10th Bt**

2 William Douglas; *b* 31 Aug 1880; Lt Col 2nd/1st Yorks Dragoons, Capt 1st Roy Dragoons, Boer War and WW I; *m* 10 Dec 1910 Frances Louise (*d* 7 April 1959, dau of W H Male, of Mount Kisco, New York, and *d* 9 June 1953, having had:

(1) Francis Husted; *b* 18 March, *d* 24 March 1912

Sir ARTHUR's er son,

Sir Arthur Grant, 10th Bt, CBE, DSO, JP, DL Aberdeenshire; *b* 14 Sept 1879; Col 5th Bn Gordon Highrs, TFR, Capt 12th Lancers, served Boer War (despatches, two medals, seven clasps) and WW I (severely wounded); *m* 12 Oct 1909 Evelyn Alice Lindsay (*d* 14 Feb 1976), yst dau of Collingwood Lindsay Wood, of Freeland, Perthshire, and *d* 21 June 1931, leaving issue:

1 **Sir Arthur Lindsay Grant, 11th Bt**, JP Aberdeenshire; *b* 8 Sept 1911; Maj Gren Gds WW II (despatches 1945); *m* 14 May 1934 Priscilla Jean Fortescue, *cr* 1970 Baroness Tweedsmuir of Belhelvie (LP, *m* 2nd 27 July 1948 2nd Baron Tweedsmuir (*qv*) and *d* 1978), yr dau of Brig Alan Fortescue Thomson, DSO, and *das* Normandy 18 July 1944, leaving issue:

(1) *Joanna Catherine; *b* 13 Feb 1935; *m* 16 Dec 1954 (*divorce* 1966) Dominick Jones, yst s of Sir Roderick Jones, KBE, and has issue:

1a *Romilly Arthur; *b* 18 Feb 1956

(2) *(Margaret) Anne [The Hon Mrs Anne Grant, 24 Amity Grove, London SW20 0LJ]; *b* 22 March 1937; *educ* LMH Oxford; *m* 17 Oct 1965 (*divorce* 1983, resumed maiden name) Nicolas Mangriotis, s of Paraskevas Mangriotis, of Athens, and has issue:

1a *Paraskevas; *b* 1971

2a *Arthuros; *b* 1974

2 FRANCIS CULLEN (Sir), **12th Bt**

1 Evelyn Mary Frances; *b* 4 Oct 1910; *m* 18 Sept 1934 Maj-Gen Cecil Martin Fothergill Deakin, CB, CBE, Gren Gds, and had issue:

(1) *Charles Cullen William; *b* 15 Nov 1939; *educ* Eton; *m* 28 July 1973 *M L, dau of Brig G L FitzGerald, of River Cottage, Longparish, Hants

(2) *Juliet Elizabeth [Lady Edmonstone, Duntreath Castle, Blanefield, Stirlingshire G63 9AJ]; *b* 1 Dec 1943; *m* 24 June 1969 *Sir Archibald Bruce Charles Edmonstone, 7th Bt (*qv*), and has issue

2 Elspeth; *b* 11 Oct 1913; *m* 24 Oct 1933 (*divorce* 1963) Richard Luis Owen Waddington and had issue:

(1) *Frances Elspeth Luise; *b* 12 Oct 1934; *m* 16 May 1961 *William Alastair Leslie Manson, of Melton Mowbray, and has issue

3 *Catherine Jean [Lady Legge-Bourke, 121 Dovehouse Street, London SW3 6JZ]; *b* 18 Aug 1917; *m* 10 June 1938 Maj Sir (Edward Alexander) Harry Legge-Bourke, KBE, MP, DL, and has issue (*see* DARTMOUTH, E)

4 *Christian Mona [Lady Bowman, The Walled Garden, Chamberlain St, Wells, Somerset BA5 2PE]; *b* 3 Dec 1920; *m* 1st 14 Nov 1942 (*divorce* 1951) Capt Michael Fife William Angas, Gren Gds (*d* 1983), s of Maj L Angas, of New York; *m* 2nd 5 Jan 1953 John Gordon Ogston Miller (*d* 1992); *m* 3rd 1993, as his 3rd w, Sir John Paget Bowman, 4th Bt (*qv*), and by her 1st husb has issue:

(1) *Auburn Carolyn Catherine; *b* 2 Aug 1945

(2) *Cherill Melmere; *b* 17 Dec 1947; *m* 10 Nov 1966 (*divorce* 1974) Charles Heckstall, of Va., USA, and has:

1a *Cyprian Carolus; *b* 5 Sept 1967

Sir ARTHUR's bro,

Sir Francis Cullen Grant, 12 Bt; *b* 5 Oct 1914; *educ* Stowe; memb Roy Co Archers, Capt RE WW II (despatches); *m* 29 June 1953 *Jean Margherita (*m* 2nd 1980 2nd Baron Tweedsmuir, *qv*), only dau of Capt Humphrey Douglas Tollemache, RN (*see* TOLLEMACHE, B), and *d* 31 Aug 1966, leaving:

1 Sir ARCHIBALD GRANT, **13th and present Bt**

2 +FRANCIS TOLLEMACHE [Francis Grant Esq, Kingston House, Kingston Bagpuize, Oxon OX13 5AX]; *b* 18 Dec 1955; heir presumptive; *m* 1993 *Virginia Elizabeth, dau of R Scott Russell, of E Hanney, Oxon, and has:

(1) +Alexander William; *b* 28 Nov 1996

(1) *Elizabeth Charlotte; *b* 1994

3 +Duncan John Cullen; *b* 26 June 1957; *m* 1985 *Maureen Cecelia, only dau of Thomas Innes of Learney (*see* INNES, Bt, of Balvenie), and has issue:

(1) +Robert Francis; *b* 1985

(2) +Thomas William; *b* 1988

(3) +Henry Douglas; *b* 1991

(4) +Alasdair John; *b* 1997

1 *Catriona Charmiane; *b* 16 May 1959; *m* 7 July 1996 *Christopher Blackwell, er s of Prof D E Blackwell

2 *Sarah Jean; *b* 19 Sept 1961

GRANT-SUTTIE

Arms: Quarterly, 1st and 4th, barry wavy of six az. and or, on a chief of the last a lion rampant naissant with two tails vert, armed and langued gu. (for SUTTIE); 2nd and 3rd, or a chevron checky gu. and of the first between three hunting-horns sa., garnished of the second, all within a bordure of the same (for SEMPLE).
Crest: A ship under full sail ppr. **Motto:** Nothing hazard, nothing have. **Creation:** Bt. (NS) 5 May 1702.

SIR JAMES EDWARD GRANT-SUTTIE, 9TH BT, of Balgone, Co Haddington [Sir James Grant-Suttie Bt, Sheriff Hall Farm, N Berwick, E Lothian EH39 5PB]; *b* 29 May 1965; *s* f 1997; *m* 1989 *Emma Jane, yr dau of Peter Craig, of Innerwick, E Lothian, and has:

1 +GREGOR; *b* 19–

2 +Andrew; *b* 19–

Lineage: Sir George Suttie, 1st Bt (NS), so *cr* 5 May 1702 , of Addiston; *m* Elizabeth, dau and heiress of John Semple of Balgone, and had, with four other sons (*d* young) and five daus:

Sir James Suttie, 2nd Bt, of Balgone; *m* Elizabeth, dau of Sir Hew Dalrymple, 1st Bt, of N Berwick (*see* 1949 edn), Lord Pres Ct of Sesson, and had an est s:

Sir George Suttie, 3rd Bt; Lt-Col, MP Haddington; *m* 7 June 1757 Agnes, 2nd dau of William Grant of Preston Grange, a Ld of Session, and *d* 26 Nov 1783, having had, with two yr sons and five daus:

Sir JAMES SUTTIE later GRANT SUTTIE (added 1818 on inheriting the Preston Grange estate from his aunt Janet Grant, Countess of Hyndford), **4th Bt**; *b* 10 May 1759; MP Haddington; *m* 17 April Katherine Isabella, 2nd dau of J Hamilton, of Bangour, and *d* 1836, having had, with two daus:

Sir George Grant-Suttie, 5th Bt; *b* 1 Aug 1797; Scots Gds; *m* 3 Sept 1829 Harriet (*d* 30 May 1858), dau of 8th Earl of Wemyss (*qv*), and *d* 19 June 1878, having had, with two daus:

1 **Sir James Grant-Suttie, 6th Bt**, DL Berwicks; *b* 25 May 1830; Lt-Col Haddington, Berwick, Linlithgow and Peebles Artillery Militia; *m* 6 Aug 1857 Lady Susan Harriet Innes-Ker (*d* 16 Oct 1909), er dau of 6th Duke of Roxburghe (*qv*), and *d* 30 Oct 1878, having had, with another s (*d* an infant):

(1) **Sir George Grant-Suttie, 7th Bt**; *b* 2 Sept 1870; *d* unm 19 May 1947

(1) Susan Harriet; *m* 1st 10 April 1878 (*divorce* 1905) 11th Earl of Stair (*qv*) and had issue; *m* 2nd 15 July 1905 Sir Neil James Menzies, 8th and last Bt (*dsp* 21 Dec 1910), and *d* 9 Feb 1946

(2) Harriet; *m* 12 July 1886 Sir Daniel Cooper, 2nd Bt, of Woollahra (*qv*), and *d* 25 April 1941, leaving issue

(3) Victoria Alberta; *m* 15 July 1896 Rev George S Smith, Min Prestonpans, and *d* 5 Jan 1900, leaving issue

2 Francis; *b* 18 Jan 1832; Capt RN; *m* 15 Jan 1877 Elizabeth (*d* 25 Dec 1945), yst dau of Donald MacIntyre, of Kayuga, NSW, and *d* 28 Feb 1884, leaving issue:

(1) George Donald; *b* 14 Oct 1877; Maj Black Watch, Boer War and WW I (ret 1920); *m* 1st 15 May 1931 Isobel Jane Campbell (*d* 6 Sept 1936), yst dau of William Murray Hosack, Crofters' Commr; *m* 2nd 27 June 1937 Marjorie Neville [Mrs Paul Underhill, Tomlinson House, Box 1236, Fredericton, NB E3B 5C8, Canada] (*m* 2nd 1944 Paul Underhill, Lt US Army), dau of Capt Cornelius Edward Carter, RN, of Barachoise, Newfoundland, and *d* 8 Nov 1940, having by her had:

1a **Sir (George) Philip Grant-Suttie, 8th Bt**; *b* 20 Dec 1938; *educ* Sussex Composite High Sch, NB, Canada, and McGill; *m* 13 Oct 1962 (*divorce* 1969) Elspeth Mary, est dau of Maj-Gen Robert Elliott Urquart, CB, DSO, of Gaidrew, by Drymen, Stirlingshire, and *d* 7 Nov 1997, leaving:

1b Sir JAMES EDWARD GRANT-SUTTIE, **9th and present Bt**

1a *Ann [Mrs Marinus Luitwieler, 56 Sunhurst Place, SE Calgary, AB T2X 1W6, Canada]; *b* 1940; *m* 1st 1958 —, and has:

1b *Susan Ann [Miss Susan McGee Grant-Suttie, 63121 2604 Kensington Rd NW, Calgary AB T2N 4S5, Canada]; *b* 1960; *educ* U of Calgary (BA); has:

1c *Nicole Noel Ann OLSON; *b* 1984

1b (cont.) Susan McGee *m* 31 Dec 1994 *Barclay Todd Redman, BEc, B Comm

1a (cont.) Ann *m* 2nd 1967 *Marinus Jan Luitwieler, and has by him:

1b *Rinus Jon; *b* 1968

2b *Melissa Ann; *b* 1970

(1) Sheila Laura Mary; *m* 15 Jan 1917 W/Cdr Douglas Austin Oliver, DSO, OBE, RN (*d* 3 Aug 1939), s of Rev Austin Oliver, of Latton, Essex, and *d* 15 Feb 1960, leaving issue

(2) Elsie Margaret Hew, BEM; *d* unm 4 Jan 1954

(3) Harriet Hamilton; *m* 8 Dec 1915 William Johnstone (*d* 23 Feb 1933) and *d* 28 Sept 1948, leaving issue

3 George; *b* 14 Dec 1835; Maj 75th Foot; *d* Jan 1875

4 Robert, JP, DL E Lothian; *b* 18 Dec 1841; barrister; *m* 2 Feb 1884 Hon Edith Mary Dawnay (*d* 15 July 1941), dau of 7th Viscount Downe (*qv*), and *d* Sept 1933, having had, with a dau (*d* unm):

(1) Hubert Francis, CBE (1940), DSO (1918), MC; *b* 15 Dec 1884; *educ* Malvern and RMA Woolwich; Col RA, served WWs I (despatches) and II, CStJ 1948; *m* 14 April 1920 Torfrida Alianore, SSStJ (*d* 30 Aug 1971), er dau of Sir Wroth Lethbridge, 5th Bt (*qv*), and had:

1a +(Robert) Ian [Ian Grant-Suttie, 17 Mountain Ave, Woodstock, VT 05091, USA]; *b* 3 Dec 1926; *educ* Wellington, Sorbonne and New Coll Oxford; late Lt Black Watch (RHR), professional Staff IMF; *m* 1 Oct 1951 *Juliet Carmen, yr dau of Nigel Eustace Philip Sutton (*see* SUTTON, Bt), and has:

1b +Francis Æneas; *b* 29 Nov 1957; *educ* Radley; *m* 22 Jan 1983 *Carolyn Forrest, er dau of Maj-Gen Robert Ginsburgh, USAF, of Chevy Chase, Md., and has issue:

1c +Ian Hamilton; *b* 1991

1c *Katherine; *b* 1988

2b +James Archibald; *b* 5 Jan 1964

1b *Atalanta Theresa; *b* 11 April 1955

2b *Roxana Idonea [Mrs Ogden Reid, Ophir West, 09 Evergreen Drive, Placitas, NM 87043, USA]; *b* 1 Nov 1961; *m* 1986 *Ogden Mills Reid, s of Ogden Rogers Reid, of Purchase, NY, and has issue:

1c *Lindsay Sutton; *b* 1990

2c *Ashley Louise; *b* 1993

3c *Natalie Mills; *b* 1995

1a Margaret Torfrida; *b* 29 May 1923; *m* 5 March 1957 *Cdr Michael Bremer Speare-Cole, RN, only s of Capt Arthur Speare-Cole, RN, and *d* 19–, leaving:

1b *Hubert Alastair; *b* 7 Sept 1959

1b *Julia Torfrida; *b* 20 Sept 1963

(2) Archibald Ronald; *b* 20 Oct 1896; 2nd Lt RHA; *kas* 23 July 1917

(1) Hilda Margaret; *d* 30 Aug 1978

(2) Ethel Mary

GRANTCHESTER

Arms: Quarterly, 1st and 4th, sa. on a fess engrailed, between in chief a fleur-de-lys between two annulets or and in base as many like annulets, a lion passant of the field (for TAYLOR); 2nd and 3rd, gu. in chief two swans rousant ppr., each crowned with an antique crown or, and in base barry wavy of six, arg. and az. (for SUENSON). **Crests:** 1 Issuant from a crown palisado or a unicorn's head sa., armed and charged on the neck with an annulet gold, and holding in the mouth an acorn, leaved and slipped ppr. (for TAYLOR), 2 Issuant from a coronet composed of eight roses gu., seeded arg. and set upon a rim or, a swan rousant ppr., crowned with an antique crown gold (for SUENSON). **Supporters:** Dexter, a unicorn sa., armed and crined or, gorged with a collar arg., charged with a bar wavy az.; sinister, a lion or, gorged with a collar of hearts gu. **Motto:** Peace and holy quiet. **Badge:** A pellet edged or, charged with an owl standing towards the sinister, gold.

Creation: B. (UK) 30 June 1953.

THE 3RD BARON GRANTCHESTER, of Knightsbridge in the City of Westminster (Christopher John Suenson-Taylor) [The Rt Hon The Lord Grantchester, Lower House Farm, Back Coole Lane, Audlem, Crewe, CW3 0ER]; *b* 8 April 1951; *s* f 1995; *educ* Winchester and LSE (BSc Econ); dairy cattle breeder and co dir; *m* 31 Oct 1973 *Jacqueline Susan, er dau of Dr Leo Jaffe, and has:

1 +JESSE DAVID JAFFE; *b* 6 June 1977

2 +Adam Joel; *b* 1987

1 *Holly Rachel Jaffe; *b* 1 Aug 1975

2 *Hannah Robin; *b* 1984

Lineage: ALFRED GEORGE TAYLOR, of Sutton, Surrey; *b* 13 May 1872; *m* 16 Oct 1892 Mary (*d* 20 Nov 1951), dau of Andrew Valentine Kirwan, barrister, and *d* 11 May 1959, leaving:

1 ALFRED JESSE, **1st Baron**

2 Harold George TAYLOR later KIRWAN-TAYLOR; FRCS Eng, hon consultant obstetric and gynaecological surgn RNVR WW I, Surgn-Lt RN WW II (despatches), Col AMS; *b* 14 April 1895; *educ* Epsom and Trin Coll Cambridge (MA, MB, ChB); *m* 21 April 1926 (*divorce* 1946) Elizabeth Mary, dau of J R J Neild, and *d* 2 Dec 1981, leaving:

(1) *(Harold) Timothy [Timothy Kirwan-Taylor Esq, 40 Zolreno Rd, Oranjiziche, Cape Town, S Africa]; late Capt RHG, Admin Offr N Rhodesia and Zambia Govts 1955–65, game research assoc 1967–68, Pncpl Assist Sec to Cabinet Lesotho 1968–70, Offr Order Menelik II Ethiopia; *b* 14 Aug 1930; *educ* Eton; *m* 4 Feb 1961 *Jackie Elizabeth Ruth, only dau of John Thomson, CBE, and has:

1a *Adam Gray; *b* 4 March 1967

1a *Catriona Nicola; *b* 20 Nov 1964

(1) *Jane [Mrs Christopher Thornton, Great House Close, Souldern, Oxon OX6 9JF]; *b* 28 Nov 1927; *m* 25 Feb 1954 *Christopher Edward Thornton, yr s of Maj Noel Shipley Thornton, DSO, MC, and has:

1a *Sarah Charlotte; *b* 9 Feb 1956

2a *Caroline Jane; *b* 4 March 1959

(2) *Shirley; *b* 20 Dec 1934; *m* 16 April 1955 *Robert Henry Vernon Moorhead, BA, only s of Col Henry Dawson Moorhead, DSO, and has:

1a *Henry Charles Dawson; *b* 14 May 1956; *educ* Marlborough

2a *Benedict Robert Kirwan; *b* 1 April 1958

3a *Thomas Samuel Nelson; *b* 21 Feb 1961

4a *Daniel Seamus Barnaby; *b* 10 Aug 1968

(3) *Caroline; *b* 30 May 1936; *m* 1 June 1957 *Robert Garnham, only s of H L Garnham, and has:

1a *Piers Alexander; *b* 3 Nov 1958

1a *Belinda; *b* 1 Nov 1961

2a *Araminta; *b* 18 Feb 1964

3a *Emily Victoria; *b* 11 April 1967

3 Ernest Edward TAYLOR, CBE (1956); Chm: British Sailors' Soc, Roy Nat Throat Nose and Ear Hosp, Inst Laryngoly and Otology Lond U, dep chm and md Unigate, jt md Cow and Gate; *b* 10 Dec 1897; *educ* Epsom; *m* 8 Sept 1920 Dorothy Eileen (*d* 9 May 1969), dau of Charles Henry Hardy, and *d* 19–, leaving:

(1) *Alfred Ernest Stephen Solfe; *b* 1 May 1929; *educ* Epsom; *m* 1 June 1950 *Penelope Anne Frances Cortlandt, dau of Cortlandt Taylor, and has:

1a *Nigel Charles Ernest; *b* 27 Sept 1951; *educ* Epsom

2a *Christopher David; *b* 25 July 1954

1a *Caroline Sarah; *b* 12 Sept 1961

(1) *Margaret Madeleine Wolfe; *b* 31 July 1921; *m* 18 April 1942 *Peter Wolfe-Taylor and has:

1a *Clive Edward Arthur; *b* 10 Jan 1947; *m* 8 April 1972 *Chantal Pagnon

1a *(Dorothea) Angela; *b* 20 Oct 1945; *m* 14 Oct 1967 *Henry Leslie Basil Falkiner, yr s of Lt-Col Sir Terence Falkiner, 8th Bt (*qv*)

(2) *Dorothea Joyce Wolfe; *b* 13 Feb 1923; *m* 1 March 1966 *William Eric Parr (formerly Roberts), est s of William James Roberts

(1) Eileen Mary Wolfe; *b* 11 July 1924; *m* 20 Sept 1951 *David Reynold Davies, s of John Davies, of Guildford

(4) Elizabeth Anne Wolfe; *b* 2 Nov 1930; *d* at sea 26 Aug 1955

4 Gordon Kirwan KIRWAN-TAYLOR; MD; *b* 19 Nov 1901; *educ* Epsom and Trin Coll Cambridge (MA 1927); *m* 1st 26 April 1934 Mae (*d* 11 Oct 1944), dau of Stephen Cozens, and had issue; *m* 2nd 3 Nov 1956 Mary (*d* 19 Jan 1998), dau of John William Dowthwaite, RN, and *d* 29 Juy 1975, leaving by his 1st w:

(1) *Roy Patrick, late 2nd Lt RA, sch master 1960; *b* 8 March 1935; *educ* Epsom; *m* 1st 2 July 1960 *Penelope Ruth, dau of Bertram Hoare Parham, and has:

1a *Julian Nicholas Hugh; *b* 29 March 1961

2a *Jeremy Robin Roy; *b* 30 June 1964

1a *Caroline Phoebe Mae; *b* 3 Nov 1962

2a *Henrietta Cecilie Ilona Penelope; *b* 14 July 1970

(1) (cont.) Roy Kirwan-Taylor *m* 2nd *Alison — and by her has:

3a *A dau, *b* 3 Aug 1979

(1) *Deirdre; *b* 6 Jan 1937

5 (William) John KIRWAN-TAYLOR, OBE (1946); FRICS, WW II: Lt-Col Rifle Bde, GSO(1) Airborne Forces, dir: Brightstone Estates, London and Yorks Tst, Bowater Paper, Br Newfoundland Corp, Churchill Falls (Labrador), Cow & Gate, Unigate; *b* 29 May 1905; *educ* Epsom and Trin Coll Cambridge (MA); *m* 1st 1929 (*divorce* 1941) Helene Charlotte de Berquely, dau of Grant Richards, and had:

(1) *Peter Robin, of Bridgehampton, NY; ACA, late 2nd Lt Rifle Bde, dir Hill Samuel, Premier Consolidated Oilfields 1975, pres Maxwell Cummings & Sons Hldgs Montreal 1976; *b* 18 Jan 1930; *educ* Winchester and Trin Coll Cambridge; *m* 1st 25 June 1952 (*divorce* 1965) Julia (*m* 2nd Viscount Lymington; *see* PORTSMOUTH, E), dau of Cdr W Graeme Ogden, DSC, RNVR, and has:

1a *Charles Patrick; *b* 8 April 1958

1a *Antonia Carmen Sybilla; *b* 7 Jan 1955

2a *Laura Madeleine Claire; *b* 22 Nov 1960; *m* 10 Aug 1996 *Keith Lloyd, s of Peter Lloyd, of Torquay

(1) (cont.) Peter Kirwan-Taylor *m* 2nd 12 March 1966 Michel Eads, dau of Robert Fulton Clarke, of Palm Beach, Florida, and by her has:

3a *Helene Aspen, *b* 14 Dec 1967

(1) (cont.) Peter Kirwan-Taylor *m* 3rd 1 Oct 1970 *Nancy Ann Normean and by her has:

2a *John Crispin Daniel; *b* 28 Dec 1971

(1) *Helene Fleur Mary Kirwan; *b* 2 Jan 1933; *m* 18 Feb 1958 *Sir Denis Mountain, 3rd Bt (*qv*), and has issue

5 (cont.) Lt-Col John Kirwan-Taylor *m* 2nd 28 June 1944 (*divorce* 1968) (Bettie) Marion, formerly w of J L Sands and dau of George Vernon Sims, and by her had:

(2) *Tessa Marianne Alexandra; *b* 1 June 1948; *educ* West Heath and Warwick U (BA), *m* 20 Sept 1969 *Edward McHale, est s of Edward McHale, and has:

1a *A dau; *b* 11 March 1970

5 (cont.) Lt-Col John Kirwan-Taylor *m* 3rd 12 May 1970 *Mrs Evelyn M McConnell, dau of George Henderson, of Canada, and *d* 1994

6 Charles Stuart TAYLOR (Sir), TD, DL (Sussex 1948); Hon Col 3rd (Sussex Bn) Mobile Def Corps 1958, WW II: Capt RA, DAAG, T/Maj 1941, MP Eastbourne 1935, Pres Grosvenor House (Park Lane) Ltd, Residential Hotels Assoc GB 1946, md Unigate, Cow and Gate, pres and v-chm Cncl Br Hotels and Restaurants Assoc to 1951, ktd 1954, Under Warden Baker's Co 1976, SBStJ; *b* 10 April 1910; *educ* Epsom and Trin Coll Cambridge (MA 1937); *m* 20 May 1936 Constance Ada, widow of Adney Gibbons and dau of Frederick E Shotter, of London, and had:

(1) *Charles Maxwell Kirwan; *b* 21 April 1937; *educ* Eton and Trin Coll Cambridge (BA 1960); *m* 2 June 1962 *Cicely Margaret, yr dau of W J V Tomlinson, and has:

1a *Jeremy William Kirwan; *b* 12 April 1963

2a *Charles Peregrine Kirwan; *b* 16 Jan 1965

1a *Elizabeth Flora Kirwan; *b* 23 Dec 1967

(2) *Alexander John Kirwan; *b* 18 March 1940; *educ* Eton; *m* 28 Nov 1964 *Gale Doreen, only dau of Charles U Caesar, of Long Island, and has:

1a *Alessandra Marquis; *b* 9 Feb 1967

(3) *Jonathan Jeremy Kirwan [Jonathan Taylor Esq, 42 Addison Road, London W14 8JH]; barrister Middle Temple 1968; *b* 12 Oct 1943; *educ* Eton and St Edmund Hall Oxford (BA 1966, MA); chm Dragon Ptnrs and Omix Country Estates Ltd, dir Gtr China Fund Inc; *m* 4 Oct 1966 *Victoria Mary Caroline, er dau of Hon John Francis McLaren, and has issue (*see* ABERCONWAY, B)

(1) *Jasmine Mary Kirwan; *b* 19 Oct 1949

1 *Hilda Joyce; *b* 19 Feb 1908; *m* 5 Sept 1935 *Stuart John Twentyman Turnbull, s of Robert Twentyman, and has:

(1) *Stuart David Twentyman; *b* 8 Oct 1936; *educ* Seaford; *m* 4 April 1963 *Dorothy Grace, dau of Fred Hare, and has:

1a *Alexandra Grace; *b* 18 Oct 1964

(2) *George Anthony Twentyman; ARICS (1964), ptnr Debenham, Tewson and Chinnocks (Surveyors) 1965, barrister Lincoln's Inn 1962; *b* 26 June 1938; *educ* Charterhouse and Ch Ch Oxford (BA 1960, MA 1965); *m* 14 June 1962 *Petronel Jonette Rene, dau of Maj James William Thursby Dunn, and has:

1a *Robert Edward Twentyman; *b* 28 Feb 1965

1a *Victoria Jonette; *b* 20 Aug 1963

(1) *Mary Victoria; *b* 5 July 1939; *educ* St Aidan's Coll Durham U (BA 1960)

(2) *Sarah; *b* 20 Feb 1947; *m* 5 Oct 1968 *Raymond Ebdon, s of Donald Ebdon

(3) *Amanda Joyce; *b* 29 March 1949

The est son,

ALFRED JESSE TAYLOR, **1st Baron Grantchester**, of Knightsbridge in the City of Westminster (UK), so *cr* 30 June 1953, OBE; *b* 14 Aug 1893; *educ* Epsom and King's Coll Cambridge (BA 1915, MA 1920); served WW I (despatches twice), barrister Middle Temple 1920, Patron Inst Atomic Info for Layman, FRSA, V-Pres UN Assoc, dir: County Fire Office Ltd 1934–68, London and Manchester Assur 1934–67 (chm 1953–61), Canal Randolph Corp USA, Pres Emeritus London Lib Pty, chm Brightstone Estates and Property Tst, FCII, memb RIIA, Govr Br Soc Internat Understanding, FRGS, V-Pres Insur Inst London, Pres Insur Inst Kent 1933–34, Brunei Order DSLJ 1966, ktd 1935; *m* 26 May 1920 Mara Henrietta (Mamie) (*d* 2 Feb 1976), 2nd dau of Albert Suenson, of Copenhagen, and had:

1 KENNETH BENT, **2nd Baron**

1 *Monica Esmé Ebba; *b* 17 Jan 1926; *educ* Queen's Coll London and Newnham Coll Cambridge (BA 1947, MA 1950); *m* 31 March 1951 (*divorce* 1965) Graeme Austin Spotswood Parish, BA, LLB, s of George Richard Parish, of The Manor House, Cossington, Somerset, and has had:

(1) Andrew Graeme Spotswood; *b* 9 Oct 1954; *educ* Westminster; *d* in an accident 1973

(1) *Alexandra Francesca Spotswood; *b* 3 Jan 1953; *m* 1987 *Nicholas Burnell and has:

1a *Joss Elliott Crystal; *b* 1987

1a *Brittany Leah; *b* 1991

The 1st BARON *d* 2 July 1976; his only son,

KENNETH BENT SUENSON-TAYLOR, **2nd Baron Grantchester**, CBE (1985), QC (1971); *b* 18 Aug 1921; *educ* Westminster and Christ's Coll Cambridge (BA 1942, MA 1946, LLB 1946, LLM 1955); Lt RA WW II, barrister Middle Temple and Lincoln's Inn 1946, lecturer company law Cncl Legal Educn 1951–72, Pres VAT Tbnl 1972–87, Recorder 1975–92, Chm: Licensed Dealers Tbnl 1976–88, Dairy Produce Quota Tbnl 1984–95, Fin Servs Tbnl 1987–91; Pres Aircraft and Shipbuilding Industs Tbnl 1980–83, Ho Lds: Dep Chm Ctees 1988–90, Speaker 1990–95; *m* 12 April 1947 *Betty, dir Littlewoods 1977–97, dau of Sir John Moores, CBE, of Freshfield, Lancs, and *d* 12 Aug 1995, leaving:

1 CHRISTOPHER JOHN SUENSON-TAYLOR, **3rd and present Baron Grantchester**

2 +Jeremy Kenneth; *b* 8 April 1951; *educ* Winchester and Liverpool U; *m* 19– *Lindsay Anne Kirby and has:

(1) +Daniel; *b* 1983

(1) *Rowan; *b* 1974

(2) *Laurel; *b* 1979

(3) *Zoë; *b* 1982

3 +James Gunnar [The Hon James Suenson-Taylor, Birches Over, Wood Lane, Weybridge, Surrey KT13 0JU]; *b* 30 Sept 1955; *educ* Eton and Kingston U (BA 1979); dir Littlewoods; *m* 12 Sept 1981 *Gillian Susan, yr dau of Peter Ayling, and has:

(1) +Andrew James; *b* 1985

(2) +Jonathan Gunnar; *b* 1991

(1) *Katharine Joyce; *b* 1988

1 *Janet Elizabeth Gudrun [The Hon Mrs Janet Grimstone, 103 Home Park Rd, London SW19 7HT]; *b* 26 June 1949; *educ* Cheltenham Ladies' Coll and St Hilda's Coll Oxford (MA), conservator paintings; *m* 23 June 1973 (*divorce* 1995) Gerald Edgar Grimstone, er s of Edgar Wilfred Grimstone, and has

(1) *Toby Stephen Gunnar; *b* 9 Oct 1975

(1) *Jenny Elizabeth May; *b* 30 May 1979

(2) *Anna Rose Yvonne; *b* 5 April 1982

2 *Deborah Katherine Louise; *b* 9 April 1957; *educ* Cheltenham Ladies' Coll and Exeter U; *m* 1st 7 July 1977 Michael Paul Jones; *m* 2nd 27 April 1996 *Ronald Stephen Cork, s of Stephen Cork, and by her 1st husb has:

(1) *Christopher Michael JONES later CORK; *b* 1987

(1) *Elizabeth Lily JONES later CORK; *b* 1992

3 *Kirsten Victoria Mary; *b* 25 Sept 1961; *educ* Cheltenham Ladies' Coll, Godolphin and Latymer, Liverpool U (BA) and London U (MA); *m* 1988 *Keith Lobban

GRANTLEY

Arms: Az. a maunch erm., over all a bend gu. **Crest:** A moor's head affrontée, couped ppr., wreathed round the temples with ivy; and round the neck a torse, arg. and az. **Supporters:** Dexter, a lion arg., gorged with a ducal coronet gold, pendant therefrom by a riband gu. an escutcheon of the arms of Norton; sinister, a griffin arg., gorged as the dexter. **Motto:** *Avi numerantur avorum* ('[My] ancestors are numbered in ancestors'). **Creation:** B. (GB) 9 April 1782.

THE 8TH LORD GRANTLEY, BARON OF MARKENFIELD, Co York (Richard William Brinsley Norton) [The Rt Hon The Lord Grantley, 8 Halsey St, London SW3 2QH]; *b* 30 Jan 1956; *s* f 1995; *educ* Ampleforth and New Coll Oxford (BA Law, MA, Pres Union 1976); Kt Honour and Devotion SMO Malta 1981, Cncllr Kensington and Chelsea 1982–86, dir Morgan Grenfell to 1997

Lineage: RICHARD NORTON, of Norton, Yorks; memb Cncl for the North *temp* HENRY VIII and EDWARD VI, Sheriff Yorks *c* 1568, joined the rising of the Northern Earls (*see* ABERGAVENNY, M); *m* 1st Susannah, dau of 2nd Lord (Baron) Latymer (*qv*); *m* 2nd Philippa, widow of Sir George Giffard and dau of Thomas Trapps, of London, and had by his 1st w, with an est s (Francis, *m* Albreda, sis and coheir of Thomas Wimbish, of Lincs, and had issue),10 yr sons and seven daus:

EDMUND NORTON, of Clowbeck, Yorks; *m* Cecilia, dau of Matthew Boynton, of Barmston, and *d c* 1610, leaving:

1 William, of Sawley, Yorks; *m* Margaret, dau and heir of William Welbury, of Newton, and was gf of:

(1) WELBURY

2 Robert, of Swinton, Yorks; *m* Catherine, dau and heir of John Staveley, and had:

(1) Maulger, of St Nicholas, Richmond, Yorks; *m* Anne, dau of Sir George Wandesford, of Kirklington, Yorks, and had:

1a Mary; *m* Sir John Yorke, of Gowthwaite

EDMUND NORTON's ggs,

WELBURY NORTON, of Sawley; living 1665; *m* Catherine, dau of Thomas Norton, of Langthorne, and had, with a yst s (John, of Carlton Hall, nr Rothwell, Yorks) and four daus:

1 William; ancestor of the NORTONs of Sawley

2 Thomas, of Grantley, Yorks; *m* Mary, dau and coheir of Thomas Fletcher, and had:

(1) Thomas, of Grantley; *m* Elizabeth, dau of William Serjeantson, of Hanlith, and *d* 22 Feb 1719, leaving:

1a FLETCHER NORTON, **1st Lord Grantley, Baron of Markenfield**, Co York (GB), so *cr* 9 April 1782, PC (1769), KC (1754); *b* 23 June 1716; barrister 1739, MP (Whig) Appleby 1756–61, Wigan 1761–68, Guildford 1768–82, Slr-Gen 1762–63, ktd 1762, Attorney-Gen 1763–65, Speaker H of C 1770–80, Recorder Guildford, LLD; *m* 21 May 1741 Grace (*d* 30 Oct 1803), est dau of Sir William Chapple, Judge King's Bench, and *d* 1 Jan 1789, having had:

1b WILLIAM NORTON, **2nd Lord Grantley, Baron of Markenfield**; *b* 19 Feb 1741/2; *m* 27 Sept 1791 Anna Margaretta (*d* 23 April 1795), dau of Jonathan Midgley, of Beverley, Yorks, and *dsp* 12 Nov 1822

2b Fletcher; Baron Exchequer Scotland; *b* 16 Nov 1744; *m* 1793 Caroline Elizabeth, only dau of James Balmain, and *d* 1820, leaving, with other issue:

1c FLETCHER NORTON, **3rd Lord Grantley, Baron of Markenfield**; High Steward Allerton and Guildford, FSA; *b* 14 July 1798; *educ* RMC Sandhurst; Gren Gds Battles of Quatre Bras and Waterloo (wounded); *m* 26 July 1825 Charlotte Earle (*d* 1 May 1878), yst dau of Sir William Beechey, and *dsp* 28 Aug 1875

2c George Chapple; Recorder Guildford, Met Police Magistrate; *b* 31 Aug 1800; granted with siblings rank of baron's daus/yr s; *m* 30 July 1827 Caroline Elizabeth Sarah (*m* 2nd 1 March 1877 Sir William Stirling-Maxwell, 9th Bt (*see* 1956 edn); *d* 15 June 1877), 2nd dau of Thomas Sheridan and gdau of Richard Brinsley Sheridan, the playwright, and *d* 24 Feb 1875, having had, with other issue:

1d Fletcher Cavendish Charles Conyers; Attaché Paris; *b* 10 July 1829; *d* 13 Oct 1859

2d THOMAS BRINSLEY, **4th Baron**

3c Charles Francis; Army Capt; *b* 4 Feb 1807; *m* 29 Dec 1831 Maria Louisa (*m* 2nd 22 May 1838 Hon Edmund Phipps (*see* NORMANBY, M); *d* 1888), est dau of Lt-Gen Sir Colin Campbell, KCB, and *d* 27 Oct 1835, leaving:

1d Charles Grantley Campbell; Maj 23rd Roy Welch Fus, Col Imp Ottoman Gendarmerie, Mil Kt Windsor; *b* 23 May 1835; *m* 1st 22 June 1870 (*divorce* 4 Nov 1879) Katharine Buckner, dau of Cdre William Henry McVickar, of New York; *m* 2nd 6 Sept 1886 Mary Elizabeth Mina (*d* 12 March 1921), dau of John Barnard Smith, and *d* 10 April 1921

1d Caroline Helen Jocelyn; *m* 6 Feb 1871 George Thomas Goodbehere and *d* 1914

4c James (Rev); *b* 27 Oct 1809; *m* 4 Oct 1838 Isabella (*d* 26 April 1877), only child of Thomas Lowndes, of Barrington Hall, Essex, and *d* 31 Oct 1853, leaving by her, with other issue:

1d Robert Thomas Lowndes NORTON later LOWNDES-STONE-NORTON, of Anningsley Park, Surrey, Brightwell Park, Oxon, and Langdon House, Devon; *b* 10 Sept 1839; Capt Gren Gds; *m* 1st 18 Sept 1862 Catherine Charlotte (*d* 11 Dec 1882), gdau and heiress of William Lowndes-Stone, and had:

1e Roger Fletcher Earle, of Brightwell Park; Maj 8th (Serv) Bn Devonshire Regt, Capt 3rd Bn; *b* 1 July 1863; *m* 18 April 1890 Agnes Selina (*d* 8 Oct 1941), dau of Rev William Thornton, Rector N Bovey, Devon, and *d* 11 July 1934, leaving:

1f Fletcher William; T/Maj Oxford and Bucks LI WW II; *b* 12 April 1908; *educ* Eton and Ch Ch Oxford (BA 1932); *m* 15 Aug 1941 (*divorce* 1945) Emma Dorothy, formerly w of Ralph Minto Wilson and dau of Henry Thomas Gager, of New York

1d (cont.) Capt Robert Lowndes-Stone-Norton; *m* 2nd 4 Nov 1891 Marie Annie, dau of George Dow, and *d* 12 Jan 1895

2d James; Lt 2nd Life Gds; *b* 6 Sept 1842; *m* 21 Feb 1871 Henrietta Clara Marie (*d* 27 June 1920), only child of Alexander Barclay, of Stockholm, and *dsp*

1d Isabel; *m* 3 March 1862 Maj-Gen William Richard Annesley (*see* ANNESLEY, E) and *d* 28 April 1927, leaving issue

2d Caroline Elizabeth Ainslie; *m* 12 Sept 1878 Charles Rankin Vickerman Longbourne, of Ripsley, Sussex, and *d* 18 Nov 1946, leaving issue. He *d* 1908

1c Grace Conyers Charlotte; *m* 3 Dec 1816 Sir Neil Menzies, Bt (*see* 1902 edn), and *d* 3 Jan 1877. He *d* 20 Aug 1844

2c Augusta Anne; *m* 9 Jan 1846 James Johnstone, of Alva, Clackmannanshire, and *d* 21 July 1859, leaving issue. He *d* 24 Feb 1888

3b Chapple; Gen; *d* 1818

4b Edward; barrister; *d* 1789

1b Grace; *m* 3rd Earl of Portsmouth (*qv*) and *d* 1831

The 3rd BARON's n,

THOMAS BRINSLEY NORTON, **4th Lord Grantley, Baron of Markenfield**; *b* 4 Nov 1831; *educ* Eton and Univ Coll Oxford; *m* 1 Aug 1854 Maria Chiara Elisa Federigo (*d* 1 Feb 1892), of Capri, and *d* 24 July 1877, leaving, with a dau (Carlotta Chiara Mary, *d* unm 21 March 1931):

JOHN RICHARD BRINSLEY NORTON, **5th Lord Grantley, Baron of Markenfield**, JP, DL Yorks; Capt Middx Yeo Cav; *b* 1 Oct 1855; *m* 1st 5 Nov 1879 his 1st cousin's former w Katharine Buckner (*d* 17 Feb 1897; *see* above) and had:

1 A son; *b* and *d* 25 Jan 1889

2 RICHARD HENRY BRINSLEY, **6th Baron**

1 Jean Mary Conyers; *m* 11 Feb 1903 Edmund Henry Bevan, JP, of Hilston Park, Mon, s of Thomas Bevan, DL, of Stone Park, Greenhithe, and *d* 22 July 1942, leaving issue (*see* SELBORNE, E). He *d* 3 Nov 1945

2 Eleanour Trehane; *d* unm 16 March 1951

3 Winifred Chapple (twin with Eleanour); *m* 26 June 1907 William Galbraith Tennant, est s of John Tennant, of The Boltons, London SW, and *d* 11 July 1914, leaving issue

4 Katharine Edith Carlotta; *d* unm 9 Feb 1961

The **5th Baron** *m* 2nd 16 Sept 1899 Alice Jones (*d* 11 May 1942), illegitimate dau of 7th Viscount Ranelagh (*see* 1885 edn), and *d* 5 Aug 1943

His only son,

RICHARD HENRY BRINSLEY NORTON, **6th Lord Grantley, Baron of Markenfield**; Capt SR Scots Gds, Staff Capt War Office 1915, WW I (wounded); *b* 2 April 1892; *m* 3 April 1919 Jean Mary (*d* 16 Jan 1945), er dau of Brig-Gen Sir David Alexander Kinloch, 11th Bt (*qv*), and *d* 17 July 1954, leaving:

1 JOHN (JOHNNY) RICHARD BRINSLEY NORTON, **7th Lord Grantley, Baron of Markenfield**, MC (1944); *b* 30 July 1923; *educ* Eton and New Coll Oxford; Capt Gren Gds WW II, memb Lloyd's, dir Leslie and Godwin Ltd; *m* 18 Jan 1955 *Lady Deirdre Elisabeth Freda Hare, only dau of 5th Earl of Listowel (*qv*), and *d* 1995, leaving:

(1) RICHARD WILLIAM BRINSLEY NORTON, **8th and present Lord Grantley, Baron of Markenfield**

(2) +FRANCIS JOHN HILARY; *b* 28 Sept 1960; heir presumptive; *educ* Ampleforth

1 *Sarah Katharine Elinor [The Hon Mrs Sarah Baring, 42 Melton Court, Old Brompton Rd, London SW7 3JH]; *b* 20 Jan 1920; *m* 1st 14 June 1945 (*divorce* 1953) 3rd Viscount Astor (*d* 8 March 1966; *qv*) and has issue; *m* 2nd 17 April 1953 (*divorce* 1965) Thomas Michael Baring (*see* NORTHBROOK, B), and has an adopted son

GRANVILLE

Arms: Quarterly, 1st and 4th, barry of eight arg. and gu., a cross flory sa. (for GOWER); 2nd, az. three laurel leaves or (for LEVESON); 3rd, gu. three clarions or (for GRANVILLE). **Crest:** A wolf passant arg., collared and lined or. **Supporters:** Two wolves arg., plain collared, a line reflexed over the back gold, and charged on the shoulder with an escutcheon gu., thereon a clarion or. **Motto:** *Frangas non flectes* ('You may break, but you will not bend me'). **Creations:** V. (UK) 12 Aug 1815, E. and B. (UK) 10 May 1833.

THE 6TH EARL GRANVILLE, Viscount Granville of Stone Park, Co Stafford, and **Baron Leveson of Stone**, Co Stafford ((Granville George) Fergus Leveson-Gower) [The Rt Hon The Earl Granville, 51 Lyall Mews, London SW1X 8DJ; Callernish, Sollas, North Uist, Inverness-shire PA51 3JH]; *b* 10 Sept 1959 (HM THE QUEEN stood sponsor); *s* f 1996; Page Honour to HM 1973; *m* 23 May 1997 *Anne, dau of Bernard Topping, of Lanark, and has:

1 *Rose Alice; *b* 16 April 1998

Granville, other creations: Sir Bevil Granville, of Stow, Cornwall, was one of the leading royalist commanders at the beginning of the Civil War but was killed in 1643, when it was barely a year old. His elder son John was created Earl of Bath in 1661 (*see* also BATH, M, preliminary remarks), but the title expired with the death of John's grandson, the 3rd Earl, in 1711. Two subsidiary titles created along with the Earldom were the Barony of Granville of Kilkhampton and Bideford and the Viscountcy of Granville of Lansdown. John Earl of Bath's youngest daughter Grace was created Countess Granville and married George Carteret, created in his turn Baron Carteret of Hawnes. Their son was the leading power in the Government between February 1741/2 and November 1744, even though the Earl of Wilmington and Henry Pelham as First Lords of the Treasury were looked on as Prime Minister. This Earldom of Granville subsequently descended with the Carteret Barony till they both expired in 1776.

Another Barony, that of Granville of Potheridge, was conferred on John Earl of Bath's second son, also called John, in March 1702/3.

John Earl of Bath's eldest daughter Jane married Sir William Leveson-Gower, Bt, and was ancestor with him of the Marquesses of Stafford (later promoted Dukes of Sutherland, *qv*), from a younger branch of whom the present Earls Granville descend.

Lineage: The 1st MARQUESS OF STAFFORD (*see* SUTHERLAND, D) had a yst s:

Lord GRANVILLE LEVESON-GOWER, **1st Earl Granville**, so *cr* 10 May 1833, as also previously 12 Aug 1814 BARON LEVESON OF STONE, Co Stafford, and VISCOUNT GRANVILLE OF STONE PARK, Co Stafford (all UK), GCB (1825), PC (1804); *b* 12 Oct 1773; *educ* Ch Ch Oxford (DCL 1799); a Ld Treasury 1800–01, Amb: St Petersburg 1804–05 and April-Nov 1807, The Hague 1823, Paris 1824–28, 1830–35 and 1835–41, Sec War July-Nov 1809; *m* 24 Dec 1809 Harriet Elizabeth Cavendish (*d* 25 Nov 1862), dau of 5th Duke of Devonshire (*qv*), and had, with other issue:

1 GRANVILLE GEORGE, **2nd Earl**

2 Edward Frederick, of Holmbury, Dorking, JP, DL Surrey; *b* 3 May 1819; *educ* Ch Ch Oxford (MA); barrister, MP Stoke-upon-Trent 1852–57 and Bodmin 1859–85; *m* 1 June 1851 Lady Margaret Compton (*d* 22 May 1858), dau of 2nd Marquess of Northampton (*qv*), and *d* 30 May 1907, leaving:

(1) George Greville (Sir), KBE (1921); *b* 19 May 1858; *educ* Balliol Coll Oxford (MA); MP (Lib) NW Staffs 1885–86 and Stoke-upon-Trent 1890–95, Priv Sec to PM 1880–85, Jr Ld Treasury 1886, Comptroller Household 1892–95, Commr Woods and Forests 1908–24; *m* 9 June 1898 Hon Adelaide Violet Cicely (*d* 21 April 1955), dau of 8th Baron Monson (*qv*), and *d* 18 July 1951, having had with two yr daus (*d* unm):

1a Iris Irma; *b* 20 Aug 1899; *m* 1st 5 Jan 1922 (*divorce* 1928) Maj-Gen William Henry Buchanan Mirrlees, CB, DSO, MC, RA (*d* 22 Oct 1964), s of William Julius Mirrlees; *m* 2nd 29 June 1938 Maj Richard Lodge Palmer, DSO, MC, RA, and *d* 2 Sept 1944

1 Susan Georgiana; *m* 2 Feb 1833 4th Baron Rivers (*see* 1880 edn) and *d* 30 April 1866, leaving issue. He *d* 28 April 1866

2 Georgiana Charlotte; *m* July 1833 Alexander George Fullerton, of Ballintoy Castle, Co Antrim, and Westwood, Hants, and *d* 19 Jan 1885, having had issue. He *d* 12 May 1907

The 1st EARL *d* 8 Jan 1846; his est s,

GRANVILLE GEORGE LEVESON-GOWER, **2nd Earl Granville**, KG (1857), PC (1846), DL; *b* 11 May 1815; *educ* Eton and Ch Ch Oxford; Attaché Paris 1835–36, MP (Lib) Morpeth 1837–40 and Lichfield 1841–46, U-Sec For Affrs 1840–41, Master Buckhounds 1846–48, Commr Railwys 1846–51, Paymaster-Gen 1848–51, V-Pres BOT 1848–51, For Sec Dec 1851–Feb 1852, 1870–74 and 1880–85, Ld Pres Cncl 1852–54, 1855–58 and 1859–66, Chllr Duchy Lancaster 1854–55, Colonial Sec 1868–70 and Feb-July 1886, Constable Dover Castle and Ld Warden Cinque Ports 1865–91, Er Bro Trin Ho 1870–91, Hon Col 3rd Bn Roy Sussex Regt, Chllr London U 1859–91, FRS 1853, DCL Oxon 1863, LLD Cantab 1864; *m* 1st 25 July 1840 Marie Louise Pellina (*d* 14 March 1860), widow of Sir Ferdinand Dalberg-Acton, 7th Bt (*see* ACTON, B), and only child of Emerich Josef Wolfgang Heribert, Duke of Dalberg; *m* 2nd 26 Sept 1865 Castalia Rosalind (*d* 12 Nov 1938), yst dau of Walter Frederick Campbell of Islay and *d* 31 March 1891, leaving:

1 GRANVILLE GEORGE LEVESON-GOWER, **3rd Earl Granville**, GCMG (1932, KCMG 1924), GCVO (1914, MVO 1904), PC (1928); *b* 4 March 1872; *educ* Eton; Dip Serv: joined as Attaché 1893, Berlin 1894, 3rd Sec 1896, Cairo 1897, 2nd Sec 1898, Vienna 1898, FO 1899, The Hague 1900, Berlin 1904, 1st Sec 1905, Brussels 1908, Counsellor 1911, Berlin 1911, Paris 1913, Min Plen 1916, Salonica 1916, Athens 1917, Envoy Extrdy 1917, Copenhagen 1921, The Hague 1926, Amb Brussels 1928–33, Ld-in-Waiting to TM QUEEN VICTORIA 1895, EDWARD VII 1905–10 and GEORGE V 1910–15, Grand Cross Dannebrog, N Star Sweden, Leopold, Concepcion Portugal; *m* 27 Sept 1900 Nina Ayesha (*d* 12 June 1955), dau of Walter Baring (*see* NORTHBROOK, B), and *dsp* 21 July 1939

2 WILLIAM SPENCER LEVESON-GOWER, **4th Earl Granville**, KG (1952), GCVO (1953, KCVO 1945), CB (1932), DSO (1919); *b* 11 July 1880; RN: Cdr and Capt WWI (despatches), V-Adml 1935, ADC to HM GEORGE V 1929, Hon Col 15th Light AA Regt 1939, Lt-Govr IOM 1937–45, Govr NI 1945–52, Pres: Amateur Fencing Assoc, All-England Fencing Club, KJStJ, Hon LLD Queen's U Belfast, Freeman Belfast and Larne, Order Redeemer Greece and St Anne Russia; *m* 24 May 1916 Lady Rose Constance Bowes-Lyon, GCVO (1953), CStJ, Hon LLD Queen's U Belfast, Freeman Belfast and Larne (*d* 17 Nov 1967), dau of 14th Earl of Strathmore and Kinghorne (*qv*), and *d* 25 June 1953, leaving:

(1) (GRANVILLE) JAMES (JAMIE) LEVESON-GOWER, **5th Earl Granville**, MC (1945), DL (Inverness-shire 1974); *b* 6 Dec 1918; *educ* Eton; V-Lt Western Isles 1976–83, Ld Lt 1983–93, Pres Navy League 1953–66, Maj Coldstream Gds (SR) WW II (twice wounded, despatches), sometime with Coutts; *m* 9 Oct 1958 Doon Aileen, yr dau of Hon Brinsley Sheridan Bushe Plunket (*see* PLUNKET, B), and *d* 31 Oct 1996, leaving:

1a GRANVILLE GEORGE FERGUS LEVESON-GOWER, **6th and present Earl Granville**

2a +NIALL JAMES; *b* 24 Aug 1963; heir presumptive

1a *Marcia Rose Aileen; *b* 10 Feb 1961; *m* 1986 *Jonathan Charles Bulmer, yst s of Edward Charles Bulmer, and has:

1b *James (Jamie) Alexander Howard; *b* 1992

2b *Hector Charles Marcus; *b* 1993

1b *Hesper Rose Constance; *b* 1990

2b *A dau; b 29 Aug 1995

(1) *Mary Cecilia; *b* 12 Dec 1917; *m* 7 July 1956 Samuel Wittewronge Clayton, MA, yr s of Brig-Gen Sir Gilbert Falkingham Clayton, KCMG, KBE, CB, and has:

1a *George Falkingham; *b* 4 Sept 1958; Page Honour to HM QUEEN ELIZABETH THE QUEEN MOTHER 1973–74

1a *Rose Cecilia; *b* 25 Jan 1960; *m* 1993 *William W Stancer, s of A J Stancer, of The Old Rectory, Wick Rissington, Glos

1 Victoria Alberta; *b* 14 April 1867; *m* 8 Sept 1896 Harold John Hastings Russell and *d* 11 Feb 1953, leaving issue (*see* BEDFORD, D)

2 Sophia Castalia Mary; *b* 25 Feb 1870; *m* 16 Aug 1892 Hugh Morrison, JP, MP, and *d* 22 March 1934, leaving issue (*see* MARGADALE, B)

3 Susan Katherine; *b* 21 Aug 1876; *d* 7 May 1878

GRATTAN-BELLEW

Arms: Quarterly : 1st and 4th, sa. fretty or, a crescent arg. for difference (for BELLEW); 2nd and 3rd, per saltire sa. and erm. a lion rampant or (for GRATTAN). **Crests:** 1 An arm embowed in armour ppr., charged with a crescent for difference, grasping in the dexter hand a sword ppr., pommel and hilt or (for BELLEW), 2 A dove ppr., holding in its dexter claw a sceptre and standing on a barrel or (for GRATTAN). **Motto:** *Tout d'en haut* ('All from above'). **Creation:** Bt. (UK) 15 Aug 1838.

SIR HENRY CHARLES GRATTAN-BELLEW, 5TH BT, of Mount Bellew, Co Galway; *b* 12 May 1933; *s* f 1948; *educ* Ampleforth; Assist Dist Offr Kenya Admin Police Res 1953–54, Dist Offr Kenya Admin 1954–55, sports administrator, journalist, radio and TV broadcaster, publisher, co dir; *m* 1st 27 April 1956 (*divorce* 1966) Naomi, yr dau of Dr Charles Cyril Morgan, of White Friars, Chester, and formerly w of Herbert Ellis; *m* 2nd 1967 (*divorce* 1974) Gillian Hulley; *m* 3rd 1978 *Elzab, Amy, only dau of Henry Gilbert Body, of Utrecht, Natal, and widow of J B Westerveld, of Pretoria, and by his 2nd w has:

1 +PATRICK CHARLES; *b* 7 Dec 1971

1 *Deirdre Sophia; *b* 1967

Lineage: MICHAEL BELLEW, of Mount Bellew, Co Galway (s of Christopher Bellew, yr bro of Sir Patrick Bellew, 1st Bt, ancestor of the Barons Bellew, *qv*); *m* 1st — Barnewall; *m* 2nd — Kelly, of Mount Kelly, and *d* 1742, leaving by his 1st w:

CHRISTOPHER BELLEW, of Mount Bellew; *m* Barbara, est dau of Lucas Dillon, of Holywell, Co Mayo, and widow of John Dillon, of Maunir, and *d* after 30 Jan 1769, leaving, with other issue:

MICHAEL BELLEW, of Mount Bellew; *m* Jane, dau of Henry Dillon, and *d* 1797, leaving an est s:

CHRISTOPHER DILLON BELLEW, of Mount Bellew; *b* 1763; *m* 27 Oct 1794 Olivia Emily (*d* Sept 1856), only dau of Anthony Nugent, of Pallas, self-styled 4th Baron Nugent (*see* WESTMEATH, E), and *d* 23 April 1826, leaving:

Sir Michael Dillon Bellew, 1st Bt (UK), so *cr* 15 Aug 1838, of Mount Bellew; *b* 29 Sept 1796; *m* 1816 Helena Maria (*d* 30 April 1865), est dau of Thomas Dillon, of Mount Dillon, Co Dublin, and Eadestown, Co Kildare, and had, with other issue:

1 **Rev Sir Christopher Bellew, 2nd Bt**; RC priest; *b* 1818; *d* 18 March 1867

2 Thomas Arthur BELLEW later GRATTAN-BELLEW (roy licence 19 March 1859), of Mount Bellew; *b* 1820; MP Co Galway 1852–57, served 34th Regt; *m* Sept 1858 Pauline (*d* 17 July 1908), dau and coheir of Henry Grattan, MP, s of Rt Hon Henry Grattan, the statesman, and *d* 24 July 1863, leaving issue:

(1) HENRY CHRISTOPHER (Sir), **3rd Bt**

(1) Mary Helena; *m* 7 July 1885 18th Lord Saltoun (*qv*) and *d* 8 Oct 1940, leaving issue.

The 2nd Bt's n,

Sir Henry Christopher Grattan-Bellew, 3rd Bt, DL Co Galway; *b* 1 June 1860; High Sheriff Co Galway 1884, Lt-Col 4th Bn Connaught Rangers, Lt 5th Dragoon Gds; *m* 11 Feb 1885 Lady Sophia Maria Elizabeth Forbes (*d* 7 Nov 1942), dau of 7th Earl of Granard (*qv*), and had issue:

1 Herbert Michael; *b* 17 June 1886; *d* unm 11 Nov 1906

2 CHARLES CHRISTOPHER (Sir), **4th Bt**

3 William Arthur, MC; 2nd Lt (T/Maj) Connaught Rangers, S/Cdr RFC WW I; *b* 15 Sept 1893; *d* 24 March 1917 from injuries recd on active service

4 Thomas Henry; Kt SMO; *b* 9 May 1901; *educ* Downside and Trin Coll Cambridge (BA); *m* 1 June 1933 Bettina Idrone Dorothy (*d* 10 March 1995), est dau of Maj John Edward Blake Loftus, of Mount Loftus, Co Kilkenny, and *d* 3 Dec 1967, leaving issue:

(1) +Patrick Edward [Dr Patrick Grattan-Bellew, 472 Edison Ave, Ottawa ONT K2A 1T9, Canada]; *b* 26 Sept 1934; *educ* Glenstal Priory, U Coll Dublin (BSc 1956), McGill (MSc 1963) and Cambridge (PhD); mineralogist; *m* 1980 *Elly Bollegraaf-Dwinger, dau of Nathan Gruner

(1) *Idrone Pauline Mary [Mrs Roger Brittain, 90 Broxash Rd, London SW11 0AB]; *b* 30 June 1936; *m* 28 June 1964 *Roger William Brittain, only s of Samson S W Brittain, of Boxted Lodge, Colchester, and has:

1a *William Henry Grattan; *b* 11 Jan 1965

2a *Charles Francis; *b* 22 May 1966

3a *James Nicholas Robert; *b* 10 March 1971

1a *Georgina Mary Idrone; *b* 28 Aug 1968

5 Arthur John (Sir), CMG (1956), QC; *b* 23 May 1903; *educ* Downside and Christ's Coll Cambridge (BA 1924); barrister Lincoln's Inn 1925, Attorney-Gen Tanganyika, Ch Sec Tanganyika 1956–59, WW II with 3rd/7th Dogra Regt IA (POW 1942–45), ktd 1959; *m* 22 July 1931 Winifred Mary, 2nd dau of Edmond Ronayne Mahony, of Marysborough, Glanmire, Co Cork, and had:

(1) +(Arthur Henry) Bertram (Bertie) [Bertram Grattan-Bellew Esq, Hole Farm, Great Waldingfield, nr Sudbury, Suffolk]; *b* 10 Feb 1937; *educ* Downside; late Lt 8th KRIH, memb Lloyd's, MFH Galway Blazers; *m* 20 June 1961 *Georgina (Georgie) Madeleine Mary, only dau of Sir (George Edward) Mordaunt Milner, 9th Bt (*qv*), and has:

1a +Charles Henry Mordaunt; *b* 11 Nov 1964

1a *Sophie Rose; *b* 14 Dec 1962; *m* 1995 *David Oliver and has issue:

1b *Edward George Mordaunt; *b* 10 July 1996

(1) *Gillian Barbara [Mrs Peter Haggard Lyster, Little Chishill Manor, Royston, Herts]; *b* 25 April 1934; *m* 29 June 1967 *Peter Haggard Lyster, late Capt City of Lond Yeo, formerly 11th Hus, yst s of Lionel Charles Lyster, of Essex, and has:

1a *Thomas Henry; *b* 1971

1a *Grania Mary; *b* 16 Jan 1968

2a *Anna Gillian; *b* 1969

1 Helena Barbara; *b* 4 April 1889

2 Moira Jane; *b* 8 May 1891; *m* 8 Jan 1920 James D'Arcy (*d* 12 May 1958), est s of Hyacinth D'Arcy, of New Forest, and *d* 20 Oct 1971, leaving issue

3 Angela Mary; *b* 11 Nov 1894

Sir HENRY *d* 20 Jan 1942; his est surv son,

Sir Charles Christopher Grattan-Bellew, 4th Bt, MC (1918); Lt-Col KRRC WW I; *b* 23 Aug 1887; *m* 21 April 1923 Maureen Peyton, niece and adopted dau of Sir Thomas George Segrave, CBE, of Shenfield, Essex, and *d* 6 Nov 1948, leaving:

1 Sir HENRY CHARLES GRATTAN-BELLEW, **5th and present Bt**

1 *Deirdre Maureen [Mrs Gerard Kiernan, 35 Priory Grove, Stillorgan, Dublin, Ireland]; *b* 21 March 1924; *m* 1946 *Gerard Kiernan and has issue:

(1) *Charles Dominick; *b* 1947

(2) *Henry Gerard; *b* 1952

(1) *Valerie Maureen; *b* 1946

(2) *Maureen Gabriel; *b* 1949

(3) *Dawn Vivien; *b* 1956

GRAVES

Arms: Gu. an eagle displayed or, ducally crowned arg., on a canton of the last an anchor ppr. **Crest:** A demi-eagle displayed and erased or, encircled round the body and below the wings by a ducal coronet arg. **Supporters:** Two royal vultures, wings close, ppr. **Motto:** *Aquila non captat muscas* ('The eagle does not catch flies'). **Creation:** B. (I) 24 Oct 1794.

THE 9TH LORD GRAVES, BARON OF GRAVESEND, Co Londonderry (Evelyn Paget Graves) [The Rt Hon The Lord Graves, Woodlands, 405 Mole Creek Rd, Deloraine, 7304 Tasmania, Australia]; *b* 17 May 1926; *s* kinsman 1994; *educ* Launceston Ch GS; *m* 13 March 1957 *Marjorie Ann, OAM (1992), dau of Dr Sidney Ernest Holder, of Wallingford, Berks, and has had:

1 +TIMOTHY EVELYN; *b* 27 March 1960; *educ* Launceston Ch GS

2 Simon Paget; *b* 29 May 1963; *educ* Launceston Ch GS; *d* 4 March 1997

1 *Wendy Susan; *b* 9 July 1958

2 *Philippa Ann; *b* 14 Feb 1962

Lineage: JAMES GRAVES, of a family reputedly long-settled in Yorks; *m* —, dau and coheir of Sir John Herdman, of Stannington, W R Yorks, and had, with other issue (including an er s Samuel, ancestor of Sir Charles Brune Graves-Sawle, Bt; *see* 1932 edn):

THOMAS GRAVES, of Thanckes, Cornwall; *b* 1680; R-Adml RN; *m* 1st 1713 — Warne (*dsp* 1718); *m* 2nd 1723 Elizabeth, dau of Rev Gilbert Budgell, DD, of St Thomas's, nr Exeter, and by her had, with an er s (William, Master in Chancery):

THOMAS GRAVES, **1st Lord Graves, Baron of Gravesend**, Co Londonderry (I), so *cr* 24 Oct 1794; *b* 23 Oct 1725; RN: R-Adml 1779, V-Adml 1787, Adml the Blue 1794, the White 1795, cdr War American Independence and fought a drawn battle against the French under de Grasse 5 Sept 1781 off the Chesapeake Capes, his failure to secure victory leading to Cornwallis's surrender at Yorktown and the collapse of the British effort in N America; C-in-C Plymouth 1786–89, 2ic under Howe (*see* HOWE, E) Glorious First of June victory over French 1794 (severely wounded), which won him his peerage and a pension of £1,000 p.a. (some £100,000 in late-1990s terms); *m* 22 June 1771 Elizabeth (*d* 1827), dau and coheir of William Peere Williams, of Cadhay, Devon, and had, with other issue:

(1) THOMAS NORTH, **2nd Baron**

(1) Elizabeth Anne; *m* 1802 William Bagwell, of Kilmore

(2) Anne Elizabeth; *m* 15 Jan 1803 Sir Thomas Hare, 1st Bt (*qv*), and *d* 11 Sept 1823

(3) Margaret Anne; *m* Capt — Nesham, RN

The 1st BARON *d* 9 Feb 1802; his est son,

THOMAS NORTH GRAVES, **2nd Lord Graves, Baron of Gravesend**; *b* 28 May 1775; *educ* Eton, Inner Temple and Univ Coll Oxford; MP (Tory) Okehampton 1812–18, Windsor 1819–20 and Milborne Port 1820–27, Ld Bedchamber to GEORGE IV 1813–27, ktd 1821, Commr Excise 1827–30; *m* 27 June 1803 Lady Mary Paget (*d* 29 April 1835), sis of 1st Marquess of Anglesey (*qv*), and *d* 7 Feb 1830, having had, with other issue:

1 WILLIAM THOMAS GRAVES, **3rd Lord Graves, Baron of Gravesend**; *b* 18 April 1804; Capt 2nd Foot Gds, ADC to Ld Lt Ireland; *m* 1st 11 Aug 1829 Sophie Thérèse (*dsp* 1 Aug 1833), widow of Gen Count Bruyére and dau of Gen Berthier; *m* 2nd 1833(?) Louise Adèle Maléne (*d* 27 Nov 1877) and *d* 20 March 1870, having by her had, with other issue:

(1) CLARENCE EDWARD GRAVES, **4th Lord Graves, Baron of Gravesend** (never established right to the title, however), JP (Cornwall); *b* 8 June 1847; *educ* Cheltenham; Lt RN 1870–72; *m* 8 June 1870 Katherine Frederica (*d* 16 May 1926), est dau of Sir Thomas William Clinton Murdoch, KCMG, and *dspms* 29 Jan 1904, having had a s and three daus (*d* unm)

(1) Jane Adèle; *m* 8 Jan 1891 William Thomas Fernie, MD, of Richmond, Surrey, and *d* 25 March 1917. He *d* Nov 1914

(2) Adèle Isabella; *m* 15 Dec 1859 George William Cume Soltau-Symons, of Chaddlewood, Devon, and *d* 27 Dec 1869, leaving issue. He *d* 1916

2 Henry Richard; *b* 9 Oct 1818; *m* 21 Oct 1843 Henrietta Wellesley (*d* 31 July 1898) and *d* 29 April 1882, leaving:

(1) HENRY CYRIL PERCY GRAVES, **5th Lord Graves, Baron of Gravesend**; *b* 10 Sept 1847; *m* 11 Oct 1870 Elizabeth Ellen (*d* 5 Jan 1914), yst dau of Henry Craven, of Wickham Hall, Kent, and *d* 13 Jan 1914, having had:

1a CLARENCE PERCY RIVERS GRAVES, **6th Lord Graves, Baron of Gravesend**; *b* 16 Aug 1871; *m* 7 Feb 1903 his cousin Mary Ada Isabel (*d* 7 Jan 1962), 3rd dau of Edward Corbett Parker by Georgiana Louisa Alice (*see* above), and *dspm* 1 March 1937, having had:

1b Cerise Evelyn Georgina; *b* 18 July 1906

2b Rosemary Audrey Alys; *b* 10 June 1910; *m* 3 Feb 1938 Maj Herbert Edward Osborne, MC (*d* 1951), s of Edward Osborne, and *d* 20 July 1996

1a Maud Evelyn; *m* 29 May 1905 John Drysdale Sandars, JP, DL, of Gate Burton Hall, Knaith Hall and N Sandsfield, Lincs, and *d* 28 March 1959, leaving issue. He *d* 18 Feb 1922

(2) William Spencer Paget; Cdr RN; *b* 21 Feb 1849; *m* 10 Aug 1882 Beatrice Mary (*d* 3 Aug 1950), 2nd dau of Robert Leake, MP, and *dsp* 6 Sept 1909

(3) Claude Thomas; *b* 21 Sept 1850; *m* 1876 Georgina, dau of Capt — Hill, and *d* 1898, leaving:

1a HENRY ALGERNON CLAUDE GRAVES, **7th Lord Graves, Baron of Gravesend**; Capt Northumberland Hus Yeo, Lt 3rd Co of London Yeo; *b* 3 Oct 1877; *m* 1909 (*divorce* 1922) Vera Blanche Neville (*d* 20 May 1953), dau of Alfred Neville Snepp, and *d* 6 Nov 1963, leaving:

1b PETER GEORGE WELLESLEY GRAVES, **8th Lord Graves, Baron of Gravesend**; *b* 21 Oct 1911; *educ* Harrow; actor; *m* 28 May 1960 Winifred Ruby (Vanessa Lee, the actress and vocalist; *d* 1992), widow of Warde Morgan and dau of Alfred Moule, and *d* 1994

1a Queena Mabel Constance; *b* 14 Oct 1880; *m* 25 Oct 1899 Edward Othon Dunne and *d* 11 June 1906

(4) Algernon Sydney George; *b* 16 Oct 1852; *m* 2 June 1880 Constance Ellen (*d* 1 Nov 1886), yr dau of Murray M Johnson, of Stone Castle, nr Dartford, and *d* 1923, leaving issue:

1a Esme; *b* 1882; *d* unm 12 Jan 1969

2a Doris; *b* 1884; *d* unm 19 Nov 1964

(5) Adolphus Edward Paget; Hon Capt Army, Maj and RTO 1916; *b* 11 Jan 1855; *m* 1st 18 March 1886 Elaine Mabelle (*d* 9 June 1887), dau of Robert Leake, MP, and had a dau (*d* an infant); *m* 2nd 17 June 1889 Katherine Louisa (*d* 13 Oct 1900), 2nd dau of Col Henry Constantine Evelyn Ward, CIE, and by her had, with other issue:

1a Evelyn Paget; Capt RFA, Maj RFC; *b* 4 June 1890; *k* in an air fight 6 March 1917

2a Alweyn Montague; AIF WW I; *b* 28 March 1892; *m* 23 Jan 1923 Kathleen Eleanor Cowley Priest (*d* 1974) and *d* 30 Aug 1950, leaving issue:

1b EVELYN PAGET GRAVES, **9th and present Lord Graves, Baron of Gravesend**

1b *Diana Wellesley [Mrs Guy Peltzer, Ravensworth, 812 Pateena Rd, Longford, 7301 Tasmania, Australia]; *b* 28 May 1934; *m* 1st 21 April 1956 (*divorce* 1974) Edgar Mark Wolfhagen, s of Ferdinand Charles Wolfhagen; *m* 2nd 1974 *Guy Paul Emile Peltzer and by her 1st husb has issue:

1c *Julian Mark; *b* 18 March 1957

2c *Martin Charles; *b* 7 Feb 1959; *m* 21 Jan 1984 (*divorce* 1993) Anita M Francoeur and has:

1d *Henry; *b* 29 June 1986

3c *Philip Garret Wellesley; *b* 10 March 1963; *m* 10 April 1993 *Catherine Sarah Waining and has:

1d *Hannah Frances Naomi; *b* 1 Oct 1991

4c *Quentin Evelyn; *b* 9 April 1969

2a *Irene; *b* 20 Dec 1897; *m* 29 March 1921 Brig Frederick Ivor de la Poer Garforth, RE, yr s of Frederick Garforth, and has issue. He *d* 8 June 1962

(5) (cont.) Adolphus Graves *m* 3rd 21 Sept 1909 Hilda May (*d* 24 April 1966), only dau of David Cruickshank, and *d* 5 Aug 1931, having by her had:

3a Vernon North, DSC; Lt-Cdr RN WW II; *b* 11 July 1911; *m* 22 March 1947 *Elizabeth Constance [Mrs Vernon Graves, 90 Stockton Lane, York YO3 0BS], dau of Capt Robert Francis Uniacke Penrose FitzGerald, RN, and *d* following a climbing accident 4 Oct 1960, leaving:

1b *Janice Penrose Iona [Mrs Christopher Rose, 18 Market Place, Kirkbymoorside, York YO6 6DA]; *b* 29 Dec 1947; *m* 1st 19 Oct 1968 (*divorce* 1974) Stephen Van Simons, s of Dennis Daniel Simons, and has issue:

1c *Isobel Jane; *b* 5 July 1972

1b (cont.) Mrs Janice Simons *m* 2nd 1980 *Christopher Bernard Rose and by him has:

1c *Thomas George; *b* 1981

2b *Sarah Frances Paget [Mrs Sarah Tamvakis, 90 Stockon Lane, York YO3 0BS]; *b* 30 Oct 1950; *m* 1979 (*divorce* 19–) Iannis Tamvakis and has:

1c *Ewan Ferenc GRAVES-TAMVAKIS; *b* 1975

1c *Charlotte Elizabeth GRAVES-TAMVAKIS; *b* 1975

(6) Augustus Edgar; *b* 11 Oct 1856; *m* 18 Sept 1889 Josephine (*d* 23 April 1924), 4th dau of Joseph Robinson, and *d* 1896, leaving issue:

1a Austin Joseph Geoffrey; Lt 1st Canadian Mounted Rifles; *b* 1893; *ka* March 1916

1a Millicent Olive; *m* 21 Oct 1912 Cdr Walter Randolph Bernard RN, s of Gerard Hawker Bernard, of Batheaston, Somerset, and *d* 5 Aug 1978, leaving issue. He *d* 18 July 1950

(7) Adrian Edward George; Capt 3rd Bn DCLI; *b* 4 May 1860; *d* 23 May 1930

(1) Henrietta Jane Caroline Florence; *m* 1881 Adolph Berto Marchi (*d* 1914)

(2) Georgina Louisa Alice; *m* 28 Aug 1868 Edward Corbett Parker and *d* 23 Nov 1905, leaving issue

(3) Mabel Mary Blanche; *m* 22 Jan 1889 Robert Bryce Hay, 93rd Highrs, and *d* 13 May 1926

3 Adolphus Edward Paget; Page Honour to WILLIAM IV 1830, Capt Coldstream Gds and 59th Regt; *b* 25 Jan 1821; *m* 27 April 1858 Caroline Glubb (*d* 14 Dec 1917), 2nd dau of Capt Samuel Wriford, RN, and *d* 1 Sept 1891, leaving:

(1) Cyril Edward Cuthbert Hare; *b* 18 June 1860; *m* 1 June 1916 Constance Katherine (*d* 12 Feb 1951), dau of François Chrysostom Mouflet, of Leamington, and *d* 16 Feb 1946, having had, with other issue:

1a *Mary Caroline Margot; *b* 4 July 1919; *m* 14 May 1942 (*divorce* 1964) Albert Arthur Puddick (*d* 1994), only s of Albert Arthur Puddick, and has:

1b *Robert Arthur Graves; *b* 1944; *educ* Cranley; *m* 1st 1967 (*divorce* 1990) Jane Margaret Ferrand and has issue:

1c *Simon Nicholas Graves; *b* 1969

2c *Julian Urling Graves; *b* 1970

1b (cont.) Robert Puddick *m* 2nd 1991 *Melanie Anne, dau of Richard Alastair Stuart-Hunt, and has issue:

3c *Charles Oscar Graves; *b* 1993

2b *David Stewart Graves; *b* 1946; *educ* Cranley; *m* 1972 *Sarah Elizabeth, dau of Antony Lamb, and has issue:

1c *Michael Antony Graves; *b* 1974

1c *Annabell Sarah; *b* 1977

3b *Christopher Nicholas Graves; *b* 1952; *educ* Cranley; *m* 1992 *Selena Ann, dau of John Thomas Hobbs

(1) Florence Mary Augusta; *m* 1st 22 Sept 1892, as his 2nd w, Edward Augustus Stewart Hobhouse (*see* HOBHOUSE, Bt); *m* 2nd 11 Aug 1909 Maj Sir Philip Arthur Sambrooke Crawley, JP, 3rd Bn The Buffs, and *d* 6 May 1936. He *d* 30 May 1933

1 Jane Anne; *m* 15 Dec 1829 Capt J W Cuthbert, of Dumbarton Manor, Isle of Thanet, and *d* 14 Sept 1881. He *d* 6 June 1874

2 Caroline North; *m* 18 Jan 1844 Maj-Gen Hugh Percy Davison, of Swarland Park, and *d* 27 Oct 1861. He *d* 5 July 1849

3 Louisa Elizabeth; *m* 28 Aug 1827 Charles Heneage, Life Gds, s of Thomas Fleschi Heneage by Hon Arabella Pelham (*see* YARBOROUGH, E), and *d* 30 June 1868, leaving issue

4 Augusta Champagne; *m* 15 March 1831 Rev Hon William Towry Law, 5th s of 1st Baron Ellenborough (*qv*), and *d* 16 Oct 1844, leaving issue

5 Hester Charlotte; *m* 4 Jan 1832 Edward Isaac Hobhouse and *d* 30 Jan 1880, leaving issue (*see* HOBHOUSE, Bt)

6 Isabella Letitia; *m* 9 June 1853 Stephen Roland Woulfe, of Tiermaclane, Co Clare, only s of Stephen Woulfe, Ld Ch Baron, and *dsp* 26 Oct 1870

GRAY

Arms: Gules a lion rampant within a bordure engrailed argent, over all a label of two points or, each point charged gyronny of eight or and sable. **Crest:** An anchor in pale or. **Supporters:** Two lions guardant gules, charged with a label as in the arms. **Motto:** Anchor fast anchor. **Creation:** L. (S) by 5 July 1445.

THE 22ND LORD GRAY (Angus Diarmid Ian Campbell-Gray) [The Rt Hon The Lord Gray, Airds Bay House, Taynuilt, Argyll PA35 1JR]; *b* 3 July 1931; *s* grandmother 1946; *educ* Eton; *m* 1st 5 Sept 1959 Patricia Margaret (*d* 1987), only dau of Capt Philip Sylvester Alexander (*see* CALEDON, E), and has had:

1 +ANDREW GODFREY DIARMID STUART, *Master of Gray*; *b* 3 Sept 1964; *educ* Trin Coll Glenalmond; *m* 1993 *Hon Lucy Elton, dau of 2nd Baron Elton (*qv*), and has:

(1) +Alexander Godfrey Edward Diarmid; *b* 7 Oct 1996

1 +Lucinda Margaret; *b* 13 May 1961

2 +Iona Doreen; *b* 4 Sept 1962

3 +(Cethlyn) Isobell; *b* 14 June 1969

The 22nd LORD GRAY *m* 2nd 1994 *Cecilia (Cilla), widow of Paul Williams

Lineage: Sir ANDREW GRAY; granted by the Crown 1314 lands of Broxmouth, Roxburghshire, later forfeited, also Longforgund, Perthshire, and a third of Craigie and Warriston, Forfarshire; presumably f of:

Sir JOHN GRAY of Broxmouth; had charters 1355 of the lands of Cragie, Kincardineshire; *d c* 1403, leaving:

Sir PATRICK GRAY of Broxmouth; had charter 1373 of the lands of Longforgund; his est s:

Sir ANDREW GRAY of Broxmouth; *m* 1st Janet, dau and heir of Sir Roger Mortimer, who brought him the lands of Foulis, Perthshire; *m* 2nd Elizabeth, dau of Sir Walter Buchanan of that Ilk, and *d* 1441, leaving by his 1st w:

ANDREW GRAY, **1st Lord Gray** (S), so *cr* by 5 July 1445; *b c* 1390; hostage with English for JAMES I 1424, Commr to England 1449 and 1451; Master Household 1452; Warden Marches 1459; *m* (contract 31 Aug 1418) Elizabeth, dau of Sir John Wemyss of Wemyss (*see* WEMYSS and MARCH, E), and *d c* 1469, having had, with other issue, including at least one dau (Margaret, *m* 1st William Murray of Tullibardine (*see* ATHOLL, D), *m* 2nd George Clephane of Carslogie):

PATRICK GRAY, *Master of Gray*; *m* 1st by 7 Feb 1439/40 Margaret (*dsp*), dau of Sir Malcolm Fleming of Biggar and Cumbernauld by Elizabeth, dau of Robert Stewart, Duke of Albany (*see* MORAY, E); *m* 2nd by 1445 Annabel, dau of 1st Lord Forbes (*qv*), and *dvp* between 23 Aug 1463 and Sept 1464, leaving (by one of his ws he was f of Janet, *m* 1st Sir Alexander Blair of Balthhayoch, *m* 2nd, as his 2nd w, 2nd Lord (Fraser of) Lovat (*qv*), *m* 3rd 9th Earl of Crawford; *see* CRAWFORD and BALCARRES, E):

1 ANDREW GRAY, **2nd Lord Gray**, PC; took part in the rebellion of JAMES IV against his f JAMES III, accordingly made Heritable Sheriff of Forfar 1488 and Justiciary Gen N of Forth 1489 and S of Forth 1506; *m* 1st Janet, dau and heir of Sir Robert Keith, bro of 1st Earl Marischal (*see* KINTORE, E), and had a s and two daus (one of whom, Elizabeth *m* 1st *c* 18 May 1487 4th Lord Glamis (*see* STRATHMORE and KINGHORNE, E), *m* 2nd just after 27 July 1511 3rd Earl of Huntly (*see* HUNTLY, M), *m* 3rd by 5 June 1525 4th Earl of Rothes (*qv*); *m* 2nd by 1483 Elizabeth, dau of John Stewart, Earl of Atholl (*see* MORAY, E), and had further issue; *m* 3rd after 1497 Margaret Houston, widow of 2nd Lord Lyle (his nephew by his sister); *m* 4th Elizabeth, widow of 2nd Earl of Huntly (*see* HUNTLY, M) and dau of 1st Earl of Erroll (*qv*), and *d* Feb 1513/4; his s by his 1st w:

(1) PATRICK GRAY, **3rd Lord Gray**; *m* between Feb 1491/2 and Feb 1492/3 Janet, dau of 2nd Earl of Huntly (*see* HUNTLY, M) and widow of Alexander Lindsay, Master of Crawford (*see* CRAWFORD and BALCARRES, E), whom she was suspected of having suffocated, and *dspl* April 1541

2 Gilbert, of Buttergask; *m* Gille, dau of Sir Laurence Mercer of Aldie, and *d* by 1541, leaving:

(1) PATRICK GRAY, **4th Lord Gray**; captured by English after their victory over the Scots of Solway Moss 24 Nov 1542 but soon ransomed for £500; vacillated between pro-English faction and that of MARY QUEEN OF SCOTS; *m* (contract 21 Sept 1537) Marion, dau of 4th Lord Ogilvy of Airlie (*see* AIRLIE, E), and *d* 1584, having had, with other issue:

1a PATRICK GRAY, **5th Lord Gray**; *b* 1538; *m* (contract 4 Jan 1556/7) Barbara, dau of 2nd Lord Ruthven (*see* CARLISLE, E), and *d* by 10 March 1607/8, leaving with at least one dau (Merion, *m* 1st Patrick, Master of Ruthven (*see* CARLISLE, E), and 2nd *c* 1561, as his 1st w, Patrick Oglivy of Inchmartine; *see* SEAFIELD, E), an est s:

1b PATRICK GRAY, **6th Lord Gray**, PC (S 1585); first supported MARY QUEEN OF SCOTS then her s JAMES VI (to whom he was Gentleman of the Bedchamber and Master of the Wardrobe 1584), thereby earning a reputation for treachery, especially as he was thought to have connived at the QUEEN's execution when Amb to England; following the latter episode he was banished from the Scottish court 1587 but returned to it and the King's favour 1589; *m* 1st (contract 18 May 1575) (*divorce* 21 May 1585) Elizabeth, dau of 8th Lord Glamis (*see* STRATHMORE AND KINGHORNE, E); *m* 2nd July 1585 Mary, dau of Robert Stewart, Earl of Orkney (*see* MORAY, E), and *d* 4 Sept 1611, leaving by her, with other issue (including Agnes; *m* 7th Earl of Menteith (*see* MONTROSE, D) and Jean, *m* 1st Earl of Wemyss; *qv*):

1c ANDREW GRAY, **7th Lord Gray**; Lt Scots Gendarmes in France 1624–54, made over the Heritable Sheriffship of Forfarshire to the Crown for 50,000 marks, which were never paid; royalist Civil War, hence fined under CROMWELL's Act of Grace 1654; also as an RC excommunicated by the Scottish Gen Assembly 1649; since by 1638 his only s was dead he obtained a regrant of his honours 8 Jan 1637/8 (though with the old precedence) to himself, then to his son-in-law and distant cousin William (*see* below), whom failing to the sons of William and Anne, the latter's w, whom failing to William's father Sir William Gray of Pittendrum and the latter's heirs male whatsoever; *m* 1st 1603, as her 2nd husb, Margaret, dau of 1st Lord Ogilvy of Deskford (*see* SEAFIELD, E) and widow of 5th Earl of Buchan (*qv*), and had issue; *m* 2nd Feb 1627/8 Mary, widow of (a) Sir John Sydenham, of Brympton, Somerset, and (b) John Baker, of Sissingham (possibly Sissinghurst) and Cranbrook, Kent, and dau of Sir John Guldeford, of Hemsted, Kent; *m* 3rd by 1639 Catherine Cadell (by whom he had a dau Frances, *m* a son of Murdoch Mackenzie, Bp of Moray and of Orkney) and *dspms* 1663, having by his 1st w had:

1d Patrick, *Master of Gray*; *d* unm 1635, *k* while besieging a town in France

1d ANNE Gray, *Mistress of Gray*; *m* William GRAY, *Master of Gray* under the regrant of Jan 1637/8 (accidentally *k* 1660 while fencing with Earl of Southesk (*see* FIFE, D)) and had, with two other sons:

1e PATRICK GRAY, **8th Lord Gray**; he too obtained a regrant of his honours since he had no surv sons, the new remainder of 27 Feb 1706/7 being direct to John Gray of Crichie (his s-in-law), with the old precedence but to the apparent exclusion of himself, the **8th Lord**, with further remainder to the heirs of the bodies of the said John and his wife, females to inherit by primogeniture, with further remainder to heirs male of the **8th Lord**; *m* 1664 Barbara, dau of 1st Lord Balvaird (*see* MANSFIELD and MANSFIELD, E), and *dspms* Jan 1711, having had, with another dau:

1f Patrick, *Master of Gray*; *b* 9 Feb 1670/1, and *d* by 30 July 1674

1f Marjorie Gray, *Mistress of Gray*; *m c* 26 Feb 1682/3 John GRAY of Crichie (*s* as **9th Lord**), 2nd s of John Gray of Crichie (yr bro of f of **8th Lord**) and gs of Sir William Gray, of Pittendrum, and *dvp* between Dec 1690 and 1707

2a James; *m* Elizabeth, dau of Sir John Beaton of Creich and widow of 4th Lord Innermeath (*see* MORAY, E)

1a Janet; *m* 1st William Ogilvy of Inchmartine (*see* SEAFIELD, E); *m* 2nd by 7 June 1566 James Sandilands of Crarie (*see* TORPILCHEN, L)

2a Agnes; *m* 1st Robert Logan of Restalrig; *m* 2nd 5th Lord Home (*see* HOME, E); *m* 3rd, as his 1st w, Sir Thomas Lyon of Auldbar (*see* STRATHMORE AND KINGHORNE, E)

The 8th LORD's s-in-law and cousin,

JOHN GRAY, **9th Lord Gray**; *s* to the peerage 1707 under the new patent and therefore in his f-in-law the **8th Lord**'s lifetime; *d* 10 Jan 1723/4; his est s:

JOHN GRAY, **10th Lord Gray**; *bapt* 15 Jan 1682/3; *m c* 1715 Helen, dau of 5th Lord Blantyre (*see* 1900 edn), and *d* 15 Dec 1738, leaving:

JOHN GRAY, **11th Lord Gray**; *b* 11 April 1716; *m* 17 Oct 1741 Margaret (*d* 23 Jan 1790), dau and heir of Alexander Blair of Kinfauns, Perthshire, and *d* 28 Aug 1782, having had, with other issue, including two er sons:

1 CHARLES GRAY, **12th Lord Gray**; *b* 1752; *d* unm 18 Dec 1786

2 WILLIAM JOHN GRAY, **13th Lord Gray**; *b* March 1754; *d* unm 12 Dec 1807

3 FRANCIS GRAY, **14th Lord Gray**; *b* 1 Sept 1765; Maj Breadalbane Fencibles 1793, PMG Scotland 1807–10, rep S peer 1812–41; *m* 17 Feb 1794 Mary Anne (*d* 31 Dec 1858), dau of Lt-Col James Johnstone, 61st Foot, and *d* 20 Aug 1842, leaving issue:

(1) JOHN GRAY, **15th Lord Gray**; *b* 12 May 1798; rep S Peer 1847–67; *m* 23 May 1833 Mary Anne (*d* 16 Feb 1882), dau of Col Charles Philip Ainslie, 14th Light Dragoons, 2nd s of Sir Philip Ainslie, of Pilton, and *dsp* Paris 31 Jan 1867

(1) MADELINA GRAY, **Lady Gray** (16th holder of the title) in her own right; *b* 11 Nov 1799; *d* unm 20 Feb 1869

(2) Margaret Gray; *m* 1820, as his 1st w, John GRANT of Kilgraston and *d* 24 April 1822, leaving an only child:

1a MARGARET Grant, **Lady Gray** (17th holder of the title) in her own right; *b* 14 April 1821; *m* 10 Nov 1840 Hon David Henry MURRAY (*d* 5 Sept 1862), s of 3rd Earl of Mansfield (*see* MANSFIELD and MANSFIELD, E), and *dsp* 27 May 1878

(3) Jane Anne; *m* 1834 (*divorce* 1843) Col C P Ainslie and *d* 4 March 1873

1 JANE Gray; *m* 28 June 1763 Francis STUART, 9th EARL OF MORAY (*qv*) and *d* 19 Feb 1786, leaving, with other issue:

(1) FRANCIS STUART, 10th EARL OF MORAY; *b* 2 Feb 1771; *m* 1st 26 Feb 1795 Lucy (*d* 3 Aug 1798), dau of Gen John Scott, and had issue:

1a FRANCIS STUART, 11th EARL OF MORAY; *d* unm 6 May 1859

2a JOHN STUART, 12th EARL OF MORAY; *d* unm 8 Nov 1867

(1) (cont.) The 10th EARL OF MORAY *m* 2nd 7 Jan 1801 Margaret Jane (*d* 3 April 1837), dau of Sir Philip Ainslie, and *d* 12 Jan 1848, having by her had,with other issue:

3a ARCHIBALD GEORGE STUART, 13th EARL OF MORAY; *d* unm 12 Feb 1872

4a GEORGE PHILIP STUART, **18th Lord Gray**, as which *s* cousin 1878, and 14th EARL OF MORAY; *b* 14 Aug 1816; *d* unm 16 March 1895

1a JANE Stuart; *m* 1st 25 Jan 1832 Sir John Archibald Drummond Stewart, 6th Bt (*dsp* 20 May 1838); *m* 2nd 25 Aug 1838 Jeremiah Lonsdale POUNDEN, MD (*d* 3 March 1887), of Brownswood, Co Wexford, and *d* 14 March 1880, leaving an only child:

1b EVELEEN Pounden, **Lady Gray** (19th holder of the title) in her own right, as which *s* her unc 1895; *b* 3 May 1841; *m* 9 May 1863 James Maclaren SMITH later SMITH-GRAY (roy licence 7 May 1897 for himself, the name GRAY only for his issue), of the Boltons, S Kensington (*d* 26 Feb 1900), and *d* 24 Dec 1918, leaving issue:

1c JAMES MACLAREN STUART GRAY, **20th Lord Gray**; *b* 4 June 1864; *educ* Pembroke Coll Cambridge (MA); Capt 5th Bn Rifle Bde; *d* unm 2 May 1919

2c Lonsdale Richard Douglas; *b* 3 March 1870; Capt 6th Dragoon Gds; *das* unm S Africa 10 June 1900

1c ETHEL EVELEEN, **Lady Gray** (21st holder of the title)

2c Thora Zelma Grace; *b* 22 Oct 1875; *m* 18 April 1911 Edward Lorne Frederick (Eric) Clough Taylor (*d* 14 May 1947), s of Lt-Col Edward Harrison Clough Taylor, of Firby Hall, Yorks, and *d* 13 April 1966, leaving:

1d +Cara Prunella [Miss Cara Clough Taylor, 19 Sherbrooke Rd, London SW6 7HX]; *b* 1919

3c Kathleen Eileen Moray; *b* 9 Aug 1878

The 20th LORD's sis,

ETHEL EVELEEN GRAY-CAMPBELL, **Lady Gray** (21st holder of the title) in her own right; *b* 16 Jan 1866; *m* 23 July 1888 Henry Tufnell CAMPBELL later GRAY-CAMPBELL (roy licence 24 April 1920, with CAMPBELL-GRAY and arms of GRAY only for their issue; he *d* 31 Jan 1945), s of John Thomas Campbell by Lady Anne Katharine, dau of 9th Earl of Lindsay (*qv*), and *d* 2 Oct 1946, having had issue:

1 Lindsay Stuart, *Master of Gray*, MC; *b* 4 May 1894; Maj Res of Offrs RFA, WW I (thrice wounded, despatches, 1914–15 star, two medals) and WW II; *m* 8 July 1930 Doreen McClymont (*d* 11 May 1948), er dau of Cyril Tubbs, of Thedden Grange, Alton, Hants, and *d* 7 Sept 1945, leaving issue:

(1) ANGUS DIARMID IAN CAMPBELL-GRAY, **22nd and present Lord Gray**

(2) Cailain Douglas; *b* 14 July 1934; *educ* Eton; granted with sisters rank of Ld of Parl's dau/yr s Nov 1950; *m* 27 April 1963 *Wendy Helen Katharine [The Hon Mrs Cailain Campbell-Gray, Fanamor, Taynuilt, Argyll PA35 1HR], yr dau of William Herbert Dunlop, of Doonside, Ayr, and *d* 4 Sept 1994, leaving:

1a +James Douglas; *b* 18 April 1966

1a +Charlotte Anne; *b* 1 Oct 1968; *m* 9 Dec 1995 *Charles White, s of Harvey White, of London

(1) Fiona Faith; *b* 12 Jan 1933; *m* 11 June 1955 Maj (Ronald Hugh) Desmond Fabling, Roy Dragoons (*d* 1974), twin s of Hugh Fabling, of Moat House, Grandborough, nr Rugby, and *d* 1991, leaving issue:

1a +Victoria Theresa Fabling; *b* 2 April 1958; *m* 1993 *Nicholas A Shugar, er s of Alan Shugar, of Bristol

2a +Fenella Mary Fabling; *b* 1 July 1963

(2) Christine Anne; *b* 17 Oct 1938; *m* 6 Oct 1960 *Lt-Col Brian Joseph Lockhart, Roy Dragoons, yr s of Maj William Arthur Joseph Lockhart, of Ballydowling, Glenealy, Co Wicklow, and *d* 1987, leaving issue:

1a +Crispin Alexander; *b* 1967; Maj Blues and Royals; *m* 22 Nov 1997 *Lucy, dau of Richard Lloyd, of Stutton, Suffolk

(2) The Hon Mrs Lockhart and Capt Lockhart also adopted:

*Edward Angus; *b* 19 Jan 1966

*Serena Emily; *b* 19 Jan 1965; *m* 14 July 1989 *Patrick James, Lord Gillford, only s of 7th Earl of Clanwilliam (*qv*), and has issue

2 Henry Bethune; *b* 1896; 2nd Lt Argyll and Sutherland Highrs; *ka* Ypres 23 Feb 1915

3 Ian Douglas; *b* 14 July 1901; Lt-Col RE WW II; *m* 7 July 1942 Diana, 4th dau of Lord Richard Cavendish (*see* DEVONSHIRE, D) and formerly w of Robert John Graham Boothby, MP (later Baron Boothby, KBE (LP; *d* 1986); *see* 1970 edn), and *dsp* 21 March 1946

1 Violet Eveleen Moray; *b* 28 May 1891; *d* unm 18 April 1942

GRAY, Bt

Arms: Barry of six arg. and az. a lion rampant gu., on a chief of the second two lymphads or. **Crest:** An anchor or in front of and supported by two lion's gambs erased gu. **Motto:** Anchor fast anchor. **Creation:** Bt. (UK) 7 July 1917.

SIR WILLIAM HUME GRAY 3RD BT, of Tunstall Manor, W Hartlepool, Co Durham [Sir William Gray Bt, Eggleston Hall, Barnard Castle, Co Durham DL12 OAG]; *b* 26 July 1955; *s* gf 1978; *educ* Aysgarth Sch Bedale, Eton and Centl London Poly (BA, DipArch); RIBA, dir Eggleston Estate Co; *m* 27 July 1984 *Catherine Victoria Willoughby, yst dau of John Naylor, of Bramley, Hants, and Mrs Richard Jerram, of Cornwall, and has:

1 +WILLIAM JOHN CRESSWELL; *b* 24 August 1986

1 *Octavia; *b* 1987

2 *Clementine; *b* 1990

Lineage: MATTHEW GRAY, of Blyth, Northumberland ship owner; *m* Ann Jane, dau of William Bryham, and had:

Sir WILLIAM GRAY, of Greatham, W Hartlepool, Co Durham, JP, DL; High Sheriff 1892, Mayor Hartlepool 1861 and 1862, 1st Mayor W Hartlepool 1887, fndr William Gray & Co, memb *Lloyd's Register* ctee, fndr S Durham Steel and Iron Co 1889, ktd 1890; *b* 18 Jan 1828; *m* 15 May 1849 Dorothy (*d* 7 Sept 1906), dau of Capt John Rall, RN, of Lewisham, and *d* 12 Sept 1898, leaving an only surv s:

Sir William Cresswell Gray, 1st Bt (UK), so *cr* 7 July 1917, JP, DL Co Durham (High Sheriff 1909), JP Devon and N Yorks; Lt-Col 10th Vol Bn Durham LI, chm William Gray & Co; *b* 1 May 1867; *m* 2 June 1891 Kate (*d* 10 Jan 1953), est dau of Charles Townshend Casebourne, CE, of Greatham House, Co Durham, and had:

1 WILLIAM (Sir), **2nd Bt**

1 Dorothy Cresswell; *m* 4 April 1918 Lt-Col Robert Napier Steuart Gordon, Sherwood Foresters, 4th s of Gen William Gordon, CIE, and *d* 25 Oct 1943, having had issue. He *d* 17 Nov 1951

2 Edith; *m* 17 Sept 1919 Stephen Godlee, est s of Arthur Godlee, and had issue. He *d* March 1940

3 Kate Irene; *m* 18 June 1925 Arthur Cyril Waddy, OBE, only s of Henry Turner Waddy, and *dsp* 26 April 1968. He *d* 21 Jan 1964

4 Margarita; *m* 22 June 1921 Sir William Guy Ropner (*see* ROPNER, Bt) and *d* 1973, leaving issue. He *d* 2 May 1971

Sir WILLIAM *d* 1 Nov 1924; his only son,

Sir William Gray, 2nd Bt, DL (Co Durham 1932); High Sheriff 1938; *b* 18 Aug 1895; *educ* Loretto; dir Eggleston Estate Co and Hartlepool Water Co, local dir Liverpool & London and Globe Insur Newcastle, Capt 3rd Bn Yorks Regt WW I (despatches, wounded, POW); *m* 1st 8 April 1929 Josephine (*d* 19 March 1943), dau of W H Eveleigh; *m* 2nd 22 March 1947 *Beryl [Beryl Lady Gray, Bryanhaven, Eype, Dorset], formerly w of Norman Scotson Henshaw and yr dau of Alfred Stott, of Crowborough, and *d* 1978, having by his 1st w had issue:

1 Willam Talbot; 9th Lancers 1950–51, dir Eggleston Estate Co, Talbot Gray and Hartlepool Water Co; *b* 4 July 1931; *educ* Eton; *m* 22 April 1954 *Rosemarie Hume [Mrs William Gray, The Cottage, Eggleston Hall, Eggleston, Co Durham DL12)AG], dau of A/Cdre Charles Hume Elliott-Smith, AFC, and *d* in a car crash 9 July 1971, leaving:

(1) Sir WILLIAM HUME GRAY, **3rd and present Bt**

(1) *Victoria Eyre [Mrs Nicholas Straker, Sough Hill, Caldwell, Darlington, Co Durham]; *b* 15 July 1958; *m* 1980 *Nicholas David Barclay Straker, 2nd s of Hugh Charles Straker, of Gaucin, Spain, and has issue:

1a *Sam; *b* 1991

1a *Jacquetta; *b* 1984

2a *Chloë; *b* 1986

(2)*Emma Mary; *b* 9 Oct 1962

2 +Nicholas Anthony; *b* 21 June 1934; *educ* Stowe; *m* 29 June 1956 *Amanda, only dau of Harold William Edwards, of Ashmore Green, Newbury, Berks, and has issue:

(1) *Daisy; *b* 1970

Gray of Contin

Creation: B. (UK, LP) 1983.

THE BARON GRAY OF CONTIN, of Contin in the District of Ross and Cromarty ((Hamish) James Hector Northey Gray, PC (1982)) [The Rt Hon The Lord Gray of Contin PC, Achneim House, Flichity, Inverness-shire IV1 2XE]; *b* 28 June 1927; *educ* Roy Acad Inverness; Queen's Own Cameron Highlanders 1945–48; co dir 1950–70; memb Inverness Town Cncl 1965–70; MP (C) Ross and Cromarty 1970–83, Assist Govt Whip 1971–73, Lord Commr Treasury 1973–74, Oppn Whip 1974–75, Oppn Spokesman Energy 1975–79, Min State: Energy 1979–83 and Scottish Off 1983–86; Ld Lt Inverness-shire 1996– (DL Inverness, Nairn and Lochaber 1989, V-Ld Lt Lochaber, Inverness, Badenoch and Strathspey 1994); *m* 1953 *Judith Waite, dau of Noel M Brydon, MBE, MICE, and has issue:

1 *James Northey David [The Hon David Gray, Pocklington School, West Green, Pocklington, Yorks YO4 2NO]; *b* 1955; *educ* Fettes and Bristol U; Head Master Pocklington Sch 1992–; *m* 1978 *Lynda Jane Harlow and has issue:

(1) *James Stuart; *b* 1991

(1) *Fiona Sally; *b* 1984

(2) *Julie Harlow; *b* 1984

2 *Peter L; *b* 1959; *educ* Fettes and Bristol U (LLB); barrister; advocate Scottish Bar; *m* 1985 *Bridget Mary Willcox and has issue:

(1) *Tom Lachlan; *b* 1994

(1) *Ishbel Mary; *b* 1989

(2) *Madelene Elisabeth; *b* 1992

1 *Sally Brydon; *b* 1957; *m* 1984 *James S Brown, FRCS, yst s of Stephen W R Brown, of Blantyre, Malawi, and has issue:

(1) *Angus; *b* 1986

(2) *Duncan James; *b* 1987

(3) *Hamish Stephen; *b* 1989

Lineage: JAMES NORTHEY GRAY, of Inverness; *m* E M— and *d* 1979, leaving:

(HAMISH) JAMES HECTOR NORTHEY, *cr* a **Baron**

Grayson

Arms: Sa. on a fess between a portcullis in chief and a lymphad in base or two ravens of the field. **Crest:** In front of a rising sun or a tower ppr., issuant therefrom a demi-lion sa., holding between the paws a spur gold. **Motto:** *Virtus tutissima turris* ('Virtue is the safest tower'). **Creation:** Bt. (UK) 12 Jan 1922.

SIR JEREMY BRIAN VINCENT GRAYSON, 5TH BT, of Ravenspoint, Anglesey [Sir Jeremy Grayson Bt, 54 Bucharest Rd, London SW18 3AR]; *b* 30 Jan 1933; *s* unc 1991; *educ* Downside; photographer; *m* 1958 *Sara Mary, dau of C F Upton, of Monte Carlo, and has had:

1 +SIMON JEREMY; *b* 12 July 1959

2 +Paul Francis; *b* 22 Nov 1965

3 +Mark Christopher; *b* 29 March 1968

1 *Caroline Mary; *b* 8 Feb 1961

2 *Anna Katherine; *b* 10 Oct 1962; *m* 1991 *Christopher William Turner

3 Mary; *b* and *d* 1964

4 *Lucy Kate; *b* 1970

Lineage: HENRY HOLDREGE GRAYSON, JP, of Birkenhead; *m* Elizabeth (*d* 1868), dau of James Mulleneux, of Liverpool, and *d* 11 Feb 1904, leaving issue:

Sir Henry Mulleneux Grayson, 1st Bt (UK), so *cr* 12 Jan 1922, KBE (1920, CBE 1920); *b* 26 June 1865; WW I: GSO 1917, Dir Ship Repairs Admlty 1916–19 (GS and Victory medals), High Sheriff Anglesey 1917–18, MP (C U) Birkenhead 1918–22, MInstNA, Hon Lt-Col RM, memb exec ctee Standing Cncl Btage, KStJ, Commr Anglesey St John Amb Bde 1939–45, life govr Princess Beatrice Hosp, Freeman Liverpool, Cdr Crown Italy, Leopold Belgium, Offr Legn Honour; *m* 1st 16 April 1891 (*divorce* 1927) Dora Beatrice (*d* 31 Dec 1946), dau of Frederick Harrington, and had:

1 **Sir Denys Henry Harrington Grayson, 2nd Bt**; *b* 10 July 1892; *educ* Harrow and Pembroke Coll Cambridge; Lt Irish Gds WW I, chm Grayson, Rollo & Clover Docks, and Liver Securities, assoc memb Standing Cncl Btage; *m* 1st 9 Feb 1916 (*divorce* 1927) Elsie May (*d* 31 May 1973), dau of Richard Davies Jones, of Cardiff, and *d* 22 Feb 1955, leaving:

(1) **Sir Ronald Henry Rudyard Grayson, 3rd Bt**; *b* 15 Nov 1916; *educ* Harrow; RAF WW II; *m* 1st 28 Dec 1936 (*divorce* 1944) Babette Vivienne, dau of Count Vivien Hollander; *m* 2nd 23 Nov 1946 *Dorothy Vera (Vicki) Hoare [Vicki Lady Grayson, 5 Cheero Point Rd, Cheero Point, NSW, Australia], dau of Charles Serrell, and *d* 1987

1 (cont.) **Sir Denys** *m* 2nd 10 Sept 1927 (*divorce* 1937) Sylvia Ironside, yst dau of Richard Keown-Boyd, of Ballydugan, Co Down; *m* 3rd 15 Sept 1951 Jeanette (*d* 8 Dec 1978), dau of John Evan Glen, of Edinburgh

2 **Sir Rupert Stanley Harrington Grayson, 4th Bt**; *b* 22 July 1897; *educ* Harrow; Kt Holy Sepulchre, novelist, Lt Irish Gds WW I (wounded twice), King's Messenger WW II, fndr memb Red Duster Syndicate; *m* 1st 13 Aug 1919 Victoria Florence, dau of Walter Henry Banks; *m* 2nd 12 Nov 1950 *Vari Colette [Vari Lady Grayson, PO Box 626, Indiantown, FL 34956, USA], only dau of Maj Henry O'Shea, Dublin Fus, of Cork, and *d* 1991

3 Brian Harrington; Capt CMP WW II, Humane Soc Silver Medal for life saving; *b* 21 Oct 1900; *educ* Harrow and Pembroke Coll Cambridge; *m* 1st 5 June 1930 (*divorce* 1946) Sofia, 4th dau of George Buchanan, and had issue:

(1) Sir JEREMY BRIAN VINCENT GRAYSON, **5th and present Bt**

(1) *Jane Angela [Miss Jane Grayson, 92 Talbot Rd, London N6 4RA]; *b* 2 April 1931

3 (cont.) Brian Grayson *m* 2nd 5 Aug 1949 Ruth, dau of Oscar Louis Anders, of Littlethorpe Hall, Ripon, and formerly w of Edwin Bernhard Gange, and *d* 1989, leaving by her:

(2) *Alicia Lorraine [Mrs Clive Rogers, 70 Wattleton Rd, Beaconsfield, Bucks HP9 1RY]; *b* 24 Feb 1953; *m* 1973 *Clive Trevor Thorne Rogers and has:

1a *Timothy Piers Thorne; *b* 1981

1a *Sophie Claire Thorne; *b* 1977

4 Tristram Hugh Harrington, OBE (1951); Col Irish Gds WW II, Dep Provost Marshal: London Dist 1947–48 and Br troops Egypt 1950–52, Commandant RMP Depot 1948–50, Provost Marshal Far East Land Forces 1952–54, Ch Constable UKAEA Constabulary 1955; *b* 15 April 1902; *educ* Harrow and Clare Coll Camb; *m* 5 Nov 1928 Barbara (*d* 1974), yst dau of Morgan Ignatius Finucane, JP, MRCS, and *d* 1984, leaving issue:

(1) +Patrick Tristram Finucane [Maj Patrick Grayson, 38 Beaufort St, London SW3 5AG]; *b* 7 July 1942; *educ* Downside and RMA Sandhurst; Maj Irish Gds, dir Defence Systems, dep chm Kroll Assocs; *m* 9 Sept 1965 (*divorce* 1989) Vivienne Mary, yr dau of Hector Rowcliffe Munro, of Alicante, and has:

1a +Mark Patrick Munro; *b* 20 Feb 1974

1a *Louise Mary Munro; *b* 8 Sept 1968

2a *Nikki Kathryn Munro; *b* 9 Dec 1970

(1) *Mary Dora Finucane [Mrs John Blaksley, The White House, Gosmore, Hitchin, Herts]; *b* 19 May 1931; *m* 1 May 1958 John Owen Blaksley (*d* 1982), only s of John Hoffham Blaksley, MC, TD, and has issue:

1a *John Patrick; *b* 21 April 1959

2a *Richard Edmund; *b* 6 July 1961; *m* 1990 *Sally-Anne, dau of Dr John Deller, and has:

1b *Thomas Percival; *b* 1992

1b *Alice Anastasia; *b* 1993

(2) *Angela Mary Finucane [Mrs Michael Drummond-Brady, Keepers Lodge, Great Chart, Ashford, Kent TN26 1JX]; *b* 7 July 1934; *m* 3 Feb 1955 *Maj Michael John Drummond-Brady, Queen's Regt, s of Bernard John Brady, and has:

1a *Simon Michael Grayson; *b* 12 Nov 1955; *m* 1988 *Nicola, dau of Peter Fletcher

2a *Mark Frederick Grayson; *b* 6 Sept 1957; BA; *m* 1984 *Susie, dau of Nicholas Fair, and has issue:

1b *Frederick Mark; *b* 1987

1b *Lucy Elizabeth; *b* 1989

1a *Emma Angela; *b* 24 Aug 1962

5 +Ambrose Desmond Harrington [Ambrose Grayson Esq, La Jachère da la Grange, St Peter Port, Guernsey]; late King's Messenger; *b* 2 Aug 1913; *educ* Downside; *m* 7 Dec 1966 *Lilian, formerly w of Dr Lydiard Wilson and dau of Gerald Westwood Potter

6 +Godfrey Ramsay Harrington; *b* 2 Aug 1913; *m* 18 Feb 1939 *Ida Nannestad, dau of Sextus Hassing, of Denmark, and has issue:

(1) +Simon Antony; *b* 25 April 1952

(1) *Karen Grethe Maria; *b* 28 April 1940; *m* 1960 *Colin Ross and has issue:

1a *Nicholas; *b* 1962

(2) *Lila Marianna; *b* 5 July 1945; *m* 5 March 1966 *Colin Michael Edmund Creswell, er s of Sir Michael Justin Creswell, KCMG

(3) *Lorna Theresa; *b* 15 Sept 1948; *m* 1972 *Vincente Romero Ramirez, of Madrid, and has:

1a *Miguel Romero Grayson; *b* 1984

1 Alisa Margaret Harrington; *m* 20 Dec 1916 Lt-Col Arthur Richard Rawlinson, OBE, s of Thomas Arthur Rawlinson, and has had issue:

(1) Michael Grayson; P/O RAF WW II; *b* 27 March 1918; *ka* 1941

(2) *PETER ANTHONY GRAYSON RAWLINSON, BARON RAWLINSON OF EWELL (LP; *qv*)

2 Nancy Doreen Harrington; *m* 29 Jan 1919 Louis Clapier Norris Drexel, yst s of Antony J Drexel, of Philadelphia, and *d* 4 Aug 1962, leaving issue. He *d* 11 Oct 1962

3 Auriol Dora Harrington; *m* 25 Nov 1927 (*divorce* 1937) Walter Bruce Harvie, s of J W Harvie, and had:

(1) John Bruce; *d* 16 June 1928
(1) *Jill Auriol [Mrs Geoffrey Hamber, The Drove, Longparish, Hants]; *b* 28 Oct 1929; *m* 1st 15 Aug 1952 Cyprian Waller-Bridge (*d* 18 April 1960), s of Horace Waller-Bridge, and has issue; *m* 2nd 19 May 1973, as his 2nd w, *Geoffrey R Hamber
(2) *Susan Dora; *b* 26 June 1933
4 Monica Shiela Harrington; *m* 1st 30 July 1925 (*divorce* 1930) Edward Charles FitzClarence and has issue (*see* MUNSTER, E); *m* 2nd 1949 Robert W Symonds, FRIBA, and *d* 5 Oct 1958. He *d* 5 Sept 1958
5 *Meryl Loraine Harrington
6 Angela Decima Harrington; *m* 1st 18 April 1934 (*divorce* 1946) Vincent Luis Dominguez (*d* 8 Dec 1965) and had:
(1) *Luis Carlos; *b* 5 Aug 1939; *m* 31 Aug 1963 *Nancy Catherine, dau of Edwin Macdougall Rhea, of Bryn Mawr, Pa., and has:
1a *Angela Harrington; *b* 14 Feb 1965
(1) *Elaine Angela; *b* 17 Nov 1935; *m* 1954, as his 2nd w, BARON RAWLINSON OF EWELL (*see* above and separate article) and has issue
6 (cont.) Mrs Angela Dominguez *m* 2nd 1946 *C Mathews Dick

Sir Henry *m* 2nd 20 Dec 1927 Louise Mary, CStJ (*d* 4 June 1954), widow of Capt Ronald Hamilton Earle (*see* EARLE, Bt) and dau of Richard John Delaney, of Warwick, and *d* 27 Oct 1951

GREEN

Arms: Vert gutté d'eau, three stags trippant or and two roses in fess arg. **Crest:** In front of a mount ppr., thereon a stag trippant or gorged with a collar gemel vert, three roses fesswise arg. **Motto:** Waste not. **Creation:** Bt. (UK) 5 March 1886.

SIR SIMON LYCETT GREEN, 5TH BT, of Wakefield, Co York, and Ken Hill, Co Norfolk, TD (1947), JP (Wakefield 1959), DL (W R Yorks 1952) [Sir Simon Green Bt TD JP DL, Cliff Bank, North Rigton, Leeds LS17 0BZ]; *b* 11 July 1912; *s* bro 1996; *educ* Eton and Magdalene Coll Cambridge (BA); QO Yorks Dragoons WW II, Lt-Col Yorks Dragoons Yeo 1947–51, Chm Greens Economiser Group 1956–83; *m* 1st 3 Jan 1935 (*divorce* 1971) Gladys (*d* 1980), est dau of Arthur Ranicar, JP, of Wigan; *m* 2nd 1971 *Mary, dau of George Ramsden, of Wakefield, and by his 1st w has:
1 *Diana Rose Frances [Mrs Ronald Wallace, Mounsey Farm, Dulverton Somerset]; *b* 26 Dec 1935; *m* 15 Jan 1964, as his 4th w, *Capt Ronald Eden Wallace (*see* LINDSAY-HOGG, Bt) and has:
(1) *David Lycett; *b* 25 Aug 1967; *m* 1991 *Emma Lisa, er dau of S R Freegard, of Langbar, N Yorks, and has:
1a *Miranda Ophelia Lycett; *b* 1993

Lineage: JOHN GREEN, of Frisinghall, Bradford, Yorks; *m* 1 Jan 1597/8 Rosamund Craven and *d* July 1643, leaving:

JONAS GREEN, of Frisinghall and Thornton; *b* 1599; had, with other issue:

JOSEPH GREEN, of Westgate Hill, Tong, Yorks; yeoman; *m* 2nd Mary (*d* April 1695), widow of Lawrence Hargreaves, of Tong, and *d* April 1692, having by his 1st w had:

JOSEPH GREEN, of Tong and Mirfield, Yorks; *b* 1657; had:

JOSEPH GREEN, of Horbury and Wakefield; *b* 12 July 1690; *m* 28 April 1720 Mary Earnshaw and *d* June 1759; his 4th s:

WILLIAM GREEN, of Wakefield; *b* 25 Nov 1729; *m* 22 Sept 1751 Grace Batty (*d* 1816) and *d* 5 Aug 1787; his est s:

THOMAS GREEN, of Wakefield; *b* 26 Oct 1753; *m* 1st 11 July 1776 Elizabeth Bargh; *m* 2nd 28 Oct 1793 Lydia Carter (*m* 2nd Christopher Andrews; *d* 16 Oct 1810) and *d* 12 Aug 1805, leaving by her a yst s:

EDWARD GREEN, of Sandal Magna, Yorks; *b* 6 Jan 1799; *m* 19 March 1821 Mary Anne (*d* 23 Aug 1866), dau of John Ironside, of Wakefield, and *d* 30 Dec 1865; his est surv s:

Sir Edward Green, 1st Bt (UK), so *cr* 5 March 1886, JP, DL Yorks, JP Norfolk; MP Wakefield 1874 and 1885–92; *b* 4 March 1831; Capt 1st W Yorks Yeo; *m* 8 Sept 1858 Mary (*d* 7 Nov 1902), dau of William Edward Lycett, of Bowden, and *d* 30 March 1923, leaving, with a yr s (Francis William, FSA, Lt-Col Yorks Dragoons IY, *b* 24 Nov 1861 *educ* Eton and Ch Ch Oxford, *d* unm 20 March 1954):

Sir Edward Lycett Green, 2nd Bt; *b* 25 May 1860; *m* 23 April 1885 Ethel Mary, OBE, DGStJ (*d* 10 April 1934), dau of Arthur Wilson, of Tranby Croft, Hull, Yorks, and had issue:
1 EDWARD ARTHUR LYCETT (Sir), **3rd Bt**
2 David Cecil Lycett; Cdr RN (emergency), chm Senior Economisers Ltd; *b* 4 June 1892; *m* 1st 8 Sept 1923 (*divorce* 1944) Angela (*d* 1992), yst dau of Edward Hubert Courage, of Kirkby Fleetham Hall, Bedale, and had issue:
(1) Richard David Rafe Lycett; *b* 4 Jan 1925; *m* 1st 13 July 1948 (*divorce* 1956) (Marie) Patricia (*d* 27 Jan 1995), widow of Capt Hon Peter Rudyard Aitken (*see* BEAVERBROOK, B) and est dau of Michael Joseph Maguire, of Melbourne, Australia; *m* 2nd 1 March 1958 *Margaret Alison, formerly w of Van Kai-Nielsen and dau of Maj Geoffrey Denis Lock, MBE, MC, and *d* 17 Dec 1969, leaving by his 1st w:
1a Richard David Edward; *b* 19 Dec 1949; *d* 13 May 1950
2a +Edward Patrick Lycett; *b* 14 Oct 1950; *educ* Stowe; *m* 1st 1971 (*divorce* 1975) Corden Sarah, dau of C B Stretton Wilson, of Stratford-on-Avon; *m* 2nd 1977 *Annette Patricia Josephine, dau of Oswald Patrick John Rochfort, of Broad Marston, Warwicks, and by her has:
1b *Charlotte Rose; *b* 1979
2b *Alice Josephine; *b* 1983
1a *Mary Angela; *b* 12 Feb 1949
(2) +Rupert William Lycett; late 2nd Lt RAC, owner Blades, the 1960s tailors; *b* 24 Oct 1938; *m* 25 May 1963 *Candida Rose, author, only dau of Sir John Betjeman (*see* CHETWODE, B), and has:
1a +David Lycett; *b* 20 Sept 1975
2a +John Peregrine Lycett; *b* 23 Oct 1978
1a *Lucy Rose Lycett; *b* 15 Dec 1964; *m* 1988 *Alexander Evelyn Giles Ward (*see* BANGOR, V)
2a *Imogen Rose Lycett; *b* 21 Sept 1966; *m* 1993 *Augustus Jack Christie, 2nd s of Sir George William Langham Christie, DL, of Glyndebourne, E Sussex
3a *Endellion Rose Lycett; *b* 29 Jan 1969
(1) *Catherine Auriol; *b* 23 April 1935; *m* 1st 22 April 1967 Raja Ranbir Singh, of The Manor, Simla, India, s of Raja Sir Maharaj Singh, of New Delhi; *m* 2nd 1981 *Patrick Field Till and by her 1st husb has issue:
1a *Xenia; *b* 9 June 1968
2a *Tamara; *b* 6 May 1970
3a *Alexia; *b* 1972
2 (cont.) Cdr David Lycett Green *m* 2nd 19 May 1948 Margery Dora Helen (*m* 3rd 12 June 1970 Alec Pilkington; *d* 1988), only dau of Lt-Col Henry Rose, CIE, OBE, IMS, and formerly w of Col Thomas Cromwell Williamson, DSO, and *d* 1 May 1960
3 Francis Denis Lycett; Lt Gren Gds WW I; *b* 2 Nov 1893; *d* unm 14 July 1959
1 Nancy Lycett, OBE (1946, MBE 1918); *m* 1st 7 Dec 1907 Capt Adrian Rose, RHG, yst s of Sir Charles Day Rose, 1st Bt, of Hardwick House and Montreal (*qv*); *m* 2nd 5 Jan 1911 4th Baron Vivian (*qv*) and *d* 6 May 1970, leaving issue
2 Phyllis Mary Lycett; *m* 21 April 1910 Brig-Gen George Francis Milner, CMG, DSO, and *d* 7 Sept 1954, leaving issue (*see* MILNER, Bt)

Sir EDWARD *d* 16 Jan 1940; his est s,

Sir Edward Arthur Lycett Green, 3rd Bt, TD, JP Norfolk; Lt-Col and Brevet-Col Yorks Dragoons Yeo, Lt 2nd Life Gds WW I; *b* 1 April 1886; *m* 17 July 1909 (*divorce* 1922) Elizabeth (*d* 3 May 1964), er dau of David Williams, barrister, and *d* 4 March 1941, leaving:
1 **Sir (Edward) Stephen Lycett Green, 4th Bt**, CBE (1964), JP (Norfolk 1946), DL (1961); *b* 18 April 1910; *educ* Eton and Magdalene Coll Cambridge (BA); barrister Lincoln's Inn 1933, Maj RA WW II, Lt-Col Norfolk HG 1952, CC Norfolk 1946–49, chm: Docking RDC 1950–57, King's Lynn Hosp Management Ctee 1948–57, Assoc of Hosp Management Ctees 1956–58, E Anglian Regnl Hosp Bd 1959–74, dep chm Norfolk QS 1948–71, High Sheriff Norfolk 1973–74; *m* 4 May 1935 Constance Mary, CC Norfolk 1958–77 (*d* 28 Feb 1996), est dau of Ven Harry Sydney Radcliffe, Archdeacon Lynn, and *d* 13 May 1996, leaving:
(1) *Livia Lycett [Mrs Robert Buscall, Carbrooke Hall, Thetford, Norfolk IP25 6TG]; *b* 23 Feb 1937; *m* 7 Oct 1961 *Robert Edmond Buscall, JP, DL, High Sheriff Norfolk 1993, only s of Victor Henley Buscall, of Carbrooke Hall, by Gwendolyn Mary Angela, yst dau of Edmond Ronayne Mahony, JP, of Marysborough, Glanmire, Co Cork, and has:
1a *Harry Charles; *b* 18 March 1963; *educ* Ampleforth and Magdalene Coll Cambridge; *m* 20 Oct 1989 *Kathryn Adrianna, yr dau of Edward William Hill, of Farnham Royal, Bucks, and has:
1b *Dominic Edward; *b* 15 Aug 1992
2b *Nicholas Edmond; *b* 7 July 1994
2a *Patrick Edward; *b* 3 Feb 1965; *educ* Ampleforth and Bristol U; *m* 12 Oct 1996 *Sarah, er dau of Adrian Hamilton QC, of Abbotsbury Rd, London
2 Sir SIMON LYCETT GREEN, **5th and present Bt**

GREEN-PRICE

Arms: Sable a chevron invected argent between three escutcheons of the last, each charged with a spear head of the first imbrued proper. **Crest:** In front of a dragon's head erased vert, holding in the mouth a dexter hand couped at the wrist gules, three escallops argent. **Motto:** *Vive hodie* ('Live today'). **Creation:** Bt. (UK) 23 March 1874.

SIR ROBERT JOHN GREEN-PRICE, 5TH BT, of Monaughty, Co Radnor [Sir Robert Green-Price Bt, Gwernaffel, Knighton, Powys LD7 1SE]; *b* 22 Oct 1940; *s* f 1964; *educ* Shrewsbury and RMA Sandhurst; Capt (ret) RCT, ADC to Govr Bermuda 1969–72, instr Concord Sch English Tokyo 1973–76, lecturer English Keio U 1977–97 and Waseda U 1986–97, Assist Prof English Chiba U Commerce 1982–97

Lineage: JOHN PRICE, of Llanrig; *m* 1st Anne, only dau and heiress of John Barnsley, of Knighton, Herefs, and had, with other issue:

1 John, of The Lodge, Leominster; barrister, Clerk in Chancery; *d* unm 1780

2 Henry; *b* 1722; *m* Elizabeth (*d* 1770), dau of Capt Thomas Foley, RN (*see* FOLEY, B), and *d* 1795, having had issue:

(1) Penelope; *m* 1794 Col Richard Lyster, MP (*d* 8 May 1819), of Rowton Castle, Salop, and *d* 1827, having had:

1a Henry; *m* 1824 Lady Charlotte Ashley (*d* 1889 aged 90), dau of 6th Earl of Shaftesbury (*qv*), and *d* 1861

JOHN PRICE *m* 2nd Elizabeth (*d* 1753), sis of Sir Richard Chace, of Hadwall, Herts, and by her had:

3 Chase; MP Leominster 1759–68 and Radnorshire 1769–77; *b* 1731; *m* 1766 Susan, dau of Evelyn Glanvile, MP St Clere, Kent, and *d* 28 June 1777, leaving:

(1) Sarah Bridget Frances; *b* 1767; *m* Bamber Gascoyne, of Liverpool, MP Childwall, W Derbys, and had issue

4 Richard, of Norton Manor, Knighton; *m* Margaret (*d* 1788), only dau and heiress of Dr Charles Humphreys, of Pennant, Montgomeryshire, and *d* 1797, having had, with other issue:

(1) Richard, of Norton Manor; MP Radnor boroughs 1794–1846; *b* 1773; *dsp* 10 April 1861

(1) Margaret; *b* 1771; *m* 13 May 1799 George GREEN (*d* 9 Jan 1819), 4th s of Jonathan Green, DD, of Ashford Hall, Salop, and *d* 3 May 1827, leaving, with three daus:

1a George; *b* 1802, *d* unm

2a RICHARD (Sir), **1st Bt**

3a Charles; *b* 1804; *m* 22 Nov 1838 Maria (*d* Dec 1870), dau of George Stevenson, of Liberty Hall, New York, and *d* 1 March 1856, leaving issue

4a Edward Jonathan (Rev); Vicar Leintwardine; *b* 1 Sept 1812; *m* 8 May 1849 his cousin Mary (*d* 1902), dau of Rev Thomas Green, of Stoke House, Salop, and *d* 1885, having had issue

RICHARD PRICE's gs,

Sir RICHARD GREEN later GREEN-PRICE (roy licence), **1st Bt** (UK), so *cr* 23 March 1874; Radnorshire: JP and DL, High Sheriff 1876, MP 1880–85; *b* 18 Oct 1803; *m* 1st 21 Feb 1837 Frances Milborough (*d* 1842), dau of Dansey Richard Dansey, of Easton Court, Herefs, and had issue:

1 RICHARD DANSEY (Sir), **2nd Bt**

1 Constance Mary; *m* 1 Aug 1863 Thomas Baskerville Mynors (*see* MYNORS, Bt) and *d* 29 May 1889

Sir Richard *m* 2nd 26 July 1844 Laura (*d* 18 March 1903), dau of Richard Henry King, MD, of Mortlake, Surrey, and by her had issue:

2 Herbert Chase (Rev), JP Herefs, MA Oxon, Rector Pembridge; *b* 17 May 1855; *m* 17 Sept 1895 Susan Alice (*d* 26 Aug 1951), dau of William Henry Barneby, of Longworth, Herefs, and *d* 24 Oct 1919, leaving issue:

(1) Francis Chase; Lt-Col IA WWs I and II; *b* 12 Aug 1896; *educ* Rossall; *m* 9 Aug 1934 Joan Atcherley (*d* 1991), 2nd of Guy Dobell, of Crickhowell, and *d* 1 Aug 1975, leaving issue:

1a Guy Chase; *b* 16 Aug 1937; *d* 18 April 1938

2a +John Chase [John Green-Price Esq, Wendover, Croyde Bay, N Devon EX33 1NP]; *b* 27 June 1947; *educ* Belmont Coll; *m* 1986 (*divorce* 1989) Susan Elizabeth, dau of Kenneth Woodyatt

1a *Susan Marion [Miss Susan Green-Price, Breezelands, Moor Lane, Croyde Bay, Braunton, N Devon]; *b* 17 Aug 1939

(2) +Richard Henry [Richard Green-Price Esq, Silvermists, RDI, Te Kuiti, NZ]; *b* 30 April 1905; *educ* Radley; *m* 17 Sept 1931 *Ruby Beatrix, dau of Robert Thomas Rowan, of Shanghai, and has issue:

1a +Anthony Chase; *b* 4 Feb 1933; *m* 1980 *Joyce Betty Schrieber

1a *Susan Anne; *b* 17 April 1943; *m* 1967 *Alfred Ian Ryder

(1) Patience Laura; *b* 16 Sept 1898; *m* 20 April 1927 Maj Robert King Holmes, RASC, only s of Lt-Col R A K Holmes, IMS

3 Francis Richard; *b* 19 Oct 1856; *d* 25 April 1885

4 Alfred Edward (Rev); Vicar Norton, Radnorshire; *b* 11 Feb 1860; *educ* Trin Coll Cambridge (MA); *m* 21 Nov 1893 Mary Louisa (*d* 17 Sept 1922), dau of Very Rev Henry Grey Edwards, Dean Bangor, and *d* 29 June 1940, having had:

(1) Enid Mary; *m* 27 Sept 1921 Capt Frank Oswald Lewis, CBE, RN (*d* 3 Sept 1962), s of Samuel Lewis, and *dsp* 28 Jan 1957

(2) Sylvia Rachel; *m* 9 Dec 1920 Capt Richard Francis John Onslow, MVO, DSC, RN (*see* ONSLOW, Bt), and *d* 15 June 1933, leaving issue

(3) Alice Monica; *b* 1907; *m* 1 April 1969 Richard Vivian Glynne Williams, s of Humphrey Glynne Williams, of Holyhead

5 George William Whitmore, JP; Chm Radnorshire QS; *b* 23 Aug 1862; *m* 11 April 1893 Rachel Georgina (*d* Jan 1946), est dau of Thomas Henry Burroughes, and *dsp* 24 March 1939

2 Fanny Laura, *d* unm 13 April 1942

3 Henrietta Margaret; *m* 7 Dec 1872 Col Arthur Lang Tickell (*d* 1904), 1st Bn Middx Regt, s of Gen Tickell, HEICS, and *d* 21 July 1937, leaving issue

4 Milburga Price; *m* 10 Aug 1871 Richard Ingram Dansey, JP (*d* 1 March 1909), of Butterley, Herefs, and *d* 14 Nov 1939, having had issue

5 Edith Mary; *m* 3 June 1875 Sir Powlett Charles Milbank, 2nd Bt (*qv*), and *d* 1 March 1928, leaving issue

6 Laura; *m* 3 Feb 1881 Harry Hills Meredith (*d* 25 Sept 1905), barrister, s of H Meredith, and *d* 31 Oct 1917, leaving issue

7 Alice Mildred; *m* 1 Sept 1892 Edgar Robert Henry Moorsom, JP, and *d* 6 March 1928, having had issue

Sir RICHARD *d* 11 Aug 1887; his est son,

Sir Richard Dansey Green-Price, 2nd Bt, JP Radnorshire and Herefs; *b* 18 Nov 1838; *m* 30 July 1863 Clara Anne (*d* 12 Oct 1917), only dau of Rev Thomas Powell, JP, Rector Dorstone, Herefs, and *d* 26 May 1909, having had:

1 Richard Clare; Natal Mounted Police; *b* 19 Nov 1864; *dvp* unm 1 Oct 1898

2 Thomas Victor; *b* 30 Oct 1867; *dvp* unm 27 March 1888

3 **Sir Robert Henry Green-Price, 3rd Bt**, JP, DL Radnorshire; High Sheriff 1930, DAQMG Egypt 1917, Shropshire Imp Yeo S Africa 1900–01, Montgomeryshire Yeo WW I (ret 1921 as Maj), MFH Teme Valley 1919–23 (Jt MFH 1932–35); *b* 6 Jan 1872; *educ* Shrewsbury; *m* 24 Nov 1906 Clara Lucile (*d* 19 Dec 1961), er dau of Frederick Gaul Potter, of New York, and *dsp* 2 Oct 1962

4 Geoffrey Cecil; Capt Natal Militia (Carabiniers) and 18th Australian Light Horse, Capt and Adj Roy Def Corps Guernsey 1914–18, Boer War 1899–1902 (wounded, two medals, seven clasps), Zulu Rebellion 1906 (medal and clasps); *b* 19 June 1877; *m* 10 Aug 1913 Alice Bertha Cox and *dsp* 12 Dec 1927

5 John Powell; *b* 19 Nov 1878; *m* 1907 Julia, dau of Manners Norman (*d c* 1959), and *d* 5 Sept 1927, leaving:

(1) JOHN (Sir), **4th Bt**

(2) +(POWELL) NORMAN DANSEY [Norman Green-Price Esq, Hivron, Bleddfa, Knighton, Radnorshire LD7 1NY]; *b* 22 July 1926; heir presumptive; *educ* Shrewsbury; High Sheriff Radnorshire 1969, late Lt Welsh Gds, MFH; *m* 1963 *Ann Stella, dau of Brig Harold George Howson, CBE, MC, TD, and has issue:

1a +Simon Richard; *b* 10 May 1964

1a *Stella Rachel; *b* 1965

6 James Llewellyn; Lt 3rd Bn S Wales Borderers and 4th Bn Worcs Regt WW I (wounded); *b* 28 July 1881; *m* 1919 Ethel Lilian, dau of C S Faram, and *d* 1962, having had:

(1) Josephine Margaret; *b* 19 April 1920; *d* unm 4 Nov 1945

(2) *Olive Maude; *b* 29 July 1922

7 Chase; *b* 1888; *d* 1889

1 Louisa Dansey; *m* 8 April 1890 Capt William Sprott, Salop RD Corps, and had issue

2 Ethel Mary; *m* 20 Aug 1889 Maj Ernest Thomas Lloyd (*d* 7 Jan 1935), barrister, formerly BCS, and *d* 12 July 1961, leaving issue (*see* LLOYD, Bt)

3 Constance Lilian; *m* 14 April 1896 John Thornton (*d* 18 Jan 1906), of Thwaite Hall, Norfolk, and *d* 22 Sept 1900, leaving issue

4 Gladys; *m* 28 July 1904 William Frederick Strick Humphreys (*d* 14 May 1947), yst s of Charles Humphreys, of Garthmyl Hall, Montgomeryshire, and *d* 14 Aug 1960, leaving issue

5 Dorothy Clara; *m* 24 June 1908 Maj John Lintorn Shore DSO, OBE, JP, Cheshire Regt (*d* 22 Dec 1947), and *d* 5 March 1963, leaving issue

6 Nesta Faith, JP Mon; *b* 1 Nov 1884; *m* 26 Sept 1912 William Humphrey Williams BA, MRCS, LRCP (*d* 2 March 1948), of St James's House, Monmouth, and *d* 8 Feb 1961, leaving issue

The 3rd Bt's nephew,

Sir John Green-Price, 4th Bt; Capt RA WW II; *b* 26 Aug 1908; *educ* Cheltenham and Gonville and Caius Coll Cambridge; *m* 1st 19 Jan 1938 Irene Marian (*d* 27 Sept 1955), est dau of Maj Sir Ernest Guy Richard Lloyd, 1st Bt (*qv*), and had:

1 Sir ROBERT JOHN GREEN-PRICE, **5th and present Bt**

1 *Roseanne [Mrs Michael Hender, Dukes, Bradninch, Devon EX5 4QN]; *b* 30 July 1943; *m* 1st 23 March 1963 Capt Richard Higginson Lowe, 1st/6th Queen's Gurkha Rifles, est s of Lt-Col Reginald Higginson Lowe, IA, and has issue:

(1) *Timothy; *b* 1963

(1) *Deborah; *b* 1965

(2) *Sophie Louise; *b* 1969

1 (cont.) Mrs Lowe *m* 2nd 1984 *Michael Hender

Sir John *m* 2nd 17 Oct 1956 *Jean Chalmers [Lady Green-Price, Gwernafel, Knighton, Powys], widow of Thomas Scott and dau of David Low Stark, of Arbroath, and *d* 30 Sept 1964

GREENAWAY

Arms: Quarterly, 1st and 4th, gu. a chevron between in chief two covered cups and in base a closed book, clasps downwards, or (for GREENAWAY); 2nd and 3rd, vert an ancient ship with three masts, sails set or, between four seagulls close ppr. (for BURDICK). **Crest:** A griffin's head erased or, semée of roses gu., barbed and seeded ppr., suspended from the beak an annulet gold. **Motto:** *Aut nunquam tentes aut perfice* ('Either never try or both try and perfect').
Creation: Bt. (UK) 23 Oct 1933.

SIR JOHN MICHAEL BURDICK GREENAWAY, 3RD BT, of Coombe, Co Surrey [Sir John Greenaway Bt, Lois Weedon House, Weedon Lois, Northants NN12 8PJ]; *b* 9 Aug 1944; *s* f 1994; *educ* Harrow, Grenoble U; Lt Life Gds 1965–70, dir Daniel Greenaway & Sons 1970–79; *m* 12 June 1982 *Susan Margaret, dau of Henry Birch, of Lion House, Tattenhall, Cheshire, and has issue:

1 +THOMAS EDWARD BURDICK; *b* 3 April 1985

1 *Camilla Helen; *b* 16 July 1983

Lineage: DANIEL GREENAWAY; had:

Sir Percy Walter Greenaway, 1st Bt (UK), so *cr* 23 Oct 1933, JP City London; *b* 11 June 1874; City London: Lt, memb Court Common Cncl 1917, Alderman 1923, Sheriff 1931–32, Ld Mayor 1932–33, Master Stationers' and Newspaper Makers' Co 1932 and 1933, Treasurer 1951, chm Daniel Greenaway & Sons, printers and stationers, Govr Irish Soc 1945, ktd 1932; *m* 17 April 1907 Lydie Amy (*d* 1 March 1962), er dau of James Burdick, and had issue:

1 DEREK BURDICK (Sir), **2nd Bt**

2 Alan Pearce, JP City London 1964; City London: memb Court of Common Cncl 1952, Sheriff 1962–63, Alderman 1965, dep chm Daniel Greenaway & Sons, Capt King's Regt, chm Central Mkts Ctee 1964; *b* 25 Nov 1913; *educ* Canford; *m* 2 Oct 1948 Patricia Frances (*d* 16 Aug 1982), yr dau of Sir Frederick Michael Wells, 1st and last Bt, of Hove, and *d* 9 Jan 1994, leaving issue:

(1) +Michael Philip [Michael Greenaway Esq, Criplands, Lindfield, W Sussex RH16 2SL]; *b* 14 Dec 1949; *educ* Harrow; *m* 1978 *Alison Robya, dau of Geoffrey Douglas Cohen, and has issue:

1a +Daniel Pearce; *b* 1981

1a *Hannah Kate; *b* 1980

2a *Rebecca Lucy; *b* 1984

(1) *Susan Mary [Mrs Alexander Cruickshank, The Doone, Byfleet Rd, Cobham, Surrey]; *b* 7 Jan 1952; *m* 1973 *Alexander Andrew Campbell Cruickshank and has issue:

1a *David Alexander; *b* 1976

2a *Benjamin Andrew; *b* 1982

1a *Sarah Frances Louise; *b* 1974

1 *Doreen Lydie, JP Kingston-upon-Thames; *m* 28 April 1936 Harold Francis Ralph Sturge (*d* 1993), Met Magistrate 1947–68, yr s of Ernest Harold Sturge, and has issue:

(1) *Martin Greenaway [Martin Sturge Esq, 3 Lower Camden Place, Bath]; *b* 1938

(2) *Simon Harold [Simon Sturge Esq, Lyndhurst, Woodhouse Lane, Holmbury St Mary, Surrey]; *b* 1940; *m* 1st 1967 Hilary Barbara Highet; *m* 2nd 1982 *Sheila Anne Jean Longsdale and by his 1st w has issue:

1a *Charles Campbell; *b* 1969

2a *Alexander James; *b* 1972

2 Jasmine Amy; *m* 1 June 1938 Charles Anthony Hinds Howell, MA, DM, FRCP, Lt-Col RAMC, 2nd s of Conrad Meredyth Hinds Howell, MA, DM, FRCP, and had issue

Sir PERCY *d* 25 Nov 1956; his er son,

Sir Derek Burdick Greenaway, 2nd Bt, TD, CBE (1974), JP (Kent 1962), DL (1973); *b* 27 May 1910; *educ* Marlborough; WW II: Capt RA 1940, Maj 1942, Hon Col 44 (HC) Signal Regt (Cinque Ports) TA 1966–67, Hon Col 36th Signal Regt (V) 1967–74, Jt MFH Old Surrey and Burstow 1958–66, pres Daniel Greenaway & Sons, Chm C Assoc Sevenoaks 1960–63 (pres 1963–66), assist treas SE Area Nat Union C and U Assocs 1966–69 (treas 1969–75, chm 1975–79), Master Stationers' & Newspaper Makers' Co 1974–75 (Silver Medal 1984), High Sheriff 1971–72; *m* 28 April 1937 *Sheila Beatrice [Sheila Lady Greenaway, Dunmore, Four Elms, Edenbridge, Kent TN8 6NE], only dau of Cyril Richard Lockett, and *d* 19 Nov 1994, leaving issue:

1 Sir JOHN MICHAEL BURDICK GREENAWAY, **3rd and present Bt**

1 *Anne Jennifer [Mrs David Hewson, 13 Abbotsbury Rd, London W14]; *b* 16 March 1939; *m* 16 June 1969 *Capt David Patrick Lewis Hewson, Blues and Royals, only s of Brig Arthur George Hewson, MC, of Attyflin, Patrickswell, Co Limerick, and has issue:

(1) *George Patrick David; *b* 1980

(1) *Annabel Mary; *b* 21 July 1971

(2) *Clare Louise; *b* 1973

GREENE OF HARROW WEALD

Creation: B. (LP, UK) 1974.

THE BARON GREENE OF HARROW WEALD, of Harrow, Greater London (Sir Sidney Francis Greene, CBE (1966)) [The Rt Hon The Lord Greene of Harrow Weald CBE, 26 Kynaston Wood, Boxtree Rd, Harrow Weald, Middx HA3 6UA]; *b* 12 Feb 1910; NUR: Union Organiser 1944, Assist Gen Sec 1954–57, Gen Sec 1957–74; JP London 1941–65; memb: NEDC 1962–75, Advsy Cncl ECGD 1967–70, (part-time) SEB 1964–77, Nat Freight Corp 1973–77; Chm: TUC Exec Ctee 1968075, Gen Cncl 1969–70 (memb 1957–75); ktd 1970; Dir: Bank of England 1970–, Trades Union Unit Tst 1970–80, RTZ Corp 1975–80, Times Newspapers Ltd 1975–80, Times Newspaper Hldgs 1980–82; FCIT; *m* 1936 *Masel Elizabeth Carter and has three daus

Lineage: FRANK JAMES GREENE, of London; *m* Alice Kerwood and had issue:

SIDNEY FRANCIS, *cr* a **Baron**

GREENHILL

Creation: B. (UK) 8 July 1950.

THE 3RD BARON GREENHILL, of Townhead in the City of Glasgow (Malcolm Greenhill) [The Rt Hon The Lord Greenhill, 28 Gorselands, Newbury, Berks RG14 6PX]; *b* 5 May 1924; *s* bro 1989; *educ* Kelvinside Acad Glasgow and Glasgow U (BSc 1944); with Telecommunications Research Establishment Malvern 1944–45, Atomic Energy Research Establishment Harwell 1945–50 and 1951–61, UK Sci Mission Washington 1950–51, UKAEA 1954–73, chartered patent agent, with MOD 1973–89

Lineage: MAURICE GREENHILL; had:

ERNEST GREENHILL, **1st Baron Greenhill**, of Townhead in the City of Glasgow (UK), so *cr* 8 July 1950, OBE (1947), JP (Glasgow 1940); *b* 23 April 1887; memb Glasgow Corp 1932, City Treas and Sr Magistrate, Hon LLD Glasgow 1963; *m* 1914 Ida (*d* 1985), dau of Mark Goodman, and *d* 18 Feb 1967, leaving:

1 STANLEY GREENHILL, **2nd Baron Greenhill**; *b* 17 July 1917; *educ* Kelvinside Acad Glasgow and Us of Glasgow, Toronto and California, MD, DPH, FACP (1959), FRSM, FRSH, instr and lecturer medicine Alberta U 1947, Br Library Info New York 1941–42, RAF WW II, dir Blood Transfusion Serv Alberta 1947–48, specialist internal medicine RCP Ottawa, FACP, Prof and Chm Dept Community Medicine 1959, FIMA 1959, Corresponding Sec Alberta Soc Specialists Internal Medicine 1960; *m* 1946 *Margaret Jean [The Rt Hon The Lady Greenhill, 10223 137th St, Edmonton, Alberta, Canada T5N 2G8], dau of Thomas Newlands, of Hamilton, Ontario, and *d* 28 Sept 1989, leaving:

(1) *Catherine Elizabeth [The Hon Mrs Youngren, # 515, 1485 Parkway Blvd, Coquitlam, BC V3E 3E6, Canada]; *b* 1948; *m* 28 April 1978 *Kenneth Orville Youngren, s of Barry Youngren

(2) *Sheila Ann [The Hon Mrs Davidson, 10336 Villa Ave, Edmonton, Alberta, Canada T5N 3T9]; *b* 1951; *m* 15 Sept 1979 *Robert Hugh Davidson, s of Hugh Davidson, of Edmonton

2 MALCOLM GREENHILL, **3rd and present Baron Greenhill**

1 Eileen Hannah; *b* 1925; *educ* St Andrews and Glasgow Us (MA 1947, DipEd); *d* 23 Oct 1971

GREENHILL OF HARROW

Arms: Vert two barrulets ermine, in chief a lion passant or, a bordure argent. **Crest:** A demi-griffin gules, semée of mullets gold, holding between the claws a mullet also gold. **Supporters:** On either side a griffin gules semée of mullets or, langued and armed azure. **Motto:** *Honos alit artes* ('Honour fosters the arts'). **Creation:** B. (LP, UK) 1974.

THE BARON GREENHILL OF HARROW, of The Royal Borough of Kensington and Chelsea (Sir Denis Arthur Greenhill, GCMG 1972 (KCMG 1967, CMG 1960), OBE (1941)) [The Rt Hon The Lord Greenhill of Harrow GCMG OBE, 25 Hamilton House, Vicarage Gate, London W8 4HL]; *b* 7 Nov 1913; *educ* Bishops Stortford Coll and Ch Ch Oxford (MA, Hon Student 1977); apprentice LNER 1935–39; WWII: RE Middle East, N Africa, Italy, India and SE Asia (despatches twice), Col 1945; FO 1946–73: 1st Sec: Sofia 1947–49, Washington DC 1949–52, FO 1952–54, IDC 1954, UK Delegn NATO Paris 1955–57, Office Commr-Gen SE Asia Singapore 1957–59; Washington DC: Counsellor 1959–62, Min 1962–64; FO/FCO: Assist U-Sec 1964–66, Dep U-Sec 1966–69, PUS 1969–73, Head Dip Serv 1969–73; Pres: Roy Soc Asian Affrs 1976–84, Anglo-Finnish Soc 1981–84; Chm: Govrs SOAS 1978–85, Cncl King's Coll Hosp Med Sch 1977–83; Dep Chm BUPA 1979–84 (Govr 1978–84); dir: Hawker Siddeley Gp 1974–84, Wellcome Fndn 1974–85, Clerical Medical and General Life Assur 1974–86, S G Warburg 1974–87 (Advsr 1987–95), BAT Industs 1974–83, Leyland Internat 1977–82; Memb: Security Commn 1974–82, Internat Advsy Ctee First Chicago Ltd 1976–81; Tstee Rayne Fndn 1974; Govr: BBC 1973–78, Wellington Coll 1974–83; Grand Cross Order Finnish Lion 1984; author: *More By Accident* (1992); *m* 1941 *Angela, dau of William Leitch McCulloch by Doris St George McCulloch (*née* Stedall), and has had:

1 *Nigel Denis St George (does not use courtesy title); *b* 1942

2 Robin James; *b* 1945; *m* 1970 (*divorce* 1975) Elizabeth, dau of Baron Roll of Ipsden (*qv*), and *d* 1986

Lineage: JAMES GREENHILL, of Ashfields, Loughton, Essex; *m* Susie Beatrice Matthews and had:

DENIS ARTHUR, *cr* a **Baron**

GREENWAY

Arms: Per pale erm. and ermines, on a chief az. a crescent between two covered cups or. **Crest:** A griffin's head or, erased gu., holding in the beak an anchor sa. **Supporters:** On either side a griffin sa., beak and claws or, holding in the beak an anchor and charged on the shoulder with a covered cup gold. **Motto:** *Labore et honore* ('With industry and honour'). **Creation:** Bt. (UK) 20 May 1919, B. (UK) 18 Jan 1927.

THE 4TH BARON GREENWAY, of Stanbridge Earls, Co Southampton, and a **Baronet** (Sir Ambrose Charles Drexel Greenway, Bt) [The Rt Hon The Lord Greenway, House of Lords, London SW1A OPW]; *b* 21 May 1941; *s* f 1975; *educ* Winchester; marine photographer and author; *m* 1985 *Mrs Rosalynne Schenk, of Devon, dau of Lt-Col Peter Geoffrey Fradgley, of Upper Manor, Rackenford, N Devon

Lineage: THOMAS GREENAWAY, of Tottenhall, parish of Colerne, Wiltshire; *m* Agnes and *d* 1609, leaving:

FRANCIS GREENAWAY, of Colerne; living 1619; *m* Elizabeth — (*d* 1665) and had:

DAVID GREENWAY, of Colerne; *m* Frances — (*d* May 1718) and *d* Feb 1725, leaving:

DAVID GREENWAY, of Colerne; *b* 1686; *m* Elizabeth — and had:

FRANCIS GREENWAY, of Colerne; *d* April 1781, leaving:

SAMUEL GREENWAY, of Corsham, Wilts; *b* 1747; *m* Betty — (*d* Jan 1822) and *d* Feb 1833, leaving:

THOMAS GREENWAY, of Corsham; *b* 1783; *m* 1 Sept 1817 Phillis Tanner (*d* Feb 1853), of Corsham, and *d* 1865, leaving:

JOHN DAVID GREENWAY, of Taunton, Somerset; *b* 1823; *m* 31 May 1853 Lucy Emily White (*d* 1901), dau of William Wiffen, of Brentwood, Essex, and *d* 16 Dec 1889, leaving:

Sir Charles Greenway, 1st Bt, so *cr* 20 May 1919, as also 18 Jan 1927 **1st Baron Greenway**, of Stanbridge Earls, Co Southampton (both UK); *b* 13 June 1857; merchant and banker, Pres Anglo-Persian Oil; *m* 5 June 1884 Mabel (*d* 24 April 1940), dau of Edwin Augustine Tower, and had:

1 CHARLES KELVYNGE, **2nd Baron**

1 Elsie Mabel; *m* 1st 17 Dec 1907 Capt William Francis Boucher Edwards, IA (*ka* Mesopotamia April 1915), and had issue; *m* 2nd 30 Aug 1916 Brig Harry Percival Currey, CBE, Roy Ulster Rifles (*d* 1969), s of Lt-Col C H Currey, 4th Dragoon Gds, and *d* 10 Aug 1965, leaving issue

2 Marjorie Phyllis; *m* 27 Nov 1915 Lt-Col John Brown Dalzell Hunter, OBE, MB, FRCS (Edin), IMS, and had issue. He *d* 7 May 1951

The 1st BARON *d* 17 Dec 1934; his only son,

CHARLES KELVYNGE GREENWAY, **2nd Baron Greenway**; *b* 24 March 1888; *educ* Charterhouse and RMC Sandhurst; Capt 26th King George's Own Light Cav, IA, Expdny Forces Mesopotamia and Aden (ret 1920); *m* 16 April 1916 Eileen Constance (*d* 8 Oct 1962), dau of Maj-Gen Sir Harry Triscott Brooking, KCB, KCSI, KCMG, and had:

1 (CHARLES) PAUL, **3rd Baron**

2 Atheling Kelvynge Brooking; Lt RNVR WW II; *b* 4 Dec 1921; *educ* Repton; *m* 22 Jan 1944 (*divorce* 1962) Stella Alice (WRNS), dau of William Joseph Jennings, of S Rhodesia, and *d* 30 Aug 1970, leaving issue:

(1) +Nigel Kelvynge Brooking [Nigel Greenway Esq, PO Box 374, Harare, Zimbabwe]; *b* 28 June 1945; *m* 1970 *Flora, dau of Lindsay Glegg, of Harare, and has issue:

1a +Timothy Kelvynge; *b* 1976

1a *Ashleigh Stella; *b* 1973

2a *Teresa Gay; *b* 1974

3a *Joanne Cordelia; *b* 1977

The 2nd BARON *d* 30 April 1963; his er son,

(CHARLES) PAUL GREENWAY, **3rd Baron Greenway**; *b* 31 Jan 1917; *educ* Winchester and Trin Coll Cambridge (BA 1938, MA 1942); memb Lloyd's, Freeman City London, 2nd Lt The Buffs 1940, Maj Parachute Regt WW II (wounded); *m* 22 Dec 1939 *Cordelia Mary [The Rt Hon Cordelia Lady Greenway, 703 Collingwood House, Dolphin Square, London SW1], yr dau of Maj Humfrey Campbell Stephen, JP, and *d* 14 Sept 1975, leaving issue:

1 AMBROSE CHARLES DREXEL GREENWAY, **4th and present Baron Greenway**

2 +MERVYN STEPHEN KELVYNGE [The Hon Mervyn Greenway, 605 Howard House, Dolphin Square, London SW1V 3PG]; *b* 19 Aug 1942; heir presumptive; *educ* Winchester; FCA 1969, Freeman City London, Liveryman Vintners' Co, stockbroker; has issue:

(1) *Philippa Mary; *b* 1980

3 +Nigel Paul [The Hon Nigel Greenway, 52 Chester Row, London SW1]; *b* 12 Jan 1944; *educ* Winchester; *m* 1979 *Gabrielle, er dau of Walter Jean Duchardt, of Obenheim, Alsace, and has issue:

(1) +Nicholas Walter Paul; *b* 1988

(2) +Philippe; *b* 1991

GREENWELL

Arms: Or two bars az. between three ducal coronets gu.
Crest: A stork statant ppr., beaked and legged gu., gorged with a wreath of laurel vert. **Motto:** *Viresco* ('I become green').
Creation: Bt. (UK) 19 July 1906.

SIR EDWARD BERNARD GREENWELL, 4TH BT, of Marden Park, Godstone, Co Surrey, DL (Suffolk 1988) [Sir Edward Greenwell Bt DL, Gedgrave Hall, Woodbridge, Suffolk IP12 2BX]; *b* 10 June 1948; *s f* 1978; *educ* Eton, Notts U (BSc) and Cranfield Inst Technology (MBA); *m* 26 Oct 1974 *Sarah Louise, yr dau of Lt-Col Philip Maitland Gore Anley, DL, of Sculthorpe House, Fakenham, Norfolk, and has:

1 +ALEXANDER BERNARD PETER; *b* 11 May 1987

1 *Belinda Clayre; *b* 30 April 1977

2 *Lucy Rose; *b* 1979

3 *Daisy Julia; *b* 1983

Lineage: JOHN de GRENWELL, of Park Yate, Wolsingham, Co Durham; *m* Catherine — and *d* by 13 Jan 1391, leaving:

JOHN de GRENWELL, of Park Yate; *d* by 6 Nov 1419, leaving:

JOHN GRENWELL, of Grenwell, Wolsingham; had a charter of lands there 1404; *m* Joan — and *d* by 21 Oct 1461, leaving:

LAWRENCE GRENWELL, of Grenwell; *d* by 21 Feb 1499, leaving:

JOHN GRENWELL, of Grenwell; *m* Agnes and *d* by 10 April 1543, leaving:

PETER GRENWELL, of Grenwell; had a yst s:

PETER GRENWELL, of Wolsingham; *d* shortly after 28 June 1573, leaving a 4th s:

ANTHONY GRENWELL, of Corbridge, Northumberland; had:

RALPH GREENWELL, of Corbridge; *m* Isabel, dau of Ralph Fenwick, of Dilston, Northumberland, and had a 3rd s:

WILLIAM GREENWELL, of Corbridge; *m* Mabel, dau of Nicholas Leadbitter, of Wardon, Northumberland, and *d* between 26 Oct and 30 Nov 1688, leaving, with other issue:

NICHOLAS GREENWELL, of Corbridge and Kingwood, Northumberland; *bapt* 17 July 1659; *m* 1st Frances — (*bur* 9 Dec 1694); *m* 2nd Hannah — (*d* by 31 Jan 1756) and was *bur* 9 Jan 1714, having had:

WHITFIELD GREENWELL, of Corbridge and Elrington, Northumberland; Capt Army; *m* 28 Feb 1713/4 Jane (*m* 2nd Ralph Redhead, of Corbridge), est dau and coheir of John Aynsley, of Threepwood, Northumberland, and was *k* in a skirmish Glenshiels Pass 10 June 1719 between Jacobites and Govt forces, leaving:

NICHOLAS GREENWELL, of Corbridge; *bapt* 5 July 1716; *m* 2nd 11 Nov 1744 Catherine Hickman and had:

JOHN GREENWELL, of the India House, London; *m* Jane (*d* 20 Sept 1832), only child of James Sheridine, of Marylebone, by Mary Thirkeld, and *d* 7 Feb 1814, having had, with other issue:

JAMES HUGO GREENWELL, of Beaumont St, Marylebone; *b* 14 June 1779; *m* 1st Livia Sophia (*d* 28 Dec 1815), dau of Col — Ward, of Bryanston Sq, and had a s (James, HEICS, *d* 1826) and dau (Livia Jane, *m* John Tweddell); *m* 2nd 1 Jan 1818 Bridget (*d* 6 Sept 1821), est dau of Edmund Lloyd, of Harley St, by Bridget, dau of John Salmon, of Holcham House, Somerset, and *d* 5 July 1838, leaving by her:

WALPOLE EYRE GREENWELL, of Upper Berkeley St; *b* 14 Nov 1819; *m* 9 Aug 1843 Eliza Theophila (*d* 1 March 1888), 3rd but sole surv dau and heiress of John Morris, of Hastings, Sussex, by Sarah, dau of Arthur Bott, and had, with four other sons:

1 James Hugo Christopher; *b* 7 May 1844; *m* 18 April 1871 Grace Frances, est dau of Frederick Scipio Clarkson, of Richmond, Surrey, and *dsp* 20 Jan 1907

2 WALPOLE LLOYD (Sir), **1st Bt**

3 Leonard; *b* 3 March 1854; *m* 3 April 1883 Emma, dau of Charles Maire, and *d* 29 Jan 1920, leaving issue

4 Donald; *b* 24 Nov 1856; *m* Rosina, dau of T B Koph

5 Edward Eyre; *b* 22 July 1859; *m* 1894 Sophie Lily (*d* 19 May 1943), dau of Felix Jones, Capt RIN, political agent Persian Gulf, and *d* 27 Nov 1938, leaving issue

6 Charles Okey; OBE (1918); Lt-Col 3rd Bn DLI; *b* 10 May 1861; *m* 26 Aug 1924 Maud Santilla (*d* 9 Feb 1934), dau of James Freeman, and *d* 3 May 1926

1 Rosa; *m* 24 April 1877 George Featherstone Griffin, of Mandeville Place, London W

2 Amy; *m* 1st 24 April 1877 Frederick Charles Caldwell, 13th Light Inf, 2nd s of Frederick William Caldwell, of Mishnish, Argyll; *m* 2nd 28 Aug 1915 Brig-Gen Sir Hugh Houghton Stewart, 4th Bt (*see* STEWART, Bt, of Athenree), and *d* 13 Sept 1924

3 Lilian; *d* unm 22 Feb 1954

WALPOLE GREENWELL *d* 13 March 1897; his 3rd s,

Sir Walpole Lloyd Greenwell, 1st Bt (UK), so *cr* 19 July 1906, of Marden Park, Godstone, Surrey, and Greenwell, Wolsingham, Co Durham, JP Surrey, High Sheriff 1903, Lt City London; *b* 9 June 1847; *m* 21 Jan 1873 Kathleen Eugenie (*d* 11 Jan 1932), V-Pres League Mercy, est dau of John Tizard, of Radipole, Dorset, and had issue:

1 BERNARD EYRE (Sir), **2nd Bt**

2 Aynsley Eyre; Maj 4th Bn Beds Regt Boer War 1900–02 and WW I; *b* 26 Nov 1876; *m* 2 Oct 1906 Beatrice Lilian (*d* 26 March 1966), 2nd dau of Rev Edward Sanderson, Rector Uckfield, Sussex, Canon Chichester Cathedral, and *d* 9 Oct 1944, having had issue:

(1) Whitfield Ava Aynsley; Lt-Cdr RNVR WW II; *b* 8 Aug 1907; *educ* Harrow and Peterhouse Cambridge; *m* 22 June 1935 Violet Rosemary Evelyn (*d* 26 March 1988), dau of Frederick Charles Turner, CIE, of The Little Place, Lyme Regis, Dorset, and *d* 10 April 1977, leaving:

1a +William Maxwell Walpole; *b* 17 Oct 1942; *educ* Harrow

1a *Eve Jennifer [Mrs Eve Greenwell DMW, Shermanbury Place, Shermanbury, W Sussex RH13 8HF]; *b* 24 March 1939; Dame of St Michael of the Wing (Portugal 1985); *m* 4 Jan 1974 (*divorce* 1981, resumed maiden name) Anthony Tullock Murly-Gotto and has:

1b *Antonia Mary Eve Alexandra; *b* 15 July 1975; *educ* Benenden and Manchester U

(2) Ivor Desmond; Lt-Cdr RNVR; *b* 28 Nov 1911; *educ* Harrow; *m* 27 Dec 1939 Diana (*d* 1991), dau of Maj John Simeon Ward, Rifle Bde, and *d* 1993, leaving:

1a *Jane Elizabeth; *b* 27 Feb 1954

2a *Mary Claire; *b* 27 Feb 1954

(3) Michael; *b* 14 May, *d* 24 May 1913

(4) Basil Evelyn; Lt RNVR; *b* 23 July 1915; *educ* Cheltenham; *m* 1st 14 Sept 1948 (*divorce* 1952) Phyllis Joyce, only dau of K L Weatherall Pepper; *m* 2nd 22 July 1955 *Sarah [Mrs Basil Greenwell, Tanners, River, Petworth, Sussex GU28 9AY], yst dau of Capt Hon Walter Seymour Carson, RN, of The Manor House, Stratton-on-Fosse (*see* 1935 edn CARSON, B), and *d* 1990, leaving by her:

1a +Simon Lloyd [Simon Greenwell Esq, Tanners, River, Petworth, Sussex GU28 9AY]; *b* 5 April 1956; *educ* Harrow and Oxford; *m* 1986 *Caroline Posner and has:

1b +Thomas Basil; *b* 1990

1b *Louise; *b* 1986

2b *Emma; *b* 1989

1a Giles Henry; *b* 1 Dec 1957; *educ* Harrow; *d* 1990

1a *Joanna Beatrice Taswell; *b* 14 Jan 1962; *m* 1986 *Rupert Clevely

2a *Virginia Annette; *b* 3 Jan 1965

(5) Walpole Edward; F/O RAFVR; *b* 27 Nov 1920; *educ* Harrow; *m* 1963 (*divorce* 1972) Rosemary Heather, formerly w of Douglas Bunn and yr dau of John Pares-Wilson, of Little Shelford, Cambs, by Lady Daniels, and *d* 1992, leaving:

1a +Rupert John Walpole [Rupert Greenwell Esq, Boxwood House, Amberley, W Sussex]; *b* 8 March 1964

(1) Verona Beatrice; *b* 7 Sept 1910; *m* 29 April 1935 Maurice Arthur Pryor (*d* 20 Dec 1969), only s of Maj John Arthur Pryor, of Bentworth Hall, Alton, Hants, and *d* 10 March 1992, leaving issue

3 Ronald Eyre; served WW I; *b* 27 Dec 1883; *m* 1917 Thomasine Elizabeth (*d* 23 March 1950), dau of James Boorer, of Taunton, and *dsp* 4 April 1960

4 Evelyn Eyre; Lt RNVR; *b* 14 Nov 1886; *d* unm 23 Feb 1919

5 Geoffrey Eyre; Capt Roy Mon RE WW I; *b* 18 Oct 1894; *m* 25 Feb 1922 *Mildred (*m* 2nd 1956 —), dau of J Evans, and *d* 13 June 1949, leaving:

(1) +John Evelyn [John Greenwell Esq, East Field, Henfold Hill, Beare Green, Surrey RH5 4RW]; *b* 28 Jan 1924; *educ* King's Canterbury; RAFVR WW II; *m* 12 May 1956 *Frances Valerie Anne, dau of Marnix Cremer, and has:

1a +Andrew John; *b* 9 Oct 1959

1a *Jane Frances; *b* 7 April 1963

1 Winifred Eyre, MBE (1918); *m* 1st 26 May 1896 Lt-Col Charles Montagu Crompton-Roberts, JP, DL, of Drybridge, Mon, 2nd s of Charles Henry Crompton-Roberts, JP, and had issue. He *d* 11 April 1931. She *m* 2nd 5 April 1932 Sir Oswald Vivian Bosanquet, KCSI, CIE, s of Arthur Bosanquet, JP, of Cleddon Hall, Trelleck, Mon, and *d* 6 Jan 1944. He *d* 6 Nov 1933

2 Cecil Eyre; *m* 14 June 1897 Rev Frederick Archibald Gresham Leveson-Gower and *d* 6 July 1939, leaving issue (*see* SUTHERLAND, D)

3 Mildred Eyre; *m* 1 Oct 1908 Rev Octavius John Loynes, s of E B Loynes, of Wells, Norfolk, and *dsp* 26 Nov 1909

4 Aubrey Eyre; *m* 13 Dec 1904 Geoffrey Averill Daniell, E Kent Regt, of White Hall, Sandwich Bay, Kent, and Knightsbridge, and *d* 24 Oct 1965, leaving issue. He *d* in a fire 26 Sept 1950

5 Kathleen Eyre; *m* 17 Feb 1903 Col Sir Robert Arthur Johnson, KCVO, KBE, TD, er s of Rev Arthur Henry Johnson, and *d* 9 Sept 1972, leaving issue. He *d* 2 March 1938

6 Margery Eyre; *m* 29 July 1915 Frank Somerville Beauford, Capt 17th Bn Roy Fus, only s of William Frederick Beauford, of Horeham Grange, Sussex. He *d* 12 April 1959

7 Gwendolin Eyre; *d* unm 12 April 1971

8 Sybil Eyre; *m* 25 April 1912 Geoffrey St John Strutt, CBE and *d* 9 Feb 1975 aged 84, leaving issue (*see* RAYLEIGH, B)

Sir WALPOLE *d* 24 Oct 1919; his son,

Sir Bernard Eyre Greenwell, 2nd Bt, MBE (1919); Chm Co of London Electric Supply Co Ltd, Maj Hants Yeo Boer War 1900–01 (medal with four clasps); *b* 29 May 1874; *m* 19 Nov 1902 Anna Elizabeth (*d* 22 June 1957), er dau of Adml Sir Francis Leopold McClintock, KCB, and had:

1 PETER MCCLINTOCK (Sir), **3rd Bt**

1 *Joyce Marjorie; *b* 1903; *m* 15 Sept 1927 Maj Walter Harold Miles, MBE (*d* 1986), Dorsetshire Regt, er surv s of Alfred Henry Miles, CMG, ISO, of Bournemouth, formerly of Kingston, Jamaica, and has issue:

(1) *Christopher Richard [Christopher Miles Esq, Court Lodge, Bletchingley, Surrey]; *b* 1 Aug 1928; *m* 11 Feb 1956 *Jean Mary, 2nd dau of Maj Anthony Buxton, DSO, JP, DL (*see* BUXTON, Bt), and has:

1a *Richard John; *b* 26 April 1957; *m* 1986 *Juliet Caroline Frances, dau of Brig John Rigby, of Hill House, Long Melford, Suffolk, and has:

1b *David John; *b* 1989

2b *William Richard Christopher; *b* 1992

1b *Rebecca Rose; *b* 1987

2a *Hubert Christopher; *b* 19 Sept 1959; *m* 1986 *Madeline, dau of Capt William Loftie, and has issue:

1b *Robert William; *b* 1988

2b *Alastair James; *b* 1990

1b *Laura Caroline; *b* 1992

1a *Mary Anna Theresa; *b* 2 Oct 1960

2a *Sophia Mary; *b* 1 March 1967

(2) *Philip David [Philip Miles Esq, Hinton Hall, Lea Cross, Salop]; *b* 20 March 1931; *m* 6 1st Feb 1960 Hon Julian Isabella Joan Chetwynd (*d* 1981), 2nd dau of 9th Viscount Chetwynd (*qv*); *m* 2nd 1985 *Hon Christine Helena, est dau of 7th Baron Forester (*qv*) and formerly w of 7th Baron Bolton (*qv*), and by his 1st w has:

1a *Charles Philip Chetwynd; *b* 15 Oct 1962

1a *Sara Isabella; *b* 6 Jan 1961

(1) *Rosemary Joyce [Mrs Michael Gow, Drummonie, Bridge of Earn, Perth PH2 9HN]; *b* 31 May 1935; *m* 1 June 1957 *Michael Harper Gow, 2nd s of Brig John Wesley Harper Gow, CBE, DL, and has issue:

1a *Christopher Michael Harper; *b* 28 Feb 1961

2a *Benjamin Fergus Harper; *b* 29 Nov 1965

1a *Lucinda Rosemary [Mrs William Collins, House of Craigie, by Kilmarnock, Ayrshire KA1 5NA]; *b* 21 Jan 1959; *m* 1979 *William Noel Collins (*see* DONOUGHMORE, E) and has issue:

1b *Emily Lucinda Julian; *b* 1981

2b *Melissa Daisy; *b* 1984

2a *Amelia Jean; *b* 6 April 1967; *m* 1994 *Peter Schaebbicke and has:

1b *Felix Michael Otto; *b* 27 Oct 1997

2 *Barbara Patience; *b* 1906; *m* 1st 24 April 1929 Capt Newton James Wallop William-Powlett, DSC, RN and has issue (*see* PORTSMOUTH, E); *m* 2nd 22 Jan 1966 her late husb's bro V-Adml Sir Peveril Barton Relbey Wallop William-Powlett, KCB, KCMG, CBE, DSO

3 *Elisabeth Kathleen; *b* 1908: *m* 28 July 1931 Capt Roddie Casement, OBE, RN (*d* 1987), 2nd s of Adml John Moore Casement, CB, of Cronoe, Ashford, Co Wicklow, and has:

(1) *Michael Bernard, OBE [Cdr Michael Casement OBE RN, Dene Cottage, W Harting, Hants]; *b* 1933; *educ* Winchester; *m* 1956 *Christina Rose, 3rd dau of Capt John Cassilis Maclean, RN, and has:

1a *William Rory John; *b* 1961; *m* 1989 *Rachel, yst dau of John Berry, and has:

1b *Daisy; *b* 1992

2b *Rosanna Isobel; *b* 1994

1a *Rachel Christina; *b* 1957; *m* 1985 *Charles James Middleton, er s of Brig R C Middleton, and has issue:

1b *Jemima Louise Mary; *b* 1988

2b *Imogen Ayesha; *b* 1991

2a *Flora Susan; *b* 1959; *m* 1991 *Hon Henry Lyttelton Alexander Hood, est s of 7th Viscount Hood (*qv*), and has issue

(2) *Patrick John [Patrick Casement Esq, 122 Mansfield Rd, London NW3 2JB]; *b* 1935; *educ* Winchester and Trin Coll Cambridge (MA); *m* 1966 *Margaret Rose, dau of Anthony George Lloyd and formerly w of Peter Jens McCowen, and has issue:

1a *Hanna; *b* 1968

2a *Isabella; *b* 1970

(1) *Elisabeth Ann [Mrs Anthony Howard, Drove Cottage, Nelbridge, Cadnam, Hants SO40 2NL]; *b* 1942; *m* 1963 *Anthony John Howard and has issue:

1a *Tom Peter; *b* 1967

1a *Kate Elisabeth; *b* 1965; *m* 1990 *Stuart Judd and has issue:

1b *George William; *b* 1993

2b *Jack Anthony; *b* 1995

2a *Emma; *b* 1967; *m* 1997 *Martin Roger Smith

(2) *Susan Henrietta [Mrs William Acworth, Little Hidden Farm, Hungerford, Berks]; *b* 1944; *m* 1964 *William Farquhar Acworth and has issue (*see* BUZZARD, Bt)

4 *Anna Margaret [Mrs Geoffrey Wilks, 60 Oxford Gardens, London W10]; *b* 1913; *m* 1st 25 July 1940 Sir James Henderson-Stewart, 1st Bt (*qv*), and has issue; *m* 2nd 29 July 1965, as his 2nd w, Geoffrey Walford Wilks, CBE, TD (*d* 1987), s of William Alfred Wilks

5 *Ruth Veronica [Mrs Peter Birchall, Cotswold Farm, Cirencester, Glos]; *b* 1916; *m* 1st 17 Dec 1936 William Reginald Colquhoun (*d* 2 Jan 1971), s of Capt William Jarvie Colquhoun, DSO; *m* 2nd 1972 *Peter Birchall and by her 1st husb has issue:

(1) *(William) Patrick [Patrick Colquhoun Esq, 2 Thornton Close, Girton, Cambs CB3 0NQ]; *b* 3 May 1939; *educ* Eton and Trin Coll Oxford; *m* 1971 *Frances Elspeth, only dau of Archibald Cameron, and has issue:

1a *Anna Elizabeth; *b* 1973; *m* 1997 *Matthew Richard John Purver, er s of William Purver, of Holmestall, Hertingfordbury, Herts

2a *Rhona Frances; *b* 1978

(2) *Alastair Peter, Capt RE; *b* 3 May 1941; *educ* Eton, RMA Sandhurst and Magdalene Coll Cambridge; *m* 1977 *Elisabeth, er dau of Capt Geoffrey Stanning, DSO, RN, of Mildenhall House, Mildenhall, Wilts, and has issue:

1a *Andrew John; *b* 1983

1a *Mary Louise; *b* 1979

(3) *John Humphrey [John Colquhoun Esq, Brooke House, Frocester, nr Stonehouse, Glos]; *b* 8 Oct 1943; *educ* Eton and Trin Coll Cambridge; *m* 1969 *Susan Elizabeth, er dau of Michael Ingram, of Driffield Manor, Cirencester, and has:

1a *Mark Humphrey; *b* 1973; *m* 1997 *Katherine Rosemary, er dau of James Woodrow, of Ladyhole House, Ashbourne, Derbys

2a *James Arthur; *b* 1975

1a *Auriol Emma; *b* 1982

(4) *Neil Robert; *b* 16 Dec 1947; *educ* Eton and Oxford; *m* 1975 *Rosemary Elizabeth, dau of Archibald Colville (*see* GIBSON-CRAIG-CARMICHAEL, Bt), and has issue:

1a *William Alexander; *b* 1976

2a *Nicholas Peter; *b* 1978

3a *Robert; *b* 1983

4a *Hamish Patrick; *b* 1985

(1) *Anna Margaret [Mrs Nigel McNair Scott, 1 Edwardes Square, London W8]; *b* 21 May 1946; *m* 11 May 1968 *Nigel Guthrie McNair Scott, yr s of Maj Ronald Guthre McNair Scott, of Huish House, Old Basing, Hants, by Hon Mary Cecilia, est dau of 1st Viscount Camrose (*qv*), and has issue

Sir BERNARD *d* 28 Nov 1939; his only son,

Sir Peter McClintock Greenwell, 3rd Bt; *b* 23 May 1914; *educ* Winchester and Trin Coll Cambridge (BA); Capt RA (TA) WW II (despatches, POW), JP Suffolk 1950–57, High Sheriff 1966; *m* 12 Feb 1940 *Jean Henrietta Rose (*m* 2nd 1985 Hugh Kenneth Haig, of Broomy Hall, Dalton, Newcastle-upon-Tyne), 2nd dau of Peter Haig-Thomas (*see* NORMANTON, E), and *d* 2 Dec 1978, leaving:

1 Sir EDWARD BERNARD GREENWELL, **4th and present Bt**

2 +James Peter [James Greenwell Esq, Boyton House, Boyton, Suffolk IP12 3LH]; *b* 27 May 1950; *educ* Eton; late Maj Blues & Royals; *m* 1979 *Serena Jane, yr dau of Maj Hon Colin James Dalrymple (*see* STAIR, E), and has:

(1) +Andrew Peter; *b* 1983

(1) *Davina Louise; *b* 1984

1 *Julia Henrietta [Mrs Alexander Trotter, Charterhall, Duns, Berwickshire]; *b* 2 Feb 1946; *m* 1 June 1970 *Alexander R Trotter, DL, s of Maj Henry Trotter, and has issue:

(1) *Henry Peter; *b* 1972

(2) *Edward John; *b* 1973

(3) *Rupert James; *b* 1977

GREENWOOD

Arms: Gu. on a chevron erm. between three saltires as many portcullises or. **Crest:** A demi-lion per fess gu. and sa., resting the sinister paw on a portcullis or. **Supporters:** On either side a lion rampant per fess gu. and sa., supporting a staff or, flowing therefrom a banner arg., that on the dexter charged with a rose gu., barbed and seeded ppr., and that on the sinister charged with a maple leaf also ppr. **Motto:** Law and loyalty. **Creations:** Bt. (UK) 8 Feb 1915, B. (UK) 31 Aug 1929, V. (UK) 16 Feb 1937.

THE 2ND VISCOUNT GREENWOOD, of Holbourne, Co London, **Baron Greenwood**, of Llanbister, Co Radnor, and a **Baronet** (Sir David Henry Hamar Greenwood, Bt) [The Rt Hon The Viscount Greenwood, c/o 63 Portsea Hall, Portsea Place, London W2 2BY]; *b* 30 Oct 1914; *s* f 1948; *educ* privately and Bowers Gifford; FRGS, chm The London Cremation Co 1973–

Lineage: JOHN GREENWOOD, farmer, of Llanbister, Radnorshire; *b* 1754; *m* 1st Sarah — and had a s and a dau (Sarah, *bapt* 19 Sept 1790); *m* 2nd Mary — (*b* 1758; *d* 9 Jan 1830) and *d* 4 May 1842, having by her had a s and dau; his s by his 1st w:

WILLIAM GREENWOOD, farmer, of Cantel Hall Farm, Llanbister, and King's Head Inn, Knighton; *bapt* 13 Jan 1793; *m* 25 Feb 1816 Mary Hamar (*b* 10 Nov 1795; *d* 28 Sept 1838), of Temple, and *d* 14 June 1882, having had, with an est s, a yst s and nine daus:

JOHN HAMAR GREENWOOD, of Knucklass Road, Knighton, and Spencer House, Whitby, Ontario; migrated Canada 1850, called Canadian Bar 1894; *bapt* 26 Jan 1829; *m* 14 Sept 1865 Charlotte Churchill (*d* July 1903), dau of Thomas Churchill Hubbard, and *d* July 1903, having had, with two other sons and four other daus:

1 (THOMAS) HAMAR, **1st Viscount**

2 William Hamar; *b* 11 Jan 1872; *m* Bessie Tamblyn and *d* Oct 1924, leaving two daus

1 (Adeliza) Florence Louise Hamar, CI (1945); CStJ; *b* 1885; *m* 16 Nov 1910 Leopold Charles Maurice Stennett Amery, PC, CH, DCL, LLD, er s of Charles Frederick Amery, of Middle Coombe, Lustleigh, S Devon, and *d* 18 Feb 1975, leaving issue. He *d* 16 Sept 1955

2 Gladys Cecil Hamar; *m* 7 Feb 1922 Hon Charles Christian Simon Rodney, 3rd s of 7th Baron Rodney (*qv*), and *dsp* 22 Jan 1966

The est son,

Sir (Thomas) Hamar Greenwood, 1st Bt, so *cr* 8 Feb 1915, as also 31 Aug 1929 BARON GREENWOOD, of Llanbister, Co Radnor, and 16 Feb 1937 (**1st) Viscount Greenwood**, of Holbourne, Co London (all UK), PC (GB 26 April 1920, I 6 May 1920), KC (1919), JP Middx; *b* 7 Feb 1870; *educ* Toronto U (BA 1895, Hon LLD 1938); with Dept Ag Ontario, Offr Canadian Militia, barrister Gray's Inn 1906, NB 1913 and Australia 1913, Gray's Inn: Bencher 1917, Treas 1930, V-Treas 1931; MP (Lib) York 1906–10, Sunderland 1910–22 and (C) E Walthamstow 1924–29, PPS to Home Sec 1906–10; Lt King Edward's Horse 1902–05, Capt 1905–12, Capt Gen Res Offrs 1913, with Dept Recruiting War Office 1914, Lt-Col 1914, raised and cmded 10th Bn S Wales Bdrs 1914, BEF 1915–16, DAAG War Office 1916, Hon Col Winnipeg Gren, Parly Under-Sec Home Dept 1919, Parly Sec Overseas Tde 1919, Ch Sec Ireland (with Cabinet seat) and Chllr Order St Patrick 1920–22, Hon Treas C Party 1933–38; Pres Br Iron and Steel Fedn 1938–39 (memb Prest's Ctee 1939), chm Dorman, Long & Co, Redpath, Brown & Co, Lewis Berger & Sons, Aerated Bread, chm: Anglo-Egyptian Chamber Commerc, Exec Ctee Pilgrims (Pres 1948); Grand Cordon Ismail Egypt; *m* 23 May 1911 Margery, DBE (1922), OStJ (*d* 24 April 1968 aged 81), dau of Rev Walter Spencer, of Fownhope Court, Herefs, and *d* 10 Sept 1948, leaving issue:

1 DAVID HENRY HAMAR GREENWOOD, **2nd and present Viscount Greenwood**

2 +MICHAEL GEORGE HAMAR [The Hon Michael Greenwood, 63 Portsea Hall, Portsea Place, London W2 2BY]; *b* 5 May 1923; heir presumptive; *educ* Eton and Ch Ch Oxford; Roy Corps Signals WW II, actor

1 *Angela Margo Hamar [The Hon Mrs Delevingne, 22 Ovington Street, London SW3] ; *b* 8 July 1912; *m* 4 Nov 1937 (Edward) Dudley Delevingne (*d* 7 Nov 1974), FRSA, FALPA, Capt Roy Fus, s of Edward Charles Delevingne, and has had:

(1) *Edward Hamar [Edward Delevingne Esq, Lime Tree Cottage, Dorking, Surrey]; *b* 7 July 1939; *m* 1982 *Fiona, dau of Donald Cameron, and has:

1a *Katherine; *b* 1985

(2) *Charles Hamar [Charles Delevingne Esq, Paddock House, Spencer Park, London SW18]; *b* 25 June 1949; *m* 1983 *Pandora Anne, er dau of Jocelyn Edward Greville Stevens (*see* SHEFFIELD, Bt), and has:

1a *Chloe Jane; *b* 1984

2a *Poppy Angela; *b* 1986

3a *Cara Jocelyn; *b* 1992

(1) Anne Venetia Charlotte; *b* 6 June 1938; *m* 1985 *Edward Lavender and *d* 1987

(2) *(Elizabeth) Caroline Felicia [Mrs Thomas Elek, The Bell House, Swinbrook, Oxon]; actress; *b* 2 June 1953; *m* 1978 *Thomas G Elek, s of Dr Imre Elek, of Millom, Cumbria, and has:

1a *Charles Thomas Hamar; *b* 1986

2a *George Dudley Hamar; *b* 1990

1a *Edwina Mary Angela; *b* 1980

2a *Flora Tamsin Elizabeth; *b* 1982

2 *Deborah Hamar, JP (Gtr London 1965); *b* 9 May 1917; *m* 9 Nov 1940 (*divorce* 1970) G/Capt Patrick David de Laszlo, MA, BLitt, 4th s of Philip Alexius Laszlo de Lombos, MVO (*see* GUINNESS, Bt), of Ardeley, Virginia Water, and has:

(1) *Damon Patrick; late 1st Bn Gren Gds, Capt 21 SAS (Artists) (V); *b* 8 Oct 1942; *educ* Gordonstoun; *m* 18 July 1972 *Hon Sandra Daphne, er dau of 2nd Baron Hacking (*qv*), and has:

1a *Lucy Deborah; *b* 1975

(1) *Stephanie Gay, barrister Gray's Inn 1966; *b* 9 March 1945; *m* 19– *Roger Williams, s of S G Williams

(2) *Meriel Perpetua; *b* 19 April 1950; *m* 19– *James Kitson

(3) *Grania Tiffany; *b* 1 Jan 1953; *m* 16 June 1979 *Simon Blake Phillips, only s of Edward Phillips, of The Old Place, Boveney, Berks

(4) *Charmian Deborah; *b* 9 Oct 1957

GREGSON

Creation: B. (LP, UK) 1975.

THE BARON GREGSON, of Stockport in Greater Manchester (John Gregson, DL (Greater Manchester 1979)) [The Rt Hon The Lord Gregson DL,12 Rosemont Road, Richmond-upon-Thames, Surrey TW10 6QL; The Spinney, Cragg Vale, Mytholmroyd, Hebden Bridge, W Yorks HX7 5SR; 407 Hawkins House, Dolphin Square, London SW1V 3XL]; *b* 29 Jan 1924; joined Fairey Engineering Stockport 1939, R and D Team 1946, dir 1966, md 1978–94; part-time memb British Steel Bd 1976–94; Chm Finance and Industry Gp Lab Party 1978–; Pres: Def Mfrs Assoc 1984–, Parly and Scientific Ctee 1986–89, Stockport Youth Orchestra; memb: Ho Lds Select Ctee Sci and Technology 1980–, memb Ho Lds European Community Ctee's Sub-Ctee on Energy, Industry and Tport 1994–97, Electra Corp Ventures 1989, Bd NRA 1992–, Ct Manchester U Inst Science and Technology 1976–; non-exec dir: Fairey Gp 1989–94, Otto-Simon Caves Ltd; AMCT; CBIM; Hon FIProdE 1982, Hon Fell Manchester Poly 1983; Hon FEng 1986; DU OU 1986; Hon FICE 1987; Hon DSc Aston 1987; Hon DTech Brunel 1989; RCMS 1990

Lineage: JOHN GREGSON; had:

JOHN, *cr* a **Baron**

GRENFELL

Arms: Gu. on a fess between three organ rests or a mural crown of the field. **Crest:** On a mural crown gu. a gryphon passant or, holding in the beak a sprig of laurel ppr. **Supporters:** Dexter, an Egyptian cavalry soldier habited, accoutred and supporting in the exterior hand a lance ppr.; sinister an Egyptian infantry soldier, habited, accoutred and supporting in the exterior hand a rifle with bayonet fixed, also ppr. **Motto:** *Loyal devoir* ('Honest duty').
Creation: B. (UK) 19 July 1902.

THE 3RD BARON GRENFELL, of Kilvey, Co Glamorgan (Julian Pascoe Francis St Leger Grenfell) [The Rt Hon The Lord Grenfell, 24 rue Chaptal, 75009 Paris, France]; *b* 23 May 1935; *s f* 1976; *educ* Eton and King's Coll Cambridge (BA 1959, Pres Union 1959); Dep Dir World Bank Gp 1973–, Special Rep World Bank to UN 1974–81, Sr Advsr External Affrs 1983–90, Head External Affrs Europe 1990–95, Capt Queen's Westminsters (KRRC) (TA), 2nd Lt KRRC (60th Rifles) 1954–56, programme writer and commentator ATV, film and TV advsr Encyclopaedia Britannica Ltd 1961–64; *m* 1st 3 April 1961 (*divorce* 1970) Loretta Maria Olga Hildegarde, est dau of Alfredo Reali, of Florence, and has issue:

1 *Isabella Sarah Frances; *b* 1 May 1966; *m* 27 May 1995 *Luigi Pianini Mazzucchetti, s of Mario Pianini Mazzucchetti, of Rimini

The 3rd BARON *m* 2nd 10 Dec 1970 Gabrielle Katharina (*divorce* 1987), only dau of Dr Ernest Raab, of Berlin; *m* 3rd 1987 Mrs Elizabeth Porter, dau of Buford Scott, of Richmond, Va.; *m* 4th 1993 *Mrs Dagmar Langbehn Debreil, dau of Dr Carl Langbehn, of Berlin, and by his 2nd w has:

2 *Katharina Elizabeth Anne; *b* 14 May 1973; *m* 18 Jan 1997 *Patrick Haven O'Connor, s of Thomas O'Connor, of Florida

3 *Vanessa Julia Claire; *b* 18 May 1976

Lineage: PASCOE GRENFELL (s of John Grenfell of St Just's, Cornwall); *b* 1692; merchant Penzance; *m* 1st 29 Nov 1718 Mary Edwards (*dsp* 1719); *m* 2nd Mary, dau of John Maugham, of Marazion, Cornwall, and *d* 1752, leaving with an est s, two yst sons and two daus:

PASCOE GRENFELL, of Marazion; Dutch Consul; *b* 1729; *m* 13 Dec 1758 Mary, dau of William Tremenheere, and *d* 27 May 1810, leaving, with three yr sons and four daus:

PASCOE GRENFELL, of Taplow House, Bucks; MP Marlow and Penrhyn, DCL; *b* 3 Sept 1761; *m* 1st 26 Aug 1786 his cousin Charlotte Granville (*d* 2 May 1790) and had issue:

1 George Granville; *b* 10 Feb 1789; *dsp* 3 June 1853

2 Charles Pascoe, of Taplow Court; MP Preston; *b* 4 April 1790; *m* 22 June 1819 Lady Georgiana Isabella Frances Molyneux (*d* 28 June 1826), est dau of 2nd Earl of Sefton (*see* 1970 edn), and *d* 21 March 1867, leaving:

(1) Charles William; Capt 2nd Middx Militia, MP Sandwich 1847–52 and Windsor; *b* 17 March 1823; *m* 20 July 1852 Georgina Caroline (*d* 2 Feb 1911), gdau of 2nd Earl of Harewood (*qv*), and *dvp* 4 May 1861, leaving, with other issue:

1a WILLIAM HENRY GRENFELL, 1st and last BARON DESBOROUGH, of Taplow, Bucks (UK), so *cr* 30 Dec 1905, KG (1928), GCVO (1925, KCVO 1908, CVO 1907), JP, DL Bucks, JP Berks, DL Tower Hamlets; *b* 30 Oct 1855; *educ* Harrow and Balliol Coll Oxford (BA 1879, MA 1936, Hon Fell 1928); High Steward Maidenhead, MP Salisbury 1880–82 and 1885–86, Hereford 1892–93 and Wycombe 1900–05, High Sheriff Bucks 1890, Hon DCL Oxon 1938, Parly Groom-in-Waiting 1882, Hon Lt-Col and Cmdt London RASC Motor Tport Vols 1918–21, Capt Yeomen Gd 1924–29, chm: Thames Conservancy Bd 1905–37, Ctee on Police Serv England, Scotland and Wales, Ctee Freshwater Fish WW I, Pres London Chamber of Commerce, KGStJ, Order Redeemer Greece; *m* 17 Feb 1887 Ethel (Ettie) Anne Priscilla, Extra Ldy Bedchamber to HM QUEEN MARY (*d* 28 May 1952), dau of Hon Julian Henry Charles Fane (*see* WESTMORLAND, E), and *dspms* 9 Jan 1945, when the Barony expired, having had:

1b Julian Henry Francis, DSO; Capt 1st Roy Dragoons WW I (despatches), poet; *b* 30 March 1888; *d* 26 May 1915 of wounds recd in action

2b Gerald William; T/Lt 8th (Service) Bn Rifle Bde; *b* 29 March 1890; *ka* 30 July 1915

3b Ivo George Winfred; Lt Res Offrs Gren Gds; *b* 5 Sept 1898; *d* 8 Oct 1926 following a car crash

1b Monica Margaret; Red Cross nurse France WW I; *b* 4 Aug 1893; *m* 2 June 1924 Marshal of the RAF Sir John Maitland Salmond, GCB, CMG, CVO, DSO, DCL, 2nd s of Maj-Gen Sir William Salmond, KCB, RE, and *d* 17 June 1973, leaving issue (*see* POWERSCOURT, V). He *d* 16 April 1968

2b Alexandra Imogen Clair; *b* 11 Feb 1905; *m* 26 Feb 1931 6th Viscount Gage (*qv*) and *d* 3 Jan 1969, leaving issue

2a Charles Molyneux, of Blackwell Hall, Chesham, Bucks; Lt 10th Hus; *b* 3 June 1857; *m* 12 Jan 1887 Hon Mabel Blanche Mills (*d* 8 Oct 1936), 2nd dau of 1st Baron Hillingdon (*see* 1970 edn), and *d* 15 Oct 1915, leaving issue:

1b Sylvia Caroline; *m* 20 Nov 1912 Capt Arthur Egerton Watts-Russell (formerly Birch), Res Offrs Coldstream Gds, s of Sir Arthur Birch, KCMG, JP, FRGS, and *d* 27 June 1969, leaving issue. He *d* 2 March 1923

3a Claude George, Lt Thornycroft's Horse; *b* 20 Aug 1858; *ka* Spion Kop Boer War 24 Jan 1900

1a Caroline Georgina; *m* 13 April 1880 Hon Sir Robert Henry Meade, GCB, and *d* 5 March 1881, leaving issue (*see* CLANWILLIAM, E)

2a Constance Isabella; *m* 21 Jan 1890 Col Frederick Arthur Aylmer, and *d* 14 Oct 1923, leaving issue (*see* AYLMER, B)

(2) Henry Riversdale, of Bacres, Henley, JP; MP Stoke-on-Trent, Dir and Govr Bank England, Lt City London; *b* 5 April 1824; *m* 25 July 1867 Alethea Louisa (*d* 18 April 1923), dau of Henry John Adeane, MP Cambridge, of Babraham, and *d* 11 Sept 1902, leaving:

1a EDWARD CHARLES GRENFELL, 1st BARON SAINT JUST (*qv*)

1a Maud Alethea Louisa; *d* unm 8 Dec 1955

(1) Maria Georgiana; *m* 26 Nov 1856 Col Frederick Paget (*see* ANGLESEY, M) and *d* 27 Sept 1900

(2) Louisa Henrietta; *m* 12 Jan 1876 Theodore Walrond, CB, Civ Serv Commr, and *d* 11 Aug 1911

1 Charlotte Granville; *m* 16 May 1811 Thomas George French, of Marino, Co Cork, and *d* 27 March 1845

PASCOE GRENFELL *m* 2nd 15 Jan 1798 Hon Georgiana St Leger (*d* 12 May 1818), yst dau of 1st Viscount Doneraile (*qv*), and *d* 23 Jan 1838, having by her had, with other issue:

3 PASCOE ST LEGER

4 Riversdale William, of Ray Lodge, Maidenhead; *b* 29 Nov 1807; *m* 20 March 1834 Charlotte Adelaide (*d* 12 Dec 1840), dau of John Elliot, of Pimlico Lodge, and *d* 1 June 1871, having had issue:

(1) Charles Seymour, of Elibank, Taplow, Bucks, JP; *b* 14 Sept 1839; *m* 30 Sept 1862 Elizabeth (*d* 6 Oct 1930), 4th dau of William Graham, of Tamrawer, Stirling, and *d* 11 Jan 1924, leaving issue:

1a Riversdale Francis John, JP London; High Sheriff 1903, Coldstream Gds; *b* 20 Aug 1864; *educ* Eton and RMC Sandhurst; *m* 1st 9 June 1888 Cecil Blanche (*d* 8 Oct 1931), 2nd dau of Henry James Lubbock, DL (*see* AVEBURY, B); *m* 2nd 3 Aug 1933 Olive Isabel (*d* 18 July 1961), formerly w of Gerald Macleay Browne, OBE, and yst dau of Lt-Col Sir Gerald Smith, KCMG, and *d* 1 Dec 1954, having by his 1st w had issue:

1b Geoffrey Seymour; Lt-Cdr RN WW II; *b* 2 June 1898; *m* 1st 30 April 1924 (*divorce* 1936) Sybil Mary, dau of Hugh Peacock, of Greatford Hall, Stamford, and had:

1c Elizabeth Mary; *m* 4 July 1953 (Charles) Brian Lascelles and *d* 1978, leaving issue (*see* HAREWOOD, E)

1b (cont.) Lt-Cdr Geoffrey Grenfell *m* 2nd 21 Sept 1938 Anne Catherine Tredick (*m* 3rd 22 Sept 1950 Don Stuart Mommand; *d* 1977), formerly w of 6th Earl of Carnarvon (*qv*) and er dau of Jacob Wendell, of New York, and was *ka* 8 June 1940

1b Esmé Winifred Mary; *m* 1st 17 Jan 1914 Lt-Col Walter Robert Stewart, DSO, MC, Rifle Bde, only surv s of Maj-Gen Hon Alexander Stewart, and has issue (*see* GALLOWAY, E); *m* 2nd 29 Jan 1929 Maj Joseph Anthony Douglas Bell, RASC, s of Robert Cragie Bell, of Edinburgh. He *d* 1 Aug 1956

2b Jean Doris; *m* 14 April 1920 Christopher William Gurney, est s of Cyril Gurney, of Henlow Grange, Beds, and *d* 31 Jan 1958, leaving issue. He *d* 31 Aug 1939

1a Mildred Louisa; *m* 31 March 1902 Brig-Gen Henri Gustave Joly de Lotbinière, DSO, RE, s of Sir Henri Gustave Joly de Lotbinière, KCMG, and *d* 5 Feb 1953, leaving issue. He *d* 15 Feb 1960

2a Alice Lilian, OStJ; *m* 26 July 1906 1st Baron Mildmay of Flete and *d* 22 March 1960, leaving issue (*see* ST JOHN MILDMAY, Bt)

3a Cicely Mary; *m* 26 Feb 1897 Lord Charles Cavendish-Bentinck, DSO, and *d* 30 Jan 1936, leaving issue (*see* PORTLAND, E)

(1) Georgina Adelaide; *m* 3 Aug 1859 Prof Friedrich Max-Muller, PC, MA, LLD, DCL, of Oxford U, only s of Wilhelm Muller, poet, and *d* 17 July 1916, leaving issue. He *d* 28 Oct 1900

(2) Charlotte Elliot; *m* 17 Nov 1859 Theodore Walrond, CB, and *d* 12 May 1872, leaving issue. He *d* 17 June 1887

2 Henrietta Maria Jane; *m* 1 March 1848 Robert Myrtens Bird, BCS, and *d* 21 Feb 1897

3 Marianne; *m* 17 March 1823 1st Baron Wolverton (*qv*) and *d* 30 March 1892, leaving issue

4 Emily Charlotte; *m* 29 May 1834 Rev Lord Sydney Godolphin Osborne, bro of 8th Duke of Leeds (*see* 1963 edn), and *d* 19 Dec 1875, leaving issue. He *d* 9 May 1889

5 Caroline Temple; *m* 30 Jan 1839 John Ashley Warre, MP, and *dsp* 9 April 1886. He *d* 18 Dec 1860

6 Charlotte Maria French; *m* 3 Oct 1849 James Anthony Froude, the historian, and *d* 12 April 1860. He *d* 1894

7 Frances Eliza; *m* 7 Jan 1844 Rev Charles Kingsley, Rector Eversley, the writer and Christian socialist, Chaplain to HM QUEEN VICTORIA, and *d* 12 Dec 1891. He *d* 1875

PASCOE GRENFELL's 3rd s (but est by 2nd w),

PASCOE ST LEGER GRENFELL, of Maesteg House, Swansea, Glam, JP, DL; *b* 5 Nov 1798; *m* 1st 15 Oct 1824 Catherine Anne (*d* 20 Jan 1845), dau of James Dupré, MP, of Wilton Park, Bucks, and had, with five daus:

1 Pascoe Du Pré, of Wilton Park; *b* 4 July 1828; *m* 13 May 1858 his cousin Sophia (*d* 19 Aug 1898), dau of V-Adml John Pascoe Grenfell, Brazilian Navy, and *d* 29 Nov 1896, having had:

(1) Pascoe St Leger; *b* 11 June 1861; *k* Matabele War 1896

(2) Cecil Alfred, TD: MP Bodmin Jan-Dec 1910, Lt-Col Bucks Yeo, T/Lt-Col Remount Serv 1917, Boer War 1900 and WW I; *b* 13 Feb 1864; *m* 8 Oct 1898 Lady Lilian Maud Spencer-Churchill (*d* 4 Jan 1951), dau of 8th Duke of Marlborough (*qv*), and *d* 11 Aug 1924, leaving:

1a Iris Consuelo; *b* 7 Oct 1900

2a Daphne Mary; *b* 26 Sept 1901; *d* unm 7 Feb 1969

3a A dau; *b* and *d* 13 Jan 1907

(3) Reginald Du Pré; Lt 17th Lancers; *b* 10 July 1866; *d* unm 10 March 1889

(4) John Pascoe; Lt Col Bucks Yeo TFR, Lt RN, Boer War 1900, WW I; *b* 21 March 1869; *m* 2 Aug 1905 Adeline Octavia (*d* 12 June 1958), dau of Gustavus William Lambart, of Beau Parc, Co Meath (*see* 1970 edn LAMBART Bt), and *d* 6 Oct 1948, leaving issue:

1a Harold Francis Pascoe, DSC; Cdr RN WW II, chm Messina Transvaal Devpt, V-Pres RNLI; *b* 8 Sept 1906; *educ* RNC Dartmouth; *m* 1st 24 July 1937 Miriam Perenna (*d* 31 March 1967), only dau of Thomas Owen, and had:

1b *David Thomas Pascoe; Midshipman RN; *b* 4 Aug 1945; *educ* Eton and RNC Dartmouth

2b Nicholas Pascoe Mariano; *b* 28 March 1950; *educ* Eton; *d* 27 Oct 1971 following an accident

1a (cont.) Cdr Harold Grenfell *m* 2nd 3 Aug 1972 *Mrs Edith Russell-Roberts

2a Cecil John; Cdr RN WW II; *b* 2 Jan 1908; *m* 8 Sept 1939 (*divorce* 1967) Diana Susan (*m* 2nd 1969 Clive Walter Edwin Windsor-Richards) [Mrs Clive Windsor-Richards, Golf Lodge, Steepways, Hindhead, Surrey GU26 6PQ], dau of Stephen Clement Paston-Cooper, of Hambleton Hall, Rutland (*see* COOPER, Bt, of Gadebridge), and *d* 19–, leaving issue:

1b *John Stephen [Lt-Cdr John Grenfell RN, 58 Heath Rd, Petersfield, Hants]; *b* 10 July 1940; *educ* Oakham Sch, HMS *Britannia* and RNC Dartmouth; *m* 19 Aug 1967 *Stephanie Ann (Sophie), dau of Capt James Richard Marigold, RN, AMIEE, and has issue:

1c *James Christopher; *b* 31 Oct 1969

2c *Nicholas Ian; *b* 31 Oct 1969

3c *Alastair Mark; *b* 3 Sept 1974

2b *Richard Francis [Richard Grenfell Esq, Grindlestone Court, Whittinghame Lane, Goosnargh, Lancs PR3 2AU]; *b* 28 July 1944; *educ* Oakham Sch; *m* 19– *Jennifer Hogg

3b *Michael Gerrard; *b* 30 Sept 1947; *educ* Oakham Sch

1b *Sally Angela; *b* 30 Sept 1947; *m* 1980 *Francis Robert Gugen and has issue:

1c *Lucy Francesca; *b* 1981

3a Victor Cyril, DSO, DL (Caithness 1977); Cdr RN (ret 1956) WW II (despatches), FO 1956; *b* 26 Sept 1909; *educ* RNC Dartmouth; *m* 1st 6 Dec 1944 (*divorce* 1958) Mary June Herron, widow of F/O Donald Little, AAF, and dau of Frederick William Herron Weaver; *m* 2nd 4 May 1962 *Jeanette Patricia Mary, only dau of H W May and Mrs S P A Henderson, and by his 1st w had:

1b *Victoria; *b* 20 Feb 1946

1a *Cynthia Maud; *b* 19 Feb 1912

2a *Hersey Constance; *b* 2 Dec 1913; *m* 2 Aug 1947 John Eaton Nevill Russell (*d* 15 July 1970), yr s of Maj Leonard Russell, of Gravesend, and has:

1b *Harold John; *b* 6 Jan 1950; *m* 16 Oct 1971 *Hilda Matar

(5) Harold Maxwell, CMG, MVO; Col and Hon Brig-Gen 3rd Dragoon Gds, 1st Life Gds, and 17th Lancers, Bde Cdr 1916, served Egypt 1898, Boer War 1899–1902, WW I; *b* 17 Aug 1870; *m* 1st 28 May 1906 Lady Muriel Frances Mary Parsons (*d* 10 April 1927), only dau of 4th Earl of Rosse (*qv*); *m* 2nd 30 April 1928 Elizabeth (*d* 30 April 1947), widow of John Sheilds Crawford, of Melton Mowbray, and dau of Alexander Walker, of Troon, Ayrshire, and *d* 26 April 1929, having by his 1st w had:

1a Elizabeth Mary; *b* 10 May 1908; *m* 1st 12 March 1929 (*divorce* 1938) Philip Tyson-Woodcock, only s of Rev Edward Tyson-Woodcock, Rector Ozleworth, and had a dau; *m* 2nd 27 Sept 1938 John Davies, s of E E Davies, and by him had:

1b *Julian David Grenfell; *b* 17 April 1942; *educ* Repton, RAC Cirencester; *m* 19 Aug 1964 *Valerie Joan Cosnett, of Johannesburg, and has:

1c *Christine Michelle; *b* 2 July 1966

2c *Jacqueline Anne; *b* 2 Oct 1967

2a *Joan Sophie; *b* 9 July 1912; *m* 1st 25 Sept 1935 Maj Douglas James Bailey, Roy Fus, est s of Lt-Col Frederick George Glyn Bailey, RA (*see* INCHCAPE, E), and has issue; *m* 2nd 29 April 1950 *Capt John de Moraville, MC, s of John de Moraville, and has further issue

3a *Cassandra Lorna; *b* 8 June 1915

(6) Arthur Morton DSO (1916), TD; Col Roy Bucks Hus WW I, 9th Lancers, RAG (wounded twice, despatches three times); *b* 21 Oct 1873; *educ* Eton; *m* 1st 23 July 1901 Lady Victoria Sybil Mary Grey (*d* 3 Feb 1907), dau of 4th Earl Grey (*qv*), and had issue:

1a Reginald Pascoe; Lt-Col KRRC; *b* 1 Nov 1903; *m* 12 Dec 1929 Joyce Irene, OBE (Joyce Grenfell the comedienne), dau of Paul Phipps

2a Harry St Leger, OBE (1955), MC; Lt-Col RA (TA), OStJ; *b* 19 Aug 1905; *educ* Eton and New Coll Oxford

1a Sybil Vera, CBE (1961), MVO (1945), Ldy-in-Waiting to HRH PRINCESS ALICE COUNTESS OF ATHLONE 1943–45, Chm Nat Assoc Mixed Clubs and Girls' Clubs 1949–60, V-Pres Nat Assoc Youth Clubs, Sec Northcote Children's Emigration Fund Australia; *b* 21 July 1902

(6) (cont.) Arthur Grenfell *m* 2nd 23 Feb 1909 Hilda Margaret, OBE (*d* 10 June 1972), 2nd dau of Gen Sir Neville Gerald Lyttelton, GCB, PC (*see* COBHAM, V), and *d* 24 Nov 1958, having by her had:

2a Mary Hermione; *b* 25 Dec 1909; *m* 22 Oct 1930 12th Earl Waldegrave (*qv*) and had issue

3a *Katherine Florita [Mrs Patrick Lort-Phillips, Rosehill, Lawrenny, Kilgetty, Dyfed]; *b* 29 May 1912; *m* 1st 18 April 1934 Pascoe Anthony George Glyn, Gren Gds, 4th s of Maurice George Carr Glyn, and has issue (*see* WOLVERTON B); *m* 2nd 23 Sept 1936 Lt-Col Patrick Lort-Phillips, DSO and bar, DL, FRGS, Gren Gds (*d* 1979), only s of Thomas Herbert Shoubridge, CB, CMG, DSO, and has further issue

4a *Frances Olivia, DCVO (1990, CVO 1977) [Dame Frances Campbell-Preston DCVO, The Turret Cottage, Inverawe, Taynuilt, Argyll PA35 1HU]; Woman Bedchamber to HM QUEEN ELIZABETH THE QUEEN MOTHER 1965–, WRNS WW II, memb Argyll CC 1960–64, chm Children's Panel Argyle and Argyll and Bute 1970–80; *b* 2 Sept 1918; *educ* St Paul's; *m* 2 Dec 1938 Lt-Col (George) Patrick Campbell-Preston, MBE, The Black Watch, 2nd s of Col Robert William Piggott Clarke Campbell Preston, JP, DL, of Ardchattan Connel, Argyl, and has issue. He *d* 14 March 1960

5a Laura Margaret; *b* 14 April 1920; *m* 22 Nov 1950 Baron Ballantrae (*see* FERGUSSON, Bt) and *d* 1979, leaving issue

(7) Robert Septimus; Lt 12 Lancers; *b* 16 Aug 1875; *ka* Omdurman 4 Sept 1898

(8) Francis Octavius, VC; Capt 9th Lancers Boer War 1902 and WW I (wounded, despatches); *b* 4 Sept 1880; *ka* 24 May 1915

(9) Riversdale Nonus; Capt Bucks Yeo; *b* 4 Sept 1880; *ka* France 14 Sept 1914

(1) Maria Dolores; *d* unm 5 May 1956 aged 96

(2) Maraquita Masini; *m* 10 Oct 1889 John George Bulteel, of Pamflete, Devon, and *d* 3 Oct 1895, leaving issue. He *d* 8 May 1920

(3) Juanita Gertrude; *m* 21 July 1887 Lionel Bulteel, 3rd s of John Bulteel, of Pamflete, and *d* 4 Dec 1953, leaving issue. He *d* 26 March 1954

(4) Florita Catherine; *m* 4 July 1899 Col Guy Stewart St Aubyn (*see* SAINT LEVAN, B), and *d* 7 Sept 1925. He *d* 25 April 1924

2 St Leger Murray; *b* 1830; *m* 7 Feb 1853 Georgiana Currie Wilson (*d* 16 Oct 1898), dau of Col W Campbell, and *d* 22 Feb 1860, leaving two daus

3 Arthur Riversdale, of Butler's Court, Beaconsfield, JP; *b* 12 Sept 1831; *d* unm 1 Nov 1895

4 FRANCIS WALLACE, **1st Baron**

PASCOE ST LEGER GRENFELL *m* 2nd 20 Sept 1847 Penelope Frances (*dsp* 8 Jan 1868), dau of Rev Dr Spencer Madan, Chllr Peterborough, and *d* 28 March 1879

The 4th son,

FRANCIS WALLACE GRENFELL, **1st Baron Grenfell**, of Kilvey, Co Glamorgan (UK), so *cr* 19 July 1902, GCB (1898), GCMG (1892, KCB 1886, CB 1885), PC (I 1904); *b* 29 April 1841; 60th Rifles 1859, expdn to Griqualand W 1875, Kaffir War 1878, Zulu War 1879, QMG Transvaal 1881–82, Col 1882, ADC to HM QUEEN VICTORIA 1882–89, Egyptian Expdn 1882, Nile Campaign 1884, Sirdar Egyptian Army 1885–92, Maj-Gen 1889, cmded forces Suakim and Toski 1889, Inspr-Gen: Aux Forces War Office 1894–97 and Recruiting 1896, cmded Egypt Khartoum Expdn 1897–98, Govr and C-in-C Malta 1899–1903, cmded 4th Army Corps 1903–04, C-in-C Ireland 1904–08, Gen 1904, FM 1908, Col Cmdt KRRC, Hon Col King's Own Malta Regt, Col 1st Life Gds, LLD Cantab, DCL Edin, Freeman City London; *m* 1st 26 May 1887 Evelyn (*dsp* 21 June 1899), dau of General Robert Blucher Wood, CB; *m* 2nd 8 Aug 1903 Margaret Aline, Maid Honour to HM QUEEN VICTORIA (*d* 24 Aug 1911), only dau of Lewis Ashhunt Majendie, MP, of Castle Hedingham, Essex, and by her had:

1 PASCOE CHRISTIAN VICTOR FRANCIS, **2nd Baron**

2 Arthur Bernard John; Maj 10th Hus WW II; *b* 24 June 1908; *m* 18 Sept 1933 *Eleanor Dorothy Alice [Mrs Brian Malyon, Chapmansford, Hurstbourne Priors, Hants GR28 7RR] (*m* 2nd 20 March 1944 Capt Brian Herbert Malyon, 10th Hus), only dau of Hon Sir John Francis William James, of Saltash, Cornwall, and was *ka* Middle East 23 Jan 1942, leaving issue:

(1) +FRANCIS PASCOE JOHN [Francis Grenfell Esq, Lenton House, Lenton, Grantham, Lincs NG33 4HB]; *b* 28 Feb 1938; heir presumptive; *educ* Eton and Ch Ch Oxford; *m* 31 Dec 1977 *Elizabeth (Liza) Katharine, dau of Hugh Kenyon (*see* THOMPSON, Bt, of Park Gate)

(2) John St Leger; Cheshire Yeo; *b* 26 May 1940; *m* 24 April 1965 *Pauline Mary, SRN [Mrs John Grenfell, Cwm Merwydd, Horeb, Llandyssul, Dyfed SA44 4J2], dau of Tom Westmorland Edward Walton, and *d* 6 Sept 1995, leaving:

1a +Richard Arthur St Leger; *b* 4 Nov 1966

2a +Julian Francis; *b* 4 Feb 1971

1a *Sarah Marion; *b* 18 Dec 1968

2a *Sophie Elizabeth; *b* 27 March 1975

(1) *Margaret [Mrs Simon Smail, Melcombe Newton Farm, Melcombe Bingham, Dorset]; *b* 30 May 1935; *m* 28 May 1960 *Simon Trevor Smail (*see* HEATHCOAT-AMORY, Bt) and has issue:

1a *Thomas Patrick; *b* 14 Aug 1964

1a *Lucy Jane; *b* 4 Aug 1962

1 Madelina Victoria Margaret;*b* 1 Oct 1904; *m* 8 Dec 1937 Archibald Julian Lucas, 2nd s of William Louis Lucas, and has issue. He *d* 23 Sept 1946

The 1st BARON *d* 27 Jan 1925; his est son,

PASCOE CHRISTIAN VICTOR FRANCIS GRENFELL, **2nd Baron Grenfell**, CBE (1974), TD (1951); *b* 12 Dec 1905; *educ* Eton; Lt-Col KRRC WW II (despatches), Hon Col 8th Bn Herts and Cambridge Mobile Def Corps 1956–59 (ret as Col), US Legn Merit, Dep Speaker Ho Lds; *m* 1st 25 July 1932 (*divorce* 1946) Elizabeth Sarah Polk [Mrs Derek Lawson, 78 Melton Court, Old Brompton Rd, London SW7 3JH] (*m* 2nd 1946 Maj Berkeley Buckingham Howard Stafford, KRRC (*d* 1966); *m* 3rd 1969 (*divorce* 1976) Trevor Walton King; *m* 4th 1983 Cdr (Arnold) Derek Arthur Lawson, of Passenham Manor, Stony Stratford, Bucks, who *d* 1984), only dau of Capt Hon Alfred Shaughnessy (*see* SHAUGHNESSY, B, and Section Polk AMERICAN PRESIDENTIAL FAMILIES, 1994, Morris Genealogical Books SA), and had:

1 JULIAN PASCOE FRANCIS ST LEGER GRENFELL, **3rd and present Baron Grenfell**

1 *Caroline Sarah Aline [The Hon Mrs Mieczkowski, Rose Cottage, Henley Park, Henley-on-Thames, Oxon RG9 6HY]; *b* 28 July 1933; *m* 26 July 1965

*Zbyszek Leon Mieczkowski, only s of Stefan Mieczkowski de Zagloba vel Zagroba, of Dzierzanowo, Poland, and has issue:

(1) *Stefan Pascoe St Leger; *b* 23 March 1967; *m* 29 March 1996 *Jocelyn, er dau of Arthur Kee, of Stranorlar, Co Donegal, Ireland

(1) *Helena Elizabeth Caroline; *b* 26 March 1970

The **2nd Baron** *m* 2nd 23 Jan 1946 Irene Lilian (*d* 1993), er dau of Harry Augustus George Cartwright, of Buenos Aires, and *d* 24 Sept 1976, having by her had issue:

2 Jane; *b* 28 Oct 1946; *d* 27 Feb 1947

3 *Aline Mary; *b* 17 Feb 1950

GRETTON

Arms: Quarterly, per fess indented or and gu., in the second quarter an anchor in bend sinister of the first, in the third an antique lamp also or, fired ppr. **Crest:** An arm embowed ppr., vested above the elbow arg., holding in the hand a torch erect fired, a sickle in bend sinister, both also ppr. **Supporters:** Dexter, a bull sa.; sinister, a chestnut horse ppr., each gorged with a chain, pendant therefrom an anchor or. **Motto:** Steadfast. **Creation:** B. (UK) 27 Jan 1944.

THE 4TH BARON GRETTON, of Stapleford, Co Leicester (John Lysander Gretton) [The Rt Hon The Lord Gretton, Somerby House, Somerby, Leics LE14 2PZ]; *b* 17 April 1975; *s* f 1989; *educ* Shrewsbury and RAC Cirencester

Lineage: JOHN GRETTON, of Bladon House, Burton-on-Trent; *b* 1793, *m* July 1832 Mary Sutton and *d* 30 Dec 1867, leaving:

JOHN GRETTON, of Stapleforth Park (bought 1894 from James Hornsby), Leics, DL; *b* 27 April 1836; *educ* Appleby Magna and UCL; *m* 27 June 1866 Marianne Louisa (*d* 5 Jan 1891), dau of Maj John Richard Molineux, of Brook House, Compton, Surrey, and *d* 2 Oct 1899, leaving issue:

1 JOHN, **1st Baron**

2 Hugh Frederick, of Donington Hall, Leics; Maj Derbys Yeo; *b* 12 May 1869; *d* 19 July 1928

3 Rupert Harold; Capt Beds Regt; *b* 8 Nov 1886; *educ* Marlborough; *ka* Ypres 18 Dec 1915

1 Katherine Louisa; *m* 8 Oct 1903 Sir John Montagu Burgoyne, 10th and last Bt, of Sutton Park, and *dsp* 26 Nov 1938. He *d* 19 March 1921 (*see* 1921 edn)

2 Alice; *d* July 1892

3 Ethel Mary; *m* 15 Feb 1906 Capt A J Campbell, DSO, and *d* Sept 1932

4 Christine Rose; *d* 22 Nov 1966

5 Muriel Elise; *d* May 1962

The est son,

JOHN GRETTON, **1st Baron Gretton**, of Stapleford, Co Leicester (UK), so *cr* 27 Jan 1944, CBE (1919), VD, TD, PC (1926), JP, DL Leics, Derbys; *b* 1 Sept 1867; *educ* Harrow; chm Bass, Ratcliff and Gretton, Burton-on-Trent brewers, 1908–45, Lt-Col and Hon Col (1907) 6th Bn N Staffs Regt, T/Lt-Col 1914, Lt-Col Res Offrs 1920–22, MP (C) Derby S 1895–1906, Rutland 1907–18 and Burton 1918–43 OStJ; *m* 19 April 1900 Hon Maud Helen Eveleigh-de-Moleyns (*d* 29 July 1934), 4th dau of 4th Baron Ventry (*qv*), and had issue:

1 JOHN FREDERIC, **2nd Baron**

1 Kathleen Fanny; *m* 9 April 1929 Brig Sir Henry Robert Kincaid Floyd, 5th Bt (*qv*), and *d* 3 May 1976, leaving issue

2 Mary Catherine Hersey; *m* 19 July 1933 Capt Edward William Brook, 20th Hus, only s of Lt-Col Charles Brook, of Meltham Mills, Yorks, and Kinmount House, Dumfries, and *d* 6 Feb 1972, having had issue. He *d* 20 Jan 1963

The 1st BARON *d* 2 June 1947; his only son,

JOHN FREDERIC GRETTON, **2nd Baron Gretton**, OBE (1950); *b* 15 Aug 1902; *educ* Eton; MP (C) Burton 1943–45, dir Bass, Mitchells & Butlers, Bass Ratcliff & Gretton and Worthington & Co (ret 1967); *m* 6 May 1930 *(Anna Helena) Margaret, JP (1943) Staffs [The Rt Hon Margaret Lady Gretton JP, The Old Rectory, Ufford, Lincs], er dau of Capt Henrik Loeffler, of 51 Grosvenor Square, London W1, and *d* 26 March 1982, having had issue:

1 JOHN HENRIK GRETTON, **3rd Baron Gretton**; *b* 9 Feb 1941; *educ* Shrewsbury; farmer; *m* 17 Oct 1970 *Jennifer Ann [The Rt Hon The Lady Gretton, Holygate Farm, Stapleford, Leics LE14 2XQ], only dau of Edmund Moore, of York, and *d* 1989, leaving issue:

(1) JOHN LYSANDER GRETTON, **4th and present Baron Gretton**

(1) *Sarah Margaret; *b* 7 Dec 1971

2 Anthony David Erik; *b* 25 July 1945; *educ* Eton and Hammersmith Coll of Art and Building; *d* unm 13 Nov 1982

1 *Mary Ann Maud Sigrid [The Hon Mrs Wragg, Manor House, Stapleford, Leics]; *b* 5 Jan 1939; breeder and judge Arab horses; *m* 1986 *Thomas Henry Wragg, s of T L Wragg, of Hinckley, Leics

2 *Elizabeth Margaret [The Hon Mrs Meynell, Bergh Apton Hall, Norwich, Norfolk]; *b* 25 July 1945; *m* 12 Oct 1968 *Christopher Mark Meynell (*see* HALIFAX, E) and has issue

GREY, Earl

Arms: Gu. a lion rampant within a bordure engrailed arg., in dexter chief point a mullet or. **Crest:** A scaling ladder or, hooked and pointed sa. **Supporters:** Dexter, a lion guardant purpure, ducally crowned or; sinister, a tiger guardant ppr. **Motto:** *De bon vouloir servir le roy* ('To serve the king with good will'). **Creations:** Bt. (GB) 11 Jan 1745/6, B. (UK) 23 June 1801, E. and V. (UK) 11 April 1806.

THE 6TH EARL GREY, Viscount Howick, Co Northumberland, **Baron Grey of Howick**, Co Northumberland, and a **Baronet** (Sir Richard Fleming George Charles Grey, Bt) [The Rt Hon The Earl Grey, House of Lords, London SW1A 0PW]; *b* 4 March 1939; *s* cousin 1963; *educ* Hounslow Coll and Hammersmith Coll of Building; *m* 1st 1966 (*divorce* 1974) Margaret Ann, est dau of Henry G Bradford, of Ashburton, Devon; *m* 2nd 17 Aug 1974 *Stephanie Caroline, formerly w of Surgn-Cdr Neil Leicester Denham, RN, and only dau of Donald Gaskell-Brown, of Newton-Ferrers, Devon

Lineage: Sir THOMAS de GREY, of Heton in Islandshire, Northumberland; *m* Agnes — and *d* just prior to 12 March 1343/4, leaving:

Sir THOMAS GREY; author: *Scalacronica*; *m* Margaret, dau of William de Pressene, of Presson, Northumberland, and *d* just prior to 22 Oct 1369, leaving:

Sir THOMAS GREY, of Berwick and Chillingham; *b c* 1359; *m* Jane or Joan, dau of 1st Duke of Norfolk of the 1397 *cr* (*see* MOWBRAY, SEGRAVE and STOURTON, B), and *d* late 1400, leaving, with an est s (Thomas, beheaded 1415 for treason):

1 Sir JOHN GREY, *cr* COUNT OF TANCARVILLE/TANQUERVILLE/TANKERVILLE 31 Jan 1418/9 by HENRY V (one of a number of such titles bestowed by HENRYs V and VI on predominantly English subjects but with French placenames and fiefs as part of a policy of planting a loyal nobility in English-occupied France towards the last phase of the Hundred Years War), KG (1418), of Heton and Wark-on-Tweed; *b* after 1384; fought Battle of Agincourt 1415, Capt Mortagne Oct 1417, granted castle and seigneurie of Tilly by HENRY V Nov 1417; *m* Joan, er dau of Sir Edward Cherleton, and was *ka* Battle of Beaugé, 22 March 1420/1, leaving:

(1) HENRY GRAY, 2nd and last of the Anglo-French COUNTs OF TANCARVILLE; *b c* autumn 1418; ktd 1426; *m* Antigone, illegitimate dau of Humphrey, Duke of Gloucester (yst s of HENRY IV), and *d* 13 Jan 1449/50, about which time Tancarville was recovered by the French anyway

2 THOMAS (Sir)

3 William, Dean York, Bp London 1426 and Lincoln 1431

4 Henry (Sir), of Ketteringham, Norfolk

1 Matilda; *m* Sir Robert Ogle

The 2nd son,

Sir THOMAS GREY, of Werke; *m* Lady Alice Nevill(e), dau of 1st Earl of Westmorland of the 1397 *cr* (*see* ABERGAVENNY, M), and had, with other issue:

Sir RALPH GREY; *m* Elizabeth, dau of Henry, Lord (Baron) Fitzhugh, and was ggf of:

Sir RALPH GREY, of Chillingham; *m* Isabel, dau and coheir of Sir Thomas Grey, of Horton, Northumberland, and had issue:

1 Thomas (Sir); *dsp* 1590

2 Ralph (Sir); *m* Anne, dau of William Ardington, of Ardington, and had an est s:

(1) Sir WILLIAM GREY, 1st Bt, so *cr* 1619 and 11 Feb 1623/4 BARON GREY OF WARKE, Co Northumberland (both E), both titles expiring with the 4th Baron 1706

3 EDWARD (Sir), of whom presently

4 Henry, of Newminster Abbey, Northumberland; *m* Mary, dau of John Widdrington, of Widdrington, and left issue:

(1) Isabel; *m* 1612 John Pemberton, of Aislaby, Co Durham

The 3rd son,

Sir EDWARD GREY, of Howick, Northumberland; *m* Catherine, dau of Roger le Strange, of Hunstanton, Norfolk, and *d* 1632, leaving issue:

PHILIP GREY; *m* — Westwood, of Westwood, Northumberland, and had:

EDWARD GREY, of Howick; *m* — , dau of Martin Fenwick, of Kenton, and *d* 1653, leaving:

1 Philip, of Howick

2 John, of Acton, Northumberland; *m* Dorothy Lisle, of Acton, Northumberland, and had:

(1) JOHN

(1) Margaret; *m* Charles Brandling

(2) Susan; *m* — Bell

(3) Dorothy; *m* Robert Ogle

(4) Mary; *m* George Tawrey

3 Edward; *d* unm

4 Martin, of Overgrass, parish of Felton; *m* Elizabeth — and left issue

EDWARD GREY's gs,

JOHN GREY, of Howick; *m* — Pearson and had:

1 HENRY (Sir), **1st Bt**

2 Thomas; *d* unm

3 John, of Morwick, Northumberland; *m* Anne, dau of Edward Grey, of Aynwick, and had, with other issue:

(1) Charles, of Morwick; *m* Katherine, dau of Rev John Skelley by Lady Betty Gordon (*see* HUNTLY, M), and *d* 1814, leaving issue:

1a John (Sir), KCB, of Morwick; Maj-Gen; *m* 1830 Rosa Josefa Louisa, dau of Capt Henry Evelyn Sturt, and *d* 19 Feb 1856

The est son,

Sir Henry Grey, 1st Bt (GB), so *cr* 11 Jan 1745/6, of Howick; High Sheriff Northumberland 1736; *bapt* 4 Dec 1691; *m* 19 April 1720 Hannah (*bur* 19 July 1764), dau of Thomas Wood, of Falloden, Northumberland, and had, with other issue:

1 **Sir Henry Grey, 2nd Bt**; MP Northumberland 1754–68; *bapt* 15 Nov 1722; *d* unm 30 March 1808

2 Thomas; *k* in a duel with Lord Pomfret (*see* HESKETH, B)

3 CHARLES, **1st Earl**

Sir HENRY was *bur* 6 May 1749; his 3rd son,

Sir Charles Grey, 3rd Bt, and **1st Earl Grey**, so *cr* 11 April 1806, as also VISCOUNT HOWICK, Co Northumberland, and earlier 23 June 1801 BARON GREY OF HOWICK, Co Northumberland, KB (1783), PC (1797); *b* 23 Oct 1729; Maj-Gen 1777, Lt-Gen 1782, Gen 1796; *m* 8 June 1762 Elizabeth (*d* 26 May 1822), dau of George Grey, of Southwick, and had issue:

1 CHARLES, **2nd Earl**

2 Henry George (Sir), GCB, GCH; Gen, Col 13th Light Dragoons; *b* 25 Oct 1766; *m* 20 Aug 1812 Charlotte (*d* 12 Feb 1882 aged 93), only dau of Sir Charles des Voeux, Bt (*see* 1940 edn), and *d* 11 Jan 1845

3 Sir GEORGE GREY, 1st Bt, of Fallodon (*qv*)

4 William; Lt-Col; *b* 20 Oct 1777; *m* Maria (*d* 4 Aug 1857), dau of Gen William Shirreff, and *d* 10 Aug 1817, leaving issue:

(1) William Thomas; *b* 22 April 1807; *m* 7 Jan 1841 Maria Georgiana (*d* 19 Sept 1906), 2nd dau of Adml William Henry Shirreff, RN, and *dsp* 13 March 1864

(2) Charles Conrad; Capt RN; *b* 2 Jan 1817; *m* 23 April 1844 Caroline Nesbit (*d* 11 Oct 1854), est dau of Maj Turner Macan, of Carriff, Co Armagh, and *d* 29 May 1848, leaving:

1a Edward Codrington William; MA Oxon, barrister; *b* 21 Feb 1845; *d* unm 6 Aug 1905

1a Maria; *m* 18 Aug 1870 12th Earl of Home (*qv*) and *d* 25 May 1919, leaving issue

(1) Maria Susannah; *d* unm 4 Aug 1859

(2) Emily Hannah; *m* 21 Sept 1837 James Duberly (*d* 3 March 1864), of Gaynes Hall, St Neots, Hunts, and *d* 30 March 1883, leaving issue

5 Edward (Rt Rev); Bp Hereford, Preb Westminster; *b* 25 March 1782; *m* 1st 21 March 1809 Charlotte Elizabeth (*d* 26 May 1821), dau of James Croft, of Greenham, Berks, and had:

(1) Edward; Lt RN; *b* 11 June 1810; *d* 24 Aug 1836

(2) Charles; *b* 13 June 1812; *m* 7 April 1838 Sarah, 2nd dau of William Gyde, of Cheltenham, and *d* 1 July 1839, leaving:

1a Charles William; Lt Army; *d* 8 Dec 1860 aged 21

(3) Leopold James Henry; Bengal CS; *b* 28 Jan 1816; *m* 1st 29 July 1839 Wilhelminia Emily (*d* 19 Jan 1842), dau of Mathew Law; *m* 2nd 14 Nov 1842 Emily Maria (*d* 15 Jan 1866), dau of Lt-Col William R C Costley, and *d* 10 Aug 1845, having by his 1st w had issue:

1a Leopold John Herbert, CSI (1877); Col IA, served Indian Mutiny and Bhutan Expdn; *b* 1 July 1840; *m* 12 May 1864 Josephine Catherine (*d* 16 Aug 1915), dau of Gen H C Van Cortlandt, CB, and *d* 1921, having had:

1b Frederick William; *b* 7 April 1873; *m* 1st 1892 Agnes Annie (*d* 1917), dau of Peter Gow, MP, Sheriff of Wellington, Ontario, Canada, and had:

1c Frederick Arthur Herbert; *b* 1895; *m* 1919 Adelaide Suchan (*d* 1949), and *d* 1973, leaving issue:

1d +Frederick [Frederick Grey, 1826 Peninsula Verde Drive, Lomita, CA 90717, USA]; *b* 1921

1d +Beverley [Mrs Lou Kennedy, 8100 Bleriot St, Los Angeles, CA 900045, USA]; *b* 1924; *m* 19– *Lou Kennedy

2c Charles Cecil; *b* 1898; *m* 1922 *Ruth, only dau of Blandry Jack Huston, and *d* 8 Sept 1965

3c +Robert Maxwell; *b* 1903; *m* 1929 *May Dawn, dau of Joseph George Washington Brand, and has issue:

1d *Barbara Anne; *b* 25 Dec 1934; *m* 25 Feb 1951 (*divorce* 1963) Truman Derwood Anderson, s of John Washington Anderson, of Dumas, Texas, and has issue:

1e *Truman Derwood, Jr; *b* 21 Nov 1951

1e *Elizabeth Ann; *b* 22 Oct 1953

2e *Rebecca Anne; *b* 8 Oct 1956

2d *Jane Ellen [Mrs Harold Whitney, 609 South 12th Street, Nederland, Texas, USA]; *b* 19 Feb 1940; *m* 26 Feb 1959 *Harold Caleb Whitney, Jr, s of Harold Caleb Whitney, of Kittery, Maine, and has:

1e *Robert Maxwell; *b* 25 Sept 1962

1e *Katherine Marie; *b* 26 Jan 1961

3d *Joyce Elaine; *b* 19 Feb 1940; *m* 29 Dec 1962 *Charles Frederick Theriot, USAF, and has issue:

1e *Charles Frederick, Jr; *b* 27 Sept 1970

1e *Angelique Elaine; *b* 11 Oct 1963

4c Leopold John; *b* 1905; *m* 1920 *Ruth Aleen, dau of Charles Christian Elmiger, and *d* 4 April 1968, leaving issue:

1d +Ronald John [Ronald Grey, 23652 Lagarto St, Mission Viejo, CA92691, USA]; US Army Korean War 1951–53; *b* 1930; *educ* U of S California (BE 1957); *m* 11 June 1954 *Nell Hope, dau of John Fletcher Adams, of Port Charlotte, Florida, USA, and has issue:

1e +Kenneth Alan; *b* 1962

1e *Julia Lynn; *b* 30 Aug 1959; *m* 1983 *Douglas Harlow, of Austin, Texas

2d +Joel Edward; late 257th US Army Res Med Corps; *b* 21 Oct 1944; *educ* U of California (BS 1966, MPH 1969); *m* 8 Sept 1968 *Kathryn Lee, dau of Paul Fralic, of Van Nuys, California, and has issue:

1e +Adam Brady; *b* 1973

1e *Lauren Emily; *b* 1977

5c +Henry James; *b* 1906; *m* 1930 *Alice Mary, dau of Alphonse Joseph Samson, and has issue:

1d *Doris Arlene; *b* May 1932; *m* 14 Feb 1952 *Louis Frederick Repucci, s of Louis Frederick Repucci, of Boston, Mass., and has:

1e *Louis Frederick; *b* 20 Dec 1953

1e *Arlene Doris; *b* 8 May 1954.

2d *Harriet Alice; *b* Aug 1940; *m* 17 March 1957 *John Ford, s of Arthur Ford, of Los Angeles, and has:

1e *Kenneth John; *b* 22 Nov 1957

2e *Laurence Robert; *b* 16 Jan 1959

1e *Jill Elaine; *b* 18 June 1960

3d *Janice Carole; *b* 26 Feb 1949

1b (cont.) Frederick Grey *m* 2nd 13 Sept 1919 *Mary Harriet, er dau of Edward Molsaint, of Santa Emilia, San Salvador, and *d* 2 June 1950, leaving:

1c *Mary Catherine; *b* 29 July 1923; *m* 27 Feb 1943 *Capt Archibald Bauer MacDonald, USNR (ret), and has issue:

1d *Bruce Grey; *b* 10 July 1946

2d *James Douglas; *b* 14 July 1948

3d *John Mark; *b* 22 Nov 1950

4d *Craig William; *b* 19 July 1962

1d *Ellen Mary; *b* 7 April 1952

2b Arthur James Herbert; Lt-Col IA (Pol Dept); *b* 26 May 1880 *m* 1st 16 Oct 1911 (*divorce* 1924) Cecile Ruth, dau of François Pogaceniq, Lt Italian Army; *m* 2nd 22 Dec 1925 *Anna [Mrs Clarence Frayn, 125, 8403–142 St, Edmonton, Alberta, Canada] (*m* 4th 16 Sept 1963 Cyril Denzil Branch, barrister (*d* 1976); *m* 5th Jan 1978 Clarence V Frayn, of Edmonton (*d* August 1978)), only dau of Axel Vennerston, Grand Marshal Court of Sweden, of Stockholm, and formerly w of (a) Gosta Otto Rudolf Axelson von Schoultz and (b) Per Hugo Huitfeldt, and *d* 2 Sept 1960, having by her had:

1c +Axel Robert Henry (Rev); *b* 30 Jan 1933; *educ* Wellington, St Andrews Coll, S Africa, and St Paul's Theological Coll, Grahamstown, S Africa (LTh 1958); *m* 14 Dec 1954 *Zenith Catherine, dau of James Gallagher, of Gwelo, Rhodesia, and has issue:

1d +Paul; *b* 28 April 1958; *m* 1978 *Bernadine Veronica, dau of Ralph George Seewalt

1b Nina Emily Katherine; *m* 15 Aug 1891 Capt Maidion Byron Bicknell, RA, and *d* 22 Dec 1891

2b Wilhelmina Katherine; *m* 16 June 1894 Maj Robert Cecil Harbottle, 18th Hus, and *d* 8 Dec 1894

3b Gertrude Sybil; *m* 29 July 1895 Capt A H Barclay, 18th Hus, and *d* 25 Aug 1902, having had issue

4b Lillian Muriel, MBE (1919); *m* 29 Sept 1903 Lt-Col John Stirling Rivett-Carnac (*see* RIVETT-CARNAC, Bt) and *dsp* 22 Sept 1955

(4) William (Sir), KCSI; Lt-Govr Bengal, Govr Jamaica; *b* 26 March 1818; *m* 1st 8 July 1845 Margaret Hungerford (*d* 13 Nov 1862), dau of Welby Jackson, and had issue:

1a Leopold James Henry; Lt-Col Bengal, SC; *b* 6 Jan 1847; *m* 10 June 1871 Clara (*d* 1 June 1879), dau of Maj-Gen George Vener, and *d* 5 July 1891, leaving issue:

1b *Clare; *m* 1 May 1909 Lt-Col John Arthur Claude Kreyer, DSO, 28th Light Cav, IA (*d* 19 Sept 1950), and had issue

2a William Francis Hungerford; Lt-Col IA; *b* 18 Feb 1849; *m* 31 Dec 1879 Isabella Harriett (*d* 1922), dau of A A Swinton, BCS, and *d* 14 March 1929, leaving issue:

1b William Archibald Swinton; Capt 33rd Punjabis, IA, Assist Commr Burma; *b* 17 July 1883; *m* 29 April 1919 Kathleen Mary (*d* 1949), yst dau of William Paulson, LRCP, of Mountsorrel, Leics, and *d* 17 June 1942, leaving issue:

1c +William Ronald [William Grey, Salisbury Cottage, 13 Robinson Rd, Kenilworth, Cape Town, S Africa]; *b* 14 Nov 1920; *m* 6 Nov 1945 *Florence Margaret, dau of John Martin, and has issue:

1d +David Swinton [David Grey, 6 Cyprian Court, Sophia St, Orangezicht, Cape Town, S Africa]; *b* 27 July 1946; *m* 1975 *Joy Bowen and has:

1e +Alistair James Egbert; *b* 1978

1d *Margaret Ann [Mrs Alan Stewart, 122 Ladies Mile Rd, Bergvliet 7800, S Africa]; *b* 1949; *m* 19– *Alan Stewart

2d *Jennifer Frances; *b* 1951; *m* 19– (*divorce* 19–) Simon Sutton and has:

1d *Warrick; *b* 19–

1c *Lillian Mary; *m* 11 Jan 1921 Francis Ashburner Richards, s of Francis Gardiner Richards, of the Cove, Boston, USA

3a Arthur Elphinstone; *b* 4 Feb 1854; *d* unm

1a Caroline Charlotte; *m* 9 March 1869 Maj-Gen Henry Hamer Stanfeld, Bengal Army, and had issue

(4) (cont.) Sir William *m* 2nd 26 Jan 1865 Georgina Chicheley (*d* 9 Dec 1936), dau of T C Plowden, and *d* 15 May 1878, having by her had issue:

4a Charles (Robin) Jocelyn Eden, DSO (1919); Capt and Brevet Maj Gren Gds and RAF WW I (Legn Hon); *b* 28 June 1872; *d* 15 May 1921

5a Trevor Spencer; *b* 28 April 1877; *d* unm 31 Jan 1907

2a Sybil Frances, OBE (1920); DGStJ; *m* 20 July 1886 Sir William Eden, 7th Bt (*see* EDEN OF WINTON, B), and *d* 17 June 1945, leaving issue

3a Dorothy Evelyn; *m* 5 Aug 1909 2nd Viscount Selby (*qv*) and *d* 22 July 1951, leaving issue

(1) Elizabeth; *m* 18 Aug 1836 Rev Henry William Maddock, Vicar Kington, Herefs, and *d* 10 Feb 1895, leaving issue

(2) Charlotte; *m* 7 May 1840 Andrew Wilson (*d* 23 Oct 1868) and *d* 18 Sept 1890, leaving issue

(3) Mary; *m* 10 Sept 1839 Maj W Alexander (*see* CABLE- ALEXANDER, Bt) and *d* 2 Sept 1897

(4) Harriet; *m* 17 Oct 1843 Rev H R Lloyd (*d* 30 Jan 1880) and *d* 7 Aug 1887 aged 68, leaving issue

(5) Hannah Jane; *m* 29 Aug 1861 Rev John Sansom, Rector Buslingthorpe, Lincs (*d* 1885), and had issue

5 (cont.) The Rt Rev Edward Grey *m* 2nd 9 Sept 1824 Elizabeth (*d* 28 Sept 1829), dau of Sir Robert Adair, GCB, and by her had, with other issue:

(5) Francis Douglas; Lt-Col 37th Regt; *b* 11 April 1828; *m* 10 Aug 1854 Sarah (*d* 8 Aug 1901), est dau of Francis Mowatt, MP, and *d* 4 Nov 1901, leaving:

1a Arthur CIE (1910); barrister, Col cmdg Punjab Light Horse; *b* 3 July 1855; *m* 1st 18 Oct 1884 Florence Intaglio (*d* 15 Jan 18–), widow of Thomas Duncan, and yst dau of John Intaglio Donlevy, of New York, and had:

1b Francis Temple; MA Oxon, MB, ChM, MRCP, barrister Lincoln's Inn 1924, Surgn RN; *b* 10 Feb 1886; *m* 17 April 1928 Eglantine (*d* 1989), yst dau of Maj Edward Charles Ellice, DSO, of Invergarry, Inverness-shire, and *d* 23 Jan 1941, leaving:

1c Egerton Francis; Capt Queen's Own Cameron Highrs, Maj TA; *b* 11 May 1930; *educ* St Edward's Oxford and RMA Sandhurst; *m* 1961 *Elizabeth Mary [Mrs Egerton Grey, Garry Cualach, Invergarry, Inverness-shire], yr dau of Peter Blackburn, of Roshvan, Lochailort, Inverness-shire, and *d* 1993, leaving issue:

1d +Simon Temple; *b* 14 Jan 1962

2d +John Egerton; *b* 26 Jan 1966; *m* 1990 *Joanne Mary, dau of William McAskill, of Inverness, and has issue:

1e +Angus John; *b* 1992

1e *Jennifer Ishbel; *b* 1993

1d *Francis May *b* 27 June 1963

2d *Jane Elizabeth Catherine; *b* 25 Nov 1965; *m* 1988 *Peter Gregory Issacson, and has issue:

1e *John Alexander; *b* 1992

1e *Sophie Claire; *b* 1990

2c +Robin Douglas, QC (1979) [Robin Grey Esq QC, Dun Cottage, The Marsh, Hungerford, Berks]; barrister Gray's Inn 1957, Recorder 1979; *b* 23 May 1931; *educ* Eastbourne Coll and King's Coll London (LLB 1954); *m* 1st 12 July 1968 (*divorce* 1972) Gillian, dau of Maj Esme Austin Reeves Porch; *m* 2nd 1972 Berenice Anna Adams, dau of Denis Wheatley; *m* 3rd 1993 *Mrs Annick Regnault, dau of Henri Kerbiriou, and by his 2nd w has:

1d *Louise Katherine; *b* 1973

3c +John Edward [John Grey Esq, Ballachulish House, Argyll, Scotland]; *b* 21 Nov 1932; *educ* Epsom Coll; *m* 1965 *Elizabeth Anne, only dau of Lt-Col- Francis Patrick St Maur Sheil, DSO, and has issue:

1d Patrick John; *b* 28 June 1966; *educ* Keil Sch and Stirling U (BSc); *k* in a climbing accident on Ben Nevis 1993

2d *Seamus Edward; *b* 1971

3d *Ian Michael; *b* 1974

1d *Clare Alexandra; *b* 29 Aug 1967

4c +Alan Arthur [Alan Grey Esq, 12 Hough St, Deane, Bolton, Lancs BL3 4LX]; *b* 4 June 1934; *educ* Epsom Coll and Durham U (BSc); *m* 1966 (*divorce* 1985) Jocelyn Elizabeth, dau of John Anthony Cooper (*see* EDEN OF WINTON, B), and has:

1d *Melanie Jane; *b* 1967

2d *Rebecca Frances; *b* 1968

3d *Iona Marau; *b* 1972

4d *Lorna Johane; *b* 1978

5c +Harry George [Harry Grey Esq, 1 Lantana St, Warrego, nr Tennant Creek, Northern Territory 5760, Australia]; *b* 13 March 1937; *educ* Allhallows Sch

6c Alexander; *b* 9 March 1939; *educ* Eastbourne Coll and Wadham Coll Oxford (MA); *m* 17 Sept 1966 (*divorce* 1992) Eleanor, dau of Leonard White, and *d* 1993, leaving:

1d +Thomas [Thomas Grey Esq, 75 Elms Crescent, London SW4 8QF]; *b* 1972

1d *Anna; *b* 10 Oct 1967

2d *Lucy; *b* 6 May 1969

1c *Elizabeth Adair [Mrs Hermann Fox, 22 Ingrams St, Forest Hill Garden, New York, NY 11375, USA]; *b* 27 March 1929; *educ* Bryn Mawr Coll, Pa. (BA 1950); *m* 19– *Hermann R I Fox and has issue:

1d *Ian Michael

2c *Joane Eglantine [Mrs Michael Whitmore, 78 Sandford Walk, Exeter, Devon EX1 2ET]; *b* 26 Sept 1935; *educ* Edinburgh U (MA 1961); *m* 8 Sept 1956 Michael Mervyn Whitmore, BSc, MRCVS (*d* Dec 1959), and has:

1d *James Temple; *b* June 1958

2d *William Rupert; *b* July 1959; *m* 1984 *Kim Milward and has:

1e *Thomas; *b* 1985

1e *Jerry; *b* 1990

2b Egerton Charles; *bapt* 10 July 1887; *dsp* 10 Aug 1928

1a (cont.) Arthur Grey *m* 2nd 8 Dec 1895 Julia Maria (*dsp* 1900), widow of Col W H Stopford, Indian Staff Corps, and dau of Granado Chester, HEICS; *m* 3rd 10 Aug 1907 Margaret Rosalie Teresa Mary (*d* 5 July 1945), dau of Rev Arthur Osborne Gibbes Alleyne, Rector St Edmund's, Exeter, and *d* 13 Oct 1924, having by her had:

3b Paul Francis (Sir), KCMG (1963, CMG 1951); Dip Serv 1947–68: Counsellor Lisbon 1949, Min Moscow 1951–54, Assist U-Sec FO 1954–57, Amb Prague 1957–60 and Berne 1960–64; *b* 2 Dec 1908; *educ* Charterhouse and Ch Ch Oxford; *m* 27 Oct 1936 *Agnes Mary [Lady Grey, Holmwood House, Elstead, Godalming, Surrey], only dau of Richard Shireburn Weld-Blundell (*see* YARBOROUGH, E), and *d* 1990, leaving:

1c +Nicholas Richard [Dr Nicholas Grey, Ryehurst Farm, Binfield, Bracknell, Berks]; *b* 17 Aug 1937; *educ* Ampleforth and Ch Ch Oxford (DPhil); *m* 25 July 1964 *Mary Cecilia, dau of Frederick Hugh Hughes, of Newcastle, and has issue:

1d +Stephen Hugh Francis; *b* 7 April 1968

2d +Benedict Justin; *b* 1971

1d *Clare Philomena; *b* 17 March 1965

2d *Eleanor Mary Grace; *b* 27 April 1966

2c +Richard Charles Edward [Richard Grey Esq, The Old Farmhouse, Elstead, Surrey]; *b* 17 June 1939; *educ* Ampleforth and Ch Ch Oxford (BA); *m* 18 April 1964 *Hilary Marguerite Térèse, 4th dau of S/Ldr Malcolm Francis Ogilvie Forbes, of Esseborne Manor, Hurstbourne Tarrant, Hants, and has:

1d +Dmitri Malcolm Paul; *b* 23 June 1965

2d +Malcolm Dominic Anthony; *b* 17 April 1967

1d *Eloise Teresa Mary; *b* 20 June 1968

2d *Annabelle Lucy; *b* 23 June 1971

3d *Saskia Bernadette; *b* 1973

3c +Timothy [Timothy Grey Esq, Poundsbridge Manor, Penshurst, Kent]; *b* 2 Oct 1943; *educ* Ampleforth

4b Arthur Christopher; Physician to Imperial College, MRCS, LRCP 1937, Lt-Col RAMC WW II; *b* 30 Aug 1911; *educ* Wellington and BNC Oxford (BA, BM, BCh); *m* 1st 21 Aug 1941 Diana Marjorie (*d* 31 March 1971), 3rd dau of Rupert Sackville Gwynne, JP, MP (*see* RIDLEY, V); *m* 2nd 1973 *Diana, JP [Mrs Edward Roberts, The White House, Bembridge, IoW], High Sheriff IoW 1984 (*m* 3rd 1984, as his 2nd w, Rt Rev Edward James Keymer Roberts, Bp Ely), dau of Ewen Cameron Bruce, DSO, MC, and widow of Anthony Seymour Bellville, and *d* 1982, leaving by his 1st w:

1c +Rupert Christopher [Rupert Grey Esq, Hampshire Farm Cottage, S Harting, Hants]; *b* 8 Sept 1946; *educ* Wellington and UCL (LLB); slr 1976; Roy Humane Soc Vellum Award 1963; *m* 1977 *Audrey, dau of Donald Vaughan Sinclair, MRCVS, of Southwood Hall, Thirsk, Yorks, and has issue:

1d *Katherine Diana; *b* 1981

2d *Carmody Theresa Sinclair; *b* 1983

3d *Rosemary Audrey Sinclair; *b* 1986

2c +Jonathon [Jonathon Grey Esq, Fyning Copse, Rogate, Hants GU31 5DH]; *b* 10 March 1951; *educ* Wellington and Architectural Assoc (AA Dipl 1977); *m* 1978 *Rebecca Hall, dau of Libby Turner, of Australia, and has issue:

1d +Harry; *b* 1984

2d +Felix; *b* 1987

3d +Benedict; *b* 1995

1d *Augusta; *b* 1990

3c +Stephen [Stephen Grey Esq, 7 Cunningham St, Maraville, NSW, Australia]; *b* 27 June 1954; *educ* Wellington and Brunel U (BA)

4c +Edward Christopher [Edward Grey Esq, Love Cottage, 20 Chapel St, Petersfield, Hants GU32 3DZ]; *b* 11 May 1957; *educ* Wellington and Imp Coll London (BSc); *m* 19– *Sonhilde, dau of Chauncey Kelley-Paterson, and has:

1d +Rowan Tagore; *b* 1992

1c Diana Christabel; *b* 19 Dec 1952; *d* unm 1990

5b Martin; WW II with RASC, Maj HQ, BLA (despatches twice), slr 1936, Commr for Oaths 1946; *b* 3 April 1913; *educ* Wellington; *m* 12 Oct 1943 *Wendy Ursula [Mrs Martin Grey, East End House, Ditchling, Sussex], dau of Charles Creasy Wray, and *d* 1975, leaving issue:

1c +David Anthony [David Grey Esq, East End Cottage, Ditchling, Sussex]; *b* 23 Dec 1946; *educ* Allhallows Sch and Brighton Coll of Architecture; Chartered Accountant; Dip Arch; *m* 1975 *Pamela Joan, dau of John George Baxter, and has issue:

1d +Thomas Charles; *b* 1979; *educ* Ardingly

2d +Charles Edward; *b* 1981

1c *Priscilla Jane; *b* 29 Dec 1949; *m* 1974 *David John Dyer Lewis

6b +Douglas OBE (1961); joined Imperial Airways 1933, subsequently BOAC, Dep Traffic and Sales Dir BEA; *b* 13 March 1915; *educ* Wellington and abroad; *m* 1st 19 Sept 1935 (*divorce* 1945) Elinor Violet, dau of Col D'Arcy Hemsworth Kay, DSO; *m* 2nd 21 Jan 1950 *Emelainne Clementine, only dau of Hector Leon Marie van Coppenolle, of Ghent

1b Diana Mary; *b* 4 Feb 1910; *m* 29 July 1937 Maj Uvedale Henry Hoare Lambert, of South Park, Bletchingley, Surrey, only s of Alfred Uvedale Miller Lambert, JP, of South Park, and was *k* by enemy action 29 July 1944, leaving issue

2a Douglas Charles Campbell; Chf Engr Bd Works Ireland; *b* 1 Feb 1861; *m* 16 June 1886 Alice Mary Fawconer (*d* 4 April 1930), dau of Thomas D Galpin, of Bristol House, Roehampton, and *d* 23 Dec 1912, leaving:

1b Spencer Douglas Adair, DSO; Cdr RN, W/Cdr RNAS, WW I (despatches), Croix de Guerre, Order Leopold Belgium, US DSM; *b* 10 Feb 1889; *m* 1st 21 July 1915 (*divorce* 1934) Dorothy, dau of Lionel Ashton Dering (*see* 1970 edn DERING, Bt); *m* 2nd 1934 *Florence Mercedes Cassidy Carnick, of Wilkes Barre, Pa., and *d* 8 Oct 1937

1b Dorothy Vernon; *b* 19 Aug 1887; *m* 26 Oct 1912 Cdr Sir Aylmer Newton George Firebrace, CBE, RN, Ch Offr London Fire Bde (*d* June 1972), s of Lt-Col George Firebrace, RA and *d* 13 July 1952, leaving issue

3a Egerton Spencer, CB (1922); barrister, Controller Clearing Office (Germany), Administrator Austrian, Hungarian and Bulgarian Property under 1919 Peace Treaties, Dir Russian Claims Dept 1923–25, Offr Legn Hon; *b* 4 April 1863; *m* 23 April 1890 Ethel Harriet (*d* 20 July 1949), dau of Sir Frederick Wigan, 1st Bt (*qv*), and *d* 11 May 1950, leaving:

1b Nigel Francis Egerton; Lt RFA WW I; *b* 21 May 1891; *educ* Winchester and Trin Coll Oxford; *m* 1st 1921 (*divorce* 1949) Eileen Sybil Lyttelton (*d* 4 Feb 1960), dau of Francis Ludlow Holt, and had issue:

1c *Ann [Mrs Peter Staheyeff, Pale Green Cottage, Helions Bumpstead, nr Haverhill, Suffolk]; *b* 1922; *m* 17 March 1955 Peter Staheyeff (*d* 1987) and has issue:

1d *Nicholas; *b* 15 Sept 1957; *m* 1st 1988 (*divorce* 1990) Antoinette Fionna Stagnetto; *m* 2nd 1993 *Christine Elisabeth, dau of William Reiter, of Geneva and has:

1e *Sophie Ann; *b* 1994

2e *Alexandra Grace; *b* 1995

2d *Michael Peter; *b* 11 Aug 1961; *m* 1989 *Rosemary, dau of Hugh Stafford, OBE, of Wells, Somerset

1b (cont.) Nigel Grey *m* 2nd 15 Dec 1949 Mary Rose (*d* 21 Dec 1962), formerly w of Roderic Miles Doughty Theisiger (*see* CHELMSFORD, V) and yst dau of Hon Guy Lawrence Charteris (*see* WEMYSS, E); *m* 3rd 1970 Marion (*d* 1971), dau of Cdr Robert Tennant-Park, OBE, RNR, and widow of Anthony Alfred Harmsworth Marlowe, QC, and *d* 1974, leaving by his 2nd w:

1c +Francis John [Francis Grey Esq, Pounds Cottage, Cowley, Glos GL53 9NJ]; *b* 16 June 1951; *educ* Nautical Coll Pangbourne; *m* 1979 *Frances Jane Cutler, dau of Cdr George Wayne Harper Jr, USN, of Guernsey, CI, and has:

1d *Telesflora; *b* 1983

2d *Mary Rose; *b* 1986

2b Cecil Charles Frederick; Capt RN; *b* 29 May 1893

3b Aubrey Arthur Douglas; Cdr RN WW I (wounded, POW), Stanhope Gold Medal; *b* 4 Sept 1894; *m* 1928 Joan Fabian (*d* 1975), dau of C H Dickinson, and *d* 1979, leaving issue:

1c +Aubrey Jeremy Spenser [Aubrey Grey Esq, The Coach House, 4 Beech Ave, Worcs WR3 8PZ], late Capt Roy Hants Regt attd 2nd Bn Parachute Regt; late Maj Fus (TA); *b* 23 Feb 1929; *educ* Gordonstoun and RMA Sandhurst; *m* 20 Sept 1958 *Jennifer M, dau of V J Keyte, of Minchinhampton, Glos, and has:

1d +Charles Spenser [Charles Grey Esq, Grimelundsveien 70, Slendal 0387, Oslo, Norway]; *b* 4 Aug 1959; *m* 1988 *Berit, dau of Ivar Stokke, of Oslo, and has issue:

1e +James Axel; *b* 1990

2e +Edward Ivar; *b* 1990

3e +William Per; *b* 1997

2d +James Aubrey; *b* 1 April 1961

1d *Annabel Clare; *b* 12 July 1963; *m* 1993 *James R Chester Walsh and has:

1e *Jack Richard Chester; *b* 14 Oct 1996

1e *Emma Clare; *b* 13 Jan 1995

2c Timothy Bryan Richard; formed Timothy Grey Film Partnership Ltd 1968; *b* 5 June 1931; *educ* Gordonstoun; *m* 1st 19 March 1955 (*divorce* 1960) Pamela Anne, only dau of Col Denys Fitzgerald Murphy, MC, FRCS(E), IMS, of Bristol; *m* 2nd 1960 *Gillian Annys (*m* 2nd 7 June 1997 *Capt Robert Anthony Lunnon), only dau of E R Hillman, of St Albans, and *d* 1992, leaving by her:

1d +Richard Nicholas Aubrey; *b* 27 Oct 1961

1d *Susannah Emma Jane; *b* 8 Sept 1963; *m* 1993 *Capt Martin J Price, RM

3c +Michael Francis Adair [Michael Grey Esq, 47 New St, Fleur de Lys, Somerset West 7130, Cape Town, S Africa]; *b* 14 May 1940; *educ* Beaudesert Park Sch Minchinhampton, Stanbridge Earls; *m* Aug 1975 Elizabeth (*d* May 1987), dau of Ivor Lean, QC

4b Geoffrey Ernest Adair, CBE (1954), MC; Assist Sec Treasury, Capt RFA WW I (despatches twice, wounded twice); *b* 26 Oct 1895; *educ* Winchester; *m* 24 Sept 1931 *Marjorie Myburgh, only dau of Arthur Henderson, of Cobham

5b John; FRIBA, AADip, FRSA, 2nd Lt Rifle Bde WW I; *b* 8 July 1899; *educ* Winchester; *m* 6 Oct 1926 Nancy Augusta (*d* 1984), yr dau of Vivian Nickalls, of The High House, Newbury Berks and *d* 1979, having had:

1c +John Egerton, CB (1981) [John Grey Esq CB, 51 St Peter's Rd, W Mersea, Colchester, Essex CO5 8LL]; Clerk Assistant Ho Lds 1974–88, BCL, barrister Inner Temple 1954; *b* 8 Feb 1929; *educ* Blundell's and BNC Oxford (MA); *m* 7 Jan 1961 his cousin *Patricia Grey, yr dau of Col Walter Francis Hanna, MC, RE (*see* below)

2c William; 2nd Lt Cameronians; *b* 27 April 1932; *educ* Blundell's; *das* Malaya 27 Nov 1951

1b Kathleen Ethel Madeline; *b* 7 June 1897; *m* 29 Sept 1923 Col Walter Francis Hanna, MC, RE (*d* 1 March 1963), and had issue (*see* above)

1a Elizabeth Adair; *m* 10 Nov 1885 Sir Frederick William Wigan, 2nd Bt (*qv*), and *d* 12 Nov 1902, leaving issue

2a Isabel; nun; *d* 17 Nov 1927

3a Lucy Alithea; *m* 1 June 1889 Maj W Hampden Evans Lawless, 8th Hus, of Ardmeen, Co Dublin, and *d* 20 Jan 1905, leaving issue

5 (cont.) The Rt Rev Edward Grey *m* 3rd 1 Dec 1831 Eliza (*d* 16 Feb 1871), dau of John Innes, and *d* 24 July 1837, having by her had:

(6) Alfred; Lt-Col Northumberland Militia; *b* 7 Feb 1834; *m* 9 June 1859 Christina Henrietta Victoria (*d* 29 June 1877), only child of Rev Calvert R Jones, and *d* 23 Sept 1899, having had, with other issue:

1a Raleigh (Sir), KBE (1919), CMG (1896), CVO (1910); Lt-Col cmdg S Rhodesian Vols, Capt and Brevet Maj 6th Dragoons, MLC Rhodesia, Greek Consul Salisbury, Rhodesia, 1914, Boer War 1900–01 (despatches twice, brevet); *b* 24 March 1860; *m* 10 July 1901 Mary Isabel (*d* 10 Oct 1936), widow of Alexander Henry Browne, of Callaly Castle, Northumberland, and dau of Cadogan Hodgson Cadogan, of Brinkburn Priory, Northumberland, and *d* 10 Jan 1936

1a Annie Trevelyan; *d* unm 3 June 1939

1 Elizabeth; *m* 1789 Samuel Whitbread (*d* 6 July 1815), MP Southill, and *d* 28 Nov 1846, leaving issue (*see* WALDEGRAVE, E)

2 Hannah Althea; *m* 1st 24 Aug 1807 Capt — Bettesworth, RN (*ka* off Bergen 25 May 1808); *m* 2nd 30 Oct 1809 Rt Hon Edward Ellice, MP, and *d* 28 July 1832

The 1st EARL *d* 14 Nov 1807; his s,

Sir Charles Grey, 3rd Bt (as which *s* unc 1808), and **2nd Earl Grey**, KG (1831), PC (1806); *b* 13 March 1764; *educ* Eton and Trin Coll Cambridge; MP (Whig) Northumberland 1786–1807, Appleby May–July 1807 and Tavistock July–Nov 1807, 1st Ld Admlty Feb–Sept 1806, For Sec Sept 1806–March 1807, PM and 1st Ld Treasury 1830–34; *m* 18 Nov 1794 Mary Elizabeth (*d* 26 Nov 1861), only dau of 1st Baron Ponsonby of Imokilly (*see* BESSBOROUGH, E), and *d* 17 July 1845, having had, with five daus (*see* REVELSTOKE, B, and ST JOHN-MILDMAY, Bt):

1 HENRY GEORGE GREY, **3rd Earl Grey**, KG (1863), GCMG (1869), PC (1835); *b* 28 Dec 1802; MP (Whig) Winchelsea 1826–30, Higham Ferrers 1830–31, Northumberland 1831–32, N Northumberland 1832–41 and Sunderland 1841–45, Sec War 1835–39, Sec State War and Colonies 1846–52, Ld Lt Northumberland 1847–77; *m* 9 Aug 1832 Maria (*d* 14 Sept 1879), dau of Sir Joseph Copley, 3rd Bt, of Sprotsborough (*see* 1883 edn), and *d* 9 Oct 1894

2 Charles; Gen, Col 71st Regt, Priv Sec to HRH THE PRINCE CONSORT and (also Equerry) HM QUEEN VICTORIA; *b* 15 March 1804; *m* 26 July 1836 Caroline Eliza, VA (*d* 4 Nov 1890), Extra Bedchamber Woman to HM QUEEN VICTORIA, dau of Sir Thomas Harvie Farquhar, 2nd Bt (*qv*), and *d* 31 March 1870, having had:

(1) Charles; *b* 6 April 1850; *d* 23 June 1855

(2) ALBERT HENRY GEORGE GREY, **4th Earl Grey**, GCB, GCMG (1904), GCVO (1908), PC (1908); *b* 28 Nov 1851; *educ* Trin Coll Cambridge (MA, LLM); Ld Lt Northumberland 1899–1904, Administrator Rhodesia 1894–97, dir Chartered Co 1898–1904, Govr-Gen Canada 1904–11, Chllr Order St Michael and St George 1916–17, pres Armstrong Coll 1911–17, MP (Lib) S Northumberland 1880–85 and Tyneside 1885–86, Hon Col 6th Bn Northumberland Fus; Hon DCL Oxford, Hon LLD Camb, McGill and Queen's U, Ontario; KGStJ; *m* 9 June 1877 Alice, LGStJ (*d* 22 Sept 1944), 3rd dau of Robert Stayner Holford, MP, of Westonbirt, Glos, and Dorchester House, Park Lane, and *d* 29 Aug 1917, leaving:

1a CHARLES ROBERT GREY, **5th Earl Grey**, DL Northumberland; *b* 15 Dec 1879; *educ* Eton and Trin Coll Cambridge (BA 1901); Hon Col Cmdt Northumberland Vol Regt, Lt 1st Life Gds, Maj, GSO(3) 1915 WW I; *m* 16 June 1906 Lady Mabel Laura Georgiana Palmer, CBE (1919), JP (*d* 15 July 1958), only dau of 2nd Earl of Selborne (*qv*), and *d* 2 April 1963, having had:

1b *Mary Cecil; *b* 5 May 1907; *m* 24 April 1935 1st Baron Howick of Glendale (*qv*), and has issue

2b Elizabeth Katherine *b* 13 Oct 1908; *m* 26 July 1932 Lt-Col Ronald Dawnay (*see* DOWNE V) and *d* 25 Feb 1941, leaving issue

1a Victoria Sybil Mary; *b* 9 June 1878 (HM QUEEN VICTORIA stood sponsor); *m* 23 July 1901 Lt-Col Arthur Morton Grenfell and *d* 3 Feb 1907, leaving issue (*see* GRENFELL, B)

2a Sybil, OBE, (1918); *b* 15 July 1882; *m* 21 Sept 1922 Lambert William Middleton (*see* MIDDLETON, Bt) and *d* 4 June 1966, leaving issue

3a Evelyn Alice; *b* 14 March 1886; *m* 23 Nov 1912 Sir Lawrence Evelyn Jones, 5th Bt, and *d* 15 April 1971, leaving issue (*see* LAWRENCE JONES, Bt)

4a Lilian Winifred; *b* 11 June 1891; *d* 7 April 1895

(1) Sybil Mary; *m* 20 June 1867 10th Duke of Saint Albans (*qv*) and *d* 7 Sept 1871, leaving issue

(2) Victoria Alexandrina Elizabeth (HM QUEEN VICTORIA stood sponsor); granted with her sisters rank of earl's dau 16 April 1895; *m* 6 June 1877 Col Hon Lewis Payan Dawnay (*see* DOWNE, V) and *d* 15 Jan 1922, leaving issue

(3) Louisa Jane, VA; Ldy Bedchamber to TM QUEENs VICTORIA and ALEXANDRA; *m* 1 June 1875 6th Earl of Antrim (*qv*) and *d* 2 April 1949, having had issue

(4) Mary Caroline, CI; DGStJ; *m* 28 July 1883 4th Earl of Minto (*qv*) and *d* 14 July 1940, having had issue

3 Frederick William (Sir), GCB; Adml; *b* 23 Aug 1805; *m* 20 July 1846 Barbarina Charlotte (*d* 23 March 1902), dau of Rev Frederick Sullivan (*see* SULLIVAN, Bt), and *dsp* 2 May 1878

4 George; Adml, King of Arms Order Bath; *b* 16 May 1809; *m* 20 Jan 1845 Jane Frances (*d* 13 Nov 1892), dau of Gen Hon Sir Patrick Stuart, and *d* 3 Oct 1891, having had issue:

(1) Charles; *b* 31 March 1846; *m* 3 Nov 1874 Constance, dau of Charles W Goad, and *dsp* 29 Nov 1896

(2) Harry George (Rev); Vicar Holy Trinity Oxford 1877–85, missionary India 1887–1900 and 1905–09, Pncpl Wycliffe Hall Oxford 1900–05 and 1910–18, Examining Chaplain to Bp Liverpool 1900–05 and 1910–23; *b* 1 Oct 1851; *educ* Wadham Coll Oxford (MA); *d* 22 Jan 1925

(3) Frederick Bryan; *b* 24 Dec 1852; *m* 22 June 1883 Mary (*d* 14 Jan 1935), dau of Rev Canon William Greenstock, and *d* 6 Jan 1927, leaving issue:

1a Sybil Frances; *m* 12 April 1910 Cdr Philip Walter Kent, RN, er s of Sir Walter George Kent, CBE, of Stanmore, and had issue

(4) George Walter; *b* 7 Dec 1857; *d* 11 Feb 1894

(5) Francis William, LLD Ottawa U 1908; *b* 8 Jan 1860; *m* 22 Dec 1885 Jessie Macleod (*d* 4 June 1928), dau of Charles Rolland, Seigneur of St Marie de Manoir, Quebec, and *d* July 1939, having had issue:

1a George Archibald; *b* 12 Dec 1886; *m* 1st 30 Oct 1905 (*divorce* Canada 1919) Margery Berridge Stuart (*d* 25 July 1952), dau of Wilfred Campbell, LLD, poet, of Kilmorie House, City View, Ottawa, and had issue:

1b Albert Harry George Campbell; Trooper Canadian Army Tanks WW II; *b* 23 June 1912; *m* 1938 Vera Helen Louise (*d* 16 Nov 1964), dau of William Harding, and *das* 1942, leaving issue:

1c RICHARD FLEMING GEORGE CHARLES GREY, **6th and present Earl**

2c +PHILIP KENT [Philip Grey Esq, Valley Cottage, Belle Cross Road, Kingsbridge, S Devon]; *b* 11 May 1940; heir presumptive; Navigating Offr Royal Fleet Aux; Master Mariner, licensed Trin House Sea Pilot; *m* 23 March 1968 *Ann Catherine, yr dau of Cecil Applegate, of Shute Farm, S Milton, Devon, and has issue:

1d +Alexander Edward; *b* 20 Dec 1968

1d *Vanessa Catherine; *b* 1975

1b *Diana Sybil [Mrs Lawrence Burford, Room 105, Bradford House, Island Lodge, Porter's Island, Ottawa K1N 5M2, Canada]; *b* 1906; *m* 7 Aug 1957 Lawrence Frederick Burford (*d* 1979), s of Thomas William Burford

2b *Janice Evelyn; *b* 1909; *m* 1936 *Cdr Boris Luts, USN, and has issue:

1c *Boris Michael; *b* 26 May 1937; *m* 1960 *Sandra Lynne, dau of Edward Lee Burch, of Texas, and has:

1d *Indrik Edward; *b* 26 Sept 1963

1d *Tania Lynne; *b* 13 April 1961

1c *Dorothy Tania Jane Grey; *b* 1 June 1944; *m* 26 Aug 1967 *Juri Elno Taalman

3b *Margery Mary Maidland; *b* 1910; *m* 1938 *Edgar Cunliffe Price and has:

1c *Rodney Frederick Walter; *b* 14 June 1940; *educ* St Bees and Manchester U (BSc Tech 1961)

1a (cont.) George Grey *m* 2nd 1919 (*divorce* 1927) Gladys Helen Complin and *d* 1952, having by her had:

2b +Rodney York; Offr of Finance Canada, WW II in RCAF; *b* 1921; *educ* Queen's U Ontario (BA 1941) and Toronto U (MA 1948), PhD London 1953; added the name of DE CHARMOY before GREY 1970; Assist Dep Min Dept Fin Ottawa; *m* 1st 1945 (*divorce* 1952) Margaret Eileen, dau of Colin Hawley, of Bristol, and has issue:

1c +Christopher John; *b* 1946

2c +David York; *b* 1947

2b (cont.) Rodney de Charmoy Grey *m* 2nd 1952 (*divorce* 1970) Roslyn, dau of Max Marcus, of Rothesay, NB; *m* 3rd 1970 *Cozette, dau of Louis Roger Guy d'Emmerez de Charmoy, and by his 2nd w has issue:

3c +Simon Alexander; *b* 1958

4c *Marcus Edward; *b* 1960

1c *Mary Stewart; *m* H James

(6) William Edward; Clerk H of C; *b* 11 May 1866; *d* unm 17 Sept 1911

(1) Mary Elizabeth; *d* unm 24 Oct 1936

(2) Katherine Louisa; *d* unm 18 Feb 1909

(3) Jane; *m* 18 May 1870 Wenman Aubrey Wykeham-Musgrave, DL (*d* 13 Nov 1915), of Thame Park, Oxon, and *d* 23 Feb 1933, leaving issue

(4) Louisa Georgiana; *d* 7 May 1870

(5) Helen Diana; *d* unm 3 March 1902

5 John (Rev), MA, DD, Canon Durham, Rector Houghton-le-Spring; *b* 2 March 1812; *m* 1st July 1936 Lady Georgiana Elizabeth Charlotte Hervey (*d* 16 Jan 1869), 2nd dau of 1st Marquess of Bristol (*qv*); *m* 2nd 11 April 1874 Helen Mary (*dsp* 24 Dec 1907), dau of John Eden Spalding, and *d* 11 Nov 1895, having by his 1st w had:

(1) Charles Frederick (Rev); Rector Gladestry, Herefs; *b* 8 April 1842; *d* 29 July 1930

(2) Frederick Thomas (Rev); Vicar Wendens Ambo, Essex; *b* 28 Feb 1844; *m* 1888 Kate, dau of Maj — Ibbetson, and *dsp* 22 April 1892

(1) Mary Katherine; *d* unm 27 May 1908

6 Francis Richard (Rev); MA, Hon Canon Newcastle, Rector Morpeth, Northumberland; *b* 31 March 1813; *m* 12 Aug 1940 Lady Elizabeth Dorothy Howard (*d* 11 May 1891), 5th dau of 6th Earl of Carlisle (*qv*), and *dsp* 22 March 1890

7 Henry Cavendish; Army Capt; *b* 16 Oct 1814; *d* 5 Sept 1880

8 William George; Sec Legation Paris; *b* 15 Feb 1819; *m* 20 Sept 1858 Theresa Catherine (*m* 2nd 5 July 1873 Duke d'Otrante and *d* 21 June 1901, leaving issue), Bedchamber Woman to HM QUEEN ALEXANDRA when PRINCESS OF WALES only dau of Maj-Gen Count Stedink, Inspr-Gen Cav Sweden, and *dsp* 19 Dec 1865

GREY, Baron

Arms: Quarterly, 1st, argent a lion rampant gules (for LEGH); 2nd, ermine a lion rampant gules, crowned or, a bordure engrailed sable bezanty (for CORNWALL); 3rd, per pale azure and vert, on a fess dancetté between three mural crowns or a crescent gules between two torteaux (for WALKER); 4th, barry of six argent and azure (for GREY). **Crest:** A demi-lion rampant gules, collared or and charged for distinction on the shoulder with an ermine spot.
Supporters: On either side a demi-lion rampant gules, crowned and charged on the shoulder with an ermine spot and conjoined with the wings and tail of a wyvern erect or. **Motto:** Play fair.
Creation: B. (E) 17 Sept 1397.

THE 6TH LORD (BARON) **GREY** (of Codnor, Derbys) (Richard Henry Cornwall-Legh, DL (Cheshire 1995)) [The Rt Hon The Lord Grey DL, High Legh House, Knutsford, Cheshire WA16 0QR]; *b* 14 May 1936; *s f* 1996; *educ* Stowe; late RN (Gen Serv Medal); High Sheriff Cheshire 1993; *m* 28 Sept 1974 *Joanna Storm, dau of Maj Sir Kenelm Henry Ernest Cayley, 10th Bt (*qv*), and has:

1 +RICHARD STEPHEN CAYLEY; *b* 24 March 1976

2 +Kenelm Michael; *b* 12 April 1978

3 +George Henry; *b* 25 Feb 1982

1 +Caroline Philadelphia; *b* 11 March 1983

Lineage (of Grey): HENRY de GREY; bought the Manor of Thurrock, Essex (later called Thurrock Grey), from Isaac the Jew and his s Josce; held the Manor of Codnor, Derbys, by 1201; granted by HENRY III 1216 the Manor of Grimston, Notts; *m* Iseaude/Isolda (*m* 2nd Reynold de Meurdre), dau of Hugh Bardolf by his w Isabel, and *d* 1219, leaving:

1 RICHARD

2 John (Sir), of Shirland, Derbys; Justice Chester; *m* 1st apparently Emma, dau and coheir of Geoffrey de Glanville, and by her had a s (Reynold, apparently *dsp*) and dau (Emma, *m* William de Huntingfield); *m* 2nd Emma, dau of Roger de Cauz and seemingly widow of John de Segrave (*dsp* 1230); *m* 3rd Oct 1251 Joan, widow of Paul Peyver/Piper, King's Steward, and *d* by 18 March 1265/6, leaving by his 2nd w:

(1) REYNOLD De GREY, 1st LORD (Baron) GREY (of Wilton), so *cr* (according to later doctrine) by writ of summons to Parl 24 June 1295 (although the assembly in question is not now recognised as a bona fide Parl; he had, however, attended the assembly called a full Parl of 29 May 1290); held the Manors of Brogborough, Thurleigh and Wrest, Beds; Gt Brickhill, Snellson and Water Eaton or Waterhall, Bucks; Hemingford, Toseland and Yelling, Hunts; Kempleigh, Glos; Purleigh, Essex; Rushton, Cheshire; Ruthin, Denbighs; Shirland; and Wilton, Herefs; Sheriff Notts and Derbys and Constable Nottingham Castle March 1265/6; Constable Northampton Castle June 1267–Jan 1267/8; Justice Chester, Constable Chester Castle and Sheriff Cheshire 1270–74; Justice Chester 1281; granted 1282 Ruthin Castle; present English victory over Scots Falkirk 1298; *m* Maud, dau of Sir Henry de Longchamp, of Wilton, Herefs, and *d* 5 April 1308, leaving:

1a JOHN De GREY, 2nd LORD (Baron) GREY (of Wilton); *b c* 1268; had granted 1311 Ruthin Castle to himself for life then to his yr s Roger; at Battle of Bannockburn 1314; Justiciar N Wales Feb 1314/5; *m* 1st allegedly Anne, dau of Sir William Ferrers, of Groby, Leics, and had:

1b HENRY De GREY, 3rd LORD (Baron) GREY (of Wilton); *b* 28 Oct 1281 or 1282; *m* allegedly Anne, dau of Ralph de Rockley, and *d* 10 or 16 Dec 1342, leaving:

1c REYNOLD GREY, 4th LORD (Baron) GREY (of Wilton); *b* 1 Nov 1311; *m* by 10 Jan 1327/8 Maud, allegedly dau of Sir John de Botetourt, of Weo(b)ley, Worcs, and *d* 28 May or 4 June 1370, leaving:

1d HENRY GREY, 5th LORD (Baron) GREY (of Wilton); *b c* 1340; *m* by 3 Feb 1379/80 Elizabeth, dau of 3rd Lord (Baron) Talbot (*see* SHREWSBURY and WATERFORD, E), and *d* 22 April 1396, leaving:

1e RICHARD GREY, 6th LORD (Baron) GREY (of Wilton); *b c* 1393; served Agincourt Campaign France 1415; *m* 1st allegedly Blanche, dau and coheir of Sir Philip de la Vache; *m* 2nd 1427 Margaret (*m* 2nd her former husb's cousin 1st and last BARON OF

RICHEMOUNT GREY; *see* below), dau of William, (probably 6th) Lord (Baron) Ferrers (of Groby), and *d* 13 or 20 Aug 1442, leaving by his 1st w:

1f REYNOLD GREY, 7th LORD (Baron) GREY (of Wilton); *b c* 1421; fought for EDWARD IV at Yorkist victory of Mortimer's Cross 2 or 3 Feb 1460/1; *m* by 6 Oct 1447 Tacine/Thomasine, illegitimate dau of John Beaufort, Duke of Somerset (*see* BEAUFORT, D), and *d* 22 Feb 1493/4, leaving:

1g JOHN GREY, 8th LORD (Baron) GREY (of Wilton); *m* 1st his cousin Anne, dau of 1st EARL OF KENT (*see* below); *m* 2nd Elizabeth (*m* 3rd 1st Lord (Baron) Mo(u)nteagle; *see* DERBY, E), dau of Thomas Vaughan and widow of Sir Thomas Cokesey *alias* Grevil(l)e, and *d* 3 April 1499, leaving by his 1st w:

1h EDMUND GREY, 9th LORD (Baron) GREY (of Wilton); *b c* 1469; *m* by May 1505 Florence, est dau of Sir Ralph Hastinges, himself yr bro of 1st Lord (Baron) Hastings of the Feb 1461/2 *cr* (*see* HUNTINGDON, E), and *d* 5 May 1511, leaving:

1i GEORGE GREY, 10th LORD (Baron) GREY (of Wilton); *b c* 1493; *dsp* by 15 Jan 1514/5

2i THOMAS GREY, 11th LORD (Baron) GREY (of Wilton); *b c* 1496; *dsp* 30 Oct 1517

3l RICHARD GREY, 12th LORD (Baron) GREY (of Wilton); *b c* 1505; *dsp* of plague by 14 Oct 1523

4i WILLIAM GREY, 13th LORD (Baron) GREY (of Wilton), KG (1557); *b c* 1509; campaigned for much of his life in northern France; Ch Capt and Seneschal, Ch Leader and Govr all armies in Boulogne and Boullonnais 1546, Capt-Gen of Horse Battle of Pinkie 1547; captured by the French at their taking of Guines (till then an English-held town) Jan 1557/8, having surrendered the castle; Govr Berwick-on-Tweed 1560, Warden E and Middle Marches 1560; *m* Mary, dau of 1st Marquess of Worcester (*see* BEAUFORT, D) by his 2nd w, and *d* 14 or 15 Dec 1562, leaving:

1j ARTHUR GREY, 14th LORD (Baron) GREY (of Wilton), KG (1572); *b* 1536; campaigned with his f in France and Scotland; ktd 1560; keen Protestant; Ld Dep Ireland 1580–82; *m* 1st *c* 1553 Dorothy, illegitimate dau of 9th Lord (Baron) Zouche (of Haryngworth) (*qv*), and had:

1k Elizabeth; *m* Sir Francis Goodwin and had:

1l Arthur; had:

1m Jane; *m* 4th Lord (Baron) Wharton (*qv*) and had issue

1j (cont.) The 14th LORD *m* 2nd Jane Sibell, dau of Sir Richard Morrison and widow of Edward, Lord Russell (*see* BEDFORD, D), and *d* 14 Oct 1593, leaving by her:

1k THOMAS GREY, 15th and last LORD (Baron) GREY (of Wilton); *b c* 1575; *educ* Univ Coll Oxford; a Puritan; ktd 1599, served in Low Countries against Spain; implicated in the Bye Plot (a conspiracy to kidnap JAMES I) 1603, hence attainted, when his titles were forfeited, and condemned to death but reprieved and *dsp* Tower of London 9 July 1614

2k Bridget; *m* Sir Rowland Egerton, 1st Bt (*see* GREY EGERTON, Bt, and WILTON, E)

1e Margaret; *m* 1st 5th Lord (Baron) Darcy de Knayth (*qv*); *m* 2nd by 12 July 1421, as his 2nd w, Sir Thomas Swinford and *d* 1 June 1454

1a (cont.) The 2nd LORD *m* 2nd Maud, allegedly dau of Sir Ralph Basset, of Drayton, Staffs, and *d* 28 Oct 1323, leaving:

2b ROGER De GREY, 1st LORD (Baron) GREY (of Ruthin) (E), so *cr* (according to later doctrine) by writ of summons to Parl 10 Oct 1325; *m* Elizabeth, dau of 1st Lord (Baron) Hastings (*qv*) by his 1st w, and *d* 6 March 1352/3, leaving, with at least one dau (Elizabeth, *m* as his 2nd w Sir Philip Okeover; *see* WALKER-OKEOVER, Bt), an est surv s:

1c REYNOLD De GREY, 2nd LORD (Baron) GREY (of Ruthin); *b c* 1319; *m* by 29 Nov 1360 Alianore, dau either of 5th Lord (Baron) Strange (of Knokyn) (*see* SAINT DAVIDS, V) or John, 2nd Lord (Baron) Strange (of Blackmere) (*see* SAINT DAVIDS, V), and *d* late July-early Aug 1388, leaving, with possibly at least one dau (Ida, *m* Sir John Cokayne, of Hatley Cokayne, Beds; *see* CULLEN OF ASHBOURNE, B), an est s:

1d REYNOLD GREY, 3rd LORD (Baron) GREY (of Ruthin); *b c* 1362; *m* 1st shortly after 25 Nov 1378 Margaret, dau of 7th Lord (Baron) De Ros (*qv*) of Helmsley, and had:

1e John (Sir), KG (1436); served Agincourt Campaign 1415; *m* by 24 Feb 1412/3 Constance, dau of John de Holand, 1st Duke of Exeter, and *dvp* 27 Aug 1439, leaving:

1f EDMUND GREY, 4th LORD (Baron) GREY (of Ruthin) and 1st EARL OF KENT (E), so *cr* 30 May 1465; *b* 26 Oct 1416; initially a Lancastrian Wars of Roses but switched sides Battle of Northampton 10 July 1460, thus probably being chief cause of the Yorkist victory then; *m* by Jan 1458/9 Lady Catherine Percy, dau of 2nd Earl of Northumberland (*see* NORTHUMBERLAND, D), and *d* 22 May 1490, having had had, with an est s (*dsp* & *vp*), a yst s and two daus (Elizabeth, *m* Sir Robert Greystoke and had issue (*see* DACRE, B); Anne, *m* 8th LORD (Baron) GREY (of Wilton); *see* above):

1g GEORGE GREY, 5th LORD (Baron) GREY (of Ruthin) and 2nd EARL OF KENT, KB (1483), JP (Hunts and Northants 1480, Beds 1483, Bucks 1494, Kent 1496); fought for HENRY VII Battle of Stoke 1487 and 1497 against rebels at Blackheath; *m* 1st in or after 1483 Lady Anne Woodville (*d* 30 July 1489), widow of Sir William Bouchier, dau of 1st Earl Rivers and sis of ELIZABETH, w of EDWARD IV, and had:

1h RICHARD GREY, 6th LORD (Baron) GREY (of Ruthin) and 3rd EARL OF KENT, KG (1505), JP (Beds, Bucks and Hunts 1504); *b c* 1478; Capt in HENRY VIII's French expdn 1513–14; *m* 1st Elizabeth, sis of 1st and last Lord (Baron) Hussey (of Sleaford) (*see* also below); *m* 2nd *c* 23 Jan 1520/1 Margaret, widow of (a) John Dawes, London Alderman, and (b) Oliver Curteys, and dau of James Fynche, London citizen, and *dsp* 3 May 1523

1g (cont.) The 5th LORD *m* 2nd by 1 Oct 1490 Lady Catherine Herbert (*d* by 8 May 1504), dau of 1st Earl of Pembroke of the 1468 *cr* (*see* POWIS, E), and *d* 16 Dec 1503, having by her had with possibly a dau (Tacy, *m* John de Gyse; *see* GUISE, Bt):

2h HENRY GREY, 7th LORD (Baron) GREY (of Ruthin) and *de jure* 4th EARL OF KENT (he did not assume the/either(?) title due to poverty, his half-bro and predecessor having dissipated most of the family wealth), JP (Beds 1512), of Wrest, Beds; granted various monastic lands 1542; *m* Anne (*d* between 6 March and 26 May 1565), dau of John Blennerhasset, of Frens, Norfolk, and *d* 24 Sept 1562, having had with possibly a dau (Tacy, m John de Gyse; see GUISE, Bt):

1i Henry, *b* 1520, *m c* 20 June 1538 Margaret, dau of John St John, of Bletso, Beds, and *dvp* 1545, leaving:

1j REYNOLD GREY, *de jure* (presumably later *de facto*) 8th LORD (Baron) GREY and initially *de jure* later *de facto* 5th EARL OF KENT; MP Weymouth 1563–67; applied to be recognised as EARL OF KENT 1571 and was called to the Ho Lds 28 March 1571/2, taking his seat 8 May 1572; *m* Susan, dau of Richard Bertie by Catherine, Baroness Willoughby de Eresby (*qv*) in her own right, and *dsp* 17 March 1572/3

2j HENRY GREY, 9th LORD (Baron) GREY (of Ruthin) and 6th EARL OF KENT, JP (Beds 1585); *b* 1541; ktd 1570, intermittently Ld Lt Beds 1585–1616; *m* Mary, dau of Sir John Cotton (*see* COMBERMERE, V) and widow of 3rd Earl of Derby (*qv*), and *dsp* 31 Jan 1614/5

3j CHARLES GREY, 10th LORD (Baron) GREY (of Ruthin) and 7th EARL OF KENT; *b c* 1545; Ld Lt Beds Feb 1614/5; *m c* 1580 Susan, dau of Sir Richard Cotton, of Bedhampton, Hants, and *d* 28 Sept 1623, leaving an only s:

1k HENRY GREY, 11th LORD (Baron) GREY (of Ruthin) and 8th EARL OF KENT; *b c* 1583; ktd 1603; MP Beds 1614, Jt Ld Lt Beds 1621–23 and 1625–26; *m* 16 Nov 1601 Lady Elizabeth Talbot (*d* 7 Dec 1651), dau and coheir of 7th Earl of Shrewsbury and Waterford (*qv*), but *dsp* 21 Nov 1639

1k SUSAN Grey; *m* 12 Aug 1611 Sir Michael LONGUEVILLE, of Wolverton, Bucks, and *dvp* (*bur* 13 Dec 1620), having had:

1l CHARLES LONGUEVILLE, 12th LORD (Baron) GREY (of Ruthin), as which recognised 5 Feb 1640/1; *bapt* 21 April 1612; *m* Frances (*d* 22 May 1668), dau and coheir of Edward Nevill, of Keymer, Sussex, and *dspm* 17 June 1643, having had an only dau and heir:

1m SUSAN Longueville, *de jure* BARONESS GREY (of Ruthin) in her own right; *b* by 1634; *m* Sir Henry YELVERTON, 2nd Bt, of Easton Mauduit, Northants, MP Northants 1660 (*d* 30 Oct 1670), and *d* 28 Jan 1676, leaving:

1n Sir CHARLES YELVERTON, 3rd Bt, as which s f, and 14th LORD (Baron) GREY (of Ruthin), as which *s* mother; *b* 21 Aug 1657; *d* unm of smallpox 17 May 1679

2n Sir HENRY YELVERTON, 4th Bt, and 15th LORD (Baron) GREY (of Ruthin), also *cr* 21 April 1690 VISCOUNT DE LONGUEVILLE (E); *b c* 1664; *educ* Eton; supported WILLIAM III 1688; *m* 11 July 1689 Barbara (*d* 31 Jan 1763 aged *c* 92), dau and coheir of Sir John Talbot, of Lacock, Wilts (*see* SHREWSBURY and WATERFORD, E), and *d* 24 March 1703/4, having had, with another s and four other daus:

1o Sir TALBOT YELVERTON, 5th Bt, 16th LORD (Baron) GREY (of Ruthin), 2nd VISCOUNT DE LONGUEVILLE and 1st EARL OF SUSSEX (E), so *cr* 26 Sept 1717, with remainder to his bro, KB (1725), PC (1727); *b* 2 May 1690; *educ* Ch Ch Oxford; Ld Bedchamber 1722–27, Dep Earl Marshal 1725–31; *m* by 1 Nov 1726 Lucy (*d* 1730), dau of Henry Pelham (*see* CHICHESTER, E), and *d* 27 Oct 1731, leaving:

1p Sir GEORGE AUGUSTUS YELVERTON, 6th Bt, 17th LORD (Baron) GREY (of Ruthin) and 2nd EARL OF SUSSEX etc; *b* 27 July 1727; *educ* Westminster; *d* unm 8 Jan 1758

2p Sir HENRY YELVERTON, 7th and last Bt, 18th LORD (Baron) GREY (of Ruthin) and 3rd and last EARL OF SUSSEX etc; *b* 7 July 1728; *educ* Westminster and Hertford Coll Oxford; Cornet 7th Dragoons 1752, Lt 1755, Capt 31st Foot 1756–59, Col 1779; *m* 1st 17 Jan 1757 Hester, dau of John Hall, of Mansfield Woodhouse, Notts; *m* 2nd 29 Jan 1778 Mary, dau of John Vaughan, of Bristol, and *dspm* 22 April 1779, when the Earldom, Viscountcy and btcy expired, leaving by his 1st w:

1q BARBARA Yelverton; *b* 19 June 1760; eloped aged 15 and *m* at Gretna Green Oct 1775 Col Edward Thoroton GOULD, Notts

Militia (*d* 15 Feb 1830), of Mansfield Woodhouse, and *dvp* 8 April 1781, leaving, with an er dau (*d* unm):

1r HENRY EDWARD GOULD later YELVERTON (roy licence 21 Feb 1800), 19th LORD (Baron) GREY (of Ruthin); *b* 8 Sept 1780; *m* 21 June 1809 Anna Maria (*m* 2nd 18 Jan 1820 Hon and Rev William Eden, *see* HENLEY, B), dau of William Kelham, farmer, of Ryton-on-Dunsmore, Warwicks, and *dspm* 29 Oct 1810, leaving an only dau:

1s BARBARA Yelverton, BARONESS GREY (of Ruthin) in her own right; *m* 1st 2nd Marquess of Hastings and had issue (*see* SAINT DAVIDS, V); *m* 2nd Adml Sir Hastings Reginald HENRY later YELVERTON, GCB, and had further issue (*see* CHURSTON, B)

1r Mary; *m* 15 Oct 1807 Hon Rev Frederick Powys and *d* 19 Jan 1837, leaving issue (*see* LILFORD, B)

1o Barbara; *m* Reynolds Calthorpe, of Elvetham, Hants, and had issue (*see* 1970 edn CALTHORPE, B)

3n Christopher

1n Frances; *m* by 27 Dec 1675, as his 2nd w of three, 1st Viscount Hatton of Gretton and *d* 15 May 1684

1i Katherine, *m* 1st — Spencer; *m* 2nd — Slayton; *dsp*

3h George; *d* unm

4h Anthony, of Brancepeth, Co Durham; had an only s:

1i George; *m* Margery, dau of Gerard Salvaine, of Croxdall, Co Durham, and *d* on or after 6 March 1564/5, leaving an only s:

1j Rev ANTHONY GREY, 9th EARL OF KENT; *b* 1557; Rector Aston Flamviller with Burbage, Leics, 1590–1643; *m c* 1590 Magdalen, dau of William Purefoy, of Caldecote, Warwicks, and *d* 9 Nov 1643, leaving:

1k HENRY GREY, 10th EARL OF KENT, JP (Essex 1644–45 and 1647); *b* 24 Nov 1594; MP Leics 1640–43, Parliamentarian Civil War, Parly Commr Gt Seal 1643, Ld Lt Rutland 1644 and Beds 1646, Commr Martial Law 1644, Speaker Ho Lds 1645 and 1647–49; *m* 1st 14 Oct 1641 Mary, dau of Sir William Courteen, of London; *m* 2nd 1 Aug 1644 Amabel, dau of Sir Anthony Benn, Recorder London, and widow of (a) Anthony Fane (*see* WESTMORLAND, E) and (b) — Douce, and *d* 28 May 1651, leaving by his 1st w a 2nd but est surv s:

1l ANTHONY GREY, 11th EARL OF KENT; *b* 11 June 1645; *educ* Trin Coll Cambridge; *m* Baroness Lucas of Crudwell (*qv*) in her own right and had issue

1h Anne; *m* as his 2nd w 1st and last Lord (Baron) Hussey (of Sleaford) and *d* between 1 March 1544/5 and 11 Feb 1545/6

2f THOMAS GREY, 1st and last BARON OF RICHEMOUNT GREY (E), so *cr* 25 June 1450, JP (Bucks 1453–58 and Beds 1455); ktd by Feb 1440/1; *m* by 14 Feb 1445/6 Margaret, dau of William, Lord (Baron) Ferrers (of Groby) and widow of 6th LORD (Baron) GREY (of Wilton); attainted Nov 1461 following the Lancastrian defeat at Towton 29 March 1461, when his titles and estates were forfeited, and was executed shortly after

1d The 3rd LORD *m* 2nd *c* 1406 Joan, widow of Thomas Raleigh and dau and heir of Sir William de Astley, 4th Lord (Baron) Astley (*see* HASTINGS, B), and *d* 20 Sept 1440, leaving by her:

2e EDWARD GREY; called to Parl by writ 1446 in right of his w as 5th LORD (Baron) FERRERS (of Groby), also 6th LORD (Baron) ASTLEY(?), if at all, through inheritance from his mother Edward; (both these Baronies, if extant, would have expired on the attainder and execution of Edward's gggs Henry Grey, Duke of Suffolk, in Feb 1553/4); *m* Elizabeth, gdau of 5th Lord (Baron) Ferrers (of Groby), and had issue (*see* HASTINGS, B, SAINT DAVIDS, V and 1970 edn STAMFORD, E)

3 William, of Cavendish, Landford and Sandiacre; had issue (*see* WALSINGHAM, B)

4 Henry

The est son,

RICHARD de GREY, of Codnor; Warden Guernsey and Jersey 1226 and 1254, Sheriff Essex and Herts 1239, Steward Gascony c 1248 and 1253; sided with Simnon de Montfort in the Barons' War 1258 on; Keeper Dover Castle on behalf of the baronial party, Keeper Rochester after Battle of Lewes 1264; later taken prisoner by HENRY III and his lands confiscated but these were shortly afterwards restored to him; *m* by 1223 Lucy, dau and heiress of John de Humez, and *d* by 8 Sept 1271, having had, with two daus (Agnes, *m* Sir William Fitzwilliam; Isabel, *m* William, s of Henry de Fauconberg):

JOHN de GREY; *m* Lucy, dau of Sir Reynold de Mohun, of Dunster, Somerset, by Hawise, dau and heir of William Fleming, and *d* by 5 Jan 1271/2, leaving:

Sir HENRY de GREY, of Codnor, Grays, Aylesford and Hoo, both Kent; *b c* 1256; campaigned Gascony 1294–97; in EDWARD I's army at Siege of Carlaverock 1300 and campaigned in Scotland as late as 1306; summoned to an assembly which met 1298/9–16 Aug 1308 and which by certain past rulings has been designated a Parl, although neither knights nor burgesses were summoned and under the more rigorous rules of evidence required today would not constitute a sitting such as could give rise to a peerage creation; *m* 1st allegedly Eleanor, sis of 1st Earl of Devon (*qv*) of the Feb 1334/5 *cr*; *m* 2nd by 6 June 1301 Joan, widow of Sir Ralph de Cromwell (*see* CROMWELL, B), and *d* Sept 1308, leaving by his 1st w, with a yr s (Nicholas, of Rydale, Derbys) and a dau (Luce, *m* a s of Roger de Somery):

Sir RICHARD de GREY; *b c* 1281–82; called to Parl 4 March 1308/9–23 Feb 1334/5 but under the more rigorous rules of evidence required today the lack of proof of an actual sitting has been held to militate against the ascription of an actual peerage creation; pardoned 1321 for any action of his hostile to EDWARD II's favourites the Despensers (*see* FALMOUTH, V); Steward Gascony 1324; Constable Nottingham Castle 1325–30; *m* Joan, dau of Sir Robert FitzPayn, 1st Lord (Baron) FitzPayn, and *d* just prior to 10 March 1334/5, leaving:

1 JOHN, for whom *see* below

2 Robert de GREY later FitzPAYN, of Cary Fitzpaine, Charlton Mackrell, Cheddon Fitzpaine, Staple Fitzpaine, Somerset, and Wraxall, Dorset, which manors he inherited from his unc Sir Robert FitzPayn 1354; *b c* 1321; accompanied EDWARD III on the campaign in France 1359–60; *m* between 16 Aug 1351 and 16 Oct 1354 Elizabeth, dau and coheir of Sir Guy de Briene, of Laugharne, Carmarths, and Walwyn's Castle, Pembs, and *dspm* 21 May 1393, leaving an only dau and heiress:

(1) Isabel; *b c* 1364; *m* Sir Richard de Poynings, 3rd Lord (Baron) Poynings, of Poynings, Sussex, and *d* 11 April 1394, leaving:

1a ROBERT de POYNINGS, 4th LORD (Baron) POYNINGS, PC (March 1410/1), JP (Surrey 1413); *b* after 3 Dec 1382; ktd by June 1404; campaigned in France 1423–24 during last phase of Hundred Years War, being present at English victory over French of Verneuil Aug 1424; *m* 1st —; *m* 2nd by June 1434 Margaret, er dau and in her issue coheir of Thomas Squery, of Westerham, Kent, and *d* 2 Oct 1446, having by his 1st w had:

1b Richard (Sir); ktd by 1423; MP Sussex 1423; *m* 1st Joan, dau of Henry Seamer; *m* 2nd Eleanor, dau of Sir John Berkeley, of Beaverstone, Glos, and widow of 14th/7th Earl of Arundel (*see* NORFOLK, D), and was *k* 10 June 1429 nr Orleans while campaigning in the final phase of the Hundred Years War, leaving:

1c ELEANOR de Poynings, *de jure* BARONESS POYNINGS according to later doctrine; *b c* 1422; *m* by 25 June 1435 2nd Earl of Northumberland of the 1415/6 *cr* (*see* NORTHUMBERLAND, D) and had issue

The er son,

Sir JOHN de GREY, KG; summoned to Parl 1 April 1335–23 Nov 1392 but again with no proof of his sitting; campaigned Scotland, Flanders and France, present Crécy and Siege of Calais 1346–47; Keeper Rochester Castle 1359; *m* 1st by 4 Sept 1325 Eleanor —; *m* 2nd by 20 Oct 1330 Alice, dau of Sir Warin de Lisle, of Kingston Lisle, and *d* 14 Dec 1392, leaving by her:

1 Henry (Sir); *m* Joan, dau of Sir Reynold de Cobham, KG, 1st Lord (Baron) Cobham (of Sterborough) (*see* COBHAM, V, preliminary remarks), by Joan, dau of 3rd Lord (Baron) Berkeley of the 1295/1308 *cr* (*see* BERKELEY, B), and *dvp*, leaving:

(1) RICHARD, **1st Baron**

2 John

1 Alice; *m* by 28 Jan 1353/4 William, s of 2nd Lord (Baron) Everingham, and had issue

Sir JOHN's gs,

Sir RICHARD de GREY, **1st Baron Grey** of Codnor (E), so *cr* by writ of summons to Parl 17 Sept 1397, KG (1404); *b c* 1371; Adml Fleet from Thames Estuary to the North 1401; King's Chamberlain and Keeper Brecknock and Hosrton (Derbys) Castles 7 Aug 1405; Dep Constable and Marshal of England 12 Aug 1405; granted lands in Wales and recommended by Parl March 1405/6 for reward for his part in suppressing Owen Glendower's uprising; Constable Nottingham Castle and Master Forester Sherwood 1406, Justice S Wales 1407, envoy France and Scotland, Capt Argentan Castle Normandy 1417; *m* by 1378 Elizabeth, yr dau and coheir of Ralph, 1st Lord (Baron) Basset (of Sapcote), and *d* 1 Aug 1418, leaving:

1 Sir JOHN de GREY, **2nd Baron Grey** of Codnor; *b c* 1396; Lt of Ireland March 1426/7–30; *m* allegedly Joan — and *dsp* 14 Sept 1430

2 Sir HENRY de GREY, **3rd Baron Grey** of Codnor; *b c* 1404; *m* by 5 May 1434 Margaret (*m* 2nd Sir Richard Vere, yr s of 12th Earl of Oxford (*see* SAINT ALBANS, D), and *d* 1474), dau of Sir Henry Percy, of Atholl (*see* NORTHUMBERLAND, D), and *d* 14 July 1444, leaving an only child:

(1) HENRY de GREY, **4th Baron Grey** of Codnor; *b c* 1435; fought on Lancastrian side at their victory of St Albans Feb 1460/1; licensed 1463 to pursue alchemical experiments, though should he succeed in transmuting base metals to gold by philosophical labours any access of riches was to be reported to the Crown; Steward all roy castles in N Ireland March 1472/3; *m* 1st just after 31 Aug 1454 Catherine, dau of Sir Thomas Strangways by Catherine, dau of Ralph Nevill(e), Earl of Westmorland (*see* ABERGAVENNY, M), and widow of John Mowbray, Duke of Norfolk (*see* MOWBRAY, SEGRAVE and STOURTON, B); *m* 2nd by 1474 Margaret —; *m* 3rd between 1486 and 5 May 1492 Catherine, dau of William, Lord (Baron) Stourton (*see* MOWBRAY, SEGRAVE and STOURTON, B), and *dspl* 1496, leaving three illegitimate sons (Richard; 'Greater' Harry, both by mother or mothers unknown; and (by Katherine Fynderon) 'Little' Harry), when the Barony fell into abeyance between his aunts or their reps

2 William; Bp Ely; *d* 1478

1 Elizabeth; *m* Sir John La Zouche, of Bulwick, Northants, 2nd s of 5th Lord (Baron) Zouche (of Haryngworth) (*qv*), and *d* 1460, leaving issue (*see* also SHEFFIELD, Bt)

2 Eleanor; *m* Sir Thomas Newport, of High Ercall, Salop, and had issue

3 LUCY de Grey; *m* as his 2nd w Sir Rowland LENTHALL, JP (Berks and Oxon) (*d c* 1451), of Bessels Leigh Manor, Berks, and Maenan Hall, Caernarvs, and had:

(1) Rowland; *m* Isabella, dau of Sir Walter Devereux, and *dsp c* 1488

(2) John; *m* Anne, dau of Humphrey Bessels, of Bessels Leigh, Berks, and *dsp* 1498

(1) Eleanor; *dsp* before 1498

(2) ELIZABETH, for whom *see* below

(3) Katherine Lenthall; *m* 6th Lord (Baron) Zouche (*qv*) and had issue

4 Jane; *m* 1st Sir William de Harcourt (*see* VERNON, B); *m* 2nd Ralph de Ferrers

The 2nd dau,

ELIZABETH Lenthall; *m* Sir Thomas CORNWALL (6th feudal Baron of Burford, Sheriff Salop 1459; Lancastrian, hence attainted 1461 and his estates confiscated; *d* 1473) and had, with other issue, including a yr s (Richard/Rowland (Sir)):

Sir EDMUND CORNWALL, KB (1483); 7th feudal Baron of Burford, his estates being restored him 1473; *m* Margaret/Maria, dau of Thomas Hoorde, Attorney-Gen to HENRY VII, and *d* 1489, leaving, with other issue, an only s:

Sir THOMAS CORNWALL; *b* 1468; 8th feudal Baron of Burford; ktd 1497; Sheriff Herefs and Salop; *m* Anne, dau of Sir Richard Corbet, and *d* 1538, leaving, with three daus, an only surv s:

RICHARD CORNWALL; *b* 1493; 9th feudal Baron of Burford; *m* Janet, dau and sole heiress of Henry Wogan, and *d* 1569, leaving, with two daus and an er s (Edmund, *b* 1537, 10th feudal Baron of Burford, Sheriff Salop 1579, *d* unm 1585):

THOMAS CORNWALL; *b* 1538; 11th feudal Baron of Burford; *m* Katherine, dau of John Hartley, and *d* 1615, leaving an est s:

Sir THOMAS CORNWALL; *b* 1573; 12th feudal Baron of Burford; ktd 1603; Sheriff Salop 1634; *m* Anne, dau of Sir Gilbert Lyttelton, and *d* 1638, leaving an est s:

Sir GILBERT CORNWALL; *b* 1598; 13th feudal Baron of Burford; ktd 1620; *m* Elizabeth, dau of Sir Thomas Reade (*see* READE, Bt), and *d* 1671, leaving an est s:

THOMAS CORNWALL; 14th feudal Baron of Burford; royalist Civil War; *m* his 1st cousin Anne, dau of Thomas Reade, and *d* 1686, leaving an er s:

THOMAS CORNWALL; *b* 1651; 15th feudal Baron of Burford; *m* Katherine Read and *d* 1724, leaving an est s:

FRANCIS CORNWALL; *b* 1685; 16th and last Baron of Burford, which was sold to pay his debts; *m* Mary, dau and heiress of James Woodhouse, of Woodhouse, and *d* 1727, leaving an only surv child:

ANNA MARIA Cornwall; *bapt* 1711; *m* (settlement 26 March 1731) George LEGH, JP (*d* 26 Jan 1780), of High Legh, Cheshire, and Furnivall's Inn, and *d* 7 July 1741, leaving:

HENRY CORNWALL LEGH, of High Legh; *b* 24 May 1743; *educ* Wadham Coll Oxford; High Sheriff Cheshire 1786; *m* 1761 Elizabeth (*d* April 1808), dau and coheir of Robert Hopkinson, of Heath Hall, Yorks, and *d* March 1791, leaving, with an est s (*d* an infant), a yst s (Henry Cornwall, Capt, *ka* Maroon War Jamaica Sept 1785) and two daus (Elizabeth Dorothea, *d* unm; Anna Maria, *m* 3 Jan 1788 Thomas Pitt, of St James's):

GEORGE JOHN LEGH, of High Legh, DL (Cheshire); *b* 26 May 1769; *educ* Oxford (DCL); High Sheriff Cheshire 1805; *m* 14 July 1803 Mary, dau of John Blackburne, MP, of Hale Hall, Lancs, and *d* 17 March 1832, having had:

1 George Cornwall, JP, DL Cheshire; *b* 30 Aug 1804; *educ* Eton and Ch Ch Oxford; Col 2nd Roy Cheshire Militia; High Sheriff Cheshire 1838; MP N Cheshire 1841–47 and 1848–68, Mid-Cheshire 1868–73; *m* 5 July 1828 Louisa Charlotte, 2nd dau of Edward Taylor, of Bifrons, Kent, and *dsps* 16 June 1877, having had:

(1) George Cornwall; *b* 1847; *d* 1848

2 Henry Cornwall (Rev); *b* 14 Aug 1811; *educ* Eton and BNC Oxford (MA); Rector Welsh Hampton, Salop; *m* 7 March 1839 Mary (*d* 21 March 1887), dau of Martin Williams, of Bryngwyn, Montgomerys, and *d* 24 Nov 1847, leaving:

(1) Henry Martin Cornwall, of High Legh, JP, DL Cheshire; *b* 14 Nov 1839; Lt-Col Gren Gds; High Sheriff Cheshire 1884; *m* 22 Jan 1896 Constance Anna (*d* 27 May 1912), dau of Henry Ashton Case, of Thingwall Hall, Lancs, and widow of Philip Ainslie Walker, of S Kensington, and *dsp* 30 Oct 1904

(1) Gertrude Mary Cornwall (twin); *m* 4 Aug 1875 Charles Walker, barrister (*b* 12 March 1830; *d* 5 Feb 1893), yst s of G J A Walker, JP, DL, of Norton, Worcs, and *d* 21 Nov 1923, leaving:

1a Charles Henry George WALKER later CORNWALL LEGH (deed poll 19 Oct 1926), of High Legh, which he inherited from his cousin (*see* below); *b* 5 June 1876; *educ* Newton Abbott and Keble Coll Oxford; *m* 19 Jan 1901 Geraldine Maud (*d* 9 July 1957), dau of Lt-Col Arthur James Shuldam, Roy Inniskilling Fus, and *d* 16 Oct 1934, leaving:

1b CHARLES LEGH SHULDAM, **5th Baron**

2b Evelyn Henry Shuldam WALKER later CORNWALL LEGH (deed poll on his f's inheriting the High Legh estate); 5 July 1905; Capt The Buffs WW II (invalided); *m* 15 Aug 1946 *Olga Frieda [The Hon Mrs Evelyn Cornwall Legh, Mill House, High Legh, Cheshire WA16 6LS], er dau of Heinrich Bodmer, of Zürich, and *d* 1975, having had:

1c +Barbara Katherine [Mrs Giles Whittome, Legh House, Denstone, Suffolk, CB8 8PW]; *b* 29 July 1947; *m* 1st 1969 (*divorce* 1973) John James Stewart Farmer and has:

1d +Katherine Frederica; *b* 1971

1c (cont.) Mrs Barbara Farmer *m* 2nd 1978 *Giles Heathcote Whittome

2a Arthur Edmund Legh (Rev); *b* 2 Nov 1878; *educ* Hatfield Hall Durham (BA 1903) and Ely Theol Coll; Vicar St Mary's Aston Brook Birmingham 1915–37 and Feckenham Worcs 1937–50, RD Feckenham 1944–50; *m* 14 June 1911 Evelyn Constance (*d* 9 Feb 1929), 2nd dau of Edward Hosking, ICS, and *d* 15 July 1962, leaving:

1b +Edward Charles Cornwall (Rev) [The Rev Edward Walker, Gt Amwell Vicarage, Ware, Herts]; *b* 24 May 1918; *educ* Denstone, Selwyn Coll Cambridge (BA 1939, MA 1943) and Cuddesdon Theol Coll Oxford; Vicar Gt Amwell 1948–81, Chaplain Christs's Hosp Hertford 1953; *m* 7 Aug 1946 *Jean Drummond, only dau of Rev Andrew Drummond Harcus, OBE, DD, and has had:

1c +(Charles) Legh [Legh Walker Esq, Barters Farmhouse, Chapmanslade, Wilts]; *b* 18 May 1947; *educ* Denstone and Oaklands Coll St Albans; *m* 1979 *Diana, dau of Rev Philip Reginald Wilton Tidmarsh, of Presteigne, Powys, and has:

1d +Andrew Philip Cornwall; *b* 4 Nov 1982

1d +Anna Clair; *b* 1985

2c Drummond Harcus; *b* 5 Nov, *d* 13 Nov 1952

3c +Drummond Alban Cornwall [Drummond Walker Esq, Zypressenstrasse 26, 33699 Bielefeld, Germany]; *b* 22 June 1959; *educ* Haileybury and Trin Coll Music London; *m* 1987 *Diana Carol, dau of Nelson Amos, of Michigan, and has:

1d +Catherine Carol Cornwall; *b* 1991

1c +Claire Cornwall [Mrs Nigel Fairley, Clark's Cottage, 61 The Green, Christian Malford, Wilts]; *b* 4 July 1950; *m* 1971 *Maj Nigel Craig Fairley, Roy Signals, s of Maj John Craig Fairley, and has:

1d +Duncan Craig; *b* 1973; *educ* Haileybury and City U

2d +Alastair Murray; *b* 1975; *educ* Haileybury

2c +Mary Cornwall [Mrs Richard Haines, 40 Alexandra Rd, Ash, Aldershot, Hants]; *b* 8 May 1961; *m* 1987 *Richard David Eliot Haines, 3rd s of Harry Haines, of Churt, Surrey, and has:

1d +George Arthur; *b* 1989

1d +Holly Nicola; *b* 1988

1a Mary Ellen; *b c* 1877; *d* unm 3 June 1962

2a Gertrude Mary Augusta

(2) Eveline Cornwall; *bapt* 1841; *d* unm 24 Dec 1919

(3) Frances Elinor Cornwall; *bapt* 1843; *m* 24 Aug 1869 George Henry Brooks, of Doctors' Commons, and *d* 29 Nov 1914, having had:

1a George Beilby Ernest Cornwall; *b* and *d* 1870

2a George William Desborough Cornwall; *b* 1872; *m* 1899 Annie Edith Lucy Walker and *d* 1937, leaving:

1b George Edward Keble Cornwall; *b* 1906; *m* 1937 Edna Mary Blyth and *dsp* 1978

1b Audrey Hester Mary Edith Cornwall; *b* 1904; *d* unm 1985

3a Edmund Hatfield Leslie Cornwall; *b* 1874; *m* 1907 Constance Sara (*d* 1948), dau of Thomas Cook, of Wellingborough, Northants, and *d* 1934, leaving:

1b John Edmund Hatfield; *b* 1909; *m* 1945 *Honoria O'Donnell [Mrs John Brooks, 71 Tennyson Way, Melton Mowbray, Leics LE13 1LJ], dau of Aloysius O'Donnell, of Co Limerick, and *d* 1966, leaving:

1c +(John) Nicholas Hatfield; *b* 1946

2c Edmund Hugh Cornwall; *b* 1949; *m* 1st 1980 (*divorce* 1987) Barbara, dau of Peter Freckingham, of Ab Kettleby, Leics; *m* 2nd 1988 *Sally Ann [Mrs Edmund Brooks, 4 All Saints Clo, Asfordby, Leics], dau of John Taylor, of Leicester, and was *k* in a car crash 1990, leaving:

1d +John Edmund Cornwall; *b* posthumously 1990

1b +Constance Theodora [Mrs Edward Corner, Rose Villa, High St, Foulsham, Norfolk NR20 5RJ]; *b* 1911; *m* 1932 Edward Stanley Corner (*d* 1984) and has:

1c +Greta Madeline [Mrs John Allen, Manor Farm, Barnham Broom, Norwich]; *b* 1933; *m* 1961 *John Allen and has:

1d +Andrew William; *b* 1963

2d +David Edward; *b* 1965

2c +Catherine Jill [Mrs Nigel Armstrong, 3 Squires Ct, Main St, Bretforton, Worcs WR11 5QD]; *b* 1937; *m* 1964 *Nigel Armstrong and has:

1d +Iain; *b* 1965

2d +Timothy; *b* 1969

1d +Amanda; *b* 1966

2b Katharine Madeline; *b* 1917; *m* 1942 John Cloutte (*d* 1982) and *d* 1989, leaving:

1c +Colin David [Colin Cloutte Esq, 93 Wetherill St, Goole, Humberside DN14 6EE]; *b* 1944

1c +Penelope Jane [Ms P Cloutte, 40a Huddlestone Rd, London N7 0AG]; *b* 1946; has:

1d *Dora Sara; *b* 1983

2c +Hilary Juliet [Mrs Nigel Forde, The Gate House, Burnby Lane, Pocklington, Yorks YO4 2UL]; *b* 1950; *m* 1968 *Nigel Forde, broadcaster, and has:

1d +Victoria Louise; *b* 1968

2d +Sara Tamsin; *b* 1973

4a Cecil Thomas Edgar; *b* 28 Jan 1877; *m* 20 Jan 1909 Hilda McMahon (*d* 1968) and *d* 1952, leaving:

1b Cecil Geoffrey Theodore; *b* 1907; *m* 1st 1932 (*divorce* 1945) Jeanne, dau of Higham Phillipson, of Yorks, and had:

1c +Michaela Theodora Diana [Mrs Richard Edridge, Thatched House, 267 Hillbury Rd, Warlingham, Surrey CT3 9TL]; *b* 1934; *m* 1954 *Richard Edridge and has:

1d +Richard Tilden Hurley; *b* 1960

1d +Annalisa; *b* 1963; *m* 1985 *Martin Parrot, of Caterham, and has:

1e +Kira; *b* 1987

1d +Katarina; *b* 1969

2c +Wendy Angela Suzanne [Ms Wendy Brooks, 205 52 Aspland St, Nambour, Qld 4560, Australia]; *b* 1936; *m* 1960 (*divorce* 19–, resumed maiden name) Stanley Eduard Hoffman and has:

1d +Dahl Wendell Eduard; *b* 1961

2d +Bradney Stan Theodore; *b* 1964

1d +Kyla Jeanell Alicia; *b* 1963; *m* 1988 *Mark Douglas Summers

1b (cont.) Cecil Brooks *m* 2nd 1946 (*divorce* 1967) Winifred Mary (Anne), dau of Frederick Augustin Coupe, of Banwell, Somerset, and by her had:

3c +Angela Valerie Alicia [Mrs Ronald Frank, 383 St Vincent Rd, Nudgee, Qld 4014, Australia]; *b* 1945; *m* 1963 *Ronald Carl Frank and has:

1d +Karl Geoffrey; *b* 1968

1d +Bethany Anne; *b* 1973

4c +Jennifer Anne Christine; *b* 1949; *m* 1974 *Francis Martin Balkwill and has:

1d +Michael Peter; *b* 1976

1d +Sarah Louise; *b* 1977

1b (cont.) Cecil Brooks *m* 3rd 1977 Mrs Eileen Bell (*d* 1982) and *d* 1980

2b Desborough Sutherland George; *b* 1913; *m* 1st 1937 Molly (*d* 1969), dau of Thomas Edwin Morgan, surveyor, and had:

1c +Christopher Desborough Colin [Dr Christopher Brooks, 83 Lake Geneva Place, Calgary SE, Alberta, Canada T2J 2S3]; *b* 1938; *educ* U Coll Sch, Emmanuel Coll Cambridge (MA) and St Thomas's Hosp (MB, BChir), LRCP, MRCS; *m* 1979 (*divorce* 1990) Mrs Linda Foster, of Chattanooga, Tenn., and has:

1d +Amanda ; *b* 1981

2c +Jonathan Henry [Jonathan Brooks Esq, 21 Northway, London NW11]; *b* 1948; *educ* Univ Coll Sch, Emmanuel Coll Cambridge and St Thomas's Hosp (FRCS, MRCOG); *m* 1974 *Janet Ruth, dau of Walter Leggott, of Burtoft, Lincs, and has:

1d +George Morgan; *b* 1980

2d +Jack Christopher; *b* 1987

1d +Tabitha Molly; *b* 1983

2d +Henrietta Jane; *b* 1985

1a Angela Mary Eveline; *m* 1895 Sandford Ffolliott Pierpont Moore and had:

1b Edward Sandford; *b* 1905; *m* 1931 Emily Joan, dau of Francis Cherucca Wheeler, of St Ives, Cornwall, and had:

1c +Jennifer Anne; *b* 1943; *m* 1970 3rd Baron Gretton (*d* 1989) and has issue

1b Joyce Mary Theodora; *b* 1907; *m* 1939 John Guise Malpas and *d* 1981, leaving:

1c +Felicity [Mrs David Isaac, 8 Durnsford Way, Cranleigh, Surrey GU6 7LN]; *b* 1939; *m* 1963 *David Isaac

(4) Maria Agnes Cornwall; *b* 1844; *d* unm 1862

3 John Cornwall; *b* 8 June 1814; *d* 25 March 1815

4 John Cornwall; *b* 27 July 1815; *d* 26 Oct 1823

5 Richard Cornwall; *b* 10 June 1818; *educ* BNC Oxford; Attorney-Gen Malta; *m* 28 June 1852 Thomassina Antonia (*d* 21 March 1884), dau of Frederick Sedley by Caterina, dau of 2nd Marquis della Taffia (*see* 1956 edn Maltese Titles Section), and *d* 10 Jan 1876, having had issue (with three daus who *d* in inf):

(1) Hubert Cornwall, of High Legh, JP, DL Cheshire; *b* 21 March 1858; *educ* Marlborough and RMC Sandhurst; Lt-Col 16th Bn London Regt, Maj KRRC, Afghan War 1878–80, Transvaal 1880–81, Baluchistan and Egyptian campaigns 1882, WWI as Bde Cdr; *m* 24 May 1893 Edith Selina Cavendish (*d* 23 Feb 1949), er dau and coheir of Henry Cavendish Cavendish, of Chyknell, Salop, and *dsp* 5 April 1926

(2) Sydney Cornwall, of High Legh; *b* 31 Oct 1861; *educ* Oxford and Harvard (BA); Lt RN; made High Legh over to his cousin Charles Henry George Walker (*see* above) 13 Nov 1926; *d* unm 12 April 1952

(3) Arthur Cornwall; *b* 24 July 1872; *m* 14 Dec 1895 Harriet Beatrice Lucy (*d* 29 Jan 1960), yst dau of Rev Alfred Jones, DD, and *dsp* 12 Nov 1917

6 Edmund Cornwall, CB; *b* 14 Oct 1821; Brig Crimea (2 i/c Ladder Party Gt Redan 8 Sept 1855), Lt-Col 1856, Indian Mutiny (Lucknow and Kaiserbagh), Col cmdg 97th Regt, Brig 1859; *m* 20 July 1852 Julia (*d* 21 Jan 1907), 2nd dau of Neville Parker, Master of the Rolls, of Fredericktown, New Brunswick, and *d* June 1859, leaving:

(1) Neville Edmund Cornwall; *b* 16 Jan 1854; *d* unm 21 June 1902

(1) Mary Helena Cornwall; *b* 20 May 1857; fndr St Barnabas Mission to Lepers, Kusatu, Japan; 6th Cl Order Sacred Treasure Japan; *d* unm 18 Dec 1941

1 Mary; *b* 19 Nov 1805; *d* 1886

2 Anna Elizabeth; *b* 1807; *d* 1808

3 Anna Elizabeth; *b* 28 Dec 1808; *m* 8 March 1832 Sir Philip de Malpas Grey Egerton, 10th Bt (*qv*), and had, with other issue:

(1) Sir PHILIP GREY-EGERTON, 11th Bt; had, with other issue:

1a Sir PHILIP GREY-EGERTON, 12th Bt; had by his 1st w, with other issue:

1b Cecily Alice Grey; *m* Lt-Col Denys Prideaux-Brune, DSO and bar, Rifle Bde, and *d* 1981, leaving:

1c +Philip Egerton Edmund [Philip Prideaux-Brune Esq, Plumber Farmhouse, Sturminster Newton, Dorset]; *b* 15 Sept 1921; *educ* Harrow; W/O RAF WW II; *m* 14 Oct 1944 *Pamela Maud, dau of Capt George Norman Ferrers-Guy (*see* AVEBURY, B), and has:

1d +Richard John Ferrers; *b* 5 Jan 1946; *educ* Harrow

2d +Denys Edmund Charles; *b* 9 May 1947; *educ* Harrow

3d +Brian Philip George; *b* 13 June 1948

4d +Timothy Rowland; *b* 1953

1d +Philippa Anne Madeleine [Mrs Mark Railing, 43 Winchendon Rd, London SW6 5DH]; *b* 1961; *m* 1985 *Mark John Railing and has:

1e +Maximilian John Prideaux; *b* 1987

2e +Philip James; *b* 1989

3e +Alexander Peter; *b* 1990

2c +Rowland Denys Charles [Rowland Prideaux-Brune Esq, 500 Dorchester Rd, San Matao, CA, USA]; *b* 24 Sept 1925; *educ* Eton, Calif Inst Technology and Magdalene Coll Cambridge (MA); Capt Rifle Bde 1943–47; *m* 1957 *Genevieve Poett, dau of Richard Ashe McLaren, of San Matao, and has:

1d +Cynthia Mary Dean; *b* 1958

2d +Diana Evelyn; *b* 1960

1c +Cynthia Mary Denise, JP [Mrs Brian Stephens JP, Tollgate House, Wing, Bucks]; *b* 26 April 1919; *m* 20 Jan 1942 *Brian Alexis Fenwick Stephens and has:

1d +Nicholas Edward Egerton [Nicholas Stephens Esq, Grafton Lodge, Montford Bridge, Salop]; *b* 1946; *educ* Charterhouse; *m* 1970 *Avril Rose, yr dau of Lt-Col Morgan Henry Birch-Reynardson, of Jersey, and has:

1e +Samantha; *b* 1974

2e +Clare; *b* 1976

2d +Hugh Offley Prideaux; *b* 1956; *educ* Charterhouse

1d +Cecely Isobel Rich; *b* 1958

4 Frances; *b* 26 Dec 1809; *m* 24 June 1833 Rev Beilby Porteus Hodgson and *dsp* 16 Dec 1877

5 Harriot; *b* 25 Jan 1813; *m* 23 April 1838 Capt Herbert Taylor, 85th LI, est s of Edward Taylor, of Bifrons, Kent, and *d* 2 July 1886, leaving issue

6 Emma; *b* 25 Dec 1819; *d* unm 1905

7 Caroline; *b* 16 May 1824; *d* unm 15 March 1883

8 Elinor; *b* 28 Aug 1826; *d* April 1827

CHARLES CORNWALL LEGH's er son,

CHARLES LEGH SHULDHAM CORNWALL-LEGH, **5th Baron Grey** of Codnor, as which recognised on termination of abeyance 1989, CBE (1977, OBE 1971), AE (1946), JP (Cheshire 1938–74), DL (Cheshire 1949); *b* 10 Feb 1903; *educ* King's Sch Bruton and Hertford Coll Oxford; WW II with AAF and RAF; High Sheriff Cheshire 1939, CC Cheshire 1949–77, Chm Cheshire Police Authority 1957–74, Chm New Cheshire CC 1974–76, Hon Alderman 1977; *m* 1930 Dorothy Catherine Whitson (*d* 1993), dau of John Whitson Scott, of Seal, Kent, and *d* 23 Dec 1996, leaving:

1 RICHARD HENRY CORNWALL-LEGH, **6th and present Baron Grey** of Codnor

1 +Rosemary [The Hon Mrs Laing, 5 Ditchfield Lane, High Legh, Cheshire WA16 0QN]; *b* 11 March 1932; *m* 1959 *Maj Hugh Charles Desmond Laing, Scots Gds, only s of Capt Hugh Desmond Bertram Laing, of London, and adopted:

*Camilla Catherine Harvey; *b* 1964

2 +Julia Margaret [The Hon Mrs Prola, The Croft, High Legh, Cheshire WA16 0NQ]; *b* 4 Dec 1939; *m* 1978 *Max Prola, DPhil (Psych), of New York, only child of Joseph Prola, formerly of Aglie, Italy

Lineage (of Legh): EDWARD de LEGA, of Lega (later Legh, later still High Legh), Rostherne, Cheshire; living *temp* WILLIAM II; had:

HUGH de LEGA; had, with other issue (including a dau Cicely, *m* Candelan de Lega *temp* HENRY II):

THOMAS de LEGA; had:

THOMAS de LEGA; living *temp* HENRY III; had:

ADAME de LEGA/Legh, of which feudal Ld 1228–37; *m c* 1245 Margery, dau of Henry de Hulgreve, and *d c* 1250, leaving, with a yr s (Richard):

HUGH de LEGH; *m* Alice de Stanwyg and *d* 1295, leaving an er s:

JOHN de LEGH; *m* by 1312 Joan, dau of Matthew de Somerville, feudal Ld of Alpraham, Cheshire, and had, with other issue:

1 William; *d c* 1349, leaving:

(1) John; *m* Margaret, dau of John Wasteneys, and *d c* 1378, leaving, with other issue, an only s:

1a Hugh; *m* Isolda, dau of William de Bromley, and *d* 1403, leaving an er s:

1b John; *m* Isabel, dau of Sir John Poole, of Poole, and *d c* 1440, leaving an er s:

1c Henry; *m* 1st —; *m* 2nd Ellen, dau of John Bruen, of Tarvin, Cheshire, and widow of Sir Geoffrey Warburton, of Arley, Cheshire, and *d c* 1466, leaving by her:

1d Nicholas; *m* Matilda/Maude, dau of Richard Legh, of West Hall, Legh, and *d c* 1496, leaving:

1e Ralph; *m* Joan, dau of Robert Grosvenor (*see* WESTMINSTER, D), and *d c* 1507, having had a s (*dsp* & *vp*) and three daus

2 John, of Northwood Hall, Legh; feudal Ld of Alpraham 1329; *m* Isabel — and had an er s:

(1) Thomas, of Northwood; living 1363; *m* Joan — (*m* 2nd Richard Harper) and *d* by 1402, leaving:

1a Thomas, of Northwood; *m* 1st Isabel —; *m* 2nd — and had:

1b Thomas, of Northwood; *m* Joan — and *d* by June 1458, leaving an only s:

1c Thomas, of Northwood; *m* Elizabeth, dau of Geoffrey Millington, of Appleton, Cheshire, and *d c* 1502, leaving an est s:

1d Thomas; inherited the High Legh estate *c* 1510 after the failure of male heirs in the senior branch, though not without litigation involving members of that branch; *m c* 2 Jan 1464 Margaret, dau of Richard Chollerton, and *d* 16 Dec 15–, having had, with three daus:

1e ROBERT

3 Matthew; ancestor of the LEGHs of Swinehead

The only s,

ROBERT LEGH, of High Legh; *m c* 2 June 1502 Alice, dau of Hugh Starkey, of Oulton, Cheshire, and *d* by Aug 1559, leaving an er s:

THOMAS LEGH, of High Legh; Alnager (official inspr of cloth) Lancs; *m* Isabel, dau of George Trafford and coheir of her bro Ralph Trafford, of Garrett Hall, Lancs, and *d* 16 Dec 1589, having had an only s:

ROBERT LEGH; *m c* 14 Oct 1540 Eleanor, dau of Randle Spurstow, of Spurstow, Cheshire, and *dvp*, leaving an est s:

GEORGE LEGH, of High Legh; *m* 1st *c* 1581 Elizabeth, 2nd dau and coheir of Peter Leycester, of Tabley, Cheshire (*see* 1967 edn LEICESTER, Bt), and had issue; *m* 2nd *c* 1587 Anne, dau and coheir of John Booth, of Barton, Lancs, and by her was ancestor of the LEGHs of Barton; *m* 3rd *c* 1601 Elizabeth, dau of (11th Lord?) Baron Audley, and *d* 24 March 1617; his s by his 1st:

THOMAS LEGH, of High Legh; *m* 6 Dec 1596 Townsend, dau of Thomas Brooke, of Norton, Cheshire (*see* BROOKE, Bt, of Norton Priory), and was *bur* 4 Feb 1628 after drowning in his own moat, having had an est s:

HENRY LEGH, of High Legh; *bapt* 23 Nov 1611; Col royalist Horse Civil War, helped defend Chester and Worcester against Parly forces; estates sequestrated but he recovered them by paying a fine; *m* 30 Jan 1631 Dorothy, dau and sole heiress of Gregory Turner, DD, of Manley, Cheshire, and *d* Feb 1665, leaving an est s:

RICHARD LEGH, of High Legh; *bapt* 4 Dec 1631; High Sheriff Cheshire 1695; *m* Mary, dau of Thomas Legh, of Adlington, Cheshire, and *d* Dec 1705, leaving, with four daus:

HENRY LEGH, of High Legh; *bapt* 6 June 1680; *m* 17 Oct 1701 Letitia (*d* 1756), dau of Sir Richard Brooke, 2nd Bt, of Norton Priory (*qv*), and *d* Nov 1757, leaving:

GEORGE LEGH; *m* Anna Maria Cornwall (*see* above) and had issue

Lineage (of Corn(e)wall): KING JOHN; *m* 2nd 24 Aug 1200 Isabella, only dau and sole heiress of Aymer Taillefer, Count of Angoulême, by Alice, dau of Pierre de Courtenay (yst s of LOUIS VI OF FRANCE; *see also* DEVON, E), and by her had a 2nd s:

RICHARD, COUNT OF POITOU by 18 Aug 1225 (renounced *c* Dec 1243), 1st EARL OF CORNWALL (E), so styled from 21 Aug 1227 and KING OF THE ROMANS (*i.e.*, heir presumptive to the Holy Roman Empire), so elected at Frankfurt 13 Jan 1256/7 and crowned at Aachen 17 May 1257 but soon ejected and returned to England, three of the Electors apparently having thrown him over because his monetary inducements to them were too small, PC (1253); *b* 5 Jan 1209; Constable Wallingford Castle 1216; ktd Feb 1224/5 and granted by his bro HENRY III 13 Feb 1224/5 the County of Cornwall during the King's pleasure, following which he was presumably invested as Earl of that county; Lt of Guienne 1226–27; Amb to HOLY ROMAN EMPEROR FREDERICK II 1237 and POPEs INNOCENT IV and ALEXANDER IV 1250 and 1259 respectively; went on Crusade 1240–41; Co- or sole Regent during his bro HENRY III's campaigns in Gascony 1253–54, fought with his bro HENRY III against Simon de Montfort's barons Battle of Lewes 1264, where captured; *m* 1st 30 March 1230/1 Isabel, 3rd dau of William Marshal, 1st Earl of Pembroke (*see* PEMBROKE and MONTGOMERY, E, preliminary remarks) and widow of Gilbert de Clare, 5th Earl of Hertford (*see* HERTFORD, M, preliminary remarks) and (2nd Earl of) Gloucester, and had three sons (all *d* young or *sp*); *m* 2nd 22 Nov 1243 Sancha, sis of his bro HENRY III's w ELEANOR and 3rd dau and coheir of Raymond Berengar V, Count of Provence, and by her had two or three further sons (also *d* young or *sp*, including the 2nd and last EARL OF CORNWALL); *m* 3rd 16 June 1269 Beatrice, 2nd dau of Walram de Fauquemont (or Valkenberg, nr Maastricht), Seigneur de Montjoie and br of Engelbert Archbp Cologne, and *d* 2 April 1272, leaving by Jeanne de Valletort an illegitimate s:

RICHARD de CORNWALL; granted 1283 by his half-bro 2nd EARL OF CORNWALL the Manor of Thunnock, Lincs; *k* Siege of Berwick 1296, leaving, with an er s (Sir Edmund):

Sir GEOFFREY CORNWALL; 1st feudal Baron of Burford, Salop; *m* by 1309, as her 1st husb, Margaret (*b* 14 Sept 1295; *m* 2nd William de Evereys and *d c* Dec 1345), yr dau and coheir of Hugh de Mortimer, 1st and last Lord (Baron) Mortimer of the Feb 1298/9 *cr* (*see* ZOUCHE, B), and *d* by June 1335, leaving, with other issue, including an est s (Geoffrey):

Sir RICHARD CORNWALL; 2nd feudal Baron of Burford; *b* 1313; *m* Joan — and *d* 1343, leaving:

1 GEOFFREY (Sir)

2 A son

3 John (Sir); *m* —, niece of the Duke of Brittany, and had:

(1) Sir JOHN CORNWALL, 1st and last BARON OF FANHOPE, Co Hereford, so *cr* 17 July 1432 by proclamation before Parl (later confirmed by patent 12 Nov 1432), as also 1st and last BARON OF MILBROKE, Co Bedford (both E), so *cr* also before Parl 30 June 1441/2 but not confirmed by patent, KG (1409); Constable Shepey [*sic*] Castle 1402, MP Salop 1402 and 1407; fought at Agincourt and was left in command of the English forces in France on HENRY V's subsequent return to England; participated also Siege of Rouen 1418–19; *m* by 12 Dec 1400 Elizabeth, 2nd dau of John of Gaunt (s of EDWARD III), widow of John Holand, Duke of Exeter, and sis of HENRY IV, she having allegedly lost her heart to him when he triumphed at a tournament earlier the same year, and *dspsl* 10 or 11 Dec 1443, when his titles expired, having by his w had:

1a John (Sir); *b c* 1404; *dvp*, *k* Siege of Meaux in Hundred Years War Dec 1421

The est s,

Sir GEOFFREY CORNWALL; *b* 1335; 3rd feudal Baron of Burford; *m* Cecilia Seymour and *d* 1365, leaving, with other issue, including an er s (Bryan (Sir), *b* 1355, 4th feudal Baron of Burford, Sheriff Salop 1378–80 and Staffs 1378, *m* Matilda — and *dsp* 1400):

RICHARD CORNWALL; *b* 1360; 5th feudal Baron of Burford; *m* Cecilia, dau of Sir John Merbury, and *d* 1443, having had an er s:

EDMUND CORNWALL; *m* 1st —; *m* 2nd Elizabeth, dau of Thomas de la Barre, and *dvp* Cologne 1435, leaving an est s:

THOMAS CORNWALL; *m* Elizabeth Lenthall (*see* **Lineage (of Grey)** above) and had issue

GREY, Bt

Arms: Gu. a lion rampant within a bordure engrailed arg., a mullet for difference. **Crest:** A scaling ladder in bend sinister or, hooked and pointed sa. **Motto:** *De bon vouloir servir le roy* ('Serving the king with good will'). **Creation:** Bt. (UK) 29 July 1814.

SIR ANTHONY DYSART GREY, 7TH BT, of Fallodon [Sir Anthony Grey Bt, 86 Kingsway Gardens, 38 Kings Park Road, West Perth, Western Australia 6005]; *b* 19 Oct 1949; *s* gf 1974; *educ* Guildford GS Perth; Inspr Dept Industl Affrs Govt W Australia; *m* 1970 (*divorce*) Donna, dau of Donald Daniels, of Mayfair

Lineage: The 1st EARL GREY (*qv*) had a 3rd s:

Sir George Grey, 1st Bt (UK), so *cr* 29 July 1814, KCB; Capt RN; *b* 10 Oct 1767; Resident Commr Portsmouth Dockyard, Marshal Barbados; *m* 18 June 1795 Mary (*d* 9 May 1858), dau of Samuel Whitbread by Mary, sis of 1st Marquess Cornwallis (*see* CORNWALLIS, B), and *d* 3 Oct 1828, having had, with five daus (including Jane, *m* as his 1st w 1st Baron Northbrook *qv*):

1 **Sir George Grey, 2nd Bt**, PC, GCB; *b* 11 May 1799; *educ* Oriel Coll Oxford; barrister 1826, MP (Whig, then Lib) Devonport 1832–47, N Northumberland 1847–52 and Morpeth 1853–74, Under Sec Colonies 1834 and 1835–39, Judge Advocate Gen 1839–41, Chllr Duchy Lancaster 1841 and 1859–61, Home Sec 1846–52, 1855–58 and 1861–66, Colonial Sec 1854–1855; inherited 1846 the Fallodon estate from his unc Henry (*see* GREY, E); *m* 14 Aug 1827 Anna Sophia (*d* 8 July 1893), est dau of Rt Rev Hon Henry Ryder (*see* HARROWBY, E), and *d* 9 Sept 1882, having had issue:

(1) George Henry; Equerry to PRINCE OF WALES, Lt-Col Northumberland Militia, Capt Gren Gds; *b* 21 March 1835; *m* 20 Nov 1860 Harriet Jane (*d* 1 June 1905), yst dau of Lt-Col Pearson, and *dvp* 11 Dec 1874, having had issue:

1a **Sir Edward Grey, 3rd Bt**, and 1st and last VISCOUNT GREY OF FALLODON, Co Northumberland (UK), so *cr* 27 July 1916, KG (1912), PC (1902), JP, DL; *b* 25 April 1862; *educ* Winchester (Fell 1929) and Balliol Coll Oxford (Chllr 1928); MP (Lib) Berwick 1885–1916, U-Sec For Affrs 1802–95, For Sec 1905–16, Tstee Br Museum 1911, Hon DCL Oxon and Durham, Hon LLD Cantab, T/Amb USA 1919, Pres Armstrong Coll Newcastle 1918, author: *Fly-Fishing* (1899); *m* 1st 20 Oct 1885 Dorothy (*dsp* 4 Feb 1906), est dau of Shalcross FitzHerbert Widdrington, of Newton Hall, Northumberland; *m* 2nd 4 June 1922 Pamela (*d* 18 Nov 1928), widow of 1st Baron Glenconner (*qv*) and yst dau of Hon Percy Scawen Wyndham (*see* EGREMONT, LECONFIELD and, B), and *dsp* 7 Sept 1933, when the Viscountcy expired and the btcy passed to his cousin

2a George; *b* 14 July 1866; *d* unm 3 Feb 1911

3a Alexander Harry (Rev); Vicar St Jude's Arima Trinidad; *b* 10 June 1870; *m* 28 July 1900 Ethel Mabel Gertrude (*d* 29 March 1923), dau of Rev Canon — Huggins, Rector San Fernando, Trinidad, and *dsp* 24 Oct 1914

4a Charles, MC; WW I (despatches); *b* 23 Aug 1873; *d* unm 28 Sept 1928

1a Alice Emma; *b* 9 March 1865; *m* 30 July 1889 Charles Larcom Graves, s of Bp Limerick, and *d* 4 Nov 1936, leaving issue

2a Jane; *b* 29 Oct 1868; *m* 28 Nov 1891 Rev Charles Evelyn Cambridge de Coetlogon, Chaplain Indian Ecclesiastical Establishment, and *d* 17 Aug 1949, leaving issue. He *d* 13 Oct 1926

3a Constance Mary, JP Salop; *b* 31 Jan 1872; *m* 18 Jan 1905 Edward Beaumont Cotton Curtis and *d* 22 June 1958, leaving issue (*see* CURTIS, Bt)

2 Charles Samuel; Paymaster Civil Servs Ireland; *b* 22 Jan 1811; *m* 1st 10 Nov 1840 Laura Mary (*d* 24 March 1848), 4th dau of Sir Charles Abraham Elton, 6th Bt (*qv*), and had issue:

(1) Charles Francis Baring; Maj RHA; *b* 8 Sept 1841; *m* 6 Dec 1881 Mirabel Jane (*d* 1 Feb 1922), dau of Gen Sir William Knollys, KCB (*see* KNOLLYS, V), and *dsp* 17 May 1903

(2) George Arthur Gordon; Cdr RN; *b* 9 Feb 1846; *d* 20 April 1886

(3) Robert Elton; Capt 3rd Hus; *b* 17 March 1848; *m* 1889 Mildred Clare (*d* 14 June 1943), yst dau of Capt H B Dickinson, of Ashton Keynes, Wilts, and *d* 22 July 1914, leaving issue:

1a Monica Elton; *b* 2 Jan 1890; *m* 20 Nov 1917 Rev Jasper Mead, Vicar St Mary's, Dorchester. He *d* 8 Jan 1934

(1) Laura Jane; *m* 15 Sept 1875 Edward Ralph Blackett, MD, and *d* March 1913, leaving issue. He *d* 1893

(2) Katherine Maude; *d* 18 Nov 1925

2 (cont.) Charles Grey *m* 2nd 9 April 1850 Margaret Dysart (*d* 1877), yst dau of Gen Sir Martin Hunter, GCMG, GCH, and *d* 12 June 1860, leaving by her:

(4) Harry George; Capt RN; *b* 25 May 1852; *m* 9 Sept 1879 Charlotte Cockburn (*d* 14 Dec 1926), dau of Capt George Forbes, Madras Cav, and *d* 2 March 1931, having had issue:

1a **Sir Charles George Grey, 4th Bt**; Sr MO Nigeria, W African Medical Staff, Medical Examiner Recruits, FRSTMH, LMSSA, LSA, CTM Lond; *b* 26 June 1880; *m* 3 Oct 1910 Jessy Elizabeth (*d* 5 Feb 1966), er dau of Paton Sutherland, of Port Elizabeth, S Africa, and *dsp* 12 Dec 1957

2a **Sir Harry Martin Grey, 5th Bt**; Maj RAMC WW I, MRCS, LRCP 1908; *b* 12 March 1882; *m* 27 Jan 1920 Gwladys, yst dau of William Maxwell, and *dsp* 12 Dec 1960

3a George Forbes; *b* 21 March 1885; *m* 29 June 1932 Clementine Blanche, er dau of Mark H Knowles, of Little Oxendon, Leics, and *dsp* 15 June 1959

1a Charlotte Dysart; *b* 25 Aug 1886; *d* 29 Nov 1887

(5) Edward George; *b* 25 Oct 1858; *m* 1885 Annette Marie (*d* 26 April 1937), dau of Col S Franck, and *d* 11 Nov 1935, leaving issue:

1a ROBIN EDWARD DYSART (Sir), **6th Bt**

1a Annette Dysart; *b* 1890; *m* 1928 Arthur Fraser Sutton, MBE, Capt RAAMC

(3) Mary Elizabeth; *d* 1887

(4) Eleanor Margaret; *d* 4 May 1880

The 5th Bt's cousin,

Sir Robin Edward Dysart Grey, 6th Bt; *b* 12 Nov 1886; *educ* Rockhampton GS Qld; with Union Bank Australia Ltd; *m* 16 Oct 1918 Maude, dau of Wesley George Wilson, of Toowoomba, Qld, and *d* 2 June 1974, having had issue:

1 Edward Elton; *b* 12 Sept 1920; *m* 5 July 1946 *Nancy [Mrs Edward Grey, 86 Kingsway Gdns, 38 Kings Park Rd, W Perth, W Australia 6005], yst dau of Francis John Meagher, of Winning Station, W Australia, and *d* 1962, leaving:

(1) Sir ANTHONY DYSART GREY, **7th and present Bt**

(1) *Diana; *b* 4 July 1947

GREY OF NAUNTON

Arms: Bendy argent and azure, two lion's faces in pale, issuing from either flank of the shield a cross formy flory dimidiated gules. **Crest:** A sheathed sword erect gules, garnished hilt and pommel or, each quillon ending in a kiwi's head erased gold, the scabbard supported by two lion's gambs erased gules, winged azure, semy of bccs volant or. **Supporters:** Dexter, a lion or; sinister, a crested crane proper, each gorged with an ancient crown, flowing therefrom a mantle gules lined vair. **Motto:** *Servir de bon gré* ('Serving with good will'). **Creation:** B (LP, UK) 1968.

THE BARON GREY OF NAUNTON, of Naunton, Co Gloucester (Sir Ralph Francis Alnwick Grey, GCVO 1973 (KCVO 1956), GCMG 1964 (KCMG 1959, CMG 1955), OBE (1951)) [The Rt Hon The Lord Grey of Naunton GCMG GCVO OBE, Overbrook, Naunton, Glos GL54 3AX]; *b* 15 April 1910; *educ* Wellington Coll NZ, Auckland U Coll (LLB) and Pembroke Coll Cambridge; barrister and slr Supreme Ct NZ 1932; Probationer Colonial Admin Serv 1936; Admin Serv Nigeria: cadet 1937, Assist Fin Sec 1949, Admin Offr 1st Cl 1951, Devpt Sec 1952–53, Sec to Govr-Gen and Cncl Ministers 1954, Ch Sec Fedn 1955–57, Dep Govr-Gen 1957–59; Govr and C-in-C: Br Guiana 1959–64, Bahamas 1964–68, Turks and Caicos Islands 1965–68; Govr NI 1968–73; Pres: Scout Cncl NI 1968–93, Chartered Inst Secs NI 1970–, Britain-Nigeria Assoc 1983–89, Overseas Serv Pensioners' Assoc 1983–; memb: Bristol Regnl Bd Lloyds Bank 1973–81, Cncl Cheltenham Ladies' Coll 1975–87; Dep Chm Cwlth Devpt Corp 1973–79 (Chm 1979–80); Chllr: New U of Ulster 1980–84, Ulster U 1984–93; Grand Pres Roy Over-Seas League 1993– (Chm Gen Cncl 1976–81, Pres 1981–93); Kt Cdr Commandery of Ards 1968–77, Bailiff of Egle 1975–87, Chllr Order 1987–88; GCStJ, Ld Prior OStJ 1988–91; Hon Life Memb NI Chamber Commerce and Industry 1970; Hon Pres Lisburn Chamber Commerce 19720; Hon Bencher: Inn of Court NI 1970, Gray's Inn 1991; Hon Freeman: Belfast 1972, Lisburn 1975, London 1980; Hon LLD: Queen's U Belfast 1971, Nat U Ireland 1985; Hon D Litt New U Ulster 1980; Hon DSc Ulster U 1985; GC Merito Melitense 1989; *m* 1944 Esme Mae, DstJ (*d* 22 March 1996), dau of Albert Victor Kerry Burcher, of Remuera, Auckland, NZ, and widow of P/O Kenneth Kirkcaldie, RAFVR, and has:

1 *Jolyon Kenneth Alnwick [The Hon Jolyon Grey, Upper Swell Farm, Stow-on-the-Wold, Glos GL54 1EW]; *b* 1946; *educ* Marlborough and Pembroke Coll Cambridge (MA); barrister Inner Temple 1968; *m* 1971 *Sarah Jane, dau of Lt-Col Samuel Brian Digby Hood, TD (*see* HOOD, V), and has:

(1) *Tobias Alnwick; *b* 1973

(2) *Matthew Samuel; *b* 1976

2 *Jeremy Francis Alnwick; *b* 1949; *educ* Marlborough and RAC Cirencester; Lt-Col King's Roy Hus; Bursar Rendcomb Coll; *m* 1973 *Susan Elizabeth Louise, dau of Duncan Richard Fraser, CBE, of Nairobi, and has issue:

(1) *Barnaby Nicholas Alnwick; *b* 1976

(2) *Sebastian Jonathan Alnwick; *b* 1979

1 *Amanda Mary Alnwick; *b* 1951; *educ* St Mary's Sch Calne and Bedford Coll London U (BA Hons); *m* 1975 *Jose das Neves

Lineage: FRANCIS ARTHUR GREY; *m* Mary Wilke Spence and had an only son: RALPH FRANCIS ALNWICK, *cr* **a Baron**

GREY EGERTON

Arms: Quarterly, 1st and 4th, arg. a lion rampant gu. between three pheons sa. (for EGERTON); 2nd and 3rd, barry of six arg. and az., a label of five points gu. (for GREY). **Crests:** 1 Three arrows, two in saltire arg. and one in pale point downwards or, barbed and feathered sa., banded with a ribbon gu., 2 On a dexter glove arg. a falcon rising or. **Supporters:** Dexter, a lion arg., ducally crowned or; sinister, a wyvern or; each gorged with a plain collar az., pendant therefrom an escutcheon gu., charged with three pheons arg. **Motto:** *Virtuti non armis fido* ('I trust not in arms, but in valour'). **Creation:** Bt. (E) 5 April 1617.

SIR (PHILIP) JOHN CALEDON GREY EGERTON, 15TH BT, of Egerton and Oulton, Co Chester [Sir John Grey Egerton Bt, Meadow House, W Stafford, Dorset DT2 8AQ]; *b* 19 Oct 1920; *s f* 1962; *educ* Eton; Capt Welsh Gds WWII in N Africa and Italy; *m* 1st 4 June 1952 Margaret Voase (*d* 19 Oct 1971), widow of S/Ldr Robert Alexander Ashton Ullman, RAF, and er dau of Rowland Rank, of Aldwick Place, Aldwick, W Sussex (*see* 1970 edn RANK, B); *m* 2nd 1986 *Frances Mary, dau of Col Robert Maximilian Rainey-Robinson, of Broadmayne, Dorset, and widow of S/Ldr William Dudley Williams, DFC, RAF

Lineage: DAVID le CLERC de MALPAS, JP (Cheshire); Sheriff Cheshire 1252; held three knight's fees in Cheshire; his 2nd s:

PHILIP, surnamed GOCH ('The Red'); Ld Manor Egerton; ancestor in the 7th generation of:

PHILIP EGERTON, of Egerton; *m* Margery, dau of William Mainwaring, and *d* 1474, leaving:

1 JOHN, his successor

2 Ralph (Sir); had:

(1) Ralph (Sir), of Ridley, Cheshire; had an illegitimate s by Alice Spark, allegedly his housemaid:

1a Sir THOMAS EGERTON, 1st VISCOUNT BRACKLEY, so *cr* 7 Nov 1616, as also earlier 21 July 1603 1st BARON OF ELLESMERE (both E), PC (1596); *b* 1540; *educ* BNC Oxford; barrister Lincoln's Inn 1572, Slr-Gen 1581–92, MP Cheshire 1584–87, Attorney-Gen 1592–94, kt 1594, Master of the Rolls 1594–1603, Ld Chllr 1603–March 1616/7; *m* 1st by 1576 Elizabeth, dau of Thomas Ravenscroft, of Bretton, Flintshire, by Catharine, dau of Richard Grosvenor, of Eaton, Cheshire (*see* WESTMINSTER, D), and had issue; *m* 2nd *c* 1596 Elizabeth, widow of (a) Richard Polsted and (b) Sir John Wolley and dau of Sir William More, of Loseley, Surrey; *m* 3rd 20 Oct 1600 Alice, widow of 5th Earl of Derby (*qv*) and dau of Sir John Spencer, of

Althorp, Northants (*see* MARLBOROUGH, D), and *d* 15 March 1616/7, having had by his 1st w:

1b Thomas (Sir); ktd 1597; *m* Elizabeth, dau of Thomas Venables, and *dspm* & *vp* Aug 1599, leaving at least one dau (Mary, *m* 1st Baron Leigh of Stoneleigh; *see* LEIGH, B)

2b JOHN EGERTON, 2nd VISCOUNT BRACKLEY and 1st EARL OF BRIDGWATER (a promotion allegedly pledged to his f), so *cr* 27 May 1617, KB (1603), PC (1626); MP Callington 1597–98 and Salop 1601, ktd 1599, Baron Exchequer Chester 1599–1605, Ld Pres of Wales (during his journey to Ludlow to take up which post his dau was lost in a forest, an incident which inspired Milton's *Comus*, itself first performed to celebrate Lord Bridgwater's appointment) and Ld Lt Herefs, Mon, Salop and Worcs 1631–34; *m c* 1601 Frances, dau of 5th Earl of Derby by his stepmother Alice, and *d* 4 Dec 1649, having had, with two er sons (*d* young) and at least one dau (Mary, *m* 2nd Baron Herbert of Chirbury of the 1629 *cr*; *see* POWIS, E):

1c JOHN EGERTON, 2nd EARL OF BRIDGWATER, PC (Feb 1666/7); *b* June 1623; Ld Lt: Bucks 1660–86, Chester and Lancs 1670–76 and Herts 1681–86; *m* 22 July 1641 Lady Elizabeth Cavendish, dau of 1st Duke of Newcastle-upon-Tyne (*see* DEVONSHIRE, D) by his 1st w, and *d* 26 Oct 1686, leaving:

1d JOHN EGERTON, 3rd EARL OF BRIDGWATER, KB (1661), PC (1691); *b* 9 Nov 1648; MP (Whig) Bucks 1685–86, Ld Lt Bucks 1686–87 and 1689–1700/1, First Ld Trade 1690–91, Speaker Ho Lds 1697 and 1700, First Ld Admlty 1699–March 1700/1; *m* 1st 17 Nov 1664 Lady Elizabeth Cranfield, dau of 2nd Earl of Middlesex, and had a s *d* young; *m* 2nd 2 April 1673 Lady Jane Powlett, est dau of 1st Duke of Bolton (*see* WINCHESTER, M) by his 2nd w Mary, illegitimate dau of Emanuel le Scrope, Earl of Sunderland, and *d* 19 March 1700/1, having had, with an est s by his 2nd w (*d* young with his er half-bro in a fire that destroyed Bridgwater House, in the Barbican, City of London, on the site of which Bridgwater Square was afterwards built) and other issue:

1e SCROOP EGERTON, 4th EARL OF BRIDGWATER and 1st DUKE OF BRIDGWATER, Co Somerset, so *cr* 18 June 1720, as also MARQUESS OF BRACKLEY, Co Northampton (both GB); *b* 11 Aug 1681; Ld Lt Bucks 1702–11 and 1714–28; *m* 1st 9 Feb 1702/3 Lady Elizabeth Churchill (*d* 22 March 1713/4), 3rd dau of 1st Duke of Marborough (*qv*), and had issue:

1f John, *Viscount Brackley*; *b* 3 Feb 1703/4; *d* 30 Jan 1718/9

1f Anne, *m* 1st 22 April 1725 3rd Earl of Jersey (*qv*) and *d* 16 June 1762, leaving issue

1e (cont.) The 1st DUKE *m* 2nd 4 Aug 1722 Rachael (*m* 2nd 14 Dec 1745 Sir Richard Lyttelton, KB (*see* COBHAM, V), and *d* 22 May 1777), dau of 2nd Duke of Bedford (*qv*), and *d* 11 Jan 1744/5, having by her had, with other issue:

2f Charles, *Marquess of Brackley*; *b* 27 July 1725; *d* 2 May 1731

3f JOHN EGERTON, 2nd DUKE OF BRIDGWATER; *b* 29 April 1727; *d* unm 26 Feb 1747/8

4f FRANCIS EGERTON, 3rd and last DUKE OF BRIDGWATER; *b* 21 May 1736; pioneer of canal construction; *d* unm 8 March 1803, when the Dukedom and Marquessate expired, leaving the Brackley estate, the Worsley estate, Lancs, the canal network which brought in some £75,000 p.a. (just under £2,360,000 in late-1990s terms), Bridgwater House, St James's (later renamed Stafford House, later still Lancaster House) and his magnificent art collection (valued even then at £150,000, say £4.75m in late-1990s terms) to his nephew 1st Duke of Sutherland (*qv*)

1f Louisa; *b* 30 April 1723; *m* 28 March 1748 1st Marquess of Stafford and *d* 14 March 1761, leaving issue (*see* SUTHERLAND, D)

2f Diana; *b* 3 March 1731/2; *m* 9 March 1753 6th Baron Baltimore and *d* 13 Aug 1758. He *dsp* 4 Sept 1771

2e Henry; Bp Hereford; *m* 18 Dec 1720 Lady Elizabeth Ariana Bentinck, dau of 1st Earl of Portland (*qv*), and *d* 1 April 1746, having had:

1f John; *b* 30 Nov 1721; Bp Durham; *m* 1st 21 Nov 1748 Lady Anne Sophia Grey, dau and coheir of 1st Duke of Kent of the 1710 *cr* (*see* LUCAS OF CRUDWELL, B), and had issue; *m* 2nd 31 March 1782 Mary, sis of Sir Edward Boughton, but *d* 18 June 1787, having had no issue by her; his issue by his 1st w:

1g JOHN WILLIAM EGERTON, 7th EARL OF BRIDGWATER; *b* 14 April 1753; Col 7th Light Dragoons 1793, Col 14th Light Dragoons 1797–1823, Gen 1812; MP (Tory) Morpeth 1777–80 and Brackley 1780–1803; *m* 14 Jan 1783 Charlotte Catherine Anne, only dau and heir of Samuel Haynes, and *dsp* 21 Oct 1823, leaving his estates in Beds, Bucks, Cheshire, Durham, Flints, Herts, Middx, Northants, Oxon, Salop and Yorks to his great-nephew John, *Viscount Alford* (*see* below), provided the latter had managed to get made Duke or Marquess of Bridgwater, or was next heir to such titles (for example, by his father or great-uncle having managed to get promoted in the peerage to such ranks, with in the case of the great-uncle suitable remainder to John); if these provisos were not met (which they were not) the estates were to go to the next heir; but these provisos were ajudged illegal and *Viscount Alford*'s son the 2nd Earl Brownlow (*see* BROWNLOW, B) succeeded to the estates from 1851, though not till after lengthy, complex and divisive litigation

2g FRANCIS HENRY EGERTON, 8th and last EARL OF BRIDGWATER; *b* 11 Nov 1756; *educ* Eton and Ch Ch Oxford; Fell All Souls, Preb Durham 1780, Rector Middle, Salop, 1781 and Whitchurch, Salop, 1797, FRS 1781, FSA 1791; an eccentric who peopled (if that is the right word) his Paris mansion with cats and dogs which he dressed in human clothes and gave dinners to at the table; left the sum of £8,000 (almost £340,000 in late-1990s terms) for the most cogent essay ('The Bridgwater Treatise') demonstrating God's goodness as apprehendable through Creation; *d* unm 11 Feb 1829, when his titles expired

1g Amelia; *m* Sir Abraham Hume, Bt, of Wormleybury, Herts, and had:

1h Amelia; *b* 23 Jan 1772; *m* 28 May 1793 1st and last Baron Farnborough of Bromley Hill Place (*dsp* 17 Jan 1838) and *d* 15 Jan 1837

2h Amelia Sophia; *b* 31 July 1788; *m* 24 July 1810, as his 1st w, 1st Earl Brownlow (*see* BROWNLOW, B) and *d* 21 Feb 1814, leaving:

1i John Hume CUST later HOME-CUST later still EGERTON, *Viscount Alford*; beneficiary of his great-uncle's will; f of 2nd Earl Brownlow, also (ultimate) beneficiary

2d William; *b* 15 Aug 1649; *m* as her 1st husb Honora, sis of 2nd Baron Leigh of Stoneleigh of the 1643 *cr* (*see* LEIGH, B), and had, with a s (*d* young) and three other daus (*d* unm):

1e Honora; *b* 11 Aug 1685; *m* Thomas Arden Bagot, of Pipe Hall, Staffs

3d Thomas, of Tatton Park, Cheshire; ancestor of the Barons Egerton of Tatton (*see* 1956 edn)

1b Mary; *m* Sir Francis Leigh, of King's Newnham, Warwicks, and had:

1c Sir FRANCIS LEIGH, 1st Bt, so *cr* 24 Dec 1618, as also 1st EARL OF CHICHESTER, Co Sussex, so *cr* 3 June 1644 for life, with remainder to his son-in-law Thomas, Earl of Southampton, and the latter's heirs male of the body, as also 31 July 1628 BARON DUNSMORE, Co Warwick (all E), with remainder, failing heirs male of the grantee's body, to his stepson John Anderson, PC (1641); MP Warwick 1625–26, Col royalist cav regt Civil War, Capt Gentlemen Pensioners 1644–46; *m* 1st 31 July 1617 Susan (*dsp*), dau of Richard Northam and widow of — Banning; *m* 2nd 1617 or 1618 Audrey, dau of 1st Baron Boteler of Brantfield by Elizabeth Villiers, sis of 1st Duke of Buckingham (*see* JERSEY, E) and widow of Sir Francis Anderson, and *dspm* 21 Dec 1653, when the Barony expired by reason of his stepson's prior death, leaving:

1d Elizabeth; *m c* 24 April 1642, as his 2nd w, Thomas Wriothesley (*dspms* 16 May 1667, when all his titles expired), 4th/2ndEarl of Southampton and 2nd EARL OF CHICHESTER under terms of special remainder mentioned above

The er son,

JOHN EGERTON, of Egerton; *m* Elizabeth, dau and heir of Hugh Done, of Oulton, Chester, and gdau maternally of James Touchet, Lord (Baron) Audley (*see* 1970 edn); and *d* 1483, leaving an only s:

PHILIP EGERTON, of Egerton and Oulton, Cheshire; *m* Joan, widow of Richard Winnington and dau and coheir of Gilbert Smith, of Cuerdley, Lancs, and *d* 1534, leaving an only s:

Sir PHILIP EGERTON; *m* Eleanor, dau of Sir Randle Brereton, of Malpas, and *d* 1563, leaving:

JOHN EGERTON; *m* Jane, dau of Piers Mostyn (*see* MOSTYN, Bt), and *d* 1590, leaving:

Sir JOHN EGERTON, of Egerton and Oulton; *b* 1551; *m* Margaret, dau of Sir Rowland Stanley, of Hooton, and had, with other issue:

1 ROLAND (Sir), **1st Bt**

2 John; *k* by Edward Morgan in a duel 20 April 1608

3 Peter; *m* Margaret, dau of Sir Thomas Hayes

Sir JOHN *d* 27 April 1614; his est surv son,

Sir Roland Egerton, 1st Bt (E), so *cr* 5 April 1617, of Egerton and Oulton; *m* Bridget (*d* 28 July 1648), sis and coheir of 15th and last Lord (Baron) Grey (of Wilton; *see* GREY, B), and was *bur* 3 Oct 1646, having by her had, with four other sons (*dsp*):

1 **Sir John Egerton, 2nd Bt**; *m* Anne (*d* 1681), dau of George Wintour, of Dyrham, Glos, and *d* 1674, having had:

(1) **Sir John Egerton, 3rd Bt**; *m* 1st Elizabeth (*d* 31 May 1701), sis and sole heir of Edward Holland, of Heaton, Lancs, and had, with other issue:

1a **Sir Holland Egerton, 4th Bt**; *m* 27 March 1712 Eleanor (*m* 2nd 1732 John Brooke, s of Sir Thomas Brooke, 3rd Bt, of Norton Priory (*qv*), and *d* 26 Sept 1734), yst dau of Sir Roger Cave, 2nd Bt (*see* CAVE-BROWNE-CAVE, Bt), and *d* 25 April 1730, having had, with other issue:

1b **Sir Edward Egerton, 5th Bt**; *d* unm 16 Feb 1743/4

2b **Sir Thomas Grey Egerton, 6th Bt**; MP Newton; *m* 14 June 1748 Catherine (*d* 30 May 1791), dau of Rev John Copley, and *d* 7 Aug 1756, having had an only surv s:

1c **Sir Thomas Egerton, 7th Bt**, and 1st EARL OF WILTON OF WILTON CASTLE (*qv*), so *cr* 26 June 1801, as also VISCOUNT GREY DE WILTON (both GB), with remainder, in default of male issue, to the Hon Thomas Grosvenor, 2nd s of his dau Eleanor and successively to all her yr sons; also *cr* 15 May 1784 BARON GREY DE WILTON, Co Hereford (GB), with the usual remainder to heirs male of his body; *b* 14 Aug 1749; *m* 12 Sept 1769 Eleanor, yst dau and coheir of Sir Ralph Assheton, 3rd Bt, of Middleton (*see* below), and *dspm* 23 Sept 1814, when the Barony exired, having had, with other issue:

1d Eleanor; *m* 28 April 1794 2nd Earl Grosvenor (*see* WESTMINSTER, D) and *d* 29 Nov 1846, leaving issue, the yr s succeeding to the Earldom of Wilton (*qv*)

1c Mary; *m* Sir Ralph Assheton, 3rd Bt (*see* CLITHEROE, B), and had issue:

1c Eleanor; *m* her cousin **Sir Thomas Egerton, 7th Bt** (*see* above)

2a John; *d* 19 Dec 1704

3a William (Rev), Rector Farthingoe, Northants; *m* Mrs — Bateman and had:

1b Frances

(1) (cont.) The **3rd Bt** *m* 2nd Anne (*d* 12 April 1726), dau and heir of Francis Wolferstan, of Statfold, Staffs, and *d* 4 Nov 1729

(1) Bridget; *m* 1st 1663 Ralph Thickness, of Balterley, Staffs; *m* 2nd Timothy Hildyard, of Lincoln

(2) Margaret; *m* Windsor Finch, of Rushock, Worcs

(3) Anne; *m* John Gardener

2 Philip (Sir), of Oulton; *m* Catherine, dau and sole heir of Piers Conway, of Hendre, Flintshire, and was *bur* 15 Aug 1698, leaving issue:

(1) John; *dsp*

(2) Philip (Rev); DD, Rector Astbury, Cheshire; *m* Frances, dau of William Offley, and greatniece maternally of Miss Jane Lane, later Lady Fisher, to whom CHARLES II owed his safety after the Battle of Worcester 1651, and *d* 6 March 1726, having had, with five daus:

1a Philip, of Oulton; *m* Frances, dau and co-heir of Sir Griffith Jeffreys, of Acton, but *dsp*

2a JOHN

3a Rowland

(1) Mary; *m* by 1682, as his 1st w, 3rd Viscount Bulkeley of Cashe (*see* WILLIAMS-BULKELEY, Bt)

Dr PHILIP EGERTON's 2nd son,

JOHN EGERTON, of Broxton and Oulton; *m* Elizabeth, dau and heir of William Brock, of Upton, and *d* 1770, leaving, with other issue:

1 Philip, of Oulton; *m* his cousin Mary, sis and sole heiress of Sir John Haskin Eyles Styles, 4th Bt, and was *bur* 15 May 1786 aged 54, having had, with other issue:

(1) Sir JOHN EGERTON later GREY-EGERTON, **8th Bt**, of Oulton; *b* 14 May 1749; *m* 9 April 1795 Maria (*bur* 23 Aug 1830), dau and sole heir of Thomas Scott Jackson, a Dir Bank of England, and *dsp* 24 May 1825

(2) PHILIP (Sir), **9th Bt**

(3) William, of Gresford Lodge, Denbighs; *b* 2 Feb 1770; *m* 23 Nov 1807 Sibella (*d* 1883), dau of Robert Boswell, and *d* 13 Dec 1827, having had, with other issue:

1a William; Bengal Native Inf; *b* 26 Sept 1815; *m* 1 Oct 1837 Mary Anne, dau of Lawford Tronson, and *d* 7 June 1841, leaving issue:

1b Sibella; *d* 12 May 1922

2a Philip Henry; ICS; *b* 9 Aug 1824; *m* 1st 15 July 1857 Mary (*d* 4 June 1878), dau of Sir William Marjoribanks, 2nd Bt (*see* 1902 edn); *m* 2nd 20 Oct 1886 Mary Louisa (*d* 12 April 1889), widow of 4th Baron Erskine (*see* BUCHAN, E) and dau of Col Alexander Campbell, CB; *m* 3rd 3 Sept 1890 Maud Mary Wedderburn (*d* 1 Dec 1924), dau of Samuel Clarke-Jervoise (*see* 1933 edn JERVOISE, Bt), and *d* 17 Jan 1893, having by his 1st w had:

1b John MARJORIBANKS-EGERTON, of Lochton, Berwicks; Chamberlain to HH POPE PIUS X, Kt SMO Malta, Kt Cdr Order St Gregory the Great, Rector Rode, Cheshire; *b* 16 April 1858; *educ* Keble Coll Oxford (MA); *m* 18 May 1899 Maud Geraldine Mary (*d* 25 Feb 1969), 2nd dau of William Henry Chambers, of Chalksole, Dover, and *d* 6 March 1931, leaving issue:

1c John Louis Gerard; Lt-Col Roy Irish Fus WW II, Kt Honour and Devotion SMO Malta 1928; *b* 24 Feb 1901; *educ* Oratory Sch Edgbaston; *m* 10 Sept 1936 Cecilia Mary Penelope (*d* 13 Nov 1974), only dau of Maj John Baillie Barstow, and *d* 27 Oct 1965, leaving:

1d +John Caledon Richard [John Marjoribanks-Egerton Esq, Sneaton Hall, Sneaton, Yorks]; *b* 14 July 1940; *educ* Ampleforth; *m* 1980 *Helen Elizabeth, dau of Frank Neville Hammond Dicks, of Amersham, Bucks, and has:

1e +John Stephen; *b* 1981

1d *Mary Penelope [Mrs John Bannister, 7 Mann St, Cottesloe, WA 6011, Australia]; *b* 30 June 1938; *educ* St Anne's Coll Oxford (MA) and Alberta U (MSc); *m* 28 Dec 1963 *John L Bannister, marine biologist, s of W P Bannister, of Burford, Oxon, and has:

1e *William John Egerton; *b* 22 July 1967

1e *Katharine Penelope; *b* 13 Oct 1964

2e *Caroline Nancy; *b* 16 Nov 1968

2e *Sarah Cecilia Geraldine; *b* 20 July 1942; *educ* St Anne's Coll Oxford (MA); *m* 5 Sept 1964 *Charles B Strouts, AMICE, and has:

1f *Henry Gerard Egerton; *b* 19 Feb 1966

1f *Emma Louise Penelope; *b* 12 April 1968

3e *Frances Mary Caroline; *b* 25 Jan 1948

2c Philip Morys, MBE (1945), JP Co Armagh; Lt-Col Roy Irish Fus, mil historian, Kt Honour and Devotion SMO Malta 1929; *b* 4 Dec 1903; *educ* Oratory Sch Edgbaston; *m* 28 Dec 1933 Adeline Barbara (*d* 1986), 2nd dau of Maj Osborn Augustin Chambers, Roy Warwicks Regt, of Manor House, Sandgate, Kent, and *d* 18 Jan 1969, leaving:

1d *Philippa Anne Mary [Mrs Philippa Szymusik, 24 Wesley Avenue, Peverell, Devon PL3 4RA]; *b* 7 May 1936; *m* 1st 7 Nov 1959 (*divorce* 1976) Brian Edgar Ford; *m* 2nd 1977 William Ernest Richards (*d* 1978); *m* 3rd 1979 (*divorce* 1984) Albin W Piotr Szymusik and by her 1st husb has issue:

1e *Philip Richard; *b* 6 July 1963

1e *Elizabeth Anne [Mrs Steven Hodgkinson, 56 St Maurice View, Plympton, Devon]; *b* 15 Nov 1960; *m* 1980 *Steven Hodgkinson and has issue:

1f *John; *b* 1984

1f *Laura; *b* 1988

2e *Sarah Jane; *b* 3 July 1964

3e *Susan Lillian; *b* 8 Nov 1965

2b George; *b* 26 Dec 1859; *educ* Jesus Coll Cambridge (BA); *m* 1892 Beatriz, dau of Antonio D'Almeida Campos, and *d* 20 May 1921, having had issue:

1c Philip Graham; Capt 3rd Bn Black Watch; *b* 18 March 1894; *d* 18 Oct 1918 of wounds recd in action

3b Graham; lawyer Naval Dept Washington, DC; *b* 6 May 1861; *m* 1886 Julia Donegan, dau of T Easley, of Dickson, Tenn., and *d* 3 April 1922, leaving issue:

1c John George; Ch Electrician USN; *b* 1890; *ka* 1917

2c William Graham; WW I with USAF; *b* 10 Jan 1896; *m* *Rebecca Crenshaw White, of Ky., and had, with two daus:

1d +William Graham; *b* 19–

2d +John; *b* 19–

3d +Philip Marjoribanks; US Dept Agriculture; WW I with USNAF; *b* 12 July 1899; *m* 19– *Susan Candler, of Corinth, Miss.

1c Mary

4b Philip, CBE (1919), DL Sutherland; Capt RN (emergency list); *b* 3 May 1866; *d* 19 May 1927

5b William; ICS, Fin U-Sec Govt Bengal 1895, Kaisar-i-Hind 1st Cl gold medal 1908; *b* 6 June 1870; *m* 19 Oct 1895 Louise Mary (*d* 29 Aug 1923), dau of Edward Algernon Le Mesurier and *d* 27 June 1917, leaving:

1c William le Belward; Political Dept Govt India; *b* 1 Dec 1901; *educ* Eton and Trin Coll Cambridge (MA); *m* 12 Sept 1931 Angela Doreen Loftus (*d* 15 Oct 1973), dau of Brig-Gen Edward Humphry Bland, CB, CMG, RE, and *d* 23 March 1947, leaving issue:

1d +Stephen Loftus (Sir), KCMG (1988, CMG 1978); 2nd Lt 60th Rifles (KRRC) 1952–53, For Serv 1956–92, Private Sec to Parly U-Sec For Affrs 1961–62, 1st Sec (Oriental) Baghdad 1963–67, 1st Sec UK Mission UN 1967–72, Counsellor Tripoli 1972–73, Head Energy Dept FCO 1973–77, Consul-Gen Rio de Janeiro 1977–80, Amb Iraq 1980–82, Saudi Arabia 1986–89, Italy 1989–92 and Albania (non-resident) 1992, Assist U-Sec FCO 1982–86, consultant Enterprise Oil plc, dir St Andrew's Tst Lambeth Palace 1994–, Order King Feisal bin Abdul Aziz 1st Cl 1987, Grand Cross Italian Republic 1990; *b* 21 July 1932; *educ* Eton and Trin Coll Cambridge (BA 1956, MA 1960); *m* 15 March 1958 *Caroline, er dau of Maj Eustace Thomas Edward Cary-Elwes, TD, Roy Norfolk Regt (TA), and has:

1e +William Luke Le Belward, LVO (1994); *b* 23 Aug 1966; *educ* Eton and Trin Coll Cambridge; Dip Serv 1988, 2nd Sec Moscow 1991–94

1e *Louisa Charlotte; *b* 31 March 1963; dir Lane Fox & Co

1d *Susan Kirsteen [Mrs Jeremy Cohen, Wiston Mill, Nayland, Essex CO6 4LX]; *b* 23 Dec 1936; *educ* Reading U (BA 1959); *m* 24 March 1962 *Jeremy Sandford Cohen, yr s of Judge Nathaniel Arthur Jim Cohen, and has:

1e *Thomas William Otway; *b* 5 June 1965; *educ* Leeds U (BA); mktg manager Swire Pacific Canton

1e *Lucy Jane; *b* 1 April 1968; *educ* Bath U (BA)

2c Henry Majoribanks; Legal Adviser MAFF; *b* 28 Feb 1911; *educ* St Paul's and Trin Coll Cambridge (BA); *m* 1st 9 Sept 1939 Marjorie Mason (*d* 14 Jan 1951); *m* 2nd 31 March 1954 *Mary Florence Howse and *dsp* 19 March 1967

1c Mary Elizabeth; MB, BS, FRCOG; *b* 9 July 1906; *d* 3 Feb 1993

1b Alice; *m* 19 April 1887 Nicholas Francis Mervyn Archdale, 5th s of Nicholas Montgomery Archdale, JP, DL, of Co Fermanagh, and *dsp* May 1889

2b Ruth; *d* unm 29 May 1955

3b Mary; *m* 15 Aug 1893 Maj-Gen Sir Gerard Moore Heath, KCMG, CB, DSO, RE (*d* 9 Jan 1929), Engr-in-Ch BEF 1917–18, s of Adm Sir Leopold Heath, KCB, and *d* 14 Nov 1954, leaving issue

3a Robert Eyles (Sir), KCSI, CIE, JP, DL Denbighs; Lt-Govr Punjab 1877–82; *b* 15 April 1827; *m* 1st 18 April 1853 Mary Warren (*d* 11 July 1882), dau of William Hickey, HEICS, the diarist, and had issue:

1b William Henry; Indian Fin Dept; *b* 2 March 1854; *d* unm 25 April 1889

2b Robert Walter, JP Denbighs; Ch Engr PWD India; *b* 3 July 1855; *m* 25 June 1887 Flora Augusta (*d* 13 Jan 1927), dau of Gen Richard Shubrick, and *d* 30 April 1933, having had:

1c Robert Randle; Lt RE; *b* 20 March 1888; *ka* 6 Nov 1914

3b Raleigh Gilbert (Sir), KCB, KCIE; Lt-Gen IA, Hazara Expdn 1888, Isazai Expdn 1892, Waziristan 1894–95 and 1901–02, Chitral 1895, Dongola 1896 and WW I, cmded 7th Inf Bde Indian Expdny Force 1914–16, a Div Mesopotamia Expdny Force 1916–17 and 3rd IA Corps 1917–19 (despatches twice), Serbian Order Karageorge, Col Guides Cav (10th QVO, FF) and 5th Bn QVO Corps of Guides, 12th FFR 1929–30; *b* 25 Sept 1860; *m* 1st 22 Aug 1894 Bridget Watson (*dsp* 23 Nov 1894), est dau of Watson Askew-Robertson, of Pallinsburn House, Northumberland, and Ladykirk, Berwicks; *m* 2nd 21 March 1903 Maud Helen (*d* 9 Dec 1935), only dau of Sir George Rendelsham Prescott, 4th Bt (*see* 1956 edn PRESCOTT, Bt, of Theobalds Park), and *d* 2 May 1931, leaving:

1c David George; Lt-Col Probyn's Horse, IA; *b* 20 June 1904; *m* 4 Dec 1947 *Jane Tweedie Adams, dau of John Marshal McKean, of Cornhill-on-Tweed, Northumberland, and *dsp* 9 June 1961

1c *Joanna Mary; *b* 14 Dec 1905; MRCS, LRCP; *m* 8 Dec 1934 Kenneth Hampden Pridie, MD, FRCS (*d* 4 May 1963), and has issue:

1d *Jonathan George Egerton; commercial helicopter pilot; *b* 31 July 1939; *educ* King's Sch Bruton

2d *David Mark Hampden; 2nd Mate Merchant Navy; *b* 5 April 1942; *educ* King's Sch Bruton

3d *Angus Kenneth; *b* 23 March 1945; *educ* Clifton and Bristol U Med Sch, MB, BS, FFRCS

4d *Diccon Charles; *b* 28 June 1947; *educ* Clifton, BDS

5d *William Raleigh; *b* 24 Aug 1949; *educ* Clifton; ACP, FCP

1d *Patricia Philippa [Mrs J Benson, 9 Church Steps, Minehead, Somerset]; *b* 30 Sept 1935; *m* 19– *Dr J Benson and has issue

2d *Judith Joanna [Mrs Bernard Halse, Totterdown Farm, Timberscombe, Somerset]; *b* 24 June 1937; *m* 1964 *Bernard Thomas Halse

4b Charles Philip; Lt-Col IA; *b* 7 March 1863; *m* 16 Nov 1889 Lilian Isabel (*d* 7 June 1950), 4th dau of Lt-Gen Hugh Rose, Bengal Staff Corps, and *d* 24 Nov 1943, leaving issue:

1c Rowland Philip; *b* 25 Nov 1891; *m* 6 Nov 1918 *Constance Alice, dau of Edward Courtney Pratt, of Montreal, and had issue:

1d +Piers Brian Philip; *b* 5 March 1927; *m* 1948 *Lorna, dau of Lorne Green, of Ottawa, and has:

1e +Brian; *b* 23 May 1949

2e +John ; *b* 9 May 1951

2c Brian Raleigh; Lt RE; *b* 18 Nov 1897; *ka* 23 Oct 1918

3c Robert Charles; CEng, MIEE, Lt RE; *b* 12 Aug 1903; *educ* Sherborne; *m* 2 Nov 1929 Mary Elizabeth Shaw (*d* 2 June 1997), dau of Rev Charles Morris Townsell, Rector Gidleigh, Devon, and *d* 1969, leaving:

1d +Julian Robert; *b* 5 June 1940; *educ* King's Coll Sch Wimbledon and Imp Coll Sci and Tech London (BSc, MSc, DIC 1966, PhD 1968); ACGI (Chem Eng), Research Offr with Australian Consolidated Industs Sydney from 1968; *m* 11 March 1967 *Kay Lewis, dau of George Michie Stewart, of Sydney

1d *Una Mary; MCSP; *b* 8 June 1939; *m* 20 July 1963 *Peter John Bayley Wassell, Hong Kong Police, s of John Wassell, of Dudley, Worcs, and has issue:

1e *Mark Peter Egerton; *b* 19 Feb 1966

1e *Amanda Claire; *b* 6 Feb 1969

2e *Victoria Jane; *b* 1970

1c Grace Lilian; *b* 5 Jan 1893; *m* 19 Dec 1914 Ernest Arthur Greswell (*d* 15 Jan 1962), Punjab Forest Dept, s of C H Greswell, of Somerset, and had issue

1b Frances Mary; *m* 21 April 1881 Sir William Mackworth Young, KCSI (*d* 10 May 1924), and *d* 8 March 1932 leaving issue (*see* YOUNG, Bt, of Formosa Place)

2b Katherine Flora; a Sister of St Mary of Wantage; *d* 27 June 1934

3b Margaret Rebecca; a Sister of St Mary of Wantage; *d* unm 18 March 1912

1a Elizabeth Frances; *m* 24 Nov 1846 Lt-Gen Sir Richard Wilbraham, KCB (*see* SKELMERSDALE, B), and *d* 23 May 1849, leaving a dau (*see* BAKER-WILBRAHAM, Bt)

(4) Charles Bulkeley (Sir), GCMG, KCH; Gen; *b* 5 June 1774; *m* 29 Nov 1809 Charlotte (*d* 1 Jan 1849), dau of Adml Sir Thomas Troubridge, 1st Bt (*qv*), and *d* July 1857, having had:

1a Charles Troubridge; *d* unm 15 Feb 1839

2a Thomas Graham, Col, *ka* Sebastopol April 1855

3a Francis; Capt RN; *m* 5 Aug 1863 Georgiana Augusta (*d* 28 April 1912), est dau of Rev G Pitt, Vicar Audlem, Cheshire, and *dsp* 2 March 1893

(5) Francis; Lt RN; *d* West Indies, 1799

(6) Thomas; Maj; *d* unm 1812

(7) Rowland EGERTON-WARBURTON (Rev) (added 1813); *b* 9 March 1778; *m* 13 Oct 1803 Emma (*d* 16 Sept 1881), dau and coheir of James Croxton, of Norley Bank, Cheshire, by Emma, 2nd dau of Sir Peter Warburton, 4th Bt, of Arley, and *d* 20 May 1846, having had, with other issue:

1a Rowland Eyles, of Warburton and Arley, JP, DL Cheshire; High Sheriff 1833, author: *Hunting Songs* (1846) and other verses; *b* 14 Sept 1804; *educ* Eton and Corpus Christi Coll Oxford; *m* 7 May 1831 Mary (*d* 21 April 1881), est dau of Sir Richard Brooke, 6th Bt, of Norton Priory (*qv*), and *d* 6 Dec 1891, having had issue:

1b Piers, of Warburton, and Arley, JP, DL; Col Earl of Chester's Yeo Cav, MP Mid-Cheshire 1876–85; *b* 22 May 1839; *educ* Eton and Ch Ch Oxford (BA); *m* 30 Sept 1880 Antoinette Elizabeth (*d* 24 Sept 1918), dau of 3rd Baron de Saumarez (*qv*), and *d* 24 March 1914, leaving:

1c John, of Warburton and Arley; Capt Scots Gds; *b* 13 Dec 1883; *educ* Eton and Ch Ch Oxford; *m* 11 June 1908 Hon Lettice Legh, JP (*m* 2nd 6 Feb 1919 Lt-Col John Dallas Waters, CB, DSO, DL, Roy Fus (*d* 31 Jan 1967), and *d* 30 April 1968), est dau of 2nd Baron Newton (*qv*), and *d* 30 Aug 1915 of wounds recd in action, leaving:

1d *Elizabeth; *b* 21 Sept 1911; *m* 8 Nov 1934 10th Viscount Ashbrook (*qv*) and has issue

2d *Priscilla [Mrs Frederick Fryer, Vernon Hill House, Bishop's Waltham, Hants]; *b* posthumously 5 Nov 1915; *m* 1st 16 July 1936 Viscount Wolmer (*kas* 2 Oct 1942), est s of 3rd Earl of Selborne (*qv*), and has issue; *m* 2nd 6 July 1948 4th Baron Newton (*qv*) and has further issue; *m* 3rd 1994 *Frederick Charles Horace Fryer (*see* PEEL, E)

2c Geoffrey, DSO (1918), TD, JP Cheshire; V-Lt 1939 (previously DL), Lt-Col and Brevet-Col Cheshire Yeo WW I (despatches), Hon Col 1951, ARIBA 1927, barrister Inner Temple 1914; *b* 18 Feb 1888; *educ* Eton and Ch Ch Oxford (BA 1910); *m* 28 Sept 1927 Georgiana Mary, MBE (*d* 23 Sept 1955), est dau of 14th Baron Dormer (*qv*), and 1 Aug 1961, leaving:

1d +Peter [Maj Peter Egerton-Warburton, Mulberry House, Bentworth, Hants GU34 5RB; 54 Prince's Gate Mews, London SW7 2RB]; Maj Cheshire Yeo, Capt Coldstream Gds; *b* 17 Jan 1933; *educ* Eton and RMA Sandhurst; *m* 1st 29 Jan 1955 (*divorce* 1958) Belinda Vera, dau of James R A Young; *m* 2nd 10 Nov 1960 (*divorce* 1967) Sarah Jessica, er dau of Maj Willoughby Rollo Norman (*see* NORMAN, Bt), and by her has:

1e +Charles Piers; *b* 9 Nov 1961; *m* 1989 *Fiona Clare, only dau of Robin Desmond Bonham-Carter, and has:

1f +Piers; *b* 1992

2f +Marcus; *b* 1994

2e +James Willoughby; *b* 1 Oct 1963; *m* 1993 *Elizabeth Boughton, est dau of Vincent Riggio, of Long Island, NY

1d (cont.) Maj Peter Egerton-Warburton *m* 3rd 6 June 1969 *Hon Marya Anne Noble, 2nd dau of Baron Glenkinglas (*see* NOBLE, Bt, of Ardkinglas), and by her has issue:

3e +Christopher Geoffrey; *b* 19 Jan 1971; *m* 28 Feb 1998 *Sarah, dau of Jeremy Russell

1e *Louisa Jane; *b* 19 Jan 1971

1d *Anne [Mrs James Irvine, School House, Caulcott, Oxon OX6 3NE]; *b* 26 June 1928; *m* 24 July 1954 *His Hon James Eccles Malise Irvine, JP, 2nd s of Brig-Gen Alfred Ernest Irvine, CB, CMG, DSO, and has issue:

1e *David Peter Gerard; *b* 20 May 1963; *educ* Stowe, Oakham, Berks Coll of Ag, RMA Sandhurst and RAC Cirencester; BSc Buckingham; Actg Capt Gren Gds 1987–91 (Gulf War Medal), Capt (TA) Roy Wessex Yeo (Roy Glos Hus) 1992 and 6th (Northumberland) Roy Regt Fus 1997

1e *Susan Caroline Jane; *b* 28 Jan 1961; *educ* St Mary's Wantage, Oakham and Aberdeen U (MA 1982)

2d *Jane, LVO [Miss Jane Egerton-Warburton LVO, Crossways, Woodgreen, Fordingbridge, Hants]; *b* 1931, Ldy-in-wating to HRH PRINCESS ALICE, DUCHESS OF GLOUCESTER to 1984, Extra Ldy in Waiting 1984–; *b* 20 Feb 1931

1c Dorothy; *d* unm 5 Nov 1954

2c Eveline; *m* 24 July 1940 Rt Rev Mark Rodolph Carpenter-Garnier, DD (*d* 11 Oct 1969), Bp Colombo, 3rd s of John Carpenter-Garnier, JP, DL, of Rookesbury Park, Wickham, Hants, and *dsp* 23 Nov 1967

3c Margery Antoinette; *d* unm 15 July 1963

4c Lettice; *d* unm 27 July 1983

1b Mary Alice; *m* 13 Sept 1859 William Edward Brinckman, 2nd s of Sir Theodore Brinckman 1st Bt (*qv*), and *d* 27 Jan 1901, leaving issue

2b Mary; *m* 1st 6 Sept 1860 Robert Newcomen Gore-Booth, est s of Sir Robert Gore-Booth, 4th Bt (*qv*); *m* 2nd 4 Nov 1865 John Ussher (*d* 8 Dec 1909) and *d* 17 March 1923, having had issue

2a James Francis (Rev); *b* 15 April 1807; *m* 19 Feb 1839 Anne (*d* 13 March 1886), 2nd dau of George Stone, of Blisworth, Northants, and *d* 12 Sept 1849, leaving, with other issue:

1b George; *b* 24 Feb 1844; *m* 14 Oct 1886 Ruth (*d* 18 Feb 1924), dau of Hon Arthur Lascelles (*see* HAREWOOD, E), and *d* 27 Oct 1923

2b Geoffrey (Rev); Rector Warburton, Cheshire; *b* 7 April 1846; *educ* St Mary Hall Oxford (BA); *m* 4 July 1878 Adela Georgina Victorine (*d* 3 Dec 1939), widow of H T Kelsey, and dau of B G Goode, and *d* 23 July 1925

3b Arthur; *b* 3 Jan 1848; *m* 8 July 1874 Edna (*d* 7 May 1901), dau of James Stowe, and *d* 3 Oct 1927, having had:

1c Arthur Francis; *b* 11 Nov 1879; *m* 2 Sept 1908 Beatrice, dau of Samuel Ward, of Pitsmoor, Sheffield, and *dsp* 5 Dec 1959

2c Piers; *b* 16 Sept 1881; *d* unm 11 June 1905

1c Edna Margaret; *d* young 6 Aug 1884

2c Ruth; *m* 16 Jan 1952 Edgar Hunt (*d* 8 April 1959)

3a Henry William; Maj 47th Foot; *b* 16 Aug 1808; *m* 27 May 1835 Harriette Elizabeth (*d* 14 March 1895), dau of Maj-Gen Thomas Evans, CB, and *d* 27 Feb 1868, having had issue:

1b Rowland Henry; *b* 20 March 1840; *d* unm Feb 1861

1b Harriette Sophia; *m* 21 July 1860 Thomas Bennett, Staff-Surgn-Maj, and had issue

2b Charlotte Edith

3b Emma Isabella; *m* 12 Sept 1877 Very Rev Charles Saul Bruce, Dean Cork

4a Peter, CMG; Maj IA, Col Vols S Australia; *b* 15 Aug 1813; *m* 8 Oct 1838 Alicia (*d* 1892), dau of Henry Mant, of Bath, and *d* 1889, leaving issue:

1b Richard; *b* 31 May 1840; *d* 7 July 1917

2b Rowland James; *b* 4 Feb 1846; *m* 14 May 1872 Annie (*d* 1 Dec 1913), dau of John Hart, CMG, and *d* 1918, leaving issue:

1c John; *b* 11 Feb 1873; *m* 1913 Winifred Vaughan and *d* 1943, leaving issue:

1d +Richard John [Richard Egerton-Warburton Esq, 10 Palmer Ave, Myrtle Bank, S Australia]; Capt AIF Res of Offrs; *b* 1917; *m* 1946 *Audrey Doreen Roberts, of Melbourne, and has:

1e *Jill Rosalind; *b* 1948

2e *Elizabeth Jane; *b* 1952

3e *Bronwyn Grey; *b* 1954

1d *Margaret [Mrs Maxwell Dunn, 18 Superba Parade, Mosman, Sydney, NSW, Australia]; *b* 1919; *m* 1st 1940 Lt Robert Paine (*ka* New Guinea 1943); *m* 2nd 1947 Maxwell Dunn (*d* 1966) and by her 1st husb has:

1e *Frances Margaret; *b* 1941

2c Peter Augustus; Imp Light Horse Boer War 1899–1902 (Queen's medal with four clasps); *b* 28 Sept 1877; *m* 12 March 1906 Ellen (*d* 1949), dau of William Fountain, of Saffron Walden, and *d* 9 Sept 1944, leaving:

1d Wilbraham; RAAF WW II; *b* 17 Sept 1911; *m* *Olive Foureur

1d *Elizabeth [Mrs Frank Mosey, Anlaby, via Eudunda, S Australia 5374, Australia]; *b* 4 March 1909; WW II as Nursing Sister AANS; *m* *Frank Mosey

3c Wilbraham; Lt AIF; *b* 14 May 1882; *das* France 25 July 1918

4c Rowland; *b* 8 Oct 1885; *m* 1914 Isabel (*d* 1957), est dau of W F Langdon, and *d* 1963, leaving:

1d +Francis [Francis Egerton-Warburton Esq, 42 Hortense St, Burwood, Victoria, Australia]; *b* 29 April 1917; F/Lt RAAF; *m* 1944 *Joan, dau of P A Ewing, of Bridgetown, W Australia, and has:

1e *Anne; *b* 1945; *m* 1966 *Herbert Timothy Lee-Steere, of Esperance, W Australia, and has issue:

1f *Peter Timothy; *b* 1968

2f *Christopher Ian; *b* 1969

1f *Wendy Anne; *b* 1972

1d *Annie Isabel [Mrs Harold Bray, 27 Clydesdale Street, Como, W Australia]; *b* 1915; *m* 1939 *Harold Vernon Bray and has issue:

1e *Robert Harold; *b* 1942; *m* 1968 *Margaret Esme, dau of T W Maxwell, of Como
2e *Ian Michael; *b* 1943
1e *Marjorie Alison; *b* 1940; *m* 1963 *William Francis Richardson, of Mardella, W Australia, and has:
1f *Michael James; *b* 1966
1f *Felicity Jane; *b* 1970
2e *Gillian Margaret; *b* 1948
1c Margaret
2c Katherine
3b William; *b* 5 Sept 1847; *m* 1877 Edith, dau of W M Sandford, and *d* 1906, leaving:
1c Richard Sandford; Lt AIF Res of Offrs; *b* 1880; *m* 1908 Emily Meredith (*d* 1965), dau of Bayfield Moulden, and *d* 1959, leaving:
1d Peter Bayfield; *b* 1909; 2nd AIF; *m* 1937 Roma Ballands Hosking (*d* 11 April 1997), dau of Frank Becker, of Adelaide, and *d* 31 Dec 1997, leaving:
1e +Richard Francis [Richard Egerton-Warburton Esq, 17A Macquarie Rd, Pymble, NSW 2073, Australia]; *b* 1940; *m* 1966 *Susan Elizabeth, of Perth, Australia, and has issue:
1f +Bayfield James; *b* 1970; *m* 9 Jan 1998 *Emma Louise, dau of D Bradshaw, of NSW
2f +Matthew Robert; *b* 1973
1e *Elizabeth Louise [Mrs Ian Giles, 159 Gover St, N Adelaide, S Australia 5006]; *b* 1938; *m* 1962 *Ian Wesley Giles and has:
1f *Benjamin-Peter Wesley; *b* 1969
1f *Anna Louise; *b* 1963
2f *Sally Elizabeth; *b* 1964
2d Edward Howard; Lt AIF WW II; *b* 1910; *m* 1938 *Margaret Newland [Mrs Edward Egerton-Warburton, 94 Gardner St, Como, W Australia 6152], and *d* 1974, leaving:
1e +Peter Ridgeway; *b* 1941; *m* 3 Feb 1966 (*divorce* 1993) Vanda Sue (*m* 2nd 1995 Philip Langham, of Geraldtown, W Australia), dau of J B Wood, of Bunbury, Australia, and has:
1f +David Peter [David Egerton-Warburton Esq, PO Box 45, Meekatharra, WA 6642, Australia]; *b* 24 Oct 1967; *m* 1st 1990 (*divorce* 1995) Gena Huck; *m* 2nd 1997 *Dr Kathryn Lisa Ford, dau of Ken Ford, of Sydney, NSW, and by his 1st w has:
1g +David William; *b* 1989
2f +Edward James; *b* 1976
1f *Deena Sue; *b* 1969
2f *Rosa Margaret; *b* 1972
1e *Ann; *b* 1946; *m* 17 Jan 1969 *James William Clarke and has:
1f *Benjamin James; *b* 1970; *m* 1990 *Tara Hotham Jenkins
3d William Arnold; *b* 1918; *m* 1940 Letty Dorian Parsons (*d* 1977), and *d* 1976, leaving issue:
1e +Michael; *b* 1948
1d *Meredith; *b* 1913; *m* 1936 *Donald Thomas Mitchell and has issue:
1e*Alan; *b* 1940
1e *Jean Meredith; *b* 1938
2e *Frances Egerton; *b* 1943
2d *Alice Elizabeth Grey [Mrs Robert Bull, 22 Pleasant View Crescent, Glen Waverley, 3150 Victoria, Australia]; *b* 1924; *m* 1947 Robert C Bull (*d* 1987) and has issue:
1e *Hugh; *b* 1954
1e *Helen; *b* 1948
2e *Barbara; *b* 1950
3e *Judy; *b* 1952
2c Philip; *b* 1882; *m* 1912 Olive Rigarlsford, dau of Alfred Palmer, of Kapunda, S Australia, and *d* 1965, leaving:
1d *Patience Anne; *b* 1916
2d *Cecily; *b* 1918
1c Ethel; *b* 1878; *m* 1900 Frank von Doussa (*d* 1928), and *d* 17 April 1961, leaving issue
2c Mary; *m* 1909 Herbert Wilfred Pownall and had:
1d *Robert Alfred; *b* 1913
1d *Elizabeth; *b* 1910
2d *Frances Mary; *b* 1917
1b Eva; *d unm*
2b Ethel Catherine; *m* 1871 Henry Augustus Short (*d* 1904), of Buttamuc, est s of Rt Rev Augustus Short, DD, 1st Bp Adelaide, and had issue
3b Mary; *m* 1893 Rev Pymar Dodd (*d* April 1906)
5a George Edward, 51st Regt; *b* 25 March 1819; *m* 1st 23 Nov 1842 Augusta (*d* 14 Nov 1871), yst dau of Sir Richard Spencer, RN, and had:
1b George Grey; *b* 9 Oct 1843; *m* 23 May 1872 Amy, dau of Edward Hester, JP, and *d* 1913, leaving issue:
1c Grey; *b* 1877; *m* 1901 Verna Grace (*d* 1939), dau of S J Rowe, of Perth, W Australia, and *d* 15 Sept 1954, leaving:
1d +Geoffrey Grey [Geoffrey Egerton-Warburton Esq, Yeriminup, RMB 219, Cranbrook, W Australia 6321, Australia]; *b* 1911; *m* Jan 1940 *Marjorie Vere, dau of Nelson Hamilton-Taylor, of Mount Barker, W Australia, and has:
1e +Arley Geoffrey; *b* Dec 1940; *m* 1970 *Patricia, dau of Philip George Champion de Crespigny, of Ararat, VICT, Australia, and has:
1f +Richard Geoffrey; *b* 22 Aug 1974
1f *Jane Emmeline; *b* 13 Sept 1971
2e +Colin Yorke; *b* 1947; *m* 1978 *Jillian Mae, dau of Robert Pugh, of Carmendale, Narrikup, WA, and has:
1f +Grant Geoffrey; *b* 1979
2f +Jonathan Yorke; *b* 1985
1f *Diana Elizabeth; *b* 1981
1e *Ione Vere; *b* 1942 [Mrs Barry Levinson, Reedy Creek, Glen Thompson, Victoria, Australia]; *m* 1964 *Barry Robert Levinson, s of Robert Francis Levinson, of Perth, W Australia, and has:
1f *Jeremy Barry; *b* 1967
2f *Robert Geoffrey; *b* 1972
1f *Samantha Ione; *b* 1965; *m* 19– *Bruce Derek Doery, of West Mere, Victoria, and has:
1g *Arabella Emma; *b* 1995
2g *Georgia Phoebe; *b* 1997
2f *Joanna Bronte; *b* 1970
2e *Vivienne Gay; *b* 1944; *m* 1965 *Graeme Bruce Stewart, s of John Maurice Stewart, of Kojowup, W Australia, and has:
1f *Andrew Graeme; *b* 1966; *m* 1994 *Alexandra Gellard, of Perth, and has:
1g *Brodie Andrew; *b* 1995
1f *Natasha Egerton; *m* 1995 *Richard Archie Burt, of Claremont, W Australia, and has:
1g *James Stewart; *b* 1996
2g *Mitchell Archie; *b* 1997
2f *Kimberley; *b* 1970
3e *Caroline Marjorie; *b* 11 June 1952; *m* 1977 Dr James William Annear, s of Rev Frank Annear, of Perth, W Australia, and has:
1f *Matthew James; *b* 1979
1f *Katherine Jane; *b* 1981
2f *Josephine Hermione; *b* 1986
2d +Ronald Grey [Ronald Egerton-Warburton Esq, Tambellilup, Frankland River, W Australia]; *b* 1914; *m* 1937 *Edith Mabel, dau of G J A Swiney, of Albany, W Australia, and has issue:
1e +Alexander; *b* 1938; *m* 1st 20 June 1968 (*divorce* 1984) Sheila, dau of Donald La Clair, of Vancouver; *m* 2nd 1986 *Pauline Anne Maxwell and by his 1st w has:
1f +John Alexander; *b* 1973
1f *Brooke Elizabeth; *b* 1971
2e +Michael George [Michael Egerton-Warburton Esq, Mirinup, Frankland River, W Australia]; *b* 1941; *m* 25 May 1966 *Lois Elizabeth, dau of H O Grimbly, of Perth, W Australia, and has:
1f +Antony Michael Grey; *b* 6 Dec 1967
2f +Grey Edward; *b* 1972
3f +Roland George; *b* 1977
3e +David Ronald; *b* 1945; *m* 31 May 1968 *Margaret Elizabeth, dau of A E Challenor, of Dandallup, W Australia, and has:
1f +Joshua David; *b* 1975
1f *Blanceh Elizabeth; *b* 1971
2f *Edwyna Margaret; *b* 1974
1e *Jennifer Mary; *b* 1940; *m* 1964 *John W Mattiske, of Norla Kojonup, W Australia, and has issue:
1f *Peter Rex; *b* 1972
1f *Marie Louise; *b* 20 Aug 1966
2f *Jane; *b* 30 Sept 1968
2e *Diana Margaret; *b* 1943; *m* 1972 *Ivan Johnson, of Perth, W Australia, and has issue:
1f *Daniel Slade; *b* 1981
1f *Joanna; *b* 1974
2f *Jennifer Lee; *b* 1977
1d *Dorothy Antoinette [Mrs George Swiney, Franklands, Frankland River, W Australia]; *b* 1909; *m* 1934 *George Alexander Swiney, and has issue:
1e *Wayne Haig Egerton; *b* 1935
2e *Graham Haig; *b* 1940
1c Georgia; *b* 1874; *m* 20 Dec 1900 Leslie Peel Hall, of the Audit Office, Perth, WA
2c Mary August; *b* 1875
3c Winifred Amy; *b* 1880; *m* 1st 12 Jan 1907 (*divorce* 1926) Jock Hassell and had issue; *m* 2nd 1932 Thomas Elliott
2b Rowland; *b* 14 Nov 1845; *m* 1881 Mary, dau of John McKail, and *d* 5 Nov 1902, leaving, with three daus:
1c Rowland; AIF WW I; *b* 1883
2c Reginald John; *b* 1885
3c Cecil Edward; AIF WW I; *b* 1887
4c Piers; AIF WW I; *b* 1892; *ka* 1915
5c Philip Augustus; AIF WW I; *b* 1894; *m* 1928 Alice Mary Price (*d* 1995), and *d* 1981, leaving:
1d +Rowland; *b* 1928; *m* 1953 *Laurel Gloria Ferguson and has:
1e +Graeme; *b* 1954; *m* 1984 *Raylene Holding and has:
1f +Peter; *b* 1990
1f *Emma; *b* 1992
2e +Trevor; *b* 1958; *m* 19– (*divorce* 19–) Louise —
1e *Maxine; *b* 1955; *m* 1976 *Gregory Beaton and has issue:
1f *Joseph Finlay; *b* 1978
2f *Donald Peter; *b* 1980
2d +Ross [Ross Egerton-Warburton Esq, RMB 228, W Pingelly, WA 6308, Australia]; *b* 1931; *m* 1954 *Wilma Joan Smoker and has issue:
1e +Dean Ross; *b* 1961; *m* 1985 *Diane Fay Roberts and has:
1f+Justin Roy; *b* 1990
2f +Troy Aron; *b* 1994
1f *Kristy Ann; *b* 1992

2e +Evan Mark; *b* 1966; *m* 1992 *Roslyn Gail Cowcill and has:
1f +Jared Evan; *b* 1996
2f +Blake Adam; *b* 1997
1e *Alison Joy; *b* 1955; *m* 1st 1974 (*divorce* 1989) Bruce Edward Dowsett; *m* 2nd 1991 *Robert Kevin Lee and by her 1st husb has:
1f *Ashley Michael; *b* 1977
2f *Narelle Marie; *b* 1974
2e *Robyn Lois; *b* 1957; *m* 1976 *Arthur Raymond Lines and has:
1f *Craig Philip; *b* 1979
2f *Maree Karen; *b* 1981
3e *Coral Janet; *b* 1960; *m* 1986 *Robert Martin Miles and has:
1f *Jackson Ross; *b* 1990
2f *Alex Stephen; *b* 1992
3f *Eric Gregory; *b* 1993
3d +Philip [Philip Egerton-Warburton Esq, Clayton Rd, Narrogin, WA, Australia]; *b* 1934; *m* 1959 *Georgina May, dau of H F J Higginson, of Pingelly, W Australia, and has:
1e +Michael Philip; *b* 1959; *m* 1982 *Jillian Steer and has issue:
1f +Benjamin Michael; *b* 1986
2f +Nicholas Jeremy; *b* 1990
1f *Rebecca Therese; *b* 1985
2f *Rachel Holly; *b* 1988
2e +Brett Francis; *b* 1970; *m* 1992 *Candice Allan
1e *Debra Suzanne; *b* 1961; *m* 1990 *Peter Evelyn-Liardet and has issue:
1f *Christopher Luke Egerton-Warburton; *b* 1982
1f *Jennifer Kate; *b* 1992
4d +Peter (twin); *b* 1934
6c Farquhar Grey; *b* 1896
3b Horace; *b* 9 Nov 1848; *m* 19 Aug 1875 Selina (*d* 1917), dau of John McKail, and *d* 2 June 1917, leaving:
1c John Le Belward; *b* 1882; *m* 1913 Blanche Josephine van Zuilecom (*d* 24 July 1950) and *d* 1 March 1949, leaving:
1d +John [John Egerton-Warburton Esq, Box 20, Kojonup, WA, Australia]; *b* 1916; *m* 1939 *Celia Maltby, dau of Allan Douglas Robinson, of Subiaco, Perth, W Australia, and has issue:
1e +Quentin [Quentin Egerton-Warburton Esq, Korellup, RMB328, Kojonup 6395, WA, Australia]; *b* 17 Oct 1942; *m* 27 Nov 1965 *Mary Heath, only dau of John Warwick Rowe, of Perth, Western Australia, and has:
1f +David Grey [David Egerton-Warburton Esq, RMB 338, Kojonup 6395, W Australia]; *b* 1970
2f+Robert John Quentin; *b* 1972; *m* 11 Oct 1997 *Natalie Michelle, dau of William Coleman, of Wilgermar Estate, Katanning, W Asutralia 6317
1f *Megan Ann; *b* 24 Nov 1967; *m* 1993 *Bruce Alexander
2e +Alan [Alan Egerton-Warburton, Yeenyellup, Box 20, Kojonup, WA 6395, Australia]; *b* 2 April 1947; *m* 1971 *Cynthia Margaret, dau of C D Lee, of Royston Park, Kojonup, and has:
1f +George Thomas; *b* 1988
1f *Rachael Margaret; *b* 1972
2f *Emily Jane; *b* 1974
3f *Diana Elizabeth; *b* 1986
1e *Celia Ruth; *b* 1940; *m* 10 Dec 1960 her cousin +Anthony Randle Egerton-Warburton (*see below*) and has issue
2c Horace Grey; *b* 1891; *m* 1st 1915 Ruth (*d* 1918), dau of Randle Egerton-Warburton (*see below*), and had:
1d *Mary Ruth; *b* 1916; *m* 1st 1941 Edward Henry Finch, RAAF (*ka* 1943), and has issue:
1e *Penelope; *b* 1942
1d Mrs Edward Finch *m* 2nd 1946 *Vernon Wells, RAAF, and has further issue:
1e *Grey Egerton; *b* 1947
2e *Peter Randell Scott; *b* 1950
2e *Diana Ruth; *b* 1948
2d *Joan [Mrs HenryAmbleside, Albany Highway, Armadale, W Australia]; *b* 1918; *m* 1941 *Henry Graham Johnson, AIF, and has:
1e *Richard Grey; *b* 11 Oct 1944; *m* 26 April 1969 *Diane Nevine Skinner
2e *Antony Egerton; *b* 26 April 1959
2c (cont.) Horace Egerton-Warburton *m* 2nd 1920 *Vera [Mrs Horace Egerton-Warburton, St Werburgh's, Mount Barker, W Australia], dau of Charles F Lake, of Melbourne, and *d* 1956, having by her had:
1d +Edward Grey; *b* 1928; *m* 20 Aug 1960 *Elizabeth Rose, dau of J Wade, of Perth, W Australia, and has:
1e +Grey Piers [Grey Egerton-Warburton, PO Box 44, Mt Barker, W Australia]; *b* 1962; *m* 1992 *Jennifer Anne, dau of Dr P Nash, of Perth, W Australia, and has:
1f *Angela Grace; *b* 1993
2f *Mia Susan; *b* 1996
2e +Robin; *b* 1967
1e *Rosemary Carlene; *b* 10 Sept 1961
3d *Yexley Selina [Mrs Gordon Maitland-Roberts, Chelsea, Moora, W Australia]; *b* 1921; *m* 1946 *Gordon Maitland-Roberts, AIF, of Moora, W Australia, and has:
1e *Wade Maitland; *b* 1947
2e *Bruce Gordon; *b* 1950
1e *Helen Ena; *b* 1948
4d *Patricia Ann [Mrs William Chaffey, 119 FitzRoy Street, Tamworth, NSW, Australia]; *b* 6 Nov 1923, SRN; *m* 29 Jan 1946 *Maj William Adolphus Chaffey, MLA, s of Maj Frank Augustus Chaffey, of Tamworth, NSW, and has:
1e *David Frank Egerton; *b* 13 Oct 1957
1e *Mary Ann; *b* 25 Nov 1946
2e *Elizabeth Patricia; *b* 3 Oct 1949
5d *Ann Vera [Mrs Donald Collins, 47 Martin Street, Mount Barker, W Australia]; *b* 28 Dec 1928, twin with her brother; *m* 3 Oct 1952 *Donald Charles Keir Collins and has issue:
1e *Bradford Kier; *b* 9 May 1958
2e *Scott Charles Egerton; *b* 1 April 1962
1e *Joanne Margaret; *b* 12 July 1953; *m* *Robert Leslie Patient, of Auckland, NZ, and has issue:
1f *Robert Donald
2f *Shone William; *b* 11 Nov 1972
1f *Rebecca Faith; *b* 10 Dec 1973
2e *Jacqueline Ann; *b* 7 Oct 1955; *m* 19– *Robert Huisman, of Qld, and has issue:
1f *Saul Simon; *b* 4 Dec 1980
6d *Helen Maud [Mrs John Arnold, Selsey Downs, Kojonup, W Australia]; *b* 1931; *m* 1957 *John Halley Arnold and has issue:
1e *Richard John Halley; *b* 1960
2e *Brooke Egerton Halley; *b* 1962
1e *Amanda Jane; *b* 1958
2e *Michelle Tracey; *b* 1959
7d *Carlene Alice [Mrs John Penn, Parsons St, Mount Barker, W Australia]; *b* 1931 (twin); *m* 1957 *John Ronald Penn and has issue:
1e *Fiona Carlene; *b* 1958
2e *Sally Louise; *b* 1960
1c Maude Mary; *m* 1897 George Mullens (*d* 1906) and has issue
2c Augusta Henrietta; *m* 1903 Montrose Graham, of W Australia, and has issue
3c Sybil Florence; *m* 11 Jan 1905 Rev Frank Collett Carr, Rector Limington, Somerset, and had issue
4c Helen Constance
4b Augustus; *b* 26 March 1850; *m* 20 May 1880 Fanny Augusta (*d* 1927), dau of Edward Hester, and *d* 2 April 1937, leaving:
1c George Edward; *b* 29 Sept 1883
2c Angus; *b* 29 Dec 1891; *m* 1925 *Dorothy [Mrs Angus Egerton-Warburton, RMB 406, Euretta, Kononup, W Australia], dau of John Weston, of Eastwood, Notts, and *d* 1960, leaving issue:
1d +Brian Wayne; *b* 1933
2d +Ian Angus; *b* 27 July 1942; *m* 1965 *Robin, dau of Dr Robert Elphick, of Shenlon Park, and has issue:
1e +Barney; *b* 1968
1e *Simone Elissa; *b* 1966
1d *Joan Irma [Mrs John Money, South Parkfield, N Danalup, W Australia]; *b* 1926; *m* 1st 1950 Ross Bovell (*d* 1950); *m* 2nd 1955 John G Money (*d* 1962)
2d *Evelyn Isabel [Mrs Frank Devine, Hillside, Frankland River, W Australia]; *b* 1928; *m* 1953 *Frank Devine and has:
1e *Peter John; *b* 1954
2e *Christopher James; *b* 1956
3e *Garry Matthew; *b* 1962
1e *Leonie Frances; *b* 1957
3d *Margaret; *b* 1931
4d *Dorothy June [Mrs John Kitto, 55 Mary Street, Como, W Australia]; *b* 1937; *m* 6 May 1961 *John Kitto and has:
1e *Johnson Grey; *b* 27 Jan 1966
2e *Grantham Angus; *b* 17 Sept 1968
3c Reginald Hubert; *b* 4 June 1894; *m* 1925 *Lena Mary Lambe [Mrs Reginald Egerton-Warburton, Woolareen, Kojonup, W Australia], of Bassendean, W Australia, and *d* 1962, leaving issue:
1d +Rex [Rex Egerton-Warburton Esq, Woolareen, Kojonup, W Australia]; *b* 1928; *m* Jan 1946 *Muriel Faith, dau of — Weise, of Austral Terrace, Katanning, W Australia, and has issue:
1e *Diane [Mrs John Partridge, Priory Park, Kojonup, W Australia]; *b* 1946; *m* 1968 *John William Partridge and has:
1f *Craig John; *b* 1969
1f *Cindy Karen; *b* 1968
2e *Denise [Mrs Hall, Lower King Rd, Albany, W Australia 6330]; *b* 1947; *m* 1st 1965 Kevin William Brown; *m* 2nd *— Hall and by her 1st husb has issue:
1f *Darrin Kevin; *b* 1965
2f *Gavin William; *b* 1967
3f *Byron Rex; *b* 1971
3e *Marie; *b* 1953; *m* 1971 *John James Matthews and has issue:
1f *Chad James; *b* 1972
2f *Damon John; *b* 1974
1f *Lisa Maree; *b* 1979
1d *Dawn [Miss Dawn Egerton-Warburton, Cherryton, Kojonup, W Australia]; *b* 1926
1c Blanche; *b* 27 Feb 1881
2c Mabel Augusta; *b* 16 Oct 1885; *m* 1906 Thomas Stead Merfield and had issue
3c Isabel Frances; *b* 15 May 1887
4c Jessie; *b* 4 June 1893; *m* 5 Oct 1921 Capt Frederick William Cox, MC, 10th Australian Light Horse Regt, and had:
1d Charles Ian; F/O RAAF WW II; *b* 1 July 1922; missing N Borneo 25 March 1945

2d *Frederick George; MB, BS, MRCOG, F/O RAAF WW II 1942–45 with RAF Bomber Cmd; *b* 24 Feb 1924; *m* 1961 *Judith Pinder and has issue:
1e *Andrew Whitworth; *b* 29 Jan 1965
3d *Reginald Egerton; P/O RAAF WW II 1943–45; *b* 4 Aug 1925
5b Reginald; *b* 27 June 1855; *d* unm 1890
6b Philip; *b* 28 Aug 1856
7b Randle; *b* 17 Sept 1860; *m* 1890 Eva (*d* 1931), dau of Edward Hester, and *d* 1938, leaving issue:
1c Piers Edward; 10th Australian Light Horse Palestine WW I; *b* 25 Nov 1895; *m* 1920 Winsome (*d* 1971), dau of John Ewing, MLC, of W Australia, and *d* Oct 1961, having had issue:
1d Judith; *b* 28 Feb 1922; *d* 10 Feb 1927
2d *Diana; *b* 17 Nov 1924; *m* 1945 *Julian B Goyder and has issue:
1e *Piers Bruce; *b* 1950
1e *Melody Anne; *b* 1946
2e *Elizabeth ; *b* 1947
3d *Pamela [Mrs Samuel Clarkson, 57 Irvine St, Peppermint Grove, Perth, W Australia]; *b* 21 June 1929; *m* 1953 *Samuel Forster Clarkson and has issue:
1e *Simon Nicholas; *b* 3 Dec 1957
1e *Eve [Dr Eve Clarkson, 7c Keane St, Peppermint Grove, Perth, W Australia]; *b* 11 May 1954; *m* 1976 *Andrew Steven Stavrianou and has:
1f *Christopher Andrew Steven; *b* 20 Sept 1980
1f *Angela Eve; *b* 1 Oct 1982
2f *Winsome Mary; *b* 5 Oct 1985
4d *Jenefer; *b* 21 Nov 1933; *m* 19– *Ian P Johnston, of Dardanup, W Australia, and has issue:
1e *Ian Justin; *b* 1958
1e *Julia; *b* 1956
2e *Andrea; *b* 1963
3e *Diana; *b* 1965
5d *Angela [Mrs John Roberts, 51 Saunders St, Mosman Park, W Australia]; *b* 10 May 1941; *m* 1964 *John Charles Roberts and has:
1e *Andrew Timothy; *b* 1966
2e *Timothy Andrew; *b* 1970
1e *Denby Emma; *b* 1976
2c Randle Norman; *b* 1 Nov 1897; *d* June 1898
3c George Grey; *b* 24 May 1899; *m* Feb 1929 *Ethel Vernon, dau of Edmund Vernon Drake-Brockman, JP, and *d* 1975, leaving issue:
1d +Anthony Randle [Anthony Egerton-Warburton Esq, Brackenhurst, PO Box 80, Bridgetown 6255, Western Australia]; *b* 23 Sept 1935; *m* 10 Dec 1960 *Celia Ruth, only dau of John Egerton-Warburton (*see* above), and has:
1e +Randle [Randle Egerton-Warburton Esq, Brackenhurst, Bridgetown, W Australia]; *b* 1 March 1963
2e +Nicholas [Nicholas Egerton-Warburton Esq, 44 Alfred St, Waratah, Newcastle, NSW, Australia]; *b* 25 Feb 1966; *educ* U of W Australia (B Comm); *m* 4 Oct 1992 *Ann Guthrie, 2nd dau of Justice John Bryson, of Pymble, NSW
1e *Belinda Jane [Mrs Andrew Viner, 89 Lyall St, Kalgoorlie, W Australia]; *b* 5 Nov 1961; *educ* Curtin U W Australia (B Social Work); *m* 1984 *Andrew John Viner, 2nd s of Hon Ian Viner, QC, of Cottesloe, W Australia and has:
1f *Jack Randle; *b* 1986
1f *Fleur Ruth; *b* 1988
2f *Rosemary Jane; *b* 1993
2e *Belinda Ruth [Miss Belinda Egerton-Warburton, 96 King St, E Freemantle, W Australia]; *b* 1967
2d +Vernon Grey; *b* 13 May 1938; *m* 1970 *Jeanny Vlahov and has:
1e +George; *b* 1971
2e +Anton; *b* 1972
1e *Virginia; *b* 1974
1d *Dorothy Vernon [Mrs John Boyle, 40 Tyrell Street, Nedlands, W Australia 6009, Australia]; *b* 3 Nov 1929; *m* 9 Sept 1954 *John Gordon Boyle, 7th Gurkha Rifles, 2nd s of Rev John Boyle, of Bellaghy, Co Derry, and has issue:
1e *Angela Egerton; *b* 5 Nov 1955; *educ* U of Western Australia (BA, Dip Ed); *m* 1989 *Anthony Francis Phillips, MPhil, and has:
1f *Ariane Margaret Emerald; *b* 1991
2f *Genevieve Georgia Elizabeth; *b* 1993
2e *Erica Egerton; *b* 4 March 1960; *educ* U of NSW (BLArch); *m* 1987 *Antony Luke Radunovich, BMechEng, and has issue:
1f *Marcus John; *b* 1989
2f *Antony Michael; *b* 1990
1f *Miranda Adelaide; *b* 1992
2d *Fleur [Mrs John Aitken, Han-ora, Havelock North, Hawkes Bay, New Zealand]; *b* 6 July 1932; *m* 1956 *John Aitken and has:
1e *Timothy Murray; *b* 1957; *m* 1986 *Susan Loffler and has:
1f *Richard George Murray; *b* 1988
2f *Andrew Robert; *b* 1990
3f *Michael Timothy; *b* 1992
2e *Hamish; *b* 29 March 1960; *m* 1993 *Susan Goodman
1e *Judith Jill; *b* 29 Feb 1962; *m* 1989 *Bruce Thomas Wagg and has issue:
1f *Timothy Guy Thomas; *b* 1991
1c Bertha Evelyn; *b* 22 Nov 1890; *m* 1926 Ulick Lord Daly, s of Ulick A Daly, of Victoria, and has issue
2c Cecily Alice; *b* 26 July 1892; *m* 22 July 1919 Maitland John Drake Brockman (*d* 1969) and had:
1d *Egerton Charles [Egerton Brockman Esq, Laverton Downs, Laverton, W Australia]; *b* 23 June 1927; *m* 1948 *Daphne Anderson and has issue:
1e *John; *b* 9 Nov 1949
2e *Philip; *b* Nov 1950
1e *Viki; *b* April 1954
2e *Elizabeth; *b* 1961
1d Mollie Agatha; *b* 30 March 1920; *m* 8 Oct 1949 *Brig James Roy Anderson, CBE, Roy Sussex Regt, and *d* 1997, leaving:
1e *Hamish Warburton Findlater; *b* 22 Sept 1952
1e *Sheena Fiona Egerton; *b* 17 Sept 1954
2d *Cecily Jean; *b* 3 July 1921; *m* 1st 1 June 1944 (*divorce* 1955) Richard Smallpiece Whitington; *m* 2nd 1962 (*divorce* 1972) Maj-Gen Paul Alfred Cullen, CBE, DSO, ED, and by her 1st husb has:
1e *Richard Mark [Richard Whitington Esq, 28 Harcourt St, Dublin 2, Ireland]; *b* 2 Jan 1947
2e *James Jerome; *b* 15 July 1951
3d *Francis Margaret [Mrs John Fenwick, Dempster Street, Esperance, W Australia]; *b* 22 March 1923; *m* 1951 *John Fenwick and has issue:
1e *Jane Deborah; *b* 1959
3c Ruth; *b* 14 May 1894; *m* 1915 her cousin Horace Grey-Egerton-Warburton and *d* 1918 (*see* above)
4c *Margaret Augusta; *b* 9 April 1903; *m* 1st 3 Sept 1932 Robert Willgress, BSc, FRIC (*d* 23 Feb 1956); *m* 2nd 19– *William Francis Dudley Allison, MIMechE, Br Colonial Serv
5c Kathleen Sybil; *b* 9 July 1904; *d* 27 Jan 1905
8b Edward; *b* 25 Sept 1867; *d* 7 Feb 1931
1b Alice; *m* 13 March 1870 Rev Waldyve Willington Tarleton (*d* 1894) and *d* 28 Sept 1931, leaving issue
2b Mary; *m* 25 July 1870 Cecil Rogers, of Torquay, and *d* 6 Aug 1930
3b Emma; *d* unm 22 Nov 1918
4b Ann; *m* 1884 William Wallace Mitchell (*d* 1929), of Albany, W Australia
5a (cont.) George Edward Egerton-Warburton *m* 2nd 14 April 1873 Emma (*d* 1896), dau of Rev James Coghlan, and *d* 1889, leaving by her:
9b Francis Joseph; barrister; *b* 3 March 1876; *educ* Keble Coll Oxford (MA); *m* 1920 *Edith Evelyn, dau of Henry Prest, of Wallasey, Cheshire, and *d* 8 Jan 1923
10b Cecil William, TD; Lt-Col TAR WW I and War Office; *b* 20 Nov 1878; *educ* Trin Coll Oxford (MA); *d* 30 July 1934

The 8th Bt's bro,

Rev Sir PHILIP EGERTON later GREY-EGERTON (roy licence 1825), **9th Bt**, of Egerton and Oulton Rector Tarporley; *b* 6 July 1767; *m* 14 Sept 1804 Rebecca (*d* 11 June 1870 aged 90), yst dau of Josia Du Pré, of Wilton Park, Bucks, and *d* 13 Dec 1829, having had:

1 **Sir Philip de Malpas Grey-Egerton, 10th Bt**; *b* 13 Nov 1806; Tstee Br Museum and Senate London U, MP Chester and Cheshire; FRS; *m* 8 March 1832 Anna Elizabeth (*d* 26 Nov 1882), 3rd dau of George John Legh (*see* GREY, B), and *d* 5 April 1881, having had issue:
(1) **Sir Philip le Belward Grey-Egerton**, 11th Bt, DL (Cheshire); *b* 28 March 1833; Hon Lt-Col 4th Bn Cheshire Regt, Capt Coldstream Gds and Rifle Bde; *m* 18 July 1861 Henrietta Elizabeth Sophia (*d* 15 July 1924), dau of 1st Baron Londesborough (*qv*), and *d* 1 Sept 1891, having had, with other issue:
1a **Sir Philip Henry Brian Grey-Egerton, 12th Bt**, JP, DL; Maj and Brevet Lt-Col TFR, formerly Earl of Chester's Yeo, Capt 4th Bn Cheshire Regt; *b* 29 April 1864; *m* 1st 4 Jan 1893 (*divorce* 1906) Mary Carolyn Campbell (*d* 9 Nov 1950), dau of Maj J Wayne Cuyler, of the USA, and had issue:
1 Philip de Malpas Wayne; Lt 19th Queen Alexandra's Own Roy Hus; *b* 4 April 1895; *educ* Eton and Cambridge; *ka* 8 Oct 1918
2 Rowland le Belward; 2nd Lt Roy Welch Fus; *b* 4 April 1895; *educ* Wellington; *ka* 30 Oct 1914
1 Cecily Alice Grey, MBE (1920), JP Dorset; *m* 30 July 1918 Lt-Col Denys Edward Prideaux-Brune, DSO and bar (*d* 4 June 1952), 2nd s of Col Charles Robert Prideaux-Brune, of Prideaux Place, Cornwall, and had issue
1a (cont.) **Sir Philip** *m* 2nd 26 April 1910 Aimée Mary (*d* 25 Nov 1958), formerly w of Sir Rupert Turner Havelock Clarke, 2nd Bt (*see* CLARKE, Bt, of Rupertswood), and dau of Hon Thomas Forrest Cumming, of Victoria, MLC, and *dspms* 4 July 1937
1a Violet Edith Grey; *b* 1 May 1870; *m* 3 Aug 1897 3rd Baron Romilly (*see* 1970 edn) and *d* 1 March 1906, leaving issue
(2) Rowland; Lt-Col Rifle Brigade; *b* 23 Oct 1838; *d* 2 April 1923
(1) Anna Mary Elizabeth; *m* 8 May 1855 Henry Reginald Corbet (*d* 4 May 1902), of Adderley, Salop, and *d* 3 March 1927, leaving issue (*see* 1970 edn CORBET, Bt)
(2) Cecily Louisa; *m* 29 June 1878 6th Earl of Selkirk (*qv*) and *d* 10 Jan 1920
2 Charles Du Pré; *b* 4 Jan 1809; Lt-Col Rifle Bde; *d* unm 30 June 1855
3 John Francis; Maj HEIC's Horse Artillery; *b* 10 Aug 1810; *ka* 23 Jan 1845
4 William Henry Egerton (Rev); MA Oxon, Rector Whitchurch, Salop, Preb Lichfield; *b* 13 Nov 1811; *m* 11 March 1840 Louisa (*d* June 1902), dau of Brooke Cunliffe (*see* CUNLIFFE, Bt), and *d* 16 March 1910, having had:
(1) William Willoughby; Lt-Col 2nd Bn Liverpool Regt; *b* 4 May 1842; *d* unm 8 March 1899
(2) Rev Sir BROOKE de MALPAS EGERTON later GREY-EGERTON, **13th Bt**; *b* 19 Aug 1845; *educ* BNC Oxford (MA); Rector Stoke-on-Terne, Salop, RD Hodnet; *m* 26 June 1878 Alice Catherine (*d* 8 March 1913), dau of Rev Edward Rose Breton, MA, and *dsp* 5 Nov 1945
(3) John Francis; Lt-Col Worcs Regt; *b* 7 Nov 1846; *d* unm 26 Dec 1898
(4) Frederick Philip; *b* 8 Aug 1853; *d* unm 22 Sept 1906

(1) Mary; *d* unm 18 Dec 1920
(2) Mabel; *m* 13 Nov 1893 Robert Peel Ethelston (*d* 9 May 1906), of Hinton, Salop, and *d* 9 Feb 1927
5 Caledon Richard; Maj-Gen 89th Regt, DAG, Mil Sec; *b* 28 July 1814; *m* 30 March 1843 Margaret (*d* 7 Sept 1900), 3rd dau of Alexander Cumming, of the Island of St Vincent, and *d* 27 May 1874, having had issue:
(1) Richard; barrister, RM Jamaica; *b* 10 July 1844; *m* 21 June 1892 Caroline Mary (*d* 20 May 1926), er dau of Rev David Phillips Lewis, Rector Llandrinio, Montgomeryshire, and *d* 6 Oct 1900, having had issue:
1a Caledon Richard; *b* 23 Jan 1895; *d* 28 June 1900
(2) Caledon Philip; Col cmdg 39 Regt Dist, Col Dorset Regt, Mashsud Waziri Expdn 1881 (despatches); *b* 4 Aug 1846; *m* 21 Oct 1884 Caroline Blanche (*d* 28 March 1912), dau of Rev Reginald Southwell Smith (*see* SMITH-MARRIOTT, Bt), and *d* 4 Oct 1930, leaving:
1a PHILIP REGINALD BELWARD (Sir), **14th Bt**
(3) Charles Comyn (Sir), GCB (1904), DSO (1891); FM IA, Col 23rd Cav IA 1904, memb India Cncl 1907–17, Afghanistan, India, Egypt and Somaliland; *b* 10 Nov 1848; *m* 7 Aug 1877 Anna Wellwood (*d* 17 Dec 1890), dau of James Lawson Hill, WS, of Edinburgh, and *d* 20 Feb 1921, leaving:
1a Wion de Malpas, DSO (1917); V-Adml, ADC to HM GEORGE V 1928, WW I (despatches), WW II in RNR as Cdre Convoys; *b* 1879; *m* 2 Sept 1913 Anita Adolphine (*d* 1972), only dau of Albert Rudolph David, of Eastfield, Grimsby, and was *ka* 1 Jan 1943, leaving issue:
1b +David Boswell, CB (1968), OBE (1956), MC (1940) [Maj-Gen David Egerton CB OBE MC, Campion Cottage, Cheselbourne, Dorset DT2 7NT], Maj-Gen late RA, FIMechE, WW II, Dir-Gen Artillery MOD 1964–67, V-Pres and Sr Army Memb Ordnance Bd 1967–69, Pres 1969–70, Col Cmdt RA to 1975; *b* 24 July 1914; *educ* Stowe and RMA Woolwich; *m* 10 April 1946 *Margaret Gillian, yst dau of Rev Canon Charles Cuthbert Inge, of Streatley, Berks, and has issue:
1c +William de Malpas [William Egerton Esq, Northdown Farmhouse, Sutton Rd, Sutton Poyntz, Weymouth, Dorset]; *b* 27 April 1949; *educ* Sherborne; MA Cambridge; *m* 1971 *Ruth, only dau of Rev George Watson, and has:
1d +Matthew Robert; *b* 1977; *educ* Stanbridge Earls
2d +Richard John; *b* 1980; *educ* Sherborne
1c *Charlotte Mary [Mrs Stephen Dixon, 58 Abinger Ave, Cheam, Surrey]; *b* 12 Aug 1950; BA Oxon; *m* 1987 *Stephen William Dixon, FIA, and has issue:
1d *John David William; *b* 1988
1d *Rose Margaret Elizabeth; *b* 1991
2c *(Margaret) Caroline [Ms Caroline Egerton, 2 Park Farm Rd, Kingston-upon-Thames, Surrey KT2 5TQ]; *b* 30 July 1955; *educ* Oxford (MA) and Lancaster U (MA); *m* 1984 *Martin George White, BSc, FIA, and has:
1d *Philip Martin; *b* 1987
2d *Robert Charles; *b* 1989
3d *Oliver Richard; *b* 1992
1b *Penelope [Mrs Penelope Ibberson, 38A High St, Puddletown, Dorset]; 2nd Offr WRNS WW II; *b* 1 Dec 1919; *m* 29 Aug 1955 (*divorce* 1967) Maj John Michael de Burgh Ibberson, 16th/5th Queen's Roy Lancers, and has:
1c *Erika Mary; *b* 25 April 1956; *m* 1985 *— and has issue:
1d *Owen Robert; *b* 1986
2d *Inigo John; *b* 1987
2c Clare Anita; *b* 29 Sept 1959; *d* 1971
2b *Alison [Mrs Richard Gregory, Rosslyn, Charmouth Rd, Lyme Regis, Dorset DT7 3DW]; WW II as 3rd Offr WRNS; *b* 4 Dec 1922; *m* 30 Aug 1955 *Lt-Col Richard Boutcher Gregory, RA, s of Capt Ernest Forster Gregory, CBE, RN, of Freshwater, IoW, and has issue:
1c *Andrew Richard; *b* 19 Nov 1957; Lt-Col RA; *m* 1986 *Sally Sheard and has issue:
1d *Rupert James; *b* 1987
2d *Charles Henry; *b* 1990
1c *Jane Patricia; *b* 15 Aug 1960; *m* 20 May 1989 *Maj David Christopher Wicks, RLC, and has:
1d *Toby Edward; *b* 1991
1d *Rebecca Mary; *b* 1994
2a James Boswell; Maj 23rd Cav IA, Waziristan 1901–02 (despatches, medal with clasp), Somaliland 1903–04 (despatches, medal with two clasps) and WW I, Croix de Guerre; *b* 4 Nov 1880; *ka* 27 Oct 1918
3a Charles Caledon; Lt W R Regt, Staff Capt 13th Bde BEF WW I (despatches twice); *b* 17 Nov 1886; *m* 28 Dec 1914 Madaleine (*d* 24 Sept 1965), er dau of Edward Miles Clayton, CB, of Cleaghmore, Ballinasloe, Co Galway, and was *ka* 18 April 1915
(4) Reginald Arthur (Sir), CB (1904); Sec to the Post Office Ireland 1897–1912, ktd 1911; *b* 22 Sept 1850; *m* 23 Jan 1877 Margaret (*d* 5 Aug 1919), dau of Hon J Baker, of Morialta, S Australia, and *d* 17 Nov 1930, leaving:
1a Reginald Francis Le Belward; *b* 31 March 1880; *m* 1907 Elsie Lilian Rose Harris and *d* 16 July 1927, leaving:
1b +Rowland Le Belward [Rowland Egerton, 1165 Bay St, Apt 10, San Francisco, CA 94123, USA]; *b* 11 Aug 1914; *m* 1945 *Denise, dau of Capt Denis Hayes, MBE
2a Wilfrid Allen, CMG (1919); R-Adml, ADC to HM GEORGE V 1930, Boer War 1899–1900 with Naval Bde (medal, five clasps), WW I (despatches, Legn Hon, Order St Stanislas Russia 2nd Cl with swords, 3rd Cl Order Sacred Treasure Japan); *b* 17 May 1881; *m* 20 June 1916 Helen (*d* 9 Jan 1964 aged 88), dau of Charles J Cunningham, DL, of St Boswells, and *d* 18 July 1931
3a Philip; *b* 18, *d* 21 March 1884
4a Hugh; *b* 19 May 1885; *d* an infant
5a Robert, MC; Capt Roy Irish Fus, Sqdn Cdr RFC WW I (despatches twice); *b* 26 Aug 1892; *ka* 23 Dec 1917
6a Thomas Graham (Dom Philip); *b* 23 Sept 1889; *educ* St Benet's Hall Oxford (BA); Lt RN WW I; monk
1a Mary Caledon; nun Convent of Poor Clares, Baddesley Clinton, Knowle, Warwicks; *b* 1 Feb 1878
2a Winefride Annie le Clerc; Sister of Charity of St Vincent de Paul; *b* 14 Feb 1879; *d* 11 Feb 1953
3a Hilda Dupré; Sister of Mercy; *b* 25 Jan 1883; *d* 19–
4a Dorothy; *b* 5 Nov 1886; *d* an infant
(5) George le Clerc (Sir), KCB (1910, CB 1897); Adml, C-in-C Cape of Good Hope Station 1908–10, 2nd Sea Ld 1911, C-in-C Plymouth Station 1913–16, ADC, Arctic Expdn 1875–76 (medal), Ch Staff Benin Expdn 1897 (despatches); *b* 17 Oct 1852; *m* 1st 5 Dec 1882 Frances Emily (*d* 5 Jan 1926), dau of Murray Gladstone, and had:
1a William Markham Le Clerc, DSO (1916); Cdr RNVR, served WW I as Cdr Hood Bn RN Div (wounded twice, despatches); *b* 28 Oct 1883; *educ* Wellington; *m* 7 Jan 1919 Ethel Daisy (*d* 22 Nov 1956), widow of Capt Alexander Cecil Graham, Gren Gds, and dau of Harry Kent Paxton, of Kensington, and *dsp* 29 May 1969
2a Brian, JP Hants 1938; R-Adml, Naval ADC to HM GEORGE V 1935; *b* 15 March 1886
1a Dorothy; *b* 18 July 1887; *m* 24 Jan 1911 Adml Philip Wylie Dumas, CB, CVO (*d* 12 Dec 1948), s of H J P Dumas, JP, and had issue
(5) (cont.) Sir George Egerton *m* 2nd 22 Oct 1932 *Margaret Stella, widow of Reginald Wickham Prentice, of Beauworth Manor, Alresford, and dau of Col Charles Albert Maunsell, and *d* 30 March 1940
(6) Francis William; Lt Col ISC; *b* 28 Dec 1854; *m* 1st 1 Jan 1887 Margaret Josephine (*d* 4 Sept 1899), dau of Col Thomas Heaton Lovett, of Belmont; *m* 2nd 1 Sept 1904 Alice Emily Marriott (*m* 2nd 30 April 1929 George Henry Blore, est s of Rev Canon G J Blore, DD), er dau of Col Walter William Marriott Smith, RA (*see* SMITH-MARRIOTT, Bt), and *d* 25 Feb 1908, having by his 1st w had:
1a Hubert Le Clerc; *b* 1888; *d* an infant.
(7) Brian (Sir), KCIE (1914, CIE 1906); Punjab Police, Afghan War 1880–81 (medal), Cont-Gen of Paigahs Hyderabad; *b* 27 Nov 1857; *educ* Cheltenham; *d* 12 June 1940
(1) Florence Maud; *d* unm 11 Dec 1953 in her 94th year
(2) Edith Rebecca; *d* unm 15 Jan 1943
6 Frederic Arthur; Cdr RN; *b* 30 April 1816; *m* 26 June 1848 Juliet Olivia (*d* 20 March 1881), dau of William Shelton Burnett, and *d* 2 May 1857, leaving:
(1) Frederick Philip; *b* 1853
(1) Juliet Rebecca; *m* 23 March 1875 Roger Assheton Ramsbotham (*d* 8 Nov 1884), of Ebnal Grange, Malpas, Cheshire, and *d* 8 March 1925, leaving issue
(2) Mary Cotton; *m* 26 Aug 1884 Petley Lloyd Augustus Price, and *d* 1946, leaving issue (*see* RUGGE-PRICE, Bt)
7 George Henry (Rev); MA Oxon, Rector Myddle, Salop, Preb Lichfield; *b* 20 Feb 1822; *m* 1st 4 Aug 1846 Mary (*d* 16 July 1876), widow of Sir William Marjoribanks, 2nd Bt, of Lees (*see* 1935 edn TWEEDMOUTH, B), and dau of Henry Stone; *m* 2nd 12 May 1881 Clara (*d* 1945), dau of J T Oswald, of Dunnikier, Fife, and *d* 12 July 1905, leaving:
(1) Arthur Oswald; Lt Salop LI; *b* 5 Aug 1890; *ka* 25/26 Sept 1915
(1) Bridget Ellin; *b* 14 May 1888; *m* 8 June 1920 Maurice Cowper Johnson, 5th s of Canon W Cowper Johnson, Rector Yaxham, Norfolk
1 Mary Anne Elizabeth; *b* 26 May 1841 Charles Robert Cotton and *d* 5 July 1902, leaving issue (*see* COMBERMERE, V)
2 Madelina
3 Eglantine; *d* 31 July 1835
4 Fanny Sarah; *d* 28 Jan 1835
5 Catherine Rebecca; *d* 7 May 1840

The 13th Bt's cousin,

Sir Philip Reginald Le Belward Grey Egerton, 14th Bt, JP, DL Cheshire; High Sheriff 1941, Sudan CS, Hon Col 521 LAA Regt, RA (TA) 1947, Lt 3rd Bn Salop LI, Order Nile 4th Cl; *b* 3 Sept 1885; *m* 1st 15 Jan 1916 Dorothy Aveys (*d* 26 April 1952), er twin dau of Brig-Gen John Henry Balguy, RA, of Brockhampton, Dorset, and had:
1 Sir PHILIP JOHN CALEDON GREY EGERTON, **15th and present Bt**
2 +BRIAN BALGUY LE BELWARD [Brian Egerton Esq, Regency Lodge, 56 Braidley Rd, Bournemouth, Dorset, BH2 6JY]; *b* 5 Feb 1925; heir presumptive; *educ* Repton
1 Mary Blanche Aveys; Section Offr WAAF WW II; *b* 3 Dec 1916; *m* 1 Aug 1939 Vincent Akroyd Palliser Costabadie, FRCS Ed, DOMS (*d* 14 Feb 1959)

Sir Philip *m* 2nd 11 Oct 1961 Kathleen, widow of Brian Thorburn Dickson, and dau of Peter Crook, of Borwick Lodge, nr Ambleside, Lancs, and *d* 9 June 1962

GRIDLEY

Arms: Gu. three bendlets enhanced and in base a portcullis chained or. **Crest:** A wyvern az. semée of lozenges or, resting the dexter claw on a grid iron gu. **Supporters:** Dexter, a wyvern az. semée of lozenges or; sinister, a lion gu. semée of grid irons gold.
Motto: *Devant si je puis* ('To the fore if I can').
Creation: B. (UK) 10 Jan 1955.

THE 3RD BARON GRIDLEY, of Stockport, Co Palatine of Chester (Richard David Arnold Gridley) [The Rt Hon The Lord Gridley, 79 Purbrook Gdns, Purbrook, Hants PO7 5LE]; *b* 22 Aug 1956; *s* f 1996; *educ* Monkton Coombe and Portsmouth Poly; *m* 1st 28 July 1979 (*divorce*) Amanda Jane, dau of Ian Mackenzie; *m* 2nd 1983 *Suzanne Elizabeth Ripper and by her has:

1 +CARL RICHARD; *b* 5 Feb 1981

1 *Danielle Lauren; *b* 1983

Lineage: JOSEPH GRIDLEY, of Bristol; *b* 1801; *m* Charlotte Bucknole and had: EDWARD GRIDLEY, of Bristol; *b* 1842; *m* Emily Mary (*d* 20 Jan 1882), dau of Thomas Babb, and *d* 20 Oct 1932, having had:

1 Edward Thomas; *d* unm NZ 1910

2 ARNOLD BABB, **1st Baron**

1 Florence Amelia; *m* W Lang

2 Mabel Gertrude; *m* F Edmonstone

3 Emily Mary, *d* Canada April 1965

The yr son,

ARNOLD BABB GRIDLEY, **1st Baron Gridley**, of Stockport, Co Palatine of Chester (UK), so *cr* 10 Jan 1955, KBE (1920); *b* 16 July 1878; *educ* Bristol GS and Clifton Laboratories; consulting engr, MIEE, Dir Electric Mfg, Controller Electric Power Supply Min Munitions 1916–19, Special Duties Home Office Jan-Sept 1919, MP (C) Stockport 1935–50 and Stockport S 1950–55, chm C Members Ctee 1946–51, pres Assoc Br Chambers Commerce 1946–48; *m* 10 Aug 1905 Mabel (*d* 5 July 1955), dau of Oliver Hudson, of Fakenham, Norfolk, and *d* 27 July 1965, leaving:

1 ARNOLD HUDSON GRIDLEY, **2nd Baron Gridley**; *b* 26 May 1906; *educ* Oundle; Colonial Serv 1928, served Malaya, interned by Japanese Changi Gaol Malaya 1941–44, Actg Dep Comptroller Fedn Malaya 1956–57, memb Cncl Overseas (Serv) Pensioners Assoc 1966, Somerset CC Appeal Tbnl 1966, dir New Homes Bldg Soc 1963, Lawdon Ltd 1968, chm then life pres Cascom Ltd, consultant Care for the Wild 1990–96,Tstee Far East Prisoners of War & Internees Fund 1973, ktd 1957; *m* 4 Dec 1948 *(Edna) Lesley Winifred [The Rt Hon Lesley Lady Gridley, Coneygore, Stoke Trister, Somerset BA9 9PG], dau of Leslie Richard Wheen, of Shanghai, China, and Penselwood, Somerset, and *d* 15 June 1996, leaving:

(1) RICHARD DAVID ARNOLD GRIDLEY, **3rd and present Baron Gridley**

(1) *Susan Lesley [The Hon Mrs Woods, 127 Sound Beach Ave, Old Greenwich, CT 06870, USA]; *b* 23 Jan 1950; *m* 1st 29 Jan 1975 John Philip Bruce Scott, s of R E Scott, of Reigate; *m* 2nd 1983 *Andrew Kinderbee Woods and by her 1st husb has issue:

1a *Edward Harry Gridley; *b* 20 Mar 1977

1a *Carrie Elizabeth Anne; *b* 14 Oct 1979

(2) *Alison Elizabeth Vivienne [Mrs Alison Hall, 81 Finsbury Park Rd, London N4]; *b* 27 June 1953; *educ* Oxford (BA 1974); *m* 2 Aug 1975 (*divorce* 1978) Michael John Hall, s of Peter Hall, of Reigate

(3) *Vivienne Nicola [The Hon Mrs Harvey, 1 Place des Freres, Tissandier, Croissy sur Seine 78290, France]; *b* 6 Feb 1955; *m* 5 Aug 1978 *John Clavert Harvey, s of William Harvey, of Sanderstead, Surrey, and has issue:

1a *William Marc Gridley; *b* 1986

1a *Hannah Louise; *b* 1983

2 Eric Howard; *b* 19 Dec 1911; *educ* Oundle and Roy Coll Science London; *m* 18 July 1936 Florence Sybil (*d* 1979), dau of Charles Darnell Bacon, of Loftus, Yorks, and *d* 30 March 1946, leaving issue:

(1) +Peter Arnold Charles [Peter Gridley Esq, Bigmore Cottage, Bigmore Lane, Stokenchurch, Bucks HP14 3UP]; *b* 5 April 1940; *educ* Nautical Coll Pangbourne; *m* 1966 *Padmani Marie, dau of Maj P D Pelpola, MBE, of Gampola, Sri Lanka

(2) +Howard Eric; plant breeder Uganda; *b* 8 April 1945; *educ* Fettes, Glasgow U (BSc) and Selwyn Coll Cambridge (DipAgS)

1 Elsa Joan, OBE (1963), JP (Lancs 1953); *b* 15 Aug 1907; *m* 5 Nov 1929 Col Gerald Collingwood, TD, CEng, FIMechE, yst s of Sir William Collingwood, KBE, and *d* 15 Oct 1973, leaving issue:

(1) *Annette Elizabeth; *b* 27 Dec 1933; *m* 9 June 1962 *Colin Campbell, s of Dr Richard Campbell, and has issue:

1a *David Richard Collingwood; *b* 23 Aug 1966

1a *Helen Mary; *b* 2 Nov 1963

(2) *Angela Geraldine; *b* 1 June 1937; *m* 3 Feb 1962 *Paul Ion Warnick, er s of Paul Warnick, of Hamilton, Ontario, and has:

1a *Mark Scott; *b* 29 Sept 1964

1a *Gail Margaret; *b* 12 July 1962

2a *Lynne Michelle; *b* 30 Dec 1966

2 Enid Kathleen *b* 16 Sept 1909; *m* 6 June 1936 Alec Frederic Plummer, MC, s of Frederick William Plummer, JP, of Luton, and *d* 19–

3 *Geraldine [The Hon Mrs Field, Fair Acres, White Hill, Bilting, Kent]; *b* 16 March 1918; *m* 1 Sept 1939 *Lt-Col Norman John Lascelles Field, OBE, Roy Fus, s of Capt Hassel Dyer Field, RAMC, and has:

(1) *Richard Clive [Richard Field Esq, Windover House, Birch Close, Lewes Rd, Haywards Heath, W Sussex]; MCIM, MIPR; *b* 31 July 1947; *educ* Oakham; *m* 1976 *Susan Rosemary Hunter, 2nd dau of Peter Hunter Pearson, of E Sussex, and has issue:

1a *James Peter; *b* 1978

2a *Christopher Guy; *b* 1981

(1) *Anne Jacqueline; *b* 10 July 1942; *m* 22 July 1967 *Anthony Edward Vicar-Miles, s of Maj Arthur Leonard William Vicars-Miles, and has issue:

1a *Sarah Elizabeth; *b* 18 July 1969

2a *Katherine Julie; *b* 1972

GRIERSON

Arms: Gu. on a fess or, between three fetterlocks arg., a mullet az. **Crest:** A fetterlock as in the arms. **Motto:** *Hoc securior* ('Safer by this'). **Creation:** Bt. (NS) 25 March 1685.

SIR MICHAEL JOHN BEWES GRIERSON, 12TH BT, of Lag, Co Dumfries [Sir Michael Grierson Bt, 40C Palace Rd, London SW2 3NJ]; *b* 24 July 1921; *s* cousin 1987; *educ* Warden House Sch Deal and St Edmund's Sch Canterbury; RAF WW II; civil engr, LGO (ret 1986); *m* 1971 *Valerie Anne, dau of Russell Wright, of Gidea Park, Essex, and has:

1 *Sarah Anne; *b* 1973

Lineage: GILBERT (2nd s of Malcolm, 11th feudal Ld of Macgregor, *alias* Gregorson (*d* 1374)); took the name GRIERSON in accordance with charters granted 1400 by 9th Earl of Dunbar/March (*see* DUNBAR, Bt, of Mochrum) conveying the lands of Airde, Tyrcrome, Overholm, Netherholm and Dalgarnock in the (territorial) Barony of Tybris to him and his heirs male by the surname of GRIERSON; granted by his cousin Henry, Earl of Orkney, a charter of the lands of Lag 6 Dec 1408 to be held in exchange for an annual gift to the Earl at Dumfries Castle of a pair of gilt spurs; granted 1410 a charter from Archibald, Earl of Douglas, to whom he was armour bearer, of the lands of Drumjoan; *m* Janet, dau of Sir Simon Glendinning of Parton by Mary, dau of 4th Earl of Douglas by Margaret (dau of ROBERT III), and had, with other issue, including a 2nd s (William, of Dalton, ancestor of the GRIERSONs of Dalton and Castlemaddie):

GILBERT GRIERSON of Lag; *m* 14 Nov 1412 Isabel, dau and coheir of Sir Duncan Kirkpatrick of Rocall (subsequently Rock Hall), Dumfriesshire, and *d c* 1444; his est s:

VEDAST GRIERSON of Lag; built Lag Tower 1460; held Bordlands by 1465, Glencain by charter 1467, Windiehill by 1468 and charter of Rocall from the Duke of Albany 1437 and of Drumjoan from JAMES III 1475; *m* 1st —; *m* 2nd Margaret Glendonwym and had (probably by his 1st w), with three yr sons (Cuthbert, f of Roger; Vedast; Gilbert, *dvp* 1472, leaving a dau Annabella, who *m* George Muirheid):

ROGER GRIERSON of Lag, of which granted a charter by JAMES III 1473; *m* 1473 Isabel, dau of Winfred Kirkpatrick (*see* KIRKPATRICK, Bt), and was *k* Battle of Sauchieburn 1488, having had, with an est s (Cuthbert, had sasine of Lag 10 Oct 1490 and Rock Hall 2 May 1505, *dsp*1513) and two yst sons (Robert, living 10 Sept 1510; Gilbert, had a charter from his cousin William, Earl of Orkney, 6 Nov 1486), a 2nd s:

ROGER GRIERSON; had sasine of Windiehill 10 May 1513; *m* Agnes, 3rd dau of James Douglas, 5th of Drumlanrig (*see* QUEENSBERRY, M), and was *k* Flodden 9 Sept 1513, having had:

1 Cuthbert; *m* Isabel of Allanton and was *k* Flodden 1513, leaving issue:

(1) Roger; had:

1a John; last Provincial of the Dominicans in Scotland; turned Protestant; *d* 1564

(2) John; *m* Elizabeth, dau of Gordon of Lochinvar

2 Gilbert, of Collin; had issue

3 JOHN (Sir)

1 Jonet; *m* Thomas Kirkpatrick of Closeburn and had issue (*see* KIRKPATRICK, Bt)

2 Margaret; *m* John Lindsay of Colvington

ROGER GRIERSON's 3rd son,

Sir JOHN GRIERSON of Lag; had sasine of Rock Hall 7 Nov 1514 and Lag 9 Nov 1514; *m* 1st 1529 Nicola, dau of Robert Herries of Mabie, and had:

1 William, of Lag; had sasine 10 Aug 1549; *m* 1550 Elizabeth, dau of James Gordon of Lochinvar, and *d* 1562; his only s John *dsp*

1 Nicola; *m* (contract 13 Feb 1548) Sir John Charteris of Amisfield (*see* WEMYSS, E)

2 Jonet; *m* John Schaw, s of John Schaw of Haly

Sir JOHN *m* 2nd Egidia, dau of Sir John Kennedy of Culzean (*see* GALLOWAY, E), and *d* 1566, having by her had:

2 ROGER

3 Thomas (Sir), of Dalgoner; living 1628; *m* Maisie, dau of John Kirkhaught of Bognie, and had issue

4 John, of Dalskaville; living 1625; *m* Elizabeth, dau of Sir James Gordon of Lochinvar, and was ancestor of the GRIERSONs of Bargatton

The 2nd son,

ROGER GRIERSON of Lag and Rock Hall; *m* 1st 21 April 1566 Helen, dau of Sir James Douglas, 7th of Drumlanrig (*see* QUEENSBERRY, M); *m* 2nd Margaret Chalmers and *d* Aug 1593, leaving by his 1st w:

Sir WILLIAM GRIERSON of Lag; ktd 1608; had sasine of Larglanley 11 May 1597, Windiehill 16 May 1609 and Capenock 26 June 1616; *m* 9 May 1593 Nicola, dau of 4th Lord Herries of Terregles (*qv*), and *d* 1629, having had, with other issue (including a dau Agnes, *m* John Laurie of Maxwelton; *see* LAURIE, Bt):

1 ROBERT (Sir)

2 Alexander, of Barnbachill; *m* 1629 Margaret Glen and *d* 1655

3 William, of Broeco; *m* Agnes, dau of James Grierson of Penfillan, and had issue

4 John, of Capenoch, Dumfriesshire; *m* Elizabeth, dau of Sir James Murray of Cockpool, and had issue

5 James (Sir), of Capenoch and Rock Hall, Northumberland; *m* Mary dau of Rev John Browne, of Glencarn, and *d* 1666; ancestor of the GREERs of Grange, Tullylagan, and Sea Park, Ireland, and the GRIERSONs of Co Meath and Dublin, also of Illinois, USA

6 Lancelot; *m* (contract 6 March 1626) Jean, dau of Nicol Thomson

The est son,

Sir ROBERT GRIERSON of Lag; MP Dumfriesshire 1628–48; *m* 1622 Margaret, est dau of Sir James Murray of Cockpool, and *d* 1654, having had, with other issue:

1 John (Sir), of Lag; *m* 1st Jane, dau of John Fleming, and had:

(1) Margaret; *m* Sir James Carmichael of Bonnington

(2) Jean; *d* unm 7 July 1664

1 (cont.) Sir John *m* 2nd Isabel, dau of 6th Lord Boyd (*see* KILMARNOCK, B) by his 2nd w Christian, and *d* April 1658, having by her had, with other issue:

(1) Robert, of Lag and Rock Hall; *d* 17 March 1666

(3) Nicola; *m* David Scott of Scotstarvet and had issue (*see* MANSFIELD and MANSFIELD, E)

2 William, of Barquhar; *m* June 1654 Margaret (*m* 2nd John Grierson), dau of Sir James Douglas of Mouswald, and *d* 1661, leaving:

(1) ROBERT (Sir), **1st Bt**

3 James; *m* Margaret, dau of John Corsane of Meikleknox, and was ancestor of the GRIERSONs of Baldonell

Sir ROBERT's gs,

Sir Robert Grierson, 1st Bt (NS), so *cr* 25 March 1685, with remainder to his heirs male whatsoever, of Lag and Rock Hall; MP Dumfriesshire 1678–86; *b* 1655; *m* Henrietta, dau of 2nd Earl of Queensberry (*see* QUEENSBERRY, M), and *d* 15 April 1736, having had:

1 **Sir William Grierson, 2nd Bt**; MP Dumfriesshire 1709–11; *m* 1720 Anne (*d* 16 Dec 1749), dau of Sir Richard Musgrave, Bt, of Hayton (*see* 1875 edn), and *dsp* 1760

2 James; *m* Elizabeth Fergusson and *d c* 26 March 1722, having had, with other issue:

(1) **Sir Robert Grierson, 3rd Bt**; *dsp* 1765

3 GILBERT (Sir), **4th Bt**

4 John, of Dalgoner; *dsp* 1730

1 Henrietta; *m* Sir Walter Laurie, 3rd Bt, of Maxwelton (*see* LAURIE, Bt)

Sir ROBERT's unc,

Sir Gilbert Grierson, 4th Bt; *m* Elizabeth (*d* 8 April 1788), dau of Col Robert Maitland, Coldstream Gds, and *d* 7 Feb 1766, leaving:

Sir Robert Grierson, 5th Bt; Lt 11th Foot; *m* 1778 Margaret, est dau of 7th Earl of Carnwath (*see* 1940 edn), and *d* 8 Aug 1839 aged 106, leaving, with other issue:

1 ALEXANDER GILBERT (Sir), **6th Bt**

2 William; *b* 7 Aug 1778; Lt-Col; *m* Jane, dau of Thomas Beattie, of Crieve, Dumfriesshire, and *d* 30 Nov 1865, leaving issue:

(1) Thomas Beattie; *d* in Indian Mutiny 1857

(1) Margaret Elizabeth; *m* 1st 25 Jan 1860 (*divorce*) David Baird Hope-Johnstone (*see* LINLITHGOW, M); *m* 2nd 21 April 1871 John Henry Gordon and *d* 26 March 1918

1 Mary; *m* Maj Hamilton Maxwell, 43rd Bengal Inf, 3rd s of Sir William Maxwell, 4th Bt, of Monreith (*qv*), and had issue

2 Elizabeth; *m* 14 Nov 1810 James Crichton of Friarscarse

Sir ROBERT's er son,

Sir Alexander Gilbert Grierson, 6th Bt; *m* his cousin Elizabeth, only dau of Richard Dalzell, est s of Alexander Dalzell (who but for the attainder of 1716 would have been 6th Earl of Carnwath; *see* 1940 edn), and *d* 1840, having had, with other issue:

1 **Sir Richard Grierson, 7th Bt**; *m* Helen Bell (*m* 2nd 8 Oct 1850 Alexander Buchanan (*d* 18 Dec 1855) and *d* 2 Oct 1854) and *d* 1846, having had a s (*d* an infant)

2 **Sir Alexander William Grierson, 8th Bt**; Offr 78th Ross-shire Highrs; *m* Anne (*d* 3 Jan 1891), yst dau of Robert Day, of Hants, and *dsp* 27 Dec 1879

3 William Charles; *b* 12 July 1815; Cdr RN; *m* 3 Oct 1854 Emma Sophia (*d* 7 Jan 1900), dau of Michael Comerford, of Portsmouth, and widow of Thomas West, and *d* 8 Feb 1871, leaving:

(1) ALEXANDER DAVIDSON (Sir), **9th Bt**

(2) Gilbert William Frederick; *b* 29 July 1861; Lt Scottish Bdrs Militia; *m* 2 March 1889 Margaret Rose (*m* 2nd 18 June 1912 her former sis-in-law's widower Lt-Col Ponsonby Glenn Huggins, CB, DSO, IA (*d* 4 Jan 1925), est s of Horatio James Huggins, Ch Justice Sierra Leone), est dau of John Eaton McLeod Wylie, and *dsp* 15 Feb 1906

(1) Elizabeth Sophia; *m* 1883 Lt-Col Ponsonby Glenn Huggins, CB, DSO (*see* above), and *d* 2 May 1893, leaving issue

1 Elizabeth; *d* 1871

2 Judith; *m* 14 June 1844 William James Davidson, of Ruchill, Lanarks, and *d* 7 June 1845, leaving issue

Sir ALEXANDER's nephew,

Sir Alexander Davidson Grierson, 9th Bt, JP Dumfriesshire; *b* 30 Nov 1858; Maj and Hon Lt-Col 3rd Bn Scottish Borderers Boer War; *m* 7 Sept 1882 Fannie (*d* 1 Feb 1941), dau of Maj George White, of Westcombe Park, Blackheath, and *d* 1 April 1912, having had issue:

1 **Sir Robert Gilbert White Grierson, 10th Bt**; *b* 27 Sept 1883; Maj 1st/5th Bn KOSB, Lt Roy Scots, ADC Personal Staff, WW I; *m* 13 Sept 1911 Hilda (*d* 17 May 1962), 2nd dau of James Stewart, and *d* 16 June 1957, leaving:

(1) **Sir Richard Douglas Grierson, 11th Bt**; *b* 25 June 1912; *educ* ISC; jnlst; *d* 1987

2 Alexander George William; *b* 27 Oct 1884; Lt-Col RM WW I (despatches), Order St Anne of Russia; *m* 1920 Violet Ethel (*d* 1980), dau of Lt-Col Arthur Edward Bewes, CMG, and *d* 29 March 1951, leaving issue:

(1) Sir MICHAEL JOHN BEWES GRIERSON, **12th and present Bt**

(1) *Pamela Violet [Mrs Pamela Vernon, Park Lodge, 46 Park Rd, Aldeburgh, Suffolk IP15 5EU]; *b* 23 April 1925; *m* 8 Jan 1955 *Richard Wallace Vernon (*see* VERNON, Bt) and has issue

3 Frederick Vedast; *b* 28 Nov 1888; Lt 5th Bn KOSB WW I (despatches); *m* 1909 Frederica (*d* 23 Oct 1941), dau of Arthur Frederick Skipp, of Cheltenham, and *d* 14 Feb 1922, leaving:

(1) *Lorna Mary Sheila; *m* 31 May 1941 (*divorce* 1951) Carl Berger

GRIFFITHS

Creation: B. (LP, UK) 1985.

THE BARON GRIFFITHS, of Govilon, Co Gwent (Sir (William) Hugh Griffiths, MC (1944), PC (1980)) [The Rt Hon The Lord Griffiths MC PC, House of Lords, London SW1A 0PW]; *b* 26 Sept 1923; *educ* Charterhouse and St John's Coll Cambridge (BA 1946, MA); WWII: Capt Welsh Gds; barrister Inner Temple 1949, Recorder: Margate 1962–64, Cambridge 1964–70, QC 1964, Treas Bar Cncl 1968–69, Judge: High Court Queen's Bench 1970– 80, NIRC 1973–74; Memb: Advsy Cncl Penal Reform 1967–70, Chllr's Law Reform Ctee 1976–93; Chm Tbnl Inquiry on Ronan Point 1968; V-Chm Parole Bd 1976–77; Pres Senate Inns of Court and Bar 1982; Ld Justice Appeal 1980–85, Ld Appeal in Ordinary 1985–93; Chm: Security Commn 1985–92, Ld Chllr's Advsy Ctee Legal Educn and Conduct 1991–93; ktd 1971; Pres MCC 1990–91, Capt Roy and Ancient St Andrews 1993–94; Hon Fell: St John's Coll Cambridge 1985, American Judicial Admin 1985, American Coll Trial Lawyers 1988; Hon Memb Canadian Bar Assoc; Hon LLD: Wales 1987, De Montfort 1993; *m* 1949 *Evelyn, dau of Col K A Krefting, and has issue:

1 *David Hugh; *b* 1958; *educ* Eton and Magdalene Coll Cambridge; *m* 1983 *Henrietta, dau of David Hall and Mrs Julian Wellesley, and has issue:

(1) *Thomas; *b* 1984

(1) *Eloise; *b* 1986

(2) *Jessica; *b* 1988

1 *Anne Serena; *b* 1951; *m* 1976 *Peter William Urquhart, s of Maj-Gen Ronald Walton Urquhart, CB, DSO, DL, and has issue:

(1) *James; *b* 1980

(1) *Katherine; *b* 1978

(2) *Flora; *b* 1981

(3) *Serena; *b* 1984

2 *Carolyn (Carly) Jane; *b* 1952; *m* 1st 1974 (*divorce* 1984) Justin Bygott-Webb and has issue:

(1) *Mark William; *b* 1976; *educ* Shrewsbury

(2) *Samuel John; *b* 1978; *educ* Shrewsbury

2 (cont.) The Hon Mrs Carly Bygott-Webb *m* 2nd 1986 *Douglas Christopher Patrick McDougall, s of Patrick McDougall, and by him has:

(1) *Fiona Maria; *b* 1987

(2) *Mary Helen; *b* 1990

3 *Emma Elizabeth; *b* 1964; *m* 1991 *Duncan H R Matthews, s of M Matthews and Mrs N J Hunter, and has issue:

(1) *George; *b* 1994

Lineage: Sir HUGH ERNEST GRIFFITHS, CBE; MS, FRCS; *m* Doris Eirene, dau of W H James, and *d* 1961, leaving an only s:

(WILLLIAM) HUGH, *cr* a **Baron**

GRIFFITHS OF FFORESTFACH

Creation: B. (LP, UK) 1991.

THE BARON GRIFFITHS OF FFORESTFACH, of Fforestfach, Co W Glamorgan (Brian Griffiths) [The Rt Hon The Lord Griffiths of Fforestfach, House of Lords, London SW1A 0PW]; *b* 27 Dec 1941; *educ* Dynevor GS and LSE (BSc, MSc); LSE: Assist Lecturer Economics 1965–68, Lecturer Economics 1968–76; Visiting Prof Rochester U USA 1972–73; City U: Prof Banking and Internat Finance 1977–85, Dir Centre for Banking and Internat Finance 1977–82, Dean Business Sch 1982–85; Prof Ethics Gresham Coll 1984–87; Dir Bank of England 1984–86 (memb Panel Academic Consultants 1977–86); Head PM's Policy Unit 1985–90; Chm: CPS 1991–, Sch Exam and Assessment Cncl 1991–93; Internat Advsr Goldman Sachs 1991–; dir: Thorn-EMI 1991–, Hermann Miller 1991–, Times Newspapers Ltd 1991–, Servicemaster 1992–, Telewest 1994; author: *Is Revolution Change?* (ed and contrib, 1972), *Mexican Monetary Policy and Economic Development* (1972), *Invisible Barriers to Invisible Trade* (1975), *Inflation: The Price of Prosperity* (1976), *Monetary Targets* (ed with G E Wood, 1980), *The Creation of Wealth* (ed with G E Wood, 1984), *Morality the Market Place* (1989); *m* 1965 *Rachel Jane, dau of Howard Jones, and has issue:

1 *James Brian; *b* 1970

1 *Aeronwen Jane; *b* 1968

2 *Owenna Mary Ruth; *b* 1973

Lineage: IVOR WINSTON GRIFFITHS; *m* Phyllis Mary Morgan and had issue:

BRIAN, *cr* a **Baron**

GRIMSTON OF WESTBURY

Arms: Quarterly,1st and 4th, arg. on a fess sa. three rowels of six points or pierced gu., in the dexter chief an erm. spot sa. (for GRIMSTON); 2nd, sa. a fess dancettée between two leopard's faces or (for LUCKYN); 3rd, arg. three bugle horns sa., stringed gu. (for FORRESTER). **Crest:** A stag's head erased ppr., attired or. **Supporters:** Dexter a stag regardant ppr., attired or; sinister, a horse regardant arg. **Motto:** *Mediocria firma* ('Moderate things are stable'). **Creation:** Bt. (UK) 11 March 1952, B. (UK) 11 Dec 1964.

THE 2ND BARON GRIMSTON OF WESTBURY, of Westbury, Co Wilts, and a **Baronet** (Sir Robert Walter Sigismund Grimston, Bt) [The Rt Hon The Lord Grimston of Westbury, The Old Rectory, Westwell, Oxon OX18 4JT]; *b* 14 June 1925; *s f* 1979; *educ* Eton; Lt Scots Gds WW II, chm Gray's Inn (Underwriting Agency) Ltd 1970–88, Freeman City London 1981, Freeman Gold and Silver Wyre Drawers' Co 1981, dir: Hinton Hill and Coles 1962–83, Stewart & Hughman Ltd 1983–90; *m* 21 June 1949 *Hon June Mary Ponsonby, er dau of 5th Baron de Mauley (*qv*), and has:

1 +ROBERT (ROBIN) JOHN SYLVESTER [The Hon Robert Grimston, Elm Farm, Sibford Ferris, Banbury, Oxon OX15 5AA]; Capt Roy Hus (PWO); *b* 30 April 1951; *educ* Eton and Reading U (BSc 1973); CA 1984; *m* 1984 *Emily Margaret, dau of Maj John Evelyn Shirley (*see* FERRERS, E), and has issue:

(1) *Charlotte Elgiva; *b* 23 March 1991

(2) *Philippa Margaret; *b* 7 Oct 1995

2 +Gerald Charles Walter [Maj The Hon Gerald Grimston, c/o Midland Bank, 69 Pall Mall, London SW1]; *b* 4 Sept 1953; *educ* Eton and Exeter U (BA 1976); late Maj Scots Gds (served NI, Falklands), dir Grimston Hldgs, J O Hambro, Conning Grimston, Woodcote Grove Estates; *m* 10 May 1980 *Katherine Evelyn, only dau of Maj Rupert Kettle, DL, 5th Roy Inniskilling Dragoon Gds, and has issue:

(1) +Edward Charles Luckyn; *b* 1985

(2) +Alexander Rupert Ponsonby; *b* 1989

(1) *Lucy Katherine Elgiva; *b* 1982

1 *Georgiana Mary; *b* 7 Sept 1961; *educ* Bristol U (BSc); *m* 1992 *Robin Pike, yst s of Thomas Pike, and has issue:

(1) *Jack Augustus Thomas; *b* 1994

(2) *Patrick Belisarius Robert; *b* 1 Jan 1996

Lineage: The 2nd EARL OF VERULAM (*qv*) had a 3rd s:

Canon ROBERT GRIMSTON; MA; had:

Sir Robert Villiers Grimston, 1st Bt (UK), so *cr* 11 March 1952, as also 11 Dec 1964 **Baron Grimston of Westbury**, of Westbury, Co Wilts (both UK); *b* 8 June 1897; *educ* Repton and London U (BSc); ACGI, Lt RGA WW I, MP Westbury 1931–64, PPS to: Parly U-Sec Home Dept 1933–34, Fin Sec War Office 1934–35, Parly U-Sec Dominion Affrs 1935–36, Parly Sec Min Ag 1936, Min Pensions 1936–37, Assist Whip 1937, Ld Commr Treasury 1937–38, V-Chamberlain Household 1938–39, Treas Household 1939–42, Assist PMG 1942–45, Parly Sec Min Supply May–July 1945, Dep Chm Ways and Means and Dep Speaker 1962–64, memb UK Delegn Gen Assembly UN 1960, Cdr Parly HG 1941–42, Pres UDCs Assoc 1949; *m* 24 Oct 1923 Sybil Rose (*d* 19 Nov 1977), est dau of Sir Sigmund Neumann, 1st Bt, of Newmarket (*qv*), and *d* 8 Dec 1979, leaving:

1 ROBERT WALTER SIGISMUND GRIMSTON, **2nd and present Baron Grimston of Westbury**

2 +Cecil Antony Sylvester [The Hon Cecil Grimston, Wellingham Vane, Ringmer, Sussex BN8 5SN]; FRICS, FRSA, late Coldstream Gds; *b* 28 Feb 1927; *educ* Eton and Cambridge (MA); *m* 11 July 1958 *Dawn Monica Ann, only dau of Guy Janson, of Fair Hall, Southover, Lewes, and has issue:

(1) +Guy Antony Edward; *b* 11 Jan 1963

(2) +John Lionel Charles; *b* 22 Oct 1968

3 Michael John Harbottle; *b* 5 Jan 1932; *educ* Eton; *m* 1st 7 Feb 1957 (*divorce* 1978) Julia Mary, 3rd dau of Sir George Werner Albu, 2nd Bt (*qv*); *m* 2nd 1982 *Denise Angove [The Hon Mrs Michael Grimston, 3 Trevethan Rd, Falmouth, Cornwall] and *d* 15 March 1997, leaving by his 1st w:

(1) +Simon Harbottle; *b* 21 March 1960

(2) +Giles Villiers; *b* 22 July 1961

(1) *Katharine Flavia; *b* 11 Oct 1962

(2) *Sybella ('Zambi') Jane; *b* 1 Jan 1966

1 *Rosemary Sybella Violet [The Hon Mrs Rowse, 75B Flood St, London SW3]; *b* 4 March 1929; *m* 10 Feb 1953 (*divorce* 1964) (Charles) Edward Underdown (*d* 1989), actor and former jockey, only s of Harry Charles Baillie Underdown, JP; *m* 2nd 1984 *Antony Herbert David Rowse, s of Herbert James Rowse

2 *Ella Zia [The Hon Mrs Humphreys, Ferne Park Cottage, Berwick St John, Dorset]; *b* 4 May 1937; *m* 12 Jan 1972 Humphrey K Humphreys (*d* 1984), s of Prof H F Humphreys, and has issue:

(1) *Catherine Sybella; *b* 25 March 1977

GRIMTHORPE

Arms: Gu. a fess between three boar's heads couped erminois. **Crest:** A boar's head couped or, pierced by a cross pattée-fitchée erect gu. **Supporters:** On either side a boar erminois gorged with a collar, pendant therefrom an escutcheon gu. charged with a cross pattée-fitchée or. **Motto:** *Prodesse civibus* ('To benefit one's fellow citizens') **Creations:** Bt. (UK) 2 Nov 1813, B. (UK) 17 Feb 1886.

THE 4TH BARON GRIMTHORPE, of Grimthorpe, in the East Riding, Co York, and a **Baronet** (Sir Christopher John Beckett, Bt, OBE (1958), DL (E R Yorks 1969, N Yorks 1969) [The Rt Hon The Lord Grimthorpe OBE DL, Westow Hall, York YO6 7NE]; *b* 16 Sept 1915; *s* f 1963; *educ* Eton; 2nd Lt 9th Lancers 1936, WW II, Lt-Col cmdg 9th Queen's Roy Lancers 1955–58, Brig RAC, HQ Western Cmd 1961–64, Dep Cdr Malta and Libya 1964–67, ADC to HM THE QUEEN 1964–68, Col 9th/12th Lancers (PWO) 1973, dir: Standard Broadcasting Corp (UK) 1972–, Yorkshire Post Newspapers 1973 and Thirsk Racecourse Ltd 1972; *m* 17 Feb 1954 *Lady Elizabeth Lumley, DCVO (1995, CVO 1983), Ldy Bedchamber to HM QUEEN ELIZABETH THE QUEEN MOTHER 1973, 2nd dau of 11th Earl of Scarbrough (*qv*), and has:

1 +EDWARD JOHN; *b* 20 Nov 1954; *educ* Harrow; *m* 1992 *Mrs Carey Elizabeth McEwen, yr dau of Robin Graham, and has issue:

(1) +Harry Maximilian; *b* 28 April 1993

2 +Ralph Daniel, 2nd Lt 9th/12th Royal Lancers (PWO); *b* 11 April 1957; *educ* Harrow and RMA Sandhurst; *m* 1987 *Susanna, er dau of Colin Townsend-Rose, and has issue:

(1) +Frederick John; *b* 31 March 1990

(2) +Thomas Ralph; *b* 30 Oct 1992

(1) *Flora Katharine; *b* 17 June 1997

1 *Harriet Lucy [The Hon Mrs Smyly, The Old Glebe House, Sparsholt, Wantage, Oxon OX12 9PU]; *b* 18 Feb 1961; *m* 1985 *Capt (Richard) Mark Smyly, 16th/5th Queen's Roy Lancers (*see* 1928 edn BUCKLAND, B), and has issue:

(1) *Hugo Richard Seymour; *b* 15 June 1990

(2) *George William Dennis; *b* 2 March 1992

Lineage: GERVASE BECKETT, of Barnsley; gf of:

Sir John Beckett, 1st Bt (UK), so *cr* 2 Nov 1813, of Leeds, Yorks, and Somerby Park, Gainsborough, Lincs; *b* 30 April 1743; *m* 3 March 1774 Mary (*d* 21 Feb 1833), dau of Christopher Wilson, Bp Bristol, and *d* 18 Sept 1826, having had, with other issue:

1 **Sir John Beckett, 2nd Bt**, PC; FRS, MP Cockermouth 1818 and 1920–21, Haslemere 1926–32 and Leeds 1835–7, JAG; *b* 17 May 1775; *m* 20 Jan 1817 Lady Anne Lowther (*d* 8 Nov 1871), dau of 1st Earl of Lonsdale (*qv*) and *dsp* 31 May 1847

2 **Sir Thomas Beckett, 3rd Bt**; *b* 1 Jan 1779; *m* 3 March 1825 his cousin Caroline (*d* 22 Jan 1878), dau of Joseph Beckett, of Barnsley, and *d* 17 Nov 1872, leaving:

(1) Mary, *d* unm 21 Feb 1915

(2) Elizabeth; *m* 17 March 1853 Sir Henry Hickman Bacon, 10th Bt (*qv*), and *d* 29 Nov 1885, leaving issue

3 Richard; Capt Gds; *b* 18 June 1782; *ka* Talavera 28 July 1809

4 EDMUND (Sir), **4th Bt**

5 William; MP Leeds and Ripon; *b* 3 March 1784; *d* 26 Jan 1868

6 Henry; *b* 11 April 1791; *m* Mary (*d* Nov 1829), dau of James Lyle, of Philadelphia, and *d* 11 Sept 1871, having had:

(1) James; *d* young

(2) Hamilton; *b* 15 Oct 1829; *m* 14 Dec 1854 Sophia Clarence (*d* 25 Dec 1911), dau and coheir of 1st and last Baron Lyndhurst (*see* 1863 edn), and *d* 1883, having had issue:

1a Henry Lyndhurst; *b* 8 April 1857; *d* 1896

1a Constance Mary; *m* 10 Feb 1880 2nd Baron Aberdare (*qv*) and *d* 8 Feb 1932, leaving issue

(1) Marianne; *m* 10 July 1839 Sir Thomas Whichcote, 7th Bt (*see* 1949 edn), and *dsp* 10 May 1849. He *d* 17 Jan 1892

1 Anne; *m* 7 Jan 1811 Gen Thomas Marriott, of Pershore, Worcs, and *d* 20 Oct 1867, leaving issue. He *d* 16 March 1847

The 3rd Bt's bro,

Sir EDMUND BECKETT later BECKETT-DENISON (roy licence 8 Sept 1816 under terms of his w's great-great aunt's will; *see* below) later still BECKETT again (roy licence 9 Dec 1872), **4th Bt**; MP W R Yorks 1841–59; *b* 29 Jan 1787; *m* 14 Dec 1814 Maria (*d* 27 March 1874), dau of William Beverley, of Beverley, and ggn of Lady Denison (widow of Sir Thomas Denison, Justice King's Bench 1741–65), and *d* 24 May 1874, having had issue:

1 Sir EDMUND BECKETT-DENISON later (on *s* f) BECKETT, **5th Bt**, and **1st Baron Grimthorpe**, of Grimthorpe, in the East Riding, CoYork (UK), so *cr* 17 Feb 1886, with remainder, in default of male issue of his body, to the heirs male of the body of his f, QC (1854), JP (Herts and W R Yorks); *b* 12 May 1816; *educ* Eton and Trin Coll Cambridge (BA 1838, MA 1841, LLD 1863); barrister Lincoln's Inn 1841, Bencher 1854, Treas 1876; Chllr and Vicar-Gen York 1877–1900; *m* 7 Oct 1845 Fanny Catherine (*dsp* 8 Dec 1901), dau of Rt Rev John Lonsdale, DD, Bp Lichfield, and *dsp* 29 April 1905

2 Christopher BECKETT later BECKETT-DENISON, DL W R Yorks; MP W R Yorks East 1868–80, Bengal CS 1845–65; *b* 9 May 1825, *dsp* 30 Oct 1884

3 William BECKETT later BECKETT-DENISON, of Nun Appleton, Yorks, DL; MP E Retford 1876–80, Bassetlaw 1885; *b* 10 Sept 1826; *m* 17 Feb 1855 Hon Helen Duncombe (*d* 22 Nov 1896), 3rd dau of 2nd Baron Feversham (*qv*), and *d* 23 Nov 1890, leaving issue:

(1) ERNEST WILLIAM, **2nd Baron**

(2) Sir (WILLIAM) GERVASE BECKETT, 1st Bt (*qv*)

(3) Rupert Evelyn BECKETT, JP, DL W R Yorks; Hon LLD Leeds, Hon Treas Leeds U, Maj Yorks Hus, dir Westminster Bank; *b* 2 Nov 1870; *educ* Eton and Trin Coll Cambridge; *m* 21 Dec 1896 Muriel Helen Florence, CBE (1918) (*d* 20 April 1941), dau of Lord Berkeley Charles Sidney Paget (*see* ANGLESEY, M), and *d* 25 April 1955, having had:

1a Gwladys Helen; Mayor Nairobi 1938–39; *m* 1st 8 Dec 1920 (*divorce* 1928) Sir Charles Markham, 2nd Bt (*qv*), and had issue; *m* 2nd 28 May 1928 3rd Baron Delamere (*qv*) and *d* 22 Feb 1943

2a Violet Consuelo (Viola); *d* unm 15 Aug 1975

3a Marjorie Nell (Diana); *m* 1st 18 July 1923 Capt Albany Kennett Charlesworth, MC (*k* plane crash 1 Feb 1945), of Grinton Lodge, Richmond, Yorks, and had issue; *m* 2nd 21 Dec 1948 Lord George Hugo Cholmondeley, OBE, MC, yr s of 4th Marquess of Cholmondeley (*qv*), and *d* 10 Feb 1965

4a Pamela Thetis; *m* 1st 6 March 1929 (*divorce* 1930) James Roy Notter Garton, s of William Garton, of Bursledon, Hants. He *d* 1939. She *m* 2nd 13 Dec 1932 Maj-Gen Sir Stewart Graham Menzies, KCB, KCMG, DSO, MC, s of John Graham Menzies, and *d* 13 March 1951, leaving issue. He *d* 29 May 1968

(1) Helen Louisa; *b* 25 Feb 1858; *d* 26 April 1935

(2) Adeline Gertrude Denison; *b* 14 May 1859; *m* 19 Oct 1880 Sir Frederick George Milner, 7th Bt (*qv*), and *d* 7 July 1902, leaving issue

(3) Violet Katharine; *b* 25 July 1860; *m* 7 March 1882 Reginald Walkelyne Chandos Pole, of Radbourne Hall, Derbys, and *d* 18 March 1882, leaving issue. He *d* 20 Oct 1930

(4) Maud Augusta; LGStJ; *b* 12 June 1864; *m* 20 Oct 1886 3rd Marquess of Abergavenny (*qv*) and *d* 15 July 1927, leaving issue

1 Mary; *m* 21 June 1837 Charles Wilson Faber, JP, DL, of Northaw, Herts, and *d* 30 May 1902, having had issue. He *d* 1 April 1878

2 Elizabeth; *m* 25 March 1841 William Frogatt Bethell, of Rise, Yorks and *d* 26 July 1870, leaving issue. He *d* 7 March 1879

3 Sophia; *m* 19 Aug 1847 Rev Thomas Bradley Paget, Vicar Welton, Preb York, and *d* 23 Sept 1906, having had issue. He *d* 20 Feb 1893

4 Augusta; *d* unm 24 May 1916 aged 92

The 1st BARON's n,

ERNEST WILLIAM BECKETT-DENISON later (1886) BECKETT, **2nd Baron Grimthorpe**; MP Whitby 1885–1905, Maj and Hon Lt-Col York Hus, DAG ImpYeo 1900, sr ptnr Beckett & Co, Leeds bankers; *b* 25 Nov 1856; *m* 4 Oct 1883 Lucy (*d* 9 May 1891), only child of William Tracy Lee, of New York, and had:

1 RALPH WILLIAM ERNEST, **3rd Baron**

1 Lucy Katherine; *b* 10 July 1884; *m* 27 July 1903 (judical separation 31 Oct 1914 Austria, *divorce* 1920 Czechoslovakia) Count Otto Czernin von und zu Chudenitz, of Dimokur, Austria, and had issue; *m* 2nd 29 June 1926 (*divorce* 1941) Capt Oliver Harry Frost, MBE, MC, s of Robert Frost

2 Helen Muriel; *b* 23 Aug 1886; *d* unm 16 June 1916

The 2nd BARON *d* 9 May 1917; his only son,

RALPH WILLIAM ERNEST BECKETT, **3rd Baron Grimthorpe**, DL (N R Yorks); *b* 3 May 1891; *educ* Eton and Univ Coll Oxford; Lt Yorks Hus WW I (despatches) and as Lt-Col cmdg 1936–40 WW II (despatches), T/Lt RAF, PPS to Parly U-Sec War 1919–20, MFH Middleton 1921–27 and 1931–39, Steward Nat Hunt Ctee 1952; *m* 1st 3 Sept 1914 (*divorce* 1945) Mary Alice (*d* following a road accident 28 April 1962), dau of Lt-Col Mervyn Henry Archdale, 12th Lancers, and had:

1 CHRISTOPHER JOHN BECKETT, **4th and present Baron Grimthorpe**

2 +Oliver Ralph [The Hon Oliver Beckett, 55 Carlisle Ave, St Albans, Herts AL3 5LX]; *b* 21 Aug 1918; *educ* Eton and Trin Coll Cambridge, FRSA; *m* 6 April 1944 *Hélène Agnes, formerly w of Richard Tasker-Evans and dau of Constantine Fessas, and has issue:

(1) *Sarah Christine; *b* 20 Feb 1946; artist; *m* 15 July 1966 (*divorce* 1977) Jonathan Hugh Spiers Crook, s of Cdr J H Crook, of Palma de Majorca, and has:

1a *John Henry; *b* 1967

1a *Tara Leonie; *b* 1968

2a *Sarah Aline; *b* 1968

(2) *Juliet Mary; *b* 25 May 1949

3 Bryan Rupert; *b* 24 July 1922; *k* car crash 11 March 1943

1 *Lucy Clare [The Hon Mrs Crewdson, Oak House, Otley, nr Ipswich, Suffolk]; *b* 5 Sept 1926; *m* 12 July 1957 *Wilson Peregrine Nicholas Crewdson, est

s of Brig Wilson Theodore Oliver Crewdson, CBE, by Albinia Joane, 2nd dau of Sir Nicholas Henry Bacon, 12th Bt (*qv*), and has had issue:

(1) *Giles Wilson Mervyn; *b* 11 June 1959; Lt 9th/12th Roy Lancers; *m* 1990 (*divorce* 1993) Hon Aurelia Margaret Amherst Cecil, only dau of 4th Baron Amherst of Hackney (*qv*)

(1) *Diana Constance Mary; *b* 11 June 1959; *m* 1980 *Christopher J M Langley, yr s of Lt-Col James Langley, and has:

1a *Venetia Margaret Clare; *b* 1983

2a *Edwina Chantal Elizabeth; *b* 1985

3a *Rose Katharine Lucy; *b* 1988

(2) Elizabeth Ann Joan; *b* 20 April 1961; *d* 17 Sept 1963

(3) *Virginia Clare; *b* 24 Oct 1964; *m* 1991 *Giles J G Appleton, only s of G/Capt James Appleton

The **3rd Baron** *m* 2nd 25 March 1945 Angela (*d* 1992), formerly w of Cdr David Cecil Lycett Green, RN (*see* GREEN, Bt), and yst dau of Edward Hubert Courage, of Kirkby Fleetham Hall, Yorks, and *d* 22 Feb 1963, leaving by her:

4 +William Ernest; *b* 30 June 1945; *educ* Eton; 2nd Lt 9th/12th Roy Lancers; *m* 15 June 1968 *Virginia Helen Clark, only dau of Alan Michael Clark Hutchinson, MP, and has issue:

(1) +Ralph Michael; *b* 24 June 1971

(1) *Serena Angela Anne; *b* 12 Jan 1974

GROTRIAN

Arms: Gu. a wyvern or, in chief two roses arg., barbed and seeded ppr. **Crest:** A wyvern or, resting the dexter leg upon a rose arg., barbed and seeded ppr. **Motto:** *Animo et fide* ('By courage and faith'). **Creation:** Bt. (UK) 28 June 1934.

SIR (PHILIP) CHRISTIAN BRENT GROTRIAN, 3RD BT, of Leighton Buzzard, Co Bedford [Sir Christian Grotrian Bt, RR3, Mansfield, Ontario LON 1MO, Canada; Calle Ample 2, Regencós, Gerona, Spain]; *b* 26 March 1935; *s* unc 1984; *educ* Eton and Trin Coll Toronto; *m* 1st 1960 Anne Isabel, dau of Robert Sieger Whyte, of Toronto, and has:

1 +(PHILIP) TIMOTHY ADAM BRENT [Timothy Grotrian Esq, 28 Bishop St, Toronto, Ontario, Canada M5R 1N2]; *b* 1962

Sir CHRISTIAN *m* 2nd 1979 *Sarah Frances, dau of Reginald Harry Gale, of Montreal, and has by her:

2 +John Hugh Brent; *b* 1982

1 *Frances Elizabeth; *b* 1980

Lineage: FREDERICK L C GROTRIAN, of London; had:

FREDERICK BRENT GROTRIAN, of W Hill House, Hessle, E Yorks, and Ingmanthorpe Hall, Wetherby, Yorks; *b* 1838; *m* 1862 Elizabeth (*d* 4 Aug 1930), dau of John Hunter, of Felixkirk, Yorks, and *d* 8 April 1905, leaving:

1 Frederick, of Branksome Dene Glen, Bournemouth, Hants, and Pennington House, Lymington, Hants, *b* 1869; *m* 1890 Nellie, dau of Stephen Martin, of Bishopshalt, Hillingdon, and *d* 1942, leaving issue:

(1) Frederick Stephen, MC, of Teneglertown, Maxwelltown, Dumfriesshire; Col RA; *b* 1896; *m* 1924 Eileen Gertrude (*d* 1974), dau of Dermond Deane, of Dublin, and *d* 1954, leaving issue:

1a *John Stephen Martin [John Grotrian Esq, Lake House, Lake, Salisbury, Wilts]; *b* 16 Sept 1925; *educ* Ampleforth; Capt Grenadier Gds 1944–49; *m* 25 April 1953 *Clodagh, dau of Maj Richard Shaw de Courcy Bennett, and has issue:

1b *Jeremy Brent; *b* 7 Sept 1959

1b *Amanda Mary Clodagh; *b* 9 July 1955; *m* 23 April 1978 *William James Brownlow, only s of James Christy Brownlow, of Ballydaugan House, Downpatrick, Co Down

2b *Emma Shane; *b* 6 March 1963

2a *Patrick Brent; *b* 1927; *m* and has issue

3a *Mark; *b* 1936

(2) Frederick Brent; *b* 1905; *d* 1968, leaving issue

(1) Betty; *b* 1901; had issue

2 HERBERT BRENT (Sir), **1st Bt**

3 Harold Hunter, of Munstead Rough, Godalming, Surrey; *b* 1871; Maj; *m* 23 Jan 1912 Phyllis Catherine (*d* 10 June 1974), est dau of Rev Charles Aubrey Durrant, of Wetherby, Yorks, and *d* 17 May 1950, leaving issue:

(1) *Michael; *b* 9 Dec 1912

(2) *Paul Reginald; *b* 1 April 1916; *m* 5 Jan 1961 *Betty, widow of Lt-Col A B S Clarke

(1) *Ursula Catherine; *b* 24 March 1914; *m* 5 May 1936 *Martin Yorke Watson, CBE, s of Ven Archdeacon A H Watson, and has issue:

1a *William Martin; *b* 16 Jan 1942; *educ* King's Canterbury, Ch Ch Oxford (MA) and LSE

2a *Simon Andrew; assist master Haberdashers' Aske's Sch 1968; *b* 28 Oct 1943; *educ* Ch Ch Oxford (BA 1965, MA) and Lond Inst Educn; *m* 4 Jan 1969 *Katherine Isobel Rose, dau of Robert Archibald Wolverson, of Cambridge

3a *James Yorke; *b* 9 April 1946

1a *Catherine Amanda [Mrs Samuel Lloyd, 30 Wessels Road, Kenilworth, Cape, S Africa]; *b* 9 Aug 1938; *m* 4 Feb 1961 *Samuel Mark Lloyd, s of S L Lloyd, of Newlands, Cape, S Africa

(2) Rachel; *b* 7 May 1918; *m* 1st (*divorce*) Michael Humphrey Wilkins; *m* 2nd 8 June 1949 Brig Hugh Nugent Leveson Gower (*see* SUTHERLAND, D) and *d* 1981

4 Edgar, of Knapton Hall, Malton, Yorks; *b* 14 Sept 1872; *m* 27 April 1905 Elsie Mary (*d* 12 Oct 1960), only dau of William Frazer, of Bournemouth, and *d* 30 March 1949, leaving:

(1) *Edgar William Brent; *b* 2 Oct 1910; *educ* Harrow; *m* 1939 *Barbara Ewing Macfie and has issue:

1a *Andrew William; *b* 5 Nov 1944; *educ* Harrow; *m* 19– *Sarah, dau of — Allen, and has issue:

1a *Caroline Barbara; *b* 13 Nov 1941; *m* 19– *Maj George Stephen, RSG, and has issue:

1b *A son; *b* 3 Sept 1970

2a *Rosanna Mary; *b* 3 Feb 1948

(1) Rosemary Brent; *b* 25 Feb 1906; *m* 1st 1927 (*divorce* 1940) Maj Eric Arthur Staniland, 8th KRI Hus, and has:

1a John Eric [John Staniland Esq, Tithe Barn, Crowcombe, nr Taunton, Somerset]; *b* 16 Dec 1928; *m* 14 April 1953 *Magdalene Cecilia, er dau of Col Francis Michael Benedict Cary Boylan, MBE, RA, of Collierstown House, Bellewstown, Co Meath, and *d* 18 July 1978, leaving:

1b *Christopher John; *b* 22 Jan 1960

1b *Anna Patricia; *b* 6 Dec 1955

(1) (cont.) Mrs Rosemary Staniland *m* 2nd 11 Sept 1940 Sir John Edmond Noel O'Brien, 5th Bt (*qv*), and had further issue

(2) *Suzanne Elsie; *b* 20 Feb 1914; *m* 1940 *Capt Francis Jack Cartwright, CVO, OBE, RN, s of Lt-Col Francis John Winsor Cartwright, DSO, and has:

1a *Michael Francis; *b* 21 Aug 1941

2a *Hugh William; *b* 23 Dec 1946

(3) *Angela Mary; *b* 3 Feb 1916; *m* 21 Nov 1946 *Lt-Col Richard Page, RAEC, of Glanwysg, Crickhowell, Breconshire, only child of Richard Page, of Singapore, and has issue:

1a *Richard; *b* 13 Dec 1953

1a *Carole Mary; *b* 11 Oct 1955

1 Ethel; *m* 1909 Maj Robert Stanley Pearson, OBE, JP, DL, BA, LLB, 3rd Dragoon Gds and Yorkshire Hus, of Brandsby Hall, York, and *d* 31 May 1952. He *d* 21 April 1953

2 Hilda; *m* 19 April 1900 Sir Philip Bealby Reckitt, 3rd Bt, OBE (*see* 1940 edn), and *d* 24 Feb 1935, leaving issue. He *d* 17 Nov 1944

3 Bessie; *m* 20 Nov 1906 Capt Appelbe Chisholm Adams, Gren Gds, of Woolston Hall, Chigwell, Essex, and *d* having had issue. He *d* 1969

4 Gwendolen; *m* 1903 James McBryde, MRCS, LRCP, and had issue. He *d* 1904

The 2nd son,

Sir Herbert Brent Grotrian, 1st Bt (UK), so *cr* 28 June 1934, KC (1925), JP, DL Herts; *b* 29 March 1870; *educ* Trin Coll Oxford (BCL, MA); barrister Inner Temple 1894, Recorder Scarborough 1918–46, Dep Chm Herts QS, Beds: High Sheriff 1931 and Chm QS, MP (C) SW Kingston-on-Hull 1924–29; *m* 14 Jan 1902 Mary Lilian (*d* 26 June 1971), dau of Robert Adams, barrister, of Hamilton, Ontario, and *d* 28 October 1951, having had issue:

1 Charles Herbert Brent, TD, JP; barrister, Maj RA (TA) WW II; *b* 7 Nov 1902; *educ* Trin Coll Oxford (BCL, MA); *m* 28 Feb 1936 Aileen Georgina (*d* 1987), only dau of George Ernest Etlinger, and was *ka* Burma 9 May 1944, leaving:

(1) *Charlotte Elizabeth [Miss Charlotte Grotrian, 17 Hogarth Rd, Hove, Sussex BN3 5RH]; *b* 9 Nov 1941

2 **Sir John Appelbe Brent Grotrian, 2nd Bt**; *b* 16 Feb 1904; *educ* Eton and Trin Coll Oxford; served WW II (despatches); *d* unm 6 Feb 1984

3 Robert Philip Brent; MA Oxon, S/Ldr RAF WW II; *b* 21 Oct 1908; *m* 1st 10 Dec 1931 (*divorce* 1940) Elizabeth Mary (*m* 2nd 1947 William Percy George (*d* 1955), US For Serv, and had further issue), only dau of Maj Herbert Hardy-Wrigley, and had issue:

(1) Sir (PHILIP) CHRISTIAN BRENT GROTRIAN, **3rd and present Bt**

3 (cont.) Robert Grotrian *m* 2nd 21 Dec 1940 *Margaret (3rd 28 Jan 1950 Geraint Rees, er s of Rev R J Rees, of Pwllheli, N Wales), formerly w of Roland Max Chaudoir, of Highgate, and yst dau of George Green, and *das* Far East 7 Sept 1945, having by her had issue:

(1) *Jane Felicity [Mrs Peter Andrews, Old Timbers, Shere Rd, W Horsley, Surrey KT24 6EW]; *b* 2 Oct 1942; *m* 4 April 1964 *Peter Lewis Andrews, only s of Kenneth Andrews, and has issue:

1a *Philip Kenneth; *b* 29 Dec 1964; *m* 1987 *Caroline Jane, dau of Raymond Woodcock, of Wivenhoe, Essex, and has:

1b *Lucy Jane; *b* 1991

2b *Emily Sarah; *b* 1993

1a *Sarah Jane; *b* 30 Aug 1967; *m* 1st 1993 Nicholas James Hughes, s of David Hughes, of Woldingham, Surrey; *m* 2nd Dec 1995 *Darren Robert

William Houghton, s of Robert Houghton, of Sutton Coldfield, and by him has:
1b *William Jack; *b* 21 Dec 1996
1 *Lilian Désirée [Miss Lilian Grotrian, 10 New Yatt Rd, Witney, Oxon]; *b* 1 July 1914
2 Mary Joizelle Elizabeth Pearl; *b* 16 June 1918; *m* 29 Nov 1947 *John Gifford Ormerod [John Ormerod Esq, 142 Tuffley Avenue, Gloucester GL1 5NS], yst s of Lt-Col George Milner Ormerod, DSO, and *d* 6 Jan 1997, leaving:
(1) Elizabeth Mary; *b* 1949; SRN; *d* 6 Jan 1997
(2) *Caroline Anne [Mrs Michael Blandford, 6 Rochester Rd, Southsea, Hants PO4 9BA]; *b* 1955; *m* 1977 *Michael James Blandford and has issue:
1a *Alan James; *b* 1979
1a *Joanne Mary; *b* 1982

GROVE

Arms: Erm. on a chevron engrailed gu. three escallops, the centre one or, the other two arg. **Crest:** A talbot statant sa., collared arg. **Motto:** *Ny dessux ny dessoux* ('Neither above nor below'). **Creation:** Bt. (UK) 18 March 1874.

SIR CHARLES GERALD GROVE 5TH BT, of Ferne, Wilts; *b* 10 Dec 1929; *s* bro 1974

Lineage: JOHN de GROVE, of Chalfont St Giles, Bucks; *d* 1353; gggf of:

THOMAS GROVE; High Sheriff Bucks 1434; had:

Agnes; *m* William Brudenell, of Aynho, Northants (*see* AILESBURY, M)

THOMAS's n,

JOHN GROVE; settled Wilts 1450; *m* Joan, dau and heir of John Burhill, of Shaftesbury, Dorset, and had:

THOMAS GROVE, of Berry Court, Wilts; living 1522; *m* Isabel, dau of John Luyshe, and had, with an er s (Thomas) and a dau (Lucie, *m* thrice):

ROBERT GROVE; MP, feodary (equivalent to escheator, a roy offr implementing escheats, or cases of property reverting to the Crown in the event of the failure of an heir) for Wilts; *m* Joane, dau of John Combe, Dorset, and had:
1 WILLIAM
2 Matthew, of Staple Inn
3 Walter, of Honiton, Devon, *c* 1623
1 Mary; *m* Hugh Kete, of Chesilborn, Dorset

The est son,

WILLIAM GROVE, of Gray's Inn; MP Shaftesbury 1557; bought Ferne 1563 and Sedgehill 1578; *m c* 1563 Thomasin, dau and heir of Edward Mayhew, of Fonthill, and *d* 1582, having had, with two er sons, a yr s (Hugh, ancestor of the GROVEs of Zeals House, Wilts) and four daus:

ROBERT GROVE; *m* 1st Gertrude (*dsp*), dau of Cuthbert Hartgill, of Cucklington, Somerset; *m* 2nd 1608 Honor South, of Swallowcliffe, Wilts, and by her had, with two daus:
1 THOMAS
2 Robert; Fell New Coll Oxford; *d* 1663 aged 50
3 William, of Morden, Dorset; living 1653, had:
(1) Robert; Bp Chichester; *b* 1634; *m* Elizabeth Cole, of Dover, and *d* 1696

The est son,

THOMAS GROVE; MP; *m* 1st 1630 Mary, dau of John Lowe, of New Sarum, and widow of John Grove; *m* 2nd Elizabeth, dau and coheir of Edward Lambert, of Corton, Wilts, and by her had, with two er sons (*d* young):

ROBERT GROVE, of Ferne; *m* 1st 1661 Mary (*d* Oct 1688), dau of John Hanham, of Wimborne Minster, Dorset, and sis of Sir William Hanham, 1st Bt (*qv*), and had two sons and two daus; *m* 2nd Feb 1692 Tryphena, widow of Richard Lloyd, of London, and *d* 1695, leaving further issue; his er s by his 1st w:

THOMAS GROVE, of Ferne and Martin, Wilts; MP; *b* 5 Feb 1664; *m* 7 Sept 1686 Elizabeth (*d* 28 Nov 1726), sis and coheir of Sir Hele Hooke, Bt, of Tangier Park, Hants, and *d* 14 March 1738, leaving, with other issue:

JOHN GROVE, of Ferne; *b* 1696; *m* 1st *c* 1751 Eleanor, dau of Sir William Hanham (*see* HANHAM, Bt), and had a s (William, *d* an infant); *m* 2nd *c* 1755 Philippa, est dau of Walter Long, of Preshaw, Hants, and Close Gate, Sarum, and *d* 1769, having by her had, with two daus:

THOMAS GROVE, of Ferne; *b* 1759; *m* Feb 1781 Charlotte (*d* 12 April 1828), dau of Charles Pilfold, of Effingham, Surrey, and *d* 22 April 1847, having had, with three daus:
1 Thomas; *b* 25 Dec 1783; *m* 1st 1 Jan 1807 Henrietta (*dsp* 15 Feb 1821), dau of James Farquharson, of Langton, Dorset; *m* 2nd 19 April 1824 Elizabeth, dau of Jeremiah Hill, of Bristol, and *dvp*, leaving issue:
(1) Mary; *m* 10 April 1849 Adml Cospatrick Baillie-Hamilton and *d* 17 Nov 1897, leaving issue (*see* HADDINGTON, E)
2 JOHN
3 William, of Netherhampton House, Wilts; Capt RN; *b* 21 Jan 1790; *m* Frances (*d* 27 March 1865), dau of Charles Grove, of Salisbury, MD, and sis of William Chafyn Grove, of Salisbury, later Zeals, and *d* 1 Aug 1855
4 George, of E Hayes, Wilts; *b* 25 Sept 1793; *m* Charlotte Louisa (*d* May 1882), dau and coheir of William Eyre, of New House, Downton, Wilts, and *dsp* 23 May 1838
5 Charles Henry (Rev); Rector Sedgehill, Wilts; *b* 29 Oct 1794; *m* 14 Feb 1820 Eliza (*d* 1 May 1866), dau of Edward Hopkins, of Alresford, Hants, and *d* 14 July 1878, having by her had surv issue four daus

The 2nd son,

JOHN GROVE, of Ferne; *b* 4 Dec 1784; *m* 17 Jan 1818 Jean Helen (*d* 8 Oct 1869), dau of Sir William Fraser, 1st Bt (*see* 1970 edn FRASER, Bt, of Ledeclune), and had:
1 THOMAS FRASER (Sir), **1st Bt**
2 John, of Mudeford, Hants; *b* 12 March 1825; *m* 13 May 1851 Clara Cicely Sarah (*d* 5 Nov 1857), dau of Joseph Ashton Burrow, of Carleton Hall, Cumberland, and *d* 16 Feb 1859, having had issue
1 Henrietta; *m* 10 Jan 1839 James Hussey (*d* 1880), of The Close, Salisbury, and had issue
2 Louisa Jean; *m* 15 Jan 1851 Frederick Augustus Selwyn, Adml RN, s of Rev Townshend Selwyn, Rector Kilmington, Somerset, Canon Gloucester, and *d* 11 Oct 1866. He *d* 1881
3 Helen Sophia; *m* 7 Jan 1864 Col John Stephen Ross, BSC, and *d* 28 March 1929. He *d* 1896, leaving issue
4 Emma Philippa; *d* unm 1 March 1925

JOHN GROVE *d* 14 April 1858; his er son,

Sir Thomas Fraser Grove, 1st Bt (UK), so *cr* 18 March 1874, DL Wilts; High Sheriff 1863, MP S Wilts 1865–74 and Wilton 1885–92, Lt-Col Wilts Yeo Cav, Capt 6th Dragoons; *b* 27 Nov 1823; *m* 1st 16 Jan 1847 Katherine Grace (*d* 8 June 1879), 2nd dau of Hon Waller O'Grady (*see* 1953 edn GUILLAMORE, V), and had:
1 WALTER JOHN (Sir), **2nd Bt**
2 Thomas Hele Hooke; *b* 21 Dec 1862; *m* 11 June 1929 Leocadia (*d* 1947), widow of Felipe Crosthwaite, of Santa Rosa, and dau of Benedito Dodero, of San Jose del Cabo, Lower California, Mexico, and *dsp* 18 April 1948
1 Grace Kathleen; *m* 1st 12 Nov 1867 Hervey John de Montmorency, of Castlemorres, Co Kilkenny, and had issue. He *d* 20 Jan 1873. She *m* 2nd 7 Oct 1896 Gen Frank Hamilton, Scots Fus, and *d* 3 Feb 1940
2 Edith Eleanor; *m* 4 Aug 1874 Edmund Benson Foster, of Clewer Manor, Berks, and *d* 29 Nov 1921, leaving issue. He *d* 1 Nov 1917
3 Charlotte Augusta; *m* 9 June 1904 Gilbert Michael Warren Davis, of Mullock, Corfe Mullen, Dorset, s of Gilbert W Warren Davis, and *dsp* 1 April 1939
4 Emily Kathleen; *m* June 1885 Lt-Col Edmund Morton Mansel-Pleydell and *d* 30 March 1945, leaving issue (*see* MANSEL, Bt)

Sir Thomas *m* 2nd 19 Sept 1882 Frances Hinton (*d* 9 Aug 1912), widow of (a) Capt Herbert Edward George Crosse, 59th Regt, and (b) Capt Hon Frederick Barnewall Best (*see* WYNFORD, B), and dau of Henry Northcote, of Okefield, Crediton, Devon, and *d* 14 Jan 1897, having by her had:
5 Olivia Frances; *m* 14 July 1910 Capt William Lewis Rowland Paul Blennerhassett, DSO, OBE, yst s of Sir Rowland Blennerhassett, 4th Bt (*qv*), and *d* 2 Jan 1953, leaving issue

His er son,

Sir Walter John Grove, 2nd Bt, JP Wilts, Dorset; Capt Roy Wilts Yeo; *b* 9 Sept 1852; *m* 20 July 1882 Agnes Geraldine (*d* 7 Dec 1926), dau of Lt-Gen Augustus Henry Lane Fox Pitt (*see* STANLEY OF ALDERLEY, SHEFFIELD and, B), and *d* 9 Feb 1932, having had issue:
1 **Sir Gerald Grove, 3rd Bt**, JP Dorset; *b* 18 Dec 1886; *educ* Sherborne and privately abroad in France and Germany; served Br S African Police Rhodesia 1911–17, German SW and E African Campaigns WW I (invalided 1918), Lt KAR 1917–19, Extra ADC to Govr-Gen S Africa 1918, FO 1920–21, Priv Sec to Govr Victoria 1922; *d* unm 3 March 1962
2 Terence; *b* 9 Dec 1893; *d* 15 May 1902
3 Walter Peel; *b* 30 March 1904; *m* 26 March 1926 (*divorce* 1933) Elena Rebecca, dau of Felipe Crosthwaite, of Lower California, and *d* 2 April 1944, leaving:
(1) **Sir Walter Felipe Grove, 4th Bt**; *b* 18 March 1927; *d* unm 1974
(2) Sir CHARLES GERALD GROVE, **5th and present Bt**
(3) +HAROLD THOMAS; *b* 6 Dec 1930; heir presumptive
1 Honor; *m* 30 May 1911 Maj-Gen Nikolai Golejewski, Imp Russian GS, and *d* 13 Dec 1944, leaving issue
2 Œnone; VAD and WRAF WW I, Min Labour 1921–23, YWCA Cairo 1923–25, LAAS 1939–41; *b* 1 March 1889; *d* unm 21 Jan 1956

GUILFORD

Arms: Az. a lion passant or between three fleurs-de-lys arg. **Crest:** A dragon's head erased sa., ducally gorged and chained or. **Supporters:** Two mastiffs ppr. **Mottoes:** 1 *La vertu est la seule noblesse* ('Virtue is the only nobility'), 2 *Animo et fide* ('With courage and fidelity'). **Creations:** B. (E) 27 Sept 1683, E. (GB) 8 April 1752.

THE 9TH EARL OF GUILFORD and **Baron of Guilford**, Co Surrey (Edward Francis North, JP (Dover and E Kent 1971), DL (Kent 1976))[The Rt Hon The Earl of Guilford JP DL, Home Farm House, Waldershare Park, Dover, Kent CT15 5BA]; *b* 22 Sept 1933; *s* gf 1949; *educ* Eton; FRSA; *m* 15 Sept 1956 (Osyth) Vere Napier, OStJ (*d* 1992), dau of Cyril Napier Leeston, of W Malling, Kent, and has issue:

1 +PIERS EDWARD BROWNLOW, *Lord North*; *b* 9 March 1971; *m* 1994 *Michèle, dau of Gilbert Desvaux de Marigny, of Curepipe, Mauritius, and Mrs Eric Story, of Durban, S Africa

Earldom of Guil(d)ford: In 1660 Elizabeth, daughter of the 1st Earl of Denbigh of the 1622 creation (*see* DENBIGH and DESMOND, E) and widow of the 1st Viscount Boyle of Kinalmeaky (*see* CORK and ORRERY, E) was created Countess of Guildford for life. This was presumably out of gratitude by CHARLES II for the Countess's services as Principal Lady of the Bedchamber to his mother HENRIETTA MARIA. Like CHARLES, the Countess converted to Catholicism.

One of the subsidiary titles of the 1st and last Duke of Lauderdale (*see* LAUDERDALE, E), virtual ruler of Scotland in CHARLES II's reign, was Earl of Guilford, so created in 1674.

Lineage: ROGER NORTH; living *temp* HENRY V; *m* Alice, dau of John Harcourt, of Oxon, and *d* 1471, having had, with a dau (Ellen, *m* John Parker, of Norton Lees, Derbys; *see* PARKER, Bt, of Shenstone Lodge):

THOMAS NORTH, of Walkeringham, Notts; had:

ROGER NORTH, of Walkeringham; *d* 1495, leaving, with an er s (Thomas, ancestor of the NORTHs of Walkeringham):

ROGER NORTH, London merchant; *m* Christian, widow of Ralph Warren and dau of Richard Warcup, of Sinnington, Yorks, and *d* by 29 Nov 1509, leaving:

EDWARD NORTH, 1st LORD (Baron) NORTH (E), so *cr* by writ(?) (?)17 Feb 1553/4(?), PC (Feb 1546/753); *b c* 1496; *educ* St Paul's and Caius or Peterhouse Cambridge; Clerk Cncl City London, Clerk of Parl 1531–40, King's Serjeant-at-law 1536, Treas Court Augmentations 1540 (Chllr 1544–48), ktd 1542, Cambs: Sheriff (with Hunts) 1540–43, MP 1542–44, 1547–52 and 1553, Ld Lt 1559; *m* 1st *c* 1528 Alice, widow of (a) Edward Myrfin, skinner, s of Sir Thomas Myrfin, Ld Mayor London 1518–19, and (b) John Brigandine, and dau and heir of Oliver Squire, of Southby, Hants, and had:

1 ROGER, 2nd LORD (Baron) NORTH

2 Thomas (Sir); translated Plutarch's *Lives*

1 Christian; *m* 3rd Earl of Worcester (*see* BEAUFORT, D)

2 Mary; *m* 9th Lord (Baron) Scrope (of Bolton)

The 1st LORD (Baron) NORTH *m* 2nd *c* 1561 Margaret (*d* 2 June 1575), dau of Richard Butler, of London, and widow of (a) Sir David Brooke, (b) Robert Chertsey, London Alderman, and (c) Andrew Francis, and *d* 31 Dec 1564

His er son,

ROGER NORTH, 2nd LORD (Baron) NORTH, KB (Jan 1558/9), PC (1596); *b* 27 Feb 1530/1; *educ* Gray's Inn; Cambs: MP 1555, 1559 and 1563–64, Commr Musters 1565, Ld Lt 1588, High Steward Cambridge 1572, Amb France 1574, Treas Household 1596–1600, as a memb English forces in Low Countries was Govr Flushing and Harlingen and Provisional Govr Utrecht 1586; *m* Winifred, widow of Sir Henry Dudley and dau of 2nd Baron Rich (*see* 1970 edn RICH, Bt), and *d* 3 Dec 1600, having had, with a yr s (Sir Henry, of Mildenhall, Suffolk; gf of Sir Henry North, 1st Bt, so *cr* 1660):

Sir JOHN NORTH; *educ* Peterhouse and Trin Coll Cambridge; MP Cambs 1584, 1586, 1588, ktd 1596; *m* Dorothy (*m* 2nd 23 May 1604 Sir James Ouchterlony), dau and coheir of Dr Valentine Dale, and *dvp* 5 June 1597, leaving, with other issue:

DUDLEY NORTH, 3rd LORD (Baron) NORTH; *bapt* 18 Sept 1582; *educ* Cambridge, Lt Cambs, Parliamentarian Civil War; *m* between 22 and 28 Nov 1600 Frances, dau and coheir of Sir John Brocket, of Brocket Hall, Herts, and *d* 16 Jan 1665/6, leaving an est s:

DUDLEY NORTH, 4th LORD (Baron) NORTH, KB (1616); *b c* 1 Nov 1602; *educ* Cambridge and Gray's Inn; MP Horsham 1628–29, Cambs April-May 1640 and 1640–48 and Cambridge 1660; *m* 24 April 1632 Anne, dau and coheir of Sir Charles Montagu (*see* MANCHESTER, D), and *d* 24 June 1677, having had, with four daus and four other sons:

1 CHARLES NORTH, 5th LORD (Baron) NORTH and 1st LORD (Baron) GREY (of Rolleston), so *cr* by writ 24 Oct 1673; *b* 1 Oct 1635; *educ* Cambridge; ktd by 1667, Govr Portsmouth 1681; *m c* 6 April 1667 Catharine (*m* 3rd Col Francis Russell; *see* BEDFORD, D), widow of Sir Edward Mosley, 2nd Bt of the 1640 *cr* (*see* RAVENSDALE, B), and dau of 1st Baron Grey of Warke, and *d* Jan 1690/1, leaving an est s:

(1) WILLIAM NORTH, 6th LORD (Baron) NORTH and 2nd LORD (Baron) GREY (of Rolleston), PC (1711–14); *b* 22 Dec 1678; *educ* Magdalene Coll Cambridge; Capt Foot Gds 1702, Col 10th Foot 1703–15, fought Blenheim 1704 (lost right hand), Brig-Gen Feb 1704/5, Maj-Gen 1709, Lt Gen 1710, Govr Sheerness 1705, Portsmouth 1711–14, Ld Lt Cambs 1711–15, FRS 1720, lukewarm Jacobite at time of 1715 Rising (recd commission from titular James III but was not actively involved), *cr* 5 Jan 1721/2 by James Earl North (E), imprisoned Tower London 1722 for high treason, out on bail 1723; *m* Oct 1705 Maria Margaretta (*m* 2nd 1735 7th Lord Elibank (*qv*); *d* 6 June 1762), dau of Cornelius de Yong, Ld of Elmeet, Utd Provinces, and *dspl* 31 Oct 1734, when the Barony of Grey and Jacobite Earldom expired, leaving:

1a William GREYSON; *b c* 1724

2 FRANCIS NORTH, **1st Baron of Guilford**, Co Surrey (E), so *cr* 27 Sept 1683, PC (1679), KC (1668); *b* 22 Oct 1637; *educ* St John's Coll Cambridge; barrister Middle Temple 1661, MP King's Lynn 1672/3–75, Slr-Gen 1671–73, Attorney-Gen 1673–82, Ch Justice Common Pleas 1675–82, Speaker Ho Lds 1678, Ld Keeper Gt Seal 1682–85; *m* 5 March 1671/2 Lady Frances Pope (*d* 4 Nov 1699), 2nd dau and coheir of 3rd Earl of Downe, who brought him Wroxton Abbey, Oxon, and *d* 5 Sept 1685, leaving issue:

(1) FRANCIS NORTH, **2nd Baron of Guilford**, PC (1712–14); *b* 14 Dec 1673; *educ* Winchester and Trin Coll Oxford; Ld Lt Essex 1703–05, Ld of Tde 1712–13, 1st Ld of Tde 1713–14; *m* 1st 25 Feb 1694/5 Elizabeth Greville (*d* 4 Nov 1699), 3rd dau of 5th Baron Brooke of Beauchamps Court (*see* WARWICK, BROOKE and, E), but had no surv issue; *m* 2nd *c* 8 July 1703 Alice, 2nd dau and coheir of Sir John Brownlow, 3rd Bt (*see* BROWNLOW, B), and *d* 17 Oct 1729, leaving an only s:

1a FRANCIS, **1st Earl**

3 Dudley; Turkey merchant; *m* Anne, widow of Sir Robert Gunning and dau of Sir Robert Cann, Bt, and *d* 31 Dec 1691, leaving, with a yr s (John):

(1) Dudley, of Glemham, Suffolk; *m* Catherine, dau and coheir of Elihu Yale, the benefactor of Yale U, Ct., and had, with two sons (Dudley, Elihu) and a yr dau (Mary):

1a Anne; *m* Hon Nicholas Herbert, 3rd s of 8th Earl of Pembroke and (5th Earl) of Montgomery (*qv*), and had issue

4 John; DD, Clerk Closet to CHARLES II, Preb Westminster, Fell Jesus Coll Cambridge (where tutor to his bro Roger), Master Trin Coll Cambridge; *d* unm 1682

5 Montagu; *m* Mary, dau of Sir Robert Geers, of Stoke, Windsor, and *d* 1710, having had two sons and five daus

6 Roger, of Rougham, Norfolk (an estate he bought 1690), KC (1682); *b* 3 Sept 1653; *educ* Thetford Sch Norfolk and Jesus Coll Cambridge; barrister Middle Temple 1675 (Bencher 1682), Steward Diocese of Canterbury 1678, Slr-Gen to Duke of York 1684, Attorney-Gen to QUEEN MARY OF MODENA 1686, MP Dunwich 1685, Recorder Bristol, author: *Memoires of Musicke* (1728), *Examen* (*i.e.*, defence [of Charles II] 1740), *Autobiography*, *The Lives of the Norths* (1742, 1744) and other works; *m* Mary, dau of Sir Robert Gayer, of Stoke Poges, Bucks, and *d* 1 March 1733/4, having had issue:

(1) Roger, of Rougham; *bapt* 26 Jan 1703; *m* 1st —; *m* 2nd Jane, dau of W Lake, of Heacham, and by her had, with two daus:

1a Fountain, of Rougham; *b* 14 March 1749; *m* Arabella, dau of Isaac Strutt, of Hampstead, and had issue:

1b Francis Frederick, of Rougham; *b* 2 July 1778; *educ* Westminster; *m* 5 March 1799 Elizabeth (*m* 2nd 24 Nov 1824 Gloucester Wilson; *d* 1853), dau of Rev William Whitear, Preb Chichester, and *d* 8 Oct 1821, having had, with other issue:

1c Frederick, of Rougham, JP, DL Norfolk; MP Hastings; *b* 2 July 1800; *educ* Harrow and St John's Coll Cambridge; *m* 16 June 1825 Janet (*d* 17 Jan 1855), widow of Robert Shuttleworth, of Gawthorn Hall, Lancs, and dau of Sir John Marjoribanks, 1st Bt (*see* 1888 edn), and *d* 29 Oct 1869, leaving:

1d Charles, of Rougham, JP, DL Norfolk; MA, barrister Inner Temple, Capt Norfolk Artillery Militia; *b* 25 March 1828; *educ* Eton and Trin Coll Camb; *m* 16 March 1859 Augusta (*d* 17 Feb 1917), est dau of Rev Hon Thomas Robert Keppel (*see* ALBEMARLE, E), and *d* 10 May 1906, having had issue:

1e Frederick Keppel, JP, of Rougham Hall; barrister Inner Temple, Chllr dioceses of Norwich, St Edmundsbury and Ipswich, Chm: Norfolk QS, Norwich and Colchester Munitions Tbnl, memb Ch Assembly Norwich, Commr Union of Benefices Act, V-Pres Soc Chm QSs Westminster; *b* 7 May 1860; *educ* Eton and Trin Coll Cambridge (BA, LLB); *m* 21 April 1898 Grace (*d* 11 May 1946), dau of Gen Hon Sir Percy Robert Basil Feilding, KCB (*see* DENBIGH and DESMOND, E), and *d* 24 March 1948, leaving issue:

1f Roger, JP; barrister Inner Temple 1925, Chm Norfolk QS 1962, memb Roy Inst; *b* 10 Dec 1901; *educ* Eton and Trin Coll Cambridge (BA 1923, MA 1962, LLB 1924); *m* 20 Sept 1934 Pamela Susan (*d* 6 Dec 1997), yst dau of Rev Henry William Leycester O'Rorke, MA, of The Manor House, N Litchfield, Hants, and *d* 1985, leaving:

1g +Thomas Frederick [Thomas North Esq, Rougham Hall, King's Lynn, Norfolk; 18 Moreton Place, London SW1]; barrister Inner Temple 1966; *b* 17 Jan 1942; *educ* Eton and Trin Coll Cambridge (BA); *m* 10 Aug 1974 *Sally Catherine, only dau of Lt-Col George Miles Strover, of Leigh Delamere House, Chippenham, Wilts, and has had:

1h Charles; *b* 1976; *d* 1993

2h +Alec Roger; *b* 1979

1h *Amy; *b* 25 April 1977

2h *Sophie; *b* 1983

1g *Valerie Susan [Mrs John Guinness, East Barsham Manor, East Barsham, Norfolk NR21]; *b* 5 Jan 1937; *m* 15 July 1967 *John Ralph Sidney Guinness (see GUINNESS, Bt), and has issue

2g *Christine; *b* 21 Sept 1938 [Mrs Alan Blakemore, Hatchford Park Nurseries, Cobham, Surrey]; *m* 1 May 1963 *Alan Blakemore, s of E R Blakemore, and has issue:

1h *Emily Jasmine Alice; *b* 10 March 1964

2h *Flora Marianne Sophie; *b* 11 March 1966

3h *Lily Isabella Katherine Bonnie; *b* 15 Dec 1968

4h *Jessie Mary Cassandra; *b* 1972

3g *Grace Elizabeth [Mrs Alan Barlow, Janet Cottages, Rougham, Norfolk]; *b* 6 May 1946; *educ* New Hall Cambridge (BA 1967) and St George's Hosp London (MB, BChir); *m* 1975 *Alan Barlow and has issue:

1h *Edward Francis; *b* 1978

1h *Katherine Clare; *b* 1980

2f Charles Percy Frederick; Air Min, Min Tport; *b* 18 April 1906; *educ* Eton and Trin Coll Cambridge (BA 1928); *m* 11 March 1937 Judith (*d* 1991), only dau of Harry Leon Hamlin, of Long Island, NY, and *d* 10 Nov 1971, leaving issue:

1g *Mary Grace [Mrs William Clow, 30 Sutton Place, New York 10022, NY, USA]; *b* 4 Sept 1939; *m* 28 May 1969 William Ellsworth Clow II (*d* 1970), s of Kent Sarver Clow, of Lake Forest, Ill., and has issue:

1h *Miranda Judith; *b* 1980

2g *Melissa Judith [Mrs Michael Chassay, 17 Powis Terrace, London W11 1JJ]; *b* 3 Feb 1944; *m* 10 March 1976 *Michael Edmund Nicholas Chassay, RIBA, s of Arthur Arcade Chassay and Mrs Margot Aptaker, and has issue:

1h *Clancy Charles Arcade; *b* 1980

1h *Dixie Cleopatra; *b* 1976

2e Roger Townshend; *b* 30 Jan 1863; *d* 13 April 1864

3e Marjoribanks Keppel; MICE, engrg inspr Min Health, Capt RE WW I (despatches); *b* 17 Nov 1865, *educ* Marlborough; *m* 19 July 1905 Edith Beatrice, JP Bucks (*d* 21 Oct 1973), only dau of Sir George John Armytage, 6th Bt (*qv*), and *d* 27 March 1949, leaving:

1f George Montagu; Traffic Dept BR, Capt RE WW II; *b* 4 June 1906; *educ* Eton; *m* 22 Feb 1940 *June Margaret (*m* 2nd 1956 Robert Burton Kenward), dau of Francis Edward Harrison, OBE, of York, and *d* 16 Feb 1953, leaving issue:

1g *Lavinia Keppel [Mrs Peter Jeffries, Brownings House, Ide Hill, Kent TN14 6JT]; *b* 11 Dec 1940; *m* 5 Sept 1970 *Peter Jocelyn Jeffries, and has issue:

1h *Charles Jocelyn; *b* 1973

1h *Alexandra Keppel; *b* 13 Aug 1971

1f *Arabella; Ch Cdr ATS WW II; *b* 12 May 1909; *m* 18 Oct 1950 *Louis Euan Babington Morgan, s of Ernest Roderick Morgan, of Montreal

4e Charles Keppel; *b* 5 Dec 1870; *d* 30 Jan 1881

5e Anthony Dudley Keppel; *b* 22 April 1874; *d* Oct 1886

6e Thomas Keppel, OBE (1918); manager Vickers; *b* 28 March 1876; *d* unm 10 Feb 1919

1e Marianne Eva; *m* 28 Jan 1880 Robert Charles Otter, of Royston Manor, Clayworth, yr s of Henry Otter, of Swinton House, Rotherham, Yorks, and *d* 4 Jan 1916, leaving issue. He *d* 25 Oct 1939

2e Arabella Valerie Keppel; *m* 7 Nov 1885 her cousin 12th Lord (Baron) North (*see* 1970 edn) and *d* 3 Aug 1965 aged 97, leaving issue. He *d* 10 Dec 1938

3e Frances Hilda, CBE (1926); *m* 16 Jan 1889 Maj Pandia John Zigomala, 19th Hus, and *d* 16 June 1946, having had issue. He *d* 26 Nov 1933

4e Dora Hermione; *m* 4 Feb 1908 Hon Reginald Hastings Marsham (*see* ROMNEY, E), and *d* 14 Aug 1923, having had issue

5e Augusta Louisa; BRC Italy, Scottish Women Hosp Unit Serbia WW I (British and Serbian medals), ARP and WVS WW II; *b* 1878

1d Marianne; *d* unm 30 Aug 1890

2d Janet Catherine; *m* 10 Nov 1864 John Addington Symonds, the poet and art historian, and *d* 6 Sept 1913, leaving issue. He *d* 1893

2c Charles William (Rev); *d* unm

3c Dudley; *b* 1805; *m* 1839 Sarah, dau of Maj — Lockyer, of Lockyersleigh, NSW, and *d* 1845, leaving, with three daus:

1d Dudley, CB; Col N Lancs Regt Ashanti War and Zhob Valley; *b* 8 Oct 1840; *d* unm 22 Nov 1917

2b Charles Edward (Rev); Rector Child Okeford, Dorset

1b Arabella; *m* Sir John Meade

2a Edward Roger (Rev); Rector Ringstead, Norfolk

The 2nd BARON's s,

FRANCIS NORTH, **1st Earl of Guilford** (GB), so *cr* 8 April 1752, and 7th LORD (Baron) NORTH (*s* cousin 1734); *b* 13 April 1704; *educ* Eton and Trin Coll Oxford; MP (Tory) Banbury 1727–29; Ld Bedchamber to FREDERICK PRINCE OF WALES 1730–51, Govr PRINCE GEORGE (later GEORGE III) OF WALES 1750–51, Treas to QUEEN CHARLOTTE 1773–90; *m* 1st 17 June 1728 Lady Lucy Montague (*d* 7 May 1734), dau of 1st Earl of Halifax of the 1715 *cr* (*see* HALIFAX, E, preliminary remarks), and had:

1 FREDERICK NORTH, **2nd Earl of Guilford**, KG (1772), PC (1766); *b* 12 April 1732; *educ* Eton and Trin Coll Oxford (DCL 1772, Chllr 1772); MP (Tory) Banbury 1754–90, a Ld Treasury 1759–65, Jt Paymaster-Gen 1766–67, Chllr Exchequer 1767–82, PM 1770–82, Home Sec (in a Whig Ministry) April–Dec 1783, Freedom Exeter 1782, LLD Cantab 1769, Er Bro Trin Ho 1771–92 and Master 1773–75, Ld Lt Somerset 1774–92, FSA 1776, Ld Warden Cinque Ports 1778–92; *m* 20 May 1756 Anne (*d* 1797), dau and heir of George Speke, of White Lackington, Somerset, and *d* 5 Aug 1792, leaving:

(1) GEORGE AUGUSTUS NORTH, **3rd Earl of Guilford**; *b* 11 Sept 1757; *educ* Eton and Trin Coll Oxford; MP (Tory) Harwich 1778–84, (Whig) Wootton Bassett 1784–90, Petersfield 1790 and Banbury 1790–92, U-Sec Home Office April–Dec 1783; *m* 1st 24 Sept 1785 Lady Maria Frances Mary Hobart (*d* 23 April 1794), dau of 3rd Earl of Buckinghamshire (*qv*), and had, with a s (*d* young):

1a Maria; *m* 29 July 1818 2nd Marquess of Bute (*qv*) and *dsp* 11 Sept 1841

(1) (cont.) The **3rd Earl** *m* 2nd 28 Feb 1796 Susan (*d* 24 Sept 1837), dau of Thomas Coutts, banker, and *dspms* (another s by his 2nd w having *d* young) 20 April 1802, when the Barony of North fell into abeyance between his daus, having by her had:

2a SUSAN North, BARONESS NORTH in her own right from 1841, when the death of her sister automatically terminated the abeyance; *b* 6 Feb 1797; *m* 18 Nov 1835 Col John Sydney DOYLE later NORTH (roy licence 20 Aug 1838), PC (1886), MP Oxon 1852–55 (*b* 28 May 1804; *d* 11 Oct 1894), 2nd s of Lt-Gen Sir Charles William Doyle, KCB, and *d* 5 March 1884, leaving issue (*see* 1970 edn NORTH, B)

3a Georgiana; *b* 6 Nov 1798; *d* unm 25 Aug 1835

(2) FRANCIS NORTH, **4th Earl of Guilford**; *b* 25 Dec 1761; *educ* Eton; Cornet 2nd Dragoons 1777, Maj 83rd Foot 1783, Lt-Col 1794, author: *The Kentish Barons* (play, 1817); *m* 19 July 1810 Maria, 5th dau of Thomas Boycott, of Rudge Hall, Salop, and *dsp* 11 Jan 1817

(3) FREDERICK NORTH, **5th Earl of Guilford**, GCMG (1819); *b* 7 Feb 1766; *educ* Eton and Ch Ch Oxford (DCL 1793 and 1819); Chamberlain Exchequer 1779–1826, became a Greek Orthodox Christian 1791, MP (Whig) Banbury 1792–94, Comptroller London Customs 1794–1812, Sec State Corsica 1795–97, Govr and V-Adml Ceylon 1798–1805, Chllr U of Corfu 1819–27, FRS 1794, LLD Cantab 1821; *d* unm 14 Oct 1827

(1) Catherine Anne; *b* 16 Feb 1760; *m* 25 Sept 1789 1st and last Baron Glenbervie and *d* 6 Feb 1817

(2) Anne; *m* 20 Jan 1798 1st Earl of Sheffield (*see* STANLEY OF ALDERLEY, SHEFFIELD and, B), and *d* 18 Jan 1832, leaving issue

(3) Charlotte; *m* 2 April 1800 Lt-Col Hon John Lindsay (*see* CRAWFORD and BALCARRES, E) and *d* 25 Oct 1849

1 Lucy; *b* 1734

The **1st Earl** *m* 2nd 24 Jan 1735/6 Elizabeth (*d* 21 April 1745), dau of Sir Arthur Kaye, 3rd Bt (*qv*), and widow of George Legge, Viscount Lewisham (*see* DARTMOUTH, E), and by her had, with other issue:

2 Brownlow (Rt Rev); DD, Bp: Lichfield 1771, Worcester 1774 and Winchester 1781; *b* 17 July 1741; *m* 17 Jan 1771 Henrietta Maria (*d* 16 Nov 1796), dau and coheir of John Bannister, and *d* 12 July 1820, leaving issue:

(1) FRANCIS, **6th Earl**

(2) Brownlow; *b* 1778; *d* 28 Sept 1829

(3) Charles Augustus (Rev); Preb Winchester; *b* 23 June 1785; *m* 11 March 1808 Rachel (*d* 25 March 1856), 2nd dau of Thomas Jarvis, of Laverstoke House, Hants, and *d* 18 Aug 1825, leaving issue:

1a Brownlow, of Dallas House, Morayshire; *b* 6 Jan 1810; *m* 12 Dec 1828 Grace Anne (*d* 29 May 1889), dau of Rev Thomas Coffey, DD, of Kinvara, Co Galway, and *d* 9 Nov 1875, leaving issue:

1b Charles Augustus; *b* 10 Nov 1829; *m* 1st 27 April 1865 Rachel Elizabeth (*d* 1 Feb 1871), dau of Sir Francis Grant, PRA; *m* 2nd 11 Nov 1873 Elizabeth (*dsp* 25 March 1878), est dau of James Hayward, and *d* 1893, having by his 1st w had issue:

1c Frederic Dudley, CMG (1902), JP W Australian Govt Serv; U-Sec Colonial Office 1902, Comptroller Gen Prisons 1912–21; *b* 9 Nov 1866; *educ* Rugby; *m* 19 Jan 1887 Flora Frances (*d* 1950), yst dau of Edward Hamersley, of Pyrton, W Australia, and *d* 22 Aug 1921, leaving:

1d Charles Frederick John; Capt RAF, barrister Middle Temple 1912, Supreme Court W Australia, MLA Claremont 1924–56, Speaker 1946–53, Silver Jubilee Medal 1935, Coronation Medal 1937; *b* 14 Sept 1887; *educ* Rugby and Oriel Coll Oxford (BA 1909); *m* 1916 Bessie (*d* 1964), dau of William Saddington, of Cheshire, and *d* 1979, leaving:

1e *Muriel Elvia Joan; *b* 10 July 1917; *m* 1942 *Roy Wilson Parr, USN

2e *Rachel Mary June [Mrs Thomas Cassidy, 4 Forrerst St, Cottesloe, W Australia]; *b* 17 April 1930; *m* 1st 22 Feb 1955 (*divorce* 1966) Garth Murray Denny; *m* 2nd 1967 *Thomas Nolan Cassidy and by her 1st husb has issue:

1f *David North Murray; *b* 5 March 1958

1f *Julie Elizabeth; *b* 15 March 1961

2d George Eustace Dudley; Lt 1st Life Gds WW I (wounded), ADC to Govr W Australia; *b* 9 April 1893; *educ* St Peter's Coll Adelaide and Jesus Coll Camb; *m* 1920 Florence Ethel Yeo, of Perth, W Australia, and *d* 1960, leaving issue:

1e *Mary Elizabeth [Mrs Geoffrey Russell, Dunkathel, Glanmire, Co Cork, Ireland]; *b* 20 Feb 1925; *m* 12 Oct 1948 Geoffrey Norreys Russell (*d* 1987), yst s of Col Henry Thompson Russell, RFA, of Milford House, Limerick, and has issue:

1f *John Norris Grant; *b* 1951; *educ* Harrow and Trin Coll Dublin; *m* 1988 *Anabel, dau of Capt Peter Tyrrell, of Glanmire, and has:

1g *Marcus Richard Grant; *b* 1989

1g *Georgina Natalia Anabel; *b* 1991
2f *Francis Guilford; *b* 1953; *educ* Harrow; *m* 1980 *Manon Regina, er dau of James Mackay Henry Millington-Drake (*see* INCHCAPE, E)
3f *Philip Brownlow; *b* 1959; *educ* Harrow and RAC Cirencester; *m* 1988 *Mary Jane, yr dau of Capt Alan Ireland, and has:
1g *Robin Geoffrey Alan; *b* 1992
1g *Tarka Elizabeth; *b* 1989
1d Margaret Frances Emily Muriel; *m* 1st 15 Nov 1919 Capt P B Shute, IA, cmdg 15th Co Burma Sappers and Miners (*d* 1 Sept 1932 following a boating accident); *m* 2nd 17 Jan 1940 George Albert Tong, RAF (*d* 1945 in a cyclone); *m* 3rd 1947 John Westley Ainsco, US Merchant Marine, and *d* 1956
2d Wilhemina Mary Isabel Flora; *m* 1920 Astley Bertram Cornelius Hamersley, Lt 10th Light Horse AIF, and *d* 1950, leaving issue
2c Brownlow Francis Gordon; Lt RAMC WW I; *b* 4 May 1869; *d* of wounds recd in action 11 Nov 1917
1c Mary Isabella; *b* 2 Feb 1868; *m* 9 Oct 1888 (*divorce* 1902) Sir William Edmund Garstin, GCMG, GBE, and *d* 2 Feb 1953, leaving issue. He *d* 8 Jan 1925
2c Rachel Elizabeth; *b* 24 Jan 1871; *m* 7 Feb 1893 Capt Henry Montague Clifton Hawkes, 2nd Bn E Yorks Regt. He *d* 1896
2b Brownlow John Jarvis; *b* 24 Feb 1831; *m* 1st 14 June 1849 Margaret Frances Byng Macdonald (*d* 5 Jan 1863), 2nd dau and coheir of Keith Macdonald MacAlister, of Inistrynich, Argyll; *m* 2nd 14 Oct 1871 Merielina Sophia (*d* 22 Feb 1906), widow of Rev Frederick Haggit, and *d* 20 Aug 1874, having by his 1st w had issue:
1c Brownlow Hamilton; *b* 10 March 1854; *m* 1 Dec 1879 Elizabeth Martha (*d* 28 March 1886), dau of John Warren Ryan, and *d* 1886, leaving:
1d Brownlow John Frederick; *b* 1883
2d George Dudley Guilford; *b* 1884; *m* 1st 19– —; *m* 2nd 1921 Jane Berkeley (*m* 2nd Oct 1937 Austin Benedict Caston; *d* 1977), dau of Charles Nathaniel Gregg, and *d* April 1937, leaving by his 2nd w:
1e Dudley Charles Guilford; *b* 1923; accidentally drowned 1944 India
1e *Patricia Grace Eileen [Mrs Jackson Askey, 7710 Fitzpatrick Drisve, Liverpool, NY 13088, USA]; *b* 1922; *m* 1944 *Jackson Samuel Askey and has issue
2e Jean Dorothy; *b* 1928; *m* 1948 Daniel Vegard (*d* 1978) and *d* 1968, leaving issue:
1f *James Dudley; *b* 1948; *m* 1971 *Jennie Abrunzo
1f *Deborah Ann; *b* 1951
2f *Victoria Jane; *b* 1954; *m* 1993 *Frederick Herbert Ahrens and has issue:
1g *James Frederick; *b* 1993
3e *Barbara Violet [Mrs James Semple, 8201 Golden Bear Loop, Port Richey, FL 34668, USA]; *b* 1931; *m* 1957 *James Edward Semple and has issue:
1f *Cathy Barbara; *b* 1958; *m* 1982 *Stephen Andrew Dock and has issue:
1g *James Matthew; *b* 1987
1g *Melissa Jean; *b* 1985
2g *Carolyn Jane; *b* 1991
2f *Jane Alice; *b* 1962; *m* 1988 *Delano Bookings Trott
1d Elizabeth Grace Margaret
2d Violet Hope O'Ryan
1a Rachel; *m* James Hayward, of Loudwater House, Herts. He *d* Oct 1876
2a Henrietta Maria; *d* unm
3a Caroline Augusta; *m* 13 Oct 1840 Rev Erskine Knollys, Rector Quedgeley, Glos, and *d* 1878
4a Louisa Frederica; *m* 21 Oct 1841 John Samuel Bowles, of Milton Hill, Berks, and *d* 1847
(1) Henrietta; *m* 9 June 1797 Rev William Garnier, MA, Preb Winchester, and *d* 10 Oct 1847, having had issue. He *d* 18 March 1835
(2) Lucy; *d* unm 20 Feb 1850
(3) Elizabeth; *m* 1802 4th Baron Walsingham (*qv*) and *d* 18 May 1845
2 Louisa; *m* 15th Lord (Baron) Willoughby de Broke (*qv*) and *d* 1798

The **1st Earl** *m* 3rd 13 June 1751 Katherine (*d* 22 Dec 1766), dau and coheir of Sir Robert Furnese, 2nd Bt, of Waldershare Park, Kent, and widow of 2nd Earl of Rockingham (*see* 1970 edn SONDES, E), by whom he had no issue, and *d* 4 Aug 1790

The 5th EARL's cousin,

FRANCIS NORTH, **6th Earl of Guilford**; *b* 17 Dec 1772; *educ* Eton and Ch Ch Oxford; Master St Cross Hosp Guildford, Rector: St Mary's, Southampton, and Old Alresford, New Alresford and Medstead; *m* 1st 20 Feb 1798 Esther (*dsp* 10 Aug 1823), dau of Rev John Harrison; *m* 2nd 4 May 1826 Harriet (*m* 2nd 10 Feb 1863 John Lettsom Elliot (*d* 17 Sept 1898); *d* 16 April 1874), only dau of Lt-Gen Sir Henry Warde, GCB, of Dean House, Hants, and by her had, with other issue:
1 Dudley, *Lord North*; *b* 7 Aug 1829; *m* 17 Oct 1850 Charlotte Maria (*m* 2nd 10 July 1861 Maj A G Dickson, 13th Lt Dragoons, MP Dover (*d* 4 July 1889); *d* 6 Feb 1909), 3rd dau of Rev Hon William Eden (*see* HENLEY, B), and *dvp* 28 Jan 1860, leaving issue:
(1) DUDLEY FRANCIS, **7th Earl**
(2) Morton William; *b* 31 Oct 1852; granted with siblings rank of earl's dau/yr s; *m* 3 April 1879 Hilda Hylton (*d* 19 Feb 1902), gdau of 1st Baron Hylton (*qv*), and *d* 26 April 1895, leaving:
1a Dudley John; Lt 3rd Bn Norfolk Regt; *b* 9 Jan 1880; *m* 3 July 1914 Natalie Helen, dau of John Adye Alston and *d* 14 Dec 1926
2a Hylton George Morton; *b* 13 Sept 1885; *m* 1915 —, widow of James Tulloch McQuaida, of Pope's Villa, Twickenham, and New York
3a Roger; *b* 24 Sept 1888; *m* 1912 Alice Amy Legros
(3) Cecil; *b* 25 April 1855; *d* 1882
(1) Flora Mildred; *m* 28 Dec 1880 Sir Robert Rodney Wilmot, 6th Bt (*qv*), and *d* 1 March 1886 aged 25, leaving issue
2 Frederick Henry; Dip Serv: 3rd Sec Berlin; *b* 1 July 1834; *d* unm 17 Nov 1917
3 Charles; Lt Rifle Bde; *b* 29 Dec 1840; *m* 26 April 1865 Amy Louisa (*d* 28 Dec 1902), yst dau of Rev J T Maine, MA, and *dsp* 10 Nov 1871
1 Harriet; *m* 28 Aug 1862 Lt-Col George Warde, JP, of Squerryes Court, Westerham, Kent, and *dsp* 27 Aug 1922. He *d* 23 Jan 1877
2 Frances; *m* 11 Nov 1862 Henry Jeffreys Bushby, barrister, Recorder Colchester 1863–70, and *d* 12 Dec 1925, leaving issue. He *d* 27 Aug 1903

The 6th EARL *d* 29 Jan 1861; his gs,

DUDLEY FRANCIS NORTH, **7th Earl of Guilford**; *b* 14 July 1851; *educ* Eton; Lt RHG, Hon Col Roy E Kent Yeo Cav; *m* 4 May 1874 Georgiana (*d* 13 May 1931), 2nd dau of Sir George Chetwynd, 3rd Bt (*qv*), and *d* 19 Dec 1885, having had:
1 Dudley Francis, *Lord North*; *b* 3 May, *d* 4 May 1875
2 FREDERICK GEORGE NORTH, **8th Earl of Guilford**, TD, JP, DL Kent; Lt-Col Roy E Kent Yeo; *b* 19 Nov 1876; *m* 25 June 1901 Mary Violet (*d* 8 Dec 1947), dau of William Hargrave Pawson, of Shawdon, Northumberland, and *d* 9 Nov 1949, leaving issue:
(1) Francis George, *Lord North*; 2nd Lt 2nd Life Gds, Maj Surrey and Sussex Yeo 1939–40; *b* 15 June 1902; *m* 9 June 1927 Joan Louise (*m* 2nd 25 June 1947 Charles Harman Hunt, JP), er dau of Sir Merrik Raymond Burrell, 7th Bt (*qv*), and was *k* in an accident 25 Aug 1940, leaving issue:
1a **EDWARD FRANCIS NORTH, 9th and present Earl of Guilford**
1a *Barbara Joan [The Lady Barbara Bossom, 97 Cadogan Lane, London SW1X 9DU]; *b* 28 Sept 1928; granted Nov 1950 with her sis rank of earl's dau; OStJ; *m* 28 Sept 1951 *Maj Hon Sir Clive Bossom, 2nd Bt (*qv*), and has issue
2a *Angela Mary [The Lady Angela Whiteley, 10 Henning St, London SW11 3DR]; *b* 28 May 1931; *m* 18 July 1955 *Peter John Henry Whiteley, est s of Brig John Percival Whiteley, OBE, TD, MP, of The Grange, Bletchley, Bucks, and has issue:
1b *Simon William Alastair; *b* 9 April 1958; *m* 7 April 1988 *Winifred, yst dau of Alex Wu, CBE, of Hong Kong
2b *Justin Henry Francis; *b* 9 March 1964; *m* 9 April 1988 *Juliette Margaret, only dau of Philip Howard (*see* HOULDSWORTH, Bt), and has issue:
1c *Henry James Edward; *b* 31 Oct 1989
2c *Charles Hamish Reginald; *b* 13 March 1992
3c *Thomas; *b* 17 Dec 1995
1b *Emma Louise; *b* 19 Dec 1959; *m* 7 Aug 1993 *Henry Campbell Bellingham (*see* BELLINGHAM, Bt)
(2) John Montagu William; engr; *b* 28 Feb 1905; *educ* RNCs Osborne and Dartmouth; *m* 1st 30 April 1927 (*divorce* 1939) Muriel Norton (*d* 1989), yr dau of Sir William Norton Hicking, 1st Bt (*see* NORTH, Bt); *m* 2nd 23 June 1939 (*divorce* 1949) Marion Dyer (*d* 1992), yst dau of Frank Irving Chase, of Boston, Mass., and by his 1st w had issue:
1a +William Jonathan Frederick (Sir); *b* 1931, *s* maternal gf as 2nd Bt (*see* NORTH, Bt)
1a *Georgiana Mary; *b* 4 April 1928; *m* 19 March 1960 Esmond Unwin Butler, CM, CVO (*d* 1989), Sec to Govr-Gen Canada, s of Rev Thomas Bertram Butler, of Ontario, and has issue:
1b *Mark William; *b* 30 March 1961
1b *Clare Martine; *b* 19 Feb 1963
(2) (cont.) The Hon John North *m* 3rd 1951 (*divorce* 1960) Polly, dau of Dick Peabody, of USA; *m* 4th 1961 *Wendy Alexandra [The Hon Mrs John North, 2 La Brecque Phillippe, Alderney, CI], yst dau of Francis Robert Peters, and *d* 1987, leaving by his 3rd w:
2a *Serena Laura Peabody [Mrs Charles Colchester, 53 Romney St, London SW1P 3RF]; *b* 1952; *m* 1976 *Charles Meredith Hastings Colchester, s of Rev Capt Halsey Sparrowe Colchester, CMG, OBE, and has issue:
1b *Alexander North Peabody; *b* 1981
2b *Benjamin Medhurst Pawson; *b* 1983
3b *Zachary Wheatland Maynard; *b* 1988
1b *Tamara Sarah Sparrowe; *b* 1985
2b *Chloë Talitha Jacob; *b* 1991
3b *Zoë Tatiana Francesca; *b* 1995
(3) +Charles Evelyn [The Hon Charles North, Shepherds Cottage, Waldershare Park, Dover, Kent CT15 5BB]; F/Lt RAFVR WW II; *b* 18 March 1918; *educ* Eton and London U (BSc 1939); *m* 1st 12 Sept 1942 (*divorce* 1957) Maureen O'Callaghan, yr dau of Maj Francis Charles Brian Baldwin; *m* 2nd 10 March 1959 *Joan Aston, dau of Maj Frederick Bertram Booker, of Edenmore House, Raheny, Co Dublin, and by his 1st w has issue:
1a +Peter David; *b* 20 Oct 1943; *educ* Dover Coll
1a *Susan Caroline; *b* 6 Aug 1947
(1) Cynthia Mary Noel; *b* 25 Dec 1908; *m* 1 June 1935 Lt-Col Max Wells Williams, s of William Stanley Williams, and was *k* in an accident 25 Aug 1940, leaving issue
1 Muriel Emily; *b* 16 April 1879; *d* unm 15 March 1937

GUINNESS

Arms: Quarterly, 1st and 4th, per saltire gules and azure a lion rampant or, on a chief ermine a dexter hand couped at the wrist of the first, a crescent for difference (for GUINNESS); 2nd and 3rd, argent on a fess between three crescents sable a trefoil slipped or (for LEE). **Crests:** 1 A boar passant quarterly or and gules, a crescent for difference (for GUINNESS), 2 On a pillar argent encircled by a ducal coronet or, an eagle preying on a bird's leg erased proper (for LEE). **Supporters:** On either side a stag gules, attired and gorged with a collar gemmel or, pendant therefrom by a chain gold an escutcheon, the dexter charged with the arms of GUINNESS, the sinister with the arms of LEE. Certain features of the Guinness coat of arms occur in that of the MAGENNISes of Co Down, although there is no proof at all of any kinship, despite assertions to the contrary by various writers, including Sir Bernard Burke in the mid-19th century. Nevertheless the GUINNESSes of Dublin and Kildare were using the dexter hand couped on a chief of ermine and a lion rampant or, together with the crest of a boar passant quarterly or and gules, apparently without authorisation, as early as 1781. In 1814 The Rev Hosea Guinness sought a grant from the deputy Ulster King of Arms and Chief Herald of All Ireland confirming the GUINNESSes' right to use the Magennis arms. He won not a confirmation but a fresh grant. When a Guinness was ennobled for the second time, on the occasion of Edward Cecil Guinness's being raised to the peerage in 1891, he chose the title Baron Iveagh of Iveagh, Co Down, and when in 1909 he was promoted, that of Viscount of Iveagh, echoes of the title conferred on Sir Arthur Magennis when James I made him Viscount Magennis of Iveagh in 1623. It was the research carried out by Henry Seymour Guinness and Brian Guinness, embodied in *The Guinness Family* (1953), that corrected the more fanciful pedigrees of older writers. The supporters to the Guinness coat of arms were granted by Royal Warrant in May 1867 to **Sir Benjamin Guinness, 1st Bt**, and subsequent baronets of the creation in recognition of his public spiritedness and generosity in restoring St Patrick's Cathedral, Dublin. **Motto:** *Spes mea in Deo* ('My hope lieth in the Lord'). **Creation:** Bt. (UK) 15 April 1867.

SIR KENELM ('TIM') ERNEST LEE GUINNESS, 4TH BT, of Ashford, Co Galway, and St Stephen's Green, Co Dublin [Sir Kenelm Guinness Bt, Rich Neck, Claiborne, MD 21624, USA]; *b* 13 Dec 1928; *s* unc 1954; *educ* Eton and MIT (BSc); late Lt RHG, with Internat Bank for Reconstruction and Devpt, Washington, DC, 1954–75, engrg consultant; *m* 3 June 1961 *Jane, dau of Ethelbert Paul Nevin, of New York, and formerly w of Robert Bruce Dickson, and has:

1 +KENELM EDWARD LEE; *b* 30 Jan 1962; *educ* Embry-Riddle Aeronautical U (BSc); commercial pilot

2 +Sean St Lawrence Lee; *b* 21 March 1966; *m* 6 Sept 1997 *Christine Leslie only dau of John O'Hara Black, of Denville, NJ

Lineage: RICHARD GUINNESS, of Celbridge, Co Kildare; *b c* 1690; described in a Bill in Equity Exchequer 10 Feb 1746 as 'Richard Guinis, Agent or Receiver to the Most Rev Arthur Price, Archbishop of Cashel', is therein authorised to demise episcopal lands; *m* 1st Elizabeth (*b* 1698; *d* 28 Aug 1742), dau of William Read, of Hutton Read or Oughterard, Co Kildare, and had, with other issue:

1 ARTHUR GUINNESS (I)

2 Benjamin; *b c* 1730; *d* unm 1778

3 Richard; *m* Anne Forster and *d* 1806, having had issue:

(1) Jane; *m* Edward Stanley and had issue

(2) Matilda; *m* William Owen and had issue

(3) Elizabeth Anne; *b* 1784; *m* 1st Joseph Hewen; *m* 2nd George O'Grady and *d* 1860, having had issue by her 2nd husb

(4) Olivia; *m* Rev — Powell and *dsp*

4 Samuel, of Dublin; *b c* 1727; goldbeater; *m* 6 Aug 1753 Sarah (*b* 1732; *d* Aug 1794), dau of Henry Jago, of Dublin, and *d* 24 Jan or 3 Feb 1795, having had:

(1) Richard; *b* 6 Sept 1755; barrister, Freeman Dublin 1802; *m* 25 Sept 1783 Mary (*d* 15 Oct 1836), est dau of John Darley, of Dublin and Kilternan, and *d* 10 Sept 1829, having had issue:

1a Samuel; *b* 1784; *d* 1785

2a George Gore; *b* 1788; *d* 1790

3a Robert Rundell, of Stillorgan, Co Dublin; *b* 12 Dec 1789; barrister, fndr with John Ross Mahon of Guinness Mahon, first a land agency, later developed as a bank by Robert's sons Richard Seymour in London and Henry (*see* below) in Dublin; *m* 1st 2 Nov 1822 Mary Anne (*d* July 1837), 6th dau of Rev John Crossley Seymour, of Castletown House, Queen's Co (now Co Laois), and had issue:

1b Richard Seymour, of 16 Rutland Gate, London SW; *b* 28 April 1826; *educ* Trin Coll Dublin; joined Guinness Mahon 1841, ptnr 1845; *m* 30 July 1857 his cousin Elizabeth Jane, dau of Rev John Darley by Susanna, herself dau of Arthur (II) Guinness, and *d* 2 Dec 1915, having had issue:

1c Robert Darley, JP (Warwicks), of Wootton Hall, Wootton Wawen, Warwicks; *b* 3 Oct 1858; *educ* Harrow and Trin Coll Cambridge (BA 1880); barrister, High Sheriff Warwicks 1924, chm finance ctee Warwicks CC; *m* 30 July 1887 Lydia Lucy Lyster (*d* 22 Nov 1947), dau of Henry Matthew Smyth, JP, of Barbavilla House, Co Westmeath, and *d* 13 Aug 1938, having had issue:

1d Richard Smyth, of Lodge Park, Co Kildare; *b* 13 June 1888; *educ* Eton and Trin Coll Cambridge (BA 1910); Lt RNR and RNVR WW I, with Br Mannesmann Tube Co, chm James Beresford & Son of Birmingham; *m* 24 Oct 1929 Esmé Patricia, er dau of Brig-Gen Archibald John Chapman, CB, CMG, CBE, Legn Hon, of Willersey, Worcs, by Annie Evelyn, yr dau of George Orr Wilson, of Dunardagh, Co Dublin, and *d* 1979, leaving issue:

1e *Robert Chapman [Robert Guinness Esq, Lodge Park, Straffan, Co Kildare, Ireland]; *b* 4 Feb 1937; *educ* Eton; Irish Gds 1957–59, Govr Rotunda Hosp; *m* 16 Oct 1963 *Sarah Jane, er dau of Miles Herman de Zoete, of Ackworth House, E Bergholt, Suffolk, and has:

1f *Richard de Zoete; *b* 22 July 1981; *educ* Eton

2f *Samuel Walter; *b* 8 Feb 1985; *educ* Eton

1f *Louisa Brigid; *b* 3 Oct 1965

2f *Clare Elizabeth; *b* 26 June 1967; *m* 4 May 1992 *Hugo Nicholas Jacobs and has two sons

3f *Katharine Geraldine; *b* 26 Sept 1970

1e *Meryl Susanna; *b* 7 Jan 1933; *m* 1st 22 Jan 1955 (*divorce* 1972) John Brabazon Booth, only s of Lt-Col Edward Brabazon Booth, DSO, and has:

1f *Edward Richard Brabazon; *b* 27 June 1959; *m* 8 Feb 1981 *Roisin Toner and has issue

2f *Grania Patricia Jane; *b* 11 March 1956; *m* 5 Nov 1983 *John Wilson Furness and has issue (*see* FURNESS, Bt)

3f *Rosanna Meryl; *b* 14 Nov 1961; *m* 6 Sept 1986 *Lord Andrew Arthur George Hay and has issue (*see* TWEEDDALE, M)

4f *Caragh Victoria; *b* 2 June 1964

1e (cont.) Mrs Meryl Booth *m* 2nd 10 May 1975 *Thomas Fields Long, MFH, only s of Alfred Thomas Long, of Pennsylvania and Florida

2e *Shaunagh Christine; *m* 16 Sept 1961 *Col (John) Antony Aylmer, Irish Gds, yr s of Maj John Wyndham Aylmer, MC, of Courtown, Kilcock, Co Kildare, and has issue:

1f *Patrick Anthony Richard; *b* 21 Dec 1963; *m* 7 Dec 1996 *Philippa Hansard

1f *Mary Susanna; *b* 14 Sept 1962; *m* 3 June 1995 *Andrew Post

2f *Rose Antonia Lucy; *b* 22 May 1972; *m* 4 July 1998 *Steven Bonsey

3e *Deirdre Veronica; *b* 1 July 1944; *m* 1st 18 Sept 1971 (*divorce* 19–) (Luis) Alberto Neyra, MSc, MBA, civil engr, yr s of Alberto Neyra, of Lima, Peru, and has issue:

1f *Charles Richard Raymond; *b* 30 Dec 1977; *educ* Radley

1f *Maria Isabel; *b* 28 July 1975

3e (cont.) Mrs Deidre Neyra *m* 2nd 5 Feb 1997 *Egerton Grey d'Estouteville Skipwith, yr s of Sir Grey Skipwith, 11th Bt (*qv*)

1d Elizabeth Muriel Smyth; *b* 20 Jan 1892; *m* 12 July 1924 Maj John Adrian Frederick March Philipps de Lisle, DL (*d* 4 Nov 1961), Leics Yeo, of Stockerston Hall, Uppingham, Rutland, est s of Edwin Joseph Lisle Philipps de Lisle, DL, MP, FSA, of Charnwood Lodge, Leics, and *d* 30 March 1974, leaving issue:

1e *Everard John Robert March Phillips, DL [Maj Everard de Lisle DL, Stockerston Hall, Uppingham, Leics LE15 9JD; 4 Hereford Mansions, Hereford Rd, London W2 5BA]; *b* 8 June 1930; *educ* Eton and RMA Sandhurst; Maj RHG (Adj Household Cav Regt 1955–58, Instr Sandhurst 1958–60, ret 1962); *m* 2 April 1959 *Hon Mary Rose Peake, yst dau of 1st Viscount Ingleby (*qv*), and has issue

2e *Julian Peter Alexander; *b* 2 Feb 1936; *educ* Eton; RHG 1955–56, Leics and Derbys Yeo thereafter

1e *Alathea Henriette Mary; *b* 14 May 1925; *m* 25 July 1953 *George Hamilton Boyle (*see* CORK and ORRERY, E), and has issue

2e *Elizabeth Catherine Denise; *b* 19 Aug 1927; *m* 24 Jan 1951 *Jeremy Anthony White, s of Brig Christopher White (*see* SCOTT, Bt, of Beauclerc), and has issue

2c Gerald Seymour, of Dorton House, Thame, Oxon; *b* 1862; *educ* Charterhouse and Trin Coll Dublin; *m* 5 Aug 1897 Eleanor Grace (*d* 11 May 1926), 3rd and yst dau of Capt Arthur Watson de Capell Brooke, JP, of Loddington Hall, Kettering, Northants, himself yr s of Sir William de Capell Brooke, 3rd Bt (*see* 1967 edn), by Hon Catherine Watson, in her turn yr dau of 2nd Baron Sondes (*see* MONSON, B), and *d* of deliberately self-inflicted gunshot wounds 5 Sept 1933, having had issue:

1d Gerald Richard de Capell Brooke, of Astrop Park, Banbury, Oxon; *b* 15 May 1889; *educ* Eton; Capt Coldstream Gds WW I, barrister (called Lincoln's Inn 1924); *m* 23 April 1932 Desirée Ann Eda, 3rd dau of Lt-Col Sir Alfred Welby, KBE, MP (*see* WELBY, Bt), and *d* 29 June 1975, leaving issue:

1e *Hugh Welby De CAPELL BROOKE GUINNESS, of Great Oakley Hall, Corby, Northants (inherited from his paternal grandmother Eleanor's cousin Sir Arthur de Capell Brooke, 5th Bt and 1st and last Baron Brooke of Oakley; *see* 1967 edn); *b* 2 Oct 1937; *educ* Eton, Trin Coll Cambridge (BA 1959) and Leeds U; added De Capell Brooke to his original surname by deed poll 1976; *m* 17 Sept 1966 *Bianca Carla, 2nd dau of Col Renzo and Donna Isabella della Pura Onorati, of Florence, and has issue:

1f *Alexander Edward GUINNESS; *b* 27 May 1968

2f *Caroline Isabella GUINNESS; *b* 22 Aug 1970

2e *David Gerald Charles GUINNESS [David Guinness Esq, 18 Savernake Rd, London NW2 2JP]; *b* 3 Aug 1939; *educ* Eton, Trin Coll Cambridge (BA 1963, MA 1967) and MIT

1e *Jessica Sybil; *b* 6 May 1933

2d Anthony Wentworth; *b* 4 Aug 1907; *educ* Eton and Ch Ch Oxford; *m* 1st Oct 1929 (*divorce* 1938) Juliette Frances Josephine D'Aven, yst dau of Godfrey Herbert Joseph Williams, of Aberpergwm, Glam, and had issue:

1e *Antonia Miriam; *b* 1930; *m* 1 Oct 1960 *(Edward) Patrick Baring (*see* NORTHBROOK, B) and has issue

2e *Bronwyn; *b* April 1936; *m* 2 March 1957 *Peter De Wyckoff Byrams, s of Mortimer Byrams, of Rye, New York, and Mrs Julius O'Rickman, of Teheran, Iran, and has issue 2 s

2d (cont.) Anthony Guinness *m* 2nd 1938 *Diana Barbara, yr dau of Maj Charles A Boone, of Toronto, and *d* 9 April 1960, leaving issue:

1e *Michael Damon; *b* 20 March 1943

3e *Shaunagh Mary; *b* May 1947

1d Hermione Grace; *b* 25 May 1898; *m* 1st 26 June 1918 Lt-Col Herbert Francis George Carter, MC (*das* 28 Feb 1919), KOYLI, s of Gen Francis Carter, and had a dau; *m* 2nd 8 May 1923, as his 1st w, Marshal of the RAF Sir John Cotesworth Slessor, GCB, DSO, MC, DL (*d* 1979), and *d* 4 Sept 1970, having had issue, with a dau:

1e *John Arthur Guinness, CVO (1995), DL (Hants 1989) [Group-Captain John Slessor CVO DL, Grateley Lodge, Chapel Lane, Grateley, Andover, Hants SP11 8JP]; *b* 14 Aug 1925; *educ* Eton and Ch Ch Oxford; joined RAF 1943: served WW II N France, Staff Coll 1959–60, USAF Acad Colorado 1960–62, OC 83 Sqdn (V-Force) 1962–65, Jt Servs Staff Coll 1965, MOD 1966–68 and 1976–77, air attaché Madrid 1968–70, OC RAF Odiham 1971–73, Ch Intell Offr RAF Germany 1973–75, ret 1978 with rank of G/Capt, Gent Usher to HM THE QUEEN 1978–, sec Overseas Rels HQ St John's Ambulance 1978–79, pres Alton Div St John's Ambulance 1988–, govr Alton Coll 1990–, CStJ 1990 (OStJ 1981); *m* 6 Oct 1951 *Ann Dorothea, dau of George Gibson, and has issue:

1f *Anthony J R; *b* 1954; *educ* Eton; Maj

1f *Catherine; *b* 1955

2d Georgina Elizabeth; *b* 1903; *m* 1933 Arthur Rawlins (*d* 3 Oct 1950), s of William Rawlins, and *d* 26 July 1940, having had a dau

3c Arthur Eustace Seymour, JP, of Green's Norton Hall, Towcester, Northants; *b* 2 Dec 1867; *educ* RMA Woolwich; High Sheriff Northants 1921, MFH Grafton; *m* 14 Sept 1897 Wilhelmine Augusta (*d* 1 Nov 1943), dau of William Henry Forester, and *d* 4 Sept 1955, leaving:

1d Barbara Elizabeth; *b* 30 April 1899; *m* 21 Jan 1930 (*divorce* 1949) Capt William Hamilton Grant (*d* 30 Aug 1953), Black Watch, yr s of Adml Alfred Ernest Albert Grant, JP, and had issue

4c Benjamin Seymour, of New York; *b* 18 Nov 1868; RN 1882–91 (ret as Lt), went to USA, where dir: New York Tst Co, Lackawanna Steel Co, Kansas City Southern Rlwy, Seaboard Air Line, Duquesne Light Co, Pittsburgh, Utd Rlrds of San Francisco, ret 1929; *m* 1st 9 Dec 1902 Bridget Henrietta Frances (*d* 5 Jan 1931), only dau of Sir Richard Williams-Bulkeley, 11th Bt (*qv*), and had issue:

1d (Thomas) Loel Evelyn Bulkeley, OBE (1942); *b* 9 June 1906; *educ* RMC Sandhurst; Lt Irish Gds and Gp Capt RAAF WW II (despatches five times), Cdr Order of Orange Nassau, Offr Legn Hon, Croix de Guerre, MP (U) Bath 1931–45 (contested Whitechapel gen election 1929 and by-election 1930) and PPS to Sir Philip Sassoon as Parly U-Sec for Air 1931–35; *m* 1st 4 July 1927 (*divorce* 1936) Hon Joan Barbara Yarde-Buller (*d* 25 April 1997), est dau of 3rd Baron Churston (*qv*) and had:

1e Patrick Benjamin ('Tara'); *b* 10 March 1931 (HM QUEEN INGRID OF DENMARK stood sponsor); *educ* Eton; Lt RHG (Blues); *m* 22 Oct 1955 *Countess Dolores Maria Agatha Wilhelmine Luise, dau of Count Franz Egon von Fürstenberg by his ('Tara"s) stepmother the 3rd Mrs Loel Guinness, and was *k* in a car crash 5 Oct 1965, leaving issue:

1f *Loel Patrick [Loel Guinness Esq, Ave de Rumine 37, 1005 Lausanne, Switzerland]; *b* 22 Oct 1957

2f *(Maria) Alexandra [Countess Foulques de Quatrebarbes, Les Cassivettes, 1173 Fechy, Switzerland]; *b* 24 Aug 1956; *m* 1979 *Count Foulques de Quatrebarbes and has issue:

1g *Foulques Patrick; *b* 1981

1g *Laétitia; *b* 1983

2g *Aurelia; *b* 1984

3g *Olivia; *b* 1985

3f *Victoria Christina [Mrs Philippe Niarchos, 2 Rue de Chanaleilles, 75007 Paris, France]; *b* 30 Jan 1960; *m* 1984 *Philippe Niarchos, est s of Stavros Niarchos, and has issue:

1g *Stavros; *b* 1985

2g *Eugeni; *b* 1986

1d (cont.) Loel Guinness *m* 2nd 24 Nov 1936 (*divorce* 1951) Lady Isabel Manners, yr dau of 9th Duke of Rutland (*qv*), and had issue:

2e *William Loel Seymour [William Guinness Esq, 10 Bourne St, London SW1]; *b* 28 Dec 1939; *educ* Eton; Lt Irish Gds 1959–61, farmer; *m* 5 Nov 1971 *(Agnes Elizabeth) Lynn, dau of Ian T M Day, of Natal, S Africa, and subsequently of Brampton Ash, Northants, and has issue:

1f *Sheridan William [Sheridan Guinness Esq, Arthingworth Manor, Market Harborough, Leics LE16 8JT]; *b* 23 Aug 1972; *educ* Eton

2f *(Thomas) Seymour; *b* 1973

1e *Serena Belinda ('Lindy') Rosemary [The Most Hon The Marchioness of Dufferin and Ava, Clandeboye, Bangor, Co Down, N Ireland; 4 Holland Villas Rd, London W14]; *b* 25 March 1941; *m* 21 Oct 1964 5th Marquess of Dufferin and Ava (*d* 1988; *see* DUFFERIN AND CLANEBOYE, B)

1d (cont.) Loel Guinness *m* 3rd 7 April 1951 Gloria (*d* 1980), dau of Raphael Rubio, of Mexico, and formerly w of Count Franz von Fürstenberg and Ahmed Fakhry, and *d* 31 Dec 1988

1d *Meraud Michel Wemyss; *b* 1904; *m* 23 Jan 1929 Alvaro Guevara (*d* 11 Oct 1951), portraitist, s of Luis Guevara, of Chile, by his w Ida Reimers, of Denmark, and has a dau

2d *Tanis Eva Bulkeley; *b* 27 Dec 1908; *m* 1st 19 Feb 1911 (*divorce* 1935), as his 1st w, Hon William Drogo Sturges Montagu, 2nd s of 9th Earl of Sandwich (*qv*), and has issue; *m* 2nd 16 Jan 1937 (*divorce* 1951) Howard Dietz, head of publicity for MGM, and has issue; *m* 3rd 21 July 1951 *Lt-Cdr (Charles) Ed(ward) Harold John Phillips, RNVR, of Biarritz

4c (cont.) Benjamin Guinness *m* 2nd 2 April 1936 Marchesa Maria Nunziante Di Mignano, dau of Mariano Nunziante, Duca di Mignano, and *d* 15 Dec 1947

5c Richard ('Dick') Sidney; *b* 4 March 1873; *educ* Harrow; chm: Mercantile & Gen Insur Co, Anglo-American Debenture Corp, Railway Debenture & Gen Tst Co, Railway Share Tst Agy Co, London & Scottish Assur Assoc, Debenture & Capital Investment Tst, Share & Gen Investment Tst and Sterling Tst; *m* 1st 1895 (*divorce* 1912) Emilie, only child of Capt Charles Weimar, German Imperial Gds; *m* 2nd Beatrice, formerly w of Nico Jungman, by whom she was mother of Zita and Teresa ('Baby') Jungman, but had no issue by her; *m* 3rd Ursula Frances Rose, er dau of Maj William Francis Tremayne, JP, of Cardew, Cornwall, and widow of Eustace William Blois, OBE (*see* BLOIS, Bt), and *dsp* 14 Jan 1949

6c Herbert Frederick; *b* 22 Jan 1876; RN; *m* 1904, as her 1st husb, Violet Catherine Adele (*m* 2nd 1924 Capt Herbert Reginald Norbury, CB, RN (*d* 15 March 1867), s of Inspr-Gen Sir Frederick Norbury, KCB, MD, FRCS), dau of Adrian Elias Hope, and *dsp* 30 May 1922

1c Annabel Mary; *b* 1860; *d* unm 23 Feb 1948

2c Adeline Elizabeth; *m* 1884 Rev Robert William Barber (*d* 1928), Rector St Mary Stoke, Ipswich, Vicar Stuntney, Cambs, and *d* 2 Jan 1955, leaving issue

3c Helen Jane; *m* 1888 Robert Miller (*d* 1930), MLC India, and had issue

4c Anna Theodosia; *m* 20 Sept 1899 Archibald John Thomas Francis Aitchison, only s of Gen Sir John Aitchison, GCB, of Devonshire Place, London W, and *dsp* 12 Sept 1900

2b Henry, of Burton Hall, Stillorgan, Co Dublin; *b* 16 March 1829; ptnr Guinness Mahon 1850; *m* 11 Feb 1858 Emmelina (*d* 4 Oct 1906), dau of James Brown, of Edinburgh, and *d* 30 Dec 1893, having had issue:

1c Henry Seymour, of Burton Hall; *b* 24 Nov 1858; *educ* Winchester and Roy Indian Engrg Coll; engr Public Works Dept India 1880–95, Lt Burma State Railway Vol Rifles 1884 (Burma medal and three clasps), AMICE 1894–1934, High Sheriff Co Dublin 1899, memb Cncl Alexandra Coll Dublin 1899–1940 and V-Warden 1913–40, dir: Gt Northern Rlwy Ireland 1902–24 and Bank of Ireland 1910–24 (Govr 1922–24), memb Roy Irish Acad 1911, rep Church Body Ireland 1916–31, Irish Free State Senator 1922–34, assist md Arthur Guinness, Son & Co 1924–30, author: (with Brian Guinness) *The Guinness Family* (1953); *m* 20 Nov 1900 Mary Middleton (*d* 1 Aug 1954), dau of Robert Stagg Bainbridge, of Keverstone, Co Durham, and *d* 4 April 1945, leaving:

1d Moira Emeline; *b* 28 Jan 1902; *m* 29 Nov 1923 Arthur Lafone Frank Hills, s of Arnold Frank Hills, of Penshurst, Kent, and had a s and a dau (*m* Sir David Oglivy, 13th Bt; *qv*)

2d *Rachel Ursula Isolde; *b* 15 July 1906; *m* 26 Nov 1931 Prince John Bryant Digby de Mahé, only s of Prince Charles Digby Mahé de Chenal de la Bourbonnais, of Totnes, S Devon, and has two daus

3d *Patricia; *b* 20 Feb 1909; *m* 30 April 1945 *Frederick Charles Leopold Ullstein, only s of Herman Heinrich Ullstein, of Grünewald, Prussia, and has issue:

1e *Augustus Rupert Patrick Anthony QC (1992) [Augustus Ullstein Esq QC, 74 Duke's Ave, London W4 2AF; 29 Bedford Row, London WC1]; *b* 21 March 1947; *educ* Bradfield and LSE (LLB); barrister (Inner Temple 1970), Assist Recorder 1993, dir Saxon Radio 1980–87, Freeman City London 1982, Liveryman Bowyers' Co, author: *The Law of Restrictive Trade Practices and Monopolies* (2nd supplement to 2nd edn 1973) and *Matrimonial and Domestic Injunctions* (1982); *m* 1 Sept 1970 *Pamela Margaret, dau of Claude Wells, of Woodford, Essex, and has issue:

1f *William; *b* 3 July 1980

2f *George; *b* 29 April 1983

1f *Elizabeth; *b* 1 June 1977

2f *Caroline; *b* 28 Oct 1978

2e *Bartholomew William Henry; *b* 10 March 1948; *m* 4 Sept 1971 *Susan Jane, er dau of Dr Geoffrey Smerdon, of Alresford, Essex

4d Heather Seymour; *b* 14 Aug 1910; *m* 1st 12 Oct 1935 Clifton Penn-Hughes (*d* 11 July 1939), of Hersham, Surrey, s of W W Hughes, of S Africa, and had two daus; *m* 2nd 17 Nov 1942 *John Henning, s of John Thomas Henning, of Toronto, and *d* 24 Oct 1952, leaving a s and another dau

2c Eustace, DSO; *b* 14 June 1860; Boer War; *m* 14 July 1898 Isabel Gertrude (*d* 19 Nov 1954), 2nd dau of Charles Loraine Bell, JP, DL, of Woolsington Hall, Northumberland, and was *k* S Africa 30 Oct 1901, leaving:

1d Eustace Francis; *b* 21 Jan 1900; *educ* Trin Coll Dublin and New Coll Oxford; Irish Gds, sr ptnr Escombe, Campbell & Co (stockbrokers)

2d Humphrey Patrick; *b* 24 March 1902; *educ* Eton and RMC Sandhurst; Col Roy Scots Greys WW II; *m* 16 July 1946 *Gladys Ellen, er dau of May William Eward Gatacre, KOYLI, and formerly w of William Maxwell Evelyn Denison

3c Howard Rundell, of Clandon Regis, W Clandon, Surrey; *b* 22 March 1868; ptnr Guinness Mahon; *m* 12 April 1887 his cousin Mary Alice ('May'; *d* 16 Nov 1949), dau of Rev William Newton Guinness and *d* 9 May 1937, having had:

1d (Henry) Samuel Howard; *b* 22 June 1888; *educ* Winchester and Balliol Coll Oxford (BA 1909); dir: Provincial Bank of Ireland 1918, Nat Discount Co 1926, Electro Tst and Viking Tanker (later merged with Guinness Mahon to form Guinness Mahon Hldgs) 1953, hon fin advsr FO 1919–20, ptnr Guinness Mahon merchant bankers 1923–71 (sr ptnr 1937–68), Chev Olav Norway 1947; *m* 8 Oct 1913 Alfhild (*d* 1983), Chev Olav Norway 1947 (conferred simultaneously with that to her husb), 2nd dau of Otto Christian Holter, of Christiania, Norway, and *d* 10 April 1975, having had:

1e George Francis Howard; *b* 4 May 1915; *educ* Shrewsbury; *d* by misadventure while cleaning a gun 7 Aug 1930

1e Helga Mary; *b* 30 Sept 1916; *m* 1st 24 Oct 1934 (*divorce* 1948), as his 1st w Sir Hugh Carleton Greene, KCMG, OBE, Dir-Gen and Govr BBC, chm Bodley Head, yst s of Charles Henry Greene, FRHistS, of Crowborough, E Sussex, and had:

1f *Graham Carleton, CBE (1986) [Graham Greene Esq CBE, K1 Albany, London W1V 9RQ]; *b* 10 June 1936; *educ* Eton and Univ Coll Oxford; merchant banker 1957–58, publisher: Secker & Warburg 1958–62, Jonathan Cape 1962–90 (md 1966–88), dir: Chatto, Virago, Bodley Head & Jonathan Cape Ltd 1969–88 (chm 1970–88), Jackdaw Publicns (chm 1964–88), Cape Goliard Press 1967–88, Guinness Mahon Hldgs 1968–79, Australasian Publishing Co Pty 1969–88 (chm 1978–88), Sprint Productions 1971–80, Book Reps (New Zealand) 1971–88 (chm 1984–88), CVBC Services (chm 1972–88), Guinness Peat Gp 1973–87, Grantham Book Storage (chm 1974–88), Triad Paperbacks 1975–88, Chatto, Virago, Bodley Head & Jonathan Cape Australia Pty (chm 1977–88), Greene King plc 1977–, Statesman & Nation Publishing 1980–85 (chm 1981–85), Statesman Publishing Co 1985–88 (chm 1980–85), Nation Pty Co (chm 1981–87), New Society (chm 1984–87), Random House Inc 1987–88, Random House UK 1988–90 and American Friends of BM 1990–, chm: Br Museum Co 1988–, Br Museum Devpt Tst 1986–, Jupiter Internat Green Investment Tst 1989–, Henry Sotheran 1990–, Ed Victor Ltd 1991–, Rosemary Sandberg Ltd 1991–, Libra KFT (Budapest) 1991– Nat Bk League 1974–76 (dep chm 1971–74) and GB-China Centre 1986–97, pres: Publishers Assoc 1971–79 (memb cncl 1969–88) and BM Fndn Inc 1989–90, memb: Book Devpt Cncl 1970–79 (dep chm 1972–73), Internat Ctee Internat Publishers Assoc 1977–88 (on exec ctee 1981–88), Groupe des Editeurs des Livres de la CEE 1977–86 (pres 1984–86), Arts Cncl Working Pty Sub-Ctee on PLR 1970, Paymaster Gen's Working Pty on PLR 1970–72, Bd Br Cncl 1977–88 and Gen Ctee Roy Lit Fund 1975, tstee: Br Museum 1978– (dep chm devpt fund 1993–, chm tstees 1996–), Open Coll of Arts 1990–, Chevalier de l'Ordre des Arts et des Lettres (France); *m* 1st 1957 (*divorce* 1975), as her 1st husb, Hon Judith Margaret Gordon-Walker, dau of Baron Gordon-Walker, CH, PC (*see* 1970 edn); *m* 2nd 1976 *Sally Georgina Horton, dau of Sidney Wilfred Eaton, and has by her:

1g *Alexander; *b* 19 Feb 1978

2f *James Carleton; *b* 20 Jan 1938; *educ* Eton and New Coll Oxford; author: *Dead Man's Fall* (poems, 1980)

1e (cont.) Mrs Helga Greene *m* 2nd 19 Nov 1963 *(Henry) Stuart Connolly, est s of H S Connolly, of Bramshall, Cheshire

2e *Marit Victoria [Mrs Marit Guinness Aschan, 25 Chelsea Park Gdns, London SW3 6AF; Studios 3 and 4, Moravian Close, 381 King's Rd, London SW10 0LP]; *b* 28 Jan 1919; *educ* Munich, Florence and Paris; WW II Min of Inf, enamellist as Marit Guinness Aschan, Pres Artist Enamellers 1969–90, author: *Modern Jewellers*, *The Art of Jewellery* (1968) and *Enamels* (ed, 1985); *m* 21 July 1937 (*divorce* 1963) Carl Nils Gunnar William Aschan, only s of Judge Nils Aschan, of Stockholm and Baroness Elsa Djurklov, of Sweden, and has issue:

1f *(John Laurence) David [David Aschan Esq, 25 Chelsea Park Gdns, London SW3 6AF]; *b* 1 May 1943; *educ* Eton; banker; *m* 1st 20 Sept 1967 (*divorce* 1968), as her 1st husb, Pennant Elfrida, only child of Thomas Iremonger, MP (C) Ilford N 1954–Feb 1974 and Redbridge, Ilford N Feb-Sept 1974; *m* 2nd 25 June 1970 (*divorce* 1978) Penelope Jane, 2nd dau of Robert Eward Arnsby Wilson, of London, NW, and has issue:

1g *Patrick Howard John Laurence; *b* 17 July 1971

1g *Charlotte Emily Helen; *b* 16 Sept 1974

1f (cont.) David Aschan *m* 3rd 19– (*divorce* 1981) Emma Mary, dau of Robert Alistair Henderson, chm Kleinwort-Benson 1987–88, dep chm BA 1985–89 and Cadbury Schweppes 1983–92, and by her has:

2g *Clare Louise; *b* June 1979

3g *Elizabeth Beatrice; *b* 5 Feb 1981

1f *Juliet Marit Gabriel; *b* 1 Dec 1946; pictures conservator, md Grand Tours 1976–87; *m* 1980 (*divorce* 1990) Randle Brooks, of Peover Hall, Knutsford, Cheshire, and has:

1g *Henry; *b* 13 Sept 1980

1g *Serena Mary; *b* 12 July 1983

3e *Ingrid Louise; *b* 12 Aug 1922; *m* 15 Dec 1948 Winston Alison Williams (*d* by his own hand 12 March 1971), s of Dr Saunders Alexander Williams, JP, of Jamaica, and has issue:

1f *Winston Guinness Andrew [Winston Williams Esq, 3 Chelsea Towers, Chelsea Manor Gdns, London SW3 5PN]; *b* 25 April 1953; *educ* Eton

1f *Deirdre Ingrid; *b* 29 Sept 1949; SRN

2d Edward ('Ned') Douglas, CBE (1946); *b* 19 April 1893; *educ* Rugby; Capt RNR WWs I and II, ptnr Guinness Mahon, dir and chm Sheldom Gp; *m* 1st 15 Sept 1931 (*divorce* 1970) Martha Letière, dau of John Eccleston Sheldon and formerly w of C Richard Goss, Gren Gds, and had issue:

1e *Howard Christian Sheldon (Sir), VRD (1953) [Sir Howard Guinness VRD, The Manor House, Glanvilles Wootton, Sherborne, Dorset DT9 5QF]; *b* 3 June 1932; *educ* Eton; midshipman RN, Lt-Cdr RNR, Union Discount Co of London 1953, Guinness Mahon 1953–55, S G Warburg 1955–85 (exec dir 1970–85), dir: Harris & Sheldon Gp 1960–81, Youghal Carpets (Hldgs) 1972–80 (also dep chm), Quality Milk Producers 1988–, chm: N Hants Conservative Assoc 1971–74 and Wessex Area C Assoc 1975–78 (v-chm 1974, treas 1978–81), memb cncl English Guernsey Cattle Soc 1963–72, ktd 1981; *m* 17 Nov 1958 *Evadne Jane, only dau of Capt Evan Llewellyn Gibbs (*see* ALDENHAM and HUNSDON OF HUNSDON, B), and has:

1f *Christopher Edward Howard; *b* 9 Jan 1961; *educ* Eton

2f *Dominic Evan Mark; *b* 20 June 1966; *educ* Eton

1f *Annabel Evadne; *b* 20 Sept 1959; *m* 1987 *William Rollo (*see* ROLLO, L) and has issue

2e *John Ralph Sidney, CB (1985); *b* 23 Dec 1935; *educ* Rugby and Trin Hall Cambridge; Union Discount Co 1960–61, Overseas Devpt Inst 1961–62, FO (later FCO) 1962–80 (Ec Rels Dept 1962–63, 3rd Sec UK Mission to UN New York 1963–64, seconded to UN Secretariat 1964–66, 1st Sec Br High Commn Ottawa 1969–72, seconded to Centl Policy Review Staff Cabinet Office 1972–75 and 1977–79, Cnsllr 1974, Alternate UK Rep Law of Sea Conference 1975–77), Dept Energy (having transferred to Home Civ Serv 1980): U-Sec 1980–83, Dep-Sec 1983–91, Perm Sec 1991–92, Govr Oxford Energy Inst 1984–92, chm Br Nuclear Fuels plc 1992–, memb: E Anglia Regnl Ctee Nat Tst 1989–, Cncl Business in the Community 1992–, Cncl Prince's Youth Business Tst 1992–; *m* 15 July 1967 *Valerie Susan, est dau of Roger North, JP, gggggg of Roger North, KC, MP, the 17th-century memoirist (*see* GUILFORD, E), and has:

1f *Rupert Edward Roger; *b* 9 Nov 1971

2f Peter John Charles; *b* 25 March 1974; *d* following a car crash 28 Aug 1978

1f *Lucy Arabella; *b* 21 March 1970; m 3 Aug 1996 *Olav Ostin, only s of Jacques Ostin, of Grenoble, France

2d (cont.) Capt Edward Guinness *m* 2nd 7 April 1970 Mrs Jeanne Amy Thompson and *d* 1983

3d Arthur Rundell (Sir), KCMG (1949); *b* 26 May 1895; *educ* Winchester; Capt and Adj Manchester Regt WW I (wounded Ypres 1915), Lt-Col cmdg 27th Bn Hants Home Gd 1942–45, ptnr Guinness Mahon from 1923, dir Guinness Mahon Representation Co Inc New York, Pres Internat Chamber of Commerce 1947–49 (V-Pres 1945–47, chm Br Nat Ctee 1943–47, memb Cncl 1938), memb: Overseas Trade Devpt Cncl 1944–45, Grand Cncl Fedn Br Industry, Chinese Govt Purchasing Commission London (also Treasurer), Exec Ctee Help Holland Cncl 1945–46, League of Nations Special Jt Ctee on Private Foreign Investment 1945 and Cncl ESU, Liveryman Goldsmiths' Co; *m* 5 Dec 1923 (Frances) Patience, dau of Edward Fortescue Wright, CMG, of Chudleigh, Devon, and Kingston, Jamaica, and *d* 12 March 1951, leaving issue:

1e *James Edward Alexander Rundell, CBE (1986) [James Guinness Esq CBE, Coldpiece Farm, Hound Green, Basingstoke, Hants RG27 8LQ]; *b* 23 Sept 1924; *educ* Eton and New Coll Oxford; RNVR 1943–46, joined Guinness Mahon 1946, ptnr 1953, chm: Guinness Mahon Hldgs 1968–72 and Public Works Loan Bd 1979–90 (Commr 1960–90), dep chm: Guinness Peat Gp 1977–84 (dir 1973–87, jt chm 1973–77) and Provident Mutual Life Assur Assoc 1983–89; *m* 5 Nov 1953 *Pauline Vivien, yr dau of Lt-Col Howard Vivien Mander, of Congreve Manor, nr Penkridge, Staffs, and has issue:

1f *Hugo Arthur Rundell; *b* 12 Sept 1959; *educ* Eton; advertising copy writer

1f *Miranda Vivien; *b* 9 Jan 1955; edtl assist *Harper's and Queen*; *m* 19– *Keith Payne

2f *Sabrina Jane; *b* 9 Jan 1955; sometime production assist with British Lion films, projects dir Youth Cable TV

3f *Anita Patience; *b* 7 Dec 1957; *m* 1981 Hon Amschel Rothschild (*d* 8 July 1996), s of 3rd Baron Rothschild (*qv*)

4f *Julia Aline; *b* 12 Sept 1959; *m* 1980 *Hon Michael Samuel, yr s of 4th Viscount Bearsted (*qv*), and has issue

2e Ivan Douglas Rundell; *b* 27 June 1927; *educ* Winchester; Irish Gds; *m* 2 Oct 1952 *Mairead, only dau of Michael FitzGerald, of Killiney, Co Dublin, and *d* 14 Aug 1956, leaving issue:

1f *Kevin Michael Rundell; *b* 20 Nov 1953; *educ* Winchester

1e *Pamela Patience; *b* 25 Sept 1925; *m* 7 Oct 1944 *Cdr Michael Beauchamp St John, DSC, RN (*see* SAINT JOHN OF BLETSO, B), and has issue

4d Frederick Roberts ('Bobs'); *b* 23 April 1900; *educ* Rugby; chm Dreyfus & Co S Africa; *m* 15 Jan 1925 (Emma) Nora (*d* 13 Aug 1975), yst dau of Grantley Deane Shelton, of Rossmore House, Co Limerick, and *d* 1979, leaving issue:

1e *Howard Michael Shelton; *b* 31 Jan 1929; *m* 29 Aug 1953 *Jacqueline, dau of Henri Frederick Brink, of Cape Town, and has:

1f *Peter Brian; *b* 1957

1f *Caroline Alice; *b* 23 July 1954

2e *Jeremy; *b* 8 May 1931; *m* 7 April 1955 *Heather, dau of Hector Macphie, of Toowomba, Queensland, Australia, and has issue:

1f *Timothy Roberts; *b* 25 April 1956

2f *Christopher; *b* 1960

4d (cont.) Frederick R Guinness also had:

1e *Patricia SCARBOROUGH

5d Brian Cecil; *b* 10 July 1903; *educ* Rugby and Trin Coll Oxford, author: (with Henry Seymour Guinness) *The Guinness Family* (1953); *m* 10 Feb 1938 Catherine Cordelia (d 9 Dec 1996), yst dau of Lucian Oldershaw, of Maidenhead, Berks, and had issue:

1e *Geoffrey Neil; *b* 27 Dec 1938; *educ* Rugby and Trin Coll Oxford; with Barclays Bank International; *m* 28 April 1962 *Jillian Ruth, er dau of John Sidney Powell, of Monmouth, and has issue:

1f *Dominic Alexander; *b* 21 Oct 1969

1f *Antonia Sophia; *b* 6 April 1963

2f *Freya Caroline; *b* 29 April 1966

2e *Lucian Francis; *b* 1 Aug 1940; *educ* Rugby and King's Coll Cambridge; *m* 5 Oct 1968 *Dr Elizabeth Cosgrave, dau of Dr C P Cosgrave, of Bishopston, Glamorgan, and has issue:

1f *Paul Rohio; *b* 20 Sept 1969

2f *Richard Mackay; *b* 24 Dec 1970

1f *Lucy Frances; *b* 10 May 1973

4c Geoffrey Gwynne; *b* 17 April 1864; *m* 1886 Severine Macelle (*d* 23 July 1923), dau of Celestin Curntchet, of Buenos Aires, and *d* 10 May 1923, leaving issue:

1d Victor Edward Gwynne; *b* 26 July 1890; *educ* Wellington and RMA Woolwich; RE WWs I and II, ret as Col 1945 (Ch Engr Scottish Command 1939, subsequently Ch Engr N Ireland District); *m* 25 June 1938 *Stella, dau of Gerald Howsin, of Southport, Lancs, and had issue:

1e *David Robert Mancknois; *b* 23 Jan 1948; *m* 25 March 1972 *Carol, dau of Ivor Humphreys, of Southport

1e *Ann Severine; *b* 18 July 1939; *m* 23 Feb 1963 *Richard Henry Salter, s of Capt Eric Salter, of Dogmersfield, Hants, and has issue:

1f *Richard James; *b* 22 July 1965

1f *Annabel Victoria; *b* 5 Feb 1967

2d Robert Celestin; *b* 1893; *educ* Wellington; Lt Roy Fus; *m* 1929 Dorothy Hilda, dau of — Bingham and formerly w of — Hyem, and *dsp* 29 June 1970

5c (Richard) Noel, JP (Co Dublin); *b* 22 Dec 1870; *educ* Uppingham and Trin Coll Oxford (BA 1893); slr, Commissioner Irish Lights, ptnr Guinness Mahon, chm Guinness & Mahon 1942; *m* July 1894 Mary (*d* 3 June 1939), 3rd dau of Henry Stokes, ICS, of Howth, Co Dublin, and *d* 30 Sept 1960, leaving issue:

1d Henry Eustace; *b* 22 Sept 1897; *educ* Winchester; Lt RA WW I, ptnr Guinness Mahon, md Guinness & Mahon 1942 (later chm), memb Irish Senate; *m* 4 Sept 1924 Beatrice Maud Hill, yr dau of Col George Murray Boothby, RA, and second cousin of 1st and last Baron ('Bob') Boothby (*see* 1970 edn), and *d* 19 Feb 1972, leaving issue:

1e *(Anthony) Peter Boothby [Peter Guinness Esq, Chapel Farm, Hyde Lane, Hyde End, Great Missenden, Bucks HP16 0RF]; *b* 11 Aug 1925; *educ* Eton, Trin Coll Cambridge and RNC Greenwich; Sub-Lt RNVR WW II, late dep md Arthur Guinness (ret 1984), late md Guinness Mahon, memb ctee management RNLI; *m* 1st 18 Sept 1948 (*divorce* 1953) Rissa, er dau of Capt Hon Trevor Parker, DSC, RN, est s of Baron Parker of Waddington, PC (*see* 1970 edn) and er bro of Baron Parker of Waddington of the 1958 *cr* (*see* 1970 edn), by Marie, 4th dau of Herman Greverus Kleinwort, er bro of Sir Alexander Kleinwort, 1st Bt (*qv*), and has:

1f *Anthony Jack [Anthony Guinness Esq, 7A Moncur St, Woollahra, NSW 2025, Australia]; *b* 28 Nov 1949; *educ* Eton and Trin Coll Dublin (BA 1972); md Ag Investments Australia, management consltant rural investment; *m* 31 Oct 19– *Barbara Caroline, dau of Barry W Muldowney, of S Coogee, NSW

1e (cont.) Peter Guinness *m* 2nd 14 July 1954 *Susan Petronella, yr dau of George Henry Carbutt, and by her has:

2f Christopher Jens; *b* 30 Aug 1957; *educ* Shiplake Coll; *d* 9 Oct 1992

1f *Lucinda Claire; *b* 1 April 1959

2e John Henry; *b* 10 April 1935; *educ* Eton; served RN, chm Guinness Mahon, dir: Guinness Peat Gp, Heiton McFerran, Irish Shoe Supplies, McNeill Gp and Telectron; *m* 9 April 1959 *Mary Jennifer [Mrs John Guinness, Censure House, Barly, Co Dublin, Ireland], dau of Lt-Col James B Hollwey, of Cabinteely, Co Dublin, and d 28 Feb 1988, leaving:

1f *Ian Richard; *b* 15 March 1961; *m* 1987 *Mary Paula Diggin and has:

1g *Henry Christopher; *b* 1990

2g *Frederick Peter; *b* 1991

1g *Freya Mary; *b* 1994

2g *Imogen Mary; *b* 1997

1f *Gillian Sarah; *b* 8 July 1962

2f *Tania Caroline; *b* 10 Feb 1966

1d Margaret Aideen, of Ceanchor House, Co Dublin; *b* 1895; *d* unm 2 Dec 1973

1c Ethel Mary; *m* 1885 Charles Frederic Hill (*d* 14 June 1945), of Vincent Sq, London SW, and Queensland, Australia, and *d* 11 April 1940, leaving a s and two daus

2c Amy Henrietta; *m* 28 May 1889 Edward Wills Sandford-Wills, JP (*d* 14 Feb 1923), of Cashlieve, Ballinlough, Co Roscommon, and *d* 3 Nov 1955, leaving issue:

1d Lucy Eleanor

2d Mary Grace; *m* 2 Feb 1924 Sydenham Harvey Brancker Blandy (*d* 18 May 1925), 5th s of Adam Fettiplace Blandy, JP, of Abingdon, Berks, and had a dau

3c Mary Katherine; *m* 1895 Col John Alexander Wright Falls and had a s and a dau

4c Eva Frances; *d* unm

5c Lucy Madeleine; *b* 1870; *m* 1900 Philip Alexius Laszlo de Lombos, MVO, FRS, PRBA, RSPP (the portraitist Philip De Laszlo; *d* 22 Nov 1937), and *d* 27 Dec 1950, having had five sons

6c Beatrice Grace; *m* 1911 John Christopher Peter du Toit (*d* 26 July 1942), s of Andries du Toit, of S Africa, and *d* 8 Nov 1944, having had a s and a dau

7c Constance Ellen; *b* 1876; *m* 9 Sept 1903 Brig-Gen Ernest Craig-Brown, DSO (*d* 22 April 1966), est s of Thomas Craig-Brown, of Selkirk, and *d* 22 Dec 1964, leaving a s and two daus

1b Mary Catherine; *b* 1823; *m* 16 Aug 1848 Sir Samuel Ferguson, QC, LLD, FRS (*d* 9 Aug 1886), Dep Keeper Public Records in Ireland and Pres Roy Irish Acad, s of John Ferguson, of Cider Court and Collon House, Co Antrim, and *d* 5 March 1905

3a (cont.) Robert Rundell Guinness *m* 2nd 27 June 1840 Mary Anne (*d* 7 Oct 1889), dau of Rev Thomas Ottiwell Moore, of Leskinfere, Co Wexford, and *d* 7 March 1857, having had issue:

3b Robert (Rev); *b* 25 April 1841; *educ* Queen's Coll Oxford (BA 1863 MA 1867); ordained 1864, Vicar: S Banbury 1869–74, St Andrew's Leicester 1874–85 and Market Harborough 1885–1911; *m* 17 April 1866 Grace Harriet (*d* 1929), est dau of Very Rev William John Butler, DD, Dean Lincoln, and *d* 17 March 1918, leaving issue:

1c Arthur Robert Henry (Rev); *b* 1880; *educ* Marlborough and Keble Coll Oxford; ordained 1910, Rector Warehorne, Kent, 1917–22 and Vicar: Tenterden 1922–26 and Tong 1926–35; *m* 1925 Maud Frances, dau of William Sharp, of Cheltenham, and *dsp* 16 Nov 1953

2c William Ernest; *b* 1882; *educ* Malvern; Maj Manchester Regt and Hon F/Lt RAFVR, Boer War 1901, N Nigeria (Lt Imp Yeo) 1908–09 and WW I (despatches); *m* 1st 1922 Dorothy (*d* 1923), dau of James Campsie Dalgleish, of Campsie, Co Derry; *m* 2nd 11 Feb 1944 Dorothy, dau of Henry Mundy, of Australia

1c Elizabeth Maude; V-Pncpl Roy Holloway Coll London and Cheltenham Ladies' Coll; *d* unm 14 Aug 1960

2c Avice Mary; *b* 1870; *d* unm 14 March 1950

3c Henrietta Darley; *d* unm 22 Feb 1963

4c Geraldine; *m* 1893 James Alfred Fort (*d* 24 June 1934), 2nd Master of Winchester Coll, and *d* 10 March 1933, leaving issue

5c Mary Grace; *d* 1899

2b Susan Rachel; *b* 1843; *d* unm 19 Feb 1892

3b Margaret Sophia; *b* 1845; *d* unm 1913

4b Elizabeth Anne; *b* 1847; *d* unm 9 April 1918

5b Henrietta; *b* 1848; *d* unm

6b Emily Maria; *b* 1850; *m* 1888 George Wale, MD, of Croydon, and *d* 8 July 1921, leaving issue

7b Edith Anne; *b* 1852; *d* unm 19 May 1919

4a Richard Samuel, of Deepwell, Co Dublin; *b* 17 June 1797; MP Kinsale and Barnstaple; *m* 25 Nov 1833 Katherine Frances (*d* 20 Nov 1881), 2nd dau of Sir Charles Jenkinson, 10th Bt (*qv*), and *d* 1857, having had:

1b Charles Wolfran Nugent, CB (1887); *b* 10 Oct 1839; 72nd Highrs 1860 (Capt 1869, Maj 1880), Lt-Col Seaforth Highrs 1881 and Col 1885, served Afghan War 1878–80 (despatches, medal with four clasps, bronze star, 4th class Osmanieh), cdr 83rd Regtl Dist 1889–90 and 1st Regtl Dist thereafter; *d* unm 1894

2b Arthur Cecil Cope Jenkinson; *b* 1841; *m* 1st 1862 Marion Jane (*d* 1885), dau of William Forlongs, of Melbourne, Australia, and had issue:

1c Mabel Constance; *m* 1882 Walter Lang (*d* 1912), broker, of Bombay, and had four sons and a dau

2c Katherine; *m* 1882 John Brennand, Ld Manor of Baldersby, Yorks, and had issue

2b (cont.) Arthur Guinness *m* 2nd 3 Aug 1886, as her 1st husb, Agnes Mary (*m* 2nd 1905 George Brodie, slr, of Albert Gate, London SW, and *d* 31 Dec 1924), dau of Capt Gordon Gilchrist, RA, and *d* 1 June 1897, leaving:

1c John Cecil Cope Jenkinson; *b* 1 June 1890; Coldstream Gds WW I, with Bleacher's Assoc; *m* 26 July 1923 Betty, est dau of Arthur Knowles Davies, and *d* 14 Oct 1970, leaving issue:

1d *(Cecil) Edward; *b* 1924; *m* 19– Elizabeth Thompson and has three daus

2d *Robin Arthur; *b* 26 Sept 1925; *educ* Stowe; Lt-Cdr RNR and Fleet Air Arm, sales dir Crockett & Jones; *m* 29 Oct 1952 Judith Anne, dau of Clifford Pitts Hare, of Scarcroft Manor, Thorner, nr Leeds, and has issue:

1e *Andrew Arthur Clifford; *b* 11 Aug 1961

1e *Alina Doone; *b* 1963

3d *(Iveagh) Perry; *b* 1927; *m* 1st 19– Heather Robinson; *m* 2nd 19– Daphne Pollard and has by her:

1e *Rupert; *b* 1962

4d Richard Iveagh; *b* 19 Dec 1938; *educ* Stowe and St John's Coll Cambridge; 11th Hus 1958–59

1d *Mary Carol; *b* 1928; *m* 19– *Pieter Robert Geoffrey Graham, MRCS, LRCP, and has three s and a dau

3c Agnes Mildred; *b* 4 May 1893; *m* 1916 (*divorce* 1921) Capt Eric McEvoy Gunning and *dsp* 2 Jan 1975

3b Reginald Robert Bruce (Sir), JP, DL (Dublin); *b* 9 Sept 1842; dir Arthur Guinness, Son & Co, ktd 1897; *m* 4 April 1866 Thomasina Anne Bloomfield (*d* 21 March 1921), yr dau of George Studdert, of Glenwood and Kilnamona, Co Clare, and *d* 9 July 1909, leaving issue:

1c Jane Agnes Maud; *b* 1867; *m* 29 Aug 1891 Maj Henry Anstruther Kinloch, KRRC (*d* 20 Feb 1903), 2nd s of Sir Alexander Kinloch, 10th Bt, of Gilmerton (*qv*)), and had issue; *m* 2nd 18 July 1905 Capt Walter Traversari Legge (*see* DARTMOUTH, E), and *d* 19 Oct 1953

4b Claude Hume Campbell, of Knockmaroon House, Co Dublin; *b* 1852; *m* 1st 5 May 1887 Gladys Helen Louisa (*d* 23 March 1891), 2nd dau of Col Hon Hercules Langford Boyle Rowley, 2nd s of 2nd Baron Langford (*qv*), and had:

1c Marjorie Gladys; *b* 11 Feb 1888; *m* 11 Feb 1909 Brig-Gen Hon Alexander Russell, CMG, MVO, yst s of 1st Baron Ampthill (*qv*), and *d* 28 April 1949, leaving issue

4b (cont.) Claude Guinness *m* 2nd 14 June 1892, as her 1st husb, Baroness Zoë Virginie (*m* 2nd 3rd Baron Manners, *qv*), 2nd dau of Baron Albert Llewellyn Nugent, RN (*see* WESTMEATH, E), and *d* 18 April 1895, having had:

2c Grace Zoë; *b* 13 Oct 1893; *m* 5 Sept 1916 2nd Viscount Daventry (*qv*) and *d* 1978, leaving issue

1b Mildred; *b* 1835; *d* unm

2b Edith Frances Sheridan; *b* 1837; *m* 1st 14 Oct 1856 Rev Robert Charles Thomas Pearse (*dsp*); *m* 2nd 31 Dec 1872 Capt Christopher Campbell Oldfield, JP, 85th Regt LI, of South Warnborough Lodge, Hants, 4th s of Col Henry Swan Oldfield, HEICS, of Farley Hill House, Berks, and *d* 1899, leaving issue:

1c Bertram Gerald Robert; *b* 31 March 1874; Lt 4th Bn Rifle Bde; *m* 1904 Margery, dau of John Lee, of Trehill, Exeter, and *d* 1912, leaving:

1d *Richard Bertram; *b* 1907

1c Sybil Christine; *m* 7 June 1900, as his 1st w, Capt John Sherard Reeve, JP, DL (*d* 20 April 1955), of Leadenham, Lincs, only s of Lt-Col John Reeve, JP, by Edith, sis of 5th Viscount Melville (*qv*), and *d* 31 Oct 1929, leaving:

1d William, JP, DL (Lincs 1950); *b* 18 May 1906; *educ* Eton and RMC; Lt-Col Gren Gds 1947, Armament Inspection, Experimental and Design Depts 1939–48, High Sheriff Lincs 1957; *m* 15 April 1936 Merial Catherine Dalrymple, dau of Sir Godfrey Dalrymple Dalrymple-White, 1st Bt (*qv*), and had issue:

1e *John [John Reeve Esq, West Chase, Bower Chalke, Salisbury, Wilts SP5 5LR]; *b* 12 Jan 1937; *educ* Eton; *m* 1st 25 April 1964 (*divorce* 19–) Penelope Anne, dau of AVM Alan Boxer, CB, DSO, DFC, and has issue:

1f *Philip John; *b* 11 July 1967

1f *Alexandra Penelope; *b* 3 Aug 1965; *educ* St Mary's Calne; *m* 19– *Charles — and has issue:

1g *A son; *b* 1993

1e (cont.) John Reeve *m* 2nd 26 June 19– (*divorce* 19–) Priscilla Ruth, dau of David Hardham, of Cirencester, and by her has:

2f *Matthew Welby; *b* 12 Aug 1976

3f *Jonathan Sherard; *b* 4 Dec 1979

2f *Merial Elizabeth; *b* 1 Sept 1974

3f *Nicola Mary Clare; *b* 6 Dec 1977

1e (cont.) John Reeve *m* 3rd 8 Aug 1988 *Esme Jane, dau of William Francis Briggs, of Winchester, and by her has:

4f *Harry William John Briggs; *b* 8 Jan 1990

4f *Francesca Jane Briggs; *b* 17 Nov 1994

2e *Christopher William [Christopher Reeve Esq, Falkland Cottage, Oddington Rd, Stow-on-the-Wold, Glos GL54 1AN]; *b* 2 April 1944; *educ* Gordonstoun and Mons OCS; Served Gren Gds 1964–67; *m* 1st 1969 (*divorce* 19–) Margaret, dau of — Godfrey, of Wimbledon, and has issue:

1f *Catherine Jane; *b* 4 Feb 1972

2e (cont.) Christopher Reeve *m* 2nd 19 Dec 1974 (*divorce* 19–) Patricia Anne, dau of Ven Evan James Gwyn Rogers, Archdeacon Doncaster 1967–69, and by her has:

2f *Alice Eleanor; *b* 17 April 1975

3f *Lucy Harriet Isobel; *b* 17 July 1980

2e (cont.) Christopher Reeve *m* 3rd 8 April 1991 *Linda Patricia, dau of Gordon Newell Done, of Kinnerley, Salop

3e *Peter Richard; *b* 15 June 1947; *educ* Gordonstoun; *m* 8 Sept 1978 *Henrietta Mary Louise, only dau of Maj (Francis) James Johnston, Coldstream Gds, by his 1st w Caroline Louise (*see* WILLS, Bt, of Blagdon), and has:

1f *William Francis; *b* 22 May 1980; *educ* Eton

2f *James Henry; *b* 6 Oct 1981; *educ* Eton

1f *Caroline Mary Louise; *b* 18 Nov 1983; *educ* Heathfield

2f *Eleanor Susan Katherine; *b* 4 June 1985

1d Susan Edith; *b* 28 Feb 1901; *m* 22 April 1925 Maj John Richard Chaplin Rawnsley, MC, 12th Roy Lancers, s of Maj Walter Hugh Rawnsley, of Well Vale, Alford, Lincs

2d Eleanor; *b* 17 July 1903; *m* 1924 John Hector Maxwell Gordon and *d* 31 March 1941

2c Norah Edith; *d* unm

3b Geraldine Henrietta; *b* 1838; *m* 1st 6 June 1865 Capt George Kingston Olliver (*d* 10 Feb 1868) and had issue; *m* 2nd 12 Oct 1869 Rev Beauchamp Kerr-Pearse and had further issue

4b Adelaide Maria; *b* 1844; *m* 20 May 1873 her cousin 1st Earl of Iveagh (*qv*) and *d* 16 Feb 1916, having had issue

5a Richard; *b* 1802; *d* 1804

1a Jane; *b* 1785; *m* Thomas Dixon and *d* 1827, leaving issue

2a Sarah; *b* 1786; *m* Henry Darley, MD, and *d* 1877, having had issue

3a Mary; *b* 1791; *m* George Hill and *d* 1816, leaving issue

4a Frances; *b* 1792; *d* unm 1888

5a Elizabeth; *b* 1794; *m* John Thompson and *d* 1860, having had issue

6a Olivia; *b* 1795; *d* 1797

7a Henrietta; *b* 1799; *m* William Livingstone and *d* 1877, having had issue

(2) Samuel; *b* 1761; *m* Mary Eccles and *dsp* 1826

(1) Mary; *b* 1759; *m* Alexander Stillas, Dublin merchant, and *dsp*

1 Frances; *m* 1st John Darley; *m* 2nd Michael Raye and *d* by 1795

2 Elizabeth; *m* Benjamin Clare

RICHARD GUINNESS *m* 2nd *c* 1752 Elizabeth Clare, a widow, and is said to have run a coaching inn at Celbridge; *d* after 1766

RICHARD GUINNESS's est s,

ARTHUR (I) GUINNESS, of Beaumont, Co Dublin; *b* 12 March 1725; founded the family brewery business, first at Leixlip, Co Kildare, in 1756 then at St James's Gate, Dublin, in 1759 on a 9,000–yr lease, Warden (later Master) Dublin Corp of Brewers 1763; *m* 29 May 1761 Olivia (aged 19 in 1761; *d* March 1814), dau and co-heir of William Whitmore, of Dublin, by Mary, dau of John Grattan, of Clonmeen, Co Kildare, by his w Martha Mason, who descended from William of Wykeham, Bp Winchester and founder of the College of Winchester and New Coll Oxford, and *d* 23 Jan 1803, having had:

1 Hosea (Rev); *b* 1765; *educ* Winchester, Oxford and Trin Coll Dublin (BA, LLD); rector St Werburgh's Dublin and Chllr St Patrick's Cathedral Dublin; *m* 18 Jan 1794 Jane, dau of Lt-Col Simon Hart, HEICS, and *d* 5 March 1841, leaving issue, with three other sons and four other daus, all unmarried:

(1) Arthur (Rev); *b* 2 April 1796; Curate Loughall, Co Armagh, then incumbent of Seaton Carew, Co Durham; *m* 26 April 1821 Catherine Laughton, dau of Rev Thomas Paul, and *d* 1831, having had issue:

1a Arthur Hart; *b* 9 Sept 1827; Proctor and Notary Public Ecclesiastical and Probate Courts; *m* 14 Aug 1856 Ellen (*d* 1919), est dau of John Galloway, of Monkstown, Co Dublin, and *d* 1901, having had, with two daus (*d* unm):

1b Arthur Percy; *b* 1858; *m* Marie Bedford and *d* 1919, leaving issue:

1c Arthur; *b* 1894; *d* 1929

2c William Andrews; *b* 1895; *m* Violet Martin and had issue:

1d *Sylvia; *b* 1930; *m* *Louis Pottier Smith

2b Thomas Archibald; *b* 1859; *m* Edith Stacy Marks and *d* 1913, leaving:

1c Arthur Henry; *b* 1886; *m* 1st Bertha Freytag (*d* 1922) and had issue:

1d Arthur Cyril; *b* 1916; *m* Enid Diana Hills and *d* 1973, leaving:

1e *Kevin John; *b* 1950; clerk DHSS London; *m* *Maureen Haley

1c (cont.) Arthur H Guinness *m* 2nd Kathleen Hiscock, widow, and *d* 1944

1c Eileen Edith; *m* William Cowie and had issue

3b Lewis Hart; *b* 1867; *m* Robina J Hatton and *d* 1929, leaving issue:

1c Terence Hart; *b* 1900; *d* unm 1961

1c Gytha Hart; *b* 1893; *m* Herbert Vincent Mathias

2c Elsie Hart; *b* 1895

3c Marjorie Hart; *b* 1896; *m* Duncan Leslie Rutherford

4c Sybil Hart; *b* 1898

5c Phyllis Hart; *b* 1902

4b Bertram Hart; *b* 1873; *d* unm 1933

2a Thomas Hosea, JP; *b* 10 Sept 1831; *educ* Cheltenham; *m* 31 Aug 1859 Mary (*d* 14 March 1925), only dau and heiress of Charles Davis, JP, of Cloragh and Tibradden House, Rathfarnham, Co Dublin, and *d* 22 Sept 1888, leaving issue:

1b Charles Davis; *b* 25 June 1860; *educ* Eton; Brevet-Col RA Boer War 1899–1902 (despatches), High Sheriff Co Louth 1918; *m* 13 Nov 1899 Hon Lucy Matilda Anne Massy (*d* 12 April 1941), est dau of 6th Baron Massy (*qv*), and *d* 7 Feb 1939, having had, with three other sons and two other daus (*d* unm):

1c Hugh Spencer; *b* 7 Oct 1890; *educ* Harrow; assist Chinese Maritime Customs; *d* unm 20 Sept 1922

2c Owen Charles, OBE (1919), of Tibradden and St Thomas, Co Dublin; *b* 14 Sept 1894; *educ* Uppingham and RMC Sandhurst; Maj Worcs Regt WW I (severely wounded) and War Office Casualty Branch WW II, Instructor RMC Sandhurst 1928–32, ret 1935; *m* 23 June 1927 Katherine Doris, yst dau of William Charles Henry Alston Smith-Ryland, JP, of Barford Hill, Warwicks, and *d* 11 Dec 1970, leaving issue:

1d *Charles Spencer, of Tibradden and St Thomas, Co Dublin; *b* 1 June 1932; *educ* Winchester and New Coll Oxford (BA 1954, MA 1959); 2nd Lt Roy Signals, sch master: Eton and St Columba's (Ireland)

2d *Paul Dennis; *b* 4 Feb 1941; *educ* Winchester and New Coll Oxford (BA 1963); slr 1967; *m* 31 May 1968 *Susan Elizabeth Jennifer, est dau of Garrett Gill, SC, of Dun Laoghaire, Co Dublin, and has had:

1e *Niall Owen Shane; *b* 15 May 1972

2e Aidan Hugh Darragh; *b* 25 Feb, *d* 17 Nov 1974

1e *Selina Karen Elizabeth; *b* 30 Dec 1970

1 b Mary Catherine; *b* 1865; nurse with BEF WW I (Croix de Guerre), painter; *d* 1955

1a Anne Elizabeth; *b* 182–; *d* unm 1844

2a Jane; *d* unm
3a Mary; *m* Rev Robert Holmes-Orr and had issue
4a Margaret; *m* Rev Archibald Robertson and *dsp*
(2) Benjamin Hart; *b* 1806; *m* Anne Shepherd and *dsp*
(3) Francis Hart Vicesimus; *b* 1819; Sub-Insp Police Canterbury, NZ, 1858–62 and RM Ahaura then Ashburton, both NZ, 1871–91; *m* Catherine Marianne Richardson (*d* 1891) and *d* 1891, having had, with four other sons, all of whom but the yst *m* and left issue, and two daus, both of whom *m* and left issue:
1a Arthur Robert (Sir); *b* 1846; barrister, Speaker NZ Ho Reps 1903–13 (formerly memb), ktd 1911; *m* Elizabeth Westbrook and *dsp* 10 June 1913
(1) Olivia; *b* 1794; *m* Rev William Archer and had issue
(2) Jane; *b* 1803; *m* Robert Richmond and had issue
(3) Elizabeth Augusta; *b* 1804; *m* William Thomas Waller (*b* 1811) and *d* 1873, having had issue
2 ARTHUR (II) GUINNESS
3 Edward; *b* 1772; founded an ironworks at Palmerston and Lucan, Co Dublin, but went bankrupt 1811; *m* 1 April 1796 Margaret (*d* 13 Aug 1839), dau of James Blair, of Lucan, Co Dublin, and *d* 20 Aug 1833, having had, with four sons and three other daus (all *d* unm):
(1) Elizabeth; *b* 1813; *m* her cousin **Sir Benjamin Lee Guinness, 1st Bt**, and *d* 22 Sept 1865, having had issue
4 Benjamin, of Brookville, Dublin; *b* 1777; *m* 27 March 1804 his er bro's sis-in-law Rebecca (*d* 1819), dau and coheir of Benjamin Lee, of Merrion, Co Dublin (*see* below against Arthur (II) Guinness), and *d* 19 May 1836 leaving issue:
(1) Susan Jane; *b* 1805; m, as his 1st w, her cousin Rev William Smythe Lee-Grattan-Guinness and *d* 1861, having had issue
5 William Lunell; *b* 1779; participated in management of the St James's Gate brewery, ret 1839; *m* Susanna Newton (*d* 1842) and *d* 1842, leaving issue:
(1) William Newton (Rev); *b* 1811; Rector Collooney, Co Sligo, and S Yarra, Melbourne, Australia; *m* 1st 31 March 1835 Harriet (*d* 1839), only dau of Rear-Adml Hon William Trench, 3rd s of 1st Earl of Clancarty (*qv*), by his (the Adml's) 1st w, and had a s (*dsp*) and two daus; *m* 2nd Elizabeth D Percival (*d* 1845) but had no issue by her; *m* 3rd Harriet F Day (*d* 1897) and *d* 1894, having had by her, with three other sons (two of whom *m* and had issue) and a dau Mary Alice ('May'), who *m* her cousin Howard Rundell Guinness (*see* above):
1a Henry William Newton, CB (1900); *b* 5 Aug 1854; *educ* Newton Abbot Coll; joined 18th Regt 1873, Capt Roy Irish Regt 1881, Brevet Maj 1885, Lt-Col 1889, AAG 1905–09, served Afghan War 1880 (medal), Nile Expedn 1884–85 (despatches, medal and clasp, Khedive's Star), Boer War 1900–01 (despatches, medal and three clasps, King's medal and two clasps); *m* 8 April 1893 Frances Helen, dau of Henry West, QC, of Loughlinstown House, Co Dublin, and *d* 5 Aug 1925, having had three sons (the est of whom, Alan, *m* as his 1st w and as her 2nd husb his 1st cousin Barbara, dau of Robert C Guinness, but had no issue)
5a Ernest Whitmore; *b* 1865; *m* Annie Macnaught and *d* 1948, leaving:
1b Eustace John, DSC; *b* 1897; Capt RN; *m* 31 Oct 1946, as her 2nd husb, Angela Beryl, only dau of Henry Hoare, JP (*see* BRISTOL, M), and had:
1c *Timothy Whitmore; *b* 1947; with Guinness Mahon & Co; *m* 19– *Beverly Anne — and has issue:
1d *Edward Benjamin Newton; *b* 19–
1d *Mary Elizabeth; *b* 19–
2d *Catherine Alice; *b* 19–
2b Dennys Robert; *b* 1903; Col RE; *m* Elizabeth Howland, of Philadelphia, and had issue:
1c Dennys Key; *b* 1933; Maj; *m* 195– Veronica Terry and *d* by his own hand 5 July 1978, leaving four children
Ic *Ann; *b* 1935; *m* *Stephen Sparks
(1) Anne Rebecca; *b* 1819; *m* Dr William C Beatty and *d* 1881, having had issue
6 John Grattan; *b* 1783; Capt HEICS; *m* 1st Susanna (*d* 1826), dau of Alderman Hutton, of Dublin, and had two sons, both of whom *m* and had issue, and three daus, all of whom *dsp*; *m* 2nd 5 Jan 1829 Jane Mary Lucretia (*d* 15 Sept 1868), dau of William Cramer and widow of Capt John Neville Norcott D'Esterre, RN, and had issue, with a 2nd s of this 2nd marriage who *m* and had two sons and a dau (none of whom themselves had issue), also a 3rd s and only dau of this 2nd marriage who were childless, an est s of this 2nd marriage:
(1) Henry Grattan (Rev); *b* 1835; *m* 1st Fanny E FitzGerald (*d* 1898) and had, with a yr s (*m* and had issue) and five daus:
1a Henry Grattan; *b* 1861; MD; *m* Anne Reed and *d* 1915, leaving, with four er sons (*m* and had issue), three yr sons (only the two er of whom *m* and had issue) and two er sisters (of whom only the senior sis *m* and had issue):
1b Ruth Eileen; *b* 15 April 1900; *m* 1917 Sir Ronald Aylmer Fisher, FRS, DSc (*d* 1962), and *d c* 1971, having had two sons (the er of whom was *ka* 1943) and six daus
1 Elizabeth; *b* 1763; *m* Frederick Darley, Ld Mayor Dublin, and *d* 1847, having had issue
2 Olivia; *b* 1775; *d* unm
3 Louisa; *b* 1781; *m* Rev William Deane Hoare (*d* 1823) and *d* 1809, leaving:
(1) Olivia; *m* Rev Samuel Emery Day, of Bristol, and had issue:
1a Arthur Benjamin (Rev); Vicar Fishponds, Bristol; *m* his cousin Adelaide Rebecca, er dau of Rev William Smythe Lee-Grattan-Guinness, and *d* 30 Oct 1890, having had issue
4 Mary Anne; *b* 1787; *m* Rev John Burke and had issue

RICHARD GUINNESS's 2nd s,

ARTHUR (II) GUINNESS, of Beaumont, Co Dublin, JP, DL; *b* 12 March 1768; dir Bank of Ireland 1808 (later Govr) and Pres Dublin Chamber of Commerce; *m* 1st 7 May 1793 Anne (*b* 1774; *d* 21 Feb 1817), est dau and co-heir of Benjamin Lee, of Merrion, Co Dublin, by Susanna, dau of Rev John Smyth, Chllr Connor (bro of Arthur Smyth, ArchBp Dublin); Anne Lee was also er sis of Mrs Benjamin Guinness (*see* above), and had:

1 William Smyth GUINNESS later LEE-GRATTAN-GUINNESS (roy licences GRATTAN 28 Feb 1856 and LEE 10 March 1857) (Rev), of Beaumont and Park Annesley, Co Wexford; *b* 13 June 1795; MA, Rector Rathdrum, Co Wicklow; *m* 1st 9 March 1826 his cousin Susan Jane (*b* 1805; *d* 24 Dec 1861), only child of Benjamin Guinness, and had:
(1) Arthur William Grattan; *b* 12 Oct 1827; barrister; *m* 18 Aug 1862 Emily Olivia (who *m* 2nd Col Sir Morgan George Lloyd, KCB, Roy Irish Regt, and *d* 1912), dau of Thomas Bell, of Brook Hill, Co Wexford, and *dsp* 1 March 1869
(2) Benjamin Grattan; *b* 27 Jan 1829; *d* unm 8 Dec 1868
(3) William; *b* 1 Sept 1830; *d* 6 Aug 1844
(4) Edward; *b* 6 Feb 1833; *d* 15 Dec 1834
(5) Frederick John Darley; *b* 25 June 1840; *d* unm from inadvertent self-poisoning 5 June 1869
(1) Adelaide Rebecca; *b* 25 Aug 1841 or 1843; *m* 29 May 1863 her cousin Rev Arthur Benjamin Day and *d* 19 May 1884, leaving issue
(2) Anna Louisa; *b* 15 Aug 1843; *d* unm 1 May 1905
1 (cont.) The Rev William LEE-GRATTAN-GUINNESS *m* 2nd 1 June 1863 his 1st cousin Susan Rebecca, dau of Frederick Darley, and *d* 21 May 1864
2 Arthur Lee, of Stillorgan House, Co Dublin; *b* 1797; *d* unm 1862 or 1863
3 BENJAMIN LEE (Sir), **1st Bt**
1 Susanna; *b* 1804; *m* her 1st cousin Rev John Darley, Fell Trin Coll Dublin and Rector Arboe, Co Tyrone, and *d* 1836, leaving, with other issue:
(1) Elizabeth Jane; *m* 1857 her cousin Richard Seymour Guinness (*see* above)
2 Mary Jane; *b* 1808; *m* Rev David Pitcairn, DD, and *d* 1870, having had issue
3 Louisa; *b* 1810; *d* unm 1856
4 Anne; *b* 1812; *d* unm
5 Elizabeth; *b* 1813; *m* Rev William Jameson
6 Rebecca; *b* 1814; *m* 13 June 1844, as his 2nd w, Sir Edmund Waller, 4th Bt (*qv*), and *d* 22 Nov 1870, having had issue

ARTHUR (II) GUINNESS *m* 2nd 1821 Maria Barker (*b* 1783; *d* 1837), of Dublin, and *d* 9 June 1855

ARTHUR (II) GUINNESS's 2nd s,

Sir Benjamin Lee Guinness, 1st Bt (UK), so *cr* 15 April 1867, of Ashford Castle, Co Galway, JP, DL; *b* 1 Nov 1798; started work at Arthur Guinness aged 16, ptnr aged 22, Ld Mayor Dublin 1851, bought from the Commrs of Encumbered Estates for £2,500 (approximately £90,000 in late-1990s terms) what was to become known as Iveagh House, St Stephen's Green, Dublin (subsequently given to the State, after which it housed the Dept of For Affrs), an Ecclesiastical Commr for Ireland, MP (C) City of Dublin 1865–68; Ashford was originally a Georgian shooting lodge belonging to Lord Oranmore and Browne, one of whose successors in the title was to marry a Guinness heiress, and was sold by the Encumbered Estates Court 1855 to Benjamin Guinness, who then added to it and altered the whole to resemble a French château; Benjamin Guinness also paid for the restoration of St Patrick's Cathedral, Dublin; *m* 24 Feb 1837 his cousin Elizabeth (*d* 1866), 3rd dau of Edward Guinness by his w Margaret, *née* Blair, and *d* 19 May 1868, having had issue:

1 **Sir Arthur Edward Guinness, 2nd Bt**, and 1st and last BARON ARDILAUN OF ASHFORD, Co Galway (UK), so *cr* 1 May 1880, Ardilaun being an island on Lough Corrib, at the head of which the castle stands; Lord Ardilaun developed the 35,000-acre estate into what was considered to be the premier woodcock shoot in the world; he also added the massive Victorian-Baronial structure to his father's 'Château d'Ashford' for which, under the sturdily Anglo-Saxon name of Ashford Castle, the property is celebrated today (though chiefly because of its prominence as one of Ireland's premier country-house hotels rather than for its association with the Guinness family, despite the colossal cipher 'A' and baron's coronet over the heavily fortified gateway and the Guinness motto carved on an oak chimney-piece in one of the principal reception rooms); DL (Cos Galway, Kerry and Dublin and City of Dublin); *b* 1 Nov 1840; *educ* Eton and Trin Coll Dublin (BA 1863, MA 1866, Hon LLD 1891), MP (C) City of Dublin 1868–69 (unseated 1869 for bribery through his agents although personally not found guilty of corrupt practices) and 1874–80; Lord Ardilaun also acquired St Stephen's Green, in Dublin, from private owners and presented it to the Irish nation; newspaper proprietor: Dublin *Daily Express*, *Morning Mail*, *Evening Mail* and *Weekly Warder*; *m* 16 Feb 1871 Lady Olivia Charlotte Hedges-White (*b* 27 Aug 1850; *d* 13 Dec 1925), 2nd dau of 3rd Earl of Bantry (*see* 1891 edn), and *d* 20 Jan 1915, when the Barony expired
2 (Benjamin) Lee, DL; *b* 4 Aug 1842; Capt RHG (Blues); *m* 6 Sept 1881 Lady Henrietta Eliza St Lawrence (*b* 1851; *d* 22 Aug 1935), dau of 3rd Earl of Howth, KP, and *d* 2 Feb 1900, leaving issue:
(1) **Sir Algernon Arthur St Lawrence Lee, 3rd Bt**; *b* 11 May 1883; *educ* Eton; Actg Lt-Cdr RNVR WW I and F/Lt RAFVR (Air-Sea Rescue) WW II (despatches), Steward RAC, bankrupt 1911; *m* 10 July 1928 Winifred (*d* 11 May 1978), dau of John George Hall, of Hamilton, Ontario, and formerly w of Bernard George Mounteney, and *d* 26 Oct 1954, leaving issue:
1a *Susan (Shoonan) Rosemary Lee [Mrs Keith Hall, Weir House, Kibworth Beauchamp, Leics]; *b* 28 Oct 1931; *m* 1st April 1953 (*divorce* 1956) Samuel Charles Gillchrest; *m* 2nd May 1958 Keith Rawlings Hall, TD, and has issue:
1b *Simon Patrick Rawlings; *b* 18 Aug 1959
2b *Timothy Mark Lee; *b* 30 Aug 1967
1b *Susan Felicity; *b* 28 Oct 1960
2b *Jennifer Margaret; *b* 7 Feb 1963
(2) Kenelm ('Bill') Edward Lee, MBE (1920); *b* 16 Aug 1887; Lt RNVR, holder of World Land Speed record in early 1920s, inventor of an innovative sparking plug (KLG plug) and a hydro-pulsator for use in dental treatment; *m* 26 Jan 1928 (*divorce* 1936) Josephine (*d* 1989), yr dau of Sir Thomas Strangman, of 3 Buckingham Gate, London SW, and *d* by his own hand 10 April 1937, leaving:
1a Sir KENELM ERNEST LEE GUINNESS, **4th and present Bt**
1a *Geraldine ('Dina') St Lawrence Lee [Mrs Michael Essayan, 6 Chelsea Square, London SW3 6LF]; *b* 24 Sept 1930; *m* 24 May 1956 *Michael Essayan, QC, Bencher Middle Temple 1983, memb Gen Cncl Bar 1987–88 and hon pres Calouste Gulbenkian Fndn Lisbon 1992– (memb bd of admin

1982–), s of Kevork Loris Essayan (Calouste Gulbenkian's secretary) and Rita Sirvante, herself dau of Calouste Gulbenkian and formerly w of Kevork Loris Essayen, and has issue:

1b *Martin Sarkis [Martin Essayan Esq, 86 Wyatt Drive, London SW13 8AL]; *b* 16 Nov 1959; *educ* Eton

1b *Joanna Consuelo; *b* 22 May 1958

(3) Nigel Digby Lee; *b* 27 May 1892; *m* 1 Aug 1920 Ruby Laura Minnie Mary (*d* 23 Feb 1964), est dau of Frederick Blackham, of Wrentham Hall, Southwold, Suffolk, and *d* 196– or 197–, having had issue:

1a Joan Henrietta Mary Lee; *b* 24 July 1921; *d* unm 23 April 1937

3 EDWARD CECIL GUINNESS, 1st EARL OF IVEAGH (*qv*)

1 Anne Lee; *b* 1839; *m* 11 June 1863 4th Baron Plunket (*qv*) and *d* 8 Nov 1889, leaving issue

GUISE

Arms: Gu. seven lozenges vair, conjoined three, three and one; on a canton or a mullet pierced sa. **Crest:** Out of a ducal coronet or a swan rising ppr., collared and chained gold. **Supporters:** Dexter, a swan arg. crusily and langued gu., beaked and membered sa., collared and chained or; sinister, a bear sa. billetty, collared and chained or, langued and armed gu. **Motto:** *Quo honestior eo tutior* ('The honester the safer'). The supporters, an unusual addition to a baronet's coat of arms, were granted by roy warrant 12 July 1863 to **Sir John Guise, 3rd Bt**, in recognition of his distinguished service in the Peninsular War half a century earlier.
Creation: Bt. (GB) 9 Dec 1783.

SIR JOHN GRANT GUISE, 7TH BT, of Elmore Court, Gloucester [Sir John Guise Bt, Elmore Court, Glos GL2 6NT]; *b* 15 Dec 1927; *s* f 1970; *educ* Winchester and RMC Sandhurst; Capt 3rd King's Own Hus 1948–61; *m* 1992 *Sally, dau of Cdr H G C Stevens, RN

Lineage: NICHOLAS de GYSE; *m c* 1262–, a relation of Hubert de Burgh, Earl of Kent, and acquired through her the manor and Ldship of Elmore; their s:

Sir ANSELM de GYSE, had the grant of the manor of Elmore confiirmed 1274; assumed the arms of de BURGH differenced by a canton; ancestor of:

JOHN de GYSE; *m* Alice, only child and heir of Sir John de Wysham by Margaret Beauchamp, only dau and heir of the 2nd and last Lord de Beauchamp, Baron of Kidderminster, and had an est s:

Sir JOHN de GYSE, KB, High Sheriff Glos 1453; *m* Agnes, dau of — Berkeley, of Stoke Gifford, and had:

JOHN de GYSE; *m* Tacy, dau of (7th?) Lord (Baron) Grey (of Ruthin) (*see* GREY, B), and had, with an er s (Anselm, d 1563):

WILLIAM GYSE; ancestor of:

Sir WILLIAM GUISE, of Elmore, High Sheriff Glos *c* 1609; *m* —, est dau and coheir of Christopher Ken, of Ken, Somerset, and *d* 19 Sept 1642, leaving an only s:

WILLIAM GUISE, of Elmore, Glos: Sheriff 1647, MP 1654–55; *m* 20 Feb 1616/7 Cecilia, dau of John Dennis, of Pucklechurch, and *d* 26 Aug 1653, having had, with three daus:

1 Sir CHRISTOPHER GUISE, 1st Bt (E), so *cr* 10 July 1661, of Elmore, Brockworth and Rendcombe, Glos; *b c* 1620; *m* 1st Elizabeth (*dsp*), dau of Sir Lawrence Washington, of Garsdon, Wilts (*see* AMERICAN PRESIDENTIAL FAMILIES, Morris Genealogical Books S.A., 1994); *m* 2nd by 1654 Rachel, dau of Nicholas Corsellis, London merchant, and *d* 1670, leaving:

(1) Sir JOHN GUISE, 2nd Bt, of Elmore, Brockworth and Rendcombe; *b c* 1654; *educ* Ch Ch Oxford; MP Glos 1679–95, Col Foot 1688, Mayor Gloucester 1690; *m* by 1678 Elizabeth, dau of Sir John Grubham-Howe, of Compton-in-the-Hole, Glos, by Lady Arabella Scrope, illegitimate dau (but granted rank of earl's dau 1 June 1663) and heir (to the Langar, Notts, estate) of 1st and last Earl of Sunderland of the 1627 *cr*, and *d* 19 Nov 1695, leaving:

1a Sir JOHN GUISE, 3rd Bt, of Elmore and Rendcombe; *b c* 1678, MP Glos 1705–10 and Gt Marlow 1722–27; *m* 1st *c* 4 June 1696 Elizabeth, dau of Sir Nathaniel Napier, 2nd Bt, of Crichel, Dorset, and had issue; *m* 2nd *c* 2 Jan 1710/1 Anne (*d* 22 Feb 1735), widow of (a) Sir Henry Every, 3rd Bt (*qv*), and (b) Richard Lygon, of Beauchamp's Court, Worcs, and dau and coheir of Sir Francis Russell, 3rd Bt, of Strensham, and *d* 16 Nov 1732; leaving by his 1st w:

1b Sir JOHN GUISE, 4th Bt, of Elmore and Rendcombe; *b c* 1701; *educ* New Coll Oxford; MP Aylesbury 1722–27, Col Gds; *m c* 1731 Jane, only dau and heir of John Saunders, of Mongewell, Oxon, and *d* by 1769, leaving:

1c Sir WILLIAM GUISE, 5th and last Bt, of Elmore and Rendcombe; *bapt* 26 July 1737; *educ* Queen's Coll Oxford and Lincoln's Inn; MP Glos 1770–83; *dsp* 6 April 1783, when the btcy expired

1c Jane; *m* Rt Rev Shute Barrington, DD, Bp Durham

1a Annabelle Anne; *m* Edward Blount, of Blagdon/Blackdown, Devon and had issue (including Mary, *m* 9th Duke of Norfolk, *qv*; Henrietta, *m* 1st Peter Proll and 2nd Philip Howard, yr bro of 9th Duke of Norfolk, *qv*)

2a Rachel; *m* Col Sir Roger Bradshaigh, 3rd Bt, of Haigh, Lancs

2 John, of Sandhurst, JP Glos; *m* Hester, dau of William Stratford, of Farmcote, Glos

3 William; *d* unm

4 Henry, of Winterborne, Glos; *m* Philippa (*d* 4 Feb 1764), sis of Sir Thomas Brydges, of Keynsham, Somerset, and had, with other issue:

(1) William, of Winterborne; *b* 1648; *m* Dorothy (*d* 12 June 1738), dau and heir of John Snell, of Uffeton, Warwicks, and *d* 28 Aug 1716, having had, with other issue:

1a Henry, of Upton St Leonards; *m* Mary (*d* 21 Aug 1750), dau and heir of Edward Cooke, of Highnam, Glos, and *d* 23 Oct 1749, having had, with other issue:

1b JOHN (Sir), **1st Bt**

1b Theodosia; *m* Denis Cooke, of Highnam

(2) Christopher, of Abbot's Court, Glos; *m* Elizabeth, dau of Col — Long, of Whaddon, Wilts, and had issue:

1a Eleanor; *m* Robert Mann, of Linton, Kent

The great great-nephew of the 1st Bt of the 1661 *cr*,

Sir John Guise, 1st Bt (GB), so *cr* 9 Dec 1783, of Highnam; *b* 1733; Lt-Col Roy S Glos Militia; *m* 28 June 1770 Elizabeth, dau and heir of Thomas Wright, and *d* 2 May 1794, having had:

1 **Sir Berkeley William Guise, 2nd Bt**, MP Glos; *b* 14 July 1775; *d* unm 23 July 1834

2 JOHN WRIGHT (Sir), **3rd Bt**

3 Powell Colchester (Rev); Rector Craike, Yorks; *b* 18 Dec 1778; *m* 13 Oct 1808 Maria (*d* 14 June 1863), dau of Nathaniel Clifford, of Frampton Court, Glos, and *d* 9 May 1835, having had, with seven daus:

(1) William Christopher; *d* 1834

(2) George Clifford (Rev); MA, Rector Pulverbach, Salop, RD; *b* 6 Dec 1816; *m* 29 Jan 1874 Caroline, 3rd dau of Joseph Venables Lovett, DL, of Belmont, Salop, and *dsp* 18 March 1883

(3) Frederick Charles (Rev); MA, Rector Longhope, Glos; *b* 22 Oct 1826; *m* 7 June 1877 Mary (*d* 1897), 2nd dau of Edward Stanley, MP, of Ponsonby Hall, Cumberland, and *d* July 1899

4 Martin George; V-Adml of Peru; *b* 12 March 1780; *m* 1827 Dona Juana Maria del Valle Reistera and was *k* in the Peruvian War of Liberation 1828, leaving:

(1) Isabel Maria Monica; *d* unm

(2) Maria Mercedes Carlotta; *m* John Dartnell, est s of Edward Russell Dartnell, of Lima

1 Maria; *d* unm

2 Jane Mary Catherine; *m* 27 July 1807 Edward Webb and *d* 1814

The 2nd Bt's bro,

Sir John Wright Guise, 3rd Bt, GCB (GCB 1863, KCB 1841, CB 1831); *b* 20 July 1777; Ensign 70th Foot 1794, tfd 3rd Foot Gds 1795, Lt and Capt 1798, Capt and Lt-Col 1805, regtl 1st Maj 1814, served Ferrol, Vigo and Cadiz 1800, Egypt 1801 (medal), Hanover 1805–06, Portugal 1809 (Busaco, Fuentes d'Onoro), Peninsula 1812–14: cmded 1st Bn 3rd Gds Salamanca, taking of Madrid, Siege of and retreat from Burgos, Vittoria, Bidassoa, Nive, Adour, Bayonne (where cmded 2nd Bde Gds), Maj-Gen 1819, Lt-Gen 1841, Col 85th LI 1847, Gen 1851; *m* 12 Aug 1815 Charlotte Diana (*d* Feb 1835), yst dau of John Vernon, of Clontarf Castle, Co Dublin, and had issue:

1 WILLIAM VERNON (Sir), **4th Bt**

2 Henry John; Maj 13th Bengal Irregular Cav HEICS; *b* 25 Aug 1817; *m* 20 Feb 1855 Frederica (*d* 1909), dau of Sir William Verner, 1st Bt, MP (*see* 1970 edn), and was *k* Indian Mutiny *d* 4 June 1857, leaving issue:

(1) William Verner; *b* 1 Oct 1856; *m* 1879 Emilie Annie (*d* 23 June 1921), dau of Lee Viner, of Ceylon, and *d* 12 Oct 1935, leaving issue:

1a Anselm Verner Lee, CBE (1918); Maj, Order Leopold Belgium; *b* 15 Feb 1881

(2) Henry John Wright; Maj Liverpool Regt, ADC to Govr S Australia; *b* 12 Nov 1857

3 Francis Edward; MA, barrister, Recorder Hereford, Clerk Peace Glos; *b* 20 April 1820; *m* 13 June 1848 Henrietta (*d* 17 Dec 1897), 2nd dau of Sir James Rivett Carnac, 1st Bt (*qv*), and *d* 20 Jan 1893, leaving issue:

(1) Reginald Edward; FRGS, Lt The Buffs; *b* 2 June 1850; *d* unm 8 Nov 1902

(2) Rivett Francis; Bengal Police; *b* 24 April 1853; *m* 1st 1881 Mary (*d* 1886), dau of W Deare, and had issue:

1a Jack Francis Vernon; Lt-Cdr RN; *b* 1882; *m* 22 Jan 1917 Catherine Renée (*d* 1970), er dau of Gilbert Ireland Blackburne, of Redland, Bristol, and *d* 30 March 1964, leaving issue:

1b John Nicholas; *b* 8 April 1920; *m* 1st 1946 (*divorce*) Valerie, dau of Ronald Parker, of Warrie Station, W Australia, and had issue:

1c +Anthony John; *b* 16 June 1951

1c *Nikki; *b* 10 Dec 1952

2c *Judith Anne; *b* 18 June 1955

1b (cont.) John Guise *m* 2nd Beverley (*d* 1982), dau of James Parker, of Maida Vale, W Australia, and *d* 1981, leaving further issue:

2c +James Nicholas; *b* 1969

2b +Christopher Rivett; *b* 18 April 1921; *m* 1948 *Marion Florence, dau of — Strang, of Kalgoorlie, W Australia, and *d* 1991, leaving issue:

1c +Christopher John [Christopher Guise, 8 Stevens St, High Wycombe, WA 6057, Australia]; *b* 7 Aug 1949; *m* 1969 *Daphne Jean, only dau of Edgar Mackie, of Kalgoorlie, WA, and has issue:

1d +David Johnathan; *b* 1977

1d *Dianne Elizabeth; *b* 1974

1c *Georgina Elizabeth; *b* 2 Sept 1951; *m* 1st 1968 (*divorce*) Peter Dowding; *m* 2nd 1988 *Marian Zupan, of Bassendean, WA, and by her 1st husb has issue

2c *Penelope Jane [Mrs Ljubo Tolj, 3 Salisbury Rd, Rivervale, WA 6103, Australia]; *b* 21 March 1955; *m* 1971 *Ljubo Tolj and has issue

3b Reginald Ireland; *b* 4 June 1923; *m* 20 Oct 1951 *Gladys Constance [Mrs Reginald Guise, 15 McLintock Way, Karrinyup, WA 6018, Australia], only dau of Robert Alexander Baxter, and *d* 1978, leaving issue:

1c +Larry Steven [Larry Guise, 100 Lucy Victoria Ave, Clifton Park, Australind, WA 62230, Australia]; *b* 15 Jan 1958; *m* 1984 *Susan, only dau of Peter Gunning, and has issue:

1d *Megan Isabella; *b* 1987

2d *Simone Renée; *b* 1989

3d *Caitlin Ruth; *b* 1992

2c +Neil Reginald [Neil Guise, PO Box 266, Harvey, WA 6220, Australia]; *b* 26 July 1960; *m* 1984 *Amanda Frances, er dau of Michael Seabrooke, and has issue:

1d +Samuel Benjamin; *b* 22 April 1996

1d *Holly Rebecca; *b* 1992

3c +David Nigel [David Guise, 15 McLintock Way, Karrinyup, WA 6018, Australia]; *b* 4 June 1970

1c *Wendy Nola; *b* 22 Dec 1954

1b *Marguerite Renee [Mrs Ralph Lang, 288 Summer Lakes Parade, Ballajura, WA 6066, Australia]; *b* 8 April 1918; *m* 19– *Ralph James Lang and has issue

2b *Diana Mary [Mrs Graham Johnson, 2 Gabor Rd, Wattle Grove 6107, W Australia]; *b* 23 Dec 1925; *m* Graham Johnson (*d* 1992), s of — Johnson, of Perth, W Australia, and has issue

3b *Tacy Avena [Mrs Bernard Kelly, 23 Kooham Way, Balga 6061, W Australia]; *b* 8 Dec 1927; *m* 1st 19– (*divorce*) Thomas Turbett, of Perth, W Australia, and has issue; *m* 2nd 19– *Bernard Kelly and has further issue

4b *Georgina Frances; *b* 12 April 1930; *m* 19– *Jack Pritchard, of Kalgoorlie, and has issue

2a Harry Rivett Cecil, OBE (1919), MC (1918); Indian Police, Capt IA WW I (despatches), Indian Police Medal and Bar; *b* 1883; *m* 23 Feb 1909 Enid Marie (*d* 1 Sept 1962), dau of Lt-Col — Zohrab, IMS, and *d* 26 Dec 1926, leaving issue:

1b Mary Dulcie; *b* 26 May 1910; *m* 8 July 1939 Lt-Col Charles Henry Edmund Wright, s of Gerald Goodhall Wright, of High Hall, Norton, Bury St Edmunds, Suffolk, and *dsp* 5 Oct 1956

1a *Gladys Mary; *b* 26 Feb 1885

(2) (cont.) Rivett Guise *m* 2nd 1888 Mary Eliza Maud (*d* 2 Oct 1936), yst dau of Maj John William Boissier, 37th Regt, and *d* 3 Jan 1908, leaving by her:

3a Francis Edward Boissier; Capt 42nd Delhi Regt IA; *b* 21 Dec 1892; *m* 1st 7 Nov 1914 Ethel Mary (*d* 25 July 1943), dau of Edward Valentine Holme, of Naples; *m* 2nd 11 Jan 1944 *Gertrude Joyce [Mrs Francis Guise, 10 Harrow Rd, Brislington, Bristol BS4 3NE], dau of E F Taylor, and *d* 14 Dec 1970, leaving by her:

1b +Christopher Francis [Christopher Guise Esq, 4 Blackthorn Close, Marford, Clwyd LL12 8LB]; *b* 10 Jan 1945, late RN; *m* 1973 *Gwynneth Hancock, of Bristol, and has issue:

1c *Nicola; *b* 1974

2c *Rhian; *b* 1974

1b *Penelope Catherine [Mrs Nigel Wilkinson, 2 Melford Gardens, Old Kempshott Lane, Basingstoke, Hants]; *b* 12 April 1946; *m* 11 June 1966 *Nigel Wilkinson, only s of Kenneth E Wilkinson, of Brislington, Bristol, and has issue:

1c *Simon; *b* 1970

2c *Nicholas; *b* 1972

2b *Elizabeth Anne [Mrs David Fynn, 50 Littledean, Yate, nr Bristol]; *b* 11 Aug 1950; *m* 1973 *David Richard Fynn and has issue:

1c *Colin Richard; *b* 1980

1c *Deborah Caroline; *b* 1982

3b *Rosemary Caroline [Mrs Michael Hills, Cain Valley Hotel, High St, Llanfyllin, Powys SS2 5AQ]; *b* 1 Oct 1954; *m* 1979 *Michael Anthony Hills and has issue:

1c *Jennifer Claire; *b* 1983

4a John William, Lt-Col IA; *b* 20 Feb 1894; *m* 11 July 1924 (*divorce* 1937) Dorothy Alma, dau of Theodore Hewitt English, and *d* June 1963, leaving:

1b *Patricia Frederica; *b* 1929

5a Reginald Edward, MC, Lt Roy Glos Hus; *b* 1896; *ka* 29 June 1918

6a Christopher Probyn, Nyasaland Police, Lt 15th Sikhs IA; *b* 1899; *m* 1st 17 March 1931 (*divorce* 1956) Hope (*d* 1983), yr dau of Francis Gordon Percival Neison, of Lahore; *m* 2nd 1959 (*divorce* 1963) Catherine Elizabeth de Villiers, and *d* 14 Dec 1965, and by his 1st w had:

1b +Anselm Neison [Anselm Guise, 21 Motukaraka Point, Grays Rd, Pauatahanui, RD1, Porirua 6221, New Zealand]; *b* 29 March 1935, RN (ret 1964); *m* 18 July 1959 *Eileen Mary, only dau of Col Patrick Henry Cummins, IMS (*see* LAUDERDALE, E), and has issue:

1c +Edward William; *b* 27 Sept 1962

2c +Christopher Patrick; *b* 12 April 1973

1c *Laura Joan [Mrs William Sommer, 45 Victory Crescent, Tawa, New Zealand]; *b* 20 June 1960; *m* 1984 *W/Cdr William John Sommer, RNZAF, and has issue:

1d *Michael Patrick; *b* 1990

2d *Jamie; *b* 1997

3d *Scott; *b* 1997

2c *Susan Mary [Mrs Owen Bieleski, 9 Jan Higgins, Howick, Auckland, NZ]; *b* 20 June 1965; *m* 1986 *F/O Owen Philip Bieleski, RNZAF, and has:

1d *David Owen; *b* 1989

2d *Andrew Craig; *b* 1993

1d *Linda Jean; *b* 1995

2b +John Francis; *b* 12 June 1947

1b *Dinah Gabrielle [Mrs Peter Maunder, Crebor Cottage, Dunmere, Bodmin, Cornwall]; *b* 15 Oct 1936; *m* 3 Aug 1957 Peter Maunder (*d* 1988), s of John Maunder, of Newquay, Cornwall

7a Rivett Arthur; *b* 1902; *m* 23 Sept 1924 Beatrice Geraldine (*d* 1979), 2nd dau of Edward Charles Rudge, DL, JP, of Abbey Manor, Evesham, and *d* 16 March 1965, leaving:

1b +Peter Rivett John [Peter Guise Esq, Highnam, 4 Cae Castell, Builth Wells, Powys LD2 3BE]; *b* 5 Oct 1928; *m* 26 June 1953 *Morfydd Meredydd, dau of Lewis Morris, and has issue:

1c Meredydd Rivett; *b* 9 Jan 1955; *d* 30 April 1973

1b *Sheila Mae [Mrs Francis Collis, Badgers, 12 Heathfield Close, Binfield Heath, Oxon]; *b* 14 Oct 1925; *m* 20 Sept 1952 Francis Brian Collis (*d* 1987), er s of Ivor Collis, and has issue:

1c *David Brian [David Collis Esq, 8 Ashcroft Close, Caversham Heights, Berks RG4 7NU]; *b* 1 Nov 1954; *m* 1978 *Kerry Alison Elizabeth, dau of Derek Alfred Preece, and has:

1d *Oliver Thomas Richard Rivett; *b* 1985

1d *Elizabeth Louisa Mae; *b* 1982

2c *Simon Christopher [Simon Collis Esq, 10 Borderside, Yateley, Hants]; *b* 6 July 1957; *m* 1983 *Jane Constance Hutchins, dau of Trevor Thomas Farmiloe, and has issue:

1d *Max Christopher; *b* 1985

2a Henrietta Mae, b 21 May 1907; *m* 9 April 1931 Charles Montagu Webster, s of Edward Montagu Webster, and *d* 8 Oct 1968, leaving issue

(3) John Wright; Registrar Newnham County Court, Capt and Hon Maj Devon Artillery; *b* 28 June 1855; *m* 1st 3 June 1884 Helen Edith (*d* 1885), 5th dau of Judge Charles Sumner, of Hempstead Court, Glos; *m* 2nd 27 Nov 1888 Charlotte (*d* 29 Jan 1931), 2nd dau of Edwin Crawshay, JP, of Blaisdon Hall, Glos, and *d* 19 March 1916, having by her had issue:

1a John Berkeley Charles; *b* March 1897; *d* Sept 1899

1a Lesa Frances; *b* June 1893; *m* 4 Feb 1920 Capt Kingsmill Foster Manley Power, MC, Glos Regt Reserve (*d* 12 May 1963), s of Manley Kingsmill Manley Power, of Aston Court, Ross, Herefs, and *d* 19 June 1971, leaving:

1b *Manley Anselm; *b* 1920

1b *Charlotte Lesa; *b* 1922

(4) Hubert Charles; Lt 3rd Bn Glos Regt; *b* 4 July 1860; *dsp* 18 May 1898

(1) Emily Charlotte; *m* 12 Aug 1879 Francis H Lyel and *d* 1887

4 Vernon George (Rev); Rector Longhope, Glos; *b* 5 Sept 1823; *m* 2 Dec 1852 Mary Harriet (*d* 1886), yr dau of Robert Lane, and *d* 10 March 1861, leaving by her:

(1) Vernon Lane (Rev); MA Oxon, Rector Stopham, Pulborough; *b* 2 April 1854; *m* 1 June 1882 Edith Henrietta Mary (*d* 13 Feb 1955 aged 96), dau of Preb William Pulling, Rector Eastnor, Herefs, and *d* 31 Oct 1925, leaving:

1a Vernon Robert, OBE (1927), MC (1919); Maj RA WW I (Mesopotamia 1915–16); *b* 30 May 1885; *m* 4 Feb 1919 Nadine Alice (*d* 1977), 4th dau of Capt Andrew Charles Armstrong (*see* ARMSTRONG, Bt), and *d* 17 Nov 1939, leaving issue:

1b *Veronica Louise [Mrs Alan Falconer, 71 Alexander Park Rd, London N10]; *b* 13 Jan 1921; *m* 7 Aug 1946 *Alan Scott Falconer, FRCS, MRCOG, Surgn-Lt-Cdr RN, est s of Dallas Scott Falconer, MB, FRCS, and has:

1c *John Hedley; *b* 2 Sept 1951

2c *Alastair Robert; *b* 28 Dec 1955

1c *Jennifer Anne; *b* 30 Dec 1947

2c *Catherine Scott; *b* 20 Nov 1949

2b *Elizabeth Mary Joanna [Mrs Francis Mennell, Woden Law, Firs Road, Kenley, Surrey]; *b* 11 May 1923; *m* 5 June 1954 *Francis John Clark Mennell, s of Robert Oscar Mennell, and has issue:

1c *Andrew Guise; *b* 14 Jan 1955

1c *Susan Lilias; *b* 10 Aug 1956

(2) Julian (Rev); MA Oxon, Rector Addington Kent 1883–1927; *b* 29 Feb 1856; *m* 5 Oct 1886 Elizabeth Lucy (*d* 26 Aug 1915), dau of Rev F George Francis Master, Rector Stratton Glos and *d* 3 May 1932

(3) Howard, Maj RA; *b* 17 Sept 1858; *m* 2 June 1891 Georgina Maud (*d* 14 Nov 1945), dau of John Wingfield-Stratford (*see* POWERSCOURT, V), and *d* 29 Sept 1904, leaving issue:

1a Jane; *b* 1893; *m* 18 Oct 1927 Rev Charles Flavell Blood, Vicar Tintinhull, Somerset, and *d* 7 Aug 1966, leaving issue

5 John Christopher, VC, CB, JP, of St Waleran, Gorey, Wexford; Lt-Gen, Col Leics Regt, formerly 90th Light Inf; *b* 27 July 1826; *m* 18 Sept 1861 Isabella (*d* 29 Sept 1921), only surv dau of Rev Arthur Newcombe by Hon Catherine Wingfield, dau of 4th Viscount Powerscourt (*qv*), and *d* 5 Feb 1895, leaving:

(1) John Henry Wingfield; Capt The Cameronians, Scottish Rifles; *b* 7 Dec 1865; *d* unm 13 Nov 1899

(2) Arthur St Valery Beauchamp; Hon Capt Army, Priv Sec to Ld Lt Ireland and Govr-Gen Canada; *b* 20 Feb 1868; *educ* Wellington; *m* 15 Sept 1910 Florence Hazel Herbert, dau of Charles Mackintosh, and *d* 1 May 1923

(1) Catherine Isabella; *d* unm 4 June 1936

(2) Mary Emily; *m* 19 Aug 1899 Capt Frederick Ulick Vernon-Wentworth, CB, RN, and *d* 8 Nov 1948, leaving issue. He *d* 21 Sept 1947

1 Georgiana Maria; *m* 24 April 1845 Capt Hon Henry Thomas Howard (see SUFFOLK and BERKSHIRE, E), and *d* 23 Nov 1859, leaving issue

2 Jane Elizabeth; *m* 10 Dec 1844 John Wingfield Stratford and *d* 20 Feb 1897, leaving issue (*see* POWERSCOURT, V)

The 3rd Bt *d* 1 April 1865; his est son,

Sir William Vernon Guise, 4th Bt, FLS, FGS, Col-Cmdt Roy S Glos Militia; *b* 19 Aug 1816; *m* 27 June 1844 Margaret Anna Maria (*d* 10 Nov 1903), est dau of Rev Daniel Henry Lee-Warner, of Tyberton Court, Herefs, and Walsingham Abbey, Norfolk, and had issue:

1 Anselm Edward Henry; *b* 26 Sept 1847; *d* 8 April 1863

2 WILLIAM FRANCIS GEORGE (Sir), **5th Bt**

3 Christopher Dering; Lt-Col and Hon Col cmdg 3rd Bn Glos Regt, Hon Maj, Staff Offr Boer War 1900–02, BRCS WW I; *b* 3 April 1855; *educ* Eton; *m* 30 July 1903 Ella Emily Letitia (*d* 5 Oct 1928), dau of V-Adml Gerard John Napier, and *d* 1 Feb 1926, leaving issue:

(1) Valérie Napier; *b* 16 Jan 1907; *d* unm 20 March 1997

1 Charlotte Anne Elizabeth; *d* unm 8 Jan 1903

2 Henrietta Margaret; *d* 10 Dec 1920

3 Jane Isabella; *d* unm 12 Feb 1882

4 Mary; *d* an infant

5 Margaret Mary Catherine; *d* unm 3 March 1946

6 Georgiana Victoria; *d* unm 16 Oct 1942

7 Elizabeth Frances; *d* unm 28 June 1950

Sir WILLIAM *d* 24 Sept 1887; his est son,

Sir William Francis George Guise, 5th Bt, DL, JP, Glos; High Sheriff 1899, Hon Col, Lt-Col 3rd Bn Glos Regt; *b* 14 Dec 1851; *m* 23 Aug 1887 Ada Caroline (*d* 10 April 1945), 2nd dau of Octavius Edward Coope, MP, and had issue:

1 ANSELM WILLIAM EDWARD (Sir), **6th Bt**

2 Henry George Christopher; Lt 5th Bn Glos Regt; *b* 16 May 1893; accidentlly *kas* 6 May 1915

1 Diana Vernon Constance; *m* 14 Oct 1920 Lt-Col Ardern Arthur Hulme Beaman, DSO, JP, Roy Glos Hus Yeo, only s of Sir Clement Frank Offley Beaman, ICS, Puisne Judge Bombay, and *d* 16 July 1945, leaving issue. He *d* 26 Aug 1950

Sir WILLIAM *d* 17 Jan 1920; his only surv son,

Sir Anselm William Edward Guise, 6th Bt, of Elmore Court, JP Glos 1922, High Sheriff 1926, Capt Gloucestershire Yeo; *b* 18 Sept 1888; *educ* Eton; *m* 23 Jan 1924 Nina Margaret Sophie (*d* 1991), dau of Sir James Augustus Grant, 1st and last Bt, of Househill, Nairn (see 1932 edn), and *d* 12 Sept 1970, leaving:

1 Sir JOHN GRANT GUISE, **7th and present Bt**

2 +(Christopher) James [James Guise Esq, Easton Town Farm, Sherston, Wilts; 106 Claxton Grove, London W6]; *b* 10 July 1930; *educ* Stowe; *m* 7 Nov 1969 *Carole Hoskins, formerly w of Charles Edward Riou Benson and est dau of Jack Hoskins Master, and has issue:

(1) +Anselm Mark; *b* 7 Feb 1971; *m* 19 July 1997 *Hannah, dau of John Bruce, of Sculthorpe

(1) *Ruth Victoria Margaret; *b* 1972

1 *Philippa Margaret [Mrs Alastair Fraser, Moniack Castle, Kirkhill, Inverness-shire]; *b* 10 June 1926; *m* 1 July 1950 Maj Alastair Hugh Joseph Fraser, MC (*d* 1986), (*see* LOVAT, L), and has issue

GULL

Arms: Azure a serpent nowed or between three seagulls proper, with as honourable augmentation a canton ermine, thereon an ostrich feather argent, quilled or, enfiled by the coronet which encircles the badge or plume of the PRINCE OF WALES, gold. **Crests:** 1 (dexter) (honourable augmentation) A lion passant-guardant or, supporting with the dexter forepaw an escutcheon azure, thereon an ostrich feather argent, quilled or, enfiled with a like coronet, 2 (sinister) Two arms embowed, vested azure, cuffs argent, the hands proper, holding a torch or fired proper. **Motto:** *Sine Deo frustra* ('Existence without God is purposeless'). **Creation:** Bt. (UK) 8 Feb 1872.

SIR RUPERT WILLIAM CAMERON GULL, 5TH BT, of Brook Street, in the parish of St George, Hanover Sq, Middlesex [Sir Rupert Gull Bt, 2 Harcourt Rd, Claremont, Cape Town, S Africa]; *b* 14 July 1954; *s* f 1989; *educ* Diocesan Coll Cape Town and Cape Town U; *m* 1980 *Gillian Lee, dau of Robert Howard Gordon MacFarlaine, and has issue:

1 *Victoria Yvonne; *b* 1984

2 *Katie Alexandra; *b* 1986

3 *Olivia; *b* 1993

Lineage: THOMAS GULL, of Thorpe-le-Soken, Essex; *b* 1744; *m* Mary May (*d* Feb 1823) and *d* 26 June 1821, leaving issue:

JOHN GULL, of Thorpe-le-Soken; *b* 1779; *m* Elizabeth Chilver (*d* 1850) and *d* 6 Sept 1827, having had, with three daus:

1 John, of Ipswich; *b* 5 March 1804; *m* 30 June 1830 Sarah, dau of William Hempson, and had issue

2 Thomas; *b* 23 March 1809; *d* 1838

3 **Sir William Withey Gull, 1st Bt** (UK), so *cr* 8 Feb 1872; *b* 31 Dec 1816; Physician in Ordinary to HM QUEEN VICTORIA, LLD Camb, FRS, MB London 1841, MD 1846; FRCS (Lond) 1848, memb Senate London U 1859, Hon DCL Oxford 1868, Fullerian Prof Physiology Roy Inst 1847–49, consultant physician Guy's Hosp 1871; *m* 18 May 1848 Susan Anne (*d* 2 Jan 1894), dau of Col J Dacre Lacy, of Carlisle, and *d* 29 Jan 1890, leaving issue:

(1) Sir WILLIAM CAMERON, **2nd Bt**

(1) Caroline Cameron; *m* 12 April 1888 Theodore Dyke Acland MD (*d* 16 April 1931), and *d* 20 March 1929, leaving issue (*see* ACLAND, Bt, of Columb John)

Sir WILLIAM's only s,

Sir William Cameron Gull, 2nd Bt, OBE, JP Berks; CA Berks, MP NW Devon 1895–1900; *b* 6 Jan 1860; *educ* Eton and Ch Ch Oxford (MA 1887); High Sheriff Devon 1908, barrister, memb London Sch Bd 1891–94; *m* 1st 28 April 1886 Hon Annie Clayton Lindley (*d* 27 Sept 1908), 2nd dau of 1st and last Baron Lindley, and *d* 15 Dec 1922, having had issue:

1 Francis William Lindley; *b* 1 Nov 1889; *educ* Eton and Ch Ch Oxford; Capt (T/Maj) Rifle Bde; *m* 4 Sept 1914 Elizabeth Hope Bine (*d* 19 Feb 1969) (*m* 2nd 16 Dec 1922 Hon Robert William Morgan-Grenville (*see* KINLOSS, L)), dau of Sir Charles Bine Renshaw, 1st Bt, and was *ka* 25 Aug 1918

2 RICHARD CAMERON (Sir), **3rd Bt**

1 Mary Edith; *b* 23 July 1887; *m* 1st 20 April 1911 William Herbert Watney (*ka* 10 May 1915), er s of Herbert Watney, MD, of Pangbourne, Berks; *m* 2nd 20 Jan 1926 William Houldsworth McConnel (*d* 1943), of Heath End, Basingstoke, and had issue:

(1) *William Roger; *b* 6 Aug 1929; *m* 2 July 1955 *Susan Ingersoll, dau of W T Lyall, of Montreal, Canada, and has issue:

1a *William Timothy; *b* 21 April 1957

2a *Andrew James; *b* 1967

1a *Patricia Heidi; *b* 8 Nov 1960

2a *Robyn Ingersoll; *b* 9 Sept 1962

2 Amy Beatrice; *b* 1888; *m* 11 Nov 1913 Charles Henry Goschen (*see* GOSCHEN, V) and *dsp* 9 Nov 1971

3 Jessie Katherine; *b* 17 Dec 1892; *d* 17 June 1894

4 Dorothea Susan; *b* 5 Oct 1897; *m* 17 April 1923 Maj Vernon Cyprian Knollys, Rifle Bde (ret) and had issue:

(1) *David Cyprian [David Knollys Esq, The Cottage, Thorpe Satchville, nr Melton Mowbray, Leics]; *b* 8 May 1925; *m* 17 May 1952 *Pamela Jane Sharman and has issue:

1a *Deborah Claire; *b* 23 May 1954

2a *Catherine Anne; *b* 13 Oct 1956

3a *Elizabeth Fay; *b* 24 Nov 1959

4a *Veronica Francis; *b* 8 Jan 1963

5a *Caroline Louise; *b* 22 Aug 1964

(1) *Susan Anne; *b* 7 Nov 1927; *m* 19 Nov 1949 Brig Peter Hudson, MBE, The Rifle Bde, and has issue:

1a *Jessica Rosemary; *b* 23 Aug 1963

(1) Mrs David Knollys also have an adopted s and dau:

*Simon David; *b* 27 Sept 1960

*Sarah Jane; *b* 27 Dec 1958

Sir William *m* 2nd 3 Dec 1910 Evelyn Louise (*d* 2 April 1914), dau of His Honour Judge Sir Thomas Snagge, DL, and by her had issue:

3 John Evelyn, MC; *b* 26 March 1914; *educ* Eton and Trin Coll Cambridge (BA); Coldstream Gds, WWII (despatches); *m* 27 April 1957 *Margaret Colquhoun [Mrs John Gull, Trowley Hill Farm, Flamstead, nr St Albans, Herts AL3 8DZ], yr dau of late Capel Berger, of Far End, Travellers Lane, Hatfield, Herts, and *d* 7 Nov 1997, leaving:

(1) +Angus William John; *b* 24 Dec 1963; *m* 1988 *Jacqueline Mary, dau of Gerald Edgar Ford

3 Mr and Mrs John Gull also adopted:

*Mark Capel James; *b* 26 April 1962; *m* 1993 Lene Tang Rasmussen, of Aarhus, Denmark

*Lucinda Jane Evelyn; *b* 15 March 1961; *m* 1983 *Doko Gorov, of Macedonia, and has issue

5 *Rosemary Violet [Mrs Richard Schreiber, Campsea Ashe House, Woodbridge, Suffolk]; *b* 12 Feb 1912; *m* 13 May 1954 Maj Richard Shuldham Schreiber (*see* MARLESFORD, B)

The 2nd Bt's 2nd s,

Sir Richard Cameron Gull, 3rd Bt; *b* 18 March 1894; *educ* Eton, Ch Ch Oxford, and RMC Sandhurst; Capt Rifle Bde WW I (wounded, despatches), WW II Lt Gen List; *m* 19 July 1917 Dona Eva Swinnerton (*d* 19 Nov 1973), er dau of Sir Thomas Swinnerton Dyer, 11th Bt (*qv*), and *d* 5 Sept 1960, leaving:

1 **Sir Michael Swinnerton Cameron Gull, 4th Bt**; *b* 24 Jan 1919; *educ* Eton; 2nd Lt Scots Gds (SR); *m* 1st 30 May 1950 Yvonne, only dau of Dr Albert Oliver Macarius Heslop, of Cape Town, and formerly w of Harold Maurice Bawtree; *m*

2nd 19– *Margaretha Catherine Johanna [Dowager Lady Gull, Wedgeport, Bertha Ave, Newlands, Cape Town, S Africa], dau of Charles Henry Adrian Pentz, of Cape Town, and *d* 1989, having had by his 1st w:

(1) Sir RUPERT WILLIAM CAMERON GULL, **5th and present Bt**

(1) *Katherine Dona Mary; *b* 8 July 1951; *m* 19– and has issue

1 *Pamela Dona Anne; *b* 3 June 1922; *m* 5 Oct 1946 Col Alistair James Strang Martin, CBE (*d* 1992), QO Highrs, only s of Brig Gen Cuthbert Thomas Martin, DSO and bar, HLI, and has issue:

(1) *Christopher Thomas; *b* 24 July 1948; *educ* Downside

(2) *Michael Richard Alistair; *b* 13 Dec 1953; *educ* Downside

GUNNING

Arms: Gu., on a fess erminois between three doves arg. as many crosses formée per pale of the first and az. **Crest:** A dove holding in the dexter claw a caduceus ppr. **Motto:** *Imperio regit unus æquo* ('He rules alone with impartial sway').
Creation: Bt. (GB) 3 Sept 1778.

SIR CHARLES THEODORE GUNNING, 9TH BT, of Eltham, Kent, CD (1964) [Lt-Cdr Sir Charles Gunning Bt CD RCN (ret), 2940 McCarthy Rd, Ottawa, Ontario K1V 8K6, Canada]; *b* 19 June 1935; *s f* 1989; *educ* Canadian Mil Coll, RNEC (Plymouth) and Tech U Novia Scotia; CEng, BEng, AIMIMechE, AMIMarE, Queen's Canadian Dirk 1954, sr consultant Eyretechnics Ltd (Ottawa), V-Chm RCS Nat Cncl Canada 1980–; *m* 1st 1969 (*divorce* 1982) Sarah, dau of Col Patrick Arthur Eaton, of Tonbridge, Kent; *m* 2nd 1989 *Linda, dau of Theodore Kachmar, of Montreal, and by his 1st w has issue:

1 *Caroline Anne; *b* 1971

Lineage: A senior line of GONNINGs, as the family was spelled then, lived for several generations at Tregonning, Cornwall, but died out when Sir John Gonning dsp 1587.

THOMAS GONNING, of Tregonning, had:

WILLIAM GONNING, of N Stoke, Somerset, living *c* 1401; *m* Alice Long and *d* 1458, leaving an only s:

JOHN GONNING, of N Stoke; *m* Jane Wilshere and had, with a dau:

THOMAS GONNING, of N Stoke and Swanswick; gf of:

JOHN GONNING, of Swanswick and Cold Aston, Glos; *m* Mary, dau of William Dodington, of Todington, and *d* 1562, having had, with a dau (Mary; *m* — Stokes, of Cold Aston):

1 Thomas, of Turney's Court, Cold Aston, ancestor of the GUNNINGs of Langridge; *d* 1603

2 Robert, of N Stoke; ggf of:

(1) Robert (Sir), of Bristol and Cold Aston; *m* Anne, only dau of Sir Robert Cann, Bt, MP Bristol, and *dsp* 1682

(1) Elizabeth; *m* Sir Thomas Langton, Mayor Bristol 1666; ancestors of the LANGTONs of Newton Park, nr Bath

3 William, of Todington; *m* Ann Savage and *dsp* 1609

4 Peter (Rev), of Brookland, Kent, later Ash, Kent; *m* Elizabeth Alchorn and *d* 1667, leaving an only s:

(1) Thomas, of Ash; *b* 1554; *d* 1630, having had, with four daus (*d* unm):

1a Peter, Vicar Hoo; *m* 1612 Ellen (*m* 2nd Edward Henshaw, *d* 1643), dau of Francis Tracy, of Hoo, and *d* 6 Dec 1615, leaving an only s:

1b Peter, Bp Ely; *b* 11 Jan 1613; *d* unm 6 July 1684

2a Thomas, of Southfleet; *dsp* 20 Feb 1634

3a Robert, of Meopham; *m* 8 Nov 1631 Dorothy Barham and d 20 Oct 1648, leaving four sons

4a Richard; *b* 1587; moved to Ireland had:

1b John, of Castlecoote, Co Roscommon; *m* Margaret, dau of Edward Malone, of Castlecoote, and had issue:

1c Barnaby, of Castlecoote; *m* Sarah Geraghty and had issue

2c John; *m* Mary, dau of William Mason, of Dublin, and had an only s:

1d Robert; *m* 1734 his cousin Catherine, dau of John Edwards, and *d* 1750, leaving:

1e ROBERT (Sir), **1st Bt**

2e William; Army Offr; *b* 1736; *m* — Christie, of Stirling, and was *ka* capture Guadeloupe 1757, leaving issue

JOHN GUNNING's er son,

Sir Robert Gunning, 1st Bt (GB), so *cr* 3 Sept 1778, KB, of Horton, Northants; *b* 8 June 1731; Min Plen Berlin and St Petersburg; *m* 1st 1 April 1752 Elizabeth (*d* 14 April 1752), dau of John Harrison; *m* 2nd 14 Feb 1757 Anne (*d* 30 June 1770), only dau of Robert Sutton, of Scofton, Notts, and *d* 22 Sept 1816, having by her had, with two daus (Charlotte Margaret, Maid Honour to QUEEN CHARLOTTE, *m* 3 Jan 1790 Col Hon Stephen Digby (*see* DIGBY, B) and *d* 1794, leaving issue; Barbara Evelyn Isabella, *m* 1795 Maj-Gen — Ross):

Sir George William Gunning, 2nd Bt; *b* 15 Feb 1763; MP Wigan 1800–1802, Hastings 1802–06 and E Grinstead 1812–18; *m* 10 Feb 1794 Elizabeth (*d* 5 May 1810), dau of 1st Baron Bradford (*see* BRADFORD, E), and *d* 7 April 1823, having had, with other issue:

1 **Sir Robert Henry Gunning, 3rd Bt**; *b* 26 Dec 1795; MP Northampton 1830–31, High Sheriff Northants 1841–42; *d* unm 22 Sept 1862

2 George Orlando; Lt 10th Hus; *b* 18 Dec 1796; *k* Waterloo

3 **Rev Sir Henry John Gunning, 4th Bt**; MA, Rector Knockyn, Incumbent Horton, Wigan, RD; *b* 17 Dec 1797; *m* 1st 27 Feb 1827 Mary Catherine (*d* 25 May 1877), 2nd dau of William Ralph Cartwright, of Aynho, Northants, and had issue; *m* 2nd 23 Oct 1878 Frances Rose (*d* 24 Dec 1927), dau of Rev Hon William Spencer, MA (*see* CHURCHILL, V), and *d* 30 June 1885; his s by his 1st w:

(1) **Sir George William Gunning, 5th Bt**, JP Lancs, JP and CA Northants; MA Oxon, Maj 4th Bn Northants Regt; *b* 10 Aug 1828; *m* 15 May 1851 Isabella Mary Frances Charlotte (*d* 12 May 1910), est dau of Col William Chester-Master, of Knowle Park, Bristol, and The Abbey, Cirencester, and *d* 21 Oct 1903, having had issue:

1a Robert Henry; Lt-Col KRRC; *b* 17 July 1852; *m* 31 July 1880 Fanny Julia (*m* 2nd 12 Sept 1903 Adml Sir Ernest Rice, KCB (*d* 15 April 1927); *d* 20 Aug 1923), est dau of Clinton George Dawkins, Consul-Gen Venice, and was *ka* cmdg his Regt Talana, S Africa, 20 Oct 1899

2a **Sir Frederick Digby Gunning, 6th Bt**, JP Northants; *b* 13 Nov 1853; *d* unm 21 July 1906

3a **Sir Charles Vere Gunning, 7th Bt**, CB (1918), CMG (1917), JP, DL Northants; Boer War (despatches, medals), Maj Res Offrs, Remount Staff Offr 1914–16 (despatches), T/Brig-Gen cmdg Remount Command Canada and N America 1916–19, Hon Brig-Gen 1927, Capt 1st Bn DLI; *b* 31 Oct 1859; *m* 17 Oct 1888 Ethel Beatrice (*d* 23 Feb 1958), dau of Rev William Robert Finch Hatton (*see* WINCHILSEA and NOTTINGHAM, E), and *dspm* 29 Jan 1950, leaving:

1b Essex Vere; *m* 23 Sept 1919 Basil Gerald Brooke, Lt 17th Lancers, s of Sir George Frederick Brooke, 1st Bt of Summerton (*qv*), and *d* 16 Dec 1996, leaving issue

4a Henry William Maude (Rev); Rector Abington, Northants; *b* 21 April 1865; *educ* Ch Ch Oxford (MA); *m* 9 May 1905 Gertrude Alga (*d c* 1920), yr dau of Rev Canon James Tufton Bartlet, and *d* 1 Oct 1916

1a Emma Louisa; *m* 2 Oct 1890 Christopher Smyth, JP, DL, barrister Inner Temple, only s of Rev Christopher Smyth, and *d* 24 Aug 1933, leaving issue. He *d* 8 Feb 1934

2a Georgina Mary; *d* unm 5 Nov 1932

4 Orlando George GUNNING later GUNNING-SUTTON (roy licence 1850), of Blendworth, Hants; Capt RN; *b* 12 May 1799; *m* 22 June 1830 Mary Dorothea (*d* 31 March 1900), sis of Sir John Hobart Culme Seymour, 2nd Bt (*qv*), and *d* 5 May 1852, leaving issue:

(1) Mary Diana; *m* 1852 2nd Earl of Ravensworth (*see* RAVENSWORTH, B) and *d* 1890

5 Spencer Greswolde (Rev), JP; *b* 27 Oct 1800; *m* 20 March 1839 Anne Janette, dau of James Connell, of Conheath, and *d* 29 May 1867

6 John; Maj HEICS; *b* 21 Dec 1801; *m* 8 Sept 1827 Jessie (*d* 1881), dau of Rev Charles Maitland Babington, and *d* 13 Oct 1845, leaving, with four daus:

(1) Charles George; Maj Madras SC; *b* 27 Feb 1834; *m* 12 Jan 1859 Emma Cameron (*d* 31 Jan 1933), dau of Lt-Gen A S Logan, and *d* 13 June 1878, leaving:

1a Charles Archibald John; Collector Pemba, Zanzibar Govt Serv, 2nd Cl El Aliyeh Order, Boer War 1900 (medal); *b* 15 Oct 1849; *m* 16 Oct 1900 Beatrice Constance (*d* 5 Nov 1947), yst dau of Robert Raaff Purvis, and *d* 26 March 1910, leaving issue:

1b ROBERT CHARLES (Sir), **8th Bt**

1b Josephine; *b* 30 June 1904

2a George Hamilton, DSO (1918); Col Cmdt PAVO Cav IA, Tirah Expdn 1897, Waziristan 1901–02 and 1919–20, WW I (despatches thrice, Brevet Lt-Col), Afghan War 1919; *b* 3 Nov 1876; *m* 1st 2 June 1906 (*divorce* 1925) Wynifred Florence Langton (*d* 22 Sept 1930), yst dau of Rev Walter David Challice, MA, of Hove; *m* 2nd 1926 Sybil Viola (*d* 1938), dau of H P Ashton, and *d* 6 Dec 1936, having by his 1st w had:

1b Jack Hamilton; Maj Bombay Gren IA; *b* 5 Feb 1907; *m* 1st 2 July 1938 Judith Clowes (*d* 10 May 1942), yst dau of Capt Norton Clowes Castle, 18th Roy Irish Regt, of Froxmere Court, Worcs; *m* 2nd 4 Aug 1951 Kathleen Irene (*d* 1993), dau of P W A Wilson, and *d* 26 Nov 1956, having by his 1st w had:

1c *Cherry Hamilton [Mrs John Underwood, 9 Linkfield, East Molesey, Surrey KT8 9SD]; *b* 8 Sept 1939; *m* 19 May 1962 *Capt John Benjamin Lionel Underwood, King's Own Royal Border Regt (ret), only s of Lt-Col J B Underwood, and has issue:

1d *Michael John Benjamin; *b* 30 Aug 1966; *m* 18 Oct 1995 *Joanne Lesley, dau of Stuart Foster, of Gosnells, nr Perth, Australia, and has:

1e *Oliver Francis; *b* 4 May 1994

2e *Louis Hamilton; *b* 5 Aug 1995

1d *Catherine Louise; *b* 2 March 1964; *m* 1992 *Mark George Beatty and has issue:

1e *Benjamin George; *b* 1994

2e *Samuel George; *b* 21 Feb 1996

2d *Jennifer Elizabeth; *b* 15 Aug 1967

2b Anthony; *b* 14, *d* 20 March 1914

3a Spencer Octavius; *b* 28 Dec 1877; *d* 4 Jan 1878

(2) John Campbell; Col IA, Burma War 1887–89, Chin Lushai 1889–90; *b* 19 June 1835; *m* 1865 Mary Anne (*d* 16 Feb 1935), dau of J R Boyson, and *d* 27 Feb 1910, having had issue:

1a Charles John; Capt IA; *b* 3 Dec 1865; *d* 1 Nov 1919

2a Orlando George, CMG, DSO; Lt-Col and Brevet Col 35th Sikhs IA, Miranzai 1891 (medal with clasp), Dongola (two medals), Malakand Expdns 1897–98 (severely wounded, despatches twice, medal with clasp) and WW I 1914 (despatches, brevet), Order St Stanislaus Russia 3rd Cl with swords; *b* 31 July 1867; *m* 1 Nov 1902 Margaret Cecilia (*d* 31 Dec 1950), dau of Clinton George Dawkins, and *d* 14 Nov 1917, leaving issue:

1b (Orlando) Peter (Sir), CMG (1956); Dep Govr E Nigeria 1956–58, Chm Uganda Public and Police Service Commrs 1959–62, F/Lt RAFVR WW II, ktd 1959; *b* 1 Oct 1908; *educ* Haileybury and Trin Coll Cambridge (BA 1930, MA 1960); *m* 19 Oct 1940 *Patricia Mary [Lady Gunning, 42 Upper Cheyne Row, London SW3], dau of Capt Dermot Patrick O'Connor, MC, and *d* 4 Nov 1964, leaving issue:

1c *Susan Mary; *b* 20 May 1944

2c *Diana Rosemary [Mrs Patrick Durnford, Stoney Down, Corfe Mullen, Dorset]; *b* 11 July 1947; *m* 1971 *Patrick Durnford and has issue:

1d *Richard Peter Henry; *b* 1974

2d *James Edward; *b* 1976

3d *Nicholas John; *b* 1980

1d *Clare Susannah; *b* 1978

1b *Elizabeth Margaret Mary [Mrs Rupert Thursfield, North Barn House, Lower Froyle, Alton, Hants]; *b* 25 Jan 1905; *m* 29 Sept 1934 Rupert Macnaghten Cecil Thursfield (*d* 12 July 1979), er s of Rev Richard Cecil Thursfield, and has issue:

1c *John Richard; *b* 2 Oct 1937; *educ* Rugby; *m* 29 April 1961 *Sarah, est dau of Charles Clinton Dawkins

2c *Anthony Cecil; *b* 15 June 1941; *educ* Rugby and Sidney Sussex Coll Cambridge

2b *Lilian Jessie Isabella; *b* 8 Nov 1906

3a Guy Campbell; *b* 1868; *d* unm 1 Nov 1904

4a Henry Ross; Capt Devonshire Regt, Boer War 1899 (wounded), WW I (wounded); *b* 30 April 1879; *educ* Clifton; *m* 1st 1905 Charlotte Henrietta (*d* 16 July 1908), dau of Anthony Harley Bacon, and had:

1b Henrietta Marion; b 1905

2b *Evelyn Briliana [Miss Evelyn Gunning, Flat 4, 7 Burlington Place, Eastbourne, E Sussex BN21 4AS]; *b* 1907

4a (cont.) Capt Henry Gunning *m* 2nd 27 Aug 1914 Violet Gwendoline (*d* 1973), dau of William Robert Cubitt, and *d* 18 Feb 1951, having by her had:

1b John Robert; *b*.4 Aug 1916; *m* 1941 *Eleanor, dau of John William Elley, of Dublin, and Windsor, Ontario

2b +Richard Ross [Richard Gunning, 58–901 Kentwood Lane, Victoria, BC, Canada] *b* 1 Oct 1928; *m* 2 July 1951 *Hilda, dau of John Ronald Staniforth, and has issue:

1c +Christopher John Ross; *b* 10 July 1955; has issue:

1d *Jennifer Christina; *b* 1976

2c +Timothy Robin; *b* 2 March 1959; has issue:

1d +Brodie Adam; *b* 1982

1c *Heather Jean; *b* 13 July 1954

1a Jessie Helen; *m* 24 Sept 1891 Col Leonard Wilkinson Kerrick, 28th Light Cav IA, and *d* 7 Jan 1949, leaving issue

The 7th Bt's cousin,

Sir Robert Charles Gunning, 8th Bt, of Eltham, Kent; *b* 2 Dec 1901; *educ* St Paul's and Leeds U, T/Capt 50th (Northants Regt), AA Bn RE (TA), WW II; *m* 15 Sept 1934 *Helen Nancy [Helen Lady Gunning, Box 6602, Peace River, Alberta T8S 1S4, Canada], only dau of V-Adml Sir Theodore John Hallett, KBE, CB, and *d* 1989, leaving issue:

1 Sir CHARLES THEODORE GUNNING, **9th and present Bt**

2 +John Robert; *b* 17 Sept 1944; *educ* Peace River Catholic Sch; *m* 1969 *Alina Tylicki and has:

(1) +Derek John Robert; *b* 1972

(2) +Kevin Philip; *b* 1976

(1) *Lori-Ann; *b* 1969

3 +Joseph Jeremy; *b* 26 May 1946; *educ* Peace River Catholic Sch; *m* 1968 *June Smith and has issue:

(1) *Diana Elizabeth; *b* 1968

(2) *Theressa Kathleen; *b* 1971

(3) *Michelle Wendy; *b* 1973

4 +David Laurence; *b* 9 Aug 1948; *m* 1978 *Claudette Dubois and has issue:

(1) *Leslie Anita; *b* 1978

(2) *Kristina Jaclyn; *b* 1980

5 +Henry Michael [Henry Gunning Esq, 37 Mearns Dve, Stonehaven, Aberdeenshire]; *b* 6 Sept 1949; *m* 1970 *Rita Bruneau and has issue:

(1) *Holly Michelle; *b* 1970

(2) *Melanie Dawn; *b* 1975

6 +Bernard Christopher [Bernard Gunning, 47 Helene Ave, Dartmouth, Nova Scotia B2X 1G5, Canada]; *b* 28 Jan 1951; land surveyor; *m* 1979 *Elizabeth McLaughlin

7 +George Peter [George Gunning, Box 6626, Peace River, Alberta T8S 1S4, Canada]; *b* 1 Sept 1953; apiarist; *m* 1974 *Pauline Maud Karpiak and has issue:

(1) +George Bryce; *b* 1975

(1) *Angela Marion; *b* 1977

8 +Anthony Andrew Simon; *b* 18 Jan 1955

1 *Iseault Sara; *b* 18 Dec 1936; *m* 1970 (*divorce* 1977) Klaus Krey and has issue:

(1) *Andrew Lee; *b* 1974

91) *Suzanne Nicole; *b* 1972

2 Marion Josephine; *b* 21 Dec 1937; *d* 7 Aug 1939

3 *Elaine Beatrice [Mrs Arnold Jones, Box 772, High Prairie, Alberta, Canada]; *b* 25 Nov 1939; *m* 26 Nov 1958 *Arnold Nelson Jones, s of Charles Ernest Jones, and has issue:

(1) *Michael Robert; *b* 8 Sept 1959

(2) *Charles Mark; *b* 28 Aug 1960

(3) *George Marion; *b* 23 Dec 1961

(4) *Bruce Gordon; *b* 26 Feb 1963; *m* 1984 *Kathleen Margaret Barnes

(5) *Christopher John Peter; *b* 1971

(1) *Kathryn Ann; *b* 13 March 1967

GUNSTON

Creation: Bt. (UK) 1 Feb 1938.

SIR JOHN WELLESLEY GUNSTON, 3RD BT, of Wickwar, Co Gloucester [Sir John Gunston Bt, 8 Leathwaite Rd, London SW11 1XQ]; *b* 25 July 1962; *s* f 1991; *educ* Harrow and RMA Sandhurst; photojnlst, FRGS 1988; *m* 1990 *Rosalind, yst dau of Edward Gordon Eliott, of Bowers Mill House, nr Guildford, Surrey, and has issue:

1 +RICHARD ST GEORGE; *b* 1992

Lineage: THOMAS BERNARD GUNSTON, of 39 Prince's Gardens, London SW; *b* 21 Oct 1813; *m* Marion, dau of Robert Wilson, and *d* 24 April 1889, leaving:

1 Henry Cecil; *m* 28 Sept 1870 Constance Laura (*d* 20 March 1931), dau of George Lear Curtis (*see* CURTIS, Bt), and *dsp* Dec 1905

2 Thomas White

3 BERNARD HAMILTON

1 Isabel

2 Jessie Wilson; *m* 1884 Capt Geoffrey Stanley Phipps Hornby, JP (*d* 9 Nov 1927), of Lordington, Sussex, est s of Adml of the Fleet Sir Geoffrey Thomas Phipps Hornby, GCB, of Little Green, and Lordington, Sussex, and *d* 15 Oct 1937, leaving issue

3 Ellen Marion; *m* Rev Sidney Charles Saunders (*d* 1934)

THOMAS GUNSTON's 3rd s,

BERNARD HAMILTON GUNSTON; Maj 5th Dragoon Gds; *m* 31 May 1883 Ethel Caroline Jane (*d* 8 May 1953) (who *m* 2nd 28 July 1909 Sir George Francis Fleetwood Cradock-Hartopp, 8th Bt (*qv*)), 6th dau of Col William Henry Charles Wellesley (*see* WELLINGTON, D), and *d* 2 June 1908 leaving issue:

1 Cecil Bernard, MC; *b* 1885; Capt Coldstream Gds; *m* 19 Oct 1922 *Lady Doris Gwendoline Hamilton-Temple-Blackwood, est dau of 2nd Marquess of Dufferin and Ava (see DUFFERIN AND CLANEBOYE, B), and *d* 8 Dec 1934, leaving issue:

(1) *Hermione Hamilton [Lady Luttrell, Court House, East Quantoxhead, Bridgewater, Somerset]; *m* 23 Dec 1942 Col Sir (Geoffrey) Walter Fownes Luttrell, KCVO, MC, er s of Geoffrey Luttrell, of Dunster Castle, Somerset

(2) *Sonia Helen, JP (Berks 1957), T/Ldy Bedchamber to HM THE QUEEN 1967–71; *m* 17 April 1951 13th Lord Fairfax of Cameron (*qv*) and has issue

2 **Sir Derrick Wellesley Gunston, 1st Bt** (UK), so *cr* 1 Feb 1938, MC; *b* 26 Feb 1891; *educ* Harrow and Trin Coll Cambridge (BA 1913); Maj 7th Bn Glos Regt (TA) and Capt Res of Offrs Irish Gds, WW I, MP Thornbury 1924–45, PPS to: Parly Sec Min Health 1926–29, Chllr Exchequer 1931–36 and Jt U-Sec War 1940–42, memb Parly Mission to Newfoundland 1943, chm S Glos C Assoc 1950–52; *m* 18 Oct 1917 Evelyn (Gardenia) Bligh, OBE (1944), er dau of Howard Bligh St George (*see* ST GEORGE, Bt), and had issue:

(1) John St George; *b* 17 Feb 1919; *educ* Harrow and Trin Coll Cambridge; Capt Irish Gds attd 2nd SAS Regt WW II; *ka* Italy March 1944

(2) **Sir Richard Wellesley Gunston, 2nd Bt**; *b* 15 March 1924; *educ* Harrow and Clare Coll Cambridge; RAF (aircrew) 1942–46, Colonial Admin Serv 1946, N Nigeria 1948–51, Nyasaland 1951–63, Bechuanaland 1964–65, Colonial Office 1966, Assist Sec Centl Cncl Care Chs & Cathedrals Advsy Ctee 1967; *m* 1st 31 July 1947 (*divorce* 1956) Elizabeth Mary, est dau of Sir Arthur Colegate, of Redbourne Hall, nr Gainsborough, Lincs, and had:

1a *Caroline Jane; *b* 13 Sept 1950; *m* 23 Feb 1971 *Jonathan Robert Felton Peel, s of Denys Peel, of 36 Eaton Sq, London SW1, and has issue:

1b *Edmund Robert Felton; *b* 7 Aug 1979

1b *Victoria Mary; *b* 1972

(2) (cont.) **Sir Richard** *m* 2nd 1959 Joan Elizabeth Marie (*divorce* 19–) , only dau of Reginald Forde, of Inanda, Johannesburg, and Mrs Marie Louise Walker, of Somerset West, CP, S Africa, and formerly w of H B Coldicott, and by her had:

1a Sir JOHN WELLESLEY GUNSTON, **3rd and present Bt**

(2) (cont.) **Sir Richard** *m* 3rd 1976 *Veronica Elizabeth [Veronica Lady Gunston, The Arboretum, Tidebrook, Wadhurst, E Sussex TN5 6NY], dau of Maj — Haynes and widow of Capt Vivian Graham Lloyd, and *d* 1991

1 Sheelah Hamilton; *d* unm 4 July 1960

2 Irene Hamilton; *d* unm 14 March 1971

GUTHRIE

Arms: Per chevron argent and azure, in chief two eagles displayed of the second, and in base a lymphad with oars and sail furled of the first, pennons flying gules. **Crest:** A cubit arm in armour proper, charged with two crosses-patée fitchée in pale azure, holding in the hand proper a grenade sable, fired also proper. **Motto:** *Fidenter ago* ('I act faithfully'). **Creation:** Bt. (UK) 6 Feb 1936.

SIR MALCOLM CONNOP GUTHRIE, 3RD BT, of Brent Eleigh Hall, Co Suffolk [Sir Malcolm Guthrie Bt, Brent Eleigh, Belbroughton, Stourbridge, Worcs DY9 0DW]; *b* 16 Dec 1942; *s f* 1979; *educ* Millfield; *m* 30 Sept 1967 *Victoria, only dau of Douglas Willcock, of Little Brookfield, Belbroughton, and has:

1 +GILES MALCOLM WELCOME; *b* 16 Oct 1972; *educ* Shrewsbury

1 *Islay Mary Welcome; *b* 24 Sept 1968

Lineage: Sir Connop Thirwall Robert Guthrie, 1st Bt (UK), so *cr* 6 Feb 1936, KBE (1918); *b* 6 July 1882; Capt Gren Gds (SR) WW I 1914–15 (wounded) and Security Div WW II 1941–45, Special Rep in USA of Min Shipping 1916–19, memb USA Govt Shipping Control Ctee 1918–19, Chev Legn Hon, Cdr Crown Italy, DSM USA, Hon Air Cdre No 905 Co Surrey (Balloon) Sqdn AAF; *m* 14 Oct 1913 Mary Islay (*d* 18 Nov 1963), dau of Sir Malcolm Donald McEacharn, of Galloway House, Wigtownshire, and *d* 28 Sept 1945, leaving:

1 Sir GILES CONNOP McEACHARN, **2nd Bt**

1 *Diana Mary; *b* 1919

Sir CONNOP's only s,

Sir Giles Connop McEacharn Guthrie, 2nd Bt, OBE (1946), DSC (1941), JP (W Sussex 1955); *b* 21 March 1916; *educ* Eton and Magdalene Coll Cambridge; Lt-Cdr (A) RNVR WW II, winner (with late C W A Scott) Portsmouth-Johannesburg Air Race 1936, merchant banker, chm Air Transport Insur SA Lausanne, chm and ch exec BOAC 1964–68, memb bd BEA 1959–68, md Brown Shipley and Co, dep chm N Centl Finance, dir: Prudential Assur, Radio Rentals, Wallace Bros, Sassoon Bank (Jersey) 1974, Jersey Gen Investment Tst 1974, govr London Hosp 1965 and v-chm 1968; *m* 17 July 1939 *Rhona Leslie [Rhona Lady Guthrie, Les Vaux, Vallée de Rozel, St Martin, Jersey JE3 6AJ, CI], only dau of Frederic Stileman, of Charlwood Manor, Charlwood, Surrey, and *d* 31 Dec 1979, having had:

1 Neil; *b* 9 Nov, *d* 17 Nov 1940

2 Sir MALCOLM CONNOP GUTHRIE, **3rd and present Bt**

3 Alastair Peter; *b* 7 Aug 1944; *educ* Eton and Magdalene Coll Cambridge; *m* 22 March 1966 *Elizabeth Dorothy Margaret [Mrs Alastair Guthrie, Stanley Mill, Chippenham, Wilts], yr dau of Valentin Schaposchnikoff, of 33 Bryanston Sq, London W1, and *d* 1986, leaving issue:

(1) +Alexander Valentine Connop; *b* 7 July 1966

(2) +Barnaby Giles; *b* 28 April 1969

HABGOOD

Arms: Per pale azure and gules a cross ermine floretty or between in dexter chief and sinister base a key in pale wards outwards and in sinister chief and dexter base a lion's head erased also or that in chief langued azure and that in base langued gules. **Motto:** *Per aspera virtus* ('Virtue through hardships'). **Creation:** B. (LP, UK) 1995.

THE BARON HABGOOD, of Calverton, Co Buckingham (Rt Rev John Stapylton Habgood, PC (1983)) [The Rt Rev and Rt Hon The Lord Habgood PC, 18 The Mount, Malton, N Yorks YO17 0ND]; *b* 23 June 1927; *educ* Eton, King's Coll Cambridge (Fell 1952–55, Hon Fell 1986) and Cuddesdon Theological Coll Oxford (PhD); demonstrator pharmacology Cambridge U 1950–53, Curate St Mary Abbots Kensington 1954–56, V-Pncpl Westcott House Cambridge 1956–62, Rector St John's Jedburgh 1962–67, Pncpl Queen's Coll Birmingham 1967–73, Bp Durham 1973–83, Archbp York 1983–95; Hon DD: Durham 1975, Cambridge 1984, Aberdeen 1988, Huron 1990, Hull 1991, Oxford, Manchester and York 1996; author: *Religion and Science* (1964), *A Working Faith* (1980), *Church and Nation in a Secular Age* (1983), *Confessions of a Conservative Liberal* (1988), *Making Sense* (1993) and *Faith and Uncertainty* (1997); *m* 1961 *Rosalie Mary Anne Boston and has:

1 *Francis John Stapylton; *b* 19 Nov 1964; *m* 28 July 1990 *Dr Nicolette Tamsin Campbell and has:

(1) *Elliott; *b* 15 June 1993

(2) *Sebastian; *b* 31 July 1995

2 *Adrian George Chetwynd; *b* 20 Sept 1971

1 *Laura Caroline; *b* 12 June 1963; *m* 5 April 1997 *Dr Virgilio Calderon Joya, s of Dr V Moncada Joya and Sra Calderon de Joya, of Tegucicalpa, Honduras

2 *Ruth Barbara; *b* 17 June 1967; *m* 6 July 1991 *Mark Kenyon-Slade and has:

(1) *Lawrence; *b* 25 July 1997

Lineage: *See* CHETWYND, V

HACKING

Arms: Arg. on a chevron az. between three roses gu., barbed and seeded ppr., two bird bolts of the field feathered or. **Crest:** In front of an oak tree eradicated two axes in saltire, all ppr. **Supporters:** On either side a griffin gu., on the shoulder an escutcheon arg. charged with a blue-bottle (cyanus) stalked and leaved ppr. **Motto:** *Dominus providebit* ('The Lord will provide'). **Creation:** Bt. (UK) 27 June 1938, B. (UK) 2 July 1945.

THE 3RD BARON HACKING, of Chorley, Co Lancaster, and a **Baronet** (Sir (Douglas) David Hacking, Bt) [The Rt Hon The Lord Hacking, 27 West Sq, London SE11 4SP]; *b* 17 April 1938; *s f* 1971; *educ* Charterhouse and Clare Coll Cambridge (BA 1961, MA 1968); Lt RNR (ret), barrister Middle Temple 1963–76, attorney New York State 1975, slr Supreme Court England and Wales 1977, Freeman Merchant Taylors' Co and City London 1962, FCIArb 1997; *m* 1st 31 July 1965 (Rosemary) Anne, est dau of Francis Penrose Forrest, FRCSE, and has:

1 +DOUGLAS FRANCIS; *b* 8 Aug 1968; *educ* Berkhamsted, Dundee U and Exeter Coll Oxford; MB, MRCP; Registrar neonatal intensive care unit Mercy Hosp Melbourne, Australia

2 +Daniel Robert; *b* 27 May 1972

The 3rd BARON *m* 2nd 30 April 1982 *Tessa Margaret, MB, MRCP, FRCA, er dau of Roland C C Hunt, CMG, and by her has:

3 +Alexander Roland Harry; *b* 1984

4 +(Maxwell David) Leo; *b* 1987

5 +Christian Eric George; *b* 1989

1 *Belinda Anne; *b* 31 July 1966; *educ* Cavendish Sch, St Andrews and Plymouth U; PhD; clinical psychologist U Coll Hosp

Lineage: JAMES HACKING, of The Grange, Clayton-le-Moors, Lancs; *b* 1821; *m* 24 May 1844 Ann Bulcock (*d* 1897) and *d* 1866, leaving:

JOSHUA HACKING, of Henfield House, Clayton-le-Moors, JP; *b* 1846; *m* 12 Oct 1870 Eliza Simpson Boyle (*d* 24 June 1928) and *d* 22 April 1925, having had, with other issue:

Sir Douglas Hewitt Hacking, 1st Bt, so *cr* 27 June 1938, and **1st Baron Hacking**, of Chorley, Co Lancaster (both UK), so *cr* 2 July 1945, OBE (1919), PC (1929), JP, DL Surrey; *b* 4 Aug 1884; *educ* Giggleswick Sch and Manchester U; served WW I (despatches), MP (U) Chorley 1918–45, PPS to: Fin Sec Admlty 1920–21 and Sec State War 1921–22, V-Chamberlain Household 1922–24 and Nov 1924–25, Sec Dept Overseas Tde, Parly Sec BOT, Parly U-Sec: For Affrs 1927–29, Home Dept 1933–34 and Dominion Affrs 1935–86, Fin Sec War Office, memb Army Cncl 1934–35, Chm C Party Orgn 1936–42, memb GMC 1932–47, V-Chm Nat U Assoc 1930–31, Chllr Primrose League 1931, fndr Travel Assoc GB and Ireland 1929, memb Surrey TAA 1943, Govr Cranleigh Sch, chm Cornhill Insur; *m* 15 April 1909 Margery Allen, OBE (1956) (*d* 1984), est dau of Henry Hargreaves Bolton, MBE, JP, and had issue:

1 DOUGLAS ERIC, **2nd Baron**

2 +Edgar Bolton, MBE (1943), TD (1950) [The Hon Edgar Hacking MBE TD, Leeming, Alice Rd, Claremont, Cape, S Africa]; MRCS 1954, LRCP, DA, Fell Assoc Anaesthetists 1951, Memb Faculty Anaesthetists, Sr Assist Anaesthetist Groote Schuur Hosp Cape Town, Maj RAMC (TA) WW II; *b* 31 May 1912; *educ* Charterhouse and Clare Coll Cambridge (BA 1932, MA 1937, MB and BCh 1937); *m* 1st 3 April 1943 (*divorce* 1950) Winifred Mary, dau of John Christie Kelly, of Uitenhage, S Africa, and has issue:

(1) *Elizabeth Anne; *b* 9 Aug 1944; *m* 1966 *—

(2) *Susan Margaret; *b* 23 April 1946

2 (cont.) The Hon Edgar Hacking *m* 2nd 5 July 1950 *Evangeline Grace, dau of Percival Burtsal Shearing, of Cape Town, and by her has had:

(1) +Douglas Percival Bolton; *b* 3 Oct 1955; *m* 1984 *Mary, yr dau of Cyril Puttergill, of Indwe, CP

(2) +Geoffrey Edgar; *b* 6 March 1958; *m* 1983 *Elizabeth, only dau of Edward Hiles, of Somerset W, CP

(3) *Margery Ethel; *b* 31 May 1952; *m* 1973 *George du Plessis, s of V du Plessis, of Cape Town

(4) Janet Patricia; *b* 24 Jan, *d* 27 April 1954

1 *Elizabeth Margery, JP (Hants 1968) [The Hon Lady Waller, Hatchway, Hatch Lane, Kingsley Green, Haslemere, Surrey]; late JP Newcastle; *b* 4 May 1916; *m* 2 April 1936 *Rt Hon Sir George Stanley Waller, OBE, W/Cdr RAFVR, MA Cantab, Judge Queen's Bench, only s of James Stanley Waller, and has:

(1) *George Mark (Sir); *b* 13 Oct 1940; LLB; barrister Gray's Inn 1964, Recorder 1986, Judge Queen's Bench 1989, ktd 1989, Ld Justice Appeal 1996–; *m* 29 April 1967 *Rachel Elizabeth, er dau of Judge Christopher Beaumont, MBE, and has had:

1a *Charles James; *b* 4 Nov 1968; *d* 8 Sept 1997

2a *Richard; *b* 1969; *m* 26 July 1997 *Katie, dau of Stephen Walduck

3a *Philip; *b* 1973

(2) *(James) Irvin [Prof Irvin Waller, 136 Brighton Ave, Ottawa, Ont, Canada K1S OT4]; Prof Criminology Ottawa U; *educ* Cambridge (BA 1965, DipCrim 1966, PhD 1971); research assoc Center Criminology U of Toronto; *b* 24 July 1944; *m* 1st 10 Sept 1966 *Myriam, est dau of Prof Pierre de Bie, of Brabant, and has:

1a *Ann-Virginie; *b* 4 June 1968

2a *Marie-Katherine; *b* 1970

(2) (cont.) Prof Irvin Waller *m* 2nd 1983 *Susan Gwen, dau of Byron Chester Tanner, of Edmonton, Alberta, and has by her:

1a *James Byron Tanner; *b* 1984

2a *Mark Patrick Byron Tanner; *b* 1986

(1) *Elizabeth Tessa [Mrs John Hedley-Whyte, 355 Fairhaven Rd, Concord, MA 01742 4404, USA], MB, BS Durham, Prof neuropathology Harvard, MD Newcastle, AM (Hon) Harvard; *b* 17 Jan 1937; *m* 19 Sept 1959 *Prof John Hedley Whyte, er s of Col Angus Hedley Whyte, DSO, TD, MB, MS, FRCS, LRCP

The 1st BARON *d* 29 July 1950; his er son,

DOUGLAS ERIC HACKING, **2nd Baron Hacking**; *b* 7 Dec 1910; *educ* Charterhouse and Clare Coll Cambridge (MA); slr 1935, ptnr Baileys, Shaw and Gillett, consultant Wedlake, Letts & Bird, Pres Nat Deaf Children's Soc, dir Gen Accident Fire and Life Assur Corp, Chm Cncl Tst Houses Gp, Tstee and Chm Governing Body Whiteley Village, memb Cncl Br Travel and Holidays Assoc, memb Pilgrims, Maj RA WW II, Freeman City London, memb Court Playing Cards Makers' Co; *m* 19 Feb 1936 Daphne Violet (*d* 21 June 1998), est dau of Robert Finnis, of Kensington, and *d* 7 Nov 1971, leaving:

1 (DOUGLAS) DAVID HACKING, **3rd and present Baron Hacking**

2 +(Leslie) Bruce [The Hon Bruce Hacking, Burchetts, Moushill Common, Milford, Surrey]; *b* 16 June 1940; *educ* Eton; Memb Ct Assistants Haberdashers' Co; *m* 23 Sept 1967 *Hon Fiona Margaret Noel-Paton, yst dau of Baron Ferrier, TD, DL (LP; *see* 1970 edn), and has issue:

(1) +Matthew Bruce; *b* 28 June 1969

(1) *Joanna; *b* 1972

1 *Sandra Daphne [The Hon Mrs de Laszlo, A2 Albany, Piccadilly, London W1V 9RD; Pelham Place, Newton Valence, Hants GU34 3 NQ]; *b* 10 June 1950; *m* 1972 *Damon Patrick de Laszlo (*see* GREENWOOD, V) and has:

(1) *Robert Damon; *b* 1977

(2) *William Patrick; *b* 1979

(1) *Lucy Deborah; *b* 1975

2 *Carina Gillian [The Hon Mrs du Preez, 8 Winters Wynd, Newlands 7700, CP, S Africa]; *b* 28 May 1956; *m* 1981 *Jacob Jacobus du Preez

HADDINGTON

Arms: Quarterly, 1st and 4th grand quarters, gules, on a chevron between three cinquefoils argent, a buckle azure between two spots of ermine, all within a bordure or, charged with eight thistles vert (for HAMILTON of Byres); 2nd and 3rd, argent a fess wavy between three roses gules, barbed and seeded proper (for MELROSE); 2nd and 3rd grand quarters, sable, the sun in his glory betwixt nine stars three, two, three and one argent (for BAILLIE of Jerviswood). **Crests:** 1 Two dexter hands issuing out of clouds conjoined fesswise and holding betwixt them a branch of laurel erect, all proper, 2 A crescent or. **Supporters:** Two talbots argent, plain collared gules. **Mottoes:** 1 (over HAMILTON Crest) *Praesto et persto* ('I undertake and persevere'), 2 (over BAILLIE Crest) *Major virtus quam splendor* ('Virtue is greater than splendour'). **Creations:** L. (S) 19 Nov 1613, E. and L. (S) 20 March 1619.

THE 13TH EARL OF HADDINGTON, Lord Binning and Lord Byres and Binning (John George Baillie-Hamilton) [The Rt Hon The Earl of Haddington, Mellerstain, Gordon, Berwickshire TD3 6LG; Tyninghame, Dunbar, East Lothian]; *b* 21 Dec 1941; *s f* 1986; *educ* Ampleforth; *m* 1st 1975 (*divorce* 1981) Prudence Elizabeth, dau of Andrew Rutherford Hayles; *m* 2nd 1984 *Susan Jane Antonia, 2nd dau of John Heyworth, of Burford, Oxon, and by her has issue:

1 +GEORGE EDMUND BALDRED, *Lord Binning*; *b* 27 Dec 1985

1 *Susan Moyra; *b* 1988

2 *Isobel Joan; *b* 1990

Lineage: WALTER Fitz GILBERT, 1st of Cadzow (*see* ABERCORN, D); had a 2nd s:

JOHN Fitz WALTER; living 17 Feb 1383/4; *m* Elizabeth, dau of Sir Alan Stewart of Darnley and Crookston, had a charter from her bro John (confirmed 15 Jan 1369) of the lands of Ballencrieff, in the Barony of Bathgate, Lothian, and had:

ALEXANDER HAMILTON of Ballencrieff and Innerwick; *m* (dispensation 15 Sept 1381) Elizabeth, dau and coheir of 2nd Earl of Angus (*see* HAMILTON and BRANDON, D), had 1389 a charter of the lands of Innerwick from her sis Margaret, Countess of Angus and Mar, and was f of:

Sir ARCHIBALD HAMILTON of Innerwick and Ballencrieff; had a charter 10 May 1458 from John Stewart, Lord Darnley (*see* MORAY, E), of the lands of Ballencrieff; allegedly *m* Margaret, dau of John Montgomerie of Thornton, and had:

ALEXANDER HAMILTON of Innerwick; had a charter of Ballencrieff 18 Nov 1465; *m* Isobel Shaw and *d c* 1505, having had, with three er sons (Hugh, ancestor of the HAMILTONs of Innerwick (*see* STRATHMORE AND KINGHORNE, E); John; Alexander, living 1503):

THOMAS HAMILTON of Priestfield (bought 1523), in Duddingston, and Orchardfield (bought 1522); Burgess Edinburgh; *m* Margaret, sis of Adam Cant of Priestfield, and *d c* 1537, leaving:

THOMAS HAMILTON of Priestfield; Burgess Edinburgh 29 April 1541; *m* Elizabeth (*m* 2nd William Hutson), dau of Robert Leslie of Innerpeffer, and was *k* Battle of Pinkie 10 Sept 1547, leaving, with a yr s (John, secular priest, settled Paris 1573, Prof Philosophy Coll of Navarre, tutor to Cardinal de Bourbon 1576, Rector Paris U 1584; left France after HENRY IV's accession 1594, returned to Scotland 1600, arrested 1609 and imprisoned Tower London, where *d* 1610):

Sir THOMAS HAMILTON of Priestfield; had charter of Balbyn, Drumcairn and Priestfield 1597, Ld of Session as Lord Priestfield 1607–08 (resigned in favour of 2nd s); *m* 1st 1558 Elizabeth, dau of James Heriot of Trabroun, Haddingtonshire; *m* 2nd Elizabeth (*bur* 23 Nov 1612), dau of Sir Andrew Murray of Blackbarony (*see* MURRAY, Bt, of Blackbarony) and widow of James Borthwick of Newbyres, and *d c* 1612, having had, with other issue:

1 THOMAS, **1st Earl**

2 Andrew (Sir), of Redhouse; a Ld of Session 1608; *m* Jean, dau and heir of John Laing of Redhouse, and *d* 1634, leaving issue

3 John (Sir), of Magdalens, Co Linlithgow; Ld of Session and Ld Register Scotland 1622; *m* (contract 26 June 1602) Agnes, dau of William Hamilton, of Edinburgh, and *d* 28 Nov 1632, leaving six daus

4 Patrick (Sir), of Little Preston; *m* (contract 18 March 1613) Elizabeth, dau of Ninian Macmorran, and *d* 1662, leaving issue

5 Alexander; Gen Artillery, served under GUSTAVUS ADOLPHUS KING OF SWEDEN Thirty Years War; *m* 1st —, dau of Thomas Dalziel of Binns (*see* DALYELL, Bt); *m* 2nd —, dau of Cochrane; *m* 3rd (contract 13 Jan 1649) Elizabeth, dau of Sir David Crichton of Lugton, and *d* 26 Nov 1649, leaving issue

The est s,

Sir THOMAS HAMILTON, **1st Earl of Haddington**, so *cr* (as EARL OF MELROSE) 20 March 1619 but exchanged for the present title (on death 28 Feb 1625/6 of 1st and last Viscount of Haddington (*see* DALHOUSIE, E)) by patent of 17 Aug 1627, with original precedence and remainder to heirs male bearing the name and arms of Hamilton, as also LORD BYRES AND BINNING and earlier 19 Nov 1613 LORD BINNING (all S); *b* 1563; *educ* Edinburgh High Sch and Paris U; advocate 1587, Ld of Session as Lord Drumcairn 1592–1626, one of the eight Commrs of Treasury called Octavians Jan 1595/6, King's Advocate Jan or Feb 1595/6, ktd 1603, Ld Clerk Register 1612, Sec State Scotland 1612–26, Ld Pres Court Session 1616–26, Ld Privy Seal 1627–37; *m* 1st *c* 1588 Margaret (*d* Dec 1596), only child of James Borthwick of Newbyres, and had issue:

1 Christian; *m* 1st (contract 26 Jan 1610) Robert, Lord Lindsay of the Byres (*see* LINDSAY, E), and had issue; *m* 2nd (contract 9 Dec 1617) Robert, Lord Boyd (*see* KILMARNOCK, B), and had further issue

2 Isabel; *b* 18 Feb 1595/6; *m* (contract 22 Nov 1610) 1st Earl of Airlie (*qv*) and had issue

The **1st Earl** *m* 2nd May-Aug 1597 Margaret (*d* 31 May 1609), dau of James Foulis of Colinton, and had, with other issue:

1 THOMAS, **2nd Earl**

2 James (Sir), of Priestfield; served La Rochelle Expdn and in Sweden; *m* (contract Sept 1623) Anna, dau of Sir Patrick Hepburn of Waughton, and *d c* 1666, leaving issue

3 John (Sir), of Trabroun; *b* 3 Nov 1605; *m* Aug 1621 Katherine, only child of Alexander Peebles of Middleton and Skirling, and *dvp*, leaving issue (*d* young)

3 Margaret; *b* 5 April 1598; *m* 1st 28 Sept 1613 David, Lord Carnegie (*dvp* 25 Oct 1633), est s of 1st Earl of Southesk (*see* FIFE, D); *m* 2nd 31 Jan 1647 1st Earl of Hartfell (*see* ANNANDALE AND HARTFELL, E)

4 Jean; *b* 5 Feb 1607; *m* (contract 7 Jan 1622) 6th Earl of Cassillis and *d* 15 Dec 1642, leaving issue (*see* AILSA, M)

The **1st Earl** *m* 3rd Sept 1613 Julian (*bur* 30 March 1637), dau of Sir Thomas Ker of Ferniehurst (*see* LOTHIAN, M) and widow of Sir Patrick Home of Polwarth (*see* POLWARTH, L), and by her had:

4 Robert, of Wester Binning; *b* 14 May 1615; *k* Dunglass Castle unm 30 Aug 1640

The 1st EARL *d* 29 May 1637; his er son,

THOMAS HAMILTON, **2nd Earl of Haddington**; *b* 25 May 1600; Covenanter; *m* 1st (contract 27 Feb 1621/2) Catherine (*d* 5 Feb 1635), dau of John, Earl of Mar (*qv*), and had, with other issue (*d* young):

1 THOMAS HAMILTON, **3rd Earl of Haddington**; *b* 1626; *m* (contract 13 May 1643) Henrietta, a celebrated beauty of her day with literary aspirations (*m* 2nd (*divorce* 9 Aug 1661) Gaspard de Champagne, Count de la Suze, a Hugenot, herself turned Catholic and *dsp* Paris 10 March 1673), est dau of Gaspard de Coligny, Marshal of France, and ggdau of the celebrated Adml de Coligny, but *dsp* a minor 8 Feb 1645

2 JOHN, **4th Earl**

The **2nd Earl** *m* 2nd 14 Jan 1639/40 Jean (*d* 1655), dau of 2nd Marquess of Huntly (*qv*), and was *k* 30 Aug 1640 in a gunpowder explosion at Dunglass Castle, Haddington (of which he was Govr), deliberately set off by an English servant, Edward Paris, having by her had:

1 Margaret; *b* 15 Jan 1641; *m* 24 April 1662 1st Earl of Kintore (*qv*)

The 3rd EARL's bro,

JOHN HAMILTON, **4th Earl of Haddington**; *b* 1626; *m* 13 April 1648 Christian (*d* 26 Oct 1704), 2nd dau of 1st Earl of Lindsay (*qv*), and *d* 31 Aug 1669, having had, with other issue (*d* young):

1 CHARLES, **5th Earl**

1 Margaret; *m* 31 Dec 1668 John Hope of Hopetoun (drowned 5 May 1682) and *d* Dec 1711, leaving issue (*see* LINLITHGOW, M)

2 Helen; *m* (contract 5 July 1677) Sir William Anstruther and had issue (*see* ANSTRUTHER, Bt)

3 Susanna; *m* (contract 13 March 1679) Adam Cockburn of Ormiston, Ld Justice Clerk, and had issue

The 4th EARL's son,

CHARLES HAMILTON, **5th Earl of Haddington**; *b c* 1650; *m* 8 Oct 1674 Margaret (*d* 20 Aug 1700), Countess of Rothes in her own right, whose title passed to their est s, while to prevent the two Earldoms being held together that of Haddington was diverted to their 2nd s, and *d* May 1685, leaving, with an er s (*see* ROTHES, E):

THOMAS HAMILTON, **6th Earl of Haddington**, KT (1717); *bapt* 5 Sept 1680; rep S peer 1716–34; on his bro's resignation obtained a new patent of the Earldom of Haddington 25 Feb 1687, ratified by another patent 22 Oct 1702; Hereditary Keeper Holyrood Park 1691; *m* 1696 his cousin Helen (*d* 19 April 1768), sis of 1st Earl of Hopetoun (*see* LINLITHGOW, M), and *d* 28 Nov 1735, having had:

1 Charles, *Lord Binning*; *b* 1697; Kt Marischal of Scotland 1718; *m c* 1719 Rachel (*d* 24 March 1773), dau and ultimate heir of George Baillie of Jerviswoode and Mellerstain by Lady Grizel Hume, est dau of Lord Polwarth (*qv*), and *dvp* 27 Dec 1732, leaving:

(1) THOMAS HAMILTON, **7th Earl of Haddington**; *b* 1721; *m* 1st 28 Oct 1750 Mary (*d* 7 Sept 1785), dau of Rowland Holt, of Redgrave, Suffolk, and widow of Gresham Lloyd, and had:

1a CHARLES HAMILTON, **8th Earl of Haddington**; *b* 5 July 1753; Ld Lt Haddingtonshire 1804–23, rep S peer 1807–12; *m* 30 April 1779 Sophia (*d*

8 March 1813), dau of 2nd Earl of Hopetoun (*see* LINLITHGOW, M), and *d* 17 March 1828, leaving:

1b THOMAS HAMILTON, **9th Earl of Haddington**, KT (1853), PC (1814); *b* 21 June 1780; *educ* Edinburgh U and Ch Ch Oxford (BA); MP (Tory) St Germains 1802–06, Cockermouth Jan-April 1807, Callington 1807–12, St Michael 1814–18, Rochester 1818–26 and Yarmouth IoW 1826–27; *cr* 24 July 1827 BARON MELROSE OF TYNINGHAME, Co Haddington (UK), Ld Lt Ireland 1834–35, 1st Ld Admlty 1841–46, Ld Privy Seal Jan-July 1846; *m* 13 Nov 1802 Maria (*d* 11 Feb 1861), only surv child of 4th Earl of Macclesfield (*qv*), and *dsp* 1 Dec 1858, when the UK Barony expired

2a Thomas; *b* 23 Sept 1758; *d* 1 Aug 1774

(1) (cont.) The **7th Earl** *m* 2nd 6 March 1786 Anne (*m* 2nd 1796 James Dalrymple and *d* 21 June 1840), est dau of Sir Charles Gascoigne, and *d* 19 May 1794, having by her had:

1a Charlotte; *d* an infant 3 May 1793

(2) George HAMILTON later BAILLIE (on inheriting maternal gf's estates), of Jerviswoode and Mellerstain; *m* 1759 Eliza (*d* 24 April 1799), dau of John Andrews, and *d* 16 April 1797, having had, with other issue:

1a George, of Jerviswoode and Mellerstain; *b* 8 Oct 1763; MP Berwick 1796–1818; *m* 13 July 1801 Mary (*d* 28 Oct 1865), yst dau of Sir James Pringle, 4th Bt (*qv*), and *d* 11 Dec 1841, having had, with three other sons and another dau:

1b GEORGE, **10th Earl**

2b Charles; *b* 3 Nov 1804; granted with siblings rank of earl's dau/yr s; Ld of Session as Lord Jerviswood 1859–74; *m* 27 Dec 1831 Anne (*d* 15 Aug 1880), 4th dau of 6th Lord Polwarth (*qv*), and *d* 23 July 1879, having had issue

3b John (Rev); *b* 3 Jan 1810; MA; Canon Residentiary York; *m* 4 April 1837 Cecilia Mary (*d* 23 Sept 1903), est dau of Rev Charles Hawkins (*see* HAWKINS, Bt), and *d* 7 Aug 1888, leaving:

1c Hugh John; *b* 28 April 1838; *m* 1st 15 Sept 1873 Sarah (*d* 3 Aug 1890), dau of J F Heather, and had:

1d John Cecil George; *b* 10 May 1888

1c (cont.) Hugh Baillie *m* 2nd 6 Feb 1902 Maria, dau of William Nevin Wallace, JP, DL, of Downpatrick, and widow of Donald Ross, FRSE, and *d* 1923

2c Thomas George (Rev), *b* 30 Jan 1842; Rector Kingsland, Herefs; *m* 1st 18 Sept 1867 Ellen Isabella (*d* 1909), 3rd dau of Richard Gregson, of Sydney, NSW, and had:

1d Richard George; *b* 31 Dec 1869; *m* 1915 Maud Gertrude (*d* 2 Dec 1952), only dau of Edward Hadley, barrister, and *d* 11 May 1945, leaving:

1e +John Robert Edward, MC (1945) [Brig John Hamilton-Baillie MC, Rectory House, Stanford-in-the-Vale, Faringdon, Oxon]; *b* 4 March 1919; *educ* Sidney Sussex Coll Cambridge (MA); MICE, Brig (ret 1974) RE WW II, ADC to HM THE QUEEN 1972–74; *m* 27 Sept 1947 *Lettice Mary, yr dau of Charles Ernest Pumphrey, of Belsay, Northumberland, and has had:

1f +Thomas Richard; *b* 29 Dec 1948; *educ* Winchester; Lt-Col RGJ; *m* 31 May 1975 *Marina J A S, dau of General Dr Ferdinand von Senger und Etterlin, of Rieden am Wald, Uhlingen-Birkendorf, Germany, and has:

1g *Isobel Ebba; *b* 27 Feb 1979

2g *Daisy Ernestine; *b* 12 March 1982

3g *Cecily Marina; *b* 23 March 1985

2f John Lawrence; *b* 31 May, *d* 28 Aug 1954

3f +Benjamin Robert; *b* 4 July 1955; *m* 1988 *Jennifer, dau of Leslie Hill of Pinner, Middx, and has:

1g +Laurence Benjamin; *b* 1990

1g *Agnes Laetitia; *b* 1992

1f *Griselda Mary; *b* 7 Nov 1950; Tstee Roy Acad; *m* 3 Aug 1983 *William Raleigh Kerr (*see* LOTHIAN, M)

2f *Katherine Maud; *b* 29 March 1957

2d John Gordon; *b* 16 June 1872; *m* 7 Oct 1911 Margaret (*d* 22 June 1956), only dau of Henry Fellows, barrister, of Wimbledon, and *d* 21 Feb 1947

3d Robert; *b* 9 Sept 1878; 9th AIF; *ka* Sept 1915

4d Charles Jerviswoode; *b* 11 Jan 1882; *m* 1915 Dora Lizzie (*d* 1973), dau of James Dunn-Smith, of N Chapel, Sussex, and *d* 1973, leaving:

1e Robert Alastair; *b* 1919; *m* 1954 *Elizabeth Amy [Mrs Robert Baillie, Suite 15, 980 Gilford St, Esher Court, Vancouver, BC, Canada V6G 2N7], dau of Alexei Chernoff, of Tiflis, Russia, and *d* 1984, leaving:

1g +Dexter Robert [Dexter Baillie Esq, Box 945, Whistler, BC, Canada V0N 1B0]; *b* 1958; *m* 19– *Kristin Grace, day of Ross Bradford, of Warwick, Australia

1e *Eve Silvia; *b* 1946; *m* 1968 *John Edward Sample and has issue

2e *Angeline Cecelia; *b* 1950; *m* 1974 *Roy Albert Derrick, only s of Raphael Derrick, and has issue

5d Thomas Claude Noel; *b* 25 Dec 1885; presumed *d* in Argentina

1d Cecilia Mary; *b* 12 March 1871

2d Katherine Grisell; *b* 5 Aug 1874; *m* 19 Sept 1899 Harold W Hayes (*d* 1932)

3d Edith Georgina; *m* 1st 18 Nov 1903 Henry L Satow (*d* 1911) and had issue; *m* 2nd 1920 Theo R Buckworth (*d* Jan 1965) and *d* 16 July 1955

4d Ellen Ruth Gertrude; *b* 19 May 1877; *m* 1902 H Weston

5d Rachel; *b* 4 July 1880; *m* 14 Feb 1911 (*divorce* 1925) George Eustace Ridley Shield and had issue

6d Beatrice Louisa; *b* 23 July 1884; *m* 18 Nov 1907 (*divorce*) Alberto Boccardo, s of Jose Boccardo, of Caracas, Venezuela, and had issue

2c (cont.) The Rev Thomas Baillie *m* 2nd 1911 Violet Amy Kate, dau of F W Dunn, and *d* 11 June 1917, leaving by her:

7d *Violet Georgina Eila; *b* 1912; *m* 18 June 1931 Albert Ranney Chewett (*d* Sept 1965), s of William Cameron Chewett, MD, of Toronto

1c Augusta Margaret; *m* 17 Feb 1863 Thomas Edward Yorke (*d* 24 March 1923), of Halton Place, Yorks, yr s of John Yorke, of Bewerley Hall, and *d* 13 April 1879

2c Mary Georgina; *m* 14 April 1874 Rev Walter Folliott Scott (*d* 1 Jan 1924), of Elidon Grove, Melrose, Rector Jedburgh, Roxburghshire, and *d* 17 April 1927

3c Cecilia Clementina; *m* 26 Dec 1871 Henry Clements Barstow, BCS, yst s of Thomas Barstow, of Garrow Hill, Yorks, and *d* 14 Dec 1914

4c Louisa Rachel; *d* 15 Sept 1867

5c Beatrice Mary Anne; *m* 6 April 1875 Thomas Mackay, LLD (*d* 23 Feb 1912), er s of Lt-Col Aeneas J Mackay, HEICS, and *d* Oct 1889

6c Katherine Grissell; *m* 20 Jan 1915 8th Lord Polwarth (*qv*) and *d* 14 Aug 1938

1b Elizabeth; *m* 23 Nov 1821 2nd Marquess of Breadalbane and *d* 28 Aug 1861 (*see* 1970 edn BREADALBANE AND HOLLAND, E)

2b Mary; *m* 5 Nov 1840 5th Earl of Aberdeen and *d* 3 April 1900, having had issue (*see* ABERDEEN AND TEMAIR, M)

3b Georgina; *m* 11 Nov 1835 7th Lord Polwarth (*qv*) and *d* 2 April 1859, leaving issue

4b Catherine Charlotte; *m* 8 Jan 1840 4th Earl of Ashburnham (*d* 22 June 1878; see 1924 edn) and *d* 6 Feb 1894, leaving issue

2a Charles (Ven); *b* 27 Nov 1764; Archdeacon Cleveland; *m* 16 April 1797 Charlotte (*d* 4 Dec 1866), 3rd dau of 9th Earl of Home (*qv*), and *d* 19 June 1820, having had:

1b George (Sir), KCH; *b* 4 Oct 1798; Envoy-Extrdy and Min Plen Florence; *d* Sept 1850

2b Charles John BAILLIE-HAMILTON; *b* 4 Jan 1800; MP Aylesbury; *m* 23 Jan 1821 Lady Caroline Bertie (*d* 12 March 1870), dau of 4th Earl of Abingdon (*see* LINDSEY and ABINGDON, E), and *d* 25 Aug 1865, having had, with other issue:

1c Peregrine Charles; *b* 23 May 1823; *m* 12 July 1848 Mary Elizabeth (*d* 30 July 1875), dau of Edward Way, and *d* 21 Feb 1860, leaving issue:

1d George James (Rev); *b* 1 March 1851; *educ* Cambridge (BA); Vicar Wowerton, Cheshire; *m* 6 July 1875 Eliza (*d* 24 Jan 1931), dau of Rev Lucius Fry, and *d* 14 July 1904, having had issue:

1e George Leslie; *b* 1877; Capt 13th Bn RSG; *m* 1st 10 Aug 1906 Florence Maud Robinson (*d* 28 July 1912) and had:

1f +George Leslie; *b* 29 March 1909

1e (cont.) George Baillie-Hamilton *m* 2nd 1918 Katherine Ida Pennicard and by her had:

2f +David Lincoln; *b* 1922; *m* 1956 *Maud Mary Phillips, dau of Samuel George Augustus Schwenke and widow of Ralph Phillips

1f *Ella Faith; *b* 1919

2f *Jean Elizabeth; *b* 1921

2e Charles Douglas; *b* 1880; *ka* 1916

3e Arthur Vivian; *b* 1881; *m* 1906 Ida Maud Harrison and had issue

4e Lucius Hugh Noel; *b* 1886; *d* 1952

5e Patrick Stephen; *b* 1890; *m* 1st 1924 Elizabeth A Nation (*d* 1944); *m* 2nd 1945 Elizabeth (Mary) Burden (*d* 1980) and *dsp* 1973

1e Edith Mary; *b* 1876; *m* 12 Feb 1919 James Herbert Crompton (*d* 1944), 2nd s of J B Crompton, of Bolton

2e Aline Melrose; *b* 1879; *d* unm 1975

3e Nora Constance; *b* 1883; *m* 20 April 1909 Norman Bennett-Powell (*d* 17 July 1913), MRCS, est s of C E Bennett-Powell, of Harlesden, Middx, and *d* 5 May 1927

4e Ethel Gordon; *b* 1885; *m* 14 Jan 1914 Lionel Walter Kennedy Scargill, MD, BC, s of Frank C Scargill, of Beaufort, Co Kerry, and had issue

5e Madeline Violet; *b* 1888; *m* 6 March 1913 Arthur Hammond Jones, of Sandringham Estate, Agrapatana, Ceylon, s of Rev Canon David Jones, and had issue

6e Helen Margaret; *d* unm 16 July 1929

1d Lesa Baillie; *m* 5 Aug 1874 John Ball, of Putney Heath and Dorking, and had issue

1c Caroline Sophia Elizabeth; *m* 1844 Count Francis Caissott de Roubion (*d* 10 April 1882) and *d* 1854

2c Emily Eleanor; *m* 10 March 1847 Count Giorgio Agnes des Geneys, of Genoa, and *d* 10 Oct 1904

3b William Alexander; *b* 6 June 1803; Adml, Sec to Admlty; *m* 15 May 1836 Lady Harriet Hamilton (*d* 19 March 1884), only sis of 1st Duke of Abercorn (*qv*), and *d* 1 Oct 1881, having had issue:

1c George; *b* 5 March 1837; *d* 18 Jan 1840

2c William Alexander (Sir), KCMG (1897), CB (1892); *b* 6 Sept 1844; barrister Inner Temple 1871, Ch Clerk Colonial Office 1896–1909, Gentleman Usher Blue Rod Order St Michael and St George 1911–20, Offr at Arms, Lt-Col and Hon Col Lothians and Berwicks Imp Yeo, Priv Sec to Ch Sec Ireland and Sec State Colonies 1886–92; *m* 21 June 1871 Mary Aynscombe (*d* 6 Oct 1919), only dau of Rev John Mossop, Rector Hothfield, Kent, and *d* 6 July 1920, having had issue:

1d George Douglas, OBE (1929); *b* 26 Sept 1875; Maj RSG Boer War, WW I (wounded); *m* 14 Jan 1914 Helen Georgina (*d* 26 April 1951), dau of Cdr Hon Henry Baillie-Hamilton (*see* below), and *d* 8 April 1934

2d Walter Stuart; *b* 9 Aug 1880; Capt Gen Staff WW I (despatches), WW II as Maj Intell Serv (despatches, French and Belgian Croix de Guerre, Order Crown Belgium and Legn Hon); Priv Sec to Govr S Australia; *d* unm 28 March 1953

3c Charles Robert; *b* 24 Sept 1848; Clerk Treasury; *d* 28 July 1927

4c James; *b* 24 April 1850; *m* 10 Aug 1886 Lady Evelyn Campbell (*d* 22 March 1940), dau of 8th Duke of Argyll (*qv*), and *d* 28 May 1921

1c Harriet Eleanor; *m* 22 Sept 1863 Henry Samuel King, JP (*d* 17 Nov 1878), of Chigwell, Essex, and *d* 1920, leaving issue

2c Laura Frances; *m* 19 Oct 1901, as his 2nd w, Surgn-Lt-Col Ralph Gooding, VD, JP, DL, MD (*d* 17 Aug 1922), of Blackheath, Kent, and *d* 17 Jan 1922, leaving issue

4b Ker BAILLIE-HAMILTON, CB; *b* 13 July 1804; Govr Newfoundland 1852, Govr-Gen Leeward Islands 1855–67; *m* 19 April 1834 Emma (*d* 29 Oct 1890), dau of Charles Blair, and *d* 6 Feb 1889, having had, with other issue:

1c Clementina Georgina; *m* 21 July 1855, as his 2nd wife, 4th Baron Lilford (*qv*) and *d* 7 April 1929

2c Florence Charlotte Emma; *m* 6 Feb 1867 Col Frederic Bayly, Madras Staff Corps (*d* 16 Sept 1877), and *d* 11 May 1899

3c Emma Evangeline Ker; *m* 14 Feb 1888 Col Alfred Molyneux Crammer Byng (*see* TORRINGTON, V) and *d* 7 April 1924

5b Thomas; *b* 1805; *m* 18 April 1838 Anne Maria (*m* 2nd 1843 Maj Joseph Scott Phillips, Bengal Artillery), 2nd dau of William Reynolds, of Milford House, Hants, and *dsp* 30 Oct 1838

6b Gerard; *b* 17 March 1808; 7th Fus; *m* 23 Sept 1833 Augusta (*d* 8 April 1880), 4th dau of Col Anderson Morshead, of Widey Court, Devon, and *d* 2 Feb 1886, having had, with three other sons and three other daus:

1c John Baillie BAILLIE-HAMILTON later BUCHANAN-BAILLIE-HAMILTON, JP, DL Perths; *b* 20 Jan 1837; *m* 14 Jan 1869 Catherine Elizabeth Grace (*d* 13 Jan 1932), of Arnprior, Cambusmore, Callander, and Strathyre, Perthshire, only dau and heiress of Alexander Buchanan of Arnprior, and *d* 20 March 1908, having had issue:

1d Alexander Walter; *b* 8 Aug, *d* 28 Sept 1872

2d John Edmonstone; *b* 11 Sept 1874; *m* 16 April 1925 Bridget Everitt (*d* 1971), est dau of John E Baker, LLB, and *d* 12 Oct 1957, leaving:

1e +John Neil [John Buchanan-Baillie-Hamilton Esq, Cambusmore, Callander, Perthshire]; *b* 12 March 1926; *educ* Winchester; Capt (ret) Black Watch, ADC to Govr Sind 1946–48; *m* 1st 8 Jan 1955 Hon Caroline (Carol) Barbara Coupar Barrie (*d* 28 Feb 1978), yst dau of 1st and last Baron Abertay (*see* 1940 edn); *m* 2nd 1981 *Gillian, former w of Roderick Macdonald, and has by his 1st w:

1f +John Michael; *b* 14 Sept 1958; *educ* Oxford (MA); *m* 22 Oct 1994 *Paula Frances, 2nd dau of John Hickman, of Hendon, Middx, and has:

1g +Angus John; *b* 2 Jan 1996

2g +Bruce Charles; *b* 6 May 1997

2f +Alexander Neil; *b* 8 Sept 1963; Capt Black Watch, Equerry to HRH THE DUKE OF YORK 1990–92

2e +James Angus [James Buchanan-Baillie-Hamilton Esq, South Farm, Shipton Oliffe, Glos]; *b* 25 Nov 1927; Lt RN (ret), High Sheriff Glos 1984, now farmer; *m* 3 April 1954 *Prudence, only dau of Cdr Wenman Humfrey Wykeham-Musgrave, RN (ret), of Barnsley, Glos, and has issue:

1f +Charles Wenman; *b* 27 Aug 1957; *educ* Marlborough

2f +Simon James; *b* 13 Aug 1963

1f *Jane [Mrs Alastair Dickson, West Kennacott, Newton Tracey, Barnstaple, N Devon]; *b* 14 July 1955; MB, BS; *m* 1979 *Alastair James Dickson and has issue

2f *Sally; *b* 3 June 1961; *m* 1987 *James Hippisley Kidner, s of Dr Patrick Gerald Kidner, of Manaton, Devon

3e +Alexander [Alexander Buchanan-Baillie-Hamilton Esq, Knowle Croft, Shoppenhangers, Maidenhead, Berks]; *b* 2 Nov 1932; *educ* Trin Coll Glenalmond and Aberdeen U (MB, ChB 1956); DIM; *m* 15 Dec 1964 *Lilia Julia Mary, dau of Alan Peter, of Castries, St Lucia, WI, and formerly w of — Eaton, and has:

1f *Fiona Mary; *b* 1 Nov 1966

2f *Alexandra Helen; *b* 28 May 1969

3d Arthur; *b* 2 June 1876; Lt Seaforth Highrs Boer War, Kano-Sokoto Expdn 1903, WW I; *m* 8 March 1906 Ina Erskine (*d* 11 May 1941), dau of Sir Malcolm McNeil, CB, of Edinburgh; *ka* 9 May 1915

4d Morshead Buchanan; *b* 11 Feb 1878; Capt RN; *d* 2 Oct 1937

5d Neil Alexander; *b* 25 Nov 1880; Col Black Watch, Boer War, DAA & QMG WW I 1916, Iraq 1920, NW Frontier India 1923, Cdr 127th (Manchester) Inf Bde 1934–37; *m* 5 April 1927 Mary, dau of Judge William Musgrove Hopley, of Cape Town, and widow of Charles Duff Leslie, of S Africa, and *dsp* 7 Aug 1943

1d Elizabeth; *b* 9 Nov 1869; *d* unm 18 Jan 1962

2d Nannie Katherine; *b* 4 June 1871; *d* 28 Sept 1921

3d Grisell Baillie; *b* 19 Aug 1886; *d* 19 Feb 1978

2c Thomas; *b* 16 March 1844; *m* Feb 1878 Emily Finn, of Belfast, and *d* 17 Feb 1880, leaving:

1d Augusta Emmeline; *b* 21 June 1878; *m* 12 June 1906 Maj Arthur Claude Willcocks, TD, AMICE, and *d* 16 May 1957, leaving:

1e *Violet Baillie; *b* 29 Feb 1908; *m* 23 June 1944 *Rev John Francis Walmsley, MA, Chaplain RN, of Elsted Rectory, Midhurst, Sussex, and has issue:

1f *John Gerard; *b* 27 Sept 1945; *educ* Rossall (BSc 1969); Lt RN, matriculated with the Lord Lyon 3 March 1961 by reason of his mother's heirship in this line of the family the arms of Walmsley quartering Hamilton, Melrose and Baillie, all within a bordure gules, charged with a martlet argent in dexter chief

3c George Gustavus; *b* 1 Aug 1847; *m* 1882 Helen Price and *d* 10 Dec 1932, having had issue:

1d George; *b* 1883; Lt 28th Bn London Regt WW I; *m* 15 April 1921 Nita (*m* 2nd 30 June 1931 George Edington Bell, of Queen's Gate), yst dau of Maj Hugh J Mackay, JP, of Halkirk, Caithness, and *d* 25 Dec 1929

7b Cospatrick BAILLIE-HAMILTON; *b* 27 Feb 1817; Adml, Kt Medjidie 4th Cl; *m* 10 April 1849 Mary (*d* 17 Nov 1897), only child of Thomas Grove (*see* GROVE, Bt), and *d* 27 Jan 1892, leaving:

1c Mary; *m* 18 July 1872 Rev Spencer Compton Hamilton Spencer Smith and *d* 23 March 1923, having had issue (*see* SPENCER-SMITH, Bt)

2c Charlotte Elizabeth; *m* 25 June 1878 Richard Arthur Hamilton Seymour and *d* 4 Jan 1931, having had issue (*see* CULME-SEYMOUR, Bt)

1b Eleanor; *m* July 1833 Rev Hon William Hugh Scott and *d* 4 Sept 1853, leaving issue (*see* POLWARTH, L)

2b Charlotte Augusta; *m* 9 Aug 1821 Evan Baillie of Dochfour (*see* BURTON, B) and *dsp* 1822

3b Clementina (Hon); Maid of Honour to HM QUEEN VICTORIA; *m* 10 July 1845 Rt Rev Edward Denison (*d* 6 March 1854), DD, Bp Salisbury, and *d* 12 May 1894

(3) Charles; *b* 3 Oct 1727; Lt-Col 1st Dragoon Gds and Govr Blackness Castle 1792–1806; *d* unm 28 Sept 1806

(1) Grizel; *m* 25 July 1745 2nd Earl Stanhope (*d* 7 March 1786) and *d* 28 Dec 1811, having had issue (*see* 1967 edn STANHOPE and CHESTERFIELD, E)

(2) Rachel; *d* unm 20 Oct 1797

2 John; advocate; *m* 8 Dec 1728 Margaret (*d* 27 Dec 1779), dau of Sir John Home, 3rd Bt, of Blackadder (*qv*), and *d* 11 Feb 1772, having had issue:

(1) Margaret; *m* J Buchanan, of Drumpellier

(2) Catherine; *m* 19 Nov 1758 15th Earl of Morton (*qv*) and *d* 25 April 1823, leaving issue

(3) Helen; *m* 3 Dec 1758 4th Earl of Selkirk (*qv*) and *d* 28 Nov 1802, leaving issue

(4) Mary; *m* 1764 Sir John Halkett, 4th Bt (*see* ROSSLYN, E), and *d* 3 Dec 1803, leaving issue

1 Margaret; *d* unm 22 Feb 1768

2 Christian; *m* (contract 17 Dec 1725) Sir James Dalrymple, 2nd Bt, of Hailes (*see* STAIR, E), and *d* 30 June 1770, leaving issue

The 9th EARL's cousin,

GEORGE BAILLIE later BAILLIE-HAMILTON (roy licence 24 March 1859), **10th Earl of Haddington**, DL Haddington; *b* 14 April 1802; rep S peer 1859–70, Ld HC Gen Assembly Ch Scotland 1868, a Ld in Waiting 1867–70; *m* 16 Sept 1824 Georgina (*d* 26 Feb 1873), dau of Ven Robert Markham, Archdeacon York, and *d* 25 June 1870, having had, with other issue:

1 GEORGE, **11th Earl**

2 Robert; *b* 8 Oct 1828; Maj 44th Regt, MP Berwicks 1874–80; *m* 18 July 1861 Mary Gavin (*d* 11 April 1912), dau of Sir John Pringle, 5th Bt (*qv*), and *dsp* 5 Sept 1891

3 Henry, JP Berwicks; *b* 20 Aug 1832; Cdr RN, Kt Medjidie; *m* 17 Oct 1872 his cousin Hon Harriet Frances Scott (*d* 18 March 1925), 3rd dau of 7th Lord Polwarth (*qv*), and *d* 20 Nov 1895, leaving issue:

(1) Georgina; *b* 22 and *d* 23 April 1873

(2) Helen Georgina; *b* 5 June 1874; *m* 14 Jan 1914 her cousin Maj George Douglas Baillie-Hamilton, OBE (*see* above), and *d* 26 April 1951

(3) Amabel Georgina; *b* 1 July 1876; *m* 28 April 1904 Rev Charles Joseph Harland and *d* 20 June 1947, leaving issue

(4) Katherine Ada Georgina; *b* 1879; *d* unm 3 June 1904

(5) Gena Mary; *b* 12 Nov 1882; *d* unm 15 June 1959

(6) Margaret Ellinor Georgina; *b* 14 June 1885; *m* 13 April 1920 Alexander Gibson Kennedy and had issue

4 Arthur Charles (Rev), JP (Suffolk); *b* 16 Feb 1838; *educ* Durham U (MA); Rector Coombs, Vicar Badley; *m* 1866 Alice Anne (*d* 16 Jan 1908), yst dau of Sir David Baird, 2nd Bt, of Newbyth (*qv*), and *d* May 1910, leaving issue:

(1) Margaret; *d* unm 4 Dec 1940

1 Mary; *m* 7 June 1855 Rev Hon Henry Douglas, 3rd s of 18th Earl of Morton (*qv*), and *d* 29 March 1904, leaving issue

2 Georgina Sophia; *m* 17 Oct 1861 Sir Harry Foley Vernon, 1st Bt (*d* 1 Feb 1920; *see* 1940 edn), of Hanbury Hall, Worcs, and *d* 17 Jan 1928, leaving issue

The 10th EARL's est son,

GEORGE BAILLIE-HAMILTON later BAILLIE-HAMILTON-ARDEN (roy licence 31 Dec 1858), **11th Earl of Haddington**, KT (1902), TD, JP Cheshire; *b* 26 July 1827; rep S peer 1874–1917, Ld Lt Haddingtonshire 1876, V-Lt Berwicks, High Sheriff Cheshire 1871, ADC to HM QUEEN VICTORIA, Capt Roy Co Archers, Hon Col Lothians and Border Horse; *m* 17 Oct 1854 Helen Catherine (*d* 29 May 1889), dau of Sir John Warrender, 5th Bt (*see* BRUNTISFIELD, B), and *d* 11 June 1917, having had issue:

1 George, *Lord Binning*, CB, MVO, DL Haddington; *b* 24 Dec 1856; *educ* Trin Coll Cambridge (BA); Lt-Col and Brevet Col cmdg RHG (Blues), T/Brig-Gen while Bde Cdr 1916–17, Egyptian campaign 1882 (medal with clasp, Khedive's Star), Sudan 1884–85 (two clasps), Black Mountain Expdn 1889 (despatches, medal with clasp); Ld Lt and Pres TFA Berwicks; *m* 21 Sept 1892 Katharine Augusta Millicent (*d* 23 Feb 1952), only child of William Severin Salting, and *dvp* 12 Jan 1917, leaving issue:

(1) GEORGE, **12th Earl**

(2) Charles William; *b* 22 May 1900; granted with sis 26 Jan 1918 rank of earl's dau/yr s; MP Bath 1929–31; *m* 17 July 1929 (*divorce* Scottish Courts 1932) Wanda, only dau of Norman Holden, and *dsp* 24 April 1939

(1) Helen; *b* 10 Oct 1893; *m* 23 April 1925 Capt Hon Henry Barnaby O'Brien, MC (*d* 7 Jan 1969), yst surv s of 14th Baron Inchiquin (*qv*), and *d* 17 Sept 1959, leaving issue

2 Richard; *b* 28 Aug 1858; 77th Regt and Lt Rifle Bde; *d* 12 Aug 1881

3 Henry Robert BAILLIE-HAMILTON later BAILLIE-HAMILTON-ARDEN (deed poll 1918), JP (Cheshire); *b* 4 Oct 1862; Capt Coldstream Gds; *d* unm 14 March 1949

1 Ruth; *b* 4 Sept 1855; *d* unm 27 Jan 1941
2 Isabel; *d* an infant, 17 Nov 1859
3 Grisell; *b* 23 April 1861; *d* unm 27 April 1957
4 Cecely; *b* 13 July 1868; *d* unm 24 Oct 1950

The 11th EARL's gs,

GEORGE BAILLIE-HAMILTON, **12th Earl of Haddington**, KT (1952), MC, TD, JP (Berwicks 1952), JP E Lothian; *b* 18 Sept 1894; *educ* Eton; Capt 2nd Dragoons (Scots Greys) WW I (wounded), WW II as W/Cdr RAFVR, Maj 19th (Lothians and Border Horse) Armoured Car Co (TA) and Res of Offrs; rep S peer 1922–58, E Lothian: Ld Lt 1952–70 (V-Lt 1946–52, DL 1929–46), Capt Roy Co Archers, Hon LLD Glasgow 1957, Tstee Nat Library Scotland 1963–86, Chm Tstees Nat Museum Antiquities Scotland, Pres Scottish Georgian Soc; *m* 10 Oct 1923 Sarah (*d* 14 Dec 1995), yst dau of George William Cook, of Westmount, Montreal, and *d* 1986, leaving:

1 JOHN GEORGE BAILLIE-HAMILTON, **13th and present Earl of Haddington**

1 *Mary [The Lady Mary Russell, Combe Manor, Newbury, Berks]; *b* 13 Jan 1934; *m* 1st 21 July 1954 (*divorce* 1965) John Adrian Bailey, er s of Ronald Graham Bailey, of London, and has issue:

(1) *William Anthony; *b* 22 Aug 1957

(2) *Philip Graham; *b* 4 Feb 1959 (HRH PRINCESS ALEXANDRA stood sponsor)

(1) *Arabella Sarah Lucy; *b* 21 April 1955

1 (cont.) Lady Mary Bailey *m* 2nd 1 Oct 1965 *David Russell, s of Brig Hugh Edward Russell, DSO, and has by him:

(3) *Jason Dominic; *b* 2 May 1966; *m* 27 April 1996 *Sybille, er dau of Christopher Gray, of Higginsbrook, Co Meath

(2) *Mariana; *b* 16 June 1968

Seat: Mellerstain, Gordon, Berwicks. The current structure is the work of what turned out to be a father-and-son team of William and Robert Adam, though their work on it was separated by half a century. William had been brought in to build a relatively compact house in the Palladian style for Lady Grizel Baillie (mother-in-law of Lord Binning, father of the **7th Earl**) back in 1725. The result was the twin wings enclosing the forecourt of the present house — unpretentious, somewhat rugged rectangles flanking minute courtyards, that on the east being for the humans, that on the west for the horses (and their human attendants). It was a scheme which would have appealed to Lady Grizel's contemporary and fellow-versifier Swift in that equine quadrupeds and featherless bipeds were placed, as it were, almost on all fours with each other. In some ways the horses seem to have been better accommodated: the east block contains only poky rooms and a cramped staircase.

Following Robert's involvement a more elegant building took shape. He joined the residential quarters to the stables by a central block, a crenellated affair above rather slablike elevations that does not show his talents to advantage. (His father had planned a central block too, something sumptuously baroque after Wren, but it was never started.) Inside things are an entirely different matter. Even Robert Adam's attempts at the gothic come off there (the vaulted ceiling of the long southern passage, for instance). But the predominant style internally is neo-classical, with creamy pistachio- and pale strawberry-mousse-hued ceilings in delicate plasterwork, generous friezes depicting episodes from the Homeric poems, ionic pilasters and other low-relief ornamentation and a medley of delicate motifs such as tazze, wands of Aesculapius, shells, lyres, hautbois, lovers' knots, garlands and even the odd mildly epicene eagle.

HADEN-GUEST

Arms: Sable two flaunches or, three Welsh triple harps in fess counter-changed. **Crest:** A caladrius displayed sable, beaked, legged and charged on the breast with a sun in splendour gold. **Supporters:** Dexter, a leopard sable semée of roundels and grasping in the interior paw a quill gold; sinister, a leopard or semée of roundels and grasping in the interior paw a quill sable. **Motto:** *Non nobis solum nati sumus* ('Not for ourselves alone do we come into the world'). **Creation:** B. (UK) 2 Feb 1950.

THE 5TH BARON HADEN-GUEST, of Saling, Co Essex (Christopher Haden-Guest) [The Rt Hon The Lord Haden-Guest, 253A 26th St, Suite 300, Santa Monica, CA 90402, USA; HC-64 Box 8018, Ketchum, Idaho 83340, USA]; *b* 5 Feb 1948; *s f* 1996; actor (films include *Spinal Tap*); *m* 1984 *Jamie Lee Curtis, actress, dau of the actors Tony Curtis and Janet Leigh, and has adopted:

*Thomas; *b* March 1996

*Anne; *b* 1986

Lineage: ALEXANDER HADEN GUEST; Dr, surgn; had:

LESLIE HADEN GUEST, **1st Baron Haden-Guest**, of Saling, Essex (UK), so *cr* 2 Feb 1950, MC; *b* 10 March 1877; *educ* William Hulme's GS Manchester, Owen's Coll Manchester and Lond Hosp; civil surgn Boer War 1901, Maj RAMC WW I, WW II, MP (Lab) N Southwark 1923–27 and N Islington 1937–50, Chm Nat Medical Manpower Bd 1945–55, Ld in Waiting 1951, MRCS (Eng), LRCP (Lond) 1900, OStJ; *m* 1st 1898 (*divorce* 1909) Edith (*d* 1944), dau of Max Low, of London, and had:

1 STEPHEN HADEN GUEST, **2nd Baron Haden-Guest**; *b* 7 June 1902; *educ* St John's House Sch, Institut St Cyr France and UCL (BA 1922); Br Info Servs 1941–45, edtl advsr American Geographical Soc 1948–54, trans and ed scientific works; *m* 1948 (*divorce* 1954) Barbara Ann, dau of James Harvey Pinson, of W Virginia; *m* 2nd 1968 Dorothy, dau of Thomas Roseberry Good, of Princeton, and *d* 21 Dec 1974, leaving by his 1st w:

(1) *Hadley; *b* 1949; *educ* City U New York (BA 1977)

2 RICHARD HADEN GUEST, **3rd Baron Haden-Guest**; *b* 1904; *educ* Bembridge; *m* 1st 1926 (*divorce* 1934) Hilda, dau of Thomas Russell-Cruise, and had issue:

(1) Susan Elizabeth; *b* 12 April 1930; *m* 27 Nov 1953 *John Orr Stanley, s of Charles Orr Stanley, CBE, of Lisselan, Clonakilty, Co Cork, and had:

1a *Charles Orr Nicholas; *b* 3 Oct 1954

2a *Martin David Anthony; *b* 9 Aug 1956

3a *Shaun Richard; *b* 21 April 1958; *m* 14 July 1984 *Fanny Ann, dau of Hon John Fremantle, only s of 4th Baron Cottesloe (*qv*)

4a *Philip Thomas; *b* 23 Jan 1962

2 (cont.) The **3rd Baron** *m* 2nd 1934 Olivie Maria, dau of Anders Gotfrid Nilsson; *m* 3rd 1949 *Marjorie Douglas [The Rt Hon Marjorie Lady Haden-Guest, 3 Chemin des Crêts-de-Champel, 1206 Geneva, Switzerland], dau of Dr Douglas F Kennard, and *d* 1987, having by his 2nd w had issue:

(1) Brian; *b* 1935; *d* at sea Sept 1951

The **1st Baron** *m* 2nd 1910 Muriel Carmel (*d* 1943), dau of Col Albert Goldsmid; *m* 3rd 10 Jan 1944 Edith Edgar (*d* 1977), MA, PhD, dau of George MacQueen, of Montrose, Angus, and *d* 20 Aug 1960, having by his 2nd w had:

3 David; *k* Spanish Civil War

4 PETER HADEN GUEST, **4th Baron Haden-Guest**; *b* 29 August 1913; *educ* City of London Sch and New Coll Oxford (BA 1934, MA 1938); Lt RCNVR WW II, dancer (as Peter Michael) 1935–41 with Markova-Dolin Ballet, Ballet Divertissement, Ballet Theatre, Ballet Jooss and Repertory Dance Theatre, editorial and theatrical work 1934–42, ed UN Lake Success 1946–50, UN Official 1946–72, Office Conference Servs 1964, Ch Editorial Control UNHQ New York, Ch Ed Dir-Gen UNO's Office Geneva 1967–96, Ch Repertory Editing Gp UNHQ New York; *m* 1st 1939 (*divorce* 1945) Mrs Elizabeth Louise Ruth Coker, est dau of Paul Wolpert, and had:

(1) *Anthony [The Hon Anthony Haden-Guest, Garden Apt, 67 East 80th St, New York, NY 10021, USA]; *b* 1937; *educ* Gordonstoun and St John's Coll Cambridge; jnlst

4 The **4th Baron** *m* 2nd 1945 *Jean Pauline, V-Pres CBS Casting and Talent, dau of Dr Albert George Hindes, and *d* 15 April 1996, leaving:

(2) CHRISTOPHER HADEN GUEST, **5th and present Baron Haden-Guest**

(3) +NICHOLAS [The Hon Nicholas Haden-Guest, 10831 Acama St, N Hollywood, CA 91602, USA]; *b* 5 May 1951; heir presumptive; *educ* New School for Social Research (BA), American Coll Paris, Stella Adler Inst, Herbert Berghof Studio; actor; *m* 1st 1980 (*divorce* 1989) Jill Ellen, dau of Harry Demby, USAF, of S Orange, NJ, and has:

1a *Julia Demby; *b* 1988

(3) (cont.) The Hon Nicholas Haden-Guest *m* 2nd 1989 *Mrs Pamela Ann Rack, dau of Lt Joseph G Seamon, USN, of Akron, Ohio, and formerly w of Thomas John Rack, and has issue:

2a *Elizabeth Ann; *b* 1990

(1) *Elissa; *b* 10 Jan 1953; *m* 1981 *Nicholas Carey Smith, s of Corlies Morgan Smith, and has issue:

1a *Nathanael Haden; *b* 1988

1a *Gena Haden; *b* 1984

1 Angela Haden; MD (1945), MPh (1948); *m* 1948 *Orlando Martinez and was *k* in a car crash 27 Nov 1965

HAGART-ALEXANDER

Arms: Quarterly, 1st and 4th, per pale arg. and sa. a chevron between a fleur-de-lys in chief and a crescent in base all counterchanged, within a bordure per pale gu. and or (for ALEXANDER of Ballochmyle); 2nd, per bend az. and arg., in chief a star of sixteen points or and in base another star of as many points of the first, on a bend sa. a lion passant of the second between two crosses moline of the third (for HAGART of Bantaskine); 3rd, gu. two straight swords in saltire, points downwards ppr., hilted and pommelled or, between two fleur-de-lys in chief and base of the second and two mullets in the flanks arg. (for McCAUL). **Crests:** Dexter, an elephant passant ppr. (for ALEXANDER); sinister, a lion rampant ppr. (for HAGART). **Mottoes:** 1 (over dexter crest) *Perseverantia vincit* ('Perseverance conquers'), 2 (over sinister crest) *Sans peur* ('Without fear'). **Creation:** Bt. (UK) 13 Feb 1886.

SIR CLAUD HAGART-ALEXANDER, 3RD BT, of Ballochmyle, JP (Cumnock and Doon Valley 1983) [Sir Claud Hagart-Alexander Bt JP, Kingencleuch House, Mauchline, Ayrshire KA5 5JL]; *b* 6 Jan 1927; *s gf* 1945; recognised in surname HAGART-ALEXANDER of Ballochmyle by Lord Lyon King of Arms 15 Dec 1948; *educ* Sherborne and Corpus Christi Coll Cambridge (BA 1948); V-Ld Lt Ayrshire and Arran 1983 (DL Ayrshire 1973), MInstMC 1980; *m* 16 April 1959 *Hilda Etain, yr dau of Miles Malcolm Acheson (*see* SAINT ALBANS, D), and has:

1 +CLAUD [Claud Hagart-Alexander Esq, 3820 West 17th Ave, Vancouver, BC, Canada V6S 1A4]; *b* 5 Nov 1963; *educ* Trin Coll Glenalmond and Glasgow U (BSc); *m* 1994 *Elaine Susan, only dau of Vincent Park, of Winnipeg

2 +Boyd John; *b* 11 April 1966; *educ* Trin Coll Glenalmond and Liverpool U

1 *Helenora Etain; *b* 22 May 1960; *m* 1983 *Carl C Smith and has issue:

(1) *Christon Claud William; *b* 1987

(2) *Aidan Boyd Angus; *b* 1988

2 *Anna Joanna Elizabeth; *b* 18 Nov 1961; *m* 14 Jan 1984 *Michael C L Adam, s of C L Adam, and has issue:

(1) *James Robert; *b* 1991

(1) *Charlotte Etain; *b* 1989

Lineage: JOHN ALEXANDER; tenant Paisley Abbey 1472.

A certain JOHN ALEXANDER (possibly kin to or identical with the above) had a s:

ALEXANDER ALEXANDER; held the lands of Candren 1522; *d* in or after 1552, leaving, with an er s (John, living 1552):

ROBERT; bought 1579 a property called Paisley Tak ('Tak' from its being on lease, or in Scotland 'tack'?); *m* Janet Matthie and had:

JOHN ALEXANDER; *m* 1598 Elizabeth Carswell and had, with other issue:

ROBERT ALEXANDER of Blackhouse and Boghall, Ayrshire, and Newton, Renfrewshire; *b* 1604; Baillie Paisley; *m* 1st 1633 Marion, dau of Claud Hamilton of Blackhole by Janet Orr, and had, with other issue:

1 James (Rev), of Boghall; *b* 1634; *m* Mary, dau of John Maxwell of Southbar by Elizabeth, dau of William Cuninghame of Craigends, and had issue

2 CLAUD

ROBERT ALEXANDER *m* 2nd Janet, coheir of David Henderson by Isobel Algeo, and had:

3 Robert; Pncpl Clerk Court of Session; *m* Janet, dau of Alexander Smith of Reidston by Margaret, dau of Maj Hugh Buntein of Kilbryde, and had two daus

4 John; settled Carolina

The 2nd son by the first marriage,

CLAUD ALEXANDER of Newton; *b* 1645; *m* 1677 Jean, dau of William Ralstoun of that Ilk by Ursula, dau of William Mure of Glanderstoun, and had, with other issue:

ROBERT ALEXANDER of Newton; *b* 1681; *m* 1720 his cousin Margaret, dau of Robert Alexander, Yr. of Blackhouse, and *d* 1738, leaving:

CLAUD ALEXANDER of Newton; *b* 1724; *m* 1746 Joanna, dau of Alexander Cuninghame of Craigends by Anne, dau of Sir John Houston of Houston, Bt, and *d* 1772, leaving, with other issue, including two er sons (Robert, *dsp*; Alexander, *d* unm) and a dau (Wilhelmina, Burns's 'Lass of Ballochmyle'):

CLAUD ALEXANDER of Ballochmyle, Ayrshire (bought by him 1783); HEICS; *b* 1752; Paymaster-Gen Forces India; *m* 1788 Helenora, dau of Sir William Maxwell of Springkell, 2nd Bt (*see* HERON-MAXWELL, Bt), and *d* 1809, leaving, with five daus:

1 Claud, of Ballochmyle; *b* 1789; Offr 1st Gds; *m* Elizabeth, dau of Col — Keatinge by Lady Martha Brabazon, dau of 8th Earl of Meath (*qv*), and *dsp* 1845

2 William Maxwell, of Southbar; *b* 1790; *d* unm 1853

3 Boyd, of Ballochmyle and Southbar; *b* 1796; *m* 17 Jan 1828 Sophia Elizabeth (*d* 19 Oct 1859), dau of Sir Benjamin Hobhouse, 1st Bt (*qv*), and had, with other issue:

(1) CLAUD (Sir) **1st Bt**

(2) John Hobhouse Inglis, of Southbar, CB; Capt RN, ADC to HM QUEEN VICTORIA, Offr Legn Hon; *b* 1832; *m* 23 Jan 1860 Isabella Barbara (*m* 2nd April 1881 John Archibald Shaw Stewart (*see* SHAW-STEWART, Bt); *d* 1883), dau of Thomas Cochran Hume, and *d* 22 Nov 1875, leaving issue

BOYD ALEXANDER *d* Oct 1861; his est son,

Sir Claud Alexander of Ballochmyle, 1st Bt (UK), so *cr* 13 Feb 1886, JP, DL Ayrshire and Renfrewshire; Maj-Gen Gren Gds Crimea, MP S Ayrshire 1874–1885; *b* 15 Jan 1831; *m* 12 Feb 1863 Eliza (*d* 16 July 1927), only dau of Alexander Spiers, of Elderslie, MP, by Eliza, *née* Hagart of Bantaskine, and *d* 23 May 1899, leaving:

Sir Claud Alexander, 2nd Bt, JP Ayrshire; Lt 3rd Bn Roy Scots Fus; *b* 24 Feb 1867; *educ* New Coll Oxford (BA); *m* 1st 14 Dec 1889 (*divorce* 1894) Lady Diana Montgomerie (*d* 27 Oct 1914), yst dau of 14th Earl of Eglinton and (2nd Earl of) Winton (*qv*), and *d* 18 March 1945, leaving:

1 Arnulph Claud; *b* 6 Sept 1891; *d* 6 Jan 1892

2 Wilfrid Archibald; Consular Serv China; *b* 6 Oct 1892; *m* 17 Nov 1919 Mary Prudence (*d* 25 July 1960), dau of Guy Francis Hamilton Acheson, Commr Customs China, and *d* 26 March 1927, leaving issue:

(1) Sir CLAUD HAGART-ALEXANDER, **3rd and present Bt**

(1) Mary Primrose; *b* 17 Dec 1921; *m* 30 Dec 1947 Lt-Col John Edward Margesson, MBE, S Wales Bdrs, only s of Maj Edward Cuninghame Margesson, and had issue:

1a *Richard William; *b* 10 Dec 1948; *educ* Wellington and Bristol U

2a *John Bertram; *b* 27 Oct 1950; *educ* Wellington

3a *Hugh David; *b* 25 March 1954; *educ* Wellington

(2) *Penelope Marion Acheson [Lady Head, 63 Chantry View Rd, Guildford, Surrey GU1 3XU]; *b* 9 Aug 1924; *m* 25 Jan 1967, as his 2nd w, *Sir Francis David Somerville Head, 5th Bt (*qv*)

Sir Claud *m* 2nd 28 Jan 1896 Rachel Belasyse (*d* 1 Feb 1944), yst dau of Rev Henry Holden, DD, and by her had:

3 Claud; Lt-Col REME WW II (despatches four times); *b* 4 June 1897; *educ* Eton; *m* 1st 1 Feb 1928 Maude (*d* 23 March 1936), only dau of Lt-Col John Oswald Clazey; *m* 2nd 8 Nov 1949 *Peggy, formerly w of Bernard Lawrence Silley (*see* SAINT ALBANS, D) and dau of Ewart Raby Le Mare, of Birchington, Kent, and *d* 1976, leaving by his 1st w:

(1) +John Oswald Claud, CB (1991), OBE (1974); *b* 23 March 1936; *educ* Marlborough and RMA Sandhurst; Maj-Gen Roy Signals; *m* 22 Dec 1962 *Mary Jean, dau of Col Derek Grant Birkett, OBE, RA, and has issue:

1a *Liza Jane; *b* 3 Oct 1964

2a *Sharon Louise; *b* 3 July 1968

4 Boyd; *b* 3 Dec 1902

1 Wilhelmina; *b* 18 May 1907

HAIG

Arms: Az. a saltire between two mullets in chief and base, and a decrescent and increscent in fess arg. **Crest:** A rock ppr. **Supporters:** Dexter, a bay horse caparisoned, thereon mounted a trooper of the 7th (QO) Hussars, habited, armed and accoutred; sinister, a bay horse caparisoned, thereon mounted a lancer of the 17th (Duke of Cambridge's Own) Lancers, habited, armed and accoutred, all ppr. **Motto:** Tyde what may. **Creation:** E. V and B. (UK) 29 Sept 1919.

THE 2ND EARL HAIG, Viscount Dawick and **Baron Haig**, of Bemersyde, Co Berwick (George Alexander Eugene Douglas Haig, OBE (1966), DL (Ettrick, Lauderdale and Roxburghshire 1977–, Roxburghshire and Berwickshire 1952–67)) [The Rt Hon The Earl Haig OBE DL, Bemersyde, Melrose, Roxburghshire TD6 9DP]; *b* 15 March 1918; *s* f 1928, also as 30th of Bemersyde; *educ* Stowe and Ch Ch Oxford (BA 1939, MA 1950); Page of Hon to HM GEORGE VI Coronation 1937; 2nd Lt 1938, Hon Maj HG 1958, Capt RSG WW II 1939–42 (POW), memb Roy Co Archers; memb: Roy Fine Art Commn Scotland 1958, Scottish Arts Cncl 1969–75; pres: Border Area Br Legion 1955–61, Scottish Craft Centre 1950–75, Br Cwlth Ex-Services League 1960–96, Earl Haig Fund Scotland 1980–86 and Offrs' Assoc Scotland 1987–96 (chm 1977–87); Nat Cm Br Legion Scotland 1962–65 (Pres1980–86); chm SE Scotland Disablement Advsy Ctee 1960–73; tstee: Scottish Nat War Meml 1961–96 (chm Bd 1983–96) and Nat Galleries Scotland 1962–72; FRSA 1951, Assoc Roy Scottish Academy 1988, V-Lt Berwickshire 1967–70, KStJ 1977; *m* 1st 19 July 1956 (*divorce* 1981) Adrienne Thérèse, only dau of Derrick Morley, of Wickhambreux, Kent; *m* 2nd 1981 *Gerolama Lopez y Royo di Taurisano and by his 1st w has issue:

1 +ALEXANDER DOUGLAS DERRICK, *Viscount Dawick*; *b* 30 June 1961; *educ* Stowe

1 *(Adrienne) Rainà; *b* 19 Feb 1958

2 *(Elizabeth) Vivienne Thérèse; *b* 1 March 1959

Lineage: JOHN HAIG, of Cameron Bridge, Fife, JP, 6th in descent from Robert Haig, of St Ninian's (2nd s of James Haig, 17th of Bemersyde); *b* 24 Oct 1802; *m* 20 Aug 1839 Rachel Mackerras (*d* 21 March 1879), dau and coheir of Hugh Veitch, of Stewartfield, and *d* 20 March 1878, having had, with other issue:

DOUGLAS HAIG, **1st Earl Haig**, so *cr* 29 Sept 1919, as also VISCOUNT DAWICK and BARON HAIG, of Bemersyde, Co Berwick (all UK), KT (1917), GCB (1916, KCB 1913, CB 1900), OM (1919), GCVO (1916, KCVO 1909, CVO 1903), KCIE (1911), DL Co Glasgow; *b* 19 June 1861; *educ* Clifton, BNC Oxford (Hon Fell 1915), RMC Sandhurst and Staff Coll; joined 7th Hus 1885, Capt 1891, Brevet Maj 1889, Egyptian Cav 1897–98, Nile Expdn 1898, present Battles of Atbara and Khartoum (despatches, Egyptian medal with two clasps), Boer War 1899–1902 (despatches, Queen's medal with seven clasps, King's medal), Brevet Lt-Col 1900, Lt-Col cmdg 17th Lancers 1901, Extra ADC to HM EDWARD VII 1902, Inspr-Gen Cav India 1903, Maj-Gen 1904, Dir Mil Trg 1906, Dir Staff Duties 1907, Ch Staff India 1909–11, GOC-in-C Aldershot Cmd 1912–14, Lt-Gen 1914, ADC Gen to HM GEORGE V 1914, cmded 1st Army Corps BEF 1914, 1st Br Army France 1914–15, C-in-C BEF Dec 1915–19, FM 1917, GOC-in-C GB 1919; Col: 17th/21st Lancers, RHG, KOSB, Hon Col 14th Bn Lond Regt (London Scottish) (TA), Hon LLD St Andrews, Glasgow, Aberdeen, Edin, Cantab, U of Wales, Sheffield, Manchester, Leeds, Durham and Bristol, DCL Oxford, Chllr St Andrews 1922; *m* 11 July 1905 Hon Dorothy Maud (*d* 18 Oct 1939), DGSt, Maid of Hon to TM QUEENs VICTORIA and ALEXANDRA, 2nd dau of 3rd Baron Vivian (*qv*), and *d* 30 Jan 1928, leaving issue:

1 GEORGE ALEXANDER EUGENE DOUGLAS HAIG, **2nd and present Earl Haig**

1 Alexandra Henrietta Louisa; *b* 9 March 1907 (HM QUEEN ALEXANDRA stood sponsor); *m* 1st 10 June 1941 (*divorce* 1954) R-Adml Clarence Dinsmore Howard-Johnston, CB, DSO, DSC, s of John Howard-Johnston by Countess Pierre de Breuil de St Germain; *m* 2nd 4 Oct 1954 *Baron Dacre of Glanton (LP, *qv*) and *d* 15 Aug 1997, leaving by her 1st husb:

(1) *James Douglas; *b* 12 March 1942 (HRH THE DUCHESS OF GLOUCESTER stood sponsor); *educ* Eton and Ch Ch Oxford (Jr Lecturer 1966), DPhil 1971; U Lecturer Byzantine History 1971, memb (Lab) Oxford Cncl 1972; *m* 24 June 1978 *Angela Maureen, novelist as Angela Huth, er dau of Harold Huth and formerly w of Quentin Crewe (*see* 1940 edn CREWE, M), and has:

1a *Eugenie; *b* 1981

(2) *Philip Peter Dawyck [Philip Howard-Johnston Esq, 4 Craiglockhart Ave, Edinburgh EH14 1DG]; *b* 25 Sept 1950 (HRH THE DUKE OF EDINBURGH stood sponsor); *educ* Clifton; *m* 1990 *Mrs Jaqueline J Mathieson, yr dau of Dr James Robert Kyles, of Lundin Links, Fife, and has issue:

1a *Jessica Emily; *b* 1993

(1) *Xenia Violet [Mrs Lyle Dennen, 92 Vassall Rd, London SW9 6JA]; Ed Russian Christian mag; *b* 11 March 1944; *educ* Cranborne Chase, St Anne's Coll Oxford (BA, MA) and London U (MSc); *m* 5 Nov 1977 *Rev Lyle Dennen, yr s of Ernest Dennen, of Beverly Hills, California, and has issue:

1a *Richard Sergei John; *b* 1980

2a *John Dawyck Alexei; *b* 1982

2 Victoria Doris Rachel; *b* 7 Nov 1908 (HRH PRINCESS VICTORIA stood sponsor); *m* 10 Aug 1929 (*divorce* 1951) Brig Claud Andrew Montagu-Douglas-Scott, DSO (*see* BUCCLEUCH and QUEENSBERRY, D), and *d* 1993, leaving issue

3 *Irene Violet Freesia Janet Augusta; *b* 7 Oct 1919; CStJ, hon life memb Cwlth Press Union 1985; *m* 4 Oct 1945 2nd Baron Astor of Hever (*qv*) and has issue

HAILSHAM OF ST MARYLEBONE

Arms: Argent three boar's heads erased azure, langued gules, between two flaunches azure, each charged with a crescent of the field. **Crest:** Out of an eastern crown argent an oak-tree fructed proper, pendant therefrom an escutcheon azure, charged with a dexter arm embowed in armour, the hand grasping an arrow in bend sinister, the point downwards, also proper. **Supporters:** On either side a ram argent armed and unguled or, gorged with a baron's coronet, the dexter supporting a representation of the Lord High Chancellor's mace, the sinister a representation of the Lord High Chancellor's purse, with the initials of Her Majesty Queen Elizabeth II, proper. **Motto:** *Dat gloria vires* ('Glory gives strength'). **Creation:** B. (UK) 5 April 1928 and (LP, UK) 3 June 1970 , V. (UK) 4 July 1929.

THE BARON HAILSHAM OF ST MARYLEBONE, of Herstmonceux, Co Sussex (Sir Quintin McGarel Hogg, KG (1988), CH (1974), PC (1956)) [The Rt Hon The Lord Hailsham of St Marylebone KG CH PC, House of Lords, London SW1A 0PW]; *b* 9 Oct 1907; *s* f as 2nd Viscount Hailsham 1950, disclaimed titles for life 20 Nov 1963; *educ* Eton and Ch Ch Oxford (MA, Hon Student 1962); Fell All Souls 1931–38 and 1962–; barrister Lincoln's Inn 1932, QC 1953, Bencher 1956; WW II: commissioned Rifle Bde TA, Maj 1942; MP (Nat C) Oxford City 1938–58, St Marylebone 1963–70; Jt Parly U-Sec Air 1945, First Ld Admlty 1956–57, Min Educn 1957, Dep Leader Ho Lds 1957–60; Ld Pres Cncl 1957–59 and 1960–64, Chm C Party Organisation 1957–59, Ld Privy Seal 1959–60, Sec State DES 1959–64, Leader Ho Lds 1960–63, Ld Chllr 1970–74 and 1979–87; Rector Glasgow U 1959; Pres Classical Assoc 1960–61; Chllr Buckingham U 1983–91; Hon Bencher NI Inn of Court 1981; Hon DCL: Westminster Coll Fulton, Mo., 1960, Newcastle 1964, Oxford 1974; Hon LLD: Cantab 1963, Delhi 1972, St Andrews 1979, Leeds 1982; Hon DLitt Ulster 1988; FRS 1973, Hon FICE 1963, Hon FIEE 1972, Hon FIStructE 1960, Hon Freeman Merchant Taylors' Co 1971; *m* 1st 1931(*divorce* 1943) Natalie Antoinette (*d* 1987), dau of Alan Sullivan, of Sheerland House, Pluckley, Kent, formerly of Toronto; *m* 2nd 18 April 1944 Mary Evelyn (*d* 10 March 1978 in a riding accident), only child of Richard Martin, of Ross, Co Galway, and Kensington (n of Violet Martin, the 'Ross' of Somerville and Ross), and by her has:

1 +DOUGLAS MARTIN, PC (1992), QC (1990) [The Rt Hon Douglas Hogg QC, MP, House of Commons, London SW1 0AA]; *b* 5 Feb 1945; *educ* Eton and Ch Ch Oxford; barrister Lincoln's Inn 1968; MP (C) Grantham 1979–97 and Sleaford and N Hykeham 1997–, Assist Govt Whip 1983–84, Home Office: Parly U-Sec 1986–89, Min State 1986–90, Min State FCO 1990–95, Min MAFF with Cabinet seat 1995–97; *m* 1968 *Baroness Hogg (*qv*) and has:

(1) +Quintin John Neil Martin; *b* 12 Oct 1973; with Lazard's corp fin dept
(1) *Charlotte Mary; *b* 26 Aug 1970

2 +James Richard Martin; *b* 1951; *educ* Eton; Capt Gren Gds; *m* 1987 *D Clare, yr da of Maurice Raffael, of Wimbledon

1 *Mary Claire, DBE (1995) [The Hon Mrs Justice Hogg, DBE, Royal Courts of Justice, Strand, London WC2A 2LL]; *b* 15 Jan 1947; *educ* St Pau's Girls' Sch; barrister Lincoln's Inn 1968, Assist Recorder 1986–90, QC (1989), Recorder 1990–95, High Court Judge Family Div 1995–; *m* 1987 *Eric Koops, est s of Leendart Koops, of Hellingly, Sussex, and has:
(1) *William Quintin Eric; *b* 1991
(1) *Katharine Mary; *b* 1989

2 *Frances Evelyn, JP [The Hon Mrs Hoare JP, Tangier House, Wootton St Lawrence, Hants RG23 8PH]; *b* 11 Nov 1949; *educ* St Paul's Girls' Sch and Homerton Coll Cambridge; *m* 19 Oct 1970 *Richard Quintin Hoare, s of Quintin Vincent Hoare, and has issue:
(1) *Alexander Richard Quintin; *b* 1973
(2) *Charles Martin Richard; *b* 1976
(1) *Elizabeth Mary; *b* 1 June 1978

3 *Katharine Amelia; *b* 18 Oct 1962; *educ* Roedean and St Peter's Coll Oxford; *m* 1993 *Richard A Collins, s of C A Collins, of Penarth, S Glam

The BARON HAILSHAM OF ST MARYLEBONE *m* 3rd 1986 *Deirdre, er dau of Capt Peter Shannon by Mrs Margaret Briscoe

Lineage: DOUGLAS McGAREL HOGG, **1st Viscount Hailsham**, of Hailsham, Co Sussex, so *cr* 4 July 1929, as also 5 April 1928 BARON HAILSHAM, of Hailsham, Co Sussex (both UK), PC (1922), KC (1917), JP (E Sussex); *b* 28 Feb 1872 (s of Quintin Hogg; *see* HOGG Bt); *educ* Eton; with a firm of West India merchants, served Boer War 1900–01, barrister Lincoln's Inn 1902, Bencher 1920, ktd 1922, Recorder Kingston-upon-Thames 1924–28, Attorney-Gen to HRH THE PRINCE OF WALES, Memb Cncl Duchy Cornwall 1920–22; MP (C) St Marylebone 1922–28, Attorney-Gen 1922–24 and 1924–28; Actg PM Aug-Sept 1928, Ld Chllr 1928–29 and 1935–38, Leader Oppn Ho Lds 1931, Sec State War and Leader Ho Lds 1931, Ld Pres Cncl 1938; Hon LLD Birmingham, Cantab and Queen's U Belfast, Hon DLitt Reading, Hon DCL Oxford; *m* 1st 14 Aug 1905 Elizabeth (*d* 1925), dau of Judge James Trimble Brown, of Nashville, Tenn., Govr Tenn. and US Amb Russia 1853, and widow of Hon Archibald John Marjoribanks (*see* 1935 edn TWEEDMOUTH, B), and had:

1 QUINTIN McGAREL HOGG; **2nd Viscount Hailsham**; disclaimed hereditary peerages 1963; *cr* a **Baron**

2 (William) Neil McGarel; *b* 1910; *educ* Eton; Dip Serv; *d* 13 Feb 1995

The **1st Viscount** *m* 2nd 3 Jan 1929 Mildred Margaret (*d* 1964), dau of Rev Edward Parker Dew, Rector and Patron Breamore, Hants, and widow of Hon Alfred Clive Lawrence (*see* OAKSEY, TREVETHIN and, B), and *d* 16 Aug 1950

HALIFAX

Arms: Quarterly, 1st and 4th, azure three naked savages ambulant in fess proper, in the dexter hand of each a shield argent charged with a cross gules, in the sinister a club resting on the shoulder, also proper; on a canton erminois three lozenges conjoined in fess sable (for WOOD); 2nd and 3rd, paly bendy or and azure, a canton ermine (for BUCK). **Crest**: A savage as in the arms, the shield sable charged with a griffin's head erased argent. **Supporters**: On either side a gryphon sable gorged with a collar, pendant therefrom a portcullis or. **Motto**: I like my choice. **Creations:** Bt. (GB) 22 Jan 1784, V. (UK) 21 Feb 1866, B. (UK) 22 Dec 1925), E. (UK) 11 July 1944.

THE 3RD EARL OF HALIFAX, Viscount Halifax of Monk Bretton, in the W Riding of the Co of York, **Baron Irwin**, of Kirby Underdale, Co York, and a **Baronet** (Sir (Charles) Edward Peter Neil Wood, Bt, JP (Wilton Beacon 1985)) [The Rt Hon The Earl of Halifax JP, Garrowby, York YO4 1QD]; *b* 14 March 1944; *s* f 1980; *educ* Eton and Ch Ch Oxford; V-Ld Lt E R Yorks 1996–, KStJ, dir: Hambros Bank 1978– and Yorkshire Post Newspapers 1985–96, fought (C) Dearne Valley Feb and Oct 1974 gen elections, High Steward York Minster 1988–, DL (Humberside 1983–96); *m* 17 Nov 1976 *Camilla, dau of Charles Frank Johnston Younger, DSO, TD (*d* 6 June 1995), of Painsthorpe Hall, Kirby Underdale, York, and formerly w of Richard Eustace Parker-Bowles (*see* MACCLESFIELD, E), and has issue:

1 +JAMES CHARLES, *Lord Irwin*; *b* 24 Aug 1977
1 *Joanna Victoria; *b* 15 Jan 1980

Earldom of Halifax: There have been three other creations under this designation, none of whose holders have been related to the WOODs who hold the present title. The earliest creation was that of 1679, conferred on George Saville [*sic*] (1633–95), a remote cousin of the Savile Earls of Mexborough (*qv*) who had been created Viscount Halifax 18 months earlier. Saville was an MP and is thought to have won his peerage for his parents' enthusiastic royalism during the Commonwealth and Protectorate periods. He was shortly afterwards promoted Marquess of Halifax and is known to history as the 'Trimmer', from his changing position so often, though Macaulay put up a strong argument for his being reckoned a consistent moderate. He was the Jotham of Dryden's *Absalom and Achitophel*. This Earldom expired in 1700.

The second creation was that of 1714, conferred on Charles Montague (1661–1715), a grandson of the 1st Earl of Manchester (*see* MANCHESTER, D) and Chancellor of the Exchequer 1694–99, in which capacity he reformed the coinage, as well as First Lord of the Treasury 1697–99 and 1714–15. Montague was an expert in public finance and originator not only of the national debt and the Bank of England but exchequer bills. One of his political opponents was Charles Duncombe, so it is a curious coincidence that a daughter of the 1st Earl of Halifax of the present creation should have married Duncombe's collateral desendent Lord Feversham (*qv*). Another coincidence is that whereas it was a Montague Lord Halifax who as Chancellor of the Exchequer imposed the window tax in 1695/6 it was a Wood Lord Halifax who as Chancellor of the Exchequer abolished it in 1851.

Charles Montague's nephew George Montague was created Earl of Halifax three weeks after his uncle's death. George's son, another George, was Lord Lieutenant of Ireland 1761–63, briefly First Lord of the Admiralty in 1762 and Lord Privy Seal 1770–71. On his death the Earldom expired.

The 1st Earl of Halifax of the present creation has gone down to history as the foreign secretary who carried out with Neville Chamberlain the deluded policy of appeasement towards Hitler in the late 1930s. He was reckoned to be a possible contender for the premiership on Chamberlain's fall in 1940 but after Churchill took over was sent off to Washington as ambassador. Andrew Roberts's biography of him, *The Holy Fox* (1992), is a partial rehabilitation.

Lineage: GEORGE WOOD, of Monk Bretton, near Barnsley, West Riding, a manor he bought *c* 1610; had:

GEORGE WOOD, of Monk Bretton; *d* 1638 leaving, with other issue, including two yr sons (John, settled at Smithies, Yorks, and was ancestor of Sir George Wood (1743–1824), Baron of the Exchequer and MP Haslemere 1796–1806; Peter, *k* at one of the six sieges of Leipzig during the Thirty Years War):

ROBERT WOOD, of Monk Bretton; *d* 1676, leaving, with other issue, including an er s (William, of Monk Bretton):

HENRY WOOD, of Barnsley, Yorks; *b* 5 July 1645; *m* as his 3rd w Elizabeth, dau of William Simpson, of Stainforth, Yorks, and Babworth, Notts, by Elizabeth, dau of William Lindley and sis of Francis Lindley, of Bowling Hall, Yorks, and *d* 4 May 1720, leaving, with six daus, an est s (Henry, *d* 1741) and a yst s (Simpson, Lt Foot Gds, *d* 1746):

FRANCIS WOOD, of Barnsley, JP, DL Yorks; *bapt* 23 July 1696; *m* 1st Mary Dorothy, dau of Rev Charles Palmer, DD, Rector Long Marston, Preb York (2nd s of Sir William Palmer, of The Hill, Beds, by Anne, dau of Sir Stephen Thompson (*see* MEYSEY-THOMPSON, Bt)); *m* 2nd Rebecca (*dsp*), dau of William Ellison, and *d* 30 March or Aug 1775, having by his 1st w had, with two daus (*d* unm):

1 Henry (Rev); *bapt* 22 Feb 1726; *educ* Cambridge (DD); Vicar Halifax, Rector and Ld Manor Hemsworth, Yorks, chaplain to Br Factory, Oporto, Portugal; *m* 17– Elizabeth, dau and coheir with her sis Florence, w of 3rd Earl Cowper (*see* LUCAS OF CRUDWELL, B), of Charles Gore, of Horkstowe, Lincs, and *dsps* 27 Oct 1790

2 **Sir Francis Wood, 1st Bt** (GB), so *cr* 22 Jan 1784, with remainder to issue of his f , of Barnsley, Yorks; *bapt* 2 Jan 1729; *m* 5 June 1779 Elizabeth, dau and heiress of Anthony Ewer, of The Lea, of Bushey Hall, Herts, and Swine in Holderness, E R Yorks (which passed on her death to the 5th Earl of Shaftesbury, *qv*), and *dsp* 1 or 9 July 1795

3 Charles, of Bowling Hall, nr Bradford, which he inherited 1770 from his kinsman Thomas Pigot; *bapt* 13 Feb 1731; Capt RN; *m* 6 Jan 1770 Caroline (*d* 30 May 1814), dau and coheir of Thomas Lacon Barker, of Otley, Yorks, and *d* 9 Oct 1782 of wounds recd in action off Madras, leaving:
(1) FRANCIS LINDLEY (Sir), **2nd Bt**
(2) Henry; Maj 3rd Dragoons
(1) Caroline; *m* 1800 William Bousfield, JP, DL (*d* 12 Sept 1851), of Upwood, and *dsp* 8 April 1839
(2) Dorothea; *m* Charles Armstrong, of Twyford, Berks
(3) Elizabeth; *m* Edward O'Reilly and *d* Feb 1845

4 John; Offr under his relative Gen Wolfe; *ka* against the French at Halifax, NS, 5 June 1760

The 1st Bt's n,

Sir Francis Lindley Wood, 2nd Bt, of Bowling Hall; *b* 16 Dec 1771; *educ* Emmanuel Coll Cambridge (BA 1793, MA 1796); High Sheriff Yorks 1814–15; *m* 15 Jan 1798 Anne (*d* 11 Jan 1841), dau and coheir of Samuel Buck, of New Grange, Yorks, Recorder Leeds, and *d* 31 Dec 1846, having had, with a yr s (Samuel Francis, *b* 1 Aug 1809, *d* unm 22 April 1843) and a dau (Anne, *m* 29 March 1824 John Walbanke Childers, MP, of Cantley, Yorks, and *d* 24 June 1863, leaving issue):

Sir Charles Wood, 3rd Bt, and **1st Viscount Halifax of Monk Bretton**, in the West Riding of the County of York (UK), so *cr* 21 Feb 1866, GCB (1856), PC (1846); *b* 20 Dec 1800; *educ* Eton and Oriel Coll Oxford (BA 1821, MA 1824); MP (Whig, later Lib): Gt Grimsby 1826–31, Wareham 1831–32, Halifax 1832–65 and Ripon 1865–66, Jt Sec Treasury 1832–34, Sec Admlty 1835–39, Chllr Exchequer 1846–52, Pres Bd Control India 1852–55, 1st Ld Admlty 1855–58, Sec State India

1859–66, Ld Privy Seal 1870–74; *m* 30 July 1829 Lady Mary Grey, CI (*d* 6 July 1884), 5th dau of 2nd Earl Grey (*qv*), and *d* 8 Aug 1885, having had:

1 CHARLES LINDLEY, **2nd Viscount**

2 Francis Lindley; *b* 17 Oct 1841; Capt RN; *d* 14 Oct 1873

3 Henry John Lindley, DL (W R Yorks); *b* 12 Jan 1843; *educ* Cambridge (BA); Lt-Col 12th Lancers Ashanti Campaign 1874, Cyprus 1878, Zulu War 1879; *m* 2 March 1897 Laura Adeline (*d* 25 Sept 1926), dau of Ernest Thellusson and widow of James Montagu, of Melton Park, Doncaster, and *d* 5 Jan 1903, leaving:

(1) Emily Mary Marguerite, MBE (1943), JP (W R Yorks); *b* 29 Sept 1899; VAD Cmdnt WW II; *d* unm 5 Nov 1969

4 Frederick George Lindley WOOD later MEYNELL (roy licence 8 Feb 1905), of Hoar Cross, Burton-on Trent, Staffs; *b* 4 June 1846; *educ* Cambridge (BA); barrister, High Sheriff Staffs 1910; *m* 9 May 1878 Lady Mary Susan Felicie Lindsay (*d* 27 Nov 1937), 3rd dau of 25th Earl of Crawford and (8th Earl of) Balcarres (*qv*), and *d* 4 Nov 1910, leaving:

(1) Francis Hugo Lindley, DSO (1917), JP, DL (Staffs), of Hoar Cross; *b* 14 April 1880; Lt-Col RFA (TA) 1914–17 (wounded, despatches), Hon Col 1935; *m* 3 Oct 1907 Lady Dorothy Legge, OBE (1945) (*d* 28 July 1974), er dau of 6th Earl of Dartmouth (*qv*), and *d* 16 Dec 1941, having had issue:

1a Hugo, MC (1943), JP, DL; *b* 1 Nov 1909; *educ* Eton and Ch Ch Oxford; Col Staffs Yeo WW II (despatches); *m* 25 June 1936 Dorothy Jean Hosta Henriette (*d* 1993), est dau of Sir Edward Henry Goschen, 2nd Bt (*qv*), and *d* 22 June 1960, leaving issue:

1b Nicholas Edward Hugo; *b* 27 Oct 1937; *educ* Eton; *m* 5 Jan 1966 (*divorce* 1987) Hon Alexandra Rachel Mary Catherine Angelica Lampson, er dau of 2nd Baron Killearn (*qv*), and *d* 1988, leaving issue:

1c +Hugo Graham Nicholas; *b* 24 Feb 1970

2c +Alexander Frederick Miles; *b* 6 June 1972

2b +David Christian Francis [David Meynell Esq, Hollybush Park, Newborough, Burton-on-Trent, Staffs DE13 8SF]; *b* 14 Jan 1940; *educ* Eton; *m* 29 Sept 1962 *Susan Lesley, only child of George M Garfield-Jones, of The Mount, Shrewsbury, and has issue:

1c +Charles Christian George; *b* 1964; *educ* Eton; Capt Life Gds; *m* 1992 *Elizabeth (Liz) Zoë, yst dau of Dr Patrick Lawrence, of Iffley, Oxford, and has issue:

1d +Cosmo Frederick Charles; *b* 2 April 1995

2c +Edward David Lindley; *b* 6 April 1971; *educ* Eton

1c *Melissa Alexandra Elizabeth Susanna; *b* 1968

3b +Frederick James [Frederick Meynell Esq, Oaklands Cottage, East Tytherley, Wilts SP5 1LL]; *b* 14 July 1944; *educ* Eton; *m* 1st 15 April 1969 (*divorce* 1973) Charmian Joy, yst dau of Maj Harcourt Michael Scudamore Gold, MC, TD, of West Stratton House, Winchester, by his 2nd w Hon Jocelyne Mary Boot, 2nd dau of 2nd and last Baron Trent (*see* 1956 edn); *m* 2nd 1975 *Mary Anne, dau of Trevor Leslie Harris, of Romsey, Hants, and by her has:

1c *Sophie Louise; *b* 1980

2c *Lucinda Mary; *b* 1983

1b *(Karen) Elizabeth Mary [The Hon Mrs George Jeffreys, Cotswold House, Condicote, Glos GL54 1ES]; *b* 27 Feb 1947; *m* 3 April 1967 *Capt Hon George Christian Darell Jeffreys, bro of 2nd Baron Jeffreys (*qv*), and has:

1c *Christopher George Hugo; *b* 1984

1c *Zara Serena; *b* 1972

2c *Susannah Elizabeth; *b* 1975

2b *Alexandra Dorothy Jean [The Rt Hon The Lady Tollemache, Helmingham Hall, Stowmarket, Suffolk IP14 6EF]; *b* 17 July 1949; *m* 24 Feb 1970 *5th Baron Tollemache (*qv*) and has issue

2a Frederick; *b* 23 July 1911; *d* 25 March 1920

3a +Mark (Rev) [The Rev Canon Mark Meynell, 2 Double St, Framlingham, Suffolk IP13 9BN]; *b* 19 Feb 1914; *educ* Eton and Ch Ch Oxford (MA); Rector Marlesford with Campsea Ashe, St Edmundsbury and Ipswich 1949–56 and Cogenhoe, Northants, 1956–65, Vicar Leamington Hastings 1965, Canon Theologian Emeritus Coventry; *m* 4 July 1940 *Diana Mary, 2nd dau of Col Sir Charles Edward Ponsonby, 1st Bt (*qv*), and has:

1b +Christopher Mark [Christopher Meynell Esq, Bergh Apton Hall, Bergh Apton, Norwich NR15 1AX]; *b* 18 Aug 1941; *educ* Eton; *m* 12 Oct 1968 *Hon Elizabeth Margaret Gretton, yr dau of 2nd Baron Gretton (*qv*), and has:

1c +Mark John Henryk; *b* 22 Dec 1970; *m* 12 April 1997 *Rachel, er dau of Graham Carr, of Uganda

2c +Guy Francis; *b* 28 April 1973

2b +Andrew Francis (Rev) [The Rev Andrew Meynell, 34 Dobbins Lane, Wendover, Bucks HP22 6 DH]; *b* 6 Nov 1943; *educ* Eton; *m* 11 Dec 1971 *Caroline Anne, 2nd dau of Sir John Gardiner Sumner Hobson, OBE, TD, PC, QC, JP, sometime MP (C) Warwick and Leamington, and has:

1c +Aidan Jonathan Charles; *b* 1974

1c *Francesca Clare; *b* 29 Oct 1976

3b +Peter John; *b* 25 Nov 1947; *educ* Eton; *m* 1973 *Judith, dau of Sir Neil Marten, PC, late MP (C) Banbury, and has:

1c +Marten Charles; *b* 11 Nov 1977

1c *Anna Louise; *b* 1979

2c *Clea Diana; *b* 1982

1b *Anna Mary Barbara [Mrs Louis de Soissons, Ivy Farm, Witton, Norfolk NR28 9TT]; *b* 6 Jan 1960; *m* 1986 *Louis Thomas de Soissons, est s of Brian de Soissons, of Swafield Hall, Norwich, and has:

1c *Alexander Thomas; *b* 1988

2c *Hugo Charles; *b* 1991

3c *Guy Louis; *b* 18 Dec 1996

1a Dorothy Emily, CVO (1959, MVO 1955); *b* 24 Sept 1908; Ldy-in-Waiting to HRH THE DUCHESS OF GLOUCESTER 1947–59, Extra-Ldy-in-Waiting thereafter, served BRC WW II (despatches); *d* unm

2a *Rachel [Mrs John Winter, Audmore House, Gnosall, Staffs]; *b* 27 June 1917; *m* 18 Oct 1941 *John Kift Winter, MA, est s of William de L'Epée Winter, of Grantchester, Cambs, and has issue:

1b *Mark John [Mark Winter Esq, via San Pio Quinto 20, Turin, Italy]; *b* 24 Sept 1948; *educ* Eton; *m* 1985 *Angelisa, dau of Vittorio Gualco, of Alessandria, Italy, and has issue:

1c *Julia Anna; *b* 1987

2c *Margherita; *b* 1989

2b *Giles Meynell [Giles Winter Esq, The Old Rectory, Rectory Rd, Wood Norton, Norfolk NR20 5AZ]; *b* 18 Oct 1950; *educ* Eton; *m* 1976 *Joanna Tilney, dau of Lt-Col John Cooper, of Anglesey, and has issue:

1c *Edward John Cochran; *b* 1985

1c *Flora Rachel; *b* 1978

2c *Emily Margaret; *b* 1979

3c *Poppy Lucinda; *b* 1982

1b *Julia; *b* 11 Nov 1944; *m* 1st 1975 (*divorce* 1976) Ali Demir Akel, of Istanbul; *m* 2nd 1983 her cousin +Anthony Charles Meynell (*see* below) and by him has issue

(2) Robert Alexander Lindley, OBE (1919); *b* 28 Jan 1883; *educ* Charterhouse; Maj 5th Service Bn Salop LI WW I (wounded); *m* 7 Aug 1907 Cora T S, yst dau of James W Riches, of Johannesburg, and *d* 28 Aug 1932

(3) Everard Charles Lindley (Sir), OBE (1919), MC (1918); *b* 19 June 1885; Capt RFA, TF, WW I (despatches), Br Resident Buenos Aires 1919 and Treasury Rep there, ktd 1946; *m* 21 July 1914 Rose (*d* 28 Dec 1975), only dau of Lionel Bulteel, of Yewden Manor, Henley-on-Thames, and *d* 22 May 1956, having had issue:

1a Francis Everard, MBE (1962); *b* 24 April 1917; *educ* Eton; Lt-Cdr RN WW II; *m* 25 Feb 1956 *Janet Penelope [Mrs Francis Meynell, 13 Spilhaus Ave, Constantia 7800, Capetown, S Africa], 2nd Offr WRNS, est dau of Engr R-Adml Albert Kingsley Dibley, CB, of Court Barn, Lee-on-the-Solent, Hants, and *d* 18 Feb 1996, leaving:

1b *Rosemary Janet; *b* 25 June 1960; *m* 1984 George Walter Bishop, est s of Frank Bishop, of Natal, and has:

1c *Charles Andrew Meynell; *b* 1986

1c *Sarah Rose; *b* 1989

2c *Mary Janet; *b* 1992

2b *Elizabeth Anne; *b* 21 July 1961; *m* 1984 *Dr Derek Montague Brink, s of Dr Johannes Brink, and has:

1c *Nicholas Francis Meynell; *b* 1990

2c *Jonathan James Meynell; *b* 1992

3c *Derek Anthony Meynell; *b* 1994

4c *Peter Andrew Meynell; *b* 1996

3b *Anne Penelope [Mrs Anthony Blumer, 13 Spilhaus Ave, Hohenort, Constantia, CP 7800, S Africa]; *b* 19 May 1964; *m* 1987 *Capt Anthony David Blumer, Roy Australian Regt, yr s of Dr John Blumer, of Sydney, and has:

1c *Natasha Anne; *b* 1993

2c *Emma Katherine; *b* 1995

1a Rose Mary; *d* 14 March 1924

2a *Clare [Mrs John Hallward, 1745 Cedar Ave P4, Montreal, Quebec H3G 1A7, Canada]; *b* 11 Oct 1932; *m* 28 Dec 1956 *John Marsham Hallward, of Montreal, s of Bernard Marsham Hallward, DSO, by Hon Alice Hamilton Graham, dau of 1st and last Baron Atholstan (*see* 1938 edn), and has issue:

1b *Peter Marsham; *b* 29 April 1968

2b *Christopher Graham; *b* 1973

1b *Jennifer Rose; *b* 14 March 1963

2b *Julia Anne; *b* 17 June 1965

3b *Mary Clare; *b* 21 Nov 1966

4b *Katherine Rosemary; *b* 19 Jan 1972

3a *Mary [Mrs Robert Clother, 15 Grosvenor Sq, London W1; Martlets, Rodmell, Lewes, E Sussex BN7 3HF]; *b* 4 July 1935; *m* 4 July 1974 *Robert Leonard Clother, only s of L Clother

(4) Charles Wilfrid Lindley; *b* 9 Aug 1890; Capt RN WWs I and II (despatches); *m* 19 April 1917 Ida Beatrice (*d* 1977), dau of Rt Hon Ernest George Pretyman, DL, MP, of Orwell Park, Suffolk, by Lady Beatrice Adine Bridgeman, OBE, est dau of 4th Earl of Bradford (*qv*), and *d* 13 April 1976, leaving:

1a +Richard Walter [Richard Meynell Esq, Berry Hall, Berrys Lane, Honingham, Norfolk NR9 5AX]; *b* 6 Jan 1923; *educ* Eton; FCA, Lt RNVR WW II; *m* 20 Sept 1950 *Countess Ilse Therese, dau of Lt-Gen Count Theodor von Sponeck, of Schloss Bachingen, Bavaria, and has issue:

1b +Anthony Charles [Anthony Meynell Esq, Old Hall Farm Cottages, North Tuddenham, Norfolk]; *b* 23 July 1952; *educ* Eton; *m* 1983, as her 2nd husb, his cousin *Julia, dau of John Winter (*see* above), and has:

1c +Wilfrid; *b* 1986

1c *Rachel; *b* 4 Jan 1984

2b +Charles Humphrey; *b* 23 Oct 1954; *educ* Eton

1b *Patricia Rose [Mrs Sharad Jain, 1002 Asbury Ave, Evanston, IL 60202, USA]; *b* 8 July 1960; *m* 1986 *Sharad Jain, s of Prof S P Jain, of New Delhi

1a *Beatrice Mary [Mrs John Whitcombe, 12a Long St, Devizes, Wilts]; *b* 10 Jan 1918; *m* 28 Sept 1945 Maj John Henry Whitcombe, RA (*d* 1985), er s of Maj-Gen Philip Sidney Whitcombe, CB, OBE, of The Grange, Lake, Wilts, and has:

1b *Sarah Rose; *b* 14 Aug 1946; *m* 1973 *Rev Barry Thorley, of Kingsley Holt, Staffs, and has issue:

1c *Thomas Edward; *b* 1984

2b *Clarissa Beatrice [Mrs Robert Gosling, Pulham Cottage, Wetherden, Suffolk IP14 3LQ]; *b* 1 Jan 1949; *m* 12 July 1969 *Robert Anthony Gosling, yst s of Robert Alexander Bennett Gosling, of Mutton Hall, Wetherden, Suffolk, by Angela, yst dau of Hon Victor Russell, CBE, JP (*see* AMPTHILL, B), and has issue

(1) Mary Margaret Desirée, CBE (1946); *b* 25 Oct 1894; *m* 17 March 1915 8th Viscount Falmouth (*qv*) and *d* 1985

1 Emily Charlotte; LJStJ; left her nephew 1st Earl of Halifax the Tudor-Jacobean mansion of Temple Newsam, Leeds (birthplace of Lord Darnley (*see* SOMERSET, D), 2nd husb of MARY QUEEN OF SCOTS), which Lord Halifax sold to that city 1925, and a town house at 88 Eaton Square, Belgravia, London SW1; *m* 11 Aug 1863 Hugo Francis Meynell Ingram, MP (*d* 26 May 1871), of Hoar Cross, Staffs, and *dsp* 21 Dec 1904

2 Alice Louisa; *m* 2 Aug 1870 Hon John Charles Dundas (*see* ZETLAND, M) and *d* 3 June 1934, having had issue

3 Blanche Edith; *m* 21 Sept 1876 Col Hon Henry William Lowry-Corry (*see* BELMORE, E) and *d* 21 July 1921, leaving issue

The 1st VISCOUNT's est s,

CHARLES LINDLEY WOOD, **2nd Viscount Halifax of Monk Bretton**, DL (W R Yorks); *b* 7 June 1839; *educ* Eton and Ch Ch Oxford (BA 1863, MA 1865); Groom Bedchamber to HM EDWARD VII when PRINCE OF WALES 1862–77, Pres English Church Union 1866–1920, Capt 1st W R Yorks Yeo Cav, FSA 1880, compiler: *Lord Halifax's Ghost Book*, Ecclesiastical Commr England 1886; *m* 22 April 1869 Lady Agnes Elizabeth Courtenay (*d* 4 July 1919), only dau of 11th Earl of Devon (*qv*), and *d* 19 Jan 1934, having had issue:

1 Charles Reginald Lindley; *b* 7 July 1870; *educ* Eton and Ch Ch Oxford; *d* 6 Sept 1899

2 Francis Hugh Lindley; *b* 21 Sept 1873; *educ* Eton; *d* 17 March 1889

3 Henry Paul Lindley; *b* 25 Jan 1879; *d* 6 June 1886

4 EDWARD FREDERICK LINDLEY, **1st Earl**

1 Alexandra Mary Elizabeth; *b* 25 Aug 1871 (HM QUEEN ALEXANDRA stood sponsor); *m* 15 Sept 1898, as his 2nd w, Maj-Gen Hugh Clement Sutton, CB, CMG (*see* SUTTON, Bt), and *d* 10 March 1965, leaving issue

2 Mary Agnes Emily, JP (W R Yorks); *b* 25 March 1877; *m* 17 Sept 1903 1st and last Baron Bingley (*d* 11 Dec 1947; *see* 1940 edn) and *d* 25 March 1962, leaving issue

The 2nd VISCOUNT's est surv s,

EDWARD FREDERICK LINDLEY WOOD, **1st Earl of Halifax**, so *cr* 11 July 1944, as also 22 Dec 1925 BARON IRWIN (UK), of Kirby Underdale, Co York (both UK), KG (1931), OM (1946), GCSI (1926), GCMG (1937, also Grand Master of Order), GCIE (1926), TD, PC (25 Oct 1922); *b* 16 April 1881; *educ* Eton and Ch Ch Oxford (BA, Fell All Souls 1903, MA 1906); MP (C) Ripon 1910–25, KJStJ, Lt-Col QO Yorks Dragoons Yeo 1915–17 (despatches), Hon Col Yorks Dragoons 1935, Assist Sec (Dep Dir Labour Supply) Min Nat Serv 1917–18, Parly U-Sec Colonies 1921–22, Pres Bd Educn 1922–24 and 1932–35, Min Ag and Fish 1924–25, Viceroy India 1926–31, Sec State War and Pres Army Cncl June-Nov 1935, Ld Privy Seal and Ldr Ho Lds 1935–37, Ld Pres Cncl 1937, For Sec Feb 1938–Dec 1940, Amb USA 1941–46, Sec For Correspondence RA 1941, High Steward Westminster 1947, Chm BBC Gen Advsy Cncl 1947–52, MFH or Jt-MFH Middleton 1932–59, pres: Bldg Socs Assoc 1947–55 and Pilgrims 1950–58, Hon LLD: Leeds 1923, Oxford, Cambridge, Sheffield and St Andrews 1931, Toronto 1932, Durham 1933, Liverpool, Dublin and London 1934, also Harvard, Princeton and Yale, Hon Dr U of Grenoble, Chllr: Oxford U 1933–59, Order Garter 1943–59 and U of Sheffield Dec 1947–59, author: *John Keble* (biography, 1909), *The Great Opportunity* (with Sir George Lloyd, *c* 1919) and *Fullness of Days* (autobiography, 1957); *m* 21 Sept 1909 Lady Dorothy Evelyn Augusta Onslow, CI, DCVO (1953), JP, Hon LLD Leeds, DGStJ, Extra Ldy of the Bedchamber to HM QUEEN ELIZABETH THE QUEEN MOTHER, yr dau of 4th Earl of Onslow (*qv*), and *d* 23 Dec 1959, having had issue:

1 CHARLES INGRAM COURTENAY, **2nd Earl**

2 (Francis Hugh) Peter Courtenay; *b* 5 Oct 1916; *educ* Eton; Maj QO Yorks Dragoons WW II; *ka* Egypt Oct 1942

3 +RICHARD FREDERICK WOOD, BARON HOLDERNESS (LP, *qv*)

1 Mary Agnes; *b* 31 July, *d* 3 Aug 1910

2 Anne Dorothy, OBE (1980, MBE 1950), JP (N R Yorks 1958); *b* 31 July 1910; *educ* Queen's Coll Harley Street, London; worked with WRVS, MFH Sinnington (N Yorks) 1963–85 and Jt-MFH with her husb 1950–63, 1st female memb Ctee Masters of Foxhounds Assoc, chm hound show Gt Yorks Show from 1980, author: *Strange Stories of the Chase* (1972); *m* 9 May 1936 3rd Earl of Feversham of Ryedale (*see* FEVERSHAM, B) and *d* 25 March 1995, having had issue

The 1st EARL's er surv s,

CHARLES INGRAM COURTENAY WOOD, **2nd Earl of Halifax**, JP (E R Yorks 1963-68); *b* 3 Oct 1912; *educ* Eton and Ch Ch Oxford (BA 1934); 2nd Lt RHG 1934–37, Capt Middle East WW II and Reserve of Offrs thereafter, MP (U) York 1937–45, Jt-MFH or MFH Middleton to 1980, Sr Steward Jockey Club 1950–51 and 1958–59, Ld Lt Humberside 1974–80 (E R Yorks 1968–74, DL E R Yorks and Kingston upon Hull 1955–68), Chm E R CC 1968–74, KStJ 1970, High Steward York Minster 1970–80, Pro-Chllr Hull U 1974–80; *m* 25 April 1936 Ruth Alice Hannah Mary, JP (E R Yorks 1956) (*d* 1989), only child of Rt Hon Neil James Archibald Primrose, MC (*see* ROSEBERY, E), and *d* 1980, leaving:

1 (CHARLES) EDWARD PETER NEIL WOOD, **3rd and present Earl of Halifax**

1 *Caroline Victoria [The Lady Caroline Gosling, The Claw, Brushford, Dulverton, Somerset]; *b* 10 Sept 1937; *m* 1st 29 April 1958 (*divorce* 1970) Randle Joseph Feilden, est s of Maj-Gen Sir Randle Guy Feilden, KCVO, CB, CBE, DL (*see* HAMPDEN, V), and has issue:

(1) *Randle Charles Roderick; *b* 19 Jan 1961

(1) Virginia Mary; *b* 6 June 1959; *d* 1994 following a skiing accident in France

(2) *Fiona Caroline; *b* 26 Jan 1965; *m* 1991 *James D E Bryant, s of J M Bryant, of Whaplode, Lincs, and has issue:

1a *Sarah Elizabeth; *b* 1993

1 (cont.) Lady Caroline Feilden *m* 2nd 1970 *John Valentine Gosling

2 *Susan Diana [The Lady Susan Watson, Bossall Hall, Barton-le-Willows, York]; *b* 22 Sept 1938; *m* 10 Oct 1959 *Brig Ian Darsie Watson, CBE, TD, only s of Darsie Watson, and has issue:

(1) *David Charles Darsie [David Watson Esq, Flat B9 Lloyds Wharf, w Mill St, London SE1 2BD]; *b* 29 July 1960; *educ* Eton

(2) *Richard Ian [Richard Watson Esq, Bossall Hall, Bossall, York YO6 7NT]; *b* 30 Jan 1962; *m* 1990 *Henrietta, only dau of Anthony Butterwick, of Pinckneys Green, Berks

HALL of Burton

Arms: Vert on a fess or, between in chief a cross crosslet fitchée between two talbot's heads erased argent collared and ringed gules, and in base a like talbot's head, three escallops sable. **Crest:** A talbot's head erased sable, ears argent, gorged with a chaplet or, garnished with roses gules, between two cross crosslets fitchée or. **Motto:** *In Deo fides* ('Trust in God'). **Creation:** Bt. (UK) 18 Sept 1919.

SIR JOHN BERNARD HALL, 3RD BT, of Burton Park, Sussex [Sir John Hall Bt, Penrose House, Patmore Heath, Herts SG11 2LT]; *b* 20 March 1932; *s* f 1962; *educ* Eton and Trin Coll Oxford; Lt Roy Fus (TARO), dir: Schroder Wagg 1967–73, Antofagasta and Bolivia Rlwy Co 1967–73 and Bank of America 1974–83 (v-pres 1982), chm Nikko Bank 1992–95 (md 1990–92), Anglo-Colombian Soc 1978–81, Ld Manor Burton; *m* 19 Oct 1957 Delia Mary (*d* 7 Nov 1997), dau of Lt-Col James Archibald Innes, DSO, of Horringer Manor, Bury St Edmunds, Suffolk, and has:

1 +DAVID BERNARD [David Hall Esq, Rose Cottage, Holly Lane, Haughton, Staffs ST18 9JS]; *b* 12 May 1961; *educ* Eton and York U

1 *Caroline Evelyn; *b* 26 July 1959; *educ* Cobham Hall and Durham U; *m* 23 Sept 1995 *Martin Dixon-Ward, only s of Frank Dixon-Ward, CBE, of Beckenham, and has:

(1) *Katharina Louise; *b* 25 July 1996

2 *Julia Nancy [Miss Julia Hall, 15 Ellington St, London N7 8PP]; *b* 25 Sept 1965; *educ* Cobham Hall and Edinburgh U

Lineage: RICHARD HALL, of Casterne in Ilam, Staffs; owned land there *temp* EDWARD IV; *d* 22 April 1506, leaving, with other issue:

RICHARD HALL, of Hilderstone, Staffs; *m* Margaret — and *d* 1557, leaving issue:

JEFFREY HALL, of Spott Grange, Stone, Staffs; *m* Margery — and *d* April 1597, leaving, with other issue:

THOMAS HALL, of Spott Grange; *m* Agnes — (*d* Nov 1635) and *d* Dec 1636, leaving, with other issue:

THOMAS HALL, of Spott; *m* Sarah — (*d* Aug 1663) and *d* 1661, leaving issue:

THOMAS HALL, of Stanton in Ellastone, Staffs; *m* Mary — and had issue:

RICHARD HALL, of Stanton; *b* 1681; *m* Prudence — (*d* 1744) and *d* Jan 1756, leaving issue:

JOHN HALL, of Ellastone; *b* 1710; *m* Ann — and had issue:

JOHN HALL, of Oakamoor, Staffs; *b* 1736; *m* Ann — and *d* 1827, having had, with other issue:

JOHN HALL, of Cheadle, Staffs ; *b* Sept 1772; *m* Mary Titley and *d* 6 July 1838, leaving a yr s:

BERNARD HALL, of Villa Mariposa, Cannes, JP; *b* 1813; Lt Kingston Regt of Foot, Mayor Liverpool; *m* 1st 1843 Mary Ann (*d* 1857), est dau of William Titley, of Kingston, Jamaica, and had, with other issue:

1 Alexander Titley (Rev); Vicar Appleby Lincs 1892–1913; *educ* Magdalen Coll Oxford (MA); *d* 25 May 1929

BERNARD HALL *m* 2nd 1860 Margaret (*d* 14 March 1902), 5th dau of William Calrow, JP, DL, of Walton Lodge, Walton-le-Dale, Lancs, and *d* May 1890, having by her had, with other issue:

2 **Sir Douglas Bernard Hall, 1st Bt** (UK), so *cr* 18 Sept 1919, JP (Sussex); *b* 24 Dec 1866; High Sheriff Sussex 1907; MP (C) IoW 1910–22, Lt RNR and Capt RE, Ld Manors Barlavington, Burton and Crouch; *m* 16 Oct 1890 Caroline (*d* 12 March 1941), only dau of Thomas James Montgomery, of Larchmont Manor, NY, USA, and *d* 30 June 1923, leaving:

(1) **Sir Douglas Montgomery Bernard, 2nd Bt**, DSO (1918); *b* 30 Dec 1891; *educ* Eton and RMC Sandhurst; Lt-Col Coldstream Gds and cmdg 4th Bn N Staffs Regt WW I (wounded twice, despatches thrice), WW II raised HG Argyll 1940, Zone Cdr 1940–43, King's Messenger 1945–47 and 1949–51, Ld Manors Barlavington, Burton and Crouch; *m* 1st 17 July 1915 (*divorce* 1923) Mary, only dau of Capt William Alexander Grant, 13th Hus, and had:

1a Pamela Mary; *b* 6 June 1916; *m* 1st 26 June 1936 (*divorce* 1944) Richard Haliburton Bentley, s of H H Bentley; *m* 2nd 1944 (*divorce* 1948) Ivan Lorn Buchanan; *m* 3rd 14 Feb 1949 Norman Percy Hackforth (*d* 1996), s of Percy Hackforth, and *d* 6 Oct 1995

(1) (cont.) **Sir Douglas** *m* 2nd 20 May 1925 (*divorce* 1950) Nancie Walton (*d* 23 Jan 1998), only dau of Col John Edward Mellor, CB, JP, DL; *m* 3rd 13 Jan 1951 Hon Diana Joan (*d* 23 June 1975), only dau of 4th Baron Sackville (*qv*) and formerly w of 4th Baron Romilly (*see* 1970 edn), and *d* 30 Aug 1962, leaving by his 2nd w:

1a Sir JOHN BERNARD, **3rd and present Bt**

HALL of Dunglass

Arms: Az. a chevron arg. between three crane's heads erased at the neck or, an inescutcheon or charged with a lion rampant gu. within a double tressure flory counter-flory of the last. **Crest:** A stork sitting on a mount in a watching posture ppr. **Motto:** *Cura quietem* ('Keep the peace'). **Creation:** Bt. (NS) 8 Oct 1687.

SIR DOUGLAS BASIL HALL, 14TH BT, of Dunglass, Haddingtonshire, KCMG (1959, CMG 1958), JP (Devon 1964) [Sir Douglas Hall Bt KCMG JP, Barnford, Ringmore, Devon TQ7 4HL]; *b* 1 Feb 1909; *s* bro 1978; *educ* Radley and Keble Coll Oxford (BA 1929, MA 1965); OCS as cadet for Govt N Rhodesia 1930, Dist Offr 1932–50, Sr Dist Offr 1950–53, Prov Commr 1953, Admin Sec 1955–56, Sec Native Affrs N Rhodesia 1956–59, Govr and C-in-C Somaliland Protectorate 1959–60, Gen Commr Income Tax Stanborough and Coleridge 1965, memb Police Authority Devon and Cornwall 1971–79; *m* 25 April 1933 Rachel Marion (*d* 1990), dau of Maj Ernest Gartside-Tippinge, RA, and has had issue:

1 Basil James; *b* 28th June; *d* 12 Sept 1935

2 +JOHN DOUGLAS HOSTE [John Hall Esq, Brook Mill, Buckfastleigh, S Devon TQ11 0HL]; *b* 7 Jan 1945; *educ* Dover Coll, Gonville and Caius Coll Cambridge (BA) and Southampton U (Cert Ed); V-Pncpl (Acad) Dartington Coll of Art; *m* 1972 *Angela Margaret, dau of George Keys, of Buckfastleigh, and has:

(1) +Thomas James; *b* 10 Dec 1975

(2) +Bernard Neville; *b* Feb 1979

1 *Marion [Mrs John Fuller-Sessions, Orchard Farm, Parwich, Derbys DE6 1QB]; *b* 18 July 1940; *educ* Trin Coll Dublin (BA 1963); *m* 10 July 1965 *John Francis Fuller-Sessions and has:

(1) *Nicholas Francis Blair; *b* 2 Jan 1974

(1) *Ruth; *b* 5 Sept 1967

(2) *Sara; *b* 22 July 1969

2 *Ruth [Mrs Anthony Cragg, PO Box 60, Umhlanga Rocks, Natal 4320, S Africa]; *b* 4 March 1942; *m* 6 July 1963 *Anthony Bernard Cragg, of Salisbury, Rhodesia, and has issue:

(1) *Stephen Browning; *b* 8 Aug 1966

(2) *Christopher Douglas; *b* 12 March 1968

(3) *Timothy Hugh; *b* 27 Aug 1970; *m* 6 Aug 1996 *Philippa Thompson

(1) *Anne Louise; *b* 16 Feb 1965; *m* 22 Feb 1992 *Christopher Charles Peter Latham and has issue:

1a *Alfred Michael; *b* 1992

2a *Joseph Anthony; *b* 1996

1a *Emily Rachel; *b* 1993

Lineage: JOHN HALL of Dunglass; *m* Janet Higgins and had:

Sir John Hall, 1st Bt (NS), so *cr* 8 Oct 1687, of Dunglass, Haddingtonshire; *m* 1st Catherine, dau of James Loch of Drylaw and widow of John Mein of Craigcrook; *m* 2nd Margaret, dau of George Fleming of Kilconquhar, and was *bur* 18 Oct 1695, leaving by his 1st w:

Sir James Hall, 2nd Bt; *m* 1st 1698 Anne (*dsp*), dau of 1st Lord Polwarth (*qv*); *m* 2nd Margaret, dau of Sir John Pringle, 2nd Bt (*qv*), and *d* 1742, leaving, with a yr s (William) and two daus (Isabella; Katherine, *m* 1743 William Hamilton of Bangour):

Sir John Hall, 3rd Bt; *m* 1759 his cousin Magdalen (*d* 1763), dau of Sir Robert Pringle, 3rd Bt (*qv*), and *d* 3 July 1776, having had, with other issue:

Sir James Hall, 4th Bt; MP St Michael's; Pres Roy Soc Edinburgh; architectural and scientific writer; *m* 9 Nov 1786 Lady Helen Douglas (*d* 12 July 1837), 2nd dau of 4th Earl of Selkirk (*qv*), and *d* 23 June 1832, having had issue:

1 **Sir John Hall, 5th Bt**; *b* 16 Sept 1787; FRS; *m* 28 Jan 1823 Julia (*d* 3 Oct 1874), dau of James Walker, of Dalry, Ayrshire, and *d* 2 April 1860, having had issue:

(1) **Sir James Hall, 6th Bt**; *b* 1824; *d* unm 7 May 1876

(2) Douglas; *dsp*

(3) **Sir Basil Francis Hall, 7th Bt**, DL Berwick and Haddington; *b* 1 June 1832; *m* 10 March 1877 Adelaide Catherine (*d* 2 Feb 1926), dau of Robert Kerr Elliot of Harwood and Clifton, Roxburghshire, and *dsp* 13 Jan 1909

(4) **Sir Henry John Hall, 8th Bt**; *b* 26 Sept 1835; *d* unm 25 March 1913

(5) Julian Hamilton; *b* 17 Jan 1837; Lt-Gen Coldstream Gds Crimea; *m* 5 July 1864 Augusta Wilhelmina Louisa (*d* 1 March 1906), dau of Maj-Gen John Fremantle, CB (*see* COTTESLOE, B), and *d* 15 Aug 1911, leaving issue:

1a **Sir John Richard Hall, 9th Bt**, CBE; *b* 14 Nov 1865; Lt-Col Irish Gds, Maj Coldstream Gds; author: *The Coldstream Guards in the Boer War* and works on French history; *m* 1 Jan 1903 Sophia Mary (*d* 30 March 1952), dau of Henry Duncan and widow of Capt Spencer Alwyne Oliver, DSO, and *dsp* 15 Feb 1928

2a Ralph Henry Seymour; *b* 12 June 1868; *m* 25 Sept 1902 Annie Charlotte (*m* 3rd John Flix Riley and *d* 8 Feb 1913), dau of Gen E S Claremont, CB, and widow of Capt Cecil William Thorold (*see* THOROLD, Bt), and *dsp* 29 Jan 1903

3a **Sir Martin Julian Hall, 10th Bt**, OBE (1918); *b* 23 March 1874; *educ* Radley; Bechuanaland CS, Ch Reconstruction Offr Scotland Min Labour, Dir Food Section Min Munitions WW I; *m* 9 Dec 1905 Alice Mary (*d* 4 July 1952), dau of William Wyndham Hasler, JP, of Aldingbourne House, Sussex, and *d* 31 Jan 1958, leaving:

1b **Sir Julian Henry Hall, 11th Bt**; *b* 22 Feb 1907; *educ* Eton and Balliol Coll Oxford (BA); WW II with Intelligence Corps and Special Forces; actor Norwich Players; ed: *Colour* 1931–32, Home Talks Dept BBC 1948–51, drama critic and obituarist *The Times*; author: *Laura Seaborne*, *The Senior Commoner* and *Two Exiles*; *d* unm 28 Jan 1974

1a Agnes Helen; *d* unm 22 Sept 1954

(1) Anna; *d* unm

2 Basil; *b* 31 Dec 1788; Capt RN; author; *m* 1 March 1825 Margaret (*d* 8 Feb 1876), dau of Sir John Hunter, Consul-Gen Spain, and *d* 11 Sept 1844, leaving:

(1) Basil Sidmouth De Ros; *b* 8 Aug 1833; Capt RN; *m* 4 May 1864 Grace (*d* 26 June 1923), yst dau of Maj-Gen Sir William Reid, GCB, GCMG, and *d* 11 July 1871, leaving:

1a Basil William Reid; *b* 31 Oct 1865; Capt RN; *m* 1st 8 May 1894 Cecil Mary (*d* 8 Feb 1919), 2nd dau of John W Ashburnham, of Claremont, Cape of Good Hope; *m* 2nd 9 Feb 1920 Mary Esther (*d* 28 April 1950), dau of Sir Arthur Blomfield, ARA, and *dsp* 10 Aug 1942

2a Lionel Erskine; *b* 18 July 1868; Capt 4th S Staffs Regt; *m* 21 April 1897 Jane Augusta (*d* Sept 1949), dau of Thomas Leetham Reynolds, and *d* 8 March 1948, leaving issue:

1b **Sir Lionel Reid Hall, 12th Bt**, MC; *b* 1 Feb 1898; Col Roy Signals WW I (despatches, wounded), NWF India 1935 (medal), WW II (despatches); *m* 29 March 1921 Mary Marjoribanks Moore, dau of Maj-Gen Sir Gerard Moore Heath, KCMG, CB, DSO, and widow of Capt James Douglas Gaussen MacNeece, MC, RFA, and *dspm* 22 April 1975, leaving issue:

1c *Mary Jane Rosamond; *b* 6 Jan 1922; WW II as 3rd Offr WRNS; *m* 1 May 1946 *Mark Peter Whitlock, TD, slr, Sudan Political Serv, and has:

1d *John Mark; *b* 9 April 1955; *educ* Downside

2d *Paul Mark; *b* 20 Nov 1957

3d *Martin Mark; *b* 8 Aug 1959

1d *Mary Louise; *b* 10 Nov 1947

2d *Jane Frances Mary; *b* 16 Nov 1949

2c *Elizabeth Katherine Marion [Mrs Oliphant Jackson, Little Stagenhoe, Horningtoft, Norfolk NR20 5ED]; *b* 16 Oct 1925; BSc Vet Sci Edin, MRCVS; *m* 29 March 1949 Oliphant Fairburn Jackson, PhD, MRCVS (*d* 1991), Lt RNVR, and has:

1d *James Ellis; *b* 21 July 1959

2d *Anthony Oliphant; *b* 11 April 1961

3d *Rosemary Frances; *b* 6 Nov 1955

3c *Teresa Madeleine [Mrs Herbert Constantine, Fyning House, Rogate, Hants GU31 5EF]; *b* 19 June 1930; *m* 3 Jan 1952 *Herbert Norman Constantine, of Tanton Grange, Stokesley, and has:

1d *Robert Francis; *b* 16 Jan 1953; *educ* Eton

2d *Nigel Loudon; *b* 26 June 1954; *educ* Eton

3d *Neville Egerton; *b* 27 Aug 1959; *educ* Eton

1d *Serena Mary; *b* 1 Aug 1963

2b **Sir Neville Reynolds Hall, 13th Bt**; *b* 16 Feb 1900; *educ* Oundle and Keble Coll Oxford (BSc 1930); ARCS, master RNC Dartmouth; *m* 22 June 1957 *Dorothy Maud [Dorothy Lady Hall, Ash Cottage, Ash, Dartmouth, S Devon], dau of William Lawrence Jones, and *d* 1978

3b Sir DOUGLAS BASIL HALL, **14th and present Bt**

1a Helen Sara Margaret; *d* 25 Dec 1882

(1) Eliza Jane; *m* 19 June 1845 R-Adml — Chamberlain (*d* 27 Feb 1878) and *d* 29 Aug 1856

(2) Frances Emily; *m* 5 May 1855 Alfred Christian, CMG (*d* 1887), of Malta, and *d* 3 April 1905, having had issue

3 James; *dsp*

1 Magdalen; *m* 1st 1815 Sir William Delancy, QMG Waterloo (*ka*); *m* 2nd 1819 Henry Harvey

2 Elizabeth; *m* 1824 Rev G P Boileau Pollen

3 Katherine; *m* Sir James Russell, KCB, of Ashiestiel, and *d* 14 May 1872

HALL of Graffham

Arms: Sable a cross moline between in the first and fourth quarters a talbot's head erased and in the second and third a chaplet of oak or. **Crest:** A demi-gryphon sable holding between the paws a portcullis or. **Motto:** *Paratus* ('Prepared'). **Creation:** Bt. (UK) 5 March 1923.

SIR (FREDERICK) JOHN FRANK HALL, 3RD BT, of Graffham, Surrey [Sir John Hall Bt, 29 Embercourt Rd, Thames Ditton, Surrey KT7 0LH]; *b* 14 Aug 1931; *s* f 1949; *educ* Bryanston; dir Thomson McLintock Assocs 1976–87, fndr chm KPMG Career Consultancy Servs 1983–93; ptnr KPMG Peat Marwick 1987–93; dir Roffey Park Inst 1978–90 (v-chm 1983–85, chm 1985–87); *m* 1st 3 April 1956 (*divorce* 1961) Felicity Anne, dau of Edward Rivers-Fletcher and Mrs L R Galloway; *m* 2nd 3 June 1961 (*divorce* 1967) Patricia Ann, yr dau of Douglas Atkinson, of Carlisle, and by her has issue:

1 *Nicola Jane; *b* 3 Sep 1962
2 *Samantha Mary; *b* 10 Feb 1965

Sir JOHN *m* 3rd 9 Nov 1967 his 1st w *Felicity and by her has:

3 *Antonia Anne; *b* 19 Aug 1970; *m* 16 May 1998 *Philippe Robert Calame, er s of Henri Calame, of Switzerland
4 *Victoria Joy; *b* 16 April 1973

Lineage: Sir Frederick Hall, 1st Bt (UK), so *cr* 5 March 1923, KBE, DSO, JP Surrey; Hon Col 53rd (Lond) AA Bde TA, Lt-Col RFA, MP (C) Dulwich 1910–32, dir Robert Gardner Mountain & Co Ltd, chm and md Mercantile Marine Finance Corp, memb Lloyd's and Baltic Exchange, raised 17 Artillery Batteries WW I (despatches); *b* 7 Oct 1864 (s of Herbert William Hall); *m* 16 April 1892 Annie Ellen (*d* 19 Feb 1929), dau of Henry Hall, MD, of Plaistow, and *d* 28 April 1932, leaving:

1 FREDERICK HENRY (Sir), **2nd Bt**
2 Cecil Mortimer; *b* 8 June 1905; *m* 1st 9 Sep 1933 (*divorce* 1947) Emily Margaret, yr dau of Walter Shelley Walkden, of Colchester; *m* 2nd 30 July 1947 Alma Agnes, yst dau of William Moore, of Felixstowe, Suffolk; *dsp*
1 Mildred Constance; *m* 1st 12 Aug 1918 (*divorce* 1929) Horace Owen Whelan and had issue; *m* 2nd Henry Alexander Hewat and *d* 15 Feb 1963
2 Anne Elsie; *m* 16 April 1926 Maurice Henry Drake, er s of Courtenay Henry Drake, MD, FRCS, and had:
(1) *Derek Courtenay [Derek Drake Esq, Kiln Cottage, Southend, Oxon RG9 6JP]; *b* 24 March 1928; *educ* RNC Dartmouth and Pembroke Coll Cambridge (BA); *m* 25 Aug 1956 *Angela, dau of AVM Sir Tom Ince Webb-Bowen, KCB, CMG, of Haverfordwest, Pembs, and has issue:
1a *Tom Courtenay; *b* 25 March 1959
2a *William Derek; *b* 7 Feb 1962
3a *James Edward; *b* 15 Sep 1967
(2) *(Frederick) Richard Maurice [Richard Drake Esq, The Red House, Standon, Herts SG11 1LA]; *b* 8 Dec 1929; *educ* Marlborough; underwriting memb Lloyd's; *m* 19 April 1955 *Cynthia Kathleen, dau of Walter George Turner, of St Saviours, Jersey, and has issue:
1a *Peter Richard Maurice; *b* 29 Jan 1956
1a *Susan Jane; *b* 10 Oct 1957
2a *Amanda Louise; *b* 15 Jan 1967

Sir FREDERICK's est s,

Sir Frederick Henry Hall, 2nd Bt; *b* 11 April 1899; *educ* Marlborough, RMC Sandhurst and Pembroke Coll Cambridge; 8th Hus WW II, underwriting memb Lloyd's; *m* 1st 24 Sep 1924 (*divorce* 1945) Olwen Irene, yr dau of Alderman Frank Collis, of Stokeville, Staffs, and Deganwy, Llandudno; *m* 2nd 26 June 1947 Constance Phyllis (*d* 6 Jan 1954), dau of Cyril Hugh Slatter, of Evesham, Worcs, and formerly w of Malcolm Duff, and *d* 22 June 1949, leaving by his 1st w:

1 Sir (FREDERICK) JOHN FRANK HALL, **3rd and present Bt**
2 +DAVID CHRISTOPHER [David Hall Esq, 6 Coniston Close, Heatherside, Camberley, Surrey GU15 1BE]; *b* 30 Dec 1937; heir presumptive; *educ* Glebe House, Cheveley, nr Newmarket; *m* 24 Nov 1962 (*divorce* 1987) Irene, only dau of William Duncan, of Aberdeen; *m* 2nd 31 Dec 1991 *Annie Madeline Renée Olivier, adopted dau of Bottemanne Raould, of Thieusies-Lez-Soignies (Mons), Belgium, and by his 1st w has:
(1) +John Christopher; *b* 22 May 1965
(1) *Olwen Evelyn; *b* 24 Sept 1967
1 *Olwen Mary Primrose; *b* 1928; *m* 1st 1958 (*divorce* 1977) Carlyle Herbert Peter Gardner (*d* 1992); *m* 2nd 1977 *James Alexander Macrae and by her 1st husb has:
(1) *Alan Frederick Peter; *b* 1952; *m* 1st 1972 (*divorce* 1993) Pamela Susan Wheal; *m* 2nd 1994 *Christine Penelope Metcalfe and by his 1st w has:
1a *Geoffrey Alan Peter; *b* 1973
1a *Nicola Susan; *b* 1975
(2) *Marcus Hillier Clive; *b* 1958
(3) *Crispin John Stuart Hyde; *b* 1961
(4) *Jonathan Carlyle Heiko; *b* 1963
(5) *Jason Peter Alan; *b* 1965
(6) *Matthew Reginald Saul; *b* 1967
(1) *Merrily Mary Susan; *b* 1955; *m* 1986 *Anthony Willis
(2) *Josephine Juliet; *b* 1956; *m* 1978 (*divorce* 1993) Jonathan Peter Matich
(3) *Susannah Mary Ann; *b* 1962

HALSBURY

Arms: Sa., three lozenges conjoined in fess erm. **Crests:** 1 Out of a coronet arg. a demi-lion gu. holding a lozenge as in the arms, 2 A moorcock's head ppr., in the beak a trefoil vert. **Supporters:** Two swans erm., beaked and legged gu., suspended from the neck by a ribbon of the last a shield of the arms. **Motto:** *Ne vile velis* ('Form no vile wish'). **Creations:** B. (UK) 26 June 1885, V. and E. (UK) 17 Jan 1898.

THE 3RD EARL OF HALSBURY, Viscount Tiverton, of Tiverton, Co Devon, and **Baron Halsbury**, of Halsbury, Devon ((John) Anthony Hardinge Giffard) [The Rt Hon The Earl of Halsbury, 4 Campden House, 29 Sheffield Terrace, London W8 7NE]; *b* 4 June 1908; *s* f 1943; *educ* Eton and London U (BSc 1935), chartered engr, with Lever Bros 1935–42 and Brown-Firth Research Labs 1942–47, dir Research Decca Records 1947–49, md Nat Research Devpt Corp 1949–59, consultant and dir Joseph Lucas Industs 1959–74, Distillers 1959–78, Head-Wrightson Ltd 1959–78; chm: Sci Museum Advsy Cncl 1951–65, Ctee on Decimal Currency 1961–63, Inst Cancer Research 1961–77, Meteorological Ctee 1970–82, Review Body Doctors' and Dentists' Pay 1971–74 and Deptl Ctee Enquiry Pay Nurses, Midwives, Speech Therapists and Professions Supplementary to Medicine 1974–75; Pres: Instn Production Engrs 1957–59, Devon Assoc 1960–61, Roy Inst Philosophy 1961–90, Instn Nuclear Engrs 1963–65, Machine Tool Industry Research Assoc 1964–77, Nat Cncl for Christian Standards in Soc 1986– and All-Party Parly and Sci Ctee 1963–66; Govr: LSE 1959–60, Manchester U Inst of Sci & Tech 1956– and BBC 1960–62; memb: Standing Cmmn Museums and Galleries 1960–76, Nationalised Tport Advsy Cncl 1963–67, MRC 1972–77, All-Party Family and Child Protection Gp, Roy Acad Engrg, Saddlers' Co; 1st Chllr Brunel U 1966, Hon DTech Brunel, Hon DU Essex, FIEE, FRIC 1947, FInstP, MIProdE, FRS 1969, Hon FIB, Hon FICE 1975, Hon FRSC, FEng 1976, Hon Memb Soc Public Analysts; *m* 1st 1 Oct 1930 (*divorce* 1936) Ismay Catherine (*d* 1989), er dau of Lord Ninian Edward Crichton-Stuart (*see* BUTE, M), and has:

1 + ADAM EDWARD, *Viscount Tiverton* but does not use courtesy title [Adam Giffard Esq, New Mills, Snapper, N Devon EX32 7JZ]; *b* 3 June 1934; *educ* Stowe, Jesus Coll Cambridge (MA 1956) and OU (BSc 1995); *m* 1st 1 Aug 1963 *Ellen, formerly w of Matthew Huxley and dau of Brynjolf Horde; *m* 2nd 1976 *Joanna Elizabeth, dau of Frederick Harry Cole, and by her has:
(1) *Sarah Cole; *b* 1976
(2) *Emma Cole; *b* 1978

The 3rd EARL *m* 2nd 2 Dec 1936 Elizabeth Adeline Faith (*d* 6 June 1983), dau of Maj Harry Crewe Godley, DSO (*see* ANNESLEY, E), and by her has:

1 *(Elizabeth) Caroline Elinor Evelyn [The Lady Caroline Blois, 22 Conduit Mews, London W2 3RE]; *b* 4 March 1939; *m* 2 Nov 1968 (*divorce* 1992) Rodney John Derek Blois (*see* BLOIS, Bt) and has issue

2 *Clare Rohais Antonia Elizabeth [The Lady Clare Lindsay, Brookwood House, Brookwood, Surrey GU23 0NX]; *b* 23 June 1944; *m* 27 Oct 1964 *Col Oliver John Martin Lindsay, CBE (*see* LINDSAY, Bt), and has issue

Lineage: OSBERN de BOLEBEC; *m* Avelina (sis of Gundra, w of RICHARD I DUKE OF NORMANDY) and had issue, who regularly bore the surname GIFFARD.

ROBERT GIFFARD (yr bro of Gerard Gifford, of Fonthill); *m* —, sis and sole heir of Gilbert de Warenne, thus acquiring large estates in Devon centred on Weare (which in consequence became known as Weare Giffard), and had:

1 Walter; confirmed by charter his f's grants to Tavistock Abbey and added his own 1155–62; made grants of land to Plympton Priory jointly with his mother; with his w and bro Roger as witnesses confirmed his uncle's grant of the Church of Bridgerule to Tavistock Abbey 1161–62; *m* Matilda — and had issue:

(1) William; had:

1a Walter; *d* 1218, leaving issue:

1b Walter; *m* Alice, dau of Henry St George, and had issue:

1c Emma; *m* Hugh de Widworthy and had issue:

1d Emma; *m* Robert de Dinham and *dsp* 1289/90

1a Cecilia, mother of Emma de Radford

2a Rohesia; *m* Ralph Daumari; heir with her sis in their issue of the Weare Giffard estate, Cecilia's half passing eventually to the FORTESCUEs Earls Fortescue (*qv*)

2 ROGER

3 Osbert, ancestor of the GIFFARDs of Bickington and through them GIFFARDs of Helland, Cornwall

4 Robert, of Whitchurch *temp* HENRY II

The 2nd son,

ROGER GIFFARD; *m* Mazra, sis of Henry de Secheville, and had, with a yr s (Bartholomew, *m* Joanne fitz Payne, of Methe, and had a s Roger (*dsp*)):

BALDWIN GIFFARD, of Clovelly, which his descendants held of the GIFFARDs of Weare, who held the manor of de Umfraville; claimed 1196–97 with his cousins Jordan Dabernon and Margaret de Pilland, Prioress of Cannington, the Manor of Goodleigh in opposition to William Briewer, close associate of KING JOHN, in right of his mother Mazra, as heir to her bro Henry de Secheville and her unc Gilbert de Albamara; *d c* 1200, leaving:

1 Roger; Ld Manors of Clovelly, Goodleigh, Methe and Awliscombe, S Devon, 1242, Coroner Devon; *d* 1253, leaving:

(1) Bartholomew; *m* Mabel — and *d* 1256/7, leaving issue:

1a Mathew; campaigned in Wales, Flanders, Scotland and Gascony; *m* Edith, widow of Richard de Bideford, and *dsp c* 1298

1a Isabella, coheir of her bro; *m* Robert de Mandeville

2a Beatrice, coheir of her bro; *m* Geoffrey de Stanton

2 Baldwin; enfeoffed by Oliver de Dinham of land at E and W Clifford in the Manor of Hartland, and by William de Marisco of land at Hundreswalles on Lundy Island; his estates were confiscated in the French War of 1215 but subsequently restored; *d* by 1238, leaving:

(1) ROGER

(2) Walter, of Clifford; had four sons (Floer; Gervaise, ancestor of the GIFFARDs of Abbotsham and Yeo Vale; Robert, priest; Baldwin, of Blagdon)

The er son,

ROGER GIFFARD; enfeoffed his bro Walter of land at Clifford; also held a life tenure of the Awilscombes from his cousins the GIFFARDs of Clovelly; *m c* 1249 Joan, dau of Martin Prudhomme, and *d* by 1268, leaving, with three yr sons (Philip, of Payhembery; Martin; Walter, DD):

BARTHOLOMEW GIFFARD; *m* Jone, dau of Peter de Halsbiri, and sole heir to her bro Peter de Halsbiri, and *d* 1314, leaving, with a yr s (Robert, *m* 1284 Katherine, dau of Nicholas Monketon, of Lannowmure, Cornwall):

BALDWIN GIFFARD, of Halsbury; living 1325; *m* Jone — and had issue:

JOHN GIFFARD, of Halsbury; living 1385; *m* Sybel — and had issue:

WALTER GIFFARD, of Halsbury; *m* Isabel — and had issue:

JOHN GIFFARD, of Halsbury; living 1414; *m* Jone, dau of Richard Deneclif, and had, with a yr s (Andrew, ancestor of the GIFFARDs of Thewborough):

THOMAS GIFFARD, of Halsbury; *m* Wilmot Knight and had issue:

JOHN GIFFARD, of Halsbury; *m* Elizabeth, dau and coheir of John Dabernon, and *d* 1491, leaving:

THOMAS GIFFARD, of Halsbury; *b* 1461; *m* 1st Avis, dau of John Dennis, of Orleigh, and had:

1 John, of Halsbury; *b* 1483; *m* Joan, dau of John Sidenham, of Orchard, and *d* 1528, leaving:

(1) Thomas, of Halsbury; *b* 1506; *m* Margaret, dau of Anthony Monk, of Potheridge, and *d* 1550, leaving:

1a John, of Halsbury; *bapt* 6 Nov 1547; *m* 1573/4 Alice, dau of Walter Smith, of Totnes, and was *bur* 15 Nov 1620, leaving:

1b John, of Halsbury; recusant; *b* 1584/5; *m* Elizabeth, dau of John Tremaine, of Collacombe, and *d* 1624/5, leaving:

1c Thomas, of Halsbury; *b* 1606; *m* Katherine, dau of Sir Simon Leach, of Cadleigh, and *dsp* 1648

2c John, of Halsbury; *b* 1612; *m* Elizabeth, dau of Arthur Champernowne, of Dartington, and *dsp* after 1666, having settled the Halsbury estate (improverished by fines paid for recusancy) on his kinsman Roger Giffard, yr s of Col John Giffard, of Brightley (*see* below)

2a Thomas

2 Thomas

THOMAS GIFFARD *m* 2nd Ann, 2nd dau of John Coryton, of Newton St Quethlock, and *d* 17 March 1513, having by her had:

3 Roger (Sir); *b* 1490; *m* Margaret, dau and sole heir of John Cobleigh, of Brightley, parish of Chittlehampton, and Tapleigh, Westleigh, and *d* 1547, leaving, with two other sons and six daus:

(1) JOHN

(2) Hugh; *m* Jone Bampfylde (*see* POLTIMORE, B), and was ancestor of the GIFFARDs of Instow

(3) Roger, of Tiverton Castle; *b* 1533; *m* 1st Audria, widow of William Yeo, of Braunton, and dau of Sir Lewis Stuckley; *m* 2nd Agnes, widow of John Duke, of Otterton, and dau of J Grindall; *m* 3rd —, widow of Richard Waldron and dau of John Prouz, of Tiverton

Sir ROGER's est son,

JOHN GIFFARD, of Brightleigh; *b* 1525; *m* Mary, dau of Sir Richard Grenville, of Stow, Cornwall, by Matilda, dau and coheir of John Beville, of Gwarnock, Cornwall, and had, with other issue, including a yr s (Achilles, *m* — Ackworth, of Kent, and had issue):

JOHN GIFFARD, of Brightleigh; Sheriff Devon *temp* JAMES I; *m* Honor, dau of Walter Erle, of Charborough, Dorset, and *d* 1622, having had, with six daus (Alice, *m* Thomas Addington, of Harleberrie, Essex; Honor, *m* John Garland, of Whitefield, in Marwood; Maria, *dsp*; Elizabeth, *m* George Broughton, of Warbrightsleigh; Joan, *m* her cousin John Giffard; Margaret, *m* Angel Madock, of Exeter):

ARTHUR GIFFARD, of Brightleigh; *b* 1580; *m* Anne, dau of Thomas Leigh, of Borough in Northam, Devon, and *dvp* 1616, leaving with other issue, including a yr s (Arthur (Rev), Fell Exeter Coll, Rector Bideford and Westleigh; *b* 1605, *m* Mary Harris, of Hayne, and *d* 1668) and three daus (Mary, *m* Hugh Wyatt, of Braunton; Honor; Elizabeth, *m* Arthur Harris, Recorder Gt Torrington):

JOHN GIFFARD, of Brightleigh; *b* 1602; Col cmdg royalist Devon pikemen Battle of Lansdowne Hill, accordingly had his property sequestrated and was imprisoned; after the Restoration he was one of the projected Kts of the Royal Oak; *m* Joan, dau of Sir John Wyndham, of Orchard Wyndham, Somerset, and *d* 1666, having had, with other issue, including two yr sons (Roger, of Halsbury, *b* 1645; *m* thrice, *dsp* 1724; Henry, *d* 1658) and a dau (Margaret, *b* 1648, *m* 1st John Keigwin, of Mousehole, Cornwall, *m* 2nd Robert Young (*d* by 1740)):

JOHN GIFFARD, of Brightleigh; *b* 1639; *m* 1st Susan, sis of Sir Copleston Bamfylde, 1st Bt (*see* POLTIMORE, B); *m* 2nd Frances Fane (*see* WESTMORLAND, E) and *d* 1712, having by her had, with a yr s (Caesar, of Brightleigh, *m* Mary Melhuish, of Exeter, and was drowned 1715 in the Torridge, leaving a dau Frances (*m* Capt Thos Kenny, RN, and left issue)):

HENRY GIFFARD, of Wotton, Devon; *b* 1675; present sea Battle of La Hogue 1692; disinherited by f; *m* Martha, dau of Edward Hill, Judge Admlty and Treasurer Virginia, by Elizabeth, dau of Sir Edward Williams, and *dvp* 1709, leaving, with two yr sons (Roger, of Halsbury, *m* Eliza Giffard, of Court, and *d* 1763; Henry, of High Buckington, Coroner Devon, *m* Mary, dau of Rev George Fairchild, Rector Atherington, and had a s Henry, Lt RN, who *m* a dau of — Martin, of Awliscombe, and had a dau Mary Ann, who *m* her cousin Stanley Lees Giffard (*see* below)):

JOHN GIFFARD, of Wotton and Great Torrington; disinherited of the greater part of his patrimony by his gf at the instigation of his unc Caesar; won court judgment in his favour but *d* soon after, leaving an infant s, who was raised through the charity of his mother's family, and who failed to pursue the claim; Coroner Devon; *m* 1745 Dorcas, widow of Francis Robinson, of Dublin, and dau of Arthur Murphy or Morchoe, of Oulardleigh, Co Wexford, Head of the Sept of O'Morchoe of the Clan MacMorrogh, formerly Kings of Leinster, and Elizabeth Knox, dau of Thomas Knox, of Tagunnan, Co Wexford, and descendant of Andrew Knox, DD, Bp of Raphoe, and *d* Nov 1746, leaving an only s:

JOHN GIFFARD, of Dromartin Castle, Co Dublin; *b* 14 Feb 1746/7; Capt Dublin Militia 1788, Accountant-Gen Customs Dublin, High Sheriff Dublin 1794; *m* June 1769 Sarah, dau of William Morton, of Ballynaclash, Co Wexford, and *d* May 1827, leaving:

1 Ambrose Hardinge (Sir); Ch Justice Ceylon; *b* 1771; ktd 1819; *m* 1808 Harriet, dau of Lovell Pennell, of Lyme Regis, and *d* April 1827, leaving, with another s:

(1) George (Sir), KCB; Adml; *d* 8 March 1895

(2) Edward; *b* 1812; Sec Tport Bd; *m* 1844 Rosamund C Dennel and had:

1a John Harding; *b* 1847; Clerk Admlty, dir Greenwich Hosp

2a Edward Walter; *b* 1861; *m* 1902 his cousin Evelyn, dau of **1st Earl of Halsbury** (*see* below)

2 John; *d* young

3 William; Lt 82nd Regt; *k* during the 1798 Uprising in Ireland

4 STANLEY LEES

1 Harriet; *m* 1st Maj — King, 7th Fus (*k* Battle of New Orleans 1814); *m* 2nd Rev James Phelan and *d* 24 Dec 1858

2 Mary; *m* Rev Richard Ryan and had issue

The 2nd surv son,

STANLEY LEES GIFFARD; LLD, barrister; *b* 1788; *educ* Trin Coll Dublin; fndr/ed *The Standard* newspaper; *m* 1st 1814 Susanna Meares, dau of Francis Moran, JP, of Downhill, Co Mayo, and had, with other issue:

1 John Walter de Longueville, barrister Inner Temple 1843, Judge County Courts; *b* 1817; *educ* Merton Coll Oxford (MA); *m* Emilie (*d* 28 March 1909), 2nd dau of D B Scott, of Ingham, Norfolk, and *d* 23 Oct 1888, leaving, with other issue:

(1) Hardinge Frank, FSA, barrister, Priv Sec to Ld Chllr, Sec to Commrs in Lunacy 1895–1900, Commr in Lunacy 1900–08; *b* 1860; *educ* Merton Coll Oxford (MA); *m* 19 June 1900 Evelyn Alice, 5th dau of Sydney Chambers, of Crete Hill, Nutfield, Surrey, and *d* 11 Oct 1908, leaving issue:

1a Roger Granville, Cdr RN; *b* 23 May 1905; *m* 30 Jan 1936 *Phyllis, dau of Brig-Gen Wilfred Ellershaw, RA, and *dsp* 16 Feb 1982

1a *Ingaret Stella; *b* 5 Feb 1902; *m* 1st 2 July 1931 Gordon Arthur James Young (they added on marriage the name GIFFARD); *m* 2nd Sir Laurens van der Post, CBE (*d* 1997)

(1) Magdalene G de Longueville; *m* 1904 Rev Arthur Bernard Littlewood, MA, Vicar E Farleigh, Kent

2 Francis Osbern (Rev); Vicar Long Sutton and Hartley Wintney, Hants, Rector Deane, Hants; *b* 27 Sept 1818; *educ* St John's Coll Oxford (BA); *m* 10 Dec 1851 Anna Maria (*d* 15 Jan 1893), dau of Rev Richard Ryan, and *d* 23 Dec 1894, leaving, with other issue:

(1) John Hardinge Leigh (Rev); Rector Cowley, Glos; *b* 10 Sept 1854; *d* 1930

3 HARDINGE STANLEY, **1st Earl**

1 Sara Lees; *m* J Houston Browne, barrister

STANLEY GIFFARD *m* 2nd 1830 his distant cousin Mary Anne, dau and coheir of Henry Giffard, RN (descended from Henry Giffard, of High Bickington, 3rd s of Heny Giffard and Martha Hill; *see* above), and *d* Nov 1858, leaving, with other issue:

4 Harry Stanley; barrister Inner Temple, Registrar Bankruptcy High Court; *b* 1832; *m* 1865 Alice (*d* 1900), dau of J Adams, and *d* 12 Oct 1912

2 Mary Lees Fane; *m* Rajendra Chandra Chandra, Surgn, Prof Medical Coll Calcutta, and *d* 1885

The 3rd son,

HARDINGE STANLEY GIFFARD, **1st Earl of Halsbury**, so *cr* 17 Jan 1898, as also VISCOUNT TIVERTON, of Tiverton, Co Devon, and earlier 26 June 1885 BARON HALSBURY, of Halsbury, Devon, PC (1885), QC (1865); *b* 3 Sept 1823; *educ* Merton Coll Oxford (BA 1852, MA 1855, Hon DCL 1891); barrister Inner Temple 1850, Bencher 1865, Treasurer 1881, Slr-Gen 1875–80, Ld Chllr 1885–86, 1886–92 and 1895–1905, Constable Launceston Castle 1883, High Steward Oxford U 1896, MP (C) Launceston 1877–85, Hon LLD Cantab 1908; *m* 1st 28 Aug 1852 Caroline (*dsp* 30 Sept 1873), dau of W C Humphreys; *m* 2nd 14 Oct 1874 Wilhelmina (*d* 22 Dec 1927), dau of Henry Woodfall, of Stanmore, Middx, and *d* 11 Dec 1921, having had, with two daus (Lynie May Rohais, *b* 25 Aug 1875, *d* 15 April 1879; (Constance Mary) Evelyn, *m* 21 April 1902 her cousin Edward Walter Giffard (*d* 8 March 1938), of Charts Edge, Westerham, Kent, 2nd s of Edward Giffard (*see* above), and *d* 3 July 1962):

HARDINGE GOULBURN GIFFARD, **2nd Earl of Halsbury**, KC 1923; *b* 20 June 1880; BA Oxon; barrister Inner Temple 1906, Recorder Carmarthen 1923–35, Maj RAF (pioneer WW I of what came to be called operational research); *m* 7 Aug 1907 Esme (*d* 19 Sept 1973 aged 89), dau of James Stewart Wallace by Lucy (*see* DUFF GORDON, Bt), dau of Douglas Sutherland, and *d* 15 Sept 1943, leaving:

1 JOHN ANTHONY HARDINGE GIFFARD, **3rd and present Earl of Halsbury**

1 *Flavia Joan Lucy; Medaille de Vermeil de la Reconnaissance Française 1946; *b* 20 Sept 1910; *m* 14 Nov 1933 James Alasdair Anderson (*d* 1982), only surv s of James Scott Anderson, of Tulichewan Castle, Dunbartonshire, and has issue:

(1) *Douglas Hardinge [Douglas Anderson Esq, 56036 Palaia, Prov di Pisa, Italy]; portrait painter; *b* 8 Aug 1934; *educ* Eton; *m* 1st 3 Jan 1962 (*divorce* 1969) Mary Elizabeth Siani, only dau of John Jenkins, of Palmers Farm, Hawkenbury, Kent, and has issue:

1a *James Henry Wallace; *b* 7 Sept 1964; *m* 1992 *Beatrice Isabella, dau of Adriano Versolato

1a *Lucy Elizabeth; *b* 26 July 1962; *m* 1985 *Bevil Charles Symondson and has issue (*see* INNES, Bt, of Balvenie)

(1) (cont.) Douglas Anderson *m* 2nd 1974 *Veronica Margaret, dau of John Edward Markes, of Recess House, Recess, Co Galway, and has issue:

2a *Sophia Esme; *b* 1977

(1) *Margaret Minette Rohais [Lady Campbell, Crarae Lodge, by Inveraray, Argyll PA32 8YA]; *b* 4 July 1937; *m* 22 July 1961 *Sir Ilay Mark Campbell of Succoth, 7th Bt (*qv*), and has issue

HALSEY

Arms: Arg. on a pile sa. three griffin's heads erased of the field. **Crest:** A dexter cubit arm erect ppr., sleeve gu., cuff arg., holding a griffin's claw erased or. **Motto:** *Nescit vox missa reverti* ('The spoken word cannot be recalled'). **Creation:** Bt. (UK) 22 June 1920.

SIR JOHN WALTER BROOKE HALSEY 4TH BT, of Gaddesden, Co Hertford [Brother John Halsey, The Hermitage, 23 Manse Rd, Roslin, Midlothian EH25 9LF]; *b* 26 Dec 1933; *s* f 1970; *educ* Eton and Magdalene Coll Cambridge (BA 1957); Deacon 1961, Curate Stockbridge 1961–65, Priest 1962, Monk 1965–

Lineage: JOHN HALSEY, of the Parsonage, Gt Gaddesden, Herts; living 1512; had:

WILLIAM HALSEY, of the Parsonage; *m* Alice — and *d* 1556, leaving:

WILLIAM HALSEY, of the Golden Parsonage; *m* Ann — and was *bur* 16 May 1596, leaving, with other issue:

ROBERT HALSEY, of Gt Gaddesden; *m* Dorothy, dau of William Downes, of Linslade, Bucks, and was *bur* 12 Oct 1618, leaving:

WILLIAM HALSEY, of Gt Gaddesden; *b* June 1590; *m* Lettice, dau and coheir of Henry Stringer, of London, and *d* Nov 1637; his est surv s:

Sir JOHN HALSEY, of Gt Gaddesden; Master Chancery; *b* Dec 1615; *m* Judith (*d* 25 April 1658), est dau and coheir of James Necton, and *d* 29 June 1670, having had, with other issue :

THOMAS HALSEY, of Gt Gaddesden; MP, High Sheriff Herts; *m* Anne, dau and heiress of Thomas Henshaw, of Kensington and Pulham, Dorset, and *d* 25 May 1715, leaving, with an er s (Henshaw Halsey, *dsp* 13 Jan 1738):

CHARLES HALSEY, of Gt Gaddesden; High Sheriff Herts 1746; *m* Agatha (*d* 26 Feb 1782 aged 75), dau of Frederick Dorrien, of London, and had issue:

1 Frederick Halsey, of Gt Gaddesden; Commissary-Gen Army Germany, ADC to Prince of Brunswick; *d* unm 24 Aug 1762

2 THOMAS

1 Elizabeth; *m* Thomas Herbert Noyes

2 Anne; *m* 1st Rev George Dutens; *m* 2nd Rev James Willis, Rector Sopley, Hants

3 Sophia; *m* 2 April 1766 Richard Bingham, of Melcombe Bingham, Dorset, and *d* 1773, leaving issue. He *d* 1823

4 Theodosia; *m* 1st Rev John Pery, Rector Wyton, Hunts; *m* 2nd Robert Sparrow, of Worlingham Hall, Suffolk. He *d* 6 April 1748

CHARLES HALSEY's 2nd son,

THOMAS HALSEY, of Gt Gaddesden; MP Herts 1768, 1774 and 1780; *b* 4 Feb 1731; *m* 18 March 1784 Sarah, yst dau of John Crawley, of Stockwood, Beds, and *d* 9 Oct 1788, having had, with a s (Thomas, *b* 21 April, *d* 30 Dec 1788):

SARAH Halsey, of Gt Gaddesden; *m* 1st 3 Aug 1804 Joseph Thompson WHATELY later HALSEY, 3rd s of Rev Joseph WHATELY later HALSEY (Act of Parl 1805), LLD, of Nonsuch Park, Surrey (*d* 1818), and had:

1 Thomas Plumer; MP Herts 1846, 1847, 1852; *b* 26 Jan 1815; *m* 26 Jan 1839 Frederica, dau and heiress of Gen Frederick Johnson, of Hilton, and was lost at sea with her in the SS *Ercolano* 24 April 1854, having had:

(1) THOMAS FREDERICK (Sir), **1st Bt**

(2) Ethelbert Arthur Sackville

1 Mary Elizabeth; *m* 11 Sept 1826 Thomas Herbert Noyes and *d* 14 Jan 1890

2 Jane; *m* 14 Aug 1827 Rev George Tyrwhitt-Drake and *d* 28 May 1864, leaving issue

3 Emma; *m* 22 Aug 1832 Lt-Col William Tyrwhitt-Drake and *d* 2 Sept 1897, leaving issue

4 Fanny; *d* 13 Nov 1886

SARAH (Mrs Joseph) HALSEY *m* 2nd 6 Feb 1821 Rev John Fitz MOORE later MOORE-HALSEY (added on marriage; *d* 24 April 1864), est s of Richard Moore, of Hampton Court Palace, and *d* 25 April 1869, leaving issue:

5 Georgiana Theodosia; *m* 3 Nov 1846 Col Leopold Grimston Paget (*see* ANGLESEY, M), and *d* 28 Feb 1919, leaving issue

SARAH's gs,

Sir (Thomas) Frederick Halsey, 1st Bt (UK), so *cr* 22 June 1920, PC, JP; *b* 9 Dec 1839; *educ* Eton and Ch Ch Oxford (BA 1861, MA 1864); Ld Manors Hemel Hempstead, Flaunden and Bovingdon, Lay Rector Gt Gaddesden, Herts: V-Lt, Chm CC and QS, MP 1874–85 and W Herts 1855–1906, Maj and Hon Lt-Col Herts Yeo; *m* 28 Sept 1865 Mary Julia (*d* 8 Dec 1922), 4th dau of Hon Frederick Octavius Wells, BCS, Ch Justice Agra, and had:

1 WALTER JOHNSTON (Sir), **2nd Bt**

2 Arthur, CBE (1919); Capt RN, Boer War (despatches) and WW I; *b* 31 July 1869; *m* 1st 14 April 1909 Blanche Helen Kerr (*d* 25 Feb 1917), dau of Adml Mark Robert Pechell (*see* 1970 edn PECHELL, Bt); *m* 2nd 3 Jan 1922 Dorothy Mary (*d* 12 Dec 1950), 4th dau of Samuel Gurney Leatham, of Hemsworth Hall, Yorks, and *d* 15 Aug 1957, having by his 1st w had:

(1) Lettice; *d* unm 21 Feb 1956

3 Frederick (Rev Canon); Hon Canon St Albans, Chaplain to Bp St Albans 1928; *b* 29 Nov 1870; *educ* Eton and Magdalen Coll Oxford (MA 1897); *m* 27 July 1901 Audrey Katharine (*d* 14 Jan 1969 aged 93), only dau of Lt-Col William Marsden, of Cedar Court, Farnham, Surrey, and Chelmorton, Derbys, and *d* 31 Jan 1952, leaving:

(1) Patrick Johnston; *b* 17 Feb 1905; *educ* Eton and Magdalen Coll Oxford (BA 1927); *d* 22 Oct 1988

(2) Guy Marsden, TD, JP (Herts 1949, Somerset 1963); Lt-Col Herts Regt (TA) WW II (despatches); *b* 15 Nov 1908; *educ* Eton; *m* 23 Sept 1939 *Mary Juliet Gough [Mrs Guy Halsey, Whitehouse Farm, Gaddesden Row, Hemel Hempstead, Herts HP2 6HG], dau of Capt Robert Wemyss Muir Arbuthnot, MC (*see* ARBUTHNOT, Bt, of Edinburgh), and *d* 28 Oct 1990, leaving issue:

1a +Nicholas Guy, TD, DL (Herts 1998) [Nicholas Halsey Esq TD DL, The Golden Parsonage, Gaddesden Row, Hemel Hempstead, Herts HP2 6HG]; *b* 14 June 1948; *educ* Eton and RAC Cirencester (MRAC); Maj RGJ (V), Dep Hon Col (Herts) Roy Anglian Regt (TA) 1996, High Sheriff Herts, FRICS; *m* 7 Aug 1976 *Viola Georgina Juliet, only dau of Maj George Thorne, MC, DL (*see* PEEL, E), and has issue:

1b +Guy Francis Johnston; *b* 4 Oct 1981

2a +Robert Frederick (Robin), FCA; *b* 13 Feb 1950; *educ* Eton and RAC Cirencester; *m* 2 Oct 1976 *Elizabeth Virginia, yr dau of John Holman, and has issue:

1b +Daniel John; *b* 26 Dec 1978

2b +Samuel Treve; *b* 16 March 1983

(1) *Katherine Audrey [Miss Katherine Halsey, 7 Chestnut Close, Potten End, Berkhamsted, Herts]

(2) *Barbara [Mrs John Curgenven, Old House Cottage, Combe, Witney, Oxon]; *m* 15 Sept 1961 John Parr Curgenven (*d* 1982), er s of Sir Arthur Joseph Curgenven

4 Lionel (Sir), GCMG, GCVO, KCIE, CB, JP, DL; *b* 26 Feb 1872; Boer War 1899–1900 and WW I (despatches), ADC to HM GEORGE V 1914–17, 4th Sea Ld 1916–17, 3rd Sea Ld 1917–18, R-Adml 1917, cmdg Australian Fleet 1918–19, V-Adml 1921 (ret 1922), Adml 1926, Memb Cncl Duchy Cornwall 1920, Comptroller and Treas to HRH THE PRINCE OF WALES 1920–36, Extra Equerry to TM GEORGE V 1921–36, EDWARD VIII 1936 and GEORGE VI 1937–49, CA Beds, Chm Navy League 1941–46 (Pres 1946), Hon Cdre Sea Cadet Corps 1941, Legn Honour, Orders Rising Sun Japan 1st Cl, St Vladimir and St Anne Russia, Grand Cordon Order Nile, American DSO; *m* 24 Jan 1905 Morwenna (*d* 20 Feb 1959), dau of Maj Bevil Granville, JP, of Wellesbourne Hall, Warwicks, and *d* 26 Oct 1949, leaving:

(1) *Joan, JP (Denbigh 1951–59, Herts 1960) [Mrs George Wood JP, The Old Schoolhouse, Whipsnade, Beds]; *b* 1910; *m* 26 May 1933 George Lockhart Wood (*d* 21 June 1959), only s of Capt John Lockhart Wood, DSO, 18th Hus, and has issue:

1a *John Lockhart, JP [John Wood Esq JP, The Hoo, Great Gaddesden, Hemel Hempstead, Herts]; *b* 22 Aug 1935; *educ* Eton and Trin Coll Cambridge (BA); High Sheriff Herts 1988; *m* 26 Oct 1963 *Rosemary Sonia Despard, dau of Richard Graham Hensley Hopkins, and has issue:

1b *George Edmund Richard; *b* 16 Sept 1966; *m* 7 Aug 1993 *Caroline Trevor, dau of Canon Anthony Johnson

1b *Kirstin Rebecca; *b* 5 Aug 1968

2a *Lionel David [Lionel Wood Esq, Manor Farm, Milcombe, Oxon]; Lt Welsh Gds, Extra Equerry to HRH THE DUKE OF EDINBURGH 1965–67; *b* 25 March 1938; *educ* Eton; *m* 8 Oct 1960 his cousin *Belinda Mary, er dau of Gilbert Graham Balfour by Jean, 2nd dau of **Sir Walter Johnston Halsey, 2nd Bt** (*see* below), and has issue:

1b *James Lionel Norman; *b* 19 May 1963

1b *Sarah Morwenna; *b* 16 Sept 1961

2b *Alexandra Louise; *b* 23 Oct 1965

3a *Richard George [Richard Wood Esq, Markham House, Badminton, Glos GL9 1DG]; *b* 4 Oct 1939; *educ* Eton; *m* 14 Dec 1963 *Penelope Gay, est dau of Lt-Col John Bertie Harris Daniel, MBE, MC, RA, and has issue:

1b *Andrew John; *b* 21 July 1966; *m* 1991 *Rachel Claire Morris and has:

1c *Angus Richard; *b* 1993

1c *Elinor Claire; *b* 1991

1b *Emma Ruth; *b* 7 Feb 1965

4a *Edmund Michael [Edmund Wood Esq, The Old Rectory, Holwell, Herts SG5 3SP]; *b* 7 Sept 1943; *educ* Eton; *m* 1971 *Elizabeth Ann, dau of S/Ldr Robert Roland Patrick Fisher, RAF, and has issue:

1b *Sarah Georgina; *b* 1974

2b *Ann Louise; *b* 1977

1a *Ruth Mary [Mrs James Ritchie, Drissaig House, Lochavich, by Taynuilt, Argyll]; *b* 8 July 1945; *m* 1973 *James Henry Wood Ritchie and has issue:

1b *Fiona Mary; *b* 1975

2b *Margaret Jean; *b* 1976

(2) *Ruth [Miss Ruth Halsey, Parsonage Piece, Whipsnade, Beds]

5 Reginald; Maj and Brevet Lt-Col Herts Yeo, RA (TA); *b* 10 Aug 1873; *m* 16 April 1910 Marion Lindsay (*d* 27 Dec 1927), widow of Capt Henry Gerald Leigh, 1st Life Gds, and dau of Hugh Lindsay Antrobus (*see* ANTROBUS, Bt), and *d* 30 May 1927

6 Gerald (Rev); MA Oxon, Rector St Fillan's Scottish Episcopal Church Comrie; *b* 21 Jan 1881; *educ* Eton and Magdalen Coll Oxford (MA 1906); *m* 11 Aug 1920 (Constance) Dove (*d* 23 Oct 1958), er dau of Rev Canon Arthur Fitzgerald Evans (*see* SALT, Bt, of Saltaire), and *dsp* 26 Dec 1960

7 Gavin George; MA Oxon, barrister; *b* 5 Sept 1888; *d* unm 23 Oct 1918

1 Florence; *d* unm 21 June 1918

2 Mary Cecilia; *m* 21 Nov 1899 Walter Edward Barnett, of Red Hall, Croxley Green, Herts, and *d* 18 March 1957, leaving issue. He *d* 31 Aug 1944

3 Edith; *m* 15 Jan 1903 Lt-Col Bernard Granville, DSO, Warwicks Yeo, formerly 3rd Hus, of Wellesbourne Hall, Warwicks, and *d* 14 June 1952, leaving issue. He *d* 4 Nov 1933

Sir FREDERICK *d* 12 Feb 1927; his est son,

Sir Walter Johnston Halsey, 2nd Bt, OBE (1920), JP, DL Herts, JP Middx, CA Herts; *b* 1 June 1868; *educ* Eton and Magdalen Coll Oxford (BA); Lt-Col 4th Bn Beds Regt, WW I as Staff Capt DAAG and AAG (despatches three times), chm Legal Insur; *m* 28 July 1896 Agnes Marion (*d* 14 Sept 1954), yr dau of William MacAlpine Leny, and had issue:

1 THOMAS EDGAR (Sir), **3rd Bt**

2 William Edmund; Lt-Cdr RN; *b* 8 Jan 1903; *m* 16 May 1931 Barbara Dorothea (*d* 1993), dau of Charles Lindsay Orr Ewing (*see* ORR EWING, Bt), and *d* 1986, having had:

(1) Gavin Charles; *b* 1 July 1932; *d* following a car crash 4 Nov 1953

(1) *Bridget; *b* 4 June 1934; *m* 18 Jan 1958 *Edward Alfred Heycock, er surv s of Morris Sadler Heycock, MC, and has issue:

1a *Susan Mary; *b* 15 March 1959; *m* 19– *William Kennedy McConnel (*see* MONTAGU-POLLOCK, Bt)

2a *Caroline Bridget; *b* 22 Nov 1960

3a *Jennifer Lucy; *b* 27 March 1966

1 Marion Blanche; *m* 2 June 1925 Thomas Selwyn Pryor, MC, 2nd surv s of Selwyn Roberts Pryor, and had issue. He *d* 27 June 1929

2 Jean; *m* 17 Feb 1931 Gilbert Graham Balfour, est s of Sir Graham Balfour, MA, LLD, and had issue:

(1) *Belinda Mary; *b* 1 May 1937; *m* 8 Oct 1960 Maj Lionel David Wood, 2nd s of George Lockhart Wood by Joan, er dau of Adml Sir Lionel Halsey (*see* above), and has issue

(2) *Elisabeth Rhoda; *b* 24 Nov 1938; *m* 30 Aug 1971 David Robert Shelley, yst s of V-Adml Richard Benyon, CB, CBE (*see* SHELLEY, Bt)

3 *Agatha; *m* 26 May 1942 (*divorce*) Alan Edmondson Bainbridge, RHA, yst s of J P Bainbridge, of Melbourne, Australia, and has issue:

(1) *Thomas Howard; *b* 9 July 1943; *educ* Geelong GS; *m* 1977 *Isabel Frances Collins

(2) *Andrew Halsey; *b* 31 Oct 1944; *educ* Geelong GS; *m* 1973 *Helen Brown and has:

1a *Alexander James; *b* 19–

1a *Elizabeth Anne; *b* 19–

(3) *David James Macalpine; *b* 5 Jan 1950; *educ* Geelong GS; *m* 1974 *Judith Roslyn Manley and has issue:

1a *Fiona; *b* 1979

2a *Megan; *b* 19–

(1) *Patricia Mary; *b* 1946; *m* 1976 *John Bruce McBride

(2) *Jean Vivien; *b* 1955

4 *Evelyn Cecilia [Mrs Frederick De Butts, Church Cottage, Hoggeston, Bucks]; *m* 8 July 1944 *Brig Frederick Manus De Butts, CMG, OBE, DL, Somerset LI, only s of Brig Frederick Cromie De Butts, CB, DSO, MC, of Coolnakilly House, Gleneay, Co Wicklow, and has issue:

(1) *David Frederick; *b* 1950; *m* 1977 *Barbara Elizabeth Scott Hooper and has issue:

1a *Richard Frederick; *b* 1978

2a *Michael McCrea; *b* 1980

1a *Lucy Katherine; *b* 1983

(1) *Caroline Mary; *b* 1952; *m* 1974 *Anthony Hugh Bond and has issue:

1a *Jonathan James Hughes; *b* 1977

2a *Rupert Charles; *b* 1980

1a *Victoria Jane; *b* 1984

Sir WALTER *d* 2 Sept 1950; his er son,

Sir Thomas Edgar Halsey, 3rd Bt, DSO (1940), JP (Herts 1950); V-Lt 1957 (DL 1948–57); *b* 28 Nov 1898; *educ* Eton; Capt RM, served WWS I and II (despatches); *m* 20 Dec 1926 Jean Margaret Palmer (*d* 12 Sept 1970), est dau of Capt Bertram Willes Dayrell Brooke, Taun Muda of Sarawak, and *d* 30 Aug 1970, having had:

1 Sir JOHN WALTER BROOKE HALSEY, **4th and present Bt**

1 Sarah Anne; *b* 17 Feb 1929; *d* 19 Jan 1937

2 *Margaret Anne [Mrs John Farnon, Old Bell House, Market Lavington, nr Devizes, Wilts]; *b* 25 Feb 1938; *m* 29 July 1961 *John Farnon, s of Leo Farnon, and has issue:

(1) *Jennifer Anne; *b* 7 June 1962

(2) *Nicola Jane; *b* 29 Jan 1964

(3) *Alison Sarah; *b* 26 Feb 1966

HAMBLEDEN

Arms: Arg. on a chevron az. between three oak leaves vert, each charged with an acorn or, as many leopard's faces jessant-de-lys of the field. **Crest:** A cubit arm erect, habited az., cuffed and charged with three mascles in chevron arg., holding in the hand ppr. three branches of oak vert, fructed or. **Supporters:** Dexter, a sea-lion vert, langued gu., semée of escallops, gorged with a collar and pendant therefrom by a chain a portcullis, all or; sinister, a wyvern gu., langued az., semée of mullets, gorged with a chain and pendant therefrom a portcullis, all or. **Motto:** *Deo non fortuna fretus* ('Relying on God, not on fortune'). **Creation:** V. (UK) 10 Nov 1891.

THE 4TH VISCOUNT HAMBLEDEN, of Hambleden, Co Buckingham (William Herbert Smith) [The Rt Hon The Viscount Hambleden, The Estate Office, Hambleden, Oxon]; *b* 2 April 1930; *s* f 1948; *educ* Eton; *m* 1st 21 Feb 1955 (*divorce* 1988) Donna Maria Carmela Attolico di Adelfia, dau of Count Bernardo Attolico, of Rome; *m* 2nd 1988 *Mrs Lesley Watson and by his 1st w has:

1 +(WILLIAM) HENRY BERNARD [The Hon Henry Smith, The Manor House, Hambleden, Oxon; 109 Eccleston Mews, London SW1]; *b* 18 Nov 1955; *m* 17 Sept 1983 *Sara Suzanne, dau of Joseph F Anlauf, of Palos Verde Estates, Calif., and Mrs Suzanne K Anlauf, of Oak Park, Ill., and has:

(1) *Sara Marie Celeste; *b* 1986

(2) *Alexandra Patricia; *b* 1989

2 +Bernard James; *b* 17 May 1957

3 +Alexander David; *b* 11 March 1959

4 +Nicolas Robin Bartolomeo [The Hon Nicholas Smith, Wellington Sq, London SW3]; *b* 17 Aug 1960; investment banker; *m* 19– *Yumi —, of Japan, and has:

(1) +Taro; *b* 1993

(1) +Kenji; *b* 1996

5 +Lorenzo Patrick Harold; *b* 8 Aug 1962

Lineage: FREDERICK DAWES DANVERS, of Bushey, Herts; *d* 21 Oct 1867, leaving:

EMILY Danvers, **Viscountess Hambleden**, of Hambleden, Co Buckingham (UK), so *cr* 10 Nov 1891, with remainder to the issue male of her 2nd husb; *m* 1st 22 July 1854 Benjamin Auber Leach (*d* 20 July 1855) and had:

1 Mary Auber; *m* 1879 R-Adml William Codrington, CB, and *d* 19 Feb 1930, leaving issue (*see* SALTOUN, L)

The **Viscountess Hambleden** *m* 2nd 13 April 1858 William Henry SMITH, PC (1877), DCL, MP (C) Westminster 1868–85 and Strand 1885–91 (*b* 24 June 1825, joined f's firm 1841, jr ptnr 1846, memb 1st London School Bd 1871, Sec Treasury 1874–77, 1st Ld Admlty 1877–80, Sec for War 1885–86 and 1886–87, Ch Sec Ireland 1886, 1st Ld Treasury and Ldr H of C 1887–91, Constable Dover Castle, Ld Warden Cinque Ports, *d* 6 Oct 1891), only s of William Henry Smith, bookseller, of Walton House, Bournemouth, Hants, and The Strand, London (*d* 28 July 1865), and had issue:

1 Henry Walton; *b* 1 Oct 1865; *d* Feb 1866

2 WILLIAM FREDERICK DANVERS, **2nd Viscount**

2 Emily Anna; *m* 7 July 1887 Sir William Alison Dyke Acland, 2nd Bt, of Oxford (*qv*), and *d* 28 Jan 1942, leaving issue

3 Helen; *m* 16 April 1896 Henry Sydney Seymour and *d* 17 Jan 1944, leaving issue (*see* SOMERSET, D)

4 Beatrice Danvers; DGStJ; *m* 30 July 1885 Col Alfred Dyke Acland, CBE, JP, yst s of Sir Henry Wentworth Acland, 1st Bt, of Oxford (*qv*), and *d* 4 Dec 1942, leaving issue

5 Mabel Danvers, DBE (1919); *m* 16 Nov 1887 5th Earl of Harrowby (*qv*) and *d* 27 March 1956, leaving issue

The VISCOUNTESS *d* 13 Aug 1913; her only surv son,

WILLIAM FREDERICK DANVERS SMITH, **2nd Viscount Hambleden**, DL Devon; *b* 12 Aug 1868; BA Oxon; MP Strand 1891–1910, Hon Col 96th (Devon Yeo) Bde, RFA (TA), Hon Col 43rd (Wessex) Div Train RASC (TA), Lt-Col TFR, Lt-Col Roy 1st Devon Yeo, Chm King's Coll Hosp, Treas King's Coll London, KGStJ; *m* 26 July 1894 Lady Esther Georgina Caroline Gore, DGStJ (*d* 11 Oct 1955), 3rd dau of 5th Earl of Arran (*qv*), and had:

1 WILLIAM HENRY, **3rd Viscount**

2 James Frederick Arthur, OBE (1945); *b* 27 Jan 1906; *educ* Eton and Oxford; CStJ, Hon FRCM, Lt-Col Gen List WW II (despatches), Assist Mil Sec to Cdr 2nd Army 1944–45, Govr Sadler's Wells Fndn, dir W H Smith & Son (Hldgs) and W H Smith & Son Ltd

3 David John, CBE (1964), JP (Berks 1946); *b* 20 May 1907; *educ* Eton and Oxford, Ld Lt Berks 1959–76, High Steward Wallingford, Hon DLitt 1973, Hon Col, Dep Hon Col 2nd Bn Wessex Regt (Vols) TAVR, chm W H Smith & Son (Hldgs) to 1972, dir Lloyds Bank and Union Discount, memb Delegacy King's Coll Lond and Cncl Bradfield Coll, Maj RA (TA) WW II; *m* 22 July 1931 *Lady Helen Pleydell-Bouverie, OBE (1946) [The Lady Helen Smith, King's Copse House, Bucklebury, Berks], yst dau of 6th Earl of Radnor (*qv*), and *d* 25 Nov 1976, leaving:

(1) +Julian David [Julian Smith Esq, 6 The Hermitage, London SW13 9RF]; *b* 5 Sept 1932; *educ* Eton; *m* 2 Feb 1966 *Eleanor, er dau of John Eustace Blyth, MBE, of Ham Common, Surrey, and has issue:

1a +Dickon Julian Henry; *b* 1972

1a *Alexandra Esther Helen; *b* 29 May 1969

(2) +Antony Frederick [Antony Smith Esq, Bouverie, PO Box 155, Mount Barker, W Australia]; *b* 24 May 1937; *educ* Eton; *m* 24 Feb 1962 *Alison Priscilla, 3rd dau of Lt-Col John Clark Pyper, OBE, IMS, of Westbury, Tasmania, and has issue:

1a +James Antony David; *b* 4 Dec 1962

2a +Philip Henry; *b* 3 March 1964

1a *Harriet Frances; *b* 17 April 1967

2a *Helen Sarah; *b* 9 July 1969

(3) +Peter Henry [Peter Smith Esq, Leighton House, Goodmanham, York YO4 3HX]; *b* 15 Aug 1939; *educ* Eton; *m* 1st April 1967 *Scilla Ann, est dau of Peter Bennett, chm W H Smith 1977–82, of Dene House, Little Dene, nr Glynde, Sussex, and has issue:

1a +Charles Henry; *b* 5 Nov 1968; *educ* Eton; *m* 20 July 1997 *Amanda, dau of Geoffrey Smith, of Titchfield, Hants

1a *Clare Scilla; *b* 12 July 1971

2a *Catherine Ann; *b* 30 April 1975

(4) +David Michael [David Smith Esq, 21 Wallingford Rd, Cholsey, nr Wallingford, Oxon]; *b* 13 Nov 1947; *educ* Eton; *m* 1st 1 Aug 1970 (*divorce* 1992) Caroline, er dau of R H Ardill; *m* 2nd 1992 *Dr Clare Stephenson and by his 1st w has:

1a +Jack Robert; *b* 1977

1a *Rachel Charlotte; *b* 1973

(1) Esther Joanna; *b* 16 May 1934; *d* unm 31 Dec 1992

1 Edith Mabell Emily (Dede); *b* 20 July 1901; *d* unm 8 June 1973

2 Margaret Esther Lucie, JP Wilts; *b* 1 Aug 1908; *m* 16 Oct 1928 1st Baron Margadale (*qv*) and *d* 1980, leaving issue

The 2nd VISCOUNT *d* 16 June 1928; his est son,

WILLIAM HENRY SMITH, **3rd Viscount Hambleden**; *b* 25 July 1903; *educ* Eton and New Coll Oxford (MA 1939); memb House Laity Ch Assembly 1939, Chm: W H Smith & Son and King's Coll Hosp; *m* 26 Sept 1928 Patricia (*d* 1994), only dau of 15th Earl of Pembroke and (12th Earl of) Montgomery (*qv*), and *d* 31 March 1948, leaving:

1 WILLIAM HERBERT SMITH, **4th and present Viscount Hambleden**

2 +Richard Edward; *b* 10 April 1937; *m* 1973 *Christine Hickey and has:

(1) +Christopher Richard; *b* 1975

3 +Philip Reginald [The Hon Philip Smith, Campden House, Chipping Campden, Glos]; *b* 7 Sept 1945 (HM QUEEN ELIZABETH THE QUEEN MOTHER stood sponsor); *educ* Eton; Maj RGJ, High Sheriff Glos 1992; *m* 2 June 1973 *Mary, yst dau of John E M Roberts, of Bottom Farm, Checkendon, Oxon, and has issue:

(1) +Thomas William; *b* 1976

(2) +James Edmund Philip; *b* 1983

(1) *Clare Elizabeth; *b* 30 Nov 1974

(2) *Emily; *b* 1980

1 *Laura Caroline Beatrice [The Hon Mrs Brand, 6 Howley Place, London W2]; *b* 9 Sept 1931; *m* 27 July 1953 *Lt Michael Charles Brand, Coldstream Gds (*see* HAMPDEN, V) and has issue

2 *Katharine Patricia [The Hon Mrs Townend, 122 Hurlingham Rd, London SW6]; *b* 17 Aug 1933; *m* 1st 22 Sept 1961 Ivan Moffat, s of Curtis Moffat and Countess Ledebur; *m* 2nd 1973 *Peter Robert Gascoigne Townend and by her 1st husb has issue:

(1) *Jonathan David; *b* 2 Jan 1963; *m* 1986 *Carmel J B, 2nd dau of L M Sawle, of Perth, W Australia

(2) *Patrick Nichols; *b* 29 July 1968 (HRH PRINCESS MARGARET COUNTESS OF SNOWDON stood sponsor)

HAMBLING

Arms: Argent a sword erect sable between two flaunches azure, each charged with a hank of cotton of the field. **Crest:** A falcon supporting with the dexter claw a distaff proper, and charged on the body with a bezant. **Motto:** Discern and decide.
Creation: Bt. (UK) 27 Feb 1924.

SIR (HERBERT) HUGH HAMBLING, 3RD BT, of Yoxford, Suffolk [Sir Hugh Hambling Bt, 1219 Evergreen Point Rd, Medina, WA 98039, USA]; *b* 3 Aug 1916; *s* f 1966; *educ* Eton; F/Lt RAF WW II, with Br Airways 1937–39, joined BOAC 1947, representing BOAC with The Boeing Co, Seattle, 1961; *m* 1st 23 Sept 1950 Anne Page (*d* 1990), er dau of Judge Hugo Edmund Oswald, of Seattle; *m* 2nd 1991 *Helen Seymour, er dau of Donald Mackinnon, of Marida Yallock, Victoria, Australia, and widow of David Maitland Gavin, of Chelsea, and has by his 1st w:

1 +(HERBERT) PETER HUGH [Peter Hambling, 2108 92nd Ave NE, Bellevue, WA 98004, USA]; *b* 6 Sept 1953; *educ* Washington U (BSc); co-fndr and ch exec Digital Control (Inc), of Washington; *m* 1st 1982 (*divorce* 1989) Jan Elizabeth, dau of Stanton Frederick, Jr, of Seattle; *m* 2nd 1991 *Lorayn Louise, dau of Frank Joseph Koson, and by her has:

(1) +Colin Hugh; *b* 1991

(1) +Austin Peter; *b* 1993

Lineage: WILLIAM HAMBLING, of Snape, Suffolk; *b* 1746; *m* Sarah Cotton and *d* 1795, leaving issue:

COTTON HAMBLING, of Snape, Rendham and Earl Soham, Suffolk, *d* 13 Nov 1858, leaving issue:

WILLIAM JAMES HAMBLING, JP, of Dunstable, Beds; *b* 27 Feb 1831; Lt-Col; *m* 21 July 1853 Elizabeth Woodruffe (*d* 1 June 1867) and *d* 25 Sept 1898, leaving, with other issue:

Sir (Henry) Herbert Hambling, 1st Bt (UK), *cr* 27 Feb 1924, JP (Herts), DL (Suffolk); *b* 8 July 1857, High Sheriff Suffolk 1924, Lt City London, fin memb Min Munitions WW I, dep chm: Barclays Bank, Barclays Bank (Dominion, Colonial and Overseas) and Barclays Bank (France), dir: Barclays Bank SAI, N Br and Mercantile Insur and Ocean Marine Insur, pres Inst of Bankers 1923–25, dir Imperial Airways 1924–30 (formed following report presented 1923 by Hambling Ctee of which he chm), ktd 1917; *m* 1st 2 Nov 1882 Thirza (*d* 8 July 1891), dau of William George Twigg, slr; *m* 2nd 10 Oct 1893 Isabella Mary (*d* 4 March 1916), dau of Frederick Brown, of Clapham, and *d* 19 Jan 1932, leaving by his 1st w:

1 **Sir (Herbert) Guy Musgrave Hambling, 2nd Bt**; *b* 12 Aug 1883; Capt Canadian Inf WW I, slr 1907; *m* 29 April 1911 Olive Margaret Gordon, JP (Suffolk 1937) (*d* 23 Oct 1969), only dau of Edwin Carter, of Leeds, and *d* 13 Feb 1966, leaving:

(1) Sir (HERBERT) HUGH HAMBLING, **3rd and present Bt**

(1) *Margherita; *b* 20 Jan 1912; *m* 27 Sept 1937 Maurice Hare (*d* 1993), yst s of Maj-Gen Sir Steuart Welwood Hare, KCMG, CB, of Blairlogie, Stirlingshire, and has issue:

1a *David Steuart [David Hare Esq, 23 Vale Rd, Claygate, Surrey KT10 0NL]; *b* 10 March 1942; *educ* Eton; *m* 1st 1969 (*divorce* 1983) Julie, dau of Walter Pierre Courtauld, and has issue:

1b *Lucas Welwood Bruno; *b* 1971

2b *Samuel James; *b* 1974

3b *Fergus Lincoln; *b* 1977

1a (cont.) *David Hare *m* 2nd 1986 *Pippa, only dau of R I McDonald, and has issue:

1b *Poppy Helen; *b* 1988

2a *Robin Gordon [Robin Hare Esq, Fordley Hall, Middleton, Suffolk]; *b* 3 Dec 1944; *educ* Eton; *m* 1st 1973 (*divorce* 1987) Caroline Mary, dau of Edward Felix Mason and formerly w of William Oscar Watson; *m* 2nd 1989 *Margaret Julia, dau of Leo William Ritchie and formerly w of (a) Mark Leigh Scorer and (b) John Stewart Bassett, and has by his 1st w:

1b *Reuben Edward; *b* 1975

1b *Rachel Veronica; *b* 1978

1a *Philippa [Mrs Simon Courtauld, Inglewood Lodge, Kitbury, Berks]; *b* 7 June 1938; *m* 1st 9 June 1959 (*divorce* 1965) Timothy Peckover Burrill, yr s of Lionel Peckover Burrill, and has issue:

1b *Rebecca Nina; *b* 8 Feb 1961

1a (cont.) *Mrs Philippa Burrill *m* 2nd 5 Sep 1967 *Simon Pierre Courtauld, er s of Walter Pierre Courtauld, of S Kensington, and has issue:

1b *Kim Guy Augustine; *b* 1973

1b *Leila Alice; *b* 1975

2a Mollie Gordon; *b* 3 Sept 1915; *m* 28 June 1958 Robert Geoffrey Smith (*d* 19 Jan 1996), only s of Robert William Smith, of Ipswich, and *d* 17 March 1996

2 William Claude; *d* 1914

HAMBRO

Creation: B. (LP, UK) 1994

THE BARON HAMBRO, of Dixton and Dumbleton, Co Gloucester (Charles Eric Alexander Hambro) [The Rt Hon The Lord Hambro, Dixton Manor, Gotherington, Glos GL52 4RB]; *b* 24 July 1930; *educ* Eton; Lt Coldstream Gds 1949–51; Hambros bank: joined 1952, md 1957, dep chm 1965, chm 1972–83, chm Hambros plc 1983–97 and GRE Assur 1988– (dir 1968–, dep chm 1974–88); dir: P&OSN Co 1987–, Taylor Woodrow 1962–97, General Oriental Investments, San Paolo Bank Hldgs 1989–; *m* 1st 1954 (*divorce* 1976) Rose Evelyn, dau of Sir Richard Cotterell, 5th Bt (*qv*), and has:

1 *Charles Edward; *b* 20 Nov 1959; *educ* Eton and RMA Sandhurst; 2nd Lt Coldstream Gds; *m* 1986 *Nicole J, only dau of Dr James A Nicholas, of Westchester, New York, and has issue:

(1) *Charles James; *b* 1991

(1) *Christiana; *b* 1988

(2) *Alissa Katherine; *b* 1989

(3) *Marina Isabella Kimberly; *b* March 1995

2 *Alexander Robert; *b* 17 Jan 1962; *m* May 1984 *Harriet, dau of David Ward-Jones, and has:

(1) *Benjamin Jake Alexander; *b* Feb 1996

(1) *Jemima Rose Amice; *b* 29 March 1997

1 *Clare Evelyn; *b* 4 June 1957; *m* 1989 *Eivind Rabben, only s of Knut Rabben, of Oslo, and has issue:

(1) *Edward Olav; *b* 1992

(2) *Alexander Haakon; *b* 1994

BARON HAMBRO *m* 2nd 1976 *Cherry Felicity, dau of Sir John Huggins, GCMG, MC

Lineage: CALMER JOACHIM HAMBRO; *b* 1747 in Rendsburg; raised Hamburg; settled Copenhagen 1778; fndr C J Hambro & Son, silk and clothing merchants; *m* 1778 Thobe Levi (*d* 1820), dau of a merchant who had acquired Danish citizenship 1751, and *d* 1806, leaving:

1 JOSEPH

2 Isach; *b* 1782; *d* 1865; ancestor of the Norwegian HAMBROs

3 Simon; *b* 1782; *d* 1831; ancestor of the Danish HAMBROs

1 Zipora (thus named when *b* 1779, but *bapt* Hanne Sophie 1808); *m* 1st 1799 (*divorce* 1805) Lazarus Raphael Leidesdorf (*d* 1833), Copenhagen merchant, and had two children; *m* 2nd 1806 Wulf Marcus Wulf (*d* 1809), merchant, and by him had three children; *m* 3rd 1813 Niels Borup (*d* 1860), lawyer, and *d* 1852, leaving by him:

(1) Julius Theodor; *b* 1814; cleric; *m* 1848 Marie Rosa Trier (*d* 1897), bapt dau of M L Nathanson, and *d* 1904, leaving:

1a Johan; *b* 1853; fndr Borup's Folk High Sch Copenhagen; *m* 1810 Eline Schousboe (*d* 1943) and *d* 1946, leaving issue

The est s,

JOSEPH HAMBRO, of Upper Portland Place, London W; *b* 2 Nov 1780; merchant and banker Copenhagen 1800–39, Cncllr Danish Court 1821; moved to London 1840; *m* 14 Jan 1807 Marianne (*d* 1838), dau of Wulf Lewin von Halle, and *d* 3 Oct 1848, leaving:

CHARLES JOACHIM HAMBRO, Baron Hambro, so *cr* by patent of Danish Crown 6 Oct 1851, of Milton Abbey, Dorset, which he bought 1852; *b* 2 Dec 1807, *bapt* 1821; *educ* Trin Coll Cambridge; US Consul Denmark 1834–39; London banker 1839, naturalised UK citizen 10 Aug 1843; *m* 1st 12 Dec 1833 Caroline Maria (*d* 1852), dau of M Gostenhofer; *m* 2nd 1861 Eliza Frances (*d* 1919), dau of T Turner, Bengal CS, and widow of Hervey Greathed, Bengal CS, and *d* 19 Nov 1877, having by his 1st w had, with a dau (*d* a child):

1 Charles Joseph Theophilus, of Milton Abbey, JP, DL Dorset; *b* 2 Oct 1834; *educ* Trin Coll Cambridge; MP Weymouth 1868–74 and Dorset S 1886–91, Col Dorset Yeo Cav, High Sheriff Dorset 1882; *m* 1857 Susan Amelia, dau of Ven Hon Henry Reginald Yorke (*see* HARDWICKE, E), and *d* 11 April 1891, leaving two daus

2 Percival Lewis, of Stapleton, Blandford, Dorset; *b* 29 Jan 1836; with C J Hambro & Son 1857–69; *m* 1st 13 March 1869 Grace (*d* 1870), dau of Maj Henry Otway Mayne, and had:

(1) Henry (Harry) Charles Thomas, of The Hyde, nr Luton, Beds, JP Beds, Dorset; *b* 21 Dec 1869; *educ* Eton; inherited Milton Abbey 1891 but sold it 1900 to his unc Sir Everard; Lt Dorset Yeo, ptnr C J Hambro & Son 1898, Prime Warden Goldsmiths' Co 1925–26, High Sheriff Beds 1929; *m* 18 June 1896 Edith Gertrude, dau of Sir Henry Bonsor, 1st Bt (*qv*), and *d* 14 Feb 1933, having had:

1a Percival; *b* 5 Aug 1898; *educ* Eton; *kas* 22 March 1918

2a John (Jack) Henry, CMG (1944), of The Hyde; *b* 7 July 1904; *educ* Eton; chm Hambros bank 1963–65, dir John Dickinson & Co, md UK Commercial Corp 1940–45; *m* 1st 23 April 1930 (*divorce* 1947) Elizabeth Therese, dau of Jersey de Knoop, of Calveley Hall, Cheshire, and had:

1b (David) Jocelyn Jersey, of The Hyde; *b* 1 March 1936; *educ* Eton; *m* 20 Dec 1958 *Helen, only dau of Hugh Boyson, and *d* 1 May 1997, leaving:

1c *Elizabeth Helen; *b* 30 Dec 1962

2c *A dau; *b* 19–

1b *Theresa Mary; *b* 15 May 1931; *m* 4 April 1961 *Harry Hanak, s of O Hanak, of Finchley, and has:

1c *Martin Paul Otto; *b* 30 March 1962

2c *A son; *b* 16 Oct 1964

2a (cont.) John Hambro *m* 2nd 30 April 1947 Linnet Pamela Millicent, only dau of Maj Edgar Mortimor Lafone, OBE, and *d* 1965

1a Cecily Edith; *b* 13 Dec 1899; *m* 23 May 1922 Rupert Greaves Williams-Ellis and had issue

(2) Percival Otway (Sir), KBE (1921), CB (1919), CMG (1918); *b* 10 Dec 1870; *educ* Eton; Col 15th Hus, Boer War 1899–1900 WW I, Mesopotamia 1920–21, Army HQ India 1921–23, Maj-Gen cmdg Admin Aldershot 1925–27, N Midland Div TA 1927–31, ret 1931, Croix de Guerre, Orders Avis Portugal, St Vladimir Russia and Ag Merit France; *m* 2 Aug 1911 Marjorie Henrietta (*d* 1965), 3rd dau of Brig-Gen Edmund George Henry Bingham, RA, and *d* 25 Nov 1931, leaving:

1a Everard Bingham, MBE (1944), of Durrington House, Essex; *b* 16 Sept 1916; *educ* Eton; Lt-Col 15th/19th Hus WW II, dir Samuel Montagu; *m* 22 Feb 1944 his yr sister's sis-in-law Mary Charlotte, only dau of Maj Charles George Lyon, JP, of Whitley Lodge, Whitley Bridge, Yorks, and *d* 1971, leaving:

1b *Peter Charles Percival [Peter Hambro Esq, Durrington House, Old Harlow, Essex CM17 0NE]; *b* 18 Jan 1945; *educ* Eton and U of Aix-Marseille; md Smith St Aubyn Hldgs to 1983, Richco Bullion 1982–83, Peter Hambro plc 1990–, dir Mocatta & Goldsmid 1985–90 and City of Oxford Investment Tst; *m* 1968 *Karen Guinevere Gould, dau of Capt George Brodrick, of Dunley Manor, Whitchurch, Hants, and has:

1c *Evy Piers George; *b* 20 April 1972

2c *George Jay; *b* 25 Sept 1975

3c *Leo Percival; *b* 10 June 1977

2b *Anthony Everard George [Anthony Hambro Esq, 108 St George's Sq, London SW1V 3QY]; *b* 21 May 1947; *educ* Eton; with Grindlays Bank; *m* 1971 (*divorce* 19–) Nathalie Maroussia Bacou and has:

1c *Eric; *b* 19–

1c *Maya; *b* 19–

1a (Beatrice) Susan; *b* 26 July 1912; *m* 12 Sept 1939 Lt-Col Christopher Fuller (*see* FULLER, Bt) and *d* 1977, leaving issue

2a Patricia Marjorie; *b* 16 Sept 1916; *m* 1st 1 March 1938 Lt John Scott Limnell Lyon, QO Yorks Dragoons (*ka* 25 Nov 1941), er s of Maj Charles Lyon (*see* above), and had:

1b *Charlotte Anne; *m* 1st (*divorce* 19–) Michael Taylor; *m* 2nd Sir Kerry Johnston

2a (cont.) Mrs Patricia Lyon *m* 2nd 6 Aug 1943 F/Lt Colin Edward Livingstone Tapley, RCAF, s of Harold Livingstone Tapley, CMG, of NZ, and by him had two sons

(1) Grace Mary; *m* 3 Aug 1898 Maj George St John Mildmay (*see* ST JOHN-MILDMAY, Bt) and *dsp* 20 Dec 1920

2 (cont.) Percival Hambro *m* 2nd 4 Feb 1875 Arabella Marianne, dau of Henry Norman, of Bromley Common, Kent, and *d* 16 April 1885, having by her had, with two daus:

(3) Norman Joachim; *ka* Boer War

(4) Bertram Emil; *b* 11 March 1880; *educ* Eton; Lt Interpreter France WW I; *m* 24 April 1912 Margaret Constance Nevile (*m* 2nd 15 May 1919 Lt-Col Charles Boyle, MC; *see* CORK and ORRERY, E), dau of Sir Nevile Lubbock, KCMG (*see* AVEBURY, B), and *das* 25 April 1915, leaving:

1a Diana Margaret; *b* 8 Feb 1913; *educ* Girton Coll Cambridge; V-Pncpl Queens Gate Sch London; *m* 23 Oct 1945 (*divorce* Mexico 1955) Alexis Christopher Ladas, s of Christo Ladas, of Athens, and had:

1b *Andrea Alexis [Andrea Ladas Esq, 2 Coombe Rd, London W4 2HR]; *b* 4 Sept 1947; *educ* Eton

2a Faith Marianne; *b* 3 April 1914; *m* 17 April 1936 Nicholas Norman Norman-Butler, s of Arthur Francis Norman-Butler, OBE, and had two sons and three daus

3 Everard Alexander (Sir), KCVO (1908), of Hayes Place, Kent, and Milton Abbey, JP Kent, Surrey, DL Dorset, City London; *b* 11 April 1842; *educ* Trin Coll Cambridge; ptnr C J Hambro & Son 1869, sr ptnr 1877, Dir Bank England 1879–1925, 1st chm Hambros Bank (of Northern Commerce) 1920–25; *m* 1st 23 Oct 1866 Gertrude Mary, dau of Henry Stuart (*see* BUTE, M); *m* 2nd 16 June 1911 Ebba Harline d'Iberville Le Moyne (*d* 5 Nov 1961, having *m* 2nd 14 Feb

1927 Robert Stanhope Dormer; *see* DORMER, B), 8th dau of Charles Cecil Beresford Whyte, of Newton Manor and Hatley Manor, Co Leitrim, and *d* 26 Feb 1925, leaving, with a dau:

(1) (Charles) Eric (Sir), KBE (1919), JP Dorset, of Pickhurst Mead, Hayes, Kent, later Manwood Court, Sandwich, Kent; *b* 30 Sept 1872; *educ* Eton and Trin Coll Cambridge; MP Surrey 1900–07, Dir Bank England, Dep Govr Roy Exchange Assur, chm Hambros Bank 1925–32; inherited Milton Abbey 1925 but sold it 1932; *m* 1st 17 July 1894 (*divorce* 1929) Sybil Mary Martin (*d* 1942), 3rd dau of Martin Ridley-Smith, and had, with two daus:

1a Charles Jocelyn (Sir), KBE (1941), MC, DL City London, of Dixton Manor; *b* 3 Oct 1897; *educ* Eton; Capt Coldstream Gds WW I, Dir: Bank England 1928–63, Provident Mutual Life Assur Assoc, Union Corp, Bay Hall Tst (chm) and Hellenic and Gen Tst (chm), Sheriff Co London 1933 (High Sheriff 1956), Col Gen Staff War Office WW II (Exec Ch SOE 1942–43), chm Hambros Bank 1961–63; Kt Cdr St Olav Norway and Dannebrog Denmark, Cdr Order Vasa Sweden and US Legn Merit; *m* 1st 22 Oct 1919 Pamela (*d* 1932), dau of John Dupuis Cobbold, of Holywells, Suffolk, and had:

1b CHARLES ERIC AXEL later ALEXANDER, *cr* a **Baron**

1b Cynthia; *b* 13 Feb 1921; *m* 31 July 1943 Maj Michael Ian Leslie Melville (*see* LEVEN and MELVILLE, E) and *d* 1986, leaving issue

2b *Diana; *b* 27 Jan 1922; *m* 10 Jan 1942 *Baron Gibson-Watt (*qv*) and has issue

3b *Pamela; *b* 31 Dec 1925; *m* 1st 6 April 1945 (*divorce* 1951) Capt Robin William Lowe, Gren Gds, s of John Loder, of New York, and has a s; *m* 2nd 23 July 1951 *Andrew James Gibson-Watt and by him has two sons and a dau

1a (cont.) Sir Charles *m* 2nd 15 Feb 1936 Dorothy Helen, dau of Alexander Mackay and formerly w of Marcus Wallenberg, and *d* 28 Aug 1963, having by her had a dau

2a Richard Everard; *b* 29 Dec 1900; *educ* Eton and Trin Hall Cambridge; *m* 1st 23 Nov 1927 Edith Mary (*d* 1950), dau of Arthur Davenport, of Montevideo, and had:

1b *Everard Nigel; *b* 5 Sept 1928; *educ* Stowe

1b *Valerie Edith; *b* 12 April 1930; *m* 14 Feb 1953 *Michael Scott Hardie, s of Col Alan Scott Hardie, OBE, TD, DL, of Dechmont House, Dechmont, W Lothian, and has:

1c *Nicholas Alan Scott; *b* 19 Jan 1955

2c *Christopher Richard Scott; *b* 25 Feb 1957

3c *Charles Michael Scott; *b* 14 Nov 1961

2a (cont.) Richard Hambro *m* 2nd 23 March 1957 *Vida Agnes, dau of Capt William Lancefield and formerly w of Lt-Cdr Thomas Henry Morrogh Chillingworth, RN

(1) (cont.) Sir Eric *m* 2nd 11 Dec 1929 his stepmother's yr sis Edith Estelle Ermyntrude le Poer, JP (*d* 1975), dau of Charles Cecil Beresford Whyte (*see* above) and widow of Capt Leonard Elger, and *d* 28 Dec 1947

(2) Harold Everard, CBE (1919), JP, DL Suffolk, of Coldham Hall, Bury St Edmunds, Suffolk; *b* 20 Jan 1876; *educ* Eton; Brevet Lt-Col RA WW I, MFH Suffolk 1922–38, High Sheriff Suffolk 1930, dir Hambros bank 1931–45; *m* 1st 29 April 1902 Katharine Alethea (*d* 1938), est dau of William Charles Scott, of Thorpe, Surrey, and had:

1a Nigel Harold, TD (1945); *b* 18 Jan 1915; *educ* Eton; Maj RA TA WW II; *m* 30 Oct 1938 *Marjorie Caroline, est dau of Col James Archibald Innes, DSO, of Horringer Manor, Bury St Edmunds, and had:

1b *Carl Nigel Ivan; *b* 26 Feb 1946; *m* 1973 *Gwen Biddle and has:

1c *Charles Nigel; *b* 1975

1c *A dau; *b* 19–

1b *Olga Diana; *b* 9 April 1944

(2) (cont.) Col Harold Hambro *m* 2nd 31 March 1941 Lilian (*d* 1971), widow of 6th Earl Cadogan (*qv*), and *d* 5 Aug 1952

(3) Angus Valdemar, JP, DL Dorset, or Merly House, Dorset; *b* 8 July 1883; *educ* Eton; MP S Dorset 1910–22 and N Dorset 1937–45, PPS to Sec State Air 1918; Capt Dorset Yeo WW I 1917–21; Dorset: CA, High Sheriff 1934, V-Chm CC; dir Hambros Bank 1945–54; *m* 1st 1 July 1907 Rosamund Maud (*d* 1914), 3rd dau of Maj Robert Wilson Kearsley, of Stapeley, Cheshire, and had, with a yr s:

1a Robert Alexander; *b* 7 July 1910; *educ* Eton; Maj Recce Corps WW II; *m* 6 Nov 1934 Barbara Jessica Hardy, yr dau of Ernest Walter Hardy Beaton, and *d* of wounds 8 Aug 1943, leaving:

1b *Alexandra Mary; *b* 5 Aug 1935; *m* 26 June 1957 *Michael Francis Rutherford Lamb, s of Algernon Joseph Rutherford Lamb, and has issue

2b *Rosamund Anne; *b* 27 Sept 1939; *m* 10 Sept 1962 *Sir Erskine William Gladstone, 7th Bt (*qv*)

(3) (cont.) Angus Hambro *m* 2nd 2 March 1916 Vanda Dorothy Julia (*d* 1981), dau of St John Charlton, of Shotton Hall, Salop, and *d* 19 Nov 1957, having by her had:

1a Patricia; *b* 17 March 1917; *m* 10 Sept 1939 *Lt-Col John William Richard Woodroffe, dir Hambros bank 1954, only s of Brig-Gen Charles Richard Woodroffe, CVO, CMG, CBE (*see* DUCIE, E, also below), and had:

1b *Simon; joined Hambros Bank 1962

2a Elizabeth; *b* 22 Oct 1920; *m* 7 March 1942 Sir Bryan Bonsor, 3rd Bt (*qv*), and *d* April 1995, leaving issue

3a * Jean Frances, CVO (1953) [Mrs John Woodroffe CVO, Arnbarrow, Laurencekirk, Kincardineshire; Maryland, Worplesdon, Guildford, Surrey]; *b* 22 Feb 1923; *m* 1st 19 Sept 1942 Hon Vicary Gibbs (*ka* 20 Sept 1944; *see* ALDENHAM and HUNSDON OF HUNSDON, B) and has issue; *m* 2nd 29 May 1946 Rev Hon Andrew Charles Victor Elphinstone (*see* ELPHINSTONE, L) and has further issue; *m* 3rd 1980 her er sister's widower *Lt-Col John Woodroffe

4a *Rachel Mary; *b* 18 Sept 1925; *m* 28 April 1945 Maj William Napier Seymour (*see* HERTFORD, M) and has issue

(4) Ronald Olaf, JP Kent, of Kidbrook Park, later Linton Park, also of Port Logan, Wigtown; *b* 1 Dec 1885; *educ* Eton and Trin Coll Cambridge; Capt Coldstream Gds and GSO(3) WW I (despatches), Hon Col 139th Regt RA 1939, md 1921 and chm 1932–61 Hambros Bank, Govr London Assur, High Sheriff Sussex 1930; *m* 17 Feb 1917 his est bro's sis-in-law Winifred Emily (*d* following a boating accident 25 Aug 1932), 5th dau of Martin Ridley-Smith (*see* above), and *d* 25 April 1961, leaving:

1a Jocelyn Olaf, MC (1944), of Waverton House, Glos, previously of Coopersale House, Essex; *b* 7 March 1919; *educ* Eton and Trin Coll Cambridge; Maj Coldstream Gds WW II, md then (1965–72) chm Hambros Bank, chm Hambros Ltd 1972 and Phoenix Assur 1978; *m* 1st 28 March 1942 Ann Silvia (*d* 1972), dau of Rowland Huntley Muir, of Binfield, Berks, and had:

1b *Rupert Nicholas [Rupert Hambro Esq, 10 Park Place, London SW1A 1LP]; *b* 27 June 1943; *educ* Eton and Aix-en-Provence; dir Hambros Bank 1969 (joined 1964), chm 1983–86; dir: Anglo-American Corp S Africa 1981–97, The Telegraph PLC 1986–, Pioneer Concrete Hldgs 1989–; chm: J O Hambro 1994–96 (gp md 1986–94), Wilton's (St James's) 1987–, J O Hambro Magan Irby Hldgs 1988–, Mayflower Corp 1988–, Internat Advsy Bd Montana AG Vienna 1988–, Fenchurch plc 1993–97, CTR Gp 1990–97, Longshot Ltd 1996–; *m* 1970 *Mary Robinson Boyer and has:

1c *Jonathan Christopher; *b* 1974

1c *A dau

2b *Richard Alexander; *b* 1 Oct 1946; *educ* Eton and Munich U; dir Hambros Bank 1979 (joined 1966); chm J O Hambro Investment Management 1986–, I Hennig & Co 1982–, Lynton Gp Inc 1986–, Hattron 1992–; dir Wilton's (St James's) 1982–, J O Hambro & Co 1986–; *m* 1st 1973 (*divorce* 1982) Hon Charlotte Soames (*see* MARLBOROUGH, D) and has a dau; *m* 2nd 1984 (*divorce* 1992) Juliet Grana Mary Elizabeth, *née* Harvey (*see* LEICESTER, E); *m* 3rd 1993 *May James, *née* Briggs

3b *James Daryl [James Hambro Esq, 15 Elm Park Rd, London SW3 6BP; Manor Farm, Kimberley, Norfolk NR9 4DT]; *b* 22 March 1949; *educ* Eton and Harvard Business Sch; Hambros Bank 1970–85 (dir 1979, exec dir 1982–85), md J O Hambro 1994– (joined 1986); *m* 1981 *Diana, yst dau of David Cherry, of Kimberley, Norfolk, and has three daus

1a (cont.) Jocelyn Hambro *m* 2nd 1976 Margaret Elisabeth (*d* 1983), dau of Frederick McConnel and formerly w of (a) Lt-Col James Church, MC, and (b) 9th Duke of Roxburghe (*qv*); *m* 3rd 28 Jan 1988 *Margaret Anne, dau of Charles Michael Stratton (*see* DUNMORE, E, and PERTH, E) and formerly w of 7th Earl Fortescue (*qv*), and *d* 19 June 1995

2a *Anthony Martin; *b* 14 Oct 1921

3a *Simon Everard; *b* 15 Feb 1924

(1) Violet Mary, MBE; *b* 1884; Co-organiser WVS Herts 1938–50, Chm WLA Herts 1939–46; *m* 1906 Everard Reginald Martin Smith (*d* 1938) and *d* 1965, leaving, with four other children:

1a Julian; *m* Susan Pearson Gregory and has:

1b *Andrew; joined Hambros Bank 1975

1a Mary; *m* Dennis Hill-Wood and had:

1b *Peter; dir Hambros Bank 1968

HAMILTON of Marlborough House and Trebinshun House

Arms: Quarterly, 1st and 4th, gu. three chinquefoils pierced erm.; 2nd and 3rd, arg. a lymphad with her sails furled sa. **Crest:** Out of a ducal coronet or an oak-tree ppr., fructed or, traversed with a frame-saw, also ppr. **Motto:** *Sola nobilitas virtus* ('Virtue is the only nobility'). **Creations:** Bt. (GB) 24 or 26 Aug 1776 and (UK) 26 Jan 1819.

SIR EDWARD SYDNEY HAMILTON, 7TH BT, of Trebinshun House, Co Brecon, and **5th Bt**, of Marlborough House, Hants [Sir Edward Hamilton Bt, The Cottage, Fordwater Rd, E Lavant, W Sussex PO18 0AL]; *b* 14 April 1925; *s f* 1966; *educ* Canford; RE 1943–47 and 1st Roy Sussex HG 1953–56

Lineage: WILLIAM HAMILTON, of Chilston Park, Kent, DL, bro of 6th Earl of Abercorn (*see* ABERCORN, D); *m* Margaret (*d* 19 Oct 1736), 2nd dau of Sir

Thomas Colepeper, of Hollingborne, Kent, and was *bur* 20 July 1737, leaving, with another s (Edward, of Geneva, *m* — Vasserot):

JOHN HAMILTON, of Chilston Park; High Sheriff Kent 1719; *m* 1715 Mary, dau of John Wright, MD, of London, and had, with other issue:

Sir John Hamilton, 1st Bt (GB), so *cr* 24 or 26 Aug 1776 for gallantry Siege Quebec 1775, of Trebinshun, RN; *bapt* 21 Feb 1725/6; *m* 3 Oct 1763 Cassandra Agnes (*d* 26 Oct 1821), dau of Edmund Chamberlayne, of Maugersbury, Glos, and *d* 24 Jan 1784, leaving:

1 **Sir Charles Hamilton, 2nd Bt**, KCB; Adml the Red, Govr Newfoundland 1820; *b* 25 May 1767; *m* 19 April 1803 Henrietta Martha (*d* 10 March 1857), only dau of George Drummond (*see* PERTH, E), and *d* 14 Sept 1849, leaving:

(1) **Sir Charles John James Hamilton, 3rd Bt**, CB; Col Scots Gds; *b* 3 April 1810; *m* 14 Dec 1833 Catherine Emily (*d* 25 May 1879), dau of William Wynne, of Dublin, and *dsp* 23 Jan 1892

2 **Sir Edward Joseph Hamilton, 1st Bt** (UK), so *cr* 26 Jan 1819, KCB, of Marlborough House, Adml; *b* 12 March 1772; ktd and awarded gold medal for cutting out HMS *Hermione* from under the batteries of Porto Cavallo, S America; Freeman City London, presented with a sword, value £300 (over £7,650 in late-1990s terms), by the Jamaicans; *m* 1 Nov 1804 Frances (*d* 27 March 1840), dau of John Macnamara, of Langoed Castle, Breconshire, and *d* 20 March 1851, having had:

(1) John James Edward; Lt 83rd Regt; *b* 11 July 1808; *m* 7 April 1842 Favoretta (*d* 3 Jan 1887), only dau of Panton Corbett, MP, of Longnor Hall, Salop, and *dvp* 2 Nov 1847, having had:

1a EDWARD ARCHIBALD (Sir), **4th and 2nd Bt**

1a Hermione Lucy; *m* 25 Feb 1868 Walter Lacy Rogers, barrister (*d* 18 April 1885), of Rainscombe, Wilts, yr s of F I N Rogers, QC, and *d* 8 Feb 1869, leaving issue

2a Favoretta Frances; *m* 29 July 1875 Albert Alexander de Steiger, of Meadowcroft, Sutton, Surrey, yst s of Baron Alexander de Steiger, of Berne, and *d* 6 July 1932, leaving issue. He *d* 4 May 1906

3a Agnes Henrietta; *m* 27 July 1882 Hugh Hamon George William Carruthers Massy (*see* MASSY, B) and *dsp* 5 Nov 1907

(2) Arthur; RN; *b* 14 March 1810; *d* at sea 22 June 1836

(1) Frances Mary; *m* 15 Aug 1831 William Henry, Baron von Donop, of Westphalia, and *d* 24 Jan 1833, leaving issue. He *d* 15 Oct 186

(2) Agnes Catherine Annabella; *m* 13 Jan 1844 Richard Jennings, of Gellideg, Carmarths, and *d* 16 May 1974, leaving issue. He *d* 8 Dec 1891

The 3rd Bt of Trebinshun's cousin (and 1st Bt of Marlborough's gs),

Sir Edward Archibald Hamilton, 4th Bt, of Trebinshun, and **2nd Bt**, of Marlborough House; Capt Coldstream Gds; *b* 26 Jan 1843; *m* 28 May 1867 Mary Elizabeth, LStJ (*d* 9 May 1912), only dau of Joseph Gill, of Trewern, Salop, and Burley, Yorks, and *d* 19 Oct 1915, leaving:

1 **Sir (Charles Edward) Archibald Watkin Hamilton, 5th** and **3rd Bt**; Lt National Reserve, Hon Recruiting Offr Selsey and dist, Assist Mil Rep 35th Regtl Dist, Lt 4th Bn Roy Sussex Regt; *b* 10 Dec 1876; *m* 1st 18 Dec 1897 (*divorce* 1902) Olga Mary Adelaide (*d* 15 Oct 1928), only dau of R-Adml Sir Adolphus Augustus Frederick FitzGeorge, KCVO, and gdau of HRH THE 2nd DUKE OF CAMBRIDGE (gs of GEORGE III), and had issue:

(1) George Edward Archibald Augustus FitzGeorge; Lt Gren Gds; *b* 30 Dec 1898 (TM GEORGE V and QUEEN MARY and HRH 2nd DUKE OF CAMBRIDGE stood sponsors in person); *ka* 18 May 1918

(1) A dau; *b* and *d* 5 May 1902

1 (cont.) **Sir Archibald** *m* 2nd Nov 1906 Algorta Marjory Blanche (*d* 1927), only dau of George Child, of Widford, Herts; *m* 3rd 1927 Lilian Maud (*d* 26 Feb 1964), dau of William Austen, of Sydenham, and *d* 18 March 1939

2 **Sir (Thomas) Sydney Perceval Hamilton, 6th** and **4th Bt**; *b* 1 April 1881; *educ* Cheltenham; London Regt WW I; *m* 29 April 1920 Bertha Muriel (*d* 16 Dec 1961), dau of James Russell King, of Honnington Hall, Shipston-on-Stour, Warwicks, and *d* 26 Feb 1966, leaving:

(1) Sir EDWARD SYDNEY HAMILTON, **7th and 5th (and present) Bt**

1 Favoretta Sydney Annina; *m* 10 Sept 1941 W/Cdr Roy Stuart Kingsford, RAF, s of Gerald Montague Kingsford, of Oast Garden, Canterbury, Kent, and *d* Sept 1991, leaving:

(1) *Colin Roy; *b* 18 Nov 1942; *educ* Bradfield

(2) *Michael Ian; *b* 9 May 1950; *educ* Bradfield

(1) *Sandra Diana; *b* 27 Jan 1946

HAMILTON of Silverton Hill

Arms: Gu. a gillie flower stemmed and leaved ppr. between three cinquefoils erm., all within a bordure or. **Crest:** A horse's head and neck couped arg., maned or. **Motto:** *Stimulis majoribus ardens* ('Keen for yet greater thrills'). **Creation:** Bt. (NS) 1646.

SIR (ROBERT CHARLES) RICHARD CARADOC HAMILTON, 9TH BT, of Silverton Hill, Co Lanark [Sir Richard Hamilton Bt, The Old Rectory, Walton, Warwicks CV35 9HX]; *b* 8 Sept 1911; *s f* 1959; *educ* Charterhouse and St Peter's Coll Oxford (MA); Intell Corps 1940–45, assist master Ardingly 1946–60, chm Warwicks Br CLA 1979–83; *m* 16 April 1952 *Elizabeth Vidal, yr dau of Sir William Pell Barton, KCIE, CSI, of Lower Lodge, Ardingly, Sussex, and has:

1 +ANDREW CARADOC; *b* 23 Sept 1953; *educ* Charterhouse and St Peter's Coll Oxford (MA); *m* 1984 *Anthea Jane, dau of Frank Huntingford, of Hindhead, Surrey, and has issue:

(1) *Alice; *b* 1986

(2) *Harriet; *b* 1989

(3) *Imogen Rose; *b* 1993

1 *Susanna Eve; *b* 20 Sept 1956; *m* 1990 *Richard Andrew Freeman and has:

(1) *Gabriella Eve Hamilton; *b* 1993

2 *Sophia Louisa; *b* 13 July 1964

3 *Penelope Catherine; *b* 3 Oct 1966; *m* 1989 *Trevor Wells and has:

(1) *Anna Elizabeth; *b* 26 Jan 1996

Lineage: ALEXANDER HAMILTON (2nd s of Sir James Hamilton, 5th of Cadzow; *see* ABERCORN, D); had a charter 1449 of 'Quhitecamp' (later Silverton Hill) from 4th Earl of Crawford (*see* CRAWFORD and BALCARRES, E); had, with a 2nd s (William, ancestor of the HAMILTONs of Westport):

JAMES HAMILTON of Silvertonhill; *m* — Douglas, who brought him the Newton estate, in the territorial Barony of Drumsarguard, and had, with a dau (*m* James Livingstone, ancestor of the 1st and last Viscount Teviot of the 1696 *cr*; *see* TEVIOT, B, preliminary remarks), and had:

JOHN HAMILTON of Newton; living 1531; granted by his cousin the Earl of Arran the rest of the Silvertonhill estate; *m* —, dau of Sir John Somerville of Camnethan, and *d* 1535, having had:

ANDREW; *dvp*, leaving:

1 Andrew of Silvertonhill; living 1541; *m* —, dau of James Hamilton of Stanehouse, and *d c* 1553, leaving:

(1) Andrew, of Silvertonhill; *m* Elspeth Baillie of Carfin and had a surv s:

1a Francis, of Silvertonhill; *d c* 1641 unm

2 Alexander of Silvertonhill but for some time called of Goslingtown, an estate he had got from his f; *m* Catherine Hamilton and had:

(1) Andrew (Sir), of Goslingtown; fought for MARY QUEEN OF SCOTS Battle of Langside 1568, for which later attainted (restored by terms of Treaty of Perth 1572); *d* 1592, leaving:

1a Robert (Sir), of Goslingtown; *m* Elizabeth, dau and sole heir of Sir William Baillie of Provan, Ld Pres Court of Session, and *d* 1642, leaving, with a dau (*m* Sir John Somerville of Camnethan):

1b EDWARD

2b James; *d* 1655; ancestor of the HAMILTONs of Newton

The er son,

EDWARD HAMILTON of Balgray, later of Silvertonhill; *m* Margaret, dau of James Mure of Caldwell, and *d* 1649, having had, with a dau (Jean, *m* — Stewart of Minto):

Sir Robert Hamilton, 1st Bt (NS), so *cr* 1646 (though patent not recorded in Gen Register due to Civil War), of Silvertonhill; MP Lanark; sold Provan to the City of Glasgow when in financial difficulties; *m* Anne, 2nd dau of 1st Lord Belhaven and Stenton (*qv*), and had, with a yr s (Thomas, *dsp* France) and four daus (Margaret, *m* 2nd Lord Belhaven and Stenton (*qv*); Anne, *m* Sir William Craigie of Garnie; Elizabeth, *m* Capt John Livingstone; Mary):

Sir Robert Hamilton, 2nd Bt, of Silvertonhill; Col; *m* 1st Aurelia Katherine van Hettingen; *m* 2nd Isabel, dau of John Hamilton of Boggs, and *d* 1708, having by his 1st w had, with an est s (James, Army Offr, *ka vp*) and a yst s (William, Offr Dutch Serv, *m* — Athinscuby and had four sons: John, Lt-Col; Robert, Capt; William, Maj Dutch Gds; George):

Sir John Hamilton, 3rd Bt; *m* 1st Mary Lewers; *m* 2nd Rachael Lempriere and *d* 1748, leaving, with a yr s (George, Capt RN, *dsp* 1763) and two daus (Mary; Aurelia):

Sir Robert Hamilton, 4th Bt; Lt-Gen, Col: 108th Foot and 40th Regt 1763; *m* 1st Mary (*d* 15 Jan 1777), sis of Sir Hutchins Williams, 1st Bt, of Clapton, and had issue; *m* 2nd 6 Feb 1778 Anne, dau of Sir John Heathcote, 2nd Bt, of London (*qv*), and *d* 10 Aug 1786; his s by his 1st w:

JOHN WILLIAM; Capt 54th Regt, U-Sec War Ireland; *m* Mary Anne, dau of Richard St George, of Kilrush, Co Kilkenny, and *dvp* 1779, having had, with other issue:

1 FREDERIC (Sir), **5th Bt**

1 Charlotte; *m* 29 Sept 1792 Sir Charles Drake Dillon, 2nd Bt, of Lismullen (*see* 1970 edn) and *dsp* 23 June 1793

2 Frances; *m* 1800 Lt-Gen Sir George Anson, GCB (*see* LICHFIELD, E), and *d* 24 Feb 1834, leaving issue

The 4th Bt's gs,

Sir Frederic Hamilton, 5th Bt; *b* 14 Dec 1777; HEICS; *m* 20 Feb 1800 Eliza Ducarel (*d* 11 Feb 1841), yst dau of John Collie, of Calcutta, MD, and *d* 14 Aug 1853, having had issue:

1 ROBERT NORTH COLLIE (Sir), **6th Bt**

2 Arthur; BCL; *b* 2 Feb 1806; Chaplain HEICS; *d* 1858

3 Frederic William, of Northaw, Herts, JP Herts, Middx; *b* 31 Jan 1810; Capt 60th Rifles and 12th Lancers; *m* 30 March 1844 Emily Maria (*d* 21 July 1892), dau of T Carvick, of Yorks and Middx, and *d* 17 Jan 1866, having had:

(1) Howden Anson Philip; *b* 23 Oct 1846; *m* 7 March 1876 Caroline Alice (*d* 7 June 1899), yst dau of Thomas Faulconer, JP, DL, of Hampstead, and *d* 18 April 1898, leaving, with other issue:

1a Frederic Howden Faulconer; *b* 30 Jan 1877; *m* 1st 17 Aug 1899 Jessie Jean (*d* 1 Nov 1929), er dau of W McMinn, of Borgue, Kirkcudbrightshire; *m* 2nd 23 Feb 1930 Beatrice Agnes (*d* 19 Jan 1955), only dau of Samuel Banfield, of Exeter, Devon, and *d* 27 Jan 1959, leaving by his 1st w:

1b Howden McMinn; *b* 19 July 1900; *m* 1 Nov 1935 *Patricia Campbell [Mrs Howden Hamilton, 42 Fieldway, Wavertree Garden Suburb, Liverpool L15 7LU], only child of Matthew Currie, of Ayr, and *d* 1988, leaving:

1c *Gloria Constance Barbara; *b* 26 Sept 1937; *m* 14 June 1956 *Edward Watson and has:

1d *Andrew Charles Howden; *b* 12 Aug 1958

2b +Frederic William Seymour [Frederic Hamilton Esq, 42995 Adams Rd, RR1, Sardis, BC BOX 170, Canada]; *b* 29 Dec 1906; *m* 1930 Florence Maud (*d* 1982), dau of George John Saby, of Cambs, and has issue:

1c *Kathleen Anita; *b* 1931

2c *Barbara Joanne; *b* 1933; *m* 1955 *Oscar Mitchell Taylor, of Delta, BC, Canada, and has:

1d *Keith Donald; *b* 1958; *m* 1979 *Penny Dawn Miller and has:

1e *Allan Keith; *b* 1981

2e *Carl Brian; *b* 1984

1e *Stephanie Anne Mary; *b* 1987

2d *Colleen Susan; *b* 1956; *m* 1978 *Vincent James Lee, of Perth, Australia, and has issue:

1e *Dennis James; *b* 1981

1e *Vanessa Joanne; *b* 1983

2e *Deborah Janette; *b* 1987

1b Constance; *b* 5 Nov 1912; *m* 10 Nov 1941 *Richard Haugh [Richard Haugh Esq, Screel, Fishers Brae, Coldingham, Berwicks TD14 5NJ], s of Robert Haugh, of Castle Douglas, Kirkcudbrightshire, and *d* 10 May 1996, leaving:

1c *Howden Hamilton; *b* 13 May 1950; *m* 1977 *Amanda, dau of Stanley Bragg, of Gilderson, Leeds, and has:

1d *Helen Kirsty; *b* 1978

2d *Shona Ann; *b* 1980

2c *Robert Seymour; *b* 13 May 1950; *m* 1974 *Marion Henderson Cunningham, only dau of Frederich Lenz, of Schönlanke, Niekosken, and Livingstone, W Lothian, and has issue:

1d *Julia Lenz; *b* 1978

2a Henry Rudston HAMILTON later STUART-HAMILTON (deed poll 19 June 1920); *b* 10 Feb 1883; Capt Gordon Highrs, served WWs I and II, Dip Serv; *m* 24 June 1920 Mabel Mary (*d* 21 June 1968), dau of Rev Edmund Milnes Ellerbeck, and *d* 24 Sept 1962, having had issue:

1b Michael Hamish Alastair, MC and bar; *b* 15 July 1921; Capt Black Watch (RHR) WW II; *m* 14 Feb 1944 *Esther Lynette Sutherland, VAD (*m* 2nd 19 Feb 1946 (Ronald) David Stewart-Brown (*see* BROWN, Bt) and has issue), only dau of Maj James Reay Sutherland Mackay, and *das* 12 June 1944

2b +Donald Maclaren [Donald Stuart-Hamilton Esq, The Shooting Greens, Potarch, Banchory AB31 4BL]; *b* 1 July 1926; *educ* Harrow and King's Coll Cambridge (MA 1964); Capt Black Watch (RHR), TA; MIMSM; *m* 1 June 1956 *Jill, MSAOT, yr dau of Col David Guy Porteous, OBE, JP, of St Cyrus, by Montrose, and has issue:

1c *Clova Claire Ducarol [Mrs Michael Stinton, 92 Walton St, Oxford OX2 6EB]; *b* 17 Oct 1959; *m* 1988 *Michael Andrew Stinton and has:

1d *Hector George Donald; *b* 1997

1d *Pandora; *b* 19—

1d *Cecilia Violet; *b* 19—

2c *Alison Fenella; *b* 9 Feb 1967

1a Alice Constance; *b* 23 April 1884; *m* 12 Oct 1906 Sydney James Ching (*d* 20 June 1942), RTC, and *d* 8 Aug 1969, having had issue

(2) William Edward Seymour; *b* 2 April 1851; Maj Cape Mounted Rifles; *m* 21 March 1878 Charlotte Mary, dau of Thomas Beck, and *dsp* 14 June 1897

(1) Emily Maryanne; *m* 23 Dec 1876 Edwin Stead, and *d* 1905

(2) Kathleen Eliza Georgina; *d* 19 July 1926

(3) Constance Eliza Prescott; *d* unm 9 July 1931

(4) Agnes Ann; *d* unm 21 Aug 1934

4 Henry Charles, CSI; *b* 23 Sept 1811; Bengal CS; *m* 1st 9 Oct 1837 Frances Isabella, yst dau of James Gane, of Frome (*see* below); *m* 2nd 5 July 1869 Letitia (*d* 23 June 1917), dau of R-Adml Charles Simeon (*see* SIMEON, Bt), and *d* 26 Oct 1872, leaving by his 1st w:

(1) Henry Charles; *b* 7 March 1843; Lt-Col 2nd Cav Hyderabad Contingent; *m* 7 March 1882 Emily Agnes (*d* 18 April 1943), dau of Maj-Gen John Norman Hector Maclean, of Coll, Argyll, and *d* 9 May 1888, leaving issue:

1a Charles Norman Maclean; *b* 19 Oct 1885; MIEE, Capt RGA WW I (despatches twice); *m* 9 Nov 1926 Molly Eileen (*d* 1986), only dau of Daniel Crowe, MB, BCh, of Blackrock, Dublin, and *d* 7 July 1957, leaving issue:

1b *Anne Maclean [Miss Anne Hamilton, 24 Oakleigh Court, Station Rd West, Oxted, Surrey RH8 9EY]; *b* 31 Aug 1927

2a Vivian Claude; *b* 22 April 1887; Lt RFA WW I; *m* 3 Sept 1919 Catherine, est dau of Capt John Lynch, Remount Depot Bangalore, and *d* 18 Feb 1929

1a Isabel Maude Mary (Isma); *m* 14 July 1910 Douglas Mappin and *d* 19 Aug 1948, leaving issue

(2) John Angus Lushington; *b* 10 May 1846; Capt 2nd West India Regt; *m* 17 May 1873 Myra Emily Wood (*m* 2nd 19 April 1883 Sir Arthur Wing Pinero, the playwright (*d* 23 Nov 1934), and *d* 29 June 1919), 2nd dau of Beaufoy A Moore, and *d* 16 Dec 1879, leaving issue:

1a John Angus Lushington Moore, FRGS; *b* 19 Feb 1874; *m* 14 Sept 1906 Helen Frances, dau of George Stiles Reilly, WO, and *d* 14 June 1913

1a Myra Emily Moore; *m* 4 June 1908 Claude Neville Hughes, 2nd s of Philip Hughes, WO, and *d* 17 July 1941

(3) Robert St George Harding; *b* 11 Jan 1852; Lt 65th Foot; *m* 1875 Jane (*m* 2nd Maj F G Pollock, 7th Bengal Cav, and *d* 1923), only dau of Gen Harry Smith Obbard, Bengal Army, and *d* April 1878, leaving issue:

1a Constance Isabella; *m* 2 Nov 1898 Edwin Ashby Phelps, ICS, and had issue

(1) Frances Isabella; *m* 22 Feb 1859 Capt G W Savage (*d* 3 Dec 1869), 37th Foot, and *d* Jan 1892

(2) Eliza Ducarol Constance; *m* 15 Dec 1859 Gen Charles Samuel Stewart and *d* 19 July 1902, leaving issue (*see* SHAW-STEWART, Bt)

(3) Katherine Elspeth Maude; *m* 25 April 1888 Arthur Augustus Helyer Webster-Wedderburn and *d* 5 June 1907, leaving issue (*see* OGILVY-WEDDERBURN, Bt)

5 Charles Dillon (Rev); *b* Oct 1818; Sr Chaplain Bengal Establishment, Vicar Loxley; *m* 15 May 1862 Harriet Mary, dau of Henry Heyman, Capt 13th Light Dragoons, and *d* 12 Sept 1873

1 Eliza Anne; *m* Charles Harding, HEICCS, 2nd s of W Harding, of Barset House, Warwicks, and *d* his widow 13 May 1859

Sir FREDERICK's est son,

Sir Robert North Collie Hamilton, 6th Bt, KCB, JP, DL Warwicks; *b* 7 April 1802; ICS, Agent to Govr-Gen Centl India, memb Supreme Cncl 1859; High Sheriff Warwicks 1866; *m* 6 Oct 1831 Constantia (*d* 28 Nov 1842), 3rd dau of Gen Sir George Anson, GCB (*see* LICHFIELD, E), and *d* 31 May 1887, having had, with other issue:

1 FREDERIC HARDING ANSON (Sir), **7th Bt**

2 Francis Henry; *b* 7 April 1840; Capt 5th Lancers; *m* 12 April 1867 Maria Theresa (*d* 1912), dau of Charles Crosbie and widow of Maj George Ernest Rose, Rifle Bde, and *d* 29 Nov 1891, having had, with other issue:

(1) Francesca Teresa; *m* Feb 1894 Gen G Victor Bitossi, 2nd Italian Grenadiers, and had issue

(2) Pyne; *m* 18 Aug 1890 Morris Wickersham Gowen, of Philadelphia

(3) Ruby; *m* 1895 Alfred Wilson Hamilton Barrett (*d* 1945), of Pebworth House, Glos, and *d* 22 July 1954, leaving issue

1 Constance Eliza Ann; *m* 19 March 1853 Maj-Gen Alexander Ross Eliot Hutchinson, IA (*d* 19 Oct 1908), and *d* 5 April 1919, leaving issue

2 Isabella Frances; *m* 8 June 1854 Capt William Rose Shakespear (*d* 31 May 1861), Madras Cav, and *d* 1906, leaving issue

3 Louisa Catherine Emma; *m* 26 July 1864 Charles Raymond Pelly (*see* PELLY, Bt) and *d* 12 Nov 1938, leaving issue

Sir ROBERT's er son,

Sir Frederic Harding Anson Hamilton, 7th Bt; *b* 24 Sept 1836; Maj 60th Roy Rifles; *m* 28 Sept 1865 Mary Jane (*d* 22 April 1918), dau of H Willan, and *d* 19 Sept 1919, leaving:

1 ROBERT CARADOC (Sir), **8th Bt**

2 Frank; *b* 12 Feb 1878; served Boer War and WW I; *m* 16 April 1913 Mary Elizabeth (*d* 8 Aug 1961), est dau of John Williams Batterham, MB, FRCS, and *d* 22 April 1934, leaving:

(1) Ian Frank Howden; *b* 30 Dec 1916; Capt SAAF WW II; co dir; *m* 1950 *Zelma (*d* 27 May 1997) dau of Laurence Theodore Snyman, and *d* 24 May 1982, leaving:

1a +Paul Howden [Paul Hamilton Esq, The Red House, New St, St Dunstan's, Canterbury, Kent CT2 8AU]; *b* 24 Dec 1951; *m* 1980 *Elizabeth Anne Harrison, and has issue:

1b *Alexandra Isabel; *b* 13 April 1983

2b *Annabelle Kate; *b* 30 Aug 1985

2a +Mark Howden [Mark Hamilton Esq, 9 Noreen Ave, Claremont 7700, Cape, S Africa]; *b* 5 June 1955; *m* 1983 *Sally Anne Macklin, and has issue:

1b +Guy Howden; *b* 1 Oct 1991

3a +Warwick Howden [Warwick Hamilton Esq, No 3 16th Street, Parkhurst 2193, Johannesburg, S Africa]; *b* 10 Sept 1959; *m* 1990 *Jacqueline, dau of Frederick Arthur Smith, of Lyon House, Lynsted, Kent

(2) Frederick Campbell; *b* 1918; Lt SAAF WW II; *das* 1944

(3) Arthur Hugh Claud; *b* 12 May 1925

(1) *Joan Mary [Mrs Stanley Silson, 15 Fairydene Village, 18 Stapleton Rd, Sarnia 3610, S Africa]; *b* 30 May 1915; *m* 1941 *Stanley A Silson and has:

1a *Ian Frank; *b* 1943; *m* 1976 (*divorce* 19–) Barbara Thompson

2a *Raymond Robert Hamilton; *b* 1946

3a *Simon Hathcard; *b* 1957; *m* 1982 *Sophia Stallbom

1a *Mary Elizabeth Joy [Mrs David Rocke, 12 Pearson Rd, Everton 3610, Natal, S Africa]; 1952; *m* 1983 *David Anthony Rocke, FRCP

1 Constance Ida; *m* 19 April 1911 Alexander Boswell Campbell (*ka* 30 Sept 1917) and *d* 12 Oct 1954

2 Mary Louisa; *d* unm 2 Aug 1956

3 Cerise; *m* 13 Jan 1910 Adolphus Carl Theobald Meyer (*d* 2 Nov 1923), of Ceylon, and *d* 28 March 1951

4 Ann Eileen; *m* 10 March 1906 Edward Cowan (*d* 29 Feb 1952), 2nd s of Maj — Cowan, of Alveston, Warwicks (*see* 1956 edn COWAN, Bt), and *d* 1965

Sir FREDERICK's er son,

Sir Robert Carodoc Hamilton, 8th Bt; *b* 22 March 1877; Maj 3rd Bn Roy Warwick Regt, formerly Norfolk Regt, Boer War (two medals and three clasps) and WW I; *m* 24 July 1907 Irene (*d* 24 Oct 1969), 2nd dau of Sir Charles Mordaunt, 10th Bt (*qv*), and *d* 15 Feb 1959, having had:

1 Sir (ROBERT CHARLES) RICHARD CARADOC HAMILTON, **9th and present Bt**

2 Oliver Anson; *b* 23 Feb 1916; *m* 25 May 1957 *Barbara Mary [Mrs Oliver Hamilton, 10 Buddle Close, Tavistock, Devon PL19 0EG], 2nd dau of Frank Willcox, of Perranporth, Cornwall, and *d* 13 Feb 1997

1 Cynthia; *b* 18 June 1909; *d* 8 Feb 1985

HAMILTON and BRANDON

Arms: Quarterly, 1st and 4th grand quarters counter quartered, 1st and 4th, gules three cinquefoils ermine (for HAMILTON); 2nd and 3rd, argent a lymphad sable, sails furled proper, flagged gules (for Earldom of Arran); 2nd and 3rd grand quarters, argent a man's heart gules, ensigned with an imperial crown or proper, on a chief azure three stars of the first (for DOUGLAS). **Crests:** 1 On a ducal coronet an oak tree, fructed and penetrated transversely in the main stem by a frame saw proper, the frame or (for HAMILTON), 2 On a chapeau gules doubled ermine a salamander in flames proper (for DOUGLAS). **Supporters:** Two antelopes argent, armed, unguled, ducally gorged and chained or. **Mottoes:** Through (for HAMILTON), *Jamais arrière* ('Never behind') (for DOUGLAS). **Creations:** L. (Abernethy and Jedburgh Forest), E. (Angus) and M. (Douglas) (S) 14 June 1633; D. (Hamilton), M. (Clydesdale), E? (Arran and Cambridge?), L. (Aven and Innerdale) (S) 12 April 1643; E. (Lanerick/Lanark) and L. (Machansyre and Polmont) (S) 31 March 1639 regrant (effectively new creation?) 15 June 1661; D. (Brandon) and B. (Dutton) (GB) 10 Sept 1711; D(?). (France) 20 April 1864(?).

THE 15TH DUKE OF HAMILTON AND 12TH DUKE OF BRANDON, Co Suffolk, **Marquess of Douglas, Marquess of Clydesdale, Earl of Angus, Earl of Arran** (?), **Earl of Cambridge** (?), **Earl of Lanark, Lord Abernethy and Jedburgh Forest, Lord Aven and Innerdale, Lord Machansyre and Polmont** and **Baron of Dutton**, Co Chester, also possibly **Duke of Châtellerault** in France (Angus Alan Douglas-Hamilton) [His Grace The Duke of Hamilton and Brandon, Archerfield Home Farm, By Dirleton, E Lothian EH39 5EH]; *b* 13 Sept 1938; *s f* 1973, also as premier Earl of Scotland, Hereditary Keeper of Holyroodhouse and hereditary bearer of the Crown of Scotland (in Parl); *educ* Eton and Balliol Coll Oxford (MA Engrg); F/Lt RAF (invalided 1967), test pilot 1971–72, memb Roy Co Archers 1975–, KStJ 1975 (Prior Scotland 1975–82); CEng, MIMechE, FBIS; *m* 1st 23 June 1972 (*divorce* 1987) Sarah Jane (*d* 1994), only dau of Maj Sir Walter Scott, 4th Bt, of Beauclerc (*qv*), and has issue:

1 +ALEXANDER DOUGLAS, *Marquess of Douglas and Clydesdale*; *b* 31 March 1978

2 +John William; *b* 2 Oct 1979

1 *Eleanor; *b* 10 Aug 1973

2 *Ann; *b* 14 May 1976

The 15th DUKE *m* 2nd 1988 *Jillian, dau of Noel Robertson, of Sydney, NSW, and formerly w of (a) Martin Page and (b) Edward, s of Sir Edward Hulton

Other creations by the same name: A. ANGUS. One of the Mormaerships (*see* BUCHAN, E) covering pre-medieval Scotland north of the Clyde and Forth, Angus became an earldom in roughly the second decade of the 12th century. Its original holder as Earl was, however, probably descended from the Mormaer of Angus two hundred years before. The first such Earl was a certain Dufugan. His successor, who may or may not have been a relation, was called Gillbride. Thereafter the succession passed mostly from father to son, though once via a brother, till the mid-13th century, ending with Maud, regarded as Countess of Angus in her own right. Maud married three times. Her first husband was definitely looked on as Earl of Angus in right of his wife, the second one only possibly so, the third (illegitimately grandson of KING JOHN OF ENGLAND) apparently not at all. Nevertheless it was her son by her second husband, Gilbert de Umfreville (the same name his father had borne), who became 8th Earl of Angus, being so referred to in contemporary sources by mid-1267. The status of the Earldom of Angus now became bedevilled by the question of who was rightful King of Scotland, whether a summons to an English Parliament made out in the name of a holder of a Scottish earldom was valid and whether such a writ of summons did not even create an Earldom of Angus in the English peerage wholly distinct from that in the Scottish peerage. Meanwhile from 1329 to 1377 the Stewarts of Bonkyl (*see* MORAY, E) held the Earldom of Angus. The sister of the 3rd and last of these was Margaret, Countess of Angus in her own right and by the 1st Earl of Douglas illegitimately mother (probably an unmarried one at the time) of the 1st Earl of Angus of the 1389 creation (*see* below **Lineage (of Douglas)**).

B. BRANDON. Ellis, widow of (a) the 7th Viscount Mayo (*see* MAYO, E) and (b) the 14th Lord (Baron) Athenry, was created Countess of Brandon, Co Kilkenny, for life in 1758. On her death in 1789 the title expired. The 1st Earl of Macclesfield of the 1679 creation (*see* MACCLESFIELD, E, preliminary remarks) was made Viscount Brandon, Co Suffolk, on the same date. He had earlier been created Baron Gerard of Brandon, allegedly selecting the 'Brandon' (his surname was already Gerard and he had a remote connection with the Barons Gerard, *qv*) because Charles Brandon had been made a Duke (of Suffolk) by his brother-in-law HENRY VIII. The Viscountcy expired on the death of the 3rd and last Earl of Macclesfield of that creation in late 1702.

C. DOUGLAS. See subsidiary titles featuring Douglas in articles HOME, E, MORTON, E, QUEENSBERRY, M, and WEMYSS and MARCH, E.

D. HAMILTON. The James Stewart created Earl of Arran in 1581 (*see* MORAY, E) was also granted as a subsidiary title the Lordship of Parliament of Avane and Hamilton.

A certain Hugh Hamilton, of Co Tyrone, thought to have been son of an Archbishop of Cashel, was in the first half of the 17th century a soldier of fortune in Sweden, where he was given the title Baron Hamilton de Deserf. On settling again in Ireland at the Restoration he was created Lord Hamilton, Baron of Glenawly, in the Irish peerage. On the death of his only son, the 2nd Lord Hamilton, in February 1680/1, the title expired.

For other titles with the name Hamilton *see* HAMILTON OF DALZELL, B, also ABERCORN, D, BELHAVEN AND STENTON, L, and BOYNE, V.

Lineage (of Douglas): GEORGE DOUGLAS, 1st EARL OF ANGUS (S), so *cr* 9 April 1389, with remainder to the heirs of his body then to his aunt Elizabeth (his mother's sis and w of Sir Alexander Hamilton of Innerwick) and the heirs of her body; *b* by 1378 (for his ancestry *see* QUEENSBERRY, M, and MORAY, E); *m* (contract 24 May 1397) MARY (*m* 2nd 1404 Sir James Kennedy, Yr., of Dunure; (*see* AILSA, M); *m* 3rd Sir William Graham (*see* MONTROSE, D); *m* 4th Sir William Edmonstone of Duntreath (*see* EDMONSTONE, Bt)), dau of ROBERT III, and *d* of plague in England shortly after his capture at the English victory over the Scots of Homildon Hill 14 Sept 1402, having had, with a dau (Elisabeth, *m* 1st 1st Lord Forbes (*qv*), *m* 2nd Sir David Hay of Yester; *see* TWEEDDALE, M):

WILLIAM DOUGLAS, 2nd EARL OF ANGUS; Amb England 1430, Warden Middle March; led the Scots to victory over English at Piperden 10 Sept 1435; *m* (dispensation 1425) Margaret, dau of Sir William Hay of Yester and sis of Sir David Hay above-mentioned, and *d* Oct 1437, having had:

1 JAMES DOUGLAS, 3rd EARL OF ANGUS; *d* unm by 9 Sept 1446

2 GEORGE, 4th Earl

3 William, of Cluny, Fife; *dsp* 1475

4 Hugh, Rector St Andrews 1466

1a Elene/Helen; *m* 1st 2nd Lord Graham (*see* MONTROSE, D); *m* 2nd 1st Lord Ogilvy of Airlie (*see* AIRLIE, E)

The 3rd EARL's bro,

GEORGE DOUGLAS, 4th EARL OF ANGUS; Amb England 1451; supported JAMES II against the rebel last Earl of Douglas 1454 and was granted large tracts of Douglas lands; defeated English at an encounter at Alnwick, Northumberland, 1462; *m* probably by 1446 Isabel (*m* 2nd by 1447 John Carmichael of Balmedie, *m* 3rd Robert Douglas of Lochleven; *see* MORTON, E), dau of Sir John Sibbald of Balgony, and *d* 14 Nov 1462 or 12 March 1462/3, having had, with a dau (Janet, *m* 1st David Scott, Yr. of Buccleuch (*see* BUCCLEUCH and QUEENSBERRY, D), *m* 2nd 2nd Earl of Rothes, *qv*), an est s:

ARCHIBALD DOUGLAS, 5th EARL OF ANGUS, known as 'Bell the Cat' (for his courage in initiating opposition to JAMES III's favourites) or 'The Great Earl', PC; *b c* 1453; Warden E Marches 1481, High Chllr Scotland 1493–98; *m* 1st 4 March 1467/8 Elizabeth, dau of 1st Lord Boyd (*see* KILMARNOCK, B), and had:

1 George, *Master of Angus*; *m* 1488 Elizabeth, dau of 1st Lord Drummond (*see* PERTH, E) and widow of Sir David Fleming, and was *k* Battle of Flodden 9 Sept 1513 *vp*, having had issue:

(1) ARCHIBALD DOUGLAS, 6th EARL OF ANGUS; *b c* 1490; memb Cncl Regency 1517–21 and 1523–26, wielding supreme power in Scotland 1526–28 (High Chllr 1527) till the young JAMES V broke free and judicially confiscated his erstwhile mentor's lands and titles; DOUGLAS thereupon withdrew to England (where made PC) but returned to Scotland on JAMES V's death 1542, thereafter playing a leading role in the Battles of Ancrum

Muir 1545 and Pinkie 1547; was regranted his Earldom 31 Aug 1547 to himself and his heirs male and assigns whomsoever; *m* 1st (contract 26 June 1509) Margaret/Mary Hepburn (*dsps* 1513), dau of 1st Earl of Bothwell (*see* BUCHAN-HEPBURN, Bt); *m* 2nd 4 Aug 1514 (*divorce* 11 March 1526/7) MARGARET, widow of JAMES IV and sis of HENRY VIII, and by her had an only child:

1 Margaret; *m* 6 July 1544 4th Earl of Lennox (*see* MORAY, E) and was gf of JAMES VI and I

(1) (cont.) The 6th EARL *m* 3rd 9 April 1543 Margaret, dau of 4th Lord Maxwell (*see* MAXWELL, Bt), and *d* Jan 1556/7, having by her had no surv issue

(2) George (Sir), of Pittendriech; *m* Elizabeth, dau and heir of David Douglas of Pittendriech, and *d* Aug 1552, having had issue:

1a DAVID DOUGLAS, 7th EARL OF ANGUS; *b c* 1515; *m* (contract 8 May 1552) Margaret (*m* 3rd Sir Patrick Whitelaw of that Ilk), dau of Sir John Hamilton of Clydesdale (illegitimate son of 1st Earl of Arran; *see* ABERCORN, D) and widow of James Johnstone, Yr. of Johnstone (*see* ANNANDALE AND HARTFELL, E), and *d* June 1557, leaving:

1b ARCHIBALD DOUGLAS, 8th EARL OF ANGUS and 5th EARL OF MORTON (as which *s* unc (also his guardian) under special remainder of 22 April 1543, confirmed 2 June 1564), called the 'Good Earl'; *b c* 1555; *m* 1st 13 June 1573 Lady Mary Erskine (*dsp* 3 May 1575), dau of 1st Earl of Mar (*see* MAR and KELLIE, E); *m* 2nd 25 Dec 1575 (*divorce* 1587) Lady Margaret Leslie, dau of 4th Earl of Rothes (*qv*); *m* 3rd (contract 29 July 1587) Jean (*m* 3rd 1593 1st Lord Spynie; *see* CRAWFORD and BALCARRES, E), dau of 8th Lord Glamis (*see* STRATHMORE AND KINGHORNE, E) and widow of Robert Douglas, Yr., Master of Morton (*see* MORTON, E), and *dspm* 4 Aug 1588, having by her had a dau Margaret (*d* unm)

1b Margaret; *m* 1st (contract 19 June 1567/8) Sir Walter Scott of Buccleuch (*see* BUCCLEUCH and QUEENSBERRY, D); *m* 2nd Francis Stewart, Earl of Bothwell (*see* MORAY, E), and *d* 1640, leaving issue

2b Elizabeth; *m* 1st 17 Feb 1571/2 7th Lord Maxwell (*see* MAXWELL, Bt); *m* 2nd Sir Alexander Stewart of Garlies (*see* GALLOWAY E); *m* 3rd Sir John Wallace of Craigie and *d* 1637

2a JAMES DOUGLAS, 4th EARL OF MORTON (*qv*), title to which confirmed in a grant of 2 June 1564; *m* 1543 Elizabeth, yst dau of 3rd Earl of Morton; beheaded 2 June 1581

(3) William; Abbot of Holyrood House; *d* 2 Oct 1528

(1) Elizabeth; *m* 1509 3rd Lord Hay of Yester and had issue (*see* TWEEDDALE, M)

(2) Alison; *m* 1st 1511 Robert Blackadder; *m* 2nd 25 June 1996 Sir David Hume of Wedderburn and had issue

(3) Janet; *m* 1st 6th Lord Glamis and had issue (*see* STRATHMORE AND KINGHORNE, E); *m* 2nd Archibald Campbell of Skipnish, 2nd s of 2nd Earl of Argyll (*see* ARGYLL, D); burned 17 July 1537 on a charge of threatening the life of JAMES V by sorcery

(4) Margaret; *m* 1513 Sir James Douglas, 7th of Drumlanrig (*see* QUEENSBERRY, M) and had three daus

2 William (Sir); had charter of the lands of Genane, Ayr, 1493, and Braidwood, Lanarks, 1510; ktd 1511; *m* 1501 Elizabeth, dau and heir of James Auchinleck of Glenbervie, son and heir of Sir John Auchinleck, and by her acquired Glenbervie; *k* Flodden 9th Sept 1513, leaving an only s:

(1) Archibald (Sir), of Glenbervie, whose lands were erected into the Barony of Glenbervie 1538 and 1542; *m* 1st Agnes (*d c* 1548), dau of 3rd Earl Marischal (*see* KINTORE, E), and had, with four other daus:

1a Sir WILLIAM DOUGLAS, 9th EARL OF ANGUS, as which sustained claim 7 March 1588/9 against JAMES VI (heir of line); *b c* 1532; *m* (contract 14 Feb 1551/2) Egidia/Gille, dau of Sir Robert Graham of Morphie, and *d* 1 July 1591, having had, with other issue:

1b WILLIAM DOUGLAS, 10th EARL OF ANGUS; *b c* 1552; turned RC when young and was involved in a grand design 1592 (the 'Spanish Blanks') to re-establish Catholicism in Scotland, hence his title forfeited; *m* April-June 1585 Elizabeth (*m* 2nd by 1619 James Hamilton), dau of 4th Lord Oliphant, and *d* Paris 3 March 1611, having had issue:

1c WILLIAM DOUGLAS, **1st Marquess of Douglas**, so *cr* 14 or 17 June 1633, as also EARL OF ANGUS and LORD ABERNETHY AND JEDBURGH FOREST (all S); *b* 1589; royalist Civil War; *m* 1st 1601 Margaret (*d* 11 Sept 1623), dau of 1st Lord Paisley (*see* ABERCORN, D), and had, with other issue:

1d Archibald, *Earl of Angus*, PC (S 1636); *b c* 1609; Extrdy Ld of Session 9 Feb 1638/9 and again 13 Nov 1641, High Chamberlain Coronation in Scotland 1 Jan 1651 of CHARLES II, who intended to *cr* him 3 April 1651 Earl of Ormond, Lord Bothwell and Hartside, with remainder to his heirs male by his 2nd w, but the patent did not pass the Great Seal owing to CROMWELL's invading Scotland; *m* 1st (contract Nov 1629 and May 1630) Lady Anne Stuart (*d* 16 Aug 1646), 2nd dau of 3rd Duke of Lennox (*see* MORAY, E), and had, with another s and two daus:

1e JAMES DOUGLAS, **2nd Marquess of Douglas**, PC; *b* 1646; *m* 1st (contract 7 Sept 1670) Lady Barbara Erskine (*d* Aug 1690), dau of 20th/14th Earl of Mar (*qv*), and had issue:

1f James, *Earl of Angus*; *b* 1671; Col Cameronians; *dvp* unm, *k* Battle Steinkirk 3 Aug 1692

1e (cont.) The **2nd Marquess** *m* 2nd (contract 13 Dec 1692) Mary (*d* 21 Jan 1736), dau of 1st Marquess of Lothian (*qv*), and *d* 25 Feb 1700, having had further issue:

2f William, *Earl of Angus*; *b* 15 Oct 1693; *d* 23 March 1694

3f ARCHIBALD DOUGLAS, **3rd Marquess** and 1st and last DUKE OF DOUGLAS, so *cr* 10 April 1703 (aged nine), as also MARQUESS OF ANGUS AND ABERNETHY, VISCOUNT OF JEDBURGH FOREST and LORD DOUGLAS OF BONKILL, PRESTOUN AND ROBERTOUN (all S); *bapt* 13 Oct 1694; Ld Lt Forfarshire 1715–61, supported Govt in 1715 Uprising, fighting at Battle of Sheriffmuir 13 Nov 1715; *m* 1 March 1758 Margaret (*d* 24 Oct 1774), est dau of James DOUGLAS (formerly CAMPBELL) of Mains, Dunbartonshire, and *dsp* 21 July 1761, when all the titles *cr* 1703 expired

1f Jane; *b* 17 March 1698; *m* (secretly) 4 Aug 1746, as his 2nd w, Sir John Stewart, 3rd Bt, of Grandtully (*d* 14 June 1764), and *d* 22 Nov 1753, having had, with a yr twin s:

1g ARCHIBALD JAMES EDWARD STEWART later DOUGLAS (9 Sept 1761 on being served heir of entail to his uncle **3rd Marquess**), 1st BARON DOUGLAS OF DOUGLAS, Co Lanark (GB), so *cr* 8 July 1790, of Bothwell and Douglas Castles, Lanarks; *b* 10 July 1748; *educ* Rugby and Westminster; ajudged rightful heir to Douglas estates by Ho Lds 1769 (the lawsuit called the 'Douglas Cause'), reversing the 1767 decision against him of the Court of Session, following objections by the Duke of Hamilton (heir male to the **3rd Marquess**) that he was not the son of his mother (certainly twins born to a woman of 51 was an improbability, and the consensus of opinion since then is that the Duke and Court of Session were probably in the right); MP (Tory) Forfarshire 1782–90, Ld Lt Forfarshire 1794–1827; *m* 1st 13 June 1771 Lady Lucy Graham, dau of 2nd Duke of Montrose (*qv*), and had:

1h ARCHIBALD DOUGLAS, 2nd BARON DOUGLAS OF DOUGLAS; *b* 25 March 1773; *educ* Eton; *d* unm 27 Jan 1844

2h CHARLES DOUGLAS, 3rd BARON DOUGLAS OF DOUGLAS; *b* 26 Oct 1775; barrister Lincoln's Inn 1802, MP (Tory) Lanarks 1830–32; *d* unm 10 Sept 1848

1g (cont.) The 1st BARON *m* 2nd 13 May 1783 Frances, sis of 3rd Duke of Buccleuch (*see* BUCCLEUCH and QUEENSBERRY, D), and *d* 26 Dec 1827, having by her had, with an er s (*d* young):

3h Rev JAMES DOUGLAS, 4th and last BARON DOUGLAS OF DOUGLAS; *b* 9 July 1787; *educ* Ch Ch Oxford; Rector Marsh Gibbon, Bucks, 1819–48 and Broughton, Northants, 1825–48; *m* 18 May 1813 Wilhelmina, 2nd dau of Gen Hon James Patrick Murray, 5th s of 4th Lord Elibank (*qv*), and *dsp* 6 April 1857, when the title expired

1d (cont.) The *Earl of Angus m* 2nd 26 April 1649 Jean (*m* 2nd 11 Aug 1659 15th Earl of Sutherland (*qv*), and *d* Jan 1715), dau and coheir of 2nd Earl of Wemyss (*qv*), and *dvp* 16 Jan 1655, having by her had, with other issue:

2e ARCHIBALD DOUGLAS, 1st EARL OF FORFAR, so *cr* 2 Oct 1661, as also LORD WANDELL AND HARTSIDE (S), with precedence of his f's patent of 3 April 1651, PC (S); *m c* 19 Aug 1679 Robina (*d* 20 March 1741), dau of Sir William Lockhart of Lee, Amb France, by his 2nd w Robina (dau of John Sewster by Anne, sis of OLIVER CROMWELL), and *d* 11 Dec 1712, having had an only son:

1f ARCHIBALD DOUGLAS, 2nd and last EARL OF FORFAR; *b* 25 May 1692; Envoy Prussia 1714; *d* unm 8 Dec 1715 of wounds recd at Battle of Sherriffmuir during 1715 Jacobite Uprising, when his titles expired or became dormant

1e Margaret; *b* Sept 1651; *m* 3 Aug 1686 1st Viscount Kingston and *dsp* Oct 1699

2d James; *b* 1617; Col Scots Regt in the French serv; *d* unm (*k* at Douai) 21 Oct 1645

3d A son

1d Margaret; *m* 1629 William, Lord Alexander (*dsp* 18 May 1638), est s of 1st Earl of Stirling, and *d* 1 Jan 1660, leaving issue

2d Jean; *m* 1632 1st Lord Bargeny and *d* 1669, leaving issue

3d Grizel; *m* (contract 23 March 1635) William, Master of Carmichael (whose s was *cr* Earl of Hyndford), s of 1st Lord Carmichael, and had issue

1c (cont.) The **1st Marquess** *m* 2nd 15 Sept 1632 Mary (*d* 1674), dau of 1st Marquess of Huntly (*qv*), and *d* 19 Feb 1659/60, having had, with other further issue:

4d WILLIAM DOUGLAS later DOUGLAS-HAMILTON, 1st EARL OF SELKIRK, so *cr* 4 Aug 1646, as also LORD DAER AND SHORTCLEUCH, with remainder to heirs males (resigned by him and regranted 6 Oct 1688 to his son Charles), and 20 Sept 1660 DUKE OF HAMILTON, MARQUESS OF CLYDESDALE, EARL OF ARRAN, LANARK AND SELKIRK, LORD AVEN, MACHANSIRE [*sic*], POLMONT AND DAER for life (all S), KG (1682), PC (S Feb 1660/1, E 1687); *b* 24 Dec 1634; Commr Treasury Scotland 1686–89, Extrdy Ld Session 1686–89 and 1693–94, Pres Convention in Edinburgh 14 March 1688/9 which declared throne vacant following JAMES II's flight; *m* 29 April 1656 Anne, **Duchess of Hamilton** in her own right (*see* below **Lineage (of Hamilton)**), and *d* 18 April 1694, when his life peerages expired, leaving issue

5d GEORGE DOUGLAS, 1st EARL OF DUNBARTON, so *cr* 9 March 1674/5, as also LORD DOUGLAS OF ETTRICK (both S), KT (1687); *b c* 1635; Maj-Gen French service; Col 1st Foot 1665–88; cmded army Scotland which defeated pro-Monmouth forces under Earl of Argyll (*see* ARGYLL, D) 1685; *m* Anne, dau of Robert Wheatley, of Bracknell, Berks, and sis of Duchess of Northumberland (*qv*), and *d* 20 March 1691/2, leaving:

1e GEORGE DOUGLAS, 2nd and last EARL OF DUNBARTON; *b c* April 1687; *dsp* shortly after 7 Jan 1748/9, when his titles seem to have expired

4d Henrietta; *m* (contract 29 May 1645) 1st Earl of Annandale (*see* ANNANDALE AND HARTFELL, E), and *d* 1 June 1673, leaving issue

5d Catherine; *m* Sir William Ruthven of Douglas, and had issue

6d Isabel; *m* 1st Marquess of Queensberry (*qv*), and had issue

7d Jean; *m* 18 Jan 1670 4th Earl of Perth (*qv*), and had issue

8d Lucy; *m* (contract 25 March 1669) 4th Earl of Nithsdale (*see* HERRIES OF TERREGLES, L) and *d* 8 Jan 1713, having had issue

2c JAMES DOUGLAS, of Mordington, Berwicks; *b c* 1591; apparently Provost Abernethy by 1608; ktd 1625–27, captured by Parliamentarians after Battle of Worcester 1651, at which he had fought for CHARLES II; *m* 1st by July 1624 his cousin Anne, only dau and heir of line of 5th Lord Oliphant, in right of whom he unsuccessfully claimed the Lordship of Oliphant but was in compensation *cr* 14 Nov 1641 jointly with her LORD AND LADY MORDINGTON, with precedence of the Lordship of Oliphant; he *d* 11 Feb 1656, leaving issue (extinct in the male line, the title having been dormant since 1755)

3c Francis (Sir), of Sandilands; *dsp*

1c Catherine; contracted to *m* 28 Nov 1600 Sir Andrew Ker, Yr. of Ferniehurst, but *dvp* unm

2c Mary; *m* (contract 17 Oct 1620) 2nd Earl of Linlithgow (*see* LINLITHGOW, M) and had issue

3c Elizabeth; *m* (contract 13 Sept 1627) Sir John Campbell of Cawdor (*see* CAWDOR, E)

2b Robert (Sir), of Glenbervie; ancestor of the DOUGLAS Bts of Glenbervie (*see* 1970 edn)

3b Gavin, of Raquarrell; ancestor of the DOUGLASes of Bridgeford; *m* 1st (contract 27 Oct 1698) Jean, sis of Robert Menzies of Aberdeen and widow of Gilbert Menzies of Auldquhat; *m* 2nd Elizabeth Keith and *d c* 1 Oct 1616, leaving issue

4b John, of Barras; *m* Jean Fraser and *d* 15 March 1618, leaving issue

1b Margaret; *m* (contract 5 Jan 1567/8) William Forbes of Monymusk and had issue (*see* STUART-FORBES, Bt)

2b Jean; *m* (contract 31 May 1576) John Wishart of Balisycht

3b Sarah; *m* 1st (contract 5 April 1586) Robert Strachan; *m* 2nd George Auchinleck of Balmamo

1a Elizabeth; *m* (contract 1 June 1543) Alexander Falconer, Yr. of Halkerton (*see* KINTORE, E)

2a Christian; *m* (contract 23 May 1555) Alexander Irvine, Yr. of Beltie

3a Joane; *m* James Skene, Yr. of Skene, and had issue

4a Isabel; *m* (contract 1 March 1562) James Melville, Yr. of Dysart, and *d* 18 Jan 1582, leaving issue

5a Alice; *m* (contract 28 Dec 1567) Alexander Guthrie, Yr. of Kincaldrum

(1) (cont.) Sir Archibald *m* 2nd *c* 28 Jan 1553/4 Margaret, dau of John Carmichael of Meadowflat; *m* 3rd Elizabeth, dau of Alexander Irvine of Drum, and *d* 18 Sept 1570, leaving by her, with another s and two daus:

2a James; Minister Glenbervie; gf of:

1b Robert; Bp Dunblane 1684; *d* 1716; ancestor of the DOUGLASes of Brigton, Forfar, also of:

1c SYLVESTER DOUGLAS; 1st and last BARON GLENBERVIE, Co Kincardine (I), so *cr* 30 Nov 1800, PC (I and GB 1794), KC 1793; *b* 24 May 1743; Ch Sec Ireland 1794–95, MP (Tory) St Canice 1794–96 (I Parl), Fowey 1795–96, Midhurst 1796–1800, Plympton 1801–02 and Hastings 1802–06, Commr Bd Control 1795–1806, a Ld Treasury 1797–1800, Jt Paymaster-Gen 1801–03, V-Pres BOT 1801–04; *m* 25 Sept 1789 Catherine Anne, dau of 2nd Earl of Guilford (*qv*) and *dspms* 2 May 1823, when the title expired

3a John; ancestor of the DOUGLASes of Cruixton, Quarrelholes and Blackmill

3 Gavin; *b c* 1475; Bp Dunkeld 1515; author: *The Palace of Honour* (allegorical poem, finished 1501, 1st edn 1553) and probably *Conscience*; translated Virgil's *Æneid*; *d* Sept 1522

4 Archibald (Sir), of Kilspindie; *m* 1515 Isabel Hoppar and *d c* 1536, leaving issue (extinct in the male line)

1 Marion/Mariot; *m* (contract 24 June 1492) 3rd Earl of Glencairn (*see* CUNINGHAME, Bt) and had issue

2 Elizabeth; contracted to *m* 19 June 1493 2nd Lord Lyle

3 Janet; *m* 1495 2nd Lord Herries of Terregles (*qv*)

The 5th EARL *m* 2nd *c* 1498 Janet, dau of 2nd Lord Kennedy (*see* AILSA, M), formerly w or mistress of Sir Alexander Gordon and certainly former mistress of JAMES IV (who had by her James Stuart, *cr* 1501 Earl of Moray, *qv*); *m* 3rd 1 June 1500 Katherine, dau of Sir William Stirling of Keir (*see* HERON-MAXWELL, Bt), and *d* between 29 Nov 1513 and 31 Jan 1513/4

Lineage (of Hamilton): JAMES HAMILTON, 2nd EARL OF ARRAN (*see* ABERCORN, D); had a 3rd s:

JOHN HAMILTON, 1st MARQUESS OF HAMILTON, so *cr* 17 April 1599, as also EARL OF ARRAN, LORD AVEN '&c' [*sic*] (all S), PC (S 1585); *b* probably *c* 1535; *m* by 10 Feb 1577/8 Margaret, dau of 7th Lord Glamis (*see* STRATHMORE AND KINGHORNE, E) and widow of 4th Earl of Cassillis (*see* AILSA, M), and *d* 6 April 1604, having had (with a dau, Margaret, *m* 8th Lord Maxwell, *see* MAXWELL, Bt) an only legitimate s:

JAMES HAMILTON, 2nd MARQUESS OF HAMILTON, KG (Feb 1622/3), PC (S 1613, E 1617); *b* 1589; *s* unc 1609 as 4th EARL OF ARRAN (insofar as the grant to his f of that title in 1599 did not constitute a fresh creation, which is debatable) and LORD HAMILTON; *cr* 5 May 1608 LORD ABERBROTHWICK (S) and 16 June 1619 EARL OF CAMBRIDGE and BARON OF INNERDALE (both E); Ld Steward Household 1624–25; *m c* 30 Jan 1602/3 Anne, dau of 7th Earl of Glencairn (*see* CUNINGHAME, Bt), and *d* 2 March 1624/5, leaving:

1 JAMES HAMILTON, **1st Duke of Hamilton**, so *cr* 12 April 1643, as also MARQUESS OF CLYDESDALE, EARL OF ARRAN AND CAMBRIDGE (whether these last two Earldoms were simply mentioned by the clerk drawing up the patent because the grantee possessed them already in the English peerage or whether they are to be regarded as new creations in the Scottish peerage is debatable), LORD AVEN AND INNERDALE (all S), with special remainder, failing heirs male of his body, to his bro William and the heirs male of his body, with remainder to the est heir female of his own (*i.e.*, the grantee's) body, and the heirs male of her body bearing the name and arms of HAMILTON, with remainder to his own (again the grantee's) legitimate heirs whatsoever, KG (1630), PC (March 1632/3); *b* 19 June 1606; *educ* Exeter Coll Oxford; Master Horse 1628–44, Gentleman Bedchamber 1628, ktd 1630, cmded as Gen 7,000 men 1631 in expdn to help GUSTAVUS ADOLPHUS OF SWEDEN in Thirty Years War in Germany; cmded troops against Covenanters 1639; Hereditary Keeper Holyrood Ho 1646; cmded pro-royalist Scottish army in defeat by CROMWELL at Preston 1648; *m* 1620 Lady Margaret Feilding (*d* 10 May 1638), dau of 1st Earl of Denbigh (*see* DENBIGH AND DESMOND, E), and *dspms*, being beheaded 9 March 1648/9 for having invaded England the previous year, when the Lordships of Hamilton and Aberbrothwick became dormant, having had, with other issue:

(1) Charles, *Earl of Arran*; *d* young; *bur* 30 April 1640

(1) ANNE, **Duchess of Hamilton** in her own right, as which *s* unc (**2nd Duke**, *see* below) 12 Sept 1651

(2) Susannah; *m* (contract 20 Dec 1668) 7th Earl of Cassillis (*d* 23 July 1701), and had issue (*see* AILSA, M)

2 WILLIAM HAMILTON, **2nd Duke of Hamilton**, KG (Jan 1649/50), PC (1640); *b* 14 Dec 1616; *cr* 31 March 1639 EARL OF LANERICK (*i.e.*, Lanark), LORD MACHANSYRE AND POLMONT; MP Portsmouth 1640, Sec State Scotland 1640–44 and 1646–49; Covenanter 1644, Parly Commr to CHARLES I 1647 but held a royalist command in Scotland 1648, joining CHARLES II in exile at The Hague 1649, Lt-Gen royalist army in Scotland 1651; *m* 26 May 1638 Lady Elizabeth Maxwell (*m* 2nd 19 June 1655 Thomas Dalmahoy and was *bur* 2 Sept 1659), dau and coheir of James, Earl of Dirletoun, and *dspms* 12 Sept 1651 of wounds recd at the Battle of Worcester nine days earlier, when the Earldom of Arran became dormant and the Marquessate of Hamilton, the Earldoms of Cambridge and Lanerick, the Barony of Innerdale and the Lordships of Machanshyre and Polmont expired, having had issue:

(1) James; *d* an infant, *bur* 12 March 1647/8

(1) Anne; *m* 5 July 1664 3rd Earl of Southesk (*see* FIFE, D)

(2) Elizabeth; *m* 1st 30 Sept 1662 Lord Kilmaurs (*dsp* & *vp* 30 May 1664), s of 9th Earl of Glencairn (*see* CUNINGHAME, Bt); *m* 2nd Sir David Cunningham of Robertland

(3) Mary; *m* 1st 25 Aug 1663 2nd Earl of Callendar (*dsp* August 1685); *m* 2nd 28 June 1690 Sir James Livingston, Bt, of Westquarter; *m* 3rd 3rd Earl of Findlater (*see* SEAFIELD, E) and *dsp*

(4) Margaret Hamilton; *m* March 1666 William Blair of Blair

1 Anne; *m* (contract 13 April 1631) 7th Earl of Eglinto(u)n (*see* EGLINTON and WINTON, E), and *d* 16 Oct 1632, leaving a dau

2 Margaret; *m* 1640 17th Earl of Crawford and Lindsay (*see* CRAWFORD and BALCARRES, E), and had issue

3 Mary; *m* (contract 4 June 1630) 2nd Earl of Queensberry (*see* QUEENSBERRY, M), and *dsp* 29 Oct 1633

The 2nd MARQUESS OF HAMILTON had illegitimately by Anne Stewart, dau of 1st lord Blantyre (*see* 1900 edn) and widow of 8th Lord Saltoun (*qv*) of Abernethy:

4 Margaret; *m* 1st Lord Belhaven and Stenton (*qv*)

The 2nd DUKE's niece (and 1st DUKE's dau),

ANNE Hamilton, **Duchess of Hamilton**; *b* Jan 1631/2; *m* 29 April 1656 William DOUGLAS later DOUGLAS-HAMILTON, 1st EARL OF SELKIRK (*see* above, also separate article), 4th s of **1st Marquess of Douglas** (*see* **Lineage (of Douglas)** above), resigned her titles 9 July 1698 for regrant to her est s and *d* 17 Oct 1716 (outliving her est s), having had issue (who bore, at any rate initially, the surname HAMILTON):

1 JAMES, **4th Duke**

2 William; *dsp* by 1688

3 CHARLES HAMILTON later DOUGLAS (1688), 2nd EARL OF SELKIRK, as which *s* f on latter's resignation under a regrant 6 Oct 1688 to himself and his four yr bros successively and their heirs male, whom failing to the other heirs male of the Duke of Hamilton with a proviso that if Charles or any of his bros or the heirs male of their bodies should succeed to the Dukedom, the Earldom should always descend to the next yr bro of the Duke so succeeding and to the heirs male of his body, with remainder over as aforesaid, PC (1733); *b* 3 Feb 1662/3; Col 1st Horse Nov–Dec 1688, Ld Bedchamber 1689–1702 and 1714–March 1738/9, Burgess Edinburgh Feb 1692/3, Ld Clerk Register Scotland 1696–1702 and 1733–39, Sheriff Pncpl Lanarks, rep S peer 1713–15 and 1722–39, Govr Edinburgh Castle 1737–38; negotiated with French govt 1713–14 settlement of family claim to Dukedom of Châtellerault in the sum of 500,000 livres (which was never paid him); *dsp* 13 March 1739

4 JOHN HAMILTON, 3rd EARL OF SELKIRK and 1st EARL OF RUGLEN, so *cr* 25 April 1697, as also VISCOUNT OF RICCARTOUN and LORD HILLHOUSE (all S), with remainder to heirs male, whom failing, to the heirs general of his body, PC (S 1696); *bapt* 26 Jan 1664/5; Gen of the Mint 1694, Commr Scottish Exchequer 1696, Commr to audit Scottish Treasury accounts 1697 and Scottish Admlty accounts 1698; *m* 1st (contract 21–26 June 1694) Anne, dau of 7th Earl of Cassillis (*see* AILSA, M), and had issue:

(1) William, *Lord Daer*; *b* 1696; Capt Roy Scots and 1st Regt of Horse; *dvp* unm 20 Feb 1742

(1) ANNE Hamilton, COUNTESS OF RUGLEN in her own right; *b* 5 April 1698; *m* 1st 2nd Earl of March (*d* 7 March 1730/1; *see* QUEENSBERRY, M) and had issue; *m* 2nd 2 Jan 1746/7 Anthony Sawyer (*dsp*), Deputy Paymaster-Gen Forces Scotland, and *d* 21 April 1748

(2) Susan; *b* 1 Nov 1699; *m* (contract 6 Oct 1738) 8th Earl of Cassillis (*see* AILSA, M) and *dsp* 8 Feb 1763

4 (cont.) The 3rd/1st EARL *m* 2nd 22 March 1700/1 Elizabeth (*d* 10 March 1734), dau of Charles Hutchinson, of Owthorpe, Notts, and widow of John, Lord Kennedy (*see* AILSA, M), and *d* 3 Dec 1744

5 GEORGE HAMILTON, 1st EARL OF ORKNEY (*qv*)

6 Basil; *bapt* 16 Dec 1671; *m* 1691 Mary Dunbar of Baldoon (*see* HOPE-DUNBAR, Bt) and was drowned 27 Aug 1701, having had:

(1) William, of Baldoon; *d* unm *c* Nov 1703

(2) Basil, of Baldoon; *b* 9 Sept 1696; Jacobite 1715, hence sentenced to death 1716 but reprieved and restored 1732; MP Stewartry of Kirkcudbright 1741; *m* 14 March 1791 Isabella (*d* 6 April 1725), dau of Col Hon Alexander Mackenzie, 2nd s of 4th Earl of Seaforth (*see* CROMARTIE, E), and *d* 14 Nov 1742, having had, with other issue:

1a DUNBAR HAMILTON later DOUGLAS (1744), 4th EARL OF SELKIRK; *b* 1 Dec 1722; rep S peer 1787–99, Ld Lt Stewartry of Kirkcudbright; *m* 3

Dec 1758 Helen (*d* 28 Nov 1802), dau of Hon John Hamilton and gdau of 6th Earl of Haddington (*qv*), and *d* 26 May 1799, having had, with other issue:

1b Sholto Basil, *Lord Daer*; *b* 3 Sept 1759; *d* 4 July 1760

2b Basil William, *Lord Daer*; *b* 16 March 1763; *d* 9 Nov 1794

3b John, *Lord Daer*; *b* 24 May 1765; *d* 9 July 1797

4b Dunbar; *b* 9 July 1766; Capt RN; *d* 29 Oct 1796

5b Alexander; *b* 12 Dec 1767; Capt 38th Foot; *d* Guadaloupe 7 June 1794

6b THOMAS DOUGLAS, 5th EARL OF SELKIRK; *b* 20 June 1771; rep S peer 1806–18, Ld Lt Stewartry of Kirkcudbright 1807–20, fndr various settlements in Canada; *m* 24 Nov 1807 Jean, only surv dau of James Wedderburn-Colvile of Inveresk, and *d* 8 April 1820, leaving issue:

1c DUNBAR JAMES DOUGLAS, 6th EARL OF SELKIRK; *b* 22 April 1809; *educ* Eton and Ch Ch Oxford; rep S peer 1831–85, Ld Lt Stewartry of Kirkcudbright 1844–85, Keeper Gt Seal of Scotland Aug-Dec 1852 and 1858–59; *m* 29 June 1878 Cicely Louisa (*d* 10 Jan 1920), 2nd dau of Sir Philip de Malpas Grey Egerton, 10th Bt (*qv*), and *dsp* 11 April 1885

1c Isabella Helen; *m* 26 Oct 1841 Hon Charles Hope and *d* 4 July 1893, leaving issue (*see* LINLITHGOW, M)

2c Katherine Jane; *m* 23 Jan 1849 Loftus Wigram, QC, MP (*d* 19 Sept 1889), s of Sir Robert Wigram, 1st Bt (*qv*), and *dsp* 30 Sept 1863

1b Helen Hamilton; *m* 9 Nov 1786 Sir James Hall, 4th Bt, of Dunglass (*qv*), and *d* 12 July 1837, leaving issue

2b Elizabeth; *m* 1 Aug 1804 Sir James Montgomery, 2nd Bt (*qv*), and *d* 28 Oct 1814, leaving issue

3b Katherine; *m* 6 July 1815 John Halkett (*see* ROSSLYN, E) and *d* 31 March 1848, leaving issue

1a Mary; *b* 8 May 1720; *m* Ranald Macdonald, 17th of Clanranald (*d* 2 Oct 1776), and *d* 11 May 1750, leaving issue

(1) Eleanor; *m* 31 Dec 1711 John Murray of Philliphaugh and *d* 27 Dec 1783, leaving issue

(2) Catherine; *m* Oct 1727 6th Earl of Dundonald (*qv*) and *d* 13 April 1779, having had issue

7 Archibald, of Riccartoun and Pardovan, Linlithgow, and Confey Castle, Co Kildare; *bapt* 17 Feb 1673; Capt RN; MP Lanarks 1708–10 and 1718–34, Queenborough 1735–41 and Dartmouth 1742–47, a Ld Admlty, Govr Greenwich Hosp, Govr Jamaica; *m* 1st Anne (*dsp* 1709), dau of 2nd Lord Lucas of Shenfield (*see* LUCAS OF CRUDWELL, B) and widow of Edward Cary (*see* FALKLAND, V); *m* 2nd 17 Dec 1718 Anne (*dsp* 29 March, *bur* 4 April 1719), dau and heir of Claud Hamilton and widow of Sir Francis Hamilton, 3rd Bt, of Castle Hamilton (*see* SEMPHILL, L); *m* 3rd 29 Sept 1719 Lady Jane Hamilton (*d* 6 Dec 1753), dau of 6th Earl of Abercorn (*see* ABERCORN, D), and *d* 5 April 1754, having by her had issue:

(1) Charles; *m* Mary Catherine, dau of Colonel Dufresne, and *d* 10 Sept 1751, leaving an only dau

(2) Frederic (Rev); *b* 1728; Vicar Wellingborough, Northants, Archdeacon Raphoe 1757–72; *m* 11 June 1757 Rachael Daniel and *d* 19 Feb 1811, leaving:

1a Elizabeth; *m* April 1777 3rd Earl of Aldborough (*d* 7 March 1823; *see* 1875 edn) and *d* 29 Jan 1846, leaving issue

(3) Archibald; accidently drowned 30 May 1744

(4) William (Sir), KB (1772), PC (1791); *b* 13 Dec 1730; foster-bro of GEORGE III; Amb Naples 1764–1800, DCL, FRS; *m* 1st 25 Jan 1758 Catherine (*d* 25 Aug 1782), est dau of Hugh Barlow, of Lawrenny Park, Pembs; *m* 2nd 6 Sept 1791 Amy (better known as Emma (Hart), Nelson's mistress, and *d* 15 Jan 1815), dau of Henry Lyon, of Nesse, and *dsp* 6 April 1803

(1) Elizabeth; *m* 1st 15 May 1742 1st Earl of Warwick (*see* WARWICK, BROOKE and, E) and had issue; *m* 2nd Gen Robert Clerk (*d* by 26 May 1797) and *d* 24 Feb 1800

(2) Jane; *m* 24 July 1753 9th Lord Cathcart (*see* CATHCART, E) and *d* 13 Nov 1771, leaving issue

1 Mary; *b* 30 April 1657; *d* unm by 1683

2 Catherine; *m* (contract 24 April 1683) 1st Duke of Atholl (*qv*) and *d* 11 Jan 1707, leaving issue

3 Susan; *m* 1st (contract 17 Nov 1684) 2nd Earl of Dundonald (*qv*) and had issue; *m* 2nd *c* 1694 3rd Marquess of Tweeddale (*qv*) and *d* 7 Feb 1736/7, leaving issue

4 Margaret; *m* 5 Feb 1687 James Maule, 4th Earl of Panmure (*dsp* 22 April 1723), and *dsp* 6 Dec 1731

The DUCHESS's est son,

JAMES HAMILTON, **4th Duke of Hamilton** (as which *s* mother in her lifetime; *see* above) and **1st Duke of Brandon**, Co Suffolk, so *cr* 10 Sept 1711, as also BARON OF DUTTON, Co Chester (both GB), with special remainder to the heirs male of his parents; was refused a seat as of right in the Ho Lds (though he sat there as a rep S peer 1708–12) under the 23rd article of the Act of Union (of E and S Parls 1707), which forbade a peer of Scotland after the Union being made one of Britain, KG (1712), KT (1687), PC (1710); *b* 11 April 1658; Gentleman Bedchamber 1679–88 and 1699–1702, Envoy Paris 1683–85 and 1686, Col 6th Horse 1685–88 and Oxford Regt of Horse (later RHG) Nov–Dec 1688, Master Gt Wardrobe 1688–89, Brig Gen 1688, Lt Gen 1693, suspected of involvement in Jacobite plots at time of attempted French invasion of Scotland March 1707/8 but no evidence found to justify a trial for high treason; Ld Lt Lancs 1710–12, Master Gen Ordnance 1712; *m* 1st by 5 Jan 1686/7 Lady Anne Spencer (*dsps* 2 July 1690), dau of 2nd Earl of Sunderland (*see* MARLBOROUGH, D); *m* 2nd 17 July 1698 Elizabeth (*d* 13 Feb 1743/4), dau and sole heir of 5th Baron Gerard of Gerard's Bromley (*see* MACCLESFIELD, E, preliminary remarks), and was *k* 15 Nov 1712 in a duel in Hyde Park with Lord Mohun (also *k* then) shortly after having been apptd Amb to Paris, his death before taking up that post being regarded by Jacobites as a considerable blow since it was thought he could have been of considerable help to them in it; Gen Macartney, Lord Mohun's second, was suspected of having contributed to the death of his principal's opponent (one source alleges he stabbed the **Duke** when Mohun was already down) and a reward of £500 was offered for his capture; Macartney gave himself up, was tried 18 June 1716 and acquitted of murder but found guilty of manslaughter; the **Duke** left issue:

1 JAMES HAMILTON, **5th Duke of Hamilton** and **2nd Duke of Brandon**, KT (1726); *b* 5 Jan 1702/03; *educ* Winchester and Ch Ch Oxford; Capt Gen Roy Co Archers 1724–43, a Ld Bedchamber 1727–33; *m* 1st 14 Feb 1722/3 Lady Anne Cochrane (*d* 14 Aug 1724), dau of 4th Earl of Dundonald (*qv*), and had:

(1) JAMES HAMILTON, **6th Duke of Hamilton** and **3rd Duke of Brandon**, KT (1755); *b* 5 July 1724; *educ* Winchester and St Mary Hall Oxford; *m* 14 Feb 1752 Elizabeth (*bapt* 7 Dec 1733; a famous beauty of her day; Ldy Bedchamber to QUEEN CHARLOTTE 1761–84; *m* 2nd 3 March 1759 5th Duke of Argyll (*qv*) and had issue (who eventually *s* to her Barony), having been *cr* 20 May 1776 BARONESS HAMILTON OF HAMELDON, Co Leicester (GB), with remainder to the heirs male of her body; *d* 20 Dec 1790), 2nd dau of Col John Gunning, of Castle Coote, Co Roscommon, by Hon Bridget Bourke, 3rd dau of 6th Viscount Bourke of Mayo, and *d* 17 Jan 1758, having had:

1a JAMES GEORGE HAMILTON, **7th Duke of Hamilton** and **4th Duke of Brandon**, also **4th Marquess of Douglas** etc, as which *s* cousin 1761 (*see* **Lineage (of Douglas)** above); *b* 18 Feb 1755; *educ* Eton; *d* unm 7 July 1769

2a DOUGLAS HAMILTON, **8th Duke of Hamilton** and **5th Duke of Brandon**, KT (1785); *b* 24 July 1756; *educ* Eton; Keeper Linlithgow Palace 1777; ajudged entitled to sit in Ho Lds as a GB peer 1782, Ld Lt Lanarks 1794–99, Col 1798; *m* 5 April 1778 (*divorce* 1794) Elizabeth Anne (*m* 2nd 19 Aug 1800 1st Marquess of Exeter (*qv*) and *d* 17 Jan 1837), dau of Peter Burrell, of Langley Park, Beckenham, Kent, and sis of 1st Baron Gwydir, and *dspl* 2 Aug 1799, leaving by Harriet Pye Bennett, actress, w of (a) Lt James Ester, RN, and (b) Maj John Scott Waring, MP, an illegitimate dau (Anne, *m* 1820 as his 1st w 2nd/3rd Baron Rossmore; *qv*), to whom he bequeathed as much in the way of unsettled possessions as possible, including the chattels at Hamilton Palace (these, however, were later bought back by a subsequent Duke of Hamilton)

1a Elizabeth; heiress of her bros; *m* 23 June 1774 12th Earl of Derby (*qv*) and *d* 14 March 1797, leaving issue

1 (cont.) The **5th/2nd Duke** *m* 2nd 1727 Elizabeth (*dsp* 3 Nov 1729), dau and coheir of Thomas Strangways (*see* ILCHESTER, E); *m* 3rd 21 Aug 1737 Anne (*m* 2nd 23 Dec 1751 Hon Richard Savage Nassau, s of 3rd Earl of Rochford, and *d* 9 March 1771), dau and coheir (with her sis, Elizabeth, w of Sir James Dashwood, 2nd Bt, of Kirtlington Park, *qv*) of Edward Spencer, of Rendlesham, Suffolk, and *d* 2 March 1742/3, having by her had:

(2) ARCHIBALD HAMILTON, **9th Duke of Hamilton** and **6th Duke of Brandon**; *b* 15 July 1740; *educ* Eton; MP Lancs 1768–72, Ld Lt Lanarks 1799–1802; *m* 25 May 1765 Lady Harriet Stewart (*d* 3 Dec 1788), dau of 6th Earl of Galloway (*qv*), and *d* 16 Feb 1819, having had:

1a ALEXANDER HAMILTON, **10th Duke of Hamilton** and **7th Duke of Brandon**, KG (1836), PC (1806); *b* 3 Oct 1767; *educ* Harrow and Ch Ch Oxford; MP (Whig) Lancaster 1802–06, Ld Lt Lanarks 1802–52, FRS 1802, FSA 1802, Amb St Petersburg 1806–07; called up to Ho Lds 4 Nov 1806 *vp* in f's Barony of Dutton; *m* 26 April 1810 Susan Euphemia Beckford (*see* HUNTLY, M) and *d* 18 Aug 1852, leaving:

1b WILLIAM ALEXANDER ANTHONY ARCHIBALD HAMILTON, **11th Duke of Hamilton** and **8th Duke of Brandon**; *b* 19 Feb 1811; *educ* Eton and Ch Ch Oxford; Kt Marischal Scotland 1846–63, Ld Lt Lanarks 1852–58; *m* 23 Feb 1843 PRINCESS MARIE AMELIE ELIZABETH CAROLINE (*d* 17 Oct 1888), yst dau of KARL LUDWIG FRIEDRICH, GRAND DUKE OF BADEN, by Stéphanie Louise Adrienne de Beauharnais (dau of Count Claude de Beauharnais, whose 1st cousin Vicomte Alexandre de Beauharnais was 1st husb of the EMPEROR NAPOLEON's 1st w JOSEPHINE, and NAPOLEON's adopted dau), and 3rd cousin of the EMPEROR NAPOLEON III, and *d* Paris 15 July 1863, having had:

1c WILLIAM ALEXANDER LOUIS STEPHEN HAMILTON later DOUGLAS-HAMILTON, **12th Duke of Hamilton** and **9th Duke of Brandon**, also probably 8th EARL OF SELKIRK, being deemed to hold it in fiduciary fee following yr bro's death 1886, KT (1878); *b* 12 March 1845; *educ* Eton and Ch Ch Oxford; NAPOLEON III issued 20 April 1864 a decree purporting to confirm him in the title of Duke of Châtellerault conferred in 1548 on the 2nd Earl of Arran (*see* ABERCORN, D) but in the circumstances (which were that the **12th/9th Duke** was neither heir of line nor heir male to the 2nd Earl) such a decree must be looked on as equivalent to a fresh creation, though with what limitation is unclear; Col Roy Lanarks Militia, Hon Col 3rd Bn HLI, Hon Col Yeo Cav, Kt Marischal Scotland; *m* 10 Dec 1873 Lady Mary Montagu, OBE (1918) (*m* 2nd 29 July 1897 Richard Carnaby Forster (*d* 23 June 1925) and *d* 10 Feb 1934), est dau of 7th Duke of Manchester (*qv*), and *d* 16 May 1895, having had issue:

1d Mary Louise, OBE (1918); *b* 1 Nov 1884; *m* 14 June 1906 6th Duke of Montrose (*qv*) and *d* 21 Feb 1957, leaving issue

2c CHARLES GEORGE ARCHIBALD DOUGLAS-HAMILTON, 7th EARL OF SELKIRK, as which *s* cousin 1885; *b* 18 May 1847; Lt 11th Hus; *dsp* 2 May 1886

1c Mary Victoria; *m* 1st 21 Sept 1869 (*annulled* 1880) ALBERT, PRINCE OF MONACO, DUKE OF VALENTINOIS (*d* 26 June 1922), and had issue; *m* 2nd 2 June 1880 Count Tassilo Festetics de Tolna, GCVO, Austrian Imp Gd (*cr* 21 June 1911 a Hungarian Prince and *d* 4 May 1933), and *d* 14 May 1922, having had issue

1b Susan Harriet Catherine; *m* 1st 27 Nov 1832 (*divorce* 1850) afterwards 5th Duke of Newcastle (*see* LINCOLN, E); *m* 2nd 2 Jan 1860 M Opdebeck, of Brussels, and *d* 28 Nov 1889

2a Archibald; MP Lanarks; *b* 16 March 1769; *d* unm 28 Aug 1827

1a Anne; *d* unm 10 Oct 1846

2a Charlotte; *m* 24 June 1800 11th Duke of Somerset (*qv*) and *d* 10 June 1827, leaving issue

3a Susan; *m* 3 Aug 1803 5th Earl of Dunmore (*qv*) and *d* 24 May 1846, leaving issue

(3) Spencer; *b* June 1742; Lt-Col Gds; *d* unm 20 March 1791

(1) Anne; *m* 11 Nov 1761 1st Marquess of Donegall (*qv*) and *d* 11 Nov 1780, leaving issue

2 William; MP Lanark; *m* 30 April 1733 Frances (*m* 2nd 19 May 1735 2nd and last Viscount Vane and *dsp* 31 March 1788), dau and heir of Francis Hawes, of Purley Hall, Berks, and *dsp* 11 July 1734

3 Anne (named after his f's god-mother QUEEN ANNE); *b* 12 Oct 1709; *m* Oct 1742 Anna Charlotte Maria (*d* 26 July 1791), only child of Charles Powell, of Pen-y-bank, Carmarths, and *d* 25 Dec 1748, leaving issue:

(1) James; *b* 18 Jan 1746; *m* 29 July 1767 Lucy (*d* Sept 1790), dau of Sir Richard Lloyd, of Hintlesham, and widow of Sir John Barker, Bt, and *d* 22 Jan 1804, having had, with a son:

1a Lucy Charlotte; *m* 16 March 1799 Brig-Gen Robert Anstruther, s and heir of Sir Robert Anstruther, 3rd Bt (*qv*)

(2) Charles Powell; *b* 26 Dec 1747; Adml; *m* May 1777 Lucretia, dau of George Augustus Prosser, and *d* 12 March 1825, leaving:

1a Hamilton Charles James; *b* 29 July 1779; Envoy Extrdy and Min Plen Brazil; *m* 13 April 1826 Maria Susannah, 2nd dau of Lt-Gen Sir Frederic Philipse Robinson, GCB, Govr Tobago and *dsp* 15 Dec 1856

2a Augustus Barrington Price Anne Powell, of Fir Hill, Droxford, Hants; *b* 22 May 1781; *educ* St John's Coll Cambridge; Lt RN; *m* 2 April 1805 Maria Catherine, dau and coheir of John Hyde, DD, Judge Supreme Court Bengal, Dean Wells, Canon Windsor, Chaplain in Ordinary to GEORGE III, by Mary, est dau of Very Rev Lord Francis Seymour (*see* SOMERSET, D), and *d* 27 Aug 1849, having had issue:

1b Augustus John; *b* 25 May 1807; *d* 1826

2b Charles Henry; *b* 7 Oct 1808; Capt RN; *m* 1st 1 Dec 1854 Anna (*dsp* Feb 1856), 3rd dau of Rev — Apthorp; *m* 2nd 31 Jan 1860 Elizabeth Ann (*d* 27 June 1867), only dau of Ven Justly Hill, Archdeacon Bucks, and had:

1c ALFRED, **13th/10th Duke**

1c Helen Augusta Charlotte Constance Sidney; granted with sis rank of duke's dau 1896; *m* 1 June 1899 Rev Sir Robert Acland-Hood, 3rd Bt (*d* 23 April 1912), and *d* 4 Aug 1950, having had issue (*see* 1970 edn ST AUDRIES, B)

2c Isobel Frances Ulrica Iris; *m* 8 July 1897 Capt Cyril John Ryder and *d* 1 Oct 1941, having had issue (*see* HARROWBY, E)

3c Flora Maria Ida; *m* 29 Sept 1898 Brig-Gen Robert Montagu Poore, CIE, DSO, JP, DL (*see* POORE, Bt) and *dsp* 27 Jan 1957

2b (cont.) Capt Charles Hamilton *m* 3rd 21 Oct 1873 Sarah Julia (*d* 29 Feb 1880), dau of Capt Samuel Spence, 28th Foot, and *d* 30 Nov 1873

3b Francis Seymour; *b* 19 Jan 1811; Col RA; *m* 6 Sept 1834 Emma Catherine Frances (*d* 7 Jan 1868), 2nd dau of Thomas Darby Coventry, of Greenlands, Bucks, and *d* 1 June 1874, leaving, with other issue:

1c Archibald Barrington Seymour; *b* 3 Nov 1840; accidentally drowned in Switzerland 18 Jan 1876

2c Algernon Percy; *b* 22 June 1844; *m* 4 Nov 1874 Idonia (*d* 26 Aug 1910), dau of Capt Douglas Ryves Douglas-Hamilton (*see* below), and *d* 31 May 1891, having had issue:

1d Percy Seymour; *b* 2 Oct 1875; Lt RASC; *m* 1st 20 July 1901 Edith Anne Hamilton (*d* 22 Aug 1927), er dau of Sir Frederick Wills, 1st Bt (*see* DULVERTON, B); *m* 2nd 20 April 1929 Barbara Margherita (*d* 1975 having *m* 2nd 25 April 1946 David George Arbuthnot; *see* ARBUTHNOT, Bt, of Edinburgh), 2nd dau of Francis Chiappini, of Wynberg, Cape Colony, and *d* 6 Feb 1940, leaving by her:

1e +John Percy [John Douglas-Hamilton Esq, Hillcrest, Forest Ave, Bishopscourt, Cape, S Africa]; *b* 14 Feb 1930; *m* 1955 (*divorce* 1980) June Mary Clifton Michler, of Rondebosch, CP; *m* 2nd 1980 *Delia Rose Davies, *neé* Bilbrough, and has by his 1st w:

1f +John Gavin; *b* 1957

1f *Tessa Jeanne; *b* 1958

2f *Debra Anne; *b* 1959

3f *Diana Barbara; *b* 1959

1e *Diana Barbara; *b* 1 July 1932; *m* 1954 Ian Emslie Austin (*d* 1973), of S Africa, and has issue

1d Constance Idonia Violet; *m* 17 June 1908 Rev John Stern (*d* 4 June 1923), Vicar Fowey, Cornwall, and *d* 16 June 1962, leaving issue

2d Edith Lena Catherine; *m* 8 Sept 1903 Rev James Boyle (*d* 16 Nov 1941), Vicar Wembdon, Somerset, and *d* 27 July 1965, leaving issue

3d Ethel Jessie; *d* unm 25 Oct 1906

3c Aubrey Reginald; *b* 21 April 1851; Lt 57th Regt; *m* 24 July 1878 Lucy (*d* 5 Oct 1939), yst dau of Hon Robert Fitzgerald, MLC, of Sydney, and *d* 21 April 1933, leaving issue:

1d Kenneth Aubrey Fitzgerald Seymour; *b* 22 April 1879; *educ* Radley and Lincoln Coll Oxford; Lt Roy Fus, Capt Lancs Fus, Boer War (medal and five clasps), WW I (despatches, three medals); *m* 28 Oct 1916 (*divorce* 1921) Maude Mary, only child of A Travail Phillips, and *dsp* 16 Aug 1944

2d Lesley Reginald Coventry; *b* 30 June 1881; *educ* Radley; Capt Cameron Highrs, Maj 1916, Boer War (medal with five clasps), WW I (three medals, severely wounded at Loos); *kas* Somme 24 July 1916

3d Herbert Eustace Seymour; *b* 2 June 1886; *educ* Uppingham; Lt 3rd Bn Black Watch WW I, Gunner Canadian Field Artillery; *m* 27 Feb 1912 Ruth (*d* 1974), 3rd dau of Cuthbert Harrison, of Gateshead-on-Tyne, and *d* June 1963, leaving:

1e +Cecil Seymour [Cecil Douglas-Hamilton Esq, Apt 304, 2020 Belwood Ave, Burnaby, BC, Canada V5B 4P8]; *b* 18 Aug 1916; *m* 1 May 1943 *Ada Louise, 4th dau of Orie Donily, of Calgary, Alberta

1e *Doreen; *b* 6 June 1914; SRN (1939); *m* 18 Oct 1941 (*divorce* 1962) Alan Ogg Davidson, est s of Robert Alan Davidson, of Vernon, BC, and has issue:

1f *Ian Hamilton; *b* 26 Nov 1945

1f *Sheila Margaret; *b* 4 Jan 1944; *m* 3 July 1965 *Hugh Charles Strathan, and has issue:

1g *Grant Douglas; *b* 3 Jan 1969

2f *Joan Lesley; *b* 13 July 1952

4d Claud Archibald Aubrey, MBE (1920); *b* 26 May 1889; *educ* Uppingham and Trin Coll Cambridge (BA 1910); Egyptian CS, Order Nile 4th Cl; *m* 8 Oct 1915 Evelyn Addison, dau of Thomas Addison Chater, and *d* 25 Jan 1961, leaving:

1e *(Evelyn) Daphne; *b* 19 July 1916; SRN 1940; *m* 1st 6 June 1940 Rev Jack Rawlins, CF, Vicar Northwood, Stoke-on-Trent (*d* 9 July 1946), only s of Joseph Rawlins, of Wigan; *m* 2nd 5 Oct 1956 *Hedley Boardman, MB, ChB, DPH, s of Frank Boardman, of Glossop, Derbys, and by her 1st husb has:

1f *Michael David [Prof Michael Rawlins, 29 The Grove, Gosforth, Newcastle-upon-Tyne; Shoreston House, Shoreston, nr Seahouses, Northumberland]; *b* 28 March 1941; *educ* Uppingham and St Thomas's Hosp (BSc 1962, MB, BS 1965) MD, FRCP, FRCPE, MRCP 1968; *m* 3 Aug 1963 *Elizabeth Cadbury, only dau of Edmund Henry Hambly, MB, BS, FRCS (Eng), LRCP, of Treharrock Manor, Port Isaac, Cornwall, and has issue:

1g *Victoria Jane; *b* 6 Feb 1964

2g *Lucy Sarah; *b* 9 Dec 1965

2f *Christopher John [Christopher Rawlins Esq, 8 Glen Hill Lane, Wilton, CT 06897, USA; Windfall Cottage, E Prawle, nr Kingsbridge, Devon]; *b* 20 Aug 1945; *educ* Uppingham and Luton Coll of Technology (BSc Lond 1968); publisher Stockton Press; *m* 31 May 1969 *Mary Joan, (BSc Lond 1968), dau of Donovan William Goodchild, of Harpenden, Herts, and has:

1g *Jeremy Mark; *b* 19 Feb 1974; *educ* Lincoln-Sudbury RHS, USA and Leeds U Med Sch (MB, ChB 1997)

1g *Sarah Elizabeth; *b* 10 Jan 1972; *educ* Durham Sch and Worcester Coll Further Educn (BA Coventry U 1993)

2g *Penelope Jane; *b* 7 July 1977; *educ* Elmhurst Ballet Sch and Guildford Sch of Acting

1d Irene Lucy; *d* unm 9 April 1934

1c Rosabel Georgiana Maria; *m* 21 Sept 1876 Albert Charles Hadland (*d c* 1922), and *d c* 1917

4b Douglas Ryves; *b* 5 Jan 1814; *m* Feb 1843 Frances (*d* 1897), dau of Hugh Ryves Graves, of Fort William, Co Limerick, and *d* 1894, leaving:

1c Alexander

2c Patrick; *dsp*

3c Frederick; *b* 1852; *m* 1887 Elizabeth White

1c Idonia; *m* 4 Nov 1874 Algernon Percy Douglas-Hamilton (*d* 31 May 1891) and *d* 26 Aug 1910, having had issue (*see* above)

2c Bertha; *m* 1885 George Dawson, of Qld, Australia, and had issue

5b Frederic; *b* 12 May 1815; Min Resident and Consul-Gen Ecuador; *m* 25 Feb 1843 Marina (*d* 20 Sept 1871), est dau of James Norton, and *d* 15 May 1887, leaving issue:

1c Frederick Robert Vere; *b* 7 Dec 1843; *m* 1873 Joesephine Baumann, and *d* by 1918

2c Augustus Maitland Ronald; *b* 2 Sept 1847; Lt RN; *m* 1880 (*divorce* 1895) Therese Maude, dau of Capt W B C Wentworth, 78th Highrs, and *d* 1906, leaving issue:

1d *Marina Norton

3c Archibald Douglas Schomberg; *b* 1 Oct 1861; Capt 4th Bn Roy Welch Fus; *m* 16 Dec 1903 Margaret Eleanor, 2nd dau of late Henry Pemberton-Binns, of New York, and *dsp* 22 Jan 1908

1c Annie Marina Augusta; *b* 23 Oct 1845; *m* 4 Oct 1873 Stephen Dix (*d* Jan 1880), of Wickham, Kent, s of Charles Dix, and *d* 9 Oct 1900, leaving issue

2c Augusta Caroline Octavia; *b* 12 Oct 1856; *d* unm 24 March 1929

6b Adolphus (Rev); *b* 5 July 1816; MA; *m* 22 May 1847 Henrietta Charlotte (*d* 6 Jan 1901), yst dau of Adml Sir B H Carew, GCB, of Beddington Park, Surrey, and *d* 12 Sept 1893, leaving, with other issue:

1c Florence Ann Hallowell; *m* 13 Feb 1890 Edmund Arundel Laurence Gerald Peel (*d* Dec 1918), 2nd s of Maj Robert Peel, and *d* 11 March 1937, leaving issue

2c Mary Geraldine; *m* 1896 Henry Steuart (*d* Sept 1936), and *d* 23 Nov 1923, leaving issue

3c Eva Bertha Gwendoline; *m* 14 Sept 1884 George Wallace (*d* 18 Jan 1928), s of Rev Allan Wallace, and *d* 2 Oct 1954, leaving issue

7b Alfred, JP, DL; *b* 21 April 1818; MA, barrister; *m* 1st 17 July 1845 Adelaide (*d* 17 April 1870), 2nd dau and coheir of Alexander Black, of Gidea Hall, and had, with other issue:

1c Alfred Hamilton Douglas; *b* 27 Jan 1856; *m* 14 Jan 1914 Katherine (*d* 16 Nov 1938), only dau of George Combermere Gould, of Ashbourne, Derbys, and widow of Edward Richardson, of Birchington, and *d* 22 July 1942

2c William Arthur Rev); *b* 6 Sept 1864; *educ* Cambridge (BA); *m* 12 April 1923 Alice Georgina (*d* 1 Feb 1958), 5th dau of Rev Augustus George Legge (*see* DARTMOUTH, E), and *dsp* 17 April 1948

1c Annie Laura; *m* 11 Nov 1876 Capt Everard Strangways Neave and *d* 18 Oct 1877, leaving issue (*see* NEAVE, Bt)

2c Nina Susannah; *m* 30 July 1878 Sir William Cospatrick Dunbar, 9th Bt, CB, of Mochrum (*qv*), and *d* 19 Jan 1943

7b (cont.) Alfred Douglas-Hamilton *m* 2nd 27 Oct 1874 Harriette Amy Blackburne (*d* 15 Nov 1929), yst dau of W H Peters, DL, of Harefield Devon, and *d* 25 March 1895, having by her had:

3c Evelyn Mary; *d* unm 4 Sept 1955

4c Amy Janet; *d* unm 29 March 1961

7b Octavius; *b* 15 Feb 1821; Maj-Gen; *m* 29 June 1852 Katherine Augusta Westenra (*d* 30 Nov 1902), dau of Capt Donald Macleod, CB, RN, and *d* 14 Aug 1904, leaving, with other issue:

1c Hamilton Anne (Ven); *b* 28 May 1853; *educ* Trin Coll Cambridge (MA); Rector Marlesford, Suffolk, Hon Canon St Edmundsbury and Hon Chaplain to Bp St Edmundsbury, Archdeacon Kimberley; *m* 1st 26 Oct 1875 Lillie (*d* 26 May 1918), dau of J Bowles, and had issue:

1d Basil Sholto Anne; *b* 11 Aug 1876; Capt ASC; *m* 11 Sept 1912 Dorothy Campbell, only dau of Robert Campbell Franks, and *d* 12 April 1920

2d James Angus; *b* 13 Aug 1890; Cdr RN, WWs I and II; *m* 20 Jan 1938 Joan Mary (*d* 17 Oct 1975), dau of Surgn-Lt J S D MacCormac, RN

1d Ilta; *m* 14 May 1915 Henry L R Watt, Capt 10th Bn Seaforth Highrs (*d* 29 Nov 1940), er s of H A Watt, of Elgin, and *d* 10 March 1957, leaving issue

1d Mary Hamilton; *m* 29 Sept 1915 Maj Christopher Martin Ingoldby, RAMC (*d* 22 June 1927), s of F Ingoldby, of Westgate House, Louth, and had issue

1c (cont.) Canon Hamilton Douglas-Hamilton *m* 2nd 24 Oct 1922 Hon Agnes Rosamund Bateman-Hanbury (*d* 11 April 1947), dau of 2nd Baron Bateman (*see* 1931 edn), and *d* 22 Aug 1929

2c Augustus Maynard; *b* 29 Nov 1854; Capt 4th Bn E Surrey Regt; *m* 4 Aug 1909 Frances Wilhelmina (*d* 30 Aug 1938), yst dau of Dirk Cloete, of Alphen, Wynberg, Cape Colony, and *d* 19 Aug 1928

3c Charles Reginald Sydney; *b* 5 Oct 1856; Capt Gordon Highrs; *m* 10 Sept 1890 Mary Isabel Hammond (*d* 5 Jan 1948), dau of Capt George Alexander Whitla, of Ben Eadan, and *d* 8 Feb 1935, leaving issue:

1d Elsie Muriel; *b* 21 Aug 1891

1c Angus Falconer, VC; *b* 20 Aug 1863; Lt-Col 6th QO Cameron Highrs, Maj 79th Cameron Highrs Sudan Expdns 1884–85 and 1885–86 and WW I (despatches); *m* 1 Aug 1894 Anna Watson (*d* 15 Feb 1945), yst dau of Capt Alexander Watson Mackenzie of Ord, Ross-shire, formerly 91st Highrs, and was *kas* Loos 26 Sept 1915, leaving:

1d Camilla Beatrice; *b* 9 Aug 1895; *d* unm 23 May 1957

1c Katherine Seymour; *d* unm 17 April 1944

1b Alexandrina Idonia Charlotte Susan; *m* 29 March 1851 Maj Robert Peel, 13th LI, and had issue

2b Lucretia Charlotte Susanna; *m* Capt Stephen Briggs, RN, and had issue

1 Elizabeth; *d* 2 April 1702

2 Catherine; *d* 22 Dec 1712

3 Charlotte; *m* 1 May 1736 Charles Edwin (*d* 29 June 1750), of Dunraven, Glam, and *d* 5 Feb 1777

4 Susan; *m* 3 Aug 1736 Anthony TRACY later TRACY-KECK, of Great Tew, Oxon, and *d* 3 June 1755, leaving issue (*see* WEMYSS, E)

The 12th/9th DUKE's cousin,

ALFRED DOUGLAS DOUGLAS-HAMILTON, **13th Duke of Hamilton** and **10th Duke of Brandon**, also 9th EARL OF SELKIRK, which held in fiduciary fee, TD, DL (Lanarks); *b* 6 March 1862; Lt RN; Hon Lt-Col 4th Bn HLI, Hon Col 6th Bn Scottish Rifles; *m* 4 Dec 1901 Nina Mary Benita, DGStJ, Pres Animal Defence and Anti-Vivisection Soc (*d* 12 Jan 1951), 3rd dau of Maj Robert Poore (*see* POORE, Bt), and *d* 16 March 1940, having had issue:

1 DOUGLAS, **14th/11th Duke**

2 GEORGE NIGEL, 10th EARL OF SELKIRK (*qv*)

3 Malcolm Avondale, OBE, (1943), DFC (1944); *b* 12 Nov 1909; *educ* Eton; W/Cdr RAFVR WW II, Cmdt ATC Scotland 1945; MP Inverness and Ross and Cromarty 1950–54, memb Roy Co Archers, Dir Gordonstoun and Aberlour Schs, Chm Outdoor Trg Ctee, Central Cncl Physical Recreation Scotland; *m* 1st 18 April 1931 (*divorce* 1952) Clodagh Pamela, only dau of Lt-Col Hon Malcolm Bowes-Lyon (*see* STRATHMORE AND KINGHORNE, E), and had issue:

(1) +Alasdair Malcolm [Alasdair Douglas-Hamilton Esq, Lessudden, St Boswells, Roxburghshire TD6 0BH]; *b* 10 Sept 1939; *educ* Gordonstoun and Edinburgh U (BL); *m* 24 July 1965 *Angela Kathleen, 2nd dau of John Molony Longley, of The Old Rectory, W Knoyle, Wilts, and has issue:

1a +Angus Gavin; *b* 1968; *m* 18 Nov 1995 *Justine Levene and has:

1b *Siana; *b* 21 May 1997

2a +Geordie Fergus; *b* 15 May 1969

1a *Fenella Mairi; *b* 19 May 1966; *m* 23 Sept 1994 *H Igor Zevenbergen and has:

1b *Caspar; *b* 9 April 1991

1b *Mara; *b* 11 Nov 1996

2a *Tessa Catherine; *b* 1980

(2) Niall David; *b* 15 June 1943; *educ* Gordonstoun; *k* with f in an air crash on Mt Cameroon 21 July 1964

(1) *Diana Mairi [Mrs Diana Younger, Friarshawmuir, Midlem, Selkirk TD7 4PZ]; *b* 13 Feb 1932; *educ* North Foreland Lodge, Edinburgh Coll of Art (Dip Drawing and Painting 1953) and Bristol Poly (Dip Sculpture 1978); exhibitor Edinburgh, London and Cardiff; Maid of Hon Assembly Holyrood Ho 1954; *m* 18 June 1955 (*divorce* 1973) Gavin William Younger, est s of Maj Henry Johnston Younger, of Baro, Haddington, E Lothian, and has:

1a *Douglas Henry; *b* 31 May 1956; *m* 1979 *Alison Susan, 2nd dau of Guy Urwick Goodbody, and has:

1b *Harry Neil; *b* 1981

2b *Samuel Guy; *b* 1984

3b *Nicholas William; *b* 1986

2a *Hugh Patrick; *b* 5 March 1958; *m* 1986 *Sophie Helen, er dau of Felix Benjamin Engel, and has:

1b *Joshua Hugh Gaskell; *b* 1988

2b *Dominic William; *b* 1990

3b *Peter Finn; *b* 1992

4b *Benedict Gavin; *b* 1995

3a *Malcolm James; *b* 22 Sept 1959; *m* 1989 *Sophie Anne Marlton, 2nd dau of Michael Dowse, and has:

1b *Anna Cecilia; *b* 1994

2b *Eliza Victoria; *b* 1997

4a *Robert William; *b* 28 June 1964; *m* 1994 *Elizabeth, er dau of Thomas Smeaton

1a *Alexandra Katharine Anna; *b* 11 April 1963; *m* 1991 *Simon James Milne, yr s of Denis Stanley Maitland Milne, and has:

1b *Geordie Alexander Maitland; *b* 1995

(2) *Fiona Margaret; *b* 26 April 1935; *educ* Edinburgh U (MA 1968); *m* 15 Sept 1973 *Jeremy Blackstone Wise (*d* 22 May 1990), est s of Cdr G H Wise, RN, of Titchfield, Hants

3 (cont.) Lord Malcolm Douglas-Hamilton *m* 2nd 4 Jan 1953 *Natalie, CBE [The Lady Malcolm Douglas-Hamilton CBE, Apt 10, 174 East 74th St, New York, NY, USA], dau of Maj Nathaniel Brackett Wales, of New York and Boston, widow of Edward Bragg Paine and formerly w of Kenelm Winslow, and was *k* in an air crash on Mt Cameroon 21 July 1964

4 David; *b* 8 Nov 1912; *educ* Harrow, Balliol Coll Oxford (BA) and St Andrews (MA); S/Ldr RAFVR WW II; *m* 15 Oct 1938 *Ann Prunella (OBE 1980) [Mrs Brian Power OBE, 14 Gertrude St, London SW10 0JN] (*m* 2nd 22 July 1950 Alfred Gustave Albers, FRCS (*d* as the result of a mountaineering accident 24 March 1951), only s of N W Albers, of S Africa; *m* 3rd 15 May 1964 *Brian St Quentin Power, 2nd s of Stephen St Quentin Power, of Guerrin, Co Clare), only dau of Capt Edward Hugh Bagot Stack, 2nd/8th Gurkha Rifles, and was *kas* 2 Aug 1944, leaving issue:

(1) +Diarmaid Hugh [Diarmaid Douglas-Hamilton Esq, 729 Cabot St, Beverly, MA 01915, USA]; *b* 17 June 1940; *educ* Gordonstoun, Balliol Coll Oxford (BA) and Harvard U (MA); *m* 1st 14 Oct 1967 (*divorce* 1982) Margaret Barlow, dau of William Matthew Hambrecht, of Lakeville, Conn.; *m* 2nd 1983 *Margaret Murray, est dau of Duncan MacGlashan Spencer, of New York

(2) +Iain, OBE (1993); *b* 16 Aug 1942; *educ* Gordonstoun and Oriel Coll Oxford (BA Zoology); elephant problems adviser to Tanzania National Parks; *m* 1971 *Oria, dau of Lt Col Mario Rocco, of Kenya, and has issue:

1a +Saba Iassa; *b* 1970; *educ* St Andrews

1a +Dudu Mara; *b* 1971; *educ* Cape Town U

1 Jean; *b* 11 June 1904; *m* 1st 8 April 1927 (*divorce* 1946) Charles Ernest Whistler Mackintosh, est s of F/Lt Charles Mackintosh, and had issue; *m* 2nd 24 May 1947 Maj Leo Zinovieff (*d* following a railway accident 21 Sept 1951), s of Leo Zinovieff, of Shalford, Surrey; *m* 3rd 20 Oct 1972 *W/Cdr Vivian Norton Bell

2 Margaret; *b* 13 Oct 1907; *m* 1 Feb 1930 Maj James Drummond-Hay of Seggieden, Coldstream Gds, est s of Col James Adam Gordon Richardson Drummond-Hay of Seggieden, and had issue

3 Mairi Nina; *b* 27 Aug 1914 (HM QUEEN MARY stood sponsor); *d* 27 May 1927

The 13th/10th DUKE's est surv son,

DOUGLAS DOUGLAS-HAMILTON, **14th Duke of Hamilton** and **11th Duke of Brandon**, KT (1951), GCVO (1946), AFC (1935), PC (1940); *b* 3 Feb 1903; *educ* Eton and Balliol Coll Oxford; WW II in RAF (despatches); MP (C) E Renfrewshire 1930–40; Dep Govr Br Linen Bank, Chm Norwich Union Life and Fire Insur Soc Scotland, dir Scottish Union and Nat Insur, Scottish Aviation Ltd and Securicor Scotland, Pres Bldg Socs Assoc; Chllr St Andrews U 1948–73, Ld Steward Household 1940–64, memb Roy Co Archers, Ld HC Gen Assembly Ch Scotland 1953–55 and 1958, LLD St Andrews and Edinburgh, FRGS, FRCSE, Freeman Hamilton and Prestwick Burghs, Pres BALPA, Ch Pilot Houston Everest Expdn 1933, in 602 Sqdn RAAF, first man to fly over Everest, Pres Air League Br Empire, Roy Victorian Chain 1964, co-author: *The Pilots' Book of Everest* (1936), Pres Boys' Bde, amateur boxer (Known as 'the Boxing Marquess' before *s* to the Dukedom), worked as 'Mr Hamilton' down coal mines and obtained Union card 1935, recd a parachute visit 1941 during WW II by HITLER's Deputy Rudolf Hess with object of negotiating peace; *m* 2 Dec 1937 *Lady Elizabeth Ivy Percy, OBE, DL [Her Grace The Dowager Duchess of Hamilton and Brandon OBE DL, North Port, Lennoxlove, Haddington, E Lothian EH41 4HH], er dau of 8th Duke of Northumberland (*qv*), and *d* 1973, leaving:

1 ANGUS ALAN DOUGLAS DOUGLAS-HAMILTON, **15th and present Duke of Hamilton and 12th and present Duke of Brandon**

2 +JAMES ALEXANDER DOUGLAS-HAMILTON, briefly 11th EARL OF SELKIRK, later BARON SELKIRK OF DOUGLAS (*qv*)

3 Hugh Malcolm; *b* 22 Aug 1946; *educ* Eton and U of S Carolina; *m* 1st 3 July 1971 (*annulled* 1991) June Mary, dau of T J Curtis, and had issue:

(1) +Brendan Thomas; *b* 29 Oct 1974

(1) *Catherine Bride; *b* 1976

3 (cont.) Lord Hugh *m* 2nd 1994 *Sheilagh Ellis and *d* 21 June 1995

4 +Patrick George [The Lord Patrick Douglas-Hamilton, 107 Eccleston Mews, London SW1X 8AQ]; *b* 2 Aug 1950; *educ* Lancing; *m* 1989 (*divorce* 1997) Cecilia F M, er dau of Capt T G Usher, of Crossford, Fife, and has:

(1) *Isabel Rose; *b* 1991

5 +David Stephen; *b* 26 Dec 1952; *educ* Eton

Seat: Lennoxlove, Haddington, E Lothian. A somewhat modest dwelling for a duke, Lennoxlove is not even in origin a Hamilton (or Douglas-Hamilton) property. It was anciently a Maitland one (*see* LAUDERDALE, E) and its chief attractions to visitors (the death mask of MARY QUEEN OF SCOTS and an avenue of limes called the 'Politician's Walk' which was planned by William, her confidential adviser), commemorate the Maitland tenancy. The house started as a tower in the mid-14th century and was extended by another Maitland, the Duke of Lauderdale (virtual ruler of Scotland in the late 17th century). In the early 18th century the estate, called till then Lethington, was bought by the 5th Lord Blantyre (*see* 1900 edn) with an ample inheritance bequeathed him by his cousin Frances, Dowager Duchess of Richmond and Lennox (*see* MORAY, E). In gratitude he rechristened the place Lennoxlove.

In late spring 1997 a fire inflicted damage estimated at up to £100,000's worth, chiefly to oil paintings of the Stewarts (holders of the Lordship of Blantyre) in the Oak Room. It is thought to have been caused by a discarded cigarette after a corporate banquet. (The present Duke no longer lives on the premises, which are hired out for such events.)

HAMILTON OF DALZELL

Arms: Gu. an annulet or, between three cinquefoils pierced ermine (for ORBISTON). **Crest:** An antelope ppr., armed and unguled or. **Supporters:** Dexter, an antelope ppr. gorged with a ducal crown and a chain thereto hanging or; sinister, a savage ppr., wreathed head and middle with laurel, holding over the sinister shoulder a club or. **Motto:** *Quis occursabit* ('Who will oppose?'). **Creation:** B. (UK) 14 Aug 1886.

THE 4TH BARON HAMILTON OF DALZELL, Co Lanark (James Leslie Hamilton, DL (Surrey 1993)) [The Rt Hon The Lord Hamilton of Dalzell DL, Stockton House, Stockton, Salop TF11 9EF; Betchworth House, Betchworth, Surrey RH3 7AE]; *b* 11 Feb 1938; *s* f 1990; *educ* Eton; Lt Coldstream Gds 1956–58, memb London Stock Exchange 1967–80, dir Rowton Hotels 1978–84, Govr Queen Elizabeth's Fndn for Disabled People (chm 1989–), Drapers' Co 1997; *m* 29 March 1967 *(Ann Anastasia) Corinna (Helena), DL (Surrey 1996), High Sheriff Surrey 1995–96, Pres St John Amb Surrey, yr dau of Sir Pierson John Dixon, GCMG, CB, and has issue:

1 +GAVIN GOULBURN; *b* 8 Oct 1968; *educ* Eton and Buckingham U (BSc); *m* 12 April 1997 *Harriet, yr dau of Thomas and Elizabeth Roskill

2 +Robert Pierson; *b* 29 July 1971; *educ* Eton and Buckingham U (LLB)

3 +John Duff; *b* 29 July 1971; *educ* Eton and Durham U (BA)

4 +Benjamin James; *b* 5 Nov 1974; *educ* Eton and Newcastle U (BSc); Page Honour to HM THE QUEEN 1986–88

Lineage: Sir JAMES HAMILTON, 5th of Cadzow (*see* ABERCORN, D); had a 4th s:

GAVIN HAMILTON, 1st of Orbieston; *b* by 1441; *m* Jean, dau of — Hamilton, of Woodhall, and *d* by 1493, having had, with four yr sons (Archibald; John, of Ferguslee; Patrick; David of Bothwellhaugh, ancestor of Hamilton of Bothwellhaugh who shot the Regent Moray 1570):

GAVIN HAMILTON, 2nd of Orbieston; *m* Marion Wallace, of Cairnhill, and *d* by 22 July 1558, having had, with five yr sons (David; Arthur; James; Archibald, migrated to France after 1575, Prof U of Paris, *d* by 20 Nov 1589; Robert, *educ* St Mary Coll St Andrews, joined Reformers 1559 and accompanied John Knox to Berwick in a mission to ELIZABETH I's PC, Minister Hamilton 1562, St Andrews 1565, Moderator 1571–73, Pncpl St Mary's New Coll St Andrews 1574, *d* 15 April 1581):

JOHN HAMILTON, 3rd of Orbieston; *m* Margaret, dau of — Hamilton of Haggs, and was *k* 14 May 1568 fighting for MARY QUEEN OF SCOTS Battle of Langside, after which his estates were confiscated by the Regent Moray and Orbieston House burned by the English 1570; had, with other issue, including two yr sons (Gavin, Bp Galloway; Robert, MA St Andrews 1592, Min Ruthven 1594, *b c* 1570, *d* 30 Dec 1594) and three daus (Isobel, *m* Robert Hamilton of Barncluith; Marjory, *m* — Dundas of Duddingstoun; Margaret, *m* John Robertoun of Earnoch):

JOHN HAMILTON, 4th of Orbieston, to whom the family estates were restored 1585; had a charter 1604 from his bro Gavin of the lands of Orbieston, Carnbrow, Unthank; *m* Christian, dau of Robert Dalzell of that Ilk (ancestor of the Earls of Carnwath; *see* 1940 edn), and *d* 1621, having had, with other issue:

1 John (Sir), 5th of Orbieston, Ld Justice Clerk; bought among other properties the (territorial) Barony of Erskine in Renfrewshire and Dumbartonshire (formerly property of the Erskine Earls of Mar); his descendants became extinct when his gs William, 7th of Orbiston, *d*

2 JAMES

1 Marion; *m* John Hamilton of Bangour

2 Margaret; *m* John Walkinshaw of that Ilk

3 Janet; *m* 1st Gavin Cupar of Boiggs; *m* 2nd Gavin Waddell

4 Agnes; *m* — Bruce of Newat

5 Grissell, contracted to Hugh Sanders, but *d*

The 2nd son,

JAMES HAMILTON, 1st of Dalzell; prospered by trade, in particular army contracts during Cromwellian wars; Burgess Glasgow 1632; granted 1647 territorial Barony of Dalzell, resigned by the Earl and Countess of Carnwath; Commr Supply Lanarks 1655; *m* 1st Beatrice Fleming (living 1629) and had four sons and two daus; *m* 2nd *c* 1646 Jean Henderson, of Fordel (*d* July 1653), and by her had three sons and two daus (the er, Anne, *m c* 24 July 1666 David Boswell of Auchinleck and *d* 1713, leaving issue); *m* 3rd Isobel (*d c* May 1715), widow of Robert Hamilton of Millburn and dau of Sir James Hamilton of Brownhill, and by her had three other sons (James, of Hallside; William, author *Manuscript on the Hamiltons of Orbiston and Dalzell*, now in the Br Museum; Sir David Hamilton, MD, FRS, *educ* Leyden and Rheims (MD 1686), physician to WILLIAM III and QUEEN ANNE, ktd 1708, ruined in the South Sea Bubble, *b c* 1663, *d* 29 Aug 1721); the middle s by the 2nd w:

ALEXANDER HAMILTON, 2nd of Dalzell (assigned him 1668 and confirmed 1672 by his half-bro Robert Hamilton of Monkland); Commr 1668 to raise three regts of Lanarks militia; *m* his cousin Bethia, widow of John Robertson of Earnoch and dau of Sir William Henderson of Fordel, and *d* Jan 1691, having had, with other issue:

JAMES HAMILTON, 3rd of Dalzell and 8th of Orbieston; *educ* Glasgow U; *b* Dec 1670; *m* 7 June 1693 Margaret (*d* 22 March 1704 aged 38), est dau of Sir Archibald Hamilton of Rosehall, and *d* 1727, having had, with other issue:

1 ARCHIBALD

2 James, of Muirhouse; Collector Supply Lanarks 1722; *b c* 1697; *educ* Glasow U; *d* 9 June 1788

1 Margaret; *b c* 1700; *m* — Hamilton and *d* 7 April 1797

2 Anne; *b* 1703; *m* — Hamilton and *d* 15 April 1796

The er son,

ARCHIBALD HAMILTON, 4th of Dalzell and 9th of Orbiston; *educ* Glasgow U; retoured lawful heir to the (territorial) Barony of Rosehall 1757; *b* 1694; *m* 19 March 1732 Marion, dau of Hugh Dalrymple of Dromore, and *d* 28 Dec 1774, having had, with other issue, including an ests (James, 5th of Dalzell and 10th of Orbieston, *b* 1773, *d* 6 Dec 1814), a 3rd s (Robert, *b* 1746, *dsp* 6 June 1790) and a dau (Anne, *d* unm 22 July 1793):

JOHN HAMILTON, of Motherwell, 6th of Dazell and 11th of Orbieston, Gen; obliged to sell Orbieston and Rosehall after the failure of a commune there (known locally as 'Babylon') run chiefly by his bro; *b* 1742; *m* 1790 Anne, dau of Dr R Mathews, and *d* 9 Feb 1834, having had, with a yr s (Robert, *b* 7 Aug 1796, *d* 1845) and a dau (Marion, *m* Lt-Col David Rattray and *d* 1 May 1818):

ARCHIBALD JAMES; served Scots Greys Waterloo; *b* 28 Oct 1793; *m* 1st Margaret (*dsp* 24 Aug 1824), dau of William Ramsay; *m* 2nd Ellinor (*d* 16 Sept 1856), dau of Daniel Hamilton of Gilkercleugh, and *dvp* 11 Jan 1834, leaving, with a dau (*d* an infant):

JOHN GLENCAIRN CARTER HAMILTON, **1st Baron Hamilton of Dalzell**, Co Lanark (UK), so *cr* 14 Aug 1886, JP; V-Lt Lanarks, Ld-in-Waiting 1892–94, Capt 2nd Life Gds, Col Queen's Own Glasgow and Lanarks Yeo, MP (Lib) Falkirk Burghs 1857059, S Lanarks 1868–74 and 1880–86; *b* 16 Nov 1829; *m* 29 March 1864 Lady Emily Eleanor Leslie-Melville (*d* 11 Nov 1882), dau of 10th Earl of Leven and (7th Earl of) Melville (*qv*), and *d* 15 Oct 1900, having had issue:

1 Archibald John; *b* 24 May 1868; *d* 20 May 1870

2 GAVIN GEORGE HAMILTON, **2nd Baron Hamilton of Dalzell**, KT (1909), CVO (1908), MC; *b* 20 June 1872; *educ* Eton and RMC Sandhurst; Ld Lt Lanarks, Maj Scots Gds WW I, Ld-in-Waiting 1905–10 and 1910–11, Assist Mil Sec 1917–19, Chm Roy Fine Art Commn Scotland 1932, Hon Col 10th Bn Cameronians (TA) 1939, Tstee Ascot Authority 1945; Orders White Eagle Russia 1st Cl, St Olav Norway, SS. Maurice and Lazarus Italy, Chev Legn Hon; *m* 24 July 1912 Sybil Mary (*d* 3 May 1933), formerly w 3rd Baron Burnham (*qv*) and dau of Lt-Gen Sir Frederick Marshall, KCMG, and *dsp* 23 June 1952

3 Leslie d'Henin MVO; Maj Coldstream Gds, Boer War 1899–1902 and WW I; *b* 19 Dec 1873; *m* 9 Sept 1905 Amy Cecil (*d* 29 Sept 1941), er dau of Col Horace Ricardo, CVO, Gren Gds, of Bramley Park, Surrey, and was *ka* 29 Oct 1914, leaving:

(1) JOHN D'HENIN, **3rd Baron**

4 John David; Lt 12th Lancers; *b* 23 Dec 1878; *dsp* 22 May 1900

1 Ellinor, OBE (1919); *m* 18 Jan 1890 Col Charles William Trotter, CB, of Barton Hartshorne Manor, Bucks, and *d* 15 Jan 1957, leaving issue. He *d* 27 July 1931

2 Alice Susan; granted 7 Feb 1921 rank of baron's widow; *m* 15 Jan 1895 Capt Hon John Beresford Campbell, est s of 3rd Baron Stratheden and Campbell (*qv*), and *d* 25 Jan 1949, leaving issue

3 Helena Mabel; *m* 2 Aug 1899 Lt-Col Henry Heywood Heywood-Lonsdale, DSO, of Shavington, Market Drayton, and *d* 21 May 1930, leaving issue. He *d* 1 Nov 1930

4 Adele Emily Anna; *m* 17 April 1912 Rev Clement Eustace Macro Wilson, Rector Ightfield with Calverhall, Salop, s of Rev Canon William Reginald Wilson, MA, and *d* 26 Aug 1946, leaving issue (*see* STEPHENSON, Bt)

The 2nd BARON's n,

JOHN D'HENIN HAMILTON, **3rd Baron Hamilton of Dalzell**, KCVO (1981), MC (1945), JP (Guildford 1957); *b* 1 May 1911; *educ* Eton and RMC Sandhurst; Surrey: Ld Lt 1973–90 (V-Lt 1957–73), Ld in Waiting 1968–81, Maj Coldstream Gds (Res Offrs) WW II (wounded), Chm: Surrey Ag Exec Ctee 1957–68, Guildford New Cathedral Cncl 1957–69, Cncl Social Serv Surrey 1960–90, Guildford Bench 1968, Ctee Legal Aid 1972–79, Liaison Offr Min Ag 1961–64, memb Cncl Tbnls 1964–72, Pres Nat Assoc Probation Offrs 1964–90; *m* 4 March 1935 Rosemary Olive (*d* 1993), er dau of Maj Hon Sir John Spencer Coke, KCVO, 7th s of 2nd Earl of Leicester (*qv*), and *d* 1990, leaving:

1 JAMES LESLIE HAMILTON, **4th and present Baron Hamilton of Dalzell**

2 +Archibald Gavin (Sir), PC (1991) [The Rt Hon Sir Archibald Hamilton MP, House of Commons, London SW1 0AA]; Lt Coldstream Gds 1960–63, memb Kensington and Chelsea Cncl 1968–71, MP (C) Epsom and Ewell April 1978–, PPS to: Sec State Energy 1979–82 and PM 1987–88, Assist Govt Whip 1982–84, Ld Commr Treasury 1984–86, Parly U-Sec Def Procurement 1986–87, Min State Armed Forces 1988–93, ktd 1994, Chm 1922 Ctee 1997–, Govr Westminster Fndn for Democracy; *b* 30 Dec 1941; *educ* Eton; *m* 14 Dec 1968 *Anne Catharine, yr dau of Cdr Trevylyan Michael Napier, DSC, RN, and has issue:

(1) *Laura Katherine; *b* 6 Dec 1969

(2) *Iona Janet *b* 23 March 1971

(3) *Alice Rose Alethea; *b* 30 June 1975

1 *Janet [The Hon Mrs Lane Fox, Kingsley Mill, Black Torrington, Beaworthy, Devon EX21 5HS]; *b* 8 Sept 1936; *m* 11 June 1960 *Richard Sackville Lane Fox, yr s of Lt-Col Francis Gordon Ward Lane Fox, of Bramham Park, Boston Spa, Yorks, and has:

(1) *Andrew Ward Jackson; *b* 17 Feb 1969

(1) *Harriot; *b* 18 May 1966

HAMILTON-DALRYMPLE

Arms: Quarterly, 1st and 4th, grand quarters, or on a saltire azure, between two water-bougets on the flanks sable, nine lozenges of the first (for DALRYMPLE); 2nd and 3rd grand quarters, quarterly, 1st and 4th, gules three cinquefoils ermine; 2nd and 3rd, argent a lymphad with sails furled sable, all within a bordure componée argent and azure charged alternately with hearts gules and mullets argent (for HAMILTON). **Crest:** A rock proper. **Supporters:** Dexter, a lion guardant gules; sinister, a falcon proper. **Motto:** Firm. **Creation:** Bt. (NS) 29 April 1698.

SIR HEW FLEETWOOD HAMILTON-DALRYMPLE, 10TH BT, of North Berwick, Co Haddington, KCVO (1985, CVO 1974) [Sir Hew Hamilton-Dalrymple Bt KCVO, Leuchie, N Berwick, E Lothian EH39 5NT]; *b* 9 April 1926; *s f* 1959; *educ* Ampleforth; commissioned Gren Gds 1944, Adj 3rd Bn 1951–54, Staff Coll Camberley 1957, DAAG HQ 3rd Div 1958–60, Regtl Adj 1960–62, ret 1962; dir: Scottish & Newcastle Breweries 1967–86 (v-chm 1983–86), Scottish American Investment 1967–93 (chm 87–93); Ld Lt E Lothian 1987– (V-Lt 1973–87, DL 1964–73), Capt Gen Roy Co Archers and Gold Stick Scotland 1996–; *m* 25 Sept 1954 *Lady Anne-Louise Mary Keppel, yst dau of 9th Earl of Albemarle (*qv*), and has:

1 +HEW RICHARD [Hew Dalrymple Esq, Blackdykes, North Berwick, E Lothian]; *b* 3 Sept 1955; *educ* Ampleforth, Corpus Christi Coll Oxford (MA), Clare Hall Cambridge (MPhil) and Birkbeck Coll Lond (MSc); ODI Fell Swaziland 1982–84; *m* 1987 *Jane Elizabeth, yr dau of Lt-Col John Morris, and has:

(1) +Hew John Lucien; *b* 28 Aug 1990

(1) *Hero Cecilia; *b* 1989

(2) *Theophania Mary Anne; *b* 1992

(3) *Lydia Jane Diana; *b* Jan 1996

2 +John James; *b* 14 Oct 1957; *educ* Ampleforth and Queen's Coll Oxford; RC Priest

3 +Robert George [Robert Dalrymple Esq, Bolton Old Manse, by Haddington, E Lothian]; *b* 19 Aug 1959; *educ* Ampleforth; *m* 1984 *Anna Mary, dau of Maj David Gibson, of Ross-on-Wye, Herefs and has issue:

(1) +David Fleetwood; *b* 1993

(1) *Effie Charlotte; *b* 1986

(1) *Sophia Louise; *b* 1988

(3) *Honor Rose; *b* 1991

4 +William Benedict [William Dalrymple Esq, 1 & 2 Pages' Yard, Church St, London W4 2PA]; *b* 20 March 1965; *educ* Ampleforth and Trin Coll Cambridge (MA 1993); author: *In Xanadu* (1989), *City of Djinns* (1993), *From the Holy Mountain* (1997); FRSL and FRGS 1995; *m* 1991 *Olivia Mary Juliet, 3rd dau of Simon Joseph Fraser (*see* LOVAT, L), and has:

(1) +Samuel Hew Tantallor; *b* 21 Feb 1997

(1) *Elizabeth Kashmir; *b* Feb 1995

Lineage: The 1st VISCOUNT OF STAIR (*see* STAIR, E); had a 3rd s:

Sir Hew Dalrymple, 1st Bt, (NS), so *cr* 29 April 1698, of N Berwick; *b c* 1653; advocate 1677, MP (S Parl) New Galloway 1696–1702 and N Berwick 1702–07; Ld Pres Court Session 1698–1737, Commr: Union S and E Parls 1706, improving Scottish fisheries and mfrs; *m* 1st 12 March 1682 Marion, dau of Sir Robert Hamilton of Pressmennan, and had, with other issue:

1 Robert (Sir), of Castleton; advocate 1714; *m* 1st 23 Feb 1707 Johanna, dau of John Hamilton, Master of Bargeny, and had, with other issue:

(1) HEW (Sir), **2nd Bt**

(2) John DALRYMPLE later HAMILTON (on inheriting the Bargeny estate after prolonged litigation); *b* 4 Feb 1715; advocate 1735, MP Wigton Burghs 1754; *m* 1st Anne, dau of 4th Earl of Wemyss (*qv*); *m* 2nd 1772 Margaret, dau of Alexander Montgomerie of Coyisfield, and *dsp* 12 Feb 1796, when the Bargeny estate passed to his n **Sir Hew, 3rd Bt** (*see* below)

(1) Marion; *m* 1732 4th Lord Reay (*qv*) and *d* 1740

(2) Anne; *m* 24 Oct 1749 5th Earl of Balcarres (*see* CRAWFORD and BALCARRES, E) and *d* 29 Nov 1820, leaving issue

1 (cont.) Sir Robert Dalrymple *m* 2nd Anne (*d* 23 Jan 1776), est dau of Sir William Cunningham of Caprington, Bt, and *dvp* 21 Aug 1734, having had, with three other sons:

(3) Charles; *m* 1738 Elizabeth, dau and heir of John Edwin, and had:

1a Elizabeth; *m* 1 June 1780 6th Earl of Balcarres (and *de jure* 23rd Earl of Crawford, *qv*) and had issue

2 Hew, of Drummore; *b* 30 Nov 1690; Ld of Session 1726 and of Justiciary 1745 as Lord Drummore; *m* Anne, dau and heir of John Horn of Horn and Westhall, and *d* 18 June 1755, having had, with other issue:

(1) Hew; *b* 7 Jan 1717; *m* Anne, dau of Sir John Inglis of Crammond, Bt, and *dsp* 26 July 1740

(2) Robert; ancestor of the ELPHINSTONE-DALRYMPLE, Bts (*see* STAIR, E)

(3) David; *b* 27 Aug 1719; Ld of Session as Lord Westhall 1777; *m* 1761 Jane (*d* 23 April 1780), dau of Alexander Aberdeen of Cairnbulg, and *d* 26 April 1784, leaving issue

(4) Campbell; *b* 27 Aug 1725; Lt-Col 3rd Dragoons, Govr Guadaloupe 1753; *m* Margaret Douglas and *d* 1767, having had, with other issue:

1a James, of North Berwick; Capt 57th Regt; *m* Feb 1796 Anne (*d* 21 June 1840), dau of Sir Charles Gascoyne and widow of 7th Earl of Haddington (*qv*), and *dsp* 1831

2a George; Col 19th Regt; *m* Martha Willett Miller, and had, with another s and dau:

1b William Henry Clarence; Capt HEICS; *m* 1830 Margaret, dau of Lt-Col Oswald Werge, and *d* 1838, leaving:

1c Mary Martha; *m* 1855 Thomas Eustace Smith, of Lyndhurst, Hants, and had issue

2c Ellen Arbuthnot; *m* 1857 Capt Edward Jackson Bruce, RA

1b Margaret; *m* 1st Capt — Burn; *m* 2nd James Wardrop, MD, and *d* 13 Jan 1867

2b Martha Willett; *m* 23 March 1831 9th Earl of Stair (*qv*) and *d* 5th June 1869, leaving issue

3b Louisa Mary Minchin; *m* 9 Feb 1832, as his 2nd w, Adml Sir Henry William Bruce, KCB (*see* BRUCE, Bt, of Downhill), and *d* 1834, leaving issue

3a Hew; Lt-Col 49th Regt; *m* Marianne, only child of James Straker, barrister, and had, with other issue:

1b Campbell James; Lt-Col, Commr suppression slave trade Havana; *m* Rosina, dau of John Walton, and *d* 17 July 1847, having had, with other issue:

1c James Pilgrim; had issue

1c Harriet Farre; *m* Chevalier Crol, Govr Dutch W Indies

2c Elizabeth Rosina; *m* J D Crol

3c Anne Walton; *m* W H Rink van Dromondt

2b Hew Manners; Lt 1st Foot; *m* Anne, only child of George Elliot, and left issue

1b Elizabeth Pilgrim; *m* Capt Colin Buchanan, 62nd Regt, and had issue

3 John; *b* 17 April 1692; Capt Enniskillen Dragoons; *m* Mary (*m* 2nd Sir James Adolphus Oughton, KB), dau of Alexander Ross of Balkail, and *d* 1753, leaving:

(1) Sir HEW WHITEFORD DALRYMPLE, 1st Bt (UK), so *cr* 6 May 1815; Lt-Gen, Col 57th Regt; *m* 16 May 1783 Frances, dau and co-heir of Lt-Gen Francis Leighton (*see* LEIGHTON, Bt), and *d* 9 April 1830, leaving, with other issue:

1a Sir ADOLPHUS JOHN DALRYMPLE, 2nd and last Bt; Gen; *m* 23 June 1812 Anne (*d* 10 May 1858), dau of Sir James Graham, 1st Bt, of Kirkstall (see 1902 edn), and *dsp* 3 March 1866, when the btcy expired

1a Charlotte Elizabeth; *m* 1816 V-Adml Sir John Chambers White, KCB, and *d* 1830, leaving issue (*see* DALRYMPLE-WHITE, Bt)

4 William; *b* 19 Oct 1693; Army Capt; his w was murdered 1746 by a footboy in her Cavendish Sq house

5 James, of Nunraw; Army Capt; *d* Sept 1737; had issue (now extinct)

1 Margaret; *m* 1700 Sir John Shaw, Bt, of Greenock

2 Anne; *m* Sir James Steuart, Bt, of Goodtrees (*see* 1850 edn)

3 Elizabeth; *m* Sir James Suttie, Bt (*see* GRANT-SUTTIE, Bt)

4 Eleanor; *m* Sir Thomas Hay, Bt, of Alderston (*see* 1949 edn)

5 Marion; *m* Sir Ludovic Grant of Grant, 7th Bt (*see* STRATHSPEY, B)

Sir Hew *m* 2nd by 1712 Elizabeth (*dsp* 21 March 1742), dau of John Hamilton of Olivestob and widow of James Hamilton of Bangour, Linlithgowshire, and *d* 1 Feb 1737

His gs,

Sir Hew Dalrymple, 2nd Bt; *b c* 1710; advocate 1730; MP Haddington Burghs 1742–47 and 1761–68 and Haddington 1747–61, King's Remembrancer Scotland 1768; *m* 1st 12 July 1743 Margaret (*d* 31 Dec 1749), dau of Peter Sainthill, surgn, of Garlick Hill, London, and had issue; *m* 2nd 17 Aug 1756 Martha (*d* 12 Sept 1782), dau of Charles Edwin, barrister Lincoln's Inn, and *d* 23 Nov 1790, leaving by his 1st w an est surv s:

Sir HEW DALRYMPLE later HAMILTON-DALRYMPLE (after inheriting Bargeny estate of his unc John Hamilton (formerly Dalrymple; *see* above) 12 Feb 1796), **3rd Bt**; *b c* 1746; Army Offr, MP Haddingtonshire 1780084 and 1784–86, Auditor Exchequer 1786; *m* by 1773 his 2nd cousin Janet, dau of William Duff of Crombie, Ayrshire, by Elizabeth (sis of **Sir Hew, 2nd Bt**), and *d* 13 Feb 1800, leaving, with another s and three other daus:

1 Sir HEW DALRYMPLE later HAMILTON-DALRYMPLE later still DALRYMPLE-HAMILTON (on *s* to the btcy), **4th Bt**; *b* 3 Jan 1774; served Gds and Dra-

goons; MP Haddingtonshire 1795–1800, Ayrshire 1803–06, 1806–07, 1811–12 and 1812–18 and Haddington Burghs 1820–26; *m* 19 May 1800 Hon Jane Duncan (*d* 7 March 1852), sis of 1st Earl of Camperdown (*see* 1933 edn), and *dspm* 23 Feb 1834 , leaving:

(1) Henrietta Dundas; inherited the Bargeny estate; *m* 16 June 1822 Augustin Louis Joseph Casimir Gustave de Franquetot, Duke de Coigny (*d* Paris 2 May 1865) and had issue (*see* STAIR, E, and 1953 edn MANVERS, E)

2 JOHN (Sir), **5th Bt**

3 James; *m* 1815 Mary Christina, 3rd dau of Sir James Nasmyth, Bt, and had:

(1) Jemima; *d* 1832

1 Janet; *m* 1st Earl of Camperdown (*see* 1933 edn) and *d* his widow 17 May 1867

The 4th Bt's bro,

Sir John Hamilton-Dalrymple, 5th Bt; *b c* 1776; Maj-Gen, MP Haddington Burghs 1805–06; *m* 30 July 1806 Charlotte (*d* 14 April 1871), only dau of Sir Patrick Warrender, 3rd Bt (*see* BRUNTISFIELD, B), and *d* 26 May 1835, having had, with other issue:

1 **Sir Hew Hamilton-Dalrymple, 6th Bt**, DL; *b* 21 Nov 1814; Lt-Col 71st Foot 1847–52; Convener Haddington 1861; *m* 27 July 1852 Frances Elizabeth (*d* 28 Feb 1894), only dau of Robert Arkwright, of Sutton Scarsdale, Derbys, and *dsp* 27 April 1887

2 JOHN WARRENDER (Sir), **7th Bt**

1 Helen Jane; *m* 14 Feb 1833 Alexander Maclean of Ardgour, Argyll (*d* 28 Nov 1872), and *d* 4 Jan 1882, leaving issue

2 Georgina; *m* 1831 Lt-Gen Sir W H Sewell, KCB (*d* 13 March 1862), and *d* 1 May 1872

3 Charlotte Sophia; *m* 15 Dec 1836 Maj-Gen John Clark, KH (*d* 22 March 1865), and *d* 1864, leaving issue

4 Janet; *m* 29 April 1847 Rev James George Curry Fussell (*d* 1883) and had issue

The 6th Bt's bro,

Sir John Warrender Dalrymple, 7th Bt, DL; *b* May 1824; Bengal CS 1842–72, Civil and Sessions Judge Hooghly 1856–60; *m* 7 June 1847 Sophia (*d* 16 June 1911), yr dau of James Pottle, Bengal CS, and *d* 28 Dec 1888, having had:

1 Hew; *b* 21 April 1848; *d* March 1868

2 WALTER (Sir), **8th Bt**

1 Virginia Julian; *m* 12 Sept 1876 Sir Francis Henry Champneys, 1st Bt (*d* 30 July 1930), and *d* 18 April 1922, leaving issue (*see* 1949 edn DALRYMPLE-CHAMPNEYS, Bt)

Sir JOHN's surv son,

Sir WALTER DALRYMPLE later HAMILTON-DALRYMPLE (roy licence 1889), **8th Bt**, JP, DL; *b* 6 Jan 1854; *m* 7 Nov 1882 Alice Mary (*d* 8 April 1927), dau of Maj-Gen Hon Sir Henry Hugh Clifford, VC, KCMG, CB (*see* CLIFFORD OF CHUDLEIGH, B), and *d* 29 Nov 1920, having had issue:

1 HEW CLIFFORD (Sir), **9th Bt**

2 John Raphael; *b* 24 Oct 1889; Lt and Adj 2nd Bn KOSB; *ka* 23 April 1915

1 Agnes Mary; *m* 28 Nov 1914 Cdr Richard Eustace Hollings, RN (*d* 1928), 2nd s of Herbert John Butler Hollings, DL, and *d* 8 Nov 1945, leaving issue

2 Marjorie, RRC; *d* 16 Dec 1939

3 Sybil (Mother Mary St Hugh, of the Order of the Holy Child); *d* 9 Oct 1968

Sir WALTER's only surv son,

Sir Hew Clifford Hamilton-Dalrymple, 9th Bt, JP (E Lothian); *b* 11 Aug 1888; memb Roy Co Archers; *m* 3 Sept 1919 Ann Dorothea Dyce Nicol, JP, yst dau of Augustus Thorne, JP, DL, of London, and *d* 12 March 1959, having had:

1 Sir HEW FLEETWOOD HAMILTON-DALRYMPLE, **10th and present Bt**

2 +John David (Rev); *b* 8 April 1928; RC priest

1 *Elsie Margaret Mary [Mrs Martin Gibbs, Sheldon Manor, Chippenham, Wilts]; *b* 10 June 1922; *m* 17 Jan 1947 Maj Martin Anthony Gibbs (*see* ALDENHAM and HUNSDON OF HUNSDON, B) and has issue

2 Jean Marion; *b* 14 Dec 1923; *m* 4 March 1946, as his 1st w, *Maj-Gen Lord Michael Fitzalan-Howard, GCVO, CB, CBE, MC (*see* NORFOLK, D), and *d* 28 July 1947, leaving issue

HAMLYN

Creation: B. (LP, UK) 1 Jan 1998.

THE BARON HAMLYN, of Edgeworth, Co Gloucester (Paul Bertrand Hamlyn, CBE (1993)) [The Rt Hon The Lord Hamlyn CBE, House of Lords, London SW1A 0PW]; *b* 12 Feb 1926; *educ* St Christopher's Sch Letchworth; fndr Hamlyn Publishing Gp 1968, dir IPC 1965–70, chm IPC Books 1965–70, jt md News Internat 1970–71 (dir 1971–86), started Paul Hamlyn Fndn 1972, dir: Reed Book Publishing 1971–, TVAM 1981–83, Reed Internat Books 1983–, Michelin House Devpt 1985–, Bibendum Restaurant 1986–, Reed Internat 1987–, Brandchart 1987–, Château de Bagnols 1988–, Michelin House Investment Co 1989–, Reed Elsevier 1993–, fndr/chm: Octopus Publishing Gp 1971–, Mandarin Offset Ltd 1971–, chm Heinemann Publishers 1985–, Octopus Books 1971–, Hamlyn Publishing Gp 1986–, Book Club Assocs 1993–, co-fndr/dir: Sundial Publications 1973–, Octopus Books Internat BV 1973– and Conran Octopus 1973–; Chllr Thames Valley U 1993–; *m* 1st 1952 (*divorce* 1969) Eileen Margaret (Bobbie), dau of Col Richard Watson, and has a s and dau; *m* 2nd 1970 *Mrs Helen Guest

Lineage: RICHARD HAMBURGER; Prof; *m* L Hamburg and had:

1 *Michael Peter Leopold, OBE (1992) [Dr Michael Hamburger OBE, Marsh Acres, Middleton, Suffolk IP17 3NH; c/o Johnson Ltd, 45/47 Clerkenwell Green, London EC1R 0HT]; *b* 22 March 1924; *educ* Westminster and Ch Ch Oxford; served WW II and to 1947, assist German lecturer UCL 1952–55, Lecturer then Reader German Reading U 1955–64 and Mt Holyoke Coll Mass. 1966–67, Visiting Prof State U New York 1969 and 1971, Visiting Prof U of SC 1973 and Boston U 1975–77, Lecturer U of Calif. San Diego 1973, part-time Prof Essex U 1978, author: *Poems of Hölderlin* (trans 1943), *C Baudelaire, Twenty Prose Poems* (trans 1946), *Flowering Cactus* (poems 1950), *L van Beethoven, Letters, Journals and Conversations* (trans 1951), *G Trakl, Decline* (trans 1952), *Poems 1950–51* (1952), *The Dual Site* (poems 1952), *Weather and Season* (poems 1952), *A Goes, The Burnt Offering* (trans 1956), *Reason and Energy* (1957), *H von Hofmannstahl, Poems and Verse Plays* (collaborative trans, 1961), *B Brecht, Tales from the Calendar* (trans 1961), *J C F Hölderlin, Selected Verse* (trans 1961), *Modern German Poetry 1910–1960* (trans, with C Middleton, 1962), *H von Hofmannstahl, Selected Plays and Libretti* (collaborative trans 1964), *From Prophecy to Exorcism* (1965), *G Büchner, Lenz* (trans 1966), *H M Enzensberger, Poems* (trans 1966), *G Grass, Selected Poems* (trans, with C Middleton, 1966), *J C F Hölderlin, Poems and Fragments* (trans 1967), *H M Enzensberger, The Poems of Hans Magnus Enzensberger* (trans, with J Rothenberg and H M Enzensberger, 1968), *H M Enzensberger, Poems For People Who Don't Read Poems* (trans 1968), *Feeding the Chickadees* (poems 1968), *P Bichsel, And Really Frau Blum Would Very Much Like To Meet The Milkman* (trans 1968), *G Eich, Journeys* (trans 1968), *N Sachs, Selected Poems* (trans 1968), *G Grass, The Poems of Günter Grass* (trans, with C Middleton, 1969), *Travelling* (poems 1969), *The Truth of Poetry* (1970), *Peter Bichsel, Stories for Children* (trans 1971), *Paul Celan, Poems* (1972), *Hugo von Hofmannstahl* (1973), *A Mug's Game* (1973), *Travelling, I-V* (poems 1973), *Ownerless Earth* (poems 1973), *Peter Huchel, Selected Poems* (trans 1974), *Art as Second Nature* (1975), *Travelling VI* (poems 1975), *German Poetry 1910–1975* (trans 1977), *Helmut Heissenbüttel, Texts* (trans 1977), *Real Estate* (poems 1977), *Moralities* (poems 1977), *Franco Fortini, Poems* (trans 1978), *An Unofficial Rilke* (trans, 1981), *Variations* (poems 1981), *A Proliferation of Prophets* (1983), *Peter Huchel, The Garden of Theophrastus* (trans 1983), *Goethe, Poems and Epigrams* (trans 1983), *Collected Poems* (1984), *After the Second Flood* (1986), *Trees* (poems 1988), *Selected Poems* (1988), *Testimonies, selected shorter prose 1950–1987* (1989), *Roots in the Air* (poems 1991), *Günter Eich, Pigeons and Moles* (trans 1991), *H M Enzensberger, Selected Poems* (trans 1994), *Collected Poems 1941–1994* (1995), *Late* (long poem, 1997); *m* 1951 *Anne Ellen File and has a s and two daus

2 PAUL BERTRAND HAMBURGER later HAMLYN, *cr* a **Baron**

HAMMICK

Arms: Paly of four or and vert a bordure erm. charged with seven hurts, on a chief az. a lion passant arg. **Crest:** A demi-lion per pale or and vert, holding an escarbuncle gold. **Motto:** *Laudari a laudato* ('Being praised by one already praised').
Creation: Bt. (UK) 25 July 1834.

SIR STEPHEN GEORGE HAMMICK, 5TH BT, of Cavendish Square, London, DL (Dorset 1989) [Sir Stephen Hammick Bt DL, Badgers, Wraxall, Dorset DT2 0HN]; *b* 27 Dec 1926; *s f* 1964; *educ* Stowe and RAC Cirencester; RN 1945–48, memb (C) Dorset CC 1958– (V-Chm 1985–88, Chm 1988–93), High Sheriff Dorset 1981–82; *m* 16 April 1953 *Gillian Elizabeth, yr dau of Maj Pierre Elliot Inchbald, MC, RA, of Wraxall Manor, and has:

1 +PAUL ST VINCENT [Paul Hammick Esq, Butterfly Cottage, Lower Wraxall, Dorset DT2 0HL]; *b* 1 Jan 1955; *educ* Sherborne and RAC Cirencester; *m* 11 July 1984 *Judith Mary, dau of Ralph Ernest Reynolds, of Wareham, Dorset

2 +Jeremy Charles [Jeremy Hammick Esq, Ebenezer Cottage, Meerhay, Dorset DT8 3SB]; *b* 3 Feb 1956; *m* 11 Oct 1997 *Mrs Melanie Louise Stock, of Herts

1 *Wendy Jane [Mrs Bob Koster-Hammick, Voorsterweg 52A, 6971 KB Brummen, Holland]; *b* 25 Sept 1960; *m* 1990 *Bob Koster, s of Jacob Koster, and has:

(1) *Daniel; *b* 29 Jan 1991

(1) *Sophie; *b* 15 Oct 1992

Lineage: STEPHEN HAMMICK; Alderman Plymouth (only s of Capt Stephen Hammick, RN); *m* 1776 Elizabeth Margaret, only child of John Love, of Plymouth Dock, and had, with two yr sons (John Love, Lt RN, *d* unm on service in Jamaica; Frederick Love, MD, *d* unm in Poland) and two daus (Elizabeth, *m* Capt William Henry Douglas, RN; Charlotte Love, *d* 17 June 1859):

Sir Stephen Love Hammick, 1st Bt (UK), so *cr* 25 July 1834; *b* 28 Feb 1777; 1st Surgn RN Hosp Plymouth, memb Senate London U, FRCS, MD; *m* 7 Feb 1800 Frances (*d* 1829), only dau of Peter Turquand, London merchant, by Eliza, dau of

Thomas Hicks, of Blackheath, and *d* 15 June 1867, having had, with an er s (Stephen Love, MD, *b* 9 Nov 1804, *d* unm 9 Dec 1839) and a dau (Frances, *d* 3 July 1871):

Rev Sir St Vincent Love Hammick, 2nd Bt; *b* July 1806; MA, Fell Exeter College Oxford; Vicar Milton Abbot, Devon; *m* 6 April 1837 Mary (*d* 17 July 1902), 2nd dau of Robert Alexander, Madras CS, memb Cncl Madras, n of 1st Earl of Caledon (*qv*), and *d* 19 Feb 1888, leaving:

1 **Sir St Vincent Alexander Hammick, 3rd Bt**; *b* 10 April 1839; BA Oxon; Col Oxon LI NZ War 1864–65 (medal, special mention); *m* 1st 20 Oct 1869 Penelope Sarah Blanche (*d* March 1886), dau of Charles William Beauclerk (*see* SAINT ALBANS, D), and had issue:

(1) Stephen Frederick; Capt Oxon LI; *b* 2 Feb 1871; *m* 6 June 1906 Muriel Katharine (*d* 2 Oct 1924), dau of Capt Andrew Hamilton Russell, of Petersfield, and *dvp* 18 April 1916 of wounds recd in action, leaving:

1a *Penelope Katherine [Miss Penelope Hammick, 46 Castle Rd, Salisbury, Wilts]; *b* 1910, MB, BS Lond 1945, MRCS, LRCP 1941, Tuberculosis Registrar Salisbury Gp Hosps 1949–53, Assist Chest Physician Reading 1956–, GP

2a Pamela Blanche, MBE (1945); Jr Cdr and T/Ch Cdr ATS WW II; *m* 28 Oct 1947 Maj-Gen Alec Wilfred Lee, CB, MC, only s of Wilfred Lee, of Tregwyn, Blisland, Bodmin, Cornwall

(1) Blanche *b* 20 May 1872; *m* 24 July 1894 Col Montague Bertie Gosset Jackson, RA, and *d* 16 June 1946, leaving issue. He *d* 21 June 1929

(2) Grace; *b* 25 April 1875; *m* 17 Jan 1900 Eustace Ralph Bankes and *d* 8 July 1948. He *d* 9 Dec 1929

1 (cont.) **Sir St Vincent** *m* 2nd 7 Jan 1890 Elinor (*d* 22 March 1942), 2nd dau of Rev Sir Gilbert Frankland Lewis, 3rd Bt, and *dspms* 8 Nov 1927

2 Robert Frederick, V-Adml; *b* 23 Oct 1843; *m* 1884 Grace Caroline, dau of William Longman, of Ashlyns, Herts, and *d* Dec 1922, having had issue:

(1) GEORGE FERDERICK (Sir), **4th Bt**

(2) Alexander Robert, R-Adml WW I; *b* 1887; *educ* HMS *Britannia*; *m* 17 Dec 1918 Nancy (*d* 22 Nov 1964), est dau of Dennis Ross-Johnson, and *d* 13 Feb 1969, having had issue:

1a Roger Alexander; Lt 6th Airborne Div WW II; *b* 4 Dec 1922; *d* following a car crash Singapore 12 Oct 1945

1a *Anne Felicity [Miss Anne Hammick, The Old House, Lodsworth, Sussex]; *b* 2 Nov 1919

(3) Maurice Hubert Love, Midshipman RN; *b* 4 Dec 1894; *d* 13 Jan 1913

(1) Ida Grace; *m* 21 July 1921 Very Rev Algernon Giles Seymour (*see* CULME-SEYMOUR, Bt), and *d* 1971, leaving issue

3 Stephen, JP Devon; Bombay CS; *b* 9 May 1846; *m* 9 April 1885 Constance (*d* 5 Jan 1937), only dau of Lt-Gen Frederick Schneider, Bombay SC, and *d* 4 Feb 1934, leaving issue:

(1) St Vincent Frederick; Maj IA; *b* 11 Aug 1886; *m* 18 Dec 1919 Annie Caroline Massingberd (*d* 3 Dec 1978), yr dau of Aubone Aldrich Pyke, of The Hermitage, Netley Abbey, and *d* 1976, leaving issue:

1a +Stephen Aubone, DSC [Cdr Stephen Hammick DSC RN (ret), Bursledon Lodge, Bursledon, Hants]; *b* 9 Sept 1922; Cdr RN WW II; *m* 12 June 1943 *Mary Elizabeth, est dau of John Laurence Westmacott (*see* HAMILTON-SPENCER-SMITH, Bt), and has issue:

1b +Stephen Timothy John; *b* 2 June 1946; *educ* Blundell's and RNC Dartmouth; *m* 1969 *Raymonde, dau of Maj Eugene I J Cowson, of S Africa, and has issue:

1c *A dau; *b* 26 Dec 1968

1b *Susan Patricia Mary; *b* 28 March 1945; 1973 *Henry James Craven Smith and has issue:

1c *Henry Stapleton; *b* 1975

1c *Jane Rachel Anne; *b* 1977

2a Aubone St Vincent; Lt-Cdr RN; *b* 27 Aug 1925; *m* 19 Aug 1948 *Cynthia Florence Katherine, est dau of William George Shiell (*see* 1970 edn AIREDALE, B) and *d* 1992, leaving:

1b *Marion [Mrs Ian Pickett, 57 Salisbury Ave, St Albans, Herts]; *b* 20 Dec 1949; *m* 1967 *Ian Donald Pickett, FCII, only s of Maj William David Pickett, MBE, RA, and has issue:

1c *Melissa Juliette; *b* 31 Dec 1967

2c *Eleanor Theresa; *b* 31 Dec 1967

2b *Imogen Kate; *b* 16 Aug 1952; *m* 1st 1972 John Blandford; *m* 2nd 1977 *David Megginson and by him has:

1c *Edward; *b* 1985

1c *Katherine Rose; *b* 1980

3b *Miranda Jane; *b* 23 April 1958; BA; has issue by Jonathan Parkinson:

1c *Martha Louise; *b* 1993

1a *Mary Désirée Massingberd [Mrs Colin Foster, 6365 Elm Street, Vancouver, BC, Canada]; *b* 26 May 1930; *m* 1953 *Colin Edward Foster and has:

1b *Michael Colin; *b* 23 Dec 1953.

2b *Christopher John; *b* 18 Aug 1956

1b *Caroline Antonia; *b* 6 Sept 1957

2a *Adrianne Elaine Patricia; *b* 24 Aug 1937; *m* 18 July 1964 *Vincent George Jarvis Ball, only s of Lt-Col Osborn Vincent Ball, OBE, of Chandlers Ford, Hants, and has issue:

1b *Anthony St Vincent; *b* 21 Aug 1965

2b *Stephen Jarvis; *b* 18 March 1967

3b *David Jonathan; *b* 1971

(2) Eustace, MC; Capt IA, Chev Crown Belgium; *b* 19 Nov 1888; *d* 8 Oct 1918 of wounds recd in action

(3) Ernest Lumley; Lt IA; *b* 1890; *das* 16 May 1916

(1) Mary Caroline, JP (W Sussex 1940); *m* 24 June 1916 R-Adml Francis Alexander Waddilove Buller, DSO, 4th s of Adml Sir Alexander Buller, GCB, and *d* 25 Oct 1965. He *d* 14 July 1943

4 William Maxwell, JP Wilts and Salisbury; Mayor Salisbury 1886; *b* 3 March 1848; *m* 17 June 1879 Jane Hussey (*d* 1882), 2nd dau of George Barnard Townsend, of The Close, Salisbury, and *d* 24 Feb 1915, leaving issue:

(1) Robert Townsend, DSO (1917), DL Wilts; Chm Wilts TAA, Col (Hon Brig 1938) RA Gen Staff WW I, Order Nile 3rd Cl; *b* 10 Aug 1882; *d* unm 26 Nov 1947

(1) Georgina Mary; *m* 1st 9 May 1905 Capt Edmund Nelson Fisher, Manchester Regt, only s of Ven Edmund Henry Fisher, Archdeacon Southwark, and had issue. He *d* 1 June 1909. She *m* 2nd 2 July 1928 Col Warburton Edward Davies, CMG, CBE, DSO, Rifle Bde, s of Byam Martin Davies, and *d* 3 Jan 1965. He *d* 3 Dec 1957

(2) Jane Alexander; ARRC; *m* 14 Nov 1922 Lt-Col Charles Moorsom Longmore, DSO, RA (*d* 10 Jan 1933), yst s of Sir Thomas Longmore, CB, and *d* 27 Dec 1973 aged 92, leaving issue:

1a *Thomas Robert William [Thomas Longmore Esq, Gofts House, Byworth, W Sussex]; Nigerian Admin Serv 1948–60, slr 1964; *b* 24 July 1925; *m* 21 July 1954 *Nancy Catherine, dau of Russell A Gatehouse

5 Ernest Austen (Ven); Rector Elford, Staffs, Canon St Saviour's Cathedral, Pietermaritzburg, Archdeacon Durban then Zululand, Vicar St James Durban; *b* 3 Jan 1850; *m* 28 Sept 1897 *Mary Elizabeth Amy, widow of William Popham, JP, of Bray Hill, Natal; *d* 2 Sept 1920

6 John Eustace; *b* 4 Nov 1852; *d* unm 1943

7 Murray (Sir), KCSI (1911), CIE (1901); Fell King's Coll London, ICS 1876–1913, Inspr-Gen Madras Police 1894, Ch Sec Madras Govt 1906, memb Exec Cncl 1908–12, Govr Madras 1912, memb Cncl of Sec State India 1915–22; *b* 11 May 1854; *m* 11 Dec 1883 Ada Constance (*d* 3 Feb 1950), dau of Maj-Gen Arthur Thaddeus Searle, ISC, and *d* 4 March 1936, having had issue:

(1) Henry Alexander, OBE (1945), MC; Maj 6th Bn Manchester Regt WW I, Ch Engr Iraq Petroleum; *b* 1890; *educ* Charterhouse; *m* 8 Jan 1919 Mabel Emily (May) (*d* 1990), only dau of Sir Philip Edward Pilditch, 1st Bt (*qv*), and *d* 6 Aug 1968, leaving issue:

1a +Henry Edgar Murray [Lt Henry Hammick RNVR, 9 Newenham Rd, Lymington, Hants]; WW II; *b* 9 Nov 1919; *educ* Charterhouse; *m* 20 April 1949 *Eleanor Macleod, er dau of Cdr Patrick Bruce Lawder, RN, and has:

1b *Elizabeth Helen Macleod; *b* 9 April 1951; *m* 1992 *Mark William Scott, and has issue:

1c *Chloë Eleanor; *b* 1992

2b *Anne Olivia Mary; *b* 8 April 1953

2a Charles Cyril Willmott; ACIS, Maj Gren Gds, Para Regt 1947–48 and Trucial Oman Scouts 1957–58; *b* 24 Oct 1927; *educ* Sherborne; *m* 1st 13 June 1953 (*divorce* 1959) Mary Rose, only dau of Col Walter Hugh Crichton, CIE, MB, ChB, and has issue:

1b +Piers St Vincent Charles; *b* 21 July 1954; *educ* Stanbridge Earls

1b *Charlotte Emily Dorothea; *b* 4 Dec 1956; *m* 1985 (*divorce* 1987) Michael P Dennis, and has issue:

1c *Oliver Charles Frederick; *b* 1986

2a (cont.) Charles Hammick *m* 2nd 24 Oct 1961 Georgina (writer as Georgina Heyman), er twin dau of Maj Gen George Douglas Gordon Heyman, CB, CBE, of Mead House, Appleshaw, nr Andover, Hants; *m* 3rd 1984 *Carol Elspeth [Mrs Charles Hammick, Higher Waterson Farm, Puddletown, Dorset DT2 7SW], dau of Brig Richard Montagu Villiers, DSO (*see* CLARENDON, E), and formerly w of Gerald Charles Mordaunt (*see* MORDAUNT, Bt), and *d* 1990, leaving by his 2nd w:

2b +Thomas Henry Heyman St Vincent; *b* 6 Sept 1963

2b *Katherine Emily Amanda; *b* 19 Nov 1965

3b *Rose Sophia; *b* 2 Oct 1970

3a +Alexander Philip [Alexander Hammick Esq, The Priory, Woodbury, Exeter, Devon]; *b* 21 Oct 1928; *educ* Sherborne; *m* 1954 *Pamela Mary, yr dau of C Prosper-Liston, of Penang, Malaya, and has issue:

1b +Murray Philip St Leger, Capt 14th/20th Hus; *b* 12 Jan 1957; *educ* Sherborne; *m* 1984 *Alexandra-Carolin, yr dau of C H Preuss, of Buckholz, Hamburg, and has issue:

1c +Alexander Charles Frederick Prosper Love; *b* 1988

2c +Philip Henry Murray St Vincent Love; *b* 1990

1c *Catherine Edwardina Pamela Mary Love; *b* 1993

1b *Melinda Mary; *b* 7 Oct 1955; *m* 1981 *Richard Guy Hilliard, only s of R G Hilliard, and has issue:

1c *Alexandra Carey; *b* 1985

2c *Georgina Mary; *b* 1988

2b *Victoria Rosanne; *b* 5 Nov 1958; *m* 1982 *Capt John Gale and has:

1c *Emily Caroline; *b* 1984

2c *Amanda Catherine; *b* 1987

3b *Nicola May *b* 30 May 1961; *m* 1989 *Anthony Alexander de Nouaille Rudge, er s of Anthony Rudge, and has:

1c *Alexander William Edward Findlay de Nouaille; *b* 1992

1c *Serena Mary Kate Felizarda; *b* 1991

2c *Felicity; *b* 1995

3c *Josephine; *b* 1997

1a *Anthea Elizabeth Eve [Mrs Dennis Shepherd, Honeywood, Westley Rd, Bury St Edmunds, Suffolk]; *b* 5 Aug 1922; *m* 22 Oct 1949 *Dennis John Dale Shepherd, s of Henry John William Shepherd, and has issue:

1b *Justin Philip William; *b* 16 Feb 1952

1b *Miranda Dorothy Emilia; *b* 20 April 1950

2b *Zoë Alexandra Denise; *b* 3 July 1954

3b *Isobel Anthea; *b* 30 Oct 1956

4b *Melissa May; *b* 7 Nov 1966

(2) John Murray; *b* 8 Sept 1901; *d* July 1902

(1) Lorna Mary; *m* 28 Oct 1911, Capt Norman Dalrymple Shaw, Lt QO Cameron Highrs, s of J C Shaw, of Chelsea, and *d* 20 March 1956, leaving issue. He *d* 15 Oct 1961

(2) *Dorothy Constance [Mrs Alexander Mackinnon, 1 Serpentine, Pinelands, Cape Town, S Africa]; *m* 7 May 1921 Col Alexander Charles

Broughton Mackinnon, CBE, 9th Gurkhas Rifles (*d* 6 May 1942), s of Col Walter Carr Mackinnon, 87th Royal Irish Fus and 3rd Buffs, and has issue:

1a Mairi Cynthia; *b* 18 Nov 1924; *m* 18 Sept 1954 *James Arnold Adams, FRCS, and has issue

(3) *Lucy Mabel, MBE (1920)

1 Frances Grace; *m* 9 April 1863 George Andrew Spottiswoode, yr s of Andrew Spottiswoode, MP, of Broom Hall, Surrey, and *d* 5 Feb 1933, leaving issue. He *d* 8 Feb 1899

2 Mary Caroline; *d* unm 2 March 1934

3 Rachel; *m* 25 Jan 1877 Everard Allen Ford, OBE, s of Rev Joseph Ford, of Hampstead, and *d* 14 May 1935, leaving issue. He *d* 16 Jan 1928

The 3rd Bt's n,

Sir George Frederick Hammick, 4th Bt; Lt RNVR, Midshipman RN, memb Devon War Ag Ctee and Area Officer Special Constabulary; *b* 24 Sept 1885; *m* 1st 29 Sept 1916 Eileen Laura (*d* 17 Dec 1920), er dau of Col Francis John Newton King, Oxon LI; *m* 2nd 5 May 1925 Mary Adeliza, er dau of Lt-Col Henry Welch-Thornton, of Stover, Newton Abbot, and *d* 12 April 1964, leaving issue:

1 Sir STEPHEN GEORGE HAMMICK, **5th and present Bt**

HAMPDEN

Arms: Az. two swords in saltire arg., hilts and pommels or, between three escallops, one in chief and two in fess or. **Crest:** Out of a crown vallory or a leopard's head arg., semée of escallops and gorged with a collar gemel gu. **Supporters:** Dexter, a wolf arg., gorged with a radiated collar with line reflexed over the back or; sinister, a bull gu., armed, unguled, ducally gorged and line reflexed over the back or. **Motto:** *Pour bien désirer* ('Wishing well'). **Creations:** V. (UK) 4 March 1884.

THE 6TH VISCOUNT HAMPDEN OF GLYNDE, Co Sussex (Anthony David Brand, DL (E Sussex 1986)) [The Rt Hon The Viscount Hampden DL, Glynde Place, Glynde, Lewes, Sussex BN8 6SX]; *b* 7 May 1937; *s f* 1975; *educ* Eton; chm Sussex CLA 1985–88, Govr Emmanuel Sch 1985–; *m* 1st 27 Sept 1969 (*divorce* 1988) Caroline, est dau of Capt Claud Proby, Irish Gds (*see* PROBY, Bt); *m* 2nd 1993 *Sally Snow, sis of Baron Hambro (*qv*), and by his 1st w has:

1 +FRANCIS ANTHONY; *b* 17 Sept 1970

2 +Jonathan Claud David Humphrey; *b* 25 Aug 1975

1 *Saracha Mary; *b* 7 March 1973

Hampden, previous creations: John Hampden, called 'the Patriot' for among other things opposing CHARLES I's supposedly arbitrary attempt to make inland counties contribute to national defence along the coasts (the 'Ship Money' episode), had, with a third and youngest dau Mary (*see* BUCKINGHAMSHIRE, E), a second daughter Ruth. She married Sir John Trevor, whose probable ancestor was a younger son of the TREVORs eventually created Barons Trevor (*qv*). The elder son of this marriage, John Trevor, of Plas Teg, Flintshire (which eventually passed to Cadwallader Trevor-Roper (*see* TEYNHAM, B), through the Dacre connection), was ancestor through his granddaughter of the Brands Viscounts Hampden of Glynde (*see* below). The younger son of Sir John and Lady Trevor, Thomas, was created Baron Trevor of Bromham in 1712 and his son, the fourth Baron, was promoted to a viscountcy, that of Hampden, in 1776. (He also changed his name from Trevor to Hampden.)

The Viscount Hampden of this earlier creation had inherited the estates of his great-grandfather the 'Patriot', and the name Hampden was certainly of sufficient historical importance to warrant its being kept alive. But the 'Patriot' had had only one son, whose own son was found guilty of high treason and died in 1696, leaving in his turn two sons, neither of whom had issue. Accordingly by the last third of the 18th century only descendants through female lines survived. So when after the 3rd and last Viscount Hampden of the 1776 creation died without issue in 1824 (having come into the title a mere twenty days earlier) it was natural for Henry Brand, who had been ten at the time, to try and resuscitate the name in his own choice of title on his ennoblement sixty years later.

Lineage: The 21st LORD (Baron) DACRE (*qv*) had a 2nd s:

HENRY BOUVERIE WILLIAM BRAND, **1st Viscount Hampden of Glynde**, Co Sussex (UK), so *cr* 4 March 1884, and 23rd LORD (Baron) DACRE (as which *s* er bro 1890), GCB (1881), PC (1866); *b* 24 Dec 1814; *educ* Eton; MP (Lib) Lewes 1852–68 and Cambs 1868–84, a Ld Treasury 1855–8, Parly Sec Treasury 1859–66, Speaker H of C 1872–84, Ld Lt Sussex 1886–92; *m* 16 April 1838 Eliza (*d* 9 March 1899), dau of Gen Robert Ellice, and *d* 14 March 1892, having had, with other issue (*see* DACRE, B):

HENRY ROBERT BRAND, **2nd Viscount Hampden of Glynde** and 24th LORD (Baron) DACRE, GCMG (1899), JP, DL Sussex, JP Herts; *b* 2 May 1841; *educ* Rugby; Capt Coldstream Gds, MP (Lib U from 1886) Herts 1868–74 and Stroud July-Dec 1874 (unseated) and 1885–86, Surveyor-Gen Ordnance 1883–85, Govr and C-in-C NSW 1895–99, CA Herts, KGStJ; *m* 1st 21 Jan 1864 Victoria Alexandrina Leopoldine (*dsp* 20 July 1865), dau of Sylvain Van de Weyer, Belgian Min to UK; *m* 2nd 14 April 1868 Susan Henrietta (*d* 16 Oct 1909), yr dau of Lord George Henry Cavendish (*see* DEVONSHIRE, D), and *d* 22 Nov 1906, having had, with other issue (*see* DACRE, B):

THOMAS WALTER BRAND, **3rd Viscount Hampden of Glynde** and 25th LORD (Baron) DACRE, GCVO (1935), KCB (1921, CB 1917), CMG (1915), JP Herts; *b* 29 Jan 1869; *educ* Eton and Trin Coll Cambridge; 10th Hus: joined 1889, Capt 1898, Boer War 1899–1901 (despatches, Queen's Mdal 6 clasps), Maj 1903–04, Col 1935–39; WW I: Lt-Col 1st Bn Herts Regt TF 1913–15 (Hon Col TA 1930) (despatches eight times, Legn Honour); Col and Hon Brig-Gen TFR 1919–21, Ld Lt and CC Herts, ADC to HM GEORGE V 1920–31, Ld-in-Waiting 1924–36, KStJ; *m* 29 April 1899 Lady Katharine Mary Montagu-Douglas-Scott, JP Herts (*d* 7 March 1951), dau of 6th Duke of Buccleuch and (8th Duke of) Queensberry (*qv*), and *d* 4 Sept 1958, having had, with other issue (*see* DACRE, B):

1 THOMAS HENRY BRAND, **4th Viscount Hampden of Glynde** and 26th LORD (Baron) DACRE, CMG (1943); *b* 30 March 1900; *educ* Eton; Lt Rifle Bde, Page of Honour to HM GEORGE V 1913–16, Br Ch Exec Offr Combined Production and Resources Bd, Washington, DC, 1942–44, Chm: Supplies for Liberated Areas Ctee 1944–45 and Issuing Houses Assoc 1953 and 1954, md Lazard Bros 1931–65; *m* 26 July 1923 Leila Emily (*d* 27 Oct 1996), only dau of Lt-Col Frank Evelyn Seely, JP, DL (*see* SEELY, Bt), and *dspm* 17 Oct 1965, having had had four daus, between the surv two of whom the Barony of Dacre (*qv*) fell into abeyance

2 DAVID FRANCIS BRAND, **5th Viscount Hampden of Glynde**; *b* 14 June 1902; *educ* Eton and Trin Coll Cambridge; Lt-Col Herts Regt WW II, DAA&QMG Madagascar (despatches); *m* 14 July 1936 *Hon Imogen Alice Rhys [The Rt Hon Imogen Viscountess Hampden, The Old School House, Glynde, E Sussex], only dau of 7th Baron Dynevor (*qv*), and *d* 4 Sept 1975, leaving, with other issue (*see* DACRE, B):

(1) ANTHONY DAVID BRAND, **6th and present Viscount Hampden of Glynde**

Seat: Glynde Place, Glynde, E Sussex. A Tudor house laid out so as to surround a courtyard, though the inside was remodelled in the 18th century. The gardens are noted for their roses.

HAMPTON

Arms: Per chevron sa. and arg., in chief three mullets or pierced of the first, in base as many garbs, one and two gu., banded of the third. **Crest:** A demi-hare az., charged on the shoulder with four bezants, one, two and one. **Supporters:** Dexter, an elephant or, charged on the shoulder with a mullet pierced sa.; sinister, a talbot arg., charged as the dexter. **Motto:** *Par viribus virtus* ('Valour equals strength'). **Creations:** Bt. (UK) 13 July 1846, B. (UK) 6 March 1874.

THE 6TH BARON HAMPTON OF HAMPTON LOVETT AND OF WESTWOOD, Co Worcester, and a **Baronet** (Sir Richard Humphrey Russell Pakington, Bt) [The Rt Hon The Lord Hampton, The Flat, Moorlands, Bovey Tracey, Devon TQ13 9EP]; *b* 25 May 1925; *s f* 1974; *educ* Eton and Balliol Coll Oxford; RNVR 1944–47, Lib Pty Spokesman NI 1977–87, Pres S Worcs Lib Assoc 1978–88, jt author (with f): *The Pakingtons of Westwood* (1975); *m* 25 Oct 1958 *Jane Elizabeth Farquharson, er dau of Thomas Frank Arnott, OBE, TD, MB, ChB, of Moorlands, Bovey Tracy, and has:

1 +JOHN HUMPHREY ARNOTT; *b* 24 Dec 1964; *educ* Shrewsbury and Exeter Coll of Art and Design (BA); photographer; *m* 4 Oct 1996 *Siena, yr dau of Remo Caldato of Rome

1 *Catherine Mary Grace; *b* 25 March 1960; *educ* Worcester GS for Girls and Bristol U (MSc)

2 *Sarah Jane Auriol; *b* 25 Nov 1961; *educ* Ellerslie Malvern and Bedford Coll London (BA)

Lineage: ROBERT PAKINGTON, living *temp* HENRY IV; had:

JOHN PAKINGTON; *d* in or after 1436, leaving:

JOHN PAKINGTON; *m* Elizabeth, dau and heir of Thomas Washbourne, of Stanford, Worcs, and had:

1 John (Sir); Chirographer (an official, now obsolete) Court Common Pleas 1509, Lent Reader 1520, Treas Inner Temple 1529, Serjeant-at-law 1532, Justice N Wales 1535 and S Wales 1542, granted all the manors formerly belonging to Westwood Monastery, Worcs (by 1560 held 31 manors); *m* Anne (*d* 22 Aug 1563), widow of — Tychbourne, and dau of — Rolle, and *d* 1560, leaving:

(1) Ursula; *m* Sir John Scudamore

(2) Bridget; *m* Sir John Lyttelton (*see* COBHAM, V)

2 ROBERT

3 Humphrey; London merchant; Ld Manor Chaddesley Corbett, Worcs; *m* Elizabeth Harding and had:

(1) John, of Harvington, Worcs; *m* Elizabeth Newport and had:

1a Humphrey Pakington, of Chaddesley Corbett; *m* Abigail Sacheverell and had:

1b Mary; *m* Sir John Yate, 2nd Bt

2b Anne; *m* Sir Henry Audley

4 Austin

The 2nd son,

ROBERT PAKINGTON; MP London *temp* HENRY VIII; *m* Catherine, dau and coheir of Sir John Baldwin, Ld Ch Justice Common Pleas, by Agnes, dau of William Dormer, of Wycombe, Bucks, through whom the PAKINGTONs acquired the manors of Aylesbury and Dundridge, Bucks, and was murdered in the street 1537, having had:

1 THOMAS

2 John; living *temp* EDWARD VI

1 Elizabeth; *m* 1st John Lane; *m* 2nd Alderman Sir Richard Mallory, of London

2 Anne; *m* Richard Cupper, of Glympton, Oxon

3 Margaret; *m* 1st Benedict Lee, of Burston, Bucks; *m* 2nd Sir Thomas Scot, of Yorks

The son and heir,

Sir THOMAS PAKINGTON; Sheriff Worcs 1561; *m* Dorothy (*m* 2nd Thomas Tashmarsh), dau of Sir Thomas Kitson, of Hengrave, Suffolk, and *d* 2 June 1571, leaving surviving issue, with three daus (Mary, *m* Sir Walter Long, MP, of Wraxall and Draycot, Wilts; Catherine, *m* 1st John Davis, of Wilts, *m* 2nd Sir Jasper Moore, *m* 3rd Sir — Mompesson, of Teddington; Margaret, *m* Thomas Litchfield):

Sir JOHN PAKINGTON, KB, PC, of Westwood Park, Worcs; Ld Lt Worcs; *m* 1 Nov 1598 Dorothy (*m* 3rd 1st Viscount Kilmorey (*see* KILMOREY, E), *m* 4th 1st Earl of Kellie (*see* MAR and KELLIE, E), *d* 1639), widow of Benedict Barnham, London Alderman (and mother by him of Alice, w of Francis Bacon; *see* VERULAM, E), and dau of Humphry Smith, of Cheapside, and *d* 18 Jan 1625, having had, with two daus (Anne, *m* 1st 9 Feb 1618 Sir Humphrey Ferrers, of Tamworth, *m* 2nd 1st Earl of Chesterfield (*see* 1967 edn CHESTERFIELD and STANHOPE, E); Mary, *m* Sir Robert Brooke, of Nacton, Suffolk):

Sir JOHN PAKINGTON, 1st Bt (E), so *cr* 22 June 1620, of Aylesbury; *b c* 1600; MP Aylesbury; *m* Frances (*m* 2nd 29 Dec 1626 Robert Leasly), dau of Sir John Ferrers, of Tamworth, and *dvp* Oct 1624, leaving, with a dau (Elizabeth, *m* 1st Henry Washington (*see* Section Washington AMERICAN PRESIDENTIAL FAMILIES, 1994, Morris Genealogical Books SA); *m* 2nd Col Samuel Sandys, (*see* SANDYS, B; *d* 1699):

Sir JOHN PAKINGTON, 2nd Bt; royalist Civil War (imprisoned Tower London, fined £5,000 (well over £200,000 in late-1990s terms), estate confiscated, house in Bucks demolished, fought Battle Worcester 1651 (where captured by Cromwellian troops), fined again, this time £7,670 (nearly £310,000 in late-1990s terms), and forced to alienate part of his Aylesbury property, though this forced alienation annulled at the Restoration), MP Worcs 1675 and Aylesbury; *m* Dorothy dau of 1st Baron Coventry (*see* COVENTRY, E), and was *bur* 3 Jan 1679/80, having had, with two daus (*m* Anthony Eyre, of Rampton, Notts; *m* William Godfrey, of Lincs):

Sir JOHN PAKINGTON, 3rd Bt; MP Worcs 1685–87; *m* 17 Dec 1668 Margaret, dau of Sir John Keyt, 1st Bt, of Ebrington, Glos, and was *bur* 28 March 1688, leaving:

Sir JOHN PAKINGTON, 4th Bt; MP Worcs 1690–1727; *b* 16 March 1671; *m* 1st 28 Aug 1691 Frances, est dau of Sir Henry Parker, 2nd Bt, of Honington, Warwicks, and had two sons and three daus (including Margaret, *m* — Dowdeswell; Frances, *m* c 30 Aug 1688, as his 2nd w, 5th Viscount Tracy of Rathcoole; *see* HANBURY, B); *m* 2nd 26 Aug 1700 Hester, dau and sole heir of Sir Herbert Perrott, of Haroldston, Pembs, and *d* 13 Aug 1727, having by her had issue:

Sir HERBERT PERROTT PAKINGTON, 5th Bt; MP Worcs 1727–41; *m* June 1721 Elizabeth (*d* July 1758), dau of John Conyers, of Walthamstow, Essex, and *d* 24 Sept 1748, having had:

1 Sir JOHN PAKINGTON, 6th Bt; *m* 1761 Mary (*d* 23 Feb 1812), dau of Henry Bray, of Bromyard, Herefs, and *dsp* 30 Nov 1762

2 HERBERT PERROTT (Sir), 7th Bt

1 Hester

2 Cecilia

The 6th Bt's bro,

Sir HERBERT PERROTT PAKINGTON, 7th Bt; *m* 1759 Elizabeth (*d* June 1783), widow of Herbert Wylde, of Ludlow, Salop, and dau of Caesar Hawkins, and *d* 2 May 1795, having had, with another s (*dsp*) and two other daus:

1 Sir JOHN PAKINGTON, 8th and last Bt; DCL; *b* 1760; *dsp* 6 Jan 1830, when the btcy expired, the estates passing to his sisters

1 ELIZABETH Pakington; *m* William RUSSELL, of Powick, Worcs, and *d* May 1813, having had, with an er s (William, *d* young) and three daus (including Elizabeth Ann Pakington, *m* 1 Dec 1825 Ferdinand Hanbury Williams, of Coldbrook Park, and *d* 30 May 1850, having had issue; Mary, *m* Rev Henry Barry Domvile, Rector Pencombe, Herefs, and had issue):

(1) Sir JOHN SOMERSET RUSSELL later PAKINGTON (roy licence 31 March 1831), **1st Bt** (UK), so *cr* 13 July 1846, as also 6 March 1874 **Baron Hampton of Hampton Lovett and of Westwood**, Co Worcester, PC (1852), GCB (1859); *b* 20 Feb 1799; *educ* Eton and Oriel Coll Oxford; MP (C) Droitwich 1837–74, Chm Worcs QS 1834–58, Sec State Colonies March–Dec 1852, 1st Ld Admlty 1858–59 and 1866, Sec State War 1867–68; *m* 1st 14 Aug 1822 Mary (*d* 6 Jan 1843), only child of Moreton Aglionby Slaney, of Shifnal, Salop, and had issue:

1a JOHN SLANEY RUSSELL later PAKINGTON, **2nd Baron Hampton of Hampton Lovett and of Westwood**, DL Worcs; *b* 13 July 1826; MA Oxon; *m* 4 July 1849 Lady Diana Boyle (*d* 1 Jan 1877), dau of 4th Earl of Glasgow (*qv*), and *dsp* 26 April 1893

(1) (cont.) The **1st Baron** *m* 2nd 4 June 1844 Augusta (*d* 23 Feb 1848), dau of Rt Rev George Murray, DD, Bp Rochester (*see* ATHOLL, D), and by her had issue:

2a HERBERT PERROTT MURRAY, **3rd Baron**

1a Edith; *b* and *d* 7 April 1845

(1) (cont.) The **1st Baron** *m* 3rd 5 June 1851 Augusta Anne (*d* 8 Feb 1892 aged 92), widow of Col Thomas Henry Hastings Davies, MP, of Elmley Castle, Worcs, and dau of Thomas C Champion de Crespigny (*see* 1949 edn CHAMPION DE CRESPIGNY, Bt), and *d* 9 April 1880

The 2nd BARON's half bro,

HERBERT PERROTT MURRAY PAKINGTON, **3rd Baron Hampton of Hampton Lovett and of Westwood**, JP, DL Worcs; MA Oxon, barrister; *b* 12 Feb 1848; *m* 23 Aug 1877 Evelyn Nina Frances (*d* 19 Aug 1904), dau of Sir George Baker, 3rd Bt (*see* BAKER WILBRAHAM, Bt), and *d* 17 March 1906, having had:

1 John Evelyn Russell; *b* 27 Sept 1880; *d* 27 April 1897

2 HERBERT STUART PAKINGTON, **4th Baron Hampton of Hampton Lovett and of Westwood**, CBE (1962), DSO (1919), DL Worcs 1922–46; Ch Commr Boy Scouts Assoc; *b* 15 May 1883; *educ* Wellington and RMC Sandhurst, Maj Worcs Yeo, Lt Rifle Bde, WW I (despatches twice); *d* unm 30 Oct 1962

3 Hugh Charles Swinton; *b* 23 Jan 1887; *d* unm 27 March 1907

4 HUMPHREY ARTHUR, **5th Baron**

1 Mary Augusta MBE (1920); dramatist, BRCS and CD WW II; *b* 21 June 1878; *d* unm 25 Sept 1949

2 Edith Frances; *b* 14 Aug 1879; *m* 12 Aug 1913, Ernest William Hopewell, Headmaster Queen Elizabeth's School, Hartlebury, s of James Hopewell, of Rugby, and *d* 4 April 1953. He *d* 18 Oct 1919

3 Dorothy Alice; *b* 15 Feb 1882; *m* 26 June 1912 Arthur Mayger Hind, OBE, LLD, FRA, Keeper Prints and Drawings, Br Museum, Slade Prof Fine Art Oxford, Norton Prof Poetry Harvard, 2nd s of Henry Robert Hind, and *d* 1 April 1966 leaving issue. He *d* 22 May 1957

4 Eleanor Gertrude *b* 5 July 1884; *m* 18 April 1917 Rev Roger Harry Bertie Roberts, MA, Rector St Martin's, Worcester, s of Capt William Bertie Roberts, of Swan Walk, Chelsea, and *d* 19–, leaving issue. He *d* 8 Feb 1949

5 Hester Murray; *b* 17 March 1893; *m* 21 April 1914 Rev Gervase Vanneck Blois, yst s of Sir John Ralph Blois, 8th Bt (*qv*), and *d* 14 Oct 1973, leaving issue

The 4th BARON's bro,

HUMPHREY ARTHUR PAKINGTON, **5th Baron Hampton of Hampton Lovett and of Westwood**, OBE (1942), DL Worcs 1953; *b* 8 Sept 1888; *educ* HMS *Britannia*, RNC Greenwich and Architectl Assoc Sch (ARIBA 1925, FRIBA 1932); Cdr RN 1920, rejoined 1939, served WW II, Pres Architectl Assoc 1934–35, author novels and architectural studies (*How the World Builds, An Introduction to Architecture, English Villages and Hamlets*); *m* 26 March 1913 Grace Dykes (*d* 18 May 1959), 3rd dau of Sir Albert Spicer, 1st Bt (*qv*), and *d* 17 Feb 1974, leaving:

1 RICHARD HUMPHREY RUSSELL PAKINGTON, **6th and present Baron Hampton of Hampton Lovett and of Westwood**

1 *Hilary Evelyn Spicer [The Hon Mrs Bevan, Kingsland, Bledington, Oxon OX7 6UX]; *b* 24 May 1914; *m* 6 Aug 1938 David John Vaughan Bevan, TD (*d* 1986), assist master Shrewsbury, 2nd s of Prof Penry Vaughan Bevan, Fell Trin Coll Camb, and has issue:

(1) *Timothy David Vaughan [Brig Timothy Bevan, 13 Whyte Rd, Chichester, W Sussex PO19 2HN]; *b* 1939; *m* 1964 (*divorce* 1988) Jill, er dau of Leslie Murrell, of Harpford, nr Sidmouth, Devon; *m* 2nd 1988 *Penelope Edyth, dau of Douglas Lavers, of Kohimarama, Auckland, NZ, and by his 1st w has issue:

1a *Simon David Vaughan; *b* 1970

1a *Charlotte Hilary Vaughan; *b* 1968

(2) *Nicholas Vaughan; *b* 1942; Headmaster Shiplake Coll Oxon; *m* 1st 1967 (*divorce* 1977) Penelope Jane, dau of Col D H Tildesley, of Tettenhall Court, Tettenhall, Staffs, and has:

1a *Edward Duder Vaughan; *b* 1971

1a *Katherine Jane Vaughan; *b* 1969

(2) (cont.) Nicholas Bevan *m* 2nd 1978 *Anne Marie, er dau of John Timothy O'Connor, of Leongatha, Vict, Australia, and has by her:

2a *Oliver David; *b* 1979

2a *Emily Grace; *b* 1982

(3) Richard Vaughan [Richard Bevan, 1145 17th Ave E, Seattle, WA, USA]; *b* 1943; *m* 1st 1972 (*divorce* 1980) Christine, er dau of B G Harte, of Bromley, Kent; *m* 2nd 1991 *Lesley Burvill-Holmes and by her has:

1a *Nicholas; *b* 1992

(1) *Jennifer Jill Vaughan; *b* 1946; *m* 1 Nov 1975 *Gerry Leslie Hayward, s of F E Hayward, and has issue:

1a *James Fulton; *b* 1979

2a *Thomas Seaborne; *b* 1980

(2) *Margaret Hilary Vaughan; *b* 1953; *m* 1987 *Aidan John Kelly and has:

1a *David John; *b* 1988

2a *Peter Richard; *b* 1990
2 *Anne; *b* 15 Oct 1919; *educ* Somerville Coll Oxford (MA)
3 *Auriol Mary Grace; *b* 8 Dec 1922; SRN, SCM

HAMWEE

Creation: B. (LP, UK) 1991.

THE BARONESS HAMWEE, of Richmond upon Thames, London (Sally Rachel Hamwee) [The Rt Hon The Baroness Hamwee, 101a Mortlake High St, London SW14 8HQ]; *b* 12 Jan 1947; *educ* Manchester High Sch for Girls and Girton Coll Cambridge (MA); slr 1972, ptnr Clintons; memb Cncl Parents for Children 1977–86; memb Richmond-upon-Thames Cncl 1978– (Chm Planning Ctee 1983–87, V-Chm Policy and Resources Ctee 1987–92); Legal Advsr Simon Community 1980–; memb: NEC Lib Party 1987–88, Fed Exec Lib Dem 1989–91; Chm London Planning Advsy Ctee 1986–94; V-Chm Assoc Lib Dem Cncllrs' 1988–96; memb: Joseph Rowntree Fndn Inquiry Planning for Housing 1992–94, Cncl Family Policies Study Centre 1994–; cncl Refuge 1991–; dir: In Harmony 1994–, Xfm Ltd 1996–

Lineage: ALEC HAMWEE; *m* Dorothy Saunders and had:

SALLY RACHEL, *cr* a **Baroness**

HANHAM

Arms: Quarterly or and gu., on a bend engrailed sa. three crosses-patée fitchée of the first. **Crest:** A griffin's head erased. **Motto:** *Esse quam videri* ('To be, rather than to seem'). **Creation:** Bt. (E) 24 May 1667.

SIR MICHAEL WILLIAM HANHAM, 12TH BT, of Dean's Court, Dorset, DFC (1945) [Sir Michael Hanham Bt DFC, Deans Court, Wimborne, Dorset BH21 1EE]; *b* 27 Dec 1922; *s* cousin 1973; *educ* Winchester; Lt RASC, F/Lt RAFVR WW II; *m* 27 Feb 1954 *Margaret Jane, dau of W/Cdr Harold Thomas, RAF, and has:

1 +WILLIAM JOHN EDWARD [William Hanham Esq, 48 Lexham Gdns, London W8 5JA]; *b* 4 Sept 1957; *educ* Winchester and Courtauld Inst of Art (BA); *m* 1st 4 Sept 1982 (*divorce* 1986) Elizabeth Anne, yr dau of Paul Keyworth, of Farnham; *m* 2nd 15 June 1996 *Jennifer Tess, dau of Harold Sebag-Montefiore, of Kensington
1 *Victoria Jane; *b* 8 March 1955; *educ* Frensham; *m* 1987 *David L Gross, s of Dr Joseph Gross, of Chippaqua, New York, and has issue:
(1) *Hugo Augustus William; *b* 1989
(1) *Dulcie Harriet Jane; *b* 1992

Lineage: WILLIAM HANHAM, of Horsington, Somerset; *m c* 1487 Margaret, 2nd dau of John Long, of Purse Caundle, Dorset, and *d* between 20 July and Oct 1505, leaving, with a yr s (William):

RICHARD HANHAM, of Horsington; *b c* 1488; *m* Ricarda, dau of John Triptry, of Somerset, and *d* 25 July 1549, leaving:
1 William, of Purse Caundle; *b c* 1511; *m* Elizabeth, 2nd dau of Richard Dyer, of Wincanton, Somerset, and had:
(1) James, of Purse Caundle; *d* 1597
(2) William, Fell King's Coll Cambridge
(3) Benjamin; *d* abroad, 1581
(4) Sylvester
(1) Dorothy; *m* Thomas Brokesby, of Great Bradley, Suffolk
(2) Mary; *m* John Giffard, of Boreham, Warminster, Wilts
2 JOHN
1 Margaret; *m* William Webbe

The yr son,
JOHN HANHAM; MP Poole 1547; *m* Alice (*d* between 12 Jan 1559/60 and 8 Feb 1560/1), dau and heir of John(?) Orange, of Wimborne Minster (probably John Orange, MP Wareham 1529), and *d* 9 Sept 1559, leaving, with two daus:
1 Richard; *b* by 28 April 1543; *m* Bridget, dau of Sir John Newton, of Barrs Court, Glos, and *d* 1 Nov 1572, leaving:
(1) John; *d* 29 Oct 1579 aged 13
(1) Anne; *m* by 15 June 1582 Sir Walter Vaughan, of Falstone, Wilts, and *d* by 1593, leaving issue
2 THOMAS

The yr son,
THOMAS HANHAM, of Wimborne; Recorder Weymouth, Melcombe Regis 1571 and Bristol 1585, Serjeant-at-law 1589, MP Melcombe Regis 1572, Bristol 1584–93; *m* Penelope (*bur* 6 March 1621/2), est dau of Sir John Popham, Lord Ch Justice, and *d* 30 Aug 1593, leaving issue:
1 John (Sir); ktd 1603, MP E Looe 1601 and Weymouth 1604–11, High Sheriff Dorset 1614; *b* 1574; *m* Joan (*bur* 3 Aug 1615), widow of V-Adml Charles Trevanion and dau of Robert Wichalse, of Chudleigh, Devon, and *d* 28 Aug 1624, leaving:
(1) Eleanor; *m* her cousin John Pyne, of Curry Mallet, s of Thomas Pyne by Amy Hanham, and *d* 1662 aged 53, leaving issue
2 THOMAS
3 Henry; *b* 1583; *d* unm 1648
1 Amy; *m* 1595 Thomas Pyne and *d* 1640, leaving issue. He *d* 1610
2 Jane; *m* Sir John Horton, of Elkstone, Glos, and had issue
3 Mary; *d* unm
4 Anne; *m* by 17 Jan 1605/6 Martin White, of Fittleford, Dorset, and *d* 1611, leaving issue

The second son,
THOMAS HANHAM; sea-captain, co-cdr voyage of exploration off the coast of Maine 1606, MP Minehead 1642–44; *b* 1576; *m* 1610 Elizabeth, widow of William Frampton, of Moreton, and 2nd dau and coheir of Robert Broughton, of Sampford Beckfield, Somerset, and *d* 1 Aug 1652, having had issue:
1 JOHN
2 Thomas; barrister 1645; *b* 1617; *m* 28 April 1646 Margaret, dau of Sir William Dodington, of Breamore, Hants, and *dsp* 17 June 1650
1 Penelope
2 Jane; *b* 1618; *m* 1637 William Constantine, of Merly, and *d* 1654, leaving issue

The er son,
JOHN HANHAM, of Dean's Court, Wimborne; *b c* 1612; *m* 1640 Frances (*bur* 28 Sept 1659), dau of Sir William Dodington, of Breamore, Hants, and was *bur* 9 Dec 1661, having had:
1 WILLIAM (Sir), **1st Bt**
2 James; *bur* 1 June 1658
3 John; *bapt* 10 Nov 1646; *d* unm 1670
4 Edward; *bapt* 23 Nov 1648; *d* young
5 Richard; *bapt* 27 Dec 1649
6 Thomas; *bur* 27 Dec 1656
1 Mary; *m* 1661 Robert Grove, of Ferne, Wilts, and *d c* 1688, leaving issue (*see* GROVE, Bt)
2a Frances; *bapt* 25 Nov 1647; *m c* 9 July 1672 Thomas Penruddocke, of Compton Chamberlain, Wilts, and had issue
3 Margaret; *bur* 29 Oct 1654

The est son,
Sir William Hanham, 1st Bt (E), so *cr* 24 May 1667, of Dean's Court, Wimborne; *m* Jan 1665/6 Elizabeth (*d c* 1722), dau of George Cooper, of Clarendon Park, Wilts, and n of 1st Earl of Shaftesbury (*qv*), and *d* 21 June 1671, leaving:

Sir John Hanham, 2nd Bt; *m* Jane (*d* 1707), dau of William Eyre, of Neston Park, Wilts, and *d* between 26 June 1709 and 28 June 1710, having had, with four yr sons (John, *educ* Winchester, *bur* 6 Dec 1711; Thomas, *d c* 1721; Charles, *d c* 1721; Edward, *d* 1701) and a dau (Jane):

Sir William Hanham, 3rd Bt; *m* June 1717 Mary (*d* 22 Dec 1774), est dau of William Norris, of Nonsuch, Wilts, and *d* 28 March 1762, having had issue:
1 **Sir William Hanham, 4th Bt**, Lt-Col Dorset Militia, DL Dorset; *b c* 1718; *educ* New Coll Oxford; *m* 1st March 1744 Anne (*dsp*), dau of James Jennings, of Shiplake, Oxon; *m* 2nd June 1762 Mary (*d* Oct 1764), dau of Very Rev William Lynch, Dean of Canterbury, and had issue:
(1) **Sir William Thomas Hanham, 5th Bt**; *b* 1763; *d* unm 19 Aug 1791
(1) Mary Ann; *d* an infant
1 **Sir William** *m* 3rd Dec 1765 Harriott (*dsp* 2 April 1786), 3rd dau of Henry Drax, of Charborough, Dorset, and *d* 11 Feb 1776
2 Thomas; *b* 1723; *educ* Oriel Coll Oxford
3 John; *d* 1748
4 JAMES (Rev Sir), **6th Bt**
1 Eleanor; *m c* 1754 John Grove (*see* GROVE, Bt)

The 5th Bt's uncle,
Rev Sir James Hanham, 6th Bt; Rector Winterborne Zelston 1754–1806; *b c* 1726; *educ* Oriel Coll Oxford (BA 1748); *m* 1757, Jane, n and sole heir of William Phelips, of Corfe Mullen, Dorset, and *d* 11 March 1806, having had, with two other sons and six other daus:
1 JAMES (Rev Sir), **7th Bt**
2 Charles; *m* Anne, dau of — Ahier, of Jersey, and had issue:
(1) Charles Edward, of Clair Val, Jersey; *m* Jane, dau of John Ley, of Cornwall, and had issue:
1a Jane; *m* Capt Philip Aplin, 3rd Regt of Foot
1 Maria; *m* Sept 1806 Richard Bentley, of Raymill, Herts, and *d* 1811

The est son,
Rev Sir James Hanham, 7th Bt; Rector Winterborne Zelston 1806–49; *b* 10 March 1760; *m* 1st 16 April 1793 Anne (*d* 15 July 1801), dau of Edward Pyke, RN, and *d* 2 April 1849, having had, with three other sons and two daus:

1 **Sir William Hanham, 8th Bt**; Capt RN; *b* 8 May 1798; *m* 6 Nov 1823 Harriet (*d* Feb 1838), dau of G Morgan, of Mount Clare, Surrey, and *dsp* 27 March 1877

Sir James *m* 2nd 14 Dec 1815 Eliza Dean (*d* 5 June 1877), dau of Lt William Patey, RN, and by her had, with another s:

2 John; Capt 9th Regt and Adj 11th Depot Bn Staff; *b* 14 Jan 1823; served Sutlej campaign; *m* 11 Aug 1853, Amy Ursula (*m* 2nd 17 Aug 1872, Camille Felix Desire Caillard, JP, DL, County Court Judge, who *d* 1 May 1898, leaving issue, and *d* 14 Jan 1909), yr dau and eventual sole heir of Alexander Copland, of Wingfield Place, Berks, and *d* 16 Sept 1861 of a gunshot wound inflicted by a soldier of the 32nd Regt at Preston, leaving:

(1) **Sir John Alexander Hanham, 9th Bt**, JP, DL; CC Dorset; *b* 5 July 1854; MA Oxon; barrister Inner Temple 1881, Apparitor-Gen Province and Diocese Canterbury; *m* 18 July 1896 Hon Cordelia Lucy Lopes (*d* 18 April 1945), 2nd dau of 1st Baron Ludlow (*see* ROBOROUGH, B), and *d* 21 Feb 1911, leaving:

1a **Sir John Ludlow Hanham, 10th Bt**, JP, DL Dorset; *b* 23 Jan 1898; *educ* Winchester and Magdalen Coll Oxford (MA 1926); Dorset: CC, CA 1948, barrister Inner Temple 1926, Apparitor-Gen Province and Diocese of Canterbury, Capt Gren Gds, ADC to Govr-Gen NZ 1930–32, served WW I (wounded) and WW II; *d* unm 30 April 1955

2a **Sir Henry Phelips Hanham, 11th Bt**; *b* 6 April 1901; *educ* Winchester and Magdalen Coll Oxford; RA WW II; *d* unm Nov 1973

1a Cordelia Amy Maud; *d* unm Feb 1974

(2) Phelips Brooke; Col RA, Assist Inspr Roy Arsenal Woolwich 1916, served WW I; *b* 27 March 1858; *m* 9 Sept 1884 Gertrude Frances (*d* 16 Sept 1922), dau of Lt-Col Patrick Lewis Cole Paget (*see* ANGLESEY, M), and *d* 20 Feb 1917 of illness contracted on service, having had:

1a Richard John Phelips; *b* 1885; *d* 1890

2a Esmond Henry Paget; *b* 12 March 1887; *educ* Wellington; *d* unm 25 Aug 1954

3a Patrick John; Lt RASC WW I; *b* 16 Oct 1893; *educ* Clifton; *m* 1st 14 Dec 1921 (*divorce* 1943) Dulcie, widow of Lynn Hartley and yr dau of William George Daffarn, of Valewood, Haslemere; *m* 2nd 6 Aug 1947 Emmeline Mary (*d* 1967), yst dau of Ernest Charles Wynter, and *d* 23 Feb 1965, having by his 1st w had issue:

1b Sir MICHAEL WILLIAM HANHAM, **12th and present Bt**

(1) Amy; *b* 6 July 1855; *m* 24 June 1875 Duncan William Hume Skrine (*d* 27 July 1928), of Horsley Court, Glos, 2nd s of Henry Duncan Skrine, JP, DL, of Warleigh and Claverton Manors, Somerset, and *d* 8 Nov 1945, leaving issue

(2) Eliza Frances, OBE (1918); DGStJ, Gd Cordon Shefakat; *b* 15 Sept 1859; *m* 16 June 1881 Sir Vincent Henry Penalver Caillard, of Wingfield House, Trowbridge, Wilts, and *d* 15 March 1926, leaving issue. He *d* 18 March 1930

5 Thomas Barnabas; Cdr RN; *b* 11 June 1825; *m* 1st 8 May 1847 Emily Annie (*dsp* 3 Oct 1853), dau of Edward Castleman, of Chettle, Dorset; *m* 2nd 30 Oct 1854 Josephine Ida Dodson (*d* 6 Jan 1866), only child of William Henry Scott, of Paris; *m* 3rd 1 Dec 1868 Edith Mary (*d* 30 July 1876), widow of Maj John Swinburne, 18th Regt, and *d* 27 Nov 1883, having by his 2nd w had issue:

(1) Maud Phelips Agatha; *d* 1870

1 Elizabeth Marianne; *d* young, 10 July 1825

HANKEY

Arms: Per pale az. and gu. a wolf salient erm. vulned on the shoulder of the second, a bordure wavy of the third. **Crest:** A wolf's head erased at the neck erm., gorged with a collar wavy az. **Supporters:** Dexter, a fallow deer resting the sinister hind foot ppr. on a millrind sa.; sinister, an alpine chamois resting the dexter hind foot ppr. on a like millrind. **Motto:** *Per sagitatem pax cum justitia* ('Peace with justice through wisdom'). **Creation:** B. (UK) 3 Feb 1939.

THE 3RD BARON HANKEY, of The Chart, Co Surrey (Donald Robin Alers Hankey) [The Rt Hon The Lord Hankey, 34 Sunray Ave, London SE24 9PX]; *b* 12 June 1938; *s* f 1996; *educ* Rugby and UCL (Dip Arch); RIBA; *m* 1st 14 Dec 1963 (*divorce* 1974) Margaretha, yr dau of Henrik Thorndahl, of Copenhagen; *m* 2nd 27 Sept 1974 (*divorce* 1994) Eileen Désirée, yr dau of Maj-Gen Stuart Hedley Molesworth Battye, CB, of Furacre House, Ascot, Berks; *m* 3rd 1994 *June, dau of Dr Leonard Taboroff, and by his 2nd w has issue:

1 *Fiona Bevyl; *b* 19 Aug 1975

2 *Beatrice Eileen; *b* 22 April 1978

Lineage: WILLIAM ALERS later ALERS HANKEY (roy licence 16 Dec 1815), of the City of London and Hackney; banker; *b* 1771; *m* 1797 Mary Marten (*d* 1851) and *d* 1859, having had, with other issue:

JOHN ALERS HANKEY, of Egham Lodge, Surrey; Govr Bank of England; *b* 1803; *m* 16 Sept 1829 Sarah Andrews (*d* 26 Dec 1885), dau of William Jameson, of Clapham, and *d* 15 Jan 1872, having had, with other issue:

ROBERT ALERS HANKEY, of Warcowie, S Australia, later Brighton; *b* 1838; *educ* Rugby and Trin Coll Cambridge; *m* 1865 Helen (*d* 9 Sept 1900), dau of William Bakwell, of Shirley, nr Adelaide, and *d* 28 Dec 1906, having had issue:

1 Hugh Martin Alers; Lt Roy Warwicks Regt, Egyptian Army 1897–98, Boer War 1899–1900 with Mounted Inf; *b* 27 Nov 1872; *ka* Paardeburg *c* 18 Feb 1900

2 Clement Theodore Alers; Capt Roy Sussex Regt, author, Sec Athenaeum 1920–30; *b* 1875; *educ* Rugby and Balliol Coll Oxford (BA 1900); *m* 29 June 1907 Amabel Julia (*d* 20 May 1951), dau of J E Bush, slr, of Brighton, and *d* 12 June 1966, leaving issue:

(1) Lancelot Hugh Alers; Headmaster Clifton Coll Prep Sch ; *b* 11 Feb 1909; *educ* Rugby and Balliol Coll Oxford (BA 1931, MA 1945); *m* 2 Jan 1943 Victoria Elisabeth (*d* 20 June 1997), dau of Edmund King, of Clifton

(2) *Oliver Clement Alers; Lt-Cdr RNVR WW II; *b* 19 April 1912; *educ* Rugby; *m* 27 June 1940 *Mildred, dau of Robert Kerkham, of Terrington St Clement, Norfolk, and has issue:

1a *Robin Noel Alers; *b* 16 Dec 1944; *educ* Rugby, Balliol Coll Oxford (BA 1967) and St Andrews

1a *Gillian Sarah Alers; *b* 11 Sept 1948

3 MAURICE PASCAL ALERS, **1st Baron**

4 Donald William Alers; 2nd Lt, author: *A Student in Arms*; *b* 27 Oct 1884; *ka* Flanders 12 Oct 1916

1 Gertrude Helen Alers; *m* 4 Sept 1902 Rev Arthur Patrick Spelman, BA Dublin, Vicar Burwash Weald, Sussex, and *d* 14 Jan 1938, leaving issue

2 Hilda Mary Alers; *d* unm following a road accident 19 July 1949

The 3rd son,

MAURICE PASCAL ALERS HANKEY, **1st Baron Hankey**, of The Chart, Co Surrey, so *cr* 3 Sept 1939, GCB (1919, KCB 1916), GCMG (1929), GCVO (1934), PC (1939); *b* 1 April 1877; *educ* Rugby (Govr 1920–46) and RNC Greenwich; Col RMA, Naval Intell Dept 1902–07, Assist Sec 1908–12 and Sec CID 1912–38, Sec War Cabinet 1916 and Imp War Cabinet 1917–18, Br Sec Peace Conf 1919, Sec: Cabinet 1920–38, Imp Confs 1921, 1923, 1926, 1930 and 1937, Br Sec Washington and Genoa Confs 1921–22, Sec London Conf of Reparation 1924, Clerk to PC 1923–38, Sec-Gen: Hague Conf 1929–30, London Naval Conf 1930 and Reparation Conf Lausanne 1932, memb Perm Mandates Commn Geneva June-Aug 1939, Min without Portfolio War Cabinet 1939, Chllr Duchy Lancaster 1940, Paymaster-Gen 1941–42, Br Govt Dir Suez Canal Co 1938–39 and 1945–58, dir: London Bd Roy Insur 1938–39 and 1945–63, Jorehaut Tea Co 1945 and Nile Insur (Egypt) 1947–56, Grand Offr Legn Hon, Grand Cross Crown Italy and Belgium, Rising Sun Japan 1st Cl; recd after WW I thanks of Parl and £25,000 (over £450,000 in late-1990s terms), Hon LLD Birmingham 1919, Edin 1921 and Cantab 1932, Hon DCL Oxon 1934, Hon MIEE 1943, FRS 1942; *m* 16 Sept 1903 Adeline Hermine Gertrude Ernestine (*d* 1979), dau of Abraham de Smidt, Surveyor-Gen Cape Colony, and *d* 25 Jan 1963, leaving:

1 ROBERT MAURICE ALERS HANKEY, **2nd Baron Hankey**, KCMG (1955, CMG 1947), KCVO (1956); *b* 4 July 1905; *educ* Rugby and New Coll Oxford (BA 1926); Dip Serv 1927–65, Priv Sec to For Sec 1933, 1st Sec Warsaw 1936, Bucharest 1939, Cairo 1941 and Teheran 1942, FO 1943–45 and 1946, Counsellor Warsaw 1945, Chargé d'Affaires Spain 1949–51, Min Hungary 1951–53, Amb Stockholm 1954–60, Perm UK Rep OEEC (Chm Paris 1960), memb OECD 1961–65 (Chm Ec Policy Ctee 1960–65), V-Pres European Inst Business Admin Fontainebleau 1962–80, memb Internat Cncl Utd World Colls and Cncl Internat Baccalaureati Orgn Geneva 1966–78, dir Alliance Bldg Soc 1970–83, Pres Anglo-Swedish Soc 1970–78, Grand Cross N Star (Sweden) 1956; *m* 1st 27 Sept 1930 Frances Bevyl (*d* 31 Dec 1957), er dau of Walter Erskine Stuart-Menteth (*see* STUART-MENTETH, Bt), and had:

(1) DONALD ROBIN ALERS HANKEY, **3rd and present Baron Hankey**

(2) +Alex(ander) Maurice Alers [The Hon Alexander Hankey, Hethe House, Cowden, Kent TN8 7DZ]; *b* 18 Aug 1947; *educ* Rugby, Trin Coll Cambridge and Stanford U California; Fell MIT 1969; *m* 19 Dec 1970 *Deborah, dau of Myron Benson, of Newton, Mass.

(1) *Juliet Alers [The Hon Mrs Alchin, Parkstone, Clenches Farm Road, Sevenoaks, Kent]; *b* 15 Oct 1931; *m* 23 Feb 1957 *Peter John Wrensted Alchin, MA, only s of Judge Gordon Alchin, DFC, and has issue:

1a *Gordon David; *b* 10 May 1961; *educ* Sevenoaks Sch

1a *Vanessa Frances; *b* 14 Sept 1962

2a *Chloe Sylvia; *b* 10 Jan 1965

(2) *Adele Bevyl Alers [The Hon Mrs Adele Anggard, Banergatan 77, 115 53, Stockholm, Sweden]; *b* 31 July 1933; *m* 15 May 1964 (*divorce* 1987) Dr Erik Emil Anggard, of Stockholm, 2nd s of Dr Gosta Anggard, and has issue:

1a *John Mikael; *b* 22 March 1967

1a *Eola Anni; *b* 11 Sept 1965

2a *Irene Malin Adele; *b* 2 Nov 1970

1 (cont.) The **2nd Baron** *m* 2nd 2 Oct 1962 Joanna Riddall (*d* 1991), dau of Rev James Johnston Wright, of Perthshire; *m* 3rd 1992 *Mrs Stephanie Langley [The Rt Hon Stephanie Lady Hankey, Hethe House, Cowden, Kent TN8 7DZ], dau of Brig Percy Paulet King and Mrs Kenneth Ford, of W Wittering, and *d* 28 Oct 1996

2 +Christopher Alers, OBE (1958) [The Hon Christopher Hankey, New Cottage, French Street, nr Westerham, Kent]; Maj RM WW II, with Min Labour 1946–61, Dept Technical Co-opn 1961–64, Pncpl Min Overseas Devpt 1964–72; *b* 27 April 1911; *educ* Rugby, New Coll Oxford (BA 1932, MA 1947) and London U (BSc 1939); *m* 1st 31 Oct 1945 (*divorce* 1957) Prudence May, er

dau of Keith Alfred Brodribb, of Tasmania, by Laura Bright, only dau of Loudoun Hector Macleod, of Raasay, and has issue:

(1) *Felicity Laura [Mrs Henry Edgell, Dennistoun, Bothwell, Tasmania 7030, Australia]; *b* 16 June 1947; *m* *Henry R Edgell, s of Geoffrey Edgell, CBE, and has issue:

1a *Thomas; *b* 1971

2a *Edward; *b* 1981

1a *Chloe; *b* 1975

2 (cont.) The Hon Christopher Hankey *m* 2nd 5 Sept 1958 *Helen Christine, yr dau of Alexander John Cassavetti, of Oxted, Surrey, and by her has:

(1) +Rupert Christopher Alers; *b* 4 Aug 1960; *m* 1984 *Jane Elizabeth, est dau of Ian Bruce and Mrs Alan Pote, of The Priory, Rothwell, Northants

3 +Henry Arthur Alers, CMG (1960), CVO (1959) [The Hon Henry Hankey CMG CVO, Llandaff Barn, 11 Thames St, Eynsham OX8 1HF]; joined FO 1937, 1st Sec Madrid 1945, Rome 1946 and Santiago 1953, FO 1949, Consul San Francisco 1950, Counsellor 1956, Beirut 1962–66, Amb Panama 1966–69, U-Sec FCO 1969–74, author: *Archaeology: artifacts and artification* (1985); *b* 1 Sept 1914; *educ* Rugby and New Coll Oxford (BA 1935); *m* 1 Jan 1941 Vronwy (*d* 11 May 1998), only dau of Rev Thomas Frederic Fisher, Rector Stilton, Peterborough, and has:

(1) +(Christopher) Ceri Alers [Ceri Hankey Esq, Route du Gros Chêne, Argonay, 74000, France]; architect; *b* 25 March 1944; *educ* Rugby and Trin Coll Cambridge (BArch); *m* 1st 12 Sept 1970 Eleanor G C, only dau of C J C Beckett; *m* 2nd 1980 *Annick, only dau of Robert Perrucon, of Annecy, and by her has:

1a +Jonathan Ceri Alers; *b* 1980

2a +Jason Henry Alers; *b* 1989

1a *Deborah Marie Alers; *b* 1982

(2) +(Maurice) Peregrine Alers [Peregrine Hankey Esq, The Green, Northmoor, Oxon]; *b* 30 Aug 1945; *educ* Rugby and New Coll Oxford; *m* 3 Jan 1970 *Juliet Caroline, yr dau of Anthony Ross Moore, CMG, and has:

1a +Anthony Thomas; *b* 1977

2a +David Henry; *b* 1988

1a *Rose Vronwy; *b* 1975

(3) +Peter John Alers [Peter Hankey Esq, Le Lassy, 73410 St Germain La Chambotte, France]; *b* 2 Aug 1951; *educ* Rugby; *m* 1981 *Margaret Catherine, only dau of John D Walker, and has issue:

1a +Robert; *b* 1984

2a +William Walker Alers; *b* 1991

1a *Katherine Claire Alers; *b* 1987

(1) *Veronica Vronwy Alers [Mrs Timothy Newman, Wester Golford, Moyness, Nairn IV12 5QQ]; *b* 2 May 1957; *m* 1980 *S/Ldr Timothy C M Newman, RAF (ret), er s of W/Cdr A T Newman, and has issue:

1a *Thomas Robert Minôt; *b* 1990

1a *Elena Vronwy Margaret; *b* 1987

1 *Ursula Helen Alers [The Hon Lady Benn, 15 The Waldrons, Oast Rd, Hurst Green, Oxted, Surrey RH8 9DY]; *b* 5 Feb 1909; *m* 23 July 1929 Sir John Andrews Benn, 3rd Bt (*qv*), and has issue

HANMER

Arms: Arg. two lions passant guardant az., armed and langued gu.
Crest: On a chapeau az. doubled erm. a lion guardant-sejant arg.
Motto: *Garde l'honneur* ('Maintain honour').
Creation: Bt. (GB) 21 May 1774.

SIR JOHN WYNDHAM EDWARD HANMER, 8TH BT, of Hanmer, Co Flint, JP (Flintshire 1971) DL (Clwyd 1978) [Sir John Hanmer Bt JP DL, The Mere House, Hanmer, Salop SY13 3DG]; *b* 27 Sept 1928; *s* f 1977; *educ* Eton; High Sheriff Clwyd 1977, late Capt Roy Dragoons; *m* 17 July 1954 *Audrey Melissa, er dau of Maj Arthur Christopher John Congreve, of Westering, Yeoman's Lane, Newton, Berks, and has:

1 +(WYNDHAM RICHARD) GUY [Guy Hanmer Esq, The Stables, Bettisfield Park, Whitchurch, Salop SY13 2JZ]; *b* 27 Nov 1955; *educ* Wellington and RMA Sandhurst, late Blues and Royals; *m* 9 Aug 1986 *Elizabeth, yr dau of Neil Taylor, of Frampton-on-Severn, Glos, and has issue:

(1) +Thomas Wyndham William; *b* 10 May 1989

(2) +George Hugh Richard; *b* 1992

(1) *Alicia Marina; *b* 1994

2 +Edward Hugh; *b* 12 July 1957; *educ* Wellington; Capt late Blues and Royals

Lineage: Sir THOMAS de MACCLESFIELD; living 1294; offr under EDWARD I; settled in Maelor Saesneg, Flints; had a grant of waste land in Hanmer by 1300; had:

JOHN UPTON; living 1313; Vicar Hanmer; *m* Hawis, dau of Einion ap Gwilym, and had, with two yr sons (Owain, *dsp*; Dafydd):

PHILIP HANMER; granted lands in Is-coed 1331; *m* Annes, dau and heir of Dafydd ap Rhirid ab Ynry, and had, with a yr s (Dafydd Foel ('The Bald')) and two daus (Myfanwy; Margaret):

Sir DAVID HANMER; Serjeant-at-law 1377, Judge King's Bench 1383, ktd 1387; *m* Angharad, dau of Llewelyn Ddu ('The Black') ap Gruffudd, of Bryncunallt, and *d* by 22 July 1387 (possibly by June 1386), having had, with an est s (Gruffudd, whose lands were confiscated for his support of Owen Glendower 1400/1, though he was pardoned 1410), a yst s (Philip, *b* 1397, *d* 1415) and two daus (including Margaret, *m* Owen Glendower, the celebrated Welsh patriot):

JENKIN HANMER; negotiated a treaty with CHARLES VI OF FRANCE on behalf of his bro-in-law Owen Glendower; pardoned by HENRY IV 1411; *m* 1st Margaret, dau and heir of Dafydd ap Bleddyn Fychan, of Llwynderw, by whom he acquired lands in Englefield, Flints, and had:

1 Gruffudd ap Jenkin Hanmer, of Yr Owredd, Hanmer, Flints; *m* by Feb 1424/5 Elen, dau of Sir Piers Dutton, of Cheshire, and had, with a yr s (Jenkin, ancestor of the HANMERs of Lee) and six daus (plus two illegitimate ones):

(1) Richard, of Hanmer; of age by 1462; *m* by 25 March 1471 Margaret, dau of Sir Roger Kynaston, of Hordley, Salop, by Elizabeth, dau of 2nd and last Count of Tancarville (*see* GREY, E), and *d c* 1507, having had, with four yr sons (David, of Ellesmere; John; Christopher; Humphrey) and three daus:

1a Thomas (Sir), of Yr Owredd; ktd 1513; *m* (1st?) between 7 Nov 1489 and 10 Feb 1489/90 Joan, dau of Sir Randle Brererton, of Malpas, Cheshire; may have *m* 2nd Matilda —; *d* 10 Feb 1546, having had, with four yr sons (Randle, of Penley, Flints, ancestor of the HANMERs of Penley, Maesbrook and Tregyffin; Richard, *dsp*; Humphrey; John) and seven daus (including Elinor, *m* her distant cousin WILLIAM HANMER, of The Fenns, *see* below):

1b Thomas (Sir), of Yr Owredd, Hanmer; ktd 1547; *m* probably after 15 April 1518 Catherine, dau of Thomas Salter, of Oswestry, Salop, and *d* 5 April 1583, having had, with three yr sons (Thomas, *dsp*; William, *dsp*; Randle) and a dau (Maudlen, *d* 1 Oct 1660):

1c John (Sir); ktd 1603; *m* between 20 April and 12 July 1564 Jane, dau of Sir John Salesbury, of Lleweni, Henllan, Denbighs, and had, with two yr sons (John, of Penley, *m* Jane, dau and heir of John Decka; Edward, Capt, ktd by the Duke of Florence, *dsp* Italy):

1d Thomas (Sir); ktd 1603; *m* 1st after 18 Nov 1585 Anne, sis of 9th Earl of Shrewsbury and Waterford (*qv*), and had a dau (Catherine, *d* unm aged 22); *m* 2nd between 31 Aug 1597 and 6 May 1598 Catherine, dau of Sir Thomas Mostyn (*see* MOSTYN, B), and *d* 18 April 1619, having by her had, with two yr sons (Thomas, *m* Mary, dau of Osmeri Hill and widow of Francis Charlton, of Apley, and *dsp*; Roger, *d* 1673) and five daus:

1e Sir JOHN HANMER, 1st Bt (E), so *cr* 8 July 1620; *b c* 1590; BA Oxon; MP Flints 1621, memb Cncl Wales 1624; *m* Dorothy, dau and coheir of Sir Richard Trevor, of Trefalun or Allington, Denbighs, and *d* between 10 June 1624 and 30 Sept 1629, leaving, with two yr sons (John, royalist Capt of Horse Civil War, *k* Little Dean, Glos, 1643; David, *dsp*) and two daus (Mary; Katherine):

1f Sir THOMAS HANMER, 2nd Bt; *b c* 1612; MP Flintshire, cup-bearer to CHARLES I; *m* 1st St Thomas's Day 1631 Elizabeth, Maid of Honour to QUEEN HENRIETTA MARIA, only dau of Sir Thomas Baker, of Whittingham, Suffolk, and had, with an only dau (Trevor, *m* after 3 June 1659 Sir John Warner, Bt, of Parham Suffolk):

1g Sir JOHN HANMER, 3rd Bt; MP Flintshire, Gentleman Privy Chamber to CHARLES II, Commr Navy, Col Williamite Regt Battle of the Boyne 1690, Maj-Gen; *m* Mary, dau and heir of Joseph Alston, of Netherall, Suffolk, and *dsps* 1701 (*k* in a duel), having had a dau (Mary, *d* young)

1f (cont.) Sir THOMAS *m* 2nd by 9 June 1655 Susan, dau of Sir William Hervey (*see* BRISTOL, M), and *d* 1678, leaving by her:

2g William; *b* Angers, France, *c* 1648; naturalised 1651; *m* after 10 May 1675 Peregrine, dau of Sir Henry North, 1st Bt (*see* GUILFORD, E), and had issue:

1h Sir THOMAS HANMER, 4th and last Bt; *b* 24 Sept 1677; MP Thetford 1701–02 and 1705–08, Flintshire 1702–05 and Suffolk 1708–27, Speaker H of C 1713; *m* 1st 14 Oct 1698 Isabella, widow of 1st Duke of Grafton (*qv*); *m* 2nd Elizabeth (*dsp*), only dau and heir of Thomas Folkes, of Barton, Suffolk, and *dsp* 7 May 1746, when the btcy expired, the Hanmer estates passing to his cousin William (*see* below)

3g Thomas (Sir), of the Inner Temple; *b c* 1650; *dsp* by 2 May 1688

JENKIN HANMER *m* 2nd Efa, dau of Dafydd ap Gronwy, of Llai, nr Wrexham, and *d* after 1 Oct 1427, having by her had:

2 John, of Lee and Halton, *b* 1426, Steward Maelor Saesneg; *d* 1475

3 EDWARD

4 Richard, of Bettisfield; ancestor of the HANMERs of Bangor Is-coed, Flints

JENKIN HANMER's 3rd s (but 2nd by his 2nd w),

EDWARD HANMER, of The Fenns, Hanmer; m Margaret, dau of Morus and had, with a yr s (Philip):

GRUFFUDD FYCHAN ('The Younger') HANMER, of The Fenns; *m* Margaret, dau of Maredudd Llwy ap Madog Llwyd, and *d* 1501, having had, with five yr sons

(Dafydd; William; Lawrence; Edward, priest; Mathew, of the King's Buttery) and four daus:

JENKIN HANMER, of The Fenns; *m* Margaret, dau of Thomas Dymock, of Willington, Flints, and had, with four daus:

WILLIAM HANMER, of The Fenns; *m* after 14 Oct 1519 but probably before Whitsun 1524 his distant cousin Elinor, dau of Sir Thomas Hanmer, of Yr Owredd, and *d* 1570, having had, with six yr sons (Thomas, *b* 1544; Humphrey, *b* 1545; Gruffudd, *b* 1550; John, *b* 1552; Christopher, *b* 1554; Harry, *b* 1560), certainly four daus (Mawd, *b* 1542; Margaret, *b* 1546; Elen, *b* 1547; Catherine, *b* 1559) and possibly two others (Anne; Jane):

WILLIAM HANMER, of The Fenns; *b* 1536; *m* after 12 June 1556 Margaret, dau and heir of David Kynaston, of Crickot, Salop, and had, with thee daus (including Margaret, *b* 1559; Ellen):

Sir WILLIAM HANMER, of The Fenns; *b* 1569; arms confirmed and crest granted by Clarenceux King of Arms 1581; *m* 1st after 2 Sept 1581Eleanor, dau of Edward Dymock, of Willington; *m* 2nd Elinor (*m* 3rd Sir Richard Egerton, of Ridley, Cheshire), dau and heir of John Jenkes, of Bridgnorth, Salop, and widow of Thomas Bromley, of Halne, Salop, and *d* 24 Sept 1620, having had, with two er sons (*d* young or *sp*), a yst s and a dau:

Sir THOMAS HANMER, of The Fenns; *b c* 1589; *m* after 29 July 1621 Catherine, dau and coheir of Thomas Puleston, of Lightwood, Flints, who brought him the manor of Moreton or Moreton Say, Salop, and *d* 11 March 1624/5, having had:

WILLIAM HANMER, of The Fenns; *b c* 1620; royalist Civil War; *m* 1st Elinor, only dau of Peter Warburton, of The Lodge, Crowley, and had a s; *m* 2nd Mary, dau and coheir of Ralph Sneyd, of Keel, and *d* 1669, having by her had two sons (William; John); his s by his 1st w:

THOMAS HANMER, of The Fenns; *m* between 24 May 1673 and 25 May 1674 Jane, est dau of Sir Job Charlton, of Ludford, Herefs, Serjeant-at-law, Speaker H of C, and *d* after 24 June 1682, having had issue:

1 William, of The Fenns; *m* Esther, sis and heir of Charles Jennens, of Gopsall, Leics, and had:

(1) Thomas, of The Fenns; MP; *m* after 11 April 1733 Catherine, dau of 1st Earl of Egmont (*qv*), and *dsp* 1737

(2) William, of The Fenns; inherited Hanmer from Sir THOMAS HANMER, 4th and last Bt; *m* his cousin Elizabeth, dau of Charles Jennens, and *dspm*, having had an only dau:

1a Esther; *m* 23 Feb 1756 1st, as his 1st w, Viscount Curzon of Penn (*see* HOWE, E) and *d* 21 July 1764

(3) Humphrey; *m* Catherine Quartermain and *dsp* April 1773, when The fenns and Hanmer passed to **Sir Walden Hanmer, 1st Bt** (*see* below)

2 Job; *bapt* 17 Jan 1677; Bencher Lincoln's Inn; *m* Susan, dau and heir of Thomas Walden, of Simpson's Place, Bucks, and *d* 2 March 1739, having had issue:

(1) **Sir Walden Hanmer, 1st Bt** (GB), so *cr* 21 May 1774; barrister and Bencher Lincoln's Inn, Treas 1774, DCL Oxon, MP Sudbury; *bapt* 19 March 1717; *m* Anne (*d* 2 Feb 1778), yst dau and coheir of Henry Vere Graham, of Holbrook Hall, Suffolk, and had issue:

1a THOMAS (Sir), **2nd Bt**

2a Job, of Holbrook Hall; *b* 4 Dec 1749; *m* Maria (*d* 8 May 1784), dau of John Syer, of Lavenham, and *d* April 1814, leaving, with other issue:

1b Thomas Job Syer; Capt RN; *b* 5 July 1781; *m* 1st 13 May 1823 Harriet (*d* 10 Oct 1831), dau of Thomas Dawson, and had, with other issue:

1c Harriet Anne; *m* 30 Aug 1849 Henry Leslie, of Seaport Lodge, Co Antrim, and *d* 7 Feb 1887, leaving issue. He *d* 7 July 1864

2c Caroline Augusta; *m* 4 June 1863 James Mitchell, DL, of Holbrook Hall, Sudbury, and *d* 14 March 1913, having had issue. He *d* 21 June 1895

1b (cont.) Capt Thomas Hanmer *m* 2nd 1835 Charlotte Sophia, dau of John Blagrave, of Calcot Park, Berks, and *d* 18 Aug 1842, leaving by her:

1c John Graham Job; R-Adml; *b* 1836; *m* 30 June 1864 Mary Caroline (*d* 18 Oct 1925), dau of Rev John Cobbold Aldrich, and *d* 21 May 1919, leaving issue:

1d Lambert Alfred Graham, DSO (1918); Lt-Col 21st Cav; *b* 21 Oct 1868; *m* 17 Dec 1901 Ethel Elizabeth (*d* 16 Feb 1964 aged 97), yst dau of Lt-Col Thomas Heaton Lovett, JP, of Belmont, Salop, and *d* 29 April 1918 of wounds recd in action, leaving:

1e Richard Graham; Lt-Col PAVO; *b* 5 Nov 1906; *educ* Wellington; *m* 26 April 1939 *Helen Jean [Mrs Richard Hanmer, Forbury Farm, Kimbolton, Leominster, Herefs], yr dau of Dr Alfred Walter Campbell, of Sydney, NSW, and *d* 1986, leaving:

1f +David Graham [David Hanmer Esq, Yew Tree Cottage, Kimbolton, Leominster, Herefs]; Capt (ret) Roy Dragoons; *b* 15 Aug 1940; *educ* Wellington and RMA Sandhurst; *m* 1st 11 Dec 1968 (*divorce* 1984) Susan Evelyn, only dau of Brig Ian M Christie; *m* 2nd 1988 *Bo White and by his 1st w has:

1g +Piers Christie Graham; *b* 21 May 1971

1g *Eugenie Claire; *b* 25 Oct 1973

1f *Rosemary Elizabeth; *b* 6 Jan 1905

2d Thomas Walden, JP; Inspr Stock Dept Ag Sydney, NSW; *b* 31 July 1875; *m* 1903 Ida (*d* 29 Oct 1961), 2nd dau of A Whitby-Simpson, of Armidale, NSW, and *d* 17 July 1949, leaving issue:

1e +John Walden, ED, JP [John Hanmer Esq ED JP, Claremont, Oaklands, nr Corowa, NSW, Australia]; AIF WW II, Greek Medal 1979; *b* 25 July 1915; *m* April 1949 *Jean Eileen Davies, dau of Arthur Archibald Sterling Nixon, of NSW, and has issue:

1f *Ruth Madeleine; *b* 1950

2f *Jean Anne; *b* 1955

3f *Patricia Margaret; *b* 1957

1e *Helen Walden [Mrs Ernest Charles Stumm, 20 Bertha Road, Cremorne, Sydney, NSW, Australia]; *b* 27 Nov 1903; *m* 2 Aug 1958 Ernest Charles Stumm (*d* 1974), only s of Albert Louis Stumm, of Brisbane

2e *Mildred Walden; *b* 25 Feb 1905; *m* 22 Feb 1932 Douglas Melliar Phelps (*d* 25 Aug 1964), 4th s of Samuel Thomas Phelps, of Sydney, and has issue:

1f *Michael Melliar; *b* 5 April 1942

3e *Beatrice Walden; Capt AANS WW II; *b* 1 Oct 1910

1d Alice Mary; *m* 28 July 1926 Rev Harry Munday Shuttleworth, Rector Wickham St Paul's, Essex, and *d* 13 May 1951. He *d* 11 Oct 1932

2d Helen Caroline; *d* unm 6 Aug 1942

3d Charlotte Edith; *d* unm 26 July 1950

3a Graham (Rev); Vicar Hanmer; *b* 16 Jan 1754; *m* Elizabeth Marple, dau of John Child, and had, with other issue:

1b Anne Eleanor Isabella; *m* 25 Aug 1806 William Selby-Lowndes, MP, of Whaddon Hall, and *d* 30 April 1852, leaving issue. He *d* 18 May 1840

(4) Edward; barrister; *b* 16 July 1758; *m* Arabella (*d* 1828), dau of Thomas Pennant, and *dsp* 24 July 1821

(5) Walden Hanry; Clerk in Chancery; *b* 30 Jan 1761; *dsp*

(1) Anne Eleanor; *m* Rev George Turnor

Sir WALDEN *d* 20 Oct 1783; his est son,

Sir Thomas Hanmer, 2nd Bt; *b* 5 April 1747; *m* 3 Dec 1779 Margaret (*d* 6 Nov 1830), est dau and coheir of George Kenyon, of Peel, Lancs, and *d* 4 Oct 1828, having had issue:

1 Thomas, of Bettisfield Park, Salop; *b* 12 April 1781; Lt-Col; *m* 14 July 1808 Arabella Charlotte (*d* 3 Sept 1862), est dau and coheir of Thomas Skip Dyott Bucknall, MP, by Jane Wyndham, of Cromer, and *dvp* 5 Nov 1818, leaving:

(1) **Sir John Hammer, 3rd Bt**, 1st and last BARON HANMER OF HANMER AND FLINT, both Co Flint (UK), so *cr* 1 Oct 1872; *b* 22 Dec 1809; *educ* Eton and Ch Ch Oxford; MP (C) Shrewsbury 1832–37 and Hull 1841–47 and (Lib) Flint Burghs 1847–72; *m* 3 Sept 1833 Georgiana (*d* 21 March 1880), yst dau of Sir George Chetwynd, 2nd Bt (*qv*), and *dsp* 8 March 1881, when the Barony expired

(2) WYNDHAM EDWARD (Sir), **4th Bt**

(3) Thomas; barrister; *b* 1813; *d* 1869

(4) Henry (Rev); MA Oxon, Rector Grendon; *b* 24 May 1814; *m* 11 Feb 1847 Sybella Elizabeth (*d* 17 Dec 1892), dau of George Gordon, of Olveston and Wincombe, Wilts, and *d* 11 Oct 1904, having had issue:

1a Charles Henry; *b* 1852; *d* 1864

2a John, JP Kent; *b* 27 Nov 1854; *m* 26 Aug 1890 Constance Catherine (*d* 19 June 1954), dau of Alexander Busby, of Cassillis, NSW, and *d* 17 April 1936, having had issue:

1b Henry Ivan, DFC and bar; G/Capt RAF, served WWs I and II, Order Nile; *b* 5 Feb 1893; *m* 1st 5 Aug 1937 Margaret Florence Mary (*d* 8 Sept 1947), only dau of Rev Henry Kenneth Warrand, of Westhorpe Hall, Southwell, Notts, and had:

1c +John Henry Warrand [John Hanmer Esq, Stubbins Farm, Stubbins Lane, Southwell, Notts]; *b* 19 Aug 1938; *educ* Eton; Capt 17th/21st Lancers, High Sheriff Notts 1981; *m* 3 Oct 1964 (*divorce* 1989) Penelope Clare, only dau of Sir Denis Le Marchant, 5th Bt (*qv*), and has:

1d +Thomas Stephen; *b* 28 Dec 1971

1d *Isobel Jane; *b* 8 Oct 1965

2d *Harriet Mary; *b* 22 Nov 1969

2c +(William) Richard; *b* 21 May 1945; *educ* Gresham's and Balliol Coll Oxford; *m* 1976 *Maria Paula Vianna, of Sao Paulo, and has:

1d +David Henry Vianna; *b* 1981

2d +Alexander Richard Vianna; *b* 1983

1c *Flora Elizabeth [Mrs Frederick Sasse, Hendy, Afonwen, Mold, Clwyd CH7 5UP]; *b* 26 Nov 1939; *m* 7 Oct 1967 Frederick John Sasse Jr (*d* 18 Nov 1994), s of Frederick John Sasse, of Linthicum Heights, Md., and has issue:

1d *Stephen John; *b* 28 Aug 1968

2d *Matthew Alexander; *b* 30 May 1974

3d *David Edward Jeremy; *b* 28 May 1979

1d *Selina Margaret; *b* 9 Jan 1970; *m* 7 Sept 1996 *Hon Edward James Frederick Penny, yst s of 3rd Viscount of Marchwood (*qv*)

1b (cont.) Henry Hanmer *m* 2nd 10 July 1954 *Lady Frances Jane Cole [The Lady Frances Hanmer, 1 Church Way, Grendon, Northants], 2nd dau of 5th Earl of Enniskillen (*qv*), and *d* 1984, having had by her:

3c Thomas Edward Trevor; *b* 28 May 1956; *d* 1980

2b Alexander John, MC; Lt E Kent Regt WW I (despatches, wounded); *b* 1896; *d* 7 Oct 1916 of wounds recd in action

3b Charles Gordon; Lt IA, WW I 1916–18, WW II 1940–43; *b* 14 July 1898; *educ* Gresham's; *m* 31 Aug 1940 *Winifred Beatrice, dau of Reginald Walter Harvey, of Stone, Tenterden, Kent, and adopted:

*John Charles Christopher [John Hanmer Esq, Nyanga Downs, Box 15, Troutbeck, Zimbabwe]; *b* 12 Dec 1954; *m* 20 Aug 1977 *Patricia Lesley Donnington, dau of Leslie John Donnington, of Stourport-on-Severn, Worcs, and has:

1b *Debbie Leigh Caroline; *b* 7 April 1988

*Jennifer Anne [Mrs Theodore Kloppenburg, 326 Eikenhof 1872, S Africa]; *b* 27 Aug 1946; *m* 1st 3 Feb 1965 (*divorce* 1967) Michael E Mallon; *m* 2nd 30 Nov 1968 *Theodore John Kloppenburg, s of T J Kloppenburg, of Nijmegen

4b William Francis Busby; Lt 97th (Kent Yeo) Bde (TAR); *m* 1st 15 Oct 1927 Margaret (*d* 28 Aug 1967), yst dau of Archibald Cameron Norman (*see* WAKE, Bt); *m* 2nd 19– *Bethia Ann, dau of Joseph Condy, of Umtali, and *d* 1980, leaving by his 1st w:

1c +John Anthony; *b* 27 Sept 1928; *m* 1st 1952 (*divorce* 1973) Margaret May, dau of I G Morrison, of Cape Town, and has:

1d +Quentin William; *b* 1952; *m* 1976 *Colleen, dau of J Campbell-Morrison, of Umtali

2d +Andrew Ian; *b* 3 July 1958

1d *Deborah Anne; *b* 1954; *m* 1974 *Muller Maas, of Umtali

1c (cont.) John Hanmer *m* 2nd 1973 *Dale Bernice, dau of J A Dickinson, of Johannesburg, and has issue:

2d *Julia Mary; *b* 1976

2c +Richard Norman Montagu, AMSAIMech E, PEng (Nova Scotia), MEIC; *b* 19 April 1937; *educ* Cape Town U (BSc Eng); *m* 1st 10 Aug 1963 Joyce Catherine (*d* following a car crash 3 Sept 1973), yr dau of Ernest Bawdon Philpot; *m* 2nd 1974 *Mrs Myrna Dorothy Tanner, dau of A G Plumb, of Bulawayo, and by his 1st w has issue:

1d +Anthony David; *b* 13 Jan 1967

1d *Gillian Margaret; *b* 22 Sept 1964; *m* 1985 *Way Choy and has:

1e *Jessica Joyce; *b* 1987

2e *Vanessa Mei Lei; *b* 1992

1c *Phoebe Margaret [Sister Phoebe Hanmer, Community of St Mary the Virgin, Wantage, Berks]; *b* 18 May 1931; Priest 1997

2c *Janet Virginia [Mrs Charles Sutherland, 24 Pine St, Buderim, Qld 4556, Australia]; *b* 28 June 1932; *m* 1971 Charles George Davies Sutherland (*d* 13 April 1995), and has issue:

1d *George Francis Hanmer; *b* 1972; *educ* Queensland U (BEng)

3c *Catherine Yvonne [Mrs Keith Allen, Old Presthayes, Eccliffe, Gillingham, Dorset SP8 5RE]; *b* 20 Jan 1936; *m* 8 Feb 1958 *Keith Allen, yr s of Guy Allen, of Chertsey, Surrey, and has issue:

1d *John Hanmer [John Allen Esq, Cranfield Cottage, Pyrford Rd, Pyrford, Surrey GU22 8UT]; *b* 3 Nov 1958; *m* 1984 *Jane Louise Ward-Lee, of Greenfield Hall, Laleham, Middx, and has:

1e *Hayley Claire; *b* 1986

2e *Olivia Catherine; *b* 1988

2d *Charles William [Charles Allen Esq, C4-13th flr, Greenery Gdns, 2A Mt Davis Rd, Pokfulam Rd, Hong Kong]; *b* 12 Aug 1960; *m* 1985 *Helen Frances Jones, of Mold, Clwyd, and has issue:

1e *Joanna Rachel; *b* 1988

2e *Catherine Rebecca; *b* 1992

3d *Stephen Guy [Stephen Allen Esq, 129 New Haw Rd, Addlestone, Surrey KT15 2DA]; *b* 14 Sept 1963; *m* 1988 *Giselle Victoria Margaret Becker, of Shepperton, Middx, and has:

1e *Guy Robert; *b* 1990

1e *Georgia Giselle; *b* 1993

2e *Phoebe Claire; *b* 14 March 1997

1d *Caroline Elizabeth [Mrs Craig Allan, 7360 Forney Hill Rd, Denver, NC 28037, USA]; *b* 8 Dec 1965; *m* 1991 *Craig James Allan, PhD, of Winnipeg, and has:

1e *Genevieve Catherine Armande; *b* 1994

2e *Skye Elizabeth; *b* 26 April 1996

5b Edward Glyndwr; *b* 10 Nov 1901; *d* 17 March 1917

1b Beatrice Mary Etheldreda; *b* 17 Oct 1891; *d* unm 2 Dec 1945

2b Dora Caroline; *b* 1894; *m* 3 Dec 1916 George Keith Homfray Hayter, Capt RFA (*d* 22 Dec 1968), est s of Rev Thomas Miller Hayter, Vicar E Acton, and *d* 8 Dec 1972, leaving issue:

1c *Richard; Lt RA WW II, Dir Productions West of England Theatre 1955–57, Resident Producer Guildford Theatre 1958–59, teacher Eng Lit Okehampton GS; *b* 16 March 1920; *educ* Bradfield and Christ's Coll Cambridge (BA 1947); *m* 9 Jan 1946 *Faith, dau of Lt-Col A S Bobby, RE, of Pulborough, Sussex, PWD, Ceylon, and has issue:

1d *David Keith; *b* 31 Jan 1950; *educ* Queen Elizabeth's Crediton

2d *Patrick Richard; *b* 14 Mar 1952; *educ* Queen Elizabeth's Crediton

1c *Diana Mary; *b* 28 Aug 1917; *m* 5 March 1946 *Henry Charles Ralph Fulford Williams, Colonial Admin Serv, s of Rev Henry Frank Fulford Williams, of Ideford Rectory, Newton Abbot, Devon, and has issue:

1d *Henry John; *b* 7 May 1954

1d *Catherine Claire; *b* 4 Feb 1948

2d *Mary Caroline; *b* 1 July 1949

2c *Sylvia Margaret [Mrs Adrian Longley, West Meon House, Petersfield, Hants]; *b* 2 July 1926; *m* 14 Dec 1957 *Adrian Reginald Longley, slr, s of Evelyn Longley, of Reigate Hill, Surrey, and has issue:

1d *Anne Mary Theodosia; *b* 25 March 1959

2d *Joanna Evelyn Clare; *b* 30 Nov 1960

3d *Melissa Frances Rose; *b* 27 Oct 1963

3c *Rosamond Clare [Mrs David Townshend, 15 Victoria Road, Sidcup, Kent]; *b* 15 July 1929; *m* 7 Aug 1954 *Maj David William Townshend, RE, s of Edmund Townshend, of Winchcombe, Glos, and has issue:

1d *Christopher Thomas Hayter; *b* 27 June 1956

2d *Richard Edmund; *b* 1 Nov 1967

1d *Gemma Mary; *b* 25 Jan 1959

2d *Helen Elizabeth; *b* 10 Nov 1960

3a Edward Wingfield; *b* 3 June 1856; *m* 1885 his cousin Catherine (*d* 19 May 1939), dau of Humphrey Hanmer (*see* below), and *d* 28 Feb 1901, leaving issue:

1b (Edward) Henry John, MC, MM; Lt RE WW I (despatches twice); *b* 1888; *m* 20 April 1922 Aileen Ethel (*d* 29 Aug 1954), dau of John Agnew Finley, of Belfast and Rio de Janeiro, and *d* 23 Aug 1969, leaving issue:

1c +John Richard; *b* 1925

2b Humphrey Richard; *b* 1890; *d* 23 Nov 1918

1b Evelyn Mary Harriet; *b* 1887; *m* 2 Nov 1916 Arthur Guy Durrant Scott, Lt Roy Fus, and *d* 3 May 1969, leaving issue. He *d* 18 Jan 1960

2b Florence Catherine Alicia; *b* 1895; *m* 5 April 1921 Lt Philip Tudor Newling, RFC, only s of Maj H T Newling, RAMC, of Paignton, Devon, and had issue

4a Thomas; *b* 13 Oct 1857; *m* 19 June 1891 Edith Mary (*d* 14 April 1905), dau of George Alfred Brittain, of The Lilies, Aylesbury, and 29 Dec 1923, leaving issue:

1b Guy Thomas; Hon Lt-Col 15th/19th Hus, Capt 19th Roy Hus, Maj 7th Bn Gloucester Regt (TA), served WWs I (wounded, despatches) and II (POW); *b* 22 Nov 1894; *m* 9 Aug 1919 Nancy (*d* 5 July 1976), widow of John Wilfred Munroe and yr dau of Duncan Anderson, and *d* 19 April 1951

1b Frances Sybella; *b* 21 March 1893; *m* 6 Sept 1916 Capt Edward Williams Hamilton Brookfield, RN, s of Col A M Brookfield, JP, and *d* 18 Sept 1964, leaving issue. He *d* 8 Feb 1965

2b Joan Florence, twin with her brother; *m* 1st 24 July 1917 Capt John Theobald Milne, MC, RFC, est s of Jack Milne, of The Brook House, Sutton Courtenay, Berks. He was reported missing 24 Oct 1917. She *m* 2nd 8 Feb 1923, as his 2nd w, Stuart Eddington Gay, yr s of William Gay, of Rye, and *d* 17 Dec 1975, leaving issue. He *d* 20 Aug 1967

5a Richard, JP Leics; *b* 21 April 1859; *m* 1st 22 July 1890 Catherine Alicia Louisa (*d* 5 June 1921), est dau of Maj Frederick Wollaston, 6th Dragoon Gds, of Shenton Hall, Leics; *m* 2nd 18 Oct 1923 Margaret (*d* 23 Aug 1960), er dau of Capt John Compton-Braceberidge, of Atherstone Hall, Warwicks, and *d* 28 Aug 1944, having by his 1st w had:

1b Dorothy Kathleen; *b* 27 June 1893; *m* 10 June 1930 Maj Henry Hawkins, OBE, JP, MFH, of Everdon Hall, Daventry, Northants, only s of Henry Ashurst Hawkins, and *d* 1 Jan 1957, leaving issue. He *d* 12 Aug 1930

2b Sybella Gwyneth; *b* 17 Dec 1894; *d* 5 June 1903

6a Hugh (Rev); Rector Selattyn 1927–31, RD Oswestry 1927–34; *b* 21 Jan 1862; *educ* St John's Coll Cambridge (MA); *m* 22 Aug 1894 Margaret Maude (*d* 19 Oct 1943), yr dau of Robert Peel Ethelston, JP, of Hinton, Salop, and *d* 21 Nov 1939, leaving issue:

1b Robert Hugh, OBE (1944), MC, DL Salop 1952; G/Capt RAF, Lt Roy Welch Fus WW I (despatches, wounded), WW II (despatches); *b* 25 Aug 1895; *m* 19 Dec 1922 Mary Helen (*d* 19 Sept 1945), yst dau of Nathaniel Spens (*see* SPENS, B), and *d* 18 Jan 1971, having had issue:

1c +Hugh Niel [Hugh Hanmer Esq, Fontevrault, Letcombe Regis, Oxon OX12 9JP]; *b* 23 April 1926; *educ* Corpus Christi Coll Cambridge (MA); *m* 22 Aug 1953 *Diana MacGeagh, only dau of Robert J MacGeagh Hurst, of Beckamoor, Lustleigh, Devon, and has issue:

1d +Robert David [Robert Hanmer Esq, 15C Brussels Rd, London SW11 2AF]; *b* 6 Dec 1957; *m* 1989 *Isabel, dau of John de Meur, of Sydney, NSW, and has issue:

1e *Daisy; *b* 1994

1d *Lucia Caroline; *b* 12 June 1956

1c Joan Margaret; *m* 7 Nov 1953 *Maj John Patrick Craw, RA, only s of Sir Henry Hewat Craw, KBE, CIE, and *d* 20 Aug 1954

2b Arthur Richard, MBE (1944), TD; Lt-Col Roy Welch Fus (TA), served WWs I and II; *b* 23 Jan 1899; *educ* Pembroke Coll Cambridge (BA); *m* 4 April 1929 Violet Millicent (*d* 19 Nov 1968), est dau of Maj William John Corbett Winder, of Vaynor Park, and *d* 10 May 1976, leaving issue:

1c +John Richard Lyon; *b* 12 July 1940; *educ* Eton

1c *Sara Elizabeth [Mrs Charles Michell, 10 Wandon Rd, London SW6 2JF]; *b* 10 March 1938; *m* 9 Nov 1973 *Charles Henry Wroughton Michell (*see* CARDEN, Bt, of Wimpole St), s of A H Michell, of Eye, Suffolk, and has:

1d *Samuel Richard Alfred; *b* 20 July 1979; *educ* Eton

3b Edward Alfred; *b* 19 March 1901; *d* 4 May 1903

4b Stephen Henry, TD; Hon Maj TAR Offrs Durham LI WW II (wounded); *b* 22 Sept 1906; *educ* Shrewsbury and St John's Coll Cambridge (BA); *d* 19–

5b John Michael, DSO (1945), OBE (1952); Brig Durham LI WW II (despatches), Chev Crown Belgium with palm, Belgian Croix de Guerre with palm; *b* 29 Sept 1907; *educ* Shrewsbury and RMC Sandhurst; *m* 29 Sept 1934 *Esther [Mrs John Hanmer, Tarrant Monkton Cottage, Blandford, Dorset], yst dau of Reginald Adam Black, JP, DL, of Prees Hall, Whitchurch, Salop, and *d* 17 June 1977, leaving:

1c +Michael David Adam [Michael Hanmer Esq, The Old Granary, Gt Wilbraham, Cambs]; late 2nd Lt Durham LI, *b* 30 May 1935; *educ* Stowe and Clare Coll Cambridge (BA 1958); *m* 4 Jan 1964 *Judy Carol, yr dau of Cecil Jack Fairchild, of Tunbridge Wells, and has issue:

1d *Clare Lucinda; *b* 27 Sept 1965; *educ* Clare Coll Cambridge (BA)

2d *Julia Caroline; *b* 17 May 1968; *educ* BNC Oxford (BA)

2c +Richard John (Rev) [The Rev Canon Richard Hanmer, 52 The Close, Norwich, Norfolk NR1 2EG]; late 2nd Lt Durham LI; *b* 6 April 1938; *educ* Peterhouse Cambridge (BA 1961, MA 1965) and Scholae Cancellarii Lincoln; *m* 1972 *Sheila, only dau of Robert King, of Wolverhampton, and has issue:

1d +Jonathan James; *b* 1 Feb 1974; *educ* Kingston U (BA 1996)

2d +Adam Robert; *b* 4 Jan 1976; *educ* Sheffield U (BSc 1997)

1d *Frances Rachel; *b* 1982

3c Henry; *b* 23 March 1943; *educ* Shrewsbury; *m* 1972 *Cristina Beatriz [Mrs José Oliveri-Biagiani, Av Gral Santander 1782, Apt 202, Carrasco, Montevideo, Uruguay] (*m* 2nd 1991 José Oliveri-Biagiani), dau of Prof Hector D'Elia, of Montevideo, and *d* 1989, leaving issue:

1d +Edward John; *b* 1974

2d +Stephen Patrick; *b* 1975

1b *Margaret Evelyn, CBE (1957); *b* 4 Oct 1896; *m* 24 Sept 1936 Maj Bertie Edward Parker Leighton (*see* LEIGHTON, Bt)

2b *Ruth Henrietta; *b* 24 May 1905; *m* 24 April 1934 Fitzherbert Edward Shallcross Jackson, of Tedsmore Hall, Oswestry, and has issue

7a Stephen Trevor; *b* 2 May 1863; *d* 20 July 1937

1a Sybella; *d* an infant

2a Arabella Frances; *b* 24 April 1900 Rev Arthur Wellesley Batson, BMus Oxford, Rector Ringstead, Norfolk, and *d* 9 Oct 1913

3a Mary Henrietta; *d* unm 30 Jan 1930

4a Alicia Georgina; *m* 3 June 1879 Rev Henry Hepworth Allott, Rector Stifford, Essex, and *d* 9 Sept 1930, leaving issue. He *d* 1913

5a Sybil Christiana; *m* 10 Oct 1906 Rev Henry Fortescue Ostrehan, Vicar Whatton-in-the-Vale 1906–09, Barholm with Stowe 1909–24 and W Tisted 1924–27, and *d* 17 Feb 1945, leaving issue
6a Evelyn Anna; *d* unm 17 June 1954
7a Ada Cecilia; *d* unm 28 July 1928
(1) Charlotte Emma; *m* 22 Oct 1839 Lord Charles Lennox Kerr and *d* 10 April 1887, leaving issue (*see* LOTHIAN, M)
(2) Margaret Maria; *m* 27 Nov 1837 Richard Baker Wingfield Baker, MP, of Orsett Hall, Essex, and *d* 25 April 1873, leaving issue. He *d* 25 April 1880
(3) Caroline; *d* unm 4 Sept 1908 aged 90
2 Job Walden, of Lincoln's Inn, barrister; *d* 1850
3 John (Rev); MA, Vicar Hanmer; *b* 28 Feb 1784; *m* 19 Sept 1816 Catherine (*d* 27 June 1860), dau of Sir Thomas Whichcote, 5th Bt (*see* 1949 edn), and *d* 4 Oct 1850, leaving issue:
(1) Anthony John; *b* 1817; *d* unm 1 Nov 1909
(2) Francis Henry; Col Indian Service; *b* 20 Oct 1825; *m* 16 Oct 1860 Mary Ann Catherine (*d* 9 June 1879), dau of Charles Gordon, and *d* 2 Feb 1876, leaving issue:
1a Walden Henry John; *b* 11 July 1861; *d* 14 Aug 1876
2a Norman Gordon Whichcote; *b* 3 Aug 1863; *d* 8 July 1924
1a Flora Emmeline Mary; *m* 23 Aug 1887 Charles Thomas Gordon, DL, of Cairness, Aberdeenshire, and *d* 4 Oct 1951, leaving issue. He *d* 27 March 1938
(3) Humphrey, of NZ; *b* 1827; *m* 1856 Harriet (*d* 2 June 1912), dau of George Batterbee, and *d* 1892, leaving:
1a George; *b* 1859; *m* 1885 Ruth (*d* 1946), dau of C Percy Cox, of Christchurch, NZ, and *d* 15 June 1934, leaving:
1b Humphrey George; *b* 1886; *m* 1st 2 June 1914 (*divorce* 1924) Beatrice Winifred, dau of George Sumpter, of NZ; *m* 2nd 30 Sept 1925 Muriel Emma (*d* 1985), dau of George Henry Bostock, of Staunton Springs, W Australia, and *d* 24 Nov 1936, leaving by her:
1c *Elizabeth Muriel; *b* 5 Sept 1929; *m* 1951 Arthur Cecil John Coates (*d* 1958), and has issue:
1d *David John [David Coates Esq, 8 Weldon Way, City Beach, 6015 Perth, W Australia]; *b* 1953; *m* 1983 *Julie Howard, and has:
1e *Christopher Michael; *b* 1985
1e *Ellen Margaret; *b* 1987
1d *Anne Muriel; *b* 1955
2b John Percy; AIF WW I; *b* 1889; *ka* Gallipoli 1916
3b Anthony Hugh; NZ Expdny Force; *b* 1890; *ka* Gallipoli 1916
1b Dorothy Harriet; *b* 28 Jan 1888; *d* 22 Aug 1918
2b Madeline Ruth; *b* 18 Sept 1890; *m* 18 Dec 1912 Reginald Percy Wilder and had issue. He *d* 9 Aug 1960
3b Municent Clara; *b* 1891; *m* 16 Nov 1917 Lt-Col Vincent Lee Dean, VD, Rlwy Dept Govt India, of Lahore, and had issue. He *d* 21 July 1942
1a Catherine; *m* 1885 her cousin Edward Wingfield Hanmer and *d* 19 May 1939, leaving issue (*see* above)
(4) Philip; *m* 12 Nov 1863 Frances, dau of James Tipping, and *dsp* 3 Nov 1878
(5) George; *b* 4 Sept 1833; *m* 13 July 1871 Margaret Eliza (*d* 1918), dau of Rev William Spencer Edwards, of Lewes, and *d* 16 Feb 1906, leaving issue:
1a Thomas Anthony; *b* 17 April 1872; *d* unm 22 July 1958
(1) Sophia; *m* John Lees Ainsworth and *d* 1882, leaving issue
(2) Catherine; *m* James Holmes and *d* 1845, leaving issue
4 George Edward (Rev); Rector Loddington and Overstone, Northants; *b* 28 Aug 1786; *dsp* 3 Aug 1857
5 Henry; Lt-Col KH, MP; *b* 23 Jan 1789; *m* 27 Jan 1815 Sarah Serra (*d* 29 June 1847), only dau of Sir Morris Ximenes, and *dsp* 2 Feb 1868
6 William; barrister Inner Temple; *b* 28 Feb 1792; *m* 7 Feb 1820 Euphemia Mary, only dau and heir of John Forbes, of Bodnod Hall, Denbighs, and *d* 26 Aug 1872, having had, with two daus (*d* unm):
(1) William, of Bodnod, JP; Maj 87th Fus; *b* 1824; *d* unm 26 May 1894
(2) Thomas, of Talgai, Australia; *b* 22 July 1827; *m* 1857 Fanny (*d* 14 Feb 1912), 2nd dau of George West, of Dromore House, Co Leitrim, and *d* 1892, leaving issue:
1a Thomas William; *b* July 1888; *m* 12 Oct 1911 Ivy Mira Frances (*d* 1 July 1965), only dau of Charles John Dodd, and *d* 15 Sept 1950, having had:
1b Patrick William Talgai; Capt RN WW II, Sec to Hon Co Edinburgh Golfers, Muirfield (Hon Life Memb); *b* 9 June 1915; *educ* Nautical Coll Pangbourne; *m* 1992 *Mrs Sadie Rydings, of Broombrough, Wirral, and *d* June 1995
2b +Nicholas Brian, MBE (1961) [Maj Nicholas Hanmer MBE, Westholme West, Cumberland St, Woodbridge, Suffolk]; Maj Roy Sussex Regt WW II (seconded Para Regt 1943–49), Sr DC Colonial Serv; *b* 18 July 1921; *educ* Nautical Coll Pangbourne; *m* 1st 7 Jan 1944 Felicity Mary (*d* 23 April 1967), only dau of Frank William Sly, of Bruton, Somerset; *m* 2nd 1970 *Betty May, dau of Harry Smith, of Sudbury Hill, and by his 1st w has:
1c +David Nicholas Frank [Maj David Hanmer, Buckland, Slapton, Kingsbridge, Devon]; Maj Para Regt; *b* 7 Sept 1944; *educ* Nautical Coll Pangbourne; *m* 1st 1968 (*divorce* 1977) Susan, dau of George Inverarity, DFC, of Brighton; *m* 2nd 1978 *Sarah, dau of Dr Roger Blackney, of Kirkham Babbacombe, Torquay, Devon, and by his 1st w has had issue:
1d Guy David; *b* 1971; *d* 1989
1d *Emma Jane; *b* 1969
2d *A dau; *b* 1973
2c +Oliver William; *b* 22 Sept 1955; *m* 1st 1977 (*divorce* 1989) Christine Ann, dau of Jeffrey Benjamin Woodin, of N Walsham, Norfolk; *m* 2nd 1994 *Melinda Lee, dau of Colin Zweck, of Henty, NSW, and by his 1st w has issue:
1d +Gavin Edward; *b* 1982
1d *Claire Louise; *b* 1980
1c *Jill Elizabeth [Mrs Jill Peachey, 23 Eugarie St, Noosa Heads, Qld 4567, Australia]; *b* 5 Oct 1951; *m* 1st 1978 (*divorce* 1981) Iain Murray; *m* 2nd 1981 (*divorce* 1996) Christopher Kenneth Peachey, only s of Kenneth Cavalier Peachey
1b Moyra Frances; WW II as 3rd Offr WRNS; *b* 8 Aug 1912; *m* 20 Feb 1943 Capt Markham Henry Evelegh, MVO, RN, Sec Roy Yacht Sqdn, only s of Markham Aldridge Evelegh, and had:
1c *Patrick John Markham; 2nd Offr P&O SS *Orcades*; *b* 27 Jan 1944; *educ* Nautical Coll Pangbourne
1c *Nicola Anne Moyra; *b* 2 June 1950
2b *Sheila Helen; WW II in ATS; *b* 2 Oct 1913; *m* 1st 8 March 1941 (*divorce*1946) 2nd Lt Donald Harry Munro, RA, s of H T Munro, of Hove; *m* 2nd 1958 *Ronald Coleridge
3b *Denys Beryl [Mrs Peter McLaughlin, 111–1485 Garnet Rd, Victoria, BC V8P 5K9, Canada]; *b* 27 May 1917; *m* 1st 1 Aug 1939 (*divorce* 1942) Maj Charles Harry Campbell, IA (*d* 1944); *m* 2nd 23 Aug 1943 Maj Peter Michael Harry Dalzel McLaughlin (*d* 1971), CD, IA, and Canadian Army, s of Lt-Col H D McLaughlin, of BC, and by him has issue:
1c *Kevin Michael Dalzell [Kevin McLaughlin, 204–830 Shamrock St, Victoria, BC V8X 2V1, Canada]; *b* 9 Jan 1949; *m* 15 Feb 1969 *Bonnie Shirley, dau of Ralph Douglas Davies, of Victoria, BC, and has issue:
1d *Dalzell Michael Talgai; *b* 1969; *m* June 1996 *Kelly May, dau of Rheal Sauriol and has:
1e *Dallas Eric Dalzall; *b* 6 Aug 1997
1d *Maya Denys Shirley; *b* 1972; *m* 1991 *John Russell Battiste Carter, and has issue:
1e *Malia Rebecca; *b* 20 Nov 1992
2e *Cheyenne Jessica Frances; *b* 10 Feb 1994
3e *Tanisha Brooke; *b* 23 Sept 1996
2d *Kara Bonnie Shawne; *b* 1980
3d *Dana Michelle Tami; *b* 21 July 1982
2c *Shawn Denys Dalzell [Shawn McLaughlin, 4621 Pipeline Rd, Victoria BC, Canada]; *b* 23 May 1955
1c *Maureen Daphne Hanmer [Mrs David Carter, 866 Latoria Road, Victoria, BC, Canada]; *b* 17 July 1944; *m* 11 Mar 1967 *David Walter Carter, only s of L C Carter, of Woodstock, Ontario, and has:
1d *Blair Alexander; *b* 1974
1d *Elektra Arlene; *b* 1980
2c *Meira Patricia [Mrs Logan Mathison, 4807 Townsend Drive, Victoria, BC, Canada]; *b* 2 Dec 1951; *m* 1st 1970 (*divorce* 1984) Gary Wayne Tennent; *m* 2nd 1987 *Logan Eric Mathison and by her 1st husb has:
1d *Leah Michelle; *b* 1975
2d *Stephanie Annette; *b* 1977
4b Daphne Veda; *b* 18 June 1918; *d* 3 May 1938
1a Fanny Madeline Jane; *m* 1st 6 Oct 1898 Lt-Col George Leonard Thomson, 1st Roy Sussex Regt (*dsp* 14 Oct 1898); *m* 2nd 13 Nov 1900 Augustus William West, of Leixlip House, Co Kildare, and *d* 5 Aug 1920, leaving issue
(3) John, twin with Thomas; *d* unm 1862
(4) Kenyon James; *b* 6 Aug 1829; *d* unm 7 Sept 1858
(1) Margaret; *m* 25 March 1851 T C Sandars, and *d* 1873
(2) Arabella Elizabeth; *m* 12 April 1860 G Everett, and had issue
(3) Emma Georgina; *m* 21 Nov 1868 Edward Bromley, yst s of Adml Sir Robert Howe Bromley, 3rd Bt (*qv*), and *dsp* 1891
1 Margaret; *m* 1 Feb 1803 2nd Baron Kenyon (*qv*) and *d* 24 Feb 1815, leaving issue

The 3rd Bt's bro,

Sir Wyndham Edward Hanmer, 4th Bt, JP, DL Flintshire and Beds; Maj RHG, High Sheriff Flintshire 1885; *b* 24 Dec 1810; *m* 1st 10 March 1842 Maria Louise Victoire (*d* 9 Feb 1866), yr dau of Sir John Conroy, 1st Bt (see 1900 edn), and had issue; *m* 2nd 2 Oct 1877 Harriet Frances (*dsp* 17 May 1911), est dau of Col Hon Henry Hely-Hutchinson (*see* DONOUGHMORE, E), and *d* 25 Aug 1887 leaving by his 1st w:

Sir Edward John Henry Hanmer, 5th Bt; *b* 15 April 1843; *m* 31 Oct 1865 Mary Elizabeth (*d* 19 Dec 1914), dau of Col Richard Cottenham Fosse, and had issue:
1 WYNDHAM CHARLES HENRY (Sir), **6th Bt**
2 Owen Herbert John; *b* 8 July 1873; *d* 9 Jan 1874
1 Florence Victoria Caroline Mary; *m* June 1894 Charles Osbaldeston Firman, of Quarry Cottage, Norton, Malton, and *d* 28 May 1926, leaving issue

Sir EDWARD *d* 3 May 1893; his only surv son,

Sir Wyndham Charles Henry Hanmer, 6th Bt, JP, DL Flintshire; High Sheriff 1902, Maj Gen List Supt Remount Service 1915–18; *b* 17 Sept 1867; *m* 16 April 1890 Essex (*d* 7 Dec 1952), est dau of William Selby-Lowndes, of Whaddon Hall, and Winslow, Bucks, and had issue:
1 GRIFFIN WYNDHAM EDWARD (Sir), **7th Bt**
1 (Victoria) Violet Essex; *m* 16 June 1917 Dagium John William Fletewode Selby-Lowndes, MC, Gren Gds, s of Rev Octavius William Cotton Selby-Lowndes, Rector Mursley, Winslow, Bucks, and *d* 7 Jan 1974 aged 81, leaving issue. He *d* 13 Nov 1939
2 Marguerite Frances; High Sheriff Montgomeryshire 1946; *d* unm 16 Dec 1975
3 Heather; WW I with VAD and YMCA, and WW II, Hon Sec and Treas Kidderminster Branch Br Sailors' Soc to 1955; *d* unm 26 April 1977 aged 80
4 Myrtle Evelyn; Ambulance Driver WW II and Leamington Borough Police Force 1942–46; *m* 12 Oct 1940 Lt-Col Arthur Graves Leech, DSO, Legn Hon, LLD, RA, est s of H Broughton Leech, LLD, of Yew Park, Clontarf, Co Dublin, and *dsp* 11 Dec 1960. He *d* 17 Feb 1953

Sir WYNDHAM *d* 3 June 1922; his only son,

Sir (Griffin Wyndham) Edward Hanmer, 7th Bt, JP (Salop 1921); High Sheriff 1932; *educ* Wellington; Lt-Col Capt Shropshire Yeo and RAF, memb Nat Hunt Ctee, Sr Steward Jockey Club 1944–45, MFH Sir Watkin Williams-Wynn's Hounds 1946–53; *b* 30 Aug 1893; *m* 1st 25 Aug 1921 Aileen Mary (*d* 26 Sept

1967), er dau of Capt John Edwin Rogerson, OBE, of Mount Oswald, Durham, and had issue:

1 Sir JOHN WYNDHAM EDWARD HANMER, **8th and present Bt**

1 *Joan Essex; *b* 25 July 1922

2 *Pamela Aileen [Pamela Lady Wilson, Lillingstone Lovell Manor, Bucks MK18 5BQ]; *b* 24 Aug 1923; *m* 16 June 1947 Capt Sir Thomas Douglas Wilson, 4th Bt of Airdrie (*qv*), and has issue

3 *Evelyn Mary; *b* 3 Feb 1926

Sir Edward *m* 2nd 23 Nov 1968 Angela Mary (*d* 27 Sept 1977), widow of Richard Nightingdale Bromley and dau of Frederick William Morley, of Cossington Hall, Leics, and *d* 1 Jan 1977

HANSON, Baron

Arms: Vert, in fess point a rose argent barbed and seeded proper between six like roses three and three in pale. **Crest:** On a wreath or and vert a demi-chestnut horse proper, charged on the shoulder with a rose argent, barbed, seeded, slipped and leaved proper. **Supporters:** Dexter, a bulldog in trian aspect with a Viking helmet of the 7th century gilded and verde antico on his head proper; sinister, an American bald eagle also proper. **Motto:** *Prima peto* ('I seek what is foremost'). **Creation:** B. (LP, UK) 1983.

BARON HANSON, of Edgerton, Co of West Yorkshire (Sir James Edward Hanson) [The Rt Hon The Lord Hanson, 1 Grosvenor Place, London SW1X 7JH]; *b* 20 Jan 1922; served WW II; chm Hanson plc 1965–97 (chm emeritus 1998–), dir Hanson Tport Gp 1965–; Freeman City London 1964, Liveryman Saddlers' Co 1964, ktd 1976, Memb Court Patrons Roy Coll Surgeons 1991; Tstee Hanson Fellowship Surgery Oxford U, Fell Cancer Research Campaign; Hon LLD Leeds, Hon DBA Huddersfield, Hon Fell St Peter's Coll Oxford, FRSA, CIMgt; *m* 1959 *Geraldine Kaelin and has:

1 *Robert William; *b* 1960; *educ* Eton and St Peter's Coll Oxford; dir Hanson plc 1992–97, chm Hanson Transport Gp, formerly with N M Rothschild

2 *(John) Brook (does not use courtesy title); *b* 1964; *educ* Pangbourne

Lineage: ROBERT HANSON, CBE, of Huddersfield, Yorks; *m* Louisa Anne (Cis) Rodgers and had:

JAMES EDWARD, *cr* a **Baron**

HANSON, Bt

Arms: Arg. three lions rampant in chevron between as many mascles az. **Crest:** A lion rampant az., holding in the dexter forepaw an antler or and resting the sinister paw upon two mascles fessways and interlaced of the last. **Motto:** *Semper parare* ('Always preparing'). **Creation:** Bt. (UK) 6 July 1918.

SIR (CHARLES) RUPERT PATRICK HANSON, 4TH BT, of Fowey, Co Cornwall [Sir Rupert Hanson Bt, 125 Ditchling Rd, Brighton BN1 4SE]; *b* 25 June 1945; *s* f 1996; *educ* Eton; *m* 16 April 1977 *Wanda Julia, dau of Arturo Larrain, of Santiago, Chile, and has issue:

1 +ALEXIS CHARLES; *b* 25 March 1978

Lineage: JOSEPH HANSON, of Fratton, Hants; *b* 13 Feb 1768; *m* 5 March 1804 Sarah Thorp (*d* 21 Sept 1859) and *d* 28 May 1827; his only s:

JOSEPH HANSON, of Fowey, Cornwall; *b* 22 Dec 1820; *m* Mary Anne, dau of William Hicks, of Fowey, and was drowned at sea 3 Jan 1868, leaving an est s:

Sir Charles Augustin Hanson, 1st Bt (UK), so *cr* 6 July 1918, JP, DL Cornwall, JP City London; High Sheriff Cornwall 1907, Lt City London, Alderman Broad Street and City of London 1909–21, Sheriff 1911–12, Ld Mayor 1917–18, MP (U) Bodmin 1916–22, Col Cmdt 4th City of London Vols 1915, KGStJ, chm Gresham Life Assur, ptnr Coates, Son & Co, Order Franz Josef 1908, Redeemer Greece, Rising Sun Japan, Grand Offr Crown Italy, Cdr Legn Hon; *b* 11 Sept 1846; *m* 16 June 1869 Martha Sabina (*d* 8 Jan 1924), yst dau of James Appelbe, JP, of Trafalgar, Halton, Canada, and had:

1 CHARLES EDWIN BOURNE (Sir), **2nd Bt**

1 Alice Maud Appelbe, Order of Mercy; *m* 28 Nov 1906 Maj-Gen Sir Frederick Cuthbert Poole, KBE, CB, CMG, DSO, JP, DL, of Torfrey, Par, Cornwall, s of Rev R H Poole, Rector Rainton, Co Durham, and *d* 12 June 1952, leaving issue. He *d* 20 Dec 1936

Sir CHARLES *d* 17 Jan 1922; his only son,

Sir Charles Edwin Bourne Hanson, 2nd Bt; *b* 17 May 1874; *educ* Clare Coll Cambridge (MA); Lt City London, High Sheriff Cornwall 1939, memb London Stock Exchange, ptnr Coates, Son & Co, Maj 3rd W R Regt Boer War 1899–1902 (two medals, three clasps) and WW I; *m* 29 April 1908 Violet Sybil (*d* 8 Jan 1966), 3rd dau of John B Johnstone, and *d* 7 Sept 1958, leaving issue:

1 **Sir (Charles) John Hanson, 3rd Bt**; *b* 28 Feb 1919; *educ* Eton and Clare Coll Cambridge; Capt DCLI WW II, memb London Stock Exchange, ptnr Simon and Coates 1947–80; *m* 1st 22 Jan 1944 (*divorce* 1968) Patricia Helen, only child of Adml Sir (Eric James) Patrick Brind, GBE, KCB, and had:

(1) Sir (CHARLES) RUPERT PATRICK HANSON, **4th and present Bt**

(1) *Bridget Clare; *b* 11 April 1948; *m* 23 Aug 1969 *Michael Grahame Cloete Graham-Cloete, s of M D C Graham, and has issue:

1a *James Montrose Stuart; *b* 11 May 1975

1a *Hermione Clare; *b* 28 April 1977

1 (cont.) **Sir John** *m* 2nd 7 Nov 1968 *(Violet) Helen [Helen Lady Hanson, 11 Osborne Ct, Lime Tree Rd, Norwich NR2 2NN], formerly w of Capt Philip Cecil Landon Yorke, OBE, RN (*see* HARDWICKE, E), and only dau of Charles Ormonde Trew, and *d* 30 March 1996

1 *(Violet Alice) Rosalind [Mrs Rosalind Poole, Mount Pleasant, Tellisford, nr Bath BA3 6RL]; *b* 11 March 1909; *m* 3 April 1930 (*divorce* 1970) Capt Robert Godmond Poole, RN, s of Rev Francis Oswald Poole, Rector Mucklestone, and has had:

(1) Scilla Rosalind; *b* 27 Sept 1935; *m* 9 May 1964 (*divorce* 1982) Anthony Francis Raikes, er s of Julian Henry Raikes, and *d* 1991, leaving:

1a *Simon Anthony [Simon Raikes Esq, 2 Plato Rd, London SW2 5UR]; *b* 28 March 1965; *m* 1989 (*divorce* 19–) Hon Tamsin Margaret Jay, dau of Baroness Jay of Paddington (*qv*)

1a *Vanessa Rosalind; *b* 1972

(2) *Serena Mary; *b* 16 Feb 1944

2 Edwina Marjorie Clare; *b* 11 May 1912; *m* 8 Aug 1940 Maj-Gen Ralph Cyril Cruddas, CB, DSO and bar, DCLI, s of Rev William Sandwith Cruddas, Rector Withiel, Cornwall, and had issue:

(1) *Sarah Joslyn; *b* 27 May 1942; *m* 25 May 1968 *Ronald Murray Brown, 3rd s of Ronald Havelock Scothern Brown, and has issue:
1a *Katherine Rose; *b* 31 May 1969
(2) *Julia Rose; *b* 1 April 1949
(3) *Joanna Clare; *b* 30 June 1951

HANWORTH

Arms: Az. three fleurs-de-lys within a bordure engrailed or, on a chief erm. two portcullises of the second. **Crest:** A boar passant quarterly or and vert, pierced through the sinister shoulder with an arrow ppr. **Supporters:** On either side a bear or, muzzled, collared and chained sa. **Motto:** *Audacter et strenue* ('Boldly and strenuously'). **Creation:** Bt. (UK) 27 Nov 1922, B. (UK) 28 Jan 1926, V. (UK) 17 Jan 1936.

THE 3RD VISCOUNT HANWORTH, **Baron Hanworth**, of Hanworth, Co Middlesex, and a **Baronet** (Sir David Stephen Geoffrey Pollock, Bt) [The Rt Hon The Viscount Hanworth, 12 Gladsmuir Rd, London N19 3JX]; *b* 16 Feb 1946; *s* f 1996; *educ* Wellington, Guildford Tech and Sussex U; Reader econometrics London U; *m* 19 Oct 1968 *Elizabeth Liberty, dau of Lawrence Vambe, of Harare, Zimbabwe, and has issue:

1 *Cecile Abigail Shona; *b* 5 Aug 1971
2 *Charlotte Anne Catherine; *b* 1973

Lineage: GEORGE FREDERICK POLLOCK; barrister (*see* POLLOCK, Bt); had a 4th s:

Sir Ernest Murray Pollock, 1st Bt, so *cr* 27 Nov 1922, as also 28 Jan 1926 **Baron Hanworth**, of Hanworth, Co Middlesex, and 17 Jan 1936 **1st Viscount Hanworth** (all UK), KBE (1917), PC (1922), KC (1905), JP Herts; *b* 25 Nov 1861; *educ* Charterhouse and Trin Coll Cambridge (MA); barrister Inner Temple 1885 (Treas, Bencher 1914), MP (U) Warwick and Leamington 1910–23, Slr-Gen 1919–22, Attorney-Gen March-Oct 1922, Master Rolls 1923–35, Recorder Kingston-upon-Thames 1911–23, High Steward Stratford-on-Avon 1934, Hon LLD Cambridge and Warsaw, Offr Legn Hon and SS. Maurice and Lazarus Italy; *m* 12 April 1887 Laura Helen (*d* 16 Feb 1954), est dau of Sir Thomas Salt, 1st Bt, MP, of Weeping Cross (*qv*), and *d* 22 Oct 1936, having had:

1 Charles Thomas Anderson; Capt Inns of Court OTC, attd 1st/4th E Yorks; *b* 12 April 1889; *educ* Trin Coll Cambridge (BA); *m* 19 Jan 1915 Alice Joyce (*d* 6 Dec 1950), er dau of John Henry Becher, and was *ka* 31 March 1918, leaving:

(1) DAVID BERTRAM POLLOCK, **2nd Viscount Hanworth**; *b* 1 Aug 1916; *educ* Wellington and Trin Coll Cambridge (BA 1939); CEng, MIMechE, FIEE, FIQA, FRPS, barrister Inner Temple 1958, Lt-Col RE WW II, Assist Dir Consumer Cncl, author books on colour photography; *m* 27 April 1940 *Isolda Rosamond, JP, DL, yr dau of Geoffrey Parker (*see* MACCLESFIELD, E), and *d* 31 Aug 1996, leaving:

1a (DAVID) STEPHEN GEOFFREY POLLOCK, **3rd and present Viscount Hanworth**

2a +(RICHARD) CHARLES STANDISH, TD (1986) [Maj The Hon Charles Pollock TD, Brook House, North End, Gt Dunmow, Essex CM6 3PQ]; *b* 6 Feb 1951; heir presumptive; *educ* Wellington and Trin Coll Cambridge; Maj Roy Yeo T&AVR; *m* 1982 *Annette Louise, dau of Peter Lockhart, and has issue:

1b +Harold William Charles; *b* 1988
2b +Frederick Thomas Charles; *b* 1988

1a *Gillian Isolda Josephine [The Hon Mrs Gillian Sarson, 8 Gatcombe Rd, London N19 4PT]; *b* 1 April 1944; *m* 24 Aug 1963 (*divorce* 1991) Timothy von Weber Sarson, s of H S R Sarson, FDS, RCS Edin, LDS, RCS Lond, and has issue:

1b *Cosmo Harold Anthony; *b* 1971
2b *Alexander; *b* 1977
1b *Emma Isolda; *b* 1964; *m* 1984 (*divorce* 1997) Hugh Davies, only s of Lt-Col R M W Davies, MC, and has issue:
1c *Bryn; *b* 1987
2c *Holly; *b* 1989
2b *(Ellen Georgina) Hester; *b* 1975

1 Marjorie Laura; *m* 16 Jan 1926 Sir (Walter) Leslie Farrer, KCVO, 2nd s of Bryan Farrer, of Binnegar Hall, Wareham, and had:

(1) *(Charles) Matthew (Sir), GCVO (1994, KCVO 1983, CVO 1973) [Sir Matthew Farrer GCVO , 6 Priory Avenue, London W4 1TX]; *b* 3 Dec 1929; *educ* Bryanston and Balliol Coll Oxford; ptnr Farrer & Co, slrs, 1959–94, slr to HM THE QUEEN 1965–94, Tstee Br Museum 1989– and Lambeth Palace Library 1991–, Commr Roy Commn Historical MSS. 1991–, memb Br Library Bd 1994–; *m* 4 Jan 1962 *Johanna Creszentia Maria Dorothea, yst dau of Prof Dr Hans-Hermann Bennhold, and has:

1a *Luke Leslie; *b* 22 July 1970
1a *Jenett Mabella; *b* 14 Oct 1965

(1) *Laura Leslie Jenett [Mrs Edward Garden, Norwood, 91 Millhouses Lane, Sheffield S7 2HD]; *b* 28 March 1932; *educ* St Andrews (MA); *m* 8 April 1961 *Prof Edward James Clarke Garden, DMus, FRCO, s of Thomas Clarke Garden, and has:

1a *Jonathan Matthew Kenneth; *b* 5 June 1962
1a *Nicola Laura Jean; *b* 6 Aug 1963

HARBERTON

Arms: Or a lion rampant gu., armed and langued az., holding between the paws an apple ppr. **Crests:** A lion rampant gu., holding between the paws an apple ppr. **Supporters:** Two wolves; the dexter, ppr., sinister, arg., both plain-collared and chained or. **Motto:** *Virtutis fortuna comes* ('Fortune is the companion of valour'). **Creation:** B. (I) 10 Oct 1783, V. (I) 5 July 1791.

THE 10TH VISCOUNT HARBERTON and **Baron Harberton of Carbery**, Co Kildare (Thomas de Vautort Pomeroy) [Lt-Col The Rt Hon The Viscount Harberton, 2 Hazely Manor, Rohais, Guernsey, CI]; *b* 19 Oct 1910; *s* bro 1980; *educ* Eton; Lt-Col (ret) RAOC, Lt Welsh Gds; *m* 1st 2 Feb 1939 (*divorce* 1946) Nancy Ellen, only dau of C A Penoyer, of San Francisco; *m* 2nd 4 Sept 1950 Paula Stafford (*d* 11 May 1971), only dau of Wilfred Sydney Baker, of Stoke, Plymouth, Devon; *m* 3rd 1978 *Wilhelmine (Vilma), dau of Heinrich Wahl and widow of Sir Alfred Butt, 1st Bt (*qv*)

Lineage: RALPH de la POMERALI (other subsequent variations are Pomerlo, de Pomeri, de la Pomeral as well as the current Pomeroy), follower of WILLIAM I (THE CONQUEROR) in latter's invasion of England 1066; granted 58 lordships in Devon. A principal manor, indeed it would seem the chief seat, was Berry Pomeroy, Devon. RALPH was ancestor of:

Sir THOMAS POMEROY; sold Berry Pomeroy Castle to the Duke of Somerset 1548; a leader Western Rising 1549, for which heavily fined. A line of POMEROYs of Tregony Pomeroy, Cornwall, descended from Hugh, yr brother of Sir Thomas. Other principal lines were those of St Columb and St Neot, Cornwall, and Sandbridge, Brixham and Ingeson (Ilsington), Devon, the last deriving from the original Berry Pomeroy line.

ROBERT POMEREY, of Ingesdon Manor (later Ilsington), Devon; *m* Elizabeth, only dau and heir of John Beaumont, of Ingesdon, and *d* 3 Jan 1517, leaving:

ST CLEER POMEREY, of Ingesdon; *m* Joanna Young (living 15 June 1533) and had:

JOHN POMEREY, of Ingesdon; *m* Elizabeth — and *d* 1532/3, leaving:

HUGH POMEREY; *b* by 1521; *m* 1st 5 Feb 1543 Barbara, dau of John Southcott, of Indiho, Bovey Tracy; *m* 2nd 1568/9 Agnes —, and was *bur* 3 March 1602, leaving by his 1st w, with other issue:

THOMAS POMEREY, of Bradford, Devon, and Ingesdon; *b* 1550; *m* Elizabeth, dau and coheir of John Henscott, of Henscott, Bradford, and was *bur* 25 April 1610, leaving, with other issue:

1 Richard; *m* Anne, dau of Henry Copleston, of Bowden, and was *bur* 31 Aug, leaving, with other issue:

(1) Thomas, of the Inner Temple, inherited Ingesdon; *m* 1st Mary, dau of Sir John Drewe; *m* 2nd Jane — and by her had, with other issue:

1a Thomas; sold Ingesdon to John Stowell 9 Oct 1662

2 John; *m* Mary, dau of Arthur Seccombe by his 1st w Grace Bligh, and had, with a dau (Dorothy, *m* Sir James Langham, 2nd Bt (*qv*), *dsp* 1713):

(1) Arthur (Very Rev); *educ* Westminster and Trin Coll Cambridge (BA 1660, Fell 1661, MA 1664, DD 1676), Chaplain 1672 to Ld Lt Ireland, Dean Cork; *m* Elizabeth, 2nd dau of Sir Richard Osborne, 2nd Bt (*qv*), and *d* 1710, having had, with a dau (Mary, *m* Richard, est s of Sir Richard Cox, Bt, Ld Chllr Ireland):

1a John (Ven); Archdeacon Cork 1717–25; *educ* Westminster and Trin Coll Dublin (MA 1700); *m* Elizabeth, dau of Edmund Donellan, of Cloghan, Co Roscommon, and had:

1b ARTHUR, **1st Viscount**

2b John, PC; Lt-Gen, Col 64th Foot (later N Staffs Regt); *d* unm

The Archdeacon's er son,

ARTHUR POMEROY, **1st Viscount Harberton**, so *cr* 5 July 1791 (the choice of title commemorating Harberton, Devon, a ldship that had been acquired by the POMEROYs through marriage with a de Valletort heiress 1207), as also 10 Oct 1783 BARON HARBERTON OF CARBERY, Co Kildare (both I); *b* 16 Jan 1723; *educ* Trin Coll Dublin (BA); High Sheriff Co Kildare 1752, MP Co Kildare 1761–83; *m* 20 Oct 1747 Mary, dau and heir of Henry Colley/Cowley (*see* WELLINGTON, D), and *d* 9 April 1798, having had, with other issue:

1 HENRY POMEROY, **2nd Viscount Harberton**; *b* 8 Dec 1740; *educ* Ch Ch Oxford and Lincoln's Inn, barrister King's Inn 1775, MP Strabane 1776–97, FSA 1806; *m* 20 Jan 1778 Mary (*d* 22 Jan 1823), dau of Nicholas Grady, of Grange, Co Limerick, and *d* 30 Nov 1829, having had:

(1) Henry; *b* 28 Nov 1788; *d* 10 March 1804

2 ARTHUR JAMES POMEROY, **3rd Viscount Harberton**; *b* 3 March 1753; *educ* Eton; Maj 5th Dragoons; *m* Oct 1800 Elizabeth (*d* Nov 1862), dau of Thomas Kinsley, of Dublin, and *dsp* 27 Sept 1832

3 JOHN POMEROY, **4th Viscount Harberton**; *b* 19 Dec 1758; *educ* Trin Coll Dublin (MA 1783); Rector Loughgilly and 1788 Urney, Co Tyrone, Preb St Patrick's Dublin 1783–1822; *m* 31 Oct 1785 Esther (*d* 3 Jan 1840), est dau and coheir of James Spencer, of Rathangan, Co Kildare, and had, with a dau (*d* unm):

(1) JOHN JAMES, **5th Viscount**

(2) Arthur William (Rev); Rector Desertmartin, Co Derry; *b* 17 July 1795; *m* 20 Dec 1837 Frances Letitia (*d* 7 Sept 1889), dau of Rt Rev Hon William Knox (*see* RANFURLY, E), and *d* 12 Dec 1867, having had:

1a John Arthur, of Salt Hill, Mount Charles, Co Donegal, JP Cos Tyrone, Fermanagh and Donegal; *b* 26 July 1839; *m* 19 Jan 1869 Louisa Letitia Jane (*d* 4 March 1929), est dau of Gartside Gartside-Tipping, of Rossferry, Co Fermanagh, and Little Bolton, Lancs, by June Margaret, dau of Robert Fowler, of Rahinston, Meath, and Jane Anne, sis of 3rd Earl of Erne (*qv*), and *d* 21 Feb 1922, leaving issue:

1b Arthur Gartside; *b* 20 Feb 1870; *educ* Uppingham and Trin Coll Dublin (MA and CE 1894); *m* 30 Oct 1916 Gertrude Louise (*d* 23 Dec 1946), widow of Robert Tunstall-Kitching, of Benguelia, SW Africa, and *dsp* 18 March 1954

2b Edmund John, DSO (1919); Lt-Col West India Regt, Boer War 1899–1902 (Queen's medal with three clasps and King's medal with two clasps) and WW I (despatches), fndr, dir and chm Sunday River Citrus Corp; *b* 5 May 1871; *m* 3 Aug 1911 Dorothy Maud (*d* 5 Nov 1949), only child of Hon Alfred Edmund Wigan, of Hartlands, Jamaica, and *d* 15 May 1945, leaving:

1c Alice Letitia; *b* 13 Nov 1922; *d* 1989

3b Louis William Henry; *b* 13 Sept 1873; *d* 26 Feb 1895

4b Francis Knox; Maj RAPC, Connaught Rangers, Boer War 1899–1902 (severely wounded Queen's medal with five clasps, King's medal with two clasps) and WW I; *b* 22 Feb 1876; *educ* Berkhamsted; *m* 25 July 1906 Helen (*d* 9 July 1955), only dau of Arthur Cinnamond, of St Helens, Belfast, and *d* 10 Aug 1962, leaving issue:

1c Arthur John Cinnamond; WW II (despatches three times); *b* 20 May 1907; *educ* Rugby; *m* 11 Jan 1962 *Rowena Mary Vesey [Mrs Arthur Pomeroy, 39 River Rd, Cantley, PQ J84 2Z7, Canada], yr dau of V-Adml Reginald Vesey Holt, CB, DSO, MVO, of Moonhills Cottage, Beaulieu, Hants, and *d* 1995, having had:

1d Hugh Reginald Arthur; *b* 30 June 1963; *d* following an accident 1986

2d +John Francis Vesey; *b* 22 March 1965

2c (Jocelyn Francis) Brian; dir Smith St Aubyn & Co; *b* 24 March 1912; *educ* Rugby; *m* 22 June 1940 Lucy Margaret (*d* 1993), only dau of Robert Hayne, of Weymouth, and *d* 1991, leaving issue:

1d +Thomas [Thomas Pomeroy Esq, Avon House, Hartley Wintney, Hants]; banker; *b* 2 Aug 1941; *educ* Eton and Trin Coll Cambridge (MA); *m* 25 April 1967 *Belinda Jane, only dau of Maj-Gen John Sheffield, CB, CBE, by Mary Patience, only dau of Lt-Col Charles Vere Nicoll, and has issue:

1e *Emily Jane; *b* 4 April 1971

2e *Rosalind Lucy; *b* 13 May 1973

3e *Laura Patience; *b* 13 May 1973

2d +Simon Robert Valentine [Simon Pomeroy Esq, The Old Vicarage, Winscombe, Avon]; *b* 7 June 1943; *educ* Eton and Keble Coll Oxford (BA), FCA; *m* 12 Aug 1972 *Ursula Jean, yr dau of John Barclay, of The Cottage, Shere, Surrey, and has issue:

1e *Patricia Margaret (Daisy); *b* 26 Feb 1974

2e *Elizabeth Frances Mary; *b* 10 May 1976

3e *Catherine Harriet; *b* 1981

1d *(Frances) Louise [Lady Heathcoat Amory, Calverleigh Court, Tiverton, Devon]; *b* 20 Oct 1947; *m* 10 June 1972 *Sir Ian Heathcoat-Amory, 6th Bt (*qv*), and has issue

1c *(Helen) Mary Ursula [Mrs Archibald Hodgson, St George's Nursing Home, Cobham, Surrey]; Jr Cdr ATS WW II; *b* 27 Nov 1909; *m* 18 Sept 1943 Lt-Cdr Archibald Richard Sanford Hodgson, DSC, RNVR (*d* 1990), yst s of Archibald Sanford Hodgson, of Westons Place, Warnham, Sussex, and has issue:

1d *Nicholas Pomeroy Sanford [Nicholas Hodgson Esq, The Old Rectory, Oldstock, Wilts SP6 4JA]; *b* 20 Jan 1945; *educ* Eton; *m* 22 June 1974 *Melissa, yr dau of Donald B Prouty, of Littleton, Mass., and has:

1e *Christopher Prouty Sanford; *b* 23 June 1980; *educ* Eton

2e *Geoffrey Peter Sanford; *b* 16 May 1986

1e *Alexandra Louise Pomeroy; *b* 13 Dec 1978

2e *Olivia Cinnamond; *b* 10 June 1983

1d *(Helen) Rose Sanford; *b* 2 May 1947; *m* 1979 *Capt Ian Cameron de Sales La Terrière, of Dunalastair, Perthshire, and has issue:

1e *Hugh William; *b* 1982

2e *Robert Duncan; *b* 1984

2d *(Ursula) Virginia Sanford [Miss Virginia Hodgson, 7 Bedford St, Oxford OX4 1SU]; *b* 22 Nov 1952

5b Eustace Crichton, Private ASC; *b* 2 June 1877; *d* 7 Feb 1917

1b Janet Mildred; *d* unm 2 Nov 1964, aged 89

2b Anna Grace Edith; *d* unm 2 Aug 1960

2a William Knox; *b* 28 May 1843; *d* 23 Aug 1926

(3) George Francis POMEROY later POMEROY COLLEY (roy licence 1830), of Ferney, Stillorgan, Co Dublin; Cdr RN; *b* 11 Nov 1797; *m* 22 July 1825 Frances (*d* 1 March 1871) n of 1st Baron Ashtown (*qv*), and *d* 9 May 1879, having had:

1a Henry FitzGeorge, of Mount Temple, Dublin; *b* 1 July 1827; *m* 12 Aug 1858 Elizabeth Isabella (*d* 18 Nov 1903), est dau of Rev Hon William Wingfield (*see* POWERSCOURT, V), and *d* 24 Nov 1886, leaving issue:

1b George Pomeroy Arthur; MA Dublin; *b* 6 March 1866; *m* 20 Jan 1909 Edith Maud Olivia (*d* 1975), er dau of Col Henry Thomas Finlay, DL, of Corkagh, Co Dublin, and *d* 23 Feb 1933, leaving issue:

1c George Dudley; *b* 19 Sept 1911; *m* 16 April 1947 *Anne Patricia [Mrs George Pomeroy Colley, The Mill House, Kilmatead, Clondalkin, Co Dublin, Ireland], dau of William Burns, of Kingswood, Clondalkin, and *d* 25 Feb 1959, leaving:

1d +Finlay FitzGeorge; *b* 18 Feb 1948

2d +Anthony William [Anthony Pomeroy Colley Esq, The Loft, Kilmatead, Clondalkin, Co Dublin, Ireland]; *b* 3 Feb 1951; *m* 1973 *Mary, dau of Hugh Kelly, and has issue:

1e +Dudley Hugh; *b* 1975

2e +Jeffrey Andrew; *b* 1978

1e *Amy Alexandra; *b* 1984

2c Henry John; RAF WW II; *b* 28 June 1918; *m* 27 March 1943 *Eileen Patricia, dau of Joseph John Lennon, and *das* S Africa 7 Jan 1944

1c Noreen Helen; *b* 1 April 1910; *m* 24 Feb 1940 *George Gilbert Butler (*see* DUNBOYNE, B) and *d* 11 Oct 1997, leaving issue

2c *Veronica Maud [Mrs Derrick Hall-Dare, 23 Whitebarn Rd, Churchtown, Dublin 14, Ireland]; *b* 14 April 1913; *m* 1st 10 July 1935 (*divorce* 1968) Maj Jeffry Ardern Patrick Lefroy, MBE (*d* 1985), MA, Lt-Col QO Yorkshire Dragoons, Inspr Educn, er s of George Frederic Lefroy, of Ochard House, Pilton, Barnstaple; *m* 1972, as his 2nd w, Lt-Col Derrick Arthur Hall-Dare, OBE (*d* 1985), RA, of Cliff, Rathfarnham, Co Dublin, and by her 1st husb has issue:

1d *Jeffry George [Maj Jeffry Lefroy, Carrigglas Manor, Co Longford, Ireland]; Maj Roy Irish Fus/Rangers (ret 1976); *b* 24 May 1936; *educ* Balliol Coll Oxford (BA); *m* 1 Feb 1964 *Teresa (Tessa) Margaret, only dau of Henry Alwyn White, DL, of Orange Hill, Tandragee, Co Armagh, and has:

1e *Jeffry Peter Langlois; *b* 4 Sept 1965

2e *Edward Christian Perceval [Edward Lefroy Esq, 29 Elizabeth St, London SW1]; *b* 19 Dec 1967

1d *Laetitia Mary [Miss Laetitia Lefroy, 40 Ailesbury Lawn, Dundrum, Dublin 16, Ireland]; *b* 18 Sept 1937; *educ* Trin Coll Dublin and Birmingham U

3c *Valerie Edith [Mrs William Hone, Kilmatead, Clondalkin, Co Dublin, Ireland]; *b* 10 Oct 1914; *m* 18 March 1947 William Patrick Hone, MC (*d* 1976), Capt RE, yst s of William Hone, of Killiney, Co Dublin, and has issue:

1d *Christopher Patrick George; *b* 1949; *m* 1981 *Mary Josephine, dau of Raymond Jennings, of Riversdale House, Craughwell, Co Galway, and has:

1e *Timothy Raymond Patrick; *b* 24 June 1995

4c *Rosemary [Mrs Nicholas Crocker, Kilmatead, Clondalkin, Co Dublin, Ireland]; *b* 4 Oct 1916; *m* 5 July 1947 (Henry) Nicholas Crocker (*d* 1982), er s of Henry J Crocker, of Hill House, Llandeilo, Wales, and has issue:

1d *(Henry) Alistair Nicholas [Alistair Crocker Esq, Clifton Hill Cottage, Constitution Hill, Clifton, Bristol BS8 1DE]; *b* 1949; *m* 1975 *Christina, dau of William McMillan, of Glasgow, and has issue:

1e *Ursula Margaret Rosemary; *b* 1985

2e *Roberta Harriet; *b* 1988

2d *Roderick John [Roderick Crocker Esq, 138 Marlborough Ave, Hull]; *b* 1954; *m* 1980 *Irena, dau of Dr Jerzy Kuroski, of Hull, and has:

1e *Alexandra Ruth; *b* 1982

1d *Virginia Helen [Mrs Edward Mustard, The Butts, Middle Woodford, Wilts]; *b* 1948; *m* 1971 *S/Ldr (James) Edward Mustard, DFC, RAF (ret), and has issue:

1e *James Edmond Alexander; *b* 1974

1e *Eleanor Clare; *b* 1981

2b William Wingfield (Rev); Rector Bonnington-cum-Bilsington Kent 1930–39; *b* 20 Aug 1868; *educ* Trin Coll Cambridge; *m* 2 Sept 1915 Helen Isabel (*d* 1974), dau of Rev Duncan John Brownlow (descended from Rev Francis Brownlow, bro of 1st Baron Lurgan, *qv*), and *d* 1947, leaving:

1c Elisabeth Margaret; *b* 8 April 1918; *d* 19 Feb 1991

2c *Esmé Florence Helen [Miss Esmé Pomeroy Colley, Carbery, 12 Albany Court, Ballybrack, Co Dublin, Ireland]; *b* 18 June 1920

3b Gerald Henry; RM Co Tipperary, Maj 3rd Bn Roy Irish Regt Boer War 1900–02 (Queen's medal with five clasps, and King's medal with two clasps); *b* 31 March 1870; *m* 20 June 1906 Dorothy Evelyn (*d* 25 Aug 1929), dau of Col James Addie, of Calder Park, Lanarks, and *d* 12 Nov 1923, leaving:

1c Patricia; *b* 18 March 1907; *m* 25 April 1930 Kenneth Hastings Nethersole, s of H R Nethersole, and has issue

4b Edward; BA Dublin, CE; *b* 15 April 1875; *d* 15 April 1912

1b Elizabeth Maria; *m* 18 Jan 1883 Frederick Selwyn Copleston, BCS, and *d* 27 Aug 1895. He *d* 23 Oct 1935

2b Frances Maud Caroline; *d* unm 15 Jan 1949

3b Florence Isabella; *m* 10 April 1890 Henry Cole Bowen, of Bowen's Court, Co Cork, and *d* 23 Sept 1912, leaving issue. He *d* 27 May 1930

4b Laura Emily; *d* unm 26 Feb 1942

5b Constance Helena; MD; *d* unm 15 Deb 1912

6b Gertrude Theodosia; *m* 9 Oct 1895 Alberic Arthur Twisleton-Wykeham-Fiennes and *d* 12 Nov 1934, leaving issue (*see* SAY AND SELE, B)

2a John Thomas; *b* 31 July 1828; *d* 27 Jan 1855

3a George POMEROY COLLEY later POMEROY-COLLEY (roy licence 8 May 1880) (Sir), KCSI, CB, CMG; Col Kaffir War 1858–60, China Campaign 1860; *b* 1 Nov 1835; *m* 14 March 1878 Edith Althea (*m* 2nd 17th Feb 1891 1st Baron Allendale (*see* ALLENDALE, V); *d* 19 May 1927), est dau of Maj-Gen Henry Meade Hamilton, CB, and was *k* Battle of Majuba, Natal, 27 Feb 1881

1a Maria Esther; *m* 17 Nov 1957 John Edward Vernon, of Erne Hill, Co Cavan, and *d* 8 May 1899, leaving issue. He *d* 7 March 1887

2a Elizabeth; *d* unm 28 Sept 1910

(4) Spencer Stewart; *b* 9 March 1803; *d* 23 June 1812

(5) Henry; *b* 20 Sept 1805; *m* 7 Feb 1829 Elizabeth (*d* 26 May 1881), 3rd dau of Rev Robert Holt Truell, DD, of Clonmannon, Co Wicklow, and *d* 18 May 1833, leaving issue:

1a Robert Henry; Bengal CS; *b* 1830; *d* at Ghazepoore, 1 Aug 1857

1a Editha Augusta Mary; *m* 4 April 1850 Rev Henry Bond, Vicar S Petherton, Somerset, and *d* 12 Dec 1899, leaving issue. He *d* 27 Sept 1875

(6) William Knox; *b* 15 June 1813; d 1 Nov 1874

(1) Elizabeth Esther; *m* 26 April 1842 Rev Cecil Russell, Vicar Drumcree, Co Meath, and *d* 3 Oct 1893. He *d* 1881

The 4th VISCOUNT *d* 4 July 1833; his est son,

JOHN JAMES POMEROY, **5th Viscount Harberton**; *b* 29 Sept 1790; *m* 1 March 1822 Caroline (*d* 4 May 1886 aged 85), 6th dau of Rev Sir John Robinson, Bt, and had:

1 John; *b* 28 Oct 1828; *d* 3 Dec 1830

2 Arthur James; *b* 30 March 1831; *d* 26 Jan 1840

3 JAMES SPENCER, **6th Viscount**

1 Mary Ann; *m* 24 March 1856 William Knox Wigram and *d* 19 April 1883, leaving issue (*see* WIGRAM, Bt)

2 Esther Caroline; *d* unm 29 June 1923

The 5th VISCOUNT *d* 5 Oct 1862; his only surv son,

JAMES SPENCER POMEROY, **6th Viscount Harberton**, JP Herefs and Surrey; *b* 23 Nov 1836; MA Cantab; *m* 2 April 1861 Florence Wallace (*d* 30 April 1911), only dau of William Wallace Legge, of Malone House, Co Antrim, and *d* 4 Dec 1912, having had issue:

1 ERNEST ARTHUR GEORGE POMEROY, **7th Viscount Harberton**; 20th Hus and 3rd Bn Roy Dublin Fus Boer War 1900 (medal); *b* 1 Dec 1867; *m* 1 March 1932 Fairlie (*d* 13 Jan 1945), dau of Col Charles D'Oyly Harmar, of Ramridge, Andover, and *dsp* 22 April 1944

2 RALPH LEGGE, **8th Viscount**

1 Aline Florence; *d* 11 Aug 1880

2 Hilda Evelyn; *m* 5 Oct 1892 (*annulled* 1902) Thomas Arthur Carless Attwood, FSA, MA, of Malvern Wells, Worcs, and *dsp* 28 Oct 1948. He *d* 21 April 1937

The 7th VISCOUNT's yr bro,

RALPH LEGGE POMEROY, **8th Viscount Harberton**, OBE (1919), JP Northants; *b* 31 Dec 1869; *educ* Balliol Coll Oxford (BA); Maj Gen Res Offrs 5th Dragoon Gds, Boer War 1899–1902 (severely wounded, Queen's medal with three clasps, King's medal with two clasps) and WW I; *m* 25 June 1907 Mary Katherine, (*d* 10 Oct 1971), only dau of Arthur William Leatham, JP, of Smallfield Place, Smallfield, Surrey, and *d* 4 July 1956, leaving issue:

1 HENRY RALPH MARTYN POMEROY, **9th Viscount Harberton**; *b* 12 Oct 1908; *educ* Eton; *d* 1980

2 THOMAS DE VAUTORT POMEROY, **10th and present Viscount Harberton**

3 Robert William; *b* 29 Feb 1916; *educ* Eton; Maj Welsh Gds (ret 1960) WW II; *m* 28 April 1953 *(Winifred) Anne [The Hon Mrs Robert Pomeroy, Rockfield House, Nunney, Somerset], 2nd dau of Sir Arthur Colegate (*see* WORSLEY, Bt), MP, and *d* 5 April 1997, leaving:

(1) +HENRY ROBERT [Henry Pomeroy Esq, Rockfield Stables, Nunney, Somerset BA11 4NP]; *b* 23 April 1958; heir presumptive; *m* 27 Oct 1990 *Caroline Mary, dau of Jeremy Grindle, of Viking Cottage, Bosham, W Sussex, and has:

1a +Patrick Christopher; *b* 10 May 1995

2a +Hugh William; *b* 18 April 1997

(2) +Richard Arthur [Richard Pomeroy Esq, 22 Stockwell Park Rd, London SW9 0AJ]; *b* 18 May 1960; *m* 21 May 1987 *Helena Claire, yr dau of Andrew Watt Drysdale, of Pitcombe Farm House, Bruton, Somerset, and has issue:

1a *Alice Tallulah; *b* 30 Aug 1992

2a *Isabella Xanthe; *b* 8 Sept 1995

1 *Rosamund Mary [The Hon Rosamund Pomeroy, The Cottage, Swain's Lane, Bembridge, IOW]; *b* 29 Feb 1916; ATS WW II

HARDIE

Creation: B. (LP, UK) May 1997.

THE BARON HARDIE, of Blackford, in the City of Edinburgh (Andrew Hardie, QC (Scotland 1985)) [The Rt Hon The Lord Hardie QC, 4 Oswald Rd, Edinburgh EH9 2HF]; *b* 8 Jan 1946; *educ* St Modan's High Sch Stirling and Edinburgh U; slr 1971, memb Faculty Advocates 1973, Advocate Depute 1979–83, Dean Faculty Advocates 1994–97 (Treas 1989–94), Ld Advocate 1997–, Hon Bencher Lincoln's Inn 1998–; *m* 1971 *Catherine Storrar Elgin and has two sons and a dau

Lineage: ANDREW RUTHERFORD HARDIE; *m* Elizabeth Currie Lowe and had:

ANDREW, *cr* a **Baron**

HARDING OF PETHERTON

Arms: Arg. on a bend az. between two lions passant guardant gu., as many kukris in saltire ppr. between two martlets or. **Crest:** Out of a mural crown gu. a cubit arm in armour, the hand gauntleted, grasping a Field Marshal's baton in bend sinister ppr. **Supporters:** Dexter, a private of the 1st Life Gds of the early-19th century; sinister, a Somerset Light Infantryman of the late-18th century, both habited and accoutred ppr. **Motto:** Vigilant and resolute. **Creation:** B. (UK) 15 Jan 1958.

THE 2ND BARON HARDING OF PETHERTON, of Nether Compton, Co Dorset (John Charles Harding) [The Rt Hon The Lord Harding of Petherton, Barrymore Farm House, Pict's Hill, Langport, Somerset TA10 9EZ]; *b* 12 Feb 1928; *s* f 1989; *educ* Marlborough and Worcester Coll Oxford (BA); Maj 11th Hus (PAO) (ret 1968); *m* 20 June 1966 *Harriet, 2nd dau of Major-Gen James Francis Hare, CB, DSO, of 35 Ovington Street, London SW3, and has issue:

1 +WILLIAM ALLAN JOHN; *b* 5 July 1969

2 +David Richard John; *b* 22 June 1978

1 *Diana Mary; *b* 9 Nov 1967; *m* 28 Oct 1995 *John David Penrose

Lineage: FRANCIS EBENEZER HARDING; *m* Elizabeth Ellen Anstice and had:

1 JOHN, **1st Baron**

1 Dorothy Ella; *m* W H Hebditch and had:

(1) *John; *m* *M Lang

(2) *Geoffrey; *b* 1 Jan 1921; *m* 19 Sept 1943 *Dorothy Mary, dau of Douglas Caple, and has:

1a *Norman Geoffrey (Brian Lee); *b* 1 July 1947

1a *Angela Jean; *b* 23 May 1945; *m* 19– *Gordon Draper and has:

1b *Paul Geoffrey; *b* 23 March 1969

1b *Nicola Mary; *b* 31 Dec 1970

(3) *David; *m* H M Mason (*d* 198–)

(4) *Michael; *m* *M E Peach

2 *Margaret Anstice; *m* Douglas Fendall Prentice (*d* 10 Jan 1969) and has:

(1) *Margaret Trenchard [Mrs J Hone, 33 Harfield Road, Sunbury-on-Thames, Middx]; *b* 27 Aug 1931; *educ* London U (BA); *m* 9 Oct 1954 *J G E Hone, BSc, ARCS, s of H J E Hone, of Hampton Hill, Middx, and has issue:

1a *Marcus John Elliott; *b* 17 July 1955

2a *Matthew Tom Elliott; *b* 22 Feb 1958

3a *Adrian Michael Elliott; *b* 6 Oct 1960

(2) *Valerie May; *b* 10 May 1934; *m* 1st 2 April 1956 (*divorce* 198–) W J Alsford; *m* 2nd *Sam Richards, and by her 1st husb has:

1a *Amanda Louise; *b* 20 Dec 1957

2a *Katherine Anne Valerie; *b* 30 Jan 1960

3a *Lucy Margaret; *b* 9 April 1964

4a *Emma Mary Madeline; *b* 1 March 1966

(3) *Cicely Helen; *m* 4 July 1942 *Frank Douglas Goodchild and has:

1a *Michael Frank; *b* 24 Feb 1944
1a *Jane Elizabeth; *b* 29 March 1946
FRANCIS HARDING's son,
ALLAN FRANCIS (JOHN) HARDING, **1st Baron Harding of Petherton**, of Nether Compton, Co Dorset (UK), so *cr* 15 Jan 1958, GCB (1951), CBE (1940), DSO (1941) and two bars (1943), MC (1917); *b* 10 Feb 1896; *educ* Ilminster GS; Hon DCL Durham 1959, Somerset LI WW I (wounded twice, despatches), Capt 1923, Maj 1935, Brevet Lt-Col 1938, Lt-Col 1939, WW II: Brig 1940, Maj-Gen 1942, Lt-Gen 1943 (despatches twice); Gen 1949, FM 1953, CIGS 1952–55, dir: National Provincial Bank, Standard Bank, Western Gazette, Williams (Hounslow) Ltd, chm: Plessey, Sausmarez Carey & Harris, Cncl for Br Casino Assoc 1973–89, Horserace Betting Levy Bd 1961–67, Govr and C-in-C Cyprus 1955–57, Col Life Gds, Gold Stick to HM THE QUEEN 1957–64, Col Somerset LI 1953–59 and Somerset and Cornwall LI 1959–60, Col 6th Queen Elizabeth's Own Gurkha Rifles 1951–61, ADC Gen to TM GEORGE VI 1950 and THE QUEEN 1952–53, KStJ 1955, Cdr US Legn Merit, Legn Hon, Croix de Guerre; *m* 21 April 1927 Mary Gertrude Mabel (*d* 1983), dau of Joseph Wilson Rooke, JP, of Knutsford, Cheshire, and *d* 1989, leaving:
1 JOHN CHARLES HARDING, **2nd and present Baron Harding of Petherton**

HARDINGE

Arms: Gu. on a chevron arg. fimbriated or, three escallops sa. **Crest:** A mitre gu., thereon a chevron, charged and fimbriated as in the arms. **Supporters:** On either side a lion ppr., the dexter murally crowned or and supporting a flagstaff ppr., therefrom flowing to the dexter a flag or; the sinister crowned with a eastern crown and supporting a like staff, therefrom flowing to the sinister a flag also or. **Motto:** *Mens æqua rebus in arduis* ('A mind equal to difficulties'). **Creation:** Bt. (UK) 4 Aug 1801, V. (UK) 2 May 1846.

THE 6TH VISCOUNT HARDINGE OF LAHORE AND KINGS NEWTON, Co Derby, and a **Baronet** (Sir Charles Henry Nicholas Hardinge, Bt) [The Rt Hon The Viscount Hardinge, Broadmere House, Broadmere, Hants RG25 2JA]; *b* 25 August 1956; *s f* 1984 in Viscountcy and cousin in btcy 1986; *educ* Upper Canada Coll, Trin Coll Sch and McGill; *m* 1985 *Mrs Julie Therese Sillett, est dau of Keith Sillett, of Sydney, Australia, and has issue:
1 *Emilie Charlotte; *b* 1986
2 *Olivia Margaux; *b* 1989

Lineage: NICHOLAS HARDYE [*sic*]; described as a yeoman 25 June 1564; *d* on or after 25 May but before 4 June 1582, leaving, with apparently four daus:

ROBERT HARDY; *d* 1596, leaving, with an er s (Robert, *m* 1607 Elizabeth, dau of Robert Brunskill, London merchant, *dsp* 8 Dec 1613):

NICHOLAS HARDIE; *m* Isabel (*m* 2nd Bryan Beauley), dau of Edward Web, of Austrey, Warwicks, and *d* 1631, leaving:

Sir ROBERT HARDING, of King's Newton Hall, Derbys; *b* 1621; royalist Civil War (raised a troop of horse), Master in Chancery, entertained CHARLES II at King's Newton Hall, ktd 1674; *m* Anne (*d* 19 July 1673), dau of Sir Richard Sprignell, Bt, of Highgate, Middx, and *d* Nov 1679, leaving, with at least nine other children:
1 Robert, of King's Newton; *b* 1654; *m* 1st Jane (*d* 1692), dau of William Buxton, of Youlgreave; *m* 2nd Elizabeth — (*bur* 1706) and *d* by 17 Oct 1709, leaving, with four daus:
(1) John, of King's Newton; *bapt* 26 Sept 1685; Remembrancer Exchequer; *m* 12 April 1711 Alice, dau of Thomas Coke (*see* LOTHIAN, M, section **Seat**); *dsp* Jan 1728
2 Gideon (Rev); Vicar Kingston, Surrey; *d* 1712, leaving:
(1) NICHOLAS
(2) Caleb; MD, Physician to THE QUEEN (ANNE?); *dsp*
(1) Mary; *m* Sir John Stracey (*see* STRACEY, Bt)
Sir ROBERT's gs,
NICHOLAS HARDINGE; barrister, Clerk H of C, Sec Treasury, MP Eyre, Recorder Kingston; *b* 7 Feb 1669; *m* 19 Dec 1738 Jane, sis of 1st Earl Camden (*see* CAMDEN, M), and *d* 9 April 1758, having had:

1 George, KC; JP Glam, Brecon and Radnor; *b* 1743; Attorney-Gen to QUEEN CHARLOTTE, w of GEORGE III; *m* Lucy, dau and coheir of Richard Long, and *dsp* 26 April 1816
2 Henry (Rev); Rector Stanhope, Co Durham; *b* 2 Sept 1754; *m* 4 June 1779 Frances, dau of James Best, and *d* 7 Sept 1820, having had:
(1) **Rev Sir Charles Hardinge, 2nd Bt**; *b* 22 March 1780; Rector Crowhurst; *m* 13 June 1816 Emily Bardford (*d* 8 Dec 1878), 2nd dau of Kenneth Callander of Craigforth, Stirling, and *d* 3 Feb 1864, having had, with six daus (*d* unm or young):
1a **Sir Henry Charles Hardinge, 3rd Bt**; *b* 26 July 1830; *d* unm 13 Nov 1873
2a **Sir Edmund Stracey Hardinge, 4th Bt**, JP, DL Kent; *b* 27 March 1833, *m* 7 Feb 1877 Evelyn Stuart (*d* 17 April 1926), 2nd dau of Maj-Gen Evan Maberly, CB, and *d* 8 April 1924, having had:
1b **Sir Charles Edmund Hardinge, 5th Bt**; *b* 15 Nov 1878; *educ* Harrow and Trin Coll Cambridge; *d* unm 29 Oct 1968
1b Evelyn Violet; *b* 30 Dec 1877; *d* 31 July 1921
2b Marion Laura; *b* 10 April 1882; *d* unm 26 April 1960
3b Muriel Emily; *b* 23 Jan 1884; *m* 27 Sept 1911 John Christie MacLeod (*d* 2 Oct 1947), er s of Col Kenneth MacLeod, and had issue
3a Robert James; *b* 2 July 1834; *m* 1854 Martha, dau of Maj Sadler, of Sopwell Hall, Kingston, Canada, and *d* 14 Dec 1877, having had:
1b Charles Herkomer; *b* 1856; *m* 1905 Catherine Ida (*d* 8 Sept 1952), dau of Francis Henry Burslem, of Dubbo, NSW, and *dsp* 5 April 1938, leaving an adopted dau
2b Edmond Cecil; *b* 1860; *m* 1884 Harriet, dau of James Fontaine, of Dakota City, Nebraska, and was *k* on the Canadian Pacific Railway 1890, leaving:
1c **Sir Robert Hardinge, 6th Bt**; *b* 3 Dec 1887; *m* 1st 1911 (*divorce* 1938) Emma Vera, dau of Charles Arnold, and had issue; *m* 2nd 1947 Nellie May, formerly wife of — Houser, and *d* 1973; his s by his 1st w:
1d **Sir Robert Arnold Hardinge, 7th Bt**; *b* 9 Sept 1914; *d* 1986
1c Jacqueline Estelle; *b* 1913; *m* 1940 Ivan Jones
1c Georgia Garnett; *b* 1886; *m* 1916 Daniel J Wallace and had issue
1b Emily Bligh; *m* 26 Nov 1887 Bernard Wiltshire Tolhurst, of Tunbridge Wells, and had issue. He *d* 28 Nov 1935
1a Caroline Bradford; *m* 31 July 1839 Ven R W Browne, MA, Archdeacon Bath, Canon Wells, and had issue
(2) George Nicholas; Capt RN; *b* 11 April 1781; *ka* cmdg HMS *Fiorenzo* after capturing a Piedmontese frigate
(3) HENRY, **1st Viscount**
(4) Richard, KH; Maj-Gen RA; *b* 14 April 1790; *m* 1st 1815 Anne (*d* 1819), est dau of Thomas Papillon, of Acrise, Kent, and had:
1a Henry; Lt-Col Rifle Bde, Gentleman-at-Arms to HM QUEEN VICTORIA, served Kaffir Wars (wounded) and Crimea; *b* 26 July 1817; *d* unm 6 Feb 1898
1a Frances Anne; *b* 1819; *d* unm 15 Sept 1891
(4) (cont.) Gen Hardinge *m* 2nd 15 Aug 1827 Caroline Johnson (*d* 4 Jan 1874), yst dau of Kenneth Callander, of Craigforth, nr Stirling, and *d* 20 July 1864, having by her had:
2a George Nicholas; Maj Bengal Army, Cmdt 3rd Oude Irregular Cav, DAQMG Defence Lucknow; *b* 12 Aug 1828; *d* unm 1859
3a Edward, CB; Adml (medal with two clasps, Legn Honour, 5th Cl Medjidie); *b* 19 May 1830; *m* 15 Sept 1875 Lilia Matilda (*d* 31 July 1928), dau of Thomas Papillon, of Crowhurst Park, Sussex, and *d* 2 May 1894, leaving:
1b Dorothy Caroline; *b* 6 Feb 1877; *m* 24 April 1907 Capt Evelyn à Court Bergne, TD, yr s of Sir John Henry Gibbs Bergne, KCB, KCMG, and *d* 25 June 1945. He *d* 11 March 1952
4a Bradford; Bengal CS; *b* 21 March 1833; *m* 16 Nov 1864 Caroline Jane Christina (*d* 27 Jan 1926), dau of William Edwards, BCS, Judge Supreme Court Agra, and *d* 31 July 1871, leaving issue:
1b George Nicholas; *b* 3 Sept 1865; *educ* Harrow and Trin Coll Camb (BA); *m* 4 Oct 1923 Lilian Frances (*d* 1974), sis of 5th Earl of Norbury (*qv*), and *d* 10 Oct 1943, leaving:
1c +Nicholas William [Nicholas Hardinge Esq, Lock Cottage, Bear St, Nayland, Essex]; *b* 11 Oct 1928; *educ* Radley; *m* 17 March 1973 Anne (*d* by 11 April 1998), dau of Lt-Col W T Delamain, and has:
1d +Philip; *b* 19–
1d *Emma; *b* 19–
1c *Phyllis Lilian [Miss Phyllis Hardinge, Rose Cottage, Bramdean Common, Alresford, Hants]
1b Emma May; *m* 2 May 1911 George Lawrence Stewart, 3rd s of Alexander John Robert Stewart, of Ards, Co Donegal, and *d* 17 March 1955. He *d* 7 Sept 1950
5a Herbert Richard; Lt-Col 32nd Regt; *b* 14 May 1840; *m* 1 Oct 1884 Margaret Emelia (*d* 28 Aug 1934), dau of William Adair Bruce, of Ashley, Box, Wilts, and *dsp* 7 April 1917
2a Emma Augusta; twin with Herbert; *d* unm 24 Jan 1892
(5) Frederick, of Coatham Hall, Co Durham; *b* 27 Feb 1801; *m* 10 Sep 1829 Hannah Elizabeth, est dau of Warren Maude, of GreenBank, Darlington, and *d* 3 Oct 1875, having had, with other issue:
1a Henry Charles; Capt 26th Regt; *b* 7 Jan 1832; *m* 22 July 1868 Eleanor (*m* 2nd 1891 Darcy Francis Mark Milbank (*see* MILBANK, Bt); *d* July 1914), est dau of James Lord, barrister, and *d* 14 June 1870, leaving:
1b Henry Charles Maurice; playwright and novelist; *b* 12 March 1870; *d* unm 12 July 1954
1a Frances; *m* 30 Sept 1852 Thomas Fenwick-Clennell, of Harbottle Castle, Northumberland, and *d* 16 March 1895, having had issue. He *d* 1893
2a Hannah Isabella; *m* 4 Jan 1866 Rev William Eade, Rector Wolviston, Co Durham, and had issue. He *d* 1885
(1) Frances; *m* Rev Stephen Woodgate, of Pembury, Kent, and had issue. He *d* 1844

(2) Caroline; *m* Feb 1829 Maj-Gen Henry Palliser, RA, and had issue

(3) Juliana Elizabeth; *m* Thomas Bates, of Wolsingham, and *dsp* 10 Dec 1808

3 **Sir Richard Hardinge, 1st Bt** (UK), so *cr* 4 Aug 1801, with remainder to the heirs male of his f, of Belleisle, Co Fermanagh (acquired through his 1st w); *b* 10 Nov 1756; *m* 1st 6 May 1793 Mary (*dsp* 1824), illegitimate dau of 1st and last Earl of Ross of the 1772 *cr* (see GORE, Bt); *m* 2nd 14 March 1826 Caroline Munster (*m* 2nd 23 Oct 1828 Henry Taylor-Jones (*see* LAWRENCE-JONES, Bt) and *d* 4 June 1858, leaving issue), dau of Maj-Gen Wulff, and *dsp* 5 Nov 1826

1 Jane; *b* 17 Nov 1740; *m* Henry Cressett-Pelham, of Crowhurst, Sussex, ggs of Sir Thomas Pelham, 2nd Bt (*see* CHICHESTER, E)

2 Caroline; *b* 1747; *d* unm 23 April 1826

3 Juliana

The 2nd Bt's yr bro,

HENRY HARDINGE, **1st Viscount Hardinge of Lahore and Kings Newton**, Co Derby, so *cr* 2 May 1846 with the thanks of Parl and a state pension of £3,000 p.a. (well over £125,000 in late-1990s terms) for him and the next two holders of the title plus an income for life of £5,000 p.a.(well over £200,000 in late-1990s terms) from the HEIC, GCB (1844, KCB 1815), PC (GB 1828, I 1830); *b* 30 March 1785; joined Army 1799, Maj 1809, Lt-Col 1811, Col 1821, Maj-Gen 1830, Col 97th Foot 1833–43 and 57th Foot 1843–56, Lt Gen 1841, Gen 1854, DQMG Portuguese Army 1809–14 (in which capacity credited with main role in Victory of Albuera 1811), also fought Vimiera 1808, Vittoria 1813 and Quatre Bras 16 June 1815 (wounded all three, lost left hand at last of these), MP (Tory) Durham 1820–30, St Germans July-Dec 1830, Newport Cornwall 1830–32 and Launceston 1832–44, Clerk Ordnance 1823–27 and Feb–Aug 1828, Sec at War 1828–30 and 1841–44, Ch Sec Ireland with seat in Cabinet July–Nov 1830 and 1834–35, Govr-Gen India 1844–48, during which time he helped (under Sir Hugh Gough; *see* GOUGH, V) defeat the Sikhs in the 1st Sikh War, principally at the Battles of the Sutlej Dec 1845–Feb 1846; Master-Gen Ordnance May–Sept 1852, *s* 1st Duke of Wellington (*qv*) as Gen C-in-C 28 Dec 1852, FM 1855, Hon DCL Oxon 1820, Gold Cross with five clasps 1815, Waterloo Medal 1816, Kt 3rd Cl Willem of Netherlands, Kt Tower and Sword Portugal, Kt St Ferdinand Spain, Kt Grand Cross Red Eagle Prussia; *m* 10 Dec 1821 Lady Emily Jane (*d* 18 Oct 1865), widow of John James (2nd s of Sir Walter James, Bt) and dau of 1st Marquess of Londonderry (*qv*), and had:

1 CHARLES STEWART, **2nd Viscount**

2 Arthur Edward (Sir), KCB, CIE; Gen, Col Coldstream Gds, Col cmdg KRRC, C-in-C Bombay Army 1881–85, Govr Gibraltar 1880–90, Chev Legn Honour and Medjidie, Equerry to HM QUEEN VICTORIA; *b* 2 March 1828; *m* 30 Dec 1858 Mary Georgiana Frances (*d* 10 Jan 1917), est dau of Col Hon Augustus Frederick Ellis (*see* HOWARD DE WALDEN, B), and *d* 15 July 1892, leaving issue:

(1) Arthur Henry (Sir), GCMG (1910), KCB (1904), PC (1913); *b* 12 Oct 1859, MA Oxon, Fell All Souls 1881; barrister Inner Temple, Dip Serv 1884 on: Political Agent and Consul-Gen Zanzibar 1894–1900, Envoy Extrdy and Min Plen Teheran 1900–06, Brussels 1906–11 and Lisbon 1911–13, Amb Madrid 1913–19, Grand Cross Charles III Spain; *m* 4 Nov 1899 Alexandra Mina (*d* 23 March 1949), 3rd dau of Gen Sir Arthur Edward Augustus Ellis, GCVO, CSI (*see* HOWARD DE WALDEN, B), and *d* 27 Dec 1933, having had issue:

1a Henry Arthur Mina; *b* 1 Oct 1903; *d* 29 June 1925

2a Edward William George; *b* 4 Oct 1905 (HM EDWARD VII stood sponsor); *d* 6 Jan 1906

3a George Granville Douglas; *b* 13 Jan 1912; *d* 30 July 1927

1a *Mary Pamela; barrister Inner Temple 1940

(1) Alberta Mary; *m* 1st 9 March 1882 Hon Evelyn Henry Ellis and had issue (*see* HOWARD DE WALDEN, B); *m* 2nd 29 April 1919 Schomberg Kerr Trefusis (*see* CLINTON, B) and *d* 26 Dec 1942

(2) Mary; Maid-of-Honour to HM QUEEN VICTORIA; *m* 17 July 1894 Lt-Col Ivone Kirkpatrick, CBE, South Staffs Regt, and *d* 10 Nov 1931, having had issue. He *d* 20 Nov 1936

(3) Alice; *d* unm 2 April 1897

1 Frances Elizabeth, CI; *m* 13 Sept 1845 Gen Sir Arthur Thurlow Cunynghame, GCB, 3rd s of Sir David Cunynghame, 5th Bt (*qv*), and *d* 9 July 1894, leaving issue

2 Emily Caroline; *d* 4 Sept 1876

The 1st VISCOUNT *d* 24 Sep 1856; his er son,

CHARLES STEWART HARDINGE, **2nd Viscount Hardinge of Lahore and Kings Newton**, VD, DL; *b* 2 Sept 1822; Hon Col 1st Vol Bn Roy W Kent Regt, ADC to HM QUEEN VICTORIA, MP (C) Downpatrick 1851–56; *m* 10 April 1856 Lady Lavinia Bingham (*d* 15 Sept 1864), dau of 3rd Earl of Lucan (*qv*), and had issue:

1 HENRY CHARLES, **3rd Viscount**

2 CHARLES HARDINGE, 1st BARON HARDINGE OF PENSHURST (*qv*)

3 Arthur Stewart; Maj Roy Scots Fus; *b* 19 May 1859; *dsp* 5 June 1899

4 Robert Nicholas; *b* 5 Aug 1863; *m* 8 March 1892 Mary (*d* 25 Aug 1955), yst dau of Sir Robert Lynch-Blosse, 10th Bt (*qv*), and *d* 21 Aug 1946, having had:

(1) Patrick Robert, MC; Maj Cameronian Scottish Rifles WW I (despatches); *b* 11 Feb 1893; *d* 17 June 1916 of wounds recd in action

5 George Arthur; Capt RN; *b* 1 Sept 1864; *d* unm 28 July 1910

1 Lavinia; *d* unm 17 May 1943

2 Emily Maude; *m* 20 July 1893 George Hanbury Field (*d* 24 July 1901), of Ashurst Park, Kent, and *d* 28 Nov 1960, leaving issue

3 Mary Hilda Madelina; *m* 29 Oct 1890 Rev Ernest Wild, Rector Barming Kent 1912–20, 3rd s of James Anstey Wild, and *d* 31 Oct 1936, leaving issue. He *d* 16 Sept 1931

The 2nd VISCOUNT *d* 28 July 1894; his est son,

HENRY CHARLES HARDINGE, **3rd Viscount Hardinge of Lahore and Kings Newton**, CB, JP, DL Kent; *b* 1 Aug 1857; ADC to HM, Nile Expdn 1885 with Mounted Inf Camel Corps (Khedive's star, medal with two clasps), Col cmdg 6th Bn Rifle Bde, Capt Rifle Bde, ADC to C-in-C 1902–04; *m* 8 July 1891 Mary Frances, Order of Mercy with bar (*m* 2nd 18 Oct 1928 3rd Marquess of Abergavenny (*qv*)), 3rd dau of Hon Ralph Nevill (*see* ABERGAVENNY, M), and had:

1 Henry Ralph; Lt Rifle Bde; *b* 13 Oct 1895; *ka* 9 May 1915

2 CARYL NICHOLAS CHARLES, **4th Viscount**

1 Ruby, JP; *b* 31 July 1897; *m* 1 March 1928 Maj-Gen Frederick George Beaumont-Nesbitt, CVO, CBE, MC, Gren Gds, only surv s of Edward John Downing Beaumont-Nesbitt, OBE, JP, of Penton Lodge, Andover, and *d* 22 July 1977, leaving issue. He *d* 14 Dec 1971

2 Sybil Mary, OStJ; *b* 4 Dec 1898; *m* 1st 25 April 1922 (*divorce* 1941) 4th Baron Penrhyn (*qv*); *m* 2nd 8 Aug 1941 6th Earl Fortescue (*qv*) and *d* 1985

The 3rd VISCOUNT *d* 30 April 1924; his son,

CARYL NICHOLAS CHARLES HARDINGE, **4th Viscount Hardinge of Lahore and Kings Newton**, MBE (1946); *b* 25 Dec 1905; *educ* Harrow and RMC Sandhurst; Maj 7th Hus, ADC to Govr-Gen Canada 1926–28, Mil Assist to AG to Forces 1941–45; *m* 15 Sept 1928 Margaret Elizabeth Arnot (*d* 1993), only child of Hugh Percy Fleming, of Wynyards, Rockcliffe, Ottawa, and had issue:

1 HENRY NICHOLAS PAUL, **5th Viscount**

1 *Carolyn Mary Wynard [The Hon Mrs Worsley, RR2, Uxbridge, Ont, Canada]; *b* 5 March 1932; *m* 16 Jan 1954 *John Arthington Worsley (*see* WORSLEY, Bt)

2 *Gay [The Hon Mrs Raymond, Stage Coach Rd, Brome, Prov Quebec, Canada]; *b* 13 Aug 1938; *m* 9 Nov 1963 *Pierre Raymond, yr s of AVM Adelard Raymond, CBE, ED, ADC, of Senneville, Quebec, and has issue:

(1) *A son; *b* 24 Jan 1965

The 4th VISCOUNT *d* 1979; his son,

HENRY NICHOLAS PAUL HARDINGE, **5th Viscount Hardinge of Lahore and Kings Newton**; *b* 15 Aug 1929; *educ* Harrow; Hon Lt 7th QOH, Assist Gen Manager Roy Bank Canada; *m* 1st 13 Oct 1955 (*divorce* 1982) Zoe Ann (*m* 2nd 13 Dec 1983 Christopher M H Murrey, of Jersey), only child of Senator Hartland de Montarville Molson, OBE, of Montreal, and had:

1 CHARLES HENRY NICHOLAS HARDINGE, **6th and present Viscount Hardinge of Lahore and Kings Newton**

2 +ANDREW HARTLAND [The Hon Andrew Hardinge, 20 Niton St, London SW6 6NJ]; *b* 7 Jan 1960; heir presumptive; *educ* The Gow Sch and Trin Coll Sch; *m* 1990 *Sophia Mary, only dau of Capt (William) David Armstrong Bagnell (*see* WILTON, E), of East Worldham House, Alton, Hants, and has issue:

(1) +Thomas Henry de Montarville; *b* 19 June 1993

(2) +Jamie; *b* 4 Nov 1996

3 +Maximilian Evelyn; *b* 19 Jan 1969

The **5th Viscount** *m* 2nd 17 Sept 1982 *Florence [Mrs Martin Shelley, 24 Stafford Terrace, London W8 7BH] (*m* 2nd 1993 Martin Graham Shelley, s of John Shelley, of St Boswells, Roxburghshire), dau of Baron Harold von Oppenheim, of Cologne, and *d* 1984, leaving by her:

1 *Georgia Victoria; *b* 1984

HARDINGE OF PENSHURST

Arms: Gu. on a chevron arg., fimbriated or, three escallops sa. (honourable augmentation), on a chief wavy of the second a frigate, wholly dismasted, with the French flag flying beneath the British ensign, towed towards the dexter by a frigate of apparently inferior force in a shattered state, the British colours hoisted all ppr. **Crests:** 1 (of augmentation) A dexter hand, couped above the wrist, vested in the uniform of a British naval officer and grasping a sword erect ppr., pommel and hilt or, surmounting a Dutch and French flag in saltire; on the former inscribed 'Atalanta', on the latter 'Piedmontaise'; the blade of the sword passing through a wreath of laurel near the point, and a little below through another of cypress, all also ppr., 2 A mitre gu., garnished or, thereon a chevron charged and fimbriated, as in the arms (for HARDINGE). **Supporters:** Dexter, a brown bear; sinister, a Bengal tiger, both ppr. **Motto:** *Pro rege et patria* ('For King and country'). **Creation:** B. (UK) 21 July 1910.

THE 4TH BARON HARDINGE OF PENSHURST, Co Kent (Julian Alexander Hardinge) [The Rt Hon The Lord Hardinge of Penshurst, Flat 2/L, 115 Broomfield Dve, Glasgow G11 7NA]; *b* 23 Aug 1945 (HM THE QUEEN stood sponsor); *s* f 1997; *educ* Eton and Trin Coll Cambridge; Page of Honour to HM THE QUEEN 1959–62

Lineage: The 2nd VISCOUNT HARDINGE (*qv*) had a 2nd s:

CHARLES HARDINGE, **1st Baron Hardinge of Penhurst**, Co Kent (UK), so *cr* 21 July 1910, KG (1916), GCB (1910, CB 1895), GCSI (1910), GCMG (1905), GCIE (1910), GCVO (1905), ISO (1906), PC (1904), DL Kent; *b* 20 June 1858; *educ* Harrow and Trin Coll Cambridge (BA 1880, Hon LLD); Dip Serv 1880–1910: 3rd Sec Constantinople 1882, Berlin 1884 and Washington 1885, 2nd Sec Constantinople 1888 and Paris 1893, Sec Legn Teheran 1896, Sec Embassy St Petersburg 1898–1903, Assist U-Sec 1903–04, Amb St Petersburg 1904–06, PUS 1906–10 and 1916–20, Viceroy India 1910–16, Amb Extrdy and Plen Paris 1920–22, Chm Roy Commn Rebellion Ireland 1916, Pncpl Del for India Geneva 1923 and 1924, memb Jt Ctee Indian Constitutional Reform 1933–34, Roy Victoria Chain, Grand Cross Our Lady of Conception Portugal, Order Crown Italy, Order Redeemer Greece, Order Charles III Spain, Dannebrog Denmark, Order Vasa Sweden, St Olaf Norway, St Alexander Nevsky Russia, Legn Hon, White Eagle Germany, Leopold Austria, KGStJ; *m* 17 April 1890 Hon Winifred Selina Sturt, CI and Kaisar-i-Hind Gold Medal, Extra Ldy Bedchamber to HM QUEEN ALEXANDRA (*d* 11 July 1914), 2nd dau of 1st Baron Alington (*see* 1940 edn), and had issue:

1 Edward Charles, DSO, Lt 15th King's Hus WW I (despatches), Page Honour to HM EDWARD VII; *b* 3 May 1892; *dvp* 18 Dec 1914 of wounds recd in action

2 ALEXANDER HENRY LOUIS, **2nd Baron**

1 Diamond Evelyn Violet; *b* 8 June 1900; *m* 12 June 1923 Maj Sir Robert Alexander Abercromby, 9th Bt (*qv*), and *d* 11 Jan

The 1st BARON *d* 2 Aug 1944; his only surv son,

ALEXANDER HENRY LOUIS HARDINGE, **2nd Baron Hardinge of Penshurst**, GCB (1943), GCVO (1937), MC, PC (1936); *b* 17 May 1894; Maj Gren Gds, IA, ADC to Viceroy India 1915–16, Equerry and Assist Priv Sec to HM GEORGE V 1920–36, Assist Keeper Privy Purse 1935–36, Priv Sec and Extra Equerry to TM EDWARD VIII 1936 and GEORGE VI 1936–43, Extra Equerry 1943–52, Grand Offr Legn Hon; *m* 8 Feb 1921 Helen Mary, author (*d* 1979), dau of Lord Edward Herbert Gascoyne Cecil (*see* SALISBURY, M), and *d* 29 May 1960, leaving:

1 GEORGE EDWARD CHARLES HARDINGE, **3rd Baron Hardinge of Penshurst**; *b* 31 Oct 1921 (HM GEORGE V stood sponsor); *educ* Eton and RNC Dartmouth; Page Honour to TM GEORGE V 1933–36, EDWARD VIII 1936 and GEORGE VI 1937–38, Lt-Cdr (S) RN; publisher with Collins 1951–57 and 1961–68, Longmans 1957–61 and Macmillan 1968–86, consultant Headline 1986–87; author: *An Incomplete Angler* (1976) and (as George Milner) *Stately Homicide* (1953), *Shark Among Herrings* (1954) and *The Crime Against Marcella* (1963); *m* 1st 22 July 1944 (*divorce* 1962) Janet Christine Goschen, JP (E Sussex 1960) (*d* 18 March 1970), dau of Lt-Col Francis Cecil Campbell Balfour, CIE, CBE, MC (*see* BALFOUR, E), and had:

(1) JULIAN ALEXANDER HARDINGE, **4th and present Baron Hardinge of Penshurst**

(2) + HUGH FRANCIS [The Hon Hugh Hardinge, Albion Villa, Church End, Ouer, Cambs CB4 5NH]; *b* 9 April 1948; heir presumptive; *educ* Eton

(3) + Edward Frederick; *b* 25 Oct 1958; *educ* Gordonstoun

1 (cont.) The **3rd Baron** *m* 2nd 1966 *Margaret, formerly w of Derek Trezise and dau of William Thomas Jerrum, of Hastings, Sussex, and had by her:

(4) + Charles Alexander; *b* 17 May 1967; *educ* Eastbourne Coll and Bradford U (BEng)

1 (cont.) The **3rd Baron** *d* 14 July 1997, having adopted the s of his 2nd w: *Dane

1 *Winifred Mary [The Hon Lady Murray, Woodmancote Manor, Cirencester, Glos]; *b* 2 May 1923, WRNS WW II; *m* 10 July 1943 *Maj Sir (John) Anthony Jerningham Murray, CBE, Gren Gds, s of John Challenger Murray, of Oaksey House, Wilts, by Cecilia Annette Mary, only child of Sir Henry Stafford Jerningham, 11th and last Bt (*see* STAFFORD, B), and has:

(1) *(George) Alexander John [Alexander Murray Esq, 24 Ackman Road, London SW6]; *b* 8 Dec 1947; *educ* Eton; City Ed *Sunday Telegraph*; *m* 19 July 1975 *Caroline, dau of John Miller

2 Elizabeth Rosemary, JP (Berks); *b* 3 April 1927 (HM QUEEN ELIZABETH THE QUEEN MOTHER stood sponsor); WRNS 1945–48; *m* 4 Nov 1949 *Lt-Col Sir John Frederick Dame Johnston, GCVO, MC [Lt-Col Sir John Johnston GCVO MC, Studio Cottage, Windsor Great Park, Berks SL4 2HP], late Gren Gds, Comptroller Ld Chamberlain's Off 1981–87, s of Frederick Horace Johnston, and *d* April 1995, leaving:

(1) *Christopher Michael [Christopher Johnston Esq, 26 Chester Place, Malvern, Worcs WR14 1RQ]; *b* 20 Aug 1951; *educ* Ampleforth; *m* 1993 *Julia Southwell

(1) *Joanna Elizabeth; *b* 11 Nov 1953

HARDWICKE

Arms: Arg. on a saltire az. a bezant. **Crest:** A lion's head, erased ppr., collared gu., on the collar a bezant. **Supporters:** Dexter, a lion rampant-guardant or, collared gu., the collar charged with a bezant; sinister, a stag ppr., attired and unguled or, collared as the lion.
Motto: *Nec cupias, nec metuas* ('Neither covet nor fear').
Creations: B. (GB) 23 Nov 1733, V. and E. (GB) 2 April 1754.

THE 10TH EARL OF HARDWICKE, Viscount Royston, Co Cambridge, and **Baron Hardwicke**, of Hardwicke, Co Gloucester (Joseph Philip Sebastian Yorke) [The Rt Hon The Earl of Hardwicke, 12 Lansdowne Rd, London W11 3LW]; *b* 3 Feb 1971; *s* gf 1974

Lineage: SIMON YORKE, of Dover, merchant; *d* 1682, leaving, with other issue:

1 Philip, of Dover; slr; *m* Elizabeth, dau and heir of Richard Gibbon, of Dover, and widow of Edward Gibbon, of Westcliffe, Kent, and *d* 18 June 1721, leaving an only s:

(1) PHILIP, **1st Earl**

2 Simon; *m* Anne, sister and heir of John Mellor, of Erddig, Denbighshire, and was ancestor of Simon Yorke, of Erddig Park

SIMON YORKE'S gs,

PHILIP YORKE, **1st Earl of Hardwicke**, so *cr* 2 April 1754, as also VISCOUNT ROYSTON, Co Cambridge, and earlier 23 Nov 1733 BARON HARDWICKE, of Hardwicke, Co Gloucester (reflecting his buying of the manor and estate there 1725 for *c* £24,000 [over £1.3m in late-1990s terms]), PC (1733); *b* 1 Dec 1690; *educ* Middle Temple and Lincoln's Inn (Bencher 1724); barrister 1715, Recorder Dover, MP (Whig) Lewes 1719–22, Seaford 1722–33, Slr-Gen 1720–24, ktd 1720, Attorney-Gen 1723/4–33, Speaker Ho Lds Feb 1734 and Feb 1736, Ch Justice King's Bench 1733–37, Ld Chllr Feb 1736/7–56, Ld High Steward 1746 for trials of Earls of Kilmarnock and Cromartie and Lords Balmerino and Lovat following the '45; a Ld Justice (Regent) of the Realm during GEORGE II's absence 1740, 1743, 1745, 1748, 1750, 1752, High Steward Cambridge U 1749–64, LLD Cantab 1753, FSA by 1751, FRS 1753, Tstee Br Museum 1757–64; *m* 16 May 1719 Margaret, dau of Charles Cocks (*see* SOMERS, B) and widow of John Lygon, and *d* 6 March 1764, having had:

1 PHILIP YORKE, **2nd Earl of Hardwicke**, PC, FRS, FSA, LLD Camb, MP Reigate 1741–47, Cambs 1747–64, Ld Lt Cambs, High Steward Cambridge U 1764–90; bought the Wimpole estate, Cambs, from Edward Harley, Earl of Oxford, for £100,000 (nearly £5.5m in late-1990s terms) in 1740; *b* 9 Dec 1720; *m* 22 May 1740 Lady Jemima Campbell (*d* 10 Jan 1797), Baroness Lucas of Crudwell (*qv*) and Marchioness Grey, both in her own right, and only dau of 3rd Earl of Breadalbane (*see* 1970 edn), and *dspm* 16 May 1796, leaving:

(1) AMABEL Yorke, COUNTESS DE GREY OF WREST, Co Bedford (UK), in her own right, so *cr* 25 Oct 1816 with remainder to her sister and her issue, also (*s* mother as) BARONESS LUCAS OF CRUDWELL (*qv*); *b* 22 Jan 1751; *m* 16 July 1772 Alexander, Viscount Polwarth (later (1776) *cr* (1st) Baron Hume of Berwick; *dsp* & *vp* 9 March 1781; *see* POLWARTH, L), est s of last Earl of Marchmont, and *dsp* 4 May 1833

(2) Mary Jemima; *m* 17 Aug 1780 2nd Baron Grantham and *d* 7 Jan 1830, leaving issue

2 Charles, KC (1754); *b* 30 Dec 1722; *educ* Corpus Christi Coll Cambridge, Middle Temple 1735 and Lincoln's Inn (barrister Feb 1745/6, Bencher 1754), Jt Clerk Crown in Chancery 1747, MP Reigate 1747–68 and Cambridge U 1768, Counsel HEIC 1751, Slr-Gen 1756, Attorney-Gen 1762–63 and 1765–66, Recorder Dover and Gloucester 1764, Ld Chllr for three days 17–20 Jan 1770; *m* 1st 19 May 1755 Catherine, only child and heir of William Freeman, of Aspeden, Herts, by Catherine, dau of Sir Thomas Pope Blount, 2nd Bt, of Tittenhanger, and had:

(1) PHILIP YORKE, **3rd Earl of Hardwicke**, KG (1803), PC (1801); *b* 31 May 1757; LLD, FRS, FSA, MA Cantab, Col, Ld Lt Cambs 1790–1834, MP Cambs 1780–90, Ld Lt Ireland 1801–06 *m* 24 July 1782 Elizabeth (*d* 26 May 1858), dau of 5th Earl of Balcarres (*see* CRAWFORD and BALCARRES, E), and *dspms* 18 Nov 1834, having had, with other issue:

1a Philip, *Viscount Royston*, MP Reigate 1806–08; *b* 7 May 1784; lost in a storm off Lubeck 7 April 1808

2a Charles James, *Viscount Royston*; *b* 21 July 1797; *dvp* 30 April 1810
1a Anne; *m* 29 Aug 1807 3rd Earl of Mexborough (*qv*) and *d* 17 July 1870, leaving issue
2a Catherine Freeman; *m* 16 Oct 1811 2nd Earl of Caledon (*qv*) and *d* 8 July 1863, having had issue
3a Elizabeth Margaret; *m* 6 Feb 1816 Baron Stuart de Rothesay and *d* 23 June 1867, leaving issue (*see* BUTE, M)
4a Caroline Harriet; *m* 4 Feb 1815 2nd Earl Somers (*see* SOMERS, B) and *d* 27 May 1873, leaving issue

2 (cont.) The Hon Charles Yorke *m* 2nd 30 Dec 1762 Agneta, dau and coheir of Henry Johnston, of Gt Berkhamsted, Herts, and was found dead at his desk 20 Jan 1770 with a patent creating him Baron Morden in front of him which he as Ld Chllr had forbidden to have validated with the Gt Seal as, he said, he 'hoped it was no longer in his custody', having by her had, with a dau (Caroline, *m* 1790 1st Earl of Saint Germans (*qv*), *dsp* 26 July 1818):
(2) Charles Philip, PC; Teller Exchequer, 1st Ld Admlty, FRS, FSA; *b* 12 March 1764; *m* 1 July 1790 Harriott, dau of Charles Manningham, and *dsp* 13 March 1834
(3) Joseph Sydney (Sir), KCB; V-Adml, MP; *b* 6 June 1768; *m* 1st 29 March 1798 Elizabeth Weake (*d* 29 Jan 1812), dau of James Rattray of Atherston, and had:
1a CHARLES PHILIP, **4th Earl**
2a Henry Reginald (Ven); MA, Archdeacon Huntingdon, Canon Ely, Rector Wimpole and Aspeden; *b* 30 Oct 1803; granted with his siblings rank of earl's dau/yr s; *m* 19 Nov 1833 Flora Elizabeth (*d* 12 Jan 1852), 3rd dau of Gen Sir Alexander Campbell, 1st Bt, KCB (*see* COCKBURN-CAMPBELL, Bt), and *d* 26 Sept 1871, having had issue:
1b Philip Sydney; Col 19th Bengal Lancers; *b* 31 Dec 1834; *m* 19 May 1881 Alice Hopwood Schofield, dau of William Dudley Coddington, of Wycoller, nr Blackburn, and *dsp* 7 Dec 1881
2b Henry Eliot; *b* 4 July 1841; *d* 16 July 1864
3b Reginald Beauchamp; *b* 29 Aug 1845; *m* 30 April 1867 Caroline Augusta (*d* 8 Nov 1878), 2nd dau of John Christian Curwen Boyd, of Merton Hall, Wigtownshire, and *dsp* 15 May 1881
4b Horatio Arthur (Sir), CB; Lt-Col RE, Ch Inspr Rlwys BOT 1900–13, served Afghanistan and Nile Expdns; *b* 3 June 1848; *m* 26 July 1893 Rebecca Caroline (*d* 9 March 1943), dau of Rev Anthony Garstin, Rector Redmile, Leics, and *d* 10 Dec 1930
5b Alexander Campbell (Rev); Rector Falmere, Cambs; *b* 12 Jan 1852; *m* 16 April 1885 Cecil Charlotte (*d* 17 March 1931), dau of Henry Stuart Russell, and *d* 7 June 1925
1b Flora Caroline; *m* 13 Dec 1859 Henry William Currie, only s of William Currie, of W Horsley Place, and *d* 22 Oct 1901, having had issue. He *d* 24 Sept 1904
2b Susan Amelia; *m* 1857 Charles Joseph Theophilus Hambro, MP (*see* HAMBRO, B), and *d* 9 July 1887, leaving issue
3a Eliot Thomas, DL; MP Cambs 1834–65; *b* 20 April 1805; *m* 31 Jan 1833 Emily Anne Millicent (*d* 1 Jan 1894), only dau of Emilius Henry Delmé Radcliffe, of Hitchin Priory, Herts, and *dsp* 3 May 1885
4a Granthan Munton (Very Rev); DD, Dean Worcester; *b* 14 Feb 1809; *m* 10 March 1830 Marian Emily (*d* 9 Sept 1895), est dau of Sir Henry Cunningham Montgomery, 1st Bt, of The Hall, Co Donegal, and *d* 2 Oct 1879, leaving, with other issue:
1b Joseph Augustus; barrister; *b* 22 Sept 1831; *m* 3 Feb 1862 Florence Mary Eliza (*d* 1920), dau of Thomas Chambré, and *d* 14 Feb 1881, leaving:
1c Lilian Maud; *m* 10 June 1891 William John Levi, of Woughton House, Bletchley, Bucks. He *d* 5 Nov 1921
1b Alice Susan; *m* 6 Oct 1863 Rev Hon Wingfield Stratford Twisleton-Wykeham-Fiennes (*see* SAYE AND SELE, B) and *d* 17 Feb 1922, leaving issue
2b Constance Ellen; *m* 5 Feb 1880 Rev Hon William Henry Lyttelton (*see* COBHAM, V) and *d* 24 Dec 1920
1a Agneta Elizabeth; *m* 24 Feb 1836 Robert Cooper Lee Bevan, of Fosbury House, Wilts, and Trent Park, Middx, and *d* 8 July 1851, leaving issue. He *d* 22 July 1890
(3) (cont.) Sir Joseph *m* 2nd 22 May 1813 Lady Urania Annie (*d* 27 Dec 1843), widow of (a) 1st Marquess of Clanricarde (*see* SLIGO, M) and (b) Col Peter Kington and dau of 12th Marquess of Winchester (*qv*), and was accidentally drowned 5 May 1831

3 JOSEPH YORKE, 1st and last LORD DOVER, BARON OF THE TOWN AND PORT OF DOVER, Co Kent (GB), so *cr* 18 Sept 1788, KB (1761), PC (1768); *b* 24 June 1724; ADC to DUKE OF CUMBERLAND Battle of Fontenoy 1745 and GEORGE II 1749–58, Col 9th Foot 1755–59, 8th Dragoons 1759–60, 5th Dragoons 1760–87, 11th Light Dragoons 1787–89, 1st Life Gds 1789–92, Maj-Gen 1758, Lt Gen 1760, Gen 1777, Sec Embassy Paris 1749–51, Min Hague 1751–61, Amb Hague 1761–80, MP (Whig) E Grinstead 1751–61, Dover 1761–74 and Grampound 1774–80; *m* 23 June 1783 Christiana Charlotte Margaret (*d* 2 March 1793), only dau of Johan Henrik, Baron de Stöcken, of Denmark, and *dsp* 2 Dec 1792, when the Barony expired

4 John; *b* 27 Aug 1728; *m* 1 Jan 1762 Elizabeth (*d* 1766 aged 24), dau of Reginald Lygon (*see* 1970 edn BEAUCHAMP, E), and *d* 4 Sept 1801, leaving:
(1) Jemima; *m* 18 Nov 1784 Reginald Pole Carew and *d* 16 July 1804, leaving issue (*see* CAREW POLE, Bt)

5 James (Rt Rev); DD, Bp Ely; *b* 9 March 1730; *m* 29 June 1762 Mary, dau of Rt Rev Isaac Madocks, Bp Worcester, and *d* 26 Aug 1808, leaving, with other issue:
(1) Joseph; *b* 5 May 1765; *m* 17 Nov 1800 Catherine (*d* 3 March 1830), dau of James Cocks, bro of 1st Baron Somers (*qv*), and *d* 9 Dec 1830, leaving issue:
1a Joseph, of Forthampton Court, Glos; High Sheriff 1844–45; *b* 11 Jan 1807; *m* 31 Dec 1834 Frances Antonia (*d* 27 Feb 1889), dau of Reginald Pole Carew (*see* CAREW POLE, Bt), and *d* 4 Feb 1889, leaving issue:
1b John Reginald, of Forthampton Court, JP, DL Worcs; High Sheriff 1892, JP Glos, MP Tewkesbury 1864–68 and 1885–86 and E Glos 1872–85; *b* 25 Jan 1836; *m* 1st 4 March 1862 Augusta Emmeline (*d* 19 Feb 1863), dau of Gen Sir Thomas Monteath Douglas, KCB, and had issue:
1c Augustus; Lt Gloucester Yeo Cav; *b* 11 Feb 1863; *d* unm 29 June 1891
1b (cont.) John Yorke *m* 2nd 11 Jan 1868 Sophia Matilda (*d* 4 Aug 1905), dau of Baron Vincent de Tuyll de Serooskerken, and *d* 27 March 1912, having by her had issue:
2c Vincent Wodehouse, JP Glos; Capt Gloucester Imp Yeo, MA Cantab, Fell King's Coll Cambridge, Order Redeemer Greece; *b* 21 May 1869; *m* 24 Aug 1899 Hon Maud Evelyn Wyndham (*d* 22 July 1963), dau of 2nd Baron Leconfield (*see* EGREMONT, LECONFIELD and, B), and *d* 26 Nov 1957, having had issue:
1d Philip; *b* 4 Aug 1900; *d* 28 July 1917
2d Gerald Joseph; Maj Roy Glos Hus; *b* 10 Dec 1901; *educ* Eton and Trin Coll Cambridge (BA); *m* 21 July 1937 Angela Vivien (*d* 1988), er dau of Maj-Gen Sir John Duncan, KCB, CMG, CVO, DSO, and *d* 29 April 1983, leaving:
1e +John Sarne [John Yorke Esq, Forthampton Court, Glos GL19 4RD]; *b* 12 Oct 1938; *educ* Eton and Trin Coll Cambridge (BA 1960); ACA 1965; *m* 1st July 1967 Jean Victoria (*d* 1989), yr dau of Anthony Reynolds, of Sintra, Portugal; *m* 2nd 1992 *C Julia, dau of Herbert M Allen, and by his 1st w has issue:
1f *Anabel; *b* 1971
2f *Sara; *b* 5 April 1974
2e +Vincent James [Vincent Yorke Esq, The Stalls, Bushley, Glos]; *b* 16 Feb 1942; *educ* Eton, Slade Sch of Art and UCL; *m* Dec 1970 *Francine, dau of F W Barker, of The White House, Hythe, and has:
1f *Griselda Rose; *b* 1973
2f *Hester Mary; *b* 14 July 1974
3f *Sophie Catherine; *b* 17 June 1977
3e +Michael Piers [Dr Michael Yorke, 31 Downside Crescent, London NW3 2AN]; *b* 26 Jan 1944; *educ* Eton, Edinburgh U and London U (MPhil 1972, PhD 1976); *m* 1 July 1972 *Valerie Margaret, dau of H Peter B Cox, of Chislehurst, Kent, and has issue:
1f +Marcus Hugo Maddox; *b* 1983
1f *Jessica Claire; *b* 1980
3d Henry Vincent; author (as Henry Green): *Blindness* (1926), *Living* (1929), *Party* (1939), *Loving* (1945), *Back* (1946), *Concluding* (1948), *Nothing* (1950), *Doting* (1952) and an autobiography *Pack My Bag* (1940), md H Pontifex & Sons, Chm Br Chemical Plant Mfrs' Assoc; *b* 29 Oct 1905; *educ* Eton and Magdalen Coll Oxford; *m* 25 July 1929 Hon Adelaide ('Dig') Mary Biddulph (*d* 1985), er dau of 2nd Baron Biddulph (*qv*), and *d* 13 Dec 1973, leaving:
1e +Sebastian; *b* 24 Jan 1934; *educ* Eton and Trin Coll Oxford; *m* 1st 18 Nov 1957 (*divorce* 1962) Hon Emma Christina Tennant, er dau of 2nd Baron Glenconner (*qv*), and has issue:
1f +Matthew Henry; *b* 24 Nov 1958
1e (cont.) Sebastian Yorke *m* 2nd 1969 *Evelien, formerly w of R M Gilbert and dau of Lewis Barrau, of The Hague
3c Charles Joseph; *b* 24 June 1872; *d* unm 28 Sept 1904
4c Ralph Maximilian, CMG (1919), DSO (1917); Lt-Col Gloucester Yeo, Capt 11th Hus, Hon Brig-Gen 1921, served Boer War 1902 and WW I (despatches), Order St Maurice and St Lazarus Italy, Cdr Order Crown Romania; *b* 22 Oct 1874; *m* 4 Oct 1906 Hon Muriel Fanny Herschell (*d* 26 Oct 1956), dau of 1st Baron Herschell (*qv*), and *d* 25 Feb 1951, leaving:
1d *Adela Sophie; *b* 22 July 1907
2d *Daphne Elizabeth; *b* 21 Dec 1910; *m* 24 April 1948 David Alan Fullerton, only s of Alan Weston Fullerton, of Rye, Sussex. He *d* 10 April 1965
1c Dorothy Constance Emily, CVO (1937); Ldy-in-Waiting to TRH PRINCESS PATRICIA OF CONNAUGHT 1917–19 and THE PRINCESS ROYAL 1919–39 (Extra Ldy-in-Waiting 1939–46); *b* 30 July 1879; *d* unm 20 Nov 1946
2a James Charles; Capt 5th Dragoon Gds; *b* 6 Feb 1816; *m* 31 Oct 1839 Georgiana Augusta (*d* 6 Dec 1901), dau of Rev Charles Hawkins (*see* HAWKINS, Bt), and *d* 5 Jan 1867, having had, with other issue:
1b James Charles, of Langton, Dwrbach, Pembs, JP; High Sheriff 1896; *b* 28 Oct 1847; *m* 1878 Katharine Ellen (*d* 23 Sept 1936), dau of Robert Langdon, of NZ, and *d* 20 Jan 1932, having had issue:
1c James Hamilton Langdon, MC (1918); Capt Pembroke Yeo, BA Oxford; *b* 1884; *m* 1 Dec 1910 Violet Mary (*d* 22 Oct 1963), dau of James Edmund Vincent, Chllr Diocese of Bangor, and was *ka* 27 Dec 1917, leaving issue:
1d James John Simon, DSC and bar, DL (Pembs 1959); High Sheriff Pembs 1962, Capt RN WW II; *b* 1 Sept 1912; *m* 29 July 1938 *Bridget Essex [Mrs James Yorke, Constant, Nevern, Newport, Pembrokeshire], dau of Adml Sir Alban Thomas Buckley Curteis, KCB, and *d* 30 April 1963, leaving issue:
1e +James Hamilton Simon, MBE [Lt-Cdr James Yorke MBE RN, 2831 S Columbus St, Arlington, VA 22206, USA]; *b* 9 Sept 1939; *educ* Wellington and RNC Dartmouth; *m* 1st 14 May 1966 (*divorce* 1984) Elizabeth Ann, er dau of Col John Leeper Anketell Macafee, CBE; *m* 2nd 1989 *Jean Anne, dau of C Richard Louis, of Trenton, Michigan, and by his 1st w has issue:
1f +Simon Anketell Hamilton; *b* 23 Feb 1967
2f +Patrick James Langdon; *b* 10 Aug 1968
1f *Rebecca Mary Annabel; *b* 26 Nov 1970
2f *Annabel Lucy Elizabeth; *b* 1972
2e +Nicholas Roger [Nicholas Yorke Esq, Lower Fishguard, Dyfed]; *b* 13 Oct 1944; *educ* Wellington; ag engr; *m* 1st 10 May 1969 (*divorce* 1976) Kathleen Prentice, 2nd dau of Kent Sanger, of Duxbury, Mass.; *m* 2nd 1977 (*divorce* 1989) Carole Crossman, yr

dau of Eldon F le Poer Power, of Ashfield, Beauparc, Co Meath, and by her has:
1f +Philip David Emerson; *b* 15 Sept 1983
1f *Louisa Harriet; *b* 26 May 1979
1e *Philippa Mary Essex [Mrs Roger Morrall, Lower Boddington, Daventry, Northants]; *b* 25 Sept 1947; *m* 5 Oct 1968 *Rcger Morrall, yr s of Cyrus Roger Morrall, of Kenya, and has issue:
1f *Thomas Simon Neil; *b* 1978
1f *Bridget Essex; *b* 1973
1d *Susannah Mary [Mrs Allen Malcolmson, 331 The Street, Holt, Trowbridge, Wilts BA14 6QH]; *b* 1 Nov 1915; *m* 1st 23 Dec 1934 Maj Gerald Hartas FitzGerald, IMS (*d* 28 Jan 1937), s of Alexander FitzGerald, and has issue:
1e *Anne Sara [Mrs Richard Eastham, Dolau Dwrbach, Scleddau, Fishguard, Dyfed]; *b* 2 Dec 1935; *m* July 1959 *Richard Michael Johnston Eastham, and has issue:
1f *Cedric Gerald; *b* Nov 1960
1f *Jane Francesca; *b* April 1962
1d (cont.) Mrs Gerald FitzGerald *m* 2nd 7 July 1938 *Maj Allen Forbes Malcolmson TD, RE, only surv s of Capt James Grant Malcolmson, Gordon Highrs, and has by him:
2e *Jean Sheila [Mrs Peter Robjant, 32 Hilperdon Rd, Trowbridge, Wilts]; *b* 8 Aug 1942; *m* 14 Aug 1971 *Peter Robjant, s of R W D Robjant and Mrs F E K Jordan, and has issue:
1f *David Allan; *b* 1973
1f *Mary Anna Susan; *b* 1975
2c Robert Langdon; ICS (ret 1947); Judge Ch Court Oudh 1938 and High Court Allahabad 1943; *b* 1887; *educ* Lincoln Coll Oxford (BA); *m* 1914 Enid Cicely Nugent (*d* 5 Feb 1974 aged 81), dau of Cecil Eddis Furlong Meares, ICS, of Bedford, and *d* 12 June 1955, having had issue:
1d Patrick Langdon; Maj Roy Corps Signals (TA) WW II; *b* 1916; *educ* Clare Coll Cambridge (BA); *m* 21 Oct 1939 *Pamela Mary (*m* 2nd 22 July 1950 Robert Michael Clive and has further issue), dau of Lt-Col Harold Rudgard, OBE, and *d* of wounds 5 March 1945, leaving issue:
1e +Robert Anthony [Robert Yorke Esq, Silver Birches, Bashurst Hill, Itchingfield, W Sussex RH13 7NY]; *b* 27 June 1944; *educ* Marlborough and Clare Coll Cambridge (MA); *m* 17 May 1975 *Morag, dau of John S McDow, of Helensburgh, and has:
1f +Andrew Patrick; *b* 1982
1f *Sarah Catherine; *b* 1978
1e *Caroline Gillian Ann [Mrs Peter Chamberlain, 60 Rock Rd, Cambridge]; *b* 14 Aug 1941; *m* 26 July 1969 *Peter Chamberlain, and has issue:
1f *Juliet Catherine; *b* 1970
2f *Rachel Claire; *b* 1972
3c Joseph Hugh Langdon; Cdr RN; *b* 1888; *m* 24 Feb 1916 Ursula Mary Vere (*d* 5 June 1959), dau of Col Robert Oliver Lloyd, CB, RE, of Trefgarne Hall, Pembs, and *d* Kenya Aug 1936, leaving issue:
1d George Cockburn; Lt (A) RN WW II (despatches); *b* 24 Dec 1921, drowned as the result of a sailing accident in Moray Firth 1 May 1948
1d *Josephine Mary [Mrs Luis Nicolin y Martinez del Campo, Bolivar 8, 402 Mexico City 1, DF, Mexico]; *b* 9 April 1917; *m* 1st 12 Dec 1945 Maurice Newton (*d* 8 April 1949), only s of Cap R A Newton; *m* 2nd 17 April 1959 *Luis Nicolin y Martinez del Campo, 2nd s of Manuel Nicolin y Gutierrez Estrada, of Mexico City
2d *April Ursula [Sister Mary of the Sacred Heart, Carmelite Monastery, Bridge Lane, London NW11]; *b* 1 April 1919
4c Hardwicke Langdon; Sub-Lt RN; *b* 1891; *d* 8 Jan 1913
5c Worthington Langdon; *b* 8 May 1901; *m* 23 July 1934 *Irene Rebecca [Mrs Worthington Yorke, 352-12720 111th Ave, Edmonton, Alberta, Canada T6H 4K8], est dau of George Oscar Britney, of Alberta, and *d* 1983, leaving:
1d +Frederick Alton; *b* 16 Aug 1935
1d *Katherine Anne [Mrs Walter Yakimets, 4803 Lansdowne Drive, Edmonton, Alberta, Canada T6H 4K8]; *b* 27 Jan 1937; *m* 1959 *Walter William Yakimets, and has issue:
1e *Walter John; *b* 1961
2e *Stephen George; *b* 1963; *m* 1986 *Marilyn Joan Mitchell
3e *Neil Edward; *b* 1969
1e *Dawn-Marie Rebecca; *b* 1968
2d *Dianne Marie; *b* 16 June 1945; *m* 1968 *Walter Herman Henry Petersen and has:
1e *Kevin John; *b* 1966
2e *Gary Michael; *b* 1968
3e *Brian Langdon Benjamin; *b* 1971
6c Philip Cecil Langdon, OBE (1941); Capt RN WW II; *b* 23 July 1903; *m* 1st 22 April 1936 Elsie Margaret (*d* 6 July 1945), dau of Frank Davis; *m* 2nd 23 July 1946 (*divorce* 1960) Violet Helen, only dau of Charles Ormonde Trew; *m* 3rd 18 Aug 1961 Mrs Margaret Rose Ross (*d* 22 May 1966), yst dau of A Rubenstein, of Knightsbridge, and *d* 19 Jan 1970, leaving by his 2nd w:
1d *Clare Amabel [Mrs Jonathan Barclay, The Old Vicarage, Stoke Holy Cross, Norfolk NR14 8AB]; *b* 15 March 1948; *m* 28 June 1969 *Jonathan Robert Barclay (*see* BARCLAY, Bt) and has issue
1c Georgiana Margaret; *m* 1st 14 April 1909 Hugh Mortimer Thomas, MRCS, LRCP, 3rd s of Lt-Col J R Thomas, Dep-Govr Sierra Leone, and had issue. He *d* 25 Sept 1925; *m* 2nd 28 Feb 1927 Maj Herbert David Johns, MC, s of Rev T Johns, of Manorowen, and *d* 1 Sept 1967. He *d* July 1963
2c Katherine Olive; *m* 3 Sept 1918 Sir (Francis Charles) Rupert Ford, 5th Bt (*see* ST CLAIR-FORD, Bt), and had issue
3c Marianna Augusta; *d* unm 12 March 1926
4c Sophie Cecilia; *m* 29 Feb 1928 Maj-Gen George Oswald Crawford, CB, CBE, RAOC, er s of Col Arthur Gosset Crawford, of Nailsworth, Glos, and *d* 10 July 1974, leaving issue
2b Reginald Somers; *b* 10 June 1854; *m* 10 Feb 1886 Emmeline (*d* 23 April 1935), sis of Sir Malby Crofton, 3rd Bt (*qv*), and *d* 29 Jan 1916, leaving:
1c Reginald Henry Crofton; Lt RGA FIA WW I; *b* 7 Sept 1897; *educ* King's Coll Cambridge (MA); *m* 9 July 1927 *Gwendolen Maude, dau of Frank Watkinson, and accidentally drowned 27 Aug 1947, leaving:
1d +John Reginald [John Yorke Esq, 9 Mornington Road, London E4]; *b* 23 May 1928; *educ* Bradfield and King's Coll Cambridge; *m* 18 April 1959 *Catherine Stewart, dau of Frank William Borthwick, of W Ham, and has:
1e *Margaret Helen; *b* 27 Feb 1967
2e *Jennifer Francis; *b* 1970
1d *Elizabeth Mary; *b* 20 Oct 1930
1c Emmeline Dorothea; Master Nenagh Harriers 1936–46; *educ* Roedean; *m* 1st 21 Aug 1915 (*divorce* 1927) Vernon Garrold Bell (*d* 1928) and had issue; *m* 2nd 15 Dec 1927 Maj-Gen Frederick William Brooke Koe, CB, CMG (*d* 6 Feb 1935), est s of John Heber Pemberton Koe, of Youghal Lodge, Nenagh, Co Tipperary; *m* 3rd 17 Feb 1940 Capt John Anthony Bulger, RFA, Dist Offr Nigerian Admin Serv, and *d* 1967. He *d* 7 July 1961
3b Algernon Joseph; *b* 29 June 1856; *m* 24 March 1888 Violet Lucy Grahame (*d* 29 July 1926), dau of James Henry Spring Branston, and *d* 15 Jan 1932, leaving issue:
1c Simon Algernon; Lt-Col LAA, RA (TA), Capt PP Canadian LI WW I and WW II; *b* 15 Feb 1920; *educ* Harrow and Clare Coll Cambridge; *m* 2 Feb 1920 *Annie Paton, dau of J P Fyfe, JP, of Greenock, and *d* 1977, having had:
1d +Joseph Algernon; *b* 19 Oct 1922; *m* 23 Oct 1945 *Mary Robertson, dau of Alexander Brown, of Fife, and has:
1e *Marianne Alexandra; *b* 18 Sept 1946
2e *Josephine Mary Bunty; *b* 17 Feb 1948
2d Alexander Peden; Midshipman RN WW II; *b* 23 Jan 1924; *ka* 17 Jan 1942
3d Josephine Annie; *b* 31 Jan 1921; *d* 17 Sept 1922
2c Harold Branson; *b* 25 March 1890; *m* 11 Feb 1920 Stella Catherine (*d* 3 Oct 1968), yst dau of R-Adml Henry Compton Aitchison, of Shrubs Hill, Lyndhurst, and *d* 6 Jan 1949, leaving issue:
1d *Therese [Mrs Michael Stirling, 6 Old Farm Rd, Nether Stowey, Bridgwater, Somerset]; *b* 1925; *m* 1963 as his 2nd w *Michael Charles Stirling
2d *Joan Felicity [Countess Bizzarri, via Galla e Sidami 49, Rome 00199, Italy]; *b* 1933; *m* 27 April 1957 *Count Mario Bizzarri and has:
1e *Flaminia Stella Gianninia Maria; *b* 24 Feb 1958; *m* 1990 *Mario di Pilla
2e *Alessandra Luisa Teresa Cristina Maria; *b* 1959; *m* 1993 *Ben Heijmen
3e *Paola Maria Augusta Audreina Giovanna; *b* 1960
4e *Giovanna; *b* 1963
5e *Carla; *b* 1966
3d *Christine Anne [Mrs Alan White, Primrose Lodge, Duddleswell, Uckfield, E Sussex TN22 3JN]; *m* 5 July 1958 *Alan Neville White, s of Harry Eric William White, and has issue:
1e *Richard Neville; *b* 10 July 1964; *m* 1996 *Helen Bernadette O'Connor
1e *Margaret Lesley; *b* 24 April 1959; *m* 1991 (*divorce* 1994) Peter Bowden
2e *Helen Mary; *b* 26 Nov 1960; *m* 1990 *Dr David Halpin
3c Vivian Joseph; *b* 25 July 1895; *m* 5 June 1929 *Elizabeth Selina Frances Witcher
1c Una Violet; *b* 2 June 1891; *d* unm 4 Feb 1943
1b Catherine Anna Cockburn; *m* 20 April 1871 Rev William Batley and *d* 24 Nov 1928, leaving issue. He *d* 1909
2b Frances Annesley; *m* 31 Aug 1871 Rev John Langhorne, Vicar Lamberhurst, Kent, and *d* 12 July 1920, having had issue. He *d* 10 Dec 1911
3b Georgina Emma; *m* 6 Nov 1876 Alfred Tucker, MLC, and *d* 29 Oct 1923, leaving issue
4b Harriett Elizabeth; *m* 19 Sept 1877 Col W Raffles Tucker, RE, and *d* 18 May 1928, having had issue. He *d* 1881
5b Dorothea Agnes; *m* 10 Feb 1882 Charles Ward, MRCS, and *d* 1886, leaving issue
6b Louisa Adelaide; *m* 23 June 1886 Sir Edmund Ernest Nott-Bower, KCB, and *d* 6 Sept 1925, leaving issue. He *d* 13 Sept 1933
1a Catherine Harriett; *m* 12 Aug 1834 Col Henry Morgan Clifford, of Llantilo, Mon, and *d* Feb 1898, leaving issue. He *d* 12 Feb 1884
(2) Philip (Rev); Preb Ely; *b* 24 Feb 1770; *m* 4 Dec 1797 Hon Anna Maria Cocks (*d* 27 July 1835), dau of 1st Baron Somers (*qv*), and *d* 29 May 1817, leaving, with other issue:
1 a Philip James; Col, FRS; *b* 13 Oct 1799; *m* 27 April 1843 Emily (*d* 16 Sept 1869), yst dau of William Morgan Clifford, of Perrystone, Herefs, and *dsp* 14 Dec 1874
2a Charles Isaac (Rev); Rector Shenfield, Essex; *b* 7 Oct 1801; *m* 17 Dec 1840 Ellen, yst dau of John Leigh, and *d* 25 July 1863, having had issue:
1b Philip Charles; Lt-Col 1st Bn KO Loyal Lancs Regt; *b* 13 April 1844; *m* 11 April 1872 Emily Marion (*d* 28 April 1936), dau of Henry Raikes, of Llwynegrin, Flintshire, and *d* 27 Jan 1895, leaving issue:
1c Henry Reginald, MC (1918); *b* 29 May 1874; Boer War 1899–1902 with Imp Yeo, Maj Warwicks Yeo WW I (despatches); *m* 28 Oct 1903 Beatrix Victoire (*d* 8 Oct 1960), yr dau of Capt George Staunton Lynch-Staunton, 14th Hus, of Purbrook House, Hants, and *d* following an accident 15 March 1944, leaving issue:

1d +Philip [Philip Yorke Esq, 3 Crowsbury Close, Emsworth, Hants PO10 7TS]; *b* 31 Dec 1905; *educ* Harrow; *m* 30 April 1945 *Elsie May, dau of E Heasman, of Brighton

2d Charles Anthony; Cdr (E) RN WW II; *b* 17 July 1910; *k* in a motor-cycle accident 27 June 1949

3d David Christopher, DSO (1940); G/Capt RAFO WW II (despatches); *b* 5 Sept 1913

2c Philip Gerard, DSO (19019), JP (Somerset 1943); Brig RHA, Cdr RA 49th (W R) Div 1934–35, Brig RA S Cmd India 1935–39, served WW I (despatches) and WW II, Merite Militaire Spain 1909, memb Lloyd's; *b* 9 Jan 1882; *educ* Wellington; *m* 7 Aug 1914 Beryl Emila (*d* 14 May 1982 aged 96), 4th dau of Brig-Gen Arthur Henry Croker Philpotts, RHA, and *d* 28 Jan 1968, leaving issue:

1d (Arthur Philip) Denys, MC (1945); Lt-Col RA WW II; *b* 16 March 1915; *educ* Wellington; *m* 19 Jan 1957 *Mary Elizabeth (*m* 2nd 1983 Jeffrey Michelmore), er dau of John Henry Lionel Glasbrook, of Childe Okeford Manor, Blandford, Dorset, and *d* 1971, leaving issue:

1e +Michael Philip; *b* 15 Feb 1959

2e +Nicholas Simon; *b* 25 Nov 1961; *m* 1991 *Esther Victoria, only dau of Barry Desmond Watkins, and has:

1f +Robert Maximilian Philip; *b* 1991

1e *Delia Mary; *b* 2 Feb 1964

1d *Amabel Marion [Mrs Robert Carr, Nethercote, Church Lane, Mottisfont, Hants SO51 0LL]; *b* 1924; *m* 14 Sept 1963 *Brig Robert Michael Carr, MBE, DFC, RA, est s of D L Carr, and adopted:

*Peter Robert; *b* 27 May 1965

*Philippa Amabel; *b* 30 Nov 1966

2b Reginald; *d* Oct 1871

1b Harriot; *d* 1 Oct 1930

3a Reginald; R-Adml; *b* 24 Nov 1803; *m* 30 Nov 1854 Harriet (*d* 16 Oct 1906), dau of John Walker, of Purbrook Park, Hants, and *d* 17 Dec 1870, having had issue:

1b Edmund Walker; Cdr RN, Harbour Master Wei-Hai-Wei, China; *b* 31 July 1857; *m* 1896 Beatrice Isabel (*d* 25 April 1932), dau of Gen Sir Francis William Thomas, KCB; RMLI, and *dsp* 8 Dec 1912

2b Reginald Frederick; MIEE; *b* 18 Nov 1862; *m* 13 April 1893 Constance Eleanor, FRGS, MRI, FRSA (*d* 27 Dec 1948), est dau of Rev Frederick Arnold, and *dsp* 6 March 1906

3b Philip Chesney; MA Oxon, Licencie-es-Lettres U of Paris, FRHistS; *b* 28 Aug 1865; *d* unm 24 Oct 1943

1b Emily Henrietta; *d* 19 Oct 1878

2b Olivia Juliana; *m* 4 Oct 1904 Harry Christopher Minchin, yst s of Rev Henry Charles Minchin, and *d* 1948. He *d* 30 Oct 1941

3b Anna Maria Antonia; *d* unm 11 June 1946

1a Anna Maria; *m* 27 Nov 1838 Sir Edmund Head, 8th and last Bt, and *d* 25 Aug 1890, having had issue. He *d* 28 Jan 1868

1 Elizabeth; *b* Aug 1725; *m* 25 April 1748 George, Lord Anson, and *dsp* 1 June 1760 (*see* LICHFIELD, E)

2 Margaret; *m* 22 June 1749 Sir Gilbert Heathcote, 3rd Bt, of London (*qv*), and *dsp* 10 Aug 1769

The 3rd EARL's nephew,

CHARLES PHILIP YORKE, **4th Earl of Hardwicke**, PC; DCL Oxon, LLD Cantab, FRS, Adml, MP Reigate 1831–32 and Cambs 1832–34, Ld Lt Cambs 1834–73, PMG 1852, Ld Privy Seal 1858–59; *b* 2 April 1799; *m* 14 Oct 1833 Susan (*d* 22 Nov 1886 aged 76), 6th dau of 1st Baron Ravensworth (*qv*), and *d* 17 Sept 1873, having had issue:

1 CHARLES PHILIP YORKE, **5th Earl of Hardwicke**, PC, DL Cambs; Comptroller Household 1866–68, Master Buckhounds 1874–80, MP Cambs 1863–73, Lt 11th Hus; *b* 23 April 1836; *m* 16 Feb 1863 Lady Sophie Georgiana Robertina Wellesley (*d* 3 June 1923), yr dau of 1st Earl Cowley (*qv*), and *d* 18 May 1897, leaving:

(1) ALBERT EDWARD PHILIP HENRY YORKE, **6th Earl of Hardwicke**, DL Cambs; Parly U-Sec India 1900–02 and 1903–04 and War 1902–03, CC Marylebone 1897–1901, Hon Attaché Vienna 1886–91, Capt 3rd Bn Duke of Edinburgh's Wilts Regt; *b* 14 March 1867 (HM EDWARD VII stood sponsor); *d* unm 29 Nov 1904

(1) Feodorowna; *m* 25 June 1883 2nd Baron Alington (*see* 1940 edn) and *d* 27 June 1934, leaving issue. He *d* 30 July 1919

(2) Magdalen; *m* 10 Dec 1885 Sir Richard Henry Williams-Bulkeley, 12th Bt (*qv*), and *d* 27 Jan 1940, leaving issue

2 JOHN MANNERS, **7th Earl**

3 Victor Alexander; Lt RA; *b* 24 March 1842; *d* 23 Dec 1867

4 Elliot Constantine, DL Cambs; Equerry to HRH THE DUKE OF EDINBURGH, Capt Cambs Militia, MP Cambs; *b* 13 July 1843; *m* 11 Feb 1873 Annie (*d* 21 Nov 1926), 2nd dau of Sir Anthony de Rothschild, 1st Bt (*see* ROTHSCHILD, B), and *dsp* 21 Dec 1878

5 Alexander Grantham, CVO; MA Oxon, Groom-in-Waiting to HM QUEEN VICTORIA 1884–1901, Extra Groom-in-Waiting to HM EDWARD VII 1901–10, Equerry to HRH THE DUKE OF ALBANY 1874–84, Capt 4th Bn Suffolk Regt; *b* 20 Nov 1847; *d* unm 17 March 1911

1 Elizabeth Philippa, VA; Extra Woman Chamber to HM QUEEN VICTORIA; *b* 15 Nov 1834; *m* 1st 5 June 1860 Henry John Adeane, DL, JP, of Babraham, Cambs, and had issue. He *d* 17 Feb 1870; *m* 2nd 16 July 1877 1st Baron Biddulph (*qv*) and *d* 13 Jan 1916

2 Mary Catherine; *b* 19 May 1837; *m* 20 July 1857 William George Craven (*see* CRAVEN, E) and *d* 14 Dec 1890, leaving issue

3 Agneta Harriett; Ldy Bedchamber to HRH PRINCESS CHRISTIAN; *b* 13 Dec 1838; *m* 28 Nov 1867 R-Adml Hon Victor Alexander Montagu (*see* SANDWICH, E) and *d* 12 March 1919, leaving issue

The 6th EARL's unc,

JOHN MANNERS YORKE, **7th Earl of Hardwicke**, JP, DL Cambs; Capt RN Baltic 1854, Black Sea 1855, Inspr Coastguard Folkestone 1870–74; *b* 30 Oct 1840; *m* 9 Jan 1869 Edith Mary (*d* 27 July 1930), yr dau of Alexander Oswald, of Auchencruive, Ayrshire, and *d* 13 March 1909, leaving:

1 CHARLES ALEXANDER YORKE, **8th Earl of Hardwicke**; Lt RNVR WW I; *b* 11 Nov 1869; *m* 1st 27 April 1911 (*divorce* 1927) Ellen, CBE (1918) (*d* 16 Feb 1968), dau of James Russell, of Auckland, NZ, and had:

(1) Elizabeth Mary, CVO (1965); Ldy Bedchamber to HM THE QUEEN 1953; *b* 10 March 1912; *m* 1 Oct 1931 5th Earl of Leicester (*qv*) and *d* 1985, leaving issue

1 (cont.) The **8th Earl** *m* 2nd 20 Aug 1930 Mary Radley (*m* 2nd 5 July 1938 W E L Jennings, Dist Offr Nyasaland; *d* 16 July 1938), dau of Edward Robert Twist, of Liverpool, and *dspm* 1 Feb 1936

2 Alfred Ernest Frederick; Lt Gren Gds (SR),5th Bn Inniskilling Fus and 23rd Bn Royal Fus WW I; *b* 11 July 1871; *m* 22 July 1905 (*divorce* 1918) Gladys Dunlop, OBE (1920) (*d* 6 Nov 1933), only child of Andrew Vans Dunlop Best, and *d* 24 Aug 1928, leaving issue:

(1) PHILIP GRANTHAM, **9th Earl**

3 Claude John; PWD Cairo 1897–1907; *b* 17 Oct 1872; *m* 28 April 1914 Fay (*d* 13 May 1928), only child of John Michel Zarifi, of Mayfair, and *d* 15 Sept 1940, having had issue:

(1) Richard Charles John; *b* 25 July 1916; *d* 1992

(2) David John Napier Edward, JP (W Sussex 1965); *b* 17 Oct 1919; *educ* Eton and Jesus Coll Cambridge; barrister Middle Temple 1949, Underwriting Memb Lloyd's; *m* 1st 2 Feb 1950 Anne Margaret (*d* 1984), yr dau of Denis George Mackail (*see* 1926 edn BURNE-JONES, Bt); *m* 2nd 1990 *June Rose Charlotte Rachel [Mrs David Yorke, Gatewick, Steyning, W Sussex BN44 3RS], only dau of Daniel Walter Thomas Gurney, MC (*see* TROUBRIDGE, Bt), and widow of Robert Duncan Fyfe, and *d* 12 July 1997, leaving by his 1st w:

1a +CHARLES EDWARD [Charles Yorke Esq, Flat 4, 3 Vicarage Gate, London W8 4HH]; *b* 18 March 1951; heir presumptive; *educ* Eton and Ruskin Sch of Drawing and Fine Art Oxford; caricaturist

2a +James Alexander [James Yorke Esq, 64 Peterborough Rd, London SW6 3EB]; *b* 30 March 1954; *educ* Eton, Balliol Coll Oxford (BA 1977) and Birkbeck Coll London U (BA 1983); *m* 1986 *Primrose Alexandra Mary, only dau of Brig Harold Kitson, CBE, and has issue:

1b +Philip Prospero Alexander; *b* 1987

2b +Henry Cosimo Frederick; *b* 1991

(1) Mary Susan; *b* 4, *d* 5 April 1915

4 Bernard Elliot; Lt Gren Gds (SR); *b* 5 June 1874; *d* unm 23 Dec 1943

1 Susan; Area Organiser NE Essex WVS WW II; *b* 7 May 1881; *m* 1st 7 April 1910 Capt Augustus Arthur Cornwallis FitzClarence (*ka* 28 June 1915; *see* MUNSTER, E); *m* 2nd 23 June 1920 Maj Wyndham Birch, DSO, MBE, yr s of Sir Arthur Birch, KCMG, and *d* 21 Aug 1965, leaving issue. He *d* 16 April 1950

The 8th EARL's nephew,

PHILIP GRANTHAM YORKE, **9th Earl of Hardwicke**; *b* 9 April 1906; *educ* Eton and RMC Sandhurst; Maj RA, AAC, Lt Life Gds; *m* 1st 12 June 1934 Sarah Katharine (*d* 8 Nov 1965), 3rd dau of Sir Francis Oswald Lindley, GCMG, CB, CBE, PC, and had issue:

1 Philip Simon Prospero Lindley Rupert (Pips); *b* 20 April 1938; *educ* Eton; *m* 20 Nov 1968 Virginia Anne (*d* 1988), est dau of Geoffrey Lyon, and *d* 1 Jan 1973, leaving issue:

(1) JOSEPH PHILIP SEBASTIAN YORKE, **10th and present Earl of Hardwicke**

(1) *Jemima Rose; *b* 17 May 1969; granted rank of earl's dau by roy warrant 1977

1 *Amabel Mary Maud; *b* 2 April 1935; *m* 16 Dec 1955 Hon Patrick Lindsay (*d* 1986), 2nd s of 28th Earl of Crawford and (11th Earl of) Balcarres (*qv*), and has issue

2 *Victoria Mary Verenia Braganca [The Lady Victoria Waymouth, 36 Elms Rd, London SW4]; *b* 22 Feb 1947; interior decorator; *m* 17 Sept 1976 (*divorce* 1998) Nigel Waymouth, s of W/Cdr T G Waymouth, and has:

(1) *Louis Alexander Philip; *b* 14 April 1978

(2) *Adam Django Joseph; *b* 1981

3 *Rose Mary Sydney; *b* 10 July 1951; *m* 1st 19– (*divorce* 19–) Kenneth Delbray; *m* 2nd 1981 (*divorce* 1985) Herbert Richard Vaughan (*d* 1987); *m* 3rd 1990 *Tony Turner and has issue by David Thompson:

(1) *Katharine Sarah Tahlita Valour THOMPSON; *b* 1985

The **9th Earl** *m* 2nd 27 April 1970 *Enid Munnick, dau of Pieter Grunwald, of S Africa, and formerly w of Roy Boulting, and *d* 31 Dec 1974

HARDY

Arms: Arg. on a bend invected plain cotised gu. three catherine wheels or, on a chief of the second as many leopard's faces of the third. **Crest:** A dexter arm embowed in armour ppr., garnished or, entwined by a branch of oak vert, charged with two catherine wheels, one above the other below the elbow gu., the hand grasping a dragon's head erased ppr. **Motto:** *Armé de foi hardi* ('Armed with robust faith'). **Creation:** Bt. (UK) 23 Feb 1876.

SIR RICHARD CHARLES CHANDOS HARDY, 5TH BT, of Dunstall Hall, Co Stafford [Sir Richard Hardy Bt, Springfield House, Gillingham, Dorset SP8 5RD]; *b* 6 Feb 1945; *s f* 1997; *educ* Eton; *m* 7 Oct 1971 *Venetia Wingfield, yr dau of Simon Wingfield Digby, TD, DL, MP, of Haydon Gate, Sherborne, and has issue:

1 *Arabella Venetia Jane; *b* 1976

2 *Jacquetta Anne; *b* 21 Sept 1977

3 *Georgina Charlotte; *b* 1982

4 *Henrietta Alicia Diana; *b* 1986

Lineage: JOHN HARDY, of Bradford, Yorks, *m* 19 Nov 1770 Annis Atkinson (*d* Oct 1774) and *d* 3 June 1806, leaving:

JOHN HARDY, of Dunstall Hall, Staffs, and Inner Temple; MP Bradford 1833–47; *m* 16 Aug 1804 Isabel, dau of Richard Gathorne, of Kirkby Lonsdale, Westmorland, and had, with other daus:

1 JOHN (Sir), **1st Bt**

2 Charles, of Chilham Castle, Kent, and Odsall House, Bradford, JP, DL; *b* 21 Jan 1813; *m* 14 June 1838 Catherine (*d* 5 Jan 1874), dau of James Orr, of Hollywood House, Co Down, and *d* 16 March 1867, having had:

3 GATHORN HARDY, 1st EARL OF CRANBROOK (*qv*)

1 Annis Elizabeth; *m* 29 Oct 1833 John Wood, of Thedden Grange, Hants, and *d* 17 Nov 1861. He *d* 1 March 1871

2 Emily; *m* 16 Jan 1839 Rev Francis Hewson, of Killarney, Co Kerry, and *d* 14 April 1866, leaving issue

3 Eliza; *m* 24 Aug 1848 Rev Charles Welfitt Blathwayt, Vicar Chelmarsh, Salop

The est son,

Sir John Hardy, 1st Bt (UK), so *cr* 23 Feb 1876, of Dunstall Hall, JP, DL; High Sheriff Staffs 1878, MP Midhurst 1859, Dartmouth 1860–68 and S Warwicks 1868–74; *b* 23 Feb 1809; *m* 13 Aug 1846 Laura (*d* 19 Jan 1885), 3rd dau of William Holbech, of Farnborough, Warwicks, and had issue:

1 REGINALD (Sir), **2nd Bt**

2 Henry John; Lt Rifle Bde; *b* 12 Dec 1850; *d* Natal 4 Oct 1879

3 Gerald Holbech, of Foston Hall, Derbys, JP, DL Derbys; High Sheriff 1910, MA Oxon, Maj Staffs Imp Yeo, Cmdg 6th Bn Sherwood Forresters 1916–19, barrister; *b* 7 July 1852; *d* unm 21 March 1929

4 Laurence, PC, of Sandling Park, Hythe, Kent, JP, DL, JP W R Yorks; MA Oxon, CA Kent, MP S Kent 1892–1918, Ecclesiastical Cmmr 1918, Dep Chm Ways and Means H of C 1905, Hon Seneschal Canterbury Cathedral 1930; *b* 14 April 1854; *m* 2 Dec 1886 Evelyn Emily (*d* 27 Sept 1911), dau of John Gathorne Wood, of Thedden Grange, Hants, and *d* 21 Jan 1933, leaving issue:

(1) Arthur Evelyn; Maj Coldstream Gds WW I (star, two medals); *b* 19 Aug 1893; *educ* Eton; *m* 27 June 1918 Nancy Marion (*d* 1983), dau of Horace George Devas (*see* CAWDOR, E), and *d* 1986, having had issue:

1a Julian; *b* 25 March 1922; *d* 28 March 1925

2a +GERALD ALAN; *b* 4 April 1926; heir presumptive; *educ* King's Sch Bruton; *m* 20 June 1953 *Carolyn, dau of Maj-Gen Arthur Charles Tarver Evanson, CB, MC, of Chilverton Elms, nr Dover, and has issue:

1b *Sarah [Mrs William Hurley, Pedlinge Farm, Hythe, Kent]; *b* 7 June 1957; *m* 1972 *William John Hurley and has:

1c *Kathryn Jane; *b* 1985

2c *Susannah Evelyn; *b* 1988

3c *Lucinda Barbara; *b* 1990

2b *Jane [Miss Jane Hardy, Sandling Park, Hythe, Kent]; *b* 24 Dec 1958

1a *Ruth, JP (Kent 1968) [Mrs Charles Tuff JP, Hogs Green, Sandling, Hythe, Kent]; *b* 9 July 1919; *m* 20 Jan 1940 *Col Charles Reginald Tuff, The Buffs (ret), only s of Maj Sir Charles Tuff, and has issue:

1b *Timothy Charles; *b* 29 April 1947; *educ* Eton and Dalhousie U Nova Scotia

2b *Geoffrey; *b* 6 Feb 1954; *educ* Eton

1b *Prunella Primrose; *b* 19 April 1942

(2) Maurice John, MBE ; *b* 17 April 1902; *educ* Eton and Ch Ch Oxford; WW II as Maj RE; *m* 8 June 1926 Rosalie Kathleen (*d* 1979), er dau of Brig-Gen Tyrell Other William Champion de Crespigny (*see* 1949 edn CHAMPION DE CRESPIGNY, Bt), and *d* 10 March 1991, having had:

1a Christopher John; *b* 9 Feb 1928; *educ* Eton; *d* 19–

1a *Jane [Mrs Peter Eckersley, Fox Hollow, Sandhurst Lane, Rolvenden, nr Cranbrook, Kent]; *b* 31 Aug 1931; *m* 3 Sept 1955 Peter Leonard Eckersley (*d* 1988), er s of Lt Peter Thorpe Eckersley, JP, MP, RNVR and Mrs Henry David Makgill-Crichton-Maitland (*see* LAUDERDALE, E), and has issue:

1b *Peter David Charles; *b* 16 Dec 1957; *m* 21 Feb 1987 *Juliet Emma Margaret, dau of Derek Graham Blundell Knight, of Little Dane, Biddenden, Kent, and has:

1c *Peter Maurice Percival; *b* 29 Jan 1989

1c *Cliantha Florence Beatrice; *b* 25 April 1991

2c *Evangeline Violet Margaret; *b* 20 April 1993

1b *Clare Arabella; *b* 19 June 1960; *m* 12 Sept 1981 *David Richard Stapylton Fairbank (*see* CHETWYND, V) and has issue

2b *Suzanne Jane; *b* 1 Oct 1962; *m* 9 Oct 1982 *Charles Roderick Roberts and has:

1c *Edmund Robert; *b* 26 Dec 1986

1c *Samantha Rosalie; *b* 1 Oct 1985

(1) Edith Annis

Sir JOHN *d* 9 July 1888; his est s,

Sir Reginald Hardy, 2nd Bt, JP, DL Staffs; MA Oxon, barrister Inner Temple 1873, Staffs: High Sheriff 1893, CA, Chm CC 1920–27 and QS, Hon Col and Lt-Col cmdg Staffs Imp Yeo; *b* 15 Sept 1848; *m* 29 April 1876 Lucy Marion (*d* 4 Oct 1921), yst dau of Capt John Neilson Gladstone (*see* GLADSTONE, Bt), and had:

1 BERTRAM (Sir), **3rd Bt**

2 Eustace; *d* young 1880

3 Leonard Henry, MC, JP Derbys; High Sheriff 1936, Lt-Col Life Gds WW I (wounded, despatches); *b* 12 May 1882; *educ* Eton and New Coll Oxford (BA); *m* 31 Oct 1938 *Diana O'Carroll (*m* 3rd 24 Jan 1956 W/Cdr Cedric Charles Boyd (*d* 22 April 1964)), widow of Edward Mark Philips, OBE, of Alsopen-le-Dale Hall, Derbys, and est dau of Jonathan Charles Darby, of Leap Castle, Co Offaly, and *d* 27 Oct 1954

4 Eric John, DSO (1917), JP, DL Staffs; CC 1937–52 (V-Chm 1941–43, Chm 1943–46), CA 1943, Dep Chm QS 1939–56, Chm Standing Jt Ctee 1936–47; 2nd Lt 4th Bn N Staffs Regt 1903–05, Maj RSG 1905–25 (despatches WW I), memb House Laity Church Assembly 1951, Chm Lichfield Diocesan Bd Finance 1955–60; *b* 6 Dec 1884; *educ* Eton; *d* unm 10 Dec 1965

1 Una; *d* unm 25 Sept 1965

Sir REGINALD *d* 6 Aug 1938; his est son,

Sir Bertram Hardy, 3rd Bt; *b* 11 Feb 1877; *educ* Eton and Trin Hall Cambridge; Staffs: High Sheriff 1925, Maj Yeo WW I; *m* 26 Oct 1899 Violet Agnes Evelyn (*d* 4 Nov 1972 aged 97), author: *Touched by the Sun* and *As it Was*, est dau of Hon Sir Edward Chandos Leigh, KCB, KC (*see* LEIGH, B), and *d* 16 Sept 1953, leaving:

1 **Sir Rupert John Hardy, 4th Bt**; *b* 24 Oct 1902; *educ* Eton and Trin Hall Cambridge (BA 1925); Maj 1940, Lt-Col Life Gds WW II (ret 1957); *m* 2 June 1930 *Hon Diana Joan Allsopp [The Hon Lady Hardy, Gullivers Lodge, Guilsborough, Northants NN6 8RB], er dau of 3rd Baron Hindlip (*qv*), and *d* 22 March 1997, leaving issue:

(1) Sir RICHARD CHARLES CHANDOS HARDY, **5th and present Bt**

(1) *Rosemary Diana [Mrs Rosemary Black, Redmoor Lodge, Guilsborough Rd, W Haddon, Northants NN6 7AD]; *b* 5 April 1931; *m* 22 Oct 1953 (*divorce* 1972) Maj Robert David Black (later Sir Robert David Black, 3rd Bt (*qv*))

2 Hugh Bertram; Staffs Yeo 1930–41, Maj 3rd Hus (ret as Lt-Col); *b* 1 May 1907; *m* 24 July 1933 *Joan Stella Gwendolyn [Mrs Hugh Hardy, Box 148, Limuru, Kenya], formerly w of James Alexander Guthrie and dau of Charles Hammond Dracott, and *d* 1988, leaving issue:

(1) *Audrey Elizabeth Una [Mrs Charles Backhouse, c/o Bank of Montreal, Calgary, Alberta, Canada]; *b* 6 May 1936; *m* 1965 *Charles Frederick Backhouse and has issue:

1a *David Hugh; *b* 9 July 1971

1a *Isabelle Joan; *b* 1969

HARDY OF WATH

Creation: B. (LP, UK) 2 Aug 1997.

THE BARON HARDY OF WATH, of Wath, Co S Yorks (Peter Hardy, DL (S Yorks 1997)) [The Rt Hon The Lord Hardy of Wath DL, 53 Sandygate, Wath-upon-Dearne, Rotherham, S Yorks S63 7LU]; *b* 17 July 1931; *educ* Wath-upon-Dearne GS (Chm Govrs 1969–80), Westminster Coll London, Sheffield U and Leeds U; RAF 1949–51, sch master S Yorks 1953–70; memb Wath-upon-Dearne UDC 1960–70 (Chm Cncl 1968–69); Pres Wath-upon-Dearne Lab Pty 1960–68, MP (Lab) Rother Valley 1970–83, Wentworth 1983–97, PPS to: Sec State Environment 1974–76, For Sec 1976–79, Chm PLP Energy Ctee 1974–92, Parly attachment RAF 1992–93, Hon Sec All-Party Gp Energy Studies 1992–97; memb: UK Delegn Cncl Europe 1976–97, Lab Delegate CSCE 1992–97, Leader UK Lab Delegn Cncl Europe and WEU 1983–96, Chm Cncl Europe Ctee Environment 1986–89, V-Chm Socialist Gp 1983–96; memb: Cncl RSPB 1984–89, Centl Exec Ctee NSPCC 1985–92; V-Pres S Yorks Fndn 1993; Patron Yorks Wildlife Tst; hon memb Kennel Club; memb Bd Landscape Fndn; author: *A Lifetime of Badgers* (1975); DLit (London); *m* 1954 *Margaret Anne Brookes and has two sons

Lineage: LAWRENCE HARDY, of Wath upon Dearne; *m* Ivy — and had:

PETER, *cr* a **Baron**

HARE

Arms: Gu. two bars and a chief indented or. **Crest:** A demi-lion rampant arg., gorged with a ducal coronet or. **Motto:** *Non videri sed esse* ('Not seeming, but being'). **Creation:** Bt. (UK) 14 Dec 1818.

SIR PHILIP LEIGH HARE, 6TH BT, of Stow Bardolph, Norfolk [Sir Philip Hare Bt, The Nettings, Hook Norton, Oxon OX15 5NP]; *b* 13 Oct 1922; *s* kinsman 1993; *educ* privately and RAC Cirencester; *m* 4 Nov 1950 *Anne Lisle, 2nd dau of Maj Geoffrey Nicholson, CBE, MC (*see* ANNESLEY, E), and has issue:

1 +NICHOLAS PATRICK [Nicholas Hare Esq, Manor Farm, Culkerton, Glos GL8 8SS]; *b* 27 Aug 1955; *educ* Bryanston; *m* 21 Aug 1982 *Caroline Keith, dau of Terence Playfair Keith Allan, of Elsted Green, W Sussex, and has:

(1) +Thomas Edward; *b* 7 Aug 1986

(2) +Robert Leigh; *b* 17 Dec 1987

1 *Louisa Kathleen; *b* 27 Aug 1955; *m* 1981 *Benson Whittle, of Utah, and has:

(1) *Charlotte; *b* 1981

Lineage: Sir NICHOLAS HARE; Speaker H of C, Master Rolls, Commr to execute office of Ld Chllr and Keeper Gt Seal 1555; bought Stow Bardolph, Norfolk, 1553; his ggn:

Sir JOHN HARE; ktd 1617; *m* Elizabeth, only dau of 1st Baron Coventry by his 1st w (*see* COVENTRY, E), and had, with other issue:

1 RALPH (Sir), 1st Bt

2 John, of Bromsthorp, Norfolk; *m* Susan, dau and coheir of John Walpole, of Bromsthorpe, and had issue

3 Nicholas; *m* Catherine, dau of William Gery, of Bushmead, Beds, and had issue

1 Elizabeth; *m* 1st Woolley Leigh, of Addington, Surrey; *m* 2nd Sir John Lowther (*see* LONSDALE, E)

2 Anne; *m* Sir John Sydenham, 1st Bt, of Brimpton, Somerset

Sir JOHN *d* 1638; his est son,

Sir RALPH HARE, 1st Bt (E), so *cr* 23 July 1641, of Stow Bardolph; MP Norfolk 1654–58 and 1661–71 and King's Lynn 1660; *m* 1st *c* 26 Oct 1647 Mary, dau and coheir of Sir Robert Crane, 1st Bt, of Chilton, Suffolk, and had, with other issue:

1 THOMAS (Sir), 2nd Bt

Sir RALPH *m* 2nd 30 Aug 1660 Vere (*dsp*), sis of 1st Viscount Townshend (*see* TOWNSHEND, M); *m* 3rd *c* Feb 1671 Elizabeth Chapman and by her had:

2 John; *b* posthumously; *d* in infancy

Sir RALPH *d* 12 July 1671; his son,

Sir THOMAS HARE, 2nd Bt; *m* Elizabeth (*d* 1750), sister of Sir Robert Dashwood, 1st Bt, of Kirtlington Pk (*qv*), and *d* 1 Jan 1693, having had, with other issue:

1 Sir RALPH HARE, 3rd Bt; *b c* 1680; *m* Susan (*bur* 15 July 1730), dau and coheir of Walter Norborne, of Calne, Wilts, and *dsp* 22 Sept 1732

2 Sir THOMAS HARE, 4th Bt; *b c* 1686; *m* Rosamond (*d* 1773), dau of Charles Newby, of Hooton, Yorks, and *d* 21 Feb 1760, leaving:

(1) Elizabeth; *d* unm

(2) Mary; *m* Sir Thomas Harris, Sheriff London, and *dsp* 24 March 1791. He *d* 15 June 1782

3 Sir GEORGE HARE, 5th and last Bt; *b c* 1691; Maj Dragoons; *d* unm 18 March 1764, when the btcy expired

1 Elizabeth; *m* 30 May 1710 Sir Thomas Robinson, 3rd Bt, of Kentwell, Suffolk, who *dsp* 21 April 1743

2 MARY Hare; *m* Thomas LEIGH, of London, 2nd s of Edward Leigh, of Iver, Bucks (*d* by 1689), descended in common with the Stoneleigh Abbey family, whose arms he bore, from the Cheshire family of that name, and had:

(1) Thomas, of Iver; *m* Anne, dau of Rt Rev Robert Clavering, Bp Peterborough, and had issue:

1a THOMAS (Sir), **1st Bt**

1a Anne; *m* 1773 Maj Robert Williams, Queen's Light Dragoons

2a Mary; *m* — Trewren, of Trevadrava, Cornwall

The 5th and last Bt's nephew,

Sir THOMAS LEIGH later HARE, **1st Bt** (UK), so *cr* 14 Dec 1818; *m* 1st 30 March 1779 Mary (*dsp* 1801), dau of Adml Sir Francis Geary, Bt; *m* 2nd 15 Jan 1803 Anne Elizabeth (*d* 11 Sept 1823), dau of 1st Baron Graves (*qv*), and *d* 12 Feb 1834, leaving, with a dau (Elizabeth Anne, *d* 17 Sept 1868):

Sir Thomas Hare, 2nd Bt, JP, DL; Capt 2nd Life Gds; *b* 18 July 1807; *m* 1 Oct 1864 Grace Norman (*d* 16 Jan 1879), dau of Hon George Vaughan (*see* LISBURNE, E), and *d* 14 Nov 1880, leaving:

1 **Sir (George) Ralph Leigh Hare, 3rd Bt**, JP Norfolk, DL; High Sheriff 1906, Capt Suffolk Yeo Cav, Lt 2nd Life Gds; *b* 16 March 1866; *m* 3 Dec 1891 Lady Florence Mary Constance (*d* 4 Oct 1054), only dau of 4th Earl of Romney (*qv*), and *d* 19 May 1933, leaving:

(1) **Sir Ralph Leigh Hare, 4th Bt**; Maj Coldstream Gds; *b* 19 Jan 1903; *m* 1st 1 Feb 1928 (*divorce* 1944) Doreen Pleasance Anna, est dau of Maj Sir Richard Ludwig Bagge, DSO, of Gaywood Hall, King's Lynn, and had issue:

1a **Sir Thomas Hare, 5th Bt**; QALAS, Coldstream Gds 1948–50, Lt RARO; *b* 27 July 1930; *educ* Eton and Magdalene Coll Cambridge (MARICS) *m* 16 Sept 1961 *Lady Rose Amanda Bligh [The Lady Rose Hare, Stow Bardolph, Kings Lynn, Norfolk PE34 3HU], 2nd dau of 9th Earl of Darnley (*qv*), and *d* 1993, leaving issue:

1b *Lucy Rose; *b* 20 Sept 1962

2b *Elizabeth Florence; *b* 21 July 1964; *m* 1992 *William Nicholas Esse, s of David Charles Scott Esse, of Horsley, Glos, and has issue:

1c *Barnaby Samuel Hare; *b* 1993

1a *Jean Bridget [Mrs Jean Wallis, 11 Lady Jane Court, Cavendish Ave, Cambridge]; *b* 31 Jan 1929; *m* 1st 1949 (*divorce* 1957) Nigel E Beard and has:

1b *Jeremy Nigel Thomas; *b* 16 June 1953

1b *Laraine Susan; *b* 20 May 1950

1a (cont.) Mrs Jean Beard *m* 2nd 1957 Richard John Wallis (*divorce* 1971), s of Leonard John Wallis, and by him has:

2b *Robin John; *b* 9 July 1961

(1) (cont.) **Sir Ralph** *m* 2nd 27 July 1945 (*divorce* 1958) Natalie Alexandria Elizabeth Julia, only child of Capt Baron Gerard de Langue, attd 3rd Hus, and Mrs Edward Vincent Irwin, and by her had issue:

2a *Angela Florence Natalie; *b* 1 Feb 1948; *m* 1971 *Terence Ronald Duke and has:

1b *Simon; *b* 1976

1b *Penelope Jane Deirdre; *b* 1974

3a *Lorna Lillianne Katrina; *b* 3 March 1957; *m* 1975 *Michael Page and has:

1b *David; *b* 1976

2b *Jonathan; *b* 1980

3b *Andrew; *b* 1981

4b *Thomas; *b* 1982

(1) (cont.) **Sir Ralph** *m* 3rd 29 April 1960 *Barbara Mary Theodora (Ann) [Ann Lady Hare, Stow Bardolph, Kings Lynn, Norfolk PE34 3HU], yst dau of Joseph Arthur Walton, and *d* 30 Oct 1976, leaving by her:

4a *Mary Anne; *b* 10 July 1961; *m* 1993 *Anthony Jacklin

(1) Grace Constance Leigh; *d* unm 25 Nov 1969

(2) Mary Leigh

(3) Marjorie Florence Rhoda Leigh; *m* 14 April 1923 Col James Alexander Charles Pennycuick, DSO, RE, s of Charles Edward Ducat Pennycuick, CMG, Ceylon CS, and *d* 22 Feb 1966, leaving issue

(4) *Joan Muriel Leigh [Miss Joan Hare, The Patch, Green Lane, Ilsington, S Devon TQ13 9RB]

2 Thomas Leigh; *b* 1867; *d* unm

3 Edward Philip Leigh; Capt Imp Yeo 1902, Capt 18th Buffs 1914–15, Staff Capt 72nd Bde, Capt Res Regt RHG 1915–19, attd Gds Div, Boer War 1902 (medal with three clasps), WW I; *b* 24 Feb 1869; *m* 1st 23 Oct 1906 (*annulled* 1910) Mabel Newton, est dau of John Taylor, of Brookdale, Newton Heath, Manchester; *m* 2nd 13 Feb 1914 (*divorce* 1920) Iris Trelawny Rutherfurd, dau of William Rutherfurd Lamb, of Ryton Hall, Northumberland, and had issue:

(1) George Leigh; Capt RA WW II; *b* 8 July 1917; *educ* Eton and RMA Woolwich, *ka* July 1944

(1) *Elizabeth Mildred Leigh [Miss Elizabeth Hare, 4 Old Museum Court, Haslemere, Surrey GU27 2JR]; *b* 17 Feb 1915

3 (cont.) Edward Hare *m* 3rd 29 Dec 1920 Lady Kathleen Florence Mary (*d* 1971), widow of Edward John Harry Eden Morant and dau of 9th Earl of Harrington (*qv*), and *d* 31 Jan 1954, having by her had issue:

(2) Sir PHILIP LEIGH HARE, **6th and present Bt**

1 Mary Leigh; *m* 1874 Anthony Hamond, JP, DL (*d* 30 March 1895), of Westacre, Norfolk, and *d* 14 May 1925

HAREWOOD

Arms: Sa. a cross patonce within a bordure or. **Crest:** A bear's head couped at the neck erm., muzzled gu., buckled or, collared of the second, rimmed and studded gold. **Supporters:** Two bears erm., muzzled and collared gu., buckled and chained, the chain reflexed over the back, or, the collar studded and rimmed gold, pendant therefrom an escutcheon sa. charged with a cross patonce gold.
Motto: *In solo Deo salus* ('In God alone is salvation').
Creations: B. (GB) 18 June 1796, V. and E. (UK) 7 Sept 1812.

THE 7TH EARL OF HAREWOOD, Co York, **Viscount Lascelles** and **Baron Harewood**, of Harewood, Co York (Sir George Henry Hubert Lascelles, KBE (1986)) [The Rt Hon The Earl of Harewood KBE, Harewood House, Leeds, Yorks LS17 9LG]; *b* 7 Feb 1923 (TM GEORGE V and QUEEN MARY stood sponsors); *s f* 1947; *educ* Eton and King's Coll Cambridge (BA 1948); Capt Gren Gds WW II in Italy (wounded, POW), ADC to Govr-Gen Canada 1945–46, ed *Opera* magazine 1950–53, Dir ROH Covent Gdn 1951–53 and 1969–72, Chm ENO 1986–95 (md 1972–85), artistic dir Edinburgh, Leeds, Adelaide Festivals, md ENO North 1978–81, Govr BBC 1985–87, Pres Br Bd Film Classification 1985–96, Hon LLD Leeds 1959, Aberdeen 1966 and Bradford 1983, Hon DMus Hull 1962, Dr U of York 1982, Hon RAM 1983, Janácek Medal 1978, Chllr U of York 1962–67, Austrian Order of Merit 1959, author: *Kobbé's Complete Opera Book* (ed, 1953), *The Tongs and the Bones* (autobiography, 1981), *Kobbé's Illustrated Opera Book* (ed, 1989); *m* 1st 29 Sept 1949 (*divorce* 1967) Maria (Marion) Donata Nanetta Paulina Gustava Erwina Wilhelmina, former concert pianist (*m* 2nd 1973 (John) Jeremy Thorpe, PC (*see* NORTON-GRIFFITHS, Bt)), only dau of Erwin Stein, and has:

1 +DAVID HENRY GEORGE, *Viscount Lascelles* [Viscount Lascelles, Harewood House, Leeds, Yorks LS17 9LG]; *b* 21 Oct 1950; *educ* Westminster; film and TV producer (including *Tibet — a Buddhist Trilogy* 1977–79, *Inspector Morse* 1989–90 (BAFTA Award for Best TV Series 1990), *Wide-eyed and Legless* 1992–93, *Richard III* 1995, *Moll Flanders* 1996, *The Wisdom of Crocodiles* 1997–98), chm: Harewood House Tst, Photo98 (The Year of Photography); *m* 1st 12 Feb 1979 (*divorce* 1989) Margaret Rosalind, dau of Edgar Frank Messenger; *m* 2nd 11 March 1990 *Diane Jane, dau of John Prince Howse, and by his 1st w has issue:

(1) *Benjamin George; *b* 19 Sept 1978

(2) +Alexander Edgar; *b* 13 May 1980

(3) +Edward David; *b* 19 Nov 1982

(1) *Emily Tsering; *b* 23 Nov 1975

2 +James Edward; *b* 5 Oct 1953; *educ* Westminster; keyboard player with It's A Small World folk/jazz band, memb Footsbarn travelling theatre gp; *m* 1st 4 April 1973 (*divorce* 1985) Fredericka (Freddy) Ann, dau of Prof Alfred Duhrrson, of Deya, Majorca, and has issue:

(1) +Rowan Nash; *b* 6 Nov 1977

(1) *Sophie Amber; *b* 1 Oct 1973

2 (cont.) The Hon James Lascelles *m* 2nd 4 May 1985 *Lori (Shadow), dau of John Rupert Lee, of Seligman, Arizona, and formerly w of John Porter, and has further issue:

(2) +Tewa Ziyan Robert George; *b* 8 June 1985

(2) *Tanit; *b* 1 July 1981

3 +Robert Jeremy Hugh; *b* 14 Feb 1955 (does not use courtesy title); *educ* Westminster; *m* 4 July 1981 *Julie, dau of Robert Bayliss, of Mildenham Mill, Claines, Worcs, and has:

(1) +Thomas Robert; *b* 7 Sept 1982

(1) *Ellen Mary; *b* 17 Dec 1984

(2) *Amy Rose; *b* 26 June 1986

The 7th EARL *m* 2nd 31 July 1967 *Patricia Elizabeth, violinist, formerly w of Athol Shmith and only dau of Charles Tuckwell, of Sydney, NSW, and by her has:

4 *Mark Hubert; *b* 5 July 1964; *educ* Bryanston; *m* 1992 *Andrea Kershaw and has:

(1) *Charlotte Patricia; *b* 24 Jan 1996

(2) *Imogen Mary; *b* 3 Jan 1998

Lineage: JOHN de LASCELLES, of Hinderskelfe, Yorks; living 1315; *m* Joanna — and had:

JOHN de LASCELLES, of Hinderskelfe; living 1392; had:

WILLIAM de LASCELLES, of Hinderskelfe; living 1428; had:

WILLIAM de LASCELLES, of Hinderskelfe; living *temp* HENRY VI; had:

WILLIAM de LASCELLES, of Ganthorpe, N R Yorks; had:

ROBERT LASCELLES, of Ganthorpe and Eryholme Grange, Hovington, Yorks; *m* Dorothy Newport and *d* 1556, leaving a 4th s:

FRANCIS LASCELLES, of Stank Hall and Northallerton, in right of his wife; *m* Elizabeth, dau and coheir of John Charter, of Northallerton, and *d* 1628, leaving an est s:

WILLIAM LASCELLES; *m* Elizabeth, dau of Robert Wadeson, of Yafforth, Yorks, and *dvp* (*bur* 16 Nov 1624), having had an est s:

FRANCIS LASCELLES, of Stank and Northallerton, JP Yorks; MP N R Yorks 1653, Col Parly Army; *bapt* 23 Aug 1612; *m* Frances (*bur* 20 Sept 1658), dau of Sir William St Quinton, 1st Bt, of Harpham, Yorks, and was *bur* 28 Nov 1667, leaving:

DANIEL LASCELLES, of Stank and Northallerton; High Sheriff Yorks 1719, MP Northallerton; *b* 6 Nov 1655; *m* 1st Margaret (*bur* 20 Dec 1690), dau of George Metcalfe, of Northallerton, and had, with other issue (*d* young):

1 George, of Stank; *bapt* 2 March 1681; *m* Mary (*d* 1723), dau of William Doldren, and *dvp* 12 Feb 1728/9, leaving issue

2 Henry, of Harewood and Northallerton; MP Northallerton, Dir HEIC; *bapt* 20 Dec 1690; *m* 1st 8 April 1711/2 Mary, dau and coheir of Edwin Carter, of Barbados; *m* 2nd 1731 Janet (*dsp* 22 April 1754), dau of John Whetstone, of Barbados, and *d* 16 Oct 1753, having by his 1st w had, with two sons (*d* young):

(1) EDWIN LASCELLES, 1st and last BARON OF HAREWOOD, Co York (GB), so *cr* 9 July 1790; MP (Whig, later Pittite) Scarborough 1744–54, Northallerton 1754–61 and 1780–90 and Yorks 1761–80; *bapt* 5 Feb 1712–13; *m* 1st 5 Jan 1746/7 Elizabeth (*d* 31 Aug 1764), dau and heir of Sir Darcy Dawes, 4th Bt; *m* 2nd 31 March 1770 Jane (*d* 11 April 1813), widow of Sir John Fleming, 1st and last Bt, and dau of William Colman, of Garnbay, Devon, and *dsp* 25 Jan 1795, when the Barony expired

(2) Daniel, of Goldsborough, Yorks; MP Northallerton; *bapt* 20 May 1714; *m* 17– (*divorce* 1751) Elizabeth Southwick and *dsp* 24 May 1784

(3) Henry; Capt HEICS; *b* 18 Aug 1716; *m* Jane (*d* June 1784), dau of John Raine, of Scarborough, and *dsp* 14 July 1786

DANIEL LASCELLES *m* 2nd Mary (*d* 28 Oct 1734), dau of Edward Lascelles, and *d* 5 Sept 1734, having by her had:

3 Edward; Collector Customs Barbados; *bapt* 25 Feb 1702; *m* 1 Jan 1732 Frances (*m* 2nd Adml of the White Francis Holburne and *d* 18 May 1761), dau of Guy Ball, of Barbados, and *d* 31 Oct 1747, having had, with two sons (*d* young):

(1) EDWARD, **1st Earl**

(2) Francis; Gen, Groom Bedchamber to GEORGE III; *b* 1 Nov 1744; *d* unm 1799

DANIEL LASCELLES's gs,

EDWARD LASCELLES, **1st Earl of Harewood**, Co York, so *cr* 7 Sept 1812 , as also VISCOUNT LASCELLES and earlier 18 June 1796 BARON HARWOOD, of Harewood, Co York; *b* 7 June 1739/40; *s* to the estates of his cousin 1st and last Baron of Harewood; Col, MP (Whig) Northallerton 1761–74 and (Tory) 1790–96; *m* 12 May 1761 Anne (*d* 22 Feb 1805), dau of William Chaloner (*see* GISBOROUGH, B), and had:

1 Edward; *d* unm 3 June 1814

2 HENRY, **2nd Earl**

1 Frances; *m* 4 Oct 1784 Hon John Douglas, 2nd s of 14th Earl of Morton (*qv*), and *d* 31 March 1817, leaving issue

2 Mary Anne; *m* 20 April 1801 Richard York, of Wighill Park, and *d* 10 June 1831, leaving issue. He *d* 27 Jan 1843

The 1st EARL *d* 3 April 1820; his only surv son,

HENRY LASCELLES, **2nd Earl of Harewood**; Ld Lt and custos rotulorum W R Yorks, High Steward Allerton; *b* 25 Dec 1767; *m* 3 Sept 1794 Henrietta (*d* 15 Feb 1840), est dau of Lt-Gen Sir John Saunders Sebright, 6th Bt (*qv*), and had:

1 Edward, *Viscount Lascelles*; *b* 13 July 1796; *m* 1st 3 Nov 1818 Ann Elizabeth Rosser (*d* 19 Aug 1831); *m* 2nd 10 Sept 1831 Philippine Munster, widow of Baron Testa, and *dsp* 17 Dec 1839

2 HENRY, **3rd Earl**

3 William Saunders Sebright, PC; *b* 29 Oct 1798; MP; *m* 14 May 1823 Lady Caroline Georgiana Howard (*d* 27 Nov 1881), est dau of 6th Earl of Carlisle (*qv*), and *d* 2 July 1851, leaving issue:

(1) Claud George William; Maj RA; *b* 4 Oct 1831; *d* unm Nov 1903

(2) Edwin; *b* 27 Sept 1833; *d* 23 March 1877

(3) Frank Cavendish (Sir), GCB (1897), GCMG (1892), GCVO (1904), PC; Dip Serv 1861–1908, Agent and Consul-Gen Bulgaria 1879–86, Envoy Extrdy and Min Plen Romania 1887–91 and Persia 1891–94, Amb St Petersburg 1894–95 and Berlin 1895–1908; *b* 23 March 1841; *m* 25 June 1867 Mary Emma (*d* 3 April 1897), est dau of Sir Joseph Francis Olliffe, MD, Physician to The Br Embassy Paris, and *d* 2 Jan 1920, leaving issue:

1a William Frank; Maj Scots Gds; *b* 21 March 1863; *m* 4 Nov 1889 Lady Sybil Evelyn de Vere Beauclerk (*d* 20 Sept 1910), 2nd dau of 10th Duke of Saint Albans (*qv*), and *d* 8 March 1913, leaving:

1b (Vreda Esther) Mary (Molly); *b* 17 Sept 1900; *m* 21 April 1921 8th Duke of Buccleuch and (10th Duke of) Queensberry (*qv*) and *d* 1993, leaving issue

2b Diana; *b* 12 April 1904; *m* 1 March 1927 (*divorce* 1950) Maj Denis Bowes Daly, MC, RHG, of Dunsandle, Athenry, Co Galway, and *d* 7 Nov 1971, leaving issue

2a Gerald Claud; V-Consul Tangier; *b* 19 July 1869; *m* 1899 Cecil (*d* 30 Nov 1960), dau of Count Joseph Raffo, and *d* 26 June 1919

1a Florence Caroline; *m* 1 June 1904 Sir Cecil Arthur Spring Rice, GCMG, GCVO, PC (*see* MONTEAGLE OF BRANDON, B), and *d* 9 Dec 1961, leaving issue

(4) Henry Arthur, MVO; Lt-Col Rifle Fde Indian Mutiny and Ashanti War; *b* 4 Dec 1842; *m* 14 Aug 1883 Caroline Maria (*d* 6 Nov 1945), dau of Hon Charles Alexander Gore (*see* ARRAN, E), and *d* 29 July 1913, leaving issue:

1a Edward Charles Ponsonby, OBE (1920); *b* 8 Oct 1884; *m* 19 April 1911 Leila Winifred Leonor, DGStJ (*d* 1979), only dau of Sir Vincent Kennett-Barrington, of The Manor House, Dorchester, and *d* 3 Feb 1956, leaving:

1b +(Henry) Anthony, CB (1967), CBE (1962, OBE 1945), DSO (1944) [Maj-Gen Anthony Lascelles CB CBE DSO, Manor Farm Cottage, Hedgerley Green, Bucks]; Maj-Gen RTR WW II (despatches twice), Gen Staff, HQ Far East Land Forces 1963–66, ret 1967, Dir-Gen Winston Churchill Memorial Tst 1967–80, Pres Br Water Ski Fedn 1980; *b* 10 Jan 1912; *educ* Winchester and Oriel Coll Oxford (BA); *m* 5 March 1941 *Ethne Hyde Ussher, yr dau of Norman Charles, of Chard, Somerset

1b *Alice Leila [Miss Alice Lascelles, The Plough, Redford, Midhurst, Sussex GU29 0QF]; *b* 4 April 1914; *educ* Lond U (BSc (Econ) 1936)

2a Henry Francis; Welsh Gds WW I, Croix de Guerre; *b* 7 July 1886; *m* 14 May 1918 Rose Caroline Georgiana (*d* 19 March 1976), dau of Col Frederick Arthur Aylmer, RA (*see* AYLMER, B), and *d* 31 Aug 1937, leaving issue:

1b John David; *b* 2 March 1919; *d* unm 7 Nov 1952

2b +Oliver, MBE (1950), DSC (1943), JP; Cdr RN WW II ; *b* 5 March 1921; *m* 7 Sept 1963 *Pamela Margaret Enid, dau of Robert William Whillis and Mrs M G MacLeod, of Parsons Mead, Beaulieu, Hants, and has:

1c *Harriet Caroline; *b* 13 Oct 1964; *m* 1989 *Anthony William Vaughan Fairbank and has issue (*see* CHETWYND, V)

2c *Nicola Jane; *b* 7 July 1966

1b Anthea Caroline; *b* 28 Feb 1930; *m* 6 July 1950 *William Ralph Merton, 3rd s of Sir Thomas Ralph Merton, FRS, and *d* 25 Feb 1976, leaving:

1c *Michael Ralph; *b* 22 April 1951; *educ* Eton

2c *Rupert Ralph; *b* 2 July 1953; *educ* Eton

3c *Jeremy Ralph; *b* 15 Feb 1961

3a Francis William (Sir), KCB (1954, CB 1937), MC; Clerk Parls Ho Lds 1953–58, Capt Sussex Yeo WW I (wounded); *b* 23 March 1890; *educ* Winchester and Ch Ch Oxford (BA 1912, MA 1953); *m* 30 Sept 1924 *Esmée Marion, est dau of Charles Arthur Bury, of Downing, Salins, Co Kildare, and *d* 1979, leaving issue:

1b +(Charles) Brian [Brian Lascelles Esq, Bank House, Glenfarg, Perthshire]; dir John Menzies 1973; *b* 5 Sept 1926; *educ* Wellington; *m* 1st 4 July 1953 Elizabeth Mary (*d* 1978), only dau of Lt-Cdr Geoffrey Seymour Grenfell, RN (*see* GRENFELL, B); *m* 2nd 1986 *Margaret Anne, yst dau of Alec Maskell Mitchell (*see* KINROSS, B) and formerly w of Ronald Patrick Thornton, FRICS, and by his 1st w has:

1c +Charles Riversdale; *b* 17 April 1954

2c +James Dominic [James Lascelles Esq, 6 Merthyr Terrace, London SW13]; *b* 19 March 1956; *m* 1984 *Diana Elizabeth, dau of James Okolo, of Lagos, Nigeria, and has issue:

1d +James Theodore Grenfell; *b* 1988

1d *Lucy Elizabeth; *b* 1985

3c +Tobias Francis; *b* 5 July 1965

2b (Henry) Giles Francis; *b* 2 Oct 1931; *educ* Wellington; *m* 1 June 1957 *Caroline Venetia [Mrs Giles Lascelles, 119 Hambalt Rd, London SW4], dau of Esmond Charles Baring, OBE (*see* ASHBURTON, B), and *d* 20 April 1998, leaving

1c +Hugo Giles; *b* 31 Oct 1958; *m* 1986 *Joanna Catherine, yr dau of Maj Christopher Roland Philipson, of Lofts Hall, Essex (*see* 1935 edn WOOLAVINGTON, B), and has issue:

1d *Rose; *b* 1988

2d *Camilla; *b* 1991

2c +Peregrine Simon; *b* 10 April 1962

1c *Sophie Caroline; *b* 31 Oct 1958; *m* 9 April 1983 *Lord (Richard) Bruce Dundas, yst s of 3rd Marquess of Zetland (*qv*)

4a John Frederick, MC; 2nd Lt Rifle Bde and RFC WW I (despatches); *b* 13 Nov 1895; *ka* 31 July 1915

(1) Georgiana Caroline; *m* 20 July 1852 Charles William Grenfell, MP, and *d* 2 Feb 1911, leaving issue (*see* GRENFELL, B)

(2) Henrietta Frances; *m* 24 July 1849 2nd Baron Chesham (*qv*) and *d* 21 May 1884, leaving issue

(3) Mary Louisa, Maid-of-Honour to HM QUEEN VICTORIA 1865–81; *d* unm 4 Aug 1917 aged 81

(4) Emma Elizabeth (Hon); Maid-of-Honour to HM QUEEN VICTORIA, Ldy Bedchamber to HRH PRINCESS CHRISTIAN; *m* 3 Aug 1865 Lord Edward Cavendish, MP, and *d* 24 Sept 1920, leaving issue (*see* DEVONSHIRE, D)

(5) Beatrice Blanche; *m* 24 Aug 1876 Most Rev Frederick Temple, DD, Archbp Canterbury, and *d* 2 April 1915, having had issue. He *d* 22 Dec 1902

4 Edwin; MP, DCL; *b* 25 Dec 1799; *d* 26 April 1865

5 Arthur, of Norley Bank, Cheshire; Maj Earl of Chester's Yeo Cav; *b* 25 Jan 1807; *m* 18 Nov 1834 Caroline Frances (*d* 8 Jan 1895), dau of Sir Richard Brooke, 6th Bt, of Norton Priory (*qv*), and *d* 19 July 1880, leaving issue:

(1) Walter Richard, of Norley Bank, JP, DL; Col Rifle Bde; *b* 30 Oct 1837; *m* 6 June 1861 Ellen (*d* 1 Feb 1920), dau of Charles Kane Sivewright, and *d* 23 May 1906, leaving issue:

1a Walter Edward; Capt Rifle Bde; *b* 21 March 1862; *m* 2 Sept 1891 Mabel Gwendoline (*d* 1 Nov 1931), dau of Lt-Col Richard Hasell Thursby, Coldstream Gds, yst bro of Sir John Hardy Thursby, 1st Bt (*see* 1940 edn), and *dvp* 23 Jan 1897, leaving:

1b Violet Rachel; *b* 10 June 1892

2b Constance Gertrude; *b* 6 Oct 1894; *m* 7 Nov 1922 James Ogilvy Fairlie, JP, of Myres Castle, Fife, and had issue. He *d* 29 April 1960

2a George Reginald, CVO (1934), OBE (1919); Hon Lt-Col Roy Fus, Lt-Col 7th Bn, Exon Yeomen Gd 1912–32 and Ensign 1932–37, ADC to GOC Western Dist 1890–95 and Govr S Australia 1899, Boer War 1899–1900 and WW I; *b* 14 April 1864; *m* 25 June 1895 Beatrice (*d* 22 Sept 1958), dau of Rev Richard Thomas Pulteney, Rector Ashley, Northants, and *d* 26 Feb 1939, leaving issue:

1b John Norman Pulteney; Lt-Col Coldstream Gds, ADC to Govr-Gen S Africa 1925–28 and GOC London Dist 1930–32, served WW I (wounded) and WW II; *b* 16 May 1898; *m* 25 Jan 1932 Elizabeth Katharine Joan (*d* 25 Jan 1978), only child of Lt-Col Lord Robert William Orlando Manners, CMG, DSO (*see* RUTLAND, D), and *das* 11 Oct 1939, leaving:

1c +Rupert John Orlando [Rupert Lascelles Esq, Giffords Hele, Meeth, Devon EX20 3QN]; late Lt Coldstream Gds; *b* 24 Feb 1935; *educ* Eton; *m* 1st 25 Nov 1963 (*divorce* 1988) Jeanne Gordon, only dau of Norman Gordon Farquharson, of Johannesburg; *m* 2nd 1990 *Hon Mrs Susan Geraldine Uniacke, only dau of 20th Baron Willoughby de Broke (*qv*), and by his 1st w has:

1d +Robert Norman; *b* 7 April 1965

1d *Frances Sarah Elizabeth; *b* 14 Feb 1970

1b Joan; *b* 13 April 1896

1b *Barbara Judith; *b* 28 March 1903; *m* 18 Nov 1925 Edward William Seymour (*see* SOMERSET, D)

3a Ernest OBE (1919); Lt-Col 10th Serv Bn Rifle Bde WW I (despatches); *b* 19 May 1870; *m* 18 Jan 1898 Flora Evelyn (*d* 5 Jan 1956), dau of John Bulteel, of Pamflete, Devon, and *d* 1948, having had issue:

1b Guy Ernest; 2nd Lt Rifle Bde; *b* 27 Nov 1898; *ka* 24 March 1918

2b Frederick; *b* 10, *d* 15 Nov 1900

1b Faith Evelyn; *b* 27 Jan 1903; *d* 1997

4a Alfred; Lt RHA; *b* 1 Sept 1873; *dsp* 16 May 1900

5a Richard; *b* 9 March 1883; *d* 19 Feb 1916

1a Gertrude; *m* 28 July 1897 Maj William Gerald Dease KM, JP, of Co Westmeath, and *d* 21 Feb 1954, leaving issue. He *d* 9 Sept 1946

(2) Arthur George; *b* 31 July 1855; *d* 8 March 1929

(3) Brian Piers; *b* 30 Aug 1859; *d* 13 Jan 1922

(1) Clare Henrietta; *m* 6 Dec 1860 Capt Arthur Edmund Mansel (*see* MANSEL, Bt) and *d* 10 Nov 1917, having had issue

(2) Gertrude; *d* unm 23 April 1889

(3) Selina; *m* 4 Feb 1869 6th Baron Dynevor (*qv*) and *d* 16 Dec 1889, leaving issue

(4) Catherine; *m* 30 Dec 1868 Granville Edwin Lloyd Lloyd-Baker, DL, of Hardwicke Court, Glos, and *d* 22 July 1890, leaving issue. He *d* 3 Oct 1924

(5) Amy; *d* unm 18 Dec 1888

(6) Eleanor Frances; *m* 29 Sept 1868 Cecil Thomas Molineux-Montgomerie, of Garboldisham, Norfolk, and *d* 21 Jan 1941, having had issue. He *d* 17 April 1901

(7) Ruth; *m* 14 Oct 1886 George Egerton Warburton (*see* GREY EGERTON, Bt) and *d* 18 Feb 1924

1 Harriet; *m* 6 June 1825 2nd Earl of Sheffield (*see* STANLEY OF ALDERLEY, SHEFFIELD and, B) and *d* 1 Jan 1889, having had issue

2 Frances Anne; *m* 2 March 1835 John Thomas Hope (*see* LINLITHGOW, M) and *dsp* 6 Dec 1855

3 Emma; *m* 16 June 1827 1st Viscount Portman (*qv*) and *d* 8 Feb 1865, leaving issue

4 Louisa; *m* 4 July 1835 Lord George Henry Cavendish, MP (*see* DEVONSHIRE, D), and *d* 10 March 1886, leaving issue

The 2nd EARL *d* 24 Nov 1841; his son,

HENRY LASCELLES, **3rd Earl of Harewood**; Ld Lt and custos rotulorum W R Yorks; *b* 11 June 1797; *m* 5 July 1823 Lady Louisa Thynne (*d* 7 Nov 1859), 2nd dau of 2nd Marquess of Bath (*qv*), and had issue:

1 HENRY THYNNE, **4th Earl**

2 Egremont William, DL; MP Northallerton 1866–68, Capt Gren Gds; *b* 26 July 1825; *m* 11 Dec 1856 Jessie (*d* 11 Jan 1900), dau of Neil Malcolm of Poltalloch, and *d* 27 Oct 1892, leaving issue:

(1) Marion; *m* 10 May 1881 Capt Henry Dent Brocklehurst, 2nd Life Gds, of Sudeley Castle, Winchcombe, Glos (*see* 1970 edn BROCKLEHURST, Bt), and *d* 10 Aug 1938, leaving issue. He *d* 15 Aug 1932

(2) Clare; *d* 1883, aged 22

3 George Edwin, JP N R Yorks; barrister, Registrar of Deeds, CA, NR Yorks; *b* 19 Oct 1826; *m* 21 July 1851 Lady Louisa Nina Murray (*d* 30 Dec 1909), dau of 4th Earl of Mansfield (*qv*), and *d* 9 March 1911, leaving issue:

(1) David Arthur George, of Leeming Garth, Northallerton, Yorks; Capt 47th and Roy Scots Lothian Regt; *b* 30 April 1852; *m* 8 Oct 1885 Edith Maud (*d* 7 March 1938), er dau of Charles John Galloway, of Thorneyholme, Knutsford, and Hauson House, Cheshire, and *d* 5 Jan 1930, leaving issue:

1a Gladys Maud; *b* 21 July 1886; *m* 12 Dec 1907 Maj John Redmond Hutton-Squire, of Holtby Hall, Leeming Bar, Northallerton, s of Robert Hutton-Squire, JP, of Holtby Hall, Yorks, and *d* 23 April 1961, leaving issue. He *d* 26 March 1954

(2) Alfred George (Sir), KC; *b* 12 Oct 1857; BA Oxon, barrister Inner Temple 1885, Ch Justice Ceylon 1911–14; *m* 26 Oct 1911 Isabel Carteret (*d* 12 Aug 1965), dau of Francis John Thynne (*see* BATH, M), and *d* 9 Feb 1952, having had issue:

1a Francis Alfred George, DFC; W/Cdr RAF WW II; *b* 5 Aug 1912; *k* on air operations Aug 1941

1a *Ursula [Mrs Alan Ormiston, Coln Orchard, Arlington, Glos GL7 5ND]; *b* 9 June 1914; *m* 28 Sept 1946 Alan George Ross Ormiston (*d* 13 Nov 1996), and has:

1b *James Christopher Ross; *b* 13 March 1949; *educ* Eton and Worcester Coll Oxford

1b *Lavinia Anne Ross; *b* 15 April 1952; *m* 1978 *3rd Baron Rathcreedan (*qv*) and has issue

2a *Kathleen Louisa Isabel [Mrs Kathleen Bellamy, Manor Cottage, Coln St Aldwyn, Glos GL7 5AD]; *b* 23 June 1916; *m* 11 Oct 1940 (*divorce* 1953) Brig Robert Hugh Bellamy, CBE, DSO and bar (*d* 27 Nov 1972), 1st Parachute Bde, yst s of Lt-Col Robert Bellamy, DSO, and has issue:

1b *Martin Hugh; *b* 21 May 1946; *educ* Stowe; *m* 1979 *Elizabeth Burton, and has issue

1b *Vivien Patricia; *b* 16 Feb 1943; *m* 20 May 1967 Anthony John Wyndham Owston (*d* 1992), barrister, er s of (Alfred) John Owston (*see* BROMLEY, Bt), and has issue:

1c *Gavin Anthony; *b* 1970

1c *Vanessa Rosemary; *b* 4 Dec 1968

3a Hermione Constance; *b* 20 July 1917; *m* 1st 3 Feb 1948 Lt-Gen Walter David Alexander Lentaigne (*d* 24 June 1955), CB, CBE, DSO, s of Mr Justice Benjamin Plunket Lentaigne, of Stackallan Glebe, Navan, Co Meath, and had issue; *m* 2nd 18 July 1959 Gerald Maclean (*d* 14 May 1968), 2nd s of Montague Francis Maclean, of The Chantry, Ross, Herefs, and *d* 11 Nov 1968

(3) Edward George; *b* 6 Feb 1859; *m* 25 July 1891 Minna (*d* 1950), 3rd dau of Rev John Boyle, Vicar Ashby Folville, Leics, and *d* 28 July 1938, having had:

1a Evelyn Herbert; WW I as 2nd Lt KRRC and RFC (wounded); *b* 1893; *m* 24 Jan 1923 Colleen Una (*d* 1986), dau of John Taylor, of Rockwood Station, Queensland, and *d* 1982, leaving issue:

1b John Edward, JP; *m* 24 Jan 1946 *Isabelle Christine Graham Maxwell, of Gordonvale, N Queensland, and *d* 1975, leaving issue:

1c +David John; *b* 23 Jan 1948; *m* 1986 (*divorce* 1989) —

2c +Peter James [Peter Lascelles Esq, The Counthouse, Wheal Kitty, St Agnes, Cornwall]; *b* 17 Oct 1952; *m* 1981 *Mary Louise O'Donovan, of Bega, NSW, and has issue:

1d +Sean Henry; *b* 1981

2d +Brennan James Maxwell; *b* 1985

3d +Marcus Peter; *b* 1990

3c +Stephen Charles [Stephen Lascelles Esq, 11 Tipuana Drive, Capalaba, Qld 4157, Australia]; *b* 1954; *m* 1991 *Theresa Louise Walter, of Brisbane

1c *Isabelle Diana; *b* 1957; *m* 19– *Rodney Phillip Spillane, of Brisbane

2b +Geoffrey George, JP [Geoffrey Lascelles Esq, 164 Esplanade, Pt Vernon, Hervey Bay, Qld 4655, Australia], WW II in RAN; *b* 14 May 1927; *m* 10 May 1951 *Gwen Martin, of Yandina, Queensland, and has issue:

1c +Scott [Scott Lascelles Esq, 60 Battye Ave, Beverley Park, Sydney, NSW, Australia]; *b* 17 Nov 1952; *m* 1981 *Lynne Jennifer Boultwood, of Earlwood, Sydney, and has issue:

1d +Robert Scott; *b* 1986

1d *Elinor; *b* 1983

2c +Kent [Lt-Cdr Kent Lascelles, 2 Caffyn Place, Garran, Canberra, ACT, Australia]; *b* 28 Oct 1954; Lt -Cdr RAN; *m* 1st 1975 (*divorce* 1980) Ann Maarie Ludwigsen, of Bellvue Park, Southport, and has issue:

1d *Tamara; *b* 1975

2c (cont.) Kent Lascelles *m* 2nd 1985 *Vicki Ann Harris, of Wagga Wagga, NSW, and has issue:

2d *Ashleigh Mary; *b* 1988

3d *Georgia Erin; *b* 1994

1c *Fiona Janne; *b* 25 July 1962; *m* 1991 *Paul Longworth, of Farnworth, Lancs, and has issue:

1d *Jack Lascelles; *b* 1993

1d *Cara Lascelles; *b* 1996

2a Geoffrey Edward; *b* 1895; *d* 11 Jan 1910

(4) Maurice George (Rev); MA Oxon, Vicar Harewood, Hon Canon Ripon; *b* 29 May 1860; *m* 8 July 1891 Jane Barbara (*d* 23 Jan 1933), er dau of Robert Ballard Woodd, of Hampstead, and *dsp* 6 June 1940

(5) Arthur George; *b* 4 Dec 1869; *d* unm 12 Oct 1946

(6) Ernest George; Lt RHA; *b* 6 March 1874; *m* 4 Aug 1926 Mrs Edna M Kidd and *dsp* 8 Sept 1946

(1) Evelyn Louisa, OBE (1918); *b* 22 June 1853; *d* unm 13 Sept 1951

(2) Alice Margaret; *b* 23 April 1855; *m* 8 July 1875 Rev J Thorneycroft Hartley, Hon Canon Ripon, and *d* 18 March 1946. He *d* 21 Aug 1935

(3) Blanche; *b* 6 Jan 1864; *m* 5 March 1889 Sir Charles Edward Smith-Dodsworth, 5th Bt (*qv*), and *dsp* 28 Aug 1949

(4) Agnes Nina; *b* 5 June 1868; *m* 18 May 1904 Arthur Wentworth Chivers Bower and *d* 8 Dec 1959, having had issue. He *d* 20 Jan 1946

(5) Margaret Emily; *b* 18 Jan 1876; *m* 16 Sept 1911 Charles Arthur Lovegrove, AMICE, Assist Dir Public Works Ceylon, and had issue. He *d* 9 June 1927

4 Algernon Francis; *b* 21 Jan 1828; *d* 28 March 1845

5 Alfred; *b* 26 Feb 1829; *d* 20 March 1845

6 James Walter (Rev); MA Oxon, Rector Goldsborough, Canon Ripon; *b* 14 Nov 1831; *m* 15 July 1856 Emma Clara (*d* 30 April 1911), dau of Sir William Miles, 1st Bt (*qv*), and *d* 25 Nov 1901, leaving issue:

(1) William James; Lt Rifle Bde; *b* 22 Aug 1858; *d* 6 Feb 1921

(2) Cecil Henry; *b* 19 Jan 1865; *m* 1892 Euphemia Carr (*d* 5 Aug 1954), dau of W Robinson, and *d* 17 Nov 1899, leaving:

1a Cecil Elizabeth; *b* 29 May 1894; *m* 11 July 1927 (*divorce* 1936) Conrad Hal Waddington, CBE, DSc, FRS, and *d* 6 March 1977, leaving issue. He *d* 26 Dec 1975

2a Ruth Carr; *b* 12 Aug 1895

(3) Walter Charles, DSO; Capt Durham LI; *b* 5 July 1867; *m* 20 Nov 1902 Louisa Gertrude (*d* 10 June 1954), only dau of Col Charles Home Cuff Knox, DL, JP, of Creagh, Co Mayo, and *dsp* 18 May 1911

(4) Reginald Francis; *b* 6 Dec 1868; *educ* Marlborough

(1) Edith Katherine; *m* 31 Oct 1882 Walter Pleydell Bouverie and *d* 23 Aug 1902, leaving issue (*see* RADNOR, E)

(2) Rachel Blanche; *m* 15 April 1884 Hugh Francis Seymour (*see* HERTFORD, M) and *d* 4 Nov 1946, leaving issue

(3) Catherine Maria; *m* 30 July 1891 Maj Charles Bateson Harvey, 10th Hus (*ka* Boer War 4 Jan 1900), and *d* 26 Jan 1929, having had issue (*see* 1931 edn HARVEY, Bt, of Langridge)

(4) Emma; *m* 19 Oct 1900 Rev William Travis Travis, Rector Ripley, Yorks. He *d* 2 May 1924

(5) Mabel Louisa; *m* 9 Aug 1882 Albert Meysey Thompson, QC, and *d* 24 Dec 1941, having had issue (*see* MEYSEY-THOMPSON, Bt)

7 Horace Douglas; Cdr RN; *b* 20 Sept 1835; *d* 15 June 1869

1 Louisa Isabella; *m* 25 Aug 1853 1st Baron Hillingdon (*see* 1970 edn) and *d* 30 Nov 1918, having had issue. He *d* 3 April 1898

2 Susan Charlotte; *m* 4 July 1855 1st Earl of Wharncliffe (*qv*) and *d* 18 May 1927

3 Blanche Emma; *m* 12 July 1859 5th Earl of Shannon (*qv*) and *d* 26 Dec 1863, leaving issue

4 Florence Harriet; *m* 21 Jan 1861 Lt-Col John Francis Cust (*see* BROWNLOW, B) and *dsp* 18 Nov 1901

5 Mary Elizabeth; *m* 19 April 1865 Hon Sir Robert H Meade, KCB, s of 3rd Earl of Clanwilliam (*qv*), and *d* 7 Feb 1866, leaving issue

6 Maud Caroline; Lady Imp Order of the Crown of India; *m* 28 Nov 1871 Lord George Hamilton, GCSI, PC, and *d* 14 April 1938, leaving issue (*see* ABERCORN, D)

The 3rd EARL *d* 22 Feb 1857; his est son,

HENRY THYNNE LASCELLES, **4th Earl of Harewood**; *b* 18 June 1824; *m* 1st 17 July 1845 Elizabeth Joanna (*d* 26 Feb 1854), est dau of 1st Marquess of Clanricarde (*see* SLIGO, M), and had issue:

1 HENRY ULICK, **5th Earl**

2 Frederick Canning; Cdr RN; *b* 6 May 1848; *m* 17 June 1878 Frederica Maria (*d* 17 March 1891), dau of Hon Sir Adolphus Frederick Octavius Liddell, KCB, QC (*see* RAVENSWORTH, B), and *d* 31 Dec 1928, having had issue:

(1) Guy Frederick Thomas; *b* 23 Aug 1884; *d* young

(2) Alan Frederick (Sir), GCB (1953, KCB 1944), GCVO (1947, MVO 1926), CMG (1933), MC, PC (1943); *b* 11 April 1887; *educ* Marlborough and Trin Coll Oxford (BA 1909, MA 1915, Hon Fellow 1948); Capt 105th (Beds Yeo), Field Brig RA (TAR) WW I (despatches), Sec to Govr-Gen Canada 1931–35, Assist Priv Sec to HRH THE PRINCE OF WALES 1920–29 and TM GEORGE V 1935–36, EDWARD VIII 1936 and GEORGE VI 1936–43, Priv Sec 1943–52, Priv Sec to HM THE QUEEN 1952–53, Extra Equerry to HM 1954–81, Keeper Roy Archives 1945–53; dir Midland Bank and Midland Bank Executor and Tstee Co 1954, Chm: Historic Buildings Cncl (England) 1953–63, Pilgrim Tst 1954–59; Hon LLD Bristol 1954 and Durham 1958, Hon FRAM 1961, Hon DCL Oxon 1963; *m* 16 March 1920 Joan Frances Vere Thesiger (*d* 15 May 1971), est dau of 1st Viscount Chelmsford (*qv*), and *d* 1981, having had:

1a John Frederick; Capt Gren Gds WW II (wounded); *b* 11 Jan 1922; *d* unm 11 Sept 1951

1a *Lavinia Joan [Mrs David Hankinson, 12A Barkston Gardens, London SW5]; *b* 27 June 1923 (HRH THE late DUKE OF WINDSOR stood sponsor); *m* 1st 30 March 1946 (*divorce* 1960) Maj Edward Westland Renton, Black Watch (RHR), and has issue; *m* 2nd 1 Feb 1962 (*divorce* 1964) Gavin Maxwell (*see* MAXWELL, Bt); *m* 3rd 1969 *David Hankinson and by her 1st husb has:

1b *Nicholas John; *b* 1946; *m* 1975 *Caroline Mary, dau of Kennedy Mayo Harrow, of NZ, and has issue:

1c *Alan Edward Mayo; *b* 1976

1c *Zoë Eleanor; *b* 1979

2b *Simon Anthony [Simon Renton Esq, 33 Church St, London SW13]; *b* 1948; *m* 1977 *Amanda Jane, dau of David Schrie, of Cape Town, and has issue:

1c *Julia Esther; *b* 1979

2c *Claudia Jessamine; *b* 1981

2a *Caroline Mary [The Hon Mrs David Erskine, Felsham House, Felsham, Suffolk]; ARCM; *b* 15 Feb 1927; *m* 1st 20 May 1949 2nd Viscount Chandos (*qv*); *m* 2nd 1985, as his 2nd w, *Hon David Hervey Erskine, bro of 13th Earl of Mar and Kellie (*qv*), and by her 1st husb has issue

(1) Helen Elizabeth; *b* 10 Oct 1879; *m* 8 July 1913 Sir Eric Robert Dalrymple Maclagan, CBE, Dir and Sec V&A, s of Rt Hon and Most Rev William Dalrymple Maclagan, Archbp York, by Augusta Anne, dau of 6th Viscount Barrington (*see* 1970 edn), and *d* 19 Oct 1942, having had issue. He *d* 14 Sept 1951

(2) Blanche Isabella (Hon); Maid of Honour to HM QUEEN ALEXANDRA 1905–11, Ldy-in-Waiting to HRH THE PRINCESS ROYAL 1941–45 (Extra Ldy-in-Waiting 1945), V-Pres Nursing Divs St John Jerusalem 1942, Pres Merchant Navy Comforts Serv 1941–45, Chm Women's Branch C Assoc 1945–48, DGStJ; *b* 8 Oct 1880; *m* 13 Nov 1911 1st Baron Lloyd, GCSI, GCIE, DSO, PC, and *d* 30 Dec 1969, leaving issue. He *d* 4 Feb 1941 (*see* 1970 edn)

(3) Maud Frederica; *b* 28 Jan 1882; *m* 1 Aug 1912 Lt-Col Fergus Brinsley Nixon, DSO, Inniskilling Dragoons, and had issue

(4) Margaret Mary, OStJ; *b* 4 April 1883; *m* 1st 18 April 1907 Maxwell Christian Livingstone Learmonth (*d* 31 March 1912); *m* 2nd 27 Nov 1914 Maj Melville Balfour, MC, RA, and *d* 22 May 1972, having had issue. He *d* 4 Oct 1962

3 Gerald William, CB (1914); BA Cantab, Dep Surveyor New Forest; *b* 26 Oct 1849; *m* 9 Feb 1875 Constance Augusta Mary FitzClarence (*d* 5 Nov 1934), dau of John Burton Phillipson, of Sunninghill, Berks, and *d* 11 Feb 1928, having had:

(1) Gerald Hubert; *b* 23 April 1876; *d* 13 July 1928

(2) John Beilby; *b* 19 Feb 1884; *d* unm 13 Nov 1907

(3) Richard; *b* and *d* 30 Nov 1887

(1) Cynthia Rachael; *b* 29 Aug 1885; *m* 10 March 1910 4th Baron Poltimore (*qv*) and *d* 6 Sept 1961, leaving issue

4 Charles George; Lt 9th Lancers, Capt Yorks Hus, ADC to Ld Lt Ireland; *b* 23 Jan 1851; *d* 19 Feb 1886

1 Constance Mary, CI; *m* 14 May 1872 3rd Baron Wenlock, GCSI, GCIE, KCB (*see* 1932 edn), and *d* 23 Aug 1932, having had issue. He *d* 15 Jan 1912

2 Margaret Joan; *m* 19 July 1876 5th and last Earl of Desart, KP (*see* 1934 edn), and *d* 19 Sept 1927, leaving issue. He *d* 4 Nov 1934

The **4th Earl** *m* 2nd 21 April 1858 Diana Elizabeth (*d* 4 March 1904), dau of Col John George Smyth, MP, of Heath, Yorks, and had:

5 Edwin Harry, Capt 7th Hus; *b* 3 Aug 1861; *d* 16 Jan 1924

6 Daniel Harry; *b* 1 Aug 1862; *d* unm 28 Nov 1904

7 George Algernon, Hon Maj Essex Regt, Capt 3rd Bn Princess of Wales's Own Yorks Regt; *b* 2 Aug 1865; *m* 4 Jan 1905 Mabel Caroline Elcocke (*d* 23 Nov 1951), 2nd dau of Francis Elcocke Massey, of Poole Hall, Nantwich, and *d* 25 May 1932, leaving:

(1) *Sybil Mary; WW II with WAAF (despatches twice); *b* 20 May 1907; *m* 24 May 1935 Col Humphrey Bradshaw Mellow Wright, RA

8 William Horace, JP Norfolk; *b* 15 Feb 1868; *m* 8 April 1899 Madeline (*d* 8 Dec 1950), dau of Rev Gerrard Barton, of Fundenhall, Norfolk, and *d* 7 May 1949, leaving issue:

(1) Daniel William (Sir), KCMG (1954, CMG 1946); Envoy Extrdy and Min Plen Addis Abba and Consul-Gen Ethopia 1948–49, Amb Extrdy 1949–51, Amb Extrdy and Plen Kabul 1953; *b* 19 March 1902; *educ* RNCs Osborne and Dartmouth and Balliol Coll Oxford; *d* unm 17 Oct 1967

(2) John Edward; slr, Lt Lincolnshire Regt; *b* 9 June 1911; *educ* Peterhouse Cambridge (BA); *m* 18 Dec 1954 *Kathleen Elizabeth, only dau of C E Ransom, and *d* 26 Jan 1955

(1) *Mary Madge [Miss Mary Lascelles, Valley House, Cley-next-the-Sea, Holt, Norfolk]; *b* 7 Feb 1900; *educ* LMH Oxford, Fell Somerville Coll Oxford 1932 (Hon Fell 1967), FBA 1962, BLitt 1927, BA 1922, MA 1931

(2) *Pamela Diana; *b* 19 March 1902

(3) *Susan Olivia [Miss Susan Lascelles, Valley House, Cley-next-the-Sea, Holt, Norfolk]; *b* 26 May 1907; ARCA

9 Francis John; *b* 29 Dec 1871; *m* 30 Nov 1905 Gertie, est dau of Robert Anstice Stradling, of Knowle, Bristol, and *d* 9 May 1925, leaving issue:

(1) Norah Gertrude; *b* 5 Sept 1906; *m* — de Chanaz and *d* 11 Feb 1972

10 Eric James; *b* 2 March 1873; *d* unm 24 June 1901

3 Susan Elizabeth; *b* 21 May 1860; *m* 21 July 1881 Francis Richard Hugh Seymour Sutton (*see* SUTTON, Bt) and *d* 22 Jan 1925, leaving issue

4 Mary Diana; *b* 24 May 1877; *m* 30 April 1898, as his 1st w, Robert Wentworth Doyne, of Marton Hall, Baschurch, Salop, and *d* 23 July 1930, leaving issue. He *d* 25 Sept 1942

The 4th EARL *d* 24 June 1892; his est son,

HENRY ULICK LASCELLES, **5th Earl of Harewood**, GCVO (1922, KCVO 1908), TD, JP Yorks; Ld Lt, custos rotulorum and Pres TAAF (W R); Hon LLD Leeds, Hon Col Yorks Hus Yeo, ADC to HM, Capt Gren Gds, ADC to Viceroy India, KGStJ; *b* 21 Aug 1846; *m* 5 Nov 1881 Lady Florence Katharine Bridgeman, DJStJ (*d* 5 May 1943), dau of 3rd Earl of Bradford (*qv*), and had issue:

1 HENRY GEORGE CHARLES, **6th Earl**

2 Edward Cecil, DSO (1918), MC; WW I: Capt and Brevet Maj, 5th Bn Rifle Bde (despatches), Staff Capt 1915–16, GSO(3) 1916, Bde Maj 1916–17 and GSO(2) 1917–18, Priv Sec to 1st Earl of Balfour (*qv*) 1919; *b* 28 July 1887; *m* 11 March 1915 Joan Eleanor Campbell (*d* 10 May 1939), 2nd dau of Col Eustace James Anthony Balfour (*see* BALFOUR, E), and *d* 18 Aug 1935

1 Margaret Selina, CBE (1920), JP; *b* 11 Aug 1883; DGStJ, Hon LLD Leeds 1951; *m* 4 Oct 1906 9th Viscount Boyne (*qv*) and *d* Dec 1978, having had issue

The 5th EARL *d* 6 Oct 1929; his er son,

HENRY GEORGE CHARLES LASCELLES, **6th Earl of Harewood**, KG (1922), JP, DL Suffolk, DL Co Galway; Lord Lt and custos rotulorum W R Yorks, Pres TAA, GCVO (1934), DSO (1918), TD, Hon LLD Sheffield 1928 and Leeds 1935, Grand Master English Lodge 1942, Personal ADC to HM GEORGE V; Hon Attaché Dip Serv 1905–07, Roy Tstee Br Museum 1930–47, Pres Inst Medical Psychology 1936, Pres Roy Patriotic Fund Corp 1942, Chllr Sheffield U 1944, Capt Gren Gds, Maj Yorkshire Hus Yeo WW I (wounded twice, despatches, Croix de Guerre), Hon Col 1st Bn City London Regt (TA) and 5th Bn W Yorks Regt (Prince of Wales's Own) TA, Hon A/Cdre 609 (W R) Bomber Sqdn AAF, KJStJ, Order Olav Norway, Grand Cross Order Mahomet Ali Egypt; *b* 9 Sept 1882; *m* 28 Feb 1922 HRH THE PRINCESS ROYAL (*d* 28 March 1965), only dau of HM GEORGE V (*see* Royal Family Section), and *d* 24 May 1947, leaving:

1 GEORGE HENRY HUBERT LASCELLES, **7th and present Earl of Harewood**

2 Gerald David; *b* 21 Aug 1924 (HM QUEEN ELIZABETH THE QUEEN MOTHER and HRH THE DUKE OF WINDSOR stood sponsors); *educ* Eton; Capt Rifle Bde WW II, Pres Br Racing Drivers' Club 1964–91, dir Silverstone Circuit, FIMI (Pres 1969–73 and 1975), chm Swedholm; *m* 1st 15 July 1952 (*divorce* 1978) Angela, dau of Charles Stanley Dowding, of Dulwich, and had:

(1) +Henry Ulick; *b* 19 May 1953; *educ* Eton; *m* 25 August 1979 *Alexandra Clare Ruth, dau of Peter Morton, and has:

1a +Maximillian John Gerald; *b* 19 Dec 1991

2 (cont.) The Hon Gerald Lascelles *m* 2nd 17 Nov 1978 *Elizabeth Evelyn [The Hon Mrs Gerald Lascelles, Les Croux, Monbazillac, 24240 Sigoules, France], only dau of Brig Sydney Collingwood, CMG, CBE, MC, of The Croft, Dedham, Essex, and *dd* 27 Feb 1998, leaving by her:

(2) *Martin David; *b* 9 Feb 1962; *educ* Bryanston; pop song lyricist ('Desire' no. 3 in charts autumn 1996) and producer; has

1a *Georgina Elizabeth; *b* 22 Dec 1988

Seat: Harewood House, Leeds. The architects were Robert Adam and John Carr, and the climax of the building they designed is a front elevation with a classical pediment surmounting six pillars with two other half-pillars to either side. The work was undertaken throughout the entire 1760s, Carr coping with the initial project and superintending the stables, while Adam put finishing touches to the building later on following a stay in Italy. In the early 1770s Capability Brown reshaped the grounds. Harewood so far was pure Palladian, but in the next century Charles Barry added extra storeys and dismantled part of Adam's internal decorations. Nevertheless the hall today displays some of Adam's best work, particularly the plasterwork. Other plasterwork is by Joseph Rose, adorned by Angelica Kauffmann painting.

HARFORD

Arms: Sa. two bendlets arg. between three cross-crosslets fitchée in pale of the last. **Crest:** In front of flames, issuant therefrom a phoenix ppr., two cross-crosslets fitchée in saltire arg.
Motto: *Inter utrumque tene* ('Hold between the two').
Creation: Bt. (UK) 29 June 1934.

SIR (JOHN) TIMOTHY HARFORD, 3RD BT, of Falcondale, Co Cardigan [Sir Timothy Harford Bt, South House, South Littleton, Worcs WR11 5TJ]; *b* 6 July 1932; *s f* 1967; *educ* Harrow, Worcester Coll Oxford and Harvard Business Sch; dir: Singer and Friedlander 1970–87, Wesleyan Assur Soc 1972– (chm 1993–); *m* 12 May 1962 *Carolyn Jane, only dau of Brig Guy John de Wette Mullens, OBE, of North House, Weyhill, Hants, and has:

1 +MARK JOHN; *b* 6 Aug 1964

2 +Simon Guy; *b* 24 Sept 1966

1 *Clare Elizabeth; *b* 24 March 1963; *m* 1989 *Nicholas Clatworthy, yr s of Peter Clatworthy, and has:

(1) *Guy Peter; *b* 1992

(2) *Laura Jane; *b* 1995

Lineage: WILLIAM HARFORD, of Marshfield, Glos, *temp* ELIZABETH I; had:

MARK HARFORD, of Marshfield; *bapt* 7 March 1569; *m* 1st 15 Jan 1601 Ellen Alsoppe (*dsp, bur* 8 Oct 1626) and was *bur* 12 Nov 1652, leaving by a 2nd w:

CHARLES HARFORD, of Bristol; *bapt* 17 May 1631; *m* 1st 22 March 1656 Mary Bushe and had issue; *m* 2nd 16 April 1671 Eliza Cox (*d* 6 March 1706) and *d* 6 Dec 1700; his s by his 1st w:

EDWARD HARFORD, of Bristol; *b* 5 May 1658; *m* 10 Oct 1689 Elizabeth (*bur* 7 June 1758), dau of Charles Jones, gs of Hugh Jones, 1st Protestant Bp Llandaff, and *d* 28 Aug 1705, having had, with other issue:

EDWARD HARFORD, of Bristol; *b* 12 Sept 1691; *m* 15 Oct 1716 Elizabeth (*d* 16 June 1729), dau of Edward Lloyd, and *d* 24 Dec 1779, leaving an only s:

EDWARD HARFORD, of Frenchay, nr Bristol; *b* 25 Dec 1720; *m* 7 March 1747 Sarah (*d* 1776), dau and heir of John Scandrett, of York, and *d* 28 April 1806, leaving an only s:

JOHN SCANDRETT HARFORD, of Blaise Castle, Glos; *b* 10 April 1754; *m* 9 Feb 1780 Mary (*d* 29 July 1830), dau of Abraham Gray, of Tottenham, Middx, and *d* 23 Jan 1815, having had, with other issue:

ABRAHAM GRAY HARFORD later HARFORD-BATTERSBY (Act of Parliament 1815 on inheriting his kinsman William Battersby's estate), of Stoke House, Glos; *b* 1 Nov 1786; *m* 11 May 1816 Elizabeth (*d* 23 Jan 1823), yst dau of Maj-Gen Dundas (*see* ZETLAND, M), and *d* May 1851, leaving, with other issue:

JOHN BATTERSBY HARFORD, of Falcondale, Cards, JP Cards and Glos, DL Glos, High Sheriff 1855; *b* 29 Nov 1819; MA Oxon; *m* 4 April 1850 Mary Charlotte (*d* 17 Feb 1919), dau of Christian Charles Josias, Baron de Bunsen, Prussian Envoy Extrdy and Min Plen to UK, by Frances, dau of Benjamin Waddington, of Llanover, Mon, and had:

1 JOHN CHARLES (Sir), **1st Bt**

2 Frederic Dundas, CVO (1906) JP, DL Cards, of Holme, Yorks; *b* 8 Feb 1862; *m* 29 Sept 1896 Amy Mary Josephine (*d* 14 March 1954), yr dau and coheir of Henry Joseph Stourton (*see* MOWBRAY, SEGRAVE and STOURTON, B), and *d* 28 April 1931, leaving:

(1) Joan Mary; *m* 12 May 1920 Sir Alexander Bannerman, 11th Bt (*qv*), and had issue

1 Alice Mary Elizabeth; *d* unm 9 April 1927

2 Constance Emilia; *m* 23 April 1878 John Baird and *d* 13 Aug 1914, having had issue (*see* KINTORE, E)

3 Mary Edith; *m* 13 July 1878 Capt Alban Gwynne, of Monachty, Cards, and *d* Feb 1917, leaving issue. He *d* 20 Feb 1904

4 Charlotte Louisa; *d* unm 10 May 1930

5 Agnes Clementina; *d* unm 23 Oct 1936
6 Eleanor Dorothy; *m* 23 April 1889 John Iltyd Dillwyn Nicholl, MBE, JP, DL, of Merthyr Mawr House, Bridgend, Glam, and *d* 6 May 1946, leaving issue. He *d* 20 Sept 1935

JOHN HARFORD *d* 11 Feb 1875; his est s,

Sir John Charles Harford, 1st Bt (UK), so *cr* 29 July 1934, JP Glos, JP, DL Cards; High Sheriff 1885, Ld Manor Lampeter, Maj Pembs Yeo; *b* 28 July 1860; *m* 11 April 1893 Blanche Amabel (*d* 28 Aug 1904), 2nd dau of Henry Cecil Raikes, PC, and had issue:

1 John Henry; Lt 1st Bn S Wales Borderers; *b* 7 Feb 1895; *ka* 26 Oct 1916
2 (GEORGE) ARTHUR (Sir), **2nd Bt**
3 William; *b* 29 June, *d* 4 July 1899
1 Mary Amabel; *m* 20 June 1916 (*divorce* 1944) Charles Loraine Hill, JP, est s of Charles Gathorne Hill, JP, and *d* 21 Jan 1966, leaving issue. He *d* 14 Dec 1976

Sir JOHN *d* 16 July 1934; his only surv son,

Sir (George) Arthur Harford, 2nd Bt, OBE; *b* 29 Dec 1897; *educ* Harrow and RMC Sandhurst; 17th/21st Lancers 1917–23 (Hon Lt-Col), WW II Gen Staff, High Sheriff Cards 1938; *m* 9 April 1931 Anstice Marion (*d* 1993), yst dau of Sir Alfred Ernest Tritton, 2nd Bt (*qv*), and *d* 18 Dec 1967, leaving:

1 Sir (JOHN) TIMOTHY HARFORD, **3rd and present Bt**
2 +Piers Scandrett [Piers Harford Esq, Church Farm, Gt Somerford, Wilts]; *b* 9 Sept 1937; *educ* Eton and Worcester Coll Oxford; *m* 1st 22 July 1961 (*divorce* 1972) Hyacinthe Cecilia, est dau of Lt-Col Nigel Walter Hoare, OBE, TD, RE (TA) (*see* PORTAL, Bt), and has issue:
(1) +Henry Scandrett; *b* 19 July 1963
(1) *Charlotte Anstice; *b* 12 June 1965
2 (cont.) Piers Harford *m* 2nd 1975 *Patricia Jane, only dau of A/Cdre Patrick Burnett, and by her has:
(2) +William Patrick; *b* 5 March 1976
1 *Robina Elspeth [Mrs Jeremy Glyn, Upton Farm, Upton, Hants SP11 0JS]; *b* 28 Oct 1934; *m* 8 Dec 1956 Jeremy Christopher Glyn (*see* WOLVERTON, B) and has issue

HARINGTON

Arms: Sa. a fret arg. **Crest:** A lion's head erased or, langued and collared gu. and buckled gold. **Motto:** *Nodo firmo* ('With a firm knot'). **Creation:** Bt. (E) 29 June 1611.

SIR NICHOLAS JOHN HARINGTON, 14TH BT, of Ridlington, Co Rutland [Sir Nicholas Harington Bt, 99 Clarendon Road, London, W11 4JG; Ring O'Bells, Whitbourne, Worcs WR6 5RT]; *b* 14 May 1942; *s* uncle 1981; *educ* Eton and Ch Ch Oxford (MA); barrister 1969

Lineage: OSULPHUS or OSWULF; had:

ROBERT de HEVERINGTON; feudal Ld Harrington/Haverington/Heverington, Cumberland; also held the Manor of Flemingby *temp* RICHARD I; ggf of:

Sir ROBERT de HAVERINGTON, initially of Harrington etc; settled *temp* EDWARD I at Aldingham, Lancs, which he acquired on marrying Agnes (*d* 1293), dau of Robert de Cansfield by Aline (sister and heir of Sir Michael le Fleming or Furness, of Michelland or Muchland in Furness, an area of Furness whose chief place was Aldingham), and *d* 1297, having had, with an er s (Michael, *dsp*):

Sir JOHN de HA(VE)RINGTON, 1st LORD (Baron) HARINGTON (E), so deemed by later doctrine to have been *cr* by writ of summons to Parl 3 Dec 1326; *b c* 1281; ktd 1306; memb of faction opposed to EDWARD II's favourite Piers Gaveston; *m* by 1326 Joan, probably dau of ? Dacre, and *d* 2 July 1347, having had, with three yr sons (John, Thomas, Michael):

Sir ROBERT; ktd by 1331; *m* by 1327 Elizabeth, dau of Thomas de Multon, and *dvp* by 1334, leaving issue:

1 JOHN de HAVERINGTON, 2nd LORD (Baron) HARINGTON; *b* by 1315; *m* (?)Joan, dau of Walter de Bermingham(?), and *d* 28 May 1363, leaving issue:
(1) Sir ROBERT de HAVERINGTON, 3rd LORD (Baron) HARINGTON; *bapt* 28 March 1356; ktd 1377; *m* 1st *c* 1376 Alice de Greystoke (*dsp*), dau of 2nd Lord (Baron) Greystock; *m* 2nd *c* 1383 Isabel (*d* 21 Aug 1400), widow of Sir William Cogan, of Bampton, Devon (*d* 1382), and dau of Sir Nele Loring, KG, and *d* 21 May 1406, having by her had:
1a JOHN de HARINGTON, 4th LORD (Baron) HARINGTON; *b* by 1484; *m* 1411 Lady Elizabeth Courtenay (*m* 2nd Oct 1427 1st Lord (Baron) Bonville, of Chewton (beheaded 18 Feb 1460/1), and *d* 18 Oct 1471), dau of 3rd Earl of Devon (*qv*) of the Feb 1334/5 *cr*, and *d* 11 Feb 1417/8
2a Sir WILLIAM HARINGTON, 5th LORD (Baron) HARINGTON; *b c* 1390; *m* by 1423 Margaret, dau of Sir John Hill, Judge King's Bench, and *dspm* 3/10 March 1457/8, having had:
1b Elizabeth; *m* by 1442 William BONVILLE (*dvp* 31 Dec 1460, *ka* Battle of Wakefield), s and heir of 1st Lord (Baron) Bonville, of Chewton (*see* above), and *dvp*, leaving:
1c WILLIAM BONVILLE, 6th LORD (Baron) HARINGTON; *b* by 1442; *m* by 1458 Lady Katherine Nevill(e), 5th dau of Richard, Earl of Salisbury (*see* ABERGAVENNY, M), and was *ka* Battleof Wakefield 31 Dec 1460, leaving:
1d CECILY Bonville, BARONESS HARINGTON and Baroness Bonville, both in her own right; *b c* 1461; *m* 1st Thomas GREY, 1st Marquess of Dorset (with the attainder and beheading in 1554 of whose gs, the 3rd Marquess and 1st and last Duke of Suffolk of the 1551 *cr*, both Baronies expired; *see* also GREY, B); *m* 2nd Henry Stafford, Earl of Wiltshire (*see* STAFFORD, B), and *d* 12 May 1529
2 ROBERT (Sir)
3 Simon, ancestor of the HARINGTONs of Bishton

The 1st LORD (Baron) HARINGTON's 2nd gs,

Sir ROBERT de HARINGTON; *m* Mary Kirkby and had:

JOHN de HARINGTON; *m* Agnes, dau of Laurence Flete, of Flete, Lincs, and *d* 1421, leaving:

ROBERT de HARINGTON; *m* —, dau and coheir of John de la Laund, and had:

JOHN de HARINGTON; *m* Catherine, dau and heir of Sir Thomas Colepepper, through whom he acquired the estate of Exton, Rutland, and had:

ROBERT HARINGTON, of Exton; High Sheriff 1492 and 1498; *m* Maud, dau of Sir John Prisett, Ch Justice Common Pleas, and *d* 1501, leaving:

Sir JOHN HARINGTON, of Exton; High Sheriff Rutland; *m* Alice, dau of Henry Southill, and had:

Sir JOHN HARINGTON, of Exton; Treasurer to the Army of HENRY VIII at Boulogne; *m* Elizabeth, dau and heir of Robert Moton, of Peckleton, Leics, and had:

Sir JAMES HARINGTON, of Exton; *m* Lucy, dau of Sir William Sidney (*see* D'LISLE, V), and *d* Jan 1591/2, having had, with two other sons (*d* unm):

1 JOHN HARINGTON, 1st BARON HARYNGTON OF EXTON, Co Rutland (E), so *cr* 21 July 1603; ktd Jan 1583/4, Mp Rutland 1571, 1593, 1597–98 and 1601 and Warwicks 1586–88, High Sheriff Rutland 1594–95, 1598–99 and 1602–03, Tutor to PRINCESS ELIZABETH, dau of JAMES I; *m* by 6 March 1580/1 Anne, dau of Robert Kelway, and *d* 23 Aug 1613, leaving a 2nd but only surv s:
(1) JOHN HARINGTON, 2nd and last BARON HARYNGTON OF EXTON, KB (Jan 1604/5); *bapt* 3 May 1592; *d* unm 27 Feb 1613/4, when the Barony expired
(1) Lucy; *m* 3rd Earl of Bedford (*see* BEDFORD, D)
(2) Frances; *m* Sir — Chichester
2 Henry (Sir); Seneschal and Ch Ruler of O'Byrne's country (now Co Wicklow), Ireland; granted land in Cos Kildare, Wexford and Westmeath; *m* 1st Cecilia, dau and coheir of John Agar, of Elmsthorpe, Leics; *m* 2nd Ruth, dau and coheir of James Pilkington, Bp Durham, and had issue by her; by his 1st w he had:
(1) John (Sir); had:
1a Sarah; *m* April 1630, as his 2nd w, 1st and last Baron Frescheville of Staveley and *dsp* 12 Nov 1717
(2) James (Sir), of Elmsthorpe; *m* Mary Offley
3 **Sir James Harington, 1st Bt** (E), so *cr* 29 June 1611, of Ridlington, Rutland, High Sheriff Rutland *c* 1593; *m* 1st Frances (*d* Sept 1599), dau and coheir of John Sapcote, of Elton, Hunts, and had issue:
(1) EDWARD (Sir), **2nd Bt**
(2) Sapcote (Sir); *m* 1st Jane (*dsp* 1677), dau of Sir William Samwell, of Upton, Northants, and had, with other issue:
1a James; Groom Bedchamber to CHARLES I, author *Oceana*
(2) (cont.) Sir Sapcote *m* 2nd Jane, dau of Sir John Woodward, by whom he had other issue
(3) John; *m* Frances, dau of Terringham Norwood, of Astwood, Bucks, and *dsp*
(1) Bridget; *m* Sir Anthony Markham, of Sedgebrook, Lincs, and had issue
3 (cont.) **Sir James** *m* 2nd Anne, widow of John D'Oyley, of Merton, Oxon, and dau of Francis Bernard, of Abington, Northants, and *d* 2 Feb 1613
1 Sarah; *m* 1st Francis, Lord Hastings, s of 4th Earl of Huntingdon (*qv*); *m* 2nd Sir George Kingshill; *m* 3rd 11th Lord (Baron) Zouche (*qv*) (of Haryngworth); *m* 4th Sir Thomas Edmunds

His est son,

Sir Edward Harington, 2nd Bt; High Sheriff Rutland 1622 and 1637; *m* 24 Sept 1601 Margery (*d* 12 Dec 1658), dau and coheir of John D'Oyley, of Merton (*see* above), through whom he obtained that estate, and *d* 1653, having had, with a dau (Bridget, *m* Sir John Gore, of Geldeston (*d* 3 Nov 1659)):

Sir James Harington, 3rd Bt; MP Middx 1654; a Commr for trial of CHARLES I; after the Restoration he was excepted from the general pardon but not actually condemned to death; *bapt* 30 Dec 1607; *m* 2 Aug 1632 Catherine (*d* 15 June 1675), dau and coheir of Alderman Sir Edward Wright, Ld Mayor London, and *d* April 1680, leaving, with other issue:

1 **Sir Edmund Harington, 4th Bt**; *m* 1st (settlement 20 Aug 1679) Sarah, dau and heir of Penning Alston, of London; *m* 2nd 6 April 1697 Abigail (*bur* 31 Aug 1709), dau of Joseph Venour, and *dspms* 1708
2 **Sir Edward Harington, 5th Bt**; *bapt* 10 Oct 1639; *dsp* 27 March 1716
3 Henry, of Cornhill, London; *d* in or after 1704/5, leaving:

(1) Richard, of Iver, Bucks; *m* 2 March 1705/6 Margaret, dau of William Lane, of Cowley, Middx, and *d* 13 June 1717, leaving:

1a JAMES (Sir), **6th Bt**

The 5th Bt's great-nephew,

Sir James Harington, 6th Bt, of Burton, Oxon; *m* 1st Catherine (*bur* 19 April 1732), dau of William Boucher, of the Middle Temple; *m* 2nd Elizabeth (*d* Oct 1794), widow of William Moore, and by his 1st w had issue:

1 JAMES (Sir), **7th Bt**

2 Richard (Rev); Rector Powderham, Devon; *b* 11 April 1729; *m* 1st Jane (*bur* 16 Jan 1768), dau and heir of Arthur Champernowne, of Dartington, Devon, and had issue:

(1) Arthur HARINGTON later CHAMPERNOWNE, of Dartington, MP Saltash 1806, High Sheriff Devon 1811; *b* 30 Dec 1767; *m* 11 Sept 1806 Louisa (*d* 31 Dec 1870), dau of John Buller, of Morval, Devon, and *d* 7 June 1819, leaving, with other issue:

1a Henry, of Dartington; *b* 14 Sept 1815; *m* 24 April 1838 Charlotte (*d* 28 Oct 1899), 6th dau of Sir Antony Buller, of Pound, Yelverton, Devon, and *d* 24 May 1851, having had, with other issue:

1b Arthur, of Dartington Hall, Devon, JP; MA; *b* 19 March 1839; *m* 11 Oct 1870 Helen Elizabeth Caroline (*d* 4 June 1922), dau of Michael Linning Melville, of Hartfield Grove, Sussex, and *d* 1887, having had issue:

1c Arthur Melville, of Dartington Hall, Devon, JP; BA Oxon, barrister; *b* 16 Aug 1871; *m* 25 Sept 1907 Helen Iris (*d* 23 Oct 1950), er dau of Lt-Col Herbert John Ouchterlony Walker, RA, and *d* 6 Dec 1946, leaving issue:

1d Arthur Gawen; *b* 14 July 1909; *educ* Trin Coll Cambridge (BA); *m* 18 Sept 1946 *Eileen Ann Strachan [Mrs Arthur Harington, 15 Rossetti Gardens Mansions, London SW3], dau of Harold E H Sternbridge, and *dsp* 5 Feb 1947

1d *Katharine Iris; *b* 16 May 1912; *m* 27 May 1949 W/Cdr Adrian Henry Paull, AFC, RAF (*d* 17 Sept 1965), only s of Archibald Paull, and has:

1e *Angela Iris Constance; *b* 30 July 1951

2c Henry Harington; Lt DCLI; *b* 27 July 1872; *d* unm 17 April 1897

3c Amyas Walter; *b* 19 Sept 1873; *m* 21 Feb 1906 Olive (*d* 30 Jan 1959), est dau of Harry Woodhill, and *d* 1940

4c Robert Anthony; *b* 6 Jan 1882; *d* unm 1923

5c Gilbert Raleigh; BA Oxon; *b* 24 March 1884; *m* 9 April 1938 *Honor Irene, Bsc, PhD, dau of Marshall Broomhall, and *dsp* 18 Nov 1959

6c Edward Buller; *b* 8 Oct 1885; *m* 22 July 1919 Violet Mary (*d* 29 July 1944), 2nd dau of Thomas Edward Studdy, and *dsp* 4 Feb 1966

1c Charlotte Elizabeth; *d* unm 1 April 1968 aged 93

2c Elinor Marcia; *m* 25 June 1913 Dr Richard Laycock Routh and *dsp* 12 Nov 1961 aged 85. He *d* 17 Dec 1916

3c Helen Frances; *m* 26 April 1906 Arthur Edmund Spender, est surv s of Edward Spender, and *d* 21 April 1956, leaving issue. He *d* 1923

4c Agnes Dorothy; *m* 5 Aug 1920 Alexander Napier Melville, 6th s of Judge — Melville, and *d* 26 Sept 1964. He *d* 12 April 1950

2b Henry, of Pound; Col RE; *b* 21 May 1840; *m* 30 Aug 1880 Elizabeth Charlotte (*d* 7 Aug 1928), dau of Maj-Gen Thomas Andrew Lumsden Murray, (*see* MURRAY, Bt, of Blackbarony), and *dsp* 20 Sept 1917

3b Walter (Rev), of Pound; MA Oxon; *b* 3 Sept 1848; *m* 14 Nov 1905 Elizabeth Mary (*d* 14 March 1949), dau of George Andrew Spottiswoode, and *d* 4 Feb 1929

1b Margaret; *b* 29 Aug 1850; *m* 22 April 1908 Rev John Henry Copleston, Rector Onwell, Devon, and *d* 8 April 1932. He *d* 1918

2a Richard (Rev); Rector Dartington; *b* 4 Sept 1817; *m* 2 May 1848 Elizabeth (*d* 6 March 1870), est dau of Rev Thomas Keble, of Keble House, Fairford, Glos, and *d* 22 Oct 1890, having by her had issue:

1b Richard Keble (Rev); *b* 2 June 1850; *dsp* 14 Dec 1883

2b Philip Henry; Maj 5th Vol Bn Rifle Bde, BA Oxon; *b* 17 Oct 1859; *m* 6 April 1893 Katharine Theresa Vidal (*d* 30 July 1939), dau of John Alexander Radcliffe, and *d* 16 Oct 1935, leaving issue:

1c Richard Harington Radcliffe; Cadet RMC; *b* 7 Oct 1897; *d* 7 March 1917

1c Doris; *m* 7 Feb 1923 William Roy Upton Litton, s of Henry Litton, and *d* 19 April 1971, having had:

3b Francis Gawayne; MA Oxon, Bursar Keble Coll, barrister; *b* 22 April 1866; *m* 31 Aug 1911 Isabel Mary (*d* 10 June 1969 aged 84), dau of George Burvill Rashleigh (*see* DARNLEY, E), and *d* 29 May 1921, leaving issue:

1c +David Gawen [David Champernowne Esq, 25 Worts Causeway, Cambs CB1 4RJ]; Fell Trin Coll Camb, Fell King's Coll Cambridge 1937–48, Prof Statistics Oxford 1948–59; *b* 9 July 1912; *educ* Winchester and King's Coll Cambridge (MA); *m* 30 March 1948 *Wilhelmina Barbara Maria, dau of Petrus Ludovicus Dullaert, of Holland, and has:

1d +Arthur Francis; *b* 1 June 1949; *educ* Bedales and Churchill Coll Cambridge

2d +Richard Peter; *b* 19 June 1953; *educ* Bedales; *m* 1986 *Jackie, dau of Bill Wills, of Petersfield, Hants

4b Thomas Arthur; *b* 2 April 1868; *m* 24 June 1919 Gertrude Isabel (*d* 29 Nov 1956), widow of Cdr Cecil Halstead France Hayhurst, RN, and dau of Adml Sir Archibald Douglas, GCVO, KCB, and *dsp* 1944

5b John Edward (Rev); Vicar Modbury S Devon 1909–21; *b* 5 March 1870; *educ* Keble Coll Oxford (MA); *m* 30 Sept 1902 Audrey Eliza (*d* 1 June 1951), 3rd dau of Joseph Russell Evans, of Hilden Manor, Tonbridge, and *d* 18 Aug 1935

1b Mary Elizabeth; *m* 28 April 1881 Rev Thomas Woodman and *d* 1882

2b Sarah Louisa; *m* 16 April 1885 Rt Rev George Kestell-Cornish, DD, Bp Madagascar, and *d* 17 May 1934. He *d* 23 June 1925

3b Agnes Charlotte; *d* unm *c* 1939

4b Edith Alicia; *m* 1895 James Frederick Williams and *d* 24 Jan 1934, leaving issue. He *d* 1915

5b Cecilia Margaret; *m* 1890 Charles Wigan and *d* 19 June 1950, leaving issue. He *d* 21 June 1937

1a Jane; *m* 12 Aug 1828 Rev William Martin, Vicar Staverton (*d* 10 April 1850), and *d* 1892, leaving issue

2a Caroline; *m* 22 June 1842 Rev Isaac Williams and *d* 1896, leaving issue. He *d* 1 May 1865

3a Maria; *m* 8 March 1836 Charles Herbert Mallock, and *d* 1893, leaving issue. He *d* 20 April 1873

2 (cont.) The Rev Richard Harington *m* 2nd Hannah Hussey, of Truro, Cornwall; *m* 3rd Elizabeth (*d* 21 Nov 1783), widow of William Hallett and dau of Abraham Chambers, of Totteridge, Herts, and *d* June 1812

Sir JAMES *d* 24 Jan 1782; his er son,

Sir James Harington, 7th Bt; *b* 6 Aug 1726; *m* Anna (*d* 26 June 1822), dau of James Ashenhurst, of Park Hall, Staffs, and *d* 17 Jan 1793, having had, with other issue, including an er s (James, *d* young):

Sir John Edward Harington, 8th Bt; HEICS; *b* 1760; *m* 10 April 1787 Marianne (*d* 20 Dec 1824), dau of Thomas Philpot, and *d* 9 June 1831, having had issue:

1 **Sir James Harington, 9th Bt**; Judge Jessore, India; *b* 30 Sept 1788; *m* 2 April 1817 Sophia (*d* 21 Oct 1859), 3rd dau of Charles Steer, and was *bur* 5 Jan 1835, leaving issue:

(1) **Sir John Edward Harington, 10th Bt**, DL Middx; Lt Coldstream Gds; *b* 22 May 1821; *educ* Ch Ch Oxford (BA); *m* 26 Oct 1846 Jane Agnes (*d* 17 April 1891), dau of John Studholme Brownrigg, MP Boston (Lincs), and *dsp* 9 Feb 1877

2 Edward John; HEICS; *bapt* 25 Dec 1793; *d* unm 10 Oct 1857

3 Richard (Rev); DD Oxon; Rector Old, Northants, Pncpl BNC Oxford; *b* 26 April 1800; *m* 1st 1 Aug 1833 Cecilia (*d* 18 June 1844), 4th dau of the Rev Samuel Smith, DD, Dean Ch Ch Oxford, and had, with other issue (*d* young):

(1) RICHARD (Sir), **11th Bt**

(2) Charles (Rev); Rector Stoke Lacey, Herefs; *b* 17 June 1837; *m* 12 April 1864 Alice (*m* 2nd 20 July 1872 Maj Robert Biscoe, of Quendon Court, Essex (*d* 9 Jan 1905), and *d* 23 Jan 1931), dau and coheir of Alexander Cotton, of Landwade, Cambs, and *dsp* 9 Feb 1868

3 (cont.) The Rev Richard Harington *m* 2nd 2 July 1846 Mary (*d* 18 Feb 1886), dau of Rev Samuel Woodfield Paul, Rector Finedon, Northants, and *d* 13 Dec 1853, having by her had, with other issue:

(3) Robert; *b* 1851; *d* 1855

4 Robert; Capt 12th Lancers, Maj Lanarks Militia; *b* 22 Sept 1801; *m* 10 July 1830 Charlotte (*d* 11 Feb 1867), yst dau of Andrew Stuart, of Castlemilk and Torrance, E Kilbride, Lanarks, and *d* 18 March 1864, having had issue:

(1) Robert Edward Stuart HARINGTON later HARINGTON-STUART (20 Nov 1879), of Torrance, VD, JP, DL; Capt Rifle Bde, Col 2nd Vol Bn Cameronians; *b* 9 Nov 1834; *m* 1st 28 April 1863 Louisa Alice (*d* 27 Feb 1898), dau of Hon Robert Arthur Arundell (*see* 1940 edn ARUNDELL OF WARDOUR, B); *m* 2nd 7 Oct 1902 Alice Sidney (*d* 7 Sept 1951), dau of Henry Robarts Madocks (*see* NAPIER OF MAGDALA, B), and *dsp* 27 Dec 1911

(2) Alexander Stuart; Rifle Bde; *b* 6 May 1839; *m* 11 Dec 1875 Ellinor, widow of Thomas Walker, of Eastwood Hall, Notts, and dau of R C Bourne, and *dsp* 2 Sept 1878

(1) Susan; *m* 17 Oct 1865 Lt-Col James Davidson, 1st Roy Lanark Militia, and *dsp* 6 Nov 1912. He *d* 2 Feb 1878

1 Maria; *m* 1 July 1826 Charles Balfour and *d* his widow 4 July 1876 aged 73, having had issue (*see* BALFOUR OF INCHRYE, B)

The 10th Bt's cousin,

Sir Richard Harington, 11th Bt, JP, DL Herefs, JP Warwicks and Worcs; MA and BCL Oxford, barrister Lincoln's Inn 1858, Met Police Magistrate 1871–72, County Court Judge 1872–1905, CA and Chm QS Herefs; *b* 20 May 1835; *m* 5 June 1860 Francis Agnata (*d* 20 May 1915), 2nd dau of Rev Robert Biscoe, Preb Hereford, Rector Whitbourne, Herefs, and had issue:

1 RICHARD (Sir), **12th Bt**

2 Charles (Rev); Vicar Hanley Castle, Worcs; *b* 23 May 1862; *educ* Selwyn Coll Cambridge (MA); *m* 28 July 1896 Audrey Emma (*d* 10 Nov 1958), dau of Rev Robert Burges Bayly, Vicar Hampton Bishop, and *d* 12 Nov 1921, leaving:

(1) Charles Robert (Sir), KBE (1962); ktd 1948, FRS, Prof Chemical Pathology London U 1931–42, ed *Biochemical Journal* 1931–42, Dir Nat Inst Medical Research 1942–62; *b* 1 Aug 1897; *educ* Malvern, Magdalene Coll Cambridge (BA 1919, MA 1930, Hon Fell 1944, Hon DSc 1949) and Edinburgh U (PhD 1922); *m* 1 Aug 1923 Jessie McCririe (*d* 19 April 1975), yr dau of Rev James Craig, and *d* 4 Feb 1972, leaving issue:

1a +Michael [Michael Harington Esq, 69 Waterford Rd, London SW6 2DT]; *b* 23 Sept 1924; *educ* Trin Hall Cambridge and UCH Medical Sch (MA, MB, BChir, FRCP); *m* 22 Feb 1958 *Marta, er dau of S Rosenfeld, of Vienna, and has:

1b +Robert Michael; *b* 15 Sept 1963; *educ* Trin Coll Oxford (PhD); *m* 1988 *Pamela, dau of P Nadash, of Columbia, Md.

1b *Amanda; *b* 14 March 1967; *educ* St Paul's Girls' Sch and St John's Coll Cambridge; barrister Inner Temple 1989

1a *Alison Mary [Mrs Derek Bangham, 4 Crown Close, Mill Hill, London NW7 4HN]; *b* 11 March 1927, MB, BCh; *m* 5 July 1952 *Derek Raymond Bangham, MB, BS, FRCP, yr s of Dr D H Bangham, and has issue:

1b *Charles Richard Mark; *b* 25 April 1955; BM, BCH, MRCP, PhD, MRCPath; *m* 1990 *Jocelyne Marie Ragody Hughes, PhD, and has issue:

1c *George Richard Derek; *b* 1991

1c *Madeleine Edith Marie; *b* 1993

2c *Florence Clara Jocelyne; *b* 1 June 1997

2b *Humphrey Bernard; *b* 18 Oct 1957; *m* 1980 *Elizabeth Mary Stafford Baker, and has issue:

1c *Charles Stafford; *b* 1987

2c *Guy Nicholas; *b* 1992

1c *Olivia Charlotte; *b* 1989

1b *Celia Elizabeth; *b* 3 Jan 1954; MB, ChB, DROCG; *m* 1995 *David Charles Lowe

2b *Jessica Frances; *b* 14 July 1961; *m* 1990 *John Graham Lawrence and has:

1c *Anna Mary; *b* 6 June 1996

2a *Margaret Jane [Miss Margaret Harington, 43 Upton Lovell, Warminster, Wilts]; *b* 19 Feb 1931

(2) John Edward; *b* 3 Sept 1901; *dsp* 6 May 1930

3 Edward, JP Herefs; barrister, County Court Judge 1905–35; *b* 25 Oct 1863; *educ* Ch Ch Oxford (BA); *m* 20 Oct 1906 Lousia Muriel (*d* 8 Jan 1963), only dau of Herbert Charles Erskine Vernon, and *d* 19 Jan 1937, leaving issue:

(1) (Edward Henry) Vernon, JP Herefs; barrister Inner Temple 1930, Priv Sec to Ld Chllr, Dep Serjeant-at-Arms Ho Lds 1934–40, Maj Coldstream Gds WW II, War Office 1944–45, Austrian Control Commn 1945, Assist Sec to Ld Chllr for Commns of the Peace 1946, Dep Judge Advocate 1946, Assist JAG 1955, Dep Chm Herefs QS 1969–72, Recorder Crown Court 1972–75, Chm Hereford, Worcester, Warwicks and W Midlands Ag Wages Ctee 1976–81, memb Malvern Hills DC 1979, Gold Staff Offr Coronation 1937; *b* 13 Sept 1907; *educ* Eton; *m* 1st 20 July 1937 (*divorce* 1949) Mary Elizabeth, dau of Louis Edwin William Egerton, and had issue:

1a Veronica Mary; *b* 29 April 1938; *d* unm Jan 1967

2a *(Victoria) Jane [Mrs Sidney Whitteridge, Inverlael Lodge, Loch Broom, by Ullapool, Ross-shire]; *b* 10 July 1941; *m* 1973 *Sidney Morgan Whitteridge, VRD, MRCS, LRPC, and has issue:

1b *(Ashley Edward) John; *b* 1976

1b *Mary Ruth; *b* 1974

(1) (cont.) Maj Vernon Harington *m* 2nd 11 April 1950 *(Mary) Johanna Jean, JP (Herefs 1969), only dau of Lt-Col Ralph George Snead Cox, MC (*see* CLYDESMUIR, B), and *d* 26 Dec 1995, having by her had issue:

3a *(Marie) Louisa [Mrs Robin Taylor, The Pulpits, Little Hereford, Salop SY4 4AU]; *b* 19 Oct 1951; *m* 1979 *Robin Pagan Taylor, and has issue:

1b *William Vernon; *b* 1980

2b *Philip Edward; *b* 1984

4a *Susan Anne Jean [Mrs David Scott, Upper Hamnish Farm, Leominster, Herefs]; *b* 31 Aug 1953; *m* 1984 *David Robert Geoffrey Scott

(2) +Kenneth Douglas Evelyn Herbert, JP [Maj Kenneth Harington JP, Bakers Cottage, Gt Rissington, Glos GL54 2LP]; Actg Dep Chm QS Gtr London 1966–67, Met Stipendiary Magistrate 1967–84, barrister Inner Temple 1952, Maj Coldstream Gds WW II, Hon Attaché Stockholm 1930–32; *b* 30 Sept 1911; *educ* Stowe; *m* 1st 8 March 1939 Lady Cecilia Bowes-Lyon (*d* 20 March 1947), er dau of 15th Earl of Strathmore and Kinghorne (*qv*); *m* 2nd 28 July 1950 Maureen Helen (*d* 1992), 2nd dau of Brig-Gen Sir Robert Chaine Alexander McCalmont, KCVO, CBE, DSO, of Glen Lodge, Strandhill, Co Sligo, and by her has had issue:

1a +Michael Kenneth [Michael Harington Esq, Bakers Cottage, Gt Rissington, Glos GL54 2LP]; *b* 9 Aug 1951; *educ* Eton and Ch Ch Oxford; barrister Inner Temple 1974; *m* 1984 *Deirdre Christine Kehoe, and has issue:

1b +Robert John Michael; *b* 1988

1b *Charlotte Mary Ann; *b* 1985

2b *Caroline Lucy Christine; *b* 1991

2a +Jonathan Edward McCalmont; *b* 14 March 1955; *educ* Eton and RMA Sandhurst; 2nd Lt Coldstream Gds; *m* 1st 17 Sept 1983 (*divorce* 1986) Lucinda Margaret, dau of Maj William Lloyd (John) Baxendale (*see* FORTESCUE, E); *m* 2nd 1989 *Susan Antonia, yst dau of Anthony Walter Fenwick, of Eaton Grange, Eaton, Lincs, and by her has:

1b *Antonia Lucy Diana; *b* 1991

2b *Katherine Rose Caroline; *b* 1994

1a A dau; *b* and *d* 6 Oct 1953

4 Robert (Rev); Rector Whitbourne, Herefs; MA Clare Coll Cambridge; *b* 26 April 1868; *d* 28 Dec 1933

5 John, CB (1927), CMG (1919), DSO (1915), JP Salop; FRGS, Col, Hon Brig-Gen 1930, 3rd and 2nd Bns Rifle Bde, Brig Cdr 1918–19, T/Col Staff and Inspr-Gen KAR 1923, cmdg 139th (Sherwood Foresters) Inf Bde 1928–30, served Nile Expdn 1898 (two medals with clasp), Boer War 1899–1902 (two medals, five clasps), Somaliland 1903–04 (medal with two clasps), Nandi E Africa 1905–06 (clasp) and WW I (despatches four times, wounded three times, Brevet Lt-Col, Legn Honour, reward for distinguished servs 1933); *b* 10 April 1873; *m* 4 April 1908 Lady Frances Aline Temple Gore Langton (*d* following an accident 20 March 1952), 4th dau of 4th Earl Temple of Stowe (*qv*), and *d* 11 April 1943, having had:

(1) John Temple, DSO and MBE (1945); Maj Rifle Bde WW II, ADC 1939; *b* 16 Dec 1909; *educ* Winchester; *m* 10 July 1946 Catherine Mary (*d* 16 July 1997), est dau of Lt-Col Donald Cameron, OBE, MC, of Tasmania, and *d* 8 May 1983, leaving:

1a +Richard Donald John [Richard Harington Esq, Wester Baldoon, Ardross, Alness, Ross and Cromarty]; *b* 3 Sept 1948; *educ* Winchester and Hertford Coll Oxford; *m* 1974 *Jane Pickin, dau of Peter Wellburn Bayliss, of Burcher Court, Titley, Herefs, and has issue:

1b +Alastair Peter John; *b* 1983

1b *Lucy Aline; *b* 1979

2b *Miranda Jane; *b* 1980

1a *Serena Catherine Lucy [Mrs Julian Barrow, 33 Tite Street, London SW3 4JP]; *b* 2 May 1947; *m* 28 Sept 1971 *Julian G Barrow, artist, and has issue:

1b *Cecilia Margaret; *b* 1974

2b *Eugenie Catherine; *b* 1977

2a *Cecilia Aline [Mrs Jacques Richard, 60 rue Doudeauville, 75018 Paris, France]; *b* 24 Feb 1953; *m* 1994 *Jacques Richard

(2) Richard James; *b* 29 Jan 1911; *d* 15 April 1917

(1) *Aline Lucy [The Hon Mrs Walter Keppel, Barton House, Meonstoke, Hants]; *b* 27 Feb 1918; *m* 5 Nov 1941 *Lt-Cdr Hon Walter Arnold Crispian Keppel, DSC, RN (*see* ALBEMARLE, E), and has issue

1 Margaret Agnata; *b* 23 June 1871; *m* 25 Sept 1900 George Hume Pollock (*see* POLLOCK, Bt) and *d* 10 Jan 1954

2 Frances Cecila; *b* 4 May 1874; *m* 5 Jan 1904 Rev Cecil George Stokoe, Chaplain Srinagar, Kashmir, 1924–48, s of Rev T H Stokoe, DD, and had issue. He *d* 12 March 1948

Sir RICHARD *d* 6 Feb 1911; his est son,

Sir Richard Harington, 12th Bt; *b* 3 March 1861; *educ* Ch Ch Oxford (MA); barrister Inner Temple 1886, Judge High Court Calcutta 1899–1913; *m* 5 Sept 1899 Hon Selina Louisa Grace Dundas (*d* 3 Dec 1945), er dau of 6th Viscount Melville (*qv*), and *d* 1 Feb 1931, leaving:

1 **Sir Richard Dundas Harington, 13th Bt**; *b* 16 Oct 1900; *educ* Eton and Sidney Sussex Coll Camb; *d* unm 1981

2 John Charles Dundas, QC (1957), JP (Herefs 1953); barrister Inner Temple 1928, Recorder Banbury 1951–56 and Windsor 1956–58, Chm Herefs QS 1957, Judge Co Courts Hants Circuit 1958, N Staffs Circuit 1961–67, Wolverhampton Circuit 1967, Lt-Cdr RNVR WW II; *b* 27 June 1903; *educ* RNCs Osborne and Dartmouth; *m* 30 April 1941 Lavender Cecilia (*d* 20 Sept 1982), dau of Maj Ernest Wriothesley Denny, DSO (*see* DARTMOUTH, E), and had:

(1) Sir NICHOLAS JOHN HARINGTON, **14th and present Bt**

(2) +DAVID RICHARD [David Harington Esq, 7 Vale Grove, London W3 7PQ]; *b* 25 June 1944; heir presumptive; *educ* Westminster and Ch Ch Oxford; *m* 1983 *Deborah Jane, est dau of Maurice William Catesby, MC, of Long Compton, Warwicks, and has issue:

1a +John Catesby; *b* 7 Jan 1984

2a +Christopher; *b* 1986

(1) *Susan Alexandra [Mrs Anis Nacrour, 38 rue du Roseau, 78610 Le Perray-en-Yvelines, France]; *b* 6 Feb 1948; *m* 17 Sept 1977 *Anis Nacrour, and has issue:

1a *Aurélien-Antoine John Mourad; *b* 1985

2a *Alexandre Philippe; *b* 1988

HARLECH

Arms: Quarterly, 1st and 4th, gu. a fess between three cross-crosslets fitchée or (for GORE); 2nd and 3rd, gu. a bend between six cross-crosslets or (for ORMSBY). **Crests:** 1 A heraldic tiger rampant arg. (for GORE), 2 A dexter arm embowed in armour, the hand grasping a human leg also in armour, couped at the thigh, all ppr. and garnished or (for ORMSBY). **Supporters:** Dexter, a heraldic tiger arg., maned and tufted sa., ducally gorged or; sinister, a lion or. **Motto:** *In hoc signo vinces* ('In this sign thou shalt conquer'). **Creation:** B. (UK) 14 Jan 1876.

THE 6TH BARON HARLECH, of Harlech, Merioneth (Francis David Ormsby Gore) [The Rt Hon The Lord Harlech, The Mount, Racecourse Rd, Oswestry, Salop SY10 7PH]; *b* 13 March 1954; *s f* 1985; *educ* Worth; *m* 1986 *Amanda Jane, dau of Alan Thomas Grieve, of Stoke Lodge, Ludlow, Salop, and has issue:

1 +JASSET DAVID CODY; *b* 1 July 1986

1 *Tallulah Sylvia; *b* 1988

Lineage (of Gore): WILLIAM GORE, of Woodford, Co Leitrim, MP 1703–29, 3rd s of Sir Arthur Gore, 1st Bt, of Newtown Gore, Co Mayo (*see* ARRAN, E); *m* 1696 Catherine (*d* 14 Jan 1747), dau of Sir Thomas Newcomen, 5th Bt, and *d* by 12 March 1729, leaving issue:

1 William, of Woodford; MP Co Leitrim 1729–60 and 1762–69; *m* 1 April 1733 Sarah, sis of 1st Earl of Darnley (*qv*), and *dsp* by 20 Nov 1769

2 Robert; *m* 18 May 1740 Lettice, dau of Henry Brooke (*see* BROOKEBOROUGH, V), and had:

(1) WILLIAM

1 Sarah; *m* 4 July 1724 Sir Arthur Newcomen, 7th Bt, and had issue. He *d* 25 Nov 1759

WILLIAM GORE's gs,

WILLIAM GORE, of Woodford; inherited his uncle William's estates; MP Co Leitrim 1783–90; *b* 11 Aug 1744; *m* 10 Feb 1778 Frances Jane Gorges, dau and heiress of Ralph Gore, of Barrow Mount, Co Kilkenny, MP, and widow of Sir Haydocke Evans Morres, Bt, and *d* 2 April 1815, leaving:

WILLIAM GORE later ORMSBY-GORE (roy licence on marriage), of Porkington, Salop, JP, DL; MP Co Leitrim 1806–07, Carnarvon 1830–31 and N Salop 1835–57; *b* 14 March 1779; *m* 11 Jan 1815 Mary Jane, only dau and heiress of Owen Ormsby, of Willowbrook, Co Sligo; and Porkington, and *d* 4 May 1860, having had, with two daus:

1 JOHN RALPH ORMSBY-GORE, **1st Baron Harlech**, of Harlech, Co Merioneth (UK), so *cr* 14 Jan 1876, with special limitation, in default of his own male issue, to his only surv bro, JP, DL Salop; *b* 3 June 1816; MP Caernarvs 1837–41 and N Salop 1859–76, Groom-in-Waiting to HM QUEEN VICTORIA; *m* 4 June 1844 Sarah (*d* 17 Jan 1898), yst dau of Sir John Tyssen Tyrell, Bt (*see* 1877 edn), of Boreham House, Essex, and *d* 15 June 1876, leaving:

(1) Fanny Mary Katherine; *m* 1st 21 July 1863 Hon Lloyd Kenyon (*see* KENYON, B) and had issue; *m* 2nd 24 Aug 1880 Rev Thomas Mainwaring Bulkeley Owen, of Tedsmore Hall, Salop, and *dsp* 25 Nov 1927. He *d* 5 June 1910

2 WILLIAM RICHARD, **2nd Baron**

3 Owen Arthur; Capt 43rd LI; *b* 3 Oct 1820; *k* Kaffir War 6 April 1852

The 1st BARON's bro,

WILLIAM RICHARD ORMSBY-GORE, **2nd Baron Harlech**, JP, DL Salop and Co Sligo, Lt and custos rotulorum Co Leitrim, High Sheriff 1857, MP Cos Sligo 1841–52 and Leitrim 1858–76, Maj 13th Light Dragoons; *b* 3 March 1819; *m* 10 Sept 1850 Lady Emily Charlotte Seymour (*d* 10 Jan 1892), sis of 5th Marquess of Hertford (*qv*), and had:

1 William Seymour; *b* 27 Dec 1852; *d* May 1853

2 GEORGE RALPH CHARLES, **3rd Baron**

3 Henry Arthur; Maj 11th Hus; *b* 18 March 1857; *d* 12 March 1921

4 Seymour Fitzroy; MA Oxford, FRGS, Capt 3rd Kent Art Vols and 4th Bn Oxford LI 1885–89, MP Gainsborough 1900–06; *b* 18 Jan 1863; *d* unm 19 Nov 1950

1 Mary Georgina; Ldy-in-Waiting to TRH THE DUCHESS OF CONNAUGHT and PRINCESS PATRICIA OF CONNAUGHT 1917; *m* 10 Oct 1878 Col Sir Alfred Mordaunt Egerton, KCVO, CB, RHG, and *d* 28 Aug 1937, having had issue (*see* 1956 edn EGERTON OF TATTON, B). He *d* 26 May 1908

2 Emily, CBE (1920); Extra Ldy Bedchamber to HM QUEEN MARY; *m* 15 July 1886 4th Earl Fortescue (*qv*) and *d* 12 July 1929, leaving issue

The 2nd BARON *d* 26 June 1904; his est surv son,

GEORGE RALPH CHARLES ORMSBY-GORE, **3rd Baron Harlech**, KCB, TD, JP Co Leitrim; Hon Col Salop Yeo, cmdg Salop Imp Yeo, Welsh Gds and Regtl Dist 1915, Capt Coldstream Gds, Constable Harlech Castle 1927–38, MP Oswestry 1901–04, High Sheriff Co Leitrim 1885, Ld Lt Merioneths, Chm Salop TAA; *b* 21 Jan 1855; *m* 25 July 1881 Lady Margaret Ethel Gordon, JP Salop, Pres Salop BRCS and SSAFA (*d* 25 April 1950), 4th dau of 10th Marquess of Huntly (*qv*), and *d* 8 May 1938, leaving:

WILLIAM GEORGE ARTHUR ORMSBY-GORE, **4th Baron Harlech**, KG (1948), GCMG (1938), PC (1927), JP, DL Salop; Ld Lt Merioneths, Constable Harlech Castle, MP Denbigh 1910–18 and Stafford 1918–38, Capt TFR, Assist Sec War Cabinet 1918, U-Sec Colonies 1922–24 and Nov 1924–29, PMG 1931, First Commr Works 1931–36, Sec State Colonies 1936–38, Chm Wheat Commn 1938; *b* 11 April 1885; *educ* Eton and New Coll Oxford (BA 1908, Hon Fell 1936), Hon DCL 1937, Hon LLD U of Wales 1947, Pro-Chllr U Wales and Chm Us Bureau Br Empire, Hon LLD Edin 1953, memb Arts Cncl GB to 1948, Chm Welsh Ctee,Tstee: Nat Gallery 1927–34 and 1936–41, Tate Gallery 1933–38 and Br Museum 1937–47, Chm Advsy Cncl V&A Museum, Pres Nat Museum Wales, Chm Ancient Monuments Bd England, Pres Nat Library Wales 1952 on, memb Standing Commn Museums and Galleries 1947 (Chm 1949), Chm: Midland Bank, Bank of Br West Africa, FSA, Hon Col 10th Bn Roy Welch Fus 1939, Regnl CD Commr NE Dist 1939–41, CStJ, High Commr Basutoland, Bechuanaland Protectorate and Swaziland, Union S Africa 1941–44, Constable Caernavon Castle 1945, carried standard of Wales at Coronation 1953; *m* 12 April 1913 *Lady Beatrice Edith Mildred Gascoyne-Cecil, DCVO (1947), er dau of 4th Marquess of Salisbury (*qv*), and had issue:

1 Owen Gerard Cecil; *b* 30 July 1916; *d* 3 Oct 1935

2 (WILLIAM) DAVID, **5th Baron**

3 John Julian Stafford; Capt Coldstream Gds; *b* 12 April 1925; *educ* Eton and New Coll Oxford

1 *Mary Hermione [The Hon Lady Mayall, Sturford Mead, Warminster, Wilts]; *b* 7 Sept 1914; *m* 1st 7 July 1936 (*divorce* 1946) Capt Robin Francis Campbell, DSO (*d* 1985), only s of Sir Ronald Hugh Campbell, GCMG, PC, and has:

(1) *Gerard Francis [Gerard Campbell Esq, 491 Fulham Rd, London SW6]; *b* 1937; *m* 1964 *Theadora Elizabeth, dau of Col Sir Roderick (Napoleon) Brinckman, 5th Bt (*qv*), and has issue:

1a *Tarquin; *b* 1966

2a *Casper; *b* 1967

(2) *Charles; *b* 1939; *m* 1963 *Philippa, dau of C J H Le B Croke and has:

1a *Phineas; *b* 1965

2a *Orlando; *b* 1967

1 (cont.) The Hon Mrs Mary Campbell *m* 2nd 24 Jan 1947, as his 2nd w, Sir (Alexander) Lees Mayall, KCVO, CMG (*d* 1992), V-Marshal Dip Corps, s of Alexander Mayall, of Bealings End, Woodbridge, Suffolk, and by him has:

(3) *Robert George Lees [Robert Mayall Esq, 13 St Mark's Place, London W10]; *b* 1954; *educ* Eton

(1) *Cordelia Isobel; *b* 1948; *m* 1969 (*divorce* 19–) John Nelson Summerscale, s of Sir John Percival Summerscale, KBE, and has:

1a *Aaron Piers; *b* 1969

2a *Gideon; *b* 1970

(2) *Alexandra Beatrice; *b* 1949; *m* 1st 1971 (*divorce* 1978) John Culme-Seymour (*see* CULME-SEYMOUR, Bt); *m* 2nd 1992 *Dominic Paul Morland, 2nd s of Sir Oscar Charles Morland, GBE, KCMG

2 *Katharine Margaret Alice (Dame), DBE (1974) [Viscountess Macmillan of Ovenden DBE, 9 Warwick Sq, London SW1]; V-Chm C Party 1968; *b* 4 Jan 1921; *m* 22 Aug 1942 Viscount Macmillan of Ovenden, PC, MP (*d* 1984), only s of 1st Earl of Stockton (*qv*), and has issue

3 *Elizabeth Jane [The Hon Mrs William Pease, 29 Upper Addison Gdns, London W14 8AJ; Lepe House, Exbury, Hants]; *b* 14 Nov 1929; *m* 26 Oct 1962 *Hon William Simon Pease, yr s of 1st Baron Wardington (*qv*)

The 4th BARON *d* 14 Feb 1964; his er son

(WILLIAM) DAVID ORMSBY-GORE, **5th Baron Harlech**, KCMG (1961), PC (1957), DL (Salop 1961); *b* 20 May 1918; *educ* Eton and New Coll Oxford (Hon Fell 1964); Maj 1945 WW II, MP (C) Oswestry 1950–61, memb UK Delegn UN Assembly 1951 and 1954, Parly U-Sec For Affrs 1956, Min State 1957–61, Amb Washington 1961–65, Chm Kennedy Meml Tst, Exec Nat Tst and Pilgrim Tst, Pres Pilgrims UK, Pres Br Bd Film Censors 1965, Dep Leader Oppn Ho Lds 1966–67, chm Harlech TV 1967, dir Frost and Reed Hldgs 1976, KStJ 1961, Hon LLD Manchester, Hon DCL U Pittsburg 1962, Hon LLD Brown U 1963, U of New York 1964, William and Mary Coll 1965, Farleigh-Dickinson U 1965, Berks Yeo 1939; *m* 1st 9 Feb 1940 Sylvia (*k* car crash 30 May 1967), dau of Hugh Lloyd Thomas, CMG, CVO (*see* BELLEW, B), and had:

1 Julian Hugh; *b* 23 Dec 1940; *educ* Eton and McGill; *d* unm 5 Nov 1974

2 FRANCIS DAVID ORMSBY-GORE, **6th and present Baron Harlech**

1 *Jane Teresa Denyse [The Hon Mrs Jane Rainey, Brogyntyn Home Farm, Oswestry, Salop]; *b* 13 Dec 1942; *m* 24 Sept 1966 (*divorce* 1984) Michael Sean O'Dare Rainey, s of Maj Sean Rainey and Mrs Marion Wrottesley, and has:

(1) *Saffron; *b* 27 Feb 1967

(2) *Gawaine O'Daire; *b* 1971

(1) *Rose Soley; *b* 1969

(2) *Ramona Alba; *b* 1973

2 *Victoria Mary [The Hon Mrs Lloyd, The Glebe, Leixlip, Co Kildare, Ireland]; *b* 20 Nov 1946; *m* 1972 *Julian Richard Leslie Lloyd (*see* CHETWYND, V) and has issue

3 Alice Magdalen Sarah; *b* 22 April 1952; *d* April 1995

The **5th Baron** *m* 2nd 11 Dec 1969 *Pamela [The Rt Hon Pamela Lady Harlech, 14 Ladbroke Rd, London W11 3NJ], only dau of Ralph F Colin, of New York, and *d* 1985 following a car crash, having by her had issue:

4 *Pandora Beatrice; *b* 19 April 1972; *educ* Wycombe Abbey and Guildhall Sch Music and Drama; bass guitarist with all-girl punk band 'Fluffy'

Lineage (of Owen): HWFA Ap CYNDDELW, of Llifon, Anglesey; *b* probably *c* 1090; had:

MATUSALEM, of Prysaeddfed; had:

MAREDUDD Ap MATUSALEM; had:

IORWERTH Ap MAREDUDD; *m* Gwenhwyfar, dau of Ieuaf, and had:

GRUFFUDD Ab IORWERTH; living 1308; *m* Gwenllian, dau of Rhirid Flaidd, and had:

IOWERTH Ap GRUFFUDD Ab IORWERTH; living 1305; *m* Gwladus, dau of Hywel Goeg ab Iorwerth, and had, with an other s (Llywelyn, living 1352), an illegitimate s:

IORWERTH DDU Ab IORWERTH; *m* Gwenllian, dau of Maredudd Benhir ap Maredudd, and had:

HYWEL Ab IORWERTH DDU; *m* Angharad, dau of Hywel ap Cynwrig Fychan, of Ysbyty Ifan, Denbighs, and had:

HWLCYN Ap HYWEL; living 1398; *m* Erddylad, dau of Dafydd ab Iorwerth, of Amlwch, Anglesey, and had:

LLYWELYN Ap HWLCYN, of Prysaeddfed, Bodedern, Anglesey; living 1451; *m* Mali, dau of Ieuan Llwyd ap Gruffudd, of Gorddinog, and had:

MEURIG Ap LLYWELYN, of Bodeon, Llangadwaladr, Anglesey, and Bodsilin, Aber, Caernarvs; *b* 1430; *m* Margaret, dau of Ieuan Fychan ab Ieuan, of Pengwern, Llangollen, and *d* 1489, leaving:

JOHN Ap MEURIG; *m* Angharad, dau of Gruffudd ap Hywel, of Llanystumdwy, Caernarvs, and had:

ROBERT Ap JOHN, of Bodsilin, Malltraeth, Anglesey; *m* Gwenhwyfar, dau of William ap Maredudd, of Llanfairfechan, Caernarvs, and had:

OWAIN Ap ROBERT, of Bodsilin; *m* Angharad, dau of Dafydd ap William ap Gruffudd, of Cochwillan, and had, with three er sons (Robert; Owen, MA, Archdeacon Anglesey, Rector Burton Latimer, Northants, *d* 1592; William, incumbent Heneglwys and Llangwyfan, Anglesey):

JOHN OWEN; Sec to Sir Francis Walsingham; *m* by 15 Sept 1599 Elin (*m* 2nd Sir Francis Eure, Ch Justice N Wales Circuit, and was *bur* 14 Sept 1626), dau and coheir of William Morris, MP Anglesey 1601, of Clenennau, Dolbenmaen, Caernarvs (s of Sir William Mor(r)is by Margaret, dau and heir of John Wyn Lacon, of Porkington (modern Brogyntyn), Selatyn, Salop), and had, with a yr s (William, Col, of Porkington, Constable Harlech Castle; *dsp* 1670):

Sir JOHN OWEN, of Clenennau; *b c* 1600; V-Adml N Wales, royalist Govr Conway Castle Civil War, ktd 1644; *m* Jonet, dau of Gruffudd Vaughan, of Corsygedol, Merioneths, and *d* 1666, leaving, with two daus:

WILLIAM OWEN, of Porkington, Clenennau and Llanddyn; *b* 1624; *m* 25 March 1648 Catherine (*d* 1685), only child of Lewis Anwyl, of Parc, Llanfrothen, Merioneths, and was *bur* 30 Jan 1677/8, having had, with another s (Lewis) and three daus:

Sir ROBERT OWEN, of Porkington, Clenennau and Llanddyn; *b* 1658; ktd 1678, MP Merionethshire 1681 and Caernarvs 1689–97; *m* Margaret (*d* 10 April 1727), dau and coheir of Owen Wyn, of Glyn Cywarch, Talsarnau, Merioneths, and Ystymcegid, Carnarvs, and *d* 1698, having had, with other issue:

1 WILLIAM, of Porkington

2 Lewis (Rev); Rector Barking and Wrexham; *b* 23 Sept 1696; *m* Elizabeth, dau and heir of Richard Lyster, of Penrhos and Moynes Court, Montgomeryshire and Mon, and *d* 1746, leaving issue:

(1) John, of Penrhos and Moynes Court; *b c* 1741; *d* unm 18 Dec 1823, leaving his Mon estates to John Lyster and the rest of his property to his 1st cousin once-removed MARY JANE (*see* below)

(1) Margaret; *d* unm 1816

1 Elizabeth; *m* Sir Thomas Longueville, Bt

The est son,

WILLIAM OWEN, of Porkington, Clenneney, Glyn and Llanddyn, High Sheriff Merioneths 1712–13 and Caernarvs 1756; *m* Mary, sister and sole heir of 2nd and last Baron Godolphin of Helston and dau of Henry Godolphin, DD, Dean St Paul's and Provost Eton (bro of Sidney, 1st Earl of Godolphin, Ld High Treasurer), and *d* 14 Feb 1767 aged 79, having had:

1 Robert Godolphin, of Porkington; High Sheriff Merioneths 1768–69 and Caernarvs 1769–70; *d* unm 1792 aged 59

2 Francis; MP Helston; *d* unm 1774

3 MARGARET Owen; *b* Jan 1738; *m* 1777 Owen ORMSBY, of Willow Brook, Sligo (s and heir of William Ormsby, MP Co Sligo, by Hannah, dau of Owen Wynne, of Haslewood), and *d* 2 March 1806, leaving an only child:

(1) MARY JANE Ormsby; *b* 17 Sept 1781; *m* 11 Jan 1815 William GORE, MP, later ORMSBY GORE (*see* **Lineage (of Gore)** above)

HARMAR-NICHOLLS

Arms: Per pale and per chevron gules and sable two arrows with broad heads pilewise, the shafts argent, the feathers and heads or, overall a chevron engrailed gold. **Crest:** Gules and sable two keys in saltire, wards upwards argent, supporting a Davy lamp proper, all tied about with a Stafford knot, the strands gules and sable, the tassels also gules. **Motto:** *Perseverantia vincit* ('Perseverence wins through'). **Creation:** Bt. (UK) 1960, B. (LP, UK) 1974.

THE BARON HARMAR-NICHOLLS, of Peterborough, Co Cambridge, and a **Baronet**, of Darlaston, Co Stafford (Sir Harmar Harmar-Nicholls, 1st Bt, JP (Staffs)) [The Rt Hon The Lord Harmar-Nicholls JP, Abbeylands, Weston, Stafford ST18 0HX]; *b* 1 Nov 1912; *educ* Queen Mary's GS Walsall; Lt RE India and Burma WW II; dir: J & H Nicholls (Paints) Ltd 1945–, Nicholls and Hennessy Gp Ltd, Radio Luxembourg (London) Ltd 1963– (chm 1983–), Cannon Insur; MP (C) Peterborough 1950–74, PPS to Assist PMG 1951–55, Parly Sec: MAFF 1955–57, Min Works 1957–60; memb European Assembly 1979–84; Chm Malvern Festival Theatre Tst; underwriting memb Lloyd's; *m* 1940 *Dorothy Elsie, dau of James Edwards, of Tipton, Staffs, and has:

1 *Judith Ann; *b* 1941; *m* 1973 *Alan Aspden

2 *Susan Frances Nicholls; *b* 1943; actress (as Susan Nicholls); *m* 1993 *Mark Eden, actor

Lineage: CHARLES EDWARD CRADDOCK NICHOLLS, of Walsall, Staffs; *m* Sarah Anne — and had:

Sir HARMAR NICHOLLS later HARMAR-NICHOLLS, **1st Bt** (UK), so *cr* 1960, as also a **Baron**

HARMSWORTH, Baron

Arms: Az. two rolls of paper in saltire or banded in the centre gu. between two bees volant in pale and as many trefoils in fess of the second. **Crest:** A cubit arm erect, the hand holding a roll of paper fesswise ppr. between two ostrich feathers or. **Supporters:** On either side a deep-sea fisherman ppr. **Motto:** *Bene qui sedulo* ('He does well who works diligently'). **Creation:** B. (UK) 4 Feb 1939.

THE 3RD BARON HARMSWORTH, of Egham, Surrey (Thomas (Tom) Harold Raymond Harmsworth) [The Rt Hon The Lord Harmsworth, The Old Rectory, Stoke Abbott, Dorset DT8 3JT]; *b* 20 July 1939; *s* unc 1990; *educ* Eton and Ch Ch Oxford (MA); 2nd Lt RHG 1957–59; *m* 26 June 1971 *Patricia Palmer, dau of Michael Palmer Horsley, of Waltham House, Brough, N Humberside, and has:

1 +DOMINIC MICHAEL ERIC; *b* 18 Sept 1973

2 +Timothy Thomas John; *b* 1979

1 *Philomena Hélène Olivia; *b* 10 Feb 1975

2 *Abigail Patricia Thérèse; *b* 14 June 1977

3 *Pollyanna Mary Clare; *b* 1981

Lineage: ALFRED HARMSWORTH (*see* ROTHERMERE, V); had a 3rd s:

CECIL BISSHOPP HARMSWORTH, **1st Baron Harmsworth**, of Egham, Surrey (UK), so *cr* 4 Feb 1939; *b* 28 Sept 1869; *educ* Marylebone GS and Trin Coll Dublin (BA, Sr Moderator Modern Lit 1891, MA 1911); MP (Lib) Droitwich 1906–10 and Luton 1911–22, PPS to: Pres Bd Ag and Fish 1911–14 and Pres BOT 1914–15, Parly U-Sec Home Dept 1915 and For Affrs 1919–22, memb PM's Secretariat 1917–19, Actg Min Blockade 1919, memb Supreme Ec Cncl, dir Amalgamated Press, chm: Associated Newspapers, Commons, Footpath and Open Spaces Preservn Soc, Cncl Town and Country Planning Assoc, author: *Pleasure and Problem in S Africa* (1908), *Immortals at First Hand* (1933), *A Little Fishing Book* (1942); Hon LLD 1938; *m* 28 April 1897 Emilie Alberta (*d* 4 May 1942), 4th dau of William Hamilton Maffett, barrister, of Finglas, Co Dublin, and *d* 13 Aug 1948, having had, with other issue:

1 CECIL DESMOND BERNARD HARMSWORTH, **2nd Baron Harmsworth**; *b* 19 Aug 1903; *educ* Eton and Ch Ch Oxford (MA); *m* 10 Dec 1926 Dorothy Alexander (*d* 1990), dau of Hon Joseph Charles Heinlein, of Bridgeport, Ohio, and *d* 1990, leaving issue:

(1) *Margaret Askew Alexander [The Hon Mrs Phillips, 15 Square de Chantillon, Paris 75014, France; Lime Lodge, Egham, Surrey]; *b* 31 Oct 1928; painter and sculptor; *m* 1st 1949 Wendell Holmes McCulloch, s of Wendell McCulloch, of Bowling Green, Ky.; *m* 2nd 2 Feb 1960 *Frank Gibson Phillips, s of Henry Gibson Phillips, and by her 1st husb has:

1a *Kevin Desmond Harmsworth [Kevin McCulloch Esq, Lime Lodge, Egham, Surrey]; *b* 1950; *educ* Harrow

(1) (cont.) The Hon Mrs Phillips also has by Fredi Re'em:

2a *Dan Eric Harmsworth [Dan McCulloch, 369 Montezuma Ave, Suite No 110, Sante Fé, NM 87501, USA]; *b* 1951; *educ* Bedales; interior designer, photographer and fine art print publisher; *m* 1st 1978 (*divorce* 1983) Donna Maria Santoro and has:

1b *Francesca Prembindu; *b* 1978

2a (cont.) Dan McCulloch *m* 2nd 1992 *Yana Halouzka and has by her:

1b *Angelo Halouzka; *b* 1993

2 Eric Beauchamp Northcliffe; FLCM 1965, Press Censor Min Info WW II (Sr Press Censor 1944); *b* 28 Aug 1905; *educ* Eton and Ch Ch Oxford (MA); *m* 15 June 1935 Hélène Marie (*d* 21 June 1962), er dau of Col Jules Raymond Dehove, of France; *m* 2nd 4 April 1964 Helen Gordon (*d* 8 April 1996), formerly w of Lt-Col Charles Arthur Norman Hudson, Black Watch, and only dau of Maj-Gen Granville George Loch, CMG, CB, DSO, and *d* 1988, leaving by his 1st w:

(1) THOMAS HAROLD RAYMOND HARMSWORTH, **3rd and present Baron**

(1) *Madeleine Thérèse Margaret [Miss Madeleine Harmsworth 15 Sudeley St, London N1 8HP]; *b* 10 July 1941; *educ* Poles Convent and Somerville Coll Oxford; jnlst

1 Stella Mary; *b* 7 Oct 1899; *d* in infancy

2 Daphne Cecil Rosemary; *b* 7 July 1901; *m* 1st 14 March 1928 (*divorce* 1937) Capt Colin David Brodie, Middx Regt, 2nd s of George James Brodie; *m* 2nd 12 May 1938 Lt-Col Harold Macneile Dixon, RASC, s of Prof William Macneile Dixon, LLD, LittD, and *d* 24 Oct 1993, leaving issue

HARMSWORTH, Bt

Arms: Az. two rolls of paper in saltire or, banded in the centre gu., between four bees volant of the second. **Crest:** Issuant out of a coronet composed of three roses set upon a rim or, a cubit arm erect, the hand holding a roll of paper fesswise ppr.
Motto: *Bene qui sedulo* ('He does well who works diligently').
Creation: Bt. (UK) 21 June 1922.

SIR HILDEBRAND HAROLD HARMSWORTH, 3RD BT, of Freshwater Grove, in the Parish of Shipley, Co Sussex [Sir Hildebrand Harmsworth Bt, Ewlyn Villa, 42 Leckhampton Rd, Cheltenham, Glos GL53 0BB]; *b* 5 June 1931; *s* f 1977; *educ* Harrow and Trin Coll Dublin; *m* 10 Aug 1960 *Gillian Andrea, only dau of William John Lewis, of Tetbury, Glos, and has issue:

1 +(HILDEBRAND ESMOND) MILES; *b* 1 Sept 1964; *educ* Dean Close Sch and Crewe and Alsager Coll; *m* 23 Dec 1988 *Ruth Denise, dau of Dennis Miles, of Cheltenham, and has issue:

(1) +Hildebrand Laurence; *b* 16 July 1994

(1) *Alice Katherine Elspeth; *b* 23 March 1990

(2) *Grace Hester Elaine; *b* 28 Dec 1991

1 *Claire Elen Mary; *b* 15 March 1961

2 *Kirsten Elizabeth Ashley; *b* 19 June 1963

Lineage: ALFRED HARMSWORTH (*see* ROTHERMERE, V); had a 5th s:

Sir Hildebrand Aubrey Harmsworth, 1st Bt (UK), so *cr* 21 June 1922; *b* 15 March 1872; *educ* Merton Coll Oxford; ed *New Liberal Review* 1901–04, fought Gravesend (Imperial Lib) 1900 and Wellington Salop (Tariff Reform) 1906; *m* 4 July 1900 Kathleen Mary (*d* 16 Dec 1966), dau of Edwin Denny Berton, MB, CM Edin, of St John's, New Brunswick, and had:

1 HILDEBRAND ALFRED BERESFORD (Sir), **2nd Bt**

2 Ronald Aubrey Leicester; *b* 22 Nov 1902; *educ* Harrow; *m* 27 Sept 1935 *Elizabeth Bertram, er dau of William Wallace Mackay, of Boksburg, S Africa, and *dsp* 26 Jan 1946

3 (Chamberlain) Michael Hildebrand; *b* 3 Dec 1903; *educ* Harrow and Pembroke Coll Camb; *m* 1st 2 June 1931 Barbara Irene (*d* 4 May 1941), dau of Henry Savile Dean, and had issue:

(1) *Josephine Angela; *b* 15 April 1932

(2) *Melanie Barbara; *b* 29 May 1934

3 (cont.) Michael Harmsworth; *m* 2nd 8 Dec 1945 *Lucette Charlotte, only dau of Jean Riché, of Paris, and *d* 29 Aug 1955, leaving by her:

(1) +John Hildebrand; *b* 4 May 1949

(2) +Charles Hildebrand; *b* 6 Aug 1951

4 Perceval Anthony Thomas Hildebrand, QC (1965); barrister Middle Temple 1936, Dep Chm W Sussex QS 1961–68; *b* 29 Dec 1907; *educ* Harrow and Merton Coll Oxford; *m* 1st 8 Dec 1930 Pansy Nina, dau of Maj William Graham Chambers, of Edinburgh; *m* 2nd 1961 *Marie Dorothy, dau of R H Miller, of Jersey, and *dsp* 27 March 1968

Sir HILDEBRAND *d* 18 April 1929; his s,

Sir Hildebrand Alfred Beresford Harmsworth, 2nd Bt; *b* 27 May 1901; *educ* Harrow; *m* 4 June 1925 *Elen [Elen Lady Harmsworth, Aucassin, Le Vallon, St Clair, Lavandou, France], dau of Nicolaj Billenstein, of Denmark, and *d* 15 Nov 1977, leaving:

1 Sir HILDEBRAND HAROLD HARMSWORTH, **3rd and present Bt**

1 *Ingeborg Kathleen Elen [Mrs Thomas Johnson, Chiffley Grange, Staplefield, Sussex]; *b* 6 Sept 1926; *m* 1 Sept 1951 Capt Thomas James Johnson, RA (*d* 18 Feb 1963), only s of Maj T J L Johnson, MC, and has:

(1) *Ingeborg Caroline Kathleen Elen; *b* 17 Oct 1952

(2) *Melissa Eugenie Ingebor Thomasine; *b* 29 Dec 1954

(3) *Atalanta Kathleen Ingeborg Elen; *b* 29 July 1962; *m* 1989 *Raymond Clive Wright

HARRINGTON

Arms: Quarterly, erm. and gu. **Crest:** A tower az., a demi-lion rampant issuant from the battlements or, holding between the paws a grenade fired ppr. **Supporters:** Dexter, a talbot guardant arg., guttée-de-poix; sinister, a wolf erminois; each gorged with a chaplet of oak, ppr. **Motto:** *A Deo et rege* ('From God and the king').
Creations: B and V. (GB) 3 July 1717 (Stanhope of Elvaston and Stanhope of Mahon respectively), B. (GB) 6 Jan 1729/30 (Harrington), V. (Petersham of Petersham) and E. (GB) 9 Feb 1741/2.

THE 11TH EARL OF HARRINGTON, Co Northampton, **Viscount Stanhope of Mahon** in the island of Minorca, **Viscount Petersham of Petersham**, Co Surrey, **Baron Stanhope of Elvaston**, Co Derby, and **Baron Harrington**, Co Northampton (William Henry Leicester Stanhope) [The Rt Hon The Earl of Harrington, The Glen, Ballingarry, Co Limerick, Ireland]; *b* 24 Aug 1922; *s* f 1929 in Earldom of Harrington, Viscountcy of Petersham of Petersham and Barony of Harrington and kinsman (*see* 1967 edn CHESTERFIELD and STANHOPE, E) 1967 in Viscountcy of Stanhope of Mahon and Barony of Stanhope of Elvaston; *educ* Eton and RMC Sandhurst; Capt 15th/19th King's Roy Hus (RAC) WW II; *m* 1st 5 Feb 1942 (*divorce* 1947) Eileen, only child of Sir John Foley Grey, 8th Bt, of Enville Hall, Stourbridge (*see* LAMBERT, Bt), and has had issue:

1 +CHARLES HENRY LEICESTER, *Viscount Petersham* [Viscount Petersham, Mount St John, Felixkirk, Thirsk, N Yorks YO7 2DT]; *b* 20 July 1945; *educ* Aysgarth and Eton; *m* 1st 14 Sept 1966 (*divorce* 1983) Virginia Alleyne Freeman, dau of Capt Harry Freeman Jackson, of Cool-na-Grena, Mallow, Co Cork; *m* 2nd 1984 *Anita Robsahm, formerly w of 21st Earl of Suffolk and (14th Earl of) Berkshire (*qv*) and dau of Robin Robsahm Fuglesang, of Laycock, Wilts, and by his 1st w has issue:

(1) +William Henry Leicester; *b* 14 Oct 1967; *educ* Aysgarth and Aiglon Coll

(2) *Serena; *b* 1 March 1970; *m* 1993 *David Albert Charles, Viscount Linley, only s of 1st Earl of Snowdon (*qv*) by HRH THE PRINCESS MARGARET (*see* ROYAL FAMILY)

1 Jane; *b* 25 Nov 1942; *m* 29 Sept 1965 *Anthony Cameron and *d* as a result of a road accident Jan 1974, leaving issue:

(1) *James William; *b* 1967

(1) *Henrietta Jane; *b* 1970

2 *Avena Margaret Clare; *b* 29 March 1944; *m* 12 July 1969 *Adrian James Maxwell, only s of Maj James Kennedy Maxwell, of Buckby Folly, E Haddon, Northants, and has issue:

(1) *Sacha Jane; *b* 1974

(2) *Kerry Alice; *b* 1978

The 11th EARL *m* 2nd 24 Jan 1947 (*divorce* 1962) Ann Theodora, only dau of Maj Richard Arenbourg Blennerhassett Chute, of Dooneen, Patrickswell, Co Limerick, and by her has issue:

2 +Steven Francis Lincoln [The Hon Steven Stanhope, Dooneen Stud, Patrickswell, Co Limerick, Ireland]; *b* 12 Dec 1951; *educ* Eton; *m* 1978 *Maureen Elizabeth Irvine, dau of Maj Harold William Cole, of Poundbury, Dorset, and has:

(1) +Ben; *b* 1978

(1) *Tara; *b* 1979

3 *Trina Maria; *b* 30 Dec 1947

4 *Sarah Sue [The Lady Sarah Barry, Mellon Stud, Kildimo, Co Limerick, Ireland]; *b* 12 Dec 1951; *m* 11 Aug 1970 *Robert John Barry, est s of J C Barry, of Adelaide House, Bruff, Co Limerick, and has issue:

(1) *Tristan James; *b* 1975

(2) *Guy William; *b* 1975

The 11th EARL *m* 3rd 14 Oct 1964 *Priscilla Margaret, only surv dau of Hon Archibald Edward Cubitt (*see* ASHCOMBE, B), and by her has:

3 +John Seymour; *b* 20 Aug 1965

5 *Isabella Rachel; *b* 1 Oct 1966; *m* 21 Oct 1994 *7th Earl Cawdor (*qv*)

Lineage: Sir JOHN STANHOPE, of Elvaston, Derbys, half bro of 1st Earl of Chesterfield (*see* 1967 edn CHESTERFIELD and STANHOPE, E); MP Derbys *temp* JAMES I and CHARLES I, High Sheriff Derbys *c* 1630; *m* 1st 1608 Olivia, dau and heir of Edward Beresford, and had an only dau; *m* 2nd Mary, dau of Sir John Radclyffe, of Orsdal, Lancs, and *d* 29 May 1638, leaving an est s:

JOHN STANHOPE, of Elvaston; *m* Jane (*d* 14 April 1652), dau of Sir John Curzon, 1st Bt (*see* SCARSDALE, V), and *d* 26 March 1662, leaving an only s:

JOHN STANHOPE, of Elvaston; *m* Dorothy, dau and coheir of Charles Agard, of Foston, Derbys, and had issue:

1 Thomas, of Elvaston; MP Derbys; *m* Jane (*d* 4 Dec 1764), widow of Charles Stanhope later Wotton, 2nd s of 1st Earl of Chesterfield (*see* 1967 edn STANHOPE and CHESTERFIELD, E), and dau and coheir of Gilbert Thacker, of Repton, Derbys, and *dsp* 10 April 1730

2 Charles, of Elvaston; Sec Treasury and Treasurer Chamber *temp* GEORGE I; *d* unm 1760

3 WILLIAM STANHOPE, **1st Earl of Harrington**, Co Northampton, so *cr* 9 Feb 1741/2, as also VISCOUNT PETERSHAM OF PETERSHAM, Co Surrey, and earlier 6 Jan 1729/30 BARON HARRINGTON, Co Northampton (all GB), PC (1727); *b c* 1683; *educ* Eton; barrister Inner Temple 1704, Gen of Foot 1747, MP (Whig) Derby 1715–22 and 1727–30 and Steyning April-July 1727, Envoy: Madrid 1717–18 and 1720 and Turin 1718–20, Amb Madrid 1721–27 and Congress Aix-la-Chapelle 1727, V-Chamberlain 1727–30, Sec State N Dept 1730–Feb 1741/2 and 1744–46, Ld Pres Cncl Feb 1741/2–Jan 1744/5, Ld Lt Ireland 1746–50; *m c* 1718 Anne (*d* 18 Dec 1719), dau and heir of Col Edward Griffith, a Clerk Comptroller Green Cloth, and had:

(1) WILLIAM, **2nd Earl**

(2) Thomas; *d* unm 12 Jan 1743

The 1st EARL *d* 8 Dec 1756; his only surv son,

WILLIAM STANHOPE, **2nd Earl of Harrington**; *b* 18 Dec 1719, Gen 1770 (fought Fontenoy 1745), Col 2nd Troop Horse Gren Gds; *m* 11 Aug 1746 Lady Caroline FitzRoy (*d* 26 June 1784), est dau of 2nd Duke of Grafton (*qv*), and had:

1 CHARLES, **3rd Earl**

2 Henry FitzRoy; Capt 1st Foot Gds; *b* 1754; *m* Elizabeth Falconer and *d* 20 Aug 1828, leaving:

(1) Robert Henry, Capt RN; *b* 21 April 1802; *m* 29 March 1830 Elizabeth Rosamund (*m* 2nd 8 June 1841 Charles Thomas Stanley (*d* 1883)), est dau of James Ward, of Willey Place, Surrey, and *dsp* 2 March 1839

(1) Harriet; *m* 23 Feb 1826 3rd Baron Southampton (*qv*) and *dsp* 23 Oct 1860

1 Caroline; *m* 7 Oct 1765 1st and last Earl of Seaforth of the 1771 *cr* (*see* CROMARTIE, E) and *d* 9 Feb 1767, leaving issue

2 Isabella; *m* 27 Nov 1768 1st Earl of Sefton (*see* 1970 edn) and *d* 29 Jan 1819, leaving issue. He *d* 31 Jan 1795

3 Amelia; *m* 16 April 1767 6th Earl of Barrymore and *d* 5 Sept 1780, leaving issue. He *d* 1 Aug 1733

4 Henrietta; *m* 20 March 1776 2nd Baron Foley (*qv*) and *d* 2 Jan 1781, leaving issue

5 Anna Maria; *m* 1st 2 May 1782 10th Earl of Lincoln (*qv*), and had issue; *m* 2nd 7 Feb 1800 Gen Sir Charles Gregan Craufurd, GCB (*see* CRAWFURD, Bt), and *d* 18 Oct 1834

The 2nd EARL *d* 1 April 1779; his est son,

CHARLES STANHOPE, **3rd Earl of Harrington**; *b* 17 March 1753; Gen, Col 1st Life Gds, Capt, Govr and Constable Windsor Castle, Kt Grand Cross Royal Hanoverian Guelphic Order; *m* 23 May 1779 Jane (*d* 3 Feb 1824), dau and coheir of Sir John Fleming, Bt, of Brompton Park, and *d* 5 Sept 1829, having had issue:

1 CHARLES STANHOPE, **4th Earl of Harrington**; Maj-Gen; *b* 8 April 1780; *m* 7 April 1831 Maria (*d* 27 Dec 1867), dau of Samuel Foote, and *d* 3 March 1851, having had issue:

(1) Charles, *Viscount Petersham*; *b* 13 Dec 1831; *dvp* 8 April 1836

(1) Jane St Maur Blanche; *m* 17 June 1854 3rd Marquess Conyngham (*qv*) and *d* 28 Nov 1907, having had issue

2 Lincoln Edwin Robert, CB; Maj-Gen; *b* 26 Nov 1781; *d* 29 Feb 1840

3 LEICESTER FitzGERALD CHARLES STANHOPE, **5th Earl of Harrington**, CB; Kt Grecian Order of the Redeemer, Col; *b* 2 Sept 1784; *m* 23 April 1831 Elizabeth (*d* 24 Dec 1898), only child and heir of William Green, of Jamaica, and *d* 7 Sept 1862, having had issue:

(1) Algernon Russell Gayleard; *b* 1838; *d* 1847

(2) SEYMOUR SYDNEY HYDE STANHOPE, **6th Earl of Harrington**; *b* 27 Sept 1845; *d* 22 Feb 1866

(1) Anna Carolina; *m* 13 Nov 1850 Edward Sacheverell Chandos-Pole, of Radborne Hall, Derbys, and *d* 9 April 1913, having had issue. He *d* 30 Nov 1873

(2) Geraldine Evelyn; *m* 19 Oct 1871 6th Earl of Milltown, KP (*see* 1970 edn), and *dsp* 5 Jan 1914. He *d* 30 May 1890

4 FitzRoy Henry Richard (Rev); Dean and Rector St Buryan, Cornwall, Rector Catton, Yorks; *b* 24 April 1787; *m* 8 Nov 1808 Caroline Wyndham (*d* 11 Feb 1876) and *d* 11 April 1864, leaving issue:

(1) CHARLES WYNDHAM, **7th Earl**

(2) Percy; *b* 27 Aug 1828; *m* 15 Dec 1858 Helenora (*d* 14 July 1874), only dau of Joshua S Crompton, of Sion Hill, and Azerley, Yorks, and *d* 29 Sept 1874, leaving issue:

1a Percy Seymour; Capt Oxfordshire LI; *b* 22 July 1865; *m* 1897 Anne, dau of G T Stallard, and *dsp* 4 March 1909

(1) Mary Alexandrina; *d* unm 4 May 1941

5 Francis Charles (Sir), KCH; Maj 1st Life Gds; *b* 29 Sept 1788; *m* Hannah (*d* 25 Oct 1863), dau and coheir of James Wilson, of Parsonstown Manor, and Dunboyne Castle, Co Meath, and *d* 9 Oct 1862, having had issue:

(1) Russell Charles; Lt 13th LI; *m* 14 Dec 1854 Ellinor Avena (*d* 27 Nov 1906), yst dau of John Ireland Blackburne, of Hale, Lancs, and *d* 15 Sept 1866, having had issue:

1a Leicester Charles; *b* 26 Oct 1855; *d* unm 7 July 1906

2a Aubrey Charles; *b* 24 Oct 1857; *d* 20 Oct 1937

3a Russell Charles; *b* posthumously 24 Dec 1866; *m* 25 April 1894 Augustine Madeline (*d* 1 July 1916), dau of De Laureal Thompson, and *d* 1945, leaving issue:

1b Aubrey Charles; *b* 17 Jan 1895; *m* 1st 11 Aug 1919 Paulette Bordier du Raincey (*d* 10 April 1922) and had:

1c +Aubrey Charles; *b* 8 June 1920, Lt-Col USAF WW II, DFC (USA); *m* 4 Sept 1941 *Muriel Grace, dau of William Anderson Lauther, of Truro, Nova Scotia, and has issue:

1d *Paulette Beatrice; *b* 13 April 1946; *m* 1968 *Gilbert Mark Rollo (*see* ROLLO, L) and has issue

1c *Marie Annick [Mrs Richard Davis, 1606 Golf View Drive, Urbana, IL, USA]; *b* 1 Aug 1921; *m* 16 June 1953 Lt-Col Richard Davis USAF (*d* 1977), of Kansas City

1b (cont.) Aubrey Stanhope *m* 2nd 19– —, of the USA, and by her had:

2c +Jonathan; *b* 19–

2c *Christian; *b* 19–

1b (cont.) Aubrey Stanhope *m* 3rd 1931 Evelyn Wadsworth (*d* 1981), of New York, and *d* 20 April 1953, leaving by her:

3c +Noel; *b* 1946

2b Russell Charles; *b* 7 June 1899; *m* 1934 *Jean Kennedy, of New York, and *d* 19–, leaving:

1c *Michelle; *b* 1945; *m* 1976 *Frank Converse Sparks and has:

1d *Kristin; *b* 1978

2d *Ashley; *b* 1980

3d *Nicole; *b* 1983

2c *Celeste; *b* 1947; *m* 27 Feb 1965 *John Nicholas Pierce and has:

1d *Michela Stanhope; *b* 8 Dec 1965

2d *Elizabeth; *b* 1971

3b Leicester de Maclot; *b* 9 Jan 1901; *m* 1930 Rose Mary Farmer, of New York, and *d* 1978, leaving issue:

1c +Leicester [Leicester Stanhope, 3633 Tangier Terr, Sarasota, FL, USA]; *b* 1932; *m* 1955 *Priscilla Carrington Young, of Connecticut, and has issue:

1d +Leicester de Maclot; *b* 1957

2d +Russell Charles; *b* 1958

1d *Margot; *b* 1960

2d *Jennifer; *b* 1961

2c +Philip [Philip Stanhope, Hidden Harbor Rd, Sarasota, FL 33578, USA]; *b* 1939; *m* 19– *Bonnie — and has:

1d +Philip; *b* 1973

2d +Sean; *b* 1980

3d +Justin; *b* 1982

1c *Nina; *b* 1931; *m* 19– —

1b *Violet Augustine [Mrs Robert Rollo, 3 Russell Terr, Russell St, Wilton, Wilts SP4 0BG]; *b* 1912; *m* 30 July 1936 Maj Robert Duncan Rollo (*see* ROLLO, L) and has issue

1a Avena Beatrice; *d* unm 12 Jan 1865

2a Isabella Olave; despatches and two medals WW I; *m* 21 Nov 1885 William Henry Wilson-FitzGerald, JP, DL, of Adelphi, Co Clare, and Chalcombe, nr Banbury, 2nd s of Richard Bassett Wilson, of Cliffe Hall, Yorks, and *d* 28 Nov 1941, leaving issue. He *d* 17 April 1932

(1) Frances Anna Jane; *m* 1st 16 March 1841 Col James Hughes, CB, brother of 1st Baron Dinorben. He *d* 26 Nov 1845. She *m* 2nd 15th June 1861 Rt Hon Sir William Hutt, KCB, MP Gateshead, Paymaster-Gen and V-Pres BOT, and *d* 26 Sept 1886. He *d* 24 Nov 1882

(2) Augusta Mary; *m* 11 April 1849 1st Baron Hemphill (*qv*) and *d* 12 April 1899, leaving issue

6 Henry William (Rev); Rector Gawsworth, Cheshire; *b* 2 Aug 1790; *m* — (*d* 9 Aug 1886) and *dsp* 21 June 1872

7 Augustus; *b* 25 March 1794; *d* 8 Dec 1831

1 Anna Maria; *m* 8 Aug 1808 7th Duke of Bedford (*qv*) and *d* 3 July 1857, leaving issue

2 Caroline Anne; *m* 21 June 1841, as his 2nd w, Edward Ayshford Sanford, JP, DL, FRS, of Nynehead Court, Somerset, and *dsp* 25 Nov 1853. He *d* 1 Dec 1871

3 Charlotte Augusta; *m* 16 June 1818 3rd Duke of Leinster (*qv*) and *d* 15 Feb 1859, leaving issue

The 6th EARL's cousin,

CHARLES WYNDHAM STANHOPE, **7th Earl of Harrington**, DL; *b* 16 Aug 1809; *m* 16 Feb 1839 Elizabeth Still (*d* 6 Feb 1912), dau of Robert Lucas de Pearsall, of Wartensee Castle, Switzerland, and *d* 26 June 1881, having had, with other issue:

1 CHARLES AUGUSTUS STANHOPE, **8th Earl of Harrington**, DL Derbys; *b* Jan 1844; ADC to TM EDWARD VII and GEORGE V 1907–17, Hon Col Cheshire Yeo (sometime cmdg), MFH S Notts 1881–1917; *m* 5 July 1869 Hon Eva Elizabeth Carington (*d* 20 June 1919), yst dau of 2nd Baron Carrington (*qv*), and *dsp* 5 Feb 1917

2 FitzRoy William Whitbread; *b* 25 Dec 1845; *m* 1st 30 Oct 1869 Jessie Marion Hawkins Hamilton (*d* 1 June 1885), yst adopted dau of J H Gell, of Ickenham; *m* 2nd 20 July 1886 Ethel (*d* 21 June 1925), dau of Peter Godfrey Chapman, and *dsp* 9 Dec 1913

3 Lincoln Edwin; Lt 7th Dragoon Gds; *b* 6 April 1849; *m* 22 July 1885 Helene de Bravura (*d* 4 Dec 1919), dau of Countess de Galve (by her 1st husband, Leon de Bravura), and was accidentally drowned 1 July 1902, leaving issue:

(1) Eva Barbara Edwina; *b* 19 March 1890; *m* 15 Sept 1921 Bertram Marion-Crawford, 2nd s of Francis Marion-Crawford, novelist, and gs of Thomas Crawford, American sculptor, and *d* 14 June 1977. He *d* 1952

4 Wyndham Edward Campbell; *b* 17 June 1851; *m* 30 Oct 1877 Camille Caroline (*m* 2nd 8 Jan 1884 Col Walter Adye, CB, who *d* 3 Sept 1915), dau of Edward Reyloff, and *dsp* 27 July 1883

5 DUDLEY HENRY EDEN, **9th Earl**

1 Caroline Margarite; *m* 15 Dec 1867 James Penrose Ingham, er s of Sir James Taylor Ingham, of Sugwas Court, Herefs, and *d* 7 Aug 1906, leaving issue. He *d* 28 Nov 1879

2 Leicester Philippa; *m* 6 Sept 1883 William Sharp Waithman, of Merlin Park, Co Galway, and *d* 20 July 1920, leaving issue. He *d* 8 Nov 1922

3 Jane Harriet Charlotte; *m* 7 Feb 1874 4th Baron Wallscourt (*see* 1917 edn) and *d* 8 Sept 1889, leaving issue. He *d* 22 July 1918

4 Blanche Georgina; *d* unm Feb 1939

The 8th EARL's only surv bro,

DUDLEY HENRY EDEN STANHOPE, **9th Earl of Harrington**; *b* 13 Jan 1859; *m* 26 April 1883 Kathleen (*d* 6 Aug 1949), dau of Joseph Carter Wood, of Falcourt, Sussex, and had issue:

1 CHARLES JOSEPH LEICESTER, **10th Earl**

2 Talbot FitzRoy Eden; Lt Rifle Bde; *b* 23 Nov 1896; *ka* 9 May 1915

1 Kathleen Florence Mary; *m* 1st 15 Jan 1907 Edward John Harry Eden Morant, JP, of Brockenhurst Park, Hants, and had issue. He *d* 20 Jan 1910. She *m* 2nd 29 Dec 1920 Capt Edward Philip Leigh Hare, 3rd s of Sir Thomas Hare, 2nd Bt (*qv*), and had further issue

The 9th EARL *d* 13 Nov 1928; his son,

CHARLES JOSEPH LEICESTER STANHOPE, **10th Earl of Harrington**, MC, DL Derbys; *b* 9 Oct 1887; Capt and Brevet Maj Res of Offrs 15th Hus; *m* 23 April 1919 Margaret Trelawney (*d* 15 Sept 1952, having *m* 2nd 14 July 1934 Capt Luke Theodore Lillingston, Leics Yeo (*das* of wounds 11 Aug 1944) and *m* 3rd 23 July 1949 Maj Stephen Cecil Johnson, 16th/5th Lancers, only s of Capt and Brevet Maj Harry Cecil Johnson, DSO, DRRC), 2nd dau of Maj H H D Seaton, of Bulford, Salisbury, and *d* 16 Nov 1929, having had:

1 Charles; *b* 19–; *d* 23 Jan 1921

2 WILLIAM HENRY LEICESTER STANHOPE, **11th and present Earl of Harrington**

HARRIS, Baron

Arms: Vert on a chevron embattled erminois, between three hedgehogs or, as many bombs sa., fired ppr.; a chief of augmentation thereon, the gates and fortress of Seringapatam, the drawbridge let down, and the Union flag of Great Britain and Ireland hoisted over the standard of Tippoo Sahib, all ppr. **Crest:** On a mural crown or a royal tiger passant-guardant vert, striped or, spotted of the first, pierced in the breast with an arrow of the last, vulned gu., charged on the forehead with a Persian character for Hyder and crowned with an Eastern coronet, both of the first. **Supporters:** Dexter, a Grenadier soldier of the 73rd Regt in his regimentals ppr., supporting with his exterior hand a flagstaff, thereon hoisted the union flag of Great Britain and Ireland over that of the standard of Tippoo Sahib, and beneath the tri-coloured flag entwined, inscribed with the word 'République'; sinister, a Malay soldier in his uniform ppr., supporting a like staff, thereon hoisted the flag of the East India Company arg., striped barwise gu. with a canton over the standard of Tippoo Sahib with the tri-coloured flag entwined beneath, as on the dexter, inscribed with the word 'Française', all ppr. **Motto:** My prince and my country.

Creation: B. (UK) 11 Aug 1815.

THE 8TH BARON HARRIS OF SERINGAPATAM AND MYSORE, in the East Indies, **AND OF BELMONT**, Co Kent (Anthony Thomas Scott Harris) [The Rt Hon The Lord Harris, 1 Linkenholt Mansions, Stamford Brook Ave, London W6]; *b* 8 March 1942; *s* f 1996; *m* 1966 *Antice, dau of Alfred Winter, and has issue:

1 *Isabel; *b* 1973

2 *Laura; *b* 1976

Lineage: JOHN HARRIS; *m* Rachel (*d* 19 March 1729), dau of William Bull, goldsmith, of Tower Hill, and was *bur* 1 May 1731; his yst s:

Rev GEORGE HARRIS; *educ* Corpus Christi Coll Cambridge (BA 1738/9); Curate Brasted, Kent; *m* Sarah, dau of George Twentyman, of Braintree, Cumberland, and *d* 1759, having had, with two other sons and three daus:

GEORGE HARRIS, **1st Baron Harris of Seringapatam and Mysore**, in the East Indies, **and of Belmont**, Co Kent (UK), so *cr* 11 Aug 1815, GCB (1820); *b* 18 March 1746; *educ* Westminster and Woolwich Mil Acad; Gen 1812, Col 73rd Highrs 1800–29, served War American Independence, also India 1790–91, C-in-C Madras Presidency 1797–1800, defeated Tippoo Sahib at Battle of Seringapatam 4 May 1799 and annexed Mysore; *m* 9 Dec 1779 Anne Carteret (*d* 30 July 1833), yst dau and coheir of Charles Dickson, of Bath, and *d* 19 May 1829, having had, with other issue:

1 WILLIAM GEORGE HARRIS, **2nd Baron Harris of Seringapatam and Mysore and of Belmont**, KCH (1833), CB (1815); Lt-Gen 1837, Col 73rd Foot; *b* 19 Jan 1782; with his f at capture Seringapatam, cmded 2nd/73rd Regt Waterloo (wounded); *m* 1st 17 Oct 1809 Eliza Serena Anne (*d* 25 Jan 1817), dau of William Dick, MD, of Tullimet North Britain House, Perthshire, by Charlotte Maclaren (coheir of the last Chief of Maclaren), and had issue:

(1) GEORGE FRANCIS ROBERT HARRIS, **3rd Baron Harris of Seringapatam and Mysore and of Belmont**, GCSI (1866); *b* 14 Aug 1810; *educ* Ch Ch Oxford (BA 1832), DCL 1863, Govr Trinidad 1846 and Madras 1854, a Ld-in-Waiting 1860–63, Chamberlain to HRH THE PRINCESS OF WALES 1862–72; *m* 16 April 1850 Sarah (*d* 6 March 1853), 2nd dau of Ven George Cummins, AM, Archdeacon Trinidad, and *d* 23 Nov 1872, leaving:

1a GEORGE ROBERT CANNING HARRIS, **4th Baron Harris of Seringapatam and Mysore and of Belmont**, GCSI (1895), GCIE (1890), TD, JP, DL; V-Lt Kent 1914–16; *b* 3 Feb 1851; *educ* Eton and Ch Ch Oxford (BA); U-Sec India 1885–86 and War 1886–90, Govr Bombay 1890–95, Ld-in-Waiting to HM QUEEN VICTORIA 1895–1901, ADC to HM, Hon Col and Co Cmdt Kent Vol Regt, Hon Col 4th Bn The Buffs, Lt-Col Roy E Kent Yeo, AAG Imp Yeo Boer War 1900–01, a celebrated cricketer, author: *A Few Short Runs*; *m* 8 July 1874 Hon Lucy Ada Jervis, CI (*d* 12 Feb 1930), 2nd dau of 3rd Viscount Saint Vincent (*qv*), and *d* 24 March 1932, leaving:

1b GEORGE ST VINCENT HARRIS, **5th Baron Harris of Seringapatam and Mysore and of Belmont**, MC, JP (Kent 1919), DL (1936); *b* 3 Sept 1889; *educ* Eton and Ch Ch Oxford (BA 1914, MA 1968); V-Lt Kent 1948–84, Capt Roy E Kent Yeo, Supreme Grand Master OStJ, Grand Master England (Mark), Chm Kent Police Authority 1945–64 and Jt Standing Ctee, Commr St John Amb Bde Kent 1940–45, served WW I (despatches, wounded); *m* 27 July 1918 Dorothy Mary (*d* 1981), Ch Cmdt ATS 1938–40, Order Mercy, 5th dau of Rev John William Crookes, Vicar Borden, Kent, and *d* 1984, leaving issue:

1c GEORGE ROBERT JOHN HARRIS, **6th Baron Harris of Seringapatam and Mysore and of Belmont**; *b* 17 April 1920; *educ* Eton and Ch Ch Oxford; Capt RA; *dsp* 17 Sept 1995

1a Frances Charlotte; *m* 9 April 1874 Lt-Col Arthur Balfour Haig, CMG, CVO, JP, and *d* 15 Dec 1939, having had issue (*see* HAIG, E)

(2) William Lushington Thomas; Fell All Souls 1836–40, Rector Wilton, Wilts, 1840; *b* 18 Jan 1814; *educ* Oriel Coll Oxford (BA); *d* unm 24 Nov 1840

(1) Charlotte Reid; *d* Dec 1818

(cont.) The **2nd Baron** *m* 2nd 28 May 1824 Isabella Helena (*d* 10 Jan 1861), only child of Robert Handcock Temple, of Waterston, Co Westmeath, by Louisa, dau of William Stearne Tighe, of South Hill, Co Westmeath, and *d* 30 May 1845, having by her had issue:

(3) Reginald (or Robert) Temple HARRIS later HARRIS TEMPLE (added 1852 on his inheriting the estate of his maternal gf), of Waterston, JP, DL Kent and Co Westmeath; High Sheriff 1860; *b* 6 May 1830; *educ* Ch Ch Oxford (BA); *dsp* 24 Feb 1900

(4) Arthur Ernest HARRIS later HARRIS-TEMPLE (roy licence 25 April 1900), JP (Co Westmeath), of Waterston; Capt 43rd Foot; *b* 31 Jan 1835; *m* 25 July 1871 Jane (*d* 11 May 1891), widow of Capt Arthur Chaigneau, of Enown House, Co Westmeath, and dau of Rev Richard Butler Bryan, and *d* 12 Aug 1906, having had issue:

1a Arthur Reginald, of Waterston, JP, DL; *b* 1 Aug 1874; *m* 28 Oct 1898 Clare (*d* 1951), dau of Alan Cameron, AIG RIC, and *d* 29 Oct 1928, leaving:

1b Arthur Temple; Lt RA WW II; *b* 15 March 1904; *educ* Radley; *m* 1946 *Mrs Thelma Crafter, BA, dau of John Lester, of Springfield, Mass., and *d* 4 Jan 1981

1b Nilah Clare; *b* 25 Nov 1899; *m* 1921 Capt Arthur Vivian Wood, Border Regt

2b Dita Helena; Jr Cdr ATS; *b* 7 June 1901; *m* 1st 1920 (*divorce* 1942) Capt Ingoldsby Philip Massy, IA, and had issue; *m* 2nd 1945 (Jared Douglas) Eric Troop, F/Lt RCAF, and *d* 21 Sept 1954

(2) Louisa Matilda; *m* 10 Feb 1857 4th Baron Castlemaine (*qv*) and *d* 31 Jan 1892, leaving issue

2 Michael Thomas; Madras CS 1799–1824; *b* 13 Sept 1783; *m* 23 March 1807 Emma Martha (*d* 11 Feb 1866), dau of William Money, Consul-Gen Venice, and *d* 17 May 1824, leaving issue:

(1) Thomas Inglis Parish; Madras CS 1831–66; *b* 10 July 1811; *m* 19 Feb 1838 Emily (*d* 26 Jan 1899), dau of Robert Burnside, and *d* 28 June 1867, leaving, with other issue:

1a Thomas; Lt-Col Middx Regt, Mil Sec to Govr Bombay 1892–95; *b* 8 May 1845; *m* 23 Dec 1880 Lilias Annie (*d* 29 Sept 1954), 3rd dau of William Turney Cole, and *d* 28 March 1918, leaving issue:

1b Thomas Guy Marriott, OBE (1919); Maj IA; *b* 7 March 1882; *m* 5 Dec 1912 Beryl (*d* 1960), dau of Col Frederick Alexander Wilson, IA, and *d* 6 Nov 1955, leaving issue:

1c DEREK MARSHALL HARRIS, **7th Baron Harris of Seringapatam and Mysore and of Belmont**; *b* 23 July 1916; Maj Duke of Wellington's Regt; *m* 1st 16 Aug 1938 (*divorce* 1968) Laura Cecilia, est dau of Maj Edmund Thomas William McCausland, Gurkha Rifles; *m* 2nd 1987 Mrs Pauline Elisabeth Skinner (*d* Nov 1997) and *d* 30 June 1996, leaving by his 1st w:

1d ANTHONY THOMAS SCOTT HARRIS, **8th and present Baron Harris of Seringapatam and Mysore and of Belmont**

1d *Amanda Cecilia [Mrs Amanda Harris, 55 Clissold Crescent, London N16]; *b* 8 Jan 1953; *m* 1974 (*divorce* 1984 resumed maiden name) Jeremy Mainwaring and has issue:

1e *Guy; *b* 1975

1e *Rosie; *b* 1980

2b George Scott; *b* 17 April 1883; *d* unm

1b Lilias Olive; *b* 1892

2a Charles Walter; Lt-Col IA; *b* 16 Dec 1856; *m* 18 April 1897 Edith Jane Frederica, er dau of Capt Frederick William Crohan, ISC, and *d* 16 Jan 1905, leaving issue:

1b Monica Fay; *b* 19 June 1898

3a Edmund Archibald Taylor; *b* 28 Oct 1861

1a Maria Eugenia; *m* 9 March 1861 Maj-Gen Archibald George Douglas Logan, Madras Army, and *d* 2 Aug 1882, leaving issue. He *d* 20 Dec 1891

2a Ellen Lushington; *m* 28 Oct 1865 Dep-Surgn-Gen John Henderson, MD, and had issue

3a Edith Godfrey; *m* 12 June 1872 Horace Spelman Marriott and *d* 8 May 1917, leaving issue. He *d* 7 Feb 1891

4a Laura Beatrice

(2) George Anstruther; Madras CS 1831–60; *b* 31 Aug 1812; *m* 1st 7 Sept 1833 Fanny (*d* 13 Dec 1850), dau of Thomas Gahagan, MCS, and had, with other issue:

1a George Lucian Taylor; BCS; *b* 24 May 1836; *m* 2 Dec 1871 Fanny Elizabeth Anne (*d* 16 Feb 1919), dau of George Alderson, and *d* 30 Sept 1903, leaving issue:

1b George Temple James; Rhodesian CS, Boer War 1899–1900 (medal with clasp); *b* 31 May 1876; *m* 27 April 1910 Eva (*m* 2nd 8 June 1933 Randle North Kenyon (*d* 10 Aug 1968), 3rd s of Rev Hon William Trevor Kenyon (*see* KENYON, B), and *d* 14 March 1942), dau of Lt-Col Henry Green-Wilkinson, Scots Gds, and *d* 11 Sept 1929, leaving:

1c Ronald George Temple; *b* 5 Sept 1911; WW II as 1st Offr ATA, late 2nd Lt The King's Regt; *m* 1st 1936 (*divorce* 1958) Simone, dau of — Hogbin, of Folkestone; *m* 2nd 1958 *Beryl [Mrs Ronald Harris, 9 Dunning Court, Dowell St, Honiton, Devon EX14 8FQ], dau of George Brown, of Fakenham, Norfolk, and *d* 31 Dec 1994

2c +ANTONY JOHN TEMPLE, OBE (1963) [Cdr Antony Harris OBE RN (ret), Hawthorns, Wickham, Fareham, Hants]; *b* 5 Aug 1915; heir presumptive; *m* 25 April 1940 *Doris, only child of Frank Dufford Drake, of Florida, and has:

1d +Michael George Temple [Rear-Adml Michael Harris RN, c/o Clothworkers Hall, Dunster Court, Mincing Lane, London EC3R 7AH]; *b* 5 July 1941; *educ* Nautical Coll Pangbourne, RNC Dartmouth; cmded HM Submarines *Osiris* 1970–72, *Sovereign* 1975–77 and HM ships *Cardiff* 1980–82 and *Ark Royal* 1987–89, Clerk Clothworkers' Co 1992–, Liveryman 1997–, Yr Bro Trin Ho 1989; *m* 1970 *Caroline Sandra Pietre Katrina, dau of Gp Capt Patrick George Chichester, OBE (*see* CHICHESTER, Bt), and has issue:

1e *Tamsin Caroline Temple; *b* 22 Nov 1971

2e *Rebecca Eva Temple; *b* 29 Aug 1973

3e *Emily Vesta Temple; *b* 11 Jan 1979

2d +John Frank Temple [John Harris Esq, 24 Manor Close, Wickham, Hants PO17 5BZ]; *b* 21 Aug 1944; *educ* Sherborne; *m* 14 Feb 1972 *Mrs Sandra Dobson, dau of C Stones, of Bishops Auckland, Co Durham

1c *June Rosemary Temple [Miss J R T Harris, 4 Dale Ave, Hassocks, W Sussex BN6 8LW]; *b* 6 Feb 1928

2b Harry Thomas Hopkinson; Capt 92nd Punjabi Regt IA; *b* 17 Aug 1882; *ka* Mesopotamia 21 Jan 1916

1b Fanny Maria Elinor; *m* 6 July 1896 Lt-Col John Cane Crawford, Manchester Regt, and *d* 22 Feb 1962, leaving issue. He *d* 1933

2a Charles John Birch; Col ISC, Consular Agent Karikhal and Pondicherry; *b* 7 Nov 1840; *m* 8 Dec 1874 Florence (*d* 28 May 1938), dau of Thomas Goodwyn Archer, of King's Lynn, and *d* 22 Dec 1892, leaving, with two other sons (*d* young unm):

1b Hugh Anstruther; Lt 64th Pioneers IA; *b* 5 May 1882; *m* 1922 Ada Miller (*d* 1966) and *d* 1951, leaving issue:

1c *Nina Denise; *b* 1924; *m* Oct 1946 *Donald R Miller and has:

1d *Michael Jeffrey; *b* 3 April 1947

2d *Gary Lee; *b* 9 Feb 1949

3d *Jeffrey Hugh; *b* 12 June 1952

1d *Wendy Louise; *b* 5 June 1954

2d *Julie Diane; *b* 25 April 1962

1b Nina Florence; *d* unm 23 April 1963

2b Ethel Harvey

1a Fanny Laura Mary; *m* 1860 Maj-Gen George Hearn and *d* 10 Aug 1906. He *dsp* 24 Aug 1888

2a Sybella Flora Conway; *m* 31 Oct 1866 Rev William Bassett Powell, Rector Stocklinch, Ilminster, and had issue. He *d* 21 June 1909

(2) (cont.) George Harris *m* 2nd 18 Aug 1852 Eliza Margaret (*d* 24 Jan 1854), dau of Capt William Douglas Harington, and by her had issue:

3a Henry Harington (Rev); MA Cantab, Rector Poynings Sussex 1839–1917; *b* 19 July 1853; *m* 18 July 1894 Mary Caroline, dau of Rev Canon Richard Norris Russell (*see* EGMONT, E), and *d* 15 May 1936, leaving:

1b Harry Perceval Harington; Capt IA, RFA, WW I; *b* 17 May 1895; *d* 12 June 1929

(2) (cont.) George Harris *m* 3rd 1 Feb 1855 Emma (*d* 1 March 1913), dau of Richard Rutherfoord, and *d* 24 Aug 1891, leaving by her, with other issue:

4a Frederick Rutherfoord; MD, LRCP, MP Dulwich 1903–06, memb Cape Parl for Kimberley 1894–96 and 1898; *b* 1 May 1856; *m* 25 Nov 1884 Florence (*d* 19 Dec 1920), dau of William Ling, and *d* 1 Sept 1920

5a Francis Anderson; Lt Indian Staff Corps; *b* 26 Oct 1857; *d* 1912

6a Hermann Gundert; *b* 26 Jan 1859; *educ* London U (BA); *m* 7 March 1895 Alice Uniacke (*d* 1927), dau of William Uniacke Townsend (*see* COOTE, Bt), and *d* 1950, having had:

1b +Eric Townsend; *b* 6 Jan 1902; Canadian Expdny Force WW I, PR Dir of Screen Actors Guild; *m* 1st 30 May 1920 (*divorce* 1927) Marjorie Peggy, dau of Charles Vokes, of Winnipeg, and has issue:

1c *Joan Patricia; *b* 21 June 1922; *m* — French

2c *Elizabeth Anne; *b* 9 June 1926; *m* — Cregar

1b (cont.) Eric Harris *m* 2nd 19 Jan 1946 *Helen, dau of Howard Francis Bidwell, of Boston and New York, and by her has:

3c *Patricia Anne; *b* 9 Feb 1950

2b George Rutherford; *b* 9 Oct 1903; *m* April 1927 *Olive, dau of — Hall, of Saskatchewan, and had:

1c +Gerald Rutherford; *b* 1928; *m* 30 June 1955 *Vernette Harris and has:

1d +Scott; *b* 2 Oct 1960

1d *Shelley Ann; *b* 19 April 1957

2c +Alfred James [Alfred Harris Esq, Box 17, Nanton, Alberta, Canada]; *b* 1942; RCM Police; *m* 4 Sept 1965 *Alexandra Konopelka and has issue:

1d +Dwayne Stephen; *b* 2 Feb 1966

1d *Suzanne Marie; *b* 21 Dec 1967

1c *Lucille Olive [Mrs William Spaidal, 1044 Charland Street, New Westminster, BC, Canada]; *b* 1930; *m* 19 April 1951 *William A Spaidal, and has issue:

1d *Richard Arnold; *b* 30 May 1952

2d *William Randle; *b* 18 June 1957

3d *Robert Matthew; *b* 9 May 1968

1d *Linda Lucille; *b* 1963

2c *Violet Joyce [Mrs Donald Watkins, 612 Vermouth Avenue, Cooksville, Ontario, Canada]; *b* 1935; *m* 20 June 1959 *Donald Watkins and has:

1d *Norman Douglas; *b* 1963

2d *Steven Patrick; *b* 1964

3b Edward Hermann; WW II in RCAF; *b* 12 Oct 1906; *m* 24 June 1944 *Alice Maud, dau of W T Duke, Rifle Bde, and *d* 8 Oct 1963

1b Ruth Maidie; *b* 1 Feb 1896; *d* 1926

2b *Doris Emma [Mrs Albert Snook, Apt 307, 409 Ash St, New Westminster, BC, Canada V3M 3NI]; *b* 7 April 1900; *m* 1910 Albert Snook (*d* 1966) and has:

1c *Glen Townsend [Glen Snook Esq, c/o Island Trust Council, Denman Island, BC, Canada]; *b* 1924; WW II with RCN; *m* 1950 *Mae Millar, dau of Charles Pihan, of Langle, BC, and has issue:

1d *Lloyd Glen; *b* 1951

2d *Brian; *b* 1954

1d *Deborah Ann; *b* 1957

7a Alfred Herschel; memb Wilts CC and Calne and Chippenham RDC, Commr Chinese Maritime Customs Canton, Order Double Dragon and Chia Ho China; *b* 29 Oct 1863; *m* 18 Jan 1894 Suzanne Amèlie (*d* 1955), dau of Edward B Anstie, and *d* 1953, leaving issue:

1b Lawrence Anstie, CBE (1945), DSO (1937), MC (1917); Brig RA (ret 1948), WWs I and II; *b* 13 Dec 1896; *educ* Tonbridge and RMA Woolwich; *m* 1st 2 Oct 1924 Dorothy Mary (*d* 1962), dau of F A England, of Rathgar, Dublin; *m* 2nd Jan 1965 *Mrs Marjorie S Bayley, dau of Henry Sydney Powell, of Pocklington, Yorks, and *d* 198–

2b Robert Louis Anstruther; actor; *b* 28 March 1900; *educ* Sherborne and New Coll Oxford; *d* 18 May 1995

3b Christopher Money, JP Glos; *b* 26 Sept 1907; *educ* Sherborne and Trin Coll Oxford (MA 1933); Fndr Chm Assoc Prof Foresters; FRSA; WW II with RAFO; *m* 22 Nov 1935 *Ruth Cunliffe, yst dau of George Harwood, MP, of Bolton, and *d* 7 April 1997, leaving:

1c +Robert Julian Brownlow [Robert Harris Esq, 57 Elizabeth St, London SW1]; *b* 10 June 1943; *educ* Eton; *m* 21 Jan 1971 (*divorce* 1976) Lady Camilla Dorothy Godolphin Osborne (*m* 2nd 1977, as his 2nd w, Nigel Dempster; *see* also QUEENSBERRY, M), only child of 11th and last Duke of Leeds (*see* 1963 edn), and has:

1d *Emily Kate Godolphin; *b* 1972

1c *Phoebe Georgina; *b* 28 May 1950; *m* 19 Nov 1970 *Guy Rudolf Bentinck (*see* PORTLAND, E) and has issue

3a Marion Fanny; *m* 4 Nov 1891 George Babington Michell, OBE, Consul-Gen Milan, and *d* 26 July 1946, leaving issue. He *d* 11 Jan 1936

4a Katherine; *m* 14 Nov 1899 George Ernest Macleod, MB, Surgn-Cdr RN, and *d* 1957. He *d* 10 Nov 1949

(1) Emma Money; *m* 14 June 1831 Capt Archibald Douglas, Madras Service, and *d* his widow 19 March 1880

(2) Frances Martha; *m* 31 Dec 1831 Lt-Gen Archibald Spiers Logan, Madras Army, and *d* 17 June 1890, leaving issue. He *d* 10 May 1873

(3) Ellen; *m* 3 Nov 1840 Baron Henri de Sainte Marie and *d* June 1911, having had issue. He *d* March 1891

(4) Maria Jane; *m* 25 Sept 1841 Henry Fearon Baber and *d* 26 Oct 1891, leaving issue. He *d* 1860

(5) Eugenia Emma; *m* 12 April 1838 Maj-Gen George Logan, Madras Army, and *d* 1 March 1891, leaving issue. He *d* 4 Nov 1870

3 Charles; Capt 85th LI; *b* 14 Dec 1793; *d* 8 Jan 1815 of wounds recd Battle of New Orleans

4 Musgrave Alured Henry (Rev); *b* 5 Sept 1801; *m* 16 June 1835 Georgina, dau of William Fosbery, and *dsp* 16 Aug 1836

1 Anne Elizabeth; *m* 9 Dec 1797 Rt Hon Stephen Rumbold Lushington, MP, and *d* 25 March 1856, leaving issue. He *d* 5 Aug 1868

2 Sarah; *b* 13 Sept 1785; *m* 2 Oct 1809 Rev John Hodgson, Vicar St Peter's Thanet 1835–57, and *d* 28 March 1844, leaving issue. He *d* 28 Nov 1870

3 Mary Jane; *m* 3 Sept 1822 Francis Bradley Dyne, of Gore Court, Kent, and *d* 22 Sept 1862, leaving issue. He *d* 13 Nov 1866

HARRIS, Bt

Creation: Bt. (UK) 14 Jan 1932.

SIR JACK WOLFRED ASHFORD HARRIS, 2ND BT, of Bethnal Green, in the County of London [Sir Jack Harris Bt, Flat 2602, Peninsula Tower, 37 Glen St, Milson's Point, Sydney, NSW 2061, Australia]; *b* 23 July 1906; *s* f 1952; *educ* Shrewsbury and Trin Hall Cambridge (BA); Pres Wellington Chamber Commerce; NZ Forces WW II; *m* 16 Sept 1933 *Patricia, only dau of Arthur P Penman, of Wahroonga, NSW, and has issue:

1 +CHRISTOPHER JOHN ASHFORD [Christopher Harris Esq, 21 Anne St, Wadestown, Wellington, New Zealand]; *b* 26 Aug 1934; *m* 24 April 1957 *Anna Karen, only dau of F H T de Malmanche, of Auckland, and has issue:

(1) +Andrew Frederick Ashford; *b* 17 March 1958

(1) *Charlotte Anna; *b* 1 Aug 1960

2 +Paul Percy Ashford [Paul Harris Esq, 28 Middlehead Rd, Mosman, NSW, Australia]; *b* 6 March 1945; *m* 1969 *Gail, dau of Arthur Stewart, of Manchester, and has issue:

(1) +Mark Percy; *b* 1970

(2) +Nicholas; *b* 1978

(3) +Samuel; *b* 1980

(1) *Sophie; *b* 1973

1 *Margaret; *b* 1939

Lineage: WOLF HARRIS, of 197 Queen's Gate, London; Warden New West End Synagogue; *b* 1834; *m* 1872 Elizabeth (*d* 14 Sept 1928), dau of David Nathan, of Auckland, NZ, and *d* 20 March 1926, leaving, with an er s (Leslie Wolfred, *b* 2 June 1873, *m* 1898 and had issue):

Sir Percy Alfred Harris, 1st Bt (UK), so *cr* 14 Jan 1932, PC (1940), DL; *b* 6 March 1876; *educ* Harrow and Trin Hall Cambridge (BA 1897, MA 1927); barrister Middle Temple, memb LCC 1907–34 and 1946–52 (Dep Chm 1915–16), Hon Assist Dir Vol Serv War Office 1916, MP (Lib) Harborough 1916–18 and SW Bethnal Green 1922–45, Ch Lib Whip 1935–45; *m* 2 April 1901 Marguerite Frieda (*d* 5 Nov 1962), yr dau of John Astley Bloxham, FRCS, of Old Malt House, Little Marlow, and *d* 28 June 1952, leaving issue:

1 Sir JACK WOLFRED ASHFORD HARRIS, **2nd and present Bt**

2 +Thomas Nicholas Robinson; artist, Lt RNVR WW II; *b* 25 Feb 1908; *educ* King's Sch Bruton and Trin Hall Cambridge; *m* 24 Feb 1942 *Lucille (Lisle), only child of D H Jonas, of Melbourne and Sydney, and has issue:

(1) +Antony Guy David Bloxham; *b* 11 Jan 1943

HARRIS OF GREENWICH

Creation: B. (LP, UK) 1974.

THE BARON HARRIS OF GREENWICH, of Greenwich in Greater London (John Henry Harris) [The Rt Hon The Lord Harris of Greenwich, House of Lords, London SW1A 0PW]; *b* 5 April 1930; *educ* Pinner GS Middx; jnlst; memb Cncl Harlow Essex 1957–63 (Chm 1960–61, Leader Lab Gp 1961–63); PA to Leader Oppn 1959–62; Dir Publicity Lab Party 1962–64; Special Assist to: For Sec 1964–66, Home Sec 1966–67, Chllr Exchequer 1967–70; political correspondent *Economist* 1970–74; Min State Home Office 1974–79; memb Exec Ctee Britain in Europe 1975; Chm Parole Board England and Wales 1979–82; Tstee Police Fedn 1980–; Pres Nat Assoc Sr Probation Offrs 1983–92; memb Ho Lds Select Ctee Murder and Life Imprisonment 1988–89; Spokesman (Lib Dem) Home Affrs Ho Lds 1988–94, Ch Whip (Lib Dem) Ho Lds 1994–; PC 1998–; *m* 1st 1952 (*divorce* 1982) Patricia Margaret, dau of George Neuby Alstrom, and has issue:

1 *Francis Oliver Alstrom; *b* 1961

1 *Deborah Jane Alstrom; *b* 1958

BARON HARRIS OF GREENWICH *m* 2nd 1983 *Angela Smith

Lineage: ALFRED GEORGE HARRIS; *m* May — and had issue:

JOHN HENRY, *cr* a **Baron**

HARRIS OF HIGH CROSS

Creation: B. (LP, UK) 1979.

THE BARON HARRIS OF HIGH CROSS, of Tottenham, Greater London (Ralph Harris) [The Rt Hon The Lord Harris of High Cross, 5 Cattley Close, Wood St, Barnet, Herts EN5 4SN]; *b* 10 Dec 1924; *educ* Tottenham GS and Queens' Coll Cambridge (MA); lecturer political economy St Andrews 1949–56; leader-writer *Glasgow Herald* 1956; Gen Dir IEA 1957–87, Chm 1987–89, Fndr Pres 1992–; Chm FOREST 1987–; Independent Nat Dir Times Newspaper Hldgs 1991–; *m* 1949 *Jose Pauline, dau of Roger Frederick Jeffery, and has had:

1 Julian Paul; *b* 1956; *d* 1992

1 *Angela Caroline; *b* 1951; *m* 1977 *Roland Triponel and has issue

HARRIS OF PECKHAM

Arms: Vert a chevron argent between in chief two rolls of carpet in cross section or and gules and in base a horse statant argent. **Crest:** On a wreath or and vert a demi horse rampant argent on its head a plume of three feathers vert and resting its sinister forefoot on a tenterhook erect gules. **Supporters:** On either side a horse sable standing on a mount of grass proper issuing therefrom sprigs of broom vert flowering or and grasping in the mouth a like sprig of broom. **Motto:** *Caritas fructum habet* ('Charity bears fruit').

Creation: B. (LP, UK) Nov 1995

THE BARON HARRIS OF PECKHAM, of Peckham, London Borough of Southwark (Sir Philip Charles Harris) [The Rt Hon The Lord Harris of Peckham, House of Lords, London SW1A 0PW]; *b* 15 Sept 1942; *educ* Streatham GS; chm: Harris Queensway plc 1964–88 (ch exec 1987–88), Harris Ventures 1988–, C W Harris Properties 1988–, Carpetright plc 1993–; dir Harveys Hldgs 1986–, GUS 1986–; memb: Br Show Jumping Assoc 1974–, Cncl Govrs UMDS Guy's and St Thomas's Hosps 1984–, Court Patrons RCOG 1984–, V-Chm Lewisham Hosp NHS Tst 1993–, Chm Generation Tst 1984–, Dep Chm C Party Treasurers 1993–; ktd 1985; *m* 1960 *Pauline Norma Chumley and has three sons and a dau

Lineage: CHARLES WILLIAM HARRIS, MC; *m* Ruth Ellen Ward and had:

PHILIP CHARLES (Sir), *cr* a **Baron**

HARRISON of Bugbrooke

Creation: Bt. (UK) 6 July 1961.

SIR MICHAEL JAMES HARWOOD HARRISON, 2ND BT, of Bugbrooke, Co Northampton, JP (1993) [Sir Michael Harrison Bt JP, 35 Paultons Sq, London SW3 5DT; Rise Cottage, Hasketon, Suffolk IP13 6JA]; *b* 28 March 1936; *s* f 1980; *educ* Rugby; late 17th/21st Lancers, Underwriting Memb Lloyd's 1964–96, Cncl memb Sail Trg Assoc 1966– (Dep Chm Tall Ships 1995–), V-Pres Assoc of Combined Youth Clubs, patron and Ld Manor Bugbrooke, Freeman City London, Liveryman Mercer's Co (Master 1986–87), Chm Berrite Ltd; *m* 22 July 1967 *(Rosamund) Louise, only dau of Edward Buxton Clive, of Swanmore Lodge, Swanmore, Hants, and has:

1 +EDWIN MICHAEL HARWOOD; *b* 29 May 1981

2 +Tristan John; *b* 22 April 1986

1 *(Auriol) Davina; *b* 27 May 1968

2 *Priscilla Caroline; *b* 30 April 1971

Lineage: Rev ROBERT HARRISON; *educ* Queen's Coll Oxford (MA 1660); Rector Wyfordby, Leics; *m* Katherine — (*d* 1696) and *d* 21 Sept 1692, leaving:

Rev ROBERT HARRISON; *b* 1666; *educ* Magdalen Hall Oxford (BA 1687); Rector Nether Broughton 1710, Min Dalby-on-the-Wolds, Leics; *m* Barbara — (*d* 1730) and *d* 1740, having had, with 11 other children:

LEWIS HARRISON, of Stony Stratford, Bucks; *b* 27 Oct 1711; Supervisor Excise Serv; *m* 1st 1738 Mary (*d* 1743), dau of Henry Bagshaw, of Frolesworth, Leics; *m* 2nd 1747 Prudence Kingston, of Crowland, Lincs, and by his 1st w had:

HENRY BAGSHAW, of Daventry; *b* 1740; attorney; *m* 22 June 1762 Catherine (*d* 12 Sept 1820), dau of Samuel Wymant, Bailiff Daventry 1727 and 1742, and *d* 16 Feb 1801, leaving with other issue:

1 HENRY BAGSHAW (Rev)

2 Samuel Wyment, DL Northants; *b* 1767; *d* 1842

3 William Bagshaw (Rev); *b* 1769; Vicar Goudhurst; *m* Charlotte Tonkin (*d* 1853) and *d* 1849, leaving two sons and seven daus

1 Catherine; *m* Rev William Benson, DD, Fell Queen's Coll Oxford

The est son,

Rev HENRY BAGSHAW HARRISON, DD, Patron and Rector Bugbrooke, Northants; *b* 27 Aug 1764; *educ* Rugby and Magdalen Coll Oxford (MA 1788, DD 1821); *m* Sarah (*b* 28 Feb 1760; *d* 23 Oct 1812), dau of Rev James Harwood, of The Vicarage House, Dartford, Kent, by Rebecca Chase, of Bromley, Kent, and *d* 5 Sept 1830, having had, with two other sons:

1 JAMES HARWOOD (Rev)

2 William (Rev); Rector Warmington, Warwicks; *b* 17 Jan 1800; *m* Mary Anne Harrison and had four sons and five daus

1 Mary Anna; *b* 29 Oct 1801; *m* Rev Richard Rocke, Rector Lynton, Rutland, and *d* 18 March 1832, leaving issue

The est surv s,

Rev JAMES HARWOOD HARRISON, JP; Patron and Rector Bugbrooke; *b* 1799; *educ* Rugby and Merton Coll Oxford (BA 1823, MA 1825); *m* 1st Gertrude Maria, dau of Capt Hickman Leland Rose, of Bath, and had, with two other sons:

1 (JAMES) HARWOOD (Rev)

2 Henry Leland (Sir); ktd 1887, Bengal CS, Commr Police and Chm Corp Calcutta; *b* 5 Feb 1837; *educ* Ch Ch Oxford (Pres Union, Racquets Blue); *m* Fanny Matilda, dau of Gilbert a Becket, and *d* 5 May 1892, leaving seven children

3 William John Rose; *b* 12 April 1840; *m* Adela A, dau of Dr — Hunt, of Bath, and *d* 1 Oct 1878, leaving issue

1 Gertrude Rose; *b* 23 July 1835; *m* 1862 Lt-Col Henry Thomas Salmon, JP, DL, of Tockington Manor, Olveston, Glos, er s of Thomas Stokes Salmon, of Tockington, and *d* 1906, leaving issue. He *d* 10 Dec 1900

The Rev JAMES HARRISON *m* 2nd Charlotte (*d* 1848), yst dau of Edward Grant, of Lichborough Hall, Northants; *m* 3rd 1863 Charlotte Maule (*d* 10 Aug 1887) and *d* 7 Feb 1890

The est son,

Rev (JAMES) HARWOOD HARRISON; Patron and Rector Bugbrooke; *b* 10 March 1834; *educ* Harrow and Magdalen Coll Oxford (MA 1859); *m* his cousin Emily Wade Holden (*d* 29 April 1879), dau of Lt-Col Holden Rose JP, DL, 9th/17th Lancers, of Wivelsfield, Sussex, and *d* 5 June 1895, having had, with three er sons (*d* young):

1 ERNEST WIVELSFIELD

2 Arthur Rocke (Rev); *b* 23 Sept 1874; *educ* Clare Coll Cambridge; *d* 23 Feb 1936

1 Emily Gertrude; *b* 3 Sept 1865; *m* 25 April 1900 William Henry Long, of The Manor House, Bugbrooke, and *d* 28 Oct 1950, leaving a s and dau

The est surv s,

Rev ERNEST WIVELSFIELD HARRISON; CC Northants 1907–19, Patron and Rector Bugbrooke 1900–20, RD 1915–20; *b* 29 Oct 1870; *educ* Uppingham, RAC Cirencester and Cambridge U (non-collegiate) (BA 1898, MA 1902); *m* 9 June 1904 Edith Eliza (*d* 4 June 1971), dau of William Foard Tribe, of Broadwater Manor, Worthing, Sussex, and *d* 31 Oct 1920, leaving:

1 (JAMES) HARWOOD (Sir), **1st Bt**

2 Charles Laud (Rev Canon); Rector Bugbrooke 1938–75, RD 1960, non-Residentary Canon Peterborough 1963, Chaplain RAFVR WW II, Curate-in-Charge Heyford 1949–51; *b* 12 March 1909; *educ* Northampton GS and Exeter Coll Oxford (BA 1931, MA 1938); *m* 18 Nov 1947 Jean McClean (*d* 4 Sept 1990), dau of Rev Elliot Wilkins Perry, of Clifton, Bristol, and *d* 9 Nov 1977, leaving:

(1) *Ernest Charles; *b* 28 Jan 1950; *educ* Marlborough; *m* 10 Nov 1971 *Anne Claire, dau of Thomas B Siddell, of Pinner, Middx

3 Ernest William; Lt Durham LI WW II; *b* 22 Oct 1910; *educ* Northampton GS and St John's Coll Oxford; *ka* unm France May 1940

4 Henry Holden Rose; company dir, C of E lay reader; *b* 14 Oct 1915; *educ* Eastbourne Coll; *m* 26 June 1958 *Margaret Joyce, dau of William Hedley Perry, of Cyncoed, Cardiff, and *d* 9 Sept 1975, leaving:

(1) *Paul Hedley Rose; *b* 22 Oct 1959; *educ* Oundle, Merton Coll Oxford (MA) and Edmonton U (PhD); *m* 1st 1984 (*divorce* 19–) —; *m* 2nd 17 Sept 1994 *Kary Kathleen, dau of John W McCahill, of Dundas, Ontario, and has by her:

1a *Simon John McCahill; *b* 6 Nov 1994

(1) *Rosemary Jane; *b* 19 Jan 1964

The est son,

Sir (James) Harwood Harrison, 1st Bt (UK), so *cr* 6 July 1961, TD (1948) and two bars (1948 and 1951); *b* 6 June 1907; *educ* Northampton GS and Trin Coll Oxford (BA 1928, MA 1946); memb Ipswich Borough Cncl 1935–46, Chm: Mental Hospital Ctee 1938–39, Daventry Jr Imp League 1929–31, Treas Woodbridge Jr Imp League 1933–38, MP (C) Eye 1951–79, PPS to Sec State Housing 1953–54, Assist Govt Whip 1954–56, Ld Commr Treasury 1956–59, Comptroller Household 1959–61, commnd 4th Bn Suffolk Regt TA 1935, Capt 1939, Maj 1940 WW II, Lt-Col cmdg 4th Suffolks 1946–51, Brevet-Col 1951, TARO 1951, Pres Ipswich and Dist Far East POW Fellowship 1953, Chm: Eastern Area C Assoc 1956–59 (Pres 1963–66), U Club 1966, Cdre H of C Yacht Club 1969, Chm Select Sub Ctee Def and Overseas Affrs 1971–79; *m* 16 Jan 1932 Peggy Alberta Mary (*d* 3 Dec 1993), dau of Lt-Col Vivian Denman Stenhouse, TD, JP, of Windy Corner, Minehead, Somerset, and *d* 11 Sept 1980, leaving issue:

1 Sir MICHAEL JAMES HARWOOD HARRISON, **2nd and present Bt**

1 *Joanna Kathleen [Mrs William Sanders, Nine Chimney House, Balsham, Cambs CB1 6ES]; *b* 16 Nov 1939; *m* 16 April 1966 *William Ashton Sanders, s of Rev John Kingsley Sanders, and has issue:

(1) *James William Ashton; *b* 19 June 1968; *educ* Eton and Exeter Coll Oxford (MA 1993)

HARRISON of Eaglecliffe

Arms: Per chevron az. and or., in chief two demi-lions rampant of the second, and in base a lymphad sa. **Crest:** Upon a fernbrake a falcon rising ppr., belled and charged on the sinister wing with a fleur-de-lys or. **Motto:** *Dum spiro spero* ('While I breathe, I hope'). **Creation:** Bt. (UK) 15 June 1922.

SIR (ROBERT) COLIN HARRISON, 4TH BT, of Eaglescliffe, Co Durham [Sir Colin Harrison Bt, Stearsby Hall, Stearsby, York YO6 4SA]; *b* 25 May 1938; *s* bro 1955; *educ* Radley and St John's Coll Cambridge (BA); late 5th Roy Northumberland Fus, chm John Harrison (Stockton) Ltd, v-chm Darlington Bldg Soc, Gen Tax Commr; *m* 27 July 1963 *Maureen Marie, er dau of Ernest Leonard Chiverton, JP, of Garth Corner, Kirby Moorside, Yorks, and has issue:

1 +JOHN WYNDHAM FOWLER; *b* 4 Dec 1972

1 *Rachel Deborah; *b* 22 April 1966; *m* 1991 *Alistair G Waddell, er s of W Waddell, of Troon, Ayrshire

2 *Claire Grace; *b* 1974

Lineage: THOMAS HARRISON, of Stockton-on-Tees; *d* 25 July 1870, leaving:

JOHN HARRISON, of Stockton-on-Tees; *b* 1827; *m* Sarah (*d* 1870), dau of William Spence, of Helmsley, Yorks, and *d* 1887, leaving issue:

Sir John Harrison, 1st Bt (UK), so *cr* 15 June 1922, JP; Mayor Stockton-on-Tees 1903, 1906, 1916, 1917 and 1918, Chm Stockton Mil Tbnl and Food Control Ctee WW I, ktd 1919; *b* 27 Dec 1856; *m* 10 Oct 1892 Clara Elizabeth (*d* 19 Jan 1945), dau of Jonathan Fowler, of Eaglescliffe, and had issue:

1 JOHN FOWLER (Sir), **2nd Bt**,

1 Mabel; *m* 16 Feb 1922 Raymond C Taylor, shipbuilder (*d* 1953)

2 Marjorie; *m* 29 April 1926 Cyril E M Robinson, s of Matthias Robinson, and had issue

Sir JOHN *d* 14 Feb 1936; his son,

Sir John Fowler Harrison, 2nd Bt; *b* 8 Feb 1899; *m* 29 April 1930 Kathleen (*d* 1993), dau of Robert Livingston, of The Gables, Eaglescliffe, Co Durham, and *d* 24 May 1947, leaving:

1 **Sir (John) Wyndham Harrison, 3rd Bt**; *b* 13 Jan 1933; *educ* Radley and Loughborough Tech; *d* unm 24 June 1955

2 Sir ROBERT COLIN HARRISON, **4th and present Bt**

1 *Judith May *b* 7 Aug 1935; *m* 28 April 1962 *Paul Standing, s of Hugh Standing, of Hove, and has issue:

(1) *Christopher Hugh; *b* 4 Feb 1965

(1) *Jane Kathleen; *b* 18 Aug 1963

HARROWBY

Arms: Quarterly, 1st and 4th, az. three crescents or, on each an erm. spot sa. (for RYDER); 2nd and 3rd, gu. three lapwings or, within a bordure arg. (for TERRICK). **Crest:** Out of a mural coronet or a dragon's head arg., on the neck an erm. spot sa. **Supporters:** Two griffins, wings elevated arg., on the shoulder of each an erm. spot sa., each gorged with a plain collar az., charged with three crescents or, chained of the last. **Motto:** *Servata fides cineri* ('Faith kept with the ashes of ancestors'). **Creations:** B. (GB) 20 May 1776, E. and V. (UK) 19 July 1809.

THE 7TH EARL OF HARROWBY, Co Lincoln, **Viscount Sandon**, of Sandon, Co Stafford, and **Baron Harrowby**, of Harrowby, Co Lincoln (Dudley Danvers Granville Coutts Ryder, TD) [The Rt Hon The Earl of Harrowby TD, 5 Tregunter Rd, London SW10 9LS; Sandon Hall, nr Stone, Staffs ST18 OBZ; Burnt Norton, Chipping Campden, Glos GL55 6PR]; *b* 20 Dec 1922; *s f* 1987; *educ* Eton; Lt-Col RA (TA) WW II with 59th Inf Div 5 Parachute Bde NW Europe (wounded), India and Java (Pol Offr) 56 Armoured Div 1941–45, OC 254 (City of London) Field Regt RA (TA) 1962–65; md Coutts & Co 1949–70 (dep chm 1970–89), dir: Nat Provincial Bank 1964–69, Nat Westminster Bank 1968–87 (dep chm 1971–87, chm: Internat Nat Westminster Bank 1977–87 and Nat Westminster Investment Bank 1986–87), Olympia Gp 1968–73, Sheepbridge Engrg 1977–79 and UK Provident Inst 1955–86, Memb: Bd Govrs Keele U 1956–58, Kensington Borough Cncl 1950–65, Kensington and Chelsea Borough Cncl 1965–71, Pres Wolverhampton SW C and U Assoc 1959–68, Hon Treas Staffs Soc 1947–51 (Pres 1957–59, Chm 1957–59), Chm: Inst of Psychiatry and Bethlem Royal and Maudsley Hosps, Dowty Gp plc 1986–91, Powell Duffryn Gp 1981–86 (dir 1976–86), Dep Chm: Teaching Hosps Assoc 1968–69, Lond Postgraduate Ctee, Family Welfare Assoc 1951–65 and S Kensington C Assoc 1953–56, Hon Treas Centl Cncl Care of Cripples 1953–60, Gen Commr Income Tax 1954–71, memb Ld Chllr's Advsy Investment Ctee for Court of Protection 1965–77, Bd Govrs Roy and Maudsley (Postgraduate Teaching) Hosps 1955–73 (Chm 1965–73), Tstee Psychiatry Research Tst 1982–, Hon FRC Psych 1983; *m* 14 June 1949 Jeanette Rosalthé (*d* 27 Jan 1997), yr dau of Capt Peter Johnston-Saint, MA, FRS Edin, FZA, CStJ, and has issue:

1 +DUDLEY ADRIAN CONROY, *Viscount Sandon* [Viscount Sandon, c/o Sandon Estate Office, Sandon, nr Stone, Staffs ST18 0DA]; *b* 18 March 1951; *educ* Eton, U of Newcastle-upon-Tyne and Magdalene Coll Cambridge (MA); dir Compton Street Securities 1988–, V-Pres Staffs CPRE 1988–95, Patron Guild of Handicraft Tst 1991–, Pres Staffs Soc 1995–97, govr John Archer Sch Wandsworth 1986–88, FRICS; *m* 1st 16 July 1977 Sarah Nichola Hobhouse (*d* 29 Dec 1994), only dau of Capt Anthony Denys Phillpots Payne; *m* 2nd 2 May 1998 *Mrs Caroline Coram James, dau of Geoffrey Markes, and by his 1st w has:

(1) +Dudley Anthony Hugo Coventry; *b* 5 Sept 1981

(2) +Frederick (Freddie) Whitmore Dudley; *b* 1984

(3) +Henry Mansell Dudley; *b* 1985

(1) *Emily Georgina Hobhouse; *b* 1992

1 *Rosalthé Frances [The Lady Rosalthé Rundall, Greater Aston Farmhouse, Aston-sub-Edge, Glos]; *b* 1 May 1954; *m* 23 June 1976 *Francis Richard Seton Rundall, yr s of Frank Lionel Montagu Rundall, of Stonleigh House, Longborough, Glos, and has issue:

(1) *(Francis) Thomas Mansell; *b* 1981

(2) *Mark Dudley Ridgway; *b* 1982

(3) *John William Nathaniel; *b* 1987

Lineage: ROBERT RYDER, of Wisbech, Cambs; had:

Rev DUDLEY RYDER, of Bedworth, Warwicks; MA; non-conformist Minister; *b* 1628; *m* Anne, n of Sir Francis Bickley, 1st Bt, and dau of Richard Bickley, of Hallaughton, Warwicks, and *d* 1682, leaving a 2nd s:

RICHARD RYDER, of Hackney, Middx; skinner, Master Skinners' Co 1717; *b* Aug 1657; *m* 2nd Elizabeth, dau of William Marshall, of Lincoln's Inn, and *d* Jan 1735, leaving a 2nd s:

Sir DUDLEY RYDER; *b* 4 Nov 1691; *educ* at a dissenting acad at Hackney; MP St Germans 1733 and Tiverton 1733–54, barrister, Slr-Gen 1733, Attorney-Gen 1737 (as which he was the chief prosecutor of the leading Jacobites involved in the '45), Ch Justice King's Bench 1754–56; *m* 1 Nov 1733 Ann (*d* 9 May 1774), dau of Nathaniel Newnham, MP, of Streatham, Surrey, and *d* 25 May 1756 the day after a warrant to ennoble him had been signed, leaving:

NATHANIEL RYDER, **1st Baron Harrowby**, of Harrowby, Co Lincoln (GB), so *cr* 20 May 1776; *b* 3 July 1735; *educ* Clare Hall Cambridge; MA, MP (Whig) Tiverton 1756–76, bought the Sandon estate; *m* 22 Jan 1762 Elizabeth (*d* 24 Aug 1804), est dau and coheir of Richard Terrick, DD, Bp London, and had issue:

1 DUDLEY, **1st Earl**

2 Richard, PC, of Westbrook Hay, Bovingdon, Herts; MP; Home Sec 1809–12; *b* 5 July 1766; *m* 1 Aug 1799 Frederica (*d* 8 Aug 1821), dau of Sir John Skynner, and *dsps* 18 Sept 1832

3 Henry (Rt Rev); Bp Lichfield and Coventry; *b* 21 July 1777; *m* 15 Dec 1802 Sophia (*d* 30 Aug 1862), 2nd dau of Thomas March Phillipps, of Garendon Park, Leics, and *d* 31 March 1836, having had, with other issue:

(1) Henry Dudley (Rev); Canon-Residentiary Lichfield; *b* 13 Oct 1803; *m* 1st 8 May 1828 Cornelia Sarah (*d* 16 April 1840), dau of George Cornish, of Salcombe, and had, with other issue:

1a Louisa Cornelia; *m* Dec 1859 John George Cope Lewis Newnham, Consul Amsterdam, and *d* 14 March 1917, aged 83, leaving issue. He *d* 1882

(1) (cont.) The Rev Henry Ryder *m* 2nd 27 March 1841 Eliza Julia (*d* 11 Feb 1897), dau of Lt-Col John Tucker, and *d* 19 Jan 1877, having by her had issue:

1a Harry Lefevre; Lt RN; *b* 1844; *m* 21 March 1872 Frances Elizabeth (*d* 28 April 1901), dau of John Blackie, and *dsp* 14 June 1880 aboard HMS *Atalanta*

2a Edith; *m* 18 April 1882 Sir George Lisle Ryder, KCB (*see below*), and *dsp* 18 Nov 1920. He *d* 30 June 1905

(2) George Dudley; *b* 11 April 1810; *m* 5 June 1834 Sophia Lucy (*d* 21 March 1850), yst dau of Rev John Sargent, and *d* 19 June 1880, having had issue:

1a Henry Ignatius Dudley (Very Rev); RC Priest, Superior the Oratory Edgbaston; *b* 12 Jan 1837; *d* 7 Oct 1907

2a George Lisle (Sir), KCB; Chm Bd Customs 1899–1903; *b* 29 Dec 1838; *m* 18 April 1882 his cousin Edith (*d* 18 Nov 1920), dau of Rev Henry Ryder (*see above*), and *dsp* 30 June 1905

3a Charles Edward (Rev); RC priest; *b* 30 April 1842; *d* 2 May 1912

4a Cyril (Rev); RC priest; *b* 15 July 1844; *d* 1 Feb 1931

1a Caroline Alice; *m* 17 Oct 1860 Henry Clutton and *d* 10 April 1934, leaving issue. He *d* 1893

2a Cecilia Mary; nun; *d* 7 March 1939

3a Beatrice Mary; *m* 24 Nov 1874 Richard Hurrell Froude, of Chelston Cross, Devon, and *d* 1877 aged 28, leaving issue

(3) William Dudley; Arbitrator Mixed Court New York; *b* 13 Oct 1813; *d* unm 11 April 1894

(4) Thomas Dudley; Registrar Diocese of Manchester; *b* 17 April 1815; *d* 23 Jan 1886

(5) Alfred Phillips (Sir), GCB; Adml of the Fleet, Kt Medjidie; *b* 27 June 1820; *m* 29 June 1852 Louisa (*d* 1855), est dau of Henry Dawson, of Launde Abbey, and *d* 30 April 1888, having had issue:

1a Edward Lisle; *b* 1853; *m* 14 June 1877 Agnes Augusta, dau of J L Bickley, and *d* 28 Sept 1877

(6) Spencer Charles Dudley; Lt-Col BSC; *b* 29 June 1825; *m* 22 Nov 1849 Julia (*d* 27 March 1902), est dau of Rev William Money, and *d* 3 March 1873, having had, with other issue:

1a Edward Dudley; RN; *b* 15 June 1866; lost in HMS *Captain* 7 Sept 1870

2a Wilfred Ironside; Lt-Col IA, served Sikkim 1888, Waziristan 1894, Tirah 1897 (Brevet Maj), Boer War 1900–01 and WW I; *b* 24 June 1866; *m* 22 Aug 1901 Tempé Rosa Ridhalgh (*d* 13 March 1942), dau of Maj-Gen James Edmund Bacon Parsons, BSC, and *d* 23 Dec 1948, leaving issue:

1b *Joan Tempé [Mrs Francis Maitland, Pullens End Cottage, Pullens Lane, Headington, Oxon]; *b* 15 Oct 1902; *m* 9 July 1945 Francis Edward Maitland (*d* Dec 1963)

2b *Margery Julia [Mrs Margery Meeres, Boult's Lodge, Boult's Lane, Marston, Oxford]; *b* 16 Jan 1904, ARIBA; *m* 29 Aug 1934 (*divorce* 1948) Capt Charles Oliver Meeres, RFA, s of Col A D Meeres, JP, of Forder House, Moretonhampstead

3a Charles Henry Dudley, CB (1922), CIE (1915), DSO (1905); FRGS , Col RE China, Tibet and WW I; *b* 28 June 1868; *m* 27 Dec 1892 Ida Josephine (*d* 25 July 1948), est dau of Lt-Col Edward Evans Grigg, ISC, and *d* 13 July 1945, leaving:

1b Lisle Charles Dudley; Maj Norfolk Regt WW II; *b* 31 Aug 1902; *educ* Cheltenham; *m* 22 Feb 1938 Enid Helen Constance (*d* 1977), only child of Maj Robert Ralston-Patrick, of Trearne and Roughwood, Ayrshire, and was *ka* May 1940, leaving:

1c +Ralston Patrick Dudley [Ralston Ryder Esq, 7518 Knickerbocker Rd, Ontario, NY 14519, USA]; *b* 22 June 1939; *educ* Harrow

2b Ernle Terrick Dudley; Maj 1st Gurkha Rifles WW II; *b* 18 April 1906; *m* 12 Sept 1936 *Daphne Joan Pillans [Mrs Ernle Ryder, Fox Covert Cottage, Priory Lane, Warfield, Berks], only child of John Greig, and was *ka* at sea off Sumatra on or shortly after 28 Feb 1942, leaving:

1c *Elizabeth Jean [Mrs James Vernon, Briarwood, East End, Lymington, Hants]; *b* 8 March 1938; *m* 12 Sept 1959 *James John Vernon, MA, late Headmaster Hordle House Prep Sch, s of James Anthony Vernon, MRCS, LRCP, and has:

1d *James Michael; *b* 16 June 1960; *m* 1994 *Mhairi Patricia, est dau of Maj John Nisbet, of Blackadder, Berwicks

2d *Peter John; *b* 10 March 1963; *m* 1988 *Patricia Jean, dau of J C N Nicol, and has issue:

1e *Kate Elizabeth Ryder; *b* 1992

2e *Philippa Carolyn Nicol; *b* 1994

3d *William Ernle Hardy; *b* 25 May 1965; *m* 1988 *Emma Mary, yst dau of Sir John Barry Salusbury-Trelawny, 13th Bt (*qv*) and has:

1e *Thomas Lisle Trelawney; *b* 1 Oct 1997

1e *Elizabeth; *b* 19–

1d *Julia Elizabeth; *b* 5 Oct 1961; *m* 1992 *Jonathan Denton, er s of John Denton, and has:
1e *Douglas John; *b* 1994
2e *Edward James; *b* 1996
2c *Anthea Daphne [Mrs Donald Brown, 357 Boston Rd, Ontario, NY 14519, USA]; *b* 15 May 1940; *m* 28 Nov 1968 *Donald Leroy Brown and has issue:
1d *Andrew Kevin; *b* 28 Sept 1972
3b Robert Edward Dudley, VC (1942); Capt RN, MP (C) Merton and Morden Feb 1950–May 1955, served WW II (despatches four times, Legion of Honour and Croix de Guerre), explorer: Pacific and Atlantic in small boat, cmded ship transporting Rymill expdn to Antarctic 1934–37; Polar Medal; *b* 16 Feb 1908; *educ* Cheltenham; *m* 26 April 1941 (Constance) Hilaré Myfanwy (*d* 1982), 3rd dau of Rev Lumley Green-Wilkinson (*see* 1940 edn EDWARDS, Bt), and *d* 1986, leaving:
1c +Lisle Robert Dudley [The Rev Canon Lisle Ryder, 1 Holywell Hill, Henwick Rd, Worcs]; late Sub-Lt RN; *b* 3 Jan 1943; *educ* Eton and Selwyn Coll Cambridge (BA 1968, MA); Dip Pastoral Studies Birmingham, Hon Canon Worcester 1989; *m* 19 March 1977 *Olivia Elvira, dau of Col Roland Stephen Langton, MVO, MC, and has issue:
1d +Philip Robert Dudley; *b* 1982
1d *Harriet Elvira; *b* 1980
1c *Susan Myfanwy Prudence [Mrs Martin Bates, 17 Queen's Gate Place, London SW7 5NY]; *b* 14 March 1944; *m* 2 Oct 1965 *Martin Graves Bates (*see* BATES, Bt, of Bellefield) and has issue
1b Ida Margaret Clare; *b* 16 Sept 1893; *m* 9 Nov 1915 Lt-Col Claude Phineas Bookey Riall, E Yorks Regt, est s of Cdr Arthur George Roberts Riall, RN, and *d* 14 June 1954, leaving issue. He *d* 10 June 1952
2b Enid Muriel Money; *b* 13 May 1895; *m* 1st 7 Oct 1919 Lt-Col Neil Alister Henry Campbell (*see* CAWDOR, E); *m* 2nd 1956 Maj Wigram Money (*d* 1959)
3b Violet Constance; *b* 23 Nov 1898; *m* 30 Dec 1931 Lt-Col Geoffrey Walter Lawson, Somerset LI, s of William Edward Lawson, JP, and *d* 28 March 1995, leaving:
1c *Julian Richard; *b* 1933; *m* 1977 *Beverley Ann, dau of C T Coleman, of Isca, Brecon, Powys
1a Una Sophia; *d* unm 17 March 1941
(1) Anna Sophia; *m* 14 Aug 1827 Sir George Grey, 2nd Bt (*qv*), and *d* 8 July 1893 aged 88, having had issue
1 Elizabeth; *d* 29 Oct 1830
2 Anne; *d* 1801

The 1st BARON *d* 20 June 1803; his son,

DUDLEY RYDER, **1st Earl of Harrowby**, Co Lincoln, so *cr* 19 July 1809, as also VISCOUNT SANDON, of Sandon, Co Stafford (both UK), PC (1790); *b* 22 Dec 1762; *educ* St John's Coll Cambridge; MA, LLD, DCL and FSA, Tstee Br Museum, High Steward Tiverton, MP (Tory) Tiverton 1784–1803, Under For Sec 1789, Comptroller Household 1790–91, Paymaster Gen 1790, Treasurer Navy 1799–1801, For Sec 1804–06, Chllr Duchy Lancaster 1805–06, Amb Berlin 1805–06, Pres India Bd 1809, Ld Pres Cncl 1812–27; *m* 30 July 1795 Lady Susan Leveson-Gower (*d* 26 May 1838 aged 66), dau of 1st Marquess of Stafford (*see* SUTHERLAND, D), and *d* 26 Dec 1847, having had:

1 DUDLEY RYDER, **2nd Earl of Harrowby**, KG (1859), PC (1855); *b* 19 May 1798; *educ* Ch Ch Oxford; DCL, FRS, memb Ecclesiastical Commn, MP (Tory) Tiverton 1819–31 and Liverpool (Tory, then Peelite, later (as a peer) Lib, lastly C) 1831–47, Chllr Duchy Lancaster 1855, Ld Privy Seal 1855–57, Pres Br Assoc; *m* 15 Sept 1823 Lady Frances Stuart (*d* 29 March 1859), 4th dau of 1st Marquess of Bute (*qv*), and *d* 19 Nov 1882, having had, with other issue:
(1) DUDLEY FRANCIS STUART RYDER, **3rd Earl of Harrowby**, PC (1874), JP, DL, Staffs; *b* 16 Jan 1831; *educ* Harrow and Ch Ch Oxford; Chm Staffs CC, MP (Lib) Lichfield 1856–59 and (C) Liverpool 1868–82, V-Pres Ctee Cncl on Educn 1874–78, Pres BOT 1878–80, Ld Privy Seal 1885–86; *m* 3 Oct 1861 Lady Mary Frances Cecil (*d* 27 July 1917), est dau of 2nd Marquess of Exeter (*qv*), and *dsp* 26 March 1900
(2) HENRY DUDLEY, **4th Earl**
2 Granville Dudley, of Westbrook Hay, Bovingdon; MP Tiverton 1830–32 and Herts 1841–46, Lt RN; *b* 26 Nov 1799; *m* 30 May 1825 Lady Georgiana Augusta Somerset (*d* 30 March 1865), 3rd dau of 6th Duke of Beaufort (*qv*), and *d* 24 Nov 1879, having had, with five daus and another s (*d* young):
(1) Dudley Henry, of Westbrook Hay, JP Herts; *b* 7 Feb 1830; *m* 1 Dec 1857 Georgiana Emily (*d* 10 July 1915), dau of John Hales Calcraft, MP (*see* MANCHESTER, D), and *d* 8 Sept 1911, having had issue:
1a Dudley Granville Richard, of Westbrook Hay, JP Herts; *b* 30 Sept 1858; Lt-Col KRRC; *m* 24 Oct 1889 Ada Carr (*d* 1950), dau of Lt-Gen Sir John Plumptre Carr-Glyn, KCB (*see* GLYN, Bt), and *d* 27 June 1926
2a Cyril John; Capt KRRC; *b* 8 July 1863; *m* 8 July 1897 Lady Isobel Douglas-Hamilton (*see* HAMILTON and BRANDON, D) and *d* 28 Dec 1907, leaving:
1b Dudley Claud Douglas; Maj 5th Bn Dorset Regt (TA); *b* 27 April 1901; *educ* Sherborne and Pembroke Coll Cambridge (BA); *m* 1st 27 Oct 1927 (*divorce* 1938) Nancy Edith (*d* 1985), dau of Edgar Morris Baker, and had:
1c +James Calcraft Dudley [James Ryder Esq, Rempstone Hall, Corfe Castle, Dorset]; 2nd Lt KORR; *b* 19 May 1934; *educ* Sherborne and RAC Cirencester; *m* 1st 9 July 1966 (*divorce* 1979) Sarah Victoria, only dau of Michael Guy Bircham; *m* 2nd 1984 *Georgina Susan, only dau of Edward George Adrian Farnham, of Quorn House, Quorn, Leics, and formerly w of Charles Howard Cole, and by his 1st w has:
1d *Lara Caroline Dudley; *b* 7 March 1968
2d *Melanie Isobel; *b* 1970
3d *Emma Katherine; *b* 1974
2c +Benjamin Guy Dudley [Benjamin Ryder Esq, The Old Farmhouse, Rempstone, Dorset]; *b* 19 May 1934; *educ* Sherborne; *m* 8 Oct 1960 *Philippa Mary, dau of Alan Maitland Cunningham, of Compton House, Wareham, Dorset, and has issue:
1d +Douglas Alan Dudley; *b* 25 Jan 1963; *m* 1988 (*divorce* 1997) Rosemary Victoria Clara Pemble
2d +Guy; *b* 11 Jan 1968; *m* 16 March 1997 *Julia Mercedes, dau of David Grynyer, of Alveston Ho, Winterbourne Zelston, Dorset
1d *Vanessa Frances; *b* 26 Sept 1965
1c *Gabriel Nancy [Lady Coghill, Sourden, Rothes, Aberlour, Banffshire AB38 7AE]; *b* 16 Aug 1928; *m* 12 April 1958 Sir Egerton James Nevill Tobias (Toby) Coghill, 8th Bt (*qv*), and has issue
2c *Jenifer Cherry [Mrs Jeremy Browne, Higher Houghton, Blandford, Dorset]; *b* 20 Aug 1929; *m* 4 July 1953 *Jeremy Charles Browne, yst s of Lt-Col William Percy Browne, MC, JP, and has had issue:
1d Rupert Michael; *b* 26 Nov; *d* 30 Nov 1954
2d *Simon Jeremy; *b* 26 June 1957
1d *Katherine Richenda; *b* 8 Jan 1956
2d *Sarah Caroline; *b* 17 March 1960
3d *Emily Charlotte; *b* 7 Feb 1965
3c *Jacqueline Iris; *b* 13 Nov 1930; *m* 4 May 1957 (*divorce* 1969) Thomas Ralph Winser, only s of James Knight Winser and Mrs Joan Sanderson, and has had issue:
1d Hugh James; *b* 27 Nov 1958; *d* 1992
1d *Polly Joan; *b* 30 Oct 1959
2d *Tamsin Jacqueline; *b* 12 July 1962
1b (cont.) Maj Dudley Ryder *m* 2nd 14 Oct 1938 Vera Mary (*d* 1980), formerly w of George Mervyn Anstey Hamilton-Fletcher, JP, and er dau of Sir Herbert Frederick Cook, 3rd Bt, of Richmond (*qv*), and *d* 1986, leaving:
3c +Richard Hood Jack Dudley; *b* 3 July 1940; *educ* Sherborne, Pembroke Coll Cambridge (MA, PhD), Columbia U New York and Edin U (Dip Clin Psychology 1967); Sr Clinical Psychologist Warneford Hosp Oxford 1967–84, Chm RSPCA 1977–79 (V-Chm 1990–91, memb cncl 1972–), fought (Lib) Buckingham 1983, Teignbridge 1987 gen elections, parly consultant Political Animal Lobby Ltd 1991–; *m* 1974 *Audrey Jane, dau of Frank Rae Arthur Smith, and has:
1d +Henry Arthur Woden Calcraft Dudley; *b* 1981
1d *Emily Nancy Charlotte; *b* 10 Dec 1978
1b Iris Katharine; *b* 10 Aug 1899
2b Patience Evelyn; *b* 22 June 1905; *d* unm 1944
3a William Henry; Midshipman RN Egypt 1882 (medal and star); *b* 7 Jan 1865; *m* 1st 1 Aug 1888 Catherine Mabel (*d* 21 Sept 1900), dau of Rev Augustus Sutton (*see* SUTTON, Bt), and had:
1b Dudley William; Lt RN WW I; *b* 1893; *das* 1917
3a (cont.) William Ryder *m* 2nd 1 July 1903 Florence Frances Augusta (*d* 6 Aug 1930), dau of Capt Frederick Augustus Campbell (*see* CAMPBELL, Bt, *cr* 1815), and *d* 24 Feb 1933, having by her had:
2b Frederick Granville Dudley; Cdr RNVR WW II, 2nd Lt Herts Regt TA; *b* 28 May 1905; *m* 1st 11 Jan 1929 (*divorce* 1934) Gillian Eleanor (*d* 10 Oct 1956), only dau of Charles Henry Bourne Quennell, of Berkhamsted, and had:
1c +Richard Peter Guy Dudley [Richard Ryder, Hardway House, 3411 Poinciana Avenue, Miami, FL, USA]; admin staff Miami-Dade Jr Coll; *b* 24 Dec 1929; *educ* U of Miami (MA); *m* 24 Nov 1955 *Angela Joan, dau of Morris Melotti, of Johnstown, Pa., and has issue:
1d +Christopher Frederick Dudley; *b* 23 Nov 1959
2d +Mark Campbell Dudley; *b* 11 July 1963
2b (cont.) Cdr Frederick Ryder *m* 2nd 2 Jan 1939 (Muriel) Eleanor (*d* 29 May 1975), dau of William S Corby, of Washington, DC, and *d* 14 Feb 1970
4a Charles Edward Henry; *b* 17 Sept 1868; *ka* Boer War 6 Oct 1900
5a Cosmo Alan Cuthbert; *b* 29 Aug 1870; *d* 20 May 1917
6a John Claud Dudley (Rev); MA Cantab; missionary; *b* 24 Sept 1873; *dsp* 1 June 1900
1a Katherine Susan; *d* 24 March 1922
2a Evelyn Georgiana; *d* unm 1940
3a Caroline Katharine; *m* 8 Jan 1891 Robert Armitage, JP, MP Centl Leeds 1906–22, of Farnley Hall, Leeds, and Dinish Island, Kenmare, Co Kerry, and *d* 14 Feb 1933, leaving issue. He *d* 10 Feb 1944
(2) Granville Richard; MA Oxon, barrister, MP Salisbury 1874–80; *b* 22 Sept 1833; *m* 19 March 1864 Sibylla Sophia (*d* 15 Oct 1901), yr dau of Rt Hon Sir Robert Grant, GCH, and *dsp* 3 Aug 1901
(3) Henry Stuart; Lt Rifle Bde; *b* 10 Feb 1835; *ka* Sebastopol 8 Sept 1855
3 Frederick Dudley; MA; FO; *b* 11 July 1806; *m* 14 Aug 1839 Marian Charlotte Emily (*d* 31 March 1873), only child of Thomas Cokayne, of Ickleford House, Beds (*see* CULLEN OF ASHBOURNE, B), and *d* 19 Nov 1882, leaving, with another s (*d* young):
(1) Hugh Cuthbert Dudley; Capt RN; *b* 10 Feb 1843; *m* 17 Feb 1887 Ada Julia (*d* 24 June 1931), only dau of Col Sir Proby Thomas Cautley, KCB, and *dsp* 14 Jan 1898
(2) John Edward Dudley; *b* 17 Nov 1844; *d* 31 July 1926
(3) Algernon Charles Dudley (Rev); MA Cantab, Rector Maresfield Sussex; *b* 14 Feb 1847; *m* 5 July 1889 Constance Eugenia (*d* 24 Oct 1915), dau of Rowland Smith, of Duffield Hall, Derbys, and *d* 19 Jan 1943, leaving:
1a Algernon Frederick Roland Dudley, MC and bar; BA Cantab, Clerk Ho Lds, Maj RFA WWs I (wounded four times) and II; *b* 25 May 1891; *m* 19 March 1921 Olive (*d* 22 Aug 1973), dau of John Baillie, of Montreal, and *d* 16 April 1957, leaving:
1b *Dione Frances [Mrs James Graham-Watson, Falconers, Shipley, nr Horsham, Sussex]; *b* 9 Aug 1924; *m* 1 Oct 1954 *(Claud Andrew) James Graham-Watson, only surv s of Capt Claud Boothby Graham-Watson, DSO, RN, of Lairg, Sutherland, and has issue:
1c *Frederick Paul; *b* 4 Sept 1957; *m* 1987 *Catherine, er dau of Reginald Rimington Wilson, of Sussex and W R Yorks, and has issue:
1d *Rory William; *b* 1990

2d *Angus James; *b* 1991
3d *Thomas Henry; *b* 1993
1d *Isobel Serena; *b* 1996
1c *Iona Mary; *b* 6 Dec 1955
2c *Sanda Susan [Mrs James Friend, Winnington Grange, Market Drayton, Salop TF9 4DW]; *b* 7 Oct 1959; *m* 7 June 1986 *James Irvine Hinchliffe Friend, s of Irvine Friend, of Mucklestone Old Rectory, Market Drayton, and has had:
1d Harry James Hinchliffe; *b* 27 March 1988; *d* 28 March 1988
2d *Alexander James Hinchliffe; *b* 1 March 1989
3d *Nicholas Andrew Irvine; *b* 20 March 1995
1d *Georgina Mary Flavia; *b* 18 June 1991
2d Louisa Dione Frederica; *b* 24 Oct 1992; *d* 2 Nov 1992
2b *Xanthe Veronica [Mrs Michael Dalglish, 142 Priory Lane, London SW15]; *b* 15 May 1926; *m* 27 April 1949 Michael Dalglish (*d* 1976), s of Lt-Cdr Kenneth Park Dalglish, RN, and Mrs Guy Reynolds, and has issue:
1c *James Thomas Macdonell; *b* 23 Feb 1950; *educ* Ampleforth; *m* 1974 *Avril Elizabeth Smith and has:
1d *Lucas Timothy Frederick; *b* 1984
2d *Dominic Benet; *b* 1986
2c *Charlie Baillie Campsie; *b* 2 June 1953; *educ* Ampleforth; *m* 1976 *Miranda Lehmann, and has issue:
1d *Kenneth Michael; *b* 1981
1d *Rachel Sarah; *b* 1985
2d *Rowan Diana; *b* 1989
1c *Clare Mary; *b* 2 Feb 1956; *m* 1986 *William Kenneth Jest and has:
1d *Julian Ryder; *b* 1991
2d *Douglas Michael; *b* 1994
3b *Charis Elizabeth; *b* 20 March 1930
2a Hugh Granville Leveson Dudley, TD; Assist Mil Attaché Athens 1943–45, Lt-Col RA (TA) WW II (despatches); *b* 26 Jan 1900; *m* 1st 2 March 1926 Diana Vivian (*d* 12 Dec 1951), est dau of Sir Paul Augustine Makins, 2nd Bt (*qv*); *m* 2nd 12 June 1955 *Patricia Geraldine [Mrs Hugh Ryder, 66 Whitelands House, Cheltenham Terrace, London SW3], widow of Maj (Basil Arthur) John Peto (*see* PETO, Bt, of Barnstaple) and yst dau of Gerald Macleay Browne, OBE, and *d* 9 March 1983, having by his 1st w had:
1b Hugh Adrian Dudley; *b* 4 Aug 1930; *d* 10 Feb 1931
1b *Jane Christine [Mrs Denzil Ffennell, Haylands, Martyr Worthy, Hants]; *b* 19 May 1927; *m* 10 June 1955 Denzil Walter Hugh Ffennell (*d* 1977), s of Walter Waldemar Ffennell and Lady Delmé-Radcliffe, of Hitchin Priory, Herts, and has:
1c *Simon Walter Hugh; *b* 10 Dec 1956; *m* 1986 *Lucinda, er dau of Lt Cdr Christopher John Ringrose-Voase, MBE, RN, of Alnaby House, Upham, Hants, and has:
1d *Jessica; *b* 1989
2d *Georgina; *b* 1992
1c *Diana Elizabeth; *b* 17 April 1963
1a *Mary Constance Eugenia; *b* 18 April 1890; *m* 7 July 1921 Rev Maurice Rooke Kingsford, MA, BLitt, Rector Nuneham Courtenay, Oxon, yst s of R E Kingsford, MA, LLB, and has issue
2a Cecily Blanche Dorothy; *b* 28 April 1893; *educ* Lond U (BA); *m* 1 Aug 1933 Charles Francis Lovell Piggott, s of Walter Piggott, and *d* 17 May 1962, leaving issue. He *d* 1964
3a Philippa Constance Marian, JP; *b* 23 March 1895; *d* unm 9 Oct 1982
4a Joan Florence Helena; *b* 9 March 1897; *m* 11 Oct 1928 Rt Rev Bertram Pollock, KCVO (*see* POLLOCK, Bt), and had issue
5a Dorothy Evelyn Frances; *b* 26 Jan 1900. *m* 31 March 1921 Lt-Col Sir Ronald Deane Ross, 2nd Bt, MC (*d* 31 Jan 1958; *see* 1956 edn)
(4) Lionel George Dudley; *b* 23 May 1849; *m* 31 Oct 1895 Priscilla Campbell (*d* 25 Dec 1912), dau of William Betts, of Frenze Hall, Norfolk, and *dsp* 10 Oct 1905
(5) Stewart Leveson Dudley; *b* 6 Dec 1850; *m* 30 June 1881 Anna Maria Campbell (*d* 23 Feb 1929), dau of William Betts (*see* above), and *d* 31 March 1943, having had issue:
1a Aubrey Leveson Dudley; Lt 5th Bn KRRC WW I (wounded); *b* 22 Sept 1891; *m* 1925 Vera Hope, dau of Colin Garside Blake Gouldesbrough, of Highfield, Notts, and *dsp* 9 March 1967
1a Helen Dorothea Wildman; *b* 17 June 1882; *d* 10 March 1883
2a Evelyn Margaret; *b* 4 Sept 1884; *m* 25 Jan 1930 C V L Hooman, of Charlwood Court, Horley, Surrey, and *dsp* 30 Dec 1947
3a Susan Marjorie; *b* 12 March 1886; *d* unm 24 Nov 1961
4a Lilian Beatrice; *b* 18 Oct 1887; *d* unm 26 July 1936
(1) Marian Frances Georgiana; *m* 3 Aug 1864 Rev Arthur Brooking, Vicar Bovingdon, Herts, and *d* 1 Feb 1925, having had issue. He *d* 1890
(2) Beatrice Mary Frederica; *m* 26 June 1875 Rev Arthur Henry Delmé-Radcliffe, MA, s of Frederick Peter Delmé Radcliffe, of The Priory, Hitchin, and *d* 13 April 1909, leaving issue. He *d* 11 Aug 1896
(3) Frederica Constance Dorothy; *m* 20 June 1874 Augustus Richard Davies and *d* 19 Oct 1908, leaving issue. He *d* 1 Nov 1878
(4) Helena Augusta Cockayne; *d* unm 19 June 1950
1 Susan; *m* 4 July 1817 2nd Earl Fortescue (*qv*) and *d* 30 July 1827, leaving issue
2 Mary; *m* 15 July 1828 Adml Edward Saurin, s of Rt Hon William Saurin, and *d* 5 Aug 1900, leaving issue. He *d* 28 Feb 1878
3 Georgiana Elizabeth; *m* 12 Dec 1825 2nd Baron Wharncliffe and *d* 22 Aug 1844, leaving issue (*see* WHARNCLIFFE, E)
4 Harriet Charlotte Sophia; *m* 15 Aug 1839 Rev Lord Charles Hervey, DD, and *d* 27 Sept 1899, leaving issue (*see* BRISTOL, M)
5 Louisa; *m* 19 Feb 1833 Hon George Fortescue (*see* FORTESCUE, E) and *d* 9 Jan 1899, having had issue

The 3rd EARL's brother,

HENRY DUDLEY RYDER, **4th Earl of Harrowby**, JP, DL; sr ptnr Coutts & Co; *b* 3 May 1836; *educ* Harrow and Ch Ch Oxford; *m* 17 May 1859 Susan Juliana Maria Hamilton (*d* 18 March 1913), only dau of Villiers Dent, of Barton Court, Hants, and had issue:

1 JOHN HERBERT DUDLEY, **5th Earl**
2 Archibald Dudley; Lt Beds Regt; *b* 26 July 1867; *m* 26 April 1898 Eleanor Frederica (*d* 31 Dec 1958), est dau of Edward Fisher Rowe, and *d* 19 Jan 1950, leaving:
(1) Archibald Stuart Dudley; Cdr RN, served WWs I and II (despatches), memb Naval Mission to Turkey 1941–43, Harbour Master and Marine Court Magistrate Hong Kong 1945–47, Actg Consul Formosa 1947–48; *b* 26 Oct 1899; *m* 28 May 1936 *Viola Maria, 2nd dau of Ur Janos Kantor, of Budapest, and *dsp* 28 Feb 1976
(2) Richard Dudley, OBE (1947); *b* 20 March 1904; *educ* Eton; *m* 18 Dec 1945 Pamela Gertrude (*d* 1982), Jr Cdr ATS, only dau of Aubrey Hammick Ford, of Wortham, Crowborough, Sussex, and *d* 1987, leaving issue:
1a *Victoria [Mrs Simon Connell, Riverside Cottage, Beaminster, Dorset]; *b* 4 April 1948; *m* 1976 *Simon J C Connell
(3) Douglas Dudley, JP; *b* 26 Nov 1905; *educ* Oundle; *m* 4 Feb 1931 *Sheilah Moore [Mrs Douglas Ryder, 16 St John Garden, Cassia Drive, Port Elizabeth, S Africa], dau of S H Gillespie, of S Africa, and *d* 1984, having had issue:
1a +Hugh Donald Dudley [Hugh Ryder Esq, 44 Princes Rd, Claremont, Cape Town, S Africa]; *b* 1936; *m* 1st 12 Oct 1963 (*divorce* 1969) Pamela Joan, only dau of S O Butow, of East London; *m* 2nd 1969 *Maria, dau of Max Pitterman, of Bielefeld, Germany, and by her has:
1b +Axel Dudley; *b* 1970
2b +Douglas Dudley; *b* 1971
2a +Atholl Graham Dudley [Atholl Ryder Esq, 50 Stella Londt Drive, Port Elizabeth, Cape, S Africa]; *b* Feb 1938; *m* 25 April 1964 *Irène, only dau of J J van Duuren, of Sunridge Park, Port Elizabeth, and has issue:
1b +Gary Dudley; *b* 15 Feb 1966
2b +Peter Dudley; *b* 8 Oct 1968
1b *Jennifer Rosemary; *b* 1979
1a Eleanor Rosemary; *b* 5 May 1932; *d* 2 Jan 1944
(4) +Atholl Dudley [Atholl Ryder Esq, 502-85 Fiddler's Green Rd, London, Ontario, Canada N6H 4TI]; *b* 10 Oct 1909; *m* 20 Jan 1940 *Kathleen Esther, yst dau of Robert Pearson, of London, Ontario, and has both an adopted s and issue:
*Lawrence Dudley [Lawrence Ryder Esq, Box 209, 421 Green St, Port Elgin, Ontario, Canada N0H 2CO]; *b* 1949; *m* 1st 1973 (*divorce* 1981) —; *m* 2nd 1984 *Kathryn Elspeth, dau of Warren Shular, of Southampton, Ont, and by his 1st w has:
1b *Leigh Janice; *b* 1977
1a +Peter Douglas Dudley [Peter Ryder Esq, 10 Matthew Dr, Guelph, Ont, Canada N1H 7L7]; *b* 24 June 1952; *m* 1976 *Michelle, dau of Derek Foreman, of London, Ont, and has issue:
1b +Andrew Douglas Dudley; *b* 1985
2b +James Richard Dudley; *b* 1985
1b *Sarah Michelle; *b* 1982
2b *Jennifer Elizabeth; *b* 1984
(5) Peter Hugh Dudley, MBE (1944); Hon Lt-Col TAR RAC, PID FO; *b* 28 April 1913; *m* 29 May 1940 *Sarah Susannah, dau of Capt Geoffrey Francis Bowes-Lyon (*see* STRATHMORE AND KINGHORNE, E), and *d* 1993, leaving:
1a +Adrian Dudley [Adrian Ryder Esq, Bracken, Blackheath, nr Guildford, Surrey]; *b* 17 March 1941; *educ* Loretto and Durham U BA (Econ); *m* 1976 *Katrina Olga, est dau of Dr Socrates Christie, PhD, and has issue:
1b *Peter Socrates Dudley; *b* 9 Jan 1984
1b *Lara Erasmia; *b* 1982
2b *Tanya Serena; *b* 1989
2a +Bruce Dudley [Bruce Ryder Esq, Crix, Hatfield Peverel, Essex CM3 2EU]; *b* 14 May 1942; *educ* St Bees; *m* 6 Sept 1969 *Charlotte Olivia, only dau of Mark Frederic Strutt, MC, TD (*see* RAYLEIGH, B), and has had:
1b +Mark Reedham Dudley; *b* 14 Dec 1970
2b +Oliver Hugh Dudley; *b* 20 Sept 1974
1b Emily Anne; *b* 15 July, *d* 6 Sept 1973
2b *Leonora Mary Charlotte; *b* 23 Dec 1978
1a *Sandra Anne [Mrs Dimitris Pepelasis, Palaion Patron Germanou, Davaki, Philothei, Athens, Greece]; *b* 3 March 1954; *m* 1978 *Dimitris Pepelasis and has:
1b *Diamandis; *b* 1979
2b *Alexander; *b* 1984
(1) Victoria; *b* 11 Nov 1901; *d* unm 4 May 1966
(2) *Sarah, JP; *b* 16 Jan 1908; *m* 9 Jan 1936 G/Capt Cuthbert John Collingwood, OBE, DFC, RAF, 2nd s of Col Cuthbert George Collingwood, CB, and has issue
3 Edward Alan Dudley; *b* 22 Oct 1869; *m* 19 July 1893 Lady (Mary) Maud Anson, OBE (22 Sept 1961), 3rd dau of 2nd Earl of Lichfield (*qv*), and *d* 4 April 1949, leaving issue:
(1) Henry Dudley, MC; CC East Sussex 1944, CA 1952, Maj RFA WW I; *b* 30 Nov 1894; *educ* Harrow; *m* 21 Feb 1918 Dorothy Marion, dau of Sidney Streatfeild, and *d* 19 March 1958, leaving issue:
1a Edward Dorrien Dudley; Capt Irish Gds WW II, chm Cater Ryder 1976–84; *b* 20 Aug 1924; *educ* Harrow; *m* 20 March 1948 *Valerie Nina [Mrs Edward Ryder, 22 St Mary Abbots Terrace, London W14 8NX], only dau of James Beecroft Soames, of Kenya, and Mrs N H Drury, and *d* 1984, leaving:
1b +Nicholas Henry Dudley; *b* 10 June 1960
1b *Jennifer Davina [Mrs George Pilkington, Sainfoin House, Wash Common, Newbury, Berks]; *b* 19 July 1949; *m* 15 Dec 1971 Charles Berkeley Johnston Dingwall (*see* GALWAY, V); *m* 2nd 1990 *George William Pilkington and by her 1st husb has:

1c *Sophie; *b* 10 Nov 1972
2c *Anthea Lucy; *b* 1977
3c *Amelia Sarah; *b* 1978
2b *Vanessa [Mrs Paul Cole, Whatcombe, Wantage, Oxon OX12 9NW]; *b* 14 April 1951; *m* 1976 *Paul F Irvine Cole, and has:
1c *Alexander James; *b* 10 Nov 1977
2c *Oliver Nicholas; *b* 1980
3c *Mark Edward; *b* 1986
1a *Maud Marion; *b* 21 Nov 1919
2a *Dorothy Joan [Mrs Alan Horton, RR1, Box 1424, Randolph, NH 03570, USA]; *b* 18 Dec 1921; *m* 17 Jan 1951 *Alan Williams Horton, only s of Dr Douglas Horton, of Randolph, and has:
1b *James McAfee; *b* 26 Nov 1954; *m* 1976 *Nancy, dau of Roger Eastman, of Hanover, NH, and has:
1c *Oliver McAfee; *b* 1989
1c *Jenna Beth; *b* 1985
2b *Edward Alan Douglas; *b* 17 April 1957; *m* 1991 *Zoë Jane, er dau of Ian Wilkinson, of Esher, and has:
1c *Lily Azella; *b* 1992
2c *Eliza Joan; *b* 1994
1b *Carol Ryder; *b* 8 March 1952
(1) Evelyn Maud; *b* 7 Jan 1897; *d* unm 25 March 1960
(2) Katharine; *b* 16 Jan 1899; *m* 17 July 1924 Capt Hon Reginald Coke, DSO, s of 2nd Earl of Leicester (*qv*), and *d* Nov 1977, leaving issue
4 Robert Nathaniel Dudley; Maj 8th Hus, ADC to Govr S Australia, served Boer War 1900–02 and WW I; *b* 7 Dec 1882; *m* 16 Sept 1908 Beryl (*m* 2nd 20 Feb 1945 Lt-Col William Baring du Pré, JP, DL, of Wilton Park, Beaconsfield (*d* 23 Aug 1946), and *d* 7 Dec 1970), dau of Charles Angas, of Linsay Park, Angaston, S Australia, and was *ka* 30 Nov 1917, leaving:
(1) Geoffrey Dudley; *b* 8 Aug 1909; *d* unm 14 June 1972
(1)*Rosemary Beryl [Lady Loehnis, 12 Eaton Place, London SW1]; *b* 8 Aug 1909; *m* 17 April 1929 Cdr Sir Clive Loehnis, KCMG, RN (*d* 1992), Dep Chm Civ Serv Selection Bd 1967, only s of Herman William Loehnis, barrister, and has had:
1a *Anthony David, CMG (1988) [Anthony Loehnis Esq CMG, 11 Cranleigh , 139 Ladbroke Rd, London W11 3PX]; *b* 12 March 1936; *educ* Eton and New Coll Oxford; *m* 7 Aug 1965 *Jennifer Forsyth, 2nd dau of Sir Donald Forsyth Anderson (*see* LLEWELLYN, Bt), and has:
1b *Dominic Anthony; *b* 31 Aug 1967
2b *Alexander Garrett; *b* 12 May 1969
3b *Barnaby David; *b* 21 July 1971
2a Peter John; *b* 25 March *d* 3 Aug 1940
1a *Serena Jane [The Rt Hon the Lady Remnant, Bear Ash, Hare Hatch, Reading, Berks RG10 9XR]; *b* 23 May 1932; *m* 24 June 1953 *3rd Baron Remnant (*qv*) and has issue
1 Margaret Susan; *b* 11 Sept 1860; *d* unm 17 Sept 1932
2 Angela Mary Alice, MBE; *b* 1 March 1863; *m* 9 May 1890 1st Baron Colgrain (*qv*) and *d* 10 Nov 1939, leaving issue
3 Constance Susan Euphemia, JP Somerset; *b* 4 April 1871; *d* unm 24 Feb 1950
4 Adelaide Audrey; *b* 19 Nov 1875; *m* 27 Oct 1902 Maj Hon Henry James Anson (*see* LICHFIELD, E) and *d* 23 Dec 1956

The 4th EARL *d* 11 Dec 1900; his est son,

JOHN HERBERT DUDLEY RYDER, **5th Earl of Harrowby**, JP London; Hon Col 61st (N Midland) Field Bde RA, TA, Lt Staffs Yeo, MP (C) Gravesend 1898–1900, Alderman Staffs CC, Ld Lt Staffs 1927–48, ptnr Coutts & Co, Hon Freedom of Stoke-on-Trent 1945; *b* 22 Aug 1864; *m* 16 Nov 1887 Hon Mabel Danvers Smith, DBE (1919) (*d* 27 March 1956), dau of Viscountess Hambleden (*qv*), and *d* 30 March 1956, having had, with three daus (*d* unm):

DUDLEY RYDER, **6th Earl of Harrowby**, JP (Staffs 1929), DL (1925); *b* 11 Oct 1892; *educ* Eton and Ch Ch Oxford (BA); Maj RA WW I (wounded), WW II, Col Cmdt Staffs Army Cadet Force 1946–50, Assist Priv Sec to Sec State Colonies 1919–20, PPS to Sec State for Air 1922–23, MP Shrewsbury 1922–23 and 1924–29, Alderman LCC 1932–37, Memb: LCC Dulwich 1937–40 and Roy Commn Historical MSS. 1935–66, author: *England at Worship* (1928) and *Geography of Everyday Things* (1932), Hon DLitt Oxon 1964; *m* 31 Jan 1922 Helena Blanche Coventry (*see* COVENTRY, E), and *d* 1987, leaving issue:
1 DUDLEY DANVERS GRANVILLE COUTTS RYDER, **7th and present Earl of Harrowby**
2 +John Stuart Terrick Dudley ; *b* 12 April 1924; *educ* Eton; W/O RAF WW II 1942–45 (wounded); *m* 24 July 1946 Dorothy Ethel (*d* 20 June 1991), dau of J T Swallow, of Mansfield, Notts, and has issue:
(1) +John Robert; *b* 21 June 1947; *m* 1970 *Rosemary Rita Tester and has:
1a *Claire Jane; *b* 1970; *m* 1989 *David Gain and has:
1b *Sasha; *b* 1990
2b *April; *b* 1992
3b *Courtney; *b* 1996
2a *Sara Helena Louise; *b* 1973
(2) +David Anthony; *b* 26 March 1951; *m* 1973 *Judith Jean Sinclair, of Sydney, NSW, and has issue:
1a +John David Dudley; *b* 1979
1a *Jessica Judith Jean; *b* 1983
1 *Frances Virginia Susan [The Lady Frances Berendt, 34 The Marlowes, London NW8 1NA]; *b* 20 June 1926; *educ* St Hugh's Coll Oxford; *m* 20 Dec 1949 *Frank Ernest Berendt, s of Siegfried Berendt, of London, and has issue:
(1) *Anthony Peregrine Dudley [Anthony Berendt Esq, 56 Lancaster Rd, London W11 1QR]; *b* 25 Jan 1957; *educ* Ampleforth; *m* 1988 *Julia Rosemary, only dau of Derek Alistair Bigham (*see* FORTESCUE, E), and has:
1a *Hermione Helena; *b* 6 June 1995
(1) *Susan Venetia [Mrs Paul Williams, Walnut Tree House, 20A Lower Teddington Rd, Hampton Wick, Middx]; *b* 7 May 1952; *m* 8 Jan 1977 *Paul Joseph Williams and has:
1a *Christopher James Dudley; *b* 1980
2a *Gavin Dominic; *b* 1986
3a *Paul Gerard Quentin; *b* 1988
4a *Hew Anthony John; *b* 1990
1a *Emma Louise; *b* 1977
2a *Joanna Frances; *b* 1981
3a *Helena Lucy; *b* 1983

HARTWELL

Arms: Arg. three bars gu., overall a pile erm. **Crest:** A griffin sejant regardant sa., collared or. **Supporters:** Dexter, a stag; sinister, a wolf ppr.; both collared or and standing on a compartment with a well between paving to the dexter and grass sinister. Creation: B. (LP, UK) 19 Jan 1968.

THE BARON HARTWELL, of Peterborough Court, in the City of London, and a **Baronet** (Sir (William) Michael Berry, Bt, MBE (1945), TD) [The Rt Hon The Lord Hartwell MBE TD, 18 Cowley St, London SW1P 3LZ; Oving House, Whitchurch, Bucks HP22 4HN]; *b* 18 May 1911; *s* bro as 3rd Viscount Camrose and 3rd Baron Camrose 1995, but disclaimed those peerages for life, also in btcy; *educ* Eton and Ch Ch Oxford (BA 1933, MA 1954); ed Glasgow *Sunday Mail* 1934–35, man ed *Financial Times* 1937–39, 2nd Lt City London Yeo 1938, served WW II (despatches twice), Capt and Maj 1940, Lt-Col 1944, chm Amalgamated Press 1954–59, chm and ed-in-chief *Daily Telegraph* 1954–87 and *Sunday Telegraph* 1961–87, dir then dep chm LWT 1968–81, tstee Reuters 1962–89, dir Telegraph plc to 1995, author: *Party Choice* (1948), *William Camrose, Giant of Fleet Street* (1992); *m* 7 Jan 1936 Lady Pamela Margaret Elizabeth Smith (*d* 7 Jan 1982 aged 67), yr dau of 1st Earl of Birkenhead, GCSI, KC, PC (*see* 1970 edn), and has:
1 +ADRIAN MICHAEL [The Hon Adrian Berry, 11 Cottesmore Gdns, London W8]; *b* 15 Jun 1937; *educ* Eton and Ch Ch Oxford; jnlst (sci correspondent) *Daily* and *Sunday Telegraph*; *m* 4 Jan 1967 *Marina Beatrice, dau of Cyrus Sulzberger, of Paris, and has:
(1) +Jonathan William; *b* 26 Feb 1970; *m* 14 Dec 1996 *Aurélie, dau of Jean-Pierre Molin, of Paris
(1) *Jessica Margaret; *b* 11 Feb 1968
2 +Nicholas William [The Hon Nicholas Berry, 22 Rutland Gate, London SW7]; *b* 3 July 1942; *educ* Eton and Ch Ch Oxford; *m* 1977 *Evelyne, dau of Jacques Prouvost and Countess de la Rozière, and has:
(1) +William Alexander; *b* by 25 June 1978
1 *Harriet Mary Margaret [The Hon Mrs Cullen, 117 Cheyne Walk, London SW10]; *b* 8 Nov 1944; *m* 16 May 1981 *Martín Cullen s of Martín Cullen and Mercedes Artayeta Uriburn de Cullen, and has:
(1) *Miguel; *b* 2 March 1982
(2) *Domingo; *b* 28 July 1983
2 *Eleanor Agnes [Miss Eleanor Berry, 21 River Mill Flats, 151 Grosvenor Rd, London SW1]; *b* 6 May 1950; *educ* Wycombe Abbey and Sussex U; novelist

Lineage: JOHN MATHIAS BERRY, of Gwaelodygarth, Merthyr Tydfil, Glam, JP; *b* 2 May 1847; *m* 24 May 1870 Mary Ann (*d* 6 June 1922), dau of Thomas Rowe, of Pembroke Dock, and *d* 9 Jan 1917, having had issue:
1 HENRY SEYMOUR BERRY, 1st and last BARON BUCKLAND, of Bwlch, Co Brecknock (UK), so *cr* 16 July 1926; *b* 17 Sept 1877; colliery owner, chm GKN and John Lysaght Ltd, High Sheriff Brecknockshire 1924, KStJ; *m* 5 Sept 1907 Gwladys Mary, est dau of Simon Sandbrook, of the Hawthorns, Merthyr Tydfiland, and *dspm* 23 May 1928, *k* in a riding accident
2 WILLIAM EWERT, **1st Viscount**
3 JAMES GOMER BERRY, *cr* VISCOUNT KEMSLEY (*qv*)
1 A dau; *m* D J Berry-Jones and had:
(1) Vivian Ewert; dir Kemsley Newspapers Ltd; *b* 1900; *m* 1929 Olga (*d* 19 Aug 1971), dau of C E Thelwall, of Tynemouth, and *d* 25 Aug 1954, leaving:
1a *Ewert Michael; *m* 18 Aug 1959 *Mrs G Maria Story, only dau of R J Cole, of Coulsdon, Surrey
1a Mary Elizabeth; *m* 14 Oct 1953 Michael John Farmiloe (*see* CONGLETON, B) and *d* 1980, having had issue
(1) Doris; *m* D G Phillips and had issue

The 2nd son,

Sir William Ewert Berry, 1st Bt, so *cr* 4 July 1921, and 20 Jan 1941 **1st Viscount Camrose**, as also earlier 19 June 1929 BARON CAMROSE, of Long Cross, Co Surrey (all UK), DL Hants; *b* 23 June 1879; fndr *Advertising World* 1901, ed-in-ch *The Sunday Times* 1915–36, ch proprietor and ed-in-ch *Daily Telegraph* 1928–54 and the *Daily Telegraph and Morning Post* 1937–54, chm: Financial Times Ltd 1919–45, Allied Newspapers Ltd 1924–36, Amalgamated Press Ltd, Pncpl Advsr Min Info 1939, author: *British Newspapers and their Controllers* (1947), Hon LLD Bristol, V-Cdre RYS; *m* 1905 Mary Agnes (*d* 9 Oct 1962), est dau of Thomas Corns, of 2 Bolton St, W, and *d* 15 June 1954, leaving issue:

1 JOHN SEYMOUR BERRY, **2nd Viscount Camrose**, TD; *b* 12 July 1909; *educ* Eton and Ch Ch Oxford; chm then dep chm *The Daily Telegraph and Morning Post* (ret 1987), v-chm Amalgamated Press 1942–59, Yr Bro Trin Ho, Maj City London Yeo RA (TA) WW II N Africa and Italy (despatches), MP (C) Hitchin 1941–45; *m* 1986 Joan (*d* 25 April 1997), est dau of 3rd Baron Churston (*qv*) and formerly w of (a) W/Cdr (Thomas) Loel Evelyn Bulkeley Guinness, OBE (*see* GUINNESS, Bt), and (b) Prince Aly Khan, and *dsp* 15 Feb 1995

2 (WILLIAM) MICHAEL, **present Baron Hartwell** and briefly before his disclaimer **3rd Viscount Camrose**

3 Rodney Mathias, TD, Lt Roy Berks Regt (TA)WW II (wounded), dir Associated Iliffe Press; *b* 29 April 1917; *educ* Eton and Hertford Coll Oxford; *m* 1st 4 Jan 1955 *Susan Jenifer [Mrs Susan Middleton, 7 Wedderburn Ho, Lower Sloane St, London SW1W 8B2] (*m* 2nd 8 Jan 1964 (*divorce* 1978) Henry Lambert Middleton; *see* MIDDLETON, Bt), er dau of William Arthur Fearnley-Whittingstall, TD, QC, JP, of The Old Manor Ho, Melbourn, Cambs, and *d* 10 March 1963, having adopted:

*Emma Louise; *b* Jan 1961; *m* 1984 *Jeremy N Oakley, s of Capt Neville Oakley, of Golf Drive, Camberley, Surrey, and has issue:

1a *Joshua; *b* 1986

1a *Georgia Alice; *b* 1988

4 Julian, OBE (1959), JP (Hants 1966); *b* 24 May 1920; *educ* Eton; Lt-Col cmdg RHG 1958–60, Col cmdg Household Cavalry and Silver Stick in Waiting 1960, ret 1964, served WW II and Cyprus, US Bronze Star, Chevalier Order Crossed Swords Sweden; *m* 31 July 1946 *Janet Frances Denise [The Hon Mrs Julian Berry, The Old Rectory, Tunworth, Hants RG25 2NA], late WRNS, er dau of Maj John Leslie Rowan-Thomson, of Sayers, Gt Somerford, Wilts, and *d* 1988, leaving:

(1) +Simon Ewert [Simon Berry Esq, The Old Rectory, Tumworth, Hants RG25 2NA]; *b* 29 Nov 1955; *educ* Eton; *m* 1981 (*divorce* 1997) Martha Davidson, yst dau of Louise Davidson Sage, of New York, and has issue:

1a *Lucy Elizabeth; *b* 1985

2a *Tara Edwina; *b* 1988

3a *Alexa Eloise; *b* 1992

(1) *Caroline Denise [Mrs Jeremy Wagg, 25 Lansdowne Gdns, London W8]; *b* 3 March 1948; *m* 9 July 1969 *Jeremy James Wagg (*see* HORLICK, Bt) and has:

1a *Julian James; *b* 14 March 1972

1a *Katharine Denise; *b* 1974

1 Mary Cecilia; *b* 1906; *m* 22 Jan 1930 Maj Ronald Guthrie McNair Scott, yst s of Robert Frederick McNair Scott, and *d* 24 June 1996, leaving:

(1) *Thomas Michael [Thomas McNair Scott Esq, Highfield House, Augerez, St Peter, Jersey, CI]; *b* 22 Jan 1935; *educ* Eton; *m* 10 Sept 1959 Susannah (*d* 1993), only dau of Frederick Leslie Hodges, of Jersey, and has issue:

1a *Simon Guthrie; *b* 12 May 1960; *m* 1st 1988 (*divorce* 1991) Hon Camilla Birgitta Davidson, 3rd dau of 2nd Viscount Davidson (*qv*); *m* 2nd 19– *Natasha Stevenson and has by her:

1b *Charlotte; *b* 8 May 1997

1a *Sarah [Mrs Richard Haszard, Milford Hall, Stafford ST17 0UL]; *b* 27 May 1966; *m* 1990 *Richard Byrd Levett Haszard, s of Richard Haszard, and has issue:

1b *William Richard Levett; *b* 1994

1b *Francesca Rosamund Cecilia; *b* 1991

(2) *Nigel Guthrie; *b* 6 Sept 1945; *educ* Eton and Ch Ch Oxford; *m* 11 May 1968 *Anna Margaret, only dau of William Reginald Colquhoun (*see* GREENWELL, Bt), and has issue:

1a *Robert William; *b* 20 March 1970

2a *Alastair Nigel; *b* 1972

3a *David Ronald; *b* 1973

4a *Benjamin Guthrie; *b* 1976

(1) *Gillian Mary; *b* 9 July 1931; *m* 14 April 1951 Charles Ivor Mervyn Williams, MC (*d* 1989), yr s of Lt-Col Mervyn Gwynne Joseph Williams, JP, and has issue:

1a *Oliver Mervyn; *b* 11 March 1953; *educ* Eton

2a *Richard Charles; *b* 27 Feb 1955

3a *(Samuel) Thomas Morgan; *b* 20 April 1959; *m* 1983 his cousin *Mrs (Isabel) Tara Mary Gilroy, est dau of William Perine Macauley, and has issue (*see* below)

1a *Lucinda Mary; *b* 30 Nov 1956; *m* 1982 *Philip Carspecken and has:

1b *Gabriel; *b* 1983

(2) *(Alison) Linda [Mrs Laurence Kelly, 44 Ladbroke Grove, London W11]; *b* 1 Oct 1936; *m* 20 April 1963 *Laurence Charles Kevin Kelly, yst s of Sir David Victor Kelly, GCMG, of Tara Ho, Inch, Co Wexford, and has issue:

1a *Nicholas Tara; *b* 24 Nov 1967; *m* 1997 *Mehreen Saigol and has:

1b *Nadia; *b* 1997

1a *Rosanna Mary; *b* 21 May 1964; *m* 1993 *Sergei Reviakin and has:

1b *Alexander Ronald; *b* 1997

2a *Rachel Sophia; *b* 19 Sept 1965; *m* 1993 *(Edward) Sebastian Grigg (*see* ALTRINCHAM, B)

(3) *Valerie Susan; *b* 13 Nov 1939; *m* 23 July 1964 *Thomas Frank Dermot Pakenham, est s of 7th Earl of Longford (*qv*), and has issue

2 Sheila; T/Ldy-in-Waiting to HRH PRINCESS MARINA, DUCHESS OF KENT, 1949–53; *m* 1 May 1935 2nd Earl of Birkenhead (*see* 1970 edn; he *d* 10 June 1975), and had issue:

(1) FREDERICK WILLIAM ROBIN SMITH, 3rd and last EARL OF BIRKENHEAD; *b* 17 April 1936; *educ* Eton and Ch Ch Oxford; market devpt consultant and co dir; author (as Robin Furneaux): *The Amazon* 1969, *William Wilberforce* 1974 (Heinemann Award 1975); memb cncl RSL 1975; *d* 1985, when his titles expired

(1) *Juliet Margaret, LVO (1981) [The Lady Juliet Townsend LVO, Newbottle Manor, Banbury, Oxon OX17 3DD]; *b* 9 Sept 1941; a Ldy-in-Waiting to HRH THE PRINCESS MARGARET, COUNTESS OF SNOWDON, 1965–71, Extra Ldy-in-Waiting 1971–; *m* 1970 *John Richard Townsend and has issue:

1a *Eleanor Mary; *b* 1971

2a *Alice Jane; *b* 1974

3a *Margaret Ann; *b* 1978

3 Molly Patricia; *b* 1915; *m* 1st 19 May 1936 Capt Roger Charles George Chetwode (*d* 14 Aug 1940), only s of FM 1st Baron Chetwode (*qv*), and had issue; *m* 2nd 23 March 1942 (*divorce* 1948) 1st Baron Sherwood (*see* 1970 edn); *m* 3rd 21 July 1958, as his 2nd w, Sir Richard Charles Geers Cotterell, 5th Bt (*qv*), and *d* by Sept 1995

4 Diana Phyllis; *b* 1924; WRNS WW II; *m* 7 April 1948 William Perine Macauley, MA, MH (*d* 1990), s of Timothy Alfred Macauley, of Montreal, and *d* by March 1995, leaving:

(1) *William Francis; *b* 30 Sept 1953; *m* 1992 *Nicola Jane, er dau of Eric D Thompson, and has issue:

1a *Nico (son); *b* 1993

(2) *Mark Justin; *b* 10 April 1956

(3) *Rupert Timothy; *b* 9 June 1962; *m* 1989 *Julie M, only dau of Berkeley Baker, and has issue:

1a *Alastair Mark Justin; *b* 1991

2a *Hamish Edward Dominic; *b* 1992

(1) *(Isabel) Tara Mary [Mrs Thomas Williams, 6 Dewhurst Rd, London W14 0ET]; *b* 17 Feb 1949; *m* 1st 25 Aug 1972 (*divorce* 19–) Desmond Gilroy, er s of Dr P J Gilroy, of Blaima, Mon, and has issue:

1a *Caspar Alexander; *b* 1973

(1) (cont.) Mrs Tara Gilray *m* 2nd 1983 her cousin *(Samuel) Thomas Morgan Williams and has further issue:

2a *Francis Edward Morgan; *b* 1988

1a *Alice Rose; *b* 1983

(2) *Virginia Margaret Diana; *b* 1 Nov 1950; *m* 1974 *Hon Alastair James Harold Hoyer Millar (*see* INCHYRA, B)

(3) *Mary Rosalind [Mrs Jonathan Heale, Aymerstrey Court, Aymestrey, Herefs HR6 9SV]; *b* 30 Sept 1953; *m* 1st 13 May 1978 Dominic Sasse, poet (*k* Kathmandu air disaster 28 Sept 1992); *m* 2nd 3 Jan 1998 *Jonathan Malcolm Heale, s of Anthony Vernon Glen Henle, and has by her 1st husb:

1a *Joshua Seymour; *b* 9 Dec 1987

1a *Lydia Nevis; *b* 24 Nov 1982

HARTWELL, Bt

Arms: Sa. a buck's head cabossed arg. attired or, between the attires a cross patée fitchée of the last, in chief a lion passant-guardant per pale of the 2nd and 3rd, on a canton erm. two bars per pale az. and gu. **Crest:** On a mount vert within seven pales or, the 2nd and 5th charged with a spear's head sanguinated arg., a hart lodged, the dexter foot on a well of the last and in the mouth a sprig of oak vert. **Motto:** *Sorte sua contentus* ('Contented with his lot'). **Creation:** Bt. (UK) 26 Oct 1805.

SIR (FRANCIS) ANTHONY CHARLES PETER HARTWELL, 6TH BT, of Dale Hall, Essex [Sir Anthony Hartwell Bt, Trevean, 14 Highlands Rd, Barton-on-Sea, Hants BH25 7BL]; *b* 1 June 1940; *s* f 1993; *educ* Thames Nautical Training Coll, HMS *Worcester*, Cadet RNR, joined P&O Shipping Co 1957, Navigating Offr, Master Mariner 1971, U of Southampton (Sch of Navigation), Merchant Navy 1958–75, MRIN, MNI, MCIT, port management, marine surveyor and consultant; *m* 26 Oct 1968 (*divorce* 1989) Barbara Phyllis Rae, est dau of Henry Rae Green, of Pymble, Sydney, NSW, and has issue:

1 TIMOTHY PETER MICHAEL CHARLES; *b* 8 July 1970; *educ* All Hallows Sch and Nene Coll Northampton (BA Hons Leicester)

Lineage: WILLIAM HARTWELL; soldier Ireland before 1649; Mayor Limerick 1659, 1676 and 1677; granted 1666 877 acres in Co Limerick and 72 acres in King's Co; had:

Capt SAMUEL HARTWELL; *m* Anne (*m* 2nd Very Rev William Jephson, Dean Kilmore, by whom she was grandmother of Murrough, Marquess of Thomond (*see* INCHIQUIN, B)), dau of Redmond Barry, of Rathcormac, Co Cork, and sis of Catherine, 1st w of 1st Viscount Midleton (*qv*), and was *k* Battle of Landen 1693, leaving, with two daus (Catherine, *m* Isaac Gervais, Dean Lismore; Barbara, *m* Rev Thomas Revett):

Rev BARRY HARTWELL; sold estates in Co Limerick; Rector Rathcormac 1712 and Kilmurry 1715; *m* Mary, 2nd dau of Matthew Spierin, of Rower, Co Limerick, and *d c* 1742, leaving an er s:

BRODRICK HARTWELL; Capt RN, Lt-Govr Greenwich Hosp; coheir to estates of the BARRYs of Rathcormac; had:

Sir Francis John Hartwell, 1st Bt (UK), so *cr* 26 Oct 1805; Adml, Col Deptford and Woolwich Vols, Dir Greenwich Hosp; *b* 15 Feb 1757; ktd 1802; *m* 1st 12 Feb 1781 Anne Charlotte Maria (*d* 6 June 1809), est dau of Capt John Elphinstone, RN, C-in-C Russian Fleet, and had issue:

1 Houlton (Rev); MA; Chaplain to THE PRINCE REGENT; *b* 12 Feb 1783; *m* 29 Feb 1812 Ruth (*m* 2nd Joseph Jackson, of St Vincent's), dau of David Ball, of Bishop's Hall, and *d* 24 Feb 1819, leaving issue:

(1) BRODRICK (Sir), **2nd Bt**

(2) Sydney Houlton; *b* 25 May 1817; *m* 1840 Judith St Martin and *d* 1873, leaving issue

Sir Francis *m* 2nd 27 Jan 1812 Louisa (*d* 1843), dau of John Aldridge, of New Lodge, Sussex, and by her had issue:

1 Louisa; *d* Naples.

He *d* 28 June 1831; his gs,

Sir Brodrick Hartwell, 2nd Bt; *b* 17 July 1813; *m* 28 Oct 1834 Alicia (*d* 24 April 1859), est dau of Rev William Gunthorpe, of Antigua, and *d* 11 Dec 1888, having had issue:

1 **Sir Francis Houlton Hartwell, 3rd Bt**, JP Somerset; Capt 17th Regt (Crimean and Turkish medals); *b* 18 Sept 1835; *m* 20 Aug 1861 Emma Jane (*d* 6 Jan 1922), only child of Sir Henry Dymoke, 1st and last Bt, 28th of Scrivelsby, Lincs, and *d* 26 Sept 1900, having had issue:

(1) Mabel; *d* unm 1956

(2) Edith; *m* 26 Oct 1922 Maj Ashton Lovett Tennyson-D'Eyncourt (*see* TENNYSON-D'EYNCOURT, Bt) and *d* Sept 1943

(3) Florence; *d* unm June 1958

2 Edward Hughes Brodrick; Capt RN, Consul S Italy; *b* 6 Sept 1837; *m* 1st 4 Dec 1873 Augusta Henrietta (*d* 22 July 1883), est dau of Stewart Henry Paget (*see* ANGLESEY, M), and had issue:

(1) BRODRICK CECIL DENHAM ARKWRIGHT (Sir), **4th Bt**

(1) Ruth Julia Augusta; *b* 17 Feb 1875; *m* 1895 W Picton Phillips and *d* Jan 1901, leaving issue

2 (cont.) Edward Hartwell *m* 2nd 24 June 1885 Ella (*d* 21 Feb 1895), dau of John Miller, CE, of Edinburgh, and *d* 14 Jan 1895

3 Sydney Charles Elphinstone; *b* 30 April 1844; *m* 18 Oct 1876 Jeannette Marion (*d* 13 April 1937), dau of Col John Hadow Jenkins, and *d* 30 Dec 1899, leaving issue:

(1) Barry; Capt IA; *b* 2 Dec 1880; *m* 1 June 1912 Emily Maybell, 2nd dau of Joseph Dobbs, of Coolbawn House, Castlecomer, Co Kilkenny, and was *ka* 30 Oct 1914, leaving issue:

1a *Evelyn Patricia; *b* 1 March 1913

(2) John Redmond, CB (1949), DSO (1916); Maj-Gen IA, served WW I (despatches) and WW II; *b* 7 May 1887; *educ* Radley; *m* 1st 28 Feb 1911 (*divorce* 1921) Nina Oliver, dau of Gen George Francis William St John, CB, RA, and had:

1a *Diana Marion; *b* 25 Aug 1912; *m* 1st 30 April 1934 Lt-Col Sidney Clive Blaber, RA (*ka* Oct 1944), and has:

1b *Marcus; *b* 1942

1b *Carol Ann; *b* 1940; *m* 1973 *Charles Bruce Nairn (*see* NAIRN, Bt)

1a (cont.) Diana Blaber *m* 2nd 24 May 1951 *Stephen Terrell, OBE, TD, DL, QC, LLB, BSc, and has further issue:

2b *Peter; *b* 14 Oct 1951

3b *Paul; *b* 12 Jan 1953

(2) (cont.) Maj-Gen John Hartwell *m* 2nd 5 April 1929 Hazel Hay (*d* 5 March 1945), widow of Capt R C C Liston, IA, and dau of Sir John Benton, KCIE; *m* 3rd 22 Sept 1946 *Edith Elizabeth [Mrs John Hartwell, 4A De Walden Court, Eastbourne, Sussex], dau of F W Fosdyke, and *d* 19 Sept 1970, leaving by his 2nd w:

1a Barry Benton; Cdr RN; *b* 19 Jan 1933; *m* 1st 11 Aug 1956 (*divorce* 1968) Lois Maureen, yst dau of Capt Eric C Bratt, and had:

1b *Karen Fiona; *b* 1 May 1961

1a (cont.) Cdr Barry Hartwell *m* 2nd 1970 *Elizabeth Linley, yst dau of Linley Underwood, of Linden House, Countesthorpe, Leics, and *d* 19–, leaving by her:

1b +Jonathan Barry; *b* 1975

2b *Charlotte Linley; *b* 1973

(1) Mignonne Louise Julia; *d* unm 1957

(2) Dorothy Effie Marion; *m* 24 Aug 1915 F W Bartholomew, Lt 9th Res Bn Beds Regt, and *d* 1957. He *d* 6 Oct 1952

4 Frederick Edward; *b* 13 Dec 1856; *m* 1881 Susan Mary Ann, dau of William Green, of Victoria, Australia, and had four sons (Frederick Sydney, *b* 31 May 1896; Brodrick William, *b* 23 Oct 1899; John Maclean, *b* 10 June 1902; George Rollen; *b* 4 Aug 1905) and four daus (Ada Wilhemina, *b* 19 Feb 1887; Frances Mary Anne, *b* 24 Feb 1895; Julia Sarah; *b* 18 Aug 1901; May Alicia, *b* 3 May 1908)

1 Julia Margaret; *m* 16 July 1863 Harry Neale Lightfoot and *d* 1894, leaving issue. He *d* 1881

2 Nina Jeanetta; *d* unm 1873

3 Ada Maria Wilhelmina; *m* 1st 9 April 1874 Roger William Stapylton Burnet (*d* 3 Nov 1880), and had issue; *m* 2nd 4 Nov 1885 Jules de Bonnières and *d* 15 July 1907

4 Lawrence Alicia; *m* 1870 William Evans Morrell and *d* 6 Oct 1923, leaving issue

The 3rd Bt's nephew,

Sir Broderick Cecil Denham Arkwright Hartwell, 4th Bt; Lt-Col 1st Garrison Bn Oxon and Bucks LI, Capt Leics Regt Boer War 1900 (medal and two clasps), WWI; *b* 10 July 1876; *m* 1st 18 July 1902 (*divorce* 1907) Georgette Madeleine, dau of George Pilon-Fleury, of Algiers, and had issue:

1 *Leila Ruth Madeleine; Croix de Guerre; *m* 1st 27 May 1925 (*divorce* 1928) Charles St Clair Parsons, est s of Horace Parsons, of Toronto; *m* 2nd 16 Aug 1928 Andre Beaufré, Offr Legn Honour, Col French Army; *m* 3rd 1950 *Jean-Edouard Bennet

Sir Broderick *m* 2nd 16 May 1908 Joan Amy (*d* 12 May 1962), only dau of Robert Milne Jeffrey, of Vancouver Island, and by her had issue:

1 BRODRICK WILLIAM CHARLES ELWIN (Sir), **5th Bt**

2 Kathleen Edith Doreen Augusta; *m* 22 July 1940 Lt Michael William Bramston Hicks-Beach, DSC, RNVR (*see* SAINT ALDWYN, E), and *d* 1985, leaving issue

Sir BRODRICK *d* 24 Nov 1948; his only son,

Sir Brodrick William Charles Elwin Hartwell, 5th Bt; *b* 7 Aug 1909; *educ* Bedford Sch; WW II with Leics Regt, Capt 1943, P/O RAF; *m* 1st 13 March 1937 (*divorce* 1950) Marie Josephine, dau of Simon Peter Mullins, and had:

1 Sir FRANCIS ANTHONY CHARLES PETER HARTWELL, **6th and present Bt**

Sir Brodrick *m* 2nd 1951 *Mary Maude, MBE [Mary Lady Hartwell MBE, 50 High St, Lavendon, Bucks MK46 1HA], dau of J W Church, of Bedford, and *d* 1993, having by her had:

1 Penelope Kathleen; *b* 11 Oct 1952; *k* in a motor accident 16 Dec 1958

HARVEY

Creation: Bt. (UK) 19 Jan 1933.

Charles Richard Musgrave Harvey; *b* 7 April 1937; *s* f 1978 as 3rd Bt but does not use title; *educ* Marlborough and Pembroke Coll Cambridge; *m* 1967 *Celia Vivien, dau of George Henry Hodson, and has issue:

1 +PAUL RICHARD; *b* 2 June 1971

1 *Tamara Catherine; *b* 1977

Lineage: Rev Canon RICHARD HARVEY, of College Green, Gloucester; *d* 27 June 1889, leaving:

Rev CHARLES MUSGRAVE HARVEY; Vicar Hillingdon, Preb St Paul's Cathedral; *b* 11 May 1837; *m* 13 Aug 1863 Frances Harriet (*d* 10 Feb 1917), dau of James Brewster, of Ashford Lodge, Halstead, Essex, and *d* 2 Nov 1917, having had:

1 Richard Charles Musgrave (Ven); Canon Emeritus Wakefield Cathedral, Archdeacon Halifax; *b* 8 Sept 1864; *educ* Keble Coll Oxford (MA); *m* 17 June 1902 Laura (*d* 12 March 1931), dau of Henry Thomas Willmer, JP, of Eastleigh, Hants, and *d* Oct 1944

2 John Musgrave (Sir); Ch Justice NSW 1933, Chllr Arch-Diocese of Sydney 1935; *b* 22 Dec 1865; *educ* Keble Coll Oxford (BA); *m* 4 Jan 1896 Pauline Beatrice, dau of E Grant Ward, Registrar-Gen NSW, and *d* June 1904, leaving issue

3 ERNEST MUSGRAVE (Sir), **1st Bt**

4 Bernard Musgrave; *b* 25 Nov 1872; *d* unm June 1897

1 Mary Frances Musgrave; *m* 28 July 1898 Rev Charles James Sharp (*d* 9 Dec 1933), Vicar Ealing, and *d* 30 Jan 1959, leaving issue (*see* 1970 edn SHARP, B)

2 Ethel Musgrave; *d* unm 19 Dec 1958

3 Dorothy; *d* unm 11 April 1924

4 Margery Musgrave; *m* 11 April 1901 Rev Aubrey Baskerville Mynors (*see* MYNORS, Bt) and *d* 28 July 1974

Preb CHARLES MUSGRAVE HARVEY's 3rd son,

Sir Ernest Musgrave Harvey, 1st Bt (UK), so *cr* 19 Jan 1933, of Threadneedle Street, City of London, KBE (1920, CBE 1917); Dir and Dep-Govr Bank of England, Lt City of London, Fell Royal Empire Soc, Chev Legion Honour, Order Leopold Belgium; *b* 27 July 1867; *m* 9 April 1896 Sophia (*d* 30 Dec 1952), 6th dau of Capt Catesby Paget (*see* ANGLESEY, M), and *d* 17 Dec 1955, leaving:

1 RICHARD MUSGRAVE (Sir), **2nd Bt**

1 Joan Musgrave; *d* unm 20 Dec 1949

2 *Ruth Musgrave [Mrs Ruth Harper, 945 Arlington Ave, Berkeley, CA, USA]; *b* 1902; *m* 26 Sept 1930 (*divorce* 1953) George Macgowan Harper, 2nd surv s of James Harper, MD, and has issue:

(1) *Jane Alison; *b* 1932; *m* 1959 Lt-Col Justus Michael Molitor Lenschau (*d* 1993), US Army, and has issue:

1a *James Gabriel Molitor; *b* 1961; *m* 1989 *Angelina Renee, dau of Mrs Shirley Huddleston Rover, of Memphis, Tenn., and has issue:

1b *Alexandra; *b* 1993

1a *Katherine Jane; *b* 1963

3 *Eleanor Paget Musgrave [Mrs Edward Karslake, 13 Duke St, S Molton, N Devon]; *b* 1905; *m* 1 Oct 1930 Edward Kent Haliburton Karslake (*d* 1988), 2nd s of Lt-Col John Burgess Preston Karslake, JP (*see* DARELL, Bt), and has:

(1) *Antony Edward Kent [Brig Antony Karslake, Nymet St George House, George Nympton, S Molton, Devon]; *b* 1932; Brig late RGJ; *m* 1956 *June Pauline, er dau of Henry William Harris Eastwood, and has issue:

1a *John Burgess [John Karslake Esq, 3 Montolieu Gdns, London SW15]; *b* 1956; *m* 1983 *Naomi Celia, est dau of Rt Hon Sir Timothy Hugh Francis Raison (*see* 1970 edn CUNARD, Bt), of Hillbreak, Brill, Bucks, and has:
1b *Samuel Kent; *b* 1990
2b *Matthew; *b* 1997
1b *Eleanor Veldes; *b* 1985
2b *Clare Laura; *b* 1988
2a *William Edward Kent [William Karslake Esq, 109 Hopton Rd, London SW16 2EL]; *b* 1963; *m* 1989 *Sarah Ann, dau of William G Hynard, and has:
1b *Emma Kate; *b* 1992
2b *Lucy Olivia; *b* 1995
1a *Caroline Sarah; *b* 1960; *m* 1989 *Luis Talavera Corona, s of Agustin Talavera Becerril, of Mexico City, and has:
1b *Thomas; *b* 1990
2b *Alexander; *b* 1992
3b *Dominic; *b* 1996
2a *Henrietta Sarah; *b* 1965; *m* 1993 *James B Forsyth and has:
1b *Rebecca Anne; *b* 1995
(1) *Sophia Susan [Mrs Sophia Brown, 14 Duke St, S Molton, N Devon EX36 3AL]; *b* 1935; *m* 1964 (*divorce* 1983) Donald Watkins Brown and has:
1a *Stephen Scott; *b* 1969; *m* *Katharine Mary, dau of Samuel Brian Crawford
2a *Geoffrey Mark; *b* 1972
1a *Bridget Joan; *b* 1967; *m* *Nicholas J Salmon
(2) *Mary Leonora [Mrs Andrew Goodhart, 35 Mount Park Rd, London W5]; *b* 1944; *m* 1966 *Andrew Nicholas Dakin Goodhart and has:
1a *Gavin John; *b* 1976
1a *Rachel Mary; *b* 1970
2a *Catherine Jervis Ruth; *b* 1973

Sir ERNEST's est son,

Sir Richard Musgrave Harvey, 2nd Bt; Lt-Cdr RN; *b* 1 Dec 1898; *educ* RNCs Osborne and Dartmouth; *m* 14 July 1930 *Frances Estelle, er dau of Lindsay Crompton Lawford, of Montreal, and *d* 1 Sept 1978, leaving issue:
1 CHARLES RICHARD MUSGRAVE HARVEY, **3rd and present Bt**
1 *Joanna Musgrave [Mrs Angus MacIntyre, 8 Linton Rd, Oxford]; *b* 29 Aug 1934; *educ* Cranborne Chase and RCM (ARCM); *m* 5 Sept 1958 *Angus Donald MacIntyre, MA, DPh, Fell Magdalen Coll Oxford, est s of Maj Francis Peter Macintyre, OBE, 14th/20th Hus, and has issue:
(1) *Benedict Richard Pierce; *b* 25 Dec 1963; *m* 1993 *Katherine Muir
(2) *Magnus William Lachlan; *b* 1971
(1) *Katherine Cressida Eve; *b* 25 Feb 1962

HARVEY OF TASBURGH

Arms: Erminois, on a chief indented gu. between two crescents arg. a representation of the gold medal presented to Sir Robert John Harvey for his services at the Battle of Orthes, pendant from a ribbon gu., fimbriated az., beneath the word 'Orthes', between two crescents arg. a canton erm., thereon a representation of a badge of the order of the tower and sword pendant from a ribbon az.
Crest: Out of a mural crown or a dexter cubit arm erect ppr. above a crescent arg., between two branches of laurel also ppr.
Supporters: Dexter, a lion or; sinister, a cock or.
Motto: *Alteri si tibi* ('If true to yourself you are true to others').
Creation: Bt. (UK) 8 Dec 1868, B. (UK) 3 July 1954.

THE 2ND BARON HARVEY OF TASBURGH, of Tasburgh, Co Norfolk, and a **Baronet** (Sir Peter Charles Oliver Harvey, Bt) [The Rt Hon The Lord Harvey of Tasburgh, Crownick Woods, Restronguet, Mylor, Cornwall TR11 5ST]; *b* 28 Jan 1921, *s f* 1968; *educ* Eton and Trin Coll Cambridge; RA WW II, FCA; *m* 25 April 1957 Penelope Anne (*d* 8 June 1995), yr dau of Lt-Col Sir William Vivian Makins, 3rd Bt, JP (*qv*), and has:

1 *Juliet Annora Christine; *b* 9 March 1958; *m* 1996 *Richard Lee
2 *Miranda Jean; *b* 4 April 1960; *m* 1987 (*divorce* 1995) Timothy H Smithies

Lineage: JOHN HARVIE, of Beachamwell, Norfolk; *d* by 1569, leaving:

JOHN HARVEYE, of Beachamwell; *d* by 1602, leaving:

JOHN HARVEYE, of Beachamwell; *d* by 1670, leaving:

ROBERT HARVEY, of Beachamwell and Shingham, Norfolk; *d* by 1695, leaving:
1 JOHN
2 Robert, of Hilborough, Norfolk; *m* Mary, only dau of William Nurse, of Hilborough, and had:
(1) John; Lt RN; had:
1a Edward, of Watton, Norfolk; *m* Mary, dau of John Longe, and *d* 1771, leaving issue:
1b Robert, of Watton; *m* Charlotte, dau of Charles Purdy, and *d* 1820, leaving issue:
1c Charlotte Mary; *m* 5 June 1815 her cousin Sir Robert John Harvey, KCB (*see* below)

The er son,

JOHN HARVEY, of Beachamwell and St Clement's, Norwich; High Sheriff Norfolk 1720, Mayor Norwich 1727; *b* 16 Aug 1666; *m* 1st Anne (*d* 1706), dau of William Stalham, and had:
1 ROBERT
2 Peter; *m* Elizabeth (*d* 18 Oct 1741), dau of John Ives, of Norwich, and 1751, leaving issue
3 Thomas, of Norwich; *m* Lydia, dau of Jeremiah Ives, of Norwich, and *d* 1772, leaving issue
4 Samuel; Mayor Norwich; *m* 1st Mary, dau of Dr — Evans, of King's Lynn; *m* 2nd Sarah, dau of Dr — Hepburn, of King's Lynn, and *d* 1772
5 William (Rev); Rector Fineham; *d* 1747, leaving issue

JOHN HARVEY *m* 2nd — and *d* 28 Sept 1742, having had further issue

The est son,

ROBERT HARVEY, of St Clement's; High Sheriff Norfolk 1727, Mayor Norwich 1738; *b* 1697; *m* Lydia (*d* 1759), dau of John Black, Mayor Norwich, and *d* 1773, leaving an only s:

ROBERT HARVEY, of Catton, Norfolk, and St Clement's; Mayor Norwich 1776 and 1809; *m* Judith (*d* 1 May 1810), sis of Rev Charles Onley, of Stisted Hall, Essex, and *d* 29 Jan 1816, having had:
1 Robert, of Catton and Stoke Holy Cross, Norfolk, and Surrey House, Norwich, JP, DL; Mayor Norwich 1785, Lt-Col E Norfolk Militia, Col-Cmdt Norwich Regt Vols 1808; *b* 8 Feb 1753; *m* Ann (*d* 28 Aug 1801), dau of Jeremiah Ives, Mayor Norwich, and *dsp* 13 Jan 1820
2 JOHN
3 Charles Henry HARVEY later SAVILL ONLEY (with arms)
1 Sarah; *m* Archibald Morrison, of Eaton, Norwich

The 2nd s,

JOHN HARVEY, of Thorpe Lodge, Norwich, JP Norfolk and Suffolk, JP, DL, Norwich; Lt-Col 3rd E Norfolk Yeo Cav, Mayor Norwich 1792, High Sheriff Norfolk 1785 and 1825; *b* 5 May 1755; *m* 27 Dec 1782 Frances (*d* 2 July 1809), dau of Sir Roger Kerrison, of Brooke House, Norfolk, and had, with other daus:
1 ROBERT JOHN (Sir)
2 George, of Thorpe Grove, Norwich; *b* 4 June 1793; *m* 25 April 1816 Marianne (*d* 4 Sept 1856), only child of Dr — Beevor, DD, and n of Sir Thomas Beevor, Bt (*qv*), and *d* 4 Oct 1831, having had issue
3 Roger Kerrison, of Thorpe, nr Norwich, and Bath, JP, DL Norfolk; Capt E Norfolk Militia and E Norfolk Yeo Cav; *b* 15 April 1802; *educ* Trin Coll Cambridge (MA); *m* 28 March 1826 Eliza Beecroft (*d* 17 April 1881), dau of Sir Edmund Knowles Lacon, 2nd Bt (*qv*), and *d* 13 Nov 1882, having had issue
1 Fanny; *m* 26 Nov 1811 Rev Edward Bellman and *d* 8 March 1867, leaving issue. He *d* 26 Dec 1843
2 Marianne; *m* 10 June 1806 Rev Charles Day and *d* 18 March 1812, leaving issue
3 Caroline Mary; *m* 16 April 1818 her cousin Onley Savill Onley, of Stisted Hall, Essex, and *d* 29 Oct 1845, leaving issue
4 Harriot; *m* 9 Aug 1827 Capt Thomas Blakiston, RN, and had issue. He *d* 30 April 1855
5 Rosa; *m* 26 Nov 1824 John Ranking and *d* 5 Dec 1865, leaving issue
6 Augusta; *m* 1st 2 Aug 1827 (*divorce* 1841) Sir Harry Dent Goring, 8th Bt (*qv*), and had issue; *m* 2nd Edward John Trelawney
7 Charlotte; *m* 9 Aug 1838 Robert Blake Humfrey, DL, of Wroxham, Norfolk, and *d* 16 Oct 1894, leaving issue. He *d* 15 Oct 1886

Col HARVEY *d* 9 Feb 1842; his est son,

Sir ROBERT JOHN HARVEY, CB, JP, DL, of Mousehold House, Norwich; Kt Tower and Sword, Kt Cdr St Bento d'Aviz, Gen, ktd 1817, ADC to Duke of Wellington Battles of Oporto, Busaco, Salamanca, Vittoria, Nive, Nivelle, Orthes and Toulouse, and Sieges of Ciudad Rodrigo, Badajoz, Burgos and St Sebastian; *b* 21 Feb 1785; *m* 5 June 1815 Charlotte Mary (*d* 22 March 1869), dau and heiress of Robert Harvey, of Watton, Norfolk (*see* above), and had, with other issue:
1 ROBERT JOHN HARVEY (Sir), **1st Bt**
2 John; *b* 2 April 1822
3 Edward Kerrison, JP Norwich and Suffolk, of Montague House, S Lowestoft, and Grey Friars, Norwich, twice Mayor Norwich; *b* 21 Dec 1826; *m* 1st 27 March 1856 Emma Susanna (*d* 1886), dau of Rev Clement Chevallier, Rector Badingham and Cransford, Suffolk, and had issue; *m* 2nd 1896 Sophia Elizabeth, dau of Rev William Smythies Beevor, of Bury St Edmunds, and *d* 2 Dec 1906
1 Julia; *m* 1st 14 Nov 1837 Maj Samuel Ives Sutton (*d* 3 Feb 1850), est s of R-Adml Sutton; *m* 2nd 4 Nov 1858 Peter Wells, of Windsor Forest, Berks, and *d* 7 Jan 1893

2 Charlotte Emma; *m* 18 Sept 1838 Rev Henry Churchman Long, Rector Newton and Swainsthorpe, 2nd s of Rev Robert Churchman Long, of Dunston Hall, Norfolk, and *d* 25 Dec 1895, leaving issue. He *d* 21 April 1884

Sir ROBERT *d* 18 June 1860; his est son,

Sir Robert John Harvey Harvey, 1st Bt (UK), so *cr* 8 Dec 1868, of Crown Point, Trowse, Norfolk; *b* 16 April 1817; MP Thetford 1865–68; *m* 1 Aug 1845 Henrietta Augusta (*d* 3 July 1874), gdau of 7th Earl of Cavan (*qv*), and had:

1 Robert Lambart Sutton; *b* 12 Sept 1847; *d* 4 Sept 1864

2 CHARLES (Sir), **2nd Bt**

3 Lambart Edward; *b* 5 Oct 1850; *d* 20 Jan 1871

1 Henrietta Julia; *m* 9 May 1868 Sir Edmund Broughton Knowles Lacon, 4th Bt (*qv*), and *d* 3 Sept 1876

2 Ida; *m* 15 Feb 1876 Thomas Keppel (*see* ALBEMARLE, E) and *d* 2 May 1931, leaving issue

3 Alicia Menella; *m* 9 June 1874 Henry Keppel (*see* ALBEMARLE, E) and *d* 8 Jan 1892, leaving issue

Sir ROBERT *d* 19 July 1870; his son,

Sir Charles Harvey, 2nd Bt, of Rainthorpe Hall, Norwich, JP; Col 4th Bn Norfolk Regt; *b* 25 Feb 1849; *m* 1st 6 March 1870 Jane Ann (*d* 13 Dec 1891), dau of Benjamin Green, of Newcastle, and had issue:

1 **Sir Charles Robert Lambart Edward Harvey, 3rd Bt**; *b* 16 April 1871; *m* 1st 29 Dec 1891 Jessie (*d* 1913), dau of Ebenezer Turnbull, of Smedley, Manchester, and had issue:

(1) John Carlton; *b* 31 March, *d* 1895

(1) Dorothy; *b* 22 July 1892

1 (cont.) **Sir Charles** *m* 2nd 1921 Lydia Alexievna, dau of Alexis Vladimirovitch Konshine, of Moscow, and *d* 15 Nov 1954

1 Sibyl Henrietta, CStJ; *m* 26 Aug 1906 Lt-Col James Campbell Ouseley FitzMaurice (*see* ORKNEY, E) and *dsp* 9 May 1949

2 Christabel Katherine; *d* young 2 May 1894

3 Gabrielle Jean; *m* 7 Sept 1909 Philip Henry Napier (*see* NAPIER and ETTRICK, L) and *d* 3 Feb 1936, leaving issue

Sir Charles *m* 2nd 1 Feb 1893 Mary Anne Edith (*d* 20 March 1929), dau of G F Cooke, of Holmwood, Norwich, and *d* 30 Jan 1928, leaving by her:

2 **Sir Oliver Charles Harvey, 4th Bt**, and **1st Baron Harvey of Tasburgh**, of Tasburgh, Co Norfolk (UK), so *cr* 3 July 1954, GCMG (1948, KCMG 1946, CMG 1937), GCVO (1950), CB (1941); *educ* Malvern and Trin Coll Cambridge (BA); WW I in France, Egypt and Palestine (despatches), FO 1919, 2nd Sec 1920, Rome 1922, FO 1925, 1st Sec 1926, Athens 1929, Paris 1931, Counsellor and Pncpl Priv Sec to For Sec 1936–39 and 1941–43, Envoy Extrdy and Min Plen Paris 1940, Assist U-Sec State 1943–46, Dep U-Sec 1946–47, Amb Extrdy and Plen Paris Jan 1948–April 1954, Tstee Wallace Collection 1954, Chm Franco-Br Soc 1956–63, Govr St Mary's Hosp 1956–58, Memb Reviewing Ctee Export Works of Art 1959–64, Grand Cross Legn Hon; *b* 26 Nov 1893; *m* 8 April 1920 Maud Annora (*d* 21 Feb 1970), est dau of Arthur Watkin Williams-Wynn (*see* WILLIAMS-WYNN, Bt), and *d* 29 Nov 1968, leaving:

(1) PETER CHARLES OLIVER HARVEY, **2nd and present Baron Harvey of Tasburgh**

(2) John Wynn; WW II 1942–46 with KRRC and Essex Regt; *b* 4 Nov 1923; *educ* Eton, Westminster and Trin Coll Cambridge; *m* 25 April 1950 *Elena Maria Teresa [The Hon Mrs John Harvey, Coed-y-Maen, Meifod, Powys SY22 6BT; 7a Frieze Green House, Chelsea Manor St, London SW3], yr dau of Giambattista, Marchese Curtopassi, of Rome, and *d* 1989, leaving:

1a +CHARLES JOHN GIUSEPPE [Charles Harvey Esq, 162 East Dulwich Grove, London SE22]; *b* 4 Feb 1951; heir presumptive; *educ* Eton; *m* 1979 *Margaret (Maggie), dau of Cecil Walter Brown, and has issue:

1b +John; *b* 1993

1b *Elena; *b* 1982

2b *Nina; *b* 1985

4b *Stephanie; *b* 1989

2a +Robert Lambart; *b* 21 Aug 1953; *educ* Eton; *m* 1981 *Jane Louisa, est dau of E Alan Roper, of The Manor, S Brent, Devon, and has issue:

1b +Oliver John Edward Giuseppe; *b* 1988

3a *Antonella Sophia Gabrielle Maria; *b* 24 Dec 1957; *m* 1988 *Al-Sharif Abdullah bin Al-Hussein and has issue:

1b *Abdulillah; *b* 1992

2b *Hassen; *b* 1994

1b *Badia; *b* 1990

HARVIE-WATT

Arms: Quarterly, per fess wavy, 1st, per pale ermine and azure upon a mound in base vert a tower proper, masoned sable roof gules, between two oak trees, also proper, fructed or; 2nd, argent fretty sable, a grenade azure inflamed of nine flames, seven or and two gules; 3rd, barry wavy argent and azure a portcullis gules; 4th, barry wavy gules and or a dexter hand proper issuing from a manche fessways sable. **Crest:** A lion's gamb issuing from the torse argent, armed gules, grasping a writing quill paleways or, feathered sable. **Motto:** Serve the highest. **Creation:** Bt. (UK) 5 Sept 1945.

SIR JAMES HARVIE-WATT, 2ND BT, of Bathgate, Co Linlithgow [Sir James Harvie-Watt Bt, 15 Somerset Sq, London W14 8EE]; *b* 25 Aug 1940; *s f* 1989; *educ* Eton and Ch Ch Oxford (MA); ACA 1965, FCA 1975, Lt 1st Bn London Scottish Regt (TA) 1959–67, Coopers and Lybrand 1962–70, exec BET 1970–78, md Wembley Stadium Ltd 1973–78, memb: exec ctee London Tourist Bd 1977–80 and Sports Cncl 1980–88 (v-chm 1985–88), chm Crystal Palace Nat Sports Centre 1984–88, OStJ 1964, dir Penna Hldgs plc and other cos 1995–; *m* 28 May 1966 *Roseline Gladys Virginia, yr dau of Baron Louis de Chollet, of Switzerland, and Mrs Foster J Tate, of Maryland, and has:

1 +MARK LOUIS; *b* 19 Aug 1969; *educ* Eton and Yale; *m* 7 Dec 1996 *Miranda, only dau of Martin Thompson and Mrs Robin Astell

1 *Isabelle Frances; *b* 19 March 1967; *educ* St Mary's Ascot and Edinburgh U; *m* 21 Oct 1995 *Marchese Carlo Claverino, s of Marchese Roberto Claverino, of Genoa, and has:

(1) *Elena Roseline Maria; *b* 15 July 1997

Lineage: JAMES McDOUGAL WATT, of Woodlands Ho, Armadale, W Lothian; *b* 1856; *m* 1899 Jessie Jack Harvie and *d* 1943, leaving:

Sir GEORGE STEVEN WATT later HARVIE-WATT, **1st Bt** (UK), so *cr* 5 Sept 1945, TD (1942), QC (KC 1945), of Bathgate, Linlithgow, JP London 1944–56, DL Surrey 1942–66 and Gtr London 1966–89; *b* 23 Aug 1903; *educ* George Watson's Coll Edinburgh and Glasgow and Edinburgh US; barrister Inner Temple 1930, Brig: RE (TA), cmded 31st Bn 1939–41, 6 AA Bde 1941 and 63 AA Bde (TA) 1948–50, MP (C) Keighley 1931–35 and Richmond, Surrey, 1937–59, PPS to: Parly Sec BOT 1937–38 and PM 1941–45, Assist Govt Whip 1938–40, memb Roy Co Archers, ADC to TM GEORGE VI 1948–52 and THE QUEEN 1952–58, memb Kensington Cncl 1934–45, City London TAA, dir: GWR 1948, Consolidated Goldfields, Midland Bank, Standard Bank, Clydesdale Bank and Eagle Star Insur, pres Printers' Pensions Corp 1957, chm: Monotype Corp 1960–69 and Caledonian Club 1953–60 (hon v-pres 1960–89), author: *Most of my Life* (1980), OStJ, FRSA 1973, Hon Freeman City London 1976; *m* 4 Jan 1932 *Jane Elizabeth [Bettie Lady Harvie-Watt, Sea Tangle, Earlsferry, Fife KY9 1AD], only dau of Capt (S) Archibald Taylor, OBE, RN, and *d* 1989, leaving:

1 Sir JAMES HARVIE-WATT, **2nd and present Bt**

2 +Euan [Euan Harvie-Watt Esq, 333 E 56th St, NY City, USA; Yarborough Cottage, Earlsferry, Fife KY9 1AD]; *b* 24 Dec 1942; *educ* Eton; late 2nd Lt 1st Bn London Scottish Regt (TA); pres Sedgwick Internat Mktg Servs Inc; *m* 11 March 1967 (*divorce* 1979) Olivia Mason, only dau of William Mason Smith, of NYC, and has issue:

(1) *Katrina; *b* 28 Feb 1968; *educ* Wycombe Abbey, Georgetown U and George Washington U; *m* 13 Aug 1994 *Marc A Faerber, s of Frederick Faerber III and Mrs Eric Champion

(2) *Jennifer; *b* 20 Oct 1969; *educ* Benenden and Claremont McKenna U

1 *Rachel [Mrs Iain Fraser, 20 Lynedoch Pl, Edinburgh EH3 7PY]; *b* 31 May 1944; *educ* Sherborne, Perugia U, Italy, St Andrews U and Edinburgh U (MA 1967); *m* 20 March 1970 *Iain Gordon Fraser, WS, yr s of Dr Donald Fraser and Dr Janet Fraser, of Inverness, and has issue:

(1) *Duncan; *b* 1972; *educ* Trin Coll Glenalmond and St Andrews U

(1) *Olivia; *b* 1974; *educ* Sherborne and Newcastle U

HASKEL

Creation: B. (LP, UK) 1993.

THE BARON HASKEL, of Higher Broughton, Metropolitan County of Greater Manchester (Simon Haskel) [The Rt Hon The Lord Haskel, House of Lords, London SW1A 0PW]; *b* 9 Oct 1934; *educ* Salford Coll Advanced Technology; Perrotts: joined 1961, chm Perrotts Gp 1973–97; Lab Pty: Sec 1972 Industry Gp 1976–81, Sec Fin and Industry Gp 1981–90 and Chm 1990–94; V-Chm Inst Jewish Policy Research 1991–; Oppn Whip 1994–97, Trade and Industry Spokesman 1995–97, memb Sci and Tech Select Ctee 1994–97, Ld in Waiting (Govt Whip) 1997–; FRSA 1979; *m* 1962 *Carole Lewis, of New York, and has a s and dau

Lineage: ISAAC HASKEL, of Kaunas, Lithuania; *m* Julia— and had:

SIMON, *cr* a **Baron**

HASLAM

Creation: B. (LP, UK) 1990.

THE BARON HASLAM, of Bolton, Greater Manchester (Sir Robert Haslam) [The Rt Hon The Lord Haslam, House of Lords, London SW1A 0PW]; *b* 4 Feb 1923; *educ* Bolton Sch and Birmingham U (BSc); joined Manchester Collieries 1944; NCB: mining engr 1947, Personnel Dir 1960; ICI: dir Nobel Div 1963 (dep-chm 1966), dep-chm Plastics Div 1969 (chm 1971), chm Fibres Div 1971; Chm ICI Americas Inc 1978–81; dir: ICI 1974 (dep-chm 1980–83), Fibre Industries Inc 1971–75, Imperial Metal Industries 1975–77, AECI 1978–79, Carrington Viyella 1982–83, Cable and Wireless 1982–83, Bank of England 1985–93; Chm: Man-Made Fibres Producers Ctee 1972–74, Nationalized Industries Chm's Gp 1985–86 (memb 1983–90), Tate and Lyle plc 1983–86 (dir 1978–86), BSC 1983–86, British Coal 1986–90 (dep chm 1986), Bechtel Ltd 1991–94, Wasserstein Perella & Co Internat 1991–, Br Occupational Health Research Fndn 1991–; memb BOTB 1981–85 (chm N American Advsy Gp 1982–85), NEDC 1985–89; advsy dir Unilever 1985–93; Chm: Cncl Manchester Business Sch 1985–90, Govrs Bolton Sch 1990–; ktd 1985, Pres IMinE 1989–90, Hon FIMinE 1987, Hon DTech Brunel 1985, Hon DEng Birmingham 1987, CEng, Freeman City London; *m* 1947 Joyce (*d* 1995), dau of Frederick Quinn, and has issue:

1 *Roger J; *b* 1948; *educ* Westminster and Dundee U (BSc); *m* 1972 *Astrid, dau of Kristian Rognoy, of Norway, and has:

(1) *Sara Caroline Rognoy; *b* 1974

(2) *Roberta Louise Rognoy; *b* 1980

2 *Nigel R [The Hon Nigel Haslam, 17 Blithfield St, London W8 6RH]; *b* 1952; *educ* Westminster and Birmingham U (BA); *m* 1988 *Alison Vanessa, dau of Alec Raymond Gourd Knight, of Cornwall, and has:

(1) *James Robert Alexander; *b* 1990

(1) *Sophie Antonia; *b* 1988

BARON HASLAM *m* 2nd 29 July 1996 *Hon Mrs Michael Sieff (*see* MARKS OF BROUGHTON, B)

Lineage: PERCY HASLAM; *m* Mary — and had:

ROBERT, *cr* a **Baron**

HASTINGS

Arms: Quarterly, 1st, az. a cinquefoil pierced erm. within a bordure engrailed or (for ASTLEY); 2nd, arg. a lion rampant gu., ducally crowned or (for CONSTABLE); 3rd, gu. two lions passant arg. (for LE STRANGE); 4th, or a maunch gu. (for HASTINGS). **Crest:** Out of a ducal coronet or a plume of five feathers arg. **Supporters:** On either side a lion gu., ducally crowned and gorged with a collar or, therefrom pendant an escutcheon of the arms of Hastings. **Motto:** *Justitiæ tenax* ('Tenacious of justice'). **Creations:** B. (E) 29 May 1290/24 June 1295, Bt (E) 25 June 1660.

THE 22ND LORD (BARON) **HASTINGS** and a **Baronet** (Sir Edward Delaval Henry Astley, Bt) [The Rt Hon The Lord Hastings, Seaton Delaval Hall, Whitley Bay, Northumberland NE26 4QR]; *b* 14 April 1912; *s* f 1956; *educ* Eton and abroad; a Ld in Waiting 1961–62, Maj (Res of Offrs) Coldstream Gds WW II, Jt Parly Sec Min Housing and Local Govt 1962–64, memb Parly Delegn West Indies 1958, Govr Br Inst Florence 1959–97 and Roy Ballet 1971–93, memb Cncl Roy Cwlth Soc for Blind 1963–, Pres Br Epilepsy Assoc 1965–93, Chm: Br Italian Soc 1957–62 (Pres 1972–), Roy Ballet Benevolent Fund 1966–84, Dance Teachers Benevolent Fund 1982–, Italian People Flood Appeal 1966–67, Grand Offr Italian Order Merit 1968; *m* 7 July 1954 *Catherine (Cecilia) Rosaline Ratcliffe, yr dau of Capt Harold Virgo Hinton, of Walton-in-Gordano, Somerset, and Mrs Ratcliffe-Hinton, of Hurstpierpoint, Sussex, and formerly w of Vernon William Coats (*see* 1970 edn GLENTANAR, B), and has issue:

1 +DELAVAL THOMAS HAROLD [The Hon Delaval Astley, 39 Colville Gdns, London W11]; *b* 25 April 1960; *educ* Radley and Hatfield Coll Durham; *m* 26 July 1987 *Veronica M, er dau of Richard A Smart, of Chester, and has:

(1) +Jacob Addison; *b* 5 Sept 1991

(1) +Molly; *b* 1993

(2) +A dau; *b* 21 June 1996

2 +Justin Edward [The Hon Justin Astley, Thornage Hall, Holt, Norfolk]; *b* 22 April 1968

1 +Harriet Marguerite [The Hon Harriet Astley, Mill Farmhouse, Thornage, Holt, Norfolk]; *b* 15 March 1958

Barony of Hastings: A Barony of Hastings (of Inchmahome), that is to say a barony other than the one that is the principal subject of this article, is mentioned in the **Lineage of Hastings** section below. In addition a Barony of Hastings (of Hastings) was created by writ of summons (or possibly patent) in 1461. The beneficiary was Sir William Hastinges, of Kirby, Leics, who belonged to a cadet branch of the family dealt with below. At that time the Barony of Hastings which is the subject of this article was thought to be at best dormant, more probably extinct, so no confusion between identically named titles would have arisen. It is this Lord Hastings of the 1461 creation whom RICHARD III had executed, the episode forming a scene in Shakespeare's play of that name.

His son was recognised as Lord Hastings despite the charge of treason brought against the father, but known also as Lord Hastings of Hungerford, which seems therefore to have been a separate peerage title altogether (*see* SAINT DAVIDS, V, for genealogical details). (To add to the confusion, a younger son of Sir William of Kirby was created Lord Hastings of Welles or Lord Welles in 1482, though he later styled himself Lord Willoughby to avoid confusion with earlier holders of the Barony of Welles.) The son of the 2nd Baron Hastings (of Hastings) of the 1461 creation was created Earl of Huntingdon (*qv*) and both Baronies of Hastings descended with that title for 250 years. In 1817 the then holder of the two Hastings Baronies was created Marquess of Hastings, but the Marquessate expired with the death of its fourth holder just over half a century later (*see* LOUDOUN, E). Between 1558 and 1572 the third son of the 1st Earl of Huntingdon was created Baron Hastings of Loughborough. Again, no confusion could have existed in the minds of contemporaries between it and the title chiefly dealt with in this article because the latter was deemed to be dormant or extinct.

Lineage (of Hastings): DAVID, EARL OF HUNTINGDON (*qv*) and bro of WILLIAM THE LION KING OF SCOTS, had a fourth dau:

Ada; *m* Sir Henry de HASTINGES, of Ashill, Norfolk (*d* just before 9 Aug 1250) and had issue:

Sir HENRY de HASTINGES, of Ashill; one of the cdrs under Simon de Montfort (*see* LEICESTER, E, preliminary remarks) Battle of Lewes 1264, Constable Winchester Castle 1265, wounded and captured Battle of Evesham 1265; *m* Joan, sis and coheir of Sir George de Cauntelo (*see* ABERGAVENNY, M, preliminary remarks), through whom the early Lords Hastingses became feudal Lords of Bergavenny (*see* again ABERGAVENNY, M), and *d* just before 5 March 1268/9, leaving issue:

1 Sir JOHN de HASTINGES, **1st Lord** (Baron) **Hasting(e)s** (E), so *cr* by writ 24 June 1295 according to later doctrine (although in the petition presented by Sir Jacob Astley, Bt, in 1840 which resulted in his being called to Parl as 16th Lord Hastings a date of 29 May 1290 was put forward as constituting the moment when Sir John de Hastinges was first present at an assembly which might be regarded as a Parl and precedence of this earlier date was assigned the Barony of Hastings; the assembly of 1290 would not now be regarded as a valid Parliament); *b* 6 May 1262; feudal Ld of Abergavenny; one of the three competitors for the Crown of Scotland 1290 in right of his grandmother Ada, Lt and Seneschal Gascony 1302; *m* 1st 1275 Isabel de Valence (*d* 5 Oct 1305), dau of William, styled but never invested as Earl of Pembroke (*see* PEMBROKE and MONTGOMERY, E, preliminary remarks), and had issue:

(1) William; *dsp*

(2) JOHN de HASTINGES, **2nd Lord** (Baron) **Hasting(e)s**; *b* 29 Sept 1286; fought Battle of Bannockburn 1314; *m* Juliane (*m* 2nd 1326 Thomas le Blount; *m* 3rd 1328 William de Clinton, Earl of Huntingdon, and *d* 1367), dau of Sir Thomas de Leybourne, and *d* 20 Jan 1324/5, leaving issue:

1a LAURENCE de HASTINGES, **3rd Lord** (Baron) **Hasting(e)s** and recognised as EARL OF PEMBROKE 13 Feb 1339 by virtue of his descent from Isabel, sis of Aymer de Valence, 1st and last Earl of Pembroke of that family; *b* 20 March 1319/20; fought naval Battle of Sluys against French 1340 and present Siege of Tournai which followed, also Siege of Calais 1346; *m* just after 29 May 1328 Agnes de Mortimer (*m* 2nd John de Hakelut and *d* 25 July 1368), dau of 1st Earl of March, and *d* 29 or 30 Aug 1348, leaving an only son:

1b JOHN de HASTINGES, **4th Lord** (Baron) **Hasting(e)s** and 2nd EARL OF PEMBROKE, KG (1370); *b* 29 Aug 1347; ktd 1369, Lt English army Aquitaine 1372, captured by Spaniards and held prisoner by them 1372–75 following defeat in a sea battle near La Rochelle 1372; *m* 1st 1359 Margaret (*dsp* 1361), 4th dau of EDWARD III; *m* 2nd *c* July 1368 Anne de Mauny (*d* 3 April 1384), dau of Walter, 1st Lord (Baron) Mauny, KG, and by subsequent doctrine entitled to be regarded as BARONESS MAUNY in her own right following her f's death Jan 1371/2, and *d* 16 April 1375, leaving an only son:

1c JOHN de HASTINGES, **5th Lord** (Baron) **Hastinges** and 3rd and last EARL OF PEMBROKE, also according to later doctrine 3rd and last BARON MAUNY; *b* 11 Nov 1372; ktd 1381; *m* 1st 24 June 1380 (*divorce* 1383) Elizabeth, dau of JOHN OF GAUNT, DUKE OF LANCASTER, and gdau of EDWARD III; *m* 2nd Philippa (*m* 2nd 11th/4th Earl of Arundel (*see* NORFOLK, D); *m* 3rd Thomas de Poynings, Lord (Baron) St John of Basing), dau of 3rd Earl of March, but *dsp* 30 Dec 1389 after being injured while practising for a tournament, when the Earldom of Pembroke reverted to the Crown, the Barony of Mauny expired and the Barony of Hastings became dormant

(1) Elizabeth; *m* 1st Lord (Baron) Grey (of Ruthin) (*see* GREY, B), and had, with an er s (John, *dvp*):

1a REYNOLD De GREY, 2nd LORD (Baron) GREY (of Ruthin); *b c* 1319; *m* by 29 Nov 1360 Alianore, dau either of 5th Lord (Baron) Strange (of Knokyn) (*see* SAINT DAVIDS, V) or John, 2nd Lord (Baron) Strange (of Blackmere) (*see* SAINT DAVIDS, V), and *d* 1388, leaving issue:

1b REYNOLD GREY, 3rd LORD (Baron) GREY (of Ruthin); heir general to his 2nd cousin's son the **5th Lord** (Baron) **Hasting(e)s** and 3rd and last EARL OF PEMBROKE and as such won a judgement in the Court of Chivalry 1421 (after an action that had lasted 20 years) over Sir Edward Hastinges (*de jure* 8th LORD (Baron) HASTINGS according to later legal judgement) in a dispute as to which of them had the right to the undifferenced arms of the feudal Lords of (A)Bergavenny, *viz*, gules a maunche or (a device still born by the current Lords Hastings (*see* above under **Arms**)); styled himself 'Lord Hastynges' in a petition to Parl 1425; *m* 1st just after 25 Nov 1378 Margaret de Ros, dau of Thomas, 4th Lord (Baron) De Ros (*qv*) of Helmsley; *m* 2nd *c* 1406 Joan, only dau and heiress of William, 4th Lord (Baron) Astley and widow of Thomas Raleghe or Raleigh, of Farnborough, Warwicks (*see* GREY, B) and below under **Lineage (of Astley)**), and *d* 20 Sept 1440, having by his 1st w had issue:

1c John (Sir), KG (1436); *m* by 24 Feb 1412/3 Constance, dau of John de Holand, 1st Duke of Exeter, by Elizabeth, 2nd dau of JOHN OF GAUNT, DUKE OF LANCASTER, and *dvp* 27 Aug 1439, leaving issue:

1d EDMUND GREY, 4th LORD (Baron) GREY (of Ruthin) and 1st EARL OF KENT of the 1465 *cr*, who in confirmations of his Earldom in 1484 and 1486 was styled 'Baron and Lord of Hastinges'; *m* by Jan 1458/9 Lady Catherine Percy, dau of 2nd Earl of Northumberland of the 1415/6 cr (*see* NORTHUMBERLAND, D), and *d* 22 May 1490, having had issue (*see* GREY, B, and LUCAS OF CRUDWELL, B)

1 (cont.) The **1st Lord** (Baron) **Hasting(e)s** *m* 2nd Isabel (*d* 4 Dec 1334), dau of Hugh le Despenser, Earl of Winchester (*see* FALMOUTH, V), and *d* 10 Feb 1312/3, having had further issue:

(3) Thomas; *dsp* 1333

(4) Hugh (Sir), of Sutton Scotney, Hants; *b c* 1310; fought Battle of Sluys 1340, Capt and Lt English army in Flanders 1346, fought Battle of Crécy 1346; *m* by 18 May 1330 Margery, sis and coheir of Richard Foliot, of Gressenhall and Weasenham, Norfolk, and *d* 29 or 30 July 1347, leaving:

1a JOHN de HASTINGES, of Elsing, Norfolk, and Fenwick, Yorks, *de jure* 6th LORD (Baron) HASTINGS; *b c* 1328; *dsp* 31 Aug 1393

2a Hugh (Sir); allegedly *m* Margaret de Everingham and *dvf* 1369(?), leaving:

1b Hugh (Sir); *m* by 1 Nov 1376 Anne, 3rd dau of 1st Lord (Baron) Le Despenser (*see* FALMOUTH, V), and *d* 6 Nov 1386, leaving issue:

1c HUGH HASTINGES, *de jure* 7th LORD (Baron) HASTINGS; *b c* 1376; *m* Constance (*m* 2nd Sir John Sutton, of Dudley, Staffs), dau of Sir Walter Blount, but *dsp* 2 Nov 1396

2c Sir EDWARD HASTINGES, *de jure* 8th LORD (Baron) HASTINGS; *bapt* 21 May 1382; ktd by 6 Nov 1399, imprisoned in Tower of London 1403, possibly because of involvement in the rebellion of Hotspur and others (*see* NORTHUMBERLAND, D) against HENRY IV, imprisoned there again 1413 and yet again *c* 1417, this time in the Marshalsea, for debt after he refused to pay the costs of his failed heraldic lawsuit in the Court of Chivalry against his cousin REYNOLD, LORD GREY (of Ruthin) (*see* above), remaining there, it seems, till his death; *m* 1st Muriel, dau of Sir John de Dinham; *m* 2nd Margery (*m* 2nd 1440 Sir John Wymondham or Wyndham, of Felbridge and Runton, Norfolk, and *d* 1456), dau of Sir Robert Clifton, and *d* 6 Jan 1437/8, having by his first w had an only surv son:

1d JOHN HASTINGS, *de jure* 9th LORD (Baron) HASTINGS; *b c* 1411; Constable Norwich Castle 1441, Sheriff Norfolk 1474–75; *m* after 21 April 1434 Anne, dau of Thomas, Lord Morley, and *d* 9 April 1477, leaving issue:

1e Sir HUGH HASTINGS, *de jure* 10th LORD (Baron) HASTINGS; *b c* 1447; Sheriff Yorks 1479–80; *m* by 12 April 1455 Anne, dau of Sir William Gascoigne, of Gawthorpe, Yorks, and *d* 7 June 1488, leaving issue:

1f Sir JOHN HASTINGS, *de jure* 11th LORD (Baron) HASTINGS; *b c* 1466; *m* 1st by March 1489/90 Isabel (*dsp* 1495), dau and heir of Sir Ralph Babthorpe; *m* 2nd Katherine, dau of Sir John Aske, of Aughton, Yorks, and *dsps* 12 July 1504

2f Sir GEORGE HASTINGS, *de jure* 12th LORD (Baron) HASTINGS; *b c* 1474; *m c* 27 Nov 1493 Joan, dau of Roger Brabason, and *d* 11 June 1511, leaving issue:

1g JOHN HASTINGS, *de jure* 13th LORD (Baron) HASTINGS; *b c* 1497–98; *d* unm 10 Feb 1513/4

2g Sir HUGH HASTINGS, *de jure* 14th LORD (Baron) HASTINGS; *b c* 1505; *m* 24 April 1523 Katherine (*bur* 2 Feb 1558), er dau and coheir of Robert Le Strange, of Hunstanton, Norfolk (*see* SAINT DAVIDS, V, section **Lineage of Strange (of Knokyn)**), and *d* 29 Dec 1540, having had issue:

1h JOHN HASTINGS, *de jure* 15th LORD (Baron) HASTINGS; *b* 27 July 1531; *d* unm 8 Jan 1541/2, when by subsequent doctrine the Barony fell into abeyance between his sisters

1h Anne; *m* William Browne, of Elsing, Norfolk, bro of 1st Viscount Montagu, and had issue

2h ELIZABETH, of whom presently

3g Martyn; *dsp* 25 Oct 1574

2 Sir EDMUND De HASTINGES, 1st and last LORD (Baron) HASTINGS (of Inchmahome) (E), so *cr* by writ 1299–1313; *m* Isabel, Countess of Menteith, dau and heir of Sir John Russel by Isabel, Countess of Menteith in her own right, and widow of William Comyn (the marriage being arranged by EDWARD I, who was then in the position of being able to enforce his overlordship of Scotland); as one of the leading nobles of Scotland swore allegiance to EDWARD I 1296, took part on the English side Battle of Falkirk 1298 and Siege of Carlaverock 1300; *dsp* 24 June 1314, *k* fighting on the English side Battle of Bannockburn

The *de jure* 15th LORD HASTINGS's yr sis and coheir,

ELIZABETH Hastings; *b* 1533; *m* Hamon Le STRANGE, of Hunstanton, Norfolk (*d* 7 Oct 1580), and *d* 1580, leaving a 2nd s:

Sir NICHOLAS Le STRANGE; *b c* 1562; MP Norfolk *c* 1547; *m* 1st 1582 Mary, dau of Sir Robert Bell, Ch Baron Exchequer; *m* 2nd 1591 Anne, widow of Sir George Chaworth and dau of Sir William Paston, and *d* 15 Dec 1591, leaving:

Sir HAMON Le STRANGE, of Hunstanton; *b c* 1584; MP Norfolk; *m* 1601 Alice, dau and coheir of Richart Stubbe, of Sedgeford, Norfolk, and *d* 31 May 1654, leaving an est s:

Sir NICHOLAS Le STRANGE, 1st Bt (E), so *cr* 1 June 1629, of Hunstanton; *bapt* 27 March 1604; *m* 26 Aug 1630 Ann (*d* 15 July 1663), dau of Sir Edward Lewkenor, of Denham, Suffolk, and *d* 24 July 1655, leaving an est s:

1 Sir HAMON Le STRANGE, 2nd Bt; *dsp* 15 Feb 1655/6

2 Sir NICHOLAS Le STRANGE, 3rd Bt; *bapt* 17 Oct 1632; *m* 1st Mary, dau of John Coke (*see* LEICESTER, E); *m* 2nd 16 Oct 1662 Elizabeth (*bur* 6 Aug 1689), dau of Sir Justinian Isham, 2nd Bt (*qv*), and *d* 13 Dec 1669, leaving an est s:

(1) Sir NICHOLAS Le STRANGE, 4th Bt; MP; *b* 2 Dec 1661; *m* 2 Dec 1686 Anne, dau of Sir Thomas Wodehouse (*see* KIMBERLEY, E), and *d* 18 Dec 1724, having had, with another s and dau:

1a Sir THOMAS Le STRANGE, 5th Bt; *m* 27 July 1721 Anne, dau of Sir Christopher Calthorpe, KB, and *dsp* 8 Nov 1751

2a Sir HENRY Le STRANGE, 6th Bt; *m* Mary, dau of Rt Hon Roger North (*see* GUILFORD, E), and *dsp* 2 Sept 1760

1a Armine; *m* Nicholas Styleman, of Snettisham, Norfolk, and *d* 29 May 1768, leaving issue. He *d* 6 Jan 1746

2a LUCY; *m* 1721 **Sir Jacob Astley, 3rd Bt** (*see* below)

3 Roger; had:

(1) Sir ROGER Le STRANGE, 7th and last Bt; *dspm* 21 April 1762, when the btcy expired

Lineage (of Astley): Sir THOMAS de ASTLEY, of Astley, Warwicks; *k* Battle of Evesham 1265 fighting with Simon de Montfort, Earl of Leicester, against HENRY III; *m* 1st Joan, dau of Ernald du Bois, and had issue (with a dau Isabel):

1 ANDREW De ASTLEY, 1st LORD (Baron) ASTLEY, so *cr* by writ of summons to Parl 24 June 1295 according to later doctrine; *m* Sybil — and *d* just before 18 Jan 1300/1, leaving issue:

(1) NICHOLAS De ASTLEY, 2nd LORD (Baron) ASTLEY; *b c* 1276; captured by the Scots Battle of Bannockburn 1314; *dsp* 1325

(2) Giles (Sir); *m* Alice, 2nd dau and coheir of Sir Thomas Wolvey, and *d* by 1316, leaving issue:

1a THOMAS De ASTLEY, 3rd LORD (Baron) ASTLEY; *m* by 1336/7 Elizabeth, dau of Guy de Beauchamp, 10th Earl of Warwick (*see* WARWICK, BROOKE and, E), and *d* on or after 3 May 1336, leaving, with three yr children:

1b WILLIAM De ASTLEY, 4th LORD (Baron) ASTLEY(?); *b* by 1344/5; never called to Parl; *m* Joan, dau of 2nd or 3rd Lord (Baron) Willoughby de Eresby (*qv*), and *dspm*, when whatever peerage may be deemed to have been *cr* by the writ of summons of 1295 would have passed according to later doctrine to his only dau and heiress:

1c JOAN, BARONESS ASTLEY in her own right; *m* 1st Thomas Raleghe or Raleigh, of Farnborough, Warwicks, but had no surv issue by him; *m* 2nd, as his 2nd w, REYNOLD, 3rd LORD (Baron) GREY (of Ruthin) (*see* above), and had (with other issue):

1d EDWARD GREY; called to Parl by writ 1446 in right of his w as LORD (Baron) FERRERS OF GROBY, also 6th LORD (Baron) ASTLEY(?), if at all, through inheritance from his mother. Both these Baronies, if extant, would have expired on the attainder and execution of Edward's gggs Henry Grey, Duke of Suffolk, in Feb 1553/4

2b Thomas (Sir); ancestor of the Astley Bts of Patshull, Staffs (*see* 1970 edn)

Sir THOMAS *m* 2nd Editha, dau of Peter Constable, of Melton Constable, Norfolk, and had, with an est and yst s:

2 Ralph; ancestor in the 7th generation of:

(1) John, of Hill Morton and Melton Constable, Warwicks; *m* Frances, dau and heiress of John Cheyney, of Sittingbourne, Kent, and had an only surv s:

1a Isaac; *m* Mary, dau of Edward Waldegrave, of Lawford, Essex, and had:

1b THOMAS, of whom presently

2b JACOB ASTLEY, 1st BARON ASTLEY OF READING, Berks (E), so *cr* 4 Nov 1644; ktd 1624, Govr Plymouth 1638, Serjeant Maj Gen royalist army start of Civil War 1642, wounded Battle of Edgehill 1642, Govr Reading, Cdr royalist Inf Battle of Naseby 1645, captured by Parliamentarians 1646; *m* Agnes, dau of Henry Imple, a German, and *d* Feb 1651/2, leaving, with four yr sons (all *dsp*):

1c ISAAC ASTLEY, 2nd BARON ASTLEY OF READING; ktd Feb 1642/3; *m* 27 Dec 1650 Anne, dau of Sir Francis Stydolfe, and *d* 1662, leaving an est s:

1d JACOB ASTLEY, 3rd and last BARON ASTLEY OF READING; *b* by 1654; *educ* St John's Coll Cambridge; *m* his cousin Frances (*d* 11 July 1692), dau and coheir of Sir Richard Stydolfe, Bt, and *dsps* 1668, when the Barony expired

1c Elizabeth; *m* her cousin Sir Edward Astley (*see* below)

ISAAC ASTLEY's er son,

THOMAS ASTLEY; *m* Frances, dau and coheir of George Deane, of Tilney, Norfolk, and had issue:

1 Francis (Sir); *dsp*

2 Sir ISAAC ASTLEY, 1st and last Bt (E), so *cr* 21 Jan 1641/2; *m* 1st Rachel, dau of Augustine Messenger, of Hackford, Norfolk; *m* 2nd Bridget, dau of John Coke (*see* LEICESTER, E), and *dsp* 7 Sept 1659, when the btcy expired, while the Hill Morton and Melton Constable estates passed to his nephew

3 Edward; *m* his cousin Elizabeth Astley, dau of 1st BARON ASTLEY OF READING (*see* above), and *d* 15 March 1653, leaving issue:

(1) **Sir Jacob Astley, 1st Bt** (E), so *cr* 25 June 1660; inherited the entailed lands of his maternal gf, Lord Astley, as well as those of his paternal unc; MP Norfolk 1685–1722; *m* 6 Feb 1661 Blanch, est dau of Sir Philip Wodehouse, 3rd Bt (*see* KIMBERLEY, E), and *d* 17 Aug 1729, leaving issue:

1a **Sir Philip Astley, 2nd Bt**; *b* 20 July 1667; *m* 2 Dec 1690 Elizabeth (*d* 30 March 1738), dau and heiress of Thomas Bransby, of Caistor, Norfolk, and *d* 7 July 1739, having had, with other sons (*dsp*) and two daus:

1b **Sir Jacob Astley, 3rd Bt**; *b* 3 Jan 1691/2; *m* 1st 1721 Lucy (*d* 25 July 1739), sis and coheir of her bro Sir HENRY Le STRANGE, 6th Bt (*see* above), and had, with other issue:

1c EDWARD (Sir), **4th Bt**

2c John (Rev); *m* 1762 Catherine, dau of Philip Bell, of Wallington, Norfolk, and *d* 1803, leaving two daus

1c Blanch; *m* Edward Pratt, of Ryston, Norfolk, and had issue

1b (cont.) **Sir Jacob** *m* 2nd 1 May 1740 Judith (*dsp* 7 March 1742/3), widow of Gresham Page, of Saxthorpe, and dau of Isaac Watlington, MP; *m* 3rd 14 July 1744 Sarah (*dsp* 9 Aug 1764), dau of Christopher Bedingfeld

Sir JACOB ASTLEY, 3rd Bt, *d* 5 Jan 1760; his est son,

Sir Edward Astley, 4th Bt; MP Norfolk 1768–90; *bapt* 26 Dec 1729; *m* 1st 1751 Rhoda (*d* Oct 1757), est surv dau of Francis Blake Delaval, of Seaton Delaval, Northumberland, and sis of 1st and last Baron Delaval of Redford (who was also 1st and last Baron Delaval of Seaton Delaval), and had issue:

1 JACOB HENRY (Sir), **5th Bt**

2 Francis; *k* aboard frigate *Arethusa* in engagement off isle of Bars 1778

Sir Edward *m* 2nd 24 Feb 1759 Anne (*d* 11 July 1792), yst dau of Christopher Milles, of Nackington, Kent, and by her had:

3 Edward John; Col 1st Life Gds; *b* 11 June 1761; *m* Anne Little and *dsp* 3 June 1806

4 Bernard (Rev); Rector Little Snoring, Norfolk, and Binston, Somerset; *b* 31 Aug 1764; *m* 1787 Anne (*m* 2nd Rev Mathew Jones; *m* 3rd Rev Horatio Dowsing and *d* 1830), dau of Edward Hase, of Sall, Norfolk, and *dsp* Nov 1789

5 Henry Nicholas (Rev); *b* 5 Jan 1767; *m* 20 Feb 1798 Sarah, dau of Rev J Pitman, and *d* 16 Sept 1822 or 14 Aug 1854, leaving, with another s and dau (*d* unm):

(1) Henry L'Estrange Milles (Rev); Rector Foulsham, Norfolk; *b* 27 Dec 1804; *m* 18 May 1841 Dulcibella, dau of Col W Gouch, of Carleton, Yorks, and had issue

(1) Jane Mary; *m* 1 Oct 1833 Rev William Frank Cubitt, DD, Rector Fritton, Suffolk, and *d* 16 Aug 1903, having had issue. He *d* 22 June 1882

(2) Anne; *m* 15 Oct 1835 Rev Canon Henry James Lee-Warner, of Thorpland Hall, Norfolk, and *d* 26 May 1878, having had issue. He *d* 22 June 1885

Sir Edward *m* 3rd Elizabeth Bullen (*dspm* 1810) and *d* 27 March 1802

His est son,

Sir Jacob Henry Astley, 5th Bt; *b* 12 Sept 1756; MP Norfolk 20 years; *m* 14 Jan 1789 Hester (*d* 13 Jan 1855), yst dau and coheir of Samuel Browne, of King's Lynn, and had, with other issue:

1 JACOB, **16th Lord**

2 Edward; *b* Jan 1799; *d* 4 April 1846

3 Francis L'Estrange; Lt-Col; *b* 27 Feb 1810; *m* 1st 28 July 1836 Charlotte (*d* 29 July 1848), dau of Nathaniel Micklethwait, of Taverham, Norfolk, and had:

(1) Francis Nathaniel; Capt 6th Dragoon Gds (Carabiniers); *b* 26 May 1837; *m* 25 March 1863 Jane, est dau of W H Binney, and *d* 1868, leaving:

1a Francis Jacob L'Estrange; *b* 17 April 1866; *dsp* 1919

2a Edward Henry Nathaniel; *b* 25 Nov 1868; *dsp* 1948

1a Charlotte Mabel; *b* 21 Dec 1867; *d* 19 April 1915

(2) Frederic Bernard; *b* 18 Aug 1843; *m* 4 Oct 1866 Emma Augusta (*m* 2nd 25 Jan 1879 Maj L M Carmichael and *d* 1883), er dau of Charles Schreiber (*see* MARLESFORD, B) and *d* 19 Aug 1876, leaving issue:

1a Delaval Graham L'Estrange, CB (1941), JP, DL Norfolk; Maj N Somerset Yeo Cav, Lt Welch Regt, CA Norfolk; *b* 7 Dec 1868; *m* 1 July 1897 Kate (*d* 23 Dec 1961), 2nd dau of John Kerr Clark, of NSW and Bath, and *d* 17 May 1951, leaving:

1b Joan Doreen; *b* 19 Jan 1901; *m* 26 April 1928 Gerald Josselyn Royce Tomkin, s of Col J W Royce Tomkin, of Norton, Suffolk, and had issue

2b Betty L'Estrange; *b* 8 Oct 1902; *m* 16 Oct 1930 1st Viscount Muirshiel (*see* 1970 edn) and *dsp* 28 June 1974

2a Bernard Armine Frederick, JP Devon; T/Lt Devon Regt, CC Devon; *b* 4 Aug 1873; *d* 31 March 1934

1a Lilian Augusta Muriel; *m* Charles H B Gaine, 4th Hus, and *d* 1916

2a Blanche Rhoda Delaval; *m* 2 Dec 1897 Thomas John Green, of The Old House, Boxmoor, Herts, and had issue

(1) Charlotte Laura; *m* 12 Feb 1867 Hon Graham Edward Henry Manners-Sutton and *d* 18 Nov 1905, leaving issue (*see* RUTLAND, D)

3 (cont.) Col Francis Astley *m* 2nd 7 Sept 1854 Rosalind Alicia (*d* 27 Aug 1900), dau of Sir Robert Frankland Russell, 7th Bt, and *d* 9 April 1866, leaving by her:

(3) Bertram Frankland ASTLEY later FRANKLAND-RUSSELL-ASTLEY (roy licence 1901), of Chequers Court, Bucks, JP, DL; Lt Rifle Bde; *b* 27 Feb 1857; *m* 30 April 1887 Lady Florence Conyngham (*d* 28 Jan 1946, having *m* 2nd 17 June 1905 Maj Hon Claud Heathcote-Drummond-Willoughby; *see* WILLOUGHBY DE ERESBY, B), yst dau of 3rd Marquess Conyngham (*qv*), and *d* 11 Feb 1904, leaving:

1a Henry Jacob Delaval, of Chequers Court; Lt 3rd Dragoon Gds; *b* 3 March 1888; *m* 29 Oct 1909 Mary Ruth (*m* 2nd 8 July 1914 (*divorce* 1922) Shirley Falcke; *m* 3rd 28 Nov 1922 Vinton A Muller, MD, of Reno, Nevada, s of Carl L Muller, MD, of Nevada City, Calif.), dau of William Kinder, of Philadelphia, and *d* 21 Sept 1912

1b Olive Joan; *b* 26 June 1893; *m* 15 Dec 1927 George Grenville Fortescue (*see* FORTESCUE, E) and *d* 11 March 1976

(4) Hubert Delaval; MA Oxon; Rector Ellesborough, Bucks; *b* 14 July 1860; *m* 30 July 1895 Constance Edith (*d* 1 Sept 1940), widow of Sir Richard Francis Sutton, 5th Bt (*qv*), and dau of Sir Vincent Rowland Corbet, 3rd Bt (*see* 1970 edn), and *d* 26 May 1925, leaving:

1a Philip Reginald, CBE (1945, OBE 194–), MC; Col Life Gds, formerly 12th Roy Lancers, WWs I and II (despatches twice), US Legion Merit; *b* 9 June 1896; *m* 1st 26 Aug 1931 (*divorce* 1940) Edith Madeleine (the actress Madeleine Carroll, who *d* 1987), dau of Prof John Carroll; *m* 2nd 4 July 1949 *Penelope Joan McKerrow, OBE (1946) [Mrs Philip Astley, 15/161 Fulham Rd, London SW3 6SN], dau of Trevor Percy Bright, and *d* 24 Dec 1958, leaving:

1b +Richard Jacob [Richard Astley Esq, 20 Staverton Rd, Oxford OX2 6XJ]; *b* 31 May 1950; *educ* Eton, BA London; *m* 1974 *Rosanna, est dau of Sir (John) Anthony Quayle, CBE, the actor, and has issue:

1c +Thomas Jacob; *b* 14 Sept 1975

2c +Harry Richard; *b* 19 Nov 1977

1c +Jenny Miranda; *b* 1980

1a Ruth Constance; *b* 5 March 1900; *m* 14 April 1920 Col Hon Everard Humphrey Wyndham, MC, and has issue (*see* EGREMONT, LECONFIELD and, B)

(5) Reginald Basil; *b* 8 Jan 1862; *m* 1st 27 Jan 1913 Caroline Douglas (*d* 5 Aug 1921), widow of Sir Walter Corbet, 4th Bt (*see* 1970 edn), and only child of Capt James Affleck Stewart, 11th Hus; *m* 2nd 8 Oct 1931 Kathleen Mary, CBE (*d* 28 Oct 1973), widow of Hon Wilfred Thesiger, DSO (*see* CHELMSFORD, V), and dau of Thomas Mercer Cliffe Vigors, and *d* 6 Oct 1942

1 Anne; *m* 1820 Thomas Potter Macqueen, MP, of Ridgemont, Beds, and *d* 1833, leaving issue

2 Editha; *m* 23 March 1825 Warden Sergison, of Cuckfield Park, Sussex, and *d* 1871, leaving issue. He *d* 22 May 1868

3 Hester; *m* June 1825 Rev Augustus Dashwood (*see* DASHWOOD, Bt, of Kirtlington Park), and *d* 31 Aug 1867, having had issue

4 Agnes; *m* Sept 1825 Rev John Henry Sparke, Canon Ely, Rector Gunthorpe, Norfolk, est s of Bp of Ely, and *d* his widow 30 July 1872, having had issue

Sir JACOB *d* 28 April 1817; his est son,

Sir Jacob Astley, 6th Bt, and **16th Lord** (Baron) **Hastings** (following termination of abeyance in his favour and summons to Parl by writ 18 May 1841); *b* 13 Nov 1797; *educ* Magdalen Coll Oxford (DCL 1820); High Sheriff Norfolk 1821–22, MP (Lib) W Norfolk 1832–37, FSA 1848; *m* 22 March 1819 Georgiana Carolina (*d* 28 June 1835), 2nd dau of Sir Henry Watkin Dashwood, 3rd Bt, of Kirtlington Park (*qv*), and *d* 27 Dec 1859, leaving issue:

1 JACOB HENRY DELAVAL ASTLEY, **17th Lord** (Baron) **Hastings**; *b* 21 May 1822; *educ* Ch Ch Oxford; 2nd Life Gds 1848–51, Hon Col Norfolk Militia; *m* 19 May 1860 Frances (*m* 2nd 1873 Robert Heane, of Barnwood, Glos, and *d* 30 Dec 1884), dau of T Cosham, and *dsp* 8 March 1871

2 DELAVAL LOFTUS ASTLEY, **18th Lord** (Baron) **Hastings**; *b* 24 March 1825; *educ* Eton and Trin Coll Cambridge (MA); Vicar E Barsham, Rector Little Snoring, Norfolk; *m* 8 Aug 1848 Hon Frances Diana Manners-Sutton (*see* RUTLAND, D), and *d* 28 Sept 1872, leaving issue:

(1) BERNARD EDWARD DELAVAL ASTLEY, **19th Lord** (Baron) **Hastings**; *b* 9 Sept 1855; *educ* Eton and Trin Coll Cambridge; *d* unm 22 Dec 1875

(2) GEORGE MANNERS, **20th Lord**

(3) Henry Jacob; Lt Suffolk Yeo Cav; *b* 2 March 1867; *m* 8 July 1891 Sybil (*d* 24 Oct 1935), yr dau of Charles George Fountaine, and *dsp* 25 Aug 1909

(1) Agneta Frances Delaval; *m* 22 Oct 1891 her cousin Roland Le Strange, DL, of Hunstanton, Norfolk, and *d* 3 Oct 1918, having had issue. He *d* 20 Feb 1919

The 2nd son,

GEORGE MANNERS ASTLEY, **20th Lord** (Baron) **Hastings**, JP (Norfolk); *b* 4 April 1857; *educ* Eton and Trin Coll Cambridge; Maj 2nd Bde E Div RA, Steward Jockey Club; *m* 17 April 1880 Hon Elizabeth Evelyn Harbord (*d* 19 Feb 1957), 3rd dau of 5th Baron Suffield (*qv*), and had issue:

1 ALBERT EDWARD DELAVAL, **21st Lord**

2 Jacob John; 2nd Lt 16th Lancers; *b* 5 March 1884; *ka* 26 Sept 1917 serving with Sherwood Foresters

3 Charles Melton; Capt Northumberland Yeo, ADC Personal Staff, WW II as Capt HG; *b* 5 May 1885; *m* 30 Dec 1914 Evelyn Vere (*d* 24 Jan 1969 aged 90), widow of Leonard Stevens and er dau of Gen George Augustus Strover, HC Upper Burma, and *d* 13 Aug 1960, leaving issue:

(1) George Delaval; Maj Roy Fus (TA), Registrar Soc Authors; *b* 5 Oct 1915; *educ* Haileybury; *m* 1st 17 Jan 1942 (*divorce* 1946) Hope Shuttleworth, yr dau of Lt-Col Francis Holden Shuttleworth Rendall, DSO, DCLI; *m* 2nd 28 April 1949 *Diana Christian [Mrs George Astley, Woodhayne, Beechwood Lane, Burley, Ringwood, Hants BH24 4AR], only dau of Brig-Gen Robert Hugh Hare, CB, CMG, DSO, MVO, and *d* 1993, having by her had issue:

1a +(Delaval) Hugh [Hugh Astley Esq, 170 Arundel Av, Toronto, Canada M4K A3D]; *b* 2 Feb 1950; *educ* Aiglon Coll Switzerland; *m* 1976 *Penelope, dau of Charles Henry Underwood, and has issue:

1b +Christopher Delaval; *b* 1976

1b +Caroline Zoë; *b* 1975

2a +(Caroline) Susan [Mrs James Stymeist, Youbou, Vancouver Island, Canada]; *b* 29 Dec 1951; *m* 1st 1974 (*divorce* 1984) Charles Philip Barrington Woollett; *m* 2nd 1992 *James Stymeist and by him has issue:

1b +Alexandra Diana; *b* 1992

1 Alexandra Rhoda; *b* 28 Sept 1886 (HM QUEEN ALEXANDRA stood sponsor); *m* 16 Oct 1917 Brig George Frederick Arthur Pigot-Moodie, MC, MGC and Capt RSG (*d* 14 March 1959), and *d* 20 April 1918, leaving:

(1) John Peter; *kas* 4 Aug 1940 serving in RN

2 Bridget; *b* 8 March 1889; *d* unm 2 March 1906

3 Hester Winifred; *b* 17 May 1899; *m* 26 July 1923 Alan Houghton Broderick (*d* 1973), Chev Legn Hon, s of Alan Broderick, of Wooder Manor, South Devon, and *d* 1980, leaving issue:

(1) +John Alan St John [John Broderick Esq, 33 Chesil Court, Chelsea Manor St, London SW3]; *b* 1 July 1924

The 20th BARON *d* 18 Sept 1904; his est son,

ALBERT EDWARD DELAVAL ASTLEY, **21st Lord** (Baron) **Hastings**, JP Norfolk; Lt-Col 7th Hus, Hon Lt-Col King's Own Roy Regt Norfolk Yeo WW I (despatches twice), WW II as Lt-Col HG, V-Lt Norfolk, High Steward Norwich Cathedral 1949–56, Norfolk CC 1909–19, Pres CLA 1939, Tstee Roy Ag Soc England 1946–56, Pres N Norfolk C Assoc, Memb Indian States Ctee 1932; *b* 24 Nov 1882; *educ* Eton and RMC Sandhurst; *m* 11 Feb 1907 Lady Marguerite Helen Nevill (*d* 7 June 1975), yr dau of 3rd Marquess of Abergavenny (*qv*), and *d* 18 Jan 1956, having had:

1 EDWARD DELAVAL HENRY ASTLEY, **22nd and present Lord** (Baron) **Hastings**

2 Simon Nevill; Maj 7th Queen's Own Hus WW II (despatches), ADC to C-in-C India 1942 and Viceroy 1943; *b* 13 Aug 1919; *m* 27 Jan 1943 *Lady Joan Patricia Quirk Wavell [The Lady Joan Robertson, Willowfield House, Spanish Green, Stratfield Turgis, Hants RG27 0AD] (*m* 2nd 19 June 1948 Harry Alastair Gordon, MC (*d* 19 June 1965), yr s of Cdr Alastair Gordon, DSO, RN; *m* 3rd Maj Donald Struan Robertson, Scots Gds (*d* 1991), s of Rt Hon Sir Malcolm Arnold Robertson, GCMG, KBE), yst dau of FM 1st Earl Wavell, GCB, GCSI, GCIE, CMG, MC, PC (*see* 1953 edn), and *d* 16 March 1946 at Quetta following a motor accident, leaving issue:

(1) +Diana Jane [Mrs Robert Kellie, The King's, Oxlynch, Stonehouse, Glos GL10 3DE]; *b* 17 Dec 1943; *m* 1975 *Robert I W Kellie and has issue:

1a +Rupert Simon Chamier; *b* 1977

2a +Toby Alastair Struan; *b* 1984

1a +Tara Margaret Joan; *b* 1980

1 +Helen Elizabeth Delaval [The Hon Mrs Haw, Windermere Estate, 158 Bibra Drive, Bibra Lake, W Australia 6163]; *b* 12 Nov 1907; *m* 1st 29 April 1930 (*divorce* 1940) Ian Bulloch, s of G J Bulloch, and has:

(1) +Donald Ian [Donald Bulloch Esq, 11 Montclair Ave, Woodvale, Perth, WA 6026 Australia]; *b* 11 Feb 1931; *m* 12 May 1956 *Joyce Illman and has issue:

1a +Nevill; *b* 26 March 1959; *m* 1987 *Daria Garizio

2a +Donald; *b* 28 Oct 1961

1a +Elinor; *b* 4 June 1957; *m* 1983 (*divorce* 1993) Andrejz Misiewicz

(2) +James Angus; *b* 24 Sept 1935; *m* 1st 1956 (*divorce* 1960) Penelope Burrows and has issue:

1a +Anthea [Mrs Rohan Vos, PO Box 511, Constantia, Cape Prov 7848, S Africa]; *b* 25 June 1957; *m* 1st 1975 (*divorce* 19–) Robert Gordon Maclaggan and has:

1b +Shaun; *b* 19 May 1976

1b +Brenda; *b* 28 Sept 1978

1a (cont.) Mrs Anthea Maclaggan *m* 2nd 1982 *Rohan Vos and by him has:

2b +Bianca; *b* 13 March 1984

3b +Tiffany; *b* 13 Feb 1986

2a +Janet; *b* 16 June 1958; *m* 1984 *Alan Wale and has:

1b +Craig; *b* 25 June 1987

2b +Keith; *b* 15 Sept 1988

(2) (cont.) James Bulloch *m* 2nd 1961 *Margaret Conley and has by her:

1a +Simon; *b* 21 Dec 1961; *m* 1986 (*divorce* 1996) Sonia Linkston and has:

1b +Melissa; *b* 3 April 1989

2b +Kirsty; *b* 27 March 1994

2a +Keith; *b* 23 March 1964

(3) +Alasdair George [Alasdair Bulloch Esq, 60 Corbet St, Shelley, Perth, W Australia 6155]; *b* 13 Nov 1937; *m* 19– *Marion Mill and has issue:

1a +Samantha; *b* 1966

2a +Pepita; *b* 1969

3a +Jaye; *b* 1971

1 (cont.) Mrs Helen Bulloch *m* 2nd 1941 George Field (*d* 1941); *m* 3rd 12 Nov 1948 John David Haw (*d* 1982), only surv s of George Haw, of Hampstead

2 Armyne Margaret; Co Cdr ATS 1938–40; *b* 19 Dec 1909; *m* 16 Aug 1933 William George Broadbent Schofield (*d* 1987), er s of Capt George Arthur Schofield, of Riseley Hall, Harrogate, and *d* 1979, leaving issue:

(1) +Armyne Morar Helen [Lady Stirling, 25 Ladbroke Grove, London W11 3AY]; *b* 29 June 1934; *m* 20 June 1959 *Sir Angus Duncan Aeneas Stirling and has issue (*see* DUNMORE, E)

(2) Ann Blackstone; *b* 19 Nov 1935; *m* 19 Sept 1959 *Kinnaird St Clair Cunningham, est s of St Clair Usher Cunningham, of Hallmanor, Peebles, and *d* 27 June 1997, having adopted:

*Hugh William Kinnaird; *b* 6 May 1962

*Mark Schofield; *b* 6 July 1968

*Louise Margaret; *b* 9 July 1966

(3) +Marigold Elizabeth [Mrs John Warrington, Low Burton Hall, Masham, N Yorks HG4 4DQ]; *b* 18 April 1937; *m* 20 Oct 1962 *Capt John Anthony Cromek Warrington, Green Howards, yr s of Wilfred Joseph Warrington, and has:

1a +George Simon Cromek; *b* 20 Dec 1964.

2a +Patrick William Cromek; *b* 28 April 1966; *m* 1990 *Jane Alice Patience, dau of Joseph Andrew Christopher Hoare (*see* ANTRIM, E), and has issue:

1b +Ferdinand Joseph; *b* 6 Feb 1996

1b +Flora Lucy Christina; *b* 1991

2b +Eleanor; *b* 1993

1a +Olivia Sarah; *b* 27 Aug 1963; *m* Oct 1996 *Hon Ralph Assheton, est s of 2nd Baron Clitheroe (*qv*)

(4) +Cicely Rose [Mrs Harold Golden, 12311 Marine St, Los Angeles, CA, USA]; *b* 7 Nov 1941; *m* 29 April 1972 *Harold Irvin Golden, s of J W Golden, of Texas

3 +Jean [Mrs Mark Napier, 12 Grassmere Close, Felpham, Bognor Regis, Sussex PO22 7NU]; 3rd Offr WRNS WW II; *b* 17 April 1917; *m* 28 June 1945 Lt-Cdr Mark Napier, RN (*see* NAPIER and ETTRICK, L) and has issue

Seat: Seaton Delaval Hall. Despite the name 'Hall' Seaton Delaval is strictly speaking a villa. It was built between 1718 and 1728 by Sir John Vanbrugh for Admiral George Delaval, whose means did not match his aspirations, but designed so cunningly that it looks on a first glance or from photographs as if it were the size of Castle Howard. Many people regard it as Vanbrugh's masterpiece. The central portion, which rises three storeys to a pediment and is flanked by arcaded wings, also with pediments, burnt down in 1822 but was restored in the middle of the 19th century. Further restoration took place around the middle of the 20th.

HATHERTON

Arms: Arg. a chevron between three escallops sa. **Crest:** A stag's head cabossed sa., attired or., between the attires a buglehorn sa., garnished and pendant from two annulets, conjoined gold. **Supporters:** Dexter, a stag ppr., gorged with a collar or, therefrom pendant an escutcheon arg. charged with a bugle stringed sa.; sinister, a lion gu., gorged with a ducal coronet or, therefrom pendant an escutcheon, charged as in the dexter. **Motto:** *Ung Dieu et ung roy.*('One God and one king'). **Creation:** B. (UK) 11 May 1835.

THE 8TH BARON HATHERTON, of Hatherton, Co Stafford (Edward Charles Littleton) [The Rt Hon The Lord Hatherton, PO Box 1341-2150, Moravia, Costa Rica]; *b* 24 May 1950; *s* kinsman 1985; agronomist; *m* 1974 *Hilda Maria, dau of Rodolfo Robert, of San José, and has:

1 +THOMAS EDWARD; *b* 7 March 1977

1 *Melissa Anne; *b* 1975

2 *Valerie Anne; *b* 1981

Lineage (of Littleton): THOMAS WESTOCOTE; *m* Elizabeth, dau and heir of Thomas de Luttleton, of Frankley, Worcs, and had:

Sir THOMAS LUTTELTON/LYTTELTON/LITTLETON, KB, of Frankley; Serjeant-at-law 1453, King's Serjeant 1455, Judge Common Pleas 1466, author: *Treatise on Tenures*; *m* Joan (*d* 22 March 1505), widow of Sir Philip Chetwynd (*see* CHETWYND, V) and dau and coheir of William Burley, of Broomscroft Castle, Salop, and *d* 23 August 1481, having had issue:

1 William (Sir), of Frankley, ancestor of the Viscounts Cobham (*qv*)

2 RICHARD

3 Thomas, of Spetchley, Worcs; ancestor of Ld Keeper Lytleton *temp* CHARLES I and Sir William Littleton, Speaker H of C *temp* WILLIAM III

The 2nd son,

RICHARD LITTLETON; lawyer; *m* Alice, dau and heir of William Winesbury, of Pillaton Hall, Staffs, and *d c* 1518, having had, with three daus and an er s (Richard, *dsp*):

Sir EDWARD LITTLETON, of Pillaton Hall; Constable Stafford Castle, keeper roy parks, Bailiff Manor of Farebriggs, Staffs, for life, Sheriff Staffs *c* 1524, 1540 and 1551; *m* 1st Helen, dau of Humphrey Swinnerton, of Swinnerton, Staffs, and had, with other issue:

1 EDWARD (Sir)

1 Barbara; *m* 1st Henry Gower, of Worcs; *m* 2nd John Folliot, of Pirton

2 Constance; *m* Sir James Fuljambe

Sir EDWARD *m* 2nd Isabel Wood (*m* 3rd Ralph Egerton, of Wrinehill), widow, and sis and heir of Robert Hill, of Hounhill, Staffs, and *d* 10 Oct 1558, having had no issue by her

His son,

Sir EDWARD LITTLETON, of Pillaton Hall; Sheriff Staffs 1563; *m* Alice, dau of Francis Cockayne (see CULLEN OF ASHBOURNE, B), and had, with five daus:

1 EDWARD (Sir)

2 Thomas; *m* Cassandra, dau of Thomas Lane, of Bentley, Staffs, and had issue

3 Francis, of Melsho, Salop; *m* Gertrude, dau of Thomas Sutton, of Overhaddon, Yorks, and had issue

4 Walter, of Eccleshall, Staffs; *m* Alice, dau of John Comberford, of Staffs

5 John; *dsp*

6 James; *m* Mercy, widow of William Bowyer and dau of John Stone, of London, and left issue

7 Devereux; *m* Jane, dau of George Allen, of Woodhouse, Derbys, and had issue

Sir EDWARD *d* 19 July 1574; his est son,

Sir EDWARD LITTLETON, of Pillaton Hall; Sheriff Staffs 1583 and 1593, MP Staffs 1597; *m* Margaret, dau and coheir of Sir William Devereux, yst s of 1st Viscount Hereford (*qv*), and had issue:

1 EDWARD (Sir)

2 Thomas; *m* Elizabeth, illegitimate dau of Adam Moretton, of Wilbrighton, Staffs

1 Mary; *m* Richard Fowler, of King's Harnage, Salop

2 Annie; *m* Humphrey Salwey, of Stanford, Worcs

3 Jane; *m* Richard Knightley, of Fawsley, Northants

4 Ellen; *m* William Babington, of Curborough, Staffs

5 Margaret; *m* John Skinner, of Cofton, Worcs

6 Lettice; *m* John Fulnethy, Archdeacon Stafford

7 Constance; *m* Richard Hill, of London, gent

Sir EDWARD's er son,

Sir EDWARD LITTLETON, of Pillaton Hall; Staffs: MP 1624, Sheriff 1627; *m* 16 Jan 1598 Mary, dau of Sir Clement Fisher, of Packington, Warwicks, and had:

1 EDWARD (Sir)

2 Fisher; *bapt* 10 Dec 1600; *m* Anne, dau of John Baynton, of Wiltshire

3 Walter (Sir), Chllr Diocese of Lichfield and Coventry; *m* Priscilla, dau of Sir Lewis Pemberton, of Rushden, Northants, and had, with three other sons (*dsp*):

(1) Walter, of Lichfield; *m* as his 1st w Catherine, dau of William Talbot (*see* SHREWSBURY and WATERFORD, E) and had issue

4 William; *m* —, dau and heir of John Webster, of Amsterdam

1 Lettice; *b* 1 Jan 1601; *m* 1st William Washbourne, of Washbourne, Worcs; *m* 2nd John Clent, of Knightwick, Worcs

2 Mary; *m* Euseby Shuckburgh, of Naseby, Northants

3 Margaret; *m* 1st Sir George Browne, of Radford, Warwicks; *m* 2nd Francis Fisher (*dsp* 27 March 1692)

4 Anne; *m* 1st Sir Thomas Holt, 1st Bt, of Aston; *m* 2nd, as his 1st w, Charles, yr s of 1st Baron Leigh (*qvv*) of Stoneleigh of the 1643 *cr*, and by him had issue (*see* VALENTIA, V)

Sir EDWARD *d* 25 Aug 1630; his est son,

Sir EDWARD LITTLETON, 1st Bt (E), so *cr* 28 June 1627, of Pillaton Hall, Staffs; *bapt* 19 Dec 1599; *m* Hester (*m* 2nd Thomas Thorne, of Shelvock, Salop), dau of Sir William Courteen, of London, and had, with two other sons (*dsp*) and two daus (Anne, *m* — Cole, of Shrewsbury; Margaret, *m* Robert Napier, est s of Sir Robert Napier, of Luton Hoo, Beds):

Sir EDWARD LITTLETON, 2nd Bt; MP Staffs 1663–78; *m* 1st Mary, dau of Sir Walter Wrottesley, 1st Bt (*see* WROTTESLEY, B), and had:

1 Edward; MP Staffs 1685–87, Sheriff 1680–81; *m* Jan 1670/1 Susannah (*d* 25 Aug 1722), dau of Sir Theophilus Biddulph, 1st Bt (*see* 1949 edn), and *dvp* 24 Jan 1704, having had, with another s (*d* unm):

(1) Sir EDWARD LITTLETON, 3rd Bt; Sheriff Staffs 1712–13; *m* Mary (*d* 18 April 1761), only dau of Sir Richard Hoare, MP, and *dsp* 2 Jan 1741/2

(2) Fisher, of Pipe Ridware, Staffs; barrister; *m* Frances, est dau and coheir of James Whitehall, of Pipe Ridware, and *d* May 1740, having had issue:

1a Sir EDWARD LITTLETON, 4th and last Bt; moved from Pillaton Hall to Teddesley, Staffs; Sheriff Staffs 1762–63, MP 1784–1808; *m* Frances, est dau of Christopher Horton, of Catton, Derby, and *dsp* 18 May 1812, when the btcy expired

2a Fisher; barrister; *m* Mary, only dau and heir of Thomas Seace, of Northrepps, Norfolk, and *dsp*

1a FRANCES Littleton; *m* (by licence) 28 July 1760 Moreton WALHOUSE, of Hatherton, Staffs, and had issue (*see below*)

(1) Susanna; *m* Sir William Coryton, 3rd Bt, of Newton Ferrers Cornwall, MP, and had issue. He *d* Dec 1711

(2) Mary; *m* Edward Arblaster, of Longdon, Staffs

(3) Elizabeth; *m* Humphry Hodgetts

(4) Catherine; *m* John Floyer, son of Sir John Floyer, MD, of Lichfield

(5) Jane; *m* John Egginton, of Staffs

2 Walter, Maj; *m* Anne, dau of Nicholas Knollys (*see* KNOLLYS, V), and was *k* in a duel

1 Elizabeth; *m* Walter Chetwynd (*see* CHETWYND, V) and had issue

2 Hester; *m* 17 Aug 1681 Humphrey Persehouse, of Reynolds Hall, Staffs, and had issue

Sir EDWARD *m* 2nd his cousin Joyce Littleton, of Teddesley Hay, and *d c* 1709, having by her had, with three other sons (*d* unm):

3 Henry; Dep-Govr Cork, *dsp*

4 Fisher; barrister

5 William; Capt RN; had:

(1) Edward; *m* his cousin Joyce, est dau of Stanford Wolferstan, of Statfold, and *dsp*

3 Mary; *m* Ward Dilke, of Maxstoke Castle

4 Sarah; *m* Stanford Wolferstan, of Statfold

Lineage (of Walhouse): THOMAS WALHOUSE, of Whiston in Penkridge, Staffs; *m c* 1537 Margaret, dau of Humphrey Pynson, and had, with an est (Clement) and yst s (Roger):

RICHARD WALHOUSE, of Whiston and Gt Saredon; bought land in the manor of Hatherton also in Staffs by 6 Feb 1556; *s* to Church House, Chillington, which he sold to John Gifford 1573; *m* Elizabeth Colman and *d* 1585, leaving:

WILLIAM WALHOUSE, of Whiston, Gt Saredon and Hatherton; *m* Elizabeth (living 1618),sis of Ralph Tonkes, of Stafford, and *d* 4 July 1615, leaving:

WALTER WALHOUSE, of Hatherton; *m* by 13 Sept 1617 Margaret (*m* 2nd Walter Grosvenor, of Bushbury), dau of John Tayleur, of Longdon (now Buntingsdale), and had an only s:

JOHN WALHOUSE, of Hatherton; *m* by 1651 Mary (living 20 Feb 1673/4), 3rd dau of Matthew Moreton, of Engleton, Staffs, and sis of Edward Moreton, ancestor of the Earl of Ducie (*qv*), and *d* between 8 April 1663 and 14 April 1671, having had, with two yr sons (Matthew, William) and a dau (Elizabeth):

WALTER WALHOUSE, of Hatherton; *b c* 1651; *m* 1st Mary, dau of William Whitby, of The Grange, Lichfield; *m* 2nd Mary Croydon, of Wolverhampton, and *d* 1735, having had an er s:

JOHN WALHOUSE, of Hatherton and Birmingham; *m* 1st — and had three daus; *m* 2nd *c* 15 Jan 1728 Elizabeth (*d* 1755), dau of Moreton Slaney, of Brocton, Staffs, and *d* between 13 Feb 1737 and 4 Nov 1738, leaving an only s:

MORETON WALHOUSE, of Hatherton, High Sheriff Staffs 1790; *b c* 1731; *m* 1st 2 July 1750 Catherine, dau and heir of Edward Wilson, of Cannock, Staffs, and had an only surv s:

1 Edward Okeover WALHOUSE later OKEOVER; *m* Margaret Bowyer, of Snelston, Derbys, and *dsp* 1793

MORETON WALHOUSE *m* 2nd *c* 28 July 1760 FRANCES, sis of Sir EDWARD LITTLETON, 4th and last Bt (*see* above), and by her had, with other issue, including (James (Rev), BA, BCL Oxon, *b* 1764, *m* Elizabeth Huskisson (*d* 1876), half-sis of William Huskisson, PC, and *d* 24 Aug 1838, leaving issue):

2 Moreton, of Hatherton; High Sheriff Staffs 1820; *bapt* 20 June 1761; *m* Anne Craycroft (*d* 17 March 1843), dau of Abraham Portal, (*see* PORTAL, Bt), and had, with two other daus (*d* unm):

(1) EDWARD JOHN, **1st Baron**

(1) Charlotte Anne; *m* 26 Aug 1818 Rev George Chetwode and *d* 19 Jan 1837, leaving issue (*see* CHETWODE, B)

(2) Sophia Elizabeth; *m* 9 Dec 1820 V-Adml Hon Josceline Percy, CB, and *d* 13 Dec 1875, leaving issue (*see* NORTHUMBERLAND, D)

The only son,

EDWARD JOHN WALHOUSE later LITTLETON (roy licence 23 July 1812 on inheriting Teddesley Park from the 4th and last Bt; *see* above), **1st Baron Hatherton**, of Hatherton, Co Stafford (UK), so *cr* 11 May 1835, PC; DCL Oxon; *b* 18 March 1791; MP (Whig) Staffs 1812–32 and S Staffs 1832–35, Ch Sec Ireland 1833–34, Ld Lt Saffs 1854–62; *m* 1st 21 Dec 1812 Hyacinthe Mary Wellesley (*d* 4 Jan 1849), illegitimate dau of 1st and last Marquess Wellesley (*see* WELLINGTON, D), and had:

1 EDWARD RICHARD, **2nd Baron**

1 Hyacinthe Anne; *d* 10 July 1847

2 Emily; *m* 16 Aug 1832 Charles Evelyn Pierrepont, Viscount Newark (*see* 1953 edn MANVERS, E), and *dsp* 10 March 1851. He *d* 23 Aug 1850

3 Caroline Augusta; *m* 24 July 1838 8th Earl of Cavan (*qv*) and *d* 18 Jan 1892, having had issue

The **1st Baron** *m* 2nd 11 Feb 1852 Caroline Anne (*d* 16 May 1897), widow of Edward Davies Davenport, of Capesthorne, Cheshire, and est dau of Richard Hurt, of Wirksworth, and *d* 4 May 1863

His only son,

EDWARD RICHARD LITTLETON, **2nd Baron Hatherton**, CB (1881); *b* 31 Dec 1815; *educ* Eton and Ch Ch Oxford; MP (Lib) Walsall 1847–52 and S Staffs 1853–57, Hon Col 3rd Bn Prince of Wales's N Staffs Regt; *m* 23 Sept 1841 Margaret (*d* 15 Oct 1897), yst dau of 5th Duke of Northumberland (*qv*), and had:

1 EDWARD GEORGE PERCY, **3rd Baron**

2 Algernon Charles, JP Staffs; *b* 23 Aug 1843; R-Adml; *m* 11 Aug 1874 Lady Margaret Needham (*d* 31 July 1940), sis of 2nd Earl of Kilmorey (*qv*), and *d* 19 June 1912, leaving issue:

(1) Algernon Edward Percy; T/Capt 1914, served Boer War 1899–1900 and WW I; *b* 29 June 1881; *m* 15 June 1912 Violet Agnes Laetitia (*d* 1973), dau of Sir John William Salusbury-Trelawny, 11th Bt (*qv*), and *d* 30 June 1943, leaving:

1a Leonard Vere Algernon; WW II as Capt RA; *b* 8 April 1913; *educ* Malvern; *m* 8 Aug 1941 Sheila Miriam (*d* 1984), dau of Stanley Couldrey, of Tunbridge Wells, and *d* 23 Sept 1996

2a +Robert Joscelyn Henry, DFC (1944) [Robert Littleton Esq DFC, 3 Springfield, Ny Timber, Bognor Regis, W Sussex]; F/Lt RAF WW II; *b* 22 Jan 1915; *educ* Malvern; *m* 7 Sept 1946 *Wendy, dau of Stanley Hurdis Stevens, of Bury, Lancs, and has issue:

1b *Susan Elaine; *b* 5 March 1952

2b *Zoë Annette; *b* 19 May 1955

(2) Josceline William, MC, ED (1947); Lt-Col RCA, invalided as Sub-Lt RN 1907, served WW I (Croix de Guerre, Mons Star, two medals), WW II; *b* 9 Aug 1886; *educ* HMS *Britannia*; *m* 10 Nov 1920 Annie McKerrell (*d* 14 July 1961), dau of Arthur George Wolley-Dod, of Alberta, and *d* 16 March 1969, leaving:

1a *(Margaret) Anne [Mrs Anne Harder, 1345 W Tulare Ave, Visalia, CA 93277, USA]; *b* 8 Sept 1921; *m* 1st 19 March 1943 (*divorce* 1948) F/Lt Alfred John Smitz, DFC, RAF, and has:

1b *Peter Gerard Littleton [Peter Smitz Esq, Box 47, Site 8 RRI, Okotoks, T0L 1T0 Alberta, Canada]; *b* 24 May 1944; Constable RCMP; *m* 1969 *Carol Thew, of Richmond Hill, Ont, and has:

1c *Stephen Douglas; *b* 1975

2c *Leigh-Ann Kimberley; *b* 1971

1b *Sheila [Mrs Sheila Jones, 1165 Treadwell Lane, Sidney, BC V8L 5L2, Canada]; *b* Dec 1942; *m* 1st 19– (*divorce*) —; *m* 2nd 19– (*divorce*) Doug Jones and by her 1st husb has:

1c *Scott JONES; *b* 19–

2c *Craig JONES; *b* 19–

1a (cont.) Mrs Anne Smitz *m* 2nd 18 Nov 1948 (*divorce* 1963) Robert Boyer Leech; *m* 3rd 7 Jan 1967 (*divorce* 1974) Arthur Dale Harder, s of Jacob Harder, of Visalia, Calif., and by her 2nd husb has:

2b *Robert Timothy; *b* 17 April 1961; *m* Oct 1990 *Melissa Ann de Marco, of Calif.

2b *Marta Anne [Mrs Kerry King, 130 East Cedar, Exeter, CA 93221, USA]; *b* 16 March 1951; *m* 12 April 1969 *Kerry Wayne King, US Army, s of Leonard King, of Visalia, and has:

1c *Sara Jayne; *b* 1975

3b *Josceline Henrietta; *b* 27 Sept 1952; *m* 1st 1971 (*divorce* 1976) Mark S Wingo and has:

1c *Jason Marcus; *b* 1973

1c *Aisha Christine Gaunt; *b* 1977; has:

1d *Aarica Camilla Horner; *b* Sept 1997

3b (cont.) Mrs Josceline Wingo *m* 2nd 1979 Philip Lon (*d* 1981); *m* 3rd 1984 *John Douglas Koopman and by her 2nd husb has issue:

2c *Delaney Brie; *b* 1981

(3) Richard Charles Arthur; Cdr RN, WW I and WW II 1939–40 (invalided); *b* 1 Feb 1888; *m* 28 July 1934 Lucy Veronica (*d* 1979), dau of Rev Robert Cecil Salmon, of Chiddingstone Rectory, Kent, and *d* 21 Nov 1945 leaving:

1a *Joanna Veronica [Mrs Brian Bashall, Pondtail, Foxhill, Petworth, W Sussex]; *b* 27 July 1935; *m* 1976 *Brian Scarlin Bashall

2a *Marilyn Eve [Miss Marilyn Littleton, Chibbet, Exford, Minehead, Somerset]; *b* 2 Dec 1937

(4) Cecil Francis Henry; T/Capt Cameron Highrs WW I; *b* 12 Sept 1890; *educ* Cheltenham; *m* 21 Oct 1913 Brenda (*m* 2nd 22 July 1919 Arthur Alexander Baillie; *m* 3rd 18 Dec 1922 (*divorce* 1934) Alwyne Rory MacNamara Scrase-Dickins (*d* 1983) and *d* 1972), only dau of George Southby Hewitt, and *d* 6 May 1917 of wounds recd in action, leaving:

1a *Diana [Mrs Stephen Early, 27 Parkside, Cuddesdon, Oxford OX44 9EZ]; *b* 19 Feb 1915; *m* 19– *Stephen Early

(1) Margaret Emily; *b* 10 July 1875; *d* 16 Jan 1885

(2) Louisa Lucy; DGStJ; *b* 18 Aug 1876; *m* 1st 12 Sept 1899 Lt Col Henry Archer Clowes (*das* 8 March 1916), of Norbury Hall, Derbys, and had issue; *m* 2nd 2 July 1923 Sir Ronald Henry Amherst Storrs, KCMG, CBE (*d* 1 Nov 1955), s of Very Rev John Storrs, Dean Rochester, and *d* 1 June 1970

(3) Hyacinthe Mary Henrietta; *b* 22 Nov 1877; *d* unm 6 March 1961

(4) Isobel; *b* 28 Jan 1889; *m* 1906 Rev Thomas Salmon, Rector N Stoneham, Hants (*d* 19 Feb 1932), and had:

1a Russell; Maj Sudan Def Force WW II; *b* 6 March 1907; *das* 27 Sept 1941

2a Frank Robert, TD; Hon Lt-Col RA WW II; *b* 19 May 1910; *educ* Winchester and Birmingham U (BSc 1932, MIME); *m* 8 Nov 1940 Patricia Jean Even (*d* 1997), CC Worcs, dau of Lt-Col George R Painton, RAMC, and *d* 1997, leaving:

1b *Timothy Russell Paynton; *b* 13 Jan 1942; *educ* Winchester and Univ Coll Oxford (BA); *m* Jan 1964 *Anne-Marie Louise Madeleine, dau of Jean Edouard Herrmann, and has had issue:

1c Dominic Edouard Wellesley; *b* 8 Oct, *d* 5 Dec 1965

2c *Jean-Marc Patrick Wellesley; *b* 1966

2b *Robin Thomas Littleton; *b* 3 Oct 1943; *educ* Winchester and Magdalene Coll Cambridge (BA 1965, MA 1968)

3b *(Frank) Julian Even [Julian Salmon Esq, 65 Belsize Lane, London NW3 5AU]; *b* 1 June 1947; *educ* Winchester and Trin Coll Dublin

3a *Thomas David; Assist Slr BOT, Capt RA WW II (despatches); *b* 1 Nov 1916; *educ* Winchester and Ch Ch Oxford; *m* 1950 *Morris Patricia Reyner, dau of George S Turner, of Ilford, Essex, and has issue:

1b *Thomas Patrick Reyner; *b* 1960

1b *Susan Jane; *b* 1951

2b *Caroline Mary; *b* 1953

1a *Margaret Isabel [Mrs Reginald Williams, The Pines, North Road West, Hythe, Kent]; *b* 30 Oct 1920; *m* 1946 *Maj Reginald Williams, Argyll and Sutherland Highrs, and has issue:

1b *Anthony Peter [Anthony Williams Esq, 31 Brunswick Court, Regency Street, London SW1]; *b* 20 July 1947; *educ* Cranbrook

2b *Simon Hilary; *b* 26 Oct 1950; *educ* Cranbrook and Exeter U

(5) Blanche; *b* 1 April 1880; *m* 1 June 1907 Maj Ernest William Clowes, DSO, yr s of Samuel William Clowes, DL, of Broughton Hall, and *d* 11 Feb 1964, leaving issue. He *d* 28 Jan 1951

(6) Eleanor; *b* 6 Dec 1884; *d* unm 8 Jan 1963

3 Henry Stuart, JP Queensland; FInstPI, Capt Staffs Yeo; *b* 3 Dec 1844; *m* 15 Sept 1898 Agnes Caroline (*d* 4 July 1935), dau of Sir Michael Robert Shaw-Stewart, 7th Bt (*qv*), and *dsp* 14 March 1933

4 William Francis, CMG, DL Staffs; barrister; *b* 11 Aug 1847; *d* unm 1 May 1889

5 Cecil James (Rev); MA Oxon, Hon Canon Southwell; *b* 12 Feb 1850; *m* 29 Jan 1881 Katharine (*d* 16 April 1935), yst dau of Sir Charles Robert Rowley, 4th Bt (*qv*), and *dsp* 12 March 1912

The 2nd BARON *d* 3 April 1888; his est son,

EDWARD GEORGE PERCY LITTLETON, **3rd Baron Hatherton**, CMG (1880), JP Staffs; Maj and Col Gren Gds, Mil Sec to Govr Gen Canada, Staffs: CA, V-Lt, Chm QS 1894–1924, Chm CC 1901–20, Hon Commr in Lunacy 1890–98; *b* 15 Aug 1842; *educ* Eton; *m* 16 Aug 1867 Charlotte Louisa (*d* 19 Feb 1923), 8th dau of Sir Charles Robert Rowley, 4th Bt (*qv*), and *d* 24 Aug 1930, having had issue:

1 EDWARD CHARLES ROWLEY LITTLETON, **4th Baron Hatherton**, JP, DL Staffs; Lt 3rd Bn N Staffs Regt 1887–90, Offr in service of HH THE RAJAH OF SARAWAK 1890–96; *b* 6 Aug 1868; *m* 14 July 1897 Hester Edithe (*d* 6 Jan 1947), dau of Thomas Tarrant Hoskins, JP, MD, of Tasmania, and *d* 10 Nov 1944, having had:

(1) EDWARD THOMAS WALHOUSE LITTLETON, **5th Baron Hatherton**, DL (Staffs 1947); *b* 13 Aug 1900; *educ* Osborne and Dartmouth, Lt-Cdr RN WW I, Assist Inspr Naval Ordnance 1938, served WW II, C Whip Ho Lds 1946–49; *m* 1st 5 Sept 1925 (*divorce* 1951) Ida Gwenduolene, formerly w of Capt Henry Burton Tate (*see* TATE, Bt) and only child of Robin Legge, of Chelsea, and had:

1a *Joanna Ida Louisa [The Hon Mrs Perceval, Pillaton Old Hall, Penkridge, Staffs]; *b* 14 Oct 1926; *m* 1 Sept 1948 *Robert Westby Perceval, BA, Clerk-Assist Ho Lds, and has issue:

1b *Antony Robin Walhouse Westby PERCEVAL later LITTLETON (roy licence 1971) [Antony Littleton Esq, Old Walls, Hannington, Hants]; *b* 19 June 1950; *educ* Eton and Durham U; *m* 12 April 1980 *Hon Aileen Mary Fitzherbert, est dau of 8th Baron Stafford (*qv*), and has:

1c *Thomas Alastair Westby; *b* 1986

1c *Katrina Mary; *b* 23 July 1983

2c *Rosanna Sophie; *b* 1989

1b *Sarah Jane Modwena [Mrs Richard Dyott, Freeford Manor, Lichfield, Staffs]; *b* 5 Aug 1954; *m* 1981 *Richard Burnaby Kennedy Dyott, FRICS, only s of William Boyd Kennedy Shaw, OBE, by Eleanor, yr dau of Richard Archibald Dyott (*see* ANGLESEY, M), and has:

1c *William Richard Perceval; *b* 1987

1c *Caroline Eleanor Frances; *b* 1985

2b *Diana Mary [Mrs Peter Burden, Gwynfe House, Sutton St Nicholas, Herefs HR1 3NP]; *b* 27 March 1959; *m* 6 Sept 1980 *Peter Henry Burden and has:

1c *Edward Hugh; *b* 28 Jan 1986

2c *Archibald Robert; *b* 28 Aug 1990

1c *Alice Titania; *b* 21 June 1988

2a *Jane Anne Caroline [The Hon Mrs Wright, Meadowsweet Lodge, Uppingham, Rutland]; *b* 10 Sept 1929; *m* 24 Jan 1967 *Rev Charles Piachaud Wright

(1) (cont.) The **5th Baron** *m* 2nd 11 Jan 1952 Kathleen May (*d* 2 Aug 1983), formerly w of Maj Oscar Westendarp, RAF, and only dau of Clarence Ernest Orlando Whitechurch, of Esher, Surrey, and *d* 13 Nov 1969

(2) JOHN WALTER STUART LITTLETON, **6th Baron Hatherton**; *b* 9 Aug 1906; *m* 6 Nov 1932 Nora Evelyn (*d* May 1955), dau of R C Smith, of Edgbaston, Birmingham, and had issue:

1a *Moonyeen Meriel [The Hon Moonyeen Littleton, c/o Interserve, 325 Kennington Rd, London SE11 4QH]; *b* 4 Aug 1933

(2) (cont.) The **6th Baron** *m* 2nd 1955 *Mary Alice, Capt QAIMNS, dau of John Roberts, of Ruthin, Denbighshire, and *d* 27 June 1973, leaving by her:

1a *Richard Brownlow [The Hon Richard Littleton, Foresters Lodge, Nether Alderley, Macclesfield, Cheshire]; *b* 1949; *m* 1st 1975 (*divorce*) Shirley Margaret Adamson; *m* 2nd 1992 *Linda Hoyland and by his 1st w has:

1b *Ian Brownlow; *b* 1981

1b *Kirsty Emma; *b* 1985

2a *Jonathan Lloyd [The Hon Jonathan Littleton, Cornish Arms Cottage, The Square, W Looe, Cornwall]; *b* 1949; *m* 1970 *Maxine Elizabeth, dau of Alistair Brough Mills, of Salop, and has issue:

1b *Alexander John Walhouse; *b* 1970

1b *Rosalind Elizabeth; *b* 1972

2b *Melissa Mary; *b* 1975

2a *Modwena Louise [The Hon Mrs Orchard, Copper Beeches, 9A Hartland Rd, Epping, Essex]; *b* 1947; *m* 1st 1968 (*divorce* 1974) Edward Willison; *m* 2nd 1978 *Peter Fleming Orchard and by her 1st husb has issue:

1b *Trecia; *b* 1969

2b *Rachel; *b* 1971

(3) THOMAS CHARLES TASMAN LITTLETON, **7th Baron Hatherton**, TD (1953); *b* 6 Oct 1907; *educ* Cranleigh; Capt RA WW II; *m* 7 April 1933 Ann Scott (*d* 1994), only dau of Lt-Cdr Thomas McLeod, RN, of Hull, and *d* 1985, leaving:

1a *Hyacinthe Ann [The Hon Mrs Peterken, Claypool Farm, Hutton Henry, Castle Eden, Co Durham]; *b* 14 April 1934; LLB Newcastle; slr; *m* 10 March 1955 *Patrick Peterken, only s of A A Peterken, and has:

1b *Patrick James Littleton; *b* 26 Oct 1957

2b *Nicholas John Littleton; *b* 30 April 1960

1b *Frances Josephine; *b* 29 July 1962

(1) Joyce Marie; *b* 2 July 1898; *m* 1st 3 Nov 1923 (*divorce* 1934) James Ian Charles Orr Gairdner (*d* 1934) and had issue; *m* 2nd 1934 Samuel Prince and *d* 20 July 1968, leaving further issue

(2) Norah Hyacinthe; *b* 19 July 1899; *m* 7 June 1923 Samuel Randolph Allsopp, CBE, JP, DL, and *d* 23 Aug 1997, leaving issue (*see* HINDLIP, B)

(3) Lilah Cecila; *b* 21 Aug 1902; *m* 25 Feb 1922 (*divorce* 1949) Stewart Sandbach Harrison, MC, and had issue:

1a *Rupert; *b* 5 June 1924; *m* 1947 *Hazel Price and has issue:

1b *Roger; *b* March 1948

2b *Philip; *b* March 1949

2a *Desmond; *b* 2 May 1926; *m* 1950 *Doreen Chappell and has issue:

1b *Stephen; *b* Jan 1951

1b *Gillian Lilah; *b* Feb 1953

1a *Youla Cecilia [Mrs Leo Mieville, Orchard House, Wattisfield, Diss, Norfolk]; *b* 25 Oct 1927; *m* 1947 *Leo Claude Vaux Mieville and has:

1b *Peter Dominic Vaux; *b* Sept 1951; *educ* Westminster

1b *Claudia Cecilia Vaux; *b* May 1949

(4) Youla Edithe; *b* 13 March 1904; *m* 5 Oct 1927 (*divorce* 1938) John Elvine Harris (*d* 28 June 1965), took name WELLESLEY by deed poll 1939 and had issue

(5) *Hester Mary Modwena [The Hon Hester Littleton, Pitt Manor Cottage, Winchester, Hants]; *b* 3 May 1912; WTS/FANY WW II

2 Algernon Joshua Percy; Robert's Horse Boer War (medal with six clasps); *b* 11 April 1871; *educ* Eton and Pembroke Coll Cambridge; *m* 11 Jan 1913 Alice Maud (*d* 28 May 1954), dau of William Frederick Lewis, Consul Shanghai, and *d* 8 Sept 1951

3 Charles Christopher Josceline, DSO (1918); Lt-Col 7th Bn Middx Regt (TF), Embarkation Staff Offr 1916 WW I (despatches), Order El Nahda 3rd Cl, High Sheriff Radnorshire 1937; *b* 18 July 1872; *educ* Trin Hall Camb; *m* 1st 13 Oct 1903 Aline Beatrix (*d* 3 July 1919), 2nd dau of Sir Frederick Hervey-Bathurst, 4th Bt (*qv*); *m* 2nd 27 May 1922 Lettice Mina (*d* 6 Dec 1969), widow of Lt-Col Ronald Bernard (*see* 1970 edn BANDON, E) and dau of Gerald Paget (*see* ANGLESEY, M), and *d* 12 March 1950, leaving by his 1st w:

(1) Mervyn Cecil; *b* 10 Aug 1908; *m* 1940 *Margaret Ann [Mrs Mervyn Littleton, PO Box 3358, San José, Costa Rica], dau of Frank Sheehy, of Canada, and *d* Sept 1970, leaving issue:

1a EDWARD CHARLES LITTLETON, **8th and present Baron Hatherton**

1a *(Aileen) Pamela Hyacinthe [Mrs Roberto Odor, PO Box 2280, San Pedro Sula, Honduras]; *b* 1941; *m* 1963 *Roberto Padilla Odor and has:

1b *Roberto; *b* 1964

2b *Andreas; *b* 1968

3b *Mervyn; *b* 1971

1b *Luciana; *b* 1964

2a *Cynthia Ann; *b* 1943; *m* 1964 *Giovanni Sosto Peralta and has issue:

1b *Giovanni; *b* 1967

2b *Eugenio; *b* 1971

3b *Carlo; *b* 1972

1b *Alexandra Eugenia; *b* 1968

4 William Hugh, JP, DL Staffs; Maj 3rd Bn N Staffs Regt WW I (wounded); *b* 26 July 1882; *educ* Eton; *m* 20 April 1920 Lilian (*d* 23 March 1954), est dau of Charles Davis, of Clifton, Bristol, and *d* 21 April 1956, leaving issue:

(1) John William; WW II with RASC 1943–47; *b* 26 Sept 1924; *educ* Canford; *m* 1956 *Hilda Ruth [Mrs John Littleton, The Bridges, 92 King's Ave, Christchurch, Hants], only dau of J Pardy, of Christchurch, and *d* 1992, leaving:

1a *Deborah Jayne; *b* 24 June 1960; *m* 1981 (*divorce* 1993) Thomas Collins and has:

1b *Steven Andrew; *b* 1981

2a *Susan Jennifer; *b* 20 April 1965

(1) *Margaret Hyacinthe [Mrs Edward Dew, Highdown, Bridge Reeve, Chulmleigh, N Devon]; *b* 8 June 1921; VAD 1940–46; *m* 29 Oct 1948 *Edward Roderick Dew, CBE, only s of Dr Charles Edward Dew

1 Margaret Louisa; *b* 29 Dec 1869; *m* 12 April 1899 Sir Bertram Percy Portal, KCB, DSO (*see* PORTAL, Bt), and *d* following a car crash 7 Feb 1945, leaving issue

2 Hyacinthe Frances; *b* 7 Oct 1874; *d* unm 27 June 1951

3 Susan Helen; *b* 17 Feb 1877; *m* 19 April 1900 Rev Owen Fitzherbert Jackson, of Tedsmore Hall, Oswestry, and had issue. He *d* 13 Jan 1935

4 Mary Cecilia; *b* 8 Feb 1884

5 Edith Modwena, ARRC WW I (despatches); *b* 19 Jan 1888

HATTERSLEY

Creation: B. (LP, UK) 1997.

THE BARON HATTERSLEY, of Sparkbrook, Co West Midlands (Roy Sydney George Hattersley, PC (1975)) [The Rt Hon The Lord Hattersley PC, House of Lords, London SW1A 0PW]; *b* 28 Dec 1932; *educ* Sheffield City GS and Hull U; NHS exec 1956–64; memb Sheffield City Cncl 1957–65 (Chm Housing Ctee and Public Service Ctee); MP (Lab) Birmingham Sparkbrook 1964–97, PPS to Min Pensions and NI 1964–67, Jt Parly Sec DEP 1967–69, MOD 1969–70, Oppn Spokesman: Def 1972, Educn and Sci 1972–74, Environment 1979–80, Home Affrs 1980–83 and 1987–92, Treasury and Ec Affrs 1983–87, Min State FCO 1974–76, Sec State Prices and Consumer Protection 1976–79, Dep Leader Lab Party 1983–92; Visiting Fell: Inst Politics Harvard U 1971 and 1972, Nuffield Coll Oxford 1984–; Dir Campaign for European Political Community 1966–67; jnlst (Granada Columnist of the Year 1982); Hon DSc: Sheffield Hallam, Hon DLitt Hull, Hon DLit W Midlands; author: *Nelson* (1974), *Goodbye to Yorkshire* (1976), *Politics Apart* (1982), *Press Gang* (1983), *A Yorkshire Boyhood* (1983), *Choose Freedom: the future for Democratic Socialism* (1987), *Economic Priorities for a Labour Government* (1987), *The Maker's Mark* (1990), *In That Quiet Earth* (1991), *Skylark Song* (1994), *Between Ourselves* (1994); *m* 1956 *Edith Mary (Molly), dau of Michael and Sally Loughran, Pres Secondary Heads Assoc 1980–81, Chm Soc Educn Consultants 1994–

Lineage: FREDERICK ROY HATTERSLEY, of Sheffield; had:

ROY SYDNEY GEORGE, *cr* a **Baron**

HAVELOCK-ALLAN

Arms: Quarterly, 1st and 4th, sable a cross potent quarter pierced or, charged with four gouttes de sang; in chief two lion's heads erased of the 2nd, all within a bordure engrailed erminois, a canton ermine (for ALLAN); 2nd and 3rd, vert, a castle double-turreted argent between two fleurs-de-lys in chief, and a cross-crosslet fitchée in base or (for HAVELOCK). **Crests:** 1 A demi-lion rampant argent, ducally crowned gules, charged on the shoulder with a cross-crosslet fitchée sable, holding in the dexter paw a cross potent or, supporting in the sinister paw a rudder of the second. 2 A lion rampant gules, powdered with ermine spots and charged on the shoulder with a castle argent, sustaining a Danish battle-axe proper. **Mottoes:** 1 (under arms) *Fortiter gerit crucem* ('He bears the cross bravely'). 2 (over crest) Fedeliter ('Faithfully'). 3 (over crest) Lucknow. **Creation:** Bt. (UK) 22 Jan 1858.

SIR ANTHONY JAMES ALLAN HAVELOCK-ALLAN, 4TH BT, of Lucknow [Sir Anthony Havelock-Allan Bt, c/o Lloyds Bank Ltd, 14 Berkeley Sq, London W1 6BJ]; *b* 28 Feb 1904; *educ* Charterhouse, *s* brother 1975; film producer; *m* 1st 12 April 1939 (*divorce* 1952) (Babette) Valerie Louise (the actress Valerie Hobson), yr dau of Cdr Robert Gordon Hobson, RN, and has had:

1 Simon Anthony Henry, *b* 6 May 1944; *d* 31 Jan 1991

2 +(ANTHONY) MARK DAVID, QC (1993) [Mark Havelock-Allan Esq QC, 38 West Sq, London SE11 4SP]; *b* 4 April 1951; *educ* Eton, Durham U (BA 1972) and Trin Coll Cambridge (LLB 1974, Diploma Internat Law 1976); barrister Inner Temple 1974, FCIArb 1991, Bencher 1995, Assist Recorder 1993–97, Recorder 1997–; *m* 1st 24 March 1976 (*divorce* 1984) Lucy Clare, yr dau of Alexander Plantagenet Michell-Innes; *m* 2nd May 1986 *Alison Lee Caroline, dau of Leslie Francis Foster, and by her has issue:

(1) +Henry (Harry) Caspar Francis; *b* 6 Oct 1994

(1) *Miranda Antonia Louise; *b* 29 July 1993

(2) *Hannah Marie Josephine; *b* 18 Oct 1997

Sir ANTHONY *m* 2nd 26 June 1979 *Maria Theresa Consuela (Sara), dau of Carlos Ruiz de Villafranca, of Madrid, late Spanish Amb Chile and Brazil

Lineage: WILLIAM HAVELOCK, of Sunderland; had, with other issue, including a dau (Hannah, *m* Robert Allan, of the ALLANs of Blackwell Grange, Co Durham, and *d* 9 Jan 1837 aged 70):

WILLIAM HAVELOCK, of Ingress Park, Kent; *m* 1787 Jane, dau of John Carter, of Yarm, Yorks, by Elizabeth, dau of — Ettrick, of High Barnes, Co Durham, and had issue:

1 William, KH; Lt-Col, ADC to Count von Alten Battle of Waterloo (wounded); *m* Caroline Elizabeth (*d* 6 May 1866), dau of Acton Chaplin, and was *ka* cmdg 14th Light Dragoons Battle of Ramnugger Sikh War 22 Nov 1848, leaving issue (*see* RAMSDEN, Bt)

2 HENRY

3 Thomas; served Spain under Sir De Lacy Evans and *d* unm of fever at Vittoria 1836

4 Charles Frederick; *b* 16 Oct 1803; Lt-Col Br Army, Maj-Gen Imp Ottoman Army (Order of Medjidie), held medals or clasps for engagements at Bhurtpore, Ghuznee, Tezeen, Kabul, Moodkee, Ferozeshah (severley wounded), Sobraon and Gujerat, Brig-Gen Irregular Osmanli Cav Crimean War; *m* 14 May 1883 Mary (*d* 29 July 1889), 2nd dau of James Wemyss, and had issue

1 Helen; *d* 1825

2 Jane; *m* Capt William Creak, RN

3 Isabella; *m* John Moore Cave and *d* 1825

The 2nd son,

Sir HENRY HAVELOCK, KCB (1858, CB 1842); *b* 5 April 1795; *educ* Charterhouse and Middle Temple; commissioned Rifle Bde 1815, served India 1823 and Burmese War, Capt 1838, Afghan War, Maj 1842, Lt-Col 1844, Sikh War, cmded 2nd Div Battle of Mohammerah Persian War, Brig-Gen relief of Cawnpore and Lucknow Indian Mutiny 1857, Maj-Gen 29 Sept 1857, author: *History of the Burmese War* and *The War in Afghanistan*; *m* 9 Feb 1829 Hannah Shepherd (*d* 25 Aug 1882 aged 73, having been granted 18 Jan 1858 rank of Bt's w, and by Parl a life annuity of £1,000 (just over £45,000 in late-1990s terms), which had been planned for her husb and his son for life and which was honoured for the son too; *see* below against 1st Bt), dau of Rev Joshua Marshman, DD, of Serampore, and *d* 24 Nov 1857 just as letters patent were in preparation to create him a Bt, leaving, with four daus:

1 HENRY MARSHMAN (Sir), **1st Bt**

2 Joshua Havelock; *b* 11 Dec 1831; Capt Bombay Staff Corps, Assist-Commer Punjab; *m* 16 Dec 1858 his cousin Isabella Louisa (*d* 12 Jan 1918), 2nd dau of Capt William Creak, RN, and *d* 24 Sept 1864, leaving issue:

(1) Henry; *b* 15 Jan 1860; *educ* Magdalen Coll Oxford (MA); *d* 1918

(2) George Eric; *b* 12 Sept 1862; slr; *m* 10 April 1890 (*divorce* 1909) Elizabeth Maria Caroline, yst dau of Lewis Nancey, of Horne Hall, Co Durham, and *d* 1924, having had issue:

1a Eric Henry Edwardes, CB (1950), CBE (1943); *b* 9 July 1891; *educ* Highgate and Merton Coll Oxford (BA); FRS (Edinburgh); Sec Devpt Commn 1934–55, Admin Sec Ag Research Cncl 1934–50, Order Crown Belgium with Gold Palms; *m* 1st 28 Aug 1919 Christina Ramsey Scott (*d* 22 Nov 1958), dau of Alexander Moodie, and had:

1b *Elizabeth Kerr [Mrs Konstanty Kosciuszko, Apt C2, 1196 Eastern Parkway, Brooklyn, New York, USA]; *b* 1 June 1920; *m* 6 Aug 1946 *Konstanty Kosciuszko, Polish Forces, son of P Kosciuszko, and has issue:

1c *Stefan Henry; *b* 2 June 1959

1a (cont.) Eric Havelock *m* 2nd 19 Dec 1962 *Eileen, dau of Col John William Hastings Potts, RHA, of New Court, Athlone, and widow of Maj-Gen Walter Reginald Paul, CBE, and *d* 1974

3 Ettrick; *b* 5 Aug 1833; *d* 11 June 1834

4 George Broadfoot Havelock; *b* 5 June 1847; Prince of Wales (N Staffs Regt) (98th), 101st Roy Bengal Fus, Bengal Police; *m* 1st 23 Sept 1873 Georgina Marian (*dsp*1888), dau of James Crosby, barrister; *m* 2nd 20 Dec 1888 Annie Helen (*d* 20 May 1937), dau of Henry Browne Beresford, HEICS (*see* WATERFORD, M), and *d* 20 April 1908, leaving:

(1) Beresford Arthur Jardine; *b* 10 Oct 1889; Maj 2nd Bn Prince of Wales (N Staffs) Regt (98th), attd 7th Serv Bn Mesopotamian Expdn WW I (despatches); *m* 6 March 1916 Kathleen Margaret (*m* 2nd 15 Oct 1921 Col Daniel Frederick Bartlett, MBE, IA), yr dau of Sydney Smith, Inspr-Gen Indian Police Punjab, and was *ka* Baku 14 Sept 1918, leaving:

1a *Patricia Margaret Helen; *b* 10 Dec 1916

2a *Beresford Aileen; *b* posthumously 3 Feb 1919

The est son,

Sir HENRY MARSHMAN HAVELOCK later HAVELOCK-ALLAN (roy licence 17 March 1880 under terms of will of his cousin Robert Henry Allan, of Blackwell Grange, Co Durham), **1st Bt** (UK), so *cr* 22 Jan 1858, with remainder, in default of issue male, to the heirs male of the body of his father, VC (1857), GCB, DL; *b* 6 Aug 1830; Lt-Gen, Col Roy Irish Regt; MP Sunderland 1874–81, SE Durham 1885–92 and 1895–97; served with his f Persian War, also DAAG to his f Relief of Lucknow, cmded 1st Regt Hodson's Horse till end Indian Mutiny 1859, served subsequently Staff Canada, New Zealand and Dublin; *m* 10 May 1865 Lady Alice Moreton (*d* 22 Dec 1922), 2nd dau of 2nd Earl of Ducie (*qv*), and was *k* by the Afridis 30 Dec 1897, leaving issue:

1 **Sir Henry Spencer Moreton Havelock-Allan, 2nd Bt,** JP (Darlington (Chm Co Bench) and N R Yorks), DL (Co Durham); *b* 30 Jan 1872; Maj 17th Bn Lancs Fus, formerly 4th Bn DLI, WW I (wounded 1916); MP (Lib) Bishop Auckland 1910–18, PPS to Chllr Duchy Lancaster 1911–14, PPS to U-Sec State India 1913; *m* 1st 12 Nov 1903 Edith, OBE (1920), JP (Darlington and Co Durham) (*d* 9 Jan 1935), 2nd dau of Thomas Charles John Sowerby, of Snow Hall, Darlington; *m* 2nd 30April 1936 (*annulled* 1937) Mary Isobel (*d* 15 April 1962), dau of Henry Shape Gordon, OBE, of Yateley Place, Herts; *m* 3rd 7 Dec 1937 (Doris) Pamela, SStJ (1971) (*d* Jan 1989), 2nd dau of Sir Maurice Levy, 1st Bt, JP, DL, and *dsp* 28 Oct 1953

2 Allan, of Drax, Tilshead, Wilts; *b* 30 March 1874; Lt 1st N R Yorks Artillery; *m* 1st 26 May 1897 (*divorce* 1913) Anne Julia (*d* 10 Nov 1953), dau of Sir William Chaytor, 3rd Bt (*qv*), and had issue:

(1) **Sir Henry Ralph Moreton Havelock-Allan, 3rd Bt;** *b* 31 Aug 1899; *educ* Charterhouse; Lt Scots Gds; *d* 4 Nov 1975

(2) Clervaux; *b* 27 March 1901; *d* an infant

(3) Sir ANTHONY JAMES ALLAN HAVELOCK-ALLAN, **4th and present Bt**

(1) Hope Aline; *m* 1st 1 July 1925 (*divorce* 1933) Graeme Stewart Lockhart Whitelaw, Seaforth Highrs (*d* 5 Dec 1962), s of Graeme Alexander Lockhart Whitelaw, of Brockham Park, Betchworth, Surrey, and had issue; *m* 2nd 2 Aug 1934 (*divorce* 1947) 3rd Baron Allerton (*see* 1970 edn) and *d* 1988

(2) Barbara Jean; *m* 4 Oct 1928 John Arnold Ellert, s of Arnold Ellert, and *d* 29 Sept 1937, leaving issue

2 (cont.) Allan Havelock-Allan *m* 2nd 1914 Aline Constance Caroline (*d* 28 May 1967), 2nd dau of Edward Beresford (*see* WATERFORD, M), and *d* 7 Nov 1949, having by her had issue:

(4) +Gervaise George Michael [Gervaise Havelock-Allan Esq, 3c Stormore, Dilton Marsh, Westbury, Wilts BA13 4BH]; *b* 24 Aug 1921; *m* 1946 *Rhoda, dau of Thomas Beard, of Swansea, and has issue:

1a +Thomas Allan Spencer; *b* 30 June 1949

1a *Louise Charlotte; *b* 1954

(3) *Diana Constance [Mrs Evelyn Scott, The Nest, Robin Hatch, Pembury Rd, Tunbridge Wells, Kent TN2 4NA]; *m* 1939 Evelyn Francis Scott (*d* 1981) and has:

1a *Angus Allan Lindsay; *b* 1940

2a *Julian Peter Francis Francis; *b* 1946

3a *David Nigel; *b* 1947

4a *Mark Michael; *b* 1950

5a *Ralph Neil Allan; *b* 1958

1a *Nina Alison Margaret; *b* 1941

2a *Elaine Ruth; *b* 1953

(4) *Nancy Stella [Mrs Patrick Musters, 4 Spring Cl, Market Overton, Leics LE15 7PT]; *m* 24 March 1948 *Maj Patrick Thorvald Auchmuty Musters, RA,

2nd s of Capt John Domvile Auchmuty Musters, DSC, RN), of Brookhill House, Claremorris, Co Mayo, and has issue:

1a *Patrick Havelock Auchmuty; *b* 1952

1a *Fiona Havelock Auchmuty; *b* 1948

2a *Gillian Havelock Auchmuty; *b* 1948

3a *Nicola Havelock Auchmuty; *b* 1954

1 Alice Margaret *d* an infant 9 June 1867

2 Ethel, OStJ; *b* 1 Nov 1867; *m* 18 Oct 1886 1st Baron Gainford (*qv*) and *d* 22 Oct 1941, leaving issue

HAWARDEN

Arms: Quarterly, 1st and 4th, az. a lion rampant arg.; 2nd and 3rd, arg. three bars gemelles sa.; over all a lion rampant gu. charged on the shoulder with a cross-crosslet fitchée or. **Crest:** A lion's gamb erased and erect ppr., grasping an oak branch slipped vert. **Supporters:** Two lions rampant gu., each charged on the shoulder with a cross-crosslet fitchée or. **Motto:** *Virtute securus* ('Safe by manliness'). **Creations:** Bt. (I) 9 May 1705, B. (I) 29 June 1785, V. (I) 5 Dec 1793.

THE 9TH VISCOUNT HAWARDEN, of Hawarden, Co Tipperary, **Baron de Montalt of Hawarden,** Co Tipperary, and a **Baronet** (Sir (Robert) Connan Wyndham Leslie Maude, Bt) [The Rt Hon The Viscount Hawarden, Great Bossington Farmhouse, Adisham, Canterbury, Kent]; *b* 23 May 1961; *s f* 1991; *educ* St Edmund's Sch Canterbury and RAC Cirencester; *m* 8 April 1995 *Judith Anne, yst dau of John Bates, of Upton Wood, Kent, and has:

1 +VARIAN JOHN CONNAN EUSTACE; *b* 1 Sept 1997

Lineage: CONSTANTINE MAUDE/MONHAULT (both names being variations of Montalt, itself referring to the hill of Mold, Flintshire, from which the family took one of its titles in the form of Montalt when ennobled), of W Riddlesden, Yorks; *m* — Kighley, of Newhall, and had:

ARTHUR MAUDE, of W Riddlesden; *m* —, dau of Lawrence Townley, and had, with a dau (Agnes, *m* Stephen Paslew):

THOMAS MAUDE, of W Riddlesden; *m* Katherine, dau of Roger Tempest, of Broughton, and had:

1 Arthur, of W Riddlesden; living 1585; *m* Jane, dau of Anthony Eltoft, of Farnell, and had five daus

2 Thomas, living *sp* 1585

3 CHRISTOPHER

1 Anne; *m* Thomas Hall, of Shipden

2 Margaret; *m* Thomas Tempest, of Yellocome

3 Isabel; *m* Robert Bayldon

The 3rd son,

CHRISTOPHER MAUDE, of Hollinghall and Woodhouse; patron of Ilkely 1554; *m* Grace — and had, with a yr s (John, of Staynland) and a dau (Isabel, *m* William Curren, of Marley):

THOMAS MAUDE, of W Riddlesden; *d* 3 Jan 1633, leaving:

A dau; *m* and had:

ROBERT MAUDE, of W Riddlesden and Ripon, Yorks, and patron Ilkley 1640, all of which estates he sold, buying others in Cos Kilkenny and Tipperary, Ireland; *m* Frances, dau of Sir Christopher Wandesford, of Kirtlington, and sis of 1st Baron Wandesford and Viscount Castlecomer, and *d* 1685, leaving:

ANTHONY MAUDE, of Dundrum; High Sheriff Co Tipperary 1686, MP Cashel 1695; *m* 1st 1666 Mary Charlton (*dsp*); *m* 2nd 1671 Alice, est dau of Sir Standish Hartstong, Bt, of Bruff, Co Limerick, and had, with a dau:

Sir Robert Maude, 1st Bt (I), so *cr* 9 May 1705; MP (I Parl) Gowran, Co Kilkenny, 1703–13, St Canice 1713–27 and Bangor, Co Down, 1727030; *b* 1676; *m* Jan 1718 Eleanor, dau of Thomas Cornwallis, of Acton, Middx, and Albermarles, Carmarths, and *d* 4 Aug 1750, leaving:

1 **Sir Thomas Maude, 2nd Bt,** and 1st and last BARON DE MONTALT OF HAWARDEN, Co Tipperary (I), so *cr* 18 July 1776, PC (I 1768); *b c* 1727; MP Co Tipperary 1761–76, High Sheriff 1765, PC (I 1768); *d* unm 17 May 1777, when the Barony expired

2 **Sir Cornwallis Maude, 3rd Bt,** and **1st Viscount Hawarden,** of Hawarden, Co Tipperary, so *cr* 5 Dec 1793, as also earlier 29 June 1785 BARON DE MONTALT OF HAWARDEN, Co Tipperary (both I); *bapt* 19 Sept 1729; MP Roscommon 1783–85; *m* 1st 8 Aug 1756 Letitia (*d* 24 May 1757), dau of Thomas Vernon, of Hanbury Hall, Worcs, and had:

(1) Elizabeth Letitia; *m* 16 June 1781 John Vaughan (*see* LISBURNE, E)

2 (cont.) The **1st Viscount** *m* 2nd 10 June 1766 Mary (*d* 8 Oct 1775), only dau of Philip Allen, of Bathampton Manor, Somerset (and n of Ralp Allen, of Prior Park, Bath, benefactor to that city and allegedly model for Squire Allworthy in Feilding's *Tom Jones*), and by her had issue:

(1) THOMAS RALPH MAUDE, **2nd Viscount Hawarden;** *b* 16 April 1767; *m* 14 Dec 1798 Lady Frances Anne Agar (*d* 20 May 1839), only dau of 1st Earl of Normanton (*qv*), and *dsp* 26 Feb 1807

(2) Sophia Maria; *m* 25 June 1807, as his 1st w, George Hay Dawkins-Pennant and *d* 23 Jan 1812, leaving issue (*see* PENRHYN, B, and SUDELEY, B)

(3) Emma Mary; *m* 12 April 1794 William Ralph Cartwright, MP, of Aynho, Northants, and *d* 11 March 1808. He *d* 4 Jan 1847

2 (cont.) The **1st Viscount** *m* 3rd 3 June 1777 Anne Isabella (*d* 26 July 1851 aged 92), sis of 1st Viscount Monck (*qv*), and *d* 23 Aug 1803, leaving by her:

(2) CORNWALLIS MAUDE, **3rd Viscount Hawarden;** *b* 28 March 1780; Ld in Waiting 1841–46 and Feb-Dec 1852, rep I peer 1836–56; *m* 8 July 1811 Jane (*d* 24 March 1852), yst dau of Patrick Crawford Bruce, of Taplow Lodge, Bucks, and *d* 12 Oct 1856, leaving:

1a CORNWALLIS MAUDE, **4th Viscount Hawarden** and 1st and last EARL DE MONTALT OF DUNDRUM, Co Tipperary (UK), so *cr* 9 Sept 1886, JP, DL Dunbartonshire; *b* 4 April 1817; *educ* Eton; rep I peer 1862–1905, Lt and custos rotulorum Co Tipperary 1881–1905, Hon Col 4th Bn R Irish Regt, Capt 2nd Life Gds, Lt-Col Cmdt and Hon Col N Tipperary Militia, Ld-in-Waiting 1866–68, 1874–80 and 1885, Dep Speaker Ho Lds 1882; *m* 24 March 1845 Clementina Elphinstone (*d* 19 Jan 1865), er sis of 14th Lord Elphinstone (*qv*), and *dspms* 9 Jan 1905, when the Earldom expired, having had issue:

1b Cornwallis MAUDE later FLEMING (assumed with arms of Cumbernauld and Wigton under entail of his ancestor 6th Earl of Wigton) later MAUDE again; Capt Gren Gds; *b* 22 Oct 1852; *educ* Eton; *m* 28 Feb 1878 Eva Henrietta (*d* 8 Nov 1940, having *m* 2nd 9 June 1883 Lt-Col George Holden Hutton, Roy Welch Fus (*d* 17 Oct 1908), and had further issue), 2nd dau of Francis Richard Brooke (*see* BROOKE, Bt, of Summerton), and was *ka* Majuba Hill 27 Feb 1881, leaving:

1c Clementina Isabel; *b* 2 Dec 1878; granted with sister rank of earl's daus 30 Aug 1905, which they would have enjoyed had their f survived to inherit the Earldom of Montalt; *m* 22 July 1909 William Frederick Loftus Tottenham (*see* ELY, M) and *dsp* 15 Aug 1961

2c Eveline; *b* 17 July 1880; *d* unm 9 Jan 1968

2b Eustace Mountstuart; *d* an infant 7 Dec 1859

1b Isabella Grace; *m* 28 Jan 1869 3rd and last Baron Colchester and *dsp* 10 Nov 1927. He *d* 26 Feb 1919

2b Clementina; *b* 15 July 1847; *d* unm 10 Aug 1901

3b Florence Elizabeth; *b* 18 Nov 1849; *d* unm 25 Dec 1931

4b Kathleen; *m* 1st 10 April 1875 (*divorce* 1886) Gerald Richard Brooke (*see* BROOKE, Bt, of Summerton) and had issue; *m* 2nd 17 July 1886 Seymour Coghill Hort Bushe, KC, s of Rev Charles Bushe, of Castlehaven, Co Cork, and *d* 25 Jan 1939, having had further issue. He *d* 27 Jan 1922

5b Elphinstone Agnes; *b* 1857; *m* 17 April 1880 Hon Walter James Sugden, bro of 2nd Baron St Leonards (*see* 1970 edn), and *d* 12 Feb 1921, leaving issue. He *d* 1 Feb 1897

6b Leucha Diana, DGStJ; *m* 6 Dec 1883 Sir (Thomas) Courtenay Theydon Warner, 1st Bt (*qv*), and *d* 23 Aug 1947, leaving issue

7b Antonia Lillian; *b* 3 May 1864; *m* 30 March 1912 Maj William Augustus Adams, 5th Lancers, of Kinnea, Co Cavan, est surv s of Rev Benjamin William Adams, DD, of Kinnea, Co Cavan, and *d* 16 June 1927

1a Isabella; *m* 11 Sept 1839 Lt-Col Charles James Tottenham (*see* ELY, M) and *d* 11 July 1892 aged 78, having had issue

2a Maria Adelaide; *m* 1st 19 Dec 1831 2nd Earl of Yarborough (*qv*) and had issue; *m* 2nd 7 Aug 1869 William John, Viscount Oxenbridge (*see* MONSON, B), and *d* 24 Dec 1897

3a Florence Priscilla Alice; *m* 9 Oct 1849 5th Baron Braybrooke (*qv*) and *d* 18 March 1914, having had issue

4a Augusta; *d* unm 25 Dec 1857

(3) Robert William Henry (Very Rev); Dean Clogher, Archdeacon Dublin; *b* 21 Aug 1784; *m* 3 May 1827 Hon Martha Elizabeth Mary Prittie (*d* 25 July 1887), half-sis of 3rd Baron Dunalley of Kilboy (*qv*), and *d* 31 Oct 1861, having had, with other issue:

1a ROBERT HENRY MAUDE, **5th Viscount Hawarden;** Lt-Col 7th Roy Fus; *b* 24 June 1842; *m* 15 Dec 1881 Caroline Anna Mary (*d* 15 March 1930), dau of Maj Arthur Ogle, and *d* 6 Sept 1908, leaving:

1b ROBERT CORNWALLIS MAUDE, **6th Viscount Hawarden;** *b* 6 Sept 1890; *educ* Ch Ch Oxford (BA); Lt Coldstream Gds; *ka* 26 Aug 1914

2a Ludlow Eustace; *b* 10 Oct 1844; *m* 12 July 1870 Clara Louisa (*d* 23 Nov 1926), dau of Rev Wyndham Carlyon Madden, and *d* 6 Aug 1903, leaving:

1b EUSTACE WYNDHAM, **7th Viscount**

1b Kathleen Emily; *b* 11 June 1871; *d* unm 28 Jan 1945

2b Elinor Louisa; *b* 11 July 1872; *m* 1st 18 June 1902 Harry William Stronge (*see* STRONGE, Bt); *m* 2nd 5 Dec 1911 Sir William Smith Marriott, 8th Bt (*qv*), and *d* 18 June 1941, leaving issue

3b Dorothy Caroline; *b* 17 June 1873; *d* unm 23 July 1945

4b Alice Charlotte; *b* 20 April 1879; *m* 6 April 1927 Maj Alan Lindsay Stewart (*d* 7 Jan 1945) and *dsp* 20 Dec 1967

1a Isabel Catherine; *m* 12 April 1853 Gen John Maxwell Perceval, CB, and *d* 27 May 1887, leaving issue. He *d* 24 Jan 1900

2a Gertrude Emily; *m* 14 Oct 1857 Capt Thomas Carpendale Baird (*d* 5 Feb 1875) and *d* 22 Jan 1895, leaving issue (*see* PETO, Bt, of Barnstaple)

3a Anna Maria Victoria; *m* 23 June 1874 Edmund Champagne Jones, and *d* 21 June 1881

(4) James Ashley (Sir), CB, KCH; Capt RN; *b* 6 Nov 1786; *m* 18 Oct 1817 Albinia (*d* 20 April 1863), 2nd dau of Most Rev Charles Brodrick, Archbp Cashel (*see* MIDLETON, V), and *d* 23 Oct 1841, leaving issue

(5) John Charles (Rev); Rector Enniskillen, Co Fermanagh; *b* 16 Sept 1792; *m* 10 Sept 1813 Mary (*d* 26 Oct 1865), 2nd but est surv dau of William Cely Trevilian, of Midelney, Somerset, and *d* 21 June 1860, having had issue:

1a Charles William (Rev); Rector Munden Magna, Herts; *b* 2 Oct 1816; *m* 25 Sept 1849 Charlotte (*d* 6 Oct 1871), dau of Robert Myddleton Biddulph, of Chirk Castle, and *d* 22 March 1888, having had issue:

1b Charles Thomas; *b* May 1851; *d* 2 Oct 1892

2b Robert John; Maj Rifle Bde; *b* 14 Jan 1853; *m* 28 Dec 1893 Susan Alexandrina (*d* 1944), widow of Rev E Blomfield and dau of Gen Sir Frank Turner, KCB, and *d* 25 Nov 1906, leaving:

1c Thomas Raymond; *b* 23 June 1898; *d* 28 Feb 1834

1c Charlotte Mary; *b* 13 May 1896; *d* 30 June 1910

2c Margaret Frances; *b* 4 Nov 1899; *d* unm 1943

2a George Ashley (Sir), KCB (1887); Col RA (ret 1858), cmded RHA Troop Crimean War (severely wounded Battle of Balaclava, invalided home), Lt-Col cmdg RHA Woolwich, ADC to C-in-C 1856, Mil Attaché Russia 1856, Dep Inspr Gen RIC 1858–59, Crown Equerry to HM QUEEN VICTORIA 1859, Kt Medjidie; *b* 11 Nov 1817; *m* 5 April 1845 Katherine Katinka (*d* 1 June 1882), dau of Charles George Beauclerk (*see* SAINT ALBANS, D), and *d* 31 May 1894, leaving:

1b Charles John; Assist Paymaster-Gen; *b* 17 March 1847; *m* 14 June 1871 Sarah Maria (*d* 25 Dec 1935), only dau of Adml Sir Watkin Owen Pell, and *d* 29 April 1910, having had:

1c Hubert William; WW I with Canadian MMG, Croix de Guerre Belgium, 1914–15 Star and MM; *b* 27 June 1877; *m* 1952 *Matilda Bolster and *d* 30 Oct 1953

1c Constance Margaret; *b* 11 April 1872; *d* unm 22 July 1967

2c Marion; *b* 4 Feb 1876; *d* 24 March 1896

2b Eustace Downman, JP British Columbia; *b* 31 Aug 1848; Cdr RN; *m* 1885 Amy (*d* 1946), dau of Oliver Williams, and *d* 12 June 1930, having had issue:

1c George Ashley; Lt RNVR WW I (Mons Star, two medals); *b* 1889; *m* 19 Dec 1921 Ruth (*d* 1984), dau of Cdr Milton Updegraff, USN, and *d* 23 Jan 1973, leaving issue:

1d +George Ashley [George Maude Esq, 10137 West Saanich Road, Sidney, BC, Canada]; *b* 13 Dec 1925; *m* 1952 *Nancy Mary, dau of John Ingvard Reitan, and has issue:

1e +Anthony John Ashley; *b* 13 Dec 1954; *m* 1st 1978 (*divorce* 1980) Gale Victoria, dau of Lt-Cdr Sydney Dalton Bryant, RCN; *m* 2nd 1982 *Saryl, dau of William Edward Rusk

2e +Christopher George; *b* 23 May 1957; *m* 1982 *Pamela Mary, dau of Leonard Lang, and has issue:

1f +Curtiss John Ashley; *b* 1984

2f +Glen Douglas George; *b* 1989

3e +David Philip; *b* 12 Sept 1964

1d *Alison Beauclerk; *b* 16 Aug 1923

1c Ruth Katinka; *m* 29 Jan 1907 Harold Digby Payne and *d* 27 Sept 1914, leaving issue

2c Cyrene Maria Beauclerk; *m* 29 March 1913 Capt Cecil Henry Hulton-Sams, RN, and had issue. He *d* 1931

3c Valerie Beauclerk; VAD 1917–18 *m* 6 Aug 1925 Capt Humfrey Greenwood Hopper, DSO, RN, s of Maj Edward Hopper, RE, of Leeds, and had:

1d *John Oliver de Montalt; *b* 6 Feb 1929; *m* 5 Aug 1965 *Nellie, dau of G Galiatsatos, of Athens, and has issue:

1e *Edward Charles Mark de Montalt; *b* 20 March 1968

1d *Elizabeth Valerie Beauclerk [Mrs Donald Sweeting, Hill Farm, Little Rissington, Glos]; *b* 27 Aug 1930; *m* 25 July 1952 *Donald Furneaux Sweeting, and has issue:

1e *James Donald Furneaux; *b* 14 Dec 1954; *m* 5 March 1990 *Annabel Mary Bryant and has:

1f *Oliver James Tremayne; *b* 13 Sept 1994

1f *Rosanna Caroline Elizabeth; *b* 23 Nov 1990

2e *Gerard John Cornwallis; *b* 14 Nov 1958; *m* 9 July 1983 *Jane Dorothy Blanche, est dau of Hilary Gosling, and has issue (see CARLISLE, E)

1e *Henrietta Maria Elizabeth; *b* 31 Oct 1953; *m* 24 July 1982 *Richard Campbell Paget, and has:

1f *Harry Arthur Westwood; *b* 2 July 1986

2f *Caspian James Alexander; b 25 Nov 1991

1f *Georgina Elizabeth Beauclerk; *b* 2 June 1984

3b Ashley Henry; barrister, Clerk BOT; *b* 14 March 1850; *m* 29 April 1876 Emma Constance (*d* 1 Sept 1889), yr dau of John Snowdon Henry, DL, of Eastdene, IoW, and *d* 3 Oct 1933, having had issue:

1c Edith Frances; *b* 19 March 1877; *m* 21 Sept 1900 Arthur Maitland Ware, MD, and *d* 10 Dec 1952, leaving issue. He *d* 5 Jan 1953

2c Sybil Margaret; *b* 26 Feb 1878; *d* unm 26 Aug 1963

3c Dorothea Clara, JP; MD, MA, BS London, Order St Sava Serbia; *b* 26 Feb 1879; *m* 19 April 1917 Hugh Nasmyth, MIME, Lt RASC, and *d* 11 Dec 1959, leaving issue. He *d* 23 May 1942

4c Frances Blanche; *b* 26 April 1880; *d* unm Feb 1958

5c Alice Muriel; *b* 5 April 1881; *m* 20 Dec 1911 Rev Henry Charles Wace, MA, Fell and Bursar BNC Coll Oxford, s of Very Rev Henry Wace, DD, Dean Canterbury, and *dsp* 12 Nov 1968. He *d* 5 Oct 1938

4b Aubrey Maurice; Lt-Col Cameronians Scottish Rifles; *b* 1 Aug 1852; *m* 23 July 1885 Amy Florence (*d* 18 Dec 1931), dau of Sir Thomas Lucas, 1st Bt (*qv*), and *d* 2 Jan 1943, leaving issue:

1c Christian George, DSO, OBE, MC; Brig Educnl Corps, late Roy Fus, served WWs I and II, Dir Cultural Relations Div Control Commn Germany 1946–54; *b* 4 Sept 1884; *educ* Rugby and RMC Sandhurst; *m* 1st 7 Oct 1920 (*divorce* 1931) Hon Patience Kemp (*d* 19 Feb 1935), er dau of 1st Baron Rochdale (*qv*), and had issue:

1d Peter George Egerton; T/Capt RE; *b* 3 Oct 1926; *m* 31 July 1952 *Olivia Elizabeth [Mrs Hugh Ley, The Dower House, Burrow, Lancs LA6 2RJ] (*m* 2nd 19 May 1961 Brig Hugh Marlborough Hale Ley, CBE, DL, s of Lt-Col Arthur Edwin Hale Ley, OBE, Royal Deccan Horse), er dau of Col Hugh O Wright, of Melling, Lancs, and was *k* in the Manchester air crash 14 March 1957, leaving issue:

1e *Sarah Patience; *b* 2 June 1954

1d Bridget Diana; 3rd Offr WRNS WW II; *b* Sept 1921; *m* 17 Oct 1946 *Lt-Col (Hugh) Michael Allan Knight, MC, RAOC, 16th Punjab Regt IA, est s of Capt A A A Knight, and *d* 1979, leaving:

1e *Simon Fairfax; *b* 16 Aug 1950; *educ* St Edward's Sch Oxford

2e *Jeremy Christian; *b* 25 Nov 1955; *educ* Fettes

3e *Peter Richard; *b* 26 Nov 1957; *educ* Fettes

1e *Cunita Amanda Egerton; *b* 3 Sept 1947

1c (cont.) Christian Maude *m* 2nd 27 Jan 1931 Hester Joan (*d* 1993), dau of Charles Augustus Egerton, JP, DL, of Mountfield Court, Robertsbridge, Sussex, and *d* 13 Dec 1971, leaving by her:

2d *Gillian Mabelle Beauclerk [Mrs David Lord, Four Wells, Lower Slaughter, Cheltenham, Glos]; *b* 11 March 1932; *m* 1st 29 March 1960 Maj Estcourt Richard Cresswell (*d* 1983), MC, MA, 15th/19th King's Roy Hus, only s of Capt Herbert Pinkney Cresswell, MBE, of Charingworth Manor, Chipping Campden, Glos; *m* 2nd 1984 *(John) David Anthony Lord, s of Lt-Col John Arthur Lord, of Broadway, Worcs

3d *Priscilla Douglas; *b* 9 Sept 1934; *m* 8 Sept 1962 *Michael Frederick Tremain Maude (*see* below) and has issue

4d *Elizabeth Joan, JP [Mrs Malcolm Anson JP, Drax House, Tilshead, Salisbury, Wilts SP3 4SJ]; *b* 20 April 1940; *m* 1st 20 April 1967 Capt Christopher Evelyn Twiston Davies (*d* 1980), late 4th/7th Roy Dragoon Gds, yr s of Sir Leonard Twiston Davies, KBE, of Rockfield Park, Mon; *m* 2nd 20 June 1992 Malcolm Allinson Anson (*d* Aug 1992), er s of Sir (George) Wilfrid Anson, MBE, MC, of West Hay Wrington, Bristol, and by her 1st husb has issue:

1e *William Ashley Christopher; *b* 1969; *educ* Radley and RAC Cirencester

2e *Benjamin James; *b* 1971; *educ* Radley and St Andrews

1c Nancy; *m* 1911 Joseph Campbell (*d* June 1944) and had:

1d *Gillachrist; Lt-Col RA WW II France 1940, Malaya 1941 and Korea 1954; *b* 13 Aug 1912; *m* 1st 1949 Jean Rosemary (*d* 4 April 1951), dau of W/Cdr R G Dyer, and has issue:

1e *Caroline Jean; *b* 2 April 1951

1d (cont.) Gillachrist Campbell, *m* 2nd 4 Feb 1956 *Victoria Maria, only child of Hon Ronald John Sholto Douglas, OBE (*see* MORTON, E), and by her has issue:

2e *Maria; *b* 27 Oct 1956

3e *Sophia Frances; *b* 29 Jan 1958

4e *Catherine; *b* 5 Dec 1959

2d *Simon; *b* 28 Aug 1914; *m* 31 Oct 1946 *Lavinia Mary, dau of R-Adml Hon (Edward) Barry Stewart Bingham VC, OBE (*see* CLANMORRIS, B), and has issue:

1e *Luke Bingham; *b* 21 Jan 1948; *educ* Lancing

2e *Julian Simon; *b* 24 July 1949; *educ* Lancing

3e *Roderick Barry; *b* 29 July 1951; *educ* Lancing

4e *Nicholas Edward Angus; *b* 22 Sept 1956

5e *Thomas Neil; *b* 29 Aug 1961

3d *Flann; *b* 24 Feb 1919; *m* 1947 *Mary, widow of Lt M Francis, RN, and has issue:

1e *Christopher Patrick; *b* 1951

4d *Dominic Diarmid [Maj Dominic Campbell, Enford House, Enford, Wilts]; Maj RA, Sr Instr RA Wing, RAC Centre; *b* 14 Aug 1928; *m* 5 April 1961 *Sarah Elizabeth, est dau of Brig Richard John Streatfeild, DSO, of Hoath House, Chiddingstone, Kent, and has:

1e *Simon; *b* 24 Sept 1969; *educ* Sherborne

1e *Bridget Nancy; *b* 28 Nov 1962

1d *Diana Mary; *b* 2 Oct 1929; *m* 1971 *Lewis Gilmour Whyte

5b Alwyne Edward, Maj Serbian Army, Order St Sava; *b* 23 July 1854; *m* 1st June 1880 Katharine Lucy (*d* 1892), dau of John Campbell; *m* 2nd 2 May 1895 Louise Caroline (*d* 1 July 1936), widow of A Laurin, of Stockholm, and dau of Rector Siljestrom, memb Swedish Parl, and *d* 1 Dec 1945, having by his 1st w had issue:

1d Alwyne Esme; *b* Oct 1880; *d* Mafeking 20 Aug 1900

1d Cathleen Cecil; *b* 1881; *m* 31 July 1912 Col Cecil Charles Brinton, JP, RAOC, yst s of John Brinton, of Moor Hall, Stourport, and *d* 26 Oct 1954, leaving issue. He *d* 16 May 1970

2d Mary Charmian; *b* 1886; *d* unm 1947

6b Frederick William, JP Kent; Baron Cinque Ports, Mayor New Romney; *b* 28 Feb 1857; *m* 8 Oct 1878 Ellen Maud (*d* 3 April 1938), dau of Sir John Kelk, 1st Bt (*see* 1902 edn), and *d* 9 Feb 1923, leaving issue:

1c John William Ashley; Lt 10th Bn KRRC; *b* 12 Oct 1885; *ka* 23 Aug 1915

1c Norah Diana HANBURY-KELK (deed poll 1934); *b* 21 April 1889; *m* 27 July 1912 (*divorce* 1929) Arthur Marcus Hanbury, OBE, 2nd s of Capel Hanbury, and *d* March 1977, leaving:

1d Nicholas John Capel HANBURY, TD; Capt KRRC; *b* 3 Nov 1913; *m* 14 Feb 1946 *Eileen, dau of Richard Conway, and *d* 16 Aug 1995, leaving:

1e *John Richard Capel [John Hanbury Esq, 4 Hopetown Terrace, Sheriton Park, W Australia 6008]; *b* 18 April 1953; *m* 16 July 1979 *Julie Tasma, dau of Edwin Piper, and has:

1f *James Edwin Capel; *b* 26 Sept 1979

1f *Layla Rose; *b* 5 Oct 1982

2f *Amelia Jeanne; *b* 15 Sept 1986

1e *Danielle Elizabeth Josette [Mrs Simon Kay, 23 Church Road West, Crowthorne, Berks]; *b* 26 Oct 1947; *m* 29 Sept 1973 *Simon John Hervey Kay and has:

1f *George Nicholas Jemmett; *b* 27 Nov 1978

1f *Alice Victoria Mary; *b* 30 March 1981

2d *Benedict Frederick Philip [Benedict Hanbury Esq, Gate House Cottage, Risby, Bury St Edmunds, Suffolk]; *b* 15 Dec 1924

1d *Diana Martha Germaine [Mrs Diana Hanbury, Fen Cottage, Littlestone, New Romney, Kent]; *b* 5 Aug 1916; *m* 1st 1939 (*divorce* 1962) Arthur Henry Morris; *m* 2nd 1963 (*divorce* 1972, resumed maiden name by deed poll 1974) David R Thompson, s of J H Thompson, and by her 1st husb has:

1e *Charles Benedict [Charles Morris Esq, Paperhouse, West Harling, Norfolk]; *b* 5 Dec 1943; *m* 20 April 1980 *Rachel Norah Ceely, dau of William Hislop, and has:

1f *Frederick Edwin; *b* 24 Sept 1987

1f *Daisy; *b* 12 April 1981

2f *Jessamy Rose; *b* 5 June 1983

3f *Martha Beauclerk; *b* 24 Dec 1989

1e *Dinah Leah Carlotta [Mrs Dinah Wiener, 27 Arlington Rd, London NW1 7ER]; *b* 17 Feb 1940; *m* 21 Sept 1963 (*divorce* 1971) Patrick P M Wiener, yr s of Raymond Wiener, of Paris, and has:

1f *Daniel Patrick; *b* 26 Nov 1964; *m* 8 April 1994 *Marianna Barbara, dau of Peter Lewis, and has:

1g *Dylan Arthur Edward; *b* 30 Aug 1995

2g *Alfred Daniel Patrick; *b* 2 Jan 1997

2f *Barnaby Mark; *b* 9 Jan 1967

2d *Jan Beauclerk [Mrs Arthur Morris, Sloane Cottage, The Green, Long Melford, Sudbury, Suffolk CO10 9DT]; *b* 15 Dec 1924; *m* 1st 1952 (*divorce* 1957) William Hislop; *m* 2nd 1 June 1962 *Arthur Henry Morris, TD, and by her 1st husb has:

1e *Cordelia Margaret Beauclerk [Mrs Michael Devine, Riwaka Valley, Motueka, Nelson, New Zealand]; *b* 3 Feb 1953; m 20 April 1979 *Michael Devine, of NZ

2e *Rachel Norah Ceely [Mrs Charles Morris, Paperhouse, West Harling, Norfolk]; *b* 26 Aug 1954; m 20 April 1980 *Charles Benedict Morris and has issue

2c Katherine Elizabeth; *b* 23 March 1892; *m* 9 Sept 1915 Col Thomas Hubert Harker, DSO and bar, KRRC (*d* 12 Nov 1938), and had issue:

1d *Paul Thomas Borton; *b* 21 Jan 1920; *educ* Stowe; *m* 1947 *Maureen, widow of Maj Peter J Alers Hankey, RHA, and dau of J G Hoatson, and has issue:

1e *Andrew Peter Thomas; *b* 24 July 1952; *educ* Eton

1e *Sarah Jane; *b* 1949

2d *Matthew; Capt 60th Rifles; *b* 24 Feb 1924; *educ* Eton; *m* 1951 *Ann Powell, dau of Noel Clifton, of Hambledon, Surrey, and has:

1e *James; *b* 29 Oct 1954; *educ* Eton

2e *Simon; *b* 1957

1b Emily Diana; *m* 7 Nov 1867 Jonathan Peel Baird, 7th s of Sir David Baird, 2nd Bt, of Newbyth (*qv*), and *d* 23 Sept 1926, leaving issue

3a Maurice Cely, of Lenaghen Park, Enniskillen; *b* 25 June 1820; *m* 18 May 1860 Marie Elise (*d* 4 Nov 1895), dau of Chretien Wehren, of Switzerland, and *d* 24 Dec 1904, leaving issue:

1b Anthony Fritz, of Belgard House, Clondalkin, Co Dublin, JP Cos Fermanagh, Down and Dublin; High Sheriff 1918, Capt NI Horse; *b* Aug 1862; *m* 27 April 1895 Eva Emily (*d* 18 Feb 1960), only dau of Maj Henry Marcus Beresford (*see* WATERFORD, M), and *d* 7 June 1935, leaving:

1c Marcus Beresford, MC; Lt 4th Bn Roy Fus WW I (despatches); *b* 21 March 1896; *das* Mesopotamia 24 Jan 1921

2c Maurice Anthony; Lt RN and F/O RAF; *b* 15 June 1900; *das* cmdg RN Air Wing at Hong Kong 12 Dec 1926

3c Hugh Arthur Cornwallis; *b* 14 Sept 1904; *d* 19 March 1982

1c Sheila Cornwallis; *b* 1 Oct 1901; *m* 18 April 1931 George Tilly Rice and *d* 23 April 1970, leaving issue:

1d *Sheila Fiona; *b* 14 Feb 1933; *m* 1954 *Henry Fulton Davis, of Westwood, Mass., and has had:

1e *Henry Fulton; *b* 16 July 1956

2e *George Anthony; *b* 27 Nov 1957

1e Sheila Victoria; *b* 4 Dec 1961; *d* 1962

2e *Alexandra Rice; *b* 7 Feb 1964

2c Monica Ruth Lisalie; *b* 6 Dec 1905; *m* 17 Dec 1929 William Eric Horsbrugh Porter (*see* HORSBRUGH-PORTER, Bt)

2b Ralph Alexander; barrister, Attorney-Gen Sierra Leone, Hon Capt Army, served Matabele (medal) 1896 and Boer Wars 1900–01 (medal with clasps); *b* 26 Feb 1864; *m* 28 Sept 1910 Sarah Adelaide (*d* 18 June 1922), dau of Robert Burt, and *d* 8 Nov 1946, having had issue:

1c Cely Alexander; *b* and *d* 1911

1c *Lisalie Marion; *b* 20 Nov 1912; *m* 1954, as his 2nd w, *Campbell Singer, actor

3b Christopher Hugh, JP, DL Co Fermanagh; High Sheriff 1927; *b* 18 Oct 1867; *m* 5 Nov 1924 Mary Elizabeth Christiana (*d* 25 Aug 1952), only dau of Rt Rev James Macmanaway, DD, Bp Clogher, and *d* 6 Nov 1942, leaving:

1c Maurice Christopher; Capt KRRC (TA); *b* 18 Nov 1925; *m* 1st 20 April 1954 (*divorce* 1963) Venetia, only dau of William Patterson Doyle, of Kuwait; *m* 2nd 1967 *Susan Frances, dau of George Lepper, and *d* 30 Oct 1997, leaving by her:

1d +Christopher George; *b* 1969

4b Cely, JP Cos Tipperary, Kilkenny, Meath and Cavan; *b* 26 July 1870; *m* 8 May 1901 Jane Marian (*d* 24 Nov 1949), dau of Charles William O'Hara, JP, DL, of Annaghmore and Cooper's Hill, Co Sligo, and *d* 4 Jan 1929, leaving:

1c Kathleen Lisalie; *b* 11 May 1902; *m* 25 July 1928 Francis Mervyn Cook (*d* 1979), yr s of John Cook, and *d* 1991, leaving:

1d *John Patrick Mervyn [John Cook Esq, Lillebo, Fulbrook, Burford, Oxon]; *b* 23 July 1941; *m* 1st 8 June 1963 (*divorce* 1980) Margaret Susan, yst dau of Michael Walter Hoard, of The Forge, Pyrton, Oxon; *m* 2nd 1984 *Jennifer Wendy, dau of Joseph Eric Ellison, OBE, and by his 1st w has:

1e *Nicholas John Mervyn; *b* 20 March 1964; *m* 1994 *Fiona Melanie, dau of David Venables, and has:

1f *Milo Captain; *b* 23 Aug 1997

1f *Affrica Blaze; *b* 30 Dec 1994

2e *Julian Michael Patrick; *b* 15 March 1966; *m* 19– *Mary, dau of E D O'Mahony, and has:

1f *Matilda; *b* 1 Nov 1997

1e *Lucinda Margaret Venetia; *b* 1973

1d *Ann Veronica [Mrs Michael Spackman, Hydestile Paddock, nr Godalming, Surrey]; *b* 4 June 1929; *m* 9 Jan 1960 *Michael Kenneth Maurice Spackman and has issue:

1e *Henrietta Louise; *b* 17 Nov 1960; *m* 27 May 1995 *Peter Sleeman and has:

1f *Imogen Sophie; *b* 29 March 1996

2e *Catriona Venetia; *b* 16 Dec 1962; *m* 11 June 1993 *Angus Stovold and has:

1f *Alexander Jack Francis; *b* 20 Nov 1993

1f *Harriet Louise Francesca; *b* 25 Dec 1995

2c Venetia Marian Cely; *b* 30 Oct 1905; *d* 1994

1b Frederick Eustace Cecil; *b* 2 May 1859; *d* 17 Feb 1862

1b Frederica Letitia; *d* young 24 Feb 1864

2b Rosalie Cornelia; *m* 11 April 1888 Marcus Beresford Armstrong, JP, DL, of Chaffpool, Ballymote, Co Sligo, and Moyaliffe Castle, Thurles, Co Tipperary, and *d* 31 Jan 1956, having had issue. He *d* 12 Sept 1923

3b Rebecca Cely; *m* 9 July 1890 James Johnston, DL, of Kinlough, Co Sligo, and *d* 7 Aug 1935, leaving issue

4b Mary Cely; *m* 1st 4 Aug 1909 Edmund William Gordon Hope-Johnstone (*see* LINLITHGOW, M); *m* 2nd 2 Oct 1934 Maj Gerard Irvine and *d* 7 Aug 1935

5b Elise Marie; *m* 1916 Lt-Col Harold Echalay Welch, DSO, Salop LI (*ka* 1918)

6b Marguerite Louisa; *m* 1898 Frederick Edward Sandford Pakenham and *d* 26 Oct 1961, leaving issue (*see* LONGFORD, E)

4a Frederick Francis (Sir), GCB, VC, Legn Hon and Medjidie, Gen; *b* 20 Dec 1821; *m* 22 Feb 1853 Catherine Mary (*d* 23 Jan 1892), only surv dau of Very Rev Sir George Bisshopp, 8th Bt (*see* 1949 edn), and *d* 20 June 1897, having had:

1b Frederick Eustace Cecil; *b* 2 May 1859; *d* 17 Feb 1862

2b (Frederick) Stanley (Sir), KCB, CMG, DSO; Lt-Gen Coldstream Gds, Brig-Maj Home Dist 1897–99, Inf Brig S Africa 1900–01, Mil Sec to Govr-Gen Canada 1901–04, Priv Sec to Sec State War 1905, DAA and QMG Plymouth 1906–08, GSO(2) London Dist 1908–09, Assist Dir Mil Trg War Office 1909–12, GSO Irish Cmd 1912–14, GSO 14th Inf Brig BEF 1915, Bde Cdr 1914–15, Maj-Gen 1915, Lt-Gen and C-in-C Mesopotamian Expdn 1916, Sudan Expdn 1885 (medal with clasp, bronze star), Boer War 1899–1901 (despatches, Queen's medal with six clasps), WW I (despatches six times, promotion, Grand Offr Order Crown Italy, Cdr Legn Hon); *b* 24 June 1864; *m* 1 Nov 1893 Cecil Cornelia Marianne St Leger (*d* 15 Feb 1942), dau of Rt Hon Col Thomas Edward Taylor, (*see* HEADFORT, M), and *das* Mesopotamia 18 Nov 1917, leaving issue:

1c Edward Frederick, OBE (1944); Brig RA, served Wws I and II, Cmdt Bermuda Militia 1936–41, Lt-Col cmdg 96th (Royal Devon Yeo) Field Regt RA 1944–45, BRA Southern Army India 1945; *b* 27 Oct 1897; *educ* Lancing and RMA Woolwich; *m* 23 March 1929 Sylvia (*d* 1987), dau of Robert Brewster, of New York, and *d* 1984, leaving issue:

1d +Michael Frederick Tremain [Michael Maude Esq, Etchilampton House, Devizes, Wilts SN10 3JH]; late 2nd Lt Coldstream Gds; *b* 11 June 1935; *educ* St Paul's Sch USA and Magdalen Coll Oxford (BA); *m* 8 Sept 1962 *Priscilla Douglas, 2nd dau of Brig Christian George Maude, DSO, OBE, MC (*see* above), and has:

1e +Rupert Frederick; *b* 24 Jan 1965

2e +Andrew Tremain; *b* 27 July 1967

1e *Alexandra; *b* 31 May 1963; *m* 1993 *Maj James Nicholas John Gray, 1st Queen's Dragoon Gds, s of Col Nicholas Gray, RA, of Yalding, Kent, and has:

1f *Maximilian Oliver Arthur; *b* 2 July 1997

2e *Victoria; *b* 1970

1d *Eileen [Miss Eileen Foster, 621 Pleasant St, Boulder, CO 80302, USA]; *b* 20 Feb 1931; took name FOSTER for herself and her issue by deed poll 1959; *m* 1954 Lloyd George (*d* 1974) and has:

1e *Lloyd Edward; *b* 1955

2e *Robert Douglas; *b* 1957; *m* 1981 *Virginia Huffman and has:

1f *Robert David; *b* 1981

1f *Jennifer; *b* 1985

3e *Ronald Wayne; *b* 1957; *m* 1987 *Audrey Poage and has:

1f *Richard; *b* 1986

1f *Renée; *b* 1987
3e *Michael Daniel; *b* 1959; *m* 1984 *Christine Oberholzer and has:
1f *Daniel George; *b* 1987
1f *Laura Elizabeth; *b* 1986
1e *Laura Ellen; *b* 1956; *m* 1982 *John Grace and has:
1f *Matthew Eric; *b* 1984
2f *Jeremy Colin; *b* 1986
2d *Barbara [Mrs Barbara Marshall, 11 Southwell Gdns, London SW7 4SB]; *b* 8 Sept 1932; *m* 19 April 1958 (*divorce* 1988) William Clarkson Marshall, only s of Rev William Clarkson Marshall, of Lynchburg, Va., and has:
1e *Thomas Alan; *b* 12 Aug 1963
1e *Cynthia; *b* 26 Feb 1959
1c Stella Cecil Evelyn; *b* 5 Oct 1894; *m* 28 Nov 1928 Brevet Lt-Col Arthur Abercromby Scott-Duff, CIE, MVO, DL, 2nd s of Sir Robert William Duff of Fetteresso, and *d* 2 July 1977, leaving issue. He *d* 3 Dec 1951
2c Beryl Mary; *b* 2 July 1896; *d* 2 June 1978
1b Ada Cecil; *m* 6 June 1878 Maj-Gen Frederick Wilson Hemming, CB, 5th Dragoon Gds, and *d* 16 July 1886. He *d* 18 Dec 1934
2b Alice Emily; Cmdt Somerset Red Cross Detachment WW I; *b* 7 June 1855; *d* unm 8 Feb 1936
3b Amy Kathleen; *b* 3 March 1863; *d* unm 30 July 1937
5a Cornwallis Oswald; Lt-Gen Bombay SC, JAG Bombay Army 1876–81; *b* 24 Aug 1823; *m* 1st 1848 Jane (*d* 8 Jan 1861), dau of Maj T W Stokoe, and had issue:
1b John Cornwallis; *b* 1849; *d* 1856
2b Maurice Oswald; *b* 24 Sept 1854; *m* 1893 Euphemia Marcella (*d* 10 May 1952), dau of Charles McLean, and *d* 1921, leaving issue:
1c Emily Order Archdall
3b Frederick Viveash; *b* 4 April 1860; *m* Feb 1892 Geraldine Mary Elizabeth (*d* 29 April 1934), est dau of Col John Gerard Irvine, of Killadeas, Co Fermanagh
1b Emily Charlotte Maria; *m* Lt-Col H Stratford Tandy, cmdg 25th Bombay Rifles, and *d* 8 Feb 1891
5a (cont.) Lt-Gen Cornwallis Maude *m* 2nd 1 Oct 1867 Emily Maria Christina (*d* 25 Aug 1889), dau of R T Goddard, and *d* 9 Feb 1894, having by her had:
4b Oswald George Bannerman; Lt 4th Bn Royal Irish Regt; *b* 27 Nov 1869; *d* 11 May 1894
5b Dudley Neville Cornwallis; *b* 29 May 1871; *d* 28 July 1880
6b Cornwallis Charles Wyndham; 2nd Lt AIF, Lt Worcs Regt; *b* 1 Nov 1876; *ka* Gallipoli 1915
6a Robert Eustace; Capt 41st Foot; *b* 14 Nov 1835; *m* 2 Oct 1861 Emily Maude (*d* 2 July 1922), dau of Thomas Addison, and *d* 4 Sept 1863, leaving:
1a Eustace Addison, JP Co Wicklow; Maj Scots Greys, Lt-Col and Brev-Col NI Horse, Boer War 1899–1902 (despatches, brevet, Queen's medal with six clasps, King's medal with two clasps); *b* 5 Jan 1863; *m* 2 Oct 1889 Olivia Georgina Katherine (*d* 26 Oct 1945), only dau of John Whaley, of Thistle Lodge, Co Louth, and *d* 31 Aug 1932, having had:
1c Eustace Anthony Whaley; Capt NI Horse, ADC Personal Staff 1916; *b* 27 Feb 1895; *d* 9 Oct 1919
1c Evelyn Olivia; *b* 28 May 1891; *m* June 1914 (*divorce*) Capt Edward Stuart Hornidge, OBE, s of Richard Hornidge, of Tulfarris, Blessington, Co Wicklow, and had issue
1a Emily Mary Rebecca; *m* 15 April 1845 William Humphreys Mervyn Archdale, JP, DL, of Castle Archdale, Trillick, and Riversdale, Co Fermanagh, and *dsp* 1892. He *d* 22 June 1899.
2a Alicia Cely; *d* unm 19 Aug 1917
3a Charlotte Georgiana; *m* 13 Feb 1866 Rev Preb Lewis Richards, DD, Rector Dungannon, Co Tyrone, and *d* his widow 10 Feb 1911, leaving issue
4a Mary Sophia Juliana; *b* 6 Dec 1841; *m* 24 March 1870 Hugh de Fellenberg Montgomery, PC (NI), DL, MA, of Blessingbourne, Fivemiletown, Co Tyrone, and *d* 11 July 1928, having had issue. He *d* 8 Oct 1924
(6) Francis; Capt RN; *b* 17 Nov 1798; *m* 1st 4 Sept 1827 Frances (*d* 4 May 1832), dau of A H Brooking, and had:
1a Francis Cornwallis, VC, CB; Col RA, Consul-Gen Warsaw 1876–86, Mil Kt Windsor; *b* 28 Oct 1828; *m* 24 Jan 1860 Paulina Susannah (*d* 26 Feb 1916), only dau of Hon Paul Ivy Sterling, Actg Ch Justice Ceylon, and *d* 19 Oct 1900, leaving:
1b Francis Sterling de Montalt; Maj W African Regt, formerly Roy Garrison Regt; *b* 12 April 1867; *m* 17 Feb 1898 Violet Brenda (*d* 5 April 1952), yst dau of John Howard Ashton, JP, DL, of Hatfield Court, Herefs, and *d* 16 Sept 1940, leaving:
1c +Francis Alan de Montalt; *b* 8 Aug 1901; *m* 1929 (*divorce* 1952) Mary, dau of Matthew Donohoe Gray, MD, of Drumlish, Co Longford
1b Ionia Isabella; *b* 8 Oct 1862; *d* unm 24 Sept 1955
2b Georgiana Ivy; *b* 10 March 1864; *d* unm 10 July 1923
3b Mabel Matilda; *b* 10 March 1871; *d* unm
2a Charles Henry; Capt HM IA; *b* 21 Aug 1830; *m* 6 Oct 1859 Georgiana Henrietta Emma (*d* 8 March 1921), 2nd dau of 2nd Baron Sudeley (*qv*), and *d* 1 Jan 1908, leaving issue:
1b Cyril Francis; actor manager, Pres RADA 1936 and 1943; *b* 24 April 1862; *m* 1st 2 June 1888 Winifred (*d* 15 July 1924), only dau of Samuel Anderson Emery; *m* 2nd 12 Oct 1927 Beatrice Mary (*d* 18 June 1979 aged 101), widow of P H Trew and dau of Rev John Ellis, and *d* 20 Feb 1951, having by his 1st w had:
1c John Cyril, KC 1943; barrister Middle Temple 1925, Recorder: Devizes 1939–44, Plymouth 1944–54, Additional Judge: Mayors and City London Court 1954–65 and Centl Criminal Court 1965–68, Jr Prosecuting Counsel Treasury Centl Criminal Court 1942–43, Actg Maj Intell Corps, MP Exeter 1945–51, Chllr Diocese of Bristol 1948–50, memb: Bar Cncl 1952–54, Bd Middx Hosp 1952–62, Bencher Middle Temple 1952, Dir Old Vic Tst 1951–54, Chm: Br Drama League 1952–54, Family Service Units 1954, Govr Roy Victoria Hall Fndn 1954–60, FRSL 1952; *b* 3 April 1901; *educ* Eton and Ch Ch Oxford; *m* 1st 13 June 1927 (*divorce* 1954) Rosamund Willing, dau of Dr T Morris Murray, of Boston, Mass; *m* 2nd 20 Aug 1955 Maureen Constance (*d* 3 May 1998), formerly w of Maj Harry Alexander Desmond Buchanan, MC, Gren Gds, previously widow of 4th Marquess of Dufferin and Ava (*see* DUFFERIN AND CLANEBOYE, B) and 2nd dau of Hon Arthur Ernest Guinness (*see* IVEAGH, E), and *d* 1986, leaving by his 1st w:
1d *Anne Murray [Mrs Michael Bradstock, Whitefold, Clunas, Nairn IV12 5UT]; *b* 16 Jan 1929; *m* 3 May 1950 *Michael Hilary George Bradstock, er s of Maj George Bradstock, and has issue:
1e *James Michael Murray; *b* 12 June 1951; *educ* Eton
2e *Rupert John [Rupert Bradstock Esq, The Old Rectory, West Woodhay, Berks RG20 0BL]; *b* 8 Oct 1958; *educ* Eton; *m* 16 May 1987 *Anna, yr dau of Maj John Riley, of Trinity Manor, Jersey, CI, and has issue:
1f *James Rupert; *b* 6 Oct 1993
1f *Camilla Rose; *b* 29 June 1996
3e *Alastair George [Alastair Bradstock Esq, 14 Dawson Place, London W2 4TJ]; *b* 23 Jan 1961; *educ* Stowe; *m* 8 Oct 1995 *Helen, dau of Michael Shaw-Stewart (*see* SHAW-STEWART, Bt)
1e *Sarah Anne [The Hon Mrs David Gilmour, 27 Ann St, Edinburgh EH4 1PL]; *b* 10 Aug 1954; *m* 1975 *Hon David Robert Gilmour, est s of Baron Gilmour of Craigmillar (*qv*), and has issue
1c Margery Kathleen; *b* 29 April 1889; *m* 23 July 1917 Joseph Warren Burden, of New York, and had issue
2c Pamela Cynthia; *b* 1893; *m* 1st 1 June 1916 Maj William La Touche Congreve, VC, DSO, MC, Rifle Bde (*ka* 20 July 1916), est s of Gen Sir Walter Norris Congreve, VC, KCB, MVO, of Congreve and Chartley, Staffs, and had issue (*see* NUTTING, Bt); *m* 2nd 22 Dec 1919 Brig Hon William Fraser, DSO, MC (*see* SALTOUN, L), and *d* 20 Oct 1975
2b Ernest Henry; *b* 15 Sept 1863; *m* 3 Sept 1889 Maud (*d* 8 Sept 1931), dau of Francis Dennis Bullen, and *d* 23 Aug 1936, having had issue:
1c Robert Henry Ernest; Lt N Staffs Regt; *b* 3 Aug 1890; *d* 12 Sept 1916
3b Hubert Cornwallis; *b* 3 July 1865; *m* 12 Oct 1908 Nellie Kate, dau of George Stanley, of Highfield House, Edgbaston, and *d* 21 March 1930
4b Alwyn Julian; *b* 25 Feb 1867; *m* 15 Nov 1893 Mabel Clarice Isabelle (*d* 11 Dec 1956), dau of James Torpy, and *d* 19 June 1911, leaving issue:
1c Dudley Jack; MB, ChM, MRACP Sydney, DOMS London, DO Oxon, ophthalmic surgn, S/Ldr RAAF (Res); *b* 21 July 1897; *m* 25 April 1925 Marcia, dau of John Williamson, and *d* 1988, leaving issue:
1d +John Alwyn [John Maude Esq, Lynton, 618 Argyle St, Moss Vale, NSW 2577, Australia]; *b* 3 May 1930; *m* 26 Oct 1955 *Susan Theresa, dau of George Gildley King, of Woolahra, NSW, and has:
1e +John Philip Cornwallis; *b* 3 Feb 1959; *m* 1986 (*divorce* 1991) Helen Tatt and has issue:
1f *Angela; *b* 1989
1e *Lisa Margaret; *b* 31 Oct 1960; *m* 1984 *Martin James Bryant and has:
1f *Maximillian Quentin Hugh; *b* 1985
2f *Oscar Charles Rowsell; *b* 1987
3f *Leopold George Roy; *b* 1989
2e *Jessica Mary; *b* 1970
1d *Jacqueline Mary [Mrs Llewellyn Wheeler, 124 Ruthven St, Bondi Junction, NSW 2022, Australia]; *b* 7 Oct 1927; *m* 28 April 1956 *Llewellyn Daniel Wheeler, surgn, s of Llewellyn Andrew Wheeler, of Strathfield, NSW, and has:
1f *Andrew John; *b* 25 July 1957; *m* 1st 1982 (*divorce* 1989) Louise Elna, dau of Denis V Hansen, of Caringbah, NSW; *m* 2nd 1991 *Anne Margaret, dau of John Verschuer, and by her has:
1g *Georgiana Rhiannon; *b* 1992
2f *Daniel Julian; *b* 23 Oct 1959; *m* 1982 *Michele Anne, dau of L Bruce Harper, of Pacific Hill, Dubbo, NSW, and has:
1g *Rachel Ellen; *b* 1989
2g *Fallon Elizabeth; *b* 1990
1f *Frances Llewellyn Maude; *b* 24 Aug 1961; *m* 1988 *Andrew Philip Dudman and has:
1g *Phillip John; *b* 1995
2g *Alastair James; *b* 1997
1c Lillian Isabel; *b* 8 Sept 1894; *m* 1917 Capt Reginald Hugh Knyvett, AIF, and *dsp* 29 Oct 1951. He *d* 1918
2c Beryl Marion; *b* 2 Jan 1896; *m* 1st 1920 (*divorce* 1935) Alan Marshall, of NSW, and had issue; *m* 2nd 1936 Jack G Parkman, and *d* 9 May 1959
5b Maurice Douglas; *b* 16 Aug 1868; *m* 17 Feb 1906 Zima Irene Lily (*d* 1952), dau of John Godfrey Koch, FSI, and *d* 1953, leaving:
1c Daphne Isabel; *m* 1936 Capt Heyland Beaufort-Jones, Essex Regt, and *d* 13 Aug 1967, leaving issue. He *d* 2 May 1968
2c *Valerie Blanche; *b* 1908; *m* 1939 John Chichester Longhurst (*d* 24 Dec 1957)
3c *Cicely [Mrs Roland Cumberbatch, Middle Farm House, Sutton Ditcheat, Somerset]; *b* 1918; *m* 1948 *Roland Cumberbatch, MD, and has issue:
1d *Toby John; *b* 1949
1d *Judith Mary; *b* 1952
2d *Hyacinth Anne; *b* 1954
6b Ralph Walter, DSO (1919); T/Maj and Assist Provost Marshal 1916, Croix de Guerre; *b* 1 Oct 1873; *m* 3 June 1905 (*divorce* 1915) Alice, dau of Noel Herford Thomson, of Dinan, France, and *d* 17 Jan 1922, leaving:

1c +Ralph Henry Evelyn (Rev) [The Rev Ralph Maude, 4 Manor Court, Pewsey, Wilts]; MA St Peter's Hall Oxford 1937, Rector St James's Shaftesbury 1945–57, Vicar St Paul's Weymouth 1957–66 and St Peter's Devizes 1966; *b* 6 Jan 1909; *m* 7 Sept 1933 *Marjorie Cecilia Emily, 2nd dau of Rev Philip Harold Rogers, and has issue:

1d +Roger Philip [Roger Maude Esq, School Cottage, School Lane, Ockham, nr Ripley, Surrey]; *b* 20 Oct 1937; *m* 22 April 1972 *Penelope Joy, er dau of Christopher Rowe, slr, and has issue:

1e +Peter Timothy Daniel; *b* 7 Nov 1975

1e *Polly Emma Frances; *b* 22 Dec 1978

1d *Rachel Anne [Mrs John Cullum, 20 Gorang Rd, Westleigh, NSW 2120, Australia]; *b* 30 Sept 1934; *m* 12 Sept 1964 *John Donald Cullum, BD, and has issue:

1e *Simon Richard; *b* 29 Aug 1967

1e *Joanna Margaret; *b* 16 April 1969

1b Lilian Selina; *d* unm 10 Dec 1927

3a James Arthur (Rev), of The Brompton Oratory; *b* 10 April 1832; RC Priest; *d* 16 Feb 1899

(6) (cont.) Capt Francis Maude *m* 2nd 28 June 1849 Georgiana (*d* 2 July 1882), dau of Gervase Parker Bushe, and *d* 23 Oct 1886, having had issue:

4a Cecil William De Latham; *b* 21 April 1850; *d* 19 June 1852

5a Gerald Edward; BA Oxon, barrister, Maj 4th Bn E Surrey Regt; *b* 12 June 1851; *m* 25 July 1894 Edith Caroline (*d* 6 Oct 1922), CBE, est dau of Maj Henry Whitby Briscoe, RA, of Tinvane, Co Tipperary, and *d* 18 Jan 1934, having had:

1b Gervase Henry Francis; Lt Roy Fus; *b* 20 March 1896; *d* 9 April 1917 of wounds recd in action

6a Raymond William de Latham; *b* 27 June 1852; *m* 6 June 1878 Jenny Maria Catherine, OBE (*d* 1 Feb 1935), only dau of Otto Goldschmidt, and *d* 13 May 1897, leaving issue:

1b Victor Francis; WW I in RAF; *b* 9 Feb 1879; *educ* Winchester; *m* 7 Sept 1923 Lucy Margaret (*d* 1 June 1942), dau of Richard Hughes, MD, of Hitchin, Herts, and *dsp* 7 March 1948

2b Charles Raymond, OBE (1919), MC; BA Oxon, T/Lt-Col Loyal Regt and Gen List, Staff Capt DAAG and AAG BEF WW I (despatches); *b* 27 Feb 1882; *m* 17 May 1907 (Lillian) Nancy Bache, CBE (1950), actress (*d* 31 March 1970 aged 90), only surv dau of William Henry Price, of Rockmount, Kinver, and *d* 14 Nov 1943, leaving issue:

1c *Joan Nancy; *b* 16 Jan 1908; *m* 1st 21 Dec 1933 Frank Henry Waters (*d* 18 Oct 1954); *m* 2nd 24 April 1956 Oliver Frederick John Bradley Woods, MC (*d* 1972), and by her 1st husb has issue:

1d *Sarah Jenny [Mrs Sarah Dunsmure, 8 East St, Lewes, Sussex]; *b* 22 June 1938; *m* 24 July 1963 (*divorce* 1973) Maj James Alexander Dunsmure, Scots Gds, er s of Maj Henry Dunsmure, Scots Gds, and has issue:

1e *Rupert Alexander Frank; *b* 1969

1e *Miranda Louise; *b* 1967

2c *Elizabeth Meriel [Miss Elizabeth Maude, Turville Cottage, Turville Heath, Oxon]; *b* 3 Sept 1912

1b Gwendolen Lind; *b* 18 April 1880; *m* 31 May 1904 John Duncan Gregory, CB, CMG, only s of Sir Philip Spencer Gregory, and *d* 21 Sept 1960, leaving issue. He *d* 29 Jan 1951

1a Blanche Emily Isabella; *b* 10 July 1855; *m* 21 June 1898 George Fosbery Lyster, JP, DL, of Plas Isaf, Ruthin, and *d* 3 Aug 1933, having had issue. He *d* 11 May 1899

2a Olivia Georgiana Elizabeth; *b* 1 March 1857; *m* 12 Nov 1884 Morton Kelsall Peto, 2nd s of Sir (Samuel) Morton Peto, 1st Bt, of Somerleyton (*qv*), and *d* 23 July 1945, having had issue

(4) Isabella Elizabeth; *b* 1779; *d* unm 1859

(5) Georgiana; *b* 1781; *m* June 1806 Lord William Stuart and *d* 31 Aug 1807, leaving issue (*see* BUTE, M)

(6) Alicia; *b* 1782; *m* 21 May 1807 Lord Robert Ponsonby Tottenham (*see* ELY, M) and *d* 21 Dec 1866, leaving issue

(7) Charlotte; *b* 1783; *m* 6 Sept 1806 Peter La Touche, of Bellevue, Co Wicklow, and *d* 3 Dec 1874, leaving issue. He *d* 11 Feb 1830

(8) Mary Anne; *b* 1786; *m* 15 April 1809 3rd Viscount Lifford (*qv*) and *d* 3 Jan 1877, having had issue

(9) Emily; *b* 1794; *m* 10 Feb 1826 2nd Baron Dunalley of Kilboy (*qv*) and *dsp* 10 Feb 1884

(10) Catherine; *b* 1788; *d* young

The 6th VISCOUNT's cousin,

EUSTACE WYNDHAM MAUDE, **7th Viscount Hawarden**, JP; Maj Queen's Roy W Surrey Regt, attd Egyptian Army 1910, served WW I (despatches, two medals), Order Nile; *b* 20 Sept 1877; *m* 17 Nov 1920 Marion (*d* 1 Oct 1974), est dau of Albert Leslie Wright, of Butterley Hall, Derbys, and had issue:

1 ROBERT LESLIE EUSTACE, **8th Viscount**

2 +Henry Cornwallis [The Hon Henry Maude, Wingham Well House, Wingham, Kent CT3 1NW]; *b* 3 March 1928; *educ* Marlborough and Worcester Coll Oxford (BA 1953 MA 1957); High Sheriff Kent 1989, WW II with Queen's R Regt and as Sgt Educn Corps; *m* 8 Aug 1964 *Elizabeth Georgina, only dau of David McNaught Lockie, of Grasse, France, and has issue:

(1) +Francis Hugh Cornwallis; *b* 7 June 1966; *educ* Eton and Clare Coll Cambridge (BA 1988, MA); RIBA; *m* 30 Dec 1994 *Caroline Aish, of Dorset

(2) +Anthony Eustace David; *b* 1972; *educ* Winchester and Collingwood Coll Durham (BA)

(1) *Elizabeth Arabella Marion; *b* 16 Dec 1967; *educ* Benenden and N London Poly (BSc Hons); *m* 20 March 1993 *Andrei Majidian, of Tehran, and has:

1a *Daniel Martin; *b* 6 Sept 1996

(2) *Diana Caroline Alice; *b* 30 Jan 1971; *educ* West Heath

1 *Helen Margaretta [The Hon Mrs Baxter, Stourbridge House, Milton-on-Stour, Dorset SP8 5PZ]; WW II 1941–46 in WRNS; *b* 23 Aug 1921; *m* 10 May 1947 (Walter) Peter Baxter (*d* 1977), est son of Col Donald Baxter, MC, of Long Burton House, Sherborne, Dorset, and has issue:

(1) *Charles Peter; *b* 3 March 1950; *educ* Marlborough; *m* 1974 *Nicola Caroline, 2nd dau of Maj N S John, of Warminster, Wilts

(1) *Joanna Rosamond [Mrs Michael Falkiner, Downclose Stud, N Perrott, Somerset TA18 7SH]; *b* 30 Jan 1948; *m* 1 Aug 1970 *Michael George Patrick Falkiner (*see* FALKINER, Bt) and has issue

(2) *Margaretta Helena [Mrs John Mansfield, Rushwood Court, Derby, Kansas, USA]; *b* 27 Sept 1954; *m* 1983 *John Giles Mansfield, s of Cyril Peter Mansfield

(3) *Victoria Marion [Mrs William Cadman, Woodhouse Cross, Stock, Dorset SP8 5NP]; *b* 11 June 1956; *m* 1st 1977 (*divorce* 1985) Brian John Blundy; *m* 2nd 1986 *William Stephen Cadman

The 7th VISCOUNT *d* 6 April 1958; his er son

ROBERT LESLIE EUSTACE MAUDE, **8th Viscount Hawarden**, WW II 1945 in Coldstream Gds, memb Kent CC 1965–67 and Eastry RDC 1964–67; *b* 26 March 1926; *educ* Winchester and Ch Ch Oxford; *m* 28 Sept 1957 *Susannah Caroline Hyde [The Rt Hon Susannah Viscountess Hawarden, The Chicken House, Canterbury Rd, Wingham, Kent CT3 1BB], only dau of Maj Charles Phillips Gardner (*see* 1970 edn GARDNER, B), and *d* 1991, leaving issue:

1 (ROBERT) CONNAN WYNDHAM LESLIE MAUDE, **9th and present Viscount Hawarden**

2 +Thomas Patrick Cornwallis [The Hon Thomas Maude, Cedar Lodge, Wingham Court, nr Canterbury, Kent]; *b* 1 Oct 1964; *educ* Rudolph Steiner Sch nr Canterbury and Hadlow Ag Coll; *m* 17 April 1998 *Christine Lydia, dau of Henry Stowe

1 *Sophia-Rose Eileen [The Hon Mrs Steel, Norton Court, nr Sittingbourne]; *b* 20 Jan 1959; *m* 26 June 1982 *Tim(othy) Michael Steel, only s of Anthony Steel, of Rock House Farm, Lower Froyle, Hants, and has issue:

(1) *Anthony Nicholas Robert; *b* 16 Sept 1988

(1) *Isabella Ann Augusta; *b* 4 Aug 1984

(2) *Emily Susannah Letitia; *b* 7 Dec 1992

(3) *Oriel Sophia Rosamund; *b* 29 Aug 1995

HAWKE

Arms: Arg. a chevron erminois between three boatswain's whistles purple. **Crest:** A hawk rising erm., beaked, belled and charged on the breast with a fleur-de-lys or. **Supporters:** Dexter, Neptune, his mantle of a sea-green colour, edged arg., crowned with an eastern coronet or, his dexter arm erect, darting downwards, his trident sa., headed silver, resting his sinister foot on a dolphin ppr.; sinister, a seahorse or, sustaining in his forefins a banner arg., the staff broken ppr. **Motto:** Strike. **Creation:** B. (GB) 20 May 1776.

THE 11TH BARON HAWKE OF TOWTON, Co York (Edward George Hawke, TD) [The Rt Hon The Lord Hawke TD, House of Lords, London SW1A 0PW]; *b* 25 Jan 1950; *s* f 1992; *educ* Eton; 2nd Lt 1st Bn Coldstream Gds 1970–73, Maj QO Yeo 1973–93; FRICS; *m* 1993 *Bronwen M, dau of William T James, BVMS, MRCVS, and has:

1 +WILLIAM MARTIN THEODORE; *b* 23 June 1995

Lineage: EDWARD HAWKE, of Lincoln's Inn; barrister; *m* Elizabeth, widow of Col Ruthven and dau of Nathaniel Bladen, of Lincoln's Inn, barrister, and Hemsworth, Yorks, by Isabella, dau of Sir William Fairfax (*see* FAIRFAX OF CAMERON, L), and had an only s:

EDWARD HAWKE, **1st Baron Hawke of Towton**, Co York (GB), so *cr* 20 May 1776, KB (1749); *b* 1705; RN: joined 1720, R-Adml the White July 1747 and 1755, won Battle of Quiberon Bay over French 20 Nov 1759, V-Adml 1765, Adml and C-in-C Fleet 1768, 1st Ld Admlty 1766–71, MP Portsmouth 1747–76; *m* 1737 Catherine (*d* 28 Oct 1756), dau and sole heir of Walter Brooke, of Burton Hall, Yorks, and *d* 17 Oct 1781, leaving an est s:

MARTIN BLADEN HAWKE, **2nd Baron Hawke of Towton**; **DCL Oxford, MP Saltash 1768–74**; *b* 20 April 1744; *m* 6 Feb 1771 Cassandra (*d* 19 Nov 1813), yst dau of Sir Edward Turner, 2nd Bt (*see* DRYDEN, Bt), and *d* 27 March 1805, having had:

1 EDWARD HAWKE later HAWKE-HARVEY (roy licence 4 Aug 1798), **3rd Baron Hawke of Towton**; *b* 3 May 1774; *m* 28 Aug 1798 Frances Anne (*d* 22 Aug 1810), dau and heir of Stanhope Harvey, of Womersley Park, Yorks, and *d* 29 Nov 1824, leaving:

(1) EDWARD WILLIAM HAWKE-HARVEY, **4th Baron Hawke of Towton**; *b* 15 July 1799; *m* 1st 1 Aug 1821 Elizabeth Frances (*dsp* 26 Aug 1824), 2nd dau of Sir John Ramsden, 4th Bt (*qv*); *m* 2nd 26 April 1848 Frances (*d* 29 June 1903), est dau of Walker Fetherstonhaugh, of The Hermitage, Chester-le-Street, and *d* 8 Jan 1869, having by her had:

1a Frances Cassandra; *m* 1 Sept 1870 4th Earl of Rosse (*qv*) and *d* 9 Dec 1921, leaving issue

2 STANHOPE HAWKE-HARVEY, **5th Baron Hawke of Towton**; Capt Army; *b* 18 Jan 1804; *d* unm 5 May 1870

(3) Martin; *b* 1806; *k* in a fall from his horse while hunting 19 Nov 1857

2 Martin Bladen Edward; *b* 17 April 1777; *m* 8 March 1815 Hannah (*d* 6 April 1876), only dau of Thomas Nisbet, of Mersington, Scotland, and *d* 14 Sept 1839, having had issue:

(1) EDWARD HENRY JULIUS, **6th Baron**

(2) Bladen Edward Martin; Cdr RN; *b* 14 March 1820; *d* unm 13 Sept 1877

1 Cassandra Julia; *m* 1st 15 July 1793 Samuel Estwicke, of Barbados; *m* 2nd Sept 1800 Rev Stephen Sloane; *m* 3rd Thomas Green

2 Annabella Eliza Cassandra; *d* unm 1818

The 5th BARON's cousin,

EDWARD HENRY JULIUS HAWKE, **6th Baron Hawke of Towton**; *b* 24 Dec 1815; *educ* St Catharine's Hall Cambridge (MA); Vicar Coates, Rector Willingham Lincs 1854–75, RD; *m* 9 July 1857 Jane (*d* 3 Aug 1915), 3rd dau of Henry Dowker, of Laysthorpe, Yorks, and *d* 5 Dec 1887, having had:

1 Edward; *b* 2 Sept 1859; *d* 6 Sept 1871

2 MARTIN BLADEN HAWKE, **7th Baron Hawke of Towton**, JP W R Yorks; Col W R Vol Regt, Capt and Hon Maj 3rd Bn Princess of Wales's Own Yorkshire Regt, Hon Freeman Scarborough 1930; *b* 16 Aug 1860; *m* 1 June 1916 Marjory Nelson Ritchie (*d* 25 Jan 1936), widow of Arthur J Graham Cross and 3rd dau of W Peacock Edwards, and *dsp* 10 Oct 1938

3 Stanhope; Adml; *b* 16 April 1863; *d* unm 1 Feb 1936

4 Bladen Edward; *b* 22 Oct 1865; *d* 24 June 1875

5 Harold Brooke; Capt Leicester Regt; *b* 23 Sept 1867; *m* 9 Aug 1906 Anne (*d* 6 Aug 1912), widow of Arthur J J Bamford, of Misterton Hall, Lutterworth, and dau of John Nash, of Chicago, and *dsp* 20 July 1913

6 EDWARD JULIAN, **8th Baron**

1 Mary Catharine; *d* unm 26 Oct 1948

2 Eleanor Jane Emily; *m* 15 Jan 1921 Arthur Gordon Watney and *d* 28 Aug 1940. He *d* 19 Dec 1927

3 Alice Cassandra; *d* unm 9 March 1957

4 Catherine Isabel, JP N R Yorks; *m* 5 May 1903 Edward Grosvenor Tew, JP, of Moorlands, Haxby, York, and *d* 5 April 1942, leaving issue. He *d* 20 June 1943

The 7th BARON's bro,

EDWARD JULIAN HAWKE, **8th Baron Hawke of Towton**; Dir Nat Bank of India; *b* 16 Feb 1873; *m* 9 Oct 1900 Frances Alice (*d* 8 July 1959), 2nd dau of Col John Randal Wilmer, IA, and *d* 4 Sept 1939, leaving:

1 BLADEN WILMER HAWKE, **9th Baron Hawke of Towton**; *b* 31 Dec 1901; *educ* Winchester and King's Coll Cambridge (BA 1923, MA 1946); WW II in Min Ec Warfare and War Office, Chm Ind U Peers Assoc 1950–53, Ld-in-Waiting 1953–57, Memb Church Assembly 1955–85, Ch Cmmr 1958–85, Chm Chichester Diocesan Bd of Finance 1961, dir Initial Services Ltd and Ecclesiastical Insur Office; *m* 1 Nov 1934 *Ina Mary Faure [The Rt Hon The Dowager Lady Hawke, Faygate Place, Faygate, Sussex], er dau of Henry Faure Walker, of Highly Manor, Balcombe, Sussex, and *d* 1985, leaving:

(1) *Caroline Ina Maude [The Hon Mrs Easton, The Old Hall, Barley, nr Royston, Herts]; barrister Middle Temple 1959; *b* 13 Feb 1937; *m* 6 Aug 1960 *John Francis Easton, barrister, only s of Rev Cecil Gordon Easton, and has:

1a *Nicholas John; *b* 6 May 1961

1a *Ina Frances [Mrs Vincent Nelson, 6 Fawnbrake Ave, London SE24 0BY]; *b* 18 May 1964; *m* 17 Sept 1988 *Vincent L Nelson, s of S A Nelson, of Jamaica, and has:

1b *Oliver John; *b* 10 July 1989

2b *Edward Simeon; *b* 20 July 1994

1b *Saffron; *b* 7 March 1992

(2) *Annabel [The Hon Mrs Ridley, 29 Richmond Hill, Richmond, Surrey TW10 6RE]; *b* 27 Aug 1940; *m* 4 April 1961 *(Nicholas) Adam Ridley, MA, slr, yr s of Rev Michael Ridley, and has issue:

1a *Caspar Hawke Michael; *b* 1 April 1967; *m* 1 Jan 1997 *Rebecca, er dau of Paul Dallyn, of Gillingham, Dorset

1a *Celia Kirstin; *b* 11 March 1964; *m* 1991 *Nicholas John Willis, yr s of Dr Peter Willis, of Stillington, Yorks, and has:

1b *Jack Michael; *b* 3 April 1997

2a *Harriet Clare; *b* 3 March 1970

(3) *Cecilia Anne; *b* 13 March 1943; *m* 1st 27 July 1963 (*divorce* 1971) Sir Peter Tapsell, MP, and has had:

1a James Hawke; *b* 11 Oct 1966; *d* 1985

(3) (cont.) The Hon Mrs Cecilia Tapsell *m* 2nd 1979, as his 2nd w, *Sir Nicholas Paul Scott, KBE (1995, MBE 1964), PC (1989), JP, MP (C) Chelsea Oct 1974–97, and has further issue:

2a *Patrick Martin Iain; *b* 1982

1a *Amber Teresa; *b* 1987

(4) *Lavinia Mary [The Hon Mrs Maclean Bristol, Breacachadh Castle, Isle of Coll, Argyll]; *b* 15 June 1945; *m* 2 April 1965 *Maj Nicholas Maclean Verity BRISTOL later MACLEAN BRISTOL, OBE, DL, and has issue:

1a *Charles Bladen Maclean; *b* 15 March 1967; *m* 7 June 1997 *Kim Elizabeth, est dau of Reginald Stanley Rowland, of Westerham, Kent

2a *Alexander Stanhope Maclean; *b* 14 Dec 1970

3a *Lauchlan Neil Maclean; *b* 24 April 1974

(5) *Rowena Margaret [The Hon Mrs Sanders, Hankerton Priory, nr Malmesbury, Wilts SN16 9JZ]; *b* 23 June 1948; Ldy in Waiting to HRH PRINCESS MICHAEL OF KENT; *m* 1st 20 Feb 1971 Philip William Leatham (*see* 1928 edn BUCKLAND, B); *m* 2nd 1990 *William T Sanders and by her 1st husb has issue:

1a *Patrick Hawke; *b* 1974

2a *Frederick Bladen; *b* 1981

1a *Arabella Rose; *b* 1976

(6) *Prunella Jane [The Hon Mrs Servatius, Van Alkemadelaan 354, 2597 As Den Haag, Netherlands]; *b* 14 Dec 1951; *m* 17 Jan 1976 *Albert Hendrik Servatius, est s of De Heer Bernard Servatius, Netherlands Dip Corps, and has:

1a *Timothy; *b* 1979

2a *Julian; *b* 1982

(7) *Olivia Mary [The Hon Mrs Pethybridge, 64 Hendham Rd, London SW17 7DQ]; *b* 5 April 1955; *m* 9 July 1983 *Timothy John Pethybridge, only s of J H Pethybridge, of Barn Park, Bodmin, Cornwall, and has issue:

1a *Henry John Hawke; *b* 1989

1a *Mary-Rose Olivia; *b* 1985

2a *Flora Louise; *b* 1987

2 (JULIAN STANHOPE) THEODORE, **10th Baron**

1 *Veronica Margery [The Hon Mrs Masefield, Down Lodge, East Harting, Petersfield, Hants]; *b* 30 Jan 1915; *m* 25 June 1940 Jack Briscoe Masefield (*d* 1993), Assist Commr Police Malaya, and has had issue:

(1) Jacqueline Rosemary; *b* 13 July 1942; *d* unm 4 Oct 1966

(2) *Delphinia Frances Annie [Mrs Richard Hall, Weston Farmhouse, Weston, Petersfield, Hants GU32 3NN]; *b* 28 Jan 1947; *m* 28 June 1969 *Richard James Fairfax Hall, and has issue:

1a *Leander Arthur Caspar; *b* 1973

2a *Hereward Ambrose Bertram; *b* 1974

1a *Imogen Penelope Veronica; *b* 1977

(3) Camilla Margery; *b* 16 April 1949; *d* 1973

The 9th BARON's bro,

JULIAN STANHOPE THEODORE HAWKE, **10th Baron Hawke of Towton**; WW II as W/Cdr AAR; *b* 19 Oct 1904; *educ* Eton and King's Coll Cambridge (BA 1926); *m* 1st 17 Feb 1933 (*divorce* 1946) Angela Margaret Griselda, only dau of Capt Edmund William Bury, and had:

1 *Sarah Elizabeth Jane; *b* 10 June 1935; *m* 5 Oct 1957 *John Norris Fennell, er s of Col Harold Percival Fennell, of Hove, Sussex, and has issue:

(1) *Adrian Martin Alexander [Adrian Fennell Esq, 70 Broxash Rd, Clapham, London SW11 6AB]; *b* 1 April 1963; *m* 1990 *Anna Meriel, dau of William John Gowing, of Buxton, Norfolk, and has issue:

1a *Alexander Theo Felix; *b* 1993

(1) *Olivia Louise; *b* 21 May 1961; *m* 1993 *Hon Martin John Hunt, yr s of Baron Hunt of Tanworth (*qv*)

2 *Catherine Mary [The Hon Mrs Brook, 7 The Hermitage, Richmond, Surrey]; *b* 11 July 1940; *m* 16 March 1963 *Charles Groves Darville Brook, MD, FRCP, yst s of AVM William Arthur Darville Brook, CB, CBE, and has issue:

(1) *Charlotte Griselda Mary; *b* 30 Sept 1965

(2) *Henrietta Diana Darville; *b* 2 April 1968

The **10th Baron** *m* 2nd 22 May 1947 *Georgette Margaret [The Rt Hon Georgette Lady Hawke, Old Mill House, Cuddington, Northwich, Cheshire CW8 2TA], only dau of George Spence Davidson, of Belgravia, and *d* 1992, leaving by her:

1 EDWARD GEORGE HAWKE, **11th and present Baron Hawke of Towton**

3 *Nichola Frances [The Hon Mrs Forbes, East Cevidley, Alford, Aberdeenshire AB33 8BH]; *b* 15 Jan 1949; *m* 1981 *Hon Jonathan Andrew Forbes and has issue (*see* FORBES, L)

4 *Vanessa Nathalie Mary [The Hon Mrs Brodie, Brook Farm, Eglwys Cross, Whitchurch, Salop SY13 2JT]; *b* 20 June 1957; *m* 1985 *(Peter) Adam William Brodie, yst s of Maj-Gen Thomas Brodie, CB, CBE, DSO, and has:

(1) *Nathalie Jane; *b* 1986

(2) *Elizabeth Sarah; *b* 1989

5 Julia Georgette; *b* 1 Jan 1960; missing presumed drowned Galapagos Islands 12 Oct 1997

HAWKINS

Arms: Arg. on a saltire engrailed sa. a quatrefoil between four fleurs-de-lys or. **Crest:** Upon a mount vert a hind lodged or, the dexter forefoot resting on a gunstone. **Motto:** *Pro Deo et rege* ('For God and king'). **Creation:** Bt. (GB) 25 July 1778.

SIR HOWARD CÆSAR HAWKINS, 8TH BT, of Kelston, Somerset [Sir Howard Hawkins Bt, c/o 41 Hume Rd, Dunkeld, Johannesburg, S Africa]; *b* 17 Nov 1956; *s* f 1993; *educ* Hilton Coll S Africa; SAAF 1975

Lineage: CÆSAR HAWKINS; *b* 1593; royalist Col Civil War, Govr Greenland House, Bucks, against Parly forces; *m* 22 Dec 1622 Priscilla Wakelin and had:

CÆSAR HAWKINS; had:

CÆSAR HAWKINS; *b* 1662; had:

CÆSAR HAWKINS; *b* 1688; *m* 1710 Ann Bright and *d* 1752, leaving, with other issue:

1 CÆSAR (Sir), **1st Bt**

2 Pennell; Body-Surgn to GEORGE II, Serjeant-Surgn to GEORGE III; *b* 16 May 1716; *m* Sarah (*d* 25 Dec 1791), dau of Thomas Chetle, and had, with a dau (*m* Rev Samuel Nott):

(1) George Edward; Serjeant-Surgn to GEORGE III; *m* Louisa (*m* 2nd Adml — Bowater), dau of Thomas Lane, and had:

1a Louisa; *m* Maj-Gen Sir Henry Wheatley, Keeper Privy Purse to TM WILLIAM IV and QUEEN VICTORIA

2a Laura; *m* Sir Matthew White Ridley, 3rd Bt (*see* RIDLEY, V)

1 Elizabeth; *m* 1st Herbert Wilde, of Ludlow; *m* 2nd Sir Herbert Perrott Pakington, 7th Bt (*see* HAMPTON, B)

The er son,

Sir Cæsar Hawkins Hawkins, 1st Bt (GB), so *cr* 25 July 1778, of Kelston, Somerset; *b* 10 Jan 1711; Serjeant-Surgn to GEORGE III; *m* Sarah (*d* 17 March 1801), dau of John Coxe, and *d* 13 Feb 1786, having had, with two other sons (*d* unm):

1 John; *m* April 1779 Anne (*d* 17 March 1823), dau and coheir of Joseph Colborne, of Hardenhuish House, Wilts, and *d* 7 May 1785, leaving:

(1) **Sir Cæsar Hawkins, 2nd Bt**; *educ* Eton; *d* there 2 July 1793

(2) JOHN CÆSAR (Sir), **3rd Bt**

(3) George; *b* 17 March 1783; *m* 25 March 1814 Mary, dau of David Wedderburn Webster, and *dsp* 1865

(1) Mary Anne; *m* 12 Jan 1803 Rev John Surtees, Preb Bristol, Rector Banham, Norfolk, and *d* 29 June 1873. He *d* 23 Dec 1857

2 Charles; Serjeant-Surgn to GEORGE III; *m* 1st —, dau of — Adair, and had, with other issue:

(1) Charles (Rev); Preb and Canon residentiary York; *m* 7 Aug 1807 Augusta (*d* 11 Aug 1847), dau of Sir James Cockburn, MP, and *d* 11 April 1857, leaving:

1a Charles James (Rev); *b* 12 Jan 1809; *m* 15 Sept 1831 Annie Mason (*d* 1884), dau of Col James Dixon, of Brandsburton, and *d* 14 June 1864, having had, with other issue:

1b Cæsar Hugh; Cdr RN; *b* 4 Oct 1841; *m* 8 May 1888 Annie Beatrice (*m* 2nd 12 April 1893 Charles Hugh Babington Elliott (*d* 1943)), 4th dau of George Wills, of Clifton, and *d* 25 Aug 1888, leaving issue:

1c Cæsar Hugh George Wills; Lt RASC (MT); *b* posthumously 3 April 1889; *m* 1st 6 June 1914 (*divorce* 1926) Margaret Edith (*d* 1980), dau of James Shaw Robertson; *m* 2nd 1930 Diodata (*m* 2nd 1948 (*divorce* 1956) Archibald Laurence Lyall (*d* 1964); *m* 3rd 19– *Marco Lucic-Roki, of Venice, and *d* 1991), dau of Count Bernhard Caboga, of Dubrovnik, Ragusa, and *d* 1947, leaving by his 1st w:

1d Cæsar Charles, DSC; Lt RN WW II; *b* 17 May 1915; *m* 25 May 1937 Mary Redwood Vachell (*m* 2nd 6 July 1945 Desmond John Dudley Torrens, MBE, MB, Lt-Col RAMC, and *d* 21 Sept 1962), dau of Edmund Hann, and was *ka* in HMS *Exmouth* 21 Jan 1940, leaving:

1e *Alice Penelope [Mrs Robin Vivian, B92 Res Amiral, Marina Baie des Anges 06270, Villeneuve-Loubet, France]; *b* 8 March 1938; *m* 13 May 1961 *Robin Audley Clinton Vivian and has issue (*see* VIVIAN, B)

1d Margaret Elizabeth Ann; *b* 31 July 1917; *m* 1st 15 Oct 1940 Lt Hilliard Baxley Wilson, USNR (*d* 1961); *m* 2nd 10 Nov 1967 James Rowland Lowe (*d* 19 Dec 1969) and *d* 1986, leaving by her 1st husb:

1e *Penelope Jane [Mrs Charles Giorgi, 947 Green St, San Francisco, CA 94133, USA] ; *b* 1944; *m* 1st 1972 (*divorce* 19–) Michael McClure; *m* 2nd 19– *Charles Giorgi

1b Annie Caroline; *m* 17 April 1856 William Copley Woodhead, MRCS, of Leeds, and *d* 1903, leaving issue

2b Augusta Isabella; *m* 1861 Maj William James Watson, 8th King's Regt, and *d* March 1900, leaving issue

3b Delia Mary; *m* 11 April 1867 Capt Henry Smith Andrews, and *d* 12 Oct 1880

2a Henry Annesley (Rev); Vicar Topcliffe; *b* 1 Jan 1813; *m* 1st 15 Aug 1838 Harriet Emma (*d* 30 April 1844), dau of William Hale, of Acomb, Yorks, and had issue:

1b William Webster (Rev); Rector Hinderclay Norfolk; *b* 1842; *m* 1877 Kate (*d* 2 July 1902), dau of P Leyburn, and *d* 25 June 1918, leaving issue:

1c Charles Francis; Maj RFA Boer War 1901–02 and WW I 1914; *b* 16 Jan 1880; *ka* 25 April 1915

1c Rose Mary; twin with her brother; *d* unm Feb 1952

2c Beatrice; *m* 18 March 1912 Capt Erle Burgo Brand, MBE, RA, and Tank Corps (*d* 1956), and had:

1d *Erle Hamilton; *b* 9 March 1913

1d *Eve Annesley; *b* 10 Nov 1921

3c Harriet Emma; *m* 12 Dec 1907 Thomas Henry Bowman Whytehead (*d* Feb 1942) and had issue

4c Olive; *d* unm 1956

1b Augusta; *m* 25 April 1867 Edward Thomas Helme, of Hornchurch Lodge, Essex, and *d* 1895

2a (cont.)The Rev Henry Hawkins *m* 2nd 19 May 1846 Isabel (*d* 10 Dec 1964), dau of — Sinclair, of Escrick, Yorks, and *d* 18 Oct 1891, having by her had, with other issue:

2b Reginald; MA Cantab; *b* 1849; *m* 1880 Marguerite Wilhelmine, dau of Rev William Collings Lukis, Rector Wath, Ripon, and *d* 14 Dec 1910, leaving issue:

1c Eustace Fellowes Sinclair, DSO (1918), OBE (1949); Lt-Col RASC, Actg G/Capt RAFVR, WW I (despatches); *b* 1881; *m* 1908 Patience, dau of Capt Joseph Henderson, 12th Lancers, and *d* 1954, leaving issue:

1d Patrick Reginald Cæsar; *b* 1918

2d Honor Marie Marguerite; *b* 1913

3b Arthur Cockburn; *b* 1852; *m* 1883 Agnes, dau of H Carmichael, and had issue:

1c Henry Cecil Carmichael; *b* 1884; *m* 1907 Winifred, dau of John Robinson, and had:

1d +Cecil Arthur Robinson; *b* 1908

2d +Harold Percy; *b* 1909

1d *Winifred Agnes Ruth

2c Arthur Charles; *b* 1885

3c Reginald Cæsar; *b* 1890

1c Agnes Isabel; *b* 1889

2c Frances Kathleen; *b* 1892

5b Lancelot; *b* 1859

2b Georgiana Elizabeth

3b Mabel Anne

4b Frances Emily

5b Mary Isabel

1a Cecilia Mary; *m* 4 April 1837 Rev Hon John Baillie and *d* 23 Sept 1903, having had issue (*see* HADDINGTON, E)

2a Georgiana Augusta; *m* 31 Oct 1839 Capt James Charles Yorke and *d* 6 Dec 1901, leaving issue (*see* HARDWICKE, E)

(1) Louisa; *m* 1801 T T Clarke, of Swakeleys, Middx, and Binham Abbey, Norfolk, and *d* 1840

2 (cont.) Charles Hawkins *m* 2nd 25 Sept 1788 Harriet Truesdale and by her had two sons (*dsp*)

3 Edward (Rev); Rector Kelston, Somerset; *m* 1787 Margaret (*d* 5 Nov 1859), dau of Rev Thomas Howes, of Morningthorpe, Norfolk, and *d* 29 Dec 1805, having had, with three other sons (*d* young) and three daus (*d* unm):

(1) Edward (Rev); DD, Canon Rochester, Provost Oriel Coll Oxford; *b* 27 Feb 1789; *m* 20 Dec 1828 Mary Anne (*d* 14 Jan 1892), dau of Richard Buckle, of Chew Magna, Somerset, and *d* 18 Nov 1882, having had, with three daus (*d* unm):

1a Edward (Rev); MA Oxon; *b* 1833; *d* unm 8 Oct 1862

2a Caesar Richard; ICS, Dep Commr Amritsar; *b* 1841; *m* 16 Oct 1867 Alice (*d* 5 Sept 1882), dau of Maj-Gen Edward Norman Perkins, Bengal SC, and *d* 29 Oct 1894, leaving issue:

1b Edward Cæsar, JP; *b* 1876; *m* 1 Feb 1899 Blanche Marianne (*d* 5 Jan 1951), 3rd dau of Rev Charles Blomfield Smith, Rector Shelton, and *d* 26 Aug 1960, leaving issue:

1c Richard Pennell Cæsar; Cdr RN; *b* 27 Dec 1899; *m* 1st 12 Sept 1929 (*divorce* 1952) Enid Helen (*d* 1983), dau of Rev John Warren Corbould-Warren, of Caistor Hall, Norwich; *m* 2nd 21 April 1964 *Mary Constance Emily [Mrs Richard Hawkins, Shelton Hall, Long Stratton, Norfolk NR15 2SF], dau of Rev Frank Percy Law, Rector Shelton, and *d* 1990, leaving by his 1st w:

1d *Diana Elizabeth [Mrs Anthony Pott, 49 Bugle St, Southampton, Hants]; *b* 24 Nov 1930; *m* 3 Jan 1953 *Anthony Fred Doran Pott, and has issue

1b Maude Ellen; *m* 24 April 1896 Lt Col Owen James Obbard, IA, Assist Commr Burma, s of Gen Harry Smith Obbard, BSc, and *d* 24 Nov 1952, leaving issue. He *d* 2 Aug 1938

2b Katherine Mary Helen; *m* 20 Nov 1900 Henry Osborne Buckle, Ch Magistrate Witwatersrand, S Africa, and *d* 3 July 1914, leaving issue. He *d* 2 April 1933

(2) Francis; MD, Physician-in-Ordinary Roy Household; *b* 1794; *m* 1st 4 May 1831 Hester (*d* 11 Dec 1847), 3rd dau of Sir John Vaughan, Baron Exchequer; *m* 2nd 23 July 1859 Sarah Jane (*d* 1890), dau of G Haywood, and *d* 13 Dec 1877, having had by his 1st w, with other issue:

1a Charles Halford (Rev); MA Cantab; *b* 1838; *m* 8 Aug 1878 Susan (*d* 31 Jan 1905), dau of Lt-Gen John Colpoys Haughton, CSI, and *d* 28 Dec 1900, leaving issue:

1b Henry Vaughan; Sudan CS, Orders Nile 3rd Cl and Medjidie 4th Cl; *b* 7 Oct 1879; *m* 17 May 1906 Mary Mackenzie (*d* 26 Nov 1946), dau of Alexander Francis Mackenzie Downie, of Holybourne, Hants, and *d* 16 Jan 1940, having had:

1c Henry Francis Vaughan; *b* 1 July; *d* 14 Oct 1912

2c Christopher Alexander Vaughan; 2nd Lt E Surrey Regt, WW II 1940–42 as F/O RAF; *b* 6 Jan 1917; *ka* 21 Feb 1942

1c *Susette Henrietta Mary; *b* 26 July 1907; *m* 6 Sept 1937 *Lt-Col Theobald Frederick Stephen Church, Roy Sussex Regt, and has:

1d *Anna Caroline; *b* 9 April 1938; *m* 9 May 1959 Col Nigel Thomas Bagnall, MC and bar, 4th/7th Roy Dragoon Gds, s of Lt-Col H S Bagnall, and has:

1e *Emma Caroline; *b* 13 May 1962

2e *Sarah Jane; *b* 27 Nov 1964

2d *Jessica Jane; *b* 20 Feb 1942

2c Hester Pamela; *b* 1915; *m* 25 Aug 1954 *Cecil Lancelot Harman, MA, only s of Preb Harman, and *d* 1980

2b Charles Francis, DSO (1918), MC; Lt-Col Tank Corps WW I (despatches); *b* 1 May 1881; *m* 3 Jan 1906 Ethel Lucy Carrie, yst dau of Edmund Joel Thomas, and *d* 12 Aug 1950

3b Edmund John Edward; Maj 25th Cav FF, IA, WW I in 5th RI Lancers and RFC, Assist Co ARP Offr Hants May 1938–Dec 1945; *b* 29 Sept 1883; *educ* Winchester; *m* 1st 1910 (*divorce* 1919) Gladys Agnes, only dau of Col E W Wilson, of Montreal; *m* 2nd 20 Oct 1924 *Eileen Marion, 3rd dau of Andrew J Loughnan, of Melbourne, Victoria, and *d* 3 Sept 1962

1b Lilias Susan; *d* unm 21 Sept 1956

2a Henry Beauchamp (Rev); MA Cantab, Hon Canon Manchester, Vicar Lytham Lancs; *b* 1843; *m* 1st 8 Jan 1873 Lydia Constance (*dsp* 1 Jan 1880), dau of George Charnley Dewhurst, of Beechwood Park, Cheshire; *m* 2nd 1894 Edith Mary (*d* 13 Feb 1896), dau of Thomas Threlfall, and *d* 13 Dec 1917, having by her had issue:

1b John Beauchamp; *b* 2 Feb *d* 27 Feb 1896

(3) Cæsar Henry; FRS, Serjeant-Surgn to HM QUEEN VICTORIA, PRCS 1852 and 1862, Surgn to St George's Hosp; *b* 19 Sept 1798; *m* 1st 2 May 1847 Catherine Dolbel (*d* 21 Dec 1858); *m* 2nd 3 Dec 1861 Ellen (*d* 10 Jan 1913), dau of Henry Rouse, of Stamford Hill, and *d* 20 July 1884

(4) Robert (Rev); MA, Vicar Lamberhurst Kent; *b* 23 Sept 1805; *m* 1st 2 July 1850 Frances Julia (*d* 9 April 1864), dau of Gen Sir Jasper Nicolls, KCB; *m* 2nd 9 Aug 1866 Henrietta (*d* 18 March 1908), dau of Rev George Howes, Rector Spixworth, Norfolk, and *d* 9 Feb 1893, having had by his 1st w, with other issue:

1a Herbert Pennell, CBE (1919); MA, BCh, MD Oxford, MRCS Eng, FRCP, Lt-Col and Brev-Col RAMC (TA); *b* 30 June 1859; *m* 17 Dec 1910 Hester Vera (*d* 1972), dau of Fleetwood Rynd, of Mount Armstrong, Co Kildare, and *d* 16 April 1940, leaving:

1b +Gerald Francis Cæsar [Maj Gerald Hawkins, Newton Orchard, Pound Lane, Whitestone, Exeter EX4 2LJ]; MRCS Eng and LRCP London 1937, WW II as Maj RAMC, Radcliffe Travelling Fell 1939, MO Wellington; *b* 8 May 1912; *educ* Eton and Oxford (BM and BCh); *m* 18 May 1940 *Patricia Enid Lambart, only dau of Maj Alexander George Lambart Sladen, MC, and has had issue:

1c Nicholas John Cæsar; *b* 15 July 1941; *d* 6 July 1960

1c *Julia Margaret [Mrs Ilgvars Spruntulis, 26 Homefield Rd, Heavitree, Devon]; *b* 10 Aug 1946; *m* 1971 *Ilgvars Spruntulis and has:

1d *Ben; *b* 1979

1d *Liza Mia; *b* 1975

2a Charles Cæsar, CBE (1935); MIEE, Supt Dept Technology City and Guilds London Inst 1920–34; *b* 15 March 1864; *educ* Eton and Magdalen Coll Oxford (MA); *d* 9 Aug 1938

1a Emily Louisa Margaret; *d* unm 24 Sept 1947

1 Sarah; *m* Rev Robert Andrews

2 Mary Anne; *m* George Thornhill, of Diddington

The 2nd Bt's yr bro,

Sir John Cæsar Hawkins, 3rd Bt; MA Oxon, High Sheriff Somerset 1807; *b* 9 Feb 1782; *m* 11 Aug 1804 Charlotte Cassandra (*d* 14 Oct 1855), est dau of William Surtees, of Hedley, Northumberland, and *d* 9 Nov 1861, having had, with three daus (*d* unm):

1 John Cæsar; *b* 20 Dec 1805; *m* 7 April 1836 Louisa Georgiana Letitia (*d* 9 April 1906), yst dau of Thomas Bourke Ricketts, of Combe, Herefs, and *dvp* 8 Jan 1845, leaving, with a dau (*d* unm):

(1) **Rev Sir John Cæsar Hawkins, 4th Bt**; *b* 27 Jan 1837; *educ* Oriel Coll Oxford (MA, Hon Fell); Hon DD St Andrews, Hon Canon St Albans, Rector St Albans then Chelmsford (resigned 1880); *m* 7 July 1863 Mary Catharine (*d* 9 Dec 1924), yst dau of Thomas Ellames Withington, of Culcheth Hall, Lancs, and *dsp* 18 Jan 1929

2 George Cæsar (Rev); Rector Honnington, Suffolk; *b* 18 March 1807; *educ* Oriel Coll Oxford (BA); *m* 4 April 1838 Eleanor Barbara (*d* 6 July 1871), est dau of George Villiers Villiers, RHG, and *d* 1 Feb 1870, leaving, with four daus (*d* unm):

(1) George Villiers Cæsar; *b* 18 July 1848; *d* 19 Nov 1919

(1) Eleanor Cassandra Frances; *m* 21 April 1863 Rev Simeon Dowell Brownjohn, Rector E Lydford, and *d* 23 Jan 1876, leaving issue. He *d* 25 Dec 1904

(2) Georgiana Villiers; *m* 4 April 1861 Rev Henry Hasted, Rector Pitsea Essex, and *d* 3 Sept 1870, leaving issue. He *d* 17 Aug 1914

3 Henry Cæsar; Capt RN; *b* 19 March 1809; *m* 1st 13 Aug 1845 Mary Freeman (*d* 12 July 1859), dau of John Inman; *m* 2nd 22 Nov 1870 Ellen (*d* 4 Oct 1923), 2nd dau of W D Harding, and *dsp* 14 May 1884

4 Frederick Cæsar; Lt-Col 10th Madras NI; *b* 28 July 1811; *d* unm 31 Jan 1880

5 William Cæsar; *b* 29 Nov 1812; *d* 1867

6 Thomas Scott; Lt-Col 1st (Roy Scots) Regt; *b* 7 June 1814; *m* 18 Sept 1873 Fanny Cecilia (*d* 9 Feb 1917), dau of Evan Williams, DL, of Duffryn Frwd, Glam, and *d* 2 Oct 1889, leaving issue:

(1) **Sir John Scott Cæsar Hawkins, 5th Bt**; *b* 12 June 1875; *educ* Merton Coll Oxford (BA); *d* unm 11 Feb 1939

(2) Reginald Cæsar; Lt RN; *b* 28 Dec 1878; *d* 26 April 1913

(1) Laura Evelyn; *d* unm 21 Feb 1948

(2) Charlotte Blanche; *d* unm 26 Mar 1928

7 Arthur Cæsar; RM Richmond, Natal; *b* 4 Aug 1816; *m* 1st 8 Dec 1850 Emmeline Jane (*d* 1854), dau of Jonah Dawnay, and had issue:

(1) Henry Cæsar; *b* 17 Oct 1852; *m* 1st 31 Dec 1883 Kate (*d* 20 July 1894), widow of George Shepstone and dau of Joseph Henderson, CMG; *m* 2nd 1906 Bessie Gertrude, dau of Charles Roper, of Blisworth, Northants, and *d* 7 May 1930, having had by his 1st w:

1a Frederick Cæsar; Lt KAR; *b* 12 Oct 1887; *d* 15 Nov 1917 of wounds recd in action E Africa

2a VILLIERS GEOFFREY CÆSAR (Sir), **6th Bt**

3a Humphry Cæsar, MC; Lt RFA SR WW I (despatches); *b* 17 Nov 1891; *ka* 23 April 1918

1a Dorothy Mary, OBE (1919); *b* 27 Sept 1884; *m* 1903 Cdr Charles Tiedemann Gervers, DSO, RN, s of Francis Gervers, of Armat, Ardgay, Ross-shire, and had issue. He *d* 4 June 1927

(1) Emmeline Edith *b* 1854; *m* 1878 George Walker, JP, of High Flats, Natal, and *d* 29 Aug 1920, leaving issue. He *d* Oct 1919

7 (cont.) Arthur Hawkins *m* 2nd 1856 Louisa Jane (*d* 21 Nov 1918), dau of S Grice, of Asheldham Hall, Essex, and *d* 4 Dec 1890, having by her had, with another s and dau (*d* in infancy):

(2) Arthur Cæsar; *b* 26 Sept 1857

(3) Villiers Cæsar; *b* 11 March 1859; *ka* Isandhlwana 22 Jan 1879

(4) Scott Cæsar; *b* 20 Dec 1861

(5) Percy Cæsar; *b* 27 July 1863; *m* Catherine Ripkin (*d* 1937) and had:

1a +Rupert Cæsar; *b* 1901

2a +Oscar Cæsar; *b* 1908; *m* 19– *Zella Bunn and has issue:

1b +John Michael Cæsar

2b +Patrick Cæsar

3a +Percy Cæsar; *b* 1910

1a *Julia Louisa

2a *Kathleen Laura

3a *Cecilia Margaret

4a *Adeline Daisy

(6) Bertram Cæsar; *b* 13 April 1872

(7) George Cæsar; *b* 6 Jan 1875

(8) Cyril Cæsar; Boer War with 1st Imp Light Horse (severely wounded), WW I in German E Africa with 9th S African Horse (medals and six clasps); *b* 12 Feb 1878; *m* 29 July 1909 Lulu (*d* 1955), dau of W H E Duuring, of Holland, and *d* 1955, leaving issue:

1a *Marie; *b* 21 May 1910

(2) *Laura Georgina

(3) Ethel Marion; *m* J Beningfield and *d* July 1909

(4) Edith Charlotte; *m* Dr G C Henderson

(5) Alice Maude

(6) Kate

8 Alexander Cæsar, CB; Maj-Gen RA Crimea 1855–56; *b* 3 Nov 1823; *m* 19 Dec 1895 Janet Lucy (*d* 6 May 1922), dau of Lt-Gen Edward Arthur Williams, CB, and *dsp* 17 Dec 1916

9 Villiers William Cæsar; *b* 30 Nov 1824; *m* 15 Dec 1857 Emily (*d* 8 Jan 1878), dau of Hon John Daly, and *d* 7 Jan 1909, having had issue:

(1) Frederick Daly Cæsar; Lt-Col IMS, LRCP Edinburgh, MRCS; *b* 18 Nov 1858; *m* 14 Sept 1892 Mabel, dau of George Whitfield, JP, of Hamsey House, Lewes, and *dsp* 10 April 1943

(2) Villiers Alweyn Cæsar; *b* 1860; *m* 14 Feb 1888 Florence Celia (*d* 4 July 1947), only child of Maj J Cowper, 15th Regt, and *d* 30 March 1945, leaving:

1a Villiers Frederick Cæsar; *b* 1888; *m* 25 Nov 1922 Emma (*d* 1979), est dau of Jean Joho, of Zurich, and *dsp* 11 Jan 1970

(3) Gerald Cæsar; *b* 1861; *d* unm 23 Sept 1902

(4) Herbert Cæsar, JP Dorset; MRCS, LRCP Edinburgh; *b* 1863; *m* 1st 1890 Florence Margaret (*d* 1897), dau of William John Tonge; *m* 2nd 19 June 1902 Marianne (*d* 16 March 1920), widow of William David Lloyd and dau of Charles Frederick Murray, of Woodcote Hall, Epsom, and *d* 9 March 1947, having by his 1st w had:

1a *Kathleen Margaret

(5) Ernest Cæsar; *b* 1872; *m* 19 July 1897 Frances Mary (*d* 28 June 1953), dau of John Foy, and *dsp* 2 July 1940

1 Emily Maria

2 Mabel Edith; *m* 2 April 1898 James S Forbes Higginson and *d* 20 Sept 1937, leaving issue

The 5th Bt's cousin,

Sir Villiers Godfrey Cæsar Hawkins, 6th Bt; Capt RFA WW I; *b* 17 Aug 1890; *m* 3 March 1920 (Marjorie) Blanche, dau of Arthur Edward Hampden-Smithers, of Springs, Transvaal, and *d* 14 Feb 1955, leaving:

1 **Sir Humphry Villiers Cæsar Hawkins, 7th Bt**; MB, ChB; *b* 10 Aug 1923; *educ* Hilton Coll, Natal; WW II 1942–45 with 6th S African Armoured Div; *m*

28 June 1952 *Anita [Lady Hawkins, 41 Hume Rd, Dunkeld, Johannesburg, S Africa], dau of Charles H Funkey, of Michigan, and *d* 1993, leaving:
(1) +Sir HOWARD CÆSAR HAWKINS, **8th and present Bt**
(2) +RICHARD CÆSAR; *b* 29 Dec 1958; heir presumptive
(1) *Carol Lee; *b* 13 April 1953
(2) *Kathryn Anne; *b* 31 July 1954
(3) *Helena Julia; *b* 26 Nov 1963
1 *Joy Blanche [Mrs James Maxwell, 35 Ferguson Rd, Illovo, Sandton 2196, S Africa]; *m* 1st 1944 John Stobart Longworth; *m* 2nd 1977 *James Sloane Hume Maxwell and by her 1st husb has issue:
(1) *Humphrey John; *b* 1945; *m* 1975 *Lynne Edward
(1) *Veronica Anne; *b* 1951

HAWLEY

Arms: Vert a saltire engrailed or. **Crest:** A dexter arm in armour ppr., garnished or, holding in the hand a spear in bend sinister, point downwards also ppr. **Creation:** Bt. (GB) 14 May 1795.

(Henry) Nicholas Hawley [Nicholas Hawley Esq, No Man's Friend, New York, Lincoln LN4 4YE]; *b* 26 Nov 1939; *s* f 1988 but does not use title; *educ* Stowe

Lineage: JOHN HAWLEY, of Auler, Somerset; *m* Dorothy, sis of William Walmot, and had, with an er s (William, of Auler, ancestor of the HAWLEYs of Somerset, who held a Baronetcy (as 'of Buckland, Somerset') together with the Barony of Hawley of Duncannon in the Irish peerage between 1645 and 1790):

JEREMY HAWLEY, of Boston, nr Brentford, Middx; *m* Kynburgh, dau of Valentine Saunders, of Sutton Court, Middx, and *d* June 1593, leaving, with other issue, including a yr s (John, DD, Pncpl Gloucester Hall, Oxford, *m* Amy, dau of Thomas Studley, and had issue):

JAMES HAWLEY, of Brentford; *b* 1558; *m* twice and had an est surv s:

RICHARD HAWLEY, of London; *b* 1592; MD; *m* Dorothy, dau of Henry Ashworth, MD, of Oxford, and had:

HENRY HAWLEY, of Brentford; *b* 1629; *m* Alice, dau and coheir of Robert Curtis, of Tenterden, Kent, and *d* 1706, having had, with two daus (Curtis, *m* Thomas Cullum; Susanna, *m* Anthony Lybbe):

JAMES HAWLEY, of Brentford; *b* 1676; *m* Dorothy (*d* 1729), 2nd dau of Sir Christopher Musgrave, Bt, of Edenhall, Westmorland, and *d* 1734, leaving, with an er s (Henry, *b* 1703, *dsp* 1756):

JAMES HAWLEY, of Leybourne Grange, Kent; *b* 2 March 1705/6; MD, FRS; *m* 8 Nov 1744 Elizabeth (*d* 27 Nov 1766), est dau of Joseph Banks, of Revesby Abbey, Lincs, and aunt of Sir Joseph Banks, 1st and last Bt, and *d* 22 Dec 1777, leaving, with a dau (Elizabeth, *m* John Crawley, of Stockwood, Beds):

Sir Henry Hawley, 1st Bt (GB), so *cr* 14 May 1795, of Leybourne Grange; *b* 12 Nov 1745; *m* 1st 10 Aug 1770 Dorothy (*d* 4 Dec 1783), only dau and heir of John Ashwood, of Madeley, Salop, and had issue:
1 HENRY (Sir), **2nd Bt**
1 Dorothy Elizabeth; *m* 1809 Sir Brooke William Bridges, Bt, and *d* 1816
2 Harriott; *d* Nov 1842
3 Charlotte; *m* 1st 1810 Rev Brook John Bridges (*dsp* 3 July 1812); *m* 2nd 1823 Thomas Gardiner Bramston, of Skreens, Essex, and *d* 25 Aug 1847

Sir Henry *m* 2nd 5 Sept 1785 Anne (*d* 7 Nov 1829), est dau of William Humphreys, of Llwyn, Montgomeryshire, and by her had, with other issue:
2 James (Rev); *b* 19 July 1790; *m* 13 Oct 1831 Henrietta Margaretta (*d* 31 Jan 1870), est dau of Peter Pegus, and *d* 20 Jan 1870
4 Frances Anne; *m* 1822 Capt Charles Shaw, RN (*see* BEST-SHAW, Bt), and *d* 11 Dec 1872
5 Louisa; *m* 1825 Rev Tatton Brockman, Curate Frant, Kent

Sir HENRY *d* 20 Jan 1826; his only son,

Sir Henry Hawley, 2nd Bt; *b* 20 Oct 1776; *m* 29 Nov 1806 Catherine Elizabeth (*d* 15 March 1862), dau of Sir John Gregory Shaw, 5th Bt, of Kenward, Kent (*see* above), and *d* 29 March 1831, having had, with four daus (*dsp*):
1 **Sir Joseph Henry Hawley, 3rd Bt**; *b* 27 Oct 1814; *m* 18 June 1839 Sarah Diana (*d* 9 March 1881), 3rd dau of General Sir John Crosbie, GCH, and *d* 20 April 1875, having had, with other issue:
(1) Mildred Catherine; *m* 7 July 1869 3rd Baron Blythswood, KCB, CVO (*see* 1940 edn), and *d* 13 Aug 1902, leaving issue. He *d* 11 March 1918
(2) Morna Georgina; *m* 25 June 1874 Percy Fitzhardinge Raymond Barker, of Fairford Park, Glos, and *d* 19 Sept 1919, having had issue. He *d* 25 Feb 1895
2 **Sir Henry James Hawley, 4th Bt**; *b* 14 July 1815; *m* 1st 1837 Elizabeth (*d* 22 Sept 1871), dau of Thomas Askew; *m* 2nd 5 June 1877 Maria Selina (*d* 25 July 1877), est dau of Edward J Morant Gale, and *d* 5 Oct 1898
3 Henry Charles (Rev); Rector Leybourne; *b* 31 July 1823; *m* 21 Oct 1845 Mary Elizabeth (*d* 8 April 1911), est dau of Sir Michael Cusack-Smith, 3rd Bt (*see* 1970 edn), and *d* 16 Feb 1877, having had issue:
(1) HENRY MICHAEL (Sir), **5th Bt**
(2) Charles Cusack (Rev); MA Cantab; Rector Leybourne 1877–1914, RD Malling, Hon Canon Rochester; *b* 31 May 1851; *d* 18 Aug 1914
(3) Frederick William; *b* 8 Nov 1854; *d* 20 Oct 1936
(4) Arthur Cecil; *b* 6 Feb 1862; *d* unm 21 Jan 1945
(1) Edith Catherine; *d* unm 15 Jan 1941
(2) Ada Mary; *d* unm 27 May 1938
(3) Kathleen Augusta; *d* unm 7 Aug 1945
(4) Mary Blanche; *d* unm 14 Feb 1943
(5) Ethel Maud; *d* unm 26 Feb 1938
(6) Nina Cicely; *d* unm 17 Dec 1947
1 Catherine Anne; *m* 7 Sept 1831 George John Smart, Capt Army, and *d* 2 June 1861
2 Theodosia; *m* 1 Nov 1849 Carleton Smythies, of Old Lawn, Suffolk. He *d* June 1860
3 Augusta Harriet; *m* 6 Aug 1839 Rev John Hamilton, Vicar Linstead Kent, and *d* 11 Jan 1904, having had issue. He *d* 1891

The 4th Bt's nephew,

Sir Henry Michael Hawley, 5th Bt, JP Lincs; *b* 25 March 1848, *m* 24 Nov 1875 Frances Charlotte (*d* 10 Sept 1926), 2nd dau of John Wingfield-Stratford (*see* POWERSCOURT, V), and *d* 2 July 1909, having had:
1 **Sir Henry Cusack Wingfield Hawley, 6th Bt**; Capt Roy W Kent Regt WW I; *b* 23 Dec 1876; *m* 29 Jan 1913 Marjorie Florence (*d* 18 Nov 1957), only dau of Robert Mascall Curteis, of Piltdown, Sussex, and *dsp* 18 Nov 1923
2 Cyril Francis; Capt KRRC, GSO(3) 1914 WW I; *b* 24 June 1878; *m* 10 July 1912 Ursula Mary (*d* 18 Feb 1971), dau of Henry Percy St John (*see* BOLINGBROKE and SAINT JOHN, V), and was *ka* 2 Nov 1914, leaving issue:
(1) DAVID HENRY (Sir), **7th Bt**
(2) Anthony Charles St John; *b* 7 Sept 1914; *educ* Eton and Magdalen Coll Oxford; *m* 30 April 1949 *Joyce Elena (*m* 2nd 19 April 1958 Kenneth Alexander Bridges) [Mrs Kenneth Bridges, 13 Tritton Fields, Kennington, Ashford, Kent TN24 9HG], yr dau of Albert Edward Cox, of Ashford, and *dsp* 17 Dec 1956
3 Michael Charles; *b* 6 June 1879; *m* 17 Feb 1911 Ethel (*d* 9 Feb 1965), 6th dau of W H Williams, and *d* 19 Feb 1934, leaving:
(1) Micheline; *b* 27 Jan 1912; *d* 23 May 1938
1 Winifred Mary; *b* 14 Sept 1880; *d* 22 July 1891
2 Gladys Florence; *d* 1922
3 Olive Victoria; *b* 17 June 1887; *m* 28 July 1920 Rev Henry Cecil Marriott Spurrier, MA, Rector Roughton and Haltham, Lincs, and had issue. He *d* 7 Feb 1954

The 6th Bt's nephew,

Sir David Henry Hawley, 7th Bt, DL (Lincs 1952); High Sheriff 1962; *b* 13 May 1913; *educ* Eton and Magdalene Coll Cambridge (BA 1935, MA 1949); FRICS, FLAS, Maj KRRC WW II (POW 1940–45); *m* 28 Sept 1938 Hermione (*d* 19 June 1994), 2nd dau of Col Lancelot Mare Gregson, OBE (*see* LICHFIELD, E), and *d* 1988, leaving issue:
1 (Sir) (HENRY) NICHOLAS HAWLEY, **8th and present Bt**
1 *Margaret Serena (Peggie) [Miss Peggie Hawley, 49 Watling Crescent, Handbridge, Chester CH4 7HD]; *b* 10 July 1946
2 *Penelope Marion [Mrs Richard Mansell-Jones, 19 Astell St, London SW3 3RT]; *b* 29 June 1948; *m* 30 June 1971 *Richard M Mansell-Jones, chm Brown, Shipley and Co Ltd, only s of A M Jones

HAWORTH

Arms: Az. on a bend between two stag's heads couped or as many garbs gu. **Crest:** Issuant out of grass ppr. a stag's head gu., armed and collared with a chain or. **Creation:** Bt. (UK) 3 July 1911.

SIR PHILIP HAWORTH, 3RD BT, of Dunham Massey, Chester [Sir Philip Haworth Bt, Free Green Farm, Over Peover, Cheshire WA16 9QX]; *b* 17 Jan 1927; *s* f 1987; *educ* Dauntseys and Reading U (BSc Ag 1948); *m* 21 April 1951 *Joan Helen, dau of Stanley Percival Clark, of Ipswich, Suffolk, and has issue:

1 +CHRISTOPHER [Christopher Haworth Esq, Applegates, Queens Rd, Crowborough, E Sussex TN6 1PX]; *b* 6 Nov 1951; *educ* Rugby and Reading U (BSc); ARICS; *m* 1994 *Susan Rachel, dau of David Ives and widow of Jonathan Dent, and has:

(1) +Oliver; *b* 20 Oct 1996

2 +Mark; *b* 19 Nov 1956; *educ* Rugby

3 +Simon Nicholas; *b* 20 April 1961; *educ* Rugby and Reading U

4 +Adam Ewart; *b* 3 May 1964; *educ* Rugby and Magdalene Coll Cambridge

1 *Penelope Jane; *b* 29 June 1953; *educ* Sheffield U

Lineage: JAMES HAWORTH, of Bolton, Lancs; *b* 9 Oct 1765; *m* Ann Lomax and *d* 17 Nov 1834, having had:

SMALLESHAW LOMAX HAWORTH, of Bolton; *b* 1 Jan 1802; *m* Marrianne, dau of Evan Jones, and *d* Sept 1858, having had:

ABRAHAM HAWORTH, of Hilston House, Altrincham, Cheshire, JP; *b* 7 Feb 1830; *m* 5 Sept 1861 Elizabeth (*d* 24 March 1900 aged 71), dau of John Goodier, of Rusholme, Lancs, and *d* 9 March 1902, having had issue:

1 ARTHUR ADLINGTON (Sir), **1st Bt**

2 Alfred, JP Cheshire; *b* 7 Feb 1868; *educ* Victoria U Manchester (BA); *m* 1st 3 Oct 1895 Dora Jeanne (*d* 27 April 1897), dau of Alexander Muir, of Altrincham, and had issue:

(1) Philip Theodore; *b* 25 April 1897; *dsp* of wounds 3 May 1917

2 (cont.) Alfred Haworth *m* 2nd 28 Dec 1899 Elizabeth Anne (*d* 1 Jan 1962), 2nd dau of S Alexander MacGowan, MD, of Oldham, Lancs, and *d* 16 Sept 1946, having by her had:

(2) *Hugh Alexander; assist master Eton 1924–61; *educ* Winchester and New Coll Oxford (MA); *m* 1st 6 April 1935 Johanna Countess Bothmer (*d* 25 April 1962); *m* 2nd 18 Dec 1963 *Mrs Hertha Karoline Hildegard Crevato, dau of Richard Anton, of Vienna

(3) *Leslie; *educ* Winchester; *m* 9 Dec 1939 *Eleanor, dau of Sir Joseph Arkwright, of Purley, Surrey, and has:

1a *Giles Arkwright; *b* 16 July 1941; *educ* Gordonstoun and Durham U

2a *Richard Gault; *b* 12 May 1943; *educ* Gordonstoun, St Andrews and Queen's U Belfast

3a *Colin Goodier; *b* 12 Jan 1946; *educ* Gordonstoun

(1) *Dorothea; *educ* LMH Oxford (MA)

3 John Goodier, JP Cheshire; *b* 1 Nov 1870; MA Oxon; *m* 1st 26 June 1901 Euphemia (*d* 1915), dau of Rev Alexander Mackennal, DD, of Bowdon, and had issue:

(1) *Stephen Alexander, TD; Maj RA WW II; *b* 8 Nov 1903; *educ* Rugby and New Coll Oxford (BA); *m* 22 Sept 1934 *Katherine Joan, widow of Cdr Ivo Wyndham Laton Frewen-Laton, DSC, RN, and 3rd dau of Maj A H Bayley, and has:

1a *Timothy Goodier; ACA 1962; *b* 9 May 1936; *educ* Rugby, Trin Coll Cambridge (MA) and Grenoble U; *m* 30 March 1968 *Susan Mary, dau of John Harrison, and has issue:

1b *Melinda Katharine; *b* 27 April 1969

(2) *Arthur Maurice, JP Manchester; *b* 4 Oct 1906; *educ* Rugby and New Coll Oxford (MA); *m* 19– *Kathleen Mary Leigh, only dau of William James Orr, of Sandiway, and has issue:

1a*Susan Kathleen; *b* 30 July 1939; *m* 22 Oct 1960 *Richard Hugh Lyon Armitage, er s of Sir Robert Perceval Armitage, KCMG, MBE, and has:

1b *Stephen Lyon; *b* 24 Aug 1961

2b *Luke; *b* 18 March 1964

1b *Mary Esther; *b* 16 Feb 1963

2a *Rosalind Jean; *b* 22 Feb 1944

(1) *Margaret Goodier; *b* 2 May 1902; *m* 8 Dec 1932 *Angus Orr and has:

1a *John Niven; *b* 20 Feb 1938; *m* 17 June 1961 *Jane, dau of William Gilbert Harris, of Bowdon, and has issue:

1b *James Nicholas Niven; *b* 27 July 1965

1b *Camilla Katherine; *b* 1 Oct 1963

1a *Elspeth Margaret [Mrs John Stuart-Mills, The Manor House, Chatburn, Clitheroe, Lancs]; *b* 11 March 1935; *m* 19 March 1960 *Maj John Stuart-Mills and has issue:

1b *Andrew Barraclough; *b* 7 Jan 1961

2b *Duncan Aubrey Goodier; *b* 14 May 1963

3b *James Euan; *b* 15 July 1967

(2) *Alison Jean; *b* 12 April 1909; *m* 15 March 1937 *John Herbert Shaw and has issue:

1a *Donald William; *b* 3 Feb 1939; *m* 7 Sept 1963 *Julia, dau of Douglas Blonet, of Woodham Ferrers, and has:

1b *Simon James Blonet; *b* 23 March 1965

2a *Robert Martin; *b* 17 Jan 1941; *m* 3 Oct 1964 *Jane, dau of Kenneth Foster, of Rooksmill Green, and has issue:

1b *Joanna Elizabeth; *b* 4 Jan 1966

3a *Stephen John; *b* 10 Dec 1942; *m* 12 Sept 1964 *Caroline, dau of Michael Robbins, of London

3 (cont.) John Haworth *m* 2nd 10 May 1921 Marion Iris (*d* 14 July 1966), widow of Lt Sidney MacDougall, 6th Bn Manchester Regt, and only dau of Thomas Crompton Waterhouse, of Lomberdale Hall, Bakewell, and *d* 31 Aug 1929

4 Frank Abraham; *b* 30 April 1874; *educ* Victoria U Manchester; *m* 17 Sept 1903 Edith March (*d* 13 July 1961), dau of William Rigby, of Altrincham, and *d* 5 Oct 1934, leaving:

(1) *Christopher William; WW II as Maj Intelligence Corps; *b* 22 Nov 1904; *educ* Rugby and New Coll Oxford (MA); *m* 24 July 1948 *Margaret Joan, dau of Thomas David Richards, of Carbis Bay, Cornwall, and has issue:

1a *Charles David; *b* 16 June 1949; *educ* Rugby

1a *Priscilla March *b* 23 July 1951

2a *Annabelle Elizabeth Jane; *b* 8 Dec 1953

(2) *Frank Alexander; ACII, WW II as Lt-Cdr RNVR (despatches), memb Lloyd's; *b* 28 Aug 1909; *educ* Oxford (MA); *m* 10 Jan 1945 *Norma Irene, yr dau of Peter Murray, of Bulawayo, Rhodesia, and Aberdeenshire

(3) *Michael Goodier, CBE (1964), DSC and bar; Capt RN WW II (despatches); *b* 25 Jan 1914; *m* 10 Nov 1943 *Cynthia, WRNS, dau of Algernon Noble, of Hexham, Northumberland, and has issue:

1a *Penelope Jane [Mrs Anthony Salter, 34 Gloucester Road, Kew Green, Surrey]; *b* 28 Feb 1945; *educ* UCL (BSc 1966); *m* 19 Dec 1964 *Anthony Bruce Salter

2a *Amanda Susan; *b* 9 April 1949

(1) Elizabeth Catherine; Capt WRAC WW II; *b* 20 Oct 1906; *d* unm 15 April 1966

1 Elizabeth Goodier; *b* 5 Feb 1863; *m* 20 Dec 1896 Thomas Arnold Herbert, JP, BA, LLB Cantab, MP S Bucks, s of Rev T M Herbert, and *d* 15 April 1917. He *d* 22 Nov 1940

The est son,

Sir Arthur Adlington Haworth, 1st Bt (UK), so *cr* 3 July 1911; Hon Maj 1st Vol Bn Cheshire Regt, JP Cheshire and Salop, Jr Ld Treasury 1912, MP S Manchester 1906–12, Chm: Manchester Roy Exchange, Manchester GS and Manchester Dist League of Nations Union, formerly Chm Congregational Union of England and Wales; *b* 22 Aug 1865; *m* 5 Feb 1891 Lily, JP Lancs (*d* 15 May 1952), yst dau of John Rigby, of Altrincham, and had issue:

1 ARTHUR GEOFFREY (Sir), **2nd Bt**

1 Lois Adlington; *b* 17 July 1892

2 Mary Suzette; *b* 8 Aug 1899; *m* 17 July 1930 Harry Goodhart and had issue:

(1) *Mark Henry, Maj 14th/20th King's Hus; *b* 2 May 1931; *educ* Stowe; *m* 8 Feb 1964 *Angela May, only dau of Cdr Eric Alfred May OBE, RN, and has:

1a *Jonathan Luke Henry; *b* 24 July 1965

1a *Caroline Emma Adlington; *b* 29 April 1967

(2) *Harry James; *b* 8 May 1933; *educ* Stowe

Sir ARTHUR *d* 31 Aug 1944; his only son,

Sir (Arthur) Geoffrey Haworth, 2nd Bt, JP (Cheshire 1937–70); *b* 5 April 1896; *educ* Rugby and New Coll Oxford (BA 1919, MA 1935); Chm Cheshire NFU 1953–54, Lt Queen's Own W Kent Regt and MGC (despatches) WW I; *m* 28 April 1926 Emily Dorothea (*d* 1980), er dau of Henry Edwin Gaddum, JP, of The Priory, Bowdon, and *d* 1987, leaving:

1 Sir PHILIP HAWORTH, **3rd and present Bt**

2 +Jeremy Geoffrey [Jeremy Haworth Esq, The Bog Farm, Minsterley, Salop]; *b* 22 Jan 1931; *educ* Dauntseys and New Coll Oxford (BA 1954)

1 *Jennefer [Mrs Herbert Minnis, PO Box 1720, Nassau, Bahamas]; *b* 5 Dec 1928; *m* 12 Aug 1952 *Herbert Hilton Minnis, s of Austin Minnis, of Calabash Bay, Bahamas, and has issue:

(1) *Sterling Herbert; *b* 7 June 1953

(2) *Russell Harold; *b* 21 Aug 1954

(3) *Quentin Geoffrey; *b* 15 Oct 1963

(4) *Royan Alexander; *b*1974

(1) *Jedda Alison; *b* 12 July 1957

(2) *Sonya Jennefer; *b* 16 Dec 1960

2 *Alison [Mrs Richard Godlee, The Grange, Clay Lane, Handforth, Wilmslow, Cheshire]; *b* 25 Oct 1934; LRAM 1955; *m* 4 Oct 1958 *Richard Crosfield Godlee and has issue:

(1) *Deborah Claire; *b* 1 July 1961

(2) *Sarah Haworth; *b* 20 Nov 1965

HAY of Alderston

Arms: Quarterly, 1st and 4th, az. three fraises (for FRASER); 2nd and 3rd, gu. three bars erm. (for GIFFORD of Yester); over all upon an escutcheon of pretence arg. three escutcheons gu., in the centre a key fessways, wards downwards, sa. (for HAY). **Crest:** A goat's head erased arg., armed or. **Motto:** Spare nought.
Creation: Bt. (NS) 22 Feb 1702/3.

SIR RONALD FREDERICK HAMILTON HAY, 12TH BT, of Alderston, Co East Lothian [Sir Ronald Hay Bt, Aspendale, Victoria 3195, Australia]; *b* 1941; *s* f 1988; *m* 1978 *Kathleen, dau of John Thake, and has issue:
1 +ALEXANDER JAMES; *b* 1979
2 +Anthony Ronald; *b* 1984
1 *Sarah Jane; *b* 1981

Lineage: Sir WILLIAM HAY of Locherworth and Yester (*see* TWEEDDALE, M); had a yst s:

EDMUND HAY, of Tala, Peeblesshire, of which he had a charter 12 Aug 1439; ancestor of (as well as the HAYs of Cocklaw, Faichfield, Linplum, Mountblairy, Ranfield and Rannes):

Sir JOHN HAY of Barra; *m* 1st —; *m* 2nd Rebecca, dau of Alexander Thomson, of Duddingstone, and by her had:

THOMAS HAY of Alderston and Hermiston; *b* 1625; Clerk of Cncl and Session, Ld Clerk Register; *m* Anna, dau of Sir John Gibson, of Pentland, Co Edinburgh, and *d* 1679, leaving, with other issue:

1 **Sir John Hay, 1st Bt** (NS), so *cr* 22 Feb 1702/3, with remainder to his heirs male forever, of Alderston; *m* 27 April 1693 Catherine, dau of Sir George Suttie of Balgone, 1st Bt (*see* GRANT-SUTTIE, Bt), and *d* 1706, leaving, with other issue (including Margaret; *m* John Mackenzie of Dalrene; *see* MACKENZIE, Bt, of Coul):

(1) **Sir Thomas Hay, 2nd Bt**; Capt Dragoons; *m* 1st 26 Aug 1724 Eleanor, dau of Hon Sir Hew Dalrymple, 1st Bt, of N Berwick (*see* HAMILTON-DALRYMPLE, Bt); *m* 2nd 31 July 1740 Frances, dau of 4th Baron Berkeley of Stratton and widow of 4th Baron Byron (*qv*); *m* 3rd 14 Oct 1761 Peggy, dau of John Don, and *dsp* 26 Nov 1769

(2) Sir GEORGE HAY later HAY-MAKDOUGALL, **3rd Bt**; Lt-Col Scots Greys; *m* Barbara, heiress of Henry Makdougall of Makerstoun, and *d* 24 Feb 1777, leaving, with other issue:

1a **Sir Henry Hay-Makdougall, 4th Bt**; *b c* 1750; *m* 11 May 1782 Isabella, dau of Adml Sir James Douglas, 1st Bt, of Springwood Park (*see* 1956 edn), and *d* 13 April 1825, leaving, with other issue:

1b Anna Maria; *m* 1819 Gen Sir Thomas Makdougall-Brisbane, Bt, GCB, GCH (*dspms* 31 Jan 1860; *see* 1860 edn)

1a Ann; *m* John Scott, of Gala

2 Alexander, of Huntingdon; *b* 1675; Sheriff Depute Haddington; *m* Mary Gordon, of Lismore, and *d* 24 March 1745, leaving:

(1) Thomas; Ld of Session as Lord Huntingdon; *m* Margaret, dau of Sir David Murray of Stanhope, Bt (*see* 1878 edn), by his 2nd w Margaret, dau of Sir John Scott, of Ancrum, Bt (*see* 1902 edn), and *d* 4 Feb 1755, leaving, with other issue:

1a Alexander, of Mordington; advocate; *m* 1st 1744 Jane Douglas, dau of Alexander Hamilton of Ballincrieff and Inverwick, and had, with other issue:

1b THOMAS, of Alderston (Sir), **5th Bt**

1a (cont.) Alexander Hay *m* 2nd Joanna, dau of Alexander Pringle of Whitbank, and *d* 1788, having by her had:

2b John, of Newcastle-on-Tyne; *b* 24 Aug 1775; Capt 9th Regt; *m* Christian, dau of William Ker, of Broadmeadows, Hutton, Berwickshire, and *d* 9 March 1864, leaving issue:

1c Alexander Murray, of Ramsay, IoM; *b* 24 Jan 1799; Lt 51st Foot King's Own; *m* May 1842 Eleanor (*d* 6 May 1878), dau of Thomas Mylechreest, of Ramsay, and *d* 17 July 1864, having had:

1d Thomas Alexander; *b* 28 March 1843; *m* 1 June 1871 Harriet (*d* 1920), dau of John Edwards, and *d* 31 May 1912, leaving issue:

1e Harriet Eleanor; *b* 26 Oct 1878

2d James Shaw; *b* 27 Feb 1850; *m* 1st 21 April 1880 Charlotte Anne, dau of William Corlett, of Ramsay, and had:

1e Conran Ker; *b* 1 June 1882; *m* 30 Dec 1908 Grace (*d* 4 Nov 1960), 2nd dau of Thomas B Horsfield, of Manchester, and *d* 24 Feb 1958, leaving issue:

1f Alexander, MA; *b* 9 June 1912; teacher; *m* 1st 1939 Bernice Louise (*d* 1968), dau of Walter C Woodward, of Richmond, Ind.; *m* 2nd 1969 *Agnes Marshall, dau of George Ferguson Finnie, of Glasgow, and *d* 10 July 1997, leaving by his 1st w:

1g +Conran Alexander; *b* 30 Dec 1946
2g +Thomas Carlton; *b* 3 Aug 1951
1g *Arminal Elizabeth; *b* 1943; editor; *m* *Dare Brian and has issue

2f +Gordon Conran [Prof Gordon Hay, 689 Westmount Hills Dve, London, Ontario N6K 1B3, Canada]; *b* Nov 1919; Prof Emeritus, BA 1943, MEd; *m* 1943 *Elizabeth Jean, dau of Edward Henry Stevenson, of Renfrew, Ontario, and has:

1g +Stuart Gordon, MSc; *b* 22 Oct 1946; *m* 1975 *Christiane Morisset, of St Michel, Quebec, and has:

1h +Gregoire Alexander; *b* 1976

2g +Alexander Edward, PhD; *b* 8 June 1949; *m* 1984 *Jocelyn Hellou, of Montreal, and has:

1h +Philip Conran; *b* 1988
1h *Natasha Bronwen; *b* 1986

1g *Elizabeth Grace, BA; *b* 22 Oct 1951; *m* 1985 *Mark Fried, of Swampscott, Mass., and has:

1h *Ben Angus; *b* 1988
1h *Sochi Bess; *b* 1985

2g *Jean Anne, BMus; *b* 20 Feb 1957; *m* 1989 *Ignatius Solis, of Mexico City, and has issue:

1h *Carlos Andreas; *b* 1990
1h *Adriana Jean; *b* 1995

1f Arminal Grace; *b* 1916; *m* Oct 1951 Charles Sweeney and had:

1g *Ross Joseph; *b* 21 Feb 1957

2e Thomas Corlett, VD; *b* 17 June 1883; Maj Singapore Vol Corps; *m* 1930 Muriel, dau of Rev Charles Harry Dant, Rector Babcary, Taunton, and *d* 22 Jan 1952, leaving issue:

1f *Pamela June; *b* 1931; *m* Dec 1957 *John G Ewing and has:

1g *James Jonathan; *b* 1965
1g *Masindi Jane; *b* 1958
2g *Katherine Winifred Anne; *b* 1963

2f *Bettine Muriel; *b* 1932; SRN; *m* Nov 1962 *René Bouganon, of Johannesburg

1e Lizzie Hilda; *b* 17 June 1881; Pncpl Domestic Science Coll Trowbridge; *d* unm 1952

2d (cont.) James Hay *m* 2nd 2 Oct 1889 Arminal Walmsley (*d* 29 Oct 1948), dau of James Scotson, of Liverpool, and *d* 29 Dec 1908, having by her had issue:

2e Muriel Scotson; *b* 1891; *m* 7 Sept 1921 Georges Louis Bard, s of Henri Bard, of Geneva

2c William Ker; *b* 22 April 1800; Surgn-Gen Madras Army; *m* 24 Feb 1825 Catherine (*d* 1883), dau and coheir of Charles Swindell Norvell, and *d* 1893, leaving, with other issue:

1d Christina; *m* Col — Hennah, Madras Cav
2d Mary Loraine; *m* 27 April 1865 Henry Wilberforce Bird

3c Thomas Pasley; *b* 1 May 1801; Lt-Col; *m* 24 Feb 1824 Georgette Heine (*d* 10 Dec 1874), dau of M Arnaud, of Mauritius, and *d* 28 June 1858, leaving issue:

1d Woulfe; *b* 27 Sept 1836; Maj-Gen ISC; *m* 3 Feb 1863 Alida Maria (*d* 21 Nov 1906), dau of Surgn-Gen H W Porteous, and *d* 11 July 1910, having had issue:

1e Henry Thomas Horatio; *b* 7 Dec 1863; Lt-Col IA; *m* 8 April 1896 Mary Margaret (*d* 27 June 1940), dau of Rev George James Corser, Rector Burrington, Salop, and *d* 14 Oct 1934, leaving:

1f Douglas Woulfe, MC; *b* 31 Jan 1897; Lt Middx Regt; *ka* 28 Sept 1918

1f Alida Mary; *b* 11 Sept 1899; *m* 3 Sept 1921 Col John Kaye Tickell, RE, and had issue:

1g *Douglas John; *b* 29 Nov 1924; Lt RE WW II; *m* 20 April 1963 *Rozann, dau of George Henry Parnell, of St Leonards-on-Sea, and has issue:

1h *Alexander John; *b* 22 July 1968

2e James Douglas; *b* 26 June 1865; Boer War and WW I in Hyderabad Vol Rifles; FGS, MIMM; *m* 4 Oct 1911 Florence Louisa (*d* 30 Nov 1950), 2nd dau of Henry Habberley Price, of Glamorgan, and *d* 18 Jan 1952

3e Frederick George; *b* 30 Sept 1870; *d* unm 8 March 1904

4e Alexander; *b* 3 Sept 1872; *m* 3 June 1909 Kathleen, dau of Gordon Styles Hare, of Croydon, and *d* 5 April 1925, leaving issue:

1f +James Woulfe; *b* 31 Dec 1910; WW II in S African Medium Regt; *m* 11 Feb 1933 *Edith Mary, dau of Arthur Henry Myston, of Johannesburg, and had issue:

1g *Bertha Lillian; *b* Jan 1934
2g *Hilda Rose; *b* 4 April 1937

2f +William Henry Ker; *b* 7 Sept 1912; *m* 30 March 1938 *Violet May, dau of Harold Mortimer, of Manchester, and has issue:

1g *Lynette Florence; *b* 4 July 1939
2g *Evadne Felicity; *b* 8 March 1943
3g *Merilyn Wendy; *b* 1951

1e Mary Conran; *m* 12 Jan 1904 Charles Stansfield Hicks (*d* 15 Sept 1931), of Co Wicklow, and *d* 23 Sept 1951, leaving issue

2e Emily Henrietta; *b* 1869; RRC, QAIMNS; *d* unm 23 Jan 1959

3e Annie Ker; *b* 1875; *d* unm 19 March 1958

4e Lucy Catherine; *m* 30 March 1910 Cuthbert Collingwood, AMICE (*d* 12 Nov 1963), 3rd s of Maj-Gen Clennell Collingwood, RA, and *d* 27 Jan 1916, leaving issue

2d James Shaw (Sir), KCMG (1889); *b* 25 Oct 1839; 89th Regt, Indian Mutiny 1858, Administrator Gambia 1886–88, Govr and C-in-C Sierra Leone 1888–92 (medal and clasp) and Barbados 1892–1900 (Jubilee Medal 1897); *m* 1st Jane, dau of John Morin, of Allanton, Dumfriesshire; *m* 2nd Frances Marie (*d* 17 June 1893), dau of Jacques Polatza, of Brussels; *m* 3rd 31 Jan 1894 Isabella Graham (*d* 5 Jan 1926), dau of George Fergusson Cockburn, BCS, and *d* 20 June 1924, leaving by his 1st w:

1e Margaret Eleanor; *m* 5 Dec 1895 Maj Harold Wolstenholme Cobb (*d* 15 Oct 1909), W R Regt, and *dsp* 7 March 1955

3d Loraine Geddes; *b* 28 June 1847; 105th Regt; *m* Feb 1879 Emily Alice (*d* 3 July 1934), dau of Capt Donald Macdonald, and *d* 9 May 1904, leaving issue:

1e Loraine Macdonald; *b* 1883; Customs Dept Trinidad; *m* 1917 Mequeline Eugenie Hamel-Smith (*d* 1978) and *d* 1961, leaving:

1f Sydney Bertrand Macdonald; *b* 1918; *m* 1945 *Joan Reis and *d* 1981, leaving issue:

1g +Phillip Michael Macdonald; *b* 22 May 1946

2g +Roger Macdonald; *b* 24 May 1948

3g +Aubrey Andrew Macdonald; *b* 2 Nov 1949

4g +Edmund Macdonald; *b* 10 June 1954

5g +Anthony Macdonald; *b* 4 Aug 1956

1g *Ann Maureen; *b* 10 Jan 1951

2g *Kathleen; *b* 21 Jan 1953

1f *Denise Rita; *b* 1920; *m* 1st 1940 Rudolph Armine Moze (*d* 1942); *m* 2nd 1948 Roberto Pelgo Lopez; *m* 3rd 1954 *Rupert Loraine Hay (*see* below) and by her 1st husb has:

1g *Patricia Angela; *b* 1941; *m* 1970 Senator Conrad O'Brien and has issue:

1h *Jason Errol; *b* 1973

1h *Sharon Mary; *b* 1971

2f *Mequeline Phyllis; *b* 1922; *m* 1941 *Max Marsan

3f *Mary Mildred; *b* 1924; *m* 1948 *Alfred Mitchell and has:

1g *Alfred Bernard; *b* 1950

2g *William Joseph; *b* 1958

1g *Bernadette Mary; *b* 1949; *m* 1969 *Michael David Diaz and has issue:

1h *Pamela Bernadette; *b* 1970

2g Denise Mequeline; *b* 1951; *m* 19– *John A C Forster and has:

1h *Andrew Donald; *b* 1969

3g *Nanette Celine; *b* 1954

4g *Susan Marie; *b* 1955

5g *Sidney Debra; *b* 1959

2e James Carrington; *b* 1888; *m* 1921 Maria Cynthia Fifi (*d* 1956) and *d* 22 Aug 1961, leaving:

1f +Rupert Loraine [Rupert Hay Esq, Alderston, Smart Street, St Augustine, Trinidad, W Indies]; *b* 15 Jan 1924; *m* 1954 his cousin *Denise Rita, dau of Loraine Macdonald Hay (*see* above)

2f +Ranald Louis; *b* 24 Feb 1925; *educ* St Francis Xavier U (BSc), Antigonish, Nova Scotia (Beng) and McGill (PEng); *m* 10 Sept 1955 *Lorraine Marianné, dau of Frederick John Fecteau, of Toronto, and has:

1g +Ranald Joseph; *b* 21 June 1956

2g +Dominic Louis; *b* 11 Jan 1958

1g *Cynthia Maria; *b* 22 Feb 1959

2g *Genevieve Anne; *b* 27 Oct 1960

3g *Marianne Noel; *b* 13 Nov 1962

4g *Laurie Elizabeth; *b* 1 Jan 1965

3f +Donald Joseph [Donald Hay Esq, Smart St, St Augustine, Trinidad, W Indies]; *b* 1927; *m* 1955 *Lola Sue Martin and has:

1g +Donald Roger Paul; *b* 1956; *educ* Kent State U Ohio (BSc Arch) and Wisconsin U, Milwaukee (Masters Arch and Urban Planning); *m* 1982 *Maureen Ellen Baker, of Cleveland, Ohio

2g +Bruce Victor Joseph; *b* 1959; *educ* U of W Indies Trinidad (BSc Eng)

3g +Christopher Michael Charles; *b* 1967

1g *Paula Emily Rebecca; *b* 1966

1e Mary Georgina; *m* 1900 Arthur John Fortnum and had issue

2e Margaret Emily; *m* 1904 Clanfergal George Chantrell O'Halloran

3e Hilda Rose; *m* 1 May 1919 A R Davidson Kemp

1d Mary Elizabeth; *m* 27 Jan 1864 Charles Bathurst and *d* 28 Jan 1885, having had issue (*see* BLEDISLOE, V)

4c George Ker; 13th Bengal Inf; *d* 1828

2a Patrick (Peter); Col HEICS; *m* 24 June 1782 Sarah, 4th dau of Robert Dashwood (*see* DASHWOOD, Bt, of West Wycombe), and *d* 1 April 1822, having had, with other issue:

1b Patrick Martin; *b* 1786; Col HEICS; *m* 9 Sept 1819 Mary Susan, 2nd dau of Lt-Cdr Richard Clark, CB, and had issue

2b Thomas; *b* 1790; Capt 43rd LI; *m* Mary Newell, dau of Col Newell Maxwell, of Dumfries, and had issue

1b Anna Marcia; *m* 28 July 1817 John Ruxton, of Broad Oak, Kent, and had issue

3a Thomas; MD Edinburgh; *b* 1751; *m* — and *d* 1813, leaving issue:

1b John; MD; HEIC

2b David; MD; 26th Foot

(2) John, of Restalrig; Sec to Prince Charles Edward Stuart; attainted 1745; *d* 1781, leaving:

1a Alexander; *dsp* 1791

The 4th Bt's cousin,

Sir Thomas Hay, 5th Bt; *m* 2 Jan 1793 Anna, dau of Sheffield Howard, of New York, and formerly w of Maj —Bingham, and *d* 1832, having had, with other issue:

Sir James Douglas Hamilton Hay, 6th Bt; *b* 28 Dec 1800; Army Offr; *m* 1819 Jane (*d* 24 Feb 1888), dau of William Sanderson, of Springbank, and *d* 30 July 1873, having had issue:

1 **Sir Hector Maclean Hay, 7th Bt**; *b* 28 March 1821; *m* 1st 9 Feb 1852 Ann Charlotte (*d* 24 July 1888), dau of Dr J White, 17th Light Dragoons, and widow of Lt-Col William Charles Lewis Bird, HEICS; *m* 2nd 24 Jan 1889 Julia (*d* 14 March 1906), widow of William Johnston of Appleby; *m* 3rd 26 Sept 1906 Florence Anne (*d* 15 July 1946), widow of Maj A Dingwall Fordyce, and *dsp* 15 Sept 1916

2 William Thomas; *b* 20 Aug 1822; *m* 29 Nov 1860 Isabella, dau of Robert Charles, of Melbourne, Australia and *d* 15 Sept 1886, leaving, with other issue:

(1) **Sir William Henry Hay, 8th Bt**; *b* 30 May 1867; house painter; *d* unm Australia 3 July 1927

(2) (Sir) Edward, *de jure* 9th Bt; *b* 30 May 1870; *d* unm 1936 without having proved his succession or assumed the title

(3) Frederick Howard; *b* 20 Oct 1871; *m* 1899 May Elizabeth, dau of George Tomlinson, of Fitzroy, Melbourne, and *d* 1934, leaving issue:

1a **Sir Frederick Baden Powell Hay, 10 Bt**; *b* 24 June 1900; *m* 1935 *Henrietta Margaret, dau of Herbert William Reid, of Melbourne, and *d* 19–

2a RONALD NELSON, **11th Bt**

1a Lucy; *b* 1901

2a *Thelma Violet [Mrs Frank Coullon, Unit 38, Gleneaon, 207 Forest Way, Belrose, NSW 2085, Australia]; *b* 1914; *m* 1938 *Frank Coullon and had issue

(4) James Herbert; *b* 17 July 1873

3 Hamilton Staveley Augustus Lindley; *b* 6 May 1824; *m* 23 Oct 1853 Agnes Swinton (*d* 2 Nov 1909), dau of John Carfrae, of Edinburgh, and *d* 9 May 1884, having had:

(1) Douglas Hamilton; *b* 1854; *d* 1872

(2) Henry Campbell; *b* 1 April 1859

(1) Agnes Jane; *d* unm Jan 1911

4 Howard Augustus; *b* 3 April 1828; *m* 13 Oct 1853 Sarah (*d* 1902), dau of Henry Harris, of Bitterne, Hants, and *d* 27 Sept 1884, leaving issue:

(1) William James Henry Beachell; *b* 20 March 1856

(2) Douglas Hector; *b* 25 Aug 1869; *m* 1896 Amy Margaret, dau of Alexander Jansen, of Ridgway, Ontario, and had:

1a Douglas Howard Jerome; *b* 1898

1a Thelma Arline; *b* 1903

(1) Jane Sophia Louisa; *m* 1902 William Watts, of Brandon, Manitoba, and had issue

5 Henry Cranston; *b* 13 July 1831; *d* 1 Sept 1890

1 Anna Maria; *m* 1846 John Morison, of Dundee (*d* 1865), and had issue

2 Mary Jane; *m* 1875 Samuel Fleming Smith (*d* 21 April 1876)

3 Augusta; *m* 9 Aug 1856 St Lawrence Berford, of Canada (*d* 1895), and had issue

4 Louisa

5 Harriotte Charlotte Elizabeth; *d* unm 8 Sept 1916

Sir FREDERICK's bro,

Sir Ronald Nelson Hay, 11th Bt; *b* 9 July 1910; *m* 1940 *Rita [Rita Lady Hay, 17 Murrumbeena Crescent, Murrumbeena, VIC 3163, Australia], dau of John Munyard, and *d* 1988, having had:

1 Sir RONALD FREDERICK HAMILTON HAY, **12th and present Bt**

1 *Pamela Rosemary; *b* 1945; *m* 1972 *Michael Edward Finnegan and has:

(1) *Mark Andrew: *b* 1977

(1) *Jodie Dawn; *b* 1980

HAY of Park

Arms: Arg. three escutcheons gu., in chief an ox-yoke fessways ppr.
Creation: Bt. (NS) 25 Aug 1663.

SIR JOHN ERROLL AUDLEY HAY OF PARK, 11TH BT; *b* 3 Dec 1935; *s* f 1993; *educ* Gordonstoun and St Andrews (MA 1960)

Lineage: Sir THOMAS de la HAYE, 7th of Erroll (*see* ERROLL, E); had a 2nd s:

Sir GILBERT HAY of Dronlaw; *m* 1416 Elizabeth Reid and had, with other issue:

ALEXANDER HAY of Dronlaw; *m* Marjory Fraser, heiress of Ardendraught and Delgaty, and *d c* 30 Dec 1470, leaving:

Sir WILLIAM HAY of Ardendraught; *m* Margaret Leslie and *d c* 30 March 1502, leaving:

Sir GILBERT HAY of Delgaty and Ardendraught; *k* Battle of Flodden 1513, leaving, with two daus (Marjory, *m* Henry Cheyne, Yr. of Esslemont; Marioun, *m* George Gordon, Yr. of Methlick):

ALEXANDER HAY of Delgaty and Ardendraught; *m* 31 May 1510 Elizabeth Abernethy, dau of 3rd Lord Saltoun (*qv*) of Abernethy, and was murdered *c* 1528, leaving:

1 Alexander, of Delgaty; *m* 1st March 1532 (*divorce* 1534/5) Mariota Shaw; *m* 2nd 1545 Janet (*m* 3rd John Leslie of Balquhain), dau of 6th Lord Forbes (*qv*) and widow of 3rd Earl of Atholl (*see* ATHOLL, D), and *dsp* 1546

2 William, of Delgaty; *m* Elizabeth Barclay (*m* 2nd John Innes of Kinkell) and *dsp* 1548

3 THOMAS

1 Margaret; *m* William Johnston of that Ilk

The 3rd s,

Sir Thomas HAY of Park; Parson Spynie 1539, Canon Moray, KStJ, Sec to MARY QUEEN OF SCOTS, Abbot (later post-Reformation Perpetual Commendator) of Glenluce 1559, which he conveyed to his est s 1572; *m* Katharine, dau of David Kennedy of Culzean, 3rd s of 2nd Earl of Cassillis (*see* AILSA, M), and *d c* 1580, leaving an est s:

THOMAS HAY of Park; built 1590 the Castle of Park; *m* Janet, dau of Uchtred Macdowall of Garthland, and *d c* 12 Sept 1628, leaving, with three yr sons (Patrick; John; Alexander, of Arrewland, *d* 1636, leaving issue):

THOMAS HAY of Park; *m* Margaret, dau of Gilbert Kennedy of Genock, and had:

(Sir) THOMAS HAY of Park; *b c* 1616?; ktd 1662?; *m* Jean, dau of Sir John Hamilton of Lettrick, and *d* between March and Aug 1683, leaving:

Sir Thomas Hay, Yr. of Park, 1st Bt (NS), so *cr vp* 25 Aug 1663; *b c* 1636?; perhaps ktd by Nov 1661; *m* 1661 Mary Hamilton, illegitimate dau of James, Duke of Hamilton (*see* HAMILTON and BRANDON, D), and *dvp* between 1 May 1666 and 30 March 1667, leaving, with a dau (Elizabeth, *m* Sir William Maxwell, 1st Bt, *qv*):

Sir Charles Hay, 2nd Bt; *b* 1662; *m* 1685 his cousin Grizel, dau of Sir Andrew Agnew of Lochnaw, 3rd Bt (*qv*), and *d* 1737, having had:

1 Thomas; *m* 1708 his cousin Mary, dau of Sir William Maxwell, 1st Bt (*qv*), and *dvp* 1737, leaving, with other issue:

(1) **Sir Thomas Hay, 3rd Bt**; *b* 1730; wounded Battle of Prestonpans 21 Sept 1745 defending Col Gardiner; *m* 1747 Jean, dau of John Blair of Dunskey, and *d* 1778, having had, with other issue (*d* as infants or unm):

1a **Sir Thomas Hay, 4th Bt**; *d* unm 30 April 1794

2a Alexander; *b c* 1750; Capt Gordon Highrs; *m* Mary (*d* 22 Feb 1792), dau of Sir Alexander Maxwell, 2nd Bt (*qv*)

1a Susan; *m* 15 April 1779 Sir John Dalrymple-Hay, 1st Bt (*qv*), and had issue

2 James; MD, physician Dumfries; *m* Dorothea, only child and heiress of William Crichton of Crawfordton, and had, with two other sons (*dsp*):

(1) William, of Crawfordton; *m* 1752 Mary, dau of Ludovick Cant of Thurstone, and had, with other issue:

1a **Sir James Hay, 5th Bt**; *d* 1794, leaving:

1b **Sir William Hay, 6th Bt**; *d* unm 7 Oct 1801

2a Lewis; Lt-Col RE; *m* 1784 Barbara, dau of John Craigie of Glendoick, Perthshire, and was *ka* Helder 27 Aug 1799, having had, with six daus:

1b JOHN (Sir), **7th Bt**

(1) Lilias; *m* C Stewart of Shambelly

(2) Dorothea; *m* 1755 John Graham of Mossknowe, Dumfriesshire (*d* 1794) and *d* 1798, leaving issue

The 6th Bt's cousin,

Sir John Hay, 7th Bt; *b* posthumously 29 Aug 1799; barrister 1821, 25 years Sheriff-Substitute of Stirling; *m* 29 June 1836 Sarah Beresford, dau of John Cossins, of Weymouth, by Susannah Elizabeth Thicknesse-Touchet, dau of 19th Lord (Baron) Audley (*see* 1970 edn), and *d* 15 June 1862, having had, with other issue:

1 ARTHUR GRAHAM (Sir), **8th Bt**

2 Harry Douglas; MD; *b* 2 Nov 1845; *m* 4 April 1872 Mary Grace (*d* 5 May 1874), er dau of Walter W Veasey, of Richmond, Surrey, and *dsp* 22 Sept 1909

3 Charles Edward; *b* 2 June 1850; *m* 13 April 1886 Jessie Fulton (*d* 17 Nov 1931), only dau of James Arthur of Carlung and Barshaw (*see* GLENARTHUR, B), and widow of John Moffat, CE, and *d* 22 April 1924, leaving:

(1) Charles Edward Erroll; *b* 9 April 1893; Lt 17th Lancers; *ka* 9 Aug 1918

1 Susanna Elizabeth Tuchet; *m* 11 Oct 1871 Maj-Gen John Gordon Graham of Mossknowe (*d* 5 Feb 1911) and *d* 21 Feb 1905, leaving issue

2 Georgiana Barbara; *m* 4 May 1863 William Johnston, MP Belfast (*d* 17 July 1902), and *d* 6 Aug 1900, leaving issue

Sir JOHN's 2nd son,

Sir Arthur Graham Hay, 8th Bt; *b* 5 June 1839; Lt Galloway Militia; *m* 29 June 1864 Thomasina Isabella (*d* 30 Nov 1918), yst dau of John Brett Johnston, of Ballykilbeg House, Co Down, and *d* 18 Nov 1889, having had:

1 LEWIS JOHN ERROLL (Sir), **9th Bt**

2 Thomas James Macpherson; *b* 15 Aug 1876; drowned 1895

3 Arthur George Beresford; *b* 31 Oct 1878; *m* 30 April 1913 Louise Emily May (*d* 19 Feb 1939), dau of Col Henry Robert Carden, DL, of Fishmoyne, Templemore, Co Tipperary, and *d* 24 June 1949, leaving:

(1) *Evelyn Alice Carden [Mrs Charles Barton, c/o Barclays Bank Ltd, St Marychurch, Torquay, Devon]; *b* 6 March 1914; *m* 16 April 1945 *Charles John Barton, Palestine Police, er surv s of Maj Dennis James Barton, 52nd LI, of Stratton, Cornwall, and has:

1a *Mary Hay; *b* 30 Jan 1948

2a *Margaret Elsie; *b* 12 Dec 1952

1 Mary Elizabeth Tuchet; *b* 24 May 1865; *d* unm 8 Aug 1948

2 Gertrude Alice Brunette; *b* 25 Dec 1867; *d* unm 17 Aug 1945

3 Emily Frances Graham; *b* 14 July 1871; *d* 17 June 1923

4 Robina Margaret Catherine Violet; *b* 4 Feb 1874; *m* 25 Sept 1906 Charles James Lord (*d* 1955) and *d* 27 April 1962, leaving issue

5 Florence Grace Douglas; *b* 31 March 1875; *m* 20 Aug 1914 Donald John O'Hara, CE (*d* 3 Sept 1936), of Omagh, Co Tyrone, and *d* 16 Jan 1953

Sir ARTHUR's est son,

Sir Lewis John Erroll Hay, 9th Bt; *b* 17 Nov 1866; memb Roy Co Archers; *m* 25 Sept 1895 Lizabel Annie (*d* 27 March 1957), dau of Lachlan Macdonald, of Skeabost, Skye, and *d* 14 May 1923, having had issue:

1 ARTHUR THOMAS ERROLL (Sir), **10th Bt**

1 Marie Lizabel Macdonald; *b* 9 July 1896; *m* 16 Feb 1927 Colin Olaf MacDhonnachadh Campbell (*d* April 1951), of Kilmartin, and *d* 31 July 1938, leaving issue

2 Elspeth Minna Erroll; *b* 13 Feb 1898; *m* 30 April 1924 Colin Henry Patrick Campbell Penney, MC (*d* 9 June 1947), and had issue

3 Dorothea Violet Douglas; *b* 18 Aug 1900; *m* 17 June 1933 Lt-Col Henry Normand MacLaurin, MBE (*ka* Burma 7 April 1944), 1st Duke of York's Own Cav, and *d* 20 Oct 1961, leaving issue

4 Jean Isobel Macpherson; *b* 29 Dec 1901; *m* 30 April 1929 Frederick Foulkes Capron, RA, and *d* 2 March 1946, leaving issue

5 (Lisabel) Ailsa Macdonald; *b* 20 Nov 1903; *m* 5 Aug 1942 Thomas Pilkington Burns (*d* 18 Nov 1951), only son of John William Burns, JP, of Mortimer, Berks, and *d* 6 April 1980, having had issue

6 Lilias Erroll Audley Beresford; *b* 23 July 1906; *m* 28 Aug 1957 Rev Edward Constable Alston, of Horncastle; *d* 9 May 1986

7 (Margaret) Audrey Theresa; *b* 3 Oct 1907; *d* 7 Nov 1989

8 Betty Louise Macdonald; *b* 11 Jan 1913; *d* 13 Feb 1984

Sir LEWIS's only son,

Sir Arthur Thomas Erroll Hay of Park, 10th Bt, ISO (*c* 1970); ARIBA; *b* 13 April 1909; *educ* Fettes; *m* 1st 4 March 1935 (*divorce* 1942) Hertha Hedwig Paula Louise (*d* 27 Jan 1994), only dau of Lugwig Stölzle, of Nagelberg, Austria, and widow of Walter Biheller, of London, and had issue:

1 Sir JOHN ERROLL AUDLEY HAY, **11th and present Bt**

Sir Arthur *m* 2nd 22 Dec 1942 Rosemary Evelyn Anne (*d* 19 July 1997), only dau of V-Adml Aubrey Lambert, of Betchworth, Surrey, and formerly w of Cdr Nigel de Glanville Waymouth, RN, and *d* 3 Feb 1993

HAYHOE

Creation: B. (LP, UK) 1992.

THE BARON HAYHOE, of Isleworth in the London Borough of Hounslow (Sir Bernard (Barney) John Hayhoe, PC 1985) [The Rt Hon The Lord Hayhoe PC, 20 Wool Rd, SW20 OHW]; *b* 8 Aug 1925; *educ* Borough Poly; Min Supply: apprentice 1941–44, Armaments Design Dept 1944–54, Inspectorate of Armaments 1954–63; Head Research Section CRD 1965–70, MP (C) Heston and Isleworth 1970–74, Hounslow Brentford and Isleworth 1974–92, Hon Sec C Parly Employment Ctee 1970–71 (V-Chm 1974), Jt Hon Sec C Gp Europe 1970–73 (V-Chm 1973–76), PPS to Ld Pres Cncl and Leader H of C 1972–74, V-Chm: C Party Internat Office 1973–79 and Trilateral Commn 1977–79, Oppn Spokesman Employment 1974–79, Parly U-Sec MOD (Army) 1979–81; Min State: CSD 1981, Treasury 1981–85, Health 1985–86; memb Select Ctee: Race Relations and Immigration 1971–73 and Defence 1987–92, memb H of C Commn 1987–92 and Public Accounts Commn 1987–92; Govr Birkbeck Coll 1976–79, ktd 1987; Chm: Hansard Soc 1990–94, Guy's and St Thomas's NHS Tst 1993–95; CEng; FIMechE; *m* 1962 *Ann Gascoigne, dau of Bernard W and Hilda Thornton, and has:

1 *Crispin Bernard Gascoigne; *b* 1963
2 *Dominic Adam Scott; *b* 1965
1 *Sarah Anne Sherwood; *b* 1967

Lineage: FRANK STANLEY HAYHOE; *m* Catherine — and had issue:

BERNARD JOHN, *cr* a **Baron**

HAYMAN

Creation: B. (LP, UK) Nov 1995.

THE BARONESS HAYMAN, of Dartmouth Park, London Borough of Camden (Helene Valerie Middleweek) [The Rt Hon The Baroness Hayman, House of Lords, London SW1A 0PW]; *b* 26 March 1949; *educ* Wolverhampton Girls' High Sch and Newnham Coll Cambridge (Pres Union 1969); with Shelter 1969, Camden Cncl Soc Servs 1971, Dep Dir Nat Cncl One-Parent Families 1974, V-Chm: Bloomsbury 1988–90 and Bloomsbury and Islington Health Authorities 1991–92; fought (Lab) Wolverhampton SW Feb 1974 gen election, MP (Lab) Welwyn and Hatfield Oct 1974–79, Parly U-Sec Roads, Tport and Environment 1997–98, Health 1998–; memb: RCOG Ethics Ctee 1982–, UCL/UCH Ctee Ethics Clinical Investigation 1987–, Cncl UCL 1992–, Chm Whittington Hosp NHS Tst 1992–97; *m* 1974 *Martin Hayman and has four sons

Lineage: MAURICE MIDDLEWEEK; *m* Maude — and had:

HELENE VALERIE, *cr* a **Baroness**

HAYTER

Arms: Quarterly, 1st and 4th, az, a cross erminois, between in the 1st and 4th quarters a bezant and in the second and third a rose or (for CHUBB); 2nd and 3rd, az., a chevron between two bull's heads couped in chief and in base an escallop, all or (for HAYTER). **Crest:** In front of a demi-lion az., holding between the paws a bezant charged with a rose gu., a key fesswise, the ward upwards and to the dexter or. **Supporters:** On either side a lion az., holding in the mouth a rose gu., barbed, seeded, leaved and slipped ppr. and charged on the shoulder with a key palewise, wards downwards and to the dexter or. **Motto:** *Cavendo tutus* ('Safe by being cautious').

Creations: Bt. (UK) 20 June 1900, B. (UK) 29 Jan 1927.

THE 3RD BARON HAYTER, of Chislehurst, Kent and a **Baronet** (Sir George Charles Hayter Chubb, KCVO (1977), CBE (1976)) [The Rt Hon The Lord Hayter KCVO CBE, Ashtead House, Ashtead, Surrey KT21 1LU]; *b* 25 April 1911; *s* f 1967; *educ* Leys Sch and Trin Coll Cambridge (MA 1932); chm Chubb and Son's Lock and Safe Co, RSA 1965–66, Ec Devpt Ctee for Movement of Exports 1972–, Br Securities Indust Assoc 1973–, past Pres Roy Warrant Holders Assoc, Liveryman Weavers' Co 1934 (Upper Bailiff 1961–62); *m* 28 March 1940 *Elizabeth Anne, MBE (1974), only dau of Thomas Arthur Rumbold (*see* RUMBOLD, Bt), and has:

1 +(GEORGE) WILLIAM MICHAEL [The Hon William Chubb, Rookery Cottage, Ramsdale Rd, Monk Sherborne, Hants RG26 5HS]; *b* 9 Oct 1943; *educ* Marlborough and Nottingham U (BSc); Renter Bailiff Weavers' Co 1997–98; *m* 8 Jan 1983 *Waltaud, yr dau of J Flackl, of Sydney, Australia, and has issue:

(1) +Thomas Frederik Flackl; *b* 23 July 1986

2 +John Andrew [The Hon John Chubb, Manor Farm House, Warborough, Oxon]; *b* 20 April 1946; *educ* Marlborough and Southampton U (MA); FCA; *m* 1975 *Sandy, only dau of Alfred Ernest Brereton, of Chiswick, and has issue:

(1) +Alfred; *b* 1977
(1) *Georgia; *b* 1978

3 +Charles Henry Thomas [The Hon Charles Chubb, Tower Hill, 101 High St, Kidlington, Oxon OX5 2DS]; *b* 22 Nov 1949; *educ* Marlborough and King's Coll Cambridge (MA 1974); MB, BS (Bart's 1978), MRCGP; *m* 1979 *(Ann) Nicola, dau of Charles William Stewart French Manning, FRCS, and has:

(1) +(Mark) Henry; *b* 1980
(2) +Jack Charles; *b* 1985
(1) *Josephine Anne; *b* 1983
(2) *Alice Christine; *b* 1989

1 *Sarah Tamsen [The Hon Mrs Clark, St Peter's Rectory, 1 Leicester Rd, Oadby, Leics LE2 5BD]; *b* 30 Jan 1941; *m* 27 July 1963 *Rev David Humphrey Clark, Team Rector Oadby, Leics, and has issue:

(1) *Andrew David; *b* 5 Nov 1964
(1) *Alison Tamsen; *b* 8 Feb 1967

1 (cont.) The Rev David and Mrs Clark also adopted:

*Simon William; *b* 20 Nov 1968
*Katherine Mary; *b* 1970

Lineage: CHARLES CHUBB, of Barnsbury Park, Islington; *b* 1772; *m* Maria Hayter and *d* 1846, leaving, with other issue:

JOHN CHUBB, of Radcliffe House, Brixton; *b* 1815; *m* Priscilla (*d* 1863), dau of Godwin Withers, of Romsey, Hants, and *d* 1872, leaving issue:

1 John Charles; *d* Sept 1899, leaving issue
2 GEORGE HAYTER, **1st Baron**
3 Harry Withers, of Burlingham, Chislehurst; *b* 1857; *m* Frances Emory, dau of Rev George Crooks, and *d* 2 Dec 1905, leaving issue
1 Priscilla Jane; *m* Thomas Hogue of Bournemouth, and had issue

The 2nd son,

Sir George Hayter, 1st Bt, and **1st Baron Hayter,** of Chislehurst, Co Kent (both UK), so *cr* 20 June 1900 and 29 Jan 1927 respectively, JP Kent; Commr Roy Patriotic Fund, Chev Legn Hon, Offr Order Leopold Belgium, KGStJ; *b* 29 Aug 1848; ktd 1885; *m* 29 Dec 1870 Sarah Vanner, DGStJ (*d* 8 Nov 1940), only dau of Charles Early, JP, of Witney, Oxon, and had issue:

1 CHARLES ARCHIBALD, **2nd Baron**
2 George Herbert; Maj RFA (TF); *b* 27 May 1873; *d* unm 28 Nov 1957
1 Ethelwyn Early; *d* unm 5 April 1942
2 Helen Mary; *m* 21 Sept 1909 Harold Gabriel Morrish, MA Cantab, er s of Sir Thomas Buxton Morrish, and had issue. He *d* 18 Oct 1953
3 Priscilla Frances Vanner; *m* 3 June 1909 Alex Woodward Hill, MA, of Musleigh Manor, Ware, Herts, only s of Dr Alex Hill, Master Downing Coll Cambridge, and had issue

The 1st BARON *d* 7 Nov 1946; his er son,

CHARLES ARCHIBALD, **2nd Baron Hayter**; *b* 11 Nov 1871; *educ* Leys Sch Cambridge; md Chubb and Sons 1898–1948, sr memb Court Common Cncl City London, Lt City London, Upper Bailiff Weavers' Co 1922, 1936 and 1950, pres Planet Bldg Soc; *m* 1st 8 June 1898 Mary (*d* 4 June 1948), est dau of John Fletcher Haworth, JP, and had:

1 GEORGE CHARLES HAYTER CHUBB, **3rd and present Baron Hayter**
2 David William Early; Cdr RN WW II (despatches, POW), Naval Attaché Copenhagen 1960–62; *b* 31 May 1914; *educ* RNC Dartmouth; *m* 2 Dec 1939 *Veronica [The Hon Mrs David Chubb, St Mary's Cottage, Broughton, Hants SO20 8AB], dau of William Clifton, of Shanghai, and *d* 1993, leaving issue:

(1) +Jeremy David Knyvett; *b* 29 July 1941; *educ* Sherborne; *m* 1978 *Valerie Ann Evans, yst dau of H J Wightman, and has issue:

1a +Patrick David; *b* 1980
2a +Andrew Harry; *b* 1982

The **2nd Baron** *m* 2nd 23 March 1949 (Margaret) Alison (*d* 1986), dau of John Gimson Pickard, of Leicester, and *d* 3 March 1967

HAZLERIGG

Arms: Arg. a chevron sa. between three hazel leaves vert. **Crest:** On a chapeau gu. doubled erm. a Scot's head and shoulders couped ppr. **Supporters:** Dexter, a Cromwellian soldier holding in his exterior hand a sword, point downwards; sinister, a Coldstream Guardsman of the 17th century supporting with his exterior hand by the muzzle a musket, all ppr. **Motto:** *Pro aris et focis* ('For our altars and our hearths'). **Creation:** Bt. (E) 21 July 1622, B. (UK) 12 Feb 1945.

THE 2ND BARON HAZLERIGG, of Noseley Hall, Co Leicester and a **Baronet** (Sir Arthur Grey Hazlerigg, Bt, MC (1945), TD (1953), JP (Leics 1947), DL (Leics 1946)) [The Rt Hon The Lord Hazlerigg MC TD JP DL, Noseley Hall, Billesdon, Leics, LE7 9EH]; *b* 24 Feb 1910, *s f* 1949; *educ* Eton and Trin Coll Cambridge (BA 1932); Maj RA (TA) WW II; *m* 19 Sept 1945 Patricia (*d* 29 April 1972), est dau of John Pullar, of Durban, Natal, and has issue:

1 +ARTHUR GREY [The Hon Arthur Hazlerigg, Noseley Hall, Billesdon, Leics LE7 9EH]; *b* 5 May 1951; *educ* Tabley House; *m* 1986 *Laura, est dau of Sir William Stratford Dugdale, 2nd Bt (*qv*), and has issue:

(1) +Arthur William Grey; *b* 13 May 1987

(1) *Eliza Patricia; *b* 1989

(2) *Amelia Frances; *b* 1989

(3) *Viola Camilla Alice; *b* 1993

1 *Angela Christine [The Hon Mrs MacDowel, 22 Murrayfield Gardens, Edinburgh EH12 6DF]; *b* 22 Dec 1946; *m* 31 May 1969 Timothy Effingham MacDowel (*d* 1978), Capt, (TA) 15th/19th King's Roy Hus, only s of Lt-Col Horace St George MacDowel, of Fulbrook House, Burford, Oxon, and has issue:

(1) *Benjamin St George; *b* 1970

(2) *Richard Arthur; *b* 14 June 1973

2 *Priscilla (Scilla) Frances; *b* 30 July 1952; *m* 24 May 1975 *Hon Richard Arthur Louis Dillon, 2nd s of 20th Viscount Dillon (*qv*), and has issue

Lineage: THOMAS HESILRIGE, of Noseley Hall, Leics; *m* Ursula, dau of Sir Thomas Andrews, of Charwelton, Northants, and had issue:

Sir Thomas Hesilrige, 1st Bt (E), so *cr* 21 July 1622, of Noseley; Leics: MP 1614 and 1624–25, Sheriff 1612–13; *b* 1564; *m* Frances (*d* 1638), dau and heir of Sir William Gorges, of Alderton, and *d* 11 Jan 1629, leaving issue:

Sir Arthur Hesilrige, 2nd Bt; MP Leics 1640–45 and 1654–59; Parly Cdr and Col Regt of Cuirassiers, Govr Newcastle; *m* 1st 1625 Frances (*d* 1632), dau of Thomas Elmes, and had issue; *m* 2nd Dorothy (*d* 28 Jan 1650), sis of 2nd Baron Brooke (*see* WARWICK, BROOKE and, E), and *d* Tower of London 7 Jan 1660/1, having by her had, with other issue:

1 **Sir Thomas Hesilrige, 3rd Bt**; *b* 1625; *m* 1664 Elizabeth (*d* 30 May 1673), dau and coheir of George Fenwick, of Brenckbourne, Northumberland, and *d* 24 Feb 1680, leaving issue:

(1) **Sir Thomas Hesilrige, 4th Bt**; MP Leics 1690–95, Sheriff 1686–87; *b* 1664; *d* unm 11 July 1700

(1) Mary; *m* Francis Blith, of Allesley, Warwicks

(2) Arabella; *m* R Hart

2 **Sir Robert Hesilrige, 5th Bt**; *b* 1640; *m* 3 May 1664 Bridget (*d* 26 July 1697), dau of Sir Samuel Rolle, of Heanton, Devon, and *d* 22 May 1713, leaving an only surv child:

(1) **Sir Robert Hesilrige, 6th Bt**; Sheriff Leics 1715–16; *b* 1668; *m* 29 July 1696 Dorothy (*d* 11 Sept 1748), 2nd dau of 3rd Baron Maynard, and had issue:

1a ARTHUR, (Sir), **7th Bt**

1a Dorothy; *m* Rev — Battle

The 6th Bt *d* 19 May 1721; his son,

Sir Arthur Hesilrige, 7th Bt; *m* June 1725 Hannah Sturges (allegedly inspiration of Samuel Richardson's character Pamela; *d* 27 Feb 1765) and *d* 23 April 1763, having had, with other issue:

1 **Sir Robert Hesilrige, 8th Bt**; *m* Sarah, dau of Nathaniel Waller, of Roxburgh, New England, and had issue:

(1) **Sir Arthur Hesilrige, 9th Bt**; HEICS; *m* 1st Elizabeth Charnand, of Smyrna (*d* 1797); *m* 2nd Charlotte Elizabeth (*m* 2nd 1 Aug 1805 Capt Henry William Wilkinson and *d* at sea 8 Jan 1817), dau of Capt F E S Gray, and *dsp* 1805

(1) Sarah; *m* David Henley

(2) Hannah; *m* Rev Thomas Abbot

2 Arthur; *d* 1791

3 **Sir Thomas Maynard Hesilrige, 10th Bt**; *m* 1st 1805 Mary (*d* 13 Feb 1809), dau of Edmond Tyreil, of Gipping Hall, Suffolk; *m* 2nd 30 Nov 1811 Hon Letitia Wodehouse (*m* 2nd 15 Aug 1842 Frederick Fielding, barrister, and *d* 3 March 1864, *see* KIMBERLEY, E), and *dsp* 24 April 1817

4 Grey, JP; Col; *m* Bridget, dau of Rev Richard Buckby and *d* Oct 1810, leaving, with five daus and two other sons (*d* unm):

(1) ARTHUR GREY (Sir), **11th Bt**

(2) Charles Maynard (Rev); MA, Rector Carlton Curlieu Leics; *b* 24 Aug 1802; *m* 10 March 1829 Deborah Maria (*d* 1866), 2nd dau of Arthur Buckby, of Seagoe, Co Armagh, and *d* 4 Dec 1878, having had, with other issue:

1a Arthur; Lt 59th Regt; *b* 20 June 1834; *m* 4 June 1862 Mary Augusta (*d* 1919), dau of George John Nicholls, FRCS, of Bourne, Lincs, and *d* 14 Feb 1863, leaving issue:

1b Arthur George Maynard; ed *Debrett's Peerage* 1887–1935, consulting ed 1935–53; *b* posthumously 5 Sept 1863; *m* 2 July 1889 Amy Florence (*d* 31 May 1947), dau of M S Myers, of Chiswick, and *d* 13 April 1953, leaving:

1c Phyllis Maynard; *b* 16 Aug 1890; *m* 12 Dec 1925 Kenneth Leslie Mortimore, MC, FCA, Capt Dorset and Regt Trench Mortar Bn, yst s of Frank B Mortimore

2c Corrie Maynard; *b* 2 Feb 1893; *d* unm 7 Jan 1957

3c Violet Maynard; *b* 20 April 1900; *m* 17 March 1943 Maj George Reginald Jackson, RASC, Res of Offrs, est s of Maj J N Jackson, VD, JP. He *d* 1954

2a Charles Maynard (Rev); Vicar Weston Yorks; *b* 7 May 1838; *m* 1871 Sarah Hannah Mason (*d* 7 Jan 1902) and *d* 4 Sept 1901, leaving:

1b Grey; FRGS, sr master St Michael's Sch, Limpsfield, Surrey; *b* 1872; *m* 3 Aug 1904 Bessie (*d* 29 May 1947), dau of John Shrimpton, of Great Haseley, Oxon, and *d* 26 July 1939

2b Charles; BA London, master Bishop Auckland GS, Roy Fus WW I; *b* 1876; *m* 1st 22 May 1920 Florence (*d* 1 Dec 1937), dau of John Burn, of Stockton-on-Tees; *m* 2nd 25 July 1945 *Doris Rawlings, and *dsp* 14 Jan 1947

1b Maria; *d* unm 27 Aug 1959

3a Thomas Greville; *b* 8 Aug 1841; *m* 1871 Eliza Preston (*d* March 1925), and *d* July 1906, leaving issue:

1b Thomas Greville; *b* 1878; *m* 1st 1901 Florence Elizabeth (*d* 1919), dau of Edwin Henry Griffiths, of Mount Pleasant, Shrewsbury, and had issue:

1c Dorothy Greville; *m* 1926 Thomas Gilbert Hodgett

1b (cont.) Thomas Hesilrige *m* 2nd 1921 Gertrude May (*d* 1985), dau of William Downs, and *d* 18 Oct 1955, having by her had:

1c +Roger Greville [Roger Hazlerigg Esq, 168 Rugby Rd, Binley Woods, Leics]; *b* 1932; *m* 1 June 1957 (*divorce* 1976) Barbara Shirley, dau of Henry Edward Daniel, and has issue:

1d +Charles Greville; *b* 22 March 1958; *m* 1985 *Elizabeth June Davies, and has issue:

1e *Rebecca Lynne; *b* 1987

2b Robert Maynard; *b* 1884; *m* 1914 Dora (*d* 1969), dau of Thomas Cope, of The Lount Farm, Osbaston, and *d* 1951, leaving:

1c Isabel Maynard; *b* 20 June 1916; *m* 18 Aug 1938 *Reginald Gerald Watts [Reginald Watts Esq, Hillcrest, 89 Pioneer Ave, Desborough, Northants], s of Richard Watts, of Stoke Albany, Northants, and *d* 12 March 1997, leaving:

1d *Richard Maynard; *b* 1941

1b Laura; *b* 20 Dec 1872; *m* 27 Sept 1898 John David Wright (*d* 24 Nov 1948), of Thurlaston, Leics, and *d* 15 Nov 1950, leaving issue

2b Deborah Maria; *m* 1914 Henry James Dilworth, of Shangton, Kibworth, and *d* 18 June 1928

The 10th Bt's n,

Sir ARTHUR GREY HESILRIGE later HAZLERIGG (roy licence 8 July 1818), **11th Bt**; *m* 25 July 1811 Henrietta Anne (*d* 25 Oct 1868), dau of John Bourne, of Stanch Hall, Hants, and had, with other issue:

1 ARTHUR GREY (Sir), **12th Bt**

2 Thomas Maynard; *b* 15 April 1815; *d* young

3 Grey (Rev), of Willoughby House, Leics; nonconformist minister, Offr 48th Regt; *b* 13 March 1818; *m* 24 June 1873 Sarah Ann (*d* 27 June 1901), est dau of Thomas Clarke, and *d* 4 Oct 1912, leaving issue:

(1) Grey, OBE (1920); Lt Leicester Regt, BA, LLB Camb, DC Gold Coast 1908, Actg Assist Colonial Sec there 1909, Registrar Supreme Court Ceylon 1910, Sec Cncl Legal Educn Ceylon 1914, Rifle Bde WW I, Sec to Govr-Gen S Africa, Colonial Office 1916–19 and 1924–34; *b* 14 Jan 1879; *m* 1st 8 Dec 1908 (*divorce* 1924) Sarah Dorothy (*d* 1965), 2nd dau of Herbert Bakewell Whetstone, JP, of Ilketshall Hall, Bungay, Suffolk; *m* 2nd 8 Nov 1933 Fannie (*d* 26 Nov 1949), widow of Frederick Hardy, of Staunton Hall, Notts, and *d* 1948, having had by his 1st w:

1a Herbert William Grey; 2nd Lt IA; *b* 13 Sept 1910; *m* 1937 *Gladys Margaret [Mrs Herbert Hazlerigg, 37 Barrhill Ave, Brighton, Sussex BN1 8UE], dau of David Alan Knighton, of Ealing, and *d* 1991, leaving issue:

1b +Alexander David Grey [Alexander Hazlerigg Esq, Glanclywedo, Staylittle, Llanbrymair, Powys SY19 7BU]; *b* 1939; BSc, PhD; *m* 1961 *Rosemary, er dau of Leslie Clarence Ottewill, and has issue:

1c +David Grey; *b* 1967; *educ* Cambridge U (Bsc, PhD)

2c +Andrew Alexander; *b* 1969; BA

2b +Alan Peter Maynard; *b* 1941; BSc

3b +Arthur Richard Thomas; *b* 1945; Lt-Col Roy Logistisc Corps; *m* 1st 1967 (*divorce* 1979) Lesley — and has:

1c *Nichola Michelle; *b* 1973

3b (cont.) Arthur Hazlerigg *m* 2nd 1980 *Elaine Elizabeth, dau of John Machey Reed, and has issue:

1c +Charles Rupert Edward; *b* 1984

2c *Antonia Rebecca Alexandrina; *b* 1983

3c *Alexandra Machey Elizabeth; *b* 1986

1b *Margaret Julia; *b* 1946; *m* 1967 *John David Gilbert, BSc, PhD, and has issue:

1c *Christopher Peter; *b* 1973

1c *Susan Ruth; *b* 1971; RGN

2a +Alexander Maynard; Colonial Civ Serv Jamaica 1935, Sub-Inspr Constabulary Trinidad 1937; *b* 1914; *educ* Lewes County Sch

1a *Dorothy Mary Louise; *b* 1912

(2) Thomas Maynard, CBE (1946), MC (1918); slr 1906, Capt RASC, Assist Crown Slr Hong Kong 1920, Registrar Supreme Court 1929, Crown Slr 1935, Political Advsr BMA 1945–46, Special Advsr Govt 1946–47, MEC and MLC Hong Kong 1946–47, served WW I and N Russia 1919; *b* 1882; *m* 1st 1905 Violet Isabella (*d* 25 Oct 1941), dau of H J Price; *m* 2nd 1941 Gladys May, BEM, dau of T Cotton, and *d* 6 Nov 1961, having by his 1st w had:

1a Robert Maynard; *b* 7 March 1911; *d* 26 Feb 1913

1a Diana Margaret; *b* 3 Jan 1914; *m* 14 March 1946 Robert Edward Hope-Falkner, Malayan Police, only s of Lt-Col Percy Hope-Falkner, and *d* 4 Dec 1977, leaving:

1b *John Alexander; *b* 24 May 1947; *educ* Wellington; PR exec

2b *Patrick Miles; *b* 1 Dec 1949; *educ* Wellington; slr; *m* 1972 *Wendy M, est dau of J D Mallinson

(1) Henrietta Anne; *d* unm 11 June 1934

(2) Caroline Susan; *m* 11 April 1900 Henry Doudney Thompson, LLB, and *d* Jan 1963, aged 85. He *d* 1921

(3) Lilian Elizabeth; *m* 26 May 1900 Frank Densham and *d* 27 Sept 1948, leaving issue (*see* PROCTOR-BEAUCHAMP, Bt). He *d* 4 July 1950

(4) Dorothy Frances; *m* 1903 Wilfred Tyler. He *d* 1943

1 Henrietta Susan; *m* 15 Oct 1840 Thomas Bell, Lt 48th Regt, yst s of Maj-Gen — Bell, CB, and *d* 4 Sept 1901, leaving issue. He *d* 1863

Sir ARTHUR *d* 24 Oct 1819; his est son,

Sir Arthur Grey Hazlerigg, 12th Bt; Sheriff Leics 1837; *b* 20 Oct 1812; *m* 14 July 1835 Henrietta (*d* 13 Dec 1883), 5th dau of Charles Allen Phillipps, of St Bride's Hill, Pembs, and had:

1 Arthur Grey; Lt-Col Roy Scots Fus Crimea 1854 and Zulu War 1879–80; *b* 10 Jan 1837; *m* 9 Jan 1878 Janet Edith (*m* 2nd 25 Feb 1888 Maj Henry Pelham Burn, Rifle Bde (*d* 9 Nov 1935), and *d* 15 June 1935, leaving further issue), er dau of Sir Archibald Orr Ewing, 1st Bt (*qv*), and *dvp* 16 July 1880, leaving issue:

(1) ARTHUR GREY, **1st Baron**

2 Thomas Maynard; Maj-Gen RHA, served Afghan War 1878–80 (despatches, brevet, medal with clasp); *b* 5 Aug 1840; *m* 19 July 1869 Margaret (*d* 27 April 1918), yst dau of Lt-Gen Francis Walker-Drummond (*see* 1970 edn WILLIAMS-DRUMMOND, Bt), and *d* 5 Nov 1915, having had issue:

(1) Arthur; *b* 31 March 1873; *d* of wounds recd in action Mafeking 13 May 1900

(2) Thomas, DSO (1918); Lt-Col RASC, Boer War 1900–01, WW I (despatches); *b* 1 June 1877; *m* 17 March 1903 Edith Violet (*d* 9 July 1959), only dau of Lt-Col William Henry McCheane, RMLI, and *d* 15 March 1935, leaving:

1a Arthur William; Lt-Col RA WW II; *b* 5 Feb 1904; *educ* Uppingham, RMA Woolwich and Cambridge (MA 1947); *m* 1st 17 June 1935 (*divorce* 1946) Marjorie Dorothea, only dau of Col George Frederick Brown Turner, DSO; *m* 2nd 16 June 1947 Jane (*d* 1977), only dau of David Wilson, OBE, and *d* 1987, leaving by his 1st w:

1b +(Arthur) Robert [Robert Hazlerigg Esq, Paddock Lodge, Whitchurch-on-Thames, Berks RG8 7EX]; *b* 24 Aug 1936; *educ* Leys Sch, RMA Sandhurst and Coll of Estate Management (BSc), FRICS, Capt RHA (ret); *m* 26 July 1963 *Janet Christine Hermione, only dau of Edward Simpson Anderson, MBE, of Elgin, and has issue:

1c *Catrina Louise [Mrs Lars Jaeger, 30 Horseshoe Rd, Pangbourne, Berks]; *b* 27 April 1964; *m* 1992 *Lars Jaeger, s of Mrs L Ager-Harris, of Easingwold, Yorks, and has:

1d *Charlotte Louise; *b* 19 July 1996

(3) Greville; Capt Sherwood Foresters, Lt Cameronians, Boer War 1900–01 and WW I; *b* 12 Dec 1881; *m* 1 June 1908 Helen Margaret (*d* 9 Dec 1949), dau of Maj-Gen Newson Thomas Parsons, 103rd Fus, and *d* 7 March 1944, leaving:

1a Arthur Greville Maynard; Capt RASC, 2nd Lt Norfolk Regt (Res) WW II; *b* 7 Nov 1910; *m* 6 Oct 1941 *Nancy [Mrs Arthur Hazlerigg, Downside, North St, Mere, Wilts BA12 6AZ], yr dau of Capt John Alexander Ingles, RN, and *d* 1990, leaving:

1b +(Arthur) Patrick [Maj Patrick Hazlerigg RA, 30 West St, Bere Regis, Dorset]; *b* 25 Feb 1943; *educ* Milton Abbey, Maj RA (ret 1994); *m* 1973 *Susan Elizabeth, dau of Lt-Cdr Patrick Kenneth Truckle, RN, and has issue:

1c +Arthur Philip Greville; *b* 1978

1c *Harriet Jane; *b* 1976

1b *Diana Elizabeth [Mrs Diana Moody, Corner Cottage, Bishop's Lane, Hardington Mandeville, Somerset BA22 9PJ]; *b* 22 Sept 1947; *m* 1971 (*divorce* 1997) Col Anthony Michael Thomas Moody, Roy Irish Rangers, er s of Maj T A Moody, of Omagh, Co Tyrone, and has:

1c *Victoria Natalie; *b* 1973

2c *Alexandria Jane; *b* 1976

2b *Shelagh Marion [Mrs Andrew Bell, Firenze, Chetcombe Rd, Mere, Wilts BA12 6AZ]; *b* 27 Dec 1951; *m* 1985 *Cdr Andrew D Bell, RN, and has issue:

1c *Georgina Hazlerigg; *b* 1986

2c *Natasha Hazlerigg; *b* 1988

(1) Gwendoline Alice; *d* unm 9 Dec 1933

(2) Henrietta Mabel; *d* unm 26 Jan 1955

(3) Evelyn; *d* unm 22 Oct 1953

(4) Margaret; *m* 10 Oct 1914 Cdr (S) George Okeover Anson, RD, RNR, and *d* 19 Nov 1956

3 Charles Cecil, 26th Foot; *b* 31 July 1845; *d* unm

4 William Grenville (Rev); MA, Rector Hallaton, Leics; *b* 8 June 1847; *m* 20 April 1876 Barbara Mary (*d* 21 Feb 1911), est dau of Lt-Col Joseph Walker Pease, JP, DL, of Hesslewood House, Yorks, and *d* 1 Nov 1893, leaving issue:

(1) Roger Greville; *b* 22 Jan 1877; *m* 2 Sept 1919 Esther Rosamond (*d* 1976), dau of Lacey Nussey Everett, MA, of Rushmere Lodge, Pool, nr Leeds, and *d* 11 Jan 1952, leaving issue:

1a *Jean Mary [Mrs Kenneth Perrin, The Old Rectory, Great Comberton, nr Pershore, Worcs]; *b* 19 Dec 1921; *m* 12 July 1947 *Maj Kenneth Leonard Perrin, Intell Corps, only s of Leonard Harry Perrin

(2) Guy Maynard, MC; Maj Res of Offrs RASC, Assist DC Malindi, Br E Africa, served E Africa 1916 (despatches); *b* 8 Feb 1887; *m* 1st 15 March 1913 Erna Irene (Hendrike) (*d* 19 Jan 1924), er dau of Capt R C Heidenreihe, 5th Austrian Hus; *m* 2nd 1929 Margaret Jennie (*d* 18 Feb 1958), widow of Cyril Ashley Welbourne, of Perth, W Australia, and only dau of Thomas Austin Francis, and *d* 1963, having had by his 1st w:

1a George Maynard; *b* 25 Aug 1915; *d* 19 Aug 1916

(1) Charlotte Isabel; *m* 27 Feb 1919 William John Hilyer, MICE, Capt RE, and *d* 1 Jan 1942

(2) Barbara Henrietta; *m* 22 Feb 1908 Sir Herbert Castleman Lushington, 6th Bt (*qv*), and *d* 13 Feb 1927, leaving issue

(3) Eleanor Frances; *d* unm 22 May 1963

5 Allen Martival; *b* 28 Oct 1855; *m* 24 July 1880 Adela Louisa Julia Fanny Codrington (*d* 25 Aug 1938), dau of Capt Codrington Forsyth, CB, RN, and *d* 1949, having had issue:

(1) Martival Grey; Lt RFA TA WW I; *b* 9 Oct 1884; *m* 31 Oct 1925 *Marian [Mrs Martival Hazlerigg, Flat 1 Craddock Court, Forest Green, Nailsworth, Glos], dau of Michael Ray, and *d* 1971, leaving issue:

1a +Martival Spencer Woolf [Martival Hazlerigg Esq, 33 Belvedere Mews, St Mary's, Chalford, Glos GL6 8PF]; *b* 5 Jan 1927; RNAS 1945–47; *m* 12 July 1947 *Kitty, dau of William Johnson Bowhill, and has issue:

1b *Marilyn Kay [Mrs Roger Huckerby, 31 Bowes Rd, Walton-on-Thames KT12 3HT]; *b* 10 Sept 1952; BScEng; *m* 1976 *Roger Huckerby, BScEng

2b *Martine Grey; *b* 23 Feb 1957; *m* 1977 (*divorce* 1991) Raymond Anthony Dawson, MScEng

1a Ella Jeanette; *d* young

1 Henrietta Louisa; *m* 6 Dec 1866 George Turner and *d* 9 April 1923, leaving issue. He *d* 1910

2 Dorothy Susan; *m* 21 Nov 1861 Maj Herrick Augustus Palmer and *d* 9 Jan 1914, leaving issue (*see* PALMER, Bt, of Carlton)

3 Gwendoline Frances; *m* 3 Oct 1883 Arthur Vores, MRCS, and *d* 11 June 1906, leaving issue

Sir ARTHUR *d* 11 May 1890; his gs,

Sir Arthur Grey Hazlerigg, 13th Bt, and **1st Baron Hazlerigg**, of Noseley, Co Leicester (UK), so *cr* 12 Feb 1945, JP; Ld Lt and custos rotulorum Leics, High Sheriff 1909, CC Leics 1906 (Chm 1922–24), Memb Billesdon RDC, Chm QS, Pres Roy Ag Soc 1931, Chm Cncl Ag for England 1932, KStJ; *educ* Eton and Trin Coll Cambridge (BA 1901); Lt RNVR 1915–16, Capt Gen List 1916–18, Hon Capt RAF 1918, Hon Col 115th Field Regt RA (TA) 1940, served Cmmn Coroners and Advsy Ctee, Regnl 18B, Dep Chm Coalite and Chemical Products Ltd; *b* 17 Nov 1878; *m* 14 July 1903 Dorothy Rachel (*d* 18 Sept 1972), est dau of John Henry Buxton (*see* BUXTON, Bt), and *d* 25 May 1949, leaving:

1 ARTHUR GREY HAZLERIGG, **2nd and present Baron Hazlerigg**

2 +Thomas Heron [The Hon Thomas Hazlerigg, Caflida, Klosters, Switzerland]; *b* 17 Jan 1914; *educ* Eton and Trin Coll Cambridge (BA 1935); Maj Leics Yeo, F/O RAFVR WW II ; *m* 1st 28 March 1942 (*divorce* 1956) Audrey Cecil (*d* car crash 1994), dau of Maj Cecil Robert Bates, DSO, MC (*see* BATES, Bt, of Bellefield, Gyrn Castle and Manydown); *m* 2nd 31 Jan 1957 (*divorce* 1974) Doussa (*d* by 1 Oct 1997), formerly w of Maj Harold Stanley Cayzer (*see* CAYZER, Bt), and dau of Fahmy Bey Wissa, of Remleh, Egypt; *m* 3rd 1979 *Anne Frances Roden, er dau of Capt Roden Henry Victor Buxton, CBE, RN (*see* BUXTON, Bt), and formerly w of Henry Winterstein Gillespie, MD, and by his 1st w has:

(1) +Rupert Heron [Rupert Hazlerigg Esq, 94 Elms Rd, London SW4]; *b* 14 Jan 1943; *educ* Eton and London U; *m* 1979 *Caroline, est dau of John Burkinshaw Fitzwilliams and formerly w of John Hugh Chetwynd (*see* CHETWYND, V), and has issue:

1a *Cecilia; *b* 1980

2a *Alexandra; *b* 8 Mar 1983

(2) +Simon Martival [Maj Simon Hazlerigg, 128 Castelnau, London SW13 9ET]; *b* 14 April 1945; *educ* Eton; Maj (TA) 15th/19th King's Roy Hus 1964–68, Capt RARO 1972; *m* 1984 *Caroline Margaret Mary, yr dau of Edward Ahlberg, OBE, and has issue:

1a *Antonia Margot; *b* 23 Oct 1985

2a *Alice Olivia; *b* 11 June 1987

3 +Robert Maynard [The Hon Robert Hazlerigg, Cottons Field Farm, Noseley, Billesdon, Leics LSE7 9EB]; *b* 21 July 1916; *educ* Eton and Trin Coll Cambridge (BA 1938), QALAS, Maj RA (TA) WW II; *m* 9 Jan 1942 *Rose, dau of Charles Cox, and has issue:

(1) *Rosemary Maynard [Mrs Malcolm Connell, 18 Kenilworth Ave, London SW19 7LW]; *b* 26 Nov 1942; *educ* Edin U (MA 1964); *m* 25 Sept 1965 *Malcolm John George Connell, BSc, er s of Frank James Connell, ARIBA, BA, of Edinburgh, and has issue:

1a *Emma Aridue Henrietta; *b* 17 June 1972

(2) *Gillian Henrietta Jean [Mrs Maurice Bradley, 9 Church St, Northboro, Peterborough]; *b* 29 March 1946; *m* 1974 *Maurice Bradley, and has issue:

1a *Robert William; *b* 1987

1a *Jessica Mary; *b* 1988

1 Rachel Elizabeth; *b* 22 June 1904; *m* 17 April 1928 Lt-Col Anthony Charles Ward Kimpton, Herts Yeo, and had:

(1) *Anthony Andrew Ward, md Kimpton Bros; *b* 15 July 1931; *educ* Eton and Trin Coll Camb; *m* 12 Dec 1964 *Kathleen Margaret, yr dau of Maj James Stockley Sinnott, of Tetbury, Glos, and has issue:

1a *Archibald James Sinnott; *b* 25 Aug 1969

1a *Melissa Emily; *b* 7 Sept 1967

(1) *Rosamond Mary [Mrs Neil Mills, Upton Grey House, Upton Grey, Basingstoke, Hants; 38 Lower Belgrave Street, SW1]; *b* 25 Jan 1929; *m* 17 June 1950 *Neil McLay Mills and has:

1a *Mark Oliver McLay; *b* 22 June 1955; *educ* Eton

1a *Jemima Rachel McLay; *b* 11 June 1953

2a *Rosamond Cornelia McLay; *b* 21 Sept 1957

(2) *Diana Rachel [Mrs Diana Collins, St Mark's Vicarage, Gillingham, Kent]; *b* 15 July 1931; *m* 30 April 1955 *Rev John Theodore Cameron Bucke Collins, only s of Rev Harry Rawle Collins, and has:

1a *Andrew Dominic John Bucke; *b* 26 Dec 1956

1a *Richenda Rachel; *b* 15 Sept 1959

(3) Patricia Hazel; *b* 9 Jan 1940; *d* unm 5 May 1965

2 Dorothy Joan; *b* 29 Aug 1905; *m* 25 Oct 1930 James Nathaniel Bosanquet Alexander, er s of Edward Bruce Alexander, CMG, of Ripsley House, Liphook, Hants, and *d* 10 Nov 1962, leaving issue. He *d* 12 Nov 1964

3 Edith Bridget, JP (Leics 1954), Sr Cdr ATS WW II; *b* 30 March 1908

HEAD, Viscount

Arms: Sa. a chevron arg. between two unicorn's heads couped in chief, and in base as many arrows in saltire enfiled by a ducal coronet or. **Crest:** A unicorn's head couped sa., armed and crined or, between two arrows erect, points downwards or. **Supporters:** On either side a Staffordshire terrier sa., gorged with a dog collar or. **Motto:** Study quiet. **Creation:** V. (UK) 2 Aug 1960.

THE 2ND VISCOUNT HEAD, of Throope, Wilts (Richard Antony Head) [The Rt Hon The Viscount Head, Throope Manor, Bishopstone, Wilts SP5 4BA]; *b* 27 Feb 1937; *s f* 1983; *educ* Eton and RMA Sandhurst; Capt Life Gds 1957–66, farmer, racehorse trainer 1968–83; *m* 11 May 1974 *Alicia Brigid, er dau of Julian John William Salmond (*see* LUCAS OF CRUDWELL, B), and has issue:

1 +HENRY JULIAN; *b* 30 March 1980

2 +George Richard; *b* 1982

1 *Sarah Georgiana; *b* 1984

Lineage: JOHN HEAD, of Bury St Edmunds, Suffolk; *m* Grace — and *d* by 26 April 1647, having had, with two yr sons (Ambrose; Abraham) and a dau (Sara):

JOHN HEAD, of Bury St Edmunds; *d* by 23 Nov 1689, having had, with an est s (John, of Bury St Edmunds), a yst s (Benjamin) and two daus (Judith; Sarah):

SAMUEL HEAD, of Bury St Edmunds; *bur* 26 Sept 1727, having had with, other issue, including an est s (Samuel, of Bury St Edmunds, *m* Lydia — and was *bur* 27 Oct 1745, having had issue), two yst sons (Jeremy, *d* 1726; Benjamin) and a dau (Judith):

THOMAS HEAD, of Bury St Edmunds; *m* Anne 1 and *d* 8 Sept 1744, having had, with other issue, including two er sons (Benjamin, *b* 8 Sept 1716, *m* Alice — (*d* 22 Jan 1745) and *d* 1759, having had issue; Thomas, *b* 20 Nov 1719, *bur* 14 March 1784) and three daus (Martha, *m* 18 March 1763 Thomas Hemming, of Ipswich; Frances, *b* 14 Oct 1733, *m* —Fry; Mary, *b* 12 Aug 1736, *m* —Lambe):

JOHN HEAD, of Ipswich; *b* 28 Aug 1731; *m* Anne — (*d* 23 July 1813 aged 83) and *d* 17 Oct 1782, leaving:

1 JOHN

2 Benjamin; *b* 28 June 1763

3 Joshua; *b* 10 June 1768; *m* Isabella — (*d* 17 Oct 1841 aged 68) and *d* 17 May 1817, leaving issue

1 Anne; *b* 10 June 1758; *m* 10 Aug 1779 John Warder, of Bury Street, London, and had issue

2 Elizabeth; *b* 7 March 1769; *m* 5 Oct 1796 Richard Tapper Cadbury, of Birmingham, and had issue

The est son,

JOHN HEAD, of Ipswich; *b* 7 Sept 1759; *m* 1st Mary (*d* 9 April 1792), dau of — Leaman, of Norwich; *m* 2nd 13 Nov 1764 Caroline (*d* 14 Dec 1795), dau of Daniel Bell, of Stamford Hill, Middx, and *d* 10 April 1812, having had by his 1st w, with other issue:

JEREMIAH HEAD, of Ipswich; *b* 24 Jan 1789; *m* 12 May 1831 Mary (*d* 13 June 1882 aged 82), dau of Thomas Howard, of St Paul's Churchyard, London, and *d* 24 Feb 1866, leaving:

1 John, of Ipswich; *b* 8 Feb 1882; *m* 27 Sept 1864 Alice Catherine, dau of William Venn, of Allington House, Tottenham, Middx, and had issue:

(1) John Reginald, of Hans Place, Chelsea; *b* 15 July 1868; *m* 28 Jan 1896 Sybil (*d* 15 July 1933), yst dau of Charles Hermann Goschen (*see* GOSCHEN, V), and *d* 15 May 1949, leaving:

1a (Sybil) Ursula; *m* 7 Feb 1922 Sir Edward Robert Micklem, and *d* 22 Sept 1970, leaving issue. He *d* 13 May 1952

(1) Alice Mary; *b* 12 Aug 1865; *m* 17 Aug 1887 Maj Hon Douglas Alfred Tollemache, 8th s of 1st Baron Tollemache (*qv*), and *d* 5 Oct 1959, leaving issue

(2) Edith Beatrice; *b* 12 Dec 1866; *d* unm 25 March 1962

(3) Muriel Comber; *b* 11 Oct 1876; *m* 26 April 1906 Hugh Richard Bromley Davenport, yst s of William Bromley Davenport, of Capesthorne, Cheshire, and *d* 1956, leaving issue. He *d* 23 May 1954

2 Thomas Howard, of Stockton-on-Tees, Co Durham, and Axminster, Devon; *b* 30 March 1833; *m* 17 April 1860 Eleanor Jane (*d* 11 Aug 1890), dau of William Walker, of Sunderland, and was *bur* 11 July 1880, leaving:

(1) Stanley Howard; *b* 26 July 1869

(2) George William; *b* 22 Oct 1871

(3) Thomas Howard, of Forest Hill, Kent; *b* 26 Aug 1875; *m* 28 July 1900 Jane (*d* 25 Aug 1963), dau of Alexander Baxter, of W Hartlepool, and had:

1a *Geoffrey

2a *Eric

1a *Jean

3 HENRY, of whom presently

4 Jeremiah, of Coatham, Yorks; MICE; *b* 11 July 1835; *m* 26 Sept 1860 Rebecca Ingram (*d* 1 Sept 1899), dau of Thomas Wrightson (*see* WRIGHTSON, Bt), and *d* 10 March 1899, having had issue:

(1) William Howard; *b* 28 Sept 1864; *m* 2 Sept 1901 Zillyan Virginia, dau of Robert Aymer, of Denver, Colorado

(2) Archibald Potter; MICE; *b* 4 Aug 1866; *m* 14 June 1892 Mary, dau of Alfred Octavius Hill, of St Petersburg, Russia, and had issue:

1a Alfred Howard; *b* 5 Oct 1899

1a Gladys Amy; *b* 28 Jan 1894

2a Marguerite Mary; *b* 21 March 1897

3a *Bessie May; *b* 2 May 1901

(3) Alfred Wrightson; *b* 7 Feb 1868; *d* 30 May 1872

(4) Benjamin Wrightson; MA Cantab; *b* 12 May 1875

(1) Mary Ingram; *b* 16 Oct 1862; *m* 29 Aug 1899 Colin Campbell, of Weston-super-Mare, and *d* 5 Nov 1904, leaving issue

(2) Rebecca Helen Gilchrist; *b* 11 June 1870; *d* 17 Oct 1889

(3) Kathleen Campbell; *b* 4 July 1872

5 George Frederick; MA Cantab, Vicar Clifton 1897–1911, Hon Canon Bristol 1900; *b* 26 Aug 1836; *educ* Caius Coll Camb; *m* 3 Aug 1865 May Henrietta (*d* 1912), dau of Capt Charles Nelson Bolton, RN, of Stoke Damerel, Devon, and *d* 14 April 1912, having had issue:

(1) George Herbert, JP E R Yorks; barrister Inner Temple, Co Ct Judge; *b* 13 April 1869; *educ* Repton and Pembroke Coll Cambridge (MA); *m* 1913 Geraldine Marie, yst dau of Maj-Gen Henry Pipon, CB, Govr Tower London, and *d* 11 Feb 1927, leaving issue

(2) Charles Stanley; *b* 16 Nov 1871; *d* Aug 1873

(3) Frederick Waldegrave (Most Rev), MC and bar; Archbp Melbourne 1929–41, Chaplain to HM GEORGE V 1922–29, CF WW I; *b* 18 April 1874; *educ* Repton and Emmanuel Coll Cambridge (MA 1900, Life Fell 1927); *m* 1904 Edith Mary Colman (*d* 27 April 1962) and *d* 18 Dec 1941, leaving issue:

(1) Annie Georgina; *b* 16 Dec 1867

6 Charles Arthur, of Hartburn Hall, Stockton-on-Tees, JP, DL Co Durham and N R Yorks; *b* 21 May 1838; *m* 1st 30 Sept 1875 Justina Charlotte (*d* 9 March 1904), widow of Thomas Green, of Athelington and Wilby, Suffolk, and dau of Peter Bartholomew Long, of Ipswich; *m* 2nd 14 Dec 1906 Edith, dau of James Henry Crawford, Bombay CS, and by his 1st w had issue:

(1) Arthur Falkland Howard; *b* 7 June 1879

(1) Doris Justina; *b* 17 June 1877

(2) Joan de Lande; *b* 3 June 1881; *m* 28 Feb 1905 John Russell Hanson, of Southend, Middlesbrough, Yorks

7 Albert Alfred, of Wimbledon and Bury Hill House, Andover, Hants; *b* 4 Sept 1844; *m* 15 Feb 1876 Caroline (*d* 26 Oct 1904), dau of Cornelius Hanbury, and *d* 31 Oct 1928, having had issue:

(1) Albert Hanbury; *b* 23 Nov 1876; *d* 14 Jan 1892

(2) Alfred; *b* 23 Jan 1878; *m* 1st 14 Sept 1904 Mary Catherine (*d* 28 May 1913), dau of Rev Charles Waltman; *m* 2nd 11 July 1917 Katherine Anette Gabb (*d* 25 Feb 1958), and *d* 3 Jan 1950, having by his 1st w had:

1a *Albert Hanbury (Rev); *b* 4 June 1908; *m* 23 June 1934 *Florence May Walker Wood, and has issue:

1b *Ian Walker Hanbury, CEng, MIMechE; *b* 3 June 1938; *m* 30 June 1962 *Angela Mary, dau of J F Tilden, and has:

1c *Christopher Ian Hanbury; *b* 10 Sept 1964

2c *Andrew James Hanbury; *b* 4 Dec 1968

1c *Jacqueline Mary; *b* 3 April 1966

2b *Nicholas Hanbury; *b* 3 Aug 1944; *m* 4 June 1966 *Margaret, er dau of Victor Kilgour, and has issue:

1c *Carol Margaret; *b* 18 July 1967

2c *Lisa Anne; *b* 22 Nov 1968

1b *Gabrielle Annette [Mrs John Lang, Frampton House, Winterbourne, Dorset]; *b* 21 April 1936; *m* 21 April 1958 *Dr John Richard Lang, and has:

1c *David John; *b* 23 Feb 1959

2c *Stephen Richard; *b* 30 May 1961

3c *Simon; *b* 9 Nov 1962

2b *Lynette May [Mrs Bernard Davenport, 418 Brincliffe Edge Road, Sheffield 11, Yorks]; *b* 2 Jan 1942; *m* 30 Dec 1967 *Bernard Brian Davenport

1a *Caroline Mary (Mollie); *b* 15 Nov 1911; *m* 30 Sept 1938 *Richard Finch Mowll, MB, BS, MRCS, LRCP, of Eatonden Manor Farm, Stonegate, Wadhurst, Sussex, and has issue:

1b *Richard Hanbury; *b* 24 June 1939; *m* *Carol Ann Cannon

2b *Nicholas Rothwell; *b* 6 March 1944

1b *Carolyn Frances; *b* 5 April 1947

2a *Muriel Elizabeth; *b* 6 May 1913

1 Mary; *b* 29 Sept 1839; *m* 6 May 1863 Rev Colin Campbell, of Weston-super-Mare, and had issue

The 3rd son,

HENRY HEAD, of Old Shoreham, Sussex; *b* 20 July 1834; *m* 11 Oct 1860 Hester, dau of Richard Low Beck, of Stamford Hill, Middx, and had issue:

1 Charles Howard; *b* 28 Dec 1862; *d* 6 Dec 1876

2 Hugh Stanley; *b* 9 June 1864; *d* 4 Nov 1890

3 Francis; *bapt* 22 April 1868; *d* 11 Feb 1905

4 Christopher; *bapt* 16 Jan 1870; *m* 15 Nov 1910 Ethel Georgina Mary (*m* 2nd 20 May 1914 Gen Sir John Philip Du Cane, GCB, RA (*d* 4 April 1947), and *d* 16 Oct 1960 aged 88), est dau of Hillyar David Chapman, of Kilhendre, Salop, and was drowned in the *Titanic* 14 April 1912

5 GEOFFREY, of whom presently

6 John Alban; *bapt* 28 Dec 1873

7 Bernard; *bapt* 13 Feb 1876

8 Henry (Sir), JP Berks, of Hartley Court, nr Reading; ktd 1927, LLD Edinburgh, FRS, MRCS Eng, FRCP Lond Hosp; *b* 4 Aug 1861; *educ* Charterhouse and Trin Coll Cambridge (MA, MD, Hon Fell); *m* 28 April 1904 Mary Ruth (*d* 1939), dau of Rev Anthony Mayhew, MA Oxford, and *d* 8 Oct 1940

1 Rachel Mary; *b* 26 Aug 1865; *d* 19 Jan 1870

2 Katherine; *b* 17 Sept 1866; *d* 2 Aug 1869

3 Hester; *bapt* 28 Feb 1875; *m* 28 Aug 1900 Maj-Gen Sir Reginald John Pinney, KCB, DL, JP, of Racedown, nr Crewkerne, Somerset, and had issue. He *d* 18 Feb 1943

The 5th son,

GEOFFREY HEAD; *b* 14 April 1872; *m* 16 Dec 1902 Ethel Daisy (*d* 9 Aug 1965), dau of Arthur Flower, of S Kensington, and *d* 22 Nov 1955, leaving, with a dau (Susan, *b* 28 April 1904, *m* 25 Jan 1928 Lt-Col Mark Vanden-Bempde-Johnstone (*see* DERWENT, B) and *d* 1993, leaving issue):

ANTONY HENRY HEAD, **1st Viscount Head**, of Throope, Wilts (UK), so *cr* 2 Aug 1960, GCMG (1963, KCMG 1961), CBE (1946), MC, PC (1951); *b* 19 Dec 1906; *educ* Eton and RMC Sandhurst; Life Gds: Adj 1934–37, Staff Coll 1939, Bde Maj 20th Gds Bde 1940, Assist Sec CID 1940–41, GSO(2) Gds Armoured Div 1942, Ch Mil Planner Combined Ops 1942–43, Rep (Brig) with Dirs Plans Amphibious Operations 1943–46, MP (C) Carshalton 1945–60, Sec State War 1951–56, Def 1956–57, HC: Fedn Nigeria 1960–63 and Malaysia 1963–66, Tstee Thompson Fndn 1967, Col Cmdt SAS Regt 1968–77, Nat Inst Pres for the Blind 1968–83, OStJ; *m* 23 July 1935 Lady Dorothea (Dot) Louise Ashley-Cooper, OStJ (*d* 1987), 2nd dau of 9th Earl of Shaftesbury (*qv*), and *d* 29 March 1983, leaving issue:

1 RICHARD ANTONY HEAD, **2nd and present Viscount Head**

2 +Simon Andrew [The Hon Simon Head, 155 Cranmer Court, Sloan Ave, London SW3]; *b* 11 Nov 1944; *educ* Eton, Ch Ch Oxford (BA 1966, Sec and Librarian Oxford Union) and Berkeley U California (MA 1969); fought S Dorset (SDP-Lib Alliance) 1983; assist ed *Far East Economic Review* Hong Kong 1966–67, contributor on for affrs *New York Review of Books* 1973–, correspondent *Financial Times* SE Asia 1970–72, New York correspondent *New Statesman* 1970–76

1 *Teresa Mary [The Hon Mrs Haddon, The Granary, Fawler, Oxon OX7 3AH]; *b* 20 June 1938; *m* 29 July 1972 *Richard Deacon Haddon, assist master Eton, Lt RNR, and has had:

(1) *Edward Anthony Deacon; *b* 19 June 1973

(2) Joseph Richard; *b* 9 Dec 1974; *d* 1994 in an accident

(1) *Alice Mary; *b* 9 Dec 1974

2 Josephine; *b* 24 May 1948; *d* 9 Oct 1949

HEAD, Bt

Arms: Arg. a chevron erm. between three unicorn's heads couped sa. **Crest:** A unicorn's head, couped erm. **Motto:** Study quiet.
Creation: Bt. (UK) 14 July 1838.

SIR FRANCIS DAVID SOMERVILLE HEAD, 5TH BT, of Rochester [Sir Francis Head Bt, 63 Chantry View Rd, Guildford, Surrey GU1 3XU]; *b* 17 Oct 1916; *s* f 1924; *educ* Eton and Peterhouse Cambridge (BA 1937); Maj QO Cameron Highrs WW II (wounded, POW), Assist Mil Attaché Helsinki 1948–50; *m* 1st 11 Feb 1950 (*divorce* 1965) Susan Patricia, dau of Arthur Douglas Ramsay, OBE (*see* RAMSAY, Bt), and has issue:

1 +RICHARD DOUGLAS SOMERVILLE [Richard Head Esq, 69 High Rd, Byfleet, Weybridge, Surrey KT14 7QN]; *b* 16 Jan 1951; *educ* Eton, Magdalene Coll Cambridge (BA) and Bristol Poly (BA); *m* 1991 *Edwina, dau of Edward Mansell, of Underwood, Notts

1 *Diana Mary Frances; *b* 22 June 1954; BA; *m* 17 Sept 1983 *Michael Robert Parkin and has issue:

(1) *Zuleika Florence Rosa; *b* 1988

Sir FRANCIS *m* 2nd 25 Jan 1967 *Penelope Marion Acheson, yr dau of Wilfred Archibald Alexander (*see* HAGART-ALEXANDER, Bt)

Lineage: RICHARD HEAD, of Rainham, Kent; yeoman; had:

RICHARD HEAD, of Rochester, Kent; *m* Anne, dau of William Hartridge, of Cranbrooke and had issue:

Sir RICHARD HEAD, 1st Bt (E), so *cr* 19 June 1676; *b c* 1609; MP Rochester 1667–69 and March–July 1679, given by JAMES II an emerald ring (which was stolen from the 7th Bt) for playing host to him in his flight from London 1688; *m* 1st *c* 1640 Elizabeth, dau and coheir of Francis Merrick, Alderman Rochester, and had issue:

1 Francis; barrister; *b c* 1641; *m* 1667 Sarah (*m* 2nd Sir Paul Barrett), only dau of Sir George Ent, MD, and *dvp* 16 Oct 1678, having had:

(1) Sir FRANCIS HEAD, 2nd Bt; *b c* 1670; *educ* Trin Coll Oxford and Middle Temple; *m* 5 May 1692 Margaret, dau and coheir of James Smithsby and gdau of Sir Thomas Smithsby, and *d* Aug 1716, having had, with other issue:

1a Sir RICHARD HEAD, 3rd Bt; *b* 1693; *d* unm May 1721

2a Sir FRANCIS HEAD, 4th Bt; *b c* 1693; *educ* Ch Ch Oxford (MA); *m* June 1726 Mary (*d* 29 Oct 1792), dau and coheir of Sir William Boys, MD, and *dspm* 27 Nov 1768, having had:

1b (Maria) Wilhelmina; *m* 1753 11th Baron Teynham (*qv*) and *dsp* 1758

2b ANNA GABRIELLA; *m* 1st Moses MENDES of London, of whom presently; *m* 2nd Capt Hon John Roper (*see* TEYNHAM, B)

3b Elizabeth Campbell; *b* 1735; *m* 1st 1761 Rev Dr — Lill; *m* 2nd 1778 Capt Sir Charles Field, and *d* 1810, having had issue

3a Rev Sir JOHN HEAD, 5th Bt; *b c* 1702; *educ* Ch Ch Oxford; DD, Rector St George's Canterbury 1730–60, Burmarsh 1737, Pluckley to 1760 and Ickham 1760–69, Vicar Selling 1732, Preb Hereford 1738–69, Archdeacon 1748–69 and Preb 1759–69 Canterbury, Dep Clerk Closet to GEORGE II 1740; *m* 1st *c* 1730 Jane, dau of Rev Peter Leigh by Elizabeth, dau of Hon Thomas Egerton (*see* GREY EGERTON, Bt), and had 10 children (*d* unm & *vp*); *m* 2nd 21 April 1751 Jane, sis of Rev William Geckie, DD, and *dsps* 4 Dec 1769

1a Anne; *b* 1704; *m* Rev William Egerton, LLD, Preb Canterbury

(1) Sarah; *m* John Lynch, of Grove

(2) Elizabeth

2 Henry, whose issue is extinct

3 Merrick; DD; *b* 1644; *m* 1675 Elizabeth, dau of Preb Robert Dixon, and *d* 1686, leaving issue

1 Elizabeth; *m* Sir Robert Faunce

Sir RICHARD *m* 2nd Elizabeth Whilly/Willey, of Wrotham Kent, and had, with other issue:

4 John; London merchant; *m* Anne, dau, and coheir of John Dawes, of London, and *d* 1687, leaving issue:

(1) Dawes, of Ravenstonesdale, Westmorland; *b* 16 April 1682; *educ* Westminster; *m* Jane Taylor and *d* May 1705, having had, with three other children:

1a John; Liverpool merchant; *b c* 1701; *m* Hannah, dau of Rev Edmund Wickins, Rector Kirby Thore, Westmorland, and *d* 1739, having had, with an er s (*d* unm):

1b Sir EDMUND HEAD, 6th Bt; *b* 1733; emigrated to America, merchant Charleston, SC, *c* 1764, Pres Charleston Court Trade and Commerce, selected memb of Congress on outbreak of War of Independence but was a loyalist so banished and his property forfeit; returned to London by 1794; *m* 1st by 1771 Mary (*d* 12 June 1775), only dau of Daniel Raineau, of Dublin, and had issue; *m* 2nd 12 May 1796 Dorothy, dau of Maximilian Western, of Cokethorpe, Oxon, Dir HEICS, and *d* without further issue 21 Nov 1796; his 2nd s by his 1st w:

1c Rev Sir JOHN HEAD, 7th Bt; *b* 3 Jan 1773; *educ* Magdalen Coll Oxford and Lincoln's Inn; Rector Rayleigh Essex, bought the Wiarton Place estate, Boughton Monchelsea, Kent, by 1801; *m* 8 Oct 1801 Jane, dau of Thomas Walker, of Russell Place, Fitzrovia, and *d* 4 Jan 1838, leaving an only s:

1d Sir EDMUND WALKER HEAD, 8th and last Bt, KCB (1860), PC (1857); *b* 1805; *educ* Winchester and Oriel Coll Oxford; Fell and Pncpl Postmaster and Tutor Merton Coll 1830–37, Oxford U examiner 1834–39, Assist Poor Law Commr 1836–41, Commr 1841–47, Govr New Brunswick 1847–54 and Canada 1854–61, poet, author: *The Handbook of Spanish Painting*; *m* 27 Nov 1838 Anna Maria, day of Rev Philip Yorke (gs of 1st Earl of Hardwicke, *qv*), and *dspms* 28 Jan 1868, when the btcy expired

Sir RICHARD *m* 3rd Anne (*d* 21 Feb 1713), widow of John Boys, of Hyde, Kent, and dau of Ven William Kingsley, DD, Archdeacon Canterbury, and *d* 18 Sept 1689 without further issue

The 4th Bt's son-in-law,

MOSES MENDES, of London (gs of Fernando Mendes, who left Portugal for England and was court physician to CHARLES II's consort CATHERINE OF BRAGANZA); *m* 1753 Anna Gabriella (*d* 1771), 2nd dau and coheir of Sir Francis Head, 4th Bt (*see* above), and had:

1 FRANCIS MENDES later HEAD, of St Andrew's Hall, Norfolk; *b* 1755; *m* 1779 Justina Maria (*m* 2nd 29 Jan 1788 Gen Andrew Cowell), 2nd dau and eventual coheir of Sir Thomas Stepney, 6th Bt, and had:

(1) Frances; *b* 1780; *m* 1 Sept 1806 Rev Hon George Herbert (*see* CARNARVON E), and *d* 2 Feb 1862

2 James Roper MENDES later HEAD; *b* 1757; *m* 29 March 1781 Frances Anne, dau of George Burges by Anne, only dau of 13th Lord Somerville (*dormant* since 1870, but *see* 1970 edn), and *d* 28 Nov 1814, leaving, with other issue:

(1) George (Sir); Dep Kt Marshal to TM WILLIAM IV and QUEEN VICTORIA; *b* 1782; *d* unm 2 May 1855

(2) James; Capt HEICS; *b* 1790; *m* 23 July 1821 Cecilia Martha Harvey (*d* 31 July 1847), 3rd dau of Hon Robert Lindsay of Balcarres (*see* CRAWFORD and BALCARRES, E), and *d* 26 Aug 1824, leaving issue:

1a Elizabeth Lindsay; *m* 21 Oct 1844 Sir Nathaniel Alexander Staples, 10th Bt (*qv*), and *d* 4 Dec 1907, having had issue

(3) FRANCIS BOND (Sir), **1st Bt**

(4) Henry Erskine (Rev); Rector Feniton, Devon; *b* 9 Jan 1794; *m* 15 Dec 1823 Elizabeth Margaret (*d* 29 Nov 1873), dau of Christopher Flood, and *d* 17 May 1860, leaving:

1a Margaret Elizabeth; *m* 16 Nov 1865 Rev Edward Geoghegan, MA, and *d* 1908

MOSES and ANNA GABRIELLA MENDES's gs,

Sir Francis Bond Head, 1st Bt (UK), so *cr* 14 July 1838, KCH, PC; Maj RE, Lt-Govr Upper Canada 1835–38; *b* 1 Jan 1793; *m* 20 May 1816 Julia Valenza (*d* 23 March 1879), sis of 17th Lord Somerville (*see* 1970 edn), and had issue:

1 FRANCIS SOMERVILLE (Sir), **2nd Bt**

2 Henry Bond; Capt 2nd Dragoon Gds; *b* 27 April 1819; *d* unm 1887

3 George (Rev), MA; Rector Aston Somerville, Glos; *b* 24 July 1822; *d* unm 20 May 1893

1 Julia Maria Burges; *m* 1 Aug 1843 Capt Robert Williamson Ramsay, 42nd Highrs, and *d* 20 Nov 1909. He *dsp* 1886

Sir FRANCIS *d* 25 July 1875; his est son,

Sir Francis Somerville Head, 2nd Bt; Bengal CS; *b* 26 May 1817; *m* 12 Dec 1843 Mary Jane (*d* 15 Nov 1887), dau of Robert Garnett, of Wyreside, Lancs, and had issue:

1 ROBERT GARNETT (Sir), **3rd Bt**

2 Francis Somerville, JP Herefs; *b* 30 June 1846; *m* 16 April 1891 Charlotte Anne (*d* 14 March 1936), widow of Lt-Col John Fletcher Hathorn and dau of Sir John Dick-Lauder, 8th Bt (*qv*), and *d* 2 April 1941

3 Richard Lyon; *b* 8 Jan 1849; *d* 13 Aug 1922

4 James HEAD later CAMERON-HEAD (roy licence 21 Feb 1911), of Inverailort Castle, Inverness-shire, JP; Capt Middx Yeo Cav and 3rd Bn The Buffs, V-Chm Union Castle Line; *b* 25 April 1851; *m* 8 Sept 1888 Christian Helen Jane, JP (*d* 13 April 1941), est dau and coheir of Duncan Cameron of Inverailort, DL, Inverness-shire, and *d* 10 Dec 1922, leaving issue:

(1) Francis Somerville Cameron, JP Inverness-shire; barrister Inner Temple 1921, memb Roy Co Archers, CStJ; *b* 17 Nov 1896; *educ* Wellington and Balliol Coll Oxford (BA 1920, MA 1949); *m* 9 June 1942 Lucretia Pauline Rebecca Ann (*d* 22 June 1997), dau of Charles Bennett Farrell, of Leiter Fearn, Invergarry, and *dsp* 14 May 1957

(1) Christian Mary Cameron; *b* 17 Nov 1896; *d* unm 9 March 1956

5 Frederick William; barrister; *b* 5 Jan 1854; *m* 14 Nov 1882 Jessie (*d* 21 Sept 1954 aged 94), dau of Hon John Donald McLean, MLA Queensland, and *dsp* 29 June 1886

1 Mary Valenza; *d* 22 Dec 1864

Sir FRANCIS *d* 26 Aug 1887; his est son,

Sir Robert Garnett Head, 3rd Bt; *b* 18 March 1845; *educ* Marlborough; *m* 5 Aug 1880 Florence Julia (*d* 30 Aug 1931), dau of Robert John Pollock, 2nd s of Sir Frederick Pollock, 1st Bt (*qv*), and had:

1 ROBERT POLLOCK SOMERVILLE (Sir), **4th Bt**

2 George Burges Digby; AMIMechE, engr in Egyptian Govt Service, Exec Enger PWD India, Dep Dir Industries Punjab; *b* 2 June 1888; *educ* Wellington; *m* 1st 11 Oct 1912 Annie (*d* 25 Sept 1940), dau of William Stockill, of Tansgate; *m* 2nd 5 Jan 1946 *Olive Peggy [Mrs George Head, 212 Glenhaven, PO Box 905-932, Garsfontein, Pretoria 0042, S Africa], yst dau of George Baker, of Ealing, and *d* 10 Aug 1963, having by his 1st w had issue:

(1) Robert Digby, DSC and bar; Cdr RN (Fleet Air Arm) WW II (despatches three times); *b* 10 June 1917; *m* 23 Oct 1946 *Lorraine [Mrs Lorraine Fallon, Balgay, Dewlands Way, Verwood, Dorset BH21 6JN], ARRC (*m* 2nd 22 Sept 1967 (*divorce* 1973) William Gerald Fallon), yr dau of T Walter Dowding, and was *k* flying on duty 10 Jan 1956, leaving:

1a *Pauline Anne [Mrs Graham d'Arcy, Brick Cottage, Gorsely, Ross-on-Wye]; *b* 16 May 1948; *m* 19– *Graham d'Arcy

2a *Linda Mary [Mrs Michael Bobak, 11 Berkeley Place, London SW19 4NN]; *b* 23 May 1951; *m* 1st 1971 (*divorce* 1976) Paul Richard Wilder and has issue:

1b *Robert James; *b* 1972

1a (cont.) Mrs Linda Wilder *m* 2nd (*divorce* 1980) Stephen Robert Whitby; *m* 3rd 1982 *Michael Benjamin Bobak and by him has issue:

1b *Danielle Anne; *b* 1982

(1) Rosemary Gabriella; *b* 30 Sept 1920; *d* 23 June 1988

1 Florence Mary; *m* 17 July 1922 Percy Meyrick Morris-Davies, VD, Capt QVO Sappers and Miners (*d* 1 Jan 1934), 2nd s of Morris Davies, DL, JP, of Cards, and *d* 3 July 1979

Sir ROBERT *d* 6 March 1907; his er son,

Sir Robert Pollock Somerville Head, 4th Bt; *b* 7 April 1884; *educ* Wellington; FRGS, Attaché Dip Serv 1905, Lisbon 1907, Madrid 1907, 3rd Sec 1908, Peking 1911, 2nd Sec Vienna 1914, Petrograd 1914, Peking 1917, 1st Sec 1919, Berlin 1920; *m* 27 Oct 1915 Grace Margaret (*d* 26 May 1967), yr dau of David Robertson, of Glasgow, and *d* 21 June 1924, leaving issue:

1 Sir FRANCIS DAVID SOMERVILLE HEAD, **5th and present Bt**

2 +John Kenelm Somerville [John Head Esq, 123 First Street, NW, Medicine Hat, Alberta T1A 6H2, Canada]; WW II in RAMC and Intell Corps; *b* 30 April 1918; *educ* Wellington and Oriel Coll Oxford (BA 1939, MA 1946, DipEd 1947, BEd Calgary); *m* 20 Aug 1942 *Lilah Doreen Prittie Wingfield, dau of Lt-Col Samuel James Chatterton Prittie Perry (*see* POWERSCOURT, V), and has:

(1) +Patrick John Somerville [Patrick Head Esq, 1406-20 Ave, N Lethbridge, Alberta, T1H 4W3 Canada]; *b* 4 Oct 1943; *educ* Medicine Hat Sch; *m* 1971 (*divorce* 1986) Karen Carla, dau of Emanuel Karl Schaufele, of Schuler, Alberta, Canada; *m* 2nd 13 May 1995 *Joan, dau of Ezekiel Crawford, of Taber, Alberta, and has had by his 1st w:

1a Derek Carl Somerville; *b* 30 Jan, *d* 1 Feb 1983

1a *Kathleen Patricia [Mrs Neil Jesske, 437 Vancouver Ave N, Saskatoon, Saskatchewan, Canada]; *b* 1974; *m* 18 May 1996 *Neil Jesske, of Schuler, Alberta

2a *Sheila Nadine; *b* 1979

(2) +David Charles Somerville [David Head Esq, 2627-49 A St, Edmonton, Alberta T6L 3X2, Canada]; *b* 8 April 1949; *educ* U of Alberta (BSc 1975, BEd 1978); *m* 1978 *Constance Faye, dau of Clifford Schowalter, of Edmonton, and has issue:

1a +Philip Arthur Somerville; *b* 1983

2a +Graeme Douglas Somerville; *b* 1986

1a *Alana Christina; *b* 1991

(1) *Sarah Grace Edith [Mrs Ronald Zezulka, 331 Queensland Rd SE, Calgary T2J 3SA, Canada]; *b* 3 March 1947; *m* 1972 *Ronald James Zezulka and has:

1a *Michael John Jaroslav; *b* 1977

(2) *Angela Lilah Mary [Mrs Joseph Panter, Box 242, Clyde, Alberta T0G 0PO, Canada]; *b* 8 April 1949; *m* 1973 *Joseph Andrew Panter and has:

1a *David James; *b* 1974; *m* 16 Aug 1997 *Christine, dau of Karl Beinert, of Edmonton, Alberta

1a *Jennifer Anne; *b* 1979

1 *Angela Grace Mary [Mrs Henry Granlund, Little Weekhayne, Southleigh, Devon EX13 6JA]; *b* 22 Jan 1922; *m* 8 March 1941 Henry Paddison Granlund, DSC (*d* 1993), Lt RNVR, yr s of Rev Canon Oscar Frederick Granlund, of Alnmouth, Northumberland, and has issue:

(1) *Hew Richard Paddison [Hew Granlund Esq, 7 Bell Hill Ridge, Petersfield, Hants GU32 2DZ]; *b* 14 July 1943; *educ* Radley and RNC Dartmouth; BA, CDipAF; Lt-Cdr RN; *m* 1977 *Gillian Hazel, dau of Rev Canon J J Cresswell, of Eastleach, Turville, Glos, and has:

1a *Charles Richard Alexander; *b* 1979

2a *Angus Gordon Howard; *b* 1981

(1) *Karen Mary [Mrs Jeremy New, 3 Bythorn St, London SW9]; *b* 24 Sept 1945; *m* 1981 *Jeremy Patrick New

(2) *Margaret Jane [Mrs Christopher Peters, Fir Tree House, Rodborough Common, Stroud, Glos GL5 5BJ]; *b* 23 April 1950; *m* 1st 1973 (*divorce* 1977) Anthony Hewett-Hicks; *m* 2nd 18 March 1988 *Christopher Ian Peters and by him had:

1a *George Duncan; *b* 30 April 1990

1a (Angela) Felicity; *b* 26 Aug 1991; *d* 20 Jan 1993

HEADFORT

Arms: 1st and 4th, erm. on a chief gu. a fleur-de-lys between two boar's heads, couped and erect or (for TAYLOUR); 2nd, vert a pegasus courant, wings addorsed erm., a chief or with a crescent for difference (for QUIN); 3rd, arg. two bendlets gu., on a chief az. a lion passant of the first. **Crest:** A naked arm, couped at the shoulder embowed, holding an arrow ppr. **Supporters:** Dexter, a lion guardant or; sinister, a leopard guardant ppr.; both collared and chained arg. **Motto:** *Consequitur quodcunque petit* ('He attains whatever he seeks'). **Creations:** Bt. (I) 12 June 1704, B. (I) 6 Sept 1760 (Headfort of Headfort) and (UK) 10 Sept 1831 (Kenlis of Kenlis), V. (I) 12 April 1762, E. (I) 24 Oct 1766, M. (I) 29 Dec 1800.

THE 6TH MARQUESS OF HEADFORT, Earl of Bective, of Bective Castle, **Viscount Headfort**, of Headfort, Co Meath, **Baron Headfort**, of Headfort, Co Meath, **Baron Kenlis of Kenlis**, Co Meath, and a **Baronet** (Sir Thomas Geoffrey Charles Michael Taylour, Bt) [The Most Hon The Marquess of Headfort, Ellerslie, Crosby, IoM]; *b* 20 Jan 1932, *s f* 1960; *educ* Stowe and Christ's Coll Cambridge (BA 1955, MA 1959); ALAS 1955, FRICS, FIArb, Act P/O RAFVR 1952, 2nd Lt Life Gds 1950, commercial pilot, Freeman Guild Air Pilots and Air Navigators; *m* 1st 2 May 1958 (*divorce* IoM 1969) Hon Elizabeth Angela Veronica Rose Nall-Cain, only dau of 2nd Baron Brocket (*qv*), and has:

1 +(THOMAS MICHAEL RONALD) CHRIS(TOPHER), *Earl of Bective* [Earl of Bective, 8 Milner St, London SW3 2PU; Thodyn, Bayview, Ramsey, IoM]; *b* 10 Feb 1959; *educ* Harrow and RAC Cirencester; estate agent, ptnr Bective & Davidson, of Chelsea; *m* 1987 *Susan Jane, er dau of C Anthony Vandervell, and has:

(1) +Thomas Rupert Charles Christopher, *Baron Kenlis*; *b* 18 June 1989

(2) +Henry; *b* 1991

(1) *Natasha; *b* 6 May 1997

1 *Rosanagh Elizabeth Angela Mary [The Lady Rosanagh Dent, Newbarn Farm, Ditchley Park, Chipping Norton, Oxon]; *b* 20 Jan 1961; *m* 30 July 1983 *Andrew Congreve Dent and has:

(1) *Michael; *b* 1989

(1) *Iona Katherine; *b* 1991

2 *Olivia Sheelin Davina Anne [The Lady Olivia Waddy, Milburn, RDZ Cheviot, North Canterbury, New Zealand]; *b* 4 Oct 1963; *m* 1986 *David Charles Henry Waddy and has:

(1) *Veronica; *b* 1993

(2) *Davinia; *b* 1996

The 6th MARQUESS *m* 2nd 11 Nov 1972 *Virginia, dau of Mr Justice Nable, of Manila

Lineage: THOMAS TAYLOR, of Ringmore, Battle, Sussex; *b c* 1559; bought land at Skircorner, Stonham, Sussex; *d* Sept 1629, having had, with a 2nd s (Nicholas, of Watling, Sussex, *dsp*):

JOHN TAYLOR, of Thorndance, Battle, which he bought 1627; *b c* 1593; *d* 1658, leaving, with four daus (*d* young):

THOMAS TAYLOR; *b c* 1631; went to Ireland 1653 with his friend and college companion Sir William Petty (*see* LANSDOWNE, M), with whom he undertook the cartographic project known as the Down Survey (although the maps were published in Sir William's name alone); sold his English property and bought 1660 land in Ireland, including Kells, Co Meath; Dep Receiver-Gen 1669–70, V-Treasurer and Treasurer-at-War; *m* 1658 Anne (*d* 4 June 1687), dau of William Axtell, of Berkhamsted, Herts, and *d* 1 Aug 1682, having had, with two other sons (*d* young), and a dau (Anne, *m* 1686 Sir Nicholas Acheson, 4th Bt; *see* GOSFORD, E):

Sir Thomas Taylor, 1st Bt (I), so *cr* 12 June 1704, PC (I 1726); *b* 20 July 1662; MP Kells 1692–93, 1695–99, 1713–14 and 1727–36; *m* 20 June 1682 Anne (*d* 22 Aug 1710), dau of Sir Robert Cotton, 1st Bt (*see* COMBERMERE, V), and had, with other issue:

1 THOMAS (Sir), **2nd Bt**

2 James; *b* 10 Jan 1700; *m* 25 Nov 1737 Catharine (*m* 2nd 5 July 1755 5th Earl of Antrim (*qv*) and was *bur* 27 Sept 1794), dau of Thomas Meredith, of Newtown, Co Meath, and *dsps* 1747

1 Salusbury; *bapt* 14 Nov 1687; *m* 1st William FitzGerald, Bp Clonfert; *m* 2nd Brig-Gen James Crofts, illegitimate s of 1st and last Duke of Monmouth (*see* BUCCLEUCH and QUEENSBERRY, D)

Sir THOMAS *d* 1736; his est son,

Sir Thomas Taylo(u)r, 2nd Bt, PC (I 1753); MP Kells 1713–57; *b* 20 Nov 1686; *m* 18 Nov 1714 Sarah, dau of John Graham, of Platten, Co Meath, and *d* by 5 Nov 1757, leaving, with a dau (Henrietta, *m* 24 Feb 1741 Richard Moore, of Barne, Co Tipperary):

Sir Thomas Taylo(u)r, 3rd Bt, and **1st Earl of Bective**, of Bective Castle, Co Meath, so *cr* 24 Oct 1766, as also earlier 6 Sept 1760 BARON HEADFORT, of Headfort, Co Meath, and 12 April 1762 VISCOUNT HEADFORT, of Headfort, Co Meath (all I), KP (1783), PC (I 1785); *b* 20 Oct 1724; *educ* Trin Coll Dublin; MP Kells 1747–60; *m* 4 July 1754 Jane, est dau of Rt Hon Hercules Langford Rowley by Elizabeth, Viscountess Langford in her own right (*see* LANGFORD, B), and had, with two daus:

1 THOMAS, **1st Marquess**

2 Hercules Langford; Maj 5th Dragoon Gds, MP Kells 1781–3 and 1785–90; *b* 9 Sept 1759; *d* unm 20 May 1970

3 Robert; Gen, Col 6th Dragoon Gds, MP Kells 1970–1800; *b* 26 Nov 1760; *d* unm 23 April 1839

4 CLOTWORTHY TAYLO(U)R later ROWLEY, *cr* BARON LANGFORD (*qv*)

5 Henry Edward (Rev); *b* 13 Nov 1768; *m* 10 Feb 1807 Marianne (*d* 22 March 1859), er dau of Hon Richard St Leger (*see* DONERAILE, V), and *d* 7 June 1852, having had, with other issue:

(1) Thomas Edward, PC, of Ardgillan Castle, Co Dublin; *b* 25 March 1811; MP Co Dublin 1841–83, Capt 6th Dragoon Gds, Col Roy Meath Militia, a Ld Treasury 1858–59, Jt Sec Treasury 1866–68, Chllr Duchy Lancaster 1868 and 1874–80; *m* 12 Nov 1862 Louisa Harrington (*d* 9 April 1928), 2nd dau of Rev Hon Hugh Francis Tollemache (*see* TOLLEMACHE, Bt), and *d* 3 Feb 1883, leaving:

1a Edward Richard, of Ardgillan Castle, JP; Capt 3rd Bn Gren Gds; *b* 21 Sept 1863; *m* 9 April 1935 Ada (*d* 26 Nov 1949), dau of William Howe Bodley, and *dsp* 30 March 1938

2a Basil Reginald Hamilton TAYLOR later TAYLOUR (deed poll 1915); *b* 8 April 1865; Capt RN, FRAS, served Egyptian War 1882 and WW I 1915–18, Order Crown Italy; *m* 17 June 1903 Harriet Mary (*d* 8 April 1940), dau of Col Henry B Osgood, of USA, and widow of Maj Paul Clendenin, of USA, and *d* 3 Sept 1936, leaving:

1b Basil Richard Henry Osgood; barrister Gray's Inn 1929, advocate and slr Straits Settlements 1934; *b* 16 March 1904; *educ* Cheltenham; *m* 5 Jan 1935 Gwendoline Edith Marion (*d* 1975), dau of Judge William Evans, and *d* 1969, having had issue:

1c Basil Richard Powys Patrick Jeremy; *b* 5 Oct 1935; *educ* Trin Coll Dublin; *d* following a shooting accident 9 Sept 1956

2c +(Douglas) Terence William Lenthall [Terence Taylour, Esq, Drumman House, Milltownpass, Co Westmeath, Ireland]; *b* 12 March 1939; *m* 1 July 1964 *Marjorie Rosalind, er dau of Rev Robert Bowie Thompson, of Straffan, Co Kildare, and has had:

1d +Edward Terence; *b* 13 Oct 1966; *m* 23 Oct 1993 *Jennifer Anne, dau of Dr Francis Taylor, and has:

1e +Zachary Thomas Henry; *b* 13 Aug 1997

1e *Chloe Louise; *b* 1 May 1995

2d Robert; *b* 9 July 1969; *d* 11 Sept 1982

1d *Kenlis Jean; *b* 24 Jan 1965; *m* 6 Feb 1988 *Haus Holger Bruno, s of Adi Sircoulomb, of Tsumeb, S W Africa

2d *Gwendoline May; *b* 18 Aug 1983

2b Douglas Bective Huntingtower; *b* 10 Oct 1905; *educ* Cheltenham; Ch Engr Lake Copais Co Greece 1945–50, Maj RE WW II 1940–45; *d* unm 1966

3b Edward Winchester Tollemache, DSC and bar; Actg Lt RN WW II (despatches 1940); *b* 1 Jan 1915; *m* 11 Feb 1942 *Dorothea, dau of Vernon Ruscombe Gatcombe, and was *ka* 13 Sept 1942

1b Mary Beatrix Kenlis; *b* 10 Oct 1906; *m* 25 Nov 1933 (Joseph) John Hartland-Swann (*d* 29 Oct 1961), Head Philosophy Dept U of Malaya, and *d* 9 June 1957, leaving issue

3a Wilfrid Doneraile Stanhope; *b* 17 March 1868; *m* 24 Feb 1892 Margaret Annie (*d* 2 Jan 1940), dau of Arthur William Follett Halcombe, of NZ, and *d* 19 Dec 1954, leaving:

1b Lois Cecil Beatrix; *m* 1st 3 Sept 1914 (*divorce* 1921) Frederick Charles Kent; *m* 2nd 21 Jan 1922 (*divorce* 1942) Samuel Aldenton, and had issue

2b Aileen Marjorie, RRC, SRN (1922), Matron QARNNS; *b* 13 June 1895

3b Enid Dorothy; *m* 18 Sept 1922 Noel Whitton, MC (*d* 28 Nov 1924), and had issue

4b Edith Daphne Eunice; *m* 10 Nov 1922 Edward Morton Drummond, G/Capt RAF, Black Watch, and had issue (*see* PERTH, E)

1a Cecil Cornelia Marianne St Leger; *b* 6 Nov 1866; *m* 1 Nov 1893 Lt-Gen Sir Frederick Stanley Maude, KCB, CMG, DSO (*das* 18 Nov 1917), and *d* 15 Feb 1942, leaving issue (*see* HAWARDEN, V)

2a Beatrix Virginia Louisa Tollemache; *b* 6 Nov 1866; *m* 27 July 1889 Maj Randal Skeffington Smyth, Coldstream Gds, and *dsp* 26 Nov 1943

(2) Richard Chambre Hayes (Sir), GCB; Gen, Col Cameron Highrs, Govr RMC Sandhurst 1883–86, Adj-Gen; *b* 19 March 1819; *m* 9 June 1863 Lady Jane Hay (*d* 13 Dec 1920), 5th dau of 8th Marquess of Tweeddale (*qv*), and *d* 6 Dec 1904, leaving issue:

1a Richard Edward Montagu; Capt 3rd Bn E Surrey Regt, Hon Lt, Boer War (medal with three clasps), WW I (two medals, 1915 star); *b* 28 July 1872; *m* 2 June 1921 Florence Mary, only surv dau of John Hart, of Linthorpe, Middlesbrough, and *dsp* 10 April 1953

1a Constance Mary Jane; *m* 16 Feb 1904 Ronald William Murray (*d* 2 Jan 1917), est s of Charles Archibald Murray of Taymount (*see* MANSFIELD and MANSFIELD, E), and *d* 1 Dec 1950
2a Millicent Lilla Harriet; *d* unm Nov 1948
3a Evelyn Beatrice Charlotte; *d* unm 12 June 1944
4a Florence Virginia Mathilde; *d* unm 23 April 1952
(1) Marianne Jane; *b* 24 Oct 1809; *m* 21 April 1873 Hon St John Butler (*see* DUNBOYNE B) and *dsp* 16 April 1874
(2) Louisa Catherine; *b* 15 July 1815; *m* 16 June 1840 Hans Hamilton Woods (*d* 12 June 1879), of Milverton, Co Dublin, and *d* 26 March 1898, leaving issue

The 1st EARL *d* 14 Feb 1795; his est son,

THOMAS TAYLOUR, **1st Marquess of Headfort** (I), so *cr* 29 Dec 1800, KP (1806); *b* 18 Nov 1757; MP Kells 1776–90, Longford 1790–94 and Co Meath 1794–95, Sheriff Co Meath 1786, rep I peer 1801–29, a Ld Bedchamber 1812–29; *m* 5 Dec 1778 Mary (*d* 12 Aug 1842), only dau and heir of George Quin, of Quinsborough, Co Clare, by Mary, dau of Sir Henry Cavendish, 1st Bt (*see* WATERPARK, B), and had, with two daus:

1 THOMAS, **2nd Marquess**
2 George TAYLOUR later QUIN (roy licence 1813); *b* 10 March 1792; *m* 1st 14 April 1814 Lady Georgiana Charlotte (*d* 21 Feb 1823), 2nd dau of 2nd Earl Spencer (*qv*); *m* 2nd 9 Dec 1847 Louisa Mary Isabella (*d* 24 Aug 1872), est dau of Sir John Ramsden, 4th Bt (*qv*), and *d* 6 Feb 1888, having by his 1st w had:
(1) George Thomas; Lt RHG; *b* 16 Feb 1815; *d* unm 23 April 1838
(2) Richard Robert; R-Adml; *b* 23 Aug 1820; *m* 1st 1 June 1852 Selina Catherine Laura (*d* 31 Jan 1867), est dau of Rev David Frederick Markham, Canon Windsor; *m* 2nd 16 June 1868 Georgiana Olivia (*d* 15 Jan 1931), dau of Hon John Boyle (*see* CORK and ORRERY, E), and *d* 22 Sept 1870, having by his 1st w had issue:
1a Catherine Selina Sarah; *d* unm 25 Oct 1919
2a Georgiana Lavinia; *m* 28 June 1881 George Francis Stewart, PC, DL (*d* 12 Aug 1928), of Killiney, Co Dublin, s of James Robert Stewart, DL, of Gortleitragh, Co Dublin, and *d* 13 June 1949, leaving issue
3a Selina Gertrude; *d* unm 15 May 1937
(1) Lavinia Jane; *b* 21 March 1816; *m* 21 Dec 1839 Hon Richard Watson (*see* 1970 edn, SONDES, E), and *d* 20 Feb 1888, leaving issue
(2) Mary; *b* 10 Feb; *d* 14 April 1823

The 1st MARQUESS *d* 24 Oct 1829; his er son,

THOMAS TAYLOUR, **2nd Marquess of Headfort**, KP (1839), PC (I 1835); *b* 4 May 1787; *educ* Harrow and Trin Coll Cambridge; MP (Whig) Co Meath 1812–29, Ld Lt Co Cavan 1831–70, a Ld Bedchamber 1835–37, Col Meath Militia, *cr* 10 Sept 1831 BARON KENLIS OF KENLIS or KELLS, Co Meath (UK), a Ld-in-Waiting 1837–41; *m* 1st 29 Jan 1822 Olivia (*d* 21 July 1834), 2nd dau of Sir John Stevenson, of Dublin, and widow of Edward Tuite Dalton, of Fennar, Co Meath; *m* 2nd 5 Feb 1853 Frances (*d* 2 March 1878), 2nd dau of John Livingstone Martyn, of Co Tyrone, and widow of (a) Sir William Hay Macnaghten, 1st Bt (*qv*); and (b) Col J O McClintock, Bengal Army, and by his 1st w had, with other issue:

1 THOMAS, **3rd Marquess**
2 Robert Conolly; Capt 49th Foot, formerly Scots Fus Gds; *b* 7 Nov 1826; *d* 19 Jan 1851
3 John Henry; Maj-Gen, Lt-Col 94th Foot; *b* 12 Dec 1831; *m* 1st 12 July 1855 Mary Hammond (*d* 14 Jan 1872), dau of Robert Macfarlane, and had issue:
(1) Edward Henry Higginson; *b* 21 June 1860; *m* 6 Oct 1903 Ada Allen (*d* 28 March 1933), est dau of G T Burnett, of New Westminster, BC, and *d* 9 March 1934
(2) John Francis; *b* 11 Oct 1863; *d* 26 Jan 1864
(1) Virginia Maria Mylius; *b* 2 April 1856; *d* unm 11 March 1957
(2) Emma Adelaide Christina; *b* 25 Dec 1857; *m* 28 Nov 1881 Brig-Gen Lionel Godophin Brooke, CB, Connaught Rangers (*see* BROOKEBOROUGH, V), and *dsp* 2 July 1882
(3) Adelaide Mary; *b* 2 Oct 1865; *m* 9 April 1885 R-Adml Uvedale Corbet Singleton, CB (*d* 14 Feb 1910), and *d* 16 March 1950, having had issue
3 (cont.) Maj-Gen John Taylour *m* 2nd 4 Sept 1873 Eliza Winifred Mary (*d* 22 Oct 1928), yst dau of Rev John Llewellin, and *d* 4 Feb 1890, having by her had:
(3) George Ryefield; *b* 13 Feb 1875; Capt Roy Warwicks Regt Boer War 1899–1901 (wounded, despatches twice, medal with six clasps) and 7th Div WW I; *ka* 19 Oct 1914
(4) Alfred Robert TAYLOUR later LLEWELLIN-TAYLOUR (deed poll 17 Feb 1937); *b* 12 May 1877; MA Oxon 1923, barrister Lincoln's Inn 1903, FRSA, FRGS, memb: Holborn 1926–45 and Kensington Borough Cncls 1933–55, Ct Govrs Nat Library Wales, author legal textbooks local govt and public health, Capt 1st Bn London Regt (TF) and Staff Lt 1st Cl BEF WW I (despatches), WW II 1940–44 CD and HG; *m* 1st 12 Aug 1954 Mrs Marjorie Leonore Apperson (*d* 14 July 1968), only child of John Francis Scully, barrister, of Drishane, Co Tipperary; *m* 2nd 19– Bo (*d* 30 March 1998), formerly w of (a) H O P Evans, KS, and (b) H E K Burge, DSC, RM, and *d* 19–
(4) Madeline Llewllin; *b* 6 April 1876; *d* unm 30 June 1951
1 Olivia; *b* 8 Feb 1824; *m* 10 Aug 1853 Rev Frederic Fitzpatrick (*d* 1895), Rector Cloone, Co Leitrim, and *d* 4 Sept 1916, having had issue
2 Mary Juliana; *b* 3 April 1825; *d* unm 26 Sept 1909
3 Virginia Frances Zerlina; *b* 17 March 1828; *m* 16 July 1850 Joseph Sanders (*d* 14 March 1893), of Henley-on-Thames, MP Yarmouth 1848–52, and *dsp* 26 Jan 1922

The 2nd MARQUESS *d* 6 Dec 1870; his est son,

THOMAS TAYLOUR, **3rd Marquess of Headfort**, KP (1885), PC (I 1879); *b* 1 Nov 1822; Sheriff Cos Meath 1844 and Cavan 1846, State Steward to Ld Lt Ireland 1852–53, High Sheriff Westmorland 1853, MP (C) Westmorland 1854–1870, Ld Lt Co Meath 1876–94, Hon Col 4th Bn Princess Victoria's Roy Irish Fus; *m* 1st 20 July 1842 Amelia (*d* 4 Dec 1864), only child of William Thompson, MP, of Underley Hall, Westmorland, and had, with other issue:

1 Thomas, *Earl of Bective*, JP, DL; *b* 11 Feb 1844; *educ* Eton and Ch Ch Oxford; MP (C) Westmorland 1871–85 and Kendal 1885–92, Hon Col 4th Bn Border Regt; *m* 9 Oct 1867 Lady Alice Maria (*d* 25 Feb 1928), only dau of 4th Marquess of Downshire (*qv*), and *dvp* 15 Dec 1893, leaving issue:
(1) Olivia Caroline Amelia, DGStJ; *b* 22 Jan 1869; *m* 27 Jan 1892 Lord Henry Cavendish-Bentinck (*see* PORTLAND, E) and *d* 26 Nov 1939
(2) Evelyn Alice Estelle; *b* 10 Feb 1873; *d* 16 Sept 1875
1 Madeline Olivia Susan; *m* 2 Jan 1873 Hon Charles Crichton (*d* 20 Aug 1918), 2nd s of 3rd Earl of Erne (*qv*), and *d* 27 Jan 1876, leaving issue
2 Isabel Frances; *m* 4 April 1872 Col Sir Fitzroy Talbot Clayton, KCVO, and *d* 17 Nov 1909, leaving issue (*see* CLAYTON, Bt)
3 Florence Jane; *m* 5 Aug 1875 10th Baron Farnham (*qv*) and *d* 16 Aug 1907, having had issue

The **3rd Marquess** *m* 2nd 29 Nov 1875 Emily Constantia (*d* 16 July 1926), est dau of Rev Lord John Thynne (*see* BATH, M) and widow of Capt Eustace John Wilson Patten, 1st Life Gds, est s of 1st Baron Winmarleigh (*see* 1892 edn), and by her had issue:

2 GEOFFREY THOMAS, **4th Marquess**
4 Beatrix, CI, CBE (1920); *b* 6 Jan 1877; *m* 26 Nov 1903 Lt-Col Sir George Frederick Stanley, GCIE, CMG, PC, and *d* 3 May 1944, leaving issue (*see* DERBY, E)

The 3rd MARQUESS *d* 22 July 1894; his only surv son,

GEOFFREY THOMAS TAYLOUR, **4th Marquess of Headfort**, JP, DL Co Meath; *b* 12 June 1878; FZS 1937, Capt Gen List, ADC on personal staff WW I 1915, Lt 2nd Co of London Imp Yeo and 1st Life Gds, Staff Capt 1916–18 (despatches), Senator Irish Free State 1922–28, Pres RHS Ireland 1916–43, Fell Linnean Soc 1929; *m* 11 April 1901 Rosie, actress Gaiety Theatre (*d* 17 Aug 1958), dau of Charles (Chamberlain) Boote, of Luton, Beds, comedian, and had:

1 TERENCE GEOFFREY THOMAS, **5th Marquess**
2 William Desmond; FSA, Capt 2nd Derbyshire Yeo (TA); *b* 3 Jan 1904; *educ* Harrow and Trin Coll Cambridge (BA 1949, MA 1954, PhD 1955, Fell); *d* 19–
1 Millicent Olivia Mary; *m* 28 April 1930 (*divorce* 1936, resumed maiden name 1941) Henry Frederic Tiarks (*m* 2nd 3 Oct 1936 Ina Bell, by whom he was f of Marchioness of Tavistock; *see* BEDFORD, D), est s of Frank Cyril Tiarks, of Foxbury, Chislehurst, Kent, and *d* 24 Dec 1975, having had issue

The 4th MARQUESS *d* 29 Jan 1943; his er son,

TERENCE GEOFFREY THOMAS TAYLOUR, **5th Marquess of Headfort**, TD; *b* 1902; *educ* Harrow and Magdalen Coll Oxford; Capt Warwicks Yeo (TA), ADC to Govr S Australia 1939–40, Staff Capt Australian Mil Forces Victoria 1941–42, War Office Mil Sec's Branch 1943; *m* 1928 Elise Florence (*d* 16 May 1972), dau of James Partridge Tucker, of Devon and Sydney, NSW, and widow of Sir Rupert Turner Havelock Clarke, 2nd Bt, of Rupertswood (*qv*), and *d* 24 Oct 1960, leaving:

1 THOMAS GEOFFREY CHARLES MICHAEL TAYLOUR, **6th and present Marquess of Headfort**
1 *Olivia Elsie June [The Lady Olivia Waldron, Idleigh Cottage, nr Meopham, Kent]; *b* 20 June 1929; *m* 13 April 1955 *Victor Echevarri Waldron, s of Ernest Victor Echevarri, of London, and has issue:
(1) *Sarah Rose Echevarri [Mrs Peter Sweeny, 364 President St, Brooklyn, NY 11231, USA]; *b* 11 Jan 1956; *m* 1983 *Peter Allen Sweeny and has issue:
1a *Miles Taylour; *b* 1991
1a *Petrea Rose Echevarri; *b* 1989
(2) *Virginia Elizabeth Echevarri [Mrs Mark Clifford-Holmes, PO Box 113, Constantia, Cape Town 7848, S Africa]; *b* 17 April 1957; *m* 1st 1979 (*divorce* 1989) Anil Kumar Varma (*d* 1990), only s of Omi Varma and has:
1a *Jai Kumar; *b* 1986
1a *Lauren Devika Olivia; *b* 1985
(2) (cont.) Mrs Virginia Varma *m* 2nd 1991 *Mark D R Clifford-Holmes and has by him:
2a *David Geoffrey; *b* 1995

HEALEY

Creation: B. (LP, UK) 1992.

THE BARON HEALEY, of Riddlesden, Co of W Yorks (Denis Winston Healey, CH (1979), MBE (1945), PC (1964)) [The Rt Hon The Lord Healey CH MBE PC, Pingles Place, Alfriston, E Sussex.BN26 5TT]; *b* 30 Aug 1917; *educ* Bradford GS and Balliol Coll Oxford (MA 1945); WWII: Maj RE 1944 (despatches); Sec Internat Dept Lab Party 1945–52; Cncllr: RIIA 1948–60, Inst Strategic Studies 1958–61; MP (Lab) SE Leeds 1952–55, E Leeds 1955–92; memb: Exec Fabian Soc 1954–61, Parly Ctee Lab Party 1959–64 and 1970–74, Lab Party NEC 1970–75; Memb Shadow Cabinet: 1959–64, 1970–74, 1979–87; Sec State Def 1964–70, Chllr Exchequer 1974–79, Oppn Spokesman For and Cwlth Affrs 1980–87, Dep Leader Lab Party 1981–83; Chm IMF Interim Ctee 1977–79; Freeman Leeds 1992; Hon Fell: Balliol Coll 1979, Leeds Poly 1987; Hon DLitt Bradford 1983; Hon LLD Sussex 1991; FRSL 1993; Pres Birkbeck Coll 1993; Grand Cross Order Merit W Germany 1979; author: *The Curtain Fall* (1951), *New Fabian Essays* (1952), *Neutralism* (1955), *Fabian International Essays* (1956), *A Neutral Belt in Europe* (1958), *NATO and American Security* (1959), *The Race Against the H Bomb* (1960), *Labour, Britain and the World* (1963), *Healey's Eye* (1980), *Labour and a World Society* (1985), *Beyond Nuclear Deterrence* (1986), *The Time of My Life* (1989), *When Shrimps Learn to Whistle* (1990), *My Secret Planet* (1992); *m* 1945 *Edna May, dau of Edward Edmunds, of Coleford, Glos, and has:

1 *Timothy Blair; *b* 1949; *educ* Highgate and Balliol Coll Oxford; *m* 1972 *Joanna Margerison, dau of Ralph Broehl, of Neville Terrace, London SW7, and has issue:
(1) *Charles Edward; *b* 1984
(1) *Susanna Jade; *b* 1979
1 *Jenifer Clare; *b* 1948; *educ* Camden Sch for Girls; *m* 1971 *Derek Copsey and has issue:
(1) *Thomas; *b* 1975

(1) *Kate
2 *Cressida; *b* 1954; *educ* Camden Sch for Girls

Lineage: WILLIAM HEALEY, of Keighley, Yorks; had issue:
DENIS WINSTON, *cr* a **Baron**

HEATHCOAT-AMORY

Arms: Quarterly, 1st and 4th, arg. two bars gu., on a bend engrailed with plain cotises sa. two annulets of the field (for AMORY); 2nd and 3rd, vert three piles, one reversed in base between the others issuant from the chief, each charged with a pomme, thereon a cross of the 2nd (for HEATHCOAT). **Crests:** 1 The battlements of a tower or, therefrom issuant a talbot's head az. charged with two annulets fesswise and interlaced gold (for AMORY), 2 Upon a mount vert between two roses springing from the same gu., stalked and leaved ppr., a pomme charged with a cross or (for HEATHCOAT).
Motto: *Amore non vi* ('By love not force').
Creation: Bt. (UK) 21 March 1874.

SIR IAN HEATHCOAT-AMORY, 6TH BT, DL (Devon 1981) [Sir Ian Heathcoat-Amory Bt DL, Calverleigh Court, Tiverton, Devon EX16 8BB]; *b* 3 Feb 1942; *s* f 1982; *educ* Eton; Devon: memb CC 1973–85, JP 1980–93; *m* 10 June 1972 *(Frances) Louise, only dau of (Jocelyn Francis) Brian Pomeroy (*see* HARBERTON, V), and has:

1 +WILLIAM FRANCIS; *b* 19 July 1975
2 +Harry James; *b* 30 April 1977
3 +Patrick Thomas; *b* 29 Oct 1979
4 +Benjamin David; *b* 22 Aug 1983

Lineage: JOHN AMORY, of Taunton, Somerset; *m* —, sis of Rev Henry Grove, and had:

THOMAS AMORY, of Taunton; DD; *b* 28 Jan 1700; *m* 1742 Mary (*d* Jan 1801), dau of Samuel Baker, of Taunton and *d* 24 June 1774, leaving, with other issue:

SAMUEL AMORY, of Clapton, Middx, and Clement's Lane, London; *b c* 1747; banker; *m* Martha (*d* 9 Jan 1838), dau of Thomas Ellis, and was *bur* 18 Dec 1799, leaving, with other issue:

SAMUEL AMORY, of The Priory, Homerton, and Portland Place, London; *b* 10 Oct 1784; *m* 19 Aug 1826 Anne (*d* 1 Jan 1833), dau of — Bolham, of Devon, MP Tiverton, and *d* 17 Nov 1857, leaving, with a dau (Sarah Anne, *b* 7 July 1827, *m* 9 Jan 1847 John Ingram Travers, of Portland Place (*d* 24 June 1866), and *d* 17 April 1869, leaving issue):

Sir JOHN AMORY later HEATHCOAT-AMORY (roy licence 28 Feb 1874), **1st Bt** (UK), so *cr* 21 March 1874, JP (Devon and Tiverton), DL (Devon); *b* 4 May 1829; Maj 1st Devon Roy Vols, MP Tiverton 1868–85; *m* 6 April 1863 Henrietta Mary (*d* 8 Nov 1923), only dau of William Unwin, Colonial Office, by Jane, est dau of James Murray Grant, JP, DL, 12th of Glenmoriston, and had:

1 John Murray; *b* 27, *d* 30 March 1864
2 IAN MURRAY (Sir), **2nd Bt**
3 Harry William Ludovic Heathcoat, JP (Somerset and Tiverton), DL (Somerset); *b* 7 June 1870; Lt-Col 4th Bn Somerset LI (TFR), Capt Coldstream Gds; *m* 1st 1 Nov 1898 Evelyn Mary (*d* 16 Nov 1929), dau of Edward James Stanley, MP (*see* DERBY, E); *m* 2nd 9 April 1931 Marjorie Una (*d* 30 Oct 1973 aged 84), widow of Edward Pearkes Gundry, JP, and dau of Rev Edgar Astley Milne, JP, of Chilfrome, Dorset, and *d* 22 Dec 1945, leaving by his 1st w:
(1) Geoffrey William; *b* 1899; *d* 1900
(2) James Vesey; *b* 26 Oct 1901; *d* 3 Oct 1920
(3) Richard Frank; Lt 4th Hussars, sr ptnr Stirling Amory, Whitehead and Chown, stockbrokers, Sec Br Embassy Washington 1939–42; *b* 26 Feb 1903; *educ* Ch Ch Oxford (MA); *m* 18 July 1938 *Hon (Margaret Irene) Gaenor Scott-Ellis, JP (N Westminster 1968) [The Hon Mrs Heathcoat-Amory, Hele Manor, Dulverton, Somerset TA22 9RN], 4th dau of 8th Baron Howard de Walden (*qv*), and *d* 19 Feb 1957, leaving issue:
1a +(Ian) Mark [Mark Amory Esq, Hele Manor, Dulverton, Somerset TA22 9RN]; *b* 1 May 1941; *educ* Eton and Ch Ch Oxford; lit ed *Spectator*; *m* 1982 *Charlotte Elizabeth, dau of (Doulrish) Evelyn Louis Joll, and has:
1b *Evelyn Caroline; *b* 1985
2b *Olivia Rachel; *b* 1988
3b *Katharine Eleanor; *b* 1991
1a *Evelyn Helen [Lady Jacomb, c/o Prudential Corp plc, 142 Holborn Bars, London EC1N 2NH]; *b* 4 June 1939; *m* 30 April 1960 *Sir Martin Wakefield Jacomb, Chm Br Cncl 1992–, and has:
1b *Matthew Barnabas Wakefield; *b* 11 June 1963
2b *Thomas Richard; *b* 22 June 1964; *m* 1988 *Philippa A, yst dau of Frederick Thomas Winter, CBE, the former racehorse-trainer, of Uplands, Lambourn, Berks, and has issue:
1c *Tara; *b* 1989
2c *Saffron; *b* 1992
1b *Emma Félise; *b* 15 May 1961; *m* 1988 *Simon Jock Bruce and has issue (*see* ELGIN and KINCARDINE, E)
2a *(Rachel) Belinda [Mrs Belinda Ryan, Saddlers, Croscombe, Wells, Somerset]; *b* 24 April 1946; *m* 1973 (*divorce* 1986) Christopher Joseph Ryan, and has issue:
1b *Jessica Siobhan Elizabeth; *b* 1976
2b *Margherita; *b* 1978
(1) *Helen Winifred; *b* 25 Sept 1905; *m* 12 July 1932 *Capt Hon William Ralph Seymour Bathurst, TD, 2nd s of 7th Earl Bathurst (*qv*)
(2) *Mary Millicent, JP (Somerset 1954) [Mrs Mary Smail JP, Melcombe Newton Farm, Melcombe Bingham, Dorset]; *b* 5 June 1907; *m* 3 Oct 1930 (*divorce* 1943) Lt-Col Adam Trevor Smail, DSO, 11th Hus (*d* 15 July 1976), yr s of John Isdale Smail, of Warren Wood, Hayes, Kent, and has:
1a *Simon Trevor [Maj Simon Smail, Melcombe Newton Farm, Melcombe Bingham, Dorset]; Maj late 11th Hus; *b* 26 Dec 1934; *educ* Eton; *m* 28 May 1960 *Margaret, only dau of Maj Hon Arthur Bernard John Grenfell (*see* GRENFELL, B), and has issue:
1b *Tom Patrick; *b* 1964
1b *Lucy Jane; *b* 4 Aug 1962
4 Geoffrey; *b* 12 Nov 1877; *d* 15 Oct 1881
5 Ludovic; T/Maj Roy 1st Devon Yeo, Staff Capt RA; *b* 11 May 1881; *m* 12 July 1911 Mary Stuart (*d* 23 July 1977), er dau of James Fitzgerald Bannatyne, JP, DL, of Haldon, Devon, and *d* 25 Aug 1918 of wounds recd in action, leaving:
(1) Patrick Gerald; 2nd Lt 96th (Roy Devon Yeo) Field Bde RA (TA) WW II, barrister Inner Temple 1937; *b* 27 April 1912; *educ* Eton and Ch Ch Oxford (BA); *ka* Libya May 1942
(2) Michael Ludovic; 2nd Lt 16th/5th Lancers; *b* 19 May 1914; *educ* Eton; *k* plane crash 7 June 1936
(3) Edgar Fitzgerald; Maj 96th (Roy Devon Yeo) Field Bde RA (TA) WW II; *b* 30 Aug 1917; *educ* Eton and Ch Ch Oxford; *m* 7 Sept 1940 *Sonia Myrtle (*m* 2nd 28 April 1947 Lt-Col Roderick Heathcoat-Amory, The Royals; *see* below), only dau of Capt Edward Conyngham Denison, MVO, RN (*see* LONDESBOROUGH, B), and was *ka* Normandy June 1944, leaving:
1a +Michael Fitzgerald [Michael Heathcoat-Amory Esq, Chevithorne Barton, Tiverton, Devon]; *b* 2 Oct 1941; *educ* Eton and Ch Ch Oxford (BA 1963); dir Kingside Investment and River Plate & Gen Investment Tst 1975–, High Sheriff Devon 1985–86; *m* 1st 29 June 1965 (*divorce* 1970) Harriet Mary Sheila, only dau of Lt-Gen Sir Archibald Edward Nye, GCSI, GCMG, GCIE, KCB, MC (*see* RANFURLY, E), and has issue:
1b *Edward FitzGerald; *b* 5 July 1967; *educ* Eton and Bristol U; *m* 1994 *Alice M R, er dau of David Paget Thomson, of Little Stoke Ho, Wallingford, Oxon
1a (cont.) Michael Heathcoat-Amory *m* 2nd 1975 *(Sarah) Arabella Marjorie, dau of Raimund von Hofmannsthal (*see* ANGLESEY, M) and formerly w of Piers von Westenholz, and has further issue:
1b *Lucy Sonia Elizabeth; *b* 1977
2b *Jessica Diana Mary; *b* 1979
1a *Amanda Mary [The Rt Hon The Countess Cairns, Bolehyde Manor, Allington, Wilts SN14 6LW]; *b* posthumously 4 Dec 1944; *m* 4 Feb 1964 *6th Earl Cairns (*qv*) and has issue
1 Muriel Mary; *b* 18 June 1867; *m* 15 Oct 1891 Charles Robert Sydenham Carew (*see* CAREW, Bt) and *d* 4 March 1939, having had issue
2 Christal Anne Lucy; *b* 7 Sept 1872; *d* 25 Feb 1874
3 Dorothy Helen; *b* 25 May 1876; *m* 20 April 1899 Louis de las Casas, of Elliscombe Ho, Wincanton, s of Julian Clemente de las Casas y Iturbe, and *d* 24 May 1942, leaving issue. He *d* 9 Feb 1941
4 Mary Christal, JP Devon; Div Pres Devon BRCS, Chm Women's Branch Br Legion Tiverton; *b* 9 Sept 1882; *m* 24 July 1907 Brig-Gen Hon Lesley James Probyn Butler, CMG, DSO, Irish Gds (*d* 31 Dec 1955), 2nd s of 25th Baron Dunboyne (*qv*), and *d* following a hunting accident 27 Feb 1951, leaving issue

Sir JOHN *d* 26 May 1914; his est surv son,

Sir Ian Murray Heathcoat-Amory, 2nd Bt, CBE, JP Tiverton, JP, DL Devon; High Sheriff 1924; Alderman and V-Chm Devon CC; *b* 16 April 1865; *m* 6 June 1893 Alexandra Georgina, OBE (*d* 28 Oct 1942), est dau of V-Adml Henry George Seymour, CB (*see* HERTFORD, M), and *d* 4 Jan 1931, leaving issue:

1 **Sir John Heathcoat-Amory, 3rd Bt**, JP (Devon 1922), DL (1952); *b* 2 May 1894; *educ* Eton and Ch Ch Oxford; High Sheriff Devon 1942, Freeman Tiverton 1969, Capt TAR, 4th Bn Devonshire Regt, ADC Personal Staff 1918 WW I (despatches, two medals), pres (formerly chm) John Heathcoat and Co; *m* 6 Jan 1937 Joyce (*d* 18 Nov 1997), golfer, only dau of Herbert Newton Wethered, of Brook Corner, Brook, Surrey, and *dsp* 22 Nov 1972
2 **Sir Derick Heathcoat-Amory, 4th Bt**, and 1st and last VISCOUNT AMORY, of Tiverton, Co Devon (UK), so *cr* 1 Sept. 1960, KG (1969), GCMG (1961), TD, PC (1953), DL (Devon 1962); *b* 26 Dec 1899; *educ* Eton and Ch Ch Oxford (BA 1921); Lt-Col Gen Staff WW II, Lt-Col RA (TA); MP (C) Tiverton 1945–60, Min Pensions 1951–53, Min State BOT 1953–54, Min Ag, Fisheries and Food 1954–58, Chllr Exchequer 1958–60, HC Canada 1961–63, dir Hudson's Bay Co 1963 (Govr 1965), Pres John Heathcote & Co 1973–81, memb Devon CC

1932–51, Freeman Tiverton 1959, Hon LLD Exeter 1959, DCL Oxon 1973, Hon DC McGill 1961; *d* unm 20 Jan 1981, when the Viscountcy expired

3 WILLIAM (Sir), **5th Bt**

4 +Roderick, MC (1942) [Brig Roderick Heathcoat-Amory MC, Allington Grange, nr Chippenham, Wilts]; Brig The Royals WW II, cmded 15th Scottish Recce Regt and NI Horse 1945–46, The Royals 1949–51 and 8th Armoured Bde (TA) 1954–56, High Sheriff Yorks 1971–72; *b* 30 Jan 1907; *educ* Eton; *m* 28 April 1947 *Sonia Myrtle, widow of Maj Gerald Heathcoat-Amory (*see* above), and has issue:

(1) +David Philip, PC (1996)[The Rt Hon David Heathcoat-Amory Esq MP, 12 Lower Addison Gdns, London W14 8BQ]; *b* 21 March 1949; *educ* Eton and Ch Ch Oxford (MA, PPE); FCA 1980, MP (C) Wells 1983–, PPS to Chllr Exchequer and Home Sec, Assist Govt Whip 1988–89, a Ld Commr Treasury 1989, Parly U-Sec DOE 1989–90, Treasurer Household (Dep Ch Whip) 1992–93, Min State FCO 1993–94, Paymaster-Gen 1994–96, Shadow Ch Sec Treasury 1997–; *m* 1978 *Linda Margaret Legh, yr dau of Alec Desmond Adams, of The Old Rectory, Winchfield, Hants, and has issue:

1a +John; *b* 1980

2a +Matthew; *b* 1982

1a *Florence; *b* 1988

(1) *Bridget Alexandra [Lady Beck, Pylle Manor, Shepton Mallet, Somerset BA4 6TD]; *b* 21 May 1952; *m* 1st 1984 Michael R I Cockerell, est s of Prof Hugh A I Cockerell; *m* 2nd 1991, as his 2nd w, *Sir (Edgar) Philip Beck, and by her 1st husb has issue:

1a *Eliza Sonia; *b* 1985

2a *Alice Fanny; *b* 1987

Sir DERICK's yr bro,

Sir William Heathcoat-Amory, 5th Bt, DSO (1943); *b* 19 Aug 1901; *educ* Eton;ADC to GOC-in-C Western Command 1937, Col KRRC WW II, memb Gentlemen-at-Arms 1950–66; *m* 20 April 1935 Margaret Isabella Dorothy Evelyn (*d* 19 March 1997), yr dau of Col Sir Arthur Havelock James Doyle, 4th Bt (*see* 1970 edn), and *d* 27 Aug 1982, leaving:

1 Sir IAN HEATHCOAT-AMORY, **6th and present Bt**

2 +Charles William [Charles Heathcoat-Amory Esq, Meethe Barton, S Molton, N Devon EX36 4JA]; *b* 29 Oct 1945 (twin); *educ* Eton ; Capt RGJ; *m* 1st 7 July 1977 Harmony Joanna, yr dau of Malcolm Lyell; *m* 2nd 1988 (*divorce* 1991) Hon Angela Jane, est dau of 4th Baron Borwick (*qv*); *m* 3rd 1991 *Mrs Diana Elizabeth Mann, and by his 1st w has issue:

(1) +Simon Charles; *b* 6 Aug 1982

(2) +Toby Derick; *b* 1985

1 *Diana Chrystal [Mrs Peter Sichel, Château d'Angludet 33460, Cantenac, Gironde, France]; *b* 3 Nov 1938; *m* 24 Feb 1962 *Peter Allan Sichel and has:

(1) *Allan Gordon; *b* 1 Sept 1962

(2) *James William; *b* 25 Nov 1963

(3) *Charles Edward; *b* 25 Nov 1963

(4) *Benjamin Pierre; *b* 14 May 1966

(5) *David Mark; *b* 12 Oct 1968

(1) *Rebecca; *b* 1978

2 *Catherine Elizabeth [Mrs David Cavender, The Manor House, Dowlish Wake, Somerset]; *b* 29 Oct 1945; *m* 1st 8 July 1967 (*divorce* 1975) Michael Godfrey Melvin Groves, only s of Lt-Col Henry Basil Melvin Groves, MC and bar; *m* 2nd 1977 *David Alan Drummond Cavender and by her 1st husb has:

(1) *Alistair Michael William; *b* 14 Dec 1968

(2) *Henry Grenville Havelock; *b* 3 May 1971

HEATHCOTE of Hursley

Arms: Erm. three pomels, each charged with a cross or. **Crest:** On a mural coronet az. a pomel, charged with a cross or, between two wings displayed erm. **Motto:** *Et Dieu mon appui* ('And God my help'). **Creation:** Bt. (GB) 16 Aug 1733.

SIR MICHAEL PERRYMAN HEATHCOTE, 11TH BT, of Hursley, Hants [Sir Michael Heathcote Bt, Warborne Farm, Boldre, Hants SO41 5QD]; *b* 7 Aug 1927; *s* f 1963; *educ* Winchester and Clare Coll Cambridge; late 2nd Lt 9th; *m* 2 June 1956 *Victoria, er dau of Cdr James Edward Rickards Wilford, RD, RNR, of Ackland Cottage, Shirley Holms, Lymington, Hants, and has issue:

1 +TIMOTHY GILBERT; *b* 25 May 1957

2 +George Benjamin; *b* 2 Feb 1965

1 *(Harriet) Louise [Mrs Richard Rouse, Sea Cottage, Westfield Rd, Lymington, Hants]; *b* 6 Feb 1962; *m* 22 May 1982 *Richard J Rouse, only s of Lt Cdr R J Rouse, RN, of Tarnaut House, Tiptoe, Hants

Lineage: SAMUEL HEATHCOTE, of Hackney (2nd s of Gilbert Heathcote, thrice Mayor Chesterfield; *see* HEATHCOTE of London); *b* 1665; *m* 1691 Mary, 2nd dau of William Dawsonne, of Hackney, and *d* 13 Nov 1708, having had, with a yr s (Samuel, *m* 3 May 1720 Elizabeth Holworthy) and two daus:

Sir William Heathcote, 1st Bt (GB), so *cr* 16 Aug 1733, of Hursley, Hants; MP Buckingham 1722–27 and Southampton 1729–41; *b* 15 March 1693; *m* 7 April 1720 Elizabeth (*d* 21 Feb 1746/7), only dau of 1st Earl of Macclesfield (*qv*) (whose male-line descendants by Elizabeth are in remainder to that Earldom and its associated titles), and *d* 10 May 1751, having had, with other issue, including a yr s (Rev Henry, *d* 1803, leaving issue):

Sir Thomas Heathcote, 2nd Bt; FSA, High Sheriff 1754; *b* 23 July 1721; *m* 1st 13 Dec 1742 Elizabeth (*d* 27 Dec 1749), dau of William Hinton, of Hursley, and had, with other issue:

1 WILLIAM (Sir), **3rd Bt**

2 Thomas (Rev); Rector Stone, Kent; *m* 20 Aug 1772 Letitia (*d* 20 July 1812), dau of Sir Thomas Parker, and *dsp* 13 July 1811

Sir Thomas *m* 2nd 30 May 1765 Anne (*d* 7 Aug 1799), dau of Rev — Tollett, and by her had, with other issue:

3 Samuel, of Shaw Hill House, Wilts; *m* Elizabeth, dau of Rev William Stone, and *d* 10 Dec 1820, leaving:

(1) Thomas (Rev), of Shaw Hill; *b* 25 March 1789; *m* 12 Sept 1816 Georgiana (*d* 15 June 1881), dau of John Fuller, of Neston (*see* FULLER, Bt), and *d* 23 Jan 1859, having had:

1a Thomas Jenkyns, of Shaw Hill, JP Wilts; *b* 14 Aug 1817; *m* 29 April 1847 Mary Catherine (*d* 28 Nov 1875), est dau of Maj — Moultrie, of Aston Hall, Salop, and *d* 1886, leaving issue:

1b Thomas George Jenkyns; MA Oxon; *b* 17 Oct 1848; *d* 28 May 1926

2b Arthur Napier, DSO (1918); Capt RN WW I (despatches); *b* 6 Oct 1850; *m* 19 Sept 1877 Louisa Willoughby (*d* 8 Nov 1904), adopted dau of Neston Fuller, and *d* 2 Nov 1923, having had issue:

1c Arthur Austin; *b* 22 June 1878; *d* unm 17 June 1948

2c Thomas Guy; *b* 11 May, *d* 3 Sept 1880

3c Crawford Napier; *b* 1890; *m* 1925 Madeleine Clare Violet Wilson, dau of Ernest Charles Young, MD

1c Margaret Mary; *b* 17 June 1881; *d* unm 2 Aug 1953

2c Amy Florence; *b* 27 Sept 1882; *d* unm 1 Jan 1943

3b Herbert Moultrie; Capt RN; *b* 23 Oct 1853; *m* 1888 Charlotte Violetta (*d* 1921), dau of Rev T C Williams and *d* 31 Dec 1938

4b Walter Comyn; *b* 3 Jan 1855; *d* July 1937

5b Basil; *b* 18 May 1858; *m* 1887 Anna Kittle and *dsp* 1898

6b Henry Lucas; *b* 9 Oct 1859

7b Wyndham Selfe (Rev); BA Oxon, Unitarian Minister, Vicar All Saints, Penarth, Rector Bundaberg, Qld, and A/Chaplain Forces S Africa; *b* 22 Jan 1862; *m* 1888 Agnes (*d* 1934), dau of Rev James MacDouall and had:

1c Wyndham MacDouall; *b* 1889

1c Catherine Moultrie Maud; *b* 1891; *m* —

8b Godfrey Austen; *b* 30 June 1866

9b George Wadham Bruce, OBE; *b* 6 Oct 1868; *m* 1895 Mary, dau of Mark Bate, and *d* 27 June 1944, leaving:

1c Grace Mary; *b* 15 May 1896; *m* 1923 Thomas B Randall

1b Florence Poulteney; *d* unm 1883

2b Rose Mary; *m* 1897 Lt-Col Arthur E Hodgins (*d* 1939), Lt Royal Canadian Regt Boer War, cmded 1st Canadian Pioneer Bn, Assist Dir Light Rlys 3rd Army WW I, and had issue

3b Georgina Mary Noel; *d* 1934

2a Samuel John (Rev); *b* 8 Aug 1823; *educ* Cambridge; Vicar Williton, Somerset; *m* 27 Aug 1846 Mary Sidney (*d* 1885), dau of Sir Christopher Sidney Smith, 2nd Bt (*see* SMITH, Bt, of Eardiston), and *d* 20 April 1906, having had:

1b Samuel Sidney (Rev); Rector Bondleigh N Devon 1893–1904; *b* 31 Aug 1848; *educ* Exeter Coll Oxford (BA); *m* 29 Oct 1901 Elizabeth Lucy, only dau of Rev Edward Owen, and *d* 20 July 1933

2b John Cuthbert; *b* 24 Jan 1852; *educ* Oriel Coll Oxford (MA); *m* 2 May 1876 Lady Eva Campbell (*d* 7 July 1945), only dau of 6th Earl of Breadalbane (*see* 1970 edn), and *d* 25 July 1934, leaving issue:

1c John Robert Campbell; Lt-Col Cameron Highrs and RAF Boer War 1902 and WW I; *b* 24 April 1879; *m* 1st 24 Nov 1898 (*divorce* 1920) Margaret McClellan; *m* 2nd 4 March 1920 Mary Gertrude, dau of Oscar Brandt, and *dsp* 15 July 1947, leaving by his 1st w:

1d Evelyn Marie; *b* 1899

1c Marie Eva; *m* 2 June 1908 Capt George Drummond Fish, MBE, and *d* 5 July 1951

3b Ernest Edward Egremont (Rev); Rector Silverton Devon; *b* 17 Feb 1858; *educ* Emmanuel Coll Cambridge (BA); *m* 1893 Clare Europa Townley (*d* 14 Dec 1941), dau of Capt Frederick Townley Parker, and *d* 28 July 1936

1b Mary Georgina; *m* 20 Oct 1881 Trehawke Kekewich, DL, JP (*d* 22 April 1909), of Devon, and *dsp* 31 March 1909

2b Sophia Letitia; *m* 6 Aug 1872 Rev Edward John Gore Dupuis and *d* 11 Oct 1898, leaving issue

3b Cecilia Maria; *d* unm 11 Oct 1942

4b Ellen Augusta Maude; *d* unm 1944
3a William Neston (Rev); Rector Ditteridge; *b* 20 June 1827; *m* 1st 29 July 1858 Juliana (*d* 21 Aug 1867), dau of William H Ludlow-Bruges, MP; *m* 2nd 10 Nov 1868 Isabella Lingwood (*d* 1900), dau of Richard Duppa-Toovey, and *d* 1894, having had by his 1st w:
1b Gertrude Ellen Beatrice; *m* 16 Jan 1895 Rev George Evans Lewis (*d* 1932), and had issue
2b Agnes Blanche Evelyn; *d* unm 12 March 1929
3b Frances Maude; *d* 2 May 1912
1a Georgiana Augusta; *m* 1st 1846 Rev Charles Wadham Diggle; *m* 2nd Col — Tapp, CB, and *d* 5 Nov 1857, leaving issue
2a Louisa Dorothea; *m* 4 May 1843 Rev C F Baker (*d* 1888), Rector Tellesford, Somerset, and *d* 1 Feb 1907, having had issue
3a Frances Elizabeth; *m* 1st Rev Caleb Williams (*d* 1856); *m* 2nd 30 Sept 1857 Matthew E Habershon, and *d* 30 April 1901, having had issue
4a Mary Anne Laetitia; *m* 1st 4 May 1843 William Lye Seagram (*d* 1844), and had issue; *m* 2nd 8 June 1869 John S Thomas (*d* 7 Nov 1878)
5a Harriet Anne Lovell; *m* 19 April 1860 17th Baron Teynham (*qv*) and *d* 1917, having had issue
6a Ellen Wyndham; *d* unm 1 Feb 1859
4 Gilbert (Ven); Archdeacon Winchester; *b* Feb 1765; *m* 1st 3 Jan 1805 Sophia Elizabeth (*d* 2 June 1806), dau of Martin Wall, MD, and had:
(1) Gilbert Wall (Rev), Fell Winchester Coll; *b* 5 May 1806; *m* 20 July 1842 Clara Rosalie, dau of Ven Timothy Stonhouse, Archdeacon Gloucester, and *d* 17 July 1893
4 (cont.) The Ven Gilbert Heathcote *m* 2nd 22 Sept 1807 Anne (*d* 3 Sept 1828), dau of Rev Edwards Beadon, and *d* 19 Oct 1829, having by her had issue:
(2) George Edward; Fell New Coll Oxford; *b* 31 Jan 1809
(3) Dawsonne; *b* 31 Aug 1810; *d* 18 July 1813
(4) William Beadon (Rev); Preb Salisbury; *b* 12 Dec 1812; *m* 3 Aug 1852 Elizabeth Mary (*d* 1892), dau of Rev George Deane, and *d* 21 Aug 1862, leaving issue:
1a Cecil Hamilton; *b* 29 May 1856; *d* unm 1896
1a Agnes Mary; nun
(1) Mary; *m* 26 July 1831 her cousin Rev John Wilder and *dsp* 12 June 1856
Sir THOMAS *d* 27 June 1787; his est son,
Sir William Heathcote, 3rd Bt; MP Hants 1790–1806, MA Oxon; *b* 31 June 1746; *m* 21 May 1768 Frances (*d* 19 Aug 1816), dau and coheir of John Thorpe, of Embley, Hants, and *d* 26 June 1819, having had issue:
1 Sir THOMAS HEATHCOTE later FREEMAN-HEATHCOTE, **4th Bt**; MP Bletchingley 1807–08 and Hants 1808–20; *b* 3 Sept 1769; *m* 27 June 1799 Elizabeth (*d* 16 March 1808), dau of Thomas Edwards Freeman, of Batsford, and *dsp* 21 Feb 1825
2 William (Rev); Preb Winchester, Rector Worting Hants; *b* 1772; *m* 11 Jan 1798 Elizabeth (*d* 23 March 1855), dau of Lovelace Bigg Wither, of Manydown, Hants, and *d* 29 March 1802, leaving issue:
(1) WILLIAM (Sir), **5th Bt**
3 Samuel (Rev); *b* 1773; *m* 1st Catherine (*d* May 1815), dau of Isaac Pickering, of Foxlease, Hants; *m* 2nd Anne (*dsp* Dec 1849), est dau of Francis Brownswood Bullock, of Ardington, Berks, and *d* 27 Nov 1846, having by his 1st w had, with other issue:
(1) William Arthur, of Rolleston Manor, Wilts, JP, DL; T-Col Wilts Militia; *b* 16 June 1808; *m* 1831 Eliza (*d* 14 Feb 1879), dau of J Walsh, of Walsh Park, Co Tipperary, and *d* 22 Aug 1882, having had issue:
1a Samuel; *b* 15 Aug 1838; *d* unm
1a Eliza; *m* 29 March 1853 Rev Gilbert V Heathcote, and *d* 16 Aug 1864, leaving issue (*see below*)
2a Katharine; *m* 12 April 1860 Charles B Smith, of Shrewton Lodge, and *d* his widow 2 May 1903
3a Sophia; *m* Rev Henry Westenra Walsh, Rector Rolleston, Wilts, and had issue
4a Maria; *m* 25 Feb 1868 Hugh Wyndham (*d* 11 Dec 1898), and *d* 10 March 1904, leaving issue
(2) Edmund; Adml, C-in-C coast of Ireland; *b* 29 Jan 1814; *m* 1st 12 July 1844 Elizabeth Lucy, dau of Col — Law, KH, and had issue:
1a William Eustace; *b* 18 April 1845; *m* 1869 Alicia Page, of Hobart Town, and *d* 1884, leaving issue:
1b William Arthur; *b* Oct 1873
1b Lucie Maud; *b* Aug 1871
2a Robert Walker; Maj RM; *b* 7 April 1847; *m* 25 Oct 1877 Constance Elizabeth (*d* 30 Nov 1925), dau of Francis Shand, of Woolton Wood, Lancs, and *d* 8 April 1918, having had issue:
1b Esmond; *b* 23 July 1880; *d* 8 March 1882
1b Esme; *b* 27 Aug 1878; *d* unm 12 July 1955
2b Edith; *b* 12 Feb 1882; *d* unm 5 Jan 1943
3b Erica; *b* 8 May 1889; *d* unm 1964
(2) (cont.) Edmund Heathcote *m* 2nd 19 Aug 1852 Jessie (*d* 19 Dec 1915), dau of Charles J Hill, and *d* 29 Oct 1881, having by her had issue:
3a Arthur Cleveland, Capt RN; *b* 31 March 1854; *m* 1886 Florence Georgina (*d* 25 Feb 1938), dau of Thomas Vance, JP, of Blackrock House, Dublin, and *d* 28 Nov 1933, leaving issue:
1b Eustace Cleveland; Maj RM; *b* 3 March 1895; *educ* Haileybury; *m* 1 Feb 1926 Marie Macmurrough (*d* 1977), dau of J J Kavanagh, and *d* 1976, leaving issue:
1c +Michael Edmund [Michael Heathcote Esq, Hursley Cottage, Lake Lane, Dockenfield, Surrey GU10 4JB]; Capt RM (ret); *b* 1 April 1931; *m* 21 March 1959 *Jean, er dau of D J V Hamilton-Miller, and has issue:
1d *Kathryn Gay; *b* 22 Aug 1961; *m* 1987 *Christopher David McDonald Cann and has:
1e *Richard James Michael; *b* 21 Oct 1989
2e *James Edward; *b* 16 Sept 1991
2d *Georgina Ann; *b* 22 Aug 1961; *m* 1986 *(Alfred Joseph Gerard Robert) Alain Rey, of Beau-Bassin, Mauritius, and has issue:
1e *Olivier Michael Robert; *b* 29 June 1987
2e *Charles Michael Robert; *b* 1 Sept 1989
3e *Dominique Michael Robert; *b* 6 Oct 1991
4e *Christopher Michael Robert; *b* 9 Oct 1994
3d *Jenny Louise; *b* 31 Jan 1964
1c *Valerie; 2nd Offr WRNS; *b* 20 April 1929
(3) Eustace; Hon Lt-Col Hampshire Militia; *b* 14 April 1815; *m* 15 Dec 1849 Caroline Harriet (*d* 22 May 1897), only child of Matthew Munro, and *d* 1881, leaving issue:
1a Eustace Munro; Lt 43rd LI; *b* 22 May 1852; *d* 15 Aug 1875
1a Caroline; *d* unm 30 Jan 1912
4 Henry (Sir); Adml the Blue; *b* 20 Jan 1777; *m* 10 Nov 1799 Sarah (*d* 19 Oct 1845), dau of Thomas Guscott, and *d* 16 Aug 1851, having had issue:
(1) William Lovell; Offr Army; *b* 1802; *m* — and *d* 1855, leaving, with other issue:
1a William; had:
1b William
2a Charles; *b* 4 Nov 1833; *m* 1874 Ida Sophia Philps (*d* 3 Sept 1933) and *d* 1 Nov 1917, leaving issue:
1b Frederick Lovell; *b* 3 July 1875; *m* 10 July 1901 Minnie Ethel Ziervogel (*d* 1938), and *d* 21 May 1968, leaving:
1c Geoffrey Charles; *b* 4 March 1906; *m* 1939 *Megan Edith Pugh-Jones [Mrs Geoffrey Heathcote, Crestwood, PO Newton Park, Port Elizabeth, S Africa], and *d* 1988, leaving issue:
1d +Charles William; *b* 22 Oct 1942 [Charles Heathcote Esq, Rietfontein Farm, PO Box 7160, Newton Park, Port Elizabeth, S Africa]; *m* 1967 *Hester Conelia de Lange and has:
1e +Charles Geoffrey; *b* 1981
1e *Karen Sarah; *b* 1968
2e *Lucille Megan; *b* 1970
3e *Dianne May; *b* 1972
4e *Marian Louise; *b* 1976
2d +Warwick Geoffrey [Warwick Heathcote Esq, PO 195, Cookhouse 5820, S Africa]; *b* 15 March 1946; *m* 1969 *Helena Louisa Marais and has had:
1e Geoffrey Charles Lovell; *b* 1973; *d* 19–
1e *Elizabeth Anne; *b* 1970
2e *Caroline Louise; *b* 1987
3d +Gerard Lovell; *b* 13 Sept 1951; *m* 1975 *Laura Glenn Hughes, *née* Anderson, and has:
1e *Caleb Geoffrey Lovell; *b* 1994
1e *Olivia Megan; *b* 1980
2e *Carmen Joy; *b* 1982
1d *Eleanor May; *b* 15 Nov 1948; *m* 1968 *Lysle Horace Wilmot and has:
1e *Mark Lysle; *b* 1969
2e *David Geoffrey; *b* 1972
1e *Suzanne Megan; *b* 1969
2e *Michelle May; *b* 1978
2c Albert Ziervogel; *b* 4 July 1909; *m* 1943 *Doreen Oke Thomas [Mrs Albert Heathcote, Glenfield, PO Box 7074, Newton Park, Port Elizabeth, S Africa], and *d* 1977, leaving issue:
1d +Frederick Malcolm [Frederick Heathcote Esq, PO Box 7071, Port Elizabeth, S Africa]; *b* 8 Oct 1944; *m* 1972 *Elenor Fourie and has:
1e +Frederick Henry; *b* 1973
2e +Llewellyn Malcolm; *b* 1975
2d +Albert Dennisson [Albert Heathcote Esq, PO Box 252, Humansdorp, S Africa]; *b* 20 June 1946; *m* 1969 *Elizabeth Stoutjesdyk and has:
1e *Yvonne Sharon; *b* 1970
2e *Carol Lisé
3e *Lynne Denise; *b* 1976
4e *Hellen Delia; *b* 1980
3d +Richard John [Richard Heathcote Esq, PO Box 252, Humansdorp, S Africa]; *b* 15 Nov 1948; *m* 1969 *Finette van Gend and has:
1e *Charmaine Sunette; *b* 1969
2e *Richelle Doreen; *b* 1970
3e *Teresé Finette; *b* 1975
4e *Jacqueline Melodé; *b* 1978
1d *Hillary Oke; *b* 16 Oct 1950; *m* 1975 (*divorce* 1979) William Kirkman Allen and has issue:
1e Wilfred Gavin; *b* 1976
1c Kathleen Mary; *b* 9 Aug 1902; *m* March 1922 W A Copeman (*d* 1938), of Alexandria, CP, and had issue
2c Minnie Lovell; *b* 10 April 1904; *m* 1929 Andrew Gerald Lovemore, and had issue
3c Beryl; *b* 30 June 1907; *m* 1939 *Sydney James Gilfillan and had issue
4c *Joan; *b* 11 Oct 1910; *m* 1938 Maurice Wilmot (*d* 1986) and has:
1d *Chester George; *b* 1948
1d *Felicity Mary; *b* 1940; *m* 1964 *John St Laurence Beaufort and has issue:
1e *Sandra; *b* 1966
5c *Esme Helen [Miss Esme Heathcote, PO Box 7160, Port Elizabeth, CP, S Africa]; *b* 28 Aug 1913
2b Charles William; *b* 16 Aug 1877; *m* 1st Sophia Kichner (*d* 1910) and had:
1c Frederick Lennox; *b* 1903; *m* Mildred W Shaw (*d* 1974) and *d* 1969, leaving:

1d +Leon Geoffrey [Leon Heathcote Esq, PO Box 998, Gweru, Zimbabwe]; *b* 1934; *m* 1957 *Gillian Jean Lawson and has:
1e +Frederick Garth [Frederick Heathcote Esq, PO Box 809, Gweru, Zimbabwe]; *b* 1958
2e +Mark Andrew; *b* 18 Oct 1962
1e *Jean Pamela [Mrs Glendyn Thompson, PO Box 633, Gweru, Zimbabwe]; *b* 1960; *m* 1980 *Glendyn Stephen Delamere Thompson and has issue:
1f *Bruce Glen; *b* 1988
1f *Shay Jean; *b* 1983
2f *Donna Caron; *b* 1985
2d +Roy [Roy Heathcote Esq, 5 Farthing Hill, PO Borrowdale, Harare, Zimbabwe]; *b* 1938; *m* 27 March 1965 *Gillian Helen Dalling and has issue:
1e +Paul Roy; *b* 1971
1e *Amanda Kim; *b* 11 Feb 1968
3d +Frederick Noel [Frederick Heathcote Esq, PO Box 585, Marondera, Zimbabwe]; *b* 1945; *m* 1967 *Catherine Caryln Barry and has issue:
1e +Clive Noel [Clive Heathcote Esq, Box 992, Marondera, Zimbabwe]; *b* 1968; *m* 1992 *Susan Wolton and has:
1f +Scott Jason; *b* 1997
1f *Storme Louise; *b* 1995
2e +Wayne Douglas; *b* 1972
1e *Kelly; *b* 1980
1d *Stella Lenore [Mrs Bruce Humpage, 19 St Brelades Rd, Borrowdale, Harare, Zimbabwe]; *b* 1933; *m* 1950 *Bruce John Humpage and has:
1e *Denise Marie; *b* 1953; *m* 1971 *John Sealy and has had:
1f Gail; *b* 1971; *d* 1996
2f *Leigh-Anne; *b* 1974
2e *Carole Gail; *b* 1955; *m* 1974 *Neville Thompson
2d *Colleen [Mrs Errol Roberts, PO Box 598, Gweru, Zimbabwe]; *b* 1936; *m* 1954 *Errol Dennis Roberts and has:
1e *Cheryl Gail; *b* 1955; *m* 1979 *Stephen Milham Cloete and has:
1f *Barry James; *b* 1980
2f *Ashley; *b* 1983
2e *Melody Gaynor; *b* 1957; *m* 1984 *Roland Francis Woods and has issue:
1f *Craig Dennis; *b* 1988
2f *Wendy Frances; *b* 1986
3e *Fiona Gaylin; *b* 1958; *m* 1981 *Bryan Matthew Rabie and has:
1f *Robert Matthew; *b* 1985
1f *Tracey-Lee; *b* 1982
4e *Beverley Colleen; *b* 1959; *m* 1978 *Anthony Kreft and has:
1f *Sean Anthony; *b* 1982
1f *Nicolette Colleen; *b* 1980
3d *Cleone; *b* 1942; *m* 1963 *Rodney Erroll Roberts, of Gweru, and has issue:
1e *Shane Gavin; *b* Feb 1965
1e *Felicity Ann; *b* 1967
1c Ellen; *b* 1906; *m* 1934 *William H Cable and had issue
2c *Millicent Pearl; *b* 1908; *m* 1937 Harry Dale (*d* 1957) and has:
1d *Margaret Ann; *b* 1939; *m* 1st 1960 (*divorce* 1962) Peter Reynecke and has issue:
1e *Millicent Sharon; *b* 1961
2c (cont.) Mrs Millicent Dale; *m* 2nd 1963 *Michael Herbert Smit and has further issue:
1d *Steve Carl; *b* 1967
2d *Irene Tessa; *b* 1965
3d *Fiona Ann; *b* 1969
2b (cont.) Charles Heathcote *m* 2nd 1911 Nellie van Heerden (*d* 1918) and *d* 4 Nov 1918, having by her had:
3c *Kathleen Mary; *b* 1912; *m* 1933 *Rev Martin Luther Janse van Rensburg and has issue:
1d *Luther Calvyn; *b* 1935; *m* 1959 *Anne Elizabeath Nieuwoudt and has issue:
1e *Johanna Maria; *b* 1960
1d *Marleen; *b* 1938; *m* 1960 *Johannes Daniel Nieuwoudt, of Hoopstad, Orange Free State, S Africa
4c *Emma Ida May; *b* 1914; *m* 1937 *Jacobus Wessel Janse van Rensburg and has issue:
1d *Jacobus Hendrikus; *b* 1938
2d *Martin Luther; *b* 1946
3d *Jacobus Wessel; *b* 1949
1d *Kathleen Mary; *b* 1943
2d *Alida Jacoba; *b* 1949
3b Fitzroy Hamilton; *b* 1881; *m* 1903 Edith (*d* 1947), 3rd dau of Maj — Beamish, and *d* 1938, leaving issue:
1c *Grace Sybil Beamish [Mrs Norman Sharwood, 5 Brickmakers, Kloof, Port Elizabeth, CP, S Africa]; *b* 27 Aug 1904; *m* 1930 *Norman Sharwood and has issue:
1d *Norma Dorothy [Mrs Tristan Maynier, c/o Standard Bank, Queenstown, S Africa]; *b* 1931; *m* 1954 *Tristan McGibbon Maynier and has issue:
1e *Derek; *b* 1959
1e *Nicolette; *b* 1956; *m* 1980 *Matthew Haxton Millar Guiney and has issue:
1f *Jacquelyn Martha; *b* 1981
2f *Gillian Norma; *b* 1983
2c *Ida Beamish [Mrs William Farrant, c/o Box 375, Pretoria, S Africa]; *b* 19 May 1906; *m* 5 Oct 1932 *William Leslie Lyddon Farrant and has:
1d *Leslie Heathcote; *b* 1935; *m* 1961 *Antoinette du Toit
2d *David Heathcote [David Farrant Esq, c/o Box 375, Pretoria, S Africa]; *b* 1937
3c Olive Ellie Beamish; *b* 13 Dec 1909; *m* 1st 1927 (*divorce* 1936) Henry Southey Scott, and has issue; *m* 2nd 1937 *Keith Wynn Hill
4c *Winifred Beamish [Mrs John Mountjoy, 48 Douglas Ave, Craighall 2196, Johannesburg, S Africa]; *b* 25 Feb 1917; *m* 1st 11 Dec 1935 John Rennie (*ka* 1942), of Haining, Bedford, CP, and has issue:
1d *Myrle Allison [Mrs Paul Noake, 49 Douglas Ave, Craighall, Johannesburg, S Africa]; *b* 1938; *m* 1963 *Paul de Vere Noake and has issue:
1e *John de Vere; *b* 1964
1e *Susan; *b* 1966
4c (cont.) Mrs Winifred Rennie; *m* 2nd 1944 Patrick Diarmid Dolan (*d* 1981); *m* 3rd 1994 *John Radforth Mountjoy, and by her 2nd husb has:
2d *Elizabeth Ann [Mrs Alan Tucker, 9 Government Rd, Beauty Point, 2088 Mosman, Sydney, NSW, Australia]; *b* 1945; *m* 1965 *Alan Tucker and has issue:
1e *Robert Kidger; *b* 1967
2e *James Kidger; *b* 1969
3e *George Kidger; *b* 1971
4e *Ian Kidger; *b* 1973
5c *Edith Ann Beamish; *b* 5 Dec 1920; *m* 1st 1943 (*divorce* 1946) Gordon Sidney Langfield Shepperson; *m* 2nd 1946 (*divorce* 1956) Llewelyn Howell, DFC; *m* 3rd *Albert Goodrick, and has issue
4b Cecil; *b* 1883; *m* 1911 Engela Starr (*m* 2nd 1930 Maurice Meek, of Rhodesia, and *d* 1941), er dau of Ambrose George Campbell Shaw, and *d* 1918, leaving issue:
1c +Cecil Starr; *b* 1912; *m* 1935 *Nora Edith, dau of Walter James, and has issue:
1d Cecil Walter; *b* 1936; *m* 1st 1955 Sylvia Ann Boyd Varty (*d* 1959) and had:
1e *Susan Norah; *b* 1958; *m* 1980 *Terence André Mangnall, of Harare, Zimbabwe, and has issue:
1f *Mark John; *b* 1982
2f *Paul Ian; *b* 1985
1d (cont.) Cecil Heathcote *m* 2nd 1961 (*divorce* 1978) Jennifer Gail Brinsley; *m* 3rd 1981 *Hendrika Albertha Roos, *neé* Kotze, and *d* 1984, leaving by his 2nd w:
2e *Debbie Gaie; *b* 1962; *m* 1983 *Lionel Victor Moore and has:
1f *Rory Victor; *b* 1984
1f *Kerry Gaie; *b* 1986
3e *Carol Jean; *b* 1964; *m* 1983 *Graham Peter Rattey, of Mafeking, Bophuthatswana, and has issue:
1f *Kai Mark; *b* 1985
1f *Linda Heidi; *b* 1971
1d *Janet Mary; *b* 1949; *m* 1976 *John Marshall, of E London, S Africa, and has issue:
1e *Andrew Keith; *b* 1983
1e *Pamela Susan; *b* 1979
2c +Ambrose Carl Starr [Ambrose Heathcote Esq, Village House, PO Esigodini, Zimbabwe]; *b* 1915; *m* 1940 Dorothy (*d* 19 Oct 1990), yr dau of W B Richards, of Fort Victoria, Zimbabwe, and has issue:
1d +David Starr [David Heathcote Esq, 6 Ada Attwell Rd, Ilanda, Bulawayo, Zimbabwe]; *b* 1952
1d *Sylvia Starr [Mrs Michael Gibbons, 39 Stanley Rd, Irene 0062, S Africa]; *b* 1956; *m* 1979 *Michael Basil Gibbons and has:
1e *Richard Michael; *b* 1985
1e *Lara Kathryn; *b* 1983
1c *Mary Lesley Starr [Mrs Harry Smith, Stanhope Farm, Sonbula, Zimbabwe] ; *b* 1913; *m* 1937 *Harry Edward Smith
5b Albert Jerrold; *b* 4 Aug 1887; *m* 1st 22 June 1914 (*divorce*) Dorothy, dau of George Twycross, of De Boise, Wynberg, CP; *m* 2nd 1945 Mrs Muriel Korsten (*d* 1961) and *d* March 1964, having by his 1st w had:
1c +William Jerrold; WW II (POW Italy 1942); *b* 1915; *m* 13 June 1954 *Johanna Hofmeyr
2c +John Albert; Sgt S African Forces; *b* 1916; *m* 1944 *Mrs Rosemary Hilda Beresford Carter, dau of Oswald Beresford Lonsdale, and has:
1d +Charles John Beresford; *b* 31 Aug 1948; *m* 1978 *Anna Krystyna, dau of Jerzy Rafal Cywinski
1d *Phyllis Mary Beresford; *b* 13 Dec 1946; *m* 1968 *Lawrence A Green
2d *Rosemary Alice Beresford; *b* 1 May 1953
3c +George Twycross; *b* 1918; *m* 26 June 1943 *Elizabeth Mary Allport and has:
1d +Michael John; *b* 1 Jan 1954
1d *Dorothy Ann; *b* 13 April 1955
4c Charles (twin with George), Sgt 1st Transvaal Scottish Regt WW II; *b* 1918; *ka* 23 Nov 1941
1b Ellen Marian; *b* 10 April 1879; *m* 1903 E C Becker, of Cradock, CP, and had issue
2b Florence Ida May; *b* 31 May 1891; *m* 1st 13 June 1913 Robert Wilson, civ engr, (*d* 1924), of Cradock, CP, and had issue; *m* 2nd 1927 Izak Petrus Kruger (*d* 1961), and *d* 23 Feb 1964, leaving further issue
3b Olive Stella; *b* 12 Feb 1894; *m* 1924 Paul Michau (*d* 1946), of Cradock, and *d* 1964, leaving issue
3a Henry; *m* Laetitia Murray (*m* 2nd 19– Rev F Stewart) and *d* 1893, leaving:

1b Henry Gage; *b* 1877
2b Clifford; *b* 18–
1b Mary; *b* 18–; *m* 18– Clem Will
2b Alice Eleanor; *b* 1886; *m* 1905 Arthur James Ford, Div Sec Boy Scouts' Assocn, and had issue:
1c *John Lovell Heathcote; *b* 1906
2c *Frank Stewart Heathcote; *b* 1915
3c *Arthur Dymond Heathcote; *b* 1920
1c *Muriel; *b* 1908
2c *Evelyn; *b* 1908
3b Ine; *b* 18–
1a Sarah; *m* W C Wallis and had issue
2a Marian; *m* James Murray
3a Georgina; *m* – Gilfillen
4a Caroline; *m* James Murray and had issue
(2) Henry (Rev); *b* 1804; *m* 1832 Henrietta Maria, dau of Robert Bransby Cooper, MP Gloucester (*see* COOPER, Bt, of Gadebridge), and *d* 1874, leaving:
1a William
2a Gilbert
(3) Thomas Hamilton; *d* 1824
(4) George Gage; Lt RN; *m* Emma, yst dau of Thomas Philipps, of Lampeter, Cards, and had issue:
1a Gage Charles Edward; *b* 29 July 1842; *m* 20 Feb 1879 Hermina Alletta Fourie, dau of A Van Wych, and *d* 5 Nov 1895, leaving issue:
1b Edward Munro; *b* 11 Nov 1882
2b William; Boer War 1900–02 with 31st Coy ASC and WW I as Lt 3rd Bde Wakerstroom Commando SW African Campaign, Locomotive Inspr S African Rlwys 1937–39; *b* 24 July 1884; *m* Helena Cathrina Faure (*d* 1985) and *d* 11 May 1961, leaving:
1c +William Charles [William Heathcote Esq, Box 439, Keetmanshoop, SW Africa]; *b* 19 June 1929; *m* 19– *Connie Danie van Neikerk and has had:
1d +William; *b* 8 July 1958; *m* 19– *Annemarie van Zyl and has:
1e *Elizmarie; *b* 1988
2d Conrad; *b* 26 Aug 1960; *d* 1985
3d *Raymond; *b* 25 Sept 1964
1c *Maria Wilhelmina [Mrs Norman Venables, Lushington Park, PO Kidds Beach, East London, S Africa]; *b* 17 April 1919; *m* 2 Jan 1940 *Norman Charles Venables and has:
1d *Keith Norman; *b* 12 May 1942; *m* 23 Oct 1965 *Yvonne Valerie Frugel and has:
1e *Bevan Keith; *b* 1972
1e *Sandra Lee; *b* 3 Dec 1966; *m* 1991 *John James Ward and has:
1f *Jay Cameron; *b* 1989
2f *Ryan; *b* 1992
2e *Terri-Ann; *b* 1969
2d *Peter Kevin; *b* 10 Aug 1956; *m* 1978 *Janet Edith Ewers and has:
1e *Wesly; *b* 1981
2e *Dai; *b* 1983
1d *Bernadette; *b* 8 Oct 1945; *m* 23 March 1966 *Johan Martines Els and has issue:
1e *Hank Stuart; *b* 5 Aug 1969
1e *Dominique; *b* 26 June 1968
2c *Thora [Mrs William van Schoor, PO Box 2013, Johannesburg, S Africa]; *b* 13 June 1922; *m* *William Herbert van Schoor and has issue:
1d *Denise Thora; *b* 12 Sept 1944; *m* 3 Dec 1965 *Alva Felix Walter Oldknow
2d *Marlene Deirdre; *b* 6 Sept 1948; *m* 1969 *Lukas Matthee Auò
3c *Maureen Cathrine; *b* 21 Jan 1937; *m* 1 Dec 1961 *Petrus Jacobus Alwyn van der Merwe, son of Petrus Jacobus Alwyn Van der Merwe, of Gibeon, SW Africa, and has issue:
1d *Petrus; *b* 10 Aug 1962
2d *Randolph; *b* 20 April 1965
1d *Marina; *b* 1966
1b Aletta Cathrina; *b* 20 Nov 1879; *m* 1898 Geohardus Jacobus van der Merwe
2b Emily; *b* 30 April 1887; *m* 1902 Ernest Alfred Hornby
3b Hermina Alletta; *b* 15 May 1889; *m* 1905 William George August
2a Thomas Munro; *b* 1848; *m* 1879 Augusta Euphine, dau of E Phillips, and *d* 1890, leaving issue:
1b Emma Katherine
2b Marion
3a Edward Arthur; *b* 1853
1a Georgina Catherine; *m* A B Kennedy and *d* 1879
2a Frances Sophia; *m* 19 Dec 1862 Dr George Clarence Hyde, JP, and had issue
3a Emma Mary; *m* 1869 Henry Carlisle (*d* 1899), and had issue
(1) Frances Sarah; *m* 1 April 1817 Lt-Gen Sir Henry Somerset, KCB, and *d* 16 March 1886, leaving issue (*see* BEAUFORT, D)
(2) Leonora Macclesfield; *d* unm
(3) Susannah Maria Ouseley; *m* 1841 Maj Thomas Donovan and had issue
(4) Anne Forbes; *m* George Sanford (*d* 1843) and had issue
(5) Harriet Forbes; *m* 1st 1840 Honoratus Van Rynvelt, of Cape of Good Hope, and had issue; *m* 2nd 1857 — Van Roojen, of Diep River, Cape of Good Hope
(6) Maria Frances Digby; *m* Thomas Ouchterlony and *d* 1846, having had issue
(7) Georgiana Jamesina Somerset; *m* 2 Feb 1839 John T H Blohm and had issue

5 Gilbert; Capt RN; *b* Dec 1779; *m* Feb 1809 Anne (*d* 30 April 1854), dau of Charles Lyell (*see* LYELL, B), and *d* 20 April 1831, leaving, with other issue:
(1) Gilbert (Rev); *b* 11 July 1816; *m* 1st 15 Jan 1840 Mary (*d* 24 Dec 1843), dau of Charles Lyell (*see* LYELL, B); *m* 2nd 10 Feb 1846 Mary (*d* 2 April 1854), dau of Adml Frederick Jennings Thomas (*see* THOMAS, Bt, of Wenvoe), and had issue:
1a Thomas Charles; Lt RN; *d* 9 Nov 1875
2a Frederick Arthur; 81st Regt; *b* 1851; *m* 1887 Evelyn Constance (*d* 14 Feb 1938), dau of Frederick Elin, and *d* 23 April 1925, having had issue:
1b Frederick Gilbert; MA Oxon, Dist Offr N Nigeria; *b* 1889; drowned 23 Aug 1918
1b Gertrude Evelyn Atherley; *m* 7 July 1920 Richard Picton Rosser, MB, ChB, and had issue:
1c *John Gilbert Heathcote; *b* 1922
2c *Charles; *b* 1929
1a Mary Louisa Ann; *m* 1885 Capt Edward Payne, RN (*d* 20 Nov 1906), and *d* Aug 1914, leaving issue
2a Selina; *m* 16 April 1874 Capt A J V Collins, RN (*d* 14 Jan 1901), and *d* 10 April 1902
3a Ellen Georgiana; *d* 10 Dec 1919
(1) (cont.) The Rev Gilbert Heathcote *m* 3rd 6 Dec 1855 Eliza Julia (*d* 30 March 1908), dau of Rev Sir Godfrey Thomas, 6th Bt, and *d* 28 Oct 1876, having by her had:
4a Eliza Paulina; *d* unm 8 Dec 1941
(1) Frances; *m* 11 Oct 1831 Rev H Fox Atherley (*d* 2 Aug 1874) and *d* 10 Aug 1858, leaving issue
1 Harriet; *m* 28 April 1798 Langford Lovell and *d* 1850
2 Maria Frances; *m* June 1824 Charles Wyndham (*d* 14 March 1846), of Donhead Hall, Wilts, and *d* 9 Aug 1859, leaving issue

The 4th Bt's nephew,

Sir William Heathcote, 5th Bt, PC; DCL Oxford, MP Hants 1826–31, N Hants 1837–49 and Oxford U 1854–68; *b* 17 May 1801; *m* 1st 8 Nov 1825 Caroline Frances (*d* 3 March 1835), yst dau of 1st Baron Arden (*see* EGMONT, E), and had:
1 **Sir William Perceval Heathcote, 6th Bt**, JP; Lt 7th Hus; *b* 7 Sept 1826; *m* 5 Sept 1849 Letitia Maria (*d* 22 Aug 1910), dau of David Daly, of Dublin, and *d* 29 Oct 1903, having had:
(1) **Rev Sir William Arthur Heathcote, 7th Bt**; RC priest, SJ; *b* 22 July 1853; *d* 9 Sept 1924
(2) **Sir Gilbert Redvers Heathcote, 8th Bt**; Lt-Col 1st Bn Cameronians, JP Hants, High Sheriff 1927; *b* 25 Dec 1854; *m* 1st 15 Oct 1891 Pauline (*dsp* 3 June 1897), dau of Sir Alfred Trevelyan, 7th Bt, of Nettlecombe (*qv*); *m* 2nd 11 July 1901 Mabel (*d* 30 July 1968), yst dau of Henry Charles Silvertop, of Minster Acres, Northumberland, and *dsp* 6 Nov 1937
(1) Kathleen Ada; nun of the Sacre Coeur
(2) Isabel Frances; *d* unm 17 Jan 1932
2 George Parker; Capt 52nd Foot; *b* 24 July 1828; *m* 15 June 1869 Isabella Mararetta Elizabeth (*d* 22 Oct 1938), yst dau of Spencer Horatio Walpole, PC, MP (*see* WALPOLE, B), and *dsp* 15 Feb 1871
3 Gilbert Vyvyan (Rev); Rector W Deeping, Lincs; *b* 12 July 1830; *m* 1st 29 March 1853 Eliza (*d* 16 Aug 1864), est dau of Lt-Col William Arthur Heathcote, of Rolleston, Wilts (*see* above), and had issue:
(1) Gilbert Arthur (Rev); MA, Supernumary Diocese of Glasgow; *b* 10 Feb 1854; *m* 2 July 1878 Mary Susan (*d* 24 June 1935), dau of Maj William James Rind, Bengal Army, and *d* 10 Sept 1907, leaving issue:
1a Mary Gertrude Caroline; ARRC, Serbian Order St Sava 5th Cl, served WWs I and II; *b* 8 Sept 1884
2a Grace Mary Bertha; *b* 2 Oct 1887; *d* unm 18 Nov 1941
(2) George Wyndham; *b* 5 June 1855; *d* 1930
(3) Gerald William Yvery; FRES; *b* 28 Dec 1858; *m* 1st 28 Sept 1882 Amy (*d* 1 April 1888), dau of Rev George Davies, Vicar of Eldon, and had issue:
1a Henry Arthur Yvery; *b* 17 Dec 1887; *m* 13 June 1913 Emmeline Nydia, est dau of Josephus Taylor, of Old Charlton, Kent, and *dsp* Nov 1934
(3) (cont.) Gerald Heathcote *m* 2nd 20 June 1893 Mary Florence (*d* 31 March 1920), dau of Ven W H Turpin, and *d* 1930, having by her had issue:
1a Dorothy May; *b* 19 May 1895; *m* 1920 Wallace Atkins Westbrook, of Johannesburg, and had issue
2a Marjorie Florence; *b* 15 Sep; *d* 18 Dec 1898
(4) Godfrey Samuel Charles (Rev); Rector Molteno, Cape Good Hope; *b* 17 Sept 1860; *m* 13 Feb 1882 Marian, dau of G Underwood, and *d* 16 July 1927
(1) Gertrude Mary Selina; *b* 20 May 1856; *m* 1895 Neville M Lawrence and *d* 1930, leaving issue
(2) Gytha Mary Catherine; *d* 8 Sept 1865
3 (cont.) The Rev Gilbert Heathcote *m* 2nd 14 Nov 1865 Helen Maxwell (*d* 1882), only child of James John Cunningham, EICS, and by her had issue:
(5) William Charles Perceval; Lt Army; *b* 27 March 1867; *m* 19 Oct 1921 Ruth (*d* 4 June 1950), yst dau of Arthur Malcolm Heathcote (*see* below), and *d* 13 June 1937, leaving issue:
1a *Anne; WW II as 3rd Offr WRNS; *b* 3 July 1923; *m* 17 March 1945 *Baron Diederic Wolter van Lynden, Amb Dutch For Serv, and has issue:
1b *Jan Willem Alexander; *b* 27 Nov 1948
2b *Crel Diederic Aernout; *b* 31 Dec 1954
1b *Carola; *b* 29 July 1947; *m* 5 July 1969 *Jonkheer Alexander Gerard Beelaerts van Blokland
(6) **Rev Sir Francis Cooke Caulfield Heathcote, 9th Bt**; DD (Trin Coll Toronto), Archdeacon Vancouver 1913–41, Prolocutor Gen Synod C of E Canada 1927–34, Provincial Synod of BC 1920–40, Bp New Westminster 1941–50; *b* 20 April 1868; *m* 13 July 1901 Evelyn Margaret (*d* 3 Feb 1957), dau of J F Smith, KC, of Toronto, and *dsp* 11 Sept 1961
(7) Spencer Gilbert; *b* 14 Oct 1871; drowned Canada 24 Dec 1901

(3) Helen Mary Caroline; *b* 17 Oct 1875; *m* 10 May 1904 Lt Godfrey Edward Landon (*d* 2 March 1924), RA and India Telegraph Serv, yst s of Rev Edward Henry Landon, and *d* 30 Sept 1964, leaving issue

(4) Margaret Mary Helena; *b* 25 June 1882; *m* 26 June 1906 Col Joseph Francis Noel Baxendale, DL, JP (*d* 29 Jan 1957), of Hursley Park, and *d* 29 March 1966, leaving issue

3 (cont.) Gilbert Heathcote *m* 3rd 20 Nov 1883 Mary Henrietta (*d* 22 Nov 1937) (*m* 2nd 25 Feb 1897 Henry Gourlay (*d* 1915), of Kempshott Park, Hants), dau of Spencer Arthur Perceval (*see* EGMONT, E), and *d* 7 Feb 1890, having by her had:

(8) LEONARD VYVYAN (Sir), **10th Bt**

(9) Reginald St Alban; DM, FRCP, Lond 1932, FRCP 1937, Prof Pharmacology Us of Egypt 1922–33 and Wales 1933–51, T/Capt RAMC and T/Surgn RN WW I, WW II in HG, Order Nile 3rd Cl; *b* 17 June 1888; *educ* Winchester, New Coll Oxford (BA 1911, MA 1914) and UCH (BM, BCh 1914, DM 1920, BSc 1922); *m* 1st 15 Aug 1913 Viola (*d* 20 Jan 1947), dau and coheir of Osbert Salvin, FRS, and gdau of Antony Salvin, FSA, of Hawksfold; *m* 2nd 19 Feb 1948 Amy (*d* 18 March 1974), formerly w of Hon A/Cdr Richard Cadman, CBE, DL (*see* CADMAN, B), and yst dau of R George Howson, and *d* 19 May 1951, having by his 1st w had:

1a Antony Giles Salvin, CD; Dir Gen Medical Services, Dept Public Health Toronto, MRCS, LRCP 1945, Maj RCAMC, Militia, DPH (U of Toronto) 1954; *b* 18 Dec 1919; *educ* Winchester and New Coll Oxford (BA 1942, MA 1952); *m* 17 June 1953 *Kathleen Joan [Mrs Antony Heathcote, 276 McKee Ave, Willowdale, Ont, Canada], only dau of Harry Dawson, and *d* 9 June 1970, leaving:

1b +William Reginald Salvin; *b* 4 June 1955

2b +Andrew Henry Salvin; *b* 30 April 1962

1b *Jean Viola; *b* 25 March 1954

2b *Catherine Dawson; *b* 10 March 1959

3b *Ann Elizabeth; *b* 15 July 1960

4b *Ruth Margaret; *b* 14 Nov 1963

1 Caroline Elizabeth; *m* 17 Aug 1858 Thomas Richard Frederick Cooke-Trench (*see* ASHTOWN, B) and *dsp* 24 Nov 1910

Sir William *m* 2nd 18 May 1841 Selina (*d* 17 July 1901), dau of Evelyn John Shirley (*see* FERRERS, E), and *d* 17 Aug 1881, having by her had, with other issue:

4 Charles George, JP Hants; MA Oxon, CA Hants, Maj Northumberland Fus, Col 1st Vol Bn Hants Regt; *b* 1 Oct 1843; *m* 15 May 1884 Lucy Lyttelton, MBE (1920) (*d* 15 Jan 1934), dau of Richard Tanfield Vachell, of Coptfold Hall, and *d* 13 April 1924, having had issue:

(1) George Malcolm; *b* 25 Sept 1891

(1) Maud Lyttelton; ARRC; *b* 20 Feb 1885

(2) Sybil Annesley; *b* 25 Sept 1886; *d* 26 Sept 1898

(3) Jennetta Selina; *b* 10 Sept 1888; *d* unm March 1964

(4) Frances Gwendolen; *b* 19 Feb 1890; *m* 1921 Maj Albert Parrott, Green Howards, and had issue

(5) Lucy Helena; *b* 12 Dec 1896; *d* unm 3 March 1949

5 Evelyn Dawsonne (Rev); MA Oxon; Vicar Sparsholt Hants; *b* 11 Nov 1844; *m* 19 Dec 1876 Grace (*d* 27 March 1932), 2nd dau of James Hussey, of The Close, Salisbury, and *dsp* 1 May 1908

6 Arthur Malcolm; BA Oxon; *b* 22 April 1847; *m* 20 Aug 1879 Mary Forbes (*d* 1 Jan 1902), 2nd dau of Rev James G Young, Vicar Hursley Hants, and *d* 5 Aug 1934, having had issue:

(1) James Shirley; Lt Coldstream Gds; *b* 7 July 1887; *m* 7 Aug 1912 Agnes Ethel, dau of James Hatcher, of Brandon, Canada, and *d* 28 Aug 1917 of wounds recd in action, leaving issue:

1a Martin Shirley; Lt RA (SR) WW II 1939–40 (POW); *b* 28 Jan 1914; *educ* Sherborne; *m* 15 Jan 1948 *Mary Gertrude, widow of S/Ldr J K Macpherson, RAAF, and est dau of Dr Horace N Nowland, of Sydney, NSW, and *d* 1992, leaving:

1b +Richard Desmond [Richard Heathcote Esq, Warrawon, Tambar Springs, NSW, Australia]; *b* 1 April 1950; *m* 1973 *Carmel, dau of William Montgomery, and has had issue:

1c +James Martin; *b* 1974

2c +Samuel William; *b* 1978

3c +Benjamin Richard; *b* 1990

1c *Sophie Louise; *b* 1976

2c Amy Patricia; *b* 1982; *d* 1984

1b *Pamela Shirley; *b* 12 March 1949; *m* 1971 *Gaasper Rey I de Grief

2b *Anne Margaret; *b* 8 Feb 1956

(2) Martin Arthur, MC; Lt 10th Roy Fus WW I (despatches); *b* 15 Jan 1892; *d* 17 July 1916 of wounds recd in action

(1) Dorothy; *b* 20 Nov 1880; *m* 8 Nov 1902 Arthur Crawford Lee (*d* 1939), Capt Roy Fus, only s of Rev Godfrey Bolles Lee, Warden Winchester Coll, and *d* 29 Jan 1951, leaving issue

(2) Phyllis Young; *b* 2 May 1882; *d* 16 March 1884

(3) Marion; *b* 3 Feb 1884; *m* 1st 23 Nov 1907 Maj Robert Maxwell Grenfell Knight, RGA, Lt-Cdr RN, and had issue; *m* 2nd 1921 Cdr Ralph W B Cotesworth, RN (*d* 18 Sept 1937)

(4) Ruth; *b* 20 Nov 1885; *m* 19 Oct 1921 William Charles Perceval Heathcote (*see* above), and *d* 4 June 1950, leaving issue

The 9th Bt's half-bro,

Sir Leonard Vyvyan Heathcote, 10th Bt; *b* 7 Sept 1885; *educ* Wellington and Clare Coll Cambridge; *m* 3 Jan 1923 Joyce Kathleen (*d* 20 Dec 1967), dau of Benjamin Perryman Willis, of Calcutta, and *d* 24 June 1963, leaving:

1 Sir MICHAEL PERRYMAN HEATHCOTE, **11th and present Bt**

1 *Pamela Mary [Mrs Gilbert Jones, Walnut Tree Cottage, Harkstead, Ipswich, Suffolk]; *b* 9 Oct 1923; *m* 18 July 1945 *(John) Gilbert Jones, Dip Serv, and has:

(1) *Richard Edmund, MBE; *b* 12 Sept 1947; *educ* Westminster and U of Kent (BSc); *m* 1987 *Euphemia Photos and has issue:

1a *Alexander Xenophon; *b* 1988

2a *Michael Andronicus; *b* 1991

3a *Simon Maximian; *b* 1993

(1) *Rosemary Anne; *b* 16 Dec 1948; *m* 1975 *T J Aston and has issue:

1a *Emma; *b* 1979

HEATHCOTE of London

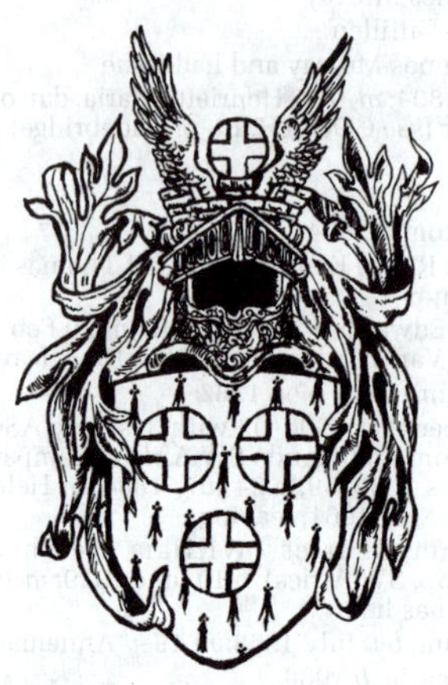

Arms: Erm. three pomeys, each charged with a cross or. **Crests:** on a mural crown az. a pomey as in the arms between two wings displayed erm. **Creation:** Bt. (GB) 17 Jan 1733.

SIR GILBERT SIMON HEATHCOTE, 9TH BT, CBE (1964, MBE 1945) [Brig Sir Gilbert Heathcote Bt CBE, The Coach House, Tillington, W Sussex GU28 ORA]; *b* 21 Sept 1913; *s* cousin 3rd Earl of Ancaster as 9th Bt 1983; *educ* Eton and RMA Woolwich; commnd RA WW II Ch of Staff Middle east Cmd 1962–66, ret 1966 as Brig; *m* 1st 28 Feb 1939 (*divorce* 1984) Patricia Margaret, dau of Brig James Travers Leslie, MC, Roy Berks Regt, of Sway, Hants, and has:

1 +MARK SIMON ROBERT, OBE (1988) [Mark Heathcote Esq OBE, c/o Upton Dean, Upton, nr Andover, Hants]; *b* 1 March 1941; *educ* Eton and Magdalene Coll Cambridge; P&O SN Co 1963–70, FCO (Counsellor) 1971–94, BP plc 1994–; *m* 15 May 1976 *Susan Mary, dau of Lt-Col George Ashley, The Cameronians, of Rosamondford Lodge, Aylesbeare, Devon, and has issue:

(1) +Alastair Robert; *b* 18 Aug 1977

(2) +Nicholas Alexander; *b* 21 July 1979

1 *Joanna; *b* 25 April 1947

Sir GILBERT *m* 2nd 2 April 1984 *Ann, widow of Brig James Frederick Charles Mellor DSO, OBE, and dau of W/Cdr J A Hatton, OBE

Lineage: THOMAS HETHCOTE, of Chesterfield, Derbys; *b c* 1440; *m* Rose — and *d* 1492, leaving, with an er s (Richard, Mayor Chesterfield 1503):

RALPH HETHCOTE, of Chesterfield; bellfounder; *m* Ellen (*d* after Oct 1496), dau of John Thompson, and *d* 1525, leaving a 3rd s:

THOMAS HEATHCOTT, of Chesterfield and Lodes in Brampton; *m* Mary — (*d* 1570) and *d* 1559, leaving, with two daus and five other sons, a 2nd s:

GEORGE HEATHCOTE, of Lodes; *m* Agnes Senior (*d* after 6 May 1610) and *d* 1601, leaving a 3rd s:

GILBERT HEATHCOTE, of Chesterfield; *m* Elizabeth Outram and *d* in or after 1634/5, leaving:

GILBERT HEATHCOTE; thrice Mayor Chesterfield; *b* Aug 1625; *m* Anne (*d* 1705), dau of George Dickins/Dickons, of Chesterfield, and *d* 24 April 1690, having had, with five other sons:

1 GILBERT, (Sir), **1st Bt**

2 Samuel; *see* HEATHCOTE, Bt, of Hursley

3 Josiah; *d* 24 Nov 1706, leaving issue:

(1) George; Ld Mayor London 1742

The est son,

Sir Gilbert Heathcote, 1st Bt (GB), so *cr* 17 Jan 1732/3; Govr Bank of England 1708, Ld Mayor London 1710, MP City London 1701–13, Hilston 1715–20, Lymington 1722–27 and St Germans 1727–33, ktd 1702; *b* 2 Jan 1651/2; *m* (licence 30 May 1682) Hester (*d* 27 Sept 1714), dau and heir of Christopher Rayner, of London, and *d* 25 Jan 1732/3, leaving:

Sir John Heathcote, 2nd Bt; MP Grantham 1715–22 and Bodmin 1733–41; *b* 1689; *m* 5 Aug 1720 Bridget (*d* 5 May 1772), dau of Thomas White (*see* WHITE, Bt, of Wallingwells), and had, with other issue:

1 GILBERT (Sir), **3rd Bt**

2 John, of Conington Castle, Peterborough, Hunts; *m* 27 Oct 1764 Lydia (*d* 14 Aug 1822), dau and heir of Benjamin Moyer, and *d* 29 July 1795, having had:

(1) John, of Conington Castle; MP Ripon; *b* 14 Nov 1767; *m* 5 Nov 1799 Mary Anne (*d* 27 July 1854), dau of George Thornhill, of Diddington, and *d* 3 May 1838, leaving issue:

1a John Moyer, of Conington Castle, DL Hunts; High Sheriff 1854; *b* 9 Nov 1800; *educ* Eton and St John's Coll Cambridge (BA 1822); *m* 11 April 1833 Hon Emily Frances Ridley Colborne (*d* 13 Oct 1849), dau of 1st and last Baron Colborne (*see* RIDLEY, V), and *d* 27 March 1892, having had issue:

1b John Moyer, of Conington Castle, JP, DL Hunts, JP Sussex; barrister, Hon Col 3rd Vol Bn Suffolk Regt, MA Cantab; *b* 12 July 1834; *m* 18 Dec 1860 Louisa Cecilia (*d* 20 Jan 1910), only dau of Norman MacLeod, 25th Chief of MacLeod, and *d* 3 Aug 1912, having had issue:

1c John Norman, of Conington Castle, JP Hunts; High Sheriff 1917, CA; *b* 21 June 1863; *educ* Trin Coll Cambridge (BA); *d* unm 16 July 1946

2c Arthur Ridley; *b* 14 Feb 1877; *m* 18 Dec 1909 Margaret Georgina (*d* 1 March 1944), dau of Horace Broke, of Gladwyns Harlow, and *d* 13 April 1951, leaving issue:

1d +John Horace Broke; *b* 28 Dec 1910; *educ* Eton and Trin Coll Cambridge (BA 1932); *m* 14 Aug 1949 *Dorelle Geraldine, dau of Lt-Col Gerald Dominic Rice, DSO, of Rocheville, Fermoy, Co Cork, and has issue:

1e *Miranda Lydia; *b* 26 Jan 1950

2e *Venetia Catherine; *b* 22 April 1951

2d +Norman Richard *b* 25 May 1914; *educ* Eton and Trin Coll Cambridge (BA); *m* 24 Aug 1946 *Margaret Enid, dau of Alan Keith Burnett, of Illovo Beach, Natal, S Africa, and has issue:

1e +Richard John; *b* 17 Jan 1951; *educ* Bembridge Sch

1e *Katherine Louise; *b* 16 Oct 1952

2e *Diana Elizabeth; *b* 16 Oct 1952

1d Ila Margaret; *b* 2 July 1912; *m* 7 May 1938 (*divorce* 1951) Lt-Cdr Walter Dermot Muspratt, RN, er s of Rev Walter Muspratt, of Brickworth Park, Whiteparish, Salisbury, and *d* 2 Aug 1961, leaving issue

1c Emily Louisa; *d* unm 25 May 1880

2c Evelyn May; *d* unm 15 April 1957 aged 91

2b William George; *b* 6 Feb 1836; *d* unm 1857

3b Charles Gilbert, JP Hants; MA Cambridge, barrister, Stipendiary Magistrate Brighton 1884–1902; *b* 2 March 1841; *m* 9 Sept 1869 Lucy Edith (*d* 19 Feb 1918), dau of Hon Walter Wrottesley (*see* WROTTESLEY, B), and *d* 15 Nov 1913, leaving issue:

1c Walter John, of Kilmeston Manor, Alresford, Hants; Consul Monastir, European Turkey 1907–08, Levant Consular Serv 1894–1908; *b* 23 Sept 1870; *d* unm 15 Nov 1936

1c Isabel Lucy; *m* 16 July 1910 Lt-Col Harry Broke, RE (*d* 23 Nov 1923), and *d* 27 Nov 1961, leaving issue

2c Mabel Frances; *m* 15 Oct 1919 Gwyn Vaughan Morgan MA, *d* 31 May 1945 (*see* 1970 edn VAUGHAN-MORGAN, Bt), and *d* 9 Jan 1955

4b Henry Francis; *b* 11 Aug 1849; *d* 1854

1b Mary Emily; *d* unm 9 June 1932

2a Robert Boothby (Rev), JP Essex, of Friday Hill, Chingford Hill, Essex; Rector Chingford; *b* 13 May 1805; *educ* Eton and St John's Coll Cambridge (BA 1827); *m* 1st 9 March 1837 Charlotte (*d* 15 Jan 1845), dau of Adml Thomas Sotheby, and had issue:

1b Robert Boothby, of Friday Hill, and Marston Hall, Leics, JP; *b* 10 Jan 1844; *m* 2 Oct 1872 Jane Vere, dau of Sir Cavendish Foster, 3rd Bt, and *dsp* Jan 1893

1b Charlotte Mary; *m* 11 April 1860 5th and last Earl of Carysfort, KP (*see* PROBY, Bt), and *dsp* 13 Jan 1918

2b Katherine Sophia Boothby; *d* unm 13 Dec 1913

2a (cont.) Robert Heathcote *m* 2nd 10 Oct 1848 Elizabeth Bridget (*d* 1894), er dau of Capt William Wells, RN, of Holme Wood, Hunts, and *d* 19 Sept 1865, having by her had:

2b William Edward Boothby, of Friday Hill; Fell Trin Coll Cambridge, barrister; *b* 11 June 1853; *d* 13 Dec 1915

3b Frederick Granville HEATHCOTE later SINCLAIR (1889), of Barrogill Castle, Caithness (which he inherited from the 15th Earl of Caithness (*qv*), adopting the latter's family name in consequence), JP, DL Caithness, JP Cambridge; *b* 8 Dec 1857; *educ* Eton and Trin Coll Cambridge (MA 1885); *m* 18 Oct 1888 Agnes Charlotte (*m* 2nd 19 Dec 1923 Rev George Leo Sinclair-Gerold (*d* 22 Feb 1933), Rector Easthope, Salop, and *d* May 1950), dau of Thomas J Barnes, barrister, and *d* 16 March 1914

3b Emily Frances; *m* 28 July 1874 1st Baron Cranworth (*qv*) and *d* 3 April 1934, leaving issue

4b Louisa Gertrude BOOTHBY HEATHCOTE; *d* unm 18 Sept 1940

3a George (Rev), JP; *b* 11 Jan 1811; *educ* Eton and St John's Coll Cambridge (BA 1833); Rector Conington, Hon Canon Ely, RD; *m* 1 July 1839 Catherine Sophia (*dsp* 1 Aug 1840), dau of Adml Thomas Sotheby, and *d* 9 March 1895

1a Mary Anne Lydia; *m* 1 Sept 1824 Lt-Col George Hussey Packe, JP, DL, MP (*d* 2 July 1874), of Prestwold Hall, Loughborough, Leics, and *d* 10 Oct 1876, leaving issue

2a Frances Catherine; *m* 16 Feb 1841Rev William Rooper and *d* 25 Jan 1882 aged 72

(1) Lydia; *m* 6 June 1811 6th Viscount Downe (*qv*) and *d* 18 March 1848

1 Bridget; *m* 31 July 1755 as his 2nd w, 14th Earl of Morton (*qv*) and had issue

2 Anne; *m* 6 Feb 1778, as his 2nd w, Sir Robert Hamilton, 4th Bt, of Silvertonhill (*qv*)

Sir JOHN *d* 5 Sept 1759; his er son,

Sir Gilbert Heathcote, 3rd Bt; MP Shaftesbury 1761–68; *m* 1st 22 June 1749 Marguerite (*dsp* 10 Aug 1796), yst dau of 1st Earl of Hardwicke (*qv*); *m* 2nd 26 Dec 1770 Elizabeth (*d* 14 July 1813), dau of Robert Hudson, of Teddington, and *d* 2 Nov 1785, having had issue:

1 **Sir Gilbert Heathcote, 4th Bt**; MP Lincs 1796–1806 and Rutland 1812–41; *b* 6 Oct 1773; *m* 1st 16 Aug 1793 Katherine Sophia (*d* 28 April 1825), est dau of John Manners, of Grantham Grange, Lincs, by Louisa Tollemache, Countess of Dysart (*qv*), and had issue:

(1) **Sir Gilbert John Heathcote, 5th Bt**, and 1st BARON AVELAND OF AVELAND, Co Lincoln (UK), so *cr* 26 Feb 1856; *b* 16 Jan 1795; Ld Lt Lincs, MP Boston 1820–30, S Lincs 1832–41 and Rutland 1841–56; *m* 8 Oct 1827 Clementina Elizabeth, Baroness Willoughby de Eresby (*qv* for further details of her issue by **Sir Gilbert**) in her own right, and *d* 6 Sept 1867, leaving with other issue:

1a Sir GILBERT HENRY HEATHCOTE later HEATHCOTE-DRUMMOND-WILLOUGHBY (roy licence 4 May 1872), **6th Bt**, 25th LORD (Baron) WILLOUGHBY De ERESBY, 2nd BARON AVELAND OF AVELAND and 1st EARL OF ANCASTER, Co Lincoln (UK), so *cr* 22 Aug 1892; had:

1b **Sir Gilbert Heathcote, 7th Bt**, 2nd EARL OF ANCASTER and 26th LORD (Baron) WILLOUGHBY De ERESBY; had, with other issue:

1c **Sir Gilbert James Heathcote, 8th Bt**, 27th LORD (Baron) WILLOUGHBY De ERESBY (in which title called up to Ho Lds *vp* 16 Jan 1951) and 3rd and last EARL OF ANCASTER, JP (Lincs 1937); *b* 8 Dec 1907; *d* 29 March 1983, when the Barony of Aveland and Earldom expired, having had issue (*see* WILLOUGHBY DE ERESBY, B)

(2) Edward Lionel; Capt RHG (Blues); *d* 17 July 1875 aged 79

(3) William Henry; *b* 29 May 1797; *m* 17 Dec 1833 Sophia Matilda (*d* 20 Nov 1880), only dau of Thomas Wright, of Upton Hall, Notts, and *dsp* 17 Oct 1880

1 (cont.) **Sir Gilbert** *m* 2nd 10 Aug 1825 Mrs Eldon (*d* 21 Oct 1842), of Park Crescent, Marylebone, and *d* 26 March 1851, having by her had issue:

(4) Arthur, of Durdan's Park, Epsom; *b* 22 June 1829; *d* unm March 1869

2 John; *d* unm 1802

3 Robert, of Lobthorpe, Lincs; *m* April 1807 Elizabeth, actress, dau of J Searle, and *d* March 1823, leaving:

(1) George Augustus Frederick, of Lobthorpe, Capt 2nd Life Gds; *b* 23 May 1809; *m* 1st Olympe (*d* 3 Jan 1839), dau of Antoine Joseph Henry d'Herculley, of Riez, and had issue:

1a Marie Olympe; *d* unm 16 Feb 1910

(1) (cont.) George Heathcote *m* 2nd 17 Nov 1841 Anna (*m* 2nd 26 Dec 1849 Baron M de Chamisso de Boncourt), dau of Jean Baptiste de Buffa, and *d* 24 July 1845, having by her had issue:

1a Robert, of Lobthorpe and Manton Hall, Oakham, Rutland, JP Lincs and Rutland; Capt Leics Yeo Cav; *b* 24 April 1843; *educ* Trin Coll Cambridge (BA); *m* 25 Aug 1877 Edith Mary (*d* 25 April 1924), only dau of John Henry Manners-Sutton (*see* RUTLAND, D), and *d* 15 July 1917, leaving issue:

1b Robert Evelyn Manners, DSO (1918), of Lobthorpe and Manton Hall, High Sheriff Rutland 1936, Hon Lt-Col 3rd Bn Roy Scots WW I, RA 1940 (wounded, despatches); *b* 4 Sept 1884; *educ* Eton; *m* 1st 6 July 1912 (*divorce* 1922) Edith Millicent, dau of William Walton, of Horsley Priory, Nailsworth, leaving issue:

1c Sir (GILBERT) SIMON HEATHCOTE, **9th and present Bt**

1c *Evelyn Valhalla Suzanne [Mrs Robert Colling, Hadcott House, West Ilsley, Berks]; *b* 11 Sept 1917; *m* 1st 21 Nov 1938 (*divorce* 1952) Henry Louis Morriss (*d* 5 April 1963), s of Henry Ernest Morriss (*see* SAMUEL, Bt); *m* 2nd 25 Sept 1952 *Robert John Colling and by her 1st husb has issue:

1d *Hugo Henry; *b* 29 Sept 1939; *educ* Downside and Univ Coll Oxford; *m* 9 Sept 1967 *Marie Diston, dau of David Scull, of Philadelphia

1d *Amanda Mary [Mrs Cosimo Prantera, via Mone Rosi 116, Rome, Italy]; *b* 23 April 1942; *m* 24 March 1965 *Cosimo Prantera, s of Cosimo Pietro Prantera, of Rome, and has issue

1b (cont.) Robert Heathcote *m* 2nd 7 July 1922 *Nesta, dau of Evan Hanbury, JP, of Braunston Manor, Oakham, and *d* 17 July 1970, having by her had:

2c *Diana Nesta; *b* 14 March 1923; *m* 24 Sept 1953 Michael James Mellows, only s of Col Arthur Holdich Mellows, TD, DL, of Bradstock, Peterborough, Northants, and has issue

3c Doria Patricia; *b* 2 April 1926; *d* unm 22 Sept 1948

1b Sibyl May Dominica; *b* 11 June 1878; *m* 15 Sept 1903 27th Earl of Mar (*qv*) and *dsp* 20 July 1958

(2) Thomas (Rev); BA Cantab, Vicar Lavington, Lincs; *b* 14 May 1810; *m* 1st Elizabeth (*dsp* 3 July 1859), dau of Rev S Halsted; *m* 2nd 24 May 1861 Lucy (*d* 10 March 1922), dau of David Joyce, and *d* 1883, leaving issue:

1a Thomas Arthur Robert, of Folkingham, Lincs, JP; *b* 2 April 1863; *m* 23 May 1894 Evelyn (*d* 1 Dec 1921), dau of Rev Thomas Todd, Rector Newton, Lincs, and *d* 7 Aug 1916, leaving issue:

1b Kathleen Evelyn

2a Frank Augustus George; *b* 20 Sept 1871; *m* 12 Aug 1902 Enid Muriel (*d* 15 Jan 1945), yst dau of Bennet Rothes Langton, JP, DL, of Langton Hall, Spilsby, Lincs, and *d* 30 Nov 1939, having had issue:

1b *Dorothy Enid; *b* 10 May 1903; *m* 5 March 1931 James Hanley, novelist, and had issue

2b Priscilla Barbara Elizabeth; *b* 1 Aug 1905; *d* 1921

3a William Lionel; *b* 18 March 1874; *m* 19 Oct 1919 Alice Mabel, dau of Rev John Dand Todd, Rector Newton, Folkingham, and *d* 19 May 1961, leaving:

1b +Gilbert Michael; *b* 9 Jan 1924; *educ* Stamford Sch; *m* 19 Sept 1953 *Dorothy Rose, dau of Henry William Pratchett, of Watford, Herts, and has issue:

1c *Jane Michele; *b* 30 Dec 1954

2c *Amanda Joy; *b* 2 July 1959

1b (cont.) Mr and Mrs Gilbert Heathcote adopted:

*Annabel Dorothy; *b* 21 Feb 1967

1a Lucy Elizabeth; *m* 12 Sept 1895 Cuthbert Edward Bradley (*d* 25 Nov 1941), of The Lodge, Folkingham, s of Rev Edward Bradley, of Lenton Vicarage, Lincs, and *d* 25 Dec 1939, having had issue

2a Louisa Gertrude; *m* 1897 Francis Herbert Schwind, of Highfield, Grantham, s of Charles Schwind, JP, of Broomfield, Derbys, and *d* 17 Sept 1910, leaving issue

3a Alice Maud; *m* 9 Sept 1903 Thomas William Stanton, MRCS, LRCP, and *d* 23 Feb 1962. He *d* 28 Sept 1962

4a Emily Sophia; *m* 1899 George Harold Schwind (*d* 13 March 1966 aged 96), of Dembleby House, nr Sleaford, Lincs, s of Charles Schwind (*see* above), and *d* 2 Aug 1928, leaving issue
5a Charlotte Victoria; *d* unm 21 June 1904
6a Edith Evelyn; *d* unm
(3) Francis; *b* 25 Dec 1812; *m* 22 June 1836 Caroline (*d* 11 Nov 1876), dau of Charles Packer, and *d* 27 Aug 1879, leaving:
1a Georgiana Elizabeth; *m* 24 Nov 1864 Rev Lyttelton Henry Powys Maurice (*d* 1915), and *d* 21 July 1902, leaving issue
2a Ida Grosvenor; *m* 17 June 1863 John Wilson Wilson (*d* 1900) and *d* 8 May 1922, leaving issue
3a Clementina Sophia; *m* 1st 4 Sept 1867 Capt John Augustus Kingston, RN (*d* 24 July 1868), and had issue; *m* 2nd 12 Aug 1876 Dr Gorgonia Petano y Mazariegos (*d* 1877), Spanish Dip Serv, and had issue; *m* 3rd 18 May 1881 Capt Claude François Abel Leon Buguet, 31st Regt French Artillery
1 Elizabeth; *m* 1797 FM Thomas Grosvenor (*see* WESTMINSTER, D)

HEMINGFORD

Creation: B. (UK) 1 Feb 1943.

THE 3RD BARON HEMINGFORD, of Watford, Hertfordshire ((Dennis) Nicholas Herbert) [The Rt Hon The Lord Hemingford, The Old Rectory, Hemingford Abbots, Huntingdon PE18 9AN]; *b* 25 July 1934; *s* f 1982; *educ* Oundle and Clare Coll Cambridge (BA 1957, MA 1960); Reuters 1956–61, Assist Washington correspondent *The Times* 1961–65, Middle E correspondent 1966–68, dep features ed 1968–70, ed *Cambridge Evening News* 1970–74, ed dir Westminster Press 1974–92 and dep ch exec 1992–, Pres Guild Br Newspaper eds 1980–81, pres Media Soc 1982, memb Br exec Intl Press Inst, hon sec Assoc Br Eds 1985–, memb E Anglian Regnl Ctee Nat Trust 1983 (chm 1990–), govr Bell Educnl Tst 1986–90, Pres Hunts Family History Soc 1985–, FRSA 1989; *m* 8 Nov 1958 *Jennifer Mary Toresen, CBE (1997), DL (Cambs 1996), only dau of Frederick William Bailey, of Harrogate, Yorks, and has issue:
1 +CHRISTOPHER DENNIS CHARLES; *b* 4 July 1973; *educ* Oundle and Victoria U Manchester
1 *Elizabeth Frances Toresen; *b* 21 Feb 1963; *educ* Durham U (BA); *m* 1994 *John Nigel Evered Witt and has:
(1) *Harry John Evered; *b* 7 Oct 1997
(1) *Alice; *b* 199–
2 *Caroline Mary Louis; *b* 4 Oct 1964; *educ* Liverpool Poly (BEd)
3 *Alice Christine Emma; *b* 1968; *m* 1992 *Christopher McManus, s of Ira McManus, of Florham Pk, NJ

Lineage: DENNIS HERBERT, of Biggleswade, Beds; *b* 1730; *m* 2 Aug 1763 Ann (*d* March 1788), dau of William Pateman, of Langford, Beds, and *d* 1803, leaving, with two est sons (George, *b* 1766, *d* 1808; Dennis, *b* 1768, *d* an infant), three yst sons (Dennis, *b* 1771; Cornelius Pateman, *b* 1772; Nathaniel Vincent) and a dau (Ann, *b* 1767, *m* G Hawkins):

WILLIAM HERBERT, of Huntingdon; *b* 1769; *m* 1st Mary, dau of John Perkins, of Huntingdon, and had five sons (*dsp*) and six daus (including Charlotte, *b* 1795, *m* 1st James Turner, *m* 2nd Walter Vavaseur and *d* 1850; Mary Ann, *b* 1796, *m* John Sweeting and *d* 1887; Rebecca Frances, *b* 1801, *m* George Morse and *d* 1870; Maria, *b* 1805, *m* Hugh Morton and *d* 1877); *m* 2nd Mary, dau of Thomas Verney Okes, MD, and *d* 1841, having by her had, with, four more daus (*d* unm):

Rev HENRY HERBERT; Rector Hemingford Abbots, Hunts; *b* 1824; *m* Mary (*d* 21 Feb 1917), dau of Rev Edward Grevile Ruddock, and *d* 11 July 1911, leaving:
1 DENNIS HENRY, **1st Baron**
2 Edward Grevile; *m* Olive Una Linton and *d* 1951, leaving:
(1) Charles Henry; *b* 1904; *m* Henrietta Begg and *d* 1957, leaving:
1a *Mary Macdonald; *m* 1962 *Dieter Doktor
2a *Caroline
3 Louis William; *m* Amy Jarvis and *d* 1955
4 Richard Charles; *m* Kathleen — and *d* 1948, leaving:
(1) *Mary Ruddock; *m* John Kent
5 George; *m* Muriel Ebsworth and *d* 1947
6 Francis Falkner; *m* Madeline King and *d* 1957, leaving:
(1) *Kenneth Falkner; *b* 1910; *m* *Kathleen Robertson and has issue:
1a *Anthony James; *b* 1940; *m* *Margaret Lowell Pelton
2a *Mark Jeremy; *b* 1948
1a *Amanda Gay; *m* *Fergus Hinds
(2) *Henry Myles; *b* 1915; *m* *Patricia Sullivan and has:
1a *Julian David; *b* 1952
2a *Robin Clive; *b* 1955
The Rev HENRY HERBERT's est s,
DENNIS HENRY HERBERT, **1st Baron Hemingford**, of Watford, Co Hertford (UK), so *cr* 1 Feb 1943, KBE (1929), PC (26 June 1933), JP, DL (Herts); *b* 25 Feb 1869; *educ* King's Sch Ely and Wadham Coll Oxford (BA 1892, MA 1901, Hon Fell 1933); slr 1895, with legal firms of Beaumont & Son and Clarke, Rawlins & Co, MP (U) Watford 1918–43, T/Chm Ctees H of C 1924–28, Dep-Chm Ways and Means 1928–29, Chm Ways and Means and Dep-Speaker Sept 1931–43, chm Equity and Law Life Assur, memb Cncl Law Soc (Pres 1941–42), CA Herts, Sr Grand Warden Utd Grand Lodge of Freemasons 1943–44 and 1944–45, Freedom of Watford 1943, author: *The Law as to Solicitors*; *m* 9 June 1902 Mary Graeme (*d* 24 July 1966), dau of Valentine Graeme Bell, CMG, and *d* 10 Dec 1947, leaving:
1 DENNIS GEORGE RUDDOCK HERBERT, **2nd Baron Hemingford**, JP (1960); *b* 25 March 1904; *educ* Oundle and BNC Oxford (MA); CC 1952 and CA Hunts 1959, Master Achimota Coll Gold Coast 1926–39, Headmaster King's Coll Budo, Uganda, 1939–47, Rector Achimota Training Coll 1948–51, chm Africa Bureau 1952–63, CC 1961–65 and V-Chm CC Huntingdon and Peterborough 1964–67 and Chm 1967–82, Ld Lt Huntingdon and Peterborough 1968–82, memb London Govt Staff Commn 1963–65; *m* 25 June 1932 Elizabeth McClare (*d* 29 July 1979), only dau of Col John McClare Clark, TD, of Ashcroft, Haltwhistle, Northumberland, by Marion, dau of Daniel Jackson, MD, of Bellister Castle, Haltwhistle, and *d* June 1982, leaving issue:
(1) DENNIS NICHOLAS HERBERT, **3rd and present Baron Hemingford**
(1) *Cecilia McClare; *b* 25 July 1939; *educ* St Hilda's Coll Oxford (MA); chm exec ctee Oxford Soc 1996–; *m* 21 May 1966 *Sir William Howard Goodhart, 2nd s of Prof Arthur Lehman Goodhart, Hon KBE, QC, of Oxford, and has:
1a *Benjamin Herbert; *b* 1972
1a *(Annabel) Frances (Fanny); *b* 30 Aug 1967; *m* 2 Sept 1995 *Jim Dallas, s of Duncan Dallas, of Chapel Allerton, Leeds
2a *Laura Christabel; *b* 1970
(2) *Catherine Grevile; *b* Sept 1942; *m* 1 Dec 1962 *Harry Traherne Moggridge, er s of Lt-Col Harry Weston Moggridge, CMG, and has issue:
1a *Geoffrey Dillwyn; *b* 8 Sept 1967; *educ* Magdalen Sch Oxford
2a *Lawrence; *b* 19 Feb 1970
1a *Harriet Fearne; *b* 23 Sept 1965; *m* 1992 *Dr Nicholas John Lawrence and has issue:
1b *Joseph Lawrence Moggridge; *b* 1993
2 Valentine Henry Okes, TD; *b* 4 June 1905; *educ* Oundle; dir and gen manager Shelton Iron, Steel and Co 1950, md 1964, WW II in RA, Lt-Col cmdg 23rd Parachute LAA and A/Tk Regt RA Ceylon and India 1942–45; *m* 1st 3 Oct 1931 Winifred Mabel (*d* 20 March 1955), dau of Sir Herbert Grayhurst Pearson; *m* 2nd 26 May 1956 Janet (*d* 1982), yst dau of Rev Gerrard Edmund Wigram (*see* WIGRAM, Bt), and *d* 1983, leaving by his 1st w:
(1) +Timothy William Okes; *b* 15 July 1936; *educ* Oundle; *m* 1977 *Erica Anne Jackson
(1) *Rosemary Ann; *b* 15 Sept 1932; *m* 17 Aug 1957 *William George Rhyll Turner, s of Lt-Col George Frederick Goodwin Turner, OBE, DCM, Mil Kt Windsor, and has issue:
1a *Valerie Jane; *b* 22 Oct 1958
2a *Penelope May; *b* 29 April 1960
3a *Susan Diana; *b* 5 Sept 1964
(2) *Silvia Valentine; *b* 11 Oct 1948; *m* 1st 16 March 1978 P Jeremy B Sayce (*d* 1980), s of P B Sayce, and has:
1a *Emily Valentine; *b* 1978
(2) (cont.) Mrs Sayce *m* 2nd 1983 *J Robin K Peile and has issue:
1a *Maxwell Herbert; *b* 1984
3 Robert John Grevile; *b* 6 Jan 1909; *d* 26 Jan 1930
4 +Oliver Hayley Dennis; *b* 14 Aug 1919; *educ* Oundle and Wadham Coll Oxford; Maj Queen's Roy Regt, attd IA, served WW II 1940–45; *m* 1976 (*annulled* 19–) Rosemary Muriel, dau of Rev Canon Roland Bate

HEMPHILL

Arms: Or on a fess gu. between two chevronels and three estoiles az. as many trefoils slipped of the field. **Crest:** A boar passant gu., charged with a chevron and a portcullis or. **Supporters:** On either side, an Irish wolfhound ppr., collared or. **Motto:** *Constanter ac non timide* ('Steadily and fearlessly'). **Creation:** B. (UK) 12 Jan 1906.

THE 5TH BARON HEMPHILL, of Rathkenny and Cashel, Co Tipperary (Peter Patrick Fitzroy Martyn HEMPHILL later MARTYN-HEMPHILL (deed poll 1959)) [The Rt Hon The Lord Hemphill, Raford House, Kiltulla, Co Galway, Ireland]; *b* 5 Sept 1928 ; *s* f 1957; *educ* Downside and BNC Oxford (MA); *m* 17 April 1952 *(Olivia) Anne, er dau of Maj Robert Francis Ruttledge, MC, of Cloonee, Ballinrobe, Co Mayo, and has issue:
1 +CHARLES ANDREW MARTIN [The Hon Charles Martyn-Hemphill, 78 Streathbourne Rd, London SW17 8QY]; *b* 8 Oct 1954; *educ* Downside and St Benet's Hall Oxford (BA); dir Morgan Grenfell Asset Management; *m* 1985 *Sarah, est dau of Richard Lumley, and has issue:
(1) +Richard Patrick Lumley; *b* 17 May 1990
(1) *Clarissa Mary; *b* 1986
(2) *Amelia Rose; *b* 1988

(3) *Marina Olivia Astrid; *b* 1992
1 *Angela Mary Martyn [The Hon Mrs Cookson, Manor Farm, Upper Slaughter, Glos]; *b* 26 Jan 1953; *m* 20 Oct 1982 *Robert Cookson and has issue:
(1) *Edward Peter; *b* 1988
(1) *Serena Louise; *b* 1986
2 *Mary Anne Martyn; *b* 29 Nov 1958

Lineage: ROBERT BOYD or HEMPHILL; migrated to the Coleraine, Co Derry, area from Ayrshire late 16th or early 17th century; ancestor of:

Rev SAMUEL HEMPHILL, of Springhill, Co Tipperary; Presbyterian controversialist; *educ* Edinburgh (MA) 1796; Minister Fethard, Co Tipperary, 1728; *m* Sarah Semple and *d* by 2 June 1761, having had, with other issue:
1 William; migrated to Lancaster, Pa.; *m* 1760
2 Edward, of Spring Hall; *b* 1735; *m* Frances, only dau of Francis Green Despard, of Killaghy Castle, Co Tipperary, and *d* 1811, leaving issue
3 JOHN
4 Samuel; Offr 14th Dragoons; migrated to Savannah, Ga., 1784

The 3rd s,

JOHN HEMPHILL, of Cashel, Co Tipperary; *b* 1741; *m* 1766 Elizabeth, dau of Edward Bacon, of Rathkenny, Co Tipperary, by Lydia Nicholson, and sis and coheir of Edward Bacon, of Rathkenny, who *d* unm 1760, and *d* 1828, having had, with three other sons and three daus:
1 John, of Cashel and Rathkenny; *b* 1777; *m* 1807 Barbara (*d* 6 May 1858), yst dau of Rev Patrick Hare, Rector Golden, Vicar-General Diocese of Cashel, and *d* 6 Sept 1833, having had issue:
(1) Edward; Lt 69th Regt; *d* unm 1 Oct 1840
(2) CHARLES HARE, **1st Baron**
(1) Mary; *m* John Atkinson, of Ely Place, Dublin, Army Agent, Capt 60th Rifles, and *d* 21 July 1888, having had issue
(2) Malvina Elizabeth; *m* Charles Morant, Offr 14th Dragoons, and *d* 5 May 1891, leaving issue
(3) Lydia; *m* 31 Aug 1835 George Morant (*d* 17 Dec 1875), of Shirley House, Carrickmacross, Gren Gds, and *d* 12 Jan 1901, leaving issue

JOHN HEMPHILL's 2nd s,

CHARLES HARE HEMPHILL, **1st Baron Hemphill**, of Rathkenny and Cashel, Co Tipperary (UK), so *cr* 12 Jan 1906, PC (I 1895), KC (1860), JP (Cos Dublin, Tipperary and Wicklow); *b* 1821; *educ* Trin Coll Dublin (BA, scholar and 1st classical gold medallist 1843); barrister 1845, Serjeant-at-law 1882, Bencher King's Inns 1882, MP Tyrone 1895–1906, Slr-Gen I 1892–95, Chm QS Cos Louth, Leitrim and Kerry; *m* 11 April 1849 Augusta Mary (*d* 12 April 1899), yr dau of Hon Sir Francis Charles Stanhope, KH, and gdau of 3rd Earl of Harrington (*qv*), and *d* 4 March 1908, having had issue:
1 STANHOPE CHARLES JOHN HEMPHILL, **2nd Baron Hemphill** , KC (1906), JP (Cos Tipperary and Dublin), DL (Dublin); *b* 13 March 1853; *educ* Trin Coll Dublin (MA); barrister Middle Temple and King's Inns; *m* 29 April 1913 Hon May Clarke Mary Nisbet Hamilton (*d* 9 Jan 1970), 2nd dau of 9th Lord Belhaven and Stenton (*qv*), and *dsp* 26 March 1919
2 Francis Bacon Russell; *b* 13 May 1854; Maj 1st Roy Berks Regt; *d* unm Malta 7 June 1891
3 FITZROY, **3rd Baron**
1 Mary Hannah Augusta; *m* 17 June 1875 Maj Edward Augustus Carter (*d* 1920), 1st Derbyshire Regt (Sherwood Foresters), only s of Augustus Carter and gs of Edward Carter, DL, of Theakston Hall, Bedale, Yorks, and *d* 20 Sept 1925, leaving issue

The 2nd BARON's bro,

FITZROY HEMPHILL, **3rd Baron Hemphill**; *b* 21 Nov 1860; memb LCC 1901–10, dep chm 1907–08, barrister Middle Temple, Capt KOSB, Chev Legion of Honour; *m* 27 Feb 1897 Mary (*d* 25 Aug 1958), only child and heiress of Andrew Martyn, JP, of Spiddal, Co Galway, and *d* 25 Nov 1930, leaving issue:

MARTYN CHARLES ANDREW HEMPHILL, **4th Baron Hemphill**; *b* 17 Feb 1901; *educ* New Coll Oxford (BA 1922); barrister King's Inns Dublin 1930 and Middle Temple 1933; *m* 10 Sept 1927 (*divorce* 1945) Emily, dau of F Irving Sears, of Webster, Mass., and *d* 19 March 1957, leaving issue:

PETER PATRICK FITZROY MARTYN MARTYN-HEMPHILL, **5th and present Baron Hemphill**

HENDERSON OF BROMPTON

Creation: B. (UK, LP) 1983.

THE BARON HENDERSON OF BROMPTON, of Brompton in the Royal Borough of Kensington and Chelsea and of Brough, Co Cumbria (Sir Peter Gordon Henderson, KCB 1975) [The Rt Hon The Lord Henderson of Brompton KCB, 16 Pelham Street, London SW7 2NG; Helbeck Cottage, Brough, Kirkby Stephen, Cumbria CA17 4DD]; *b* 16 Sept 1922; *educ* Stowe and Magdalen Coll Oxford; Scots Gds 1942–44; Clerk Ho Lds 1954–60; seconded to Treasury as Sec to Leader and Ch Whip Ho Lds 1960–63; Reading Clerk and Clerk Public Bills 1964–74; Clerk Assist 1974; Clerk of Parls 1974–83; Memb Ctee Preparation Legislation 1973–74; Govr Lake District Art Gallery and Museum Tst 1984–; Pres: New Bridge 1990–, Progress 1991–; V-Pres Nat Assoc Motor Projects 1991–; *m* 1950 *Susan Mary, dau of Richard Charles Gordon Dartford, of Swallowfield Park, Berks, and has issue:
1 *Launcelot Dinadan James, QC [The Hon Launcelot Henderson QC, 17 Carlisle Rd, London NW6 6TL]; *b* 1951; *educ* Westminster and Balliol Coll Oxford; *m* 1989 *Elaine Elizabeth, er dau of Kenneth Frank Webb, of Dringhouses, York, and has:
(1) *Peter George Galahad; *b* 1990
(2) *Arthur Frank Gabriel; *b* 1994
(1) *Matilda Jane; *b* 1992
2 *Richard Crosbie Aitken [The Very Rev The Hon Dr Richard Henderson, The Deanery, Rossearbery, Co Cork, Ireland]; *b* 1957; *educ* Westminster and Magdalen Coll Oxford; *m* 1985 *Anita Julia, dau of Antony Gerald Stroud Whiting
1 *Lucy Jess; *b* 1954; *m* 1980 *Paul Benedict Askew
2 *Mary Sophia; *b* 1965; *m* 1994 *Robert Cumming

Lineage: JAMES ALEXANDER LEO HENDERSON, of London; had:

PETER GORDON, *cr* a **Baron**

HENDERSON-STEWART

Creation: Bt. (UK) 28 March 1957.

SIR DAVID JAMES HENDERSON-STEWART, 2ND BT, of Callumshill, Co Perth [Sir David Henderson-Stewart Bt, 90 Oxford Gdns, London W10 5UW]; *b* 3 July 1941; *s* f 1961; *educ* Eton and Trin Coll Oxford; *m* 1972 *Anne, dau of Count Serge de Pahlen, and has issue:
1 +DAVID; *b* 2 Feb 1973
2 +Nicholas; *b* 1974
3 +André; *b* 1976
1 *Nathalie; *b* 1981

Lineage: JAMES STEWART; *m* Annie Henderson and had issue:

MATTHEW DEAS STEWART, of Crieff, Perthshire; *b* 2 Feb 1870; *m* 1896 Isabella Niven Stevens (*d* 11 March 1956), dau of William Todd, of Gorthy, nr Crieff, and *d* 20 Aug 1950, having had:
1 JAMES HENDERSON (Sir), **1st Bt**
2 William Todd; *b* 16 Sept 1900
3 John Henderson; *b* 12 Aug 1903
4 Valentine; *b* 14 Feb 1909; *d* 5 March 1938
5 *Ronald; *b* 24 Jan 1911
1 Sophia, actress; *b* 5 March 1905; *m* 1940 Ellis Irving, actor, s of Edward William Irving, of Sydney, NSW

The est son,

Sir JAMES HENDERSON STEWART later HENDERSON-STEWART (authority of Lord Lyon and deed poll 1957), **1st Bt** (UK), so *cr* 28 March 1957; *b* 6 Dec 1897; *educ* Morrison's Acad Crieff and Edinburgh U (BCom 1922, MA 1923), MP E Fife 1933–61, Sessional Chm Lib Nat Parl Party 1945, Jt Parly U-Sec Scottish Office 1952–57, Capt RN WW I (wounded), on Lloyd George's staff 1924–29, with Unilever 1929–33; *m* 25 July 1940 *Anna Margaret [Mrs Geoffrey Wilks, 64 Cadogan Sq, London SW1] (*m* 2nd 29 July 1965 Geoffrey Walford Wilks, CBE, TD; *d* 1987), 4th dau of Sir Bernard Greenwell, 2nd Bt (*qv*), and *d* 3 Sept 1961, leaving:
1 Sir DAVID JAMES HENDERSON-STEWART, **2nd and present Bt**
1 *Annabel [Mrs Annabel Henderson Stewart, 29 Chipstead St, London SW6 3SR]; *b* 19 June 1943; *educ* West Heath Sch Sevenoaks; *m* 20 Aug 1966 (resumed maiden name) *Andrew Alastair Borthwick, s of Sidney Guy Borthwick, and has issue:
(1) *Selena Margaret; *b* 7 Nov 1967
(2) *Emilie Anna; *b* 15 May 1970; *m* 18 Feb 1995 *Stephen Alan Crees and has:
1a *Oliver James; *b* 7 May 1996

HENLEY

Arms: Quarterly, 1st and 4th, gu. on a chevron arg. between three garbs or, banded vert, as many escallops sa. (for EDEN); 2nd and 3rd, az. a lion rampant arg., ducally crowned or, within a bordure of the second, charged with eight torteaux (for HENLEY). **Crest:** A dexter arm in armour, couped at the shoulder ppr., and grasping a garb or. **Supporters:** Dexter, a lion arg. semée of torteaux, ducally crowned or, having a plain collar of the last rimmed az., on the collar three escallops sa., and pendant therefrom a shield gold, charged with an eagle displayed with two heads sa.; sinister, a stag arg., semée of torteaux, attired or and gorged with a plain collar of the last rimmed az. and charged with three escallops sa., pendant therefrom an escutcheon also or charged with an eagle displayed with one head, also sa. **Motto:** *Si sit prudentia* ('If there only be prudence'). **Creations:** B. (I) 9 Nov 1799 (Henley of Chardstock) and (UK) 28 June 1885 (Northington of Watford).

THE 8TH BARON HENLEY OF CHARDSTOCK and **Baron Northington of Watford**, Co Northampton (Oliver Michael Robert Eden) [The Rt Hon The Lord Henley, Scaleby Castle, Carlisle, Cumbria CA6 4LN]; *b* 22 Nov 1953; *s f* 1977; *educ* Clifton and Durham U (BA 1975); barrister Middle Temple 1977, pres Cumbria Assoc Local Cncls 1981–89, chm Penrith & Border C Assoc 1989–89, Cumbria CC 1986–89, Ld in Waiting (Govt Whip) 1989, Parly U-Sec: DSS 1989–93 and Employment 1993–94, MOD 1994–95, Min State Educn and Employment 1995–; *m* 1984 *Caroline Patricia, JP, dau of A G Sharp, of Mackney, Oxon, and has issue:

1 +JOHN MICHAEL OLIVER; *b* 30 June 1988
2 +Patrick Francis; *b* 1993
3 +Edward Andrew; *b* 16 July 1996
1 *Elizabeth Caroline; *b* 1991

Henley, other creations: The 1st Earl of Northington, whose daughter married the 1st Baron Henley of the present creation, had a subsidiary title of Lord Henley, Baron Henley of Grainge. The 2nd Earl died unmarried in 1785, when the two titles expired. It must have been natural for his brother-in-law Morton Eden, the successful diplomat, to resurrect the name Henley in his own choice of title when ennobled a few years later.

Lineage: Sir ROBERT EDEN, 3rd Bt (*see* EDEN OF WINTON, B); had a yst s:

MORTON FREDERICK EDEN, **1st Baron Henley of Chardstock**, Co Dorset (I), so *cr* 9 Nov 1799, GCB (1815), KB (1791), PC (1794); *b* 8 July 1752; *educ* Eton and Ch Ch Oxford; Min Bavaria 1776–79, Copenhagen 1779–82, Dresden 1782–91, Berlin 1791–93 and Vienna 1793–94 and 1795–99, Amb Madrid 1794–95; *m* 7 Aug 1783 Elizabeth (*d* 20 Aug 1821), yst dau of 1st Earl of Northington, and had issue:

1 Frederic Morton; *b* 19 Aug 1784; *d* 5 Nov 1823
2 ROBERT HENRY, **2nd Baron**
3 William (Rev), Rector Bishopsbourne, Kent; Sr Preacher Canterbury Cathedral; *b* 9 Nov 1792; *m* 19 Jan 1820 Anna Maria (*d* 23 Oct 1875), widow of 19th Baron Grey (of Ruthin) (*see* GREY, B) and dau of William Kelham, and *d* 4 May 1859, having had, with other issue:

(1) Arthur (Rev); Vicar Ticehurst, Sussex 1851–1908; *b* 3 Jan 1825; *m* 24 Aug 1848 Alice Julia (*d* 18 Dec 1897), dau of T A Whitney, of Merton, Co Wexford, and *d* 17 Nov 1908, leaving issue:

1a William Gaven; Lt RN; *b* 26 July 1849; *m* 4 Jan 1876 Augusta Rose (*d* 13 Dec 1945), 3rd dau of Matthew Bell, of Bourne Park, Kent, and *d* 27 Jan 1931, leaving issue:

1b Cecil; *b* 3 Oct 1876; *m* 27 Jan 1914 Inez Gilmour, est dau of William Orr, and *d* 27 Jan 1963, having had issue:

1c +Cecil Gilmour Orr [Cecil Eden Esq, Estancia Santa Inez, 2609 Maria Teresa, Prov Santa Fé, Argentina]; *b* 4 June 1921; *m* 9 April 1953 *Anne Mabel, dau of George F Bridger, of Estancia Pascuala, Sandel, Argentina, and has:

1d +Robert Gilmour; *b* 1 Feb 1954
2d +David Arthur; *b* 26 April 1961
1d *Joanna Inez; *b* 17 Oct 1957
2d *Margaret Alice; *b* 26 April 1961

1c Inez Augusta; *d* 1 July 1932
2c *Edna Constance [Mrs Geoffrey Lees, St George's College Preparatory Sch, 1978 Quilmes, Argentina]; *m* 15 Sept 1956 *Geoffrey Arthur Lees and has issue:

1d *John Arthur; *b* 27 Dec 1960
1d *Elizabeth Inez; *b* 1 Oct 1958

3c Patricia Alice; *m* 12 Feb 1954 George Page and has issue:

1d *Christine Sheila; *b* 4 July 1955
2d *Angela Jean; *b* 17 Feb 1957

2b Morton; Lt 3rd Bn Roy Irish Regt; *b* 9 Dec 1881; *d* 6 June 1922
1b Constance; *m* 22 Oct 1908 Edward Percy Fairbairn and *d* 19 June 1952, leaving issue (*see* FAIRBAIRN, Bt)
2b Norah; *m* 22 Oct 1908 Edward Andrewes, 3rd s of Rev W J Andrewes, of Ontario, and had issue
3b Hilda; *m* 8 May 1915 Maj Clement Arthur Linton, RFA, and was *k* in an earthquake at San Juan,1943, leaving issue
4b Alice Nesta

2a Arthur Yelverton, of Merton, Co Wexford, JP; *b* 19 March 1856; *m* 22 Nov 1888 Fanny Spencer (*d* 4 Nov 1934), only surv child of John T L le Blanch, of Beechfield, Cheshire and *d* 5 May 1922, leaving issue:

1b Barbara Yelverton; *d* unm 1940
2b Lelgarde Edith Eleanor; *m* 3 April 1918 Geoffrey Ronald Aubert Buckland, CB (*d* 27 Dec 1968), s of Francis Oke Buckland, and had issue
3b Dulcie Flora; *d* unm 2 May 1955

1a Alice Lizzie; *m* 27 Sept 1883 William Sherrard, 2nd s of Rev William Sherrard, Rector Castlelyons, Co Cork, and had issue
2a Mary Constance; *m* 30 April 1878 Arthur Hills Cobbold, and *d* 29 March 1884, leaving issue
3a Eleanor Agnes; *m* 18 Dec 1879 V-Adml Henry Bedford Woollcombe (*d* 14 Feb 1904), and *d* 1897, leaving issue
4a Edith Amelia; *m* 1st 26 Oct 1876 Charles Davers Eden, RN (*dsp* 1895); *m* 2nd 1 June 1901 Col Arthur Frederick Eden-Perkins, VD, JP, DL (*d* 17 July 1914), of Bursledon, Hants, and *dsp* 7 April 1947
5a Flora Colcough; *d* 1 July 1919
6a Julia Augusta Maria; *m* 12 Sept 1911 Herbert Frances Edward Odell (*d* 2 Oct 1943), only s of Edward George Herbert Odell (*see* HUNTINGDON, E)

(2) Robert Charles; Lt-Col US Army, diplomat; *b* 31 Aug 1836; *m* 26 Jan 1865 Annie Gardner, yst dau of Andrew Bain, of Bonhill, Dunbartonshire, and *d* 22 Jan 1907, having had, with other issue:

1a Morton Edward; *b* 17 Sept 1867; *m* 1894 Marie Elizabeth (*d* 1900), dau of James Stewart, of Dansville, USA, and *d* 1914, leaving issue:

1b Robert Henley Stewart; *b* 1896

2a Reginald Yelverton; *b* 15 Dec 1871; *m* Sophia, dau of T Hart, of Warren, USA, and *d* 1949, leaving issue:

1b *Anne Louise; *m* Lurelle van Arsdale Guild and has issue:

1c *Cynthia Eden; *b* 1938

2b *Beatrice Elizabeth

1a Mabel Wenonah
2a Ethel Elizabeth
3a Sybil Constance

(1) Mary Yelverton; *m* 4 July 1848 Samuel Lucas Lancaster Lucas (*d* 1894), of Wateringbury Place, Kent, and had issue
(2) Charlotte Maria; *m* 1st 17 Oct 1850 Dudley, Lord North, and had issue (*see* GUILFORD, E); *m* 2nd 10 July 1861 Maj Alexander George Dickson (*d* 3 July 1889), 13th Hus, MP Dover, and *d* 6 Feb 1909, having had further issue
(3) Flora Jane; *m* 2 April 1866 John Morant (*d* 30 May 1899), of Brockenhurst Park, Hants, and *d* 3 March 1915, having had issue

1 Mary Jane; *m* 23 Sept 1824 Sir Edmund Cradock-Hartopp, 2nd Bt (*qv*), and *dsp* 12 Sept 1843

The 1st BARON *d* 6 Dec 1830; his er son,

ROBERT HENRY EDEN later HENLEY (roy licence 31 March 1831), **2nd Baron Henley of Chardstock**; *b* 3 Sept 1789; *educ* Eton and Ch Ch Oxford; barrister Lincoln's Inn 1814, MP (Tory) Fowey 1826–30, a Master in Chancery 1826–40; *m* 11 March 1824 Harriet (*d* 7 May 1869), dau of Sir Robert Peel, 1st Bt (*see* PEEL, E), and had:

1 ANTHONY HENLEY, **3rd Baron**
2 Robert (Rev); MA Oxon, Vicar Putney; *b* 7 March 1831; *m* 1 June 1852 Emily Louisa (*d* 20 Aug 1893), est dau of Robert Aldridge, of New Lodge, Horsham, and *d* 7 Aug 1910, having had issue:

(1) Robert Eden (Rev); MA Oxon, Vicar Wharton, Cheshire; *b* 10 Sept 1861; *d* unm 7 May 1933
(2) Arthur Keith (Rev); MA Oxon, Curate Putney; *b* 12 April 1863; *d* unm 16 July 1903
(3) Charles Beauclerk; Capt RIN; *b* 7 Feb 1869; *m* 26 Dec 1910 Nellie Barbara (*d* 30 July 1961), est dau of E F Stranack, of Kodai Kanal, S India, and *d* 21 Oct 1945, having had:

1a Robert Stephen, OBE, DSC; Cdr RN WW II; *b* 4 July 1917; *m* 31 July 1940 *(Cecile) Noreen Sheila [Mrs Robert Henley, Eden Lodge, Liss, Hants GU33 6JQ], only dau of Eric Hudson, of Horsham, Sussex, and Argentina, and *d* 1991, leaving issue:

1b +(Robert Anthony) Nigel [Nigel Henley Esq, Boldre Bridge House, Boldre, Hants]; *b* 23 Aug 1942; *educ* Cambridge (BA); *m* 1st 1968 (*divorce* 1986) Celia, dau of Leslie Ford, of Lusaka, Zambia, and has:

1c +Robert Alexander; *b* 1973
1c *Deborah Lucie; *b* 1971
2c *Victoria Elizabeth; *b* 1978

1b (cont.) Nigel Henley *m* 2nd 1988 *Anne, only dau of James Beadle, of Great Missenden, Bucks, and has:

2c +Richard James; *b* 1989

3c *Joanna Katharine; *b* 1992
2b +Timothy David [Timothy Henley Esq, Palings, Warboys Rd, Kingston Hill, Surrey KT2 7LS]; *b* 20 June 1945; *m* 1972 *Jane Hughes, dau of John Fisher, of Chiswick, and has issue:
1c *Sarah Margaret; *b* 1975
2c *Rachel Katherine; *b* 1978
3b +(Christopher) Basil Patrick [Basil Henley Esq, 55 Napier Ave, London SW6 3PS]; *b* 20 March 1953
4b +Jonathan Paul Sebastian [Jonathan Henley Esq, Finches Cottage, Langley, Hants GU33 7JL]; *b* 4 Jan 1956; *m* 1st 1980 (*divorce* 1986) Caroline Fiona, yr dau of D D A Beattie, of Aston Mead, Windsor; *m* 2nd 1987 *Rowena Jane, dau of Lionel David Cowan, of Cobham, Surrey, and by her has:
1c +James William; *b* 1989
1c *Clare Olivia; *b* 1991
2c *Katherine Alexandra; *b* 1993
2a Antony Basil; Lt RN WW II (despatches) *b* 3 July 1919; *ka* 12 Jan 1942
3a +David Beauclerk [David Henley Esq, Alpina, 36 Bruce Ave, Worthing, Sussex BN11 5JU]; *b* 9 June 1923; *m* 7 July 1951 *Eileen Fuller
1a *Elizabeth Barbara [Miss Elizabeth Henley, 9 Wynne's Park Cottages, Brookhouse Rd, Denbigh, Clwyd LL16 4YB]; *b* 26 Sep 1911
2a Helen Beatrice; *b* 17 April 1913; *d* 17 April 1914
3a *Violet Hope [Mrs Owen Davis, 5 Feilding House, 103 North Hill, London N6 4DP]; *b* 3 Oct 1914; *m* 13 Aug 1937 Owen Austen Davis (*d* 1992), and has issue:
1b *Nicholas Austen [Nicholas Davis Esq, 1 Meadway Gate, London NW11 7LA]; FRICS, MA; *b* 11 Feb 1940; *m* 12 June 1965 *Maria Henrietta, est twin dau of Peter Jongebreur, of NSW, and has issue:
1c *Austen Peter; *b* 1966
1c *Christa Ann; *b* 1968
2b *Antony Simon [Antony Davis Esq, 220 Douglas Drive, Toronto M4W 2C1, Canada]; *b* 24 Jan 1942; *m* 1967 *Carol Ann Neilert, and has issue:
1c *Christopher Antony; *b* 1968
2c *Amy Katharine; *b* 1970
2c *Maggie Alison; *b* 1974
(1) Constance Laura; *m* 16 April 1890 Rev Robert Stewart Gregory, MA (*d* 31 July 1912), Rector Much Hadham, Herts, and *d* 21 Dec 1930, leaving issue
(2) Beatrice Mary; *d* unm 8 Feb 1941
(3) Ethel Maud; *d* unm 27 June 1931
(4) Mildred Caroline; *d* unm 15 Dec 1951
(5) Mabel Augusta; *d* unm 28 April 1966

The 2nd BARON *d* 3 Feb 1841; his er son,

ANTHONY HENLEY HENLEY, **3rd Baron Henley of Chardstock**, JP, DL; CC Northants, High Sheriff 1854, MP (Lib, as a peer was U from 1886) Northampton 1859–74; *b* 12 April 1825; *cr* 28 June 1885 BARON NORTHINGTON OF WATFORD, Co Northampton (UK); *m* 1st 30 July 1846 Julia Augusta (*d* Feb 1862), dau of Very Rev John Peel (*see* PEEL, E), and *d* 27 Nov 1898, having had issue:

1 FREDERIC HENLEY, **4th Baron Henley of Chardstock**, JP Northants; Dip Serv 1868–73; *b* 17 April 1849; *m* 20 Oct 1900 Augusta Frederica (*dsp* 27 July 1905), yr dau of Herbert Langham, of Cottesbrooke Park, Northants (*see* LANGHAM, Bt), and *d* 23 Dec 1923
2 ANTHONY ERNEST HENLEY, **5th Baron Henley of Chardstock**; *b* 3 July 1858; CE; *m* 1st 17 Aug 1882 Georgiana Caroline Mary (*dsp* 26 Aug 1888), dau of Lt-Col Richard Michael Williams and gdau of Sir William Williams, 5th Bt, of Tregullow (*qv*); *m* 2nd 12 Sept 1889 Emmeline Stuart (*d* 22 Nov 1933), yst dau of George Gammie Maitland, and *d* 23 Oct 1925, having by her had issue:
(1) Joan Beryl; *b* 1 Aug 1893; *m* 6 Dec 1914 Lt Kildare Stucley Meager, RASC, son of D Villiers Meager, barrister, and had issue
1 Florence Mary; *d* 28 May 1866
2 Gertrude Augusta; *d* unm 14 Dec 1932
3 Evelyn; *m* 9 Aug 1881 John Langham Reed, of Thornby, Northants, s of Rev Georve V Reed, Rector Hayes, Kent, and *d* 14 Feb 1910, leaving issue

The **3rd Baron** *m* 2nd 30 June 1870 Clara Campbell Lucy (*d* 11 Nov 1922), dau of Joseph H S Jekyll, and by her had:

3 Anthony Morton, CMG (1919), DSO (1916); Hon Brig Gen (Res of Offrs), psc, barrister Inner Temple 1898, Col 5th Lancers, Adj Scots Greys 1903–06, GSO(3) War Office 1911–13, Bde Maj 2nd Cav Bde 1913–14, Priv Sec to Sec State War 1914, GSO(2) 1914–15, and GSO(1) 1915, Boer War with Compton's Horse 1900 and RSG 1900–02 (Queen's medal, three clasps, King's medal, two clasps) and WW I (despatches, brevet); *b* 4 Aug 1873; *educ* Eton and Balliol Coll Oxford (BA 1895); *m* 24 April 1906 Hon Sylvia Laura Stanley (*d* 1980), OBE (1962), 3rd dau of 4th Baron Sheffield (*see* STANLEY OF ALDERLEY, SHEFFIELD and, B), and *d* 17 May 1925, having had:
(1) Rosalind Venetia; FRS (1954); *b* 4 March 1907; *m* 14 Oct 1931 (*divorce* 1938) Capt George Henry Lane-Fox Pitt-Rivers (*d* 17 June 1966), Roy Dragoons, of Hinton St Mary, Dorset, and had issue
(2) Mary Katharine; *b* 30 Jan 1908; *m* 27 March 1936 Evan Kennedy Morton
(3) Elizabeth; *b* 18, *d* 31 Dec 1913
(4) *Juliet Olive [Mrs Juliet Daniel, 20 Fitzroy Gardens London SE19]; *b* 29 Jan 1917; *m* 25 Nov 1944 (*divorce* 1965) John Stuart Daniel, QC, barrister (*d* 1977), and has issue:
1a *Laura; *b* 12 Nov 1947
4 FRANCIS ROBERT, **6th Baron**
4 Harriet Adelaide Louisa; *b* 16 April 1871; *d* 28 March 1879

The 5th BARON's half-bro,

FRANCIS ROBERT HENLEY later EDEN (deed poll 11 Dec 1925), **6th Baron Henley of Chardstock**; *b* 11 April 1877; *educ* Harrow and Balliol Coll Oxford (BA 1900, MA 1904); FIC, Lt RNVR WW I (despatches); *m* 14 Oct 1913 Lady Dorothy Georgiana Howard (*d* 14 Sept 1968), 3rd dau of 9th Earl of Carlisle (*qv*), and had issue:

1 MICHAEL FRANCIS, **7th Baron**
2 +Roger Quentin Eden [The Hon Roger Eden, 29a Hamilton Terrace, London NW8 9RE]; *b* 18 June 1922; MRAeS, F/O RAFVR WW II; *educ* Rugby; *m* 1st 26 June 1946 Carys Wynne (*d* 1990), dau of Ifi Hywi Dyfed Davies, of Gwynedd; *m* 2nd 14 May 1994 *Barbara Daphne, dau of J F W Singleton, of Glasgow and Calcutta, and by his 1st w has:
(1) +Morton Roger [Morton Eden Esq, 59 Grove Close, Thulston, Derbys]; *b* 12 Nov 1949; *educ* Rugby and St Cuthbert's Soc Durham; *m* 1975 *Sally, dau of W H Brittain, of Redcar, Cleveland, and has issue:
1a +William Morton; *b* 1985
(2) +Elvyn Alexander [Elvyn Eden Esq, 7 Radcliffe Rd, London N21]; *b* 30 April 1954; *educ* Shiplake Coll; *m* 1982 *Claudia Marli, dau of Sid Colin, of Chiswick, and has issue:
1a *Dorcas Claudia; *b* 1983
2a *Emma Alexandra; *b* 1983
1a *Gudrun Dorothy; *b* 1989
(1) *Carol Rosamund; *b* 21 Mar 1947
(2) *Jane Rebecca [Mrs William Kellock, 432 Upper Richmond Rd, London SW15]; *b* 1 Jan 1956; *m* 1983 *William Nicholas Russell Kellock and has:
1a *Howard Nicholas; *b* 1985
2a *Christopher Charles; *b* 1989
1a *Siân Louise; *b* 1987
2a *Clara Carys; *b* 1992
1 *Barbara Dorothy [The Hon Mrs Calvocoressi, 1 Queen's Parade, Bath, Avon BA1 2NJ]; *m* 10 Sept 1938 *W/Cdr Peter John Ambrose Calvocoressi, RAF Vol Reserve, and has issue:
(1) *Paul Peter; *b* 12 Oct 1939; *educ* Eton
(2) *David Sebastian [David Calvocoressi Esq, 11a Bathwick St, Bath, Avon BA2 6NX]; *b* 21 Sept 1941; *educ* Eton; *m* 3 Aug 1971 (*divorce* 1993) Dzagbe, dau of Seth Cudjoe, of Ho, Ghana, and has issue:
1a *Nuku Vanonyi; *b* 1974
2a *Nuname Ankaret; *b* 1976
3a *Nujoji Peter; *b* 1977
2 *Griselda Rosalind [The Hon Mrs Griselda Buckman, 8 High St, W Haddon, Northampton]; *b* 16 Jan 1917; *m* 6 Sept 1939 (*divorce* 1964) S/Ldr John Buckman, RAFVR, and has issue:
(1) *Christopher Simon; *b* 4 Nov 1940; *m* 1970 *Gwendola, dau of Count de Kersaintgilly, of Poizay les Ormes, France, and has issue:
1a *Andrew Pierre; *b* 1972
1a *Sophie Rosalind; *b* 1978
(1) *Jennifer Susan; *b* 14 Jan 1944; *m* 10 Oct 1963 *John Jellis Ashby and has:
1a *Jeremy Robert; *b* 23 Sept 1964
1a *Sarah Charlotte; *b* 9 July 1966
3 *Nancy Clare; *b* 1918; 2nd Subaltern ATS WW II; *m* 22 Nov 1941 *Lt Edmund Ernest Wynne, Reconnaissance Corps, and has issue:
(1) *Robert Edmund; *b* 16 Aug 1956
(1) *Rosalind Clare; *b* 26 Aug 1942; *m* Dec 1965 *David Gow, of Eagle Heights, Madison, USA, and has:
1a *Donovan Fergus; *b* 1970
1a *Caitlin Fiona; *b* 1972
(2) *Deborah Dorothy [Mrs Michael Stagonakis, 67 Mikras Asias, Athens, Greece]; *b* 25 May 1944; *m* 17 May 1968 *Michael Stagonakis
(3) *Clare Catherine; *b* 27 April 1946; *m* 1969 *Colin Smith and has:
1a *Christian; *b* 1971
2a *Eleanor Charlotte; *b* 1975
(4) *Marilyn Anne [Mrs Stephen Padgett, 13 Priory Gate, Blackpool, Lancs]; *b* 18 Sept 1947; *m* 21 Oct 1967 *Stephen Padgett and has:
1a *Christopher Stephen; *b* 1969
2a *Richard Anthony; *b* 1970
(5) *Alexandra Mary; *b* 27 April 1953

The 6th BARON *d* 21 April 1962; his er son,

MICHAEL FRANCIS EDEN, **7th Baron Henley of Chardstock**; *b* 13 Aug 1914; *educ* Eton and Balliol Coll Oxford; Capt Life Gds WW II, Pres Lib Party 1966–67, chm 1968–77; *m* 1st 19 Nov 1943 (*divorce* 1947) Elizabeth, est dau of Sir Arthur Lawrence Hobhouse, of Hadspen House, Somerset, and had:

1 *Victoria Catherine Elizabeth; *b* 13 Sept 1944; *m* 20 Nov 1965 *Hon John Hedworth Jolliffe, yr s of 4th Baron Hylton (*qv*), and has issue

The **7th Baron** *m* 2nd 31 Aug 1949 (*divorce* 1974) Nancy Mary [Nancy Lady Henley, 10 Abbey St, Cerne Abbas, Dorset DT2 7JQ], only dau of Stanley Walton, of The Hill, Gilsland, Carlisle, and *d* 20 Dec 1977, leaving by her:

1 OLIVER MICHAEL ROBERT EDEN, **8th and present Baron Henley of Chardstock**
2 +Andrew Francis [The Hon Andrew Eden, Watford Fields House, Watford, Northampton NN6 7UR]; *b* 4 Sept 1955; *educ* Clifton; *m* 10 Oct 1997 *Liann, dau of Robert Bartlett, of NJ, and Mrs Patricia Vasbinder, of NH
2 *Ursula Nancy; *b* 25 July 1950; *educ* Badminton Sch Bristol; *m* 1978 *William Thomas and has issue:
(1) *Philip Stephen William; *b* 1982
(1) *Jessica Nadine; *b* 1978
3 *Ingaret Barbara [The Hon Ingaret Eden, 37 Fairholme Rd, London W14]; *b* 26 Dec 1951; *educ* Badminton Sch Bristol
4 *Rose Griselda; *b* 17 Nov 1957; *educ* Badminton Sch Bristol; *m* 1st 1976 (*divorce* 1978) —; *m* 2nd 1984 (*divorce* 1991) Hon Christopher James Bellew, yr s of 7th Baron Bellew (*qv*); *m* 3rd 1993 *Lawrence Emerson Foulds

Seat: Scaleby Castle, Carlisle, Cumbria. The original demesne dates back at least to the late 13th century. In the last year of EDWARD I's reign the then holder, Richard Tilliol, was given permission to fortify his dwelling; the oldest parts of the Castle at the bottom of the walls, together with the gatehouse, are of that date. The east wing is approximately a century later. About now, that is to say the mid-15th century, the property passed from the Tilliols to the Musgraves (probably the same family as MUSGRAVE, Bt, of Hartley Castle, *qv*). The early-16th century modifications to the gatehouse and one of the towers to render it polygonal were carried out under the latter family's occupancy, as was the south-facing purely domestic front (which has no crenellations, for instance) at the end of the same century.

Scaleby was subsequently acquired by a family called Colville and later still by one called Gilpin, a member of which was William Gilpin (1724–1804), the ecclesiastical biographer and author of topographical works which he illustrated himself. To his influence has largely been ascribed the growing 18th century taste for wild landscape and ancient buildings in an evocative state of decay. Naturally Scaleby was one of his earliest subjects. A generation after his death further changes were made to the Castle, with a drawing-room added on the southwest flank, it is thought by Thomas Rickman. During most of the 19th century the Standishes owned Scaleby. It was bought by the **7th Baron Henley** in 1952, having been disposed of six years earlier by the widow of Edward William Standish, who was herself aunt of the present Lord Byron (*qv*).

HENNIKER, Baron

Arms: Quarterly, 1st and 4th, three Corinthian columns or, two and one, on the top of each a ball or (for MAJOR); 2nd and 3rd, or on a chevron gu. between two crescents in chief and in base an escallop az., three estoiles arg. (for HENNIKER). **Crests:** 1 A dexter arm, embowed, habited az., cuff arg., and charged on the elbow with a plate, holding in the hand ppr. a baton or (for MAJOR), 2 An escallop or, charged with an estoile gu. (for HENNIKER). **Supporters:** Dexter, a stag arg., attired and unguled or, gorged with a chaplet of oak ppr., fructed or, therefrom pendant a shield az. charged with the crest of HENNIKER; sinister, an otter arg., ducally gorged or, pendant therefrom a shield of the arms of MAJOR. **Motto:** *Deus major columna* ('God the greater support'). **Creations:** Bt. (GB) 15 July 1765, B. (I) 31 July 1800 (Henniker and (UK) 13 July 1866 (Hartismere).

THE 8TH BARON HENNIKER OF STRATFORD-UPON-SLANEY, Co Wicklow, **Baron Hartismere** of Hartismere, Co Suffolk, and a **Baronet** (Sir John Patrick Edward Chandos Henniker-Major, Bt, KCMG (1965, CMG (1956)), CVO (1960), MC (1945), DL (Suffolk 1988)) [The Rt Hon The Lord Henniker KCMG CVO MC DL, The Red House, Thornham Magna, Suffolk IP23 8HH]; *b* 19 Feb 1916; *s* f 1980; *educ* Stowe and Trin Coll Cambridge (BA, 1937); WW II with Rifle Brigade in Western Desert and Yugoslavia (wounded), Maj 1944, Head FO Personnel Dept 1953–60, Amb Jordan 1960–62 and Denmark 1962–66, Civ Serv Commr 1966–67, Assist U-Sec FO 1967–68, Dir-Gen Br Cncl 1968–72, dir Wates Fndn 1972–78; *m* 1st 18 Dec 1946 Margaret Osla (*d* Oct 1974), dau of James William Benning, of Montreal, and has:

1 +MARK IAN PHILIP CHANDOS [The Hon Mark Henniker-Major, Thornham Hall, Thornham Magna, Eye, Suffolk]; *b* 29 Sept 1947 (HRH THE DUKE OF EDINBURGH stood sponsor); *educ* Eton and Trin Coll Cambridge (MA); LLM (London), FCIArb, MRAeS; slr; *m* 3 Nov 1973 (*divorce* June 1995) Lesley Antoinette, formerly w of — Masterton-Smith and dau of W/Cdr G W Foskett, of Fernvale, Qld, Australia, and has issue:

(1) +Frederick John Chandos; *b* 31 March 1983

(2) +Edward George Major; *b* 1985

(1) *Jessica Sarah; *b* 15 Nov 1977

(2) *Josephine Helen; *b* 1979

(3) *Harriet Laura; *b* 1981

2 +Charles John Giles [The Hon Charles Henniker-Major, Great Chilton Farm, Co Durham DL17 0JY]; *b* 2 Sep 1949; *educ* Stowe; *m* 1980 *Sally D M Kemp, er dau of Donald Newby, of Halesworth, Suffolk, and has issue:

(1) +Thomas Charles John; *b* 1982

(1) *Osla Mary; *b* 1981

(2) *Ruth Felicity; *b* 1985

1 *Janie Elizabeth [The Hon Mrs Szpiro, 124 Cambridge St, London SW1V 4QF]; *b* 6 July 1954; *m* 1st 1979 (*divorce* 1993) Richard John Grenville Spring, s of Herbert Spring, of Cape Town, and has:

(1) *Frederick John Otway; *b* 1987

(1) *Sophia Romilly Alexandra; *b* 24 Sept 1983

1 (cont.) The Hon Mrs Janie Spring *m* 2nd 23 Oct 1997 *Richard Szpiro, s of late George Szpiro

The 8th BARON *m* 2nd 8 May 1976 *Mrs Julia Marshall Poland, er dau of George M Mason, of Kew

Lineage: JOHN MAJOR, of Bridlington, Yorks; *m* Elizabeth, dau of Rev Richard Tennant, Rector Carnaby and Boynton, Yorks, and *d* at sea 1709 aged 40, leaving:

Sir John Major, 1st Bt (GB), so *cr* 15 July 1765, with remainder, in default of male issue, to his son-in-law John (*see* below), of Worlingworth Hall, Suffolk; *b* 17 May 1698; Er Bro Trin House 1741–81, Sheriff Suffolk 1754, MP Scarborough 1761–68; *m* 20 Jan 1723/4 Elizabeth (*d* 1780), only dau of Daniel Dale, of Bridlington, and *d* 22 Feb 1781, leaving, with a yr dau (Elizabeth, *m* 18 July 1767 2nd Duke of Chandos (*see* KINLOSS, L, also CHANDOS, V, preliminary remarks) and *dsp* 30 March 1813):

ANNE Major; *m* 24 Feb 1746/7 **Sir John Henniker, 2nd Bt**, and **1st Baron Henniker of Stratford-upon-Slaney**, Co Wicklow (I), so *cr* 31 July 1800 (*b* 15 June 1724 (s and heir of John Henniker (*d* 6 April 1749), Freeman London and Russia Merchant, by Hannah (*d* 1745), dau of John Swanson, of London, and gs of John Henniker, of Chatham, by Sarah Long, of Ramsgate), MP Sudbury 1761–68 and Dover 1774–78, *d* 18 April 1803) and *d* 18 July 1792, having had:

1 JOHN HENNIKER later HENNIKER-MAJOR (roy licence 27 May 1822), **2nd Baron Henniker of Stratford-upon-Slaney**; *b* 19 April 1752; *educ* Eton and St John's Coll Cambridge (MA, LLD); FRS, FSA, barrister 1777, MP (Tory) Romney 1785–90, Steyning 1794–1802, Rutland 1805–12 and Stamford 1812–18; *m* 27 April 1791 Emily (*d* 18 Dec 1819), dau of Robert Jones, of Duffryn, Glam, and *dsp* 5 Dec 1821

2 Major, of London and Streatham, Surrey; *b* 9 May 1755; *m* 24 June 1776 Mary (*d* 6 Feb 1803), dau of John Phoenix, of Rochester, and *d* 2 Feb 1789, leaving:

(1) JOHN MINET, **3rd Baron**

(2) Major Jacob, of Ashdown Park, Sussex; R-Adml, granted 1831 rank of baron's yr s; *b* 19 Aug 1780; *m* 28 April 1829 his cousin Anne Eliza (*see* HENNIKER, Bt), and *d* 5 June 1843, having had, with other issue:

1a Frederick, of Car Colston Hall, Notts, Capt 96th Regt; *b* 10 March 1842; *m* 1872 Ethelred Harriet Matilda (*d* 28 Sept 1910), dau of Maj-Gen William Johnson, and *d* 12 March 1908, having had, with other issue:

1b Charles Henry; ARSM; *b* 15 May 1880; *m* 1914 Dorothy Albinia Cecil (*d* 29 Dec 1959), dau of Rev Cecil Locke, and *d* 1966, leaving:

1c +Charles John Chandos [Dr Charles Henniker, 16 Clos de Verrières, 91, Verrières le Buisson, France]; *b* 26 April 1916; *educ* U of BC (BapSc) and Washington U (PhD); *m* 1st 1 July 1938, Ella Margaret Hemberow; *m* 2nd 1 May 1945 Helen Gray; *m* 3rd 12 June 1954 *Madeleine, dau of Albert Caton, of Marseilles, and by her has:

1d *Hélène Dorothy; *b* 1957; *m* 1983 *Baron Pierre de Prittwitz and has:

1e *Gregory Charles; *b* 1983

2e *Igor Antoine; *b* 1993

1e *Fiona Natacha; *b* 1988

2d *Eve Alice; *b* 1962

2b Augustus Major; Capt 3rd Bn Northants Regt WW I; *b* 17 Aug 1884; *m* 20 Sept 1910 Dorothy Roche (*d* 8 March 1956), dau of Lt-Col Roche Rahilly, RAMC, and *d* 29 June 1957, leaving issue:

1c +Anthony Trecothic Major [Anthony Henniker Esq, 7 Evans Avenue, Allestree, Derbys]; *b* 12 April 1912; P/O RAFVR WW II, later with Rolls Royce Aero-Service; *m* 28 Oct 1950 Ann Elizabeth Gwinnell (*d* 1993), er dau of Lt-Col George Campbell Goldney Grey, OBE, RA, of Weston-super-Mare, and has:

1d +Christopher Anthony Major [Christopher Henniker Esq, 29 Rusthall Ave, London W4]; *b* 20 Oct 1952; *educ* Bedford Sch and Manchester U (LLB); slr 1978; *m* 16 June 1979 *Bernadette, dau of F J Ball, and has:

1e *Charles Edwin Major; *b* 1984

2e *James Christopher Major; *b* 1986

1e *Rosanna Josephine Major; *b* 1989

1a Anna Cassandra; *m* 22 Aug 1865 Rev Frederick John Ramsden and *d* 5 May 1906, leaving issue (*see* RAMSDEN, Bt)

(1) Mary Anne; *m* 10 Nov 1798 Sir Francis William Sykes, 2nd Bt, of Basildon (*qv*), and *d* 27 Feb 1804, leaving issue

(2) Elizabeth Dale; *m* 7 Dec 1800 John Simon Harcourt, of Ankerwycke, Bucks (for whose early ancestry *see* VERNON, B), and *d* his widow 10 May 1811

3 Sir BRYDGES TRECOTHIC HENNIKER, 1st Bt (*qv*)

1 Anne Elizabeth; *m* 1st 24 March 1788 2nd Earl of Aldborough (*dsp* 2 Jan 1801); *m* 2nd Dec 1801 George Powell and *dsp* 14 July 1802

The 2nd BARON's nephew,

JOHN MINET HENNIKER later HENNIKER-MAJOR (roy licence 27 May 1822), **3rd Baron Henniker of Stratford-upon-Slaney**; *b* 20 Nov 1777; barrister and Bencher, Lincoln's Inn, LLD Cantab; *m* 1 Jan 1799 Mary (*d* 10 Jan 1837), est dau of Rev William Chafy, Canon Canterbury, and had issue:

1 JOHN, **4th Baron**

2 Major; Capt 2nd Life Gds; *b* 21 July 1810; *d* 8 May 1842

3 William Chafie (Rev); Rector Gt Bealings, Suffolk; *b* 13 March 1813; *m* 28 Sept 1842 Mary Eliza (*d* 4 Aug 1878), dau of Edward Farnham, of Quorndon House, Leics, and *d* 28 Aug 1845

1 Anne Eliza; *m* 1824 John Heaton (*d* 14 May 1855), of Plas Heaton, Denbighs, and *d* 19 April 1872

2 Mary; *m* 24 June 1829 John Longueville Bedingfeld, of Ditchingham, Norfolk, and *d* 12 Sept 1870

3 Emily; *m* 10 Feb 1835 Thomas Lovett (*d* 1863), of Fernhill, Salop, and 23 March 1882

4 Elizabeth; *m* 1826 her cousin Sir Augustus Brydges Henniker, 3rd Bt (*qv*), and *d* 23 May 1882

5 Frances; *m* 23 July 1839 Rev James Bedingfeld, Rector Bedingfield, Suffolk, and *d* 22 Dec 1881

The 3rd BARON *d* 22 July 1832; his est son,

JOHN HENNIKER-MAJOR, **4th Baron Henniker of Stratford-upon-Slaney**; *b* 3 Feb 1801; *educ* Eton and St John's Coll Cambridge (MA); barrister Lincoln's Inn, MP (C) E Suffolk 1832–47 and 1856–66, High Sheriff Suffolk 1853, *cr* 13 July 1866 BARON HARTISMERE, of Hartismere, Suffolk (UK); *m* 5 Jan 1837 Anna (*d* 10 May 1889), est dau of Lt-Gen Sir Edward Kerrison, Bt, of Oakley and Brome, and had, with two daus (*d* unm):

1 JOHN MAJOR, **5th Baron**

2 Edward Minet; V-Consul St Malo 1888 and 1902–19; *b* 3 Feb 1848; *m* 1869 Eveline Talavera (*d* 17 May 1926), widow of W Harvey and only dau of Capt Henri de St Maur, French Army, and *d* 20 Dec 1924

3 Arthur Henry, CB, JP Suffolk; Maj-Gen cmdg 1st Lond Div TF Coldstream Gds, BA Cantab; *b* 3 April 1855; *m* 20 June 1882 Hon Florence Ellen Hungerford Milnes (*d* 4 April 1923), dau of 1st Baron Houghton (*see* 1940 edn CREWE, M), and *dsp* 6 Feb 1912

The 4th BARON *d* 16 April 1870; his est son,

JOHN MAJOR HENNIKER-MAJOR, **5th Baron Henniker of Stratford-upon-Slaney**, VD, JP, DL Norfolk; *b* 7 Nov 1842; *educ* Eton and Trin Coll Cambridge (MA); Chm QS and CC E Suffolk, Hon Col 6th Vol Bn Suffolk Regt, Ld-in-Waiting 1877–80, 1885–86 and 1886–92, MP (C) E Suffolk 1866–70, Govr IoM 1895, FSA; *m* 14 Jan 1864 Alice Mary (*d* 19 Nov 1893), only dau of 3rd Earl of Desart (*see* 1934 edn), and *d* 27 June 1902, having had:

1 Albert Edward John, JP Suffolk; *b* 30 May 1865 (HM EDWARD VII stood sponsor); *educ* Eton and Trin Coll Cambridge (BA); ADC to Govr S Australia; *d* unm 2 March 1901

2 Otway Major; *b* 31 Oct, *d* 2 Nov 1866

3 CHARLES HENRY CHANDOS HENNIKER-MAJOR, **6th Baron Henniker of Stratford-upon-Slaney**, JP, DL Suffolk; *b* 25 Jan 1872; *educ* Eton and RMC Sandhurst; Lt-Col Rifle Bde cmdg Rifle Depot 1917–19, served NWF India 1897 and WW I; *d* unm 4 Feb 1956

4 Gerald Arthur George; *b* 3 Dec 1872; *m* 27 July 1921 Monica (*d* 28 July 1950), only dau of Hamilton Howard Curtis, of Poole, Dorset, and *dsp* 18 Jan 1955

5 Victor Alexander (Rev); Rector Worlingworth with Southolt Suffolk 1912–22 and Thornham Magna and Parva Suffolk 1927–49; *b* 8 March 1878 (HM QUEEN VICTORIA stood sponsor); *m* 5 July 1943 Mary (*d* 27 July 1971 aged 76), widow of Rev Reginald Ughtred Pilbeam and dau of Bertram Nesfield, of Guernsey, and *dsp* 20 Jan 1954

6 JOHN ERNEST DE GREY, **7th Baron**

1 Alice Margaret Mary; *b* 23 May 1870; *m* 17 Dec 1902 Julian Seymour Clifford (*d* 27 Dec 1921) and *d* 27 July 1923, having had issue

2 Ethel Elizabeth Emily; VAD WW I and WW II; *b* 30 Nov 1874; *m* 29 Sept 1920 Rev George Thomas Wilkes (*d* 1951), Rector Worlingworth, Suffolk, and *d* 18 Jan 1957

3 Cicely Anne Lucy; *b* 10 Dec 1876; *d* unm 24 June 1901

4 Lilian Bertha Aline; *b* 16 Aug 1880; *d* unm 10 Oct 1959

5 Dorothy Florence Stella; *b* 7 Jan 1885; *m* 4 Dec 1906 Baron Claude de Chassiron (*d* 5 March 1929) and *d* 8 July 1931, leaving issue

The 6th BARON's bro,

JOHN ERNEST DE GREY HENNIKER-MAJOR, **7th Baron Henniker of Stratford-upon-Slaney**; *b* 18 Jan 1883; *educ* Radley and RAC Cirencester; FLAS, Page of Honour to HM QUEEN VICTORIA 1895–99, WW I as Staff Lt 1915 and in RAF 1917, Croix de Guerre; *m* 5 Dec 1914 Molly (*d* 21 Oct 1953), yr dau of Sir Robert William Burnet, KCVO, and *d* 1980, leaving:

1 JOHN PATRICK EDWARD CHANDOS HENNIKER-MAJOR, **8th and present Baron Henniker of Stratford-upon-Slaney**

2 +Richard Arthur Otway [The Hon Richard Henniker-Major, 13 Market Cross Place, Aldeburgh, Suffolk]; *b* 20 Dec 1917; *educ* Stowe and Magdalene Coll Cambridge (BA 1939); Lt RA WW II (POW 1942–45), slr 1948; *m* 2 June 1946 *Nancy Pauline, er dau of Sir John Armitage Stainton, KCB, KBE, QC (*see* FORTEVIOT, B), and has:

(1) +David Richard [David Henniker-Major Esq, Westbourne House, 37 Northside, Hutton Rudby, nr Yarm, Cleveland]; *b* 24 June 1949; *educ* Stowe; *m* 15 Dec 1973 *Valerie Ann, er dau of Dr Francis Martin Lanigan-O'Keefe, MD, of Kenilworth, Warwicks, and has issue:

1a *Anna Natalie; *b* 23 Sept 1976

2a *Fiona Louise; *b* 2 June 1978

(2) +John Alexander [John Henniker-Major Esq, Harewell House, Stourton, Warwicks CV36 5HG]; *b* 7 March 1952; *m* 18 Sept 1976 *Mary, dau of Anders Mathiesen, and has issue:

1a +George Richard; *b* 1985

1a *Charlotte Alice; *b* 1979

1a *Rose Clementine; *b* 6 Oct 1982

(1) *Susan Rose; *b* 26 March 1947; *m* 4 Sept 1976 *Peter Croft

Seat: Thornham Hall, Thornham Magna, Suffolk. The original house on this site was remodelled during the reign of WILLIAM IV in the neo-Jacobean style by Sydney Smirke (brother of the more famous Sir Robert, architect of the British Museum, whose pupil he was). It was probably the **3rd Baron** who commissioned him.

HENNIKER, Bt

Arms: Or on a chevron gules between two crescents in chief and in base an escallop azure, three estoiles argent. **Crest:** An escallop or, charged with an estoile gules. **Motto:** *Deus major columna* ('God is a greater support'). **Creation:** Bt. (UK) 2 Nov 1813.

SIR ADRIAN CHANDOS HENNIKER, 9TH BT, of Newton Hall, Essex [Sir Adrian Henniker Bt, Llwyndu Court, Abergavenny, Gwent]; *b* 18 Oct 1946; *s* f 1991; *educ* Marlborough; *m* 1971 *Ann, dau of Stuart Britton, of Malvern Ho, Fairwater Rd, Llandaff, Cardiff, and has issue:

1 *Victoria Louise; *b* 1976

2 *Holly Georgina; *b* 1976

Lineage: The 1st BARON HENNIKER (*qv*); had a yst s:

Sir Brydges Trecothic Henniker, 1st Bt (UK), so *cr* 2 Nov 1813; *b* 10 Nov 1767; MP (I Parl) Kildare 1798–1800, Lt-Gen; *m* 25 Sept 1791 Mary (*d* 29 March 1840), dau of William Press, of Dedham, Essex, and *d* 3 July 1816, having had, with two daus:

1 **Sir Frederick Henniker, 2nd Bt**; *b* 1 Nov 1793; *dsp* 6 Aug 1825

2 **Rev Sir Augustus Brydges Henniker, 3rd Bt**; *b* 24 Jan 1795; *m* 1st Frances Amelia (*d* 17 June 1823), dau of J Henry Stewart, and had:

(1) Frances Elizabeth; *m* 19 Dec 1845 Charles Robert Bree (*d* Oct 1886), of Colchester, MD, JP, and *dsp* 19 Nov 1906

2 (cont.) **Sir Augustus** *m* 2nd 14 Feb 1826 Hon Elizabeth Henniker-Major (*d* 23 May 1882), yst dau of 3rd Baron Henniker (*qv*), and *d* 28 Jan 1849 having by her had, with other issue:

(1) **Sir Brydges Powell Henniker, 4th Bt**, JP, DL; *b* 3 Sept 1835; Capt RHG, Capt W Essex Yeo Cav, Registrar-Gen Births, Deaths and Marriages 1880–1900; *m* 14 July 1860 Justina Louisa (*d* 13 Feb 1890), dau of Thomas Hughan (*see* SAINT ALBANS, D), and *d* 12 July 1906, having had issue:

1a **Sir Frederick Brydges Henniker, 5th Bt**; *b* 12 Aug 1862; Lt-Col KRRC; *d* unm 19 Aug 1908

2a Sir ARTHUR JOHN HENNIKER later HENNIKER-HUGHAN (added 1896 under terms of will of his aunt Mrs Houghton Hughan), **6th Bt**, CB; *b* 24 Jan 1866; MP Galloway, ADC to HM GEORGE V 1914–16, Adml Supt Devonport Dockyard 1916–19, Capt HMS *Ajax* Grand Fleet WW I 1914–16, Mil Order of Avis Portugal 1st Cl; *m* 26 Jan 1904 Inger Margueretta (*d* 16 April 1923), only dau of Graham Hutchinson, of Balmaghie, Kirkcudbrightshire, and *dspm* 4 Oct 1925, leaving issue:

1b *Beryl Inger; *b* 1904

2b Rhona Mary; *m* 19 Dec 1936 W/Cdr Francis Lenox Ingall, RAuxAF, er s of Francis William Ingall, of Garth House, Hertingfordbury, Herts, by Elizabeth Margaret, dau of Rev Robert Townsend Crawley, and had issue

3b *Alison Frances; *b* 1910; *m* 29 Sept 1936 (*divorce* 1947) John Gladstone, est s of Sir Hugh Steuart Gladstone, of Capenoch, Penpont, Dumfriesshire

1a Mabel Sophia; *m* 1st 1 July 1882 Col Edward Godolphin Hastings, CB (*see* HUNTINGDON, E); *m* 2nd 2 April 1891 Charles Robert Southwell, 7th Baron Dimsdale (*cr* 1769 by CATHERINE II OF RUSSIA; *see* 1956 edn Foreign Title Section; he *d* 6 Dec 1928), and *d* 13 Dec 1942, having had issue

2a Edith Janetta; *m* 4 May 1912 Rev Lewis Gilbertson, MA, Rector St Martin's, Ludgate Hill, London EC, and *dsp* 20 Feb 1940

3a Louisa Mary, OBE (1918); DGStJ; V-Pres Essex Br BRCS; *m* 6 Jan 1891 Maj Horace Walter Calverley (*d* 22 Sept 1929), of Oulton Hall, Yorks, and *d* 1946, having had issue

(2) Augustus Henry Aldborough Stratford; *b* 23 Feb 1837; barrister, Stipendiary Magistrate NZ, Lt RN; *m* 1st 23 Aug 1859 Lillias Grant (*dsp* 2 Aug 1900), dau of Capt John Campbell, RN, and widow of Hon Joseph Holroyd, of Prince Edward's Island, MLC; *m* 2nd 30 Jan 1902 Margaretta (Daisy), dau of Edmund Wickes, JP, Westland, NZ, and *dsp* 27 Nov 1906

(2) Louisa Augusta; *m* 28 April 1862 Charles John Manning (*d* 28 Nov 1880), bro of Cardinal Manning, and *d* 15 Oct 1906, having had issue

3 Aldborough Brydges John, of Mayfurlong, Staffs; *b* 4 Jan 1797; *m* 1820 Sarah (*d* 18 Sept 1854), dau of John Jones, and *d* 6 July 1880, having had, with other issue:

(1) Aldborough, QC; *b* 6 July 1821; *m* 17 Oct 1860 Phoebe Anne (*d* 10 Jan 1900), yst dau of David Henderson, MD, and widow of Thomas Henry Winwood (*d* 1857), of Ty Glyn-Aeron, Cards, and *d* 28 Jan 1880, leaving issue:

1a Aldborough Montagu; *b* 16 Dec 1865; *d* unm 23 July 1912

1a Mary Constance; *m* 1st 22 April 1888 William George Vallancey Wetherall (*d* 21 April 1903), of Little Pelham, Herts; *m* 2nd 7 Oct 1916 Walter Forder (*d* 1927), of Cambs, and *d* 22 March 1952, having by her 1st husb had issue

2a Maude Ellen Margaret; *m* 15 Oct 1892 Raymond Bourne (*d* 17 March 1954), and *d* 3 March 1954, leaving issue

(2) John; *d* unm 1854, drowned off Sebastopol during the Crimean War

(3) Robert (Rev); *b* 1 June 1833; MA, Vicar Frocester; *m* 11 Jan 1859 Jane Livesey (*d* 27 March 1904), dau of John Leadbeater, of Blackburn, and *d* 1 Feb 1880, leaving issue:

1a John Granville, JP (Somerset); *b* 11 Jan 1862; *educ* Oxford (BA); *m* 2 Sept 1887 Margaret (*d* 29 July 1911), dau of Robert Murray, of Golspie, Scotland, and *d* 29 March 1914, leaving issue:

1b **Sir Robert John Aldborough Henniker, 7th Bt**, MC; *b* 26 May 1888; Maj Duke of Wellington's Regt (W R) WW I (wounded twice, despatches twice, 1914 star, two medals), also WW II; *m* 5 Dec 1914 Lucy Mable (*d* 13 March 1964), dau of Edward Swan Hennessy, of Hazelbrook, Co Roscommon, and *d* 19 Feb 1958, leaving issue:

1c Ann Margaret Henniker; *m* 5 Feb 1946 John Holroyd Bairstow (*d* 4 Aug 1968), BA, LLB, slr, F/O RAFVR, and had issue

1b Dorothy Margaret; *m* 18 Sept 1926 Cecil Joseph Waldron (*d* 1953) and *d* March 1964, leaving issue

2a Robert Percy; *b* 14 Dec 1863; *dsp* 10 Jan 1896

3a Frederick Chandos; *b* 2 Sept 1866; ICS, Capt Cambs Regt (TA) WW I; *m* 3 Jan 1901 Ada Russell (*d* 20 Aug 1958), dau of Arthur Pearce Howell, ICS, and *d* 12 Dec 1953, leaving issue:

1b MARK CHANDOS AUBERON HENNIKER (Sir), **8th Bt**

1b Alison Margaret; *b* 12 Oct 1909; *d* 21 Jan 1996

4a Alan, CBE (1919); *b* 24 Jan 1870; *educ* RMA Woolwich; Col RE, Boer War 1899–1902 as Dep Assist Dir Rlwys and WW I (despatches), Legion of Honour, Croix de Guerre France and Belgium, Order Crown Belgium; *m* 28 Nov 1902 Blanche Marie (*d* 12 Jan 1961), dau of James Gadsden, of Lannion, Britanny, and *d* 11 April 1949, leaving:

1b Richard (Dick); *b* 10 June 1906; *educ* Marlborough and Trin Hall Cambridge (MA); FRIBA, Maj RE WW II 1940-45; *m* 26 Feb 1938 *Daphne Irene Frederick, yr dau of Capt C J Maxwell, RSG, of Cirencester, and *d* 31 Oct 1996

1b Anne Marie; *b* 19 March 1910; VAD (attd RAMC) WW II; *d* unm 29 Nov 1960

1a Eleanor Margaret; *d* unm 31 Jan 1920

4 John HENNIKER later WRIGHT-HENNIKER-WILSON; *b* 7 June 1800; *m* 29 April 1839 Mary (*d* 6 July 1866), only child of Capt Edward Wilson and heiress of Sir Henry Wright Wilson, of Chelsea Park, Middx, and *d* Aug 1872

The 7th Bt's cousin,

Sir Mark Chandos Auberon Henniker, 8th Bt, CBE (1953, OBE 1944), DSO (1945), MC (1934), DL (Mon 1963); *b* 23 Jan 1906; *educ* Marlborough, RMA Woolwich and King's Coll Cambridge; Brig RE, served NW Frontier 1933, WW II (wounded), Malaya 1952–54 (despatches) and Near East 1956 (despatches), T/Brig 1951, ret 1958, Hon Col Parachute Engr Regt (TA) 1959–68, Hon Col REME 1963–68, author: *Memoirs of a Junior Officer* (1951), *Red Shadow over Malaya* (1956) and *Life in The Army Today* (1957); *m* 5 Sept 1945 *Kathleen Denys [Dowager Lady Henniker, 27 Wester Rd, Abergavenny, Gwent NP7 7AB], 2nd dau of John Cousmaker Anderson, of Pilgrim's Way, Farnham, Surrey, and *d* 1991, leaving issue:

1 Sir ADRIAN CHANDOS HENNIKER, **9th and present Bt**

1 *Fiona Jane [Mrs Peter Milewski, Dorney Wood, Llawhaden, Dyfed]; *b* 12 May 1951; *m* 1977 *Peter Jan Milewski, MChir, FRCS, and has issue:

(1) *Andrew Mark Jan; *b* 1982

(2) *Henry Bish Chandos; *b* 1984

(1) *Lucy Kathleen Amina; *b* 1984

(2) *Anna Denys Olive; *b* 1987

HENNIKER-HEATON

Arms: Argent on a bend sable three bull's heads couped of the first, over all on an escutcheon of pretence, quarterly of six, 1st, vert, three escutcheons argent, each charged with a bordure engrailed or (for BURRELL); 2nd, argent three battering rams fessways in pale proper headed and garnished azure (for BERTIE); 3rd, or fretty azure (for WILLOUGHBY); 4th, vert three eagles displayed fessways or (for OWEN GWYNEDD); 5th, gyronny of eight or and sable (for CAMPBELL); 6th, per pale sable and gules, on a cross between four fleurs-de-lys argent five pheons azure (for BANKS). **Crest:** Out of a crest coronet gules a bull's head argent. **Motto:** *Lux in litteris* ('Enlightenment in Literature'). **Creation:** Bt. (UK) 31 Jan 1912.

SIR YVO ROBERT HENNIKER-HEATON, 4TH BT, of Mundarrah Towers, Sydney, Australia [Sir Yvo Henniker-Heaton Bt, 7 Brendon Way, Ashby-de-la-Zouch, Leics LE65 1EY]; *b* 24 April 1954; *s* f 1971; memb NW Leics DC, chm Kegworth C Assoc 1988–94, author: *Corporate Computer Insurance* (1990); *m* 1978 *Freda, dau of Brian Jones, of The Hollies, Broughton Astley, Leics, and has:

1 +ALASTAIR JOHN; *b* 4 May 1990

1 *Julia Sermonda; *b* 1987

Lineage: Lt-Col JOHN HEATON; *b* 1810; *m* 8 May 1841 Elizabeth Anne (*d* 20 May 1868), dau of John Henniker, of Rochester, Kent, and *d* 6 May 1856, leaving:

Sir JOHN HEATON later HENNIKER-HEATON, **1st Bt** (UK), so *cr* 31 Jan 1912; *b* 18 May 1848; MP (C) Canterbury 1885–1910; *m* 16 July 1873 Rose (*d* 23 March 1920), only dau of Samuel Bennett, of Rosewarne, Camborne, Cornwall, and Mundarrah Towers, Sydney, NSW, and *d* 8 Sept 1914, leaving issue:

1 JOHN (Sir), **2nd Bt**

2 Reginald; *b* 19 Jan 1879; Capt RN; *m* 30 April 1910 Mary Isabel Dorothy Follett, dau of Maj James Houstoun, DL, of Haddington, and *dsp* 9 Aug 1958

3 Herbert (Sir), KCMG; *b* 9 Feb 1880; *educ* Eton and New Coll Oxford (BA 1901); Colonial Sec Gambia 1917, Actg Govr 1918–20, Colonial Sec Falkland Islands 1921, Actg Govr 1923–24, Colonial Sec Bermuda 1925–29 and Cyprus 1929–34, Govr and C-in-C Falkland Isles Jan 1935–41, Actg Govr 1929–32; *m* 1st 5 Aug 1909 Susan Angele Phoebe Anne (*d* 15 Aug 1922), dau of Lindsey Bertie Talbot-Crosbie, DL, of Ardfert Abbey, Co Kerry, and had issue:

(1) John Lindsey Patrick (Rev); *b* 5 July 1910; *d* unm 21 Nov 1942

(2) +(Arthur) Dermot [Dermot Henniker-Heaton Esq, 2 Manor Gdns, Kingskerswell, Devon]; *b* 11 Aug 1922; *m* 24 March 1956 Joan Townsend (*d* 1996) and has:

1a +Colin Edward Richard; *b* 16 Nov 1956

2a +Keith Patrick; *b* 8 March 1962

(1) *Rose Phoebe Anne [Mrs Norman Cameron, Beaufort House, Beaufort, Co Kerry, Ireland]; *b* 6 March 1914; *m* 10 Oct 1945 Maj Norman Keith Cameron (*d* 1971), Coldstream Gds, and has had issue:

1a Alastair; *b* 1951; *d* 1989 in the Falkland Islands

2a *Donald [Donald Cameron Esq, Beaufort House, Beaufort, Co Kerry, Ireland]; *b* 1953; *m* 1985 *Rachel Wendy Fell and has:

1b *Katherine Elizabeth Phoebe; *b* 1991

2b *Eleanor Jessica Jane; *b* 1995

1a *Jane; *b* 1950

2a *Susan; *b* 1956

(2) *Priscilla Moira Angèle [Mrs Walter Ballantyne, c/o 7 Eastville, Bath BA1 6QN]; *b* 18 Dec 1916; *m* 19 Oct 1940 Walter Ballantyne (*d* 1971) and has:

1a *Priscilla Sarah Anne [Mrs Sven Gahlin, 7 Eastville, Bath BA1 6QN]; *b* 8 Jan 1943; *m* 26 March 1967 *Sven Gahlin and has issue:

1b *Adam Hugo; *b* 1972

1b *Lucia Karin; *b* 1970; *m* 1995 *Richard Hugh Evans

3 (cont.) Sir Herbert *m* 2nd 8 June 1926 Helena Iris (*d* 17 March 1927), dau of Sir Henry McCallum, GCMG, and by her had:

(3) Christopher Robin, JP (Lokoja 1953); *b* 6 March 1927; *educ* Canford, Ontario Ag Coll and Miami U Florida (BA 1950); Sr Assist Sec Fedl Govt

Lagos 1962 (ret 1962); *m* 1st 24 April 1952 (*divorce* 1967) Elizabeth, dau of Dr C Curtis, of Tuckerstown, Bermuda, and has issue:

1a *Elizabeth Anne; *b* 12 Aug 1954; *m* 1974 *Walter — and has issue:

1b *Aaron James; *b* 1976

1b *Rebeca Elizabeth; *b* 1980

(3) (cont.) Christopher Henniker-Heaton *m* 2nd 1967 Estelle Patricia (*d* 1986), dau of Samuel John Newing, of Cheshunt, Herts, and *d* 1990

3 (cont.) Sir Herbert *m* 3rd 27 Jan 1947 Gladys Meta (*d* 23 Nov 1962), widow of Col George Going, The South Staffordshire Regt, and dau of Col Claud Francis, and *d* 24 Jan 1961

4 Arthur ; *b* 14 April 1883; Capt RN, served WW I and WW II (despatches), Order of St Maurice and St Lazarus of Italy; *m* 12 June 1913 Vera Isabel (*d* 11 Oct 1965), dau of Hamilton Atherley, and *d* Jan 1965, leaving:

(1) +Michael Hamilton; *b* 3 April 1914; Maj Roy Signals WW II; *m* 1st 1937 —; *m* 2nd 12 May 1956 Mrs Brenda Miller (*née* Morriston Davies); *m* 3rd 1957 *Elizabeth Catherine, FLA, dau of Maurice Budgett

(2) Robin John; *b* Sept 1915; Assist Treasurer Sarawak, Lt-Cdr (S) RNVR WW II (despatches); *m* 1st 16 July 1951 Sylvia Elizabeth, yr dau of Julian Charles Grumbar, MBE, of 7 Prince's Gate, London SW7; *m* 2nd 1958 *Barbara, dau of William Newman Ayers, and *d* 1985, having by her had:

1a +Anthony; *b* 15 Nov 1958

1a *Sally; *b* 26 Feb 1961

1 Elizabeth Anne; *m* 5 Jan 1909 Algernon Berkeley Paget (*see* ANGLESEY, M) and *d* 11 May 1925, leaving issue

2 Rose; author: *The Perfect Schoolgirl* and *Cruising with James*; *m* 10 March 1914 Lt-Col Adrian Sydney Morton Porter, King's Messenger (*d* 23 Dec 1954), and *d* 8 Oct 1975, leaving issue:

(1) *Leila Charlotte Evelyn Petronella; *b* 16 Jan 1917; *m* 1st 1938 (*divorce*) Courtenay Edward Stevens, Fell Magdalen College, Oxford, and has issue:

1a *Richard Paul; *b* 9 Dec 1943; *educ* Winchester and Trin Hall Cambridge (BA 1965, MA 1969)

(1) (cont.) Mrs Leila Stevens *m* 2nd 1949 Philip Strachan Buckley (*d* 4 June 1962), and has issue:

1a *Colin Damian; *b* 28 Nov 1954; *educ* Downside

1a *Rose Aylmer; *b* 8 Oct 1951

2a *Clare Lorraine; *b* 27 Feb 1953

Sir JOHN's est son,

Sir John Henniker-Heaton, 2nd Bt; *b* 19 April 1877; Capt 1st Welsh Horse, 10th Bn Imp Yeo Boer War 1900–01 (medal with three clasps); *m* 16 April 1902 Hon Catherine Mary Sermonda Burrell (*d* 24 Nov 1958), dau and heir of 5th and last Baron Gwydyr (*see* 1915 edn), and *d* 21 Feb 1963, leaving issue:

1 (JOHN VICTOR) PEREGRINE (Sir), **3rd Bt**

2 Peter Joseph; *b* 11 Dec 1909; *educ* Wellington and Corpus Christi Coll Oxford (BA 1931, MA 1965); Priv Sec to Parly and Fin Sec Admlty 1936, edtl staff *Punch* 1949–52 and *Christian Science Monitor* 1952–63, edtl consultant to Christian Science Bd of Dirs 1963–76, sr memb Br Interplanetary Soc, memb: American Astronautical Soc, New England Poetry Club, author: *Jubilee and other Poems* (1961); *b* 9 May 1907; *m* 10 Sept 1934 Rose Maddock (*d* 2 Sept 1982), only dau of Amyas Morse, PWD India, and *d* 10 Sept 1976

3 Clement Algernon Charles, CBE (1965); 14th/20th Hussars and 26th Hussars WW II 1940–44, MLC Assam, dir Br Spinners and Doublers Assoc, Fell Inst of Linguists 1960; *m* 11 July 1940 *Marjorie [Mrs Clement Henniker-Heaton, Clevemede, Goring-on-Thames, Berks], only dau of William E Speight, of Bournemouth, and *d* 4 Oct 1983, having had issue:

(1) John Anthony Willoughby Burrell; *b* 11 Oct 1941; *d* 2 April 1942

(2) +(John) Lindsey [Lindsey Henniker-Heaton Esq, Northwoods House, Northwoods, Winterbourne, Bristol BS36 1RS]; *b* 19 June 1946; *educ* Wellington and Emmanuel Coll Cambridge (MA), CEng, FIMechE; *m* 1970 *Elisabeth Gladwell, and has issue:

1a +Anthony James; *b* 1974

2a +Robert Piers; *b* 1978

(3) +Charles Peter [Charles Henniker-Heaton Esq, 206 Rue de la Limité, 1950 Krarinem, Brussels, Belgium]; *b* 20 April 1956; *educ* Eton; *m* 1989 *Julia, dau of Derek Johnson, of Much Hadham, Herts, and has issue:

1a +Alexander James Peter; *b* 1992

2a +Toby Anthony; *b* 1994

(1) *Hilary Rose; *b* 21 June 1948; *m* 1976 *Edward Holloway and has issue:

1a *Nicholas Henniker; *b* 1977

2a *William David; *b* 1980

1a *Rachel Sermonda; *b* 1983

2a *Charlotte Anne (twin); *b* 1983

1 Mary Araluen Elizabeth Anne; Registrar Rose Brumford Coll of Speech and Drama, Life Govr Roy Life Saving Soc, served WW II (Ambulance Corps)

Sir JOHN's est s,

Sir (John Victor) Peregrine Henniker-Heaton, 3rd Bt; *b* 15 Jan 1903; W/Cdr RAF WW II (despatches), APM Austria 1945, DPM Levant 1945–48; *m* 1st 19 April 1927 (*divorce* 1937) Gladys, 2nd dau of Peter E Tyson, of Alnwick, Northumberland, and had issue:

1 *Jacqueline; *b* 20 March 1931; *m* Jan 1959 *Michael Ferris and has issue:

(1) *Rory; *b* 10 Dec 1959

(2) *Michaela Jacqueline; *b* Feb 1961; *m* *Jorge de Villanova-Rattazzi

2 *Anthea Jennifer; *b* 2 May 1934

Sir Peregrine *m* 2nd 13 March 1948 *Margaret Patricia, F/O WAAF WW II (despatches), dau of Lt Percy Wright, Canadian Mounted Rifles, and *d* between 5 Oct 1971 and June 1974 (when his body was found in a locked room at his house in Ealing), leaving issue:

1 Sir YVO ROBERT HENNIKER-HEATON, **4th and present Bt**

3 *Priscilla Margaret; *b* 19 Jan 1949; *m* 1976 *Iain James Saddler Mann and has:

(1) *Alison Catriona; *b* 1977

(2) *Jessamy Robert; *b* 1980

HENRY

Creation: Bt. (UK) 26 Feb 1923.

SIR PATRICK DENIS HENRY, 3RD BT, of Cahore, Co Londonderry [Sir Patrick Henry Bt, 55 Old Park Rd, Roundhay, Leeds LS8 1JX]; *b* 20 Dec 1957; *s* unc 1997; *m* 1997 *Georgina Ravenscroft

Lineage: JAMES HENRY, of Cahore, Draperstown, had issue:

Sir Denis Stanislaus Henry, 1st Bt (UK), so *cr* 26 Feb 1923, PC, JP, DL (Londonderry 1919); *b* 7 March 1864; barrister King's Inn Dublin 1885, QC 1896 and a Bencher 1898, Slr-Gen Ireland 1918–19, Attorney-Gen Ireland 1919–21, Ld Ch Justice NI 1921–25, Sr Crown Counsel Co Westmeath, MP S Derry, memb Speaker's Ctee on Irish Redistbn 1918, Hon LLD Queen's U Belfast; *m* 1 Oct 1910 Violet (*d* 9 Jan 1966), 3rd dau of Rt Hon Hugh Holmes, Ld Justice of Appeal Ireland, and *d* 1 Oct 1925, having had issue:

1 **Sir James Holmes Henry, 2nd Bt**, CMG (1960), MC (1944), TD (1950), QC (Tanganyika 1953, Cyprus 1957); *b* 22 Sept 1911; *educ* Downside and UCL (BA 1932); barrister Inner Temple 1934, practised London 1934–39, Crown Counsel Tanganyika 1946, Legal Draftsman 1949, Cyprus: Slr-Gen 1952 and Attorney-Gen 1956–60, memb For Compensation Commn 1960–77 and chm 1977–83, Capt London Irish Rifles WW II (wounded); *m* 1st 5 July 1941 (*divorce* 1948) Susan Mary, er dau of Authur G Blackwell, of Salisbury, S Rhodesia; *m* 2nd 23 Feb 1949 *(Christina) Hilary [Lady Henry, 24 Seymour Rd, Hampton Hill TW12 1DD], est dau of Sir Hugh Oliver Holmes, KBE, CMG, MC, QC, of Alexandria, and widow of Lt-Cdr Christopher Hayward Wells, RN (*see* WELLS, Bt), and *d* 19 Feb 1997, having by her had:

(1) *Teresa Violet [Mrs Gordon Stewart, 7 Croom's Hill, London SE10 8ER]; *b* 28 Nov 1949; *m* 1982 *Gordon Stewart and has issue:

1a *Edmund James; *b* 1985

2a *Roland Valentine; *b* 1988

(2) *Christina Mary; *b* 16 March 1951; *m* 2 June 1979 *Peter William Irving Ingram, only s of Maj W A Ingram, RA, and has had issue

(3) Sarah Rose; *b* 18 Sept; *d* 21 Sept 1953

(4) *Rosemary Jane; *b* 29 May 1955; *m* 1990 *Peter Winckley, s of John Winckley, of E Aberthaw, S Glam

2 Denis Valentine; *b* 29 June 1917; *educ* Shrewsbury and Clare Coll Cambridge (BA 1939, MA 1944); Capt Roy Ulster Rifles; *m* 1956 Elizabeth (*d* 14 June 1997), dau of Rowland Walker, and *d* 1983, leaving issue:

(1) Sir PATRICK DENIS HENRY, **3rd and present Bt**

(1) *Jessica Ellen [Mrs Ian Beech, 1 Park Ave, Bridgewater, Somerset TA6 7EE]; *b* 1960; *m* 1988*Ian Beech

(2) *Martha Olive [Miss Martha Henry, 307 Bevidge Rd, Blackburn BB1 8DF]; *b* 1961

1 *Denise Olive [Miss Denise Henry, 7 Morley Rd, Farnham, Surrey]; MB, BS, DCH, MRCS, LRCP (Lond) 1936

2 *Alice Ellen [Mrs Alan Newton, 3 Oakdene, 64 Bourne Way, Hayes, Kent BK2 7HA]; BSc; *m* 26 Nov 1946 *Alan Newton and has issue

3 *Lorna Mary [Miss Lorna Henry, 7 Morley Rd, Farnham, Surrey]

HEREFORD

Arms: Arg. a fess gu., in chief three torteaux. **Crest:** Out of a ducal coronet or a talbot's head arg., eared gu. **Supporters:** Dexter, a talbot arg., eared gu., ducally gorged of the last; sinister, a reindeer gu. ppr., attired, gorged with a ducal coronet and lined or.
Mottoes: 1 *Virtutis comes invidia* ('Envy is the attendant of virtue'), 2 *Basis virtutum constantia* ('Firmness is the basis of virtue').
Creations: V. (E) 2 Feb 1549/50, Bt. (E) 25 Nov 1611.

THE 18TH VISCOUNT HEREFORD and a **Baronet** (Sir Robert Milo Leicester Devereux, Bt) [The Rt Hon The Viscount Hereford, House of Lords, London SW1A 0PW]; *b* 4 Nov 1932; *s* gf 1952, Premier Viscount of England; *educ* Eton; OStJ; *m* 11 Dec 1969 (*divorce* 1982) Susan Mary, only child of Maj Maurice Godley (*see* KILBRACKEN, B), and has issue:

1 +(CHARLES) ROBIN DE BOHUN; *b* 11 Aug 1975

2 +Edward Mark de Breteuil; *b* 8 June 1977

Hereford, previous creations: It is possible that an Earldom of Hereford existed well before the Norman Conquest, although the putative holder, Ralph, a nephew of EDWARD THE CONFESSOR, seems on the balance of probability to have been Earl of the next door county of Worcester(shire) — at any rate so early as the late 1040s. (For the lack of distinction between county town and county names in assigning early medieval earldoms *see* in particular WINCHESTER, M, preliminary remarks.) By the mid-1050s the evidence for Ralph's possessing the Earldom of Hereford itself is stronger, though by no means conclusive.

After the Conquest the Earldom was granted to William Fitz Osbern (*see* also MILFORD-HAVEN, M), a great-nephew by marriage of RICHARD I DUKE OF NORMANDY and a companion in arms of WILLIAM I THE CONQUEROR at Hastings. Fitz Osbern's son, the 2nd and last Earl of this creation, had his lands and Earldom confiscated for rebellion.

In 1141, during the struggle between the EMPRESS MAUD and STEPHEN for the throne the former conferred the Earldom of Hereford on Miles of Gloucester, so-called from his father being hereditary Constable of that shire. Only two years earlier the new Earl had supported STEPHEN, but it has been suggested that he went over to the EMPRESS in part because his overlord, the Earl of Gloucester, was one of HENRY I's many bastard sons, hence MAUD's half-brother. (Her generous gifts to Miles of land, houses and castles, in addition to the Earldom, may have helped win him over.)

The Earldom of Hereford passed to Miles's eldest son Roger (sometimes called of Gloucester and sometimes Fitz Miles) but on the latter's death in 1155 seems to have fallen into disuse. It was revived in 1200 for Miles's great-grandson Henry de Bohun, hereditary Constable of England and a close relative of both the English and Scottish reigning dynasties. He was heir to his grandmother Margaret's estates in and around Herefordshire, she being Miles's daughter and eventual coheir, hence the choice of title when he was made an earl.

The Earldom of Hereford remained with the de Bohuns for almost another two centuries, being held by them from 1236 with that of Essex and for the last dozen or so years with that of Northampton also.The 4th de Bohun Earl of Hereford, Humphrey, married EDWARD I's daughter Elizabeth but was killed at the Battle of Boroughbridge in March 1321/2 having taken up arms against his own brother-in-law EDWARD II. On the death in Jan 1372/3 without male issue of the 7th Earl of this 1200 creation the title expired but his son-in-law Henry was created Duke of Hereford in 1397 before usurping the throne two years later as HENRY IV. The new King was husband of the 7th Earl's younger daughter, Mary; that of his elder one, Eleanor, was Thomas of Woodstock, EDWARD III's youngest son. Their daughter Anne married Sir William Bourchier, whose granddaughter by her, Cecily Bourchier, was wife of John Devereux, 2nd Lord (Baron) Ferrers (*see* below).

Lineage: Sir WALTER DEVEREUX; *d* 1376, leaving:

Sir WALTER DEVEREUX, to whom RICHARD II committed the forests and castles of the Earl of Hereford 1387; *m* Agnes (*m* 2nd John Parr, of Kendal (and was great-great-grandmother of KATHERINE PARR, HENRY VIII's last w); *m* 3rd John Merbury and *d* 1436), dau of Thomas de Crophull, and was *k* fighting against Owen Glendower 1403, leaving, with four yr sons (Richard; John; Stephen; Roger) and a dau (Joan, *m* Thomas Swynford):

Sir WALTER DEVEREUX; *b* 1387; *m* Maud, dau of Sir Thomas Bromwich, and *d* 1420, leaving, with a dau (Elizabeth, *m* — Milbourne):

Sir WALTER DEVEREUX, of Bodenham and Weobley, Herefs, Branston, Cotesbach and Newbold Verdon, Leics, and Market Rasen, Lincs; *b* 1411; Chllr of Ireland 1449, granted land in Drogheda 1459, Yorkist Wars of the Roses; *m* Elizabeth, dau and heir of Sir John Merbury, Ch Justice S Wales, by his 1st w, and *d* 22 or 23 April 1459, having had, with a yr s and dau (Sir John; Anne, *m* 1st Earl of Pembroke of the 1468 *cr*; *see* PEMBROKE and MONTGOMERY, E, also POWIS, E):

WALTER DEVEREUX, 1st LORD (Baron) FERRERS (of Chartley), so *cr* (apparently by writ) 26 July 1461 (*see* also FERRERS, E, preliminary remarks), KG (1472); *b c* 1432; Yorkist, MP Herefs 1460, ktd 1461; *m* 1st by 26 Nov 1446 Anne (*d* 9 Jan 1468/9), only dau and heir of Sir William Ferrers, often known as 7th Lord (Baron) Ferrers (of Chartley); *m* 2nd Jane — (*m* 2nd Thomas Vaughan; *m* 3rd Sir Edward Blount, of Sodington, Worcs; *m* 4th Thomas Poyntz) and was *k* fighting for RICHARD III at Bosworth 22 Aug 1485, following which he was attainted posthumously, leaving by his 1st w:

1 JOHN (Sir)

2 Richard (Sir)

3 Thomas (Sir)

1 Elizabeth; *m* 1st Sir Richard Corbet, of Moeton Corbet, and had issue (*see* POWIS, E); *m* 2nd Sir Thomas Leighton (*see* LEIGHTON, Bt)

2 Isabel/Sybil; *m* Sir James Baskerville

The est son,

JOHN DEVEREUX, 2nd LORD (Baron) FERRERS (of Chartley) on reversal of attainder *c* Jan 1488/9; *b c* 1463; *m* Cecily Bourchier (*see* preliminary remarks above), sis of 2nd Earl of Essex (*see* ESSEX, E, preliminary remarks) and *d* 3 or 7 May 1501, leaving, with a dau (Anne, *m* Sir David Owen, of Midhurst, Sussex):

WALTER DEVEREUX, 3rd LORD (Baron) FERRERS (of Chartley) and **1st Viscount Hereford** (E), so *cr* 2 Feb 1549/50, KG (1523), PC (Jan 1449/50–53); *b c* 1491; *m* 1st by 15 Dec 1503 Lady Mary Grey (*d* 22 Feb 1534), dau of Thomas, Marquess of Dorset (*see* 1970 edn STAMFORD, E, and for earlier generations GREY, B), and had issue:

1 Henry; *d* unm

2 Richard (Sir); *m* Lady Dorothea Hastings, dau of 1st Earl of Huntingdon (*qv*), and *dvp* 13 Oct 1547, leaving, with other issue:

(1) WALTER DEVEREUX, **2nd Viscount Hereford** and 1st EARL OF ESSEX (E), so *cr* 4 May 1572; KG (1572); *b* 16 Sept 1539; Ld Lt Staffs 1569–76, Capt Gen and Govr Ulster 1573, Earl Marshal Ireland March 1574/5; *m* between 1560 and 1565 Lettice (*m* 2nd Robert Dudley, Earl of Leicester (*see* WARWICK, BROOKE and, E, LEICESTER, E, preliminary remarks, and DE LISLE, V); *m* 3rd Sir Christopher Blount and *d* 1634), dau of Sir Francis Knollys, KG (*see* KNOLLYS, V, and MOUNTGARRET, V), and *d* 22 Sept 1576, leaving:

1a ROBERT DEVEREUX, **3rd Viscount Hereford** and 2nd EARL OF ESSEX, KG (1588), KB (1586), PC (Feb 1592/3); *b* 19 Nov 1566; *educ* Trin Coll Cambridge; Master of the Horse 1587–1601, Ld Lt Staffs 1594–1601, Jt Lt Gen Azores Expdn and taking of Cadiz 1596, Master-Gen Ordnance 1597–1601, Earl Marshal 1597–Feb 1600/1, Ld Dep Ireland March–Nov 1599; *m* 1590 Frances (*m* 3rd 4th Earl of Clanricarde (*see* SLIGO, M) and *d* 1631), widow of Sir Philip Sidney (*see* DE L'ISLE, V) and dau and heir of Sir Francis Walsingham, Sec of State, and was beheaded for high treason 25 Feb 1600/1, when his titles were forfeited by attainder, leaving:

1b ROBERT DEVEREUX, **4th Viscount Hereford** and 3rd and last EARL OF ESSEX (restored 18 April 1604) of the 1572 *cr*, PC (Feb 1640/1); *bapt* 22 Jan 1590/1; *educ* Eton and Merton Coll Oxford; Ld Lt: Staffs 1612–46, Yorks 1641–42 and (Parly appointment) Herefs, Montgomeryshire, Salop, Staffs and Yorks 1642; cmded Cadiz Expdn 1612; Lt-Gen CHARLES I's army in the N of England 1639 but went over to Parly side *c* 1642 and served as General of the Army of the Parliament 1642–45; *m* 1st 5 Jan 1605/6 (*divorce* on offical (and apparently trumped up) charge that he was impotent Oct 1613) Frances (*m* 2nd Robert Carr, Earl of Somerset; *see* LOTHIAN, M), dau of Thomas Howard, Earl of Suffolk (*see* SUFFOLK and BERKSHIRE, E); *m* 2nd 11 March 1630/1 Elizabeth (*m* 2nd Sir Thomas Higgons and *d* 1656), dau of Sir William Paulet, of Eddington, Wilts, illegitimate s of 3rd Marquess of Winchester (*qv*), and *dsps* 14 Sept 1646, having by her had an only s (*dvp* aged five), whereupon the Earldom of Essex expired and the Baronies of Ferrers (of Chartly) and Bourchier (which the 1st Earl had inherited from his female Bourchier cousin) fell into abeyance (*see* FERRERS, E)

1b Frances; *m* 3 March 1616/7 2nd Duke of Somerset (*qv*) and *d* 24 April 1674

2b Dorothy; *m* 1st Sir Henry Shirley, 2nd Bt (*see* FERRERS, E) and had issue; *m* 2nd William Stafford, of Blatherwick, and *d* 1636

2a Walter (Sir); *m* Margaret, dau and heir of Arthury Dakyns, and was *k* Siege Rouen 1591

1a Dorothy; *m* 1st Sir Thomas Perrott, of Haroldston; *m* 2nd 3rd Earl of Northumberland of the 1557 *cr* (*see* NORTHUMBERLAND, D)

2a Penelope; *m* 1st 1st Earl of Warwick (*see* WARWICK, BROOKE and, E); *m* 2nd Charles Blount, Earl of Devon (*see* DEVON, E, preliminary remarks)

3 William (Sir), of Mirevale Abbey, Warwicks; *m* Jane, dau of John Scudamore, of Holme Lacy, and had:

(1) Barbara; *m* 1st Edward Cave; *m* 2nd Sir Edward Hastings (*see* HUNTINGDON, E)

(2) Margaret; *m* Sir Edward Littleton and had issue (*see* HATHERTON, B)

The **1st Viscount** *m* 2nd Margaret (*m* 2nd 1st Baron Willoughby of Parham (*see* WILLOUGHBY DE ERESBY, B) and *d* 1599), dau of Robert Garneys, of Kenton, Suffolk, and *d* 27 Sept 1558, leaving by her:

4 **Sir Edward Devereux, 1st Bt** (E), so *cr* 25 Nov 1611, of Castle Bromwich, Warwicks, High Sheriff 1593–94, MP Tamworth 1588–89; *m* Catherine (*d* 20 Nov 1627), est dau of Edward Arden, of Park Hall, Warwicks, and *d* 22 Sept 1622, leaving, with other issue (including two daus, Anne, *m* Robert Leighton (*see*

LEIGHTON, Bt); Mary, *m* as his 1st w Sir Hugh Wrottesley; *see* WROTTESLEY, B):

(1) **Sir Walter Devereux, 2nd Bt**, and **5th Viscount Hereford**; *b* 1578; MP Stafford 1614, Marlborough 1621–22, Worcs 1624–25 and Worcester 1624–25, Sheriff Worcs 1625–26; *m* 1st Elizabeth (*dsp*), dau and heir of Robert Baspole, of Aldeby, Norfolk; *m* 2nd by 1615 Elizabeth, widow of Thomas Martin and 2nd dau of Thomas Knightley, of Burgh Hall, Staffs, and *d* by 5 Jan 1657/8, leaving by her an est surv s:

1a LEICESTER DEVEREUX, **6th Viscount Hereford**; *b* 1617; *m* 1st 6 June 1642 Elizabeth, dau of Sir William Withypoole, and had issue:

1b Frances; *m* 4th Viscount Tracy of Rathcoole (*see* SUDELEY, B)

1a (cont.) The **6th Viscount** *m* 2nd *c* 1670 Priscilla (*bur* 12 Feb 1680/1), dau of John Catchpole, of Suffolk, and *d* 1 Dec 1676, having by her had, with other issue:

1b LEICESTER DEVEREUX, **7th Viscount Hereford**; *bur* in his ninth year 12 Feb 1682/3

2b EDWARD DEVEREUX, **8th Viscount Hereford**; *b c* 1675; *m* (licence 25 April 1690) Elizabeth (*m* 2nd 21 Feb 1716/7 John Symes Berkeley, of Stoke Gifford, and *d* Nov 1742, having by him had further issue; *see* BEAUFORT, D), dau and coheir of Walter Norborne, and *dsp* 9 Aug 1700

1b Anne: *m* Leicester Martin and had issue (*see below*)

(2) George (Sir), of Sheldon Hall, Warwicks; *m* Blanche, dau and heir of Sir John Ridge, of Ridge, Salop, and *d* 1665, leaving, with other issue:

1a George, of Vaynor, Montgomeryshire; *m* Bridget, dau and heir of Arthur Price, of Vaynor, and *d* 1682, having had, with other issue:

1b Price; *b c* 1637; *m* 1st Lettice Robinson, of Gwersylit, Denbighs (*d* 1659); *m* 2nd 1662 Damaris (*d* Dec 1663), widow of C Benyon, of Shrewsbury, and dau of Richard Sherar, of London; *m* 3rd 1664 Mary, widow of S Sherar, bro of Damaris, his 2nd w, and dau of — Stephens, and was *kvp* in the 3rd Dutch War 1673, leaving by her:

1c PRICE DEVEREUX, **9th Viscount Hereford**; *b* 1664; MP (Tory) Montgomery 1691–1700, Ld Lt Montgomeryshire 1711–14; *m c* 1693 Mary (*d* 14 Jan 1728/9), dau of Samuel Sandys (*see* SANDYS, B) and *d* 3 Oct 1740, leaving:

1d PRICE DEVEREUX, **10th Viscount Hereford**; *b* 9 June 1694; High Sheriff Breconshire 1719–20, MP (Tory) Montgomeryshire 1719–40; *m* 1st 3 Jan 1720/1 his cousin Elizabeth (*d* 26 Aug 1735), only dau and heir of Leicester Martin (*see* above); *m* 2nd 30 July 1740 Eleanora (*d* 13 June 1763), dau of Roger Price, of Rhiwlas, and *dsp* 29 July 1748

1d Mary; *m* William Price, of Rhiwlas

2b Vaughan, of Munlyn; *m* Mary Fox and *d* 1700, leaving, with other issue:

1c Arthur, of Nantcribba, Montgomeryshire; *m* 1st Bridget (*d* 1706), dau of Evan Glyn, of Glyn, Clywedog, and had issue; *m* 2nd Elizabeth (*d* 1746), dau of Richard Glyn, of Maesmawr, Llandinam, Montgomeryshire, and *d* 1711, leaving by her:

2d EDWARD, **11th Viscount**

1 Katherine; *m* Sir James Baskerville, of Erdisley

The 10th VISCOUNT's cousin,

EDWARD DEVEREUX, **11th Viscount Hereford**; *b c* 1710; *m* 13 April (?)1738(?) Catherine (*d* 22 Feb 1748/9), dau of Richard Mytton, of Garth, Montgomeryshire, and *d* 20 Aug 1760, having had, with other issue:

1 EDWARD DEVEREUX, **12th Viscount Hereford**; *b* 19 Feb 1740/1; *m* 2 June 1774 Henrietta Charlotte (*d* 23 June 1817), Maid of Honour to QUEEN CHARLOTTE, dau of Anthony TRACY later KECK, and *dsp* 1 Aug 1783

2 GEORGE DEVEREUX, **13th Viscount Hereford**; *b* 25 April 1744; *m* 15 Dec 1768 his cousin Marianna (*d* 1811), only dau and heir of George Devereux, of Tregoyd, Breconshire, and *d* 31 Dec 1804, having had, with other surv issue:

(1) HENRY FLEMING LEA, **14th Viscount**

(1) Marianne; *m* 14 Oct 1801 Sir James Cockburn, 9th Bt (*d* 26 Feb 1852), of Langton, and *d* 9 Dec 1847, leaving issue

The 13th VISCOUNT's son,

HENRY FLEMING LEA DEVEREUX, **14th Viscount Hereford**, PC (1830); *b* 9 Feb 1777; *educ* Winchester and Trin Coll Oxford; Capt: Gentlemen Pensioners 1828–30 and Gentlemen at Arms 1834–35; *m* 12 Dec 1805 Frances Elizabeth (*d* 20 Feb 1864), 3rd dau of Sir George Amyand Cornewall, 2nd Bt (*see* 1959 edn), and had issue:

1 Henry Cornewall; *b* 1807; *d* unm 14 Sept 1839

2 ROBERT, **15th Viscount**

3 Walter Bourchier; R-Adml; *b* 3 Nov 1810; *m* 10 Nov 1856 Adelaide Ellinor (*d* 30 Dec 1916), yst dau of Hugh Robert Hughes, of Bache Hall, Cheshire, bro of 1st Baron Dinorben (*see* 1852 edn), and *d* 15 May 1868, having had, with other issue:

(1) Walter de Laci; *b* 18 Dec 1864; *m* 30 May 1893 Blanche Isobel (*d* 23 Jan 1949), dau of W H Johnston, of Ealing, and *d* 17 June 1959, having had issue:

1a Humphrey William; Lt S Staffs Regt (TF); *b* 18 April 1894; *ka* 26 June 1916

2a Edmund Bourchier; F/Lt RN; *b* 28 July 1895; *das* at sea 26 Nov 1917

3a Robert de Bohun, MBE; Lt-Col Roy Scots WW I (despatches twice), WW II; *b* 19 April 1897; *m* 25 July 1925 Enid Marion (*d* 14 Jan 1976), only dau of Gen Sir Henry Bulkley Burlton Watkins, KCB, of The Old Rectory, Farnborough, Hants, and *d* 1981, leaving issue:

1b +(Robert) Humphrey Bourchier [Humphrey Devereux Esq, Woolbeding Cottage, nr Midhurst, W Sussex]; *b* 3 May 1930; *educ* Marlborough and Exeter Coll Oxford (BA); *m* 3 April 1954 Barbara (*d* 1989), only dau of Norman Heywood, of Ealing, and has issue:

1c +Robert Harold Ferrers [Robert Devereux Esq, 5 Ladbrooke Terrace, London W11 3PG]; *b* 11 April 1955; *educ* Marlborough and Downing Coll Cambridge; *m* 1983 *Vanessa, dau of Edward James Branson, of Tanyard Farm, Shamley Green, Surrey, and has issue:

1d +Noah Edward de Bohun; *b* 1987

2d +Louis Robert de Laci; *b* 1991

3d +Ivo Edmund Bourchier; *b* 1995

1d *Florence Barbara Clare; *b* 1989

2c +Godfrey Edmund de Bohun; *b* 19 Oct 1956; *educ* Marlborough; *m* 1982 *Barbara, dau of William Accousti, of Connecticut, USA, and has:

1d +Arum; *b* 1983

1c *Henrietta Marian Clare; *b* 2 June 1960

1b *Marion Blanche [Mrs Timothy Hollis, Padwicks Farm, Bepton, Midhurst, GU29 0LY]; *b* 28 Aug 1927; *m* 1 Feb 1958 *Rev Timothy Knowles Hollis and has issue:

1c *Timothy John Walter; *b* 15 Aug 1968; *m* 1991 *Michaela Francis and has issue:

1d *Ryan Arthur; *b* 1991

2d *Charlie Buster; *b* 1996

1d *Rebecca Anne; *b* 1993

1c *Jennifer Marion; *b* 15 March 1961

2c *Lucy Anne; *b* 26 Sept 1962

(1) Cicely Frances; *d* unm 10 Sept 1940

(2) Dorothy Bridget; *d* unm 4 Nov 1931

4 Humphrey Bohun, DL Herefs; ICS; *b* 29 June 1812; *m* 2 Oct 1860 Caroline (*d* 22 Dec 1903), 4th dau of Sir Edmund Antrobus, 2nd Bt (*qv*), and *dsp* 19 May 1880

5 George Talbot; Maj Gen RHA; *b* 12 Jan 1819; *m* 1st 3 March 1847 Flora (*d* 5 Nov 1884), widow of Hon Arthur Annesley (*see* VALENTIA, V) and dau of Col Reginald George Macdonald of Clanranald, JP, DL; *m* 2nd 18 June 1895 Katherine Jane (*d* 5 June 1934), only dau of Ashe Windham, of Waghen Hall, Yorks (*see* BOWYER-SMYTH, Bt), and *d* 14 Feb 1898, leaving issue:

(1) George Arthur Windham; Sub-Lt, RN; *b* 1 Jan 1894; *d* unm 13 Oct 1913, *k* in a motor accident

(1) Sheila Myfanwy; *b* 4 Oct 1896; *m* 16 Feb 1927 Capt Harold Gray King, RN (*d* 13 Sept 1967), and had issue:

1a *Christopher Windham; *b* 18 March 1928; *educ* Fettes; *m* 3 Aug 1951 *Mary Bannister and has issue:

1b *Ann; *b* 17 April 1955

2b *Joan; *b* 11 Aug 1957

3b *Jane; *b* 6 Nov 1963

1a *Margery Ann; *b* 15 Feb 1934

1 Frances Catherine, Maid of Honour to HM QUEEN VICTORIA; *m* 21 Jan 1847 Thomas Bradshaw (*d* 17 Dec 1884) and *d* 12 Jan 1857

The 14th VISCOUNT *d* 31 May 1843; his son,

Rev ROBERT DEVEREUX, **15th Viscount Hereford**; Hon Canon Durham; *b* 3 May 1809; *m* 25 Nov 1841 Emma Jemima (*m* 2nd 23 Feb 1857 Lt-Col John Ireland Blackburne, of Hale Hall, Lancs, and *d* 26 Oct 1870), dau of George Ravenscroft, and had issue:

1 ROBERT, **16th Viscount**

2 Henry de Bohun; *b* 10 Oct 1848; *m* 17 July 1872 Maud Philippa (*d* 28 Feb 1934), dau of Edward Salamon, of Bayswater, Double Bay, Sydney, NSW, and *d* 18 July 1909, leaving:

(1) Humphrey Bourchier; *b* 29 April 1873; *m* 1900 Winifred Christiana (*d* June 1937), dau of George Hosking, of Cornwall, and *d* 17 May 1921, leaving:

1a Rodney de Bohun; WW II in NZ Med Corps; *b* 13 Nov 1903; *m* 1 July 1949 *Miriam, dau of Edward Pritchett, of The Castle, Munsley, Herefs, and *dsp* 23 Dec 1963

2a Rupert Montague; *b* 1907; *m* Dec 1940 Joan Ursula (*d* 1983), dau of D W Thomas, and *d* 1974, leaving issue:

1b *(Blanche) Rosemary [Mrs Harvey Nausbaum, 61 Chichester Drive, Arundel, Qld 4214, Australia]; *b* 1943; *m* May 1966 *Harvey Nausbaum, s of C Nausbaum, of Lower Hutt, NZ, and has issue:

1c *Aaron; *b* 1972

1c *Sarah Rosemary; *b* 1974

2b *Susan Ursula [Mrs Terence Currie, 125 Koutu Rd, Rotorua, New Zealand]; *b* 1947; *m* 1967 *Terence Adrian Currie and has issue:

1c *Simon Zane; *b* 1967; *m* 1997 *Rosemary King

1c *Bridget Susan; *b* 1971

3a George Makgill de Bohun; *b* March 1909; *m* June 1937 *Olga Christina [Mrs George Devereux, 3 Mays Rd, Onehunga, Auckland SE5, New Zealand], dau of Karl S Larsen, of Auckland, NZ, and *d* 1976, leaving issue:

1b +Colin de Bohun; *b* 1941; *m* 1st 1964 (*divorce* 1976) Helen Ann, dau of K Buchanan, of Auckland, NZ; *m* 2nd 1976 *Carole Ann, dau of J Parkes, of Dannevirke, NZ, and by his 2nd w has issue:

1c +Justin de Bohun; *b* 1976

1b *Dorothy Wyn [Mrs Graham Leaning, 3 Mays Rd, Onehunga, Auckland, SE5, New Zealand]; *b* 1938; *m* 1958 *Grahame Leaning and has:

1c *Karl Stuart; *b* 1964

1c *Christine Anne; *b* 1961

2b *Marilyn Joan [Mrs Robert Hessey, 28 Littlejohn St, Hillsborough, Auckland, New Zealand]; *b* 1948; *m* 1971 *Robert Leslie Hessey and has:

1c *Steven James; *b* 1977

1c *Rachel Ann; *b* 1975

1a *Dorothy Maud Amelia; *b* 21 Jan 1902

2a Blanche Bourchier; *b* 20 Jan 1916; *m* 1955 Harry Francis Schoen (*d* 1995) and *d* 1992 leaving:

1b *Pauline Anne [Mrs Jason Akitt, 2/131 Matipo Rd, Te Atau Peninsula, New Zealand]; *b* 1957; *m* 1977 *Jason Mark Akitt and has:

1c *Hannah Marie; *b* 1986

2c *Bronwen Louise; *b* 1989

(2) Rodney Talbot; *b* 6 March 1879; *k* Boer War 1900

(3) Geoffrey de Bohun, MC; Maj NZ Inf WW I (despatches); *b* 1890; *ka* 1 Oct 1918

(4) Godfrey Vaughan; *b* 24 April 1893; *m* 1925 *Ellen, dau of John Black, of Bay of Islands, and *d* 1976, leaving:

1a +Robin Geoffrey [Robin Devereux Esq, 76 Colman Ave, Upper Riccarton, Christchurch 4, New Zealand]; Capt RNZAC; *b* 1927; *m* Nov 1953 *Glennis Fyfe, dau of T F Kerr, and has issue:

1b *Susan Lee [Mrs R Strez, 49 Sayers Crescent, Christchurch, New Zealand]; *b* 6 Nov 1956; *m* 1981 *R Noel Strez and has:

1c *Simon Geoffrey; *b* 1986

1c *Kirsten Anna; *b* 1983

2b *Vicki Anne [Mrs James Bennie, 97 Patterson Terrace, Christchurch, New Zealand]; *b* 6 Nov 1959; *m* 1982 *James Bennie and has:

1c *Rachel Zoe; *b* 1997

2a +David de Bohun [David Devereux Esq, 432 Fraser St, Tauranga, New Zealand]; *b* 1928; *m* June 1951 *Roberta Barbara, dau of F R G Souness, and has issue:

1b +Malcolm Fergus [Malcolm Devereux Esq, 8 Rowenwood Close, Christchurch 3, New Zealand]; *b* 18 March 1952; F/Lt RNZAF; *m* 1975 (*divorce* 19–) Barbara, dau of R Irwin, of Pukekohe, NZ, and has issue:

1c +Mark Robert; *b* 1978

2c +Ross Timothy; *b* 1980

1b *Wendy Anne [Mrs Ashley Philip, 3 Endeavour Ave, Tauranga, New Zealand]; *b* 28 Dec 1956; *m* 1st 1978 (*divorce* 1989) John Roy Donaldson; *m* 2nd 1990 *Ashley Richard Philip and by her 1st husb has:

1c *Matthew James; *b* 1988

1c *Melissa Joy; *b* 1983

2c *Sarah Marie; *b* 1985

3a +Francis Richard [Francis Devereux Esq, Tangowahine RD2, Dargaville, New Zealand]; *b* 25 March 1937; *m* 1978 (*divorce* 1984) Linda Jane, dau of John Wright, of Dargaville, NZ, and has issue:

1b +Richard John; *b* 1982

1a *Jennifer Mary [Mrs George Finlayson, 120A Puriri Park Rd, Whangarei, New Zealand]; *b* 27 Sept 1933; *m* 1959 *Lt-Col George Scott Finlayson, ED, CEng, MIEE, Roy NZ Corps of Signals, and has issue:

1b *George Robert; *b* 26 Oct 1960; *m* 1991 *Michelle Judith, dau of A R McLennan

2b *James Scott; *b* 6 March 1963

1b *Helen Mary; *b* 29 March 1966

2b *Judith Anne; *b* 1970

(1) Sybil Henrietta; *b* 2 May 1874; *m* 1902 Henry Edward Kempthorne (*d* 1931) and *d* 25 Nov 1955, leaving issue

(2) Muriel Ravenscroft; *b* 6 March 1876; *m* July 1897 John Edward Makgill (*see* OXFUIRD, V) and *d* 5 May 1946, leaving issue

(3) Miriam Beatrice; *b* 28 Aug 1877; *m* 1906 H J Lowe (*d* May 1937), of Wellington, NZ, and *d* March 1915

(4) Maud Guinevere; *b* 16 Dec 1880; *m* 1908 Archibald Hussey Davidson (*d* 1911), of Dunedin, NZ, and *d* 29 June 1955, leaving issue

3 Eustace; *b* 25 Sept 1849; *d* unm 1878

4 Walter de Bourchier; *b* 26 Sept; *d* 15 Oct 1850

1 Sybil Catherine; *m* 10 Jan 1867 Capt John Bayford Butler, RN (*d* Oct 1888), of 21 Alexandra Road, Bedford, and *d* 19 July 1930, having had issue (*see* BUTLER, Bt)

2 Blanche; *m* 29 Aug 1867 Thomas Francis Hazlehurst, DL (*d* 1918), of Cold Ashby Hall, Rugby, and *d* 13 Oct 1923

The 15th VISCOUNT *d* 18 Aug 1855; his est son,

ROBERT DEVEREUX, **16th Viscount Hereford**, JP, DL (Breconshire, Herefs and Radnorshire); *b* 3 Jan 1843; *m* 16 July 1863 Mary Anna (*d* 14 Aug 1924), yst dau of 1st Baron Tredegar (*see* 1963 edn), and had issue:

1 ROBERT CHARLES, **17th Viscount**

1 Muriel; *b* 11 Aug 1866; *m* 2 May 1893 Anthony Noel Denny, barrister (*d* 28 Aug 1933), of La Chripa, Puerto Oratava, Tenerife, and *d* 5 July 1924

2 Eleanor Mary; *b* 20 Sept 1868; *m* 21 Aug 1906 Albert Addams-Williams, OBE, ICS (*d* 29 June 1931), 6th s of William Addams-Williams, of Langibby Castle, and *d* 22 June 1944

3 Lillian; *b* 4 Sept 1870; *d* unm 17 Oct 1959

4 Sybil; *b* 19 Jan 1873; *d* 3 March 1892

5 Rosamond Ela; *b* 23 July 1875; *d* unm 3 Aug 1945

The 16th VISCOUNT *d* 27 March 1930; his son,

ROBERT CHARLES DEVEREUX, **17th Viscount Hereford**, JP, DL Breconshire and Herefs; *b* 11 Aug 1865; BA Oxon, chm Breconshire QS 1907–27, CA Breconshire 1898–1904, Cncllr Llyswen Div 1907–13 and Llanigon Div 1913–25, Coronation Medal 1937, KJStJ; *m* 21 Jan 1892 Ethel Mildred, DJStJ (*d* 2 June 1945), yr dau of John Shaw, of Welburn Hall, Yorks, and *d* 16 April 1952, having had issue:

1 Robert Godfrey de Bohun, JP Breconshire; *b* 24 Nov 1894; BA Oxon; OStJ, Lt Res of Offrs Welsh Gds WW I (wounded); *m* 5 Dec 1923 Audrey Maureen Leslie, CStJ (*m* 2nd 14 Nov 1961 7th Earl of Lisburne; *qv*), yr dau of James Meakin, of Westwood Manor, Staffs, and Countess Sondes (*see* MONSON, B), and *dvp* 13 July 1934, leaving issue:

(1) ROBERT MILO LEICESTER DEVEREUX, **18th and present Viscount Hereford**

(1) *(Diana) Bridget [The Hon Mrs Gaussen, 60 Alder Lodge, Stevenage Rd, London SW7; Nutbeam, Duntisbourne Leer, Glos]; *b* 25 March 1931; granted rank of viscount's dau 20 Jan 1953; *m* 16 Oct 1967 *Maj Samuel Charles Casamajor Gaussen, Welsh Gds, and has issue:

1a *Robert Casamajor; *b* 15 Dec 1968

1a *Mariana Diana; *b* 14 May 1971

1 Blanche Marion; OStJ; *m* 12 July 1927 Maj Harry Talbot Rice and *d* 13 April, leaving issue (*see* DYNEVOR, B)

2 Ursula Mary Ethel, DJStJ, Lady Supt-in-Chief St John Amb Bde Overseas 1938–50, Grand Cross Holy Sepuclchre; *m* 17 July 1922 Brig Felix Alexander Vincent Copland-Griffiths, DSO, MC, JP, DL, KStJ, Welsh Gds (*d* 10 April 1967), and *dsp* 12 Aug 1957

HERON-MAXWELL

Arms: Quarterly, 1st and 4th, arg. on a saltire sa. an annulet or, stoned az., in base a crescent of the second, all within a bordure gu. charged with eight bezants (for MAXWELL), 2nd and 3rd, gu. on a bend arg. a rose between two lions passant gu. (for HERON). **Crest:** A dexter hand ppr., holding an eagle's neck erased with two heads sa. **Supporters:** Two eagles close regardant sa. **Motto:** *Revirescat* ('May it flourish again'). **Creation:** Bt. (NS) 7 Feb 1682/3.

SIR NIGEL MELLOR HERON-MAXWELL, 10TH BT, of Springkell, Dumfriesshire [Sir Nigel Heron-Maxwell Bt, 50 Watlington Rd, Old Harlow, Essex CM17 0DY]; *b* 30 Jan 1944; *s* f 1982; *educ* Milton Abbey; Navigating Offr RFAuxS; *m* 1972 *Mary Elizabeth Angela, only dau of William Ewing, of Co Donegal, and has:

1 +DAVID MELLOR; *b* 22 May 1975

1 *Claire Louise; *b* 1977

Lineage: AYMER/EUMERUS/HOMER MAXWELL (*see* MAXWELL, Bt); had a 3rd s:

Sir JOHN MAXWELL; had from his father the lands of Netherpollok, Dryps and Calderwood in Clydesdale; Govr Dumbarton Castle; had:

Sir ROBERT MAXWELL of Pollok; had:

Sir JOHN MAXWELL of Pollok; *d c* 1360, leaving:

Sir JOHN MAXWELL of Pollok; *m* 1st Elizabeth, dau of Sir James Lindsay of Crawford (*see* CRAWFORD and BALCARRES, E), and had:

1 JOHN (Sir)

2 Robert (Sir); ancestor of the MAXWELLs of Calderwood (now extinct) and the MAXWELLs Barons Farnham (*qv*)

3 William, of Aikenhead; ancestor in the 7th generation of John Maxwell, who sold Aikenhead 1611

1 Janet; *m* Thomas Murray of Culbyne

2 Agnes; *m* Sir Gilbert Kennedy of Dunure and had issue (*see* AILSA, M)

Sir JOHN *m* 2nd Elizabeth de Saint Michel, heiress of Whitchester, Roxburghshire, but apparently *dsp* by her

His est son,

Sir JOHN MAXWELL of Pollok; fought Battle of Otterburn or Chevy Chase 1388, where he allegedly captured Sir Ralph Percy, s of the Earl of Northumberland (*see* NORTHUMBERLAND, D); *m* —, dau of John Montgomery of Eaglesham (*see* EGLINTON and WINTON, E), and had:

THOMAS MAXWELL of Pollok; living 1440; had:

1 John, of Pollok; living 1452; *d c* 1490, leaving, with two yr sons and a dau:

(1) John, of Pollok; *m* Elizabeth, dau of 11th Earl of Lennox (*see* MORAY, E), and had:

1a John, of Pollok; *m* Margaret, dau of John Blair of that Ilk, and *d* 1517, leaving, with a dau (Katherine, *m* 1515 John Fullerton of that Ilk):

1b John, of Pollok; *m* Elizabeth, dau of Patrick Houston of Houston, and had:

1c Elizabeth, heiress of Pollok; *b* 1523; *m* (dispensation 31 Aug 1535) her cousin John Maxwell of Cowglen and *d* 17 Feb 1592, having had, with other issue, including a yr s (William, of Cowglen, guardian 1624 to Grissell Maxwell (1st w of George Ross of Galston, Ayrshire, *d* 4 April 1647)):

1d John (Sir), of Pollok; *m* 1st 1569 Margaret, dau of William Cunningham of Caprington; *m* 2nd (contract 17 Sept 1592) Marjory, widow of Mungo Graham of Orchill and 2nd dau of Sir William Edmondstone of Duntreath, and was *k* Battle of Lockerby 7 Dec 1593, leaving by his 1st w, with a dau (Agnes, *m* (contract 9 March 1611) John Boyle, Yr. of Kelburne, and had issue; *see* GLASGOW, E):

1e Sir JOHN MAXWELL, 1st and last Bt (NS), so *cr* 25 Nov 1630, of Pollok; *m* 1st (contract 21 Aug 1593) Isabel (*d* 1612), dau of 1st Lord Loudoun (*see* LOUDOUN, E), and had a dau (Isobel); *m* 2nd by

1615 Grizel, widow of David Blair, 7th of Adamton, and est dau and coheir of John Blair, Yr. of that Ilk, but *dspm* 1 Nov 1647, when the btcy expired, leaving his estate to his distant cousin Sir George Maxwell of Auldhouse (*see* below)

2a Robert; Rector Torbolton 1521, Bp Orkney 1536

3a George, of Cowglen; *m* Janet Maxwell of Tinwald (*m* 2nd John Maxwell of Dargarvel and *d c* 1546) and had:

1b John (Sir), of Cowglen; *b* 1524; ktd *c* 1567; *m* his cousin Elizabeth Maxwell, heiress of Pollok (*see* above) and *d* 20 Feb 1577

4a William, of Carnwaderick; *m* Janet Culheart (*m* 2nd John Robertson of Ernock) and had:

1b John, of Carnwaderick

2 Hugh; ancestor of:

(1) John; had a charter of Auldhouse 1572; *m* —, dau of Robert Dunlop of Hapland, and had, with other issue:

1a George (Rev), of Auldhouse; Minister Mearns, Renfrewshire; *m* 1st Janet, dau of John Miller of Newton, and had:

1b John, of Auldhouse; Min Eastwood, later of the High Church of Glasgow; Rector Glasgow U; *m* (contract 8 Jan 1621) Elizabeth, dau of James Stewart, tutor (guardian) Blackhall, and *d c* 1666, having had, with four other sons and three daus:

1c George (Sir), of Auldhouse, later also of Pollok, to which *s* as mentioned above; *m* 1646 Annabella, sis of Sir Archibald Stewart 1st Bt (*see* SHAW-STEWART, Bt), and *d* April 1677, leaving:

1d Sir JOHN MAXWELL (NS), 1st Bt, so *cr* 12 April (sealed 25 May) 1682, with extension of remainder 27 March 1707 to his heirs of entail whatsoever in his lands and estates, PC (S); a Ld Commr Exchequer and Treasury, MP Renfrewshire 1690–96 and 1698, Ld of Session 1699, Ld Justice Clerk 1702; *b* 1648; *m* 23 Feb 1671 Marian (*d* 1706), dau of Sir James Stewart of Coltness and Kirkfield, but *dsp* 4 July 1732

2d George; *d* by 14 Aug 1688

1d Marian; *b* 8 Aug 1649; *m* 1st Dec 1674 James Stewart of Rosyth (*dsp*); *m* 2nd *c* 1706 Sir Charles Murray, Bt, of Dreghorn

2d Annabella; *bapt* 24 May 1657; *m* 1st *c* 28 Nov 1679 John Cathcart of Carleton; *m* 2nd *c* Jan 1686 Sir Robert Pollok of Pollok (Upper Pollok)

3d Margaret; *m c* 30 Sept 1684 Alexander Maxwell, Yr. of Calderwood, and *dsp* 1685

2c Zacharias, of Blawerthill; *m* Jean, dau of John Maxwell and widow of John Colquhoun, and *d* April 1698, leaving:

1d Sir JOHN MAXWELL, 2nd Bt; *m* 1st 8 April 1709 Lady Anne Carmichael (*d c* 1720), dau of John, Earl of Hyndford (*see* GIBSON-CRAIG-CARMICHAEL, Bt), and had, with a dau (Beatrix, *d* unm 5 April 1795):

1e Sir JOHN MAXWELL, 3rd Bt; *d* unm 14 Sept 1758

1d (cont.) Sir JOHN *m* 2nd Aug 1727 Barbara, dau of Walter Stewart, of Stewart Hall (*see* SHAW-STEWART, Bt), and by her had, with other issue:

2e Sir WALTER MAXWELL, 4th Bt; *b* 15 Feb 1732; *m* 19 Feb 1760 D'Arcy (*d* 2 July 1810), dau of Thomas Brisbane of Brisbane, and *d* 29 April 1762, leaving:

1f Sir JOHN MAXWELL, 5th Bt; *d* an infant nine weeks after his f

3e Sir JAMES MAXWELL, 6th Bt; *b* 26 March 1735; *m* (contract 19 and 23 Nov 1764) Frances (*m* 2nd 1786 Sir John Shaw-Stewart, 4th Bt (*qv*), and *d* 21 March 1818), 2nd dau of Robert Colquhoun, of St Christopher's, and *d* 3 May 1785, having had, with two daus:

1f Sir JOHN MAXWELL, 7th Bt; MP Paisley; *b* 31 Oct 1768; *m* 1788 Hannah Anne (*d* 21 July 1841), dau of Richard Gardiner, of Aldborough, Suffolk, and *d* 30 July 1844, having had, with another dau:

1g Sir JOHN MAXWELL, 8th Bt; MP Renfrewshire 1818–30 and Lanarks 1832–37; *b* 12 May 1791; *m* 14 Oct 1839 Lady Matilda Harriet Bruce (*d* 31 Aug 1857), dau of 7th Earl of Elgin and (11th Earl of) Kincardine (*qv*), and *dsp* 6 June 1865

1g ELIZABETH Maxwell; *b* 1793; *m* 1 June 1815 Archibald STIRLING of Keir (*d* 9 April 1847) and *d* 5 Sept 1822, leaving, with two daus (*d* unm):

1h Sir WILLIAM STIRLING later STIRLING-MAXWELL, 9th Bt, as which *s* unc under extended remainder of 1707, KT; *b* 8 March 1818; V-Lt Renfrewshire (previously DL), MP Perthshire, DCL, LLD, Rector Edinburgh U; *m* 1st 26 April 1865 Anne Maria (*d* 8 Dec 1874), 3rd dau of 8th Earl of Leven and (7th Earl of) Melville (*qv*), and had:

1i Sir JOHN MAXWELL (Sir), 10th Bt, KT (1929), DL (Inverness-shire and Renfrewshire); *b* 6 June 1866; *educ* Eton and Trin Coll Cambridge (BA 1894, MA 1919); V-Lt Co of City of Glasgow, MP Glasgow College 1895–1906, Tstee Wallace Collection and Nat Galleries Scotland; Scottish U Commr 1892, Chm Forestry Commn 1929–32, memb Roy Commn Ancient and Historical Monuments and Constructions Scotland 1934 (Chm 1940), Hon Col 7th Bn Scottish Rifles, Lt Lanarks Yeo Cav; Hon LLD Glasgow 1907 and Edinburgh 1934; *m* 12 Nov 1901 Ann Christian (*d* 5 April 1937), est dau of Sir Herbert Eustace Maxwell, 7th Bt, KT, PC, of Monreith (*qv*), and *d* 30 May 1956, when the btcy became dormant, leaving:

1j *Anne; *b* 8 Sept 1906; *m* 22 April 1930 *John MORETON-MACDONALD later MAXWELL MACDONALD (1930), 19th of Largie and has issue (*see* DUCIE, E)

2i Archibald STIRLING OF KEIR, of Keir, Dunblane, Perthshire, and Cawder, Lanarks, DL (Stirlingshire, Perthshire and Lanarks); MP W Perthshire 1917–18, Lt-Col Lovat Scouts, Capt Scots Gds, served Nile Expdn 1899, Boer War 1899–1902, WW I as Brig-Gen cmdg Highland Mounted Bde Gallipoli and Egypt 1915–16 (despatches); *b* 14 Sept 1867; *m* 14 April 1910 Hon Margaret Mary Fraser, OBE (1920), 4th dau of 13th Lord (Fraser of) Lovat (*qv*), and *d* 18 Feb 1931, leaving:

1j William Joseph, of Keir; Hon Lt-Col Scots Gds WW II, Chm African Medical and Research Fndn; *b* 9 May 1911; *educ* Ampleforth and Trin Coll Cambridge (BA 1932); *m* 22 Nov 1940 Susan Rachel (*d* 1983), yr dau of Lt-Col Hon Noel Gervase Bligh, DSO (*see* DARNLEY, E), and *d* 1983, leaving:

1k +Archibald Hugh [Archibald Stirling of Keir, Ochtertyre, Stirling FK9 4UN]; Lt Scots Gds 1959–62; *b* 18 Sept 1941; *educ* Ampleforth; *m* 11 Nov 1964 (*divorce* 1977) Charmian Rachel, yr dau of Lord George Francis John Montagu-Douglas-Scott (*see* BUCCLEUCH and QUEENSBERRY, D), and has:

1l +William Rory Alexander; *b* 15 Dec 1965

2l +Ludovic David; *b* 29 April 1967

1k (cont.) Archibald Stirling of Keir *m* 2nd 25 March 1982 (*divorce* 1993) (Enid) Diana Elizabeth (Dame Diana Rigg, DBE, the actress), dau of Louis Rigg and formerly w of Menachem Gueffen, Israeli artist, and by her has:

1l *Rachael Atlanta; *b* 1977

2k James Joseph; *b* 18 March, *d* 20 March 1943

3k +John Alexander; *b* 26 Feb 1948; *m* 1st 1971 Mrs Susan Burton, only dau of Edmund Black, of Johannesburg; *m* 2nd 1985 *Olivia Louise, dau of Maj Patrick Waller, and by her has:

1l +Joseph Patrick William; *b* 1985

2l +Hugh David Archibald; *b* 1993

1l *Christabel Georgia; *b* 1987

4k A son; *b* 8 Feb, *d* 9 Feb 1952

1k *Hannah Ann; *b* 29 May 1944; *m* 7 Jan 1970 *Viscount Cranborne (*see* CECIL OF ESSENDON, B) and has issue

2k *Magdalen; *b* 25 Nov 1945; *m* 1969 *Patrick Petit and has:

1k *Jonathan; *b* 1971

2k *Benjamin; *b* 1973

2j Peter John; *b* 1 Feb 1913; *educ* Ampleforth and Magdalen Coll Oxford; 1st Sec For Serv; *m* 6 Feb 1963 Mrs Mahin Khadji-Noori, dau of Hassan Mohasebel Dowleh Nast Feli

3j Archibald David (Sir), DSO (1942), OBE (1946); Hon Lt-Col Scots Gds WW II, ktd 1990; *b* 15 Nov 1915; *d* Nov 1990

4j Hugh Joseph; Lt Scots Gds WW II; *b* 4 May 1917; *ka* Libya 22 April 1941

1j Margaret Elizabeth Mary; CStJ; *b* 4 July 1914; *m* 26 June 1940 *16th Earl of Dalhousie (*qv*) and *d* 9 Feb 1997, leaving issue

2j Irene Matharine Teresa; *b* 9 March 1919; *d* 1992

1h (cont.) Sir WILLIAM *m* 2nd 1 March 1877 Caroline (*d* 15 June 1877), widow of Hon George Chapple Norton (*see* GRANTLEY, B), and *d* 15 Jan 1878

2f Robert; Army Capt; *b* 17 July 1770; *m* Margaret (*m* 2nd July 1800 John Cunninghame of Craigends), dau of Sir William Cunningham, Bt, and *dsp* 1796

1d (cont.) Sir JOHN *m* 3rd Margaret (*dsp* 25 March 1758), dau of John Caldwell of Caldwell, and *d* 24 Dec 1752

1a (cont.) The Rev George Maxwell *m* 2nd Jane, dau of William Mure of Glanderston, and by her had, with four yr sons and a dau:

2b William; acquired 1648 the territorial Barony of Kirkconnel and Springkell in Annandale; *m* (contract 20 May 1637) Jane (*d c* 1683), dau of Patrick Stewart of Roslane and Balshegray, and *d c* 1695, having had, with other issue:

1c PATRICK (Sir), **1st Bt**

2c Robert; excluded from the succession by his f and er bro 19 April 1693

1c Agnes; *m* 27 Jan 1657 Dr John Colquhoun

2c Mary; *m* (contract 3 Nov 1680) John Maxwell of Broomholm

1a (cont.) The Rev George Maxwell *m* 3rd Janet Douglas of Waterside and *d* Nov 1648, having by her had, with four other sons:

3b Hugh; ancestor of the MAXWELLs of Dalswinton

2a Patrick; living 1585; *m* Elizabeth, dau of James Boyd of Trodrig, Archbp Glasgow, and was ancestor in the 6th generation of:

1b Thomas; *b* 1812; *m* 1848 Constantia Margaret Church (*d* 26 June 1925 aged 95) and *d* 1878, leaving:

1c Patrick William; *b* 1855; *m* 1884 Kate Elizabeth Suckling and had three daus

1c Elizabeth; *m* George Brown

2c Amy Jane Marion

3c Constance Ada; *m* Scott Moncrieff Penney, advocate

4c Euphan; *m* 24 May 1902 Henry Rivers Nevill, ICS, 5th s of Ven H R Nevill, Archdeacon Norfolk

WILLIAM MAXWELL of Kirkconnel and Springkell's er s,

Sir Patrick Maxwell, 1st Bt (NS), so *cr* 7 Feb 1682/3, of Springkell; *m* 1st — (*dsp*), dau of Joseph Dacre Appleby, of Kirklinton; *m* 2nd Mary, dau of 6th Viscount Kenmure (*see* 1847 edn), and *d* April 1723, having by her had, with other issue, including a dau (Mary, *m* James Douglas, MD, s of Sir William Douglas, 1st Bt, of Kelhead (*see* QUEENSBERRY, M), and had issue):

Sir William Maxwell, 2nd Bt; *b* 10 Aug 1703; *m* 11 Oct 1725 Catherine (*d* 29 Sept 1761), est dau of Sir William Douglas, 2nd Bt, of Kelhead (*see* above), and *d* 14 July 1760, leaving, with a dau (Catherine, *d* unm 15 April 1763):

Sir William Maxwell, 3rd Bt; *b* 1 Dec 1739; *m* 26 March 1764 Margaret (*d* March 1816), dau of Sir Michael Stewart, 3rd Bt, of Blackhall (*see* SHAW-STEWART, Bt), and *d* 4 March 1804, having had, with other issue, including a dau (Catherine, *b* 7 Jan 1767, *m* 24 Sept 1787 her first cousin Sir Michael Shaw-Stewart, 5th Bt, of Blackhall (*see* above), and *d* 10 May 1849):

Sir JOHN SHAW MAXWELL later HERON-MAXWELL (added on f-in-law's death), **4th Bt**; *b* 29 June 1772; Lt-Gen, Col 23rd Light Dragoons, MP Dumfries Burghs 1803–12; *m* 4 Jan 1802 Mary (*d* 18 June 1856), only child and heiress of Patrick Heron of Heron, Kirkcudbrightshire, MP, by Lady Elizabeth Cochrane, only dau of 8th Earl of Dundonald (*qv*), and *d* 29 Jan 1830, having had:

1 William; *b* 24 Oct 1803; *d* 27 June 1810

2 **Sir Patrick Heron-Maxwell, 5th Bt**; *b* 1 Jan 1805; *d* unm 27 Aug 1844

3 JOHN (Sir), **6th Bt**

4 Michael MAXWELL later MAXWELL-HERON (added on mother's death) (Rev); *b* 8 Nov 1809; Vicar Heddon-on-the-Wall, Northumberland; *m* 24 Feb 1834 Charlotte Frances (*d* 28 Dec 1886), est dau of Capt Frederick William Burgoyne, RN, and gdau of Lt-Gen Sir John Burgoyne, 7th Bt, of Sutton Park, Beds (*see* 1877 edn), and *d* 4 April 1873, leaving issue:

(1) John Heron, of Heron and Kiroughtree, JP, DL; *b* 5 Sept 1836; Capt 1st Roy Scots, MP Kirkcudbrightshire 1880; *m* 12 Nov 1868 Marguerita (*d* 6 Sept 1925), dau of William Stancomb, of Blounts Court, Wilts, and *d* 26 Jan 1899, leaving issue:

1a Guy Heron; *b* 8 June 1871; Lt-Col 3rd Bn S Wales Borderers, Boer War (despatches twice, two medals, five clasps), WW I (medal); *m* 1st 24 Jan 1922 Hilda (*d* 10 Aug 1924), dau of G F Parker, MRCS, LLD; *m* 2nd 25 April 1928 Dorothea Rose (*d* 8 Dec 1960), dau of Capt Albert Henry Harrison, Roy Warwicks Regt, and *dsp* 29 Jan 1944

2a Basil Charles Montague; *b* 18 June 1878; Capt 4th Bn Scottish Rifles, Staff Capt 1915–16, Boer War (two medals) and WW I; *m* 1905 Mary (*d* 6 Feb 1957), dau of Garrett O'Byrne, and *d* 1916, leaving issue:

1b Guy John Ewen; *b* 1905; *m* 1st 21 July 1928 (*divorce* 1957) Vera Ismay, 2nd dau of J N Pereira, of Georgetown, Br Guiana; *m* 2nd 1957 Mrs Moira Kathleen James, yst dau of Charles Clover Brown, of St John's Wood, London, and *dsp* 22 Feb 1968

1b *Rita Steuart Mary [Mrs Anthony Nelson, 7 Sutton Court, London W4]; *b* 1905; *m* 2 July 1927 *P/O Antony William Hamilton Nelson, RAF, and has issue:

1c *John Edward Arthur Hamilton; *b* 1935

1c *Patricia Anne; *b* 1930; *m* 19– P L Braine

2c *Sheila Steuart Mary; *b* 1932; *m* 19– J C Horrocks

1a Violet Bridget Heron; *m* 23 Nov 1898 Arthur Charles Wombwell and *d* 5 Sept 1929, leaving issue (*see* WOMBWELL, Bt)

(2) Frederick William Burgoyne; *b* 13 Feb 1838; Cdr RN; *m* 4 July 1882 Louisa Annie (*d* 29 Aug 1924), dau of Maj F S Paterson and widow of Capt Albert Henry Harrison, Roy Warwicks Regt, and *d* 31 Aug 1918, leaving:

1a Charlotte Margaretta; *m* 25 Jan 1911 Cdr Charles Albert Carey, RN (*d* 8 Sept 1925), 4th s of Henry Carey, of Alicante, Spain, and had issue:

1b *Carlos George Maxwell; *b* 21 March 1912

1b *Mary Jacqueline Heron; *b* 19 Oct 1919

(1) Harriet; *d* unm 26 June 1925

(2) Stuart Mary; *d* unm 23 April 1888

5 Charles Douglas; *b* 10 Oct 1813; *d* 17 May 1824

6 Robert Heron; *b* 24 Nov 1815; *d* 3 Feb 1828

7 Edward HERON-MAXWELL-BLAIR, DL, of Teviot Bank, Roxburghshire; *b* 2 March 1821; *m* 20 Oct 1847 Elizabeth Ellen (*d* 28 June 1901), only dau of Col W H Stopford Blair, of Penninghame, Wigtownshire (*see* COURTOWN, E), and *d* 4 Sept 1890, leaving issue:

(1) John Shaw, JP, DL Wigtownshire; *b* 31 March 1850; BA Cantab; 14th Hus; *d* unm 2 Aug 1899

(2) William Henry Stopford HERON-MAXWELL, of Teviot Bank, Roxburghshire, JP; *b* 14 June 1852; Maj Roy Fus, Lt-Col SE of Scotland Artillery, Zulu War (despatches, medal, clasp), 1st Boer War 1881; *m* 26 Feb 1884 Adeline Helen, MBE (1920), JP Roxburghshire (*d* 11 May 1941), dau of Osgood Hanbury, of Holfield Grange, and *d* 23 May 1927, leaving:

1a Helen Alice; *d* unm 4 Feb 1932

2a Elizabeth Marion; *m* 7 Oct 1919 Edmund Joseph Stapleton-Bretherton (*d* 29 Aug 1946), of Cambridge

3a Nora; *d* unm 24 Dec 1935

4a Mary Adeline; *m* 10 June 1921 Lt-Col Cecil George Arkwright, MC, 5th Fus, of Rhodesia, and had issue

(3) Patrick HERON-MAXWELL; *b* 8 March 1866; *m* 1st 26 Nov 1898 Constance Violet (*d* 24 Aug 1915), dau of Sir John Ralph Blois, 8th Bt (*qv*); *m* 2nd 1919 Hilda Adelaide Eleanor (*d* 7 June 1962), 4th dau of Hon Frederick Hanbury-Tracy (*see* SUDELEY, B), and *d* 2 Feb 1949, leaving by his 1st w:

1a John Edward Blois; *b* 19 Sept 1899; *d* Kenya 20 May 1925

2a Patrick Archibald; *b* 14 Sept 1903; 2nd Lt 4th Bn Roy Berks Regt; *d* 10 Jan 1935

1a Margaret Violet; *b* 9 June 1901; *m* 23 June 1927 John P T Fisher, of Headcorn, Kent, yst s of Bishop Fisher, of Fleggburgh, Norfolk, and *dsp* 5 Feb 1962

(1) Mira; *d* unm 21 June 1931

(2) Stuart Mary; *m* 16 Dec 1880 John Clarence Pierson (*d* 29 May 1902) and *d* 1891, leaving issue

(3) Jane Elizabeth; *d* 13 April 1921

(4) Helenora Catherine; *m* 30 April 1892 George Stehn, of Kensington, and *d* 23 March 1941, leaving issue

(5) Elizabeth Alice; *d* unm 27 July 1879

(6) Margaret Emily; *m* 10 Jan 1901 Harold William Kemble, of Birchfield, Cirencester, Capt Roy Glos Hus Yeo (*d* 1920), only surv s of Charles A Kemble, of Montvale, Somerset, and *d* 31 Dec 1949, leaving issue

(7) Georgina Florence; *m* 15 Nov 1904 Lt-Col Ralph Brunton Umfreville, CMG, DSO (*d* 29 Jan 1937), Worcs Regt, s of S C Umfreville, of Ingress Abbey, Kent, and had issue

1 Elizabeth; *m* 27 Sept 1819 Sir James Dalrymple-Hay, 2nd Bt (*qv*), and *d* 14 Feb 1821, leaving issue

2 Margaret Stewart; *d* unm 17 June 1882

3 Jane Stuart; *m* 15 Aug 1827 John Shaw-Stewart (*see* SHAW STEWART, Bt), and *d* 27 Dec 1886, leaving issue

4 Mary; *m* 27 April 1836 Sir James Dalrymple-Horn-Elphinstone, 2nd Bt, and *d* 16 Nov 1876, leaving issue (*see* STAIR, E)

5 Helenora Catherine; *m* 6 Nov 1838 Hew Drummond Elphinstone-Dalrymple and *d* 2 Nov 1889, leaving issue (*see* STAIR, E)

Sir PATRICK's yr bro,

Sir John Heron-Maxwell, 6th Bt; *b* 7 March 1808; Capt RN; *m* 7 Nov 1833 Caroline (*d* 22 Oct 1896), 6th dau of Hon Montgomery J G Stewart (*see* GALLOWAY, E), and *d* 22 Aug 1885, having had:

1 JOHN ROBERT HERON (Sir), **7th Bt**

2 Robert Charles Heron; *b* 1845; *d* 1846

3 Robert Charles Heron; *b* 7 Aug 1848; barrister, Priv Sec to Secs BOT 1881–92, Comptroller Companies Dept BOT 1911–13, memb Roy Co Archers; *d* unm 31 Jan 1938

4 Arthur Wellington Heron; *b* 14 Sept 1852; *m* 28 April 1896 Alicia Blanche (*d* 27 Feb 1942), dau of Robert Thomas Buckle, and *d* 3 Dec 1923

5 Spencer Horatio Walpole Heron; *b* 7 Dec 1855; *m* 24 Jan 1891 Beatrice Maude Emilia (*d* 7 March 1927), dau of E B Eastwick, CB, MP, and widow of F L Huddart, and *dsp* 20 June 1907

1 Caroline Mary Heron; *d* 20 Nov 1922

2 Mary Katherine Dundonald Heron; *d* unm 10 May 1934

3 Louisa Susan Marlborough Heron; *m* 23 June 1863 Sir James Robert Walker, 2nd Bt, and *d* 13 Jan 1920, leaving issue (*see* WALKER, Bt, of Sand Hutton)

4 Edith Elphinstone Heron; *m* 1st 23 Nov 1882 Aucher Cornwall Taylor (*dsp* 1896); *m* 2nd 18 Sept 1900 Rev George Napier (*d* 8 June 1902), Vicar St Mary's, Westminster, and *d* 24 July 1920

5 Beatrice Ethel Heron; Lady-in-Waiting to HRH THE DUCHESS OF ALBANY; *d* unm 27 Aug 1939

Sir JOHN's est son,

Sir John Robert Heron-Maxwell, 7th Bt, JP, DL Dumfriesshire, JP Cumberland, Surrey and London; *b* 4 June 1836; Capt 15th Hus, memb Roy Co Archers, Master Merchant Taylors' Co 1905–06; *m* 7 Aug 1866 Caroline Harriette (*d* Feb 1900), 3rd dau of Richard Howard-Brooke, of Castle Howard, Co Wicklow (*see* BROOKEBOROUGH, V), and *d* 12 May 1910, having had issue:

1 IVOR WALTER HERON (Sir), **8th Bt**

1 Maud Lucia Heron; *m* 20 July 1893 William Marshall Cazalet (*d* 22 Oct 1932), JP, DL, of Tonbridge, Kent, and *d* 14 Jan 1952, having had issue

2 Gwendoline, MBE (1918); *m* 16 July 1889 Richard Bayley Chenevix Trench (*d* 5 April 1933), and *d* 9 Jan 1948, leaving issue (*see* ASHTOWN, B)

3 Kathleen Edith Heron; *d* unm 23 Oct 1950

4 Muriel Heron; *d* unm 27 May 1956

Sir JOHN's son,

Sir Ivor Walter Heron-Maxwell, 8th Bt, MC; *b* 13 Nov 1871; *educ* Trin Coll Cambridge (MA); Army Capt WW I; *m* 7 Dec 1910 Norah Henrietta (*d* 9 Aug 1971), dau of Hon Francis Parker (*see* MACCLESFIELD E), and *d* 19 Feb 1928, having had issue:

1 PATRICK IVOR (Sir), **9th Bt**

1 Jean Norah; *b* 28 Dec 1911; *m* 6 July 1938 Anthony Sancroft-Baker, of Chippenham, Wilts, and *d* 1981, leaving:

(1) *Raymond Samuel [Raymond Sancroft-Baker Esq, 4 Westbourne Park Rd, London W2 5PH]; *b* 30 July 1950; *m* 1983 (*divorce* 1993) Daphne Caroline Adams and has:

1a *Robert Thomas; *b* 7 Dec 1985

2a *Hugh Jasper; *b* 18 July 1987

(1) *Rosalind Jean; *b* 11 Jan 1946; *m* 3 Aug 1967 *Geoffrey Richard Noel Cleveland, s of Dr Francis Howard Cleveland, of Sidmouth, Devon

2 (Helen) Naomi; *b* 25 June 1913; *m* 1st 2 March 1938 Francis Cecil Harold Allen (*d* 23 Jan 1939); *m* 2nd 31 Dec 1957 (*divorce* 1967) Howard Dale Thomas, s of Nicholas James Thomas, of Oregon, USA, and *d* 1983 leaving by him:

(1) *Nicholas John; *b* 10 July 1958

3 *Rachel Mary [Mrs Roy Macnab, 9/86 Elm Park Gdns, London SW10 9PD]; *b* 30 Aug 1922; *m* 6 Dec 1947 *Roy Martin Macnab, MA, D Litt et Phil, FRSA, 2nd s of Andrew Martin Macnab, of Durban, S Africa, and has:

(1) *Simon Martin; *b* 13 Oct 1955; *educ* Eton and Oxford

(1) *Celia Mary; *b* 2 Oct 1949; *m* 1988 (*divorce* 1993) Brian John Weller

Sir IVOR's only son,

Sir Patrick Ivor Heron-Maxwell, 9th Bt; *b* 26 July 1916; *educ* Stowe; *m* 9 Dec 1942 *Dorothy Geraldine Emma [Geraldine Lady Heron-Maxwell, 9 Cowslip Hill, Letchworth, Herts], yr dau of Claud Paget Mellor, and *d* 1982, having had:

1 Sir NIGEL MELLOR HERON-MAXWELL, **10th and present Bt**

2 +Colin Mellor; *b* 5 April 1952; *educ* Down House; *m* 1976 *Angela, only dau of Sabin Nister, of Petrosani, Romania, and has:

(1) *Kirsten Diana; *b* 1982

(2) *Hayley Claudia; *b* 1983

3 +Paul Mellor; *b* 17 Aug 1957; *educ* Knights Templar

HERRIES OF TERREGLES

Creation: L. (S) by 3 Feb 1489/90.

THE LADY HERRIES OF TERREGLES (Anne Elizabeth Fitzalan-Howard) [The Rt Hon The Lady Herries of Terregles, Angmering Park, Littlehampton, West Sussex BN16 4EX]; *b* 2 June 1938; *s f* 1975; *m* 1985 *Baron Cowdrey of Tunbridge (*qv*)

Lineage: Sir DAVID HERRIES of Terregles, Kirkcudbrightshire; *m* Margaret, dau of Sir Robert Crichton of Sanquhar (*see* BUTE, M), and *d* after 26 Aug 1495, leaving:

HERBERT HERRIES, **1st Lord Herries of Terregles** (S), so *cr* by 3 Feb 1489/90; *b c* 1460; *m* 1st Mariot Carlyle, allegedly dau of 1st Lord Carlyle, and had, with other issue (including a dau, *m* 1st Lord Maxwell; *see* MAXWELL, Bt):

1 ANDREW, **2nd Lord**

2 Roger; Tutor (Guardian) to **3rd Lord Herries of Terregles** when a minor; had 5 June 1520 a charter of Maidenpaup, Galloway, which was sold by his descendants 1629

The **1st Lord Herries of Terregles** *m* 2nd by 4 June 1493 Mariot Cunningham and *d* between 14 Jan 1501/2 and 12 June 1505, having been a lunatic since 1494

His er son,

ANDREW HERRIES, **2nd Lord Herries of Terregles**; *b c* 1477; outlawed for homicide 1507 and 1508 but pardoned late latter year; *m* 1st 1494 (*divorce* after 15 Nov 1495) Beatrice Herries, dau (probably) of George Herries of Terraughtie; *m* 2nd between 25 Nov and 22 Dec 1495 Lady Janet Douglas, dau of 5th Earl of Angus (*see* HAMILTON and BRANDON, D); *m* 3rd Nicole (*m* 2nd Patrick Hepburn, yr bro of 2nd Earl of Bothwell, *see* BUCHAN-HEPBURN, Bt), dau of 2nd Lord Home (*see* HOME, E), and was *ka* Battle of Flodden 9 Sept 1513, leaving by her:

WILLIAM HERRIES, **3rd Lord Herries of Terregles**; Extrdy Ld Session 1532; *m* Catherine (*m* 2nd *c* 1545 John Wallace of Dundonald), dau of James Kennedy of Blairquhan, and *dspm* 26 Sept 1543, leaving, with two yr daus (Catherine, *m* 1st Alexander Stewart of Garlies (*see* GALLOWAY, E) and 2nd Uchreld McDowall of Mundork and *d* 8 Feb 1592/3; Janet, *m* Sir James Cockburn of Skerling and *d* Dec 1612, leaving issue):

AGNES HERRIES, **Lady Herries of Terregles** in her own right; *b c* 1534; *m* by 18 March 1547/8 Sir John Maxwell (*b c* 1512; fought for MARY QUEEN OF SCOTS Battle of Langside 1568 and remainded true to her afterwards, suffering confiscation and incarceration 1568 and 1569 respectively; *d* 20 Jan 1582/3), 2nd s of 4th Lord Maxwell (*see* MAXWELL, Bt), who obtained 8 May 1566 a new charter of the territorial Baronies of Terregles and Kirkgunzean to him and his w and the heirs male of their bodies, with further remainder to his heirs male whatsoever; he also had a seat in Parl as **Lord Herries of Terregles** from 14 April 1567; she *d* 14 March 1593/4, leaving, with other issue:

1 WILLIAM, **5th Lord**

2 Robert (Sir), of Spottis; *m* 1st Elizabeth, dau of John Gordon of Auchinresch and widow of Alexander Maclellan of Gelston; *m* 2nd Sara, sis of Sir James Johnstone of that Ilk (*see* ANNANDALE AND HARTFELL, E), and *d c* 31 Oct 1615, leaving:

(1) Sir ROBERT MAXWELL, 1st Bt (NS), so *cr* 30 June 1663, of Orchardtoun, Kirkcudbrightshire, and Ballycastle, Co Londonderry; *m* by Feb 1639/40 Anne/Marion Maclellan, only dau of 1st Lord Kirkcudbright, and *d* by 1673, leaving:

1a Sir ROBERT MAXWELL, 2nd Bt, of Orchardtoun and Ballycastle, also of Waringstown and Killyleagh, Co Down, JP (Cos Down and Londonderry 1683); ktd by 1655; MP (S Parl) Stewartry of Kirkcudbright 1669–74 and 1681–82, Sheriff Co Down 1673; *m* 1st 1668 Anne, est dau of Henry Carey, 2nd Earl of Monmouth (*see* ALDENHAM and HUNSDON OF HUNSDON, B, preliminary remarks), and widow of 1st Earl of Clanbrassill; *m* 2nd Margaret, dau of Henry Maxwell, of Mullaghatoney, Co Armagh, and *dsp* 1693, when the btcy seems to have expired or become dormant, although it was assumed by two other persons of the name of Maxwell in the 18th century

3 Edward; Commendator Dundrennan; *m* Margaret, dau of William Baillie of Lamington, and *d* 29 Sept 1598, leaving issue

1 Elizabeth; *m* 1st 1563 Sir John Gordon of Lochinvar; *m* 2nd Sir Alexander Fraser, 8th of Philorth (*see* SALTOUN, L)

2 Margaret; *m* 1st Earl of Lothian (*see* LOTHIAN, M)

3 Mary; *m* 6th Lord Hay of Yester (*see* TWEEDDALE, M)

4 Sarah; *m* 1st 1588 Sir James Johnstone of Johnstone (*see* ANNANDALE AND HARTFELL, E); *m* 2nd 1st Earl of Wigton; *m* 3rd 1st Viscount Montgomery of the Great Ardes

The est son,

WILLIAM MAXWELL, **5th Lord Herries of Terregles**; *b c* 1555; *m* by 1 July 1592 Catharine, sis of 1st Earl of Lothian (*see* LOTHIAN, M), and *d* 10 Oct 1603, leaving, with other issue, including two yr sons (Sir William, of Gribton, *m* Barbara, dau of John Johnstone of Newbie, and had issue; Sir Robert, Gentleman of the Bedchamber):

JOHN MAXWELL, **6th Lord Herries of Terregles**; *m* his cousin Elizabeth, sis of 1st Earl of Nithsdale (*see* MAXWELL, Bt, also MORTON, E), and *d* 1631, having had, with other issue:

1 JOHN, **7th Lord**

2 James, of Breconside; ancestor of the MAXWELLs of Breconside, Terraughtie, Munches and Carruchan; his descendant William Maxwell of Carruchan (*dsp* 1863) opposed 1858 the claim of Mr Constable-Maxwell to the Ldship of Herries of Terregles (*see* below)

3 Frederick; Rector Scots Seminary Madrid

1 Elizabeth; *m* 3rd Earl of Winto(u)n (*see* EGLINTON and WINTON, E)

The 6th LORD's est son,

JOHN MAXWELL, **7th Lord Herries** and 3rd EARL OF NITHSDALE, LORD MAXWELL, ESKDALE, AND CARLEILL [*sic*], as which *s* his cousin Robert Maxwell, 2nd Earl of Nithsdale (*see* MAXWELL, Bt) 1667; *m* (contract 19 Aug 1626) Elizabeth, sis of 1st Viscount Kenmure, and *d* between 16 Feb and 29 June 1677, having had issue:

1 ROBERT, **8th Lord**

2 John; *m* Elizabeth (*m* 2nd Thomas Maxwell), dau and heiress of William Glendoning of Gelston, and *d* 1658, having had:

(1) Elizabeth; *m* Robert Maxwell of Kirkhouse

3 William; *m* (contract 30 June 1674) Agnes (*m* 2nd John Lindsay of Wauchope), dau of 5th Viscount Kenmure, and *dsp* 1684

The 7th LORD's est son,

ROBERT MAXWELL, **8th Lord Herries** and 4th EARL OF NITHSDALE; *b c* Jan 1628; *m* (contract 6 and 25 March 1669) Lucy (*d* 8 Jan 1713), dau of 1st Marquess of Douglas (*see* HAMILTON and BRANDON, D), and *d* by 23 March 1682/3, leaving, with two daus (one of whom, Mary, *m* 9 Jan 1694 4th Earl of Traquair (*see* MORAY, E) and *d* 22 Sept 1759, leaving issue):

WILLIAM MAXWELL, **9th Lord Herries** and 5TH EARL OF NITHSDALE; *b* 1676; Jacobite 1715, captured Battle of Preston 14 Nov 1715; sentenced to death for high treason 19 Jan 1715/6 but escaped from the Tower of London by the time-honoured (*see* AIRLIE, E) though effective method of donning female costume (which his wife had brought him on a conjugal visit) 23 Feb 1715/6 (the eve of his intended execution); *m* Lady Winifred Herbert (*d* 1749), dau of 1st Marquess of Powis (*see* POWIS, E), and *d* 20 March 1744, his titles having been forfeited by attainder after his capture, though his estates were saved by his having made them over to his s in 1712, reserving only a life rent to himself, leaving, with a dau (Anne, *m* 13 Sept 1731 4th and last Baron Bellew of Duleek; *see* BELLEW, B):

WILLIAM MAXWELL, *Lord Maxwell* by courtesy; assumed title Earl of Nithsdale on f's death; *b* 27 June 17–; *m* 1st 27 June 1731 his cousin Lady Catherine Stewart (*d* 16 June 1765), dau of 4th Earl of Traquair (*see* MORAY, E); *m* 2nd 11 Aug 1767 Anne Fox (*d* 6 March 1773), and *dspm* 2 Aug 1776, having by his 1st w had, with another dau (Mary, *dsp* 1747):

WINIFRED Maxwell; *b c* 1736; *m* 17 Oct 1758 William CONSTABLE formerly HAGGERSTON (changed on inheriting 1746 the Everingham Park and other estates from his great-uncle Sir Marmaduke Constable, 4th Bt; *d* 30 June 1797), 2nd s of Sir Carnaby Haggerston, 3rd Bt (*see* MAXWELL SCOTT, Bt), and *d* 13 July 1801, having had, with two daus:

1 Marmaduke William CONSTABLE later CONSTABLE-MAXWELL, of Everingham Park, Yorks, and Caerlaverock Castle, Dumfriesshire; *b* 2 Jan 1760; *m* 26 Nov 1800 Theresa Appollonia (*d* 8 Nov 1846), dau of Edmund Wakeman, of Beckford, Worcs, and *d* 30 June 1819, leaving:

(1) WILLIAM, **10th Lord**

(2) Marmaduke, of Terregles; *b* 1 Jan 1806; granted with siblings 2 Aug 1858 rank of Lord of Parl's dau/yr s; *m* 1836 Mary (*d* 22 Oct 1882), only dau of Rev Anthony Marsden, of Gargrave, and *dsp* 16 July 1872

(3) Peter; *b* 7 Feb 1807; *m* 1834 Helena Mary (*d* 16 June 1851), est dau of John Peter Bruno Bowdon, of Southgate, Derbys, and *d* 27 Feb 1851, having had, with other issue:

1a Alice Clare; *m* 4 Feb 1875 Philip John Canning Howard (*see* NORFOLK, D) and *d* 22 May 1941, leaving issue (*see* below)

(4) Henry CONSTABLE-MAXWELL later CONSTABLE-MAXWELL-STUART (added 1876 on inheriting the estates of the Earls of Traquair; *see* MORAY, E), JP, DL, of Traquair, Peeblesshire; *b* 28 Dec 1809; *m* 23 July 1840 Juliana (*d* 12 Sept 1904), dau of Peter Middleton, of Stockeld (*see* below), and *d* 26 Oct 1890, leaving:

1a Herbert Joseph, of Traquair and Terregles, DL (Peeblesshire and Kirkcudbrightshire); *b* 20 July 1842; *d* 13 April 1921

2a Arthur Joseph; *b* 31 May 1845; *d* unm 7 Nov 1942

3a Charles Stanislaus; *b* 12 Feb 1851; *d* 3 Feb 1911

4a Edmund Joseph; *b* 2 Sept 1858; *m* 16 July 1884 his cousin Hon Mary Anne Constable-Maxwell (*d* 13 Dec 1941), dau of **10th Lord Herries of Terregles**, and *d* 21 July 1924, leaving:

1b Francis Joseph; *b* 17 June 1886; *educ* Stonyhurst; WW I with E R Yorks Yeo, WW II as Capt RE; *m* 24 Oct 1917 Dorothy Mary (*d* 1975), only dau of J D'Arcy Hartley, of Billesdon Coplow, Leics, and *d* 11 July 1962, leaving:

1c Peter D'Arcy Joseph; *b* 16 Nov 1922; *educ* Downside; Capt IA; md Vickers Hldgs Pty and Vickers Australia, dir Vickers Ltd 1975; *m* 1 Sept 1956 *Flora Mary [Mrs Peter Maxwell-Stuart, Traquair House, Innerleithen, Peeblesshire], only dau of Sir Alexander Morris Carr-Saunders, FBA, and *d* 1990, leaving:

1d +Catherine Margaret Mary [Mrs John Grey, Traquair House, Innerleithen, Peeblesshire]; *b* 16 Nov 1964; *m* 19– John Patrick Grey (*d* 17 March 1998) and has:

1e *Isabella Stuart; *b* 19–

2c +Michael Joseph Edmund [Michael Constable-Maxwell-Stuart Esq, Baitlaws, Lamington, Lanarks]; *b* 17 April 1932; *educ* Ampleforth; *m* 8 Aug 1970 *Kirsty Marion Forbes, est dau of Capt Harold Keith Salvesen, DL, FRSE, of Iveralmond, Cramond, Edinburgh, and has:

1d +Justin; *b* 6 Oct 1973

1d +Laura Mary; *b* 1971

1c +Madeleine Mary Josephine [Mrs John Sherbrooke, Churchen Green, E Morden, Dorset BH20 7AW]; *b* 21 Aug 1918; *m* 23 Nov 1946 *John Penn Sherbrooke, only s of Col Nevile Hugh Cairns Sherbrooke, CBE, DSO, and has:

1d +Simon [Simon Sherbrooke Esq, Bolney, Salisbury Rd, Blandford, Dorset DT11 7SP]; *b* 1947; *m* 1977 *Miranda, dau of Michael McCrea, of Kelso, and has:

1e +Archie John; *b* 1980

2e +Benedict; *b* 1984

3e +Luke; *b* 1986

4e +Edmund; *b* 1993
1e +Rosanna; *b* 1982
2d +Hugh [Hugh Sherbrooke Esq, Middle Farm, Taston, Oxon OX7 3JL]; *b* 1948; *m* 1974 *Nicola Mary Hamilton, yr dau of Anthony Andrew Francis Tabor (*see* DULVERTON, B), and has:
1e +Harry; *b* 1977
2e +Tom; *b* 1979
3d +Alexander; *b* 1957
1d +Elizabeth; *b* 1959
2c Joan Margaret Mary; *b* 2 May 1920 ; *m* 9 Dec 1943 Charles Erik Paterson (*d* 1983), s of Charles Paterson, of Edinburgh, and *d* 1987, leaving:
1d +David Francis Joseph [David Paterson Esq, 15B, 6 Po Shan Rd, Hong Kong; 30 Walpole St, London SW3]; *b* 1944; *educ* Stonyhurst and Oriel Coll Oxford; *m* 1983 *Jayne, dau of T Y Tung, of Hong Kong
2d +Michael Charles Joseph; *b* 1948; *educ* Stonyhurst and Oriel Coll Oxford; *m* 1987 *Marguerite, dau of V-Adml Sir Iwan Raikes, KCB, CBE, DSC, DL, of Brecon, and has issue:
1e +David; *b* 1990
1e +Hermione; *b* 1987
2e +Sophia; *b* 1990
1d +Caroline Mary Madeleine [Mrs Edward Serocold, 1 Morella Rd, London SW12]; *b* 1945; *m* 1975 *Edward Pearce Serocold, s of Lt-Col Walter Pearce Serocold, DSO, TD, of Highclere, Berks, and has:
1e +Charles; *b* 1976
2e +Mark; *b* 1979
3e +Henry; *b* 1985
1e +Georgina; *b* 1987
2b Henry Joseph Ignatius; *b* 21 July 1887; Lt Coldstream Gds; *ka* 1917
3b Edmund Joseph; *b* 3 Oct 1892; T/Lt RE; *ka* 26 April 1916
4b William Joseph Peter; *b* 22 July 1895; Lt Roy Sussex Regt; *m* 1st 7 July 1932 Ruth Patricia Craven (*d* 10 May 1952), yst dau of Charles Craven Sykes, of London; *m* 2nd 3 Jan 1955 *Anne Christine, dau of Peter John Williamson, of Edinburgh, and *d* 3 Oct 1964, leaving issue:
1c +Joseph Peter; *b* 24 Jan 1956; *m* 1988 *Deirdre, yr dau of John O'Neil, and has issue:
1d +Laurence; *b* 1990
1d +Rebecca; *b* 1989
2c +Julian Francis; *b* 27 Dec 1956
5b Joseph Joachim; *b* 22 Aug 1896; Lt W R Regt; *ka* 2 March 1916
6b Alfred Joseph; *b* 27 March 1898; Lt Coldstream Gds; *ka* 20 Aug 1918
7b Philip Joseph; *b* 8 March 1903; *educ* Stonyhurst; WW II with RA (POW); *d* unm 13 Dec 1975
1b Mary Josephine; *b* 6 July 1885; *m* 11 March 1918 Capt Hamish Morton Anderson, MB, ChB, RAMC (*d* 8 March 1960), est s of Hamish Morton Anderson, and *d* 1973, leaving issue:
1c Patricia Maria; *b* 1919; *m* 1988, as his 2nd w, *Sir Francis Vallat, GBE, KCMG, QC, and *d* 1995
2b Florence Mary Collette; *b* 17 June 1886; nun as Sister Mary Frances; *d* 11 June 1976
3b Marcia Mary Gertrude; *b* 10 Oct 1888; *m* 26 Oct 1920 Douglas Christopher Leng (*d* 3 June 1930), only s of C D Leng, of Sandygate, Sheffield, and *d* 9 July 1956, leaving issue:
1c +Christopher Anthony William, OBE (1987), DL (Peeblesshire 1983) [Christopher Leng Esq OBE DL, Juniper Bank, Walkerburn, Peeblesshire]; *b* 1922; *educ* Downside and Hertford Coll Oxford (BA 1947, MA 1947); WW II as Capt 27th Lancers, Middle East and Italy (despatches), Burma; *m* 1953 *Patricia, dau of W Edmund Lillywhite, of Kent, and has issue:
1d +Malcolm Simon Christopher [Malcolm Leng Esq, West Bold Farm, Walkerburn, Peeblesshire EH43 6DD]; *b* 1959; *m* 1990 *Fiona, er dau of P A Murray, of Painswick, Glos, and has issue:
1e +Christopher Marmaduke; *b* 1995
2e +Barclay Malcolm Dominic; *b* 1997
1e +Demelza Fiona; *b* 1993
2d +Rupert William; *b* 1961; *m* 1991 *Helen, dau of H A Nicholson, of Kirkmichael, and has:
1e *Julia Rosemary; *b* 1997
1d +Fiona Anne; *b* 1954; *m* 1988, as his 2nd w, *Nicholas Charles Gilmour Marshall and has issue (*see* GILMOUR, Bt)
2d +Teresa Madeleine; *b* 1955
2c +David Joseph Timothy; *b* 1924; *educ* Downside and New Coll Oxford (BA); WW II as Capt 4th Bn Gren Gds; *m* 1951 *Dorothy Lucie (*d* 1967), dau of C Seymour, of Folkestone, and has:
1d +Felicity Mary [Mrs George Whitman, 37 rue de la Bucherie, 75005 Paris]; *b* 1952; *m* *George Whitman, of USA, and has issue:
1e +Sylvia; *b* 1979
2d +Leonora Rosemary; *b* 1956
4b Emily Mary Josephine; *b* 5 May 1890; *d* unm 10 Sept 1970
5a Henry; *b* 18 Aug 1861; *m* 11 Feb 1908 Florence (*d* 19 May 1956), twin dau of William Wickham, MP, of Chestnut Grove, Yorks, and *d* 31 May 1932, leaving issue:
1b Charles Joseph; *b* 4 April 1913; Benedictine monk Ampleforth; *d* Jan 1994
1b Alice Mary; *b* 11 Feb 1909; *d* Jan 1985
2b +Clare Mary [Mrs James Cafferkey, 4 Apple Garth, Easingwold, Yorks YO6 3LZ]; *b* 9 Aug 1914; *m* 28 Sept 1938 S/Ldr James Patrick Cafferkey, RAF (*d* 1978), est s of Patrick Cafferkey, of Ardagh, Co Mayo, and has:
1c +Patrick Charles; *b* 19–
6a Philip; *b* 17 July 1864; *d* 27 May 1872
7a George; *b* 11 May 1866; *d* unm 1945
1a Laura; *d* 14 Dec 1864
2a Agnes; nun; *d* 14 Feb 1929
3a Juliana Mary; *d* unm 18 Nov 1926
4a Louisa May Josephine; *d* 10 May 1873
5a Blanche; nun; *d* 17 Aug 1937
(5) Joseph (Rev); *b* 1811; RC priest; *d* 17 Oct 1869
(1) Mary; *m* 1 May 1821 Hon Charles Langdale (*d* 1 Dec 1868), 4th s of 17th Baron Stourton, and *d* 25 Sept 1857, leaving issue (*see* MOWBRAY, SEGRAVE and STOURTON, B)
(2) Theresa; *b* 28 Feb 1802; *m* Hon Charles Thomas Clifford, of Irnham Hall, Lincs (*d* 11 Sept 1870), 2nd s of 6th Baron Clifford of Chudleigh (*qv*), and *d* 24 April 1883, leaving issue
2 William CONSTABLE later MIDLETON (on inheriting the Stockeld Park estate under terms of will of his great-uncle William Midleton); *b* 25 Dec 1760; *m* Feb 1782 Clara Louisa (*d* Feb 1832), dau of William Grace (gf of Sir William Grace, 2nd Bt, *see* 1949 edn) by Mary, dau and heiress of Richard Harford, of Marshfield, Co Dublin, and *d* 17 Dec 1847, leaving, with other issue:
(1) Peter, of Stockeld Park; *b* 1786; *m* 23 July 1812 Hon Juliana Mary Stourton (*d* 27 Nov 1861), dau of 17th Baron Stourton (*see* MOWBRAY, SEGRAVE and STOURTON, B), and *d* 3 June 1866, having had, with other issue:
1a Charles Marmaduke, JP, DL (W R Yorks, Inverness-shire and Somerset), of Myddelton Lodge, Yorks; *b* 6 Dec 1820; *m* 28 July 1858 Helen (*d* 1903), dau of Col — Fraser, of Achnagairn, and widow of George Huntly Duff, of Muirtown, Inverness-shire, and *d* 1904, leaving:
1b Marmaduke Francis; *b* 3 May 1867; *d* unm
2b Reginald John (Rev); SJ; *b* 21 Feb 1870; RC priest
3b Lionel George William; *b* 8 Jan 1872; *d* unm
1b Hilda Mary; *b* 26 May 1868; *d* unm
2a Edward, of Suirmount, Co Tipperary; *m* Emily, dau of Alfred Power, of Bellevue House, Co Waterford, and had:
1b Edith Annie; *m* 20 Jan 1900 her cousin Marmaduke Manley (*d* 9 Dec 1950), 3rd s of George William Manley, of Spofforth Hall, Yorks, and *d* 29 April 1916, leaving issue
1a Juliana; *m* 23 July 1840 her cousin Hon Henry Constable-Maxwell-Stuart (*see* above) and *d* 12 Sept 1904, leaving issue
2a Charlotte; *m* 1853 George William Manley, JP (*d* 1904), of Spofforth Hall and Buckland Manor, Somerset, and *d* 1883, leaving issue
3 Charles CONSTABLE later STANLEY; *b* 25 March 1764; *m* 1st 21 July 1793 Elizabeth (*dsp* 23 June 1797), sis and heiress of Sir William Stanley, Bt, of Hooton (*see* 1893 edn); *m* 2nd 24 Feb1800 Mary (*d* 18 Feb 1831), dau of Thomas Macdonald (s of Angus Macdonald of Gellovie, of a cadet branch of the MACDONALDs of Keppoch), and *d* 14 Sept 1844, leaving, with other issue:
(1) Thomas Angus, of Otley, JP (Yorks); *b* 16 June 1805; *m* 17 Aug 1865 Elizabeth Ducarel de la Pasture (*d* 22 Dec 1919), only dau of Henri Pierre, 3rd Marquis de la Pasture, and *d* 1891, leaving:
1a Mary; *b* 22 June 1870; *m* 26 July 1893 24th Baron Mowbray, (25th Baron) Segrave and (21st Baron) Stourton (*qv*) and *d* 9 Dec 1961, leaving issue

MARMADUKE CONSTABLE-MAXWELL's est son,

WILLIAM CONSTABLE-MAXWELL, **10th Lord Herries of Terregles**, as which recognised 23 June 1858 following reversal of attainder of 1716; *b* 25 Aug 1804; High Sheriff Yorks 1833; *m* 12 Nov 1835 Marcia Mary (*d* 13 Nov 1883), est dau of Hon Sir Edward Marmaduke Joseph Vavasour, 1st Bt (*qv*), and *d* 12 Nov 1876, having had, with other issue:

1 MARMADUKE FRANCIS, **11th Lord**
2 William; *b* 24 April 1841; *d* unm 25 Jan 1903
3 Joseph CONSTABLE-MAXWELL later CONSTABLE-MAXWELL-SCOTT, JP, DL Roxburghshire; *b* 16 Jan 1847; Rifle Bde; *m* 21 July 1874 Mary Monica (*d* 15 March 1920), dau of J Robert Hope-Scott (*see* LINLITHGOW, M), and *d* 29 Aug 1923, leaving:
(1) Sir WALTER JOSEPH CONSTABLE-MAXWELL-SCOTT, 1st and last Bt (UK), so *cr* 23 June 1932, CB (1923), DSO (1915), DL; *b* 10 April 1875; *educ* Stonyhurst; Maj-Gen Cameronians, Scottish Rifles, served Tirah Expdn 1897–98 (medal with clasp), Boer War (medal with two clasps), WW I (despatches six times, Brevets of Lt-Col and Col) and WW II (Zone Cdr Scottish HG), cmded 52nd Lowland Div (TA) 1930–34, memb Roy Co of Archers, V-Chm Cncl Scottish BRC Soc 1935–50, Offr Legn Honour, Serbian Order Karageorge 4th Cl with swords, Croix de Guerre, Hon DSc Fordham U New York 1945; *m* 1st 19 March 1918 Mairi Richmond (*d* 9 Oct 1924), 3rd dau of Lt-Col Stewart MacDougall, DL, of Lunga, Argyll, and had:
1a +Patricia Mary, OBE (1972); *b* 11 March 1921; Hon Lt WRAC WW II; *m* 8 Sept 1944 *Sir Harold Hugh Christian Boulton, 4th Bt, of Copped Hall (*qv*), and resumed maiden name by deed poll 1951
2a +Jean Mary Monica (Dame), DCVO (1984, CVO 1969) [Dame Jean Maxwell-Scott DCVO, Abbotsford, Melrose, Roxburghshire TD6 9BQ]; *b* 8 June 1923; WW II with VAD; Ldy-in-Waiting to HRH PRINCESS ALICE, DUCHESS OF GLOUCESTER 1959–
(1) (cont.) Sir WALTER *m* 2nd 19 June 1928 Marie Louise St Paul, Countess de Beaucaire (*d* 2 Oct 1969), dau of Maj John A Logan, of Washington, DC, and widow of Henri de Sincay, and *d* 3 April 1954, when the btcy expired
(2) Joseph Michael; *b* 25 May 1880; Lt RN; *d* 20 Dec 1911
(3) Malcolm Joseph Raphael, DSO (1917); *b* 22 Oct 1883; R-Adml, ADC to HM GEORGE V, served WW I (despatches, Croix de Guerre); *m* 6 Sept 1918 Fearga Victoria Mary (*d* 22 March 1969), est dau of Sir Nicholas Roderick O'Conor, GCB, GCMG, PC (*see* LINLITHGOW, M), and *d* 23 Feb 1943, leaving:
1a Sir MICHAEL FERGUS MAXWELL SCOTT, 13th Bt, of Haggerston (*qv*)
2a Ian Malcolm; *b* 18 July 1927; *m* 14 Feb 1958 *Susan Mary [Mrs Ian Maxwell Scott, 12 Kelmscott Rd, London SW11 6QY], yr dau of Sir Andrew Edmund James Clark, 3rd Bt, MBE, MC, QC, of Cavendish Sq (*see* 1970 edn), and *d* 1993, leaving:
1b +Malcolm Fergus; *b* 24 Dec 1960; *m* 1990 (*divorce* 1993) Tanya, yr dau of William Church
2b +Simon Magnus; *b* 28 Dec 1962; *m* 1986 (*divorce* 1992) Gaynor, yst dau of Daniel Jones, and has:

1c +Hector George; *b* 1986
1c +Amelia Elizabeth; *b* 1989
3b +Andrew Nicholas Hugh; *b* 25 Nov 1966
1b +Lucy Ann; *b* 26 Sept 1958
2b +Sarah Secunda; *b* 15 Oct 1959
3b +Catherine Monica Jane; *b* 25 Nov 1966
1a Elizabeth Mary; *b* 28 May 1924; *d* Nov 1991
(4) Herbert Francis Joseph; *b* 14 March 1891; Lt 48th Highrs of Canada WW I; Coronation Medal 1937; *m* 27 Feb 1924 Eileen Margaret Josephine (*d* 14 Sept 1974), yst dau of Henry Smail, of Donhead Lodge, Wimbledon, and *d* 9 Feb 1962, leaving issue:
1a +Simon Malcolm [Simon Constable-Maxwell-Scott Esq, Foss House, Strensall, Yorks]; *b* 8 May 1939; *educ* Stonyhurst: *m* 28 April 1962 *Moyna, yr dau of Satish Yeshwant Gore, of Calcutta, and has:
1b +Amanda Mary; *b* 8 Dec 1962; m 1987 *Charles John Kay, s of Dr John Anthony Kay, of York, and adopted:
*Isabella Moyna; *b* 10 Jan 1996
2b +Fiona Anne; *b* 22 Jan 1964
3b +Joanna Jane; *b* 26 Jan 1965
2a +David Darragh [David Constable-Maxwell-Scott Esq, 66 Marryat Rd, London SW19]; *b* 28 June 1944; *educ* Stonyhurst; *m* 15 Feb 1969 *(Helen) Isabel, er dau of Leonard Caplan, QC, and has:
1b +James Herbert; *b* 26 Sept 1971
2b +Charles Leonard; *b* 3 March 1975
1a +Aurea Mary Josephine [Mrs Peter Williams, 66 Valecrest Drive, Islington, Ontario, Canada, M9A 4P6]; *b* 6 March 1926; *m* 30 April 1947 Peter Humphrey Williams (*d* 1987), only surv s of Dr W Humphrey Williams, of Monmouth, and has had issue:
1b +Michael Humphrey [Michael Williams Esq, 657 Carlaw Ave, Toronto, Ontario, Canada M4K 3K6]; *b* 19 July 1948; *m* *Anne Catherine, dau of Edgar James Thomas, and has issue:
1c +Jake Peter Thomas; *b* 1988
2b +Ian Maxwell [Ian Williams Esq, 66 Valecrest Drive, Islington, Ontario, Canada, M9A 4P6]; *b* 21 April 1951; *m* *Mary Jo — and has:
1c +Christopher; *b* 19–
2c +Trevor; *b* 19–
1c +Kathleen; *b* 19–
3b +David Andrew; *b* 19 May 1955
1b Deborah Mary; *b* 5 April 1950; accidentally drowned 17 June 1956
2b +Elizabeth Anne [Mrs Jan Rzyzora, Box 889, Knowlton, Prov Quebec, Canada J0E 1V0]; *b* 19 Sept 1953; *m* 1975 *Jan Joseph Rzyzora and has:
1c +Matthew Scott; *b* 1981
2c +Simon Peter; *b* 1982
1c +Deborah Katherine; *b* 1976
2c +Andrea Jan; *b* 1978
3b +Sheila Mary; *b* 24 July 1956; *m* 1985 *Andries Johannes Stephanus van der Merwe and has:
1c +Pamela Jo; *b* 1987
2c +Stephanie Ann; *b* 1990
3c +Megan Elizabeth; *b* 1993
4b +Joanna Susan [Miss Joanna Williams, 848 Goodwin Rd, Mississauga, Ontario, Canada L5G J4T]; *b* 24 June 1958
5b Pamela Jane; *b* 5 Jan 1961; *d* 1976
2a +Susan Mary [Miss Susan Constable-Maxwell-Scott, 2 Westfield House, West Cross, Tenterden, Kent TN30 6JL]; *b* 27 Oct 1931
3a +Mary Monica (Mamo) [Miss Mary Constable-Maxwell-Scott, St Mary's House, St George's Retreat, Burgess Hill, W Sussex]; *b* 29 Oct 1945
(1) Mary Josephine; *b* 1876; *m* 21 Sept 1897 Alexander Augustus Dalglish, of Goulburn, NSW, and *d* 29 July 1922, leaving issue:
1a James Campbell; *b* 1898; gf of:
1b +John [John Dalglish, Pomeroy, Goulburn, NSW, Australia]
(2) Winifride Mary Josephine; *d* 12 March 1880
(3) Alice Mary Josephine; *m* 26 April 1905 Edward Cassidy, of Monasterevan, Co Kildare, and *d* 30 Aug 1908
(4) Margaret Mary Lucy; *d* unm 10 Dec 1912
4 Bernard, JP Inverness-shire; *b* 3 April 1848; memb Roy Co Archers; *m* 1st 8 Nov 1881 Mathilda (*d* 13 Nov 1882), 2nd dau of Alfred Dupont Jessup, of Philadelphia, and had issue:
(1) Bernard Joseph; *b* 12 Nov, *d* 4 Dec 1882
4 (cont.) Bernard Constable-Maxwell *m* 2nd 30 April 1890 Hon Alice Mary Charlotte Fraser (*d* 7 Aug 1958), 2nd dau of 15th Lord (Fraser of) Lovat (*qv*), and *d* 27 Oct 1938, having by her had:
(2) Ian Simon Joseph; *b* 15 April 1891; *educ* Downside and Trin Coll Cambridge (BA 1913, MA 1915); Capt QO Cameron Highrs, also RFC and RAF and Staff Capt 204 Bde WW I (wounded, 1914 Star); Kt SMO Malta; *m* 6 April 1937 Jeanette Louisa (*d* 4 Aug 1944), er dau of Lt-Col Wilfrid Ricardo, DSO, of Surrey, and *d* 3 Sept 1975, leaving:
1a +Jeannette Alice Norah [Miss Jeanette Constable-Maxwell, Flat 9, 12 Chelsea Embankment, London SW3]; *b* 26 April 1942
(3) Ronald Joseph Tarlagan; *b* 9 July 1892; Capt Egyptian Army, Darfur Compaign 1916 (despatches); *d* unm 4 Jan 1931
(4) Gerald Joseph, MC, DFC, AFC, AEM, DL (Hants 1957); *b* 8 Sept 1895; *educ* Downside; Maj 1st Lovat Scouts and W/Cdr RAF, WWs I and II (despatches); memb Roy Co Archers, Kt SMO Malta, Papal Chamberlain, Prime Warden Fishmongers146 Co 1956–57; *m* 8 March 1920 Caroline Burns Shumard (*d* 10 Feb 1984), dau of George Alexander Carden, of Dallas, Texas, and *d* 18 Dec 1959, having had issue:
1a William Michael; *b* 27 Sept 1926; F/Lt RAF; *k* while on flight duty Thorney Island RAF Station 29 March 1950
2a +Peter George [Peter Constable-Maxwell Esq, Les Moureaux, Neuffous, Monsegur, Aquitaine, France]; *b* 18 Jan 1944; *educ* Ampleforth; Gren Gds; *m* 30 June 1973 *Virginia Anne, dau of John Ewart, of Dial House, and has issue:
1b +Benedict Gerald John; *b* 2 April 1976
1b +Laura Katherine; *b* 10 Sept 1974
2b +Eleanor Margaret; *b* 8 March 1977
3b +Elizabeth Marsha; *b* 1983
1a +Ann Mary Teresa, CBE (1992); *b* 30 Aug 1927; Fndr/Co Chm Help the Hospices; *m* 4 July 1949 *17th Duke of Norfolk (*qv*) and has issue
2a +(Veronica) Diana Margaret [Mrs Timothy Boyd Wilson, Ardelve, Kyle of Lochalsh, Ross-shire]; *b* 15 Dec 1930; *educ* St Mary's Ascot; *m* 29 Oct 1960 *Timothy Lawrie Boyd Wilson, only s of Lt-Col J Lawrie Boyd Wilson, and has:
1b +William Lawrie Joseph; *b* 1 Dec 1963
1b +Lucy Mary Carolyn; *b* 18 Aug 1961
2b +Magdalen Margaret; *b* 30 Sept 1966
3a +Carolyn Mary; *b* 23 Aug 1938; *m* 23 July 1960 *Maj Count Charles John de Salis, Scots Gds, er s of Maj Count Anthony Denis Rodolph de Salis, FRGS, of Bath (*see* 1956 edn Foreign Titles Section), and has issue:
1b +Isobel Oriane Clare; *b* 31 Aug 1961; MB, BS; *m* 1992 *Dr Hugh J Herzig (*see* BUXTON, Bt) and has issue:
1c +Jessica Angelica Rachel; *b* 1993
2b +Frances Mary Josephine; *b* 28 March 1963
3c +Julia Mary Blanche; *b* 1968
4c +Theresa Mary Bridget; *b* 1970
4a +Rosemary Isabel; *b* 21 Aug 1941; *m* 24 July 1965 *Antony Craven Chambers, Gren Gds, only surv s of Brig Samuel Craven Chambers, and has issue:
1b +Dominic Peter Craven [Dominic Chambers Esq, 1 Dorncliffe Rd, London SW6]; *b* 4 May 1966; *m* 1992 *Nicola Marina Merry, yst dau of Maj Hon Edward Renfric Arundell (*see* TALBOT OF MALAHIDE, B)
2b +Sebastian George Craven [Sebastian Chambers Esq, 12 Quilter St, Bethnal Green, London E2 7BT]; *b* 4 Sept 1967; *m* 1989 *Maria Mercedes, only dau of John Frederick Scrope (*see* SYKES, Bt, of Sledmere)
3b +Edmund Mungo Craven; *b* 1977
1b +Antonia Mary Craven; *b* 1974
2b +Alexandra Bridget Craven; *b* 1979
(5) David CONSTABLE-MAXWELL later TURVILLE-CONSTABLE-MAXWELL (1960), TD; *b* 28 June 1904; *educ* Ampleforth; Maj RA WW II; High Sheriff Leics 1958, Kt SMO Malta; *m* 29 April 1930 Alethea Mary Elizabeth Evelyn (*d* 29 Sept 1995), 2nd dau of Lt-Col Oswald Henry Philip Turville-Petre, of Bosworth Hall, Rugby (*see* PETRE, B), and *d* 1985, leaving:
1a +Robert John, DL (Leics 1994) [Robert Turville-Constable-Maxwell Esq DL, Bosworth Hall, Husbands Bosworth, Leics LE17 6LZ]; *b* 4 Oct 1933; *educ* Ampleforth; Lt Gren Gds 1952–54, High Sheriff Leics 1991–92; *m* 23 April 1960 *Susan Mary, only dau of Capt Stephen Francis Gaisford-St Lawrence, RN, of Howth Castle, Co Dublin (*see* MOSTYN, Bt), and has:
1b +Anthony Nicholas; *b* 6 Dec 1961; *educ* Ampleforth
2b +Stephen Bernard; *b* 15 Dec 1963; *educ* Ampleforth; *m* 16 May 1992 *Louise Anne, only dau of Alan Crossland, of Wychnor, Burton-onTrent, and has:
1c +Thomas William; *b* 8 April 1998
1c +Olivia Sarah; *b* 13 Jan 1995
2c +Kate Sophie; *b* 2 Sept 1996
1b +Alice Marion; *b* 1 Aug 1969
2a +Christopher Thomas [Kit Turville-Constable-Maxwell Esq, La Silonnière, 37240 Ciran, Indre et Loire, France; Garden Cottage, Itchen Stoke, Hants]; *b* 12 Oct 1940; *educ* Ampleforth; Lt Scots Gds 1958–62, FRGS; *m* 21 Sept 1963 *Lavinia Moira (Lyn), only dau of Hubert Arthur George Howard (*see* CARLISLE, E), and has issue:
1b +Simon Hubert; *b* 15 Oct 1965
2b +Gavin Herries; *b* 22 July 1967
1a Mary Belinda; *b* 2 Nov 1931; *m* 25 Aug 1951 (*divorce* 1976) 9th Earl of Carrick (*qv*) and *d* 1993, leaving issue
2a +Jennifer Mary [Mrs Christopher Newton, Manor Park, Ripe, E Sussex BN8 6AW]; *b* 23 March 1937; *m* 12 Sept 1970 *Christopher David Newton, TD, JP, only s of James Newton, of Warlingham, Surrey, and has issue:
1b +James Nicholas Turville; *b* 16 June 1971; *educ* Eton and London U (BA)
1b +Lucinda Rosalind Mary; *b* 23 April 1975
3a +Marcia Anne Helen [Mme Howard Tanner, Château de Cheseaux, 1033 Vaud, Switzerland]; *b* 27 July 1947; *m* 1st 27 Nov 1968 Sir Everard Radcliffe, 6th Bt (*qv*); *m* 2nd 1988 *Howard Montagu Stuart Tanner
(6) Andrew Bernard, MBE (1945), MC; *b* 31 Jan 1906; Lt-Col Scots Gds (Res) and Lt Lovat Scouts (TA) WW II; Kt SMO Malta; *m* 26 Feb 1949 *Militza, dau of Mark Kerkes, of USA, and *d* 1990, having had issue:
1a Mark; *b* 14 Nov, *d* 16 Nov 1951
1a +Andreina Philomena; *b* 1950
(7) +Michael Hugh, DSO (1944), DFC (1943) [Wing Commander Michael Constable Maxwell DSO DFC, Theobalds House, Old Park Ride, Waltham Cross, Herts EN7 5HX; Newton House, Kirkhill, Inverness-shire IV5 7PU]; *b* 3 June 1917; *educ* Ampleforth and Hertford Coll Oxford (BA 1939, MA 1943); Lt 4th Bn QO Cameron Highrs (TA) 1936, tfd to RAF 1939, W/Cdr 1943, WW II (Battle of Britain) and Netherlands E Indies 1945–46 (despatches), entered Novitiate of Ampleforth Abbey 1948, returned to RAF 1952, ret 1964; Kt SMO Malta 1961, memb Roy Co Archers; *m* 20 Jan 1962 *Susan Joan, only dau of W Trevor Davies, and has issue:
1a +Hugh Peter [Hugh Constable Maxwell Esq, 34 Rumbold Rd, London SW6 2HX]; *b* 16 May 1963; *educ* Ampleforth and Digby Stuart Coll Roehampton (BSc); *m* 5 Nov 1994 *Anna Maria, est dau of Giuseppe Cruciata, of St Alcamo, Sicily, and has:
1b +Julian Edward; *b* 10 Jan 1997

2a +Thomas Bernard [Thomas Constable Maxwell Esq, Ash Mount, Husthwaite, York]; *b* 1 Dec 1966; *educ* Ampleforth, Heythrop Coll and London U (BA); *m* 1992 *Alice Ellinor Mary, only dau of Jonathan Julian Cotterell (*see* CAMOYS, B), and has issue:

1b +Helena Mary; *b* 1993

2b +Theresa Maria; *b* 10 July 1977

(1) Mary Philomena; *b* 25 Dec 1893; *m* 9 Feb 1926 Maj Anthony Buxton, DSO, JP, DL (*see* BUXTON, Bt), and *d* 16 March 1953, leaving issue

(2) Margaret Mary Ethelreda (Marjorie); *b* 16 Oct 1897

(3) Winifride Mary (Oona); *b* 20 Dec 1898; *m* 19 April 1923 Capt Ronald Arthur Charteris Foster, Rifle Bde (*d* 22 June 1977), s of Phillip Foster, of Withyham, Sussex, and *d* 1994, leaving:

1a +David Philip [David Foster Esq, Wyndford Farm, Broxburn, W Lothian EH52 6NW]; *b* 1924; *educ* Ampleforth and Trin Coll Cambridge (BA); Capt RE; ARIAS; *m* 1969 *Margaret Helen, est dau of Ian Gordon Lindsay, OBE, and has issue:

1b +Ronald Ian; *b* 1972

2b +Peter John; *b* 1976

1b +Elizabeth Mary; *b* 1970; *educ* Aberdeen U (BEngrg)

2a +Giles Anthony; *b* 1927; *educ* Ampleforth and RAC Cirencester; Lt Rifle Bde

(4) Joan; *b* 22 March 1901; *m* 30 Dec 1930 Lt-Col Hon Henry George Orlando Bridgeman, DSO, MC (*see* BRADFORD, E), and *d* 1991, having had issue

(5) Elizabeth Mary; *b* 29 May 1907

(6) +Ursula Marcia [Mrs Chalmers Davidson, Farlie House, Beauly, Invernesshire]; *b* 5 Nov 1911; *m* 3 Dec 1960 *Chalmers Davidson, MB, ChB, FRCP (Edinburgh), late Maj RAMC, est s of John Chalmers Davidson, of Falkirk

5 Walter Constable; *b* 13 Aug 1849; Maj and Hon Lt-Col 4th Bn King's Liverpool Regt; *m* 24 Nov 1898 Henrietta Maria Arienwen (*d* 5 March 1922), dau of J A E Herbert, of Llanarth, and *d* 7 Dec 1925

1 Mary Anne; *m* 16 July 1884 her cousin Edmund Constable-Maxwell-Stuart and *d* 13 Dec 1941, leaving issue (*see* above)

The 10th LORD's est son,

MARMADUKE FRANCIS CONSTABLE-MAXWELL, **11th Lord Herries of Terregles**, DL (Dumfriesshire); *b* 4 Oct 1837; *educ* Stonyhurst; Ld Lt and Custos Rotulorum Kirkcudbrightshire and E R Yorks, Hon Col E R Yorks Imp Yeo, Hon LLD Leeds, *cr* 10 Nov 1884 BARON HERRIES OF CAERLAVEROCK CASTLE, Co Dumfries, AND OF EVERINGHAM, in the East Riding, Co York (UK); *m* 14 April 1875 Hon Angela Mary Charlotte Fitzalan-Howard (*d* 1 March 1919), 2nd dau of 1st Baron Howard of Glossop (*see* NORFOLK, D), and *d* 5 Oct 1908, leaving, with a yr dau (Angela Mary, *b* 10 Dec 1877, *m* 20 April 1904 16th Earl of Perth (*qv*) and *d* 24 April 1965, leaving issue):

GWENDOLEN MARY Constable-Maxwell, **Lady Herries of Terregles** in her own right; *b* 11 Jan 1877; Grand Cross Order Holy Sepulchre; *m* 15 Feb 1904, as his 2nd w, Henry FITZALAN-HOWARD, 15th Duke of Norfolk (*qv*), and *d* 28 Aug 1945, leaving:

BERNARD MARMADUKE FITZALAN-HOWARD, **13th Lord Herries** and 16th DUKE OF NORFOLK; *b* 31 May 1908; *m* 27 Jan 1937 Hon Lavinia Mary Strutt, CBE (1971) (*d* 1995), only dau of 3rd Baron Belper (*qv*), and *d* 30 Jan 1975, leaving issue:

1 ANNE ELIZABETH Fitzalan-Howard, **present Lady Herries of Terregles**

2 +MARY KATHARINE, DCVO (1995, CVO 1982) [The Lady Mary Mumford DCVO, North Stoke Cottage, North Stoke, Arundel, W Sussex BN18 9LS; Lantonside, Glencapel, Dumfries]; *b* 14 Aug 1940; heir presumptive; Ldy-in-Waiting to HRH PRINCESS ALEXANDRA, THE HON LADY OGILVY 1964–; *m* 1986 *G/Capt Anthony Mumford, CVO, OBE

3 +Sarah Margaret, DL (W Sussex) [The Lady Sarah Clutton DL, The Dover House, Poling, Arundel, W Sussex]; *b* 28 Sept 1941; *m* 1988, as his 2nd w, *Nigel Hugh Clutton, yr s of Robert John Clutton, of Rotherfield, Sussex

4 +(Theresa) Jane; *b* 24 Jan 1945; *m* 7 June 1975 *Earl of Ancram, est s of 12th Marquess of Lothian (*qv*), and has issue

HERSCHELL

Arms: Per fess az. and sa. a fasces fesswise between three stag's heads couped or. **Crest:** On a mount vert a stag ppr., gorged with a collar gemel az., the dexter forefoot supporting a fasces in bend or. **Supporters:** On either side a stag ppr. gorged with a collar gemel az. and standing on a fasces or. **Motto:** *Celeriter* ('Quickly').

Creation: B. (UK) 8 Feb 1886.

THE 3RD BARON HERSCHELL OF THE CITY OF DURHAM (Rognvald Richard Farrer Herschell) [The Rt Hon The Lord Herschell, Westfield House, Ardington, Oxon OX12 8PN]; *b* 13 Sept 1923; *s f* 1929; *educ* Eton; Page of Honour to TM GEORGE V 1935–36, EDWARD VIII 1936 and GEORGE VI 1937–40; Train Bearer Coronation 1937, Capt Coldstream Gds WW II, Coronation Medal; *m* 1 May 1948 *Lady Heather Mary Margaret Legge, only dau of 8th Earl of Dartmouth (*qv*), and has issue:

1 *Arabella Jane; *b* 20 Feb 1955; *m* 1984 *Brig John Panton Kiszely, late SG, and has issue:

(1) *Alastair; *b* 1986

(2) *Matthew; *b* 1987

(3) *Andrew; *b* 1990

Lineage: Rev RIDLEY HENRY HERSCHELL, of Gloucester Terrace, London; *m* Helen, dau of William Mowbray, of Edinburgh, and had, with other issue:

FARRER HERSCHELL, **1st Baron Herschell of the City of Durham** (UK), so *cr* 8 Feb 1886, GCB (1893), PC, QC, DL Kent and Durham; *b* 2 Nov 1837; barrister Lincolns' Inn 1860, Bencher 1872, Recorder Carlisle 1873–80, MP Durham 1874–85, Slr-Gen 1880–85, Ld Chllr 1886 and 1892–95, Chllr London U 1893, DCL, LLD; *m* 20 Dec 1876 Agnes Adela (*d* 23 Feb 1902), 3rd dau of Edward Leigh Kindersley Porcher, of Clyffe, Dorset, and *d* 1 March 1899, leaving:

1 RICHARD FARRER HERSCHELL, **2nd Baron Herschell of the City of Durham**, GCVO; Cdr RNVR, Ld-in-Waiting 1910–19 and 1924–29, Priv Sec to Ld Lt Ireland 1905–07, served WW I, Legn Hon, Kt Grand Cross Dannebrog Denmark; *b* 22 May 1878; *m* 1 Nov 1919 Annie Vera Violet (*d* 31 March 1961), dau of Sir Arthur Thomas Bennett Robert Nicolson, 10th Bt, of that Ilk and Lasswade (dormant; *see* 1959 edn, also CARNOCK, B), and *d* 14 Oct 1929, leaving issue:

(1) ROGNVALD RICHARD FARRER HERSCHELL, **3rd and present Baron Herschell of the City of Durham**

1 Helen Mowbray; *b* 20 June, *d* 30 Nov 1879

2 Agnes Freda, OBE (1920); DGStJ; *b* 9 Oct 1881; *m* 27 Nov 1912 1st Baron Forres (*qv*) and *d* 5 May 1942

3 Muriel Fanny; *b* 4 April 1883; *m* 4 Oct 1906 Brig-Gen Ralph Maximilian Yorke, CMG, DSO and *d* 26 Oct 1956, leaving issue (*see* HARDWICKE, E)

HERTFORD

Arms: Quarterly, 1st and 4th, sable, on a bend cotised argent, a rose gules between two annulets of the first (for CONWAY); 2nd and 3rd quarterly, 1st and 4th or, a pile gules, charged with three lions of England between six fleurs-de-lys azure; 2nd and 3rd, gules two wings conjoined in lure or (for SEYMOUR). **Crests:** 1 The bust of a Moor in profile couped at the shoulders proper and wreathed about the temples argent and azure (for CONWAY), 2 Out of a ducal coronet or a demi-phoenix in flames proper (for SEYMOUR). **Supporters:** Two Blackamoors proper, wreathed about the temples or and sable, habited in a short garment or and in buskins gold, adorned about the waist and shoulders with green and red feathers, each holding in his exterior hand an antique shield azure garnished or; the dexter charged with a sun in splendour gold; the sinister with a crescent argent. **Motto:** *Fide et amore* ('By faith and love'). **Creations:** B. (E) 17 March 1702/3 (Conway of Ragley) and (I) 16 Oct 1712 (Conway and Killultagh); E. (Hertford) and V. (GB) 3 Aug 1750; E. (Yarmouth) and M. (GB) 5 July 1793.

THE 9TH MARQUESS OF HERTFORD, Earl of Hertford, Earl of Yarmouth, Co Norfolk, **Viscount Beauchamp, Baron Conway of Ragley**, Co Warwick, and **Baron Conway and Killultagh**, Co Antrim (Henry Jocelyn Seymour [The Most Hon The Marquess of Hertford DL, Ragley Hall, Alcester, Warwicks B49 5NJ]; *b* 6 July 1958 (HRH THE DUKE OF KENT stood sponsor); *s* f 1997; *m* 1990 *Beatriz, dau of Jorge Karam, of Copacabana, Rio de Janeiro, Brazil, and has:

1 +WILLIAM FRANCIS, *Earl of Yarmouth*; *b* 2 Nov 1993

2 +A son; *b* 24 Jan 1995

1 *Gabriella Helen; *b* 1992

2 *Antonia Louisa; *b* 24 July 1998

Hertford, previous creations: Gilbert de Clare was created Earl of Hertford in 1138 by KING STEPHEN two years after inheriting the vast landed possessions of his father, who in turn was great-grandson of Godfrey, illegitimate son of RICHARD DUKE OF NORMANDY. Subsequently this 1st Earl of Hertford apparently supported the EMPRESS MAUD. His successor, a brother called Roger, is usually known as Earl of Clare but nevertheless seems to have inherited the Earldom of Hertford as well. (Meanwhile a younger branch of the family became Earls of Pembroke; *see* PEMBROKE and MONTGOMERY, E, preliminary remarks.) The 3rd Earl, Roger's son Richard, was likewise better known as Earl of Clare but is most celebrated for his part in the proceedings that led up to the issuing of the Magna Carta, of which he was one of the 25 baronial guarantors. He married Amice, ultimately sole heir of the Earls of Gloucester who descended illegitimately from HENRY I, and his and Amice's own descendants were known as Earls of Gloucester (see ROYAL FAMILY, section GLOUCESTER, D) and Hertford equally until the line died out when the 7th Earl was killed in battle at the Scottish victory over the English of Bannockburn in 1314.

The title of Earl of Hertford was revived over two centuries later for Edward Seymour, later 1st Duke of Somerset (*qv*), but was forfeited on his attainder in January 1551/2. His son was created Earl of Hertford anew in January 1558/9 and the latter's grandson, who inherited the Earldom, was promoted Marquess of Hertford in 1641, while the attainder affecting the Dukedom of Somerset (though not it would seem the 1537 creation of Earl of Somerset) was lifted in 1660. With the death in 1675 of the restored Duke of Somerset's younger son John, 3rd Duke of Somerset, the Marquessate of Hertford expired, but the Earldom of Hertford continued in the line of Dukes of Somerset who were his cousins till the death without surviving male issue of the 7th Duke in February 1749/50, when it too expired.

Conway, previous creations: Sir Fulke Greville, of Beauchamp's Court, Warwicks (*see* WARWICK, BROOKE and, E), had a daughter Helen who married Sir John Conway, of Ragley, Warwicks. Their son Edward Conway was created Baron Conway of Ragley in March 1624/5 and promoted Viscount Killult in March 1626/7 and a little later Viscount Conway of Conway Castle, both at a time when he was coming to the end of his stint as Secretary of State. His son and successor the 2nd Viscount married Frances, daughter of Sir Francis Popham and aunt of the Laetitia Popham who was mother of the **1st Baron Conway of Ragley** of the present creation (*see* below). On the death of their son the 1st and last Earl of Conway in 1683 the **1st Baron** inherited the Conway estates.

Lineage: FRANCIS SEYMOUR later SEYMOUR-CONWAY (1699), **1st Baron Conway of Ragley**, Co Warwick (GB), so *cr* 17 March 1702/3 (*see* SOMERSET, D), as also 16 Oct 1712 BARON CONWAY AND KILLULTAGH, Co Antrim (I), PC (I Feb 1727/8); *b* 28 May 1679; MP (Tory) Bramber 1701, Govr Carrickfergus 1728–32; *m* 1st 17 Feb 1703/4 Lady Mary Hyde (*d* 25 Jan 1708/9), 3rd dau of 1st Earl of Rochester (*see* CLARENDON, E), and had, with three other daus:

(1) Mary; *m* Nicholas Price, of Saintfield, Co Down, and *d* 1728, leaving issue

2 (cont.) The **1st Baron** *m* 2nd 1709 Jane Bowden, of Drogheda (*d* 13 Feb 1715/6), and by her had further issue (*d* unm); *m* 3rd July 1716 Charlotte (*d* 12 Feb 1733/4), dau of John Shorter, of Bybrook, Kent, and by her had, with other issue:

(1) FRANCIS, **1st Marquess**

(2) Henry, PC 1765; FM, Col RHG, MP Higham Ferrers 1741, cmded Br Forces Germany 1761, Sec of State Northern Dept; *bapt* 12 Aug 1719; *m* 19 Dec 1747 Caroline (*d* 17 Jan 1803), widow of 4th Earl of Elgin and 3rd Earl of Ailesbury (*see* AILESBURY, M) and dau of 4th Duke of Argyll (*qv*), and *d* 9 July 1795, having by her had issue:

1a Anne; *b* 8 Nov 1748; *m* 14 June 1767 Hon John Damer (*dvp* 15 Aug 1776), er s of 1st Earl of Dorchester, and *dsp* (*see* PORTARLINGTON, E)

The 1st BARON *d* 3 Feb 1731/2; his est son,

FRANCIS SEYMOUR-CONWAY, **1st Marquess of Hertford**, so *cr* 5 July 1793, as also EARL OF YARMOUTH, Co Norfolk, and earlier 3 Aug 1750 VISCOUNT BEAUCHAMP and EARL OF HERTFORD (all GB), with special remainder, failing heirs male of his body to his bro, Henry, KG (1757), PC (I 1749/50, E 1763); *b* 5 July 1718; *educ* Eton; Ld Lt: Warwicks 1757–94, Ireland 1765–66 and Montgomeryshire 1775–76, Amb Paris 1763–65, Ld Chamberlain 1766–82, Master Horse Sept–Nov 1766; *m* 29 May 1741 Lady Isabella FitzRoy (*d* 10 Nov 1782), yst dau of 2nd Duke of Grafton (*qv*), and *d* 14 June 1794, having had, with six daus:

1 FRANCIS SEYMOUR-CONWAY later SEYMOUR-INGRAM (roy licence 18 Dec 1807), **2nd Marquess of Hertford**, KG (1807), PC (I 1765, GB 1780); *b* 12 Feb 1743; *educ* Eton and Ch Ch Oxford; MP (I Parl) Lisburn 1761–68 and Antrim 1768–76, (GB Parl, Tory) Lostwithiel 1766–68 and Orford 1768–94, Ch Sec to his f as Ld Lt Ireland 1765–66, a Ld Treasury 1774–80, Ld Chamberlain 1812–21, Ld Lt and custos rotulorum Warwicks 1816–22, Govr Co Antrim; *m* 1st 4 Feb 1768 Alice Elizabeth (*dsp* 11 Feb 1772), yst dau and coheir of 2nd Viscount Windsor (*see* PLYMOUTH, E); *m* 2nd 20 May 1776 Hon Isabella Anne Ingram Shepheard, est dau of 9th Viscount Irvine, and *d* 17 June 1822, having by her had issue:

(1) FRANCIS CHARLES SEYMOUR-CONWAY, **3rd Marquess of Hertford**, KG (1822), GCH (1819), PC (1612); *b* 11 March 1777; MP (Tory) Orford 1797–1802, Lisburn 1802–12, Co Antrim 1812–18 and Camelford 1820–22, Warden Stannaries 1812–42, Recorder of Coventry and Bodmin, Ch Steward and V-Adml Duchy Cornwall; generally recognised as the model for Thackeray's Marquess of Steyne; *m* 18 May 1798 Maria Emily (*d* 2 March 1856, nominally dau of the Marchese Fagnani by his w, allegedly a ballet dancer, but reckoned by contemporaries to have been the dau by the Marchesa of the Duke of Queensberry (*see* QUEENSBERRY, M), though her adoptive f, the dandy George Selwyn, considered her to be by him), and *d* 1 March 1842, having had issue:

1a RICHARD SEYMOUR-CONWAY, **4th Marquess of Hertford**, KG (1846); Capt 22nd Dragoons; *b* 22 Feb 1800; MP (Tory) Co Antrim 1822–26; *dspl* unm 25 Aug 1870, leaving by Agnes Wallace:

1b Sir RICHARD WALLACE, 1st and last Bt (UK), so *cr* 1866, KCB; *b* 26 July 1818; inherited from his f the assemblage of pictures gathered by the latter; these were bequeathed by Sir RICHARD's widow to the nation and make up the Wallace Collection in Manchester Sq, London; *m* 1871 Julie Amelie Charlotte, dau of Bernard Castelnau, and *dsp* 20 July 1890, when the btcy expired

2a Henry; *b* 10 Jan 1805; *d* Aug 1859

1a Frances Maria; *m* Feb 1822 Marquis de Chevigné and *d* Nov 1822

2 Henry, of Norris Castle, IoW, Jt Clerk Crown and Hanaper, King's Bench, Ireland; *b* 15 Dec 1746; *d* 5 Feb 1830

3 Robert; MP, Jt Clerk Crown and Hanaper, King's Bench, Ireland; *b* 20 Dec 1748; *m* 1st 15 June 1773 Anne (*d* 29 Nov 1804), dau of Peter Delmé; *m* 2nd 2 May 1806 Anderlechtia Clarissa (*dsp* 3 June 1855 aged 90), dau of 4th Viscount Chetwynd (*qv*), and *d* 23 Nov 1831, leaving by his 1st w issue:

(1) Henry; Serjeant-at-Arms H of C; *m* 1 July 1800 Emily (*d* 3 Sept 1824), 4th dau of 4th Viscount Torrington (*qv*), and *d* 13 Feb 1843

(1) Elizabeth; *m* 1st 10 Dec 1805 William Griffith Davies (*d* 4 July 1814), of Penlan, and had issue; *m* 2nd May 1817 Maj Herbert Evans (*d* 1848), of Highmead, Caernarvonshire

(2) Frances Isabella; *m* 2 Dec 1802 2nd Baron Southampton (*qv*) and *d* 3 June 1838, leaving issue.

(3) Anna Maria; *d* unm

(4) Gertrude; *m* 12 Nov 1812 John Hensleigh Allen, JP, DL (*d* 9 April 1843), of Cresselly, Pembs, and *d* 3 Jan 1825, leaving issue

4 Edward; Canon Ch Ch Oxford; *d* unm 1785

5 Hugh; Adml RN; *b* 1759; *m* 2 April 1786 Anne Horatio (*d* 12 June 1801), 3rd dau of 2nd Earl Waldegrave (*qv*), and *d* 11 Sept 1801, leaving, with other issue:

(1) George Francis (Sir), GCH, GCB; Adml the Fleet; *b* 17 Sept 1787; *m* Feb 1811 Georgiana Mary (*d* 1878), dau of Adml Hon Sir George Cranfield Berkeley, GCB (*see* BERKELEY, B), and *d* 20 Jan 1870, having had issue:

1a FRANCIS GEORGE HUGH, **5th Marquess**

2a Henry George, CB; V-Adml, MP Co Antrim, a Ld Admlty; *b* 20 March 1818; *m* 4 Sept 1861 Sophia Margaret (*d* 16 May 1917), er dau of Derick Hoste, of Barwick House, Norfolk, and *d* 26 July 1869, having had issue:

1b George Hoste; Lt 14th Hus; *b* 28 June 1862; *k* by lightning at Secunderabad India 28 May 1885

2b Charles Derick, of Barwick House, Norfolk, JP, DL; BA Cantab, Lt-Col TFR cmdg Norfolk Yeo; *b* 26 Aug 1863; *m* 28 Nov 1903 Mina (*d* 20 March

1950), widow of Maj Antonio Stephen Ralli (*see* RALLI, Bt) and dau of Andrew Scaramanga, and *d* 22 April 1935

1b Alexandra Georgina, OBE (1920); *m* 6 June 1893 Sir Ian Murray Heathcoat-Amory, 2nd Bt (*qv*), and *d* 28 Oct 1942, leaving issue

2b Emily Augusta; *m* 21 April 1891 Edward Lewis Birkbeck (*d* 12 Oct 1901) and *d* 14 June 1960 age 93, leaving issue

3b Horatia Anne; *d* 28 May 1919

3a William Frederick Ernest, KCVO; granted with surv siblings rank of marquess's dau/yr s 7 Feb 1871; Gen, Col Coldstream Gds, Midshipman RN, served Baltic 1854, Crimea 1856 and Egypt 1882, Lt Tower London 1902–05; *b* 8 Dec 1838; *m* 31 Aug 1871 Hon Eva Anna Caroline Douglas-Pennant (*d* 3 Jan 1934), 7th dau 1st Baron Penrhyn (*qv*), and *d* 9 Feb 1915, having had issue:

1b Edward Noel; *b* 25 Dec 1878; *d* 26 Jan 1880

1b Mabel Louisa; *m* 5 Sept 1914 Capt Wynyard Keith Brown, 5th Gurkha Rifles FF (*ka* Dardanelles 4 June 1915), son of Col F D M Brown, VC, and *d* 27 March 1951, leaving issue

2b Hazel Georgina; *m* 5 Jan 1905 Col Edward Campbell Loch, OBE, of Durtnells, Kemerton, Glos, and *d* 24 Nov 1920, leaving issue

3b Dorothy Nina; RRC, a Woman of the Bedchamber to HRH PRINCESS CHRISTIAN, WW I with VAD BRCS, WW II as Jr Cdr ATS 1939–42, Hon Sec SSAFA Dorset 1942; *m* 16 Dec 1919 Gen Sir Henry Cholmondeley Jackson, KCB, CMG, DSO (*d* 19 Oct 1972 aged 93), of West House, Piddletrenthide, Dorchester, and *dsp* 7 Jan 1953

4b Mary Freda; *m* 29 April 1919 Capt David Henry Loch (*d* 3 Sept 1941) and *d* 20 Nov 1968, leaving issue

1a Georgina Isabella; *m* 22 July 1844 Charles Corkran (*d* 1885), of Long Ditton, and *d* 4 Dec 1848, leaving issue

2a Horatia Louisa; *d* 1829

3a Emily Charlotte; *m* 10 Sept 1850 2nd Baron Harlech (*qv*) and *d* 10 Jan 1892, leaving issue

4a Matilda Horatia; *m* 22 Sept 1886 Lt-Col Cecil Rice, 72nd Highrs (*d* May 1917), of Kingscote House, Sussex, and *dsp* 11 March 1916

5a Laura Williamina; *cr* by ERNST II DUKE OF SAXE-COBURG-GOTHA 14 Jan 1861 COUNTESS Von GLEICHEN, with remainder to the heirs male of her body; *m* 26 Jan 1861 Adml HSH PRINCE VICTOR OF HOHENLOHE-LANGENBURG (*d* 31 Dec 1891), having resumed in 1886 the name of Hohenlohe-Langenburg in lieu of Count Gleichen, and *d* 13 Feb 1912, leaving issue:

1b (Albert) Edward Wilfred, KCVO, CB, CMG, DSO; Extra Equerry to TM GEORGE V 1910–36, EDWARD VIII 1936 and GEORGE VI 1937, Maj-Gen Gren Gds, attd Egyptian Army 1901–03, Mil Attaché Berlin 1903–06, Washington 1906–07, Assist Dir HQ 1907–11, cmdg 15th Inf Bde Irish Cmd 1911–14 and France 1914–15, Maj-Gen cmdg 37th Div 1915–16, served Sudan, Dongola, S Africa and WW I (despatches), Extra Equerry to TM QUEEN VICTORIA and EDWARD VII, KGStJ, Cdr Legion of Honour, Order Medjidie 2nd Cl, Dannebrog 1st Cl; *b* 15 Jan 1863; *m* 2 July 1910 Hon Sylvia Gay Edwardes, Maid of Honour to TM QUEENs VICTORIA and ALEXANDRA (*see* KENSINGTON, B), relinquished with his w and sisters German titles and was granted rank of marquess's dau/yr s by roy warrant 12 Sept 1917, and *d* 14 Dec 1937

1b Feodora Georgina Maud; *b* 20 Dec 1861; *d* unm 22 Feb 1922

2b Victoria Alice Leopoldine Ada Laura; *b* 28 Nov 1868; *m* 5 Dec 1905 Lt-Col Percy Wilfrid Machell, CMG, DSO (*ka* 1 July 1916), of Crakenthorpe Hall, Appleby, Westmorland, and *d* 10 Sept 1951, leaving issue

3b Helena Emily, OBE (1920); painter, FSA, DGStJ, Italian Bronze Medal for Valour; *b* 1 Feb 1873; *d* unm 28 Jan 1947

(2) Hugh Henry; Lt-Col; *b* 25 Sept 1790; *m* 14 May 1818 Charlotte Georgiana (*d* 24 June 1828), only dau of 1st Marquess of Cholmondeley (*qv*), and *d* 2 Dec 1921, leaving issue:

1a Hugh Horatio; *b* 15 Sept 1821; *m* 4 Nov 1846 Georgiana (*d* 12 Oct 1907), dau of Gen Robert Ellice, and *d* 4 Dec 1892, leaving issue:

1b Hugh Francis, JP Herts; *b* 23 Dec 1855; barrister; *m* 15 April 1884 Rachel Blanche (*d* 4 Nov 1946), dau of Rev Hon James Walter Lascelles (*see* HAREWOOD E) and *d* 14 June 1930, having had issue:

1c Horace James (Sir), GCMG (1946), CVO (1936); entered FO 1908, 2nd Sec Washington 1919, 1st Sec The Hague 1923, Rome 1925, FO 1927, Counsellor of Embassy 1929, Pncpl Priv Sec to For Sec 1932–36, Envoy Extrdy and Min Plen Teheran 1936–39, Assist U-Sec FO 1939–42, Amb China Feb 1942–June 1946, on Franco-Siamese Boundary Commn Washington, DC, April–July 1947, Ch UK Delegn on Balkans Commn, Salonika, Dec 1947; *b* 26 Feb 1885; *educ* Eton and Trin Coll Camb; *m* 9 April 1917 Violet Amy (*d* 11 Aug 1996), dau of Thomas Edward Erskine (*see* BUCHAN E), and *d* 8 Sept 1978, having had:

1d +Hugh Francis [Hugh Seymour Esq, Luccombe Mill, Bratton, Westbury, Wilts]; Lt KRRC WW II; *b* 14 Dec 1926; *educ* Eton and Trin Coll Camb; *m* 14 Aug 1954 *Mary Elizabeth, dau of Thomas Hunter Roberts, of Pucklechurch House, nr Bristol, and has issue:

1e +(Hugh) James [James Seymour Esq, 67 Eaton Terr, London SW1]; *b* 10 March 1956; *educ* Downside; *m* 1986 Felicity Anne (*d* 1993), dau of P H Webber, of Jincox Farm, Oxted, Surrey, and has:

1f +Hugo Frederick James; *b* 1988; *m* 1996 *Anya Susannah, dau of M W Hindmarch, of Danbury, Essex

2f +Rupert Alexander Erskine; *b* 1992

1f *Octavia Claire Camac; *b* 1990

2e +Julian; *b* 11 April 1961

3e +Francis Benedict; *b* 14 Dec 1966

1e *Charlotte; *b* 10 July 1957

2e *Sarah Catherine; *b* 20 Sept 1962

1d Jane; *d* 15 Aug 1918

2d *Virginia [Mrs William Young, The Old Bakery, Kimpton, Andover, Hants]; WW II as 3rd Offr WRNS *m* 1st 26 Jan 1945, as his 2nd w, Sir Ivo Herbert Evelyn Joseph Stourton CMG, OBE (*see* MOWBRAY, SEGRAVE and STOURTON, B); *m* 2nd 1986 *William Hilary Young, CMG, and by her 1st husb has issue

3d *Joan [Mrs Clive Thompson, 97 Forbes Rd, Orange, NSW, Australia]; WW II as Sect Offr WAAF; *m* 27 Oct 1945 F/Lt Clive Gordon Thompson (*d* 1969), DFC and bar, RAAF, and has issue:

1e *Anthony Seymour; *b* 1946

2e *Nicholas Austen; *b* 1948

3e *Jeremy; *b* 1950

2c Francis; Lt 7th Bn KRRC; *b* 30 May 1886; *m* 21 Dec 1914 Lady Barbara Ann Bootle-Wilbraham (*d* 31 Oct 1949), dau of 2nd Earl of Lathom (*see* SKELMERSDALE, B), and was *ka* 30 July 1915

1c Mabel; *d* unm 21 July 1973

2c Kathleen Georgiana; *d* unm 29 May 1946

3c (Mary) Gwendolen; VAD; *d* unm 18 Sept 1974

1b Charlotte Susan; *m* 27 May 1879 Charles Walter Campion (*d* 18 March 1926) and *d* 5 Aug 1948

(3) Horace Beauchamp (Sir), KCH; Col, MP; *b* 22 Nov 1791; *m* 1st 15 May 1818 Elizabeth Malet (*d* 18 Jan 1827), dau of Sir Lawrence Palk, 2nd Bt (*see* 1940 edn); *m* 2nd 2 July 1835 Frances Isabella, (*d* 29 Aug 1875) widow of 18th Baron Clinton (*qv*), and *d* 23 Nov 1851, leaving by his 1st w:

1a Charles Francis; Capt and Lt-Col Scots Fus Gds; *b* 13 Sept 1819; *k* at Inkerman 5 Nov 1854

2a FREDERICK BEAUCHAMP PAGET SEYMOUR, 1st and last BARON ALCESTER, of Alcester, Co Warwick (UK), so *cr* 24 Nov 1882 , GCB; entered RN 1834, Adml 1882, Priv Sec to 1st Ld Admlty 1868–70, cmded detached Sqdn 1870–72, a Ld Admlty 1872–74, cmded Channel Sqdn 1874–77 and Mediterranean Sqdn 1880–83, a Ld Admlty 1883–85, ADC to HM QUEEN VICTORIA; *b* 12 April 1821; *d* unm 30 March 1895, when the Barony expired

1a Adelaide Horatia Elizabeth; *m* 9 Aug 1854 4th Earl Spencer (*qv*) and *d* 29 Oct 1877, leaving issue

(4) Frederick Charles William; *b* 1 Feb 1797; *m* 1st 15 April 1822 Lady Mary Gordon (*d* 13 June 1825), dau of 9th Marquess of Huntly (*qv*), and had issue:

1a Conway Frederick Charles; Gentleman Usher of the Privy Chamber 1878–1901, FO Messenger 1859–1900, Capt 85th Regt; *b* 25 March 1823; *d* 1 May 1914

1a Mary Frederica, VA (3rd cl); Maid of Honour and Hon Woman Bedchamber to HM QUEEN VICTORIA; *m* 16 Feb 1857 Gen Sir Thomas Myddelton Biddulph, PC, KDB (*d* 28 Sept 1878), and *d* 23 Oct 1902, leaving issue

(4) (cont.) Frederick Seymour *m* 2nd 18 Sept 1832 Lady Augusta Hervey (*d* 17 March 1880), est dau of 1st Marquess of Bristol (*qv*), and *d* 7 Dec 1856, having by her had issue:

2a Frederick Horace Arthur; Maj -Gen Rifle Bde; *b* 9 Nov 1836; *d* 25 March 1914

3a Arthur Laurence Hervey; *b* 1838; *d* 1859

4a Horace Alfred Damer, KCB (1902, CB 1898), BA Cantab, Priv Sec to PM , a Commr Customs 1885–90, Dep Chm 1890–94, Dep Master of the Mint 1894–1902; *b* 9 April 1843; *m* 17 Feb 1880 Elizabeth Mary, Medaille de la Reine Elisabeth (*d* 17 April 1950 aged 97, having been granted by roy warrant 15 Sept 1902 rank of kt's widow, it having been intended to kt her husb when he d), dau of Col Frederick Romilly (bro of 1st Baron Romilly, *see* 1970 edn), and *d* 25 June 1902, leaving issue:

1b Ralph Frederick, CMG (1919), DSO (1916); Cdr RN WW I (despatches), Russian Order St Anne 3rd Cl with swords, Cdr Order Redeemer of Greece; *b* 6 Jan 1886; *d* 4 Oct 1922

2b Leopold Robert; WW I as Pte 31st Bn Canadian Expeditionary Force (wounded); Dept Pensions and Nat Health Canada; *b* 30 April 1888; *educ* Marlborough; *m* 23 April 1914 Mary Elizabeth (*d* Sept 1955), dau of Thomas Frayer; *m* 2nd *Henrietta Margaret Cynthia, dau of Gerald Arthur

1b Horatia Augusta Elizabeth; *d* unm 11 Nov 1966

2b Mary Gertrude, JP Co London; *m* 1 June 1904 2nd Viscount Mersey (*qv*) and *d* 1 May 1973, leaving issue

3b Cynthia Charlotte, MBE (1920); *m* 11 July 1923 Sir Milne Cheetham, KCMG (*d* 6 Jan 1938), son of J Milne Cheetham, of Eyford Park, Glos, and *d* 8 Aug 1968

4b Margaret Lily Winifred; *b* 1891; *m* 14 June 1916 Maj Cecil Francis Aleck Walker, MC, Gren Gds (*d* 27 Jan 1925), and *d* 17 May 1976

2a Eliza Horatia Frederica; Extra Ldy Bedchamber to HM QUEEN VICTORIA; *m* 1st 23 Sept 1861 3rd Viscount Clifden (*see* 1970 edn); *m* 2nd 12 Oct 1875 Col Sir Walter G Stirling, Bt, and *d* 23 April 1896, leaving issue

3a Augusta Georgiana Sophia; *m* 2 Feb 1860 Lord Charles Bruce (*d* 16 April 1897), yst s of 1st Marquess of Ailesbury (*qv*), and *dsp* 10 Feb 1901

4a Charlotte Frances Frederica, VA; *m* 8 July 1858 5th Earl Spencer (*qv*) and *d* 31 Oct 1903

(1) Horatia Maria Frances; *m* 1814 John Philip Morier, UK Min Dresden, and *d* 26 Aug 1853, leaving issue (*see* SOMERSET, D)

(2) Mary Georgiana; *m* 1825 Rt Hon George Lionel Dawson Damer (*see* PORTARLINGTON, E) and *d* 30 Oct 1848

6 William; *b* 29 April 1759; *m* 10 Nov 1798 Martha (*d* 6 July 1848), dau of James Clitherow, of Boston House, Mddx, and *d* 31 Jan 1837, leaving issue:

(1) Edward; *b* 1801; *d* 15 Dec 1853

(2) Henry, JP Bucks and Surrey; *b* 29 Nov 1802; Army Capt; *m* 16 Aug 1831 Jane, yst dau of Thomas Willan, of Twyford Abbey, Middx, and *d* 19 April 1867, having had issue

7 George; *b* 21 July 1763; *m* 20 July 1795 Isabella, dau of Rev Hon George Hamilton (*see* ABERCORN, D), and *d* 10 March 1848, leaving issue:

(1) George Hamilton (Rt Hon Sir), GCB, GCH, PC; Envoy Extrdy and Min Plen Austria; *b* 21 Sept 1797; *m* 21 July 1831 Gertrude (*d* 30 Aug 1883), dau of 21st Baron Dacre (*qv*), and *d* 2 Feb 1880, having had issue:

1a Arthur Henry; 2nd Sec Dip Serv 1861–75; *b* 25 Aug 1838; *d* unm 27 Sept 1910

2a Leopold Richard; Lt-Col Gren Gds; *b* 2 June 1841; *m* 5 July 1871 Mary Hubbard (*m* 2nd 18 July 1906 1st and last Baron Portsea (*d* 1 Nov 1948; *see* 1940 edn), and *d* 27 Feb 1942), dau of Russell Sturgis, and *d* 30 May 1904, leaving:

1b Conway Russell; *b* 24 June 1874; *m* 27 May 1897 Louisa Mary (*d* 28 March 1944), dau of Gen J A Street, CB, and *dsp* 22 Jan 1958

2b Richard Sturgis, MVO (1909); Dip Serv, Envoy Extrdy and Min Plen Siam 1919–22 and Bolivia 1924–25, author: *Rhyme Unreasoned* and *Shaded Candles*; *b* 21 Sept 1875; *educ* Eton and Magdalen Coll Oxford; *m* 20 April 1911 Lady Victoria Alexandrina Mabel (*d* 23 Nov 1969), sis of 10th Duke of Grafton (*qv*), and *d* 21 April 1959, leaving:

1c +Leopold (Leo) Richard [Leopold Seymour Esq, 2 Pembroke Gardens, London W8]; High Sheriff Herts 1964, Capt Gren Gds WW II; *b* 23 Sept 1912; *m* 13 June 1940 *Sheila, dau of Col Arnold Charles Paul Butler, CBE, of Carters Hill, Therfield, Royston, Herts, and has issue:

1d +Hugh Leopold [Hugh Seymour Esq, Home Farm, Stobo, Peebles, Scotland]; *b* 2 July 1943; *educ* Eton and Magdalene Coll Cambridge (BA 1965, MA 1969); *m* 1st 6 Jan 1971 (*divorce* 1978) Emma Mary, only dau of Robert Henderson (*see* LOWTHER, Bt); *m* 2nd 31 May 1979 *Camilla Madelaine Gerard, yr dau of Col William Henry Gerard Leigh (*see* LESLIE, Bt), and by her has:

1e *Molly Rose; *b* 3 Aug 1983

2d +Charles Richard; *b* 21 Nov 1955; *educ* Eton; *m* 1994 *Henrietta Margaret Cynthia, dau of Gerald Arthur Hobler (*see* STUCLEY, Bt), and has:

1e +A son; *b* 23 April 1997

1d *Anthea Rosemary [The Hon Mrs David Bigham, Hurston Place, Pulborough, W Sussex]; *b* 1 July 1941; *m* 2 Jan 1965 *Hon David Edward Hugh Bigham, 2nd s of 3rd Viscount Mersey (*qv*), and has issue

2d *Sarah Victoria Frances [Mrs William Ducas, 194 Village Ave, Dedham, Mass, USA]; *b* 27 June 1952; *m* 1979 *William Jay Ducas, son of Robert Ducas and Mrs Jean Weir Ducas, of Quaker Hill, Pawling, NY, USA, and has issue:

1e *Benjamin Colin; *b* 1981

2e *Patrick Leopold; *b* 1983

3e *William Alexander; *b* 1988

3d *Lavinia Sheila; *b* 8 July 1954; *m* 21 May 1977 *John Norman Gerard Leigh, er s of Col William Henry Gerard Leigh, MVO, of Bartlett House, Holyport, Maidenhead (*see* above)

2c George FizRoy, JP, DL Notts; High Sheriff 1966; 60th Rifles 1941–42 (invalided); *b* 8 Feb 1923; *educ* Winchester; Ld Manor Thrumpton; *m* 1 June 1946 *Hon Rosemary Nest Scott-Ellis [The Hon Mrs Seymour, Thrumpton Hall, Notts NG11 0AX; 25 Wimpole St, London W1], yst dau of 8th Baron Howard de Walden (*qv*), and *d* 1994, leaving:

1d +Thomas Oliver; *b* 20 Oct 1952; *educ* Radley; *m* 1989 *Sally Ward, dau of Henry P Coolidge, of Lincoln, Mass., and has:

1e +Edward Alexander; *b* 1992

2e +William; *b* 1994

1e *Charlotte Emily; *b* 1990

1d *Miranda; *b* 8 Aug 1948; *m* 1st 25 Oct 1972 (*divorce* 1986), as his 2nd w, Andrew Annadale Sinclair (*see* MELCHETT, B); *m* 2nd 1989 *Anthony John Gottlieb, s of Felix Gottlieb, of London, and by her 1st husb has:

1e *Merlin George; *b* 25 Oct 1973

1c *Alexandra Victoria [Mrs Samuel Gurney, Heggatt Farm House, Horstead, Norfolk]; *b* 24 May 1914 (HM QUEEN ALEXANDRA stood sponsor); *m* 16 Dec 1939 Capt Samuel Edmund Gurney (*d* 1990), TD, 3rd s of Sir Eustace Gurney, of Walsingham Abbey, Norfolk, and has had issue:

1d Timothy Samuel; *b* 1940; *educ* Radley and Magdelene Coll Cambridge; *k* in a motor accident 1962

2d *Richard Eustace Thomas [Richard Gurney Esq, Heggatt Farm House, Horstead, Norfolk]; *b* 1943; *educ* Radley and RAC Cirencester; *m* 1977 *Margaret Elizabeth Diana, dau of Stephen William Agnew (*see* AGNEW, Bt, of Gt Stanhope St), and has:

1e *Henry Robert Timothy; *b* 1980

2e *Oliver Samuel; *b* 1983

1e *Isabel Margaret; *b* 1979

2e *Richenda Victoria Amelia; *b* 1986

1d *Jane Mary Alexandra [Mrs Simon Macfarlane, Whitehouse Farm, Rackheath, Norfolk NR13 6LB]; *b* 1948; *m* 1970 *Simon Warren Macfarlane and has:

1e *Thomas Edward Hastings; *b* 1972

1e *Louisa Alexandra; *b* 1974

2e *Alice Victoria; *b* 1979

3b Edward (Sir), KCVO, DSO, OBE; Maj Gren Gds, Comptroller to HRH THE DUCHESS OF ALBANY 1908, GSO(2) 1916, Equerry to HM QUEEN ALEXANDRA 1923–25, Comptroller to HRH PRINCESS VICTORIA 1925–35, extra Equerry to TM GEORGE V 1935, EDWARD VIII 1936 and GEORGE VI 1937–48, served Nile Expdn 1898 (medal with clasp), Boer War 1900–02 (wounded, medal) and WW I (despatches); *b* 10 Feb 1877; *m* 29 July 1905 Lady Blanche Frances Conyngham (*d* 11 Feb 1956), est dau of 4th Marquess Conyngham (*qv*), and *d* 28 Feb 1948, leaving:

1c John Edward; Maj Gren Gds WW II (wounded), ADC to Govr Bengal 1941–42; *b* 18 Oct 1915; *educ* Eton; *m* 14 Aug 1940 *Elizabeth Norah [Mrs John Seymour, Edgedell Cottage, Martyr Worthy, Winchester, Hants], only child of Adml Hon Sir Hubert Brand, GCB, KCMG, KCVO (*see* HAMPDEN, V), and *d* S Africa 16 March 1972, leaving:

1d +Conway John Edward [Lt-Col Conway Seymour, 41 Lime Grove, London W12 8EE]; Lt-Col Gren Gds (ret 1992); *b* 13 May 1941; *educ* Eton and RMA Sandhurst; *m* 1st 10 July 1969 (*divorce* 1980) Elizabeth, dau of Maj Francis Holdsworth Hunt (*see* FORESTER, B), and has issue:

1e +Harry Edward; *b* 17 Feb 1971

1e *Arabella Elizabeth; *b* 22 Aug 1974

1d (cont.) Lt-Col Conway Seymour; *m* 2nd 1981 *Diana Elizabeth, dau of Michael Gibb, of Forge House, Taynton, Oxon, and formerly w of Hon Trevor Garro Trefgarne (*see* TREFGARNE, B), and has by her:

2e *Emily Diana; *b* 1982

2d +Richard Hubert [Richard Seymour Esq, Dell House, Chilland Lane, Martyr Worthy, Hants SO21 1EB]; *b* 17 Jan 1947; *educ* Milton Abbey; *m* 1982 *Amanda Claire, yr dau of Ian McAuslan Hardie and has issue:

1e +James Richard Edward; *b* 1985

1e *Sarah Kathleen; *b* 1987

1c Verena Mary; *b* 24 May 1906; *m* 30 Jan 1932 (*divorce* 1945) Lt-Col Robert Harry Doyne, Oxond and Bucks, LI (*d* 5 Oct 1965), only s of Maj Robert Wentworth Doyne, JP, DL, of Towcester, Northants, and *d* 2 July 1979, leaving issue

4b Beauchamp; Maj KRRC Boer War 1899–1902 (medals with five clasps) and WW I (severely wounded); *b* 6 Oct 1878; *educ* Eton and Magdalen Coll Oxford; *m* 12 April 1928 Eva Douglas (*d* 24 Dec 1949), 2nd dau of Rev Herbert Brown, of St Lawrence, Southminster, Essex, and *d* 20 Jan 1965, leaving issue:

1c +Julian Conway [Julian Seymour Esq, Waterdale House, E Knoyle, Salisbury, Wilts SP3 6BL]; *b* 11 May 1934; *educ* Eton; *m* 1st 15 July 1958 (*divorce*) Alexandra, only dau of Douglas MacLeod, of Stratton, Dorset, and has:

1d +Leopold Conway; *b* 17 Feb 1959

2d +Mark Hamilton; *b* 5 July 1960; Lt RN; *m* 1989 *Louise, est dau of W T Whittingham

1c (cont.) Julian Seymour *m* 2nd 7 Jan 1971 *Lavinia Margaret, er dau of Sir William Lawrence, 4th Bt, of Ealing Park (*qv*), and by her has:

3d +Harry William; *b* 30 Sept 1974

1d *Camilla Jane; *b* 22 March 1973

1c *Jane Mary Naomi [Mrs Jane Scarr, 3 Forge Close, Benson, Oxon]; *b* 13 Oct 1929; *m* 8 Jan 1954 (*divorce* 1976) Maj Desmond Eric Renforth Scarr, 14th/20th King's Hus, and has issue:

1d *Edward Desmond Renforth; *b* 28 April 1958

1d *Susan Renforth; *b* 26 July 1956; *m* 1989 *Richard Hamill and has:

1e *Matthew; *b* 7 June, 1990

2d *Sarah Anne Renforth; *b* 9 July 1960; *m* 1997 *Richard Berry

2c *Anne Victoria [Mrs Henry Porter, Brockham, Birlingham, nr Pershore, Worcs]; *b* 13 Oct 1929 (twin); *m* 28 July 1951 *Maj Henry Robert Mansel Porter, MBE, KRRC, 60th Rifles, Palestine 1946–48, High Sheriff Worcs 1970, est s of Lt-Col Henry Colin Mansel Porter, DSO, KRRC, and has:

1d *Henry Christopher Mansel; *b* 23 March 1953; *educ* Wellington and Manchester and Perugia Us; ed *Illustrated London News* 1987–89, jnlst with *Evening Standard* 1979–81, *Sunday Times* 1981–83, *Independent on Sunday* 1990–91; has by *Elizabeth Mary Elliot:

1e *Miranda Victoria ELLIOT; *b* 30 Oct 1985

2e *Charlotte Mary Clementine ELLIOT; *b* 22 Oct 1988

2d *Michael Beauchamp Mansel; *b* 9 July 1954; *educ* Wellington; *m* 1989 *Elizabeth, dau of Maj George Hadshar, KHS, of Woburn Sands, Beds

5b Lionel, OBE (1919); barrister; *b* 24 Feb 1889; *m* 28 Oct 1909 Catherine Moore Docking (*d* 28 Aug 1932), only dau of William Wooding, of Rugby, and *d* 11 May 1931

1b Mildred; *b* 14 Aug 1872; *d* unm 28 Aug 1930

2b Ethel; *b* 17 Jan 1881; *m* 23 May 1910 Maj Sir Eric Henry Bonham, 3rd Bt, CVO (*qv*), and *d* 7 Sept 1962, leaving issue

3a Alfred; Lt Rifle Bde; *b* 16 Feb 1843; *m* 20 April 1870 Jessie Madeleine (*d* 17 Jan 1926), dau of Hon William Macdougall, CB, of Toronto, and *d* 30 Jan 1897, leaving issue:

1b George; Hon Attaché at Tangier; *b* 10 May 1871; *dsp* 19 April 1899

2b Ralph; Lt 3rd Hus; *b* 3 March 1875; *d* 17 Dec 1916

3b Claude, DSO (1916); V-Adml (ret), served WW I (despatches twice); *b* 17 March 1876; *m* 18 June 1919 Auriel Dorothy, only dau of Richard Quin, and *dsp* 2 Dec 1941

4b Hugh; *b* 5 March 1877

5b Vere; Lt RNR; *b* 14 June 1879; *ka* 7 March 1916

6b Guy; *b* 1888; *d* young

1b Maud; *m* 15 Nov 1901 Col Herbert Mayow Fisher-Rowe, CBE, DL, Surrey Yeo (*d* 18 Jan 1938), of Thorncombe, Bramley, Surrey, and *d* 26 Nov 1959, leaving issue

2b Ruth; *m* 19 Oct 1909 Leopold George Arthur Collins (*d* 21 July 1947), and *d* 23 Nov 1959, leaving issue

4a George Evelyn; *b* 15 Nov 1848; *m* 3 Dec 1874 Evelyn Elizabeth (*m* 2nd Philip Barnett, of Yewden Manor, Henley-on-Thames, and *d* 22 Sept 1929), dau of Archibald J Campbell, of Belgravia, and *d* 11 Aug 1884, leaving:

1b Archibald George, DSO (1917), MVO 4th Cl (1921); Col 10th Hus, Lt-Col 2nd Dragoons, Hon Brig-Gen 1924, served Boer War 1899–1901 (despatches, medal with four clasps) and WW I (despatches); *b* 21 Sept 1875; *m* 30 April 1907 Ellen Mary (*d* 16 Aug 1973 aged 96), yst dau of R Corfield Bucknall, and *d* 30 Dec 1933, leaving issue:

1c Archibald Kenneth; *b* 26 Feb, *d* 2 Aug 1908

2c (Evelyn) Roger, OBE (1946), TD; Lt-Col RA (TA) WW II; *b* 26 Feb 1908 (twin); *m* 31 March 1936 *Rosemary Evelyn [Mrs Roger Seymour, Sakins, Roydon, Harlow, Essex], er dau of Maj Horace John Flower, DSO, MC, 60th Rifles, and *d* 1987, leaving issue:

1d +(Archibald) John [John Seymour Esq, Longfield, Ledburn, Beds LU7 0QB]; 10th Hus 1957–58; *b* 29 Aug 1937; *educ* Eton; *m* 10 Oct 1961 *(Lavinia Mary) Louis, 2nd dau of Christopher York, DL, of South Park, Long Marston, York, and has:

1e *Charlotte Louise; *b* 14 April 1963

2e *Susanna Clare [Mrs James Fletcher, Stragglers Lodge, Heyford Rd, Caulcott, Oxon OX6 3ND]; *b* 24 Sept 1966; *m* 1993 *James E Fletcher and has:

1f *George Arthur John; *b* 3 Nov 1995

3e *Melinda Nell; *b* 7 Sept 1969

2d +Julian Roger [Julian Seymour Esq, 37 Surrey Lane, London SW11 3PA]; *b* 19 March 1945; *educ* Eton; *m* 1984 *Diana Daniels and has:

1e +Archie Christopher; *b* 1989

1e *Rose Elizabeth; *b* 1987

3c Christopher George; Maj 10th Hus, WW II with 23rd Hus (wounded, despatches); *b* 14 Aug 1913; *educ* Radley; *m* 6 May 1940 *Honor [Mrs Christopher Seymour, Pamplins, Bentley, Farnham, Surrey], dau of Capt Cecil Leatham, of Redbourn House, Wentworth, and *d* 1983, leaving:

1d +(Christopher) Mark [Mark Seymour Esq, The Mill House, Fintry, Stirlingshire, Scotland]; *b* 10 Sept 1942; *educ* Eton and RNC Dartmouth; Lt RN; *m* 16 April 1968 *Carol Daphne, yr dau of Peter Pitman, of Muirfield Gate, Gullane, E Lothian and has issue:

1e +Thomas Mark Middleton; *b* 19 May 1972

2e +Peter Christopher James; *b* 2 Jan 1977

1e *Katherine Louise; *b* 21 June 1970

1d *Penelope Jane [Mrs Neil Kennedy, 27 Fisher Rd, Bishops Itchington, Warwicks CV33 0RE]; *b* 17 April 1944; *m* 1st 28 Sept 1966 (*divorce* 1974) (Robert Alexander) Neon Reynolds, s of F Neon Reynolds, FRCS Ed, of Mellow, Loxwood, Sussex, and has issue:

1e *Alexander Seymour; *b* 1969

1d (cont.) Mrs Penelope Reynolds *m* 2nd 1979 *Neil James Kennedy and has by him:

2e *Patrick; *b* 1978

1e *Lisa; *b* 1979

2b Reginald Henry (Sir), KCVO; Lt-Col KRRC, Equerry to TM GEORGE V 1916–36 and QUEEN MARY 1936–38, Boer War 1900–02 (wounded) and WW I (wounded); *b* 1 Aug 1878; *m* 1st 17 July 1922 Winifred (*d* 12 Dec 1925), formerly w of Lt-Col Harold Boyd-Rochfort, DSO, MC, and only dau of John Bathurst Akroyd, of Birdingbury Hall, Rugby, and had issue:

1c +George Raymond, CVO (1990, LVO 1972), DL (Berks 1992) [Maj George Seymour CVO DL, The Old Vicarage, Bucklebury, Reading, Berks; Appletrees, Swains Rd, Bembridge, IoW]; *b* 5 May 1923; *educ* Eton; Maj KRRC, High Sheriff Berks 1989, served WW II and Palestine (despatches), Train Bearer Coronation 1937, Page of Honour to TM GEORGE V 1935–36, EDWARD VIII 1936 and GEORGE VI 1937, Extra Equerry to HM QUEEN ELIZABETH THE QUEEN MOTHER 1956, Equerry 1984–, Assist Private Sec and Equerry to HM QUEEN ELIZABETH THE QUEEN MOTHER 1993–; *m* 9 Sept 1957 *Hon Mary Quenelda Stanley, widow of Robert Mervyn FitzFinnis and 3rd dau of Gen 1st and last Baron Ismay, KG, GCB, CH, DSO, PC (*see* 1956 edn), and has issue:

1d *Katharine Margaret Lucy; *b* 15 Dec 1959 (HRH PRINCESS MARGARET, COUNTESS OF SNOWDON stood sponsor); *m* 1983 *Hon John Edward Richard Harbord-Hamond, 2nd s of 11th Baron Suffield (*qv*)

2b (cont.) Sir Reginald Seymour *m* 2nd 6 Aug 1930 Lady Katharine Hamilton (*d* 1985), DCVO (1961), Extra Woman Bedchamber to HM QUEEN ELIZABETH THE QUEEN MOTHER, yst dau of 3rd Duke of Abercorn (*qv*), and *d* 2 Oct 1938, leaving by her:

2c +Henry Charles; Page of Honour to TM GEORGE VI 1949–52 and HM THE QUEEN 1952–53, served KRRC 1955–58; *b* 9 Oct 1936; *educ* Eton; *m* 1st 7 April 1960 (*divorce* 1965) Yolande, 2nd dau of Richard B Murray, of Banhoek, Stellenbosch, S Africa; *m* 2nd 19– *Alexandra Mary Hilda, dau of Maj Sir Victor Basil John Seely, 4th Bt (*qv*), and by her has had:

1d Conway Seely Reginald; *b* 14 Oct 1968; *d* 1980

1c *Mary Virginia; *b* 27 May 1932

2c Elizabeth Cynthia; *b* 2 July 1934; *d* following an accident 9 Jan 1954

3b Charles Evelyn; Capt Scots Greys WW I (despatches, Legn Hon); *b* 1882; *m* 1st 3 June 1909 Gladys Edith Muriel (*d* 18 Jan 1913), only dau of Walter Henry Hadow, of The Priory, Sudbury; *m* 2nd 25 March 1919 Eugenie Sybil (*d* 1 Nov 1950), widow of (a) Lt-Col Maxmillian David Wood, DSO, W Yorks Regt, and (b) Capt Dermot Howard Blundell-Hollinshead-Blundell, MVO, KRRC, and est dau of William Hunble Dudley Ward (*see* DUDLEY, E), and *d* 5 Jan 1943, leaving by his 1st w:

1c Michael Henry; WW II with Roy Fus (POW), memb London Stock Exchange 1931–39; *b* 21 July 1912; *m* 5 April 1950 *Dorothy Mary, formerly w of Raymond Harding Dean and 2nd dau of Henry Arthur Dennis, of Overhill Road, Dulwich, and *d* 19 Jan 1978

1a Augusta Emily; *m* 27 Dec 1860 2nd Baron Delamere (*qv*) and *d* 25 Feb 1911, leaving issue

2a Gertrude Frances; *m* 28 July 1864 Lt-Col James Frederick Dudley Crichton Stuart and *d* 2 Dec 1909, leaving issue (*see* BUTE, M)

3a Isabella; *d* unm 18 Feb 1925

1 Isabella Horatia; *m* 9 Nov 1820 1st Earl of Ravensworth of Ravensworth Castle and *d* 5 Aug 1856, leaving issue (*see* RAVENSWORTH, B)

2 Emily Henrietta; *m* 28 May 1832 4th Earl of Shannon (*qv*) and *d* 1 Dec 1887, leaving issue

The 4th MARQUESS's cousin,

FRANCIS GEORGE HUGH SEYMOUR, **5th Marquess of Hertford**, GCB (1879), PC (1874), DL (Warwicks); *b* 11 Feb 1812; *educ* Harrow; Gen 1876, Equerry to HRH THE PRINCE CONSORT 1846–58 and HM QUEEN VICTORIA 1858–70, Ld Chamberlain 1874–79, Dep Ranger Windsor Gt Park; *m* 9 May 1839 Lady Emily Murray (*d* 24 June 1902), dau of 3rd Earl of Mansfield (*qv*), and had issue:

1 HUGH DE GREY, **6th Marquess**

2 Albert Charles; Col Scots Gds; *b* 24 April 1847; *m* 22 June 1872 Sarah (*d* 30 April 1901), only child of Capt John Moore Napier (*see* NAPIER and ETTRICK, L), and *d* 24 March 1891, leaving issue:

(1) Charles Hugh Napier, DSO (1916); Lt-Col KRRC, Boer War 1899–1902, WW I (wounded, despatches) and NW Frontier India 1920; *b* 11 Nov 1874; *m* 31 Oct 1905 Mary Adelaide (*d* 12 Oct 1977), dau of William Morton Phillips, DL (*see* COURTOWN, E), and *d* 15 March 1933, leaving:

1a +William Napier [Maj William Seymour, Park House, Shaftesbury, Dorset]; *b* 8 Sept 1914; *educ* Eton; FRICS 1966, Maj Scots Gds WW II (despatches), Palestine 1936 and 1946, Burma 1941–42 and Malaya 1948; *m* 28 April 1945 *Rachel Mary, dau of Capt Angus V Hambro (*see* HAMBRO, B) and has:

1b *Carolyn Sarah [Mrs Simon Hanbury, Casa Nirvana, La Mortola, 18030 Ventimiglia, Italy]; *b* 21 March 1946; *m* 15 April 1967 *Simon Thomas Cecil Hanbury, The Life Gds (*d* 30 May 1997), est s of Capt Thomas Francis Jeune Hanbury, MC, of Downs House, Wantage, and has issue:

1c *Jonathan Cecil; *b* 1977

1c *Serena Mary; *b* 1970

2c *Melissa Jane; *b* 1971

2b *Sarah Jane; *b* 3 Oct 1947; *m* 1974 *Richard David O'Mahony Page, of Rathcon, Co Wicklow, and has issue:

1c *Dermot Michael; *b* 1976

1c *Patricia Hannah; *b* 1978

2c *Arabella Jennifer; *b* 1980

3b *Arabella Mary [Mrs Christopher Elwes, The Old Rectory, Checkendon, Oxon]; *b* 1 Jan 1952; *m* 8 Feb 1973 *Christopher Julian Elwes, yr s of Capt Robert Philip Henry Elwes, MBE, MC, of Ennistown, Kilmessan, Co Meath, and has:

1c *Rupert William; *b* 1975

2c *James Rex; *b* 1983

1c *Charlotte Vanda; *b* 1983

(2) William Walter; Col Rifle Bde, Hon Brig-Gen 1928, served WW I (despatches, Brevet, Chevalier Legn Hon), NW Frontier India 1919 and WW II; *b* 28 Nov 1878; *m* 8 Aug 1906 Muriel (*d* 29 Sept 1946), widow of Alfred Corkran Campbell and dau of Lt-Col C Walter Campbell, of Hampton Court, and *d* 12 July 1940, leaving issue:

1a Hugh Wilfred Napier; Lt Rifle Bde WW II; *b* 1 Oct 1917; *ka* June 1942

1a *Jane; *b* 18 Sept 1907; *m* 28 Oct 1933 *Michael Arther Unwin-Heathcote, er son of Maj Arthur Unwin-Heathcote, and has issue

2a Pamela; *b* 12 Dec 1908; *m* 10 June 1939 R-Adml Bryan Cecil Durant, CB, DSO, DSC, and *d* 4 Aug 1963, leaving issue

(3) Edward Victor Francis; Capt 9th Hodson's Horse, IA; *b* 5 Aug 1887; *m* 1 Feb 1915 Grace Florence Harriette, dau of Travers John Hubert Blackley, and *d* 16 April 1927, leaving issue

1a *Jane; *b* 27 July 1917; *m* 30 Oct 1951 (Charles) Christopher Short, s of Charles Wilkins Short, of Cincinnati, Ohio, by Countess Camilla Hoyos, and has issue:

1b *Camilla Jane; *b* 13 July 1953

2b *Marguerite Grace; *b* 9 July 1956

(1) Violet Cecilia Georgina; *b* 27 Oct 1876; *d* 12 Aug 1877

3 Ernest James, JP Warwicks and Worcs; Capt and Hon Maj Warwicks Yeo Cav Sub-Lt RN; *b* 10 May 1850; *m* 26 Sept 1877 Lady Georgiana Seymour Fortescue (*d* 24 Dec 1915), dau of 3rd Earl Fortescue (*qv*), and *d* 23 Jan 1930, leaving:

(1) Francis Ernest; Cdr RN WW I; *b* 7 Oct 1878; *d* unm 21 May 1952

(2) Reginal Guy; Capt and Adj Roy N Devon Yeo Hus, Hon Capt Army, Boer War 1900–01 (wounded, despatches) and WW I (wounded); *b* 15 Jan 1880; *d* unm 4 Jan 1965

(3) Arthur George, DSO (1915); Capt RN Mesopotamia WW I; *b* 19 Oct 1884; *m* 19 Feb 1930 Elizabeth Patricia (*d* 1957), widow of Lennox James Zeederbert, of Cape Town, and dau of Peter McKeand, of Airlies, Wigtownshire, and *d* 22 July 1935

(1) Ruth; *b* 16 June 1881; *m* 5 Oct 1911 Bertram Edward Petre and *d* 23 Aug 1976, leaving issue (*see* PETRE B)

(2) Eleanor Alice; *b* 22 June 1883; *d* unm 30 Aug 1975

(3) Constance Emily Mary; *b* 6 May 1887; *das* 12 Feb 1917

4 Victor Alexander (Rev); Rector Carshalton 1884–1901, Vicar St Stephen's S Kensington, 1901–29; *b* 6 March 1859 (HM QUEEN VICTORIA stood sponsor); *educ* Ch Ch Oxford (MA); *m* 23 Sept 1885 Elizabeth Margaret (*d* 8 June 1858), est dau of Albemarle Cator, of Woodbastwick Hall, Norfolk, and *d* 7 Aug 1935, leaving issue:

(1) Conway Hugh, MC; Maj Scots Gds WW I (wounded twice); *b* 27 July 1886; *m* 8 Jan 1916 Kathleen (*d* 2 Dec 1950), dau of Lt-Col Francis John Paul Butler, late 18th Hus, of Wyck Hill, Glos, and *d* 20 Oct 1931, leaving issue:

1a +Adrian John Conway [Col Adrian Seymour, Wantsley Farm, Broadwindsor, Dorset]; WW II (despatches), Lt-Col cmdg Scots Gds 1962–64; *b* 11 June 1918; *educ* Radley and Ch Ch Oxford (MA); *m* 14 Feb 1953 *Elizabeth Ann, only child of Lt-Gen Sir Edwin Otway Herbert, KBE, CB, DSO, and has issue:

1b *Virginia Kathleen [Mrs Alexander Rottenburg, 14 Sugden Rd, London SW11 5EF]; *b* 8 Oct 1955; *m* 1983 *Alexander Theodore Terence Rottenburg and has:

1c *William Alexander Seymour; *b* 1986

1c *Charlotte Elizabeth Virginia; *b* 1988

2b Angela Mary; *b* 19 Aug 1957; *d* 1979

2a +Francis Hugh; *b* 18 June 1922; *educ* Radley; *m* 31 Dec 1951 Helen Elizabeth (*d* 1986), yr dau of Rev Canon David John Cornish, of Ontario, and has:

1b +William Thomas; *b* 24 Feb 1955; *m* 1984 *Cindy Linda Marie, dau of Christian Murray, of Chicoutimi, Quebec, and has issue:

1c *Gillian Nathalie Elizabeth; *b* 1987

2c *Hilary Roseline; *b* 1990

1b *Margaret Louise; *b* 8 Oct 1953; *m* 1986 *George William Boldick, of Surrey, BC, Canada

(2) William John; Cdr RN, ADC to Govr-Gen of Australia, served WW I and WW II; *b* 7 April 1900; *m* 9 Sept 1930 Wilma (*d* 1987), MA, dau of W J Clarke, of Toorak, Australia, and *d* 5 March 1967, leaving:

1a +Conway William Hugh [Conway Seymour Esq, 43 Officers Parade, Condobolin, NSW 2877, Australia]; *b* 30 June 1934; *educ* Geelong GS; *m* 22 May 1959 *Susan Evizel, only dau of Ronald Robert Richard McKay, of Birch Street, Coonabarabran, NSW, and has issue:

1b +Conway Ronald Hugh; *b* 19 Feb 1962

1b *Susan Kristin; *b* 24 Dec 1960

2b *Jane Evizel; *b* 11 July 1965

1a *Sarah Gardenia [Miss Sarah Seymour, Flat 2, 579 Toorak Rd, Toorak 3142, Vict, Australia]; *b* 14 March 1939

(1) Jane; *b* 18 March 1890; *m* 1st 15 June 1912 Louis Edwin William Egerton, Capt Bucks Yeo (*ka* 1 Aug 1917), 2nd s of Sir Alfred Mordaunt Egerton, KCVO, CB, and had issue; *m* 2nd 11 July 1921 Maj Arthur Roland Ernest Wilberforce, DD, Bp Chichester (*d* 19 March 1955)

(2) Mary; *b* 17 Nov 1893; *d* 25 April 1899

(3) Anne Christian; *b* 30 Nov 1896; *m* 1st 8 Nov 1920 Capt Cajetan Louis Victor Marno, London Regt (*d* 18 June 1930); *m* 2nd 25 Sept 1934 Victor Frederick Engleheart (*d* 4 June 1949), yst s of Sir John Gardner Dillman Engleheart, KCB, and by her 1st husb had issue:

1a John Seymour; *b* 25 Oct 1921; Capt Irish Gds; *educ* Felsted; *m* 25 Sept 1943 *Diana Helen [Mrs John Marno, Scotts House, Hunton, Maidstone, Kent], dau of Capt Henry Christian Dunell, RA, of Ryarsh Place, West Malling Kent, and *d* 1988, leaving issue:

1b *Peter Cajetan Seymour; Lt RCT; *b* 12 Feb 1948; *educ* Lancing; *m* 1981 *Felicity Jayne, dau of Cdre T R Fisher, RAN, of Sydney, NSW, and has:

1c *Edward Christian Seymour; *b* 1983

1c *Alice Jane Thorburn; *b* 1986

1b *Julian Mary Christian; *b* 14 June 1945

2a Edward Charles; Rifle Bde; *b* 17 Aug 1923; *m* 17 Dec 1947 (*divorce* 1957) Joan Chrysogon, dau of Brig Edward William Drummond Vaughan, CB, DSO, MC, of White Knights, Newick, Sussex, and *d* 1988, leaving:

1b *Phyllida Jane [Mrs Christopher Cornfield, 55 Temple Sheen Rd, London SW14 7QF]; *b* 14 Feb 1951; *m* 1981 *Christopher William John Cornfield

3a *William Victor [William Marno Esq, Ty Watty, Rhandirmwyn, Llandovery, Dyfed]; late Capt RA ; *b* 26 Nov 1925; *m* 1st 15 July 1952 (*divorce* 1968) Daphne Christobel, dau of Douglas Doyle Jones, and has issue:

1b *Nicholas Douglas; *b* 21 July 1961

1b *Madeleine Sarah; *b* 18 Feb 1954

2b *Denise Barbara; *b* 20 July 1955

3b *Alison Jane; *b* 3 July 1958

3a (cont.) William Marno *m* 2nd 24 Jan 1969 (*divorce* 1979) Hazel Dorothy, dau of Stanley Westley; *m* 3rd 1983 *Clare Linette Mordaunt and by his 2nd w has issue:

4b *Lowri; *b* 1973

1 Frederica Georgina; *d* 12 Jan 1848

2 Horatio Elizabeth; *m* 26 June 1861 Sir Henry David Erskine, KCVO, and *d* 16 April 1922, leaving issue (*see* BUCHAN, E)

3 Florence Catherine; Maid of Honour to HM QUEEN VICTORIA; *m* 23 July 1872 Rev James St John Blunt (*see* BLUNT, Bt), and *d* 7 May 1921

4 Georgina Emily Lucy; Order of Queen Elisabeth of Belgium; *m* 23 Jan 1877 Lt-Col Henry Edward Stirling Home Drummond, JP, DL, Scots Gds (*dsp* 16 May 1911), of Blair Drummond, and *d* 22 July 1944

5 Constance Adelaide; *m* 2 Nov 1871 Lt-Col Frederick St John Barne, Scots Gds (*d* 25 Jan 1898), of Sotterley Park, and *d* 30 Nov 1915, leaving issue

6 Mary Margaret; *m* 12 Aug 1875 Sir George John Egerton Dashwood, 6th Bt, of Kirtlington Park (*qv*), and *d* 29 Dec 1948, leaving issue

The 5th MARQUESS *d* 25 Jan 1884; his est son,

HUGH DE GREY SEYMOUR, **6th Marquess of Hertford**, CB (1906), TD, PC (1879), JP (Co Antrim); *b* 22 Oct 1843; MP (C) Co Antrim 1869–74 and S Warwicks 1874–80, Comptroller Householder 1879–80, ADC to TM EDWARD VII 1902–10 and GEORGE V 1910–12, Ld Lt and custos rotulorum Warwicks, Pres Warwicks TFA, V-Chm CC, Tstee and Govr Rugby Sch, Hon Col cmdg Warwicks Yeo, Capt Gren Gds; *m* 16 April 1868 Hon Mary Hood (*d* 6 April 1909), 2nd dau of 1st Viscount Bridport (*qv*), and *d* 23 March 1912, having had issue:

1 GEORGE FRANCIS ALEXANDER SEYMOUR, **7th Marquess of Hertford**, JP, DL Warwicks; Lt Warwicks Yeo and 3rd Bn Black Watch; *b* 20 Oct 1871; *m* 27 April 1903 (*annulled* 1908) Alice Cornelia, dau of William Thaw, of Pittsburgh, and *dsp* 16 Feb 1940

2 Henry Charles, DSO (1916) and bar (1918); Ld Lt Warwicks, Col Gren Gds, Hon Brig-Gen 1930, Col 68th (S Midland) Field Bde 1934 and Warwicks Yeo 1937, served Boer War (wounded twice, despatches, Brevet, Legn Hon); *b* 18 May 1878; *m* 10 Nov 1915 Lady Helen Frances Grosvenor (*d* 21 Oct 1970), yst dau of 1st Duke of Westminster, KG (*qv*), and *d* 18 June 1939, leaving issue:

(1) HUGH EDWARD CONWAY SEYMOUR, **8th Marquess of Hertford**, DL (Warwicks 1959); *b* 29 March 1930; *educ* Eton; Lt Gren Gds; *m* 10 July 1956 *Countess Pamela Terese Louise de Caraman-Chimay, only child of Lt-Col Prince Alphonse de Chimay, TD (*see* ABERCORN, D), and *d* 22 Dec 1997, leaving:

1a HENRY JOCELYN SEYMOUR, **9th and present Marquess of Hertford**

1a *Carolyn Mary; *b* 30 Sept 1960

2a *Diana Helen; *b* 10 Dec 1963; sales coordinator The Reel Thing, blood sports outfitters; *m* 1992 * Timothy Verdon, chartered surveyor

3a *Anne Katherine; *b* 26 May 1966

(1) Margaret Katharine, DCVO (1971, CVO 1953), Ldy-in-Waiting to HRH PRINCESS ELIZABETH 1947–52, Woman of the Bedchamber to HM THE QUEEN 1953–75; *b* 9 May 1918; *m* 22 April 1948 Sir (Alan) Philip Hay, KCVO, yst son of Alan Hay, of Chetcombe House, Mere, Wilts, and *d* 24 May 1975, leaving issue:

1a *Edward Philip Gerald; *b* 22 Dec 1949 (HM THE QUEEN and HRH PRINCESS MARINA, DUCHESS OF KENT, stood sponsors); Page of Honour to HM THE QUEEN 1964–66; *educ* Harrow

2a *Andrew Nicholas John; *b* 10 Oct 1951; *educ* Eton; *m* 1977 *Virginia, dau of Mark Coats (*see* MAR and KELLIE, E) and has issue

3a *Simon Henry Peter; *b* 23 Nov 1955 (HRH PRINCESS ALEXANDRA stood sponsor); *educ* Eton

3 Edward Beauchamp, of Erindale, Ontario, Canada; Trooper Lord Strathcona's Horse, Boer War 1900–01 (wounded) and WW I; *b* 22 Nov 1879; *m* 23 May 1914 Elfrida Adelaide (*d* 10 Nov 1965), dau of Sigismund Cathcart de Trafford (*see* DE TRAFFORD, Bt), and *d* 5 Dec 1917 of wounds recd in action

4 George Frederick; Cdr RN; *b* 2 Sept 1881; *m* 12 July 1906 Norah (*d* 23 Sept 1959), only dau of Archibald Payton Skipwith (*see* SKIPWITH, Bt), and *d* 30 Oct 1940, leaving issue:

(1) Paul de Gray Horatio; S/Ldr RAF WW II; *b* 16 May 1911; *m* 16 Oct 1937 *Hilary Mary (*m* 2nd 22 Dec 1948 Ian Hamilton Barrett (*d* 1985), s of James Arthur Samuel Barrett, of Redbraes, Peebles), dau of Douglas Ernest Crickmay, OBE, of Little Green, Kirkella, Hull, and was *ka* on air operations Nov 1942, leaving issue:

1a +Andrew Conway Paul; *b* 1 Nov 1939; *educ* Stowe; A/Cdre RAF 1963; *m* 31 Oct 1964 *June Ann, est dau of Frederick A Gardner, of Long Itchington, Warwicks, and has issue:

1b *Elizabeth Jane; *b* 1972

(2) George Victor, MC; Lt-Col Roy Scots Fus WW II (wounded); *b* 5 Aug 1912; *m* 3 Aug 1946 Hilda Elizabeth (*d* 1986), formerly w of Maj Peter Mant MacIntrye Kemp and dau of Capt Harold Lionel Phillips (*see* PHILLIPS, Bt), and *d* 12 July 1953, having had issue:

1a +Nicholas George Mark [Nicholas Seymour Esq, 15 Cargill Rd, London SW18 3ED]; *b* posthumously 26 Oct 1953; *educ* Clayesmore; *m* 1978 (*divorce* 1981) Nicola Clare, dau of Walter William Burgoyne Chalwin (*see* O'BRIEN, Bt)

1a Georgina; *b* 28 Feb; *d* 1 March 1951

(3) Frank Hugh; Lt RN WW II; *b* 5 Dec 1919; *ka* July 1944

(1) Edith Patricia Mary; *b* 24 Sept 1913; *m* 23 Nov 1933 (*divorce* 1972, resumed maiden name by deed poll 25 Jan 1972) Rev Emmanuel Casdagli, est s of Theodore Emmanuel Casdagli, of Cairo, and had:

1a *David Seymour Emmanuel [David Casdagli Esq, c/o Midland Bank, Cornhill, Dorchester, Dorset]; *b* 27 Sept 1934; *educ* Harrow; *m* 2 Oct 1965 *Christine Ethne, only child of Brig Harry H Cottier, of Rottingdean, and has:

1b *Christopher Charles David; *b* 1975

(1) (cont.) Mrs Edith Seymour also adopted:

*Susan Margaret [Mrs Michael Gilligan, St Anthony's, Rousden, Lyme Regis, Dorset DT7 3XP]; *b* 7 Jan 1946; *m* 1970 *Michael Gilligan and has issue:

1b *Liam Patrick; *b* 1978

2b *Dominic Francis; *b* 1980

3b *Arran Thomas; *b* 1982

*Celia Jane; *b* 18 Feb 1948; *m* 1970 (*divorce* 1977) John de Wageneer

1 Margaret Alice; *b* 22 March 1869; *m* 10 Nov 1892 James Hainsworth Ismay (*d* 24 Jan 1930), and *d* 18 Aug 1901, leaving issue

2 Emily Mary; *b* 4 Aug 1873; *m* 10 Sept 1895 Rev Reginald Edmund Walker (*d* 23 Aug 1945), Rector Frant, Sussex, and *d* 7 Nov 1948, leaving issue (*see* WALKER, Bt, of Sand Hutton)

3 Victoria Frederica Wilhelmina Georgina; *b* 20 Oct 1874; *m* 29 May 1900 Lt-Col Charles Alan Cathcart de Trafford, Royal Warwickshire Regt (*d* 9 May 1950), son of John Randolphus de Trafford and *d* 23 April 1960, leaving issue (*see* DE TRAFFORD, Bt)

4 Jane Edith; *b* 1 April 1877; *m* 11 Aug 1904 Maj Hugh Dudley Carleton, DSO (*d* 9 Aug 1906), and had issue

Seat: Ragley Hall, Alcester, Warwicks. The house was originally designed in the late 17th century by Robert Hooke, who in the versatile spirit of that age was chiefly a scientist rather than architect; indeed Ragley is the only example of his work in the latter field. He had been commissioned by the Earl of Conway, whose family owned the estate, and although the entrance front has had a late-18th-century portico imposed on it by Wyatt, to which a double-set of steps surmounted by a terrace form the base (the work of John Tasker some hundred years later), the overall appearance is still predominantly Restoration-Williamite. Around the time of the Wyatt addition to the centre-front elevation the demolition took place of a pair of wings, separate from the main block though designed to form a single group to the eye.

Inside there are a billiard room and study decorated by James Gibbs, a Wyatt-designed dining room, saloon and drawing room and — the gem of the entire house internally — the hall, with its colourful and ornate plasterwork, the creation overall again of Gibbs. On the wall above the more southerly of the two staircases, both thought to have been late Victorian installations, is an early-1970s mural by Graham Rust depicting the **8th Marquess** and members of his family.

HERVEY-BATHURST

Arms: Quarterly, 1st and 4th, sable two bars ermine, in chief three crosses patée or (for BATHURST); 2nd and 3rd, gules on a bend argent three trefoils slipped vert, a martlet for difference (for HERVEY). **Crests:** 1 A dexter arm embowed habited in mail holding in the hand, all proper, a spiked club or (for BATHURST), 2 A leopard passant sable, bezantée collared and lined or, holding in the dexter paw a trefoil slipped vert (for HERVEY). **Mottoes:** 1 *Tien ta foy* ('Hold thy faith') (for BATHURST), 2 *Je n'oublieray jamais* ('I will never forget') (for HERVEY). **Creation:** Bt. (UK) 7 Dec 1818.

SIR (FREDERICK) JOHN CHARLES GORDON HERVEY-BATHURST, 7TH BT, of Lainston, Hants [Sir John Hervey-Bathurst Bt, Somborne Park, King's Somborne, Hants SO20 6QT]; *b* 23 April 1934; *s f* 1995; *educ* Eton and Trin Coll Cambridge (BA 1957); Lt Gren Gds (Res); *m* 7 Dec 1957 *Caroline Myrtle, only dau of Sir William Randle Starkey, 2nd Bt (*qv*), and has issue:

1 +FREDERICK WILLIAM JOHN [Frederick Hervey-Bathurst Esq, Somborne Park, King's Somborne, Hants SO20 6QT]; *b* 18 Sept 1965; *m* 27 April 1991 *Annabel Peta, yr dau of Donald Warburg, of Zurich, and has:

(1) +Frederick Benjamin Guy; *b* 9 March 1998

(1) *Eleanor Maryse; *b* 15 Aug 1995

1 *Louisa Caroline [Lady Portal, Burley Wood, Ashe, Basingstoke, Hants RG25 3AG]; *b* 25 Sept 1959; *m* 9 Oct 1982 *Sir Jonathan Portal, 6th Bt (*qv*)

2 *Sophia Selina Irene [Mrs Henry Colthurst, Asserton House, Berwick St James, Wilts SP3 4TZ]; *b* 28 April 1961; *m* 5 June 1982 *Henry Nicholas Almroth Colthurst, s of Sir Richard Colthurst, 9th Bt (*qv*)

Lineage: The Hon FELTON HERVEY (7th s of 1st Earl of Bristol (*see* BRISTOL, M) by his 2nd w); *b* 12 Feb 1711/2; *m* Dorothy (*d* 8 Nov 1761), dau of Solomon Ashley and widow of Charles Pitfield, and *d* 18 Aug 1773, leaving, with three daus:

FELTON LIONEL HERVEY; Lt RHG; *m* 2 March 1779 Selina Mary (*m* 2nd 21 Sept 1797 Sir William Henry Fremantle, GCH, PC (*see* COTTESLOE, B), and *d* 22 Nov 1841), only dau and heir of Sir John Elwell, Bt (by Selina, dau of Peter Bathurst and widow of the last Earl of Ranelagh), and *d* 9 Sept 1785, having had, with other issue:

1 Sir FELTON ELWELL HERVEY later HERVEY-BATHURST (roy licence 1801), **1st Bt** (UK), so *cr* 7 Dec 1818, with remainder to his bro Frederick, KH (1818), CB, of Lainston, Hants; *b* 24 June 1782; Col 14th Dragoon Gds, ADC to the Duke of Wellington at Waterloo, Kt Cdr St Henry (Saxony), Kt of Maximilian Joseph (Bavaria) and St George (Russia); *m* 24 April 1817 Louisa Catherine (*m* 2nd 24 April 1838 7th Duke of Leeds (*see* 1963 edn) and *dsp* 8 April 1874), 3rd dau of Richard Caton, of Maryland, USA, and *dsp* 24 Sept 1819

2 FREDERICK ANNE HERVEY (Sir), **2nd Bt**

3 Lionel Charles; *b* 1784; Col; *m* 3 May 1825 Frances Mary (*d* 2 March 1840), only dau of V-Adml Thomas Wells, of Holmewood, Hunts, and *d* 4 June 1843, having had issue:

(1) Felton Frederick William; *b* 12 March 1826; Inspr-Gen Prisons Ireland, Capt 13th Light Dragoons; *m* 4 Sept 1855 Eleanor Augusta Killowen Acheson (*m* 2nd Samuel Greg Rathbone, of Allerton, Lancs), 2nd dau of Acheson Lyle, Master in Chancery, of the Oaks, Co Londonderry, and *dsp* 31 March 1861

(2) William Frederick; *b* 21 Dec 1831; *d* 4 Aug 1840

(1) Frances; *b* 18 April 1827; *m* 30 Sept 1851 Rev Cyril Randolph, MA (*d* 1912), Rector Riverhead, Surrey, RD West Bridge, only s of Rev George Randolph, MA, Rector Eastey, Kent, and Coulsdon, Surrey, by Catherine Elizabeth, only dau of Rev Henry Roger Drummond (*see* PERTH, E), and *d* 1911, leaving issue (*see* NEPEAN, Bt)

(2) Eliza Catherine; *b* 16 Jan 1829; *m* 11 April 1860 Sir Henry Edward Francis Lambert, 6th Bt (*qv*), and *d* 17 Feb 1898, leaving issue

(3) Isabella Mary; *b* 30 April 1830; *m* 8 July 1852 Walter Drummond (*d* 23 April 1883), 4th s of Charles Drummond and *d* 21 Nov 1911, leaving issue (*see* PERTH, E)

(4) Selinah Sarah; *b* 25 Oct 1833; *m* 20 April 1865 William Wyndham Hasler, JP (*d* 5 May 1905), of Aldingbourne, and Barkfold, Sussex, and *d* 5 Feb 1900, leaving issue

Sir FELTON's yr bro,

Sir FREDERICK ANNE HERVEY later HERVEY-BATHURST, **2nd Bt**; *b* 18 June 1783; *m* Jane Douglas (*d* June 1827), dau of Joseph Hutchison, and *d* 20 Sept 1824, having had an est s:

Sir Frederick Hutchison Hervey-Bathurst, 3rd Bt; *b* 6 June 1807; *m* 1st 14 May 1832 Louisa Mary (*d* 30 Dec 1840), dau of Walter Smythe, of Bambridge House, Hants, and had:

1 FREDERICK THOMAS ARTHUR (Sir), **4th Bt**

1 Augusta Frederica; *m* 30 Jan 1872 Rev Felix John Buckley (*dsp* 20 March 1911), Hon Canon Bristol, Rector Stanton St Quinton, and *d* 12 May 1926

Sir Frederick *m* 2nd 23 Sept 1845 Clare Emily (*d* 24 Jan 1867), yst dau of Sir Richard Brooke, 6th Bt, of Norton (*qv*), and *d* 29 Oct 1881, having by her had, with four other sons and three daus:

2 Lionel HERVEY-BATHURST later PASTON-COOPER (roy licence 7 Oct 1905); *b* 7 July 1849; Lt-Col Rifle Bde; *m* 29 Jan 1885 Mary Ethel (*d* 16 Aug 1931), dau of Sir Astley Paston Cooper, 3rd Bt, of Gadebridge (*qv*), and *d* 4 May 1908, leaving issue:

(1) Sidney Lionel; *b* 15 Dec 1887; Capt Beds Regt; *m* 9 June 1927 Ermyntrude Mary (*d* 1936), dau of Henry Caley, of Hovingham, Yorks, and *d* 1934, leaving:

1a Astley Cecil Hervey; *b* 26 April 1929; *m* 7 June 1950 *Jean Louise, dau of Ch Engr Lawrence Dickinson, of 8 Dorset Ave, Welling, Kent, and *d* 15 March 1978, leaving issue:

1b +Lionel Lawrence Hervey [Lionel Paston-Cooper Esq, 33 St Mark's Rd, Teddington, Middx]; *b* 5 June 1951; *m* 1987 *Edwina Jane, dau of F Ward Smith, of Wave Crest, Whitstable, Kent, and has issue:

1c +Thomas Astley Ward; *b* 1993

1b *Sally Anne; *b* 21 Aug 1953

(2) Arthur Reginald HERVEY-BATHURST; *b* 19 Nov 1889; Lt RFA (SR) and 4th Rifle Bde; *m* 1920 Margaret Seymour and *d* 19–

(3) Cecil Annesley HERVEY-BATHURST; *b* Jan 1894 ; *d* April 1897

The 3rd Bt's est s,

Sir Frederick Thomas Arthur Hervey-Bathurst, 4th Bt, of Clarendon Park, Wilts; *b* 13 March 1833; Lt-Col Gren Gds, MP S Wilts 1861–65; *m* 24 April 1869 Ada (*d* 27 Feb 1914), only surv dau of Sir John Sheppy Ribton, 3rd Bt (*see* 1901 edn), and *d* 20 May 1900, leaving:

1 FREDERICK EDWARD WILLIAM (Sir), **5th Bt**

2 Felton Rainald George; *b* 19 March 1871; Capt Bucks Yeo; *d* 2 March 1921

3 Algernon Richard; *b* 10 Aug 1872; *m* 1st 27 April 1901 (*divorce* 1936) Elfrida Mary (*d* 27 Feb 1944), only child of Howard Miall Cockerell, of 18 Pelham St, London SW; *m* 2nd 5 Nov 1936 Margery McDougal, dau of Joseph H Faraday, and *d* 4 June 1949, having had by his 1st w:

(1) Iris Elfrida; *b* 4 June 1902; *d* unm 9 May 1958

4 Bertrand Elwell; *b* 5 Oct 1882; Maj Northumberland Fus SR, Boer War 1901–02 (Queen's medal with four clasps) and WW I 1914–15 (wounded three times); *m* 7 April 1920 Dorothy Margaret (*d* 12 Dec 1952), yr dau of Joseph William Baxendale, of Preshaw Ho, Upham, Hants, and *dsp* 31 Dec 1942

5 Reginald Mervyn; *b* 21 Feb 1885; *d* unm 4 Jan 1905

1 Cecilia Ada; *b* 14 Oct 1874; *m* 21 Aug 1906 Henry Brooke Macartney Crewe Greville and *d* 3 July 1959, leaving issue (*see* WARWICK, BROOKE and, E)

2 Aline Beatrix; *b* 15 Feb 1877; *m* 13 Oct 1903 Lt-Col Hon Charles Christopher Josceline Littleton, DSO, 3rd s of 3rd Baron Hatherton (*qv*), and *d* 3 July 1919, leaving issue

3 Violet Maude; *b* 30 March 1878; *m* 22 July 1905 Maj Robert Francis Stapleton-Cotton (*see* COMBERMERE, V) and *dsp* Aug 1959

The 4th Bt's est s,

Sir Frederick Edward William Hervey-Bathurst, 5th Bt, DSO (1917); *b* 11 Feb 1870; Maj Gen Res of Offrs, formerly Capt Gren Gds, Nile Expdn 1898 (two medals with clasp), Boer War 1899–1900 (despatches twice, Queen's medal with two clasps) and WW I on Staff (despatches three times), Order Crown Italy; *m* 1st 24 July 1901 (*divorce* 1912) Hon Moira O'Brien, 3rd dau of 14th Baron Inchiquin (*qv*), and had issue:

1 FREDERICK PETER METHUEN (Sir), **6th Bt**

Sir Frederick *m* 2nd 14 March 1919 Katharine Mary Delicia, OBE (1920) (*d* 1 April 1974), dau of Alexander Dick-Cunyngham and widow of John Henry Gaythorpe Nevill, Gren Gds, and *d* 16 April 1956, leaving by her:

2 Benjamin Alexander Frederick, OBE (1985), DL (Herefs 1967); *b* 27 March 1920; *educ* Eton and Trin Coll Cambridge (BA 1940); Maj Gren Gds and Special Forces WW II (wounded, despatches twice), Pres Herefs CLA; *m* 1st 18 Feb 1947 Hon Elizabeth Violet Virginia Somers Cocks (*d* 1986), only child of 6th Baron Somers (*qv*); *m* 2nd 1992 *Mrs Anne Pollak [Mrs Benjamin Hervey-Bathurst, Hillend House, Eastnor, Herefs HR8 1RF], only dau of Rev Thomas Vernon Garnier and formerly w of Robert Pollak, and *d* 18 Oct 1997, leaving by his 1st w:

(1) +James Felton Somers [James Hervey-Bathurst Esq, Eastnor Castle, Ledbury, Herefs HR8 1RN]; *b* 8 Dec 1949; *educ* Eton and Trin Coll Cambridge (rowing blue 1970 and 1971); *m* 25 Sept 1982 *Hon Sarah Rachel Peake, 2nd dau of Viscount Ingleby (*qv*), of Snilesworth, Northallerton, Yorks, and has issue:

1a *Imogen Elizabeth Somers; *b* 1986

2a *Isabella Katharine Somers; *b* 1990

3a *Nancy Rose Somers; *b* 3 March 1995

(2) +George Arthur Somers; *b* 31 Oct 1952; *educ* Eton and RMA Sandhurst; Lt 9th/12th Lancers

The 5th Bt's est s,

Sir Frederick Peter Methuen Hervey-Bathurst, 6th Bt; *b* 26 Jan 1903; *educ* Eton; Capt Gren Gds WW II; *m* 1st 21 June 1933 (*divorce* 1956) Maureen Gladys Diana, est dau of Charles Gordon, of Boveridge Park, Salisbury, and had issue:

1 Sir (FREDERICK) JOHN CHARLES GORDON HERVEY-BATHURST, **7th and present Bt**

1 *Maureen Anthea Selina [Mrs Henry Chaldecott, Lauristina Cottage, Lower Inkpen, Berks RG17 9DP]; *b* 15 Dec 1936; *m* 1st 19 Feb 1959 (*divorce* 1989) Brig Peter Gerald Sandeman Tower, CBE (*d* 1996) (*see* BUTLER, Bt, of Cloughgrenan); *m* 2nd 1990 (Oswald) Henry Chaldecott (*d* 1996) (*see* 1959 edn WORSLEY-TAYLOR, Bt) and has by her 1st husb:

(1) *William John [William Tower Esq, Flat 5, 24 Ormonde Gate, London SW3 4EX]; *b* 30 Sept 1963; *m* 23 June 1995 *Emma Hall

(1) *Nicola Jane [Mrs Richard Crosthwaite, 25 Lavender Gdns, London SW11 1DH]; *b* 16 Feb 1961; *m* 1987 *Richard D Crosthwaite, yr s of Tudor Derek Crosthwaite

Sir Frederick *m* 2nd 22 March 1958 Cornelia (*d* 1994), dau of Frederic White Shepard, of New York, and widow of Dr John Lawrence Riker, of Rumson, New Jersey, and *d* 27 Dec 1995

HESKETH

Arms: Quarterly, 1st and 4th, arg. on a bend sa. three garbs or (for HESKETH); 2nd and 3rd, arg. a fess sa. between three lion's heads erased gu. (for FERMOR). **Crests:** 1 A garb or banded az. (for HESKETH), 2 Out of a ducal coronet or a cock's head gu., combed and wattled gold (for FERMOR). **Supporters:** On either side a griffin or, gorged with a collar gu., thereon a fleur-de-lys gold and charged on the shoulder with a rose also gu., barbed and seeded ppr. **Motto:** *Hora e sempre* ('Now and always'). **Creations:** Bt. (GB) 5 May 1761, B. (UK) 25 Jan 1935.

THE 3RD BARON HESKETH, of Hesketh, in the Co Palatine of Lancaster, and a **Baronet** (Sir (Thomas) Alexander Fermor-Hesketh, Bt, KBE (1997), PC (1993)) [The Rt Hon The Lord Hesketh KBE PC, Easton Neston, Towcester, Northants NN12 7HS]; *b* 28 Oct 1950; *s f* 1955; *educ* Ampleforth; proprietor Hesketh Racing (Formula 1 Racing Team), winner Ferodo Trophy 1973; Ld in Waiting 1986–89, Parly U-Sec Environment 1989–90, Min State DTI 1990–91, Capt Gentlemen at Arms (Ch Whip) 1991–93, chm Br Midland Airways 1997–; *m* 21 May 1977 *Hon Claire Georgina Watson, er dau of 3rd Baron Manton (*qv*), and has:

1 +FREDERICK HATTON; *b* 13 Oct 1988

1 *Flora Mary; *b* 1981

2 *Sophia Christian; *b* 1984

Lineage (of Hesketh): RICHARD HESKETH, of Hesketh, Croston, Lancs; had:

WILLIAM HESKETH, of Hesketh; *m* Annabel, dau and heir of Richard de Stafford, and had:

ROBERT HESKETH, of Hesketh; had:

WILLIAM HESKETH, of Hesketh; *m* Albora, dau and heir of Richard de Totleworth, and had, with other issue:

Sir WILLIAM HESKETH, of Hesketh and Beconsaw; living 1276; *m* Maud, dau and coheir of Richard Fitton, of Great Harwood and Martholme, Lancs, and had:

THOMAS HESKETH, of Hesketh; *m* Alice Warren, of Bispham, Lancs, and had:

Sir JOHN HESKETH, of Hesketh and Rufford; *m* Alice, dau and sole heir of Edmond Fitton, Ld half the Manor of Rufford, Lancs, and had:

Sir WILLIAM HESKETH, of Rufford; *m* Marcella, dau and coheir of — Thwenge, of Kendal, Westmorland, and had:

THOMAS HESKETH, of Rufford; *m* Margaret, dau and coheir of Thomas Banastre, of Newton, and had:

NICHOLAS HESKETH, of Rufford; *m* Margaret (*d* 1418), dau and coheir of — Mynshull, and had issue:

Sir THOMAS HESKETH, of Rufford; *m* 1418 Sibill, dau and coheir of Sir Robert Lawrance, and *d* 1459, having had:

THOMAS HESKETH, of Rufford; *m* Margaret, dau of Hamon Massy, of Rixton, Lancs, and *d* 8 Oct 1443, leaving, with other issue:

ROBERT HESKETH, of Rufford; *m* Alice (*d* 17 Sept 1495), dau of Sir Robert Booth, of Dunham Massy, Cheshire, and *d* 1 Jan 1480, leaving, with other issue:

1 THOMAS

2 Richard; *d* 1520

3 Hugh; Bp of Man; living 1520

1 Margery; *m* Sir Henry Keighley, of Inskip, Lancs, and Keighley, Yorks

2 Maud *m* 1469 Hugh Aughton, of North Meols, and had:

(1) Richard (Sir); had a yr dau and coheir:

1a Anne; mother of:

1b Alice; *m* Hugh Hesketh (*d* 11 Dec 1520)

3 Margaret; *m* — Keighley

4 Dulcie; *m* John Nowell, of Read, Lancs

The est son,

THOMAS HESKETH, of Rufford; *m* Grace (*d* 29 June 1510), dau of Sir Richard Towneley (*see* O'HAGAN, B), and *d* 14 Aug 1523, having had a s (William, *dsp* & *vp*); he also had, with two yr illegitimate children:

Sir ROBERT HESKETH, of Rufford; *m* Grace (*m* 2nd Lawrence Habergham, of Habergham), dau of Sir John Towneley (*see* O'HAGAN, B), and *d* 8 Feb 1539, having had, with a yr s (Robert, *dsp*) and two daus (Ellen, *m* Richard Barton, of Barton Row, Lancs, and *dsp*; Jane, *m* Richard Assheton, of Croston, and had issue):

Sir THOMAS HESKETH, of Rufford; High Sheriff Lancs 1563; served Siege of Leith 1554; *m* Alice, dau of Sir Thomas Holcroft, of Holcroft, and *d* on or after 20 June 1588, leaving, with two daus and two yr sons (Thomas; Richard, executed at St Albans for alleged conspiracy to make Ferdinando, 5th Earl of Derby (*qv*), King):

ROBERT HESKETH, of Rufford; MP Lancs 1597–98; *m* 1st Mary (*d* by 1613), dau and heir of Sir George Stanley, Marshal Ireland (*see* DERBY, E), and had:

1 Thomas, of Rufford; *m* 1st Susan, dau of Thomas Powys; *m* 2nd Jane Edmundson; *m* 3rd Katharine, dau of Alexander Briers, of Lathom, and *dsp* Nov 1646

2 ROBERT

3 Henry; *dsp*

4 George; *m* Jane, widow of — Sherburne, and had issue

5 John; *m* Mary, dau of — Haydock, of Pheasantford, and had:

(1) Robert

1 Holcroft; *m* 1st Lawrence Rawstorne, of New Hall; *m* 2nd Roger Dodsworth, Chllr York

2 Jane; *m* 1st Edward Raynall; *m* 2nd — Heneage

3 Mary; *m* 1st Richard Barton, of Barton; *m* 2nd Thomas Stanley, of Eccleston, and had issue

ROBERT HESKETH *m* 2nd Blanch (*dsp*), dau and coheir of Henry Twyford, of Kenwick; *m* 3rd Jane (*m* 2nd Richard Hoghton), dau of Thomas Spencer, of Rufford, and by her had:

6 Cuthbert; *d* 1620

His 2nd son,

ROBERT HESKETH, of Rufford; *m* Margaret, dau of Alexander Standish, of Standish, by Elizabeth, dau and heir of Adam Hawarden, and *d* Jan 1653, leaving:

ROBERT HESKETH; *m* Lucy (*m* 2nd John Molyneux), dau of Col Alexander Rigby, of Middleton, and *dvp* Sept 1651, having had, with other issue:

THOMAS HESKETH, of Rufford; *m* Sydney (*m* 2nd Col — Spencer), yst dau of Sir Richard Grosvenor, 2nd Bt (*see* WESTMINSTER, D), and had, with other issue:

1 Robert; *m* Elizabeth, dau of Hon William Spencer (*see* MARLBOROUGH, D), and had:

(1) Elizabeth; *m* 11th Earl of Derby (*qv*)

2 Thomas, of Rufford; *m* Ann, dau of Sir Reginald Graham, 2nd Bt, of Norton Conyers (*qv*), and had issue:

(1) Thomas, of Rufford; MP Preston 1722–27; *m* Martha, dau and coheir of James St Amand (by Elizabeth, dau and in her issue heir of Sir William Juxon, 1st Bt, of Little Compton, Glos), and *d* 18 April 1735, having had, with other issue:

1a **Sir Thomas Hesketh, 1st Bt** (GB), so *cr* 5 May 1761, with special remainder, failing heirs male of his body, to his bro Robert; *b* 21 Jan 1727/8; *m* Harriet (*d* 10 Jan 1807), dau and coheir of Ashley Cowper, cousin of the poet Cowper and grandniece of 1st Baron Cowper, and *dsp* 4 March 1778

2a Sir ROBERT HESKETH later JUXON (took name and arms of his maternal ggf, Sir William Juxon, 1st Bt, for life 1792), **2nd Bt**, of Rufford; *b* 23 April 1729; *m* 19 April 1748 Sarah (*d* 1792), dau of William Plumbe, of Wavertree, Lancs, and *d* 30 Dec 1796, having had:

1b Thomas; *b* 1750; *m* Jacintha (*d* 7 Jan 1802, having *m* 2nd Thomas Winckley, of Brockholes, Lancs, and had further issue; *see* SHELLEY, Bt), dau of Hugh Dalrymple, Attorney-Gen Grenada, and *dvp* 13 Jan 1781, leaving:

1c THOMAS DALRYMPLE (Sir), **3rd Bt**

1c Harriet Anne; *m* Lt-Gen John Despard, 5th s of William Despard, of Coolrain and Curtown, Queen's Co, and Killaghy Castle, Co Tipperary, and had issue

2c Dorothea; *m* Arthur Barry Shears and *dsp*

3c Jacintha Catherine; *m* 14 May 1796 Sir Thomas Lethbridge, 1st Bt (*qv*), and *d* 31 Aug 1801, leaving issue

4c Anne Charlotte; *m* 22 Feb 1796 Hon Rt Rev Edmund Knox (*see* RANFURLY, E) and *d* 2 Oct 1837, leaving issue

5c Lucy; *m* Edward Pearson and *d* 1836

2b Robert; *b* 23 July 1751; *dvp* unm (*k* Bunker's Hill) 17 June 1775

1b Anne; *b* 28 Feb 1748/9; *m* Henry Byrne, of Carshalton

The 2nd Bt's gs,

Sir Thomas Dalrymple Hesketh, 3rd Bt; *b* 13 Jan 1777; *m* 1st 1 Feb 1798 Sophia (*d* 8 Feb 1817), only dau of Rev Nathaniel Hinde, and had:

1 THOMAS HENRY (Sir), **4th Bt**

1 Harriet; *m* 6 Nov 1832 Rev Joshua Thomas Horton (*d* May 1845), of Howroyde, Yorks, and *d* 10 May 1836, leaving issue

2 Sophia Elizabeth; *m* 6 Aug 1840 Rev J S Hodgson, Rector Brinklow, Warwicks, and *d* 3 Feb 1886, leaving issue

3 Emma Susette; *m* E Honzecker

Sir Thomas *m* 2nd 15 Sept 1821 Louisa Allemand (*d* 6 Sept 1832) and *d* 27 July 1842, having had further issue

His est son,

Sir Thomas Henry Hesketh, 4th Bt; *b* 11 Feb 1799; *m* 3 April 1824 Annette Maria (*d* 17 Dec 1879), est dau of Robert Bomford, of Rahinstown House, Co Meath, and *d* 10 Feb 1843, leaving, with a dau (Maria Harriet, *m* 15 Nov 1845 1st Baron Haldon (*d* 22 March 1883; *see* 1939 edn) and *d* 18 Dec 1905, leaving issue):

Sir THOMAS GEORGE HESKETH later FERMOR-HESKETH (roy licence 8 Nov 1867), **5th Bt**; Col 2nd Lancs Militia, Sheriff Lancs 1848, MP Preston 1862–72; *b* 11 Jan 1825; *m* 10 March 1846 Lady Anna Maria Arabella Fermor (*d* 25 Feb 1870), est dau of 4th Earl of Pomfret (*see* **Lineage (of Fermor)** below), and *d* 20 Aug 1872, having had, with other issue:

1 **Sir Thomas Henry Fermor-Hesketh, 6th Bt**; *b* 9 Jan 1847; *d* unm 28 May 1876

2 THOMAS GEORGE (Sir), **7th Bt**

3 Hugh Robert; *b* 11 June 1850; *d* 1879

1 Edith Elizabeth; *m* 10 Aug 1871 Lawrence Rawstorne, DL (*d* 11 Nov 1938), of Penwortham Priory and Hutton Hall, Lancs, and *d* 27 Dec 1931, leaving issue

The 6th Bt's bro,

Sir Thomas George Fermor-Hesketh, 7th Bt; Hon Col 3rd and 4th Bns King's Liverpool Regt, formerly Ensign Rifle Bde; *b* 9 May 1849; *m* San Francisco 23 Dec 1880 Florence Emily (*d* 25 Sept 1924), dau of William Sharon, of Nevada, Senator, and *d* 19 April 1924, having had, with a yr s (Frederick, Lt 9th Lancers, *b* 24 Sept 1883, presumed *d* on or after 29 Oct 1910):

Sir Thomas Fermor-Hesketh, 8th Bt, and **1st Baron Hesketh**, of Hesketh, in the Co Palatine of Lancaster (UK), so *cr* 25 Jan 1935, JP Lancs and Northants; Capt Lancs Hus, Lt RHG, Hon Maj TA; *educ* Trin Coll Cambridge (BA); High Sheriff Northants 1932, MP Enfield 1922–23; *b* 17 Nov 1881; *m* 3 Sept 1909 Florence Louise (*d* 4 March 1956), dau of John Witherspoon Breckinridge, of San Francisco, and gdau of Gen J C Breckinridge, V-Pres USA, also stepdau of Frederick W Sharon, of San Francisco, and had issue:

1 Thomas Sharon; Lt and Adj Scots Gds; *b* 7 Oct 1910; *d* unm 21 June 1937 as the result of an aeroplane accident

2 FREDERICK, **2nd Baron**

3 John Breckinridge; Maj RE WW II; *b* 7 March 1917; *educ* Eton and Magdalen Coll Oxford (BA 1938, MA 1944); *m* 1st 18 Dec 1946 (*divorce* 1947) Patricia Mackaskie, formerly w of Y B L Huggins and dau of Coleridge Henry Tillerade Cole, of Knotty Green, Beaconsfield, by Dorothy Cunnigham Mackaskie; *m* 2nd 7 April 1958 Joan Isabel (*m* 3rd 3 Sept 1966 Capt Michael Frederick Laud Robinson (*d* 16 May 1971), only surv s of Sir Frederick Villiers Laud Robinson, 10th Bt, of London (*qv*)), formerly w of Richard Sydney Edridge and dau of Vernon James Reveley, of Furzedown, Upper Warlingham, Surrey, and *dsp* 8 Nov 1961

1 Louise; *b* 15 Dec 1911; *m* 24 July 1937 Sir Edmund Villiers Minshull Stockdale, 1st Bt (*qv*), and *d* 1994, leaving issue

2 Florence; *b* 23 Feb 1913; *m* 1st 1 March 1934 (*divorce* 1944) 4th Baron Revelstoke (*qv*) and had issue; *m* 2nd 12 April 1944 Lt-Cdr Derek Lawson, JP, RNVR, yr s of Sir Arnold Lawson, KBE, MD, FRCS, and *d* 15 Sept 1970, leaving by him:

(1) *Arabella Ann [Mrs Steven Spurrier, Bayonne, 83, Bagnals-en-Foret, France]; *b* 14 Aug 1946; *m* 31 Jan 1968 *Steven Hugh Walthall Spurrier

(2) *Caroline; *b* 23 Sept 1953

The 1st BARON *d* 20 July 1944; his er surv son,

FREDERICK FERMOR-HESKETH, **2nd Baron Hesketh**, DL (Northants 1950); *b* 8 April 1916; *educ* Eton and Magdalene Coll Cambridge; Maj Scots Gds (resigned, Hon Maj 1946); *m* 22 Nov 1949 *Christian Mary, OBE (1984), DL (Northants), Hon LLD Leicester U 1982, High Sheriff Northants 1981 [The Rt Hon The Dowager Lady Hesketh OBE DL, Pomfret Lodge, Towcester, Northants NN12 7HT; 20A Tregunter Rd, London SW10], only dau of Capt Sir John Helias Finnie McEwen, 1st Bt (*qv*), and *d* 10 June 1955, leaving:

1 (THOMAS) ALEXANDER FERMOR-HESKETH **3rd and present Baron Hesketh**

2 Robert; *b* 1 Nov 1951; *educ* Ampleforth; *m* 1979 *Jeanne [The Hon Mrs Robert Fermor-Hesketh, 70 Drayton Gardens, London SW10], dau of Leo Herbert (Patrick) McDowell, of Co Clare, and *d* 2 Feb 1997 in a motor accident in California, leaving:

(1) +Blaise Isambard Robert; *b* 1987

3 +John [The Hon John Fermor-Hesketh, 53 Old Church St, London SW3 5BS]; *b* 15 March 1953; *educ* Ampleforth; *m* 1st 2 Dec 1980 (*divorce* 19–) Anna, only dau of Hamish Wallace, of Old Corrimony, Glen Urquhart, Inverness-shire; *m* 2nd 14 July 1986 *Helena Marian, only dau of Robert Hunt, of Petropolis, Brazil, and by her has:

(1) *Alice Mary Louisa; *b* 5 March 1987

Lineage (of Fermor): THOMAS RICARDS *alias* FERMOUR, of Witney, Oxon; *m* 1st Alice — and had a s (Laurence, of Minister Lovell, Oxon, f of William (*dsp*) and Mary, *m* Thomas Benoit, Clarenceux King of Arms (*d* 8 May 1534)); *m* 2nd Emmotte (*d* his widow), widow of Henry Wenman, of Blewbury, Berks, and dau of Simkin Hervey, of Herefs, and *d* between 9 Sept and 8 Nov 1485, having by her had, with a yr (3rd) s (William, of Summertown, Oxon, Clerk of the Crown; *m* four times and *dspm* 20 Sept 1552):

RICHARD FERMO(U)R, of Easton Neston, Towcester, Northants; Merchant Staple Calais; *m* Anne (*d* his widow), dau of Sir William Brown, Ld Mayor London, and *d* 17 Nov 1552, having had, with two other sons (*d* in infancy):

1 JOHN (Sir)

2 Thomas, of Summertown Oxford; MP Chipping Wycombe 1563; *m* Bridget — and *d* 8 Aug 1580, leaving a s (Richard, of Summertown, had issue) and dau (Mary, *m* Francis Plowden and had issue; *see* PLOWDEN, B)

3 Jerome; *m* Jane — and *d* 7 Sept 1602, leaving a s (Nicholas)

1 Joan; Maid of Honour to Princess MARY (later QUEEN MARY); *m* 1st Robert Wilford, merchant tailor, of London; *m* 2nd *c* 3 Dec 1545 2nd Lord (Baron) Mordaunt (*see* MORDAUNT, Bt); *m* 3rd *c* 20 Dec 1571, as his 3rd w, Sir Thomas Kempe, of Boughton Aluph and Chilham Castle, Kent, and *d* by 24 April 1592

2 Anne; *m* William Lucy and had issue (*see* RAMSAY-FAIRFAX-LUCY, Bt)

3 Elizabeth; *m* Thomas Lovet, of Astwell, Northants

4 Ursula; *m* Richard Fiennes, *de jure* 6th Baron Saye and Sele (*qv*) and had issue

5 Mary; *m* Sir Richard Knightley, of Fawsley, Northants, and *d* 27 Sept 1573

The est son,

Sir JOHN FERMOR, of Easton Neston; MP Northants, Sheriff Northants 1557–58; *m* Maud (*d* 14 April 1569), dau of 1st Baron Vaux of Harrowden (*qv*), and *d* 12 Dec 1571, leaving, with an intermediate s (*d* unm):

1 GEORGE (Sir)

2 Richard; *m* Dionysia, dau of Robert Tanfield, of Burford, Oxon, and had:

(1) Catherine; *m* 1st Philip Godard; *m* 2nd Sir Richard Wenman, of Thame, Oxon

1 Catherine; *m* 1st Michael Poulteney, of Misterton, Leics; *m* 2nd Sir Henry Darcy (*see* DARLY DE KNAYTH, B) and had issue

2 Anne; *m* Sir Edward Leigh, of Shawel, Leics

3 Mary; *m* Sir Thomas Lucas, of St John's, Colchester, Essex, and *d* 5 July 1613

The est son,

Sir GEORGE FERMOR, of Easton Neston; served Netherlands against Spaniards, ktd 1586; *m* Jan 1572 Mary (*d* 12 Oct 1628), dau and heir of Thomas Curson, of Addington, Bucks, and *d* 1 Dec 1612, having had, with six other sons (*dsp*) and three other daus (*d* unm):

1 HATTON (Sir)

1 Agnes; *m* 1st Viscount Wenman and was *bur* 4 July 1617, leaving issue

2 Elizabeth; *m* 1st Sir William Stafford, of Blatherwick, Northants; *m* 2nd Sir Thomas Chamberlain, of Oxon

3 Jane; *m* Sir John Killigrew, of Falmouth Castle, Cornwall

4 Catherine; *m* William Hobby, of Hales, Glos

5 Mary; *m* 1st 16 April 1608 8th Lord Crichton Sanquhar (*see* BUTE, M); *m* 2nd 17 July 1615 6th Earl of Thomond and was *bur* 13 April 1675, leaving issue (*see* INCHIQUIN, B)

The 2nd son,

Sir HATTON FERMOR, of Easton Neston; *m* 1st Elizabeth (*dsp*), dau of Sir Edmund Anderson, Ld Ch Justice Common Pleas; *m* 2nd Anna (*d* 1665), dau of Sir William Cokayne, Ld Mayor London, and *d* 28 Oct 1640, having by her had, with three other sons and three other daus (all *d* young or unm):

1 WILLIAM (Sir), 1st Bt

2 Hatton; royalist Maj of Horse; *ka* Culham Bridge, nr Oxford, 11 Jan 1644/5 aged 19

1 Mary; *m* Sir Charles Compton, 2nd s of 2nd Earl of Northampton (*see* NORTHAMPTON, M), and *d* 1660

2 Anne; *m* Jonathan Cope (*d* 1670), of Ranton Abbey, Staffs, 2nd s of Sir William Cope, 2nd Bt, and had issue

3 Catherine; *m* 1st 18 Dec 1656 Sir John Shuckburgh, 1st Bt (*qv*), and had issue; *m* 2nd 12 May 1663 Sir Roger Norwich, 2nd Bt, and *d* 19 May 1681

The est son,

Sir WILLIAM FERMOR, 1st Bt (E), so *cr* 6 Sept 1641, of Easton Neston; royalist Civil War; *m* Mary (*d* 18 July 1670), widow of Henry Noel, 2nd s of 2nd Viscount Campden (*see* GAINSBOROUGH, E), and dau of Hugh Perry, of London, and *d* 14 May 1661, leaving, with four yr sons (d unm) and two daus (d young or unm):

Sir WILLIAM FERMOR 2nd Bt, and 1st BARON LEOMINSTER (E), Co Hereford, so *cr* 12 April 1692; *m* 1st Jane, dau of Andrew Barker, of Fairford, Glos, and had a dau (Elizabeth, *d* unm March 1705); *m* 2nd Hon Catherine Poulett, dau of 3rd Baron Poulett (*see* 1970 edn POULETT, E), and by her had a dau (Mary, *m* Sir John Wodehouse, 4th Bt (*see* KIMBERLEY, E), and *d* 24 Oct 1729); *m* 3rd Sophia (*d* 8 Dec 1746), widow of Donatus, Lord O'Brien, s and h of 7th Earl of Thomond (*see* INCHIQUIN, B), and 6th dau of 1st Duke of Leeds (*see* 1963 edn), and *d* 7 Dec 1711, having by her had, with a yr s (William) and four daus (Sophia, *d* young; Catherine, *d* unm 11 April 1719; Bridget, *d* unm; Matilda, *m* Edward Conyers, of Copthall, Essex, and *d* 1741):

THOMAS FERMOR, 1st EARL OF POMFRET (*i.e.*, Pontefract), Co York, so *cr* 27 Dec 1721, KB (1725); Master of the Horse to QUEEN CAROLINE 1727, Ranger and Keeper St James's Park 1751; *m* 14 July 1720 Hon Henrietta Louisa Jeffreys, Lady of the Bedchamber to QUEEN CAROLINE (*d* 15 Dec 1761), only dau and heir of 2nd and last Baron Jeffreys of Wem (*see* JEFFREYS, B), and *d* 8 July 1753, having had, with three yr sons (*d* young or unm):

1 GEORGE, 2nd Earl

1 Sophia; *b* 29 May 1721; *m* 1744 1st Earl Granville (*qv*) and *d* 1745, leaving issue

2 Charlotte; Governess to GEORGE III's children; *b* 14 Feb 1725; *m* 9 Aug 1746 William Finch, PC, 2nd s of 7th Earl of Winchilsea and (2nd Earl of) Nottingham (*qv*), and *d* 11 July 1813, leaving issue

3 Henrietta; *b* 29 Sept 1727; *m* 13 Jan 1747 John Conyers (*d* 7 Sept 1775), of Copthall, Essex, and *d* 25 Nov 1793, leaving issue

4 Juliana; *b* 21 May 1729; *m* Aug 1751 Thomas Penn, of Stoke Park, Bucks

5 Louisa, Lady of the Bedchamber to PRINCESS AMELIA; *b* 23 Feb 1731; *m* 24 Sept 1767 William Clayton, of Harleyford, Bucks, 2nd s of Sir William Clayton, 1st Bt (*qv*), and *d* 30 June 1809, leaving issue

6 Anne; *m* 15 July 1754 1st Viscount Cremorne (*see* 1933 edn DARTREY, E) and *d* 1 March 1769

The est son,

GEORGE FERMOR, 2nd EARL OF PROMFRET; Ld Bedchamber to GEORGE III; Ranger Little Park Windsor; *b* 1722; *m* 30 April 1764 Anna Maria Drayton (*d* 23 Sept 1767) and *d* 9 June 1785, leaving:

1 GEORGE FERMOR, 3rd EARL OF POMFRET; *b* 6 Jan 1768; *m* 29 Aug 1793 Mary (*d* 17 Sept 1839), dau and heir of Thomas Trollope Browne, of Gretford, Lincs, and Besthorpe, Norfolk, and *dsp* 1830

2 THOMAS WILLIAM FERMOR, 4th EARL OF POMFRET; Lt-Gen; *b* 22 Nov 1770; *m* 13 Jan 1823 Amabel Elizabeth (*m* 2nd May 1834 Rev William Thorpe, DD, of Belgrave Chapel, Pimlico), est dau of Sir Richard Borough, 1st Bt (*see* 1879 edn), of Basildon, and *d* 29 June 1833, leaving issue:

(1) GEORGE WILLIAM RICHARD FERMOR, 5th and last EARL OF POMFRET; *b* 31 Dec 1824; *d* unm 8 June 1867, when his titles expired

(2) Thomas Hatton George; *b* 1832; *d* 4 March 1864

(1) Anna Maria Annabella; *m* 10 March 1846 **Sir Thomas Hesketh, 5th Bt**, and had issue (*see* above)

(2) Henrietta Louisa; *m* 7 Aug 1856 Col Thomas Wedderburn Ogilvy, of Ruthven, Forfarshire (*see* OGILVY-WEDDERBURN, Bt)

1 Charlotte; *b* 20 Nov 1766; *m* 1 Aug 1787 Peter Denys, of Hans Place, Chelsea, and Fremington, Yorks, and *d* Nov 1835, leaving issue (*see* SHUCKBURGH, Bt)

Seat: Easton Neston, Towcester, Northants. The only country mansion by Hawksmoor, Easton Neston was nevertheless meant by its creator to be in a style (and on a scale) after Vanbrugh. Hawksmoor had worked under Vanbrugh on both the Blenheim (*see* MARLBOROUGH, D) and Castle Howard projects, so this was not surprising. Certainly the size of the planned array of buildings at Easton Neston was of similarly ambitious proportions. There was to have been a gigantic forecourt in the shape of a squat but elephantine inverted T, roughly three times the length of the current main block in depth and twice it in width. Some of this did get built: the entrance pillars, the main block and two wings either side of the main block, of which that housing the stables survives.

Wren had been called in to advise on the original plans but is thought never to have worked on site and to have done no more than dash off a preliminary draft in the way of design. Certainly Hawksmoor thought little of the supposedly Wren-created portion, even though it was a recommendation by Wren, under whom he had also worked, that won him his commission from Lord Leominster. The south wing, opposite what for want of a better term is called the Wren one, was pulled down a couple of generations after Easton Neston was completed, or at any rate as much of the planned palace as Lord Leominster by then cared to fund. Leominster was probably only able to undertake the project at all through having married an heiress. His earlier plans had hung fire, it is thought for want of funds.

The completion date has been put at 1702 or 1713, in other words the year of QUEEN ANNE's accession or the year before her demise. The Queen's Anglican enthusiasm was a source of considerable employment to Hawksmoor as he was made surveyor of the scheme projected in her last years to build 50 new churches and he was noted in his ecclesiastical work for a love of armorial emblems (and often ridiculed for it). That aspect of his personality is also on display at Easton Neston, where a huge representation of Lord Leominster's achievement (the Fermor arms currently in use to the dexter) forms the artistic climax to the portico on corinthian pillars over the main door. Lord Leominster bought some of the Arundel marbles (*see* NORFOLK, D) and intended to embellish his new mansion with them but they were afterwards lodged in a greenhouse and either neglected or subjected to amateurish attempts at restoration by Leominster's son Lord Pomfret.

HEWETT

Arms: Gules on a chevron embattled argent, between three owls of the second, on the head of each an eastern crown or, as many bombs fired proper. **Crest:** Out of a mural crown or the stump of an oak tree with branches, thereon a hawk proper gorged with an eastern coronet and belled of the first. **Supporters:** Dexter, a tiger proper gorged with an eastern crown or; sinister, a buffalo charged on the shoulder with a trefoil slipped proper. **Motto:** *Ne te quæsiveris extra* ('Seek nothing beyond your sphere'). **Creation:** Bt. (UK) 6 Nov 1813.

SIR PETER JOHN SMITHSON HEWETT, 6TH BT, of Nether Seale, Leicestershire, MM (1957) [Sir Peter Hewett Bt MM, PO Box 15669, Nairobi, Kenya]; *b* 27 June 1931; *s f* 1990; *educ* Bradfield and Jesus Coll Cambridge (BA 1953); barrister Gray's Inn 1954, later advocate Kenya; *m* 14 Feb 1958 *Jennifer Ann Cooper, dau of Emrys Thomas Jones, OBE, of Limuru, Kenya, and has:

1 +RICHARD MARK JOHN [Richard Hewett Esq, 118 Lovibonds Ave, Orpington, Kent BR6 8EN]; *b* 15 Nov 1958; *educ* Bradfield and Jesus Coll Cambridge (BA)

2 +David Patrick John [David Hewett Esq, PO Box 15669, Nairobi, Kenya]; *b* 24 June 1968; *educ* Bradfield, Reading U (BSc) and St Hugh's Coll Oxford (MSc); *m* 13 Sept 1997 *Kate Suzanne Elizabeth, er dau of Dr Keith Leslie Ormand, of Ruiru, Kenya

1 *Joanna Yuilleen [Mrs Patrick Blundell, 10 Robinson Rd, Darlington, W Australia]; *b* 6 May 1960; *m* 1990 *Patrick Fitzgerald Blundell, er s of Maj Alan F Blundell, of Gooseberry Hill, W Australia, and has:

(1) *Michael Benjamin Patrick; *b* 19 May 1995

Lineage: WILLIAM HEWETT, of Dunton Bassett (s of William Hewett, of Dunton, formerly of Millbrook and Ampthill, Beds); High Sheriff Leics 1647; *m* Frances, dau of Edward Nele, and *d* 1662, leaving:

NEALE HEWETT, of Dunton Bassett; had:

SHUCKBURGH HEWETT, of Melton Mowbray; *b* 1719; Maj; *m* Ann Ward, of Harborough, Leics, and *d* 10 Dec 1759, leaving:

Sir George Hewett, 1st Bt (UK), so *cr* 6 Nov 1813, GCB; *b* 11 June 1750; Gen, Col 61st Foot, C-in-C India and Ireland; *m* July 1785 Julia, dau of John Johnson, of Blackheath, Kent, and gdau of Sir Christopher Musgrave, Bt, and *d* 21 March 1840, having had, with three other sons and six daus:

1 GEORGE HENRY (Sir), **2nd Bt**

2 William; *b* 2 July 1795; Lt-Col Rifle Bde; *m* 21 June 1826 Sarah (*d* 1883), 2nd dau of Gen Sir James Duff, and *d* 26 Oct 1891, having had, with three daus:

(1) William; Capt RN; *d* unm Bermuda *c* 1860

(2) James Duff; emigrated to NZ

(3) Charles (Rev); *b* 18 Nov 1796; *m* 26 Sept 1837 Frances Sophia, 4th dau of C W Cator, of Guildford St, London, and *d* 10 Nov 1871

(4) Philip (Rev); *b* 7 Sept 1799; *m* 10 Dec 1828 Anne (*d* 22 Nov 1898), yst dau of Gen Sir James Duff, and *d* 15 Dec 1879, leaving:

1a Philip George; *b* 22 May 1834; Lt-Col 1st W York Militia, Capt 20th Regt; *m* 20 May 1857 Emily Janet (*d* 1912), dau of Rev C U Barry, and *d* 29 Nov 1900, leaving, with four daus (*d* unm):

1b Paul, CBE (1919); *b* 15 April 1858; Capt RN WW I (despatches); *d* 13 March 1934

2b Godfrey; *b* 12 Aug 1859; Consul Paramaribo; *d* 14 Jan 1932

3b Leonard; *b* 1 Aug 1866; *d* 3 July 1912

Sir GEORGE's est s,

Sir George Henry Hewett, 2nd Bt; *b* 18 May 1791; Col 1838, served Peninsular War and India; *m* 26 July 1816 Louisa (*d* 25 Sept 1880), dau of Rt Rev Henry William Majendie, DD, Bp Bangor, and *d* 20 May 1862, having had, with two daus:

1 GEORGE JOHN ROUTLEDGE (Sir), **3rd Bt**

2 Frank William, of The Grove, Bridgnorth, Salop; *b* 10 May 1820; *m* 25 Sept 1849 Julie Minna (*d* 2 Oct 1915), dau of Vicomte Carl von Douallier, Capt Prussian Army, and *d* 22 Oct 1911, having had issue:

(1) Henry Frank Oscar; *b* 13 Sept 1854; RM Wynberg, Cape Colony; *m* 1884 Henrietta, dau of H C Blundell, of Port Alfred, Cape Colony, and had issue:

1a William Henry Routledge; *b* 1884; S African Inf; *ka* 1916

2a Frank Harald; *b* 1886; *m* 10 June 1931 *Dorothy, dau of Edwin Heymanson, of Johannesburg, and *d* 1936

1a Minnie Mabel Majendie; *d* 1911

(2) Charles William; *b* 14 Jan 1858; *educ* Wellington; Capt RIN WW I; *m* 1893 Marianne Ellen (*d* 4 July 1946), dau of Rev G S Munn, and *d* 4 Dec 1942, leaving:

1a William George, OBE (1941), MC and bar; *b* 4 Sept 1894; Brig Welch Regt, WW I (despatches five times, Brevet Maj, wounded, Croix de Guerre) and WW II, Dist Army Welfare Offr 1946, rd safety organiser Glos; *m* 1st 19 April 1922 (*divorce* 1931) Louise Susan, dau of Francis R Wolfe, and had:

1b +Richard William; *b* 22 Oct 1923; Maj RA WW II and Malaya 1953 (despatches), chm and md Readers Digest UK, dir int ops Readers Digest USA 1986–; *m* 24 July 1954 *Rosemary, yr dau of Basil E Cridland, MC, TD, of The Old Laundry, Fernhurst, Sussex, and has:

1c *Vanessa Annabel; *b* 23 April 1957

2c *Virginia Carolyn Rose [Mrs Dominc Wheatley, 64 Orbain Rd, London SW6 7JY]; *b* 4 Feb 1960; *m* 1985 *Dominic Marius Dennis Anthony Wheatley, er s of Dennis Anthony Marius Thomas Wheatley, of Ridgeway Gdns, Wimbledon, and has:

1d *A son; *b* 1991

1d *Charlotte Rose; *b* 1989

1a (cont.) Brig William Hewett *m* 2nd 11 June 1932 Beatrice (*d* 3 Feb 1961), only dau of Lt-Col James Francis Donegan, CB, LLD, RAMC, and *d* 1973, having by her had issue:

1b *Sarah Margaret Arianwen; *b* 4 July 1942

(3) George Stuart, CBE (1919), JP; *b* 27 Feb 1863; Capt RIN and RN, Dep Dir RIM Calcutta, 1st Cl Magistrate, served WW I, Legion of Honour; *m* 23 Dec 1899 Maude Mary Brind (*d* 20 Feb 1958), 3rd dau of Surgn-Gen Henry Kendall, AMD, and *d* 12 Jan 1937, having had issue:

1a George Kendall Shuckburgh; *b* 30 June 1904; *educ* Haileybury; Lt-Col RASC

2a +Neale Brind Stuart, JP (NZ) [Cdr Neale Hewett JP, Villa 29, Mary Doyle Trust, Karanema Dve, Havelock North, New Zealand]; *b* 24 Aug 1906; Cdr RINR; *m* 25 Feb 1930 Thecla Edana (*d* 1993), er dau of Arthur John Davis, and has issue:

1b +Neale John Patrick, BEM (1953) [Neale Hewett Esq BEM, PO Box 357 Seven Hills, NSW 2147, Australia]; *b* 5 Feb 1931; *educ* Ampleforth; in operations against Mau-Mau Kenya 1953, Ag Dept Uganda 1959–65; *m* 9 April 1960 (*annulled* 19–) Felicity Ann, only dau of Bernard H Kerby, and has issue:

1c +Matthew Patrick George; *b* 3 Dec 1969

1c *Merri Bernard Neale; *b* 15 Jan 1961

2c *Felicity Sheena; *b* 2 May 1968

3c *Anita Noreen; *b* 12 July 1967
2b +George Andrew Kendall [George Hewett Esq, 5 Rosalind Road, Glenfield, Auckland 10, New Zealand]; *b* 19 Nov 1942; *educ* St Patrick's Coll Wellington; precision engr; *m* 4 March 1967 *Sharron-Rose, yst dau of W Souster, of Auckland, NZ, and has issue:
1c +Jason Conrad Neale; *b* 1969
2c +Brind Nicholas Andrew; *b* 1974
1b *Jeanne Marie Thecla; *b* 24 Oct 1933; *m* Dec 1955 *Alan Dever and has issue:
1c *Neale Alan Kendall; *b* 5 March 1958
2c *Alan Guy; *b* 21 Jan 1961
1c *Wendy Janet Thecla; *b* 24 Sept 1956
2c *Penelope Jeanne; *b* 28 March 1959
3c *Catherine Adelaide; *b* 28 Nov 1967
3a Jack Patrick Majendie; *b* 12 July 1909; F/O RAF; *m* 4 June 1938 *Mary Elinor Rothero, yst dau of Engr R-Adml Frederick George Haddy, MVO, of White Gates, Farnham Royal, Bucks, and was *kas* April 1940
1a Nancy Maude Neville; *b* 3 Oct 1900; *d* 8 July 1901
(4) John Routledge; *b* 10 April 1864; *d* 1 Jan 1891
(1) Mary Bianca; *b* 12 Nov 1851; *d* 9 Oct 1854
(2) Minnie Louisa; *b* 13 Feb 1856; *d* 5 Jan 1912
(3) Eda Mary; *b* 25 Nov 1860; *d* unm 20 Nov 1894
(4) Julia Emma; *b* 30 Nov 1866; *m* 3 Sept 1896 Robert Henry Lloyd (*d* 4 Dec 1940), s of Rev George Lloyd, Rector Westhill, Devon, and *d* 28 April 1938, leaving issue
(5) Clara Ethelinda; *b* 4 March 1868; *d* unm 1904

Sir GEORGE's est s,
Sir George John Routledge Hewett, 3rd Bt; *b* 21 Sept 1818; *m* 1st 30 Oct 1856 Clara (*d* 24 Nov 1867), yst dau of Wilhelm von Pochammer, Gen Prussian service, and had issue:
1 HARALD GEORGE (Sir), **4th Bt**
2 Edbert Ansgar, CMG, JP; *b* 5 Sept 1860; Supt P&O Co Hong Kong, unofficial memb Exec and Legislative Cncls Hong Kong, China war medal 1900, Cross Order of Orange Nassau, Iron Cross Austria 3rd Cl, Japanese Order Sacred Treasure 4th Cl; *m* 2 Feb 1893 Ruth Jeannette (*d* 3 Oct 1912), 2nd dau of Quentin K McKendrick, of New York, and *d* 24 Nov 1915
3 George Henry; *b* 20 Nov 1865; V-Consul Tuxpam, Mexico, 1915–19; *d* unm 30 Nov 1930
1 Anna; *m* 21 Sept 1878 Carl Ernst Gotthard, Baron von Richthofen (*d* 26 Aug 1915), est s of Bolko, Baron von Richthofen, of Gross Rosen, Silesia, and *d* 1 Dec 1884, having had issue
2 Helga Louisa; *m* 22 Aug 1885 Ernst, Baron von Richthofen (*d* 9 June 1933), and *d* 13 May 1954, leaving issue
3 Mary Ethelinda; *d* unm 1873
4 Hilda Henrietta; *d* unm 18 Aug 1945
5 Hulda Emilie; *d* unm 7 Aug 1928

Sir George *m* 2nd July 1873 Sophia Harriette (*d* 31 Dec 1921), dau of Robert Godwin-Austen, of Shalford, and *d* 15 April 1876, having by her had:
4 Bertram Henry Majendie; *b* 23 Dec 1874; ch engr Mersey Tunnel, FRGS; *m* 4 Oct 1911 Theodore (*d* 1946), widow of Alexander Weir, of New Jersey, and *d* 14 Nov 1933
5 Gerard Shuckburgh; *b* 1 Nov 1875; *d* 17 Feb 1922

Sir GEORGE's est s,
Sir Harald George Hewett, 4th Bt; *b* 24 Oct 1858; Capt and Hon Maj Edinburgh RGA Militia; *m* 1st 10 Nov 1887 Emma (*d* 23 Oct 1889), dau of T Pope, of Portlemouth, S Devon, and had issue:
1 Mary Hilda; *b* 15 Sept 1888; *d* unm 19 March 1947
2 Hulda Emma; *b* Oct 1889; *d* unm 19 Dec 1920

Sir Harald *m* 2nd 30 Jan 1892 Eleanor Margaret (*d* 2 April 1946), er dau of Cdr Henry Studdy, RN, and *d* 5 March 1949, having by her had issue:
1 Harald, MC; *b* 22 Oct 1892; Capt Roy Berks Regt and RFC WW I; *kas* 4 Jan 1918
2 **Sir John George Hewett, 5th Bt**, MC (1919); *b* 23 Oct 1895; *educ* Cheltenham; Capt 4th KAR, served WW I 1914–15 in Br E Africa as Trooper in Bowker's Horse; *m* 22 Dec 1926 *Yuilleen Maude, only surv child of Samuel Frederick Smithson, of Lauriston, Camberley, and *d* 1990, leaving issue:
(1) Sir PETER JOHN SMITHSON HEWETT, **6th and present Bt**
(2) +Richard Harald [Richard Hewett Esq, PO Box 15033, Nairobi, Kenya]; *b* 10 Feb 1933; Sgt Kenya Regt during Mau-Mau Ops; *educ* Gordonstoun; *m* 6 June 1959 *Bridget Elizabeth Anne, only dau of Alistair John Kirkman Finlay, and has had issue:
1a Anthony John Finlay; *b* 8 Aug 1962; *d* 1982
1a *Julia Caroline [Mrs Michael Hyde-Duder, Box 24460, Nairobi, Kenya]; *b* 19 Sept 1960; *m* 1984 *Michael Hyde-Duder and has issue:
1b *James; *b* 1986
2b *Ross Finlay; *b* 16 May 1997
1b *Siana Nicole; *b* 1985
3 George Neale; *b* 1901; FIEE, RN WW I; *m* 7 Nov 1931 *Margaret Skaife, est dau of G T Denis de Vitré, of Newbury, Berks, and *d* 1972, leaving issue:
(1) +Denis Neale [Dennis Hewett Esq, PO Box 246, Keri Keri, Bay of Islands, New Zealand]; *b* 15 Sept 1932; Lt RN (ret)
(2) +Jeremy Patrick Neale; *b* 28 March 1935; *educ* Oxford (MA); *m* 13 July 1963 *Shirley Norma Garnett, dau of William Rodolph Smith, of Victoria, BC, Canada, and has issue:
1a +Geoffrey Alexander; *b* 20 Nov 1966
1a *Kari Denise; *b* 1964
3 Margaret; *b* 1894; *m* 1922 Joshua Rupert Ingham Brooke, MBE (*d* 11 July 1934), est s of Rev Ingham Brooke, and has issue

HEWITT

Arms: Sa. a chevron, in chief three owls or. **Crest:** Upon the battlements of a tower arg. an owl ppr. **Motto:** *Semper eadem* ('Always the same'). **Creation:** Bt. (UK) 15 Jan 1921.

SIR NICHOLAS CHARLES JOSEPH HEWITT, 3RD BT, of Barnsley, West Riding Co York [Sir Nicholas Hewitt Bt, Colswayn House, Huttons Ambo, Yorks YO6 7HJ]; *b* 12 Nov 1947; *s* f 1973; *m* 1969 *Pamela Margaret, only dau of Geoffrey J M Hunt, TD, of Broadacres, Scalby, Scarborough, and has issue:
1 +CHARLES EDWARD JAMES; *b* 15 Nov 1970
2 +Michael Joseph; *b* 1973
1 *Victoria Alexandra Margaret; *b* 1978

Lineage: ALFRED HEWITT, of Barnsley, had issue:

Sir Joseph Hewitt, 1st Bt (UK), so *cr* 15 Jan 1921, JP Barnsley; ktd, Hon Lt-Col, slr and colliery owner; *b* 14 Oct 1865; *m* 21 April 1891 Margaret Eliza (*d* 23 Nov 1950), dau of George Guest, of Barnsley, and had issue:
1 George Alfred Guest; Capt 1st/5th Bn Yorks and Lancs Regt; *b* 14 Feb 1893; *ka* 27 Nov 1917
2 JOSEPH (Sir), **2nd Bt**
1 Margaret Elizabeth; *b* 7 March 1894; *m* 7 Sept 1922 Maj Thomas Thornton, MC
2 Kathleen; *b* 3 June 1896; *m* 6 Oct 1921 Maj Hugh Parry Smith (*d* 9 Oct 1956), of Wellcroft, Worsborough, Barnsley, and has issue
3 Winifred Mary; *b* 26 Jan 1901
4 Joan Christine; *b* 3 Dec 1903; *m* 6 Oct 1927 Eric Hinton Stewart and *d* 23 Dec 1957, leaving issue (*see* STEWART, Bt, of Strathgarry)

The 1st Bt *d* 8 Feb 1923; his only surv son,
Sir Joseph Hewitt, 2nd Bt; *b* 8 Sept 1907; *educ* Uppingham; T/Maj RA WW II; *m* 20 Oct 1940 *Marguerite [Marguerite Lady Hewitt, Lebberston Hall, nr Scarborough, Yorks], yr dau of Charles Burgess, of Deepdene, Filey, and *d* 1 Oct 1973, leaving issue:
1 Sir NICHOLAS CHARLES JOSEPH HEWITT, **3rd and present Bt**
2 +Timothy George; *b* 25 April 1950
1 *Elizabeth Margaret; *b* 23 May 1945

HEYGATE

Arms: Gules two bars argent, on a bend or a torteau between two leopard's faces azure. **Crest:** A wolf's head erased gules.
Mottoes: 1 *Boulogne et Cadiz*, 2 *Souvenez St Quentin* ('Remember St Quentin'). Both mottoes recall military successes in which Thomas Heygate and his s, also Thomas, took part (*see* **Lineage**).
Creation: Bt. (UK) 30 Sept 1831.

SIR RICHARD JOHN GAGE HEYGATE, 6TH BT, of Southend, Essex [Sir Richard Heygate Bt, 29 Rossetti Gdns Mansions, Flood St, London SW3 5QX]; *b* 30 Jan 1940; *s* bro 1991; *educ* Repton and Balliol Coll Oxford; *m* 1st 1968 (*divorce* 1972) Carol Rosemary, dau of Cdr Richard Michell, RN, of Leith Ho, Amberley, W Sussex; *m* 2nd 1974 (*divorce* 1988) Jong-Ja Hyun, dau of In Suk, of Seoul, S Korea, and has issue:

1 *Eun-Hee Isobella Gage; *b* 1977

Sir RICHARD *m* 3rd 1988 *Susan Fiona, dau of Robert Buckley, of Peasmarsh, E Sussex, and by her has issue:

1 +FREDERICK CARYSFORT GAGE; *b* 28 June 1988
2 +Robert George Liam; *b* 1991

Lineage: This is a branch of the HEYGATEs of Essex and Suffolk.

THOMAS HEYGATE, of Hayes, Middx; Provost-Marshal-Gen of the English army which in alliance with the Spaniards besieged St Quentin (held by the French) in 1557, also Provost-Marshal in Scotland; *m* Elizabeth, dau of Thomas Stonor, of Stonor (*see* CAMOYS, B), and *d* 1576, leaving issue:

THOMAS HEYGATE, JP (Middx), of Hayes; Provost-Marshal-Gen capture of Cadiz 1596; *m* Margery, dau of Ralph Skipwith, of Parkbury, Herts (of the family of Skipwith of St Albans), and had issue:

1 Thomas, of Hayes; barrister; *d* 1658, leaving an only dau:
(1) Sophia; *m* — Lancaster, barrister
2 RALPH
1 Elizabeth Anne; *m* E Heylyn, of Minster Lovel
2 Katherine; *m* Robert Tyrwhitt, Master of the Buckhounds to CHARLES I
3 Letitia; *m* Dr Peter Heylyn, Preb Westminster

THOMAS HEYGATE's 2nd s,
RALPH HEYGATE; settled in London; *m* 1st — (*dsp*); *m* 2nd Anne, dau of Nicholas Spicer, of Exeter, and had an er s:

NICHOLAS HEYGATE; memb Court Assists Merchant Taylors' Co; *m* Elizabeth, dau of Thomas Cotton, of Loughton, and gdau of Edward Shuckburgh, of Naseby, Northants, and had an only child:

ROBERT HEYGATE, of Husband's Bosworth; *m* Anne, dau of John Freeman, and *d* 1736, leaving an only s:

NICHOLAS HEYGATE, of West Haddon, Northants; *b* 7 Sep 1705; *m* Mary Anne (*d* 20 July 1794), dau of John Cooke, of Hill Morton, Warwicks, and *d* 20 July 1774, having had, with three er sons and three daus:

JAMES HEYGATE, of Aldermanbury, Hackney and Southend, Essex; *b* 11 Jan 1747; banker; *m* 11 Jan 1781 Sarah (*d* 2 Feb 1801), 2nd dau of Samuel Unwin, of Sutton-in-Ashfield, Notts, and *d* 11 April 1833, leaving, with a yr s (James, *b* 15 Feb 1784, *m* 20 Aug 1814 Anna (*d* 9 Sept 1867), dau of Edward Longdon Mackmurdo, and *d* 22 July 1873, leaving issue):

Sir William Heygate, 1st Bt (UK), so *cr* 30 Sept 1831; *b* 24 June 1782; MP Sudbury, Alderman City London (Ld Mayor 1822); *m* 19 May 1821 his sis-in-law Isabella (*d* 7 Oct 1859), 4th dau of Edward Longdon Mackmurdo, of Upper Clapton, and *d* 28 Aug 1844, having had issue:

1 FREDERICK WILLIAM (Sir), **2nd Bt**
2 William Unwin, JP, DL, of Roecliffe Hall, Leics; *b* 12 March 1825; *educ* Eton and Merton Coll Oxford (BA 1847, MA 1850), MP Leicester 1860–65, Stamford 1868 and S Leics 1870–80, Capt Leics Yeo Cav; *m* 6 July 1852 Constance Mary (*d* 7 Oct 1929), only dau of Sir George Beaumont, 8th Bt (*qv*), and *d* 2 March 1902, leaving issue:

(1) William Howley Beaumont, JP (Leics 1883–90); *b* 20 May 1854; *educ* Eton and RMA Woolwich; Capt RA, Hon Maj 1916 WW I; *m* 27 July 1881 Helen Frances (*d* 3 Nov 1939), dau of James Dalglish, and *d* 21 Sept 1928, leaving:
1a Gerald, DSO (1918), JP (Leics 1924); *b* 1 Aug 1882; *educ* Radley and RMA Woolwich; Lt-Col RA WW I (despatches); *m* 15 June 1916 Cynthia (*d* 4 July 1963), dau of Charles Darley, of Doncaster, and 7 Sept 1954, leaving:
1b *(Katherine) Raymonde Anne [Mrs Raymonde Horner, c/o Nat West Bank, 185 Sloane St, London SW1]; *b* 26 July 1917; *m* 24 Oct 1940 (*divorce* 1953) Lt-Col John Bayley Middleton Horner, only s of Maj John Fitz Lloyd Horner, OBE, JP, of Fitz Manor, Shrewsbury, and has issue:
1c Sarah Elizabeth Raymonde Anne Horner; *b* 13 Jan 1942; *m* 12 Sept 1962 *Virgil Pomfret [Virgil Pomfret Esq, 25 Sispara Gdns, London SW18 1LG], only s of Virgil Pomfret, of Kilchrenan, Argyll, and *d* 18 June 1994, leaving:
1d Virgil Alexander Dominic; *b* 19 Aug 1966; *d* 21 June 1994
1d *Emma-Louise; *b* 11 June 1965
2b *Felicity Cynthia June [Mrs Charles Owen, Flat 31, 15 Portman Sq, London W1]; *b* 27 June 1926; *m* 14 Feb 1950 *Lt-Cdr Charles Alexander Headon Owen, DSC, RN, s of William Owen, and has issue:
1c *Rupert Charles [Rupert Owen Esq, 91 Cambridge St, London SW1V 4PY]; *b* 3 April 1956; *m* 1988 *Astrid Bigbie and has:
1d *Charles William; *b* 1990
2d *Henry Beaumont; *b* 1991
1c *Caroline Angela [Mrs James Knox, Martnaham Lodge, by Ayr, Ayrshire]; *b* 4 April 1954; *m* 1983 *James Richard Dunsmuir Knox and has:
1d *Bryce William Dunsmuir; *b* 1992
1d *Constance Felicity Rose; *b* 1992
2a Claud Raymond; *b* 27 July 1886; Capt Yorks LI WW I; *ka* 2 July 1916
3a Lionel Clement; *b* 20 Feb 1893; Maj DCLI WW I (wounded), ADC to Govr and C-in-C Gold Coast 1929; *m* 1st 22 May 1918 Janet Leigh (*d* 25 Aug 1923), only dau of Richard Jeston Ogle, of Christchurch, NZ, and had:
1b *(Diana) Juliet Beaumont [Mrs John Rush, 1 Eastwell Barn Mews, Tenterden, Kent]; *b* 13 Jan 1920; *m* 6 July 1946 Lt-Col John Francis Rush, RASC (*d* 1992), yr s of Francis James Rush, of West Norwood, and has issue:
1c *Charles Burlison RUSH later OGLE-RUSH (deed poll 10 June 1968); *b* 30 April 1947; *educ* Uppingham; *m* 1977 *Melanie Elizabeth Roche, dau of Austin Hasslacher, of Bowler's Farm, Dockenfield, Surrey, and has:
1d *Michael Pellew Roche; *b* 1980
1d *Sophie Elizabeth; *b* 1982
1c *Diana Louise; *b* 30 Sept 1949; *m* 1972 (*divorce* 1977, later took by deed poll name OGLE-RUSH) Michael Bailey
3a (cont.) Maj Lionel Heygate *m* 2nd 25 Sept 1935 (*divorce* 1943) Yvonne Sylvia, 2nd dau of William Ferdinand Tyler, and *d* 25 Feb 1947, having by her had issue:
2b *Marilyn Jennifer [Mrs John Fountaine, Moor Farm, Great Bircham, Norfolk PE31 6QP]; *b* 14 March 1938; *m* 8 Oct 1966 *John Brigg Charles Fountaine, yr s of V-Adml Charles Algernon Andrew Fountaine, CB, JP, DL, of Narford Hall, Norfolk, and has issue:
1c *Alexandra Juliet Catherine; *b* 1973
2c *Auriole Diana Eleanor; *b* 1975
(2) Reginald Beaumont; *b* 10 Oct 1857; *educ* King's Coll Cambridge (MA); *d* unm 5 Jan 1903
(3) Harry Beaumont; *b* 8 Feb 1872; Lt RN; *d* unm 20 July 1897
(1) Mary Florence; *b* 16 Jan 1861; *m* 20 May 1890 Rev John Nigel Philpott, Rector Cole Orton, Leics, s of Rev R S Philpott, Preb Wells, and *d* 1 July 1929, having had issue

3 Edward Nicholas, JP, DL, of Buckland, Leominster; *b* 23 June 1827; *educ* RMA Woolwich; Hon Maj RE; *m* 24 Sept 1857 Mary Jane (*d* 9 Sept 1914), only child of John Leonard Hammond, of Dinsdale Hall, Yorks, and *d* 30 May 1896, having had:
(1) Edward Leonard Aspinall, JP and DL (Herefs), of Buckland; *b* 29 Sept 1858; *educ* Wellington; Capt Roy W Kent Regt; *m* 20 July 1897 his cousin Henrietta Constance (*d* 21 Sept 1933), dau of Sir Frederick Heygate, 2nd Bt, and widow of Samuel Maxwell Alexander, of Roe Park, Co Londonderry, and *d* 26 Dec 1922
(2) Richard Lionel, JP (Herefs); *b* 25 Oct 1859; *educ* Wellington; Maj RA; *m* 17 July 1895 Eleanor Mary Gwenllian (*d* 11 Aug 1958), dau of Edward James Evans, and *d* 26 Nov 1926, leaving issue:
1a Mary Ursula; *b* 7 Aug 1896; *m* 4 July 1930 Capt Eustace King-King (*d* 7 Jan 1975) and *d* 17 April 1976, leaving issue
2a Gladys Henrietta; *b* 28 Nov 1898; *m* 1st 9 Aug 1924 Maj Brereton Ockleston Rigby (*d* 2 June 1931), s of Thomas Arthur Rigby, of Liverpool, and has issue:
1b *Richard Arthur; *b* 1926; *m* 1950 *Margaret Stocker and has issue:
1c *Janice Anita; *b* 1951
2c *Yvonne Linda; *b* 1953
2b *Walter Oswald; *b* 1931
2a (cont.) Mrs Brereton Rigby *m* 2nd 28 Sept 1933 Richard Thomas, s of Richard Thomas, of Ffan Hall, Llandewy, Radnorshire, and has by him:
3b *Harold Mostyn; *b* 1936; *m* 1960 *Kathleen Ada Hughes and has:
1c *Richard Edward; *b* 1963
2c *Roger Harold; *b* 1970
1c *Elizabeth Mary; *b* 1960
(3) Walter Beaumont; *b* 31 July 1861; *educ* Wellington and Trin Coll Cambridge (MA); *m* 15 April 1902 Edith Maud (*d* 20 March 1947), dau of Stephen Robinson, of Lynhales, Herefs, and *d* 17 May 1940, leaving issue:
1a Edward Stephen, MC; *b* 16 July 1906; *educ* Wellington and RMC Sandhurst; Lt-Col Roy W Kent Regt, served Palestine 1938 (despatches) and WW II; *m* 1st 30 Nov 1938 Margaret Victoria Moss (*d* 28 Dec 1961), dau of

Hugo Wilhelm Koch, of Mecklenburg; *m* 2nd 8 Dec 1962 *Joyce Marion, dau of Charles Henry Gerrard, and *d* 19–

4 Robert Henry John, JP; *b* 28 March 1830; MA; *m* 13 June 1866 Isabella Dorothea (*d* 9 Feb 1929), only surv dau of George Gill Mounsey, of Castletown, Cumberland, and *dsp* 7 Jan 1890

Sir WILLIAM's est s,

Sir Frederick William Heygate, 2nd Bt, DL; *b* 4 Sept 1822; MP Co Londonderry 1859–74; *m* 26 Aug 1851 Marianne (*d* 7 July 1914), only dau and heiress of Conolly Gage, of Bellarena, Co Londonderry, and *d* 14 Nov 1894, having had:

1 **Sir Frederick Gage Heygate, 3rd Bt**, JP and DL (Co Londonderry); *b* 23 Aug 1854; *educ* Cambridge (BA); barrister, Maj Mid-Ulster Art; *m* 17 July 1888 Flora (*d* 13 July 1948), dau of John Walter, of Bearwood, Berks, and *d* 14 Jan 1940

2 Robert Henry Gage, DSO (1896); *b* 26 July 1859; Lt-Col and Brev Col Border Regt, served Dongola, Nile and S Africa; *d* 28 Aug 1923

3 Arthur Conolly Gage; *b* 18 Aug 1862; *educ* Eton and St John's Coll Oxford (MA 1891); assist master Eton 1887–1918; *m* 17 Dec 1891 Frances Evelyn Rowley (*d* 21 March 1931), only dau of Edward Nourse Harvey, of Overross, Hereford, and The Purlieu, Hythe, Hants, and *d* 30 Sept 1935, having had:

(1) Christopher Evelyn Gage; *b* 21 April 1893; *d* 11 March 1905

(2) JOHN EDWARD NOURSE (Sir), **4th Bt**

(1) Elizabeth Sophia Frances,; *b* 8 March 1898; *m* 28 Nov 1918 (*divorce* 1944, resumed maiden name 1945) Maj Gerald Bryans Wolfe, RA (*d* 27 Aug 1961), and *d* 18 Jan 1966, leaving a son

1 Henrietta Constance; *m* 1st 22 April 1884 Samuel Maxwell Alexander (*dsp* 10 June 1886), of Roe Park, Co Londonderry; *m* 2nd 20 July 1897 Capt Edward L A Heygate (*see* above) and *d* 21 Sept 1933

2 Isabella Mary Anne; *d* 22 March 1938

3 Rosamond Anna; *b* 1859; *m* 23 Dec 1879 Lt-Col Thomas Edward John Lloyd, CB, DL (*d* 31 Jan 1937), of Plas Tregayan, Anglesey, and *d* 25 Feb 1948, having had issue

4 Maud Alice; *m* 24 Oct 1895 William Alexander Ingram (*d* 13 May 1943), of Walworth, Limavady, Londonderry, and *d* 11 Jan 1931

Sir FREDERICK's n,

Sir John Edward Nourse Heygate, 4th Bt; *b* 19 April 1903; *educ* Eton and Balliol Coll Oxford (BA); WW II in CD and as Bombardier RA; Assist News Ed BBC, writer in UFA film studios, journalist and novelist, author: *These Germans* (1940), *White Angel, A House for Joanna, Love and Death* and *Kurumba*; *m* 1st 7 Aug 1930 (*divorce* 1936) Hon Evelyn Florence Margaret Winifred, yst dau of 1st and last Baron Burghclere (*see* 1921 edn) and formerly w of Evelyn Waugh (*see* CARNARVON, E); *m* 2nd 28 Feb 1936 (*divorce* 1947) Gwyneth Eliot, 2nd dau of John Eliot Howard Lloyd, and by her had:

1 **Sir George Lloyd Heygate, 5th Bt**; *b* 28 Oct 1936; *educ* Repton and Trin Coll Cambridge (BA 1960); *m* 23 Dec 1960 *Hildegard Mathilde, est dau of August Anton Kleinjohann, of Duisburg, Germany, and *d* 1991, having had:

(1) A son; *b* July 1973; *d* late Jan 1974

(1) *Joanna; *b* 1977

(2) *Catherine; *b* 1977

2 Sir RICHARD JOHN GAGE HEYGATE, **6th and present Bt**

Sir John *m* 3rd 8 Dec 1951 Dora Luz (*d* 18 June 1968), 3rd dau of John Harvey, of Malin Hall, Co Donegal, and former w of Lt-Col Robert Rollo Gillespie, OBE, MC, and *d* 18 March 1976

HEYTESBURY

Arms: Quarterly, 1st and 4th, barry wavy of six, or and az., in a canton gu. a lion of England passant guardant or (for HOLMES); 2nd and 3rd, per fess or and paly of six erminois and az., in chief an eagle displayed sa., beaked and membered gu., charged on the body with two chevronels arg. (for À COURT). **Crests:** 1 Out of a naval crown or an arm embowed in armour, the hand ppr., grasping a trident az., headed or (for HOLMES); 2 An eagle displayed sa., charged with two chevronels or, beaked and legged gu., holding in the beak a lily, slipped, ppr. (for À COURT). **Supporters:** On either side an eagle, wings elevated sa., beaked and membered gu., each holding in the beak a lily, slipped, ppr. **Motto:** *Grandescunt, aucta labore* ('Increased by labour, they grow large').
Creations: Bt. (GB) 4 July 1795, B. (UK) 23 Jan 1828.

THE 6TH BARON HEYTESBURY OF HEYTESBURY, Co Wilts, and a **Baronet** (Sir Francis William Holmes À Court, Bt) [The Rt Hon The Lord Heytesbury, Manor House, Tarrant Keyneston, Dorset]; *b* 8 Nov 1931; *s* f 1971; *educ* Bryanston and Pembroke Coll Cambridge (BA 1954); *m* 22 Sept 1962 *Alison,est dau of Michael Graham Balfour, CBE, of Hampstead, and has:

1 +JAMES WILLIAM; *b* 30 July 1967

1 *Sarah Camilla [The Hon Mrs Dobell, 73 Montagu Mansions, London W1H 1LG]; *b* 20 April 1965; *m* 1989 *James T C Dobell, and has issue:

(1) *Edward; *b* 1993

Lineage: JOHN À COURT, of Raddon; *m* Mary, dau of Robert Pierce, of Bath, MD, and had:

PIERCE À COURT, of Ivy Church, Wilts; MP Heytesbury 1722–24; *m* 1705 Elizabeth, dau of William Ashe, of Heytesbury, by Anne, dau of Alexander Popham, of Littlecote, Berks, and *d* 20 March 1724, leaving, with other issue:

WILLIAM À COURT later ASHE À COURT (under terms of will of his great-uncle, Edward Ashe, of Heytesbury); Col 11th Foot, Gen, MP Heytesbury; *m* 22 Feb 1746 Annabella, dau and coheir (with her sister Matilda, w of Charles Repington, of Amington Hall, Warwicks) of Thomas Vernon, of Twickenham Park, and *d* 1781, leaving an only s:

Sir William Pierce Ashe à Court, 1st Bt (GB), so *cr* 4 July 1795; MP Heytesbury, Col; *b* 1747; *m* 1st Catherine (*dsp* 23 Sept 1776), dau of Lt-Col John Bradford; *m* 2nd 30 Oct 1777 Letitia (*d* 2 Aug 1821), dau of Henry Wyndham, of Salisbury, and by her had, with four daus:

1 WILLIAM, **1st Baron**

2 Edward Henry À COURT later À COURT REPINGTON (on inheriting the Amington Hall estate); V-Adml RN, MP Tamworth; *b* 10 Dec 1783; *d* 22 Sept 1855

3 Charles Ashe À COURT REPINGTON, CB; Lt Gen, Kt Guelphic Order; *b* 17 June 1785; *m* 10 May 1815 Mary Elizabeth Catherine (*d* 21 Jan 1878), only dau of Abraham Gibbs, and *d* 19 April 1861, leaving issue:

(1) Charles Henry Wyndham, of Amington; MA Cantab, MP Wilton 1852–55; *b* 14 Oct 1819; *m* 5 Aug 1854 Emily (*d* 28 Feb 1916), est dau of Henry Currie, of West Horsley Place, Surrey, and *d* 29 Oct 1903, leaving issue:

1a Charles, CMG (1900), of Amington and Maryon Hall, Hampstead; Lt-Col Rifle Bde, Mil Attaché Brussels and The Hague 1900, Cdr Order Leopold, Offr Legn Hon, Afghan War 1878 (medal with clasp), Burma 1889, Nile Expdn 1898 (despatches twice) and Boer War 1899–1900 (despatches twice); *b* 29 Jan 1858; *m* 11 Feb 1882 Melloney Catherine (*d* 13 May 1934), dau of Col Henry Sales Scobell, and *d* 25 May 1925, having had, with other issue (*d* young):

1b Melloney Catherine Isabel; *b* 25 Feb 1891; *m* 10 Nov 1910 Maj Gilbert Ireland Blackburne, er s of Col Robert Ireland Blackburne, CB, DL, of Hale Hall, Lancs, and *d* 13 May 1965, leaving issue. He *d* 28 April 1973

2b Elizabeth Frances; *b* 1892; *m* 10 Jan 1923 Thomas Henry Ratcliffe and *d* 17 Dec 1950, leaving issue

2a Sidney À COURT; civ engr; *b* 5 Aug 1862; *m* 28 June 1893 Florence Maud (*d* 5 June 1957), only dau of Lawrence Harrison, of Chelsea, and *d* 20 Feb 1951, having had issue

1a Margaret; *m* 21 June 1881 Maj Sir Edwin Frederick Wodehouse, KCB, KCVO, RA, and *d* 2 Nov 1927, leaving issue (*see* KIMBERLEY, E)

(1) Elizabeth; *m* 12 Aug 1846 1st Baron Herbert of Lea and *d* 30 Oct 1911, leaving issue (*see* PEMBROKE and MONTGOMERY, E)

Sir WILLIAM *d* 22 July 1817; his est son,

Sir William à Court, 2nd Bt, and **1st Baron Heytesbury of Heytesbury**, of Heytesbury, Wilts (UK), so *cr* 23 Jan 1828, GCB, PC; *b* 11 July 1779; Amb Extrdy and Plen St Petersburg 1828–32, nominated Govr Gen India 1834 but govt fell before he installed, Ld Lt Ireland 1844–46; *m* 3 Oct 1808 Maria Rebecca (*d* 6 Oct 1844), 2nd dau of Hon William Henry Bouverie (*see* RADNOR, E), and had issue:

1 WILLIAM HENRY ASHE, **2nd Baron**

2 Frederick Ashe; *b* 15 Dec 1818; *d* 28 Jan 1840

1 Cecilia Maria; *m* 27 Dec 1845 Hon Robert Daly, 5th s of 1st Baron Dunsandle and Clanconal (*see* 1911 edn), and *d* 25 Dec 1889 aged 78, leaving issue. He *d* 15 Jan 1892

The 1st BARON *d* 31 May 1860; his est son,

WILLIAM HENRY ASHE À COURT later HOLMES À COURT, **2nd Baron Heytesbury of Heytesbury**; *b* 11 July 1809; *m* 3 Oct 1833 Elizabeth (*d* 30 June 1874), est dau and heir of Sir Leonard Thomas Worsley Holmes, 9th Bt, of Westover, IoW, and *d* 21 April 1891, having had, with other issue:

1 William Leonard, DL IoW; *b* 19 Jan 1835; *m* 24 Sept 1861 Isabella Sophia (*d* 24 Sept 1908), dau of Rev Richard à Court Beadon, Vicar Cheddar, and *dvp* 16 Dec 1885, leaving:

(1) WILLIAM FREDERICK HOLMES À COURT, **3rd Baron Heytesbury of Heytesbury**, JP Wilts; *b* 25 June 1862; *m* 19 Nov 1887 Margaret Anna (*d* 7 Jan 1920), 2nd dau of J Nixon Harman, of Tadmarton, Oxon, and *d* 15 Aug 1903, having had:

1a William Leonard; *b* 14 Aug *d* 16 Nov 1889

1a Margaret Elinor; *b* 22 Aug 1888; *m* 4 April 1907 Ven Henry Edward Fitz-Herbert, yst s of Rev Sir Richard FitzHerbert, 5th Bt (*qv*), and *d* 3 March 1957, leaving issue

(2) LEONARD, **4th Baron**

(3) Richard Henry; *b* 23 Jan 1866; *d* unm 7 Jan 1930

(4) Charles; *b* 16 Dec 1867; *m* 1st 13 April 1893 Marion May (*d* 17 Feb 1913), est dau of Walker Busfeild, JP, 68th DLI, of Charlton, Somerset; *m* 2nd 7 March 1918 Lydia Gertrude (*m* 2nd 4 July 1927 V-Adml Hon Herbert Edward Holmes à Court (*see* below) and *d* 19 Nov 1967), 2nd surv dau of William Manning, of Wing, Bucks, and *d* 21 Dec 1922, having by his 1st w had:

1a Richard William Herbert; Capt (Gen Res of Offrs), Lt Rifle Bde WW I (wounded); *b* 25 Sept 1897; *d* unm 31 Jan 1939

(5) Herbert Edward; V-Adml; *b* 16 Feb 1869; *m* 4 July 1927 Lydia Gertrude (*d* 19 Nov 1967), widow of Hon Charles Holmes à Court (*see* above), and *d* 21 Oct 1934

(6) Alfred, JP Dorset; *b* 24 April 1870; *m* 4 Oct 1900 Constance Isabel (*d* 1963), dau of Charles John Newton, and *d* 18 Jan 1941, leaving issue:

1a *Bridget, OBE (1944); Ch Cdr ATS WW II; *b* 27 Aug 1901

(7) Henry Worsley, *b* 1 Sept 1871; *m* 23 April 1901 Evelyn Spencer (*d* 31 Jan 1947), 3rd dau of W Edward Woolley, of The Red House, Loughborough, and *d* 5 Oct 1924, leaving issue:

1a +Robert Anthony Pierce; WW II S African Forces; *b* 7 July 1905; *m* 6 March 1930 *Mrs Edith Clarice Mason, dau of J W Elworthy

2a Peter Worsley; WW II in RNR; *b* 15 April 1912; *m* 1st 2 Oct 1936 (*divorce* 1950) Ethnee Celia, dau of H R Cumming, of Gwelo, S Rhodesia; *m* 2nd 12 June 1951 *Hilda Rose Hunt and *d* 23 July 1966, having had by his 1st w:

1b (Michael) Robert (Robin) Hamilton; *b* 27 July 1937; *educ* Michaelhouse, Natal, and U of W Australia, Perth (LLB 1965); *m* 18 May 1966 *Janet Lee [Mrs Robin Holmes à Court, 22 The Esplande, Peppermint Grove 6011, W Australia; Heytesbury Stud, Keybsrook 6206, W Australia], BSc, theatre proprietor, dau of F H Ranford, of Perth, W Australia, and *d* 1990, leaving issue:

1c +Peter Michael Hamilton; *b* 1968; *educ* Geelong GS, Middlebury Coll, Vermont, USA (BA) and Pembroke Coll Oxford (MA); investment banker New York, fndr Back Row Productions; *m* 17 June 1995 *Divonne Jarecki, lawyer, of New York

2c +Simon Antony; *b* 1972

3c +Paul William; *b* 1973; *educ* Middlebury Coll

1c *Catherine Elizabeth; *b* 1969; *educ* U of W Australia (BA); with accounts dept Stoll Moss

2b +Simon Roger; game ranger 1959; *b* 26 Oct 1939; *educ* Michaelhouse, Natal

1a *Majorie Sophia, MBE (1961); *b* 23 July 1903

(1) Emily Caroline; *b* 16 July 1864; *d* 14 Aug 1892

(2) Edith Mary; *b* 24 April 1874; *m* 31 Dec 1907 Frederick John Press, of Clifton, and *d* 15 Sept 1961, leaving issue. He *d* 26 Sept 1944

(3) Elizabeth Anne; *b* 28 April 1878; *m* 12 July 1900 Arthur Stanley Rogers, and *d* 10 Nov 1962, leaving issue. He *d* 1916

2 Frederick; Lt 85th Foot; *b* 24 Aug 1839; *d* 1919

3 Henry; Capt RN; *b* 26 June 1841; *d* 4 Jan 1885

4 Charles George; *b* 8 Dec 1843; *m* 1st 8 April 1874 Mary (*d* 22 Feb 1875), dau of John Henry Anderson, and had:

(1) Alexander Charles; *b* 22 Feb *d* 24 Nov 1875

4 (cont.) Charles Holmes à Court *m* 2nd 12 April 1877 Mary West (*d* 29 Oct 1889), only child of William Howe, of Glenlee, NSW; *m* 3rd 1 Jan 1895 Martha (*dsps* 22 June 1899), dau of Herbert W Clowes; *m* 4th 26 June 1901 Mary Rae Johnstone (*d* 28 Dec 1944), widow of Henry Ralfe, barrister, and dau of R L Jenkins, of Nepean Towers, NSW, and *d* 10 Jan 1924, having had by her:

(2) Harold Charles; *b* 1 Jan 1878; *d* 2 March 1882

(3) Reginald Ashe, MC; Capt 54th Canadian Bn 2nd Centl Ontario Regt WW I (wounded); *b* 7 Dec 1879; *m* 8 April 1911 Gwladys Mary Eyre (*d* 1971), only dau of Henry Ralfe, barrister (*see* above), and *d* 8 Aug 1973, leaving issue:

1a Mary Gwladys Vaughan Ashe; *m* 28 Nov 1936 John William Jocelyn McClintock, of Little Norton Mill, Norton-sub-Hamdon, Somerset, and had:

1b *William Ashe; *b* 6 Oct 1942; *educ* Sherborne; *m* 16 July 1966 *Caroline, dau of Kenneth Ronald Munro Williams, of Bridge House, West Chinnock, Somerset

2b *John Neill; ARICS; *b* 15 Feb 1948; *educ* Milton Abbey

3b *Peter Miles; BSc (Eng) ACGI; *d* 14 Oct 1950; *educ* Sherborne

2a *Ruth Vaughan Ashe [Mrs George Walsh, Colts Close, E Burton, Wool, Wareham, Dorset]; Jr Cdr ATS WW II; *m* 3 Nov 1944 Maj-Gen George Peregrine Walsh, CB, CBE, DSO, RA (*d* 5 Feb 1972), and has issue:

1b *David Peregrine [David Walsh Esq, Claypits Farm, Winfrith Newburgh, Dorchester, Dorset]; 2nd Lt 1st Queen's Dragoon Gds 1968; *b* 18 Feb 1949; *educ* Sherborne and Fitzwilliam Coll Cambridge (MA); *m* 1980 *Harriet Glen, of Sydney, NSW

2b *Jonathan à Court Peregrine; *b* 15 Oct 1950; *educ* Sherborne; commissioned 16th/5th Queen's Roy Lancers 1972; *m* 1977 *Diana Susan, dau of William Ernest Jones, and has issue:

1c *Charles Peregrine; *b* 1980

2c *Thomas William Peregrine; *b* 1983

1c *Rebecca Jane à Court; *b* 1979

1b *Anne à Court Peregrine [Mrs T Colquhoun, Higher Norris Hill, Brockhampton, Dorchester, Dorset]; *b* 3 March 1952; *m* 1976 *Maj T A Colquhoun and has issue:

1c *Alastair George; *b* 1979

1c *Emma Louise; *b* 1980

(4) Alan Worsley; MD (Sydney), FRCP (Lond), Pres RACP 1950–52, Lt-Col AAMC WW I (despatches), Medaille des Epidemies; *b* 19 June 1887; *m* 3 June 1913 *Eileen, dau of Arthur Rouse, of Sydney, NSW, and *d* 16 April 1957, having had:

1a Brian; F/O RAAF WW II; *b* 1922; *ka* 1943

2a +Peter; RAAF WW II; *b* 1925; *educ* Sydney U (B Civil Eng 1950); *m* 1950 *Margaret Brown, dau of Col Eric Campbell, DSO, of Young, NSW, and has:

1b +Alan William; *b* 1953

2b +Campbell Worsley; *b* 25 Aug 1958

1b *Penelope; *b* 1951

2b *Juliet Helen; *b* 9 Aug 1955

1a *Pamela; *b* 1921; *m* 1945 *Mark Russell Glasson, RAAF, and has issue:

1b *David Alan Russell; *b* 17 April 1949

1b *Anne Russell; *b* 1 Aug 1946; *m* 16 March 1968 *William Howard Pendrill Charles, and has issue

2b *Jillian Russell; *b* 3 July 1951

5 Edward Alexander; Ch Constable Oxon, Lt-Col KSLI; *b* 23 Oct 1845; *m* 21 Dec 1880 Adelaide Sophie (*d* 6 May 1945), yst dau of Hugh Hamersley, of Pyrton Manor, Oxon, and *d* 23 June 1923, leaving issue:

(1) Rupert Edward, DSO (1917); Col Salop LI Boer War 1900–02 and WW I (wounded), DAA and QMG 1915, Col in Charge Admin NI 1939; *b* 6 Feb 1882; *educ* Haileybury; *m* 1 Dec 1917 Linda Katharine Cecil (*d* 18 Aug 1935), dau of Rev Cecil E Smith, and *d* 1958, leaving issue:

1a *Linda Rosemary; *b* 2 May 1919; *m* 1 June 1940 *Richard Paton Pollitt, Salop Yeo, and has issue:

1b *George Edward Paton; *b* 18 Feb 1947

2b *Andrew Gerald Paton; *b* 12 March 1949

1b *Linda Susan; *b* 13 Oct 1941

2b *Rosemary Caroline; *b* 10 March 1943

(1) Adelaide Emily; *b* 29 April 1883; *m* 22 April 1909 Sir John Walter Barrington Simeon, 6th Bt (*qv*), and *d* 3 Sept 1934, leaving issue

(2) Ruth Mary; *b* 4 June 1885; *m* 1st 20 Aug 1910 Maj Charles Evelyn Forrest DSO (*ka* Mesopotamia 22 Nov 1915), Oxon and Bucks LI; *m* 2nd 9 July 1919 Col Ernest Astley Edmund Lethbridge, CMG, DSO, and *d* 29 Aug 1960, leaving issue (*see* LETHBRIDGE, Bt)

6 Arthur Wyndham; Surveyor Public Works Antigua 1872–1903; *b* 7 May 1848; *m* 23 Oct 1873 Ann Berkeley (*d* 7 April 1935), 2nd dau of Hon Thomas Berkeley Hartman-Berkeley, CMG, V-Pres Gen Cncl Leeward Islands, and *d* 2 Oct 1915, leaving issue:

(1) Arthur Worsley; Strathcona's Horse Boer War 1899–1901, Canadian Expdny Force WW I (gassed and wounded); *b* 17 Sept 1876; *m* 17 June 1904 Sarah Eleanor, dau of John Mawson, of Saskatoon, Canada, and *d* 23 Dec 1919 from wounds recd in action

(2) William Alexander Russell; Lt Princess Patricia's LI WW I (severely wounded); *b* 19 April 1878; *m* 15 March 1916 Priscilla (*m* 2nd 10 July 1954 Reginald Victor Miles (*d* July 1956), and *d* 13 Feb 1955), est dau of Charles Gray, of Bosham, nr Chichester, and *d* 6 Aug 1942, leaving:

1a William Charles; Sgt Roy Canadian Artillery WW II; *b* 8 Dec 1918; *m* 1st 1943 (*divorce* 1946) Joan Patricia, only dau of J Lindsay Ellis; *m* 2nd 17 July 1946 *Elizabeth Ann [Mrs William Holmes à Court, 7920 Croydon Ave, Winnipeg, Canada R3M OY5], yr dau of Eric Tayleur, of Winnpeg, and *d* 29 March 1967, leaving by his 2nd w:

1b +William Walter [William Holmes à Court Esq, 532 Ave F South, Saskatoon, Canada SFM 1T7]; *b* 13 Oct 1948; *m* 1975 (*divorce* 1981) Catherine Anne Bannister

2b +Phillip John [Phillip Holmes à Court Esq, Box III, Caronport, Sask, Canada 50H 050]; *b* 11 May 1960; *m* 1988 *Deborah Anne Haachman

3b Eric Robert; *b* 25 Sept 1963; *d* 1985

1b *Margaret Anne [Mrs Ronald Chevrefils, Box 571, Pine Falls, Manitoba, Canada]; *b* 20 March 1951; *m* 1973 *Ronald Chevrefils, and has:

1c *Lawrence; *b* 1980

2c *Kevin; *b* 1983

2b *Deborah Mary [Mrs Francis Nogier, 134 Forester Rd, Saskatoon, Sask, Canada]; *b* 11 Oct 1953; *m* 1976 *Francis Richard Nogier and has:
1c *William Charles Heathcote; *b* 1973
1c *Margaret Elisabeth; *b* 1978
2c *Stacy Annette; *b* 1979
3c *Melissa Lee Anne; *b* 1982
3b *Barbara Jane; *b* 25 June 1955; *m* 1980 *A Ross Russell and has:
1c *Christopher; *b* 1982
2c *Nicholas; *b* 1984
2a Walter Alexander; F/O RCAF WW II; *b* 10 Feb 1923; *ka* over Berlin 2 Jan 1944
1a *Priscilla Ann [Mrs Herbert McCloy RR1, Prince Albert, Saskatchewan, Canada S6V 5P8]; *b* 22 Feb 1917; *m* 10 April 1948 *Herbert Samuel McCloy, s of S B McCloy, of Prince Albert, and has issue:
1b *Samuel Boyd [Samuel McCloy Esq, RR1, Prince Albert, Saskatchewan, Canada S6V 5P8]; *b* 22 April 1952; *m* 1976 *Elaine Joyce, dau of Raymond Smith, of Holbein, Saskatchewan, and has issue:
1c *Janet Kyle; *b* 1983
2b *Russell Alexander [Russell McCloy Esq, Box 421, Prince Albert, Saskatchewan, Canada S6V 5R7]; *b* 31 March 1954; *m* 1st 1973 (*divorce* 1980) Elaine June, dau of Albert Aalbers, of Prince Albert, and has issue:
1c *Jason Albert; *b* 1974
2b (cont.) Russell McCloy *m* 2nd 1987 *Janet Muriel Crosland Shane-Alexander and has by her:
2c *Shane Alexander; *b* 1987
1c *Bethany Jane; *b* 1990
3b *James Andrew; *b* 7 July 1959; *m* 1978 *Sherri Dawn, dau of Peter Dyck, of Prince Albert, and has issue:
1c *Benjamin John; *b* 1978
2c *Ryan James; *b* 1981
1c *Kristin Dawn; *b* 1981
1b *Constance Gail [Mrs Kent Walters, Box 434, Prince Albert, Saskatchewan, Canada]; *b* 22 June 1961; *m* 1980 *Kent Mark Walters and has:
1c *Matthew Adam; *b* 1983
2c *Brock Carl; *b* 1987
1c *Amy Monelle; *b* 1989
(3) Thomas Edward; *b* 23 Sept 1879; *m* 15 Oct 1918 Violet Constance Lahay, dau of Templeton Vincent Blackwell, of Poona, Bombay, and *d* 12 July 1943, having had issue:
1a Edward Templeton Berkeley; *b* 22 Nov 1919; *d* 4 Aug 1921
2a Thomas Berkeley; Merchant Navy WW II; *b* 25 April 1921; *d* at sea as a result of enemy action 1940
3a Humphry Berkeley; *b* 6 Aug 1922; *d* 9 Sept 1932
1a *Constance Ann Berkeley; *b* 4 Dec 1924
(4) Leonard Wyndham Daly, MBE (1930); Maj cmdg Antigua Def Force; *b* 26 Sept 1881; *m* 1 Oct 1909 Helen Marjorie (*m* 2nd 1947 W Walwyn, of Estridge, St Kitts, WI), 2nd dau of Robert Allman Hardtman, of Stapleton, St Kitts, and *d* 19 June 1934, having had issue:
1a Arthur Leslie; *b* 25 Sept 1910; *d* 11 July 1911
2a Robert Douglas Hardtman, QPM; Colonial Police Medal for Meritorious Service (1952), Assist Commr Police Malawi; *b* 9 April 1913; *educ* Haileybury; *m* 2 May 1941 *Sheila Gwendolyne [Mrs Robert Holmes à Court, 3 Belmont Rd, Mowbray 7700, S Africa], dau of Hugo Hauffman Gibbon, of Trinidad, and *d* 26 Feb 1983, leaving issue:
1b +Robert Leonard [Robert Holmes à Court Esq, 104 Forest Lodge, Main Rd, Rondebosch 7700, S Africa]; *b* 3 July 1946; *educ* Haileybury and U of Cape Town (MSc Elec Eng); *m* 21 June 1997 *Astrid, dau of Henry Dirk Jackson, of Melbourne, Australia
1b *Sheila Lou [Mrs Alan Lowes, 441 Cowper Rd, Blyth, Northumberland NE24 5NF]; *b* 26 Feb 1942; *m* 1st 2 May 1964 (*divorce* 1997) Nigel Gordon Armstrong; *m* 2nd 28 June 1997 *Alan Lowes and by her 1st husb has:
1c *James Douglas; *b* 17 May 196–; *m* 19– *Deborah — and has:
1d *Flora; *b* 19–
1c *Quinta Evelyn; *b* 10 April 1966; *m* 19– *Kevin —
1a *Dorothy Kathleen; PO WRNS; *b* 27 Aug 1911; *d* 1986
(1) Anne Berkeley Ashe; *b* 7 Feb 1875; *m* 19 Oct 1910 Gerald Edward Friend, MA, FRCS, LRCP, MO Christ's Hospital Horsham, and *d* 3 Nov 1944, leaving issue
1 Elizabeth; *m* 16 June 1859 Edward Wilkes Wand, JP, of Manston Hall, son of Edward Wand, of Manston Hall and Chester Court, Yorks, and *d* 20 Aug 1902, leaving issue
2 Emily; *m* 21 Aug 1862 14th Baron Inchiquin (*qv*) and *d* 3 Jan 1868, having had issue
3 Gertruda Anne; *m* 25 Jan 1882 Hugh Hamersley, DL, of Pyrton Manor, Oxon, and *d* 1 Sept 1933. He *d* 2 Nov 1884
4 Margaret; sister St Mary's Home, Wantage; *d* 21 Feb 1933

The 3rd BARON's bro,

LEONARD HOLMES À COURT, **4th Baron Heytesbury of Heytesbury**; Lt-Col and Brevet Col Duke of Edinburgh's Wiltshire Regt, Boer War 1900–01 and WW I, Col Wiltshire Regt 1919; *b* 11 June 1863; *m* 9 Sept 1896 Sybil Mary (*d* 20 April 1937), dau of Capt Frank B Morris, Bengal Army, and had issue:
1 WILLIAM LEONARD FRANK, **5th Baron**
1 Sybil Nancy; *b* 20 June 1897; *m* 12 May 1933 Lt-Col Geoffrey Richard Marriott Bowly, Roy Warwicks Regt (ret), of Manor Lodge, Aller, nr Langport, Somerset, and *d* 4 Jan 1970, leaving issue
2 *Betty Mary; *b* 9 June 1902; *m* 1st 31 July 1923 (*divorce* 1946) Cdr Vivian John Robinson, RN, and has issue:
(1) *Anthony Leonard à Court; *b* 7 March 1927; *m* 26 Jan 1952 *Sheila Ann, er dau of Capt Richard Stratford Lovatt, OBE, RN, and has issue:
1a *Anthony Henry; *b* 3 July 1957
1a *Ann Sophia; *b* 20 March 1953
2a *Caroline Jane; *b* 22 March 1960
(2) *Kenyon John à Court; *b* 2 Feb 1929
(1) *Jill à Court; *b* 14 July 1924; *m* May 1947 (*divorce* 1968) Robert William Burt and has:
1a *Benjamin William; *b* 24 March 1948
2a *Daniel Robert; *b* 22 Dec 1949
1a *Nancy Elizabeth; *b* 3 July 1951
2a *Sally Jane; *b* 25 Feb 1953
2 (cont.) The Hon Mrs Betty Robinson added the name À COURT 1946; *m* 2nd 18 Sept 1956 *Alfred Esmond Robinson, CBE, MC, only s of Alfred Roberts Robinson, JP, of Blackwell House, Somerset

The 4th BARON *d* 2 Feb 1949; his only son,

LEONARD FRANK HOLMES À COURT, **5th Baron Heytesbury of Heytesbury**; *b* 17 April 1906; *educ* Pembroke Coll Cambridge (BA 1928); *m* 11 May 1926 Beryl (*d* 8 Oct 1968), yst dau of Albert Edward Bredin Crawford, DCL, LLD, of Aston Clinton House, Bucks, and *d* 27 Nov 1971, leaving:

FRANCIS WILLIAM HOLMES À COURT, **6th and present Baron Heytesbury**

HEYWOOD

Arms: Arg. three torteaux in bend between two bendlets gu., on a canton of the last a cross-patée or. **Crest:** On a mount vert the trunk of a tree with two branches sprouting therefrom and entwined with ivy, thereon a falcon, wings displayed ppr. **Motto:** *Alte volo* ('I fly high'). **Creation:** Bt. (UK) 9 Aug 1838.

SIR PETER HEYWOOD, 6TH BT, of Claremont, Co Lancaster [Sir Peter Heywood Bt, 64 Newbridge Rd, Weston, Bath BA1 3LA]; *b* 10 Dec 1947; *s f* 1992; *educ* Bryanston and Keble Coll Oxford (BA 1969); *m* 11 July 1970 *Jacqueline Anne, dau of Sir Robert Frederick Hunt, CBE, of Maple House, Withington, Glos, and has:
1 *Vanessa Jane; *b* 1975
2 *Annabel Sarah; *b* 1976

Lineage: JOHN HEYWOOD, of Bolton, Lancs, allegedly of a yr branch of the HEYWOODs of Heywood, Lancs (who had held land in Bury from Peter Heywood (*b* 1164) to the 18th century); *m* — Seddon, of Prestolee, and had issue:

OLIVER HEYWOOD, of Little Lever, Bolton; *b* 1556; *m* Alice, sis of Adam Hulton, of Breightmet, and *d* 1628, leaving:

RICHARD HEYWOOD, of Little Lever; *m* 1st Alice Critchlow, of Longworth (*d* 1657); *m* 2nd Margaret Brereton (*dsp*) and *d* 1 March 1677, leaving, with four daus:
1 Oliver (Rev); ejected from Coley, Halifax, Yorks, 1662; *educ* Trin Coll Cambridge (MA); *d* 1702, having had issue
2 NATHANIEL
3 John, of Barbados; had issue
4 Josiah, of Barbados; *dsp* April 1664

The 2nd son,

Rev NATHANIEL HEYWOOD; MA, Vicar Ormskirk; *b* 1633; ejected 1662; *m* Elizabeth Parr and *d* 1677, leaving issue:

NATHANIEL HEYWOOD, of Ormskirk; *b* 1659; *m* 1st Isabel Lynford, of Brinscawes, nr Blackburn (*d* 1687); *m* 2nd Rebecca Angier (*dsp*), of Warrington, and *d* 26 Oct 1704, leaving:

BENJAMIN HEYWOOD, of Drogheda; merchant; *m* Anne, dau of Arthur Graham, of Ballyherridan, Co Armagh, and sis of Brig-Gen William Graham, of Armagh, and *d* 1725, having had, with other issue:
1 Arthur, of Liverpool; banker; *b* 1719; *m* 1st Sarah, dau of Samuel Ogden, of Mossley Hill, Lancs, and had issue; *m* 2nd 26 April 1750 Hannah, dau of Richard Milnes, of Wakefield, and *d* 11 Feb 1795, having had further issue
2 BENJAMIN
3 Nathaniel; Lt-Col Coldstream Gds, Gentleman Bedchamber to HRH THE DUKE OF GLOUCESTER; *m* 1st Anna Maria, dau of Gen — Bowles; *m* 2nd

Mary (*d* 7 Aug 1824), dau of Sir Richard Hughes, and *d* 17 June 1808, leaving issue

1 Mary; *m* Patrick Stewart

2 Elizabeth; *m* 1732 Charles Caldwell, of Dublin, and was mother of Adm Sir Benjamin Caldwell, GCB

The 2nd son,

BENJAMIN HEYWOOD, of Liverpool, later Manchester; merchant and banker; *m* 1751 Phoebe (*d* 25 May 1810 aged 81), 2nd dau of Samuel Ogden, of Mossley Hill, by Phoebe, dau and coheir of John Pemberton, of Liverpool, and *d* Aug 1795 aged 72, leaving, with other issue:

1 Samuel; Serjeant-at-law, Ch Justice Wales; *b* 8 Oct 1753; *m* 1 Jan 1781 Susan (*d* 19 Jan 1822), dau of John Cornwall, of London, and *d* 11 Sept 1828, leaving issue

2 Benjamin Arthur, of Claremont, Liverpool and Manchester; banker; *b* 24 Aug 1755; *d* unm 19 Nov 1828

3 Nathaniel, of Manchester; banker; *b* 8 July 1759; *m* 24 June 1791 Ann (*d* 13 July 1847), dau of Thomas Percival, of Manchester, MD, FRS, and had issue:

(1) BENJAMIN (Sir), **1st Bt**

(2) Nathaniel

(3) Thomas, of Hope End, Herefs; *b* 3 Sept 1797; *m* 2 Oct 1823 Mary Elizabeth (*d* 12 Nov 1870), dau of John Barton, of Swinton Park, Lancs, and *d* 20 Nov 1866, leaving issue

(4) Richard, of Banner House, Bath; *b* 6 March 1799; *m* 1st 16 Dec 1822 Jane (*d* 14 Jan 1844), dau of Most Rev William Magee, DD, Archbp of Dublin, and had issue; *m* 2nd 1 June 1849 Frances (*dsp* 14 July 1875), dau of Henry Harford, of Down Place, Windsor, and *d* 20 Feb 1867

(5) James, of Kensington Palace Gardens; MP N Lancs, FRS; *b* 28 May 1810; *m* 11 June 1853 Anne (*d* 17 July 1872), widow of Albert Escher and dau of John Kennedy, and *d* 1897, leaving issue:

1a Anne Sophia; *d* unm

(1) Elizabeth; *m* 6 Nov 1818 her cousin Benjamin Heywood Bright, of Bristol, and *dsp* 31 May 1819

NATHANIEL HEYWOOD *d* 2 April 1815 aged 56; his est son,

Sir Benjamin Heywood, 1st Bt (UK), so *cr* 9 Aug 1838; FRS; *b* 12 Dec 1793; MP Lancs; *m* 22 Oct 1816 Sophia Ann (*d* 25 Aug 1852), only dau of Thomas Robinson, of Woodlands, and had, with other issue:

1 THOMAS PERCIVAL (Sir), **2nd Bt**

2 Oliver, JP, DL Lancs; High Sheriff 1888; *b* 9 Sept 1825; *m* 7 Sept 1847 Eleanor (*d* 14 Sept 1877), dau of Richard Watson Baron, of Springwood, Lancs, and *dsp* 17 March 1892

3 Arthur Henry, JP Lancs and Westmorland; *b* 21 Dec 1826; *m* 1st 25 Jan 1853 Alice (*d* 16 July 1855), est dau of William Langton, of The Rookery, nr Manchester, and had issue:

(1) Alice Sophia; *m* 17 May 1899 Samuel Henry Gladstone (*d* 14 Jan 1932), of Manchester, and *dsp* 20 Dec 1939

3 (cont.) Arthur Heywood *m* 2nd 10 Jan 1861 Margaret Helen (*dsp* 9 Dec 1918), yst dau of John Frederick Foster, DL, JP, and *d* 11 March 1901

4 Edward Stanley, JP Lancs; *b* 22 Dec 1829; *m* 30 Dec 1856 Louisa (*d* 26 Sept 1910), est dau of John Peel, MP Tamworth, of Middleton Hall, Warwicks, and *d* 19 Jan 1914, leaving issue:

(1) Mary Beatrice; *m* 6 July 1882 Francis Buller Howell, DL, JP (*d* 1918), of Ethy, Lostwithiel, Cornwall, and *d* 6 May 1954, leaving issue (*see* SHAKERLEY, Bt)

5 Henry Robinson (Rev); MA, Vicar Swinton, Hon Canon Manchester; *b* 18 Aug 1833; *m* 19 May 1858 Ella Sophia (*d* 15 Aug 1928), est dau of Rev William Gibson, Rector Fawley, Hants, and *d* 12 March 1895, leaving:

(1) Henry Arthur; *b* 19 June 1859; *m* 5 Jan 1899 Katharine Louisa (*d* 21 Jan 1937), dau of Rev Canon Ernest Alured Waller (*see* 1970 edn WALLER, Bt, of Braywick Lodge), and *d* 2 July 1943, leaving:

1a Geoffrey Henry, CBE; FRICS; *b* 22 Aug 1903; *educ* Repton; *m* 7 July 1931 Magdeleine Jeanne Georgette Marie (*d* 1987), yr dau of Jean Herpin, of Paris, and *d* 1986, leaving issue:

1b +Claude Geoffrey [Claude Heywood Esq, 1626 Verling Ave, Saanichton, BC V8M 1W8, Canada]; Dep Min Labour Prov of BC 1989–96; Overseas Civ Serv Kenya 1957–62; *b* 18 March 1933; *educ* Repton and Gonville and Caius Coll Cambridge (MA); *m* 10 Dec 1960 *Anne Helen, dau of Theron Wilding-Davies, of Fayre Ways Stud Farm, Dorstone, Herefs, and has:

1c +James Claude; *b* 19 May 1962; *m* 1995 *Susan Anne Amesbury, of Manchester

2c +Peter Geoffrey; *b* 15 Jan 1965; *m* 1989 *Heather Joan, er dau of Barry Gill, of Brentwood Bay, BC, and has:

1d +David Geoffrey; *b* 21 Feb 1996

1d *Erin Heather; *b* 23 May 1994

1c *Sarah Anne; *b* 20 Sept 1963; *m* 1991 *Colin Derek Ewart and has:

1d *Annie Magdeleine; *b* 29 Sept 1993

2d *Lucy Rose; *b* 6 July 1996

1b *Claire Margaret [Mrs Alexander Ferguson, Bernisdale, Hook Heath, Woking, Surrey GU22 0LE]; *b* 5 Aug 1938; *m* 23 Sept 1961 (*divorce* 1968) Mark Hugh Learoyd Piercy; *m* 2nd 1973 *Alexander Campbell Newton Ferguson and by her 1st husb has issue:

1c *Giles Hugh Scott; *b* 16 July 1966; *m* 1994 *Camilla Anne, est dau of Giles Sim, of Littles Farmhouse, Shalford Green, Essex

1c *Emma Magdeleine; *b* 1 Sept 1963; *m* 1989 *Edward Vincent Knox, of Godalming, Surrey, and has:

1d *Amy Claire; *b* 21 Dec 1994

2a Charles Richard (Rev); Rector Tarporley Cheshire 1945–62, Vicar Bakewell Derbys 1962–75; *b* 5 Jan 1908; *educ* Repton and Gonville and Caius Coll Cambridge (BA 1929, MA 1933); *m* 5 Sept 1939 *Alice Ruth [Mrs Charles Heywood, 5 Stoney Furlong Rd, Baslow, Bakewell, Derbys], yr dau of Dr William Henry Dobie, of Chester, and *d* 1979, having had:

1b +Richard Henry Norman [Richard Heywood Esq, 142 Clarkfield, Mill End, Rickmansworth, Herts WD3 2FJ]; *b* 5 Dec 1946; *educ* Worksop Coll; MIMS, MICFM, Sec Gen Jaycees Intl 1983–85; head fundraising EEIBA; *m* 1971 (*divorce* 1987) Melody Dawn, er dau of Col J A H Nicholson, DL, of Quinton, Bamford, Sheffield, and has:

1c *Tamsin Melody; *b* 24 June 1975

2c *Nicola Dawn; *b* 19 July 1977

1b Katharine Susan; *b* 25 Nov 1944; *d* 30 March 1950

2b *Margaret Anne; *b* 19 March 1950

(2) Hugh Sumner; *b* 9 June 1860; *d* 25 July 1871

(3) Basil; *b* and *d* 2 March 1864

(4) Charles Christopher; MA, MB, BC Cambridge MRCS, MRCP (Lond), LSA, Lt-Col 2nd/9th Bn Manchester Regt and Maj RAMC WW I; *b* 3 May 1865; *m* 7 Sept 1893 Mildred Ella (*d* 22 May 1957), est dau of Capt Percy Reid Lempriere, RA, and *d* 10 March 1948, leaving issue:

1a Hugh Christopher Lempriere (Very Rev); Fell and Dean Gonville and Caius Coll Cambridge 1928–45, examining Chaplain to Bps Southwark 1932 and Southwell 1942, Provost Southwell 1945–69, Select Preacher Cambridge 1932, 1933, 1938, 1940, 1945, 1949 and Oxford 1942, 1943, 1944 and 1963, Jr Proctor 1934–35 and 1943–44, U Lecturer 1933–45, Hulsan Preacher Cambridge 1957, Capt IA WW I (wounded, despatches); *b* 5 Nov 1896; *educ* Haileybury and Trin Coll Cambridge (BA 1925, MA 1929); *m* 14 Jan 1920 Margaret Marion (*d* 1982), only dau of Herbert Vizard, of Whitepost House, Redhill, and *d* 1987, leaving issue:

1b +Peter [Peter Heywood Esq, 2 Dalemoor Gardens, Aspley Park Drive, Nottingham, NG8 3EB]; Capt Oxfordshire and Buckinghamshire LI 1945–48, assist master: Worksop Coll Notts 1949–52, The Leas, Hoylake, Cheshire 1952–58, Roy Masonic Jr Sch Bushey 1958–60 and Manvers Sch Nottingham 1960–68, Headmaster William Sharp Bilateral Sch 1968–87; *b* 18 March 1922; *educ* Haileybury and Gonville and Caius Coll Cambridge (BA 1948, MA 1951); FCP

1b *Ann Rosemary [Mrs Thomas James, The Mill House, 32 Mill Lane, Linton, Cambridge CB1 6JY]; *b* 8 Feb 1930; *m* 16 Jan 1954 *Thomas Strachan James and has issue:

1c *Christopher William; *b* 26 March 1955; *educ* The Leys Sch

2c *Timothy Robert; *b* 12 May 1956; *educ* Langley Sch

1c *Pamela Susan; *b* 17 June 1961

2a Everard Lempriere; Maj Middlesex Regt, served 1917–47; *b* 26 Aug 1898; *educ* Haileybury; *d* unm 6 May 1967

3a Alan Lempriere; Lt Middx Regt; *b* 7 Dec 1899; *educ* Haileybury; *m* 12 Sept 1925 Constance (*d* 1988), dau of Fred Swales, of Melbourn Villa, Simla, India, and *d* 5 March 1960, leaving issue:

1b +Denys Guy Lempriere [G/Capt Denys Heywood, Deddington Manor, Deddington, Oxon]; G/Capt RAF, served on Fighter Sqdns in Palestine, Iraq and Egypt 1947–50 and Germany 1954–58, Staff Coll 1961, cmded No 94 (F) Sqdn and No 617 (The Dambusters) Sqdn, SACEUR Rep to Jt Strategic Target Planning Staff at SAC HQ, Nebraska, USA; Bursar Tudor Hall Banbury 1977–88; *b* 10 Nov 1926; *educ* Denstone and Gonville and Caius Coll Camb; *m* 12 Oct 1957 *Elisabeth Ann, dau of J Jeffrey Baker, of Windyridge, Altwood Rd, Maidenhead, and has issue:

1c +Robin Guy; *b* 22 July 1958; *m* 1984 *Mitchiko, dau of John Cole, of Deddington

2c +Simon John; *b* 19 May 1966; *m* 1992 *Alison, dau of Garry Cook, of Adderbury, Oxon

1c *Annabel Jane; *b* 20 Feb 1961

2c *Carol Elizabeth; *b* 13 Oct 1962; *m* 1992 *Charles Skinner, of Winchester

2b +Adrian Christopher Lempriere [Adrian Heywood Esq, c/o The Willows, Sandown Park, Tunbridge Wells, Kent], RA 1947–49, 2nd Lt 1948; *b* 20 Jan 1928; *educ* Denstone and Selwyn Coll Cambridge (BA 1952, MA 1953); *m* 13 Jan 1962 *Patricia Mollie Gardner, dau of Guy Goulden, and has issue:

1c +Christopher Lempriere; *b* 23 Nov 1962; *m* 1991 *Lisa Mary Buckley, of Oldham, Lancs

2c +Guy Lempriere; *b* 14 Feb 1965; *m* 1993 *Tracy Jane McCormack, of Melbourne, Australia

4a Basil Lempriere; WW II 1942–45 in RAF Regt; *b* 2 Nov 1903; *educ* Haileybury; *m* 17 Sept 1930 *Phyllis Miriam [Mrs Basil Heywood, 6 Pheasant Field, Hale, Liverpool L24 5SD], dau of John Orchard, barrister, of Haighmoor, Topsham, Exeter, and *d* 1989, leaving issue:

1b +John Basil Summer [John Heywood Esq, 6 Pheasant Field, Hale Village, Liverpool L24 5SD]; RAF 1952–57, memb Inst of Trg Offrs, Trg and Personnel Offr with Plessey Co 1957–93; *b* 6 Sept 1933; *educ* Holt High Sch, Liverpool and Liverpool Coll of Technology; CEng, MIEE

2b +Christopher Richard [Christopher Heywood Esq, Rozel, Ditchling Rd, Haywards Heath, W Sussex RH17 7RF]; *b* 22 March 1949; *educ* Liverpool Coll; *m* 1971 *Susan Rosa, dau of Thomas William Howarth, of Tynwald, The Moorings, Preston Brook, Cheshire, and has:

1c +Christopher David; *b* 1979

1c *Nicola Jane; *b* 1974

1b *Diana Ruth [Mrs Brian Woodcock, 6 Pheasant Field, Hale Village, Liverpool L24 5SD]; *b* 6 Nov 1937; *m* 1st 24 Aug 1963 Michael John Evans (*d* 1988); *m* 2nd 1991 (*divorce* 1995) Brian Victor Woodcock, and by her 1st husb has:

1c *(Andrew) Michael [Michael Evans Esq, 1 Highway Cottages, Basingsoke Rd, Winchester, Hants SO20 6DP]; *b* 22 Sept 1964; *educ* Girton Coll Cambridge (MA); *m* 1993 *Sheelagh Marie Jones and has:

1d *Effie Elizabeth; *b* 1994

2c *(Christopher) Philip [Philip Evans Esq, 44 Croftlands, Bigrigg, Egremont, Cumbria CA22 2UX]; *b* 18 April 1966; *educ* Bath U (BSc)

1c *Jennifer Lesley [Mrs Martin Croxford, 28 Mayfield Rd, Oldfield Pk, Bath BA2 3QA]; *b* 16 Aug 1968; *educ* Bath (BSc) and Surrey Us (MSc); *m* 1996 *Martin Gordon Croxford

1a Ella Marjorie Lempriere; WW II with QAIMNS; *b* 12 Dec 1906; *d* 199–
2a Mildred Ursula Lempriere; WW II as Petty Officer WRNS; *b* 28 Aug 1909; *d* 199–
(5) Geoffrey George Temple (Rev); MA Cantab; *b* 3 Nov 1869; *d* unm 3 June 1902
(6) Bernard Oliver Francis (Rt Rev); Bp Southwell 1926–28, Hull 1930–34 and Ely 1934–40, Canon St Albans, Assist Bp to Bp St Albans 1942–51; *b* 1 March 1871; *educ* Harrow and Trin Coll Cambridge (MA, DD); *m* 17 Oct 1895 Marion Maude (*d* 23 Oct 1957), dau of Capt Percy Reid Lempriere, RA, and *d* 13 March 1960, leaving issue:
1a Michael Henry Lempriere; *b* 3 Aug 1900; *educ* Haileybury; *m* Aug 1941 *Marjorie [Mrs Michael Heywood, The Hollies, Barningham, Richmond, Yorks DL11 7DW], dau of Charles Batty Wood, of Sheffield, and *d* 1990, leaving:
1b +Charles Michael Lempriere [Charles Heywood Esq, Rowantree House, Butterknowle, Bishop Auckland, Co Durham DL13 5JL]; *b* 16 May 1942; *educ* Barnard Castle Sch; *m* 11 May 1963 *Robina Anne, dau of John Robert Pattison, of Cleatham, Co Durham, and has:
1c +Benjamin Michael Lempriere; *b* 1971
1c *Lucy Catherine Adamson; *b* 1977
2b +Peter Bernard Martin; *b* 28 April 1946; *educ* Barnard Castle Sch
3b +David Mark; *b* 4 Dec 1947; *educ* Barnard Castle Sch
1b *Margaret Adamson; *b* 30 May 1944
2a Oliver Martin; Headmaster Barnes Lodge 1951–61 and Fonthill Sch East Grinstead 1962; *b* 14 June 1904; *educ* Haileybury and Selwyn Coll Camb; *m* April 1946 *Eileen Maud [Mrs Oliver Heywood, Virginia Cottage, Church Rd, Rotherfield, E Sussex], dau of Dr Martin Liebert, of Bradford, and *d* 1982, leaving issue:
1b +Timothy David Lempriere [Timothy Heywood, PO Box 25335, Abu Dhabi, United Emirates]; *b* 2 Feb 1948; *educ* Haileybury; *m* 1st 1972 (*divorce* 1986) Kathleen Ellen, dau of J L Waldman, of Caracas, and has:
1c +Benjamin Michael; *b* 1973
2c +Nicholas Anthony; *b* 1976
1b (cont.) Timothy Heywood *m* 2nd 1986 *Jane, dau of Julian Sherrard, of Tunbridge Wells, Kent, and by her has:
1c *Sophie Henrietta; *b* 1986
2c *Jessica Jane; *b* 1989
3c *Joanna Clare; *b* 1989
2b +Jonathan Martin [Jonathan Heywood Esq, Scripp, Foxhunt Green, Waldron, E Sussex]; *b* 2 Feb 1948; *educ* Haileybury; *m* 1982 *Elizabeth Mary, dau of Thomas Wilks, of Laggan, Isle of Islay, Argyll, and has:
1c +Thomas Martin; *b* 1985
1c *Emma Caroline; *b* 1983
2c *Kate Elizabeth Bridget; *b* 1993
3a +Charles Bernard Mark [Charles Heywood Esq, 21 St Andrews Drive, Charmouth, Dorset DT6 6LN]; WW II as Capt Oxon and Bucks LI; *b* 17 Feb 1906; *educ* Haileybury and Emmanuel Coll Cambridge (MA); *m* 13 Dec 1941 Julia Veronica (*d* 1977), dau of John Denis Cronin, of Cork, and adopted:
*Myra Anne; *b* 6 Feb 1929; *m* 1st Feb 1951 James Munro Lyall (*d* 7 Dec 1962), son of James Munro Lyall, of Wessels Nek, Natal; *m* 2nd 19 June 1964 Angus Douglas Stewart Rose, MA, and by her 1st husb has issue:
1c *Sally Bernice; *b* 8 May 1952
2c *Teresa Jane; *b* 8 Aug 1954
3c *Katherine Bridget; *b* 9 Dec 1959
4a Francis Melville; assist master Haileybury 1931–35; Fell, Assist Tutor and Praelector Trin Hall Cambridge 1935–39, Headmaster Marlborough 1939–52, Warden Ld Mayor Treloar Coll, Froyle, Hants 1952–69; *b* 1 Oct 1908; *educ* Haileybury and Gonville and Caius Coll Cambridge (BA 1931, MA 1934); *m* 28 Dec 1937 Dorothea Kathleen (*d* 1983), est dau of Sir Basil Edgar Mayhew, KBE (*see* PAGET, Bt, of Harewood Place), and *d* 2 Nov 1995, having had:
1b Simon Paget; *b* 18 Jan 1945; *educ* Marlborough, New Coll Oxford (BA 1966, DPhil), Inst of Educn Lond U, and Harvard (Kennedy Memorial Scholar 1967); *m* 29 July 1967 (*divorce* 1972) Sheila Madeleine, only dau of Sir Frank Stannard Gibbs, KBE, CMG, and *d* 1984
1b *Susan Frances; *b* 8 March 1939; *m* 1st 25 Nov 1965 (*divorce* 1984) Jean-Marc Duquesne, yr s of Leon Duquesne, of Roubaix, France; *m* 2nd 10 Jan 1990 *— and by her 1st husb has:
1c *Marc Dominic; *b* 9 Dec 1966; *m* 25 June 1994 *Sylvie Bisson
2c *Benjamin Piers; *b* 25 June 1969; *m* 1 Jan 1993 *Florence Pauline Annette Leotard and has:
1d *Martin Jean Marc Maurice; *b* 19 Sept 1994
3c *Sebastian Paul; *b* 5 Nov 1972
2b *Janion Lempriere [Mrs John LeQuesne, Bruce Rd RD5, Te Awamutu, New Zealand]; BSc (Lond), MB, BS, MRCS, LRCP; *b* 26 Oct 1947; *m* 1972 *John LeQuesne, MB, BS, MRCS, LRCP, and has issue:
1c *Nicholas Robert Page; *b* 1981
1c *Katherine Amy; *b* 1977
2c *Rebecca Janion; *b* 1978
4a (cont.) Mr and Mrs F M Heywood also adopted:
*Michael Patrick; *b* 24 Feb 1941; *educ* Trin Hall Cambridge (BA)
5a Percival Meredith; LRAM, musical dir Rydal Sch, Colwyn Bay, assist master Leys Sch 1937–45; *b* 26 March 1912; *educ* Haileybury, King's Coll and Trin Hall Cambridge (BA 1933, MA 1937); *d* unm 8 Jan 1975
1a Maude Lempriere; *b* 27 Jan 1897; *m* 4 April 1923 Rev Herbert Bowman, Hon CF, Vicar St Marks, Leeds (*d* 10 Dec 1930), and had:
1b *Iris Margaret Lempriere; *b* 3 April 1924; *educ* Leeds GHS and Edin U (MB, ChB 1947); *m* 28 March 1951 *Michael Atkinson, MD, FRCP, and has issue:
1c *Gillian Lempriere; *b* 9 Jan 1953
2c *Catherine Veryran; *b* 24 March 1955
3c *Judith Margaret; *b* 24 March 1955
4c *Alison Clare; *b* 6 July 1962
2a Ella Marion; *b* 25 Oct 1898; *m* 1 Aug 1923 Rev Canon Thomas Arnold Lee, MA (*d* 1973), and *d* 1993, leaving:
1b *John Richard Crispin; Sub-Lt RNVR 1956–57, Dep Govr Borstal; *b* 19 May 1933; *educ* Durham Sch and Emmanuel Coll Cambridge (BA 1955, MA 1959); *m* 17 Sept 1960 *Elizabeth Mary (MCSP), dau of Arthur Pring Farmer, MB, BSc, of Rochester, Kent, and has issue:
1c *Benjamin Mark; *b* 8 March 1962
2c *Crispin Oliver; *b* 13 Dec 1963
1c *Philippa Claire; *b* 7 March 1967
1b *Ruth Patricia Heywood; *b* 21 June 1924; *educ* London U (BSc); *m* 1 Oct 1949 *Michael John Bridgman, BSc, ANZIC, ANZIM, s of George Bridgman, of Wellington, NZ, and has issue:
1c *Tamsin Jane Lee; *b* 8 March 1953
1b (cont.) Mr and Mrs M J Bridgman also adopted:
*David Nicholas; *b* 10 Jan 1957; *educ* Selwyn Coll, Australia
2b *Tamsin Margaret Romanis, MB, ChB, DCH, DRCOG; *b* 14 Feb 1926; *m* 27 Nov 1959 Lt-Col Adrian Goodenough Hayter, MBE, MC, s of Graham Hayter, of Takaka, NZ, and has issue:
1c *Sarah Ann Lee; *b* 12 Sept 1960
2c *Rebecca Margaret; *b* 27 Aug 1963
3b *Frances Mary Cotchett; *b* 1 Dec 1927; *educ* London U (BSc Econ 1948)
(1) Mary Ella Sophia; *b* 13 Oct 1876; *d* unm 13 Feb 1931
(2) Dorothy Katherine Alice; *b* 22 May 1879; *d* unm 25 Aug 1967

Sir BENJAMIN *d* 11 Aug 1865; his est son,

Sir Thomas Percival Heywood, 2nd Bt, JP, DL Staffs, JP Lancs; High Sheriff 1852; *b* 15 March 1823; *m* 19 May 1846 his cousin Margaret (*d* 30 Jan 1894), est dau of Thomas Heywood, and had:
1 ARTHUR PERCIVAL (Sir), **3rd Bt**
2 Francis Graham; *b* 19 Jan 1854; *d* 7 May 1865
3 Bertram Charles Percival, TD, JP Staffs; MA Cantab, Col TF (Res), Hon Col 6th Bn Manchester Regt, cmdg Manchester Inf Bde BTF 1906–11, Boer War 1900–01 (medal and three clasps); *b* 10 Nov 1864; *m* 30 April 1889 Florence Maude (*d* 21 March 1943), 2nd dau of Edward David Meynell, of Kirk Langley, and *d* 28 Oct 1914
4 Gerald Graham Percival, TD; Lt-Col TAR, 1st/6th Bn Manchester Regt; *b* 12 Jan 1867; *educ* Winchester; *m* 14 July 1898 Mary (*d* Aug 1948), only dau of Ven Hon Berkeley Lionel Scudamore Stanhope (*see* HARRINGTON, E), and *d* 28 July 1954, leaving issue:
(1) Graham Scudamore Percival; Dir Roy Observatory Hong Kong, FRMS; *b* 5 July 1903; *educ* Winchester and New Coll Oxford (BA 1925, BSc 1926, MA 1934); *m* 4 June 1937 Valerie Rose Isabel (*d* 1992), dau of Lt-Col John Railton Wyatt, of Heathmere, Locks Heath, Hants, and *d* 1985, leaving issue:
1a *Susan Mary [Mrs Michael Knight, Oakwood, Itchen Abbas, Hants SO21 1AX]; *b* 15 July 1938; *m* 14 Jan 1961 *(John) Michael Knight, and has:
1b *Timothy John; *b* 3 June 1963; *m* 3 Aug 1991 *Lynda Marie, dau of Keith Seymour, of Bradford, Yorks, and has:
1c *Thomas Daniel; *b* 18 May 1997
1c *Catherine Louise; *b* 25 Nov 1994
1b *Nicola Susan; *b* 14 March 1962; *m* 15 July 1989 *Glenn Allan Royall, of Ulladulla, NSW, Australia, and has issue:
1c *Lachlan Allan; *b* 5 Nov 1992
2c *Jack Duncan; *b* 11 June 1995
1c *Charlotte Louise; *b* 5 Feb 1991
2b *Deborah Ann; *b* 27 Jan 1965
3b *Bridget Julia; *b* 29 April 1970
2a *Veronica Anne; *b* 24 Feb 1942
1 Isabel Mary, OBE (1930); *d* unm 23 Feb 1940
2 Etheldred Sophia Ann; *d* unm 7 Oct 1925
3 Hilda Margaret; *d* unm 5 Sept 1897
4 Mary Monica; *d* unm 10 Nov 1951

Sir PERCIVAL *d* 26 Oct 1897; his est son,

Sir Arthur Percival Heywood, 3rd Bt, JP Staffs and Derbys; MA Cantab; *b* 25 Dec 1849; *m* 14 Aug 1872 Margaret Effie (*d* 18 Aug 1921), est dau of Rt Rev George Henry Sumner, Bp Suffragan Guildford, and *d* 19 April 1916, having had:
1 **Sir Graham Percival Heywood, 4th Bt**, CB, DSO (1918), TD, JP, DL Staffs; MA Cantab, CA Staffs, chm Staffs TAA, High Sheriff 1922, barrister Inner Temple, Lt-Col cmdg Staffs Yeo 1916–18 and 1920, served WW I (despatches twice, wounded); *b* 14 July 1878; *d* unm 30 June 1946
2 Cecil Percival, CB (1933), CMG (1918); DSO (1916); Maj-Gen Coldstream Gds (Adj 1904–7), ADC to HM GEORGE V 1931–32, Boer War 1900–02 (wounded, two medals, seven clasps), Sudan 1908 (medal and clasp) and WW I (wounded, despatches six times, two brevets, Croix de Guerre); *b* 17 May 1880; *m* 12 Dec 1917 Margaret Vere (*d* 25 Oct 1958), er dau of Arthur Herbert Kerr (*see* LOTHIAN, M), and *d* 20 Oct 1936, leaving issue:
(1) OLIVER KERR (Sir), **5th Bt**
(1) *Joan Margaret [Mrs John Preston, Boxhanger Cottage, Box, Glos GL6 9HF]; *b* 1 March 1919; *m* 19 Dec 1950 *John Marsden Preston, s of John Preston, of San Francisco, and has issue:
1a *Nicolas; *b* 1952; *educ* Lycée Français London
3 Arthur George Percival; MA Cantab; Maj 6th Bn Manchester Regt WW I; *b* 1885; *d* 12 Sept 1918 of wounds recd in action
1 Muriel Annette Margaret; *m* 24 Jan 1899 Frederick Warren Markham, 2nd s of Rev Charles Warren Markham, and *d* 26 Feb 1924
2 Ella Mary Effie; *m* 3 July 1901 Col Percy Theodosius Denis de Vitre, DSO, DL, JP (*d* 8 Aug 1940), RE, s of Maj-Gen Denis de Vitre, RA, and *d* 12 June 1953, leaving issue
3 Dorothy Alice; *d* unm 10 March 1957

4 Evelyn Mary; *m* 2 Sept 1913 Lt-Col Robert James Rees-Mogg, DSO (*see* REES-MOGG, B), and *d* 8 Dec 1970, leaving issue

5 Margaret Sophia; *m* 23 Aug 1913 Lt-Col James Ernest Stewart, GC, MC (*d* 3 May 1946), RE, 6th surv s of James Stewart, of Tientsin and Pei-tai-ho, N China, and *d* 13 Oct 1940, leaving issue

6 Guendolen Constance; *d* an infant 1888

7 Isabel Effie

The 4th Bt's nephew,

Sir Oliver Kerr Heywood, 5th Bt; *b* 30 June 1920; *educ* Eton and Trin Coll Cambridge (BA 1940); Capt Coldstream Gds WW II (despatches); *m* 28 March 1947 *Denise [Dowager Lady Heywood, Rose Cottage, Elcombe, Glos], formerly w of 11th Baron Strabolgi (*qv*) and yr dau of Jocelyn William Godefroi, MVO, and *d* 1992, leaving:

1 Sir PETER HEYWOOD, **6th and present Bt**

2 +MICHAEL; *b* 10 Dec 1947; heir presumptive; *educ* Bryanston and Keble Coll Oxford (BA 1969); *m* 1972 *Carolyn Awdry, est dau of Ian Joseph Greig, of High Trees, Gustard Wood, Herts, and has:

(1) +Daniel Oliver; *b* 1979

(1) *Katie May; *b* 1977

3 +(James) Philip; film maker; *b* 5 June 1951; *educ* Bryanston; *m* 1978 *Alizen, dau of Reginald Merryweather, FRCS, of Painswick, Glos, and has issue:

(1) +Jack Theyre; *b* 1981

(2) +Barnabas Timothy; *b* 1985

(1) *Lucy; *b* 1979

HICKMAN

Arms: Per saltire sa. and or two leopard's faces jessant-de-lys in pale and as many fleurs-de-lys in fess, all counterchanged. **Crest:** A phoenix issuing out of flames, transfixed through the mouth by a tilting spear erect ppr., each wing charged with two annulets interlaced paleways or. **Motto:** *Igne et ferro* ('By fire and sword'). **Creation:** Bt. (UK) 25 Aug 1903.

SIR (RICHARD) GLENN HICKMAN, 4TH BT, of Wightwick, Tettenhall, Staffs [Sir Glenn Hickman Bt, Manor Farm House, Liddington, Wilts SN4 0HD]; *b* 12 April 1949; *s f* 1979; *educ* Eton; *m* 1981 *Heather Mary Elizabeth, dau of Dr James Moffett, of Westlecot Manor, Swindon, Wilts, and has issue:

1 +CHARLES PATRICK ALFRED; *b* 5 May 1983

2 +Edward William George; *b* 1990

1 *Elizabeth Margaret Ruth; *b* 1985

Lineage: JOSEPH HICKMAN, of Bilston, Staffs; *m* Sarah Rushbury and had:

GEORGE RUSHBURY HICKMAN, of Tipton, Staffs, JP; *b* 31 Jan 1795; *m* 18 June 1822 Mary (*d* 28 Feb 1872), only dau of Benjamin Haden, of Old Hall, Tipton, and *d* 25 Jan 1854, leaving, with an er s (George Haden) and a dau (Sarah Haden, *m* Rev E H L Noott, Vicar St John's Dudley):

Sir Alfred Hickman, 1st Bt (UK), so *cr* 25 Aug 1903, of Wightwick, Wolverhampton, Staffs, JP, DL; MP W Wolverhampton 1885–86 and 1892–1906, ktd 1891; *b* 3 July 1830; chm Alfred Hickman; *m* 10 June 1850 Lucy Owen (*d* 30 Sept 1914), only dau of William Smith, of Portsea, Hants, and had, with other issue:

1 Alfred William, of Goldthorn Hill, Wolverhampton, JP Staffs; *b* 10 March 1851; *m* 30 April 1879 Mary Whitby (*d* 19 Oct 1946), dau of William Hickin, JP, of Audmore House, Stafford and *dvp* 21 Aug 1902, having had:

(1) ALFRED EDWARD (Sir), **2nd Bt**

(2) William Christie; 2nd Lt RFA (SR); *b* 23 March 1888; *educ* Caius Coll Cambridge (BA); *m* 28 April 1912 Elizabeth (*d* 1934), dau of Frederick A Mumford, of Kingston-on-Thames, and was *ka* 17 July 1916

(3) Arthur; Capt TAR Worcs Yeo, Lt-Col Roy Pioneer Corps, WW I and II; *b* 20 June 1891; *m* 8 Sept 1914 Dorothy Gwendolen RRC (*d* 18 Aug 1957), dau of Edward Charles Rudge, JP, DL, of Abbey Manor, Evesham, and *d* 28 Sept 1959, leaving:

1a *Christine Gwen, TD [Maj Christine Hickman TD, 308A Barkham Rd, Wokingham, Berks]; *b* 8 Jan 1920; Maj WRAC (TAR), WW II with ATS 1942–46

2a *Pamela Jill [Miss Pamela Hickman, 308A Barkham Rd, Wokingham, Berks]; Lt WRAC Reserve, WW II with ATS 1942–46; *b* 14 Nov 1921

(1) Phillis Lucy, MBE (1918); *m* 25 June 1908 Maj James Deane, CMG, JP, DL, Roy Highrs (*d* 14 Nov 1942), of Goldington Bury, Beds, s of William Henry Deane, of Fareham House, Fareham, Hants, and *d* 29 March 1970, leaving issue

(2) Evelyn Julia; *m* 1st 23 April 1907 Charles Francis Simonds (*ka* 29 June 1916), of The Crofts, Shinfield, Berks, Maj 13th Bn KRRC, and had issue; *m* 2nd 5 Oct 1917 Capt Bernard James Fuller, KAR

2 Thomas Edgecumbe, CB (1900), DSO (1889), DL Staffs; Brig-Gen cmdg 109th Inf Bde 1914, Worcs Regt, Hon Col 6th Bn S Staffs Regt 1909, attd Egyptian Army 1884–94, 1896 and 1897–1900, Govr Dongola Prov Sudan 1899–1900, served Sudan Expdn 1884–85, Suakin 1888, Sudan 1888–89, Dongola Expdn 1896, Nile Expdn 1897, 1898 and 1899, Boer War 1899–1902 and WW I (despatches three times), MP S Wolverhampton 1910–18 and Bilston 1918–22; *b* 25 July 1859; *m* 8 Oct 1907 Elizabeth Maud Mackenzie (*d* 26 March 1960), yst dau of Surgn-Maj James Alexander Smith, DSO, and *d* 23 Oct 1930, leaving issue:

(1) Thomas Alfred Kenneth; Capt Cameronians, 13th/18th Hus, WW II; *b* 30 July 1912; *educ* Eton and RMC Sandhurst; *m* 30 April 1936 *Leila Philippa [Mrs Eric Scott, Holme Cottage, Church St, Nunnington, York YO6 5US] (*m* 2nd 25 March 1945 Maj Eric Inman Scott, MC (*d* 1967)), est dau of Lt-Col Montagu Martindale Parry-Jones, MC (*d* 1969), Roy Fus (*see* 1939 edn BORROWES, Bt), and was *ka* 27 May 1940, leaving issue:

1a +Thomas Montague [Maj Thomas Hickman, 60 Acre Lane, London SW2 5SP]; late Maj Life Gds; *b* 18 Feb 1940; *educ* Eton and RMA Sandhurst; *m* 1st 1967 (*divorce* 1974) Lieselotte Brandstetter, of Vienna, and has:

1b +Thomas Michael; *b* 1972

1b *Lucinda Ann; *b* 14 June 1970; *m* 1991 *Anthony Kenneth Noel Terry and has:

1c *Anna

2c *Emily Constance; *b* 9 Nov 1996

1a (cont.) Maj Thomas Hickman *m* 2nd 1977 *Christina, dau of Lt-Cdr Kenneth Alston Cradock-Hartopp, MBE, DSC, RN (ret) (*see* CRADOCK-HARTOPP, Bt), and has further issue:

2b +Alexander Kenneth; *b* 1980

2b *Louise Amy; *b* 1978

1a *Mary Elizabeth [Mrs Richard Graham, Cedar Hill, Roscrea, Co Tipperary, Ireland]; *b* 14 Dec 1937; *m* 1st 1 Sept 1962 (*divorce* 1975) Timothy Haworth, s of Maj Philip Knight Haworth, MC, of Filey, Yorks; *m* 2nd 1975 *Richard Malise Graham and by him has:

1b *Lileth Rosamund Anne; *b* 1975

2b *Ruth Leila Margaret; *b* 1977

(2) Michael; *b* 11 Dec 1922; *educ* Eton and RMC Sandhurst; Lt 11th Hus (PAO) WW II (wounded); *m* 1st 22 Sept 1944 (*divorce* 1948) Vivienne Loraine, yr dau of Lt-Col Maurice Isacke Clutterbuck, TD, DL, of Windmill House, Rowington, Warwicks; *m* 2nd 19 May 1951 *Phyllis, dau of W R Robinson, of Sheffield

(1) Elizabeth Ann; *b* 3 March 1915; *m* Oct 1939 Patrick George Grey, s of Sir John Grey, 8th Bt (*see* 1949 edn), and had issue

3 Edward, of Danes Court, Wolverhampton, Staffs, JP; *b* 6 Dec 1860; *m* 9 Aug 1887 Cecilia (*d* 26 Feb 1958), est dau of Thomas Charles Thompson, JP, of Milton Hall, Cumberland, and *d* 2 Jan 1941, leaving issue:

(1) Charles Edward; Maj RFA WW I (wounded, despatches); *b* 24 Dec 1890; *m* 1st 12 June 1915 Edith Barbara (*d* 22 June 1915), dau of Frank Spencer, JP, of Harrow-on-the Hill; *m* 2nd 7 Dec 1921 Dorothy (*d* 16 June 1966), dau of W Deans Forster, of Ponteland, Newcastle-on-Tyne, and *d* following a car crash 10 June 1963, having by her had:

1a +David Michael Roy [David Hickman Esq, Tower House, West Castle St, Bridgnorth, Salop]; *b* 11 April 1930; *m* 1st 8 Aug 1959 (*divorce* 1967) Eileen Elizabeth, yr dau of Brian Robert Boyd, of Belfast; *m* 2nd 1978 *Valerie Beatrice, er dau of Frank Victor Collins, of Wolverhampton, and by his 1st w has issue:

1b +Charles John; *b* 2 June 1960

2b +Timothy Robert [Timothy Hickman Esq, Ilex Trees, Mickleham, Surrey RH5 6EH]; *b* 17 Oct 1964; *m* 1990 *Vanessa Caroline, est dau of Lt-Col R A Latchford, of Düsseldorf, Germany, and has issue:

1c *Camilla Beatrice; *b* 1990

2c *Holly Olivia; *b* 1994

3b +Peter Richard; *b* 17 Oct 1964

1a Daphne Cecilia; WW II 1941–45 in WRNS; *b* 14 Sept 1922; *m* 1st 7 June 1947 Capt James Charles Critchell-Bullock (*d* 31 March 1953), 18th KGO Lancers, IA, and had issue; *m* 2nd 26 Oct 1954 (*divorce* 1961) Leslie George Pitt-Moore and *d* 1 Dec 1968

2a *Catherine Elaine [Mrs Patrick Hall, Cae Grugog, Trearddur Bay, Holyhead, Anglesey LL65 2UD]; LRAM; *b* 5 March 1926; *m* 1st 1 June 1949 Giles Reid Walker and has issue (*see* WALKER-OKEOVER, Bt); *m* 2nd 14 June 1955 *Patrick Campbell Hall, s of John Hall, of Charnes Hall, Eccleshall, Staffs, and by him has issue:

1b *Andrew Campbell; *b* 22 May 1957

(2) Wilfred Haden; Capt 1st/6th S Staffs Regt WW I; *b* 18 June 1892; *m* 5 June 1915 Kathleen Mary Stuart (*d* 1978), yr dau of Edward Noel Nason, MD, of Nuneaton, Warwicks, and *d* 1973, leaving issue:

1a +Wilfred Ian Edward, JP (Warwicks) [Wilfred Hickman Esq JP, Clifton Manor, Clifton-upon-Dunsmore, Rugby, Warwicks]; *b* 28 April 1916; *educ* Shrewsbury; *m* 3 Feb 1940 *Muriel Claire, dau of William Horsnall, of Nuneaton

2a Denis Stewart, MC; Capt RASC WW II Italy (Africa and Italy stars, POW); *b* 28 Feb 1918; *educ* Shrewsbury; *m* 1st 13 Oct 1947 (*divorce* 1964) Peggy Barbara (*d* 19–), formerly w of Alfred James McAlpine (*see* 1970 edn McALPINE, Bt) and est dau of John Ernest Saunders, of Glen Alyn, Gresford, Denbighs; *m* 2nd 25 March 1965 *Jean [Mrs Denis Hickman, 28 Kingham Rd, Churchill, Oxford OX7 6NE], yst dau of A Urwin, of Tynemouth, Northumberland, and *d* 30 March 1995, having by her had:

1b *Tara Jane; *b* 3 April 1966

2b *Rona Stuart; *b* 20 Feb 1967
3b *Anya Lucy; *b* 28 Aug 1969
3a +Christopher Wolf Arden [Christopher Hickman Esq, Barnhill, Nauton, Stow-on-the-Wold, Glos]; RASC 1944–46; *b* 30 Oct 1925; *educ* Shrewsbury; *m* 18 April 1949 *Daphne Esther, dau of John Alec Clift, of The Orchards, Loxley, Warwicks, and has issue:
1b *Rachael [Mrs Peter Austin, Ludbridge Mill, East Hendred, Oxon OX12 8LN]; *b* 11 June 1951; *m* 1979 *Peter Austin, and has issue:
1c *William Michael; *b* 1980
2c *James Peter; *b* 1983
1c *Claire Poppy Rosina; *b* 1986
2b *Rosemary Kathleen; *b* 7 July 1953
3b *Gillian Esther; *b* 23 Aug 1955
4b *Joanna Elizabeth; *b* 10 Dec 1964
1a Jocelyn Cecilia; *b* 27 May 1919; *m* 6 July 1946 Brian Shawe-Taylor, of Brockhampton, Glos, and had issue:
1b *Richard Arland; *b* 16 April 1951
2b *John Stewart; *b* 29 Oct 1953
3b *Desmond Edward Philip; *b* 30 Sept 1955
2a *Rona Kathleen [Mrs Reginald Smith, Green Farm Cottage, Farmborough, nr Bath, Somerset]; *b* 22 April 1921; WRNS WWII; *m* 1943 *Reginald Alfred Henry Reardon Smith, and has issue:
1b *Christopher Harry Reardon [Christopher Smith Esq, 139 Learag St, Coolum, Queensland, Australia]; *b* 18 May 1946; *m* 1967 *Frances Barnes, and has issue
1c *David Harry Reardon; *b* 1978
1c *Paula Maria; *b* 9 Oct 1967
2c *Tina Georgina; *b* 1971
2b *William Jeremy Reardon; *b* 3 March 1949; *m* 1st 19– (*divorce* 19–) Margaret Harrap; *m* 2nd 19– *Judith —
1b *Anthea Kathleen; *b* 26 Nov 1944; *m* 1st 1967 (*divorce* 19–) Michael Monks; *m* 2nd 19– *Richard Holborrow, of Tetbury, Glos, and by her 1st husb has issue:
1c *Emma Katherine; *b* 1969
2b *Janice Caroline; *b* 19 June 1953; *m* 1979 *Antony Collins and has:
1c *Timothy Gerald; *b* 1980
1c *Sarah Jocelyn; *b* 1983
(1) Dorothy Violette; *m* 20 March 1915 Capt Percy Myles Reese (*d* 24 Dec 1933), RFA
(2) Lucy, MBE (1939), JP (1939) Staffs
(3) Amy Cecilia; *d* unm 22 Sept 1977
4 Victor Emmanuel, JP Staffs, BA Cantab; *b* 25 Dec 1863; *m* 3 Aug 1889 Ethel Margaret (*d* 12 March 1969 aged 103), dau of Edward Brown Fitton, of Fair Lea, Gt Malvern, and *d* 15 Dec 1935, leaving issue:
(1) Geoffrey Victor, DSC; Cdr RN, navigator and 2ic HMS *Broke*, served WW I (despatches) and WW II; *b* 1 May 1890; *m* 1st 2 April 1914 Josephine Helen (*d* 17 Jan 1933), dau of Lt-Col Walter Reginald Fox, RA; *m* 2nd 1 Sept 1939 *Gwendoline Dorothy, dau of W H Miell, and *d* 1975, leaving by his 1st w:
1a +Hugh Geoffrey; WW II as Lt S Staffs Regt; *b* 15 Sept 1916
1a *Geraldyne Rosemary Margaret [Mrs Richard Wiltshire, 4 Claverdon Close, Solihull, Warwicks]; *b* 8 Nov 1917; *m* 1946 *Richard Wiltshire and has issue:
1b *Hugh Richard; *b* 1947; *m* 1970 *Barbara Gwyneth Price and has issue
(2) Philip Gregory; Lt 6th Bn S Staffs Regt; *b* 19 July 1897; *d* 31 Oct 1917 of wounds recd in action
(1) Isabel Katherine; *b* 13 June 1891; *m* 16 Sept 1914 Cecil Martin, and had issue
(2) Clare Mary; *b* 29 Aug 1892
(3) Margaret Hilda May; *b* 4 June 1894; *m* 22 March 1917 Lt-Col Richard Dalrymple Lauder (*d* 1961), The Roy Scots, s of John Lauder, of Colinton, Midlothian, and had issue
5 John Owen, of Micklefield Green, Rickmansworth; barrister; *b* 13 June 1870; *m* 15 April 1903 Nancy (*d* 23 April 1963), dau of Harry Barlow, of Goldthorn Hill, and *d* 10 Dec 1949, leaving issue:
(1) John Barlow; *b* 13 Sept 1904; *m* 9 Sept 1925 *Joan, dau of Kyrtle Chatfield Hankinson, and *d* 26 May 1932, leaving issue:
1a +John Kyrle, CMG (1977) [John Hickman Esq CMG, 48a Fitzgeorge Ave, London W14]; Dip Serv: 1st Sec Madrid 1966–67, Consul-Gen Bilbao 1967–69, Counsellor and Dep HC Singapore 1969–71, Head SW Pacific Dept FCO 1971–74, Counsellor Dublin 1974–77, Amb: Ecuador 1977–81, Chile 1982–87; dir Anaconda (S America) Inc 1988–; author: *The Enchanted Islands: the Galapagos Discovered* (1985); *b* 3 July 1927; *educ* Tonbridge and Trin Hall Cambridge (BA 1948); *m* 4 April 1956 *Jennifer Olive, yr dau of Reginald Kendall Love, and has:
1b +Matthew John Kyrle; *b* 21 Jan 1964; *m* 1994 *Andrea, dau of D J P Hudson and Adriana Kimber, of Santiago, Chile
2b +Andrew Giles Lovell; *b* 23 Jan 1966
1b *Catherine Lucy; *b* 6 Dec 1960; *m* 1987 *Tom Owen Edmunds
2a +Richard Malim [Richard Hickman Esq, The Malt Shovel, Vigo, Burcot, Bromsgrove, Worcs]; Colonial Serv 1954–64 (DC Kenya), Lt RA (TA); *b* 24 July 1930; *educ* Tonbridge and Pembroke Coll Cambridge (BA 1954, MA 1966); *m* 23 June 1962 *Judy Penelope Sylvia, 2nd dau of Brig Charles Douglas Armstrong, CBE, DSO, MC, and has issue:
1b +Marcus Sebastian Charles; *b* 7 April 1963
2b +Jonathan Edward Barlow; *b* 28 June 1964
1a *Dinah [Mrs John Saunders, Trehu, Pulla Cross, Truro, Cornwall]; *b* 8 Jan 1929; *m* 22 April 1953 *John Frederick Saunders; and has:
1b *Richard Neville; *b* 18 April 1955
1b *Joanna Elizabeth; *b* 27 Jan 1958
(2) +Michael Ranulf [His Honour Michael Hickman, The Acorn, Bovingdon, Herts]; *b* 2 Oct 1922; *educ* Wellington and Trin Hall Cambridge (BA); late F/Lt RAF, barrister Middle Temple 1949, Circuit Court Judge 1974–93; *m* 16 Jan 1943 *Diana, dau of Col Derek Charles Houghton Richardson, 10th Hus, and has issue:
1a +Peter Derek; *b* 25 May 1951; *educ* Uppingham; *m* 1974 *(Hilary) Clare, dau of Don Sadler, of Gwelo, Zimbabwe, and has issue:
1b +Richard Ranulf; *b* 1977
2b +Adam Derek; *b* 1980
1a *Susan Marilyn [Mrs Aris Zarpanely, 2 Old Dock Close, Kew Green, Surrey]; *b* 8 July 1948; *m* 1972 *Aris Alexander Pierre Zarpanely and has:
1b *Petros Alexander; *b* 1975
1b *Rene Diana; *b* 1977
(1) Vera Charlotte Nancy; MRCVS; *b* 10 Feb 1908; *d* 6 Aug 1985
(2) Audrey Violet Elsie; MRCVS; *b* 3 March 1912; *m* 19– Geoffrey May and *d* 21 July 1991
(3) Angela Mary Dolsome; *b* 18 Jan 1924; *m* 1st 1943 Charles Gordon Richards (*ka* 1943); *m* 2nd 1948 William Freshwater (*d* 1989) and *d* 21 July 1995, leaving by him:
1a *Michael David Latimer; *b* 1950
2a *Martin Walter James; *b* 1958
1a *Jane Elizabeth Mary; *b* 1948
2a *Christina Ella Janey; *b* 15 April 1962
1 Louisa; *m* 18 April 1877 William Mathias Noott (*d* 29 Nov 1927), MRCSE, and *d* 21 May 1936, leaving issue
2 Lucy; *m* 12 Dec 1877 Col Stewart John Le Poer Trench (*see* ASHTOWN, B) and *d* 13 June 1936, leaving issue
3 Mary Violette; *m* 13 Dec 1881 Sir William Henry Mahoney Christie, KCB, FRS, FRAS, Astronomer Royal (*d* 22 Jan 1922), s of Professor S H Christie, FRS, and *d* 13 Dec 1888, leaving issue
4 Margaret Sarah; *m* 30 April 1879 Thomas Fisher (*d* 20 Aug 1887) and *d* 31 Dec 1938, having had issue
5 Katherine Josephine; *m* 1st 7 April 1888 Rupert Edward Cooke Kettle (*d* 15 Oct 1908), Met Police magistrate; *m* 2nd 29 April 1912 Walter Leveson Byrd Levett (*d* 8 Jan 1935), yst s of Richard Byrd Levett, DL, of Milford Hall, Staffs, and *d* 21 April 1938
6 May; *m* 5 Oct 1910 Brig-Gen Hugh Gregory Fitton, CB, DSO, ADC (*d* 20 Jan 1916 of wounds recd in action), and *d* 1 March 1954
7 Lilian Frederica Violette Lucy; *m* 23 Jan 1917 Capt Frederic Bouhier Imbert-Terry, MC (*d* 20 Jan 1963), Devonshire Regt, yr s of Sir Henry Machu Imbert-Terry, 1st Bt (*qv*), and *dsp* 4 Sept 1949

Sir ALFRED *d* 11 March 1910; his gs,

Sir Alfred Edward Hickman, 2nd Bt; Maj Shropshire Yeo (TA), Capt 4th/7th Dragoon Gds WW I France (wounded); *b* 8 May 1885; *m* 1st 16 Jan 1919 (*divorce* 1940) Lilian Brenda (*d* 16 Aug 1969), only dau of Benjamin Howard Mander, of Trysull Manor, Wolverhampton, and had issue:
1 ALFRED HOWARD WHITBY (Sir), **3rd Bt**
2 +Patrick Nelson [Patrick Hickman Esq, Hale Park, Fordingbridge, Hants; 65 Onslow Gardens, London SW7]; F/Lt RAFVR WW II, memb Fishmongers' Co, Freeman City London; *b* 13 March 1921; *m* 1st 13 April 1944 (*divorce* 1950) Leontine Mariette (Marylena), yr dau of Capt James Allen Dyson Perrins, MC and bar, JP, Welsh Gds, and has:
(1) +(Patrick) Rupert COTTRELL (deed poll 1953) [Rupert Cottrrell Esq, Old Larcombe Court, Exford, Somerset TA24 7PF]; *b* 14 June 1945; *educ* Gordonstoun; *m* 1st 19 Oct 1968 (*divorce* 1989) Claire, est dau of Lt-Col James Gray Round, OBE, JP, DL, of Hellens, Birch, Colchester, Essex; *m* 2nd 1989 (*divorce* 1997) Anne, only dau of Arthur Ralph Holbrook, of Mahon House, Cropwell Butler, Notts, and by his 1st w has issue:
1a +Nicholas Rupert Round; *b* 21 Aug 1970
1a *Jessica Victoria; *b* 1974
(1) *Rozanna Mariette COTTRELL (deed poll 1953); *b* 11 Nov 1946; *m* 8 Nov 1969 *Michael John Hardy Hammond and has:
1a *James David Hardy; *b* 1972
2a *Matthew Charles Perrins; *b* 1975
2 (cont.) Patrick Hickman *m* 2nd 28 Dec 1953 *(Margaret) Gail, dau of Col Cassell Ryan St Aubyn, 60th Rifles, of Paris, and by her has issue:
(2) +(Patrick) Sloan; *b* 29 Nov 1955; *educ* Eton; *m* 1993 *Candida R d'Ombrain, dau of Dr Roderick William Grant, of Alderholt Park, Fordingbridge (*see* 1915 edn ARDILAUN, B)
(2) *Vivien Anne [Mrs Edmund MacDonald, 88 West Clay Park, San Francisco, CA 94121, USA]; *b* 22 Nov 1957; *m* 1983 *Edmund B MacDonald, Jr, s of Edmund B MacDonald, of San Francisco, and has issue:
1a *Angus Nelson; *b* 1987
2a *Kenneth Reid; *b* 13 Oct 1996
1a *Fiona Margaret; *b* 1990

Sir Alfred *m* 2nd 5 April 1940 *(Nancy) Beryl [Dowager Lady Hickman, Holmbush House, Faygate, nr Horsham, W Sussex], est dau of Capt Trevor George Morse-Evans, JP, barrister Inner Temple, MFH, of The Parc, Bridgend, Glam, and *d* 11 March 1947

His er son,

Sir (Alfred) Howard Whitby Hickman, 3rd Bt; AIBAE; *b* 29 Jan 1920; *educ* Eton; *m* 24 Jan 1948 Margaret (*d* 1996), formerly w of Denis Thatcher (later Sir Dennis Thatcher, 1st Bt; *qv*), and only dau of Leonard Kempson, of Potters Bar, Middx, and *d* 1979, leaving:
1 Sir RICHARD GLENN HICKMAN, **4th and present Bt**

HIGGINS

Creation: B. (LP, UK) 2 Aug 1997.

THE BARON HIGGINS, of Worthing, Co W Sussex ((Sir) Terence Langley Higgins, KBE (1993), PC (1979), DL (W Sussex 1989)) [The Rt Hon The Lord Higgins KBE PC DL, House of Lords, London SW1A 0PW]; *b* 18 Jan 1928; *educ* Alleyns Sch Dulwich (Govr 1995–) and Gonville and Caius Coll Cambridge (BA Hons 1958, MA 1963); Staff NZ Shipping Co 1948–55; Lecturer Ec Principles Yale U 1958–59; economist Unilever 1959–64; MP (C) Worthing 1964–97, Sec C Party Fin Ctee 1965–66, Oppn Spokesman: Treas and Ec Affrs 1966–70 and 1974, Trade 1974–76, Min State Treasury 1970–72, Fin Sec Treasury 1972–74, Chm C Party Ctee: Sport 1979–81, Tport 1979–91, Chm Select Ctee: Procedure 1980–83, Treasury and Civ Serv 1983–92 (memb 1980–92), Chm H of C Liaison Ctee 1984–97; memb: Cncl RIIA 1979–85, Cncl IAM 1979–97, Exec Ctee 1922 Ctee 1980–97, Public Accts Commn 1984–97; Tstee Industry and Parly Tst 1985–91; Govr NIESR 1989; chm Lex Pension Fund Tstees 1994–97; dir Lex Service Gp 1980–92 (consultant 1992–), First Choice Holidays 1992–; hon memb Keynes Coll Kent U 1976–; Special Fell PSI 1986 (memb Cncl 1989–); *m* 1961 *Rosalyn Higgins, DBE (1995), QC (1995), JSD, FBA (1995), Judge Internat Ct Justice 1995–, Prof Internat Law LSE 1981–, dau of Lewis Cohen, and has a s and a dau

Lineage: REGINALD HIGGINS, of Dulwich; *m* Rose Longley and had:

TERENCE LANGLEY (Sir), *cr* a **Baron**

HILL, Viscount

Arms: Quarterly, 1st and 4th, erm. on a fess sa. a castle triple towered arg. (for HILL); 2nd and 3rd, per pale sa. and az. a cross-crosslet crossed between two acorns in bend dexter and as many fleurs-de-lys in bend sinister arg. (for CLEGG). **Crests:** 1 A tower, arg., surmounted with a garland of laurel ppr. (for HILL), 2 In front of two branches of oak fructed in saltire ppr. a cross-crosslet crossed or (for CLEGG). **Supporters:** Dexter, a lion arg., murally crowned or, gorged with a wreath of oak fructed ppr.; sinister, a horse arg., bridled and saddled ppr., murally gorged gu. **Motto:** *Avancez* ('Forward'). **Creations:** Bt. (GB) 20 Jan 1727, B. (UK) 16 Jan 1816, V. (UK) 27 Sept 1842.

THE 8TH VISCOUNT HILL OF HAWKSTONE AND OF HARDWICKE, Co Salop, **Baron Hill of Almarez and of Hardwicke**, Co Salop, and a **Baronet** (Sir Anthony Rowland Clegg-Hill, Bt) [The Rt Hon The Viscount Hill, House of Lords, London SW1A 0PW]; *b* 19 March 1931; *s* f 1974; *educ* Kelly Coll and RMA Sandhurst; late Capt RA; Freeman Shrewsbury 1957; *m* 1st 10 Aug 1963 (*divorce* 1976) Juanita Phyllis, dau of John W Pertwee; *m* 2nd 1989 *Elizabeth Harriet, dau of Ronald L Offer, of Salisbury, Wilts

Lineage: HUMPHREY HILL, of Buntingale; living *temp* HENRY V; *m* Agnes, dau and coheir of John Bird, and had, with an est s (William, ancestor of the HILLs of Court Hill, Salop) and a yst s (Thomas, f of Sir Rowland, Ld Mayor London):

RALPH HILL; *m* —, dau of Thomas Green, of Green's Norton, and had, with an er s (William, of Bletchley):

HUMPHREY, of Adderley; ggf of:

ROWLAND HILL, of Hawkestone; *m* Margaret, dau of Richard Whitehall, and had issue:

1 Rowland; *d* unm

2 Richard (Sir), PC; diplomat *temp* WILLIAM III, QUEEN ANNE and GEORGE I; *d* unm, leaving much of his wealth to hs nephews Samuel Barber and Thomas Harwood, who both took the name HILL, the latter being f of Noel Hill, 1st Baron Berwick of Attingham, though the Hawkestone estate passed to **Sir Rowland, 1st Bt**

3 John, of Lightrick; *m* 12 Feb 1699 Sarah, dau of John Stubbs, of Shaw, Kingsley, Staffs, and had:

(1) ROWLAND (Sir), **1st Bt**

ROWLAND HILL's gs,

Sir Rowland Hill, 1st Bt (GB), so *cr* 20 Jan 1727, with remainder, in default of male issue, to three other nephews of his said uncle, namely Samuel Hill, of Shenstone, Thomas Hill, of Tern (f of 1st Baron Berwick), and Rowland Hill, his bro; MP Lichfield 1734; *m* 1st 1732 Jane, dau of Sir Brian Broughton, 3rd Bt, of Broughton (*qv*); *m* 2nd 1776 Mary (*m* 3rd J Foster Barham), widow of Thomas Powys and dau of German Pole of Radbourne, Derbys, and *d* 1783, leaving by his 1st w, with other issue:

1 **Sir Richard Hill, 2nd Bt**; *d* unm 28 Nov 1809

2 JOHN (Sir), **3rd Bt**

3 Rowland (Rev); *b* 12 Aug 1744; *educ* St John's Coll Cambridge (BA); *m* 27 May 1773 Mary (*d* 17 Aug 1830), sis of Clement Tudway, of Wells, Somerset, and *dsp* 11 April 1833

4 Robert (Rev); *b* 17 May 1746; *m* 13 Aug 1772 Mary (*d* April 1824), dau and sole heir of John Wilbraham, and *d* 1 Feb 1831, leaving:

(1) Robert Wilbraham Bromhall (Rev); Rector Waters Upton, Salop; *b* 8 Feb 1774; *m* Eliza (*d* March 1849), dau of Edward Greene, and *d* 13 Jan 1815, leaving:

1a Robert Greene, of Hough, Cheshire; *b* 21 June 1801; *m* 1st Jan 1829 Mary (*d* 26 Feb 1938), dau of — Beckett, of Audlem, Cheshire, and had issue:

1b Robert Greene; *b* 27 Nov 1829; *m* 1st 26 Aug 1852 Mary Ann (*d* 1889), dau of Thomas Hassall; *m* 2nd 5 Jan 1899 Elizabeth Louisa Sprake Day, of Weston Manor, Corscombe, Dorset

2b Clement John, of Natal; *b* 15 Sept 1835; *m* Ellen Maria (*d* 16 Jan 1906), dau of William Gillett, and *d* 16 Aug 1909, having had:

1c Rowland Wilbraham; *b* 18 April 1857; *dsp*

2c Robert Greene; *b* 21 Dec 1858; *m* 1887 Minna Field Orchard (*d* 31 Oct 1933) and *d* 11 Nov 1943, leaving:

1d Ivy Ellen Greene; *m* 9 Aug 1910 Robert Bloy (*d* 1959), of Natal, and had issue

2d Gladys Irene

3d Vivienne Constance; *b* 31 Dec 1893; *m* 23 April 1919 Douglas Wise, JP (*d* 30 Oct 1966), and had:

1e *Vivienne Daphne; *b* 27 June 1923; *m* 14 April 1956 Melvyn William Pigg (*d* 24 Jan 1968)

3c Clement William Noel; *b* 24 Nov 1862; *m* 1898 Sarah Catherine (*d* 24 Oct 1957), dau of P Zeitsman, and *d* 10 July 1903, leaving:

1d Clement John; *b* 1899; *m* 26 July 1924 *Marion, dau of William Cuthbertson, of Sarina, Natal, and *d* 28 April 1972, leaving:

1e William Clement Noel, BSc Geology; *b* 28 Sept 1929; *m* 8 April 1958 *Felicity-Ann, dau of C H Gierke, of Tongaat, Natal, and had:

1f +Bradley John Sheldon; *b* 3 May 1960

1f *Lianne; *b* 22 Sept 1958

2e +Rowland Robert; *b* 22 Jan 1937; *m* 1st 16 July 1960 (*divorce* 1964) Joan Merie, dau of R Laing, of Malvern, Natal, and has issue; *m* 2nd 1 April 1967 *Jeanette Colla, dau of Wauld Paton, of Grosvenor, Bluff Durban, Natal, and by her has issue:

1f +Rowland David; *b* 11 April 1969

2f +Brendan Clement; *b* 24 June 1972

1e Daphne Kathleen; *b* 11 June 1925; *m* 1947 *Llewellyn Tennyson Fisher, and had issue:

1f *Donald Malcolm; *b* 21 July 1951

1f *Dawn Collen; *b* 5 Dec 1949

2f *Kenylwynne Craig; *b* 12 Sept 1954

3f *Sharonene Marion; *b* 30 June 1957

2e *Joey Catherine; *m* 8 June 1942 *Patrick Broughton Fenn, s of Rev L H Fenn, of Colchester, Essex, and has:

1f *Evelyn Marion; *b* 24 Dec 1943

2f *Judy Anne; *b* 14 July 1945

4c Harry Francis; *b* 8 Sept 1867; *d* young

1c Ellen Eliza; *m* 17 Dec 1885 Thomas Payne St James (*d* 17 Sept 1924), and *d* 1937, leaving issue

2c Marie Anne Frances; *m* 14 Sept 1897 Harrie George Pearson, of Durban, and had:

1d Eliza Jane; *m* 18 Sept 1861 Thomas Bower, of Brookbank, Nantwich

1a (cont.) Robert Hill *m* 2nd Eleanor (*d* 18 April 1869), dau of — Young, of Bristol; *m* 3rd 24 Oct 1872 Marian, dau of W R Grieve, and *d* 20 Feb 1874, having had by his 2nd w:

3b Henry Daniel; *b* 22 June 1844; *m* 16 Jan 1868 Elizabeth Harriet, widow of William Salmon and dau of John Speakman, and *d* 12 May 1920, leaving:

1c Rowland Wilbraham; *b* 26 Oct 1868; *d* 20 June 1937

2c Henry Laurence Noel, BA Camb; *b* 30 Jan 1870; *d* unm

3c Richard Bryan; *b* 18 Jan 1873; *d* 4 Sept 1946

4c Robert Greene; *b* 24 Sept 1876; *m* 30 July 1924 Maud Marianne, dau of Frederick Terry, of Lydd, Kent

5c Randle Edward; *b* 5 May 1881; *ka* 4 Nov 1918

6c Roger Wilbraham; *b* 7 March 1883; *m* 24 April 1912 Mary Ann (*d* 1971), dau of James Sadler, of Acton, Cheshire, and *d* 1962, leaving:

1d +Gerald Roger [Gerald Hill Esq, Hough Gates, Hough, Crewe, Cheshire]; *b* 6 Jan 1921; *m* 29 July 1953 *Jane Elizabeth, JP, dau of Frank Haighton, of Elm House, Nantwich, Cheshire, and has issue:

1e +Gerald Robert Wilbraham; *b* 1958

1e *Elizabeth Mary; *b* 1955; PhD

1d *Sheila Mary; *b* 26 April 1913; *m* 26 April 1939 *Lionel Churchill Wood, and has issue:

1e *Elizabeth Anne; *b* 12 May 1941; *m* *Richard Wilson Hocknell, and has issue:
1f *Sarah Ann; *b* 3 Aug 1967
1c Lucy Wilbraham; *d* unm 5 Sept 1946
2c Katherine Harriette
3c Mary Wilbraham
4b Thomas Laurence; *b* 22 Feb 1848; *d* unm
5b Francis Robert Wilbraham; *b* 20 March 1852; *m* 12 Aug 1880 Mary Anne Bennett (*d* 1912), dau of Daniel Boote, of Edstaston Hall, Salop, and *d* 1936, leaving issue:
1c John Francis; Natal Police, Boer War 1902 (medal with two clasps), Natal 1908 (medal and clasp) and WW I (star, two medals); *b* 1882; *m* 1916 Natalie Ivy (*d* 16 June 1967), dau of Thomas Payne St James (*see above*), and *d* 14 March 1948, leaving:
1d Alaric Bryan; AMIFE, AFICD, SAAF 1939–46, Ch Territorial Fire Adviser Tanganyika Govt 1958–60; *b* 1921; *m* 1948 *Elizabeth Margaret Allen [Mrs Alaric Hill, 49 Crown St, Dubbo, NSW 2830, Australia], and *d* 1992, leaving:
1e +Dallas John [Dallas Hill Esq, PO Box 283, Kokstad, E Griqualand, S Africa]; *b* 1950; *m* 1975 *Bronwyn Lucie van der Leeuw, and has issue:
1f +Christopher John; *b* 1975
2f +Rowland John; *b* 1978
3f +Dallas Joseph; *b* 1989
1e *Carol Elizabeth [Mrs Gordon Bell, 12 Gibson Close, Singleton Heights, NSW 2330, Australia]; *b* 1953; *m* 1974 *Gordon Redvers Bell, and has issue:
1f *Julian Redvers; *b* 1978
1f *Cherie Elizabeth; *b* 1974
1d *Ellen Maryan [Mrs Thomas MacMillan, 12A Coombes Rd, Remuera, Auckland 1005, New Zealand]; *b* 25 March 1920; *m* 5 March 1946 *Thomas Duncan MacMillan, ACIS, formerly 2nd Transvaal Scottish, and has issue:
1e *Bruce Warwick Hugh [Bruce MacMillan Esq, Farmlet Rd, Hastings, New Zealand]; *b* 27 Oct 1951; BSc, DipEd; *m* 1973 (*divorce* 1980) Deborah Suzanne Cathey, and has issue:
1f *Fiona Louise; *b* 1978
1e *Brenda Caroline Dale [Mrs Gary Filer, 131 Crossfield Rd, Glendowie, Auckland 5, New Zealand]; *b* 2 Feb 1955; *m* 1979 *Gary Malcolm Filer, Dip Opt, and has issue:
1f *Natalie Jean Caroline; *b* 1983
2f *Claire Bridget Alice; *b* 1985
2d *Vivette Natalie [Mrs Johan Moll, 15 Straker Ave, Gun Hill, Harare, Zimbabwe]; *b* 1925; *m* 8 Jan 1949 *Johan Heinrich Moll, BSc, FMIMechE, and has issue:
1e *Victor Derek [Victor Moll, Box 1309, Oranjemund, Namibia]; *b* 1954; *m* 1984 *Patricia Du Randt
1e *Coleen Yvonne; *b* 1951, BSocSc, BCom; *m* 1975 (*divorce* 1983, resumed maiden name) Roger Charles Peplow, MSc, of Durban
2c Robert Wilbraham; *b* 1886
1c Beatrice Margery; *b* 1884; *m* 1921 George Francis Hearnden (*d* 3 May 1969), and *d* 14 April 1969
2c Mary Doris Maud; *b* 1888; *m* 1915 Percy Harold Lewin, and had issue
2b Eleanor Mary; *m* 26 May 1880 Robert Hime, and had issue
1a Mary Meeke; *m* 9 June 1836 William Salmon, and *d* 8 May 1877, leaving issue
(2) John, of Standish Hall, Wigan; *b* 26 Feb 1775; *m* 1801 Elizabeth (*d* 28 Aug 1860), dau of Thomas Wilkinson, and *d* 4 April 1849, leaving issue:
1a Thomas Wilkinson; barrister; *b* 20 May 1804; *d* unm 23 Jan 1853
2a John Wilbraham (Rev); Rector Waverton, Cheshire *b* 2 Sept 1806; *m* 28 Nov 1843 Maria Frances, dau of H R Wood, of Hollin Hall, and *dsp*
3a Rowland; Col Bengal Army; *b* 12 Dec 1807; *d* unm 12 Dec 1854
1a Frances Emily; *m* 9 April 1861 William Denison Wilkinson (*dsp* 20 April 1874)
2a Henrietta Amelia
3a Louisa Charlotte; *m* 5 Sept 1839 E G Fawcett (*d* 23 Sept 1875) and *d* 23 June 1863, leaving issue
(3) Rowland Alleyne (Rev); MA Oxon; *b* 8 Aug 1776; *m* — (*d* 4 Feb 1861) and *dsp* 7 Nov 1844
(4) Samuel; *b* 28 Dec 1777; *m* Anne Frances Wright, and *dsp* 1850
(5) Richard; *b* 1 Feb 1779; *m* 1806 Anne (*d* 1811), dau of Richard Mytton, of Garth, and *d* 17 May 1834, leaving:
1a Richard Devereux (Rev); *b* 5 Feb 1807; *d* unm 23 April 1839
2a George Mytton; Lt-Gen Bengal Army; *b* 25 May 1810; *m* 23 Oct 1841 Harriet Mary Benyon (*d* 10 Jan 1908), dau of M T Whish, and *d* 1883, leaving:
1b George Michell Devereux; Lt-Col IA; *b* 3 Jan 1845; *m* 3 April 1874 Kate Gough Clynn, and *d* 1889, leaving:
1c Mary Glynn Mytton; *b* 1875
2b Arthur; Col cmdg 3rd Bn Cheshire Regt Boer War (medal, three clasps); *b* 27 Sept 1851; *m* 4 June 1879 Katharine Emily (*d* 2 April 1949), dau of Thomas Morris, MD, and *d* 21 Aug 1950, leaving issue:
1c Arthur Rowland; Maj Cehsire Regt; *b* 23 July 1880; *m* 1908 Kathleen, dau of C James Todd, of Hull, and was *ka* 6 Oct 1915, leaving:
1d Christina Mary; BA Oxon; *b* 17 June 1909; *m* 9 Feb 1933 *2nd Baron Riverdale (*qv*) and *d* 1991, leaving issue
2d *Alison Kathleen [Mrs Henry Morley, Fife House, Heath Drive, Walton-on-the-Hill, Surrey KT20 7QQ]; *b* 28 July 1911; *m* 6 Sept 1934 Henry Seaward Morley, MD, FRCP (*d* 5 July 1961), only s of Henry Forster Morley, MD, of Church Hill House, Midhurst, Sussex, and has issue:
1e *John Henry [John Morley Esq, Derwent Lodge, Oldfield Rd, Maidenhead, Berks]; *b* 5 Nov 1936; *educ* Wellington and Downing Coll Cambridge (MA); *m* 1963 *Felicity Faith Beryl, est dau of John Peile, of Grindleford, Sheffield, and has issue:
1f *Rupert Oliver Henry; *b* 10 June 1965
2f *Benjamin William Mervyn; *b* 28 Feb 1969
2e *Timothy Rowland; MB, BCh, FRCS, LRCP; *b* 18 March 1939; *educ* Wellington, Downing Coll Cambridge (MA) and UCH; *m* 20 Aug 1966 *Mary Elspeth Holborn, dau of Noel Frederick Adeney, FRCS, and has:
1f *David Mark Rowland; *b* 1969; *educ* London U (BA)
1f *Nicola Susie Gray; *b* 22 Aug 1968; *educ* Leeds U (BSc); *m* 1993 *Andrew Philip Martello Gray
3d Brenda Rowland; *b* Sept 1915; *d* 24 June 1917
2c George Mytton; Cdr RN; *b* 20 June 1883; *m* 22 July 1919 Olive Odell (*d* March 1966), yst dau of William Millar, of Eskbank, and *d* 10 July 1935, leaving issue:
1d *Doreen Odell Mytton [Mrs Hector Reith, 78B Granville Rd, Sevenoaks, Kent]; *b* 9 June 1920; *m* 7 Oct 1950 *Maj Hector McNeill Tytler Reith, RA, 3rd s of Rev George Murray Reith, of Edinburgh, and has issue:
1e *Douglas McNeill Mytton; *b* 14 Oct 1953; *educ* St George's Sch Tonbridge and Webber Douglas Acad of Dramatic Art
3c Harold Brian Cunningham, FRGS; *b* 27 Feb 1887; *educ* Harrow; *m* 19 June 1920 Elise (*d* 1971), dau of Julius Jeppe, JP, Consul-Gen Greece and Romania and Sr Danish Consul S Africa, and *d* 1980, having had:
1d Rowland Mytton; P/O RAF WW II; *b* 1 Nov 1921; *ka* 1 Nov 1941
2d +Noel Brian [Noel Hill Esq, Balneath Manor Farm, S Chailey, E Sussex BN8 4AP]; *b* 26 Dec 1926; *educ* Eastbourne Coll; *m* 7 July 1958 *Gladys Rosa, widow of Laurie Edward Richard Umney and dau of Sidney George West, MBE, of Morden, Surrey, and has issue:
1e *Nicola Anne [Mrs Paul Woodley, Broadoak, Copthorne, Sussex]; *b* 3 Dec 1959; *educ* Moira House and Warwick U (BA); *m* 1985 *Paul Jonathan Woodley, BA, ACA, and has:
1f *Christopher Benjamin; *b* 1989
1f *Daisy Anne; *b* 19–
2e *Philippa Jane; *b* 3 Oct 1962; *m* 1989 *Colin Hatcher
2d (cont.) Mr and Mrs N Hill also adopted:
*Jill Adrienne [Mrs James Jackson, Balneath Manor, S Chailey, E Sussex]; *b* 1953; *educ* Moira House and Sussex U (BA); *m* 1996 *James Leonard Jackson
3d +Julian [Julian Hill Esq, Huntsland Cottage, Huntsland Lane, Crawley Down, Sussex RH10 4HB]; Lt Cheshire (22nd) Regt, with 1st Bn in Egypt 1953–54; md Julian Hill and Scanhill Ltd; Freeman City of London; FBIM; MinstM; FIOD; *b* 9 Aug 1932; *educ* Eastbourne Coll; *m* 30 March 1956 *Ruth Monica, yst dau of Paul Sekvens Toll, of Stockholm, and has issue:
1e +Rowland Paul [Rowland Hill Esq, 16 Ashley Mansions, London SW1]; *b* 27 Nov 1956; *educ* Eastbourne Coll; ACA, dir Hill Samuel Investment Management
2e +Michael Mytton [Michael Hill Esq, La Ruelle, 62770 Le Fresnoy, France]; *b* 19 May 1960; *educ* Eastbourne Coll, W Surrey Coll Art & Design (BA) and Duncan of Jordanstone Coll of Art Dundee (MA); *m* 1990 *Priscilla, yst dau of Frank Morgan, and has issue:
1f +Christopher Robert; *b* 1993
2f +Joshua Julian; *b* 1996
1e *Anne Louise [Mrs Paul Hottinger, 5 Linzee Rd, London N8 7RG]; *b* 5 Nov 1963; *educ* Moira House, St Claire's Hall Oxford and Edinburgh U (MA); *m* 1995 *Paul Hottinger and has:
1f *Rory Alexander HILL-HOTTINGER; *b* 1996
4c Reginald Herbert; *b* Nov 1889; *educ* Wellington; *m* 1st 3 Dec 1914 Elizabeth Wallace, dau of A S Coubrough, JP, of Blanefield, Stirlingshire, and has issue:
1d *Kathleen Agnes [Mrs George Burrell, 2760 Burdick Avenue, Victoria, BC, Canada]; *b* 20 May 1916; *m* 16 Nov 1946 *George Elden Burrell, and has issue:
1e *Robin Elden Adair; *b* 5 March 1951; *m* 1982 *Katharine Regina, dau of Colin D McCullough, of Victoria, BC
2e *Keith Edgar; *b* 23 Oct 1953; *m* 1981 *Leslie Jean, dau of Ian C Colquhoun, of Vancouver, BC, and has:
1f *Scott Thomas; *b* 1983
1e *Wendy Evelyn [Mrs Bruce McConnan, 2481 Central Ave, Victoria, BC, Canada]; *b* 20 April 1948; *m* 1969 *Bruce Ronald McConnan, and has issue:
1f *Brock Stewart; *b* 1976
1f *Kelly Evelyn; *b* 1973
2d *Winifred Evelyn [Mrs Charles Humphrys, 3613 Nico Wynd Drive, Surrey, BC V2A 2W3, Canada]; *b* 9 May 1920; *m* 1945 *Charles M Humphrys, and has issue:
1e *Daphne Mary; *b* 31 July 1946; *m* 1968 *Douglas James Lovick, of Vancouver, BC, and has issue:
1f *Heidi Marie; *b* 1970
2f *Cynthia Evelyn; *b* 1973
3f *Anna Marjory; *b* 1983
2e *Sheila Elizabeth; *b* 16 Aug 1947; *m* 1969 *Brian Paul Jagger, and has issue:
1f *Brigham Humphry; *b* 1976
2f *Ryan Selwyn; *b* 1978
1f *Christina Catherine; *b* 1974
2f *Stephanie Elizabeth; *b* 1980
3e *Brenda Ann; *b* 29 June 1948; *m* 1974 *David William Haskett, of Calgary, Alberta, Canada, and has issue:

1f *Kevin; *b* 1983
1f *Kathryn Jane; *b* 1982
2f *Kelly Evelyn; *b* 1988
4e *Nancy Maureen; *b* 4 June 1953; *m* 1981 *Douglas Alan Leard, of Vancouver, BC, and has issue:
1f *James Douglas; *b* 1984
2f *Kerry Alana; *b* 1986
4c (cont.) Reginald Hill *m* 2nd 1931 *Gertrude, dau of J Perry, of Tavistock, and *d* 1978, having by her had:
1d +(Arthur) Brian Montague [Brian Hill, 2545 Rolling Hills Court, Alamo, CA 94507, USA]; *b* 9 Sept 1932; *m* 10 Sept 1960 *Brenda Margaret, dau of William Arthur Murray, of Wirral, Cheshire, and has had issue:
1e Susan Josepha; *b* 3 April; *d* 17 April 1968
1d (cont.) Mr and Mrs Brian Hill also adopted:
*George Mytton; *b* 1969
3b Rowland Mytton; *b* 1847; *d* 1863
4b Martin Mackinnon; Lt 14th Regt; *b* 1853; *d* 1877
1b Emma Monteath; *m* 5 Dec 1862 Seaburne May Moens (*d* 1881), BCS, and *d* 14 Sept 1922, leaving issue
2b Lucy Anne; *m* 28 May 1866 Maj G M Bowie (*d* 1876), Madras SC, and *dsp* 1912
3b Harriette Alice; *m* 1st 31 May 1868 Capt John Gregory (*d* 7 Feb 1871) and had issue; *m* 2nd 4 April 1873 Col W L N Knyvett (*d* 1904), IA, and *d* 1925
4b Jessie Isabel; *m* 1st 6 Sept 1870 Alexander Benning Shekleton (*d* 1884), and had issue; *m* 2nd 1888 George William Bronte Branwell (*d* 1903)
5b Florence Augusta; *m* 1895 Rev Arthur Burnell (*d* 1905), MA, Br Chaplain Compiegne, France, and had issue
(1) Margaret; *m* 13 Feb 1900 John Leigh (*d* 26 Dec 1841), of Codsall, Staffs and *d* 20 May 1859, leaving issue

Sir RICHARD's yr bro,

Sir John Hill, 3rd Bt; *b* 1 Aug 1740; *m* 27 Sept 1768 Mary (*d* 8 March 1806), dau and coheir of John Chambré, of Petton, and *d* 21 May 1824, having had, with other issue:
1 John, of Hawkstone; Col; *b* 10 Oct 1769; *m* 16 Nov 1795 Elizabeth Rhodes (*d* 16 Dec 1842), dau of Philip Cornish, and *dvp* 26 Jan 1814, leaving issue:
(1) ROWLAND, **2nd Viscount**
(2) John (Rev); MA, Curate Weston-under-Red Castle, Salop; *b* 11 March 1802; *m* 17 Dec 1833 Charlotte (*d* 14 Jan 1884), dau of Hon Thomas Kenyon (*see* KENYON, B), and *d* 15 June 1891, having had issue:
1a John, JP Salop; *b* 23 July 1840; BA Oxon; *m* 12 July 1865 Mary (*d* 25 Oct 1928), dau of James Gothorp, JP, of Mowbray Hill, Bedale, and *d* 8 Feb 1928, leaving issue:
1b John Kenyon; Capt King's Salop LI, dir Ex-Service Farm Settlement under Min of Ag, Boer War 1900–02 (Queen's medal with three clasps, King's medal with two clasps) and Br E Africa WW I; *b* 13 Jan 1869; *m* 10 Dec 1906 Mary Ruby, only dau of Frank Watkins, of Nairobi, and *d* 9 Dec 1944, having had issue:
1c +John Rowland Clement; *b* 8 June 1908
2c Brian Geoffrey; *b* 14 March 1914; *d* 22 April 1915
3c Thomas Kenyon; *b* 1 Nov 1916; *d* 1937
1c *Mary Sybil [Mrs Mary MacKenzie, Box 269, Graskop 1270, E Transvaal, S Africa]; *b* 31 Dec 1909; *m* Sept 1935 (*divorce* 1947) S/Ldr Colin Alexander MacKenzie, RAFVR, and has issue:
1d *Ewen Rowland Francis [Ewen MacKenzie, PO Box 269, Graskop 1270, E Transvaal, S Africa]; *b* 5 Aug 1936; *educ* St Lawrence Coll and Reading U (BSc)
2c *Muriel Rachel [Mrs John Harris, Tantoni, PO Box 63, Kilifi, Kenya]; *b* 6 Sept 1911; *m* 1934 *Maj John Wilson Lichfield Harris, MFH, and has issue:
1d *Charles John; *b* 1935
2d *David Lichfield; *b* 1942
1d *Mary Victoria; *b* 1940
3c Helen Georgina; *b* 16 Feb 1913; *m* 24 Oct 1942 *Patrick Campbell MacDougall Watson, s of George Watson, of Wigtownshire
2b Frederick Rowland, JP Salop; *b* 27 Jan 1870; *m* 22 Nov 1910 Theodora Ann (*d* 16 May 1961), only dau of Rev R H Quick, and *d* 9 June 1947, leaving:
1c +Richard Hebert (Rev Preb) [The Rev Richard Hill, 4 Old School, Henley Rd, Ludlow, Salop SY8 1RA]; Vicar and RD Bromyard, Herefs, 1961, Rector Ledbury 1972–1978, CF WW II, Freeman Shrewsbury 1959, Preb Putson Minore Herefs 1965, Preb Emeritus Hereford; *b* 27 Oct 1911; *educ* Wrekin Coll; *m* 9 May 1945 *Suzanne, dau of Dr Horace Gooch, of Ragleth House, Church Stretton, and has issue:
1d +Frederick Peter Gooch [Frederick Hill Esq, Springbank, Well Lane, Little Witley, Worcs WR6 6LN]; *b* 24 June 1946; *educ* Worksop Coll and Grey Coll Durham; Freeman Shrewsbury; slr 1972; *m* 1975 *Diana Mary, dau of Richard Ekin, and has issue:
1e +Matthew Anthony; *b* 1982
1e *Mary Elizabeth; *b* 1976
2d +Richard Stephen [Richard Hill Esq, The Old Vicarage, Cockshutt, Salop SY12 0JQ]; *b* 2 July 1949; *educ* Worksop Coll and Sheffield Poly (Bsc); FRICS; Freeman Shrewsbury; *m* 1976 *Susan, dau of Ronald Wren, of NZ, and has:
1e +Nicholas Anthony Owen; *b* 1979
2e +Jeremy David Rhydian; *b* 1981
2c Rowland Edward (Rev Canon); CF 1944–47, Rector Holy Trinity, Ayr, Canon St Mary's Cathedral Glasgow 1959–62, Vicar Cirencester 1962, Freeman Shrewsbury 1959; *b* 26 April 1913; *educ* Shrewsbury and Trin Coll Oxford (BA 1937, MA 1940); *m* 5 Sept 1939 Elizabeth (*d* 1981), dau of Capt Roland Maddison Valsey, RFA, of Tring, Herts, and *d* 1981, leaving:
1d +David Rowland [David Hill Esq, 9 Relugas Rd, Edinburgh EH9 2NE]; *b* 15 Oct 1940; *educ* Trin Coll Glenalmond, Keble Coll Oxford (MA), DipEd, BA, MSc, and Inst for Applied Language Studies, Edinburgh U; Freeman of Shrewsbury; *m* 1st 1969 (*divorce* 1984) Sonya, dau of Stuart McClusky, and has:
1e *Charlotte Ruth; *b* 1973
1d (cont.) David Hill *m* 2nd 1984 *Janet Elizabeth, dau of Harold John Powell, and has issue:
1e +Christopher Rowland; *b* 1989
2e *Katharine Martha; *b* 1987
2d +Nigel John [Nigel Hill Esq, 32 Colebrooke Ave, London W13 8JY]; Inspr Met Police; Freeman Shrewsbury; *b* 19 Dec 1943; *educ* Trin Coll Glenalmond and U Coll Durham (BA 1966); *m* 27 July 1968 *Gillian Mary, yr dau of Ian Heath Stock, MC, of Darlington, Co Durham, and has issue:
1e +Oliver Rowland Vaisey; *b* 1972
1e *Clarissa Mary; *b* 1969
2e *Rosanna Seymour; *b* 1978
3d +James Geoffrey [James Hill Esq, The Priory, 11 Friars Lane, Lanark ML11 9EL]; *b* 30 April 1948; *educ* Trin Coll Glenalmond, U Coll Durham (BA) and Birmingham U (MB, ChB); Freeman Shrewsbury; *m* 1974 *Eileen Frances Rachel, dau of Charles Rodney Webster, WS, of Edinburgh, and has issue:
1e *Katriona Helen; *b* 1976
2e *Anna Elizabeth; *b* 1979
3e *Sara Frances; *b* 1983
4e *Nicola Margaret; *b* 1985
4d +Andrew Vaisey [Andrew Hill Esq, 17 Cockle Crescent, Clovelly, CP, S Africa]; *b* 26 Aug 1950; *educ* Shrewsbury and U Coll Durham (BA); Freeman Shrewsbury; *m* 1st 1974 (*divorce* 19–) Zaria Caroline Annabel, dau of Maj Joseph Theodore Knowles, Wilts Regt; *m* 2nd 19— — and by his 1st w has issue:
1e +Jonathan Rowland Vaisey; *b* 1980
1e *Rowena Jane Imogen; *b* 1977
3c +James Carthew (Rev), Rector Newport Salop 1962, Freeman Shrewsbury 1959, Missioner Shrewsbury Sch Mission 1942–53; *b* 10 Feb 1915; *educ* Shrewsbury; *m* 30 March 1954 *Muriel Beatrice, dau of Rev Roland James Peake, MBE, of Aylesford, Kent
1c Mary Bertha; *b* 22 Jan 1916; *d* 24 Sept 1937
1b Bessie Georgina Jane; *b* 1866; *d* unm 22 Nov 1954
2b Charlotte Helen; *b* 1867; *m* 22 Dec 1903 William Gilchrist (*d* 1954), of Mowbray, Marshbrook, Church Stretton, Salop, s of John Gilchrist, of Ballonack, Skelmorlie, Ayrshire, and *d* 1942, having had issue
2a George William; V-Adml; *b* 20 July 1843; *m* 1st 7 Nov 1882 Mary Caroline (*d* 1896), 2nd dau of Adml Morgan Singer and gdau of Most Rev Joseph Henderson Singer, PC, DD, Bp Meath and Primate Ireland (*see* CROFTON, of Mohill, Bt), and had issue:
1b Cyril John Percy; Cdr RN, served WW I and WW II (despatches), Assist Inspr Kenya Police Reserve in state of emergency; *b* 14 Feb 1884; *m* — and *d* 23 April 1965, leaving issue
2b Hubert George Morgan, JP Salop; Cdr RN, served WW I and WW II 1939 (invalided); *b* 11 Feb 1888; *m* 1 March 1932 Marjorie Perenna (*d* 9 June 1966), 4th dau of Thomas Bate, of Kelsterton, Flints, and *dsp* 15 Nov 1961
3b Guy Charles Dunlop; Lt 2nd Bn King's Salop LI; *b* 21 Nov 1890; lost at sea 4 May 1917
1b Gladys Frances Charlotte; *d* unm 3 Aug 1945
2b Gwendoline Mary Kenyon; *d* unm 15 Oct 1960
3b Eileen Edith Singer; *b* 11 Aug 1896; *m* 25 March 1931 Rev Brian Golland Crowley, yst s of Rev Cedric E Crowley, and *d* 28 feb 1980, having had:
1c *John Christopher Golland; *b* 8 Nov 1933; *educ* Keble Coll Oxford (MA 1963); *m* 15 July 1961 *Elisabeth Julia Donkin Read, BA Oxon (1960), and has:
1d *Jonathan Mark; *b* 14 March 1963
1d *Catherine Elisabeth; *b* 29 Sept 1965
2c *Brian Nicholas Hill [Brian Crowley Esq, 25 Linkway, Crowthorne, Berks RG45 6ES]; *b* 7 June 1942; *educ* Bradfield and Keble Coll Oxford (BA 1964, MA 1969); *m* 12 June 1965 *Celia Robson and has:
1d *Nicola Louise Hill; *b* 12 July 1969; MB ChB 1993
2d *Philippa Charlotte Hill; *b* 26 March 1973; *m* 20 July 1996 *David Llewellyn Bulpin
1c *Mary Elspeth Singer [Mrs David Langford, 56 Springfield Grove, Bristol BS6 7XE]; *b* 16 Oct 1935; *educ* St Michael Sch Petworth and Dorset House Sch Oxford; MAOT 1957; *m* 19 May 1962 *David Hyde Langford and has:
1d *Robin Charles [Robin Langford Esq, 56 Springfield Grove, Bristol BS6 7XE]; *b* 13 Oct 1964; *educ* Bristol Cathedral Sch and Leicester Poly (BA Hons 1986)
1d *Sarah Caroline [Mrs Gary Reynolds, 8 Standbury Ave, Fishponds, Bristol BS16 5AN]; *b* 10 March 1967; *educ* Colstons Sch Bristol and Hull U (BA 1988); *m* 22 Oct 1994 *Gary Edward Reynolds and has:
1e *James Charles Edward; *b* 19 June 1995
2a (cont.) George Hill *m* 2nd 15 Nov 1898 Helen Maude (*d* 14 Oct 1954), dau of Frederick Woodman, of Bedford House, Upper Deal, and *d* 25 Sept 1905, having by her had issue:
4b Geoffrey Frank Kenyon; Lt RN; *b* 12 Jan 1900; *d* 14 July 1924
3a Clement Lloyd (Sir), KCB, KCMG; FRGS, MP Shrewsbury 1906–13, Clerk FO 1867, Priv Sec to U-Sec State For Affrs 1885–86, Assist Clerk and

Actg Sec Dip Serv 1886, Commr Haiti 1886–87, Head African Dept FO 1894, Supt African Protectorates 1900–05; *b* 5 May 1845; *m* 1st 15 May 1889 Charlotte Eliza Mary Jane (*d* 11 Jan 1900), widow of Charles Waring and dau of Sir George William Denys, 2nd Bt (*see* 1956 edn), and had issue:

1b Rachel; *b* 29 Dec 1891; *d* 28 Dec 1892

3a (cont.) Sir Clement *m* 2nd 6 Dec 1906 Muriel Mary (*d* 4 Aug 1958), er dau of Colin Glencairn Campbell (*see* MACNAGHTEN, Bt), and *d* 9 April 1913, having by her had issue:

1b Clement Walter Rowland; *b* 22 Feb 1909; *educ* Eton; Maj QO Cameron Highrs WW II (wounded three times); Freeman Shrewsbury; *m* 1st 1 Feb 1935 (*divorce* 1941) Violet (*d* 1988), er dau of Charles Phillimore (*see* PHILLIMORE, B); *m* 2nd 5 Feb 1947 Elizabeth Theresa (*d* 10 Jan 1970), formerly w of John Henry Hambro, CMG (*see* HAMBRO, B), and 3rd dau of Capt Jersey J J De Knopp, of Calveley Hall, Tarporley, Cheshire, by Evelyn, dau of Charles John Fletcher, of Dale Park, Sussex; *m* 3rd 1971 Kathleen (*d* 1982), dau of Frank Dickie, of Truro, Nova Scotia, and widow of Norman Walduck, and *d* 29 Nov 1997, leaving by his 1st w:

1c *Carolyn Mary [The Rt Hon Carolyn Countess Fortescue, The Old Rectory, Bradoc, Lostwithiel, Cornwall PL22 ORN]; *b* 26 Jan 1937; *m* 1st 24 June 1968 (*divorce* 1983) Edward C Lockwood; *m* 2nd 1989, as his 3rd w, 7th Earl Fortescue (*qv*) and by her 1st husb has:

1d *Richard Rowland; *b* 1971

1d *Louisa Elizabeth; *b* 10 Dec 1969

2c *Joanna Clementine [Mrs Charles Bastin, 14 Avenue de Grande Bretagne, 98000 MC, Monaco; Larroque, 47370 Tournon d'Agenais, France]; *b* 28 Aug 1939; *m* 1965 *Charles C Bastin, only s of Charles A Bastin, of Louisville, Ky., and has issue:

1d *Alexander Charles; *b* 12 Aug 1969

2d *Nicholas Rowland; *b* 11 Nov 1970

2b Primrose Agnes; *b* 13 Dec 1907; *d* 1971

4a Brian Hubert; *b* 4 June 1847; *m* 8 Aug 1861 Alice Mary, dau of Charles Langton, of Barkhill, Liverpool, and *d* 1893, leaving:

1b Nina; *b* 1892

(3) Richard Frederick, JP, DL; Lt-Col, Col 3rd Bn Salop LI; *b* 14 Jan 1804; *m* 3 April 1835 Maria Jane (*d* 13 Oct 1880), dau of Lt-Col J D Bringhurst, and *d* 9 Jan 1890, leaving:

1a William Frederick; Lt-Col 73rd Regt; *b* 8 Sept 1843; *d* 1885

2a Henry Philip; *b* 13 July 1845; *m* 27 April 1870 Nora Alice, dau of Maj H A Scott, and *d* 6 Jan 1924, leaving:

1b Henry Alan; Boer War and WW I; *b* 10 March 1877; *m* 14 Jan 1920 Marjory Stewart, er dau of James Tyhurst, and *d* 29 Aug 1940, leaving:

1c Henry James; Lt 17th/21st Lancers; *b* 23 March 1921; *educ* Wellington; *m* 1953 *Ina Philpott [Mrs Henry Hill, El Refugio, 2852 E Carbo, Entre Rios, Argentina], and *d* 1985, leaving issue:

1d +Henry John [Henry Hill, El Refugio, 2852 E Carbo, Entre Rios, Argentina]; *b* 8 Jan 1962

1d *Virginia; *b* 1954; *m* 1975 *Ronald Joffre Bain and has:

1e *Joffre Enrique; *b* 1978

2e *Alan; *b* 1980

1e *Karen Irene; *b* 1976

2d *Margaret Ina; *b* 1956; *m* 1980 *Christian Dowgall

3d *Christina Marion; *b* 27 Dec 1959

2b Reginald Frederick; *b* 10 May 1881; *m* Sept 1912 *Nesta Gwendoline Hinds Howell, and *d* 12 Sept 1957

3b Rowland Philip; *b* 28 Feb 1888; *m* Nov 1912 Ruth (*d* 1976), dau of C H Stott, and *d* 1979, leaving issue:

1c +Brian Henry Rowland [Brian Hill Esq, 7 Thompson Rd, Napier, New Zealand]; *b* 1917; DDM Sydney (1950), WW II Middle East with RNZMC, Fell American Coll of Allergists 1950; *educ* Christ's Coll Christchurch NZ and Otago U (MB ChB 1943); *m* 1945 *Marjorie Virginia, dau of Capt Euan Dickson, DSC, DFC, RFC, of Epsom, Auckland, NZ, and has issue:

1d +Heathcote Henry Rowland; *b* 1949

2d +Simon Phillip; *b* 1951

1d *Angela Francesca; *b* 1946; *m* 1977 *Kim Campbell and has:

1e *Benjamin; *b* 1980

1b Alice Isabel; *m* 1910 Gerald Markham Bowen (*d* 1930), s of Hon Sir Charles Christopher Bowen, KCMG, and had issue

2b Ella Mary; *m* 1910 William Harry Helmore (*d* 1915) and *d c* 1968, leaving issue

1a Fanny Melita; *m* 25 March 1856 Thomas Kynnersely Kynnersley (*d* 10 Feb 1919), of Leighton Hall, nr Ironbridge, Salop, and *d* 15 Sept 1913, leaving issue

2a Mary Rhoda; *m* 10 April 1860 Sir Thomas Charlton Meyrick, 1st Bt, KCB (*qv*), and *d* 4 Oct 1924, leaving issue

3a Selina Rachel; *m* 12 April 1864 Rev William Wingfield (*d* 1913), of Worfield, Shrewsbury, Vicar Leighton, Salop, and *d* 25 July 1927

4a Annette Catharine; *m* 28 Dec 1875 Vere Francis John Somerset (*see* BEAUFORT, D) and *d* 5 Oct 1889, leaving issue

(4) Philip; Col; *b* 12 July 1806; *m* 19 Dec 1833 Charlotte Catherine Emma (*d* 16 Feb 1877), est dau of John George Norbury, and *d* 10 Dec 1861

(5) Clement Delves; Capt RHG; *b* 3 Jan 1808; *m* 26 June 1841 Harriet (*d* Nov 1885 aged 66), est dau of John Mytton, and *d* 1883, having had:

1a Godfrey Clement; *b* 24 May 1842; left issue

(1) Rachel Stephenson; *m* 19 Sept 1820 Sir Andrew Vincent Corbet, 2nd Bt (*see* 1970 edn), and *d* 4 April 1875, leaving issue

(2) Mary Emma; *m* 1823 Andrew William Corbet (*d* 1856), of Sundorne Castle, Salop, and *d* 31 July 1864

2 ROWLAND HILL, **1st Viscount Hill of Hawkestone and of Hardwicke,** Co Salop, so *cr* 22 Sept 1842, as also earlier 17 May 1814 BARON HILL OF ALMARAZ and of HAWKESTONE, Co Salop, and 16 Jan 1816 BARON HILL OF ALMARAZ AND OF HARDWICKE, Co Salop (all UK), with in the first and last cases remainder, failing male issue of his body, to his n Rowland; *b* 11 Aug 1772; Gen, served Peninsular War, C-in-C 1828–42; *d* unm 10 Dec 1842, when the 1814 Barony expired

3 Richard (Rev); *b* 17 Sept 1773; *d* 3 Sept 1821

4 Robert Chambré (Sir), CB, of Prees Hall, Salop; Col; *b* 25 March 1778; *m* 5 Feb 1801 Eliza (*d* 7 Jan 1861), dau of Henry Lumley, and *d* 5 March 1860, having had:

(1) George Stavely; *b* 20 Nov 1801; *m* 3 May 1832 Jane (*d* 28 Jan 1894), dau of Thomas Borough, of Chetwynd Park, and *d* 22 March 1873, having had issue

(2) Alfred Edward; Col; *b* 19 March 1810; *m* 9 April 1839 Anne Howard (*d* 18 Dec 1888) and *d* 24 Oct 1890, leaving:

1a Alfred; *b* 11 Feb 1840; *d* unm 25 Dec 1858

2a Rowland; Lt-Col 2st Bn Dorsetshire Regt; *b* 17 June 1841; *m* 5 April 1879 Amy Caroline (*m* 2nd 4 June 1925 Robert Edward Chichester (*d* 7 Jan 1927), of Inglside, Budleigh Salterton, and *d* 19 March 1962), dau of Maj-Gen John Octavius Chichester, and *d* 12 Aug 1892, having had issue:

1b Emily Constance; *b* 7 Feb 1880; *d* unm 1 July 1966

2b Ada Blanche; *d* an infant

3a Robert; barrister; *b* 12 March 1847; *m* 10 Jan 1894 Ethel Murdoch (*d* 27 Feb 1930), dau of W F Brabant, and *d* 15 Dec 1930, having had:

1b Alfred Brabant; *b* 25 May 1896; *m* 20 Oct 1933 Frances (*d* 1986), est dau of Edward Pooley, and *d* 1979, leaving:

1c +John Richard; *b* 7 June 1935; *educ* U of BC (BSc 1960) and McGill (PhD)

2c +Peter Robert [Peter Hill, 1840 Nigel Court, Vienna, VA 22182, USA]; *b* 7 Jan 1937; *educ* U of BC (BA, BSc 1961); *m* 1st 27 July 1968 Mary Lynn (*d* 1993), only dau of Keller Smith, of Knoxville, Tenn.; *m* 2nd 1994 *Joyce Ann Ralston, dau of Robert E Prowty, and by his 1st w has issue:

1d +Peter Brabant; *b* 1970

2d +Charles Edward Keller; *b* 1980

1d *Molly Cochran; *b* 1972

1b Margaret Anne; *b* 29 Sept 1894; *m* 23 June 1946 Edwin W Fletcher (*d* 8 Nov 1964)

2b Mary; *b* 6 Dec 1908; drowned while helping to save a playfellow 24 July 1920

1a Emily; *d* 1860

(3) Percy, CB; Lt-Gen, Lt-Col Rifle Bde; *b* 24 Dec 1817; *m* 1846 Harriet Cecilia (*d* 2 March 1901), dau of Capt John Steuart, and *d* 24 April 1880, leaving:

1a Percy Graham; Capt Rifle Bde; *b* 31 Jan 1848; *m* 1st 18 April 1872 Margaret Anne Hamilton (*dsp* 1879), dau of Lt Charles Stewart, Bengal Artillery; *m* 2nd 21 June 1892 Alice Margaret (*dsp* 20 Dec 1897), est dau of Rev Canon Henry Brown, Rector Woolwich; *m* 3rd 1899 Elizabeth Ann (*m* 2nd 1927 Charles Beaufoy Wright (*d* 1944) and *d* 9 Feb 1960), dau of George Raworth, and *d* 8 May 1923, having by her had issue:

1b Percy; *b* 10 July 1900

2b Rowland Graham, OBE (1956), MBE; Lt-Col Dorset Regt WW II; *b* 18 Feb 1912; *m* 6 June 1941 *Doris Lucy Frances, formerly w of Lt George Maitland Edye, 7th Hus, and er dau of Sir Francis Dundas Couchman, KBE, of Beaudesert Park, Henley-in-Arden and *d* 1943

1b *Florence Cecilia; *b* 2 March 1906; *m* 2 Jan 1926 Lt-Col Julian Edward Wright, Sherwood Foresters (*d* Dec 1967), s of Charles Beaufoy Wright (*see* above), and has issue:

1c *Juliet Ann Cecilia; *b* 19 Dec 1928; *m* 22 Sept 1960 *Peter Oswald Gatehouse and has issue:

1d *James Peter Wright; *b* 9 April 1963

1d *Elizabeth Ann Cecilia; *b* 10 March 1965

1a Florence Julia; *m* 1st 20 Nov 1877 Thomas Henry Bennett (*d* 25 Sept 1900), of Cobham Court, Surrey; *m* 2nd 23 Oct 1901 Charles Gawen Roberts-Gawen (*d* 9 Sept 1940), of Sharnbrook House, Beds, and *dsp* 9 Dec 1938

(1) Mary Julia; *d* unm 3 Oct 1850

5 Francis Brian; Kt Portuguese Order of Town and Sword 2nd Cl; *b* 21 April 1779; *m* 1st 22 April 1804 Johanna Caroline Hilebina (*d* 31 Oct 1806), 4th dau of Christian Falbe, of Copenhagen, and had issue; *m* 2nd 6 Oct 1819 Emily Lissey (*d* 13 Feb 1840), yst dau of Thomas Jelf Powys, and *d* 4 April 1842, having by her had issue

6 Clement Delves; Maj-Gen *b* 6 Dec 1781; *d* unm 20 Jan 1845

7 Thomas Noel (Sir), KCB; Col; *b* 14 Feb 1784; *m* 27 July 1821 Anna Maria (*d* 25 Feb 1886 aged 88), 2nd dau of 1st Baron Teignmouth (*see* 1970 edn), and *d* 8 Jan 1832, leaving, with other issue:

(1) Charles Rowland; Maj-Gen RA; *b* 21 July 1829; *m* 6 Oct 1874 Elizabeth (*d* 11 June 1934), dau of John Matthew Ridley, of Walwick Hall, Northumberland, and *d* 30 Oct 1898, leaving issue:

1a Rowland Clement Ridley, DSO (1918); Col RE, Hon Brig 1935, served Aden 1904 and WW I (despatches three times); *b* 3 Sept 1879; *educ* Clifton; *m* 6 Jan 1920 Margaret, dau of Percy Vickers, of Wilmslow, Cheshire, and *dsp* 7 Oct 1967

2a Geoffrey Noel, DSO (1918); Lt-Col RA WW I (despatches five times) and Waziristan 1920 (despatches); *b* 6 Jan 1881; *m* 25 Sept 1934 Josephine (Jessie), est dau of John McIntyre, of Theakston Hall, Bedale, Yorks, and *dsp* 7 Sept 1947

1a Florence Mary; *m* 31 July 1902, Rev Harry Morton Gorham (*d* 7 Feb 1957), Chaplain to Earl Ferrers, est s of Rev H S Gorham, and *d* 23 April 1962, leaving issue

2a Louisa Susan Violet; *m* 1st 1 Aug 1912 Hugh Alfred Cholmley (*d* 25 July 1944), er s of Alfred John Cholmley, DL, of Place Newton, Yorks, and had issue; *m* 2nd 4 Jan 1947 John Clapham Radcliffe (*d* 1962), of Beverley House, Malton, Yorks, and *d* 5 Jan 1969

(1) Anna Maria; *m* 9 Oct 1851 Rev William J Trevenen (*d* 17 Nov 1864), and *d* 13 March 1917, having had issue

The 1st VISCOUNT's nephew,

Sir Rowland Hill, 4th Bt (as which *s* gf 1824), and **2nd Viscount Hill of Hawkestone and of Hardwicke**; *b* 1800; MP (Tory) Salop 1821–32 and N Salop 1832–42;

m 21 July 1831 Anne (*d* 31 Oct 1891), only child of Joseph Clegg, of Peplow Hall, Salop, and gdau and sole heir of Arthur Clegg, and *d* 2 Jan 1875, leaving, with a yr s (Geoffrey Richard Clegg, JP, DL, Maj RHG, *b* 14 April 1837, *m* 9 Dec 1880 Frances Jessie (*see* SHREWSBURY and WATERFORD, E) and *dsp* 4 May 1891):

ROWLAND CLEGG HILL later CLEGG-HILL (roy licence 7 Feb 1874), **3rd Viscount Hill of Hawkestone and of Hardwicke**, DL Salop; MP (C) N Shropshire 1857–65, bankrupt 1894; *b* 5 Dec 1833; *m* 1st 3 May 1855 Mary (*d* 7 Jan 1874), dau of William Madax and formerly serving maid to her husb's mother, and had:

1 ROWLAND RICHARD CLEGG-HILL, **4th Viscount Hill of Hawkestone and of Hardwicke**, JP Salop, DL Co London; Capt 3rd Bn Royal Warwicks Regt WW I; *b* 12 Feb 1863; *m* July 1890 Ann (*d* 10 Jan 1937), dau of William Irwin, of Tanrago, Co Sligo, and *dsp* 19 Dec 1923

2 FRANCIS WILLIAM CLEGG-HILL, **5th Viscount Hill of Hawkestone and of Hardwicke**, JP Radnorshire; *b* 4 Nov 1866; *m* 5 Sept 1905 Caroline Anna (*d* 29 June 1941), 2nd dau of Capt Frank Corbett, of Greenfield, Presteigne, Radnorshire, and *dsp* 6 July 1924

The **3rd Viscount** *m* 2nd 29 April 1875 Hon Isabella Elizabeth Wynn (*d* 29 July 1898), 5th dau of 3rd Baron Newborough (*qv*), and *d* 30 March 1895, leaving by her:

3 CHARLES ROWLAND, **6th Viscount**

4 Arthur Reginald, DSO; Actg Lt-Col cmdg 2nd Bn Cheshire Regt, Lt 3rd Bn Cheshire Regt Boer War and WW I (despatches three times), Croix de Guerre with Palms; *b* 15 June 1877; *m* 4 July 1905 Evelyn Hilda Sinclair, dau of Rev William Charles Bell, Sr Indian Chaplain, Vicar Northmoor, Oxford, and was *ka* 18 Sept 1918, having had:

(1) Evelyn Mary; *b* 15 Oct 1909; *d* 8 Dec 1910

(2) Aline Rosemary; *b* 1, *d* 7 Jan 1912

5 Gerald Spencer, JP Salop; Capt N Staffs Regt, served Boer War 1900–02 and WW I; *b* 4 March 1879; *m* 3 April 1907 Dorothy (*d* 18 Jan 1978), 3rd dau of Rev Sir George Boughey, 5th Bt (*qv*), and *d* 4 April 1930, leaving:

(1) *Anne Selina Elizabeth [Mrs Janusz Juhre, Aqualate Hall, Newport, Salop]; WW II in WRNS, Polish Order of Merit 1960; *b* 18 Feb 1915; *m* 1st 17 July 1940 (*divorce* 1947) Edward Hanbury Carrington David Lloyd-Davis (*d* 20 June 1968), of Brewood, Staffs; *m* 2nd 16 April 1947 *Janusz Maria Stanislaw Eugeniusz Juhre, civ engr, 2nd Lt Polish Army, and by him has:

1a *Tadeusz Maria Gerald Alexander [Tadeusz Juhre Esq, Aqualate Hall, Newport, Salop]; *b* March 1951

1a *Maria Jadwiga Teresa [Mrs Andrew Maryniák, 181 Pitshanger Lane, London W5]; *b* Jan 1948; *m* 21 July 1973 *Andrew Maryniák, est s of Ludwick Marynaik, of Ealing, and has issue:

1b *Richard; *b* 1977

2b *Martin; *b* 1980

3b *Stefan; *b* 1982

1b *Joanna Maria; *b* 8 Oct 1974

2a *Jadwiga Maria Teresa Celina [Mrs Richard Saller, 92 Grove Ave, London W7]; *b* Oct 1949; *m* 30 Dec 1972 *Richard Antoni Saller, MSc, and has:

1b *Michael; *b* 1976

2b *Andrew; *b* 1976

3b *Jan Fryderyk; *b* 1983

1b *Teresa; *b* 1974

2b *Monika; *b* 1990

3a *Anna Zofia Maria [Mrs Anna Behnke, 18 Parkcroft Rd, Westbridgeford, Notts]; *b* May 1954; *m* 1974 (*divorce* 1991) Dr George Behnke, and has:

1b *Wojciech; *b* 1983

1b *Margaret; *b* 1980

2b *Kathryn; *b* 1981

1 Evelyn Isabella; *b* 26 June 1880; *m* 28 June 1905 Justinian John Edwards-Heathcote (*d* 1 March 1937), of Betton House, Market Drayton, est son of Capt Justinian Heathcote Edwards-Heathcote, of Apedale Hall, Staffs, and *dsp* 13 Jan 1940

The 5th VISCOUNT's half-bro,

CHARLES ROWLAND CLEGG-HILL, **6th Viscount Hill Hawkestone and of Hardwicke**, DSO, JP, DL Salop; Maj and Brevet Lt-Col Roy Welch Fus, Boer War 1899–1902 (wounded, despatches twice) and WW I (wounded, despatches, Croix de Guerre with Silver Star); *b* 5 May 1876; *m* 1st 6 Jan 1903 Mildred (*d* 29 Jan 1934), dau of Thomas Bulteel, of Radford, S Devon, and had issue:

1 GERALD ROWLAND CLEGG-HILL, **7th Viscount Hill of Hawkestone and of Hardwicke**; *b* 31 March 1904; *educ* Shrewsbury; Maj Roy Welch Fus WW II; *m* 1st 7 Oct 1930 (*divorce* 1942) Elizabeth Flora (*d* 19 March 1967), yr dau of Brig-Gen George Nowell Thomas Smyth-Osbourne, CB, CMG, DSO, DL, of Ash, Iddesleigh, N Devon, and had issue:

(1) ANTHONY ROWLAND CLEGG-HILL, **8th and present Viscount Hill of Hawkestone and of Hardwicke**

(2) Gerald William; 2nd Lt RTR; *b* 26 Aug 1932; *educ* Kelly Coll and RMA Sandhurst; *d* unm 12 July 1962

1 (cont.) The **7th Viscount** *m* 2nd 30 Nov 1942 *Catherine Mary (Molly), only dau of Dr Rowland Venables Lloyd Williams, of Malford, nr Denbigh, and *d* 4 May 1974

2 Frederic Raymond; Maj King's Salop LI WW II (despatches) (with 1st Bn N Rhodesian Regt 1938–44); *b* 10 Aug 1909; *m* 18 Nov 1938 *Alice Dorothy [The Hon Mrs Frederic Clegg-Hill, The Old Forge, Stone in Oxney, nr Tenterden, Kent], dau of R-Adml Cuthbert Godfrey Chapman, MVO (*see* NEWBOROUGH, B), and was *ka* Germany 13 April 1945, leaving issue:

(1) +PETER DAVID RAYMOND CHARLES; *b* posthumously 17 Oct 1945; heir presumptive; *educ* Tabley House Sch; *m* 1973 *Sharon Ruth, adopted dau of — Deane, of Kaikohe, New Zealand, and has issue:

1a +Paul Andrew Raymond; *b* 4 May 1979

2a +Michael Charles David; *b* 1988

1a *Catherine Anne; *b* 22 Dec 1974

2a *Jennifer Louise; *b* 9 July 1976

3a *Susan Dorothy; *b* 1980

4a *Rachel Emma; *b* 1984

5a *Melissa Jane; *b* 1986

The **6th Viscount** *m* 2nd 18 Jan 1936 Berthe Maria Emilie (*d* 31 Dec 1959), dau of Alphonse Schmidt-Immer, of Strasbourg, and *d* 3 May 1957

HILL of Bradford

Arms: Or on a fess between three leopard's faces sable as many roses argent, barbed and seeded proper. **Crest:** In front of a rock, thereon a merino ram statant all proper, two roses as in the arms. **Motto:** *Ne tenta vel perficite* ('Attempt not, or else accomplish'). **Creation:** Bt. (UK) 13 Jan 1917.

SIR JAMES FREDERICK HILL, 4TH BT, of Bradford, DL (W Yorks 1994) [Sir James Hill Bt DL, Roseville, Moor Lane, Menston, W Yorks LS29 6AP]; *b* 5 Dec 1943; *s* f 1976; *educ* Wrekin Coll and Bradford Inst of Tenchology; *m* 9 Sept 1966 *Sandra Elizabeth, only dau of John Crosland Ingram, of Lenner House, Beamsley, Yorks, and has:

1 +JAMES LAWRENCE INGRAM; *b* 22 Sept 1973

1 *Juliet Clare; *b* 3 July 1969; *m* 1st 1989 (*divorce* 1996) James Christopher Kaberry, er s of Hon Sir Christopher Donald Kaberry, 2nd Bt (*qv*), and has issue; *m* 2nd 1996 *Richard Morton, er s of Kenneth Morton, of Harrogate

2 *Georgina Margaret; *b* 1971

3 *Josephine Valerie; *b* 1973

Lineage: Sir James Hill, 1st Bt (UK), so *cr* 13 Jan 1917, JP and Alderman Bradford; *b* 11 March 1849; MP (Lib) Bradford Centl 1916–18, Ld Mayor 1908 and 1909, Freeman City of Bradford 1921; wool merchant, fndr Sir James Hill and Son 1891, chm local dirs Barclays Bank (also on London Advisory Bd); *m* 24 Feb 1875 Alice (*d* 21 June 1936), dau of Joshua Knight, and *d* 17 Jan 1936, having had:

1 Arthur James; *b* 13 Jan 1876; *m* 6 July 1898 Eleanor Beatrice Hindle, dau of Thomas Duxbury, FCS, AMICE, of Darwen, and *d* 1 Aug 1935, leaving issue:

(1) Annie Dulcie; *b* 1900; *m* 1st 4 Aug 1923 (*divorce* 1946) Cdr Robert Derek Stawell Crosse, OBE, RN (*d* 8 April 1967); *m* 2nd 10 Dec 1946 Paul William Manzi-Fe (*d* Jan 1993), of Borwick Lodge, Outgate, Westmorland, and *d* Oct 1979, leaving issue by her 1st husb

(2) Eleanor Kathleen; *b* 1904; *d* Feb 1981

(3) Nellie Elizabeth Audrey; *b* 1907; *m* 1st 26 Sept 1931 (*divorce* 1939) Peter Sime Douty (*d* 1948), yr s of Ceasar Colston Douty, of Langton Manor, Knaresborough, Yorks, and had issue:

1a *Juliette Eleanor Sime [Mrs John Lindley, Theberton Grange, nr Leiston, Suffolk]; *b* 30 June 1934; *m* 10 Dec 1955 *Lt John Gordon Lindley, RN, and has issue:

1b *Charles Arthur; *b* 23 July 1965

1b *Antonia Eleanor; *b* 2 Sept 1957

2b *Bridget Alexandra; *b* 7 Nov 1959

(3) (cont.) Mrs Nellie Douty *m* 2nd 27 July 1949 Cecil Denbigh Hannam, MC (*d* Oct 1975), slr, of Leeds, s of William Simpson Hannam, of Moor House, Burley-in-Wharfdale, Yorks and *d* Feb 1988

(4) *Noeline Etrenne [Lady Aarvold, The Coach House, Crabtree Lane, Westhumble, Surrey RH5 6BQ]; *b* 1909; *m* 8 July 1934 Judge Sir Carl Douglas Aarvold, JP, OBE (1945), TD (1950), DL (Surrey 1973), Recorder London (*d* 1991), and has issue:

1a *Christopher Olaf [Christopher Aarvold Esq, Watcomb Farmhouse, Godmonstone, Dorset DT1 1PX]; *b* 22 Sept 1943; *educ* Marlborough; *m* 1981 *Sandi Gazzard and has:

1b *Tobias Carl; *b* 1981

2b *Dominic Ralph Ole; *b* 1983

1b *Camilla Louise; *b* 1984

2a *James Hillary [James Aarvold Esq, Foxbury, Westhumble, Surrey RH5 6BQ]; *b* 1946; *educ* Marlborough; *m* 1976 *Dr Jillian Stanley Jones and has:

1b *Daniel Alexander; *b* 1977

2b *Thomas William; *b* 1982

1b *Eleanor Pippin; *b* 1980

3a *John Merriman [John Aarvold Esq, Thanington, Chichester Rd, Dorking, Surrey RH4 1LR]; *b* 9 Sept 1947; *educ* Marlborough; *m* 1976 *Elizabeth Rumball, of Johannesburg, and has:

1b *Robert John Douglas; *b* 1978

2b *Angus David Merriman; *b* 1984

3b *Douglas Henry Eric; *b* 1984

2 **Sir Albert Hill, 2nd Bt**; *b* 4 Nov 1877; *m* 11 July 1900 Ellen, dau of Thomas Sowden, of Bradford, and *d* 13 May 1946, having had:

(1) JAMES (Sir), **3rd Bt**

(1) Alice Edna; *b* 19 July 1902; *m* 7 Sept 1926 George F Carlton and *d* 17 July 1943, leaving issue

1 Annie; *b* 11 Feb 1880; *m* 7 April 1903 Fred Ambler (*d* 8 Nov 1932), of Chellow Grange, Bradford, and *d* 15 June 1964, leaving issue

Sir ALBERT's s,

Sir James Hill, 3rd Bt; *b* 29 May 1905; *educ* Wrekin Coll; chm Sir James Hill and Son, of Bradford; *m* 23 Sept 1930 *Marjory, JP (Bradford 1954) [Marjory Lady Hill JP, Brea House, Trebetherick, Cornwall], dau of Frank Croft, of Brocka, Lindale, Grange-over-Sands, and *d* 1976, leaving issue:

1 Sir JAMES FREDERICK HILL, **4th and present Bt**

1 *Anita Joan; *b* 20 Nov 1931; *m* 14 July 1953 Michael John Riley (*d* 1988) and has:

(1) *Peter James Wynne; *b* 20 May 1956

(2) *Christopher John; *b* 5 Nov 1960

(1) *Wendy Jeanne; *b* 19 Aug 1954

2 *Judith Mary; *b* 29 Dec 1933; *m* 8 Oct 1960 *Dixon Donkin and has:

(1) *Dixon; *b* 10 Aug 1961

(1) *Deborah Marjory; *b* 17 Dec 1963

(2) *Nicola Dawn; *b* 20 May 1969

3 *Ellen Barbara [Mrs Edward Robson, Windrush, Apperley Bridge, nr Bradford, Yorks]; *b* 10 April 1936; *m* 27 Jan 1960 *Edward Norman Robson and has:

(1) *Susan Joy; *b* 2 Oct 1960

(2) *Jacqueline Ann; *b* 27 Nov 1963

(3) *Penelope Jane; *b* 3 March 1967

4 *Florence Margaret [Mrs Florence Coombs, Windsor Mews, Windsor Rd, Vincent, E London, South Africa]; *b* 5 Dec 1943; *m* 20 Jan 1965 (*divorce* 19–) Terence John Coombs and has:

(1) *Tessa Annette; *b* 9 Oct 1965

(2) *Linda Margaret; *b* 8 May 1967

(3) *Tracey Elizabeth; *b* 1973

HILL of Brook Hall

Arms: Sa. a chevron erminois between three leopard's faces arg. **Crest:** A talbot's head, couped sa., guttée d'eau, collared gu., studded and ringed or. **Motto:** *Ne tentes aut perfice* ('Accomplish or else try not at all'). **Creation:** Bt. (I) 17 Aug 1779.

SIR JOHN ALFRED ROWLEY HILL, 11TH BT, of Brook Hall, Co Londonderry [Sir John Hill, Bt, 12 Ledbury Close, Oadby Grange, Leicester LE2 4SR]; *b* 1940; *s* half-bro 1992; *m* 1966 (*divorce* 1981) Diana Anne Walker

Lineage: SAMUEL HILL, of Bucks and later Coleraine, Co Derry; Treasurer Ireland *c* 1642; granted land in Cos Armagh, Tyrone, Antrim and Derry; Burgess of Londonderry; *m* Sarah, dau of Michael Beresford, and *d* on or after 25 August 1688, leaving, with a yr s (Jonathan, Maj during Siege of Derry):

JOHN HILL; *m* 17 July 1642 Mary, dau of Thomas Wilson, of Kilkenny, thus acquiring property in E Smithfield, London, and had:

SAMUEL HILL, of Culmore, Co Derry; *m* Mary, dau and coheir of Hugh Rowley, of Culmore, by Mary, dau of Edward Rowley, of Castle Roe, MP Londonderry, by Lettice, dau and coheir of Viscount Massereene (*qv*), leaving, with other issue, including a yr s (Hugh (Rev), DD, of Mount Hill, Co Armagh; *m* Elizabeth, dau of Edward Hall, of Mount Hall, Co Down, and had issue):

ROWLEY HILL; MP Derry; *m* 9 Feb 1726 Sophia Beresford, sis of Sir Marcus Lowther-Crofton, 1st Bt (*see* CROFTON, B), and had, with three daus and a yr s (George, Lt RN, *b* 15 April 1729, lost in hurricane E Indies):

Sir Hugh Hill, 1st Bt (I), so *cr* 17 Aug 1779; MP Derry; *b* 1 Jan 1727; *m* 1st 27 Dec 1754 Mary (*d* 16 July 1760), dau of John Hodgson, of Ballynascreen, Co Derry, and had a dau (Elizabeth, *m* 19 Nov 1774 Very Rev Stewart Blacker, of Carrickblacker, Co Armagh); *m* 2nd 17 June 1762 Hannah, dau of John McClintock (*see* RATHDONNEL, B) and widow of J Spence, of Co Leitrim, and by her had, with other issue:

1 **Sir George Fitzgerald Hill, 2nd Bt**, PC (UK); *b* 1 June 1763; Col Londonderry Miltitia, MP Derry, Clerk I H of C, a Ld Irish Treasury 1806, V-Treasurer Ireland 1817, Govr St Vincent and Trinidad; *m* 10 Sept 1788 Jane (*d* 2 Nov 1836), 3rd dau of Rt Hon John Beresford (*see* WATERFORD, M), and *d* 8 March 1839

2 John Beresford (Rev); Rector Langfield, Preb St Patrick's Cathedral Dublin; *b* 16 Nov 1765; *m* 7 April 1803 Laetitia (*m* 2nd Capt — Steel, 43rd Regt, and *d* Oct 1855), 2nd dau of Dominick McCausland, of Daisy Hill, Co Derry, and *d* 4 Dec 1806, leaving:

(1) **Sir George Hill, 3rd Bt**; *b* 15 Jan 1804; *m* 30 April 1831 Elizabeth Sophia (*d* 23 July 1900), est dau of John Rea, of St Columbs, Co Derry, by Louisa, 4th dau of Very Rev Stewart Blacker, of Carrickblacker, Co Armagh, and *d* 15 Dec 1845, having had, with other issue:

1a **Sir John Hill, 4th Bt**; Maj, Capt 17th Lancers Indian Mutiny; *b* 4 Feb 1833; *m* 9 June 1863 Charlotte Isabella (*m* 2nd 5 July 1879 William Fuller and *d* 19 Dec 1892), dau of Henry David Blyth, of Hamilton Place, Piccadilly, and *d* 30 July 1872, having had:

1b **Sir George Hill, 5th Bt**; *b* 22 March 1866; *d* 17 Oct 1878

2b **Sir Henry Blyth Hill, 6th Bt**, DSO; Capt and Brevet Maj Roy Irish Fus, Govr Berber and Bahr el Gazal, attd Egyptian Army 1898–1908, served Nile Expdn 1898, present Khartoum (despatches) and subsequent operations against Ahmed Fedil (despatches, Brevet Maj), Nile Expdn 1899 and ops resulting in defeat of the Khalifa (despatches), Order Medjidie 4th Cl and Osmanieh 3rd Cl, WW I (despatches twice); *b* 31 March 1867; *m* 26 Aug 1907 Eliza Maud (*d* 14 Nov 1959), dau of George Bowdler Gipps, of Howletts, nr Canterbury, and *d* 2 May 1929, having had:

1c Patrick John; *b* 11 June 1909; *d* 22 Feb 1910

3b John; *b* 25 June 1869; *d* unm 1 Dec 1907

4b Hugh Rowley; *b* 31 Aug 1870; *d* 19 Jan 1871

1b Charlotte Elizabeth; *m* 19 June 1894 Maj Henry Philip Oldfield (*d* 9 Dec 1950), of Steep Hill, Harrow-on-the-Hill, and *d* 24 Jan 1959, leaving issue

2b Letitia Catherine; *m* 7 June 1894 Lionel Stuart (*d* 1920), of Weemalle, Ceylon, and *d* 10 Feb 1951

3b Mary Maud; *d* unm 10 Feb 1944

4b Louisa Isabella; *b* posthumously; *m* 19 Nov 1896 James Bruce Rennie (*d* 1921), of Galaha, Ceylon, and *d* 6 Nov 1941, leaving issue

2a Rowley (Rt Rev); DD, Vicar Sheffield, Canon York, Bp Sodor and Man 24 Aug 1877; *b* 22 Feb 1836; *m* 1st 30 April 1863 Caroline Maud (*d* 6 April 1882), 2nd dau of Capt Alfred Chapman, RN (see MACNAGHTEN, Bt), and had:

1b **Sir George Rowley Hill, 7th Bt**; *b* 28 April 1864; *m* 16 Jan 1890 Alice Estelle Harley (*d* 27 May 1940), dau of Edward Bacon, of Elywood, Kington, Herefs, and *d* 30 June 1954, leaving:

1c **Sir (George) Cyril Rowley Hill, 8th Bt**, of Brook Hall; *b* 18 Dec 1890; *educ* Wellington and abroad; jnlst; *m* 15 July 1919 Edith Muriel, dau of W O Thomas, of Oakhurst, Liverpool, and Bryn Glas, Mold, and *dsp*

2b Marcus Rowley, CBE (1919); V-Adml, Offr Legn Hon; *b* 13 March 1867; *m* 17 Nov 1808 Ellen Mabel (*d* 1 Jan 1942), dau of John William Mellor, PC, MP, and *d* 8 Feb 1925

3b Alfred Rowley; *b* 24 Dec 1868; *m* 1893 Jean (*d* 14 Nov 1943), dau of J Cunninghame, and *d* 22 April 1946, leaving:

1c **Sir George Alfred Rowley Hill, 9th Bt**; WW II as Lt RNVR, formerly Lt IA; *b* 11 Oct 1899; *educ* Melville Coll Edinburgh; *m* 1st 20 Dec 1924 (*divorce* 1938) Rose Ethel Kathleen, MBE, dau of William Richard Spratt, of Portsmouth, and had issue:

1d **Sir Richard George Rowley Hill, 10th Bt**, MBE; Maj KOSB, Lt Roy Fus and Sikh Regt IA; *b* 18 Dec 1925; *educ* Clayesmore and Glasgow U; *m* 2 March 1954 *Angela Mary, only dau of Lt-Col Stanley Herbert Gallon, TD, of St Duthus, Berwick-upon-Tweed, and *d* 1992, leaving:

1e *Charlotte Mary Rowley; *b* 1976

2e *Georgina Emma Rowley; *b* 1977

1c (cont.) **Sir George** *m* 2nd 1938 Jessie Anne (*d* 1995), dau of —Roberts, of Leics, and *d* 1985, leaving:

2d Sir JOHN ALFRED ROWLEY HILL, **11th and present Bt**

1d *Margaret Anne Rowley; *b* 1942

1c Maud Elizabeth Anne; *m* 22 Feb 1917 Raymond Arundell Leakey, of Longwood Chase, Little Baddow, nr Chelmsford, Essex, 2nd s of Rev Arundell Leakey, Rector Bassingham, Lincs, and *d* 18 June 1941, leaving issue

4b Edmund Rowley; *b* 19 Feb 1873; *m* 7 Aug 1913 Rosamira Murray, dau of Ven Francis W Austin, Archdeacon Demerara, Br Guiana, and *dsp* 1 Oct 1947

1b Letitia Caroline Rowley; *m* 20 July 1901 Rev Canon David Buxton Barclay (*d* 17 Jan 1954), Canon Emeritus Chelmsford, 2nd s of Robert Barclay, of High Leigh, Hoddesdon, and *d* 8 March 1957, leaving issue

2b Elizabeth Madeline Rowley; *b* 13 Feb 1882; *d* unm 31 March 1969

1a (cont.) The Rt Rev Robert Hill *m* 2nd 11 June 1884 Alicia Eliza (*d* 1 Oct 1930), dau of George Probyn (*see* MACNAGHTEN, Bt), and *d* 27 May 1887

(2) Rowley John; Capt Bengal Irregular Cav; *b* 1 Sept 1806; *m* 2 Jan 1835 Caroline Catherine (*d* 1 Aug 1890), 2nd dau of Maj-Gen Sir Robert Sale, GCB, Col 13th Inf, and *d* 12 Nov 1850, leaving issue:

1a Marcus, 42nd Highrs; *b* 8 Dec 1836; *m* 10 Dec 1872 Maria Payne (*d* 1890), and *d* 1917, leaving issue:

1b Rowley John; *b* 5 Dec 1873; *m* 1896 Anne Elizabeth Morrow (*d* 1912), and *d* 1960, leaving issue:
1c Leslie Thomas; *b* 1897; *m* 1920 Irene Howlett and *d* 1958, leaving:
1d *Joan Maria; *b* 1925; *m* 1945 *Leslie Bailey and has:
1e *Kenneth Leslie; *b* 1946
1e *Cheryl Larraine; *b* 1948
2d *Dorothy Irene; *b* 1928; *m* 1947 *Herbert Alfred Morley and has:
1e *Christopher John; *b* 1950
1e *Carol Anne; *b* 1948
2c Claude Adam James; *b* 1901; *m* 1928 *Ruby Alice Mallett [Mrs Claude Hill, 8 Lancaster Rd, Mooroolbark, Vict, Australia], dau of Robert Mallett, and *d* 1991, leaving issue:
1d +ALLAN CLAUDE JAMES [Allan Hill Esq, 18/20 Havelock St, Lawrence, NSW 2460, Australia]; *b* 1936; heir presumptive; *m* 1970 (*divorce* 1978) Rachel St Just, dau of Geoffrey Filsell, and has:
1e +Marcus Adam James; *b* 1974
1e *Sonya Rachel Anne; *b* 1972; *m* 1995 (*divorce* 1997) Ian Scott Thomson and has:
1f *Ian Clarence James; *b* 1994
1f *Natasha Dawn Anne; *b* 1993
1d *Joyce Patricia [Mrs Geoffrey Paul, 8 Lancaster Rd, Mooroolbark, Vict, Australia]; *b* 1934; *m* 1951 *Geoffrey Paul and has:
1e *Allan Geoffrey; *b* 1952
1e *Cheryl Therese [Mrs Andrew Rhodes, 112 Chirnside St, West Footscray, Vict, Australia]; *b* 1955; *m* 1987 *Andrew Rhodes and has:
1f *Gene Paul; *b* 1987
3c Marcus George; *b* 1904; *m* 1929 *Lydia May Liddle and *d* 1993, leaving:
1d George Frederick; *b* 1930; *m* 1951 *Jean Craggel and *d* 1991, having had:
1e +Anthony Rowland; *b* 1961
1e *Debra; *b* 1964
2e Sallyanne; *b* 1966; *d* 1989
2d +Kevin Leslie [Kevin Hill Esq, 49 Fraser St, Sunshine, Vict 3020, Australia]; *b* 1935; *m* 1959 *Wendy Chandler and has:
1e +Mark; *b* 1961; *m* 1986 *Caryn Geddes and has:
1f +Joshua Mark; *b* 1992
2e +Paul; *b* 1964; *m* 1989 *Tina-Jane Pinchen and has:
1f +Jason Paul; *b* 1997
1d *Patricia Miriam [Mrs Rolf Ludviksen, 26 Poole St, Deer Park, Vict 3023, Australia]; *b* 1932; *m* 1954 *Rolf Ludviksen and has:
1e *John Kenneth [John Ludviksen Esq, 75 Tarella Drive, Keilor Downs, Vict 3038, Australia]; *b* 1955; *m* 19– *Tracey Ruth, dau of John McLoone, and has:
1f *Michael John; *b* 1991
2f *Daniel James; *b* 1994
2e *Brett; *b* 1972
1e *Leanne Michelle [Mrs Leanne Borg, 16 Locke St, Essendon, Vict 3040, Australia]; *b* 1959; *m* 1977 (*divorce* 1983) Allan Borg and has:
1f *Melinda Amy; *b* 1979
2d *Dawn Ann; *b* 1939; *m* 1963 *John Justin and has:
1e *Kenneth; *b* 1964
2e *Darren; *b* 1966
3e *Glen; *b* 1971
3d *Lorraine Margaret; *b* 1941
4c Cyril Edward; *b* 1908; *m* 1939 *Mary Elizabeth [Mrs Cyril Hill, Unit 16/2, High Field Rd, Canterbury, Vict 3126, Australia], dau of Francis Tinker, and *d* 1988, leaving issue:
1d +James Rowland Edward [James Hill Esq, Lot 7, 9 Arnold St, Kilsyth, Melbourne, Vict, Australia]; *b* 1943; *m* 1969 *Lynette Jean, dau of — Berry, and has:
1e +Jason James; *b* 1972
2e +Christopher Eric; *b* 1974
1d *Janice Ann [Mrs Ronald Haynes, 39 Sandy St, Nunawading, Vict 3131, Australia]; *b* 1940; *m* 1962 *Ronald Arthur Haynes and has:
1e *Diane Mary; *b* 1964
2e *Michelle Lucy; *b* 1966
3e *Joanne Lisa [Mrs Carl Gittins, 4/34 Oak St, Seymour, Vict 3660, Australia]; *b* 1969; *m* 1990 *Carl Gittins
4e *Belinda Jane; *b* 1975
2d *Elizabeth Dianna [Mrs Constantine Politis, 16 Russell Ave, Mooroolbank, Vict, Australia]; *b* 1945; *m* 1967 *Constantine Politis, and has:
1e *Andrew Edward; *b* 1973
1e *Jeanette Ann; *b* 1969
2e *Debra Lee; *b* 1971
5c +Albert John; *b* 1912; *m* 1935 *Annie Melba, dau of Edgar William Johnstone
1c *Vera Maria; *b* 1902; *m* 1st Tim Burke (*d* 1957); *m* 2nd 1957 Francis Hill
2b Marcus George; *b* 1878
3b Robert Joseph; *b* 1880
4b James Henry Sale; *b* 1885; *m* 1910 Ethyl Woodbury (*d* 1967), of Albury, NSW, and *d* 1954, leaving:
1c +Roy Ernest [Roy Hill Esq, 381 Rau Street, Albury, NSW, Australia]; *b* 1914; *m* 1935 *Phyllis Allen, of Ringwood, Vict, and has:
1d *Lorres Ann; *b* 1938; *m* 19—, *Robert E Johnson, of Launceston, Tasmania, and has:
1e *Antony; *b* 1964
2e *David; *b* 1970
1e *Elizabeth; *b* 1966
2c +James Herbert; *b* 1916; *m* 1936 *Charlotte Ethel Bastion
1c *Olive May; *b* 1915; *m* 1933 *Allan Klinberg, of Albury, NSW
5b Philip Ernest; *b* 1887; *m* 1913 Hilda Maria Ambrosina Copper (*d* 1966) and *d* 1960, leaving:
1c +Clem Ernest; *b* 1913
2c +Stanley George [Stanley Hill Esa, 27 Summerhill Ave, E Malvern, Melbourne 3145, Vict, Australia]; *b* 1935; *m* 1964 *Patricia Ann McLellan and has:
1d +Philip William Adrian; *b* 1966
2d +Paul Timothy; *b* 1968
3d +Michael John; *b* 1975
1d *Catherine Elizabeth; *b* 1979
1c *Phyllis May [Mrs George Robinson, 49 Hardy Ave, Wagga Wagga, NSW, Australia]; *b* 1917; *m* 1938 *George Lewis Robinson and has:
1d *Helen; *b* 1940; *m* 1960 *—
2d *Shirley; *b* 1942; *m* 1962 *—
3d *Dawn; *b* 1950
4d *Maree; *b* 1956
2c *Thelma Rose [Mrs Ronald Wheeler, 61 Gormley Avenue, Wagga Wagga, NSW, Australia]; *b* 19–; *m* *Ronald Charles Wheeler and has:
1d *Garry; *b* 19–
2d *Robert; *b* 19–
1d *Janet; *b* 19–
1b *Caroline Maud
2b *Florentia Maria
2a Rowley Sale HILL later SALE-HILL (1889) (Sir), KCB; Gen, Hon Col 1st Gurkha Rifles (Majaun Regt), served Indian Mutiny, Bhutan Expdn, Hazara Expdn, Malay Expdn, Afghan War, Akha Expdn; *b* 6 Nov 1839; *m* 30 March 1873 Caroline Sophia (*d* 6 Feb 1932), dau of Lt-Col Robert Henry Sale, and *d* 23 March 1916, leaving:
1b Alan Rowley; Maj Somerset LI Boer War 1900–01 and WW I (wounded); *b* 8 Dec 1877; *m* 1st 8 Aug 1914 Elizabeth Caroline (*d* 1 July 1924), widow of William John Wallace, and dau of Hon Albert Yelverton Bingham, DL (*see* CLANMORRIS, B); *m* 2nd 7 March 1925 Mary Eliza (*d* 1 June 1948), yst dau of William Holmes Sullivan, and *d* 17 Sept 1936
1b Lena Maud; *m* 25 Nov 1902 Lt-Col Robert Frederick Ewart, DSO, IA, son of Col C H Ewart, ISC, and *d* 9 July 1933, leaving issue
2b Effie Caroline; *m* 19 Sept 1899 Maj George A Meakin (*d* 1 July 1949), 15th Hus, est son of H G Meakin, of Poona, and *d* 29 Jan 1954
3b Ella Florentia; *m* 30 Jan 1907 Lt-Col Guy Lee, DSO, MC, The Buffs, E Kent Regt, yst son of Harry Wilmot Lee, of Charterhouse, EC, and of Monks Horton Park, Kent, and *d* 13 Sept 1908, leaving issue
3a George Henry; *b* 26 Aug 1842; *m* 11 May 1868 Ellen Sarah, dau of Thomas Daly, of Ealing, and had:
1b Marcus Henry Sale; *b* 13 Feb 1870; *m* 1903 Emma Frances, dau of Harry Kenton, of Lower Harbour, Port Chalmers NZ, and *d* 1946, having had:
1c Wilfred Henry; *b* 1906; *m* 1936 *Thelma Mattingly, of Anderson's Bay, Dunedin, NZ, and *d* 1972, leaving:
1d +Robert Maxwell; *b* 1938; *m* 1962 *Wendy Cross and has:
1e +Christopher; *b* 19–
1e *Robyn; *b* 1962
2e *Julie; *b* 1965
2d *Lesley Robin Gael; *b* 1949; *m* 1966 *Gavan McEntee and has:
1e *Gavan Chayne; *b* 1966
2e *Brett Owen; *b* 1968
3e *Stephen Robert; *b* 1969
1d *Dawn Adeline; *b* 1937; *m* 1963 *Raymond Wilkins and has:
1e *Lionel David; *b* 1964
1e *Deborah Margery; *b* 1967
2e *Dionne Beryl; *b* 1970
2c Henry George; *b* 1909; *m* 1940 *Eileen Webb, of Port Chalmers, Otago, NZ, and *d* 1988, leaving:
1d +Harold Alexander; *b* 1941; *m* 1st 19– (*divorce* 19–) Fay Ogarman; *m* 2nd 19– (*divorce* 19–) Cynthia John Letherland
2d +Francis John; *b* 1941; *m* 1963 *Margaret — and has:
1e +David John; *b* 1963; *m* 1986 *Joanne — and has:
1f *Cheryl Maree; *b* 1987
2e +Brett Christopher; *b* 1966
1e *Yvonne Clare; *b* 1970
3d +Owen Patrick; *b* 1943
4d +Mervyn George; *b* 1945; *m* 1967 *Janet Murgatroyd and has:
1e +Aaron Mervyn; *b* 1967
2e +Adrian Bevan; *b* 1974
1e *Leanne Marie; *b* 1968
2e *Deborah Anne; *b* 1970
5d +Michael David; *b* 19–; *m* 1974 *Robyn — and has:
1e +Allan Paul; *b* 1981
1e *Jocelyn; *b* 1979
1d *Sharon Joy; *b* 1947; *m* 1966 *David Dick and has:
1e *Steven Kidmond; *b* 1968
1e *Tracey Joy; *b* 1969
2d *Angela Fay; *b* 19–; *m* 1975 *Ian Page and has:
1e *Steven; *b* 1979
1e *Anita; *b* 1981
3d *Eileen Christine; *b* 19–; has:

1e *Tania Marie; *b* 1974
3c +Edward Albert; *b* 1911; *m* 1935 Jessie Margaret McWilliam, dau of Robert Wilson, of NZ, and has:
1d +Edward Wilson Sale; *b* 1936
2d +Robert George; *b* 1940
3d +Leonard James; *b* 1943
4d +Marwyn Albert; *b* 1955
1d *Margaret Elizabeth; *b* 1938
4c Leonard Graham; *b* 1911; *m* 1935 *Christina Agnes Allan Wilson [Mrs Leonard Hill, Section 3, Awakaponga, RD Whakatane, New Zealand], and was *ka* 1942, leaving:
1d +Graham Robert Marcus; *b* 1936; *m* 1958 *Shirley Fay Whan, of Sydney, NSW, and has issue:
1e +Michael Peter John; *b* Jan 1960
2e +Leonard Graham; *b* Dec 1960
3e +Warren Stephen; *b* 1962
4e +Stanley Norman; *b* 1963
1e *Deborah Joy; *b* 1964
2d +Allan Henry [Allan Hill Esq, 3 Windsor Rise, Whakatane, New Zealand]; *b* 1938; *m* 1959 *Raewyn Alice Smith, of Whakatane, NZ, and has:
1e +Douglas Allan; *b* 1960; *m* 1986 *Linda Duncum, of Rotorua, NZ
2e +Gordon France; *b* 1962; *m* 1990 *Deborah Hunter, of Rotorua, NZ, and has:
1f +Rory Nathan; *b* 1991
2f *Krystal Moira; *b* 1984
3e +Rowley Wilson; *b* 1964; *m* 1993 *Sharon Naylor, of Warwick, Qld
4e +Murray Richard; *b* 1967; *m* 1991 *Leah Longdon, of Rotorua
5c +Russell Sale; *b* 1913; *m* 1945 *Pearl Iris, dau of Lewis Septimus Civil, of Pukekohe, NZ, and has:
1d *Marie June; *b* 1946; *m* 1968 *David Ivor Jones, of Manawahe, Bay of Plenty, NZ, and has:
1e *Glenn David; *b* 1969
1e *Justine Joanne; *b* 1971
1d *Carolyn Leslie; *b* 1947; *m* 1982 *Gerry McGillicuddy, of Mongonui, Northland, NZ
6c Ernie Parker; *b* 1916; *m* 1946 *Jessie May Court [Mrs Ernie Hill, Deborah Bay, Port Chalmers, New Zealand], and *d* 1992, leaving:
1d +Malcolm Ross; *b* 1947; *m* 19– (*divorce* 19–) Clare McAlley and has:
1e *Sarah-Jane Frances; *b* 1978
2e *Rebecca Ailsa; *b* 1981
2d +Donald Graeme; *b* 1962
1d *Janice Audrey; *b* 1950; *m* 1st 1970 (*divorce* 19–) Lindsay Wilson and has:
1e *Jocelyn Anne; *b* 1971
2e *Deborah Kaye; *b* 1973
1d (cont.) Janice Wilson; *m* 2nd 1974 *Neville Billington and has:
1e +Philip John; *b* 1975
2e +Craig Neville; *b* 1978
2d *Nellie May; *b* 1952; *m* 1976 (*divorce* 19–) Stephen Rayson and has:
1e *Michael Alexander; *b* 1979
3d *Barbara Ann; *b* 1959; has issue:
1e *Kelly Marie; *b* 1978
1c Eva Frances
2c Rita
3c Muriel
4c *Thelma Alice [Mrs Walter McLay, 9 Islington St, Te Aroka, N Island, New Zealand]; *b* 1920; *m* 1940 Walter James McLay (*d* 1986), and has:
1d *Ernest James; *b* 1941; *m* 1961 *Sylvia May Rolf and has:
1e *Stephen James; *b* 1962; *m* 1984 *Linda Quigley and has:
1f *Christopher James; *b* 1988
2e *Kenneth Stuart; *b* 1963; *m* 1987 *Sarah Ash
3e *Peter Ernest; *b* 1967
1e *Donna Ann; *b* 1964
2d *Douglas Stuart; *b* 1942; *m* 1969 *Carol Jean Grice and has:
1e *Jason Stuart Marshall; *b* 1971
2e *Scott Douglas; *b* 1971
3e *Katrina Maree; *b* 1969
3d *Alastair David; *b* 1946; *m* 1980 *Bronwen Roger and has:
1e *Joanne Beth; *b* 1981
2e *Heather Ruth; *b* 1983
3e *Rebecca Lois; *b* 1986
4d *Trevor Sale; *b* 1947; *m* 1982 *Carol Cunningham
5d *Norman Walter; *b* 1951; *m* 1982 *Sandra Grubber and has:
1e *Bradley Walter; *b* 1984
2e *Jonathan David; *b* 1986
6d *Ian Murray; *b* 1956; *m* 1984 *Fiona Mary Lowery and has:
1e *James Murray; *b* 1987
1d *Sheryl Joy; *b* 1949; *m* 19– *Hugh Kay Stueistrup and has:
1e *Shawn Kay; *b* 1971
2e *Darrell Boyes; *b* 1974
1e *Kassandra Joy; *b* 1972
5c *Myra Edith [Mrs Bruce Bannerman, 10 Wigan St, Gore, Southland, New Zealand]; *b* 1922; *m* 1945 Bruce Bannerman (*d* 1991) and has:
1d *Kevin Bruce [Kevin Bannerman Esq, 50 Caulfield St, Ranfurly, New Zealand]; *b* 1947; *m* 1976 *Cheryl McLeod and has:
1e *Dwayne Marcus; *b* 1983
1e *Natalie Ann; *b* 1981
2d *Andrew Henry; *b* 1950; *m* 1973 (*divorce* 1994) Shirley Newlove and has:
1e *Brendon Peter; *b* 1974
2e *Shane Bruce; *b* 1976
1e *Jenny Marie; *b* 1979
3d *Neville William; *b* 1955
1d *Nola Mae [Mrs Norman Anderson, Ashley Downs, Clinton, S Otago, New Zealand]; *b* 1946; *m* 1967 *Norman Russell Anderson and has:
1e *Ernest Keith; *b* 1973
2e *James Bannerman; *b* 1976
1e *Diane Marie; *b* 1969
2e *Glenys Mae; *b* 1970
2d *Marion Frances; *b* 1949; *m* 1st 1967 Ian Ross Lamberth (*d* 1985); *m* 2nd 1985 *Gerald Delahunt and by her 1st husb has:
1e *Steven Ross; *b* 1968
2e *Warren George; *b* 1974
1e *Susan Margaret; *b* 1970; *m* 1993 *Geoffrey Townsend and has:
1f *Damian Jay KENNY; *b* 1988
1f *Kylie Renée KENNY; *b* 1987
2f *A dau; *b* 1994
3d *Loraine Jay; *b* 1953; *m* 1st 1972 (*divorce* 19–) Peter Donaldson; *m* 2nd 1992 *Phillip Wright and by her 1st husb has:
1e *Aaron Mark; *b* 1973
2e *Joanne Robyn; *b* 1973
3e *Philippa Marie Wright; *b* 1988
4d *Denise Myra; *b* 1966; *m* 1982 *Claude Gemell and has:
1e *Bruce; *b* 1982
2e *Shaun Jason; *b* 1989
1e *Sasha Rose; *b* 1984
2e *Regan Dallas; *b* 1987
3e *Hami Jade; *b* 1991
6c *Dorothy Loraine; *b* 1924; *m* 1956 (*divorce* 19–) James Barclay and has:
1d *Bruce Lindsay; *b* 1957; *m* 1977 *Pauline Joy Adams, of Palmerston, NZ, and has:
1e *Patrick Allan; *b* 1978
2e *Kevin Philip; *b* 1981
2d *Christopher Warren; *b* 1958
1d *Sandra Kaye; *b* 1961; *m* 1979 *Stewart James Wallis, of Camden, NSW, Australia, and has:
1e *Joleen Lisa Wallis; *b* 1979
2e *Logan James; *b* 1981
2b George Rowley Sale; *b* 9 April 1874; *m* Elizabeth Attfield (*d* 1941), and *d* 1936, having had issue
3b Arthur William Gordon; *b* 3 April 1876
4b Louis; *b* 1878; *m* Elizabeth Walker and had issue
5b Percy Graham; *b* 1883; *m* 1905 Mary Ellen Wilson and *d* 1953, leaving:
1c +George Arthur Graham; *b* 1905; *m* 1931 *Kathleen Geary and has:
1d +David Graham; *b* 1931
2d +Donald Percival; *b* 1937
3d +Russell George; *b* 1942
4d +Douglas John; *b* 1943
1d *Valerie May *b* 1946
2c +Percival Thomas; *b* 1913; *m* 1939 *Maude Monk
1c *Helen Caroline; *b* 1910; *m* 1927 William Robert Lewis (*d* 1981) and has:
1d *William Leonard [William Lewis Esq, Wallacetown, Southland, New Zealand]; *b* 1932; *m* 1956 *Jeanette McGregor and has:
1e *Bruce David; *b* 1958; *m* 1985 *Anne Marie Glendening and has:
1f *Scott William; *b* 1988
2e *Donald Percival; *b* 1959; *m* 1981 *Nicola Ann Dennison and has:
1f *Bradley Donald; *b* 1984
3e *Rodney William; *b* 1961; *m* 1987 *Heather Woods
1e *Susan Gaye; *b* 1960; *m* 1984 *George Paul Hastings
2c *Mary Catherine [Mrs Maxwell Murphy, 49 Peel St, Westport, New Zeland]; *b* 1928; *m* 1952 *Maxwell Maurice Murphy and has:
1d *Brian William; *b* 1955; *m* 1981 *Kathryn Margaret Peick, of Westport, NZ, and has:
1e *Thomas Brian; *b* 1988
1e *Jacinta Kathryn; *b* 1985
2e *Emma Grace; *b* 1992
2d *Anthony Maxwell; *b* 1958; *m* 1981 *Marcia Dianne Tipping and has:
1e *Samuel Maurice; *b* 1982
2e *Andrew William; *b* 1984
3e *James Anthony; *b* 1992
1e *Rebekah May; *b* 1988
3d *Patrick Thomas; *b* 1961; *m* 1988 *Cathy Ann Talbot and has:
1e *Cody Allan; *b* 1993

2e *Brandon Maxwell; *b* 1994
1e *Teagan Rae; *b* 1990
1d *Helen Margaret; *b* 1954; *m* 1973 *Anthony John Robertson and has:
1e *Blair Anthony; *b* 1979
2e *Glen Francis; *b* 1981
1e *Mia Catherine; *b* 1985
2d *Gloria Mary; *b* 1957; *m* 1983 *Bernard John Hutchinson and ha s had:
1e *Maxwell Connell; *b* 1997
1e *Hannah Louise; *b* 1992
2e Caitlin Rose; *b* and *d* 1995
3d *Kathleen Ann; *b* 1963; *m* 1986 *Andrew Robin Hobern and has:
1e *Michael; *b* 1990
2e *Sean Maxwell; *b* 1994
1e *Clare Alyce; *b* 1992
4d *Julie Maureen; *b* 1964
3c *Vera Joy, JP [Mrs John Walsh JP, Menzies Ferry No 3 RD, Wyndham, Southland, New Zealand]; *b* 1930; *m* 1954 *John J Walsh and has had:
1d Kevin Gerard; *b* and *d* 1958
1d *Angela Mary; *b* 1956; *m* 1979 *Russell Caldwell and has:
1e *Hayden James; *b* 1983
2e *Kieran John; *b* 1985
3e *Ryan Gerard; *b* 1987
1e *Nadia Lauren; *b* 1981
2e *Olivia Leah; *b* 1989
2d Jillian Caroline; *b* 1960; *d* 1986
3d *Maree Jane; *b* 1962; *m* 1983 *Maurice John Crawford and has:
1e *Matthew John; *b* 1984
2e *Braden Walsh; *b* 1991
1e *Krystal Jillian; *b* 1987
2e *Jorelyn Deanna; *b* 1992
4d *Leanne Ruth; *b* 1966; *m* 1987 *Ross McLeod and has had:
1e Daniel Ross; *b* and *d* 1984
2e *Jeremy Ross; *b* 1992
3e *Cameron John; *b* 1994
4e *Hadley Daniel; *b* 1996
5d *Denise Louise; *b* 1968; *m* 1990 *David William Dunlop and has:
1e *Heath William; *b* 1991
2e *Dane Joseph; *b* 1992
1e *Brenna Walsh; *b* 1995
4c *Lorna Ellen [Mrs Desmond Wright, 49 Tees St, Oamaru, New Zealand]; *b* 1939; *m* 1958 *John Desmond Wright, and has issue:
1d *Darrell John [Darrell Wright Esq, 106A Eden St, Oamaru, New Zealand]; *b* 1959; *m* 1982 *Carol Margaret Blair, and has issue:
1e *Christopher John; *b* 1988
1e *Michelle Leigh; *b* 1987
2d *Graham Norman; *b* 1960
3d *Paul Robert; *b* 1961
5c *Dawn Margaret [Mrs Stuart Gray, 61 Forth St, Mataura, Southland, New Zealand]; *b* 1942; *m* 1961 *Stuart Gray, and has issue:
1d *David Andrew; *b* 1962; *m* 1st Oct 1990 (*divorce* 1994) Sonya Jane Fraser; *m* 2nd 1994 (*divorce* 1997) Karen Ann Marie P— and by his 1st w has:
1e *Graham William; *b* 12 Feb 1991
1d *Julie Margaret Irene [Mrs Nigel Blackler, 166 Kana St, Matawa, New Zealand]; *b* 1964; *m* 1986 *Nigel John Blackler and has:
1e *Holly Margaret; *b* 1988
2e *Cristelle Irene; *b* 1990
3e *Paige Marie; *b* 1994
6c *Sonia Carol [Mrs Alexander Kelly, 20 Gretna St, Invercargill, Southland, New Zealand]; *b* 1947; *m* 1965 *Alexander George Kelly and has:
1d *Allan Peter; *b* 1966; *m* May 1992 *Donna Margaret Mclellan and has:
1e *Joshua William; *b* 13 April 1996
1e *Lauren Margaret; *b* 22 June 1994
1d *Katrina May; *b* 1969; *m* Nov 1990 *Logan Maxwell and has:
1e *Benjamin George; *b* 2 Feb 1996
1e *Kate Hannah; *b* 21 March 1994
1b Carline
2b Florentia
3b Ellen
4b Charlotte; *m* 1st Edward Crawley; *m* 2nd William Bennett
5b Margaret Mary (Pear); *m* George Victor Percy (*d* 1955) and had issue
4a Robert Sale; *b* 10 Oct 1850; *m* 1st 1886 Sarah Randolph (*d* 1891), dau of Frederick W Foote, of New York, and had:
1b Robert Sale; WW I (wounded); *b* 19 Sept 1888; *m* 1920 Ruth Gertrude, yst dau of J W Edy, of Chiswick, and *dsp* 18 Sept 1953
4a (cont.) Robert Hill *m* 2nd 1893 Helen Troup (*d* 7 Oct 1933), dau of G L Harrison, of Baltimore, USA, and *d* 5 April 1922
1a Florentia; *d* young
(1) Mary; *m* 1st 6 Oct 1829 Rev John Potts (*d* 1835), 2nd s of D Potts, of Roscommon, and had issue; *m* 2nd March 1884 Joseph Trumperant Potts, 2nd s of William J Potts, of Correen Castle, Co Roscommon, and *d* 13 June 1879

HILL-NORTON

Arms: On a bend gules, between in chief a terrestrial sphere proper and in base three cannon balls sable within an annulet azure, four anchors or. **Crest:** Out of a naval crown or on a mount vert a springbok trippant proper. **Supporters:** On either side a hippocampus holding in the tail an anchor proper. **Motto:** Try harder. **Creation:** B. (LP, UK) 1978.

THE BARON HILL-NORTON, of South Nutfield, Co Surrey (Sir Peter John Hill-Norton, GCB (1970, KCB 1967, CB 1964) [Admiral of the Fleet The Rt Hon The Lord Hill-Norton GCB, Cass Cottage, Hyde, Hants SP6 2QH]; *b* 8 Feb 1915; *educ* RNCs Dartmouth and Greenwich; RN: joined 1936, WW II Arctic and NW Approaches, Admlty Naval Staff, Cdr 1948, Capt 1952, Naval Attaché 1963–55, cmded HMS *Decoy* 1956–57, HMS *Ark Royal* 1959–61, Assist Ch Naval Staff 1962–64, Flag Offr 2ic Far East Fleet 1964–66, Dep CDS 1966, 2nd Sea Ld 1967, V-Ch Naval Staff 1967–68, Adml of the Fleet and C-in-C Far East Forces 1969–70, First Sea Ld 1970–71, CDS 1971–74; Chm NATO Mil Ctee 1974–77; Pres: Sea Cadets Assoc 1977–84, Def Mfrs' Assoc 1980–84, Br Maritime League 1982–85, V-Pres RUSI 1977–90; Liveryman Shipwrights' Co 1973 (memb Court 1979), Freeman City London 1973; author: *No Soft Options* (1978), *Sea Power* (1982); *m* 1936 *Margaret Eileen, dau of Carl Adolph Linstow, and has:

1 *Nicholas John (Sir), KCB (1991); *b* 1939; *educ* Marlborough, RNC Dartmouth and US Naval War Coll Newport RI; RN 1957–95, V-Adml, Dep CDS 1992–95; defence advsr GEC-Marconi; *m* 1966 *(Ann) Jennifer, dau of V-Adml Dennis Mason, CB, CVO, and has:
(1) *Simon Nicholas Sebastian; *b* 1967; *m* 1997 *Tamara Franks
(2) *Peter Tom; *b* 1975
(1) *Claudia Genevieve Jane; *b* 1969; *m* 1994 *Thomas M Bradby and has:
1a *Jack; *b* 1996
1a *Louisa; *b* 8 Oct 1997
1 *Carla Ann; *b* 1943; *m* 1st 1966 Christopher Thomas Jowett; *m* 2nd 1974 *Graeme McLintock, of Old Beith House, Milland, Hants, and has had by her 1st husb:
(1) *Benjamin; *b* 1967; *m* 1995 (*divorce* 1996) Ingrid — and has:
1a *Kai; *b* 1996
(2) James; *b* 1969; *d* 1991

Lineage: Capt MARTIN JOHN NORTON; *m* M— B— and had issue:
PETER JOHN, *cr* a **Baron**

HILL-WOOD

Arms: Quarterly, 1st and 4th, sa. on a bend between two roses arg., seeded or, three fleurs-de-lys gu. (for WOOD); 2nd and 3rd, per chevron or and vert, in chief two acorns leaved and slipped, and in base a cross-bow bent, all counterchanged (for HILL). **Crests:** 1 Issuant from a crown vallary or an oak tree ppr., fructed gold (for WOOD), 2 Upon a mount vert a bugle-horn, stringed gu. (for HILL). **Motto:** *Omne bonum Dei donum* ('Every good thing is the gift of God'). **Creation:** Bt. (UK) 25 Jan 1921.

SIR DAVID BASIL HILL-WOOD, 3RD BT, of Moorfield, Glossop, Co Derby [Sir David Hill-Wood Bt, Dacre Farm, Farley Hill, Berks RG7 1XJ; 58 Cathcart Rd, London SW10]; *b* 12 Nov 1926; *s* f 1954; *educ* Eton; Gren Gds 1945–48; with Morgan Grenfell & Co Ltd 1948–55, Myers & Co (stockbrokers) 1955–71 (sr ptnr 1971–74), dir Capel-Cure Myers Ltd 1974–77, dir Guinness Mahon & Co 1977–, Aust Rep FA Cncl 1978–, High Sheriff Berks 1982; *m* 11 July 1970 *Jennifer Anne McKenzie Stratmann (took surname by deed poll 1960), 2nd dau of Peter McKenzie Strang, of Adelaide, Australia, and has issue:

1 +SAMUEL THOMAS; *b* 24 Aug 1971
2 +Edward Charles; *b* 22 April 1974
1 *Emma Victoria; *b* 21 Aug 1972

Lineage: SAMUEL WOOD, JP, of Moorfield, Glossop, Derbys (*see* 1970 edn WOOD, Bt, of Hengrave); *b* 24 Jan 1819; *m* 21 April 1869 Anne Kershaw (*d* 8 March 1914), dau of William Sidebottom, of Etherow Ho, Cheshire, and *d* 8 April 1888, leaving:

Sir SAMUEL HILL WOOD later HILL-WOOD (roy licence 30 March 1912), **1st Bt**, so *cr* 25 Jan 1921, JP, DL Derbys, Herefs; *b* 21 March 1872; *educ* Eton; Maj TAR, MP (C) High Peak 1910–29; *m* 12 April 1899 Hon Rachel Anne Selina Decima Bateman-Hanbury (*d* 10 Dec 1971), 6th dau of 2nd Baron Bateman (*see* 1931 edn), and had:

1 BASIL SAMUEL HILL (Sir), **2nd Bt**
2 Wilfred William Hill (Sir), KCVO (1976), CBE (1946); *b* 8 Sept 1901; *educ* Eton and Trin Coll Cambridge; md Morgan Grenfell, memb Advsy Cncl Morgan Grenfell, dir Anglo-American Securities Corp, Bucklersbury Securities Corp, N Atlantic Securities Corp, Torola Ltd, Commercial Union Assur, Harris and Ptnrs Ltd, Toronto Morgan Nominees, R A Stephen and Co, Br Sugar Corp, Warfield Investment Tst and Nucleonic Investments 1965; *m* 30 April 1947 Diana Marian, dau of Maj Hugh Wyld, of Beverstone Old Rectory, Tetbury, Glos, and widow of W/Cdr Harry Manners Mellor, MVO, RAF
3 Denis John Charles Hill, MC (1943); *b* 25 June 1906; *educ* Eton and Ch Ch Oxford (BA 1930, MA); Maj 4th Co London Yeo (TA) WW II 1939–43 (despatches, wounded); chm Arsenal FC; *m* 1 Dec 1932 Mary Cecilia, JP (Hants 1951) (*d* June 1997), est dau of Capt Everard Reginald Martin-Smith, JP, of Codicote Lodge, Herts, and *d* 4 May 1982, leaving issue:
(1) +Peter Denis [Peter Hill-Wood Esq, 13 Smith's Terrace, London SW3]; *b* 25 Feb 1936; *educ* Eton; late 2nd Lt Coldstream Gds; dir Hambros Bank, Cavenham Ltd and Hellenic & Gen Tst 1977–; *m* 1971 *Sarah H (Sally), dau of Albert O'Beirne Andrews, of Wilton, Conn., and has issue:
1a +Julian Peter; *b* 16 Jan 1974
2a +Charles Denis; *b* 21 April 1976
1a *Sarah Frances; *b* 5 July 1972
(1) *Angela Mary, JP (Essex 1967) [Mrs Mark Smith JP, Ballacurn, Ballaugh, IoM]; *b* 4 Sept 1933; *m* 12 May 1956 *Mark Eric Smith, FRCS, yst s of Capt Evan Cadogan Eric Smith, MC, of Ashfield, Sussex, and has issue:
1a *Matthew Eric; *b* 23 Nov 1960; *m* 1989 (*divorce* 1992) Hon Melanie Francis Broughton, yr dau of 3rd Baron Fairhaven (*qv*), and has:
1b *Shamus Oliver Eric; *b* 1990
2a *Luke Eric; *b* 30 March 1968
1a *Amanda Mary; *b* 26 Feb 1957; *m* 1984 *Matthew Frewer, of Los Angeles
2a *Lucinda Rachael; *b* 8 July 1958
(2) *Rachael Vivien; *b* 31 July 1940; *m* 1972 Anthony Wood (*d* 1989), of Hartley Wintney, Hants, and has issue:
1a *Cheska Mary; *b* 16 April 1974
2a *Selina Rachel; *b* 1976
4 Charles Kerrison Hill; *b* 5 June 1907; *educ* Eton and Ch Ch Oxford (BA 1930, MA); Lt-Col Coldstream Gds WW II; *m* 8 July 1936 Cecilia Katharine (*d* 16 June 1988), 3rd dau of Capt Everard Reginald Martin Smith, JP, of Codicote Lodge, Hitchin, Herts, and *d* 21 Sept 1988, leaving issue:
(1) +Michael Kerrison; *b* 3 Sept 1946; *educ* Milton Abbey; *m* 1st 30 May 1970 (*divorce* 1991) Patricia Guy, of Stainland, Yorks; *m* 2nd 1991 *Patricia Ann Caldon, of Biggleswade, Beds, and by his 1st w has issue:
1a +Steven Guy; *b* 1977
1a *Susan Michelle; *b* 1974
(2) +Ian Charles [Ian Hill-Wood Esq, The Bury, Barton-Le-Clay, Beds]; *b* Oct 1947; *educ* Milton Abbey
(1) Jane Cecilia; *b* 17 Oct 1937; *m* 2 Oct 1976, as his 2nd w, Capt Caledon Alexander, 7th QOH, of Crudwell Ct, Malmesbury, Wilts, er s of Capt Francis John Alexander, RN
(2) *Georginia Sarah [Mrs Richard Holt, 3 Caroline Place Mews, London W2]; *b* 23 June 1940; *m* 29 Sept 1962 *Richard Basil Holt, only s of James Alwyn Holt, of Rockbourne, Hants, and has issue:
1a *Nicholas James; *b* 17 April 1965
1a *Camilia Katherine; *b* 30 Jan 1967
2a *Susannah Rachael; *b* 26 Feb 1969
3a *Caroline Lucinda; *b* 1972
(3) *Diana Susan [Mrs Ian Phillips, 18 Campion Rd, London SW15]; *b* 2 July 1943; *m* 1st 4 June 1966 (*divorce* 1971) Lestock Harold George Livingstone-Learmonth, er s of Lestock Brian Livingstone-Learmonth, and has issue:
1a *Lestock Alexander Iain; *b* 25 Sept 1969
(3) (cont.) Mrs Diana Susan Livingstone-Learmonth *m* 2nd 6 June 1975 *Ian P M Phillips, er s of R M Phillips, and by him has:
2a *Alastair Patrick Markham; *b* 1980
3a *Simon Richard Markham; *b* 1982

Sir SAMUEL *d* 4 Jan 1949; his est son:

Sir Basil Samuel Hill Hill-Wood, 2nd Bt; *b* 5 Feb 1900; *educ* Eton and Trin Coll Cambridge; Capt Gren Gds; *m* 18 Feb 1925 Hon Joan Louisa Brand (*d* 20 April 1996), est dau of 3rd Viscount Hampden (*qv*), and *d* 3 July 1954, having had issue:

1 Sir DAVID BASIL HILL-WOOD, **3rd and present Bt**
1 *Anne Katherine [Miss Anne Hill-Wood, Knipton Lodge, Grantham, Lincs]; *b* 2 Sept 1928

HILTON OF EGGARDON

Arms: Azure between two bees in fess and volant upwards and outwards proper, growing from a grassy mount in base and protected by palings about its trunk, an oak tree, also proper and fructed gold. **Supporters:** Dexter, on a grassy mount growing therefrom two dog roses proper, a crested newt statant erect vert, holding by its inner forefoot a tipstaff proper; sinister, on a grassy mount, growing therefrom two dog roses proper, a griffin statant erect argent, armed, winged and tail tufted or, grasping in its inner foreclaw a serpent entwined about the foreleg, also proper. **Motto:** *Poursuivre raison avec resolution* ('To follow right with resolution'). **Creation:** B. (LP, UK) 1991.

THE BARONESS HILTON OF EGGARDON, of Eggardon, Co Dorset (Jennifer Hilton, QPM (1989)) [The Rt Hon The Baroness Hilton of Eggardon QPM, House of Lords, London SW1A 0PW]; *b* 1936; *educ* Bedales, Manchester U (BA Psych 1970, MA 1971) and London U (Dip Criminology 1972, Dip Hist Art 1982); offr Metropolitan Police 1956–90 (Cdr 1984–90); Oppn spokesperson environment 1991–97, Memb: European Community Sub-Ctee Environment 1991– (Chm 1995–), Sci and Tech Ctee 1993–95 (Memb Forensic Sci Ctee 1993–95); author: *The Gentle Arm of The Law* (1967, 2nd edn 1973), *Individual Development and Social Experience* (with Sonya Hunt, 1975, 2nd edn 1981)

Lineage: JOHN ROBERT HILTON, CMG; *m* — and had issue:

JENNIFER, *cr* a **Baroness**

HINDLIP

Arms: Sable three pheons in chevron or between as many doves rising argent, each holding in the beak an ear of wheat of the second. **Crest:** Upon a pheon a dove close, in the beak an ear of wheat, all or. **Supporters:** On either side a fox-hound gorged with a pair of couples all proper. **Motto:** *Festina lente* ('Hasten carefully'). **Creation:** Bt. (UK) 7 May 1880, B. (UK) 16 Feb 1886.

THE 6TH BARON HINDLIP OF HINDLIP, Co Worcester, and of Alsop-en-le-Dale, Co Derby, and a **Baronet** (Sir Charles Henry Allsopp, Bt) [The Rt Hon The Lord Hindlip, The Cedar House, Inkpen, Berks RG15 ODT; 18 Chester Sq, London SW1W 9HS]; *b* 5 Aug 1940; *s* f 1993; *educ* Eton; Coldstream Gds 1959–62, gp chm Christie's 1996– (dir 1970–, dep chm 1985, chm 1986), dir Wilts Faber & Dumes 1977– and Christie's Internat 1986– (Chm 1996–); *m* 18 April 1968 *Fiona Victoria Jean, only child of Hon William Johnston McGowan (*see* McGOWAN, B), and has:

1 +HENRY WILLIAM; *b* 8 June 1973
1 *Kirstie Mary; *b* 31 Aug 1971
2 *Sophia Atherley; *b* 1980
3 *Natasha Fiona; *b* 1986

Lineage: SAMUEL ALSOP, of Derby; *m* 1681 Mary (living 20 Oct 1706), widow of Edward Wast, of Derby, and *d* between 14 Nov 1728 and 25 Feb 1729, having had, with other issue:

SAMUEL ALLSOPP, of Worcs; *bapt* 10 June 1688; *m* Bridget (*d* 1747), est dau of Thomas Bearcroft, of Upton-on-Severn, Worcs, and *dvp* 3 March 1716, having had, with other issue:

THOMAS ALLSOPP, of Derby and Birlingham Hall; *bapt* 2 Feb 1706; *m* 8 Dec 1733 Anne (*d* May 1786), dau of William Challinor, of Faulde, Staffs, and *d* Dec 1783, leaving a yst s:

JAMES ALLSOPP, of Derby and Birlingham Hall; *bapt* 23 July 1751; *m* 30 June 1778 Anne (*d* 2 Sept 1845), only dau of Benjamin Wilson, of Burton-on-Trent, and *d* 24 April 1800, leaving, with two other sons and three daus:

SAMUEL ALLSOPP, of Burton-on-Trent; *b* 12 Aug 1780; *m* 6 Sept 1804 Frances (*d* 12 June 1862), only dau of Charles Fowler, of Shrewsbury, and *d* 26 Feb 1838, having had, with other issue, including two er sons (Charles James, of Burton-on-Trent, *b* 5 June 1805, *m* 29 Dec 1836 Sarah Emma (*m* 2nd 5 May 1852 Rev William Belcher, of Wensley, Derbys, and *d* 1879), dau of John Drewry, and *dsp* 20 Oct 1844; William, *b* 7 June 1809, *d* 21 Oct 1815):

Sir Henry Allsopp, 1st Bt, and **1st Baron Hindlip of Hindlip**, Co Worcester, and of Alsop-en-le-Dale, Co Derby (both UK), *cr* 7 May 1880 and 16 Feb 1886 respectively, JP (Staffs, Worcs and Derbys), DL (Staffs and Worcs); *b* 19 Feb 1811; MP (C) E Worcs; *m* 21 Aug 1839 Elizabeth (*d* 19 Aug 1906), 2nd dau of William Tongue, of Comberford Hall, Staffs, and *d* 3 April 1887, having had issue:

1 SAMUEL CHARLES, **2nd Baron**

2 William Henry; *b* 9 Nov 1843; *educ* Oxford (MA); Hon Lt-Col 3rd Bn Worcs Regt; *d* unm 20 Feb 1909

3 George Higginson, JP (Staffs, Derbys and Worcs 1885–1906), DL (Staffs and Derbys); *b* 28 March 1846; *educ* Trin Coll Cambridge (MA); *m* 16 July 1895 Lady Mildred Georgiana Ashley (*d* 4 March 1958), 3rd dau of 8th Earl of Shaftesbury (*qv*), and *d* 9 Sept 1907, having had issue:

(1) Anthony Victor George; *b* 7 Sept 1899; Midshipman RN; *ka* 22 Sept 1914, lost in HMS *Aboukir*

(1) Winifred Violet; *b* 6 May 1896; *m* 1st 20 Sept 1916 (*divorce* 1928) Reginald Arthur Walter and had issue; *m* 2nd 1930 Edward Hazlehurst-Cherry, CBE, and *d* 26 July 1965, leaving further issue

4 Ranulph; *b* 27 July 1848; Maj RA, Lt-Col HAC, Veteran Co; *m* 5 Jan 1898 Margaret (*d* 30 July 1941), 2nd dau of William Whitbread, and *d* 25 Dec 1911, leaving:

(1) Samuel Ranulph, CBE (1954, MBE 1944), DL (Essex 1946); *b* 7 March 1899; *educ* Eton and King's Coll Cambridge (MA); High Sheriff 1955, Maj 12th Bn Essex HG WW II, OC 12th Essex Cadet Bn (Army Cadet Force) 1945–48, chm Hops Marketing Bd; *m* 7 June 1923 Hon Norah Hyacinthe Littleton (*d* 23 Aug 1997), 2nd dau of 4th Baron Hatherton (*qv*), and *d* 10 March 1975, leaving issue:

1a +Michael Edward Ranulph [Michael Allsopp Esq, Little Coxwell Grove, Faringdon, Oxon SN7 7LW]; *b* 9 Oct 1930; *educ* Eton; Capt Roy Wilts Yeo, chm London Discount Market Assoc 1974–76; *m* 16 July 1953 *Patricia Ann, only dau of Geoffrey Hugh Berners, JP, of Little Coxwell Grove, and had:

1b A son; *b* and *d* 1 Oct 1966

1b *Frances Jane Berners [Mrs David Woodd, The Homestead, Little Coxwell, Faringdon, Oxon]; *b* 26 May 1955; *m* 26 April 1975 (*divorce* 1980) Dermot Michael Claud Chichester (*see* DONEGALL, M); *m* 2nd 1984 *Maj David John Basil Woodd, 14th/20th King's Hus, and by him has:

1c *Matilda Elizabeth; *b* 1990

2c *Tabitha Ann; *b* 1991

2b *Carolyn Ann Berners; *b* 30 Sept 1957

3b *Davina Hayacinthe Berners; *b* 5 April 1960; *m* 1987, as his 2nd w, *Sir Nicholas Folliott Douglas Powell, 4th Bt (*qv*), and has issue

4b *Jessica Elizabeth Berners [The Hon Mrs Edward Leigh-Pemberton, Longcot House, Longcot, Faringdon, Oxon]; *b* 5 April 1960; *m* 1984 *Hon Edward Douglas Leigh-Pemberton, PC, 3rd s of Baron Kingsdown (*qv*), and has issue

2a +David Samuel [David Allsopp Esq, 37 Cadogan Place, London SW1]; *b* 14 March 1933; *educ* Eton; *m* 1st 22 Oct 1960 (*divorce* 1968) Tan Doris May, er dau of Frederick J Arnold; *m* 2nd 8 Jan 1972 *Sally, dau of V H Thirkell, of High Tilt Farm, Cranbrook, Kent, and by her has:

1b +James Samuel; *b* 17 July 1972

1b *Melanie Angela; *b* 20 Dec 1977

1a *Juliet Modwena; *b* 30 Dec 1924; *m* 27 Sept 1952 *Samuel Arthur Scott, 2nd s of Col Sir Jervoise Bolitho Scott, 1st Bt, of Rotherfield (*qv*), and has issue

2a *Charmain Hyacinthe Allsopp [Mrs David FitzHerbert, Sycamore House, Tissington, Derbys]; *b* 13 April 1926; *m* 4 Oct 1962 Maj Rev David Henry FitzHerbert, MC (*see* FitzHERBERT, Bt), and has issue

(2) John Ranulph; *b* 12 Jan 1908; *educ* Eton and Magdalene Coll Cambridge; Hon Attaché Brussels and Madrid, Capt OTC and Gren Gds WW II; *m* 10 April 1934 Audrey Carteret Priaulx (*m* 2nd 29 July 1944 Oliver van Oss, of Headmaster's House, Charterhouse, Godalming, Surrey, and *d* 19 April 1960), dau of Maj E G Fellows, and was *ka* N Africa 17 March 1943, leaving:

1a Mark Ranulph; *b* 14 Sept 1938; *educ* Eton; *m* 3 Sept 1960 *Tania Anna [Mrs Mark Allsopp, Portishead House, Mistley, Manningtree, Essex], only child of Capt John Eustace-Smith, of Northumberland, and *d* 15 Sept 1996, leaving:

1b +Jonathan Ranulph; *b* 9 Feb 1962; *educ* Harrow

2b +Richard Mark; *b* 7 Nov 1963; *educ* Eton and RMA Sandhurst; *m* 1990 *Alexandra Dominica, dau of Maj Johnnie Grosch, of Stoke-by-Nayland, Suffolk, and has issue:

1c +Milo Johnnie Mark; *b* 27 Sept 1996

1c *Matilda May Cornelia; *b* 11 Oct 1993

3b +Charles Samuel; *b* 27 June 1970; *educ* Eton and RMA Sandhurst

1b *Arabella Sarah Georgiana; *b* 29 July 1972; *educ* North Forland Lodge

2a +Peter William [Peter Allsopp Esq, Mill Barn, Mill Lane, Bramley, Surrey]; *b* 2 May 1940; *educ* Eton; *m* 13 Oct 1962 *Pepita, er dau of Lt-Cdr Peter E Mason, DSC, of Redford, Sussex, and has issue:

1b *Amanda Caroline; *b* 21 Jan 1964; *m* 1988 *John Howard Perry

2b *Sophie Victoria; *b* 26 May 1967

3b *Katherine Pepita; *b* 18 May 1970; *m* 1993 *Timothy Scott Ireland, 2nd s of Donald Ireland, of N Rocks, NSW

(1) Sybil Maud Elizabeth; *b* 28 Jan 1901; Sr Cdr ATS; *m* 17 Jan 1924 Frederick Ronald Oliver, Gren Gds, and had issue

5 Herbert Tongue, of Walton Bury, Staffs, JP; *b* 5 Dec 1855; Capt 10th Roy Hus; *m* 11 Aug 1891 Edith Mary (*d* 4 Sept 1935), 4th dau of Haughton Charles Okeover (*see* WALKER-OKEOVER, Bt), and *d* 31 Jan 1920, leaving issue:

(1) Cynthia Bridget; *b* 18 Sept 1895; *d* unm 14 May 1974

6 Frederick Ernest; *b* 21 Sept 1857; T/Maj, Capt RA; *d* unm 20 Dec 1928

7 Alfred Percy, JP (Worcs), DL (Staffs); *b* 26 Aug 1861; Mayor Worcester 1892, 1894 and 1909, T/Capt and GSO(3) 1915, MP Taunton 1887–95; *m* 23 July 1890 Lillian Maud (*d* 29 Oct 1962 aged 91), dau of Rev John Stanley Chesshire, Rector Hindlip, and *d* 22 Feb 1929, leaving issue:

(1) Dorothy; *b* 25 April 1891; *m* 9 Nov 1915 Brig Charles Richard Britten, MC, Gren Gds, 2nd s of R-Adml Richard Frederick Britten (*see* COLVILLE OF CULROSS, V), and had issue

8 Henry; *b* 23 Feb 1864; *d* 11 May 1865

1 Frances Elizabeth; *m* 23 Aug 1877 Rev Melville Russell Moore (*d* 31 May 1923), Vicar Preston, Glos, s of Rev Charles Moore, of Garlewick House, Cornwall, and *d* 13 Dec 1932

2 Elizabeth Sydney; *m* 7 July 1874 Thomas Edes Walker (*d* 13 Jan 1899), of Studley Castle, Worcs, MP E Worcs 1874–80, and *d* 10 Dec 1928, leaving issue

3 Ada Katherine; *m* 10 Feb 1881 Edward Waldron Haywood, JP, DL (*d* 28 Feb 1908), of Sillins, Redditch, and *dsp* 2 Jan 1903

The 1st BARON's est s,

SAMUEL CHARLES ALLSOPP, **2nd Baron Hindlip of Hindlip**, JP (Derbys, Worcs and Staffs), DL (Staffs); *b* 24 March 1842; *educ* Trin Coll Cambridge (MA); MP (C) E Staffs 1873–1900 and Taunton 1882–87; *m* 28 April 1868 Georgina Millicent (*d* 15 Jan 1939), est dau of Charles Rowland Palmer-Morewood (*see* BYRON, B), and *d* 12 July 1897, having had, with an er s (Henry, *b* 27 March, *d* 7 Nov 1876):

CHARLES ALLSOPP, **3rd Baron Hindlip of Hindlip**, OBE (1919), JP (Worcs and Derbys), DL (Worcs); *b* 22 Sept 1877; *educ* Cambridge (BA), FRGS, FZS, CC; Capt 5th Bn Worcs Regt, Lt 8th Hus, Boer War (medal with three clasps), GSO WW I (despatches twice, Legn Hon), ADC to Govr Victoria, Jr U Whip Ho Lds 1907–14;

m 19 April 1904 Agatha Lilian (*d* 11 Dec 1962), 2nd dau of John Charles Thynne (*see* BATH, M), and *d* 2 Dec 1931, having had:

1 CHARLES SAMUEL VICTOR ALLSOPP, **4th Baron Hindlip of Hindlip**; *b* 5 Nov 1906; *educ* Eton; Maj RASC, Lt RA (TA), WW II (despatches); *m* 1st 23 Feb 1932 (*divorce* 1934) Bridget, dau of Harold Nickols; *m* 2nd 16 Feb 1939 Hansina Elfrida Cecilia (Tulla) (*d* 1988), dau of Frederick William Harris, and *d* 30 March 1966, having had:

(1) *Penelope Jane [The Hon Mrs Velissaropoulos, Taxilis 75, Athens 15771, Greece]; *b* 2 April 1940; *m* 1 July 1965 *Theodore Demetrios Velissaropoulos, est s of Demetrios Velissaropoulos, of Athens

(2) *Elizabeth Tulla [The Hon Elizabeth Allsopp, 40 Bloomfield Terrace, London SW1W 8PQ]; *b* 20 June 1942

2 HENRY RICHARD, **5th Baron**

1 *Diana Joan [The Hon Lady Hardy, Gullivers Lodge, Guilsborough, Northants NN6 8RB]; *b* 19 Dec 1908; *m* 2 June 1930 *Sir Rupert John Hardy, 4th Bt (*qv*), and has issue

2 *Nancy Marion; *b* 15 Oct 1910; *m* 27 July 1936 *Peter Geoffrey Brooke, s of Maj-Gen Geoffrey Francis Hereman Brooke, CB, DSO, MC, and has issue:

(1) *Michael Peter; *b* 1937; Maj 16th/15th Lancers; *m* 1970 *Susan Rhona Martin, yr dau of A W Peacop, of Blue Hills, Finchampstead, Berks

The 4th BARON's yr bro,

HENRY RICHARD ALLSOPP, **5th Baron Hindlip of Hindlip**, JP (Wilts 1957), DL (1956); *b* 1 July 1912; *educ* Eton and RMC Sandhurst; Maj (ret 1948) Coldstream Gds WW II, US Bronze Star; *m* 12 April 1939 *Cecily Valentine Jane [The Rt Hon Cecily Lady Hindlip, Tytherton House, E Tytherton, Chippenham, Wilts], only dau of Lt-Col Malcolm Borwick, DSO (*see* BORWICK, B), and *d* 1993, leaving:

1 CHARLES HENRY ALLSOPP, **6th and present Baron Hindlip of Hindlip**

1 +John Peter [The Hon John Allsopp, Vern Leaze, Colne, Wilts]; *b* 16 Nov 1942; *educ* Eton; *m* 1976 *Daryl, yst dau of Leonard Shawzin, of CP, S Africa, and has issue:

(1) +James Leonard; *b* 26 Jan 1978

(1) *Kathryn Sarah; *b* 1981

(2) *Camilla Rose; *b* 1990

1 *Sarah Cecily [The Hon Mrs Myddelton, 139 Holland Park Ave, London W11]; *b* 13 March 1944; *m* 27 July 1967 *Hugh Robert Myddelton (*see* LANSDOWNE, M) and has issue

(1) Joyce Evangeline; *b* 28 May 1899; *d* 11 Jan 1900

(2) Pamela Mary; *b* 5 Oct 1901; *m* 14 Dec 1927 Arthur Frederick Vavasour McConnell, JP (*d* 17 Sept 1961), est s of Frederick Vavasour McConnell, of Camfield Place, Hatfield, Herts, and has issue

(3) Evangeline Gratiana; *b* 11 Nov 1904; *m* 15 Nov 1927 Philip William John Fryer, MBE, MA, of Browick Hall, Wymondham, Norfolk, and has issue

(4) Rosemary Sybil; *b* 29 July 1909; *m* 5 Jan 1937 Col George William Browning, OBE, Welsh Gds (*d* 1981), est s of Rev Berthold Alexander Browning, Vicar Pakenham, Suffolk, and *d* 10 May 1995, leaving:

1a *John Montague George [John Browning Esq, Weatherhill Farm, Icklingham, Bury St Edmunds, Suffolk]; *b* 11 Aug 1944; *m* 1970 *Mary-Grace Feachem and has issue:

1b *Christopher George John; *b* 1972

2b *Timothy Robert; *b* 1974

1a *Mary Joan; *b* 12 Nov 1938; BEM (1992); *m* 8 Sept 1962 *Rev Andrew Alexander Macintosh, BD, Dean St John's Coll Cambridge, s of Rev Felix Macintosh, of Black Notley, Essex, and has issue:

HIVES

Arms: Or on a chevron sable three beehives of the field. **Crest:** In front of a sun in splendour or an eagle rising proper. **Supporters:** Dexter, the figure of a mechanic proper, overalls azure, holding in the exterior hand a micrometer; sinister, the figure of a draughtsman proper, coat argent, holding under the exterior arm a set-square and a T-square, also proper. **Motto:** *Sic vos non vobis mellificatis apes* ('You do not make honey for yourselves thus').
Creation: B. (UK) 7 July 1950.

THE 3RD BARON HIVES, of Duffield, Co Derby [Matthew Peter Hives, House of Lords, London SW1 0AP]; *b* 25 May 1971; *s* unc 1997

Lineage: JOHN WILLIAM HIVES; had:

ERNEST WALTER, **1st Baron Hives** (UK), of Duffield, Co Derby, so *cr* 7 July 1950, CH (1943), MBE (1920); *b* 21 April 1886; *educ* Redlands Sch Reading; chm and md Rolls-Royce, Rotal Ltd and Park Ward, chm Regnl Ctee for Resettlement Offenders, Hon DSc Nottingham, Hon LLD Cantab, CStJ; *m* Feb 1913 Gertrude Ethel (*d* 20 Sept 1961), 2nd dau of John A Warwick, of Derby, and *d* 24 April 1965, leaving:

1 JOHN WARWICK HIVES, **2nd Baron Hives**, CBE (1989), JP (Derbys 1967); *b* 26 Nov 1913; *educ* Derby Sch; *m* 1st 1937 Olwyn Protheroe Llewellin (*d* 16 June 1972); *m* 2nd 1972 *Gladys Mary [The Rt Hon The Lady Hives, Langdale House, Sutton on the Hill, Derbys DE6 5JA], dau of Alfred Seals, and *dsp* 8 Oct 1997

2 Edward; *b* 1915; F/O RAF; *ka* Battle of Britain 1940

3 Peter Anthony; *b* 21 Jan 1921; *educ* Derby Sch and Cambridge; Lt RNVR; *m* 1956 *Dinah [The Hon Mrs Hives, Harrier Garry, Harrier Green Lane, Welwyn, Herts], dau of F Wilson-North, of Walcott, Norfolk, and *d* 26 May 1974, leaving:

(1) MATTHEW PETER HIVES, **3rd and present Baron Hives**

(1) *Julie Laura; *b* 1957; *m* 1st 1979 Thomas J MacNab (*d* 1988) and has:

1a *Robert Thomas Peter Campbell; *b* 1982

1a *Camilla Laura

(1) (cont.) Mrs Thomas MacNab *m* 2nd 1990 *Dr Anthony Reed, of Mardley Bury Manor, Knebworth, Herts, s of Dr E S Reed, MBE, of Shalford, Surrey, and by him has:

2a *Frederick Anthony Spencer; *b* 1992

2a *Clemintine Florence; *b* 1991

(2) *Liza Joanna; *b* 1963; has issue:

1a *Oscar; *b* 1992

1a *Alice; *b* 1993

(3) *Sophie Josephine; *b* 1964

4 +Michael Bruce [The Hon Michael Hives, Fairfield, The Pastures, Duffield, Derbys]; *b* 1926; *educ* Repton; *m* 20 Oct 1951 *Janet Rosemary, 2nd dau of Wilfred E Gee, of Duffield, and has issue:

(1) +Robert George [Robert Hives Esq, The Meadows, Church Lane, Barrow Upon Trent, Derby]; *b* 1953; *m* 1975 *Annabelle Vicars and has issue:

1a +William Duncan; *b* 1977

2a +Jeremy Robert; *b* 1982

3a +Thomas Francis; *b* 1985

1a *Victoria Jane; *b* 1980

(2) +Paul Michael; *b* 1963; *m* 1987 *Ellen, dau of J M Kaufman, of New York

(1) *Jillian Sarah [Mrs Kevin Titterton, 6 Keats Ave, Littleover, Derbys]; *b* 1955; *m* 1988 *Kevin Titterton and has:

1a *Grace Sarah; *b* 1989

2a *Ruth Catherine; *b* 1992

5 +David Benjamin [The Hon David Hives, Cumberhill House, Duffield, Derbys DE56 4HA]; *b* 1931; *educ* Repton; S/Ldr RAF; *m* 24 Feb 1954 *Shirley, est dau of Harold Walker, of Cumberhill House, and has:

(1) +Nigel Edward Ian; *b* 16 July 1960; *m* 1983 *Helen Louise, dau of W N K Rowley, of Derby, and has:

1a +Lawrence Ernest William; *b* 1987

1a *Imogen Jean; *b* 1990

(1) *Sally Margaret; *b* 10 Aug 1955; *m* 16 Dec 1978 *Malcolm Howard Lambie and has issue:

1a *Peter Benjamin; *b* 1984

2a *William Ian; *b* 1985

1a *Hannah Louise; *b* 1989

(2) *Sandra Dawn; *b* 4 July 1958; *m* 1990 *Col Jack M W Stenhouse, OBE, MVO, Gordon Highs, er s of Lt-Col D R Stenhouse, MBE, and has issue:

1a *Catriona Rose; *b* 1991

2a *Elizabeth Maitland; *b* 1993

1 *Joan Mary [The Hon Mrs Gee, 9 Chestnut Close, Duffield, Derbys]; *b* 1917; *m* 1939 *Adrian Gee and has:

(1) *Wendy Elizabeth [Mrs Thomas Neville, Beech Tree House, Audlem, Cheshire]; *b* 30 Sept 1943; *m* 4 May 1963 *Thomas Neville and has issue:

1a *Alexander William; *b* 10 Oct 1965

1a *Sally Ann; *b* 27 Feb 1968

(2) *Jane Anne [Mrs John Berry, Bunystone Cottage, Bunnison Lane, Colston Bassett, Notts NG12 3FF]; *b* 9 Sept 1945; *m* 9 Sept 1967 *John Hodgson Berry, er s of J T W Berry, of The Manor House, Ashley, Leics, and has issue:

1a *Duncan Gee; *b* 11 Dec 1968

2a *Nicholas Gee; *b* 1970

2 *Ruth Margaret [The Hon Mrs Riley, 7 Avenue Rd, Duffield, Derbys]; *b* 1922; *m* 1941 *Joseph Graham Riley and has:

(1) *Michael Edward; *b* 1947

(2) *John Andrew; *b* 1947

3 *Philippa Ann [The Hon Mrs Morrison, 17 Eastward Dve, Littleover, Derbys]; *b* 1928; *m* July 1978 *His Honour Judge Alexander John Henderson Morrison

HOARE of Annabella

Arms: Sa. a double-headed eagle displayed within a bordure engrailed arg. **Crest:** A deer's head and neck ppr., erased arg. **Mottoes:** 1 (over the crest) *Venit hora* ('The hour approches'), 2 (under the arms) *Dum spiro spero* ('While I breathe I hope').
Creation: Bt. (I) 10 Dec 1784.

SIR TIMOTHY EDWARD CHARLES HOARE, 8TH BT, of Annabella, Co Cork, OBE (1996) [Sir Timothy Hoare Bt OBE, 10 Belitha Villas, London N1 1PD]; *b* 11 Nov 1934, *s f* 1969; *educ* Radley, Worcester Coll Oxford (MA) and Birkbeck Coll London (MA); late Lt Green Jackets, sometime 60th Rifles (Nat Service Commn), dir: New Metals & Chemicals 1966–, Careerplan 1970– and World Vision UK 1983–95, memb: Gen Synod C of E 1970–, Crown Appointments Commn 1987–92 and Church and State Commn 1970–; *m* 1 March 1969 *Felicity Anne, only dau of Peter Boddington, of Stratford-on-Avon, and has issue:

1 +CHARLES JAMES; *b* 15 March 1971

1 *Louisa Hope; *b* 13 Oct 1972

2 *Kate Annabella; *b* 17 Oct 1972

Lineage: THOMAS HORE, of Green's Norton, Northants; *m* Elizabeth — and *d* 1526, leaving, with other issue:

THOMAS HORE, of Green's Norton; *m* Agnes — and *d* May 1573, leaving, with an er s (James, of Green's Norton, *d* Dec 1629, leaving issue):

JOHN HOARE, of Green's Norton; *m* twice and *d* July 1613, leaving, with other issue:

1 William; *b* 1565

2 George; *b* 1566

3 Thomas; *b* 1569

4 James, of Green's Norton; *m* 8 Aug 1601 Audrey, dau of William Hope, of Stafford, and had:

(1) James, of the Tower of London; Controller Mint, alleged fndr at the sign of the Golden Bottle, Cheapside, of Hoare's Bank, handling among other people's OLIVER CROMWELL's finances; *m* Elizabeth, dau of Martin Trinder, of Cham Court, Gloucester, and *d* 30 Nov 1696, leaving issue

5 Edmund, of Green's Norton; *m* 1st 18 Feb 1599 Elizabeth Rowe (*d* March 1616) and had issue; *m* 2nd Mary (*d* May 1941), dau of Robert Elliott, of Green's Norton, and by her had, with with other issue:

(1) Edward, of Togher Castle, Co Cork; Maj; *m* Mary (*d* 27 Aug 1690), yr dau of Capt John Woodcock, of Dublin, and Kilcragin, Co Kilkenny, by Margaret, dau of Richard Bennett, of London, and *d* 3 July 1690, leaving, with other issue:

1a EDWARD

2a Joseph; ancestor of Viscount Templewood (*see* 1959 edn)

The er son,

EDWARD HOARE, of Dunkettle, and Factory Hill, Co Cork; banker and merchant; Sheriff Co Cork 1684, Mayor Cork city 1686; bought estates in Cos Cork and Limerick; *m* 25 March 1676 Sarah (*bur* 6 Oct 1715), est dau and coheir of Richard Burnell, of Dublin, and had, with other issue:

1 EDWARD

2 Richard; barrister; *m* 1st 1708 Elizabeth (*dsp* 1709), dau of Benjamin Burton; *m* 2nd 17 Jan 1711/2 Elizabeth, dau and coheir of Gamaliel Purefoy, and *d* 23 Jan 1724/5, leaving issue

3 Robert, of Factory Hill, Co Cork; Town Clerk Cork; *m* 1 Oct 1721 Jane, est dau of Thomas Newenham, of Coolmore, Co Cork, and was *bur* 24 Nov 1764, leaving issue

4 John, of Drumcar, Co Kerry; *bapt* 28 March 1687; *m* 1st Anne, dau of Maskelyne Alcock; *m* 2nd Anne, dau of Samuel Blennerhassett, and had issue by his 1st w

EDWARD HOARE *d* 3 Nov 1709; his est son,

EDWARD HOARE, of Dunkettle and Factory Hill; Sheriff Co Cork 1708, Mayor Cork City 1710, MP Cork 1710–27; *m* 1st 1703 Grace (*d* 8 Aug 1709), 2nd dau of Benjamin Burton, MP Dublin 1703 and Ld Mayor 1706, and *d* 20 July 1765, having had:

1 Edward; barrister; *bapt* 31 Aug 1704; *m* Sarah (*d* 26 Nov 1741), dau and coheir of Edward Worth, and *dsp* 16 Dec 1740

2 Francis Conynghamm; *b* 4 Jan 1706; *d* unm 1732

3 JOSEPH (Sir), **1st Bt**

1 Grace; *m* 26 Sept 1725 Thomas Spaight, of Bunratty, Co Clare, and had issue

EDWARD HOARE *m* 2nd 27 Aug 1715 Anne, dau of Thomas Grant, of Cork, and by her had surv issue:

4 Samuel; *bapt* 8 July 1719; *m* Jane (*dsp* 25 June 1802), dau of John Simpson, and *d* 29 Sept 1791

The 3rd son,

Sir Joseph Hoare, 1st Bt (I), so *cr* 10 Dec 1784, of Annabella, Co Cork; barrister, MP Askeaton, Co Limerick, 1761–1800; *b* 25 Dec 1707; *m* Catherine, dau of Sir James Somerville, 1st Bt, of Cookstown, Co Dublin (*see* 1970 edn), and had:

1 EDWARD (Sir), **2nd Bt**

1 Catherine; *m* William Hume, MP, of Humewood, Co Wicklow

2 Anne; *m* John Peyton, of Co Roscommon

3 Elizabeth; *m* 1st Dominick Blake, of Castlegrove; *m* 2nd Col James Bulkeley, of Huntley Hall

Sir JOSEPH *d* 24 Dec 1801; his only son,

Sir Edward Hoare, 2nd Bt; MP Carlow, Capt 13th Light Dragoons; *b* 14 March 1745; *m* 14 Sept 1771 Clotilda (*d* 3 Sept 1816), 2nd dau and coheir of William Wallis, of Ballycrenan Castle, Co Cork, and had, with other issue:

1 JOSEPH WALLIS (Sir), **3rd Bt**

2 Edward Wallis; Adml; *b* 1 May 1778; *m* Mary Aubrey (*d* 6 Dec 1868), 3rd dau of Robert Uniacke Fitzgerald, MP, and *d* 6 Jan 1870, leaving issue:

(1) Louisa Frances; *m* 30 March 1841 Capt Thomas Burton Maynard, RN, and had issue

(2) Clotilda Henrietta; *m* 14 Dec 1842 Adml James Beckford Lewis Hay and had issue

3 Thomas (Rev); *b* 20 April 1779; *m* 20 Dec 1806 Mary Anne (*d* 17 April 1865), est dau of Henry Jesse Lloyd, of Castle Iney, Tipperary, and *d* 15 Dec 1835, leaving, with four daus:

(1) Edward; *b* 28 March 1809; *m* 16 June 1864 Cornelia (*d* 9 Feb 1925), dau of Bernard Robert Shaw, of Monkstown Castle, Co Cork, and *d* 1893, leaving:

1a Thomas Edward, of Glenanore, Castletownroche, Co Cork; barrister; *b* 27 April 1865; *d* 19 April 1926

2a Edward Lloyd; *d* Feb 1956

3a William Wallis; MD Brussels 1901, FRCS Edin 1916, MRCS and LRCP 1893, Hon Capt AAMC (Res Offrs); *b* 17 Jan 1871; *m* 1903 Kathleen Mary Bolton, of Qld, and had:

1b +Edward Bryan; *b* 1905

1b Geneeta Kathleen; *b* 1904; *d* unm 1955

1a Rebecca Elizabeth; *m* 14 Aug 1909 Maj Henry Charles Mansergh (*d* 29 July 1911), 27th Inniskilling Fus, of Rock Savage, Castletownroche, Co Cork

2a Mary Anne Cornelia; *d* 4 June 1937

(2) William Jesse; Capt 59th Regt and 7th Roy Fus; *b* 1826; *m* 1st 25 Sept 1854 Anna (*d* 1856), only dau of Frederick Lidwill, of Dromard, and had issue:

1a Anna Maria; *d* Aug 1925

(2) (cont.) Capt William Hoare *m* 2nd 1857 Mary Elizabeth (*d* 1920), est dau and coheir of John Henry Gamble, and *d* 1881, having by her had:

1a Thomas; *b* 1858

2a Henry; *b* 1859; *d* May 1932

3a Edward Wallis; FRCVS; *b* 9 Oct 1863; *m* 30 Aug 1899 Emily, BA, RUI (*d* 5 March 1961), dau of Henry Lindsay Helen, of Dublin, and *d* Nov 1920, leaving issue:

1b Edward William Wallis; *b* 14 June 1902; *m* 6 April 1936 Elizabeth (*d* 1977), dau of Angus Baillie, of Newlands, Glasgow, and *d* 1966, leaving:

1c *Elizabeth McClean [Miss Elizabeth Hoare, 1a Sinclair Dve, Helensburgh, Dunbartonshire G84 9BB]; *b* 1937

2c *Margaret Wallis; *b* 1941; *m* July 1965 *Duncan Macpherson Muir, BDS, and has issue

3c *Barbara [Mrs Paul Green, 10 Ranelagh Dve North, Liverpool L19 9DS]; *b* 1948; *m* 1st 1979 (*divorce* 1984) Geoffrey Goddin; *m* 2nd 1987 *Paul Green, and by her 1st husb has issue:

1d *Alastair William; *b* 1979

1b Alma Violet Lloyd; BA; *b* Aug 1900; *m* 10 July 1941 Desmond Fitz-Maurice, of Co Cork

2b Emily Alexandra; BA; *b* July 1903

3b Freesia Helen; *b* April 1909

4b *Cecilia Viola [Mrs Richard Gorsuch, 6811, 236th St, RR6, Langley, BC, Canada]; *b* Dec 1913; *m* 1939 *Richard Roberts Gorsuch and has:

1c *Diarmuid Roberts; with BC Forest Serv; *b* 29 Dec 1941; *m* 1970 *Jane, er dau of Arthur Stanley Peacock, of Vancouver

2c *Terence Richard; electronic technician Dept Tport; *b* 22 Sept 1947; *educ* BC Inst of Technology; *m* 26 April 1969 *Patricia Ann, dau of Arthur Stanley Peacock, of Vancouver, BC

1c *Deirdre Cecilia; *b* 24 Oct 1943; *educ* U of BC (BHE 1965); *m* 1970 *Michael le Bell

5c *Maeve Emily; *b* 24 Jan 1946; *educ* U of BC; *m* 1972 *Keith Harrison, of Ch Ch, NZ

5b *Myrtle Jesse; *b* Feb 1918; *m* 1st 1940 William Henry Hall (*d* May 1951); *m* 2nd June 1956 *Basil Lionel Baker, s of A L Baker, Civil Commr Bulawayo, S Rhodesia, and adopted:

*Aidan Lee; *b* June 1959

4a Joseph (Rev), MA, TCD; *b* 1867; *d* unm April 1905

2a Eliza; *d* unm Jan 1933

Sir EDWARD *d* 30 April 1814; his est son,

Sir Joseph Wallis Hoare, 3rd Bt; *b* 9 March 1775; *m* 17 April 1800 Harriett (*d* 1 May 1851), sis of 3rd Marquess of Thomond (*see* INCHIQUIN, B), and had, with six other daus:

1 EDWARD (Sir), **4th Bt**

2 William O'Bryen, Capt RN; *b* 23 March 1807; *m* 2 May 1834 Caroline (*d* 9 Jan 1891), dau of John Hornby, of Hook, Hants, and *d* 26 March 1886, leaving:

(1) Harriot Jane; *d* unm

(2) Elizabeth Clotilda; *d* unm 10 Dec 1910

(3) Mary Louisa; *d* unm 20 Dec 1907

3 Joseph James Parish; *b* 22 March 1811; *m* 17 April 1834 Helen Moritz Dillon (*d* 10 July 1879), dau of Henry N Hardman, of Mount Hardman, Grenada, and *d* 17 Dec 1889, leaving issue:

(1) James O'Bryen Richard Dott; MA Cantab, Vicar Papanui, NZ; *b* 12 March 1835; *m* 1st 23 Feb 1865 Frances Eleanor (*d* 15 Feb 1911), dau of Rev Thomas Henderson, Vicar Messing, Essex; *m* 2nd 1912 Vera Mary Martell (*d* 1950) and *d* 1914, leaving by his 1st w:

1a Arthur, of Bombay; *b* 1865; CE

2a Philip O'Bryen, MBIM Sc; *b* 1871; *m* 1896 Florence Evans and had:

1b Donovan O'Bryen; NZ Navy; *b* 1899; *das* 1917

3a John; *b* 1873; *m* 1904 Margaret Jane Leversedge (*d* 1959) and *d* 1954, leaving:

1b James OBryen; WW II as Maj RIASC; *b* 1910; *m* Jan 1941 Helen Dorey Hardie (*d* 1991) and *d* 5 Feb 1967, leaving:

1c +Richard James O'Bryen [Richard Hoare Esq, 242 Hurstmere Rd, Takapuna, Auckland, New Zealand]; *b* 1947; *m* 1971 *Sally Ann, dau of John Cornwell, of Northcote, NZ, and has issue:

1d +David O'Bryen; *b* 1974

2d +Matthew James; *b* 1976

1d *Rosemary Jane; *b* 1978

2c +Stewart John [Stewart Hoare Esq, 27 Morvern Rd, Mt Eden, Auckland, New Zealand]; *b* 1949; *m* 1976 *Marcelle, dau of Elie Bitoun, of Paris, and has:

1d +Andrew James; *b* 1982

1c *Janet O'Bryen [Mrs William Richardson, 45 St Leonard's Rd, Mt Eden, Auckland 4, New Zealand]; *b* Nov 1941; *m* 16 Jan 1965 *William Frank Richardson, son of G W Richardson, of Epsom, NZ, and has:

1d +Michael George; *b* 1970

1d *Diana Helen; *b* 10 Feb 1967

2b John Leslie; *b* 1919; *m* 1945 *Maxine Heaslip and *d* 1991, leaving:

1c *Susan Elizabeth [Mrs Michael Quinnell, Lot 8, Rosleigh Court, Yugar, Qld, Australia]; *b* 1946; *m* 1970 *Michael Clifford Quinnell, of Qld, and has:

1d *Mark Alexander; *b* 1976

2c *Jane Victoria; *b* 1950; *m* 1977 *Marion Lester Woods, of Brisbane, and has:

1d *Clare Marcello; *b* 1980

2d *Caroline Elizabeth; *b* 1983

3d *Hannah Victoria; *b* 1987

1b *Joan Mary Frances [Mrs Harry Cameron, c/o 63 Greentrees Ave, Brookfield, Qld, Australia]; *b* 1905; *m* 1931 Harry Albert Cameron (*d* 1983) and has:

1c *John Bruce [John Cameron Esq, 63 Greentrees Ave, Brookfield, Qld, Australia]; *b* 1933; *m* 1961 *Jennifer Dines Mackay and has:

1d *Christine Louise [Mrs Geoffrey Crozier, Tulip Garden, Singapore]; *b* 1962; *m* 1987 *Geoffrey Douglas Crozier and has:

1e *James Allen; *b* 1992

1e *Louise Jane; *b* 1990

2d *Fiona Judith [Mrs David Finney, 1 Furrow Close, Cairns, Qld, Australia]; *b* 1963; *m* 1992 *David Hubert Finney and has:

1e *Kate Elizabeth; *b* 1994

3d *Belinda Anne; *b* 1965; *m* 4 June 1994 *Mario Ricardo Crismani and has:

1e *Suzanna Jane; *b* 6 Oct 1996

1c *Margaret Anne [Mrs Grahame Barry, 361 Warners Bay Rd, Charlestown, NSW, Australia]; *b* 1932; *m* 19– *Grahame Iliff Barry and has:

1d *David Bruce [David Barry Esq, 23 Bilba Cresent, Marylands, NSW, Australia]; *b* 1955; *m* 1985 (*divorce* 19–) Gillian Howie and has:

1e *Dean Cameron; *b* 1987

1e *Lisa Danielle; *b* 1988

2d *Richard John [Richard Barry Esq, 19 Broulla St, Baulkham Hills, NSW, Australia]; *b* 1961; *m* 1992 *Julie Maguire

1d *Helen Margaret [Mrs Matthew Gooden, 147 Castle Hill Rd, Castle Hill, NSW, Australia]; *b* 1957; *m* 1980 *Matthew Gooden and has:

1e *Alexander Matthew; *b* 1981

2e *Daniel Benedict; *b* 1983

3e *Dominic Thomas; *b* 1988

4e *Jerome Patrick; *b* 1990

1e *Cecily Rita; *b* 1986

2e *Prudence Jane; *b* 1992

2c *Diana Molly [Mrs Jules Le Lievre, 150 Old West Coast Rd, RD6, Christchurch, New Zealand]; *b* 1943; *m* 1st 19– (*divorce* 1981) Kevin Patrick Shone; *m* 2nd 1982 *Jules Le Lievre, and by her 1st husb has:

1d *Robert; *b* 1970

2d *Michael; *b* 1973

3d *Jonathan; *b* 1976

2b Margaret Alice; *b* 1912; *m* 1943 Jack Steane Comport (*d* 28 Nov 1961) and *d* 28 Nov 1994, leaving:

1c *Stephen [Stephen Comport Esq, 15 The Grange, E Malvern, Vic, Australia]; *b* 1944; *m* 1st 1966 (*divorce* 1972) Mary Boyd Thomson; *m* 2nd 1973 *Gillian Elizabeth Sinton and by her has:

1d *David John; *b* 1980

2d *Michael Douglas; *b* 1982

3b *Molly Gertrude [Mrs Patrick Shine, 59 Sofala Ave, Lane Cove, NSW, Australia]; *b* 1913; *m* 1942 Patrick Shine (*d* 1985) and has:

1c *John [John Shine Esq, 2 Mayfield Ave, Woolwich, NSW, Australia]; *b* 3 July 1946; Prof; *m* 1969 *Kathleen Mary Morgan and has:

1d *Michael Patrick; *b* 1972

1d *Rebecca Kathleen; *b* 1970

2c *Richard [Richard Shine Esq, 30 Farnell St, Boronia Park, NSW, Australia]; *b* 7 June 1950; *m* 1978 *Terri Sue Griffith, of Pennsylvania, and has:

1d *James Macquarie; *b* 1982

2d *Benjamin Griffith; *b* 1984

1c *Judith Mary [Mrs Joseph Ohana, 62 Hamilton St, Lane Cove, NSW, Australia]; *b* 23 April 1948; BA (1968); *m* 1971 *Joseph Ohana, of Beersheba, Israel, and has:

1d *David Patrick Yaniv; *b* 1978

1d *Yael Simma; *b* 1973

4a Denys, JP; *b* 1875; FPA (NZ), FICS; *m* 1906 Frances York (*d* 1959) and *d* 1958, leaving:

1b Norah Frances O'Bryen; *m* 1940 John Edward Buxton (*d* 1981) and *d* 1995, leaving:

1c *Joanna Elizabeth [Mrs Christopher Leefe, West Farm House, Harriotts Lane, Ashtead, Surrey KT21 2QE]; *b* 31 Oct 1941; *m* 1964 *Maj Christopher Timothy Rawdon Leefe, s of Maj Thomas Leefe, of Malton, Yorks, and has:

1d *Mark Rawdon; *b* 25 Oct 1966

2d *Thomas Rawdon; *b* 20 June 1968

2c *Frances Jane [Mrs John Holford, Kings Cottage, Elmdon, Saffron Walden, Essex]; *b* 13 Nov 1944; *m* 1 April 1967 *John Edward Holford and has:

1d *Rebecca Jane; *b* 25 Dec 1968

2d *Melanie Sarah; *b* 1970

3d *Elizabeth Alice; *b* 1975

3c *Annabel Mary [Mrs Michael Foster, Tadworth Cottage, Tadworth St, Tadworth, Surrey]; *b* 23 May 1948; *m* 1971 *Michael Bonhote Rodney Foster and has:

1d *James Edward Bonhote; *b* 1982

1d *Lucy Annabel Henrietta; *b* 1974

2d *Harriet Mary Emma; *b* 1976

2b Kathleen Hannah

1a Mary; *m* 1917 Alfred Long (*ka* 1918) and *dsp* 1947

2a Janet; *m* 1900 Geoffrey John Phillips, engr, of S Africa, and had issue

3a Helen; *m* 1910 H M Trevor (*d* 1927), of Ohakuner, NZ, and had issue

(2) Joseph George Wallace; Paymaster RN; *b* 26 July 1840; *m* 1st 1 June 1865 Susan Mary (*d* 13 Sept 1874), only child of Capt Frederick William Paul, RN, and had:

1a Ernest Frederick Wallis; *b* 29 Aug 1866; *d* unm 1902

2a Wallace Suttie; *b* 28 Oct 1873; *d* unm 1900

1a Helen Susan Kathleen; *b* 21 Nov 1867; *m* 2 April 1894 John Meek (*d* 6 Oct 1907), er son of John Meek, of Liverpool, formerly of Perth, and *d* 16 April 1935, leaving issue

2a Lily; *b* 12 June 1869; *d* unm 5 Jan 1943

3a Daisy; *b* 8 Dec 1870; *d* unm 19 April 1907

4a Edith Mary; *b* 19 June 1872; *m* Fritz Furhop (*d* 12 Nov 1946), of Hamburg, and *d* 11 Nov 1946

(2) (cont.) Joseph Hoare *m* 2nd 9 April 1878 Mary Martha (*d* 24 June 1928), 2nd dau of Henry White England, of Kingsbury, Somerset, and *d* 1884, having by her had:

5a Marie Violet; *b* 16 Feb 1879

6a Olive Buchanan; *b* 24 June 1881; *m* 21 June 1904 William Gerald Morris (*d* 25 March 1959), and *d* 9 Sept 1951, leaving issue

(3) Arthur Calvert; *b* 24 March 1840; *m* 29 Jan 1869 Charlotte Rosina, dau of J Robinson, of Banffshire, and *d* 4 April 1898, having had:

1a Arthur Carrick Dickson; Lt RNVR; *b* 23 Oct 1872; *m* 17 March 1921 Ursula Audrey Mary, only child of Frank Pacy, of Kensington, and has:

1b *Jacqueline FitzMaurice O'Bryen; *b* 27 March 1922

1a Helen Brownlow; *m* 21 Sept 1904 W E G Solger, 7th E Prussian Inf

2a Brenda Marie; *m* 18 Oct 1905 Charles Henry Dorward Moberly and had issue

3a Sydney Josephine FitzMaurice; *m* 1909 Walter Granville Warburton, and *d* 12 July 1912

(4) Charles Campbell William; Inspr Factories; *b* 31 Dec 1841; *m* 25 July 1867 Blanche (*d* 4 May 1913), dau of Frederick Richard Phayre, of Killoughran, Co Wexford, and *d* 20 June 1921, leaving:

1a Carl Frederick; *b* 21 Sept 1869

1a May Annesley; *m* 1890 Charles F Edwards (*d* 1908) and *d* 26 Aug 1959

2a Blanche Evelyn; *m* 1915 Maj Ernest St George Anson, OBE (*d* 1946), 2nd Bn E Surrey Regt

(5) Oliver William Simpson; Capt Lanark Militia; *b* 3 Oct 1843; *m* 27 Oct 1864 Catherine Annie (*d* 1 June 1881), dau of George James, of Ridgway, Hants, and *d* Oct 1902, leaving:

1a Oliver George St Clair; *b* 18 Sept 1865; *m* 1892 Helen, dau of Robert Lloyd Peel, and *d* 12 Nov 1934

2a Basil O'Bryen; *b* 1 March 1870

3a Walter James; *b* 4 Oct 1871; *d* 1910

4a Gerald Robin O'Bryen; *b* 1878; *d* 1941

1a Annie Frances Isabella; *m* 1st 1887 Isaac Beeman Oyler (*d* 16 Oct 1916); *m* 2nd 31 Jan 1920 Baron van Tuyll van Serooskerken, of Promek Haus, St Wolfgang, Upper Austria, and *d* 9 Nov 1943

2a Constance Helen; *m* 1901 Maj Philip L Stevenson, 5th Lancers

3a Geraldine Erin; *m* 26 Sept 1893 Edmund Beverley Blair McKean

(6) Henry Douglas Martin; *b* 26 Sept 1849; *d* 1906

(7) Edward Senior; *b* 15 July 1851; *m* 16 Aug 1870 Sophia Elizabeth (*d* July 1913), dau of Rev J G Hird, and *d* Aug 1895, having had:

1a Cyril Bertie Edward; *b* 29 Sept 1882; *m* 24 Oct 1907 Isabel Mary, yr dau of Edward Fielder, and *d* 16 Jan 1940, leaving:

1b Bertie Rex O'Bryen, DSO (1942) and bar (1944), DFC and bar; W/Cdr RAF WW II (despatches three times); *b* 6 June 1912; *educ* Harrow; *m* 22 Dec 1945 Lucy, S/O WAAF (*d* 21 June 1970), dau of Richard Nimmo Watson, MRCS, LRCP, of Harrogate, and *d* 26 March 1947 following an air accident, leaving:

1c *Rosemary Verity O'Bryen [Mrs Nicholas Russell, Box 14357, Nairobi, Kenya]; *b* posthumously 1 Nov 1947; *m* 19– *Nicholas Russell and has:

1d *Samantha O'Bryen; *b* 1980

1b Hermione Sophia O'Bryen; *b* 27 Feb 1910; *m* 18 July 1952 (*divorce* 1954) 2nd Baron Colwyn (*qv*) and *d* 1989

(1) Marion Maria Dorothy; *m* 20 Feb 1855 John Turner Turner (*d* 8 Feb 1874), only s of John Thorp Burton Phillipson, of Bramshaw House, Hants, and had issue

4 John Lynam Parish; Maj 13th Bombay NI; *m* 4 May 1840 Jane Ellis (*d* 9 Aug 1891), est dau of Lt-Col Charles Payne, and *dsps* 12 June 1882

1 Harriet; *m* 1826 Francis Hunt Sitwell (*see* SITWELL, Bt)

Sir JOSEPH *d* 26 Nov 1852; his son,

Sir Edward Hoare, 4th Bt; *b* 23 Dec 1801; *m* 24 April 1824 Harriet (*d* 25 Jan 1880), 2nd dau and coheir of Thomas Hercey Barritt, of Garbrand Hall, Ewell, Surrey, and had issue:

1 Edward Barritt; *b* 1825; *ka* Gujarat 21 Feb 1849

2 JOSEPH WALLIS O'BRYEN (Sir), **5th Bt**

1 Anne; *m* 4 June 1856 Thomas Leslie, barrister (*d* 15 Feb 1880), s of Rt Rev John Leslie, DD, Bp Kilmore, and *d* 24 Feb 1910, leaving issue

Sir EDWARD *d* 15 Nov 1882; his only surv son,

Sir Joseph Wallis O'Bryen Hoare, 5th Bt, JP, DL Hants; Lt RE 1847–49, Maj 5th Middx Militia, KStJ; *b* 11 Nov 1828; *m* 6 Aug 1857 Cecilia Eleanor Selina (*d* 7 Jan 1888), 4th dau of James Ede, of Ridgeway Castle, Hants, and had:

1 Edward Wallis O'Bryen; *b* 22 Feb 1859; *dvp* unm 29 Oct 1892

2 SYDNEY JAMES O'BRYEN (Sir), **6th Bt**

1 Kathleen Henriette; *d* unm 3 April 1937

2 Norah Cecile Helen; *d* unm 26 June 1949

Sir JOSEPH *d* 30 April 1904; his only surv son,

Sir Sydney James O'Bryen Hoare, 6th Bt; Lt 2nd/5th Bn E Surrey Regt, Lt 5th Middx Militia; *b* 2 July 1860; *m* 1st 16 June 1896 Mabel (*d* 12 May 1916), dau of Maj O'Bryen Taylor, Standard Bearer Gentlemen-at-Arms, and had issue:

1 EDWARD O'BRYEN (Sir), **7th Bt**

2 Terence O'Bryen; F/Lt RAFVR; *b* 21 Jan 1904; *m* 10 Oct 1939 Elizabeth, dau of William James Cambridge

1 Violet Hester O'Bryen; *b* 4 May 1897; *d* 7 Nov 1900

Sir Sydney *m* 2nd 8th Feb 1917 Mona Gwendoline (*d* 27 Oct 1955), dau of Capt John Pitt Taylor, Seaforth Highrs, and *d* 8 Oct 1933

His er son,

Sir Edward O'Bryen Hoare, 7th Bt; *b* 29 April 1898; *educ* Charterhouse; Maj RASC, Lt Suffolk Regt; *m* 1 Oct 1932 Nina Mary (*d* 15 Oct 1995), er dau of Charles Nugent Hope-Wallace, MBE (*see* LINLITHGOW, M), and *d* 4 Dec 1969, leaving:

1 Sir TIMOTHY EDWARD CHARLES HOARE, **8th and present Bt**

1 *Catherine Mary; *b* 27 July 1937; *m* 19 Jan 1963 *David James Clark and has:

(1) *David Noah; *b* 24 Oct 1966

(2) *Ezra David; *b* 20 March 1968

(3) *Abel David; *b* 1971

(1) *Hester Catherine; *b* 1973

HOARE of Barn Elms

Arms: Sa. a double-headed eagle displayed arg., charged on the breast with an ermine spot, a bordure engrailed of the second. **Crest:** An eagle's head erased arg., charged with an ermine spot. **Motto:** *In ardua* ('For arduous undertakings'). **Creation:** Bt. (GB) 27 June 1786.

SIR PETER RICHARD DAVID HOARE, 8TH BT, of Barn Elms, Co Surrey [Sir Peter Hoare Bt, Crèdit Andorrà, Avinguda Princep Benlloch 25, Andorra la Vella, Principality of Andorra]; *b* 22 March 1932; *s* f 1973; *educ* Eton; High Sheriff Devon 1955; *m* 1st 2 Sept 1961 (*divorce* 1967) Jane, only dau of Daniel Orme, of Bulleigh Barton, Ipplepen, S Devon; *m* 2nd 1978 (*divorce* 1982) Katrin Alexa, dau of Erwin Bernsteil and formerly w of Sir Michael Robin Adderley Hodson, 6th Bt (*qv*); *m* 3rd 1983 *Angela Francesca de la Sierra, yr dau of Fidel Fernando Ayarza, of Santiago, Chile

Lineage: Sir RICHARD HOARE (s of Henry Hoare and gs of Henry Hoare, of Walton, Bucks); ktd 1702, Ld Mayor London 1712, MP City London 1710–23; *b* 1648; *m* (licence 27 July 1672) Susannah (*d* 24 Sept 1720), dau of John Austin, of Brittons, Essex, and had, with other issue:

1 RICHARD; ancestor of the HOAREs of Ellisfield

2 HENRY

3 John; *b* 13 April 1682; *m* Elizabeth (*d* 1723), dau and heiress of Robert Hookes, of Conway, and *d* 18 May 1721, leaving issue

4 Benjamin, of Boreham, Essex; *b* 11 July 1693; *m* Ellen (*d* Feb 1747/8), dau of Benjamin Richards, and *d* 12 Jan 1749/50, leaving issue

Sir RICHARD *d* 6 Jan 1718; his 2nd son,

HENRY HOARE, of London, later Stourhead, Wilts; banker; *b* 21 July 1677; *m* 19 May 1702 Jane (*d* 25 June 1741), dau of Sir William Benson, of Bromley, and *d* 12 March 1724/5, having had, with three daus:

1 Henry, of Stourhead; *b* 7 July 1705; *m* 1st 11 April 1726 Anne (*d* 4 March 1727), est dau of 1st Baron Masham of Otes; *m* 2nd 6 July 1728 Susan (*d* 17 May 1743), dau and heiress of Stephen Colt, and *d* 8 Sept 1785, leaving, with other issue:

(1) Susannah; *m* 1st 11 May 1753 Charles, Viscount Dungarvan, and had issue (*see* CORK and ORRERY, E); *m* 2nd 7 Feb 1761 1st Earl of Ailesbury (*see* AILESBURY, M) and *d* 4 Feb 1783, leaving issue

(2) Anne; *m* 20 March 1756 her cousin **Sir Richard Hoare, 1st Bt**, and *d* 5 May 1759, leaving issue (*see* below)

2 Richard (Sir); Ld Mayor London 1745, ktd 1745; *b* 2 March 1709; *m* 1st 24 April 1732 Sarah (*d* 20 Sept 1736), dau and heiress of James Tully, and had:

(1) RICHARD (Sir), **1st Bt**

2 (cont.) Sir Richard *m* 2nd 30 June 1737 Elizabeth (*d* 29 June 1752), dau of Edward Rust, of Crutched Friars, London, cooper, and *d* 12 Oct 1754, having by her had issue:

(2) Henry; *b* 13 June 1744; *m* 25 June 1765 Mary (*d* 15 Jan 1820), dau of William Hoare, RA, of Bath, portrait painter, and *dsps* 20 Feb 1785

(1) Jane; *d* young

(2) Elizabeth; *d* unm

The est son,

Sir Richard Hoare, 1st Bt (GB), so *cr* 27 June 1786, of Barn Elms; *b* 7 March 1734/5; *m* 1st 20 March 1756 his cousin Anne (*d* 5 May 1759), dau of Henry Hoare, of Stourhead (*see* above), and had issue:

1 **Sir Richard Colt Hoare, 2nd Bt**; FRS, FSA, FLS; *b* 9 Dec 1758 *m* 18 Aug 1783 Hester (*d* 22 Aug 1785) est dau of 1st Baron Lyttelton (*see* COBHAM, V), and *d* 19 May 1838, having had issue:

(1) Henry; *b* 17 Sept 1784; *m* 20 Feb 1808 Charlotte (*d* 14 Feb 1839), only dau of Sir Edward Dering, 7th Bt (*see* 1970 edn), and *dvp* 18 Sept 1836, leaving:

1a Anne; *m* 26 March 1835 Sir George Benvenuto Buckley Mathew, KCMG, CB (*d* 22 Oct 1879), Envoy Extrdy and Min Plen Brazil, and *d* 17 Jan 1872, leaving issue

Sir Richard *m* 2nd 7 May 1761 Frances Ann (*d* 10 Sept 1800), dau of Richard Acland, bro of Sir Hugh Acland, 6th Bt, of Columb John (*qv*), and *d* 11 Oct 1787, having by her had issue:

2 **Sir Henry Hugh Hoare, 3rd Bt**, of Wavendon House, Bucks; *b* 27 Feb 1762; *m* 25 Aug 1784 Maria Palmer (*d* 31 Jan 1845), dau of Arthur Acland, 2nd s of Sir Hugh Acland, 6th Bt, of Columb John (*qv*), and *d* 17 Aug 1841, having had, with other issue:

(1) **Sir Hugh Richard Hoare, 4th Bt**; *b* 27 Nov 1787; *m* 22 April 1819 Anne (*d* 23 March 1847), 2nd dau of Thomas Tyrwhitt-Drake, LLD, of Shardeloes, Bucks, and *dsp* 10 Jan 1857

(2) Henry Charles; *b* 30 Jan 1790; *m* 6 Oct 1821 Anne Penelope (*d* 30 March 1887 in her 101st yr), widow of Capt John Prince and sis of Sir Robert Sharpe Ainslie, 1st Bt (*see* 1858 edn), and *d* 15 Jan 1852, having had, with other issue:

1a **Sir Henry Ainslie Hoare, 5th Bt**, DL Somerset; MP Chelsea 1868–74; *b* 14 April 1824; *m* 15 April 1845 Augusta Frances (*d* 12 April 1903), 2nd dau of Sir East George Clayton East, 1st Bt, of Hall Place, Berks (*see* 1932 edn), and *d* 7 July 1894, having had:

1b Charles Peregrine; *b* 27 Sept 1846; *d* 4 Aug 1854

1b Augusta Frances Anne; *m* 1st 22 Feb 1868 William John Nettleship Angerstein (*d* 23 Feb 1892), of Weeting Hall, Norfolk, and had issue; *m* 2nd 1894 Col J St Aubyn Hastie (*d* 1901), and *d* 7 Nov 1922

(3) Richard; Capt RN *b* 1 Sept 1793; *m* 1st 15 March 1823 Matilda Ottley (*d* 27 Sept 1826), dau of R-Adml Sir William Charles Fahie, KCB; *m* 2nd 27 March 1834 Elizabeth (*dsp* 15 June 1860), est dau of William Praed, of Tyringham, Bucks, and *d* 5 Dec 1850, having had by his 1st w:

1a Hugh Richard Fahie; *d* 29 March 1840 aged 13

1a Maria Palmer; *m* 3 June 1848 Count Pompeo Troili

2a Renee Elizabeth Lavina; *m* 25 Aug 1853 Edward Heneage (*d* 25 June 1880), of Stag's End, Herts, and *d* 14 March 1871, leaving issue

(4) Henry Arthur, of Wavendon House, JP Bucks; High Sheriff 1865; *b* 20 March 1804; *m* 20 July 1859 Julia Lucy (*d* 27 Aug 1916), est dau of Thomas Veale Lane and gdau of 2nd Viscount Exmouth (*qv*), and *d* 6 Nov 1873, leaving:

1a **Sir Henry Hugh Arthur Hoare, 6th Bt**, JP Wilts; *b* 19 Nov 1865; *educ* Harrow; High Sheriff Wilts 1915, Lt 3rd Bn Beds Regt; *m* 4 Oct 1887 his cousin Alda (*d* 25 March 1947), dau of William Henry Purcell Weston, and *d* 25 March 1947, having had:

1b Henry Colt Arthur; Capt 1st Dorset QO Yeo; *b* 30 July 1888; *d* 20 Dec 1917 of wounds recd in action

1b Renée Julia; *m* 1889 (*divorce* 1903) Charles Cunninghame Church, of Hinton House, Northants, and *d* 1953, leaving issue

(1) Julia; *b* 9 Jan 1800; *m* 15 March 1827 Sir John Hesketh Lethbridge, 3rd Bt (*qv*), and *d* 29 May 1850, leaving issue

3 Charles, of Luscombe House, Devon, and London; banker; *b* 25 Aug 1767; *m* 7 May 1790 Frances Dorothea, dau of Sir George Robinson, 5th Bt, of London (*qv*), and *dsp* 16 Nov 1851

4 Henry Merrik; *b* 20 July 1770; *m* 13 Aug 1807 Sophia (*d* 8 Nov 1824), dau of Henry Thrale, and *dsp* 22 June 1856

5 Peter Richard, of Kelsey Park, Beckenham, Kent; *b* 13 Oct 1772; *m* 23 Sept 1799 Arabella Penelope Eliza (*d* 26 April 1865 aged 84), dau and coheir of James Greene, of Turton Tower and Clayton Hall, Lancs, and *d* 10 Sept 1849, having had, with other issue:

(1) Peter Richard, of Luscombe House; High Sheriff Devon 1860; *b* 8 May 1803; *m* 17 April 1837 Lady Sophia Marsham (*d* 4 Jan 1863), est dau of 2nd Earl of Romney (*qv*), and *d* 30 May 1877, having had issue:

1a Peter Merrik, of Luscombe Castle, Dawlish, Devon; MP Southampton 1868–74; *b* 29 Oct 1843; *m* 1st 29 June 1865 Edith Augusta (*d* 20 Oct 1880), est dau of Rev Edmond Strong, Rector Clyst St Mary, Devon; *m* 2nd 13 Aug 1881 Marguerite Johanna (*d* 16 April 1912), dau of John Bell, and *d* 22 Feb 1894, having had by his 1st w:

1b Peter Arthur Marsham, of Luscombe Castle; ptnr Messrs C Hoare and Co; *b* 1 Sept 1869; *m* 28 April 1897 Norah Alicia Beresford (*d* 2 Jan 1909), yst dau of W Stewart Falls, MD, of Bournemouth, and *d* 3 Dec 1939, leaving:

1c PETER WILLIAM (Sir), **7th Bt**

1c Joyce Norah

2b (Henry) Lennox Merrik Noel Colt; *b* 14 May 1871; *m* 26 Nov 1895 Evelyn Augusta (*d* 25 Jan 1952), dau of Thomas Gerard, of Claughton, Cheshire, and *d* 26 Oct 1924, leaving issue:

1c Dorothy Augusta Edith; *m* Dec 1920 Capt F N Mitchell (*d* 6 Dec 1927), IAR, attd 126th Baluchistan Inf, and had:

1d *Jane; *b* 3 Sept 1923; *m* 7 Aug 1954 Capt John Charles Montague, RE, and has issue

2d *Ruth; *b* 18 Aug 1926; *m* 1st 12 Feb 1949 (*divorce* 1965) Charles Derek Sydney Wintle and has issue:

1e *David Michael Charles; *b* 1961

2d (cont.) Mrs Ruth Wintle *m* 2nd 1965 *Roger John Mules, MB, BS, and has by him:

2e *Anthony John; *b* 29 May 1966

1e *Frances Jane; *b* 3 March 1968

2c *Alda Evelyn [Mrs Henry Shewell, Bramble Down, Denbury, Devon]; *m* 29 Jan 1929 Brig Henry Anthony Lampen Shewell, OBE (*d* 1974), RE, and has issue:

1d *John Michael Henry [Maj John Shewell, The Lindens, Hutton Rd, Ash Vale, Hants GU12 5EY]; *b* 26 Jan 1931; Maj ACC (ret); *m* 4 April 1959 *Alison Averil, dau of Maj-Gen Basil Douglas Jones, CB, CBE, of Sutton Courtenay, Berks, and has issue:

1e *Christopher John Henry; *b* 13 Jan 1961

2e *Anthony Martin Edward; *b* 29 Oct 1962

2d *Alda Mary [Mrs John Mousley, Norleigh House, Widecombe-in-the-Moor, Devon TQ13 7TF]; *b* 27 Nov 1933; *m* 16 June 1962 *John Charles Allday Mousley and has issue:

1e *Peter John Hunter; *b* 2 June 1963; *m* 1991 *Jacqueline Frances Shelbourne and has:

1f *Thomas Barnanbas Hunter; *b* 1996

1e *Claire Alda Louisa [Mrs Neil Polley, Grantsfield, Kimbolton, Hunts]; *b* 12 Nov 1964; *m* 1987 *Lt-Col Neil Guy Trepess Polley, King's Roy Hus, and has:

1f *Lucy Alda Elspeth; *b* 1991

2f *Alicia Charlotte Oenone; *b* 1994

1b Evelyn Sophia; *d* 13 Aug 1867

2b Norah Lillian Augusta; *m* 9 Dec 1914 Francis Herbert Awdry (*d* 9 Jan 1951), of Brynteg, Towyn, Merioneths, 3rd s of Rev Walter Herbert Awdry, and *d* 7 Oct 1951

2a Charles Arthur Richard, of Hall Place, Hants; *b* 18 May 1847; *m* 17 July 1867 Margaret (*d* 7 Oct 1899), yst dau of Francis Baring Short, of Bickham, Devon, and *d* 22 May 1908, having had issue:

1b Hugh Richard Francis; *b* 13 April 1868; *d* 9 Nov 1880

2b Wilfrid Arthur Richard; *b* 17 March 1876; *m* 15 June 1915 Helen Adria, only dau of Col Harry Hepenstall Rose Heath, CB, of Devon, and *d* 1971, leaving issue:

1c +Richard Michael St George; *b* 23 April 1918; *m* 15 Jan 1947 *Gladys Margaret Tyzack and has issue:

1d +Richard Charles; *b* 21 Oct 1947; *m* 19– *Helen — and has issue:

1e +Michael John; *b* 19–

2d +Nigel; *b* 26 Aug 1949

3d +John Michael; *b* 3 Sept 1950

1c *Jacquetta Adria Margaret [Mrs Dudley Fisher, Sorley Farm, Kingsbridge, S Devon]; *b* 28 June 1916; *m* 1st 1940 (*divorce* 1946) Lt Terence Stafford, RAPC, and has issue:

1d *Rebecca; *b* 19–; *m* 19– — and has issue

2d *Bridget; *b* 19–

1c (cont.) Mrs Jacquetta Stafford *m* 2nd 1946 Dudley Fisher (*d* 19–) and has further issue:

1d *Noel Hugh; *b* 1949

3d *Philippa Jacquetta; *b* 1949

4d *Heather Sophia; *b* 1953

3b Reginald Arthur; *b* 13 July 1878; *m* 23 Feb 1909 Una Mildred (*d* 27 March 1951), dau of Thomas C Williams, of Wellington, NZ, and was *ka* 1918, leaving issue:

1c Merrick Colt Temple; *b* 10 Nov 1912; *d* 30 May 1917

2c +Reginald Merrick [Reginald Hoare Esq, Blue Cottage, Lower Froyle, Hants]; *b* 22 June 1918; *m* 1st 31 Aug 1950 Barbara Jean (*d* 1984), dau of Francis John Buckland (*see* MELCHETT, B); *m* 2nd 1984 *Meriel Karen, dau of Michael Gold, and by his 1st w has issue:

1d +Charles Mark; *b* 6 Sept 1961; *m* 1984 *Morag White

2d +Paul Reginald Richard; *b* 18 Aug 1963

1d *Diana Charlotte [Mrs William Taunton, 27 Longburton, nr Sherborne, Dorset]; *b* 10 Feb 1956; *m* 1978 *William Taunton and has:

1e *Matthew William; *b* 1984

1e *Rebecca Charlotte; *b* 1982

2d *Clare Githa; *b* 24 April 1958

1c *Anne Temple Githa [Mrs Vere Tweedie, Old Larkhayes, Dalwood, Axminster, Devon]; *b* 19 Jan 1916; *m* 5 June 1945 *Vere Justin Tweedie, MC, yst s of Adml Sir Hugh Justin Tweedie, KCB, JP, DL, and has issue:

1d *Simon Vere; *b* 26 May 1954

1d *Sarah Patricia; *b* 4 Feb 1947; *m* 1 June 1968 *Edward Charles Townsend, only s of R-Adml Michael Southcote Townsend, CB, DSO, OBE, DSC and bar, of Tor-y-Mynydd Farm, Devauden, Mon

2d *Amanda Jane Anne; *b* 2 Nov 1948

4b Ralph Francis; *b* 2 June 1881; *m* 3 Jan 1906 Katherine Hallen (*d* 1969), dau of R J Sumner Drinkwater, of Northbrook, Orillia, Canada, and *d* 1956, leaving:

1c Hugh John Francis; *b* 14 June 1911; *m* 1947 *Margaret Edith Williams and *d* 1979

2c +Eric Reginald; *b* 8 April 1918; *m* 9 July 1949 *Rosemary Brodie Hallowell, dau of Francis Vickerman Lumb, of Vancouver, and has:

1d +Geoffrey Charles Brodie; *b* 28 July 1953

2d +Richard Sumner Anthony; *b* 13 July 1955

1d *Wendy Pamela; *b* 3 Feb 1961; *m* 1989 *Gerald Timothy Griffin, s of James Griffin, of Edmonton, Alberta

3c +Peter Richard [Peter Hoare Esq, 204 Park St, Orillia, Ontario L3V 5V8, Canada]; *b* 1920; *m* 1960 *Beverley Jean, dau of Arthur Frederick Hessel, and has:

1d *Barbara Lynne; *b* 1965; *m* 1992 *James Arthur Orell, s of Arthur F Orell, of Toronto, and has:

1e *Conner James; *b* May 1997

2d *Deborah Katherine Jean; *b* 1969; *m* 1994 *Jeffrey Brian John Richardson, s of Brian John Aghmuty Richardson, of Pickering, Ontario

1c *Margaret Katherine Dorothy [Mrs William Gill, Apt 103-S, 412 Muskoka Rd, Orillia, Ontario L3V 6M5, Canada]; *b* 27 July 1907; *m* 1938 William Stephens Gill (*d* 1951), and has:

1d *Peter William [Peter Gill Esq, Edgewood Farm, RR2, Orillia, Ontario, Canada]; *b* 1939; *m* 1967 *Angela Patricia, dau of Ernest D Gillezeau, of St Vincent, WI, and has:

1e *Jeremy David Hallen; *b* 1968

2e *Nicholas Anton Stephens; *b* 1971

2d *Ralph John David [Ralph Gill Esq, 42 Andrea Crescent, Orillia, Ontario L3V 6W5, Canada]; *b* 1947; *m* 1976 *Marlene Elsie, dau of Hugh Doyle, of Orillia, and has:

1e *Trevor William Hugh; *b* 1981

2e *Ryan David; *b* 1984

1d *Margaret Natalie Katherine [Mrs Bruce Budd, 10534 26th Ave, Edmonton, Alberta, T6J 4B9, Canada]; *b* 1944; *m* 1965 *Bruce Teague Budd, s of Luther H Budd, of Montreal, and has:

1e *Teague William Garth; *b* 1971
1e *Donicka Anne Evelyn; *b* 1966
2e *Tehranna Margaret Katherine; *b* 1969
2c *Natalie Kathleen Grove [Miss Natalie Hoare, Apt 412, 55 Broadway Ave, Toronto, Canada]; *b* 1915
1b Agatha Margaret Sophia; *b* 8 July 1869; *d* unm 6 Dec 1952
1a Isabella Mary; *b* 29 Nov 1840; *d* unm 27 March 1918
2a Charlotte Anne; *b* 28 May 1841; *m* 28 Jan 1863 Algernon Augustine de Lille Strickland and *d* 1890, having had issue (*see* STRICKLAND-CONSTABLE, Bt)
(1) Isabella Dorothea; *b* 12 June 1810; *m* 28 April 1852 Very Rev James Allen, Dean St David's, and *d* 18 July 1860
(2) Henrietta Ann; *b* 12 April 1812; *m* 16 June 1863 Richard Grindale Festing (*d* 16 March 1869)
(3) Sophia; *b* 13 Sept 1814; *m* 25 Aug 1842 Rev Henry Burney (*d* 16 July 1893), Rector Wavendon, Bucks, and *d* 24 Sept 1872, leaving issue
1 Henrietta Anne; *m* 1st 4 July 1785 Sir Thomas Dyke Acland, 9th Bt, of Columb John (*qv*), and had issue; *m* 2nd 6 June 1795 Capt Hon Matthew Fortescue, RN, and *d* 5 Sept 1841, leaving issue (*see* FORTESCUE, E)

The 6th Bt's cousin,

Sir Peter William Hoare, 7th Bt, of Luscombe, Devon; *b* 22 July 1898; *educ* Harrow, WW I 1917–19 as Lt RGA (wounded), managing ptnr C Hoare and Co, dir Hoare Tstees and Eagle Star Insur, Life Govr Roy Soc of St George, memb Cncl Dr Barnardo's Homes; *m* 10 July 1929 Laura Ray (*d* 1992), only dau of Sir John Esplen, 1st Bt, KBE (*qv*), and *d* 29 May 1973, leaving issue:
1 Sir PETER RICHARD DAVID HOARE, **8th and present Bt**
2 +DAVID JOHN [David Hoare Esq, Luscombe Castle, Dawlish, S Devon]; *b* 8 Oct 1935; *educ* Eton; *m* 1st 20 April 1965 (*divorce* 1978) Mary Vanessa, yst dau of Peter Gordon Cardew, of Westhanger, Cleeve, Somerset; *m* 2nd 1984 *Virginia Victoria Labes, dau of Michael Menzies, of Long Island, NY, and by his 1st w has issue:
(1) +Simon Merrick; *b* 11 Oct 1967

HOBART

Arms: Quarterly, 1st, sable an estoile of six rays or between two flaunches ermine (for HOBART); 2nd, argent a saltire gules between four eagles displayed azure (for HAMPDEN); 3rd, argent three battering-rams fesswise in pale proper, armed and garnished azure (for BERTIE); 4th, quarterly gules and or, in the 1st quarter a mullet argent (for VERE). **Crest:** A bull statant per pale sable and gules bezanté, in his nose a ring or. **Motto:** *Auctor pretiosa facit* ('The giver makes the gift valuable'). **Creation:** Bt. (UK) 14 July 1914.

SIR JOHN VERE HOBART, 4TH Bt, of Langdown, Southampton [Sir John Hobart Bt, Shore End, 63 Queen's Rd, Cowes, IoW PO31 8BW]; *b* 9 April 1945; *s* f 1988; heir presumptive to Earldom of Buckinghamshire (*qv*); *m* 1980 *Kate, only dau of George Henry Iddles, of Cowes, and has issue:
1 +GEORGE HAMPDEN; *b* 10 June 1982
2 +James Henry Miles; *b* 1986

Lineage: The 3rd EARL OF BUCKINGHAMSHIRE (*qv*); had a 4th s:

Very Rev HENRY LEWIS HOBART; DD; had an er s:

Sir Robert Henry Hobart, 1st Bt (UK), so *cr* 14 July 1914, KCVO (1902), CB (1885), JP (Middx, London and Hants), DL (Middx); *b* 13 Sept 1836; *educ* Cambridge (LLB); civ serv War Office 1860–1900, Sec to Earl Marshal for Coronation (coronation medal) 1902, Gold Staff Offr Coronation 1911 (coronation medal), MP (Lib) New Forest 1906–10, Official Verderer New Forest 1907–28; *m* 13 May 1869 Hon Julia Trollope (*d* 11 Aug 1931), er dau of 1st Baron Kesteven (*see* TROLLOPE, Bt), and *d* 4 Aug 1928, having had, with a dau (Irene Marguerite, SSStJ, Coronation Medal 1902, served BRC Serbia 1915, Serbian Order Mercy and Red Cross Medal, *d* unm 7 Nov 1961 aged 89):

Sir (Claud) Vere Cavendish Hobart, 2nd Bt, DSO, OBE, JP (London and Hants), DL (Hants and IoW); *b* 12 March 1870; Lt-Col cmdg 8th Bn Hants Regt, Maj Gren Gds, Uganda 1897–99 (despatches, medal with clasp), DAAG S African Field Force 1899–1900 (medal with clasp), Staff BEF WW I (despatches three times, 1914 Star, two medals), CD WW II, Gold Staff Offr 1902 and 1911 Coronations; *m* 1st 10 Dec 1900 Violet Verve, MBE, Medaille de la Reine Elisabeth (*d* 28 Jan 1935), 2nd dau and coheir of John Wylie, of West Cliff Hall, Hants; *m* 2nd 18 April 1936 Lois Anne (*d* 15 May 1947), est dau of Rev Albert Popham, of Ilfracombe, and *d* 29 Nov 1949, leaving by his 1st w:

Sir Robert Hampden Hobart, 3rd Bt; JP (1954); *b* 7 May 1915 (HRH THE PRINCESS BEATRICE stood sponsor); *educ* Wixenford and RNC Dartmouth; Lt-Cdr RN WW II (wounded), invalided 1950, CC IoW 1950; *m* 1st 10 Sept 1942 Sylvia Laughton (*d* 25 May 1965), only dau of Henry Airth Argo, of Durban; *m* 2nd 1975 *Caroline Fleur [Dowager Lady Hobart, The Boat House, Cowes, IoW], yr dau of Col Henry Monckton, artist, and widow of (a) 11th Duke of Leeds (*see* 1963 edn) and (b) Peter Hendrick Peregrine Hoos (*see* BROWNLOW, B), and *d* 1988, leaving by his 1st w:
1 Sir JOHN VERE HOBART, **4th and present Bt**
2 +Robert Henry [Robert Hobart Esq, 12 Brunswick Gdns, London W8]; *b* 2 July 1948; *educ* Harrow; *m* 19– *Diana (Baba), only dau of Archibald Trevor Parker (*see* MACCLESFIELD, E), and has:
(1) *Sophie Camilla; *b* 26 June 1978
(2) *Jessica; *b* 1980
3 +Anthony Hampden; *b* 24 Jan 1956; *m* 1985 *Katherine Anne, 3rd dau of Robert Noel Willis Fleming, of Acorn Hse, St Helens, IoW, and has issue:
(1) *Charles Hampden; *b* 1986
1 *Penelope Diana; *b* 5 Dec 1954; *m* 1979 *Robert Maunsell Hunter-Jones, s of Michael Hunter-Jones, of Burmington House, Shipston-on-Stour, Warwicks

HOBHOUSE

Arms: Per pale azure and gules three crescents argent, issuant therefrom as many estoiles irradiated or. **Crest:** Out of a mural crown per pale azure and gules an estoile irradiated as in the arms. **Motto:** *Spes vitæ melioris* ('The hope of a better life'). **Creation:** Bt. (UK) 22 Dec 1812.

SIR CHARLES JOHN SPINNEY HOBHOUSE, 7TH BT, of Broughton-Gifford, Bradford-on-Avon, and Monkton Farleigh, Wilts [Sir Charles Hobhouse Bt, The Manor, Monkton Farleigh, Wilts BA15 2QE]; *b* 27 Oct 1963; *s* f 1991; *educ* Eton; *m* 1993 *Katrina, dau of Maj-Gen Sir Denzil Macarthur-Onslow, CBE, DSO, ED (*see* ONSLOW, E)

Lineage: JOHN HOBHOUSE, whose family originated in Drewsteignton, Devon, but settled at Minehead, Somerset; *m* Ann Madox (*bur* 8 Feb 1722), of Norton in Gower, Glamorgan, and was *bur* 11 July 1711, leaving:

BENJAMIN HOBHOUSE, of Minehead; *bapt* 14 Dec 1682; *m* Mary Spragge (*bur* 10 Oct 1745) and was *bur* 4 Feb 1748/9, leaving:
1 JOHN
2 Henry, of Clifton; ancestor of Baron Hobhouse of Hadspen (*see* 1904 edn)
1 Betty; *m* John Maidman

The er s,

JOHN HOBHOUSE, of Westbury College, Glos; *b* 1712; *m* 1st Mary Medley, of Hereford (*d* 1759), widow of — Smith; *m* 2nd 30 Oct 1761 Susannah Gwatkin (*dsp* 29 June 1789) and *d* 21 May 1787, having had, with an er s (Isaac, *m* 1st 10 Nov 1791 Mary (*d* 1803), dau of George Hardwick; *m* 2nd 5 April 1807 Mary, dau of William Royston, and *d* 29 Sept 1810):

Sir Benjamin Hobhouse, 1st Bt (UK), so *cr* 22 Dec 1812, of Chantry House, Bradford-on-Avon, Wilts; *b* 29 March 1757; barrister, MP Bletchingley 1797, Grampound 1802 and Hendon 1806–18, Ch Sec Bd Control India 1801–03 and 1808–07; *m* 1st 12 Sept 1785 Charlotte (*d* 25 Nov 1791), dau and heir of Samuel Cam, of Chantry House, Bradford-on-Avon, Wilts, and *d* 15 Aug 1831, having had, with a dau (*d* unm):
1 **Sir John Cam Hobhouse, 2nd Bt**, and 1st and last BARON BROUGHTON OF BROUGHTON-DE-GYFFORD, Wilts, so *cr* 26 Feb 1851, GCB (1852), PC (1832); *b* 27 June 1786; *educ* Westminster and Trin Coll Cambridge (where a friend of Byron's; *see* BYRON, B); MP (radical, later Whig/Lib) Westminster 1820–33, Nottingham 1938–47 and Harwich 1849–51, Sec for War 1832–33, Ch Sec Ireland 1835, 1st Commr Woods and Forests 1834, Pres Bd Control 1835–41 and

1846–52, FRS 1814, ptnr Whitbread & Co, brewers; *m* 28 July 1828 Lady Julia Hay (*d* 3 April 1835), yst dau of 7th Marquess of Tweeddale (*qv*), and *d* 3 June 1869, when the Barony expired, having had:

(1) Julia Hay; *d* unm 5 Sept 1849

(2) Charlotte; *m* 27 July 1854 4th and last Baron Dorchester (*see* 1897 edn) and *d* 11 June 1914

(3) Sophia; *m* 31 July 1851 5th Earl of Roden (*qv*) and *d* 3 Dec 1916, leaving issue

2 Benjamin; Capt 69th Regt; *k* Waterloo 18 June 1815

3 Henry William; HEICS; *b* 8 Aug 1791; MP Hereford 1841; *m* 1814 Mary Anne (*d* 14 Dec 1879), dau of John Palmer, of Calcutta, and *d* 22 May 1868, having had, with other issue:

(1) John Byron; *b* 29 March 1817; Lt 13th Light Inf; *ka* Afghanistan Jan 1842

(2) CHARLES PARRY (Sir), **3rd Bt**

Sir Benjamin *m* 2nd 18 April 1793 Amelia (*d* Jan 1880), dau of Rev Joshua Parry and aunt of Sir Edward Parry, and by her had, with seven daus:

4 Edward Isaac; *b* 12 April 1804; Capt Coldstream Gds, Priv Sec to his half-bro 1st and last BARON BROUGHTON, at War Office, Irish Office and Bd Control, Gentleman Usher to HM QUEEN VICTORIA; *m* 4 Jan 1832 Hester Charlotte (*d* 30 Jan 1880), 4th surv dau of 2nd Baron Graves (*qv*), and *d* 16 May 1854, leaving:

(1) Edward Augustus Stewart; *b* 23 April 1833; *m* 1st 19 Sept 1882 Elizabeth (*dsp* 5 May 1891), dau of George Samuel Norris, of Brighton; *m* 2nd 22 Sept 1892 Florence Mary Augusta (*m* 2nd 11 Aug 1909 Capt Sir Philip Arthur Sambrooke Crawley, 4th Bn Lancs Fus (*d* 30 May 1933), and *d* 6 May 1936), dau of Hon Adolphus Edward Page Graves (*see* GRAVES, B), and *dsp* 3 Aug 1908

5 Thomas Benjamin; *b* 19 June 1807; MP Rochester 1837–41 and Lincoln 1848–52, barrister; *d* unm 31 Dec 1876

1 Catherine; *m* 30 Nov 1826 Lt-Col John William Fane (*d* 19 Nov 1875) JP, DL, DCL, MP Wormsley, Oxon, est s of John Fane, DCL, MP Wormsley, and *d* 6 Nov 1828, leaving issue

2 Joanna; *m* 10 June 1834 Rev Frederick Adrian Fane, 2nd s of John Fane (*see* WESTMORLAND, E), and *d* 8 April 1878, leaving issue

The 2nd Bt's n,

Sir Charles Parry Hobhouse, 3rd Bt, JP (Wilts and Somerset); *b* 2 Jan 1825; Bengal CS 1844–72, Judge High Court Calcutta 1867–70; *m* 1st 15 Jan 1855 Edith Lucy (*d* 7 Dec 1867), yr dau of Sir Thomas Turton, 2nd Bt, of Felcourt, and *d* 30 Dec 1916, having had issue:

1 **Sir Charles Edward Henry Hobhouse, 4th Bt**, TD, PC, JP (Wilts); *b* 30 June 1862; CC Wilts 1891–1919, MP (Lib) E Wilts 1892–95 and E Bristol 1900–18, Assist Priv Sec to Parly U-Sec Colonies 1892–95, Ch Estates Commr 1906–07, Parly U-Sec India 1907–08, Fin Sec Treasury 1908–11, Chllr Duchy Lancaster 1911–14, PMG 1914–15, Hon Col and Lt-Col cmdg 6th Bn Glos Regt, Capt 7th Bn KRRC, Lt 60th Rifles; *m* 1st 24 April 1890 Georgina Fleetwood (*d* 17 Dec 1927), only dau of George Pargiter Fuller (*see* FULLER, Bt); *m* 2nd 18 June 1931 Aimee Gladys (*d* 7 Dec 1965), widow of Benjamin Adams Brendon, ICS, and 2nd dau of David Charles Ballinger Griffith, of Huntworth, Beds, and *dsp* 26 June 1941

1 Ethel Mary; *b* 5 July 1856; *m* 8 Aug 1877 Sir Charles Edmund Fox, KCSI (*d* 9 Oct 1918), Ch Justice Lower Burma, and *d* 25 Feb 1945

2 Ada Margaret; *b* 12 Nov 1857; *m* 15 Feb 1886 William Lloyd Thomas (*d* 19 Oct 1929), of Tredilion Park, Mon, and *d* 3 Sept 1931, leaving issue

3 Florence Evelyn; *b* 21 Aug 1859; *d* unm 27 Dec 1902

4 Edith Amy; *b* 11 Nov 1864; *m* 5 Sept 1911 Edward Lewis Agassiz (*d* 23 Sept 1933), of Chelmsford, and *d* 13 Oct 1938

5 Constance Eleanor; *b* 10 May 1866; *m* Sept 1891 Sigismund Raynor Arthur and *d* 27 Oct 1947, leaving issue (*see* ARTHUR, Bt)

6 Mabel Ella; *b* 31 July 1867; *d* unm 15 Sept 1940

Sir Charles *m* 2nd 9 Sept 1868 Anna Maria (*d* 13 May 1923), 3rd dau of Alexander Sawers, of Calcutta, and *d* 1916, having by her had:

2 REGINALD ARTHUR HOBHOUSE (Sir), **5th Bt**

7 Lilian Jane; *b* 21 Aug 1869; *m* 17 Jan 1900 James Thornton, JP (*d* 31 March 1939), 4th s of John Thornton, of Petrograd, Russia, and *d* 1 Dec 1953, leaving issue

8 Mary Fitzroy; *b* 6 June 1871; *m* 18 April 1900 Maj Hugh Cochrane Mactier (*d* 19 May 1940), Hants Regt, and *d* 25 Oct 1943, leaving issue

9 Ina Millicent; *b* 17 May 1873; *d* unm 16 Sept 1947

10 Annie Violet; *b* 8 May 1875; *d* unm 16 Sept 1903

The 4th Bt's half-bro,

Sir Reginald Arthur Hobhouse, 5th Bt, JP (Somerset); *b* 4 May 1878; High Sheriff 1932, Coronation Medal 1937, Chm Somerset War Ag Exec Ctee; *m* 26 April 1905 Marjorie Chisholm, JP (*d* 18 March 1967 aged 89), est dau of Frederick Spencer, of Somerset, and *d* 9 July 1947, leaving issue:

1 CHARLES CHISHOLM HOBHOUSE (Sir), **6th Bt**

2 +John Spencer, AFC [John Hobhouse Esq AFC, Farleigh Court, Farleigh Hungerford, Somerset]; *b* 15 Nov 1910 *educ* Eton; S/Ldr RAFVR WW II; *m* 29 May 1940 Mary (*d* 1991), dau of Dr Llewelyn Roberts, of Porthcawl

3 Benjamin Arthur; *b* 25 April 1914; *educ* Bryanston; Lt Somerset LI WW II; *m* 14 Nov 1942 Valeria Cuthbertson (*d* 1990), yst dau of Dr John Cuthbertson Walker, of Barnwell, Troon, Ayrshire, and *d* 1970, leaving:

(1) +John Cam; *b* 25 June 1947; *educ* privately; *m* 1971 (*divorce* 1982) Mary Angela Deakins, dau of Arthur George Newton, and has:

1a *Thomasina

2a *Louise

(1) *Carol Ann [Mrs George Rogers, 35 Sunnyhill Rd, Salisbury, Wilts SP1 3QJ]; *b* 12 Oct 1943; *m* 18 June 1964 *George Rogers and has:

1a *Bruce Andrew; *b* 29 Aug 1967

4 Hugh Cam; *b* 11 Sept 1917; *educ* Eton; Maj N Somerset Yeo (TA) WW II; *m* 1st 5 Sept 1939 (*divorce* 1947) Diana, 2nd dau of Philip George, and had issue:

(1) +Mark Cam; *b* 24 June 1940; *educ* Eton; Lt RAC; *m* 1975 *Stephanie, dau of Capt K E Buxton, and has:

1a +Benjamin Alexander Cam; *b* 1979

1a +Matthew Jack; *b* 1979

4 (cont.) Hugh Hobhouse *m* 2nd 1949 (*divorce* 1965) Aline Rosemary, only dau of Lt-Col David Walter Hunter Blair (*see* HUNTER BLAIR, Bt) and formerly w of Lt-Col David Theodor Dobie, DSO, Parachute Regt, and by her had:

(2) +James Charles; *b* 15 Sept 1951; *educ* Millfield; *m* 1974 *Sarah, dau of David Sladen, and has issue:

1a *Rebecca Sarah; *b* 1980

2a *Nicola; *b* 19–

(3) +Martin Hugh John; *b* 6 May 1955; *educ* Eton; *m* 1981 *Julia Isobel, dau of Dr David Andrew Young Craig, and has issue:

1a +Hugh; *b* 19–

2a +Alexander; *b* 1986

1a +George; *b* 1991

1a *A dau; *b* 19–

(1) *Julia Mary; *b* 26 Sept 1956; *m* 1985 *Henry G Buckmaster and has issue:

1a *(Eleanor) Rose; *b* 1986

2a *Camellia Aline; *b* 1988

3a *Lily Henrietta; *b* 1990

4 (cont.) Hugh Hobhouse; *m* 3rd 7 May 1965 *Judy Margaret, only dau of J D Tisdall, of Butcombe, Somerset, and *d* 1987, leaving by her:

(2) *Sophia; *b* 28 May 1967

1 Mary Elspeth; *b* 30 Nov 1908; *m* 24 June 1930 Lt-Col Hon Alexander Burdett Money-Coutts, OBE, 2nd s of 6th Baron Latymer (*qv*), and has issue

2 *Audrey [Mrs Audrey Firbank, Old Mill, Bourton, Gillingham, Dorset]; *b* 12 Nov 1912; *m* 20 Nov 1934 (*divorce* 1952) Maj-Gen Cecil Llewellin Firbank, CB, CBE, DSO, Somerset LI (*d* 1985), 2nd s of Godfrey Firbank, of Aldwick Court, Wrington, Somerset, and has issue:

(1) *Simon Christopher; *b* 8 June 1937; *educ* Wellington and RMA Sandhurst; Lt Somerset and Cornwall LI; *m* 30 June 1962 (*divorce* 1988) Caroline Anne, only dau of Maj — Howard, of Cornwall, and has:

1a *Rupert; *b* 6 April 1964

2a *A son; *b* 19–

1a *Henrietta

The 5th Bt's est son,

Sir Charles Chisholm Hobhouse, 6th Bt, TD; *b* 7 Dec 1906; *educ* Eton; Hon Col N Somerset Yeo (TA), commissioned 1927, Maj WW II 1940; *m* 1st 27 Nov 1946 Mary (*d* 20 May 1955), dau of John Park, of Benton, Northumberland, and widow of Walter James Hodgson Horrocks, MC, of Salkeld Hall, Cumberland; *m* 2nd 18 July 1959 *Elspeth Jean (Jo) [Elspeth Lady Hobhouse, South Wing, The Manor, Monkton Farleigh, Wilts BA15 2QE], yr dau of Thomas George Spinney, of Mazagan, Morocco, and *d* 1991, leaving by his 1st w:

Sir CHARLES JOHN SPINNEY HOBHOUSE, **7th and present Bt**

HODGE

Arms: Sable an eagle, wings addorsed and inverted or, between three crescents argent. **Crest:** An eagle as in the arms supporting with the dexter claw an increscent argent and looking at the rays of the sun issuant from clouds proper. **Motto:** *Præmium virtutis gloria* ('Glory is the reward of virtue'). **Creation:** Bt. (UK) 3 March 1921.

SIR ANDREW ROWLAND HODGE, 3RD BT, of Chipstead, Co Kent [Sir Andrew Hodge Bt, 12 Clyde Rd, Menora, Perth, W Australia 6050, Australia]; *b* 4 Dec 1968; *s* f 19–; *educ* Stella Maria Coll Malta and Benjamin Britten High Sch Suffolk

Lineage: ROWLAND HODGE, of Newcastle (*see* WYFOLD, B); *m* Jane Cram and had a 2nd s:

JOHN ROWLAND HODGE, of Newcastle; *b* 23 Aug 1819; *m* 21 March 1857 Emily (*d* 18 March 1916), dau of Edward Dean Davis, of Newcastle, and *d* 4 July 1868, leaving, with two daus (Emily Madge, *b* 14 April 1858, *d* unm 9 July 1942; Dora Blanche, *b* 15 March 1861, *d* 4 May 1938):

Sir Rowland Frederic William Hodge, 1st Bt (UK), so *cr* 3 March 1921; *b* 15 Sept 1859; fndr Northumberland Shipbuilding Co, chm Eltringham's; *m* 1st 28 March 1895 Mabel (*d* 10 Aug 1923), dau of William Edward Thorpe; *m* 2nd 30 Sept 1930 *Vera Estelle, dau of John Fraser, of Cape Town, formerly w of 5th Earl Cathcart (*qv*) and previously widow of Capt Henry de Grey Warter, 4th Dragoon Gds, and *d* 21 Sept 1950, leaving by his 1st w :

1 JOHN ROWLAND HODGE (Sir), **2nd Bt**

2 Peter Rowland; *b* 24 Oct 1915; 2nd Commando Bde; *m* 1st 5 May 1940 (*divorce* 1945) Mia, yr dau of Sir Noel Campbell Macklin; *m* 2nd 12 July 1951 *Margaret Norma, dau of Harold Plow, of Broadway, Barnton, Cheshire, and *d* 1982, leaving by her:

(1) *Jacqueline Jane [Mrs Richard Jesse, Copyhold Cottage, Lock Lane, Partridge Green, W Sussex RH13 8EF]; *b* 1954; *m* 1991 *Richard A D Jesse and has issue:

1a *Lawrence Rowland; *b* 1992

2a *Alexander Peter; *b* 27 July 1995

1a *Ellena Joy; *b* 27 July 1995

(2) *Bridgitte Michele; *b* 1956; *m* 1989 *Patrick L Field

1 Margaret Viola; *b* 16 July 1908; *m* 1st 11 June 1927 Jorge Yvan Lage, est s of Jorge Lage, of Santa Cruz, Rio de Janeiro; *m* 2nd 20 April 1938 Sir Robert Spencer Isaacson, KBE, CMG, Amb Berne, and by her 1st husb had:

(1) *Elaine Margaret Elizabeth; *b* 16 July 1928; *m* 7 Feb 1951 Thomas Payne, s of Randolph de Payen Payne, of Buenos Aires, and has issue:

1a *Vivien Elizabeth Lage; *b* 20 Oct 1953

2 *Vivien Rosemary [Mrs Hugh Murton-Neale, The Old Tannery, Smallhythe Rd, Tenterden, Kent]; *b* 19 May 1911; *m* 1st 10 April 1930 (*divorce*) St John Legh Clowes (*d* 1951), only s of Capt Phillip Cecil Clowes (*see* CLANMORRIS, B); *m* 2nd 6 May 1941 *Hugh Gordon Murton-Neale, of Malta, and has by her 1st husb:

(1) *Timothy Legh; *b* 1932

(1) *Susan Carol; *b* 1935

Sir ROWLAND's est son,

Sir John Rowland Hodge, 2nd Bt, MBE (1940); *b* 1 May 1913; *educ* Wrekin Coll, FRHistS; 2nd Lt Oxon and Bucks LI, Lt-Cdr RNVR WW II; *m* 1st 1 March 1936 (*divorce* 1939) Peggy Ann, only dau of Sidney Raymond Kent, of New York; *m* 2nd 5 Dec 1939 (*divorce* 1961) Joan, only dau of Sydney Foster Wilson, and by her had:

1 *Wendy Madeleine [Mrs John Kidd, 3 Hereford Mews, London W2 5AN]; *b* 8 Nov 1941; *m* 6 July 1962 (*divorce*) Michael Dennis Whiting, only s of D R Whiting, of Grittleton, Wilts, and has issue:

(1) *Nicholas D'Arcy; *b* 29 Dec 1962

(1) *Deborah Joanna; *b* 31 Jan 1964

1 (cont.) Mrs Wendy Whiting *m* 2nd 1973 *John Edward Aitken Kidd and has further issue (*see* BEAVERBROOK, B)

2 *Sally Joan [Miss Sally Hodge, 6601 E Hummingbird Lane, Scottsdale, AZ, USA]; *b* 2 June 1943

3 *Vicki Alexandra; *b* 17 Oct 1946; *m* 4 Dec 1969 (*divorce* 1980), as his 1st w, (George) Ian Alexander Heath (*d* 1 Jan 1996), s of Sir Barry Heath, chm GKN

Sir John *m* 3rd 22 June 1962 (*divorce* 1967) Jeanne Wood Anderson, only dau of Cdr W E Buchanan, of Edinburgh; *m* 4th Nov 1967 *Vivienne, dau of Alfred Knightley, of Norwood, and *d* 19– , leaving by her:

1 Sir ANDREW ROWLAND HODGE, **3rd and present Bt**

4 *Louise Vivien [Miss Louise Hodge, PO Box F1473, Freeport, Bahamas]; *b* 13 Aug 1970

HODSON

Arms: Sable a chevron between three martlets or. **Crest:** A dove close azure, beaked and membered or, holding in the beak an olive branch proper. **Motto:** *Pax et amor* ('Peace and love'). **Creation:** Bt. (I) 28 Aug 1789.

SIR MICHAEL ROBIN ADDERLEY HODSON, 6TH BT, of Holybrooke House, Co Wicklow [Sir Michael Hodson Bt, The White House, Awbridge, Hants SO51 0HF]; *b* 5 March 1932; *s* f 1972; *educ* Eton and RMA; Capt (ret) Scots Gds; *m* 1st 16 Dec 1963 (*divorce* 1978) Katrin Alexa, dau of Erwin Bernstiel; *m* 2nd 1978 *Catherine, dau of John Henry Seymour and formerly w of Ralph Denne, and by his 1st w has issue:

1 *Tania Elizabeth; *b* 19 May 1965

2 *Alexa Adderley [Mrs Christopher Chambers, 12 Tynemouth St, London SW6]; *b* 13 July 1966; *m* 1990 *Christopher Michael Chambers, s of W M Chambers, of Chipping Camden, Glos, and has issue:

(1) *Lara Adderley; *b* 1992

(2) *Gemma Marlis; *b* 1994

3 *Jane Katrina; *b* 24 Feb 1970

Lineage: The Rt Rev JOHN HODSON; Bp Elphin; *m* Abigail, dau of Robert Madden, of Donore, Co Dublin, and *d* 14 Feb 1686, leaving, with another s:

Rev WILLIAM HODSON; Rector Annagh, Co Cavan; *m* Elizabeth Pearce, of Woburn, and had issue:

WILLIAM HODSON, of Tuitstown, Co Westmeath; *m* Mary, dau of John L'Estrange, and *d* 1713, having had, with a dau (Elizabeth):

WILLIAM HODSON; *m* Mary, dau of John Cooke, of Cookstown, Co Westmeath, and had, with a dau (Letitia, *m* Charles William Wall, of Co Waterford):

WILLIAM HODSON, of Tuitstown; *b* 1721; *m* 1st Eleanor, dau of Robert Adair, of Holybrooke, Co Wicklow, and had, with two other daus:

1 ROBERT (Sir), **1st Bt**

1 Mary; *m* 1 Jan 1765 Garrett Neville (*d* 1823), of Marymount, Co Kilkenny, and had issue

WILLIAM HODSON *m* 2nd Harriet, dau of Hartley Hutchinson, and *d* 1768, leaving by her:

2 William; *b* 1757; barrister; *m* Margaret, est dau of Andrew Armstrong, of Clara House, King's Co, and *d* 1815, leaving issue

3 Hartley, of Old Connaught; *b* 1759; *m* Elizabeth, dau of John Copley, and *d* 1839, leaving issue

The est s,

Sir Robert Hodson, 1st Bt (I), so *cr* 28 Aug 1789, of Holybrooke House, Co Wicklow; *m* 1st Anne, only dau and heiress of Forster Adair, MP, of Holybrooke, but by her had no surv issue; *m* 2nd 1799 Jane, est dau of Brent Neville, of Ashbrook, Co Dublin, and *d* 19 July 1809, having had issue, with two daus:

1 **Sir Robert Adair Hodson, 2nd Bt**; *b* 14 March 1802; *d* unm 19 Oct 1831

2 **Sir George Frederick John Hodson, 3rd Bt,** JP (Cos Dublin and Wicklow), DL (Co Wicklow); *b* 25 Oct 1806; *m* 15 Sept 1852 Meriel Anne (*d* 17 March 1906), 3rd dau of Rev Richard Neville, Rector Clonpriest, Co Cork, and *d* 2 April 1888, having had:

(1) **Sir Robert Adair Hodson, 4th Bt,** JP, DL; *b* 29 Sept 1853; Hon Col cmdg 4th Bn Roy Irish Fus; *m* 20 April 1911 Emily Frances Louisa (*d* 14 Feb 1933), yst dau of Col George John Beresford (*see* WATERFORD, M), and *d* 3 Jan 1921

(2) George Frederick John; *b* 26 Nov 1854; Lt 24th Foot; *ka* 22 Jan 1879 Zulu War

(3) Richard Edmond, of Coolfadda House, Bandon, JP Co Cork; *b* 1 Dec 1856; *educ* Trin Coll Dublin (BA); FSI; *m* 8 June 1892 Margaret (*d* 31 Aug 1950), dau of Rev Stanley Pemberton, MA, and *d* 8 July 1915, leaving:

1a EDMOND ADAIR (Sir), **5th Bt**

2a Gilbert Stanley; *b* 21 May 1895; *educ* Marlborough and Pembroke Coll Cambridge; Lt RE (TF) WW I; *m* 29 June 1948 Felicity Margaretta (*d* 2 Jan 1995), yr dau of Lt-Col Hon Claud Maitland Patrick Brabazon, OBE (*see* MEATH, E), and *d* 26 Aug 1972, leaving issue:

1b *Kathleen Margaret [Mrs Gerald Dalby, Dalbie House, Castle Donnington, Leics DE74 2PP]; *b* 9 Sept 1949; *m* 1980 *(Charles) Gerald Dalby (*see* SMILEY, Bt) and has:

1c *Edward Charles Gerald; *b* 15 Sept 1982

1c *Lucy Margaretta Hyacinthe; *b* 8 April 1981

2b *Marion Felicity; *b* 17 Oct 1951; *m* 1989 *Bruce Swanhuyser, of White Salmon, Washington, USA, and has:

1c *Robin Adair; *b* 1990

1c *Emma Paige; *b* 1993

3a +Cecil George [Cecil Hodson Esq, Crocnaran House, Kingstown, Moyard, Co Galway, Ireland]; *b* 1 Oct 1900; *educ* Uppingham; *m* 30 Jan 1934 *Betty Estelle, yst dau of Capt Arthur Jewell North, MC, of Vale Mascal, Bexley, Kent

(4) Gilbert Neville; *b* 7 Dec 1859; *m* 5 Dec 1900 Etheldreda Marjory (*d* 4 Nov 1961, having *m* 2nd 25 May 1929 Francis Montagu-Douglas-Scott; *see* BUCCLEUCH and QUEENSBERRY, D), 2nd dau of Rev Thomas Lane Coulson Bridges, Rector Warkton, Northants, and *d* 8 Nov 1918, leaving:

1a *Eva Meriel Violet; *m* 1 Jan 1927 Rev Charles Sydney Hardy (*d* 1965) and has issue

2a *Audrey Lutterell; *m* 30 Sept 1938 Dudley Charles Carew, of Gratham House, Broad Oak, Rye, Sussex

3a *Vera Constance Marjory

(1) Meriel Anne; *m* 28 Nov 1907 Markham Richard Leeson-Marshall, DL (*d* 13 Dec 1939), of Callinafercy, Co Kerry (*see* 1970 edn MILLTOWN, E), and *d* 16 May 1944

Sir ROBERT's n,

Sir Edmond Adair Hodson, 5th Bt, DSO (1917); *b* 22 March 1893; *educ* Marlborough and Trin Coll Cambridge (MA); Maj Rifle Bde (Prince Consort's Own), served WW I (despatches) and WW II; *m* 28 July 1928 Anne Elizabeth Adderley, yr dau of Lt-Col Hartopp Francis Charles Adderley Cradock, of Hill House, Sherborne St John, Hants, and *d* 7 Sept 1972, leaving issue:

1 Sir MICHAEL ROBIN ADDERLEY HODSON, **6th and present Bt**

2 +PATRICK RICHARD [Patrick Hodson Esq, Shipton Slade Farm, Woodstock, Oxford OX7 1QQ]; *b* 27 Nov 1934; *educ* Eton; heir presumptive; Capt (ret) Rifle Brigade; *m* 8 April 1961 *June, only dau of Herbert Michael Shepherd-Cross, JP, of The Old Rectory, Brandsby, Yorks, and has issue:

(1) +Mark Adair [Mark Hodson Esq, 52 Orbain Rd, London SW6]; *b* 9 April 1964; *m* 1991 *Kathleen (Kate) Mary Florence, only dau of William Rippon Bissill (*see* NUNBURNHOLME, B)

(2) +James Patrick; *b* 7 June 1966; *m* 1993 *Fiona Marion, 2nd dau of Michael Herbert Johnson-Ferguson (*see* JOHNSON-FERGUSON, Bt), and has:

1a +George Patrick; *b* 3 July 1996

1a *Flora Anne; *b* 4 March 1998

(3) +Rupert Edward; *b* 1972

HOFFMANN

Creation: B. (LP, UK) Feb 1995.

THE BARON HOFFMANN, of Chedworth, Co Gloucester (Sir Leonard Hubert Hoffmann, PC (1992) [The Rt Hon The Lord Hoffmann PC, Surrey Lodge, 23 Keats Grove, London NW3 2RS]; *b* 8 May 1934; *educ* S African Coll Sch Capetown, U of Cape Town and Queen's Coll Oxford (Hon Fell 1992); advocate S Africa Supreme Court 1958–60, barrister Gray's Inn 1964, Bencher 1984, QC 1977, Judge CI Appeal Courts 1980–85, High Court Judge Chancery 1985–92, ktd 1985, Ld Justice of Appeal 1992–95, a Ld of Appeal in Ordinary 1995–, non-perm Judge Hong Kong Court Final Appeal 1998–; Pres Br-German Jurists Assoc 1991–, Hon DCL City U 1992 and UWE 1995; *m* 1957 *Gillian Lorna Sterner and has two daus

Lineage: B W HOFFMANN; *m* G — and had:

LEONARD HUBERT (Sir), *cr* a **Baron**

HOGG, Baroness

Creation: B. (LP, UK) 1995.

THE BARONESS HOGG, of Kettlethorpe, Co Lincoln (The Hon Sarah Elizabeth Mary Boyd-Carpenter) [The Rt Hon The Baroness Hogg, House of Lords, London SW1A 0PW]; *b* 14 May 1946; *educ* St Mary's Convent Ascot and LMH Oxford (Hon Fell 1994); edtl staff *Economist* 1967 (lit ed 1970, econmics ed 1977), economics ed *Sunday Times* 1981, presenter Channel 4 News 1982–83, economics ed and dep exec ed fin and indust *The Times* 1984–86, assist ed and business and city ed *Independent* 1986–89, economics ed *Daily Telegraph* and *Sunday Telegraph* 1989–90, head PM's Policy Unit 1990–95; dir LSE 1995–, F&C Smaller Cos Investment Tst 1995–, Nat Provident Instn 1996–, Internat Advsy Bd Natwest Bank 1995–, Advsy Bd Bankinter 1995–; memb Ho Lds Select Ctee Sci and Tech 1996–; Fell Eton 1996–, Hon MA OU 1987, Hon DLitt Loughborough 1992; author: *Too Close to Call* (with Jonathan Hill, 1995); *m* 1968 *Rt Hon Douglas Hogg, QC (*see* HAILSHAM OF ST MARYLEBONE, B) and has issue

Lineage: *See* BOYD-CARPENTER, B

HOGG, Bt

Arms: Arg. three boar's heads erased az., langued gu., between two flaunches of the second, each charged with a crescent of the field. **Crest:** Out of an eastern crown arg. an oak tree fructed ppr., pendant therefrom an escutcheon az., charged with a dexter arm embowed in armour, the hand grasping an arrow in bend sinister, point downwards, also ppr. **Motto:** *Dat gloria vires* ('Glory gives strength').

Creations: Bt. (UK) 20 July 1846.

SIR MICHAEL DAVID HOGG, 8TH BT, of Upper Grosvenor Street, Co Middx [Sir Michael Hogg Bt, 19 Woodlands Road, London SW13 0JZ]; *b* 19 Aug 1925; *s f* 1995; *educ* Sherborne and Ch Ch Oxford (BA 1950, MA 1953); Capt Gren Gds WW II, late jnlst with *Daily Telegraph*; *m* 21 Jan 1956 *Elizabeth Anne Thérèse, est dau of Lt-Col Sir Terence Edmond Patrick Falkiner, 8th Bt (*qv*), and has:

1 +PIERS MICHAEL JAMES [Piers Hogg Esq, 49 Bramley Rd, London W5 4QT]; *b* 25 April 1957; *m* 1982 (*divorce* 1996) Vivien, yr dau of Dr Philip Holman, of Kew, Surrey, and has:

(1) +James Edward; *b* 11 Sept 1985

(1) *Sarah Alice; *b* 1988

2 +Adam Charles; *b* 9 Aug 1958; *m* 1987 *Alison Pauline, dau of Nicholas Selby, of Putney, and has:

(1) +Daniel Richard; *b* 1988

(1) *Madeleine Victoria; *b* 1989

3 +Oliver John; *b* 27 June 1961

Lineage: WILLIAM HOGG, of Lisburn, Co Antrim, whither he migrated from Scotland or Northern England late 17th century; *m* 1st 1677 Mary Podefield; *m* 2nd 11 June 1680 Elizabeth Wilson and *d* 1716, having by her had, with two yr sons (James; Jacob):

WILLIAM HOGG; *m* 1718 Abigail Higginbothom and *d* 1726, leaving:

1 William; *m* 1766 Esther, dau of Rev John O'Neill, of Largy, and had issue

2 EDWARD

3 James; *m* 1 Feb 1764 Mary (*d* 1818 aged 88), yr dau of Jonathan Greer, of Redford, Co Tyrone, and *d* 23 Aug 1781, leaving issue

1 Ruth; *m* John Richardson (*d* 1759), of Eagerlougher, Co Armagh, and had issue

The 2nd son,

EDWARD HOGG, of Lisburn; *b* 1722; *m* 1752 Rose (*d* 30 June 1813 aged 102), dau of Rev John O'Neill, of Largy, and *d* 1809, leaving issue:

1 WILLIAM

2 James; *b* 1756; *m* 3 Oct 1822 Mary (*d* 13 June 1828), dau of Jacob Hancock, of Lisburn, and *dsp* 9 May 1847

1 Abigail; *b* 1757; *m* John Bolton, of Wexford, and *d* 28 Oct 1846, leaving issue

2 Mary; *b* 1764; *m* John Barnett, of Belfast, and *dsp* 28 Feb 1856

The er son,

WILLIAM HOGG; *b* 1754; *m* 31 Dec 1783 Mary (*d* 28 Feb 1856 aged 92), dau of James Dickey, of Dunmore, Co Antrim, and *d* 25 July 1824, leaving issue:

1 JAMES (Sir), **1st Bt**

2 Charles; *b* 8 Jan 1799; *m* 1st 1825 Lucy (*d* 1827), dau of Ralph Marshall, of Ballymcadam, Co Kerry, and had issue; *m* 2nd 11 Dec 1831 Louise Fleming (*d* 4 July 1882), dau of William Trower, and *d* 5 Oct 1873, leaving further issue

1 Mary; *b* 1703; *d* unm

2 Clara; *b* 1795; *m* 1820 Dr Alexander Jaffrey Nicholson and *d* 17 Feb 1874, leaving issue

3 Rosina; *b* 1797; *m* 1st 21 Jan 1826 Edward Maxwell (*dsp* 19 Aug 1826), of Ballyroley; *m* 2nd Dr William Thompson and had issue

4 Lily Anne Maria; *b* 1801; *m* 1st 1821 Augustus Charles Floyer (*dsp* 21 Aug 1832); *m* 2nd 14 Jan 1837 James Robert Campbell and had issue by him

The er son,

Sir James Weir Hogg, 1st Bt (UK), so *cr* 20 July 1846, PC (1872); barrister, Registrar Supreme Court and V-Admlty Court Calcutta 1815–33, MP (C) Beverley 1834–47 and Honiton 1847, Dir HEIC Sept 1839 (twice chm), memb Indian Cncl; *b* 7 Sept 1790; *m* 26 July 1822 Mary Claudine (*d* 26 June 1874), 2nd dau of Samuel Swinton, HEICS, of Swinton, Berwicks, and *d* 27 May 1876, having had:

1 Sir JAMES MACNAGHTEN HOGG later McGAREL-HOGG (roy licence 8 Feb 1877 under terms of will of his bro-in-law, Charles McGarel, of Magheramorne, Co Antrim), **2nd Bt**, and 1st BARON MAGHERAMORNE OF MAGHERAMORNE, Co Antrim (UK), so *cr* 5 July 1887, KCB (1874); *b* 3 May 1823; *educ* Eton and Ch Ch Oxford; chm Metropolitan Bd of Works 1870–89, Lt-Col 1st Life Gds, MP (C) Bath 1865–68, Truro 1871–85 and Hornsey 1885–87; *m* 31 Aug 1857 Hon Caroline Elizabeth Emma Douglas Pennant (*d* 1 June 1924), est dau of 1st Baron Penrhyn (*qv*), and *d* 27 June 1890, leaving:

(1) **Sir James Douglas McGarel-Hogg, 3rd Bt**, and 2nd BARON MAGHERAMORNE OF MAGHERAMORNE; *b* 16 Jan 1861; Lt Derbyshire Yeo Cav, Capt 1st Life Gds, ADC to Ld Lt Ireland; *m* 23 Oct 1889 Lady Evelyn Harriet Ashley (*m* 2nd 1 March 1905 Hon Hugh Baring (*see* REVELSTOKE, B) and *d* 22 Jan 1931), 2nd dau of 8th Earl of Shaftesbury (*qv*), and *d* 10 March 1903, leaving:

1a Norah Evelyn; *b* 1 Sept 1890; *m* 7 June 1919 (*divorce* 1933) Lt-Col Edward Julian GROVES later McGAREL-GROVES (deed poll 22 March 1926), DSO, MC, Scots Gds, 2nd s of Col John Edward Trimble Groves, CMG, TD, JP, and *d* 30 Jan 1967, leaving issue

(2) **Sir Dudley Stuart McGarel-Hogg, 4th Bt**, and 3rd BARON MAGHERAMORNE OF MAGHERAMORNE; *b* 3 Dec 1863; *educ* Radley; *d* unm 14 March 1946

(3) **Sir Ronald Tracy McGarel-Hogg, 5th Bt**, and 4th and last BARON MAGHERAMORNE OF MAGHERAMORNE; *b* 28 July 1865; *d* unm 21 April 1957, when the Barony expired

(4) Archibald Campbell; chartered architect; *b* 21 Sept 1866; *d* unm 10 Feb 1945

(5) Gerald Francis; Lt 4th Bn Royal Welch Fus, WW I as Lt and Assist Adj10th County of London Vol Regt, Hon Lt 1920; *b* 6 Aug 1868; *educ* Eton; *d* unm 29 June 1942

(1) Edith Mary; *b* 25 May 1859; *m* 3 Aug 1881 Hon Arthur Saumarez (*d* 14 Aug 1933), 2nd surv s of 3rd Baron de Saumarez (*qv*), and *d* 31 Aug 1939, having had issue

2 Charles; Administrator-Gen Bengal; *b* 3 Oct 1824; *m* 29 Dec 1860 Harriet Anne (*d* 6 April 1919), yr dau of Sir Walter George Stirling, 2nd Bt, and *d* 16 March 1870, leaving issue:

(1) Guy Weir, JP; Sheriff St Helena, Consul there for Portugal, Sweden and Norway, V-Consul for Russia, Actg Consul for Germany and Denmark, Br V-Consul at Monaco, md SA Advertising Contractors, Cape Town, gen manager Uganda Co, twice Pres Uganda Chamber of Commerce; *b* 24 Oct 1861; *m* 8 Nov 1892 Constance Piercy (*d* 1 Jan 1920), est dau of Henry Joseph Marsden, and *d* 5 April 1943, leaving issue:

1a **Sir Kenneth Weir Hogg, 6th Bt**, OBE (1946); Lt-Col Irish Gds WW I (wounded), ret 1933, re-employed 1939, AAG Directorate Recruiting and Demobilisation War Office 1941; *b* 13 Sept 1894; *educ* Haileybury and Ch Ch Oxford; *m* 11 June 1936 Hon Aline Emily Partington, only dau of 2nd Baron Doverdale (*see* 1949 edn), and *dsp* 1985

1a Maybird later Mavis Constance (deed poll 20 Nov 1930), JP Middx 1935; MP W Willesden 1931–35 and Frome 1935–45; *b* 17 Aug 1893; *m* 1st 9 Aug 1915 (*divorce* 1925) Capt Gerald Ewart Gott (*d* 26 July 1966), Beds Regt, er s of Col George Arthur Gott, of Will Hall, Alton, Hants; *m* 2nd 22 Aug 1925 (*divorce* 1944) Capt Henry Burton Tate (*see* TATE, Bt), and *d* 5 June 1947

(2) Ernest Charles, RN; *b* 12 June 1863; *m* 16 Aug 1893 Lucy (*d* 29 June 1924), 3rd dau of William Felton Peel, of Wistaston Hall, Cheshire, and *d* 2 April 1907, leaving issue:

1a **Sir Arthur Ramsay Hogg, 7th Bt**, MBE (1945); *b* 24 Oct 1896; *educ* Sherborne and Ch Ch Oxford (BA 1921, MA 1929); Capt 7th Bn QO Roy W Kent Regt WW I (wounded twice), WW II as Maj Gen List; *m* 28 Feb 1924 Mary Aileen Hester Lee (*d* 1980), dau of Philip Herbert Lee Evans, and *d* 31 Oct 1995, leaving:

1b Sir MICHAEL DAVID HOGG, **8th and present Bt**

2b +Mark Arthur Philip [Mark Hogg Esq, 27 Thorncliffe Rd, Oxford OX2 7BA]; ARIC; *b* 6 March 1928; *educ* Sherborne and Ch Ch Oxford (BA 1949, BSc 1950, MA 1953); *m* 1st 1 Jan 1955 (*divorce* 1977) Jennifer Mary, dau of Michael Farrer Spurrell, of Greenhayes, Reigate, Surrey; *m* 2nd 1977 *Jane Margaret, dau of Rev Alan James Sutherland Symon and formerly w of David R Lawrence, and by his 1st w has:

1c +Stephen Mark; *b* 16 April 1960; *m* 1986 *Deborah, er dau of Cyril Skipworth, and has issue:

1d *Charlotte Katherine; *b* 1988

1c *Philippa Mary; *b* 13 May 1956; *m* 1979 *Jeremy James Leon and has:

1d *Frances Clare; *b* 1983

2d *Nicola Robyn; *b* 1987

2c *Sally Elizabeth; *b* 5 June 1958; *m* 1985 *Simon Hamling

3c *Nicola Frances; *b* 20 Nov 1962

3b +Simon Charles [Simon Hogg Esq, Meadow Cottage, Church St, Beckley, Oxon OX3 9UT]; *b* 20 June 1936; *educ* privately; Alan Nabarro medal 1987

1b *Anthea Aileen [Mrs Ian Carmichael, Harracott House, Harracott, N Devon]; *b* 20 June 1936; *m* 5 Oct 1957 *Ian Stewart Gordon Carmichael, s of Col D R Gordon Carmichael, and has had:

1c Donald Malcolm; *b* 11 Jan 1961; *d* 1984

1c *Alison Fiona; *b* 21 Sept 1958; *m* 1982 *Nigel J Llewelyn-Price

2c *Victoria Anthea; *b* 6 March 1966; *m* 1989 *Giles E Gordon Brown and has:

1d *Emily Megan; *b* 1991

1a Irene Constance; *b* 14 July 1898

2a Winifred Lucy; *b* 25 Nov 1903; *m* 3 June 1925 Maj Camille des Clayes, OBE (*d* 2 Aug 1966), and *d* 15 May 1959, leaving issue

(1) Mary Alice; *m* 17 Feb 1885 Col Robert George Wardlaw-Ramsay (*d* 22 April 1921), DL, of Whitehill and Tillicoutry, and *d* 15 Jan 1951, leaving issue (*see* SALTOUN, L)

(2) Violet Caroline Stuart; *d* unm 3 Nov 1949

3 Fergusson Floyer; Bengal CS; *b* 3 Aug 1829; *m* 18 Nov 1861 Elizabeth Helen (*d* 5 Dec 1862), est dau of Hon Laurence Parsons (*see* ROSSE, E), and *dsp* 19 Dec 1862

4 Stuart Saunders (Sir); ktd, Bengal CS 1853–78, chm Magistrates Calcutta 1866, Commr Police Calcutta, MLC Bengal 1874–78; *b* 17 Feb 1833; *m* 27 Dec 1860 Selina Catherine (*d* 3 March 1927), est dau of Rt Hon Sir Thomas Erskine Perry, and *d* 23 March 1921, leaving:

(1) Stuart James; *b* 6 July 1865; *educ* Winchester; *m* 9 Sept 1890 Margaret Alice (*d* 28 Nov 1943), est dau of Andrew Muir, and *d* 2 March 1947, leaving:

1a Alison Mary; *m* 26 Dec 1914 Philip Hope Edward Bagenal, CBE, DCM, FRIBA, and had issue

2a Margaret Erskine; *m* 8 Aug 1917 Lt-Col Joseph Herbert Brett, Suffolk Regt, s of Albert Charles Brett, of Exeter House, Sheerness, and had issue

(2) Alan Frederick; BA Cantab, barrister, Attorney-Gen Nyasaland Protectorate 1914–18 and Uganda Protectorate 1918, Actg Ch Sec and Dep Govr 1922; *b* 30 Oct 1868; *d* unm 6 Dec 1934

(1) Evelyn Louisa; *m* 15 April 1880 Hugh Gurney Barclay, MVO (*d* 9 March 1936), and *d* 22 Oct 1899, leaving issue

(2) Selina; *d* 1873

(3) Lucy Isabel; *m* 1st 20 Aug 1890 Maj J C Arthington Walker (*ka* 1 April 1902), 2nd Dragoon Gds; *m* 2nd 23 Aug 1918 Maj Arthur Edward John Legge (*see* DARTMOUTH, E) and *dsp* 7 Oct 1940

5 Frederick Russell (Sir), KCIE, CSI; Bengal CS 1856–89, Dir-Gen Post Office India 1882–89; *b* 29 Oct 1836; *m* 1st 31 Oct 1857 (*divorce* 1873) Emily, 3rd dau of Gen — Eckford, and had, with other issue:

(1) Frederick Stapleton Dickey; MRCS, LRCP; *b* 19 Sept 1859; *m* 1895 Maude Amelia (*d* 18 April 1918), widow of R Maxwell Keith and dau of Arthur Wynnson Howes, and *d* 5 April 1937 having had issue:

1a Saville Weir Bensley; *b* 24 Jan 1901; *d* unm 9 May 1937

(2) Charles John Haldane; PMG UP India, Lt Art Militia; *b* 9 July 1861; *educ* Marlborough and Edin U; *m* 16 Dec 1892 Annie Evelyn (*d* 29 Oct 1945), dau of Rutherford Haldane, MD, LLD, and *d* 14 Oct 1940, leaving issue:

1a Nancy Evelyn Lowthorpe; *b* 29 Sept 1893

(1) Margaret Eleanor; *b* 18 Sept 1867; *m* 12 Feb 1889 Lt-Col Stewart Douglas Gordon, IA, of Sundial Cottage, Croxley Green, Herts, and *d* 1942, leaving issue

5 (cont.) Sir Frederick Hogg *m* 2nd 12 Aug 1885 Harriett Venn (*d* 6 Sept 1930), dau of William Stephens Dicken, and *d* Sept 1923, having by her had, with other issue:

(3) Esmond Popham; Lt-Cdr RN WW II (POW); *b* 10 May 1886; *m* 8 June 1927 Mary Gertrude Irene, dau of Hugh Boyle, and *dsp* 31 Jan 1962

6 Stapleton Cotton; Assist Fin Sec India Office; *b* 4 Dec 1839; *d* unm 25 March 1918

7 Quintin; *b* 14 Feb 1845; *m* 16 May 1871 Alice Anna (*d* 5 Aug 1918), est dau of William Graham, JP, DL, of Burnsfields, Renfrewshire, and *d* 17 Jan 1903, leaving:

(1) DOUGLAS McGAREL HOGG, *cr* VISCOUNT HAILSHAM (*see* HAILSHAM OF ST MARYLEBONE, B)

(2) Ian Graham, DSO; Lt-Col 4th Hus, Boer War, S Nigeria, Aro and Kano-Sokoto Expdns and WW I; *b* 2 Feb 1875; *d* France 2 Sept 1914 of wounds recd in action

(3) Malcolm Nicholson (Sir); ktd 1920, dep chm Bombay Chamber Commerce 1915–19 (later chm) and MLC Bombay 1915–17, memb Viceroy's Legislative Cncl 1917–19, dir and dep chm Forbes, Campbell and Co Ltd, London, East India merchants, and Westminster Bank Ltd, dir Union Bank of Australia Ltd, Beaumont Property Tst Ltd, Rohilkand and Kunaon Railway Co Ltd and Bengal and N Western Railway Co Ltd, memb Cncl of India 1920–25; *b* 17 Jan 1883; *educ* Eton and Balliol Coll Oxford (BA 1904); *m* 20 Dec 1910 Lorna (*m* 2nd Cdr N B Deare and *d* 1978), yr dau of Sir Frank Clement Offley Beaman, Judge High Court, Bombay, and *d* 14 Feb 1948, leaving:

1a +John Nicholson (Sir), TD [Sir John Hogg TD, The Red House, Shedfield, Hants SO32 2HN]; ktd 1963, High Sheriff Co London 1960, Maj KRRC (TA) WW II Greece, Crete, W Desert, N Africa and NW Europe; memb Cwlth War Graves Commn 1958–64, dep chm Gallaher Ltd 1964–78 and Williams & Glyn's plc 1970–83, dir Prudential Corpn plc 1964–85, Nat and Commercial Banking Gp Ltd, The Roy Bank of Scotland Gp plc 1965–82 and Honeywell Ltd 1972–80, chm: Glyn Mills Co, Export Credits Guarantee Dept Advsy Cncl 1962–67, Abu Dahbi Investment Bd 1967–75 and Banque Francaise de Credit Intl Ltd 1972–83; *b* 4 Oct 1912; *educ* Eton

(Fell 1951–70) and Balliol Coll Oxford; *m* 28 Oct 1948 *Barbara Mary Elisabeth, widow of Viscount Garmoyle (*see* CAIRNS, E) and yr dau of Capt Arden Franklyn, of New Place, Shedfield, Hants, and has issue:

1b +Malcolm David Nicholson [Malcolm Hogg Esq, Lanterns, Mapledurwell, Hants RG25 2LU]; *b* 14 Sept 1949; *educ* Eton and York U; *m* 1975 *Mary Clare, only dau of Maj Richard Francis Preedy, RE, and has:

1c *Richard John Nicholson; *b* 1982

1c *Lucy Mary Arden; *b* 1977

2c *Alice Emily Geraldine; *b* 1979

1b *Susan Elisabeth [Mrs Jeremy Rae, The Ponts Cottage, S Moreton, Oxon OX11 9AG]; *b* 13 Jan 1954; *m* 1980 *Jeremy A J F Burnett Rae and has:

1c *Henry Oliver; *b* 1985

2c *Charles Frederick; *b* 1986

1c *Emma Louise; *b* 1983

1a *Vivien Yzabel Suzanne Nicholson [Mrs Thomas Walters, 23 Christchurch Rd, London SW14]; *b* 29 May 1915; *m* 1st 9 July 1939 (*divorce* 1946) Cdr Henry Morland, RIN, only s of Capt Henry Morland, CIE, RIN; *m* 2nd 19 Sept 1947 (*divorce* 1954) John R Caldwell, only s of W H G Caldwell, of Newton of Belltrees, Loch Winnoch, Renfrewshire; *m* 3rd 4 Jan 1955 Thomas Melmoth Walters (*d* 1974), and by her 1st husb has:

1b *Michael Henry, Lt RN; *b* 17 March 1941; *educ* Radley

2b *Miles Quintin [Miles Morland Esq, 6 Hereford Square, London SW7]; *b* 18 Dec 1943; *educ* Radley and Lincoln Coll Oxford; md The First Boston Corp; writer; *m* 1972 *Ghislaine, only dau of Guy Vincent Chastenet de la Maisoneuve and Countess de Chamberet, and has:

1c *Catherine Natasha; *b* 29 Aug 1973

2c *Georgia Susanna; *b* 1976

(1) Elsie Florence; *m* 5 Nov 1901 Maj Vincent Robertson Hoare (*ka* 15 Feb 1915), 12th Bn London Regt (The Rangers), of Highfields, Ware, s of Rev Walter Marsham Hoare, Rector Colkirk, Norfolk, and *d* 8 Nov 1965 aged 92, leaving issue

(2) Ethel Mary, CBE (1920); Sec London War Pensions Ctee 1914–21, chm Domestic Servants' Inquiry Ctee 1923, Govr Regent Street Poly, pres WI; *b* 29 June 1876; *m* 14 Feb 1907 Maj Herbert Frederick Wood (*d* 12 Dec 1918), 9th Lancers, RFC, s of Lt-Col David E Wood, of Kibworth, Leics, and *d* 29 June 1970, leaving issue

1 Isabella; *m* 19 Oct 1848 1st Baron Tweedmouth (*see* 1935 edn) and *d* 20 March 1908, leaving issue. He *d* 4 March 1894

2 Mary Rosina; *m* 1856 Charles McGarel (*d* 10 Oct 1876), of Magheramorne, Co Antrim, and *dsp* 22 April 1913

3 Letitia; *d* young 1837

4 Amy; *m* 13 Sept 1860 James William MacNabb, JP (*d* 22 Nov 1915), of Arthurstone, Binfield, Berks, and *d* 5 Dec 1871, leaving issue

5 Annie Claudina; *d* 21 Aug 1921

6 Florence; *m* 8 May 1865 George William Campbell (*d* Dec 1892), 6th son of Colin Campbell, of Colgrain, Dunbartonshire, and *d* 1914, having had issue

7 Constance; *m* 19 April 1866 Francis Augustus Bevan, s of Robert Cooper Lee Bevan, of Fosbury House and Trent Park, and *d* 15 Oct 1872, leaving issue

HOGG OF CUMBERNAULD

Creation: B. (LP, UK) 2 Aug 1997.

THE BARON HOGG OF CUMBERNAULD, of Cumbernauld, N Lanarks (Norman Hogg) [The Rt Hon The Lord Hogg of Cumbernauld, House of Lords, London SW1A 0PW]; *b* 12 March 1938; *educ* Causewayend Sch Aberdeen, Ruthrieston Secondary Sch Aberdeen; local govt offr Aberdeen Town Cncl 1953–67, Dist Offr NALGO 1967–79, MP (Lab) Dunbartonshire E 1979–83, Cumbernauld and Kilsyth 1983–97, memb Select Ctee Scottish Affrs 1979–82, Chm Scottish Parly Lab Gp 1981–82, Scottish Lab Whip 1982–83, Dep Ch Oppn Whip 1983–87, Spokesman Scottish Affrs 1987–88, memb: Chairman's Panel 1988–97, Public Accts Ctee 1991–92, Ld H C to 1998 Gen Assembly Ch of Scotland, V-Pres Cncl Christians and Jews 1997–; *m* 1964 *Elizabeth McCall Christie

Lineage: NORMAN HOGG, CBE, JP, DL, LLD; *m* Mary Wilson and had:

NORMAN, *cr* **a Baron**

HOLCROFT

Arms: Argent a cross engrailed between in the first and fourth quarters an eagle, wings elevated sable, preying upon an infant proper, swaddled gules, banded or. **Crest:** Upon a log lopped proper a raven sable, holding in the dexter claw a sword erect, also proper. **Motto:** *Constans et fidelis* ('Constant and faithful'). **Creation:** Bt. (UK) 12 Jan 1921.

SIR PETER GEORGE CULCHETH HOLCROFT, 3RD BT, of Eaton Mascott, Berrington, Co Salop, JP (Salop 1934 and 1976) [Sir Peter Holcroft Bt JP, Berrington House, Berrington, Salop SY5 6HA]; *b* 29 April 1931; *s f* 1978; *educ* Eton; High Sheriff Salop 1950 and 1969–70; *m* 21 July 1956 (*divorce* 1987) Rosemary Rachel, yr dau of George Nevill Deas (*see* ANGLESEY, M), and has:

1 +CHARLES ANTHONY CULCHETH; *b* 22 Oct 1959; *m* 1986 *Mrs Elizabeth Carter, yr dau of John Raper, of Four Crosses, Powys, and has:

(1) +Toby David; *b* 1990

(1) *Samara Elisabeth; *b* 1988

2 +Thomas Marcus Culcheth; *b* 12 April 1967; *m* 31 May 1997 *Camilla, yr dau of Brian Marr, of Sutton Scotney, Hants

3 +Alexander James Culcheth; *b* 27 Feb 1969

1 *Tania Melanie; *b* 4 Nov 1961

Lineage: THOMAS HOLCROFT, of Brierley Hill, Staffs; *b* 29 Nov 1794; *m* 26 Nov 1815 Phoebe (*d* 28 Aug 1832), dau of William Sedgley, of Brierley Hill, and *d* 20 April 1865, leaving with other issue, including a yr s (Sir CHARLES HOLCROFT, 1st and last Bt (UK), so *cr* 28 July 1905, of The Shrubbery, Kingswinford, Staffs, *b* 16 July 1831, Hon LLD Birmingham U, *d* unm 11 March 1917, when the btcy expired):

WILLIAM HOLCROFT, of Prescot House, Old Swinford, Worcs, JP (Staffs); *b* 10 March 1826; *m* 1 March 1847 Mary (*d* 3 March 1860), dau of John Guest, of Tipton, Staffs, and *d* 29 Jan 1903, leaving, with other issue:

Sir George Harry Holcroft, 1st Bt (UK), so *cr* 12 Jan 1921, JP (Worcs and Staffs); *b* 14 Aug 1856; *educ* Exeter Coll Oxford (MA); Ld Manor Berrington, Salop, High Sheriff Staffs 1913; *m* 11 Oct 1893 Annie Gertrude (*d* 2 March 1929), dau of Rev Jeremiah Coombes, Vicar Portwood, Cheshire, and *d* 19 April 1951, having had:

1 Gilbert Culcheth; *b* 23 Oct 1894; 2nd Lt 2nd Bn Durham LI; *ka* Hooge 9 Aug 1915

2 REGINALD CULCHETH (Sir), **2nd Bt**

3 John Culcheth; *b* 1 March 1905; Lt 3rd Co London Yeo WW II; *m* 8 Sept 1932 Beatrice Mathewson (*d* 1985), dau of George F Feathers, and was *ka* N Africa 19 Nov 1941, leaving issue:

(1) +Timothy Gilbert Culcheth; *b* 2 June 1934; *educ* Radley and RMA Sandhurst; Capt (ret) 11th Hus (PAO); *m* 1st 5 June 1958 Joanna Eve (*d* 13 Dec 1983) only child of Adml Sir Stuart Sumner Bonham-Carter, KCB, CVO, DSO, of Ardmoy, Petersfield, Hants; *m* 2nd 1982 *Charmian Joy, only dau of Maj Harcourt Michael Scudamore Gold, MC (*see* 1956 edn TRENT, B), of W Stratton Hse, Winchester, Hants, and formerly w of (a) Frederick James Meynell (*see* HALIFAX, E) and (b) James Richard Nicholson (*see* NICHOLSON, Bt), and by his 1st w has:

1a *Alexandra Jane; *b* 22 May 1962; *m* 1986 *Andrew Fion Bethune Norman, only child of Alexander Vesey Bethune Norman, CBE, Master Armouries Tower London, and has:

1b *Natasha; *b* 1992

2a *Caroline Joanna; *b* 28 Dec 1966; *m* 1993 *Charles J D Todhunter, only s of Michael John Benjamin Todhunter, of The Old Rectory, Farnborough, Oxon

(1) *Tania [Mrs Mark Cory-Wright, Tilhill House, Tilford, Surrey]; *m* 10 April 1956 *Mark Richard Geoffrey Cory-Wright, yst s of Sir Geoffrey Cory-Wright, 3rd Bt (*qv*), and has issue

1 Doris Mary Gertrude; *d* unm 2 Nov 1955

2 Phyllis Evelyn

Sir GEORGE's only surv s,

Sir Reginald Culcheth Holcroft, 2nd Bt, TD; *b* 6 April 1899; *educ* Radley, RMC Sandhurst and Exeter Coll Oxford; Maj Salop Yeo (TA), Lt 23rd Cav (FF) IA; *m* 1st

26 July 1928 Mary Frances (*d* 4 July 1963), yst dau of William Swire, CBE, of Longden Manor, Shrewsbury; *m* 2nd 20 Oct 1965 Maybel Elizabeth (Betty), 2nd dau of Raymond Playfair, of Nairobi, Kenya, and formerly w of 5th Earl of Bandon (see 1970 edn), and *d* 1978, having by his 1st w had:

1 Sir PETER GEORGE CULCHETH HOLCROFT, **3rd and present Bt**

2 +Michael William Culcheth [Lt-Cdr Michael Holcroft RN, Wrentnall House, Pulverbatch, Salop SY5 8ED]; *b* 31 May 1935; *educ* Radley; *m* 31 Aug 1968 (*divorce*) Amanda Victoria, dau of W/Cdr Ian Roy Cardew Macpherson, DFC, AFC, of Winterbourne Abbas, Dorset

1 *Ann Cherida [Mrs John Lake, The Old Mill, South Moreton, Berks]; *b* 12 May 1929; *m* 26 April 1952 *John Dewe Neville Lake, yr s of Capt Henry Neville Lake, DSO, DSC, RN (*see* WALSHAM, Bt), and has:

(1) *Christopher John Neville; *b* 9 Jan 1954

(2) *Timothy Michael David; *b* 17 Dec 1955

2 *Mary Virginia [Mrs William Trotter, The Deanery, Staindrop, Co Durham DL2 3LD]; *b* 18 June 1939; *m* 6 Aug 1960 *Maj William Kemp Trotter, CBE, DL, 11th Hus (PAO), er twin s of Lt-Col William Dale Chaytor Trotter, of The Deanery, and has:

(1) *James William Dale; *b* 18 Jan 1964; *m* 19– *Nicola, est dau of Vivian Mahaffy, and has:

1a *Hebe Florence; *b* 1994

2a *Lavinia Althea; *b* 27 Jan 1997

(2) *Henry Edward Dale; *b* 21 Aug 1966

(3) *Philip George Dale; *b* 6 April 1969

(1) *Victoria Mary; *b* 10 July 1962; *m* 1989 *Maj Nicholas J Thomas, QRH, s of Maj T J Thomas, of Hey House, Heytesbury, Wilts, and has:

1a *Ivo James; *b* 14 Aug 1994

1a *Letitia Mary; *b* 26 May 1992

HOLDEN of Oakworth House

Arms: Or a chief azure, over all a bend nebuly between two roses gules. **Crest:** Issuant from a chaplet of oak vert an eagle's head erased or, gorged with a collar gemel az. **Motto:** *Extant recte factis premia* ('Rewards wait on actions performed righteously'). **Creation:** Bt. (UK) 1 July 1893.

SIR EDWARD HOLDEN, 6TH BT, of Oakworth House, Keighley, Co York [Sir Edward Holden Bt, 40 South End, Osmotherley, N Yorks DL6 3BL]; *b* 8 Oct 1916; *s* f 1962; *educ* Leys Sch Cambridge, Christ's Coll Cambridge (MA) and St Thomas's Hosp (MRCS and LRCP 1942); DA Eng 1946, FRCA, FFARCS 1958; *m* 17 Oct 1942 *Frances Joan, er dau of John Spark, JP, of Ludlow, Stockton-on-Tees, and adopted:

*Christopher John; *b* 14 Sept 1947; *educ* Giggleswick Sch and Middlesbrough Coll of Art

*Anthony Richard Norman; *b* 26 Sept 1948; *educ* Giggleswick Sch and Lanchester Tech

Lineage: ISAAC HOLDEN, of Gunends, Alston, Cumberland; *m* Mary Forest (*d* 1850), of Alston, and *d* 1826, having had:

Sir Isaac Holden, 1st Bt (UK), so *cr* 1 July 1893, of Oakworth House, Keighley, Yorks, JP, DL (W R); *b* 7 May 1807; MP (Lib) Knaresborough 1865–68, W R Yorks N Div 1882–85, Keighley 1885–95; *m* 1st 6 April 1832 Marion (*d* 4 April 1847), dau of Angus Love, of Paisley; *m* 2nd 5 April 1850 Sarah (*d* 3 May 1890), dau of John Sugden, of Dockroyd, Keighley, and *d* 13 Aug 1897, having had issue:

1 **Sir Angus Holden, 2nd Bt**, and 1st BARON HOLDEN, of Alston, Co Cumberland (UK), so *cr* 4 July 1908, JP (Bradford); *b* March 1833; MP (Lib) E Bradford 1885–86 and Buckross 1892–1900, Mayor 1878–80 and 1886; *m* 23 May 1860 Margaret (*d* 24 April 1913), dau of Daniel Illingworth, of Bradford, and *d* 25 March 1912, having had:

(1) Alfred; *b* 23 May, *d* 12 Dec 1861

(2) **Sir Ernest Illingworth Holden, 3rd Bt**, and 2nd BARON HOLDEN, JP (W and N Rs); *b* 8 Jan 1867; *m* 1st 19 May 1897 Ethel Eden (*d* 26 May 1913), dau of Maj William Cookson, 80th Regt, and had:

1a **Sir Angus William Eden Holden, 4th Bt**, and 3rd and last BARON HOLDEN; *b* 1 Aug 1898; Hon Ensign Coldstream Gds, Lt RNVR, Hon Attaché Holy See 1918, Madrid 1921–24 and Berlin 1924–26, Speaker and Dep Chm Ho Lds 1947; *d* unm 6 July 1951, when the Barony expired

2a Mostyn Ernest Eden; *b* 23 Dec 1900; *d* 10 Oct 1902

(2) **Sir Ernest** *m* 2nd 17 Feb 1914 Edith Isabel (*d* 25 March 1957), yst dau of Bertram George Scott Judd, of Rickling, Essex, and *d* 30 Jan 1937, leaving by her:

1a Donna Diana; *b* 5 Jan 1916

(1) Annie Elizabeth; *m* 13 July 1897 Tatton Henry Bower (*d* 14 May 1931) and *d* 17 April 1950, leaving issue

2 Edward, of Lynwood, Park Avenue, Southport, Lancs; *b* 14 Jan 1835; *m* 3 Dec 1863 Maria Elizabeth (*d* 6 July 1932), dau of Peter Wood, MD, of Southport, and *d* 11 Oct 1913, leaving:

(1) ISAAC (Sir), **5th Bt**

(2) Peter Wood; *b* 11 July 1872; *educ* Leys Sch and Clare Coll Cambridge (BA); *m* 19 June 1901 Margaret Jane (*d* 11 Dec 1946), 3rd dau of Utrick Alexander Ritson, JP, DL, of Calf Hall, Muggleswick Park, Co Durham, and *d* 9 Feb 1965, leaving:

1a Duncan; *b* 1 Feb 1907; *m* 4 Jan 1930 *Helen, only dau of Kinross White, of Napier, NZ, and *d* 1985, leaving:

1b +Peter Ritson [Peter Holden Esq, Forest Gate Onga Onga, Hawkes Bay, New Zealand]; *b* 14 Sept 1933; *m* 1958 *Juliet, dau of Keith de Castro, of Christchurch, NZ, and has:

1c +Duncan Dudley; *b* 1963

2c +Matthew Keith; *b* 5 Sept 1967

1c *Deborah Elizabeth; *b* 1959

2c *Caroline Jane; *b* 1961

1b *Diana Margaret [Mrs John Williams, Kaiaua Station, Tolaga Bay, New Zealand]; *b* 24 Nov 1930; *m* 1955 *John Morris Williams, 2nd s of Charles Kenneth Williams, of Gisborne, NZ, and has:

1c *Michael Duncan; *b* 25 April 1956

2c *Philip John; *b* 28 June 1960

1c *Fiona Margaret; *b* 21 April 1958

2c *Jennifer Lillian [Mrs David Gordon, 114 White Swan Rd, Mt Roskill, Auckland, New Zealand]; *b* 8 Dec 1961; *m* 1987 *David John Gordon, only s of Rev David Bruce Gordon, CBE, of Auckland, and has:

1d *Michael Charles; *b* 6 Sept 1991

1d *Grace Margaret; *b* 21 April 1994

(1) Eliza Marion; *b* 7 Oct 1864; *m* 12 July 1888 Samuel Rathbone Edge (*d* 27 Sept 1936), of Pitfield House, Newcastle, MP Newcastle-Under-Lyme, and *d* 19 Oct 1936, leaving issue

(2) Clara Maria; *b* 8 Dec 1865; *m* 15 April 1896 Robertson Lawson, CA (*d* 1917), and *d* 23 Dec 1950

1 Mary; *b* 26 Nov 1838; *m* 23 May 1860 Henry Illingworth, JP (*d* 1895), of Layde Royde Hall, Bradford, and *d* 29 Oct 1908, leaving issue

2 Margaret; *b* 2 July 1842; *m* 8 Aug 1866 Alfred Illingworth (*d* 1907), of Daisy Bank, Bradford, MP Bradford, and *d* 15 Feb 1919, leaving issue

The 4th Bt's 1st cousin once-removed,

Sir Isaac Holden Holden, 5th Bt, JP (Lancs 1909); *b* 8 July 1867; *educ* Leys Sch and Christ's Coll Cambridge (MA); *m* 1st 7 June 1905 Marian (*d* 10 May 1908), dau of Peter A Keevney, of Salford, Lancs; *m* 2nd 1913 (Alice) Edna (*d* 13 Jan 1971), dau of George F Byrom, of Droylesden and Hyde, Cheshire, and *d* 5 Jan 1962, leaving by her:

1 Sir EDWARD HOLDEN, **6th and present Bt**

2 +PAUL [Paul Holden Esq, Glenside, Rowhills, Heath End, Surrey GU9 9AU]; *b* 3 March 1923; heir presumptive; *educ* Leys Sch; F/Lt RAFVR WWII 1942–46; *m* 5 Sept 1950 *Vivien Mary, yst dau of Hedley Broxholme Oldham, of Allesley, Coventry, and has:

(1) +Michael Peter [Michael Holden Esq, 1 Greenways, Pembroke Rd, Woking, Surrey GU22 7DT]; *b* 19 June 1956

(1) *Judith Margaret; *b* 15 Jan 1952; *m* 1st 1974 (*divorce* 1979) Robert Forrest; *m* 2nd 19– *— Tumelty

(2) *Susan Diana; *b* 6 Dec 1953; *m* 19– *— Aked

1 *Ruth; *b* 3 March 1915

2 *Helen; *b* 1918; *m* 11 Dec 1947 *William Herbert Chapman, MB, ChB, and has:

(1) *Andrew; *b* 3 Dec 1948

(2) *Richard Holden; *b* 26 Nov 1953

(1) *Bridget; *b* 11 Dec 1950; *m* 1971 *Peter Herbert Stone

(2) *Ann; *b* 4 Dec 1957

3 *Janet [Mrs George Welsh, 12 Bylands, White Rose Lane, Woking, Surrey]; *b* 1920; *m* 27 June 1946 *Capt George Richmond Aagaard Welsh, RAOC, and has:

(1) *Geoffrey Peter; *b* 16 Feb 1948

(2) *Raymond Michael; *b* 12 May 1949

(3) *Malcolm Nigel; *b* 20 Dec 1950

HOLDEN of The Firs, Leigh, Lancs

Arms: Sa. on a pale erm. between two chevrons or a covered cup of the last. **Crest:** In front of a rising sun in its splendour or a moorcock sa., jelloped and wattled gu. **Motto:** *Deo omnia debeo* ('I owe all things to God'). **Creation:** Bt. (UK) 19 Sept 1919.

SIR JOHN DAVID HOLDEN, 4TH BT, of The Firs, Leigh, Co Lancaster [Sir John Holden Bt, 13 Sterne Ave, Tang Hall, York YO3 0TF]; *b* 16 Dec 1967; *s* gf 1976; *m* 1987 *Suzanne Cummings, of York, and has:

1 *A dau
2 *A dau
3 *A dau

Lineage: Sir John Henry Holden, 1st Bt (UK), so *cr* 19 Sept 1919, JP; *b* 25 Jan 1862; Mayor Leigh 1911–13; *m* 26 Aug 1885 Emma (*d* 31 May 1946), dau of Thomas Cawkwell, of Sands House, Keyingham, Yorks, and *d* 4 May 1926, having had issue:

1 John; *b* 15 Dec 1886; *d* 1 July 1888
2 GEORGE (Sir), **2nd Bt**
3 Henry; *b* 14 March; *d* 24 July 1893
4 Arthur; *b* 7 Aug 1897; *m* 1st 2 June 1920 Laura (*d* 14 May 1949), dau of H Williams, of Cardiff; *m* 2nd 14 June 1949 *Dorothy [Mrs Arthur Holden, Agincourt, Woodlands Ave, Rustington, Sussex], dau of Nathan Seddon, of Eccles, and *d* 1993, leaving by his 1st w:
(1) Arthur John; *b* 30 June 1921; *m* 21 June 1949 *Ethel Hall [Mrs Arthur Holden, Eagley Bank, Andrew Lane, Bolton, Lancs], and *d* 2 Feb 1996
(2) Henry David; *b* 2 June 1922; *m* Aug 1947 *Marjorie Brown [Mrs Henry Holden, Anglezarke, Belmont Rd, Penn, W Midlands] and *d* 1980, leaving:
1a +David Lawrence; *b* 1948; *m* 1971 *Sharon Joyce, dau of A C W Mobbs, of Perton, and has:
1b *Robert Arthur; *b* 1972
1b *Emma Jane; *b* 1974
2a +Andrew Charles [Arthur Holden Esq, Cote Leasowe, Heath House Lane, Codsall, Wolverhampton]; *b* 1949; *m* 1972 *Susan, dau of J W Dicken, of Bilston
3a +William John [William Holden Esq, Knights Close, Penkridge, Staffs]; *b* 1953; *m* 1975 *Patricia Joan, dau of R C Knight, of Wolverhampton
1a *Madeline Julie [Mrs David Haynes, 5 Ayrton Close, Perton, Wolverhampton]; *b* 27 May 1967; *m* 1989 *David Raymond Haynes and has issue:
1b *Lauren Victoria; *b* 1991
5 John; *b* 21 June 1900; *m* 17 June 1925 *Rita, only dau of H Walton, of Reedley, Burnley, and *d* 1977, leaving:
1 +Derek John [Derek Holden Esq, 5 Greystoke Court, 29 Abermarle Rd, Beckenham, Kent BR3 2HL]; *b* 1 Jan 1927; *m* 24 Nov 1951 *Patricia Kathleen, dau of F Mansfield, of Heaton Moor, and has issue:
1a +Richard John; *b* 1960; *m* 1982 *Atie, dau of G Nieuwenhuis, of Durban N, S Africa
1a *Elizabeth Anne; *b* 1955
(2) +Norman Michael [Norman Holden Esq, 7 Trafford Ave, Westville, Durban, S Africa]; *b* 26 Aug 1928; *m* 1957 *Enid Natalie, dau of M Smith, of Adelaide, S Australia, and has issue:
1a +Christopher Derek; *b* 15 March 1959
2a +Peter James; *b* 30 June 1960
(1) *Gillian Nancy [Mrs Dennis Cox, White Ladyes, Woodman Lane, Chingford, Essex]; *b* 26 June 1935; *m* 3 June 1964 *Dennis George Cox and has:
1a *Gordan Michael; *b* 12 Aug 1967
1a *Julia Alison; *b* 21 May 1965
1 Emma; *m* 17 Sept 1913 Henry Pemberton, of Westfield, Leigh, Lancs, and *d* 19–, leaving issue
2 Ada; *m* 24 June 1914 Vincent Fairclough and *d* 29 Oct 1958, leaving issue
3 Gertrude *b* 16 Feb 1895; *d* 6 May 1901

Sir JOHN's est s,

Sir George Holden, 2nd Bt, JP; *b* 16 April 1890; Mayor Leigh; *m* 11 June 1913 Margaret Adamson (*m* 2nd 28 Feb 1946 Joseph Harold Wright, of Chorlton, Manchester), dau of Thomas Smith, JP, of The Lingards, Astley, Lancs, and *d* 26 Sept 1937, leaving:

1 GEORGE (Sir), **3rd Bt**
2 John; *b* 18 June 1918; *educ* Oundle; WW II with Manchester Regt (TA); *m* 12 Feb 1940 Margaret Lois (*d* 1985), dau of Ivan Sharpe, of Southport, and *d* 1985, leaving:
(1) +Robin John [Robin Holden Esq, Tall Trees, Barry Rise, Bowdon, Altrincham, Cheshire WA14 3JS], ACA 1964; *b* 22 May 1942; *educ* Oundle; *m* 19 Sept 1964 *Margaret Susan, dau of G I Rushton, of 53 Westbourne Road, Birkdale, Southport, Lancs, and has:
1a +Richard Ingham; *b* 10 Dec 1966
2a +Jonathan Robin; *b* 26 April 1969
(2) +Anthony Ivan [Anthony Holden Esq, c/o Rogers Coleridge White, 20 Powis Mews, London W11 1JN]; *b* 22 May 1947; *educ* Oundle and Merton Coll Oxford (MA); jnlst with *Hemel Hempstead Evening Echo* 1970–73, *Sunday Times* 1973–79 (Atticus 1977–79), *Observer* 1979–81, *Punch* 1979–81, *The Times* 1981–82, *Today* 1985–86, author: *The St Albans Poisoner* (1974), *Charles, Prince of Wales* (1979), *Their Royal Highnesses* (1981), *Of Presidents, Prime Ministers and Princes* (1984), *The Queen Mother* (1985), *Don Giovanni* (1987), *Olivier* (1988), *Charles* (1988), *Big Deal* (1990), *A Princely Marriage* (1991), *The Oscars* (1993), *The Tarnished Crown* (1993), *Tchaikovsky* (1995), *Diana* (1997); broadcaster; *m* 1st 1971 (*divorce* 1988) Amanda Juliet, MA, LGSM, LRAM, ARCM, dau of Sir Harold Brian Seymour Warren, MRCS, LRCP, of Chelsea, and has:
1a +Samuel Ivan; *b* 1975
2a +Joseph Anthony; *b* 1977
3a +Benajmin John; *b* 1979
(2) (cont.) Anthony Holden *m* 2nd 1990 *Cynthia, dau of Mrs George Blake, of Brookline, Mass.
3 +James Temple [James Holden Esq, The Firs, 22 Lambs Rd, Thornton, Blackpool, Lancs FY5 5JJ]; *b* 23 Nov 1922; *educ* Oundle; late RA; *m* 1st 17 Jan 1948 (*divorce* 1956) Olive, dau of Henry Thompson Kirby, of Southport, Lancs, and has:
(1) +Peter James; *b* 16 Nov 1954
(1) *Jacqueline Peta; *b* 10 May 1950
3 (cont.) James Holden; *m* 2nd 23 March 1957 *Golda Bracey, dau of Clifford Shirley, of Thornton-le-Fylde, Lancs, and by her has:
(2) +Carl Temple; *b* 20 Sept 1963; LLB; *m* 1992 *Caroline Anne, dau of Stanley Gould, of Llanferres, and has:
1a +James Joseph; *b* 27 Feb 1997
1 *Margaret [Mrs E Webster, Green Banks, Beechwood Lane, Culcheth, Cheshire]; *b* 15 May 1916; *m* 1 June 1942 Maj E R Webster, Roy Signals, and has:
(1) *Pamela Pixie Anne [Mrs Timothy Cahill, Glen House, Upper Rochestown, Co Cork, Ireland]; *b* 1946; *m* 1970 Timothy Joseph Cahill, FRCS (*d* 1988), and has:
1a *Timothy Joseph; *b* 1977
2a *Bryan Anthony Ernest; *b* 1979
3a *Jeremy James; *b* 1981
1a *Joanne Amanda; *b* 1971
2a *Rachel Louise; *b* 1972
(2) *Carol Yvonne Margaret; *b* 1949; *m* 1973 *Kenneth G Wilcock and has:
1a *Ian Michael; *b* 1977
2a *James Richard; *b* 1982
1a *Jennifer Louise; *b* 1975

Sir GEORGE's est s,

Sir George Holden, 3rd Bt; *b* 6 Dec 1914; *educ* Oundle; London Area Manager L&G Fire Appliance Co; *m* 5 June 1937 Betty, dau of William Shaw, of Portland Place, London W1, and *d* 1976, having had:

1 David George; *b* 19 April 1938; *educ* St Columba's Coll Dublin; *m* 13 June 1964 *Nancy [Mrs David Holden, Woodhouse Grange, Sutton-in-Derwent, Yorks], 2nd dau of H W D Marwood, of Bodnor Hse, Whenby, Yorks, and *d* 1971, leaving:
(1) Sir JOHN DAVID HOLDEN, **4th and present Bt**
2 Christopher William; *b* 5 Jan 1940; *m* 19– *June (*m* 2nd 1970 Barry Hargreaves Beaumont, of Manor Farm, Wyton, Hull), dau of Stephen Carrington, of Keighley, Yorks, and *d* 26 April 1968
3 +BRIAN PETER JOHN; *b* 12 April 1944; heir presumptive; *m* 1984 *Bernadette Anne Lopez, dau of George Gerald O'Malley, of Manchester
1 *Patricia Margaret Anne [Mrs David Mitchell, 60 Scott Lane West, Riddlesden, Keighley, Yorks]; *b* 14 Oct 1942; *m* 1963 *David Coates Mitchell and has:
(1) *Kieron [Kieron Mitchell Esq, 14 Moorthorpe Ave, Bradford Moore, Bradford, W Yorks]; *b* 1970; *m* 1991 *— and has:
1a *James Declan; *b* 1992
2a *Kyle Patrick; *b* 1993
(1) *Deborah Mitchell [Mrs David Petty, 45 Airedale Rd, Undercliffe, Bradford, W Yorks]; *b* 1964; *m* 1989 *David John Petty
2 *Deirdre Rosemary [Mrs David Marsh, 23 Impstone Rd, Pamber Heath, Tadley, Hants RG26 3EQ]; *b* 22 Jan 1949; *m* 1969 *David Marsh and has:
(1) *Andrew David; *b* 1974; *educ* U of Hertfordshire (BSc Hons)
(2) *Christopher George; *b* 1986
(1) *Nicola Catherine; *b* 1972; *educ* Birmingham U; MB ChB

HOLDER

Arms: Per pale dancettée or and gu. three chevronels erm., in chief two trefoils slipped counterchanged. **Crest:** Upon the battlements of a tower, per pale or and arg., charged with a cross couped gu., a lion sejant per pale dancettée az. and gu., resting the dexter forepaw on an anchor arg. **Motto:** *Nisi Dominus frustra* ('It is in vain without the Lord'). **Creation:** Bt (UK) 10 March 1898.

SIR (JOHN) HENRY HOLDER, 4TH BT [Sir Henry Holder Bt, 47 St Paul's Rd North, West Walton Highway, Wisbech, Cambs PE14 7DN]; *b* 12 March 1928; *s f* 1986; *educ* Eton and Birmingham U (Dip Malting and Brewing), prodn dir and head brewer Elgood & Son (Wisbech) 1975–93, chm East Anglian Section Incorporated Brewers' Guild 1981–83, dip memb Inst of Brewing; *m* 1st 10 Sept 1960 Catherine (Kate) Harrison (*d* 30 Aug 1994), yr dau of Leonard Baker, of Stone Lane, Kinver, nr Stourbridge, Worcs; *m* 2nd Sept 1997 *Josephine Mary, dau of A Elliott and widow of G Rivett, and by his 1st w has:

1 +NIGEL JOHN CHARLES; *b* 6 May 1962; *educ* Wisbech GS and The Isle Coll Wisbech

2 +Hugo Richard; *b* 6 May 1962; *m* 1991 *Barbara, only dau of Walter Plenk, of Munich, and has:

(1) +Alexander John; *b* 1993

(1) *Stephanie; *b* 1995

1 *Bridget Georgina; *b* 16 Sept 1965; *m* 1991 *Christopher L T Davis, only s of L F Davis, of Burrough Green, Newmarket, Suffolk, and has:

(1) *Thomas Henry Frederick; *b* 1993

Lineage: CHARLES HOLDER, of Bishop's Cleeve, Glos; *m* 22 May 1810 Martha Hone and *d* 14 Jan 1866, leaving, with other issue:

HENRY HOLDER, of Lansdowne House, Malvern; *b* 21 Nov 1811; *m* 17 Oct 1837 Maria Purser (*d* 14 May 1893), and *d* 27 Jan 1880, leaving:

Sir John Charles Holder, 1st Bt (UK), so *cr* 10 March 1898, JP, DL Worcs, JP Birmingham; High Sheriff Worcs 1903, KGStJ; *b* 10 Dec 1838; *m* 29 Aug 1872 Geraldine Augusta Baynton (*d* 27 Nov 1943), dau of John Williams Knipe, of Worcester, and had:

1 HENRY CHARLES (Sir), **2nd Bt**

2 John Alexander; Capt MVC; *b* 21 Aug 1876; *m* 5 Oct 1904 Ida Muriel Sybil (*d* 6 June 1969), yst dau of Very Rev Robert William Forrest, DD, Dean Worcester, and *d* 28 June 1957, leaving:

(1) John Terence; *b* 5 Nov 1905

(1) Muriel Lettice; *b* 6 July 1912

3 Alfred Ernest, of Hood Manor, Totnes, S Devon; *b* 1879; *m* 23 June 1909 Gwendoline Louisa Ryland (*d* 1976), est dau of Sir Thomas Chavasse, MD, and *d* 29 April 1963, having had:

(1) Charles Frederic Chavasse; Lt-Col RA; *b* 3 July 1910; *educ* Cheltenham; *m* 10 Sept 1951 *Margaret [Mrs Charles Holder, Balsam House, Wincanton, Somerset BA9 9HT], yst dau of A E Wrigley, of Gaines, Whitbourne, Worcester, and *d* 1989, leaving:

1a *Lucy Margaret [Mrs David Badham-Thornhill, Holton House, Wincanton, Somerset]; *b* 3 Jan 1953; *m* 21 March 1987 *David B Badham-Thornhill, s of Maj D G B Badham-Thornhill, of Cheltenham, and has had:

1b *Thomas Charles George; *b* 1989

2b *Edward David; *b* 1993

3b *Mark Frederick; *b* 1995

1b Ruth Elizabeth; *b* and *d* 1991

2b *Helen; *b* 1991

2a *Judith Mary; *b* 14 March 1954

(2) Arthur Thomas Chavasse; *b* 7 Nov 1916; *d* 16 March 1928

(3) Richard John Chavasse; Lt Dorset Regt attd 3/4th Gurkha Rifles; *b* 30 March 1921; *d* of injuries recd Middle East March 1944

(1) *Gwendoline Mary Chavasse [Mrs Sidney Knight, 59 Victoria Rd, Topsham, Exeter, Devon]; *b* 26 Dec 1913; *m* 16 June 1943 Lt Sidney Lawry Knight, RA, s of W U Knight, of Wintringham Hall, St Neots, Hunts, and has:

1a *William; *b* 1945

1a *Caroline; *b* 1944

(2) *Phyllis Margaret Chavasse [Mrs Matthew Wood, The Orchard, Bishopsteignton, Teignmouth, Devon]; *b* 27 May 1918; *m* 1st 27 Aug 1956 (*divorce* 1967) William Raymond John Evelyn WHATELEY later BALFOUR, only s of William John Balfour; *m* 2nd 1967 *Lt-Col Matthew Wakefield Drury Evelyn Wood (*see* PAGE-WOOD, Bt)

4 Norman Francis; Lt Warwicks Regt; *b* 15 Aug 1884; *m* 26 Sept 1916 Georgette Sara, widow of David Llewellyn Patric Jones and dau of Ernest Schwarz, and *dsp* 12 Sept 1955

1 Geraldine Mabel; *m* 23 Jan 1898 Rev John St Clair Mayne, Rector Wilmslow Cheshire 1903–11, and *dsp* 1946

2 Flora Constance Maria

3 Edith Mary; *m* 29 Oct 1918 Capt Charles Henry Hirst Walker, Border Regt, and *d* 7 July 1970. He *d* 1920

4 Kathleen Isabel; *m* 1 June 1905 Maj William Henry Booth, DSO, OBE, only s of Maj-Gen William Booth, RA, and *d* 1960. He *d* 3 June 1950

5 Isabella Dorothea; *m* 25 Nov 1922 Robert Newall Mayne, 2nd s of Joseph Mayne, and *d* 7 May 1957. He *d* 7 Oct 1951

6 Gladys Evelyn Austin; *m* 15 Jan 1923 Phillippe Cosmo Henri de Satgé and *d* 5 May 1969 aged 82, leaving issue. He *d* 1943

Sir JOHN *d* 26 April 1923; his est son,

Sir Henry Charles Holder, 2nd Bt, JP Worcs; *b* 1 May 1874; *educ* BNC Oxford (MA); *m* 23 June 1898 Evelyn (*d* 5 July 1956), 3rd dau of Col Sir Robert Ropner, 1st Bt, of Preston Hall, Stockton-onTees (*qv*), and had:

1 JOHN ERIC DUNCAN (Sir), **3rd Bt**

2 Henry Nigel, of Burghclere, Berks; *b* 4 April 1906; *m* 1st 25 Sept 1929 Anne, only dau of Lewis Harris Kittredge, of Cleveland, Ohio; *m* 2nd 16 April 1946 Kathleen Mary, dau of A R Pratt, and *d* 19–

1 Kathleen Joyce; *b* 5 April 1902; *m* 10 April 1945 Frank Osborne Cooke (*d* 1959), s of H J Cooke, and *d* 19–

2 Geraldine Evelyn Marjorie; *b* 9 May 1903; *d* unm 30 Nov 1961

3 Nancy Lillian; *b* 18 Nov 1907; *d* unm 1996

Sir HENRY *d* 3 Aug 1945; his er son,

Sir John Eric Duncan Holder, 3rd Bt; *b* 2 Aug 1899; *educ* Uppingham and BNC Oxford (MA); WW II as F/Lt RAFVR; *m* 1st 27 April 1927 (*divorce* 1948) Evelyn Josephine (*d* 16 Oct 1994), er dau of William J F Blain, of The Old Manor House, Combe Florey, Somerset; *m* 2nd 1971 *Marjorie Emily [Marjorie Lady Holder, Clare Park, Crondall, Surrey GU10 5DT], dau of Frank Reynolds Markham, of Cape Town and London, and *d* 1986, leaving by his 1st w:

1 Sir JOHN HENRY HOLDER, **4th and present Bt**

1 *Anthea Josephine [Mrs Peter Swayne, The Barn, Stockham, W Bagborough, Somerset, TA4 3EU]; *b* 8 April 1930; *m* 8 April 1961 *Peter Wilbraham Swayne, yr s of Philip Coney Swayne

2 *Meryl Evelyn [Miss Meryl Holder, The Tudor House, Charlynch, Somerset TA5 1BL]; *b* 20 Sept 1936; *educ* Charlotte Mason Coll, Ambleside, Westmorland (Teaching Cert 1958); Manchester U Teaching Cert; late assist pncpl and headmistress Manor House PNEU Sch, Gt Durnford, Wilts

HOLDERNESS, Baron

Arms: Quarterly, 1st and 4th, az., three naked savages ambulant in fess ppr., in the dexter hand of each a shield arg., charged with a cross gu., and in the sinister a club resting on the shoulder also ppr., on a canton erm. three lozenges conjoined in fess sa. (for WOOD); 2nd, or three torteaux gu., differenced with a label az. (for COURTENAY); 3rd, or a lion rampant az., in the centre a mullet gu. **Crest:** A savage as in the arms, the shield sa., charged with a griffin's head erased arg. **Supporters:** Dexter, an officer of the King's Royal Rifle Corps *c* 1904; sinister, a boar sa., armed, unguled and bristled or, gorged with a collar arg., thereon Cornish choughs ppr., pendant threfrom a cinquefoil arg., resting the inner rear leg on an anchor. **Motto:** I still like my choice. **Creation:** B. (UK, LP) 1979.

THE BARON HOLDERNESS, of Bishop Wilton, Co Humberside (Richard Frederick Wood, PC (1959), DL (E R Yorks 1967)) [The Rt Hon The Lord Holderness PC DL, Flat Top House, Bishop Wilton, York YO4 1RY; La Cheneraie, 83310 Grimaud, France]; *b* 5 Oct 1920; *educ* Eton and New Coll Oxford; Hon Attaché Rome 1940, Lt KRRC 1941–43 (severely wounded), Hon LLD: Sheffield 1962, Leeds 1978 and Hull 1982, MP (C) Bridlington 1950–79, PPS to: Min of Pensions 1951–53, Min of State Bd of Trade 1953–54 and Min of Ag and Fish 1954–55, Jt Parly Sec: Min Pensions and NI 1955–58 and Min Labour 1958–59, Min Power 1959–63 and Pensions and NI 1963–64, Min Overseas Devpt 1970–74, Hon Col: Queen's Roy Rifles 1962– and 4th (V) Bn RGJ 1967–89, dir: Hargreaves Gp 1974–86 and FJC Lilley & Co, regnl dir Yorks and Humberside regnl bd Lloyds Bank 1981–90, chm Disablement Servs Authority 1987–91 and Advsy Gp Rehabilitation Dept of Health 1991–, pres Queen Elizabeth's Fndn for Disabled 1983–96; *m* 15 April 1947 *Diana, Pres Queen Elizabeth's Fndn for Disabled 1996–, only dau of Col Edward Orlando Kellett, DSO, MP (*see* McGOWAN, B), and has:

1 *Edward Orlando Charles, JP [The Hon Edward Wood JP, Town Green House, Settrington, N Yorks]; *b* 14 Aug 1951; *educ* Eton; chartered accountant; *m* 1st 19 Dec 1977 (*divorce* 1993) Joanna H (*m* 2nd 22 Dec 1995 Charles Hausard), er dau of John Pinches, MC, by Rosemary, proprietress of Heraldry Today (bookshop specialising in genealogy, family history and heraldry), of Parliament Piece, Ramsbury, Wilts, and has:

(1) *Leonora Sarah Clare; *b* 1982

1 (cont.) The Hon Edward Wood *m* 2nd 1993 *Katherine Maria, yst dau of Brig Denis Leonard Ormerod, CBE, of High Halden, Kent, and has by her:

(2) *Georgia Emily Rosanna; *b* 1995

1 *Emma Myrtle Mary Anne [The Hon Lady Brooksbank, Ryton Grange, Malton, N Yorks YO17 0RY]; *b* 13 Feb 1949; *m* 17 Dec 1970 *Sir Nicholas Brooksbank, 3rd Bt (*qv*), and has issue

Lineage: *See* HALIFAX, E

HOLDERNESS, Bt

Creation: Bt. (UK) 16 Feb 1920.

SIR RICHARD WILLIAM HOLDERNESS, 3RD BT, of Tadworth, Surrey [Sir Richard Holderness Bt, 1 Tollhouse Close, Chichester, W Sussex PO19 1SE]; *b* 30 Nov 1927; *s* f 1968; *educ* Dauntsey's Sch and Corpus Christi Coll Oxford (MA); ARICS 1976; Overseas Civil Serv N Rhodesia 1955–65, estate agent with Whitehead and Whitehead, Bognor Regis, 1967–86; *m* 14 Nov 1953 *Pamela Mary, only dau of Eric Chapman, CBE, of Guildford, and has:

1 +MARTIN WILLIAM; *b* 24 May 1957; *educ* Bradfield; *m* 1984 *Elizabeth, BSc DipVH, dau of Dr William Thornton, of Belfast, and has:

(1) +Matthew William Thornton; *b* 23 May 1990

(1) *Tessa Elizabeth Mary; *b* 8 Sept 1992

2 +Andrew James; *b* 15 Feb 1962; *m* 1989 *Charlotte, er dau of Michael Broadbent, of Shrewton, Wilts, and has:

(1) +Edward Thomas James; *b* 15 March 1995

(1) *Henrietta Emily Alice; *b* 12 Nov 1993

1 *Jane Carleton [Mrs Richard Pailthorpe, The Chase, Charlton, W Sussex]; *b* 20 March 1955; *m* 1 May 1976 *Richard David Bruce Pailthorpe, BSc, and has:

(1) *Nicholas Richard Bruce; *b* 1980

(1) *Victoria Emma Carleton; *b* 1983

Lineage: Sir Thomas William Holderness, 1st Bt (UK), so *cr* 16 Feb 1920, GCB (1917, KCB 1914), KCSI (1907, CSI 1898); *b* 11 June 1849; *educ* Cheltenham and Univ Coll Oxford (BA 1872); ICS 1873–1901, India Office: Sec Revenue and Statistics Dept 1901 and PUS 1912–19; *m* 14 March 1885 Lucy (*d* 20 Jan 1948), dau of George Robert Elsmie, CSI, and *d* 16 Sept 1924, leaving, with a dau (Helen Alice, *m* 5 April 1913 Lt-Col Sir (Charles) Max Page, KBE, CB, DSO, MB, MS, FRGC, FRCS, RAMC (*d* 1963), and *d* 16 Jan 1973, leaving issue):

Sir Ernest William Elsmie Holderness, 2nd Bt, CBE (1950); *b* 13 March 1890; *educ* Radley and Corpus Christi Coll Oxford; barrister Inner Temple 1920, Assist Sec Home Office; *m* 7 Jan 1926 Emily Carleton (*d* 19 Aug 1950), yst dau of Arthur Frederick Hale McQuade, of Sydney, NSW, and *d* 23 Aug 1968, leaving issue:

1 Sir RICHARD WILLIAM HOLDERNESS, **3rd and present Bt**

1 *Margaret Carleton [Mrs William Southwood, 1 Aldwick Ave, Bognor Regis, W Sussex], MB, ChB, Edin (1954), FFARCS (1959), consultant anaesthetist Utd Bristol Hosps; *b* 8 June 1929; *m* 1 May 1965 *William Frederick Walter Southwood, MD, MCh, FRCS, and has:

(1) *Robert William; *b* 9 Aug 1966

(2)*John Carleton; *b* 7 Nov 1967

HOLLENDEN

Arms: Arg. a leopard's head jessant-de-lys sa. between three griffin's heads erased gu. **Crest:** A demi-gryphon arg., wings elevated erm., holding between the claws a leopard's head jessant-de-lys as in the arms. **Supporters:** On either side a stag ppr., chained around the neck and suspended therefrom an anchor or. **Motto:** *Tenax propositi* ('Tenacious of purpose'). **Creation:** B. (UK) 9 Feb 1912.

THE 3RD BARON HOLLENDEN, of Leigh, Co Kent (Gordon Hope Hope-Morley) [The Rt Hon The Lord Hollenden, Hall Place, Leigh, Kent TN11 8HH]; *b* 8 Jan 1914; *s* unc 1977; *educ* Eton; Maj Black Watch (RHR) WW II, Alderman City London 1954–58, with I and R Morley Ltd 1933–67 (ret as chm), King Haakon of Norway Liberation Medal; *m* 27 Oct 1945 *Sonja, dau of Thorolf Sundt, of Bergen, Norway, and has:

1 +IAN HAMPDEN [The Hon Ian Hope-Morley, c/o Hampden Estate Office, Gt Hampden, Gt Missenden, Bucks HP16 9PT]; *b* 23 Oct 1946; *educ* Eton; *m* 1st 29 April 1972 (*divorce* 19–) Beatrice Saulnier, dau of Baron Pierre d'Anchald, of Paris, and has:

(1) +Edward; *b* 9 April 1981

(1) *Juliette; *b* 13 June 1974

1 (cont.) The Hon IAN HOPE-MORLEY *m* 2nd 1988 *Caroline, only dau of Kim Ash, of Johannesburg, and by her has:

(2) +Alastair Kim; *b* 1990

(3) +Henry Gordon; *b* 1993

2 +Robin Gordon [The Hon Robin Hope-Morley, Flat 2, 159 Ebury St, London SW1 9QN]; *b* 9 June 1949; *educ* Brickwall, Northiam

3 +Andrew James Sundt [The Hon Andrew Hope-Morley, Flat 5, 33 Cathcart Rd, London SW10 9JG]; *b* 16 Sept 1952; *educ* Eton

Lineage: JOHN MORLEY, of Hackney, Middx (est s of Samuel Morley, of Sneinton, Notts, living 1775, by Mary —); *b* 1768; *m* 18 Oct 1798 Sarah (*d* 29 Oct 1840), dau of Richard Poulton, of Maidenhead, Berks, and *d* 10 May 1848, having had, with er sons:

SAMUEL MORLEY, of Hall Place, Leigh, Tonbridge, Kent, JP, DL; MP Nottingham 1865–66 and Bristol 1868–85; *b* 15 Oct 1809; *m* 19 May 1841 Rebekah Maria, dau of Samuel Hope, of Liverpool, and had, with other issue:

1 SAMUEL HOPE, **1st Baron**

2 Charles, of Shockerwick, Bath, JP Berks, Somerset and Wilts; MA Cantab; MP Brecknock 1895–1906, Hon Sec RCM 1882–1917; *b* 27 Nov 1847; *d* 27 Oct 1917, leaving three sons and a dau

3 Arnold, PC; MA Cantab, memb U Senate, barrister Inner Temple 1873, MP Nottingham 1880–85 and Nottingham E 1885–95, Patronage Sec Treasury 1886, PMG 1892–95; *b* 18 Feb 1849; *m* 30 June 1911 Elsie Waite (*d* 3 Oct 1912), widow of James Runyon, of New York, and dau of David H Touzalin, of Boston, USA, and *d* 16 Jan 1916

SAMUEL MORLEY *d* 5 Sept 1886; his est s,

SAMUEL HOPE, **1st Baron Hollenden**, of Leigh, Co Kent (UK), so *cr* 9 Feb 1912, JP, DL Kent, JP Co London; *b* 3 July 1845; *educ* Trin Coll Cambridge (MA); High Sheriff Co London 1893, Lt City London; sr ptnr I and R Morley, Dir Bank England (Dep Govr 1901–02, Govr 1903–04); *m* 6 March 1884 Laura Marianne (*d* 28 Oct 1945), dau of Rev G Royds Birch, MA, and *d* 18 Feb 1929, leaving:

1 GEOFFREY HOPE MORLEY later HOPE-MORLEY (deed poll 24 Oct 1923), **2nd Baron Hollenden**, JP (1927); *b* 28 Jan 1885; *educ* Eton and Trin Coll Cambridge; High Sheriff Co London 1917; Prime Warden Fishmongers' Co 1938–39, Pres Clothing Inst; *m* 1st 19 Dec 1914 (*divorce* 1928) Hon Mary Sidney Katharine Almina Gardner (*d* 1982), 3rd dau of 1st and last Baron Burghclere (*see* 1921 edn), and had:

(1) *Mary Joan Fenella Hope [The Hon Mrs John, Thornfield Grange, Thropton, Northumberland NE65 7HX]; *b* 21 Sept 1915 (HRH THE late PRINCESS ROYAL stood sponsor); *m* 1st 28 May 1941 (*divorce* 1965) David Babington Smith (*d* 1989), yst s of Sir Henry Babington Smith, GBE, CH, KCB, CSI; *m* 2nd 4 Feb 1965 *Geoffrey Hugh Pendril John, s of William Davies John, MRCS, and by her 1st husb has:

1a *Catherine; *b* 3 March 1952; *m* 1979 *Maj John McMorrough Carr-Ellison (*see* BUXTON, Bt) and has:

1b *Thomas Ralph; *b* 1987

2b *A son; *b* 1991

1b *Lucy Emma; *b* 1986

2b *Hannah Mary; *b* 1989

(2) Elspeth Rachel Marianne Winifred Hope; *b* 10 March 1917; *m* 20 June 1942 *Sir David Francis Muirhead, KCMG, CMG, CVO, Amb Peru, s of David Muirhead, of Kippen, Stirlingshire, and *d* 1989, leaving:

1a *David Nicholas Geoffrey [David Muirhead Esq, 3354 Stratfield Dve, Atlanta, GA 30319, USA]; *b* 15 Jan 1946; *educ* Eastbourne Coll; *m* 21 June 1969 *Emma Cecilia Borrero, of Cali, Colombia

2a *Mark Robert Gavin [Mark Muirhead Esq, 3354 Stratfield Dve, Atlanta, GA 30319, USA]; *b* 2 May 1951; *educ* Lancing and Markham Coll, Lima

1a *Mary Elizabeth Janet [The Hon Lady David Gore-Booth, 27 Wetherby Mansions, Earls Court Sq, London SW5 9BH]; *b* 1 Feb 1949; *m* 1st 9 July 1969 Enrico Gambetta de Patrantonio, of Lima, Peru; *m* 2nd 7 Oct 1977, as his 2nd w, *Hon David Alwyn Gore-Booth (*see* GORE-BOOTH, Bt), and by her 1st husb has:

1b *Riccardo (Rick); *b* 19–

1 (cont.) The **2nd Baron** *m* 2nd 6 May 1929 Muriel Ivy (*d* 6 June 1962), yst dau of Sir John Evelyn Gladstone, 4th Bt (*qv*); *m* 3rd 7 Jan 1963 *Violet Norris [The Rt Hon Anne Lady Hollenden, Valley Farm, Duntisbourne Hill, nr Cirencester, Glos], widow of Frank Dutch Howitt, CVO, MA, MD, FRCP, and dau of Alfred Leverton, of Glapthorn, Peterborough, and *dspm* 19 Oct 1977

2 Claude HOPE later HOPE-MORLEY (deed poll 24 Oct 1923); High Sheriff Co London 1938, Capt Gren Gds (SR); *b* 5 June 1887; *educ* Eton; *m* 6 July 1911 Lady Dorothy Edith Isabel Hobart-Hampden-Mercer-Henderson (*d* 15 Dec 1972), est dau of 7th Earl of Buckinghamshire (*qv*), and *d* 8 April 1968, leaving:

(1) GORDON HOPE-MORLEY, **3rd and present Baron Hollenden**

(1) *Ann Rosemary Hope [The Hon Lady Newman, Blackpool House, Dartmouth, S Devon]; *b* 10 Aug 1916; Jr Cdr ATS WW II; *m* 12 June 1946 Sir Ralph Alured Newman, 5th Bt, of Mamhead (*qv*), and has issue

(2) *Stella Hope [The Hon Mrs Robinson, 107 Old Church St, London SW3]; *b* 15 April 1919; 2nd Offr WRNA WW II; *m* 21 Oct 1950 *Neville Whiteoak Robinson, yr s of David Whiteoak Robinson, of Richmond Court, Edgbaston, Birmingham, and has:

1a *Anthony David Whiteoak; *b* 11 March 1953; *educ* St Edward's Oxford; *m* 1982 *Claire Milligan and has:

1b *Michael Humphrey Whiteoak; *b* 1988

2a *Brian Robert Whiteoak; *b* 1 Nov 1956; *m* 1988 *Jayne Connelly

1a *Julia Mary; *b* 10 Sept 1954

(3) *Lorna Margaret Dorothy, JP; *b* 25 Feb 1929; *m* 30 April 1957 *Sir Michael Bowen Hanley, KCB, s of Prof James Alec Hanley, PhD, of Cumberland, and adopted:

*Peter Michael; *b* 28 Dec 1968

*Sarah Margaret; *b* 26 July 1967; *m* 1992 *Simon L H Ash, yst s of Michael Ash, of Trowbridge, Wilts

HOLLICK

Creation: B. (LP, UK) 1991.

THE BARON HOLLICK, of Notting Hill, Royal Borough of Kensington and Chelsea (Clive Richard Hollick) [The Rt Hon The Lord Hollick,14 Kensington Park Gdns, London W11]; *b* 20 May 1945; *educ* Taunton's Sch Southampton and Nottingham U (BA); joined Hambros Bank Ltd 1968, dir 1973–; ch exec MAI plc 1974–96; chm: Shepperton Studios Ltd 1976–84, Garban Ltd (USA) 1983–97, Galleon Tst 1992–; dir: Logica plc 1987–91, Avenir Havas Media SA 1989–92, Satellite Information Systems Ltd 1990–94, Meridian Broadcasting 1992–96, Br Aerospace 1992–97, Anglia TV 1994–; memb: NBC 1984–91, Advsy Ctee Dept Applied Economics Cambridge U 1989–, Financial Law Panel 1993–; Special Advsr Pres BOT 1997–; Founding Tstee Inst for Public Policy Research 1988–; apptd head of European Movement-backed campaign for UK entry to European Single Currency 1998; Hon LLD Nottingham 1993; *m* 1977 *Susan Mary Woodford, dau of H E P L U Cross, of Trinidad and Tobago, and has:

1 *Caroline Daniela; *b* 1975

2 *Georgina Louise; *b* 1979

3 *Abigail Miranda; *b* 1981

Lineage: LESLIE GEORGE HOLLICK, of Southampton; *m* Olive Mary Scruton and has:

CLIVE RICHARD, *cr* a **Baron**

HOLLIS OF HEIGHAM

Creation: B. (LP, UK) 1990.

THE BARONESS HOLLIS OF HEIGHAM, of Heigham, City of Norwich (Patricia Lesley Wells, DL (Norfolk 1994)) [The Rt Hon The Baroness Hollis of Heigham DL, 30 Park Lane, Norwich]; *b* 4 May 1941; *educ* Plympton GS Plymouth, Cambridge U (MA 1965), U of Calif Berkeley, Columbia U NY and Nuffield Coll Oxford (DPhil 1968); Harkness Fellow 1962–64, Nuffield Scholar 1964–67, Reader Modern History UEA 1967–, Sr Fell and Dean English and American Studies 1988–90, Lab Parly candidate Gt Yarmouth 1974 and 1979; memb: Norwich City Cncl 1968–91 (Leader 1983–88), Norfolk CC 1981–85, E Anglia Ec Planning Cncl 1975–79, Govt Commn Housing 1975–77, RHA 1979–83, BBC Regnl Advsy Ctee1979–83, Press Cncl 1989–90; Nat Commr English Heritage 1988–91; Oppn Whip 1990–97, Labour front bench spokesman social security and environment, Parly U-Sec DSS 1997–; V-Pres: ADC 1990–, AMA 1990–, Environmental Health Officers 1992, NFHA 1993–; FRHistS; Hon DLitt Anglia Poly U; author: *The Pauper Press* (1970), *Class and Conflict 1815–50* (1973), *Pressure from Without* (1974), *Women in Public 1850–1900* (1979), *Robert Lowery: Radical and Chartist* (with Dr B H Harrison, 1979), *Ladies Elect: Women in English Local Government 1865–1914* (1987), *Jennie Lee* (1997); *m* *(James) Martin Hollis and has:

1 *Simon; *b* 1969

2 *Matthew; *b* 1971

Lineage: HARRY LESLEY GEORGE WELLS, of Norwich; *m* Queenie Rosalyn — and had:

PATRICIA LESLEY, *cr* a **Baroness**

HOLME OF CHELTENHAM

Creation: B. (LP, UK) 1990.

THE BARON HOLME OF CHELTENHAM, of Cheltenham, Co Gloucester (Richard Gordon Holme, CBE (1983)) [The Rt Hon The Lord Holme of Cheltenham CBE, Rio Tinto plc, 6 St James's Sq, London SW1Y 4LD]; *b* 27 May 1936; *educ* Royal Masonic Sch, St John's Coll Oxford (MA) and Harvard Business Sch (PMD); 2nd Lt 10th Gurkha Rifles Malaya 1954–56; V-Chm Lib Party Exec 1966–67, Pres Lib Party 1980–81; Dir Campaign Electoral Reform 1976–85; Sec Parly Democracy Tst 1977–; Lib Dem Spokesman NI Ho Lds 1992; Hon Treas Green Alliance 1978–90; dir: AVI Hldgs 1987–, Political Quarterly 1988–; Chm: Constitutional Reform Centre 1984–, Threadneedle Publishing Gp 1988–, DPR 1988–, Black Box Publishing 1988–95, Hollis Directories 1989–, Prima Europe 1992–, Data Mgmt Servs Gp 1995–; Visiting Prof Business Admin Middx Poly 1990–94; assoc memb Nuffield Coll 1985–89; exec memb Campaign for Oxford 1990–; v-chm Hansard Soc for Parly Govt 1991; Chm English Coll Fndn Prague 1991, dir Rio Tinto plc 1995–; author: *No Dole for the Young* (1975), *A Democracy Which Works* (1978), *The People's Kingdom* (1987), *1688–1988: Time for a New Constitution* (jt ed, 1988); *m* 1958 *Kathleen (Kay) Mary, dau of Vincent Powell, and has:

1 *Richard Vincent; *b* 1966; *m* 1992 *Caroline Elizabeth, dau of Michael Holman, of Hazlemere, Bucks

2 *John Gordon; *b* 1966

1 *Nicola Ann; *b* 1959; *m* 1989 *Nicholas Hardy

2 *Penelope Jane; *b* 1962; *m* 1992 *Roger Kirman, s of Peter Kirman, of Wimbledon

Lineage: JACK RICHARD HOLME; *m* E M Eggleton and had:

RICHARD GORDON, *cr* a **Baron**

HOLMPATRICK

Arms: Gu. a mullet arg. between three cinquefoils pierced erm., on a chief or a heart of the first. **Crest:** A demi-antelope arg. armed and unguled or, charged with a mullet gu., holding between the hoofs a human heart as in the arms. **Supporters:** Dexter, an antelope arg., attired or; sinister, a lion gu., each having pendant from a collar flory counterflory or a shield erm., charged with a heart gu. **Motto:** *Qualis ab incepto* ('I continue as I begin'). **Creation:** B. (UK) 27 July 1897.

THE 4TH BARON HOLMPATRICK, of Holm Patrick, Co Dublin (Hans James David Hamilton) [The Rt Hon The Lord Holmpatrick, 67 Vicarage Rd, St Agnes, Cornwall TR5 0JH]; *b* 15 March 1955; *s* f 1991; *educ* Harrow; *m* 19 July 1984 *Mrs Gill Francesca Anne du Feu, est dau of S/Ldr Kenneth James (Toby) Harding, DFC, RAF (*d* 1990), of Binisafua, Minorca, and has:

1 *James Hans Stephen; *b* 6 Oct 1982

Lineage: JOHN HAMILTON, of Coronary, Co Cavan, and Monilla or Hamilton Bawn, Co Armagh (4th s of Rev Hans Hamilton, Vicar Dunlop, and bro of 1st Viscount Claneboye; *see* DUFFERIN AND CLANEBOYE, B); *m* 1617 Sarah, dau of Anthony Brabazon (*see* MEATH, E), and *d* 4 Dec 1639, having had, with other issue:

1 Sir HANS HAMILTON, 1st and last Bt (I), so *cr* 6 April 1662, of Monilla and Hamilton Bawn; MP Armagh; *m* Magdalen, dau of Sir Edward Trevor, and *dspm* 15 Feb 1681, when the btcy expired, leaving:

(1) Sarah; *m* Sir Robert Hamilton, 1st Bt, of Manor Hamilton, and had issue

2 James, of Baillieboro', Co Cavan; *m* 1639 Jane, dau and heiress of William Baillie, DD, Bp Clonfert, and had, with a yr s (Hans):

(1) Henry, of Baillieboro; *m* Rebecca Blackwell (*m* 2nd 1694 Daniel Falkiner, of Dublin) and was *k* Siege of Limerick, having had:

1a JAMES

2a John, of Holm Patrick; MP Wendover and Dundalk; *m* — Ligoe and had issue

1a Mary; *m* — Ligoe

The er s,

JAMES HAMILTON; MP Carlow; *m* Anne Hall and had, with two er sons and six daus:

JAMES HAMILTON, of Sheephill and Holm Patrick; Dep-Prothonotary Court King's Bench; *b* 1727; *m* 1st 1750 Hannah Phillips and had, with other issue:

1 HANS

2 Henry, of Ballymacoll, Co Meath; *b* 16 July 1760; *m* Mary, dau of John Wetherall, of Dublin, and *d* Nov 1844, leaving issue

3 James, of Dunboyne Castle; *b* 1761; *d* 24 May 1800, leaving issue

4 John, of Hacketstown, Co Dublin; *m* Eliza, dau of Sir William Alexander, Bt (*see* CABLE-ALEXANDER, Bt), and *dsp*

5 Robert, of Clonsilla; *m* 1797 Catherine, dau of Sir William Alexander, Bt (*see* CABLE-ALEXANDER, Bt), and had five sons and three daus

6 Francis, of Dublin; *m* 1797 Rebecca, dau of Col William Reynell, of Castle Reynell, Co Westmeath, and had four sons and three daus

JAMES HAMILTON *m* 2nd Alice, dau of John Hamilton, of Derby, and by her had, with two daus:

7 Charles

8 Richard (Rev); Rector Culdaff and Cloncha, Co Donegal; *m* 1815 Catherine, dau of Edward Tipping, of Bellergan Park, Co Louth, by Hon Mary Blayney, sis of 11th Baron Blayney (*see* 1874 edn), and *d* 1847, leaving issue

9 Christopher; Maj-Gen 97th Foot; *m* 1817 Hon Sarah Handcock (*see* CASTLEMAINE, B) and *d* 1842, leaving issue

JAMES HAMILTON *m* 3rd Jane, 2nd dau of Rev William Candler, DD, and widow of (a) Capt S Barrett and (b) Oliver Grace and *d* 1800, having had 36 children in all

The eldest son,

HANS HAMILTON, of Sheephill; Capt 5th Dragoons, MP Co Dublin 30 years, High Sheriff 1803; *m* 1st June 1787 Sarah, dau of Joseph Lynam, of Dublin, and had two daus (Sarah, *m* 7 Jan 1812 George Woods, of Winter Lodge and Milverton; Jane, *m* Michael Law and *dsp* 1821); *m* 2nd Anne, dau of Hugh Henry Mitchell, MP, of Glasnevin, Dublin, and *d* Dec 1822, having by her had, with other issue:

1 JAMES HANS

3 Frances Caroline; *m* 3 June 1837 Richard Howard-Brooke (*see* BROOKEBOROUGH, V) and had issue

4 Harriet; *m* 28 Oct 1834 Robert Clayton Browne, of Browne's Hill

The son,

JAMES HANS HAMILTON, of Abbotstown (*alias* Sheephill), Co Dublin, and Holm Patrick, DL, JP Co Dublin; *b* Feb 1810; MP 1841–63, High Sheriff Co Dublin 1832; *m* 1833 Caroline (*d* March 1845), dau of John Frederick Trant, of Dovea, Co Tipperary (*see* BROOKEBOROUGH, V), and *d* 29 June 1863, having had, with an er s (Hans James, *b* 21 Sept 1835, *d* 8 Nov 1862):

ION TRANT HAMILTON, **1st Baron Holmpatrick**, of Holm Patrick, Co Dublin (UK), so *cr* 27 July 1897, PC (I 1887), JP, DL, Lt City and Co of Dublin 1892; *b* 14 July 1839; *educ* Trin Coll Cambridge (MA); MP (C) Co Dublin 1863–85; *m* 6 Sept 1877 Lady Victoria Alexandrina Wellesley (*d* 31 July 1933), sis of 3rd Duke of Wellington (*qv*), and had:

1 HANS WELLESLEY, **2nd Baron**

1 Margaret Augusta; *d* unm 1 Feb 1905

2 Georgina, OBE (1920); *m* 12 Nov 1902 Maj Cecil Henry Anderson-Pelham, OBE (*see* YARBOROUGH, E), and *d* 20 Dec 1960

3 Sybil Evelyn; *d* unm 22 Apr 1958

4 Winifred; *m* 25 Oct 1906 3rd Baron Swansea (*qv*) and *d* 3 Sept 1944, leaving issue

5 Clare; *m* 26 Nov 1919 Charles Armine Willis, CBE, Sudan CS, s of John Armine Willis, Sr Insp Schs, and *d* 13 Oct 1935, leaving issue

The 1st BARON *d* 6 March 1898; his son,

HANS WELLESLEY HAMILTON, **2nd Baron Holmpatrick**, DSO, MC, DL; *b* 8 Aug 1886; Capt 16th Lancers, GSO(3) 1917 WW I (wounded, despatches); *m* 27 Oct 1925 Lady Edina Dorothy Hope (*d* 13 April 1964), formerly w of Sir Thomas Ainsworth, 2nd Bt (*qv*), and dau of 4th Marquess Conyngham (*qv*), and had:

1 JAMES HANS, **3rd Baron**

1 *Caroline [The Hon Mrs Bonham, Trumroe, Castle Pollard, Co Westmeath, Ireland]; *b* 21 Oct 1926; *m* 10 April 1951 *Maj John Henry Hamilton Bonham, late DLI, er s of Maj John Wroughton Bonham, of Ballintaggart, Colbinstown, Co Kildare, and has:

(1) *Oliver John Hans [Oliver Bonham Esq, 2472 Calmino La Fuente, Las Condes, Santiago, Chile]; *b* 4 March 1954; *educ* St Columba's, Trin Coll Dublin (BA) and Dalhousie U Novia Scotia (MSc); *m* 1979 *Ann, dau of Michael Proulx, of Gainsborough, Lincs, and has issue:

1a *Michael John; *b* 1985

1a *Patricia Ann; *b* 1981

2a *Elizabeth Mary; *b* 1983

(2) *Francis Richard Hamilton [Francis Bonham Esq, 40 The Fairway, South Ruislip HA4 0R7]; *b* 11 June 1956; *educ* St Columba's and Trin Coll Dublin (BA, MSc); *m* 1983 *Christine, dau of George Hunter, of Blackrock, Co Dublin, and has issue:

1a *Kate Caroline Jytte; *b* 1990

(3) *John Arthur Norris; *b* 12 July 1961; *educ* St Columba's; *m* 1990 *Amanda, dau of David Potterton, of Dunboyne, Co Meath, and has issue:

1a *Richard David; *b* 1993

2a *Andrew James; *b* 1996

The 2nd BARON *d* 5 Sept 1942; his s,

JAMES HANS HAMILTON, **3rd Baron Holmpatrick**; *b* 29 Nov 1928; *educ* Eton; 16th/5th Lancers 1947–52; *m* 22 May 1954 *Anne Loys Roche, only dau of Cdr John Ernest Padwick Brass, RN, of Haroldston House, Haverfordwest, Pembs, and *d* 1991, leaving issue:

1 HANS JAMES DAVID HAMILTON, **4th and present Baron Holmpatrick**

2 +ION HENRY JAMES [The Hon Ion Hamilton, The Steward's Lodge, Ballinlough, Clonmellon, Co Westmeath, Ireland]; *b* 12 June 1956; heir presumptive; *educ* Harrow

3 +Evelyn William James; *b* 28 April 1961; *educ* Rannoch; *m* 1990 *Nicola Jane Fullerton and has issue:

(1) *Ross Andrew James; *b* 1990

HOME, Earl of

Arms: Quarterly, 1st and 4th grand quarters counterquartered, 1st and 4th grand quartered, 1st and 4th, vert a lion rampant argent, armed and langued gules (for HOME); 2nd and 3rd, argent three popinjays vert, beaked and membered gules (for PEPDIE of Dunglas); over all an escutcheon or, charged with an orle azure (for LANDALE); 2nd and 3rd grand quarters, quarterly, 1st, azure a lion rampant argent, armed and langued gules and crowned with an imperial crown or (for Lordship of GALLOWAY); 2nd, or a lion rampant gules, armed and langued azure, debruised of a ribbon sable (for ABERNETHY); 3rd, argent three piles gules (for Lordship of BRECHIN); 4th, or a fess chequy azure and argent, surmounted of a bend sable, charged with three buckles of the field (for STEWART of Bonkill); over all on an escutcheon argent a man's heart ensigned with an imperial crown proper, on a chief azure three mullets of the field (for DOUGLAS). **Crests:** 1 On a chapeau proper a lion's head erased argent (for HOME), 2 On a chapeau proper a salamander vert, encircled with flames of fire proper (for DOUGLAS). **Supporters:** Two lions argent, armed and langued gules. **Mottoes:** 1 (over 1st crest) *A Home, a Home, a Home*, 2 (over 2nd crest) *Jamais arrière* ('Never behindhand'), 3 (under arms) True to the end. **Creations:** L. (S) 2 Aug 1473 (Home), E. and L. (Dunglas) (S) 4 March 1604/5, B. (UK) 11 June 1875.

THE 15TH EARL OF HOME, Lord Home, Lord Dunglas [*sic*] and **Baron Douglas of Douglas**, Co Lanark (David Alexander Cospatrick Douglas-Home, CVO (1997), CBE (1991)) [The Rt Hon The Earl of Home CVO CBE, The Hirsel, Coldstream, Berwicks TD12 4LP; Castlemains, Douglas, Lanarks]; *b* 20 Nov 1943; *s f* 1995; *educ* Eton and Ch Ch Oxford; dir: Morgan Grenfell & Co 1974– (gp dir 1988–), Deutsche Morgan Grenfell Gp plc 1996–, Morgan Grenfell Internat 1972– (chm 1987–); Tstee Grosvenor Estate 1993–; Govr: Ditchley Fndn 1977–, Cwlth Inst 1988–; cncl memb RASE 1990–; Oppn Spokesman Trade 1997–; *m* 10 Oct 1972 *Jane Margaret, yr dau of Col John Francis Williams-Wynne, DSO, JP, RA (*see* WILLIAMS-WYNN, Bt), and has:

1 +MICHAEL DAVID ALEXANDER, *Lord Dunglas*; *b* 30 Nov 1987; Page of Honour to HM THE QUEEN 1998–

1 *Iona Katherine; *b* 1980

2 *Mary Elizabeth; *b* 1982

Lineage: This family derives its name from Home, Berwicks. There are descriptions of various persons as 'of Home' 1217–1385, but the exact pedigree begins with:

Sir JOHN HOME; had:

Sir THOMAS HOME of that Ilk; living 8 Feb 1385; had:

Sir JOHN HOME of that Ilk; *m* Nicole Papedy/Pepdie, who brought him the territorial Barony of Dunglas, Berwicks, and had, with two yr sons (Sir David, of Wedderburn; *see* POLWARTH, L, and HOME Bt; Patrick, of Rathburn) and a dau (Elizabeth, *m* Thomas Ker of Kershaugh):

Sir ALEXANDER HOME of Home and Dunglas; *m* Janet/Jean, dau of Sir William Hay (*see* TWEEDDALE, M), and was *ka* Battle of Verneuil 17 Aug 1424 in the Hundred Years War fighting with the French against the English, having had, with two yr sons (Thomas, of Tyninghame, living 20 June 1443; George, ancestor of the HOMEs of Spott) and at least one dau, m Ist Sir Adam Hepburn, Master of Hailes, *m* 2nd *de jure* 14th Earl of May, *qv*:

Sir ALEXANDER HOME, **1st Lord Home** (S), so *cr* 2 Aug 1473; fndr Collegiate Church of Dunglas 1450, Amb England 1459; *m* 1st by 1424 Marion, dau of John Lauder by Katherine, dau of William de Landells, and had, with other issue:

1 Alexander, *Master of Home*; Steward Dunbar; *m* (contract 2 Feb 1447/8) Agnes, sis of 1st Lord Hailes (see BUCHAN-HEPBURN, Bt), and *dvp c* 1456, leaving:

(1) ALEXANDER HOME, **2nd Lord Home**, PC (S 1488); Warden E Marches 1489–96, Keeper Stirling Castle Jan 1489/90; *m* 1st (*divorce* due consanguinity 30 May 1476) Isabel Douglas; *m* 2nd by 22 March 1492/3 Nicole (*m* 2nd *c* 1508, as his 2nd w, Sir Alexander Ramsay of Dalhousie; *see* DALHOUSIE, E), dau of George Ker of Samuelston, Haddingtonshire, and *d* 9 Sept 1506, having had, with four other sons (David, Prior Coldingham; John, *dsp*; William, executed *sp* with his bro, the **3rd Lord**; Andrew, *dsp*) and a dau (Mariot, *m* 6th Earl of Crawford; *see* CRAWFORD and BALCARRES, E):

1a ALEXANDER HOME, **3rd Lord Home**; Gt Chamberlain Scotland 1507; together with Huntly (*see* HUNTLY, M) led the van of the Scottish army at the disastrous defeat by the English of Flodden 1513; later supported the pro-English party against the Regent Albany, who had him tried for treason and executed 8 Oct 1516, his titles being forfeited; *m* between 9 Sept 1513 and 24–25 Feb 1513/4 Agnes (*m* 3rd 4th Lord Maxwell; *see* MAXWELL, Bt), illegitimate dau of James Stewart, Earl of Buchan (*see* MORAY, E) by Margaret Murray, of the MURRAYs of Philiphaugh, and widow of Adam Hepburn, 2nd Earl of Bothwell (*see* BUCHAN-HEPBURN, Bt), and *dspl*, leaving an only surv illegitimate dau:

1b Janet; inherited the Samuelston estate; *m* by 24 Aug 1531 Sir John Hamilton

2a GEORGE HOME, **4th Lord Home**, as which restored 12 Aug 1522, PC (S 1545); Warden E Marches 1543 and 1546; *m* by 30 Oct 1531 Mariot, dau and coheir of Patrick Halyburton, 5th Lord (Halyburton of) Dirletoun, and *d c* 15 April 1549, leaving, with a dau (Margaret, *m* Sir Alexander Erskine of Gogar; *see* MAR and KELLIE, E):

1b ALEXANDER HOME, **5th Lord Home**, PC (S 1561); Warden E Marches 1550 and E and Mid Marches 1557; vacillated between Reformers and Catholics, also between MARY QUEEN OF SCOTS' supporters and those of JAMES VI, accordingly convicted of treason and his titles forfeited Oct 1573; *m* 1st by 4 Feb 1557/8 Margaret, dau of Sir Walter Ker of Cessford (*see* ROXBURGHE, D), and had a dau (Margaret, *m* 5th Earl Marischal; *see* KINTORE, E); *m* 2nd by 3 May 1568 Agnes (*m* 3rd Sir Thomas Lyon; *see* STRATHMORE AND KINGHORNE, E), dau of Patrick, Lord Gray (*qv*), and widow of Sir Robert Logan of Restalrig, and *d* 1575, leaving by her, with a dau (Isabel, *m* Sir James Home of Eccles):

1c ALEXANDER HOME, **6th Lord Home**, as which restored 25 July 1578, and **1st Earl of Home** (S), so *cr* 4 March 1604/5, as also LORD DUNGLAS [*sic*], with remainder to heirs male whatsoever, PC (1603); *b c* 1566; Warden E Marches 1582–99, Sheriff Berwicks 1592; *m* 1st *c* 14 Dec 1585 Christian 2nd dau of 6th Earl of Morton (*qv*), and widow of Laurence, Master of Oliphant, by whom he had no issue; *m* 2nd by 28 June 1607 Mary, est dau of 9th Lord (Baron) Dudley (*qv*), and *d* 5 April 1619, having by her had, with two daus (Margaret, *m* 4th Earl of Moray (*qv*); Anne, *m* 1st Duke of Lauderdale; *see* LAUDERDALE, E):

1d JAMES HOME, **2nd Earl of Home**; *b c* 1607; *m* 1st *c* 2 Aug 1622 Catherine, dau of 1st Viscount Falkland (*qv*); *m* 2nd Lady Grace Fane, dau of 1st Earl of Westmorland (*qv*), and *dsp* Feb 1633

(2) John, of Ersiltoun, Whitriggs and Crailing; Amb England 1491; *m* (contract 20 March 1471/2) Margaret, dau of James Ker of Gateshaw, and *d c* 22 June 1493, having had:

1a Mungo, of Ersiltoun etc; *m* 1507 Elizabeth Stewart (*m* 2nd Patrick Sinclair), illegitimate dau of James Stewart, Earl of Buchan (*see* MORAY, E), and *d* 1513, leaving:

1b John (Sir), of Cowdenknows or Ersiltoun; ktd 1552; *m* Margaret, dau of Andrew Ker of Cessford (*see* LOTHIAN, M), and *d c* Nov 1573, having had:

1c James (Sir), of Cowdenknows; ktd 1565; *m* (contract 13 Aug 1562) Katherine, dau of John Home of Blackadder (*see* HOME, Bt), and *d* 22 April 1592, having had:

1d John (Sir), of Cowdenknows; *m* 1st Marie Sinclair, dau of John, Master of Caithness (*see* CAITHNESS, E); *m* 2nd Beatrice, dau of 1st Earl of Gowrie (*see* CARLISLE, E), and *d c* 1629, having had, with other issue:

1e James, of Whitriggs; *m* his distant cousin Anne (*d* 1621), dau and coheir of 1st Earl of Dunbar of the 1605 *cr* (*see* HOME, Bt), and *d c* 30 March 1620, leaving an only s:

1f JAMES, **3rd Earl**

2e Henry (Sir), of Herdrig; Sheriff Depute Berwicks; *m* (contract 28 Nov 1674) Katherine, dau of Thomas Nisbet and widow of Dickson of Belchester

2d James (Sir); Commendator Eccles; *m* Isobel, dau of **5th Lord Home**, and had issue

3d Harie, of Smailholm; *m* Margaret, sis of Henry Sinclair of Whitekirk, and had issue

2c Alexander, of Graden and Darnchester; living 27 Sept 1595; *m* Janet Hamilton and had issue

3c Mark; living 20 Aug 1566

4c William, of Bassendan, Berwicks; ancestor of the HOMEs of Bassendean; *m* 1st (contract 5 Oct 1568) Marion, dau of James Pringle of Whytbank and widow of George Pringle of Blyndlie, and had issue; *m* 2nd *c* 2 Jan 1576/7 —, dau of John Eamestoun of that Ilk and widow of Henry Haitlie, Yr. of Mellerstain

2b Alexander; living 5 May 1534

2a John, of Synlaws; *k* Battle of Flodden 9 Sept 1513

2 John; living 17 March 1476/7; Prior Coldingham, Dean Chapel Royal

3 George, of Aton; living 23 Feb 1489/90; had issue

4 Patrick, of Fast Castle; living 25 June 1467; envoy England and Spain, *m* twice and had issue

The **1st Lord Home** *m* 2nd by 14 July 1467 Margaret, dau of Alexander, Master of Montgomerie (*see* EGLINTON and WINTON, E), and *d* between Feb 1490 and April 1491, having by her had, with other issue:

5 Thomas (Sir), of Langshaw, Ayrshire; living 10 June 1505; *m* 1st Janet Rynd and had issue; *m* 2nd Alison Colquhoun

1 Elizabeth; *m* Sir Alexander Seton of Touch (*see* SETON, Bt, of Abercorn)

The 2nd EARL's distant cousin,

Sir JAMES HOME, **3rd Earl of Home**, PC (S Feb 1660/1); Covenanter 1638, later royalist, cmded Berwicks Regt Battle of Preston 1648 against CROMWELL; *m* by 16 July 1640 Jean, dau of 8th Earl of Morton (*qv*), and *d* Dec 1666, leaving:

1 ALEXANDER HOME, **4th Earl of Home**; Burgess Glasgow 1666, Gentleman Privy Chamber 1671; *m* 19 April 1671 Lady Anne Sackville, 5th dau of 5th Earl of Dorset (*see* SACKVILLE, B), but *dsp* 1674

2 JAMES HOME, **5th Earl of Home**; Sheriff Berwicks; *m* Anne, dau of 2nd Earl of Dalhousie (*qv*), and *dsp* 1687

3 CHARLES HOME, **6th Earl of Home**; *m c* 1680 Anne, dau of Sir William Purves, Bt, of Purves Hall, Berwicks (*see* 1970 edn HOME-PURVES-HUME-CAMPBELL, Bt), and *d* 22 July 1706, having had, with other issue:

(1) ALEXANDER, **7th Earl**

(2) James, of Ayton; Jacobite 1715, hence his estate confiscated; *m* Zerobabel Haig, of Bemersyde, and *d* 1764, leaving:

1a Marion; *m* as his 2nd w **9th Earl of Home** (*see* below) and *dsp* 30 Oct 1763

2a Jane; *m* Dr James Hunter, of Monfodd

(3) George; *d* 1777, leaving two daus

(1) Jean; *m* 1703, Patrick, Lord Polwarth, s of 1st Lord Polwarth (*qv*)

The 6th EARL's est son,

ALEXANDER HOME, **7th Earl of Home**; rep S Peer 1710–13; imprisoned Edinburgh Castle 1715–16 on suspicion of Jacobite sympathies; *m* Anne (*m* 2nd Henry Ogle and *d* 1727), 2nd dau of 2nd Marquess of Lothian (*qv*), and *d* 1720, having had, with six other children:

1 WILLIAM HOME, **8th Earl of Home**; Cornet 2nd Dragoon Gds 1735, Capt-Lt 3rd Foot Gds 1743, fought for Govt at defeat by Jacobites Prestonpans 21 Sept 1745, Maj-Gen 1755, Lt-Gen 1759, Col 48th Foot 1750–52; Govr Gibraltar 1757–61; rep S peer 1741–61; *m* 25 Dec 1742 Elizabeth, dau of William Gibbons, of Jamaica, and widow of James Laes, and *dsp* 28 April 1761

2 Rev ALEXANDER HOME, **9th Earl of Home**; *m* 1st 1757 Primrose (*d* 18 Dec 1759), 5th dau of 9th Lord Elphinstone (*qv*), and had issue:

(1) William, *Lord Dunglas*; *b* 27 Nov 1757; Lt Coldstream Gds 1778; *d* unm *vp* a few days later of wounds recd Battle of Guildford War American Independence 15 March 1781

(1) Elizabeth Eleanor; *m* 1784 Gen Thomas Dundas (*d* 1794) and *d* 10 April 1837

2 (cont.) The **9th Earl** *m* 2nd his cousin Marion (*see* above); *m* 3rd 10 Feb 1768 Abigail Brown (*d* 5 Feb 1814), dau and heiress of John Ramey, barrister, of Yarmouth, and *d* 8 Oct 1786, having by her had:

(2) ALEXANDER, **10th Earl**

(2) Caroline; *d* unm 30 April 1794

(3) Charlotte; *m* Ven Charles Baillie-Hamilton (*d* 1820), Archdeacon Cleveland, and *d* 4 Dec 1866 (*see* HADDINGTON, E)

The 9th EARL's only surv son,

ALEXANDER HOME later RAMEY-HOME (roy licence 1 March 1814), **10th Earl of Home**; *b* 11 Nov 1769; rep S peer 1807–41, Ld Lt Berwicks 1794–1841, Col Berwicks Militia; *m* 9 Nov 1798 Elizabeth (*d* 29 June 1837), 2nd dau of 3rd Duke of Buccleuch and (5th Duke of) Queensberry (*qv*), and *d* 21 Oct 1841, having had, with two yr sons (William Montagu Douglas, *b* 22 Nov 1800, *d* unm 22 July 1822; Henry Campbell, *d* in infancy):

COSPATRICK ALEXANDER HOME, **11th Earl of Home**; *b* 27 Oct 1799; *educ* Ch Ch Oxford; Attaché St Petersburg 1822–23, FO 1824–27, U-Sec For Affrs 1828–30, rep S peer 1842–74, Lt-Gen Roy Co Archers 1878–81 (Maj-Gen 1859–78), *cr* 11 June 1875 BARON DOUGLAS OF DOUGLAS, Co Lanark (UK); *m* 4 Dec 1832 Lucy Elizabeth (*d* 15 May 1877), est dau of 2nd and last Baron Montagu of Boughton, and *d* 4 July 1881, having had, with other issue:

1 CHARLES ALEXANDER DOUGLAS, **12th Earl**

2 William Sholto; *b* 25 Feb 1842; Maj-Gen, Col cmdg Gren Gds; *d* 22 Dec 1916

3 Cospatrick; *b* 2 May 1848; Maj and Hon Lt-Col 3rd Bn Roy Scots, Capt Rifle Bde; *d* 25 April 1912

4 George Douglas; *b* 4 Oct 1853; Lt Lanarks Yeo Cav; *d* 18 May 1913

1 Ada; *b* 8 Sept 1846; *m* 10 April 1880 Hon Henry Robert Hepburne-Scott (*d* 4 March 1914), bro of 8th Lord Polwarth (*qv*), and *d* 1 June 1932, leaving issue

The 11th EARL's est son,

CHARLES ALEXANDER HOME later DOUGLAS-HOME (added on mother's death 1877), **12th Earl of Home**, KT (1899), TD, DL (Berwicks and Glasgow); *b* 11 April 1834; *educ* Eton and Trin Coll Cambridge (MA); Hon Col 3rd and 4th Bns Scottish Rifles and Lanarks Yeo, ADC to HM QUEEN VICTORIA 1887–97; Ld Lt Berwicks 1879–90 and Lanarks 1890, Capt Roy Co Archers; *m* 18 Aug 1870 Maria (*d* 25 May 1919), only dau of Capt Charles Conrad Grey, RN (*see* GREY, E), and *d* 30 April 1918, leaving issue:

1 CHARLES COSPATRICK ARCHIBALD, **13th Earl**

1 Mary Elizabeth Margaret; *m* 5 Sept 1895 Richard Charles, Lord Gillford (*dvp* 14 Oct 1905), est s of 4th Earl of Clanwilliam (*qv*), and *d* 21 April 1951, leaving issue

2 Beatrix Lucy; *m* 9 Feb 1899 Sir Henry Herbert Philip Dundas, 3rd Bt, MVO (*qv*), of Arniston, and *d* 6 Nov 1940, leaving issue

3 Margaret Jane; *m* 10 Dec 1908 5th Baron Ormathwaite, MVO (*see* 1970 edn), and *d* 9 Sept 1955, leaving issue

4 Isobel Charlotte; RRC; *d* unm 8 Jan 1934

The 12th EARL's son,

CHARLES COSPATRICK ARCHIBALD HOME later DOUGLAS-HOME, **13th Earl of Home**, KT (1930), TD, JP (Lanarks and Berwicks); *b* 29 Dec 1873; *educ* Eton and Ch Ch Oxford; Hon Col Lanarks Yeo and 3rd and 4th Bns Cameronians WW I (despatches); V-Lt Lanarks 1922, Ld Lt Berwicks, Hon LLD Glasgow, Capt Roy Co Archers; *m* 14 July 1902 Lady Lilian Lambton (*d* 26 Sept 1966), 2nd dau of 4th Earl of Durham (*qv*), and *d* 11 July 1951, leaving issue:

1 ALEXANDER FREDERICK, **14th Earl**

2 Henry Montagu, MBE (1954); *b* 21 Nov 1907; *educ* Eton and Ch Ch Oxford ; Maj Gen List WW II; *m* 1st 7 July 1931 (*divorce* 1947) Lady Margaret Spencer (*d* 26 May 1996), 3rd dau of 6th Earl Spencer (*qv*), and had:

(1) (Cecil) Robin; *b* 8 May 1932; *educ* Eton; Lt Seaforth Highrs; pianist and writer; *m* 9 July 1959 (*divorce* 1965) Sandra Clare (*m* 2nd 1975 Michael Howard, QC, MP, Home Sec 1993–97), yr dau of W/Cdr Saville Paul, MRCS, LRCP, of Surrey, and *d* 15 Oct 1968, leaving:

1a +(Alexander) Sholto [Sholto Douglas-Home Esq, 38A Tite St, London SW10 9DT]; *b* 1 Sept 1962; head advertising BT, 1995–, author *Zayat Restaurant Guide to London* (1996); *m* 1992 *Alexandra, dau of Benjamin Miller, turf accountant (*see* also BRADFORD, E)

(2) Charles Cospatrick; *b* 1 Sept 1937; *educ* Eton; 2nd Lt RSG; defence correspondent *The Times* 1965, ed 1982–85; *m* 28 Jan 1966 *Jessica Violet (*m* 2nd 1993 Rodney Leach) [Mrs Rodney Leach, 63 Hillgate Place, London W8], dau of Maj John Nevile Wake Gwynne, of Knightsmill, Quenington, Glos, and *d* 1985, leaving:

1a +Tara John; *b* 8 April 1969

2a +Luke Cospatrick; *b* 2 March 1971

(1) *Fiona Margaret; *b* 7 Jan 1936; *m* 1st 25 Sept 1962 (*divorce* 1981) Gregory Martin, s of William Alexander Martin, and has:

1a *Kezia Alexandra Lilian; *b* 12 April 1970

2a *Lydia Georgiana Bridget; *b* 30 Sept 1975

(1) (cont.) Mrs Fiona Martin *m* 2nd 1993, as his 2nd w, *Sir Ian James Fraser, CBE, MC (*see* LOVAT, L)

2 (cont.) The Hon Henry Douglas-Home *m* 2nd 16 June 1947 Vera Bugge (*d* 6 June 1963), dau of Carl Herman Jensen, of Oslo, and formerly w of Ivan Johansen, and by her had:

(3) +George Erik Montagu; *b* 6 Oct 1948

2 (cont.) The Hon Henry Douglas-Home *m* 3rd 16 Feb 1966 *Felicity Betty, dau of Maj Aubrey Thomas Jonsson, Roy Irish Rifles, of Natal, S Africa, and formerly w of Hon Victor Patrick Hamilton Wills (*see* DULVERTON, B), and *d* 1980, leaving by her:

(4) +Peregrine Montagu; *b* 28 July 1967

3 William; *b* 3 June 1912; *educ* Eton and New Coll Oxford (BA 1934); Capt RAC WW II; playwright; *m* 26 July 1951 *Baroness Dacre (*qv*) in her own right and *d* 1992, having had issue

4 +Edward Charles [The Hon Edward Douglas-Home, Westnewton, Kirknewton, Wooler, Northumberland]; *b* 1 March 1920; *educ* Eton; 2nd Lt RA WW II (wounded, POW); *m* 24 July 1946 *Nancy Rose, 3rd Offr WRNS, only dau of Sir Thomas Dalrymple Straker-Smith, of Carham Hall, Berwick-on-Tweed, and has:

(1) +Simon [Simon Douglas-Home Esq, 70 Cloncurry St, London SW6]; *b* 20 Aug 1947; *educ* Eton; *m* *Sally, only dau of S/Ldr B Beard, AFC, RAF, and has:

1a +Edward; *b* 1980

1a *Joanna; *b* 16 Feb 1973

2a *Louisa; *b* 10 Feb 1976

(2) +Andrew [Andrew Douglas-Home Esq, The Lees, Coldstream, Berwickshire]; *b* 14 May 1950; *educ* Eton; *m* 1980 *Jane, dau of Maurice Oliver Pease, and has had issue:

1a +Richard; *b* 4 March 1983

2a +Nicholas; *b* 1985

3a Freddie; *b* 13 Dec 1989; *d* 27 Jan 1990

(3) +Mark [Mark Douglas-Home, 25 India St, Edinburgh EH3 6EH]; *b* 31 Aug 1951; *educ* Eton; *m* 1976 *Colette, dau of James O'Reilly and has issue:

1a +Rory; *b* 1981

1a *Rebecca; *b* 1978

5 George Cospatrick; *b* 2 Sept 1922; F/O RAF WW II; *ka* 14 June 1943

1 Bridget; *b* 4 May 1905; *d* 25 Dec 1980

2 Rachel; *b* 10 April 1910; *m* 27 April 1937 Lt-Col Lord William Walter Montagu- Douglas-Scott, MC (*d* 30 Jan 1958), 2nd s of 7th Duke of Buccleuch and (9th Duke of) Queensberry (*qv*), and *d* 4 April 1996, leaving issue

The 13th EARL's est son,

ALEXANDER (ALEC) FREDERICK DOUGLAS-HOME, **14th Earl of Home**, disclaimed peerages for life 23 Oct 1963, *cr* 1975 BARON HOME OF THE HIRSEL, of Coldstream, Co Berwick (LP, UK), KT (1962), PC (1951), JP, DL (Lanarks1960), DL (Berwicks 1944); *b* 2 July 1903; *educ* Eton and Ch Ch Oxford; Maj Lanarks Yeo TAR; MP (C) Lanark Oct 1931–June 1945 and Feb 1950–July 1951 and Perthshire and Kinross-shire Nov 1963–74, PPS to Rt Hon Neville Chamberlain 1935–40, Jt Parly U-Sec For Affrs May–July 1945, Min State Scottish Off Oct 1951–April 1955, Sec State Cwlth Rels April 1955–July 1960, Ld Pres Cncl Jan–Sept 1957 and Oct 1959–July 1960, Leader Ho Lds Jan 1957–July 1960, For Sec July 1960–63 and 1970–74, PM and First Ld Treasury 1963–64, Leader Oppn 1964–65, memb Select Ctee Procedure 1976, Chm C working party reform Ho Lds 1977, Chm Jr Imp League, Grand Master Primrose League 1966, Pres MCC 1966–67, Govr I Zingari 1977, Chllr Order Thistle 1973–92, Hon LLD Oxon 1960, Freeman Coldstream 1972; *m* 3 Oct 1936 Elizabeth Hester (*d* 1990), 2nd dau of Very Rev Cyril Argentine Alington, DD, Dean Durham, and *d* 9 Oct 1995, leaving:

1 DAVID ALEXANDER COSPATRICK DOUGLAS-HOME, **15th and present Earl of Home**

1 *(Lavinia) Caroline, DL (Berwicks 1983) [The Lady Caroline Douglas-Home DL, Heaton Mill House, Cornhill-on-Tweed, Northumberland TD12 4XQ]; *b* 11 Oct 1937; T/Woman Bedchamber to HM QUEEN ELIZABETH THE QUEEN MOTHER 1963–65, T/Lady-in-Waiting to HRH THE DUCHESS OF KENT 1966–67, Extra Ldy-in-Waiting 1967–; FSA Scot; Tstee Nat Museum Antiquities Scotland 1982–86

2 *Meriel Kathleen [The Lady Meriel Darby, Kemerton Court, Tewkesbury, Glos GL20 7HY]; *b* 27 Nov 1939; *m* 30 March 1964 *Adrian Marten George Darby, Fell, Tutor and Bursar Keble Coll Oxford, only s of Col Cyril George Darby, MC, of Kemerton Court, by Monica Clarice, yr dau of Lt-Col Edward Marten Dunne, JP, DL, of Herefs, and has issue:

(1) *Matthew George Darby; *b* 27 Aug 1967

(1) *Catherine Monica Darby; *b* 23 Dec 1964

3 *Diana Lucy; *b* 18 Dec 1940; *m* 8 June 1963 (*divorce* 1976) James Archibald Wolfe Murray and has issue (*see* MURRAY, Bt, of Blackbarony)

HOME, Bt

Arms: Quarterly, 1st, azure on a chevron three roses gules (for BLACKADDER); 2nd, vert a lion rampant argent, langed and armed gules (for HOME); 3rd, argent three popinjays vert, beaked and limbed gules (for PEPDIE); 4th, argent a cross engrailed azure (for SINCLAIR of Hermandston). **Crest:** An adder sable in pale, holding in its mouth a rose gules, leaved and stalked vert. **Supporters:** Dexter, an otter; sinister, a falcon, both proper. **Motto:** *Vise a la fin* ('Look to the end'). **Creation:** Bt. (NS) 25 Jan 1670/1.

SIR WILLIAM DUNDAS HOME, 14TH BT, of Blackadder, Co Berwick [Sir William Home Bt, 27A Oatley Rd, Paddington, NSW 2021, Australia]; *b* 19 Feb 1968; *s* gf 1992; *educ* Cranbrook Sch, Sydney; consultant tree surgn and horticulturalist, memb Internat Soc Arboriculture 1991, Aust Inst of Horticulture 1992; *m* 30 Sept 1995 *Dominique Maryl, dau of Sydney Fischer, OBE, of Sydney, NSW, and has:

1 +THOMAS JOHN; *b* 24 Nov 1996

Lineage: Sir DAVID HOME (2nd s of Sir John Home of that Ilk; *see* HOME, E), had a charter from the 4th Earl of Douglas of the lands of Wedderburn, Berwicks, part of the forfeited estates of 10th Earl of Dunbar, which was confirmed by the latter Earl on his restitution in 1413 and by JAMES I 19 April 1431; *m* Alice — and *d c* 28 Feb 1452/3, having had:

DAVID HOME of Wedderburn, Yr.; *m* Elizabeth Carmichael (*d* 1495) and *dvp c* 1450, leaving, with a yr s (Patrick, *see* POLWARTH, L) and a dau (Sibilla, *m* Henry Hatly of Mellerstains):

GEORGE HOME of Wedderburn; *m* Mariota (*m* 2nd George Ker of Samuelston), dau and coheir of Sir John St Clair of Hermandston, and was *k* 18 May 1497, having had, with a yr s and two daus:

Sir DAVID HOME of Wedderburn; *m* Isobel, dau of David Hoppringil of Smailholm, and was *k* Battle of Flodden 9 Sept 1513, having had, with three daus:

1 George; known in border song with his bros as the 'Seven Spears of Wedderburn'; *k* Flodden

2 David, of Wedderburn; ancestor of the MILNE HOMEs of Wedderburn

3 Alexander, of Manderston, Berwicks; had:

(1) Alexander, of Manderston; *m* 1552 Janet, dau of George Home of Spot, and *d* by 1593, leaving, with an est s (*d* young):

1a Alexander, of Manderston; *m* Christian, dau of Sir Alexander Erskine of Gogar, and *d* between May 1608 and 1610, leaving:

1b GEORGE HOME, *de jure* 3rd EARL OF DUNBAR; *m* 1st Isobel Home (*d* between May 1608 and Aug 1610); *m* 2nd 4 Sept 1610 Helen, dau of Sir John Arnot of Berswick [*sic*], Provost Edinburgh, and widow of Isaac Morison, Baillie Edinburgh, and *d* between 1637 and 1651, leaving by his 1st w:

1c Sir ALEXANDER HOME, *de jure* 4th EARL OF DUNBAR; *m* 1616 Margaret, dau of Isaac Morison, his stepmother's former husb, and *dspm* 1675

2c George; *dvf* by 24 Sept 1663, leaving an est s:

1d ALEXANDER HOME, *de jure* 5th EARL OF DUNBAR; Capt of Horse in Dutch service; he and/or his heirs allegedly lived in Holland, the line dying out later in the 17th century

1c Margaret; *m* 1624, as his 2nd w, Sir Archibald Stewart of Blackhall (*see* SHAW-STEWART, Bt)

2a JOHN HOME, *de jure* 2nd EARL OF DUNBAR; *m* Christian Cockburn and *dspm* on or after 23 Aug 1628, leaving:

1b Nicola; *m* Robert Dickson of Stanefauld

3a GEORGE HOME, 1st EARL OF DUNBAR (S), so *cr* 3 July 1605, with remainder to heirs male, as also earlier 7 July 1604 BARON HUME, OF BERWICK (E), with remainder to his heirs for ever (*i.e.*, any relatives he cared to nominate), KG (1608), PC (1603); Gentleman Bedchamber to JAMES VI 1585, ktd 1590, Master Gt Wardrobe Scotland 1590 and England 1603, High Treasurer Scotland 1601, Chllr Exchequer 1603–07, Keeper Holyrood Palace Jan 1609/10; *m* Elizabeth, dau of Sir Alexander Gordon of Gight (*see* HUNTLY, M), and *dspm* 20 Jan 1610/1, when his titles became dormant (and were certainly not assumed by his heirs mentioned above), leaving:

1b Anne; *m* Sir James Home and had:

1c JAMES HOME, 3rd EARL OF HOME (*qv*)

2b Elizabeth; *m* March 1611/2 2nd Earl of Suffolk (*see* SUFFOLK and BERKSHIRE, E)

2a James, of Steill; *d* by 1622, leaving:

1b John

3a William; *m* Mary Quhytlaw and *dspm* by 1616, leaving:

1b Jean

(2) Patrick, of Killknow; ancestor of the Home Bts of Renton (*cr c* 1675; extinct 1788) and the Home Bts of Lumsden (*cr* 1697, extinct 1784)

4 JOHN, for whom *see* below

5 Robert; *m* Margaret, yr dau and coheir of Robert Blackadder of that Ilk

6 Andrew; Parson of Lauder *c* 8 May 1536

7 Bartholomew, of Simprin

8 Patrick, of Broomhouse; ancestor of the LOGAN HOMEs of Broomhouse

Sir DAVID's 4th son,

JOHN HOME of Easter Blackadder; *m* 1518 Beatrix, er dau and coheir of Robert Blackadder of that Ilk, and shared the inheritance with his bro Robert, husb of the other coheir; his gs:

JOHN HOME of Blackadder; *d* 1608, leaving:

Sir JOHN HOME of Blackadder; MP Berwicks 1617–40; *m* —, dau of Haldane of Gleneagles, and had:

Sir JOHN HOME of Blackadder; MP Berwicks 1643–46; *m* Mary, dau of Sir James Dundas of Arniston, Midlothian, Govr Berwick, and *d* 1655, having had, with a yr s (Sir David, of Crossrigs, a Ld of Session as Lord Crossrigs 1689, a Ld of Justiciary 1690, *d* 12 April 1707, leaving issue):

Sir John Home 1st Bt (NS), so *cr* 25 Jan 1670/1, of Blackadder; *m* 1660 his cousin Mary (*d* 1672), dau of Sir James Dundas of Arniston, and *d* 23 Jan 1675, leaving, with a yr s:

Sir John Home, 2nd Bt; MP Berwick 1690–1706; *m* Katherine (*d* 6 June 1755), dau of Sir Robert Pringle, 1st Bt (*qv*), and *d* 4 April 1706, leaving:

1 **Sir John Home, 3rd Bt**; *m* Anne (*d* 1 Jan 1779), dau of William Nisbet of Dirleton, and had:

(1) **Sir William Home, 4th Bt**; *d* young

(2) **Sir John Home, 5th Bt**; *dsp*, *bur* 9 April 1737

(1) Margaret; *m* 8 Dec 1728 Hon John Hamilton (*d* 27 Dec 1779), 2nd s of 6th Earl of Haddington (*qv*), and *d* 11 Feb 1772, leaving issue

2 **Sir James Home, 6th Bt**, WS; *m* Catherine (*d* 30 Aug 1788), dau of George Livingstone, Dep-Clerk Session, and *d* 28 March 1755, having had, with a dau (Anne, *m* Walter Forrest), an only s:

1a **Sir George Home, 7th Bt**; V-Adml the Blue; *m* 13 Sept 1785 Helen, dau and coheir of James Buchanan, of Drumpellier, and *d* 2 May 1803, having had, with other issue:

1b **Sir James Home, 8th Bt**; *b* 17 March 1790; HEICS; *m* 12 July 1828 Anna (*d* 8 June 1866), est dau of Andrew Stirling of Drumpellier, and *d* 12 March 1836, having had:

1c **Sir John Home, 9th Bt**; *b* 4 Aug 1829; RN; *d* unm 26 March 1849

2c Sir GEORGE HOME later HOME-SPIERS (added 1878), **10th Bt**, DL Stirlingshire; *b* 23 Sept 1832; advocate Scottish Bar, Sheriff-Substitute Argyllshire; *m* 9 March 1858 Ann Oliphant (*d* 26 June 1907), only child of Robert Graham Spiers, Advocate Sheriff Midlothian, and *d* 30 July 1887, having had issue:

1d **Sir James Home, 11th Bt**; *b* 28 Sept 1861; Capt 11th (Service) Bn Highland LI 1914–16, Capt 9th Bn Cameron Highrs 1916, formerly Lt 1st Bn Black Watch, Egyptian Campaign 1882–85 (medal, five clasps, bronze star), WW I in France and Belgium (star, two medals); *m* 30 Aug 1892 Amy Eliza (*d* 28 July 1927), yr dau of William A Green, of San Francisco, and *dsp* 1 Aug 1931

2d Robert Graham Spiers; *b* 26 May 1864; lost aboard the *Louisa* between Hobart and Melbourne Dec 1882

3d JOHN HOME (Sir), **12th Bt**

1d Catherine; *m* 23 Nov 1891 Rev Alwyne Compton Howard Rice, Rector Wolverton, Norfolk, and *d* 19 July 1916, leaving issue

2d Anna Beatrice; *m* 19 Jan 1886 Col Alfred Harold Middleton (*dsp* 2 Feb 1905), Argyll & Sutherland Highrs, and *d* 20 June 1937

3d Alice Georgina; *m* 12 June 1890 James Mackenzie (*d* 3 Jan 1928), of Dumbarton, and *d* 10 Nov 1950, leaving issue

The 11th Bt's bro,

Sir John Home, 12th Bt; *b* 9 July 1872; *educ* Trin Coll Glenalmond; Dir Nat Bank of Egypt, Order Nile 2nd Cl; *m* 21 Dec 1898 Hon Gwendolina Hyacinth Roma Mostyn (*d* 22 March 1960), sis of 7th Baron Vaux of Harrowden (*qv*), and *d* 19 Oct 1938, leaving:

Sir David George Home 13th Bt; *b* 21 Jan 1904; *educ* Harrow and Jesus Coll Cambridge (BA 1925), T/Maj Argyll & Sutherland Highrs WW II, memb Roy Co Archers; dir Edin & Dundee Investment; *m* 5 Jan 1933 Sheila, dau of Mervyn Campbell Stephen, and *d* 1992, having had:

1 John; *b* 1 June 1936; *educ* Harrow and Jesus Coll Cambridge (BA 1959); *m* 6 July 1966 *Nancy Helen [Lady Gorton, 32 Parsley Rd, Vaucluse, NSW 2030, Australia] (*m* 3rd Rt Hon Sir John Grey Gorton, GCMG, AC, CH), er dau of Harry Greenlaw Elliott, of Perth, W Australia, and widow of Cdr Ian Macgregor, RAN, and *d* 1988, leaving:

(1) Sir WILLIAM DUNDAS HOME, **14th and present Bt**

(1) *Georgina Helen; *b* 30 June 1969

2 +Patrick [Patrick Home Esq, Winterfield, North Berwick, E Lothian EH39 4LY]; *b* 4 July 1941; *educ* Harrow; *m* 1984 *Catherine Mary, yr dau of James Mclaren Henderson, of Spittalrigg, Haddington, E Lothian, and has:

(1) +David McLaren; *b* 6 March 1993

(1) *Janet; *b* 11 July 1986

1 *Hermione [Hermione Lady Malcolm, Whiteholm, Gullane, E Lothian EH31 2BD]; *b* 25 Feb 1934; *educ* LMH Oxford (BA 1955); *m* 6 June 1959 *Sir David Peter Michael Malcolm, 11th Bt (*qv*), and has issue

2 Anne; *b* 14 Aug 1942; *m* 1st 3 Nov 1962 (*divorce* 19–) Michael Franks, est s of Jacob Franks, LRCS, of Step House, W Chiltington, Sussex; *m* 2nd (*divorce*) — and *d* 1986, leaving:

(1) *Lucinda Home; *b* 17 March 1964

(2) *Miranda Home; *b* 6 Feb 1966

HONYWOOD

Arms: Arg. a chevron between three hawk's heads erased az., beaked or. **Crest:** A wolf's head, couped erm. **Motto:** *Omne bonum desuper* ('All good comes from above'). **Creation:** Bt. (E) 19 July 1660.

SIR FILMER COURTENAY WILLIAM HONYWOOD, 11TH BT, of Evington, Co Kent [Sir Filmer Honywood Bt, Greenway Forstal Farmhouse, Hollingbourne, Kent ME17 1QA]; *b* 20 May 1930; *s* f 1982; *educ* Downside, RMA Sandhurst and RAC Cirencester (MRAC Dip), FRICS; 3rd Carabiniers (Prince of Wales's Dragoon Gds) 1950–51, assist surveyor MAFF 1966–73, surveyor Cockermouth, Cumbria, 1973–74, sr lands offr CEGB (SE Regn) 1974–78, regnl surveyor and valuer CEGB (SE Regn) 1978–88, Ag Compensation and Restoration Consultant to UK Nirex 1988–89, Co Sec Honywood Business Consultancy Services Ltd, land agency consultant to Nuclear Electric plc 1993–94, examiner ag Inc Soc Estate & Wayleaves Offrs 1989–95 and Soc of Surveying Technicians 1996–97; *m* 12 May 1956 Elizabeth Margaret Mary Cynthia (*d* 25 Dec 1996), 2nd dau of Sir Alastair George Lionel Joseph Miller, 6th Bt of Glenlee (*qv*), and has:

1 +RUPERT ANTHONY PAGAN [Rupert Honywood Esq, c/o Greenway Forstal Farmhouse, Hollingbourne, Kent ME17 1QA]; *b* 2 March 1957; consultant systems designer; *m* 10 Oct 1992 *Wendy, 3rd dau of Thomas Young, of Carshalton and has:

(1) +Samuel Thomas Courtenay; *b* 19 Oct 1996

2 +Simon Joseph [Simon Honywood Esq, 182 Annie St, New Farm, Qld 3005, Australia]; *b* 16 July 1958; BA, MRTPI, MRAPI, AAILA; Parks Planning Offr Brisbane City Cncl

1 *Mary Caroline [Mrs Christopher Bear, 424 Rue des Ecoles, Zutkerque, France]; *b* 18 May 1961; SRN, SCM; *m* 25 Sept 1992 *Christopher Bear, yr s of Eric Bear of Gedling, Notts, and has:

(1) *Edward James; *b* 24 Nov 1994

2 *Judith Mary Frances; *b* 30 Sept 1964

Lineage: JOHN HONYWOOD, descended from a family long resident in Kent; *m* 1st Agnes, dau and heir of Henry Martin, and had:

1 JOHN

JOHN HONYWOOD *m* 2nd a dau of — Barne, of Wye, Kent, and had by her:

2 Robert, of Charing, Kent, and Marks Hall, Essex, *m* Mary, dau and coheir of Robert Waters, of Lenham, Kent, and was ancestor both of the HONYWOODS, of Horsham, Sussex, and:

(1) Philip, of Marks Hall; Lt-Gen; willed his estates 1785 to Filmer Honywood

The er son,

JOHN HONYWOOD, of St George's Priory, Canterbury; MP Hythe *temp* ELIZABETH I; *m* Mildreda, dau of — Hales, Baron Exchequer, and had issue, with an est s (Thomas, MP Hythe, *dsp*), a yst s (Christopher, MP Hythe, *dsp*) and two daus:

JOHN HONYWOOD; *m* 1st Joanna, dau and heir of — Perry, of Chatham, and had a s; *m* 2nd Jane, dau of Peter Heyman and sole heir of her mother Mary (dau of — Tirrel, of Beches, Essex), and had a dau (Catherine, sole heir of her mother, *m* Sir Edward Scott, KB, of Scott's Hall); his s by his 1st w:

Sir THOMAS HONYWOOD, of Greenwich, *m* Jane, dau of Edward Hales, of Tenterden, and had, with three yr sons and two daus:

1 JOHN (Sir)

2 William; Sheriff London 1639

3 Edward; *m* Mary, dau of John Baker, of Withiam, Sussex, and had:

(1) Isaac, of Hampstead; *m* 1667 Rebecca, 3rd dau of William Pycheford, and had:

1a Isaac; *m* Mary Fraser and *d* 1740, leaving:

1b Frazer, of London; banker; *m* Jane, dau of Abraham Atkins, and willed his property to **Sir John Honywood, 3rd Bt**

Sir Thomas *d* 1622; his est son,

Sir JOHN HONYWOOD; High Sheriff Kent 1607–09; *m* Mary, dau of Thomas Godfrey, of Lydd, Kent, and *d* 1658, leaving:

Sir Edward Honywood, 1st Bt (E), so *cr* 19 July 1660, of Evington, Kent; *m* Elizabeth, dau of Sir John Maynard, of Tooting, Surrey, and *d* 1670, having had, with a yr s (John (Rev), MA Cantab, Rector Burwash, Kent, *d* unm Sept 1737) and a dau (Thomasine):

Sir William Honywood, 2nd Bt; MP Canterbury 1685–98; *m* 15 July 1675 Anna Christiana (*d* 26 Oct 1736), dau of Richard Newman, of Fifehead Magna, Dorset, and had, with four daus:

1 William, of Cheriton; *m* Frances, dau of William Raleigh, and *dvp* 1719, leaving:

(1) JOHN (Sir), **3rd Bt**

(1) Frances Newman; *m* Thomas Hodges, of Lacon Warehorn, Kent

(2) Martha; *m* Thomas Andrews, of Hinkshill, Kent

(3) Thomasine; *m* Thomas Randolph, DD, Pres Ch Ch Oxford

2 Edward; Judge Advocate RN; *m* Mary, dau of Thomas Wearg, of Kensington, and had:

(1) Mary; *m* James Smith, 3rd s of Trafford Smith (est s of Sir Robert Smith, Bt, of Upton)

(2) Anne

Sir WILLIAM *d* 1 June 1748; his gs,

Sir John Honywood, 3rd Bt, Sheriff Kent 1752; *s* 1754 to his kinsman Frazer Honywood's seats at Malling Abbey, Kent, and Hampstead; *m* 1st Annabella (*d* 22 July 1737), dau of William Goodenough, of Langford, Berks, and had, with three daus

1 William, of Malling Abbey; *b* 1731; *m* Elizabeth, dau of Thomas Clack, of Wallingford, and *dvp* 23 Oct 1764, leaving:

(1) JOHN (Sir), **4th Bt**

(2) William, of Lyminge, Kent, and Marks Hall, Essex; *s* to the estates of his uncle Filmer Honywood; *m* Mary, sis of James Drake Brockman, of Beachborough, and had:

1a William Philip, of Marks Hall; *m* Priscillia Hanbury, of Halstead, Essex, and *d* 22 April 1801, leaving:

1b William Philip; *b* 15 Oct 1823; *m* Frances Emma (*d* 30 Jan 1895), dau of Charles Phelips, of Briggens Park, Herts, and *d* 28 Feb 1859

1a Caroline; *m* 17 Jan 1815 Rev T H de Ripley, Vicar Wootton Bassett

2a Elizabeth

(3) Edward (Rev); LLD; Rector Honiton, Preb Exeter, *m* Sophia, dau of Rev John Long, and *d* 1 Dec 1812, leaving a s (*d* unm) and dau

(1) Annabella Christiana; *m* Robert Gorges Dobyns Yate, of Bromesberrow, Glos, and had issue

2 Edward; *d* Norwich 1752

Sir John *m* 2nd 1742 Dorothy (*d* 8 Oct 1781), dau of Sir Edward Filmer, Bt, and *d* 26 June 1781, leaving by her:

3 Filmer, of Hull Place, Kent, and Marks Hall; MP; *d* unm 2 June 1809

4 John (Rev); *b* 1745; *m* 1785 Elizabeth, dau of Rev Preb Charles Wake

1 Mary; *m* J W Emmett

His gs,

Sir John Honywood, 4th Bt; MP Steyning 1784–85 and 1788–90, Canterbury 1790–1802 and Honiton 1802–06; *m* 13 Dec 1788 Frances, dau of 2nd Viscount Courtenay of Powderham Castle (*see* DEVON, E), and *d* 29 March 1806, having had, with other issue, including three daus (Charlotte Dorothea, *m* Col Sir Frederick Grey Cooper, Bt, and *d* 1811; Annabella Christiana, *m* Sir Edward Knatchbull, 9th Bt (*see* BRABOURNE, B), and *d* 1814; Caroline, *m* 1807 Edward Temple, only s of Rev Thomas William Temple, DD, and had a s and two daus):

Sir John Courtenay Honywood, 5th Bt; *b* 1787; *m* 27 July 1808 Mary Anne (*d c* April 1841), est dau of Rev William Henry Cooper, and had, with other issue:

1 JOHN EDWARD (Sir), **6th Bt**

2 William; Hon Col Berks Yeo; *b* 4 March 1814; *m* 19 March 1844 Barbara Henrietta (*d* 8 Aug 1895), yst dau of James Whyte, of Pilton House, Devon, and *d* 6 Feb 1895

1 Mary Anne Elizabeth; *m* 4 Feb 1834 Capt Frederick Barne, 12th Lancers, of Scotterley and Dunwich, Suffolk, and *d* 18 June 1890 aged 81. He *d* March 1886

2 Louisa Lucy; *m* 4 June 1844 Rev James Whyte, Rector King's Nympton, Devon, and *d* 18 Oct 1870

Sir JOHN *d* 12 Sept 1832; his est son,

Sir John Edward Honywood, 6th Bt; *b* 16 March 1812; *m* 17 April 1834 Mary (*m* 2nd 11 July 1848 William Clark, of Oswalds, Torquay, and *d* 27 May 1884 aged 68), 2nd dau of Rev Charles Hughes-Hallett, of Higham, Kent, and had, with other issue:

1 COURTENAY (Sir), **7th Bt**

1 Frances Hallett; *m* 22 Jan 1861 Rev Thomas Stone Carnsew, Vicar Constantine, Cornwall, and *d* 7 Oct 1890, leaving issue

2 Marion Grace; *m* 9 Feb 1869 Rev John Theed Watson, Rector Woodford, Northants, and *d* 4 Dec 1915, leaving issue. He *d* 20 June 1911

3 Florence Elizabeth; *m* 22 Aug 1867 Rev Edward William Northey, JP, of Woodcote House, Epsom, and *d* 18 June 1928, leaving issue. He *d* 21 Oct 1914

The 6th Bt *d* 17 July 1845; his est son,

Sir Courtenay Honywood, 7th Bt, DL Kent; *b* 5 March 1835; *m* 23 Aug 1855 Annie Maria (*d* 27 April 1905), 2nd dau of William Paynter, of Camborne House, Richmond, Surrey, and had issue:

1 JOHN WILLIAM (Sir), **8th Bt**

2 Philip Courtenay; Lt Essex Rifles; *b* 16 July 1858; *d* unm 14 July 1902

3 Wyndham; Lt SW Bdrs; *b* 16 July 1858; *d* unm 23 March 1896

4 Arthur; Lt 66th Foot; *b* 17 Nov 1860; *ka* Kushk-i-Nakhud 27 July 1880

5 Cecil Robert; *b* 27 Dec 1862; *d* 1925
6 Reginald Ernest; Capt SS *Ismalia*; *b* 14 Dec 1863; *m* 23 July 1906 Victoria Henrietta Ezilda Carr and *d* 3 Oct 1917, leaving issue:
(1) Flora Victoria; dir Coty (England) Ltd; *m* 4 Dec 1957 Maurice Edward Grubb
7 Edward Fenton; *b* 24 Oct 1865; *d* 20 May 1891
8 Guy; *b* 7 Nov 1871; *m* 20 Sept 1900 Margaret Bennett Adamson and *d* 22 Sept 1912, leaving:
(1) Thomas Guy; *b* 28 April 1903; *m* 1st 19– — and has:
1a +Guy Thorp [Guy Honywood Esq, 15 Kelvin St, Oamaru, New Zealand]; *b* 19–; *m* 19– *Adriane —
(1) (cont.) Thomas Honywood *m* 2nd *Anne Gertrude Molloy, and *d* 1968, leaving by her:
2a +Barry [Barry Honywood Esq, Box 50 PO, Castle Hill, NSW 2154, Australia]; *b* 1932; *m* 19– *Anne — and has:
1b +Michael; *b* 19–
2b +Matthew; *b* 19–
1a *Bernadette Margaret [Mrs Nepia Maniapoto, 44 Wharenni Rd, Rotorua, New Zealand]; *b* 1936; *m* 1960 *Nepia Maniapoto, RNZA Regt Korean War, and has issue:
1b *Maru John; *b* 1967; BMS
1b *Moana Maree [Mrs William Jackson, 44 Tamaki Ave, Otahuhu, Auckland, New Zealand]; *b* 1961; LLB; *m* 19– *William Wakatere Jackson, and has issue:
1c *Kimiora Hikurangi Elijah; *b* 1990
2b *Katarina Mae [Mrs Warren Morgan, 9 Morey St, Rotorua, New Zealand]; *b* 1962; *m* 19– *Warren Ruru Morgan and has:
1c *Nepia Thomas; *b* 1986
1c *Katarina Aroha; *b* 1991
3b *Niki Ann; *b* 1964
4b *Keri Lee [Mrs David Cheer, 141 Tavistock Rd, Waipukurau, New Zealand]; *b* 1965; *m* 19–
5b Lisa Aroha; *b* 1969; BEd
1 Annie Mabel; *d* unm 6 Nov 1934
2 Violet Constance Evelyn; *d* unm 1 May 1949

Sir COURTENAY *d* 17 April 1878; his est son,

Sir John William Honywood, 8th Bt, JP Kent; Alderman Kent, CC, Lt RE Kent Yeo and 2nd Derby Militia; *b* 15 April 1857; *m* 22 Aug 1877 Zaidée Emily Iseulte (*d* 15 Oct 1893), est dau of John Bodychan Bodychan-Sparrow, of Bodychan, Anglesey, and *d* 17 June 1907, leaving:
1 **Sir Courtenay John Honywood, 9th Bt**; *b* 29 May 1880; *m* 1903 Constance Mary, OStJ (1951), fndr Honywood Hotels (*d* 9 April 1956), dau of Rev Charles Henry Vincent Pixell, MA, and *dsp* 4 July 1944
2 WILLIAM WYNNE (Sir), **10th Bt**
3 Philip Sidney, of Woodcliffe Lake, NJ; *b* 5 Sept 1893; *m* 1st 21 Aug 1916 Helen, dau of Rev Henry B Hudson, of New York; *m* 2nd 1928 Rachel Gray, dau of Dr O M Jones, of Norfolk, Va., and *d* 19–, leaving:
(1) *Elodie Constance Joyce; *b* 1935
1 Zaidée Violet; *b* 8 June 1878; *m* 29 April 1925 Laurence Naylor Hodgson Wilson, of Hexgreave Park, Southwell, Notts, s of William Wilson, and *d* 3 July 1935. He *d* 18 Oct 1933
2 Hilda Catharine; *b* 23 April 1886; *d* unm 25 June 1952

The 9th Bt's yr bro,

Sir William Wynne Honywood, 10th Bt, MC; *b* 7 April 1891; *educ* Downside; 17th (DCO) Lancers WW I (despatches three times), airship pilot 1918–19, Adj Ceylon Mounted Rifles and Ceylon Planters' Rifle Corps 1928–31, 17th/21st Lancers 1934, WW II: Brevet Maj 1939, Lt-Col 1940, Col 1945, cmded 8th Bn KSLI 1941–42, Ch Instr 210 OCTU 1944, Dep Dir Cyrenaica Dist 1945–46, Cmdt RPC Depot MELF 1946–48; *m* 9 Jan 1923 Maud Naylor (*d* 28 July 1953), dau of William Hodgson Wilson, of Hexgreave Park, and *d* 10 Aug 1982, leaving:
1 Sir FILMER COURTENAY WILLIAM HONYWOOD, **11th and present Bt**
1 *Rosamund Iseulte Mary; WW II with WRNS; *m* 18 Oct 1947 *Paul Anthony Prior, late Lt RNVR, only s of Arthur Hawtayne Prior, and has:
(1) *Jacqueline Mary; *b* 26 July 1950; *educ* Sussex U (BSc), London (PhD); *m* 1972 *Timothy Charles Feline, PhD, and has:
1a *William James; *b* 1979
2a *David Charles; *b* 1981
1a *Eleanor Ruth; *b* 1983
(2) *Helen Catherine; *b* 9 May 1953; SRN, SRCN; *m* 1976 *Aribert Wolframm, and has issue:
1a *Thomas; *b* 1980
2a *Martin Hawtayne; *b* 1982
1a *Yvonne Bianca; *b* 1978
(3) *Sarah Jane; *b* 27 Aug 1956; *m* 1975 *Leslie Howe
(4) *Emma Charlotte Claudia; *b* 10 Aug 1962; NNEB
2 *Zaidée Maud Elsie [Mrs Douglas Haywood, Downgate Cottage, N Petherwin, Cornwall PL15 8LR]; SRN, SCM Edinburgh; *b* 31 May 1926; *m* 24 April 1954 *Lt-Cdr Douglas Inglefield Haywood, RN, only s of Col Austin Hubert Wightwick Haywood, CMG, CBE, DSO, Mil Kt Windsor, and has:
(1) *Richard Douglas; *b* 29 Nov 1964; BA; *m* 1986 *Malika Dukali and has:
1a *Karima Frances; *b* 1986
2a *Aisha Zaidée; *b* 1992
(1) *Elizabeth Zaidée; *b* 11 Nov 1955; BSc, PhD
(2) *Katherine Mary; *b* 1 May 1962; SRN; *m* 1989 *Derek Moore
(3) *Patricia Anne; *b* 4 May 1967

HOOD, Viscount

Arms: Az. fretty arg., on a chief or three crescents sa. **Crest:** A Cornish chough sa. ppr., resting the dexter claw on the fluke of an anchor placed in bend sinister or. **Supporters:** Dexter, a merman, in his exterior hand a trident; sinister, a mermaid, in her exterior hand a mirror, all ppr. **Motto:** *Ventis secundis* ('With favourable winds'). **Creations:** Bt. (GB) 19 May 1778, B. (I) 2 Sept 1782 and (GB) 27 March 1795, V. (GB) 1 June 1796.

THE 7TH VISCOUNT HOOD OF WHITLEY, Co Warwick, **Baron Hood of Catherington**, Co Southampton, and a **Baronet** (Sir Alexander Lambert Hood, Bt) [The Rt Hon The Viscount Hood, Loders Court, Bridport, Dorset DT6 3RZ; 67 Chelsea Square, London SW3 6LE]; *b* 11 March 1914; *s* bro 1981; *educ* RNC Dartmouth, Trin Coll Cambridge (MA 1935) and Harvard (MBA 1937); Lt-Cdr RNVR WW II; *m* 30 April 1957 *Diana Maud, CVO (1957), est dau of Hon George William Lyttelton (*see* COBHAM, V), and has:
1 +HENRY LYTTELTON ALEXANDER [The Hon Henry Hood, 4 Alexander St, London W2 5NT]; *b* 16 March 1958; *educ* Eton; *m* 1991 *Flora Susan, yr dau of Cdr Michael Bernard Casement, OBE, RN (*see* GREENWELL, Bt), and has:
(1) +Archibald Lyttelton Samuel; *b* 16 May 1993
(2) +Atticus Michael Alexander; *b* 20 Oct 1995
2 +John Samuel [The Hon John Hood, 72 Thurleigh Rd, London SW12]; *b* 16 Oct 1959; *educ* Eton; *m* 1982 *Melissa Anne, 2nd dau of Kerry D Bell, of NSW, and has issue:
(1) +Christian Alexander; *b* 1989
(2) +Samuel Francis Wheeler; *b* 1991
(1) *Gemma Kathryn; *b* 1986
3 +James Francis Touzalin [The Hon James Hood, 86 Oxford Gardens, London W10 5UW]; *b* 15 March 1962; *educ* Eton

Lineage: Rev SAMUEL HOOD; Vicar Butleigh, Somerset, and Thorncombe, Devon, Preb Wells 1736 (2nd s of Alexander Hood, of Mosterton, Dorset; *see* 1970 edn ST AUDRIES, B); *m* Mary (*d* 10 Oct 1766), dau of Richard Hoskyns, of Beaminster, Dorset, and *d* 1777, leaving, with two yst sons (*d* young) and two daus (*d* unm):
1 SAMUEL, **1st Viscount**
2 ALEXANDER HOOD, *cr* VISCOUNT BRIDPORT (*qv*)
3 Arthur William (Rev); DD; Vicar Butleigh 1765; *b* 1731; *d* 23 Nov 1769

The est son,

Sir Samuel Hood, 1st Bt, of Catherington, Co Southampton, and **1st Viscount Hood of Whitley**, Co Warwick (both GB), so *cr* 19 May 1778 (on occasion of GEORGE III's visit to Portsmouth) and 1 June 1796 respectively, as also between whiles 2 Sept 1782 (following his part in Rodney's victory over the French off Dominica 12 Aug previously) BARON HOOD OF CATHERINGTON (I), GCB (1815); *b* 12 Dec 1724; RN: joined 1740, Lt 1746, Cdr 1754, Post Capt 1756, R-Adml the Blue 1780, V-Adml 1787, Adml the Blue 1794, the White 1795, the Red 1805; in 1759 took the French frigate *Bellona*, 32, while blockading the coast of France 1757–59, N America station 1763–67, Navy Commr Portsmouth 1778–80; MP (Tory) Westminster 1784–88 and 1790–96 and Reigate 1789–90, C-in-C: Portsmouth 1786–89 and 1791–93 and Med 1793–94 (when organised the successul attack on Toulon and the taking of Corsica), a Ld Admlty 1788–95, Govr Greenwich Hosp 1796; *m* 25 Aug 1749 SUSANNAH (*cr* 27 March 1795 BARONESS HOOD OF CATHERINGTON, Co Southampton (GB), with remainder to heirs male of her body, and *d* 25 May 1806), dau of Edward Linzee, of Portsmouth, and *d* 27 Jan 1816, leaving an only s:

HENRY HOOD, **2nd Viscount Hood of Whitley**; *b* 25 Aug 1753; *m* 10 Sept 1774 Jane (*d* 6 Dec 1847), dau and heir of Francis Wheler, of Whitley, and had, with two daus:
1 Francis Wheler; Lt-Col; *m* 11 Oct 1804 Caroline (*d* 11 March 1858), only dau of Sir Andrew Snape Hamond, 1st Bt (*see* 1970 edn HAMOND-GRAEME, Bt), and was *ka* on the heights of Aire South of France 2 March 1814, leaving:
(1) SAMUEL, **3rd Viscount**
(2) Francis Grosvenor; Lt-Col Gren Gds; *b* 4 March 1809; granted by roy licence with his sis rank of viscount's dau/yr s; *m* 8 Sept 1842 his cousin

Elizabeth Jane (*d* 15 Jan 1910), 2nd dau of Sir Graham Eden Hamond, 2nd Bt, and was *ka* in the trenches at Sebastopol 18 Oct 1854 *sp*

(1) Caroline; *m* 25 Feb 1834 Arthur Francis Gregory, of Styvichall, Warwicks, and *d* 9 May 1890

2 SAMUEL HOOD, 2nd BARON BRIDPORT (*see* BRIDPORT, V)

Th 2nd VISCOUNT *d* 15 Jan 1836; his gs,

SAMUEL HOOD later HOOD-TIBBITS (1841), **3rd Viscount Hood of Whitley**; *b* 10 Jan 1808; *m* 27 June 1837 Mary Isabella (*m* 2nd 6 May 1849 George Hall, MD, of Brighton (*d* 1854), and had issue (*see* MONSON, B); *m* 3rd 17 June 1858 Capt J Borlase Maunsell, 17th Lancers, of Thorpe Malsor, Northampton, who took by roy licence 1858 the name TIBBITS and *d* 17 Jan 1902; she *d* 18 July 1904), dau and heiress of Richard John Tibbits, of Barton Seagrave, and had, with other issue:

1 FRANCIS WHELER, **4th Viscount**

2 Albert; Lt Rifle Bde; *b* 26 Aug 1841; *m* 2 June 1868 Julia Jane (*d* 20 Aug 1906), only dau of Thomas Wynn Hornby, of Upham House, Hants, and *d* 21 Dec 1921, having had issue:

(1) Samuel Wynn Hornby; *b* 30 March 1869; *m* 29 Oct 1906 Miram Ethel North (*d* 15 Nov 1956), dau of Lionel Smith and step-dau of J S Moss, of Wintershill Hall, Bishops Waltham, and *d* 19 Oct 1935, leaving issue:

1a Evelyn Rosemary Jane; *b* 24 May 1910; *m* 11 Dec 1937 Brig Brian Wolseley Webb-Carter, DSO, OBE, Duke of Wellington's Regt (*d* 1981), s of Maj-Gen Sir John Carter, KCMG, of Ixworth Court, Beds, and *d* 1979, leaving:

1b *David Brian Wynn, OBE, MC (1967) [David Webb Carter Esq OBE, MC, Little Ashton Farm, Bishop's Waltham, Hants SO32 1FR]; late Capt Irish Gds; *b* 5 Nov 1940; *educ* Eton and RMA Sandhurst; *m* 15 Oct 1973 *Felicity Elisabeth, dau of William Lytton de Burgh Young, DL, of Ballymena, Co Antrim, and has:

1c *Oliver James Samuel; *b* 23 Oct 1975; *educ* Harrow and Warwick U

1c *Margot Olivia; *b* 14 July 1977; *educ* West Heath and Manchester U

2c *Camilla Elisabeth; *b* 11 March 1983; *educ* North Foreland Lodge

2b *Evelyn John, OBE; Maj Gen Gren Gds; *b* 30 Jan 1946; *educ* Wellington and RMA Sandhurst; *m* 20 Jan 1973 *(Anne) Celia, yr dau of 2nd Baron Wigram (*qv*), and has issue

(2) Albert Oscar, JP Wilts; FLAS, land agent to Marquess of Lansdowne, Capt 3rd Bn Irish Gds (SR), Lt 5th Bn Rifle Bde; *b* 2 April 1870; *m* 26 Nov 1912 Theresa Emily Margery (*d* 31 Dec 1970), only dau of Col Hon Everard Charles Digby (*see* DIGBY, B), and *d* 31 Jan 1952, having had:

1a +John Oscar Everard; WW II with Sudan Def Force (despatches); *b* 17 Oct 1913; *educ* Eton and Worcester Coll Oxford; *m* 18 March 1953 *Winifred Mary Milne, dau of S Gaze Ritson

2a Geoffrey Kenelm; Capt Irish Gds; *b* 21 Nov 1920; *d* unm 24 June 1946

1a *Georgina Mary [Mrs Anthony Morley, Shanks House, Cucklington, Somerset]; *b* 12 Oct 1915; *m* 14 Dec 1944 *Lt Anthony Morley, Life Gds, 2nd s of John Morley, DL, of Alcombe Manor, Box, Wilts, and has:

1b *Andrew Mark; *b* 25 Oct 1945; *educ* Stowe; *m* 1979 *Antoinette Barbara Betts and has:

1c *Samuel Anthony; *b* 1980

2c *Edward Giles; *b* 1982

2b *(Geoffrey) John [John Morley Esq, Mt Ulston, Jedburgh, Roxburghshire]; *b* 11 April 1948; *m* 1973 *Christian Aline, dau of Sir Hugh Fitzgerald Arbuthnot, 7th Bt, of Edinburgh (*qv*) and has issue

(3) Edward, TD, JP Co Kerry; Lt-Col London Regt, High Sheriff 1918, Comptroller Household to Ld Lt Ireland 1916–18, Egyptian Govt Serv, 3rd Cl Medjidie and 3rd Cl Osmanieh, WW I in France (despatches); *b* 18 July 1872; *m* 22 Oct 1900 Nora Evaleen (*d* 4 July 1951), dau of Richard John Mahony, JP, DL, of Dromore Castle, Co Kerry, and *dsp* 18 July 1951

(4) Alexander Frank; Capt Corps of Sch of Musketry; *b* 27 Jan 1874; *m* 21 June 1905 Gladys Ursula (*d* 7 March 1868), 3rd dau of Edward C Youell, of Galatz, Romania, and *d* 2 Dec 1923, leaving issue:

1a +Albert Edward; *b* 23 March 1906

2a Samuel Brian Digby, TD; Lt-Col Middx Yeo WW II (despatches twice); *b* 1 June 1910; *m* 8 April 1937 Myrtle Baron (*d* 1982), niece and adopted dau of Sir Louis Bernhard Baron, 1st Bt (*see* 1934 edn), and *d* 1988, leaving:

1b +Alexander Robert [Alexander Hood Esq, Greys Green Farm, Rotherfield Greys, Oxon RG9 4QG]; 2nd Lt Rifle Bde; *b* 9 Feb 1945; *educ* Eton; *m* Feb 1967 *Ann Marie, dau of John O'Donovan, of Greenwich, and has:

1c +Samuel; *b* 15 Oct 1967

2c +Padraig; *b* 1971

1c *Jane; *b* 18 July 1969

2c *Sarah; *b* 1972

1b *(Anne) Caroline; *b* 30 March 1938; *m* 20 Oct 1962 *Guy Smallwood, er s of Capt Edward Guy Seymour Smallwood, 4th CLY, and has:

1c *Emma; *b* 2 Jan 1965

2c *Kate; *b* 12 May 1966

2b *(Sarah) Jane [The Hon Mrs Jolyon Grey, Upper Swell Farm, Stow-on-the-Wold, Glos GL54 1EW]; *b* 9 Feb 1945; *m* 1971 *Hon Jolyon Kenneth Alwick Grey (*see* GREY OF NAUNTON, B)

3a +John Michael Alexander [John Hood Esq, 11 Shiremore Hill, Marriott, Somerset TA16 5PH]; *b* 23 Oct 1918

(5) Robert Valentine; *b* 5 Feb 1876; *m* 2 Oct 1917 Mignon (*d* 1973), only dau of John E Cooke, and *d* 19 April 1942, leaving:

1a +Robin Julian Patrick [Robin Hood Esq, 50 Pont St Mews, London SW1]; *b* 12 Aug 1919; *educ* Eton

(1) Emily Beryl Sissy; *b* 20 March 1871; *m* 19 Sept 1893 10th Baron Digby (*qv*) and *d* 28 Nov 1928, leaving issue

(2) Marguerite Jenny; *b* 20 May 1881; *m* 2 June 1928 **5th Viscount Hood** (*see* below) and *dsp* 10 May 1966

3 Alexander Frederick HOOD later GREGORY (roy licence 9 April 1910), of Styvechale, Warwicks, JP E and W R Yorks; RN and 15th Hus; *b* 20 May 1843; *m* 7 June 1870 Ethel Cecilia (*d* 21 Nov 1923), dau of Algernon Charles Heber-Percy (*see* NORTHUMBERLAND, D), and *d* 20 May 1927, having had:

(1) Alexander Nelson; Lt Centl India Horse, Boer War with Imp Yeo; *b* 21 Oct 1873; *kas* 25 Feb 1902

(2) Charles Hugh HOOD later GREGORY later still GREGORY-HOOD (deed poll 19 Oct 1927), of Loxley Hall, Warwicks, JP, DL, Maj Salop RHA, E Kent Regt, Boer War 1899–1900 as ADC to Gen Sir H L Smith-Dorrien, GCB (despatches, medal with three clasps), Aden 1904, WW I (wounded, despatches); *b* 6 Feb 1877; *m* 11 Jan 1911 Dorothy (*d* 1983), er dau of Hon Marshall Jones Brooks (*see* CRAWSHAW, B), and *d* 30 Oct 1951, leaving issue:

1a +Alexander Marshall Horace, OBE (1959, MBE, (1954), MC and bar [Col Alexander Gregory-Hood OBE MC and bar, Loxley Hall, Warwicks]; Col Gren Gds WW II (despatches, wounded); *b* 18 July 1915; *educ* Winchester; *m* 6 March 1943 (*divorce* 1949) Diana (*d* 1987), only dau of Maj Sir John Little Gilmour, 2nd Bt (*see* GILMOUR, Bt), and has:

1b +Peter Charles Freeman [Peter Hood Esq, 73 Cambridge St, London SW1]; FCO: 3rd Sec Tel Aviv 1969; *b* 12 Dec 1943; *educ* Eton and Trin Coll Camb; *m* 17 Dec 1966 *Camilla, er dau of Richard Anthony Bethell, JP (*see* RADNOR, E), and has:

1c *Clare; *b* 4 April 1968

2c *Carolyn Jane; *b* 6 June 1970

3c *Lucy; *b* 14 Dec 1973

1b *Jane [Mrs Brian FitzGerald, Sherfield Mill, Sherfield English, Hants SO51 6FN]; *b* 24 Nov 1946; *m* 16 Sept 1965 *Brian A FitzGerald, er s of Maj Desmond FitzGerald, of Chelsea, and has:

1c *Richard Derek; *b* 5 June 1967

2c *James Mark; *b* 1973

1c *Sarah Jane; *b* 2 Sept 1968

1a Rosemary; *b* 6 March 1913; *m* 1st 7 July 1932 (*divorce* 1937) Peter Kenneth Chance, er s of Kenneth Macomb Chance, of Radford Manor House, Leamington; *m* 2nd 18 Dec 1937 Capt Jack Brittain-Jones, CBE; *m* 3rd 12 Nov 1943 James Harold Lavery, Purser Merchant Navy; *m* 4th 17 Sept 1951 (*divorce* 1959) Alfred James McAlpine (*see* McALPINE, Bt), and *d* 1983, leaving issue

(3) Grosvenor Percy, Lt Centl India Horse IA; *b* 24 Sept 1882; drowned Agra 12 April 1904

(1) Edith Blanche Mary; *b* 4 July 1871; *d* 6 March 1873

(2) Sibell Ethel; *b* 16 Jan 1875

(3) Gertrude Margaret; *b* 13 March 1879; *m* 8 June 1920 Col Alan Hewlett, Centl India Horse, s of Gen T G Hewlett, CIE. He *d* 1943

The 3rd VISCOUNT *d* 8 May 1846; his est son,

FRANCIS WHELER HOOD, **4th Viscount Hood of Whitley**, JP, DL Warwicks; *b* 4 July 1838; Lt-Col Gren Gds; *m* 18 July 1865 Edith Lydia Drummond (*d* 9 March 1911), dau of Arthur W Ward, of Tunbridge Wells, and *d* 27 April 1907, having had:

1 Grosvenor Arthur Frederick; *b* 6 June 1867; *d* 2 June 1868

2 GROSVENOR ARTHUR ALEXANDER HOOD, **5th Viscount Hood of Whitley**, OBE (1919); *b* 13 Nov 1868; Lt-Col cmdg 7th Bn London Regt, Maj Gren Gds, served Ashanti 1895–96 and Boer Wars 1900–02; *m* 1st 28 Feb 1911 Primrose (*d* 5 March 1919), yst dau of Col Hon Richard Southwell George Stapleton-Cotton (*see* COMBERMERE, V); *m* 2nd 2 June 1928 his cousin Marguerite Jenny (*d* 10 May 1966), gdau of **3rd Viscount Hood of Whitley**, and *dsp* 26 April 1933

3 Horace Lambert Alexander, KCB, MVO, DSO; joined RN 1883, Sub-Lt 1889, Lt 1890, Cdr 1898, Capt 1903, R-Adml 1913, Capt RNC Osborne 1910–13, ADC to HM GEORGE V 1912–13, Naval Sec to 1st Ld Admlty 1914, Adml cmdg Dover Patrol 1914 and 3rd Battle Cruiser Sqdn 1915, served Nile 1897–98 (despatches, medal, 4th Cl Medjidie), Somaliland 1903–04 (despatches) and WW I (despatches); *b* 2 Oct 1870; *m* 19 Jan 1910 Ellen (granted style and precedence of KCB's w; *d* 1 Oct 1950), widow of George Augustus Nickerson, of Dedham, Mass., and dau of A E Touzalin, and was *ka* off Jutland 31 May 1916, leaving:

(1) SAMUEL HOOD, **6th Viscount Hood of Whitley**, GCMG (1969, KCMG 1960, CMG 1953); *b* 15 Oct 1910; *educ* Eton and Trin Coll Cambridge; Assist Priv Sec to Sec State India 1936–39, Priv Sec to Min Info 1939–41, FO 1942046, 1st Sec Madrid 1947–48, Counsellor Paris 1948–51, FO 1951–56, Assist U-Sec and UK Perm Rep Cncl WEU 1956–57, Min Washington 1957–62, Dep U-Sec 1963–69, Dep Speaker and Dep Chm Ctees Ho Lords 1971–81, Chm Advsy Cncl V&A 1975–78; *d* unm 13 Oct 1981

(2) ALEXANDER LAMBERT HOOD, **7th and present Viscount Hood of Whitley**

4 Neville Albert, CMG (1918), DSO (1917), DL Cornwall; Lt-Col RGA and Sec TAA, Boer War 1900–02, WWs I and II; *b* 4 Oct 1872; *m* 30 April 1908 Eveline Mary (*d* 31 March 1967), only dau of Herman Usticke BROAD later PENDER, of Tresilian, Falmouth, and *d* 24 Jan 1948, leaving issue:

(1) Peter Neville; Lt RNVR WW II, US Legion of Merit; *b* 4 Sept 1913; *m* 7 Nov 1936 Nancy Warrington (*d* 5 April 1968), yr dau of Tristram Warrington Haward, JP, of Abbey Lands, Alnwick, Northumberland, and *d* 25 April 1969, leaving:

1a *Sally Penelope [Mrs Edward Thompson, The Bolthole, Six Ashes, Salop]; *b* 23 July 1937; *m* 18 April 1959 *Edward Martin Amphlett Thompson, only s of Sir Edward Walter Thompson, JP (*see* COVENTRY, E), and has:

1b *Stephen Peter; *b* 18 April 1960

1b *Mary Jane; *b* 29 Jan 1963

2b *Sarah Ann; *b* 30 March 1965

3b *Rosemary Claire; *b* 21 June 1969

2a *Anna Rosemary [Mrs Anna Glazebrook, 220 Marlborough Rd, Oxford]; *b* 4 Oct 1940; *m* 27 July 1968 (*divorce* 1974) Peter Christopher Glazebrook and has:

1b *Anthony Peter; *b* 1970

2b *Daniel George; *b* 1978

3a *Eveline Jane Venetia; *b* 27 Nov 1957; has:

1b *Katherine; *b* 1992

(1) *Edith Rosemary [Mrs Rosemary Macleod, 4000 Massachusetts Ave, NW 924, Washington DC 20016, USA]; *b* 29 March 1909; *m* 1st 9 July 1931

(*divorce* 1947) Martin Ayerst Ingram, Lt RNVR, only child of William Ayerst Ingram, RI, PRBC, and has:

1a Annabelle; *b* 20 June 1933; *m* 1963 *Julian Payne Freret [Julian Freret, 5507 Parkston Rd, MD 20016, USA], and *d* 7 Aug 1967, leaving:

1b *Mary Suzanne; *b* 1964; *m* 1996 *T Norman

2b *Carol Arthemise; *b* 1965; *m* 1990 *Thierry van Bastalaer and has:

1c *Sebastian; *b* 1996

1c *Sophie; *b* 1993

2a *Margot Faye; *b* 16 Aug 1934; *m* 9 June 1959 (*divorce* 1982) John A H Shober and has:

1b *John Andrews Harris; *b* 26 Aug 1961; *m* 1st 1987 (*divorce* 1991) Dena Louise Smith; *m* 2nd 1985 *Stephanie Anderson

2b *Martin Pemberton; *b* 11 Aug 1966; *m* 1995 *Jennifer Burke

1b *Cintra Suzanne; *b* 11 May 1964; *m* 1992 *Joseph Hardcastle and has:

1c *Margot; *b* 1996

(1) (cont.) Mrs Edith Ingram *m* 2nd 19 Dec 1947 (*divorce* 1956) Capt Donald Grant, Black Watch, yr s of Kenneth Grant Macleod, of St James, CP, S Africa, and by him has:

3a *Carole Alice Grant; *b* 22 Oct 1948; *m* 1982 *Paul Noel Inman and has:

1b *Annabelle May Ruth; *b* 1983

2b *Hannah Myfanwy Mary; *b* 1986

(2) *Eveline Suzanne; *b* 8 Jan 1917; *m* 31 Oct 1945 *Henry Arthur Frederick Hohler, CMG, est s of Lt-Col Arthur Preston Hohler, DSO (*see* GORT, V), and has:

1a *Katherine Elizabeth; *b* 1948; *m* 1972 *Christopher Ernest Nelson Harries and has:

1b *Eleanor Annabel; *b* 1972

2b *Emma Susan; *b* 1975

2a *(Edith) Mabel; *b* 1952; *m* 1984 *Stephen D McLeod, er s of G R McLeod, of Bethesda, Md., and has:

1b *Robert Charles; *b* 1986

2b *Franklin Henry; *b* 1990

1b *Susan Leighann; *b* 1988

(3) Catherine Mary; *b* 4 Oct 1919; *m* 14 Dec 1940 Graham Charles George Cheverton (*d* 1982) and *d* 1993, leaving:

1a *Neville Courtenay [Neville Cheverton Esq, 30 College Gdns, Kemp Town, Brighton, Sussex]; *b* 21 May 1949

1a *Genevieve Sonia [Mrs John Fielder, Quatrieme, Les Mouriaux, Alderney, CI]; *b* 4 May 1945; *m* 1st 1966 (*divorce* 19–) David Maxwell Martin; *m* 2nd 19– *John Fielder

5 Francis George, Col RE; *b* 28 March 1880; *m* 20 Oct 1904 Helen Kendall Mouncy, est dau of Hon Edward Gawler Prior, PC (Canada), of Victoria, BC, and *d* 11 Aug 1949, leaving:

(1) Francis Basil; *b* 5 Sept 1905; *m* 1934 *Catherine Anna [Mrs Francis Hood, 302-2427 Amherst St, Sidney, BC, Canada V8L 2HI], dau of Hon Sir Richard McBride, KCMG, KC, Premier Br Columbia 1903–16, and *d* 1986, leaving:

1a +John Francis Alexander [John Hood Esq, 4533 46B St, Delta, BC, Canada V4K 2N2]; *b* 8 Dec 1935; *m* 9 Nov 1963 *Barbara Anne, dau of Cyril Cuthbert Turner, of Victoria, BC, and has:

1b *Valerie Anne; *b* 1966

2b *Christine Frances; *b* 1971

1 Mabel Edith; *m* 25 July 1889 5th Baron Ashburton (*qv*) and *d* 18 Jan 1904, leaving issue

2 Alma Margarite; *b* 12 Aug 1875; *d* 27 Feb 1877

3 Dorothy Violet; *b* 4 Sept 1877; *d* unm 28 Jan 1965

HOOD, Bt

Arms: Arg. on a mount vert an oak tree fructed ppr., a chief sa., thereon a bow stringed also ppr. **Crest:** A demi-stag ppr. resting the sinister foot on a fret or. **Motto:** Thorough.
Creation: Bt. (UK) 16 Jan 1922

SIR HAROLD JOSEPH HOOD, 2ND BT, of Wimbledon, Co Surrey, TD (1950) [Sir Harold Hood Bt TD, 31 Avenue Rd, London NW8 6BS]; *b* 23 Jan 1916; *s* f 1931; *educ* Downside; 2nd Lt 58 Middx Bn RE (AA) (TA) 1939, Lt RA (TA) 1941, WW II, circulation dir *Catholic Herald* 1961–87 and *Universe* 1953–60, ed *The Catholic Who's Who* 1952 edn, assist ed *The Catholic Directory* 1950–60 (managing ed 1959–60), Kt Cdr St Gregory the Gt 1964, Kt Grand Cross St Gregory the Great 1986, Kt Magistral Grace SMO Malta 1972; *m* 30 April 1946 *Hon Ferelith Rosemary Florence Kenworthy, dau of 10th Lord (Baron) Strabolgi (*qv*), and has had:

1 Timothy Joseph Madach; *b* and *d* 25 May 1951

2 +JOHN JOSEPH HAROLD; *b* 27 Aug 1952

3 +Basil Gervase Francis Gerard; *b* 4 Oct 1955; *educ* Ampleforth and London U (BA)

1 *Josepha Ferelith Emma Margaret-Mary; *b* 17 Oct 1953; *educ* St Mary's Convent Ascot and Bristol U (BA); *m* 1981 *Ian Murray, est s of Sir Donald Murray, KCVO, CMG, and has:

(1) *Andrew Duncan Culverwell; *b* 1985

(2) *Alasdair Angus Culverwell; *b* 1987

(1) *Kirstie Iona Culverwell; *b* 1990

2 *Margaret Marie Elizabeth Felicia; *b* 26 March 1965; *educ* St Mary's Convent Ascot; *m* 1990 *Michael Gresslin, s of Heinz Gresslin, of Badenweiler, Germany

Lineage: JOHN HOOD, of Ashby de-la-Zouch, Leics; had issue:

JOHN HOOD, of Ashby-de-la-Zouch; *b* 1839; *m* 1861 Eliza (*d* 4 Oct 1912), dau of Joseph Hood, and *d* 13 Jan 1869, leaving, with other issue:

1 JOSEPH (Sir), **1st Bt**

2 William; *b* 7 Jan 1865; *m* Jane Munton and *d* 1 May 1937, leaving a s (John William, *b* 16 April 1893) and two daus (Elizabeth Jane, *b* 10 Nov 1888; Gladys, *b* 18 Feb 1891)

The er son,

Sir Joseph Hood, 1st Bt (UK), so *cr* 16 Jan 1922, JP; MP (U) Wimbledon 1918–24, Mayor Wimbledon 1930–31, slr 1890, dep chm Br American Tobacco, assist controller Min Info 1918; *b* 31 March 1863; *m* 1st 11 May 1900 Katherine (*d* 5 March 1913), dau of Martin Kenny, of Ballindaggin, Co Wexford, and had:

1 Winifred Edith; *b* March 1901; *m* 10 Feb 1927 Basil Raymond Worthington, DFC (*d* 8 Sept 1968), yr s of Frederick Worthington, and *d* 15 Dec 1989, having had:

(1) Denis Hood; *b* 30 Nov 1932; *d* 23 Jan 1933

(1) Colleen Mary Katherine; *b* 15 Dec 1927; *d* 1979

2 Norah Mary; *b* 27 April 1903; *m* 12 Feb 1931 Maj James Hargreaves Turner, Queen's Bays, and *d* 30 Dec 1956, leaving issue

3 Kathleen Muriel; *b* 23 Oct 1905; *m* 1st 20 April 1928 (*divorce* 1938) Thomas Percival Durant Beighton, est s of Thomas Durant Beighton, ICS; *m* 2nd 26 Aug 1939 Jessel Anidjar Romain (*d* 2 Feb 1961), 2nd s of David Anidjar Romain, and *d* 15 April 1981

Sir Joseph *m* 2nd 17 April 1915 Marie Josephine (*d* 4 Jan 1956), er dau of Archibald Robinson, JP, of Dublin, and *d* 10 Jan 1931, having by her had:

1 Sir HAROLD JOSEPH HOOD, **2nd and present Bt**

2 Alan Edgar; *b* 3 March 1920; *m* 21 April 1951 Magdalen Olga Phyllis (*m* 2nd 20 July 1961 Brig John Cuthbert de Fontenne Sleeman, CBE, KStJ, KM (*d* 14 July 1971)), er dau of Capt George Edward Thomas Eyston, OBE, MC, of Park Ave, New York, and *dsp* 21 Dec 1957

3 Robin Adrian; *b* 1 Dec 1924; *educ* Downside; BA London 1969, memb London Stock Exchange 1961–64, treasurer Catholic Housing Aid Soc 1964–68 (v-chm 1968), Dir Catholic Fund for Overseas Devpt 1977–82; *m* 30 April 1949 Miriam Teresa, MA (*d* 7 July 1991) (minister counsellor Venezuelan Embassy), yr dau of Humberto Blanco Fombona, and *d* 24 Sept 1993, leaving:

(1) +Simon Joseph Paul Blanco [Simon Hood Esq, 4 Bedford Rd, London W4 1JJ]; *b* 29 June 1951; *educ* Downside; *m* 1st 1979 (*divorce* 1989) Josette Eliane, only dau of Jean Baumgartner, of Lausanne, and has:

1a *Victoria Alexandra; *b* 16 April 1984

(1) (cont.) Simon Hood *m* 2nd 1990 (*divorce* 1991) Judith Louise, dau of D W Prickett, of Kingston Hill, Surrey; *m* 3rd 23 Aug 1996 *Charlotte, only dau of Dr J Leahy-Taylor, and by her has:

1a *Natasha Lara Leahy Isabel; *b* 27 Sept 1996

(2) +Martin Joseph Blanco [Dom James Hood OSB, Downside Abbey, Stratton-on-the-Fosse]; *b* 29 Nov 1953; *educ* Downside; monk; Bursar Downside Abbey

(1) *Bernadette Marie Blanco; *b* 29 Nov 1953

(2) *Anne-Marie Elena Kathleen Blanco [Mrs Nicholas True, 114 Palewell Park, London SW14 8JH]; *b* 4 June 1957; *m* 1979 *Nicholas Edward True, CBE, s of Edward T True, of W Bridgford, and has issue:

1a *James Alexios Edward; *b* 26 Aug 1981

2a *Thomas-Leo Richard; *b* 30 May 1984

1a *Sophia Miriam Marie-Louise Blanco; *b* 10 Aug 1992

HOOPER

Creation: B. (LP, UK) 1985.

THE BARONESS HOOPER, of Liverpool and St James's in the City of Westminster (Gloria Dorothy Hooper) [The Rt Hon The Baroness Hooper, House of Lords, London SW1A 0PW]; *b* 25 May 1939; *educ* Southampton U (BA); slr 1973; ptnr Taylor Joynson Garrett 1974–84; MEP (C) Liverpool 1979–84; V-Chm European: Parly Environment and Consumer Affs Ctee 1979–84; European Democratic Gp Whip 1982–84; Baroness-in-Waiting 1985–87; Parly U-Sec: DES 1987–88, Energy 1988–89, Health 1989–92; Del Cncl Europe and WEU 1992–97, Dep Speaker Ho Lds 1993–97, Pres Canning Ho 1997–; Fell Ind and Parly Tst 1983; FRGS 1982, FRSA 1986, author: *Cases of Company Law* (1967), *Law of International Trade* (1968)

Lineage: FREDERICK HOOPER; *m* Frances — and had issue:

GLORIA DOROTHY, *cr* a **Baroness**

HOOSON

Creation: B. (UK, LP) 1979.

THE BARON HOOSON, of Montgomery in Co Powys and of Colomendy in Co Clwyd ((Hugh) Emlyn Hooson, QC (1960)) [The Rt Hon The Lord Hooson QC, Summerfield, Llanidloes, Powys SY18 6AQ]; *b* 26 March 1925; *educ* Denbigh GS and UCW; barrister Gray's Inn 1949, Bencher 1968, Treas 1986; Dep Chm QS: Flint 1960–71, Merioneth 1960–67 (Chm 1967–71); Leader Wales and Chester Circuit 1971–74; Recorder: Merthyr Tydfil 1971, Swansea 1971; Recorder Crown Court 1972–94; MP (Lib) Montgomeryshire 1962–79; Leader Welsh Lib Party 1966–79; V-Pres: Political Ctee N Atlantic Assembly 1975–79, Peace Through NATO 1985; dir Laura Ashley Hldgs 1985–96 (chm 1995–96); Pres Llangollen Internat Eisteddfod 1987–93; Govr Grassland and Environmental Research Inst 1989–92; Chm Severn River Crossing 1991–; Hon Prof Fell UCW 1971; *m* 1950 *Shirley Margaret Wynne, dau of Sir George Hamer, CBE, of Summerfield, Llanidloes, Powys, and has two daus

Lineage: HUGH HOOSON, of Colomendy, Denbighs; *m* Elsie — and had issue:

(HUGH) EMLYN, *cr* a **Baron**

HOPE

Arms: Az. a chevron or between three bezants. **Crest:** A broken terrestrial globe, surmounted of a rainbow issuing out of a cloud at each end, all ppr. **Supporters:** Two female figures representing Hope, in vestments vert, on their heads garlands of flowers, each resting her exterior hand on an anchor all ppr. **Motto:** *At spes infracta* ('But hope is unbroken'). **Creation:** Bt. (NS) 19 Feb 1628.

SIR JOHN CARL ALEXANDER HOPE, 18TH BT, of Craighall, Co Fife [Sir John Hope Bt, 9 Westleigh Ave, London SW15 6RF]; *b* 10 June 1939; *s* f 1987; *educ* Eton; *m* 29 June 1968 *Merle Pringle, dau of Robert Douglas, of Holbrook, Suffolk, and has:

1 +ALEXANDER ARCHIBALD DOUGLAS; *b* 16 March 1969

1 *Natasha Anne; *b* 1971

Lineage: JOHN HOPE; alias Petit Johnne, trompetour; *b* 1472–76 (probably at Leith); *m* (1st?) Janet Kirkpatrick and *d c* 1558, leaving:

EDWARD HOPE; Commr Edinburgh to S Parl 1560; had:

HENRY HOPE; merchant; *m* Jaqueline de Tot and had, with an est s (Henry) and a yst s (James, ancestor of the HOPEs of Amsterdam):

Sir Thomas Hope, 1st Bt (NS), so *cr* 19 Feb 1628, of Craighall; Jt Ld Advocate 1626, Ld Advocate 1628; Commr Gen Assembly Ch of Scotland 1643; *m* Elizabeth, dau of John Binning of Wallyford, and *d* Nov 1646, having had, with other issue, including a yr s (James (Sir), of Hopetoun; *see* LINLITHGOW, M) and two daus (Mary, *m* 1638 Sir Charles Erskine of Alva, *see* ROSSLYN, E; Anne, *m* 1643 2nd Lord Cardross, *see* BUCHAN, E):

Sir John Hope, 2nd Bt; Ld of Session 1632 as Lord Craighall; *m* Margaret, dau of Sir Archibald Murray, 1st Bt, of Blackbarony (*qv*), and *d* 28 April 1654, having had, with other issue:

1 **Sir Thomas Hope, 3rd Bt**, of Craighall; *b* 11 Feb 1633; *m* Elizabeth (*m* 2nd 26 March 1663 John Gibson of Durie (*see* GIBSON-CRAIG-CARMICHAEL, Bt), dau of Sir John Aytoun of that Ilk, and had:

(1) **Sir Thomas Hope, 4th Bt**; *m* Anne (*m* 2nd Sir John Carstairs of Kilconquhar), dau and eventual heir of Sir William Bruce, 1st Bt, of Kinross (*see* ELGIN and KINCARDINE, E), and had:

1a **Sir William Hope, 5th Bt**; *d* unm

2a Sir THOMAS HOPE later BRUCE-HOPE (on inheriting mother's Kinross estate), **6th Bt**; sold Craighall 1729 to his cousin Earl of Hopetoun (*see* LINLITHGOW, M); *d* unm

3a **Sir John Bruce-Hope, 7th Bt**, of Kinross; Gen, MP Kinross-shire; *m* 1st Charlotte (*dsps*), dau of Sir Charles Halket of Pitfirrane; *m* 2nd Marianne Denune, of the CADBOLEs of Ross-shire, and *d* 1766, having by her had a dau (Anne)

2 Archibald (Sir), of Rankeillor; Ld of Session 1689; *m* Margaret, dau of Sir John Aytoun of that Ilk, and *d* 10 Oct 1706, leaving, with other issue:

(1) THOMAS (Sir), **8th Bt**

(2) Charles, of Edinburgh; *m* 1st 1701 Marie, dau of Thomas Boyd, and had a s (Robert); *m* 2nd —, dau of John Corse, and had a further s (Archibald, *m* Elizabeth, dau of Rev W Robertson)

(3) Robert, of Edinburgh; MD; *bapt* 1 Jan 1687; *m* 1st *c* 1716 Marian, dau of John Glas of Sauchie, and *d* 17 Nov 1743, having had, with other issue:

1a Archibald; *bapt* 4 Nov 1723; Excise Collector Haddington; *m* 1st — and had a s; *m* 2nd — Bennet, of Chester, and *d* 1793–96, having had by her, with other issue:

1b Erskine; Col 25th Regt; had:

1c James Archibald (Sir), GCB; Gen, Col 9th Regt Hanover 1805–06, Walcheren Expdn 1809, Peninsular War 1811–13; *m* Christiana Elizabeth (*d* 20 Jan 1907) and *d* 30 Dec 1871, having had issue

2a John; MD, FRS; *b* 10 May 1725; Prof Medicine Edinburgh U; *m* Juliana, dau of John Stevenson, MD, and *d* 1786, having had, with other issue:

1b Thomas Charles; MD, FRS, FRSE; *b* 1766; Prof Chemistry Edinburgh U, discovered strontium; *d* unm 13 June 1844

2b James, WS; *b* 17 Sept 1769; *m* 1805 Jane (*d* 6 April 1822), dau of James Walker, and *d* 14 Nov 1842, leaving:

1c John; *b* 12 May 1807; *d* unm

2c James, WS; *b* 1 July 1818; *m* 16 April 1850 Hon Gertrude Elphinstone (*d* 29 March 1894), sis of 15th Lord Elphinstone (*qv*), and *d* 10 July 1903, leaving issue:

1d James Edward; *b* 6 Nov 1852; *m* 1 June 1880 Sophia (*d* 19 Feb 1924), dau of Adml Sir William Edmonstone, 4th Bt (*qv*), and *d* 8 Dec 1917, leaving:

1e James Horatio; *b* 12 March 1881; Capt and Brevet Maj HLI WW I (despatches, wounded twice, Legion Honour); *ka* Mesopotamia 17/18 April 1916

2e Reginald John; *b* 18 Jan 1884; T/Lt RNVR; *m* 30 April 1923 Eileen, dau of Roland Philipson, of Tynemouth, and *dsp* 7 Oct 1952

3e William Douglas; *b* 30 March 1886; Lt Scots Gds WW I

1e Vera Mary; *b* 7 Oct 1882

2d Cecil Arthur, JP Denbighs; *b* 28 June 1865; Lt 6th Dragoons, Capt Montgomery Yeo, Maj Lothian & Border Horse; *m* 3 Jan 1889 Eleanor Isabel (*d* 6 Oct 1950), dau of James Blare Grove, RN, of Shanstone Park, Staffs, and *d* 25 Oct 1934, leaving:

1e Arthur Clement, MBE (1919); *b* 14 July 1891; Sudan Pol Serv 1926–36, Lt-Col Scots Gds and Maj and Adj Palestine Gendarmerie, served WW I (wounded) and WW II; *m* 29 April 1933 *Elizabeth Hale, dau of Frederick Seccombe Wallace, of Redjacket, Washington, USA, and *d* 12 Aug 1961, leaving:

1f *Jean Elizabeth; *b* 11 July 1937; *m* 1960 *Sergio Pizzicaria

1d Anna Gertrude; *m* 20 Feb 1878 Francis Bertram Dalrymple, and *d* 1895

2d Mary Constance; *m* 1889 Col Otho Glynn Bolitho (*d* 26 Oct 1911), of Kenegie, Gulval, Cornwall, and had issue

3d Edith Geraldine; *d* unm 23 Feb 1904

3a Robert; *b* 18 Aug 1727; Lt Marines 1755–60, Capt 122nd Regt 1762–63, Purser RN; *m* 21 July 1761 Maria Christian, of Yarmouth (*bur* 24 Feb 1800), and *d* 14 Jan 1802, leaving:

1b Falkner; Lt 63rd Regt, Paymaster E Norfolk Militia; *m* — White and had, with other issue:

1c John Charles; Lt-Col Rifle Bde; *dsp* 12 Oct 1842

2b Robert; *b* June 1763; Lt-Col RA, attd army of Grand Vizier Egypt; *m* 19 March 1785 Elizabeth Stanwix (*d* 10 Dec 1838), dau of John Johnson, Inland Revenue, and *d* 26 June 1805, having had:

1c Robert Wallis; *b* 11 March 1787; Dep Surv-Gen Ordnance; *m* 1st Margaret — and had:

1d Robert Valentine; *b* 1811; *dvp* 4 Jan 1850, leaving:

1e Robert; *b* 1841; *d* unm 1874

1c (cont.) Robert Hope *m* 2nd Margaret — (*d* 3 May 1852) and by her had:

1d Emily Jane; *d* 6 March 1938

1c (cont.) Robert Hope *m* 3rd Eliza (*d* 11 April 1872), dau of H G Smith, and *d* 9 May 1871, having by her had:

2d Edward William, OBE (1918); MD, DSc; *b* 5 Aug 1854; Emeritus Prof Public Health Liverpool U, Ch MOH Liverpool, examiner Cambridge, Edinburgh, London, Manchester and Belfast Us, FRCP, FRCS; *m* 7 June 1899 Charlotte Rennie, JP Liverpool (*d* 23 Jan 1962), dau of John Bowring, of Liverpool, and *d* 27 April 1950, leaving:

1e John Edward Bowring; *b* 21 Dec 1901; *educ* Oriel Coll Oxford (MA); *m* 9 June 1927 Catherine Paley (*d* 7 July 1979), dau of Robert Stephen Hubbersty, MD, of Sunderland (*see* below), and *d* 5 Oct 1957, leaving:

1f +Michael Stephen Edward [Michael Hope Esq, Apt 503, Brentwood Park, Portugal Cove Rd, St Johns, Newfoundland, Canada A1B 4H9]; *b* 4 July 1928; 2nd Lt RHG; *m* 1st 22 April 1957 Edith Rosemary Byrne (*d* 23 Oct 1962), dau of Rev Victor Charles Roberts, and has:

1g +Nigel John Charles; *b* 23 Aug 1959; *m* 1983 *Janet, dau of Reginald Gordon Warner

1g *Michelle Catherine Margaret [Mrs Nicholas Devereux, 9 Poplar Rise, Little Aston, W Midlands B74 4HT]; *b* 14 Feb 1958; *m* 1981 *Nicholas Charles Devereux, and has issue:

1h *Christopher Charles; *b* 1981

1h *Jennifer Sarah; *b* 1985

1f (cont.) Michael Hope *m* 2nd 16 Feb 1964 *Catherine Emily, dau of Fred Bradshaw, of St John's, Newfoundland, and widow of William Kenneth Latham, of Newfoundland, and by her has:

2g *Catherine Charlotte; *b* 17 Dec 1964; *m* 1988 *David John Fell and has issue:

1h *James Michael; *b* 1990

2h *Thomas Charles; *b* 1993

3g *Louise Joan; *b* 22 July 1969

2f +Christopher John [Christopher Hope Esq, 1 Port Hill Drive, Shrewsbury, Salop]; *b* 6 Aug 1931; 2nd Lt King's Salop LI; *m* 25 Aug 1956 *Louise Alicia, dau of Joseph Hall, of St John's, Newfoundland, and has:

1g +Peter John; *b* 13 June 1959; *m* 1989 *Terry-Anne, dau of Denis Polkey, of Devon, and has:

1h *Katherine Jane; *b* 1990

1g *Susan Louise; *b* 5 Nov 1960

1f *Catherine Eve [Mrs Alastair Hardie, Westfield House, Thropton, Northumberland NE65 7LB]; *b* 14 Feb 1941; *m* 20 April 1963 *Alastair John Padraic Hardie, s of Rev Archibald George Hardie, of Halifax, Yorks, and has:

1g *Timothy John Alexander; *b* March 1979

1g *Jane Catherine Sheelagh; *b* 23 April 1964; *m* June 1993 *Steven Goldsmith and has:

1h *James Andrew; *b* Jan 1997

2g *Lucy Anne; *b* 12 Nov 1967

3g *Catherine Mary; *b* Oct 1980

1e Marjorie Mary; *b* 23 March 1900; *m* 25 May 1940 Francis Stephen Hubbersty, FRCS, s of Robert Stephen Hubbersty, MD, of Sunderland (*see* above), and *d* 19–

2e Elsa Rennie; *b* 4 July 1905; *m* 25 Nov 1926 Lionel Bishop Ridley (*d* 7 July 1965), s of Bishop Latimer Ridley, of Sutton, Surrey, and *d* 1997, leaving:

1f Roger Hugh; *b* 30 Aug 1929; CA; *m* 6 June 1959 *Jennifer Ann, dau of Capt W R Colbeck, RNR, FRICS, FIN, of Birkenhead Park, Cheshire, and *d* 19–, leaving:

1g *Markham Hugh; *b* 26 Sept 1960

2g *Julian Bowring; *b* 10 Jan 1963

1f *Gillian Hope; *b* 19 Aug 1934; *m* 6 July 1963 Edward Guy Swales (*d* 25 March 1965), of Yorks

2d Eleanor Adelaide; *m c* 1879 Joseph Payne Garrett (*d* 11 Nov 1934) and *d* 1 Dec 1946, leaving issue

2c John Isaac; *b* 26 Oct 1795; Col RE; *m* 10 Aug 1826 Margaret Letitia (*d* 22 July 1854), dau of Maj Edward Molesworth (*see* MOLESWORTH, V), and *d* 17 April 1860, having had, with other issue:

1d John Edward; *b* 9 Sept 1828; Maj-Gen RA,Crimea (Turkish Medal, Legn Honour, Medjidie); *m* 10 June 1880 Mary (*d* 25 Jan 1929), dau of George Urmson, of Frodsham, Cheshire, and *d* 18 Sept 1909, leaving:

1e John Urmson, DSO; *b* 25 June 1881; *educ* Wellington; Col RA,WW I (despatches), WW II as Adj ATA; *m* 27 Nov 1907 Christine Jessie Shelton, dau of Augustus Shelton Hooper, JP, of Hong Kong, and *d* 21 Oct 1967, leaving:

1f John Patrick Molesworth; *b* 17 March 1913; *educ* Wellington; Lt-Col RA WW II; *m* 30 June 1938 (*divorce* 1947) (Margaret) Clare Aida, yr dau of Lionel Walford, of Middleton Stoney, Oxon, and *d* 22 Jan 1975, leaving:

1g *Virginia Anne [Miss Virginia Hope, 4 Phillimore Gdns Close, London W8]; *b* 6 Nov 1942

1f *(Christine) Mary Shelton [Mrs Harry Sparks, 32 Moberley Rd, Salisbury, Wilts]; *b* 10 Aug 1909; *m* 1st 12 Sept 1929 (*divorce* 1934) Capt Frank Wilson Houghton, RA; *m* 2nd 20 July 1938 Maj-Gen Harry Pratt Sparks, CBE, MC, Suffolk Regt (*d* 11 Feb 1965), 3rd s of Charles Pratt Sparks, CBE, of Ormsdale, Dorking, and has:

1g *Charles Pratt; *b* 25 Oct 1941; *educ* Sherborne and Pembroke Coll Cambridge (BA); *m* 24 June 1967 *Brigette Marcelle Marie Louise Jeanneau, and:

1h *William Xavier Pratt; *b* 1972

1h *Marie-Ann Ruth; *b* 1970

1g *Jane Pauline; *b* 18 July 1939; *m* 6 June 1964 *Eric Hugh Legat, and has:

1h *Patricia Jane; *b* 15 Aug 1965

2h *Vanessa Sarah; *b* 2 May 1967

3h *Joanna Mary; *b* 1971

2e George Archibald (Rev); *b* 27 Dec 1882; *educ* New Coll Oxford (MA); Vicar Prestbury Cheshire 1936–50, YMCA Egypt and Palestine 1917–18; *m* 30 April 1929 Edith Margaret Aston, er dau of Benjamin William Martin Aston Key, OBE, MD, of Southsea, and *d* 17 March 1950, leaving:

1f +Robert Frank Molesworth; *b* 18 March 1934; *educ* Marlborough and New Coll Oxford (BA 1957); *m* 2 April 1957 *Jacqueline Pierrette Regine, only dau of Paul Marcelle Albert Forer, of Marseilles, and has:

1g +Frank George Aston; *b* 4 July 1959

2g +Patrick James Mailhe; *b* 10 Nov 1960

2f +Charles Aston; *b* 19 June 1940; *educ* Marlborough and Emmanuel Coll Cambridge (BA); slr 1968; *m* 1967 *Kathryn Elizabeth, dau of Capt Wilfred Williams, Merchant Navy, and has:

1g +Philip Aston; *b* 1968

2g +Nicholas Astley; *b* 1970

1f Margaret Mary; *b* 23 Feb 1932; *m* 26 July 1958 *Cdr Brian Thomas Tippetts, RN, of Bristol, and *d* 19–, leaving:

1g *Thomas Edward Hope; *b* 31 May 1965

1g *Rebecca Mary; *b* 3 Nov 1959

2g *Lucinda Ann Margaret; *b* 22 Sept 1961

3g *Alice Elizabeth; *b* 24 Sept 1963

2f *Elizabeth; *b* 27 Feb 1937; *m* 25 June 1966 *Rev John Nigel Rowe, BD Oxon

3f *Clare Urmson; *b* 8 April 1943

3e Edward Molesworth; *b* 20 April 1885; Offr Roy Fus; *d* unm 8 Oct 1958

4e Frank Charles; *b* 25 Oct 1891; *d* 19 Nov 1914

1d Elizabeth Stanwix; *b* 29 Aug 1836; *m* 4 Dec 1855 James B Alston (*d* 1898) and *d* 3 Dec 1894, leaving issue

1c Augusta; *b* 16 Jan 1786; *m* 14 March 1808 Maj Martin Eccles Alves, 6th Foot, and *d* 9 June 1830, leaving issue

2c Elizabeth; *b* 15 Dec 1790; *m* Donald Grant and *d* 25 Jan 1820, leaving issue

3b John; Imp India Serv *c* 1791

1 Margaret; *m* 1660 Sir Robert Pringle, 1st Bt (*qv*), and had issue

The 7th Bt's cousin,

Sir Thomas Hope, 8th Bt; agriculturalist; laid out The Meadows or Hope Park on Edinburgh's south side; *m* Margaret, est dau of Ninian Lowis, of Merchiston, and *d* 1771, having had:

1 Archibald; *b* 1703; *m* 4 April 1725 Catherine, dau of Very Rev Hugh Tod, and *dvp* 1769, leaving:

(1) ARCHIBALD (Sir), **9th Bt**

2 James, of Loudoun; *d* unm

3 Thomas; physician

4 John, of Edinburgh; *m* Isabel, dau of Sir Alexander Bannerman, 2nd Bt (*qv*), and had:

(1) Thomas; Capt 11th Regt

(2) Alexander, of Edinburgh

5 Charles; Capt RN; *d* unm

Sir THOMAS's gs,

Sir Archibald Hope, 9th Bt; *b* 1735; bought the Pinkie estate 1778 from the Marquess of Tweeddale (*qv*); *m* 1st 1757 Elizabeth (*d* 1778), dau of William Macdowall, of Castle Semple, and had, with other issue:

1 Archibald; *b* 1762; *d* a prisoner at Seringapatam 1782

2 **Sir Thomas Hope, 10th Bt**; *b* 1768; *m* — Pierce and *dsp* 1801

Sir Archibald *m* 2nd 1779 Elizabeth (*d* 1818), dau of John Patoun of Inveresk by Jean, dau of George Douglas of Friarshaw, and *d* 10 June 1794, having by her had:

3 JOHN (Sir), **11th Bt**

4 Hugh; *b* 1782; Bengal CS; *m* 1819 Isabella Gray (*d* 1858), dau of Capt Æneas Mackay of Scotstoun, and *d* 1823, leaving, with a dau (Helen, *d* 1868):

(1) Archibald Hugh; *b* 17 Jan 1820; Gen Madras Cav; *m* 8 Jan 1842 Caroline Elizabeth (*d* 7 Feb 1912), dau of Lt-Gen Sir Richard Jones, KCB, and *d* 8 March 1890, leaving:

1a Hugh Richard, CB; *b* 24 July 1844; Maj-Gen IA; *m* 25 July 1865 Frances Georgina (*d* 14 May 1903), 2nd dau of Sir Thomas Pycroft, KCSI, and *dsp* 11 May 1900

2a Archibald Godfrey; *b* 7 Jan 1848; *m* 5 Oct 1871 Adela Henrietta (*m* 2nd 1889 Perceval Kingsford and *d* 15 Sept 1923), dau of Charles William Curtis (*see* CURTIS, Bt), and *d* 17 June 1881, leaving:

1b Graham Archibald; *b* 18 July 1872; Capt RA WW I (1915 Star); *m* 19 Dec 1894 Ruby Evelyn (*d* 17 Nov 1952), dau of Col Harvey Y Murray, Bengal Army, and *d* 10 June 1932, having had:

1c Archibald Murray; *b* 2 Oct 1898; *d* Jan 1899

2c Charles Evelyn Graham; *b* 6 Dec 1900; *educ* Marlborough; Lt-Col Indian Cav WW II, Intell and Staff India and ALFSEA; novelist as Charles Graham Hope, ed *Pony* and *The Light Horse*; *m* 29 March 1930 *Beryl Maud, dau of Capt Bernard Daly, of Templeogue House, Co Dublin, and *d* 24 June 1971, having had twin sons (Michael, John, *b* 11 May 1939; both *d* in infancy)

3c Nigel; *b* 24 Aug 1907; S/Ldr RAF WW II; *m* 28 July 1936 Evelyn Di (*m* 2nd 1950 William Bryant), yr dau of Harry Arnaud Watson, of Emsworth, Hants, and *das* 30 Nov 1939, leaving:

1d *Alison; *b* posthumously 8 March 1940

2b Lucius Charles; *b* 18 July 1873; Lt-Col Dorsetshire Regt, Tirah Expdn 1897 (medal with two clasps), Boer War (medal with two clasps), WW I (severely wounded); *d* 25 May 1938

3b Richard Berwick; *b* 25 Oct 1874; Maj E Surrey Regt, Lt Roy W Kent Regt, NW Frontier India 1897 (medal), WW I (wounded, despatches); *m*

1st 29 April 1899 (*divorce* 1907) Frances Catherine Genette Douglas (*d* 1942), yst dau of Capt R Douglas Lane, 17th Lancers, and had:

1c Richard Charles Adrian; *b* 1 Aug 1900; *d* an infant

1c Betty Genette; *b* 1 Sept 1902; *m* 12 Feb 1941 Rev Philip Brandon Mercier, Vicar Batheaston, Somerset, and *d* 10 Nov 1947

3b (cont.) Maj Richard Hope *m* 2nd 1907 Mary Francis, dau of Stephen West, and *d* 13 Sept 1952, having by her had:

2c David Archibald Douglas; *b* 1908; *d* 19–

3c Alexander Erskine; *b* 15 May 1917; Lt Beds and Herts Regt WW II; *m* 11 Oct 1941 *Lilias Mary Phyllis (*m* 2nd 21 Jan 1948 Lt-Col Gerard Francis Kirkpatrick Daly, RE, s of Col Sir Clive Kirkpatrick Daly, CSI, CIE), dau of Rev William Herbert Austwick, and was *ka* 2 Oct 1944, having had:

1d +Alexander David Austwick; *b* posthumously 12 Jan 1945; *educ* Bloxham; actor

1d Juliet Mary Elizabeth; *b* 29 Nov 1942; *d* 11 Feb 1943

4c Archibald Paul; *b* 15 May 1917; 2nd-Lt Dorset Regt (SR); *d* 1958

4b Douglas Edmund; *b* 6 March 1877; Capt N Staffs Regt Boer War (medal with two clasps), WW I as RTO; *m* 18 Nov 1914 Victoria Maud, dau of John Burbridge Arnold, and *d* 1 Aug 1931

5b Adrian Lewis; *b* 3 Oct 1878; Lt BSAP Boer War; *das* unm 17 June 1902

1b Edith Adela; *m* Oct 1906 Luke Neil Robinson and *d* 14 Dec 1947, leaving issue

3a Edmund William Birch; *b* 23 June 1851; *d* unm 1876

4a Lewis Anstruther, CB (1898); *b* 4 Nov 1855; MP Reading; Col ASC, ADC to HM, AQMG N Comd Zulu Campaign 1878–79, Nile Expdn 1884–85, Khartoum Expdn 1898, Boer War, memb Roy Co Archers; *m* 3 Sept 1887 Lucy Elizabeth (*d* 21 July 1952), dau of George Palmer, and *d* 2 May 1929, having had:

1b Hugh Lewis, MC; *b* 20 June 1897; Lt RHA Res Offrs WW I (wounded three times, despatches); *m* 9 June 1921 Ethel Lilian, yr dau of Sir Henry King, and *d* 19 Oct 1921

1b Helen Jean; *d* unm 20 Feb 1952

2b Olive Georgina; *m* 17 July 1915 Lt-Col Norman Valentine Blacker, DSO, MC (*d* 13 May 1958), E Yorks Regt, 2nd s of Maj Frederick Henry Blacker, 4th Hus, of Johnstown, Co Kildare, and had issue

1a Edith Caroline; *d* 30 Jan 1869

2a Isabella Helen; *d* 18 Oct 1849

3a Sophia Montgomery; *b* 6 Feb 1857; *d* unm 15 Oct 1950

5 William; *b* 1784; Master-Attendant Calcutta; *d* unm 1837

1 Magdalen; *m* John Scott, of Gala (*d* 13 July 1873)

Sir THOMAS's half-bro,

Sir John Hope, 11th Bt, MP; *b* 13 April 1781; *m* 17 June 1805 Anne (*d* 17 March 1867), 4th dau of John Wedderburn (*see* OGILVY-WEDDERBURN, Bt), and *d* 5 June 1853, having had, with other issue:

1 **Sir Archibald Hope, 12th Bt**, DL Edinburgh; *b* 28 Feb 1808; Lt-Col Midlothian Militia; *m* 17 July 1862 Aldena (*d* 20 Oct 1908), dau of Henry Kingscote, and *dsp* 24 Jan 1883

2 **Sir John David Hope, 13th Bt**, JP Midlothian and Fife; *b* 27 April 1809; *d* unm 14 July 1892

3 Thomas; *b* 10 July 1810; R-Adml; *d* 31 Aug 1867

4 Hugh; *b* 3 June 1813; *m* 1848 Catherine (*d* 17 March 1875), dau of Lt-Col A Spens, HEICS, and *d* 15 Aug 1876

5 **Sir William Hope, 14th Bt**, KCB; *b* 12 Jan 1819; Gen Crimea with 71st Highrs (Turkish Medal, Legn Honour, Medjidie); *m* 22 Jan 1862 Alicia Henrietta (*d* 19 June 1901), dau of Sir John Wedderburn, 2nd Bt (*see* OGILVY-WEDDERBURN, BT), and *dsp* 5 Sept 1898

6 James Wedderburn; *b* 4 Sept 1823; 26th Bombay NI; *d* 9 June 1846

7 **Sir Alexander Hope, 15th Bt**, JP Midlothian; *b* 22 Oct 1824; Bengal CS; *d* unm 7 March 1918

8 Charles Augustus (Rev); *b* 7 Aug 1827; Rector Barwick-in-Elmet, Hon Canon Ripon; *m* 21 Sept 1854 Julia Sophia (*d* 1 March 1903), 2nd dau of John Watson Barton, of Stapleton Park, Yorks, and *d* 30 Dec 1898, leaving issue:

(1) JOHN AUGUSTUS (Sir), **16th Bt**

(2) Robert Philip; *b* 29 June 1873; *d* 21 June 1930

Sir ALEXANDER's nephew,

Sir John Augustus Hope, 16th Bt, OBE (1919), JP Midlothian; *b* 7 July 1869; Lt-Col Res of Offrs KRRC Boer War (medal, four clasps), WW I (wounded); MP Midlothian 1912–18 and N Midlothian and Peebles 1918–22; *m* 26 April 1910 Hon Mary Bruce, OBE, JP Midlothian, memb Eden Endowments Commn Scotland (*d* 18 Feb 1957), est dau of 10th Lord Balfour of Burleigh (*qv*), and *d* 17 April 1924, having had:

1 ARCHIBALD PHILIP (Sir), **17th Bt**

2 John Cecil, DSO, MC; *b* 9 May 1913; Lt-Col 60th Rifles, WW II; *das* April 1945

3 Hugh Alexander, OBE (1956), MC; *b* 16 July 1914; *educ* Eton and Worcester Coll Oxford; Lt-Col KRRC WW II (despatches), E Africa 1955–56 (despatches), memb Gentlemen-at-Arms; *m* 26 July 1949 *Cynthia Evelyn [Mrs Hugh Hope, 7 High St, Sherston, Wilts SN16 OLQ], 2nd dau of Lt-Col Algernon Corbet Turnor, MC, RHG, of Malmesbury, Wilts, and *d* 1982, having had:

(1) +Andrew Hugh; *b* 19 March 1951; *educ* Quantock Sch, Somerset; *m* 1982 (*divorce* 1992) Rosanna Jane, dau of Gilbert Ian Noel Johnstone, of Warminster, Wilts, and has:

1a +Oliver Hugh; *b* 1989

1a *Clara Harriet; *b* 1986

1 *Katharine Anne [Mrs Eric Rayner, The Colt House, Chieveley, Berks RG16 8XB]; *b* 10 Oct 1916; *m* 1st 29 April 1939 F/Lt Carl Raymond Davis, DFC, AAF (*das* 6 Sept 1940), of Nettlebed, Oxon, and has:

(1) *Carl Michael [Carl Davis Esq, Marymead Cottage, Chieveley, Berks RG16 8UX]; *b* 24 June 1940; *educ* Eton and Lincoln Coll Oxford (BA); *m* 1st 27 July 1963 (*divorce* 1987) Carolyn Rachel, only dau of John Campbell White, of Berkhamsted, Herts; *m* 2nd 1987 *Carolyn Jane, dau of Ernest Smith Hall, of Solihull, Warwicks, and has by his 1st w:

1a *Carl Robert; *b* 1971

1a *Helen Rachel; *b* 7 Jan 1966

2a *Julie Theresa; *b* 7 Nov 1968

1 (cont.) Mrs Carl Davis *m* 2nd 14 May 1945 Maj Eric George Ewart Rayner, RA (*d* 1978), and by him has:

(1) *Gillian Mary [Mrs Peter Cardiff, 29 Stokenchurch St, London SW6 3TS]; *b* 20 March 1948; *m* 1986 *Peter Alan Cardiff

Sir JOHN's est son

Sir Archibald Philip Hope, 17th Bt, OBE (1945), DFC (1940); *b* 27 March 1912; *educ* Eton and Balliol Col Oxford (BA 1934); G/Capt RAuxAF WW II (despatches twice); memb Roy Co Archers; md Airwork Ltd, ch exec and dir Napier Aero Engines Ltd, chm Air League 1965–68, exec English Electric Co Ltd; *m* 20 April 1938 Ruth, yst dau of Carl Raymond Davis, of Nettlebed, Oxon, and *d* 1987, leaving:

1 Sir JOHN CARL ALEXANDER HOPE, **18th and present Bt**

2 +Charles Archibald; *b* 11 April 1945; *educ* Eton, Balliol Coll Oxford (BA) and London U (MA); Research Lecturer Warburg Inst; *m* 20 Dec 1977 *Jennifer Katharine, dau of John Hadley, of Godmanchester, Hunts, and has:

(1) +Thomas; *b* 1978

HOPE OF CRAIGHEAD

Arms: Azure, on a chevron or between three besants a bay leaf between two quill pens vert. **Crest:** A broken terrestial globe proper, charged with an anchor gules, surmounted by a rainbow proper. **Supporters:** Two blackfaced rams guardant proper. **Motto:** *Spes non est fracta* ('Hope is not broken'). **Creation:** B. (LP, UK) March 1995.

THE BARON HOPE OF CRAIGHEAD, of Bamff, District of Perth and Kinross (James Arthur David Hope, PC (1989) [The Rt Hon The Lord Hope of Craighead PC, House of Lords, London SW1A 0PW]; *b* 27 June 1938; *educ* Edinburgh Acad, Rugby, St John's Coll Cambridge (Hon Fell 1995) and Edinburgh U (LLB 1965); Seaforth Highrs 1957–59, advocate 1965, Standg Jr Counsel Scotland to Bd Inland Revenue 1974–78, Advocate Depute 1978–82, QC (S) 1978, Dean Faculty Advocates 1986–89, Ld Justice Gen Scotland and Ld Pres Court Session 1989–96, a Ld Appeal in Ordinary 1996–; Pres Stair Soc 1993–, Hon Prof Law Aberdeen 1994–, Hon Memb Canadian Bar Assoc 1987, Hon Bencher Gray's Inn 1989 and Inn of Court NI 1995, Chllr Strathclyde U 1998–, Hon LLD: Aberdeen 1991, Strathclyde 1993, Edinburgh 1995; *m* 11 April 1966 *Katharine Mary, dau of W Mark Kerr, WS, and has:

1 *William Thomas Artur; *b* 19 Oct 1969

2 *James David Louis; *b* 19 Oct 1969; *m* 29 June 1996 *Maria-Pia Midenbäck, of Jönköping, Sweden

1 *Lucy Charlotte Mary; *b* 30 Dec 1971

Lineage: *see* LINLITHGOW, M

HOPE-DUNBAR

Arms: Quarterly, 1st, gu. a lion rampant arg., armed and langued az., a bordure of the second charged with ten roses of the field, barbed and seeded vert (for DUNBAR); 2nd, az. on a chevron or between three bezants a bay leaf slipped vert, a mullet of the second in chief for difference (for HOPE); 3rd, arg. a man's heart imperially crowned ppr., on a chief az. three mullets of the field (for DOUGLAS); 4th, counter-quartered, 1st and 4th, gu. three cinquefoils erm.; 2nd and 3rd, arg. a lymphad, sails furled sa., flagged gu. (for HAMILTON). **Crest:** A horse's head couped arg., bridled gu. **Supporters:** Two lions rampant guardant arg., armed and langued gu., each holding in one of the forepaws a rose slipped ppr. **Motto:** *Firmior quo paratior* ('The more prepared, the more powerful'). **Creation:** Bt. (NS) 13 Oct 1664.

SIR DAVID HOPE-DUNBAR, 8TH BT, of St Mary's Isle, Stewartry of Kirkcudbright [Sir David Hope-Dunbar Bt, Banks Farm, Kirkcudbright DG6 4XF]; *b* 13 July 1941; *s* f 1961; *educ* Eton and RAC Cirencester; ARICS, fndr Dunbar & Co, now Allied Dunbar plc; *m* 30 Sept 1971 *Kathleen Ruth, yr dau of J T Kenrick, of Edgbaston, Birmingham, and has:

1 +CHARLES; *b* 11 March 1975
1 *Philippa; *b* 1973
2 *Juliet Antonia; *b* 5 July 1976

Lineage: Sir ALEXANDER DUNBAR of Westfield (*see* DUNBAR, Bt, of Mochrum, Bt); had a 2nd s:

Sir JOHN DUNBAR of Mochrum; *m* 1st Margaret (*d* 1483), 2nd dau and coheir of Patrick Dunbar of Cumnock and Mochrum, and had issue; *m* 2nd Janet, dau of Sir Alexander Stewart of Garlies (*see* GALLOWAY, E), and *d* 1503, having by her had, with three daus and two yr sons (Gavin, Archbp Glasgow 1524, Ld Chllr Scotland 1528, fndr and 1st pres Ct of Session; James, of Glasnock):

ARCHIBALD DUNBAR; had charter 17 Feb 1533 of lands of Baldoon, Wigtownshire; *m* Janet, dau of Mure of Rowallan, and *d* 1536, having had, with three yr sons (Archibald; John, *m* 1568 Margaret, dau of Sir Patrick Vans of Barnbarroch; Alexander):

GAVIN DUNBAR of Baldoon; *m* Janet Cunningham and *d* 18 April 1618, having had, with other issue, including an er s (David, of Baldoon, *b* 25 Jan 1582, *m* 9 Feb 1615 Janet Charteris of Amisfield (*see* WEMYSS, E) and *dsp c* 1641):

ARCHIBALD DUNBAR, in Orchardton; *b* 25 July 1583; *m* Mary — and *d c* 1641, leaving:

Sir David Dunbar, 1st Bt (NS), so *cr* 13 Oct 1664, with remainder to the heirs male of his body and to his heirs of tailzie succeeding him in his lands; *b c* 1610; *m* 1st May 1641 Elizabeth, dau of John McCulloch of Myretown, and had issue; *m* 2nd 1666 Anna (*dsp*), dau of Sir Archibald Sydserf of Lowden, and *d* 12 Dec 1686, when the btcy became dormant till 1 June 1916; his s by his 1st w:

DAVID DUNBAR; *m* 1st 12 Aug 1669 Janet (*d* 12 Sept 1669), dau of 1st Viscount of Stair (*see* STAIR, E) and the model for Scott's *The Bride of Lammermoor*; *m* 2nd 1674 Eleanor (*d* Sept 1687), dau of 7th Earl of Eglinton (*see* EGLINTON and WINTON, E), and *dvp* 20 March 1682, having by her had, with a s (David, *d* 1685):

MARY Dunbar, of Baldoon; *b* 1677; *m* 1691 Lord Basil HAMILTON (*see* HAMILTON and BRANDON, D) and *d* 15 May 1760, having had, with other issue:

BASIL HAMILTON; *b* 9 Sept 1693; *m* 14 March 1719 Isabella (*d* 6 April 1725), dau of Col Hon Alexander Mackenzie (*see* CROMARTIE, E), and *d* 14 Nov 1742, having had, with a yr s (Basil, *d* young) and two daus:

DUNBAR HAMILTON later DOUGLAS (on succeeding his great-uncle as Earl 1744), 4th EARL OF SELKIRK; *b* 1 Dec 1722; *m* 3 Dec 1758 Helen, gdau of 6th Earl of Haddington (*qv*), and *d* 24 May 1799, having had, with other issue:

THOMAS DOUGLAS, 5th EARL OF SELKIRK; *b* 20 June 1771; *m* 24 Nov 1807 Jean (*d* 10 June 1871), only surv dau of James Wedderburn-Colvile of Inveresk, and *d* 8 April 1820, leaving, with a s and other dau (*see* HAMILTON and BRANDON, D)

ISABELLA HELEN Douglas; *b* 8 Jan 1811; *m* 26 Oct 1841 Hon Charles HOPE and *d* 4 July 1893, having had, with other issue (*see* LINLITHGOW, M):

JOHN HOPE, of St Mary's Isle, Kirkcudbrightshire, JP, DL; *b* 30 Jan 1843; Capt RN; *m* 13 Aug 1872 Rebecca Marion (*d* 20 June 1914), 2nd dau of Peter Blackburn, MP, of Killearn, Stirling, and *d* 27 Feb 1915, having had:

1 CHARLES DUNBAR (Sir), **6th Bt**
2 Adrian Leslie; *b* 1 Oct 1880; *d* 24 Oct 1885
1 Dorothea Jean; *b* 8 Dec; *d* 23 Dec 1874
2 Helen Jacqueline, MBE; *b* 26 Oct 1875; *m* 27 Nov 1901 Alan Burns, of Cumbernauld, Dunbartonshire, and *d* 21 April 1923, leaving:
(1) John Alan; *b* 4 Oct 1905; *educ* Harrow and Trin Hall Cambridge; Lt-Col Scots Gds, memb Roy Co Archers; *m* 6 March 1944 *Joyce Margaret [Mrs John Burns, Fairfield, 9 Cole Rd, Bruton, Somerset BA10 0DD], dau of George Alfred Bagley August, of Bedford, and *d* 16 Sept 1987, having had:
1a +Felicity Margaret [Mrs Francis Peto, Cowdenowes Mains, Earlston, Berwickshire]; *b* 24 July 1945; *m* 1974 *Francis Michael Morton Peto (*see* PETO, Bt, of Somerleyton) and has issue
2a +Marion Jacqueline [Mrs Peter Chamberlin, Drove House, Coombe Bissett, Wilts]; *b* 12 July 1948; *m* 30 Nov 1968 *Lt-Col Peter Guy Chamberlin, RGJ (ret), and has:
1b +Edward Alan; *b* 6 Feb 1974
1b +Lucinda Geraldine; *b* 3 Dec 1970; *m* 30 Nov 1996 *Giles William Stanford
2b +Vanessa Louise; *b* 24 June 1977
(2) George, JP (Dunbartonshire); *b* 1 Sept 1909; *educ* Eton and Trin Coll Cambridge; Lt-Cdr RNVR WW II; CA Dunbartonshire; *d* 1 July 1989
(3) Charles Hope; *b* 1912; *educ* Eton and RMC Sandhurst; 60th Rifles; *m* 30 April 1949 *Barbara Delscey [Mrs Charles Burns, 16 Sinclair St, Milngavie, Glasgow G62 8NU], dau of Dr E Macmillan, of Pretoria, and *d* 25 Oct 1958, leaving:
1a +Geoffrey Douglas Charles; *b* 19 Feb 1954; *m* 4 Oct 1980 *Celia, dau of Guy Kynaston, of Croxdalewood, Co Durham, and has:
1b +Kirstin; *b* 30 Dec 1981
2b +Phebe; *b* 29 June 1985
3b +Shiona; *b* 13 June 1988
1a +Delscey Hope; *b* 29 March 1951; late Head St Mary's Sch Calne
(1) +Jean Douglas; *b* 15 June 1903; *d* 1991
1 Katherine Marion; *b* 1 July 1878; *d* unm 21 June 1961

Capt JOHN HOPE's est son,

Sir CHARLES DUNBAR HOPE later HOPE-DUNBAR (1916), **6th Bt**, as which recognised 1 June 1916, JP, DL; *b* 12 July 1873; Maj RFA and Actg Lt-Col cmdg a Bde 1917, served Boer War (two medals with five clasps), WW I; *m* 1st 31 Jan 1906 Edythe Mary (*d* 27 Feb 1948), est dau of Richard Ramsden, JP, of Siddinghurst, Surrey, and had issue; *m* 2nd 21 Oct 1948 Marjorie (*d* 29 Jan 1970), dau of Hugh Chesterton Ford, of Amersham, and widow of Capt W MacRobert, of Stranraer, and *d* 6 Jan 1958; leaving by his 1st w:

Sir Basil Douglas Hope-Dunbar, 7th Bt; *b* 16 Feb 1907; *educ* Eton and RMC Sandhurst; Maj QO Cameron Highrs WW II; *m* 1st 8 Nov 1932 (*divorce* Scotland 1937) Evelyn Diana, er dau of Col George Ireland Fraser, CMG, DSO, QO Cameron Highrs; *m* 2nd 11 July 1940 Edith Maud Maclaren (*d* 1989), est dau of Malcolm Cross, of Earlston, Borgue, and *d* 21 July 1961, leaving by her:

Sir DAVID HOPE-DUNBAR, **8th and present Bt**

HORLICK

Arms: Arg. a lion rampant gu., on a chief of the last a garb of barley between two bull's heads cabossed, all or. **Crest:** In front of a garb of barley or a lion's head erased gu. **Motto:** *Labore et scientia* ('By labour and knowledge'). **Creation:** Bt. (UK) 18 July 1914.

SIR JAMES CUNLIFFE WILLIAM HORLICK, 6TH BT, of Cowley Manor, Co Gloucester [Sir James Horlick Bt, Braelangwell House, Balblair, Ross-shire IV7 8LQ]; *b* 19 Nov 1956; *s* f 1995; *educ* Eton and RMA Sandhurst; commissioned Coldstream Gds 1977, 2nd Lt 1979; *m* 1985 *Fiona Rosalie, est dau of Andrew McLaren, of Alcester, Warwicks, and Mrs Harry Digby, and has:

1 +ALEXANDER; *b* 8 April 1987

2 +Jack Orlando; *b* 3 Sept 1989

3 +Hugo Roland; *b* 1991

Lineage: JAMES HORLICK, of Ruardean, Glos; *d* 1875, leaving:

Sir James Horlick, 1st Bt (UK), so *cr* 18 July 1914, JP, DL Glos; High Sheriff 1902, Ld Manor Cowley; *b* 30 April 1844; chm and pres Horlicks Ltd; *m* 12 April 1873 Margaret Adelaide (*d* 20 Nov 1925), er dau of William Burford, of Leicester, and *d* 7 May 1921, having had:

1 **Sir Ernest Burford Horlick, 2nd Bt**; *b* 29 Feb 1880; *educ* Ch Ch Oxford (BA); Capt RAF; *m* 1st 31 Dec 1902 (*divorce* 1929) Jane Shillaber, 2nd dau of Col Cunliffe Martin, CB, Bengal Cav, and had:

(1)**Sir Peter James Cunliffe Horlick, 3rd Bt**; *b* 4 March 1908; *educ* Eton; chm Horlicks Pty, Sydney, Australia; *m* 1st 29 Oct 1931 (*divorce* 1934) Rosemary Margaret (*m* 2nd 1940 Maj Sir Henry d'Avigdor-Goldsmid, 2nd Bt (*see* 1970 edn), and *d* 13 June 1997), est dau of Lt-Col Charles Nicholl; *m* 2nd 21 April 1934 (*divorce* 1948) Beryta Kathleen Amy, formerly w of Charles Stewart Murray (*see* DUNMORE, E) and only dau of Roland Allport, of Sydney, NSW, and by her had:

1a *Natasha [Miss Natasha Horlick, Apt 16, Gaucin, Malaga, Spain]; *b* 27 Oct 1935

2a *Anna [Mrs Tim Wright, 17 The Little Boltons, London SW10]; *b* 22 Feb 1938; *m* 1st 22 Oct 1960 (*divorce* 1971) Peter Gammon, only s of J C Gammon and Mrs R G French; *m* 2nd *Tim Fraser Wright and by her 1st husb has:

1b *Anthony John; *b* 14 April 1965

1b *Tania Jane; *b* 13 Sept 1962

(1) (cont.) **Sir Peter** *m* 3rd 28 April 1948 (*divorce* 1957) Jacqueline Mary, formerly w of Charles Lurie and dau of Clement Walter Mander; *m* 4th 24 Sept 1957 his 2nd w Beryta (*d* 7 Sept 1982) and *dspm* 29 Jan 1958

(1) *Roma Ernestine; *b* 25 Nov 1903; *m* 10 April 1923 8th Earl of Dartmouth (*qv*) and has issue

(2) *Elizabeth Ann (Betsan) [Mrs John Coats, Conch, Kate St, Alexandra Headland, Qld, Australia]; *b* 15 July 1914; *m* 31 Oct 1933 John Balfour Symington Coats, s of Ernest Coats, of Sundrum Castle, Ayr, and has issue:

1a *Callum Mackenzie [Callum Coats Esq, Mail Service 591, Stewart's Rd, Wolvi via Gympie, Qld 4570, Australia]; architect, AA Dipl 1967, ARIBA 1968, ARAIBA 1969; *b* 19 July 1939; *m* 31 Dec 1966 (*divorce* 1981) Emily Jane, dau of Philip C B Archer and gdau of Lady Braintree (*see* 1956 edn); *m* 2nd 1985 *Muriel Florence Wattinne and by his 1st w has issue:

1b *Angus Orlando; *b* 4 Aug 1968

2b *Guy Oliver Balfour; *b* 1972

2a *Christopher David [Christopher Horlick, 5156 NE 5th St, Seattle, WA 98105, USA]; *b* 22 Dec 1943; *educ* St Catherine's Coll Oxford (BA 1967); *m* 17 Sept 1966 *Margaret Helen, dau of Richard Van Etten, of Monticello, NY, USA, and has:

1b *James John; *b* 1978

1b *Mercedes Jane; *b* 1970

3a *Ian Forester Mungo; *b* 1 Oct 1953; *m* 1986 *Anna Birrell

1a *Mary Manuela [Mrs Francis Skorka, 20 Essendon Rd, Anstead, Brisbane, Qld 4070, Australia]; *b* 9 Jan 1937; *m* 17 March 1959 *Francis Skorka and has issue:

1b *Lester Carl; *b* 14 Oct 1963; *m* 1987 *Tracey Ann Symons, of Redcliffe, Qld, and has:

1c *Kelly Ann; *b* 1992

2b *Darius Brian Christopher; *b* 1970

1b *Catherine Benita; *b* 3 June 1966; *m* 1984 *Lennard Thomas Walbank, of Nundah, Qld, and has:

1c *Thomas Shane Ronald; *b* 1991

1c *Katie Louise; *b* 1993

2b *Meri-Anne Kaye; *b* 1976

1 (cont.) **Sir Ernest** *m* 2nd 17 Feb 1931 Sonia Sophie, dau of George Theolesco, of Romania, and *d* 7 Oct 1934

2 **Sir James Nockells Horlick, 4th Bt**, OBE (1918), MC (1917), of Cowley Manor; *b* 22 March 1886; *educ* Eton and Ch Ch Oxford (BA 1908); Lt-Col Coldstream Gds WW I (despatches), Brevet-Maj 1917, at Peace Conf Paris 1919, Pres Horlicks Ltd, High Sheriff Berks 1938, MP Gloucester 1923–29, OStJ, Chev Legion Honour, Order White Eagle Serbia with swords and Greek MC; *m* 1st 22 March 1911 Flora Macdonald (*d* 1 Oct 1955), dau of Col Cunliffe Martin, CB, and had:

(1) JOHN JAMES MACDONALD (Sir), **5th Bt**

(1) (Rachel) Katherine; *b* 1913; *m* 1st 26 Oct 1933 (*divorce* 1946) Lt-Col Kenneth Arthur Wagg, Rifle Bde, yr s of Henry John Wagg, OBE, and had four sons (*see* WILLOUGHBY DE BROKE, B); *m* 2nd 7 March 1947 Anthony John Nicholas Christopher Photius Contomichalos, est s of Gerasimo Anthony Contomichalos, OBE, of Alexandria, Egypt, and *d* 22 Jan 1969, leaving a further s and dau

(2) *Ursula Priscilla Marie Gabrielle [Mrs John Weaver, Greywalls, Gullane, E Lothian; 47 Glebe Pl, London SW3 5JE]; *b* 29 Aug 1916; *m* 1st 15 July 1936 (*divorce* 1940) Stafford Vaughan Stepney Howard (*see* NORFOLK, D) and has issue; *m* 2nd 18 July 1940 *Lt-Col John Frederick Herron Weaver, 1st King's Dragoon Gds, s of Frederick William Herron Weaver, of Hook Heath, Woking, and by him has had:

1a Martin John Herron; *b* 10 Aug 1941; *educ* Eton; *m* 24 June 1965 *Virginia Frances, er dau of Edward Segal, of New York, and was *k* in a car crash in New Mexico 16 Jan 1971, leaving:

1b *Jesse Martin Herron; *b* 23 Nov 1970

2a *Christopher Giles Herron; *b* 4 April 1946; *educ* Eton; *m* 1974 *Rosamund Betty, yst dau of Lionel Geoffrey Mayhew, and has issue:

1b *Frederick Giles Herron; *b* 1977

2b *Jonathan Martin Herron; *b* 1986

1b *Flora Xaviere Herron; *b* 1975

2b *Johanna Kate Herron; *b* 1983

2 (cont.) **Sir James** *m* 2nd 19 Jan 1956 *Joan Isabel, dau of James Barrie MacGill, and *d* 1 Jan 1973

3 Gerald Nolekin; Maj Glos Yeo; *b* 1 Feb 1888; *educ* Eton and BNC Oxford; *das* 5 July 1918

The 4th Bt's only s,

Sir John James MacDonald Horlick, 5th Bt; *b* 9 April 1922; *educ* Eton and Babson Inst Business Admin, Wellesley Hills, Mass.; Capt Coldstream Gds, dep chm Horlicks 1968–71, ptnr Tournaig Farming Co 1973, chm Highland Fish Farmer 1978–85, OStJ 1973; *m* 2 Oct 1948 June, est dau of Douglas Cory-Wright, CBE (*see* CORY-WRIGHT, Bt), and *d* 20 Feb 1995, leaving:

1 Sir JAMES CUNLIFFE WILLIAM HORLICK, **6th and present Bt**

1 *Harriet Anne [Mrs Antony Granville, Tachbrook House, Stourton, Warwicks]; *b* 6 June 1950; BA Lond; *m* 1970 *Antony Lansdowne Granville (*see* ROSE, Bt, of Montreal (and Hardwick House)), and has issue

2 *Araminta [Mrs Rory Carson, Perseverance Cottage, Harpsden, Henley-on-Thames, Oxon]; *b* 7 June 1953; MCSP; *m* 19 April 1975 *(Edward) Rory Carson, only s of Hon Edward Carson (*see* 1935 edn CARSON, B), of Cleve Court, Minster-in-Thanet, and has:

(1) *Toby Edward; *b* 1977

(2) *Jonathan Henry; *b* 1979

(3) *Oliver James; *b* 1982

(4) *Bartholomew John; *b* 1988

HORNE

Arms: Gu. a fret vair between two boars passant, one in chief and one in base or. **Crest:** A dexter arm vested gu., cuffed or, holding in the hand ppr. a hunting horn and charged on the sleeve with a fret gold. **Motto:** *Fronti nulla fides* ('Appearances can be deceptive'). **Creation:** Bt. (UK) 25 March 1929.

SIR (ALAN) GRAY ANTHONY HORNE, 3RD BT, of Shackleford, Co Surrey [Sir Gray Horne Bt, Château du Basty, Thenon, Dordogne, France]; *b* 11 July 1948; *s* gf 1984; *m* 1980 *Cecile Rose, dau of Jacques Desplanche, of 5 rue de Cheverny, Romorantin, France

Lineage: EDGAR HORNE, of Witley, Surrey, had, with other issue:

Sir William Edgar Horne, 1st Bt (UK), so *cr* 25 March 1929, JP Co London, DL Sutherland, memb Westminster CC, Mayor 1923–24, Alderman 1925, chm Prudential Assur, Pres Surveyors' Instn, Order Dannebrog, MP (U) Guildford 1910–22; *b* 21 Jan 1856; *m* 1886 Margery (*d* 18 March 1939), dau of George Anderson May, of Elford, Staffs, and had:

1 ALAN EDGAR (Sir), **2nd Bt**

2 William Guy; served WW I (POW, 1914 star, two medals), later with 19th Roy Hus, joined 10th Hus 1921, served India and Sudan (ret as Maj 1930), WW II 1939–43 with AAF, dir Prudential Assur 1932–42, Master Clothworkers' Co 1957–58; *b* 19 Sept 1889 (twin with his bro); *educ* Eton and RMC; *m* 1st July 1920 (*divorce* 1949) Louisa Carey (*d* 1961), 6th dau of Herbert Carey Hardy, JP, of Sussex; *m* 2nd Hortense Barbiton, of Paris

1 Phyllis Margery; *b* 28 Aug 1888; *d* unm 3 May 1970

Sir EDGAR *d* 26 Sept 1941; his er son,

Sir Alan Edgar Horne, 2nd Bt, MC; *b* 19 Sept 1889; *educ* Eton and Univ Coll Oxford; Capt Surrey Yeo WW I (despatches four times, Croix de Guerre with Palm), Lt-Col Pioneer Corps WW II; *m* 1st 27 Aug 1915 Florence Etty (*d* 4 Nov 1918), dau of Arthur Wolseley Kelly, and had:

1 *Edith Margery Jay [Mrs Thomas Reddaway, Saltingsgarth, Broad Lane, Brancaster, Norfolk PE31 8AU]; Jr Cdr ATS (FANY) WW II; *m* 20 May 1944 Maj Thomas Fiddian Reddaway, MA, FSA, FRHistS, RA (*d* 26 Oct 1967), Prof History, London U, and has had:

(1) *Edgar James Fiddian; *b* 8 July 1945; *educ* Oundle and Westfield Coll London (BSc)

(2) *William Thomas; *b* 29 Jan 1948; *educ* Oundle and Bedford Coll London

(3) *Henry Sills; *b* 4 Aug 1950; *educ* Oundle and Bedford Coll London

(4) *Richard Alan; *b* 5 May 1952; *educ* Oundle and Oriel Coll Oxford

(5) Mark Andrew; *b* 16 Nov; *d* 13 Dec 1954

(6) *Michael Jay; *b* 30 June 1956; *educ* Oundle and Balliol Coll Oxford

(1) *Susan Mary; *b* 16 June 1949; *educ* St Mary's Calne, Queen Elizabeth Coll and London U

Sir Alan *m* 2nd 21 July 1924 (*divorce* 1930) Roslyn (*d* 15 May 1961), dau of John Bryan Robinson, and *d* 4 Feb 1984, leaving by her:

1 Antony Edgar Alan; F/Lt RAFVR WW II; *b* 19 May 1925; *educ* Ampleforth and Oriel Coll Oxford; *m* 28 June 1945 *Valentine Antonia [Mrs Anthony Horne, Château du Basty, Thenon, Dordogne, France], dau of Valentine Dudensing, of Thenon, and 65 E 57th St, NYC, and *d* 20 Nov 1954, leaving issue:

(1) Sir (ALAN) GRAY ANTHONY HORNE, **3rd and present Bt**

HORSBRUGH-PORTER

Arms: Arg. on a bend az. three bells of the field between in chief a portcullis and in base two keys in saltire sa. **Crest:** On a fasces fesswise a cherub, all ppr. **Motto:** *J'ayme porter secours* ('I love bringing help'). **Creation:** Bt. (UK) 22 July 1902.

SIR JOHN SIMON HORSBRUGH-PORTER, 4TH BT, of Merrion Square, City and Co of Dublin [Sir John Horsbrugh-Porter Bt, Bowers Croft, Coleshill, Bucks HP7 0LS]; *b* 18 Dec 1938; *s* f 1986; *educ* Winchester and Trin Coll Cambridge; late 2nd Lt 12th Lancers; *m* 18 July 1964 *Lavinia Rose, 2nd dau of Ralph Meredyth Turton, of Kildale Hall, Whitby, Yorks, and has:

1 +ANDREW ALEXANDER MARSHALL; *b* 19 Jan 1971; *educ* Winchester

1 *Anna Josephine; *b* 24 May 1965; *m* 18 Dec 1993 *Nicholas J F McNulty and has:

(1) *Ella Hero; *b* 9 May 1995

2 *Zoë Mary; *b* 20 July 1967; *m* 23 July 1994 *Nicholas S Curtis

Lineage: The Rev JOHN SCOTT PORTER; *b* 31 Dec 1801 (est s of Rev William Porter, of Newtown-Limavady, Co Londonderry (*d* 1843), by Mary Scott); Min 1st Presbyterian Ch Belfast, Prof Biblical Criticism and Hebrew to non-subscribing Presbyterian Assoc Ireland; *m* 1833 Margaret (*d* 1879), est dau of Andrew Marshall, MD, Surgn RN, and *d* 5 July 1880, leaving, with other issue:

Sir Andrew Marshall Porter, 1st Bt (UK), so *cr* 22 July 1902, PC (I 1883); *b* 27 June 1837; *educ* Queen's Coll Belfast (MA); barrister 1860, QC 1872, Bencher King's Inns 1878, MP (Lib) Londonderry 1881–83, Slr-Gen Ireland 1881–83, Attorney-Gen 1883, Master Rolls 1883–1906, Hon LLD Queen's U Belfast 1880, Hon LLD Dublin U 1889; *m* 12 April 1869 Agnes Adinston (added name and arms of HORSBRUGH to her married one under terms of entail; *d* 3 March 1929), dau of Lt-Col Alexander Horsbrugh of Horsbrugh and The Prin, Peeblesshire, and only sis and heir of entail of Alexander Horsbrugh of that Ilk (*d* 26 July 1911), and had:

1 JOHN SCOTT (Sir), **2nd Bt**

2 Alexander; *b* 26 Dec 1872; *m* 2 July 1904 Hon Frances Maud Gibson (*d* 5 March 1957), 3rd dau of 1st Baron Ashbourne (*qv*), and *d* 4 Feb 1946, having had:

(1) William Eric; *b* 24 Nov 1905; *m* 17 Dec 1929 Monica Ruth Lisalie (*d* 1986), yst dau of Capt Anthony Fitz Maude (*see* HAWARDEN, V), and had:

1a *Dympna Monica; *b* 8 April 1931; *m* 1st 19 Sept 1950 Patrick St John Pavier Brawn (*d* 19–), s of Maj Thomas Pavier Brawn, N Staffs Regt; *m* 2nd 1975 *Richard Jones and by her 1st husb has had:

1b *Daniel; *b* 31 July 1954

2b *Michael Patrick; *b* 16 May 1958

1b A dau; *b* and *d* 30 Dec 1952

2b *Anna Livia; *b* 13 Nov 1955

3b *Isabel Frances; *b* 1965

2a *Phyllida Ruth [Mrs Donald McAlpine, 12 Martindale Rd, London SW12]; *b* 6 March 1934; *m* 28 Jan 1956 *Donald Kenneth McAlpine, s of Frederick Charles McAlpine, of Auckland, NZ, and has:

1b *Louisa Ngaire; *b* 21 Nov 1958

2b *Fiona Caroline; *b* 13 Jan 1961

(2) John Scott; *b* 23 Jan, *d* Dec 1907

(3) Alexander Ashbourne; *b* 12 July 1911; *m* 9 July 1936 Elizabeth Mary Noreen, only child of Capt Mark Burns-Lindow, of Holmrook, Cumberland

(1) Agnes Constance; *b* 12 May 1909; *m* 24 June 1938 Barney Heron and *d* 18 April 1952, leaving issue

3 Andrew Marshall; *b* 6 Jan 1874; *ka* Boer War 5 June 1900

4 William Francis, BA Dublin; *b* 26 Aug 1878; *d* unm 24 Oct 1903

1 Helen Violet; *d* unm 12 Aug 1961

2 Margaret; *m* 28 Aug 1905 Capt Cuthbert Avenal John Vernon, MC, Irish Gds, 2nd s of Col Edward Venables Vernon, DL (*d* 1944), of Clontarf Castle, Co Dublin

Sir ANDREW *d* 9 Jan 1919; his est son,

Sir JOHN SCOTT PORTER later HORSBRUGH-PORTER (1911), **2nd Bt**; *b* 18 July 1871; *educ* Charterhouse and BNC Oxford (BA 1894, MA 1923); Sr Clerk H of C (ret 1934); *m* 1st 12 June 1906 Elaine Maud (*d* 28 Nov 1919), yst dau of Thomas Jefferies, JP, of Newbay, Co Wexford, and Los Ceibos, Buenos Aires; *m* 2nd 30 Jan 1924 Edith Dorothy (*d* 23 May 1957), er dau of Maj-Gen Richard Worsley, and *d* 7 March 1953, leaving by his 1st w:

Sir Andrew Marshall Horsbrugh-Porter, 3rd Bt, DSO (1940) and bar; *b* 1 June 1907; *educ* Winchester and RMC Sandhurst; Hon Col, Lt-Col 12th Lancers WW II (wounded, despatches); *m* 21 April 1933 Annette Mary, only dau of Brig-Gen Robert Clayton Browne-Clayton, DSO, of Browne's Hill, Co Carlow, and *d* 1986, leaving:

1 Sir JOHN SIMON HORSBRUGH-PORTER, **4th and present Bt**

1 *Susan [Lady Barlow, Bulkeley Grange, Malpas, Cheshire SY14 8BT]; *b* 17 Oct 1936; *m* 30 June 1962 *Sir John Kemp Barlow, 3rd Bt, of Bradwell Hall (*qv*), and has issue

2 *Caroline Elaine [Mrs J B Henderson, Cottage-on-the-Green, Barton-on-the-Heath, Glos GL56 0PJ]; *b* 1 June 1940; *m* 1986 *Col J B Henderson

HORSFALL

Arms: Gu. two horse's heads in chief arg., bridled az., and in base a rose of the second, barbed and seeded ppr. **Crest:** Out of a chaplet of roses gu., leaved vert, a horse's head, couped erm. **Motto:** *Labore et honore* ('By industry and honour'). **Creation:** Bt. (UK) 27 Nov 1909.

SIR JOHN MUSGRAVE HORSFALL, 3RD BT, of Hayfield, Glusburn, Co York, MC (1946), TD (1949) and clasp (1951), JP (W R Yorks 1959, N Yorks 1974) [Sir John Horsfall Bt MC TD JP, Greenfield House, Embsay, Skipton, N Yorks BD23 6SD]; *b* 26 Aug 1915; *s f* 1975; *educ* Uppingham; Maj Duke of Wellington's (W R) Regt WW II Burma, Underwriting Memb Lloyd's, late dir: Skipton Bldg Soc, J C Horsfall & Sons, Bradford Wool Exchange and Hayfield Textiles Ltd, jt md John C Horsfall & Sons, worsted spinners, dir Worsted Spinners' Fedn 1954–80 (pres 1962–64), Gen Commr Taxes 1964–90, pres Skipton C Assoc 1966–79, memb: Bradford A Gp Hosp Management Ctee 1952–69, Skipton RDC 1952–74, Wool and Allied Textile Employer Cncl 1957–75; *m* 22 Feb 1940 *Cassandra Nora Bernardine, only dau of George Wright, of Brinkworth Hall, Elvington, Yorks, and has:

1 +EDWARD JOHN WRIGHT [Edward Horsfall Esq, Long Thatch, Uffington, Oxon SN7 7RP]; *b* 17 Dec 1940; *educ* Uppingham; *m* 10 July 1965 *Rosemary, yr dau of Frank N King, of Keighley, Yorks, and has:

(1) *David Edward; *b* 3 Sept 1966; *m* 24 Aug 1996 *Maria Gloria Martin Sandoval, dau of Melinea Sandoval Rosales, of Toro, Spain

(2) *Robert Ian; *b* 31 May 1968

(3) *James Christopher; *b* 1971

2 +(Donald James) Linton [Linton Horsfall Esq, 25 Stirling Rd, Edinburgh, EH5 3JA]; *b* 3 Oct 1942; *educ* Uppingham and Jesus Coll Cambridge (BA 1964, MA 1968); *m* 4 Dec 1965 *Angela Mary, 2nd dau of Henry Firth, of Ilkley, Yorks, and has:

(1) *Peter Linton John; *b* 1970 (added John by deed poll 1982)

(2) *Richard Michael Henry; *b* 1973 (added Henry by deed poll 1989)

(1) *Elizabeth Jane; *b* 25 June 1968

1 *Henrietta Nora; *b* 1 July 1947; *m* 1987 *Arthur Eubank, of Millstone Moor, Cockermouth, Cumbria

Lineage: The family originated in a hamlet of the same name near Hebden Bridge, Yorks. WILLIAM HORSFALL, of Haworth in the adjoining parish of Bradford, mentions in his will 1 July 1536 three sons (Thomas; Richard; William); alleged ancestor of:

RICHARD HORSFALL, of Oxenhope, Haworth; bought 31 Aug 1612 lands in Weetshaw, Denholme and Bradford, and had, with an ests s (William, *d* 1664, leaving issue) and a yst s(Thomas, living at Stanbury, Haworth, 1638):

JONAS HORSFALL, of Weetshaw, Denholme; clothier; granted by his f 10 Dec 1622 part of the lands in Weetshaw; he and his bro William bought additional lands there 1636; had with three er sons and a daughter:

JONAS HORSFALL, of Hill House, Haworth, which he bought 1670; clothier; had:

THOMAS HORSFALL, of Manywells, Wilsden, Bradford; Collector Subsidy for Thornton, Bradford Dale, 1693; inherited lands in Holme Park from his great-uncle 1700; *m* 6 June 1676 Sarah, sis of John Whitaker, and *d* 1710, having had:

JONAS HORSFALL, of Westcroft Head, in Oxenhope, nr Keighley; *m* 14 April 1699 Mary Odgen, of Haworth, and *dvp* 1 Jan 1705, having had, with a yr s and a dau:

TIMOTHY HORSFALL, of Westcroft Head; *m* 22 Dec 1720 Mary, dau of William Midgley, Ld Manor Haworth, and *d* between 24 April 1776 and 8 June 1781; his 3rd s:

JONAS HORSFALL, of Westcroft Head; *bapt* 27 Feb 1735; *m* 21 Jan 1758 Hannah (*d* Oct 1790 aged 64), dau of Jonas Pearson, of Thornton, and *d* between 2 Aug 1806 and 12 Dec 1809, having had, with two daus:

JONAS HORSFALL, of Westcroft Head; *bapt* 7 April 1765; *m* 1st *c* 30 March 1791 Rebecca (*d* 15 Nov 1798 aged 38), dau of Robert Heaton, of the HEATONs of Ponden, Haworth; *m* 2nd Susanna (*dsp*) and *d* 22 Nov 1819, having had, with an er s (Jonas, *b* 9 Nov 1794, *bur* 6 April 1833, leaving issue, who settled Melbourne, Australia):

HEATON HORSFALL, of Westcroft Head; *b* 27 Oct 1798; *m* 8 Sept 1819 Mary, dau of John Foster, of Slack, Heptonstall, and *d* 23 Jan 1831, leaving, with a dau:

JOHN FOSTER HORSFALL, of Westcroft Head; *b* 11 July 1820; *m* 16 May 1844 Mary (*d* 27 Aug 1873), dau of John Cousin, of The Hall, Oldtown, Wadsworth, and *d* 4 March 1894, having had, with a yr s (William, *b* 25 May 1851, *d* unm 13 Jan 1872):

Sir John Cousin Horsfall, 1st Bt (UK), so *cr* 27 Nov 1909, JP W R Yorks; Alderman and Chm W R CC and Chm Fin Ctee 1897–1912, worsted spinner and banker, benefactor Glusburn Tech Inst; *b* 8 Dec 1846; *m* 1st 7 Dec 1870 Elizabeth Anne (*d* 8 April 1887), dau of James Hartley, of Glusburn, Yorks, and had:

1 John Eric; *b* 13 March, *d* 26 Nov 1882

1 Marian; *b* 15 July 1872; *d* unm 20 July 1954

2 Edith Maude; *b* 6 Sept 1874; *m* 5 Sept 1900 Norman Dixon Walker, of Currer Gate, Steeton, nr Keighley, and *d* 24 March 1961, leaving issue. He *d* 14 April 1923

3 Alice Dora; *b* 20 Dec 1878; *d* unm 21 April 1936

Sir John *m* 2nd 31 Jan 1889 Sarah Emily (*d* 17 April 1930), dau of John Crossley Fawcett, of Greenfield, Brearley, Yorks, and by her had:

2 Cedric Fawcett; MA Cantab, Capt 6th Bn W R Regt; *b* 15 Dec 1889; *m* 26 Nov 1915 Dora May (*m* 2nd 30 April 1928 Richard Henry Beckett, CSI, CIE, India Educnl Serv, s of Richard Beckett), dau of William T Sutcliffe, of Pendle, Buxton, and was *ka* 18 Sept 1916

3 (JOHN) DONALD (Sir), **2nd Bt**

4 William Alec; *b* 14 Oct 1894; *d* 4 Jan 1895

4 Kathleen May; *b* 1 Feb 1893; *m* 17 Dec 1919 (*divorce* 1937) Thomas Muir (*d* Jan 1944), s of Thomas Temple Muir, of Melrose, and had:

(1) *Richard Horsfall; late Capt Rifle Bde; *b* 16 Aug 1923; *educ* Uppingham and King's Coll Cambridge (BA 1947); *m* 20 Jan 1956 *Patricia Mary Braithwaite, formerly w of Humphrey Richard Adeane Lyttelton (*see* COBHAM, V) and dau of J Wellesley Gaskell, and has:

1a *Sophie Alexander; *b* 2 Nov 1962

2a *Darcy Jane; *b* 20 March 1964

Sir JOHN *d* 18 Oct 1920; his 3rd s,

Sir (John) Donald Horsfall, 2nd Bt, of Hayfield, Glusburn, JP (W R Yorks 1928); *b* 1 June 1891; *educ* Uppingham; High Sheriff W R Yorks 1927, Capt 6th Bn W R Regt, chm John C Horsfall & Sons, worsted spinners, and Skipton C Assoc 1922–37, dir Halifax Building Soc, Underwriter at Lloyd's; *m* 1st 28 Oct 1914 Henrietta (*d* 8 Dec 1936), 2nd dau of William Musgrave, of Shoebridge House, Eastburn, and had:

1 Sir JOHN MUSGRAVE HORSFALL, **3rd and present Bt**

2 Donald Fawcett, TD; Capt 6th Bn Duke of Wellington's (W R) Regt WW II, Underwriting Memb Lloyd's; *b* 26 Aug 1915 (twin); *educ* Uppingham and King's Coll Cambridge (BA 1937, MA 1941); *m* 11 Aug 1947 *Jeanne Elizabeth [Mrs Donald Horsfall, Fairleigh, Skipton, N Yorks], er dau of Col F Longden Smith, of Woodlands, Skipton, and *d* 18 May 1995, leaving:

(1) +Michael Fawcett [Michael Horsfall Esq, Waulkmill, Strachan, Kincardineshire AB3 3NS]; *b* 8 May 1948; *educ* Giggleswick; *m* 1979 *Elizabeth Anne, dau of Isaac Pickthall, of Barrow in Furness, and has:

1a +Timothy Michael; *b* 1981

2a +Luke Benjamin; *b* 1982

3a +Donald Isaac; *b* 1985

(2) +Peter John; *b* 15 May 1953; *educ* Uppingham; *m* 1978 *Lesley Jane, dau of Robert Hardy, of Lothersdale, N Yorks, and has:

1a +James Robert; *b* 1983

1a *Louise Rachel; *b* 1981

(1) *Patricia Jane; *b* 18 Nov 1950; *m* 1974 *Thomas Andrew Hoyle and has:

1a *Katie Jane; *b* 1977

2a *Harriet Louise; *b* 1979

(2) *Susan Elizabeth; *b* 18 Nov 1955

(3) *Sarah Louise; *b* 2 Aug 1966

3 Cedric Michael; Capt 1st Airborne Div WW II; *b* 26 April 1918; *educ* Uppingham; *d* of wounds recd Arnhem on or shortly after 20 Sept 1944

4 +(Patrick) David [David Horsfall Esq, The Nook, Arkholme, Carnforth, Lancs LA6 1AX]; Capt Duke of Wellington's (W R) Regt WW II, Underwriting Memb Lloyd's; *b* 5 Aug 1921; *educ* Uppingham; *m* 23 Sept 1947 *June, dau of Capt Sam H Clough, of Bailey Cottage, Skipton-in-Craven, and has had:

(1) +Christopher David [Christopher Horsfall Esq, Overslade, Sedgwick, Kendal, Cumbria LA8 0JS]; *b* 17 Sept 1948; *educ* Uppingham; *m* 1st 1970 (*divorce* 1988) Sally, dau of Frank S Greenwood, of Ingleton; *m* 2nd 31 March 1995 and by his 1st w has:

1a +Jonathan David; *b* 1973

2a +Philip Edward; *b* 1975
3a +Robert John; *b* 1981
(1) Carol Anne; *b* 25 June 1951; *m* 1975 *Anthony Raymond Collinson [Anthony Collinson Esq, The Coach House, Capernwray, Lancs LA6 1AL] and *d* 1991, leaving:
1a *John Horsfall; *b* 1980
1a *Poppy Henrietta; *b* 1983

Sir Donald *m* 2nd 24 Aug 1953 *Gladys, widow of Percy Taylor (*see* INGROW, B), of Knowle Spring House, Keighley, and dau of Robert Buck Broster, of Keighley, and *d* 1975

HORT

Arms: Az. a cross or, between in the first and fourth quarter a rose arg., barbed and seeded ppr. **Crest:** An eagle regardant, wings expanded, holding in the beak a chaplet of laurel, all ppr. **Motto:** Well win, well wear. **Creation:** Bt. (GB) 8 Sept 1767.

SIR ANDREW EDWIN FENTON HORT, 9TH BT, of Castle Strange, Middlesex [Sir Andrew Hort Bt, Westerlee, 77 Fortis Green, London N2 9JD]; *b* 15 Nov 1954; *s* f 1995; *m* 15 Nov 1986 *Mary, dau of Jack Whibley, of Spalding, Lincs, and has:
1 +JAMES JOHN FENTON; *b* 26 Nov 1989
1 *Jennifer; *b* 1987

Lineage: JOHN HORT, of Marshfield, Glos; had:

Rt Rev JOSIAH HORT; DD, Domestic Chaplain to Ld Lt Ireland 1709, Dean: Cloyne 1718 and Ardagh 1720, Bp: Ferns 1721 and Kilmore 1727, Archbp Tuam 1741–51; *b* 2 Feb 1673; *m* 19 Feb 1725/6 Elizabeth, dau of Hon William Fitz-Maurice (*see* LANSDOWNE, M), and *d* 14 Dec 1751, having had, with an er s (Josiah George, of Hortland, Co Kildare, High Sheriff 1758, *b* 1732, *m* 14 June 1766 Jane Maria, dau and coheir of John Hawks, of Pontenive, Co Longford, and *dsp* 1786) and four daus:

Sir John Hort, 1st Bt (GB), so *cr* 8 Sept 1767, of Castle Strange, Middx, and later Hortland; *b* 8 Aug 1735; BA, LLB Trin Coll Dublin, Consul-Gen Lisbon 1767; *m c* 20 Oct 1789 Margaret (*d* 15 Sept 1843), dau of Sir FitzGerald Aylmer, 6th Bt (*qv*), and *d* 23 Oct 1807, having had:

1 **Sir (Josiah) William Hort, 2nd Bt,** of Hortland, DL; High Sheriff 1818, MP Co Kildare 1831–32, MA Cambridge; *b* 6 July 1791; *m* 31 March 1823 Louisa Georgina (*d* 6 May 1856), 2nd dau and coheir with her sis Frances Arabella (*m* Maj John Colpoys Bloomfield) of Sir John Caldwell, 5th Bt, of Castle Caldwell, Co Fermanagh, Count of the HRE, and *d* 24 Aug 1876, leaving, with two daus:

(1) **Sir John Josiah Hort, 3rd Bt,** CB; *b* 14 Jan 1824; Gen, served Crimean War (Crimean medal with three clasps, Sardinian and Turkish medals, Kt Medjidie); *d* unm 5 Jan 1882

(2) **Sir William Fitzmaurice Josiah Hort, 4th Bt;** *b* 20 Jan 1827; barrister, RM Ireland 1854–82; *m* 1st 2 June 1866 Harriett Lydia (*d* 28 June 1870), est dau of Rev Charles Butler Stevenson, Rector Callan; *m* 2nd 1874 Katherine Anne Villiers (*d* 2 Dec 1925), dau of John Wade, of St Canice, Kilkenny, and *dsp* 18 Sept 1887

(3) **Sir Fenton Josiah Hort, 5th Bt,** JP Co Kildare; *b* 27 March 1836; joined Army 1857, served Ceylon Rifles and 13th Prince Albert's LI, Hon Col, Lt-Col cmdg 3rd Bn Roy Inniskilling Fus; *d* unm 3 Feb 1902

2 Fenton, of Leopardstown, Co Dublin, and later St John's Mount, Brecon; High Sheriff Co Dublin 1834; *b* 3 Aug 1794; *m* 25 April 1825 Anne (*d* 23 June 1866), est dau of Rev Anthony Collett, of Kelsall Hall, Suffolk, and *d* 18 March 1873, leaving:

(1) Fenton John Anthony (Rev); DD, LLD, DCL, Hulsean Prof and Lady Margaret Reader Divinity Cambridge, Fell Emmanuel Coll; *b* 23 April 1828; *m* 14 May 1857 Fanny Henrietta (*d* 16 May 1925), dau of Thomas John Dyson Holland, and *d* 30 Nov 1892, leaving:
1a ARTHUR FENTON (Sir), **6th Bt**
2a Francis FitzGerald (Rev); *b* 9 March 1868; *educ* Emmanuel Coll Cambridge (MA); *m* 18 April 1912 Margaret Charis (*d* 1972), dau of Rev Joseph Henry Gray, Fell Queens' Coll Cambridge, and *d* 28 Feb 1942, leaving:
1b Anthony Gilbert (Rev); MA Queens' Coll Cambridge; memb Cambridge Brotherhood of the Ascension, Delhi; *b* 11 Jan 1916; *d* 3 Aug 1944
1b *Margaret Frances [Mrs John Terry, 11 Bandon Rd, Girton, Cambridge CB3 0LU]; *b* 27 May 1913; *educ* Girton Coll Cambridge (MA 1950); *m* 5 April 1952 John Hunter Terry (*d* 1976), s of Francis John Terry, and has:
1c *Stephen John Anthony; *b* 1 Aug 1955; *educ* Magdalene Coll Cambridge (MA)
1c *Rosemary Frances; *b* 22 June 1953; *educ* Birmingham U (MA)
3a Edward Collett; FRCP (Edin), Assist Physician Italian Hosp, Dir Bacteriology Dept Addington Park War Hosp; *b* 19 May 1869; *m* 20 April 1897 Ethel Augusta (*d* 17 Feb 1939), dau of Rev Arthur Pitman Gordon, and *d* 14 Oct 1922, leaving:
1b Violet Gordon; bacteriologist, Civ Serv 1919–20; *b* 7 Feb 1898; *d* unm 27 Nov 1928
2b Joan Gabrielle; *b* 27 Sept 1913; *m* 1st 1940 Richard Westcott-Betenson; *m* 2nd Guy Downing
4a Frederick Aylmer; MA, MD, MRCS, LRCP, FZS, T/Capt RAMC WW I 1915–19; *b* 15 July 1872; *m* 17 Aug 1920 Muriel Mary (*d* 19–), dau of Rev Canon George Thompson, Rector N Bovey, Moretonhampstead, Devon, and *d* 25 Jan 1952
5a Alfred Stanley; *b* 2 Feb, *d* 21 July 1875
1a Ellen Margaret; *d* unm Feb 1945
2a Mary Dyson; *m* 8 April 1902 Rev George Jameson Chitty, Rector Worplesdon, Guildford, and *d* Sept 1947, leaving issue. He *d* March 1947
(1) Margaret Anne; *d* 16 March 1895
(2) Catherine Frances; *m* 11 Jan 1854 Rev Garnons Williams, Vicar Bettws Penpont, Preb St David's, and *d* 28 Dec 1892, leaving issue. He *d* 24 Oct 1908
(3) Louisa Josephine; *d* an infant

Sir FENTON's 1st cousin once-removed,

Sir Arthur Fenton Hort, 6th Bt; *b* 15 Jan 1864; MA, Fell Trin Coll Cambridge; master Harrow 1888–1922; *m* 20 Dec 1894 Helen Frances (*d* 14 Oct 1946), JP Middx and Hants, dau of Rev Canon George Charles Bell, Headmaster Marlborough 1876–1903, and had:
1 FENTON GEORGE (Sir), **7th Bt**
2 Aylmer Victor Dyson, MBE (1958), TD; Maj Roy Signals (TA), WW I 1916–19 and WW II; *b* 9 Nov 1897; *educ* Harrow and BNC Oxford (BA); *m* 19 July 1927 Lois Mary (*d* 1995), dau of Col W Clifford Phillips, VD, TD, DL, of Coolgreany, Malpas Newport, Monmouth, and *d* 1981, leaving:
(1) +John Aylmer Laybourne [John Hort Esq, 239 Bramcote Lane, Wollaton, Notts]; *b* 9 Sept 1931; *educ* Trin Coll Cambridge (BA 1954, MA 1962); *m* 11 Jan 1958 *Leela, dau of R G Senan, of Penang, and has:
1a +Peter Senan Aylmer; *b* 19 Nov 1958
2a +Michael John Laybourne; *b* 4 July 1960
3a +Patrick Marcus Govind; *b* 1971
(1) *Daphne Lois [Miss Daphne Hort, 36 Alanthus Close, London SE12 8RE]; *b* 18 Feb 1930; *educ* LMH Oxford (BA 1951, MA 1956); memb Guild of Physiotherapists 1987
(2) *Frances Mary [Mrs John Simpson, 38 Kidbrooke Gdns, London SE3]; SRN 1960; *b* 7 Aug 1937; *m* 1963 *John Cameron Simpson, MB, BS, FFARCS, er s of William Henry Simpson, of Chelmsford, and has:
1a *James Aylmer; *b* 29 Aug 1964
2a *David Cameron; *b* 7 June 1966
1 Iris Elizabeth; BA Oxon, FRICS, Fell Inst Housing Managers; *b* 23 Feb 1904; *d* 1980

Sir ARTHUR *d* 7 March 1935; his er son,

Sir Fenton George Hort, 7th Bt; *b* 1 May 1896; *educ* Harrow and Trin Coll Cambridge (BA); RE WW I; *m* 2 Sept 1922 Gwendolene (*d* 2 March 1982), 5th dau of Sir Walter Galpin Alcock, MVO, DMus, FRCM, FRCO, and had:
1 JAMES FENTON (Sir), **8th Bt**
2 +(Richard) Patrick Arthur [Patrick Hort Esq, Kungstensg 59 4tr, S11329, Stockholm, Sweden]; *b* 3 Jan 1931; *educ* Harrow and Trin Coll Cambridge (BA 1954, MA 1959); *m* 16 June 1956 *Agnete Maria, only dau of Nils Mannheimer, of Gothenburg, and has:
(1) +Nicholas Patrick Fenton; *b* 20 Nov 1962
(1) *Rebecca Maria; *b* 6 Nov 1957
(2) *Elsa Katinka; *b* 18 Feb 1960
3 +Robert William Lucas [Robert Hort Esq, Meentashesk, Glencolumcille, Co Donegal, Ireland]; *b* 12 May 1936; *educ* Marlborough and Trin Coll Cambridge (BA 1958); *m* 1973 *Eleanor Mary Coburn
1 *Elizabeth [Mrs Elizabeth Holmes, 36 Berkeley Vale Park, Berkeley, Glos GL13 9TG]; *b* 31 March 1925; *m* 1951 S/Ldr Eric George Holmes, MBE, RAF (*d* 1975), and has:
(1) *Helen Margaret; *b* 1 Sept 1952
(2) *Georgina Slaney; *b* 29 May 1954
2 *Barbara Anne; *b* 23 Aug 1929; *m* 1961 *George Bruce Sackville Berkeley, only s of Lt-Col Cyril Sackville Jocelyn Berkeley, OBE, of Lisbuoy House, Beragh, Co Tyrone, and has:
(1) *Sackville Hamilton; *b* 18 Jan 1964
(1) *Emma Louise Diana; *b* 29 Jan 1962
(2) *Sarah Jane Arabella; *b* 1966

Sir FENTON *d* 5 March 1960; his est son,

Sir James Fenton Hort, 8th Bt; *b* 6 Sept 1926; *educ* Marlborough and Trin Coll Cambridge (MA, MB, BCh 1950); medical dir Berk Pharmaceuticals and A H Robins Co; *m* 4 Jan 1951 *Joan, dau of Edward Peat, of Sheffield, and *d* 19 July 1995, leaving:
1 Sir ANDREW EDWIN FENTON HORT, **9th and present Bt**
2 +Tim(othy) George; *b* 15 March 1960
1 *Jane Antonia; *b* 22 Nov 1958
2 *Diana Rachel; *b* 23 March 1962

HOSKYNS

Arms: Per pale az. and gu. a chevron between three lions rampant or. **Crest:** A lion's head erased or, flames of fire issuing from the mouth ppr., crowned ducally of the first. **Motto:** *Vincula da linguae vel tibi lingua dabit* ('Bind the tongue or the tongue will bind thee'). **Creation:** Bt. (E) 18 Dec 1676.

SIR BENEDICT LEIGH HOSKYNS, 16TH BT [Sir Benedict Hoskyns Bt, Russell House, Wherry Corner, High St, Manningtree, Essex CO11 1AP]; *b* 27 May 1928; *s* bro 1956; *educ* Haileybury, Corpus Christi Coll Cambridge and London Hosp (MB, BChir 1952); DObst, RCOG 1958, house surgn London Hosp 1953, Capt RAMC 1953–56, house physician Roy Surrey County Hosp 1957 and Gen Lying in Hosp 1957; *m* 19 Sept 1953 *Ann, JP, dau of Harry Wilkinson, of London, and has:

1 +EDWIN WREN; *b* 4 Feb 1956; *educ* Nottingham U (MS, BS); MRCP 1984, FRCP 1997; Sr Chorister King's Coll Cambridge 1969; Consultant Paediatrician Leicester Gen and Leicester Roy Infirmary 1993–; *m* 1981 *Jane, dau of John Sellers, and has:

(1) +Robin Chevallier; *b* 5 July 1989

(1) *Lucy Mary; *b* 1993

2 +John Chandos; *b* 4 April 1961; *educ* Gonville and Caius Coll Cambridge (BA) and Middx Hosp

1 *Janet Mary; *b* 13 May 1954; *educ* York U (BA, CertEd, DPhil 1997); ARCM; Sr Lecturer Music in Educn U of Centl England, Birmingham; *m* 1982 *Christopher Harris

2 *Sarah Leigh; *b* 3 April 1959; *educ* Birmingham U (V-Chllr's Prize, BA) LGSM (MusTh), ARCM 1981; dir Music Therapy Guildhall Sch of Music; *m* 1989 *Julian Peter C Raphael, s of Ven Timothy John Raphael, Archdeacon Middx, and has:

(1) *Nino Timothy Benedict; *b* 1994

(1) *Dorothy Clare; *b* 1990

Lineage: JOHN HOSKYNS; MP Hereford; *m* Margery, dau of Thomas Jones, of Llanwarne, and had, with other issue, including two er sons and a yr s (John (Rev), DCL, Fell New Coll Oxford, Rector Ledbury 1612–13, Chaplain to JAMES I, *d* 30 Aug 1631):

JOHN HOSKYNS; Serjeant-at-law 1623, MP Hereford 1604–29; *educ* Westminster and Winchester (fndr's kin), MA, Fell New Coll Oxford; *b* 1566; *m* 1 Aug 1601 Benedicta, dau of Robert Moyle, of Buckwell, Kent, and *d* 27 Aug 1638, having had, with a dau:

Sir Bennet Hoskyns, 1st Bt (E), so *cr* 18 Dec 1676, of Harewood, Herefs; barrister 1631, Bencher and Treasurer Middle Temple, MP Wendover 1640, Hereford 1640–48 and Herefs 1656–59; *m* 1st 1634 Anne, dau of Sir Henry Bingley; *m* 2nd 1655 Dorothy, widow of John Abrahall, of Ingeston, and dau of Francis Kyrle, and *d* 10 Feb 1679/80, having by his 1st w had, with a yr s (William):

Sir John Hoskyns, 2nd Bt; MP Hereford 1685–87, Pres Roy Soc 1682, Master in Chancery 1676–1703; *b* 23 July 1634; *m* 29 Aug 1671 Jane (*bur* 15 Aug 1724), dau of Sir Gabriel Lowe by Agnes Hungerford, of Down Ampney, Glos, and *d* 12 Sept 1705, having had, with other issue:

1 **Sir Bennet Hoskyns, 3rd Bt**; *b* 28 Jan 1674/5, *m* 2 Oct 1707 Gertrude (*d* 23 Sept 1709), widow of Sir Peter Whitcombe and dau of 2nd Baron Arundell of Trerice, and *dsp* 17 Dec 1711

2 HUNGERFORD (Sir), **4th Bt**

3 John HOSKYNS later HOSKYNS-ABRAHALL (under terms of will of his cousin Mary Abrahall) (Rev); *b* 1692; MA Oxon, Rector Peterstow Herefs 1727–67; *m* Anne, dau of Theophilus Leigh (*see* LEIGH, B), and *d* 1 Sept 1765, having had, with other issue:

(1) James, of Ingeston, Herefs; *b* 1725; *dsp* 1786

(2) John (Rev), of Ingeston; MA Oxon, Preb Hereford, Rector Peterstow; *b* 1729; *m* Anne Cotton Wo(r)gan and *d* 1820, having had:

1a John (Rev); Curate Badgworth, Somerset, BA Oxon; *bapt* 20 Sept 1773; *m* Maria Morgan and *d* 1840, having had:

1b John Charles James (Rev); MA Oxon, Rector Butterleigh, Devon, Head Master King Edward's Sch Bruton; *b* 1800; *m* 1827 Jane, dau of Edward Dyne, of Bruton, and *d* 26 Feb 1876, leaving issue:

1c John (Rev); MA, Fell Lincoln Coll Oxford, Vicar Combe, Oxon, Prof Classics U Coll Aberystwyth, examiner ICS, Sanskrit scholar, antiquarian, author; *b* 15 Jan 1829; *m* Harriet Charlotte (*d* 4 June 1915), dau of Capt P H Bridges, RN, and *d* 26 Sept 1894, leaving, with two other daus (*d* unm):

1d John Leigh; *b* 6 Jan 1865; *educ* Eton and Magdalen Coll Oxford (PhD); *d* 12 Oct 1891

1d Gertrude Renira Wenonah; *b* 16 Sept 1858; *educ* Trin Coll Coll Dublin (MA)

2d Constance Eleanor; *m* 1894 Arthur Wright Bishop (*d* 1917), PhD, and had issue

3d Augusta Maria; *b* 28 March 1869; *d* unm 28 Aug 1888

2c James, of the War Office; *b* 1831; *m* 1862 Ellen (*d* Dec 1918), dau of Christopher Moresby, and *d* 19 April 1913, leaving:

1d John Hoskyns; Maj RMLI; *b* 9 Sept 1864; *m* 1900 Frances Elizabeth (*d* 19 Nov 1941), dau of J H Vessey, of Halton Manor, Lincs, and *d* 8 June 1924, leaving:

1e John Wren; *b* 9 Nov 1903; *d* 13 Aug 1911

1e *Barbara Mary Angela; *b* 16 Aug 1901

2e *Dorothea Frances [Mrs Alliston Hazledine, 61 Regents Park, Exeter EX1 2NZ]; *b* 11 April 1916; *m* 1st 12 Feb 1942 (*divorce* 1962) Charles Robert Gardiner, est s of Charles Gardiner, of Edinburgh; *m* 2nd 1962 *Lt-Cdr Alliston Temple Clough Hazledine, RNR, and by her 1st husb has issue:

1f *Christopher Charles [Christopher Gardiner Esq, 17 Bell St, Sawbridgeworth, Herts CM21 9AR]; *b* 1942; *m* 1st 1967 Janet Marie Lack and has:

1g *Rebekah Jane; *b* 1968; *m* 1991 *Gerald Cooper and has:

1h *Joseph; *b* 1993

2g *Alice Mary; *b* 1972

1f (cont.) Christopher Gardiner *m* 2nd 1986 *Brenda Hebb and by her has:

3g *Claire Christine; *b* 1986

2f *Peter Patrick Fairfax [Peter Gardiner, 177 Ave Louise, 1050 Brussels, Belgium]; *b* 1945; *m* 1974 *Nicole Adrienne Marie Stalleart and has:

1g *Miles Dexter; *b* 1988

1f *Catherine Juliet [Mrs Richard Sale, 23 Denmark Ave, Woodley, Berks RG5 4RS]; *b* 1944; *m* 1970 *Richard Stephen George Sale, barrister, and has issue:

1g *George William Alexander; *b* 1972

1g *Mary Margaret; *b* 1971; *m* 1993 *Philip Richards

2g *Juliet Anne; *b* 1974

3g *Jessica May Victoria; *b* 1977

4g *Fenella Grace Dorothea; *b* 1983

5g *Emily Caroline; *b* 1985

2f *Victoria [Mrs Derrick Swain, 2 Englewood Rd, London SW12 9NZ]; *b* 1947; *m* 1972 *Derrick William Swain and has:

1g *Andrew Charles; *b* 1972

1g *Christy-Anne; *b* 1974

2g *Naomi Frances; *b* 1980

2d Christopher Henry; Maj RMLI; *b* 23 July 1871; *m* 1895 Alice Maude Mary Allen and *d* 7 May 1915 of wounds recd in action Dardanelles, leaving:

1e James, MM; WW I with AIF (wounded); *b* 18 Dec 1897; *m* 1923 Minne Elizabeth Holland (*d* 1990), of Coolup, WA, and *d* 1967, leaving:

1f Christopher Leslie; *b* 1925; *m* 1947 *Phyllis Mae Sansome [Mrs Christopher Hoskyns-Abrahall, 27 Norman St, Innaloo, W Australia 6018] of Gosnells, WA, and *d* 30 April 1996, leaving:

1g +Terrence Ross [Terence Hoskyns-Abrahall Esq, 34 Donna St, Morley 6062, Australia]; *b* 1954; *m* 1978 *Beverly Ann Kealy, of Harvey, WA, and has:

1h +Shaun Ross; *b* 1981

2h +Adam James; *b* 1984

2g +Brian Leslie; *b* 1956; *m* 1984 *Kerry Nelson, of Balga, WA, and has:

1h +Joshua Andrew; *b* 1985

1g *Kathleen Elizabeth; *b* 1950; *m* 1st 1970 John Leslie Brewer, of Claremont, WA, and has:

1h *Michael John; *b* 1972

1h *Shelly Anne; *b* 1970

1g (cont.) Mrs Brewer *m* 2nd 1978 *Alan Ronald Dawson, of Carine, WA, and has:

2h *Philip Gregory; *b* 1979

2g *Lynette Jean; *b* 1953, *m* 1973 *Kevin Malcolm Langman, of Kununurra, W Australia, and has:

1h *Daniel Graham; *b* 1976

1h *Sandra Alice; *b* 1978

2f +Ernest John; *b* 1926; *m* 1948 *Margaret Winscom, of Katanning, WA, and has:

1g +Ian John; *b* 1948

2g +Douglas Frank; *b* 1950

3g +Gregory Alan; *b* 1955

1g *Mary Pauline; *b* 1954

3f +Colin James; *b* 1927

1f *Ellen Maude; *b* 1923; *m* 1946 *Leslie Charles Limbrick, of Fremantle, WA, and has:

1h *Raymond George; *b* 1948
2h *Keith Leslie; *b* 1950
3h *Kevin Colin; *b* 1951
4h *Philip John; *b* 1954
2f *Beatrice Angela; *b* 1930; *m* 1952 *Hamilton McCormick, of Gingin, WA, and has:
1h *Gary Thomas; *b* 1953
2h *Jeffrey David; *b* 1954
2e Christopher Henry; 2nd Lt, RFA, attd RFC; *b* 19 Jan 1899; *k* while flying 22 Dec 1917
1e Ellen Moresby; *b* 15 Oct 1901; *d* unm 10 Feb 1926
1d Angela Mary
3c Bennet (Rev); *b* 1832; *m* 1st Sophia (*d* 1894), dau of Rev John Partridge, of Tiverton; *m* 2nd 1896 Mary, dau of John Gisbourne, and *d* 2 Jan 1918
4c Chandos William; *b* 31 March 1806; *d* 1868
1c Jane; *m* Rev F J Bryant (*d* 8 Dec 1907), DD, Rector St Peter Tavy, Tavistock, and had issue
2c Maria; *m* 1856 Rev John Simeon Barrow (*d* 1903), Rector Rogate, Sussex, and had issue
1b Theophilus Bennet; barrister, Commr Court of Bankruptcy; *b* 21 March 1802; *educ* Wadham Coll Oxford (MA); *m* 1849 Helena, dau of Rev Henry Kingsmill, of Southampton, and *d* 2 Aug 1874, leaving:
1c Bennet, CBE (1919); Dir Investigation Branch Secretary's Office GPO 1910–21; *b* 26 Aug 1858; *educ* Keble Coll Oxford; *m* 19 Jan 1897 Edith Louise (*d* 15 Aug 1954), dau of Rev W Egerton Tapp, and *d* 1 Oct 1951, leaving:
1d Bennet Edmund; 2nd Lt RGA; *b* 30 Oct 1899; *d* 25 April 1918 of wounds recd in action
2d Anthony Leigh Egerton (Rt Rev); Lt RN, Curate St Mary's Portsea 1931–33, Chaplain Shrewsbury Sch 1933–36, Curate St Wilfrid's Harrogate 1936–39, Chaplain Tower London 1939, Vicar Aldershot 1945–54, RD 1949–54, Bp Suffragan Lancaster 1955, WW II as Chaplain RNVR; *b* 13 Oct 1903; *educ* RNCs Osborne and Dartmouth and Westcott House Theological Coll Cambridge; *m* 16 June 1937 Margaret Ada (*d* 1986), dau of Frederick George Storey, barrister, of Sunderland (*see* 1970 edn BUCKTON, B), and *d* 1982, leaving:
1e +(John) Benedict Leigh [Benedict Hoskyns-Abrahall Esq, Earby Hall, Newsham, Richmond, N Yorks]; FRICS, QALAS; *b* 13 Oct 1939; *educ* St John's Sch Leatherhead and RAC Cirencester; *m* 1970 Mary Delamain (*d* 10 March 1998), dau of Lt-Col Mansel Jackson, DSO and bar, MC, and has:
1f +Bennet Mansel Leigh [Bennet Hoskyns-Abrahall Esq, 140 Stephendale Rd, London SW6]; *b* 1971; *educ* Eton and Durham U (BA); ACA
2f +(John) Harry Wren; *b* 1975; *educ* Radley and Durham U (BSc)
3f +Edward Anthony Egerton (Bertie); *b* 1977; *educ* Eton and Newcastle U
2e +(Anthony David) Wren [Wren Hoskyns-Abrahall Esq, West Wing, Lochside, Kelso TD5 8PD]; *b* 19 May 1943; *educ* St John's Sch Leatherhead and RNC Dartmouth; Lt RN; dir Portsmouth and Sunderland Newspapers 1972–77, chm P and SN News Shops 1975–77; *m* 23 April 1965 *Phyllis Penrose, 2nd dau of R-Adml William Penrose Mark-Wardlaw, DSO, of Alyscroft, Crowthorne, Berks, and has:
1f +Mark Egerton Wren [Mark Hoskyns-Abrahall Esq, 41 W Relugus Rd, Edinburgh EH9 2PW]; *b* 22 July 1966; *educ* Sherborne and Edinburgh U (BSc); ACA; *m* 22 Aug 1992 *Fiona, dau of Alasdair Gordon, and has:
1g +Sam Oliver Wren; *b* 16 Feb 1996
1f *Sarah Katherine Phyllis; *b* 18 April 1971
1e *Janet Elizabeth Rosemary, JP [Mrs Nicholas Hurry JP, 10 Cedars Rd, London SW13]; SRN; *b* 3 July 1938; *m* 5 May 1962 *Nicholas George Hurry, s of Capt George Egerton Hurry, RN, of Croft Cottage, Liss, Hants, and has:
1f *Fiona Elizabeth; *b* 19 June 1963; *m* 16 Aug 1991 *Jeffrey P Cohen, of Miami, Fla. and has:
1g *Max Egerton; *b* 28 Sept 1994
2f *Victoria Mary; *b* 23 July 1967; *m* 19– *Patrick J Prendergast, of Melbourne, Australia, and has:
1g *Harry Nicholas; *b* 23 Aug 1997
1g *Mollie Elizabeth; *b* 2 May 1995
3d (Andrew) John Chandos; WW II as S/Ldr RAFVR (despatches), dir Unilever Ltd, chm Hindustan Lever Ltd India 1953–57; *b* 22 Aug 1905; *educ* Charterhouse and Univ Coll Oxford; *m* 11 Jan 1935 Audrey Lorraine, BEM (*d* 1992), 3rd dau of Sir Norman Alexander Leslie, KBE, and *d* 1978, leaving:
1e +John Hungerford Leslie [John Hoskyns-Abrahall, RD3, Box 3951, Reading, PA 19606, USA]; *b* 13 Feb 1945; *educ* Sherborne and Univ Coll Oxford; *m* 1973 *Winifred Scherrer, of California, and has:
1f +Alexander Philip; *b* 1978
2f *Megan Selina; *b* 1976
1e *Harriet [Ms Harriet Hoskyns-Abrahall, 1025 Lindbergh Dve, Atlanta, GA 30324, USA]; *b* 11 March 1939; *educ* Cheltenham Ladies' Coll and Edin U (BL 1960); *m* 13 Feb 1965 (*divorce* 1981, resumed maiden name 1989) Edward Brendan Lynch, WS, s of H W Lynch, of St Andrews, and has:
1f *Bahama Leslie Chandos; *b* 1977
2e *Lucinda; *b* 10 Dec 1940; *m* 1972 *Graham de Putron Tardif, of Cranbrook, Kent, and has:
1f *Benjamin Charles de Putron; *b* 1972
1f *Kate Amanda de Putron; *b* 1975
2f *Lucy Mia de Putron; *b* 1981
3e *Amanda; *b* 10 Dec 1940; *m* 1972 (*divorce* 1985) Burton K Fox, and has:
1f *Joshua Maxwell; *b* 1976
1f *Gemma Lorraine; *b* 1979
2c Chandos William; LRCP, MRCS; *b* 1859; *m* 1 Feb 1892 Gertrude (*d* 22 May 1947), dau of Robert Kearsley, and *d* 9 Sept 1899, leaving:
1d (Theo) Chandos (Sir); ktd 1950, CMG (1942), Colonial Admin Serv 1921–53: Ch Commr W Provinces Nigeria 1946–51, Lt-Govr W Regn Nigeria 1951–53, Offr Legn Hon 1950, Capt London Regt WW I (wounded), painter (one man exhibitions London and elswhere); *b* 17 Dec 1896; *educ* Epsom Coll; *m* 1st 21 Feb 1925 (*divorce* 1944) Clare Constance Maria (*d* 1990), dau of Lt-Col Richard Frederick Drury, CBE, of Brock House, Dawlish, Devon; *m* 2nd 1944 *Lois Jennet, dau of Rev Hugh Lambert Ogle, Canon Ripon, and *d* 1975, leaving by his 1st w:
1e +Robin Chandos [Robin Hoskyns-Abrahall Esq, Woodlands House, Redbourn Rd, Hemel Hempstead, Herts HP2 7BA]; *b* 25 Jan 1928; *educ* Haileybury; WW II as Lt Sherwood Foresters; dir subsidary co of Unilever; *m* 1st 1950 (*divorce* 1962) Petronella Elizabeth, yr dau of John E Cantlon, BA, of Co Carlow, and has:
1f *Scarlett [Mrs Scarlett Punthöler, 1 Marden Close, Woodingdean BN2 6NJ]; *b* 7 Dec 1952; *m* 1984 (*divorce* 1997) John Punthöler and has:
1g *Theo Alexander; *b* 1990
2f *Gail [Mrs Stephen Brendell, Jade House, Holme lacey, Hereford HR2 6LJ]; *b* 16 Sept 1955; *m* 1979 *Stephen Brendell and has:
1g *Dominic; *b* 1980
1g *Rebecca; *b* 1984
1e (cont.) Robin Hoskyns-Abrahall *m* 2nd 1962 *Margaret Angela, dau of Frank Keggins, of Knowle, Warwicks, and has:
1f +Charles Chandos [Charles Hoskyns-Abrahall Esq, 60B Heber Rd, Dulwich, London SE22]; *b* 12 Nov 1964; *educ* Haileybury; musician; *m* 19– *Teresa, dau of Prof Ricard Jordana, of Barcelona
2e Follett Peter Mark; *b* 28 June 1934; actor as Mark Follett; *m* 1960 *Carole [Mrs Follett Hoskyns-Abrahall, Hill Farm, Tendring, Essex], er dau of Edwin Alexander Marks, of Chigwell, Essex, and *d* 1983, leaving:
1f +Edwin Follett Eden; *b* 8 Dec 1965; *educ* Leys Sch
1f *Emma Clare Elizabeth; *b* 23 Aug 1963
1e *Priscilla [Mrs Frank Le Bas, 67 Lancaster Rd, St Albans, Herts]; *b* 30 Jan 1926; *m* 1951 *Frank Eric Russel Le Bas and has:
1f *Julian Robin Olavarria; *b* 22 March 1958
2f *Timothy Russell; *b* 26 Nov 1964
1f *Vanessa June *b* 22 Dec 1954
1d Irene; *b* 18 Feb 1895; *m* 8 Jan 1962 Maj George Drury Coleman (*d* 27 Dec 1968)
1c Helena; *m* 1874 Rev G E Phillips (*d* 1896), Rector Stalbridge, Dorset, and *d* 1913, leaving issue
2c Charlotte Eliza Mary; *d* unm 7 Nov 1933
3c Caroline Emily; *m* 1890 Arthur Jeffreys Hills, of Harpenden, Herts, and *d* 7 Aug 1924, leaving:
1d Mary Josephine
3b Chandos; *dsp*
4b Charles; *d* 26 Feb 1868
1b Maria; *m* Rev J Bradley Dyne, DD, Headmaster Highgate Sch, Hon Canon St Paul's

Sir BENNET's yr bro,

Sir Hungerford Hoskyns, 4th Bt; MP Hereford 1917–22; *m* 1720 Mary (*d* 9 July 1735), dau of Theophilus Leigh, of Addlestrop, Glos (*see* LEIGH, B), and *d* 21 Dec 1767, having had an er s:

Sir Chandos Hoskyns, 5th Bt; High Sheriff Hereford 1771; *bapt* 22 April 1720; *m* 1753 Rebecca (*d* 14 Aug 1782), dau of Joseph May, of Reading, and *d* 29 May 1773, leaving, with a dau (Jane, *m* 13 Jan 1784 Sir John Reade, 6th Bt (*qv*), and *d* 17 Dec 1847):

Sir Hungerford Hoskyns, 6th Bt; High Sheriff Herefs 1785; *m* 14 Dec 1774 Catherine (*d* 14 Feb 1790), dau of Edwyn Francis Stanhope, of Stanwell House, Middx (*see* 1967 edn CHESTERFIELD and STANHOPE, E), and had, with other issue:
1 HUNGERFORD (Sir), **7th Bt**
2 Bennet (Rev); Vicar Montacute, Somerset; *b* 1 May 1782; *educ* Balliol Coll Oxford (MA); *m* Sept 1815 Amelia, dau of Adml — Chamberlain, and *dsp* 18 April 1843
3 John; MD, of Morehampton, Dublin; *b* 21 Dec 1784; *m* Caroline Ellen (*d* 1854), dau and coheir of Allen Ribton, of Little Forest and Kilmartin, Dublin, and *d* 1858, leaving:
(1) Edwyn Bennet; *b* 1804, and *d* 1848, having had, with two daus:
1a John; *b* 1836; *d* 1926, having had:
1b William John; *b* 1871; *m* 1900 Caroline Borer, and *d* 1948, leaving:
1c +John [John Hoskyns, 1804 Kenmore, Grosse Pointe, MI 48236, USA]; *b* 1902; *m* 1935 *Therese Stascuk and has had:
1d A son; deceased
1c *Marian [Mrs Howard Shirkey, 3627 Millay, Troy, MI 48083, USA]; *b* 1916; *m* 1935 *Howard Shirkey and has:
1d *Howard; *b* 1942
2d *Suzanne; *b* 1936
3d *Joanne; *b* 1938
4d *Julianne; *b* 1945
5d *Christine; *b* 1950

2b Louis Charles Hoskyns; *b* 1878; *m* 1930 Irene Beck (*d* 1981), and *d* 1955, leaving issue:
1c +Louis [Louis Hoskyns III, Lan Yair Country Club, Box 18161, Spartanburg, SC, USA]; *b* 1930; *m* 1952 (*divorce* 1982) Joan Vandermale and has:
1d +Louis; *b* 1964
1d *Mary Jo [Miss Mary Jo Hoskyns, 1415 Church Hill Place, Reston VA, USA]; *b* 1952
2d *Lynn Ann [Mrs Gio Chasewski, 725 Tallwood Dve, Charleston, SC, USA]; *b* 1953; *m* 1st 1973 (*divorce* 1975) Stephen Michael Sentell; *m* 2nd 1994 *Gio Chasewski and by her 1st husb has:
1e *Colleen Elizabeth; *b* 1974
3d *Suzanne Arrian [Mrs Mitchell Peterson, 109 Longwood Dve, Spartanburg, SC, USA]; *m* 1988 *Mitchell Peterson
2c +Gordon William [Gordon Hoskyns, 1599 14th Ave, Boca Raton, FL 33486, USA]; *b* 1933; *m* 1st 1963 (*divorce* 1974) Mary Lou Foit; *m* 2nd 1976 *Leah Besch Easton
3b James Patrick; *b* 1887; *m* 1st 1908 Lena Lusk (*d* 1934), and had:
1c *Alice; *b* 1909; *m* 19– *Martin Frankhouse, and has:
1d *Jerrold; *b* 1931
2c *Helen; *b* 1912; *m* 19– *Russell Wright, and has:
1d *John; *b* 19–
1d *Janice; *b* 19–
3b (cont.) James Hoskyns *m* 2nd 19– Jane Doty and *d* 1953, leaving:
1c +James; *b* 1935; *m* 19– (*divorce* 19–) Judith McCausland, and has:
1d +James; *b* 1957
1d *Gail; *b* 1958
2a Chandos; *b* 1838; *m* 1st 18– Catherine, dau of Ira Morris Allen, MD; *m* 2nd 18– Mary — and had:
1b Edwin Allen; *b* 1871; *m* 1907 Margaret Barton (*d* 1942) and *d* 1960, leaving:
1c +Chandos Allen [Chandos Hoskyns, 923N 33W Ave, Tulsa, OK 74127, USA]; *b* 1911; *m* 1945 *Mildred McPherson
2a (cont.) Chandos Hoskyns; *m* 3rd *c* 1901 Mary Anne (*d* 1954), dau of William Hipkiss, and *d* 1929, leaving:
2b +Wesley Lucien; *b* 1903; *m* 1930 (*divorce* 19–) Marjorie Louise (*d* 1981), dau of George Joseph Fix; *m* 2nd 19– (*divorce* 19–) Alice Blythe; *m* 3rd 19– (*divorce* 19–) Catherine Akester, and by his 1st w has:
1c +Wesley Francis; *b* 1932; *m* 1958 *Caroline Frances Davis, of Idaho, and has:
1d +William Anthony; *b* 1962; *m* 1986 *Susan Patricia Bramhill and has:
1e +Spencer John Chandos; *b* 1991
1e *Alexandra Allyce Caroline; *b* 1989
2d +Robert Nicholas; *b* 1962; *m* 1985 *Nancy Paige Sailors and has:
1e +Wesley Sailors; *b* 1987
2e +Cooper Davis; *b* 1988
3e +Brick Carlos; *b* 1993
1d *Diane Carole; *b* 1960; *m* 1982 *Kevin Noble Faulkner and has:
1e *Jonathan Nobel; *b* 1985
1e *Lisa Marie; *b* 1983
2e *Caroline Elizabeth; *b* 1992
2d *Nancy Renee; *b* 1971; *m* 1992 *Thomas Christian Nienstedt
1c *Joyce Louise; *b* 1933; *m* 1952 *Kenneth Lawrence Cooper and has:
1d *Steven Alfonse; *b* 1953
2d *Donald Kenneth; *b* 1956
3d *Kenneth Lawrence; *b* 1958
4d *Michael Joseph; *b* 1961; *m* 1991 *Cheryl Ann Marquart and has:
1e *Dylan Michael; *b* 1993
5d *Thomas William; *b* 1964
3b +Chandos (Mike) [Chandos Hoskyns Esq, 58 Cayuga Creek Rd, Alden, NY 14004, USA]; *b* 1906; *m* 1942 *Eleanor Hoskins and has:
1c +Clayton Chandos [Clayton Hoskyns, 303 Broadway, Darien Center, NY 14040, USA]; *b* 1949; *m* 1974 *Barbara Sobolewski and has:
1d *Sarah Ann; *b* 1981
2d *Laura Elizabeth; *b* 1985
2c +Loren Russell [Loren Hoskyns Esq, 509 Cayuga Creek Rd, Alden NY 144, USA]; *b* 1951; *m* 1983 *Barbara Holtenhoff and has:
1d +Michael Chandos; *b* 1983
1d *Caitlyn Elizabeth; *b* 1986
1c *Nancy Elizabeth; *b* 1952; *m* 1970 *Michael Paul Noody and has:
1d *Brian Michael; *b* 1971
2d *Kevin Paul; *b* 1973
4b William James; *b* 1908; *m* 1st 1934 (*divorce* 1953) Jean Louise McMullen (*d* 1988); *m* 2nd 1959 *Margaret Norman and *d* 1983, leaving by his 1st w:
1c +William Roy [William Hoskyns Esq, 4819 W Desert Hills Drive, Glendale, AZ 85304, USA]; *b* 1936; *m* 1956 *Marilyn Jane Miller and has:
1d +Donald James [Donald Hoskyns Esq, 10030 N 49th Lane, Glendale, AZ 85302, USA]; *b* 1960; *m* 1st 1980 (*divorce* 1987) Rika Rundall, and has:
1e *Chelsea; *b* 1982
2e *Alyssa; *b* 1984
1d (cont.) Donald Hoskyns *m* 2nd 1989 *Tamra Garcia and has:
3e *Elayna; *b* 1993
1d *Brenda Jeanne; *b* 1957; *m* 1st 1975 (*divorce* 1991) Rodney Abbott; *m* 2nd 1992 *Wade Beauchaine and by her 1st husb has:
1e *Justin; *b* 1986
1e *Stacie Joy; *b* 1976
2e *Tina Winifred; *b* 1981
1c (cont.) Mr and Mrs William Hoskyns also adopted:
Robert John; *b* 1964
2c +Leslie Laing [Leslie Hoskyns Esq, 6119 Pine Wood Rd, Oakland, CA 94611, USA]; *b* 1941; *m* 1970 (*divorce* 1974) Stephanie Irene Muth
1b *Lucy Caroline; *b* 1911; *m* 1942 *Willard Wakeman English
3a Bennett
(2) Hungerford; *d* unm
(3) Chandos; *dsp*
(4) John; *b* 15 Nov 1824; *m* 10 Nov 1861 Mary Elizabeth, dau of George Duff, of Monkstown, Dublin, and *d* 1891, leaving:
1a John Chandos; *b* 1862; *d* 1863
2a Chandos; *b* 1868; *d* 1928
3a George; *b* 1871; *d* unm 6 May 1959
4a John; *b* 1872; *m* 1911 Florence May (*d* 1966), dau of Alfred Taylor, of Sydney, Australia, and *d* 1963, having had:
1b +Chandos John [Chandos Hoskyns Esq, 29 Woodcroft Ave, St Georges, Adelaide, S Australia]; *b* 1915; *m* 1938 *Harriet Anderson, dau of Andrew Anderson Sundquist, of NSW, and has:
1c +Max [Max Hoskyns Esq, Cumulus Place, Willeton, W Australia 6155], with Soil Conservation Service of NSW; *b* 1940; *m* 1964 *Lottie Jolliffe, of Manilla, NSW, and has:
1d +Wayne Gregory; *b* 9 Feb 1967
1d *Lena Gay; *b* 1965; *m* 1985 *John Kraima
2d *Mandy Jane; *b* 1969
2c *Craig [Craig Hoskyns Esq, Warners Rd, Upper Hermitage, Houghton, S Australia 5131]; *b* 1944; *m* 1962 *Beverley Joan Westbrook, of Loxton, S Australia, and has:
1d *Joanne Kaye; *b* 1962; *m* 1982 *Joseph Anthony Mamone and has:
1e *Rachel; *b* 1982
2e *Rebecca; *b* 1985
2d *Sharon Julie; *b* 1965; *m* 1987 *Martine Leigh Goldsworthy of Loxton, S Australia, and has:
1e *Benjamin Nathan; *b* 1990
3d *Natalie Ruth; *b* 1970
3c +Paul [Paul Hoskyns Esq, 20 Morland Ave, Stoneyfell, S Australia 5066]; *b* 1945; *m* 1969 *Deidre Margaret Saunders, of Adelaide, and has:
1d +Andrew John; *b* 1970
1d *Elizabeth Anne; *b* 1972
2d *Sarah Louise; *b* 1974
2b Alfred Hungerford; *b* 1919; *d* 1939
1a Lydia Benedicta; *b* 1864; *d* Nov 1935
2a Caroline; *b* 1865; *d* unm 1945
3a Mary; *b* 1866; *d* unm 1956
4a Gertrude Ada; *b* 1875; *m* 4 May 1904 John Menzies Southern, and had issue
5a Lucy; *b* 1876; *m* Yeo T Shand, of Christchurch, NZ, and *d* 22 Nov 1959, leaving issue
(1) Kate; *m* Arthur Cuthbert Baines (*d* 29 Aug 1901), of Riccarton, NZ, and *dsp* 1910
(2) Ellen
(3) Caroline
(4) Lucy; *d* 1880
1 Maria Jane; *b* 25 May 1787; *m* 6 March 1809 George Compton Reade and *d* 20 Aug 1837, leaving issue (*see* READE, Bt)

Sir HUNGERFORD *d* 10 July 1802; his est son,

Sir Hungerford Hoskyns, 7th Bt; High Sheriff Herefs 1814; *b* 12 June 1776; *m* 4 Aug 1803 Sarah (*d* 12 March 1860), yst dau of John Philips, of Bank Hall, Lancs, and *d* 27 Feb 1862, having had, with four daus:
1 **Sir Hungerford Hoskyns, 8th Bt**; barrister; *b* 19 Sept 1804; *educ* Oriel Coll Oxford (MA); *d* unm 1 Nov 1877
2 Chandos HOSKYNS later WREN-HOSKYNS (roy licence 15 April 1837), of Wroxall Abbey, Warwicks, and Harewood, Herefs; MP Hereford 1869–74, barrister, High Sheriff Warwicks 1853; *b* 15 Feb 1812; *educ* Balliol Coll Oxford (BA); *m* 1st 20 April 1837 Theodosia Anne Martha (*d* 25 Marach 1842), dau and heir of Christopher Roberts Wren, of Wroxall Abbey, and had:
(1) Catherine; *m* 17 July 1873 Rev Charles Francis Corbet Pigott (*d* 22 Jan 1888), Canon Lichfield, and *d* 12 June 1911
2 (cont.) Chandos Wren-Hoskyns *m* 2nd 9 July 1846 Anna Fane, yst dau of Charles Milner Ricketts, and *dspms* 28 Nov 1876, having by her had, with two daus (*d* unm):
(1) Hungerford Chandos; *b* 12 Sept 1852; drowned while bathing 16 June 1871
3 **Rev Sir John Leigh Hoskyns, 9th Bt**, JP Berks; *b* 4 Feb 1817; *educ* Rugby and Balliol Coll Oxford (MA); Rector Aston Tyrrold Berks 1845–1911, Fell Magdalen Coll Oxford, Hon Canon Ch Ch Oxford 1880; *m* 22 April 1846 Phyllis Emma (*d* 7 May 1914), dau of Sir John Strutt Peyton, KCH, and *d* 1911, having had:
(1) John, Lt 24th Regt; *b* 28 April 1848; *d* unm 13 March 1887
(2) **Sir Chandos Hoskyns, 10th Bt**; *b* 28 April 1848; Col RE, served Jowaki campaign 1877 (medal with clasp), Afghan campaign 1878–80 (despatches, medal with clasp) and Zhob Valley Expdn 1884; *m* 22 July 1886 Jean Bannatyne (*d* 1 Jan 1936), dau of David MacDuff Latham, DL, of Gourock, Renfrewshire, and *d* 22 July 1914, leaving:
1a Euphemia; *m* 21 Sept 1920 Col Robert Francis Hurter Wallace of that Ilk, CMG, Black Watch, er s of Col Charles Tennant Wallace, HLI, of Willowvale, Nairn, and had:
1b *Malcolm Robert; *b* 14 Dec 1921; *educ* Stowe; Lt-Col Argyll and Sutherland Highrs 1964–67, formerly Maj Black Watch, psc, WW II 1941–45

(despatches), Korea 1950–51 and 1952 and Borneo 1964–66, Regtl Sec RHQ Black Watch Balhousie Castle 1967, memb Roy Co Archers

2b Donald Charles; *b* 25 Oct 1923; *educ* Stowe and New Coll Oxford; Lt Black Watch WW II (despatches); *ka* 1 July 1944

3b *Ian Francis, RASC and Arab Legion; *b* 28 Sept 1929; *educ* Stowe and New Coll Oxford (MA); *m* 2 Feb 1963 *Teresa Hyne, yst dau of Rev Christopher Leigh Buckingham, of Priest's Cottage, Alciston, Sussex, and has:

1c *Andrew Robert; *b* 16 Feb 1964

2c *James Christopher; *b* 8 June 1969

1c *Henrietta Katherine; *b* 28 Feb 1966

2a Muriel

3a Elizabeth Mary; *m* 11 June 1914 Brig-Gen Arthur Blair (*d* 4 Feb 1947), DSO, s of Capt James J Blair (*see* ARTHUR, Bt), and *d* 7 April 1969

(3) **Sir Leigh Hoskyns, 11th Bt**, JP (Oxon); *b* 14 Feb 1850; *educ* Trin Coll Oxford (BA); High Sheriff (Oxon) 1907, barrister, Crown Prosecutor Griqualand W; *m* 17 Jan 1882 Frances Hester Frederica (*d* 20 Jan 1941), dau of John Samuel Bowles, of Milton Hill, Berks, and *dspms* 12 Sept 1923, having had:

1a Edwyn Cecil Leigh; Lt Roy Welch Fus; *b* 22 Sept 1890; *ka* 20/21 Oct 1914

1a Mary Leigh; *m* 9 Aug 1910 Maj Henry Chase Meredith (*d* 21 Sept 1957), TD, JP, only child of Henry Hills Meredith, JP, barrister, of Maraton Hall, Salop, and *d* 9 April 1966, leaving issue

2a Frances Etrenne; *m* 16 Sept 1914 Maj Henry Compton Maul (*d* 1957), er sHenry Compton Maul, of Banbury, and *d* 4 Feb 1963, leaving issue

3a Catherine Emma; *m* 10 April 1915 Ronald Herbert Acland Holbech (*d* 2 Jan 1956), OBE, of Farnborough Hall, Banbury, Warwicks, and had issue

(4) EDWYN (Rt Rev Sir), **12th Bt**

(5) Peyton, CMG, MVO; R-Adml, served Sierra Leone 1898–99 (despatches, medal) and Boer War 1902 (medal); *b* 15 Sept 1852; *m* 26 April 1882 Grace MacDuff (*d* 21 Sept 1935), dau of D MacDuff Latham, DL, of Gourock, Lanarks, and *d* 20 Dec 1919, leaving:

1a Oswald Peyton Latham; Capt and Brevet Maj Queen's Westminster Rifles, GSO(2) 1917; *b* 1883; *m* 13 June 1913 Evelyn Mary (*d* 19 Sept 1965), dau of Joseph Herbert Blacklock, of Banbury, and *d* 12 Aug 1922, leaving:

1b +John Algernon Peyton (Rev) [The Rev John Hoskyns, Tump House, Woolhope, Herefs HR1 4QP]; Rector Worplesdon, Surrey, late Maj RCOS; *b* 11 May 1920; *educ* Pembroke Coll Cambridge (BA 1941, MA 1945); *m* 1st 12 April 1944 Ann Veronica (*d* 1 June 1968), dau of C R Harrison, of The Old Rectory, Kingsworthy, Winchester; *m* 2nd 17 Jan 1970 Andrea Evelyn (*d* 1991), yr dau of Adml Sir Henry Bertram Pelly, KCVO, CB (*see* PELLY, Bt); *m* 3rd 27 May 1995 *Joan Mary Wight, only child of Capt John Jaspar Roy Peirson, DSC, RN, and by his 1st w has:

1c +Oswald Christopher Peyton [Oswald Hoskyns Esq, Hobbit House, High St, Whitmell, Ventnor IOW PO38 2QS]; *b* 30 March 1954; Police Sgt Hants Constabulary; *m* 1990 *Julie Anne, dau of Gordon Geddes, and has:

1d +Benedict Mungo Peyton; *b* 1990

2d +Fergus; *b* 1991

1c *Rachel Susan [Mrs Robert Lund, 16 Margerison Rd, Ben Rhydding, W Yorks LS29 8QU]; *b* 14 May 1946; *m* 19 July 1969 *S/Ldr Robert Lund, RAF, s of Cyril Lund, of Kuwait, and has:

1d *Mark Edward; *b* 1973

1d *Suzanne Elizabeth; *b* 1977

2c *Jane Elizabeth Carol [Mrs Rodney Sinclair, Flat 50C, Orakei Rd, Remuera, Auckland, New Zealand]; *b* 19 Dec 1947; *m* 1972 *Rodney Alexander Sinclair and has:

1d *James Lawrence; *b* 1980

1d *Charlotte Ann Hoskyns; *b* 1973

2d *Amy Elizabeth; *b* 1976

3d *Sarah Jane; *b* 1977

3c *Juliet Ann [Mrs Ian Doswell, The Old Post Office, Shapwick, Dorset DT11 9JT]; *b* 3 Feb 1951; *m* 1973 *Ian Richard Doswell, MRIPHH, and has:

1d *Ewan Rufus; *b* 1978

1d *Gwendolyn Natasha; *b* 1976

2a John Walter; Cdr RN, served WW I and WW II (wounded, despatches); *b* 19 July 1892; *m* 31 July 1917 Magdalen Rose Wyndham (*d* 1991), dau of Peter James Duff Hawker, of Longparish House, Hants, and had:

1b Hungerford Robert Leo; WW II as Lt Rifle Bd; *b* 6 May 1921; *educ* Charterhouse and Fitzwilliam House Cambridge (MA 1953), CertEd (London); *d* 25 July 1996

1b *Rosemary Eleanor Peyton [Mrs Geoffrey Stanton, 50 Greenway Lane, Bath BA2 4LW]; *b* 24 Aug 1919; *m* 1 Jan 1949 Maj Geoffrey Nelson Stanton, KOYLI (*d* 1978), only s of Capt G A Stanton, of Yarmouth, IoW, and has issue:

1c *David John Nelson; *b* 1958; *m* 1988 *Catharine Mary Crick and has issue

1c *Juliet Rose Brailsford; *b* 1952

2c *Sarah Dorothy Macduff; *b* 1955; *m* 1980 *Martin Gordon Walters, of Cambridge, and has issue

2b *Zara Stephanie Jardine [Miss Zara Hoskyns, c/o Lloyds Bank plc, 8-10 Waterloo Place, London SW1Y 4BE]; F/O WRAF 1954–63; *b* 10 Oct 1929

1a Grace MacDuff

2a Dorothea; *m* 21 Oct 1916 Capt Walter Macdonald Nash (*d* 1952), OBE, RN, and had issue

(6) Benedict George (Ven); Vicar Brighton 1902–17, RD 1907–16, Preb Chichester 1903–18, Archdeacon Hastings 1915–20, Canon Chichester 1918, Archdeacon Chichester 1920–34, Canon Residentiary Truro Cathedral 1895–1902, Fell Lancing; *b* 23 Feb 1856; *educ* Jesus Coll Cambridge (MA); *m* 15 Nov 1893 Dora Katherine (*d* 16 June 1950), est dau of H W Franklyn, of Shedfield Lodge, Hants, and *d* 11 Sept 1935, leaving issue:

1a Chandos Benedict Arden; Lt-Col Rifle Bde, Mil Sec to Govr Malta 1927–31, served WW I 1915 (wounded, despatches) and WW II; *b* 15 Sept 1895; *m* 26 July 1920 Joyce Austin (*d* 1979), 2nd dau of Austin Taylor, and *d* of wounds recd in action Calais 18 June 1940, leaving:

1b +John Leigh Austin Hungerford (Sir) [Sir John Hoskyns, c/o Child & Co, 1 Fleet St, London EC4Y 1BD]; Capt Rifle Bde; *b* 22 Aug 1927; Head PM' s Policy Unit 1979–82; Dir-Gen IOD 1984–89, chm Burton Gp plc 1990– and Emap plc 1994–; ktd 1982; *m* 1956 *Miranda, only dau of Tom Mott, and has:

1c +Barnaby Chandos Tom [Barnaby Hoskyns Esq, 214 Broomwood Rd, London SW11]; *b* 5 May 1959; *m* 1990 *Victoria, dau of Conrad Sandler, and has:

1d +Jake Austin Thomas; *b* 1990

2d +Fred Daniel Rufus; *b* 1992

2c +Benedict John Hungerford; *b* 20 May 1963; *m* 1993 *Sally, yr dau of C Hodges, of Dunton, Norfolk

1c *Benedicta Tamasine Maria; *b* 20 March 1961

2b +David Chandos Benedict [David Hoskyns Esq, The Oast House, Wittersham, Kent]; *b* 24 Dec 1929; *m* 21 June 1958 Sheelagh Marion (*d* 31 May 1996), only child of Hon Sir Patrick Redmond Joseph Barry, MC, and adopted:

*Simon Chandos; *b* Sept 1965

*Jessica Marion; *b* 6 May 1967; *m* 1989 *Iain Macdonald Johnston, er s of Alan Johnston, of Wickambrook, Suffolk, and has:

1d *Archie; *b* 19–

1d *Flora Marion; *b* 1990

1b *Benedicta Lucia; *b* 19 June 1922; *m* 4 July 1955 (*divorce* 1989) Richard Evelyn Vernon, yr s of Evelyn Vernon, of Reading, and has:

1c *Thomas Richard Adam; *b* 11 April 1958

1c *Sarah Benedicta; *b* 25 Nov 1956

1a Diana Mary Katharine; *b* 12 Dec 1899; *m* 11 Sept 1924 Rt Hon Sir Godfrey John Vignoles Thomas, 10th Bt, GCVO, KCB, CSI, PC, of Wenvoe (*qv*), and had issue

(1) Emma; *m* 13 May 1884 Charles Morrell, JP (*d* 2 Sept 1913), of Dorchester Manor, Wallingford, Oxon, and *d* 7 May 1933, leaving issue

(2) Mary; *d* unm 7 Aug 1949 aged 91

(3) Florence; *m* 30 May 1893 Rt Rev Francis Gurdon (*d* 23 Dec 1929), Bp Hull 1913–29, and *d* 23 March 1909, leaving issue

The 11th Bt's bro,

Rt Rev Sir Edwyn Hoskyns, 12th Bt; *b* 22 May 1851; *educ* Jesus Coll Cambridge (MA); DE, Bp Southwell 1904–25, Bp Suffragan Burnley 1901–04; *m* 15 Nov 1883 Mary Constance Maude (*d* 15 Jan 1939), dau of Robert Benson, and had:

1 EDWYN CLEMENT (Sir), **13th Bt**

1 Phyllis Eleanor; *m* 4 Aug 1910 Very Rev Edward Gordon Selwyn (*d* 11 June 1959), DD, Dean Winchester, Fell Corpus Christi Coll Cambridge, s of Rev Edward Carus Selwyn, DD, Headmaster Uppingham, and *d* 30 May 1941, leaving issue

2 Evelyn Mary; *m* 10 April 1918 Rev Edwin George Bucknill, Hon Canon Emeritus Carlisle, Vicar Isel, Cockermouth, Chaplain Yokohama, Japan, est s of G E Bucknill

The Rt Rev Sir EDWYN *d* 2 Dec 1925; his only son,

Rev Sir Edwyn Clement Hoskyns, 13th Bt, MC; *b* 9 Aug 1884; *educ* Jesus Coll Cambridge (MA); Pres, Fell, Dean and Librarian Corpus Christi Coll Cambridge, Hon Canon Derby, Sr Proctor Cambridge U 1921–22, Select Preacher Oxford U 1923–24, Canon Theologian of Liverpool 1932–35, WW I TCF 1915–19 (wounded, despatches); Hon DD St Andrews; *m* 27 July 1922 Mary Trym (*d* 1994), Research Fell Newnham Coll 1921–24, yr dau of Edwin Budden, MA, BSc, of Macclesfield, and *d* 28 June 1937, leaving:

1 **Sir Chandos Wren Hoskyns, 14th Bt**; *b* 14 Dec 1923; *educ* Winchester; F/O No 190 Sqdn RAFVR WW II; *k* on air operations over Norway 3 April 1945

2 **Sir John Chevallier Hoskyns, 15th Bt**; *b* 23 May 1926; *educ* Marlborough, King's Coll Cambridge and Cuddeson Coll Oxford; barrister Inner Temple 1951, Capt KRRC; *d* unm 12 April 1956

3 Sir BENEDICT LEIGH HOSKYNS, **16th and present Bt**

4 +Anthony Hungerford [Anthony Hoskyns Esq, 25 Hamilton Gardens, London NW8]; *b* 7 Aug 1932; *educ* Marlborough; Lt Roy Fus Korea 1952; *m* 30 Aug 1958 *Hon Katherine Margaret, er dau of Baron Kaldor (LP), and has:

(1) +Nicholas Clement; *b* 15 Oct 1967

(1) *Jane Frances; *b* 1 Jan 1962

(2) *Teresa Mary; *b* 1963

1 *Catherine Mary Trym [Prof Catherine Hoskyns, 6 Willes Terrace, Leamington Spa, Warwicks CV31 1DL]; Prof Coventry U; author: *The Congo since Independence, January 1960–December 1961* (1965) and *Integrating Gender* (1996); *b* 15 March 1935; *educ* Cheltenham Ladies' Coll and St Hilda's Coll Oxford (BA 1956); *m* 24 June 1967 *Sol Picciotto, Prof Lancaster, and has:

(1) *Anna Rachel; *b* 16 Dec 1968

HOTHAM

Arms: Barry of ten arg. and az., on a canton or a Cornish chough ppr. **Crest:** A demi-seaman issuing out of the water ppr., holding in his dexter hand a flaming sword erect arg., hilt and pommel or, on his sinister arm a shield of the arms of HOTHAM. **Supporters:** Two seamen habited, each holding a cutlass, the point resting on the ground, all ppr. **Mottoes:** 1 Lead on, 2 (over crest) *Pro patria* ('For my country'). **Creation:** Bt. (E) 4 Jan 1621/2, B. (I) 17 March 1797.

THE 8TH BARON HOTHAM OF SOUTH DALTON, and a **Baronet** (Sir Henry Durand Hotham, Bt, DL (Humberside 1981)) [The Rt Hon The Lord Hotham DL, Dalton Hall, Dalton Holme, Beverley, Yorks HU17 7PY; Scorborough Hall, Driffield, Yorks YO25 9AZ]; *b* 3 May 1940 (HRH THE DUCHESS OF GLOUCESTER stood sponsor); *s f* 1967; *educ* Eton and RAC Cirencester; late 2nd Lt Gren Gds, ADC to Govr of Tasmania 1963–66; *m* June 1972 *Alexandra Mary, 2nd dau of Maj Andrew Charles Stirling Home Drummond Moray, Scots Gds, of Easter Ross, Comrie, Perthshire, and has:

1 +WILLIAM BEAUMONT; *b* 13 Oct 1972

2 +George Andrew; *b* 10 Jan 1974; *educ* Harrow

1 *Elizabeth Henrietta Alexandra; *b* 10 Jan 1976

Lineage: WILLIAM de HOTHAM; had:

DURAND de HOTHAM; held two knights' fees of William Fossard 1165 and was mentioned in the Pipe Roll of 1166 as owing one mark for his land in Harthill, Yorks; possible f of:

ROBERT de HOTHAM; held two bovates of land in Cranswick *c* 1210; *m* Agnes, dau of William de Arundell and sister and coheir of Roger de Arundell, of Foston, Yorks, and had:

THOMAS de HOTHAM; Sheriff Yorks 1218; *m* Margaret — and *d c* 1221, leaving:

ROBERT de HOTHAM; held the two knights' fees formerly held by Durand de Hotham; *m* Alice — and *d* by 1252, leaving:

JOHN de HOTHAM, of Scorborough, E R Yorks; granted free-warren in his lands of Hotham, Scorborough and Birsley 16 July 1290; *d* by 1299, leaving an est s:

Sir JOHN de HOTHAM, of Scorborough; Collector Subsidies, Commr of Oyer and Terminer and Commr of Array Yorks, present Battle of Boroughbridge 16 March 1321/2; *m* Agnes, dau and heiress of Adam Daniel, of Lockington, and *d c* 1348, leaving:

Sir JOHN de HOTHAM, of Scorborough; MP Yorks 1324, Commr of Array 1335 and Collector of Subsidies for Yorks 1341; *m* Agnes, dau and eventual heir of Sir John de Heslarton, and *d* 1370, leaving, with other issue:

Sir JOHN de HOTHAM, of Scorborough; granted Manor of Carnaby by Henry de Percy 1354; *m* Matilda, dau and coheir of 4th Lord (Baron) Hilton, and *d c* 1370, having had:

Sir JOHN de HOTHAM, of Scorborough, MP Yorks 1378; *b* 1344; *d* 18 Jan 1414/5; his est s:

Sir JOHN de HOTHAM, of Scorborough; present Battle of Agincourt 1415; *b* 1386; *m* Matilda (*m* 2nd Sir John Routh), dau and coheir of William Newsome, and *d* 2 Oct 1419, leaving issue:

Sir JOHN HOTHAM, of Scorborough; ktd *c* 1453, High Sheriff Yorks 1456; *b* 1411; *m* Elizabeth, dau of Sir William Eure, and was *ka* Battle of Towton 1461, leaving:

JOHN HOTHAM, of Scorborough; *m* Isabel (*m* 2nd Sir Thomas Netham), dau of Sir Robert Hildyard, of Winstead, Yorks, and was *ka* Battle of Towton 1461, leaving:

Sir JOHN HOTHAM, of Scorborough; *b* 13 Nov 1458; High Sheriff Yorks 1498–99; *m* 2nd Lora, dau of Ralph Constable, of Halsham, Yorks, and was *ka* Battle of the Spurs 1513, leaving:

Sir JOHN HOTHAM, of Scorborough; present Battle of Flodden 1513, ktd afterwards; *m* Elizabeth Headlam (*m* 2nd Sir John Constable) and *d* 18 Oct 1524, leaving:

Sir FRANCIS HOTHAM, of Scorborough; served against Scots 1544, ktd 1544; *m* Mary, dau of Humphrey Hercy, and sis and coheir of Sir John Hercy, of Groves, Notts, and *d* 3 Dec 1546, leaving, with other issue:

JOHN HOTHAM, of Scorborough; MP Scorborough 1584 and Hedon 1586, High Sheriff 1586; *b* Sept 1540; *m* 1st Julian, dau of Sir Michael Stanhope, of Shelford, Notts (*see* 1967 edn CHESTERFIELD and STANHOPE, E); *m* 2nd Mary, dau of George Goring (*see* GORING, Bt); *m* 3rd 10 Jan 1585 Jane, dau and coheir of Richard Legard, of Rysome, Yorks, and *d* 15 June 1609, leaving by her an est s:

Sir John Hotham, 1st Bt (E), so *cr* 4 Jan 1621/2, of Scorborough; Govr (presumably Parly) Hull Civil War; beheaded with his s 2 Jan 1644/5 for communicating with royalists; *m* 1st 16 Feb 1606/7 Katherine, dau of Sir John Rodes, MP Barlborough, Derbys, and had:

1 John (Sir); *m* 1st Frances, dau of Sir John Wray, of Glentworth, Lincs, and had:

(1) **Sir John Hotham, 2nd Bt**; *m* Elizabeth, only dau of 2nd Viscount Beaumont of Swords (*see* BEAUMONT, Bt), and *d* 1689, leaving an est s:

1a **Sir John Hotham, 3rd Bt**; *b* 2 Aug 1656; *m* 5 Feb 1678 Catherine, dau of John Heron, of Beverley, Yorks, and *dspm* 1691

1 (cont.) Sir John had two other wives (one of whom was Margaret, dau of 1st Viscount Fairfax of Emmeley, *see* FAIRFAX OF CAMERON, L) but left no surv issue by them; executed 1 Jan 1644/5 (the day before his f)

2 Richard; *dsp*

Sir John *m* 2nd 16 July 1614 Anne, dau of Ralph Rokeby, of Yorks, by whom he had, with two other sons:

3 Charles (Rev); Rector Wigan, Lancs; *m* Elizabeth, dau of Stephen Thompson, of Humbleton, Yorks (*see* MEYSEY-THOMPSON, Bt), and had:

(1) CHARLES (Sir), **4th Bt**

Sir John *m* 3rd Frances, dau of John Legard, of Ganton; *m* 4th Catharine, widow of Sir Thomas Norcliff and dau of Sir William Bamburgh, 1st and last Bt; *m* 5th 7 May 1635 Sarah, dau of Thomas Anlaby, but had no surv male issue by them

The 3rd Bt's cousin,

Sir Charles Hotham, 4th Bt; Col of Dragoons, MP Beverley; *m* 1st Bridget, dau of William Gee, of Bishop Burton, and had, with other issue:

1 **Sir Charles Hotham, 5th Bt**; Col Horse Gren Gds, Groom Bedchamber, MP Beverley; *m* 1724 Lady Gertrude Stanhope, est dau of 3rd Earl of Chesterfield (*see* 1967 edn CHESTERFIELD and STANHOPE, E), and *d* 15 Jan 1738/9, leaving:

(1) **Sir Charles Hotham, 6th Bt**; Groom Bedchamber; *m* Caroline Anne (*d* 1759), dau and heiress of Thomas Clutterbuck, of Mill Green, and *dsp* 1767

2 BEAUMONT (Sir), **7th Bt**

1 Elizabeth; *m* Sir Thomas Style, 4th Bt (*qv*), and *d* 25 Oct 1737

Sir Charles *m* 2nd Lady Mildred Cecil, yst dau of 3rd Earl of Salisbury (*see* SALISBURY, M), and *d* Jan 1722/3, having by her had:

3 Richard; *d* young

The 6th Bt's uncle,

Sir Beaumont Hotham, 7th Bt; *m* Frances, dau of Rev Stephen Thompson, of Humbleton (*see* MEYSEY-THOMPSON, Bt) and *d* 1771, having had:

1 Sir CHARLES HOTHAM later HOTHAM-THOMPSON (on inheriting estate from that family), **8th Bt**; *m* 21 Oct 1752 Lady Dorothy Hobart (*d* 1 June 1798), dau of 1st Earl of Buckinghamshire (*qv*), and *dspm* 25 Jan 1794

2 **Rt Rev Sir John Hotham, 9th Bt**; DD, Bp Clogher; *m* Susanna, sis of Sir Herbert Mackworth, 1st Bt, of Gnoll Castle (*qv*), and *d* 3 Nov 1795, leaving:

(1) **Sir Charles Hotham, 10th Bt**; *dsp* 1811

3 **Sir William Hotham, 11th Bt**, and **1st Baron Hotham of South Dalton** (I), so *cr* 17 March 1797, with remainder in default of male issue to the heirs male of his deceased father; *b* 8 April 1736; *educ* Westminster and Roy Naval Acad Portsmouth; Col RM 1779–87, R-Adml 1787, V-Adml 1790, Adml: the Blue 1795, White 1799, Red 1805; *d* unm 7 May 1813

4 BEAUMONT, **2nd Baron**

5 George; Gen, Col 14th Regt of Foot; *b* 7 Jan 1741; *m* 16 Dec 1769 Diana (*d* 17 July 1817), yst dau of Sir Warton Pennyman, Bt (*see* 1852 edn), and *d* 7 Feb 1806, leaving, with other issue:

(1) George; Lt-Col 3rd Gds; *b* 18 Oct 1770; *m* 1st 1 March 1792 Caroline (*d* 23 Dec 1811), dau and coheir of Roger Gee, of Bishop Burton, and had, with other issue:

1a William, KH; Adml; *b* 30 July 1794; *d* unm 22 Feb 1875

2a George; Capt RE; *b* 11 Sept 1796; *m* 1st Caroline (*d* 27 Sept 1839), dau of Richard Watt, of Bishop Burton, and had:

1b Richard; Adj and Hon Maj 11th Middx RVC; *b* 16 Oct 1832; *m* Ellen — (*d* 19 July 1907) and *d* 23 Feb 1917

1b Harriet; *m* 1889 Philip Saltmarshe, of Saltmarshe, and *dsp* July 1897. He *d* 10 March 1912

2a (cont.) Lt-Col George Hotham *m* 2nd 11 July 1844 Amelia (*d* 10 Nov 1885), 2nd dau of Francis Ramsden Hawksworth, of Barmbro' Grange, Doncaster, Yorks, and *d* 14 April 1860, having by her had, with other issue:

2b Francis; Lt RN; *b* 21 June 1851; *dsp* Jan 1900

2b Alice; *m* 2 July 1868 Capt John Loftus Bland, 6th Dragoons, of Blandsfort, Queen's Co, and *d* 31 Jan 1898, leaving issue. He *d* 3 Dec 1908

3b Lora; *m* 14 Nov 1872 Montagu Lubbock, MRCS, and *d* 1 Aug 1882. He *d* 8 April 1925

3a John; Capt Bengal HA; *b* 29 Jan 1805; *educ* Addicombe; *m* 1st 9 April 1842 Maria Elizabeth (*d* 3 June 1853), dau of Henry Thompson, of Burton, Yorks, and had, with three daus (*d* unm):

1b Charles Frederick (Sir), GCB, GCVO; Adml of the Fleet, Jr Ld Admlty 1888–89, C-in-C Pacific station 1890, Sheerness 1897–99 and Portsmouth 1900–03, NZ and Egypt; *b* 20 March 1843; *m* 29 Feb 1872 Margaret (*d* 25 May 1918), dau of David Milne Home of Wedderburn, and *d* 22 March 1925, having had:

1c John Beaumont; BA Cantab, Clerk Senate and Assist Clerk Parl NI; *b* 15 Sept 1874; *m* 15 Aug 1905 Gladys Mary (*d* 12 Feb 1972 aged 91), 2nd dau of Col John Gerald Wilson, CB, of Cliffe Hall, Yorks (*see* INCHIQUIN, B), and *d* 29 Dec 1924, having had:

1d +(John) David Durand [David Hotham Esq, Milne Graden, Coldstream, Berwickshire]; Lt RAC (TA), late *The Times* correspondent Germany; *b* 5 Aug 1917; *educ* Eton and New Coll Oxford; *m* 11 Dec 1954 Marianne (*d* 9 July 1996), formerly wife of Siegfried Becker and dau of Louis Pollak, of Vienna

1d Dorothy Jean, MBE (1947); *b* 12 Aug 1906; V-Pres Co London Branch BRC (S), SStJ; *m* 27 July 1925 7th Earl of Donoughmore (*qv*) and *d* 29 Dec 1995, leaving issue

2d Margaret; *b* 14 Aug 1909; *m* 10 June 1933 George Anthony Harford, yst s of Hugh Wyndham Luttrell Harford, of Horton Hall, Avon, and *d* 23 Sept 1958, leaving issue

3d Ursula; *b* and *d* 2 Feb 1912

4d *Anne [The Rt Hon The Lady Howard of Penrith, Dean Farm, Coln St Aldwyns, Glos]; *b* 27 Sept 1913; *m* 1st 9 Feb 1934 Anthony Gardner Bazley (*d* 23 May 1937) (*see* BAZLEY, Bt) and has issue; *m* 2nd 1 July 1944 2nd Baron Howard of Penrith (*qv*) and has further issue

5d *Catharine Geraldine [The Rt Hon The Lady Guest, 22 Lennox St, Edinburgh]; *b* 27 Sept 1915; *m* 28 June 1941 Baron Guest (LP; *d* 1984) and has issue

2c Alan Geoffrey (Sir), KCMG (1938), CB (1923); Adml, Gentleman Usher Blue Rod Order St Michael and St George 1934; *b* 3 Oct 1876; *d* unm 10 July 1965

1c Jean; *m* 16 Sept 1897 Charles William Forbes, JP, DL, of Callendar, and *d* 5 Sept 1951, leaving issue. He *d* 31 July 1948

2b John, CB; Col and Hon Brig-Gen RA, Boer War 1900–04, WW I as CRA 20th Div 1915–16 and Inspr Gen Remounts 1916–18; *b* 31 July 1851; *m* 10 Dec 1889 Rose Florence (*d* 5 Jan 1944), dau of Gen Hon Bernard Matthew Ward, CB (*see* BANGOR, V), and *d* 16 Nov 1932, leaving issue:

1c Charles Ernest, DSC; Capt RN WW I (despatches); *b* 16 Sept 1891; *d* unm 30 Jan 1940

1c Angela Rose Emily; *b* 7 March 1902; *m* 26 Oct 1939 Brig Rintoul Edward George Carolin, Essex Regt

3a (cont.) Capt John Hotham *m* 2nd 11 Jan 1855 Mary Anne (*d* 20 June 1898), dau of Rev Danson Richardson Roundell, of Gledstone, Yorks, and *d* 11 Feb 1881, having by her had, with another dau (*d* unm):

3b George; *b* 4 April 1856; *m* 5 May 1896 Louisa Neumeister (*d* 25 Oct 1958), and *d* 15 Nov 1948, leaving:

1c +George Edward; *b* 20 March 1906

4b William, Capt Salop LI and 3rd Bn Yorks LI; *b* 17 April 1859; *dsp* Oct 1899

1b Lucy; *d* unm 7 July 1945

1a Harriet; *m* 29 June 1833 Sir John William Lubbock, 3rd Bt, and *d* 12 Feb 1873, leaving issue (*see* AVEBURY, B)

(1) (cont.) Col George Hotham *m* 2nd 29 June 1813 Rosamund (*d* 5 Sept 1826), dau of Francis Best, Rector S Dalton, and *d* 23 April 1823, leaving by her:

2a Maria; *m* 12 April 1836 William Bradley Wainman, of Carrhead, and *d* 19 July 1871

3a Gertrude; *m* 27 Dec 1830 Rev Christopher Nevile, JP, Rector Wickenby, Lincs, and Thornby, and *d* 15 Sept 1859

(2) William (Sir) GCB; Adml the Red; *b* 12 Feb 1772; *m* 1st June 1804 Anne (*d* 21 Aug 1827), dau of Sir Edward Jeynes, and had, with other issue:

1a Edwin (Rev); Rector Crowcombe, Somerset; *b* 13 Dec 1807; *m* 13 Sept 1838 Harriet (*d* 30 Dec 1891), yst dau of Sir John Geers Cotterell, 1st Bt (*qv*), and *d* 8 March 1875, leaving:

1b John; Capt Bengal NI; *b* 19 Feb 1841; *d* unm 1880

2b Edwin; Cdr RN; *b* 29 Aug 1842; *d* 27 June 1889

3b Stephen; *b* 26 Dec 1844; *d* unm 1907

4b William Charles; Cdr Royal Indian Marine; *b* 30 June 1846; *m* 21 June 1881 Aileen Agnes (*d* 19 April 1884), dau of Capt G Carew, CIE, and *d* 22 April 1889, leaving issue:

1c John Clarence; Lt Col IA WW I and Afghan War 1919, Remount Purchasing Offr Calcutta 1924–27, officiating Dir Remounts Simla 1931, cmded 9th Cadet Bn Roy Hants Regt 1942–51, Cadet Force Medal 1951; *b* 25 March 1882; *educ* Eastbourne Coll and Pembroke Coll Camb; *m* 23 June 1909 Margaret Emily Anne (*d* 12 Dec 1952), est dau of Horace Wilmer, of Church House, Brede, and *d* 23 May 1959, having had:

1d John Altham; Maj RTR, P/O RAF WW II; *b* 4 June 1913; *m* 16 May 1939 Osra Aubrey (*d* 16 Feb 1944), yr dau of W/Cdr H B Porteous, RAF, MS, and was *ka* N Africa July 1942

1d Aileen Mary Margaret; *d* unm 2 Dec 1932

2d *Diana [Mrs John Whately-Smith, Grey Cottage, Church Walk, Aldeburgh, Suffolk IP15 5PU]; *b* 1918; *m* 31 July 1948 *John Calkin Whately-Smith, yst s of Rev Ernest Whately-Smith, MC, and has:

1e *David John; *b* 5 June 1949; *m* 1982 *Penny Stone and has:

1f *Alastair Charles; *b* 1986

1f *Jessica Clare; *b* 1984

2e *Jeremy William; *b* 20 Aug 1956; *m* 1988 *Kathrin Norah Murray Prior, and has:

1f *Jonathan; *b* 1990

1e *Susan Jane [Mrs Oswald Eberhardt, Schlosshote, Rosenegg, Fieberbrunn, Tyrol, Austria]; *b* 15 Oct 1950; *m* 1973 *Oswald Eberhardt, and has:

1f *Andreas; *b* 1980

1f *Elisabeth; *b* 1978

2f *Kathrin; *b* 1978

2e *Charlotte Anne; *b* 21 Dec 1952; *m* 1978 *David Richard Charles Agnew and has issue (*see* AGNEW, Bt, of Gt Stanhope St)

2c William Montagu; Lt-Cdr RCNVR, served Boer War (two medals), WW I and WW II; *b* 4 March 1884; *educ* Eastbourne Coll; *m* 16 June 1905 Margaret Browne and *d* at sea 9 Oct 1951, leaving:

1d +Ronald St Vincent Carew; *b* 22 May 1911; *m* 30 July 1937 *Muriel Eva Marie Sheather

2d +Alan Geoffrey [Alan Hotham Esq, 1130 Channel Drive, Santa Barbara, CA, USA]; WW II in RCAF; *b* 25 Aug 1921; *educ* Brentwood Sch and U of BC (BASc); *m* 25 Oct 1951 *Kathleen, dau of Ralph Cramer Coxhead, of New York, and has:

1e +Peter Alan; *b* 9 Oct 1952

2e *Daryl; *b* 1953

1e *Lisa; *b* 1955

5b Montagu Conyers; *b* 23 Jan 1850; *m* 1883 Francisca Rosa Pizarro and *d* Nov 1931, leaving:

1c Edwin; *b* 1887

2c George, IM; *b* 1899; *m* 1932 *Adriana Maria Franco and has:

1d +Charles Edward; *b* 1934

2d +Richard Alan; *b* 1936

1c Harriett V H; *m* 1905 Edward Holroyd Doveton and has issue

1b Anna; *m* 1st 20 April 1876 John St Vincent Parker Jervis (*see* SAINT VINCENT, V); *m* 2nd 18 April 1896 Ven John Spence, DD, Archdeacon Connor (*d* 1919)

2a John William; Cdr RN; *b* 30 March 1809; *m* 1st 29 April 1838 Sarah Eliza (*d* 2 Nov 1871), dau of William Hawksley, of Bath, and had, with other issue:

1b Charles Ernest; *b* 27 March 1855; *m* 1881 Mary Louisa (*d* 13 Aug 1939), dau of Thomas Robertson, of Sydney, NSW, and *dsp* 15 Nov 1881

1b Rosetta Anne; *m* 6 Nov 1860 Coventry Warrington Carew, and *d* 26 Jan 1914, leaving issue. He *d* 1889

2b Jane Caroline; *m* 27 July 1876 Capt W H Miller Francklyn, Madras Army, and *d* 1884, leaving issue

3b Louisa Augusta; *m* 4 Oct 1873 Albert William Sergison

2a (cont.) Cdr John Hotham *m* 2nd 21 Nov 1874 Matilda Anne (*d* 1896), dau of Denis Hollingworth, of Hollingworth Hall, Cheshire, and *d* 31 Aug 1879

(2) (cont.) Sir William *m* 2nd 25 June 1835 Jane Seymour (*dsp* 30 Nov 1855), dau and coheir of Francis Colman, of Hillersdon, Devon, and widow of Roger Pettiward, and *d* 31 May 1848

The 1st BARON's bro,

BEAUMONT HOTHAM, **2nd Baron Hotham of South Dalton**; a Baron of the Exchequer; *b* 5 Aug 1737; *m* 6 June 1767 Susannah (*d* 1 Aug 1799), yr dau of Sir Thomas Hankey and widow of James Norman, and *d* 4 March 1814, having had:

1 Beaumont; Lt-Col Coldstream Gds; *b* 30 Aug 1768; *m* 20 May 1790 Philadelphia (*d* 20 May 1808), dau of Sir John Dixon Dyke, 3rd Bt (*qv*), and *dvp* Aug 1799, leaving:

(1) BEAUMONT HOTHAM, **3rd Baron Hotham of South Dalton**; Gen, present at Waterloo, war medal with four clasps for Salamanca, Vittoria, Nivelle and Nive; MP Leominster 1820–41 and E R Yorks; *b* 9 Aug 1794; *d* unm 12 Dec 1870

(2) George Frederick; R-Adml; granted rank of baron's yr s 1 Sept 1835; *b* 20 Oct 1799; *m* 12 Aug 1824 Lady Susan Maria O'Brien (*d* 25 March 1857), est dau and coheir of 2nd Marquess of Thomond (*see* INCHIQUIN, B), and *d* 19 Oct 1856, having had, with other issue:

1a Beaumont; *b* 8 Sept 1833; *d* 5 June 1848

2a CHARLES HOTHAM, **4th Baron Hotham of South Dalton**; Kt of the Medjidie; *b* 27 May 1836; *d* unm 29 May 1872

3a JOHN HOTHAM, **5th Baron Hotham of South Dalton**, DL Yorks; High Sheriff 1884, sometime RN, served on W Coast of Africa and in Crimean War 1854–56 (three medals and clasp); *b* 13 May 1838; *d* unm 13 Dec 1907

1a Susan Frances; granted rank of baron's dau 8 March 1871; *m* 6 June 1877 Rev A C Jackson, gs of Adml Sir Peter Halkett, 6th Bt (*see* 1904 edn), and *d* 24 March 1921, leaving issue. He *d* 23 Feb 1907

2 Frederick (Rev); Preb Rochester; *b* 16 Jan 1774; *m* 23 Nov 1802 Anne Elizabeth (*d* 28 Jan 1862), est dau of Thomas Hallett Hodges, of Hemsted Place, Kent, and *d* 10 Oct 1854, having had, with five daus:

(1) Charles (Sir), KCB; Capt RN, Govr Victoria; *b* 14 Jan 1806; *m* 10 Dec 1853 Jane Sarah (*m* 3rd 3 Aug 1860 Capt William Armytage, RN (*see* ARMYTAGE, Bt), and *d* 28 April 1907), widow of Hugh Holbech, of Farnborough, Warwicks, and dau of 2nd Baron Bridport (*qv*), and *dsp* 31 Dec 1855

(2) John Hallett (Rev); MA Oxon, Vicar Sutton-at-Hone Kent; *b* 25 Aug 1811; *d* unm 25 Aug 1901

(3) Henry (Rev); Vicar Woodnesborough, Kent; *b* 19 Nov 1814; *m* 10 July 1845 Mary (*d* 16 June 1887), 2nd dau of Hon John Hale, of Lower Canada, and niece of 1st Earl Amherst (*see* 1970 edn), and *d* 30 Aug 1900, leaving issue

(4) Augustus Thomas; Capt 75th Foot; *b* 25 Jan 1817; *m* 17 Aug 1858 Anne Byam (*d* 14 April 1871), 2nd dau of Rev Hon Miles John Stapleton (*see* NORFOLK, D), and *dsp* 24 Dec 1896

(5) William Francis (Rev); Rector Buckland, Surrey; *b* 28 March 1819; *m* 31 Jan 1855 Emma (*d* 28 May 1900), 5th dau of John Carbonell, and *d* 10 Sept 1883, leaving issue:

1a FREDERICK WILLIAM HOTHAM, **6th Baron Hotham of South Dalton**; *b* 19 March 1863; *m* 9 July 1902 Eliza Benita (*d* 14 Dec 1954), dau of Thomas Sanders, of Sanders Park, Charleville, Co Cork, and *d* 7 Oct 1923, leaving:

1b Sylvia Benita Frances; FLAS; *m* 24 Jan 1924 1st Baron Clitheroe (*qv*) and *d* 1991, leaving issue

2b Jocelyne Mary Emma; *b* 1908; *d* unm 25 May 1997

1a Frances Emma; granted rank of baron's dau 22 Aug 1908; *m* 8 Oct 1889 Very Rev Edward Reid Currie, DD, Dean of Battle, and *d* 8 June 1920. He *d* 4 Feb 1921

3 Henry (Sir), GCMG, KCB; V-Adml the Red; *b* 19 Feb 1777; *m* 6 July 1816 Lady Frances Anne Juliana Rous (*d* 31 Jan 1859), dau of 1st Earl of Stradbroke (*qv*), and *d* Malta while cmdg the Mediterranean Fleet 19 April 1833, having had:

(1) Henry John (Rev); MA, Fell Trin Coll Cambridge; *b* 14 Dec 1822; *d* unm 9 April 1885

(2) Frederick Harry (Rev); Rector Rushbury Salop, RD; *b* 3 Aug 1824; *m* 17 Dec 1851 Eleanor (*d* 22 April 1909), 4th dau of Robert Gosling, of Botleys Park, Surrey, and *d* 11 April 1887, having had issue:

1a Henry Edward; Capt Cameronian Scottish Rifles; *b* 1 Aug 1855; *m* 17 Dec 1896 Ethel Lindsay (*d* 10 Nov 1949), dau of Collingwood Lindsay Wood, of Freeland, Perthshire, and *d* 13 June 1912, leaving issue:

1b HENRY FREDERICK, **7th Baron**

2b Peter; Maj KOYLI; *b* 27 April 1904; *educ* Winchester; granted with sis and yr bro rank of baron's dau/yr s 1 Dec 1924; *m* 4 Oct 1934 *Margaret [The Hon Mrs Peter Hotham, Plas Newydd, Glascoed, Abergele, Clwyd], yr dau of Col Sir Robert William Herbert Watkin Williams-Wynn, 9th Bt (*qv*), and *d* 1991, leaving:

1c +Edward Durand, Capt 15th/19th King's Roy Hus; *b* 26 Aug 1944; *educ* Stowe; *m* 1982 *Susan Elisabeth, dau of Noel Tilley, of Stoke, Marlborough, Wilts

1c *Caroline Alathea; *b* 3 May 1937; *m* 5 Dec 1959 Capt Harry Llewellyn Davies (*d* 1981), RA, est son of Brig Arthur Birney Davies, CBE, of Orchards, Tatworth, nr Chard, Somerset, and has:

1d *Catherine Margaret; *b* 1962

2d *Thora Lucinda; *b* 1965

2c *Mary Elizabeth [Mrs Peter Harman, Abbey Feal Farm, Ringstead, nr Dorchester, Dorset]; *b* 1 April 1940; *m* 25 Jan 1964 *Lt-Col Peter Harman, 14th/20th King's Hus, est s of C Lancelot Harman, of Evenley, Brackley, Northants, and has:

1d *Andrew Charles; *b* 17 Jan 1967

1d *Nicola Jane; *b* 11 April 1969

3b John David, DSC; Lt Cdr RN WW II; *b* 19 April 1911; *m* 11 April 1939 *Aileen [Mrs Colin Smith, 31 Brynmaer Rd, London SW11] (*m* 2nd 27 Sept 1969 Cdr Colin Edward Hugh Smith (*d* 1975), RN (*see* below)), dau of Capt Harry Coates, Durham LI, and *d* 24 March 1962, leaving issue:

1c +Martin Patrick [Martin Hotham Esq, The Old Rectory, Drinkstone, Bury St Edmunds, Suffolk]; *b* 17 Aug 1941; *educ* Stowe; *m* 2 Oct 1965 *Erica Antoinette Strang (*see* BIBBY, Bt) and has had:

1d +Charles Beaumont David; *b* 31 March 1969

2d Henry Ralph; *b* 28 Oct 1974; *d* 1986

1d *Sophie Henrietta; *b* 12 Oct 1967

2d *Amelia Oriana Philadelphia; *b* 6 Oct 1971

1c *Henrietta Elizabeth; *b* 3 May 1944; *m* 17 June 1967 *Maj Philip Andrew Janson Wright, Gren Gds, Dep Assist Serjeant-at-Arms H of C, only s of Sir Andrew Barkworth Wright, KCMG, CBE, MC, of Knapp Farm House, Lewknor, Oxon, and has:

1d *Romayne Louise; *b* 1972

2d *Melanie Clare; *b* 1974

2c *Georgina Rose [Mrs John O'Connell, c/o Barclays Bank, 19 Fleet St, London EC4]; *b* 28 July 1947; *m* 2 Oct 1971 *Lt-Col John V E F O'Connell, Gren Gds, and has:

1d *James Alexander; *b* 1973

2d *Simon David Sebastian; *b* 1974

1d *Emily Mary Frances; *b* 1976

1b Eleanor Ethel; *m* 26 Dec 1935 John Du Preez, s of H J Du Preez, of Salisbury, S Rhodesia, and had issue

2b Elizabeth Dulcie; *m* 7 Oct 1930 Lt-Cdr Colin Edward Hugh Smith, RN (*see* above), s of V-Adml Humphrey Hugh Smith, DSO, and *d* 23 Jan 1969, leaving issue

3b Catherine Muriel; *m* 12 April 1939 Lt-Gen Sir Roger Herbert Bower, KCB, KBE (*d* 1990), KOYLI, and *d* 1996, having had:

1c Jeremy Roger; *b* and *d* 1944

1c *Anne Catherine; *b* 1940; *m* 1972 *Robert Sackville Riseley and has:

1d *Mark James; *b* 1974

2d *David Michael; *b* 1977

3b (cont.) The Hon Lady Bower adopted:

*Michael Roger; *b* 1952

2a Beaumont George; *b* 10 Feb 1859; *d* unm 14 Dec 1895

3a William; *b* 16 Nov 1861; *d* 13 Feb 1864

4a Algernon John; Capt RN; *b* 28 April 1863; *m* 12 Sept 1906 Grace Adeline Rous (*d* 6 Oct 1963), yr dau of Adml Sir Algernon de Horsey, KCB, and *d* 10 Feb 1913, leaving issue:

1b Grace Frances (took by deed poll 1958 name DE HORSEY); FRGS, Assoc Roy Photographic Soc; *b* 29 July 1907; *d* unm 12 March 1975

2b *Rachel Muriel; Lambeth Dipl Theology 1953, assoc memb Roy Yacht Sqdn [Miss Rachel Hotham, Rosetta Cottage, Cowes, IOW]; *b* 21 Sept 1909; *educ* St Anne's Coll Oxford (BA 1932, MA 1944)

5a Francis Herbert; Maj QORWKR; *b* 20 Sept 1865; *d* unm 30 Oct 1914

6a Robert Harry; *b* 24 May 1874; *d* 14 Sept 1929

1a Eleanor Frances; *m* 1 Oct 1878 Sir William St Andrew Rouse-Boughton 12th Bt (*see* 1963 edn), and *d* 4 Oct 1930, leaving issue

2a Georgina Amelia; *m* 3 Jan 1889 Arthur Devereux Cripps (*see* PARMOOR, B) and *d* 3 Jan 1922

3a Emily Harriet; *m* 5 May 1885 Lyde Ernest George Benson, barrister, of Larden Cottage, Much Wenlock, and *d* 5 Sept 1932, leaving issue. He *d* 12 Sept 1924

(3) Beaumont Williams; Capt Gren Gds, UK Consul Calais 1859–82; *b* 22 Aug 1825; *m* 13 March 1855 Charlotte Amelia (*d* 4 June 1910), yst dau of Adml George Frederick Rich, and *d* 14 July 1915, leaving:

1a Charles George Beaumont (Rev); MA Cantab; *b* 19 Sept 1858; *m* 22 Jan 1891 Laura (*d* 9 Nov 1927), dau of Sir Charles Cunliffe-Smith, and *d* 27 Dec 1927

2a John Henry Beaumont; *b* 2 May 1866; *d* 14 March 1914

1a Frances Charlotte Agnes; *m* 22 Aug 1882 Collingwood Lindsay Wood, of Freeland, Perthshire, and *d* 4 May 1923, leaving issue. He *d* 10 July 1906

2a Alice Caroline; *m* 20 Feb 1879 Col Eustace Beaumont Burnaby, 10th Regt, 3rd s of Thomas Fowke Andrew Burnaby, JP, of Brampton Manor House, Hunts, and *d* 4 Sept 1944, leaving issue. He *d* 30 Dec 1932

3a Mary Eleanor; *m* 21 March 1882 11th Lord Rollo (*qv*) of Duncrub and *d* 24 June 1929, leaving issue

4a Margaret; *m* 8 May 1890 Capt Richard Dacre Vincent, Roy Dublin Fus, and *d* 9 March 1935, leaving issue. He *d* 14 Aug 1926

1 Frances; *m* 30 March 1797 Adml Sir John Sutton, KCB, and *d* 1836

2 Amelia; *m* 19 Dec 1798 John Woodcock and *d* 8 March 1812, leaving issue

3 Louisa; *m* 1st 5 Dec 1804 Sir Charles Edmonstone, 2nd Bt (*qv*), and had issue; *m* 2nd Jan 1832 Charles Woodcock, and *d* 30 Aug 1840

The 6th BARON's cousin,

HENRY FREDERICK HOTHAM, **7th Baron Hotham of South Dalton**, CBE (1958), JP, DL E R Yorks and Kingston-upon-Hull; *b* 13 Aug 1899; *educ* Winchester and RMC Sandhurst; Maj-Gen Gds; *m* 16 Dec 1937 Lady Letitia Sibell Winifred Cecil (*d* 1992), er dau of 5th Marquess of Exeter (*qv*), and *d* 18 Nov 1967, having had:

1 Geoffrey Frederick William; *b* 26, *d* 27 Jan 1939

2 Robert; *b* and *d* 26 Jan 1939

3 HENRY DURAND HOTHAM, **8th and present Baron Hotham of South Dalton**

4 John Francis; *b* 18 June 1942; *d* as the result of an accident 17 Sept 1944

5 +Peter William; *b* 10 March 1944; *educ* Eton and Ch Ch Oxford (BA 1965); *m* 1978 *Deborah, dau of G Macdonald-Brown, of Rose Cottage, Campsall, Doncaster, and has:

(1) +Charles Peter; *b* 1982

(1) *Caroline Susan; *b* 1979

6 +Nicholas Charles Frederick; *b* 3 June 1947; *educ* Eton; *m* 1973 *Jane, er dau of D Brydon, of Thirley Beck Farm, Harwood Dale, Scarborough, Yorks, and has:

(1) +David Charles; *b* 1976

(1) *Catherine Frances; *b* 1978

HOTHFIELD

Arms: Sa. an eagle displayed erm. within a bordure wavy or. **Crest:** A sea-lion sejant arg., charged with a bendlet wavy sa. **Supporters:** On either side an eagle erm., gorged with a collar gu., pendant therefrom an escutcheon of the arms of Tufton, *viz.*, sa. an eagle displayed erm. within a bordure wavy or. **Motto:** *Ales volat propriis* ('The bird flies to its own'). **Creations:** Bt. (UK) 16 Jan 1851, B. (UK) 11 Oct 1881.

THE 6TH BARON HOTHFIELD OF HOTHFIELD, Co Kent, and a **Baronet** (Sir Anthony Charles Sackville Tufton, Bt) [The Rt Hon The Lord Hothfield, Drybeck Hall, Appleby-in-Westmorland, Cumbria CA16 6TF]; *b* 21 Oct 1939; *s* f 1991; *educ* Eton and Magdalene Coll Cambridge (MA); CEng, MICE; *m* 1975 *Lucinda Majorie, dau of Capt Timothy John Gurney (*see* 1940 edn DE BATHE, Bt) and formerly w of Capt Graham Morrison Vere Nicoll (*see* MADDEN, Bt), and has:

1 +WILLIAM SACKVILLE; *b* 14 November 1977; *educ* Eton

1 *Emma; *b* 24 April 1976

Lineage: Sir Richard Tufton, 1st Bt (UK), so *cr* 16 Jan 1851; probable illegitimate s of 11th and last Earl of Thanet (*see* LUCAS OF CRUDWELL, B), whose estates he inherited; High Sheriff Kent 1859; *b* 1813 in France but naturalised Briton 1849; *m* 22 Aug 1843 Adelaide Amelie Lacour (*d* 13 April 1902) and had:

1 HENRY JAMES, **1st Baron**

2 Alfred Charles, JP Westmorland; *b* 15 May 1852; *educ* Oriel Coll Oxford (BA); barrister; *m* 2 Aug 1876 Edith Sophia Elizabeth (*d* 23 May 1938), 2nd dau of Rev William John Deane, Rector Ashen, Essex, and *d* 21 July 1925, leaving:

(1) Harold Richard; *b* 25 June 1877; *d* unm 14 April 1952

(2) Cecil George; *b* 3 Aug 1880; *m* 1st 28 Nov 1912 Agatha Vere Ripley (*d* 20 Dec 1928), dau of Edward Ripley Dalton, barrister; *m* 2nd 18 Oct 1930 Vere Mary (*d* 27 March 1932), est dau of T P W Barnes, of Hove, and *d* 16 Oct 1957, leaving by his 1st w:

1a Richard Cecil; MA, MB, BCh Cantab 1941; Capt RAMC; *b* 20 June 1914; *d* 199–

(3) Alfred Guy; *b* 11 Sept 1889; *educ* Rugby and Oriel Coll Oxford (BA 1912); *m* 25 April 1916 Marjorie Neville (*d* 1979), dau of Frederick Charles Thompson, and *d* 27 Feb 1968, leaving:

1a Colin Charles Guy; Vicar All Saints Maidstone, Hon Canon Canterbury 1968, late Lt RM; *b* 2 May 1924; *educ* Oriel Coll Oxford (BA 1948, MA 1953); *d* 27 July 1994

1a *Barbara Marjorie [Miss Barbara Tufton, 8 Croft Ct, Croft Lane, Seaford, E Sussex BN25 1SB]; *b* 11 Oct 1920

(1) Violet Alice; *m* 3 Nov 1909 Isaac Redwood Davies, barrister, and *d* 2 April 1969, leaving issue. He *d* 1949

(2) Norah; *m* 9 April 1921 Reginald Ensor Sedgwick and *d* Nov 1968, leaving issue. He *d* 16 Sept 1944

(3) Kathleen Edith; *d* unm 24 Dec 1957

3 George Richard; Capt 5th Lancers; *b* 18 Feb 1856; *d* unm 26 Nov 1938

1 Therese Elizabeth; *m* 10 May 1870 Count de Chazelle and *d* 8 May 1922

Sir RICHARD *d* 20 June 1871; his son,

Sir Henry James Tufton, 2nd Bt, and **1st Baron Hothfield of Hothfield**, Co Kent (UK), so *cr* 11 Oct 1881, JP Kent; *b* 4 June 1844; V-Adml Cumberland and Westmorland, Westmorland: Ld Lt, custos rotulorum, Pres TAA and High Sheriff 1874; Ld-in-Waiting 1886, Mayor Appleby 1895–96; *m* 17 Dec 1872 Alice Harriot Argyll (*d* 29 June 1914), 2nd dau of Rev William James Stracey Clitherow (*see* STRACEY, Bt), and *d* 29 Oct 1926, leaving:

1 JOHN SACKVILLE RICHARD TUFTON, **2nd Baron Hothfield of Hothfield**, DSO, JP, DL Westmorland and Kent; Mayor Appleby 1936–45, Maj 3rd Bn Roy Sussex Regt, APM 1915, Lt 1st Life Gds, Boer War 1901–02 (medal with five claps), WW I (despatches, 1914–15 star, Glen Service and Victory medals), Order Leopold Belgium, Mérite Agricole, Croix de Guerre and Montenegrin medal; *b* 8 Nov 1873; *m* 1st 10 June 1896 Lady Ierne Hastings (*d* 5 Jan 1935), dau of 13th Earl of Huntingdon (*qv*), and had:

(1) HENRY HASTINGS SACKVILLE TUFTON, **3rd Baron Hothfield of Hothfield**, JP Westmorland; Lt-Col 15th Hus, Assist Dir PR Home Forces 1942, chm Tattersalls Ctee 1954; *b* 16 March 1897; *m* 18 June 1918 Dorothy (*d* 3 Dec 1981), est dau of William George Raphael, and *dsp* 20 Aug 1961

(2) Peter John Sackville, JP Kent; Capt Queen Victoria's Rifles, KRRC (TA); *b* 7 March 1906; *m* 15 Sept 1944 *Alicia Mary Julia, formely w of Roger Chitty and dau of Brig-Gen Arthur Montagu Perreau, CB, CMG, of Bank End, Appleby, Westmorland, and *dsp* 1 March 1956

(1) Patricia Irene Wilmot; *b* 18 March 1900; *m* 14 Dec 1921 Lt Col Hon George Chenevix Hill (*see* DOWNSHIRE, M, and SANDYS, B)

(2) Noreen Rosamund Anne; *b* 4 Oct 1903; *m* 11 July 1928 Lt-Col Owen Frederick Morton Tudor, 3rd KOH, s of Adml Henry Morton Tudor Tudor, JP, and had:

1a *Idonea Rosamund Ierne; *b* 26 June 1932 *m* 19 Jan 1954 *Baron Nils Taube and has issue

2a *Carole Anne; *b* 26 July 1934; *m* 10 June 1963 *Henry John William Phillips, son of Lt-Col Frank Phillips, DSO, MC (*see* ACTON, B), and has issue

3a Camilla Maryrose; *b* 15 July 1936; *d* unm 5 May 1963

1 (cont.) The **2nd Baron** *m* 2nd 31 Dec 1935 Sybil Augusta (*d* 7 June 1950), dau of John Sant, and *d* 21 Dec 1952

2 Sackville Philip, JP Westmorland; *b* 5 May 1875; *m* 1st 22 April 1911 Cicely Mary Isabel (*dsp* 26 June 1912), est dau of Capt Arthur Blundell George Sandys Hill (*see* DOWNSHIRE M); *m* 2nd 9 Dec 1913 Winifred Mary Ripley (*d* 11 Sept 1970 aged 86), er dau of Edward Ripley Dalton, barrister, and *d* 24 Jan 1936, leaving:

(1) THOMAS SACKVILLE TUFTON, **4th Baron Hothfield of Hothfield**; *b* 20 July 1916; *educ* Eton and Cambridge; *d* unm 1986

(1) Diana Mary; *b* 21 Sept 1917; *m* 13 May 1947 *Lt-Col Charles Henry Freeman Coaker, RA [Lt-Col Charles Coaker, Fairfield, Manningford Bruce, Wilts SN9 6JE], est s of Col Vere Arthur Coaker, DSO, of Richards Hill, Battle, Sussex, and *d* 3 May 1993

3 Charles Henry, CMG (1917); Assist Sec FO and Actg Counsellor Dip Serv, Priv Sec to Parly Sec For Affrs 1910–12; *b* 16 May 1879; *m* 17 Dec 1903 Stella Josephine Faudel, OBE (*d* 28 Oct 1958), yst dau of Sir George Faudel-Philips, 1st Bt (*see* 1940 edn), and *d* 23 Sept 1923, leaving:

(1) GEORGE WILLIAM ANTHONY TUFTON, **5th Baron Hothfield of Hothfield**, TD, DL (Herts 1963); *b* 28 Oct 1904; *educ* Eton and Hertford Coll Oxford (BA 1927); Lt-Col RA (TA) WW II; *m* 3 Dec 1936 Evelyn Margarette (*d* 1989), est dau of Eustace Mordaunt (*see* MORDAUNT, Bt), and *d* 1991, leaving:

1a ANTHONY CHARLES SACKVILLE TUFTON, **6th and present Baron Hothfield of Hothfield**

2a +Nicholas William Sackville [The Hon Nicholas Tufton, The Red House, Barkway, Herts SG8 8EA]; *b* 9 Jan 1946; *educ* Eton and RAC Cirencester; *m* 1978 *Meriel, dau of Maj William Acworth, and has:

1b +Richard Charles; *b* 1980; *educ* Eton

2b +Henry George; *b* 1983; *educ* Eton

1a *Jennifer Margaret [The Hon Mrs Raikes, Parsonage Oasts, Yalding, Kent]; *b* 5 Oct 1937; *m* 25 Sept 1965 *Edward Robert Raikes, yr s of Julian Henry Raikes, of Stone Lodge, Pluckley, Kent, and has issue:

1b *Jason Alexander; *b* 9 Nov 1966; *educ* Stowe and Exeter U; *m* 1992 *Emma, dau of Peter Budgen, and has:

1c *Thomas William; *b* 1994

2c *Alexander Caspian; *b* 1997

2b *Benedick Arthur; *b* 13 Jan 1969; *educ* Eton and LSE

1b *Stella Mary Evelyn; *b* 5 April 1972

(2) +Francis Charles Sackville, VRD [Lt-Cdr Francis Tufton VRD RNVR, Church Farm House, Clothall, Herts SG7 6RG]; *b* 8 Oct 1913; *educ* Eton and Trin Coll Oxford (MA); Lt-Cdr (S) RNVR WW II, slr 1946, Kt Dannebrog; *m* 10 Sept 1942 Eileen Joyce Clara (*d* 1985), yr dau of Sir Edward Henry Goschen, 2nd Bt (*qv*), and has:

1a +Edward Philip Sackville [Edward Tufton Esq, 70 Perrymead St, London SW6]; *b* 18 April 1948; *educ* Eton and Magdalene Coll Cambridge (MA)

1a *Mary Josephine [Mrs John Paxton, Church Farm, Church lane, Upwood, Cambs]; *b* 14 July 1943; *m* 1979 *John Yorkston Paxton and has:

1b *John Edward Sackville; *b* 1985

2b *Charles Thomas Yorkston; *b* 1988

(1) *Susan Stella, JP (Lincs 1958) [Mrs Thomas Coltman JP, Laigh Aldons, Girvan, Ayrshire KA26 0TB]; *b* 12 Feb 1908; *m* 30 Dec 1936 *Col Thomas Alexander Hamilton Coltman, OBE, DL, RA, er s of Maj William Hew Coltman, of Daljarrock, Ayrshire, and has:

1a *Timothy Charles [Timothy Coltman Esq, Skellingthorpe Hall, Lincs LN6 5UU]; *b* 4 July 1939; *educ* Eton and Trin Coll Cambridge (BA 1962); *m* 1st 1 July 1964 Joanna Mary (*d* 1986), only dau of John Richard Bergne-Coupland, of Skellingthorpe Hall; *m* 2nd 1989 *Anne, dau of Rt Rev Kenneth Riches, and by his 1st w has:

1b *Sarah Elizabeth; *b* 24 June 1966

2b *Mary Jane; *b* 2 May 1968

2a *David Alexander [David Coltman Esq, Haystoun House, Peebles EH45 9JG]; *b* 5 Aug 1942; *educ* Eton and Edinburgh U; *m* 1972 *Hon Mary Cecilia, 3rd dau of 1st Viscount Whitelaw (*qv*), and has issue:

1b *Susannah Mary Lavinia; *b* 1987

1 Rosamond; *b* 5 Oct 1877; *m* 1 June 1907 Stuart Gordon Anderson, yst s of Col James Anderson, and *d* 5 June 1957. He *d* 8 Sept 1923

HOULDSWORTH

Arms: Erm. the trunk of a tree in bend raguly eradicated at the base ppr., between three fox's heads erased gu. **Crest:** A stag's head erased gu., attired and collared or, the attires banded with a hank of cotton arg. **Motto:** *Flecti non frangi* ('To be bent, not broken')
Creation: Bt (UK) 20 July 1887.

SIR RICHARD THOMAS REGINALD HOULDSWORTH, 5TH BT, of Reddish, Co Lancaster, and Coodham, Symington, Ayrshire [Sir Richard Houldsworth Bt, Kirkbride, Glenburn, Crosshill, Maybole, Ayrshire KA19 7QA]; *b* 2 Aug 1947; *s* f 1989; *educ* Bredon Sch Tewkesbury and Blanerne Sch Denholm, Roxburghshire; *m* 1st 12 Sept 1970 (*divorce* 1982) Jane, only dau of Alistair Orr, of Sydehead, Beith, Ayrshire, and has:

1 +SIMON RICHARD HENRY; *b* 6 Oct 1971

2 +Nicolas Peter George; *b* 1975

Sir RICHARD *m* 2nd 1992 *Ann Catherine, est dau of Capt Jean Jacques Tremayne, MN, of Sway, Hants, and by her has:

3 +Matthew James; *b* 1992

Lineage: HENRY HOULDSWORTH, of Gonalston, Notts; *b* 1733 (s of Joseph Houldsworth, of Gonalston, by Anne Hall, of Chesterfield); *m* Anne, dau of Thomas Hooton, of Newton, Notts, and had, with other issue:

1 William, of Farnsfield, Notts, and Coltness, Lanarks; *b* 15 May 1770; *m* Sarah, dau of John Hall, of Hoveringham, Notts, and *dsp* 13 Feb 1854

2 Thomas, of Manchester and Coltness; Ld Manor Epperston, Notts; MP Pontefract and N Notts; *b* 13 Sept 1771; *d* unm 1 Sept 1852

3 Henry, of Cranston Hill, nr Glasgow, and Coltness (which he inherited from his bro), JP; *b* 28 June 1774; *m* Jane (*d* 12 Nov 1847), dau of John Richardson, of Glasgow, and *d* 10 Oct 1853, having had, with other issue:

(1) HENRY

(2) John, of Cranston Hill; *b* 12 April 1807; *d* 18 Oct 1859, leaving:

1a Henry

The er son,

HENRY HOULDSWORTH, of Coltness, JP, DL; *b* 4 June 1797; *m* 1st 25 Nov 1823 Helen (*d* 31 May 1837), dau of James Hamilton, of Glasgow, and had, with two other sons:

1 James, of Coltness, JP, DL; *b* 1 Dec 1825; *m* 12 May 1858 Catherine Jane (*d* 2 March 1931), dau of Canon — McGrath, and *d* 8 Sept 1897, leaving issue

2 WILLIAM HENRY (Sir), **1st Bt**

HENRY HOULDSWORTH *m* 2nd 18 Oct 1838 Marianne (*d* 2 Dec 1865), dau of James Burt, of Chorlton, and by her had, with other issue:

3 Arthur Hooton; *b* 11 July 1847; *d* 1890

HENRY HOULDSWORTH *d* 16 Feb 1868; his er s here mentioned,

Sir William Henry Houldsworth, 1st Bt (UK), so *cr* 20 July 1887, of Reddish, Lancs, and Coodham, Ayrshire, DL Ayrshire; *b* 20 Aug 1834; MP Manchester 1883–85 and Manchester NW 1885–1906, Hon LLD Manchester U; *m* 20 Aug 1862 Elizabeth Graham (*d* 11 Dec 1923), dau of Walter Crum, of Thornliebank, Renfrewshire, and *d* 18 April 1917, having had:

1 **Sir Henry Hamilton Houldsworth, 2nd Bt**, JP, DL; *b* 17 Sept 1867; *educ* Eton and Ch Ch Oxford (BA 1891, MA 1894); Capt and Hon Maj 4th Bn Argyll and Sutherland Highrs, Capt (SR) 1915–19, patron living of St Elizabeth's Reddish, served Boer War 1900–01 (Queen's medal with three clasps); *d* unm 18 Dec 1947

2 Walter Crum; *b* 26 Sept 1870; *d* 1880

3 WILLIAM THOMAS REGINALD (Sir), **3rd Bt**

1 Agnes Graham; *m* 24 April 1895 Lt-Col Robert George Buchanan Riddell (*see* RIDDELL, Bt) and *d* 15 March 1955, having had issue

2 Margaret Constance; *m* 26 Sept 1911 Rev Canon Edward Stevenson Gordon Saville, Chaplain to Archbp Canterbury, er s of Edward Bourchier Saville, and *d* 10 April 1952. He *d* 26 Aug 1937

3 Violet Frances Elizabeth, OBE (1920); *m* 28 June 1900 Col Sir Frances Henry Douglas Charlton Whitmore, 1st Bt (*qv*), and *d* 13 June 1927

Sir HENRY's yr bro,

Sir William Thomas Reginald Houldsworth, 3rd Bt, CBE (1946), TD, JP Essex and Ayshire, DL; *b* 24 Aug 1874; *educ* Eton and Ch Ch Oxford (BA 1897, MA 1898); Hon Col (Lt-Col cmdg 1920–23) Ayshire Yeo WW I, Order Nile 3rd Cl; *m* 20 July 1899 Ethel Mary Alberta (*d* 7 May 1937), dau of Capt Thomas Charles Douglas Whitmore (*see* WHITMORE, Bt), and had:

1 REGINALD DOUGLAS HENRY (Sir), **4th Bt**

2 +Walter William Whitmore, TD [Walter Houldsworth Esq TD, The Fold, Sheep St, Stow-on-the-Wold, Glos GL54 1AU]; Maj 149th (Sherwood Foresters) LAA Regt RA, 6th Bn Sherwood Foresters, WW II (despatches); *b* 9 Feb 1906; *m* 28 Nov 1945 *Hazell Marcella, dau of Julian Packer Shepherd, of Barbados, and has:

(1) +Charles William Shepherd [Charles Houldsworth Esq, Hailey House, Duntisbourne Abbots, Glos GL7 7JL]; *b* 19 Dec 1946; *m* 1971 (*separated* 1996) *Jacqueline, only dau of Paul Smith, of Biddestone, Wilts, and has:

1a *Zoë Anne; *b* 1974

2a *Joanna Clare; *b* 1976

(1) *Hazell Mary Fiona; *b* 15 July 1954

1 Evelyn Ethel Edwina; *b* 9 May 1902; *m* 24 April 1930 Maj Richard Edmund Davey, TD, JP, Somerset Yeo, s of Thomas Ruding Davey, JP, of Wraxall Court, Somerset, and *d* 1 March 1967, leaving a s and two daus. He *d* 24 March 1967

Sir WILLIAM *d* 31 Dec 1960; his er son,

Sir Reginald Douglas Henry Houldsworth, 4th Bt, OBE (1944), TD; *b* 9 July 1903; *educ* Shrewsbury and Trin Hall Cambridge; cmded Ayrshire Yeo 1939–42 (Hon Col 1959) and 4 Pack Group Mules 1943–45; *m* 30 April 1934 Margaret (Meg) Mary (*d* 1 Aug 1995), 4th dau of Cecil Emilius Laurie (*see* LAURIE, Bt), and *d* 1989, leaving:

1 Sir RICHARD THOMAS REGINALD, **5th and present Bt**

1 *Myrtle Janet Mary [Mrs Philip Howard, Flat 1, 47 Ladbroke Grove, London W11 3AR]; *b* 19 July 1935; *m* 17 Oct 1959 *Philip Charles Nicholas Howard, jnlst with *The Times*, er s of Peter D Howard, of Hill Farm, Brent Eleigh, Suffolk, and has:

(1) *John Henry Nicholas; *b* 12 Sept 1961

(2) *James Reginald Mark; *b* 1976

(1) *Juliette Margaret; *b* 25 July 1960; *m* 1988 *Justin Henry Francis Whiteley (*see* GUILFORD, E) and has issue

2 *Rosemary Margaret; *b* 6 Sept 1939; *m* 6 Jan 1962 (*divorce* 1990) (William) John Tevenar Usher (*see* USHER, Bt), and has issue

HOUSTOUN-BOSWALL

Arms: Quarterly, 1st and 4th, arg. on a fess sa., between two thistles in chief and a garb in base ppr. three cinquefoils of the first (for BOSWALL); 2nd and 3rd, or a chevron chequy sa. and arg., between three martlets of the second (for HOUSTOUN). **Crests:** 1 A cubit arm grasping a sword ppr. (for BOSWALL), 2 A sand-glass winged ppr. (for HOUSTOUN). **Supporters** (borne by the family in right of their being ancient hereditary Barons of Scotland): On either side a greyhound ppr., collared and chained or. **Mottoes:** 1 (over the BOSWALL crest) *Fortiter* ('Bravely'), 2 (over the HOUSTOUN crest) In time. **Creation:** Bt. (UK) 19 July 1836.

SIR (THOMAS) ALFORD HOUSTOUN-BOSWALL, 8TH BT [Sir Alford Houstoun-Boswall Bt, 18 rue Basse, Biot 06410, France; 15 E 77th St, New York, NY 10021, USA]; *b* 23 May 1947; *s* f 1982; *educ* Lindisfarne; internat economics and business consultant, ptnr Rosedale-Engel, Houstoun-Boswall Partnership, Bermuda, dir Stair and Co, NY, pres Houstoun-Boswall Inc (Fine Arts) NY, lecturer New York U and Metropolitan Museum of Art, chm The Harrodian Sch, London, and The Merlin Sch, London; *m* 1971 (*divorce* 1996) Eliana Michele, dau of Dr John Pearse, of New York, and has:

1 +ALEXANDER ALFORD; *b* 16 Sept 1972

1 *Julia Glencora; *b* 1972

Lineage: This Baronet is heir male of the HOUSTOUNs of Cotreoch, the chiefs of which were heritable Baillies and Justiciaries of the Barony of Busbie, Wigtownshire, and Calderhall, Midlothian.

ANDREW HOUSTOUN (2nd s of William Houstoun, of Cotreoch); *m* 26 July 1656 Catherine Maculloch, only dau of Mrs Mary Keie (dau of 1st Lord Jedburgh; *see* LOTHIAN, M), and had:

ANDREW HOUSTOUN of Gartland; *m* Jean, dau of Sir James Macdowell of Gartland, and had an est s:

ANDREW HOUSTOUN of Calderhall/Calderhaugh; *m* 5 Oct 1694 Isabel, est dau and eventual coheir of William Elphinston of Calderhaugh, and by her had, with a 2nd s (Alexander, of Jordanhill, ancestor of the HOUSTOUNs of Clerkington) and eight daus:

ANDREW HOUSTOUN of Calderhaugh; *b* 25 Dec 1702; *m* Nellie Waddell and *d* 28 July 1786, leaving issue:

Sir William Houstoun, 1st Bt (UK), so *cr* 19 July 1836, GCB, GCH; *b* 10 Aug 1766; Gen, Col 20th Regt; *m* 5 Nov 1808 Lady Jane Maitland (*d* 1 June 1833), widow of Samuel Long (bro of Lord Farnborough) and dau of 7th Earl of Lauderdale (*qv*), and *d* 8 April 1842, leaving, with a yr s (William, Capt 10th Hus, *b* 23 Feb 1811, *m* 1837 Matilda (*d* 1892), widow of Rev L Fraser and dau of E Jesse, and *d* 23 Oct 1872, leaving a s (George, *b* 1841)):

Sir GEORGE AUGUSTUS FREDERICK HOUSTOUN later HOUSTOUN-BOSWALL, **2nd Bt**, DL (Berwicks); Col Gren Gds; *b* 4 Oct 1809; *m* 22 Feb 1847 Euphemia (*d* 29 Dec 1882), only child of Thomas Boswall of Blackadder, and *d* 8 Jan 1886, leaving:

1 **Sir George Lauderdale Houstoun-Boswall, 3rd Bt**, DL (Berwicks); Convenor Berwicks CC; Capt Gren Gds; *b* 11 Dec 1847; *m* 1 March 1877 Phoebe (*d* 24 Dec 1904), dau of Sir Hugh Allan, and *d* 8 Feb 1908, leaving:

(1) **Sir George Reginald Houstoun-Boswall, 4th Bt**, DL (Berwicks); *b* 6 Dec 1877; Capt 4th Bn Gren Gds Boer War 1900–02 (Queen's medal with three clasps) and WW I; *m* 25 Feb 1913 Naomi Veronica (*d* 26 Nov 1970), yr dau of Col Thomas Henry Anstey, RE, and was *ka* 27 Sept 1915, having had:

1a Sheila Mary; *b* 28 Dec 1913; *d* 15 Jan 1914

2a *(Elizabeth) Phoebe; *b* 21 May 1915; *m* 25 May 1940 (*divorce* 1956) Maj John Alastair Livingston Timpson, MC, Scots Gds, yst s of Capt Lawrence Timpson, of Maizeland, Barrytown-on-Hudson, NY, and Appleton Manor, Abingdon (*see* Section Van Buren AMERICAN PRESIDENTIAL FAMILIES, 1994, Morris Genealogical Books SA), and has:

1b *Nicholas George Lawrence [Nicholas Timpson Esq, Ardington Croft, Wantage, Oxon]; *b* 21 Feb 1941; *educ* Eton; late Lt Scots Gds; *m* 1972

*Lady Selina Catherine Meade, er dau of 6th Earl of Clanwilliam (*qv*), and has:

1c *Lawrence Rupert John; *b* 1974

1c *Catherine Selina Alexandra; *b* 1979

2b *Rupert Alastair Hugh; *b* 18 June 1945; *educ* Eton; *m* 1980 *Anne, est dau of H Meigh, of Ash House, Cheltenham

3b *Gerard Brian Sebastian; *b* 29 July 1946; *educ* Eton; *m* 1972 *Siobhan Anne Southwell, dau of Maurice Fitzgerald, of Hill Place, Haywards Heath, Sussex

1b *Veronica Naomi Livingston; *b* 21 Jan 1950; *m* 1973 (*divorce* 1987) 3rd Earl Peel (*qv*) and has issue

(2) **Sir (Thomas) Randolph Houstoun-Boswall, 5th Bt**; Capt 14th Service Bn Roy Scots, formerly 3rd Bn; *b* 5 Feb 1882; *m* 8 Feb 1912 Edith Mary (*d* 30 Sept 1962), yr dau of Jarvis Salter, of Wribbenhall, Worcs, and *d* 4 Dec 1953, having had:

1a Thomas Gordon; *b* 20 Feb, *d* 7 May 1915

2a George Cleeton; Lt Roy Scots WW II; *b* 1 Sept 1920; *kas* Hong Kong 11 Dec 1941

1a *Pamela Nanine; *b* 6 June 1916; *m* 30 April 1938 William Oliver Calvert (*d* 1959), s of Capt Albert James Calvert, RSG, and has:

1b *Ian Arbuckle; *b* 1939

2b *George Arbuckle; *b* 1951

1b *Susan Arbuckle; *b* 1942

2a *Patricia Mary [Mrs Leslie Le Mottee, The Willows, 34 Kingsway, Ewell, Surrey]; *b* 16 Oct 1917; *m* 8 July 1939 *Maj Leslie Le Mottee, RA, and has:

1b *Judith Christina; *b* 1942

2b *Pamela Mary; *b* 1947

3a *Elizabeth Flora [Mrs Anthony Hawker, Honeycomb Cottage, Shalden, nr Alton, Hants]; *b* 12 May 1923; *m* 6 Dec 1941 *Maj Anthony Arthur Hawker, MC, RA (TA), yr s of Maj Arthur Edward Hawker, and has:

1b *Nicholas George James; *b* 1942

1b *Victoria Jane; *b* 1956

(1) Evelyn Mary Alice; *m* 8 Aug 1914 Maj Alexander Houstoun, late RFA, of Mayshiel, and had issue

2 William HOUSTOUN-BOSWALL later HOUSTOUN-BOSWALL-PRESTON (roy licence 7 April 1883, added under terms of will of his great-uncle Sir Henry Lindsay Preston, Bt); MA, barrister; *b* 11 April 1849; *d* unm 1885

3 Thomas Alford HOUSTOUN-BOSWALL later HOUSTOUN-BOSWALL-PRESTON (roy licence 1886), of Tweed Hill, Berwick-on-Tweed, JP, DL (Berwicks); Hon Col, Col cmdg SE Scotland Art; *b* 21 July 1850; *m* 8 May 1883 Alice Mary (*d* 9 July 1916), only dau of William Cunard (*see* 1970 edn CUNARD, Bt), and *d* 3 Jan 1918, leaving:

(1) GORDON (Sir), **6th Bt**

(2) Alistair, CBE (1920); *b* 20 Dec 1888; Maj RASC, Assist Dir Rd Tport Min Food WW II (despatches)

(1) Euphemia Constance (Effie); *b* 5 March 1884; *m* 1st 24 Oct 1906 Maj Antony Edmund Gibbs (*see* ALDENHAM and HUNSDON OF HUNSDON, B) and had issue; *m* 2nd 25 July 1934 Cyril Chester Chester-Master, 2nd s of Thomas William Chester Chester-Master, JP, of The Abbey and Knole Park, Glos, and *d* 21 April 1966. He *d* 18 April 1961

4 Robert HOUSTOUN-BOSWALL later HOUSTOUN-BOSWALL-PRESTON (roy licence 20 July 1908); *b* 11 Dec 1852; *d* unm 12 Feb 1913

5 Alfred, JP (Northumberland); Lt E Lothian Yeo Cav; *b* 13 Feb 1854; *m* 22 July 1891 Emmeline Charlotte Frances (*d* 6 June 1947), dau of Capt Robert Henry de Winton, of Graftonbury, Herefs, and *d* 29 April 1920, leaving:

(1) William Evelyn (Sir), KCMG (1949, CMG 1942), MC (1918); Br Political Rep Bulgaria 1944–47, Envoy Extrdy and Min Plen Lebanon 1947–51 (ret 1951), Capt Black Watch WW I (wounded, despatches, Croix de Guerre); *b* 5 June 1892; *m* 2 June 1921 Margaret Dorothy, OBE (*d* 15 Feb 1957), er dau of George Anson Byron (*see* BYRON, B), and *d* 2 Aug 1960, leaving:

1a *Diana Mary; *b* 2 April 1925; *m* 18 May 1961 G/Capt Charles Blundell Owen, DSO, DFC, AFC, RAF, est s of Montague Blundell Owen, of Spain, and has:

1b *William Francis Blundell; *b* 5 Jan 1963

2b *Oliver Peter Stevens; *b* 22 May 1964

(2) Charles; *b* 17 April 1894; Lt Res Offrs RSG WW I, ADC to Govr Bahamas 1933–35; *m* 2 Oct 1935 *Marguerite Yvonne Savage, dau of Herbert Pritchard, of Toronto and Nassau, and *d* 24 Feb 1946, leaving:

1a *Jane Carolyn [Mrs John Trevor, Northborough Manor, Peterborough, Cambs PE6 9BJ]; *b* 20 Aug 1936; *m* 14 Sept 1957 *John Clyfford Trevor, er s of Clyfford Trevor, and has:

1b *Mark Clyfford; *b* 4 Aug 1961; *m* 1985 *Elise Thayer, est dau of David Green, and has issue:

1c *Alexander John Houstoun; *b* 1990

1c *Natasha Thayer Houstoun; *b* 1992

2b *Richard Charles Houstoun; *b* 7 Nov 1969

1b *Carolyn Elizabeth; *b* 30 June 1959; *m* 1989 *Patrick Lahiff and has:

1c *Max Alexander Patrick; *b* 1989

2c *Jack William Oliver; *b* 1991

2b *Emma Cecil; *b* 12 Aug 1963; *m* 1991 *David Blake and has:

1c *Rory Dominic David; *b* 1993

(3) John Francis; Maj 1st Roy Dragoons (SR), WW I (despatches) and WW II, ADC to Govr S Australia 1920–22; *b* 31 May 1895; *educ* Wellington; *m* 11 Aug 1951 Cecil Marjorie (*d* 13 April 1971), yst dau of Charles James Gwyer, JP, DL, and *dsp* 20 Nov 1963

1 Evelyn Lucy; twin with Alfred; *d* unm 5 Dec 1932

The 5th Bt's cousin,

Sir GORDON HOUSTOUN-BOSWALL-PRESTON later HOUSTOUN-BOSWALL (when *s* to btcy), **6th Bt**; *b* 15 March 1887; *educ* Marlborough; Maj 1st Life Gds WW I; *m* 11 July 1916 Daisy Copeland (*d* 22 June 1965), dau of Edwin Copeland Waller, of Gt Yarmouth and Fulham, and *d* 28 Feb 1961, leaving:

1 **Sir Thomas Houstoun-Boswall, 7th Bt**; *b* 13 Feb 1919; *educ* Nautical Coll Pangbourne; P/O RAFVR WW II; *m* 1st 7 May 1945 Margaret, dau of George Bullen-Smith, of Arlington, Sussex, and had:

(1) Sir (THOMAS) ALFORD HOUSTOUN-BOSWALL, **8th and present Bt**

(1) *Amber Georgina [Mrs Alan Moore, 14 Stafford Terrace, London W8]; *b* 5 June 1946; *m* 4 Oct 1969 *Alan Moore, only s of Lionel Moore, of Jersey, and has:

1a *Thomas James; *b* 1980

1a *Georgina; *b* 1972

2a *Chloe; *b* 1977

1 (cont.) **Sir Thomas** *m* 2nd 1971 *Anne-Lucie, dau of Pierre Naquet, and *d* 16 May 1982, leaving by her:

(2) *Sophie; *b* 10 June 1973

2 +Alistair; *b* 16 Jan 1931

HOWARD

Arms: Az. two wings conjoined in lure and in chief as many cross-crosslets fitchée or, a chief or, thereon between two leaves of the india rubber tree ppr. a pale vert charged with a bezant. **Crest:** A toucan holding in the dexter claw and feeding on an apple, slipped and leaved, all ppr. **Motto:** To the core. **Creation:** Bt. (UK) 1 Dec 1955.

SIR (HAMILTON) EDWARD DE COUCEY HOWARD, 2ND BT, of Great Rissington, Co Gloucester, GBE (1972) [Sir Edward Howard Bt GBE, Courtlands, Bishops Walk, Shirley Hills, Surrey CRO 5BA]; *b* 29 Oct 1915; *s* f 1967; *educ* Radley and Worcester Coll Oxford; F/O RAFVR WW II, memb London Stock Exchange, City London: Alderman, Sheriff 1966, Ld Mayor 1971–72, Ld Lt 1976–90; chm Advance Electronics Ltd, Master Gardeners' Co 1961–62, Pres City London Sheriffs Soc 1973–, KStJ 1972, Hon DSc London; *m* 10 July 1943 *Elizabeth Howarth, dau of Maj Percy Howarth Ludlow, of Ontario, and has:

1 +DAVID HOWARTH SEYMOUR [David Howard Esq, 25 Luke Street, London EC2]; *b* 29 Dec 1945; *educ* Radley and Worcester Coll Oxford (MA); Alderman City London, Liveryman Gardeners' Co (Master 1990–91); *m* 6 June 1968 *Valerie Picton, only dau of Derek Weatherly Crosse, of Broadstairs, and has:

(1) +Robert Picton Seymour; *b* 28 Jan 1971

(2) +James Picton Seymour; *b* 1979

(1) *Caroline Picton Seymour; *b* 1970

(2) *Victoria Picton Seymour; *b* 1975

2 + John Ludlow Seymour; *b* 5 Sept 1948; *educ* Grenville Coll, Devon; *m* 14 May 1983 * Virginia, only dau of Richard Purkis, of Shirley, Surrey, and has:

(1) +Rupert; *b* 1988

(1) *Emily; *b* 1990

(2) *Harriet Elizabeth; *b* 1993

Lineage: WILLIAM HOWARD, of Gt Rissington, Glos; had:

WILLIAM ALBERT HOWARD; *b* 15 Nov 1853; *educ* Burford GS Oxon; co dir; *m* 2 May 1882 Elizabeth Mary (*d* 4 Feb 1910), dau of John Henry Seymour, of Stratford-on-Avon, and *d* 10 March 1938, leaving, with an er s (William John, *b* 4 Nov 1884, emigrated to Australia):

Sir (Harold Walter) Seymour Howard, 1st Bt (UK), so *cr* 1 Dec 1955; *b* 8 April 1886; Min Aircraft Production WW II, Lt and Alderman City London 1945–60, Sheriff 1944, Ld Mayor 1954, KGStJ 1954, Kt Cdr Mil Order Christ Portugal, ktd 1955; *m* 10 Sept 1913 Edith Maud (*d* 24 Sept 1962), dau. of Edward James Turner, of Warminster, Wilts, and *d* 15 April 1967, leaving:

1 Sir (HAMILTON) EDWARD DE COUCEY HOWARD, **2nd and present Bt.**

2 David Seymour de Coucey; *b* 5 Feb 1919; *educ* Radley and Worcester Coll Oxford; *m* 14 April 1942 (*divorce* 1949) Jean McMurdo, dau of Thomas McMurdo Heywood, and *d* 29 Nov 1954, leaving:

(1) *Jennifer Anne de Coucey [Miss Jennifer Howard, Bericote, Peachfield Rd, Malvern Wells, Worcs]; *b* Sept 1945

HOWARD DE WALDEN

Arms: Quarterly, 1st and 4th, erminois on a cross sa. five crescents arg. (for ELLIS); 2nd and 3rd, or on a bend az., a star betwixt two crescents of the field, in chief a crescent gu., all within a bordure engrailed of the last (for SCOTT). **Crests:** 1 On a mount vert a goat's head erased arg. (for ELLIS), 2 A dexter hand holding an annulet or, in which is set a carbuncle ppr. (for SCOTT). **Supporters:** On either side a lion arg., charged on the neck with three trefoils slipped vert within a collar gemel gu. **Mottoes:** 1 *Non quo sed quomodo* ('Not by whom but how'), 2 *In tenebris lux* ('Light in darkness').
Creations: B. (E) 5 Dec 1597 (Howard de Walden), and (UK) 15 July 1826 (Seaford).

THE 9TH LORD (BARON) **HOWARD DE WALDEN** and **5th Baron Seaford of Seaford**, Co Sussex (John Osmael Scott-Ellis, TD (1953)) [The Rt Hon The Lord Howard de Walden TD, Avington Manor, Hungerford, Berks RG17 0UL; Flat K, 90 Eaton Square, London SW1W 9AG]; *b* 27 Nov 1912, *s* f 1946; *educ* Eton and Magdalene Coll Cambridge (BA 1934); Maj Westminster Dragoons (TA) WW II; dir Howard de Walden Estates Ltd, Alliance Assur and Sun Alliance and London Insur, Steward Jockey Club 1955–57 and 1962–64, Sr Steward 1957, 1964 and 1976, chm Howard Ctee; *m* 1st 21 Aug 1934 Countess Irene Harrach (Nucci) (*d* 17 Jan 1975), yst dau of Count Hans Albrecht Harrach, of Munich, and has:

1 +(MARY) HAZEL CARIDWEN [The Hon Mrs Czernin, 47 Queens Gate Gardens, London SW7 5ND; White Oak House, Highclere, Berks RG20 9RJ]; *b* 12 Aug 1935; coheiress presumptive (with her three yr sisters) to Barony of Howard de Walden only (as are all females or issue of females with + against their names); *m* 20 Nov 1957 *(Count) Joseph Czernin, only s of Count Franz Joseph Czernin, and has:

(1) +Peter John Joseph; *b* 1 Jan 1966; *m* 17 Sept 1994 *Lucinda, yr dau of Richard Wright, of Wilbraham Temple, Gt Wilbraham, Cambs, and has:

1a +Audrey Serena Angela; *b* 13 Aug 1997

(1) +Charlotte Mary Sidonia [Mrs Neil Girkins, Kingston House, Kingston, Dorset BH20 5LQ]; *b* 28 Nov 1958; *m* 1986 *Neil A Girkins, s of Gerard Girkins, of Bordeaux, and has:

1a +Benedict James Seward; *b* 1992

2a +Maximilian George Seward; *b* 18 Sept 1995

1a +Emily Alexandra Mary; *b* 1991

(2) +Henrietta Mary Rosario; *b* 10 Jan 1960; *m* 1985 *C Alistair Currey and has:

1a +Camilla Rose Francesca; *b* 1986

2a +Alice Catarina Mary; *b* 1988

3a +Louisa Henrietta Anne; *b* 1990

4a +Rosanna Mariella Claire; *b* 1992

5a +Isabelle Quinta Marina; *b* 28 June 1996

(3) +Alexandra Mary Romana; *b* 6 Nov 1961; *m* 1992 *David Mark Noël Kelly and has issue (*see* NORFOLK, D)

(4) +Philippa Mary Loretta; *b* 3 July 1963

(5) +Isabelle Mary Benedicta; *b* 27 Dec 1967

2 +(BLANCHE) SUSAN FIONODBHAR [The Hon Mrs Buchan of Auchmacoy, Auchmacoy House, Ellon, Aberdeen AB41 9RB; 30 Chipstead St, London SW6 3SS]; *b* 6 Oct 1937; *m* 8 Feb 1961 *Capt David William Sinclair Buchan of Auchmacoy, only s of Capt Stephen Lloyd Trevor (*see* CAITHNESS, E), and has:

(1) +(John) Charles Augustus David; *b* 1 March 1963

(2) +James Alexander Stephen; *b* 27 Sept 1964

(3) +Thomas Richard Sinclair; *b* 22 Jan 1966

(4) +Robert Edward William; *b* 22 July 1968

(1) +Sophia Jane Elizabeth; *b* 5 March 1962; *m* 1991 *David William Hamilton Ruck and has:

1a +Matilda Rose Athena; *b* 1994

2a +Cordelia Mary Augusta; *b* 5 March 1996

3 +JESSICA JANE VRONWY [The Hon Mrs White, Farnborough Downs Farm, Wantage, Oxon OX12 8NW]; *b* 6 Aug 1941; *m* 12 July 1966 *Adrian Tancred White, er s of Dr Harold Denis White by Phyllida Mary, only dau of Alfred Robert Warren by Constance Anne Tancred (*see* LAWSON-TANCRED, Bt), and has:

(1) +Nicholas John Sebastian; *b* 29 March 1967; *m* 31 May 1997 *Cristina, yr dau of Dr Gaetano Caltagirone, of Rome

(2) +Simon James Alexander; *b* 3 June 1968

(3) +Richard Dominic Edward; *b* 3 June 1970

(4) +Michael Philip Alastair; *b* 24 May 1977

4 +CAMILLA ANNE BRONWEN [The Hon Mrs Acloque, Alderley Grange, Wotton-under-Edge, Glos GL12 7QT]; *b* 1 April 1947; *m* 16 Nov 1971 *Guy Acloque and has:

(1) +Alexander John Sebastian; *b* 8 Jan 1978

(2) +Henrietta Mary Rose; *b* 28 Aug 1979

(3) +Laura Isabella Helen; *b* 28 Aug 1979

The 9th BARON *m* 2nd 1978 *Gillian Margaret, only dau of Cyril Francis Stuart Buckley and formerly w of 17th Viscount Mountgarret (*qv*)

Lineage (of Howard): The 4th DUKE OF NORFOLK (*qv*) had by his 2nd w an est s:

THOMAS HOWARD, **1st Lord** (Baron) **Howard de Walden** (E), so *cr* by writ of summons to Parl 5 Dec 1597, also *cr* 21 July 1603 EARL OF SUFFOLK (*see* SUFFOLK and BERKSHIRE, E); *b* 24 Aug 1561; *d* 28 May 1626, leaving by his 2nd w:

THEOPHILUS HOWARD, **2nd Lord** (Baron) **Howard de Walden** and 2nd EARL OF SUFFOLK; *b* 13 Aug 1584; *d* 3 June 1640, leaving, with other issue:

JAMES HOWARD, **3rd Lord** (Baron) **Howard de Walden** and 3rd EARL OF SUFFOLK; *bapt* 10 Feb 1619/20; had by his 1st w:

1 ESSEX Howard; *m* 4 March 1666/7 Edward GRIFFIN, 1st Baron Griffin of Braybrooke (*d* Tower of London, imprisoned there for treason as a Jacobite 10 Nov 1710) and *d* on or after 31 Jan 1704/5, having had:

(1) JAMES GRIFFIN, 2nd BARON GRIFFIN OF BRAYBROOKE; *bapt* 15 Dec 1667; MP (Tory) Brackley 1685–87; *m* 29 Nov 1684 Anne (*d* 1707), dau and sole heiress of Richard Raynsford, of Dallington, Northants (est s of Sir Richard Raynsford, Ld Ch Justice, by Anne, dau of Richard Nevill(e), of Billingbear, Berks; *see* ABERGAVENNY, M), and *d* 31 Oct 1715, leaving:

1a EDWARD GRIFFIN, 3rd and last BARON GRIFFIN OF BRAYBROOKE; *bapt* 17 Oct 1693; *educ* Rugby and Ch Ch Oxford; *m* 1713 Mary, dau of Anthony Welden, of Well, Lincs, and *dspl* June 1742, when the Barony expired, leaving by Bridgett, dau of Samuel Taylor, of Stretton, Warwicks:

1b Edward; inherited his f's estates, also the Mastership of Magdalene Coll Cambridge

1a Elizabeth; *m* 1st Henry GREY, formerly NEVILLE (*see* BRAYBROOKE, B, also ABERGAVENNY, M); *m* 2nd 4 June 1741 1st Earl of Portsmouth (*qv*) and *dsp* July 1762

2a Anne; *m* William Whitwell, of Oundle, Northants, and *d* 1770, leaving:

1b JOHN GRIFFIN WHITWELL later GRIFFIN (Act of Parl 1749), **4th Lord** (Baron) **Howard de Walden** (abeyance terminated in his favour 3 Aug 1784) and 1st LORD BRAYBROOK, BARON OF BRAYBROOKE, Co Northampton (GB; *qv*), so *cr* 5 Sept 1788, with special remainder to his distant cousin Richard Aldworth Nevill(e), KB (1761); *b* 13 March 1719; *educ* Winchester; Maj Gen 1759, Lt Gen 1765, Gen 1778, FM 1796, Col 33rd Foot 1760–66, 1st Horse Gren Gds 1766–88 and 4th Dragoons 1788–97; MP (Whig) Andover 1749–84, Adj-Gen April-Dec 1778, Ld Lt Essex 1784–97; *m* 1st 9 March 1748/9 Anna Maria, dau of John, Baron Schutz; *m* 2nd 11 June 1765 Catherine, dau of William Clayton, of Harleyford, Bucks, and *dsp* 25 May 1797, when the Barony of Howard de Walden fell again into abeyance

1b Mary; *m* William PARKER later GRIFFIN (roy licence 3 June 1797), DD, and *dsp* 17 Nov 1799

The 3rd Lord (Baron) Howard de Walden *m* 2nd 13 Feb 1650 Barbara (*d* 13 Dec 1680), dau of Sir Edward Villiers (*see* JERSEY, E) and widow of Sir Richard Wentworth, and by her had issue; *m* 3rd 17 May 1682 Anne (*dsp* 19 Oct 1720), dau of 1st Earl of Manchester (*see* MANCHESTER, D), and *dspm* 7 Jan 1688/9, leaving by his 2nd w:

2 ELIZABETH Howard; *b* 1656; *m* Sir Thomas FELTON, 4th Bt (*d* 1691), of Playford, Suffolk, and *d* 1681, leaving:

(1) ELIZABETH Felton; uncuccessfully claimed Barony of Howard de Walden 1691; *m* 25 July 1695 John HERVEY, 1st Earl of Bristol (*see* BRISTOL, M), and *d* 2 May 1741, leaving an er s:

1a John, *Lord Hervey*; *b* 13 Oct 1696; *m* 29 Oct 1720 Mary (*d* 2 Sept 1768), dau of Brig-Gen Nicholas Lepell, and *dvp* 5 Aug 1743, leaving, with other issue:

1b GEORGE WILLIAM HERVEY, 2nd EARL OF BRISTOL; *d* unm 18 March 1775

2b AUGUSTUS JOHN HERVEY, 3rd EARL OF BRISTOL; *m* 4 Aug 1744 Elizabeth, dau of Col Thomas Chudleigh, and *dsp* 23 Dec 1779

3b Rt Rev FREDERICK AUGUSTUS HERVEY, **5th Lord** (Baron) **Howard De Walden** and 4th EARL OF BRISTOL; Bp Derry; *m* 10 Aug 1752 Elizabeth (*d* 15 Dec 1800), dau of Sir Jermyn Davers, 4th Bt, and *d* 8 July 1803, having had, with other issue:

1c John Augustus, *Lord Hervey*; Capt RN; *b* 1 Jan 1757; *m* 4 Oct 1779 Elizabeth (*d* 4 Sept 1818), dau of Colin Drummond, of Megginch Castle, Perthshire, and *dvp* 10 Jan 1796, leaving issue:

(1) ELIZABETH CATHERINE CAROLINE Hervey; *b* 1 Aug 1780; *m* 2 Aug 1798 Charles Rose ELLIS, **1st Baron Seaford of Seaford** (*see* below), and *d* 21 Jan 1803, leaving an est s:

1e CHARLES AUGUSTUS ELLIS, **6th Lord** (Baron) **Howard de Walden and 2nd Baron Seaford of Seaford**

Lineage (of Ellis): JOHN ELLIS, of a family from Wrexham, Denbighs; migrated to Jamaica *temp* CHARLES II; Capt 1685; memb House of Assembly for St Katherine, St George and St Mary 1688–1706; later Maj; *m* Martha 1 (*bur* 27 March 1698) and was *bur* 1 Sept 1706, having had, with other issue, including a yr s

(George, Memb for St George 1701–02, *b* 26 Aug 1677) and a dau (Martha, *b* 14 Jan 1684, *m* 16 Sept 1701 Francis March, Memb House of Assembly 1704–22):

JOHN ELLIS; Memb Assembly 1701–09 for St George, St Katherine and Port Royal; *bapt* 26 Dec 1678 aged three; *m* Elizabeth Grace (*d* 1718), dau of Col George Needham, Speaker House of Assembly (*see* KILMOREY, E), and *d* on or after 7 Feb 1710, leaving an est s:

GEORGE ELLIS; Memb Assembly for Hanover 1726–33 and Westmorland, Ch Justice Jamaica 12 Feb 1736; *bapt* 20 Nov 1704; *m* 8 Nov 1726 Elizabeth (*d* Jan 1846), dau of Peter Beckford, Speaker House of Assembly, sis of William Beckford, Lord Mayor, MP London, and aunt of William Beckford, MP, of Fonthill Abbey, Wilts (*see* HUNTLY, M), and had:

1 George; Memb House of Assembly for St George 1751; *m* Susanna Charlotte (*m* 2nd Sir David Lindsay, 3rd Bt, of Evelick), dau of Samuel Long, of Longville, Capt Queen Caroline's Dragoons, memb Cncl of Jamaica, custos precinct of Clarendon and Vere, and Keeper King's Palace Newmarket, Cambs, sis of Edward Long, historian of Jamaica, Ch Judge Admlty Court there, by Katherine Maria, w of Sir Henry Moore, 1st Bt, Lt-Govr Jamaica and Govr New York, and *d* 1753, leaving a posthumous s:

(1) George, of Sunninghill, Berks; MP Seaford; *m* 10 Sept 1800 Anne, dau of Sir Peter Parker, 1st Bt, of Basingbourn, Adml of the Fleet, and *dsp* 10 April 1815

2 JOHN

3 William Beckford; Memb Ho Assembly 1756–64 for St Mary and St George; *m* 15 Dec 1757 Susanna Addenbrooke and was *bur* 16 Dec 1764, having had:

(1) William Beckford; Memb Ho Assembly for Portland 1793; *b* 1761; *d* June 1795

(1) Anna Maria; *b* 1759; lost at sea with her uncle John Ellis 1782

4 Robert Julines; *d* under age at Eton

5 Bathsua Hering; *d* unm 1783

GEORGE ELLIS was *bur* 26 March 1740; his 2nd son,

JOHN ELLIS; Memb Ho Assembly 1752–69 for St Mary, St George and St Katherine, called to the Cncl 1769, custos precinct of St Mary and St George; *m* 13 Nov 1754 Elizabeth, dau of John Pallmer, Ch Justice Jamaica, and was lost with his w and niece en route to England 1782, leaving, with an er s (John, of Hurlingham, Middx, *b* 5 Aug 1757, *m* 1795 Antoinette (*d* Sept 1829), dau of Adml of the Fleet Sir Peter Parker, 1st Bt, of Basingbourn, and *d* 18 Feb 1832, leaving issue; *see* RIDLEY, V):

CHARLES ROSE ELLIS, **1st Baron Seaford of Seaford**, Co Sussex (UK), so *cr* 15 July 1826; *b* 19 Dec 1771; MP (Tory) Heytesbury 1793–96, Seaford 1796–1806 and 1812–26 and E Grinstead 1807–12; *m* 1st 2 Aug 1798 Elizabeth Catherine Caroline (*d* 21 Jan 1803), gdau of 4th Earl of Bristol (*see* **Lineage (of Howard)** above); *m* 2nd 2 Oct 1840 Anne Louisa Emily (*d* 2 Nov 1877), widow of V-Adml Sir Thomas Masterman Hardy, Bt, and dau of Adml Hon Sir George Cranfield Berkeley (*see* BERKELEY, B), and *d* 1 July 1845, having by his 1st w had:

1 CHARLES AUGUSTUS, **2nd/6th Baron**

2 Augustus Frederick; Lt-Col 60th Royal Rifles, MP; *b* 17 Sept 1800; *m* 25 June 1828 Mary Frances Thurlow (*m* 2nd Wilhelm, Baron von Munster, Chamberlain to the Duke of Saxe Meiningen, and *d* 12 Sept 1851), dau of Sir David Cunynghame, 5th Bt (*qv*), and *d* 16 Aug 1841, leaving:

(1) Charles David Cunynghame; Maj 60th Rifles Kaffir War 1851–53, Crimea 1855–56 and in India 1858–59 (three medals); *b* 25 July 1833; *m* 17 Nov 1859 Emily (*d* 19 Nov 1924 aged 91), dau of Maj-Gen Sir Guy Campbell, 1st Bt, CB (*qv*), and *d* 5 Dec 1906, leaving:

1a Augustus Frederick Guy; MLC Jamaica; *b* 10 Dec 1868; *m* 10 Jan 1899 Mary Agnes, widow of Hon B G Levy, of Jamaica, and dau of Hon Henry Westmorland, of Jamaica, and *d* 13 March 1927

1a Mary Pamela; *m* 2 July 1889 Col David Milne-Home, DL, RHG (*d* 19 Nov 1901), of Wedderburn, and *d* 7 Aug 1936, leaving issue

2a Helen Louisa Georgina; *m* 16 April 1885 James Grahame Stewart (*d* 5 Oct 1913) and *d* 6 Aug 1934, leaving issue

3a Lucy Emily Madeline Genevieve; *d* unm 3 Dec 1957

(2) Arthur Edward Augustus (Sir), GCVO, CSI; Serjeant-at-Arms Ho Lds 1898–1901, Maj-Gen Gren Gds, Extra Equerry to HM EDWARD VII and Comptroller Ld Chamberlain's Dept 1901–07, served Crimea 1854–56 and India 1859–66; *b* 13 Dec 1837; *m* 2 May 1864 Hon Mina Frances Labouchere (*d* 4 Sept 1917), dau and coheir of 1st Baron Taunton, and *d* 11 June 1907, leaving:

1a Arthur Henry Augustus, CB (1931); Clerk H of C; *b* 13 Feb 1866; *d* 2 June 1934

2a Gerald Montagu Augustus; Maj Rifle Bde, Gentleman Usher to TM EDWARD VII 1908–10 and GEORGE V 1910–19, Extra Gentleman Usher to TM GEORGE V 1919–36, EDWARD VIII 1936 and GEORGE VI 1937–52, Page of Honour to HM QUEEN VICTORIA, served NWF Campaign India 1897–98 (medal with clasp), Boer War 1899–1900 (wounded, medal with five clasps) and WW I (wounded twice); *b* 13 Sept 1872; *d* unm 29 May 1953

1a Mary Evelyn; *m* 17 Dec 1885 Ralph Sneyd, of Keele, Staffs, and *d* 30 Aug 1923

2a Albertha Lily Magdalen; *d* unm 15 May 1948

3a Alexandra Mina; *m* 4 Nov 1899 Sir Arthur Henry Hardinge, GCMG, KCB, PC (*d* 27 Dec 1933), and *d* 23 March 1949, leaving issue (*see* HARDINGE, V)

4a Evelyn Mary; *m* 22 June 1898 Walter W Kerr (*see* LOTHIAN, M) and *d* 10 Dec 1934

5a Dorothy; *m* 10 Aug 1899 8th Baron Wharton (*qv*) and *d* 3 Aug 1944, leaving issue

(1) Mary Georgiana Frances; *m* 30 Dec 1858 Gen Hon Sir Arthur Edward Hardinge, KCB, CIE (*d* 15 July 1892), and *d* 10 Jan 1917, leaving issue (*see* HARDINGE, V)

(2) Annie Eliza Margaret; *m* 13 June 1859 Col Sir Charles Edward Mansfield, KCMG (*d* 31 July 1907), bro of 1st Baron Sandhurst (*qv*), and *d* 21 Feb 1922, leaving issue

(3) Augusta Louisa Caroline; *m* 25 Dec 1861 8th Baron Monson (*qv*) and *d* 21 May 1936, having had issue

1 Eliza; *d* 1820

The 1st BARON SEAFORD OF SEAFORD *d* 1 July 1845; his son,

CHARLES AUGUSTUS ELLIS, **6th Lord** (Baron) **Howard de Walden** (claim granted Feb 1807) and **2nd Baron Seaford of Seaford**, GCB (1838); *b* 5 June 1799; *educ* Eton; Capt Gren Gds 1822; Br Minister Stockholm 1832, Lisbon 1833–46 (Kt Tower and Sword of Portugal) and Brussels 1846–68; *m* 8 Nov 1828 Lady Lucy Joan Cavendish-Bentinck-Scott (added by roy licence 26 Nov 1889 SCOTT to ELLIS and *d* 29 July 1899), 4th dau of 4th Duke of Portland (*see* PORTLAND, E), and had:

1 FREDERICK GEORGE, **7th/3rd Baron**

2 William Charles (Rev); MA Oxon, Rector Bothal, Morpeth; *b* 22 July 1835; *m* 16 Dec 1873 Henrietta Elizabeth (*d* 10 Feb 1915), dau of Henry Metcalfe Ames, of Linden, and *d* 20 June 1923, leaving:

(1) Henry Guysulf Bertram; barrister, BA Oxon, Lt RASC WW I; *b* 7 March 1875; *m* 5 Jan 1911 Kathleen Roberta (*d* 24 Nov 1940), only dau of William Charles Mitchell, of Marmont, Co Down, and *d* 25 March 1947, leaving:

1a William Felton; Maj RASC WW II; *b* 27 Nov 1912; *educ* Cheltenham and Trin Coll Cambridge (BA 1936); *m* 16 March 1940 Edwina (*d* 1977), dau of Maj Reginald Edwin Bond, IA, and *d* 1978, leaving:

1b +COLIN HUMPHREY FELTON [Colin Ellis Esq, Bush Farm, West Knoyle, Warminster, Wilts BA12 6AE]; *b* 19 April 1946; heir presumptive to Barony of Seaford; *educ* Sherborne; *m* 1st 2 Jan 1971 (*divorce* 1992) Susan, dau of R H Magill, of Lisnamore, Crossgar, Co Down; *m* 2nd 1993 *Penelope Mary Bastin, and by his 1st w has:

1c +Benjamin Felton Thomas; *b* 1976

2c +Humphrey Henry Guysulf; *b* 1983

1c +Harriett Fay; *b* 1973

2c +Charlotte Susan; *b* 1975

1b +Jill Kathleen [Mrs Jeremy Anderson, The Vicarage, Christchurch Rd, Epsom, Surrey]; *b* 18 March 1944; *m* 15 June 1968 *Jeremy Dudgeon Anderson, s of Maurice Anderson, of Kenya, and has:

1c +William Maurice; *b* 1973

1c +Kathleen Fleur; *b* 1971

1a Henrietta Roberta Elizabeth; *b* 30 Oct 1911; *m* 10 April 1943 *Thomas Stewart Lewis Russell [Thomas Russell Esq, 44 Churchside, Vigo Village, Meopham, Kent] and *d* 1982, leaving:

1b +David Guysulf; *b* 22 Oct 1944; *educ* Shrewsbury

2b +Peter Stuart; *b* 14 April 1948; *educ* Shrewsbury

3b +Michael Roland; *b* 8 Feb 1950; *educ* Shrewsbury

2a +Catherine Rosemary, BEM (1949) [Mrs Douglas Clarke-Smith BEM, Court House, West Milton, Dorset DT6 3SH]; Sgt FANY; *b* 22 Feb 1918; *m* 2 June 1945 Douglas Alexander Clarke-Smith, MA, FRSA (*d* 12 March 1959), s of Alexander Clarke-Smith, and has:

1b +Humphrey Douglas Bevis [Humphrey Clarke-Smith Esq, 24 Ave Y Lutens, 1150 Brussels, Belgium]; *b* 10 July 1948; *m* 1975 *Christine Quy and has:

1c +Benedict; *b* 1978

2c +Orlando; *b* 1980

1b +Lucinda Mary [Mrs Nigel Henzell-Thomas, Town Mill House, Whitchurch, Hants RG28 7LZ]; *b* 19 Feb 1946; *m* 1977 *Nigel Henzell-Thomas and has:

1c +Lucy; *b* 1978

2b +Susan [Mrs Joseph Santolini, The Stables, Milton Court, Alfriston, E Sussex RG26 5RT]; *b* 15 Sept 1950; *m* 1973 *Joseph Santolini and has:

1c +Lindsay; *b* 1979

(2) Evelyn Charles Cadogan; *b* 1 Oct 1877; *d* 1 June 1878

(3) Humphrey Cadogan, JP; WW I in RA, WW II in HG; *b* 21 Jan 1879; *d* unm 28 April 1957

(4) Frances Bevis; Capt Northumberland Fus; *b* 17 April 1883; *ka* 25 Sept 1916

(5) Roland Arthur; Capt Northumberland Fus WW I (severely wounded); *b* 7 June 1884; *d* 5 Jan 1963

(1) Lucy Henrietta Katharine; *b* April 1876; *m* 28 July 1908 4th Earl of Norbury (*qv*) and *dsp* 26 May 1966

(2) Henrietta Christobel CBE (1919, OBE 1918); *b* 15 Jan 1866; *m* 21 June 1923 Hector Munro-Ferguson (*d* 27 Sept 1951), JP, DL, of Assynt, Novar, Ross-shire, and *d* Nov 1957

3 Charles Arthur; barrister, BA Oxon; *b* Dec 1839; *d* unm 30 March 1906

4 John Charles; RN; *b* 29 Sept 1841; *d* 8 Nov 1886

5 Evelyn Henry; RN; *b* 9 Aug 1843; *m* 9 March 1882 Alberta Mary (*m* 2nd 29 April 1919 Schomberg Kerr Trefusis (*see* CLINTON, B) and *d* 26 Dec 1942), dau of Gen Hon Sir Arthur Edward Hardinge, KCB, CIE (*see* HARDINGE, V), and *d* 5 Sept 1913, having had:

(1) Arthur Evelyn Paul, MBE (1918); Capt Rifle Bde WW I (severely wounded); *b* 27 April 1894; *m* 1st 1915 (*divorce* 1920) Jessica Delma Maria (*d* 1923), dau of James Harcourt Harrington; *m* 2nd 22 Feb 1921 (*divorce* 1929) Margaret Ethel Philippa, only dau of William Campbell Durham, of Thornbury House, Windsor; *m* 3rd 12 Aug 1929 *Dorothy Mary, dau of Charles Henry Eagle, and *dsp* 1 Feb 1957

(1) Joan Mary Evelyn; *b* 9 Sept 1884; *d* 30 Nov 1886

(2) Mary, OBE (1946); MD; WW I France 1917 with Anglo-American-French Red Cross, WW II as Co-Cdr ATS 1939–41, Controller CWL Clubs, Head Organiser NW Europe 1944–46 (despatches); *b* 23 March 1888; *m* 3 Feb 1916 Maj Denis Granville Coskey Critchley-Salmonson, MC, JP, RSF, Roy Scots Fus (*das* 19 April 1943), only s of Capt Harold Basil Septimus Critchley-Salmonson, and *d* 9 Sept 1971, leaving:

1a +John Albert Miles; Maj 12th Roy Lancers Burma 1937–43 and Italy; *b* 16 Dec 1916; *educ* Downside; *m* 7 Sept 1946 *Joan Margaret, dau of Col Henry Robert Haseldine, DSO, OBE, and has:

1b +Denis Patrick Antony [Denis Critchley-Salmonson Esq, Strathmore Water, 126 W High St, Forfar DD8 1BP]; Capt Coldstream Gds; *b* 15 March 1953; *educ* Downside; *m* 1976 *Angela Jane, dau of Brig Hon (Henry Ernest) Christopher Willoughby (*see* MIDDLETON, B), and has:

1c +John Henry Guy; *b* 1986

1c +Katherine Adini Mary; *b* 1979

2c +Isabella Caroline; *b* 1981

1b +Mary-Clare; *b* 30 Nov 1947; *m* 1989 *Henry John Scrope (*see* MEXBOROUGH, E) and has:

1c +William John; *b* 1991

2b +Antonia Isabella Mary [Mrs Christopher Tregoning, The Old Vicarage, Chrishall, Royston, Herts SG9 8QU]; *b* 4 June 1949; *m* 1973 *Christopher William Courtenay Tregoning, 3rd s of Col John L Tregoning, MBE, and has:

1c +Harold John William; *b* 1976

2c +Daniel Christopher Leonard; *b* 1977

3c +Thomas Anthony Cecil; *b* 1982

3b +Henrietta Margaret Mary [Mrs Jacques Baudouin, 431 rue des Auges, Grandfresnoy, France]; *b* 7 Jan 1959; *m* 1985 *Jacques Baudouin, only s of Lt-Col Roger Baudouin, Chev Legn Hon, of Paris, and has:

1c +Alexandre John; *b* 1986

2c +Maxime Roger; *b* 1987

3c +Luke Jacques; *b* 1990

4c +Timothy Joseph; *b* 1994

2a +Peter Evelyn George, OBE [Peter Critchley Esq OBE, Dormans, Combe St Nicholas, Chard, Somerset]; Lt Roy Irish Fus and F/Lt RAF WW II; *b* 30 Dec 1919; *educ* Downside; took name CRITCHLEY by deed poll 1954; *m* 25 Sept 1948 *Grace Blanche, dau of Col J L Oliver, and has had issue:

1b Christopher; *b* 19 Aug 1949; *d* 23 March 1951

2b +Michael Shavin; *b* 1952

3b +Kim Hardinge; *b* 1954

4b +Peter Kerr; *b* 1957

5b +Mark Nicholas; *b* 1959

1a +Denise Irene Mary; WW II in ATS and WRNS; *b* 6 Nov 1918; *educ* St Mary's Convent Ascot

6 Augustus William Charles; 60th Rifles; *b* 5 Feb 1846; *d* 22 April 1882

1 Harriet Georgina; *b* 3 Sept 1831; *m* 27 May 1875 Michael Angelo Caetani, Duke of Sermoneta (*d* 12 Dec 1882), and *d* 16 April 1906

2 Charlotte Isabella; *d* 31 March 1891

The 6th/2nd BARON *d* 29 Aug 1868; his est son,

FREDERICK GEORGE ELLIS, **7th Lord** (Baron) **Howard de Walden** and **3rd Baron Seaford of Seaford**; *b* 9 Aug 1830; *educ* Eton and Trin Coll Cambridge (MA); Maj 4th Light Dragoons 1867; *m* 27 April 1876 (*judicial separation* 1893) Blanche (*m* 2nd 25 March 1903 2nd Baron Ludlow (*see* ROBOROUGH, B) and *d* 7 April 1911), est dau and coheir of William Holden, of Palace House, Lancs, and *d* 3 Nov 1899, leaving:

THOMAS EVELYN ELLIS later SCOTT-ELLIS (roy licence 21 April 1917), **8th Lord** (Baron) **Howard de Walden** and **4th Baron Seaford of Seaford**; *b* 9 May 1880; *educ* Eton and RMC Sandhurst; Hon LLD Wales, Hon Col 4th/5th Bn Roy Scots Fus, Maj and Brevet Lt-Col Roy Tank Corps (TD), Hon Col 1927, Staff Capt 1915, Bde Maj 1916, GSO(3) 1918, Lt 10th Hus, Boer War 1899–1900 and WW I, Tstee Tate Galley 1938–46; *m* 19 Feb 1912 Margherita, CBE, DStJ, FRGS (*d* 31 Dec 1974), er dau of Charles Van Raalte, JP, of Dorset and Mayfair, and *d* 5 Nov 1946, leaving:

1 JOHN OSMAEL SCOTT-ELLIS, **9th and present Baron Howard de Walden and 4th and present Baron Seaford of Seaford**

1 +Bronwen Mary [The Hon Mrs James Lindsay, Sutton Manor, Sutton Scotney, Hants SO21 3JX]; *b* 27 Nov 1912; *m* 26 April 1933 Hon James Louis Lindsay (*d* 27 Aug 1997), yr s of 27th Earl of Crawford and (10th Earl of) Balcarres (*qv*), and has issue

2 Elisabeth Gwendolen; *b* 5 Dec 1914; *m* 1st 24 July 1935 Lt-Cdr Count Serge Orloff-Davidoff, RNVR (*k* in a car crash 12 Aug 1945), only s of Count Alexis Orloff-Davidoff; *m* 2nd 31 Oct 1959 *Bernard Wheeler Robinson, DSc, and *d* 3 May 1976, leaving by her 1st husb:

(1) +Tatiana [Mrs William Mallinson, 67 Camberwell Grove, London SE5 0TQ]; *b* 9 April 1936; *m* 1972 *William John Whitworth Mallinson MB, MRCP, and has:

1a +Thecla; *b* 1973

(1) (cont.) Mrs Mallinson also has:

2a *Sophie Orloff-Davidoff; *b* 1963

(2) +Marina; *b* 30 Dec 1937; ARIBA, AADip; *m* 20 March 1964 Derek William Charles, Viscount Bury (*dvp* 8 Nov 1968), est s of 9th Earl of Albemarle (*qv*), and has issue

3 (Essylt) Priscilla; *b* 15 Nov 1916; *m* 1st 27 Sept 1945 (*divorce* 1972) Jose Luis de Villallonga y Cabeza de Vaca, Marqués de Castellvell, Grandee of Spain, est s of the Duke of Segur, of Casa Falgnera San Feliu de Llobregat, Barcelona, Spain; *m* 2nd 19– Ian Hanson (*d* 19–) and *d* 1983, leaving by her 1st husb:

(1) +Juan Alphonso de Vilallonga; *b* 22 June 1946; *m* 19– *Michelle — and has:

1a +Atalanta; *b* 1987

(1) +Susanna Carmen Margherita Beatriz [Mrs Gregory de Vilallonga Foster, 68 Ventry St, Alexandra, New Zealand]; *b* 6 Aug 1947; *m* 1975 *Gregory John Foster and has:

1a +Adam Kevin Salvador; *b* 1978

4 +Margaret Irène Gaenor, JP (N Westminster 1968) [The Hon Mrs Heathcoat-Amory JP, Hele Manor, Exebridge, Somerset TA22 9RN]; *b* 2 June 1919; *m* 18 July 1938 Richard Frank Heathcoat-Amory and has issue (*see* HEATHCOAT-AMORY, Bt)

5 +Rosemary Nest [The Hon Mrs Seymour, Thrumpton Hall, Notts; 38 Molyneux St, London W1]; *b* 28 Oct 1922; *m* 1 June 1946 George FitzRoy Seymour and has issue (*see* HERTFORD, M)

HOWARD OF PENRITH

Arms and Crests: As for Duke of Norfolk. **Supporters:** Dexter, a lion arg.; sinister, a horse arg., holding in the mouth a sprig of oak fructed ppr., each charged on the shoulder with an escutcheon barry of six arg. and az., three chaplets gu. **Motto:** *Sola virtus invicta* 'Courage alone undaunted'). **Creation:** B. (UK) 10 July 1930.

THE 2ND BARON HOWARD OF PENRITH, of Gowbarrow, Co Cumberland (Francis Philip Howard), JP (Glos 1946), DL (1960)) [The Rt Hon The Lord Howard of Penrith JP DL, Dean Farm, Coln St Aldwyns, Glos GL7 5AX]; *b* 5 Oct 1905; *s* f 1939; *educ* Downside and Trin Coll Cambridge (BA 1928); barrister Middle Temple 1932, Capt RA WW II (POW); *m* 1 July 1944 *Anne, widow of Anthony Gardner Bazley (*see* BAZLEY, Bt) and dau of John Beaumont Hotham (*see* HOTHAM, B), and has:

1 +PHILIP ESME [The Hon Philip Howard, 45 Erpingham Rd, London SW15]; *b* 1 May 1945; *educ* Ampleforth and Ch Ch Oxford; *m* 1969 *Sarah, dau of Barclay Walker, and has:

(1) +Thomas Philip; *b* 1974

(2) +Michael Barclay; *b* 1984

(1) *Natasha Mary; *b* 29 April 1970

(2) *Laura Isabella; *b* 1976

2 +Michael Edmund; *b* 19 April 1947; *educ* Ampleforth

3 +David Francis [The Hon David Howard, Glebe House, Ulcombe, Kent ME16 1DN]; *b* 29 May 1949; *educ* Ampleforth; *m* 1981 *Diana, dau of John S Radway and formerly w of Timothy Davis, and has:

(1) *Rachel Anne; *b* 1982

(2) *Alice Isabella; *b* 1983

(3) *Olivia Charlotte; *b* 1986

(4) *Frances Elizabeth; *b* 1988

(5) *Charlotte Grace; *b* 1993

4 +William John; *b* 30 May 1953; *educ* Ampleforth; *m* 1981 *Alexandra Josephine, dau of Maurice Graham, and has:

(1) *Miranda Catherine; *b* 1982

(2) *Elizabeth Clara; *b* 1984

Lineage: HENRY HOWARD, of Greystoke, Cumberland (*see* NORFOLK, D); had a 4th s:

Sir ESME WILLIAM HOWARD, **1st Baron Howard of Penrith**, of Gowbarrow, Co Cumberland (UK), so *cr* 10 July 1930, GCB (1928, KCB 1919), GCMG (1923, KCMG 1916, CMG 1906), CVO (1906, MVO 1904), PC (1919); *b* 15 Sept 1863; entered Dip Serv 1887, Consul-Gen Crete 1903–06, Counsellor Washington 1906–08 and Vienna 1908, Consul-Gen Budapest 1908–11, Envoy Extrdy and Min Plen Berne 1911–13 and Stockholm 1913–19, attd Br Delegn Paris Peace Conf and Br Civil Delegate Internat Commn to Poland 1919, Amb Madrid 1919–24 and Washington 1924–30, trooper Boer War 1900 (medal and four clasps), Hon LLD Washington 1925 and Hartford 1929; *m* 17 Nov 1898 Lady Isabella Giustiniani-Bandini (*d* 20 Jan 1963 aged 95), 5th dau of 8th Earl of Newburgh (*qv*), and *d* 1 Aug 1939, having had:

1 Esme Joseph Henry Sigismondo; *b* 17 Oct 1903; *educ* Downside; *d* 27 Nov 1926

2 FRANCIS PHILIP HOWARD, **2nd and present Baron Howard of Penrith**

3 Hubert John Edward Dominic; *b* 23 Dec 1907; *educ* Downside and Trin Coll Cambridge (BA 1928); *m* 17 Sept 1951 Donna Lelia Calista Ada Caetani, painter and gardener (inherited Ninfa on the death of her brother) (*d* 11 Jan 1977), only dau of Roffredo Caetani, 18th Duke of Sermoneta, of Palazzo Caetani, Rome

4 +Edmund Bernard Carlo, CMG (1969), MVO (1961); barrister Middle Temple 1934; Capt KRRC WW II; Dip Serv: 2nd Sec (Info) Rome 1947–51, FO 1951–53, 1st Sec Madrid 1953–57, Head Chancery and Chargé d'Affaires Bogota 1957–59, Consul Florence 1960–61, Counsellor Rome 1961–65, Consul Gen Genoa 1965–69; *b* 8 Sept 1909; *educ* Downside and New Coll Oxford (BA); *m* 1 Sept 1936 *Cécile, dau of Charles Geoffroy-Dechaume, of Valmondois, France, and has had:

(1) +Esme Francis [Esme Howard Esq, The Gallery House, Picketts Lane, Horney Common, Uckfield, E Sussex TN22 3EG]; late 2nd Lt Sherwood Foresters; *b* 29 Aug 1938; *educ* Downside and New Coll Oxford (BA); *m* 1st 20 April 1963 (*divorce* 1973) Tessa Longhurst, yr dau of Maj Kenneth Evan Meredith, Dorsetshire Regt, and Mrs Robert Hamond, of Morston Hall, Norfolk, and has:

1a +Dominic William; *b* 15 June 1964; *m* 1993 *Belinda Sarah, yr dau of Anthony Cassidy, of Albury, Surrey, and has:

1b *Eleanor Louise Tessa, *b* 2 Sept 1997

2a +Stephen Anthony; *b* 20 July 1966; *m* 1994 *Emma Louise, er dau of Adrian Platt, of Butlers Hill, Surrey

1a *Elizabeth Anne; *b* 20 June 1965; *m* 1995 *Benedict Dunhill and has:

1b *Camilla Cecile Alice; *b* 27 July 1997

(1) (cont.) Esme Howard *m* 2nd 1979 *Diane Marie Kacic, of St Louis, Mo., and by her has:

3a +Edmund Philip; *b* 1980

2a *Katherine Lelia; *b* 1984

(2) +John Edmund [John Howard Esq, 53 Mount Rd, London SW19 8ES]; *b* 2 June 1940; *educ* Downside and New Coll Oxford (BA); *m* 1971 *Gloria Cano, of Medellin, Colombia, and has:

1a Alejandro; *b* 1973; *d* 1994

2a +Francis; *b* 1985

1a *Patricia Anita; *b* 1972

2a *Caterina; *b* 1977

(3) +Anthony Richard [Anthony Howard Esq, 48 Batoum Gdns, London W6 7QD]; *b* 30 May 1947; *educ* Downside and Guildhall Sch of Music and Drama (GGSM); *m* 19 Aug 1978 *Anstice Bridget, 2nd dau of Maj Martin Antony Gibbs (*see* ALDENHAM and HUNSDON OF HUNSDON, B), and has:

1a +Geoffrey John Bernard; *b* 1986

1a *Cecily Mary Margaret; *b* 1983

(1) Anne Elizabeth; *b* 14 Aug, *d* 18 Sept 1937

(2) *Katherine Isabella [Mrs Christopher Woods, The Vicarage, Traverse St, St Helens, Lancs WA9 1BW]; *b* 17 June 1952; *m* 1977 *Rev Christopher Woods and has:

1a *Francis; *b* 1981

2a *Thomas; *b* 1983

1a *Isabella; *b* 1977

2a *Madeline; *b* 1979

3a *Lydia; *b* 1989

5 Henry Anthony Camillo, CMG (1960); Lt-Col Res Offrs Coldstream Gds, Lt KAR 1935, served WWII (despatches), Colonial Serv 1946, Administrator St Kitts, Nevis and Anguilla; *b* 3 March 1913; *educ* Downside and RMC Sandhurst; *m* 11 Sept 1937 *Adele Le Bourgeois [Mrs Henry Howard, Bushby House, Greystoke, Penrith, Cumberland], er dau of Reese Denny Alsop, of New York, and *d* 15 Oct 1977, having had:

(1) *Mary Rosalind [Mrs Ian Lowe, Spring Ford, Newton Reigny, Cumbria CA11 0AY]; *b* 6 Aug 1938; *m* 13 July 1961 *Ian Harlowe Lowe, only s of Harlowe Robert Lowe, MC, and has:

1a *Esme Charles Harlowe; *b* 21 June 1962; *educ* Ampleforth; served Coldstream Gds; *m* 1990 *Carlotta, er dau of Gian Carlo Guglielmino, and has:

1b *Cosima Anne Julia; *b* 1992

(2) Susan Isabella; *b* 4 June 1940; Canoness of St Augustine; *d* unm 10 Oct 1963

(3) *Joan Dacre [Mrs Gordon Richards, Greystoke Castle, Greystoke, Penrith, Cumbria CA11 0TG]; *b* 30 June 1946; *m* 1st 7 May 1966 (*divorce* 1979) William J Lacey, est s of Capt William J Lacey, of New York; *m* 2nd June 1980 *Gordon Waugh Richards, racehorse trainer and National Hunt jockey 1950–63, and by her 1st husb has:

1a *William John; *b* 13 Aug 1967; *m* 1993 *Claire Baker

1a *Anne Marie; *b* 1972

(4) *Adèle Cristina Sophia [The Hon Mrs Timothy Palmer, West Woodyates Manor, Salisbury, Wilts]; *b* 18 Nov 1952; *m* 1984 *Hon Timothy John Palmer (*see* LUCAS OF CRUDWELL, B) and has issue

(5) *Charlotte Fell; *b* 15 Dec 1953; *m* 1985 *Ian Mintrim

HOWARD-LAWSON

Arms: Gules on a bend between six cross crosslets fitchée argent an escutcheon or charged with a demi-lion rampant pierced through the mouth with an arrow within a double tressure flory counterflory of the first, in chief a mullet for difference and (for distinction) a cross botonny gules. **Crest:** On a chapeau gules doubled ermine a lion statant guardant, the tail extended or, ducally gorged argent, charged on the shoulder with a mullet for difference and (for distinction) on the body with a cross botonny gules.
Motto: *Sola virtus invicta* ('Courage alone undaunted').
Creation: Bt. (UK) 8 Sept 1841.

SIR JOHN PHILIP HOWARD-LAWSON, 6TH BT, of Brough Hall, Catterick, Co York [Sir John Howard-Lawson Bt, Hunter Hall, Great Salkeld, Cumbria CA11 9NA]; *b* 6 June 1934; *s* f 1990; *educ* Ampleforth; *m* 17 Sept 1960 *Jean Veronica, only dau of Col John Evelyn Marsh, DSO, OBE, and has:

1 +PHILIP WILLIAM; *b* 28 June 1961; *educ* Ampleforth; *m* 1st 1988 (*divorce* 1992) Cara Margaret, only dau of Hon Martin Michael Dominick Browne (*see* ORANMORE AND BROWNE, B); *m* 2nd 1993 *Isobel Anne Oldridge, er dau of Christopher George James Oldridge de la Hay

2 +Thomas John; *b* 2 Aug 1963

1 *Julia Frances Veronica; *b* 3 Oct 1964

Lineage: WILLIAM LAWSON; *m* Agnes, dau and coheir of William Cramlington, Northumberland, who brought him that manor by *c* 1425, and had a 2nd s:

THOMAS LAWSON, of Cramlington; *m* Isabella, dau of — Killinghall, of Middleton St George, and *d* 1489, leaving:

WILLIAM LAWSON, of Cramlington, living 1518; *m* — Horsley and had:

JAMES LAWSON, of Cramlington; merchant Newcastle-upon-Tyne; *m* Alice, dau of — Bertram, of Bentley, and had:

EDMUND LAWSON; *m* Margery, dau and heiress of Ralph Swinnow, of Rock Castle, Northumberland, and had:

Sir RALPH LAWSON; ktd 1603; *m* Elizabeth, dau and sole heiress of Roger Brough, of Brough Hall, nr Catterick, Yorks, and had, with two yr sons and two daus (Jane, *m* Thomas Rokeby, of Mortham; Alice, *m* Thomas Ingleby, of Lawkland):

ROGER LAWSON, of Heaton, Northumberland; *m* Dorothy (*d* 1632), 2nd dau of Sir Henry Constable, of Burton Constable, Yorks, and *dvp*, having had an est surv s:

HENRY LAWSON, of Brough Hall, Yorks; *m* Anne, dau of Robert Hodgson, of Heburne, Co Durham, and *d* 1636, having had, with other issue:

1 Roger; *d* young

2 Henry; *m* Catherine (*m* 2nd by 1655 1st Earl of Derwentwater (*see* NEWBURGH, E) and *d* by 1696), est dau and coheir of Sir William Fenwick, of Meldon, Northumberland, and was *k* 1644 fighting for CHARLES I at Battle of Melton Mowbray (minor royalist victory in Civil War), leaving an only dau:

(1) Isabella; *m* Sir John Swinburne, 1st Bt (*see* 1949 edn) and allegedly had 24 children

3 Sir JOHN LAWSON, 1st Bt (E), so *cr* 6 July 1665, of Brough Hall, which he inherited from his er bro 1644 but which was subsequently sequestrated and sold 1653, he being banished; *b c* 1627; royalist Capt of Horse Civil War; *m c* 1660(?1650?) Katharine (*d* 4 July 1668), sis of 1st Earl of Carlisle (*qv*), and *d* 26 Oct 1698, having had:

(1) John; said to have been 14 in Aug 1665, hence *b c* 1651, but this would make him illegitimate if the date of *c* 1660 for the 1st Bt's w is correct as above; *dvp* unm at Calais

(2) Sir HENRY LAWSON, 2nd Bt, of Brough; *b c* 1663; *m* by 1688 Elizabeth (*d c* 1735), dau of Robert Knightley, of Offchurch, Warwicks, and *d* 9 May 1726, having had issue:

1a Sir JOHN LAWSON, 3rd Bt; *b c* 1689; *m* by 1712 Mary, est dau of Sir John Shelley, 3rd Bt, of Michelgrove (*qv*), and *d* 19 Oct 1739, having had:

1b Sir HENRY LAWSON, 4th Bt; *b c* 1712; *m* by 1742 Anastasia (*d* 5 Nov 1764), yst dau of Thomas Maire, of Lart(h)ington Hall, Yorks, and Hardwick-near-the-Sea, Co Durham, and *d* 1 Oct 1781, having had issue:

1c Sir JOHN LAWSON, 5th Bt; *b* 13 Sept 1744; raised 1798 a vol infantry corps, which he commanded; *m* 1st 1 Aug 1768 Elizabeth (*d* 10 June 1801), yst dau of William Scarisbrick, of Scarisbrick, Lancs; *m* 2nd 8 Feb 1803 Monica, dau of Miles Stapleton (*see* LINDSEY and ABINGDON, E), and *dspms* 27 June 1811, leaving by his 1st w:

1d Anastasia Maria; *b* 25 May 1769; *m* 1789 Thomas STRICKLAND later STANDISH, of Sizergh, Westmorland, and *d* 22 June 1807, having had issue

2d Elizabeth; *b* 2 Nov 1770; *m* 8 Jan 1789 John Wright, of Kelvedon Hall, Essex, and *d* 7 July 1812, having had a 2nd s:

1e WILLIAM (Sir), **1st Bt**

2c Sir HENRY LAWSON later MAIRE later LAWSON again, 6th Bt, of Brough; *b* 25 Dec 1750; inherited the Maire estates from his unc John Maire, whose will allowed him to enjoy them as long as the property and title of Sir HENRY's own family remained with his er bro Sir John, but stipulated that if he succeeded to the Lawson estates those of the Maire family were to pass to his sis Catherine; as a result Sir HENRY initially assumed 1771 by roy licence the surname MAIRE but under the terms of his unc's will he later had to transfer the Maire estates to his sis on succeeding his er bro in the btcy, whereupon he resumed his original surname; *m* 1st 2 Sept 1773 Monica (*dsp* 8 Jan 1800), yst dau of Nicholas Stapleton *alias* Errington, of Carleton, Yorks (*see* NORFOLK, D); *m* 2nd 18 May 1801 Catherine, only dau of Henry Fermor, of Worcester, and *dsp* Jan 1834, when the btcy *cr* 1665 expired, although a certain Henry Lawson, later De Burgh-Lawson, styled himself 'Sir Henry De Burgh-Lawson, Bt', from 1877, claiming to be the heir to the title by virtue of legitimate male-line descent from the 4th s of Sir JOHN LAWSON, 1st Bt (*see* above); a s of 'Sir Henry De Burgh-Lawson, Bt' also assumed the title, doing so after his f's death

1c Mary; *b* 26 July 1742; nun at Bruges

2c Catherine; *b* 9 Aug 1747; *m* June 1772 John Silvertop, of Minster Acres, Northumberland, and had:

1d George, of Minster Acres; *d* unm 20 Feb 1849

2d John; *b* 3 Aug 1777; *d* young

3d Henry Thomas Maire SILVERTOP later WITHAM; eventually inherited the Maire estates

4d Charles; Col Spanish Army; *dsp*

2b Thomas; priest; *d* 1807

3b John; *m* Elizabeth, dau of Thomas William Selby, of Biddleston, Northumberland, and *d* 1791 aged 69, having had:

1c Thomas; priest

2c John, of York; MD; *m* Clarinda, est dau of John Fallow, of Cloona, Co Roscommon, and widow of William Bermingham

3c Henry; priest

1c Elizabeth; *m* John Webbe Weston, of Sutton Place, Surrey, and *d* 1791, leaving issue

1b Mary; nun at Bruges; *d* 1783

2b Bridget; nun at Bruges; *d* 1787

1a Anne; *m* William Witham, of Cliffe, Yorks

2a Elizabeth; *m* Stephen Tempest, of Broughton, Yorks (*see* LONDONDERRY, M)

(3) Charles; *dsp*

(4) William; Catholic priest and *dsp*, but claimed as ancestor by the self-styled 'Sir Henry De Burgh-Lawson' (*see* above)

(5) Philip; *dsp*

(6) Ralph; *b* after 1665; *dsp*

(7) Thomas; *b* after 1665; *dsp*

The 6th and last Bt of the 1665 creation's great-nephew,

Sir WILLIAM WRIGHT later LAWSON, **1st Bt** (UK), so *cr* 8 Sept 1841; *b* 8 May 1796; *m* 20 Oct 1825 Clarinda Catherine (*d* 10 Jan 1861), only dau and heiress of John Lawson, MD, of York, and *d* 22 June 1865, having had:

1 JOHN (Sir), **2nd Bt**

2 Henry; *b* 20 Feb 1833; drowned New Zealand 3 Jan 1857 attempting to save the life of his shepherd

3 William (Rev); *b* 22 Dec 1834; RC priest; *d* 28 Nov 1920

4 Thomas Paulinus; *b* 11 Sept 1837; Lt-Col 3rd Bn Durham LI; *m* 16 May 1878 Gertrude Sarah (*d* 17 Sept 1890), dau of James Addison and widow of Thomas Farmer Bailey, JP, DL, of Hall Place, Kent, and Sunnyside, IoW, and *dsp* 10 April 1890

1 Clarinda Mary; nun; *d* 3 May 1873

2 Eliza; nun; *d* 23 May 1897

3 Grace; nun; *d* 24 Dec 1885

The 1st Bt's est s,

Sir John Lawson, 2nd Bt, JP (Yorks), DL; *b* 17 Dec 1829; *educ* London U (BA); *m* 1st 15 Oct 1856 Mary Anne (*d* 5 Nov 1868), est dau of Frederick Sewallis Gerard (*see* GERARD, B), and had:

1 Mary; *b* 24 Aug 1857; *m* 7 April 1880 Sir George Hugh Charles Clifford, 2nd Bt (*qv*), and *dsp* 19 Dec 1880

2 Alice; *b* 9 July 1859; *d* unm 8 Sept 1945

3 Agnes; *b* 2 Feb 1861; *m* 11 Oct 1887 Henry Bernard Joseph Parker, est s of Sir Henry Watson Parker, and *d* 12 Nov 1929

Sir John *m* 2nd 5 Oct 1870 Agnes Mary Matilda (*d* 7 March 1945), est dau of Edmund Molyneux Seel and gdau of Maj Molyneux Seel, of Huyton Hey, Lancs, and *d* 10 Dec 1910, having by her had:

1 HENRY JOSEPH (Sir), **3rd Bt**

4 Charlotte Mary; *b* 22 Oct 1871; *d* 11 Dec 1919

5 Teresa; *b* 3 Jan 1874; *m* 9 Aug 1898 Francis William Joseph Macdonnell, JP (*das* 1916), of Dunfierth, Co Kildare, and *d* 5 Oct 1945, leaving issue

6 Edith; *b* 1 Feb 1875; *m* 6 Aug 1896 John Herbert Riley and *d* 23 Feb 1949, leaving issue

7 Mabel Mary; *b* 9 Sept 1876; *d* unm 16 Sept 1942

8 Beatrice Mary; *b* 30 March 1881; *d* 1 Feb 1901

9 Margaret Mary; *b* 17 Nov 1889; *m* 19 Aug 1920 Robert Kinnear Robertson, MD, only s of James Robertson, of Perth, and *d* 1967, leaving issue

The 2nd Bt's only s,

Sir Henry Joseph Lawson, 3rd Bt; *b* 25 Dec 1877; *m* 22 Nov 1899 Ursula Mary (*m* 2nd 27 April 1949 Lt-Col Hugh Levin, OBE, Green Howards, s of Maj Lionel Henry Levin, 19th Foot, and *d* 5 Jan 1960), only child and heir of Philip John Canning Howard (*see* NORFOLK, D), and *d* 21 Oct 1947, leaving:

1 **Sir Ralph Henry Lawson, 4th Bt**; *b* 27 Sept1905; *educ* Ampleforth; *m* 1st 26 Oct 1935 Lilian Mary (*d* 13 June 1968), est dau of Sir Edmund Hugh Chaytor, 6th Bt (*qv*); *m* 2nd 11 May 1970 (Helen) Beres(ford) (*d* 19–), dau of Richard Cornelius and formerly w of (a) Capt Kenyon Goode, of Nassau, and (b) Capt Edward Joseph Algernon Petre (*see* PETRE, B), and *d* 13 Feb 1975, leaving by his 1st w:

(1) *Valerie Anne [Mrs William Worthington, Wood House, Brough Park, Richmond, N Yorks]; *b* 21 July 1936; *m* 10 Dec 1960 Benjamin Worthington (*d* 1984), yr s of Lt William Greville Worthington, RNVR (*see* AYLESFORD, E), and has:

1a *Greville Thomas; *b* 22 Nov 1963; *educ* Ampleforth; *m* 1995 *Hon Sophie Stapleton Cotton (*see* COMBERMERE, V) and has:

1b *Blue (dau); *b* March 1996

1a *Ursula; *b* 16 March 1962; *m* 1988 (*divorce* 19–) Capt (Archibald) Edward Charles Edmonstone (*see* EDMONSTONE, Bt)

2a *Lucy; *b* 4 May 1967; *m* 1994 *Oliver Leatham and has:

1b *Benjamin; *b* 26 July 1996

(2) *Alethea Jill Clare [Miss Alethea Lawson, The Stallion Box, High Green, Catterick Village, N Yorks]; *b* 9 Dec 1939

2 WILLIAM HOWARD (Sir), **5th Bt**

1 Mary Catherine; *b* 25 Nov 1900; *m* 1926 Geoffrey Grosvenor Eccles Bradley (*d* 16 March 1945) and *d* 19–

2 Aurea Clare; *b* 20 Dec 1901; *m* 2 Feb 1926 Alberic Waterkeyn, 7th s of Rev Jean Pierre Waterkeyn, of Wimbledon, and had:

(1) *Denis Gerard WATERKEYN later HOWARD (roy licence June 1962); *b* 8 July 1929; *m* 18 May 1957 *Betty Plant, twin dau of Howard Greenham, and has:

1a *Francis; *b* 10 Oct 1960

1a *Catherine Anne; *b* 30 Jan 1959

(1) *Cecelia Mary; *b* 6 Nov 1926; *m* 6 Sept 1947 *Philip Marland Rambaut, DSC, MA, yr s of Dr Daniel Frederick Rambaut, and has:

1a *Michael Adrian; *b* 28 Oct 1948; *educ* Ampleforth

2a *Anthony Howard; *b* 1 Nov 1950; *educ* Ampleforth

3a *Benedict Peter; *b* 30 June 1954; *educ* Ampleforth

1a *Andrea Clare Mary; *b* 12 Oct 1957

The 4th Bt's yr bro,

Sir William Howard Lawson, 5th Bt, DL (Cumberland 1963); *b* 15 July 1905; *educ* Ampleforth; Kt SMO 1965; *m* 25 April 1933 Joan Eleanor (*d* 1989), only child of Maj Arthur Cowie Stamer, CBE (*see* STAMER, Bt), and *d* 1990, leaving:

1 Sir JOHN PHILIP HOWARD LAWSON later HOWARD (roy licence June 1962) later still HOWARD-LAWSON (roy licence 1992), **6th and present Bt**

2 +Hugh William [Hugh Lawson Esq, Croftlands, Heads Nook, Carlisle, Cumbria CA4 9AF]; *b* 5 March 1936; *educ* Ampleforth; *m* 10 June 1961 *Margaret Anne, er dau of Maj Richard Heysham Gubbins-Mounsey-Heysham, of Carlisle, by Margaret Isabel, 2nd dau of Brig William Bradley Gosset Barne, CBE, DSO, and has:

(1) +Simon David; *b* 20 April 1962; *educ* Ampleforth; *m* 1989 *Lucy Rose, dau of James Morrish, of Ham Farm, Wellington, Somerset, and has:

1a +Oliver Hugh; *b* 18 Nov 1994

2a +Sebastian James; *b* 19 June 1997

(1) *Philippa Joan; *b* 10 Dec 1964; *m* 1993 *Philip A J Leech, er s of Jeremy Leech, of Hovingham, York, and has:

1a *William Jeremy; *b* 1 Feb 1995

1a *Georgina Florence; *b* 15 Nov 1997

(2) *Pollyanne Lucy; *b* 1970; *m* 30 Aug 1997 *Julian Edward Roberts, yr s of David Edward Roberts, of Solihull

3 +(Arthur) Mark [Mark Lawson Esq, Brough House, Milton Brodie, Forres, Moray IV36 0UA]; *b* 23 Jan 1940; *educ* Ampleforth; *m* 8 June 1968 *Rosemary Veronica, dau of Samuel Parkington Vickery, of Glasgow, and has:

(1) +Henry Benedict; *b* 1970; *educ* Ampleforth

(1) *Charlotte Niamh; *b* 1975

1 *Mary Frances (Mafra) [Mrs Julian Smithers, Haversham Grange, Haversham, nr Milton Keynes, Bucks]; *b* 5 Aug 1947; *m* 14 June 1969 *Julian Rupert Smithers, er s of Rupert Langley Smithers, of Kinsbourne House, Herts, and has:

(1) *William Rupert John; *b* 1973

(1) *Louisa Jane; *b* 23 Aug 1971

Seat: Corby Castle, Wetherell, Cumbria. A family called Salkeld owned this property from at least the 13th century. Indeed a pele tower of that date still formed the core of the house when it was transformed by the new owners, the Howards, in the 17th century. The Salkelds had sold Corby in 1625 to Lord William Howard. His descendant Ursula married the 3rd Bt (*see* above), hence its acquisition by the Lawsons, later Howard-Lawsons. Before it passed out of the family via Ursula the heiress another Henry Howard, a keen student of his family's history who lived during the Regency period, drastically recast the building in the Greek Revival style, commissioning Peter Nicholson (who was employed as the county architect for Cumberland) to draw up plans.

Corby is with Castleto(w)n House, Rockcliffe, Nicholson's best work, though there are some authorities who regard Corby as in a league of its own. Nicholson's skill at mathematics made him particularly well suited to the decorative features of a neoclassical house such as Corby and his talent for relatively mundane matters such as joints and hinges is also in evidence. Nevertheless parts of the interior survive from approximately a century before the remodelling, notably the staircase and the stucco ceilings to the ground-floor rooms at the back of the house. This is slightly surprising, because if there was one speciality of Nicholson's it was beautifully turned staircase handrails.

HOWE

Arms: Quarterly, 1st and 4th, or a fess between three wolf heads couped sa. (for HOWE); 2nd and 3rd, arg. on a bend sa. three popinjays or, beaked and legged gu. (for CURZON). **Crests:** 1 Out of a ducal coronet or a plume of five ostrich feathers az. (for HOWE), 2 A popinjay rising or, collared gu. (for CURZON). **Supporters:** On either side a Cornish chough ppr., round the neck a plain gold chain. **Motto:** Let Curzon holde what Curzon helde. **Creations:** B. (GB) 19 Aug 1788 (Howe of Langar) and 13 Aug 1794 (Curzon of Penn), V. (UK) 27 Feb 1802, E. (UK) 15 July 1821.

THE 7TH EARL HOWE, Viscount Curzon of Penn, Co Buckingham, **Baron Howe of Langar**, Co Nottingham, and **Baron Curzon of Penn**, Co Buckingham (Frederick Richard Penn Curzon) [The Rt Hon The Earl Howe, Penn House, Amersham, Bucks HP7 0PS]; *b* 29 Jan 1951; *s* kinsman 1984; *educ* Rugby and Ch Ch Oxford (MA); a Ld-in-Waiting (Govt Whip) 1991–92, Govt Spokesman Employment and Tport 1991 and Environment and Defence 1992, Parly U-Sec MAFF 1992–95 and MOD 1995–97; *m* 26 March 1983 *Elizabeth Helen, DL (Bucks 1995), er dau of Capt Burleigh Edward St Lawrence Stuart (*see* CASTLE STEWART, E), and has:

1 +THOMAS EDWARD PENN, *Viscount Curzon*; *b* 22 Oct 1994

1 *Anna Elizabeth; *b* 19 Jan 1987

2 *Flora Grace; *b* 12 June 1989

3 *Lucinda Rose; *b* 12 Oct 1991

Lineage (of Curzon): Sir NATHANIEL CURZON, 4th Bt, of Kedleston (*see* SCARSDALE, V), had a 2nd s:

ASSHETON CURZON, **1st Viscount Curzon of Penn**, Co Buckingham, so *cr* 27 Feb 1802, as also earlier 13 Aug 1794 BARON CURZON OF PENN, Co Buckingham (both GB); *b* 2 Feb 1729/30; *educ* BNC Oxford; MP (Tory) Clitheroe 1754–80 and 1792–94; *m* 1st 21 Feb 1756 Esther (*d* 21 July 1764), only dau and heir of William Hanmer (*see* HANMER, Bt), and had:

1 Penn Assheton; *m* 31 July 1787 Sophia, **Baroness Howe of Langar** in her own right (*see* below), and *dvp* 3 Sept 1797, leaving:

(1) RICHARD WILLIAM, **1st Earl**

1 Esther; *m* 8 Jan 1778 Sir George Bromley, 2nd Bt, and *d* 7 Nov 1839, leaving issue (*see* 1949 edn BROMLEY-WILSON, Bt)

2 Mary; *m* 1 July 1779 2nd Baron Stawell (*see* DARTMOUTH, E) and *d* 19 Sept 1804, leaving issue

The **1st Viscount** *m* 2nd 6 Feb 1766 Dorothy (*d* 25 Feb 1774), sis of 1st Earl Grosvenor (*see* WESTMINSTER, D), and had, with other issue:

2 Assheton; *b* 1 June 1771

3 Robert; *b* 13 Feb 1774; *m* 14 Oct 1808 Baroness Zouche (*qv*) in her own right and *d* 14 May 1863

The **1st Viscount** *m* 3rd 17 April 1777 Anna Margaretta (*d* 13 June 1804), widow of Alderman Barlow Trecothick and dau of Amos Meredith, and *d* 21 March 1820, having by her had no issue

Lineage (of Howe): HENRY HOWE; living *temp* HENRY VIII; ggf of:

Sir JOHN HOWE, 1st Bt (E), so *cr* 22 Sept 1660; had the Manor of Compton, Glos, and other estates made over to him by his unc Sir Richard Grubham; *m* Bridget, dau of Thomas Rich, of N Cerney, Glos, Master in Chancery, and had:

1 Sir RICHARD GRUBHAM HOWE, 2nd Bt; *m* Anne, widow of John Dutton, of Sherborne, Glos, and dau of Dr John King, Bp London, and *d* 1703, leaving:

(1) Sir RICHARD HOWE, 3rd Bt; MP Wilts; *m* 12 Aug 1673 Mary, dau of Sir Henry Frederick Thynne, 1st Bt (*see* BATH, M), and *d* 3 July 1730

2 JOHN GRUBHAM

3 Thomas (Sir); *m* Hester, dau of Sir William Mainwaring, and *dsp*

The 2nd son,

JOHN GRUBHAM HOWE; MP Glos, Ld Manor of Langar, Notts, through his w; *m* Lady Annabella Scrope (*b* 1629; *d* 21 March 1703), illegitimate dau but coheir (and granted by roy warrant 1 June 1663 rank of earl's legitimate dau) of 11th Earl of Sunderland by Martha Jeanes, and had, with other issue:

1 SCROPE

2 John Grubham, PC, of Stowell, Glos; Paymaster-Gen; *m* Mary, widow of Sir Edward Morgan, 3rd Bt, of Llantarnam, and dau and heir of Humphrey Baskerville, of Pentrylios, Herefs, and *d* 1721, leaving:

(1) JOHN HOWE, 1st LORD CHEDWORTH, BARON OF CHEDWORTH, Co Gloucester (GB), so *cr* 12 May 1741; inherited the Compton and Wishford estates, Glos and Wilts respectively, from his cousin Sir RICHARD HOWE, 3rd Bt (*see* above); MP (Whig) Glos Feb-July 1727 and Wilts 1729; *m* Dorothy, dau of Henry Frederick Thynne (*see* BATH, M), and *d* 3 April 1742, having had, with an er s (*d* young):

1a JOHN THYNNE HOWE, 2nd LORD CHEDWORTH, BARON OF CHEDWORTH; *b* 18 Feb 1714; Ld Lt Glos 1758–62; *m* 23 Sept 1751 Martha, dau and coheir of Sir Philip Parker later Parker-a-Morley-Long, Bt, and *dsp* 9 May 1762

2a HENRY FREDERICK HOWE, 3rd LORD CHEDWORTH, BARON OF CHEDWORTH; *b* 17 Feb 1715; *d* unm 7 Oct 1781

3a Thomas (Rev); Rector Wishford; *m* Frances, dau of Thomas White, of Tattingstone Place, Suffolk, and had, with an er s (*d* young):

1b JOHN HOWE, 4th and last LORD CHEDWORTH, BARON OF CHEDWORTH; *b* 22 Aug 1754; *educ* Harrow and Queen's Coll Oxford; *d* unm 29 Oct 1804, when the title expired

(1) Mary; *m* 1st 28 March 1711 Sir Edmond Thomas, 2nd Bt, of Wenvoe (*qv*); *m* 2nd Anthony Powell, of Coytrehen, Glam

3 Charles, of Gritworth, Notts; *b* 1661; *m* Eleanor, widow of Sir Henry Dering and dau and heir of Sir William Pargiter, of Gritworth, and had:

(1) Leonora Maria; *m* Peter Bathurst (*see* BATHURST, E)

4 Emanuel Scrope; Lt Gen, Envoy to Hanover; *m* Ruperta, illegitimate dau of PRINCE RUPERT OF THE RHINE, 1st cousin of CHARLES II, and *d* 26 Sept 1709, leaving:

(1) William, of Beckenham, Lincs, Maj; *bapt* 24 March 1699/1700; *m* Elizabeth, 3rd dau and coheir of William Pauncefote, of Carswalls, Glos, and *d* 28 July 1733, leaving:

1a Mary; *b* 3 Nov 1725; *m* 18 Aug 1747 Sir George Smith, 1st Bt (*see* BROMLEY, Bt), and had issue

(2) Emanuel, Page-of-Honour; *b* 7 Jan 1701/2; *d* 3 April 1721

(3) James; *b* 25 July 1704

(1) Sophia Arabella, Maid-of-Honour to QUEEN CAROLINE; *b* 28 Dec 1698/9; *d* 4 April 1726

1 Bridget; *m c* 1 May 1673, as his 2nd w, 1st Baron Ossulston and had issue (*see* TANKERVILLE, E)

2 Elizabeth; *m* Sir John Guise, 2nd Bt, of Elmore, Glos (*qv*), and had issue

The est son,

SCROPE HOWE, 1st VISCOUNT HOWE, so *cr* 16 May 1701, as also BARON OF GLENAWLY, Co Fermanagh (both I); *b* Nov 1648; *educ* Ch Ch Oxford; ktd March 1662/3, MP Notts 1673–81, 1689–98 and 1710–13, Groom Bedchamber to WILLIAM III, Comptroller Excise 1693–1710; *m* 1st April 1672 Lady Anne Manners, 6th dau of 8th Earl of Rutland (*see* RUTLAND, D), and had issue; *m* 2nd 1698 Juliana Alington (*d* Sept 1747), dau of 3rd Baron Alington of Killard, and *d* 26 Jan 1712, leaving by her:

1 Sir EMANUEL SCROPE HOWE, 4th Bt, as which *s* cousin 3 July 1730, and 2nd VISCOUNT HOWE; *b c* 1699; MP (Whig) Notts 1722–32, Govr Barbados 1732–35; *m* 8 April 1719 Mary Sophia Charlotte (*d* 13 June 1782), est dau of Baron Kielmansegge by Charlotte Sophia, Countess of Darlington in her own right and alleged by some historians to have been mistress of GEORGE I even though as the probable dau (illegitimately) of the Elector of Brunswick she would seem to have been his half-sis, and *d* 29 March 1735, leaving:

(1) Sir GEORGE AUGUSTUS HOWE, 5th Bt, and 3rd VISCOUNT HOWE; *b c* 1724; MP (Whig) Nottingham 1747–58, Capt and Lt-Col 1st Foot Gds 1749, Col cmdg 3rd Bn 60th Foot 1757 and 55th Foot 1757–58, Brig Gen 1757; *d* unm, *k* in a skirmish with the French at Trout Brook, nr Fort Ticonderoga, N America, 6 July 1758

(2) Sir RICHARD HOWE, 6th Bt, and 4th VISCOUNT HOWE, also 1st and last EARL HOWE, and **1st Baron Howe of Langar**, Co Nottingham (both GB), so *cr* 19 Aug 1788, with remainder in the case of the Barony to female issue, also *cr* previously 20 April 1782 VISCOUNT HOWE OF LANGAR, Co Nottingham, KG (1797), PC (1765); *b* 19 March 1725/6; *educ* Westminster and Eton; MP (Whig) Dartmouth 1757–82; RN: joined 1739, cmded *Baltimore* 1746 (wounded), in command attack on Cherbourg 1758, cmded *Magnanime* Quiberon Bay 1759, Capt 1748, R-Adml 1770, V-Adml 1775, Adml 1782, Col Marines 1760–90, Gen Marines 1796–99, a Ld Admlty 1763–65, Treasurer Navy 1765–70, C-in-C Mediterranean 1770, C-in-C America and Jt Commr American Colonies 1776–78, C-in-C Channel 1782 and 1793–97 during which time he accomplished the victory of the Glorious First of June over the French 1794 and quelled the mutiny at Spithead 1797, 1st Ld Admlty Jan-April 1783 and Dec 1783–88, V-Adml of GB 1792–96, Adml of the Fleet 1796; *m* 10 March 1758 Mary (*d* 9 Aug 1800), dau of Chiverton Hartopp, of Welby, Leics, and *dspm* 5 Aug 1799, when the Earldom of Howe and Viscountcy of Howe of Langar expired, having had:

1a SOPHIA CHARLOTTE, **Baroness Howe of Langar** in her own right; *b* 19 Feb 1762; *m* 1st 31 July 1787 Hon Penn Assheton Curzon (*d* 3 Sept 1797), est s of **1st Viscount Curzon of Penn** (*see* above), and had, with other issue:

1b RICHARD WILLIAM PENN, **1st Earl Howe**

1a **Baroness Howe of Langar** *m* 2nd 1 Oct 1812 Sir Jonathan Wathen Waller, 1st Bt (*d* 1 Jan 1853), and *d* 3 Dec 1835

2a Maria Juliana; *d* unm

3a Louisa Catherine; *m* 1st 21 May 1787 1st Marquess of Sligo (*qv*) and left issue; *m* 2nd 10 April 1813 1st and last Baron Stowell of Stowell Park (*see* 1836 edn) and *d* 20 Aug 1817. He *d* 28 Jan 1836

(3) Sir WILLIAM HOWE, 7th and last Bt, and 5th and last VISCOUNT HOWE, KB (1776), PC (1782); *b* 10 Aug 1729; *educ* Eton; MP (Whig) Nottingham 1758–80; Army: joined 1746, Lt 1747, Capt Lt 20th Foot 1749/50, Capt 1750, Maj 1756, Col 1762, Maj Gen 1772, Lt Gen 1777, Gen 1793, cmded Br forces battle of Bunker's Hill, won victory of Long Island 22 Aug 1776, took New York Sept 1776 and defended Germantown Oct 1776 in War of American Independence, Jt Commr North American colonies with his er bro 1776, Col 19th Light Dragoons 1786–1814, Lt-Gen Ordnance 1782–1804, Govr: Berwick 1795–1808 and Plymouth 1808–14; *m* 2 June 1765 Frances (*d* Sept 1817), 4th dau of Rt Hon Thomas Conolly, of Castletown, Co Kildare, and *dsp* 12 July 1814, when all his titles expired

1 Mary, Maid-of-Honour to QUEEN CAROLINE (w of GEORGE II); *m* 1st 14 June 1725 8th Earl of Pembroke and (5th Earl of) Montgomery (*qv*); *m* 2nd 9 Oct 1735 Hon John Mordaunt, bro of 4th Earl of Peterborough (*see* MORDAUNT, Bt), and *d* 12 Sept 1749

2 Judith; *m* 29 May 1725 Thomas Page, of Battlesden, Beds, 2nd s of Sir Gregory Page, 1st Bt, and *dsp* 1780

3 Anne; *m* 8 May 1728 Charles Mordaunt

The Hon PENN ASSHETON CURZON and SOPHIA CHARLOTTE, **Baroness Howe of Langar**'s son,

RICHARD WILLIAM PENN CURZON later CURZON-HOWE (roy licence 7 July 1821), **3rd Baron Howe of Langar** (through his mother), **2nd Viscount Curzon of Penn** and **2nd Baron Curzon of Penn** (through his f, having *s* his gf) and **1st Earl Howe** (UK), so *cr* 15 July 1821, GCH (1830), PC (1831); *b* 11 Dec 1796; *educ* Eton and Ch Ch Oxford; *m* 1st 20 March 1820 Harriet Georgiana (*d* 25 Oct 1836), 2nd dau of 6th Earl of Cardigan (*see* AILESBURY, M), and had:

1 GEORGE AUGUSTUS FREDERICK LOUIS CURZON-HOWE, **2nd Earl Howe**; MP S Lancs; *b* 16 Jan 1821; Lt Col cmdg Prince Albert's Own Leics Vols; *m* 3 Feb 1846 Harriet Mary (*d* 29 Jan 1877), dau of Henry C Sturt (*see* AILESBURY, M), and *d* 4 Feb 1876, having had:

(1) Harriet Alice; *m* 3 Feb 1871, as his 1st w, Rev Henry Neville Sherbrooke, late 43rd LI, 2nd s of Henry Porter Sherbrooke, DL, JP (*d* 2 Oct 1916), of Oxton Hall, Notts, and *d* 13 April 1875, leaving issue

2 RICHARD WILLIAM PENN, **3rd Earl**

3 Frederick, Capt RN; *b* 16 July 1823; *d* 23 Sept 1881

4 Henry Dugdale CURZON, of E Dean, Romsey, DL and JP Hants; *b* 21 Sept 1824; *m* 22 Oct 1857 Eleanor Young (*d* 28 Aug 1887), yst dau of Maj-Gen John Swinburne, of Keynsham, Somerset, and *d* 22 March 1910, having had:

(1) Henry; *b* 31 March 1865; *m* 11 Jan 1899 Ellen (*d* 1953), dau of Samuel Hibberd, and *d* 31 March 1912, leaving:

1a Henry CURZON later CURZON-HOWE (1949); *b* 29 Oct 1899; *educ* Midhurst GS; WW II as Cpl RAF and Sgt RM Police; schoolmaster; *m* 1940 Florence Jane (*d* 14 Feb 1997), dau of Charles Stanley Skinner, of Cornwall, and *dsp* 1985

1a Ivy Eleanor; *b* 17 July 1902; *d* unm 1973

(2) Assheton; *b* 1876; *d* 13 June 1925

(1) Nina; *d* unm 6 Jan 1920

(2) Millicent; *m* 25 June 1885 John Henry Jacob, RN (*d* 8 Aug 1905), of The Close, Salisbury, and *d* 16 Sept 1944, leaving issue

(3) Eleanor; *m* 22 Sept 1888 William Henry David Boyle and *d* 15 Nov 1893, leaving issue (*see* GLASGOW, E)

(4) Sybil; *b* 25 July 1869; *d* unm 16 May 1930

5 William Henry CURZON, Maj 17th Light Dragoons Crimea (medal and clasp and Turkish medal) and Centl India (medal); *b* 1 June 1827; *m* 1st 26 Oct 1870 Beatrice Louisa Margaret (*dsp* 10 July 1873), 2nd dau of Alexander Page; *m* 2nd 3 Nov 1874 Emily (*d* 21 Dec 1924), yst dau of Frederick Cowper, DL, of Carleton Hall, Penrith, and *d* 5 Jan 1914, leaving surv issue:

(1) Hilda Georgina Susan; *m* 14 Feb 1916 Rev Gordon Miles Staveley Oldham, OBE (*d* 1948), Vicar Ramsey, Hunts, RD St Ives, and *d* 26 Nov 1963, having had issue

6 Ernest George CURZON, Col 52nd Foot, AA&QMG Aldershot 1877–82, DAG Ireland, Col staff at Shorncliffe; *b* 12 Aug 1828; *m* 14 Jan 1856 Augusta Latham (*d* 24 Dec 1917 aged 82), 3rd dau of Brig-Gen — Hallifax, and *d* 5 March 1885, leaving:

(1) Ernest Charles Penn, Maj 18th and 3rd Hus Boer War 1899–1901 (Queen's medal with three clasps); *b* 24 Nov 1856; *m* 18 Oct 1882 Edith, CBE (1918) (*d* 30 April 1943), only dau of Charles Henry Basset, of Pilton House, and Watermouth Castle, Devon (*see* WILLIAMS, Bt, of Tregullow), and *d* 12 Feb 1938, having had issue:

1a Charles Ernest Basset Lothian, Lt RNR; *b* 1885; *m* 13 Jan 1917 Geraldine Fosbery (*d* 15 Sept 1962), dau of Sir James Mills, KCMG, and *d* 23 June 1952, leaving issue:

1b James Quintin Penn, Capt Gordon Highrs, WW II 1942–45 as Lt KRRC; *b* 21 Aug 1923; *educ* Eton; *m* 1st 10 June 1966 (*divorce* 1980) Jennifer Anne, yr dau of Percy Douglas Harrison, of Southsea; *m* 2nd 1980 *Mary Anne Vere (*m* 3rd 1987 Major John David Makgill-Critchton-Maitland, *see* LAUDERDALE, E), only dau of Maj Charles Herbert Harberton Eales, MC (*see* OGILVY, Bt), and formerly w of Charles Pepler Norton, and *d* 1985, leaving:

1c +(Charles) Mark Penn; *b* 12 Nov 1967

1c *Camilla Mary; *b* 10 July 1969; *m* 1 Feb 1997 *Simon J Chambers

1b Lorna Geraldine; *b* 5 Nov 1917; *d* 30 April 1945

2b *Mary Eleanora Basset [Mrs James Hay, Edinglassie, Huntly, Aberdeenshire, Scotland]; *b* 19 June 1920; *m* 19 April 1941 Maj James Malcolm Hay (*see* TWEEDDALE, M) and has issue

1a Nina Eleonora; *b* 18 July 1883; *d* 17 May 1886

2a Lorna Katherine; *m* 1st 27 Oct 1908 Capt Quintin Dick, DL (*d* 9 Dec 1923), only surv s of Rev Quintin Dick Hume; *m* 2nd 4 Aug 1927 **4th Earl Howe** (*see* below) and *d* 24 Feb 1961

(2) Robert Lothian, DL Essex; *b* 21 Nov 1857; *d* unm 18 Nov 1899

(3) FitzRoy Edmund Penn, Lt Col 6th Service Bn Roy Irish Regt, Roy Irish Rifles, served Egyptian Campaign 1898, present Khartoum (despatches, two medals with clasp), Sierra Leone Expdn 1898–99 (medal with clasp), Boer War 1900–02 (Queen's medal with four claps, King's medal with two clasps) and WW I; *b* 23 March 1859; *ka* 9 Sept 1916

(4) Arthur Wardlaw; *b* 5 Jan 1861; *m* 1894 Charlotte Gertrude (*d* 1915), dau of Richard Radcliffe, of Ontario, and *d* 23 Feb 1934, leaving:

1a Adelina Brudenell; *d* unm 30 Oct 1929

(1) Harriet Annie Augusta; *m* 29 April 1882 Thomas George Lithgow (*d* 7 Nov 1935), FRCS, LRCP, and *d* 26 Nov 1911, leaving issue

(2) Mary Ellen; *m* 19 June 1888 Rev Arthur Lewis Whitfield (*d* 1937), Rector Englefield, Berks, s of George Whitfield, and *d* 1940, leaving issue

7 Leicester CURZON later SMYTH (Sir) (roy licence 16 Nov 1866), KCB, KCMG; Gen Rifle Bde, Kt Legn Honour and Medjidie, ADC to Lord Raglan Crimea, Mil Sec Ireland 1865–70, cmded troops Southern Dist 1889, Govr and C-in-C Gibraltar 1890; *b* 25 Oct 1829; *m* 12 Feb 1866 Alicia Maria Eliza (*dsp* 13 July 1898), er dau and heiress of Robert Smyth, DL, JP, of Drumcree, Co Westmeath, and *d* 27 Jan 1891

1 Georgiana Charlotte; *m* 3 July 1845 8th Duke of Beaufort (*qv*), and *d* 14 May 1906, leaving issue

2 Adelaide Ida; *m* 16 July 1857 12th Earl of Westmorland (*qv*), and *d* 22 March 1903, having had issue

3 Emily Mary, Woman Bedchamber to HM QUEEN ALEXANDRA; *m* 5 Feb 1856 Col Sir Robert Nigel Kingscote, GCVO, KCB (*d* 22 Sept 1908), and *d* 9 Dec 1910, having had issue

The **1st Earl** *m* 2nd 9 Oct 1845 Anne (*d* 23 July 1877), 2nd dau of Adml Sir John Gore, KCB, and *d* 12 May 1870, having by her had:

8 Montagu CURZON, Col Rifle Bde, MP N Leicester 1883–85; *b* 21 Sept 1846; *m* 19 Oct 1886 Esmé (*m* 2nd 26 Oct 1909 Rev William Arthur King, Vicar Woodhouse, Leics, and *d* 25 May 1939), yst dau of Francis Horatio FitzRoy (*see* GRAFTON, D), and *d* 1 Sept 1907, leaving:

(1) William Montagu CURZON later CURZON-HERRICK (30 Nov 1915), of Beau Manor, Leics; Lt Rifle Bde SR, High Sheriff Leics 1927; *b* 8 Sept 1891; *m* 28 July 1916 Lady Maud Kathleen Cairnes Plantagenet Hastings (*d* 8 Feb 1965), est dau of 14th Earl of Huntingdon (*qv*), and *dsp* 29 Oct 1945

(1) Mary *b* 30 Oct 1887; *m* 28 Oct 1907 (*divorce* 1937) **5th Earl Howe** (*see* below), and *d* 1 Sept 1962, leaving issue

9 Assheton Gore CURZON-HOWE (Sir), GCVO, KCB, CMG; Adml C-in-C at Portsmouth; *b* 10 Aug 1850; *m* 25 Feb 1892 Alice Anne (*d* 5 Nov 1948), est dau of Major-Gen Sir John Cowell, PC, KCB, and *d* 1 March 1911, having had:

(1) Leicester Charles Assheton St John, MVO (1935), Capt RN, Naval Attaché Washington 1938, served WW I (despatches), Silver Medal of Italy; *b* 8 July 1894; *m* 28 Feb 1923 Marguerite Graham (*d* 1977), dau of A Allan Mackenzie, of Montreal, and *das* 21 Feb 1941, leaving:

1a *Anne Rita [Mrs Ian Edwards, Inwood House, Holly Hill Lane, Sarisbury Green, Hants SO31 7AH], late WRNS; *b* 14 Dec 1923; *m* 1st 11 Feb 1955, as his 2nd w, 19th Baron Teynham (*qv*); *m* 2nd 1975 Dr Ian Edwards (*d* 1988) and by her 1st husb has issue

(2) Assheton Penn CURZON-HOWE later CURZON-HOWE-HERRICK (roy licence June 1946), JP, Lt -Col RA, Page of Honour to HM GEORGE V 1913–15, served WW I and WW II (despatches); *b* 21 Aug 1898; *m* 26 Nov 1930 *Joan Henrietta, OBE (1964) [Mrs Assheton Curzon-Howe-Herrick, The Hermitage, Thornton Watlass, Ripon, Yorks], er dau of James Windsor Lewis, Welsh Gds, and *d* 23 Feb 1959, leaving:

1a +Assheton Montagu Windsor [Assheton Curzon-Howe-Herrick Esq, Le Chastanet, Collonges, Corrèze, France]; *b* 8 Feb 1939; *educ* Eton

1a Marigold Mary Henrietta, SRN 1964; *b* 7 Oct 1934; *m* 18 Dec 1982 *Patrick Benjamin Walker and *d* 1983

(1) Victoria Alexandrina Alice; *b* 1 Sept 1896 (HM QUEEN VICTORIA stood sponsor); *d* 3 Feb 1910

(2) Joyce Mary, MBE (1982); *b* 16 July 1906; *m* 1st 1 Sept 1934 Lt Col Thomas Ethelston Hussey (*ka* Normandy 9 June 1944), RA, est s of Henry Percy Hussey, of Bricklehurst Manor, Sussex; *m* 2nd 22 June 1950 R-Adml Robert Kirk Dickson, CB, DSO (*d* 17 Sept 1952), only surv s of William Kirk Dickson, LLD, advocate, of Edinburgh, and *dsp* 24 Sept 1997

(3) Elizabeth Anne, OBE (1946); WW II in FANY; *b* 15 Nov 1909; *m* 29 April 1939 Brig David Arthur Hunt, DSO, OBE, RA (*d* 25 April 1967), and had:

1a *Sarah Constance Curzon [Mrs Michael Dangerfield, Beechmead, Alton Pancras, Dorset DT2 7RT]; *b* 12 Nov 1942; *m* 18 Aug 1962 *Maj Michael Roland Dangerfield, 4th/7th Roy Dragoon Gds, and has:

1b *Roland; *b* 4 Oct 1969

1b *Georgina Sarah; *b* 27 July 1967

4 Mary Anna; *m* 7 Jan 1869 2nd Duke of Abercorn (*qv*) and *d* 10 May 1929, leaving issue

The 2nd EARL's bro,

RICHARD WILLIAM PENN CURZON-HOWE, **3rd Earl Howe**, GCVO (1897), CB (1858); Ld Lt and custos rotulorum Leics, Gen, Col 2nd Life Gds, Hon Col Leics Yeo Cav and Gren Gds; *b* 14 Feb 1822; *m* 8 Feb 1858 Isabella Maria Katherine (*d* 29 March 1922), est dau of Maj Gen Hon George Anson (*see* LICHFIELD, E), and *d* 25 Sept 1900, having had:

1 RICHARD GEORGE PENN CURZON, **4th Earl Howe**, GCVO (1903), TD, JP Bucks; MP (C) Wycombe 1885–1900, Treasurer Household 1896–1900, Ld-in-Waiting 1900–01 and 1901–03, Ld Chamberlain to HM QUEEN ALEXANDRA 1903–25, Capt Leics Yeo, Hon Lt-Col 2nd Bn Leics Vol Regt, Roy Victorian Chain 1925, Grand Cross Saviour of Greece, St Olaf Norway, Dannebrog Denmark, Polar Star Sweden, White Eagle Poland and Charles III of Spain, Grand Cordon Order of Leopold of Belgium, Grand Offr Legion of Honour; *b* 28 April 1861; *m* 1st 4 June 1883 Lady Georgiana Elizabeth Spencer-Churchill, LGStJ (*d* 8 Feb 1906), 5th dau of 7th Duke of Marlborough (*qv*), and had:

(1) FRANCIS RICHARD HENRY PENN CURZON, **5th Earl Howe**, PC (1929), CBE, VD; *b* 1 May 1884; *educ* Eton and Ch Ch Oxford; Cdre RNVR, Jr Ld Treasury 1924–29, Tstee Imperial War Museum 1925, pres RNVR Club and Br Racing Drivers' Club, chm RNLI, V-Pres Commn Sportif Internationale Competitions Ctee RAC, Assist Gunnery Offr HMS *Queen Elizabeth* 1914–19, Sr Inspr Degassing WW II, MP (C) S Battersea 1918–29, ADC (RNVR) to HM GEORGE V 1925–28; *m* 1st 28 Oct 1907 (*divorce* 1937) his cousin Mary (*d* 1 Sept 1962), only dau of Col Hon Montagu Curzon, and had:

1a EDWARD RICHARD ASSHETON PENN CURZON, **6th Earl Howe**, CBE (1961), DL (1906), JP (1946), CA (1958) Bucks, memb CC 1949; *b* 7 Aug 1908 (HM EDWARD VII stood sponsor); *educ* Eton and Corpus Christi Coll Cambridge; WW II as Lt Cdr RNVR in HMS *Cairo* and HMS *Howe*, memb LCC for Battersea 1937–46, chm S Bucks C Assoc 1949–65, Tstee King William IV Naval Asylum, memb Management Ctee *Arethusa* Trg Ship, memb RAC Ctee, CStJ, Commr Bucks St John's Ambulance Bde 1954–56, V-Chm RAC 1973, memb Ctee Management RNLI 1976; *m* 1st 23 July 1935 (*divorce* 1943) Priscilla, only dau of Lt Col Sir Archibald Weigall, 1st and last Bt, KCMG (*see* 1949 edn), and had:

1b *(Priscilla) Mary Rose [The Lady Mary Keen, The Old Rectory, Duntisbourne Rous, Glos]; *b* 12 Feb 1940; *m* 21 July 1962 *Charles William Lyle Keen, yr s of Harold Hugh Keen, of The Old Manor, Broadwell, Glos, and has:

1c *William Walter Maurice; *b* 1970

1c *Laura Mary Catherine; *b* 1 May 1963; *m* 1990 *Hon Nicholas Duncan Beatty, yr s of 2nd Earl Beatty (*qv*)

2c *Eleanor Margaret; *b* 4 April 1965

3c *Alice Priscilla Lyle; *b* 31 Aug 1966; *m* 1994 *Peter C P Oswald, est s of Peter David Hamilton Oswald, of Fliskmillan, Fife

2b *Jennifer Jane; *b* 12 May 1941; *m* 6 Sept 1962 *Alan Joseph Ponté, est s of Capt Leo Ponté, and has:

1c *David Joseph Marcus Blundell; *b* 30 March 1964

2c *Gideon Léo FitzRoy; *b* 11 May 1965

3c *Joshua Albert Coriat; *b* 21 Aug 1970

4c *Luke Antony Archibald; *b* 4 Sept 1974

1c *Rebecca Kate Priscilla Clara; *b* 23 April 1967

1a (cont.) The **6th Earl** *m* 2nd 30 April 1946 Grace Lilian, OStJ (*d* 24 Dec 1985) formerly w of Capt A N Barker, of Durban, and est dau of Stephen Frederick Wakeling, of Durban, and *d* 29 May 1984, leaving by her:

3b *Mary-Gaye Georgiana Lorna [The Lady Mary-Gaye Shaw, Hinton Ampner, Branmdean, Hants SO24 0LA]; *b* 21 Feb 1947; *m* 1st 18 Dec 1971 (*divorce* 1976) (Kevin) Esmond (Peter) Cooper-Key (*d* 1985), and has issue (*see* ROTHERMERE, V); *m* 2nd 27 May 1977 (*divorce* 1987) John Austen Anstruther-Gough-Calthorpe and has further issue (*see* ANSTRUTHER-GOUGH-CALTHORPE, Bt); *m* 3rd 1988 (*divorce* 1994) Jeffrey Bonas, s of Harry Bonas, of Grangewood Hall, Netherseale, Burton-on-Trent, and by him has:

1c *Cressida; *b* 1989

3b (cont.) Lady Mary-Gaye Bonas *m* 4th 17 Dec 1996 *Christopher Shaw

4b *Charlotte Elizabeth Anne [The Lady Charlotte Dinan, Chalkpit House, Knotty Green, Beaconsfield, Bucks]; *b* 5 July 1948; *m* 1988 *Capt (John) Barry Dinan, Irish Gds, and has:

1c *Richard Assheton Dermot; *b* 1986

1a Georgiana Mary; *b* 7 Jan 1910; *m* 1st 27 Nov 1935 (*divorce* 1943, resumed maiden name 1944) Lt Home Ronald Archibald Kidston, RN, yr s of Capt Archibald Glen Kidston, JP; *m* 2nd 1 Nov 1957, as his 2nd w, Lt-Col Lewis Stanton Starkey (*see* STARKEY, Bt) and *d* 11 Jan 1976, leaving by her 1st husb:

1b *Glen; *b* 17 April 1937; *educ* Eton and Ch Ch Oxford

(1) (cont.) The **5th Earl** *m* 2nd 8 Feb 1937 (*divorce* 1943) Joyce Mary Mclean, dau of Charles Mclean Jack, of Johannesburg, and by her had:

2a *Frances Esmé [The Lady Frances Denman, East Heath Barn, Stream Lane, Hawkhurst, Kent TN18 4RD]; *b* 8 June 1939; *m* 1st 4 April 1962 Derek Alan Whiting and has:

1b *Francis; *b* 15 Aug 1965

2b *Alexander; *b* 27 June 1967

2a (cont.) Lady Frances Whiting *m* 2nd 26 March 1976 *Harold Denman and has further issue (*see* DENMAN, B)

(1) (cont.) The **5th Earl** *m* 3rd 8 Feb 1944 *Sybil Boyter [Mrs Graham Goodson, 23 Lee Rd, Aldeburgh, Suffolk] (*m* 3rd 27 Sept 1972 Graham Goodson, who *d* 1988), formerly w of Maj Ernest Duncombe Shafto and dau of Capt Francis Johnson, of Hove, and *d* 26 July 1964, having by her had:

3a *Sarah-Marguerite (Sally) [The Lady Sarah-Marguerite Aspinall, 64 Sloane St, London SW1X 9SH]; *b* 25 Jan 1945; *m* 1st 29 March 1966 Piers Raymond Courage (*k* motor accident 21 June 1970), est s of Richard Hubert Courage, JP, of Fitzwalters, Shenfield, Essex, and has issue:

1b *Jason Piers; *b* 10 Feb 1967

2b *Amos Edward Sebastian; *b* 26 Feb 1969; *educ* Eton and Oxford; wildlife photographer

3a (cont.) Lady Sarah Courage *m* 2nd 1972 *John Victor Aspinall and has issue:

3b *Bassa Wulfhere; *b* 1972

1 (cont.) The **4th Earl** *m* 2nd 11 Dec 1919 Florence (*d* 14 April 1925), widow of 2nd Marquess of Dufferin and Ava (*see* DUFFERIN AND CLANEBOYE, B) and dau of John H Davis, of New York; *m* 3rd 4 Aug 1927 Lorna Katherine (*d* 24 Feb 1961), widow of Capt Quintin Dick, DL, and dau of Major Ernest Charles Penn Curzon (*see* above), and *d* 10 Jan 1929

2 Frederick Graham, King's Messenger, Hon Attaché Dip Serv 1891–93, Coronation Medals 1902 and 1911; *b* 5 March 1868; *m* 11 Sept 1894 (*divorce* 1903) Minnie Ellis Gertrude (*d* 21 Jan 1943), dau of Capt Dodsworth Jeffreys, and *d* 4 Nov 1920, leaving:

(1) (Chambré) George William Penn, Cdr RN, served WW I (despatches) and WW II, actor; *b* 18 Oct 1898; *m* 24 Feb 1927 Mrs Louise Merrill Rowe (*d* 1 Jan 1942), dau of A Jackson Stone, of Paris; *m* 2nd 25 April 1950 (*divorce* 1965) Jane Victoria (*d* 13 May 1997), dau of Malcolm Mackenzie Fergusson, of Toronto, and *d* 7 May 1976, leaving:

1a FREDERICK RICHARD PENN CURZON **7th and present Earl Howe**

1a *Emma Charlotte; granted rank of earl's dau 1985; *b* 10 Feb 1953; SRN

(1) Evelyn Ellis Isabella; *b* 9 July 1897; *d* 22 Dec 1987

1 Evelyn Alice; *b* 10 April 1862; *m* 25 April 1896 John Eyre, of Three Gables, Beaconsfield, and *d* 4 Oct 1913

2 Edith Cecilia; *m* 18 April 1896 Harry Walter Franklin (*d* 14 Mar 1915), s of James Franklin, 77th Regt, The Royals, and *d* 20 Sept 1936, having had issue

HOWE OF ABERAVON

Arms: Chequy or and azure on a chief per pale vert and gules a portcullis chained or. **Crest:** Upon a howe turfed proper a wolf courant sable mantled with a fleece of a sheep sans head holding in its mouth a remnant of cloth gules. **Supporters:** Dexter, a dragon gules armed and langued azure gorged with a collar company sable and argent the sable charged with a crescent ermine the argent with a rose gules barbed and seeded proper holding in its exterior foreclaw a sword erect argent hilt pommel and quillons or; sinister, a winged lion or armed and langued gules similarly gorged and resting its interior hind leg upon a clarion also gold. **Motto:** *Tibi fidelis* ('To yourself be true'). **Creation:** B. (LP, UK) 1992.

THE BARON HOWE OF ABERAVON, of Tandridge, Co Surrey (Sir (Richard Edward) Geoffrey Howe, CH (1996), PC (1972)) [The Rt Hon The Lord Howe of Aberavon CH PC, House of Lords, London SW1A 0PW]; *b* 20 Dec 1926; *educ* Winchester and Trin Hall Cambridge (MA, LLB, Hon Fell 1992); Lt Roy Signals and E African Signals 1945–48; barrister Middle Temple 1952, Memb: Gen Cncl Bar 1957–61 and Exec Ctee Justice 1963–70, QC 1965, Dep-Chm Glam QS 1966–70, Bencher 1969; Chm Bow Gp 1955; md *Crossbow* 1957–60 (ed 1960–62); MP (C) Bebington 1964–66, Reigate 1970–74, E Surrey 1974–92, Sec C Parly Health and Soc Sec Ctee 1964–65, Oppn Spokesman: Labour and Soc Servs 1965–66, Slr-Gen 1970–72, ktd 1970, Min Trade and Consumer Affrs 1972–74, Oppn Spokesman: Soc Serv 1974–75, Treas and Ec Affrs 1975–79; Chllr Exchequer 1979–83, For Sec 1983–1989, Leader H of C, Ld Pres Cncl and Dep PM 1989–1990; Memb Cncl Surrey U 1970–; Chm: IMF Interim Ctee 1982–83, Framlington Russian Investment Fund 1994–, Project Liberty Steering Ctee 1991–; dir: Sun Alliance and London Insur 1974–79, AGB Research 1974–79, EMI 1976–79; Patron Enterprise Europe 1990–; non-exec dir: Glaxo Hldgs 1991–96, BICC 1991–97; Pres: Trinity Hall Assoc 1977–78, C Political Centre Nat Advsy Ctee 1977–79, Nat Union of C and U Assocs 1983–84, GB-China Centre 1992–, Assoc Consumer Research 1992– (Hon V-Pres 1974–92) and Acad of Experts 1996–; Jt-Pres Wealth of Nations Fndn 1991–, Special Advsr Jones, Day, Reavis & Pogue 1991–, Memb Internat Advsy Cncls: J P Morgan & Co 1992–, Inst Internat Studies Stanford U 1990–, Centre European Policy Studies 1992–; Memb Bertelsmann Fndn Bonn 1992–; Chm Advsy Bd English Centre Legal Studies Warsaw U 1992–; V-Pres: RUSI 1991–, English Coll Fndn Prague 1992–; Visitor SOAS 1991–; Visiting Fell John F Kennedy Sch of Govt Harvard 1991–92; Herman Phleger Visiting Prof Stanford Law Sch 1993; Grand Cross Order Merit Germany 1992; Hon LLD Wales 1988, Hon DCL City 1993; author: *Conflict of Loyalty* (1994); *m* 1953 *Elspeth Rosamund Morton, JP, dau of Philip Morton Shand and aunt of Mrs Camilla Parker-Bowles (*see* ASHCOMBE, B), and has:

1 *Alexander Edward Thomson; *b* 1959; *educ* Marlborough and York U; *m* Aug 1997 *Victoria McIvor

1 *Caroline; *b* 1955; *m* 1st 1977 (*divorce* 1988) Edward Thornton; *m* 2nd 1994 *Stephen Ralph and by her 1st husb has:

(1) *Christopher; *b* 1980

2 *Amanda; *b* 1959; *m* 1981 *S F Glanvill and has:

(1) *James; *b* 1989

(1) *Emma; *b* 1996

Lineage: BENJAMIN EDWARD HOWE, of Port Talbot, Glam; *m* E F Thomson, JP, and had an er s:

(RICHARD EDWARD) GEOFFREY (Sir), *cr* a **Baron**

HOWELL OF GUILDFORD

Creation: B. (LP, UK) 19 April 1997.

THE BARON HOWELL OF GUILDFORD, of Penton Mewsey, Co Hants (David Arthur Russell Howell, PC (1979)) [The Rt Hon The Lord Howell PC, House of Lords, London SW1A 0PW]; *b* 18 Jan 1936; *educ* Eton and King's Coll Cambridge; Lt Coldstream Gds 1954–56; Treasury Ec Section 1959–60; leader writer and special correspondent *Daily Telegraph* 1960; Chm Bow Gp 1961–62, ed *Crossbow* 1962–64, Dir C Political Centre 1964–66, MP (C) Guildford 1966–97, Ld Commr Treasury 1970–71, Parly Sec CSD 1970–72, Parly U-Sec: Employment 1971–72, NI 1972, Min State: NI 1972–74, Energy 1974, Sec State Energy 1979–81, Tport 1981–83, Chm: Select Ctee For Affrs 1987–97, C One Natiion Gp 1987–, UK-Japan 2000 Gp 1990–; Sr Visiting Fell Policy Studies Inst 1983–85; Visiting Fell Nuffield Coll Oxford 1993–; dir: Trafalgar House 1990–, Jardine Insur Brokers 1991–, Monks Investment Tst 1993–; Memb: Internat Advsy Cncl Swiss Bank Corp 1988–; author: *Principles to Practice* (co-author, 1960), *The Conservative Opportunity* (1965), *Freedom and Capital* (1981), *Blind Victory: a study in income, wealth and power* (1986); *m* 1967 *(Cary) Davina, yr.dau of Maj David John Wallace, KRRC (*ka* 1944), and has:

1 *Toby David; *b* 1975

1 *Frances Victoria; *b* 18 Feb 1969; *m* 4 April 1998 *George Osborne, est s of Sir Peter Osborne, 17th Bt (*qv*)

2 *Kate Davina; *b* 1970

Lineage: *See* BOWATER, Bt, of Friston

HOWICK OF GLENDALE

Arms: Az. a fess or charged with an eastern crown az. as a mark of difference, in chief a bear's head couped ppr., muzzled and ringed or. **Crest:** A mullet erminois, two of the points resting on the pinions of a pair of wings conjoined and elevated arg. **Supporters:** Dexter, a tiger guardant ppr., gorged with an eastern crown or; sinister, a lion guardant purpure crowned with a ducal coronet or and gorged with an eastern crown also or. **Motto:** *De bon vouloir servir le roi* ('To serve the King with goodwill'). **Creation:** B. (UK) 8 Feb 1960.

THE 2ND BARON HOWICK OF GLENDALE, of Howick, Co Northumberland (Charles Evelyn Baring) [The Rt Hon The Lord Howick of Glendale, Howick, Alnwick, Northumberland NE66 3LB; 42 Bedford Gdns, London W8 7EH]; *b* 30 Dec 1937; *s f* 1973; *educ* Eton and New Coll Oxford; dir Baring Bros 1969–82; memb exec ctee Nat Art Collections Fund; *m* 11 April 1964 *Clare Nicolette, yr dau of Col Cyril Darby, MC, of Kemerton Court, Tewkesbury, Glos, by Monica Clarice, yr dau of Lt-Col Edward Marten Dunne, JP, DL, of Gatley Park, and Bircher Hall, Herefs, and has:

1 +DAVID EVELYN CHARLES; *b* 26 March 1975

1 *Rachel Monica; *b* 29 June 1967; *m* 1989 *Capt (George Charles) Nicholas Lane Fox, Blues and Royals, s of George Lane Fox, of Bramham Park, Wetherby, W Yorks (*see* 1940 edn BINGLEY, B), and has:

(1) *Charles Edward; *b* 13 June 1996

(1) *Sophie; *b* 1991

2 *Jessica Mary Clare; *b* 8 Oct 1969; *m* 2 Sept 1995 *Marcus Laithwaite, est s of Paul Laithwaite, of Deeside House, Chester

3 *Alice Olivia; *b* 17 March 1971

Lineage: The 1st EARL OF CROMER (*qv*) had by his 2nd w an only child:

Sir EVELYN BARING, **1st Baron Howick of Glendale**, of Howick, Co Northumberland (UK), so *cr* 8 Feb 1960, KG (1972), GCMG (1955, KCMG 1942), KCVO (1947), DL (1968); *b* 29 Sept 1903; *educ* Winchester and New Coll Oxford (BA, Hon Fell 1960); DCL Newcastle U 1968, ICS 1926–34, Sec to Agent of Govt of India in S Africa, Govr S Rhodesia 1942–44, High Commr Basutoland, Bechuanaland Protectorate and Swaziland and for UK in Union of S Africa 1944–51, Govr and C-in-C Kenya, chm E Africa Commn 1952–59 and Cwlth Devpt Corp 1961–72 (dep chm 1960–61), dir Swan, Hunter and Wigham Richardson, md Sudan Plantation Syndicate, memb Nature Conservancy 1961 (chm 1963) and Governing Body SOAS Lond U 1961–68, pres Centre for Internat Briefing 1972, KStJ; *m* 24 April 1935 *Lady Mary Cecil Grey, er dau of 5th Earl Grey (*qv*), and *d* 10 March 1973, leaving:

1 CHARLES EVELYN BARING, **2nd and present Baron Howick of Glendale**

1 *Katherine Mary Alice [The Hon Lady Wakefield, Chillingham Castle, Alnwick, Northumberland NE66 5NJ]; *b* 30 March 1936; *m* Dec 1974, as his 3rd w, *Sir (Edward) Humphry Tyrell Wakefield, 2nd Bt (*qv*)

2 *Elizabeth Beatrice; *b* 10 Jan 1940; *m* 15 Jan 1962 Capt Nicholas Albany Gibbs (*d* 1984), 9th Roy Lancers, and has issue (*see* ALDENHAM and HUNSDON OF HUNSDON, B)

HOWIE OF TROON

Creation: B (LP, UK) 1978.

THE BARON HOWIE OF TROON, of Troon, in the District of Kyle and Carrick (William Howie) [The Rt Hon The Lord Howie of Troon, 34 Temple Fortune Lane, London NW11 7UL]; *b* 2 March 1924; *educ* Marr Coll Troon and Roy Tech Coll Glasgow (BSc); MP (Lab) Luton 1963–70, Assist Whip 1964–66, Ld Commr Treasury 1966–67, Comptroller Household 1967–68, V-Chm PLP 1968–70; Memb: CICE 1964–67, Govrs Imp Coll 1965–67, Governing Cncl City U 1968–91, Ctee Inquiry Engrg Profession 1977–80; Pres: Assoc Supervisory and Exec Engrs 1980–85, Assoc Educn and Trg Technology 1982–93, Independent Publishers' Guild 1987–93; Pro-Chancellor City U 1984–91; V-Pres PPA 1990–; MSocIS France 1978, FICE 1984 (MICE 1951), Hon DSc City U 1992, Hon LLD Strathclyde 1994, Hon FIStructE 1995; author: *Public Sector Publishing* (jt author, 1968), *Trade Unions and the Professional Engineer* (1977), *Trade Unions in Constructions* (1981); *Thames Tunnel to Channel Tunnel* (jt ed, 1987); *m* 1951 *Mairi Margaret, dau of John Sanderson, of Troon, and has:

1 *Angus; *b* 1963; *m* 1995 *Julie Bixley

2 *Alexander Robin; *b* 1965

1 *Annabel Martha; *b* 1956; *m* 1979 *Louis Gibb

2 *Alisoun Mary Kyle; *b* 1959; *m* 1991 *Luke Batterham

Lineage: PETER HOWIE, of Troon, Ayrshire; *m* Annie McGhee and had:

WILLIAM, *cr* a **Baron**

HOYLE

Creation: B. (LP, UK) 19 April 1997.

THE BARON HOYLE, of Warrington in the Co Palatine of Chester ((Eric) Doug(las) Harvey Hoyle, JP (1958)) [The Rt Hon The Lord Hoyle JP, House of Lords, London SW1A 0PW]; *b* 17 Feb 1930; *educ* Adlington C of E Sch and Horwich and Bolton Technical Coll; apprentice engr BR 1946–51, sales engr AEI 1951–53, sales engr and mktg exec Charles Weston Ltd 1951–74, memb: Manchester Regnl Hosp Bd 1968–74, NW RHA 1974–75, MP (Lab) Nelson and Colne 1974–79, Warrington 1981–83, Warrington N 1983–97; memb: Select Ctee Trade and Industry 1984–92, PLP Trade and Industry Ctee 1987–92, Nat Exec Lab Party 1978–82 and 1983–85, Govt Whip Ho Lds 1997–; Chm: ASTMS Parly Ctee 1975–76, PLP 1992–; Pres: ASTMS 1977–81 and 1985–88 (V-Pres 1981–85), MSF 1988–91 (Jt-Pres 1988–90), Adlington Cricket Club 1974–; *m* 1953 Pauline Spencer (*d* 1991) and has:

1 *Lindsay Harvey; *b* 10 June 1957; *educ* Adlington Co Sch, Lord's Coll Bolton; building firm proprietor, md textile printing firm, memb (Lab) Chorley Cncl (Dep Leader 1995–, chm Ec Devpt and Tourist Ctee), Mayor Chorley 1997–98; MP (Lab) Chorley 1997– ; *m* 1st 19– (*divorce* 1982) Lynda Anne Fowler; *m* 2nd 1994 *Catherine Swindley and has by her two daus

Lineage: WILLIAM HOYLE; *m* Leah Ellen Harvey and had:

(ERIC) DOUG(LAS) HARVEY, *cr* a **Baron**

HUGHES, Baron

Creation: B. (LP, UK) 7 Feb 1961.

THE BARON HUGHES, of Co of City of Dundee (William Hughes, CBE (1956, OBE 1942), PC (1970), JP (1943), DL (Co of City of Dundee 1960)) [The Rt Hon The Lord Hughes CBE PC JP DL, The Stables, Ross, Comrie, Perthshire PH6 2JU]; *b* 22 Jan 1911; *educ* Balfour Street Sch Dundee and Dundee Tech; Memb Dundee Town Cncl 1933–36 and 1937–61; WW II: ARP Controller Dundee 1939–43, RAOC India, Borneo and Burma 1944, Capt 1946; Hon City Treas Dundee 1946–47; Chm Scotland E Regnl Hosp Bd 1948–60; Ld Provost and Lt Co of City of Dundee 1954–60; Memb: Court St Andrews U 1954–63, Cncl Queen's Coll Dundee 1954–63, N Scotland Hydro-Electric Bd 1956–64, Ctee Civil Juries 1958–59, Ctee Enquire Registration Title to Land Scotland 1960–62, Scottish Tport Cncl 1960–64; Chm Glenrothes Devpt Corp 1960–64; Scottish Office: Jt Parly U-Sec 1964–69, Min State 1969–70 and 1974–75; Chm: E Kilbride Devpt Corp 1975–82, Roy Commn Legal Servs Scotland 1976–80; Pres: Scottish Fedn Housing Assocns 1975–, Scottish Assoc Mental Health 1975–; Del WEU and Cncl Europe 1976–87; Chevalier Legion Hon 1958, Hon LLD St Andrews 1960; *m*

22 Feb 1951 Christian Clacher (*d* 12 Nov 1994), dau of James and Sophia Gordon, and has:

1 *(Christian) Alison [The Hon Mrs Henry, Tigh-an-Lios, Ross, Comrie, Perthshire]; *b* 2 March 1952; *educ* Strathclyde U (BSc); *m* 1973 *Allan Cameron Cassels Henry and has:

(1) *Graham

(2) *Jamie

(1) *Gillian

(2) *Elaine

2 *Janet Margaret [The Hon Janet Hughes, Alltan, by Tulloes, Forfar, Angus DD8 2NE]; *b* 21 Feb 1956; *educ* Edinburgh U (BSc) and OU (BA)

Lineage: JOSEPH HUGHES; *m* Margaret — and had an est s:

WILLIAM, *cr* a **Baron**

HUGHES, Bt

Arms: Quarterly of eight, 1st, az. a lion rampant or (for HUGHES); 2nd, gu. a lion rampant regardant or (for ELISTAN GLODRYDD); 3rd az. three crowns in pale or (for BELI MAWR); 4th, per bend sinister erm. and ermines a lion rampant or (for TUDOR TREVOR); 5th or a lion rampant regardant sa. (for GWAETH VOYD); 6th per pale az. and sa. three fleurs-de-lys or (for YNYR, King of Gwent); 7th sa. a chevron between three goat's heads erased or (for ITHEL VELYN); 8th, az. a lion cowed passant guardant or (for LLEWELLYN AUR DORCHOG). **Creation:** Bt. (GB) 17 July 1773.

SIR DAVID COLLINGWOOD HUGHES, 14TH BT, of East Bergholt, Suffolk [Sir David Hughes Bt, The Berristead, Wilburton, Ely, Cambs CB6 3RP]; *b* 29 Dec 1936; *s f* 1970; *educ* Oundle and Magdalene Coll Cambridge (BA 1960, MA 1967); *m* 14 March 1964 *Rosemary Ann, MA, LLB (Cambridge), only dau of Rev John Pain, of Framfield Vicarage, nr Uckfield, Sussex, and has had:

1 +THOMAS COLLINGWOOD; *b* 16 Feb 1966

2 +Timothy John Pell; *b* 13 March 1968

3 +Benjamin Richard; *b* 30 Sept 1969

4 Anthony George David; *b* 1972; *d* in a road accident 1991

Lineage: ALAN Ap GRIFFITH; had:

JENKYN; had:

JOHN; had:

HUGH; had:

THOMAS HUGHES; *m* Katherine, dau of Matthew-Griffith ap Robert, and had:

Sir THOMAS HUGHES, of Wells, Somerset; Recorder Bath, ktd 1619; *m* 1st Hester, dau of Rev William Tonnes, DCL, Canon of Wells; *m* 2nd Frances, dau of Nicholas Mynne, of Norfolk, and *d* 1626, leaving by her, with other issue:

Capt THOMAS HUGHES, of Barnet, Middx, and Deptford, Kent; *m* Ellen (*d* 1660), sis of Thomas Harman, and *d* 1645, leaving:

HENRY HUGHES, of Deptford; *m* Mary — (*d* Aug 1705) and *d* Oct 1679, leaving, with other issue:

Capt RICHARD HUGHES, of Deptford; RN; Commr Portsmouth Dockyard; *m* Mary, dau of Isaac Loader, and *d* 11 Nov 1756, leaving, with a yr s (Robert, Adml RN; *d* 19 Jan 1774):

Sir Richard Hughes, 1st Bt (GB), so *cr* 17 July 1773; Capt RN, Commr Portsmouth Dockyard; *m* Joanne, dau of Capt William Collyer, RN, and *d* 23 Sept 1780, having had:

1 **Sir Richard Hughes, 2nd Bt**; Adml of the Red, 2ic under Lord Howe (*qv*) Relief of Gibraltar, took the *Solitaire* and won a victory over the French off Barbados 1782; *b* 1729; *m* Jane, dau of William Sloane, of S Stoneham, Hants, n of Sir Hans Sloane, and *d* 5 Jan 1812, having had, with other issue:

(1) Rose Mary; *m* 1784 Maj John Browne (*d* 1814), 67th Foot, n of the Earl of Altamont (*see* SLIGO, M), and left issue

2 ROBERT (Sir), **3rd Bt**

1 Mary; *m* 1st Capt Thomas Collingwood, RN, of Unthank; *m* 2nd Col Nathaniel Heywood

2 Sarah; *d* unm

The 2nd Bt's bro,

Rev Sir Robert Hughes, 3rd Bt; *bapt* 17 Sept 1739; Rector Trimley St Mary, Suffolk; *m* 1st Gratiana, dau of Thomas Mangles, and had:

1 **Rev Sir Richard Hughes, 4th Bt**; *b* 2 June 1768; *m* 8 Dec 1798 Sarah Perring (*d* 15 July 1848), dau of Rev Richard Sleeman, Vicar Tavistock, and *d* 3 Jan 1833, having had, with two daus (*d* unm):

(1) **Sir Richard Hughes, 5th Bt**; *b* 10 Oct 1803; barrister Middle Temple; *d* umn 16 May 1863

(2) **Sir Edward Hughes, 6th Bt**; *b* 31 March 1809; *d* unm 8 Aug 1871

(1) Sarah Catherine; *m* 8 March 1849 Rev Baldwin Leighton, n of Sir Baldwin Leighton, 6th Bt, of Wattesborough (*qv*), and *d* 21 June 1864

2 Robert (Rev); *m* Judith, dau of Robert Porteus, and *d* 1828, leaving, with other issue:

(1) **Sir Frederick Hughes, 7th Bt**; *b* 1816; *m* 1848 Matilda, dau of Edward Yates, and *dsp* 1 Feb 1889

1 Gratiana; *d* unm

Sir Robert *m* 2nd 1798 Bethia, dau of Thomas Hiscutt, and was *bur* 4 June 1814, having by her had:

3 THOMAS COLLINGWOOD (Sir), **8th Bt**

4 William; barrister; *b* 1803; *m* 1827 Jane Caroline, dau of Edward Knapman, of Bideford, Devon, and *d* Aug 1861, having had:

(1) William Collingwood; *b* 16 July 1830; *m* 16 Oct 1855 Fanny Agnes (*d* 7 Nov 1904), dau of Col James Fynmore, RMLI, and *d* 3 July 1899, leaving:

1a Collingwood James; Lt-Cdr RNVR, Paymaster Cape Colonial Division RNVR, SW Africa with S African Expdny Force 1914–15, Naval Intelligence Dept Admlty 1917–19, MP Peckham 1922–24; *b* 31 Jan 1872; *m* 11 Aug 1899 Lilian, yr, dau of John Crocker, Head RNE Coll Keyham, and *d* 25 March 1963, leaving:

1b Helen Lily Collingwood; *b* 7 March 1903

2b Diana Crocker Collingwood; *b* 13 Feb 1905

1a Fanny Jane; *d* unm 5 July 1928

2a Elizabeth Bethia

3a Grace Maud; *m* 9 Aug 1890 Mathew Melville Bawden, of Plymouth

4a Lilian Rosina

5a Eva Mary; *m* April 1895 Rev Henry Jacob Swanger Glover, and had issue

(2) Edward; *b* 1 Oct 1834; lost at sea 1874

(3) Arthur; *b* 30 Sept 1836; *m* 20 Sep 1860 Penelope Susanna (*d* 1918), dau of Henry Thwaites, and *d* 1909, having had:

1a Arthur; *b* 18 July 1861; *m* 20 Feb 1897 Louisa Grace (*d* 1950), dau of Ernest Warren, and *d* 16 Dec 1905, having had:

1b Arthur Warren Collingwood; *d* an inf

2b Richard Arthur Warren, OBE (1946); Hon DLitt U of Wales 1956, dep pncpl Priority Offr Admiralty, poet, playwright and novelist, author: *A High Wind in Jamaica* (1929), *In Hazard* (1938), *A Fox in the Attic* (1961) and *The Wooden Shepherdess*; *b* 19 April 1900; *educ* Charterhouse and Oriel Coll Oxford; *m* 8 Jan 1932 Frances Catherine Ruth (*d* 1985), 2nd dau of Gardner Sebastian Bazley (*see* BAZLEY, Bt), and *d* 28 April 1976, leaving:

1c +Robert Elystan-Glodrydd (Rev) [The Rev Robert Hughes, Clogwyn Melyn, Talsarnau, Gwynedd LL47 6TP]; MLitt Birmingham U; *b* 20 Nov 1932; *educ* Trin Coll Oxford (MA 1954); *m* 1960 *Sheila Basketts and has:

1d *Claire Frances Rosemary; *b* 1961

2d *Rachel Catherine; *b* 1964

2c +Owain Gardner Collingwood; *b* 21 Nov 1943

1c *Penelope; *b* 27 April, 1934; *educ* Somerville Coll Oxford (MA); *m* 20 Dec 1958 *Robin Paul Minney and has:

1d *Thomas; *b* 6 April 1960

2d *Hugo Benjamin Paulus; *b* 31 Jan 1962

3d *James; *b* 3 Aug 1963

4d *Richard; *b* 1967

2c *Lleky Susannah; *b* 6 Aug 1936; *m* 19– Stavros J Papastavrou, MA (decd), lecturer Byzantine and Modern Greek Cambridge, Fell Peterhouse, and has:

1d *Vassili Alexander Dimitri; *b* 1960

1d *Ekaterina Theodora Joanna; *b* 18 Feb 1966

3c *Catherine Phyllida; *b* 17 April 1940; *m* 23 July 1960 *Colin Michael Wells and has:

1d *Christopher William Llewellyn; *b* 13 May 1961

2d *Dominic Richard Alexander; *b* 7 March 1963

1b Grace Margaret Lilias; *d* an infant

2a Alfred Collingwood; *b* 22 Oct 1864; *m* 16 Oct 1897 Ada Mary (*d* 23 Sept 1940), dau of Edmond Drage, and *d* 1915, leaving:

1b +Stanley Collingwood; *b* 1903

2b +Jack Collingwood; *b* 20 Aug 1903

3b +Harry Leonard Collingwood; *b* 12 July 1906; *m* 19– *Pamela Phillips and has:

1c +A son; *b* 2 June 1943

3a Edward; *b* 16 Aug 1867; *m* 28 July 1893, Helena (*d* 2 Jan 1952), dau of John Baldwin Buckstone, and *d* Feb 1946, leaving:

1b Edward Buckstone; *b* Nov 1902; *m* 19– Agnes Katherine Weber and *d* Sept 1959

1b Helen Isabella; *m* 1915 Harry John Johnson and had:

1c Katherine Mary; *b* 1916; *m* 10 Nov 1941 Stuart Gore McCampbell and has:

1d *Stuart; *b* 10 Sept 1945

1d *Kathie; *b* 17 March 1941; *m* 23 March 1963 *Joseph R Hardiman and has:
1e *Katherine; *b* 27 July 1965
2d *Bonnie; *b* 21 Feb 1943; *m* 25 Feb 1962 *Laurence Carrington Road and has had:
1e Laurence McCampbell; *b* 27 Feb 1963; *d* 13 Oct 1966
2e *Christopher Thorburn; *b* 24 Feb 1966
2c Helen Janet; *m* 12 Sept 1941 Edward George Johnson and has:
1d *Penelope Wyatt; *b* 22 Aug 1944
2d *Karen Hughes; *b* 13 May 1946
4a Henry; *b* 3 Feb 1869; *d* unm 1 June 1888
5a Robert, MRCS, LRCP Lond 1895, Ch Sch MO Stoke-on-Trent, Capt RAMC; *b* 1 July 1870; *m* 10 Jan 1900 Ella Fanny (*d* 1953), dau of Frederick Boldero, and *d* 1929, leaving:
1b +Robert Bernard [Robert Hughes Esq, Calle Buen Aire, 26 3rd Piso B, Villa Carlos, Minorca, Spain]; *b* 23 June 1906
1b Mary Doris Winifride
2b *Margaret Rosemary [Mrs William Woodward, Residencia de Anlians, Mahon, Minorca, Spain]; *b* 1909; *m* 1938 (*divorce* 1976) John Hannaford; *m* 2nd 1979 William Woodward (*d* 1991)
1a Mary Frances; *d* 1940
2a Edith; *m* 4 Sept 1886 Herbert Innes Fripp and had issue
(4) Henry Howell; *b* 7 Jan 1841; *d* 1890
(1) Elizabeth
5 Arthur; *b* 5 July 1805; *m* 1st 1826 Frances, dau of William Burnard; *m* 2nd 16 Jan 1838 Hon Anna Maria Petre (*d* 14 Oct 1864), dau of 10th Baron Petre (*qv*), and *d* 5 Nov 1838, leaving by his 1st w:
(1) Ellen Hamilton; *d* unm 27 Dec 1915
2 Mary; *m* Rev Thomas Gibbons, Rector Peter Tavy, Devon, and *d* 1858, having had issue

The 7th Bt's uncle,

Rev Sir Thomas Collingwood Hughes, 8th Bt; *b* 12 Aug 1800; Rector Little Billing, Northants; *m* 1st 31 May 1820 Elizabeth St John (*d* 12 July 1879), dau and coheir of Robert Butcher, of Upland Grove, nr Bungay, Suffolk; *m* 2nd 20 April 1881 Mary Agnes Winwood (*m* 2nd Nov 1890 Robert Halliday Gunning, MD, LLD (*d* 22 March 1900), and *d* 19 Oct 1932), dau of Sir William Smith, 3rd Bt, of Eardiston (*qv*), and by his 1st w had issue:
1 Marcus; Lt 63rd Regt; *b* 27 July 1821; *dvp* unm India 30 July 1846
2 Robert Edgar (Rev); Fell Magdalene Coll Cambridge; *b* 11 Sept 1822; *m* 24 Oct 1857 Frances Eleanor (*d* 3 May 1902), dau of Christopher Robert Pemberton, of Newton Park, Cambridge, and *dvp* 1 Nov 1863, having had:
(1) Robert Alexander; *b* 5 June 1861; *d* unm 12 Oct 1885
(1) Beatrice Mary; *b* 31 July 1858; *m* 1st 5 Feb 1884 Jerome James Guiry, JP (*d* 5 July 1899), of Pypardstown, Co Tipperary, and had issue; *m* 2nd 2 Oct 1902 Nicholas Patten-Saunders, Roy Dublin Fus, est s of Waynflete Henry Patten-Saunders, Offr Russian Army, and *d* 20 June 1947
(2) Cecil Frances Grace; *b* 13 Dec 1859; *m* 6 Nov 1886 Col Benjamin A Donne, CB (*d* 23 Sept 1907), Roy Sussex Regt, and *d* 4 Dec 1930, leaving issue
3 ALFRED (Sir), **9th Bt**
4 Richard Thomas; Lt 66th Regt; *b* 16 Sept 1831; *d* unm India 4 May 1861
5 John William St John; Capt 66th and 8th Regts 1855–64; *b* 26 Aug 1837; *m* 1st 1863 Jessie Ann Atkinson (*d* 1879), dau of William Gardner, 2nd s of Robert Gardner, of Chaseley Hall, Lincs; *m* 2nd 1898 Ellen Sophia, dau of Surg-Maj William Deeble, and *d* 22 Jan 1921, having had by his 1st w:
(1) Frederic St John, MVO (1916), OBE (1919); Capt and Brev Maj 3rd Bn Duke of Cornwall's LI, Capt S Wales Borderers Boer War 1899–1900 (medal with six clasps) and WW I (despatches), Order St Maurice and St Lazarus Italy; *b* 22 Feb 1866; *m* 12 Dec 1908 Gertrude Mabel Jane (*d* 3 July 1965), 2nd dau of David Evans, JP, of Frwdgrech, Brecon, and *d* 3 Nov 1956, leaving:
1a Alpha Jessie Ruth; *b* 22 Jan 1910; *m* 8 Oct 1938 G/Capt James McLaughlin, DSO, DFC, RAF, and had:
1b *Deirdre; *b* 19 May 1940
2b *Rona Mary; *b* 7 Oct 1945; *m* 12 Aug 1967 *James Charles Hanna and has:
1c *James Owen; *b* 18 Dec 1970
2c *Neil Ewan; *b* 7 Aug 1972
2a Beta Mira Grace; twin with sis; *m* 15 Jan 1938 G/Capt Benjamin Heywood Jones, RAF (*ka* 3 Aug 1943), yst s of Capt B N Heywood Jones, 6th Dragoon Gds, and had:
1b *Cherry Bronwen; *b* 2 Dec 1939
2b *Gypsy Gail; *b* 20 Nov 1943
3a *April Mary [Mrs Hugh Smeddle, Ivy Cottage, Sprayton, Crediton, Devon]; *b* 1 April 1913; *m* 3 Sept 1939 *G/Capt Hugh Lomas Smeddle, DFC, RAF, and has had:
1b *Robert Adam Hughes; *b* 22 Dec 1948; *m* 1st 1972 (*divorce* 1982) Sarah Anne, dau of Maj Ernest Howarth, MBE (*see* MEATH, E), and has:
1c *William Robert; *b* 1976
1c *Vanessa Mary; *b* 1974
1b (cont.) Robert Smeddle *m* 2nd 1988 *Daryl Anne, dau of Maj R E Brookes, of West Hill Farm, Okehampton, Devon, and by her has:
2c *Samuel Edward; *b* 1988
2c *Lucy Susan; *b* 1990
1b Susan Ostara Mary; *b* 6 April 1947; *d* in a car crash 1967 on a Durham U expdn to India
(2) Alfred Collingwood; *b* 1868; *m* 1909 Margaret Ford (*d* 1935), of Blackheath, and *d* 17 Feb 1935
(1) Edith Anne Elizabeth; *m* 15 July 1908 Thomas Leighton Boyce (*d* 10 Aug 1934), and *d* 27 March 1955
(2) Grace Atkinson; *m* 19 Jan 1887 George Alfred Shenley (*d* 29 Aug 1934) and *d* 31 July 1950, leaving issue
(3) Barbara Susan
(4) Evangeline; *m* 11 Oct 1909 Brig Arthur Francis Gore Pery-Knox-Gore, CB, DSO (*d* 18 Feb 1954), and *d* 18 Feb 1967 aged 87, leaving issue (*see* LIMERICK, E)
1 Mary Emily; *b* 9 April 1826; *d* unm 12 Nov 1845
2 Gratiana Fanny; *b* 18 Dec 1827; *m* 7 Aug 1855 Rev George Cressener Tufnell, yst s of John Jolliffe Tufnell, DL, JP, of Langleys, Essex, and *d* 4 June 1859
3 Susan Elizabeth Anna; *b* 25 June 1836; *m* 18– Rev Charles Foster Garratt (*d* 21 April 1915), Rector Little Tew, Oxon, and *d* 28 Sept 1872
4 Anna Maria; *b* 26 Nov 1839; *d* unm 26 July 1860
5 Constance; *b* 3 May 1843

Sir THOMAS *d* 22 May 1889; his 3rd son,

Sir Alfred Hughes 9th Bt; 33rd Regt; *b* 3 Jan 1825; *m* 4 Sept 1851 Maria (*d* 27 Dec 1913), er dau of Col John Smith, of Ellingham Hall, Norfolk, and *d* 1 April 1898, having had:
1 Harry Scott; *b* 10 Jan 1853; *d* unm California 17 May 1888
2 **Sir (Alfred) Collingwood Hughes, 10th Bt**, JP; *b* 12 May 1854; High Sheriff 1923, Maj 4th Bn Suffolk Vol Regt WW I (despatches), Ld Manors of Old Hall and Illaries; *m* 30 Dec 1880 Elsie (*d* 25 Dec 1932), dau of John Johansson, and *d* 9 Dec 1932, leaving:
1 **Sir Reginald Johansson Hughes, 11th Bt**; *b* 22 June 1882; *d* unm 6 May 1945
1 Muriel Elsie, JP (Suffolk 1947), CC 1958, memb RDC 1946; *m* 19 Jan 1916 Adml Sir William Frederick Wake Walker, KCB, CBE, and *d* 28 Nov 1963, leaving issue (*see* WALKER, Bt, of Oakley House)
3 Hugh St John *b* 10 Feb 1857; *m* 11 June 1890, Eleanor Frances (*d* 28 Oct 1898), dau of Rev Joseph Walker, Rector Gt Billing, and *d* 6 July 1901, having had:
(1) Richard St John; *b* 7 April 1891; *d* 10 Feb 1892
4 Ralph Townsend, JP N R Yorks; *b* 29 July 1864; *m* 10 Sept 1892 Mary (*d* 1949), dau of John Addison Birkbeck, of The Priory, Grosmont, Yorks, and *d* 5 April 1925, leaving:
(1) Sybil Mary; *b* 4 Sept 1893; *m* 8 Dec 1921 William Eden Walker (*d* 21 Jan 1962) and had:
1a *Ralph Eden; Capt Royal Sigs; *b* 20 June 1923; *m* 12 Oct 1954 *Joyce Cownie and has:
1b *Charles Eden; *b* 1955
2b *Richard; *b* 1959
2a *Clive Eden; late Merchant Navy; *b* 21 March 1927
1a *Louise; *b* 29 May 1931; *m* 8 May 1954 *John Hereward Allix and has:
1b *Timothy Peter; *b* 27 May 1959
1b *Jane Catherine; *b* 30 Sept 1955
(2) Joan Kathleen; *b* 11 June 1897; *d* unm 6 March 1959
5 **Sir Robert Heywood Hughes, 12th Bt**; *b* 2 Nov 1865; *m* 7 June 1894 Edith Agnes (*d* 16 Jan 1964 aged 95), yst dau of Charles Binnie Skinner, and *d* 3 Jan 1951, having had:
(1) Elizabeth Mary Theodora; *b* 22 June 1896; *m* 28 March 1921 Cdr Sir John James Kenward Best-Shaw, 9th Bt (*qv*), and had issue
(2) Barbara Frances; *b* 21 Dec 1897; *m* 9 March 1918 Cdr Paul Alaric Masters Long, RN (*d* 8 July 1936 following an explosion at Woolwich Arsenal), and had issue
(3) Joanne Mary, JP Hants; *b* 28 Nov 1900; *m* 18 Oct 1923 V-Adml Ronald Hamilton Curson Hallifax, CB, CBE (*das* 5 Nov 1943), s of R-Adml John Salway Hallifax, of Old Alresford, Hants, and had:
1a David John (Sir) KCB, KCVO, KBE; *b* 3 Sept 1927; *educ* Winchester; Adml; *m* 8 Dec 1962 *Anne, dau of Col John Matthew Blakiston-Houston, of Beltrim Castle, Gortin, Co Tyrone (*see* BLAKISTON, Bt), and *d* 1992 leaving issue
1a *Diana Dominica *b* 18 March 1925; *m* 22 July 1948 *James Michael Sword, formerly Colonial Admin Serv, Tanganvika, s of Arthur Nicholson Sword, and has issue:
1b *Robert Arthur Hallifax; *b* 16 May 1952; *educ* Bradfield
2b *David Stephen; *b* 22 Oct 1954; *educ* Charterhouse
1b *Emma Clare; *b* 12 June 1959
2a *Elizabeth Ann; *m* 24 Aug 1957 *Sir William Richard SHELLEY later BENYON (deed poll 1964, *see* SHELLEY, Bt) and has issue
(4) Diana Margaret; *b* 12 Sept 1905; *m* 1 Nov 1927 Sir George Robert Mowbray, 5th Bt (*qv*), and d 18 Oct 1996, leaving issue
6 Hubert Edgar; *b* 23 Feb 1867; *m* 23 July 1896 Mary Charlotte (*d* 1941), dau of Charles W Harrison, of Whitmores, Beckenham, and *d* 21 Oct 1946, leaving:
(1) RICHARD EDGAR (Sir), **13th Bt**
(2) Alfred Marcus, OBE (1946); Cdr RN, WW I and II; *b* 12 Sept 1900; *m* 6 April 1934 Hope Frances (*d* 19–), dau of Arthur George Pritchard, and *d* 19–, having had:
1a Michael Hugo; *b* 4 June 1944; *educ* Berkhamsted; *d* 19 Oct 1963
1a *Pamela Mary [Mrs Colin Howgill, 1204 Wiesman Court, Wolf Trap Green, Great Falls, VA 226649, USA]; *b* 3 June 1939; *m* 9 July 1965 *Col Colin Humphrey Cowley Howgill, RM, and has:
1b *Michael Colin; *b* 3 Sept 1968
1b *Susan Rosemary; *b* 26 April 1967
(3) +Charles Collingwood [Charles Hughes Esq, 6 Renson Close, Hessett, Bury St Edmunds, Suffolk]; WW II as Capt RA; *b* 9 Feb 1907; *educ* Oundle; *m* 4 Dec 1937 *Sheila Dorothea, dau of Col Walter Henry Patrick Law, DSO, of Rougham House, Bury St Edmunds (*see* BROOKE, Bt, of Almondbury), and has:
1a +Peter Collingwood [Peter Hughes Esq, Larch House, 543 Limpsfield Rd, Warlingham, Surrey CR3 9DX]; *b* 10 Feb 1943; *educ* Oundle and Pomfret Sch, Conn.; *m* 4 Dec 1965 *Susan Elizabeth Ann, only dau of Algernon James Cubitt, and has:
1b *Natasha Sarah; *b* 6 July 1967; *m* 19– *Richard Gray and has:
1c *Francesca; *b* 1994
2b *Kate; *b* 1970
3b *Victoria; *b* 1972

(1) Joyce Evangeline; *b* 28 May 1899; *d* 11 Jan 1900
(2) Pamela Mary; *b* 5 Oct 1901; *m* 14 Dec 1927 Arthur Frederick Vavasour McConnell, JP (*d* 17 Sept 1961), est s of Frederick Vavasour McConnell, of Camfield Place, Hatfield, Herts, and has issue
(3) Evangeline Gratiana; *b* 11 Nov 1904; *m* 15 Nov 1927 Philip William John Fryer, MBE, MA, of Browick Hall, Wymondham, Norfolk, and has issue
(4) Rosemary Sybil; *b* 29 July 1909; *m* 5 Jan 1937 Col George William Browning, OBE, Welsh Gds (*d* 1981), est s of Rev Berthold Alexander Browning, Vicar Pakenham, Suffolk, and *d* 10 May 1995, leaving:
1a *John Montague George [John Browning Esq, Weatherhill Farm, Icklingham, Bury St Edmunds, Suffolk]; *b* 11 Aug 1944; *m* 1970 *Mary-Grace Feachem and has issue:
1b *Christopher George John; *b* 1972
2b *Timothy Robert; *b* 1974
1a *Mary Joan; *b* 12 Nov 1938; BEM (1992); *m* 8 Sept 1962 *Rev Andrew Alexander Macintosh, BD, Dean St John's Coll Cambridge, s of Rev Felix Macintosh, of Black Notley, Essex, and has issue:
1b *George Alexander John; *b* 16 June 1967; Welsh Gds
2b *Thomas Andrew Charles; *b* 1974
1b *Rachel Alison Mary; *b* 29 July 1964
2a *Frances Evangeline [Mrs John Rigby, Penn Cottage, Corton, Warminster, Wilts BA12 0SZ]; *b* 12 Nov 1941; *m* 7 March 1964 *Col John Granville Beaumont Rigby, OBE, Royal Fus, and has issue:
1b *Peter Alexander Beaumont; *b* 11 Dec 1965; *m* 6 June 1992 *Alexandrina Collyer and has issue
2b *Simon William Granville; *b* 1967; *m* 14 Oct 1995 *Gabriela Lederer, of Austria
(1) Evangeline Lockhart; *m* 7 Dec 1881 John Ramsay Drake, of Batchworth Hall, Herts, and *d* 26 Dec 1937, having had issue
2 Florence Mary; *m* 1881 Arthur Elliot Deane, of Minster House and Littleton House, Winchester, and *d* 30 June 1942, leaving issue
3 Gratiana Lucy; *m* 30 April 1895 Rev Samuel John Sherbrooke Banks, Canon St Edmundsbury and Ipswich, est s of Rev S Banks, Rector Cottenham, Cambs, and had issue
4 Gertrude Maria; *m* 1888 Lt-Col Frederick William Templetown Robinson, DSO, and had issue
5 Sybil Jessie; *m* 20 Aug 1890 Godolphin Henry Vane Milbank (*see* MILBANK, Bt)
6 Constance; *m* 14 Feb 1901 William Henry Bowles, JP (*d* 18 Jan 1938), barrister, 4th s of Rev Charles Bradshaw Bowles, Vicar Woking, and had issue

The 12th Bt's nephew,

Sir Richard Edgar Hughes, 13th Bt; *b* 8 June 1897; *educ* Uppingham; 2nd Artists Rifles WW I; *m* 1st 21 July 1927 Angela Lilian Adelaide (*d* 4 Feb 1967), est dau of Albert Julian Pell, DL, JP, of Wilburton Manor, Isle of Ely, Cambs; *m* 2nd 3 Oct 1967 *Jessica Florence (*d* 9 April 1998), BA, dau of B C Broomhall, FRCS, and *d* 29 Aug 1970, leaving by his 1st w:

1 Sir DAVID COLLINGWOOD HUGHES, **14th and present Bt**
1 *Elizabeth Barbara [Mrs Paul Lever, Leftwich Heyes, Davenham, Northwich, Cheshire CW9 8HN]; SRN 1958; *b* 21 May 1933; *m* 23 Sept 1964 *Paul Ronald Scott Lever, and has:
(1) *Christopher Mark; *b* 17 July 1965; *m* 1989 *Susan Elizabeth Mullin and has:
1a *James Richard; *b* 1993
(1) *Alison Clare; *b* 25 Feb 1967
(2) *Catherine Elizabeth; *b* 25 June 1969; *m* 16 Sept 1995 *Andrew Bradley

HUGHES OF ISLWYN

Creation: B. (LP, UK) 2 Aug 1997.

THE BARON ISLWYN, of Casnewydd, Co Gwent (Royston John Hughes, DL (Gwent 1992)) [The Rt Hon The Lord Islwyn DL, Chapel Field, Chapel Lane, Abergavenny, Gwent NP7 7BT]; *b* 9 June 1925; *educ* Ruskin Coll Oxford; with TGWU 1959–66; memb Coventry City Cncl 1962–66; MP (Lab) Newport (Gwent) 1966–83, Newport E 1983–97, PPS to Sec State Tport 1974–75, memb Speaker's Panel 1982–84 and 1991–97, Chm: PLP Sports Gp 1974–83, PLP Steel Gp 1978–87, Parly Gp TGWU 1979–82, Welsh Grand Ctee 1982–84 and 1991–, Oppn Spokesman Welsh Affrs 1984–88; Del Cncl Europe and WEU 1991–; exec memb IPU 1987– (Treas 1990–92); jt chm Rugby Union Gp 1993–; V-Pres: Crawshays RFC, Glamorgan CCC; *m* 1957 *Florence Marion Appleyard and has three daus

Lineage: JOHN HUGHES; coal miner; had:

ROYSTON JOHN, *cr* a **Baron**

HUGHES OF WOODSIDE

Creation: B. (LP, UK) 2 Aug 1997.

THE BARON HUGHES OF WOODSIDE, of Woodside, City of Aberdeen (Robert Hughes) [The Rt Hon The Lord Hughes of Woodside, House of Lords, London SW1A 0PW]; *b* 3 Jan 1932; *educ* Robert Gordon's Coll Aberdeen, Benoni High Sch Transvaal and Pietermaritzburg Tech Coll Natal; engrg apprentice S African Rubber Co Natal; ch draughtsman C F Wilson & Co (1932) Ltd to 1970; memb: AEU 1952–, Lab Party League of Youth 1954–57, Movement for Colonial Freedom 1955–74 (chm S Africa Ctee), Aberdeen Trades Cncl and Exec Ctee 1957–69, Aberdeen Town Cncl 1962–70 (convenor Health and Welfare Ctee 1963–68, Social Work Ctee 1969–70), Scottish Poverty Action Gp, GMC 1976–97, Parly U-Sec Scottish Office 1974–75, Ch Oppn Spokesman: Ag 1983–84, Tport 1985–88 (Jr Oppn Spokesman 1981–83); memb: Standing Ctee Immigration Bill 1971, Select Ctee Scottish Affrs 1971 and 1992–97, PLP Shadow Cabinet 1985–88; fndr memb and Aberdeen Chm CND, V-Chm: Anti-Apartheid Movement 1975–76 (Chm 1976–94), Tribune Gp 1984; chm Action for S Africa (ACTSA) 1994–; Tstee Canon Collins Educnl Tst for S Africa 1997; *m* 1957 *Ina Margaret Miller and has two sons and three daus

HUGHES-MORGAN

Arms: Quarterly, 1st and 4th, arg. a griffin segreant sa., over all a chevron of the second charged with a mullet between two fleurs-de-lys of the first (for MORGAN); 2nd and 3rd, sa. a lion rampant guardant between two fleurs-de-lys in fess or, on a chief engrailed of the second two Cornish choughs ppr. (for HUGHES). **Crests:** 1 In front of a reindeer's head erased or, collared and chained sa., a fleur-de-lys between two mullets also sa. (for MORGAN), 2 In front of a demi-lion rampant guardant arg., charged on the shoulder with a fleur-de-lys sa., two swords saltirewise ppr., pommels and hilts or (for HUGHES). **Motto:** *Heb dduw heb ddim* ('Without God, without anything'). **Creation:** Bt. (UK) 27 June 1925.

SIR DAVID JOHN HUGHES-MORGAN, 3RD BT, CB (1983), CBE (1973, MBE 1961), of Manascin, Pencelly, Co Brecon [His Honour Judge Sir David Hughes-Morgan Bt, c/o National Westminster Bank plc, 143 High Street, Bromley, Kent BR1 1JH]; *b* 11 Oct 1925; *s* f 1969; *educ* RNC Dartmouth; Maj-Gen Army Legal Corps (ret 1984), formerly Sub-Lt RN WW II, slr 1950, Brig Legal Staff HQ UKLF 1976–78, Dir Army Legal Servs BAOR 1978–80, MOD 1980–84, Recorder 1983, Circuit Judge SE Circuit 1986–98; *m* 31 March 1959 Isabel Jean Blacklock Geltatly Milne (*d* 1994), only dau of John Milne Lindsay, of Dumfriesshire, and has:

1 +(IAN) PARRY DAVID [Parry Hughes-Morgan Esq, 10 South Side, London W6 0XY]; *b* 22 Feb 1960; *m* 5 Sept 1992 *Julia Katrin, er dau of R J S Ward, of Amersham, Bucks, and has:
(1) *Isabel Florence Anne; *b* 18 Jan 1995
(2) *Rachel Francesca Jill; *b* 28 Nov 1996
2 +Jonathan Michael Vernon; *b* 22 Feb 1962; m 1996 *Gail, yr dau of Ian Melling, and has
(1) *Charlotte; b 1996
3 +Mark Richard Milne; *b* 26 July 1964; *m* 1988 *Sophia Frances, yst dau of Graham Rogers, and has issue:
(1) +Daniel; *b* 1988
(2) +Theo; *b* 1990
(3) +Felix; *b* 1992
(1) *Beatrice; *b* 1995

Lineage: MORGAN MORGAN, of Llandovery, *d* 24 Jan 1883, leaving:

DAVID MORGAN, of Henllys, Llandovery; *b* 10 May 1848; *m* 9 Aug 1870 Mary Elizabeth (*d* 21 July 1915), dau of David Davies, of Llandovery, and *d* 15 Aug 1904, leaving, with other issue:

1 DAVID (Sir), **1st Bt**
2 John James Ernest; *b* 2 Sept 1885; *m* 16 Dec 1914 Elizabeth Jane, er dau of Joshua Davies, and had issue
3 Morgan Cyril, MC; Brig Res Offrs S Wales Borderers; *m* 12 Sept 1917 Gertrude Constance Mary, dau of Cdr R Greey, RNR, and had issue
1 Mary Louisa; *m* 6 Feb 1900 Rev David Davies, Vicar Penally, Pembs, 1914, s of David Elias Davies, and *d* 11 Sept 1935
2 Sarah Anna; *m* 27 Nov 1907 Evan Williams, s of Daniel Williams, and *d* 1 June 1956. He *d* 16 Sept 1944
3 Elizabeth Gwladys; *m* 18 Sept 1909 William Herbert Bowles, s of Edwin Bowles, of Haverfordwest
4 Edith Florence; *m* 1905 Harry Vaughan Watkins, of Llandovery, and *d* 12 July 1932, leaving issue. He *d* 15 May 1945
5 Ida Blanche Enid; *m* 7 June 1910 Emile T Evans, of Bryn-teg, Aberystwyth, s of Rev Thomas Evans, JP, and *d* 1951
6 Ethel Winifred; *m* 1 Nov 1908 H Neville Taylor, MA, MD, FRCS, barrister, s of Hugh Taylor, of Norfolk
7 Olive Beatrice; *m* 30 Aug 1911 Norman Aldred Cooper, s of William Cooper, of Norwich

The est son,

Sir DAVID MORGAN later HUGHES-MORGAN (deed poll 24 Nov 1925), **1st Bt** (UK), so *cr* 27 June 1925, JP Brecon, Tenby and Pembroke; *b* 16 Aug 1871; High Sheriff Breconshire 1898, Maj 3rd Bn S Wales Borderers, ktd 1920; *m* 29 Sept 1896 (Blanche) Elizabeth Wedge (*d* 22 Nov 1965), est dau of James Buckley, of Bryn-y-caerau, and had issue:

1 JOHN VERNON (Sir), **2nd Bt**
2 David James; S/Ldr RAF WW II; *b* 26 Feb 1903; *m* 17 April 1935 Lilian Evelyn (*d* 9 Sept 1965), dau of John Windsor-Richards, of Plas Caerleon, Monmouth, and *d* 8 April 1967, leaving:
(1) *Elizabeth Dolores [Mrs John Brill, Rookhurst, Coast Hill Lane, Westcott, nr Dorking, Surrey]; *b* 12 Jan 1936; *m* 10 Sept 1960 *John Brill, er s of Eric William Brill, of Bramhall, Cheshire, and has had:
1a *Timothy John; *b* 29 June 1965
2a *Jonathan Richard; *b* 16 Dec 1966
3a *Edward James; *b* 4 May 1969
1a Catherine Anne; *b* 20 Feb, *d* 21 Dec 1964
1 Violet; *m* 17 Oct 1921 W/Cdr Brian Alexander Spencer Lewin, RAF, s of Lt-Col Robert Nicholas Spencer Lewin, DCLI, and has issue:
(1) *Joan Daphne; *b* 30 Oct 1922; *m* 22 May 1946 *S/Ldr Royston Edward Bindlos Manson, RAF, est s of W/Cdr D Manson, of Johannesburg, and has:
1a *Christopher Spencer; *b* 4 Feb 1950; *educ* Stowe
1a *Jane; *b* 21 Aug 1952
(2) *Cicely Patricia; *b* 26 Oct 1923; *m* 28 Sept 1946 *Maj Bruce Edgar Holford-Walker, RTR, yr s of Col Bruce Archibald Holford-Walker, and has:
1a *Michael O'Donnell Spencer; *b* 27 Aug 1947; *educ* Nautical Coll Pangbourne
2a *Patrick Bruce Spencer; *b* 17 Aug 1952; *educ* Wellington
1a *Suzanne Patricia Spencer; *b* 26 Aug 1950
2 Iris; *m* 1925 William Haddon Howard (*d* 16 May 1965) and had:
(1) *Richard Percival; *b* 1936; *m* 1957 *Sheila Ann, dau of — McNab and has:
1a *William; *b* 1959
2a *Andrew; *b* 1961
3a *James; *b* 1962
4a *Duncan; *b* 1967
1a *Suzanne; *b* 1958

The 1st Bt *d* 16 March 1941; his er son,

Sir John Vernon Hughes-Morgan, 2nd Bt; *b* 12 Aug 1900; *educ* Malvern; *m* 4 April 1923 Lucie Margaret (*d* 1987), only child of Thomas Parry Jones-Parry, of Llwyn Own Hall, Denbighs, and *d* 13 Jan 1969, leaving:

1 Sir DAVID JOHN HUGHES-MORGAN, **3rd and present Bt**
2 (Thomas Parry) Michael HUGHES-MORGAN later JONES-PARRY (deed poll 1 March 1961); *b* 27 April 1928; *educ* Malvern and RMA Sandhurst; Capt S Wales Borderers; *m* 24 May 1952 *Gillian [Mrs Michael Jones-Parry, White Hart Cottage, Westbrook, Boxford, Berks], yr dau of Reginald Carter Stern, and *d* 24 Feb 1982, leaving:
(1) +David Anthony; *b* 24 Oct 1954; *educ* Wellington; *m* 1983 *Jacqueline Rowland-Rouse and has:
1a +Thomas Edward; *b* 1986
2a +Matthew Nicholas; *b* 1991
1a +Gemma; *b* 1987
(1) *Caroline Anne; *b* 20 Aug 1953; *m* 1975 *Baron Hugues M F d'Achon, of Paris, 3rd s of Baron Antoine d'Achon, of Herblay, France
(2) *Sarah Margaret; *d* 6 July 1961
3 Robert Frederick Buckley; *b* 17 Sept 1933; *d* unm 11 Jan 1964

HULSE

Arms: Per fess arg. and erm. three piles, one issuing from the chief, between the others reversed sa. **Crest:** A buck's head couped ppr. attired or, between the attires a sun of the last, and charged on the neck with two bezants and a plate. **Motto:** *Esse quam videri* ('To be rather than to seem'). **Creation:** Bt. (UK) 7 Feb 1738/9.

SIR EDWARD JEREMY WESTROW HULSE, 10TH BT [Sir Edward Hulse Bt DL, Breamore House, Breamore, Hants SP6 2DF]; *b* 22 Nov 1932; *s* f 1996; *educ* Eton and RMA Sandhurst; stockbroker, Capt (ret) Scots Gds, High Sheriff Hants 1978; *m* 9 Oct 1957 *Verity Ann, only child of William Lee Pilkington, MFH, of Jersey, and has:

1 +(EDWARD) MICHAEL WESTROW; *b* 10 Sept 1959; *m* 11 Oct 1986 *Doone, dau of Iain Brotherton, of London, and has:
(1) +Edward Westrow William; *b* 4 March 1993
(2) +Samuel Arthur Michael; *b* 9 Sept 1995
(1) *Venetia Katherine; *b* 3 March 1987
(2) *Roseanne Elizabeth; *b* 2 Jan 1989
(3) *Natasha Lucy Gabriella; *b* 13 Dec 1990
1 *Camilla Ann [Mrs Luca Corona, PO Box 7003, Kathmandu, Nepal]; *b* 15 Nov 1962; *m* 1991 *Luca C Corona, son of Giuseppe Corona, of Milan, and has:
(1) *Alexander (Sasha) Tenzin; *b* 27 Sept 1991
(1) *Francesca Tara; *b* 18 July 1996

Lineage: WILLIAM HOOLSE, of Stanney, Cheshire, descended from the HULSEs of Clive, Stanney, and Norbury, Cheshire; *m* Anne (*bur* 11 Aug 1655) and was *bur* 28 April 1653, having had:

1 Richard HOOLSE/HULSE; inherited f's property at Stanney and left issue
2 EDWARD
3 John HOOLSE; *d* an infant
4 William HOOLSE; *d* an infant
1 Anne; living 1652

The 2nd son,

EDWARD HULSE, of Baldwins, Dartford, Kent; Fell Emmanuel Coll Cambridge; MD Leyden; physician Court of PRINCE OF ORANGE 1677, Fell Coll Physicians London 1677, Treasurer 1704–09; *bapt* 18 March 1631/2; *m* Dorothy, dau of Thomas Westrow, of Twickenham, MP Hythe 1645–53, by Anne, half-sis of 1st Baron Capell of Hadham (*see* ESSEX, E), and *d* 3 Dec 1711, leaving issue:

1 EDWARD, **1st Bt**
2 William, of Stone Castle, Kent; citizen and salter London; *d* Aug 1761
1 Anne; *d* unm 30 Jan 1745
2 Mary; *d* unm Oct 1721

The er son,

Sir Edward Hulse, 1st Bt (GB), so *cr* 7 Feb 1738/9; *b* 1682; *educ* Emmanuel Coll Cambridge (MD); physician to QUEEN ANNE, GEORGE I and GEORGE II; *m* 15 Jan 1712/3 Elizabeth (*d* 15 Jan 1741/2), dau of Sir Richard Levett, Ld Mayor London 1700, and *d* 10 April 1759, leaving:

1 EDWARD (Sir), **2nd Bt**
2 Richard, of Blackheath and Baldwins, Kent, JP Kent; Sheriff 1768, Dep Govr Hudson Bay Co 1799–1805; *b* 16 Oct 1727; *d* unm 27 Oct 1805
3 Westrow, Capt Dragoons; *educ* Lincoln's Inn; *b* 25 Nov 1723; *d* unm 1746
4 Thomas, of Hutton Essex; *educ* Peterhouse Cambridge (BA 1758); *b* 1735; *d* Dec 1766
5 Levett; *d* an infant
1 Elizabeth; *bapt* 16 Feb 1732; *m* 8 Sept 1757 John Calvert, MP, of Albury Hall, Herts (*see* VERNEY, Bt, of Claydon)
2 Mary; *bapt* 4 Jan 1716

The est son,

Sir Edward Hulse, 2nd Bt, of Breamore, Hants; High Sheriff 1765; *b* 21 June 1715; *m* 23 Feb 1741/2 Hannah (*d* 16 Dec 1803), dau of Samuel Vanderplank, of London, and had:

1 EDWARD (Sir), **3rd Bt**

2 Samuel (Sir), GCH, PC; FM, Col 62nd Regt, Govr Chelsea Hosp, Ranger Home Park Windsor, Treasurer to GEORGE IV as PRINCE OF WALES; *b* 27 March 1746; *m* Charlotte — (*d* 6 Feb 1842) and *d* 1 Jan 1837 aged 90
3 Westrow (Rev); Chaplain to THE PRINCE OF WALES and HEIC; *d* unm 23 April 1787
1 Dorothy; living 1803
2 Hannah; *b* 1742; *m* 3 Sept 1776 Richard Benyon, of Gidea Hall, Essex, MP, and *d* 27 April 1828, leaving issue
3 Mary Anne; *b* 1755; *m* 9 April 1785 Gen Edmund Stevens, Equerry to GEORGE IV, and *d* 1825
4 Charlotte Matilda; *b* 1765; *m* 15 June 1815, as his 2nd w, Sir Thomas Bernard, of Nether Wickendon, Bucks, and *d* 1846
5 Elizabeth; *m* 17 Aug 1772 Joseph Berens, of Hextable, Kent

Sir EDWARD *d* 1 Dec 1800; his est son,

Sir Edward Hulse, 3rd Bt; MA Oxon, Sheriff Hants 1802–03; *b* 17 Aug 1774; *m* 13 May 1769 Mary (*d* 24 Mar 1813), dau of Charles Lethieullieur, LLD, Fell All Souls Oxford, and heiress of her unc, Smart Lethieullieur, of Aldersbrook, Essex, and had issue:
1 Edward; *d* unm 9 Sept 1789
2 CHARLES (Sir), **4th Bt**
3 Richard; Maj-Gen cmdg Gds Bde Talavera; *d* Spain Sept 1813
4 Thomas; Fell All Souls; *d* 7 Oct 1853
1 Mary; *m* 22 March 1816, as his 2nd w, Edward Berkeley Portman (*see* PORTMAN V), and *dsp* 31 Oct 1852
2 Elizabeth; *d* unm 19 May 1807
3 Frances; *m* 30 June 1803 George Eyre, JP (*d* 18 Jan 1837), of Warrens, Bramshaw, Wilts, and *d* 29 April 1820, leaving issue
4 Harriet; *m* 29 June 1814, as his 2nd w, John Morval, of Morval, Cornwall
5 Charlotte; *b* July 1786; *d* 30 July 1873

Sir EDWARD *d* 30 Sept 1816; his son,

Sir Charles Hulse, 4th Bt; MP W Looe 1816–32, MA Oxon; *b* 12 Oct 1771; *m* 5 July 1808 Maria (*d* 20 Jan 1855), 2nd dau of John Buller, of Morval, and had, with other issue:
1 EDWARD (Sir), **5th Bt**
2 Charles, of Stoke Park, Guildford; Gren Gds; *b* 20 Aug 1810; *m* 3 April 1836 Georgina Amelia (*d* 18 Dec 1897), yst dau of Lt-Gen Frederick Buller, of Pelyn and Lanreath, Cornwall, and *d* 25 May 1863, leaving, with other issue:
(1) Charles Frederick; Lt-Col Rifle Bde; *b* 30 April 1843; *m* 11 Nov 1875 Jessie Marian (*d* 23 Nov 1934), est dau of Lt-Gen Joseph Edwin Thackwell, CB, and *dsp* 7 Feb 1902
(2) Samuel George; 42nd Foot; *b* 4 Jan 1845
(1) Agnes Charlotte Letitia; *m* 21 May 1873 Gilbert John Smallpiece, of Guildford, and *d* 1882, leaving issue
(2) Selina Frances; *d* unm 5 Feb 1932
(3) Augusta Julia; *b* 8 June 1850; *d* unm 12 May 1941
(4) Henrietta Eleanor; *d* unm 10 May 1915
3 Richard Samuel; Capt Coldstream Gds; *d* 27 Sept 1866

Sir CHARLES *d* 19 Oct 1854; his est son,

Sir Edward Hulse, 5th Bt; DL Hants; High Sheriff 1868, Fell All Souls 1829–53, Lt-Col S Hants Militia; *b* 2 April 1809; *m* 29 Nov 1854 Katharine Jane (*d* 23 Aug 1928), only child of Very Rev Henry Parr Hamilton, FRS, Dean of Salisbury, and *d* 11 June 1899, leaving:
1 **Sir Edward Henry Hulse, 6th Bt**, JP, DL Wilts, JP Hants; MP Salisbury 1886–97, Capt 15th Bn Imp Yeo S Africa 1900–02, Capt Roy Wilts Yeo; *b* 25 Aug 1859; *educ* Eton and BNC Oxford; *m* 1 Nov 1888 Edith Maud , only dau of 1st Baron Burnham (*qv*), and *d* 30 May 1903, leaving:
(1) **Sir Edward Hamilton Westrow Hulse, 7th Bt**; BA Oxon, Capt Scots Gds WW I (despatches); *b* 31 Aug 1889; *ka* 12 March 1915
2 Charles Westrow, JP Hants; Capt and Hon Maj Hants and IoW Artillery; *b* 25 Nov 1860; *ka* Boer War 3 June 1901
3 HAMILTON JOHN (Sir), **8th Bt**
1 Katharine Charlotte; *m* 19 Sept 1878 Andrew Coventry Maitland-Makgill-Crichton (*d* 29 July 1925) and *d* 24 Nov 1942, leaving issue (*see* LAUDERDALE, E)
2 Maria Eleanor; *m* 11 July 1883 Hon Duncombe Pleydell-Bouverie and *d* 25 Nov 1936, leaving issue (*see* RADNOR, E)

The 7th Bt's uncle,

Sir Hamilton John Hulse, 8th Bt, JP Hants; barrister Inner Temple; *b* 21 Feb 1864; *m* 27 April 1908 Estelle (*b* 13 April 1933), dau of William Lorillard Campbell, of New York, and *d* 5 Dec 1931, leaving:
1 **Sir (Hamilton) Westrow Hulse, 9th Bt**; *b* 20 June 1909; *educ* Eton and Ch Ch Oxford; barrister Inner Temple 1932, W/Cdr RAFVR WW II (despatches); *m* 1st 7 Jan 1932 (*divorce* 1937) Philippa Mabel, yr dau of Arthur James Taylor, of Strensham Court, Worcs, and had:
(1) Sir EDWARD JEREMY WESTROW HULSE, **10th and present Bt**
(2) +Richard Arthur Samuel [Richard Hulse Esq, The Old Chappel, Netton, Salisbury, Wilts SP4 6AW]; late 2nd Lt Scots Gds; *b* 22 March 1936; *educ* Eton; *m* 14 Nov 1963 *Caroline Susan Joan, only dau of Lt-Col Sir George David Elliott Tapps-Gervis-Meyrick, 6th Bt, MC (*qv*), and has:
1a +George Richard; *b* 25 March 1967
1a *Frances Caroline; *b* 30 Aug 1968
1 (cont.) **Sir Westrow** *m* 2nd 3 June 1938 Ambrosine Nellie Orr (*d* 7 Jan 1940), only dau of Capt Herbert Stanley Orr Wilson, RHA, of Dublin; *m* 3rd 25 Oct 1945 (*divorce* 1954) Dorothy (*d* 1991), widow of James Anderson McKay Hamilton, and only dau of William Durran; *m* 4th 8 July 1954 *Lucy Elizabeth Smitheyt, er dau of Col George Redesdale Brooker Spain, CMG, TD, FSA, and *d* 10 April 1996

Seat: Breamore House, Breamore, Hants. A house in red brick fronted with stone, Breamore dates from 1583. It was then owned by the Dodingtons. A son of that family murdered his mother on the premises in 1629. It was the second Hulse Baronet who bought Breamore, doing so in 1748. The house still contains much good Elizabethan fittings and furniture despite a fire in 1856 which apparently did more damage to the fabric than the contents.

HUNT

Arms: Argent a Himalayan black bear passant proper, a chief dancetty azure. **Crest:** Upon a wreath argent and azure, on two mountain peaks the first higher than the second, a chamois statant regardant proper. **Supporters:** Dexter, on a mount of grass and reedmace proper, issuant from water barry wavy argent and azure, a swan, wings elevated and addorsed proper; sinister, on a rock a buzzard, wings also elevated and addorsed proper. **Motto:** Endeavor.

Creation: B. (LP, UK) 1966.

THE BARON HUNT, of Llanfair Waterdine, Co Salop (Sir (Henry Cecil) John Hunt, KG (1979), DSO (1944), CBE (1945)) [The Rt Hon The Lord Hunt KG CBE DSO, Highway Cottage, Aston, Henley-on-Thames RG9 3DE]; *b* 22 June 1910; *educ* Marlborough and RMC Sandhurst; commissioned KRRC 1930; Indian Police 1934–35 and 1938–40, Indian Police Medal 1940; Rector Aberdeen U 1963–66; WW II: cmded 11th Bn KRRC 1944, 11th Indian Inf Bde 1944–46; Jt Staff Coll 1949; GSO HQ Allied Staff Centl European Command 1949–52; Leader Br Expdn Mt Everest 1952–53, ktd 1953; Assist Comdt Staff Coll Camberley 1953–55, ret as Hon Brig 1956; Dir Duke of Edinburgh's Award Scheme 1956–67; Memb Roy Commn Press 1974–77; Chm: Parole Board England and Wales 1967–73, Advsy Ctee Police NI 1969; Pres: Nat Assoc Youth Clubs 1954–70, Alpine Club 1956–58, Br and Nepal Soc 1960–75, Climbers' Club 1963–66, Br Mountaineering Cncl 1965–68, Cncl Vols Overseas 1968–74, Rainer Fndn 1971–85, Nat Assoc Probation Offrs 1974–80, RGS 1977–80, Cncl Nat Parks 1980–86; Nat Assoc Outdoor Educn 1991–93; Head Relief Missions Nigeria 1968–70; Hon DCL Durham 1954, Hon LLD Aberdeen 1954, London 1954, City 1976, Leeds 1979, Hon DSc Sheffield 1989, Hon Memb RGS 1984; Order 1st Cl Gurka Right Hand 1953, Indian Everest Medal 1953; Hubbard Medal US 1954; RGS Fndr's Medal 1954; Lawrence Memorial Medal RCAS 1954; King Albert I Memorial Medal Mountaineering 1994; author: *The Ascent of Everest* (1953), *Our Everest Adventure* (with C Brasher, 1954), *The Red Snows* (1959), *Life is Meeting* (1978), *My Favourite Mountaineering Stories* (ed, 1978), *In Search of Adventure* (1989); *m* 1936 *Joy, dau of Dr Mowbray-Green, and has:
1 *Sally
2 *Susan
3 *Prudence
4 *Jennifer

Lineage: Capt C E HUNT, MC; IA; *m* E H Crookshank and had:

(HENRY CECIL) JOHN (Sir), *cr* a **Baron**

HUNT OF KINGS HEATH

Creation: B. (LP, UK) 2 Aug 1997.

THE BARON HUNT OF KINGS HEATH, of Birmingham, Co W Midlands (Philip Alexander Hunt, OBE (1993)) [The Rt Hon The Lord Hunt of Kings Heath OBE, House of Lords, London SW1A 0PW]; *b* 19 May 1949; *educ* City of Oxford High Sch, Oxford Sch and Leeds U; memb: Oxford Regnl Health Bd 1972–74, Oxon AHA 1975–77, Oxford City Cncl 1973–79, Nuffield Orthopaedic Centre 1974–75, Bimingham City Cncl 1980–82, Cncl Internat Hosp Fedn 1986–91, King's Fund Inst Advsy Ctee 1991–93, Cncl Assoc for Public Health 1992– (Co-Chm 1994–), Inst Health Servs Mgmt; Sec Edgware/Hendon Community Health Cncl 1975–78; Dir NAHA 1984–90 (Assist Sec 1978–79, Assist Dir 1979–84); Ch Exec NHS Confedn; Govt Whip Ho Lds 1998–; author: *The Health Authority Member* (with W E Hall, 1978); *m* 1st 1974 (*divorce* 19–) — and has a dau; *m* 2nd *Selina Ruth Helen Stewart and by her has three sons and a dau

Lineage: Rev PHILIP LACEY WINTER HUNT; *m* 1947 Muriel — and had:

PHILIP ALEXANDER, *cr* a **Baron**

HUNT OF TANWORTH

Creation: B, (LP, UK) 1980.

THE BARON HUNT OF TANWORTH, of Stratford-upon-Avon (Sir John Joseph Benedict Hunt, GCB (1977, KCB 1973, CB 1968)) [The Rt Hon The Lord Hunt of Tanworth GCB, 8 Wool Rd, London SW20 0HW]; *b* 23 Oct 1919; *educ* Downside and Magdalene Coll Cambridge (MA, Hon Fell 1977); Lt RNVR 1940–46; joined Dominions Off 1946; Priv Sec to Parly U-Sec 1947; 2nd Sec Ceylon 1948–50, Pncpl 1949, Directing Staff IDC 1951–52; 1st Sec Canada 1953–56, Priv Sec to: Sec Cabinet 1956–58, Perm Sec Treas 1957–58; Assist Sec: CRO 1958–60, Cabinet Office 1960–62, Treas 1962–65; U-Sec Treasury 1965–68; 1st Civ Serv Commr CSD 1968–71; 3rd Sec Treasury 1971–72, 2nd Perm Sec Cabinet Off 1972–73, Sec Cabinet 1973–79; chm: Banque Nationale de Paris 1980–97; Prudential Corp 1985–90 (dir 1980–92, dep chm 1982–85); dir IBM (UK) 1980–90; advsy dir Unilever 1980–90; dep chm Prudential Assur 1982–85; Chm Disasters Emergency Ctee 1981–89, Inquiry into Cable Expansion and Broadcasting Policy 1982; Ditchley Fndn 1983–91, Tablet Publishing Co 1984–96, European Policy Forum 1992–; *m* 1st 1941 Hon Magdalen Mary Robinson (*d* 1971), dau of 1st Baron Robinson (*see* 1967 edn), and has had:

1 *Michael Anthony [The Hon Michael Hunt, 1407 Clipperton Ave, Henderson, NV 89014, USA]; *b* 1942; *m* 1st 1963 (*divorce* 19–) Rosemary Ann, only dau of Col Theodore Ernle Longridge, OBE; *m* 2nd 19– *Jennee Lynn, dau of G Thomas Baker, of Malibu, California, and has issue

2 *Martin John [The Hon Martin Hunt, 1 Ballingdon Rd, London SW11 6AS]; *b* 1962; *educ* Worth; *m* 1993 *Olivia Louise, only dau of John Norris Fennell (*see* HAWKE, B), and has:

(1) *Georgemma; *b* 24 Dec 1996

1 Charlotte Mary Magdalen; *b* 1947; *m* 1976 *Dr Herbert Gill [Dr Herbert Gill, 22230 Drums Court, Woodland Hills, CA 91364, USA] and *d* 29 Oct 1995, leaving:

(1) *Julia; *b* 1980

THE BARON HUNT OF TANWORTH *m* 2nd 1973 *Madeleine Frances, dau of Sir William Hume, CMG, FRCP, and widow of Sir John Charles, KCB, FRCP, and has a stepson and stepdaughter

Lineage: Maj ARTHUR L HUNT, MC; *m* Daphne — and had an er s:

JOHN JOSEPH BENEDICT, *cr* a **Baron**

HUNT OF WIRRAL

Arms: Azure, a stag's head caboshed argent, on a chief or a rose gules barbed and seeded proper between two ostrich feathers sable. **Crest:** Statant upon a portcullis chained or, an oyster catcher, wings elevated and addorsed proper, holding in its beak by the strings gules a bugle horn or garnished gules. **Supporters:** Dexter, a lion azure resting the dexter forepaw on an anchor or; sinister, a dragon azure resting the sinister foreclaws on a pickaxe head downwards or. **Motto:** *Pro deo et civitate* ('For God and state'). **Creation:** B. (LP, UK) 2 Aug 1997.

THE BARON HUNT OF WIRRAL, of Wirral, Co Merseyside (David James Fletcher Hunt, MBE (1973), PC (1990)) [The Rt Hon The Lord Hunt of Wirral MBE, PC, House of Lords, London SW1A 0PW]; *b* 21 May 1942; *educ* Liverpool Coll, Montpellier U, Bristol U and Guildford Coll of Law; chm Bristol U Conservatives 1964–65, Bristol City CPC 1965–68; ptnr and consultant Stanley Wasbrough & Co 1965–85; Nat V-Chm FUCUA 1965–66, YCNAC 1967–69; slr Supreme Ct Judicature 1968; Chm Bristol Fedn YCs 1970–71 (V-Pres Nat YCs 1986–88, Chm 1972–73), Br Youth Cncl 1971–74 (Pres 1978–80); memb: SW Ec Planning Cncl 1972–76, Advsy Ctee Pop Festivals 1972–75; ptnr: Stanleys and Simpson North 1977–88, Beachcroft Stanleys 1988 (sr ptnr 1995), V-Chm Nat Union C and U Assocs 1974–76, MP (C) Wirral 1976–83, Wirral W 1983–97, Chm C Shipping and Shipbuilding Ctee 1977–79, V-Chm Parly Youth Lobby 1978–80, V-Pres C Gp for Europe 1984–87 (V-Chm 1978–81, Chm 1981–82), V-Chm C Party 1983–85, PPS to Sec State: DTI 1979–81, Def 1981, Assist Govt Whip 1981–83, Ld Commr Treasury 1983–84, Parly U-Sec Energy 1984–87, Dep Ch Whip 1987–89, Min State DOE 1989–90, Sec State: Wales 1990–93, Employment 1993–94, Chllr Duchy Lancaster with responsibility Public Serv and Sci 1994–95; V-Pres: Nat Playbus Assoc 1981; Pres Tory Reform Gp 1991–; dir BET Omnibus Servs Ltd 1980–81; author: *Europe Right Ahead* (1978), *A Time for Youth* (1978); *m* 1973 *Patricia (Paddy) Margery Orchard and has two sons and two daus

Lineage: ALAN NATHANIEL HUNT, OBE; *m* Jessie Edna Ellis Northrop and has:

DAVID JAMES FLETCHER, *cr* a **Baron**

HUNTER BLAIR

Arms: Quarterly, 1st, arg.,a chevron gu. between three hunting horns vert, vested and stringed of the second (for HUNTER); 2nd, arg. on a chevron gu., between three cross crosslets fitchée sa., a fleur-de-lys or within a double tressure flory-counterflory of the second (for KENNEDY of Culzean); 3rd, arg. on a saltire sa. eight mascles of the field, in chief a star gu. (for BLAIR); 4th, arg. a shake-fork sa. and in chief a rose gu., surmounted by a mullet of the field (for CUNINGHAME of Brownhill). **Crest:** A stag's head cabossed ppr. **Supporters:** Dexter, a dog of chase salient arg.; sinister, an antelope springing ppr., gorged with an open crown and a chain hanging thereat or. **Motto:** *Vigilantia, robur, voluptas* ('Vigilance, strength, pleasure'). **Creation:** Bt. (GB) 27 June 1786.

SIR EDWARD THOMAS HUNTER BLAIR, 8TH BT, of Dunskey, Co Wigtown [Sir Edward Hunter Blair Bt, Parton House, Castle Douglas, Kirkcudbrightshire DG7 3NB]; *b* 15 Dec 1920; *s* f 1985; *educ* Eton, Balliol Coll Oxford and U of Paris; KOYLI WW II, landowner, memb: Kirkcudbrightshire CC 1970–71 and Cncl Wyndham's Tst 1992–, author: *Scotland Sings* (1981), *A Story of Me* (1981), *A Future Time* (1984), *A Mission in Life* (1987), *Nearing the Year 2000* (1990) and *Our Troubled Future* (1993); *m* 21 April 1956 *Norma (*d* 1972), er dau of Walter Sidney Harris, of Barnsdale, Cutsyke, nr Castleford, Yorks, and adopted:

*Alan Walter; *b* 20 Sept 1961

*Helen Cecilia [Mrs J B Watson, 17 Adams Rd, Cambridge]; *b* 28 March 1963; *m* 1985 *J B (James) Watson, 2nd s of Peter Watson, and has:

(1) *Emily Ann; *b* 1989

(2) *Natasha Jean; *b* 1991

Lineage: JAMES HUNTER; scion of Hunter of Hunterston; acquired Abbotshill, Ayrshire, by charter 9 May 1569; *m* Janet Neil and had:

JAMES HUNTER of Abbotshill; *m* —, dau of Campbell of Craigdow, and had:

JAMES HUNTER of Abbotshill; *d* 1617; f of:

JAMES HUNTER of Abbotshill, Provost Ayr; *m* Jane Campbell and had, with other issue:

ADAM HUNTER of Abbotshill; *m* 1st Marion, dau of Thomas Blair; *m* 2nd Janet, dau of Wallace of Mainholm, and by his 1st w had:

JAMES HUNTER of Abbotshill; *b* 5 Aug 1672; *m* 1694 Janet, dau of John Ferguson of Craigdarroch, and *d* 1 Nov 1739, having had a yr s:

JOHN HUNTER of Mainholm and Millquarter; *b* 11 Aug 1702; *m* Anne, dau of William Cuninghame of Brownhill, Ayrshire, by Anne, dau and coheir of Sir Archibald Hamilton of Rosehill, Bt, MP, and *d* 1755, having had:

1 William; Lt-Col; *b* 2 Aug 1739; *d* unm 1792

2 Sir JAMES HUNTER later HUNTER BLAIR (added 1777), **1st Bt** (GB), so *cr* 27 June 1786; *b* 21 Feb 1741; Edinburgh banker, ptnr with Sir William Forbes, Ld Provost and MP Edinburgh; *m* 1770 Jean (*d* 2 Feb 1817), dau and heir of John Blair of Dunskey (*see* AILSA, M), and *d* 1 July 1787, having had, with nine other children:

(1) **Sir John Hunter Blair, 2nd Bt**; *b* 19 Feb 1773; *d* unm 24 May 1800

(2) DAVID (Sir), **3rd Bt**

(3) James; inherited the estates of Dunskey and Robertland, Lt-Col Ayrshire Militia, thrice MP Wigtownshire; *d* unm 24 June 1822

(4) Forbes; inherited James's estates; *d* unm Feb 1833

(5) Thomas, CB; Maj-Gen, inherited bro's estates, wounded and made prisoner Battle of Talavera by French till 1814; wounded Waterloo, Lt-Col, Brig-Gen Burmese War and India; *m* 1820 Eliza (*d* 28 Aug 1858), dau of J Norris, and *dsp* 31 Aug 1849

Sir JOHN's bro,

Sir David Hunter Blair, 3rd Bt; *b* 3 Oct 1778; Col Ayrshire Militia, Convenor and V-Lt Ayrshire; *m* 1st 2 July 1813 Dorothea (*d* 22 May 1820), 2nd dau of Edward Hay MacKenzie of Newhall and Cromartie (*see* TWEEDDALE, M), and had:

1 James, MP Ayrshire 1852–54, Lt-Col Scots Fus Gds; *b* 22 March 1817; *ka* Inkerman 5 Nov 1854

2 EDWARD (Sir), **4th Bt**

1 Maria Dorothea; *m* 15 Jan 1839 Sir Walter Elliot, KCSI (*d* 1 March 1887), of Wolfelee, Roxburghshire, and *d* 24 Dec 1890, leaving issue

Sir David *m* 2nd 15 Jan 1825 Elizabeth (*d* 3 Aug 1859), 3rd dau of Sir John Hay, Bt, of Hayston by Mary Elizabeth, 2nd dau of 17th Lord Forbes (*qv*), and by her had, with other issue:

3 John; *b* 18 Oct 1825; *m* 22 April 1852 Emily Williams (*d* 9 Dec 1897), yst dau of Edward Grant, and *d* 27 March 1885, having had:

(1) Penton; *b* 5 Jan 1856; *d* 26 April 1882

(1) Caroline; *m* 1874 Walter Morgan, of Wolverton Manor, Ventnor, est s of Sir Walter Morgan (*d* 1903), Ch Justice Madras, and *d* 18 Nov 1943, leaving issue

(2) Elizabeth Montgomery; *m* 25 May 1881 Frank Napier Thorowgood, MICE (*see* below), s of John Charles Thorowgood, and *d* 24 Jan 1936, leaving issue. He *d* 24 April 1920

4 David; Lt-Col Scots Fus Gds; *b* 22 Jan 1827; *d* Rome 31 March 1869

Sir DAVID *d* 26 Dec 1857; his son,

Sir Edward Hunter Blair, 4th Bt, JP, DL Ayrshire and Wigtownshire; RN and 93rd Highrs, Col cmdg Ayrshire Artillery Vols; *b* 24 March 1818; *m* 4 June 1850 Elizabeth (*d* 5 Sept 1899), dau of George Wauchope, bro of William Wauchope of Niddrie, and *d* 7 Oct 1896, having had issue:

1 **Sir David Oswald Hunter Blair, 5th Bt**, OSB; *b* 30 Sept 1853; *educ* Eton and Magdalen Coll Oxford (MA 1878), entered Benedictine Order 1878, ordained 1886, Rector Abbey Sch Fort Augustus 1890–95, Master Hunter Blair's Hall Oxford 1889–1909, Abbot Fort Augustus 1913–17, titular Abbot Dunfermline, Privy Chamberlain to HH POPE LEO XIII, late Capt Ayr and Wigtown Militia; *d* unm 12 Sept 1939

2 James; *b* 12 Dec 1854; *d* Harrow 25 July 1870

3 George Wauchope; *b* 14 Feb 1857; *d* 8 March 1858

4 EDWARD (Sir), **6th Bt**

5 Forbes Cromartie; memb Roy Co Archers, ptnr Wauchope, Moodie & Co, of Leith, entered 4th Bn Roy Scots Fus 1885, Capt 3rd Bn 1915, Maj 1919, Comdt Combined Base Depot Egypt 1919, cmded a Bn Roy Scots; served WW I Gallipoli, Salonica and Egypt (four medals, 1914–15 star); *b* 22 Sept 1859; *educ* Repton and Trin Coll Cambridge (BA, LLB); *d* unm 27 Sept 1940

6 Walter Charles, CB (1915), CMG (1917); Maj-Gen RA, AAG War Office 1913–14, Memb Exec Cncl Malta 1916, DL and JP E Lothian, served Sudan 1898 (two medals, despatches, brevet) and WW I 1914–16, Order White Eagle Serbia 2nd Cl with swords, Cdr Legion Honour; *b* 1 Sept 1860; *educ* Fettes and RMA Woolwich; *m* 8 July 1888 Ethel Mary (*d* 27 Oct 1935), dau of David Logan, MICE, and *d* 24 Nov 1938, having had:

(1) John Wauchope; *b* 4 Aug 1903; *educ* Oriel Coll Oxford (MA); *m* 1935 *Helen, yr dau of J Ezergallis, of Liepaja, Latvia, and *dsp* 31 Dec 1964

(1) Alice Dalrymple; *b* 15 May 1889; *m* 7 Sept 1909 Lt-Col Willoughby Ewart Peel, DSO, s of William Felton Peel, of Blackwater, Hants, and *d* 8 May 1966, leaving issue. He *d* 2 March 1966

(2) Cicely Mary; DStJ; *b* 11 Feb 1891; *m* 31 Aug 1910 Maj-Gen Sir Percival Spearman Wilkinson, KCMG, CB, est s of Percival Spearman Wilkinson, JP, of Mount Oswald, Co Durham, and *d* 3 Feb 1972, leaving issue. He *d* 4 Nov 1953

7 Reginald Stanley, MBE (1919); Maj Gordon Highrs, memb Roy Co Archers, served Egypt 1882 (Battle of Tel-el-Kebir), Suakim Expdn 1884, Nile Expdn 1885 (medal with four clasps) and Boer War 1901 (medal with two clasps), GSO 1914; *b* 18 Nov 1861; *m* 17 Oct 1893 Emily Gertrude (*d* 22 Sept 1967 aged 98), dau of Robert Heaton Rhodes, of Christchurch, NZ, and *d* 11 Oct 1948, having had:

(1) David Walter; Lt-Col Gordon Highrs, memb Roy Co Archers, WW I (POW), S Russia 1919 on Mil Intell and WW II; *b* 22 July 1894; *educ* Wellington; *m* 1st 17 Dec 1919 (*divorce* 1941) Barbara (*d* 27 May 1965), er dau of George Cameron Norman, and had:

1a +John David [John Hunter Blair Esq, 34 Orange Grove Drive, Box 269, Harare, Zimbabwe]; *b* 31 Jan 1925; *educ* Eton; WW II as F/O RAF; *m* 1st 25 July 1952 (*divorce* 1978) Jennifer Mary, only dau of Leslie Hamilton Gault; *m* 2nd 1988 *Edwina Margaret, dau of James Done, of Harare, and has by his 1st w:

1b +T(h)om(as); *b* 24 April 1957; *m* 1986 *Caroline ('Pol'), only dau of D Unwin, of Coventry, and has issue:

1c +Jack David Hamilton; *b* 1989

2c +Charlie; *b* 9 Jan 1997

1c *Sophie; *b* 1991

1b *Jane; *b* 25 Feb 1956; *m* 1st 1982 William Scott Hutton and has:

1c *Oliver David; *b* 20 Aug 1982

2c *Louis Philip; *b* 1985

1b (cont.) Mrs Hutton *m* 2nd 19– *Max Wolf and by him has:

1c *Gabriella Ilse; *b* 1990

2c *Cordelia Iris; *b* 1992

2b *Sophie; *b* 2 Nov 1960; *m* 1984 *Philip John McCann

1a *Aline Rosemary; WW II in VAD; *b* 22 Dec 1921; *m* 1st 16 Dec 1944 (*divorce* 1949) Lt-Col David Theodor Dobie, DSO, Parachute Regt, est s of David Walter Dobie, of Tynemouth, Northumberland; *m* 2nd 1 Sept 1949 (*divorce* 1965) Hugh Cam Hobhouse, yst s of Sir Reginald Arthur Hobhouse, 5th Bt (*qv*), and has issue; *m* 3rd 3 April 1965 *John Alastair Livingston Timpson, MC, yst s of Lawrence Timpson, of Appleton Manor, Berks (*see* Section Van Buren AMERICAN PRESIDENTIAL AMILIES, 1994, Morris Genealogical Books SA)

(1) (cont.) Col David Hunter Blair *m* 2nd 6 Aug 1941 Hughe Thelma (*m* 3rd 1965 Adml Sir Walter Thomas Couchman, KCB, CVO, DSO, OBE, and *d* 1972), widow of Maj John Walter Williams, 2nd Punjab Regt, and dau of Capt Hugh Edward Reid, Roy Scots, and *d* 6 March 1961, having by her had:

2a Ronald David; *b* and *d* 31 March 1942

3a Neil Malcolm; 2nd Lt Gordon Highrs; *b* 7 Feb 1944; *educ* Gordonstoun; *d* 19–

(2) Alister; Lt Cameron Highlanders; *b* 25 April 1896; *ka* 9 May 1915

(3) Ronald, DSC (1919); Cdr RN, served WWs I and II, US Legn Merit 1945, memb Roy Co Archers; *b* 23 Dec 1898; *m* 18 Dec 1929 *Nancye Murray [Mrs Ronald Hunter Blair, Fiddlers Hall, Charlestown, Fife], dau of Wilfred Bruno Colbeck, of Auckland, NZ, and *d* 30 July 1968, leaving issue:

1a +Alister [Lt-Cdr Alister Hunter Blair, Gilder Lodge, Chelmsford, Essex]; *b* 22 Oct 1930; *educ* Wellington; Lt-Cdr RN served Korea 1952–53; *m* 20 March 1958 *Jennifer Shirley, er dau of Rev Basil William Greenup, of Rock, Cornwall, and has:

1b +Nicholas Patrick Alister; *b* 20 April 1959

2a +Reginald Stuart; 2nd Lt Gordon Highrs; *b* 11 Nov 1942; *educ* Nautical Coll Pangbourne and RMA Sandhurst; *m* 1968 *Jennifer Marjorie, est dau of Jack Paley Yorke, and has:

1b *Camilla Louise; *b* 5 Dec 1970

2b *Antonia Claire; *b* 12 Dec 1972

3a +Ronald Patrick; *b* 23 Oct 1944; *educ* Trin Coll Glenalmond; *m* Sept 72 *Mary Fitzhugh, dau of William T Stewart, Jr, of NJ, USA, and has:

1b +James Stewart; *b* 31 Oct 1974

2b +A son; *b* 31 Oct 1977

1a *Julia; *b* 5 Oct 1932; *m* 1st 17 Oct 1958 Charles Maitland Zane, er son of Rollin Zane, of Hartford, Conn., and has:

1b *Lucy Sarah Mackenzie; *b* 7 Oct 1960

1a (cont.) Mrs Zane *m* 2nd 1966 *Arnold J Bauer and by him has:

2b *Rebecca; *b* 1968

2a *Mary Elizabeth (twin); *b* 23 Oct 1944

(4) Reginald Eustace; *b* 27 Feb 1905; *d* unm 17 May 1931

(1) Elizabeth Anne; *b* 23 June 1909; *m* 14 Sept 1933 (Abraham) Eyre Chatterton, BA, BAI, AMInstCE, er s of Abraham Chatterton, of Kilgarron, Enniskerry, Co Wicklow, and had:

1a Michael Eyre; *b* 17 May 1937; *d* 7 March 1940

2a *Peter James; *b* 2 Aug 1941

3a *Anthony Richard; *b* 29 March 1946

1a *Lorna Laderina; *b* 6 Feb 1935

8 John; *b* 26 July 1865; *m* 1st 14 June 1890 Maude (*d* 25 June 1931), yst dau of Sandford Wills-Sandford, of Compton Castle, Somerset, and had issue:

(1) Colin Edward; WW I as Lt Scots Gds (wounded), WW II as Capt DCLI; *b* 13 Feb 1898; *educ* Eton and RMC Sandhurst; *m* 1st 1 Nov 1924 (*divorce* 1933) Olive Mary (*d* 8 July 1969), formerly w of Louis Hervé Coatalen and only dau of Henry James Bath; *m* 2nd 28 Oct 1933 Mrs Louise Thompson (*d* 24 Dec 1961), est dau of Harrison Hood and gdau of Samuel Hood, of Alford, Aberdeenshire, and *dsp* 25 Nov 1967

8 (cont.) John Hunter Blair *m* 2nd 16 Jan 1932 Mrs Evelyn Vanderburgh (*d* 26 Jan 1938), dau of Frank Maynard Gentle, and *d* 25 Jan 1937

9 Gilbert Wauchope, JP Ceylon; with Ceylon contingent Boer War 1901 (medal with three clasps); *b* 25 Oct 1868; *m* 5 Jan 1904 Muriel Frances (*d* 28 June 1977), est dau of Frank Napier Thorowgood, MICE, of Wimbledon, by Elizabeth Montgomery, yr dau of John Hunter Blair (*see* above), and *dsp* 1 Oct 1939

1 Dorothea Elizabeth Thomasina; *m* 23 July 1873 7th Earl of Glasgow (*qv*) and *d* 23 Jan 1923, leaving issue

2 Alicia Mary; *m* 7 April 1874 Sir Charles Dalrymple, 1st Bt, PC, and *d* 2 Sept 1884, leaving issue. He *d* 20 June 1916

3 Helen Constance; *m* 1st 12 July 1883 Capt Stair Hathorn Johnston Johnston-Stewart, DL, 20th Hus, of Physgill, Wigtownshire. He *dsp* 1 April 1904. She *m* 2nd 9 June 1906 Lt-Col Charles Francis Cracroft Jarvis, OBE, JP, DL, late 19th Regt, only s of Rev Francis Amcotts Jarvis, and *d* 30 April 1948, leaving issue. He *d* Jan 1957

4 Ada Selina; *d* unm 30 Dec 1886

The 5th Bt's bro,

Sir Edward Hunter Blair, 6th Bt, JP, DL Ayrshire; *b* 14 March 1858; Capt RN, ret 1898, re-employed WW I; *m* 6 July 1886 Cecilia Dora (*d* 21 Oct 1951), dau of Sir William James Farrer, of Sandhurst Lodge, Berks (*see* 1963 edn FARRER, B), and had issue:

1 JAMES (Sir), **7th Bt**

2 Gaspard Patrick; Cdr RN WW I and WW II (despatches); *b* 21 Sept 1895; *m* 12 May 1929 Sophie (*m* 2nd 18 July 1945 R-Adml Robert Cathcart Kemble Lambert, DSO (*d* 31 Oct 1950), 3rd s of Robert Carr Lambert, and *d* 19 Oct 1968), er dau of Prince Alexis Koudacheff, and was *ka* in HMS *Calcutta* June 1941, leaving:

(1) +Francis John [Francis Hunter Blair Esq, Marbrack, Carsphairn, Castle Douglas, Kirkcudbrightshire]; *b* 29 Oct 1930; *educ* RNC Dartmouth and W of Scotland Ag Coll; late Lt (S) RNVR; *m* 26 Nov 1957 *Joyce Adeline Mary, dau of Cdr James Graham, OBE, RN, and has:

1a +Patrick David; *b* 12 May 1958

2a +Michael Francis; *b* 29 Aug 1959

3a +Peter James; *b* 4 March 1961

4a +Alexander John; *b* 1974

1a *Caroline Mary; *b* 2 May 1963

(1) *Katherine Isabel [Mrs Michael Stidworthy, The Old Rectory, Caldecote, Cambs]; *b* 21 May 1933; *educ* LMH Oxford (BA 1954, MA 1958); *m* 8 Dec 1960 *Michael Stidworthy, only s of Richard E Stidworthy, of Torquay, and has:

1a *John Damian; *b* 13 March 1967

2a *Alexander Luke; *b* 19 Oct 1969

1a *Xenia Mary Gabriel; *b* 2 Oct 1961

2a *Imogen Theresa; *b* 27 Sept 1963

The 6th Bt *d* 11 April 1945; his er s,

Sir James Hunter Blair, 7th Bt; *b* 7 May 1889; *educ* Wellington, Balliol Coll Oxford (BA 1911) and Christ's Coll Cambridge (MA); Lt Seaforth Highlanders (SR) WW I (wounded), Dist Offr Forestry Commn 1920–28; *m* 1st 15 May 1917 Jean (*d* 13 Nov 1953), er dau of Thomas Walker McIntyre, of Sorn Castle, Ayrshire, and had:

1 Adam; *b* 2 Aug; *d* 19 Aug 1919

2 Sir EDWARD THOMAS HUNTER BLAIR, **8th and present Bt**

3 David Gaspard, P/O RAF WW II; *b* 30 Sept 1922; *ka* May 1942

4 +JAMES, DL (Ayrshire) [James Hunter Blair Esq DL, Blairquhan Castle, Maybole, Ayrshire]; *b* 18 March 1926; heir presumptive; *educ* Eton and Balliol Coll Oxford; late Lt Scots Gds

Sir James *m* 2nd 15 July 1954 Ethel Norah (*d* 4 Dec 1966,) formerly w of Kenneth Godfrey Collins and er dau of Herbert Edward Beyers, of Woking, and *d* 1985

HUNTINGDON

Arms: Arg. a maunch sa. **Crest:** A bull's head erased sa., gorged with a ducal coronet and armed or. **Supporters:** Two man-tigers guardant or, their visages resembling the human face, ppr. **Mottoes:** 1 *In veritate victoria* ('Victory is in truth'), 2 *Honorantes me honorabo* ('I will honour those who honour me') and 3 *Post praelia praemia* ('Reward after battle'). **Creation:** E. (E) 8 Dec 1529.

THE 17TH EARL OF HUNTINGDON (William (Bill) Edward Robin Hood Hastings-Bass) [The Rt Hon The Earl of Huntingdon, Hodcott House, West Ilsley, Berks RG16 OAE]; *b* 30 Jan 1948; *s* cousin 1990; *educ* Winchester and Trin Coll Cambridge; racehorse trainer to HM THE QUEEN 1989–; *m* 1989 *Susan Mary Gavin, dau of John Jellicoe Pelham Francis Warner, s of Sir Pelham Warner, MBE

Earldom of Huntingdon: There seems to have been an Earldom of Huntingdon before the Norman Conquest, among its holders then being KING HAROLD, according to the chronicler Florence of Worcester, and Tostig, HAROLD's brother. The first post-Conquest Earl of Huntingdon appears to have been Waltheof, son of Siward Earl of Northumberland (*see* NORTHUMBERLAND, D, preliminary remarks) and indeed Siward's successor in the latter Earldom as well. Waltheof was later beheaded for conspiring against WILLIAM THE CONQUEROR. His son-in-law Simon de St Liz was the next holder of the Earldom, the family connections of Simon's wife Maud making the transition a natural one under the terms prevailing then. Indeed the history of the Earldom over the next few decades amply illustrates the almost chattel-like nature of such a title at this time, a quasi-hereditary post which was nevertheless as often as not held from the king at pleasure and which could be transferred between members of the same family like a parcel of land.

After Earl Simon's death his widow Maud married DAVID I of Scotland, who consequently became Earl of Huntingdon too, keeping the Earldom even after he succeeded his brother as King of Scots. He sided with the EMPRESS MAUD against STEPHEN but came to terms with the latter and made the Earldom over to his son Henry. Henry swore fealty to STEPHEN but subsequently fought against him under the Scottish banner, which may account for Simon de St Liz's son, another Simon, being recognised as Earl of Huntingdon before Henry's death in 1152. Thereafter the Earldom was more or less bounced back and forth between the de St Liz family and the Kings of Scotland, first being held 1157–65 by MALCOLM THE MAIDEN and (1165–74) his brother WILLIAM THE LION, then by a Simon de St Liz (grandson of the first Simon and son of the second) from 1174 to 1184.

When the third Simon de St Liz died in 1184 he left no surviving issue and David, younger brother of the Kings of Scots just mentioned, assumed the Earldom from 1185 (on the handing over of it to him by WILLIAM THE LION) till it was taken away from him in 1215 or 1216 by KING JOHN. He got it back again in 1218, however. It is this David's daughter Ada who married Sir Henry de Hastinges, ancestor of the Lords (Barons) Hastings (*qv*) of which the current Hastings holders of the Huntingdon Earldom are cadets. David's son John was the last member of the Scottish royal family to hold the title, doing so from his father's death in 1219 till his own in 1237. A little over a century later the then Lord Clinton (*qv*) was promoted Earl of Huntingdon. Apart from his wife being widow of Lord Hastings he seems to have had no family connection with the title's previous holders. On his death without issue in 1354 the Earldom expired once more. Between 1377 and 1380 an anglicised Frenchman, Guichard d'Angle, held the Earldom as a life creation granted by RICHARD II. Eight years later it was conferred on John de Holand and from then till 1461 it shared the fortunes of the Dukedom of Exeter (*see* EXETER, M). From 1471 to 1475 Thomas Grey, Lord Ferrers of Groby and a distant relative of the Lords Hastings, held the Earldom, resigning it on being promoted Marquess of Dorset in the latter year. Eight years later William Herbert, Earl of Pembroke (*see* PEMBROKE and MONTGOMERY, E), gave up his existing Earldom to the Crown and was made in compensation Earl of Huntingdon. So even at this late date a peerage title could be treated as something which one could simply resign.

It is perhaps worth adding that despite the fondness of recent members of the Hastings family for the forenames Robin and Hood there is no evidence whatsoever that the legendary outlaw Robin Hood (even supposing he existed) held the Earldom of Huntingdon or indeed any other title.

Lineage: Sir LEONARD HASTINGES, of Kirby, Leics, and Burton Hastings, Warwicks; *m* Alice, dau of 1st Lord (Baron) Camoys (*qv*) of the 1383 *cr*, and *d* 20 Oct 1455, leaving, with three yr sons (Richard (Sir), *m* 1st Joan, *de jure* Baroness Willoughby de Eresby (*qv*) in her own right, and *dsp* 1503; Ralph, living 1462; Thomas):

Sir WILLIAM HASTINGES, 1st LORD (Baron) HASTINGS (E), so *cr* 26 July 1461, though whether by writ of summons, investiture or patent is unclear; also granted by EDWARD IV 17 Feb 1461/2 the Lordship, Barony and Honour of Hastings (which probably was a late example of a feudal tenure rather than a peerage creation, though connected with the peerage creation of the previous July rather in the same way that Earls had traditionally been created or invested with grants of lands attached for the upkeep of the dignity; *see* NORTHUMBERLAND, D, and RUTLAND, D, for a discussion of this point), KG (March 1461/2); *b c* 1431; Sheriff Warwicks and Leics 1455–56,Yorkist Wars of Roses, fought Battle of Towton 1461 (Yorkist Victory), where ktd, Receiver-Gen Duchy Cornwall 1461, Master and Worker King's Mints 1461, Chamberlain N Wales 1461, Steward Honour of Leicester and Lordships and Manors of Castle Donington, Leics, and Higham Ferrers and Daventry, Northants, also Keeper Leicester Castle and Constable Higham Ferrers and Donington Castles (where Donington Hall, the seat of the Earls of Huntingdon, was erected in 1595, remodelled in the neo-Gothic style by William Wilkins 1795, used as a POW camp WW I, as a children's charity home later in the 20th century and as a setting for the BBC TV film of *Alice in Wonderland* 1966 and acquired as a corporate HQ by Br Midland Airways 1982; LORD HASTINGS also in 1474 converted 3,000 acres to parkland at Ashby-de-la-Zouche, Leics, and constructed a castle there, which was afterwards one of the places of imprisonment of MARY QUEEN OF SCOTS and a royalist stronghold in the Civil War of the 17th century till demolished spring 1645 after a nine-months' siege); Jt Constable with his bro Ralph of Rockingham and Northampton Castles 1462; Ch Justice and Chamberlain Merioneths and Constable Harlech Castle 1464; granted 1464 the Castle and Honour of Huntingdon, recently the property of his remote cousin John Hastynges Earl of Pembroke (*see* HASTINGS, B); envoy to negotiate alliances abroad with Burgundy and Brittany 1466; fought Battle of Barnet 1471 (overthrow of Warwick the Kingmaker by EDWARD IV (*see* ABERGAVENNY, M)); Chamberlain Receipt Exchequer 1471; Lt-Gen Calais 1471; *m* by 6 Feb 1461/2 Katherine, widow of William Bonville, 6th Lord (Baron) Harington or Haverington, and dau of Richard Nevill(e), Earl of Salisbury (*see* ABERGAVENNY, M), and was beheaded at the Tower of London 13 June 1483 on a charge of treason (though not attainted), having displeased RICHARD III, when his estates were confiscated (but later restored to his son, part by RICHARD and the remainder by HENRY VII), having had, with three sons (including Richard and William) and a dau (Anne, *m* by 27 June 1481, as his 1st w, 4th Earl of Shrewsbury and Waterford, *qv*):

EDWARD HASTINGS, 2nd LORD (Baron) HASTINGS and 1st LORD (Baron) HASTINGS (of Hungerford) (E), as which called to Parl by writ 15 Nov 1482 *vp* (in the circumstances this must be regarded as a separate peerage to the almost identically named one he was to inherit the next year), KB (1475); *b* 26 Nov 1466; *m* by 18 Feb 1480/1, as her 1st husb, his 2nd cousin Mary, dau and sole heiress of Sir Thomas Hungerford and according to later doctrine Baroness Botreaux, Hungerford and Moleyns (*see* LOUDOUN, E, and SAINT DAVIDS, V), and *d* between 4 and 15 Nov 1506, leaving, with a dau (Anne, *m* by 1503 2nd Earl of Derby (*qv*) and was *bur* 17 Nov 1550):

GEORGE HASTINGS, **1st Earl of Huntingdon** (E), so *cr* 8 Dec 1529, also 3rd LORD (Baron) HASTINGS (under which title he was called to Parl 1509) and 2nd LORD (Baron) HASTINGS (of Hungerford), also on his mother's death deemed by later doctrine to have inherited the Baronies of Botreaux, Hungerford and Moleyns (*see* LOUDOUN, E, and SAINT DAVIDS, V), KB (1501), PC; *b* 1488; *m c* Dec 1509 his 3rd cousin Anne Stafford, widow of Sir Walter Herbert and dau of 2nd Duke of Buckingham (*see* STAFFORD, B), and had, with other issue:

1 FRANCIS, **2nd Earl**

2 Thomas (Sir)

3 Sir EDWARD HASTINGS, 1st and last BARON HASTINGS OF LOUGHBOROUGH, so *cr* 19 Jan 1557/8, KG (1555); *b c* 1520; MP Leicester 1545–47, Leics 1547–52 and Feb-March 1552/3 and Middx 1553–55, ktd 1547, Sheriff Warwicks and Leics 1550–51, Master Horse to QUEEN MARY 1553–57, Chamberlain Household 1557–58; as might be expected from his high favour with QUEEN MARY, a devout RC; *m*(?) Joan — and *dspl* 5 March 1571/2, leaving an illegitimate s Edward, when the Barony expired

4 Henry

5 William

1 Dorothea; *m* Sir Richard Devereux, s of 1st Viscount Hereford (*qv*)

The 1st EARL *d* 25 March 1543/4; his est son,

FRANCIS HASTINGS, **2nd Earl of Huntingdon**, KG (1549), KB (1533), PC (1550); *b c* 1514; Ld Lt Rutland 1550–59, Leics 1554–60, Derbys 1552–60 and Warwicks 1554–59, supported LADY JANE GREY but soon went over to QUEEN MARY, Capt Queen's Vanguard forces 1558, Master Harthounds 1559; *m c* 25 June 1532 Katherine (*d* 23 Sept 1576), dau and coheir of Henry Pole, Lord Montague, and gdau of Margaret, Countess of Salisbury (*see* ABERGAVENNY, M), and *d* 23 June 1560, leaving, with four er daus:

1 HENRY HASTINGS, **3rd Earl of Huntingdon**, KG (1570), KB (Feb 1546/7); *b c* 1536; *educ* Queens' Coll Cambridge; called up to Ho of Lds *vp* 23 Jan 1558/9 in his f's Barony of Hastings; a staunch Protestant, initially distrusted by Elizabeth I on account of his strong claim to the throne through his mother but supported by many Protestants on that very account, nevertheless appointed jt custodian of MARY QUEEN OF SCOTS 1569, Ld Pres of the North 1572; *m* 25 May 1533 Catherine, dau of John Dudley, Duke of Northumberland (*see* DUDLEY, B, and NORTHUMBERLAND, D, preliminary remarks), and *dsp* 14 Dec 1595

2 GEORGE HASTINGS, **4th Earl of Huntingdon**; *b c* 1540; MP (?)Derbys 1562(? and) Leics 1584–87, High Sheriff Leics 1571, ktd 1565; *m* July 1557 Dorothy (brought him Dale Abbey, Derbys; *d* 2 Sept 1607), 2nd dau and coheir of Sir John Port, of Etwal, Derbys, and *d* 30 Dec 1604, having had issue:

(1) Francis, *Lord Hastings*; *m* by 1586 Sarah (*m* 2nd Sir George Kingsmill; *m* 3rd 11th Lord (Baron) Zouche (of Haryngworth) (*qv*); *m* 4th Sir Thomas Edmonds; *d* 1620), sis of 1st Baron Harington of Exton (*see* HARINGTON, Bt), and *dvp* 17 Dec 1595, having had issue:

1a HENRY HASTINGS, **5th Earl of Huntingdon**; *b* 24 April 1586; *m* 15 Jan 1601 Lady Elizabeth Stanley (*d* 20 Jan 1633), yst dau of 5th Earl of Derby (*qv*), and *d* 14 Nov 1643, having had:

1b FERDINANDO HASTINGS, **6th Earl of Huntingdon**; *b* 18 Jan 1608/9; *educ* Emmanuel Coll Cambridge; MP Leics 1625 and 1628–29, called up to Ho of Lds *vp* Oct 1640 in his f's Barony of Hastings (*see* SAINT DAVIDS, V), nominal cdr in Parly army Civil War but inactive; *m* 7 Aug 1623 Lucy, dau and heiress of Sir John Davies, of Englefield, Berks, and *d* 13 Feb 1655/6, having had issue (with a 2nd and 3rd s between Henry and Theophilus):

1c Henry, *Lord Hastings*; *b* 16 Jan 1630; *dvp* & unm 24 June 1649

2c THEOPHILUS HASTINGS, **7th Earl of Huntingdon**, PC (Feb 1682/3–Feb 1688/9); *b* 10 Dec 1650; Capt Gentlemen Pensioners Feb 1682/3–Dec 1688; protested against Act of Settlement 1701 and one of six noblemen excepted from Act of Indemnity 1690 following Glorious Revolution; *m* 1st 19 Feb 1671/2 Elizabeth, est dau and coheir of Sir John Lewis, Bt, of Ledstone, and had issue, with two daus (*d* unm):

1d Thomas, *Lord Hastings*; *b* 12 Nov 1674; *d* an infant 2 March 1675

2d GEORGE HASTINGS, **8th Earl of Huntingdon**; *b* 22 March 1677; *educ* Wadham Coll Oxford; Lt-Col 1st Foot Gds 1697–1702, served under 1st Duke of Marlborough (*qv*) Low Countries at capture of Venloo and Ruremond (Roeremond) 1702; *d* unm 22 Feb 1704/5

2c (cont.) The **7th Earl** *m* 2nd 8 May 1690 Frances (*m* 3rd the Chevalier Mich(a)el de Ligondez, of The Auvergne, and *d* 26 Dec 1723), widow of 6th Viscount Kilmorey (*see* KILMOREY, E) and dau and sole heir of Francis Leveson Fowler, and *d* 30 May 1701, leaving further issue:

3d THEOPHILUS HASTINGS, **9th Earl of Huntingdon**; *b* 12 Nov 1696; *educ* Oxford; *m* 3 June 1728 Lady Selina Shirley, fndr The Countess of Huntingdon's Connection (*d* 17 June 1791), 2nd dau of 2nd Earl Ferrers (*qv*), and *d* 13 Oct 1747, having had, with other issue:

1e FRANCIS HASTINGS, **10th Earl of Huntingdon**, PC (1760); *b* 13 March 1728/9; *educ* Westminster and Ch Ch Oxford; Master Horse to George Prince of Wales 1756–60 and GEORGE III 1760–61, Groom Stole 1761–70, FRS 1758, FSA 1768; *dspl* unm 2 Oct 1789, when the Baronies of Botreaux, Hastings (of Hastings), Hastings (of Hungerford), Hungerford and Moleyns passed to his only surv sister Elizabeth, Countess of Moira (*see* SAINT DAVIDS, V, and LOUDOUN, E), while the Earldom of Huntingdon became dormant

1e Elizabeth, *m* 1st Earl of Moira (*see* LOUDOUN, E also SAINT DAVIDS, V)

2e Selina; engaged to her distant cousin Lt-Col George Hastings (*see* below; f of **12th Earl**) but *d* young 12 May 1763

1d Catherine Maria; *m* Rev Granville Wheler, of Otterden Place, Kent, s of Sir George Wheler, and was gmother of Granville Hastings Wheler, who inherited the Ledstone Hall estate, Yorks, from his great-aunt, Lady Elizabeth Hastings

2d Margaret; *m* Rev Benjamin Ingham, Rector Aberford, and was grandmother of Theophilus Hastings Ingham, of Marton-in-Craven, Yorks

1c Elizabeth; *m c* 18 Nov 1662 Sir James Langham, 2nd Bt (*qv*), and *dsp* 28 March 1664

2c Mary; *m* Sir William Jolliffe

2b HENRY HASTINGS, 1st and last BARON LOUGHBOROUGH OF LOUGHBOROUGH, Co Leicester (E), so *cr* 23 Oct 1643; *b* 28 Sept 1610; Leics: Ld Lt 1638 and High Sheriff 1642; royalist Civil War, raised and led own troop of horse Battle of Edgehill 1642, fought various minor engagements in Midlands, Col Gen Leics; *d* unm 10 Jan 1666/7 when the Barony expired

1b Alice; *m* Sir Gervase Clifton, Bt, of Clifton

2b Elizabeth; *m* Sir Hugh Calveley, of Lea

2a George (Sir); *m* Seymour, dau and coheir of Sir Gilbert Pryn, and had issue (*see* 1939 edn)

3a Edward; Capt RN; *d* unm 1617

1a Catherine; *m* 1st Earl of Chesterfield (*see* 1967 edn CHESTERFIELD and STANHOPE, E)

2a Theodosia; *m* Sir Francis Bodenham, of Ryal, Rutland

(2) Henry, of Woodland, Dorset; features in *Biographia Britannica*; *m* twice and had issue by his 1st w

(3) Edward (Sir); *d* unm at Vienna

(1) Catherine; *m* 1st Sir Edward Unton, of Wadley; *m* 2nd Sir Walter Chetwynd, of Ingestre (*see* CHETWYND, V)

(2) Dorothy; *m* 1st Sir James Stuart, KB; *m* 2nd, as his 2nd w, 2nd Earl of Roscommon

3 William; *dsp*

4 Edward (Sir), of Leicester Abbey; *m* Barbara, est dau and coheir of Sir William Devereux (*see* HEREFORD, V), and widow of Edward Cave, of Ingarsby, Leics, and *d* 1603, having had, with a yr s, Walter (*dsp*):

(1) Henry (Sir); Sheriff Leics 1619; *m* Mabel (*d* 1618), dau of Antony Faunt, of Foston, Leics, and *d* 1629, having had, with two daus:

1a Henry, of Hamberston, Leics; *m* Jane Goodall, of Belgrave, Leics, and had, with two other sons and five daus:

1b Henry; *b* 1643; *m* 1st 1671 Elizabeth Warren; *m* 2nd 1673 Pentecost Smalley (*d* 1705) and *dsp* 1697

2b Walter; *b* 1645; *m* Hannah Cradock and had:

1c Henry, of Castle Donington; *dsp* 1753

1c Jane; *m* Edward Holme, of Upholland

3b Richard, of Welford, Notts; *b* 1645; *m* 1st Sarah Sleath (*d* 1707); *m* 2nd — and *d* 1715, leaving by his 1st w:

1c Richard; *b* 1699; *d* an infant

2c Henry, of Lutterworth, Leics; *b c* 1701; the trustees appointed by his f dissipated much of his property; *m* 1727 Elizabeth Hudson, of Lutterworth, and *d* 1786, leaving issue:

1d Rev THEOPHILUS HENRY HASTINGS, *de jure* 11th EARL OF HUNTINGDON according to the decision of the Ho of Lds 1819 which recognised his nephew as Earl; assumed the title in any case; *bapt* 7 Oct 1728; *educ* St John's Coll Cambridge; Vicar Osgathorpe and Belton, Leics, Rector Gt and Little Leake, Notts; *m* 1st — Pratt (*d* a few months later); *m* 2nd 1798 Elizabeth Warner and *dsps* 2 April 1804

2d George; *b c* 1735; brought up with his er bro by **9th Earl of Huntingdon**; Lt-Col 3rd Foot Gds; *m* 1769 Sarah (*d* 1807), dau of Sir Richard Fowler, 2nd Bt, of Harnage Grange, Salop, and *d* 6 Feb 1802, having had, with two er sons:

1e Francis; *b* 1770; *d* 1776

2e Henry; *b* 1774; *d* 1796

3e Ferdinando; *b* 1776, *d* 1801

4e HANS FRANCIS, **12th Earl**

3d Ferdinando; *d* in his 14th year

2a Walter Hastings; Mil Kt Windsor; *d* 1672

3a Sir RICHARD HASTINGS, 1st and last Bt (E), so *cr* 7 May 1667, of Redlynch, Somerset; *m* Margaret, dau of Sir Robert Poyntz, KB, of Iron Acton, Glos; *dsp* and was *bur* 3 Sept 1668, when the btcy expired

4a Antony; *m* 1638 Anne Watkinson and *d* 1667, leaving issue:

1b Henry; *bapt* 1641; his descendants allegedly settled in Ireland; a Hastings family of Killaloe, Co Clare, at one point asserted but failed to prove a connection with the Earls of Huntingdon

2b George; *bapt* 1642; *m* 1665 Elizabeth Fleming; *dsp* 1704

3b Edward; *bapt* 1647; *m* 1678 Catherine Dale and *dspm* 1719/20

4b Anthony; *bapt* 1649; *m* 1685 Caroletta Churchill and *d* 1692, leaving with other issue:

1c Antony; *bapt* 1689; *bur* 1691/2

2c Churchill; *bapt* 1690; *bur* 1722

3c Antony; *b c* 1692; *d* 1700

5 Francis (Sir); *b c* 1545; *dsp* 1610

6 Walter; *m* 1574 Joyce Roper (*d* 1616) and *d* 1616, leaving issue:

(1) Henry (Sir); *b c* 1578; *m* 1st Dorothy Huddleston and had issue; *m* 2nd —

1 Mary; a beauty whose fame reached the ears of IVAN THE TERRIBLE, TSAR OF RUSSIA; he sent an envoy to England to negotiate for her hand in marriage, even though his 5th w Martha Nagaya was still living, holding out the prospect of an alliance with Russia to ELIZABETH I meanwhile; Lady Mary wisely preferred spinsterhood to marriage with arguably the greatest monster of the age and nothing came of it; she *d* unm

The 10th EARL's distant cousin and *de jure* 11th Earl's n,

HANS FRANCIS HASTINGS, **12th Earl of Huntingdon**; *b* 14 Aug 1779; *educ* Repton and Bettesworth's Acad Chelsea; joined RN 1793: wounded Quiberon Bay 1795, Lt 1799, Cdr 1821, Post Capt 1824, Ordnance Barrack Master IoW and Ordnance Storekeeper Enniskillen 1808–17; successfully claimed Earldom 29 Oct 1818 and was summoned 14 Jan 1819, though unsuccessful in reclaiming any of the once enormous family estates, Govr Dominica 1822–24; *m* 1st 12 May 1803 Frances (*d* 31 March 1820), dau of Rev Richard Chaloner Cobbe, Rector Gt Marlow; *m* 2nd 28 Sept 1820 Eliza Mary (*m* 3rd 26 April 1838 Col Sir Thomas Noel Harris, KH, and *d* 9 Nov 1846), widow of Alexander Thistletwayte and est dau of Joseph Bettesworth, and *d* 9 Dec 1828, having by his 1st w had, with four daus:

1 FRANCIS THEOPHILUS HENRY HASTINGS, **13th Earl of Huntingdon**; *b* 31 July 1808; *educ* Charterhouse; *m* 8 Sept 1835 Elizabeth Anne (*d* 18 Feb 1857), only surv dau of Richard Power, MP, of Clashmore, Co Waterford, and *d* 13 Sept 1875, leaving:

(1) FRANCIS POWER PLANTAGENET HASTINGS, **14th Earl of Huntingdon**; *b* 4 Dec 1841; *educ* Ch Ch Oxford; *m* 15 Aug 1867 Mary Anne Wilmot (*d* 16 Dec 1894), only child of Col Hon John Craven Westenra (*see* ROSSMORE, B), and *d* 20 May 1885, having had:

1a WARNER FRANCIS JOHN PLANTAGENET, **15th Earl of Huntingdon**, DL (King's Co); *b* 8 July 1868; Page of Honour Viceregal Court Ireland 1880–81, Lt-Col cmdg 3rd Bn Prince of Wales's Leinster Regt, served WWI; *m* 11 June 1882 Maud Margaret, V-Pres Leics Branch BRCS (*d* 26 Dec 1953), 2nd dau of Sir Samuel Wilson, MP Portsmouth, and *d* 5 April 1939, leaving:

1b FRANCIS JOHN CLARENCE WESTENRA PLANTAGENET HASTINGS, **16th Earl of Huntingdon**; *b* 30 Jan 1901; *educ* Eton and Ch Ch

Oxford (BA 1924, MA, memb Oxford polo team), CD WW II 1941–45, Parly Sec Min Ag and Fisheries 1945–50, muralist (works exhibited Chicago World Fair 1933, Birmingham U, Women's Press Club London, Buscot Park Faringdon, Marx House Clerkenwell), Pres: Soc Mural Painters 1952–55 and Solent Protection Soc 1958–68, author: *The Golden Octopus* and *Commonsense about India*; *m* 1st 21 Oct 1925 (*divorce* 1943) Cristina (*d* 22 March 1953), dau of the Marchese Casati, of Rome, and had:

1c *Moorea, JP (1995) [The Lady Moorea Black JP, 17 Lansdowne Walk, London W11]; *b* 4 March 1928; Under Warden Guild Freemen City London 1998–99; *m* 1st 22 June 1957 (*divorce* 1966), as his 2nd w, Baron Wyatt of Weeford (*d* 7 Dec 1997), and has:

1d *Pericles Plantagenet James Casati; *b* 22 Aug 1963

1c (cont.) Lady Moorea *m* 2nd 11 Jan 1967 *Brinsley Graham Black, s of Percy Irvine Victor Black, of Hampstead, and by him has:

2d *Octavius Orlando Irvine Casati; *b* 2 May 1968

1b (cont.) The **16th Earl** *m* 2nd 1 Feb 1944 Margaret, JP (Dorset 1946), authoress as Margaret Lane (*d* 1994), formerly w of Bryan Wallace and only child of Harry George Lane, of Vernham Dean, Andover, and *d* 1990, leaving by her:

2c *Selina Shirley [The Lady Selina Hastings, c/o Rogers Coleridge & White, 20 Powis Mews, London W11 1JN]; *b* 5 March 1945; author biographies of Nancy Mitford and Evelyn Waugh

3c *(Caroline) Harriet [The Lady Harriet Shackleton, c/o Coutts & Co, 16 Cavendish Sq, London W1]; *b* 12 June 1946; *m* 6 June 1970 Hon Charles Edward Ernest Shackleton (*d* 1979), only s of Baron Shackleton, OBE (LP; *see* 1970 edn), and has:

1d *David Charles; *b* 1986

1d *Emma Jane Miranda; *b* 1985

1b Maud Kathleen Cairnes Plantagenet; *b* 28 March 1893; *m* 28 July 1916 William Montagu Curzon-Herrick (*see* HOWE, E) and *d* 8 Feb 1965

2b Norah Frances; *b* 12 Sept 1894; *m* 10 Feb 1920 4th Earl of Kilmorey (*qv*) and *d* 1985, leaving issue

3b Marian Ileene Mabel; *b* 15 Sept 1895; *m* 1st 16 July 1918 Capt Patrick Keith Cameron, Cameron Highrs, est s of Keith Cameron, and had issue. He *d* 8 Feb 1933. She *m* 2nd 1943 Capt John Walter Wilson Bridges, only s of R-Adml Walter Bogue Bridges, FRGS, FRCI, of Birch, Essex, and *d* 22 April 1947. He *d* 4 Aug 1952

2a Osmond William Toome Westenra; T/Capt and Assist Supt Remount Serv 1916; *b* 7 Aug 1873; *m* 14 April 1896 Mary Caroline Campbell (*d* 12 Nov 1955), dau of Daniel Fox Tarratt, of Ellary, Argyll, and *d* 25 Oct 1933, leaving:

1b David Fox Godolphin, of Timur Beg, Upper Lambourn, Newbury, Berks; F/Lt RAF WW II; *b* 13 Dec 1909; *educ* Eton; *m* 20 Dec 1945 *Mary, widow of Edward Hunter Power, RA, and dau of Elystan Charles Jones, of Llanfair Grange, Llandovery, and *d* 19–

2b Robin Hood William Stewart, DSO (1944) and bar (1945), OBE (1945), MC, of Bramdean Manor, nr Alresford, Hants; Lt-Col Rifle Bde WW II (wounded, despatches twice); *b* 16 Jan 1917; *educ* Stowe and Ch Ch Oxford; *m* 25 May 1950 *Jean Suzanne [Mrs Robin Hastings, The Malt House, Bramdean, Hants; 2 Billing Rd, London SW10], formerly w of John Ronald Christopher Holbech and dau of Henry Palethorpe, of Stone Manor, Chaddesley Corbett, Worcs, and *d* 1990, leaving:

1c *Lucinda Ileene [Mrs Michael Waterhouse, Middleton Hall, Bakewell, Derbys]; *b* 15 July 1955; *m* 1983 *Michael Thomas Waterhouse (*see* MARLBOROUGH, D) and has issue

1b Ileene Wilmot Fox; *b* 2 Feb 1898; *m* 2 April 1918 Capt Gordon Armytage Fairbairn, 18th Hus, of Australia, only s of Lt-Col Frederick Fairbairn, of Logan Downs, Qld, and *d* 19–, leaving issue

2b Dorothy Isabel Westenra; Ldy Pres Roy Cambridge Home for Soldiers' Widows; *b* 18 May 1899; *m* 10 April 1923 2nd Marquess of Cambridge (*see* 1970 edn) and had issue

3b Helen Stewart Daubuz; *b* 26 Nov 1900; *m* 14 June 1934 Col Douglas Charles Murray Beech, MC, JP, s of Lt-Col Rowland John Beech, JP, DL, of Brandon Hall, Warwicks, and *d* 18 Dec 1964. He *d* 14 June 1944

4b Osmunda Mary, of Little Toyd Farm, Rockbourne, Fordingbridge, Hants; *b* 17 Jan 1903; *d* 19–

3a Aubrey Craven Theophilus Robin Hood; *b* 9 Jan 1878; *m* 29 April 1907 Winifred (*d* 1977), dau of Thomas Forsyth-Forest, of The Querns, Cirencester, and *d* 25 May 1929, leaving:

1b Peter Robin Hood HASTINGS later HASTINGS-BASS (deed poll 16 Feb 1954); Capt Welsh Gds WW II, racehorse trainer; *b* 16 July 1920 (twin); *educ* Stowe and Ch Ch Oxford; *m* 9 April 1947 *Priscilla Victoria [Mrs Peter Hastings, Wells Head House, Kingsclere, Berks], only child of Capt Sir Malcolm Bullock, 1st and last Bt (*see* 1963 edn), and *d* 4 June 1964, leaving:

1c WILLIAM EDWARD ROBIN HOOD HASTINGS later HASTINGS-BASS, **17th and present Earl of Huntingdon**

2c +SIMON AUBREY ROBIN HOOD HASTINGS later HASTINGS-BASS [The Hon Simon Hastings-Bass, Coronation House, Newmarket, Suffolk]; *b* 2 May 1950; heir presumptive; *educ* Winchester and Trin Coll Cambridge; granted with siblings rank of earl's dau/yr s 1992

3c +John Peter Robin Hood [The Hon John Hastings-Bass, Ashmansworth Manor, Newbury, Berks]; *b* 5 June 1954; *educ* Winchester and Trin Coll Cambridge; *m* 1982 *Sophie, only dau of Peter Ewald Scarisbrick, and has:

1d *Alice Victoria Mary; *b* 1983

2d *Lily Frances Mary; *b* 1986

1c *Emma Alice Mary [The Lady Emma Balding, Park House, Kingsclere, Berks]; *b* 28 Jan 1949; *m* 25 Aug 1969 *Ian Anthony Balding, LVO, trainer to HM THE QUEEN, s of Gerald Balding, of Weyhill House, Andover, Hants, and Mrs Martin Quirk, of Rumson, NJ, and has:

1d *Andrew Matthews; *b* 1972

1d *Clare Victoria; *b* 29 Jan 1971

1b Diana Wilmot; *b* 9 Dec 1914

2b *Joan; *b* 24 April 1917; *m* 1st 5 Sept 1942 Thomas Frank Bartlett, only s of T H Bartlett, of Surbiton; *m* 2nd 21 June 1948 Kenneth Porter (*d* 1986), of Long Island, s of Kenneth Porter, of Rockville Center, Long Island, and has:

1c *Steven Kenneth; *b* 28 April 1951; *m* 1977 *Melinda Smith and has:

1d *Whitney Kemp; *b* 1979

2d *Steven Lawrence; *b* 1981

2c *Grant Aubrey; *b* 28 April 1951; *m* 1976 *Christina French and has:

1d *Christina Chrysler; *b* 1982

3b Aubreen Heather; *b* 16 July 1920; *m* 6 May 1946 Lloyd Weinberger, of Long Island, s of Harry H Weinberger, of NJ, and *d* 1967

1a Constance Wilmot Annie; *b* 10 July 1870; *m* 17 April 1890 Maj Sir Thomas Edward Sabine Pasley, 3rd Bt (*qv*), and *d* 25 Aug 1922, leaving issue

2a Ileene Frances Cairne; *b* 20 May 1872; *m* 15 Nov 1893 Lt-Col Colin George Pelham Campbell, of Stonefield, Argyll, and *d* 15 June 1946, leaving issue. He *d* 8 Feb 1955

3a Ierne Louisa Arundel; *b* 29 Oct 1874; *m* 10 June 1896 2nd Baron Hothfield (*qv*) and *d* 5 Jan 1935, leaving issue

4a Rowena Grace Marion Selina; *b* 2 Feb 1879; *m* 29 July 1901 Graham Paterson (*d* 22 March 1938), s of William Paterson, and *d* 5 Sept 1944, leaving issue (*see* WIMBORNE, V)

5a Wilmot Ida Noreen; *b* 5 Aug 1880; *m* 9 June 1903 Sir William Arthur Hamar Bass, 2nd Bt (*see* 1909 edn), and *dsp* 25 May 1949. He *d* 28 Feb 1952

(1) Dorothea Frances; *m* 27 Oct 1869 George Dundas Yeoman, of Woodlands, nr Whitby, Yorks, and *d* 8 July 1909. He *dsp* 3 Dec 1908

(2) Selina Elizabeth Anne; *m* 3 March 1870 E G H Odell, of Carriglea, Co Waterford, and *d* 24 April 1875

(3) Louisa Arabella; *m* 8 Aug 1871 W P Maxwell, of Moore Hill, Co Waterford, and *d* 3 Feb 1873. He *d* 11 Aug 1902

2 George Fowler, CB; V-Adml, Kt Medjidie, cmded Pacific and the Nore; *b* 28 Nov 1814; *m* 14 Sept 1864 Mathilde Alice (*d* 6 July 1916), only dau of W H Hitchcock, of St Omer (took the surname Degacher 1874), and *d* 21 March 1876, having had:

(1) Hans Francis; Consul Cyclades Islands 1914, Greek Order Redeemer; *b* 23 June 1865; *m* 19 June 1900 Edyth Mary (*d* 1959), dau of George O Spratt, of Lamorna, Gibraltar, and *d* 2 March 1933, leaving:

1a George Godolphin; *b* 1905; *m* 1932 Marjory Harris, of Melbourne, Australia, and *d* 1981, leaving:

1b +Warren Francis [Warren Hastings Esq, 3/8A Mosman St, Mosman 2088, NSW, Australia]; *b* 30 April 1938; *m* 1st 9 Aug 1963 Heather Jean, dau of Collins Watson Gordon, of NSW; *m* 2nd 1968 (*divorce* 1976) Elaine Adams; *m* 3rd 1976 *Elisabeth Kay Vine-Hall and by her has:

1c +Adam Francis; *b* 1977

1c *Emma Louise; *b* 1979

1b *Edyth Leonie [Mrs Edyth Ekins, 127 Date Street, Adamstown, Newcastle, NSW, Australia]; *b* 16 July 1933; *m* 1956 (*divorce* 19–) Ross Ekins and has:

1c *David Ross; *b* 19–

2c *Russell John; *b* 19–

1c *Linda Margaret; *b* 19–

1a Alice Mary Hamilton; *b* 1 May 1901; *m* 5 April 1923 Col Colin Wilson, RAMC, of Lymington, Hants, s of F Wilson, of Keighley, Yorks, and *d* 1975, leaving:

1b *Colin David Hastings; Brig RA; *b* 7 Nov 1926; *m* Oct 1951 *Eileen Edna, dau of H W Fort, of Steeton, Yorks, and has:

1c *Christopher Colin; *b* Sept 1953; Col RA

2c *Brian David; *b* Dec 1954

1c *Sarah Jane Margaret; *b* 1963

1b *Monica Hastings [Mrs David Gibson, Woodcote Cottage, Hamstead, Yarmouth, IoW PO41 0YE]; *b* 6 Jan 1924; *m* 1 Jan 1950 *Col David Travers Worsley Gibson, MBE, Roy Signals, and has:

1c *Peter Worsley; *b* 7 June 1952

1c *Helen Morrish; *b* 3 Sept 1953

2a Edyth Cecile; *b* 7 March 1910; *m* 12 Oct 1930 Brig Geoffrey Anderton, OBE, RAMC (*d* 1981), s of Frederic Anderton, of Embsay, Yorks, and *d* 1994, leaving:

1b *Frederic Michael (Rev) [The Rev Frederic Anderton, 100 Harvist Rd, London NW6 6HL]; *b* 7 Dec 1931; *m* 1977 *Angela Robin Coulson and has:

1c *Sophia Vera Kathrin; *b* 26 Aug 1982

2b *Richard Hastings [Richard Anderton Esq, 38 Acacia Rd, Hampton, Middx TW12 3DS]; *b* 23 Sept 1946; *m* 15 June 1974 *Susan Challis, dau of J C Bousfield, of Beaconsfield, Bucks, and has:

1c *James Challis; *b* 14 May 1978

1c *Sarah Hastings; *b* 18 June 1981

1b *Cecile Mary Frances [Mrs Trevor Townsend, 18 Virgins Lane, Battle, Sussex TN33 0JH]; *b* 18 Sept 1933; *m* 1959 *Trevor Gerald Townsend and has:

1c *Michael John; *b* 1966

1c *Jane Cecile; *b* 1963

(2) Walter Henry; *b* 31 July 1868; *d* 8 March 1921

(3) William Fowler; *b* 9 June 1873; *d* 18 Aug 1935

(1) Frances Alice; *b* 26 July 1870; *m* 4 Nov 1895 Gordon George William Henry, MRCS, of Kildare Lodge, Minehead, Somerset, and *d* 3 Feb 1945, leaving issue

3 Edward Plantagenet Robin Hood; EICMS; *b* 12 Aug 1818; *m* 12 Dec 1840 Caroline Sarah (*d* 28 Jan 1890), est dau of G J Morris, HEICS, and *d* 17 Oct 1857, having had:

(1) Edward George Godolphin, CB; Lt-Col Bengal Army, Capt 21st Hus; *b* 29 Jan 1842; *m* 1 July 1882 Mabel Sophia (*d* 13 Dec 1942, having *m* 2nd 2 April

1891 7th Baron Dimsdale (*d* 6 Dec 1928); *see* 1956 edn Foreign Titles Section), dau of Sir Brydges P Henniker, 4th Bt (*qv*), and *d* Dec 1884, leaving:

1a Violet Edith Henniker; *b* 18 June 1883; *m* 3 Sept 1907 Geoffrey Clinton Baker, 4th s of William Clinton Baker, of Bayfordbury, Herts, and *d* 24 May 1947, leaving issue

(2) Alexander Plantagenet, CB; Adml, ADC to HM QUEEN VICTORIA; *b* 31 Dec 1843; *m* 29 July 1885 Edith Caroline (*d* 15 Feb 1941), dau of Col Frederic Rodolph Blake, CB, 33rd Regt, and *d* 7 Dec 1925, leaving:

1a Edward George Godolphin, CBE (1946); Capt RN; *b* 17 Nov 1887; *m* 26 April 1922 Hon Grisell Annabella Gem Cochrane-Baillie (*d* 1985), only dau of 2nd Baron Lamington (*see* 1949 edn), and *d* 1973, leaving issue:

1b Marian Hermione Grisell

2b *(Sheila) Felicity Phoebe [Mrs John Scrimgeour, Huntick Farm, Lytchett Matravers, Poole, Dorset BH16 6BB]; *b* 1925; *m* 30 April 1954 *John Humphrey Scrimgeour, TD, BSc, yr s of Humphrey Scrimgeour, of Glebe Farm, Sternfield, Suffolk, and has:

1c *Alexander John Humphrey; *b* 5 Dec 1957; *m* 1993 (*separated* 1994) *Sarah Beatrix, only dau of John Horatio (Rae) Gordon Shephard

2c *Benjamin Victor Sheddon; *b* 9 June 1960; *m* 1988 *Christian Clare, yst dau of Maj Sir Hamish Stewart Forbes, 7th Bt (*qv*), and has:

1d *Charlie Atlas; *b* 1995

1d *India; *b* 1993

1c *Sally Belinda [Mrs Graham Mitchell, 29 Pinehurst Dve, Fairways, Maraval, Port of Spain, Trinidad, W Indies]; *b* 16 March 1955; *m* 1987 *Graham Lewis Mitchell, only s of Mrs E W Hill, of Gerrards Cross, and has:

1d *James Alexander; *b* 1995

1d *Olivia Rose; *b* 1994

3b *Bridget Anne [Mrs Patrick Leigh, Ragged Lands, Glynde, Sussex BN8 6RP]; *b* 1928; *m* 29 Oct 1955 *Patrick Stephens Leigh, yr s of Lt-Col Harold Leigh, of Chislehurst, Kent, and has:

1c *William Patrick; *b* 19 Sept 1956; *educ* Eton and Ch Ch Oxford; *m* 1987 *Nancy Oliveira, dau of João Lavinsky, of Bahia, Brazil, and has:

1d *Natasha Maria; *b* 1988

2c *Edward Harold; *b* 28 April 1960; *educ* Eton; *m* 1988 *Bianca Daphne, dau of Paul Wansbrough, and has:

1d *Benjamin Patricio; *b* 1989

2d *Dominic Pablo; *b* 1991

1c *Belinda Grisell; *b* 20 Aug 1958; has:

1d *Eppie Irene; *b* 1988

2c *Annabella Hylda; *b* 10 July 1968

1a Muriel Edith; *b* 3 May 1886; *m* 5 Aug 1914 Maj Oswald Fairbanks Smith, Hodson's Horse, IA, s of Rev Lewis A Smith, Vicar Bayford, and *d* 25 Dec 1961, leaving issue. He *d* 19 June 1942

(3) Francis Theophilus Henry; *b* 9 Jan 1850; *d* unm 20 Dec 1905

(4) Godolphin Plantagent; *b* 10 Oct 1851; *dsp* 1 Nov 1892

(5) George Fowler; MA Cantab; *b* 2 Sept 1853; *dsp* 24 Oct 1899

4 Richard Godolphin Henry (Rev); Rector Hertingfordbury, Herts; *b* 26 March 1820; *m* 26 Nov 1846 Agnes (*d* 6 March 1872), 6th dau of Henry Fynes Clinton (*see* LINCOLN, E), and *d* 10 March 1865, having had:

(1) Francis Theophilus Clinton; India Office; *b* 18 April 1850; *d* 10 Oct 1912

(2) Charles Godolphin William, CIE; Inspr-Gen Police NWF; *b* 29 June 1854; *m* 27 Nov 1882 Margaret Logie (*d* 9 Oct 1920), dau of Gen Sir James Macpherson, KCB, and *d* 6 Feb 1920, leaving:

1a James Richard Godolphin; ICS; *b* 26 Aug 1883; *d* 7 Jan 1936

(3) Henry John Churchill; *b* 17 July 1856; *m* 14 Oct 1903 Edith Maria (*d* 1966), 7th dau of James Clark, of Pendock Court, Tewkesbury, and *d* 20 June 1924, leaving:

1a Henry Theophilus James; *b* 1910; *m* 3 March 1941 Muriel Hyde (*d* 1977), BA (Rand), 2nd dau of Walter Turner, of Athol Place, Banket, S Rhodesia, and *d* 1977, leaving:

1b +David Walter Theophilus [David Hastings Esq, Robin Hood Estate, Box 54, Shamva, Zimbabwe]; *b* 4 May 1947; *m* 24 July 1971 *Margaret Netta Allyson, est dau of Douglas Andrew Wilkinson, of Forrester Estate, Umvukwes, Rhodesia, and has:

1c +Ian David; *b* 1975

2c *Kate Rosemary; *b* 1973

1b Rosemary Muriel; *b* 8 July 1944; *m* 18 Sept 1965 Trevor MacRoberts, er s of W S Roberts, of Salisbury, Rhodesia, and had issue. They both *d* 23 Nov 1968

1a Katharine Edith; *b* 17 Aug 1904; *m* 1930 Bertie Leighton Henderson, of Salisbury, Rhodesia, and *d* 19–, leaving issue

2a Dorothy Agnes; *b* 15 July 1905; *m* 1930 Leslie Duncan Henderson, of Rhodesia, and *d* 19–, leaving issue

(4) Hugh Francis Plantagenet; *b* 29 June 1859; *d* 27 Jan 1860

(1) Isabel; *d* 14 Jan 1864

(2) Margaret Selina; *m* 1 Oct 1870 Henry James Davidson Horne, s of Sir William Horne, and had issue. He *d* 1883

(3) Henrietta Mabel; *d* unm 12 Nov 1929

(4) Lucy

(5) Katherine Agnes

HUNTINGFIELD

Arms: Arg. a torteau between three bugle-horns gu., stringed or. **Crest:** A bugle-horn gu., stringed or, between two wings expanded arg., tipped gold. **Supporters:** Two greyhounds erm., collared paly of six or and gu., chained gold. **Motto:** *Droit et loyal* ('Just and loyal'). **Creations:** Bt. (GB) 14 Dec 1751, B. (I) 9 July 1796.

THE 7TH BARON HUNTINGFIELD OF HEVENINGHAM HALL and a **Baronet** (Sir Joshua Charles Vanneck, Bt) [The Rt Hon The Lord Huntingfield, 69 Barrons Way, Comberton, Cambridge CB3 7EQ]; *b* 10 Aug 1954; *s f* 1994; *educ* Eton and Magdalene Coll Cambridge (MA); 2nd Lt Scots Dragoon Gds; *m* 4 Sept 1982 *Arabella Mary, est dau of Maj Alastair Hugh Joseph Fraser, MC (*see* LOVAT, L) and has:

1 +GERARD CHARLES ALASTAIR; *b* 12 March 1985

2 +John Errington; *b* 11 Jan 1988

3 +Richard Fraser; *b* 29 Sept 1990

4 +David Guise; *b* 29 Sept 1990

1 *Vanessa Clare; *b* 31 Aug 1983

Huntingfield, previous creation: A Sir William de Huntingfield, of a Lincolnshire family, was called to Parliament by writ in 1351, thereby becoming according to later doctrine Lord (Baron) Huntingfield. He served abroad during the Hundred Years War but died without surviving issue in 1376, when the notional Barony of 1351 expired.

Lineage: Sir Joshua Vanneck, 1st Bt (GB), so *cr* 14 Dec 1751 (2nd s of Cornelius Vanneck, Paymaster land forces for Utd Provinces); London merchant; *m* 20 Feb 1731/2 Mary Anne (*d* 1 Dec 1750), yst dau of Stephen Daubuz, and *d* 6 March 1777, having had:

1 **Sir Gerard Vanneck, 2nd Bt**; MP Dunwich 1768–90; *d* unm 23 May 1791

2 JOSHUA, **1st Baron**

1 Elizabeth; *m* 14 Nov 1753 Hon Thomas Walpole (*see* WALPOLE, B) and *d* 9 June 1760, leaving issue

2 Anna Maria Cornelia; *m* 7 March 1752 Henry Uhthoff and had issue

3 Gertrude; *d* unm 14 March 1798

4 Margaret; *m* 22 Nov 1758 Hon Richard Walpole (*see* WALPOLE, B) and *d* 9 May 1818, leaving issue

Sir GERARD's bro,

Sir Joshua Vanneck, 2nd Bt, and **1st Baron Huntingfield of Heveningham Hall** (I), so *cr* 9 July 1796; MP Dunwich 1790–1816; *b* 31 Dec 1745; *m* 29 Sept 1777 Maria (*d* 7 Dec 1811), 2nd dau of Andrew Thompson, of Roehampton, Surrey, and had:

1 JOSHUA, **2nd Baron**

2 Gerard; *b* 23 Aug 1786; *m* 29 Dec 1810 Charlotte (*d* 9 April 1875), 2nd dau of Robert Lovelace, and *d* 29 Dec 1829, leaving:

(1) William; *b* 1812; *dsp* July 1840

(1) Maria; *m* 13 Dec 1849 Capt Michael Henry Perceval (*d* 1890), RN, 3rd s of Michael Henry Perceval, of Quebec, MLC, by Anne, dau and coheir of Sir Charles Flower, Bt, and *d* 10 Nov 1903

(2) Caroline; *m* 18 Dec 1842 George Ernest, Count Gersdorff, and *d* 21 Dec 1849

(3) Harriet; *m* 1 July 1845 the Duke dell' Albaneto, of the Kingdom of the Two Sicilies, and *d* 10 Jan 1878

3 Tompson; *b* 27 Jan 1791; *m* 3 Nov 1816 Mary Anne Palmer, of Halesworth (*d* Nov 1833), and *d* 22 March 1855, having had:

(1) Tompson, of Montreal; *b* 1819; *m* Dec 1841 Catherine Anne, dau of J Torrance, and *dvp* 26 July 1853, leaving:

1a George Crewe; Offr 47th Regt; *b* 1842; *d* unm *c* 1872

2a John Torrance, of Montreal; *b* 6 Feb 1848; *m* 1st 1893 Amy (*dsp* 23 Nov 1900), dau of Edward Hyatt, of Baltimore; *m* 2nd 18 June 1902 Sarah (*d* 11 Dec 1908), widow of Philip Bradford Niles, of New York, and dau of Henry D Brookman, of Brooklyn, and *d* 22 Feb 1912, having by her had:

1b John; *b* 14 Jan 1908; *m* 17 May 1930 *Barbara [Mrs John Vanneck, Parsonage Point, Rye, NY 10580, USA], dau of Frank Bailey, and *d* 1974, leaving:

1c +John Bailey [John Vanneck, 1100 Park Ave, New York, NY 10128, USA]; *b* 15 April 1938; *m* 1st 30 Jan 1965 (*divorce* 1981) Isabelle Adele, dau of James Gordon Knipe; *m* 2nd 1985 *Cynthia Laney and by his 1st w has:

1d +F Bailey; *b* 1970

1d *Alexandra Knipe; *b* 5 Nov 1965; *m* 1991 *Charles Capel Smith

2d *Cynthia Gordon; *b* 4 Sept 1967

2c +William Prentice [William Vanneck, 521 Riversville Rd, Greenwich, CT 06831, USA]; *b* 15 Jan 1941; *m* 1st 4 Aug 1962 (*divorce* 1990) Nancy Walker, dau of Lanphear Buck, of Rye, NY; *m* 2nd 19– *Rebecca Heffington and by his 1st w has:

1d +John Lanphear; *b* 2 Aug 1963

2d +Richard Prentice; *b* 7 Jan 1966; *m* 1991 *Karen Elizabeth Bugniazet and has:

1e *Lindsay Bailey; *b* 1992

1d *Christine Walker; *b* 2 Aug 1963; *m* 1992 *Robert Thomas Owen and has:

1e *Sarah Ann; *b* 1992

2d *Sandra Brookman; *b* 27 Sept 1967

1c *Marion Louise; *b* 10 Jan 1937; *m* 3 Jan 1959 (*divorce* 1989) Raymond Robert Konopka and has had:

1d Raymond Robert; *b* 29 April 1961; *d* 1993

2d *Lee Bailey; *b* 15 June 1963; *m* 1987 *Ann Smith and has:

1e *Christopher Walter; *b* 1988

1e *Grace Ann; *b* 1991

3d *Steven Bailey; *b* 13 May 1966; *m* 1992 *Megan Cassidy

1d *Suzanne Louise; *b* 7 Oct 1959; *m* 1983 *Bryan M Fitzpatrick and has:

1e *Bryan Michael II; *b* 1986

2e *Morgan Bailey; *b* 1988

3e *Bryce Galvin; *b* 1989

1e *Ashley Louise; *b* 1985

2c *Barbara Anne [Mrs Barbara May, Kelleher Rd, Dorset, VT 0521, USA]; *b* 26 Aug 1946; *m* 1968 (*divorce* 1976) James S May and has:

1d *Wendy Bailey; *b* 12 Sept 1968

2d *Tanya Sheridan; *b* 1973

1 Maria; *b* 20 May 1783; *m* 1 May 1817 Charles Lovelace

2 Caroline; *b* 14 June 1788; *m* 1 May 1817 Alexander Donovan (*d* 4 Sept 1846), of Framfield Place, Sussex, and *d* 26 May 1836

Sir JOSHUA *d* 15 Aug 1816; his est son,

JOSHUA VANNECK, **2nd Baron Huntingfield of Heveningham Hall**; *b* 12 Aug 1778; *educ* Eton; MP (Tory) Dunwich 1816–19; *m* 1st 2 April 1810 Catherine (*d* 3 Aug 1815), dau of Chaloner Arcedeckne, of Glevering Hall, Suffolk, and had:

1 Joshua; *b* 19 Aug 1813; *d* unm 31 May 1835

1 Maria Louisa; *m* 14 Sept 1830 Sir Robert Charles Rowley, 4th Bt, of Tendring (*qv*), and *d* 16 March 1878, leaving issue

The **2nd Baron** *m* 2nd 6 Jan 1817 Lucy Anne (*d* 3 April 1889 aged 90), 3rd dau of Sir Charles Blois, 6th Bt, of Cockfield Hall (*qv*), and *d* 10 Aug 1844, leaving by her:

2 CHARLES ANDREW, **3rd Baron**

The 2nd BARON's yr son,

CHARLES ANDREW VANNECK, **3rd Baron Huntingfield of Heveningham Hall**, DL (Suffolk); High Sheriff 1848; *b* 12 Jan 1818; *m* 6 July 1839 Louisa (*d* 4 Feb 1898), only dau of Andrew Arcedeckne, and *d* 21 Sept 1897, having had, with five daus:

1 JOSHUA CHARLES VANNECK, **4th Baron Huntingfield of Heveningham Hall**, JP Suffolk; Col 2nd Bn Scots Gds, served Egypt 1882 and Suakim Expdn 1885; *b* 27 Aug 1842; *d* unm 13 Jan 1915

2 William Arcedeckne; *b* 30 Oct 1845; *m* 21 March 1882 Mary (*d* 5 March 1919), dau of William Armstrong, MRCS, of Toowoomba, Qld, and *d* 6 Nov 1912, having had:

(1) WILLIAM CHARLES ARCEDECKNE, **5th Baron**

(2) Rupert Chaloner Andrew; *b* 11 June; *d* 15 Oct 1889

(3) Andrew Nicolas Armstrong, MC; Capt Scots Gds (SR) WW I, WW II cmded 4th Bn Suffolk HG 1941–43; *b* 21 July 1890; *educ* Harrow; granted with surv siblings 27 April 1922 rank of baron's dau/yr s; *m* 1st 1 Sept 1930 (*divorce* 1933) Louise (*d* 10 Feb 1970), only dau of Henry Clews, of The Chateau de la Napoule, AM, France; *m* 2nd 6 April 1939 *Britta Ingeborg Nilsdotter [The Hon Mrs Andrew Vanneck, Sylchester, 2/4 Trahlee Rd, Bellevue Hill, 2023, Sydney, NSW Australia], only dau of Count Nils Bonde, of Stockholm, and *d* 20 Feb 1965, leaving by her:

1a +William Bonde [William Vanneck Esq, 31 Pymble Ave, Pymble, NSW 2073, Australia]; *b* 27 Dec 1943; *educ* Harrow; *m* 1971 *Jane Blanton and has:

1b +Mark Alexander Blanton; *b* 1979

1b *Nina Sara; *b* 1975

1a *Margita [Mrs David Wheeler, Broadlands, La Hougue Bie, Grouville, Jersey, CI]; *b* 4 Aug 1940; *m* 21 Oct 1961 *David Michael Wheeler, only s of Anthony Wheeler, of Majorca, and has:

1b *Andrew Michael; *b* 21 July 1963

2b *James Nicholas; *b* 28 Oct 1966

(1) Louisa Medora Hermione; *b* 11 Feb 1885; *m* 28 Nov 1914 Lt-Col Edward Helme Pott, DSO, MVO, 1st Lancers (Skinner's Horse) (*d* 25 Nov 1968), er s of Col William Pott, 27th Inniskilling Fus, of Knowsouth, Hawick, Roxburghshire, and had:

1a Hermione Vanneck; *b* 14 June 1919; *d* 8 Dec 1974, leaving:

1b *A dau

(2) Anne Mary Chaloner; *b* 31 Aug 1892; *m* 1st 20 Jan 1915 (*divorce* 1939) Maj Percy Rygate Borrett, Scots Gds (SR), JP (*d* 19 Sept 1963), only s of Thomas Percy Borrett, JP, of Cransford Hall, Saxmundham; *m* 2nd 29 April 1939 5th Earl of Leitrim (*see* 1953 edn) and by her 1st husb had:

1a Anthony Thomas Vanneck, MC; *b* 13 Nov 1915; *educ* Harrow; *m* 1940 *Eileen Mary (*m* 2nd 29 June 1957 *(Frederick) Rowland Cottel), dau of Geoffrey Graham Watson, and *d* 8 Jan 1954, leaving:

1b *(Antonia) Clare; *b* 3 May 1946; *m* 15 Dec 1967 *Robert Ewing, er s of John Ewing, of Johannesburg

2a John Alastair Sancroft; Capt RA; *b* 7 Dec 1918; *educ* Stowe; *m* 20 April 1957 *Constance Margaret, only dau of Maj Walter S Burfoot, and *d* 27 July 1969, leaving:

1b *Richard Thomas Shelley; *b* 21 March 1958

1a *Aurea Janet Arcedeckne; *b* 10 Oct 1916; *m* 13 Sept 1947 *Maj Owen Courtney Weeks, MBE, RA, s of Charles John Weeks, of Monkstown, Co Dublin, and has:

1b *Susan Jane Aurea; *b* 20 March 1949; *m* 25 July 1970 *Adam Duncan Paul

2b *Patricia Anne Courtney; *b* 18 Aug 1953

3 Charles Andrew; *b* 8 Jan 1848; *dsp* 12 July 1897

4 Walter; *b* 9 March 1849; *m* 24 Sept 1877 Catherine Medora (*d* 5 Aug 1932), dau of William Armstrong, MRCS, of Toowoomba, Qld, and *d* 17 Sept 1931, leaving:

(1) Joshua Walter Huntingfield; served WW I; *b* 1 Nov 1886; *m* 1 Sept 1914 *Joan Ransome, dau of Edgar Turner, of Colombo, Ceylon, and *d* 3 June 1947

(2) +Ralph Wyndham; *b* 20 Sept 1891; *m* 1st 1945 Emily Sarah (*d* 1951), dau of E A Bellow; *m* 2nd 1971 *Phyllis Evelyn, only dau of G Mitchell Hill

(1) Nesta Frances; *m* 1 Oct 1908 (*divorce* 1911, resumed maiden name) Lt-Col Horace Cocks, RAMC, and *d* 3 April 1955

(2) Hilda Arcedeckne; *m* 26 Sept 1914 Maj Eric Warneford McArthur, 13th Hus, s of Col A D McArthur, RE, and *d* 6 May 1969 aged 88, leaving issue

(3) Catherine Gladys; *m* 11 Feb 1904 Lt Harold Thomas Maryon-Wilson (*d* 27 March 1944), ASC, s of Frederick Maryon-Wilson, and *d* 1 Jan 1962, leaving issue (*see* 1970 edn MARYON-WILSON, Bt)

5 Gerard; *b* 19 April 1851; *m* 29 April 1878 Harriet Oakley Beaton (*d* Jan 1907), dau of James Ivory, of Bundanoa, Qld, and *d* 11 Aug 1904, having had:

(1) Blois Evelyn; *b* 7 Feb 1881; *d* unm 19 April 1902

(2) Albert Christian; *b* 14 Oct 1883; *d* 19 Sept 1887

(1) Harriet Louisa Cora; *d* unm 13 Jan 1931

The 4th BARON's nephew,

WILLIAM CHARLES ARCEDECKNE VANNECK, **5th Baron Huntingfield of Heveningham Hall**, KCMG (1934), JP (Suffolk); *b* 3 Jan 1883; *educ* Wellington; Capt 13th/18th Hus, Hon Air Cdre No 21 (City of Melbourne) Sqdn RAAF, MP Eye 1923–29, PPS to Parly U-Sec Home Office 1926–27 and Pres BOT 1927–28, Govr Victoria, Australia, 1934–39, Actg Govr-Gen Australia March-Sept 1938, apptd Govr and C-in-C S Rhodesia 1942 but did not proceed, Col cmdg 58 Bn Co of London HG, Freeman City London, memb Glaziers' Co, KGStJ; *m* 1st 21 Dec 1912 Margaret Eleanor, CStJ (*d* 1 March 1943), only dau of Judge Ernest Crosby, of New York; *m* 2nd 24 May 1944 Muriel Mary Georgina (*d* 13 May 1953), widow of 1st Baron Eltisley (see 1940 edn) and only dau of Col Jemmet Duke, 17th Lancers, and by his 1st w had:

1 GERARD CHARLES ARCEDECKNE, **6th Baron**

2 +Peter Beckford Rutgers (Sir), GBE (1977, OBE 1963), CB (1973), AFC (1955), AE, DL (Gtr London); [The Hon Sir Peter Vanneck GBE CB AFC AE DL, 2/10 Brompton Square, London SW3; Red House, Sudbourne, Woodbridge, Suffolk IP12 2AT]; *b* 7 Jan 1922; *educ* Geelong GS, Stowe, Trin Coll Cambridge (MA) and Harvard; Lt (P) RN WW II, 601 Sqdn RAuxAF 1950–57, Hon Air Cdre RAuxAF; OC No 3619 (Suffolk) Fighter Control Unit RAuxAF 1959–61 (Inspr 1962–73, Hon Inspr-Gen 1974–83), Hon Air Cdr No 1 MHU RAuxAF; Upper Warden Gunmakers' Co 1975–, ADC to HM THE QUEEN 1963–73, Gentleman Usher to HM THE QUEEN 1967–79, Alderman City London 1969–79, Sheriff City London 1974–75, Ld Mayor 1978–79; MEP 1979–89; High Sheriff Suffolk 1974; dir Shippams 1974–, KJStJ; Hon DSc, City U TEng (CEI); *m* 1st 8 April 1943 (*divorce* 1984) his er bro's sis-in-law Cordelia, yr dau of Capt Reginald Hugh Errington, RN (*see* below); *m* 2nd 1984 *Elizabeth Lechmere, dau of Sandys Stuart Macaskie, of Lustleigh, S Devon, and fomerly w of Spencer Malcolm Edward Forbes (*see* STUART-FORBES, Bt), and by his 1st w has had:

(1) Lois Margaret Grace; *b* 2 Dec 1944; *d* 31 Dec 1946

(2) *Charlotte Susan [Mrs Dennis Stevenson, 32 Catherine Place, London SW1E 6HL]; *b* 26 Feb 1947; *m* 15 Feb 1972 *H Dennis Stevenson, CBE, and has:

1a *Alexander; *b* 1974

2a *John Heneage; *b* 1978

3a *Charles Dennistoun; *b* 1980

4a *William Beckford James; *b* 1984

1 *Sarah Carola [The Hon Mrs Peel, Huntingfield Hall, Halesworth, Suffolk IP19 0QA]; *b* 25 Sept 1913; *m* 14 April 1936 David Arthur Peel (*see* PEEL, E) and has had issue

2 *Anne Margaret Theodosia; *b* 20 May 1918; *m* 2 March 1940 (*divorce* 1984) Peter Moro, FRIBA, s of Prof Ernest Franz Moro, of Heidelberg, and has:

(1) *Frances [Mrs Michael Molloy, 61 Annandale Rd, London SE10]; *b* 9 Dec 1945; *m* 1st 1966 (*divorce* 1979) John Barnes; *m* 2nd 1987 *Michael Edward Thomas Molloy and by her 1st husb has had:

1a Joseph; *b* 1967; *d* 1968

2a *Samuel; *b* 1968

1a *Jessie; *b* 1972

(2) *Alice [Mrs Jacek Basista, 23 Culverden Park, Tunbridge Wells, Kent TN4 9QT]; *b* 29 Sept 1948; *m* 1978 *Jacek Lech Basista and has:

1a *Tom; *b* 1984

1a *Rose Zofia; *b* 1991

(3) *Dinah; *b* 10 Sept 1960

The 5th BARON *d* 20 Nov 1969; his er son

GERARD CHARLES ARCEDECKNE VANNECK, **6th Baron Huntingfield of Heveningham Hall**; *b* 29 May 1915; *educ* Stowe and Trin Coll Cambridge (BA 1937); WW II in RAFVR, with UN Secretariat 1946; *m* 27 Oct 1941 *Janetta Lois [The Rt Hon The Dowager Lady Huntingfield, 53 Barron's Way, Comberton, Cambs CB3 7EQ], er dau of Capt Reginald Hugh Errington, RN (*see* DARTMOUTH, E), and *d* 1994, having had:

1 JOSHUA CHARLES VANNECK, **7th and present Baron Huntingfield of Heveningham Hall**

1 Sara Anne; *b* 29 Feb 1944; *m* 23 Aug 1966 (*divorce* 1976), as his 1st w, Marcus Binney, architectural historian, s of Lt-Col Francis Crofton Simms, MC, and Lady (George) Binney, of Domaine des Vaux, St Lawrence, Jersey, CI, and *dsp* 24 Jan 1979

2 *Christina Louise [The Hon Mrs Darell-Brown, The Old Rectory, Witnesham, Ipswich, Suffolk]; *b* 26 Jan 1946; *m* 8 July 1967 *Anthony Darell-Brown, RGJ, s of Lt-Col Mark Darell-Brown, DSO, and has:

(1) *Mark Philip Anthony; *b* 12 Aug 1969

(2) *Henry Robert; *b* 25 June 1971; *m* 25 April 1998 *Lindsey, dau of David Webster, of Micheldean, Glos, and Mrs Patricia Ashton, of Stonehouse, Glos

(1) *Juliet Cordelia Diana; *b* 26 March 1973

3 *Katherine Grace [The Hon Mrs Bacon, Church Gate Barn, Colston Bassett, Notts NG12 3FP]; *b* 10 Aug 1954; BA; *m* 18 Dec 1976 *Nicholas John Bacon and has:

(1) *Sara Elizabeth; *b* 1980

(2) *Frances Louise; *b* 1983

(3) *Charlotte Helena; *b* 1991

HUNTINGTON-WHITELEY

Arms: Quarterly, 1st and 4th, per fess dancetté sable and gules, in chief a pale or, thereon three bars of the second, in base a fleur-de-lys argent (for WHITELEY); 2nd and 3rd, or, on a pale between two roses in fess gules, barbed and seeded proper, a lion rampant between two water bougets of the first (for HUNTINGTON). **Crests:** 1 A stag's head couped argent, attired or, holding in the mouth a bell gold (for WHITELEY), 2 Upon a mount vert a lion's head couped at the neck or, gorged with a collar vair, between two roses gules, barbed, leaved and stalked proper (for HUNTINGTON). **Motto:** Live to live. **Creation:** Bt. (UK) 8 Feb 1918.

SIR HUGO BALDWIN HUNTINGTON-WHITELEY, 3RD BT, DL (Worcs 1972) [Sir Hugo Huntington-Whiteley Bt DL, Ripple Hall, Tewkesbury, Glos GL20 6EY; Balleure, 71240 Etrigny, France]; *b* 31 March 1924; *s* f 1975; *educ* Eton; RN WW II (despatches), FCA, High Sheriff Worcs 1971, Prime Warden Goldsmiths' Co 1989; *m* 4 April 1959 *Jean Marie Ramsay, JP, DStJ, dau of Arthur Francis Ramsay Bock, and adopted:

*Sophie Elizabeth; *b* 1 Aug 1964; *m* 1988 *Dr Steven Michael Zdatny, est s of W J Zdatny, of Florida, and has:

(1) *Samuel Oliver; *b* 1993

(1) *Isabelle; *b* 1990

*Charlotte Anne; *b* 23 Oct 1965; *m* 1993 *Andrew Philip McAuliffe, ACA, and has:

(1) *Jaspar James; *b* 1996

(1) *Matilda Kate; *b* 1994

(2) *Daisy Sarah; *b* 1997

Lineage: GEORGE WHITELEY, of May Field House, Halifax, had:

GEORGE WHITELEY, of Blackburn and Halifax; *b* 31 July 1825; *m* 13 July 1853 Margaret (*d* 19 Jan 1913), dau of James Pickop, MD, of Blackburn, and *d* 10 March 1873, having had, with an er s (GEORGE WHITELEY, *cr* BARON MARCHAMLEY, *qv*):

Sir HERBERT JAMES WHITELEY later HUNTINGTON-WHITELEY (roy licence 7 Feb 1918), **1st Bt** (UK), so *cr* 8 Feb 1918, of Grimley, Co Worcester, JP (Blackburn); *b* 8 Dec 1857; Mayor Blackburn 1892, MP (C) Ashton-under-Lyne 1895–1906 and Droitwich 1916–18, High Sheriff Worcs 1913; *m* 25 Sept 1895 Florence Kate (*d* 28 June 1948), est dau of William Balle Huntington, DL, of Woodlands, Darwen, Lancs, and had:

1 HERBERT MAURICE (Sir), **2nd Bt**

2 Eric Arthur, JP (1962); *b* 2 Aug 1903; *educ* Eton and Trin Coll Cambridge (BA 1925); W/Cdr RAuxAF WW II, Hants: CC 1950, CA 1961; *m* 1st 21 Nov 1929 (*divorce* 1938) Enid Etta Cohn (*d* 1983); *m* 2nd 21 July 1938 Evelyn Mary (*d* 14 March 1978), dau of Henry Munt and formerly w of Denis Clark, and *d* 1 Aug 1972, having had by his 1st w:

(1) +Nigel Charles [Nigel Huntington-Whiteley Esq, Highway, Cansiron Lane, Ashurst Wood, W Sussex RH19 3SD]; *b* 22 March 1931; *educ* Radley; *m* 29 June 1956 *Gillian Margaret, yr dau of Jacob Franks, MRCS, LRCP, of W Chiltington, Sussex, and has:

1a +Charles Andrew; *b* 7 May 1957, FRICS; *m* 1981 *Fiona Yvonne, dau of Alan Jackson, of Mythby, Weston Turville, Aylesbury, and has:

1b +Toby Charles; *b* 1989

1b *Rosie Alice; *b* 1987

2b *Florence; *b* 1992

2a +James Alexander; *b* 14 Aug 1963; *m* 1996 *Magdalen Lucy Ceriedwen, er dau of Martin Phillip William Evans, RIBA, of London, and has:

1b +William Joseph; *b* 21 Nov 1997

1a *Kate Elizabeth; *b* 4 Oct 1959; *m* 1984 *Peter Charles Lowry de Montfort, er s of Charles Henry Cliffe de Montfort, of Skibbereen, Co Cork, and has:

1b *Guy Alexander; *b* 1987

2b *Charles Nicholas; *b* 1989

3b *Sean Thomas, 1994

(2) +Philip Cecil [Philip Huntington-Whiteley Esq, Llangattock House, Penpergwm, Abergavenny, Gwent]; *b* 2 Nov 1933; *educ* Radley; *m* 18 May 1968 *Susan Laird, er dau of Maj-Gen George Warren Richards, CB, CBE, DSO and bar, MC, DL, of Trewarren, nr Abergavenny, Mon, and has:

1a +George Adam; *b* 31 July 1971

1a *Camilla Mary; *b* 1970

Sir HERBERT *d* 22 Jan 1936; his er son,

Sir Herbert Maurice Huntington-Whiteley, 2nd Bt; *b* 25 July 1896; *educ* Eton; MIEE; Capt RN WW I (wounded) and WW II, High Sheriff Worcs 1968; *m* 2 April 1919 Lady (Pamela) Margaret Baldwin (*d* 14 Aug 1976), 3rd dau of 1st Earl Baldwin of Bewdley (*qv*), and *d* 18 May 1975, having had:

1 Herbert Oliver (Peter); *b* 27 Feb 1920; *educ* Eton; Capt RM WW II (despatches); *ka* France Sept 1944

2 Sir HUGO BALDWIN HUNTINGTON-WHITELEY, **3rd and present Bt**

3 +(JOHN) MILES, VRD [Lt-Cdr Miles Huntington-Whiteley VRD RNR (ret), 6 Matheson Rd, London W14 8SW]; *b* 18 July 1929; heir presumptive; *educ* Eton and Trin Coll Cambridge; V-Pres Navy League; *m* 20 June 1960 *Countess Victoria Adelheid Clementine Louise zu Castell-Rudenhausen, only dau of Count Friedrich-Wolfgang zu Castell-Rudenhausen by his 1st w Princess Caroline Mathilde of Saxe-Coburg-Gotha, and has:

(1) +Leopold Maurice; *b* 15 July 1965

(1) *Alice Louise Esther Margot; *b* 22 July 1961 (HM QUEEN LOUISE OF SWEDEN and HRH PRINCE MICHAEL OF GREECE stood sponsors)

(2) *Beatrice Irene Helen Victoria; *b* 6 Sept 1962 (TRH PRINCESS IRENE OF THE NETHERLANDS and PRINCESS ALICE COUNTESS OF ATHLONE stood sponsors)

HUNTLY

Arms: Quarterly, 1st, azure three boar's heads couped or (for GORDON); 2nd, or three lion's heads erased gules, langued azure (for BADENOCH); 3rd, or three crescents within a double tressure flory counterflory gules (for SETON); 4th, azure three fraises argent (for FRASER). **Crest:** Issuing from a ducal coronet or a hart's head and neck affrontée proper, attired with ten tynes or. **Supporters:** Two deerhounds argent, each gorged with a collar gules, charged with three buckles or. **Motto:** *Animo non astutia* ('By courage, not by stratagem'). **Creations:** ?E. (S) between 30 Oct 1444 and 3 July 1445 (Huntly)? (*see* below against **3rd Marquess**), M., E. (Enzie) and L. (Gordon of Badenoch) (S) 17 April 1599, E. (Aboyne) and L. (Gordon of Strathavon and Glenlivet) (S) 10 Sept 1660, B. (UK) 11 Aug 1815 (Meldrum of Morven).

THE 13TH MARQUESS OF HUNTLY, (Earl of Huntly?), Earl of Enzie, Earl of Aboyne, Lord Gordon of Badenoch, Lord Gordon of Strathavon and **Glenlivet** and **Baron Meldrum of Morven**, Co Aberdeen (Granville Charles Gomer Gordon) [The Most Hon The Marquess of Huntly, Aboyne Castle, Aberdeenshire AB34 5JP]; *b* 4 Feb 1944; *s* f 1987; premier marquess of Scotland; *educ* Gordonstoun; Nat Ctee Scottish Georgian Soc 1976–81, memb Cncl Nat Tst Scotland 1977–80, Pres Inst Fin Accountants; *m* 1st 29 Jan 1972 (*divorce* 1990) Jane Elizabeth Angela, only dau of Lt-Col Alistair Monteith Gibb, Roy Wilts Yeo, and has:

1 +ALISTAIR GRANVILLE, *Earl of Aboyne*; *b* 26 July 1973; *educ* Harrow

1 *Amy Jane; *b* 1975

2 *Lucy Yoskyl; *b* 1979

The 13th MARQUESS *m* 2nd 1991 *Catheryn Millbourne, dau of Gay Kindersley (*see* KINDERSLEY, B), and by her has:

3 *Rose Marie-Louise; *b* 1993

Lineage: The GORDONs take their name from the lands of Gordon, Berwicks; in the late 12th century witnesses of the name of Gordon occur in charters or as benefactors to Kelso Abbey.

Sir ADAM GORDON; Justiciar Lothian 1305; represented Scottish nobility at a Cncl at Westminster during EDWARD I's partially successful attempt to conquer Scotland; later supported ROBERT I (THE BRUCE) and was granted (but found difficulty in asserting right to) the territorial Lordship of Strathbogie forfeited by the Earl of Athole (*see* ATHOLL, D, preliminary remarks); had, with a yr s (William, ancestor of the GORDONs of Lochinvar and Viscounts Kenmure (*see* 1847 edn)):

Sir ADAM GORDON of that Ilk; apparently had, with an er s (Sir John of that Ilk; imprisoned Durham 1346, released 1357; had confirmatory charter of Strathbogie 1376; *d c* 1395 and by two illegitimate sons (John (Jock) Gordon, of Scudargue, and Thomas Gordon, of Ruthven) was ancestor of GORDONs in Mar, Buchan and Strathbogie):

Sir ADAM GORDON of that Ilk; had a charter of the family's Berwicks estates; *m* Elizabeth Keith, Lady of Aboyne (*m* 2nd Sir Nicholas Erskine of Kinnoun; *m* 3rd Thomas Somerville; *d c* 1437), dau of Sir William Keith, Marischal Scotland (*see* KINTORE, E), and was *k* Battle of Homildon 1402, having had, with a s (John, *dsp* 1407):

ELIZABETH Gordon; *m* between 27 March 1407/8 and 20 July 1408 Alexander SETON (*d* between 31 Aug 1440 and 3 April 1441, *see* EGLINTON and WINTON, E) and *d* 16 March 1348/9, having had, with a yr s (William; ancestor of the SETONs of Meldrum) and a dau (Elizabeth, *m* Alexander, Lord of the Isles and Earl of Ross):

ALEXANDER SETON later GORDON (*c* 1457), **1st Earl of Huntly** (S), so *cr* between 30 Oct 1444 and 3 July 1445; had Crown grants of territorial Lordship of Badenoch (1451) and other lands in Inverness-shire and Morayshire; inherited from his grandmother Elizabeth (*see* above) Aboyne, Cluny and Glenmuick, Aberdeenshire; *m* 1st *c* 8 Jan 1426/7 Egidia/Gille, dau and heir of Sir John Hay of Tullibody, Clackmannanshire, and had a s (Alexander, *see* SETON, Bt of Abercorn); *m* 2nd by 18 March 1439/40 Elizabeth, est dau of 1st Lord Crichton, Ld Chllr Scotland, and *d* 15 July 1470, having by her had, with two yr sons (Alexander, ancestor of the GORDONs of Abergeldie; Adam, Dean Caithness, *d* 1528) and a dau (Janet, *m* Sir James Innes, 12th of that Ilk, and had issue; *see* ROXBURGHE, D):

GEORGE GORDON, **2nd Earl of Huntly**, as which he *s* his f by charter 8 Jan 1449/50 to the apparent exclusion of his er half-bro, PC (S); ktd *c* 1455, Ld Chllr S 1498–1501; granted by the Crown Schivas, Aberdeenshire, and Aboyne, Enzie and Netherdale, Banffshire; *m* 1st (contract 20 May 1445; *divorce* by 10 March 1459/60) Elizabeth, dau of James Dunbar, 4th Earl of Moray of the March 1371/2 *cr* (*see* DUNBAR, Bt, of Mochrum), and widow of Archibald Douglas, Earl of Moray (*see* QUEENSBERRY, M); *m* 2nd by 10 March 1459/60 (*divorce* 24 July 1471) Annabel, dau of JAMES I and divorced w of Louis Count of Geneva (s of Louis Count of Savoy); *m* 3rd Aug 1471 Elizabeth, dau of 1st Earl of Erroll (*qv*), and *d c* 8 June 1501, having had:

1 ALEXANDER, **3rd Earl**

2 Adam; territorial Ld of Aboyne; *m* Elizabeth, Countess of Sutherland (*qv*), and had issue

3 William; *ka* Flodden 1513; ancestor of the GORDONs of Gight (*see* HOME, Bt, and BYRON, B)

4 James; Adml of the Fleet; ancestor of the GORDONs of Letterfourie, Bts (*see* 1902 edn)

1 Catherine; *m* 1st Perkin Warbeck; *m* 2nd James Strangways; *m* 3rd Sir Matthew Cradock; *m* 4th Christopher Ashton

2 Agnes; *m* James Ogilvy of Deskford and Findlater (*see* SEAFIELD, E)

3 Eleanor; *m* John Crichton of Invernytie

The 2nd EARL's est son,

ALEXANDER GORDON, **3rd Earl of Huntly**, PC (S); granted Strathavon, Banffshire, and the Brae of Lochaber; cmded a battalion Battle of Flodden 1513 (*see* also HOME, E); memb Cncl Regency of the 1457 *cr* 1517; *m* 1st (contract 14 Oct 1474) Janet, dau of John Stewart, 1st Earl of Atholl of the 1457 *cr* (*see* MORAY, E); *m* 2nd just after 27 July 1511 Elizabeth (*m* 3rd 4th Earl of Rothes, *qv*), dau of 2nd Lord Gray (*qv*) and widow of 4th Lord Glamis (*see* STRATHMORE AND KINGHORNE, E), and *d* 21 Jan 1523/4, having by his 1st w had:

1 John, *Lord Gordon*; *m* Nov 1512 Margaret Stewart (*m* 2nd 20 Jan 1530/1 Sir John Drummond of Innerpeffray), illegitimate dau of JAMES IV by Margaret Drummond, and *dvp* 5 Dec 1517, leaving:

(1) GEORGE, **4th Earl**

(2) Alexander; titular Archbp Athens, Bp of the Isles, later of Galloway

(3) James; Chllr of Moray

2 Alexander, of Strathavon; ancestor of the GORDONs of Cluny

3 William; Bp Aberdeen 1547–77

The 3rd EARL'S gs,

GEORGE GORDON, **4th Earl of Huntly**, PC (S 1535); *b* 1513; reputed the wealthiest, wisest and most powerful subject in Scotland; Lt-Gen of the North, Ld Chllr Scotland 1546–49 and 1561–62; Kt Order St Michael France 1548; *cr* 13 Feb 1548/9 EARL OF MORAY (the Earldom in question being in the gift of the Crown from 1544; *see* MORAY, E, preliminary remarks) but this title was presently conferred by MARY QUEEN OF SCOTS on her illegitimate bro James Stewart 30 Jan 1561/2, due at least in part to **Huntly**'s tergiversation between the Reformed and Catholic parties; he consequently rebelled but was beaten and taken prisoner at the encounter of Corrichie 22 Oct 1562 by a royalist force under the new Earl of Moray, dying a few hours later, apparently from a seizure (certainly not from wounds, as he had sustained none)); *m* 27 March 1530 Elizabeth, sis of 4th Earl Marischal (*see* KINTORE, E), his titles being posthumously forfeited 28 May 1563, having had, with other issue:

1 Alexander, *Lord Gordon*; *m c* 1546 Lady Barbara Hamilton, (*m* 2nd 4th Lord Fleming and had issue; *see* LAUDERDALE, E) dau of 2nd Earl of Arran (*see* ABERCORN, D), and *dspvp* between 18 Sept 1552 and 11 Aug 1553

2 GEORGE, **5th Earl**

3 John (Sir) of Ogilvy; *m* as her 2nd husb his cousin Elizabeth, illegitimate dau of Adam Gordon, s of 1st Earl of Huntly (*see* above, also SEAFIELD, E); captured with his f at Corrichie and executed

4 Adam (Sir), of Auchindoun; captured at Corrichie but pardoned; later supported MARY QUEEN OF SCOTS in the North of Scotland; *d* 1580

5 Thomas; *m* as her 2nd husb Jean, dau of 12th Earl of Sutherland (*qv*) and widow of Alexander Innes, 16th of that Ilk (*see* ROXBURGHE, D)

1 Elizabeth; *m* 4th Earl of Atholl of the 1457 *cr* (*see* MORAY, E)

2 Jean; *m* 1st (*divorce*) 4th Earl of Bothwell (MORAY, E); *m* 2nd 11th Earl of Sutherland (*qv*); *m* 3rd Alexander Ogilvy of Boyne

The 4th EARL's 2nd son,

GEORGE GORDON, **5th Earl of Huntly**, as which restored 1567, though he had been found guilty of treason 8 Feb 1562/3 and narrowly escaped the death sentence; Chllr Scotland March 1564/5–67; *m c* 12 Aug 1558 Anne, his er bro's w and dau of 2nd Earl of Arran (*see* ABERCORN, D), and *d* 19 Oct 1576 of a seizure following a football game, having had, with a dau (Jean, *m* 5th Earl of Caithness; *qv*):

GEORGE GORDON, **1st Marquess of Huntly**, so *cr* 17 April 1599, as also EARL OF ENZIE and LORD GORDON OF BADENOCH, PC (S Feb 1598/9); *b c* 1563; Capt of the Gd 1588; rebelled 1588 in concert with Spanish forces, was captured and imprisoned for treason in Borthwick Castle 24 May 1588–Sept 1589; rebelled again 1594, overcoming a Govt force sent against him under the Earl of Argyll at Glenlivet 3 Oct but was pardoned; despite his rebellious tendencies was a favourite of JAMES VI, under whose commission to bring to book the Earl of Bothwell he had James Stewart, Earl of Moray, murdered 7 Feb 1591/2, thrusting a final dagger blow in the victim's face in person; seemingly a genuine adherent of the old Catholic form of worship (and certainly often conspiring to reestablish it), he nevertheless publicly apostatised in favour of Protestantism twice, in 1610 and 1616; *m* 21 July 1588 Lady Henrietta Stewart (*d* 2 Sept 1642), est dau of Esmé Stewart, 1st Duke of Lennox (*see* MORAY, E), and had, with other issue:

1 GEORGE, **2nd Marquess**

2 Adam, of Auchindoun

3 JOHN GORDON, 1st and last VISCOUNT OF MELGUM AND LORD ABOYNE (S), so *cr* 20 Oct 1627; *m* 1626 Sophia, 5th dau of 9th Earl of Erroll (*qv*) by his 3rd w Elizabeth, and *dspm* 9 Oct 1630 in a fire at Frendraught Tower

while staying with Sir James Crichton of Frendraught (whose w, sis of the Earl of Sutherland, may have started the fire as part of a long-standing feud against the Gordons); with his death the titles expired

1 Anne; *m* 3rd Earl of Moray (*qv*)

2 Elizabeth; *m* Alexander Livingston, 2nd Earl of Linlithgow (*see* LINLITHGOW, M, preliminary remarks)

3 Mary; *m* 1632 1st Marquess of Douglas (*see* HAMILTON and BRANDON, D)

4 Jean; *m* 1st 1632 1st/2nd Lord Hamilton, Baron of Strabane (*see* ABERCORN, D); *m* 2nd after 1641 Sir Phelim O'Neill (*see* O'NEILL, B)

The 1st MARQUESS *d* 13 June 1636; his est son,

GEORGE GORDON, **2nd Marquess of Huntly**, KB (1610), PC (1616); *cr* 20 April 1632 VISCOUNT ABOYNE (S), with remainder to his 2nd s; royalist 1639 on, though ineffectively so, possibly because he refused to take action without consulting his horoscope first; nevertheless beheaded for his royalist sympathies 22 March 1648/9, when his titles were forfeited also; *m* 1607 Lady Anne Campbell (*d* 14 June 1638), dau of 7th Earl of Argyll (*see* ARGYLL, D), and had, with other issue:

1 George, *Lord Gordon*; royalist under Marquess of Montrose (*see* MONTROSE, D) Battle of Alford 2 July 1645, where *k*

2 JAMES GORDON; 2nd VISCOUNT ABOYNE; royalist Civil War; fled to France, where he *d* unm Feb 1648/9, when the Viscountcy expired

3 LEWIS GORDON, **3rd Marquess of Huntly**, as which (and to his other titles) restored 25 March 1651; it is an open question, however, whether this was a general restoration (in which case the Earldom of Huntly would have passed to the heir general on the death of the **8th Marquess** 1836 (*see* below) and subsequently have been held by the Dukes of Richmond and Gordon, *qv*), or a regrant in favour of heirs male, in which case it would have descended with the Marquessate; *m* Oct 1644 Mary (*m* 2nd, as his 2nd w, 2nd Earl of Airlie, *qv*), dau of Sir John Grant of Freuchy, and *d* Dec 1653, having had:

(1) GEORGE GORDON, **4th Marquess of Huntly** and 1st DUKE OF GORDON, so *cr* 1 Nov 1684, as also MARQUESS OF HUNTLY, EARL OF HUNTLY AND ENZIE, VISCOUNT OF INVERNESS, LORD BADENOCH, LOCHABER, STRATHAVON, BALMORE, AUCHINDOUN, GARTHIE, and KINCARDINE (all S), KT (1687), PC (S 1686); *b* 1649; *educ* RC seminary France; joined French Army 1673, served under Turenne at Battle of Strasbourg, also under the Prince of Orange; *m* Oct 1676 Lady Elizabeth Howard (separated 1707, *d* 16 July 1732), 2nd dau of 5th Duke of Norfolk (*qv*), who was also 1st Earl of Norwich, and *d* 7 Dec 1716, having had, with a dau (Jane, *m* James Drummond, s of 4th Earl of Perth, *qv*):

1a ALEXANDER GORDON, **5th Marquess of Huntly** and 2nd DUKE OF GORDON; *b c* 1678; Jacobite 1715 but surrendered after Battle of Sheriffmuir and was for a time held in Edinburgh Castle but then set free; *m* just prior to 13 Feb 1706/7 Lady Henrietta Mordaunt (*d* 11 Oct 1760), dau of 3rd Earl of Peterborough (*see* MORDAUNT, Bt), and *d* 28 Nov 1728, having had, with other issue:

1b COSMO GEORGE GORDON, **6th Marquess of Huntly** and 3rd DUKE OF GORDON, KT (Feb 1747/8); *b c* 1721; named Cosmo after his f's close friend Cosmo dei Medici III, Grand Duke of Tuscany; rep S peer 1747–52; *m* 3 Sept 1741 Catherine (*m* 2nd March 1756 Staats Long Morris, Col 61st Foot, MP Elgin, who *d* 10 Dec 1779), dau of bro-in-law 2nd Earl of Aberdeen (*see* ABERDEEN AND TEMAIR, also below), and *d* 5 Aug 1752, having had, with other issue:

1c ALEXANDER GORDON, **7th Marquess of Huntly** and 4th DUKE OF GORDON, KT (1775); *b* 18 June 1743; *educ* Eton and allegedly Harrow too; served 89th Foot, Col 1793, rep S peer 1767–84, *cr* 7 July 1784 BARON GORDON OF HUNTLY, Co Gloucester, and EARL OF NORWICH (both GB), the latter title in an earlier creation having been held by his gggf (*see* above); Keeper Gt Seal Scotland 1794–1806; Ld Lt Aberdeenshire 1794–1808; inherited right to Barony of Mordaunt (*see* MORDAUNT, Bt) and possibly Beauchamp (of Bletso) (*cr* by writ 1363 but dormant from 1412) on death 1819 of his cousin Baroness Mordaunt in her own right, she being related to him through his grandmother Lady Henrietta Mordaunt; *m* 1st 23 Oct 1767 Jane (*d* 11 April 1812), dau of Sir William Maxwell, 3rd Bt (*qv*), and had:

1d GEORGE GORDON, **8th Marquess of Huntly** and 5th and last DUKE OF GORDON, GCB (1820), PC (1830); *b* 2 Feb 1770; *educ* Eton and St John's Coll Cambridge (MA 1791); joined army 1790, Maj-Gen 1801, Lt Gen 1808, Gen 1819, Col 92nd Foot 1796–1806, 42nd Foot 1806–20, 1st Foot 1820–34 and Scots Fus 1834–36; MP (Tory) Eye 1806–07; Govr Edinburgh Castle; called up to Ho Lds *vp* 11 April 1807 in f's Lordship of Parl of Gordon of Huntly; Ld Lt Aberdeenshire 1808–36; *m* 11 Dec 1813 Elizabeth (*d* 31 Jan 1864), dau of Alexander Brodie of Arnhall, Kincardineshire, and *dsp* 28 May 1836, when the Dukedom of Gordon and other titles *cr* with it 1684, also the Earldom of Norwich and Barony of Gordon of Huntly expired, while the Barony of Mordaunt and any right he may have had to that of Beauchamp (of Bletsoe) fell into abeyance between his sisters or their issue

2d Alexander; *b* 1785; Army Offr; *d* unm 8 Jan 1808

1d Charlotte; *m* 9 Sept 1789 4th Duke of Richmond (*see* RICHMOND and GORDON, D) and *d* 5 May 1842, leaving issue

2d Madeline; *m* 1st 3 April 1789 Sir Robert Sinclair, Bt (*see* SINCLAIR-LOCKHART, Bt), and had issue; *m* 2nd 25 Nov 1805 Charles Fysche Palmer (*d* Jan 1843) and *d* 31 May 1847

3d Susan; *m* 7 Oct 1793 5th Duke of Manchester (*qv*) and *d* 26 Aug 1828, leaving issue

4d Louisa; *m* 17 April 1795 2nd Marquess Cornwallis (*see* CORNWALLIS, B) and *d* 5 Dec 1850, leaving five daus

5d Georgiana; *m* 23 June 1803 6th Duke of Bedford (*qv*) and *d* 24 Feb 1853, leaving issue

1c (cont.) The **7th Marquess** *m* 2nd July 1820 his long-standing mistress Jane Christie (*b c* 1780; *dspl* 27 July 1824), by whom he had already had four children, and *d* 17 June 1827

2c William; Dep Ranger St James's Park; *m* 1 March 1781 Frances, dau of 9th Viscount Irvine, and *d* 1 May 1823, leaving a dau (Frances, *d* unm 2 Sept 1831)

3c George; *b* 26 Dec 1751; *educ* Eton; Lt RN, MP Inverness-shire 1774; instigated the Gordon Riots 1780 (against Popery) but was cleared of constructive subversion; converted to Judaism 1786; *d* unm 1 Nov 1793

1c Susan; *m* 1st 9th Earl of Westmorland (*qv*); *m* 2nd Lt-Col John Woodford and *d* 11 Dec 1814

2b Adam; Gen, C-in-C Scotland; *m* 2 Sept 1767 Jane, dau of John Drummond and widow of 2nd Duke of Atholl (*qv*), and *d* 1801

1b Anne; *m* as his 3rd w 2nd Earl of Aberdeen (*see* ABERDEEN AND TEMAIR, M) and *d* 25 June 1791, leaving issue

2b Elizabeth; *m* Rev John Skelly and had issue

3b Catherine; *m* 12 Sept 1745 5th Earl of Wemyss (*qv*)

(1) Anne; *m* Count de Crolly

(2) Mary; *m* 1st 1667 Adam Urquhart of Meldrum; *m* 2nd 4th Earl of Perth (*qv*) and *d* 1726

(3) Jean; *m* James Seton, 4th Earl of Dunfermline

4 CHARLES GORDON, **1st Earl of Aboyne**, so *cr* 10 Sept 1660 , as also LORD GORDON OF STRATHAVON and GLENLIVET (both S); royalist Civil War; *m* 1st Margaret (*dsp*), dau of Alexander Irvine of Drum; *m* 2nd *c* 28 Aug 1665 Elizabeth Lyon *d* March 1681), dau of 2nd Earl of Kinghorne (*see* STRATHMORE AND KINGHORNE, E), and *d* March 1681, having had, with other issue, including a dau (Elizabeth, *m* 1685 2nd Earl of Cromarty; *see* CROMARTIE, E):

(1) CHARLES GORDON, **2nd Earl of Aboyne**; *m* Elizabeth (*m* 2nd 3rd Lord Kinnaird (*see* 1970 edn); *m* 3rd Capt Alexander Grant), 2nd dau of 3rd Earl of Strathmore and Kinghorne (*qv*), and had, with three other daus (including Helen, *m* George Kinnaird and was mother of 6th Lord Kinnaird, *see* 1970 edn):

1a JOHN GORDON, **3rd Earl of Aboyne**; *m* 20 June 1724 Grace (*m* 2nd 8th Earl of Moray (*qv*) and *d* 17 Nov 1738), dau of George Lockhart of Carnwath by Euphemia, 2nd dau of 9th Earl of Eglinton (*see* EGLINTON and WINTON, E), and *d* 7 April 1732, leaving:

1b CHARLES GORDON, **4th Earl of Aboyne**; *b c* 1726 *m* 1st 22 April 1759 Margaret (*d* 12 Aug 1762), 3rd dau of 6th Earl of Galloway (*qv*); *m* 2nd 14 May 1774 Mary (*d* 25 Dec 1816), dau of 14th Earl of Morton (*qv*), and *d* 28 Dec 1794, having had:

1c GEORGE, **9th Marquess**

2c Douglas GORDON later HALYBURTON (on inheriting 1784 the Forfarshire estate of his cousin Hamilton Douglas Halyburton of Pitcur); *b* 10 Oct 1777; MP; granted 24 June 1836 rank of marquess's yr s; *m* 16 July 1807 Louisa (*d* 2 Oct 1851), dau of Sir Edward Leslie, Bt, of Tarbert, Co Kerry, and *d* 25 Dec 1841

1c Catherine; *d* young

2c Margaret; *m* 5 May 1783 William Beckford, the enormously rich eccentric, builder of the celebrated but rickety Fonthill Abbey, Wilts (the 300-foot high tower fell down twice, the second time after he had sold it), and author of *Vathek*, only s of William Beckford, Ld Mayor London, and *d* 23 May 1786, leaving:

1d Margaret Maria Elizabeth; *m* 15 May 1811, as his 1st w, Lt-Gen James Orde (*m* 2nd 11 Nov 1829 Elizabeth Susan, dau of 6th Duke of Beaufort (*qv*) and widow of Lord Edward O'Brien (*see* INCHIQUIN, B)) and *d* 7 Sept 1818, leaving two daus

2d Susan Euphemia; *b* 14 May 1786; *m* 26 April 1810 10th Duke of Hamilton and (7th Duke of) Brandon (*qv*) and *d* 27 May 1859, leaving issue

2b John; *b* 19 June 1728; Lt-Col 81st Regt; *m* 18 May 1761 Clementina (*d* 31 March 1803), dau of George Lockhart of Carnwath, and *d* 30 Oct 1778, leaving, with other issue:

1c John; *b* 8 July 1765; Maj-Gen and Col-Cmdt 2nd Bde Bengal Cav; *m* Nov 1810 Eliza, 3rd dau of Robert Morris, MP Gloucester, and *d* 1832

3b Lockhart; *b* 1732; JAG Bengal; *m* 3 Oct 1770 Catherine (*d* May 1813), sis of 2nd Earl of Portsmouth (*qv*), and *d* 24 March 1788, leaving issue

1 Henrietta; *m* 1st 1630 George, Lord Seton (*see* EGLINTON and WINTON, E); *m* 2nd 1649 2nd Earl of Traquair (*see* MORAY, E)

The 4th EARL's er son,

GEORGE GORDON, **5th Earl of Aboyne** and **9th Marquess of Huntly**, as which s cousin 1836, KT (1827); *b* 28 June 1761; *educ* Eton; Ensign 1st Foot 2 Sept 1777, Capt 61st Foot 26 Sept 1777, ADC to Ld Lt Ireland 1780, Capt and Lt-Col 35th Foot 1789, tfd to Coldstream Gds, ret 1792; rep S peer 1796–1806 and 1807–18; *cr* 11 Aug 1815 BARON MELDRUM OF MORVEN, Co Aberdeen (UK); Militia ADC to WILLIAM IV 1830–37 and HM QUEEN VICTORIA 1837–53; Col Aberdeen Militia; *m* 4 April 1791 Catherine (*d* 16 Nov 1832), 2nd dau of Sir Charles Cope, 2nd Bt, of Brewerne, and *d* 17 June 1853, leaving, with three daus:

1 CHARLES, **10th Marquess**

2 George (Rev); *b* 27 Jan 1794; MA; Rector Chesterton, Hunts; *m* 29 July 1851 Charlotte Anne (*d* 23 Aug 1879), dau of Col Thomas Wright Vaughan, of Woodstone, Hants, and *d* 25 Sept 1862

3 John Frederick GORDON later HALYBURTON, GCH; *b* 15 Aug 1799; Adml; MP; *m* 24 Aug 1836 Augusta (*d* 8 Dec 1865), sis of 1st Earl of Munster (*qv*) and widow of Hon John Kennedy-Erskine (*see* AILSA, M); *dsp* 29 Sept 1878

4 Henry; *b* 31 Aug 1802; Maj HEIC; *m* 6 March 1827 Louisa Payne (*d* 17 May 1867), and *d* 28 Aug 1865, leaving, with other issue:

(1) Leslie Charles; *b* 14 May 1852; with Probate Court; *d* unm 7 Feb 1888

(1) Sarah Elizabeth Catharine; *m* 2 Jan 1845 Rev Lord Augustus FitzClarence (*d* 14 June 1854) and *d* 23 March 1901, leaving issue (*see* MUNSTER, E)

(2) Louisa Frances Charlotte; Maid-of-Honour to HM QUEEN VICTORIA; *m* 21 July 1857 Hon Ashley George John Ponsonby and *d* 12 Feb 1910, leaving issue (*see* DE MAULEY, B)

(3) Millicent Theresa (twin with Wilhelmina); *d* unm 1 Aug 1949

(4) Wilhelmina

(5) Augusta; *m* 1st 21 July 1869 Capt William Gerard Walmesley, 17th Lancers (*d* 2 Jan 1877), and had issue; *m* 2nd 6 Feb 1879 George Nugent Ross Wetherall, 15th Hus (*d* 19 April 1893), and *d* 14 May 1881, having had further issue

5 Cecil James GORDON later GORDON-MOORE (roy licence 1850); *b* 23 Feb 1806; *m* 23 April 1841 Emily (*d* 26 April 1902), dau of Maurice Crosbie Moore, of Moresfort, Co Tipperary, and *d* 15 Jan 1878, having had:

(1) Cecil Crosbie; *b* 24 Jan 1850; RN; *m* 1st 1874 Lucy, dau of Rev Charles Hodges and widow of Capt James Westhead; *m* 2nd 1911 Anastasia Theodora Beatrix (*m* 2nd 19 Oct 1935 Maj Ernest Frank Holden, MBE, 5th Dragoon Gds (*d* 23 March 1937), and *d* 1963/4), dau of John Henry Wolseley Bourne, and *d* 3 Feb 1935

(2) Arthur Henry Wyndham; *b* 18 April 1853; Inspr-Gen Prisons Mauritius; *m* —, dau of Rev Thomas Clement Browne

(3) Hubert George; *b* 23 Jan 1858; *m* 27 Sept 1882 (*divorce* 1885) Helena, dau of Thomas White, of London

(1) Catherine Augusta; *m* 8 Feb 1869 Oriel Farnell Watson (*d* 1 Nov 1886), of Somerset, and *d* 22 May 1906, leaving issue

(2) Emily; *m* 5 June 1866 Charles Robert Besley (*d* 1896) and *d* 16 June 1921, leaving issue

(3) Edith; *m* 26 June 1876 Oscar Henry Felix Cornille and had issue

(4) Agnes; *m* 1st 25 July 1872 James Milward and had issue; *m* 2nd 6 Aug 1891 Harry Leycester Powys Keck (*see* LILFORD, B) and *d* 20 April 1926

(5) Adela Crosbie; *d* unm 19 Oct 1908

(6) Evelyn; *d* unm 16 Sept 1906

(7) Philippa Jane; *m* 1 June 1881 Thomas Dunn and had issue

6 Francis Arthur Gordon; *b* 20 Jan 1808; Lt-Col 1st Life Gds; *m* 17 April 1835 Isabel (*d* 7 Jan 1892), dau of Lt-Gen Sir William Keir Grant, KCB (*cr* a Baron of the Austrian Empire by patent 22 Jan 1831), and *d* 26 June 1857, having had:

(1) George Grant, CVO, CB, JP (Berks and Co London); *b* 29 Jan 1836; Col Scots Gds; Equerry and Comptroller Household to HH PRINCE and HRH PRINCESS (3rd dau of HM QUEEN VICTORIA) CHRISTIAN OF SCHLESWIG-HOLSTEIN; Hon Col and Lt-Col 3rd Bn Roy Scots, Lt-Col 2nd Bn Roy Scottish Res Regt; *m* 8 Aug 1863 Constance Augusta Lennox (*d* 14 April 1921), dau of Laurence Peel (*see* PEEL, Bt), and *d* 24 Jan 1912, leaving:

1a Laurence George Frank, CB, DSO; *b* 21 May 1864; Col RFA, Boer War (despatches), WWI (despatches), Hon Brig-Gen 1919; *m* 1st 1 Oct 1895 Florence Juliet (*d* 25 April 1924), dau of C A Walters and widow of Alexander McHinch, CIE, and had:

1b Thelma Esmé Florence; *b* 3 Jan 1900; *m* 1st 1918 (*divorce*) Sydney Robertson; *m* 2nd 29 Nov 1923 (*divorce* 1940) F/Lt Leslie Acton Kingsford Butt, RAF, and had issue; *m* 3rd 27 June 1940 Leonard Charles Hopwood Coventon (*m* 2nd 6 Jan 1926 Violet, dau of Charles Townsend Murdoch, MP, and widow of Ambrose Yarburgh Lethbridge; *see* LETHBRIDGE, Bt), and *d* 15 Jan 1943

2a Christian Frederic; *b* 30 Oct 1866; served WWI; *m* 1st 27 Aug 1894 (*divorce* 1901) Margaret (*d* 1920), dau of W F Humble and widow of Frederick Brooks Close, and had:

1b Cicely Margot; *b* 30 April 1899; *m* 1923 Dr Alex Le Fort, of Paris

2a (cont.) Christian Gordon *m* 2nd 5 Oct 1909 Kate Elizabeth (*d* 27 March 1969), yr dau of Henry Frederick Swan, CB, and *d* 29 July 1934, having by her had:

2b Kittie Ernestine Muriel; *b* 18 Oct 1911; *m* 1st 1934 — Loam and had:

1c *Nadia O'Connor [Ms Nadia O'Connor, Wild Rose Cottage, 8 Queens Rd, Thames Ditton, Surrey KT7 0QX]; *b* 1939; (legally adopted by stepfather); *m* 1st 1959 (*divorce* 1974) Michael John BROWN later CORY BROWN and has had:

1d Simon Nicholas; *b* 1962; *d* 1990

1d Paula Elizabeth; *b* 1960; *d* 1962

2d *Nichola Kate; *b* 1964; *m* 1991 *Paul G O'Connor and has:

1e *Marcus Michael Gerrard; *b* 1991

2e *Fergus Simon John; *b* 1997

1e *Freya Laura Ellen; *b* 1994

1c (cont.) Mrs Nadia Brown *m* 2nd 1975 (*divorce* 1984) Robin O'Connor; *m* 3rd 1991 (*annulled* 1993) Robert Wellings and resumed surname O'Connor 1992

2b (cont.) Mrs Loam *m* 2nd 3 Feb 1948 Paul Edward Weldon (*d* 26 April 1972) and *d* 1990, having by him had:

1c *Paul Frederick Edward [Paul Weldon Esq, Strouds House, Farrington, Dorset DT11 8RA]; *b* 1948; *educ* Milton Abbey and Millfield; *m* 1st 1976 (*divorce* 1989) Deborah Evelyn, dau of Richard Condon, author; *m* 2nd 1992 *Sally, dau of Anthony Campbell, of Berwick St John, Dorset, and formerly w of Charles Muspratt

1a Helena Jane; *b* 21 April 1870; *m* 17 April 1894 Rev Preb William Henry Stone (*d* 1920), Rector Chipstead, Surrey, and *d* 12 Feb 1932, leaving issue

(2) Francis Frederick; *b* 10 July 1839; with Admlty; *m* 12 Feb 1877 Helen Augusta Mariana (*d* July 1940), dau of Rawson H B Reid, of Shandarick, Ross-shire, and *d* 24 July 1925, leaving:

1a Francis Lewis Rawson, DSO (1917); *b* 28 March 1878; Lt-Col Roy Irish Rifles and Gordon Highrs, Boer War, WW I (despatches); *d* 30 Jan 1920

1a Isabel Constance Helen; *m* 12 July 1911 Gordon Stewart Duncan of Coldrach, ARSM, MIMM (*d* 22 Nov 1969), yst s of Col Patrick Duncan of Coldrach, RA, of Aboyne, and had issue

2a Nita Florence; *m* 17 Oct 1906 Eric Le Strange (*d* 22 June 1918), 3rd s of Hamon Le Strange, and *d* 5 May 1955, leaving issue

(1) Catherine; *d* unm 2 Nov 1915

The 9th MARQUESS's est son,

CHARLES GORDON, **10th Marquess of Huntly**; *b* 4 Jan 1792; *educ* St John's Coll Cambridge; MP (Tory) E Grinstead 1818–30 and (Whig) Hunts 1830–31, a Ld Bedchamber 1826–30, a Ld in Waiting 1840–41, Ld Lt Aberdeenshire 1861–63; *m* 1st 20 March 1826 Lady Elizabeth Henrietta Conyngham (*dsp* 24 Aug 1839), er dau of 1st Marquess Conyngham (*qv*); *m* 2nd 10 April 1844 Maria Antoinetta (*d* 10 Aug 1893), dau of Rev Peter William Pegus by his w, formerly Dowager Countess of Lindsey (*see* LINDSEY and ABINGDON E), and *d* 18 Sept 1863, having had:

1 CHARLES GORDON, **11th Marquess of Huntly**, PC (1881), JP, DL; *b* 5 March 1847; *educ* Eton and Trin Coll Cambridge; Capt Gentlemen-at-Arms 1881, Hon Col 7th Bn Gordon Highrs; Hon LLD Aberdeen U, Ld Rector Aberdeen U 1890–1896; ed: *Records of Aboyne*, author: *Milestones* and *Auld Acquaintance*; a Ld-in-Waiting in Ordinary to HM QUEEN VICTORIA 1870–73; *m* 1st 14 July 1869 Amy (*d* 13 May 1920), er dau and coheir of Sir William Cunliffe-Brooks, 1st and last Bt (*see* CRAWSHAW, B); *m* 2nd 26 June 1922 Charlotte Jane Isabella (*d* 17 May 1939), dau of John H Fallon and widow of (a) James MacDonald, of Cincinnati, Ohio, and (b) Bradley Campbell, and *dsp* 20 Feb 1937

2 Lewis; *b* 3 May 1848; lost at sea 7 Sept 1870

3 Bertrand; *b* 24 July 1850; *d* Sydney, NSW, 10 Aug 1869

4 Douglas William Cope; *b* 11 Oct 1851; Lt Coldstream Gds; MP W Aberdeenshire 1876–80 and Hunts 1880–85; *d* unm 4 Aug 1888

5 Esmé Stuart; *b* 12 March 1853; *m* 21 July 1874 Elizabeth Anne Phippen (*d* 16 May 1929), dau of William Brown, of Northover, Somerset, and *dspm* 29 Sept 1900, leaving:

(1) Beatrice Mary; *b* 21 July 1875; *m* 19 April 1900 (*divorce* 1923) Francis Henry Meade, CBE, and *d* 6 March 1959, leaving issue (*see* CLANWILLIAM, E)

6 Granville Armyne; *b* 14 June 1856; *m* 1st 4 Sept 1878 Charlotte D'Olier (*d* 28 May 1900), dau of Henry Roe, of Mount Anneville Park, Co Dublin, and had:

(1) Charles Henry Granville; *b* 19 June 1880; *d* unm 16 July 1899

(2) (Granville Cecil) Douglas, CVO (1918), DSO; *b* 28 April 1883; Lt-Col Welsh Gds, formerly Scots Gds, Boer War, WW I (despatches), Croix de Guerre, Chev Legn Honour 4th Cl, Order Nile, OStJ; Equerry to HRH THE DUKE OF CONNAUGHT 1921; *m* 20 April 1907 Violet Ida (*d* 15 Dec 1968), dau of Gerard Streatfield, and *d* 3 Oct 1930, leaving:

1a DOUGLAS CHARLES LINDSEY, **12th Marquess**

2a Adam Granville, KCVO (1960), MBE (1945); *b* 1 March 1909; *educ* Eton; Maj RA (TA) WW II (despatches), memb Roy Co Archers, Comptroller Household to HM QUEEN ELIZABETH THE QUEEN MOTHER and Assist Priv Sec 1953–74; granted with yr bros rank of marquess's s 20 Nov 1937; *m* 12 June 1947 *Pamela [The Lady Adam Gordon, Hethersett, Littleworth Cross, Seale, Surrey GU10 1JL], dau of Alexander Herriot Bowhill, CBE, of Inchmarlo, Banchory, Kincardineshire, and *d* 1984, having had:

1b +Adam Alexander [Adam Gordon Esq, Heatheryleys, by Glenfarg, Perthshire]; *b* 6 April 1948; *educ* Eton; memb Roy Co Archers; *m* 1979 *Jennifer Susan, est dau of William George McHardy, CVO, MBE, MC, of Woodend House, Banchory, Kincardineshire, and has:

1c +Alexander Charles Adam; 1989

1c *Joanna Mary; *b* 1986

2b +Douglas Herriot [Douglas Gordon Esq, 4 Coastguard Cottages, Sandwich Bay CT13 9PZ]; *b* 8 Jan 1951; *educ* Eton; Page of Honour to HM THE QUEEN 1965–67; memb Roy Co Archers; *m* 1977 *Susan Jennifer, dau of Anthony White, and has:

1c +James Adam Anthony; *b* 1991

1c *Alexandra Anne; *b* 26 June 1979

2c *Katherine Louisa; *b* 1981

3c *Isabella Clare; *b* 1985

3a Roderic Armyne, MBE (1943), TD ; *b* 27 Jan 1914; *educ* Stowe; Maj 72nd (Hants) AA Bde RA (TA) WW II; *m* 1st 7 Jan 1937 (*divorce* 1949) Anne (*d* 6 Jan 1997), yr dau of Lt-Col Osbert Eustace Vesey, CBE (*see* DE VESCI, V); *m* 2nd 26 Aug 1949 *Baroness Joana Alexandra, 2nd dau of Ion Bujoiu, of Bucharest, Romania, and formerly w of (a) Prince Serban Ghika and (b) Chevalier de Stuers, and *d* 1997, having had by his 1st w:

1b +David Esmé Douglas; *b* 28 Oct 1937; *educ* Sherborne; *m* 1st 4 April 1959 (*divorce* 1962) Audrey Diana, dau of E Dermot Carey; *m* 2nd 1962 Valerie Ellis, dau of Henry Charles Guy Owen; *m* 3rd 1979 *Anne, dau of Per Thor Brockdorf-Knutzon, of Copenhagen, and by his 2nd w has:

1c *Samantha; *b* 1962

2b +Angus Lindsey Eustace; *b* 13 Jan 1941; *educ* Nautical Coll Pangbourne and Bloxham; Lt RM; *m* 9 July 1966 *Diana Mary, dau of Robert C Pawlyn, of Mevagissey, Cornwall, and formerly w of Graham Clive Crockford

3b James Ian; *b* 13 Dec 1942; *d* 3 March 1943

4a +Douglas Claude Alexander , DSO (1944) [Lt-Col The Lord Douglas Gordon DSO, The Old Rectory, Stockbridge, Hants]; *b* 30 July 1916; *educ* Eton and RMC Sandhurst; Lt-Col Black Watch WW II Italy, memb Roy Co Archers, Page of Honour to HM GEORGE V 1930–33; *m* 1st 21 Dec 1940 (*divorce* 1961) Suzanne, dau of Lt-Col Arthur Houssemayne Du Boulay, DSO, and has:

1b +Andrew Granville Douglas [Andrew Gordon Esq, Elm Lodge, 230 Petersham Rd, Richmond, Surrey TW10 7AL]; *b* 13 Aug 1942; *educ* Eton; Page of Honour to HM THE QUEEN 1957–1960; *m* 1st 1963 (*divorce* 1969) Gillian Thorne and has:

1c +David; *b* 1963

2c +Jamie; *b* 5 Oct 1965

1b (cont.) Andrew Gordon *m* 2nd 1976 *Brigitte Marx, dau of Herbert Marx, and by her has:

3c +Glen; *b* 1984

1c *Kitty; *b* 1980

2b +Douglas George Alexander [Douglas Gordon Esq, 25 Coleherne Mews, London SW10 9DZ; Dunira, Comrie, Perthshire PH6 2LA]; *b* 25 Oct 1947; *educ* Gordonstoun; memb Roy Co Archers; *m* 1 March 1975 *Celina d'Orey, dau of Peter Landsberg, CBE, of Rio de Janeiro, and has:

1c +Thomas Peter Douglas; *b* 1979

2c +James Alexander Douglas; *b* 1984

1c *Georgina Violet; *b* 15 June 1976

1b *Jane Elizabeth [The Lady Robert Mercer Nairne, The Old Manse, Kinclaven,by Stanley, Perthshire; 10105 SE, 25th Bellevue, Washington,

98004, USA]; *b* 1 Sept 1950; *m* 1 Nov 1972 *Lord Robert Harold Mercer Nairne, yr s of 8th Marquess of Lansdowne (*qv*)

4a (cont.) Lord Douglas Gordon *m* 2nd 1962 *Bridget, dau of Gerald Bryan Ingham and formerly w of Maj Alexander Hutchison, and by her has:

2b *Sarah Alexandra; *b* 1963

(1) Armyne Evelyn; *b* 21 June 1879; *m* 8 April 1908 Sir Lionel Lawson Faudel Faudel-Philips 3rd Bt (*d* 12 March 1941), and *d* 16 June 1942, leaving issue (*see* 1940 edn)

6 (cont.) Lord Granville Gordon *m* 2nd 1902 Margaret (*d* 17 May 1920), dau of W F Humble and widow of Frederick Brooks Close, and *d* at sea 14 June 1907

7 Randolph Seaton; *b* 17 May, *d* 16 July 1859

1 Mary Katherine; CBE; *m* 17 April 1866 Edmund Turnor (*d* 15 Dec 1903), of Stoke Rochford, Lincs, and *dsp* 8 Sept 1930

2 Evelyn Elizabeth; *m* 14 July 1863 1st Earl of Ancaster (*d* 24 Dec 1910) and *d* 16 March 1921, leaving issue (*see* HEATHCOTE, Bt, of London)

3 Grace Cecilie; CBE (1920); *m* 27 June 1878 5th Earl of Lonsdale (*qv*) and *dsp* 12 May 1941

4 Margaret Ethel; *m* 25 July 1881 3rd Baron Harlech (*qv*) and *d* 25 April 1950, leaving issue

5 Elena Mary; *m* 28 Feb 1885 Maj George Lamplugh Wickham, RHG (Blues) (*d* 4 Nov 1919), of Wetherby,Yorks, and *d* 19 Jan 1936, leaving issue

6 Edith Blanche (twin with Elena); *d* 25 Dec 1862

7 Ethelreda Caroline; *b* posthumously Feb 1864; *m* 16 Sept 1884 Lt-Col Henry Wickham, CMG, Scots Gds (*d* 6 Feb 1933), of Oundle, Northants, yst s of Lamplugh Wickham Wickham, JP, DL, and *d* 9 May 1961, leaving issue

The 11th MARQUESS's great-nephew,

DOUGLAS CHARLES LINDSEY GORDON, **12th Marquess of Huntly**; *b* 3 Feb 1908; Lt Gordon Highrs (TA) WW II; *m* 15 March 1941 (*divorce* 1965) Hon (Mary) Pamela Berry, dau of 1st Viscount Kemsley (*qv*), and had:

1 GRANVILLE CHARLES GOMER GORDON, **13th and present Marquess of Huntly**

1 *(Pamela) Lemina [The Lady Lemina Lawson Johnston, Coldstone House, Logie Coldstone, Aboyne, Aberdeenshire AB34 5NP]; *b* 17 Dec 1941; *m* 4 April 1970 *Hon (Ian) Henry Lawson Johnston, 2nd s of 2nd Baron Luke (*qv*), and has issue

The **12th Marquess** *m* 2nd 1977 *Elizabeth Haworth Leigh [The Most Hon The Dowager Marchioness of Huntly, Hollybrook, Ewhurst Rd, Cranleigh, Surrey], dau of Lt-Cdr Frederick Haworth Leigh, RD, RNR, and *d* 1987

HURD OF WESTWELL

Creation: B. (LP, UK) 19 April 1997.

THE BARON HURD OF WESTWELL, of Westwell, Co Oxon (Douglas Richard Hurd, CH (1996), CBE (1974), PC (1982)) [The Rt Hon The Lord Hurd of Westwell CH CBE PC, House of Lords, London SW1A 0PW]; *b* 8 March 1930; *educ* Eton and Trin Coll Cambridge; Dip Serv 1952–66: Peking 1954–56, UK Mission UN 1956–60, Private Sec to PUS FO 1960–63, Rome 1963–66; CRD 1966 (Head For Affrs Section 1968), Priv Sec to Leader Oppn 1968–70, Political Sec to PM 1970–74, MP (C) Mid-Oxon 1974–83, Witney 1983–97, Oppn Spokesman Europe 1976–79, Min State: FCO 1979–83, Home Office 1983–84, Sec State NI 1984–85, Home Sec 1985–89, For Sec 1989–95; Visiting Fell Nuffield Coll Oxford 1978–86; dep chm NatWest Markets 1995–; chm: Br Invisibles 1997– and Prison Reform Tst 1997–; author: *The Arrow War* (1967), *Send Him Victorious* (with Andrew Osmond, 1968), *The Smile on the Face of the Tiger* (with Andrew Osmond, 1969), *Scotch on the Rocks* (with Andrew Osmond, 1971), *Truth Game* (1972), *Vote to Kill* (1975), *An End to Promises* (1979), *War Without Frontiers* (with Andrew Osmond, 1982), *Palace of Enchantments* (with Stephen Lamport, 1985) and *Search for Peace* (1997); *m* 1st 1960 (*divorce* 1982) Tatiana Elizabeth Michelle Eyre and has:

1 *Nicholas Richard; *b* 13 May 1962; *m* 1988 *Kim, er dau of Ray Richards, of Hartley Court, Reading, and has:

(1) *Maximillan; *b* 1991

(2) *Gus; *b* 1993

(1) *Katie Mae; *b* 29 Aug 1996

(2) *Florence Amy; *b* 29 Aug 1996

2 *Thomas Robert Benedict; *b* 22 Sept 1964; *educ* Eton and Pembroke Coll Oxford; *m* 17 Dec 1994 *Catherine, dau of Dr Daniel Roland Aubrey, of Mattingley, Hants, and has:

(1) *Benedict Julian; *b* 27 Nov 1996

(1) *Lara Juliet; *b* 27 Nov 1997

3 *Alexander Paul Anthony; *b* 7 June 1969

BARON HURD OF WESTWELL *m* 2nd 1982 *Judy, dau of Sidney and Pamela Smart, and by her has:

4 *Phillip Arthur; *b* 1983

1 *Jessica Stephanie; *b* 1985

Lineage: WILLIAM HURD, of Highgate; *b* 17 Jan 1831; slr; *m* 1859 Elizabeth (*d* 1910), dau of Rev — Angier, of Wincanton, Somerset, and *d* 1913, leaving, with other issue:

1 Percy Angier (Sir); *b* 18 May 1864; MP Frome 1918–23 and Devises 1924–25; ktd 1932; fndr-ed *The Outlook*, ed *Canadian Gazette*, London ed *Montreal Star*; *m* 5 Sept 1893 Hannah (*d* 15 Feb 1949), dau of Rev William Jackson Cox, DD, of Dundee, and *d* 5 June 1950, leaving:

(1) ANTHONY RICHARD HURD, BARON HURD, of Newbury, Co Berks (LP, UK), so *cr* 24 Aug 1964; *b* 2 May 1901; *educ* Marlborough and Pembroke Coll Cambridge; farm ed *The Field* 1924–37, ag correspondent *The Times* 1932–58, farmer Berks and Wilts 1926 on, ag advsr Min Ag WW II, MP (C) Newbury 1945–64, Chm C Ag Ctee 1951–64, ktd 1959, V-Pres Roy Ag Soc of England, Pres Guild Ag Jnlsts 1965; *m* 26 Sept 1928 Stephanie Frances (*see* 1985), er dau of Edred Mosss Corner, FRCS, of Stratton End, Beaconsfield, Bucks, and *d* 1966, having had:

1a DOUGLAS RICHARD, *cr* a **Baron**

2a John Julian; *b* 19 March 1932; *d* 3 June 1951

3a *Stephen Anthony, JP [The Hon Stephen Hurd JP, The Glebe House, Mildenhall, Marlborough, Wilts SN8 2LU]; *b* 6 April 1933; *educ* Winchester and Magdalene Coll Cambridge; *m* 1973 *Pepita Lilian, dau of Lt-Col Walter George Hingston, OBE, of Ramsbury, Wilts, and has issue

2 Archibald (Sir), of The Shaw, Brasted Chart, Kent; *b* 13 Aug 1869; jnlst *Daily Telegraph* 1899–1928, jt ed *Brassey's Naval Shipping Annual* 1921–28, chm Shipping World Co 1928, Assoc Inst Naval Architects, Hon Freeman Shipwrights' Co, ktd 1928; *m* 1st 19 Sept 1895 Anne Perrott (*d* 14 Sept 1946), dau of Albert Groser, and had:

(1) Vivyen Groser; *m* 14 June 1918 Francis Donald Holden Bremner, s of Capt Donald Bremner, of Brasted Chart

(2) Mary Barbara; *m* 21 July 1928 Sir (Henry) Gordon Willmer, OBE, TD, PC, JP, Ld Justice of Appeal 1955–69, s of Arthur Washington Willmer, JP, of The Wirral (*d* 1983), and had, with two daus:

1a *John Franklin, QC (1967) [John Willmer Esq QC, Flat 4, 23 Lymington Rd, London NW6 1HZ]; *b* 30 May 1930; *educ* Winchester and Corpus Christi Coll Oxford; 2nd Lt Cheshire Regt 1949–50, TA 1950–51, Capt Middx Regt 1951–57, barrister Inner Temple 1955, Bencher 1975, Gen Commr Income Tax Inner Temple 1982, memb panel Lloyd's Arbitrators Salvage Cases 1967–91 and Admlty Court Ctee 1980–95, Leader Admlty Bar 1992–95, Lloyd's Appeal Arbitrator Salvage Cases 1991–, Freeman Arbitrators' Co 1992; *m* 1st 1958 (*divorce* 1979) Nicola Ann Dickinson and has a s and three daus; *m* 2nd 1979 *Margaret Lilian, dau of Chester B Berryman

2 (cont.) Sir Archibald *m* 2nd Sept 1947 Beatrice Maude, 3rd dau of Alfred Stair, Inland Revenue accountant, and *d* 20 June 1959

HUSSEY OF NORTH BRADLEY

Creation: B. (LP, UK) June 1996.

THE BARON HUSSEY OF BRADLEY, of Bradley in the County of Wiltshire (Marmaduke James Hussey) [The Rt Hon The Lord Hussey of Bradley, Flat 15, 45–47 Courtfield Rd, London SW7 4DB]; *b* 1923; *educ* Rugby and Trin Coll Oxford; WW II in Gren Gds; Associated Newspapers: joined 1949, dir 1964; md Harmsworth Publicns 1967–70, ch exec and md Thomson Orgn 1971–80, dir Times Newspapers 1982–86, jt chm Gt Western Radio 1985–86, dir William Collins plc 1985–89 and Colonial Mutual Gp 1982–96, chm Ruffer Investment Management 1995– and Cadmeb Ltd 1996–, memb bd Br Cncl 1983–; chm bd govrs BBC 1986–96 and Roy Marsden Hosp 1985–; *m* 1959 *Lady Susan Katherine Waldegrave, DCVO, 5th dau of 12th Earl Waldegrave (*qv*), and has issue

Lineage: Rev JAMES HUSSEY; *m* Martha Ellen Hewett and had:

ERIC ROBERT JAMES HUSSEY, CMG (1933); *b* 26 April 1885; *educ* Repton and Hertford Coll Oxford; Sudan Civ Serv 1908–20 (DC 1912, Ch Inspr Educn Dept 1918); Dir Educn Uganda 1925 and Nigeria 1929–36, Order Nile 4th Cl; *m* 1922 Christine Elizabeth Justice, dau of A Noel Morley, and *d* 19 May 1958, leaving:

1 MARMADUKE JAMES, *cr* a **Baron**

1 Helen Justice; *d* unm 19 Dec 1997

HUTCHINSON OF LULLINGTON

Creation: B. (LP, UK) 1978.

THE BARON HUTCHINSON OF LULLINGTON, of Lullington, Co East Sussex (Jeremy Nicolas Hutchinson) [The Rt Hon The Lord Hutchinson of Lullington, House of Lords, London SW1A 0PW]; *b* 28 March 1915; *educ* Stowe and Magdalen Coll Oxford; WW II: RNVR; barrister Middle Temple 1939, Bencher 1963, QC 1961, Recorder Bath 1962–72, Recorder Crown Court 1972–76; Memb Ctee: Immigration Appeals 1966–68, Identification Procedures 1974–76; V-Chm Arts Cncl 1977–79 (memb 1974–79); Tstee: Tate Gallery 1979–84 (Chm 1980–84), Chantrey Bequest; Prof Law RA 1987–; *m* 1st 1940 (*divorce* 1966) Dame Peggy (Edith Margaret Emily) S Ashcroft, DBE, actress (*d* 1991), dau of William Worsley Ashcroft, of Croydon, and formerly w of (a) Sir Rupert Hart-Davis and (b) Theodore Komisarjevsky, and has:

1 *Nicholas St John; *b* 1946; *m* 19– *— and has:

(1) *March (dau); *b* 19–

1 *Eliza; *b* 1941; *m* 1974 *Pierre Loizeau and has:

(1) *Manon; *b* 19–

(2) *Emily; *b* 19–

The BARON HUTCHINSON OF LULLINGTON *m* 2nd 1966 *June, dau of Capt Arthur Edward Capel, CBE (*see* 1925 edn RIBBLESDALE, B) and formerly w of Franz Osborn

Lineage: ST JOHN HUTCHINSON, QC; *m* Mary, only dau of Sir Hugh Shakespear Barnes, KCSI, KCVO, BCS (*see* STRACHEY, Bt), and had an only s:

JEREMY NICOLAS, *cr* a **Baron**

HUTCHISON of Rossie

Arms: Arg. an arrow fessways vert, feathered gu. and barbed or, between two lymphads vert, sails furled gu., in chief, and a parachute az., stringed vert and ringed or, in base.
Crest: A parachute as in the arms, the ring transversed of an arrow fessways, also as in the arms. **Motto** (above the crest): *Surgam* ('I will rise'). **Creation:** Bt. (UK) 26 Jan 1956.

SIR JAMES COLVILLE HUTCHISON, 3RD BT, of Rossie, Co Perth; *b* 7 Oct 1967; *s* f 1998

Lineage: PETER ADAM HUTCHISON, Town Cncllr and Baillie of Glasgow; *b* 5 Feb 1834; *m* 18– Marion Holt and *d* 7 Sept 1899, leaving:

THOMAS HOLT HUTCHISON, Town Cncllr 1910 and Baillie 1916, Capt HLI 1890, Maj Lanarks Vols 1917; *b* 10 Feb 1861; *m* 22 Jan 1890 Florence (*d* 27 Oct 1939), dau of James Railey, and *d* 22 June 1918, leaving:

1 JAMES RILEY HOLT (Sir), **1st Bt**
2 Thomas Holt; WW I 1917 with RNAS; *b* 3 Oct 1899; *educ* Harrow; *m* 1925 Agnes Graham (*d* 13 Feb 1959), dau of James Rankin, and *d* 2 Dec 1946, leaving:
(1) *Virginia Graham [Mrs Geraint Glynn, The Cedars, Hursbourne Tarrant, nr Andover, Hants]; *b* 10 Feb 1928; *m* 26 April 1954 *Geraint David Vernet Glynn, er s of Lt-Col Rupert Trevor Wallace Glynn, MC, of Harlesford House, Tetsworth, Oxon, and has:
1a *Robert Jolyon Hutchinson; *b* 7 Feb 1960
1a *Joanna Elizabeth; *b* 12 Nov 1958
1 Marion; *b* 27 Sept 1895; *m* 28 March 1918 John Eric Glynne-Percy (*d* July 1960) and *d* 23 May 1945, leaving issue

THOMAS HOLT HUTCHISON'S est son,

Sir James Riley Holt Hutchison, 1st Bt (UK), so *cr* 26 Jan 1956, DSO (1945), TD (1928); *b* 10 April 1893; *educ* Kelvinside Acad, Stanmore Park, Harrow, and in France; WW I with Lanarks Yeo and Indian Cav, WW II with BEF, SOE and Maquis in France, Chev Legn Hon and Croix de Guerre 1945, dir: J & P Hutchison Ltd and Ailsa Shipbuilding Co Ltd 1918–33, Glasgow Shipowners Assoc 1927 and Tayside Floorcloth Co Ltd 1937, chm Hutchison & Craft, Grampian Holdings, and Glenfield and Kennedy Holdings, MP Glasgow Centl 1945–50 and Scotstoun 1950–59, Parly U-Sec and Fin Sec War Office Nov 1951–54, v-chm Scottish U Members' Ctee 1957, commnd Lanarks Yeo 1929, Hon Col 1948, Nat Pres Incorporated Sales Managers Assoc 1949, pres Assembly WEU and Assoc Br Chambers of Commerce; *m* 1st 1 March 1920 (*divorce* 1932) Dorothy Joan (*d* 25 Feb 1939), er dau of Maj Henry Siward Balliol Surtees, JP, DL, of Redworth, Co Durham; *m* 2nd 31 July 1928 Winefryde Eleanor Mary (*d* 1988), dau of Rev Richard Henry Craft, Vicar Ford, Salop, and *d* 1979, leaving:

1 **Sir Peter Craft Hutchison, 2nd Bt**, CBE (1992); *b* 5 June 1935; *educ* Eton and Magdalene Coll Cambridge (BA); Lt QO Lowland Yeo (TA) and RSG; chm Hutchison & Craft, insur brokers, Glasgow, and Bd Tstees Roy Botanical Gardens Edinburgh, V-Chm Br Waterways Bd, Bd Memb Scottish Nat Heritage 1994–98; *m* 10 Sept 1966 *Virginia [Lady Hutchison, Milton House, Milton, by Dumbarton G82 2TU; 32 Moore St, London SW3], er dau of John Millar Colville (*see* CLYDESMUIR, B), and *d* Jan 1998, leaving:
(1) Sir JAMES COLVILLE HUTCHISON, **3rd and present Bt**
1 Jancis; *b* 26 Sept 1929

HUTCHISON of Thurle

Creation: Bt. (UK) 6 July 1939.

SIR ROBERT HUTCHISON, 3RD BT, of Thurle, Parish of Streatley, Berks [Sir Robert Hutchison Bt, Hawthorn Cottage, Lower Rd, Grundisburgh, Suffolk IP13 6UQ]; *b* 25 May 1954; *s* f 1998; *educ* Marlborough; *m* 1987 *Anne Margaret, er dau of Sir (Godfrey) Michael David Thomas, 11th Bt, of Wenvoe (*qv*), and has:
1 +HUGO THOMAS ALEXANDER; *b* 16 April 1988
2 +Guy Piers Giles; *b* 30 April 1990

Lineage: Sir Robert Hutchison, 1st Bt (UK), so *cr* 6 July 1939 (4th s of Robert Hutchison and yst bro of Sir Thomas Hutchison, 1st Bt, of Hardiston, Co Kinross; *see* 1970 edn); *b* 28 Oct 1871; *educ* Edinburgh, Strasbourg and Paris Us (MB and CM Edinburgh 1893, MD 1896); MRCP Lond 1897, FRCP 1903, Hon FRCP Edinburgh 1931, Hon LLD Edinburgh and Birmingham, Hon DSc Oxford, Hon MD Melbourne, consulting physician Lond Hosp and Hosp for Sick Children, Gt Ormond Street, 1900–35, pres RSM 1934–36 and Roy College of Physicians Lond 1938–41; *m* 27 June 1905 Laetitia Nora (*d* 1964), est dau of Very Rev William Moore-Ede, DD, Dean Worcester, and *d* 12 Feb 1960, having had:

1 **Sir Peter Hutchison, 2nd Bt**; *b* 27 Sept 1907; *educ* Marlborough and Lincoln Coll Oxford (MA 1928); slr 1933, F/Lt RAFVR (Intell) WW II, Dep Clerk Peace and CC E Suffolk 1947–1971, Clerk Peace and Co Slr 1971–72; *m* 16 July 1949 *Mary-Grace [Mary-Grace Lady Hutchison, Melton Mead, Suffolk IP12 1PF], only dau of Very Rev Algernon Giles Seymour (*see* CULME-SEYMOUR, Bt), and *d* 16 Jan 1998, leaving:
(1) Sir ROBERT HUTCHISON, **3rd and present Bt**
(2) + Mark Seymour; *b* 30 April 1960; *m* 1 March 1997 *Sarah, er dau of John Nicholson, of Waltham St Lawrence, Berks
(1) *Elspeth [Mrs John Bryers, The Old Hall, Kilnwick, Yorks YO25 9JG]; *b* 25 April 1950; *m* 30 Aug 1975 *John Richard Feneran Bryers, s of Brig R H C Bryers, of Thorndon Old Rectory, Eye, Suffolk, and has:
1a *Henry Peter Newman; *b* 1977
2a *George Richard Timothy; *b* 1983
1a *Charlotte Emily; *b* 1979
(2) *Alison Margaret; *b* 28 July 1951; *m* 1990 *Peter Brendon Wintgens
2 Gerald Tait; *b* 12 June 1909; *educ* Rugby and Univ Coll Oxford; *d* 16 Nov 1928
3 +Michael Duncan, slr 1939; *b* 18 Nov 1912; *educ* Eton and Magdalen Coll Oxford (BA); *m* 1 Dec 1945 *Margery Betty, dau of Albert Victor Martin, of Leeds, and has had:
(1) David; *b* 23 Aug 1946; *educ* Charterhouse; *k* bicycle accident 3 June 1960
(2) +Paul Michael; *b* 12 Nov 1959
(1) *Sara Laetitia; *b* 18 July 1949; *m* 22 July 1976 *C William Squire
(2) *Margaret Ann; *b* 5 March 1953
1 *Ann Felicity, JP (Surrey) [Mrs Geoffrey Greenwood JP, Saxons, Frensham, Farnham, Surrey]; *b* 19 March 1917; *m* 30 June 1945 Geoffrey Martin Greenwood (*d* 1994), Dip Serv, and has:
(1) *John Gerald; *b* 3 Dec 1946; *educ* Rugby
(2) *Alan Graham; *b* 26 Oct 1948; *educ* Marlborough
(3) *Charles Duncan; *b* 12 Sept 1954
(1) *Victoria Jean; *b* 11 Sept 1950

HUTTON

Creation: B. (LP. UK) 1997.

THE BARON HUTTON, of Bresagh in the County of Down (Sir (James) Brian Edward Hutton, PC (1988)) [The Rt Hon The Lord Hutton PC, House of Lords, London SW1A 0PW]; *b* 29 June 1931; *educ* Shrewsbury, Balliol Coll Oxford (Hon Fell 1988) and Queen's U Belfast; barrister NI 1954 (English bar 1972), Bencher Inn of Court NI 1974, Jr Counsel to Attorney-Gen NI 1969, QC NI 1970, Legal Advsr to Min Home Affrs NI 1973, Sr Crown Counsel NI 1973–79, High Court Judge NI 1979–88, Hon Bencher Inner Temple 1988 and King's Inns Dublin 1988, Dep Chm NI Boundary Cmmn 1985–88, Pres NI Assoc Mental Health 1983–, ktd 1988, Ld Ch Justice NI 1988–97, Ld Appeal in Ordinary 1997–; *m* 1975 *Mary Gillian Murland and has two daus

Lineage: JAMES HUTTON, of Belfast; *m* Mabel — and had:
(JAMES) BRIAN EDWARD, *cr* a **Baron**

HYLTON

Arms: Quarterly, 1st and 4th, arg. on a pile vert three dexter hands couped of the first (for JOLLIFFE); 2nd and 3rd, arg. two bars az. (for HYLTON). **Crest:** A cubit arm erect, couped, vested vert, cuffed and the sleeve charged with a pile arg., the hand grasping a sword in bend ppr. **Supporters:** Two lions guardant az., each charged on the shoulder with three annulets two and one or. **Motto:** *Tant que je puis* ('As much as I can'). **Creation:** Bt. (UK) 20 Aug 1821, B. (UK) 9 July 1866.

THE 5TH BARON HYLTON OF HYLTON, Co Palatine of Durham, **AND OF PETERSFIELD**, Co Southampton, and a **Baronet** (Sir Raymond Harvey Jolliffe, Bt) [The Rt Hon The Lord Hylton, Ammerdown, Radstock, Somerset BA3 5SH]; *b* 13 June 1932; *s f* 1967; *educ* Eton and Trin Coll Oxford (MA); Lt Coldstream Gds (Res of Offrs); ARICS, Assoc memb Chartered Land Agent's Soc 1960, Assist Priv Sec to Govr-Gen Canada 1960–62, Tstee Shelter Housing Aid Centre 1969–76, Chm: Nat Fedn Housing Assocs 1973–76, Catholic Housing Aid Soc 1972–73, Help the Aged Housing Tst and Housing Assocs Charitable Assoc for Care and Resettlement of Offenders, memb Frome RDC, DL Somerset 1975–90; *m* 29 June 1966 *Joanna Ida Elizabeth, est dau of Andrew Ramon Dalzell de Bertodano (*see* MEXBOROUGH, E), and has:

1 +WILLIAM HENRY MARTIN; *b* 1 April 1967; *educ* Ampleforth and RAC Cirencester
2 +Andrew Thomas Peter; *b* 29 June 1969
3 +Alexander John Charles Martin; *b* 10 Feb 1973
4 +John Edward Arthur; *b* 1977
1 *Emily Sylvia Rose Elizabeth; *b* 1975

Lineage: THOMAS JOLLIFFE, of Cofton Hall, Worcs; *b* 1617; *m* 1st Margaret, dau of Richard Skinner, of Cofton; *m* 2nd Mary, dau of Sir Gabriel Lowe and widow of Edward Ducie, and *d* 1693, leaving an only surv s by his 1st w:

BENJAMIN JOLLIFFE, of Cofton Hall; *m* Mary, dau of John Jolliffe, of London, and *d* 1719, having had, with two daus (Rebecca, *m* Humphrey Lowe, of Bromsgrove; Anne, *m* Robert Biddulph, of Ledbury):

JOHN JOLLIFFE; MP Petersfield; *m* 1st Katherine, dau of Robert Michell; *m* 2nd Mary, dau and heir of Samuel Holden, and by her had:

1 WILLIAM
2 Thomas Samuel; MP; *m* 1778 Ann, dau and heir of Rev Robert Twyford, of Kilmersdon, Somerset, and had:
(1) John Twyford, of Ammerdown Park, Somerset; *dsp* 13 March 1854
(2) Thomas Robert (Rev), of Ammerdown Park; *dsp*
(3) Charles; *k* Waterloo 1815
(1) Mary Ann; *d* Dec 1869

The er son,

WILLIAM JOLLIFFE; MP Petersfield; *m* 28 Aug 1769 Eleanor, dau and heiress of Sir Richard Hylton, Bt, of Hayton Castle, Cumberland, est s (by Anne, est sis and coheir of John Hilton, of Hilton Castle, Co Durham, whose ancestors were called to Parl by writ between 1295 and probably 1399 and who therefore himself may be regarded as *de jure* 20th Lord (Baron) Hilton) of Sir Richard Musgrave, Bt, of Hayton, and had, with three daus:

1 Hylton, of Mertham, Burney, and St James's; MP Petersfield; *b* Feb 1773; *m* 7 Sept 1804 Eleanor (*d* 13 Jan 1809), illegitimate dau of 7th Earl Ferrers (*qv*), and *dsp* 1 Jan 1843
2 William John (Rev), of Merstham House, Redhill, Surrey; Ld Manor Merstham; *m* 10 Jan 1799 Julia, dau and coheir of Sir Abraham Pytches, of Streatham, and *d* 31 Jan 1835, leaving issue:
(1) WILLIAM GEORGE HYLTON, **1st Baron**
(2) Gilbert East, of Tilgate Forest; 19th Light Dragoons; *m* Aug 1823 Margaret Ellen (*d* 12 Oct 1836), dau of Sir Edward Banks, and *d* 18 Dec 1833
3 George; Lt RN; *k* Battle of the Nile 1 Aug 1798

WILLIAM JOLLIFFE *d* 28 Feb 1802; his er gs,

Sir George Hylton Jolliffe, 1st Bt, and **1st Baron Hylton of Hylton,** Co Palatine of Durham, **and of Petersfield,** Co Southampton (both UK), so *cr* 20 Aug 1821 and 9 July 1866 respectively, PC; High Sheriff Surrey 1830, Capt Army, MP (C) Petersfield 1830–32, 1837–38 and 1841–66, Parly U-Sec Home Affrs 1852, Parly Sec Treasury 1858–59; *b* 7 Dec 1800; *m* 1st 8 Oct 1825 Eleanor (*d* 23 July 1862), 2nd dau of Hon Berkeley Thomas Paget (*see* ANGLESEY, M); *m* 2nd 19 Jan 1867 Sophia Penelope (*d* 27 Aug 1882), widow of 4th Earl of Ilchester (*qv*) and dau of Sir Robert Sheffield, 4th Bt (*qv*), and had by his 1st w, with other issue:

1 Hylton; Capt Coldstream Gds; *b* 10 July 1826; *m* 1 July 1848 Leila (*d* 6 March 1904), est dau of Sir Thomas John Tyrwhitt, 2nd Bt (*see* BERNERS, B), and *dvp* before Sebastopol of cholera 4 Oct 1854, leaving:
(1) Eleanor Constance; *m* 18 July 1871 Col Frederick Hambleton Custance (*d* 29 Sept 1925), CB, of Weston, Norfolk, Gren Gds, and *d* 14 Nov 1908, leaving issue
(2) Hilda Hylton; *m* 3 April 1879 Hon Morton William North (*d* 26 April 1895), bro of 7th Earl of Guilford (*qv*), and *d* 19 Feb 1902, leaving issue
2 HEDWORTH HYLTON, **2nd Baron**
3 (William) Sydney Hylton, of Heath House, Petersfield, Hants (bought from **3rd Baron**), JP, DL Hants; Capt Scot Gds, MP Petersfield 1874–80; *b* 27 Sept 1841; *m* 9 Nov 1870 Gertrude Henrietta (*d* 13 March 1915), est dau of Richard Eaton, MP, of Stetchworth Park, Cambs, and *d* 20 Jan 1912, having had:
(1) John Cecil; Lt 3rd Bn Norfolk Regt; *b* 17 March 1873; *ka* Boer War 18 Feb 1900
(2) Conyers Herbert; Maj RAVC, Boer War 1899–1902 and WW I; *b* 16 April 1876; *d* 20 July 1951
(3) Berkeley Gerald Hylton; Maj Scots Gds, Boer War 1901–02 and WW I; *b* 31 Oct 1878; *m* 23 Jan 1919 Mary Viola (*d* 1984), only dau of Capt John Douglas Maude Guthrie, DL, of Guthrie, Forfarshire, and *d* 13 Feb 1956, leaving:
1a John Neil Hylton; *b* 21 Jan 1923; *m* 26 Oct 1957 *Eileen Mary [Mrs John Jolliffe, Barretts Farm, Corton Denham, Sherborne, Dorset], only dau of Col George Harold Absell Ing, CMG, DSO, DL, of Jerards, Sandford Orcas, Dorset, and *d* 14 Aug 1976, leaving:
1b *Sarah; *b* 6 April 1960; *m* 1981 *Dominic William Michael Nelson, 2nd s of Sir William Vernon Hope Nelson, 3rd Bt (*qv*), and has issue
2b *Lucy [Mrs Samuel Kellie-Smith, 59 Cornwall Gdns, London SW7]; *b* 19 March 1962; *m* 1992 *Samuel Anthony Kellie-Smith (*see* CHAYTOR, Bt)
1a *Cynthia Myra; *b* 20 May 1920
2a *Eileen Daphne Hylton; *b* 15 Nov 1921; *m* 1st 1946 (*divorce* 1955) Arthur Harold Morse and has:
1b *Simon Arthur Davidson; *b* 1952
1b *Lavinia May; *b* 1947
2a (cont.) Mrs Eileen Morse *m* 2nd 1955 *Richard Arthur Edwards and has by him:
2b *Chloë Annabel; *b* 1956; *m* 1985 *Hon Maurice Robson, s of Baroness Robson of Kidlington (*qv*), and has issue
3b *Miranda Bridget; *b* 1961
(1) Julia Gertrude; *m* 2 Aug 1906 Algernon Ughtred Shuttleworth, of Chetwode Grange, Bucks, and *d* 24 Aug 1917, leaving issue
(2) Maud Eleanor; twin with John Cecil; *m* 3 Feb 1910 Lt-Col William Francis George Wyndham, MVO, s of Sir Hugh Wyndham, KCMG, and *d* 2 April 1948, leaving issue
(3) Bertha Alice; *m* 23 June 1900 Capt Edward Bathurst Compton, OBE, RN (*d* 12 March 1943), and *d* 15 Dec 1950, leaving issue
4 Walter Hylton, Cdr RN; *b* 28 June 1844; *m* 20 April 1871 Amy Mary (*d* 17 Nov 1934), 2nd dau of William Watt, and *d* 22 April 1889, leaving:
(1) William Montagu Hylton; *b* 17 April 1872; *d* 4 March 1897
1 Eleanor Amelia; *b* 18 June 1828; *m* 25 Nov 1852, as his 2nd w, 4th Baron de Blaquiere of Ardkill (*dsp* 2 Jan 1871; *see* 1889 edn) and *d* 11 Jan 1894
2 Allada Harriot; *m* 17 Nov 1853 Capt Grenville Granville Wells (*d* 1901), JP, of Holmewood, Hunts, and *d* 3 March 1908, leaving issue
3 Julia Agnes; *m* 22 July 1856, Col Richard Henry Howard Vyse (*d* 12 June 1872), JP, RHG, of Stoke Place, Bucks, and *d* 30 Dec 1862, leaving issue
4 Cecil Emily; *m* 18 July 1866 4th Earl of Sefton and *d* 25 Feb 1899, leaving issue (*see* 1970 edn)
5 Mary Augusta; *m* 18 April 1865 Sir Edward Birkbeck, 1st and last Bt, KCVO, JP, DL (*dsp* 2 Sept 1908), of Horstead Hall, Norfolk, and *d* 26 Sept 1925

The 1st BARON *d* 1 June 1876; his est surv son,

HEDWORTH HYLTON JOLLIFFE, **2nd Baron Hylton of Hylton and of Petersfield**, JP, DL Somerset, JP Sussex, Cornwall, and Surrey; MP Wells 1855–68, Capt 4th Light Dragoons, and Coldstream Gds, served Crimea at Alma and Inkerman and charge Light Bde Balaclava; *b* 23 June 1829; *m* 1st 30 Dec 1858 (*divorce* 1872) Agnes Mary (*d* 7 April 1878), est dau of 2nd Earl of Strafford (*qv*); *m* 2nd 26 April 1879 Anne (*d* 30 Oct 1917), widow of 3rd Earl of Dunraven and Mount-Earl (*qv*) and dau of Henry Lambert, DL, of Carnagh, MP Co Wexford, and by his 1st w had:

1 HYLTON GEORGE HYLTON, **3rd Baron**
1 Mabel; *d* an infant Feb 1861
2 Agatha Eleanor; *b* 18 Oct 1863; *m* 9 Feb 1886 1st Baron Ailwyn, KCVO, KBE, PC, and *d* 9 July 1938, leaving issue (*see* 1970 edn)

The 2nd BARON *d* 31 Oct 1899; his only son,

HYLTON GEORGE HYLTON JOLLIFFE, **3rd Baron Hylton of Hylton and of Petersfield**, JP Somerset; *b* 10 Nov 1862; *educ* Eton and Oriel Coll Oxford (MA 1891); Dip Serv 1888–95, MP (C) Wells 1895–99, Capt N Somerset Yeo, memb Court Bristol U 1909–45, Ld-in-Waiting 1915–18, Capt Yeomen Gd 1918–24, FSA 1908; *m* 29 Aug 1896 Lady Alice Adeliza Hervey (*d* 27 Aug 1962), dau of 3rd Marquess of Bristol (*qv*), and had:

1 WILLIAM GEORGE HERVEY, **4th Baron**
2 Thomas Hedworth; *b* 6 Oct 1900; *d* 14 Sept 1918
1 Mary Lepel; *b* 25 May 1897; *d* 9 Dec 1912
2 *Elizabeth Alice Cecilia; *b* 23 Nov 1906; *m* 1st 16 Oct 1928 (*divorce* 1937) Lt-Col Edmond Joly de Lotbinière, RE (ktd 1964), er son of Brig-Gen Henri Gustave Joly de Lotbinière, DSO, RE, of Brandon Hall, Suffolk, and has issue; *m*

2nd 23 Nov 1938 (*divorce* 1947) W/Cdr Hilary Beecham Duke-Woolley, DFC, ARIBA, RAF, s of Frederick Duke-Wolley, FRCS, of London

The 3rd BARON *d* 26 May 1945; his only surv s,

WILLIAM GEORGE HERVEY JOLLIFFE, **4th Baron Hylton of Hylton and of Petersfield**, JP (Somerset); *b* 2 Dec 1898; *educ* Eton and RMC Sandhurst; Lt-Col Coldstream Gds, served WW I, ADC to Govr-Gen Canada 1921–23, Staff Capt OTC Camps and Adj Eton Coll OTC 1928–30, Bde Maj 142nd (6th Lond) Inf Bde 1931–36, DAQMG Lond Dist 1939–41, AQMG War Office 1942, Cdr Trg Bn Coldstream Gds 1943 WW II, CA Somerset, Ld Lt and custos rotulorum Somerset 1949–67; KStJ; *m* 14 Jan 1931 Lady Perdita Rose Mary Asquith (*d* 17 May 1996), sis of 2nd Earl of Oxford and Asquith (*qv*), and *d* 14 Nov 1967, leaving:

1 RAYMOND HERVEY JOLLIFFE, **5th and present Baron Hylton of Hylton and of Petersfield**

2 +John Hedworth [The Hon John Jolliffe, Church House, Chesterblade, Somerset BA4 4QX]; *b* 27 March 1935; *educ* Eton and Ch Ch Oxford (BA 1957); High Sheriff Somerset 1993, Dir: Constable & Co, Publishers 1968–74, Bain Dawes plc 1979–85, Museums and Galleries Marketing Ltd 1988– and Audiogrove Ltd 1996–; author: *Clive Pearson* (1992), *Glyndebourne, A New History* (1994) and *Duckworth, a History* (1998), ed *Raymond Asquith, life and letters* (1980); *m* 20 Nov 1965 *Hon Victoria Catherine Elizabeth Eden, est dau of 7th Baron Henley (*qv*), and has:

(1) +Hugo Conrad William; *b* 19 Nov 1966; *educ* Eton and LSE

(2) +Robert Francis Raymond; *b* 2 April 1968; *educ* Eton and Bristol U

(3) +Benedict Thomas Aldhelm; *b* 26 Feb 1970; *educ* Eton and Keble Coll Oxford

1 *(Mary) Alice; *b* 1 Nov 1937; *m* 1st 31 Jan 1959 (*divorce* 1969) John Paget Chancellor (*see* PAGET, Bt) and has issue; *m* 2nd 1969, as his 2nd w, Hon Richard Archer Alan Windsor-Clive (*see* PLYMOUTH, E)

HYLTON-FOSTER

Creation: B. (LP, UK) 1965.

THE BARONESS HYLTON-FOSTER, of the City of Westminster (Dame Audrey Pellew Clifton-Brown, DBE (1990)) [The Rt Hon The Baroness Hylton-Foster DBE, The Coach House, Tanhurst, Leith Hill, Surrey RH5 6LU; 54 Cranmer Court, Whiteheads Grove, London SW3 3HW]; *b* 19 May 1908; *educ* St George's Ascot and Ivy House Wimbledon; BRCS: Dir Chelsea Div 1950–60, Pres and Chm London Branch 1960–83, Patron 1984–, Memb Nat Cncl 1966–76, Hon Consultant Nat HQ 1984–86; Pres Research into Blindness Fund 1965–76; Convenor Cross Bench Peers 1974–95; *m* 1931 Rt Hon Sir Harry Braustyn Hylton Hylton-Foster, QC, MP, Speaker H of C 1959–65 (*d* 1965)

Lineage: 1st and last VISCOUNT RUFFSIDE (*see* BROWN, Bt); had:

AUDREY PELLEW, *cr* a **Baroness**

IDDESLEIGH

Arms: Argent three cross-crosslets in bend sable. **Crest:** On a chapeau gules, doubled ermine, a stag trippant argent. **Supporters:** Two stags proper, suspended from the neck of each by a chain or an esutcheon ermine, thereon a pinecone or. **Motto:** *Christi crux est mea lux* ('The Cross of Christ is my light'). **Creations:** Bt. (E) 16 July 1641, E. and V. (UK) 3 July 1885.

THE 4TH EARL OF IDDESLEIGH, Viscount Saint Cyres of Newton Saint Cyres, Co Devon, and a **Baronet** (Sir Stafford Henry Northcote, Bt, DL (Devon 1979)) [The Rt Hon The Earl of Iddesleigh DL, Shillands House, Upton Pyne Hill, Exeter, Devon EX5 5EB]; *b* 14 July 1932; *s f* 1970; *educ* Downside; 2nd Lt Irish Gds 1951–52, dir Devon & Exeter Steeplechases Ltd 1975– (v-chm 1990–), Gemini Radio Ltd 1993– and Orchard Media Ltd 1996–, chm SW SB 1980–83, SW Regnl chm England and Wales TSB 1983–88, dir TSB Gp plc 1986–87, United Dominions Tst Ltd 1983–88 and TV SW plc 1982–92; Kt Honour and Devotion SMO Malta; *m* 20 July 1955 *Maria Luisa (Mima) Alvarez-Builla y Urquijo (Countess del Real Agrado in Spain, *cr* 1771), OBE, DL (Devon 1987), only child of Gonzalo Alvarez-Builla y Alvera and Maria Luisa, widow of 9th Viscount Exmouth (*qv*), and has issue:

1 +JOHN STAFFORD, *Viscount St Cyres* [Viscount St Cyres, Hayne Barton, Newton St Cyres, Devon]; *b* 15 Feb 1957; *educ* Downside and RAC Cirencester; *m* 14 May 1983 *Fiona Caroline Elizabeth, dau of Paul Alan Campbell Wakefield, of Barcelona, and Mrs C A Hattrell, of The Priory Cottage, Burnham, Bucks, and has:

(1) +Thomas Stafford; *b* 1985

(2) *Elizabeth Rose Adèle; *b* 1989

1 *Mary Louise [The Lady Mary Fishwick, Lower Woodrow, Brampford Speke, Devon EX5 5DY]; *b* 14 April 1959; *m* 1981 *Maj Simon Nicholas Fishwick, 13th/18th Roy Hus, yr s of Clifford Fishwick, of Salisbury House, Topsham, Devon, and has had:

(1) *James Nicholas; *b* 1983

(2) Hugh Simon; *b* 1984; *d* 1987

(1) *Lucy Mary; *b* 1988

Lineage: GALFRIDUS, of Northcote, Devon; living 1103; had:

JOHN; presumably f of:

GALFRIDUS de NORTHCOTE; living 1118; held land from the Abbot of Tavistock, also land in Colston, Witheridge Hundred, and had, with a yr s:

WILLIAM de NORTHCOTE; *m* 1190 Margarite, dau of Robert de Afeton, and had, with an est s (Walter) and yst s (Edmund):

ANDREW de NORTHCOTE; *m c* 1289 Matilda, est dau of Peter Faber, of Bovey Tracey, Devon, and had, with two yr sons (Robert; Edmund):

WILLIAM de NORTHCOTE; *m* 1325 Matilda, dau and heir of Robert Hillion, and had, with a yr s:

JOHN de NORTHCOTE; *m* 1343 Johanna, 2nd dau and coheir of Roger Meoles by Avis, sole heir to Sir William le Prouse, and had, with a yr s (Robert):

JOHN de NORTHCOTE; High Sheriff Devon; *m* Margery, sis and heir of Thomas de Bechington and widow of John de Graas, and had:

JOHN NORTHCOTE, of Newton; had:

WALTER NORTHCOTE; had:

JOHN NORTHCOTE; had:

JOHN NORTHCOTE; had:

WALTER NORTHCOTE; gf of:

WALTER NORTHCOTE; had:

JOHN NORTHCOTE, of Crediton; living 1521; *m* Alice, dau of John Durk, and had:

WALTER NORTHCOTE, of Crediton; *m* Elizabeth, dau of Richard Hill, of Shilston, Devon, and had, with two yr sons (Robert *dsp*; Philip, *m* Julian, dau of Tresilian, of Tresilian, Cornwall):

JOHN NORTHCOTE, of Crediton; *m* Elizabeth, dau of Thomas Dowrish, of Dowrish, and had, with five daus:

1 Walter, of Hayne, Newton St Cyres, Devon; *m* Mary, dau and heiress of Edmund Drew, of Hayne, and had:

(1) Elizabeth; *m* 1st George Yard, of Churston; *m* 2nd Rt Rev Barnabas Potter, DD, Bp Carlisle

(2) Mary *m* Sir Edward Giles, of Bowdon

2 John, of Upton, Devon; *m* 1st Elizabeth, dau of Sir Anthony Rouse, of Halston, by Elizabeth, dau and heir of Thomas Southcote, of Bovey Tracey, and had, with 11 other sons and six daus:

(1) **Sir John Northcote, 1st Bt** (E), so *cr* 16 July 1641, of Hayne; Sheriff Devon 1627, MP Ashburton 1640–60, Devon 1654, 1656 and 1660 and Barnstaple 1667–76; *m* Grace, dau and heir of Hugh Halswell, of Halswell, Somerset, and had, with three daus:

1a ARTHUR (Sir), **2nd Bt**

2a John; *m* Catherine Foljambe and had issue

3a Lewis; *m* Jane Coplestone and had issue

4a Haswell; *m* Mary Crook and had issue

5a William; *m* Alice Leigh and had issue

2 (cont.) John Northcote *m* 2nd Susan, dau of Sir Hugh Pollard, of King's Nympton, and *d* Dec 1632, having by her had:

(2) Anthony; *dsp* 1619

Sir JOHN was *bur* 24 June 1676; his est son,

Sir Arthur Northcote, 2nd Bt; *bapt* 25 March 1628; *m* 1st Elizabeth, dau and heir of James Welsh, of Alvardiscott, and had two sons (*dsp* & *vp*) and a dau (*d* unm); *m* 2nd 1650 Elizabeth (*d* 1707), est dau of Sir Francis Godolphin, KB, and sis of Ld High Treasurer Godolphin, and *d* 1688, having by her had issue:

1 **Sir Francis Northcote, 3rd Bt**; *m* 26 July 1688 Anne, dau of Sir Chichester Wrey, 3rd Bt (*qv*), and *dsp* 1709

2 HENRY (Sir), **4th Bt**

3 Charles; *m* his cousin Sarah, dau of John Northcote, and *d* 1721, leaving:

(1) Arthur

(2) Charles

1 Elizabeth; *d* unm

2 Dorothy; *m* in 1685 Andrew Quick

3 Penelope; *m* John Hesket, Lancester Herald

Sir FRANCIS's bro,

Sir Henry Northcote, 4th Bt; MD Oxford; *b* 1655; *m* Penelope, dau and coheir of Robert Lovett, of Liscombe, Bucks, and Corfe, Devon, and *d* Feb 1729/30, having had, with two daus (of whom the yr *d* unm and the er, Elizabeth, *m* 1st 1734 John Incledon, of Braunton, Devon (*d* 28 June 1746), and had issue, *m* 2nd Rev John Wright and was *bur* 1758):

Sir Henry Northcote, 5th Bt, MP Exeter 1735–43; *b* 1710; *m* 16 Aug 1732 Bridget Maria (*m* 2nd 11 Sept 1754 Richard Maddon and *d* 15 Aug 1773), only dau and heiress of Hugh Stafford, of Pynes, Devon, and had issue (among whom those with + against them are in remainder to the btcy only):

1 STAFFORD (Sir), **6th Bt**

2 Henry; *bapt* 8 March 1738; *m* 1st Philippa, dau of Edward Searle, of Plympton, and had issue:

(1) Bridget; *m* Rev David Perkins, DD, Vicar Mamhead, and *d* 9 July 1835, leaving issue

2 (cont.) Henry Northcote *m* 2nd 15 Nov 1777 Sarah, dau of James Tuke, of Doncaster, and by her had:

(1) Stafford; *b* 5 May 1783; *m* 31 May 1810 Sarah, dau of John Beauchamp, and *d* 2 April 1854, leaving issue:

1a Stafford Henry; *b* 16 Sept 1813; *m* 27 Aug 1842 Isabella (*d* 1884), dau of Robert McNeill, and *d* 1889, leaving, with two other sons and two daus:

1b Stafford Charles; *b* 22 Dec 1844; *m* 15 Aug 1871 Rosa Annette (*d* 26 Sept 1906), dau of Henry Wilson, of The Poplars, Herne Hill, and *d* 9 Aug 1903, leaving issue:

1c Stafford Henry; *b* 24 Nov 1872; *m* 1st 29 March 1907 Elizabeth Hélène Louise (*d* 13 Jan 1914), est dau of Robert Philip Heligers; *m* 2nd 23 April 1921 Lucy May, widow of Herbert Laurence Vaughan, of Bournemouth, and *d* 21 April 1950, leaving by his 1st w had:

1d Stafford Charles Robert; dir Chartered Bank; *b* 23 March 1909; *educ* Brighton Coll; *m* 1st 17 May 1947 Helen Isabel (*d* 26 March 1965), dau of Herbert Nelson Hawker, of Christchurch, NZ; *m* 2nd Sheila Mary Northcote,(*d* 1986), widow of Dr Paul H Sandifer, and *d* 1977, having by his 1st w had:

1e +Stafford Robert; *b* 7 Dec 1948; *m* 1969 *Penelope Ann Tracy, dau of (Thomas) Michael Eastham, QC

1e *Helena Ann Stafford [Miss Helena Northcote, 48 Rothsay Rd, Forest Gate, London E7]; *b* 23 May 1951

2d Geoffrey Stafford; *b* 11 Jan 1912; *educ* Brighton Coll and Massey U, NZ; *m* 22 June 1938 Ruth (*m* 2nd 1975 Philip Williamson), dau of Alan McNeill, of Auckland, NZ, and *d* 1968, leaving issue:

1e +Robert Stafford [Prof Robert Northcote, 52 The Dress Circle, Athelstone, SA 5076, Australia]; *b* 9 May 1939; *educ* U of Wellington (MSc 1961) and U of Adelaide (PhD 1964), Emeritus Prof Computer & Info Sci U of S Australia; *m* 27 Dec 1963 *Patricia Margaret, dau of William Arthur Baillie, of Adelaide, Australia, and has:

1f +Roger Stafford [Roger Northcote Esq, 7 Bragg St, Hackett ACT 2602, Canberra, Australia]; *b* 11 Aug 1966; *educ* Australian Nat U (BA, LLB 1991); lawyer, Australian Customs Service, Canberra; *m* 5 Jan 1991 *Ann Lesley, dau of Arthur Taylor, of Crookwell

2f +Bruce Stephen [Dr Bruce Northcote, 61 Stonegate Rd, Chelmsford, MA 01824, USA]; *b* 30 Jan 1969; *educ* U of Adelaide (BSc 1991, PhD 1995); sr performance engr Fujitsu Nexion

1f *Michelle Patricia [Dr Michelle Winn, 14 Acacia St, Mt Barker, SA 5251, Australia]; *b* 28 Jan 1972; *educ* U of Adelaide (MB, BS 1995); medical practitioner; *m* 12 Dec 1992 *Anthony, s of Colin Winn, of Adelaide

2e +Alan McNeill [Alan Northcote Esq, 71 James Cook Dve, Welcome Bay, Tauranga, New Zealand]; *b* 19 Sept 1940; *educ* U of Wellington (BCom); ACANZ, ACIS; *m* 1963 *Mary Vesey, dau of E A Zambra, of Napier, NZ, and has:

1f +Peter Bruce; *b* 1964

2f +Stuart Paul; *b* 1966

1f *Susan Mary; *b* 1967

3e +Geoffrey John [Geoffrey Northcote Esq, 25 Spencer Rd, Mosman, NSW 2088, Australia]; *b* 5 April 1947

1e *Margaret Moralee [Ms Meg Northcote, 17 Alberta St, Pt Chevalier, Auckland 2, New Zealand]; *b* 12 Aug 1950; *m* 1971 (*divorce* 1994) Wallace Donald Thomson and has:

1f *Robert Wallace; *b* 1974

1f *Kathryn Helen;*b* 1977

1d Elizabeth Joy Stafford; *b* 16 Dec 1907; *m* 17 June 1933 (*divorce* 1953) Lt-Col Arthur Neville Browning, Artists Rifles, and had issue

2c Cyril Charles Stafford; Staff WW I 1915–18 (despatches); *b* 22 Sept 1874; *m* 6 Jan 1903 Adela (*d* 31 Oct 1963), dau of Sir William Bowyer-Smith, 11th Bt (*qv*), and *d* 9 Nov 1946, leaving issue:

1d John Wilfred Cyril Stafford; *b* 22 May 1904; *m* 1st 22 July 1933 (*divorce* 1937) Mary Caroline, yr dau of Robert Collier, FRIBA, and had issue:

1e *Jennifer Anne Stafford; *b* 18 Feb 1935; *m* 28 Dec 1955 *John Morley and has had:

1f *Robert; *b* 13 Oct 1956

2f Peter; *b* 20 Oct 1957; *d* 19–

3f *Jasper; *b* 1 Aug 1959

4f Mark James; *b* 29 Oct 1962; *d* 8 Jan 1964

5f *David John; *b* 1 Nov 1964

1f *Amanda Caroline; *b* 20 March 1966

1d (cont.) John Northcote *m* 2nd 22 Aug 1938 Grace, dau of E Carruthers Webb, of Mill Hill, Middx; *m* 3rd 1952 Janet, dau of Ronald Grose, of Manor Rd, Taunton, and *d* 6 Dec 1970, leaving by her:

1e +Martin Charles Stafford [Martin Northcote Esq, 30 Madeley Rd, London W5 2LH]; *b* 1953; *m* 199– *Lucy Patricia, dau of P A Willard, and has issue:

1f +A son; *b* 1992

1f *Nadia Mary (twin); *b* 1992

2e +Nigel John Stafford; *b* 14 Oct 1960

3e +Andrew Alexander Stafford; *b* 14 March 1964

2e *Gillian Stafford; *b* 22 Sept 1954

1d Joan Annette Fechnie Stafford; *b* 24 Sept 1907; *m* 19 May 1951 Robert Steuart-Clark (*d* 24 June 1953)

3c Wilfrid Ernest Stafford; *b* 1875; *d* 1898

4c Leonard Augustus Stafford; Cmdt Police Cyprus, Maj RASC, Maj Res of Offrs (Roy Fus) WW I in Gallipoli, Egypt and Balkans; *b* 1879; *m* 1st 1903 (*divorce* 1914) Lilian Cora, dau of J van Praagh, and had issue:

1d Denis Leonard Stafford; Maj RA; *b* 17 Aug 1904; *educ* Clifton; *m* 1st 1929 Sylvia, dau of Col I Manners Smith, VC, CIE, CVO, IA, and had issue:

1e +Willian John; *b* 1939

1e *Sylvia Alison; *b* 1930

2e *Veronica Phyllis; *b* 1932

1d (cont.) Denis Northcote *m* 2nd 1947 Beatrice Margaret (*d* 1985), dau of Robert Malcolm, of Rawalpindi, India, and *d* 1978, leaving by her:

1e *Jaquetta Stafford [Mrs Michael Philip, Bank House, Hatherton, Nantwich, Cheshire CW5 7PQ]; *b* 1941; *m* 1968 *Michael Robert Philip and has issue:

1f *Nicholas Alexander Michael; *b* 1973; *educ* Wrekin Coll

1f *Olivia Kate; *b* 1975; *educ* W Chester Coll of Art and Aberystwyth U

1d *Iris Blanche Stafford; *b* 1909; fashion ed (as Iris Ashley) *Daily Mail* (ret 1964); *m* 1st 20 June 1928 (*divorce* 19–) Maurice Ashley Brown (*d* 1978); *m* 2nd 1939 (Stanley) John Knowles (*d* 19–); *m* 3rd 1964 His Honour Desmond Harvey Weight Vowden, QC (*d* 1990), and by him has:

1e *Penelope Ann [Mrs Michael Wigram, 2 Clarendon Place, London W2 2NP]; *b* 1937; *m* 1962 *Michael John Wigram, of Madrid, and has:

1f *Lionel Nicholas Richard; *b* 1962; *educ* Eton and BNC Oxford

2f *Benjamin Peter Desmond; *b* 1970; *educ* Emanuel Sch

1f *Sophie Denia; *b* 1964; *educ* St Paul's Girls' Sch and Somerville Coll Oxford

4c (cont.) Leonard Northcote *m* 2nd 1916 Ida (*d* 9 Jan 1978), dau of 5th Marquis Testaferrata-Olivier (*see* Maltese Nobility 1956 edn), and *d* 20 Dec 1942, leaving:

2d +(Henry) James Stafford, WW II with Oxon and Bucks LI and Intell Corps Europe and SEAC, feature film technician; *b* 25 July 1922; *educ* Downside; *m* 5 March 1949 (*divorce* 1961) Sheila, dau of Capt John Manahan, of Dublin

5c Arthur Frederick Stafford, DSO (1920); Maj Devonshire Regt WW I and N Russia with Oxon and Bucks LI (despatches); *b* 1881; *m* 1st 1905 (*divorce* 1930) Constance Fanny (*d* 19–), dau of Col William Henry Salmon, IA; *m* 2nd 1930 Dora (*d* 19 July 1932), dau of Congreve Jackson, OBE, and by her had:

1d Peter Stafford; *b* 10 July; *d* 12 Dec 1932

1d *Annette Stafford [Mrs David Paterson, 365 E Queen's Rd, N Vancouver, BC V7N 1G7, Canada]; *b* 25 April 1931; *m* 1st 8 April 1952 (*divorce* 1970) Harry Alexander McPhee and had:

1e *Roderick Jody; *b* 1965; *m* 1996 *Denise Gaye Fulton

1e *Beverley Eve; *b* 1956; *m* 1990 *John Alexander Dodd and has:

1f *Jordi Michael; *b* 1993

1f *Sarah Elizabeth; *b* 1991

1d (cont.) Mrs Annette McPhee *m* 2nd 1971 David Crichton Paterson (*d* 1993) and by him has:

2f *John Leslie; *b* 1973

5c (cont.) Arthur Northcote *m* 3rd 20 July 1938 Beryl (*d* 1989), dau of Rev W H Weekes, of Devizes, and *d* 1949, having adopted:

*Eve; *b* 1 Aug 1934; *m* Dec 1953 *Maj Colin Dening Carr, MC, RE, and has issue:

1e *Peter Dening; *b* 15 Feb 1955; *educ* Cheltenham

1e *Jane Elizabeth; *b* 3 Dec 1956

2e *Mary Rose; *b* 12 Dec 1962

6c Harold Beauchamp Stafford; *b* 1884; *educ* St John's Coll Oxford (MA); assist master Dulwich Coll, Capt ASC WW I in Mesopotamia and Persia; *d* 1944

1c Gertrude Laura Stafford; *b* 1877; *m* 23 July 1906 Herbert Robert Loraine (*d* 24 Nov 1952), s of Preb Loraine, of Chiswick, and *d* c 1955, having had issue

2b Leonard Beauchamp; *b* 18–; had:

1c Henry Peter; *b* 1891; *m* 1924 Eileen, dau of Edwin Charles Irish, and *d* 1971, leaving:

1d +Edwin Charles Stafford [Edwin Northcote Esq, Alwin, The Green, Jordans, Beaconsfield, Bucks]; *b* 1926; *educ* Blundell's; *m* 1956 (*divorce* 1974) Angela, dau of James Edward Hutton, and has:

1e +Ashley James Stafford; *b* 1959

1e *Belinda Susan; *b* 1965

1d *Anne; *b* 1936; *m* 1959 (*divorce* 1972) Ernst Zumbrunn, of Interlaken, Switzerland, and has issue:

1e *Helene Diana; *b* 1963

2c Frederick Beauchamp; *b* 1893; *m* 1923 Jessie Florence (*d* 1988), dau of William James, and *d* 1937 leaving:

1d Leon Frederick James; *b* 1924; *educ* Swansea GS; WW II with RN 1942–46; *m* 1951 *Valerie May [Mrs Leon Northcote, 29 Orchard Rd, Longlevens, Gloucester], dau of Victor Thomas George Bennett, of Gloucester, and *d* 16 April 1997, leaving:

1e +Richard Leon Stafford; *b* 1952; *m* 1976 *Jeanette May, dau of Thomas Rich, of Upton St Leonards, Glos, and has:

1f +Christopher Thomas Stafford; *b* 1985

1f *Jessica Elizabeth; *b* 1981

1e *Susan Elizabeth [Mrs Peter Dove, 5 Wren Close, Saint Bridge, Gloucester]; *b* 1954; *m* 1st 19– (*divorce* 1979) — and has:

1f *Stewart Richard (adopted by stepf); *b* 1972
2f *David Grahams (adopted by stepf); *b* 1978
1e (cont.) Susan Northcote *m* 2nd 1981 *Peter William Dove and by him has:
3f *James Peter; *b* 1983
3 Hugh (Rev); Rector Upton Pyne; *bapt* 9 March 1740; *m* Elizabeth, dau of Rev George Bradford, and *d* 25 July 1787, leaving, with another s and two daus (*d* unm):
(1) Hugh (Rev); Rector Monk Oakhampton, Devon; *bapt* 26 Jan 1774; *m* 12 April 1804 Anne Lewis (*dsp* 1838), dau of Rev G Southcombe
(1) Catherine Maria; *m* Rev John Pitman
(2) Frances Anne; *m* Rev John Tally
1 Bridget Maria; *m* 11 Dec 1773 William Paynter
Sir HENRY was *bur* 28 May 1743; his est son,
Sir Stafford Northcote, 6th Bt; *bapt* 6 May 1736; *m* 17 Oct 1761 Catherine (*d* Jan 1802), dau of Rev George Bradford, Rector Talaton, and *d* 11 March 1770, having had, with two daus (Catherine Jane, *m* 1782 John Thomas Wright, of Lympstone, and *d* 1844, leaving issue; Maria Anne, *m* Maj George Bradford):
Sir Stafford Henry Northcote, 7th Bt; *b* 6 Oct 1762; *m* 6 May 1791 Jacquetta (*d* 22 Jan 1841), dau of Charles Baring (*see* NORTHBROOK, B), and had:
1 Henry Stafford; *b* 18 March 1792; *m* 1st 13 Nov 1815 Agnes Mary (*d* 9 April 1840), only dau of Thomas Cockburn, HEICS, and had, with another s (*d* young):
(1) STAFFORD HENRY), **1st Earl**
(2) Henry Moubray (Rev), of Temple Hill, E Budleigh; Rector Monk Okehampton, Devon; *b* 10 Sept 1826; *m* 1st 29 April 1851 Georgiana (*d* 10 Feb 1866), est dau of Richard Ford, and had, with two other sons (*d* young):
1a Gordon Stafford; *b* 23 Feb 1852; *m* 1 Nov 1904 Amy (*d* 6 Nov 1933), only surv dau of George Pay, and *d* 1921
2a Richard Cecil Graham; *b* 24 Jan 1858; *d* 8 April 1904
3a Francis Stafford; *b* 17 March 1859; *d* 11 June 1935
4a Moubray Stafford; *b* 22 Oct 1860; *m* 20 Jan 1886 Emily Swanton (*d* 27 Dec 1920), dau of William Dwervyhouse, merchant, of Liverpool, and *d* 8 June 1930
5a James Alfred, MBE 1919; *b* 23 Oct 1861; *m* 6 April 1893 Edith Marion (*d* 4 Jan 1905), only dau of James Dupré Lance, of Horsley Down, Canterbury, NZ, and *d* 5 May 1928, leaving issue:
1b Thomas Francis; 2nd Lt King Edward's Horse and RFC and Gunnery Instr WW I (despatches); *b* 10 April 1894; *m* 9 Sept 1924 Vera Frances, dau of Arthur Hope, of NZ, and *d* 1977 having had:
1c +[Peter Northcote Esq, Highfield, Waiau, North Canterbury, New Zealand]; *b* 30 March 1928; *m* 27 Oct 1957 Geraldine Margaret (*d* 1980), dau of Gerald Murray, and has:
1d +Hugh Stafford; *b* Oct 1960
2d +Michael John; *b* Nov 1962
1d *Margaret Anne; *b* July 1959
2c +George Arthur; *b* 1929; *m* 20 Feb 1960 *Julia Elvira Morton, dau of W Bower Watkins, and has:
1d +Charles Moubray; *b* 1 July 1961; *m* 1984 *Ynez Powers
1d *Cynthia Jane; *b* 19 Dec 1962
2d *Diana Mary; *b* 24 March 1964
1c *Frances Roma; *b* 1931; *m* 22 Sept 1956 *John Endell Wanklyn, s of D E Wanklyn, and has:
1d *David Endell; *b* Oct 1959
1d *Catherine Frances; *b* 28 Nov 1957
2d *Jacquetta; *b* Nov 1958
1b Elizabeth Marion; *b* 23 Aug 1896; *m* 17 Jan 1924 Stuart Cameron Heard and had issue
6a George Russell; MA Oxford, Fell New Coll, barrister; *b* 10 Oct 1863; *m* 27 Aug 1901 Hon Evelyn Maud Walrond, OBE (*d* 20 March 1944), dau of 1st Baron Waleran (*see* 1963 edn), and *d* 9 Dec 1920
1a Alice Mary; *m* 16 Oct 1877 Rev William Sidney Saunders, MA, and *d* 14 Oct 1879, leaving issue
(2) (cont.) The Rev Henry Northcote *m* 2nd 18 Feb 1867 Elinor (*d* 5 May 1924), widow of Rev Frederick Pitman and dau of Hugh Mallet, of Ash Ho, Devon, and *d* 6 Feb 1878, leaving by her:
7a Hugh (Rev); MA NZ U; *b* 2 Nov 1868; *d* 12 Aug 1933
8a Robert Henry (Rev), MC; PhD, RC priest, CF WW I (despatches); *b* 20 Oct 1869; *d* 16 July 1950
9a St John; *b* 9 Nov 1871; *d* unm 10 Oct 1904
10a Andrew Cockburn; *b* 25 Oct 1873; *d* unm 1956
2a Marion Agnes; *d* unm 27 Aug 1969 aged 101
3a Ruth Elinor; *m* 26 Oct 1904 Orme Joynt Morris (*d* 12 April 1934), s of Westcott Mallet Morris, and *d* 23 May 1953
(1) Henrietta; *m* 5 May 1846 Charles Manners Lushington (*d* 1864) and *d* 20 Jan 1900, leaving issue
(2) Cecilia Agnes; *m* 11 Oct 1851 Thomas Bishop (*d* 24 June 1884), MD, FRCP, and had a dau
1 (cont.) Henry Northcote *m* 2nd 6 Jan 1846 Catherine, 2nd dau of Thomas Robbins, and *dvp* 22 Feb 1850
2 Hugh Stafford; Maj 1st Roy Dragoons; *b* 22 Dec 1793; *m* 31 March 1826 Harriet Hope (*d* 14 May 1883), 3rd dau of William Cely Trevilian, of Midelney, Somerset, and *d* 19 Feb 1880, having had, with other issue:
(1) Emily; *m* 1854 Rev Lloyd Sanders (*d* 23 Dec 1898), Rector Whimple, and had issue
(2) Helen Harriette; *m* 7 Nov 1862 Lt-Gen Sir Fiennes Middleton Colvile, KCB (*d* March 1917 aged 84), Col Oxon and Bucks LI, and *d* 24 Feb 1910, leaving issue
(3) Katherine Jane; *m* 1870 James Knighton, barrister, and had issue
3 Stafford Charles (Rev); Rector Upton Pyne; *b* 31 July 1796; *m* 22 April 1830 Elizabeth Helena (*d* 30 March 1883), 3rd dau of Thomas Robbins, and *d* 19 April 1872, leaving, with a dau (*d* unm):
(1) Lewis Stafford; Capt 39th Regt; *b* 23 March 1831; *m* 4 April 1861 Isabella Mary Augusta (*d* 7 Jan 1917), dau of Capt J C R Weguelin, 16th Lancers, and *d* 21 Sept 1882, having had issue:
1a Frank Stafford; *b* 13 Feb 1862; *d* young
2a Cecil Stafford; Capt and Hon Maj 7th Bn Rifle Bde; *b* 1870; *m* 2 Aug 1906 Ida Sybil Mary (*d* 29 Sept 1963), only dau of Capt Joseph Boulderson, 68th Regt, and *d* 15 Feb 1912, having had issue:
1b Lewis Stafford; Capt RA WW II; *b* 2 May 1907; *m* 24 April 1935 Esmé (*d* 1979), only dau of Capt Arthur Robert Seignelay Lyon-Campbell, of Stockhill, Settle, Yorks, and *d* 1977 having had issue:
1c *Sarah Caroline Patricia [Mrs Patrick Sheehan, St Catherine's, East Hendred, Oxon OX12 8JT]; *b* 15 Jan 1936; *m* 22 Dec 1962 *Capt Patrick Timothy Sheehan, CBE, AMBIM, RN, yr s of Lt-Cdr Jeremiah Thomas Sheehan, MBE, RN, of Aldershot, and has:
1d *Timothy Stafford; *b* 3 Oct 1966
1d *Clare Anne; *b* 18 Nov 1963; *m* 1994 *Thomas Richard Glen Downes and has:
1e *Annabel Sarah; *b* 10 April 1996
2d *Joanna Mary; *b* 5 Sept 1965; *m* 1993 *David Charles Carreras, slr
2c *Jaqueta Seignelay; *b* 9 Jan 1937
2b +Cecil Henry Stafford, OBE (1982); *b* posthumously 8 June 1912; *educ* Douai and Queen's Coll Oxford (MA 1937); Kt SMO Malta (1957), served RAEC 1941–42, Headmaster St Bede's Sch, Staffs, memb Stafford RDC 1952 and Parish Cllr, CC Staffs (1958), chm Stafford and Stone C Assoc and Co Records & Shugborough & Co Museum Ctee, Govr King Edward VI GS, Stafford, and C of E Sch, Colwich, Staffs, High Sheriff Staffs 1981; *m* 28 Dec 1936 *Winifreda Iola Marguerite, dau of Frederick de Lobau Williams, and has issue:
1c +Amyas Henry Stafford, JP (Staffs 1969); *b* 25 Nov 1937; *educ* Ampleforth and Ch Ch Oxford (MA); Kt SMO Malta
2c +Hugh Cecil Camden Stafford [Hugh Northcote Esq, Bishton Hall, Wolsey Bridge, Staffs]; *b* 22 Nov 1938; *educ* Ampleforth and Trin Coll Cambridge (MA 1960); Kt SMO Malta; *m* 1974 *Hilary Jane, yr dau of Col R J C Evans TD, DL, of Cage Hill, Stowe-by-Chartley, and has issue:
1d +Charles Walter Hugh; *b* 1977
1d *Arabella Lucy Mary; *b* 1975
2d *Beatrice Eleanor Margaret; *b* 1979
3d *Helena Jane Alice; *b* 1980
4d *Katherine Sybil Ruth; *b* 1983
1c *Julia Marguerite Mary; *b* 17 July 1941; *educ* Assumption Bury St Edmunds and Webber Douglas Sch of Dramatic Art
1b Jaquetta Mary; *b* 3 Nov, *d* 3 Dec 1908
2b Sybil Mary; *b* 7 March 1910; *m* George Hudson (*d* 1980), and *d* 6 May 1990, leaving:
1c *Agnes; *b* 21 Jan 1955
3a Charles Montagu; Ceylon Mtd Inf Boer War 1900 and Lt RFA WW I 1915–16; *b* 1872; *m* and *d* June 1957
4a Ernest Alfred; *b* 1875; *m* 1900 Sarah (*d* 1911), dau of Col Gilbert Dwight Munson, of Ohio, and *d* 1944, having had:
1b +Oliver Stafford [Oliver Northcote Esq, 839 W Orange Grove Ave, Arcadia, CA 91006, USA]; barrister California 1933, Lt-Cdr USNR WW II; *b* 1906; *educ* Stanford U Calif (AB 1929, LLB 1932); memb legal firm Chandler, Wright, Tyler and Ward, of Los Angeles, and American, Californian and Los Angeles Bar Assocs; *m* 1933 *Dorothy Lucille, dau of James Hain, and has:
1c +Philip Stafford [Philip Northcote Esq, 2192 Raquet Hill, Santa Ana, CA 92626, USA]; *b* 1937, *m* 1966 —, dau of Henry Reichert and has:
1d +Kent Stafford; *b* 14 June 1969
1d *Kristin; *b* 26 Oct 1970
2c +Geoffrey Stafford (twin) [Geoffrey Northcote Esq, 305 Calle Paisano, San Clemente, CA 92672, USA]; *b* 1937; *m* 1964 *Sharon Ann, dau of Vachel Conn Foree Jr, and has:
1d +Douglas Stafford; *b* 19 Jan 1971
3c +John Stafford [John Northcote, PO Box 754, Carmel, CA 93921, USA]; *b* 1940; *m* 1966 *Virginia Lee Camden, dau of William Henry Wight, and has issue:
1d +Stafford Oliver; *b* 1975
1b *Katherine; *m* Nov 1935 Dr Carl Rolin, and has issue:
1c *Christopher Ernest [Christopher Rolin Esq, 2993 Haddington Dve, Los Angeles, CA 90069, USA]; *b* 15 Feb 1940; *m* 1994 *Debbie — and has:
1d *Brett; *b* 1977
1d *Whitney; *b* 1975
1c *Sarah Victoria [Mrs Bart Hackley, 3872 Sherwood Place, Sherman Oaks, CA, USA]; *b* 26 Jan 1943; *m* 19– *Bart Hackley
2b Beatrice; *d* 19–
1a Beatrice Mary; *d* unm 23 March 1934
2a Bertha Ima; *d* unm 2 Jan 1951
3a Ida Mary; *d* unm 10 May 1953
4a Sybil Monica; *b* 1872; *m* Dominic Presbiter and *d* Jan 1968
5a Nina Agnes; *d* unm
The 7th Bt *d* 17 March 1851; his gs,
STAFFORD HENRY NORTHCOTE, **1st Earl of Iddesleigh**, so *cr* 3 July 1885, as also VISCOUNT SAINT CYRES OF NEWTON SAINT CYRES, Co Devon (both UK), GCB (1880, CB 1851), PC (1866); *b* 27 Oct 1818; *educ* Eton and Balliol Coll Oxford; Priv Sec to Pres BOT (W E Gladstone) 1843–45, barrister Inner Temple 1847, Legal Sec BOT 1847, MP (I) Dudley 1855–57, Stamford 1858–66 and N Devon 1866–85, Fin Sec Treasury Feb-June 1859, Pres BOT 1866–67, Sec State

India 1867–68, Chllr Exchequer and Leader H of C 1874–80, First Ld Treasury 1885–86, Ld Lt Devon 1886–87, For Sec 1886–87, Ld Rector Edinburgh U 1883; *m* 5 Aug 1843 Cecilia Frances, CI (*d* 17 Jan 1910), sis of 1st Baron Farrer (*see* 1963 edn), and *d* 12 Jan 1887, leaving:

1 WALTER STAFFORD NORTHCOTE, **2nd Earl of Iddesleigh**, CB (1887), JP Devon; Commr, Dep-Chm and Chm Bd Inland Revenue 1877–92; *b* 7 Aug 1845; *m* 23 Sept 1868 Elizabeth Lucy (*d* 17 April 1928), est dau of Sir Harry Stephen Meysey Thompson, 1st Bt (*qv*), and *dspms* 26 May 1927, having had:

(1) Stafford Harry, *Viscount St Cyres*; Sr Student Ch Ch Oxford 1893, MA 1895, DLitt 1914, KJStJ, WW I as Sec and Counsellor Dip Serv; *b* 29 Aug 1869; *m* 9 July 1912 Dorothy, DGStJ (*d* 20 Sept 1936), yst dau of Alfred Morrison (*see* MARGADALE, B), and *dsp* 2 Feb 1926

(1) Rosalind Lucy; *d* unm 31 Dec 1950

(2) Elizabeth Mabel; *m* 6 Jan 1914 Hon Robert Robert Randolph Bruce (*d* 21 Feb 1942), DSc, LLD, of Wilmer, BC, of son of Rev Charles Bruce, of Banff, and *d* 27 Sept 1915

(3) Katharine Cecilia Rachel; *d* young, 21 Oct 1893

2 Sir HENRY STAFFORD NORTHCOTE, 1st and last Bt, and 1st and last BARON NORTHCOTE, of Exeter, Co Devon (both UK), so *cr* 23 Nov 1887 and 20 Jan 1900 respectively, GCMG (1904), GCIE (1900), CB (1880), PC (1909); *b* 18 Nov 1846; *educ* Eton and Merton Coll Oxford (MA); clerk FO 1868–80, MP (C) Exeter 1880–99, Fin Sec to War Office 1885–86, Surveyor-Gen Ordnance 1886–87, Govr Bombay 1900–03, Govr-Gen Australia 1903–08, KJStJ; *m* 2 Oct 1873 Alice, CI, DBE, DGStJ (*d* 1 June 1934), adopted dau of 1st Baron Mount Stephen (*see* 1921 edn), and *dsp* 29 Sept 1911, when his titles expired

3 John Stafford (Rev); Vicar St Andrew's, Westminster, Preb St Paul's, Hon Chaplain to TM QUEEN VICTORIA and EDWARD VII, Fell King's Coll London; *b* 3 Jan 1850; *m* 14 June 1881 Hilda Cardew (*d* 8 Jan 1908), 2nd dau of Very Rev Frederic William Farrar, DD, FRS, Dean Canterbury, and *d* 5 June 1920, leaving:

(1) Edward Stafford; Capt Roy Sussex Regt; *b* 6 Jan 1884; *ka* 3 Sept 1916

(2) Hugh Farrar; Lt IA; *b* 21 Jan 1886; *ka* 28 April 1916

(3) HENRY STAFFORD, **3rd Earl**

(1) Jaquetta, JP Salop; *b* 28 Sept 1882; granted with sisters 3 Nov 1927 rank of earl's daus; *m* 3 Feb 1909 Philip Victor Williams (*d* 10 Feb 1954), of Childs Ercall Hall, Market Drayton, s of Philip Williams, JP, of Hinstock Hall, Salop, and *d* 12 Oct 1962

(2) Mabel Stafford; *b* 20 July 1889; *m* 10 Dec 1913 Sir Arnold Henry Moore Lunn (*d* 2 June 1974), er s of Sir Henry Simpson Lunn, MD, and *d* 4 March 1959, leaving issue

4 Arthur Francis (Rev); MA Oxon, Hon Canon Bury St Edmunds 1922–32, Hon Canon Emeritus 1932; *b* 2 Nov 1852; *m* 1st 28 April 1877 Alice Caroline (*d* 28 May 1878), dau of Edward R Owen, of Oxford, and had:

(1) Frances Mary Alice; *b* 1878; *m* 28 Dec 1899 Charles Richard Jelf (*d* 8 June 1960), 2nd s of Sir Arthur Richard Jelf, QC, and *d* 21 Jan 1960, 1960, leaving issue

4 (cont.) The Rev and Hon Arthur Northcote *m* 2nd 6 April 1880 Mary Arabella (*d* 7 May 1888), yst and only surv child of S Bush Toller, QC, and by her had:

(1) Geoffry Alexander Stafford (Sir), KCMG (1935); MA Oxon, Kenya CS 1904–27, Ch Sec N Rhodesia 1927–30, Colonial Sec Gold Coast 1930–34, Govr and C-in-C Br Guiana 24 July 1934–37 and Hong Kong 1937–41, Pncpl Info Offr E African Command 1942–47, first Speaker E African Legislative Assembly April 1948, KStJ; *b* 9 Feb 1881; *m* 27 Oct 1910 Edith Juliet Mary (*d* 28 Feb 1958), only dau of Rev James Williams Adams, VC, by Alice Mary, dau of Sir Thomas Willshire, 1st Bt (*see* 1940 edn), and *d* 10 July 1948, having had:

1a +Maxwell Adams Stafford [Maxwell Northcote Esq, PO Box 827, Nairobi, Kenya]; RAF WW II 1942–46, Hon Sec Dimbula Planters Assoc 1951 and 1952; *b* 22 Nov 1911; *educ* King's Canterbury and Balliol Coll Oxford (BA); *m* 17 June 1958 *Katharine, yst dau of Charles Campbell Sheild, of NZ

2a Arthur Geoffry Stafford; *b* 30 March 1913; *d* unm 30 Sept 1962

3a Amyas Henry Stafford, MC; Maj S Lancs Regt, Lt Prince of Wales's Vols, WW II; *b* 13 Feb 1916; *m* 6 June 1941 Mollie Gordon Buchanan (*m* 2nd 17 May 1947 Anthony Russell Smallwood, er s of Maj-Gen Gerald Russel Smallwood, CB, DSO, MN, and had further issue), yr dau of Maj Gordon Buchanan Scott, and was *ka* Burma 6 March 1944, leaving:

1b *Sylvia Rosalind Stafford [Mrs Anthony Doulton, 41 Hans Place, London SW1]; *b* 5 June 1942; *m* 4 Oct 1968 *Antony Cokayne Doulton (*see* CULLEN OF ASHBOURNE, B) and has issue

(2) Dorothea Mary; *b* 5 May 1882; *m* 4 May 1914 Bryan Hook (*d* 14 March 1925), s of JC Hook, RA and *d* 13 Sept 1964, leaving three sons

(3) Beatrix Edyth; *b* 29 Nov 1884; *m* 1 Jan 1908 Percival Inglis Farrer (*d* 5 Feb 1949), s of Frederick Willis Farrer, and *d* 12 Sept 1940, leaving issue

(4) Hester Selina Mary; *b* 29 April 1888

4 (cont.) The Rev and Hon Arthur Northcote *m* 3rd 14 June 1892 Emily Catherine (*d* 8 Nov 1931), est dau of Col Samuel Blomefield Kekewich, 5th Northumberland Fus, of Tiverton, and *d* 30 Aug 1943, having by her had:

(5) Evelyn Olivia Stafford; *b* 4 April 1893; *m* 27 Feb 1938 Ronald Frederick Green, s of William Green, of Monks Eleigh, Ipswich

5 Hugh Oliver; *b* 13 Nov 1854; *m* 6 June 1883 Edith Livingston (*d* 20 Dec 1887), yst dau of Hon Hamilton Fish, of New York, and *d* 30 March 1900, leaving:

(1) Hugh Hamilton Stafford, of Chyngton Grange, Seaford; *b* 10 Dec 1887; *educ* Balliol Coll Oxford (BA); *m* 28 Feb 1925 Josephine (*d* 12 Jan 1928), yr dau of Thomas O'Shaughnessy, of Killacolla, Glin, Co Limerick, and *d* 29 Jan 1929, leaving:

1a *Mary Edith [Miss Mary Northcote, 29 Thackeray Court, Elystan Place, London SW3 3LB]; *b* 14 April 1926

(1) Cicely Julia Monica; *b* 4 May 1885; *d* unm 20 April 1904

6 Edward Louis; *b* 25 Aug 1857; *d* 3 Oct 1872

7 Amyas Stafford, JP (Bucks); *b* 25 Oct 1864; *m* 14 May 1890 Helen May (*d* 20 Nov 1936), est dau of James Garrard Dudley, of Kentucky, and *d* 11 May 1923, leaving:

(1) Dudley Stafford (Rev); Vicar St Luke's Bermondsey 1928–46, Rector Upton Pyne 1946, WW I with Oxon and Bucks LI, Relief Offr Ld Mayor's Fund Soviet Armenia 1920–25; *b* 28 April 1891; *educ* Winchester and Trin Coll Cambridge; *d* unm 28 May 1955

(1) Cecilia Helen, *d* unm 1 Aug 1977

1 Agnes Mary Cecilia; *m* 17 April 1877 Sir Reginald MacLeod of MacLeod, KCB (*d* 20 Aug 1935), and *d* 26 Oct 1921, leaving issue

2 Mabel; *d* 1851

3 Margaret Stafford; *m* 1 June 1882 Frederick Shelley, 2nd s of Rev Sir Frederick Shelley, 8th Bt (*qv*), and *d* 20 July 1947, leaving issue

The 2nd EARL's n,

HENRY STAFFORD NORTCOTE, **3rd Earl of Iddesleigh**; *b* 19 Nov 1901; *educ* Rugby and Magdalen Coll Oxford (BA 1923, MA 1927); Maj Welsh Gds WW II, dir General Life Assur; *m* 14 May 1930 Elizabeth Susan Angela Mary, JP (Devon 1951) (*d* 1991), er dau of Frederic Sawrey Archibald Lowndes, and *d* 16 Feb 1970, having had:

1 STAFFORD HENRY NORTHCOTE, **4th and present Earl of Iddesleigh**

2 +Edward Frederic [The Hon Edward Northcote, Flat 38, Westmore Court, Carlton Drive, London SW15 2BU]; Pncpl Treasury 1969–71, FSS, Maj Intell Corps (TAVR), served with Devon Regt 1955–56 and Intell Corps (Cyprus) 1956–57; *b* 29 July 1934; *educ* Downside and Trin Coll Oxford (BA 1956, MA 1961, ACWA 1961); *m* 29 June 1963 (*divorce* 1980) Vivien Sheena Hornby (*see* BRUCE, Bt, of Stenhouse) and has:

(1) +(Edward) Bede Robert Hornby; *b* 17 Aug 1964; *educ* Wimbledon Coll

(2) +(Alexander) Benet Paul Hornby; *b* 26 Jan 1971

(1) *Modwenna Vivien Hornby; *b* 29 July 1968; *m* 4 May 1996 *Hon Thomas Rees-Mogg and has issue (*see* REES-MOGG, B)

1 *Catherine Cecilia Mary; *b* 1931; Religious Order of Assumption; teacher and author

2 Hilda Susan Mary; *b* 23 July 1937; Dame Honour and Devotion SMO Malta; *m* 28 Dec 1957 *Sir Conrad Marshall John Fisher Swan, KCVO, PhD, MA, Garter King of Arms 1992–95, Kt SMO Malta [Sir Conrad Swan KCVO, Boxford House, Boxford, Suffolk CO10 5JT], 2nd s of Henry Peter Swan, MD, CM, LMCC, DRCOG, of Colchester, and was *k* 5 Dec 1995 in a road accident, leaving:

(1) *Andrew Conrad Henry Joseph [Andrew Swan Esq, Silverleigh House, Church Hill, Burstall, Ipswich, Suffolk IP8 3DU]; *b* 29 Jan 1964; *educ* Downside and Liverpool U (BSc); ACA, Kt SMO Malta; *m* 1989 *Fenella Jane, yr dau of ACM Sir John Rogers, KCB, CBE, and has:

1a *Isabelle Francis Anne; *b* 1992

2a *Amelia Mary Elizabeth; *b* 9 May 1994

3a *Alexandra Hilda Catherine; *b* 15 July 1996

(1) *(Mary) Elizabeth Magdalen [Mrs Roger Herring, Belchamps House, Hartest, Suffolk IP29 4DS]; *b* 5 Aug 1959; SRN, RM; *m* 1981 *Roger Peter Le Strange Herring, er s of Col P W Le Strange Herring, OBE, and has:

1a *John Roger Le Strange; *b* 1987

2a *Thomas Peter Le Strange; *b* 1990

3a *Rafe Henry Le Strange; *b* 1991

1a *Alice Elizabeth Le Strange; *b* 1985

(2) *(Hilda) Juliana Mary [Mrs Patrick Galvin, Longwood House, Nayland, Suffolk CO6 4JD]; *b* 16 July 1961; *m* 1982 *Patrick D T Galvin, yr twin s of Maj T D Galvin, of Nayland, and has:

1a *Thomas Paul Conrad; *b* 1984

2a *Edward Andrew Henry; *b* 1985

3a *Nicholas Patrick William; *b* 1986

4a *Alexander James Stafford; *b* 1988

5a *Frederick Mark David; *b* 1990

1a *Elizabeth Anna Mary; *b* 1982

(3) *Catherine Sylveria Mary [Mrs Jeremy Walters, The Old Rectory, Monks Eleigh Suffolk IP7 7JL]; *b* 20 Oct 1962; *m* 1986 *(John) Jeremy Walters, s of Capt Greaves Walters, DSC, RN, and has:

1a *Alfred Hugh Charles; *b* 1987

2a *Francis Henry Conrad; *b* 1991

1a *Eleanor Hilda Mary; *b* 1989

(4) *Anastasia Cecilia Mary [Mrs Peter Hatvany, 33 High St, Rode, Bath BA3 6PA]; *b* 26 July 1966; RN; *m* 1989 *Peter Galbraith Mark Hatvany, est s of Paul Imre Hatvany (Baron Hatvany de Hatvan), and has:

1a *Alexander Imre; *b* 1991

2a *Benedict Xavier; *b* 22 July 1994

1a *Alicia Mary; *b* 1993

ILCHESTER

Arms: Quarterly, 1st and 4th, sable two lions passant paly of six argent and gules (for STRANGWAYS); 2nd and 3rd, ermine on a chevron azure three fox heads erased or, on a canton of the second a fleur-de-lys of the third (for FOX). (The canton with the fleur-de-lys, a royal device, was granted Sir Stephen Fox, f of the 1st Earl, by CHARLES II in 1658 as an honourable augmentation for his services during the Interregnum.) **Crest:** On a chapeau azure doubled ermine a fox sejant or. **Supporters:** Dexter, a fox ermine, fretty or, collared dovetail azure, charged with three fleur-de-lys of the second; sinister, a fox proper, collared as the dexter. **Motto:** *Faire sans dire* ('Deeds not words'). **Creations:** B. (GB) 11 May 1741 (Ilchester, Woodford Strangways) and (GB) 12 Jan 1747 (Ilchester and Stavordale, Redlynch), E. (GB) 17 June 1756.

THE 9TH EARL OF ILCHESTER, Lord Ilchester, Co Somerset, **Baron of Woodford Strangways**, Co Dorset, and **Lord Ilchester and Stavordale, Baron of Redlynch**, Co Somerset (Maurice Vivian De Touffreville Fox-Strangways) [The Rt Hon The Earl of Ilchester, Farley Mill, Westerham, Kent TN16 1UB]; *b* 1 April 1920; *s* f 1970; *educ* Kingsbridge GS; G/Capt RAF WW II India, Staff and Air Min 1946–68, seconded Min Technology 1969, CEng, MRAeS, FINucE (Pres 1982–84), FIMgt, Hon FSE, Hon FCP, FRSA, AMBIM, MSE, Fell Br Interplanetary Soc, Pres RAF Assoc SE Area; *m* 29 Nov 1941 *Diana Mary Elizabeth, est dau of George Frederick Simpson, of Cassington, Oxon

Lineage: WILLIAM FOX, of Farley, Wilts, allegedly a footman (the source for this statement, however, is the 1st Earl of Egmont's diary, written in the mid–18th century, *i.e.*, over well over 100 years later); *m* Elizabeth, dau of Thomas Pavey, of Plaitford, Wilts, and had a yst s:

Sir STEPHEN FOX, PC, of Farley and Chiswick; *b* 27 March 1627; managed CHARLES II's household while latter in exile from 1654, being particularly adept at finding money for its upkeep; was after the Restoration nominated Clerk of the Bd of Green Cloth; Paymaster-Gen Forces 1661–80, MP Salisbury 1661, 1685 and March 1713/4, Westminster Feb 1678/9, 1691 and 1695 and Cricklade Jan 1698/9, ktd 1665, a Ld Cmmr of Treasury 1679, a fndr Roy Hosp Chelsea 1681, offered a peerage by JAMES II 1685 if he converted to Rome; *m* 1st c 1654 Elizabeth (*d* 11 Aug 1696), dau of William Whittle, of Lancs, and had (with another six sons and a dau):

1 Charles (so-called after his godfather CHARLES II); MP Salisbury, Paymaster Forces; *m* 1679 Elizabeth Carr (*d* March 1703), dau and heiress of Sir William Trollope, 2nd Bt (*qv*), and *dsp* Sept 1713

1 Elizabeth; *m* 27 Dec 1673, as his 1st w, 3rd Baron Cornwallis of Eye (*see* CORNWALLIS, B) and *d* 28 Feb 1680/1, having had issue

2 Jane; *m* 9 May 1686, as his 1st w, 4th Earl of Northampton (*see* NORTHAMPTON, M) and *d* 11 July 1721, leaving issue

Sir STEPHEN *m* 2nd 11 July 1703 Christian (*d* 17 Feb 1718/9), dau by Christian Palfreyman of Rev Francis Hopes, Rector Haceby later Aswarby, Lincs, and *d* 28 Oct 1716, having had by her:

2 STEPHEN, **1st Earl**

3 HENRY FOX, 1st BARON HOLLAND OF FOXLEY, Co Wilts (GB), so *cr* 17 April 1763, PC (1746); *b* 28 Sept 1705; *educ* Eton and Ch Ch Oxford; MP (Whig) Hindon 1735–41, Windsor 1741–61 and (Court Party) Dunwich 1761–63, Surveyor Gen Works 1737–43, a Ld Treasury 1743–46, Sec War 1746–55, Sec State South, memb Cabinet and Ldr H of C 1755–56, Paymaster Gen 1757–65 and Ldr H of C 1762–63, Clerk of the Pells (I) for his and his two sons. lifetime 1762; *m* 1st Feb 1732/3 Penelope, dau of John Dyne (Maid of Honour Feb 1724/5; *dsp* by 1744); *m* 2nd 2 May 1744 Lady Georgiana Caroline Lennox (*b* 27 March 1723; *cr* 3 May 1762 LADY HOLLAND, BARONESS OF HOLLAND (GB) with remainder to her heirs male by her husb; *d* 24 July 1744), dau of 2nd Duke of Richmond (*see* RICHMOND and GORDON, D), and *d* 1 July 1774, having had, with other issue:

(1) STEPHEN FOX, 2nd BARON HOLLAND OF FOXLEY and 2nd LORD HOLLAND, BARON OF HOLLAND; *b* 20 Feb 1745; *educ* Eton; *m* 20 April 1766 Lady Mary FitzPatrick, dau of 1st Earl of Upper Ossory, and *d* 26 Dec 1774, leaving:

1a HENRY RICHARD FOX later VASSALL FOX, 3rd BARON HOLLAND OF FOXLEY and 3rd LORD HOLLAND, BARON OF HOLLAND, PC (1806); *b* 21 Nov 1773; *educ* Eton and Ch Ch Oxford; Ld Privy Seal 1806–07, Chllr Duchy Lancaster 1830–34 and 1835–40; *m* 6 July 1797 Elizabeth, divorced (because of her adultery with Lord Holland) w of Sir Godfrey Webster, 4th Bt, and dau and heiress of Richard Vassall, of Jamaica (through which connection Lord Holland added the name VASSALL by roy licence 18 June 1800 under terms of the will of Richard Vassall's f Florentius, drawn up 1777), and *d* 22 Oct 1840, having had, with other issue (including an illegitimate s by his w when she was still Lady Webster: Gen Charles Richard Fox; archaeologist, *m* Lady Mary FitzClarence, *see* MUNSTER, E):

1b HENRY EDWARD FOX, 4th and last BARON HOLLAND OF FOXLEY and LORD HOLLAND, BARON OF HOLLAND; *b* 7 March 1802; *educ* Ch Ch Oxford; MP (Whig) Horsham 1826–27, Dip Serv 1831, Sec Legn Turin 1832–35, Attaché St Petersburg, Sec Embassy Vienna 1835–38, German Confedn 1838, Florence 1839–46; *m* 9 May 1833 Lady Mary Augusta Coventry, dau of 8th Earl of Coventry (*qv*), and *dsps* 18 Dec 1859, when his Baronies expired, having adopted a dau (possibly his illegitimate issue):

(1c) Mary; *b* 21 Dec 1850; *m* 27 June 1852 HSH PRINCE ALOIS(E) OF LIECHTENSTEIN and *d* 26 Dec 1878, leaving issue

1b Mary Elizabeth; *m* 22 May 1830 3rd Baron Lilford and had issue (*qv*)

1a Caroline; *d* 12 March 1845

(2) Charles James, the celebrated orator and Parliamentarian, PC to 1798; *b* 13 Jan 1748/9; *educ* Eton and Hertford Coll Oxford; MP Midhurst 1768, Westminster 1780–1806, a Ld Admlty 1770–72, Jr Ld Treasury 1772–74, For Sec March-July 1782, April-Dec 1783 and Feb-Sept 1806, author: *Histoy of the Early Part of the Reign of James II* (1808); *m* 28 Sept 1795 Elizabeth Bridget Cane *aka* Armistead (*d* 8 July 1842 aged 92) and *dsps* (his deaf mute illegitimate s *d* aged 15) 13 Sept 1806

(1) Louisa Amelia; *m* 4 April 1807, as his 1st w, Sir Edward Bunbury, 7th Bt (*qv*), and *d* 1828, having had issue

(2) Caroline; *m* Lt-Gen Sir William Napier, KCB (*see* NAPIER and ETTRICK, L) and *d* 26 March 1860

3 Christian (twin with HENRY); *d* unm

4 Charlotte; *m* 5 July 1729 Edward (*d* 2 Oct 1746), 3rd s of 5th Baron Digby (*qv*), and *d* Nov 1778, leaving issue

Sir STEPHEN's est s by his 2nd w,

STEPHEN FOX later FOX STRANGWAYS (added 2nd name Feb 1758 on his mother-in-law's death), **1st Earl of Ilchester**, so *cr* 17 June 1756, as also earlier 11 May 1741 LORD ILCHESTER, Co Somerset, BARON OF WOODFORD STRANGWAYS, Co Dorset, and 12 Jan 1746/7 LORD ILCHESTER AND STAVORDALE, BARON OF REDLYNCH, Co Somerset (all GB), all with remainder, in default of his own male issue, to the heirs male of his bro Henry, PC (1763); *b* 12 Sept 1704; *educ* Eton and Ch Ch Oxford; MP (Whig) Shaftesbury 1726–34 and 1735–41 and Hindon 1734–35, Jt Sec Treasury 1739–41; *m* 15 March 1735/6 Elizabeth, sis and heiress of Thomas Strangways formerly Horner, of Melbury Sampford, Dorset (*see* ESSEX, E, for earlier ancestry), and only dau of Thomas Strangways-Horner, of Mells Park, Somerset, by Susanna, dau and coheiress of Thomas Strangways, and *d* 29 Sept 1776, leaving:

1 HENRY THOMAS FOX later FOX-STRANGWAYS, **2nd Earl of Ilchester**; *b* 10 Aug 1747; *educ* Eton and Ch Ch Oxford; MP (Whig) Midhurst 1768–74, Capt 24th Foot 1771; *m* 1st 26 Aug 1772 Mary Theresa (*d* 14 June 1790), dau of Standish O'Grady, of Cappercullen, Co Limerick, and had:

(1) HENRY STEPHEN FOX-STRANGWAYS, **3rd Earl of Ilchester**, PC (1837); *b* 21 Feb 1787; *educ* Ch Ch Oxford; Capt Yeomen Gd 1835–41, Ld Lt Somerset 1837–39; *m* 16 June 1812 Caroline Leonora (*d* 8 Jan 1819), dau of Rt Rev Lord George Murray (*see* ATHOLL, D), and *d* 3 Jan 1858, having had:

1a Henry Thomas Leopold, *Lord Stavordale*; *b* 7 Jan 1816; *d* unm 11 Aug 1837

2a Stephen, *Lord Stavordale*; *b* 21 March 1817; *d* unm 25 May 1848

1a Theresa Anna Maria; *m* 20 June 1837 9th Baron Digby (*qv*) and *d* 2 May 1874

2a Caroline Margaret; *m* 23 July 1844 Sir Edward Clarence Kerrison, 2nd and last Bt (*d* 11 July 1886), and *d* 26 Jan 1895

(1) Elizabeth Theresa; *m* 1st 17 April 1796 William Davenport-Talbot, of Lacock Abbey, Wilts; *m* 2nd 24 April 1804 R-Adml Charles Feilding (*see* DENBIGH and DESMOND, E) and *d* March 1844

(2) Mary Lucy; *m* 1st Feb 1794 Thomas Mansel Talbot, of Margam; *m* 2nd 28 April 1815 Sir Christopher Cole, KCB (*d* 1836), Capt RN, Col Marines, and *d* 3 Feb 1855

(3) Harriot; *m* 1799 James Frampton (*d* 8 Feb 1855), of Moreton, Dorset, and *d* 6 Aug 1844, leaving issue

(4) Charlotte Anne; *m* Sir Charles Lemon, 2nd and last Bt (*d* 12 Feb 1868), of Carclew, Cornwall, and *dsp* 1826

(5) Louisa Emma; *m* 3rd Marquess of Lansdowne (*qv*)

1 (cont.) The **2nd Earl** *m* 2nd 28 Aug 1794 Maria (*d* 23 Sept 1842), dau of Very Rev Hon William Digby (*see* DIGBY, B), and *d* 5 Sept 1802, leaving by her:

(2) WILLIAM THOMAS HORNER FOX-STRANGWAYS, **4th Earl of Ilchester**; *b* 7 May 1795; *educ* Westminster and Ch Ch Oxford; Attaché St Petersburg 1819, Constantinople 1820, Naples 1822, The Hague 1824, Sec Legn Florence 1825–28, Naples 1828–32, Sec Emb Vienna 1832–35, U-Sec FO 1835–40, Min Frankfurt 1840–49; *m* 21 July 1857 Sophia Penelope (*m* 2nd 19 Jan 1867 1st Baron Hylton (*qv*); *d* 27 Aug 1882), 2nd dau of Sir Robert Sheffield, 4th Bt (*qv*), and *dsp* 10 Jan 1865

(3) Giles Digby Robert; *b* 26 May 1798; *d* 12 Feb 1827

(4) John George Charles, of Brickworth House, Wilts; FO, MP Calne, Gentleman Usher to QUEEN ADELAIDE; *b* 6 Feb 1803, *m* 19 Feb 1844 Amelia (*d* 9 Sept 1886), 3rd dau of Edward Majoribanks, and *d* 8 Sept 1859, leaving:

1a HENRY EDWARD FOX-STRANGWAYS, **5th Earl of Ilchester**, PC (1874); *b* 13 Sept 1847; *educ* Eton and Ch Ch Oxford; Capt Gentlemen at Arms Jan-Feb 1874, Ld Lt Dorset 1895–1905, Capt Dorset Yeo Cav; *m* 8 Feb 1872 Lady Mary Eleanor Anne Dawson (*d* 25 Oct 1935), only dau of 1st Earl of Dartrey, KP (*see* 1933 edn), and *d* 6 Dec 1905, leaving:

1b GILES STEPHEN HOLLAND FOX-STRANGWAYS, **6th Earl of Ilchester**, GBE (1950, OBE 1919), DL (Dorset to 1956); *b* 31 May 1874; *educ* Eton and Ch Ch Oxford; Capt Coldstream Gds, GSO(3) 1914 (Legn Hon); Hon DLitt, FSA, Tstee Nat Portrait Gallery 1922–59 (Chm 1941–59) and Br Museum 1931–59, Memb Roy Commn Historical Monuments 1939–59 (Chm 1943–59), Pres London Library 1940–52, Roy Lit Fund 1941–51 and Roxburghe Club 1940, Steward Jockey Club 1937–40; *m* 25 Jan 1902 Lady Helen Mary Theresa Vane-Tempest-Stewart (*d* 14 Jan 1956), dau of 6th Marquess of Londonderry (*qv*), and *d* 29 Oct 1959, having had:

1c (EDWARD) HENRY (HARRY) CHARLES JAMES FOX-STRANGWAYS, **7th Earl of Ilchester**, DL (Dorset 1957); *b* 1 Oct 1905; *educ* Eton and Ch Ch Oxford; Capt Res of Offrs RHG (Blues); *m* 27 April 1931 Helen (Nell) Elizabeth (*d* 1970), twin dau of Capt Hon Cyril Augustus Ward, MVO, RN (*see* DUDLEY, E), and *dspms* 21 Aug 1964, having had:

1d Giles Henry Holland; *b* 7 May 1934; *d* as the result of an accident 2 Sept 1947

2d (Charles) Stephen; *b* 6 May 1938; *educ* Eton; 2nd Lt RHG (Blues); *kas* Cyprus 8 July 1958

1d Teresa Jane; *b* 12 Aug 1932; *m* 1st 4 Nov 1953 9th Viscount Galway (*d* 1971) and had issue; *m* 2nd 1972 Mark Agnew and *d* 1989

2c John Denzil; *b* 21 March 1908; *educ* Eton and Ch Ch Oxford (BA 1929), Lt Coldstream Gds WW II (wounded, POW); *d* unm 28 June 1961

1c Mary Theresa; Woman of Bedchamber to HM THE QUEEN (then HRH PRINCESS ELIZABETH) 1944–48, Kaisar-i-Hind Gold Medal; *b* 23 Jan 1903; *m* 11 June 1924 Col Sir John Arthur Herbert, GCIE, DL (*d* 11 Dec 1943), of Llanover, Abergavenny, Mon, s of Sir Arthur Herbert, GCVO, of Coldbrook, Abergavenny, and *d* 26 Jan 1948, leaving issue

2c (Mabel) Edith; *b* 17 Feb 1918; Pres Northants Red Cross and Jt Ctee Red Cross and St John's Ambulance Bde Northants 1943–69, Pres Guernsey Red Cross 1982–84, memb Dendrology Soc; *m* 22 Nov 1938 2nd Viscount Wimborne (*qv*) and had issue

2b Denzil Vasey; *b* 26 Feb 1879; *d* unm 7 March 1901

1b Muriel Augusta; *b* 23 Nov 1876; *m* 5 Aug 1903 George Hugh Digby (*see* DIGBY, B) and *d* 7 Jan 1920

1a Maria Georgiana Julia; granted rank of earl's dau; *m* 4 April 1872 2nd Viscount Bridport (*qv*) and *d* 12 Oct 1922, leaving issue

2 Stephen Strangways Digby; *b* 3 Dec 1751; Lt-Col; *d* 12 March 1836

3 Charles Redlynch (Rev); Rector Rewe, Devon; *b* 27 April 1761; *m* 2 Aug 1787 Jane (*d* 8 June 1830), dau of Rev Dr Haines, and *d* 4 Nov 1836, having had:

(1) Charles; *b* 25 Dec 1789; Capt RN; *d* unm 1835

(2) Thomas; *b* 28 Dec 1790; Brig-Gen RA Crimea; *m* 20 July 1833 Sophia Eliza (granted rank of KCB's widow) and *d* 19 March 1870, est dau of Benjamin Harenc, of Foots Cray, and was *ka* Inkerman 5 Nov 1854, leaving:

1a Sophia Maria; *m* 28 April 1864 Rev Christian Frederick Newell, Rector Chiselborough, Somerset, and *dsp* 18 Jan 1900

(3) Henry (Rev); *b* 25 Feb 1793; Rector Rewe; *m* 26 June 1827 Hester Eleanor (*d* 31 Jan 1865), 7th dau of James Buller, of Shillingham and Downes, and *d* 25 Feb 1860, leaving:

1a Henry (Rev); *b* 3 May 1828; MA; Rector Silverton, Devon; *m* 15 April 1857 Charlotte Chester (*d* 3 July 1909), est dau of Francis Copleston, Madras CS, and *d* 23 Sept 1894, leaving:

1b Theodore Stephen; *b* 4 July 1862; Maj Roy Irish Rifles, Staff Capt Egypt, DAAG Boer War 1899–1900; *m* 21 April 1898 Rosamond Cleere (*d* 30 March 1958), dau of Charles Edmund Newton, of Miekleover Manor, Derbys, and *d* 19 March 1917, leaving:

1c Pamela Mary; *b* 13 Dec 1907

2b Herbert William; *b* 3 Dec 1863; *d* 1 Oct 1876

3b Francis Copleston; *b* 14 May 1870; *educ* Keble Coll Oxford (BA); *d* unm 21 March 1945

4b Henry Wentworth; *b* 1 Oct 1871; *d* 18 Feb 1935

5b Henry George (Rev); *b* 13 June 1873; Rector Kilmington, Somerset; *m* 15 Sept 1903 Isabella Mary (*d* 11 May 1937), 2nd dau of William Macartney Read, of Stockwell, Silverton, and *dsp* 11 Dec 1944

1b Alice Laura; *m* 17 Aug 1890 Albert W Searley, of Newton Abbot, and *d* 16 April 1932, leaving issue

2b Eveline Charlotte; *m* 2 Jan 1890 Rt Rev Ernest Arthur Copleston (*d* 24 Aug 1933), Bp Colombo, and *d* 26 Nov 1928

3b Margaret Christina; *d* unm 16 May 1951

4b Henrietta Frances; *d* unm 29 Jan 1930

2a Walter Aston; *b* 14 Dec 1832; Col RA, Chev Legn Hon; *m* 19 Aug 1858 Harriet Elizabeth (*d* 13 April 1903), 2nd dau of John Edward Buller, of Chase Lodge, Enfield, and *d* 26 Feb 1885, leaving:

1b Arthur Henry; *b* 14 Sept 1859; *educ* Wellington, Balliol Coll Oxford (BA and MA 1886) and Berlin; music critic *The Observer* 1925–39, fndr ed *Music and Letters* 1920–37, later translated Brahms, Strauss, Wolf and Liszt songs, assist master Wellington; *d* unm 2 May 1948

2b Maurice Walter, CSI; ICS, Fin Commr Centl Provinces and Behar 1908–13; *b* 23 March 1862; *m* 29 Dec 1886 Louisa Blanche (*d* 9 April 1940), dau of Maj-Gen George R Phillips, IA, and *d* 27 May 1938, leaving:

1c WALTER ANGELO, **8th Earl**

2c Vivian, CBE (1953); QVO Corp of Guides and Overseas CS, served WW I (despatches), and WW II (US Legion Merit 1944); *b* 29 July 1898; *educ* Winchester; *m* 1st 17 May 1927 (*divorce* 1932) Rona Heathcote, yst dau of A H Plummer, of Taunton; *m* 2nd 13 June 1934 Dorothy Margaret Sinker, yst dau of Rev William Edward Bannerman, of Levens, Westmorland, and *d* 21 Nov 1974

1c Sylvia; *b* 1890

2c Elinor; *b* 1893

3b Harold Stephen; Lt-Col IA, Dep Commr Punjab; *b* 24 Nov 1864; *m* 24 Nov 1891 Beatrice (*d* 12 Oct 1939), dau of Maj-Gen William Howey, Bengal Inf, and *d* 8 July 1912, having had:

1c Dorothy Kate; *b* 27 Aug 1892; *m* 5 Nov 1914 Maj Ernest Gardiner Collings, IA (*d* 5 Sept 1938), s of Dr Charles d'Auvergne Collings, of Guernesey, and had:

1d *Geoffrey Stephen d'Auvergne [Geoffrey Collings Esq, Hougue Foucque Farm, St Saviours, Guernsey, CI]; *b* 23 Feb 1924; *educ* Wellington and Magdalene Coll Cambridge; Lt 60th Rifles WW II; *m* 26 Jan 1966 *Rosemary, dau of G Holden, barrister, and has:

1e *A son; *b* 23 June 1968

1e *Julia Frances; *b* 23 Nov 1966

1d Barbara d'Auvergne; *b* 13 May 1920; *m* 11 March 1948 Stuart Askwith Schofield; both *k* air crash 14 April 1965, having had:

1e Richard Adrian; *b* 19 April 1950; *k* same air crash 14 April 1965

2e Nigel James; *b* 29 Nov 1951; *k* same air crash 14 April 1965

1e *Caroline Judith; *b* 16 Dec 1953

2c Marjorie; *b* 14 Jan 1894; *m* 1st 25 Jan 1917 Capt Wilfrid Harold Swift, IA (*ka* 17 April 1917), s of Harold Swift, of Budleigh Salterton; *m* 2nd 3 July 1919 (*divorce* 1936) Capt Harry Thomas Ridlington, IA (*d* 20 July 1956), s of Harry Ridlington, and has:

1d *Jack Harry; Maj Glos Regt, Capt RAOC, WW II (wounded), Korea 1951–52 (despatches, POW); *b* 18 June 1920; *m* 1 June 1941 *Brigid Mary, dau of T Myers, and has:

1e *Michael John; Capt Roy Signals; *b* 17 March 1942; *educ* Duke of York's Roy Mil Sch and Birmingham U (BA 1964); *m* 9 Sept 1967 *Rosemary Anne, only dau of Lt-Col Robin Charles Burleigh Stuart (*see* CASTLE STEWART, E)

2e *Peter Charles; *b* 18 Sept 1954

1e *Denise Mary; *b* 24 Sept 1944

2e *Pauline Anne; *b* 13 Aug 1946

3e *Jacqueline Brigid; *b* 6 Nov 1955

2d *Peter Harold; Maj Roy Signals and Bde of Gurkhas; *b* 3 Sept 1927; *educ* St Paul's Coll Cheltenham

1d *Stella Mary; *b* 30 July 1922; *m* 24 July 1948 William Procter Bell, yr s of William Proctor Bell, and has:

1e *Rosemary Annette; *b* 26 March 1951

2e *Priscilla Mary; *b* 22 March 1956

1d (cont.) Mr and Mrs W P Bell also adopted:

*Christopher John; *b* 6 May 1950

1b Violet Agnes; *d* unm 17 Oct 1903

2b Mary Beatrice; *m* 1895 Owen Gould (*d* 16 July 1929), s of John Nutcombe Gould, and *d* 1 Jan 1943, leaving issue

3a Charles Edward; *b* 13 Feb 1844; *m* 2 Sept 1868 Annie Maria (*dsp* 27 June 1898), 3rd dau of George Flory, of Ipswich, and *d* 5 March 1910

(4) George; Army Offr; *b* 1802; *d* 10 April 1858

(5) Edward (Rev); *b* 2 April 1806; *d* 31 Dec 1838

(6) Stephen; *b* 10 Aug 1811; *d* 4 March 1839

(1) Susannah; *m* 9 Oct 1830 Lt-Gen Alexander Macdonald, RA, and *d* June 1863

1 Susan Sarah Louisa; *m* (elopement) 1764 William O'Brien, of Stinsford, Dorset, and *d* 1827

2 Lucy; *m* 1771 Hon Stephen Digby, s of 5th Baron Digby (*qv*), and *d* 1787

3 Christian Henrietta Caroline; *m* 1770 Colonel Acland and *d* 1815

4 Frances Muriel; *b* Aug 1755; *m* 24 Aug 1777, as his 1st w, 1st Earl of Dunraven and Mount-Earl (*qv*) and *d* 5 March 1814

The 7th EARL's cousin,

WALTER ANGELO FOX-STRANGWAYS, **8th Earl of Ilchester**; *b* 24 Sept 1887; *educ* Charterhouse and Pembroke Coll Cambridge (BA 1911); Levant Consular Service 1910–23, V-Consul Mogador, Morocco, Special Mediterranean Intell Bureau WW I, Queen's Roy Regt WW II; *m* 8 April 1916 Laure Georgine Emilie (*d* 29 Oct 1970), dau of Evanghelos Georgios Mazaraki, treasurer Suez Canal Co, and *d* 4 Oct 1970, leaving:

1 MAURICE VIVIAN DE TOUFFREVILLE FOX-STRANGWAYS, **9th and present Earl of Ilchester**

2 +RAYMOND GEORGE [The Hon Raymond Fox-Strangways, 4 Trull Green Dve, Trull, Somerset TA3 7JL]; *b* 11 Nov 1921; heir presumptive; *educ* Exeter Sch and Seale Hayne Ag Coll; RAF 1939–48, civ serv 1949–76; *m* 15 Nov 1941 *Margaret Vera, dau of James Force, of N Surrey, BC, Canada, and has:

(1) +Robin Maurice [Robin Fox-Strangways Esq, Little Haven, Frankton, Warwicks CV25 9PL]; *b* 2 Sept 1942; *educ* Loughborough Coll; with Lloyds Bank; *m* 19 July 1969 *(Margaret) Elizabeth, dau of Geoffrey Miles, of Camberley, Surrey, and Mrs Henry Travers-Tombs, of Castle Hill House, Warwick, and has:

1a +Simon James; *b* 25 Aug 1972

1a *Charlotte Helen; *b* 1974

(2) +Paul André [Paul Fox-Strangways Esq, Cherry Orchard Yews, Trull, Somerset TA3 7LF]; *b* 2 Nov 1950; *educ* Loughborough Coll and Sussex U (BSc (Hons), MA); U lecturer

1 *Jeanne Doreen (Elisabeth) [The Lady Jeanne Livingstone, 72a Fore St, Bovey Tracey, Newton Abbot, Devon]; *b* 22 Jan 1931; fndr and pncpl Lady Elizabeth Livingstone Modelling Sch 1983; *m* 22 March 1958 (*divorce* 1969) Peter Skelton, s of Maj Edwin Skelton, of Scawinds, Willingdon, Sussex, and adopted:

*Caroline; *b* 26 Feb 1962

1 (cont.) Lady Jeanne Skelton *m* 2nd 30 July 1977 *John Livingstone

ILIFFE

Arms: Sable a lion rampant double-queued between four crosses patée flory or. **Crest:** In front of a demi-lion rampant double-queued sable, collared or, three crosses as in the arms. **Supporters:** Dexter, a scribe holding in the exterior hand an open parchment proper; sinister, a printer of the time of Caxton holding in the exterior hand in front of his body a composing-stick proper. **Motto:** *Vive ut vivas* ('Live in such a way, that you may be alive'). **Creation:** B. (UK) 22 June 1933.

THE 3RD BARON ILIFFE, of Yattendon, Co Berks (Robert Peter Richard Iliffe) [The Rt Hon The Lord Iliffe, Yattendon Park, Yattendon, Berks RG18 0UT]; *b* 22 Nov 1944; *s* unc 1996; *educ* Eton and Ch Ch Oxford; High Sheriff Warwicks 1983; chm Yattendon Estates Ltd and Yattendon Investment Tst plc; dir Br Air Tport (Hldgs) Ltd and Scottish Provincial Press Ltd; former chm Birmingham Post and Mail Ltd and Coventry Newspapers Ltd; memb cncl Roy Ag Soc 1972– (Chm 1994–); *m* 16 July 1966 *(Rosemary) Anne, twin dau of Cdr Arthur Grey Skipwith, RN (*see* SKIPWITH, Bt), and has:

1 +EDWARD RICHARD; *b* 13 Sept 1968; *m* 8 June 1996 *Teleri Rees-Evans and has:

(1) *Alys Christina; *b* 5 June 1997

2 +George Langton; *b* 16 June 1970

3 +Thomas Arthur; *b* 3 April 1973

1 *Florence Clare; *b* 3 April 1973

Lineage: WILLIAM ILIFFE, of Upper Stoke, nr Coventry, Warwicks; *b* 7 March 1812; *m* 19 Dec 1839 Mary Ann, dau of Isaac Morrall, and had, with two daus:

WILLIAM ISAAC ILIFFE, of Allesley, Warwicks, JP; *b* 1 July 1843; *m* 11 Oct 1873 Annette, dau of James Coker, of Guernsey, and *d* 5 July 1917, leaving:

1 William Coker, of Whyteleafe, Surrey; *b* 9 Oct 1874; *m* 31 May 1906 Aveline Bertha (*d* 6 Sept 1954), dau of Edward Mantell, of Golden Manor House, Hanwell, Middx, and *d* 30 Sept 1942, leaving:

(1) William Geoffrey; *m* 1st 21 Oct 1935 Edith Dorothy (*d* 28 June 1956), twin dau of Maj Herbert George Brownrigg (*see* BROWNRIGG, Bt), and had:

1a *Margaret Ann Dorothy; *b* 30 June 1939; *m* 1st 14 March 1959 (*divorce*) Lt Kurth Sprague, US Army, only s of Mortimer Ernest Sprague, of NY and Virginia, and has:

1b *Quin John; *b* 4 Dec 1959

1a (cont.) Mrs Margaret Sprague *m* 2nd 3 May 1965 Gary Lee Gardner (*d* 1995), est s of Rufus Gardner, of Maryland

(1) (cont.) William Iliffe *m* 2nd 1957 *Rosamund Lynthorne, 4th dau of James Weir, of Carrickmollen, Killiney, Co Dublin, and *d* 1958

2 EDWARD MAUGER, **1st Baron**

1 Marguerite

WILLIAM ILIFFE's yr s,

EDWARD MAUGER ILIFFE, **1st Baron Iliffe**, of Yattendon, Co Berks (UK), so *cr* 22 June 1933, GBE (1946, CBE 1918), JP (Warwicks); *b* 17 May 1877; MP Tamworth 1923–29, Pres Birmingham Post and Mail Ltd, chm Guildhall Insur, dir London Assur, memb Lloyd's, pres Shakespeare Meml Theatre, pres Queen Elizabeth Hosp for Children, chm Coventry and Warwicks Hosp, Controller Machine Tool Dept Min Munitions WW I, chm Duke of Gloucester's Red Cross and St John Fund WW II, Pres Assoc Br Chambers Commerce 1932, Internat Lawn Tennis Club and Periodical Proprietors Assoc 1935–38, Master: Coachmakers and Coach Harness Makers Co 1936, Stationers and Newspaper Makers Co 1937 and Clockmakers Co 1946, Offr Legn Hon, Hon A/Cdre RAF 1939–44, KStJ, ktd 1922; *m* 10 June 1902 Charlotte (*d* 18 Jan 1972), dau of Henry Gilding, JP, of Gateacre, nr Liverpool, and *d* 25 July 1960, having had:

1 (EDWARD) LANGTON ILIFFE, **2nd Baron Iliffe**; *b* 25 Jan 1908; *educ* Sherborne, France and Clare Coll Cambridge; F/Lt RAFVR WW II (despatches), v-chm Birmingham Post and Mail Ltd, chm Coventry *Evening Telegraph* and Cambridge *Daily News*, High Sheriff Berks 1957, Hon Freeman Coventry 1969, govr Roy Shakespeare Theatre, Tstee Shakespeare's Birthplace, memb cncl Warwick U, govr Bradfield, Pres Internat Lawn Tennis Club GB; *m* 8 Dec 1938 *Renée Merandon [The Rt Hon Renée Lady Iliffe, Basildon House, Lower Basildon, nr Reading, Berks RG8 9NR], er dau of René Merandon du Plessis, of Mauritius, and n of Lady Kemsley (2nd w of 1st Viscount), and *dsp* 15 Feb 1996

2 (William Henry) Richard; *b* 24 March 1911; *educ* Sherborne and Ch Ch Oxford; *m* 30 May 1940 *Christine Marie, dau of Alfred Eaton Baker, MD, of Hastings, and *d* 30 May 1959, leaving:

(1) ROBERT PETER RICHARD ILIFFE, **3rd and present Baron Iliffe**

(2) +John David; *b* 9 Sept 1947; *educ* Eton and Ch Ch Oxford

1 Kathleen Iliffe; *m* 15 Oct 1926 Maj Leslie Frederick Laurence, s of Sydney Mortimer Laurence, of St Ives, Cornwall, and *d* 28 March 1988, leaving issue

IMBERT-TERRY

Arms: Az. guttée d'or, on a chief of the last a bull's head cabossed between two mullets of the field. **Crest:** Issuant from the coronet of a French seigneur an eagle rising ppr., crowned with an eastern crown or. **Supporters:** Two eagles with wings displayed ppr., crowned with eastern crowns or, both looking dexterwise. **Motto:** *Ubique fecundat imber* ('Everywhere the rain fertilizes'). **Creation:** Bt. (UK) 2 July 1917.

SIR MICHAEL EDWARD STANLEY IMBERT-TERRY, 5TH BT, of Strete Ralegh, Whimple, Co Devon [Sir Michael Imbert-Terry Bt, c/o Lady Sackville, Knole, Sevenoaks, Kent TN15 0RP]; *b* 18 April 1950; *s* bro 1985; *educ* Cranleigh; *m* 21 June 1975 *Frances Dorothy, 3rd dau of Peter Scott, of Ealing, and has:

1 +BRYCHAN EDWARD; *b* 1975

2 +Jack; *b* 1985

1 *Song; *b* 1973

2 *Bryony Jean; *b* 1980

Lineage: MARIE de HEMON; lived *c* 1410; *m* as her 1st husb Jehan Eveillard, Seigneur de Fortune, Island of Noirmoutier, off the coast of La Vendée, Western France; *m* as her 2nd husb — Boulmen, bro of Perot Boulmen, and by him had:

1 Geoffroi; Prior of the Reclusage, Noirmoutier; *d* on or after 14 Nov 1480, leaving an estate to his nephew, Etienne

2 Clairette; *m* François Imbert (living 1440), Seigneur de la Roche Servière, and had:

(1) Etienne; living 1499, Officier de la Cour de Noirmoutier; possibly f of:

1a Robert; living between 1539 and 1585; almost certainly f of (together with another s Jullien, Seigneur de Retraites, and a daughter Gillette):

1b Jacques, of Paux, nr La Garnache, Province of Poitou; *m* Catherine Rivallain and *d* by 25 March 1607, leaving an ests s:

1c André, of La Garnache; living 10 May 1644; *m* Elizabeth Angiseau (*d* by 1644) and had:

1d Jacob, Seigneur de la Sorlière; *m* 10 May 1644 Catherine (*d* by 7 Oct 1681), dau of Louis Rivière, of Mouchamps, and *d* by 12 July 1681, having had:

1e Jacob; *m* Radegonde Gardenau and had issue:

1f Pierre; Conseiller du Roi, Eschevin de Poitiers; *b* 1686; *m* 1712 Marie Ingrand de Douailleur and *d* 1741, having had:

1g Pierre Isaac Imbert de la Gibautier; Conseiller du Roi; *m* Marie Barbe Françoise Chevalier and had:

1h Mario Suzanne; *m* 1773 Jean, Count Pelletier de Montigny, and had:

1i Jean, Count Pelletier de Montigny; *m* 1817 Alexandrine M M Letard de la Bouvelliere, and had:

1j Marie; *m* 1849 Jean A, Count de Mascureau, and had:

1k Paule, Count de Mascureau; *m* 1889 Jeanne Richer de Beauchamp Montlieard and had:

1l Jacques, Count de Mascureau; *m* 1945 Ghislaine de Bois David (*see* below) and had:

1m Jacqueline

2m Chantal

3m Dominique; *b* 1952

2g Jacob Jacques; Eschevin et Trésorier de France, dans la Generalité de Poitiers; *b* 1715; *m* 1741 Marie Catherine Ursule Rocquard de Combereau and *d* 1794, having had:

1h Pierre Joseph Antoine Jacques; Trésorier de France; *b* 1743; *m* 1765 Marie Cathérine Radegonde Ingrand and *d* 1825, having had:

1i Joseph Jacques; Order of St Louis; *b* 1769; *m* Aimée Thérèse-Alexandrine de Regnier and *d* 1848, having had:

1j Marie Constance; *m* 1833 Henri, Count de la Rochfoucauld-Bayers, and had:

1k Marie; *m* 1863 Armand, Marquis de Baudry d'Asson, and had:

1l Armand, Marquis de Baudry d'Asson; *m* 1906 Magdeleine Pichard du Page and had:

1m Armand, Marquis de Baudry d'Asson; *m* 1934 Louise Buring des Rosiers and had two sons (Armand; Roland) and three daus (Magdeleine; Diane; Gilles)

1m Françoise

1m Irène; *m* 1930 Count de St Priest d'Urgel

2m Annick; *m* 1932 Hubert, Count de Courtibron

2k Henriette; *m* 1864 Count de Griffon-Senejac and had:

1l Henri, Count de Griffon-Senejac; *m* 1899 Noemi Favre and had:

1m Solange; *m* 1926 Marquis de Terrasson de Montleau and had:

1n *Béatrice; *m* 1952 *Pierre Tessier Huort

2n *Yseult

3n *Gaetan; *b* 1935

2m Elizabeth; *m* 1910 Marquis de Rochefoucauld

3l Paule; *m* 1871 Baron de Bois David and had:

1m Louis, Baron de Bois David; *m* 1911 Emma Papeians de Monchoven and had:

1n Ghislaine

2e Pierre; Seigneur de la Choltière, Lt-Gen Côtes Maritimes de l'Ouest de la Capitainerie de Barre le Mont et de Beauvoir-sur-Mer; *b* 7 May 1666; *m* 2 May 1686 Charlotte Marguerite (*d* 24 April 1714), only dau of Jacques Guérin, Seigneur de Bretellière, by Louise Angelique de Privat, heiress of her uncle Alexandre Guérin de la Terrière, and *d* 31 May 1720, leaving a 3rd s:

1f Pierre Alexandre; Seigneur de la Terrière de la Sorlière, de Malescot et du Paty, Capitaine de Dragoons, Seneschal de Noirmoutier 1730 et de Challans 1737; *bapt* 2 Nov 1701; *m* 5 Aug 1727 Suzanne Thérèse (*d* 27 March 1764), dau of Jean Bouhier, Seigneur de Sableau et de Beaulieu, and *d* 1756, leaving, with two daus:

1g Alexandre Benjamin IMBERT De La TERRIÈRE; Seigneur de Malescot, du Sableau, de Breteillière et de Beaulieu, Chevalier Order St Louis, Capitaine de Cavallerie de Gendarmerie de la Garde du Roi; *b* 1732; *m* 12 Feb 1765 Suzanne Marie Anne (*d* 20 July 1814), dau of Luc Bouhier, Seigneur de la Davière, and *d* 12 June 1792, leaving:

1h Alexandre Luc Frédéric Aimé IMBERT De La TERRIÈRE, known in England as Imbert-Terry, of the Château de Bois de Breuil, Challans, La Vendée, France, Chevalier of St Louis, Page of Honour to MARIE ANTOINETTE, Seigneur de la Choltière et de la Terrière; *b* 15 Nov 1765; *m* 27 Feb 1798 Elizabeth Walters, of Air St, Piccadilly (*d* 11 Jan 1858), and *d* at Le Barbin 18 Jan 1846, leaving:

1i Henri IMBERT De La TERRIÈRE (IMBERT-TERRY), of Le Barbin, Vieillevigne, Loire Inférieure, and 17 Chester Terr, London NW; *b* 3 Oct 1800; *m* Jan 1842 Susanna (*b* 7 Aug 1820; *d* 19 Aug 1883), dau of John Henry Machu, of Oakfield Lodge, Norwood, and *d* 30 Jan 1884, leaving:

1j Frederic William, of Aston Ho, Aston, Herts; Seigneur de la Terrière; *b* 6 Feb 1843; *m* 23 Nov 1872 Louisa Sophia Elizabeth (*d* 4 May 1935), dau of William Sagon Pabe, and *d* 12 Oct 1931, leaving:

1k Alexander Frédéric Aimé, MBE; Capt 7th Hus; *b* 6 Feb 1874; *m* 1st 5 Oct 1903 Agatha Gertrude (*d* 11 March 1947), dau of Rev Charles Robert William Hardy, Vicar Canewdon, Essex; *m* 2nd Daisy Constance Adelaide (*d* 23 Nov 1959) and *d* 24 Sept 1964

1k Olive Clotilde Bouhier; *m* 25 Aug 1909 Lt-Col Josslyn Vere Ramsden, CMG, DSO, and *d* 13 Feb 1977, leaving issue (*see* RAMSDEN, Bt)

2j HENRY MACHU (Sir), **1st Bt**

3j Claude Alexander; *b* 19 Dec 1857; *m* 18 Sept 1879 Sarah Frances (*d* 10 May 1926), dau of James Tyrrel, of Hadley, Essex, and *d* 4 April 1889, leaving:

1k Claude Henry Maxwell, DSO; Lt-Col Devonshire Regt, T/Lt-Col Service Bn Yorks LI 1916, Boer War 1901–02 (medal with three clasps) and WW I (despatches twice); *b* 31 Aug 1880; *m* 29 Aug 1921 Ethel Mary, est dau of William Henry Monckton (*see* GALWAY, V), and *d* 20 March 1942

2k Douglas Philip; Lt The Buffs WW I 1915 (wounded); *b* 20 Dec 1882; *m* 1 Feb 1951 Muriel (*d* 18 March 1967), yst dau of John Alston, of Ashwells, Penn, Bucks, and *d* 4 Feb 1925

1j Mary Anne Abbot; *m* 2 Jan 1880 Rev Herbert Athill, Rector Digswell, Herts, and *d* 30 April 1935, leaving issue. He *d* 19 Dec 1919

2j Eliza Sophia; *m* 8 Oct 1885 Forbes Ernest Hallett, barrister, and *d* 2 Dec 1909, leaving issue

3j Antoinette; *b c* 1860; *d* young

The 2nd son,

Sir Henry Machu Imbert-Terry, 1st Bt (UK), so *cr* 2 July 1917, JP, DL; *b* 28 June 1854; *educ* Charterhouse; Hon Lt-Col Canadian Gen List 1917, Fell and Memb Cncl Roy Soc Literature (V-Pres 1922, Hon Treas 1930, Hon Fell 1930), chm: Nat Union C Assocs 1905–07 (and Organisation Ctee 1907–17), Jr Imp League 1906–27; Hon Sec Devonshire Yeo and Equipment Fund for Boer War, V-Chm Overseas Forces Reception Ctee WW I, author: *The Royal Courtenays* (1902), *Nashe, Satirist, The Poetical Contemporaries of Chaucer, Some Memorialists of the Restoration, A Misjudged Monarch (Charles II)* (1917), *A Constitutional King (George I), In Spacious Times* (1927), *Acid* (1928), *Doom* (1929), *Les Imbert — The Chronicle of an Ancient Family* (1930), *Nightshade* (1930), *Clay* (1931), *Weeds* (1933), KGStJ; *m* 28 June 1883 Lydia Moore Stringfield (*d* 6 March 1918), dau of Charles Duncan Roberts, of Bishopsdown, Tunbridge Wells, and had issue:

1 HENRY BOUHIER (Sir), **2nd Bt**

2 Frederic Bouhier, MC, JP Devon; Capt Devonshire Regt WW I (despatches), High Sheriff 1928; *educ* Cheltenham and Clare Coll Cambridge; *m* 23 Jan 1917 Lilian Frederica Violette Lucy (*d* 4 Sept 1949), yst dau of Sir Alfred Hickman, 1st Bt, DL (*qv*), and *d* 20 Jan 1963

Sir HENRY *d* 1 Jan 1938; his er son,

Sir Henry Bouhier Imbert-Terry, 2nd Bt, DSO (1919), MC, DL; High Sheriff Devon 1948, Seigneur de la Terrière; *b* 10 Feb 1885; *educ* Charterhouse; Lt-Col RA WW I (despatches twice), also served WW II, chm Devon and Exeter Savings Banks, KStJ; *m* 5 Oct 1910 (Mildred) Dorothy, CStJ (*d* 14 Jan 1975), only dau of Brig-Gen Edward Montagu Flint, RA, by Mildred Salome, 2nd dau of Trehawke Kekewich, DL, of Peamore, and had issue:

1 EDWARD HENRY BOUHIER (Sir), **3rd Bt**

1 *Rosanne Mildred Clothide; *b* 1913

2 Antoinette Lydia; *m* 19 Nov 1962 William Belaieff, 3rd s of Alfred Michael Belaieff, of London. He *d* 15 Oct 1964

3 *Marie Jacqueline; *b* 1923; *m* 1st 28 Feb 1947 (*divorce* 1954, resumed maiden name) MacRae Wyndham Greenhill, yr s of Pelham Benjamin Greenhill; *m* 2nd 10 March 1972 *William Maurice Williams, s of J R Williams

Sir HENRY *d* 9 Oct 1962; his only son

Sir Edward Henry Bouhier Imbert-Terry, 3rd Bt, MC (1944); *b* 28 Jan 1920; *educ* Eton and New Coll Oxford; Maj Coldstream Gds WW II; *m* 19 April 1944 *Jean, JP (1973) [The Rt Hon The Lady Sackville JP, Knole, Sevenoaks, Kent TN15 0RP] (*m* 2nd 2 Dec 1983, as his 3rd w, 6th Baron Sackville, *qv*), 2nd dau of Arthur Stanley Garton, and *d* 27 Nov 1978, leaving:

1 **Sir Andrew Henry Bouhier Imbert-Terry, 4th Bt**; Lt Life Gds; *b* 5 Oct 1945; *educ* Eton; *m* 23 Feb 1972 (*divorce* 1975) Sarah Margaret (*m* 2nd 19 Jan 1976 Maj Peter Charles Hibbert, s of K F Webster), dau of Dr W E F Evans, and *d* 1985

2 Sir MICHAEL EDWARD STANLEY IMBERT-TERRY, **5th and present Bt**

1 *Carolyn Rose [Mrs Christopher Goode, Grove Cottage, Sandy Lane, Maybury, Surrey]; *b* 1 April 1947; *m* 1st 4 Aug 1973 (*divorce* 1981) Peter Lauderdale Mackintosh, only s of Christopher Mackintosh; *m* 2nd 1984 *Christopher Goode, s of Brig Ernest Reginald Goode, CBE, of Milford, Surrey, and by her 1st husb has:

(1) *Rory Edward Christopher; *b* 1976

(1) *Catherine Rose; *b* 1977

2 *Alison Jean [Mrs Julian Sanger, TheVale House, Frostenden, Suffolk]; *b* 6 Feb 1952; late FCO; *m* 1981 *Julian Lorimer Sanger and has:

(1) *Jonathan Edward; *b* 1983

(1) *Rachel Mary; *b* 1981

INCHCAPE

Arms: Per chevron azure and argent in chief two lymphads of the second and in base a Bengal tiger proper. **Crest:** A cubit arm holding a falcon proper. **Supporters:** Dexter, a lion rampant gules supporting a pennant argent charged with a saltire also gules; sinister, a Bengal tiger proper supporting a like pennant. **Motto:** *Manu forti* ('With a strong hand'). **Creations:** B. (UK) 26 June 1911, V (UK) 21 Jan 1924 (Inchcape), E. and V. (UK) 20 June 1929.

THE 4TH EARL OF INCHCAPE, Viscount Inchcape, of Strathnaver, Co Sutherland, **Viscount Glenapp**, of Strathnaver, Co Sutherland, **Baron Inchcape**, of Strathnaver, Co Sutherland ((Kenneth) Peter Lyle Mackay) [The Rt Hon The Earl of Inchcape, Manor Farm, Clyffe Pypard, Wilts SN4 7PY; 63 Pont St, London SW1]; *b* 23 Jan 1943; *s* f 1994; *educ* Eton; late Lt 9th/12th Royal Lancers; chm: Saracen Power Ltd, Duncan MacNeill Tea Inernat and Glenapp Estate Co; dir: Inchcape Family Investments Ltd, The Assam Co, Master Grocers' Co 1993–94, 2nd Renter Warden Shipwrights Co 1997–98, Prime Warden 1998–99, Pres Inchcape Soc 1994–, memb Roy Co Archers; *m* 7 June 1966 *Georgina, dau of Sydney Charles Nisbet and Mrs G R Sutton, of Morwick Hall, Acklington, Northumberland, and has:

1 +FERGUS JAMES KENNETH, *Viscount Glenapp*; *b* 9 July 1979
1 *Elspeth; *b* 3 Nov 1972
2 *Ailsa Fiona; *b* 1 April 1977

Lineage: JAMES MACKAY, of Arbroath, Forfarshire; *m* Deborah (*d* 3 Oct 1864), dau of Alexander Lyle, and *d* 11 April 1862, leaving:

JAMES LYLE MACKAY, **1st Earl of Inchcape**, so *cr* 20 June 1929, as also VISCOUNT GLENAPP, of Strathnaver, Co Sutherland, and previously 26 June 1911 BARON INCHCAPE, of Strathnaver, Co Sutherland, and 21 Jan 1924 VISCOUNT INCHCAPE, of Strathnaver, Co Sutherland (all UK), GCSI (1924, KCSI 1910), GCMG (1902), KCIE (1894, CIE 1890), DL (Ayrshire); *b* 11 Sept 1852; Pres Bengal Chamber Commerce 1890–93, MLC Viceroy India 1891–93, Sheriff Calcutta 1892, memb Cncl Sec State India 1897–1911, Special Commr negotiate Commercial Treaty China 1901–02, ptnr Mackinnon, Mackenzie & Co, V-Pres Suez Canal Co, chm and md P&O and Br India Steam Navgn, dir Nat Prov Bank, Master Shipwrights. Co 1924, Hon Capt RNR 1927, freedom Arbroath 1922, Hon LLD St Andrews; *m* 10 July 1883 Jean Paterson (*d* 10 Nov 1937), dau of James Shanks, of Rosely, Arbroath, and *d* 23 May 1932, leaving:

1 KENNETH, **2nd Earl**
1 Margaret Cargill; *m* 24 July 1913 2nd Baron Craigmyle (*qv*) and *d* 31 May 1958, leaving issue
2 Janet Lyle, CStJ; *m* 14 July 1908 Lt Col Frederick George Glyn Bailey, RA, 2nd s of Sir James Bailey (*d* 25 Oct 1951), of Lofts Hall, Essex, and *d* 1 Jan 1972, having had issue (*see* RUMBOLD, Bt)
3 Elsie; *m* 23 May 1917 (*annulled* 1922) Dennis Wyndham, Wilts Regt; lost in aeroplane attempting Atlantic Flight E-W 13 March 1928
4 Effie; *m* 20 Jan 1920 Sir Eugen John Henry Vanderstegen Millington-Drake, KCMG, FRSA (*d* 12 Dec 1972), only s of Henry Millington-Drake, and had issue

The 1st EARL's only s,

KENNETH MACKAY, **2nd Earl of Inchcape**; *b* 25 Dec 1887; *educ* Trin Coll Cambridge (BA); barrister Inner Temple, dir P&O Steam Nav Co and William Cory & Son, chm Marine Insur, Lt 12th Lancers and MGC WW I; *m* 1st 22 Sept 1915 (*divorce* 1931) Joan (*d* 13 Feb 1933), yst dau of Rt Hon John Francis Moriarty, Ld Justice Appeal Ireland, and *d* 21 June 1939, leaving:

1 KENNETH JAMES WILLIAM, **3rd Earl**
2 +Alan John Francis [The Hon Alan Mackay, Enterkine, Annbank, Ayrshire KA6 5AL]; *b* 6 Sept 1919; *educ* Eton and Trin Coll Cambridge; *m* 1st 3 Jan 1945 (*divorce* 1946) Janet Mary, yst dau of Frederick Wallis, of Elvendon Priory, Goring-on-Thames; *m* 2nd 30 June 1948 (*divorce* 1953) Sonia Cecilia Helen, yst dau of Capt James Richard Tylden, of Milsted Manor, Kent, and Lady (Francis) Tower, of Sway, Hants, and by her had:
(1) *Siobhan Amanda [Mrs Christopher Carver, 124 Wolseley Rd, Point Piper, Sydney, Australia]; *b* 8 Nov 1949; *m* 7 April 1973 *Christopher O B Carver, s of Col R O H Carver, OBE, of Throwley Forstal, Kent
(2) *Kristina Mary; *b* 25 July 1951; *m* 1975 *Simon M F Lamb

2 (cont.) The Hon Alan Mackay *m* 3rd 7 July 1955 *Countess Lucie Catinka Christiane Julie, dau of Count Curt Ludwig Haugwitz-Hardenberg-Reventlow, of Denmark, and formerly w of John Patrick Douglas-Boswell
3 James Lyle; *b* 19 Oct 1923; *educ* Eton; *d* following an accident 20 Aug 1941
1 Patricia Margery Kathleen; *b* 18 Aug 1916; *m* 1st 12 Jan 1938 (*divorce* 1949) Maj Hugh Washington Hibbert and had issue (*see* MOWBRAY, SEGRAVE and STOURTON, B); *m* 2nd 24 July 1951 Maj Reginald Fairweather, RA (*d* 12 Jan 1959), s of Frederick Fairweather, of Steeple Court, Botley, Hants, and *d* Aug 1973

The **2nd Earl** *m* 2nd 1 June 1933 Leonora Margaret (*m* 2nd 22 March 1946 Col Francis Parker Tompkins, US Army, s of Col Frank Tompkins, US Army; *d* 26 June 1996), est dau of Sir Charles Vyner de Windt Brooke, GCMG, Rajah Sarawak 1917–46, and by her had:

4 +SIMON BROOKE MACKAY, *cr* BARON TANLAW (LP; *qv*)
2 *Rosemary [The Lady Rosemary French, Little Offley, Hitchin, Herts]; *b* 5 Nov 1936; *m* 19 Jan 1957 *Francis Martin French, s of Francis Holroyd French and Mrs Henry Morland, and has issue:
1a Ewan Alexander Francis; *b* 2 April 1959; *d* 198–
1a *Anna-Louise Rosemary; *b* 23 May 1961
2a *Nicola Catharine; *b* 16 April 1967; *m* 1993 *Lawrence Charles Reintjes, er s of Anthony Reintjes, of Herts
3a *Kirsty Elizabeth; *b* 9 Dec 1970

The 2nd EARL's est s,

KENNETH JAMES WILLIAM MACKAY, **3rd Earl of Inchape**; *b* 27 Dec 1917; *educ* Eton and Trin Coll Cambridge (BA 1940, MA 1948); Lt 12th Lancers BEF and Maj 27th Lancers CMF WW II, Dep Pres Soc for India, Pakistan and Ceylon, chm Inchcape & Co and P&O, dir Cwlth Devpt Finance Co, Nat Westminster Bank, Chartered Bank, BP, Roy Exchange Assur and Burmah Oil, Chm Cncl Middle E Trade 1963–65, Freeman and Liveryman Fishmongers' Co 1958, Prime Warden Shipwrights' Co 1967 and 5th Warden 1973–74; *m* 1st 12 Feb 1941 (*divorce* 1954) Aline Thorn (Pixie) [Mrs Aline Roe, 23 rue Pré-du-Marché, Appt 114, Lausanne, Switzerland] (*m* 3rd 1955 (*divorce* 1968) Thomas Chambers Windsor Roe (*d* 1988)), only dau of Sir Richard Arthur Pease, 2nd Bt (*qv*), and widow of F/O Patrick Claude Hannay, AAF, and had:

1 (KENNETH) PETER LYLE MACKAY, **4th and present Earl of Inchcape**
2 +James Jonathan Thorn [The Hon James Mackay, 34A Dorset Sq, London NW1 6QJ]; *b* 28 May 1947; *educ* Eton and Trin Coll Cambridge; *m* 18 July 1970 *Mary Caroline, est dau of Peter Joyce, of Dorset, and has:
(1) +Aidan James Turner; *b* 1978
(1) *Sophie; *b* 1974
1 *Lucinda Louise; *b* 13 Dec 1941; *educ* Edinburgh U and Art Coll (MA 1965); *m* 1983 (*divorce* 1987, resumed maiden name) David Bogie, Sheriff Grampian, Highlands and Islands

The **3rd Earl** *m* 2nd 13 Feb 1965 *Caroline [The Rt Hon The Dowager Countess of Inchcape, Grange Farm, Churchill, Oxon OX7 6NG], est dau of Cholmeley Dering Harrison, of Emo Court, Co Laois, Ireland, and *d* 1994, leaving by her and having adopted a s:

3 +Shane Lyle; *b* 18 April 1973
4 +Ian Cholmeley; *b* 6 May 1976
*Anthony Kenneth; *b* April 1967

INCHIQUIN

Arms: Quarterly, 1st and 4th, gules three lions passant guardant in pale per pale or and argent (for O'BRIEN); 2nd, argent three piles meeting in point, issuing from the chief gules; 3rd, or a pheon azure. **Crest:** Issuing from a cloud an arm embowed brandishing a sword argent, pommel and hilt or. **Supporters:** Two lions guardant per fess or and argent. **Mottoes:** 1 *Vigueur de dessus* ('Strength from above'), 2 (over the crest) *Lamh laidir an uachtar* ('The strong hand uppermost'). **Creations:** B. (I) 1 July 1543, Bt. (I) 9 Nov 1686.

THE 18TH BARON OF INCHIQUIN and a **Baronet** (Sir Conor Myles John O'Brien, Bt) [The Rt Hon The Lord Inchiquin, Thomond House, Dromoland, Newmarket on Fergus, Co Clare, Ireland]; *b* 17 July 1943; *s* unc 1982, also as The

O'Brien, Chief of the Name, Prince of Thomond; *educ* Eton; late Capt 14th/20th King's Hus, Adj, ADC to Cdr Br Forces Gulf, GSO(3) POLMIL Hong Kong, Corporate Offr Inter Alpha Asia (Hong Kong) 1979–81, md Dromoland Devpt Co 1983–, dir and dep chm Darvela Ltd 1987–90, dir Radisson Hotels Ireland 1991–93, chm Swift Internat Devpts 1992–; *m* 1988 *Helen, dau of Gerald Fitzgerald O'Farrell, of Curry Lodge, Newtownforbes, Co Longford, and has:

1 *Slaney Alexandra Anne; *b* 1989

2 *Lucia Jospehine Mary; *b* 1991

Lineage: The O'BRIENs, one of the few native Irish families with a peerage, descend in the male line from BRIAN BOROIMHE, Prince of Thomond (North Munster or the north part of southwest Ireland, roughly commensurate with an area centred on modern Co Clare) and Chief of the Dalgais, who became HIGH KING OF IRELAND 1002 and was *k* at the victory over the Danes of Clontarf 23 April 1014; gf of:

TURLOGH; HIGH KING OF IRELAND; *d* 1086; ancestor in the 13th generation of:

TURLOGH DONN, PRINCE OF THOMOND; *b* 1499; *m* 1st Raghnailt, dau of John Macnamara, of Clancullen, and had:

1 CONOR O'BRIEN, PRINCE OF THOMOND; *m* 1st Anabel, dau of Ulick de Burgh, of Clanricarde, and had:

(1) DONOGH O'BRIEN, 'The Fat'; *s* his unc **1st Baron of Inchiquin** (*see* below) as 2nd EARL OF THOMOND for life, which title he surrendered to EDWARD VI, being *cr* afresh 7 Jan 1551/2 (1st) EARL OF THOMOND, with remainder to heirs male of his body, as also earlier 1 July 1543 BARON OF IBRACKAN; ktd by 14 March 1541/2; *m* by 1533 Lady Helen Butler (*d* 1597), yst dau of 8th Earl of Ormonde and (1st Earl of) Ossory (*see* MOUNTGARRET, V), and *d* 1 April 1553 of wounds recd in a skirmish with followers of his bros Sir Donal and Turlough, leaving:

1a CONOR O'BRIEN, 2nd EARL OF THOMOND; *b c* 1535; initially supported the English but took up arms against them Jan 1569/70, soon submitting, however, and being pardoned late 1570; *m* 1st just after 17 July 1559 Eveleen (*d* 1581), widow of 13th Earl of Desmond (*see* DENBIGH and DESMOND, E, preliminary remarks) and dau of Donald MacCarthy (s of Cormac Ladrach MacCarthy *Mor* ['The Great' or 'The Elder']), and had issue; *m* 2nd Ownye/Una (*d* 1589), dau of Turlough O'Brien, of Arra, Co Tipperary, and *d* Jan 1590/1, leaving by her:

1b DONOUGH O'BRIEN, 3rd EARL OF THOMOND ('The Great Earl'), PC (I 1603); supported the English ascendancy; Ld Pres Munster 1605–24; *m* 1st after Sept 1577 Any/Helen (*dspm* 1583), dau of Maurice Roche, Viscount Roche of Fermoy (*see* FERMOY, B, preliminary remarks); *m* 2nd after 6 Nov 1585 Lady Elizabeth FitzGerald, dau of 11th Earl of Kildare (*see* LEINSTER, D), and *d* 5 Sept 1624, leaving by her:

1c HENRY O'BRIEN, 4th EARL OF THOMOND, PC (I); *b c* 1588; *educ* Eton and BNC Oxford; called up to Ho Lds *vp* 31 March 1613 in f's Barony; *m* 13 July 1608 Mary, only dau of 1st Baron Brereton of Leighlin, and *dspm* just prior to 22 April 1639, leaving:

1d Mary; *m* 1st Viscount Cullen (*see* CULLEN OF ASHBOURNE, B) and had issue; *m* 2nd George Blount but by him had no issue

2d Margaret; *m* as his 2nd w 2nd Marquess of Worcester (*see* BEAUFORT, D) but *dsp* 1681

3d Elizabeth; *m* 1st as his 2nd w 3rd Baron Gerard of Gerard's Bromley (*see* GERARD, B) and had issue; *m* 2nd 3rd Viscount Wenman of Tuam of the 1628 *cr* and *d* between 9 April 1656 and 30 June 1659

4d Anne; *m* her cousin 6th EARL OF THOMOND (*see* below) and had issue

5d Honora; *m* 1st Sir Francis Englefield, 3rd Bt; *m* 2nd Hon Sir Robert Howard and had issue

2c BARNABY/BRIAN O'BRIEN, 5th EARL OF THOMOND, PC (I 1639); *b c* 1590; *educ* BNC Oxford; MP (I Parl) Coleraine 1613, Carlow and Ennis 1634, ktd 1615; a document creating him Marquess of Billing passed the Privy Seal 3 May 1645 but Letters Patent were never completed and he never took up that peerage designation; having been neutral between the Confederate Irish and the English forces 1641–42, he came out in support of Parl during the full English Civil War 1646, gave up Bunratty Castle and retired to England; *m* 17 July 1615 Mary, widow of 8th Lord Crichton of Sanquhar (*see* BUTE, M) and yst dau of Sir George Fermor (*see* HESKETH, B), and was *bur* 15 Nov 1657, leaving an only s:

1d HENRY O'BRIEN, 6th EARL OF THOMOND, PC (I 1670); *b c* 1620; *educ* Exeter Coll Oxford; *m* 1st 1641 his cousin Anne (*d* Sept 1645), 4th dau of 4th EARL OF THOMOND, and had:

1e Henry, *Lord Ibrackan* or *O'Brien*, PC (I 1673); MP (I Parl) Co Clare 1661–66 and (E Parl) 1670–78; *m* 1661, as her 1st husb, Baroness Clifton (of Leighton Bromswold) in her own right (*see* also MORAY, E) and *dvp* 1 Sept 1678, leaving:

1f Donogh, *Lord O'Brien*; *bapt* 16 Sept 1663; *m* 26 May 1679 Lady Sophia Osborne, dau of 1st Duke of Leeds (*see* 1963 edn), and *dsp* 6 May 1682

2f George; *dsp*

1f Mary; *m* 18th Earl of Kildare (*see* LEINSTER, D)

2f CATHERINE O'Brien, BARONESS CLIFTON (of Leighton Bromswold) in her own right, as which *s* mother Nov 1702; *b* 23 Jan 1673; *m* 10 July 1688 3rd Earl of Clarendon (*qv*, preliminary remarks) of the 1661 *cr* and *d* 11 Aug 1706

1d (cont.) The 6th EARL *m* 2nd 1660 Sarah, widow of Sir John Reynolds and 3rd dau of Sir Francis Russell, 3rd Bt, of Chippenham, Cambs, and *d* 2 May 1691, having by her had:

2e Henry Horatio, *Lord O'Brien*; *b c* 1670; *m* 24 June 1686 Lady Henrietta Somerset (*m* 2nd 1705, as his 2nd w, her former husb's former bro-in-law 6th Earl of Suffolk), dau of 1st Duke of Beaufort (*qv*) and *d* 10 July 1690, leaving:

1f HENRY O'BRIEN, 7th EARL OF THOMOND, PC (I 1714); *b* 14 Aug 1688; MP (Whig) Arundel 1710–14; *cr* 19 Oct 1714 VISCOUNT TADCASTER, of Tadcaster, Co York (GB), Ld Lt Essex 1721/2–41; *m* 14 June 1707 Lady Elizabeth Seymour, est dau of 6th Duke of Somerset (*qv*), and *dsp* 20 April 1741, when the Viscountcy of Tadcaster expired and the Earldom and Barony fell under the attainder of his cousin (*see* below)

1f Mary; *d* unm 30 Aug 1716

1e Elizabeth; *d* unm 3 June 1688

2e Auberie Anne Penelope; *m* 6 Aug 1691, as his 1st w, 6th Earl of Suffolk (*see* SUFFOLK and BERKSHIRE, E)

3e Mary; *m* Sir Matthew Dudley, 2nd Bt, of Clapton/Clopton, Northants, and *d* 9 Nov 1735

1d Penelope; *m* 2nd Earl of Peterborough (*see* MORDAUNT, Bt)

2b Teig, of Dromore and Bohneill; proclaimed himself 1599 The O'Brien and Chief of Thomond during the O'Neill Rising, which he joined; pardoned 1601; *m* 1st Margaret, dau of Robert Talbot, of Belgard, and widow of John Talbot, of Templeogue, Co Dublin, and had two sons (Connor, *dsp*; Donogh, *dsp*) and a dau (Margaret); *m* 2nd by 13 Aug 1599 Slany, dau and coheir of Teig O'Brien, 3rd s of 1st EARL OF THOMOND (*see* below), and had by her, with an est s (Teig, *dsp* & *vp*) and five daus:

1c Dermot, of Bohneill; Col; *m* Una, dau of Donogh O'Brien, of Newtown, Co Clare, and *d c* 1649, leaving two sons (Teig, *b* 1644, *dsp* after 1650; Donogh, *dsp* after 1664)

2c Murtough; Col; *m* Joan, dau of Turlough MacMahon, of Clenagh, Co Clare, and *dspm* after 1664

3c Turlough, of Ballyslattery; Col; *m* Margaret, dau of Donough O'Brien, of Lemenagh (*see* below), and *d* 1689, leaving, with a dau (Una):

1d Connor, of Dromore; Capt; heir presumptive to Earldom of Thomond; attainted by JAMES II's Irish Parl May 1689; Equerry to PRINCE GEORGE OF DENMARK (husb of QUEEN ANNE); *dsp*, drowned crossing from England to Ireland 24 Feb 1707

2b (cont.) Teig O'Brien *m* 3rd Joan, dau of Sir Dermot O'Shaughnessy, of Gort, Co Galway, and widow of Sir William Burke (*see* SLIGO, M), and *d* after 1641

3b DANIEL/DONAL O'BRIEN, 1st VISCOUNT CLARE AND BARON MOYARTA, Co Clare (I), so *cr* 11 July 1662; ktd 1604; MP (I Parl) Co Clare 1613–14/5 and 1634–35; joined Confederate Irish; *m* just after 1600 Catherine, dau of 16th Earl of Desmond (*see* DENBIGH and DESMOND, E, preliminary remarks) and widow of 6th Viscount Roche of Fermoy, and *d* 1663, having had, with other issue (*dsp* & *vp*):

1c CONNOR O'BRIEN; 2nd VISCOUNT CLARE; *b c* 1605; *m* Honora, dau of Daniel O'Brien, of Duagh, and *d c* 1670, leaving:

1d DANIEL O'BRIEN, 3rd VISCOUNT CLARE; MP JAMES II's I Parl 7 May 1689, raised three regts for JAMES and fought Battles of Linaskea 26 July 1689 and the Boyne 1 July 1690, following which he was outlawed 1691 and his titles and estates forfeited; *m* Philadelphia, dau of 14th Lord (Baron) Dacre (*qv*), and *d* probably 1691, leaving:

1e Daniel; *ka* French defeat of Imperial (HRE, *i.e.*, Austrian) army at Marsaglia 4 Oct 1693

2e Charles; outlawed as Jacobite by 1699; cmded a French regt Battles of Marsaglia, Blenheim 1704 and Ramillies 1706, following which he *d* 23 May 1706 of wounds recd in action; *m* 9 Jan 1696/7 Charlotte, dau of Henry Bulkeley, 4th s of 1st Viscount Bulkeley of Cashel, and had:

1f Charles; would have inherited not only the Viscountcy of Clare from his f but from his cousin the Earldom of Thomond had it not been for his gf's attainder (he was in fact known in France as 'Comte de Thomond'); *bapt* 17 March 1699; cmded the French troops at Battles of Dettingen 1743, Fontenoy 1745 (when his Irish troops were instrumental in defeating the English), Landshut 1745 and Raucoux 1746, Kt Holy Ghost of France; *m* 1755 Marie Geneviève Louise, dau of François Gauthier, Marquis de Chiffreville, and *d* 9 Sept 1761, leaving:

1g Charles; *b* 1757; *d* unm 29 Dec 1774 when the attainted titles expired

1g Antoinette-Charlotte-Marie-Septimanie; *m* 3rd Duke of Choiseul-Praslin

1d Margaret; *m* Hugh O'Reilly

2d Ellen; *m* Sir Roger O'Shaughnessy, of Gort

3d Honora; *m* John FitzGerald, 13th Knight of Kerry (*see* FitzGERALD, Bt, of Valencia)

4d Catherine; *m* 1st Garrett FitzGerald, of Castle Ishen, Co Cork; *m* 2nd John MacNamara, of Moyriesk, Co Clare

5d Sarah; *m* Daniel O'Sullivan Beave

6d Mary; *m* — Power, of Dunhill, Co Waterford

2c Murrough; *m* Eleanor, dau of Richard Wingfield, of Robertstown (*see* POWERSCOURT, V), by Honora O'Brien (*see* below), and had a dau (Honora)

3c Teig; *m* Honora, dau of Gerald FitzGerald, of Ballygleaghan, Co Limerick, and had a s (Donogh, living 1694)

1c Margaret

1b Mary; *m* as his 2nd w Turlough Roe MacMahon, of Clonderalaw, Co Clare

2b Margaret; *m* as his 2nd w 2nd/12th Baron (of) Dunboyne (*qv*)

3b Honora; *m c* 1594, as his 1st w, 17th Baron of Kerry and Lixnaw (*see* LANSDOWNE, M) and *d* 1600

2a Turlough, of Fomerla, Co Clare; *m* 1st Honora O'Shaughnessy and had:

1b Any; *m* Thomas Power, of Coolfin (*see* WATERFORD, M)

2a (cont.) Turlough O'Brien *m* 2nd a dau of O'Mulrian and by her had two sons (Murrough; Connor; both *d* after 1605)

3a Teig; *m* after 1565 his cousin Móre, yr dau of Sir Donal O'Brien by his 1st w (*see* below), but *dspl* 1567

1a Margaret; *m* 1st by 1550 her cousin **2nd Baron of Inchiquin**; *m* 2nd 1553, as his 2nd w, 2nd Earl of Clanricarde (*see* SLIGO, M)

2a Honora; *m* 1st 15- — MacNamara; *m* 2nd 15- (*divorce* 15-) Donogh O'Brien, of Lemenagh, and *d* 1579

3a Móre; *m* 1st — O'Shaughnessy; *m* 2nd Donal Reagh MacNamara Reagh, Chief of his name, and *d* after 1609

4a Mary; *m* Theobald Bourke (*kvp* 19 Aug 1578 helping his f put down on the Crown's behalf an insurrection by James Fitz Maurice), est s of 1st Baron (Bourke of Castle) Connell, and had issue

(2) Donal (Sir); ktd 1542; tried to maintain the old order of succession and as such proclaimed himself 1557 Tanaiste, or designated successor to the Chief of the name (1st/2nd ('The Fat') EARL OF THOMOND) under the Brehon Law, and later, following his er bro's death, as Chief of the name O'Brien and Lord of Thomond with superior claim to that of his n the 2nd (truly hereditary) EARL OF THOMOND, ruling as such till driven out of his territory by the English Ld Deputy of Ireland the 3rd Earl of Sussex (*see* FITZWALTER, B) 1558; granted (teritorial?) Barony of Corcomroe in compensation for his claims 1564; nevertheless feuded in alliance with the 1st/2nd ('The Fat') EARL's other sons against his n 2nd (truly hereditary) EARL OF THOMOND and after the latter's rebellion against the English Crown tried again to establish himself as Chief; *m* 1st — MacNamara and had:

1a Teig; *dsp* & *vp* 1559

1a Honora; *m* Connor O'Connor Kerry, of Carrigafoyle, Co Kerry, and *d* 1558

2a Móre; *m* 1st Mahon McTurlough Mantagh O'Brien, of Aran (*d* 1565); *m* 2nd Teig O'Brien, 3rd s of 1st/2nd ('The Fat') EARL OF THOMOND, and *d* 1599

(2) (cont.) Sir Donal *m* 2nd his cousin Slany (*d* 1569), dau of **1st Baron of Inchiquin** and widow of 11th Baron of Kerry and Lixnaw (*see* LANSDOWNE, M), and *d* 10 Oct 1579, leaving by her:

2a Turlough (Sir), of Duagh and Ballinalackan; *b c* 1546; *m* 1st Anabel, dau of James Lynch, of Galway, and *d* 1 Aug 1623, leaving:

1b Teig; *m* (contract 28 April 1595) Margaret (*m* 2nd Brian MacDermot, of Carrickmacdermot, Co Roscommon, Chief of his name), dau of Richard Burke, of Derrymaclaughna, and *dsp* & *vp*

2b Donal, of Duagh; *m* Ellen, dau of Edmond FitzGerald, Kt of Glin, and was ancestor of the O'BRIENs of Duagh, later of Ennistymon, and the O'BRIENs of Glencolumkill, Co Clare

3b Donogh, of Newtown, Co Clare; *m* Mary, dau of Richard Burke, of Derrymaclaughna, and had issue

1b Slany; *m* 1st Connor McDonogh O'Brien, of Lemenagh; *m* 2nd William Lynch, of Aquirk, Co Mayo; *m* 3rd Donel O'Dowd, of Ardnaglass, Co Sligo

2b Móre; *m* Murrough O'Brien, of Ballycorick

2a (cont.) Sir Turlough *m* 2nd (*divorce*) Slany, dau of **3rd Baron of Inchiquin** (*see* below); *m* 3rd Joan, dau of Edmond Bourke, and by his 2nd w had:

3b Mary; *m* Donal O'Brien, of Annagh, Co Tipperary

3a Murtough, of Tullagh, Co Clare; *m* Mary French and *d* 31 Aug 1593, leaving issue

4a Connor, of Inchovea, Co Clare; *m* — MacMahon and had issue

5a Donogh; *dsp* & *vp* after 1567

3a Margaret; *m* Donal O'Sullivan Beave

4a Sawney; *m* Teig *Caoch* MacMahon, of Carrigaholt

5a Finola; *m* 1st, as his 2nd w (repudiated by him 1580), 15th Baron of Kerry and Lixnaw (*see* LANSDOWNE, M); *m* 2nd Owney O'Loughlin

6a Aine; *m* as his 1st w Turlough Roe MacMahon, of Clonderalaw, and *d* 1591

(1) Margaret; *m* 1st Fearganainm O'Carroll, Ld or Chief of Ely (an area extending over the western parts of modern Cos Laois and Offaly and the northern part of Co Tipperary); *m* 2nd Owney O'Loughlin, Chief of Burren, Co Clare; *m* 3rd — Bourke

(2) Slany; *m* Sir Donogh O'Grady, of Tomgraney, Archdeacon Killaloe

(3) Móre; *m* Mahon McBrien O'Brien, of Castletown

1 (cont.) CONOR O'BRIEN, PRINCE OF THOMOND, *m* 2nd by 1517 Ellice, dau of 10th Earl of Desmond (*see* DENBIGH and DESMOND, E, preliminary remarks), and *d* 1539 or 1540, certainly by 26 July 1540, when the fully independent sovereignty of the O'BRIENs may be said to have ended, leaving by her:

(3) Turlough (Sir), of Bunratty; *dspms* 1557

(4) Teig, of Ballycorick, Co Clare; Tanaiste to his half-bro Donal; *d* Aug 1582; ancestor of the O'BRIENs of Ballycorick, who survived there till 1853

(5) Murrough, of Caherminnaun, Co Cork; *d* 25 Feb 1591; ancestor of the O'BRIENs of Caherminnaun

(6) Murtough, of Dromline; *d* 1593, leaving a s (Connor, claimant to Dromline)

2 Donogh; Tanaiste of Thomond; *d* 1531; ancestor of the O'BRIENs of Ballyportry and of Binral, Co Cork

3 MURROUGH, **1st Baron**

4 Teig; *dsp* 1523, *k* by 8th Earl of Ormonde and (1st Earl of) Ossory (*see* MOUNTGARRET, V)

5 Dermod; *dsp*

1 Móre; *m* Donogh McMahon O'Brien and *d* 1527

2 Ranelt; had by Mahon O'Brien, Bp Kilmacduagh:

(1) Turlough; Bp Killaloe

TURLOUGH DONN O'BRIEN *m* 2nd Shile (*dsp* 1490), dau of Dermod MacCarthy Reagh, Ld of Carbery; *m* 3rd Ellen/Evelin, dau of 8th Earl of Desmond (*see* DENBIGH and DESMOND, E, preliminary remarks), widow of Thomas Butler of Cahir and former mistress of Edmond Butler, er bro of 8th Earl of Ormonde and (1st Earl of) Ossory (*see* MOUNTGARRET, V), and *d* 1528, leaving by her:

3 Margaret; *m* 1st Mulrony McShane O'Carroll, Ld or Chief of Ely; *m* 2nd Connor *Carrach* ('The Ill-tempered') O'Connor, of Kerry, and by her 1st husb had:

(1) Móre; *m* by 1533, as his 2nd w, 13th Earl of Desmond and *d* 1548, leaving issue

4 Any; *m* Cuvea MacNamara and had:

(1) Donal Reagh MacNamara Reagh

5 Honora; *m* John Burke, of Benmore, Co Galway

6 Slany; *m* Brian MacMahon, of Carrigaholt, Co Clare, and *d* 1579

The 3rd s,

MURROUGH O'BRIEN, **1st Baron of Inchiquin**, so *cr* 1 July 1543, as also EARL OF THOMOND (both I) in the latter case for life, with special remainder of the latter dignity to his n DONOGH (*see* above), for his life only, PC (I 1543); fought against English attempts to assert rule over Ireland till March 1541/2, when he submitted and went to England to surrender to HENRY VIII in person, on which occasion the King ennobled him; *m* Eleanor, 5th dau of Sir Thomas FitzGerald, Knight of Glyn, and *d* between June and 28 Oct 1551, having had:

1 DERMOD O'BRIEN, **2nd Baron of Inchiquin**; *m* by 1550 his cousin Margaret, est dau of 1st (truly hereditary) EARL OF THOMOND, and *d* 31 Jan 1552, leaving an only s:

(1) MURROUGH MACDERMOT O'BRIEN, **3rd Baron of Inchiquin**; *b* 1550; *m* Margaret (*m* 2nd Christopher Cruce, of The Naul, Co Meath, and *d* in or after 1610), dau of Sir Thomas Cusack, Ld Chllr and Ld Justice Ireland, and was *k* 20 April 1573 by Dermot Reagh O'Shaughnessy at the instigation of 3rd Earl of Clanricarde (see SLIGO, M), leaving:

1a MURROOGH O'BRIEN, **4th Baron of Inchiquin**; *b c* 1562; *m* Annabel/Mabel (*m* 2nd John FitzPatrick, of Castletown, Upper Ossory [now Co Laois], 2nd s of 3rd Baron of Upper Ossory), sis of 1st Earl of Westmeath (*qv**), and was *ka* 29 July 1597, drowned in the River Erne at Ballyshannon, Co Donegal, while fighting on behalf of the English against the O'DONNELLs of Ulster, leaving:

1b DERMOD O'BRIEN, **5th Baron of Inchiquin**; *b* Oct 1594; *m* by 1614 Ellen, est dau of Sir Edmond fitz John FitzGerald, of Cloyne and Ballymaloe, Co Cork, and *d* 29 Dec 1624, leaving:

1c MURROUGH O'BRIEN (*An tothaine* or 'The Incendiary'), **6th Baron of Inchiquin** and 1st EARL OF INCHIQUIN, so *cr* 21 Oct 1654, as also BARON O'BRIEN OF BURREN, Co Clare (both I), PC (I); *b* Oct 1614; V-Pres Munster 1642, defeated the forces of the 1641 Uprising at Lisacarrol 1642 and other encounters, supported Parl in Civil War 1644 but then switched to the Royalists 1648, hence his step up in the peerage; turned RC by 1654; lived abroad during Interregnum, Lt-Gen French forces, apptd Viceroy Catalonia 1654 by LOUIS XIII; *m c* 1 Oct 1635 Elizabeth (*d* 22 May 1685), dau of Sir William St Leger (*see* DONERAILE, V), and *d* 9 Sept 1674, having had:

1d WILLIAM O'BRIEN, **7th Baron of Inchiquin** and 2nd EARL OF INCHIQUIN, PC (I Jan 1670/1); *b c* 1640; Capt-Gen Tangier 1674–80, Col 2nd (Tangier) Foot 1675–80, attainted *in absentia* by JAMES II's I Parl May 1689, Govr Jamaica and V-Adml surrounding waters 1690–92; *m* 1st 1665 Lady Margaret Boyle (*bur* 27 Dec 1683), dau of 1st Earl of Orrery (*see* CORK and ORRERY, E); *m* 2nd Elizabeth (*m* 4th and last Baron Howard of Escrick (*see* SUFFOLK and BERKSHIRE, E) and *d* 3 Feb 1718), widow of 3rd Baron Herbert of Chirbury of the 1629 *cr* (*see* POWIS, E) and yst dau and coheiress of 6th Baron Chandos of Sudeley (*see* TEMPLE OF STOWE, E), and *d* Jan 1691/2, having by his 1st w had, with two yr sons (*dsp* young) and a dau (Margaret, *d* unm):

1e WILLIAM O'BRIEN, **8th Baron of Inchiquin** and 3rd EARL OF INCHIQUIN, PC; *b c* 1666; attainted by JAMES II's I Parl May 1689; Govr Kingsale 1693 and Co Clare, Col of Foot, Mayor Kilkenny 1704–05; *m* 1st Margaret (*dsp* 1688), dau of James O'Brien; *m* 2nd April 1691 Mary (*d* 17 April 1753), sis of 1st Earl of Jersey (*qv*), and *d* 24 Dec 1719, having by her had:

1f WILLIAM O'BRIEN, **9th Baron of Inchiquin** and 4th EARL OF INCHIQUIN, KB (1725), PC (I 1753); MP (Whig) Windsor 1722–27, Tamworth 1727–34, Camelford 1741–47 and Aylesbury 1747–54; *m* 1st 29 March 1720 Anne, Countess of Orkney in her own right (*d* 7 Dec 1756; *qv*), and by her had, with other issue (*dsp* & *vp*):

1g MARY, COUNTESS OF ORKNEY in her own right; *m* 5 March 1753 her cousin **10th Baron of Inchiquin** (*see* below)

1f (cont.) The **9th Baron** *m* 2nd 12 Oct 1761 Mary (*dsp* 1793), dau of 1st Viscount Mount Cashell, and *dspms* 18 July 1777

2f Charles; Lt RN; *d* unm

3f James; MP; *m* Mary, dau of Very Rev William Jephson, Dean Kilmore (by Anne, widow of Capt Samuel Hartwell and est dau of Redmond Barry), and *d* 17 Dec 1771, having had, with another s and dau:

1g MURROUGH O'BRIEN, **10th Baron of Inchiquin** and 1st MARQUESS of THOMOND, so *cr* 29 Dec 1800 (I), with special remainder to his bros, also 2 Oct 1801 BARON THOMOND OF TAPLOW, Co Bucks (UK), KP (1783), PC (I 1780); *b* 1726; Capt Gren Gds, MP (I Parl) Co Clare 1757–60 and Harristown 1761–68 and (GB Parl, Whig to 1796, Pittite thereafter) Richmond 1784–96 and Liskeard 1797–1800; *m* 1st 5 March 1753 his cousin Mary (*d* 10 May 1791), Countess of Orkney in her own right (*see* above), and had, with other issue:

1h MARY O'Brien; *s* her mother as COUNTESS OF ORKNEY in her own right; *m* Hon Thomas FitzMAURICE (*see* LANSDOWNE, M, also ORKNEY, E)

1g (cont.) The **10th Baron** *m* 2nd 25 July 1792 (at Beaconsfield, where her guardian Edmund Burke the political philosopher and MP lived) Mary (*d* 7 Sept 1820), dau of John Palmer, of Torrington, Devon, and niece and heiress of Sir Joshua Reynolds, the celebrated painter, and *d* 10 Feb 1808 after falling from his horse in Grosvenor Sq, when the UK Barony expired, leaving by her no issue

2g Edward; *m* Mary Carrick and *d* March 1801, leaving:

1h Murrough; *d* unm

2h WILLIAM O'BRIEN, **11th Baron of Inchiquin** and 2nd MARQUESS OF THOMOND, KP (1809), PC (I 1809); *b c*

1765; Capt 14th Light Dragoons 1795; rep I peer 1816–46; *cr* 3 July 1826 BARON TADCASTER, of Tadcaster, Co York (UK); *m* 16 Sept 1799 Elizabeth (*d* 3 March 1852), only dau and heiress of Thomas Trotter, of Duleck, but *dspm* 21 Aug 1846, when the UK Barony expired, leaving:

1i Susan Maria; *m* 12 Aug 1824 R-Adml Hon George F Hotham and *d* 25 March 1857, leaving issue (*see* HOTHAM, B)

2i Sarah; *m* 3 April 1830 Maj William Stanhope Taylor, s of Thomas Taylor, of Seven Oaks, and gs of 3rd Earl Stanhope (*see* 1967 edn CHESTERFIELD and STANHOPE, E), and *d* 9 Feb 1859

3i Mary; *m* 11 Oct 1836 2nd Earl of Bantry (*see* 1891 edn) and *dsp* 13 July 1853

4i Elisabeth; *m* 22 Dec 1835 Sir George Stucley Stucley, 1st Bt (*qv*), and *d* 9 May 1870, leaving issue

3h JAMES O'BRIEN, **12th Baron of Inchiquin** and 3rd and last MARQUESS OF THOMOND, GCH (1831); *b c* 1768; joined RN 1783, Midshipman 1786–89, Lt 1790, Cdr 1796, Capt 1799, R-Adml 1825, V-Adml 1837, Adml 1847; *m* 1st 25 Nov 1800 Eliza Bridgeman (*d* 14 Feb 1802), 2nd dau of James Willyams, of Carnanton, Cornwall; *m* 2nd Jane (*d* 8 Sept 1843), widow of Valentine Horsford and dau of Thomas Ottley, of St Vincent and Antigua; *m* 3rd 5 Jan 1847 Anne (*d* 22 Oct 1874), widow of R-Adml Francis William Fane (*see* WESTMORLAND, E) and sis of Sir Charles Flint, and *dsp* 3 July 1855, when the Marquessate, Earldom and 1654 Barony expired

4h Edward; Capt RN; *m* 1st 1805 Diana (*dsp* 26 Nov 1810), est dau of Gen George Hotham (*see* HOTHAM, B); *m* 2nd 11 April 1815 Gertrude Grace (*d* 1 May 1817), yst dau of Paul Cobb Methuen (*see* METHUEN, B), and by her had:

1i Gertrude Matilda; *m* 17 June 1840 her cousin Rev Thomas Plumptre Methuen (see METHUEN, B) and *d* 17 Dec 1869, leaving issue

2i Mary Catherine; *m* 20 Jan 1842 Rev John Hamilton Forsyth and *d* 10 May 1885, leaving issue

4h (cont.) Lord Edward O'Brien *m* 3rd 16 April 1822 Elizabeth Susan (*m* 2nd Gen James Orde (*d* 1850) and *d* 16 April 1876, leaving further issue), 2nd dau of 6th Duke of Beaufort (*qv*), and *d* 9 March 1824, having had a s (*d* an infant)

5h John; Capt 67th Regt; *d* unm

1h Mary; *m* 1st Sir Richard Cox, Bt; *m* 2nd Rt Hon William Saurin, Attorney-Gen Ireland, and *d* 23 Jan 1840

2h Harriet; *m* Sir Joseph Wallis Hoare, 3rd Bt, of Annabella (*qv*), and *d* 1851

1g Anne; *m* 23 March 1744 Most Rev Michael Cox, DD, Archbp Cashel, and *d* 19 Jan 1745

2g Henrietta; *m* 1st Terence O'Loughlen; *m* 2nd Sir William Vigors Burdett, 2nd Bt (*see* WELDON, Bt)

1f Henrietta; *m* 1717 Robert Sandford, of Castlerea, and *d* 1730, leaving issue

2f Mary; *m* 19th Earl of Kildare (*see* LEINSTER, D)

2d Charles; naval Capt; *dsp*, *k* at sea Siege Maastricht

3d John, of Inchiquin; Capt; *m* Honora, dau of Connla Geoghegan, and *dsp c* 1699

1d Elizabeth; *m* 1st Richard Southwell (*see* SOUTHWELL, V); *m* 2nd John MacNamara, of Cratloe, Co Clare, and *d* Sept 1688

2d Honpora; *m* 3rd Lord Bourke, Baron of Brittas, and had issue

3d Mary; *m* 1st Henry Boyle (*see* SHANNON, E); *m* 2nd R-Adml Sir Thomas Dilkes; *m* 3rd Col John Irwin

2c Henry; participated with his bro Murrough against Confederate Irish in 1641 Uprising; *dsp* 1645

3c Christopher, of Ennistymon; Col; supported Confederate Irish against his bros; *m* his cousin Honora, widow of Baltius Clancy, of Knockfin, and dau of Turlough Roe MacMahon (*see* above), and *dsp c* 1662

1c Honora; *m* Anthony Stoughton, of Rattoo, Co Kerry, and had a 3rd dau (Ellen, *m* Thomas Blennerhassett, of Littur, Co Kerry, and had an est dau, Martha, who *m* 1st Frederick Mullins (*see* VENTRY, B) and 2nd Henry Parr, of Dingle, Co Kerry)

2c Mary; *m* as his 2nd w Michael Boyle, Archbp Armagh, and had issue (*see* CORK and ORRERY, E)

1a Slany; *m* 1st (*divorce*) her cousin Sir Turlough O'Brien (*see* above); *m* 2nd Murtough O'Brien, of Arra, Bp Killaloe; *m* 3rd William Dungan, Recorder Dublin, and was living 30 Oct 1640

2 Teige McMurrough, of Smithstown; assumed headship of his branch of the O'BRIENs after his f's and er bro's deaths, keeping up the feud with the 3rd EARL OF THOMOND; 1st Sheriff Co Clare 1567–70; *m* Móre (*d* 1599), dau of Sir Donal O'Brien by his 1st w, and *d* 12 Dec 1577, leaving:

(1) Turlough, of Smithstown; *b* 1571; *dsp* 12 July 1584

(1) Honora; *b* 1571; *m* Richard Wingfield (*see* POWERSCOURT, V) and *d* after Jan 1657, leaving issue (*see* below)

(2) Slany; *b* 1575; *m* her cousin Teige, 2nd s of 3rd EARL OF THOMOND (*see* above)

(3) Aine/Amy; *b* 1578; *m* after 13 Aug 1600 Donogh McMahon O'Brien (*d* in exile in Spain 20 March 1611/2), of Cloonooaun, Co Clare, and *d* 2 Sept 1606, leaving:

1a Turlough, of Tullamore, Co Clare; *d* Oct 1650, leaving:

1b Aine; *m* Murrough O'Brien, 5th s of Donogh O'Brien, of Lemenagh

3 Donogh McMurrough, of Lemenagh and Dromoland, which lands, with their castles, he inherited, together with other lands in Co Clare, from his f; *m* 1st (*divorce*) Honora, dau of 2nd EARL OF THOMOND; *m* 2nd Slany, dau of John MacNamara Finn, of Knappogue, Chief of his name, and was hanged at Limerick 6 Sept 1581 under martial law operating there at the time, despite being under nominal protection, leaving, with a dau (Margaret):

(1) Connor McDonogh, of Lemenagh; *m* Slany (*m* 2nd William Lynch, of Aquirk, Co Mayo; *m* 3rd Donal O'Dowd, of Ardnaglass, Co Sligo), dau of Sir Turlough O'Brien, and *d* 2 Jan 1603/4, leaving:

1a Donogh, of Lemenagh; *b* 1595; *m* his cousin Honora, dau of Richard Wingfield (*see* above), and *d* 10 Jan 1634/5, leaving:

1b Connor McDonogh, of Lemenagh; *b* 1617; Col; *m* Mary *Rua* ('The Red-haired') (*m* 3rd Capt John Cooper), dau of Turlough Roe MacMahon, of Clonderalaw (*see* above) and widow of Daniel Neylan, of Tullagh and Dysert, Co Clare, and *d* 1651, leaving, with two yst sons (*dsp*):

1c **Sir Donough/Donat O'Brien, 1st Bt** (I), so *cr* 9 Nov 1686, of Lemenagh and Dromoland, PC; *b* 1642; MP; *m* 1st (contract 24 July 1674) Lucia (*d* 1676), 2nd dau of Sir George Hamilton (*see* ABERCORN, D), and had:

1d Lucius; MP Co Clare 1703–14; *m* 1701 Catherine, dau of Rt Hon Thomas Keightley, V-Treasurer Ireland, and gdau of the 1st Earl of Clarendon (*qv*, preliminary remarks) of the 1661 *cr*, and *dvp* Paris 6 Jan 1717, leaving, with a yr s (*dsp*) and two daus (*d* young):

1e EDWARD (Sir), **2nd Bt**

1c (cont.) **Sir Donough/Donat** *m* 2nd 23 July 1677 Elizabeth (*d* 16 Jan 1683/4), widow of Henry Grey, of Dublin, and dau of Maj Joseph Deane, of Cromlin, and by her had, with two other daus (*d* unm)

2e Henry, of Stonehall, Co Clare; *m* 1699 Susanna (*m* 2nd Arthur Geoghegan, of Castletown, Co Westmeath, and *d* March 1743), dau and coheir of William Stafford, of Blatherwycke, Northants, and *d* 15 Jan 1723/4, leaving, with an est and yst s (*d* young and *dsp* respectively) and another dau (*d* unm):

1f Henry, of Blatherwycke and Stonehall; *b* March 1708; *m* Nov 1730 Margaret, dau of William Stamer, of Carnelly, Co Clare, and *d* 17 March 1717, leaving:

1g Susanna; *m* Edward O'Brien, of Ennistimon

2f Donogh/Donatus, of Blatherwycke; *m* Mary, dau of J Beckett, of Barnsley, Yorks, and had:

1g Henry

2g Lucius

3g Donogh

1f Elizabeth; *m* John Rice

2f Anne; *m* Edward Butler

3f Susanna; *m* 1st June 1722 James Rice, of Mount-Rice, Co Kildare; *m* 2nd Augustine Ievers

4f Catherine; *m* 10 June 1727 Patrick French, Counsellor-at-law

5f Mary; *m* 1752 Capt James Campbell

6f Frances; *m* Hyacinth Darcy and *d* 21 Oct 1753

2c Teig; *d* after 1678, leaving:

1d Connor; living 1689

2d Donogh; living 1689

1c Honora; *m* (settlement 6 March 1662/3) Donogh O'Brien, of Ballynalacken, Co Clare

2c Mary; *m* Donogh McNamara

3c Slany

2b Dermod

3b Teig

4b Turlough

5b Murrough; *m* his cousin Aine, dau of Turlough O'Brien, of Tullamore, and had:

1c Teig/Timothy, of Smithstown; *m* Joan, dau of William Cuffe, and *d* after 1713

6b Donogh

1b Margaret; *m* Turlough O'Brien, of Ballyslattery (*see* above)

2b Mary; living 1650

(1) Margaret; *m* Brian Duff O'Brien, of Carrigogunnell, Co Limerick

1 Honora; last Abbess of Killone; *m* by papal dispensation Sir Rory O'Shaughnessy, Chief of his name

2 Aine; *m* 1st William O'Kelly (*d* 1542), of Mullaghmore, Co Galway; *m* 2nd John Burke fitz Thomas, of Derrymaclaughna, Co Galway

3 Margaret; *b c* 1535; *m* 1st (*divorce*) 2nd Earl of Clanricarde (*see* SLIGO, M); *m* 2nd — MacNamara; *m* 3rd Ross O'Loughlen and was living 1616

4 Slany; *m* 1st 11th Baron of Kerry and Lixnaw and had issue (*see* LANSDOWNE, M); *m* 2nd Sir Donl O'Brien and *d* 1569

5 Ranelt; mistress of Turlough O'Brien, Bp Killaloe

6 A dau; *m* Connor Cróne O'Brien, of Shallee and Tobermaly, Co Clare

Sir DONOUGH/DONAT *d* 17 Nov 1717; his gs,

Sir Edward O'Brien, 2nd Bt, of Dromoland; *b* 7 April 1705; MP Peterborough 1727–28 and (I Parl) Co Clare 1728–65; *m* 1726 Mary (*d* 20 Feb 1760), dau of Hugh Hickman, of Fenloe, and had, with five daus:

1 LUCIUS HENRY (Sir), **3rd Bt**

2 Donogh; *m* Mary, dau of Richard Henn, and had issue

3 Edward; *m* Charlotte, dau of Thomas Hickman, of Brickhill, Co Clare, and *d* Dec 1787, leaving, with other issue:

(1) James, of Castle Fergus, Co Clare; *b* 1775; *m* Margaret, dau of Capt William Stronge, and *d* 5 Oct 1822, leaving issue

(2) Murrough; *b* 1787; *m* 31 July 1810 Matilda, dau of Robert Norman, and *d* 1814, leaving:

1a Edward Morrough; *b* 1814; *d* 4 Jan 1895

1a Harriet Matilda; *b* 28 Feb 1812; *m* 1 June 1836 Dr Nesbit Sealy Heffernan and *d* 11 Jan 1904, leaving issue

(1) Marian; *m* 1796 Rev Thomas Ross (*d* 1818), of Rostrevor, Co Down, and had issue

(2) Anne; *m* her cousin Adml Robert O'Brien and had issue (*see* below)

1 Lucy; *m* Nov 1766 Thomas Arthur (*d* 1803), of Glanomera, Co Clare

Sir EDWARD *d* 26 Nov 1765; his est s,

Sir Lucius O'Brien, 3rd Bt, PC; *b* 2 Sept 1731; MP Ennis 1761–68 and 1790–96, Co Clare 1768–83 and Tuam 1783–90, Clerk Crown and Hanaper 1788–95, FRS; *m* 26 May 1768 Anne, dau of Robert Ffrench, of Monivea Castle, Co Galway, MP Co Galway, and had, with other issue:

1 EDWARD (Sir), **4th Bt**

2 Lucius; *m* Julia, dau of William Humphreys, and *dsp*

3 Robert; *b* 25 Oct 1776; Adml; *m* 1st Anne, dau of Edward O'Brien (*see* above); *m* 2nd —, widow of — Bermingham (*dsp* 11 Aug 1836), of Brighton, and *d* 21 Jan 1838, leaving by his 1st w, with other issue:

(1) Catherine Maria; *m* 13 Jan 1847 Robert Wogan Studdert (*d* 27 May 1897), of Cullane, Kilkishen, Co Clare, and *d* 12 April 1900, leaving issue

(2) Lucy; *m* 1854 Very Rev George Henry Johnson (*d* 1881)

4 Donough Acheson; *b* 1780; *m* 1822 Marianne Lydia (*d* 1 Jan 1843), dau of William Semple, of Dublin, and *d* 22 Oct 1847, leaving two daus

1 Nichola Maria; *m* 1 Jan 1799 her 1st cousin Robert Ffrench, JP (*d* Jan 1851), of Monivea Castle, and *d* 1848, leaving issue

2 Katherine; *m* 1813 as his 2nd w Gerald FitzGerald, DL (*d* April 1845), of Coolanowle, Queen's Co, and *d* 31 March 1819, leaving issue

3 Anne Maria; *m* 11 Sept 1810 Ven William Spooner (*d* 2 Sept 1857), Archdeacon Coventry, and *d* 24 Dec 1846, leaving issue

4 Charlotte Sophia; *m* Feb 1806, as his 1st w, Rev Hon Gerard Noel (*see* GAINSBOROUGH, E) and *d* 31 Aug 1838

Sir LUCIUS *d* 15 Jan 1795; his est s,

Sir Edward O'Brien, 4th Bt; *b* 17 April 1773; MP Ennis 1795–1800 and Co Clare 1802–26; *m* 12 Nov 1799 Charlotte (*d* 28 Sept 1856), est dau and coheir of William Smith, of Cahirmoyle, Co Limerick, and had:

1 LUCIUS, **13th Baron**

2 William (Smith), of Cahirmoyle; *b* 17 Oct 1803; MP Limerick; *m* 19 Sept 1832 Lucy Caroline (*d* 13 June 1861), dau of Joseph Gabbett, of High Park, Co Limerick, and *d* 18 June 1864, leaving, with other issue:

(1) Edward William, of Cahirmoyle, JP, DL Co Limerick; *b* 24 Jan 1837; BA Dublin; High Sheriff Co Limerick 1869; *m* 1st 8 Sept 1863 Mary (*d* 25 April 1868), sis of 2nd Baron Monteagle of Brandon (*qv*), and had:

1a William Dermod, DL Co Limerick; *b* 10 June 1865; *educ* Harrow and Trin Coll Cambridge; artist, Pres Roy Hibernian Academy 1910–45, High Sheriff Co Limerick 1916; *m* 8 March 1902 Mabel Emmeline (*d* 8 Dec 1942), 2nd dau of Sir Philip Crampton Smyly, FRCSI, and *d* 5 Oct 1945, leaving:

1b Brendan Edward; *b* 11 Jan 1903; *educ* St Bees and Trin Coll Dublin (MB, BCh 1935, MD 1950); FRCPI 1943; *m* 10 Oct 1936 Pamela Kathleen Helen (*d* 1982), only dau of Maj Harold Gordon Wilmer, 14th KGO Sikhs, and *d* 1984, leaving:

1c +Dermod Wilmer [Dermod O'Brien Esq, Glenside, Lee Rd, Carrigrohane, Co Cork, Ireland]; *b* 18 June 1941; *educ* St Columba's and Trin Coll Dublin (BA BAI 1963); *m* 6 May 1966 *Rosalind, est dau of Robert Gibson Service, RNVR, of Dolphin Lodge, Helensburgh, Dunbartonshire, and has:

1d +Jeremy William; *b* 23 Feb 1971; *educ* Bath U (BA 1992)

1d *Lucia Jane; *b* 13 Sept 1969; *m* 1994 *Michael O'Donovan and has:

1e *Elinor Mary; *b* 19–

2d *Charlotte Elizabeth; *b* 1974; *educ* Trin Coll Dublin

2c +Anthony Derek; *b* 2 May 1947; *educ* Haileybury and Trin Coll Dublin (BA 1970); *m* 1974 *Najma Madhavjee and has:

1d +Cormac Brendan; *b* 1979

2d +Murrough Idries; *b* 1983

1d *Zahara Grace; *b* 1976

2b David Lucius; *b* 6 Aug 1904; BSc, MRCVS, Maj RAVC; *m* 1st 7 Oct 1929 (*divorce* 1946) Mary Katherine Drummond (*d* 1987), er dau of Sir Arthur Herbert Drummond Steel-Maitland, 1st Bt, PC (*see* 1963 edn), and had:

1c +Michael David [Michael O'Brien Esq, Addlestead Farm, Headley, Epsom, Surrey]; *b* 15 July 1930

1c *Lucia Margaret [Miss Lucia O'Brien, 84 Colehill Lane, London SW6]; *b* 19 Aug 1932

2b (cont.) David O'Brien *m* 2nd 1954 *Shirley, dau of C P Hurford, of Worcester Park, Surrey, and *d* 1988, leaving by her:

2c +Tasman David [Tasman O'Brien Esq, 13 Harrison Close, Whitfield Park, Cairns 4870, N Queensland, Australia]; *b* 1955; *m* 1986 *Brenda Goodwin and has:

1d +Kirby; *b* 1986

2d +Conor Michael; *b* 1988

3c +Donough William [Mr Donough O'Brien, c/o Daylesford, Victoria, Australia]; *b* 1956

3b +(Horace) Donough [Dr Donough O'Brien, 30 Queen St, Burnie, Tasmania]; *b* 24 June 1911; BSc, MB, BCh, FRCSI, Lt-Col RAMC WW II (despatches), Surgn i/c Burnie Gen and Spencer Public Hosps Tasmania 1951, FRACS 1958; *m* 1st 23 July 1941 (*divorce* 1949) Pamela Charlotte, er dau of Capt Barrington Goodbody, of Cork Hill, Clara, Co Offaly, and has:

1c Caroline Phyllis Anne [Mrs Arthur Cox, 5851 Old Mountain Rd, Louisa, VA 23093, USA]; *b* 25 Oct 1942; *m* 1982 *Arthur James Cox, s of J Cox, of Pulaski, Va.

3b (cont.) Donough O'Brien *m* 2nd 25 Nov 1950 *Lucy Ann, dau of Maj Terence Edward Stafford O'Brien, of Ray Ho, Ray, Co Donegal, and by her has had:

1c John Alan Conor; *b* 10, *d* 14 May 1952

2c +Bartholomew Brendan [Dr Bartholomew O'Brien, 28 Wheaton Rd, Stepney, Adelaide 5069, S Australia]; *b* 22 Oct 1953; RGN, BN, PhD; *m* 1981 *Lauri Therese, dau of James Cadzow, and has:

1d +David Nicholas; *b* 1990

1d *Alice Louise; *b* 1986

3c +Alexander Kennedy [Alexander O'Brien Esq, 6 Barnett Terrace, Seacliffe Park, S Australia 5049]; *b* 30 March 1955; *m* 1st 1985 (*divorce* 1992) Lynley Keynes; *m* 2nd 19– *Rebecca, dau of Robert Hazelgrove, of Adelaide

1b *Mary Elinor [Mrs Bruce Flegg, St Nicholas House, Rostrevor Rd, Rathgar, Co Dublin, Ireland]; *b* 1 Feb 1907; BA 1929; *m* 3 Jan 1934 *Bruce Martin Flegg, ARIBA, S/Ldr RAF, s of Dr F A Martin Flegg, of Essex, and has:

1c *Aubrey Martin; *b* 23 May 1938; BA, PhD; *m* 2 July 1966 *Jennifer Condell, MLitt, of Dublin, and has:

1d *Nigel Patrick Martin; *b* 1970

1d *Eleanor Minta; *b* 15 Oct 1967

2c *Katherine Elinor; *b* 5 Nov 1934; ARCM; *m* 26 Sept 1964 *N Dimitrakopoulos, of Thessaloniki

2b *Rosaleen Brigid [Mrs Andrew Ganly, 6a Laurel Hill, Upper Glenageary Rd, Dun Laoghaire, Co Dublin, Ireland]; *b* 29 Jan 1909; RHA; *m* 19 May 1936 Andrew Ganly, BA, MA, FFD, RSCI, BDentSc (*d* 1982), and has:

1c *Eoghan Timothy; *b* 1938; *m* 1966 *Vera Behan and has:

1d *Brian; *b* 1967

1c *Helen Phillida; *b* 1939; *m* 1963 *Henry Brian Smith, MB, and has:

1d *Conor Melville; *b* 1967

2d *Desmond Brian; *b* 1978

1d *Kathleen Brigid; *b* 1970

1a Ellen Lucy; *d* 2 April 1925

2a Lucy Mary, CBE; *m* 24 Jan 1894 Arthur Beresford Cane, CBE (*d* 21 Dec 1939), 2nd s of Arthur Beresford Cane, of Collinstown, Clondalkin, Co Dublin, and *d* 23 April 1926, leaving issue

(1) (cont.) Edward O'Brien *m* 2nd 31 Jan 1880 Julia Mary (*d* 2 March 1907), dau of James Garth Marshall, of Monk Coniston, Ambleside, and *d* 21 Jan 1909, leaving by her:

2a Edward Conor Marshall; *b* 3 Nov 1880; Lt RNR; *m* 10 Oct 1928 Katharine Frances (*d* 27 July 1936), yr dau of Sir George Clausen, RA, and *d* 1952

3a Aubrey Ulick Marshall; *b* 7 June 1882; Capt RA; *ka* 1 Nov 1914

3a Katharine Jenny; *d unm* 13 Jan 1951

4a Margaret Ernestine; *m* 20 July 1915 her cousin Hugh Murrough Vere O'Brien, MC, Roy Munster Fus (*see* below), and *d* 1968, leaving issue

(2) Lucius Henry (Very Rev); *b* 13 Aug 1842; Dean Limerick; *m* 30 May 1872 Emily Mary Hannah (*d* 3 June 1942), est dau of Richard Thomas Montgomery, of Beaulieu, Co Louth, and *d* 25 Sept 1913, leaving:

1a Donough Richard; *b* 6 Jan 1876; Lt 5th Bn Roy Munster Fus; *m* 26 March 1914 Cicely Maud (*d* 1981), only dau of Rev Frederick Neville Carus-Wilson, and *d* 2 July 1938, leaving:

1b Lucia Elizabeth; *b* 12 March 1915; *d* 21 Jan 1918

2b Patricia Cicely; *b* 17 March 1918; *m* 14 Sept 1939 Rev John Godwin Benson, Hon CF, s of Rev R S Benson, of Co Donegal, and *d* 19 Jan 1991, having had:

1c *Donough O'Brien [Donough Benson Esq, 17 Pirie St, Newtown, Hobart, Tasmania 7008, Australia]; *b* 3 Aug 1940; has by *Carolyn Hall-Jones:

1d *Donough O'Brien; *b* 1975

1d *Lucia Patricia; *b* 1979

2c *Murrough John [Murrough Benson Esq, 37 Findlay Ave, Roseville, Sydney, NSW 2069, Australia]; *b* 2 May 1946; *m* 1969 *Eileen Joyce Cox and has:

1d *Murrough William George; *b* 1985

2d *Patrick John Godwin; *b* 1987

3c *Brian Lucius [Mr Brian Benson, 15 Murray St, Highton, Geelong, Victoria 3268, Australia]; *b* 10 Sept 1950; *m* 1975 *Jane Evelyn Martin and has:

1d *Antony Paul; *b* 1976

2d *Richard Lucius; *b* 1988

3d *Carus Edward; *b* 1989

1d *Cicely Jane; *b* 1985

2d *Brianna Maud; *b* 1991

3b Oona Charlotte; *b* 14 Sept 1919; *d* 27 Sept 1932

4b *Geraldine Mary [Mrs David Hely-Hutchinson, Parteenalax, Limerick, Ireland]; *b* 27 Feb 1922; *m* 25 Sept 1948 David Coote Hely-Hutchinson (*d* 26 April 1994; *see* DONOUGHMORE, E) and has issue

2a Charles Murrough; *b* 3 Aug 1877; *m* 1903 Agnes Purdom (*d* 1970), dau of James Wilson, of Alberta, and *d* 1939, leaving:

1b Lucius James; *b* 1904; *m* 1932 Evelyn, dau of James Storey, of Alberta

2b Donough Robert; *b* 1910; *m* 1940 *Rita Denny, dau of Rev William Musson, of Buckingham, and *d* 1991, leaving:

1c +Murrough [Murrough O'Brien Esq, 230 Hector Rd, RR3, Victoria, BC V8X 3X1, Canada]; *b* 14 Jan 1947; *m* 21 Dec 1968 *Patricia Arlene, dau of George Cyril Ellison, of N Vancouver

1c *Francine Denny [Mrs Francine Kissinger, 1736 Maple Bay Rd, RR5, Duncan, BC V9L 4T6, Canada]; *b* 9 Oct 1942; *m* 1969 (*divorce* 1991) Donald Vincent Kissinger and has:

1d *Simon Raven John; *b* 1972

1d *Sarah Tsu Emily O'BRIEN; *b* 1974

1b *Eileen Moira Agnes [Mrs Dan Heelas, 79 5550 Langley By-Pass, Langley, BC V3A 7Z3, Canada]; *b* 1912; *m* 1939 Dan Stephenson Heelas (*d* 1985), s of Dr W W Heelas, of Wolverhampton, and has:

1c *Moira Jessica [Mrs Henry Stephens, 7902 Glover Rd, RR6, Langley, BC V3A 4P9, Canada]; *b* 1942; *m* 1963 *Henry Stephens and has:

1d *Sheryl Lynn; *b* 1963; *m* 1984 *Guy Anthony Widiner and has:

1e *Brett Stephen; *b* 1990

2e *Dylan Daniel; *b* 1994

2d *Yvonne Doreen; *b* 1967

2c *Joan Zenda [Mrs Lynden Sharman, 3942 Indian River Drive, N Vancouver, BC V7G 2G9, Canada]; *b* 1944; *m* 1973 *Lynden Sharman and has:

1d *Paul Richard; *b* 1977

2d *Keith Stephenson; *b* 1980

3a William Lucius Robert; *b* 28 Jan 1889; *m* 1st 7 May 1913 Jean Graham (*d* 31 Aug 1946), yst dau of Tom Pollok, of Renfrewshire and Liverpool; *m* 2nd 1957 *Violet Fairbrother, widow of G D Mayer, and by his 1st w had:

1b *Mary Lockhart; *b* 10 Feb 1914

2b *Eileen Graham; *b* 10 Dec 1915; *m* 3 Aug 1940 *(Robert) David Eastham, 2nd s of His Hon Sir Tom Eastham, and has issue

1a Lucy Mabel; *m* 9 Dec 1902 Francis Carmichael Purser, OBE, MD (*d* 28 Feb 1934), of Dublin, and *d* 16 June 1957, leaving issue

2a Eileen

3a Honor Alice; *m* 1909 Lt-Col Walter McClellan Crosbie, DSO (*d* 2 April 1951), Res of Offrs Lancs Fus, of Co Donegal, and *d* 14 July 1947, leaving issue

4a Charlotte Grace; *m* 31 July 1912 John Charles Metge, of Alberta, and has issue

(3) Charles Murrough; *b* 24 Jan 1849; *m* 27 July 1871 Mary (*m* 2nd 1891 Canon W A Dickson and *d* 19 March 1941), dau of James Watt, of Claragh, Co Donegal, and *d* 13 Jan 1877, leaving:

1a Brian; *b* 12 July 1872; MD Dublin, Medical Inspr Local Govt Bd Ireland; *m* 1903 Mary Henrietta (*d* Nov 1968), dau of Maurice Charles Hime, LLD, of Co Donegal, and *d* 29 Oct 1915, leaving:

1b +Charles Murrough [Dr Charles O'Brien, 73 Knighton Drive, Leicester]; *b* 7 Dec 1903; *educ* Trin Coll Dublin (MB, BCh 1928); *m* 2 Oct 1930 Elizabeth Joyce (*d* 1988), dau of Ven Gerald William Peacocke, Archdeacon Kildare, and has:

1c +Brian Murrough Fergus; *b* 18 July 1931; *educ* Bedford Sch and Univ Coll Oxford (BA 1954, MA 1959); barrister Lincoln's Inn 1955

2c +David Donough; *b* 23 June 1933; *m* 1962 *Carole June Walters and has:

1d +Nicholas Charles Donough; *b* 1963; *m* 1993 *Mrs Kathryn Ann Hutchins (*née* Randle) and has:

1e *Anastasia Grace Ailne; *b* 199–

2d +Seamus Timothy Lucius; *b* 1965

2b Brian; *b* March 1908; MB, BCH Dublin 1931, DPH London 1933, W/Cdr RCAF; *m* 1 Dec 1938 Dorothea (*d* 1980), dau of John F A Simms, of Combermore, Lifford, and *d* Nov 1968, leaving:

1c +Brian Dermod [Dr Brian O'Brien, 5863 Macleod Drive, Halifax, NS B3H 1C6, Canada]; *b* 14 Jan 1942; *educ* U of Alberta, Queen's U Kingston (BSc 1963, MD, LMCC) and Dalhousie U NS (MSc 1997); FRCP 1978, Col RCAF Medical Br 1959–89; *m* 1 May 1962 *Barbara Eileen, dau of John Frederick Brennagh, of Ottawa, and has:

1d +Brian David; *b* 1 Nov 1963; *educ* Mount St Vincent U Halifax (BA, BEd); *m* 1990 *Susan Anne, dau of Francis Martin, of Halifax, and has:

1e +Christopher Keaton; *b* 5 May 1989

1e *Eliot Mary Brennagh; *b* 17 April 1992

2d +Patrick John; *b* 28 Dec 1965; *m* 1988 (*divorce* 1997) Karen Helen, dau of John Lyons, of Calgary, and has:

1e +Brian Douglas Conor; *b* 29 Sept 1997

3d +Christopher Michael; *b* 22 April 1969; *educ* Carlton U Ottawa (BA); *m* 1994 *Sheila Isobel, dau of Dr Robert Loughrey, of Brockville, Ontario

1d *Katherine Jennifer Eileen; *b* 12 Feb 1971

2c + George Lucius [Dr George O'Brien, 95 Empress Ave, N York, Ontario M2N 3T5, Canada]; *b* 19 Sept 1944; *educ* Queen's U Kingston (MSc) and Dartmouth Coll NH (AM, PhD); *m* 1976 *Elizabeth Frances, dau of Thomas Sharpless Ely, of Rochester, NY, and has:

1d +William Thomas; *b* 15 July 1982

1d *Margaret Clare; *b* 27 Dec 1984

2d *Katherine Elizabeth; *b* 19 March 1987

1c *Deirdre [Ms Deirdre O'Brien, 4534 W 3rd Ave, Vancouver, BC V6R 1N2, Canada]; *b* 24 Jan 1940; *educ* Ottawa U (BSc, MHA); *m* 24 Aug 1963 (*divorce* 1975, resumed maiden name) James Moxley Shearer, s of James Brodie Shearer, of Ottawa, and has:

1d *James O'Brien; *b* 1965

2d *George Brodie; *b* 1969

1d *Margaret Kathleen; *b* 1968; *educ* Carleton U (BA)

2d *Joan Hilary; *b* 1968

2c Ruth Brigid; *b* 16 July 1946; *d* unm 1990

1b *Mary Grainne; *b* Jan 1905; *m* 1935 Ian Galbraith Robson (*d* 1977) and has:

1c *Michael William; *b* 1948

2b *Margaret Theodora; *b* Feb 1916

1a Aline Mary; *m* 1898 George Murray KNOX later KNOX-PEEBLES (*d* 1926) and *d* 1945, leaving issue

2a Lucy Grace; *m* 1897 Capt Sam Wright Knox, LLB, Roy Irish Rifles (*d* 23 Aug 1929), and *d* 1954, leaving issue

(1) Lucy Josephine; *m* 26 June 1862 Very Rev John Gwynn, DD, Dean Derry, and *d* 3 April 1907, leaving issue

3 Edward; *b* 6 Dec 1806; *m* 15 Aug 1839 Louisa Susan, dau of James Hewitt Massy Dawson (*see* MASSY, B) and *d* 19 May 1840, leaving:

(1) Edward Arthur; *b* 1 Sept 1840; *m* 2 Jan 1877 Josephine Edith (*d* 26 May 1916), dau of C T Morey, of New York, and *dsp* 3 Oct 1912

4 Robert; granted with siblings 12 Sept 1862 rank of baron's dau/yr s; *b* 15 Oct 1809; *m* 14 Feb 1835 Elinor Jane Alicia Lucy (*d* 5 March 1889 aged 76), est dau of Sir Aubrey de Vere, 2nd Bt (*see* 1904 edn), and *d* 5 March 1870, leaving:

(1) Aubrey Stephen; *b* 4 May 1837; RM, Maj 60th Rifles; *m* 10 Aug 1871 Lucy Harriette (*d* 11 Feb 1932), only dau of Maj-Gen George Wynne, RE (*d* 18 Dec 1898), and had:

1a Robert Stephen Vere O'BRIEN later DE VERE (assumed, as did his mother, by roy licence 1899), of Curragh Chase, Adare, Co Limerick, JP; *b* 23 July 1872; LLB Cantab; 5th BN Roy Sussex Regt Boer War 1900 (Queen's medal) and WW I; barrister, Ch Justice Seychelles 1928–31 and Grenada 1931–35, Chllr Diocese of Windward Is 1932, Legal Adviser Seychelles, Jt Court Judge New Hebrides; *m* 26 Sept 1906 Isabel Catherine, only surv child of Rt Rev Handley Carr Glynne Moule, DD, Bp Durham, and *d* 15 Sept 1936

1a Eva Mary; *d* unm 15 Aug 1892

(2) Robert Vere, of Ballyalla, Ennis, and Monare, Foynes, JP Co Limerick, DL Co Clare; *b* 20 Oct 1842; barrister; *m* 10 July 1883 Florence Mary Arnold Forster (*d* 8 July 1936), dau of William Delafield Arnold, Dir Public Instruction Punjab, and adopted dau of Rt Hon William Edward Forster, MP, and *d* 30 May 1913, leaving:

1a Aubrey William Vere; *b* 29 Nov 1885; BA Oxon; *d* 7 Oct 1925

2a Hugh Murrough Vere, MC, of Monare, Foynes, Co Limerick; *b* 15 July 1887; Lt Roy Munster Fus; *m* 20 July 1915 his cousin Margaret Ernestine (*d* 1968), dau of Edward William O'Brien, DL, of Cahirmoyle, Co Limerick (*see* above), and *d* 31 May 1955, having had:

1b +Murrough Vere [Murrough O'Brien Esq, Monare, Foynes, Co Limerick, Ireland; 69 The Elms, Mt Merrion Ave, Blackrock, Co Dublin, Ireland]; *b* 15 Dec 1919; *educ* Dublin U (BA, BAI 1940) and London U (BSc 1947); ARSM, Dir Geol Survey Ireland 1952–64, Gen Man and V-Pres Tara Exploration and Devpt Co 1964, FIMM 1974, Hon Fell 1987; *m* 4 June 1945 *Zsuzánna Eva Szeréna, dau of Károly Károlyi, of Budapest, and has:

1c Colm Murrogh Vere; *b* 4 April 1947; *educ* Dublin U; represented Ireland at fencing Mexico Olympic Games 1968; *d* 1985 Miami, Florida

2c +Hugh Stephen Vere [Hugh O'Brien Esq, 10 Dungar Terrace, Dun Laoghaire, Co Dublin, Ireland]; *b* 13 Oct 1948; *educ* U Coll Dublin; architect; *m* 1983 *Alison Ann Cooke and has:

1d +Robert Murrough Vere; *b* 1991

2d +Donough Patrick Vere; *b* 1992

1d *Catherine Lucy Bebhinn; *b* 1987

1c *Sylvia Caroline Piroska [Mrs Julian Reynolds, 115 Weirview Drive, Stillorgan, Co Dublin, Ireland]; *b* 9 March 1946; *educ* Dublin (BA) and Simon Fraser Us (MSc); botanist; *m* 1971 *Julian Douglas Reynolds, Fell and Sr Lecturer Biology, Trin Coll Dublin, and has:

1d *Conor Charles O'Brien; *b* 1976

2d *Owen Ralph Douglas; *b* 1981

1d *Elinor Florence Dirny; *b* 1978

2c *Iseult Anne [Mrs Bryan Murphy, Thatch House, Adare, Co Limerick, Ireland]; *b* 30 July 1952; *m* 1981 *Bryan Fergus Murphy and has:

1d *Hugh Patrick Fergus; *b* 1982

1d *Slany Elizabeth; *b* 1985

3c *Charlotte Elinor; *b* 11 April 1962; *educ* Dublin U (BA 1984) and Imp Coll London (MSc 1985)

2b Turlogh Robert Vere; *b* 16 Nov 1923; *d* 22 Feb 1933

1b *Elinor Vere [Mrs Reginald Wiltshire, 62 Carroll Ho, Lancaster Gate, London W2]; *b* 30 May 1918; *m* 1956 Reginald Wiltshire (*d* 1968)

1a *Jane Elinor Vere, *m* 19 June 1928 Godfrey V M Hardy (*d* 21 Oct 1945) and has:

1b *Veronica Mary Rainault; *b* 1 April 1930; *m* 1960 *David N Rowe, s of Charles Rowe, of Wexford, and has:

1c *Brian Howard; *b* 8 July 1967

1c *Orla Elinor Vere; *b* 24 Feb 1963

2c *Nicola Hazel Ailve; *b* 24 Dec 1964; *m* 13 Sept 1997 *Erin McGovern

2b *Frances Pauline Eithne; *b* 16 March 1932; *m* 1957 *James Cunningham

2a *Florence Margaret Vere

(1) Mary Ellen Vere; *m* 2 Jan 1868 Charles Spencer Perceval (*see* EGMONT, E) and *d* 19 June 1924, leaving issue

(2) Charlotte Alice Vere; *d* unm 9 March 1903

(3) Eleanor Grace Katharine; *m* 25 Oct 1876 William T Monsell, RM (*d* 1887), and *d* 7 April 1920, leaving issue

5 Henry (Rev), of The Hall, Great Glen, Leics; *b* 15 April 1813; Vicar Killerskerdiney, Kilmore; *m* 23 May 1839 Harriet (*d* 1 May 1872), dau of John Godley (*see* KILBRACKEN, B), and *d* 12 Feb 1895, having had:

(1) Edward; *b* 26 July 1840; BCS, Dep Commr Punjab; *m* 1867 Mary (*d* 4 June 1939), dau of Col William Lamb, HEICS, and *d* 1894, leaving:

1a Murrough Charles, JP; *b* 1868; MD Manitoba 1897, Maj Canadian Army Med Corps; *m* 1901 Margaret Eleanor Barber (*d* 1958) and *d* 1955, leaving:

1b *Muriel Oclanis; *b* 1904; *m* 30 Aug 1932 Hamilton Stewart McKee, s of Alexander Mckee, of Belfast and Dauphin, Manitoba

2a Aubrey John, CIE (1906), CBE (1919); *b* 5 Dec 1870; Lt-Col IA, Commr Punjab, formerly N Lancs Regt; *m* 27 Oct 1906 Annie Winifred (*d* 10 May 1936), dau of James D'Arcy, of Kew, and *d* 31 Aug 1930, leaving:

1b Turlough Aubrey, CBE (1959); *b* 30 Sept 1907; *educ* Charterhouse and Ch Ch Oxford (BA 1929); Maj RA WW II, Dir PR PO 1966–68, Pres Inst PR 1965; *m* 14 July 1945 Phyllis Mary (*d* 1986), twin dau of Edward Grosvenor Tew, and *d* 7 Nov 1997, leaving:

1c +Teige Henry Patrick [Teige O'Brien Esq, 10 Fairlawn Grove, London W4 5EH]; *b* 25 April 1949; *m* 4 Sept 1976 *Sarah Catherine, dau of Henry Wilson, and has:

1d *Grania Catherine; *b* 30 Sept 1982

2d *Finola Clare; *b* 30 May 1985

2c +(Brian Edward) Nicholas [Nicholas O'Brien, 73 Craven Gdns, London SW19 8LU]; *b* 17 Aug 1951; *educ* Westminster and Ch Ch Oxford

(MA 1976); IT manager; *m* 3 Oct 1992 *Miranda Penelope Gillian, dau of Maj Jack Warren Pollock (*see* POLLOCK, Bt)

1c *Corinna Moira [Mrs Christopher Edge, 2 Kingswood Rd, London SW19 3NE]; *b* 5 Feb 1955; *m* 18 June 1993 *Christopher Edge, s of Bruce Edge

2b Edward Donough (Toby); *b* 21 Nov 1909; *educ* Stowe and Exeter Coll Oxford (BA 1931, MA 1949); Dir Press Div Br Cncl, Dir Info Servs C Centl Office, chm E D O'Brien Organisation, PR consultants; Im 1st 12 Feb 1936 Sylvia Inchbold (*d* 10 Sept 1950), yr dau of Court Denny, and had:

1c +Donough Anthony [Donough O'Brien Esq, 36 Charlwood Rd, London SW15 9IW]; *b* 23 April 1939; *educ* Stowe, Sorbonne and Munich U; Lt Irish Gds, PR consultant; *m* 1st 15 May 1969 Clare Jane Haddon, only dau of Leonard Merritt Read, of Llandaff, Cardiff, and has:

1d +Murrough Martin Donough; *b* 24 Aug 1972

1d *Katherine Abigail Thalia; *b* 20 June 1977

1c (cont.) Donough O'Brien *m* 2nd 1980 Philippa, dau of Maj-Gen Mervyn James, CB, MBE; *m* 3rd 1990 *Elizabeth, dau of Lt Gen Sir John Guise Cowley, GC, KBE, CB, and by his 2nd w has:

2d +Edmond Mahon; *b* 20 Aug 1981

1c *Natalie Deirdre [Mrs Roger Whittaker, Cubberley House, Ross-on-Wye, Herefs]; *b* 9 Aug 1941; *m* 15 Aug 1964 *Roger Henry Brough Whittaker, the singer, only s of Edward Whittaker, of Kenya, and has:

1d *(Edward) Guy; *b* 1974

2d *Alexander Michael; *b* 1978

1d *Emily Clare; *b* 1968; *m* 1991 *Stewart Malcolm Kennedy, s of S/Ldr Ewen Kennedy

2d *Lauren Marie; *b* 1970

3d *Jessica Jane; *b* 1973

2c Geraldine Moira; *b* 27 Feb 1945; *m* 28 June 1969 Rolfe Erwolder Elholm, of Bergen, Norway, and *d* 1987, leaving:

1d *Astri; *b* 1971

2b (cont.) Edward O'Brien *m* 2nd 26 Feb 1952 *Leonora Thayne [Mrs Edward O'Brien, 49 Kenway Rd, London SW5 0RE], er dau of Manning Leonard Railton, and *d* 9 Jan 1979, leaving by her:

2c +Fionn Murrough Manning [Fionn O'Brien Esq, Calle de Arzobispo, cos 15 (1a) 28027, Madrid, Spain]; *b* 14 March 1953; *educ* Stowe; regnl dir Newsweek Internat Amsterdam; *m* 1st 1973 Carole Ann, dau of William Whitlock, and has:

1d *Zoe; *b* 1973

2c (cont.) Fionn O'Brien *m* 2nd 1996 *Monica van der Eb, dau of Lt-Cdr Marinus Jacobus, Dutch Navy, and has by her:

1d +Murrough Marinus Edward; *b* 16 Feb 1997

3c +Lucius Edward [Lucius O'Brien Esq, 22 Hendrick Ave, London SW12 8TL]; *b* 1 April 1957; educ Stowe; late Lt Irish Gds, money broker; *m* 6 Sept 1986 *Caroline Veronica Mary, dau of Maj Hywel Colwyn Phillips, of Mostyn, Clwyd, and has:

1d *Caroline Louisa Maire; *b* 1992

2d *Olivia Alison Clare; *b* 1993

1b *Moira Winifred Oclanis [Mrs George Barstow, Butt House, Painswick, Glos GL6 6QS]; *b* 18 Nov 1912; *educ* St Paul's Girls' Sch; *m* 1st 7 Dec 1932 (John) Michael Orpen Barstow (*d* 1976) and has had:

1c Aubrey John O'Brien; *b* 17 April 1935; *educ* Winchester and Ch Ch Oxford; lost at sea while sailing 29 Sept 1963

1c *Elizabeth Catharine Oclanis [Mrs Charles Bevis, 15 Abbey Rd, Sheringham, Norfolk NR26 8NN]; *b* 22 Sept 1933; *educ* St Hilda's Coll Oxford (BA 1956, MA 1959); *m* 18 July 1959 *Charles Richard Cubitt Bevis, s of Leslie Cubitt Bevis, and has:

1d *Elizabeth Margaret Moira; *b* 29 Aug 1960; *m* 1982 *Julian Bryan Stevens and has:

1e *Frederick Charles Bevis; *b* 13 March 1988

1e *Harriet Lucinda Elizabeth; *b* 27 Sept 1985

2e *Olivia Catharine Anne; *b* 22 Dec 1989

2d *Maria Catharine Oclanis; *b* 6 Jan 1962; *m* 25 March 1995 *Stephen McCoy

3d *Alexandra Anne Cecilia; *b* 6 July 1963; *m* 1986 *Stephen Andrew Carl White and has:

1e *Henry Edward Bevis; *b* 15 July 1991

1e *Felicity Patricia Anne; *b* 27 June 1989

2e *Imogen Elizabeth Cecilia; *b* 7 Nov 1994

4d *Lucinda Mary Sophia; *b* 19 July 1965; *m* 1986 *Jonathan Walter David Starling and has:

1e *Anna Letitia Mary; *b* 21 Sept 1986

2e *Sophia Rachel Xanthe; *b* 26 Dec 1988

5d *Selena Penelope Beatrice; *b* 18 Sept 1969

6d *Xanthe Frances Henrietta; *b* 3 April 1972

2c *Anne Moira Olivia [Mrs Roger Beament, 74 Clarence Rd, St Albans, Herts AL1 4NG]; *b* 3 Aug 1940; *educ* St Paul's Girls' Sch and Middx Hosp; SRN 1962; *m* 1st 24 April 1965 Derek Landale Christie (*d* 1974), er s of Thomas Landale Christie, OBE, MC, and has:

1d *John Michael Landale; *b* 22 Feb 1966; *m* 1993 *Karen, dau of Michael Heaney, and has:

1e *Rachel Helen Olivia; *b* 28 April 1995

2d *Edward Hugh Landale; *b* 7 Feb 1968; *m* 6 June 1995 *Sarah, dau of John McClay, and has:

1e *Thomas Edward; *b* 11 July 1996

1d *Annabella Moira Orpen; *b* 7 Oct 1969

2c (cont.) Mrs Derek Christie *m* 2nd 1977 *Roger Beament and has by him:

2d *Emily Catherine Olivia; *b* 25 Dec 1978

3c *Mary Geraldine Sheila [Mrs Graham Finch, 38 Sion Hill, Bath, Somerset BA1 2UW]; *b* 26 July 1943; *educ* St Paul's Girls' Sch; *m* 1970 Graham Finch (*d* 1995) and has:

1d *Henrietta Lucy Anne; *b* 17 June 1975

2d *Cressida Mary Frances; *b* 3 July 1979

4c *Henrietta Penelope [Mrs Nicholas Rose, 23 All Saints Villas Rd, Cheltenham, Glos GL52 2HP]; *b* 29 Sept 1945; *educ* Exeter U (DSA 1967) and London U (DASS 1968); *m* 7 Dec 1968 *Nicholas Frank Killeen Rose, only s of Thomas Rose, and has:

1d *Thomas Michael Orpen; *b* 19 June 1978

1d *Beatrice Caroline Ellen; *b* 19 Aug 1974

5c *Brigid Evelyn Cecilia [Mrs Charles Brett, St Margaret's, 3 St Michael's Rd, Winchester, Hants SO23 9JE]; *b* 3 Nov 1947; *educ* St Paul's Girls' Sch and Hornsey Coll of Art; *m* 1973 *Charles Michael Brett and has:

1d *Aubrey Francis Patrick; *b* 7 Dec 1974

1d *Caroline Moira Cecilia; *b* 14 Jan 1977

1b (cont.) Mrs Michael Barstow *m* 2nd 24 March 1990 Capt George Baillie Barstow (*d* 1991)

2b *Winifred Mary Sheila [Sister Sheila CSJB, Convent of St John Baptist, Hatch Lane, Windsor, Berks SL4 3QR]; *b* 27 May 1918

3a Edward, CBE (1927); *b* 20 Sept 1872; Lt-Col IA and Political Dept, Kaisar-i-Hind Medal 2nd Cl 1901; *m* 1898 Mary Elma Travers (*d* 19 Nov 1952), dau of Robert William Hunter, BCS, and *d* 20 March 1965

1a Claudine Oclanis; *m* 15 Oct 1888 Col Charles James Bamber, MVO, IMS (*d* 9 Jan 1940), s of Henry J Bamber, of Bedford, and *d* Dec 1947, leaving issue

2a Oclanis; *m* 8 Sept 1902 Hubert Calvert, CSI, CIE, ICS (*d* 9 May 1961), of Devon, s of J M Calvert, of Rochdale, and *d* 27 Sept 1944, leaving issue

3a Eileen; *m* 30 Oct 1915 Capt Gilbert Kennedy, Roy Munster Fus (*d* 1918), s of Robert Muirhead Kennedy, ICS, and had issue

(2) Murrough John; *b* 10 June 1842; *m* 16 Sept 1873 Eleanor (*d* 26 Oct 1916), 3rd dau of John Waller, and *d* 22 Feb 1914, leaving:

1a Henry Eoghan, DSO (1918); *b* 1876; BSc 1898, MIEE, Lt-Col RE WW I (despatches twice); *m* 10 Jan 1905 Frances Victoria Lucy (*d* 15 Feb 1969), dau of Richard Altamount Smythe, of Court-na-Farraga, Killiney, Co Dublin, and *d* 9 Sept 1967, having had:

1b Brian Eoghan; *b* 1907; Lt-Cdr RN WW II; *m* 10 Feb 1936 Elizabeth (*m* 2nd 1949 L P Dennis (*d* 1983), of Eye, Suffolk), dau of Stuart Séguin Strahan, MA, MB, BCh, of Hong Kong, and was *ka* in HM Submarine *Thames* Aug 1940, leaving:

1c *Olivia Fiona [Mrs Sebastian Robinson, 7 Kirklee Gdns, Glasgow G12 0SG]; *b* 22 Nov 1938; *educ* LMH Oxford (MA); PhD Lond; *m* 8 Sept 1960 *(Richard Edmund) Sebastian Robinson, s of Herbert Robinson, of Storrington, Sussex, and has:

1d *James Lucius O'Brien; *b* 10 June 1962

1d *Amanda Mary Victoria; *b* 22 May 1961; *m* 1st 1983 Martyn D Smith; *m* 2nd 1996 *Adam Justin Spielman

(1) Katherine; *m* 16 May 1867 Rev Frederick Bransby Toulmin (*d* 26 March 1924), Vicar Hatfield Peverel, 2nd s of Henry Heyman Toulmin, of Herts, and *d* 16 Aug 1912, leaving issue

(2) Annabella Charlotte; *m* 14 Sept 1871 John Watt Smyth, Judge Ch Court Lahore, and *d* 20 Feb 1907, leaving issue

(3) Olivia Henrietta; *d* 21 May 1863

(4) Angelina Rose Geraldine; *m* 4 June 1873 Col John Gerald Wilson, CB, DL (*ka* Boer War 8 March 1902), of Cliffe Hall, Yorks, and *d* 18 Aug 1941, leaving issue

(5) Grace Amy Frances; *m* 26 May 1890 Maj Reginald McKerrell (*d* 4 Dec 1925), 93rd Sutherland Highrs, and *d* 28 Dec 1890

1 Harriet; 25 years Superioress House of Mercy Clewer; *m* 21 Sept 1839 Rev Charles Monsell (*d* 1851) and *d* 25 March 1883 aged 71

2 Grace; *d* 10 March 1871

3 Anne; *m* 26 Oct 1837 Rev Arthur Martineau (*d* 11 Nov 1872), Vicar Whitkirk, Yorks, Preb St Paul's Cathedral, and *d* 20 July 1872

4 Katherine Lucia; *m* 20 April 1837 Rt Rev Hon Charles Amyand Harris (*see* MALMESBURY, E) and *dsps* 31 Jan 1865

Sir EDWARD *d* 13 March 1837; his est s,

Sir Lucius O'Brien, 5th Bt, as which s f, and **13th Baron of Inchiquin**, as which recognised by Ho Lds 11 April 1862 after having *s* 9th cousin 1855; *b* 5 Dec 1800; Ld Lt Co Clare, rep I peer 1863–72; *m* 1st 21 Feb 1837 Mary (*d* 26 May 1852), est dau of William FitzGerald, of Adelphi, Co Clare, and had, with other issue:

1 EDWARD DONOUGH, **14th Baron**

1 Juliana Cecilia; *m* 30 July 1858 Col William Edward Armstrong MacDonnell (*d* 14 Nov 1883), of New Hall, Co Clare, and *d* 26 Aug 1925, leaving issue

2 Charlotte Anne; *m* 23 May 1866 Rev George Stopford Ram (*d* 19 Nov 1889), Vicar St Peter's, Bournemouth, and *d* 31 Jan 1918, leaving issue

3 Mary Grace; *m* 23 April 1874 Abel John Ram, KC (*d* 8 Aug 1920), Recorder Wolverhampton, and *d* 28 June 1912, leaving issue

The **13th Baron** *m* 2nd 25 Oct 1854 Louisa (*d* 13 Feb 1904), dau of Maj James Finucane and coheir of Andrew Finucane, of Ennistymon Ho, Co Clare, and by her had:

2 Lucius Murrough; *b* 2 Aug 1857; BA Cantab; barrister; *m* 19 Sept 1907 Rose Elizabeth (*d* 30 July 1926), widow of Maj-Gen James Graham Robert Douglas MacNeill, CB, and dau of Thomas Somers, of Mendip Lodge, Somerset, and *dsp* 16 Feb 1939

3 William Henry Ernest Robert Turlough; *b* 20 April 1863; *m* 1 June 1901 (Henrietta) Ethne (*d* 18 Dec 1950), yst dau of George Robert Browne (*see* SLIGO, M), and *d* 7 Nov 1943, leaving:

(1) Turlough George Henry; *b* 11 Dec 1907; *educ* Harrow; Lt RNVR WW II; *m* 1 April 1939 (*divorce* 1966) Catherine, dau of Dr John Watt Senter, of Edinburgh, and *d* 30 Nov 1976, leaving:

1a +Patrick Brian [Patrick O'Brien Esq, via Marco Aurelio 42, Flat 15, Rome, Italy]; *b* 25 June 1943

1a *Diana [Mrs Ronald Ostwald, 8 Cholmeley Park, London N6 5EU]; *b* 4 Jan 1941; *m* 3 Nov 1961 *Ronald Anthony Ostwald, s of Rudolf Ostwald, and has:

1b *Christian Mark Sebastian; *b* 20 May 1962; has by *Joanna Lynn Kelly:

1c *Samuel Thomas; *b* 21 Feb 1996

1c *Kitty Annabel Kelly; *b* 13 Nov 1993

1b (cont.) Christian Ostwald has by *Joanne Lillian Brown:

2c *Lewis George; *b* 25 May 1997

1b *Cassie Kate Louise; *b* 27 Aug 1978

(1) (Ethne) Lucia, *b* 27 June 1902; *m* 14 Dec 1932 G/Capt Valentine Brice Jephson Jackson, RAF (*d* 7 July 1976), yr s of Rev Canon Brice Jackson, of Belmullet, Co Mayo, and *d* 1989

4 Anastasia Kathleen Lucia; *m* 23 Oct 1879 Lt-Col Charles Arthur Madan Warde, DL (*d* 21 April 1912), of Squerryes Court, Westerham, Kent, and *d* 1 April 1938, leaving issue

5 Nora Louisa Jane; *m* 17 July 1895 Richard Hugo Douglass (*d* 28 March 1939) and *d* 26 June 1927, leaving issue

6 Blanche Louisa; *m* 23 July 1896 Rev Paget Lambart Bayly (*see* ANGLESEY, M) and *d* 19 Jan 1945

7 Alicia Amabel (twin with Blanche Louisa); Sister-of-mercy at Clewer; *d* unm 28 July 1939

8 Louisa Anna Maria (twin with William); *d* unm 28 Jan 1940

The 13th BARON *d* 22 March 1872; his est s,

EDWARD DONOUGH O'BRIEN, **14th Baron of Inchiquin**, KP (1892); *b* 14 May 1839; MA Cantab; High Sheriff Co Clare 1862, rep I peer 1873–1900, Ld Lt and custos rotulorum Co Clare 1879–1900, Hon Col 7th Bde S Irish Div RA; *m* 21 Aug 1862 Emily (*d* 3 Jan 1868), 2nd dau of 2nd Baron Heytesbury (*qv*), and had:

1 LUCIUS WILLIAM, **15th Baron**

2 Murrough, DSO, MVO; *b* 8 Nov 1866; Maj Northumberland Fus Boer War, ADC and Mil Sec to Ld Lt Ireland 1902–05, Extra Equerry to HRH PRINCESS LOUISE, DUCHESS OF ARGYLL 1912, Mil Attaché Washington 1914–17, Hon Lt-Col 1917; *m* 21 Nov 1906 Marguerite (*d* 6 Nov 1958), dau of William Lewis, of New York, and *d* 6 Sept 1934, leaving:

(1) +MURROUGH RICHARD [Maj Murrough O'Brien, Shelleys House, Wick Lane, Englefield Green, Surrey TW20 0XE]; *b* 25 May 1910; heir presumptive; *educ* Eton and Balliol Coll Oxford (MA 1931); Maj Irish Gds WW II; *m* 1st 3 June 1942 (*divorce* 1951) Irene Clarice, formerly w of (a) 10th Marquess of Queensberry (*qv*) and (b) Sir James Hamet Dunn, 1st Bt, of Bathurst (*see* 1970 edn), and only dau of H W Richards, of Regent's Park, NW1; *m* 2nd 11 Feb 1952 *Joan, widow of Capt Wolf Barnato and dau of Charles Pierre Jenkinson, and has:

1a +Conor John Anthony [Conor O'Brien Esq, Gorsefield House, Newtown, Berks RG20 9BE]; *b* 24 Sept 1952; *educ* Eton; *m* 1982 *Vivian, yr dau of Col Adrian Rouse, of Chelsea, and has:

1b +Fionn Murrough; *b* 1987

1b *Slaney Victoria; *b* 1989

1a *Melissa Jane [Mrs Jorge de Paiva Raposo, Manor Farm House, Upper Wootton, Hants]; *b* 3 May 1956; *m* 1st 1979 Nicholas Simunek, of New York; *m* 2nd 19– *Jorge de Paiva Raposo and by him has:

1b *Charles Murrough; *b* 1996

1b *Alessandra Belinda; *b* 1991

(2) +Edward Cecil, OBE (1958) [Maj Edward O'Brien OBE, The Old Barn, 1 Station Rd, Docking, Norfolk PE31 8LS]; *b* 6 April 1915; *educ* Eton; Capt Irish Gds, Maj Para Regt WW II, Kt SMO Malta; *m* 1st 30 Aug 1943 (*divorce* 1968) Elizabeth Margaret, est dau of Col Sir William Henry Dyke Acland, 3rd Bt, of Oxford (*qv*), and has:

1a *Lucia Jane [Mrs David Smith, 68 Goldington Ave, Bedford]; *b* 14 Feb 1947; *m* 1973 *David Lawrence Gilbert Smith and has:

1b *Caroline Teresa Slaney; *b* 1976

2b *Isabel Helen; *b* 1980

2a *Emily Maria Theresa [Mrs Emily Anson, 67 Courtfield Gdns, London SW5 0NJ]; *b* 30 Jan 1952; *m* 1978 (*divorce* 1997) Stephen Anson and has:

1b *Nicholas Phaedrig Charles; *b* 1989

(2) (cont.) Maj Edward O'Brien *m* 2nd 1991 *Phyllis Elsie Margaret, dau of Philip Heber-Jones and formerly w of Derek Chudleigh

3 Edward Donough, JP Co Clare; *b* 28 Dec 1867; Lt 7th Bde S Irish Div RA; *m* 4 April 1899 Lady Beatrice Mary Hare (*d* 1960), yr dau of 3rd Earl of Listowel (*qv*), and *d* 27 Dec 1943, leaving:

(1) Terence; *b* 20 Feb 1900; Capt DLI; *m* 1st 25 July 1928 (*divorce* 1946) Irene, dau of W Harle, of Newcastle; *m* 2nd 5 April 1947 *Marjorie Day and *d* 19 Feb 1970

(1) Enid Moira; *b* 4 Feb 1903; *m* 1st 2 May 1928 (*divorce* 1940) Rowland Frank Taaffe Finn, only s of Dr Taaffe Finn, of Ashwick, Somerset, and had issue; *m* 2nd 1 March 1941 Walter William Wilkinson, s of William Wilkinson

1 Geraldine Mary, MBE (1920); *b* 16 June 1863; *m* 1st 8 June 1886 Thomas George Stacpoole Mahon, DL (*d* 10 Oct 1906), of Corbally, Co Clare, and had issue; *m* 2nd 21 Oct 1908 John Blood (*d* 25 Aug 1912), of Ballykilty, Co Clare, and *d* 3 Feb 1951

The **14th Baron** *m* 2nd 29 Jan 1874 Hon Ellen White (*d* 2 March 1913), est dau of 2nd Baron Annaly (*qv*), and by her had:

4 Donough; *b* 29 Aug 1870; *educ* Winchester and Ch Ch Oxford (MA 1905); 2nd Lt Irish Gds, barrister Inner Temple 1905, author: *History of the O'Briens from Brian Boroimhe* and *Miniatures in the 18th and 19th Centuries*, FSA, FSAI, FRSA, Fell Irish Genealogical Research Soc; *m* 1st 21 Jan 1914 Patricia Alice Fedora (*d* 15 Oct 1926), dau of John Dowdeswell, of Derby; *m* 2nd 1 Oct 1928 Rose (*d* 7 June 1978), formerly w of Elie N Ades, of Alexandria, and *dsp* 23 Sept 1953

5 Henry Barnaby, MC, DL (E Lothian); *b* 9 Jan 1887; Capt Irish Gds, Staff Capt 1916, WW I (wounded, despatches); *m* 1st 23 April 1925 Lady Helen Baillie-Hamilton, OBE (*d* 17 Sept 1959), sis of 12th Earl of Haddington (*qvI**); *m* 2nd 1964 Edith Lawrie (*d* 7 Nov 1996), widow of T M Steele, and *d* 1969, having by his 1st w had:

(1) Desmond Barnaby; *b* 27 Aug 1926; *educ* Eton; memb Lloyd's; *m* 3 Feb 1955 Cherry Angela Mary (*d* 1992), yr dau of Maj (Frank) James Wriothesley Seely (*see* SHERWOOD, B), and *d* 1969, leaving:

1a *Karen [Mrs Paul Cowan, The Old Farmhouse, Weald, Bampton, Oxon OX18 2HW]; *b* 19 Dec 1956; Master Forester Delamere Forest; *m* 1978 *Paul William Cowan and has:

1b *Jonathan; *b* 1981

1b *Lara Frances; *b* 1979

2b *Nina Elizabeth; *b* 1980

3b *Molly; *b* 1988

2a *Sarah Jane; *b* 12 March 1961; *m* 1986 *Simon Cellan-Jones and has:

1b *Daniel Alexander; *b* 18 May 1996

1b *Kate; *b* 1988

(2) +Michael George; *b* 22 Dec 1928; *educ* Eton and King's Coll Cambridge (MA 1952); 2nd Lt Irish Gds, memb Lloyd's, dir H W Stutter and Ptnrs; *m* 23 April 1955 *Susan Mary Matilda, est dau of W/Cdr Robert Cecil Talbot Speir, OBE, of Linkside, Nairn, and has:

1a +Peter Thomond; *b* 14 March 1961

2a +John Michael; *b* 31 March 1964

1a *Gillian Ursula Helen; *b* 1 March 1956

2a *Rebecca; *b* 25 Oct 1957

5 (cont.) The Hon Henry O'Brien *m* 2nd 16 Nov 1964 *Edith Lawrie [The Hon Mrs Henry O'Brien, 3 Ibris Place, N Berwick, E Lothian], widow of Thomas M Steele, and *d* 7 Jan 1969

6 Desmond; *b* 14 May 1895; Lt RFC; *ka* 1915

2 Clare; *b* 17 Jan 1875; *m* 26 July 1904 Brig-Gen Noel Armar Lowry-Corry and *d* 21 Sept 1950, leaving issue (*see* BELMORE, E)

3 Moira; *b* 13 April 1876; *m* 1st 24 July 1901 (*divorce* 1912) Sir Frederick Edward William Hervey-Bathurst, 5th Bt, DSO (*qv*), and had issue; *m* 2nd 19 Sept 1918 Cdr George Russell Peckham, RN (*d* Jan 1961), s of H Thornton Peckham, and *d* 20 Nov 1957

4 Eileen; *b* 7 July 1877; *d* unm 4 March 1967

5 Maud; *b* 19 Sept 1878; *d* unm 8 Nov 1956

6 Beatrice; *b* 23 Dec 1882; *m* 1st 16 March 1905 (*divorce* 1924) Senatore Guglielmo Marconi, Hon GCVO, LLD, DSc (*d* 20 July 1937), yr s of Signor Marconi, banker, of Bologna, by Annie, only dau of Andrew Jameson, and had issue; *m* 2nd 3 March 1924 Liborio Marignoli, Marquis di Montecorona (*d* 24 Jan 1948), and *d* 10 Oct 1976, leaving further issue

7 Lilah; *b* 18 Oct 1884; *m* 1st 12 Sept 1914 Capt Hon Coulson Churchill Fellowes, er s of 2nd Baron de Ramsey (*qv*), and had issue; *m* 2nd 6 March 1925 Nobile Riccardo Assanti (*d* Feb 1957), Magistral Kt SMO Malta, Kt Order SS. Maurice and Lazarus, Kt Grand Cross Crown Italy, Capt Res Alpine Regt, s of Gen Damiano Assanti, Senator, ADC to KING OF ITALY, and *d* 19–

8 Doreen; *b* 4 March 1888; *m* 21 Dec 1907 (*divorce* 1927) Maj Hon Richard Coke, 5th s of 2nd Earl of Leicester (*qv*), and *d* 10 June 1960, leaving issue

The 14th BARON *d* 9 April 1900; his est s,

LUCIUS WILLIAM O'BRIEN, **15th Baron of Inchiquin**, JP Salop, DL Co Clare; *b* 21 June 1864; Lt Rifle Bde, Hon Col Clare RF Res Artillery, rep I peer 1900–29, memb Senate IFS 1921; *m* 14 Jan 1896 Ethel Jane (*d* 5 June 1940), medal Queen Elisabeth Belgium 1920, er dau and coheir of Johnston Jonas Foster, JP, of Moor Park, Ludlow, and Cliffe Hill, Lightcliffe, and *d* 9 Dec 1929, leaving:

1 DONOUGH EDWARD FOSTER O'BRIEN, **16th Baron of Inchiquin**; *b* 5 Jan 1897; *educ* Eton, RMC Sandhurst and Magdalen Coll Oxford; 1st and 3rd Bn Rifle Bde 1916–19 WW I, ADC to Viceroy India 1919–20, Capt 2nd Bn London Rifle Bde WW II 1939–42, Order Crown Romania; *m* 13 Dec 1921 Hon Anne Molyneux Thesiger (*d* 10 Aug 1973), 2nd dau of 1st Viscount Chelmsford (*qv*), and *d* 19 Oct 1968, leaving:

(1) * Deirdre Jane Frances [The Hon Mrs Chapin, Mizzentop No 47, Harbour Rd, Warwick WKO6, Bermuda]; *b* 6 Nov 1924; WRNS WW II 1943–45; *m* 23 April 1954 Horace Beecher Chapin, MD (*d* 19 Feb 1992), yr s of Horace H Chapin, of Batavia, NY, USA

(2) * Grania Rachel [The Hon Mrs Weir, Ballinakella Lodge, Whitegate, Co Clare, Ireland]; *b* 31 May 1928; Priv Sec to Sir Arthur Salter, PC, MP, 1947–52, social sec to: Sir John Balfour, KCMG, 1952, Sir Esler Denning, GCMG, 1954–57, Hon John Hay Whitney, US Amb UK, 1958, Sir Berkeley Gage, Amb Peru, 1958–60; *m* 17 July 1973 * Hugh William Lindsay Weir, er s of Maj Terence J C Weir, MC

2 PHAEDRIG LUCIUS AMBROSE O'BRIEN, **17th Baron of Inchiquin**; *b* 4 April 1900; *educ* Eton, Magdalen Coll Oxford (MA) and Imp Coll London; geologist, Anglo-American Corp, Maj Rifle Bde WW II 1940–45, attd E Africa Intell Corps (wounded, despatches 1941), Colonial Serv Overseas Geological Survey; *m* 19 Feb 1945 *Vera Maud [The Rt Hon Vera Lady Inchiquin, Hanway Lodge, Richards Castle, Ludlow, Salop], dau of Rev Clifton Samuel Winter, of Winton Ho, Dawlish, Devon, and *d* 1982

3 Fionn Myles Maryons; *b* 28 Oct 1903; *educ* Radley and Loughborough Coll; F/Lt RAFVR WW II 1941–45; *m* 22 June 1939 *Josephine Reine [The Hon Mrs Fionn O'Brien, 1 Dault Rd, London SW18 2NH], dau of Joseph Eugene Bembaron, of Long Ditton, Surrey, and *d* 2 Aug 1977, leaving:

(1) CONOR MYLES JOHN O'BRIEN, **18th and present Baron of Inchiquin**

(1) * Fiona Jane [Mrs Romano Obert de Thieusies, 47 Chiddingstone St, London SW6 3TQ]; *b* 23 July 1941; *m* 24 April 1965 *Romano Louis Marie Joseph Ghislain Obert de Thieusies, 2nd s of Alain Martel Marie Joseph Ghislain, Vicomte Obert de Thieusies, of Château de Thoricourt, Thoricourt, Hainaut, Belgium, and has:

1a *Patrick Conor Alain; *b* 6 June 1968

1a *Isabelle Stephanie; *b* 15 Feb 1966

2a *Sophie Patricia; *b* 6 Dec 1972

1 Katharine Beryl; *b* 19 April 1898; *m* 9 April 1929 John Francis Patrick Gallagher, LRCP, LRCSI, Capt RAFMS (*d* 22 Aug 1955), only s of Patrick Gallagher, JP, of Co Donegal, and had issue

2 Griselda Etheldreda Clodagh; *b* 19 Oct 1906; F/O WAAF WW II; *m* 14 March 1953 David Clifford Christopherson, DSC, yr s of Henry Clifford Christopherson, of Woodbury, Reigate, Surrey

3 (Finola) Helga Laetitia Monica; *b* 22 Sept 1910; Section Offr WAAF WW II, Immigration Offr Nairobi 1949–65; *m* 7 Sept 1968 Howell Effingham Davis (*d* 1 April 1974), yr s of Walter Stewart Davis, of Coglan House, Longhope, Glos, and *d* 14 June 1975

INCHYRA

Arms: Quarterly, 1st, or a cross moline azure and base barry undy gules and vert, on a chief of the third a lozenge of the first between two spur-revels, also of the first (for MILLAR); 2nd, per bend argent and vert a lion passant gules (for HOYER); 3rd, azure a chevron argent between two spur-revels in chief and a demi-moon reversed or (for VAN SWINDEREN); 4th, azure a cross argent cantoned between four roses or (for DE MAREES). **Crest:** A cubit arm, the hand erect in the act of blessing proper. **Supporters:** Two blackcock proper. **Motto:** *Manent optima coelo* ('The best things rest in heaven). **Creation:** B. (UK) 2 Feb 1962.

THE 2ND BARON INCHYRA, of St Madoes, Co Perth (Robert Charles Reneke Hoyer Millar) [The Rt Hon The Lord Inchyra, Rookley Manor, King's Somborne, Hants SO20 6QX]; *b* 4 April 1935; *s f* 1989; *educ* Eton and New Coll Oxford; *m* 1 Aug 1961 *Fiona Mary, yr dau of Edmund Charles Reginald Sheffield, JP, DL (*see* SHEFFIELD, Bt), and has:

1 +(CHRISTIAN) JAMES CHARLES [The Hon James Hoyer Millar, 29 Caithness Rd, London W14 0JA]; *b* 12 Aug 1962; *educ* Eton and Edinburgh U; *m* 3 Oct 1992 *Caroline Jane, dau of Robin Swan, of Lower Wield, Hants, and has:

(1) +Jake Christian Robert; *b* 10 July 1996

(1) *Eleanor Mary; *b* 23 Aug 1994

1 *Henrietta Julia [The Hon Mrs Villanueva Brandt, 34 Guildford Rd, London SW8 2BX]; *b* 21 Sept 1964; *m* 15 Oct 1988 *Carlos Manuel Villanueva Brandt, s of Manuel Villanueva, of Caracas, Venezuela, and has:

(1) *Alfredo Enrique; *b* 19 Feb 1993

(2) *Mateo Carlos; *b* 9 July 1996

2 *Louisa Mary [The Hon Mrs Parladé, 43 Sinclair Rd, London W14]; *b* 26 April 1968; *m* 12 Sept 1997 *Jaime Parladés of Francisco and Mary Parladé, of Banahavis, Spain

Lineage: ROBERT MILLAR, of Montrose, Angus; *b* 18 Sept 1778; timber merchant; *m* 1st Jane MacNeil, of Musselburgh, Midlothian; *m* 2nd 1 May 1806 Elsebolette (*d* 20 June 1833), dau of Christian Hoyer, of Christiansand, Norway, by Ingeborg Maria Arundreep, and *d* 1 Jan 1861, having by her had:

1 CHRISTIAN

2 Robert; *dsp*

3 William, of South Heath, Hampstead; *b* 1814; *m* 11 April 1849 Julia Matilda (*d* 1870), dau of Edward Scott, RN, of Outlands, Devonport, and *d* 1876, leaving, with seven other children:

(1) Henry Edward, of Heathdown, Hampstead; *b* 12 May 1856; *m* 20 May 1879 Ada Margaret (*d* Jan 1943), dau of Robert Rooke Prance, of Hampstead, and *d* 19 Feb 1912, having had:

1a Edric William Hoyer, CBE (1942), of Bushey Heath, Herts; Assist Sec Treasury; *b* 5 Sept 1880; *educ* Rugby and Corpus Christi Coll Oxford (BA 1901, MA 1903); *d* unm 4 March 1963

2a Cecil Robert; *b* 9 Dec 1882; *d* 29 April 1896

3a Gilbert Henry; Assist Dir Nat Physical Laboratory Teddington, RN WW I; *b* 17 July 1884; *educ* Rugby and Pembroke Coll Cambridge; *kas* 29 April 1918

4a Ion Keith; dir William Millar & Co, Lt E Surrey Regt WW I; *b* 17 June 1887; *educ* Rugby; *ka* 29 July 1916

5a Herbert Frederick; *b* 17 March 1889; *educ* Rugby; *d* unm 11 Aug 1913

6a Basil Ernest; *b* 29 May 1892; *educ* Rugby and St John's Coll Oxford (MA); *m* 23 April 1919 Janet, dau of Arthur King Smith, of Beaconsfield, Bucks, and *d* 21 March 1930, leaving:

1b Philip Henry; *b* June 1920; *d* 5 March 1981

2b *Stephen Basil [Stephen Millar Esq, 75 Heyman Rd, Suburbs, Bulawayo, Zimbabwe]; *b* 1922; *m* and has three sons and a dau

1b *Anwyn [Miss Anwyn Millar, Stone Cottage, Friars Gate, Crowborough, Sussex TN6 1XD]; *b* 1927

1a Doris Marguerite; *b* 21 Dec 1885; *m* 27 Sept 1907 Ernest Tomlin, of Hampstead, and *d* 1924, leaving five sons and a dau

2a Winifred Agnes; *b* 13 Nov 1890; *m* June 1913 Dr Ffrangcon Roberts, Fell Clare Coll Cambridge, and *d* March 1960, leaving two sons and a dau

3a Muriel Julia Beatrice; *b* 9 Dec 1893; *m* 27 April 1920 Eric Crawshay and had a dau

4a Olive Christine, CBE (1951); *b* 20 Nov 1895; *educ* Newnham Coll Cambridge; *m* 7 Sept 1916 Adml of the Fleet Sir Algernon Usborne Willis, GCB, KBE, DSO (*d* 12 April 1976), s of Herbert Bourdillon Willis, of Hampstead, and had two daus

5a Violet Helen; *b* 20 Nov 1895; *m* 10 Jan 1922 1st Earl Attlee (*qv*) and *d* 7 June 1964, leaving issue

(2) Charles Christian Hoyer, of Felden, Boxmoor; *b* 4 March 1860; *m* 15 May 1884 Beatrix (*d* 11 Nov 1913), dau of George du Maurier, the artist and novelist, and *d* 8 June 1942, leaving:

1a Geoffrey Hoyer; *b* 8 March 1885; *educ* Rugby; *m* 14 Jan 1913 (*divorce* 1919) Dorothy, only child of Frederick Cadwallader Dodsworth (*see* SMITH-DODSWORTH, Bt), and *d* 8 Feb 1945, leaving:

1b *Derrick Norman; *b* 1914

2a Guy Darracott; Cdr RN; *b* 13 Sept 1887; *educ* Clifton and HMS *Britannia*; *m* 7 April 1921 Rosalind, MBE (1962), yr dau of Charles Edward Stuart Cockburn, JP (*see* COCKBURN, Bt), and *d* 24 Aug 1940, leaving:

1b *Michael Darracott [Lt-Cdr Michael Hoyer Millar RN (ret), Flat 5 24 Palace Court, London W2]; *b* 30 May 1924; *m* 24 Oct 1945 *Rosemary Ann, dau of Sydney A Hunn, and has:

1c *Andrew Michael Talbot; *b* 8 Oct 1946; *educ* Stowe

3a Leslie Hoyer; *d* in infancy

4a Gerald Arthur, MC (1918); *b* 31 Aug 1895; *educ* Rugby; *m* 8 April 1920 Ruth, dau of Charles Hornblower Cock, of Mainstone Court, Ledbury, and had:

1b *Oliver Nicholas (Sir), GCVO (1988, KCVO 1973, CVO 1963, MVO 1953) [Sir Oliver Millar GCVO, The Cottage, Ray's Lane, Penn, Bucks HP10 8LH]; *b* 26 April 1923; *educ* Rugby and Courtauld Inst; Assist Surveyor HM's Pictures 1947–49, Dep Surveyor 1949–72, Surveyor 1972–88, Surveyor Emeritus, Tstee Nat Portrait Gallery 1972–95, memb exec ctee Nat Art Collections Fund 1986–, dir Friends Tate Gallery 1989–97, chm Patrons Br Art 1989–, FBA, FSA; *m* 21 Jan 1954 *Delia Mary, 2nd dau of Lt Col Cuthbert Henry Dawnay, MC (*see* DOWNE, V), and has:

1c *Charles James; *b* 1965; *m* 1990 *Alice Katherine, dau of John W P Martin, of E Molesey, Surrey, and has:

1d *Alfred Martin; *b* 1995

1c *Cynthia Mary; *b* 1956

2c *Lucy Anne; *b* 1958; *m* 1st 1977 (*divorce* 1982) John E L Porter and has:

1d *Roland Oliver; *b* 1979

2d *Max John; *b* 1981

2c (cont.) Mrs Lucy Porter *m* 2nd 1983 *Barnaby John Dickens and has by him:

3d *Archie; *b* 1994

1d *Marianna; *b* 1985

3c *Beatrix Jane; *b* 1961; *m* 1987 *Peter Andrew Flory and has:

1d *Oliver William; *b* 1990

2d *Nico Piers; *b* 1993

2b *Luke Benvenuto; *b* 9 Jan 1937; *educ* Rugby; *m* 1 Aug 1962 *Freda Williams and has:

1c *Jane; *b* 17 Oct 1964

1b Mary; *b* 20 May 1926; *m* 10 May 1962 Thomas Riviere Bland, er s of Charles Riviere Bland, JP, and *d* 1971

2b *Sarah [Mrs Jack Cohen, Raylands, Pleshey, Chelmsford, Essex]; *b* 20 Aug 1930; *m* 1st 1 July 1954 John Henry Manners Judd (*d* 8 Oct 1958) and has:

1c *Christopher; *b* 5 Oct 1957

1c *Isabelle; *b* 2 April 1955

2b (cont.) Mrs John Judd *m* 2nd 19– *Jack Cohen

(1) Emily; *m* William Trevor (*d* 4 April 1939), 6th s of Edward Salusbury Rose Trevor, JP, DL, and *d* Feb 1943, leaving issue

4 John; *dsp*

5 Edward, of Rossie Castle, Montrose; *b* 1822; timber merchant; *m* Margaret Buist, dau of Tyndall Johnstone, of Bridge of Allan, and *d* 23 Oct 1911, leaving, with five daus:

(1) Robert Christian Hoyer, of Montrose; timber merchant; *b* 9 Jan 1872; *educ* Fettes; Capt Black Watch WW I; *m* 8 June 1899 Muriel Rosa Lillian (*d* 3 April 1952), dau of John Foster, of Sandy Place, Beds, and *d* 2 June 1932, leaving:

1a Edward George Hoyer; Maj Black Watch; *b* 9 May 1900; *educ* Harrow; *m* 14 July 1925 Phyllis Edith Amy (*d* 1957), est dau of Brig-Gen Edward Gurth Wace, CB, DSO, RE, and d 24 Dec 1949, leaving:

1b *Gurth Christian Hoyer [Gurth Millar Esq, 27 Trevor Place, London SW7]; *b* 13 Dec 1928; *educ* Harrow and Lincoln Coll Oxford (LLB 1952); barrister Middle Temple 1956; Scottish Rugger XV 1952; chm Bonhams 1988–96; *m* 17 March 1956 *Jane Taylor, dau of Col Harold John Aldington, of Swan Wood, Henley-on-Thames, and has:

1c *Christian Gurth Hoyer; *b* 7 Jan 1959

2c *Luke Edward Hoyer; *b* 10 May 1962

1c *Eliza Jane Hoyer; *b* 11 May 1965

2a Francis Kinglake, MC (1945); *b* 14 July 1919; *educ* Uppingham; Black Watch and Parachute Regt WW II (Arnhem); FO 1949; *m* 1st 17 Oct 1947 (*divorce* 1956) Betty Lindsay, dau of V F Macpherson, and had:

1b *Lindsay Elizabeth Hoyer; *b* 27 Oct 1948
2b *Nicola Frances Hoyer; *b* 24 Feb 1951

2a (cont.) Francis Hoyer Millar *m* 2nd 30 Jan 1957 *Pamela Mary [Mrs Francis Hoyer Millar, Craig, Montrose, Angus], dau of Brig Moray M Milne Thomson and formerly w of Leslie Charles Glass, CMG (later Sir Leslie Glass, KCMG), and *d* 1993, having by her had:

1b Rob Kinglake Hoyer; *b* 13 Dec 1957; *d* 18 Jan 1966

1a (Evelyn Louisa) Elizabeth (Dane), DBE (1960, OBE 1952), JP (Angus 1968), DL (Angus 1971); *b* 17 Dec 1910; *educ* privately; VAD and WRNS WW II, Dir WRNS and ADC to HM THE QUEEN 1958–61, ret 1961; *d* unm 26 Feb 1984

(2) Edward William (Rev); *b* 14 Nov 1876; *educ* Fettes and Ch Ch Oxford (BA 1900); deacon 1903, priest 1904, Curate St Paul's Dundee 1903–06, Chaplain St Ninian's Cathedral Perth 1906–10, Domestic Chaplain to Bp St Andrews 1908–10, Rector Kinross 1910–12, St Mary's Arbroath 1912–29, Catterline with Bervie 1929–31, St Andrew's Fettercairn with Lochlee and Bervie 1931–42 and Montrose 1942, Canon St Paul's Cathedral Dundee 1927, T/CF WW I; *m* 5 June 1911 Margaret Alice Adele (*d* 6 Jan 1960), dau of Alexander Robert Duncan, of Parkhill, Arbroath, and *d* 26 March 1963, having had:

1a Basil Edward Robert (Rev); *b* 16 March 1912; *educ* King's Sch Bruton, Downing Coll Cambridge (BA 1935) and Wells Theological Coll; deacon 1936, priest 1937, Curate St John's Aberdeen 1936–40 (Rector 1940–54), Canon St Andrew's Cathedral Aberdeen 1945, Rector St Peter's Edinburgh 1954; *m* 12 Nov 1940 *Lorna Mary, dau of Arthur Trevor Nichols, CBE, of Lower Farm House, Hambledon, Surrey, and *d* 1971, leaving:

1b *Sonia Mary [Miss Sonia Millar, 117 Elm Park Mansions, Park Walk, London SW10]; *b* 20 May 1942

2b *Tessa Lorna Mary; *b* 8 June 1945; *m* 8 April 1969 *Dr Ian Macintyre, s of Rev John Macintyre, of The Manse, Strathpeffer, Ross-shire

2a Alexander Henry Hoyer; *b* 24 May 1913; *educ* King's Sch Bruton; *d* unm 1940

1a *Margaret Frances Cicily [Miss Margaret Millar, 69 Park Rd, Brechin, Angus DD9 7AM]; *b* 31 March 1915; Sch Matron Brighton Coll

2a *Marion Edmonstone [Miss Marion Millar, 69 Park Rd, Brechin, Angus DD9 7AM]; *b* 17 June 1918; SRN

3a *Audrey Elizabeth [Miss Audrey Millar, 21 Holland Rd, Marlow, Bucks]; *b* 26 March 1920; LRAM

(3) John Henry Buist; Maj RA; *b* 14 Aug 1879; *educ* Fettes; *m* 1918 *Elizabeth Anne, dau of William Alexander Mackintosh, of Inchbreyock, Montrose, and *d* 6 Feb 1946, leaving:

1a *Alison Margaret; *b* 1919; *m* 1945 *Adolph S Mantel and has a s and dau

2a *Elizabeth Mulreall Buist [Mrs John Codrington, Oakley Riding School, PO Box 94, Borrowdale, Zimbabwe]; *b* 12 Sept 1923; *m* 18 Dec 1948 John Humphrey Warren Codrington (*d* 5 April 1968), s of Col H O Warren-Codrington, of Worting House, Basingstoke, and has:

1b *Robert Ian; *b* 3 Jan 1950
1b *Denise Ann; *b* 10 Feb 1951
2b *Sheila Helen; *b* 21 Dec 1952
3b *Isabel Muireall; *b* 7 Aug 1954

ROBERT MILLAR's est son,

CHRISTIAN HOYER MILLAR, of Blair Castle, Culross, Fife; timber merchant; *b* 1 May 1807; *m* 1st 1850 Marion Marshall (*d* 1865), dau of Ebenezer Watson, of Edinburgh, by Isabella Thorburn, and had:

1 ROBERT HOYER
2 Edward Christian Hoyer; *b* 1861; *d* unm 1922
1 Marion Bolette; *b* 1856; *d* unm 1936
2 Isabella Elizabeth; *b* 1859; *m* Staff-Paymaster Herbert Lauder Warren, RN (*d* 1897), and *d* 1946, leaving two daus
3 Alice; *b* 1863; *m* Very Rev Charles Pressley Smith, Dean Argyll and the Isles, and *d* 1899, leaving three daus
4 Louisa; *b* 1864; *d* 1869

CHRISTIAN HOYER MILLAR *m* 2nd Katherine Cooke and *d* 1 Oct 1884, leaving by her:

5 Katherine; *m* William Alexander and *d* 1948, leaving two sons and a dau
6 Augusta; *d* unm 1905

The er son,

ROBERT HOYER MILLAR, of Blair Castle; timber merchant; *b* 5 July 1857; Capt attd Black Watch Boer War, Lt-Col Black Watch (TA) WW I; *m* 1886 Alice Ann Combe (*d* 2 April 1944), dau of Dr James Simson, of Edinburgh, by Margaret Combe, and *d* 29 April 1942, having had:

1 Christian Hoyer, MC, of Place of Tilliefoure, Monymusk, Aberdeenshire; *b* 26 March 1887; *educ* Rugby; *m* 13 Feb 1915 Barbara Constance, dau of John Stewart, of Wimbledon, and *d* 1964, having had:

(1) Barbara Joan; *b* 27 Dec 1915; *m* July 1958 Maj William Petty and *d* May 1962, leaving a dau

2 Jarold Watson Hoyer; *b* 4 Sept 1892; *educ* Repton; *d* unm 28 May 1914

3 FREDERICK ROBERT HOYER MILLAR, **1st Baron Inchyra**, of St Madoes, Co Perth (UK), so *cr* 2 Feb 1962, GCMG (1955, KCMG 1949, CMG 1939), CVO (1938); *b* 6 June 1900; *educ* Wellington and New Coll Oxford (BA 1922, MA 1954, Hon Fell); Dip Serv 1923, 3rd Sec Berlin 1923, Paris 1924–28, 2nd Sec Cairo 1930–34, Assist Priv Sec to For Sec 1934–38, 1st Sec Washington 1939 and Cnsllr 1941–42, Sec Br Secretariat Washington 1943–44, Counsellor and Assist U-Sec FO 1944–48, Min Washington 1948–50, UK Rep NATO 1950–53, UK HC Germany 1953–55, Amb Bonn 1955–57, PUS FO 1957–61, ret 1962; Govr Wellington, King of Arms Order St Michael and St George, memb Roy Co Archers; Chm Gen Accident Fire & Life Assur; *m* 15 April 1931 Anna Judith Elizabeth [The Rt Hon The Dowager Lady Inchyra, Inchyra House, Glencarse, Perthshire], dau of Jonkheer Reneke de Marees van Swinderen, Netherlands Min London 1913–37, by Elizabeth Lindsay, dau of Charles Carroll Glover, of Washington, DC, and *d* 1989, leaving:

(1) ROBERT CHARLES RENEKE HOYER MILLAR, **2nd Baron Inchyra**

(2) +Alastair James Harold [The Hon Alastair Hoyer Millar, 16 Pembridge Villas, London W11]; *b* 13 Nov 1936; *educ* Eton; co-owner Border Incident (race horse); *m* 20 Feb 1974 *Virginia Margaret Diana, 2nd dau of William Perine Macauley, MFH, of Ballyward House, Blessington, Co Wicklow (*see* HARTWELL, B), and has:

1a +Mark Cristian Frederick; *b* 12 March 1975
1a *Martha Harriet Alice; *b* 17 Dec 1976

(1) Elizabeth Anne Hoyer; *b* 12 July 1933; *m* 22 Oct 1965 William Euan Wallace (*d* 4 Feb 1977), yst s of David Euan Wallace, MC, PC, of Kildonan, Barrhill, Ayrshire, and *d* 1990

(2) *Annabel Alice Hoyer, LVO (1986) [The Hon Mrs Whitehead LVO, 5 Vicarage Gdns, London W8]; *b* 25 Jan 1943; T/Ldy-in-Waiting to HRH THE PRINCESS MARGARET, COUNTESS OF SNOWDON 1971–75, Extra Ldy-in-waiting 1975–92, Ldy-in-Waiting 1992–; *m* 1973 *Christopher James Bovill Whitehead and has:

1a *Robert William Bovill; *b* 1977
1a *(Christina) Daisy Elizabeth; *b* 1975

INGE

Arms: Argent on a cross nowy formy throughout gules, the limbs voided vert, a rose argent, barbed and seeded or. **Crest:** Issuant from a representation of the White Tower of London argent a phoenix or, onflamed gules. **Supporters:** Dexter, a ram or, armed, unguled and gorged with lozenges conjoined gules; sinister, a lion or gorged with lozenges conjoined gules, each supporting a Field Marshal's baton erect proper. **Compartment:** A limestone rock proper. **Badge:** In front of flames gules an eagle displayed or grasping with both feet a Field Marshal's baton fesswise proper. **Motto:** *Ingenii vis* ('The strength of ingenuity'). **Creation:** B. (LP, UK) June 1997.

THE BARON INGE, of Richmond, Co of N Yorkshire (Sir Peter Anthony Inge, GCB (1992, KCB 1988), DL (N Yorks 1994)) [Field Marshal The Rt Hon The Lord Inge GCB DL, c/o Barclays Bank, Market Place, Leyburn, N Yorks DL8 5BQ]; *b* 5 Aug 1935; *educ* Wrekin Coll and RMA Sandhurst; commissioned Green Howards 1956, ADC to GOC 4th Div 1960–61, Adj Ist Green Howards 1963–64, psc 1966, MOD 1967–69, Coy Instr Staff Coll 1973–74, CO 1st Green Howards 1974–76, Cmdt Jr Div Staff Coll 1977–79, Cdr Task Force C/4 Armoured Bde 1980–81, Ch Staff HQ 1st Br Corps 1982–83, GOC NE Dist and Cdr 2nd Inf Div 1984–86, MOD 1986–87, Cdr 1st Br Corps 1987–89, Cdr N Army Gp and C-in-C BAOR 1989–92, CGS 1992–94, CDS 1994–97; Constable Tower London 1996–, ADC Gen to HM THE QUEEN 1991–94, Col Green Howards 1982–94, Pres Army Benevolent Fund 1997–; *m* 1960 *Letitia Marion Beryl, yr dau of Trevor Thornton-Berry, JP, barrister, of Swinithwaite Hall, Yorks, and has two daus

Lineage: RAYMOND ALBERT INGE; *m* Grace Maud Caroline Du Rose and had:

PETER ANTHONY (Sir), *cr* a **Baron**

INGILBY

Arms: Sable an estoile argent within a bordure engrailed gobony or and gules. **Crest:** A boar's head, couped and erect argent, tusked or, in the mouth an estoile of the last. **Motto:** *Mon droit* ('My right'). **Creation:** Bt. (UK) 26 July 1866.

SIR THOMAS COLVIN WILLIAM INGILBY, 6TH BT, of Ripley, in the West Riding of the Co of York [Sir Thomas Ingilby Bt, Ripley Castle, Harrogate, N Yorks HG3 3AY]; *b* 17 July 1955; *s f* 1974; *educ* Eton and RAC Cirencester; ARICS 1982, CAAV 1983; *m* 25 Feb 1984 *Emma, only dau of Maj R A Thompson, of Whinfield, Strensall, York, and has:

1 +JAMES WILLIAM FRANCIS; *b* 15 June 1985
2 +Joslan Richard Ryland; *b* 1986
3 +Jack Henry Thomas; *b* 1990
4 +Richard Joseph Frederick; *b* 1994
1 *Eleanor Jame Pamela; *b* 1989

Lineage: An earlier baronetcy was conferred in 1642 on William Ingleby or Ingilby, of a gentry family that had been prominent in the Ripley area of Yorkshire since the 14th century. It expired with the death of Sir John Ingleby/Ingilby, 4th Bt, in 1772, but his illegitimate son John was granted a fresh baronetcy in 1781. Another illegitimate s of the last Bt of the 1642 *cr* (though whether out of the same mother or not is unclear) was:

Rev HENRY INGILBY, of Ripley, later Kirkleatham, Yorks; *b* 23 Feb 1761; *m* 14 Sept 1786 Isabella Jane (*d* 27 Sept 1822), est dau of Ralph Bates, of Milbourne, Northumberland, and *d* 4 Sept 1833, having had, with five other daus:

1 HENRY JOHN (Sir), **1st Bt**
2 William Bates (Sir), KCB; *b* 30 April 1791; Gen, Col RA; *d* 6 Aug 1879
3 Richard Wharton; *b* 20 Feb 1796; *d* 4 March 1855
4 Ralph Mitford Preston; *b* 14 June 1797; Capt 84th Regt; *m* 12 Oct 1826 Jane (*m* 2nd 6 July 1840 Charles Dance; *d* 2 Nov 1854), est dau of Charles Knyvett, of Sonning, Berks, and *d* 29 Aug 1831, having had issue
1 Esther; *m* 14 June 1842 Rev William Wright (*d* 22 March 1863), of Owmby-cum-Searby, Lincs, Rector Healing, Lincs, and *d* 10 March 1870

The est son,

Rev Sir Henry John Ingilby, 1st Bt (UK), so *cr* 26 July 1866; *b* 28 Jan 1790; MA; inherited estates of Sir William Amcotts Ingilby, 2nd and last Bt of the 1781 *cr* (*see* above), of Ripley and Kettlethorpe (*dsp* 14 May 1854); *m* 19 Aug 1824 Elizabeth (*d* 7 March 1869), 2nd dau of Day Hort Macdowall, of Walkinshaw, Renfrewshire, and *d* 4 July 1870, leaving:

1 **Sir Henry Day Ingilby, 2nd Bt,** JP and DL (Yorks); *b* 12 Oct 1826; MA Oxon, Fell Magdalen Coll; High Sheriff Yorks 1882; *m* 26 June 1862 Hon Alicia Margaret Robertson (*d* 15 Dec 1916), 2nd dau of 1st and last Baron Marjoribanks of Ladykirk, and *dsps* 5 Dec 1911, having had:
(1) Henry Haggerston; *b* 12 July 1869; *d* 28 Dec 1873
(1) Mary Alicia; *d* 14 Oct 1872
2 WILLIAM (Sir), **3rd Bt**
1 Wilhelmina; *d* unm 16 Dec 1902

Sir HENRY's brother,

Sir William Ingilby, 3rd Bt, JP (W R Yorks); *b* 13 Dec 1829; Lt Bengal Artillery; *m* 4 Feb 1874 Eleanor Isabella (*d* 13 May 1923), 2nd dau of Henry Macdowall, of Garthland, Renfrewshire, and had:

1 WILLIAM HENRY (Sir), **4th Bt**
2 John Uchtred Macdowall, OBE (1919), JP (W R Yorks); *b* 28 Dec 1874; Lt Col Gordon Highrs, Tirah Expdn 1897–98, Boer War 1899–1900 and WW I; *m* 3 Aug 1904 Marjorie Cecily, MBE (*d* 10 Dec 1957), est dau of William Robert Phelips, DL, of Montacute, Somerset, and *d* 14 Jan 1948, leaving:
(1) Cecily Eleanor; *b* 1 July 1905
(2) *Joan Alicia, MBE (1997) [Miss Joan Ingilby MBE, Coleshouse, Askrigg, Leyburn, Yorks DL8 3HH]; *b* 11 Dec 1911

Sir WILLIAM *d* 17 Dec 1918; his er son,

Sir William Henry Ingilby, 4th Bt, JP (Liberty of Ripon), JP and DL (W R Yorks); *b* 28 Dec 1874; Maj Scots Gds (Brevet Lt-Col Res of Offrs) Boer War 1899–1902 (two medals, eight clasps), Cmdt Gds Depot Caterham 1914; *m* 18 April 1906 Hon Alberta Diana Vivian (*d* 11 Dec 1968), 3rd dau of 1st Baron Swansea (*qv*), and *d* 20 Sept 1950, leaving:

Sir Joslan William Vivian Ingilby, 5th Bt, JP and DL (W R Yorks 1952); *b* 1 Sept 1907; *educ* Eton; Maj Scots Gds WW II; *m* 31 Jan 1948 *Diana [Diana Lady Ingilby, Ripley Castle, Harrogate, N Yorks HG3 3AY], only dau of Brig-Gen Sir George Lethbridge Colvin, CB, CMG, DSO, of Wellsbridge Cottage, Ascot, and *d* 1974, leaving:

1 Sir THOMAS COLVIN WILLIAM INGILBY, **6th and present Bt**
1 *Caroline Diana Colvin; *b* 9 Sept 1949; *m* 1986 *David Francis Wakefield, est s of F H Wakefield, of Ogston Hall, Higham, Derbys
2 *(Katherine) Benita (Bindy) Colvin; *b* 22 May 1951; *m* 15 June 1974 *Richard (Wally) Dennis Kingsmill Wallace, only s of Pierce Wallace, TD, of Kirkee, Cambusdeen, Ayr, and has:
(1) *Sally Diana; *b* 1981

Seat: Ripley Castle. Only the centre of the building is what might strictly be termed a castle — a 15th- or 16th-century tower keep (accounts differ as to its age). It is surrounded by an 18th-century dwelling house, though this is crenellated. The separate gatehouse is also 15th-century, though again accounts differ as to whether it dates from 1410 or the 1460s/70s. The gardens are laid out in 18th-century style.

INGLEBY

Arms: Sable three crosses patée argent within an orle of eight fleur-de-lys and a bordure or. **Crest:** A heart gules between two wings displayed erminois. **Supporters:** On either side a blackfaced Swaledale ram proper, holding in the mouth a rose argent, barbed, seeded slipped and leaved also proper. **Motto:** *Quae supra quaerenda* ('What is on high is worth seeking). **Creation:** V. (UK) 17 Jan 1956.

THE 2ND VISCOUNT INGLEBY, of Snilesworth, North Riding of Co York (Martin Raymond Peake) [The Rt Hon The Viscount Ingleby, Snilesworth, Osmotherley, N Yorks DL6 3QD; Flat 1, 61 Onslow Sq, London SW7]; *b* 31 May 1926; *s f* 1966; *educ* Eton and Trin Coll Oxford; Lt Coldstream Gds 1945–47, barrister Inner Temple 1955, CC N R Yorks 1964–67, dir Hargreaves Gp 1960–80 sec Hargreaves Quarries 1958–61, Chm Soc Health Educn 1973; *m* 26 Jan 1952 Susan Gladys (*d* 10 Feb 1996), er dau of Capt Henderson Russell Landale, of Ewell Manor, W Farleigh, Kent, and has had:

1 Richard Martin Herbert; *b* 7 Aug 1953; *educ* Eton; *d* unm 19 July 1975
1 *Fiona Catherine [The Hon Mrs Horton, Whorlton Cottage, Swainby, N Yorks DL6 3ER]; *b* 24 Jan 1955; *m* 23 July 1977 *(Gavin) Tobias (Toby) Alexander Winterbottom Horton, yr s of Alistair Winterbottom, of Manor Farm House, Brill, Bucks (*see* 1970 edn WINTERBOTTOM, B), and has:
(1) *George William Arthur; *b* 1983
(2) *Thomas Henry Ralph; *b* 1985
(1) *Alice Emily Rose; *b* 1978
(2) *Violet Constance Lily; *b* 1980
2 *Sarah Rachel; *b* 27 Nov 1958; *m* 1982 *James Felton Somers Hervey-Bathurst and has issue (*see* HERVEY-BATHURST, Bt)
3 *Henrietta Cecilia Imogen; *b* 23 Oct 1961; *m* 1990 *James J P McNeile, er s of Rory J McNeile, of Nonsuch, Bromham, Wilts
4 *Katherine Susan Emma; *b* 23 Dec 1963

Lineage: ROBERT PEAKE, of Burrough-on-the-Hill, Leics; *m* 26 Feb 1781 Anne (*d* 10 July 1824), widow of— Astle and dau and coheir of Thomas Copson, of Sutton Cheyney, Leics, and *d* 30 July 1806 aged 71, leaving:

ROBERT PEAKE, of Burrough-on-the-Hill; *b* 11 Dec 1781; *m* 29 Nov 1813 Mary (*d* 10 Sept 1861), dau of Thomas Cross, of Woodborough, Leics, and *d* 13 Dec 1861, leaving, with three er sons:

HENRY PEAKE, of Sleaford, Lincs; *b* 16 Oct 1821; slr; *m* 24 June 1851 Eliza (*d* 11 Sept 1902), dau of Charles Kirk, of Sleaford, and *d* 20 June 1886, having had a yr s:

GEORGE HERBERT PEAKE, of Sutton Hall, Thirsk, and Snilesworth, Northallerton, formerly of Bawtry Hall, all Yorks, JP (W R Yorks 1896 and Notts 1903), DL (Notts 1931); *b* 4 Sept 1859; Maj Sherwood Rangers Yeo 1906–16, barrister Lincoln's Inn 1887, Mayor E Retford 1903–05; *m* 26 June 1895 Evelyn Mary (*d* 26 July 1945), est dau of Hon John Charles Dundas, MP (*see* ZETLAND, M), and *d* 11 Oct 1950, having had:

1 Raymond; *b* 25 May 1896; Lt Coldstream Gds WW I; *d* of wounds recd in action 30 Sept 1916

2 OSBERT, **1st Viscount**

3 Harald (Sir); ktd 1973; *b* 28 Oct 1899; *educ* Eton and Trin Coll Cambridge (MA); A/Cdre RAF, Lt Coldstream Gds and QOY Dragoons Yeo; Dir: AAF Air Min 1938, PR Air Min 1940–41, Air Force Welfare Air Min 1942–43, Yorkshire Bank, Chm RAF Benevolent Fund; *m* 1st 31 Oct 1933 (*divorce* 1944) Resy, OBE (1946), only dau of Count Henrl de Baillet-Latour, of Brussels, and *d* 1978, having had:

(1) *David Alphy Edward Raymond [David Peake Esq, Sezincote, Moreton-in-Marsh, Glos; 15 Ilchester Place, London W14 8AA]; *b* 27 Sept 1934; *educ* Ampleforth and Ch Ch Oxford; Lt Roy Scots Greys (2nd Dragoons) 1953–55, chm: Hargreaves Gp 1974 and Kleinwort Benson Gp plc 1988–; *m* 22 Nov 1962 *Susanna, yst dau of Cyril Hugh Kleinwort (*see* KLEINWORT, Bt), and has:

1a *Edward; *b* 19 Feb 1964

1a *Katharine Sophie; *b* 27 Oct 1965; *m* 1989 *Thomas Assheton (*see* CLITHEROE, B) and has issue

3 (cont.) Sir Harald Peake *m* 2nd 24 June 1952 *Felicity Hyde, DBE (1949), AE, JP [Dame Felicity Peake DBE AE JP, Court Farm, Tackley, Oxon OX5 3AQ; Flat 5, 35 Bryanston Sq, London W1H 7LP], yr dau of Humphrey Watts, of Cheadle, and widow of P/O John Charles Mackenzie Hanbury, RAF, and *d* 25 May 1978, leaving by her:

(2) *Andrew Charles; *b* 18 April 1956; *m* 1990 *Suzette Ray, er dau of Sampson Mitchell, DL, of Woore, Salop, and has:

1a *Alexander Harald; *b* 22 June 1993

2a *George Sampson; *b* 5 March 1997

4 *Edward Charles [Edward Peake Esq, 6 Westbury Court Grange, Cambridge CB3 9BG]; *b* 19 Jan 1911; *educ* Eton and Trin Coll Cambridge (BA); barrister Inner Temple 1939; F/Lt RAFVR WW II; *m* 4 Sept 1935 *Baroness Santa Maria, only dau of Baron Alfred Carl Gustav von Henikstein, of Salzburg, and has had:

(1) Henry Alfred; *b* 13 April 1937; *educ* Ampleforth and Ch Ch Oxford; RAF 1956–58; *d* unm 1990

(2) *Robert Alexander [Robert Peake Esq, 96 Campden Hill Rd, London W8 7AP]; *b* 23 May 1938; *educ* Ampleforth and Trin Coll Dublin (BA 1968, LLB 1965, MA 1968); late Coldstream Gds; *m* 3 Feb 1968 *Meriel Elizabeth Lyon, only dau of William Vernon Lyon Bowie, of Dublin, and has:

1a *James Robert William; *b* 16 July 1978

1a *Lucy Meriel; *b* 1972; *educ* Charterhouse

(3) *Christopher George [Christopher Peake Esq, 34 Bettridge Rd, London SW6 3QD]; *b* 20 May 1951; *educ* Ampleforth, Queens' Coll Cambridge (MA), and London U (MTh); *m* 1993 *Ann Marie, only dau of John O'Rourke, of Chelsea

(1) *Marianna Clotilde [Mrs Rupert Langham, 5 Bournside Rd, Cheltenham, Glos GL51 5AL]; *b* 22 July 1939; MAOT 1961; *m* 1974 *Maj Rupert Charles Langham, Roy Corps of Signals, and has:

1a *Jonathan Charles; *b* 1975

1a *Caroline Mary; *b* 1976

(2) *Christina Maria [Mrs Peter Leadlay, 17 Clarendon Rd, Cambridge CB2 2BH]; *b* 16 Aug 1949; *m* 1974 *Dr Peter Francis Leadlay and has:

1a *Francesca Catherine; *b* 1978

2a *Louisa Clare; *b* 1980

3a *Serena Imogen Alice; *b* 1985

1 Maud Eileen; *b* 12 Aug 1904; *d* 27 Jan 1978

GEORGE PEAKE's 2nd son,

OSBERT PEAKE, **1st Viscount Ingleby**, of Snilesworth, North Riding of Co York (UK), so *cr* 17 Jan 1956, PC (1943); *b* 30 Dec 1897; *educ* Eton, RMC Sandhurst and Ch Ch Oxford (BA 1919, MA 1921); Maj Notts Yeo, Lt Coldstream Gds WW I; barrister Inner Temple 1923, MP (C) Leeds 1929–56, Chm Public Accounts Ctee 1945–48, Parly U-Sec Home Office 1939–44, Fin Sec Treasury 1944–45, Min Pensions and NI 1951–55; *m* 19 June 1922 Lady Joan Rachel de Vere Capell (*d* 1979), yr dau of 7th Earl of Essex (*qv*), and *d* 11 Oct 1966, having had:

1 MARTIN RAYMOND PEAKE, **2nd and present Viscount Ingleby**

1 *Iris Irene Adele, LVO (1957) [The Hon Mrs Dawnay LVO, Flat 5 32 Onslow Sq, London SW7 3NS; Wexcombe House, nr Marlborough, Wilts]; *b* 23 July 1923; Ldy in Waiting to HRH PRINCESS MARGARET 1952–62, Extra Ldy-in-waiting 1962–63; *m* 26 March 1963 Capt Oliver Payan Dawnay, CVO (*see* DOWNE, V), and has issue

2 *Sonia Mary [The Hon Mrs Hammond-Maude, Wychwood Lodge, Ramsden, Oxford; Amerdale House, Arncliffe, Skipton, Yorks]; *b* 12 Dec 1924; WRNS WW II; *m* 1st 26 Oct 1946 (*divorce* 1958) 12th Marquess of Tweeddale (*qv*) and has issue; *m* 2nd 27 June 1966 *Maj Michael William Vernon Hammond-Maude, JP, 5th Roy Inniskilling Dragoon Gds, only s of Capt Gerald William Edward Maude, Green Howards

3 Imogen Clarissa; *b* 18 Jan 1934; *d* 29 Oct 1937

4 *Mary Rose [The Hon Mrs Phillipps de Lisle, 4 Hereford Mansions, Hereford Rd, London W2 5BA; Stockerston Hall, nr Uppingham, Leics LE15 9JD]; *b* 23 April 1940; *m* 2 April 1959 *Maj Everard John Robert March Phillipps de Lisle, RHG (Blues) (ret), er s of Maj John Adrian Frederick March Phillipps de Lisle, JP, DL, and has:

(1) *Charles Andrew Everard; *b* 18 Aug 1960; *educ* Eton and Worcester Coll Oxford

(2) *Timothy John; *b* 25 June 1962; *educ* Eton and Worcester Coll Oxford; *m* 1991 *Amanda Helen, 2nd dau of Clive Julian Stanley Barford, of Pibworth House, Aldworth, Berks, and has:

1a *Daniel Barford; *b* 1994

(1) *Mary Rosanna; *b* 18 May 1968; *educ* St Hugh's Coll Oxford

INGLEFIELD-WATSON

Arms: Per pale argent and or, on a mount vert an oak tree proper, the whole surmounted by two bars sable. **Crest:** The stump of an oak tree with a branch sprouting from either side, each grasped by a hand issuing from a cloud, all proper. **Motto:** *Insperata floruit* ('It has flourished beyond expectation). **Creation:** Bt. (UK) 15 July 1895.

SIR JOHN FORBES INGLEFIELD-WATSON, 5TH BT, of Earnock, Hamilton, Co Lanark [Lt-Col Sir John Inglefield-Watson Bt, The Ross, Hamilton, Lanarks ML3 7UF]; *b* 16 May 1926; *s f* 1987; *educ* Eton; Lt-Col RE (ret); FA Staff Referee Instructor 1978–

Lineage: THOMAS WATSON, of Cupar, Fife; *b* 3 Feb 1760; *m* 14 March 1782 Elizabeth Dykes (*d* June 1809) and *d* Oct 1818, leaving, with other issue:

1 Thomas; *b* 12 July 1783; *d* unm 23 May 1860

2 David, of Cupar; *b* 15 June 1785; *m* 10 March 1812 Jane Smith (*d* 4 Nov 1853) and *d* 28 Jan 1866, leaving issue

3 John, of Bathville, Linlithgow; *b* 28 March 1791; *m* 1st 13 April 1816 Ann (*d* 19 Nov 1829), dau of John Hendry, of Kirkintilloch and had, with other issue:

(1) Thomas; *b* 26 Sept 1817; *d* 11 Oct 1824

(2) **Sir John Watson, 1st Bt** (UK), so *cr* 15 July 1895, JP and DL Lanarks; *b* 9 July 1819; *m* 1st 18 June 1846 Agnes (*d* 1 April 1876), dau of Robert Haig Simpson, of Glasgow; *m* 2nd 29 April 1879 Harriet Drury (*d* 22 Jan 1936), dau of Peter Mackenzie, of Glasgow, ed and prop *Reformers' Gazette*, and *d* 26 Sept 1898, having had:

1a John; *b* 19 Jan 1853; *d* 19 March 1860

2a JOHN (Sir), **2nd Bt**

3a Thomas William, of Neilsland, Hamilton, Lanarks, JP; WS Edinburgh; *b* 31 Oct 1864; *m* 23 July 1891 Lucy (*d* 2 Jan 1947), dau of William Henry Hamilton, of Broughton Park, Manchester, and *d* 23 March 1935, leaving:

1b Douglas Hamilton; *b* 12 Oct 1892; Lt 1st Roy Dragoons WW I; *d* unm 20 Nov 1958

2b Leslie Dundas; *b* 26 May 1894; *educ* Rugby and RMC Sandhurst; Capt Res of Offrs King's Dragoon Gds WW I (star, two medals); *m* 24 April 1923 Enid Margaret, only dau of Col George Hay Montgomery Conran, E Yorks Regt, and *d* 1975, leaving:

1c +SIMON CONRAN HAMILTON [Simon Watson Esq, 51 Clapham Manor St, London SW4 6DT]; *b* 11 Aug 1939; heir presumptive; *educ* Harrow; *m* 13 May 1971 *Madeleine Stiles, est dau of W Mahlon Dickerson, of New York

1c Gillian Fay Lucy; *b* 13 May 1928; *d* 1990

3b Thomas Gavin; *b* 23 Oct 1896; Lt-Col 8th Hus WW I (wounded, star, two medals), Iraq 1919–20 and WW II (despatches, A/Col and Cmdt Ceylon Def force 1942–45); *d* unm 5 Sept 1951

4b Somerled Hamilton; *b* 7 May 1899; Lt Res of Offrs Welsh Gds; *m* 3 Oct 1925 Elma Mary (*d* 1983), only dau of William Walker, of High Canons, Shenley, Herts, and *d* 14 Jan 1938, leaving:

1c +Julian Frank Somerled [Julian Watson Esq, Baythorne Park, Birdbrook, Essex]; *b* 12 Nov 1931; *educ* Harrow and RAC Cirencester

1b Jeanette Lucy Vickers; *b* 3 Dec 1902; *m* 1 June 1923 Brig-Gen James Lockhead Jack, JP, DL, DSO, Cameronian Sottish Rifles (*d* 22 Dec 1962), est s of Peter Jack, of Paisley, and *d* 22 Oct 1995, leaving:

1c *Kenneth Hamilton Muir [Kenneth Jack Esq, Abbey House, Pipewell, Northants NN14 1QY]; *b* 3 March 1931; *educ* Haileybury; Kettering Borough Cncllr; *m* 5 Nov 1959 *Bridget Sarah, 2nd dau of Lt-Col Alan Stuart Casey, Roy Dragoons, by Hon Diana Sybil, est dau of 1st Viscount Monsell (*see* 1970 edn), and has:

1d *Richard Kenneth Hamilton; *b* 15 Aug 1962; *m* 1992 *Geraldine Jennings, of Lansing, Michigan

2d *Christopher James Hamilton; *b* 1971

1d *Louise Diana; *b* 9 March 1964

2c *Angus Gavin Lockhead; *b* 8 Jan 1935; *educ* Uppingham; *m* 22 Nov 1960 (*divorce* 1970), as her 1st husb, Elizabeth Ann, er dau of Sir John Samuel Richardson, 1st Bt (*see* RICHARDSON, B), and has:

1d *Charles Watson Hamilton; *b* 5 May 1962; *m* 19-—

3 (cont.) John Watson *m* 2nd 16 Dec 1830 Jean (*d* 10 March 1894), dau of Robert Hendry, of Kirkintilloch, and *d* 7 March 1862, having by her had four sons and a dau

1 Marianne; *b* 27 Oct 1848; *m* 6 Aug 1872 Oliphant Williamson (*d* 10 March 1891), of Notting Hill, and *d* 8 Aug 1903, leaving issue

2 Agnes; *b* 9 Dec 1849; *d* 23 May 1856

3 Isabella; *b* 16 Sept 1851; *m* 14 Sept 1881 Giles Francis Kitts, of Rochester, NY, USA, and *d* 6 July 1893, leaving issue

4 Jane; *b* 6 Nov 1854; *m* 4 Aug 1874 Charles Macdonald Williamson and *d* 3 July 1890, leaving issue

5 Georgina; *b* 1 March 1856; *m* 30 Oct 1877 9th Lord Belhaven and Stenton (*qv*) and *d* 9 Nov 1940, leaving issue

6 Margaret; *b* 18 Feb 1857; *m* 19 July 1877 James Cowie Simpson (*d* 1906), of Carfin Hall, Holytown, took name WATSON SIMPSON 1924 and *d* 18 Jan 1939

7 Agnes; *b* 4 June 1859; *m* 1st 20 April 1886 Ebenezer Erskine Harper (*d* 1899); *m* 2nd 1904 Donald Macandrew Mackintosh (*d* 1917) and *d* 2 July 1946, leaving issue

8 Henrietta; *b* 28 Sept 1862; *m* 10 Dec 1896 William Brown, JP (*d* 1922), of Glasgow, and *d* 1 Jan 1944, having had issue

9 Mina Steele; *b* 12 Feb 1866; *m* 17 Sept 1890 Lt-Col Stephen Flockton Charles, 3rd Bn Lancs Fus, of Wroxham Ho, Norwich, and *d* 27 Aug 1933, leaving issue

Sir JOHN's 2nd s,

Sir John Watson, 2nd Bt; *b* 31 Aug 1860; MA Cantab; *m* 22 June 1893 Edith Jane (*d* 22 March 1926), dau of William Henry Nott, of Princes Park, Liverpool, and *d* 13 Sept 1903, having had:

1 Ian Greville; *b* and *d* 1894

2 **Sir John Watson, 3rd Bt**; *b* 24 Feb 1898; *educ* Eton and RMC Sandhurst; 2nd Lt 16th Lancers; *ka* 23 March 1918

3 DERRICK WILLIAM (Sir), **4th Bt**

1 Doreen Agnes Edith; *b* 5 Jan 1896; *m* 2 March 1921 Col Rt Hon Sir Reginald Hugh Dorman-Smith (*d* 20 March 1977), Govr Burma, s of Maj Edward Patrick Dorman-Smith, of Bellamont Forest, Co Cavan, and *d* 5 Dec 1988, leaving issue

Sir JOHN's bro,

Sir DERRICK WILLIAM WATSON later INGLEFIELD-WATSON (deed poll 1945), **4th Bt**, TD; *b* 7 Oct 1901; *educ* Eton and Ch Ch Oxford; Capt 4th Bn QO Roy W Kent Regt TARO WW II, CC Kent 1931–37; *m* 1st 15 April 1925 (*divorce* 1939) Margrett Georgina (*m* 2nd 1945 Eric William Crawley Savill), only dau of Col Thomas Stokes George Hugh Robertson-Aikman, CB, of the Ross and Broomhilton, Lanarks; *m* 2nd 1946 Therese (Terry) only dau of Prof Charles Boden, of Budapest, and *d* 27 Jan 1987, leaving:

1 Sir JOHN FORBES INGLEFIELD-WATSON, **5th and present Bt**

1 *Sheila Margrett [Mrs Dugald Graham-Campbell, 14 Murrayfield Gdns, Edinburgh EH12 6DF]; *b* 13 Feb 1931; *m* 18 Oct 1958 Dugald Graham-Campbell (*d* 14 Sept 1967), only s of John Graham-Campbell, CBE, of Shirvan, Lochgilphead, Argyll, and has:

(1) *Robert John; *b* 14 Aug 1964; *m* 1992 *Henrietta, only child of George Robert Heneage, and has:

1a *William Dugald; *b* 25 April 1996

1a *Emily Marguerite; *b* 11 Sept 1997

(1) *Sarah Alexandra; *b* 3 Dec 1960

INGLEWOOD

Arms: Azure three sinister gauntlets or. **Crest:** A dexter hand in armour couped at the wrist proper holding a sword argent, pommel and hilt or. **Supporters:** On either side a roebuck proper collared, pendant therefrom a pheon argent. **Mottoes:** 1 *Martis non cupidis* ('Not enamoured of war'); 2 Faithful unto death.
Creation: B. (UK) 30 June 1964.

THE 2ND BARON INGLEWOOD, of Hutton-in-the-Forest, Co Cumberland ((William) Richard Fletcher-Vane, DL (Cumbria 1993)) [The Rt Hon The Lord Inglewood, Hutton-in-the-Forest, Penrith, Cumbria CA11 9TH]; *b* 31 July 1951; *s* f 1989; *educ* Eton, Trin Coll Cambridge (MA) and Cumbria Coll of Ag and Forestry, ARICS; barrister Lincoln's Inn 1975; memb Lake District Special Planning Bd 1984–90 and NW Water Authority 1987–89; MEP (C) Cumbria and Lancs N 1989–94, Br C Spokesman Ctee Legal Affs Euro Parl 1989–94, Ch Whip Br C Gp 1994–95, Ld in Waiting (Govt Whip) 1994–95, Capt Yeoman Gd (Govt Dep Ch Whip) 1995–97, Parly U-Sec Nat Heritage 1995–97; *m* 29 Aug 1986 *Cressida R, photographer, yst dau of Alan Desmond Frederick Pemberton-Pigott, CMG, of Fawe Park, Keswick, and has issue:

1 +HENRY WILLIAM FREDERICK; *b* 24 Dec 1990

1 *Miranda Mary; *b* 19 May 1987

2 *Rosa Katharine; *b* 25 July 1989

Lineage: WILLIAM LYONEL VANE, JP, DL, yst bro of 9th Baron Barnard (*qv*); Col; *m* 27 Jan 1904 Lady Katharine Louisa Pakenham (*d* 9 March 1954), dau of 4th Earl of Longford (*qv*), and *d* 23 Jan 1920, having had:

WILLIAM MORGAN VANE later FLETCHER-VANE (deed poll 9 April 1931), **1st Baron Inglewood**, of Hutton-in-the-Forest, Co Cumberland (UK), so *cr* 30 June 1964, TD, DL (Westmorland 1946); *b* 12 April 1909; *educ* Charterhouse and Trin Coll Cambridge (MA 1934); Lt-Col DLI (TA) WW II (despatches), MP (C) Westmorland 1945–64, PPS to: Min Ag 1951–54, Jt Parly Sec For Affrs 1954–55 and Min Health 1956, Jt Parly Sec Pensions and NI 1958–60 and Ag 1960–62, memb Historic Bldgs Cncl England 1954–58; *m* 28 July 1949 Mary (*d* June 1982), JP (1960), CC Cumberland, Sr Cdr ATS (despatches), memb LCC, est dau of Sir Richard George Proby, 1st Bt (*qv*), and *d* 1989, leaving:

1 (WILLIAM) RICHARD FLETCHER-VANE, **2nd and present Baron Inglewood**

2 +Christopher John [The Hon Christopher Fletcher-Vane, 41 Larkspur Terrace, Jesmond, Northumberland NE2 2DT; Morton House, Morton, Calthwaite, Penrith, Cumbria CA11 9PZ]; *b* 27 March 1953; *educ* Eton and Trin Coll Cambridge (MA); barrister Inner Temple 1976; *m* 23 June 1990 *Margaret M, slr, dau of Dr Paul Eisenklam, of London, and has:

(1) +Francis William Paul; *b* 1 Nov 1992

(2) +Arthur Wladek Jocelyn; *b* 30 June 1995

(1) *Olivia Evelyn Mary; *b* 19 Aug 1991

INGLIS

Arms: Azure a lion rampant argent, armed and langued gules, on a chief argent three mullets sable. **Crest:** A demi-lion as in the arms holding in his dexter fore-paw a mullet argent. **Motto:** (above the crest) *Recte faciendo securus* ('Safe in acting rightly').
Creation: Bt. (NS) 22 Feb 1702/3.

SIR RODERICK JOHN INGLIS OF GLENCORSE, 10TH BT [Sir Roderick Inglis of Glencorse Bt, 18 Cordwalles Rd, Pietermaritzburg, Natal, S Afrca 3201]; *b* 25 Jan 1936; *s* f 1974; *educ* Winchester and Edinburgh U (MB, ChB 1960); *m* 1st 13 Sept 1960 (*divorce* 1975) Rachel Evelyn, only dau of Lt-Col Noel Meeson Morris, of Dowdstown, Co Louth, and has had:

1 Alastair Mackenzie; *b* 28 July 1961; *d* 19–

2 +IAN RICHARD; *b* 9 Aug 1965

3 +Alexander Colin; *b* 9 Aug 1965

1 *Amanda Fiona; *b* 22 June 1963

Sir RODERICK *m* 2nd 1975 (*divorce* 1977) Geraldine, yr dau of Rees Kirk, of Thaxted, Essex, and by her has:

2 *Harriet; *b* 10 Jan 1977

Sir RODERICK *m* 3rd 1986 *Marilyn, dau of A I Irwin, of Glasgow, and by her has:

4 +Harry Mackenzie; *b* 1987

Lineage: HECTOR MACKENZIE *Eachainn Ruadh* ('Red Hector') (yr s of Alexander Mackenzie of Kintail; *see* CROMARTIE, E); held part of Gairloch in the late 15th century; ancestor of:

JOHN MACKENZIE, 4th of Gairloch; had a new charter of the (territorial) Barony of Gairloch 19 Nov 1619; *d* 1628, leaving:

ALEXANDER MACKENZIE, 5th of Gairloch; *d* 1638, leaving:

KENNETH MACKENZIE, 6th of Gairloch; *d* 1669, leaving by his 2nd w:

ALEXANDER MACKENZIE, 7th of Gairloch; *m* 1670 Barbara, dau of Sir John Mackenzie of Tarbat, 1st Bt (*see* CROMARTIE, E), and *d* 1694, having had, with a dau (Anne, *m* Kenneth MacKenzie of Torridon; *see* MACKENZIE, Bt, of Coul):

Sir Kenneth Mackenzie, 1st Bt (NS), so *cr* 22 Feb 1702/3, of Gairloch; MP Ross-shire 1702; *m* 21 April 1696 Margaret, dau of Sir Roderick Mackenzie of Findon, and *d* 3 Oct 1704, leaving an est s:

Sir Alexander Mackenzie, 2nd Bt; *m* 1730 Janet, dau of Sir Roderick Mackenzie, 2nd Bt, of Scatwell (*qv*), and *d* 9 June 1766, leaving an est s:

Sir Alexander Mackenzie, 3rd Bt; *m* 1st 29 Nov 1755 Margaret (*d* 1 Dec 1759), dau of Roderick Mackenzie of Redcastle, and had an only s:

1 HECTOR (Sir), **4th Bt**

Sir Alexander *m* 2nd 26 July 1760 Jean (*d* 1766), only dau of John Gorry of Balblair, Commissary Ross, and had, with two daus:

2 John; *b c* 1764; Gen, served 1779–1814; *m* Lilias, yst dau of Alexander Chisholm of Chisholm, and *d* 14 June 1860, having had:

(1) Alastair; Offr 90th LI, Treasurer Colony of Victoria; *m* 1839 Wade Ellen, dau of George Huyler, US Consul-Gen and French Consul Bahamas, and *d* 1852, having had:

1a George William Russell (Rev); Curate Winford, Bristol; *b* 1840; *m* 2 Aug 1876 Annie Constance (*d* 1893), 2nd dau of Richard J Congreve, of Carlingwark, Scotland, and *d* 1903, leaving:

1b Dorothy Lilias; *m* H E Harvey and had issue

2b Kythé; *d* unm 1969

3b Marjorie; *m* W Lee and had issue

(1) Lilias Mary Catherine; *d* unm

3 Kenneth; Offr IA; *m* Flora, dau of Farquhar McRae and had two sons and four daus

Sir ALEXANDER *d* 13 April 1770; his est son,

Sir Hector Mackenzie, 4th Bt; Ld Lt Ross-shire; *b* Sept 1758; *m* 1st 29 July 1778 (*divorce* 22 April 1796) Cochrane, dau of James Chalmers of Fingland; *m* 2nd 9 May 1796 Christian, only child of William Henderson, and *d* 26 April 1826, having by her had:

1 **Sir Francis Alexander Mackenzie, 5th Bt**; *m* 1st 10 Aug 1829 Kythé Caroline (*d* May 1834), est dau of J Smith Wright, of Rempstone Hall, and had:

(1) **Sir Kenneth Smith Mackenzie, 6th Bt**, JP Ross-shire; Ld Lt 1881–99, Convenor and Chm CC Ross-shire; *b* 25 May 1832; *m* 11 Dec 1860 Eila Frederica (*d* 12 Oct 1923), 2nd dau of Walter Frederick Campbell of Islay, and *d* 9 Feb 1900, leaving:

1a **Sir Kenneth John Mackenzie, 7th Bt**, JP, V Lt and Convenor Ross and Cromarty, King's and Ld Treasurer's Remembrancer Scotland 1900–21, Maj 3rd Bn King's Own Cameron Highrs, Capt Rifle Bde; *b* 6 Oct 1861; *m* 8 April 1891 Lady Marjory Louisa Murray, CBE (1920), JP (*d* 18 Feb 1943), est dau of 4th Earl of Mansfield (*qv*), and *d* 4 Dec 1929, having had:

1b **Sir Hector David Mackenzie, 8th Bt**, MC, JP (1932); Ld Lt Ross and Cromarty 1936–58 (V-Lt 1935–36, DL to 1935); *b* 6 June 1893; *educ* Winchester; Capt Lovat Scouts Yeo WW I (despatches); *d* unm 10 May 1958, when the territorial Barony of Gairloch passed to his niece

2b Roderick Ian; 2nd Lt 1st Bn Black Watch (Roy Highrs); *b* 27 May 1895; *ka* 11 April 1915

1b (Marjory) Kythé, JP Ross and Cromarty; *b* 25 Jan 1892; *m* 1 June 1915 Maj Sir John Stirling of Fairburn and Monar, Ross-shire KT, MBE, JP, DL (*d* 21 March 1975), s of Maj William Stirling of Fairburn, and *d* 12 Dec 1971, leaving, with yr daus:

1c *Marjory Charlotte, Mrs Mackenzie of Gairloch, as which *s* unc (recognized by Ld Lyon warrant 1958); *m* *Brig William Alexander Stevenson Mackenzie, DSO, OBE

2a Francis Granville; *b* 31 Aug 1865; *d* 8 April 1933

1a Muriel Katharine; *d* unm 29 Dec 1952

(2) Francis Harford; *b* 5 May 1833; *d* 3 Sept 1895

1 (cont.) **Sir Francis** *m* 2nd 25 Oct 1836 Mary (*d* 8 March 1901), dau of Osgood Hanbury, of Holfield Grange, Essex, and *d* 2 June 1843, having by her had:

(3) Osgood Hanbury, of Inverewe House, Poolewe, Ross-shire, JP, DL; *b* 13 May 1842; *m* 26 June 1877 Minna Amy (*d* 19 Aug 1909), dau of Sir Thomas Edwards-Moss, 1st Bt (*qv*), and *d* 15 April 1922, leaving:

1a Mary Thyra; *b* 1 March 1879; *m* 1st 18 April 1907 Robert John Hanbury (*d* 5 April 1933), s of George Hanbury, of Blythewood, Bucks; *m* 2nd July 1935 Capt Ronald Sawyer (*d* 25 Oct 1945), s of Lt-Col William Harcourt Sawyer, and *d* July 1953

2 William; *d* unm 1858

3 Hector; Col HEICS; *m* Mary Lydia, dau of Gen Sir Hugh Fraser, of Braelangwell, and *dsp*

4 John, of Eileanach; MD; *b* 1803; *m* 28 Sept 1826 Mary Jane (*d* 1897), dau of Rev John Inglis, DD, of Edinburgh and Perthshire, and *d* 18 Dec 1886, having had:

(1) Hector; *b* 1828; Col BSC; *m* 19 May 1855 Eliza Ann Theophila, dau of Lt-Col Jamieson, and *dsp* 11 May 1907

(2) John; *dsp*

(3) Harry Maxwell; *b* 1839; Lt-Col RA; *m* 7 Sept 1872 Georgina Caroline (*d* 30 Aug 1911), dau of Capt Charles Ponsonby, ISC, and *d* 13 July 1891, leaving:

1a Hector Ian Maxwell MACKENZIE later INGLIS (1929); *b* 14 June 1875; *m* 18 Dec 1902 Dora (*d* 13 April 1919), 5th dau of Robert Mole, of Beoley Hall, Worcs, and *d* 27 Feb 1937, leaving:

1b MAXWELL IAN HECTOR INGLIS (Sir), **9th Bt**

2a Harry Ponsonby; Engr-Cdr RN; *b* 30 March 1877; *m* 22 Dec 1915 Gladys Dalziel (*d* 15 Aug 1966), yr dau of William Weatherly, of Woolongoon, Mortlake, Victoria, Australia, and *d* 4 Dec 1948, leaving:

1b +Alastair John [Lt Alastair MacKenzie RANVR (ret), Wombat Pk, RM13 3356, Daylesford, Victoria, Australia 2460]; *b* 16 Aug 1922; served WW II (despatches); *m* 1955 *Isabel Anne, dau of Capt Andrew Kelt, RAMC, of Pickdick, Brede, Sussex, and has:

1c +Roderick Andrew John; *b* 17 Feb 1962

1c *Kythé Jane; *b* 1956

2c *Iona Margaret; *b* 1957

3c *Mairi Anne; *b* 12 Dec 1959

2b +Kenneth William [Kenneth MacKenzie Esq, Trawalla, Victoria, Australia]; *b* 8 Aug 1928; *m* 8 March 1962 *Jennifer Margaret, only dau of Col Patrick Hyde, OBE, of Berrembed, Matong, NSW, and has:

1c *Caroline Margaret; *b* 26 Sept 1963; *m* Oct 1996 *Roger Pescott

2c *Elizabeth Georgina; *b* 22 March 1965

3a Kenneth Gordon; Maj Canadian Inf; *b* 6 July 1878; *m* 8 Nov 1911 Minnie Hamilton, er dau of Charles Henry Strutt, of Kamloops, BC, and was *ka* 20 Nov 1916, leaving:

1b *Cicely Kythe Mary Hamilton; WRCNS WW II; *b* 26 Oct 1916; *m* 24 Aug 1946 *S/Ldr William Anderson Beaumont, RAFVR, s of William Lionel Beaumont, of Nesbit Hall, Pudsey, nr Leeds, and has issue

4a Colin Rae; Lt Canadian Inf; *b* 7 May 1887; *m* 27 Aug 1913 Nora Constance, 2nd dau of Herbert Guernsey, JP, of Victoria, BC, and St John, New Brunswick, and has:

1b *Margaret Elaine; *b* 8 July 1914; *m* 1st 6 Feb 1937 (*divorce* 1958) Gerald Ashby Wodehouse Garland (*d* 28 July 1965), s of R H Wodehouse Garland, and has:

1c *Angela Robin; *b* 28 Feb 1938

2c *Jennifer Sarah; *b* 28 March 1942; *m* 19 June 1965 *Edward John Roberts and has:

1d *Benjamin Alexander; *b* 20 June 1966

2d *Nicholas Justin; *b* 25 Nov 1967

1b (cont.) *Mrs Margaret Garland *m* 2nd 1958 *C R Cuthbert

2b *Molly Georgina; *b* 16 Dec 1915; *m* 16 Dec 1947 *Reginald Frank John Featherstone, s of Capt R B Featherstone, of Devon, and has:

1c *Grenfell John; *b* 22 Oct 1949

2c *Devon Elizabeth; *b* 5 June 1952

3b *Nora Kythe; *b* 31 May 1917; *m* 1944 *Capt Victor Browne, RCN, s of Maj GA Browne, and has:

1c *Colin Victor Alleyne; *b* 29 Jan 1946

1c *Susan Kythe; *b* 18 Aug 1949

4b *Christine Ponsonby (uses maiden name) [Mrs Christine MacKenzie, 16 Eva St, Malvern, Melbourne 3144, Australia]; *b* 8 Aug 1928; *m* 1953 *Adrian C Boehme and has:

1c *Justine Christian; *b* 20 Oct 1959

2c *Nicholas Christian; *b* 21 May 1962

1c *Anna Kythe; *b* 1 April 1958

5a Alistair Ponsonby; *b* 25 June 1889; *d* unm 15 May 1910

1a Margaret; *d* unm 4 Jan 1958

2a Mary Lilian Kythe; *m* 1907 Alfred William Johnson (*ka* 1918), of Balquhidder, Kamloops, BC, and *d* 19 Nov 1947, leaving issue

3a Kythé; *m* 10 Sept 1913 Lt-Col John Kenneth Boyd Campbell, KOSB (*d* 29 April 1938), yr s of John Roy Campbell, of Buckfastleigh, and *d* 28 Nov 1958, leaving issue

4a Gladys Georgina; *d* unm 22 Feb 1969

(1) Mary; *b* 1827; *m* 1849 Duncan Davidson (*d* 20 Sept 1880), of Tulloch, and *d* 1867, leaving issue

(2) Christina Isabella; *b* 31 March 1831; *m* 23 Nov 1853 Charles Addington Hanbury (*d* 13 Dec 1900), of Belmont House, E Barnet, and *d* 8 March 1909, leaving issue

(3) Kythé Caroline; *m* 12 April 1865 Frank Mackenzie Ogilvy and *d* 8 July 1900, leaving issue

(4) Lisette Scott; *m* 28 June 1878 Frederick Louis Kindermann, of Aberfeldy, Perthshire, and *dsp* 11 May 1914

(5) Georgina Elizabeth; *b* 26 Jan 1842; *m* 26 Jan 1860 Lt-Col Duncan Henry Caithness Reay Davidson (*d* 29 March 1889), of Tulloch, and *d* 20 Dec 1926, leaving issue

5 Roderick; *m* Margaret, dau of Rev John Day, Rector Killalagh, Co Kerry

Sir HECTOR's cousin,

Sir Maxwell Ian Hector Inglis of Glencorse, 9th Bt (recognised by Lord Lyon 1958 in surname); *b* 18 Oct 1903; *educ* Winchester and Trin Coll Cambridge (BA 1925, MA 1959); W/Cdr RAFVR; Gold Coast political service 1928–37; Midlothian: JP 1946, memb CC 1938–67, Convenor 1946–47, Ld Lt 1964–72 (DL 1957–64), memb Roy Co Archers, Chm S of Scotland Electricity Consultative Cncl 1960–65 (Dep Chm 1948–60); *m* 13 Feb 1932 (Dorothy) Evelyn Stewart, JP (Midlothian 1960), MD (London), BS, MRCS, LRCP, only dau of Dr John Stewart, of Tasmania, and *d* 22 July 1974, leaving:

1 Sir RODERICK JOHN INGLIS OF GLENCORSE, **10th and present Bt**

INGRAM

Arms: Quarterly, argent and or guttée de poix, on a fess invected gules four escallops of the second. **Crest:** Upon a rock proper, issuant from a wreath of cinquefoils or, a gryphon's head erased quarterly gules and argent, charged on the neck with an escallop counter-changed. **Motto:** *In hoc signo vinces* ('In this sign shalt thou conquer'). **Creation:** Bt. (UK) 9 Aug 1893.

SIR JAMES HERBERT CHARLES INGRAM, 4TH BT, of Swineshead Abbey, Co Lincoln [Sir James Ingram Bt, 8 Lochaline St, London W6 9SH]; *b* 6 May 1966; *s* gf 1980; *educ* Eton and Cardiff U

Lineage: HERBERT INGRAM; *b* 1667; leader small Quaker community Boston, Lincs; *d* 1751; gf of:

HERBERT INGRAM; Controller Customs Boston; had:

HERBERT INGRAM, of Loudwater House, Rickmansworth, Herts, JP and DL (Lincs); *b* 27 May 1811; MP Boston; *m* 4 July 1843 Ann (*m* 2nd 6 April 1892 Sir Edward William Watkin, 1st Bt; *d* 26 May 1896), dau of William Little, of the Manor House, Eye, Northants, and was drowned with his est s Lake Michigan 8 Sept 1860, having had:

1 Herbert; *b* 1845; drowned with his f

2 WILLIAM JAMES (Sir), **1st Bt**

3 Charles Lewis Nathaniel, of S Kensington and Elstead House, Elstead, Surrey; Capt Surrey Militia; *b* 9 June 1849; *m* 18 Dec 1877 Lucy Frances (*d* 3 Feb 1893), dau of Francis A Davis, of Anglesea Lodge, Surbiton, and *d* 7 May 1931, having had issue

4 Walter Herbert; BA Cantab; *b* Dec 1855; *m* 27 April 1887 Ethelinda Favoretta (*d* 28 Oct 1910), yst dau of Richard Hemming, of Bentley Manor, JP Worcs, and was *k* on safari Berbera, Africa, *c* 14 April 1888, having had issue

HERBERT INGRAM's est surv son,

Sir William James Ingram, 1st Bt (UK), so *cr* 9 Aug 1893, JP (Surrey and Cinque Ports); *b* 27 Oct 1847; *educ* Winchester and Trin Coll Cambridge (BA); barrister; MP (Lib) Boston 1874–80 and 1885–95; *m* 10 Nov 1874 Mary Eliza Collingwood (*d* 8 Oct 1925), er dau of Hon Edward Stirling, MLA, of Adelaide, S Australia, and had:

1 HERBERT (Sir), **2nd Bt**

2 Bruce Stirling (Sir), OBE (1919), MC (1917); *b* 5 May 1877; *educ* Winchester and Trin Coll Oxford (BA 1897); T/Capt RGA, Lt Roy E Kent Yeo Cav WW I, ed *Illustrated London News* 1900 and *The Sketch*, ktd 1950, Offr Legn Hon 1950, D Litt 1960; *m* 1st 14 July 1904 Amy (*d* 26 Jan 1947), dau of John Foy, of S Kensington, and had:

(1) David Martin Bruce; *b* 26 Jan 1917; *d* 12 Sept 1930

(1) Averil Stirling; *b* 6 April 1905; *m* 4 Dec 1945 Capt Jean-Claude Prost (*d* 19–), 3rd s of Maurice Prost, banker, of Lons-le-Saunier (Jura), France

2 (cont.) Sir Bruce *m* 2nd 12 Nov 1947 Lily (*d* 6 Oct 1962), dau of Sydney Grundy, playwright, and *d* 8 Jan 1963

3 Collingwood; *b* 30 Oct 1880; Capt RAF WW I; *m* 17 Oct 1906 Florence Maude (*d* 1980), only child of Henry Rudolph Laing, of Chelsea, and *d* 1981, having had:

(1) Ivor Laing; *b* 1 Nov 1907; FCA, F/Lt RAFVR WW II (despatches); *m* 27 June 1936 *Winifred Edith [Mrs Ivor Ingram, 27 West Knowe, Bidston Rd, Birkenhead], only dau of William Battle Waterhouse, of Wallasey, Cheshire, and *d* 1990, leaving:

1a +John Anthony [John Ingram Esq, Wardle Old Hall, Nantwich, Cheshire]; *b* 19 Jan 1941; *educ* Shrewsbury; *m* 14 Sept 1963 *Jacqueline Ann, dau of William Alexander Lockley Cook, and has:

1b +Christopher William Ivor Lockley; *b* 15 Feb 1965

2b +Louis Anthony Lockley; *b* 1968

1a *Jennifer; *b* 1 Aug 1938; *m* 5 July 1958 *Michael Derek White, s of Charles Derrick White, of Birkenhead, and has:

1b *David Ingram; *b* 1 Feb 1965

1b *Susan Patricia; *b* 6 Nov 1961

2a *Jill Susan Rosemary [Mrs Clyde Coltart, Browfield, Dale End Rd, Barnston, Wirral, Cheshire]; *b* 20 April 1948; *m* 31 May 1969 *Clyde Dennis Gordon Coltart, only s of Albert Mounsey Coltart, of The Wirral, and has:

1b *Rupert Gordon; *b* 1971

1b *Amanda Jane; *b* 1973

(2) Mervyn Jeffry; *b* 21 March 1909; *educ* Winchester and Trin Coll Cambridge (MB, BCh); MRCS, LRCP; Capt RAMC WW II; *m* 16 Jan 1936 *Joan Doreen, twin dau of Capt (E) Arthur Philip Leslie Dupen, RN, and step-dau of Col Edward Guy Kynaston Cross, DSO, of the Fishery, Co Galway, and *d* 8 Nov 1993, leaving:

1a +Collingwood William Malcolm [Collingwood Ingram Esq, 37 Poplar Grove, London W11]; *b* 16 Aug 1939; *educ* Stowe and Trin Coll Cambridge (BA 1962); *m* 1976 *Susan Anne, dau of Dudley Love, of Solihull, and has:

1b +William Mervyn; *b* 1980

1b *Rosalind Annabel; *b* 1978

1a *Priscilla Jane [Mrs Dudley Doust, Westbrook House, West Bradley, Somerset BA6 8LS]; *b* 3 May 1937; *m* 26 Jan 1963 *Dudley Allen Doust, s of Brewster Doust, of Syracuse, NY, and has:

1b *Hannah Victoria [Mrs Sean Barrington, The Old College Arms, Stour Row, Dorset SP7 0QF]; *b* 11 Nov 1963; *m* 18 June 1990 *Sean Michael Gresham Barrington and has:

1c *Harry Jake; *b* 28 April 1997

2b *Elinor Jane; *b* 25 Feb 1966

2a *Charlotte Certhia [Mrs Charlotte Fox, Middle St Andrew's Wood, Dulford, Devon EX15 2DF]; *b* 3 Nov 1944; *m* 8 Aug 1964 (*divorce* 1993) Charles St Vigor Fox, only s of Maj William Michael Fox, of Thorn Falcon House, nr Taunton, and has:

1b *Laurence St Vigor; *b* 14 March 1965; *m* May 1995 *Nancy Basile, of New York

1b *Nina Jane; *b* 17 Sept 1970

(3) William Alastair; *b* 26 Aug 1913; *educ* Winchester; Maj RA; *m* 7 Jan 1947 *Daphne [Mrs William Ingram, 8 St James Villas, Winchester, Hants], er dau of Reginald Bramley Van Wart, OBE, MA, of Merioneths, and *d* 1975, leaving:

1a +Peter William Irving; *b* 13 Jan 1950; *educ* Winchester and Kent U (BA 1977); *m* 1979 *Christina Mary, 2nd dau of Sir James Holmes Henry, 2nd Bt (*qv*), and has:

1b *Sarah Christina; *b* 1980

2b *Corinna Alice; *b* 1983

1a *Heather Anne [Mrs Michael Bowyer, Lockerley Water House, Lockerley, Hants]; *b* 8 June 1948; *m* 18 Oct 1969 *Michael Paget Bowyer, MSc, s of Paget Bowyer, of Peake House, Corfe Castle, Dorset, and has:

1b *James William Paget; *b* 1974

1b *Caroline Sarah; *b* 1972

(1) *Certhia Mary [Mrs Charles Harden, Springhill Farm, Iden Green, Kent]; *b* 4 Jan 1917; *m* 27 April 1940 Charles Gerald Harden (*d* 1983), only s of Charles Harden, and has:

1a *Alastair Geoffrey; *b* 8 July 1943; *educ* Rugby and St Andrews (BSc 1966); *m* 1982 *Evelyn Macguire and has:

1b *Niall Charles Brendan; *b* 1983

2b *Alastair Francis; *b* 1984

1b *Marina Catherine; *b* 1990

2a *Richard Charles [Lt-Cdr Richard Harden RN, New Lindsey, Spring Lane, Burwash, E Sussex]; *b* 13 Sept 1946; *educ* Rugby; *m* 1976 *Elizabeth Catherine Lacy, er dau of Evelyn Charles Lacy Hulbert-Powell (*see* SAINT LEVAN, B), and has:

1b *Charles John; *b* 1981

1b *Annabel Mary; *b* 1977

2b *Rosemary Juliet; *b* 1979

1a *Veryan Penelope [Mrs Ernest Pollard, Springhill Farm, Benenden, Kent]; *b* 29 July 1941; *educ* Reading U (BSc); *m* 4 April 1964 *Ernest Pollard, PhD, s of A J Pollard, of Beeston, Notts, and has:

1b *John Collingwood; *b* 21 Feb 1968

1b *Tessa Mary; *b* 30 July 1966

2a *Frances Mary; *b* 31 March 1956; *m* 1980 *Paul Stryker Meier

Sir WILLIAM *d* 18 Dec 1924; his est son,

Sir Herbert Ingram, 2nd Bt; *b* 26 Sept 1875; *educ* Winchester and Exeter Coll Oxford (BA 1897); Capt Roy E Kent Yeo Cav, T/Lt-Cdr RNVR and Maj RAF WW I, WW II CD; Hon DLitt Oxon 1958; *m* 5 Feb 1908 Hilda Vivian (*d* 8 June 1968), dau of Col Carson Lake, of New York, and had:

1 HERBERT (Sir), **3rd Bt**

2 +Michael Warren, OBE (1982), JP (Glos 1949), DL [Maj Michael Ingram OBE JP DL, The Manor House, S Cerney, Glos GL1 5TT]; *b* 20 June 1917; *educ* Winchester and Balliol Coll Oxford (BA 1945); Maj Gren Gds WW II; *m* 13 Oct 1944 *Auriol Blanche, est dau of Lt-Gen Sir Arthur Francis Smith, KCB, KBE, DSO, MC (see SOMERLEYTON, B), and has:

(1) +Andrew David Michael [Andrew Ingram Esq, 30 King Henry's Rd, London NW3 3RP]; *b* 28 July 1945; *educ* Winchester and Trin Coll Oxford; *m* 28 Aug 1969 *Carole Letitia, 2nd dau of Maj John David Summers (*see* SUMMERS, Bt), and has:

1a +Matthew William Michael; *b* 27 May 1971

2a +Toby David Warren; *b* 1972

(1) *Susan Elizabeth [Mrs John Colquhoun, Brooke House, Frocester, Glos]; *b* 20 Nov 1947; *m* 26 July 1969 *John Humphrey Colquhoun, s of William Reginald Colquhoun, of Cecily Hill House, Cirencester, and has:

1a *Mark Humphrey; *b* 1973; *m* 1997 *Katherine Rosemary Woodrow

2a *James Arthur; *b* 1975

1a *Auriol Emma; *b* 1982

(2) *Nicola Mary, JP (Cornwall); *b* 16 Sept 1951; *m* 26 June 1970 *Paul Archer Tyler, CBE, s of Capt O W Tyler, of Devon, and has:

1a *Dominick Michael Archer; *b* 1975

1a *Sophie Grace Auriol; *b* 1972

(3) *Auriol Jacqueline; *b* 26 July 1957
1 Vivian Mary; *b* 21 Dec 1909; *d* 27 Oct 1919

Sir HERBERT *d* 1 June 1958; his er son,

Sir Herbert Ingram, 3rd Bt; *b* 18 April 1912; *educ* Winchester and Balliol Coll Oxford; Maj Gren Gds and REME WW II (despatches); *m* 9 Feb 1935 Jane Lindsay, dau of James Edward Palmer-Tomkinson, of Totterdown, Inkpen, Berks, and *d* 3 July 1980, having had:

1 (Herbert) Robin Ingram; *b* 13 Jan 1939; *educ* Eton; *m* 1st 24 Sept 1963 (*divorce* 1971) Shiela Rosette [Countess Shiela von der Schulenburg, 8 Pitt St, London W8] (*m* 2nd 1972 (*divorce* 1985) Count Fritz Dietlof von der Schulenburg), only dau of Charles Peczenik, of Mayfair, and had:
(1) Sir JAMES HERBERT CHARLES INGRAM, **4th and present Bt**
(1) *Frances Jane [Mrs Louis Bernon, Eagle Cottage, Tangley, Hants]; *b* 7 May 1964; *m* 19– *Louis Bernon and has:
1a *Robin; *b* 19–
1 (cont.) Robin Ingram *m* 2nd *Sallie Willoughby [Mrs Robin Ingram, Southridge House, Streatley, Berks], 2nd dau of Frank Hilary Minoprio, of Hessle Well House, Heswall, Cheshire, and *d* 1979, having by her had:
(2) +NICHOLAS DAVID; heir presumptive; *b* 12 June 1975
(2) *Caroline Robin; *b* 1979
1 *Marion Judith; *b* 18 Feb 1937; *m* 27 Nov 1969 *Graham H Harvey-Evers, er s of Prof H Harvey-Evers, of Fernwood House, Jesmond, Northumberland, and has:
(1) *Charles James; *b* 3 July 1970
(2) *David Edward; *b* 1971
2 *Vivian Helen [Mrs Oliver Turnbull, Cleabarrow, Windermere, Cumbria]; *b* 18 Feb 1937; *m* 31 Aug 1963 *Oliver Turnbull, yr s of Rev Peveril Hayes Turnbull, of The Cottage, Brandeston, Suffolk, by Lady Jane Grey, only dau of 9th Earl of Stamford (*see* 1970 edn), and has:
(1) *Harry Jonathan Peveril; *b* 1971
(1) *Jane Lucy; *b* 11 April 1965; *m* 1991 *Charles Waddington and has:
1a *Toby George; *b* 1993
(2) *Clare Catherine; *b* 27 July 1966; *m* 1990 *Edward Barham and has issue:
1a *Emily Catherine; *b* 1993
(3) *Sarah Mary; *b* 18 Oct 1968
3 *Anne Carolyn [Mrs Alan Peck, Hurst Lodge, Hurst, Berks RG10 0RB]; *b* 6 Feb 1952; *m* 20 April 1974 *Alan C W Peck, s of A F W Peck of Broomclose, Porlock, Somerset, and has:
(1) *Alexander Robin; *b* 1981
(1) *Frances Miranda; *b* 1978

INGROW

Arms: Vert two chevronels between in chief as many garbs of barley and in base a talbot sejant or, holding in the mouth an arrow in bend, the head downwards ppr. **Crest:** A demi-talbot or, holding in the mouth an arrow in bend, the head downwards ppr.
Supporters: Dexter, a shire horse arg., harnessed and bridled ppr.; sinister, a lion or, head and mane gu., gorged with a chaplet of roses arg., barbed and seeded ppr., the compartment comprising a grassy mount, growing therefrom on each side a rose arg., barbed, seeded and leaved ppr. between two sprigs of oak fructed, also ppr.
Motto: *Semper fidelis* ('Always faithful'). **Creation:** B. (LP, UK) 1982.

THE BARON INGROW, of Keighley, Co W Yorks (Sir John Aked Taylor, TD 1951, OBE (1960), JP (Keighley 1949)) [The Rt Hon The Lord Ingrow OBE TD JP, Fieldhead, Keighley, W Yorkshire BD20 6LP]; *b* 15 Aug 1917; *educ* Shrewsbury; Maj Duke of Wellington's Regt and Roy Signals WWII; Memb Keighley Town Cncl 1946–67 (Mayor 1956–57); Chm: Keighley C Assoc 1952–86 (Hon Treas 1976–86, V-Pres 1986–), Exec Ctee Nat Union C and U Assocs 1971–76 (memb 1964–83, Pres 1982–83), ktd 1972; memb Cncl Magistrates. Assoc 1957–86; chm and md Timothy Taylor and Co; Pres Yorks and Humberside TAVRA 1988–91; Gen Commr Income Tax 1965–92; Memb Ct Leeds U 1986–; Pres Cncl OStJ (KStJ 1986) S and W Yorks 1985–92; Ld Lt and Custos Rotulorum W Yorks 1985–92 (V-Ld Lt 1976–85, DL 1971); DU Bradford 1990; *m* 1949 *Barbara Mary, dau of Percy Wright Stirk, of Crestmead, Keighley, and has:
1 *Anne Elizabeth [The Hon Mrs Dent, Ribston Hall, Wetherby, Yorks]; *b* 1951; *m* 1975 *Charles Jonathan Dent, er s of John Harker Dent
2 *Diana Mary [The Hon Mrs Dent, Clock Farm, Hunsingore, Yorks]; *b* 1953: *m* 1979 *John Patrick Dent, yr s of John Harker Dent

Lineage: PERCY TAYLOR, of Knowle Spring House, Keighley; *m* Gladys Broster (*m* 2nd Sir (John) Donald Horsfall, 2nd Bt, *qv*), and had:
JOHN AKED, *cr* a **Baron**

INNES of Balvenie

Arms: Argent three mullets in chief azure. **Crest:** A dexter arm, armed and couped at the elbow, holding a broadsword in pale proper. **Supporters:** Two greyhounds argent.
Motto: *Sine crimine fiat* ('Let it be done without blemish').
Creation: Bt. (NS) 15 Jan 1628.

SIR PETER ALEXANDER BEROWALD INNES, 17TH BT, of Balvenie [Sir Peter Innes Bt, The Wheel House, Nations Hill, Kings Worthy, Hants SO23 7QY]; *b* 6 Jan 1937; *s f* 1988; *educ* Prince of Wales Sch Nairobi and Bristol U (BSc 1958); Lt-Col Engr and Transport Staff Corps RE (TA); FICE; with Scott Wilson Kirkpatrick and Co 1964– (dir 1995–, Associate 1982–87), responsible for airport projects UK, Africa and Middle East; *m* 18 July 1959 *Julia Mary, dau of Alfred Stoyell Levesley, MSc, FRSC, of Bristol, and has:
1 +(ALEXANDER) GUY BEROWALD [Guy Innes Esq, Rosebank, Church Rd, Longhope, Glos]; *b* 4 May 1960; *educ* Queen Mary's Coll Basingstoke; dir Netpro Mktg, Pncpl Alexander Residential; *m* 1986 (*divorce* 1989) Sara-Jane, dau of Dennis Busher, of Moraira, Spain; has by *Susan Barwick:
(1) *Laura Jane INNES-BARWICK; *b* 2 Sept 1997
2 +Alastair John Peter; *b* 19 May 1965; *educ* Newcastle U (BSc)
1 *Fiona Julie; *b* 22 Feb 1963; *educ* Dundee U (MA)

Lineage: WALTER INNES of Innermarkie, of which he had sasine 17 May 1486 (2nd s of Sir Robert Innes, 11th of that Ilk; *see* ROXBURGHE, D); *m* Christine Gordon and *d* by 3 Nov 1499, leaving:
1 ROBERT
2 Walter, of Toux; *m* 1st —, dau of William Forbes, Yr. of Drumallachie; *m* 2nd Janet Terrall, heiress of Inverbreaky, and was ancestor of the INNESes of Auchintoul, Calrossie and Inverbreaky
3 Patrick; *see* 1882 edn INNES, Bt, of Coxton
4 Thomas, of Elrick; *m* Margaret (*m* 2nd 7th Earl of Erroll, *qv*), dau of Alexander Robertson of Struan, and *d* by 1528
1 Elizabeth; *m* John Grant of Glenmorriston, illegitimate s of John Grant, 2nd of Freuchie (*see* STRATHSPEY, B)

The est son,

ROBERT INNES, 2nd of Innermarkie; Hereditary Constable Redcastle in Ardmannoch, a Cdr on the Borders with England 1533; *m* Lady Elspeth Stewart, dau of 1st Earl of Atholl (*see* MORAY, E), and *d c* Oct 1551, having had:
1 Robert, of Monycabok, which his f made over to him 1531; *m* Marioun (*m* 2nd Sir Alexander Robertson), dau of Alexander Ogilvy of Deskford, and *dvp* by 10 Nov 1547, leaving:
(1) Robert, 3rd of Innermarkie; *b* 1532; supported MARY QUEEN OF SCOTS, later a secret diplomatic agent; *m* June 1553 (*divorce* 19 Nov 1574) Margaret, dau of Alexander Innes, 14th of that Ilk (*see* ROXBURGHE, D), murdered 1580 his chief Alexander Innes, 18th of that Ilk and of Crommey, and in the ensuing feud was himself *k* Sept 1584, having been betrayed by his s:
1a Robert, 4th of Innermarkie; one of the murderers of the Earl of Moray 1591, for which executed 12 July 1595; *m* Jean (*d c* Oct 1607), dau of Walter Barclay of Towie-Barclay, and had:
1b **Sir Robert Innes, 1st Bt** (NS), so *cr* 15 Jan 1628, with remainder to his heirs male whatsoever, 5th of Innermarkie and 1st of Balvenie; *m* 1st Jean, dau of James Innes of Minnonie; *m* 2nd by 1607 Barbara, sis of Sir Thomas Burnett, 1st Bt, of Leys (*see* 1970 edn), and had:
1c **Sir Walter Innes, 2nd Bt**; royalist Civil War; *m* 28 April 1623 Lilias, dau of John Grant of Grant, and *d* by 10 Dec 1650, leaving:

1d **Sir Robert Innes, 3rd Bt**; *m* Janet, dau of Sir John Gordon, 1st Bt, of Haddo (*see* ABERDEEN AND TEMAIR, M), and widow of George Morrison of Pitfour, and *dspms* 8 June 1689, having had five children
1d Margaret; *m* William Farquharson and *d* Feb 1688
2d Barbara; *m* 8 Aug 1659 John Douglas of Murrastown
3d Katherine; *m* 21 April 1681 Archibald Dunbar of Newton
2c William, of Kinnermony; *m c* 1624 Elizabeth, dau of Walter Barclay of Towie-Barclay, and *dspm* May 1672, having had two daus, of whom Margaret *m* William Sutherland of Kinstairie
1c Isobel; *m* 1625 Robert Cumming of Altyre
2c Margaret; *m* Patrick Og ('The Younger') Grant of Easter Elchies
1b (cont.) **Sir Robert** *m* 3rd *c* Feb 1626 Margaret Dunbar and *d* by Feb 1642
2b Alexander, of Torrieglas
3b James, of Wester Coxton; *m* Isobel Grant and *d* by 1653, leaving:
1c James, of Denoone, Angus; Col; *m* Barbara Maxwell and *d* by 19 Aug 1670, leaving:
1d **Rev Sir George Innes, 4th Bt**, of Denoone, Angus; RC priest; *d* 2 Feb 1698
2d William; predeceased his bro *sp*
1d Isobel; *m* William Ruthven of Easter Denoone
2d Margaret; *m* Maj James Stirling, Capt Berwick
4b William, of Mayne and Orblieston; *m* Magdalene Falconer and *d* by 1634, leaving:
1c Walter, of Ortoun; Baillie Regality of Rothes; *m* 1st 2 July 1630 a dau of James Sutherland of Kinstairie and widow of John Chisholm, The Chisholm, and had:
1d Alexander, of Orblieston and Ortoun; *m* 1 June 1671 Margaret, dau of Maj George Crichton of Arveckie and widow of Hew Craigie of Gairsay, MP, and *dsp* by 1698
1d Margaret; *m* 1st 2 Nov 1660 Robert Gibson of Linkwood; *m* 2nd by 1671 James Rose of Allanbuie
1c (cont.) Walter Innes of Ortoun *m* 2nd 1661 Margaret, 4th dau of Sir William Hamilton of Ellieston, and *d* 1684, having by her had:
2d **Sir James Innes, 5th Bt**, of Balvenie and Orton; *m* 2 Dec 1699 Margaret, est dau of Thomas Fraser of Cairnbulg, s of 2nd Lord Fraser (*see* SALTOUN, L), and *d* 1722, having had:
1e **Sir Robert Innes, 6th Bt**; *b* 1702; Offr 1st Roy Dragoons; *m* 1734 Margery (*d* 30 Sept 1765), dau and heiress of Col Winram, and *d* 31 Aug 1758, leaving an only surv dau:
1f Catherine; *m* 1760 17th Lord Forbes (*qv*) and *d* 16 April 1805
2e **Sir Charles Innes, 7th Bt**; *b* 21 Feb 1704; Capt 71st Foot; *m* Isobel, dau and heir of Alexander Paton of Kinaldie, Ld Provost Aberdeen, and *dsps* 8 April 1768, having had two sons (Robert; John; both *dvp*)
3e Walter
4e **Sir William Innes, 8th Bt**; Cornet 3rd Horse Gds, Lt-Col 2nd Dragoon Gds (Queen's Bays); *m* 1st Sarah (*d* 15 May 1770), dau and heir of Thomas Hodges, of Ipswich, and had two daus (Elizabeth Charlotte, *b* 1766, *d* 14 Dec 1858; Sarah Catherine, *b* 1770, *d* 2 July 1845); *m* 2nd 22 March 1774 Mary Maria (*dsp* 1819), dau and heir of Maj Parsons, of York, and *d* 13 March 1817 aged *c* 100
5e James; Capt RN, *dsp*
1e Margaret; *b* 25 Jan 1703; *m* 4 July 1741 Sir Ludovick Grant, 6th Bt, of Dalvey
2e Mary; *m* 16 Jan 1755 Rev Alexander Watt, Min Alves, and *d* 8 April 1777
3e Jean; *m* John Geddes, and *d* 9 Aug 1788
2d Mary; *b* Jan 1663
1c Barbara; *m* 2 July 1630 James Sutherland, s of James Sutherland of Kinstairie
5b Archibald; *m* Barbara, dau of John Innes of Coxton and widow of Dumbreck of Orton, and *dspm* by 1642, leaving:
1c Margaret; *m* 13 Nov 1630 James Geddes of Auchinhalrig
1b Beatrix; *m* 1595 William Mackintosh of Borlum
2b Agnes; *m* 1612 Walter Innes of Auchlunkart
3b Isobel; *m* 1st Patrick Gordon of Proney (*d* 1624); *m* 2nd by 1628 John Gordon of Hallhead
4b Elizabeth; *m* Henry Stewart, of Ardbrodin
2 Alexander, of Ardgrane; *m* Griselda Auchinleck and *dsp*
3 John, of Edingight, Banffshire, by 1559; *m* 1545 Marjorie, dau of Alexander Leslie, 3rd of Wardis (*see* LESLIE, Bt), and had:
(1) Thomas, 2nd of Edingight; *m* 1st Janet, dau of John Seton of Auchenhuiff; *m* 2nd Janet Abercromby, widow of Ogilvy of Netherclunie; *m* 3rd Isobel Ogilvie (*m* 2nd Alistair Leslie) and *d* 1625, having by his 1st w had:
1a Thomas, 3rd of Edingight, to whom his f made it over 1611; *m c* 1611, as her 1st husb, Jean, est dau of John Innes, 2nd of Coxton (*see* INNES, Bt, of Coxton), and *dvp* by 1618, leaving:
1b John, 4th of Edingight; *m* June 1637 Christian, dau of Sir John Bruce of Airth and widow of Thomas Urquhart of Kinoudie, and *d* April 1674, leaving:
1c John, 5th of Edingight, to whom his f made it over 1659; *m* 1st Elizabeth, dau and heiress of John Gordon of Ardlogie, and had:
1d John, 6th of Edingight, which his f made over to him 1691; *b* Oct 1662; Baillie Regality of Strathisla; *m* (contract 7 Aug 1691) Helen, dau of Michael Strachan of Auchnagatt and sis of Sir Patrick Strachan of Glenkindle, and had:
1e John, 7th of Edingight; *b* Oct 1692; Baillie Regality Strathisla; *m* 30 March 1720 Jean (*d* 23 May 1776), dau of Patrick Duff of Craigston by his 1st w Ann, dau of John Innes, 5th of Edingight (*see* below), and *d* 1748, leaving:
1f John, 8th of Edingight; *b* 22 Feb 1721; Provost Banff; *m* 9 Aug 1753 Elizabeth (*d* 22 March 1803), dau of Lewis Grant of Auchterblair and Carron, and *d* 7 June 1790, having had, with three sons (*d* unm):
1g **Sir John Innes, 9th Bt**, of Balvenie and Edingight, DL (Banffshire); *b* 23 June 1757; served heir to **8th Bt** 12 Jan 1818; *m* 6 Aug 1796 Barbara, gdau of Sir John Forbes, 3rd Bt, of Monymusk (*qv*), and *d* 23 March 1829, having had, with four other daus (*d* unm):
1h **Sir John Innes, 10th Bt**, of Edingight; *b* 1801; Capt 10th Inverness-shire Militia; *d* unm 3 Dec 1838
2h **Sir James Milne Innes, 11th Bt**, of Edingight, JP, DL; *b* 24 Feb 1808; *m* 4 April 1837 Elizabeth (*d* 29 April 1899), dau of Alexander Thurburn of Keith, and *d* 11 May 1878, having had:
1i **Sir John Innes, 12th Bt**, JP, DL Christchurch, NZ; *b* 25 Nov 1840; the Balvenie arms and supporters were confirmed to him by Lyon King of Arms 20 Jan 1912, V-Lt Banffshire; *d* unm 2 May 1912
2i **Sir James Innes, 13th Bt**, JP (Banffshire); *b* 20 Jan 1846; *d* unm 7 Jan 1919
3i Robert; *b* 28 March 1847; *d* 22 Jan 1896
4i George Forbes; *b* 9 Sept 1848; *d* 9 Dec 1870
5i Thomas, of Valparaiso and Liverpool; *b* 22 Feb 1852; *m* 1880 Virginia (*d* 12 Feb 1934), dau of Col Hugh Plunket Bourchier, and *d* 23 April 1911, leaving:
1j **Sir James Bourchier Innes, 14th Bt**, JP Banffshire; *b* 27 Oct 1883; *d* unm 20 Dec 1950
1j Mary Thurburn; *m* 7 March 1912 Edward John Heneage Ash (*d* 18 Aug 1946) and *d* 28 Oct 1954
6i Hector; *b* 27 Oct 1860; *m* 20 Nov 1895 Annie Jane, dau of William Fraser, and *d* 30 Dec 1904, having had:
1j John Fraser; *b* 1896; *d* 1897
2j **Sir Walter James Innes, 15th Bt**, of Balvenie and Edingight; *b* 8 Aug 1903; *d* unm 2 Sept 1978
1j Anita Elizabeth; *m* 8 May 1920 Robert Edward Forrest, Western Telegraph Co, Montevideo, and *d* 31 July 1925, leaving issue
2j Lily Eileen; *m* 1925 Hubert Brunel Mallet and had:
1k *Myra Ana; *b* 9 March 1927; *m* 11 Jan 1952 *Oliver Miles Dawe and has:
1l *Michael Charles; *b* 12 Aug 1954
1l *Angela Katherine; *b* 11 Dec 1956
2k *Nancy Lily; *b* 20 July 1929; *m* 20 March 1951 *Charles Brandon and has:
1l *John; *b* 23 June 1956
1l *Diana Lily; *b* 20 Sept 1953
7i Edward; MB; *b* 10 Aug 1864; Surgn Nayar Bde Travancore; *d* unm 24 April 1895
1i Barbara Forbes; *m* 29 Dec 1864 her 1st cousin Edward Wood Stock, barrister, and *d* 24 March 1872, leaving issue
2i Anne Thurburn; *m* 27 Sept 1870 Edward A Thurburn, of Mayen, Rothiemay Banffshire, and *dsp* 11 March 1914
3i Elizabeth Helen; *d* unm 27 Dec 1916
1h Elizabeth; *b* 26 Aug 1798; *m* Edward Stock and had issue
2h Georgina Forbes; *b* 12 Dec 1803; *m* James Blackwood and *dsp* 1871
1g Jean; *b* 7 Nov 1754; *m* 12 Sept 1772 James Milne, yr s of Alexander Milne
2g Elizabeth; *b* 16 April 1756; *m* 1st 1774 Thomas Innes of Monellie (*see above*); *m* 2nd George Robinson of Gask
3g Anne; *b* 15 May 1762; *m* Alexander Innes of Garmouth
2f Alexander, of Cowie and Breda; *b* 12 July 1727; Commissary Aberdeen; *m* 9 Feb 1767 Elizabeth (*d* 8 July 1795), dau of William Davidson, of Midmar Castle, and *d* 30 June 1788, having had, with eight daus:
1g John, of Cowie; WS; *b* 20 Aug 1776; *m* 25 July 1802 Une Cameron Barclay Allardice (*d* 26 Sept 1809), dau of Robert Barclay of Urie, MP, and *d* 17 April 1832, having had:
1h John; *b c* 1803; *dvp* 30 March 1816
1h Cameron; *m* 8 Sept 1826 Gen Peter Augustus de Lautour, CB, KH, Col 20th Light Dragoons and 3rd Hus, 2nd s of Joseph François Louis de Lautour (*d* 11 Jan 1866), of Hexton House, Herts, and had a dau
2h Elizabeth; *m* 4 Dec 1832 Arthur Abercromby of Glassaugh
3h Margaret; *m* 4 Dec 1835 Alexander Gibbon of Johnston
2g William, of Raemoir and Cowie, Kincardineshire, JP, DL; *b* 29 March 1781; *m* 19 Oct 1809 Jane (*d* 19 June 1872), er dau and coheir of Alexander Brebner of Learney, and *d* 9 Sept 1863, leaving:
1h Alexander, of Raemoir, JP, DL; *b* 29 March 1812; memb Roy Co Archers 1841; *m* 5 April 1842 Anne Katherine (*d* Jan 1908), dau of Sir Alexander Leith, KCB (*see* BURGH, B), and *d* 29 Oct 1883, having had, with a dau (*d* unm):
1i Alexander, DL; *b* 25 April 1846; Lt 3rd Foot (The Buffs); *m* 1st 31 Aug 1871 Helen Eythan (*d* 16 Feb 1875), dau of Rev S W King, and had:
1j Alexander Berowald, of Raemoir, JP, DL; *b* 10 Sept 1872; Lt Gordon Highrs, memb Roy Co Archers; *m* 1 Dec 1910 Mary (*d* 18 May 1942), dau of Erskine Beveridge, LLD, and was *ka sp* 18 June 1915

2j James William Guy, CBE (1919), of Raemoir, JP and DL Kincardineshire; *b* 11 Sept 1873; Capt RN, Chev Legn Hon; *m* 28 Aug 1906 Anna Orrok Stronach Sheila Foster (*m* 2nd 21 Dec 1940 2nd Marquess of Aberdeen and Temair, *qv*), dau of Lt-Col John Foster Forbes of Rothiemay, JP, DL, and *d* 1 Oct 1939, leaving:

1k (RONALD GORDON) BEROWALD (Sir), **16th Bt**

2k +William Alexander Disney, JP (Banffshire 1964) [Lt-Col William Innes JP, Heath Cottage, Aberlour, Banffshire AB3 9QD]; *b* 19 April 1910; *educ* Marlborough; Lt-Col Gordon Highrs WW II; V-Lt Banffshire 1971–87 (DL 1959–71); *m* 7 June 1939 Mary Alison (*d* 13 Feb 1997), only dau of Francis Burnett-Stuart, of Howe Green, Hertford, and has:

1l +Michael Alexander [Michael Innes Esq, St Mary's Farm, Cupar, Fife KY15 4NF]; *b* 25 Feb 1954; *educ* Trin Coll Glenalmond and Durham U (BA), Dip Hort Kew; by Carolyn Ann Scott has:

1m *Rosanna Mary Scott INNES; *b* 1988

2l +Jonathan Berowald [Jonathan Innes Esq, 33 Croft Rd, Thame, Oxon OX9 3JF]; *b* 4 July 1955; *educ* Trin Coll Glenalmond, St Andrews (MA) and Reading U (MSc); *m* 1986 *Jane Angela, dau of Lt-Col John Dalton Stephenson, of Cefn Parc, Brecon

3k Thomas Guy, AFC (1953); *b* 27 June 1922; *educ* Harrow; Cdr RN; *d* car crash 21 March 1958

1k *Elizabeth Katherine Mary [Mrs Eric Mackenzie, Hill Cottage, Fressingfield, Suffolk]; *b* 22 Aug 1918; *m* 1st 16 Jan 1943 (*divorce* 1948) Lt-Col James Robertson-McIsaac, Gordon Highrs; *m* 2nd 15 Nov 1948 Col Eric Dighton Mackenzie, CMG, CVO, DSO (*d* 8 Aug 1972), yst s of Sir Alan Russell Mackenzie, 2nd Bt, of Glenmuick (*qv*), and by him has issue

1j Helen Kathleen; *d* unm 14 March 1959

1i (cont.) Alexander Innes *m* 2nd 26 June 1878 Sylvia Christina Armitage (*d* 16 Dec 1887), dau of Rev James P Garrett, of Kilgaran, Co Carlow, and *d* 13 Nov 1882, leaving by her:

3j Sydney Armitage, DSO and bar (1917); *b* 24 April 1879; Col Black Watch, Cmdt Queen Victoria Sch Dunblane 1930–39, Boer War 1899–1900 and WW I (wounded, despatches); *m* 10 Nov 1903 Constance Edith (*d* 19 April 1957), dau of Samuel Blain, and *d* 24 March 1960, having had:

1k Berowald Alfred; *b* 22 July 1904; *educ* Rugby; Lt-Col Black Watch WW II (wounded); *m* 24 Nov 1931 Betty Ida (*d* 20 Feb 1997), dau of Alastair Campbell Sandeman, of Pitlochry, and *d* 1981, having had:

1l Hector Berowald; *b* 21 Nov 1933; *d* 2 June 1935

2l +Colin Berowald [Maj Colin Innes, Easter Dunbog, Newborough, Cupar, Fife KY14 6JF]; *b* 5 June 1936; *educ* Wellington; Maj Black Watch; *m* 30 Sept 1961 *Clovannis Jane, twin dau of Lt-Col Charles Frederick Cathcart, DSO (*see* CATHCART, E), and has had:

1m Andrew Berowald; *b* 28 Dec 1963; *d* 17 March 1991

1m *Katherine Candida; *b* 30 May 1967; *m* 1994 *Giles Ernest Peppiatt, yr s of Brian Peppiatt, of Ford, Bucks, and has:

1n *Dominic Andrew Slingsby; *b* 19 March 1997

2m *Emily-Jane [Mrs Edward Taylor, 1 Cupar Rd, London SW14 4JW]; *b* 14 Jan 1969; *m* 14 June 1997 *Edward John Timothy Taylor

3l +Malcolm Alastair [Malcolm Innes Esq, 132 Wakehurst Rd, London SW11 6BS; 10 Regent Terr, Edinburgh]; *b* 27 Feb 1939; *educ* Wellington and Trin Hall Cambridge (BA 1962); late Lt Scots Gds, Capt Black Watch (TA); *m* 11 Sept 1976 *Celia Jane, LVO, er dau of Jock Wykeham Strang Steel (*see* STRANG STEEL, Bt), and has:

1m +Robert Alexander; *b* 1980

1m *Fiona Bridget; *b* 14 Oct 1983

4l +James Alexander [James Innes Esq, Newbigging Birks, Oxnam, Jedburgh TD8 6NA]; *b* 27 Feb 1939; *educ* Gordonstoun; *m* 18 Oct 1969 *Frances, yst dau of Hugh Leggat, of Pirnie House, Kelso, and has:

1m +Rory Alexander; *b* 1977

1m *Melissa Jane; *b* 1972

2k Herome Alexander, DFC; *b* 2 Nov 1912; F/O RAF, Lt (SR) Black Watch; *ka* 4 April 1940

1k *Sylvia [Mrs Frank Richardson, 4B Barnton Ave West, Edinburgh]; *b* 3 Sept 1909; *m* 4 March 1944 Maj-Gen Frank McLean Richardson, CB, DSO, OBE, MD, OStJ, RAMC (*d* 28 Aug 1996), s of Hugh Richardson, DSO, MD, of Finavon, St Andrews, and has:

1l *Hugh Alexander; *b* 1946; *m* 1981 *Zaleha Pawan, of Kuala Lumpur, and has:

1m *Christopher Johan Roland; *b* 1984

1m *Noelle; *b* 1988

2l *Alistair Neil; *b* 1953; *m* 1980 *Marianne Angela, dau of John Curry, of Co Mayo, and has:

1m *Simon Alexander; *b* 1988

1m *Saoirse Joanna; *b* 1981

1l *Jennifer Jane; *b* 1944

2i William Disney (Rev), of Cowie, DL; *b* 17 Oct 1851; *m* 12 Dec 1877 Helen Amy (*d* 1892), dau of Capt James B Burnett of Monboddo, and *d* 31 Oct 1928, leaving:

1j Alexander, of Cowie, MC, DL Kincardineshire (1953); *b* 20 March 1892; *educ* Trin Coll Glenalmond; Maj RFA, WWs I and II, memb Roy Co Archers 1949; *m* 9 Nov 1937 Alberta Laura (*d* 24 Sept 1975), dau of Capt Guy Mainwaring, RN, and widow of Walter Hargreaves Brown (*see* PIGOTT-BROWN, Bt), and *dsp* 30 Jan 1975

2h Thomas, CVO, of Learney, DL; *b* 31 Oct 1814; LLD, Lt-Col and Hon Col 3rd Bn Gordon Highrs, memb Roy Co Archers 1844; advocate 1836; *m* 22 July 1839 Helen Christian (*d* 30 Oct 1901), dau of Thomas Burnett of Park and Keppleston, and *d* 12 Nov 1912, having had:

1i William; *b* 27 May 1841; Capt RE; *ka* Passir Sala 7 Nov 1875 unm

2i Thomas; *b* 20 April 1843; *d* unm 18 June 1888

3i Francis Newell, of Learney, DL; *b* 17 Nov 1845; Lt-Col RHA, Order Medjidie; *m* 6 July 1892 Margaret Anne (*d* 15 Oct 1923), dau of Archer Irvine-Fortescue (*see* FORTESCUE, E), and *d* 12 April 1907, leaving:

1j Thomas of Learney (Sir), GCVO (1967, KCVO 1946); LLD (Hon) St Andrews, FSA Scot; *b* 26 Aug 1893; *educ* Edinburgh Acad, Edinburgh U and abroad; advocate 1922, peerage and heraldic counsel, Carrick Pursuivant of Arms 1926–35, interim Lyon Clerk and Keeper Records Lyon Court 1929 and 1939–40, Albany Herald 1935–45, Lord Lyon King of Arms and Sec to Order Thistle 1945–69, Genealogist OStJ Scotland 1947, Merchant Herald 1969–71, memb Nat Bldgs Record Scotland 1941, Chm PMG's Stamps Ctee Scotland 1956–57, Pres Scottish Ecclesiological Soc 1957–58 and 1959–60, memb Roy Co Archers, KStJ, author: *Scots Heraldry* and other works; *m* 27 Dec 1928 *Lady Lucy Buchan Sinclair [The Lady Lucy Innes of Learney, 56 Darnell Rd, Edinburgh EH5 3PJ], 3rd dau of 18th Earl of Caithness (*qv*), and *d* 16 Oct 1971, leaving:

1k +Thomas, of Learney [Thomas Innes of Learney, Learney, Torphins, Banchory AB31 4LU]; *b* 22 Jan 1930; *educ* Edinburgh Acad and Edinburgh U (BSc Ag); late Roy Signals, OStJ; Pres Deeside Field Club 1971–76; *m* 17 July 1958 *Rosemary Elizabeth, yr dau of Brig Cecil Vivian Staveley Jackson, CIE, CBE, of Burnside, Aboyne, Aberdeenshire, and has:

1l *Maureen Cecelia; *b* 1 Nov 1962; *m* 1985 *Duncan John Cullen Grant and has issue (*see* GRANT, Bt, of Monymusk and Cullen)

2k +Berowald Fortescue [Berowald Innes Esq, 18 Old Mill Lane, Inverness IV2 3XP]; *b* 25 May 1931; *educ* Melville Coll; FSA Scot

3k +Malcolm Rognvald, 16th of Edingight (family arrangement 1955) (Sir), KCVO (1990, CVO 1981) [Sir Malcolm Innes of Edingight KCVO, 35 Inverleith Row, Edinburgh]; *b* 25 May 1938; *educ* Edinburgh Acad and Edinburgh U (MA 1960, LLB 1963); Falkland Pursuivant Extraord 1957, Carrick Pursuivant 1958–72, Lyon Clerk and Keeper of the Records of Lyon Court 1966–81, WS, KStJ, FSA Scot, Marchmont Herald 1972–81, Lord Lyon King of Arms and Sec Order Thistle 1981–, memb Roy Co Archers; *m* 19 Oct 1963 *Joan, only dau of Thomas D Hay, CA, of Edinburgh, and has:

1l +John Berowald [John Innes Yr. of Edingight, Edingight, Keith, Banffshire AB55 6TD]; *b* 30 June 1965; *educ* Edinburgh Acad, Heriot Watt U (BSc) and RMA Sandhurst; Capt Gordon Highrs

2l +Colin William of Kinnairdy [Colin Innes Esq, Kinnairdy Castle, Bridge of Marnoch, Banffshire]; *b* 1 Dec 1967; *educ* Edinburgh Acad and Aberdeen U (LLB, LLM); *m* 1993 *Joanna, only dau of David Judge, of Birchwood, Hereford and Worcester, and has:

1m +Thomas David; *b* 19 Jan 1995

2m +William James Maxim; *b* 19 Jan 1997

3l +Michael Thomas, of Crommey; *b* 11 Jan 1970; *educ* Edinburgh Acad, St Andrews (MA) and Chester Law Sch; *m* 17 April 1998 *Robyn, er dau of Stewart Milne

1k *Sybil Marjorie [Miss Sybil Innes, 56 Darnell Rd, Edinburgh]; *b* 9 Jan 1934

1j Helen Christian; *b* 6 Dec 1895; *d* unm 9 March 1982

1h Christina; *m* 26 April 1842 Capt Charles Gordon, 92nd Highrs, and *dsp* 30 July 1901

3f James, of Maisly; *b* 1 Nov 1729; *m* 17 Jan 1754 Isobel, dau of John Abernethy, of Mayen, and *d* 10 March 1812, leaving:

1g John INNES later RAMSAY, of Barra, Inverurie; *m* 25 June 1785 Mary (*d* 18 Dec 1811), dau and heir of John Ramsay of Barra and Straloch, and *d* 14 April 1814, having had, with other issue:

1h John, of Barra; *b* 3 May 1786; *m* 15 Feb 1831 Susan (*m* 2nd 24 Oct 1844 Capt William Henry Nares, RN, and *d* 5 Aug 1887), dau of Alexander Innes of Pitmedden, and *d* 23 Oct 1832, leaving:

1i John, of Barra; *b* 3 Dec 1831; *m* 16 Sept 1858 Leonora Sophia (*d* 4 Feb 1862), dau of Rev Nathaniel Bond, of Creech Grange, and *d* 29 May 1895, leaving:

1j Mary Agnes, of Straloch and Barra Castle, Aberdeenshire; *m* 18 Nov 1880 Francis Hugh Forbes Irvine of Drum (*d* 25 July 1894) and *d* 13 March 1938, having had issue

2j Christina Susan Mary; *d* unm 12 Sept 1905

2h James; *b* 1797; *m* Maria, dau of Maj-Gen Duff of Carnousie and widow of Francis Garden-Campbell of Troup and Glenlyon, and had four sons (*dsp*) and four daus

3h William; *b* 1800; *m* Eliza Morley and *d* 26 Nov 1881, leaving:

1i Jessie; *b* 1828; *m* 1st 29 Aug 1853 Count Alexandre de Polignac (*d* 14 Aug 1858); *m* 2nd 1862 Charles Allanson Knight (*d* Feb 1897), 2nd s of John Knight, of Wolverley, Worcs, and *d* 1 April 1922, leaving issue

2i Ida; *b* 1833; *m* as his 2nd w Prince Michael Vlangali-Handjeri (*d* 27 July 1911), gs of Prince Handjeri, Hospodar of Wallachia, and *dsp* 1913

2g Alexander, of Pitmedden; *b* 1756; *m* Christine Susan (*d* 11 March 1834), dau of George Forbes of Boyndlie and Ladysford, and *d* 22 July 1829, having had six daus

1g Elizabeth; *b* 1762; *d* 6 June 1838

2e James; *b* 1699; Provost Banff 1744–48 and 1750–53; *m* 5 Dec 1728 Anne Garden (*d* 15 Oct 1770) and *dspm* 29 March 1757, having had two daus

3e Alexander, of Rosieburn; *b* Dec 1701; Provost Banff, Sheriff Clerk Banffshire; *m* Katherine, dau of Alexander Abercromby of Glassaugh, MP, and *d* 16 April 1761, leaving a s (Thomas, of Rosieburn, *d* unm 27 Aug 1784) and four daus

4e Thomas; *b* Jan 1705; Capt RN; *d* 1738

1e Anne; *m* 24 March 1719 James Innes, Provost Elgin (*d* June 1719)

1c (cont.) John Innes, 5th of Edingight *m* 2nd Nov 1663 Isobel, dau of John Hamiltom, of Corse of Kinnoir, and by her had:

2d James, of Thornton; *d* by 1725

3d Thomas, of Muiryfold, Banffshire; *b* 1681; Baillie Regality of Strathisla; *m* 14 Jan 1722 Mary, dau of John Gordon of Drumwhindle, and *d* 12 Sept 1754, leaving:

1e John, of Muiryfold and Netherdale; *m* 7 June 1760 Helen, dau of Patrick Gordon of Ardmeallie, and *dspl* 3 Oct 1780

2e Thomas, of Monellie; WS; *m* 3 Nov 1774 Elizabeth Innes, sis of the **9th Bt** (*see* above), and *d* 6 Sept 1779, leaving:

1f Elizabeth Mary, of Netherdale; *m* 1797 James ROSE later ROSE-INNES, advocate, and had issue

1d Ann; *m* 1687, as his 1st w, Patrick Duff of Craigston, unc of 1st Earl of Fife (*see* FIFE, D), and had issue (*see* above against John Innes, 7th of Edingight)

2d Helen; *m* 7 June 1698 William Scott, Provost Banff, and *d* 12 Nov 1758

3d Elspeth; *m* 22 Oct 1703 George Ruddoch of Blairock

4d Margaret; *m* 1707 George Geddes in Burnside (*d* 3 Feb 1726)

2a George, of Mosstown; *m* Grizel, dau of Gilbert Ogilvie of Ardrone, and had a dau (Isobel, of Mosstown)

(2) John, of Auchlunkart, Banffshire, 1578; ancestor of Walter Innes of Auchlunkart, whose dau and heiress Helen *m* 1706 Andrew Steuart of Tanachie

(3) Robert

(4) William; living 1597

(5) Jerome; had two sons (*dsp*) and three daus

4 Walter (Rev); Vicar Thurso 1554; *dsp*

5 William, of Thursater; Baillie (Magistrate) Diocese of Caithness; *d* after 1594, leaving:

(1) Robert, 2nd of Thursater; Archdeacon Caithness; *m* Margaret Sinclair, gdau of 4th Earl of Caithness (*qv*), and *d c* 1611, leaving:

1a John, 3rd of Thursater; *m* by 2 Nov 1607 Isobel, dau of William Innes of Blackhills, and had:

1b Robert, 4th of Thursater; *m* 11 July 1628 Margaret, dau of John Sinclair of Scrabster, and had:

1c James, 5th of Thursater; *m* Barbara Murray and *d c* 1693, leaving:

1d Robert, 6th of Thursater, which he sold 1693; *m* March 7 1685 Mary Furness and *dsp* by 1694

2d James, in Thrumster, Caithness; *m* a dau of James Calder of Strath and had:

1e William, in Oliclete; *b* 16 Sept 1711; *m* 1750 Janet Sinclair (*d* 1818) and had:

1f James, of Thrumster; *b* 10 April 1752; Maj 94th Regt; *m* 28 April 1790 Margaret (*d* 16 Sept 1841), dau of Gordon Clunes of Crakaig, and *d* 1832, leaving:

1g William; *b* 1791; Lt 94th Regt; *k* Badajoz Peninsular War

2g Gordon Clunes; *b* 1792; Lt 94th Regt; *k* Salamanca Peninsular War

3g John Clunes; *b* 1793; *d* unm 1814

4g Robert, 2nd of Thrumster; *b* 20 Oct 1794; *m* 29 June 1836 Henrietta, dau of Col William Sinclair Wemyss Southdun, and *dspm* 10 Jan 1852, leaving an only dau:

1h Henrietta, 3rd of Thrumster; *b* 18 May 1837; *m* 2 Dec 1856 Frederick Stocks BENTLEY later BENTLEY-INNES (*d* May 1887), barrister and memb Gentlemen-at-Arms, and *d* 1896, leaving three sons

5g James; *b* 29 April 1796; Bengal Med Serv; *m* 10 Dec 1828 Jane Alicia (*d* 2 Dec 1881), dau of Duncan McLeod of Geanies, and *d* 4 July 1846, leaving:

1h James John McLeod, VC, CB; *b* 5 Feb 1830; Lt-Gen RE; *m* 30 Oct 1855 Lucy Jane, dau of Prof Hugh Macpherson, and *d* 13 Dec 1907, having had:

1i James Edgeworth, ICS; *b* 17 March 1859; *d* unm 9 July 1881

2i Hugh McLeod; *b* 22 March 1862; *educ* Trin Coll Cambridge; *m* 1894 Margaret (*d* 1948), dau of James Bird, and *d* 13 July 1944, leaving:

1j Patrick McLeod; *b* 22 Aug 1897; Lt RGA; *ka* 30 April 1917

2j Donald McLeod; *b* 6 June 1899; Lt Black Watch; *ka* 6 Oct 1918

1j Christina McLeod; *b* 9 March 1902; *m* 14 May 1925 Frank Vigor Morley, DPhil (*d* 1980), s of Frank Morley, ScD, of Baltimore, Md., and had:

1k *John Donald Innes [John Morley Esq, 40 Hillside Close, Chalfont St Peter, Bucks]; *b* 15 March 1926; *m* 25 Aug 1962 *Alice Millicent, dau of J T Flook and widow of George Boast

2k Hugh Oliver; FRCO, ARCM; *b* 4 Dec 1928; *d* 1987

1k *Susanna Loveday [Mrs John Smithson, Corner Cottage, Jordans, Bucks]; *b* 12 May 1932; *m* 26 July 1956 *John Guthrie Smithson and has:

1l *Michael John, BSc; *b* 1957; *m* 1982 *Emilia, dau of Klimos Shaylou, of Nicosia, and has:

1m *Sophia Marina; *b* 1984

2l *Robert Hugh; BSc; *b* 1963

1l *Deborah Mary; *b* 1959; *m* 1981 *Richard Zealey and has:

1m *David John; *b* 1983

2m *Philip James; *b* 1989

1m *Christina May; *b* 1986

2k *Christina Margaret Peregrine; *b* 6 Feb 1940; *educ* OU (BA)

3i Arthur Donald; *b* 15 Sept 1863; *m* 13 Aug 1901 Helen, dau of Edward Arnold Pittis, of Lyme Regis, and *d* 19 April 1938, leaving:

1j Neil McLeod; *b* 17 Nov 1903; *educ* RNCs Osborne and Dartmouth, Haileybury and Trin Hall Cambridge (MA); Sudan Political Serv 1926–52, Min External Affrs to Sultan Muscat and Oman 1953–58, Order Nile 1941, matriculated arms at Lyon Office as rep of Innes of Thursater 5 April 1948; *m* 26 Aug 1931 Nancy Audrey (*d* 1987), dau of James Temple Stephens, of Melbourne, Australia, and *d* 1989, having had:

1k +Roderick Temple McLeod [Lt-Cdr Roderick Innes RN, Rose Cottage, Upper Swanmore, Hants SO32 2QQ]; *b* 14 Jan 1938; *educ* Marlborough and RNC Dartmouth; FRICS; *m* 22 Sept 1962 *Diana Selkirk, dau of Eric Summers Drew, of Alverstoke, and has:

1l +James McLeod; *b* 8 March 1966; *educ* Milton Abbey; ARICS

2l +Charles McLeod; *b* 27 May 1969; *educ* Sherborne and Reading U (BSc); *m* 1994 *Nathalie, dau of Giles Sharp, of Tanworth-in-Arden, Warwicks

1k *Catherine McLeod; *b* 16 July 1935; *m* Sept 1954 *Guy Francis Symondson, s of Francis Symondson, MC, of Lyme Regis, and has:

1l *Bevil Charles; *b* 12 Dec 1955; *m* 1985 *Lucy Elizabeth, dau of Douglas Hardinge Anderson (*see* HALSBURY, E), and has:

1m *Robert Michael; *b* 1986

2m *Foy Rohais; *b* 1987

1m *Minnette Elizabeth; *b* 1989

2l *Robin Francis; *b* 9 March 1957; *m* 1986 *Alison Gaddie and has:

1m *Angus John; *b* 1988

1m *Alexandra Mary Catherine; *b* 1989

3l *Alistair James Guy; *b* 11 July 1958; *m* 1st 1985 (*divorce* 1993) Mrs Rosemary Hardingham, *née* Cole; *m* 2nd 1995 Sheila McCartney (*d* 1997) and has by her:

1m *Hamish Ronald McCartney; *b* 1995

2k *Fiona McLeod; *b* 6 Aug 1939; *m* 1st 20 Feb 1960 Simon Noel Chick (*d* 1982), s of William Noel Chick, of Wynford Eagle, Dorset, and has:

1l *Theresa Nicola [Mrs Jeremy Russell, Manor Farm, Compton Valence, Dorset DT2 9ES]; *b* 23 Nov 1960; *m* 1987 *Maj Jeremy Russell, RGJ, and has:

1m *Edward Simon Chick (twin); *b* 1993

1m *Alice Elizabeth Newton; *b* 1991

2m *Camilla Louise Newton; *b* 1993

2l *Philippa Helen [Mrs Hugo James, Pigeon House, Hampton, Dorset DT2 9DZ]; *b* 27 March 1963; *m* 1986 *Hugo James and has:

1m *Grace Daisy; *b* 1992

2m *Flora Emily (twin); *b* 1992

3l *Sarah Rebecca [Miss Sarah Chick, Thrae, Compton Valence, Dorset DT2 9ER]; *b* 20 Dec 1967

2k (cont.) Mrs Simon Chick *m* 2nd 1986 Barry Gray Brookes (*d* 11 July 1995)
6g Archibald Clunes; *b* 4 May 1799; Maj 3rd Buffs; *m* 15 June 1829 Margaret, 3rd dau of Alexander Maclay, 1st Colonial Sec NSW, and *d* 20 Aug 1857, leaving, with other issue:
1h Gustavus Archibald Clunes; *b* 14 March 1838; Archdeacon Hamilton, NSW; *m* 14 July 1868 Emily Cornelia (*m* 2nd James O Maxwell and *d* 1941), dau of J Hack, of Paramatta, NSW, and *d* 9 Aug 1880, leaving:
1i George Archibald Clunes; *b* 1 March 1870; *m* 4 Nov 1900 Agnes Mary Gowthorpe (*d* 1937) and had:
1j Charles McLeod; *b* 8 Aug 1902; *m* July 1931 Elspeth Anne, dau of Charles Bilbe, of N Qld, and had:
1k +Ian; *b* 1 Sept 1933; *m* Aug 1965 *Janice Cassidy
2k +Colin; *b* 4 March 1935; *m* 12 March 1960 *Alison Mary Murra and has:
1l +Timothy Charles; *b* 12 Dec 1960
2l +John William; *b* 29 Jan 1964
1l *Elizabeth Mary; *b* 19 April 1962
2l *Susan Jane; *b* 25 July 1965
3k +James Alan; *b* 3 Nov 1947
1k *Lorraine; *b* 28 April 1932; *m* 8 Sept 1962 *Varsey Nano and has:
1l *Stephen Charles; *b* 30 Sept 1963
1l *Vivienne Anne; *b* 23 Nov 1965
2l *Belinda Ruth; *b* 1 March 1968
3l *Theresa Jane; *b* 24 March 1969
2k *Patty; *b* 4 March 1935; *m* 1960 *Paul Falconbridge Canty and has issue
3k *Mary *b* 25 Aug 1938; *m* 10 Jan 1959 *Bernard Robert Larkin, s of Robert Alan Larkin, of NSW, and has:
1l *Geoffrey Allan; *b* 18 Dec 1964
1l *Jennifer Kay; *b* 15 April 1961
2l *Louise Anne; *b* 10 Nov 1962
3l *Vicki Maree; *b* 18 Nov 1967
4k *Jillian; *b* 10 March 1941; *m* *Thomas Dalton, s of Dr Reginald Thomas Dalton, of Singleton, and has:
1l *Francis Ann; *b* 1 Aug 1962
2l *Gaye; *b* 30 Sept 1964
3l *Helen Mary; *b* 8 Nov 1965
1j Enid Emily; *b* 3 July 1904; *m* Donald James Mackay and had:
1k *Shirley; *b* 1931
2i Colridge Clunes; *b* 3 Feb 1877; *d* 1 May 1889
1i Lillian Macleod; *b* 24 Feb 1872; *m* 1889 Frank A Sweetnam, MD (*d* 9 Feb 1946), and *d* 2 July 1942, leaving issue
2i Vivienne Mary Floribel; *b* 30 Jan 1875; *m* 1906 E Hutton
7g George, of Capita, NSW; *b* 5 July 1802; *m* 1825 Lorna Campbell, illegitimate dau of 6th Duke of Argyll (*qv*), and had:
1h Annabella Alexandria Campbell; *m* 17 June 1856 Patrick Charles Douglas-Boswell, of Garallam
2h Margaret Clunes; *m* 14 Feb 1874 Hugh Campbell, 6th s of John Campbell, of Sundrum, and *dsp* 22 Dec 1902
8g Peter; *b* 20 Aug 1804; Maj-Gen HEICS; *d* unm 1871
9g Hugh Clunes; *b* 21 Aug 1806; *d* unm 1825
1g Ann Gordon; *b* 1797
2g Jane Sinclair; *b* 10 July 1805; *d* unm 1874
3g Barbara Sinclair; *b* 7 July 1808; *m* Sir George Macleay, KCMG, of Redhill, Surrey
4g Williamina; *b* 25 June 1812; *m* James Grigg (*d* 1865), Sheriff Substitute of Caithness, and *d* 1861
5g Gordina; *b* 1814; *d* unm 1832
2f John; *b* 27 Dec 1755; Maj 94th Regt; *m* Margaret, dau of Andrew Liddell, MD, and was *ka* Salamanca, leaving:
1g William; *b* 1 Jan 1806; Col HEICS; *d* 28 May 1872
2g Andrew Liddell; *b* 1808; *d* unm 26 Dec 1895
3f Peter, in Tannach, Caithness; *b* 27 Dec 1756; Capt 79th Regt; *m* 17 April 1822 Magdalen Manson and *d* 1822, having legitimated his s:
1g Robert, of Hayfield of Olrig; *b* 1 March 1804; *m* 1st Margaret Calder (*d* 1859) and had:
1h Peter, of Nova Scotia; *b* 3 May 1840; *m* 10 Oct 1888 Mary Logan (*d* 27 July 1952), dau of Robert Archibald Guild, and *d* 27 Aug 1919, leaving:
1i Robert; *b* 18 Aug 1891; Lt-Col Canadian Army; *m* 3 June 1913 Charlotte Lloyd Heming (*d* 1972) and *d* 1963, leaving:
1j Charles Heming; *b* 3 April 1915; *m* 18 April 1933 Gladys, dau of Frederick Rockwell, and *d* 1954
1j *Frances Mary, of Va., USA; *b* 15 Dec 1918; *m* 1 July 1946 James Thomas (*d* 1965)
2j Charlotte Elizabeth; *b* 19 Nov 1921; *m* 28 Aug 1939 William Young, of Nova Scotia, and had:
1k *Peter William; *b* 1949
2k *Sidney Allen; *b* 1953
1k *Patricia Kathleen; *b* 1940
2k *Charlotte Joy; *b* 1941; *m* 1961 *John Robert Wilkinson, of Nova Scotia, and has:
1l *John William; *b* 1963
1l *Debra Lee; *b* 1961
3k *Sandra Vaughan; *b* 1944; *m* 1964 *Donald Wade Perry, of Nova Scotia, and has:
1l *Shannon Rae; *b* 1965
1l *Shelley Lynn (twin); *b* 1965
3j *Margaret Joan; *b* 19 Oct 1925; *m* 1952 *Douglas Comrie and has:
1k *Laurie Douglas; *b* 1954; *m* 1979 *Marie Clare Allard
2k *Michael Raoul; *b* 1962
1k *Charlotte Ann; *b* 1953; *m* 1980 *T Jeffrey Davidson and has:
1l *John Douglas; *b* 1983
1l *Jessica Jane; *b* 1982
2k *Mary Jane; *b* 1963
2i Mary Isobel; *b* 12 Sept 1889; *m* 26 Oct 1912 Charles B Lowe, of Canada, and had issue
2h James; *b* 10 Feb 1842; *d* 13 Oct 1870, leaving a dau
1g (cont.) Robert Innes *m* 2nd Margaret Macdonald and by her had:
1h Isobel; *m* John Coghill, of Chicago
4f George, of Madras; *b* 8 April 1763; *dspl* 1806
5f William; *b* 12 Sept 1771; *dsp* 1806
3d William, WS; *m* Janet (*d* 29 Dec 1758), widow of Sir George Primrose of Dunipace and dau of Sir William Cunningham, 2nd Bt, of Caprington, and *dsp* 1746
4d George; living 1688; had:
1e James, of Tannach; had a s (Alexander, *b* 21 June 1726) but was *s* in the farm by his bro:
2e Patrick, of Tannach; *m* 1st — and had:
1f George; *b* 22 July 1747
2e (cont.) Patrick Innes *m* 2nd *c* 12 Jan 1751 Elizabeth, dau of Andrew Bremner, of Waterseat, and by her had:
2f James, of Reay Inn; *b c* 1754; *m* Margaret (*d* 26 March 1833), dau of Farquhar Mackay, of Brakside, and *d* 22 Jan 1795, leaving:
1g Donald; *b* 13 Oct 1783
2g James; *b* 18 Feb 1785; *d* Calcutta 24 Jan 1853
3g William, of Reay Inn; *b* 18 Feb 1786; *m* Elizabeth (*d* 9 June 1877), dau of — Mackay, of Sutherland, and *d* 21 April 1873, leaving:
1h William; *b* 6 Sept 1833; grazier Australia; *m* 6 Dec 1862 Jessie, 3rd dau of Duncan Mackintosh, of Culloden, Inverness, and had:
1i William James; *b* 8 Dec 1863; *d* unm Qld 20 April 1924
2i Duncan; *b* 19 Dec 1865; *m* Alicia Thomson, of Corowa (*d* 3 March 1942), and *d* 17 May 1951, leaving:
1j William John, of NSW; *b* 18 July 1907
2j Duncan, of Melbourne; *b* 18 Jan 1909; *m* 4 Dec 1945 *Ruby Martyr and had:
1k +Raymond Duncan; *b* 11 March 1947; *m* 16 March 1968 *Lois Buzza
2k +Peter Charles; *b* 30 April 1948
1j *Dorothy Ellen, of NSW; *b* 7 Sept 1911
2j *Phyllis Bessie; *b* 7 Jan 1913; *m* Oldrick Studenick, of NSW, and has:
1k *Peter William; *b* 20 June 1953
3i Joseph Percy; *b* 22 May 1867; *m* Jean Cartwright and *d* 31 Oct 1938, leaving:
1j Keith; *m* Ierna Lillyman and had:
1k *A dau; *m* William Johnston, of Nowema, New Caledonia
4i Peter; *b* 26 June 1868; *m* 22 June 1916 Alice Edith, dau of Arthur Trethowan, and *d* 18 Feb 1930, leaving:
1j +Peter Allan, of NSW; *b* 4 Sept 1918
1j *Lesley
5i Donald; *b* 9 Aug 1872; *m* Ada Grennell and *d* 26 May 1923, leaving issue
1i Bessie; *b* 14 Nov 1870; *m* 5 Aug 1902 J F Burgess (*d* Nov 1932) and *dsp* June 1948
2i Jessie; *b* 7 March 1876; *d* unm 30 Aug 1961
2h James, of Victoria, Australia; *b* 29 Sept 1838; *m* Dec 1870 Isobel, dau of Duncan Mackintosh, of Culloden, Inverness, and *d* 5 Nov 1904, leaving:
1i William; *b* Dec 1871; *d* unm 10 Oct 1891
2i Duncan; *b* 17 Aug 1873; *m* 1908 Martha Lye and *d* 10 Oct 1939, leaving:
1j Douglas; *b* 8 July 1914; *m* 1938 Millicent Ausborne and had:
1k John; *b* 1941; *d* 1948
1j Maurie; *b* 1909; *m* 1951 Kenelm Knox, of Sydney
2j Frances; *b* 1911
3i James; *b* July 1876; *m* 1908 Margaret Katherine (*d* Feb 1946), dau of Hugh Mckinnon, and *d* Aug 1962, leaving:
1j Hugh Mackinnon; *b* 1909; *m* Jessie Ammerman and had:
1k *Jean
2k *Margaret
2j James Mackintosh; *b* 1911; *d* unm 1946
3j Richard Thomas, of Melbourne; *b* 1915; *m* Rita Cooper and had:
1k +Graeme McIntosh; *b* 1947

1k *Judith Anne; *b* 1940; *m* 1963 *Douglas Bertram
2k *Heather Margaret; *b* 1943; *m* 25 April 1964 *Graham Jeffery Orr, of Victoria, and has:
1l *Andrew Richard; *b* 5 May 1968
1l *Sharron Leanne; *b* 9 Dec 1965
4i Peter John; *b* 1880; *d* 1882
5i Donald Joseph, of Sydney; *b* Jan 1882; *m* 1919 Katherine Daly and had:
1j Joan Elizabeth; *b* 16 Nov 1919; *m* 13 July 1940 *Philip John Walker North, of Killara, NSW, and had:
1k *Lawrie Elizabeth; *b* 6 Feb 1948
2k *Julia Louise; *b* 29 Sept 1957
6i Alexander Adam, of W Australia; *b* 30 Aug 1886; *m* 19 Nov 1928 Winifred (*d* 20 June 1959), dau of Ernest Finn, and had:
1j +Gordon James; *b* 13 May 1932; *m* 1955 *Laurel O'Byrne and has:
1k +Eric James; *b* 25 Jan 1956
2k +Philip; *b* 7 Dec 1957
1k *Deanne; *b* 12 July 1959
1j *Joan Margaret; *b* 12 May 1930; *m* 11 April 1953 *S/Ldr Noel Johnson, of Canberra, and has two sons and three daus
2j *Helen; *b* 9 Feb 1936; *m* 3 Oct 1959 *Jim Hancock and has two daus
7i Peter John; *b* Nov 188–; *d* unm Nov 1927
8i Thomas Mackay; *b* 1887; *m* 1924 Agatha Davidson and *d* 1965
9i Richard; *b* 1889; *m* 1929 Ethel Jones and *d* 1945, leaving:
1j +Richard Fraser; *b* 1935
1j *Dorothy; *b* 1930; *m* 1947 *Roderick Morell
2j *Jean; *b* 1932; *m* 1950 *Philip Kilketly
1i Elizabeth Ann; *b* 1875; *d* 1962
2i Jessie Margaret; *b* 1879; *m* Percy Henry Bratt and *d* 1964
3h Peter, of Orblieston, Moray; *b* 1842; *m* 1st Margaret Agnes, dau of Richard Tucker, of Holyhead; *m* 2nd 24 April 1904 Mary Birnie, dau of the Rev George Davidson, Min Logie Coldstone, Aberdeenshire, and *d* 14 Nov 1927, leaving:
1i Patrick Donald Davidson; *b* 1 July 1905; farmer at Dounreay, Caithness; *m* 7 Aug 1931 *Alexandrina, MA, dau of John Mark, and *d* Jan 1949, leaving:
1j +(Patrick) Mark Davidson; *b* 19 May 1941
2j +David Spence Davidson; *b* 1 Jan 1943
1j *Valerie Mark Davidson; *b* 27 Dec 1932; *m* 30 March 1957 *James Denny Stokes, CA, and has:
1k *Richard; *b* 28 Dec 1960
2k *Andrew; *b* 20 May 1962
1k *Katrina; *b* 20 Jan 1967
2j *Sonia Margaret Davidson; *b* 30 March 1934; *m* 12 July 1955 *Gerald John Jones, of Guildford, and has:
1k *Robert Gerald; *b* 16 Dec 1955
2k *Alan Peter; *b* 10 Oct 1958
4h John; *b* 25 July 1844; *m* Mary Finlayson, dau of Alexander Laing, and *d* 1896, leaving:
1i William; *b* 11 May 1885; *m* Margaret Wright, dau of Wellington Boyd, of Southfield, Canada, and *d* 23 May 1969, leaving:
1j Donald; *b* 1916
1j Margaret; *b* Aug 1915; *m* David Harrington, of Los Angeles, and had issue
2j *Betty Jane; *b* 1919
2i Alexander; Municipal Sec Spirit River, Alberta; *m* and *d* Aug 1950
3i Donald; *m* Mary Macdonald and had a dau
4i Joseph Adam, MC, of Isauld, Caithness; *b* 11 Jan 1894; *d* unm 1930
1i Mary; *m* Walter Gibb, of Edinburgh, and *d* Oct 1954, leaving issue
2i Elizabeth, of Isauld
5h Donald, of Isauld, Caithness; *b* 1846; *d* unm 20 Aug 1920
6h Joseph Adam; *m* Agnes — and *d* Mafeking, leaving two daus:
1i Anne Bessie; *d* young
2i Alicia; *m* Rev John Franks, Congregational Min Broadstairs, and *dsp*
1h Anne; *m* Robson Mackay and had:
1i Bessie; *m* Doctor Maclennan, of Nairn
2h Margaret; *b* 18 Oct 1835; drowned in childhood at Borlum Bridge
4g Patrick; *b* 1779; *d* 5 Jan 1822
1g Jean; *b* 1777; *m* 1794 George Innes of Brabster and *d* 1 Dec 1802, leaving issue
2g Elizabeth; *b* 5 Feb 1788; *d* young
3g Elizabeth; *b* 5 March 1792
4g Margaret; *b c* 1803; *m* Adam Sutherland, of Whelkhouse, fishcurer at Wick, and *d* April 1826, leaving issue
5g Mary; *m* Colin Sinclair, of Melvin Inn, and had issue
3f John; *b* 26 April 1759
4f Donald; *b* 9 July 1765; *d c* 1780
5d John; had an illegitimate dau:
1e Margaret; *b* 20 April 1687
1d Margaret; *m* 10 March 1681 William Sinclair of Thursater, 2nd s of John Sinclair of Brims
2d Elizabeth; *m* by 1685 Laurence Calder of Lynger
3d Janet; *m* 9 Sept 1691 John Swanson, Thurso merchant

The 15th Bt's cousin,

Sir (Ronald Gordon) Berowald Innes, 16th Bt, OBE (1943); *b* 24 July 1907; *educ* Harrow; Lt-Col Seaforth Highrs WW II (wounded), cmded 7th Bn Seaforth Highrs 1945, psc, GSO(1) WO 1946–48, OC 4th Uganda Bn KAR and OC Troops Uganda 1948–49; *m* 1st 17 Oct 1933 Elizabeth Haughton (*d* 3 Feb 1958), est dau of Alfred Fayle, of Merlin, Clonmel, Co Tipperary, and had:

1 PETER ALEXANDER BEROWALD (Sir), **17th and present Bt**
2 +George Guy Alfred [George Innes Esq, PO Box 1069, Esperance, W Australia]; *b* 11 Oct 1941; *educ* Massey U of Manawatu, NZ (Dip Agric); Kenya Regt
1 *Catherine Eythan [Mrs Donald Dawson, Lesmurdie House, Lesmurdie, W Australia]; *b* 20 Jan 1940; *m* 1st 1 Sept 1962 (*divorce* 1970) Mark Grant Oliver, of W Australia, author, est s of Cdr Rev Anthony Grant Oliver, OBE, RN, of Crowborough, Sussex, and has:
(1) *Karen Elizabeth; *b* 16 Aug 1965
(2) *Alison Mary; *b* 1967; *m* 1997 *Douglas Atkinson
1 (cont.) Mrs Catherine Oliver *m* 2nd 1974 Hugh Leslie Sanderson (*d* 1985); *m* 3rd 1993 *Donald Campbell Dawson

Sir Berowald *m* 2nd 1961 *(Elizabeth) Christian [Christian Lady Innes, The Loom House, Aultgowrie, Muir of Ord, Ross-shire IV6 7XA], er dau of Lt-Col Charles Henry Watson, DSO, and *d* 1988

INNES of Coxton

Arms: Argent three mullets within a bordure embattled azure, in dexter canton argent a saltire azure surmounted of an inescutcheon or charged with a lion rampant within a double tressure flory counterflory gules. **Crest:** A dexter arm in armour, the hand naked holding a skean in pale, both proper, issuing from an embattled tower argent, masoned sable, port gules. **Motto:** *Sine crimine fidelis* ('Faithful without blemish). **Creation:** Bt. (NS) 20 March 1685/6.

SIR DAVID CHARLES KENNETH GORDON INNES, 12TH BT, of Coxton, Co Moray [Sir David Innes Bt, 28 Wadham Close, Shepperton, Middx TW17 9HT]; *b* 17 April 1940; *s f* 1990; *educ* Haileybury, City and Guilds Coll of Imperial Coll, London U (BScEng); ACGI; electronics consultant for petro-chemical and power generation fields, technical dir Peak Technologies 1974–78, md Peak Combustion Controls 1978–81; *m* 1969 *Marjorie Alison, dau of Ernest Walter Parker, and has issue:

1 +ALISTAIR CHARLES DEVERELL; *b* 17 Sept 1970; *educ* Haileybury and Southampton U
1 *Dione Elizabeth Colquhoun; *b* 1974

Lineage: PATRICK INNES, in the Keam of Duffus, Morayshire (3rd s of Walter Innes of Innermarkie; *see* INNES, Bt of Balvenie); *m* Christian Cockburn and *d* 1547, leaving:

ALEXANDER INNES, 1st of Coxton, Morayshire, of which he had a charter 9 March 1571/2; *b* 1532; *m* 1st Janet Reid; *m* 2nd Catherine, dau of George Gordon, 2nd of Cairnborrow, and widow of James Innes, 3rd of Drainie, and *d* 5 Oct 1612, having by his 1st w had, with an est and yst s (apparently *d* unm):

JOHN INNES, 2nd of Coxton; *b c* 1565; *m* 1st 15 Dec 1586 Margaret, dau of Walter Kinnaird of Culbin, Morayshire; *m* 2nd Margaret Gordon and *d* 1634, leaving by his 1st w:

1 James, Yr. of Coxton; *m* Feb 1612 Marjory, dau of Alexander Innes of Cotts and Leuchars (*see* ROXBURGHE, D), and *dvp c* 1621, having had, with other issue:
(1) Alexander (Sir), 3rd of Coxton; *b c* 1615; *m* 1st Mary (*d* 20 Aug 1647), dau of Sir George Gordon, 6th of Gight, Aberdeenshire, by his 1st w Isobel, dau of Sir Patrick Ward of Bonnyton; *m* 2nd March 1649 Mary, sis of Sir Kenneth Mackenzie, 1st Bt, of Coul (*qv*), and *dsp*

(2) John, of Culdrain; *m* Helen, dau of Sir Adam Gordon, 1st of Park, by his 2nd w Helen Tyrie, and had:

1a **Sir Alexander Innes, 1st Bt** (NS), so *cr* 20 March 1685/6, with remainder to heirs male whatsover, 4th of Coxton (conveyed him by his unc 12 Sept 1677); *b c* 1652, MP Moray; Jacobite in campaign of Viscount Dundee (*see* DUNDEE, E, preliminary remarks); *m* 1st *c* 1678 Jean, dau of Hon Sir John Rolls, of Bannockburn, and had:

1b **Sir George Innes, 2nd Bt**, of Coxton; Jacobite 1715; *m* 10 Jan 1706 Jean, dau and (on death 18 Sept 1711 of her bro Patrick, from whom she inherited Towie-Barclay, Turriff, Aberdeenshire), eventual heiress of John Gordon of Rothiemay, by Elizabeth Barclay, heiress of Towie-Barclay, and *d c* Dec 1715, having had, with other issue:

1c Sir ALEXANDER INNES later BARCLAY-INNES, **3rd Bt**, of Coxton and Towie-Barclay; *m* 1st Helen, dau of James Duff of Crombie, and had:

1d Jane Barclay of Towie-Barclay; *b* 1727; *m* 22 July 1745 Dr Robert Dalrymple and *dsps* May 1746

1c (cont.) Sir ALEXANDER *m* 2nd Jean, dau and eventually sole heir of Patrick Ogilvy of Balpur, and *dspm* 1735/6, having by her had:

2d Isobel Barclay of Towie-Barclay, which was sold 1775; *m* Hon Charles MAITLAND later BARCLAY-MAITLAND, 2nd s of 6th Earl of Lauderdale (*qv*), and *d* 23 Oct 1761, leaving issue

2c **Sir James Innes, 4th Bt**; Jacobite 1745; *m* Margaret (*d* 17 Oct 1756), dau of James Brodie of Muiresk, and *d* 3 June 1790, having had, with other issue:

1d **Sir David Innes, 5th Bt**; Capt RM; *dsp* 8/9 Oct 1803

1d Elizabeth; *m* her cousin George Innes of Parkside (*d* 20 May 1790) and *d* 4 Jan 1823, having had issue (*see* above)

1c Elizabeth; *b* 1709; *m* William Fraser of Meunzie and *d* 3 Jan 1756

2c Ann; *m* Alexander Leslie, s of James Leslie, 8th of Kininvie

2b John; advocate 1710; *m* Jean, only dau of John Ross of Allanbuie, and *dsp*

3b James; Capt Col Pocock's Regt of Foot, Jacobite 1715 and 1745 (hence executed 21 Oct 1746), ADC to Lt Ogilvy; *m* Mary, dau of John Ramsay of Laithers, and had:

1c Mary

1b Elizabeth; *m* 29 Aug 1710 her cousin John Ord of Findochty

1a (cont.) **Sir Alexander** *m* 2nd Jean (*m* 2nd 19 Feb 1710 George Ogilvy, Queen's Limner (illuminator of manuscripts) for Scotland), dau of Patrick Neldrum of Laithers, and *d* 28 Jan 1709

2a John, 1st of Inaltrie 1688; *d* by 1706, leaving:

1b Alexander, 2nd of Inaltrie; Jacobite 1715; *m* Isobel Anderson and *d c* 1767, leaving:

1c Alexander, of Clerkseat; *b c* 1710; advocate 1748, Commissary Clerk Aberdeen, Burgess 1757; *m* Anne (*d* 28 Sept 1807), dau of Hugh Rose of Tillysnaucht, and *d* 12 March 1790, having had six sons (*dsp*) and 11 daus

2c George, of Parkside; Inspr-Gen Stamps Scotland; *m* his cousin Elizabeth (*d* 4 Jan 1823), dau of **Sir James Innes, 4th Bt**, and *d* 20 May 1790, leaving:

1d **Sir Alexander Innes, 6th Bt**; *dsp* 7 Sept 1811

2d Thomas; surgn; *d* at sea *sp* 1798

3d **Sir David Innes, 7th Bt**; *b* 1781; Lt 99th Foot; *m* 1833 Mary Anne (*d* 7 July 1884), dau of John Williamson of Stewarton, Ayrshire, and *d* 11 Aug 1866, having had, with two daus (*d unm*):

1e **Sir George Innes, 8th Bt**; *b* 1834; Lt 22nd Bombay Native Inf (ret 1859), Adj 5th Lanarks Rifle Vols 1860–65, Capt Hants Militia 1870, Musketry Instr 1871; *m* 1st 20 Jan 1855 Judith (*d* 1864), only surv dau of William Colquhoun Stirling of Edinbarnet; *m* 2nd 1865 Elsie, dau of H Watts, of Wooley, Bath, and widow of Maj Henderson, KH, 50th Foot, and *dsp* 25 Aug 1886, when the btcy became dormant

1d Margaret; *m* 1795 James Ure, Comptroller Customs Alloa

3c John; *b* 1719; dyer Turriff, Jacobite 1745

4c Patrick, of Mickle Mill of Esslemont

5c Peter; Capt RA; *dsp c* 1766

3a George, of Bogton in Pittenseir 1675

4a Patrick, of Soccoch; *m* Helen Innes and *d* Feb 1722, leaving issue

1a Jean; *m* Nov 1677 William Ord of Findochty

(2) (cont.) John Innes of Culdrain also had an illegitimate s:

1a Berowald INNES (Rev), of Inchstellie; *b c* 1644; Rector Alves, Morayshire, Chanter Diocese of Moray, ejected as a Jacobite 1693; *m* 15 Aug 1678 Jean, dau of Rt Rev Colin Falconer, Bp Moray, and *d* 27 March 1722, leaving:

1b James, of Inchstellie; *b* 30 Jan 1683; *m* Katharine, dau of Hugh Falconer, of Inverness, and had:

1b Hugh (Rev), of Parkhouse, nr Glasgow; *b* 30 July 1727; *m* Jean (*d* 1774), only surv child and eventual heiress of Thomas Graham, of Bogton of Rednock, and *d* 1765, having had, with other issue (*d* young):

1d Sir HUGH INNES, 1st and last Bt (UK), so *cr* 29 Oct 1818, of Lochalsh House, Balmacara, Ross-shire, and Coxton, Morayshire; *b* 1764; MP Ross and Cromarty 1809–12, Wick Burghs 1812–18, 1820–26, 1826–30 and Sutherland 1831; unsuccessfully claimed Btcy of INNES of Coxton before Lyon Court 1784–1811; granted armorial supporters 1819; *d* unm 14 Sept 1831, when the btcy expired

1d Catherine; *m* James Lindsay, of Glasgow, and had a surv child:

1e Hugh; *b* 1775; *m* Agnes, dau of George Crawford, writer (legal practitioner) Glasgow, and *d* 1815, leaving:

1a Catherine Innes; *b* 1811; sole heir of her great-uncle Sir HUGH INNES, 1st Bt; *m* 9 Jan 1832 Isaac William Lillingston (*d* 3 Oct 1850), est s of Abraham Lillingston (formerly Spooner), of Elmdon Hall, Warwicks, and *d* 19 Oct 1875, having had issue

2d Berowald; *d* young

1d Jean; *m* Capt Mackenzie, Scots Bde, s of Mackenzie of Allangrange

2d William, in Wester Alves; *b* 23 July 1686; *m* Margaret Mackay and had:

1e Robert, in Wester Alves 1739; *b* 28 June 1720

2e Hugh; *b* 12 Aug 1729

3e Berowald; *b* 12 Aug 1729

1e Jean; *b* 3 June 1713; *m* John Gilzean, portioner (holder of part of a once-greater parcel of land where tenure by military service had been commuted for payment in kind or other services) of Coltfield

2e Janet; *b* 26 April 1717

3d Robert; *b* 10 July 1692; merchant in Elgin

4d Hugh (Rev); *b* 31 March 1698; Episcopal clergyman; *d* unm

1d Lilias; *b* 2 June 1681

2d Jean; *b* 25 Aug 1694

(1) Marjory; *m* 16 Sept 1634 George Gordon of Over Skibo

2 Walter, of Pittenseir; *m c* 1621 Jean Gordon

3 John; living 1634; *m* by 1633 a dau of Walter Innes, 4th of Inverbreakie, and had (with an er s, William):

(1) James, of Newseat of Scurdargue; *b* 1635; Jacobite, left Scotland 1690; *m c* 1671 Elizabeth, dau of George Gordon of Tewchiens (gdau and heiress of Rev John Gordon, of Newseat of Scurdargue, DD, Min Elgin, Jr Charge 1633–39 and Port Yonne, 4th s of John Gordon, 5th of Craig), and *d* 21 Jan 1723, leaving, with another dau:

1a John; *b* 1676; sch master Andover; *m* 12 May 1713 Mary Mendham (*d* 18 March 1755) and *d* April 1762, having had, with other issue:

1b Edward (Rev); *b* 3 Oct 1719; Preb Netheravon, Salisbury, Domestic Chaplain to 4th Earl of Dunmore (*qv*); *m* 18 Dec 1755 Elizabeth (*d* 29 May 1809), dau of George Moore, and *d* 18 Nov 1788, having had, with two other sons and another dau (all *dsp*):

1c George (Rev); *b* 5 Aug 1759; Rector Hilperton, Headmaster King Henry VIII's Sch Warwick, Domestic Chaplain to 5th Duke of Roxburghe (*qv*); *m* 1793 Isabella, est dau of Capt Henry Stodart, and *d* 17 July 1842, having had, with other issue (*dsp*):

1d Elizabeth, of Islips Manor, Northolt, Middx; *m* 13 Dec 1848 George Harris, barrister Middle Temple, and *dsp* 6 Feb 1893, having settled Islips Manor on her cousin Charles Edward Innes (*see* below)

2c Charles; *b* 12 July 1763; *m* 1st Anne (*d* 19 Sept 1796), est dau of Thomas Neate, and had, with other issue (*dsp*):

1d Edward; *b* 17 Aug 1792; *m* 1st 11 June 1818 Jane Josepha (*d* 9 March 1832), dau of Samuel Lightfoot, and had:

1e CHARLES, *de jure* 9th Bt

2e Edward; *b* 6 April 1827; emigrated to Tasmania 1842, Stipendiary Magistrate Kingsborough, Tasmania, 1883–93; *m* 21 Jan 1853 Anne (*d* 20 July 1899), dau of George Stromborn Peacock, of Sorell, Tasmania, and *d* 26 Feb 1913, leaving, with other issue:

1f Edward George; *b* 9 Feb 1854; Dist Surveyor Port Cygnet, Tasmania; *m* 1st 15 Dec 1880 Jane (*d* 9 May 1884), dau of Philip Ballantyne, engr and surveyor, of Hobart, Tasmania, and had:

1g Edward David Ballantyne; *b* 24 April 1884; mining surveyor and engr, Master Mariners. Coastal Cert; matriculated arms 8 May 1944; *m* 1st 9 March 1906 Ethel Agnes Isobel (*d* 10 July 1929), dau of Charles Lucas, and had:

1h Edward Gordon; *b* 9 April 1908; *d* unm 17 March 1937

2h +John Houldsworth; *b* 28 May 1915; *m* 1960 —

3h +Robert Maxwell; *b* 1 Nov 1917; *m* *Jean Marshall and has:

1i *Barbara Ann; *b* 26 June 1944

2i *Margaret Diane; *b* 28 Nov 1946

1h Gwendolin Eleanor; *b* 10 Dec 1906

2h *Marjorie Betty; *b* 30 Sept 1913; *m* 15 June 1939 *James Benjamin Greer, of Dublin

1g (cont.) Edward David Ballantyne Innes *m* 2nd 25 Oct 1933 Viney Isobel, dau of Patrick Keogh, of Gawlis, Tasmania, and *d* 1967, having by her had:

4h +George Berowald; *b* 12 Aug 1938

3h *Jean Elizabeth; *b* 19 May 1934

4h *Pauline Margaret; *b* 23 Oct 1939

1f (cont.) Edward Innes *m* 2nd 20 July 1886 Marjorie (*d* 6 May 1946), dau of Jacob Christie, and *d* 3 Aug 1904, having by her had:

2g Vivian Oswald; *b* 3 May 1888; *m* 23 Oct 1912 Theresa, dau of Matthew Fitzpatrick, and *d* 1971, having had:

1h +Gordon Vivian; *b* 22 Feb 1922; WW II as ABQO RAN 1940–45; *m* 1 Feb 1951 *Rhonda Helen, dau of Denis Direen, of Lymington, Hants

2h +Cecil Alfred; *b* 19 Nov 1923

1h *Leila Anne [Mrs F Dillon, Glen Fern, Port Cygnet, Tasmania, Australia]; *b* 24 Nov 1913; *m* F Dillon

3g Cecil Alfred; *b* 6 Dec 1889; *d* unm 19 Dec 1905

4g Eric Edward; *b* 20 Dec 1891; *m* 1st 1917 Winifred Shelma (*d* 1 Aug 1921), dau of Edward Charles O'Brien; *m* 2nd 25 June 1925 Doris Cecilie, dau of Brian Kilmartin, and by his 1st w had:

1h +Edward George [Edward Innes Esq, Linga Longa, Port Cygnet, Tasmania, Australia]; *b* 1 Jan 1919; *m* 1942 *Ruth Minnie, dau of Ralph Norris, and has:

1i +Nigel David; *b* 1944

2i +Christopher Wayne; *b* 1948

5g Athol Rupert; *b* 4 Oct 1893; WW I with 15th Bn 1st AIF (wounded Passchendaele 1917); *m* 25 Jan 1933 Kathleen (*d* 5

Feb 1990), dau of Edward Crease, of Devon, and *d* 3 May 1973, having had:

1h +William James; *b* 5 May 1924; *m* 1st 1950 Avis Lorraine, dau of Victor Eugene Yelland, and has:

1i *Wendy Beryl Anne; *b* 1951; *m* 19– Peter Shoobridge (*d* 1997) and had issue

2i *Josephine Lilian; *b* 1953; *m* 19– (*divorce*) Anthony Friend and has issue

1h (cont.) William Innes *m* 2nd 1967 *Claire Adelaide, dau of R A Batty, of Adelaide, and by her has:

3i *Bronwyn Heather; *b* 1971

1h Sheila Jean; *b* 2 May 1927; *m* 1957 *James Flourance Turnour (*see* WINTERTON, E) and *d* 14 Feb 1980, leaving:

1i *Keppel John; *b* 1959

2i *Quentin David; *b* 1962

1i *Louise Margaret [Mrs Guy Ryan, 6 Toora St, Ivanhoe, Vict, Australia]; *b* 1958; *m* 1980 *Guy John Ryan and has issue

6g Adrian Arthur; *b* 24 Dec 1900; *m* 14 April 1927 Daisy (*d* 1 June 1996), dau of Francis Calvert Smith, and *d* 4 March 1995, leaving:

1h +Roy Edward [Roy Innes Esq, Clifton Beach Rd, Sandford, Tasmania, Australia]; *b* 7 Dec 1927; *m* 1963 *Shirley Ester, dau of Victor Richardson Clements, and has:

1i +Shane Edward; *b* 1969

1i *Kim Nyree; *b* 1972

2h +George Calvert [George Innes Esq, 1 Lanena St, Bellerive, Tasmania, Australia]; *b* 14 May 1932; *m* 1965 *Chou Seng, dau of Thar Yu Mok, and has:

1i +Andrew Gary; *b* 1969

2i +Trevor Craig; *b* 1971

1g Linda Victoria; *b* 1887; *m* John Taylor (*d* 1 April 1953) and *d* 23 Oct 1961

2g Olga Estella; *b* 1895; *m* 1st Hugh Wallace; *m* 2nd March 1925 Edward Ward (*d* 9 Aug 1949) and *d* 30 Sept 1951

3g Ismay Anne; *b* 1898

2f Charles; *b* 20 Nov, *d* 5 Dec 1855

3f William, of Devonport, Tasmania; *b* 16 Dec 1859; *m* 1887 Adelina Bianca Alexandrina (*d* 13 March 1946), dau of William Allsopp, and *d* 6 Dec 1928, having had:

1g Francis Allsopp; *b* 28 Jan 1888; WW I as Lt-Cdr RNR (Croix de Guerre with palms); *m* 3 Feb 1926 Marjorie Rolleston, dau of William Tucker Pike, and had:

1h +Berowald Francis; *b* 11 Dec 1928

2h +William; *b* 15 Sept 1935

2g William Edward Allsopp; *b* 15 Feb 1893; banker; *m* 18 Aug 1923 Lyla Alta, dau of Frederick Charles Thomson-Brown, of Launceston, Tasmania, and had:

1h +Desmond Erick; *b* 10 May 1926

1h *Patricia Joan; *b* 9 April 1925

3g Arthur Berowald; *b* 4 Aug 1899; *m* 26 July 1926 Irene Eva, dau of William Walter Eastman, and had:

1h +Graeme Alastair; *b* 22 Oct 1932

2h +Darren Arthur; *b* 20 March 1936

1h *Janet Lucille; *b* 28 March 1930

2h *Sandra Ann; *b* 5 Aug 1938

4g Gordon Tullah; *b* 5 Dec 1904; *m* 31 Aug 1931 Brunetta Grace, dau of Lawrence Harold O'Brien

1g Clotilda Adelina Leona; *b* 27 Sept 1897

4f Francis James; *b* 22 April 1861; *m* — and *d* Yokahama 19 April 1887, having had:

1g Josiah Francis; *b* 29 March 1885; *d* unm 8 Dec 1933

1g Fanny; *b* 16 Dec 1882; *m* —, of Japan, and emigrated to S America

5f Arthur Sextas; *b* 5 Aug 1863; *d* unm 30 April 1919

6f Josiah; *b* 28 Aug 1865; mining surveyor and prospector, discovered the Mount Farrell Silverlead Field 1897; *m* Maud Williams and *dsp* 9 Oct 1938

3e George; *b* 6 Jan 1832; *m* 18 Oct 1862 Emma Blyth, yst dau of George Stromborn Peacock, of Sorell, Tasmania, and *d* 8 May 1917, having had, with three daus:

1f George Peacock, of Sydney; *b* 10 Sept 1863; *m* 11 Oct 1893 Susanna Robina, dau of Robert Mills, and *d* 5 April 1936, having had:

1g George Arnold; *b* 2 July 1905; municipal engr Miniwa NSW; *m* 19 Nov 1927 *Florence Elizabeth Younger

1g Myrtle Robina; *b* 1894

2g Elizabeth Stuart; *b* 1898; Emergency Ambulance Corps 1939

2f Charles Edward; *b* 20 April 1865; *d* unm 21 Jan 1916

1d (cont.) Edward Innes *m* 2nd 20 April 1841 Emma, dau of James Webb, and by her had two daus (*d* unm)

1d Maria C; *b* 9 Sept 1796; author: *Anecdotal Memoirs of Queen Victoria*; *d* 13 Dec 1880

2c (cont.) Charles Innes *m* 2nd 12 June 1798 Mary (*d* 5 April 1845), 3rd dau of Capt Henry Stodart, and *d* 10 Nov 1824, leaving, with four other sons (*d* unm):

2d George Nigel Anthony (Rev); *b* 29 April 1803; Headmaster King's Sch NSW 1831–32; *d* 5 Sept 1832

3d James (Rev); *b* 27 Feb 1814; *m* 1st 21 May 1839 Frances (*d* 15 July 1840), 3rd dau of William Oldham, and had:

1e Charles Edward, of Islips Manor, Northolt; *b* 11 Feb 1840; Clerk War Office; *m* 1st 10 July 1872 Gertrude (*d* 20 May 1882), dau of William Henry Jackson, and had:

1f Arthur Norman, JP (Sussex 1937); *b* 2 Nov 1874; *educ* Cheltenham; Lt RDC 1916–18; memb E Sussex CC 1925–45, Mayor Lewes 1926–28, Alderman Lewes 1930–44; *m* Maud, 6th dau of Rev W E Dalton, Vicar Glynde

2f Harold Goodwin, OBE (1947); *b* 10 Aug 1876; *educ* HMS *Britannia*; RN 1890–1913, Capt 1897, Dep Ch Inspr RNLI, WW I, resumed RNLI 1918, ret 1933; matriculated arms 10 Jan 1944; *m* 27 July 1905 Ella Elizabeth Octavia (*d* 28 Nov 1948), dau of Jacob Francis Hirsch, of Oak Lodge, Hampstead

3f Charles Edward Oldham; *b* 10 Aug 1876; *d* 31 Aug 1877

1e (cont.) Charles Innes *m* 2nd Fanny Louisa (*d* 3 Feb 1899), dau of Dep Surgn-Gen Richard Pemberton, and *d* 18 Oct 1913, having by her had:

4f Melvill Stodart; *b* 26 March 1885; *educ* Dover Coll; Capt RMLI; *dsp* 22 Oct 1922

5f Richard Pemberton; *b* 6 Oct 1886; *educ* Dover Coll; RNR; *ka sp* 24 April 1917

6f Charles Douglas; *b* 20 June 1890; *d* unm 11 Jan 1916

3d (cont.) The Rev James Innes *m* 2nd 19 July 1842 Amelia Mary Anne (*d* 30 July 1860), dau of William Pitt Muston, MD, and by her had two sons and three daus (all *dsp*); *m* 3rd 10 Oct 1861 Catherine Biggs (*d* 19 Jan 1878), widow of George Cosby Harpour, of Castletown, IoM, and *d* 19 Jan 1880, having by her had, with a dau:

2e Edward Henry; *b* 30 Aug 1864; Fleet Paymaster RN; *m* 25 Aug 1885 Mary Laughlin (*d* 28 April 1921), dau of Rose Dempster Fraser, of Southampton, Bermuda; *m* 2nd 8 July 1924 Mary Emma Butter (*d* 31 July 1925) and *d* 22 Nov 1930, leaving by his 1st w (with two other sons, *dsp* infants):

1f Edward Henry; *b* 16 May 1895; *educ* Bermuda and RMC Sandhurst; Capt 1st Bn Middx Regt WW I; *m* 1st 1932 Louise, dau of Carlo Wedekind; *m* 2nd 22 Aug 1945 *Johanna Conradine, dau of Dr Louis van Hasselt, of Holland, by Baroness Anna Spiering, and *dsp* 7 Sept 1960

2f George William Holt; *b* 5 Dec 1900; *educ* Felsted, Churchers and RMC Sandhurst; Lt-Col W Yorks Regt, Kurdistan 1923, Palestine 1936, WW II, cmded 70th Bn W Yorks Regt 1941–43, 12th Bn Roy Hants Regt 1943–44, Dep Cdr Regierungsbezirk Lüneburg (CCG) 1945–46, 14 County Primary Trg Centre 1946–48, ret 1948; *m* 7 Oct 1931, as her 2nd husb, Alexandra Dunbar (*d* Dec 1977), only dau of Dunbar Marshall, of Natchez, Miss., and *d* 1983, having had:

1g *Vivien Holt [Mrs John Wagstaff, 52 Salmons Lane, Whyteleafe, Surrey CR3 0AN]; *b* 3 Sept 1932; *m* 1959 *John Kennedy Wagstaff and has:

1h *Clarissa Christine [Mrs Philip Dann, 1b Claremont Rd, Highgate, London N6 5DR]; *b* 1960; *m* 1983 *Philip John Dann and has:

1i *Isabelle Alexandra; *b* 2 Sept 1990

2i *Eleanor Louise; *b* 27 Feb 1993

2h *Martine Charis; *b* 1962; *m* 1st 1986 (*divorce* 1990) Stephen Patrick Cotton; *m* 2nd 1991 *Lawrence Michael Biddle and by him has:

1i *Thomas Lawrence; *b* 24 Jan 1993

1i *Alexandra Grace; *b* 5 July 1991

3h *Vanessa Jacynth; *b* 28 Sept 1971

2g *Valerie Evelyn; *b* 26 Nov 1935; *m* 1958 (*divorce* 1978) Mervyn Russell Chute and has:

1h *Nigel Anthony; *b* 2 June 1960

1h *Rosalind Alexandra; *b* 1 Oct 1962

1c Maria; *b* 13 June 1769; *m* 13 Jan 1794 Rev John Manning Hazeland, of Pilton, Wilts, and *d* 21 Nov 1834, leaving two sons and five daus

1a Margaret; *b* 1681; *m* — Adams (*d* 28 Dec 1732) and *d* 1769, leaving issue, who may be extant, possibly in the USA

1 Jean; *m* 1st *c* 1611 Thomas Innes, 3rd of Edingight (*see* INNES, Bt, of Balvenie); *m* 2nd by 7 Aug 1624 Robert Innes, Baillie Elgin; *m* 3rd John Ogilvie of Melton

2 Barbara; *m* 1st Dumbreck of Orton; *m* 2nd Archibald Innes of Westerton (*dspm* by 1642), bro of Sir Robert Innes, 1st Bt, of Balvenie (*qv*), and had issue

3 Grizel; *m* Oct 1631 Alexander Innes of Mathiemill (*d* 1 Nov 1636)

The 8th Bt's cousin,

CHARLES INNES, *de jure* 9th Bt; *b* 20 April 1825; *m* 20 July 1864 Adelaide Jane (*d* 14 July 1914), est dau of Col T J Deverell, 77th Foot, and *d* 15 July 1907, having had, with three daus (Adelaide Frances Jane, *b* 1865, *d* unm 23 Aug 1949; Elspeth Stuart, *b* 8 March 1867, *m* 1898 Jospeh Alexander Jekyll; Janet Marion, *b* 19 Sept 1872):

CHARLES GORDON DEVERELL INNES, *de jure* 10th Bt; *b* 1 May 1870; *educ* Haileybury; Maj 20th Middx Regt; *m* 25 June 1901 Ethel Hilda, dau of George Earle, of Barnes, Surrey, and had:

1 CHARLES KENNETH GORDON (Sir), **11th Bt**

1 *Eleanor Joan [Mrs Trevor Mimpriss, 4 Midmar Ave, Edinburgh EH10 6BS]; *b* 7 April 1913; *m* 9 July 1938 *Trevor Walter Mimpriss, MB, MS, FRCS, 2nd s of Sydney Trevor Mimpriss, slr, of Bromley, Kent, and has:

(1) *Timothy John (Rev) [Rev Dr Timothy Mimpriss, 27 Lon-y-Bryn, Bangor, Gwynedd]; *b* 18 March 1940; *educ* Charterhouse, Jesus Coll Cambridge (MA, MB, ChB, 1964) and St Thomas's Hosp; FFARCS 1969; *m* 7 April 1964 *Wendy Anne, dau of Donald Pryce, of Wimbledon, and has:

1a *Robert Charles; *b* 1 Aug 1971

1a *Rosemary Jill; *b* 13 May 1965

2a *Hilary Anne; *b* 12 June 1967

(2) *John Graham [John Mimpriss Esq, Orchard Clo, The Downs, Givons Grove, Leatherhead, Surrey]; *b* 23 March 1944; *educ* Charterhouse; airline capt, formerly FAA; *m* 20 Dec 1966 *Lorraine, dau of Donald Lovell, of Faygate, Surrey, and has:

1a *Graham Donald; *b* 9 June 1968

2a *James Christopher; *b* 18 Nov 1970

(1) *Jill Alison [Mrs David Gregory, 32 Midmar Gdns, Edinburgh]; *b* 1 March 1942; *m* 2 April 1966 *Lt-Cdr David Richard Munro Gregory, RN, er s of V-Adml Sir (George) David Archibald Gregory, KBE, CB, DSO and bar, of Guthrie Castle, Angus, and has:

1a *Peter James; *b* 1967

1a *Caroline Joan; *b* 1969

2a *Nicola Helen; *b* 1972

CHARLES INNES *d* 22 Oct 1953; his only son,

Sir Charles Kenneth Gordon Innes, 11th Bt, placed on Roll of Bts 1973; *b* 28 Jan 1910; *educ* Haileybury; WW II as Capt RA; matriculated arms at Lyon Court 29 Dec 1942; *m* 14 April 1936 Margaret Colquhoun Lockart (*d* 1992), est dau of Frederick Charles Lockart Robertson, and *d* 1990, leaving:

1 Sir DAVID CHARLES KENNETH GORDON INNES, **12th and present Bt**

1 *Daphne Margaret Colquhoun [Mrs Nigel Haig, Sparkfield House, High St, Newnham on Severn, Glos]; *b* 18 April 1948; *m* 6 March 1971 *Nigel Geoffrey Wolseley Haig, s of John Wolseley Haig, of Dorking, and has:

(1) *Jonathan Peter Wolseley; *b* 1975

(1) *Katharine Jane Innes; *b* 1976

INVERFORTH

Arms: Or on a fess azure, between in chief an escutcheon per bend sinister azure and gules charged with a bend argent and in base a lymphad, sail furled sable, pennons flying to the dexter gules, three mullets of the first. **Crest:** A dexter and sinister hand, each couped at the wrist proper, supporting a lymphad as in the arms. **Supporters:** On either side a sailor of the Mercantile Marine proper. **Motto:** *Per laborem ad honorem* ('Through toil to honour'). **Creation:** B. (UK) 5 Feb 1919.

THE 4TH BARON INVERFORTH, of Southgate, Co Middlesex (Andrew Peter Weir) [The Rt Hon The Lord Inverforth, 27 Morgan St, London E3 5AA]; *b* 16 Nov 1966; *s* f 1982; *educ* Marlborough, Trin Coll Cambridge and London Hosp Med Coll; *m* 1992 *Rachel Sian Shapland Davies and has:

1 *A dau; *b* 19–

Lineage: ANDREW WEIR, **1st Baron Inverforth**, of Southgate, Co Middx (UK), so *cr* 5 Feb 1919, PC (1919); *b* 24 April 1865; Hon Pres Cable and Wireless, Surveyor-Gen War Office 1919, Min Munitions and Supply 1919–21, Pres Andrew Weir Shipping and Trading, Chm Bank Line, American DSM 1919, Kt Grand Cross Dannebrog 1937, Diploma Grand Croix Grand Duke Gedinimas Lithuania 1938; *m* 1 Aug 1889 Anne (*d* 12 June 1941), dau of Thomas Kay Dowie, and had:

1 ANDREW ALEXANDER MORTON, **2nd Baron**

1 Annie Forrestdale Dowie; *b* 19 Jan 1891; *m* 11 Oct 1949 Cdr Ronald Langton-Jones, DSO, FRAS, FRGA, RN; *d* 9 Jan 1967

2 Janet Laing; *b* 28 April 1892; *d* 31 May 1962

3 Isabella May; *b* 17 July 1893; *m* 21 Jan 1925 William James McAlister (*d* 1 Dec 1937), of Millfield, Isle of Arran, and Mayfair, 2nd s of Donald McAlister, of Millfield, and *d* 10 Nov 1929

4 Andrina Forrestdale; *b* 14 Aug 1894; *m* 25 April 1922 Godfrey Holdsworth, MC (*d* 22 April 1934), s of Sir Charles Holdsworth, and *d* 27 April 1967, leaving a s and dau

5 Alexandra Cora Wilmer; *b* 2 March 1902; *m* 16 July 1930 Archibald Robert Cecil Fleming (*d* 5 Aug 1969), er s of Rev Dr Archibald Fleming, and *d* 9 Dec 1971, leaving:

(1) *Archibald Andrew Ian [Archibald Fleming Esq, House of Mailer, by Perth]; *b* 25 Oct 1934; *educ* Charterhouse

(2) *Alastair Morton Hamilton [Alastair Fleming Esq, Grange House, Culroy, Ayrshire KA19 8EP]; *b* 12 Sept 1936; *educ* Charterhouse; *m* 31 March 1967 *Sheila Margaret, only dau of Robert Forbes McFarlane, of E Lothian

The 1st BARON *d* 17 Sept 1955; his only son,

ANDREW ALEXANDER MORTON WEIR, **2nd Baron Inverforth**; *b* 12 Sept 1897; *educ* St Paul's; Governing Dir Andrew Weir and Co, shipowners and merchants, Cdr Order Dannebrog; *m* 26 June 1929 Iris Beryl (*d* 6 June 1996), dau of Charles Vincent, 4th Bn The Buffs, and *d* 17 Nov 1975, leaving:

1 (ANDREW CHARLES) ROY WEIR, **3rd Baron Inverforth**; *b* 6 June 1932; *educ* Malvern; *m* 26 Jan 1966 *Jill Elizabeth [The Rt Hon The Lady Inverforth, 27 Hyde Park St, London W2], only dau of John Ward Thornycroft, CBE, of Steyne, Bembridge, IoW, and *d* 6 June 1982, leaving:

(1) ANDREW PETER WEIR, **4th and present Baron Inverforth**

(1) *Clarinda Jane; *b* 22 May 1968; *m* 1994 *Jonathan S H A Kane, s of Douglas Kane

2 +(John) Vincent [The Hon Vincent Weir, 85 Whitehall Ct, London SW1A 2EI]; *b* 8 Feb 1935; *educ* Malvern; late chm Andrew Weir Gp

IRONSIDE

Arms: Per bend sable and gules, on a bend argent a bendlet wavy azure, in sinister chief a garb or, and in base a lion salient or, and in fess a dexter gauntletted hand grasping a sword paleways argent, hilted or. **Crest:** A dexter hand gauntletted, grasping a sword paleways argent, hilted and pommelled or. **Supporters:** Two bull terriers proper. **Motto:** Fear not; hold fast. **Creation:** B. (UK) 29 Jan 1941.

THE 2ND BARON IRONSIDE, of Archangel, and of Ironside, Co Aberdeen (Edmund Oslac Ironside) [The Rt Hon The Lord Ironside, Priory House, Old House Lane, Boxted, Essex CO4 5RB]; *b* 21 Sept 1924; *s* f 1959; *educ* Tonbridge; Lt RN WW II, with: Marconi Ltd 1952–60, English Electric 1960–63, Cryosystems 1963–68, Internat Research & Devpt 1968, Hon FCGI 1987; *m* 29 April 1950 *Audrey Marigold, yst dau of Col Hon Thomas George Breadalbane Morgan-Grenville, DSO, OBE, MC, JP, DL (*see* KINLOSS, L), and has:

1 +CHARLES EDMUND GRENVILLE [The Hon Charles Ironside, 46 Mayford Rd, London SW12 8SN]; *b* 1 July 1956; *m* 1985 *Hon Elizabeth Mary Law, est dau of 2nd Baron Coleraine (*qv*), and has:

(1) +Frederick Thomas Grenville; *b* 22 April 1991

(1) *Emily Charlotte Olivia; *b* 1988

(2) *Alice Octavia Louise; *b* 1990

1 *Fiona Georgina [The Hon Mrs Jack, The Old Vicarage, Lyford, Wantage, Oxon]; *b* 12 Sep 1954; *m* 24 June 1978 *Roland M Jack, yr s of Evan Jack, of Barnston Old Rectory, Gt Dunmow, Es Fiona Georgina sex, and has:

(1) *Oliver Edmund Maclean; *b* 1983

(1) *Anthea Audrey Charlotte; *b* 1985

Lineage: The IRONSIDEs take their name from a strip of land in Buchan. In the 14th century they were confined to the New Deer area, but later farmed all over Buchan.

JOHN IRONSIDE; *b* 1636; farmer Rothy, Fyvie; *m* Agnes Kennert and had an est s:

JOHN IRONSIDE; *b* 4 July 1688; his est s:

FRANCIS IRONSIDE; *b* 10 March 1733; farmer Lonehead, Old Rayne and Middlegateside, Culsalmond; *m* 27 April 1763 Elizabeth Ledingham (*d* April 1805 aged 75) and *d* 3 Sept 1816, leaving, with yr sons:

WILLIAM IRONSIDE; *b* 21 Oct 1766; *m* 1796 Elspeth Mitchell (*d* 1832 aged 52) and *d* 14 Aug 1843, leaving, with yr sons:

WILLIAM IRONSIDE; *b* Nov 1806; farmer Earlsfield, Kennethmont and Mains of Tonley; *m* Grizeal Garden (*d* 14 March 1859 aged 46) and *d* 17 Aug 1879, leaving, with yr sons:

WILLIAM IRONSIDE, of Ironside, Aberdeenshire; *b* 16 May 1836; *educ* Clatt Sch, Aberdeen U (MD) and Lond U (MD); Surgn-Maj RHA; *m* 14 Nov 1869 Emma Maria (*d* 14 May 1939 aged 94), dau of William Haggett Richards, and *d* 16 Jan 1881, leaving:

(WILLIAM) EDMUND IRONSIDE, **1st Baron Ironside**, of Archangel and of Ironside, Co Aberdeen (UK), so *cr* 29 Jan 1941, GCB (1938, KCB 1919)), CMG (1918), DSO (1915); *b* 6 May 1880; *educ* Tonbridge and RMA Woolwich; RA Boer War 1899–1902 (despatches, Queen's medal with three clasps, King's medal with two clasps) and WW I, Gen Staff cmdg Inf Bde (despatches seven times, Brevets Lt-Col and Col, 1914 star, two medals), C-in-C Allied Forces Archangel 1918–19 (Maj-Gen), cmded Ismid Forces 1920 and Br Forces N Persia 1920–21 (medal with clasp), Cmdt Staff College 1922–26, cmdg 2nd Div Aldershot 1926–28, GOC Meerut Dist India 1928–31, Lt Gen 1931, Lt Tower London 1930–33, QMG India 1933–36, Gen 1935, GOC-in-C E Cmd 1936–38, ADC Gen to HM GEORGE VI 1937–40, Govr and C-in-C Gibraltar 1938–39, Inspr-Gen Overseas Forces July–Sept 1939, CIGS Sept 1939–May 1940, C-in-C Home Forces May–July 1940, FM 1940, Col Cmdt RA 1932–59, LLD Aberdeen, KStJ, Grand Cross Legn Honour, Croix de Guerre avec Palme, Order Mil Virtue Poland, St George's Cross Russia, Kt Order St Vladimir and St Anne Russia, 3rd Cl Order Rising Sun Japan; *m* 26 June 1915 Mariot Ysobel (*d* 1984), dau of Charles Cheyne, IA (of the CHEYNEs of Inverugie, Aberdeenshire), by Eva Alice Wheeler (*see* DUCKWORTH, Bt), and *d* 23 Sept 1959, leaving:

1 EDMUND OSLAC IRONSIDE, **2nd and present Baron Ironside**

1 *Elspeth Mariot (Jane) [The Hon Mrs Hendry, 4 Easter Ferrygate, Abbotsford Rd, N Berwick, E Lothian EH39 5DD]; *b* 8 Jan 1917; *m* 15 Feb 1941 Capt (Andrew) Gilbert Hendry (*d* 1987), Black Watch (RHR), only s of Andrew Hendry, slr, of Dundee, and has:

(1) *Michael Andrew; *b* 1 May 1942; *educ* Stanbridge Earls

(2) *John Edmund Gordon; *b* 28 Sept 1949; *m* 14 July 1979 *Gillian Margaret, 2nd dau of David Young, of Shields House, Newton Hill, Kincardineshire, and has:

1a *Edmund John Ironside; *b* 1988

1a *Johanna Katherine; *b* 1981

2a *Sophia Elizabeth; *b* 1984

(3) *David Robert Charles; *b* 9 Nov 1955

IRVINE OF LAIRG

Creation: B. (LP, UK) 1987.

THE BARON IRVINE OF LAIRG, of Lairg in the District of Sutherland (Alexander Andrew Mackay Irvine) [The Rt Hon The Lord Irvine of Lairg, House of Lords, London SW1A 0PW]; *b* 23 June 1940: *educ* Inverness Roy Acad, Hutchesons' Boys' GS Glasgow, Glasgow U (MA, LLB) and Christ's Coll Cambridge (scholar, BA, LLB); barrister Inner Temple 1967, QC 1978, Bencher 1985, Recorder 1985–88, Dep High Court Judge 1987–97; Lecturer LSE 1965–69, fought (Lab) Hendon N 1970 gen election 1970; Fdr Tstee Whitechapel Art Gallery 1990–97, memb Ctee of Slade Sch of Fine Art 1990–; Shadow Ld Chancellor 1992–97, Tstee John Smith Meml Tst 1992–97, Hon Fell Christ's Coll Cambridge 1996, Ld Chllr 1997–, Hon LLD Glasgow 1997, Pres Magistrates Assoc, Church Commr, Jt-Pres: Industry and Parl Tst, Br-American Parly Gp, Cwlth Parly Assoc, Inter-Parly Union; Hon Fell Soc for Advanced Legal Studies, Tstee Hunterian Collection 1997–; *m* 1st 19– (*divorce*) Margaret Veitch, of Ayr; *m* 2nd 1974 *Alison Mary, yst dau of Dr James Shaw McNair, MD, and formerly w of Donald Dewar, Sec State Scotland, and has:

1 *David; *b* 1974

2 *Alastair; *b* 1976

Lineage: ALEXANDER IRVINE; *m* Margaret Christina, dau of Alexander MacMillan, and had:

ALEXANDER ANDREW MACKAY, *cr* a **Baron**

ISHAM

Arms: Gules a fess wavy, in chief three piles also wavy, points meeting in fess argent. **Crest:** A demi-swan with wings displayed argent, beaked sable. **Mottoes:** 1 *Ostendo non ostento* ('I show; I sham not'), 2 On things transitory resteth no glory.
Creation: Bt. (E) 30 May 1627.

SIR IAN VERE GYLES ISHAM, 13TH BT, of Lamport, Northamptonshire [Sir Ian Isham Bt, 40 Turnpike Link, Croydon, Surrey CR0 5NX]; *b* 17 July 1923; *s* 3rd cousin once-removed 1976; *educ* Eton and Worcester Coll Oxford; Capt RAC, Capt Co of London Yeo WW II NW Europe 1944, BAOR 1945–47

Lineage: HENRY ISHAM; had:

ROBERT ISHAM; had:

ROBERT ISHAM, of Pytchley, Northants; Escheator (roy official implementing reversion to overlord of feudal holding on tenant's death) Northants 1391–92, granted 22 Nov 1403 Manor of Cranford, Northants; *d* 31 March 1424, having had:

ROBERT ISHAM, of Pytchley; *b c* 1402; Escheator Northants 1438–39, attorney 1466 to Anne, sis of EDWARD IV, and EDWARD's w ELIZABETH, Controller Customs Port of London; *m* Margaret, dau and coheir of — Aston, of Knuston, Irchester, Northants, and *d* 1475, leaving, with three yr sons:

WILLIAM ISHAM, of Pytchley; *m* Elizabeth (*d* 20 Sept 1478), widow of Thomas Braunspath, of Glooston, Leics, and *d* 13 June 1510, leaving:

THOMAS ISHAM, of Pytchley; *b c* 1456; *m c* 1485 Ellen, dau of Richard Vere, of Addington and Thrapston, Northants, and had, with a yr s (John):

EUSEBY ISHAM, of Pytchley; *m* Anne, est dau of Giles Pulton, of Desborough, Northants, and *d* by 11 Dec 1546, having had, with 16 other children:

1 Gyles, of Pytchley, JP; Steward to Earl of Bedford; MP Peterborough 1553 and 1557; *m* Mary Watts (*bur* 11 June 1560), of Knotting, Beds, and *d* 31 Aug 1559, leaving three daus

2 Robert; Rector Pytchley 1548–64, Preb Peterborough 1553–59, Chaplain to QUEEN MARY; *educ* Christ's Coll Cambridge (MA 1542); *d* 5 May 1564

3 Gregory, of Braunston, Northants; merchant London, Freeman Mercers' Co, ended up a considerable landowner in Northants; *m* Elizabeth (*m* 2nd William Rosewell, of Ford Abbey, Slr-Gen to ELIZABETH I, and had further issue), dau of Matthew Dale, of Bristol, and *d* 4 Sept 1558 aged 38, leaving, with a yr s and two daus:

(1) Euseby (Sir), of Pytchley and Braunston; ktd 1603, High Sheriff Northants 1584; *b* 26 Feb 1552/3; *m* Anne (*d* by 1 Jan 1627/8), dau of John Borlase, of Little Marlow, Bucks, and *d* 11 June 1626, leaving, with other issue (including ancestors of THOMAS JEFFERSON, 3rd President of the USA; *see* AMERICAN PRESIDENTIAL FAMILIES, 1994, Morris Genealogical Books SA):

1a John, of Pytchley and Braunton; *m* 1st Anne (*d* June 1604), dau of Sir William Fitzwilliam, of Milton (*see* 1970 edn FITZWILLIAM, E), and had:

1b Anne; *m* William Lane, of Horton and Glendon, by whose family the Pytchley property is said to have been sold to the Washbourne family

1a (cont.) John Isham *m* 2nd 23 Nov 1605 Elizabeth, dau of Edmund Dunch, and *d* 11 Dec 1626

4 John, of Lamport; *b c* Aug 1525; merchant adventurer London, Freeman Mercers' Co; with his bro Rev Robert Isham bought from Sir William Cecil the Manor and advowson of Lamport 1559–60, later inheriting Robert's share; built Lamport Hall (*see* **Seat** below), High Sheriff Northants 1581; *m* 6 Oct 1552 Elizabeth, only dau of Nicholas Barker, of Sonning, Berks, and widow of Leonard Barker, and *d* by 15 May 1596, having had, with other sons:

(1) Thomas, of Lamport; *b* 11 Sept 1555, blind from *c* age 12; *m* Sept 1576 Elizabeth (*d* 9 Aug 1621), er dau of Christopher Nicholson, of Cambridge, and *d* 3 Dec 1605, leaving, with three daus:

1a **Sir John Isham, 1st Bt** (E), so *cr* 30 May 1627; *b* 27 July 1582; High Sheriff Northants 1611, ktd 1608; *m* 19 Oct 1607 Judith (*d* 25 June 1625), dau of Dr William Lewin, DCL, Judge Prerogative Court Canterbury, and sis of Sir Justinian Lewin, and *d* 8 July 1651, leaving, with two daus:

1b **Sir Justinian Isham, 2nd Bt**; *b* 20 Jan 1611; MP Northants 1661–75, FRS, royalist Civil War, as his f was, consequently heavily fined during Interregnum; *m* 1st 10 Nov 1634 Jane (*d* 4 March 1638), dau of Sir John Garrard, Bt, of Lamer, Herts, and had a s (*d* young) and four daus (of whom Elizabeth *m* Sir Nicholas L'Estrange, Bt, and Susan *m* Sir Nicholas Carew); *m* 2nd 1653 Vere, dau of 1st Baron Leigh of Stoneleigh (*see* LEIGH, B) and *d* 2 March 1675, having by her had, with four yr sons and two daus:

1c **Sir Thomas Isham, 3rd Bt**; *b* 15 March 1657; *d* unm 27 July 1681

2c **Sir Justinian Isham, 4th Bt**; *b* 11 Aug 1658; MP Northants 1685–1730; *m* 16 July 1683 Elizabeth (*d* 22 Aug 1713), only dau of Sir Edmund Turnor, of Stoke Rochford, Lincs, and *d* 13 May 1730, having had, with a dau:

1d **Sir Justinian Isham, 5th Bt**; *b* 20 July 1687; MP Northants 1734; *m* 11 Sept 1725 Mary, only surv child of Lisle Hacket, of Moxhull, Warwicks, by his 2nd w Dorothy, dau of Sir John Bridgeman, Bt, and *dsp* 5 March 1736/7

2d **Sir Edmund Isham, 6th Bt**; *b* 18 Dec 1690; *educ* Rugby and Wadham Coll Oxford (MA 1714, DCL 1723), Fell Magdalen Coll Oxford; MP Northants, Advocate Doctor's Commons, Judge Admlty Ct 1731–41; *m* 1st 17 Feb 1734 Elizabeth (*dsp* 19 July 1748), est dau of Edward Wood, of Littleton; *m* 2nd 4 May 1751 Philippa (*d* 17 Dec 1786), only dau of Richard Gee, of Orpington, Kent, and *dsp* 15 Dec 1772

3d Euseby (Rev); *b* 6 Nov 1697; MA (1721), DD (1733); Rector Lamport and Lincoln Coll Oxford; *m* 1 May 1739 Elizabeth (*d* 17 June 1808), dau of Rev Matthew Panting, DD, Master Pembroke Coll Oxford, and *d* 17 June 1755, having had, with other issue:

1e **Sir Justinian Isham, 7th Bt**; *b* 8 July 1740; *educ* Lincoln Coll Oxford (MA 1763, DCL 1793); High Sheriff Northants 1776; *m* 9 Sept 1766 Susannah (*d* 31 Aug 1823), dau of Henry Barret, and *d* 1 April 1818, having had, with other daus:

1f **Sir Justinian Isham, 8th Bt**; Lt-Col Northants Militia, Col 1830; *b* 24 April 1773; *m* 12 May 1812 Mary (*d* 26 Jan 1878), est dau of Rev Samuel Close, of Drumbanagher and Elm Park, Co Armagh, and maternal gdau of Very Rev Arthur Champagne, Dean Clonmacnoise, and *d* 23 March 1845, having had:

1g **Sir Justinian Vere Isham, 9th Bt**; *b* 7 Nov 1816; *d* unm 25 Aug 1846

2g **Sir Charles Edmund Isham, 10th Bt**, DL Northants; High Sheriff 1851; *b* 16 Dec 1819; *m* 26 Oct 1847 Emily (*d* 6 Sept 1898), dau of Sir John Vaughan, PC, a Baron Court Exchequer, by Louisa, widow of 13th Baron Saint John of Bletsoe (*qv*) and dau of Sir Charles Rouse Boughton, 9th Bt (*see* 1963 edn), of Downton Hall, Salop, and *d* 7 April 1903, having had:

1h Louisa Mary; *m* 12 July 1871 Edward Corbett, of Longnor, Salop, and *d* 11 Jan 1947, leaving issue. He *d* 8 Sept 1918

2h Emily Caroline; *m* 27 April 1881 Norman Magnus Macleod, CMG (Macleod of Macleod), Capt 74th Regt, of Dunvegan Castle, Isle of Skye, and *d* 21 March 1942, leaving issue. He *d* 5 Nov 1929

3h Isabel Vere; *d* 14 Feb 1868

1g Mary; *d* 1828

2f Vere (Rev); *b* 13 Sept 1774; Rector Lamport; *m* 4 Aug 1799 Jane, dau of John Chambers and n of Sir William Chambers, Comptroller Public Works to GEORGE III, and *d* 27 Feb 1845, leaving, with two other sons and a dau:

1g John Vere; *b* Jan 1803; *m* 1st 28 July 1830 Mary (*dsp* 26 Sept 1856), only dau of William Wood, of Brixworth; *m* 2nd 9 Jan 1862 Emily, dau of John Kinch, and *d* July 1883, leaving:

1h **Sir Vere Isham, 11th Bt**, JP Suffolk and Northants; Maj 13th Bn Sherwood Foresters, Capt 2nd Bn Suffolk Regt; *b* 10 May 1862; *m* 16 Jan 1895 Millicent (*d* 11 Aug 1961), dau of Henry Halford Vaughan, Regius Prof History Oxford, and *d* 10 Feb 1941, having had:

1i John Vere; Lt 5th Dragoon Gds; *b* 14 Nov 1895; *das* 3 June 1916

2i **Sir Gyles Isham, 12th Bt**, DL (Northants 1952); *b* 31 Oct 1903; *educ* Rugby and Magdalen Coll Oxford (Demy 1922–26, BA and MA 1930, Pres Union 1926); WW II: London Irish Rifles 1939, commissioned KRRC Feb 1940, served Middle East 1940–44, Capt 1941, Maj 1942, Lt-Col 1943, GSO(1) War Office 1945, Def Sec Offr Palestine 1945–46; stage and screen actor, CC Northants 1955–64, High Sheriff 1958, Tstee Nat Portrait Gallery 1964, Pres Assoc Genealogists and Record Agents 1968–76; *d* unm 29 Jan 1976

1i Virginia, JP Hastings; *b* 25 April 1898

2g Robert (Rev); *b* 1 Sept 1805; *educ* BNC Oxford (MA 1823); Rector Lamport; *m* 29 Oct 1832 Martha Jane Eleanor (*d* 3 June 1877), est dau of Rev William Wilson, Rector Harrington, and *d* 26 Nov 1890, leaving:

1h Martha Jane; *d* unm 26 Dec 1916

2h Eleanor; *m* 15 July 1880 Rev Henry Vere Packe, Rector Lamport, and *d* 12 July 1936 aged 100. He *d* 1903

3h Louisa; *m* 28 Oct 1856 Maj-Gen Charles Scudamore Longden, RA, and *d* 31 July 1891, leaving issue. He *d* 1894

3f Henry Charles (Rev); Rector Shangon, Leics; *b* 14 Feb 1777; *m* 19 Sept 1804 Marianna (*d* 8 July 1874), dau of Richard Buller, and *d* 1 April 1833, having had:

1g Henry; *d* unm 1825

2g Arthur (Rev); Rector Weston Turville, Bucks; *b* 23 July 1808; *m* 29 Oct 1840 Charlotte Elizabeth (*d* 29 Jan 1892), yst dau of Sir Patrick Murray, 6th Bt, and *d* 4 Feb 1892, leaving:

1h Arthur Charles; *b* 8 April 1847; *m* 11 Oct 1887 Evelyn Rose (*m* 2nd 22 Nov 1904 Rev Clement Eustace Macro Wilson (*d* 8 Feb 1944); *d* 18 July 1909), 7th dau of Richard William Selby Lowndes, of Elmers, and *d* 25 Feb 1897, leaving:

1i Vere Arthur Richard, MC; Lt-Col Staff, Capt Res Offrs Suffolk Regt WW I (despatches three times); *b* 27 Sept 1889; *m* 7 Oct 1922 Edith Irene (*d* 5 May 1973), yr dau of Harry Brown, and *d* 19 July 1968, leaving:

1j Sir IAN VERE GYLES ISHAM, **13th and present Bt**

2j +NORMAN MURRAY CRAWFORD ISHAM, OBE (1988) [Norman Isham Esq OBE, 5 Langton Way, Park Hill, Croydon, Surrey]; ARIBA, BArch; *b* 28 Jan 1930; heir presumptive; *educ* Stowe and Cape Town U; *m* 28 April 1956 *Joan, dau of Leonard James Genet, of Umtali, Rhodesia, and has:

1k +Richard Leonard Vere [Richard Isham Esq, 8 Fitzwilliam Rd, London SW4 0DN]; *b* 30 Dec 1958; *m* 1990 *Julia Claire Mary, dau of David Frost Pilkington, of Lancs, and has:

1l +Angus David Vere; *b* 26 Oct 1992

2l +Charles Vere Ian; *b* 22 Dec 1996

2k +Vere Murray Gyles [Vere Isham Esq, Hill Pasture, Broxted, Essex CM6 2B2]; *b* 11 Oct 1960; *m* 1991 *Lynne Janette, dau of Howard Warren Armishaw, of Alberta, and has:

1l +Maximiliano Vere; *b* 15 June 1991

2l +Oscar Howard Vere; *b* 18 May 1993

1k *Elizabeth Angela; *b* 20 Oct 1957; *m* 1980 *Richard Nigel Brayshaw

2i Henry Euseby Murray; sheep farmer Cape Colony, Lt Roy Warwicks Regt WW I; *b* 30 Sept 1895; *d* 5 March 1930

1i Dorothy Evelyn Vere; *m* 2 June 1917 Lt-Col Harry Norton Schofield, VC, RHA, memb Gentlemen-at-Arms, and had issue. He *d* 10 Oct 1931

2i Elizabeth Mary Victoria; *m* 25 April 1916 Neville Hollings Ogilvie, of S Africa, and *d* 26 Oct 1956, leaving issue

1h Anna; *d* unm 15 April 1930

1f Sophia; *m* Dec 1798 Thomas Palmer, est s of Sir John Palmer, 5th Bt, of Carlton (see 1949 edn), and *d* 1851, having had issue. He *dvp* June 1810

2f Louisa; *m* Ralph Caldwell, of Hilborowe, Norfolk, and had issue

Seat: Lamport Hall, Lamport, Northants. Although it ceased to be the Ishams' home in 1976, when the **12th Bt** died, it is open to the public under the auspices of the Lamport Hall Trust, which makes much of the family's long residence there, for example publicising the fact that the garden gnome was introduced in 1850 to English landscape gardening by **Sir Charles Isham, 10th Bt**. The oldest part now existing is the central block. It dates from the middle of the 17th century, when the architect John Webb was commissioned by **Sir Justinian Isham, 2nd Bt**, to create an Italian Palace. Some three-quarters of a century later Francis Smith of Warwick added two wings and altered the interior, 'improving' what is now the music room with plasterwork that is certainly splendid enough, although one may feel some regret that it was imposed at the expense of the previous classical decoration by Webb. At least Webb's fireplaces were not swept away. In the 19th century there were more changes, including an entrance on the north side of the house. The collection of Isham family portraits is particularly noteworthy.

IVEAGH

Arms: Quarterly , 1st and 4th, per saltire gules and azure, a lion rampant or, on a chief ermine a dexter hand couped at the wrist of the first (for GUINNESS); 2nd and 3rd, argent on a fess between three crescents sable a trefoil slipped or (for LEE). **Crests**: 1 A boar passant, quarterly or and gules (for GUINNESS), 2 On a pillar argent, encircled by a ducal coronet or, an eagle preying on a bird's leg erased proper (for LEE). **Supporters**: On either side a stag gules, attired and collared gemel or, resting a hind hoof on an escutcheon vert charged with a lion rampant or. **Motto**: *Spes mea in Deo* ('My hope lies in God'). **Creations**: Bt. (UK) 27 May 1885, B. (UK) 19 Jan 1891, V. (UK) 18 Dec 1905, E. and V. (UK) 30 Sept 1919.

THE 4TH EARL OF IVEAGH, Viscount Elveden, Viscount of Iveagh, Co Down, **Baron Iveagh of Iveagh**, Co Down, and a **Baronet** (Sir Arthur Edward Rory Guinness, Bt) [The Rt Hon The Earl of Iveagh, Iveagh House, 41 Harrington Gdns, London SW7 4JU]; *b* 10 Aug 1969; *s* f 1992

Lineage: Sir BENJAMIN LEE GUINNESS, 1st Bt (*qv*), had a 3rd s:

Sir Edward Cecil Guinness, 1st Bt, of Castleknock, Co Dublin, so *cr* 27 May 1885 (following HRH THE PRINCE OF WALES's visit to Ireland 7–26 April 1885 during the year in which the new Sir Edward was High Sheriff of Co Dublin), and **1st Earl of Iveagh** also VISCOUNT ELVEDEN, so *cr* 30 Sept 1919, and earlier 19 Jan 1891 BARON IVEAGH OF IVEAGH, Co Down, also 18 Dec 1905 VISCOUNT OF IVEAGH, Co Down (all UK), KP (1895), GCVO (1910), JP (Co Dublin); *b* 10 Nov 1847; *educ* Trin Coll Dublin (BA 1870, MA 1872, LLD 1886); Sheriff Dublin 1876, bought the 17,000-acre Elveden estate, Suffolk, from India Office tstees for £159,000 in 1893 (just under £8,100,000 in late-1990s terms), subsequently adding a further 6,000 acres, chm Irish U Alliance, FRS 1906, Chllr Dublin U 1908, Hon LLD Aberdeen U 1891, KStJ; *m* 20 May 1873 his 2nd cousin once-removed Adelaide Maria (*d* 16 Feb 1916), dau of Richard Samuel Guinness, MP, and *d* 7 Oct 1927, leaving to the nation the Iveagh Bequest of Old Masters and British paintings generally, also one of his London residences, Ken Wood or Kenwood, the Adam mansion lived in by the 1st Earl of Mansfield (*qv*) for the last four years of his life following the sacking of his central London house at the time of the Gordon Riots in 1780, and had issue:

1 RUPERT EDWARD CECIL LEE, **2nd Earl**

2 Arthur Ernest, JP, DL (Co Dublin); *b* 2 Nov 1876; *educ* Trin Coll Cambridge (MA); Lt LRB (1st London Vols); *m* 15 July 1903 Marie Clotilde, DGStJ (*d* 22 July 1953), dau of Sir George Russell, 4th Bt, of Swallowfield (*qv*), and *d* 22 March 1949, leaving:

(1) *Aileen Sibell Mary [Mrs Aileen Plunket, Old Mead, Elsenham, Herts]; *b* 16 May 1904; *m* 1st 16 Nov 1927 (*divorce* 1940) F/Lt Hon Brinsley Sheridan

Bushe Plunket, RAFVR (Ikas Nov 1941), 2nd s of 5th Baron Plunket (*qv*), and has issue; *m* 2nd 19 Dec 1956 (*divorce* 1965, resumed name PLUNKET) Valerian Stux-Rybar, interior decorator, s of Geza Stux-Rybar

(2) Maureen Constance; *b* 31 Jan 1907; dir Arthur Guinness, Son & Co 1949, fndr Horder Centre for Arthritics; *m* 1st 3 July 1930 4th Marquess of Dufferin and Ava (*see* DUFFERIN AND CLANEBOYE, B) and had issue; *m* 2nd 14 Sept 1948 (*divorce* 1954) Maj (Harry Alexander) Desmond ('Kelpy') Buchanan, MC, Gren Gds, s of Lt-Col James Claud Buchanan, of Hales Hall, Market Drayton, Salop; *m* 3rd 20 Aug 1955 His Hon Judge John Cyril Maude, QC (*d* 1986, *see* HAWARDEN, V), and *d* 3 May 1998, having long reverted to her 1st husb's name

(3) Oonagh; *b* 22 Feb 1910; *m* 1st 24 June 1929 (*divorce* 1936) Hon Philip Leyland Kindersley, yst s of 1st Baron Kindersley (*qv*), and had issue; *m* 2nd 29 April 1936 (*divorce* 1950) 4th Baron Oranmore and Browne (*qv*) and had further issue; *m* 3rd 1957 (*divorce* 1965) Miguel Ferreras, couturier, of Cuba and New York, resumed 2nd husb's name and *d* 2 Aug 1995

3 WALTER EDWARD GUINNESS, *cr* BARON MOYNE (*qv*)

The 1st Earl's est s,

RUPERT EDWARD CECIL LEE GUINNESS, **2nd Earl of Iveagh**, KG (1955), CB (1911), CMG (1901), DL (Surrey and Suffolk); *b* 29 March 1874; *educ* Eton (winner: Sch Sculling 1892, Ladies Plate Henley 1893 as memb Eton Eight) and Trin Coll Cambridge (winner: Diamond Sculls Henley 1895 and Diamond and Wingfield Sculls 1896); Boer War: served with Irish Hosp 1900 and as Capt 9th Vol Bn KRRC thereafter (despatches, Queen's Medal, three clasps), memb: London Sch Bd 1902–04, Metropolitan Asylums Bd 1903–04, LCC 1904–10 and London Educn Ctee 1911–13, MP (U) Shoreditch Haggerston 1908–10, SE Essex 1912–18 and Southend-on-Sea 1918–27 (Freedom of Southend 1932), Cdr RNVR WW I, ADC to HM KING GEORGE V 1916–19, Lt City London 1910, co-fndr Tuberculin Tested Milk Producers' Assoc 1920, chm: Wright-Fleming Inst Microbiology 1921, Research Inst Dairying 1920 and Arthur Guinness, Son & Co, 1927–62, Chllr Dublin U 1927, Hon LLD Trin Coll Dublin and Nat U Ireland 1928, Hon DSc Reading 1937, first honrand Roy Ag Soc's Bledisloe gold medal 1937, FRS 1964; *m* 8 Oct 1903 Lady Gwendolen Onslow, CBE (1920), MP (C) Southend-on-Sea 1927–35 and chm Women's C Organisation (Freedom Southend 1932; *d* 16 Feb 1966), er dau of 4th Earl of Onslow (*qv*), and *d* 14 Sept 1967, having had:

1 Richard; *b* 15, *d* 17 Oct 1906

2 Arthur Onslow Edward, *Viscount Elveden*; *b* 8 May 1912; *educ* Eton and Trin Coll Cambridge; memb W Suffolk CC, Maj RA (TA, then Suffolk and Norfolk Yeo) WW II; *m* 22 July 1936, as her 1st husb, Lady Elizabeth Cecilia Hare (*m* 2nd 30 Sept 1947 Edward Rory More O'Ferrall, yst s of late Dominic More O'Ferrall, of Kildangan, Co Kildare, and *d* 1990), yr dau of 4th Earl of Listowel (*qv*), and was *ka* 8 Feb 1945, leaving:

(1) ARTHUR FRANCIS BENJAMIN, **3rd Earl**

(1) *Elizabeth Maria, JP (Berks) [The Lady Elizabeth Mays-Smith JP, Chaddleworth House, Chaddleworth, Newbury, Berks]; *b* 31 Oct 1939; granted with her sis rank of earl's dau 6 Jan 1969; *m* 1st 28 Sept 1960 (*divorce* 1990), as his 1st w, David Hugh Lavallin Nugent, yr s of Sir Hugh Charles Nugent, 6th Bt (*qv*), of Ballinlough, and has issue; *m* 2nd 1992, as his 2nd w, *(Robert) Martin Mays-Smith

(2) Henrietta; *b* 19 Aug 1942; *m* 3 Feb 1978 *Luigi Marinori, of Spoleto, Umbria, Italy, and *d* by her own hand 3 May 1978, leaving by her husb:

1a *Sara; *b* 1977

1 Honor Dorothy Mary; *b* 1909; *educ* LSE; *m* 1st 14 July 1933 (*divorce* 1945) Sir Henry ('Chips') Channon, of Kelvedon Hall, Essex (*b* 7 March 1897; MP (U) Southend-on-Sea 1935–50 and Southend-on-Sea W 1950–58, dir Arthur Guinness, Son & Co 1935–53, author: *Chips, The Diaries of Sir Henry Channon* (ed Robert Rhodes James, 1967), one of the great politico-social journals of the 20th century, also *Joan Kennedy* (novel, 1929), *Paradise City* (1930) and *The Ludwigs of Bavaria* (1933), ktd 1957; *d* 7 Oct 1958), only s of Harry Channon, of Chicago, and Vesta Westover, and had:

(1) *(HENRY) PAUL GUINNESS CHANNON, *cr* BARON KELVEDON (LP, *qv*)

1 (cont.) Lady Honor Channon *m* 2nd 19 Nov 1946 F/Lt Frantisek ('Frankie') Václav Svejdar (*d* May 1977), s of Václav Svejdar, of Prague, and *d* 2 Nov 1976

2 *Patricia Florence Susan [The Rt Hon Patricia Viscountess Boyd of Merton, 2 Bloomfield Terrace, London SW1; Ince Castle, Saltash, Cornwall PL12 4RA]; *b* 3 March 1918; dir Arthur Guinness, Son & Co 1949; *m* 29 Dec 1938 1st Viscount Boyd of Merton (*qv*) and has issue

3 Brigid Katharine Rachel; *b* 30 July 1920; *m* 1st 30 July 1945 HRH PRINCE FRIEDERICH ('FRITZI') GEORG WILHELM CHRISTOPH OF PRUSSIA (*b* 19 Dec 1911; *educ* Cambridge; with Schroder's in London, interned by UK authorities 1940–41, after release served Pioneer Corps on London bomb sites, then as 'George Mansfield' as ag worker in Herts, naturalised as Br subject 1947 when renounced title, took surname von Preussen by deed poll 1951, later took dual nationality on being readmitted as German subject 1953; *d* by drowning in the Rhine 20 April 1966), 4th and yst s of CROWN PRINCE WILHELM OF GERMANY, himself est s of EMPEROR WILHELM II OF GERMANY, who in turn was gs of HM QUEEN VICTORIA, and had issue:

(1) *(Frederick) Nicholas; *b* 3 May 1946; *m* 27 Feb 1980 *Hon Victoria Mancroft, er dau of 2nd Baron Mancroft (*qv*), and has:

1a *Frederick Nicholas Stormont; *b* 11 June 1990

1a *Beatrice Victoria; *b* 10 Feb 1981

2a *Florence Jessica; *b* 28 July 1983

3a *Augusta Lily; *b* 15 Dec 1986

(2) *(William) Andrew; *b* 14 Nov 1947; *m* 2 Jan 1979 *Alexandra Blahova, formerly Blahova-Alsbitt, da of Frantisek Blaha, and has:

1a *Frederick Alexander; *b* 15 Nov 1984

1a *Tatiana Brigid Honor; *b* 16 Oct 1980; *educ* St Paul's Girls' Sch

(3) *Rupert Alexander Frederick [HRH Prince Rupert von Preussen, 53 Redington Rd, London NW3]; *b* 28 April 1955; *m* 5 Jan 1982 *Ziba, dau of Morteba Rastegar Jahaveri, of Teheran, Iran, and has:

1a *Brigid Elizabeth Soraya; *b* 24 Dec 1983

2a *Astrid; *b* 16 April 1985

(1) *Victoria Marina Cecilie; *b* 22 Feb 1952; *m* 3 May 1976 *Philippe Alphonse Achache and has issue:

1a *George Jean; *b* 8 June 1980

2a *Francis Maximilian Frederick; *b* 30 April 1982

(2) *Antonia Brigid Elizabeth Louise; *b* 28 April 1955; *m* 3 Feb 1977 *Marquess of Douro, est s of 8th Duke of Wellington (*qv*), and has issue

3 HRH PRINCESS FRIEDERICH Von PREUSSEN *m* 2nd 3 June 1967 Maj Anthony Patrick Ness (*d* 20 Aug 1993), Queen's Bays, Starter Jockey Club 1959–69, only s of Gordon Stuart Ness, and *d* 8 March 1995

The 2nd EARL's gs,

(ARTHUR FRANCIS) BEN(JAMIN) GUINNESS, **3rd Earl of Iveagh**; *b* 20 May 1937; *educ* Eton, Trin Coll Cambridge and Grenoble U; memb Irish Senate 1973–77, chm Arthur Guinness, Son & Co, subsequently pres Guinness plc, CStJ 1972; *m* 12 March 1963 (*divorce* 1984) Miranda Daphne Jane, only dau of Maj Michael Smiley, CVO (*see* SMILEY, Bt), and *d* 1992, leaving:

1 ARTHUR EDWARD RORY GUINNES, **4th and present Earl of Iveagh**

2 +RORY MICHAEL BENJAMIN; *b* 12 Dec 1974; heir presumptive

1 *Emma Lavinia; *b* 7 Dec 1963; *educ* Lincoln Coll Oxford; *m* 4 Dec 1995 *James Barnard, barrister, s of Geoffrey Barnard, and has:

(1) *Benjamin Philip; *b* 23 Oct 1996

2 *Louisa Jane; *b* 20 Feb 1967

JACKSON of Arlsey

Arms: Arg. on a fess between a goat's head couped in chief gu. and a ship in full sail in base ppr. a greyhound courant, between two pheons or, within a bordure of the second charged with eight bezants. **Crest:** A goat's head, couped arg., guttée de sang, armed and bearded or, gorged with a collar gu., charged with three bezants from the collar a line reflexed of the third, the rings gold.
Creation: Bt. (UK) 22 May 1815.

SIR ROBERT JACKSON, 7TH BT, of Arlsey, Co Bedford [Sir Robert Jackson Bt, Apartamento 601, Boulevard Artigas 266, Montevideo, Uruguay]; *b* 16 March 1910; *s* cousin 1980; *educ* St George's Coll; *m* 1943 *Maria E, dau of Leon P Casamayor, of Montevideo, and has had:

1 Victoria M; *b* 1945; *d* 19–

2 *Bertha Mary; *b* 1949

Lineage: ROBERT JACKSON, of Carlisle, Cumberland; had:

JOHN JACKSON; *d* 1665, leaving:

THOMAS JACKSON; *b* May 1649; *m* 1671 Mary Johnson and had a 3rd s:

JOSEPH JACKSON, of Carlisle; *b* 5 Oct 1681; *m* 22 May 1707 Mary Patinson and had:

ROBERT JACKSON, of Yorktown, Va.; Surgn HMS *The Captain* 1748; *m* Elizabeth Brett, of Yorktown, and was *bur* Chatham 25 April 1756, having had, with other issue (of whom Joseph, Capt RN Battle of Quiberon Bay, *b* 1731, *m* Mary Sax, *dsp* 1800):

JOHN JACKSON, of Kingston, Jamaica; Surgn RM; *m* Hannah (*d* 1788), dau of Nathaniel Coverley, and *d* 1777, having had, with two other sons (*d* unm) and three daus:

1 Samuel, of Clarendon, Jamaica; *m* Elizabeth Sarah King (*d* 1851) and *d* 1 Aug 1831, leaving issue

2 JOHN (Sir), **1st Bt**

3 Robert; *b* April 1765; V-Adml the Red; *d* unm 9 June 1852

4 Joseph; *b* 1771; barrister; *d* unm 20 Aug 1850

The 2nd son,

Sir John Jackson, 1st Bt (UK), so *cr* 22 May 1815, of Arlsey, Co Bedford; *b* Kingston, Jamaica, 30 Dec 1763; Dir HEIC; Priv Sec to Lord Keith; MP Dover; *m* 13 Feb 1797 Charlotte Spry (*d* 30 June 1807), widow of J Christian, dau of Gen Joseph Gorham, of Gorham Point, Nova Scotia, niece of William Spry, Govr Barbados, and *d* 17 May 1820, leaving:

1 **Sir Keith Alexander Jackson, 2nd Bt**; Offr 14th later 4th Light Dragoons, ADC to Govr Bombay, Order Lion and Sun Persia, served Sind Campaign; *b* 8 Jan

1798; *m* Feb 1834 Amelia (*d* 22 Sept 1872), only dau of George Waddell, Commissary-Gen Bombay Army, and *d* 21 Aug 1843, leaving:

(1) **Sir Mountstuart Goodricke Jackson, 3rd Bt**; *b* 6 Jan 1836; *educ* Eton and E India Coll; joined Bengal CS 1855; *d* Lucknow 22 Nov 1857 in Indian Mutiny

(2) **Sir Keith George Jackson, 4th Bt**; *b* 2 Aug 1842; *educ* Wye Coll and Magdalene Coll Cambridge; Lt 83rd Foot, dir Canadian Oil Wells Syndicate at Petrolia, Canada; had sheep-farming interests in Argentina; *m* 25 Feb 1875 Alice (*d* 12 Nov 1940), dau of Charles Francis Montresor, Bengal CS, and *d* Argentina 3 Sept 1916, leaving:

1a **Sir Robert Montresor Jackson, 5th Bt**; *b* 11 March 1876; *educ* Tonbridge; engr Brazilian and Argentine Rlwys 1898–1908, Dir-Gen Rlwys Dept Argentine Govt, consulting engr Buenos Aires and Rio de Janeiro, MIMechE, Assist Inspr Guns Woolwich Min Munitions WW I 1916–19; *m* 11 March 1913 Katherine (*d* 24 Oct 1959), yst dau of John Abrey, of The Glen, and Barden Park, Tonbridge, and *d* 4 Dec 1940, leaving:

1b **Sir John Montresor Jackson, 6th Bt**; *b* 14 Oct 1914; *educ* Tonbridge and Clare Coll Cambridge (BA 1936); RA (TA) WW II, memb London Stock Exchange 1948–80; *m* 28 July 1953 Enid (*d* 18 Feb 1994), formerly w of Alfred Chester Beatty and dau of Stanley Hugh Groome, of Kingston, Surrey, and *d* 31 May 1980

2b George Hauteville; P/O RAF WW II; *b* 22 Feb 1916; *educ* Tonbridge, *ka* 3 Sept 1940

1b Bernice Evelyn Abrey; *b* 24 June 1917; *m* 1st 30 Jan 1940 W/Cdr Patrick Edward Geoffrey Gunnell Connolly, RAF (*ka* 14 July 1944), est s of Col W E G Connolly, RM; *m* 2nd 12 July 1954 Frederick John Ralph (*d* 19–) and *d* 4 Sept 1994, leaving by her 1st husb:

1c *Richard Edward Geoffrey Gunnell; *b* 17 Aug 1942; *m* 1st 8 March 1969 Catherine Mary Angela, dau of Rex Keelaghan, of Park, Kinnegad, Co Westmeath, and has:

1d *Oonagh Christina; *b* 12 July 1970

2d *Kitty Catherine Amelia; *b* 3 Sept 1971

1c (cont.) Richard Connolly *m* 2nd 31 Dec 1991 *Amanda Jane, dau of Frederick Oliver, of Brighton, Sussex, and by her has:

3d *Mimi Aurora; *b* 10 Feb 1992

4d *Paloma Lola; *b* 6 June 1995

5d *Phoebe Augusta; *b* 19 Aug 1997

1c *Penelope Ann [Mrs Penelope Govett, 62 Glebe Place, London SW3 5JB]; *b* 6 Feb 1941; *m* 1st 14 Jan 1960 (*divorce* 1969) John Richard Irwin, er s of Ralph M Irwin; *m* 2nd 16 Oct 1970 (*divorce* June 1993) William John Romaine Govett, yst s of John Govett, of Newton Stacey, and has by him:

1d *Romaine Lizabeth; *b* 4 Jan 1973

2a Francis Gorham; Maj RE; *b* 11 Nov 1878; *m* 1st 1908 Anna Maria, dau of Pedro Biscar, of Montevideo, and had:

1b Sir ROBERT JACKSON, **7th and present Bt**

2a (cont.) Francis Jackson *m* 2nd 11 Feb 1919 Dorothy Hattie, 6th dau of Albert Edward Willis, of Teddington, and *d* 7 March 1942

(1) Amelia Georgina; presumed *k* 1857 Indian Mutiny

(2) Anna Madeline; *m* 21 March 1859 her cousin Elphinstone Jackson (*d* 3 Sept 1873) and *d* 31 March 1924, leaving issue (*see* below)

(3) Julia Honoria Catherine; *d* unm 5 March 1926

(4) Monimia Emily; *m* 21 May 1888 Capt Pascal N Robaglia, of Goletta, Tunis, Chev Legn Hon (*d* 16 Aug 1911), and *d* 30 Jan 1923

2 John, of Wellington, NZ; HEIC's China CS; *b* 28 April 1799; *m* 8 March 1832 Honoria Anna Maria (*d* 25 May 1869), dau of James Daniell, HEIC's China CS, and *d* 2 June 1869, leaving, with other issue:

(1) Keith Robert; *b* 1832; *d* unm

(2) Welby Charles; *b* 1839; *m* Dec 1866 Elizabeth (*d* 1926), dau of John Grace, of Wellington, and *d* 1926, leaving:

1a John Keith; *b* 1872; *m* 1914 Anna Maria Bertha (*d* 21 Oct 1953), dau of — Arnold, of Freeling, S Australia, and *d* 22 Sept 1957 leaving:

1b +KEITH ARNOLD [Keith Jackson Esq, 6 Coast Rd, Wainuiomata, New Zealand]; *b* 24 April 1921; heir presumptive; *m* *Pauline Mona, dau of B P Climo, of Wellington, NZ, and has:

1c +Neil Keith; *b* 12 May 1952; *m* 1973 *Sandra Whitehead and has:

1d +Stephen Keith; *b* 27 Sept 1973

2d +Paul Alan; *b* 1976

2c +Colin Paul; *b* 11 Aug 1954; *m* 1976 *Shirley Hair

3c +Bruce John; *b* 4 Nov 1957

4c +Kenneth Grant; *b* 1961

1c *Claire Alison (twin); *b* 11 Aug 1954; *m* 1979 *Graham John Close and has:

1d *Jason John; *b* 1980

2d *Tyrell Dan; *b* 1983

1b *Noela Grace [Mrs Arthur Lambourn, 16 Beaumont Ave, Lower Hutt, New Zealand]; *b* 1915; *m* 16 Oct 1945 *Lambourn, s of Ernest Lambourn, of NZ, and has:

1c *Graham John; *b* 31 Dec 1946; *m* 1968 *Ngaire Johnson and has:

1d *Clynton Arthur; *b* 1970

1d *Susan Barbara; *b* 1968

2a William Alfred; *b* 1878; *m* 1904 Emily (*d* 1952), dau of John Hale, of Westport, NZ, and *d* 1965, leaving:

1b *Grace Irene; *b* 1906; *m* 1937 *Stephen Frederick Louis Cooper and has:

1c *Stephen Jackson; *b* 1952

2b *Elizabeth [Mrs Arthur McKay, 62B Essex St, Masterton, Wairarapa, New Zealand]; *b* 1911; *m* 1937 *Arthur David McKay and has:

1c *Arthur Thomas; *b* 1937; *m* 1960 *Jocelyn Celia Goodwin and has:

1d *David William; *b* 1961

2d *Iain Thomas; *b* 1967

1d *Shona Margaret; *b* 1963

2c *Rex David; *b* 1953; *m* 1975 *Beverley Anne O'Dea and has:

1e *Andrew Thomas; *b* 1985

1e *Natasha Louise; *b* 1982

2e *Kate Amanda; *b* 1990

1c *Colleen Mary; *b* 1941; *m* 1963 *Philip Cotter and has:

1d *Kathryn Mary; *b* 1964

2d *Tania Elizabeth; *b* 1965

3d *Maria Louise; *b* 1967

4d *Julia Jane; *b* 1971

2c *Marie Elizabeth; *b* 1943; *m* 1974 *Maurice Doran and has:

1d *James Gerard; *b* 1976

2d *Richard John; *b* 1979

3a Sydney Leybourne; *b* 1886; *m* 1916 Daphne (*d* 1948), dau of William Halse, of Wellington, NZ, and *d* 1974 leaving:

1b *Peggy Elinor [Mrs Archibald Wallace, Remuera Gdns, 57 Richard Farnell Ave, Remuera, Auckland, New Zealand]; *b* 1917; *m* 1941 Archibald Douglas Wallace (*d* 1986) and has:

1c *James Leybourne Douglas [James Wallace Esq, Sundrum Woodbury, Rd 21, Geraldine, New Zealand]; barrister and slr; *b* 18 April 1946; *m* 1973 *Evelyn Wilder, 2nd dau of Sir (Hugh) John Dyke Acland, KBE (*see* ACLAND, Bt, of Columb-John), and has:

1d *James Ormond; *b* 1974

1d *Antonia Acland; *b* 1977

2d *Henrietta Harper; *b* 1979

2c *Simon John Lewis [Simon Wallace Esq, 87 Clyde St, Island Bay, Wellington, New Zealand]; *b* 23 Sept 1949; *m* 1st 1978 (*divorce* 19–) Anne Braithwaite; *m* 2nd 19– *Susan Patterson and by her has:

1d *George; *b* 1988

2d *Henry; *b* 1992

1c *Judith Margaret [Mrs Thomas Aldridge, 20 St Vincent Ave, Remuera, Auckland, New Zealand]; DipH Sc; *b* 18 Sept 1943; *m* 1964 *Col Thomas Arthur Aldridge, CBE, NRZ Inf Regt, and has issue:

1d *Michael Douglas Arthur; *b* 21 Dec 1966

2d *Patrick Leybourne Thomas; *b* 29 June 1970

1d *Louise Elizabeth; *b* 6 June 1965; *m* 11 April 1990 *Robert Alan Clark and has:

1e *James Alexander; *b* 2 Aug 1996

2b *Sheila; *b* 1924; *m* 1950 *Roy James Grant and has issue

4a Gordon Francis Welby; *b* 5 April 1888; *m* 26 Jan 1917 Kathleen Florence, dau of John Haldane, of Takaka, NZ, and had:

1b Gordon Haldane; *b* 1919; *d* 22 Sept 1942

2b John Richard; *b* 1924; *m* 1947 *Leslie Mackay, dau of James Mackay Heise, and *d* 1987 having had:

1c +Peter; *b* 27 Sept 1951; *m* 1991 *Guadalupe Rosales and has:

1d +Igor; *b* 1991

2c +John [John Jackson Esq, 59 Glen Rd, Kelburn, Wellington 5, New Zealand]; *b* 26 June 1956; *m* 1989 *Toni, dau of Ernest Cornish Cosgrove, of Wellington, and has:

1d +Timothy Richard; *b* 1989

1d *Lillian Jane; *b* 1991

3c +James; *b* 16 Aug 1965; has by Désirée Marie Jones:

1d +Hayden Jesse Jones JACKSON; *b* 1991

2d +Mitchell Lee Jones JACKSON; *b* 1993

1c*Margaret Gail; *b* 16 Oct 1949; *m* 1968 (*divorce* 1994) Wong Teck Sing, of Melbourne, Victoria, and has:

1d *Geoffrey Peter; *b* 27 Sept 1968

2d *Conrad Dow; *b* 1972

1d *Vera Dow; *b* 1971

2c *Kathleen; *b* 23 Jan 1954

(3) Hugh Whiteman; *b* 1842; *m* Jan 1864 Charlotte (*d* 1929), dau of A W Howard, of Wellington, and *d* 1929, leaving sons and daus

(4) Murray James Hamilton; *b* 1849; *m* 1877 Selina Spearink (*d* 1942) and *d* 3 Oct 1935, leaving:

1a William John (twin); *b* 1895; *m* 1924 Ella, dau of George Guppy, and *d* 1980, leaving:

1b +Alan Hamilton [Mr Alan Jackson, 8 Hunter Place, New Plymouth, New Zealand]; *b* 24 March 1924; *m* 12 Feb 1949 *Lynn, dau of Arthur Prichard Lindsay, and has:

1c +William Lindsay; *b* 2 Oct 1956

2c +Murray Grant; *b* 15 Nov 1959

1c *Anne Agnes; *b* 1 Oct 1953

2b +Robert John; *b* 1939; *m* 19 May 1962 *Ruth Wynita Lamb and has:

1c +Stephen John; *b* 23 April 1965

2c +Andrew Philip; *b* 1969

3c +Brenden James; *b* 1970

1c *Pauline Ruth; *b* 19 June 1963; *m* 1989 *Craig Robert Whiting

1b *Esme Ruth; *b* 1925

2b *Ella Marian [Mrs Cecil Smith, 20 Bracken Ave, Epsom, Auckland, New Zealand]; *b* 1927; *m* 1949 *Cecil Edmund Smith and has:

1c *Cecil David; *b* 1951

2c *Bruce Edmund; *b* 1953

3c *Peter Raymond; *b* 1954

4c *Paul Barry; *b* 1959

5c *Rodney John; *b* 1964

1c *Margaret Ann; *b* 1957

2c *Beverley Joy; *b* 1962

3b *Evelyn Isabel; *b* 1931; *m* 1956 *Ashley Gordon Howan and has:

1c *Lance; *b* 1959

2c *Philip; *b* 19–

1c *Cherry; *b* 1957
2a Murray Spearink (twin); *b* 1895; *m* 1921 Mary, dau of William Robinson, and *d* 197–, leaving:
1b +David Murray James; *b* 1921; Salvation Army Offr; *m* 1950 *Olive, dau of William Wilde, of Yeovil, Somerset, and has issue
1c +Paul Murray; *b* 1951
1c *Verna Elizabeth; *b* 1954
2b +Edmund Robinson [Edmund Jackson Esq, Apotu Rd, Kamo, Whangarei, New Zealand]; *b* 1923; sheep farmer; *m* 1st 1945 Viola Thelma (*d* 8 Dec 1966), dau of Hans Ries, of Pohokura, NZ, and has:
1c +Peter Edmund [Peter Jackson Esq, 129 Queen St, Pukekohe, New Zealand]; *b* 18 Feb 1948; farmer and property developer; *m* 1973 *Maria Clow and has:
1d +Quentin; *b* 1974
2d +Shaun Lewis; *b* 1976
2c +Geoffrey Kendal; *b* 10 March 1952; *m* 1974 *Glenda Murdoch and has:
1d *Dianna Jan; *b* 1974
2d *Carolyn Thelma; *b* 1975
1c *Raewyn Ada; *b* 17 Jan 1947; *m* 6 July 1968 *Alan Cole, of Kaitaia, NZ, and has:
1d *Ruth; *b* 12 June 1969
2d *Sheryl; *b* 1970
3d *Wendy; *b* 1973
2c *Linda Mary; *b* 17 Sept 1954; *m* 19– *Hamilton Stuart-Brown
3c *Zoe; *b* 1963; *m* 1982 *Graham Hughes and has:
1d *Seamus; *b* 1990
1d *Clare; *b* 1985
2d *Rachel; *b* 1987
2b (cont.) Edmund Jackson *m* 2nd 22 June 1968 *Nancy Pyle and by her has:
3c +Russell Joseph; *b* 1970
3b +Stuart Harold; *b* 1926; *m* 1961 *Eleni, dau of Savvas Michalis, of Cyprus, and has:
1c +Andros Vassilis; *b* 1962
2c +Nikos Manolis; *b* 1963
3b (cont.) Mr and Mrs Stuart Jackson also adopted:
*Kiro; *b* 19 Sept 1968
4b +Graham George; MA, MD, lecturer anthropology Auckland U; *b* 1935
1a Selina Harriett Honoria; *b* 1878; *m* 1901 William Willis (*d* 1929) and has issue
2a Minnie Catherine; *b* 1879; *m* 1904 Thomas Arden Willis (*d* 1943) and *d* 1 July 1958, leaving issue
3a Marion Marguerita; *b* 1882; *m* 1917 Frederick Thorp (*d* 1947) and had issue
4a Verna Gladys
(5) Lindsay Astell; *b* 1851
(1) Mary; *m* Dr Darby and was *k* with her husb and child in the Indian Mutiny 1857
(2) Catherine Emily
(3) Charlotte Maria
3 Welby Brown; Judge Calcutta; *b* 30 Dec 1802; *m* 1st 1 April 1823 Katherine (*d* 3 Sept 1836), dau of John Townsend Hungerford, and had:
(1) Elphinstone; Judge High Court Calcutta; *b* 14 March 1824; *m* 21 March 1859 his cousin Anna Madeline (*d* 31 March 1924), dau of **Sir Keith Jackson, 2nd Bt** (*see* above), and *d* 3 Feb 1873, leaving:
1a Mountstuart Hungerford; PWD India; *b* 28 Jan 1860; *m* 1886 Ethel Beatrice (*d* 26 Aug 1954), dau of David Cowie, of Calcutta, memb Viceroy's Cncl, and *d* 18 Nov 1925, leaving:
1b Cecil Hungerford; Col IA; *b* 7 Nov 1887; *m* 9 Feb 1916 Marian Blanche (*d* 1971), dau of Cdr Francis Wheeler, RN, and *d* 1978 having had:
1c *Audrey Madeline Hungerford [Mrs Robert Howe, The Manor House, Martock, Somerset]; *b* 10 March 1920; *m* 16 Sept 1944 *Robert Douglas Howe, MBE, SQA, ICS, s of Rev Canon Samuel Francis Howe, Rector Valentia, Co Kerry, and has:
1d *Peter Mountstuart [Peter Howe Esq, 41 Drax Ave, London SW19]; *b* 29 Jan 1948; *m* 1983 *Anne-Marie Boys, and has:
1e *Michael Mountstuart; *b* 1984
1d *Veronica Joan [Mrs James Goodford, The Old Rectory, Chilton Cantelo, Yeovil, Somerset]; *b* 21 Feb 1946; *m* 1968 *James William Goodford and has:
1e *Andrew Christopher John; *b* 1970
2e *Richard Michael James; *b* 1972
3e *Simon Charles Jasper; *b* 1979
1e *Georgina Helen Jane; *b* 1975
2b Laurence Hungerford; Col IA Survey of India; *b* 27 Sept 1889; *m* 30 July 1919 Freda Mary (*d* 1978), er dau of Col Edmund Henry Dalgety, CB, and *d* 1985, having had:
1c +Peter Hungerford [Maj Peter Jackson, Hadstock Hall, Hadstock, Cambridge]; *b* 2 Nov 1925; Maj RE; *m* 5 Sept 1953 *Joyce Thomasina, yr dau of Lt-Col V H Wells-Cole, MC, KOYLI, of Hall Farm, Abbotts Ripton, Hunts, and has:
1d *Amelia Mary Hungerford; *b* 23 May 1955; *m* 1991 *Hon Brandon, est s of Baron Brandon of Oakbrook (LP, *qv*)
2d *Catherine Ann Hungerford; *b* 21 May 1957
1b Dorothy Hungerford; *m* 30 Nov 1922 Col Spence Daer Reid, RAMC (*d* 8 Feb 1954), and had:
1c *Peter Daer, CB (1981)[Maj-Gen Peter Reid CB, The Border House, Cholderton, nr Salisbury, Wilts]; *b* 5 Aug 1925 ; Maj-Gen late Roy Dragoons; *m* 9 Aug 1958 *Catherine Fleetwood, yst dau of Wilfred Andrew Carmichael Boodle, and has:
1d *Duncan Andrew Daer; *b* 1959
2c *Ian Daer [Dr Ian Reid, 1 Cedar Crescent, Woy Woy, NSW 2256, Australia]; *educ* Edinburgh U (MB, ChB 1950); *b* 19 Dec 1927; *m* 6 Oct 1956 *Olive Jean Courtenay, dau of W Courtenay Snook, of Cornwall, and has:
1d *Hamish Ian Daer; *b* 1957
2d *Angus Courtenay Daer; *b* 1962
1d *Heather Susan Daer; *b* 1959
1c *Joan Pamela Daer; *b* 11 Jan 1924; *m* 5 April 1956 *Martin Vlaanderen, of Amsterdam, and has:
1d *Martin Richard; *b* 1957
2d *Robert Laurens; *b* 1964
1d *Rosemarie Anne; *b* 1958
2d *Fiona Veronica; *b* 1960
2b Beatrice Hungerford; *d* unm Feb 1941
2a Elphinstone; *b* 9 Oct 1868
3a Alexander Townsend; Capt Worcs Regt; *b* 18 Nov 1869; *m* 18 Dec 1900 Edith E F (*m* 2nd 2 Jan 1909 Frank Collins, MA, est s of Brig-Surgn F Collins), dau of Rev W Urquhart, and *dsp* 13 June 1903
4a Keith Hungerford; Lt-Col Indian Cav; *b* 3 Dec 1870; *m* 17 June 1918 Constance (*d* 25 Aug 1966), widow of Col W F Shore, Army Remount Dept, and dau of Col Watling, Rajputs, IA, and *d* 30 May 1930, leaving:
1b John Gordon; *d* 20 June 1923
(2) Hungerford Deedes; Lt-Col RA; *b* 2 May 1833; *d* unm 9 June 1878
(1) Margaret Hungerford; *m* 8 July 1845 Sir William Grey, KCSI, and had issue
(2) Catherine Johanna; *m* 1 May 1848 Charles F Montresor and had issue
(3) Alice Shakespeare; *m* Francis Cockerell and *d* June 1861, leaving issue
3 (cont.) Judge W B Jackson *m* 2nd 24 July 1839 Maria Margaretta (*d* 21 Aug 1843), est dau of Lt-Col George Thomas D'Aguilar, and by her had:
(3) Louis D'Aguilar; *b* 20 April 1840
(4) George D'Aguilar; Maj-Gen Bengal Cav; *b* 20 July 1843; *m* 20 May 1874 (*divorce* 1887) Margaret Springall (*d* 1920), dau of Springall Thompson, and *d* 1919, leaving:
1a Harold D'Aguilar; WW I with US Engrs in France; *b* 1877; *educ* Harrow; *m* 1903 Anna Lillian, widow of Count von Stadie, of Koenigsberg, Germany, and *d* 1942, leaving issue
1b William Douglas D'Aguilar; Col US Army; *b* 1904; *educ* California Inst of Technology and S California U; chm Research and Development Div, Office of QMG, Legion of Merit with Oak Leaf Cluster; *m* 1933 *Margaret Williams and has:
1c *Margaret Anne; *b* 1938
2c *Susan; *b* 1940
1b *Hyacinthe Lillian D'Aguilar; *b* 1908; *educ* S California U; *m* 1933 John Machell Procter (*d* 1941)
1a Isabel May D'Aguilar; *b* 1875; *educ* S California U; *m* 11 Feb 1902 Lt-Col Charles Norman Buzzard, CMG, DSO, RA (*see* BUZZARD, Bt), and *d* 1922
3 (cont.) Judge W B Jackson *m* 3rd 29 Aug 1856 Elizabeth, dau of Thomas James Ireland, of Owsden Hall, Suffolk, and *d* 17 Nov 1890, having by her had:
(5) Cecil Welby; Maj 3rd Bengal Cav; *b* 2 June 1861; *m* 24 July 1894 Violet Emily Caroline (*d* 1955), 2nd dau of Col Bolton, RHG
4 Colville Coverley; HEIC's CS Bengal; *b* 7 May 1804; *m* 1850 Mary (*d* 7 April 1872), dau of Thomas Hughes, and *d* 19 June 1858, leaving:
(1) Caroline Edith; *m* 22 April 1875 Edward Briggs Kennedy (*d* 6 Nov 1914) and *d* 29 Dec 1935, leaving issue (*see* AILSA, M)
1 Charlotte Spry; *d* unm 1819
2 Margaret Anne; *m* 24 April 1828 George Rennie, FRS, CE, and *d* 13 Aug 1881, having had issue

JACKSON of Eagle House

Arms: Argent a greyhound courant ermines between three eagle's heads erased sable. **Crest:** A demi-horse argent gutté de sang, maned and hoofed sable. **Motto:** *Chi si contenta gode* ('Whoever is content enjoys life'). **Creation:** Bt. (UK) 10 Feb 1913.

SIR NICHOLAS FANE ST GEORGE JACKSON, 3RD BT, of Eagle House, Wimbledon, Surrey [Sir Nicholas Jackson Bt, 42 Hereford Road, London W2 5AJ]; *b* 4 Sept 1934; *s* f 1979; *educ* Radley, Wadham Coll Oxford and RAM (LRAM, ARCM); harpsichordist, composer (*Mass for a Saint's Day* (1966), *20th Century Merbecke* (1967), *4 Images* (for organ) (1971), *Solemn Mass* (1977), *Divertissment* (organ) (1983), *Organ Mass* (1984), *2 Organ Sonatas* (1985), *Suite, for brass quintet and organ* (1986) and *The Reluctant Highwayman* (opera) (1992)) and organist (St Anne's Soho 1963–68, St James's Piccadilly 1971–74, St Lawrence Jewry 1974–77, organist and Master of Choristers St David's Cathedral 1977–84), musical dir St David's Cathedral Bach Festival 1979, dir Concertante of London 1987– and Bach Festival Santes Creus Spain 1987–89, memb: London Virtuosi, Music Ctee Welsh Arts Cncl 1981–, examiner Trin Coll Music 1985–, Master Drapers' Co 1994–95, Hon Fell Hertford Coll Oxford 1995; *m* 1st 2 Dec 1961 (*divorce* 1968) Jennifer Ann, dau of Francis Augustus Squire; *m* 2nd 1972 *Nadia Françoise Geneviève, dau of Georges Michard, of St Etienne, France, and has issue:

1 +THOMAS GRAHAM ST GEORGE; *b* 5 Oct 1980

Lineage: NICHOLAS JACKSON, of Duddington, Northants; restored the house there 1633; *d* 1662, leaving:

WILLIAM JACKSON, of Duddington; founded the school there; *d* 1667, leaving:

THOMAS JACKSON, of Duddington, JP (Northants); granted arms 1689; *m* Frances (*d* 5 July 1683), dau of Christopher Thursby, of Castor, Northants, and *d* 1694, having had, with three other sons and a dau, an est surv s:

FRANCIS JACKSON, of Duddington, Castor and Helpstone; *m* Frances Fairchild (*d* 15 July 1740); *bur* 24 Jan 1744, having had, with two yr sons (Francis (Rev), Rector Bulwick, Northants; Jeremiah, of Fanningstown, Co Limerick, ancestor of the GOULDs of Upwey, Dorset):

THOMAS JACKSON, of Duddington; *b* 1695; *m* 1st 22 April 1720 his cousin Sarah (*bur* 23 July 1739), dau and coheir of Thomas Burneby, of Manton, Rutland, and had issue; *m* 2nd Frances (*d* 9 July 1754), dau of Rev Hugh Cartwright, Vicar Ossington, Notts, and *d* 12 July 1771, having by her had, with a dau (Frances, *bapt* 24 Aug 1749, *m* her cousin Rev Jeremiah Jackson, Headmaster Uppingham, and *d* Sept 1809):

HUGH JACKSON, of Duddington and Stamford, Lincs; *b* 11 Oct 1745; *m* 1767 his cousin Jane (*d* 22 April 1816), dau of James Weldon by Mary, dau of Francis Jackson, of Duddington, and *d* 28 April 1829, having had:

1 THOMAS

2 William, of Stamford; *b* 12 May 1769; *m* Sarah (*d* June 1810), dau and coheir of Joseph Hawkins, of Barwell and Hinckley, Leics, and *d* 26 July 1810, leaving issue

3 Francis; *bapt* 5 July 1770; *d* 28 March 1772

4 Hugh, of Wisbech; *b* 26 July 1771; *m* 1st 25 April 1797 Anne (*d* 19 Jan 1838), dau of John Marshall, of Waldersea House, Elm, Isle of Ely, and had issue (who *s* to Duddington); *m* 2nd 1839 Elizabeth, dau of John Patrick Moore, of Aspley Guise, Beds, and *d* 1852

5 Jeremiah (Rev), JP (Cambs and Norfolk); *b* 29 July 1775; *educ* St John's Coll Cambridge (MA, Fell); Vicar Elm-cum-Emneth, Cambs, and Preb Brecon; *m* 9 June 1801 Mary Ann (*d* 8 Jan 1849), dau of Rev Robert Willan, Vicar Cardington, Beds, and *d* 24 Sept 1857, leaving issue

1 Caroline Mary; *b* 26 Aug 1782; *m* 1st John Goddard Marshall, of Ely, Cambs (*d* 10 June 1825), and had issue; *m* 2nd Rev John Russell Christopherson, LLB, Rector Gainsby and Vicar Eagle

The est s,

THOMAS JACKSON, of Stamford; *b* 20 March 1768; *m* Aug 1790 Elizabeth (*m* 2nd 10 Aug 1802 Capt John Gardner, RN; *d* 8 April 1823), dau and coheir of Tobias Hippisley, of Hambleton, Rutland, and *d* 30 June 1800, having had, with two er sons (Thomas Hippisley, of Stamford, *b* 16 May 1791, *m* 14 Feb 1820 Sarah, dau of Rev William Pochin, Rector Morcott, Rutland, and had issue; John, of Hampstead, *b* 2 Aug 1797, *m* 16 July 1825 Anne Dodsworth, dau of Sir William Beechey, RA, and had issue):

HUGH JACKSON, of Hampstead; *b* 25 May 1799; slr; *m* 31 March 1834 Elizabeth (*d* 6 March 1880), dau of Thomas Graham Arnold, MD, of Stamford, and *d* 24 April 1881, having had, with a yr s (Basil, *b* 1840, *d* 1845) and two daus (Annie Jane, *m* 26 Jan 1864 Charles Thomas Arnold, MA; Emily):

Sir Thomas Graham Jackson, 1st Bt (UK), so *cr* 10 Feb 1913; *b* 21 Dec 1835; *educ* Brighton Coll and Wadham Coll Oxford (MA, Fell 1864–80, Hon Fell 1882–1924, Hon DCL Oxon 1911); architect (pupil of Sir George Gilbert Scott), projects included Oxford Examination Schs, restoration Bodleian, new bldgs for Balliol, BNC, Corpus, Hertford, Lincoln and Trinity Colls, new Radcliffe Library, Somerville Coll, at Cambridge Sedgwick Memorial Museum and Archaeological Mueum, also new Law Library and Law Sch, restoration at Longleat, Eltham Palace, Bath Abbey, Christchurch Priory and Winchester Cathedral, new bldgs for Inner Temple, Eton, Harrow, Westminster and Rugby, ARA 1892, RA 1896, Hon LLD Cantab 1910, Associé de l'Académie Royale Belgique 1910; author: *Modern Gothic Architecture* (1873), *Dalmatia, the Quarnero, and Istria* (1887), *Wadham College, Oxford: its History and Architecture* (1893), *Byzantine and Romanesque Architecture* (1913), *Gothic Architecture in France, England, and Italy* (1915), *A Holiday in Umbria* (1917), *The Renaissance of Roman Architecture* (1921–22) and *Memories of Travel* (1923); *m* 31 March 1880 Alice Mary (*d* 21 April 1900), dau of William Lambarde, JP, DL, of Beechmont, Sevenoaks, Kent, by Harriet Elizabeth, dau of Sir James Naesmyth, 3rd Bt (*see* 1928 edn), and *d* 7 Nov 1924, leaving, with a yr s (Basil Hippisley, MC (1918), *b* 4 Feb 1887, *educ* Winchester, FRIBA, Maj W R RHA WWs I (despatches) and II, *m* 23 Nov 1950 Helen, dau of Stanley Brotherhood, of Thornhaugh Hall, nr Peterborough, and formerly w of C Nicholson):

Sir Hugh Nicholas Jackson, 2nd Bt; *b* 21 Jan 1881; *educ* Winchester; Maj RFA, Lt RW Fus, WW I; *m* 15 July 1931 *Violet Marguerite Loftus [Violet Lady Jackson, 38 Oakley St, London SW3], yst dau of Loftus St George (*see* ST GEORGE, Bt), and *d* 1 Nov 1979, leaving:

1 Sir NICHOLAS FANE ST GEORGE JACKSON, **3rd and present Bt**

1 *Louise Loftus; *b* 10 Aug 1946

JACKSON of Stansted House

Arms: Ermine on a pile azure between two fountains in base proper a sheldrake or. **Crest:** Upon a fountain proper a sheldrake or. **Motto:** *Aut mors aut victoria* ('Either death or victory'). **Creation:** Bt. (UK) 4 Aug 1902.

SIR MICHAEL ROLAND JACKSON, 5TH BT, of Stansted House, Stansted, Essex [Sir Michael Jackson Bt, Jolliffe's House, Stour Row, Dorset SP7 0QW]; *b* 20 April 1919; *s* f 1956; *educ* Stowe and Clare Coll Cambridge (MA); F/Lt RAFVR WW II, chartered engr (ret), MIEE, FIQA; *m* 1st 7 Nov 1942 (*divorce* 1969) (Hilda) Margaret (BA Girton Coll Cambridge), dau of Cecil George Herbert Richardson, CBE, of Newark, and has:

1 +THOMAS ST FELIX [Thomas Jackson Esq, 70 Marryat Rd, London SW19 5BN]; *b* 27 Sept 1946; *educ* Stowe and Southampton U (BA Hons); md Billington Jackson Advertising; *m* 1980 *Georgina Victoria, dau of George Harold Malcolm Scatliff, and has:

(1) *Lucy Harriet; *b* 1982

(2) *Charlotte Dare; *b* 1986

1 *Sally Ann; *b* 10 March 1944

Sir MICHAEL *m* 2nd 18 June 1969 *Hazel Mary, dau of Ernest Harold Edwards, of Sussex

Lineage: The ancestor of this family in Ireland came from Yorks in OLIVER CROMWELL's Army and was granted lands in Co Carlow for his services. The estate, called Mount Leinster, was sold 1745 by his descendant GEORGE JACKSON, who settled at Urker, Crossmaglen, Co Armagh, and was presumably kin to:

JOHN JACKSON, of Urker; had:

DAVID JACKSON, of Urker; *b* 4 Feb 1814; *m* 7 Feb 1838 Eliza, dau of William Oliver, of Killynure, Co Armagh, and *d* 11 Nov 1899, having had, with other issue:

1 John; *b* 28 Nov 1839; *m* Kate Maria Jane Whiting and *d* 21 July 1886, having had issue

2 THOMAS (Sir), **1st Bt**

3 Andrew Coulter Bradford; *b* 8 April 1846; *m* 1 Aug 1876 Eliza Emily Gilmore and had issue

4 James; *b* 24 Oct 1850; *m* 13 Oct 1866 Elizabeth Sarah Browne

5 David; *b* 16 Nov 1855; *m* 28 Dec 1893 Margaret Louisa Wright and *d* 27 July 1903

6 George William; *b* 20 Aug 1858; *d* 28 Nov 1859

DAVID JACKSON's 2nd s,

Sir Thomas Jackson, 1st Bt (UK), so *cr* 4 Aug 1902, JP (Hong Kong); *b* 4 June 1841; ch manager, chm and dir Hong Kong and Shanghai Bank, 1st elected rep Chamber of Commerce in Legislative Cncl Hong Kong, ktd 1899; *m* 19 Sept 1871 Amelia Lydia (*d* 10 April 1944), dau of George Julius Dare, RN, of Dorset, and *d* 21 Dec 1915, leaving:

1 **Sir Thomas Dare Jackson, 2nd Bt**, DSO and bar (1918), MVO (1912), JP (Suffolk), DL; *b* 14 June 1876; Boer War 1901–02 (despatches twice, Queen's medal, five clasps), Adj 1902–05, ADC to GOC Southern Army India 1906–08, Assist Mil Sec to GOC Gibraltar 1910–14, WW I (despatches three times): T/Lt-Col 1914–15, T/Brig-Gen and Bde Cdr 1915–16, cmded a Bn Manchester Regt 1916–17, Hon Brig-Gen 1919, Col late KORR (Lancaster); *m* 25 Jan 1919 (Mary Lilian) Vera Massy ('Mimi') (*d* 1 April 1975), est dau of Brig-Gen Samuel Eyre Massy Lloyd, CBE, JP, DL, late Suffolk Regt, and *d* 7 Feb 1954, having had:

(1) Thomas Richard Eyre; *b* 3 Feb 1921; Lt Coldstream Gds WW II; *ka* Feb 1944

(2) Julius Lloyd; *b* 6 Feb 1922; Sub-Lt RNVR WW II; drowned while bathing 31 July 1943

(1) *Nancy Amelia [Mrs Michael Bowman-Vaughan, 9 Cope Place, London W8]; *b* 24 Sept 1924; *m* 25 Sept 1948 *Michael John Bowman-Vaughan, FCA, only s of Capt John Bowman-Vaughan, Queen's Westminsters, and has had:

1a *Michael Thomas; *b* 2 July 1959

1a *Annabel Leslie; *b* 6 Aug 1949

2a *Juliet Euphrosyne; *b* 3 April 1951

3a *Venetia Mary; *b* 19 Aug 1954

4a Valerie Anne; *b* 14, *d* 19 Sept 1956

2 **Sir (George) Julius Jackson, 3rd Bt**, JP (Hants); *b* 4 June 1883; Boer War 1901–02 (medal, three clasps) and WW I (wounded), Maj KRRC; *m* 12 Jan 1909 Nesta Katherine, est dau of Hedworth Trelawny Barclay, of Gaddesby Hall, Leics, and *d* 21 Feb 1956, having had:

(1) David Thomas Trelawny; *b* 9 Aug 1917; Lt 60th Rifles WW II; *ka* Italy 7 Dec 1943

(1) *Dawn Nesta; *b* 1909 [Miss Dawn Jackson, Farthing Cottage, Gun Hill, Heathfield, Sussex]

(2) *Joyce Katherine [Mrs Joyce Walker, Nyton House, Nyton, Chichester PO20 6UL]; *b* 1910; *m* 30 Oct 1937 (*divorce* 1954) Col John Ralph Walker, er s of Alfred Alexander Walker, of Hamble, Hants, and has had:

1a Gay; *b* 1941; *d* 1986

(3) *Meryl Julian (twin) [Mrs Herbert Currie, 6 Manor Gate, St John's Ave, London SW15]; *b* 1910; *m* 12 May 1939 Capt Herbert Sharpe Currie (*d* 10 Sept 1964), s of Herbert Sharpe Currie, and has:

1a *Julian David Sharpe; *b* 8 Aug 1944; *educ* Eton; *m* 2 Aug 1969 *Lynda Barbara, dau of David Spurway

1a *Caroline Joyce [Miss Caroline Currie, 60a Waldo Ave, London SW6]; *b* 3 June 1941

(4) *Daphne Myddelton [Mrs Malcoln Gray, Garden Hill Cottage, Steep, Petersfield, Hants]; *b* 1914; *m* 1st 29 July 1939 S/Ldr Frederick Undecimus Hollins, AFC, RAF (*ka* 4 May 1942), s of William Hollins, and has:

1a *Sarah Daphne [Mrs S D James, 12 Newburgh St, Winchester SO23 8UY]; *b* 30 March 1941; *m* 25 May 1963 *John Anthony Massereene-James and has:

1b *Toby Julius; *b* 14 March 1969

(4) (cont.) Mrs Frederick Hollins *m* 2nd 7 Aug 1948 *Maj Malcolm Comrie Gray, Worcs Regt, yr s of Engr R-Adml Colin Gray, CBE, DSO, and has by him:

2a *Fiona Catherine [Mrs Edward Fairbairn, Applegarth, Bradfield, Reading RG7 6AS]; *b* 9 Sept 1949; *m* 1974 *Edward J Fairbairn, s of Patrick Y Fairbairn, and has:

1b *Miranda; *b* 1977

2b *Rosalind; *b* 1979

3 **Sir (Walter David) Russell Jackson, 4th Bt**; *b* 8 March 1890; Lt RGA WW I (despatches); *m* 15 March 1915 Kathleen (*d* 6 July 1975 aged 80), dau of Summers Hunter, CBE, of Tynemouth, and *d* 15 Dec 1956, leaving:

(1) Sir MICHAEL ROLAND JACKSON, **5th and present Bt**

4 Claude Stewart; *b* 30 Jan 1892; Capt 3rd Bn Coldstream Gds WW I (despatches, wounded); *m* 6 May 1916, as her 1st husb, Laura Emily, dau of Hon William Pearson, of Victoria, Australia, and was *ka* 9 Oct 1917

1 Kathleen McCullagh; *b* 7 July 1872; *m* 29 Oct 1910 Maj Albert Maitland Tabor, 3rd KOH, of Bovingdon Hall, Braintree (*d* 12 Nov 1941), and *d* 2 June 1959

2 Amy Oliver; *b* 27 May 1874; *m* 4 Aug 1900 Brig-Gen John Henry Lloyd, DSO, KORR (Lancaster) (*d* 5 Nov 1941), of Queensbridge, Ellesmere, s of Maj John Henry Lloyd, RA, and *d* 1962, leaving issue

3 Beatrice Minnie Shrieve; *b* 19 Dec 1879; *m* 21 Nov 1906 Lt-Col Raymond John Marker, DSO, er s of Richard Marker, JP, DL, of Combe, Honiton (*d* of wounds recd in action 4 Nov 1914), and had issue

4 Dorothy St Felix; *b* 26 July 1887; *d* unm 1964

JACKSON of The Manor House, Birkenhead

Arms: Azure a fess between two goat's heads couped in chief and a fleur-de-lys in base argent, two flaunches of the last. **Crest:** Upon a ragged staff fesswise sable a goat's head couped argent, semée of trefoils vert. **Motto:** *Fortiter, fideliter, feliciter* ('Boldly, faithfully, successfully'). **Creation:** Bt. (UK) 4 Nov 1869.

SIR (WILLIAM) THOMAS JACKSON, 8TH BT, of The Manor House, Birkenhead [Sir Thomas Jackson Bt, Fell End, Mungrisdale, Cumbria CA11 OXR]; *b* 12 Oct 1927; *s f* 1985; *educ* Mill Hill and RAC Cirencester; 2nd Lt Border Regt 1947–49 (later Lt on Gen Res), ARICS (resigned 1969), land agent to 1969; farmer; chm: Cumberland CLA 1984–86, Whitehaven NFU 1983–85; *m* 25 July 1951 *Gillian Malise, er dau of John William Stobart, MBE, of Farlam Ghyll, Brampton, Cumbria, and has:

1 +(WILLIAM) ROLAND CEDRIC [Dr Roland Jackson, Summer Hill, 14 Glebe Rd, Welwyn, Herts AL6 9BP]; *b* 9 Jan 1954; *educ* Wycliffe Coll and St Peter's Coll (MA) and Exeter Coll (DPhil) Oxford; *m* 1977 *Nicola Mary, MA, DPhil, yr dau of Prof Peter Reginald Davis, MB, BS, PhD, FRCS, of St Mawes, Cornwall, and has:

(1) +Adam William Roland; *b* 19 May 1982

(2) +James Anthony Foljambe; *b* 1984

(3) +Oliver Thomas Peter; *b* 1990

2 +Piers Anthony [Piers Jackson Esq, 26 Astral Ave, The Drive, Hipperholme, W Yorks HX3 8NN]; *b* 6 Nov 1955; *educ* Keswick Sch and Derwent Coll York (BA); *m* 1980 *Anne-Marie, er dau of Patrick Quigg, of Belfast, and has:

(1) +Carl Patrick Thomas; *b* 1981

(2) +Luke Dominic Gregory; *b* 1985

(3) +Ben Philip Joseph; *b* 1988

3 +Jolyon Thomas; *b* 12 Oct 1957; *educ* Keswick Sch and RMA Sandhurst; Lt-Col RGJ; *m* 1986 *Serena A, er dau of David Howell, of Battersea, and has:

(1) +Thomas Sebastian Esmé; *b* 1993

(1) *Alicia Sophie; *b* 1989

Lineage: JAMES JACKSON, of Middlewich, Cheshire; had:

PETER JACKSON, of Warrington, Cheshire; *b* 6 June 1772; *m* 17 Feb 1791 Sarah (*d* 22 Oct 1841), dau of Henry Mather, of Warrington, and *d* 22 May 1811, leaving, with an er s (John Somerville Mather, *m* Mary, dau of James Monk, of Bolton, widow of I Colby, and *d* 1860) and a dau (Ellen Mather, *m* Samuel Highfield and *d* 1877):

Sir William Jackson, 1st Bt (UK), so *cr* 4 Nov 1869, of The Manor House, Birkenhead, and Portland Place, Middx; *b* 28 April 1805; MP Newcastle and N Derbys; *m* 30 Oct 1829 Elizabeth (*d* 20 Jan 1875), dau of Thomas Hughes, of Liverpool, and *d* 31 Jan 1876, having had:

1 **Sir Henry Mather Jackson, 2nd Bt**, DL, QC; *b* 23 July 1831; MP Coventry 1867–68 and 1874–81, High Ct Judge 1881; *m* 8 Aug 1854 Elizabeth (*d* 2 June 1907), dau of Thomas Buddicum Blackburne, of Grange Ho, Birkenhead, and *d* 8 March 1881, leaving:

(1) Sir Henry Mather JACKSON later MATHER-JACKSON (roy licence 1886), **3rd Bt**, CBE (1918), JP, DL (Mon); *b* 19 Oct 1855; *educ* Harrow and Trin Coll Cambridge (MA 1881); Ld Lt Mon, Chm QS, barrister; *m* 3 Aug 1886 Ada Frances, CBE (1939), JP (Mon), DGStJ (*d* 17 March 1949), dau of Gen Edward Arthur Somerset, CB (*see* BEAUFORT, D), and *d* 23 March 1942, having had:

1a Henry; *b* 27 Feb 1894; Capt 9th Lancers WW I (despatches); *m* 16 June 1920 Florence (*d* 1980), dau of Grenville William Garth, of NY, and *d* 2 April 1928, leaving:

1b *Rosemary [Mrs Stanley Legouix, 2 Orchard Green, Chilton Foliat, Hungerford, Berks]; *b* 10 Aug 1924; *m* 27 June 1949 *Stanley Joe Legouix, s of Auguste Legouix, of Jersey, and has:

1c *Geoffrey John Henry; *b* 24 June 1954

1c *Susan Yvette; *b* 25 June 1950

2a **Sir Edward Arthur Mather-Jackson, 4th Bt**; *b* 8 Jan 1899; Lt Scots Gds (SR) WW I 1917–18, FO, barrister 1940–45, underwriting memb Lloyd's, resident dir Buenos Aires Gt Southern Rlwy and Buenos Aires Western Rlwy 1946–48, dep chm resident Bd of Br Argentine Rlwys, author as Edward Mather; *m* 27 Feb 1932 Cecilia (*d* 23 Aug 1949), er dau of Capt Christopher Balfour, DSO, KRRC, and *dsp* 8 Nov 1956

1a Gwladys Ada; *b* 31 May 1888; *m* 13 Sept 1923 Ven Reginald Palmer, DSO, MC, Hon CF (*d* 22 Sept 1945), yst s of John Palmer, of Belton Grange, Hampstead

2a Norah Frances; *b* 21 Jan 1890; *m* 4 Dec 1916 Capt Herbert William Clarke, MC, RE (SR) (*d* 26 Feb 1958), er s of William Edward Thompson Clarke, barrister

3a Agatha Elizabeth; *b* 23 July 1891

(2) William Birkenhead Mather, JP (Derbys); *b* 5 Oct 1864; Capt Roy Monmouth Militia; *m* 19 Dec 1892 Georgiana Catherine (*d* 19 May 1932), dau of Rev Brabazon Hallowes, of Glapwell Hall, Derbys, and *d* 30 Dec 1934, having had:

1a William Brabazon Mather; *b* 7 Oct 1893; Capt 6th Bn Sherwood Foresters; *d* 28 April 1917 of wounds recd in action

2a **Sir (George) Christopher Mather Mather-Jackson, 5th Bt**, JP (Derbys 1939); *b* 12 March 1896; *educ* Wellington; High Sheriff 1951, Lt Sherwood Foresters WW I (wounded, despatches), jt md Sheepbridge Coal and Iron Co, dir Yorks Amalgamated Collieries; *m* 18 Jan 1941 Victoria Emily Ford, dau of Indrick Freyberg, of Mitau, Latvia, and *dsp* 19 Nov 1976

3a **Sir Anthony Henry Mather Mather-Jackson, 6th Bt**, JP (Notts 1938), DL (1942); *b* 9 Nov 1899; *educ* Harrow; Lt Gren Gds (Res of Offrs); *m* 5 April 1923 Evelyn Mary, est dau of Lt-Col Sir Henry Kenyon Stephenson, 1st Bt, DSO (*qv*), and *dspm* 11 Oct 1983, leaving:

1b *Angela Mary [Mrs Angela More O'Ferrall, Sansome's Farm House, Ellen's Green, Rudgwick, Sussex RH12 3AR]; *b* 1925; *m* 1 Feb 1947 Francis Ambrose More O'Ferrall (*d* 1976), 2nd s of Dominic More O'Ferrall, and has:

1c *Susan Angela; *b* 10 Jan 1948; *m* 1974 *3rd Baron Beaverbrook (*qv*) and has issue

2c *Theresa Mary; *b* 8 March 1950; *m* 1975 *Hon Wentworth Peter Ismay Beaumont, est s of 3rd Viscount Allendale (*qv*), and has issue

3c *Emma Rose; *b* 1 April 1956

2b *Elizabeth Georgiana Mather; *m* 4 March 1953, as his 2nd w, 3rd Viscount Cowdray (*qv*) and has issue

3b *Sarah Gillian Mather [Mrs Sarah Morriss, 36 Cambridge Rd, London SW11 4RR]; *m* 30 March 1955 Henry Lester Louis Morriss (*d* 1 April 1963), s of Henry Ernest Morriss, of Banstead Manor, Newmarket, and has had:

1c James Nicholas; *b* 31 Dec 1958; *d* 1993 in Thailand

1c *Annabel Ruth; *b* 13 Jan 1957; *m* 1982 *14th Lord Fairfax of Cameron (*qv*)

2c *Henrietta Sarah; *b* 20 June 1961; *m* 1988 *James W Petit and has:

1d *William; *b* 1989

2d *Henry; *b* 1995

1d *Eliza Mary Lara; *b* 1991

(3) Hamilton Mather; *b* 31 March 1869; *d* 13 Jan 1871

(1) Gertrude Elizabeth Mather; *d* 28 Aug 1920

(2) Edith Sarah Mather; *d* unm 18 June 1944

(3) Frances Blackburne Mather; *m* 30 Sept 1891 Kevitt Rotherham, JP (*d* 26 March 1950), of Leek Wootton Ho, nr Warwick, and *d* 4 Feb 1953, leaving issue

2 William, JP (Cheshire); *b* 19 Nov 1832; *m* 21 June 1861 Therese Isabel (*d* 19 April 1915), dau of Edward Howard, of Liverpool, and *d* 8 Aug 1906, leaving:

(1) William, of Leighton Court, Neston, Cheshire, JP (Birkenhead); *b* 27 Oct 1870; *educ* Cambridge (MA); Lt Notts and Derbys Regt; *m* 29 Sept 1899 Blanche Whitworth (*d* 25 April 1953), dau of George Atkin, JP, of Egerton Park, Rock Ferry, Cheshire, and *d* 23 March 1951, leaving:

1a WILLIAM (Sir), **7th Bt**

1a Pamela Blanche; *b* 15 June 1900

(1) Caroline; *d* unm 6 March 1943

(2) Elizabeth; *m* 4 Jan 1893 Edgar Leicester Billson (*d* 19 Aug 1940), only s of Alfred Billson, MP, and *d* 3 Sept 1940, leaving issue

(3) Miriam Hermine; *m* 17 Sept 1895 Harold Stanley Inman, s of Charles Inman, of Richmond, and *d* 8 May 1934, leaving issue

(4) Maud Isabel; *m* 12 June 1889 John Glynn (*d* 29 Aug 1944) and *d* 19 Feb 1956, leaving issue

(5) Edith Jane; *d* unm

(6) Therese Alice Mary; *d* unm 16 Sept 1958

(7) Enid Ursula; *d* unm 13 Oct 1942

(8) Margery Gladys; *d* unm 19 Dec 1946

3 Thomas Hughes, JP, of The Manor Ho, Birkenhead; *b* 26 Feb 1834; *m* 24 June 1862 Hermine (*d* 29 June 1897), 3rd dau of Daniel Meinertzhagen, and *d* 3 Jan 1930, having had:

(1) Frederick Huth, PC; *b* 26 April 1863; *educ* Harrow and Balliol Coll Oxford (MA 1887); Lt City London, Sheriff London 1918, Dir Bank of England 1892–1921; *m* 11 May 1895 Clara Annabel Caroline (*d* 12 Jan 1944), dau of Sir Mountstuart Elphinstone Grant-Duff, PC, GCSI, CIE, and *d* 3 Dec 1921, leaving:

1a Frederick Huth; *b* 22 April 1896; *educ* Eton and Balliol Coll Oxford; Lt Roy Sussex Regt and RFC; *m* 1st 14 Jan 1920 Helen (*divorce* 1929), dau of Sir Paul Vinogradoff; *m* 2nd 10 May 1940 Frederica Frances (*d* 1975), dau of Duncan Tucker, and *d* 22 Feb 1966, having by his 1st w had:

1b +Patrick Huth; *b* 7 Dec 1922; *educ* Radley; late Capt KRRC

1b *Laura Huth [Mrs William Geddes, The Old Rectory, Rowberrow, Winscombe, Somerset]; *b* 3 Jan 1922; *m* 1st 1943 (*divorce* 1948) Eric Dyson; *m* 2nd 13 Feb 1954 *William Leys Geddes, late Capt 16th/5th Lancers, yr s of John Leys Geddes, of Dumfriesshire, and adopted:

*Mark Leys; *b* 15 Feb 1956

*Julia Leys *b* 7 Aug 1957

1a Konradin Huth; *b* 25 Dec 1898; *m* 26 Nov 1919 Capt Sir Arthur Lawrence Hobhouse, s of Henry Hobhouse, PC (*d* 20 Jan 1965), of Hadspen Ho, Castle Cary, Somerset, and *d* 24 July 1965, leaving issue

2a *Anne Marie Huth; *b* 15 June 1909; *educ* Cheltenham Ladies' Coll and LMH Oxford; *m* 12 Nov 1930 Hon Christopher Evelyn Fremantle (*d* 1978), 4th s of 3rd Baron Cottesloe (*qv*), and had issue

3a *Clare Annabel Huth; *b* 30 Nov 1911; *m* 23 July 1935 Lt-Col Percival Guillaume Louis Gorrerod de Loriol, Count de Loriol, late RA (*d* 27 July 1967), s of G T G de Loriol, of Cologny, Geneva, and has:

1b *Peter Gabriel Nicholas Harle [Count de Loriol, Flat 20, 117 Warwick Rd, London SW5]; *b* 6 Dec 1954

(2) William Rudolph Peter; *b* 8 May, 1867; *d* unm 23 July 1910

(3) Geoffrey Meinertzhagen, TD, JP, DL (Derbys); *b* 9 April 1869; High Sheriff 1924, Hon Brig-Gen, Lt-Col cmdg 6th Bn Sherwood Foresters, Hon Col 46th N Midland Div RCS (TA); *m* 1 March 1893 Jessie Cowper Coles (*d* 3 Sept 1945), dau of Henry Hyndman Laird, of Birkenhead, and *d* 9 Sept 1946, leaving:

1a Geoffrey Laird; *b* 10 Jan 1894; Capt Rifle Bde WW I (despatches); *ka* 9 April 1917

2a Henry Humphrey, OBE (1939), MC, TD, JP, DL (Derbys); *b* 10 March 1895; *educ* Harrow; High Sheriff 1945, Lt-Col cmdg 40th (Foresters) AA Bn RE (TA), served WWs I (despatches) and II; *m* 9 Oct 1924 Georgina (*d* 1974), yst dau of Henry Howard Middleditch, JP, of Derbys, and *d* 7 March 1969, leaving:

1b Thomas Geoffrey Henry; Lt-Col RGJ; *b* 29 March 1926; *educ* Harrow; *m* 16 Jan 1957 *Judith Margaret (*m* 2nd 1981 Colin MacPherson), yr dau of Capt Henry Mangles Denham, CMG, RN, and *d* 1979, leaving:

1c *Catherine Margaret; *b* 7 May 1958; *m* 1983 *Howard William Arthur Palmer, s of W A Palmer, and has:

1d *Thomas Howard; *b* 1988

1d *Laura Margaret; *b* 1984

2d *Emily Rose; *b* 1986

3d *Harriet Bridget; *b* 1991

2c *Victoria Georgina; *b* 16 Sept 1960; *m* 1987 *David Mark Stewart and has issue

3c *Louise Sarah; *b* 11 Feb 1966

4c *Joanna Henrietta (twin); *b* 11 Feb 1966

2b +John Guy Carmichael, JP, DL (Derbys) [John Jackson Esq JP DL, Copse Hill, Osmaston, Derbys DE6 1LU]; *b* 4 April 1931; *educ* Harrow; exec v-chm Clay Cross Co 1974; *m* 1973 *Flora Mary Margaret, dau of Lt-Col William Herbert Oliver, TD, DL, and has:

1c *Georgina Mary; *b* 1974

2c *Ann Margaret; *b* 1976

1b *Ann Georgina Laird [Mrs Colville Wemyss, West Lodge, Upham, Southampton SO31 1JP]; *b* 24 Dec 1928; *m* 16 Aug 1952 *Maj Colville Graham Wemyss, Rifle Bde, only s of Gen Sir Henry Colville Barclay Wemyss, KCB, KBE, DSO, MC, and has:

1c *Henry Graham; *b* 10 March 1956; *educ* Wellington; *m* 1984 *Diana Bridget, dau of R K Selby, and has:

1d *Nicholas Henry; *b* 1988

1d *Eleanor Rose; *b* 1986

1c *(Alice) Caroline; *b* 4 Sept 1953; *m* 1986 *Stephen Walter Hubert Lacey, s of David Lacey, and has:

1d *William David *b* 1990

1d *Alice Megan; *b* 1987

3a Guy Rolf; MC, JP (Derbys); *b* 23 June 1896; *educ* Harrow; Capt Derbys Yeo WW I (despatches, Chev Legn Hon), High Sheriff 1952; *m* 7 April 1937 *Shelagh [Mrs Guy Jackson, St Andrews, Higham, Derbys], dau of A Ignatius Tolhurst, and *d* 21 Feb 1966, leaving:

1b +Geoffrey Laird [Geoffrey Jackson Esq, Plas Newydd, Llanfair DC, Ruthin, Clwyd LL15 2EP]; *b* 17 March 1940; *educ* Ampleforth and RAC Cirencester; *m* 12 July 1963 *Ruth Clare, JP, dau of Desmond Francis Neville Campion, of NZ, and has:

1c +Jonathan Guy Campion; *b* 22 May 1964; *m* 1990 *Mary Rose M, only dau of Col Peter Arkwright, OBE

2c +Charles Desmond Bertram; *b* 24 June 1965

3c +Rupert James; *b* 22 Feb 1968

4c +William David Geoffrey; *b* 1970

2b +Robert Humphrey [Robert Jackson Esq, 14 Dewhurst Rd, London W14 0ET]; *b* 7 April 1943; *educ* Ampleforth and BNC Oxford; *m* 1971 *Margaret Letitia, dau of James Matthew Barrie, of Cornwall, and has:

1c +Guy Nicholas Barrie; *b* 1975

2c +David Geoffrey; *b* 1978

1b *Jane Mary; *b* 28 Jan 1938

1a (Hermine) Joan Carmichael, JP (Derbys); *b* 2 Dec 1900

2a Margaret Beatrice Meinertzhagen; *b* 29 March 1903; memb Chesterfield RDC 1964, Co Commr Derbys Girl Guides 1947–58

3a *(Elizabeth) Bridget Huth [Miss Bridget Jackson, Mount Hall, Llanfair Caereinion, Powys]; *b* 17 May 1909; ATS WW II, ret 1946 with hon rank of Controller

(4) Thomas Hughes; *b* 14 Oct 1872; barrister Lincoln's Inn; *m* 10 Aug 1910 Eileen (*d* 1980), dau of Edward Devery, of Gisborne, NZ, and *d* 11 Feb 1926, leaving:

1a *Hermine Catherine [Mrs George Davies, 1 St Andrews Grove, Lower Hutt, New Zealand]; *m* 10 April 1939 *Lt-Cdr (S) Davies, RNZNVR, s of William Lloyd Davies, and has:

1b *Thomas Hughes Lloyd [Thomas Davies Esq, 20 Foster Cres, Belmont, Lower Hutt, New Zealand]; *b* 1942; *m* 1st 1966 (*divorce*) Anne Mary, dau of N J McHugh; *m* 2nd 1997 *Amy Eleanor, dau of Eric Henry Leask, of Wellington, NZ and by his 1st w had:

1c Guy William Lloyd; *b* 1972; *d* 1994
1c *Caroline Jane Lloyd; *b* 1975
2b *David William Lloyd, VRD; *b* 1947; Lt RNZNVR; *m* 1970 *Alison Margaret, dau of Prof D A Kidd, of Christchurch, NZ, and has:
1c *Huw Alexander; *b* 1982
1c *Bronwen Sara Lloyd; *b* 1973
2c *Megan Kate Lloyd; *b* 1975
3c *Edwina Mair; *b* 1978
1b *Susan Hermine Lloyd [Mrs Wilhelmus Julicher, 1 St Andrews Grove, Lower Hutt, New Zealand]; *b* 1948; *m* 1974 *Wilhelmus Julicher, of Swalmen, Netherlands, and has:
1c *Justin Peter Lloyd; *b* 1979
1c *Nikki Catherine Lloyd; *b* 1977
2a *Barbara Eileen Marian [Mrs Barbara Bourke, 99 Waterloo Rd, Lower Hutt, New Zealand]; *b* 1918; *m* 8 April 1947 Lt Thomas Joseph Bourke, RNZNVR (*d* 1987), s of James Joseph Bourke, and has:
1b *Gerard Thomas Hughes [Gerard Bourke Esq, Ratanui, 92 Waterloo Rd, Lower Hutt, New Zealand]; *b* 1948; *m* *Joy Patricia, dau of R H Matthews, JP, and has:
1c *James Thomas Henry; *b* 1976
1c *Amanda Joy; *b* 1978
2c *Hannah Kathryn; *b* 1980
2b *John Patrick; *b* 1955
(5) Ernest Somerville, CMG, DSO; *b* 26 Dec 1873; Lt-Col Welch Regt WW I (despatches), 3rd Cl Medjidie and 4th Cl Osmanieh; *d* unm 10 March 1943
(6) Guy Rolf; *b* 2 Nov 1875; *d* 3 Oct 1884
(7) Maximilian; *b* 7 May 1877; *m* 1st 1901 Angela Grace Mary, dau of G E Worthington, formerly Ceylon CS; *m* 2nd 1916 Lily, dau of Richard Stubbs, of Birkenhead, and *d* 30 Dec 1924
(8) Roland Octavius, MBE (1918); *b* 26 March 1879; *d* unm 2 Nov 1955
(1) Margaret Hermine; *m* 6 June 1889 (*divorce* 1925) Charles Paxton Markham, JP (*see* MARKHAM, Bt), and *d* 9 Oct 1936
(2) Evelyn Johanna, MBE (1918), JP (Cheshire 1918); *m* 22 April 1899 Charles Maxwell Nicholson (*d* 10 Jan 1929) and *d* 17 Nov 1948
(3) Winifred Barbara Alice; *d* unm 27 July 1949
4 Hamilton; *b* 23 May 1837; *d* 12 Aug 1846
5 Edward Patten; *b* 10 Aug 1842; *m* 23 Aug 1865 Margaret Anne, dau of George Sanderson, of Green Bank, Birkenhead, and *dsp* 17 Jan 1881
6 John Peter; *b* 9 Sept 1843; *m* 22 June 1869 Florence (*d* 30 Dec 1945), dau of William Evans, and *d* 28 Feb 1899, leaving:
(1) John Bertram; *b* 1878; *educ* Harrow and BNC Oxford; Lt 3rd Bn Sherwood Foresters; *m* 27 Jan 1916 Dora Molly, dau of William Pullinger, of Alton, Hants
(1) (Edith) Millicent; *d* unm 8 Aug 1966
(2) Ethel Beatrice; *d* unm
(3) Elizabeth Beryl; *m* 11 Sept 1917 Rev Lawrence Stafford Gresley (*d* 8 Dec 1941), of The Mount, Malton, Yorks (*see* 1970 edn GRESLEY, Bt)
(4) Mary Florence; *m* 3 April 1907 Capt Clement Loftus Long, RN (*d* 6 Feb 1964), 5th son of R-Adml Samuel Long, and had issue
(5) (Margaret) Alice

The 6th Bt's cousin,

Sir William Jackson, 7th Bt; *b* 18 Sept 1902; *educ* Harrow and Balliol Coll Oxford; Maj RAC (Border Regt) TA WW II; *m* 1st 7 April 1927 Lady Ankaret Howard (*d* following a riding accident 9 April 1945), 2nd dau of 10th Earl of Carlisle (*qv*); *m* 2nd 1 Oct 1966 *Ina [Ina Lady Jackson, 8 West View, Gelt Rd, Brampton, Cumbria CA8 1QG], dau of James Leonard Joyce, FRCS, of Reading, Berks, and *d* 1985, leaving by his 1st w:
1 Sir (WILLIAM) THOMAS JACKSON, **8th and present Bt**
1 *Ankaret Tarn [Mrs Timothy Riley, Burbank House, Blencowe, Cumbria]; *b* 10 March 1934; *m* 12 April 1955 *Maj Timothy Richard Riley, 3rd Green Jackets (Rifle Bde), s of Lt-Col Hamlet Lewthwaite Riley DSO, OBE, Rifle Bde, of Enmim, Blencowe, and has:
(1) *Nicola Ankaret Katherine; *b* 11 April 1959
(2) *Antonia Elizabeth Tarn; *b* 1 April 1962; *m* 1992 *Michael Reid and has:
1a *Jennifer Tarn; *b* 1993

JACOBS

Creation: B. (LP, UK) 2 Aug 1997.

THE BARON JACOBS, of Belgravia, City of Westminster (Sir (David) Anthony Jacobs) [The Rt Hon The Lord Jacobs, 9 Nottingham Terrace, London NW1 4QB]; *b* Nov 1931; *educ* Clifton Coll and London U; chm: Nig Securities Gp 1957–72, Tricoville Gp 1961–90 and 1992–94, BSM 1973–90; Lib candidate Watford both 1974 gen elections, Jt-Treas Lib Party 1984–87, V-Pres Social and Lib Dems 1988, Chm Fedl Exec Social and Lib Dems 1988, ktd 1988; FCA; *m* 1954 *Evelyn Felicity Patchett and has a s and dau

Lineage: RIDLEY JACOBS; *m* Ella — and had:

ANTHONY, *cr* a **Baron**

JAFFRAY

Arms: Argent three pallets sable, on a fess cotised gules four mullets or. **Crest:** On a mound in front of two branches of palm in orle vert, a mullet or. **Motto:** *Post nubila Phœbus* ('After clouds the sun').
Creation: Bt. (UK) 8 Oct 1892.

SIR WILLIAM OTHO JAFFRAY, 5TH BT, of Skilts, Co Warwick [Sir William Jaffray Bt, The Manor House, Priors Dean, Petersfield, Hants GU32 1BP]; *b* 1 Nov 1951; *s* f 1953; *educ* Eton; *m* 9 May 1981 (*divorce* 1997) Cynthia Ross Corrington, of Montreal, and has:
1 +NICHOLAS GORDON ALEXANDER; *b* 18 Oct 1982
2 +Jack Henry William; *b* 3 Aug 1987
3 +William Lawrence Paget; *b* 5 March 1990
1 *Alexandra Marina Ross; *b* 18 May 1984

Lineage: ALEXANDER JAFFRAY; Provost of Aberdeen *c* 1652; diarist; alleged ancestor of:

JOHN JAFFRAY, of Stirling; *m* Agnes Wilson and had:

Sir John Jaffray, 1st Bt (UK), so *cr* 8 Oct 1892, JP (Warwicks and Worcs), DL (Warwicks), of Skilts, Warwicks, and Park Grove, Birmingham; *b* 11 Oct 1818; High Sheriff Warwicks 1888; owner *Birmingham Daily Post*, fndr Jaffray Chronic Hosp; *m* 12 Feb 1850 Anna (*d* 20 Feb 1893), dau of William Munton, of Bourne, Lincs, and *d* 4 Jan 1901, leaving:
1 WILLIAM (Sir), **2nd Bt**
2 John Munton, JP, of The Stydd House, Lyndhurst, Hants; *b* 27 Dec 1853; *m* 5 June 1877 Edith Mary Selina (*d* 27 Sept 1906), dau of Rev Thomas Edmund Franklyn, Vicar Old Dalby, Leics, by Selina Elizabeth Hope Vere (*see* LINLITHGOW, M), and *d* 23 June 1906, leaving:
(1) Edith Mabel; *m* 28 Aug 1901 Capt Frederick Claude Hynman-Allenby, CBE, RN (*d* 1 Aug 1934), and *d* 28 Jan 1956, having had issue (*see* ALLENBY, V)
(2) Gwladys Hope; *m* 6 Jan 1909 Capt Henry Roland Milvain, 12th Lancers (*d* 17 Aug 1960), and *d* 18 Nov 1909, having had issue
1 Annie; *m* 14 May 1879 Albert Cay, MBE, JP, of Woodside, Kenilworth, s of Robert Dundas Cay, of Shepperton, Edinburgh (*d* 16 Nov 1921), and *d* 6 April 1941, having had issue

The 1st Bt's er s,

Sir William Jaffray, 2nd Bt, JP, DL (Warwicks); *b* 5 June 1852; *educ* Cambridge (BA); High Sheriff Warwicks 1906; *m* 1st 28 Jan 1885 Mabel Augusta (*d* 29 April 1886), 3rd dau of Sir Francis Edward Scott, 3rd Bt, of Gt Barr, Staffs (*see* 1970 edn), and had:
1 Arthur Douglas Scott; *b* 20 April 1886; *d* 5 June 1886

Sir William *m* 2nd 11 May 1889 Alice Mary (*d* 22 Nov 1917), dau of Francis Galloway, of Hereford, and *d* 27 Nov 1914, leaving:
2 **Sir John Henry Jaffray, 3rd Bt**; *b* 9 Dec 1893; Lt Worcester Yeo; *ka* 23 April 1916
3 WILLIAM EDMUND (Sir), **4th Bt**
4 Hugh Alexander; *b* 9 Sept 1896; *educ* Eton and RMC Sandhurst; Maj 11th Hus RAC WWs I (wounded) and II 1939–43, Mil Sec to Govr-Gen NZ 1943–46, Pres Bishop Auckland C Assoc 1959–66, Jt MFH Brocklesby 1928–32, Cotswold 1932–33, Meynell 1933–37 and Zetland 1937–42; *m* 24 Oct 1924 Ruth (*d* 5 March 1983 aged 83), only dau of Lt-Col Basil Edward Spragge, DSO, of Dumfriesshire, and *d* 6 April 1972, having had:
(1) Michael John; *b* 21 Aug 1925; *educ* Eton; Capt 11th Hus (PAO) WW II 1943–45; *m* 4 Sept 1954 Sheila Aileen, yr dau of Martin Morrison, MC, of Grey Close, Yarm, Yorks; both *k* boating accident 5 June 1958
1 Mabel Violet Mary; *b* 27 Nov 1890; *m* 24 July 1916 Col Sir Charles Richard Henry Wiggin, 3rd Bt (*qv*), and *d* 25 Dec 1961, leaving issue

The 3rd Bt's bro,

Sir William Edmund Jaffray, 4th Bt, JP (Warwicks 1929), DL (Warwicks 1931), TD; *b* 29 July 1895; *educ* Eton and RMC Sandhurst; Col Warwicks Yeo (TA), Lt 1st (King's) Dragoon Gds WW I, 2nd Assist Supt Remount Serv 1918 and WW II 1940–42, Aerodrome Def 1943–44, HG Liaison Mid-West Dist HQ; *m* 1st 3

May 1923 (*divorce* 1936) Synolda Emily (*m* 3rd Guy Argles and *d* 27 June 1975), yr dau of James Augustine Harvey Thursby Pelham, of Upton Cressett, Salop, and formerly w of Sir Robert James Milo Walker, 4th Bt of Sand Hutton (*qv*); *m* 2nd 11 Oct 1950 *Anne [Anne Lady Jaffray, Flat A9 Sloane Avenue Mansions, Sloane Ave, London SW3 3JF], CC Hants 1964–80, only dau of Capt (John) Otho Paget, MC, of Thorpe Satchville Hall, Leics, author *Memories of the Shires* and other books on hunting in Leics, whose forebear Valerian Paget was granted the Manor of Ibstock, Leics, 1469, and formerly w of Sir John Godfrey Worsley-Taylor, 3rd Bt (*see* 1956 dn), and *d* 24 Oct 1953, leaving:

Sir WILLIAM OTHO JAFFRAY, **5th and present Bt**

JAKOBOVITS

Creation: B. (UK, LP) 1988.

THE BARON JAKOBOVITS, of Regent's Park, Greater London (Sir Immanuel Jakobovits) [The Rt Hon The Lord Jakobovits, Jews' College, 44A Albert Rd, London NW4 2SJ]; *b* 8 Feb 1921; *educ* London U, Jews' Coll London and Yeshivah Etz Chaim London (Dipl 1944); Min London synagogues: Brondesbury 1941–44, SE London 1944–47, Gt Synagogue 1947–49; Ch Rabbi Ireland 1949–58; Rabbi 5th Ave Synagogue New York 1958–67; Ch Rabbi Utd Hebrew Congregations Br Cwlth Nations 1967–91, ktd 1981, Emeritus Ch Rabbi 1991–; Hon DD Yeshiva U NY 1975, Fell: UCL 1984–, Assoc Jews' Coll, Hon Fell QMC 1987, Hon DLitt City 1986, DD Lambeth 1987, Hon DD Wales 1993; author: *Jewish Medical Ethics* (1959 NY, 4th edn 1975), *Jewish Law Faces Modern Problems* (1965 NY), *Journal of a Rabbi* (1966 NY, 1967 GB), *The Timely and the Timeless* (1977), *If Only My People: Zionism in My Life* (1984), *Centenary Edition of the Authorised Daily Prayer Book* (ed, 1990); *m* 1949 *Amélie, dau of Rabbi Elie Munk, of Paris, and has:

1 *Julian; *b* 1950; doctor; *m* 1973 *Michelle Tauber and has:
(1) *Nechemya; *b* 1974
(2) *David; *b* 1975
(3) *Nathan; *b* 1977
(4) *Elie; *b* 1982
(5) *Jeremy; *b* 1985
(1) *Penina; *b* 1979
(2) *Tzippora; *b* 1981
(3) *Sima; *b* 1988
2 *Samuel; *b* 1951; Rabbi; *m* 1973 *Ester Gitel Kahana and has:
(1) *Yaacov; *b* 1979
(2) *Shraga Feitel; *b* 1975
(1) *Zipora; *b* 1977
(2) *Yehudit; *b* 1988
1 *Esther; *b* 1953; *m* 1971 *Rabbi Chaim Zundel Pearlman and has:
(1) *Yehuda; *b* 1972
(2) *Eliezer; *b* 1974
(3) *Ephraim; *b* 1978
(4) *Eliyohu; *b* 1982
(5) *Daniel; *b* 1985
(1) *Zipporah; *b* 1976
(2) *Adina; *b* 1980
(3) *Sarah; *b* 1988
2 *Jeanette; *b* 1956; *m* 1977 *Norman David Turner and has:
(1) *Ezriel; *b* 1978
(2) *Yehuda; *b* 1981
(3) *Elie; *b* 1983
(1) *Hadassa; *b* 1979
(2) *Ayala; *b* 1987
(3) *Simcha; *b* 1994
3 *Aviva; *b* 1958; *m* 1978 *Dr Joseph Samuel Adler and has:
(1) *Pierre; *b* 1979
(2) *Nathan; *b* 1980
(3) *Abraham; *b* 1989
(4) *Tobi; *b* 1992
(1) *Ann; *b* 1982
(2) *Tzippora; *b* 1983
(3) *Gila; *b* 1985
4 *Elisheva; *b* 1966; *m* 1985 Sam Eli Homburger and has:
(1) *Meir; *b* 1986
(2) *Pinchos Jacob; *b* 1988
(3) *Yehoshua; *b* 1990
(4) *Isaac Aryeh; *b* 1992
(1) *Avigail Esther; *b* 1987

Lineage: Rabbi JULIUS JAKOBOVITS, of Königsberg; *m* Paula Wrescher and had:

IMMANUEL (Sir), *cr* a **Baron**

JAMES OF HOLLAND PARK

Arms: Vert between two oak trees eradicated or a bend sinister wavy argent, thereon another azure charged with a quill pen argent, the quill or, a chief azure issuant thereon a representation of Southwold Lighthouse proper. **Supporters:** On either side a tabby cat salient guardant proper, wearing a collar vert, edged, buckled and studded or, reposing the exterior paw upon an open book, the pages lettered proper edged or and bound gules, each upright on a set of two closed books edged or, their spines outward, one bound vert lying on top of the other azure. **Motto:** *Gratus erga Deum beatitudine vitae.* ('Showing gratitude to God for the blessings in one's work')
Creation: B. (LP, UK) 1991.

THE BARONESS JAMES OF HOLLAND PARK, of Southwold, Suffolk (Phyllis Dorothy James, OBE (1983), JP (Willesden (1979–82, Inner London (1984)) [The Rt Hon The Baroness James OBE JP, c/o Greene and Heaton Ltd, 37 Goldhawk Rd, London W12 8QQ]; *b* 3 Aug 1920; *educ* Cambridge High Sch for Girls; Admin NHS 1949–68; Pncpl Home Office: Police Dept 1968–72, Criminal Policy Dept 1972–79; Memb: BBC Gen Advsy Cncl 1987–88, Arts Cncl 1988–92 (Chm Lit Advsy Panel 1988–92), Bd Br Cncl 1988–93 (Lit Advsy Ctee 1988–93), Ctee Soc Authors; Chm: Booker Prize Judges 1987, Soc Authors 1984–86, Pres 1997–; Govr BBC 1988–93; Hon DLitt Buckingham 1992, London 1993, Herts 1994, Glasgow 1995; FRSL 1987, FRSA; Assoc Fell Downing Coll Cambridge 1986, Hon Fell St Hilda's Coll Oxford 1996; author (as P D James): *Cover Her Face* (1962), *A Mind to Murder* (1963), *Unnatural Causes* (1967), *Shroud for a Nightingale* (1971), *The Maul and the Peartree* (with T A Critchley, 1971), *An Unsuitable Job for a Woman* (1972), *The Black Tower* (1975), *Death of an Expert Witness* (1977), *Innocent Blood* (1980), *The Skull Beneath the Skin* (1982), *A Taste for Death* (1986), *Devices and Desires* (1989), *The Children of Men* (1992), *Original Sin* (1994), *A Certain Justice* (1997); *m* 1941 Connor Bantry White (*d* 1964) and has:

1 *Clare Bantry; *b* 1942; *m* 1963 *Lyn Flook
2 *Jane Bantry; *b* 1944; *m* 1972 *Peter Duncan McLeod

Lineage: SYDNEY VICTOR JAMES; *m* Dorothy Amelia Hone and had:
PHYLLIS DOROTHY, *cr* a **Baroness**

JANNER OF BRAUNSTONE

Creation: B. (LP, UK) 2 Aug 1997.

THE BARON JANNER OF BRAUNSTONE, of Leicester, Co Leics (Greville Ewan Janner), QC [The Rt Hon The Lord Janner of Braunstone QC, House of Lords, London SW1A 0PW]; *b* 11 July 1928; *educ* Bishop's Coll Sch Canada, St Paul's, Trin Hall Cambridge and Harvard Law Sch; Sgt RA BOAR, War Crimes Investigator; MP (Lab) Leicester NW 1970–74, Leicester W 1974–97, Chm: All-Party Industl Safety Gp 1975–, All-Party Magic Gp 1991–, All-Party Ctee for Homeless and Rootless People (Fndr 1973), Select Ctee Employment 1992–97 (memb 1982–97), V-Chm: All-Party Parly Ctee for Jews in Former Soviet Union 1971, Br-Israel Parly Gp 1983–97 (Jt V-Chm), Br-Spanish Parly Gp 1987–97 (Sec 1986), All-Party Race and Community Gp 1990–92 (Fndr 1990, Pres 1990–97), All-Party Br-Romanian Gp 1990–92, All-Party Parly Ctee for E European Jewry 1990–97, Br-India Parly Gp 1991 (Jt V-Chm 1987–91), Sec All-Party War Crimes Gp 1987–97; Pres: Nat Cncl Soviet Jewry 1979–85, Bd Deputies Br Jews 1979–85, REACH 1982, Cwlth Jewish Cncl 1983–, Jewish Museum 1985–, Bd Dirs Jt Israel Appeal 1985–, World Exec Inter-Party Cncl against Anti-Semitism (Fndr 1990, Pres 1990–97); V-Pres: Assoc for Jewish Youth 1970–, Assoc Jewish Ex-Servicemen, IVS 1983–, Guideposts Tsts 1983–; European V-Pres World Jewish Congress 1984–86 (memb World Exec 1986–, Hon V-Pres 1990–); Partner JSB

Assocs 1984–; Chm JSB Gp 1988–; non-exec dir Ladbroke plc 1986–; Chm and Fndr Maimonides Fndn 1992–; Fndr memb Internat Ctee for Human Rights USSR; Chm Holocaust Educnl Tst 1987–; Dir Jewish Chronicle Newspaper Ltd; Tstee Jewish Chronicle Tst; Visiting Law Fell Lancaster U 1985–88; hon memb Leics NUM 1986–; FIPD (FIPM 1976); Hon PhD Haifa U 1984; Sternberg Award CCU 1985; author of 64 books; *m* 1955 Myra Louise (*d* 9 Dec 1996), dau of Emmanuel Sheink, of Melbourne, Australia, and has:

1 *Daniel; *b* 19–

1 *Marion; *b* 19–

2 *Laura; *b* 19–

Lineage: JOSEPH JANNER, of Barry, Glam; *m* Gertrude — and had:

BARNETT JANNER, BARON JANNER, of City of Leicester (LP, UK), so *cr* 1970; *b* 20 June 1892; *educ* Co Sch Barry and U of Wales; RGA WW I, slr 1919, MP (Lib) Whitechapel and Stepney St George's 1931–35 and (Lab) Leicester W 1945–50 and Leicester NW 1950–70, Pres Bd Deps Br Jews 1955–64, ktd 1960, Pres Br Gp Inter-Parly Union, Chm Parly Anglo-Benelux Gp and Anglo-Israel Parly Gp, Pres Zionist Fedn GB and Ireland, V-Pres Monash Branch Br Legn, Assoc Met Authorities and Assoc Jewish Ex-Servicemen and Women, Chm Ho Lds and H of C Slrs Gp and Parly Water Safety Gp, Pres Leaseholders' Assoc GB, Life Govr Cardiff U, Govr Ben Gurion U The Negev, Freedom Leicester 1971, Cdr Orders Orange Nassau and Leopold II Belgium; *m* 1927 *Elsie Sybil, CBE, JP [The Rt Hon The Lady Janner CBE JP, 45 Morpeth Mansions, Morpeth Terrace, London SW1], V-Pres Magistrates Asoc, Pres Stonham Housing Asssoc, dau of Joseph Cohen, and *d* 1982, leaving:

1 GREVILLE EWAN, *cr* a **Baron**

2 Ruth Joan Gertrude Rahle [The Rt Hon The Lady Morris of Kenwood, 35 Fitzjohns Ave, London NW3 5JY]; *b* 1932; *educ* St Paul's Girls' Sch; slr 1956, Chm DSS Appeals Tbnl, Pres Habonim Dror, Tstee Rowan Educn tst, Dir and Tstee Womankind Worldwide; *m* 1958 *2nd Baron Morris of Kenwood (*qv*) and has issue

JARDINE of Applegirth

Arms: Argent a saltire and chief gules, the latter charged with three mullets of the first, pierced of the second. **Crest:** A spur-rowel of six points argent. **Supporters:** Dexter, a horse at liberty proper; sinister, a man in armour having a scimitar at his side proper. **Motto:** *Cave adsum* ('Beware; I am present'). **Creation:** Bt. (NS) 25 May 1672.

SIR ALEXANDER MAULE JARDINE OF APPLEGIRTH, 12TH BT [Sir Alexander Jardine of Applegirth Bt, Ash House, Thwaites, Cumbria LA18 5HY]; *b* 24 Aug 1947; *s* f 19 April 1986, also as Chief of the Name Jardine; *educ* Gordonstoun; herb farmer, memb Roy Co Archers; *m* 9 Oct 1982 *Mary Beatrice Cross (*see* CROSS, V) and has:

1 +WILLIAM MURRAY JARDINE, Yr. of Applegirth; *b* 4 July 1984

2 +John Alexander Cross; *b* 1991

1 *Kirsty Sybil; *b* 1986

2 *Jean Maule; *b* 1988

Lineage: ALEXANDER JARDINE of Applegirth, Dumfriesshire; *d* by 20 April 1691, leaving:

Sir Alexander Jardine, 1st Bt (NS), of Applegirth, so *cr* 25 May 1672 with remainder to his male heirs whatsoever; *m* by 1675 Lady Margaret Douglas (*m* 2nd Sir David Thoirs), sis of 1st Marquess of Queensberry (*qv*), and *d* between 1691 and 1699, leaving:

1 **Sir Alexander Jardine, 2nd Bt**, of Applegirth; *b* 1675; *dsp* and was *bur* 6 Feb 1699

2 **Sir John Jardine, 3rd Bt**, of Applegirth; *b* 1683; *m* 1st Jan 1712 Catherine, dau of Sir James Lockhart of Carstairs, and had:

(1) **Sir Alexander Jardine, 4th Bt**, of Applegirth; *b* 1712; turned RC, entered mil service abroad, Kt SMO; *d* unm Brussels Dec 1790

(1) Margaret

2 (cont.) **Sir John** m 2nd 1721 Jean (*bapt* 30 Aug 1694; *d* 7 Feb 1762), 5th dau of William Charteris of Brigmuir, and *d* 1737, having had, with four daus:

(2) **Sir William Jardine, 5th Bt**, of Applegirth; *m* Barbara de la Motte, of France, and *d* 17 March 1807, leaving:

1a **Sir Alexander Jardine, 6th Bt**, of Applegirth; *m* by 1799 Janet Dorcas (*d* Madeira 9 Aug 1825), dau of Thomas Maule, gs of Henry Maule, Bp Meath 1744–58, and *d* 1821, leaving, with another s (*d* young):

1b WILLIAM (Sir), **7th Bt**

2b Alexander; *b* 2 Oct 1803; Maj-Gen 75th Regt; *m* 1830 Eliza (*d* 14 March 1870), dau of Charles Curtis, of Cluna, King's Co, Ireland, and *d* 23 June 1869

3b John, of Rockhampton, Qld; *b* 5 March 1807; Capt 1st Royals; *m* 22 Aug 1837 Elizabeth (*d* 1890), dau of Capt William Henry Craig, RN, and *d* 27 Feb 1874, leaving:

1c Frank Lascelles, of Somerset and Lockerbie, N Qld; *b* 28 Aug 1841; *m* 16 Oct 1873 Sana Solia (*d* Sept 1923), n of MALIETOA KING OF SAMOA, and *d* 17 March 1919, leaving:

1d Hugh Herries Cholmondeley Lascelles; *b* Oct 1881; *d* 30 Dec 1935

2d Bertie Bootle Arthur Lascelles; *b* Jan 1884; AIF (wounded) WW I; *m* 10 Aug 1919 Bessie Duffey (*d* 1966), of Brisbane, and *d* 1973, leaving:

1e *Marie Dempster Lascelles; *b* 1920; *m* 19– —

2e *Elizabeth Margaret Lascelles [Mrs Ronald Williamson, 22 Mainsail St, Marlin Waters, Gold Coast, Qld, Australia 4223]; *b* 1927; *m* 19– *Ronald Williamson and has issue

1d Alice Maule Lascelles; *b* June 1878; *m* 1899 Herbert Graham Vidgen and *d* 12 May 1961, leaving issue

2d Elizabeth Hamilton Sana Lascelles; *b* Nov 1895; *m* 30 Dec 1919 Maj Charles Richard Sheldon, AIF (*k* by Japanese while POW 1942), s of Lt-Col Richard Edward Sheldon, Roy Australian Engrs, and had:

1e Cholmondeley Charles Lennox; *k* with his f by Japanese while POW 1942

1e *Betty Pamela [Mrs Thomas Ivy, c/o 18 Gotha St, Cleveland, Brisbane, Queensland, Australia 4163]; *b* 1920; *m* 1942 *Thomas Ivy and has issue

2c Alexander William; *b* 1843; MInstCE; *m* 1883 Charlotte Elizabeth (*dsp* 1890), dau of Archibald Mosman, and *d* 20 March 1920

3c John Robert; *b* 1847; *m* 1883 Elizabeth Catherine, 2nd dau of Hon Thomas Lodge Murray-Prior, MLC and Postmaster-Gen Qld, and *d* 21 Sept 1911, leaving:

1d John Lodge Murray; *b* 1888; *ka* WW I

2d Francis Alexander Lascelles; *b* 1893; served WW I (wounded); *m* 15 Oct 1924 Madge Dorothy Ellen, dau of Archibald Hugh Blackman, of Brisbane, and had:

1e +Murray Hugh Lascelles; *b* 23 July 1925; *m* 1950 *Alma Glenise Byrne and has:

1f *Jan Frances Lascelles; *b* 1952

2f *Mary Elizabeth; *b* 1958

4c Charles Lennox; *b* 1855; *d* unm 9 Sept 1908

1c Elizabeth Jane; *m* 19 July 1875 Col Arthur Bootle-Wilbraham (*see* SKELMERSDALE, B) and *d* 2 Feb 1925, leaving issue

2c Katherine Maule; *m* 15 July 1871 Hugh Miles Milman and *d* 1947, leaving issue (*see* MILMAN, Bt)

1b Helen; *m* 1827 Rev C S Hassells (*d* Dec 1878), of Fox Earth, Staffs, and *d* 9 Jan 1848

Sir ALEXANDER's est s,

Sir William Jardine, 7th Bt, of Jardine Hall, Dumfriesshire; *b* 13 Feb 1800; Commr salmon industries 1860; *m* 1st 28 June 1820 Janes Home (*d* 2 March 1871), dau of Daniel Lizars, of Edinburgh, and had, with four daus:

1 ALEXANDER (Sir), **8th Bt**

2 William; *b* 23 Jan 1834; Capt RN; *m* 16 June 1864 Louisa Archer (*m* 2nd 9 Dec 1876 Brig-Gen Horatio Reginald Meads, CB (*d* 11 Dec 1933) and *d* 17 June 1934), 2nd dau of George Cockburn Harvey, of Halifax, NS, and *d* 28 Oct 1869, leaving:

(1) William; *b* 6 Oct 1867; *m* 1890 Margaret Helen, dau of Dr George J Bucknall, of San Francisco, and *d* 12 May 1912, having had:

1a Dorothy Helen; *d* 1905

3 Charles John (Rev); *b* 18 May 1839; Rector Horsington, Lincs, 1894–1907; *m* 3 Nov 1870 Martha (*d* 1918), est dau of Edward Twining, MRCS, of Walthamstow, and *d* 1917, leaving:

(1) Edward William Ratcliff; *b* 10 March 1872; *m* 20 Sept 1910 May Janet, dau of Capt J Hubby, of California, and had:

1a *Dorothea Twining; *b* 1911

2a Marie Isobel; *d* unm

(2) Eric Hamilton; *b* 17 Oct 1874; *m* 18 June 1910 Alma Anderson, of New York

(3) Peter St John; *b* 1 Feb 1879; *m* 20 Feb 1919 Monica Maud, only child of Capt Leonard Head, 30th Regt, and had:

1a +Piers Leonard; *b* 1921

(1) Margaret Dorcas Mary; *m* 16 Feb 1901 Frank Fullerton Dyas, of Bolton, Ontario, and had:

1a Maxwell Wing; *b* 1902

(2) Muriel Lucy; *m* 1 Nov 1915 Stanley Clarke Parsloe (*d* 30 Oct 1932), of Hungerford, Berks, and had issue

Sir William *m* 2nd 18 Nov 1871 Hyacinthe (*m* 2nd 22 Aug 1876 Sir Joseph Dalton Hooker, OM, GCSI, CB (*d* 10 Dec 1911), Dir Kew Gdns, and *d* 8 Dec 1921), only dau of Rev William Samuel Symonds, Rector Pendock, Worcs, and *d* 9 Nov 1874

His est s,

Sir Alexander Jardine, 8th Bt, JP, DL, of Jardine Hall; *b* 10 Feb 1829; *educ* Edinburgh and Woolwich; *m* 28 Dec 1861 Henrietta (*d* 13 June 1925), 3rd dau of William Younger (*see* YOUNGER, Bt), and *d* 14 Jan 1893, leaving:

1 **Sir William Jardine, 9th Bt**, JP (Dumfriesshire), of Jardine Hall; *b* 11 June 1865; *educ* Fettes; Lt 1st Vol Bn Cheshire Regt and Calcutta Light Horse Boer War 1899–1902, Maj 3rd Bn KOSB, memb Roy Co Archers; *m* 7 Nov 1906 Eda

Georgina May (*d* 30 Dec 1960), 4th dau of Henry Johnston Younger (*see* YOUNGER, Bt), and *dsp* 13 Dec 1915
2 ALEXANDER (Sir), **10th Bt**
1 Isabel Edith; *m* 7 April 1910 Robert Young Pickering, of Conheath, Dumfriesshire, and *d* his widow 3 March 1933
2 Jane Gertrude; *m* 4 Oct 1905 Francis Claud Grey, s of Capt F L Grey, 96th Regt, and *d* 9 Sept 1919
3 Henrietta; *m* 17 April 1895 Maj Harold James Clifford Stanton, MVO (*d* 22 Feb 1927), KOSB, and *d* 5 July 1928, leaving issue
4 Janet Madeleine; *d* unm 14 April 1939
5 Catherine Dorcas Maule; *m* 20 July 1897 Maj James Rea (*d* 14 Oct 1937), KOSB, of Dundrum House, Dundrum, Co Down, and *d* 2 May 1948, leaving issue
6 Sibyl Mary; *m* 7 Jan 1896 Harry Scott (*d* 1935), s of W H Scott of Nunfield, Dumfries, and *d* 27 Sept 1947, leaving issue
7 (Margaret) Lindsay; *m* 8 April 1902 Sir George Douglas Dixie, 12th Bt (*d* 25 Dec 1948; *see* 1970 edn), and *d* 19 June 1973, leaving issue

Sir WILLIAM's bro,
Sir Alexander Jardine, 10th Bt; *b* 1 Aug 1868; *m* 10 Feb 1914 Winifred Mary Hamilton (*d* 12 Nov 1954), yst dau of Maj Thomas Young, of Lincluden House, Dumfriesshire, and *d* 27 March 1942, leaving:
1 WILLIAM EDWARD (Sir), **11th Bt**
1 *Christian Maule Jackson [Mrs Charles Anderson, Ulva Ferry, Isle of Mull, Argyllshire]; *m* 15 Oct 1940 *Lt-Col Charles Patrick Anderson, Argyll and Sutherland Highrs, s of Lt-Col William Herbert Anderson, VC, and has:
(1) *Charles Adair [Charles Anderson Esq, Ravensheugh, Selkirk]; *b* 19 Oct 1946; *educ* Trin Coll Glenalmond; *m* 1973 *Patience, dau of Joseph Crewdson Howard, and has:
1a *Lewis Adair; *b* 1978
2a *Ralph Oliver; *b* 1985
1a *Alice Selby; *b* 1976
(2) *Roderick William [Roderick Anderson Esq, Blantyre, Lenox, Mass., USA]; *b* 17 June 1950; *educ* Trin Coll Glenalmond; *m* 1983 *Evelyne Corbier
(1) *Andrena Christian [Mrs Alastair Scott-Elliot, Shorelands, Kippen, Stirlingshire]; *b* 1943; *m* 1 Nov 1969 *Maj Scott-Elliot, Argyll and Sutherland Highrs, only s of Maj-Gen James Scott-Elliot, CB, CBE, DSO, and has:
1a *Robin James; *b* 1970
2a *Simon Charles; *b* 1972
(2) *Araminta Patricia [Mrs Peter J Hall, 35 Elk Point, Durango, CO, USA]; *b* 1950 (twin); *m* 1985 *Peter John Hall

Sir ALEXANDER'S only s,
Sir William Edward Jardine, 11th Bt, OBE (1966), TD, JP (Dumfriesshire 1963); *b* 15 April 1917; Maj KOSB WW II (wounded), Lt-Col cmdg 4th/5th KOSB (TA) 1963–67, Brevet-Col 1967, memb Roy Co Archers; *m* 2 June 1944 *Ann Graham [Ann Lady Jardine of Applegirth, Little Dyke, Dalton, Dumfriesshire DG11 1DU], yr dau of Lt-Col Claud Archibald Scott Maitland, DSO, Gordon Highrs, of Dundrennan and Cumstoun, Stewartry of Kirkcudbright, and *d* 19 April 1986, leaving:
1 Sir ALEXANDER MAULE JARDINE, **12th and present Bt**
2 +William [William Jardine Esq, Driftway Cottage, Dullingham Ley, Newmarket, Suffolk]; *b* 29 April 1952; *educ* Sedbergh

JARDINE of Godalming

Arms: Gules a saltire argent charged in the centre point with a lotus flower proper, on a chief of the second six mullets of the first. **Crest:** A mullet of six points pierced gules between two palm branches proper. **Motto:** *Cave adsum* ('Beware; I am here'). **Creation:** Bt. (UK) 20 Jan 1916.

SIR ANDREW COLIN DOUGLAS JARDINE, 5TH BT, of Godalming, Co Surrey [Sir Andrew Jardine Bt, 99 Addison Road, London W14 8DD]; *b* 30 Nov 1955; *s f* 1982; *educ* Charterhouse, Reading U (BSc Hons) and RAC Cirencester; RGJ 1975–78, with C T Bowring and Co 1979–81 and Henderson Admin Gp 1981–92, dir Gartmore Investment Tst Management Ltd 1992–93, with Strutt and Parker 1996–, memb: Securities Inst and Roy Co Archers 1990–; *m* 11 Oct 1997 *Dr Claire Vyvien, only dau of Dr William Griffith, of The White House, Lyth Hill, Salop

Lineage: WILLIAM JARDINE, JP, of Dunstable, Beds; *b* Closeburn, Dumfriesshire; *m* Jane, dau of Robert Sharpe, of Ecclefechan, and had:
Sir John Jardine, 1st Bt (UK), so *cr* 20 Jan 1916, KCIE (1897), JP (Surrey), of Godalming, Surrey; *b* 27 Sept 1844; *educ* Christ's Coll Cambridge (Chllr's Medal for English poem 1864); Bombay CS 1864, Registrar High Ct Bombay 1873, Law Offr Supreme Govr 1877, Judicial Commr Burma 1878, Pres: Burma Sch Bd 1881, Asylum Workers' Assoc and Bombay Roy Asiatic Soc, Ch Sec Bombay Govt 1885, Puisne Judge High Ct Bombay 1885–97 (Ch Justice 1895), Dean Arts, Dean Law and V-Chllr Bombay U, Hon LLD Aberdeen 1906, MP (Lib) Roxburghshire 1906–18; *m* 27 Nov 1880 Minnie Dunbar (*d* 8 July 1941), dau of Jabez Hogg, MRCS, and *d* 26 April 1919, leaving:
1 **Sir John Eric Birdwood Jardine, 2nd Bt**; *b* 30 Sept 1890; *educ* Corpus Christi Coll Oxford (BA); Maj 5th Queen's Roy Regt (TA) Mesopotamia WW I (despatches); *d* unm 24 March 1924
2 COLIN ARTHUR (Sir), **3rd Bt**
3 Lionel Westropp, CIE (1939); *b* 15 Feb 1895; *educ* Charterhouse and Wadham Coll Oxford; ICS, Capt 1st/5th Bn Queen's Roy Regt Mesopotamia WW I (severely wounded, despatches), Political Offr Iraq 1919–21 (medal and clasp), NW Frontier India 1930–31 (medal with clasp), Revenue Commr NW Frontier Province India 1938–43 and 1946–47, Resident Baroda and Gujerat States 1943–44 (ret 1948); *m* 6 Nov 1922 Marjorie Mildred, only dau of Maj Richard John Woods, OBE, of Englefield Green, and *d* 1980, leaving:
(1) +John Alexander; *b* 28 Dec 1939; *educ* Charterhouse; *m* 19 June 1971 *Catherine, dau of André Trentesaux, of Lille, France, and has:
1a *Emily; *b* 1979
2a *Alice; *b* 1980
(1) *Barbara Ann [Mrs Neville Cooper, 5 Scarsdale Villas, London W8 6PT]; *b* 16 Dec 1925; *m* 11 Jan 1964 *Neville John Cooper, only s of John Edgar Cooper, of Buckland Grange, Ryde, IOW, and has:
1a *Susan Ann; *b* 14 Oct 1964; *m* 20 July 1991 *Michael Hedegaard and has:
1b *Nicholas Alexander; *b* 15 May 1997
1b *Natasha Monica; *b* 31 May 1995
2a *Henrietta Jane; *b* 25 July 1967; *m* 1 July 1995 *Neil Southard
(2) *Jean Alison; *b* 19 Feb 1928; *m* 9 Aug 1949 *Frederick Disney Rivers Currie (*see* CURRIE, Bt) and has issue
4 Kenneth William Seymour (Rev Canon); *b* 23 June 1899; *educ* Charterhouse and Corpus Christi Coll Oxford (BA 1921, MA 1926); 2nd Lt RFA WW I 1918–19, CMS missionary Pakistan and India 1938–48, Canon Lahore Cathedral 1954; *m* 15 April 1926 Katherine Frances (*d* 8 Nov 1932), er dau of William Cranswick Noad, of Mount Tabor House, Perth, and *d* 25 Oct 1960, having had:
(1) +David Eric Cranswick (Rev) [The Rev David Jardine, 81 Fraser Rd, Sheffield S8 0JH]; *b* 17 Oct 1930; *educ* Bryanston and Corpus Christi Coll Oxford (BA 1953, MA 1958, DipTh 1954); ordained 1955, Vicar Christ Church Mitcham 1965–72, and St Saviour's Iford 1972–89, Rector Ch Ch Smannell with St George Enham Alamein 1989–96; *m* 25 June 1955 Elsie Vera Susan (*d* 4 March 1996), only dau of Herbert Shanks, and has:
1a +Charles Kenneth Herbert; *b* 16 Aug 1960; *m* 26 Aug 1988 *Jacqueline Hannah and has:
1b +Ruari John; *b* 18 March 1994
1b *Catriona Louise; *b* 5 Jan 1992
1a *Katharine Shelagh Margaret; *b* 1 June 1957; *m* 29 Dec 1984 *Angus G Grandfield and has:
1b *Colin Douglas Hugh; *b* 29 March 1988
2b *Alexander David George; *b* 8 May 1992
3b *Francis Gregory Charles; *b* 14 March 1994
1a *Ruth Katriona; *b* 28 March 1986
2a *Rachel Heather Agnes [Mrs David Schoon, 81 Fraser Rd, Sheffield S8 0JH]; *b* 17 Jan 1965; *m* 23 Sept 1995 *David Julian Schoon
(2) Julian Francis; *b* 17 Oct 1932; *educ* Bryanston; E Surrey Regt 1951–53, HAC 1953–55, chartered loss adjuster with Toplis & Harding; *d* 30 Dec 1984
(1) Heather; *b* 11 Feb 1929; *m* 6 Nov 1954 *Francis Robert Howard Almond, 2nd s of Sir James Almond, and *d* 28 Sept 1958, leaving issue
5 Geoffrey David; *b* 10 June 1901; *educ* Charterhouse; Lt 5th Bn Queen's Roy Regt, Lt Indian Engrs, POW Burma WW II, ARSM; *d* unm 10 July 1959
6 Raymund Angus; *b* 1 June 1903; *educ* Charterhouse; with Hong Kong and Shanghai Bank; *d* unm 15 March 1959

Sir JOHN's bro,
Sir Colin Arthur Jardine, 3rd Bt, CB (1940), DSO (1914) and bar (1918), MC, DL (Hants 1954); *b* 24 Sept 1892; *educ* Charterhouse and RMA Woolwich; Bde-Maj 7th Inf Bde (Razmak) 1926–27, DAMS War Office 1930–34, GSO(1) TA 1939, served WWs I (three times wounded, despatches four times) and II (despatches twice), Mil Sec to C-in-C BEF 1930–40, Maj-Gen RA, Dep Govr Gibraltar 1941, Dir Army Welfare 1943, Govr Charterhouse, chm bd: Church Army, Friends of the Poor, Family Welfare Assoc and RUKBA, memb Church Assembly; *m* 1 May 1919 Jean Evelyn Livesey, only child of Maj-Gen Sir William Andrew Liddell, KCMG, CB, and *d* 24 Sept 1957, leaving:
1 IAN LIDDELL (Sir), **4th Bt**
1 *Elizabeth [Mrs John Sharpley, Field House, Fulbrook, Oxon]; *b* 14 May 1921; *m* 4 May 1946 *F/Lt John Edward Sharpley, RAF, BM, BCh, only s of Dr Christopher Wilfred Sharpley, and has had:
(1) *Mark Alastair; *b* 1947
(2) *Oliver John; *b* 1949
(1) Sarah Marilyn; *b* 1952; *d* 1992
2 *Gillian Fiona [Mrs Ian Mackenzie, Nether Kingshill, Kingswells, Aberdeenshire]; *b* 18 Dec 1930; *m* 25 Sept 1954 Ian Grant Mackenzie, MD, FRCS (Id 1986), only s of Dr Arthur Henderson Mackenzie, CSI, CIE, and has:
(1) *Alistair Grant; *b* 1955
(2) *Angus Colin; *b* 1957

(3) *Andrew Kenneth; *b* 1958

Sir COLIN's only s,

Sir Ian Liddell Jardine, 4th Bt, OBE (1966), MC (1945); *b* 13 Oct 1923; *educ* Charterhouse; Brig Coldstream Gds WW II, ADC to HM THE QUEEN 1976–78; *m* 25 Aug 1948 *Priscilla Daphne Scott-Phillips [Priscilla Lady Jardine, Teal House, Cheriton, Hants SO24 OPY], yst dau of Douglas Middleton Parnham Scott-Phillips, of Ayrshire, and *d* 25 Nov 1982, leaving:

1 Sir ANDREW COLIN DOUGLAS JARDINE, **5th and present Bt**

2 +MICHAEL IAN CHRISTOPHER [Michael Jardine Esq, 12 Graham Ave, London W13 9TQ]; *b* 4 Oct 1958; heir presumptive; *educ* Charterhouse; *m* 1982 *(Maria) Milky Pineda and has:

(1) +Oliver Michael Ian; *b* 20 Feb 1983

(2) +Adrian Douglas Francis; *b* 1986

1 *Harriet Anne; *b* 18 Aug 1949; *m* 1972 *Anthony Malcolm Douglas Palmer, RGJ, and has:

(1) *Edward Anthony Douglas; *b* 1975

(2) *Henry Arthur Douglas; *b* 1982

(1) *Alice Georgina; *b* 1976

2 *Jean Margaret; *b* 2 March 1951; *m* 1984 (*divorce* 198–) (James) Andrew Gardiner Baird (*see* BAIRD, Bt, of Saughton Hall) and has issue

JAUNCEY OF TULLICHETTLE

Arms: Or three chevronels engrailed gules, in chief two lions rampant and respectant of the second. **Crest:** An arm embowed in armour argent, holding in the gauntlet or a battle-axe in fess, also argent, the forearm environed of a wreath of laurel vert. **Supporters:** Dexter, a lion gules gorged of a collar or, charged with a chevronel engrailed gules; sinister, a buck proper, attired, collared and chained or, the collar charged with a chevronel engrailed gules. **Motto:** *Virtute majorum* ('By the courage of our ancestors') . **Creation:** B. (LP, UK) 1988.

THE BARON JAUNCEY OF TULLICHETTLE, of Comrie, in the District of Perth and Kinross (Charles Eliot Jauncey, PC (1988)) [The Rt Hon The Lord Jauncey of Tullichettle PC, Tullichettle, Comrie, Perthshire PH6 2HU]; *b* 8 May 1925; *educ* Radley, Ch Ch Oxford (MA 1953) and Glasgow U (LLB 1949); Sub-Lt RNVR WW II; advocate 1949, Standing Jr Counsel Admlty 1954, QC Scotland 1963; Kintyre Pursuivant of Arms 1955–71, Hon Sheriff-Substitute Perthshire 1962, Sheriff Pncpl Fife and Kinross 1971–74; Judge Courts Appeal Jersey and Guernsey 1972–79, Ld of Session 1979–88, Ld Appeal in Ordinary 1988–96; Memb: Roy Co Archers 1951, Historic Bldgs Cncl Scotland 1971–92; Hon Student Ch Ch Oxford 1990; *m* 1st 1948 (*divorce* 1969) Jean (*m* 2nd 8 Aug 1969 10th Lord Polwarth, *qv*), only dau of Adml Sir Angus Edward Malise Bontine Cunninghame Graham of Gartmore, KBE, CB, of Ardoch, Cardross, Dunbartonshire, and has:

1 *James Malise Dundas [The Hon James Jauncey, Altchroskie, Enochdhu, Perthshire PH10 7PB]; *b* 1949; *educ* Radley and Aberdeen U (LLB); author: *The Albatross Conspiracy* (1991), *The Mapmaker* (1994) and *The Crystal Keeper* (1996), Chm Soc Authors Scotland 1995–, memb Scottish Arts Cncl Literature Ctee 1997–; *m* 1st 1980 (*divorce* 1986) Caroline Elizabeth, dau of Charles Ede, of The Garden House, Hollington, Berks, and has:

(1) *Sophie Jean Elizabeth; *b* 1980

(2) *Eleanor Fleur; *b* 1983

1 (cont.) The Hon James Jauncey *m* 2nd 1988 *Sarah Jacqueline, yr dau of Lt-Col (David Ludovic) Peter Lindsay, DSO (see CRAWFORD and BALCARRES, E), and by her has :

(1) *Jake Ludovic Dundas; *b* 1991

(1) *Anna Maria; *b* 1989

2 *Simon Helias [The Hon Simon Jauncey, Upper Ballunie, Kettins, Coupar Angus, Perthshire]; *b* 1953; *educ* Radley and Bristol U (BA); *m* 1979 *Aurora, dau of Juan de Jesus Castaneda, of Colombia, and has:

(1) *Jeremy Cunninghame; *b* 1984

(2) *Thomas Charles; *b* 1987

1 *Arabella Bridget Rachel [The Hon Mrs Maudslay, 84 Muncaster Rd, London SW11 6NU]; *b* 1965; *m* 1989 *James H B Maudslay, yr s of Sir (James) Rennie Maudslay, GCVO MBE, and has:

(1) *Angus Charles Rennie; *b* 1993

(2) *Henry Joseph Dundas; *b* 26 April 1996

THE BARON JAUNCEY OF TULLICHETTLE *m* 2nd 1973 (*divorce* 1977) Elizabeth, widow of Maj John Ballingal, MC, and dau of Capt R H V Sivewright, DSC, RN; *m* 3rd 1977 *(Sarah) Camilla, yst dau of Lt-Col Charles Frederick Cathcart, DSO (*see* CATHCART, E), and by her has:

1 *Cressida Jane; *b* 1981

Lineage: JOHN JAUNCEY, of Fenny Stratford, Bucks; *m* Mary, dau of John Dewberry, and *d* 1698, leaving:

JOHN JAUNCEY; *b* 1658; *educ* Westminster, St Mary Hall Oxford and Clare Hall Cambridge; Rector Shenley, Berks; *m* Mary Cressy and *d* 1702, leaving:

JOHN JAUNCEY; Sec to Bp London; *m* Mary Holt and had:

Rev FYGE JAUNCEY; *b* 1736; *educ* Charterhouse, St John's Coll Cambridge and Hertford Coll Oxford; Rector Castle Camp, Cambs; *m* 8 Jan 1767 Helen, only dau of Rev John White, and *d* 1812, having had, with two yr sons:

JOHN JAUNCEY; *b* 1767; *educ* Charterhouse; Capt 69th Foot, Maj 10th Foot, served Walcheren Expdn and Peninsular War; *m* Jane (*m* 2nd R-Adml Alexander Shippard), dau of Adml Sir John Knight, KCB, and *d* 1796, leaving, with a yr s:

HENRY FYGE JAUNCEY; *b* 1789; Capt 50th Foot Peninsular War (wounded); *m* 20 Jan 1817 Arabella (*m* 2nd Richard Dawkins), dau of Rev Richard Chaloner Cobbe, and *d* 1821, leaving:

1 HENRY JOHN

2 Alexander Sidney Godolphin; Capt 11th Foot; had:

(1) Edith Frances Arabella; *m* 6 Feb 1871 Col Sir Alexander Campbell, 6th Bt, of Aberuchill (*qv*), and *d* 29 Jan 1884, leaving issue

The er s,

HENRY JOHN JAUNCEY; *b* 1827; Lt 99th (Lanarks) Regt, Capt 67th (Wilts) Regt; *m* 10 Aug 1848 Sophia, dau of Rev Henry Hubbard, and *d* 19 Jan 1899, leaving, with a yr s and a dau:

HENRY HASTINGS JAUNCEY; *b* 1851; Cdr RN; *m* 30 July 1885 Edith Blanche, yst dau of Col John Henry Pringle, Coldstream Gds, and *d* 1890, leaving, with an er s (*d* young) and a dau:

JOHN HENRY JAUNCEY, DSO and bar, of Tullichettle, Comrie, Perthshire; *b* 14 April 1889; *educ* HMS *Britannia*; Capt RN, served WWs I and II; *m* 4 Aug 1923 Muriel Charlie, est dau of Adml Sir Charles Dundas, 28th of Dundas, KCMG, and *d* 25 Sept 1958, leaving an only child:

CHARLES ELIOT, *cr* a **Baron**

JAY OF PADDINGTON

Arms: Quarterly 1st and 4th, vert a portcullis or, 2nd and 3rd, azure a lymphad with an anchor at its prow and masted or, the sail set argent and pennants flying gules, overall a fess or, to the sinister thereof a grassy mount with a hurst of oak trees and issuing therefrom passant to the dexter a wolf proper. **Motto:** *Malo laborare quam languere* ('I had rather labour than be idle'). **Creation:** B. (LP, UK) 1992.

THE BARONESS JAY OF PADDINGTON, of Paddington in the City of Westminster (Margaret Ann Callaghan) [The Rt Hon The Baroness Jay of Paddington, 44 Blomfield Rd, London W9 2PF; Elm Bank, Glandore, Co Cork, Ireland]; *b* 18 Nov 1939; *educ* Blackheath High Sch and Somerville Coll Oxford (BA); BBC TV: reporter *Panorama* 1981–86, reporter and producer *This Week* 1986–88; memb: Parkside Health Authority 1986– (V-Chm 1990–), NHS Centl R & D Ctee 1991–, Min for Health AIDS Action Gp 1991–, Min State Health and Dep Leader Ho Lds 1997–98, Ld Privy Seal, Leader Ho Lds and Min for Women 1998–; Dir Nat AIDS Tst 1988–92; Patron ReAction Tst 1991–, Memb: Cncl London Lighthouse, Management Bd Positively Women; author: *Battered—The Story of Child Abuse* (jt author, 1986); *m* 1st 1961 (*divorce* 1986) Hon Peter Jay, s of Baron Jay (LP, so *cr* 1987; Douglas Patrick Thomas Jay, Pres BOT 1964–67; *d* 1996), and has:

1 *Patrick James Peter; *b* 1971; *educ* Winchester and SOAS London U; mkt maker IG Index

1 *Tamsin Margaret; *b* 1965; *educ* St Paul's Girls' Sch and Bristol U; *m* 1989 (*divorce* 19–) Simon Anthony Raikes (*see* HANSON, Bt)

2 *Alice Katharine; *b* 1968; *educ* Bedales and Pembroke Coll Oxford

BARONESS JAY *m* 2nd 1994 *Prof Michael William Adler

Lineage: *See* CALLAGHAN OF CARDIFF, B

JEFFREYS

Arms: Ermine a lion rampant and a canton sable. **Crest:** A demi-lion or, holding in the dexter paw a laurel wreath proper. **Supporters:** On either side a lion regardant sable, crowned with an ancient crown or. **Motto:** *Pob dawn to Dduw* ('Every gift from God'). **Creation:** B. (UK) 12 July 1952.

THE 3RD BARON JEFFREYS, of Burkham, Co Southampton (Christopher Henry Mark Jeffreys) [The Rt Hon The Lord Jeffreys, Bottom Farm, Eaton, Lincs NG32 1ET]; *b* 22 May 1957; *s f* 1986; *educ* Eton; futures broker GNI 1985–90, stockbroker Raphael Zorn Hemsley 1992–; *m* 1985 *Anne Elisabeth, dau of Antoine Denarie and Mrs Derek Harry Johnson, of Boden Hall, Scholar Green, Cheshire, and has:

1 +ARTHUR MARK HENRY; *b* 18 Feb 1989

1 *Alice Mary; *b* 1986

Lineage: JOHN JEFFREYS, of Acton, Denbighs; Circuit Judge N Wales; *m* Margaret (*m* 2nd Sir Thomas Ireland, of Bewsay, Lancs; *m* 3rd Sir Thomas Trevor), dau of William Lloyd, of Haighton, Flintshire, and *d* 19 May 1622, leaving:

JOHN JEFFREYS, of Acton; *b* 1608; *m* Margaret, dau of Thomas Ireland, of Bewsay, and *d* 1691, having had:

1 John, of Acton; *m* Dorothy, dau of Sir Griffith Williams, 1st Bt (*see* WILLIAMS-BULKELEY, Bt), and *d* 1670, leaving:

(1) Griffith (Sir), of Acton; *m* 1683 Dorothy (*d* July 1729), dau of Robert Pleydell, of Ampney, Glos, and *d* March 1694, having had issue

2 Edward

3 Thomas (Sir), of Alicante, Spain; ktd 1686; *m* Laura Vaubin, of Alicante

4 Charles

5 William

6 Sir GEORGE JEFFREYS, 1st Bt, and (1st) BARON JEFFREYS OF WEM, Co Salop, so *cr* 7 Nov 1681 and 16 May 1685 respectively (both E), of Bulstrode, Hedgerley, Bucks, PC (1683–Feb 1688/9), KC (1677); *b c* 1648; *educ* Shrewsbury, St Paul's and Westminster and Trin Coll Cambridge; barrister Inner Temple, Common Serjeant 1671, ktd 1677, Slr-Gen to Duke of York (later JAMES II) 1677, Recorder London 1678–80, Ld Ch Justice King's Bench 1683–Feb 1688/9, Ld Chllr 1685–88, notorious (though unjustly) for his savage sentencing in the aftermath of Monmouth's Rebellion 1685, Ld Lt Bucks and Salop 1687–89; *m* 1st 22 May 1667 Sarah (*bur* 18 Feb 1677/8), dau of Rev Thomas Neesham, and had, with other issue:

(1) JOHN JEFFREYS, 2nd and last BARON JEFFREYS OF WEM; *b* 16 July 1673; *m* 17 July 1688 Lady Charlotte Herbert (*m* 2nd 28 Aug 1703 1st Viscount Windsor; *see* PLYMOUTH, E), only dau and heir of 7th Earl of Pembroke and (4th Earl of) Montgomery (*qv*), and *dspm* May 1702, when the btcy and Barony expired, leaving:

1a Henrietta Louisa; *m* 14 July 1720 1st Earl of Pomfret (*see* HESKETH, B)

(1) Margaret; *m* Sir Thomas Stringer, of Durance, Middx

(2) Sarah; *m* George Harnage, Col Marines, 3rd s of Edward Harnage, of Belswardyne

6 (cont.) The 1st BARON *m* 2nd *c* 6 June 1679, as her 2nd husb, Anne, dau of Sir Thomas Bludworth, Ld Mayor London 1665–66 and widow of Sir John Jones, of Fonmon, Glam (*see* BOOTHBY, Bt), and *d* Tower of London 18 April 1689 (imprisoned there 1688 after WILLIAM III's landing), having by her had further issue

7 James (Rev); *b* 1649; DD, Preb Canterbury, Rector Carmarthen 1686–89; *m* 18 April 1686 Margaret (*d* Sept 1723), 2nd dau and coheir of Sir William Wray, 1st Bt, of Ashby, Lincs, and *d* 4 Sept 1689, leaving an only surv s:

(1) John, of Lincoln's Inn Fields; *b* 1690; *educ* Oxford (MA); *m* 1711 Elizabeth (*d* 1741), dau of Edward Darell, of Putney, and *d* 20 July 1741, having had:

1a John (Rev); *b* 10 Aug 1718; DD, Canon Resident St Paul's and Ch Ch Oxford, Rector Gt Berkhamsted 1756–98; *m* 2 June 1761 Elizabeth (*d* 16 March 1805), 2nd dau of Robert Darell, of Richmond, Surrey, and *d* 20 Nov 1798, leaving:

1b John (Rev); *b* 9 Jan 1771; DD, MA; Rector Barnes, Surrey; Chaplain to PRINCE OF WALES (later GEORGE IV); *m* 21 Jan 1796 Charlotte (*d* 19 May 1858), dau of Capt Richard Byron, Coldstream Gds, and *d* 6 June 1840, having had:

1c John Edward; *b* 25 Dec 1801; *d* unm 22 June 1824

2c Frederick Thomas; *b* 26 March 1803; Lt RN; *d* unm 26 Feb 1824

3c Marmaduke Robert, JP (Wilts), of Marchmont, Hemel Hempstead, Herts; *b* 4 May 1807; *m* 25 Jan 1840 Anna Maria (*d* 21 Oct 1877), dau of John Benett, MP, of Pyt House, Wilts, and *d* 10 Nov 1898, having had issue

4c Edmund Richard

5c Henry Anthony (Rev); *b* 28 May 1810; Sr Student Ch Ch Oxford (MA), RD and Vicar Hawkhurst, Kent, Hon Canon Canterbury; *d* unm 23 June 1898

6c Arthur; *b* 1 Oct 1811; Lt RN; *m* 17 Feb 1841 Sarah (*d* 28 March 1856), dau of Robert Campbell, Duntroon, Argyll, and *d* 13 Sept 1861, having had:

1d John

2d Arthur Frederick, PC, JP, DL, of Burkham, Hants; *b* 7 April 1848; *educ* Ch Ch Oxford (BA 1872); CA Hants, barrister, MP (C) N Hants 1887–1906, Dep Chm H of C 1902–05, Parly Sec Local Govt Bd 1905; *m* 15 May 1877 Amy Constantia (*d* 28 Oct 1932), est dau of George J Fenwick, DL, of Pelton, Co Durham, and *d* 14 Feb 1906, leaving:

1e GEORGE DARELL, **1st Baron**

1e Winifred Madeline; *m* 1st 6 June 1912 Maj Chandos Leigh, DSO (*ka* 25 Aug 1914, *see* LEIGH, B); *m* 2nd 7 Oct 1925 Sir Christopher Boyd William Magnay, 3rd Bt, MC (*d* 4 Sept 1960; *see* 1959 edn), and *dsp* 28 Sept 1966

2e Sibyl Constance, JP (Hants 1942); *m* 2 June 1908 Capt G Charles Sholto MacLeod, Black Watch (Roy Highrs) (*d* of wounds recd in action 9 May 1915), and had issue

3e Eleanor Sophia Campbell; *m* 2 July 1914 Brig Harold Vincent Spencer Charrington, DSO, MC, 12th Roy Lancers (*d* 8 June 1965), only s of Spencer Charrington, of Winchfield House, Hants, and had issue

3d Robert, *b* 15 Sept 1851; *d* unm 13 March 1871

1d Sophia; *b* 15 Sept 1851; *d* in infancy

1c Charlotte Elizabeth; *b* 4 Nov 1796; *d* unm 10 March 1873

2c Elizabeth Mary; *b* 12 May 1798; *m* 24 April 1827 John Forbes (*d* 9 Nov 1830), of Ham, Surrey, and *d* 22 Jan 1872, leaving issue

3c Caroline; *b* 20 Aug 1799; *m* 30 Dec 1828 Adml Sir John Burnett Dundas, 4th and last Bt (*d* 2 Sept 1868), and *d* 20 Aug 1871

4c Harriet Margaret; *b* 16 Oct 1800; *m* 21 Aug 1834 William Henry Deedes, of London (*d* 18 Dec 1859), and *d* 21 Feb 1877, leaving issue

5c Lucy Anne; *b* 24 Oct 1804; *m* 3 July 1832 Rev William Henry Cymric Lloyd (*d* 3 Jan 1881), Rector Norbury, Staffs, and *d* 14 Feb 1843, leaving issue

6c Frances; *b* 17 Jan 1806; *m* 21 Aug 1833 Thomas Bambury Lenon (*d* 3 April 1888), of London, and *d* 28 Nov 1884, leaving issue

7c Julia; *b* 1 Nov 1813; *m* 9 Sept 1841 Thomas Byron, of Coulsdon, Surrey (*d* 7 April 1863), and *d* 8 Feb 1899, leaving issue

1 Margaret; *m* Robert Betton, of Shrewsbury

ARTHUR FREDERICK JEFFREYS' est s,

GEORGE DARELL JEFFREYS, **1st Baron Jeffreys**, of Burkham, Co Southampton (UK), so *cr* 12 July 1952, KCB (1932, CB 1918), KCVO (1924), CMG, JP, DL; *b* 8 March 1878; *educ* Eton and RMC Sandhurst; Nile Expdn 1898, Battle of Khartoum (Queen's Medal and Khedive's Medal with clasp), Boer War 1900–02 (Queen's and King's Medals, five Clasp), cmded Gds Depot 1911–14, WW I (severely wounded 1916), cmdg 2nd Bn Gren Gds 1915, T/Brig-Gen cmdg Bde 1916–17, T/Maj-Gen cmdg 19th Div 1917–19 and Light Div BAOR 1919, Maj-Gen 1919, GOC London Dist 1920–24, cmdg 43rd (Wessex) Div and Area 1926–30, Lt-Gen 1930, GOC-in-C S Cmd India 1932–36, Gen 1935, ADC Gen to TM EDWARD VIII and GEORGE VI 1936–38 (ret 1938), Col Gren Gds April 1952–60, chm Basingstoke Bench 1925–32 and 1936–52, CC Hants 1926–32 and 1937–60, chm Hants Co CD Ctee 1938–54, MP (C) Petersfield 1941–52, CA 1941–60, Organiser Hants HG 1940, Chm Hants and IoW TAA 1938–48, Col Roy Hants Regt 1945–48, Hon Col 583 (Hants) HAA Regt RA (late 48th SL Regt) 1938–48, Kt St Olaf Norway 1st Cl, St Stanislaus Russia 2nd Cl with swords, Rising Sun Japan 2nd Cl, Grand Offr Leopold Belgium, Croix de Guerre Belgium and France, Grand Cross Crown Romania, Cdr Legn Honour France and Crown Belgium; *m* 28 Feb 1905 Dorothy (*d* 21 May 1953), dau of John Postle Heseltine and widow of Viscount Cantelupe (*see* DE LA WARR, E), and *d* 19 Dec 1960, having had:

1 Christopher John Darell, MVO 5th Cl (1936); *b* 30 Dec 1907; *educ* Eton and RMC Sandhurst; Capt Gren Gds, ADC to C-in-C S Cmd India 1933–35, PA to CIGS and C-in-C BEF 1939–40; *m* 23 April 1931 Lady Rosemary Beatrice Agar, yst dau of 4th Earl of Normanton (*qv*), and was *ka* Dunkirk 28 May 1940, leaving:

(1) MARK GEORGE CHRISTOPHER, **2nd Baron**

(2) +George Christian Darell [The Hon George Jeffreys, Manor Farm Barn, Alkerton, Oxon OX15 6NL]; *b* 2 Dec 1939; *educ* Eton and RMA Sandhurst; granted rank of baron's yr s 25 Sept 1961, Capt Gren Gds, dir Seccombe, Marshall and Campion plc 1976; *m* 3 April 1967 *(Karen) Elizabeth Mary, er dau of Col Hugo Meynell (*see* HALIFAX, E), and has:

1a *Zara Serena; *b* 23 June 1972

2a *Susannah Elizabeth; *b* 9 Oct 1975

The 1st BARON's gs,

MARK GEORGE CHRISTOPHER JEFFREYS, **2nd Baron Jeffreys**; Ld Manor Burkham, Hants; *b* 1932; *educ* Eton and RMA Sandhurst; Maj Gren Gds (ret 1961); *m* 1st 24 July 1956 (*divorce* 1967) Sarah Annabelle Mary (*m* 2nd 1968 (*divorce* 1997) Alexander Edward Pennant Clarke) [Mrs Sarah Clarke, Foxhill House, Hawling, Glos GL54 5SX], only dau of Maj Henry Claude Lyon Garnett, late RHG, and had:

1 CHRISTOPHER HENRY MARK JEFFREYS, **3rd and present Baron Jeffreys**

2 +(Alexander) Charles Darell; *b* 14 May 1959; *educ* Harrow; *m* 1991 *Sonamara, MA, dau of Barry Sainsbury, of London

1 *Laura; *b* 13 Aug 1961

2 *Rose Amanda; *b* 4 Dec 1962; *m* 1993 *Dominic C Prince, er s of John Prince, of Chipping Warden, Oxon

The **2nd Baron** *m* 2nd 14 March 1967 *Anne-Louise (Annie-Lou), yr dau of His Honour Judge Sir (William) Shirley Worthington-Evans, 2nd Bt (*see* 1970 edn), and had by her:

3 *Sophie Louise [The Hon Mrs Scruton, Sunday Hill Farm, Brinkworth, Wilts SN15 5AS]; *b* 17 June 1972; *m* Dec 1996, as his 2nd w, *Prof Roger Scruton

The **2nd Baron** *m* 3rd 18 Nov 1981 *Suzanne (*m* 3rd 1990 Geoffrey C Martin), dau of James Stead, of Trowswell, Goudhurst, Kent, and formerly w of — Gilbert, and *d* 12 Feb 1986

JEGER

Creation: B. (LP, UK) 1979.

THE BARONESS JEGER, of St Pancras in Greater London (Lena May Chivers) [The Rt Hon The Baroness Jeger, 9 Cumberland Terr, Regent's Park, London NW1 4HS]; *b* 19 Nov 1915; *educ* Southgate County Sch Middx and Birkbeck Coll London U (BA); Civ Serv: Customs and Excise, Min Info and FO 1936–49; Br Embassy Moscow 1947; staff *Manchester Guardian* London 1951–54 and 1961; memb: St Pancras Borough Cncl 1945–59, LCC for Holborn and St Pancras S 1952–55; MP (Lab): Holborn and St Pancras S 1953–59 and 1964–74 and Camden Holborn and St Pancras S 1974–79; memb: Lab NEC 1968–80 (V-Chm 1978–79, Chm 1980), Chm's Panel H of C 1971, Chm Lab Party 1979–80; UK Del UN Status of Women Commn 1967; memb: Consultative Assembly Cncl Europe 1969–71, WEU 1969–71; *m* 1948 Dr Santo Wayburn Jeger, MP (*d* 1953)

Lineage: CHARLES CHIVERS; *m* Alice — and had:

LENA MAY, *cr* a **Baroness**

JEHANGIR

Arms: Azure a sun in splendour within an orle of mullets or, on a canton argent a rose gules slipped proper in bend surmounting a lotus flower in bend sinister, also slipped proper. **Crest:** Upon a mount a column, thereon flames of fire all proper. **Mottoes:** 1 (above the crest) Burning I shine, 2 (below the arms) My life is His who gave it. **Creation:** Bt. (UK) 16 July 1908.

SIR HIRJI JEHANGIR, 3RD BT, of Malabar Hill, Bombay [Sir Hirji Jehangir Bt, Readymoney House, 49 Nepean Sea Rd, Bombay, 400 036 India; 24 Kensington Ct Gdns, Kensington Ct Place, London W8 5QF]; *b* 1 Nov 1915; *s f* 1962; *educ* St Xavier's Sch Bombay and Magdalene Coll Cambridge; dir Coorla Spinning and Weaving Mill Bombay, chm Jehangir Art Gallery Bombay and United Asia Publicns, Bombay Pres Parsi Public Sch Soc, chm Cowasji Jehangir Charitable Tst; *m* 10 Aug 1952 *Jinoo, er dau of Kakushroo H Cama, of Bombay, and has:

1 +JEHANGIR; *b* 23 Nov 1953; *m* 1988 *Jasmine, dau of Beji Billimoria, and has:

(1) +Cowasji; *b* 28 March 1990

2 +Ardeshir; *b* 1 Oct 1956

Lineage: HIRJEE JEHANGIR READYMONEY; migrated from Persia to Bombay 1726; ancestor of:

Sir COWASJEE JEHANGIR, CSI, of Readymoney House, Malabar Hill, Bombay; *b c* 1812, banker and philanthropist; *d* 1878; his n and adopted s (who took his unc's name):

Sir Cowasjee Jehangir, 1st Bt (UK), so *cr* 16 July 1908; JP (Bombay); *b* 8 June 1853; shipowner and pioneer of trade between India and China, banker to HEIC, Fell Bombay U, delegate Parsee Matrimonial Ct, mill owner, Bombay landowner, philanthropist, sr memb Parsi-Panchayel; ktd 1895; special Act of India's Supreme Legislative Cncl 22 Sept 1911 ordained that his successors assume name of 1st Bt; *m* 21 March 1876 Dhunbai (Kaisar-i-Hind Gold Medal), dau of Ardeshir Hormusjee Wadia, of Lowjee Castle, Bombay, and *d* 27 July 1934, leaving:

1 COWASJEE JEHANGIR (Sir), **2nd Bt**

1 Cooverbai; *b* 30 Jan 1877; *m* Oct 1917 K A Ghaswalla, BA, barrister, of Poona

2 Meherbai; Kaisar-i-Hind Silver Medal; *b* 26 Nov 1879; *m* March 1918 A P Sabavala, BA, barrister, of Malabar Hill, and had:

(1) Sharokh Ardeshir; *b* 7 Dec 1918; jnlst; *m* 10 Feb 1947 *Roshan Jehangir Batliwalla and had issue

(2) Jehangir Ardeshir; *b* 23 Aug 1922; artist; *m* 31 Dec 1948 *Shirin Jehangir Dastur and had issue

The 1st Bt's s,

Sir Cowasjee Jehangir, 2nd Bt, GBE (1944), KCIE (1927), JP (Bombay); *b* 16 Feb 1879; *educ* St Xavier's and St John's Coll Cambridge (BA 1900); memb Bombay Corp 1904–21, chm Standing Ctee 1914–15, memb Bombay Improvement Tst, Pres Bombay Municpl Corp 1919–20, Hon Sec War Loan Ctee 1917–18, non-official memb Legislative Cncl 1917–18, actg memb Bombay Govt in charge Revenue Dept 1921–22, full memb in charge Gen Dept 1923–28, MLA (Centl) for Bombay 1930–47, chm Cowasjee Jehangir and Co, Pres Parsi Punchayet; *m* 22 Feb 1911 Hilla Hormarji, MBE, Kaisar-i-Hind Gold Medal with bar, dau of Hormarji Wadia and gdau of Sir Jamsetjee Jejeebhoy, 2nd Bt (*qv*), and *d* 17 Oct 1962, having had:

1 Jehangir; *b* 15 Nov 1911; *m* 9 April 1938 Mehru, dau of Sir Dhunjibhoy Bomanjee, and *d* following an accident in London 23 Oct 1944

2 Sir HIRJI JEHANGIR, **3rd and present Bt**

1 *Sylla Cowasjee; *b* 8 April 1914; *m* June 1946 *Richard Holmes, of Kensington

JEJEEBHOY

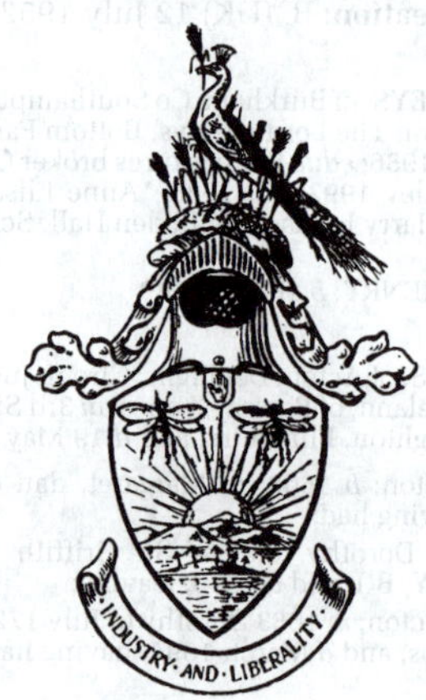

Arms: Azure a sun rising above a representation of the Ghats in base, and in chief two bees volant, all proper. **Crest:** A mount vert, thereon amidst wheat a peacock, in the beak an ear of wheat, all proper. **Motto:** Industry and liberality. **Creation:** Bt. (UK) 9 Aug 1857.

SIR JAMSETJEE JEJEEBHOY, 7TH BT, of Bombay [Sir Jamsetjee Jejeebhoy Bt, Beaulieu, 95 Worli Seaface, Bombay 400025, India]; *b* 19 April 1913; *s* cousin 1968; *educ* St Xavier's Coll Bombay (BA 1936); chm Sir Jamsetjee Jejeebhoy Charity Funds, Sir Jamsetjee Jejeebhoy Parsee Benevolent Instn, Bombay Panjrapole, Tstee Sir Jamsetjee Jejeebhoy Sch of Arts, Zoroastrian Bldg Fund, Byramjee Jeejeebhoy Parsee Charitable Instn, Deccan Coll Poona; *m* 3 Oct 1943 *Shirin, dau of Jehangir Hormusjee Cama, of Worli Seaface, and has:

1 +RUSTOMJEE; *b* 16 Nov 1957; *educ* Bombay U (Bcom, LLM); *m* 1984 *Delara, dau of Jal N Bhaisa, and has:

(1) +Jehangir; *b* 20 Jan 1986

1 *Ayesha; *b* 5 June 1952

Lineage: Sir Jamsetjee Jejeebhoy, 1st Bt (UK), so *cr* 6 Aug 1857 (by special Act of Indian Legislative Cncl all subsequent Bts were to take the 1st Bt's name), JP (Bombay Presidency); *b* 15 July 1783; Parsee merchant, ktd 1842, Freeman City London; *m* 1 March 1803 Awabai Framji (*d* 24 Feb 1870), dau of Framjee Nusserwanjee, Bombay merchant, and *d* 14 April 1859, having had:

1 CURSETJEE (Sir), **2nd Bt**

2 Rustomjee Jamsetjee; JP (Bombay Presidency); *b* 23 Jan 1824; Freeman City London, memb Govr's Cncl; *m* 24 Jan 1836 Sonabai Muncherjee and *d* 13 April 1872, leaving issue

3 Sorabjee Jamsetjee; *b* 22 Oct 1825; JP (Bombay Presidency); *m* 24 Jan 1836 Buchoobai Merwanjee, dau of Merwanjee Jejeebhoy, Bombay merchant, and had issue

1 Pirojbai Jamsetjee; *b* 2 Jan 1834; *m* 6 June 1846 Shapoorjee Dhunjeebhoy (*d* 1896) and *d* 11 May 1906

Sir JAMSETJEE's est s,

Sir CURSETJEE later JAMSETJEE JEJEEBHOY, **2nd Bt** (forename changed under provisions of Legislative Cncl Act; *see above*); *b* 9 Oct 1811; *m* 1st Deenbai (*d* 21 July 1833), dau of Dinshaw Cooverjee, Bombay merchant, and *d* 11 July 1877, having had:

1 Buchoobai Cursetjee; *b* 7 July 1831; *m* 25 Jan 1836 Jejeebhoy Dhunjeebhoy and *d* 6 June 1872

Sir JAMSETJEE *m* 2nd 29 Nov 1835 Ruttonbai Cursetjee and by her had:

2 Sir MANOCKJEE CURSETJEE later JAMSETJEE JEJEEBHOY, **3rd Bt**, CSI, JP; *b* 3 March 1851; memb Govr's Cncl; *m* 8 Feb 1869 Jerbai, dau of Shapoorjee Dhunjeebhoy, and *d* 17 July 1898, having had:

(1) Cursetjee; *b* 11 Nov 1878; *d* unm 28 July 1893

(1) Dinbai; *b* 1874; *m* 3 March 1894 Sir Dinshaw Manekjee (formerly Jejeebhoy Framjee) Petit, 2nd Bt (*qv*), and *d* 1965, leaving issue

(2) Cooverbai; *b* 1881; *m* 1901 Kavasha Sorabjee Powalla (*d* 1965) and *d* March 1968, leaving issue

3 Sir COWASJEE CURSETJEE later JAMSETJEE JEJEEBHOY, **4th Bt**, JP; *b* 29 Nov 1852; Fell Bombay U, head Parsee Community Bombay, chm Parsi Panchyat and Collector Bombay City; *m* 1869 Goolbai Rustamjee Wadia (*d* 28 May, 1926), and *d* 17 June 1908, having had:

(1) Sir RUSTOMJEE later JAMSETJEE JEJEEBHOY, **5th Bt**, KCSI; *b* 6 March 1878; Pres Parsee Community Bombay, memb Municipal Corp and Dep Pres Ind Legve Assembly 1921; *m* 22 Jan 1906 Sereenbai Jalbhoy Ardaser Sett (*d* 22 June 1939) and *d* 6 Feb 1931, leaving:

1a Sir COWASJEE later JAMSETJEE JEJEEBHOY, **6th Bt**; *b* 10 May 1909; *educ* Cathedral and John Connon High Sch Bombay and Gonville and Caius Coll Cambridge (BA 1933), JP and Hon Presidency Magistrate, co dir, memb Bombay Muncpl Corp; *m* 21 Jan 1951 Soonoo, dau of Hormusji Comissariat, of Bombay, and *d* 24 Sept 1968, leaving:

1b *Shireen; *b* 20 Jan 1952

2b *Deanna; *b* 15 Dec 1953

3b *Geeta; *b* 3 March 1955

1a Ratanbai; *b* 22 Aug 1911; *m* 5 Dec 1936 Naval Kaikushroo Dubash, MBE, ch pilot instructor Bombay Flying Club (*d* 4 Aug 1943), s of Kaikushroo N Dunbash, and had:

1b *Russi; *b* 1 Sept 1940

2b *Jimmy; *b* 16 July 1943

2a *Aimai [Mrs Nozer Pandole, Silverene, 63 Worli Swea Face, Bombay, India]; *b* 31 March 1918; *m* 1942 Nozer Erach D Pandole (*d* 1983)

(1) Soonabai; *b* 20 Oct 1873; *m* 21 March 1896 Manekjee Shapoorjee Vacha (*d* 1943) and had issue

(2) Virbaijee; *b* 22 May 1875; *m* 29 May 1903 Jehangi Dinshaw Davar, barrister, Actg Puisne Judge Bombay High Court, and *d* April 1940, leaving issue

(3) Jerbai; *b* 30 Aug 1881; *m* 1911 Dhunjibhoy Framjee Batlivala (*d* Sept 1934) and *d* July 1930

4 Jamsetjee Cursetjee, JP (Bombay); *b* 31 Aug 1860; Hon Magistrate Bombay, memb Bombay Muncpl Corp,Tstee Parsee Punchayet Funds; *m* 1882 Awabai (*d* 29 Dec 1926), dau of Shapoorjee Dhunjeebhoy, and *d* 6 May 1916, leaving:

(1) Rustamjee; *b* 1 May 1884; *m* 10 May 1908 Soonabai Rustamjee Byramjee Jejeebhoy (*d* 24 Jan 1968) and *d* 12 July 1947, having had:

1a Sir MANECKJEE RUSTOMJEE later JAMSETJEE JEJEEBHOY, **7th and present Bt**

2a Cowasjee Rustamjee; *b* 31 Aug 1914; *educ* St Xavier's (BA); *d* unm 27 Nov 1943

(2) Cursetjee; *b* 29 Sept 1897; *m* 4 April 1937 Meherbai Feroze Jehangir and *d* 1982, leaving:

1a *Pirojbai; *b* 22 July 1938; *m* 1988 *Burjor Sohrabji Cooper, of Bombay

(1) Jerbai; *b* 1883; *m* 8 March 1908 Sir Byramjee Jejeebhoy, JP (*d* 1 April 1946), s of Rustomjee Byramjee Jejeebhoy, and had issue

(2) Cursetbai; *b* 1887; *m* 24 Sept 1911 Jejeebhoy Rustomjee Byramjee Jejeebhoy and had:

1a Jamsetjee; *b* 10 Oct 1912; *educ* Bombay U (BA); *m* 1957 *Dinoo Coverjee Jussawalla and had:

1b *Jeroo; *b* 16 July 1962

2a *Rustomjee; *b* Nov 1924; *educ* Bombay U (BA); *m* 1977 *Nargeth Sapal Loriee and has:

1b *Villoo; *b* 1978

1 Jeevunbai Cursetjee; *b* 11 Oct 1840; *m* 4 June 1854 Homjee Cursetjee Dady and *d* 1 Dec 1855

2 Dhunbaijee Cursetjee; *b* 26 Sept1842; *m* 1848 Dinshawjee Jamsetjee Parakh (*d* 9 Oct 1901) and *d* 6 July 1922, leaving issue

3 Jerbai Cursetjee; *b* 28 Dec 1843; *m* 12 Feb 1857 Nowrojee Rustomjee Arda and *d* 1870, leaving issue

4 Goolbai Cursetjee; *b* 26 Feb 1845; *m* 19 April 1855 Nesserwanjee Sorabjee and *d* 31 Aug 1865

5 Heerabai Cursetjee; *b* 2 Aug 1846; *m* 17 Feb 1857 Cawasjee Dady Ghoga and *d* 4 Jan 1868, leaving issue

6 Soonabai Cursetjee; *b* 30 July 1847; *m* 1st 19 April 1855 Nowrojee Jewajee Manekjee (*d* 1897); *m* 2nd 1899 Furdoonjee Jamsetjee Parakh, JP (*d* 1925), of Bombay, and *d* 18 May 1936

7 Jaijee Cursetjee; *b* 4 Aug 1848; *m* 25 May 1864 Heerjeebhoy Nowrojee Burjorjee (*d* 1909), of Bombay, and *d* 26 Dec 1936, leaving issue

8 Chandanbai Cursetjee; *b* 23 Oct 1855; *m* 1st 1869 Homjee Cursetjee Dady (*d* 1884); *m* 2nd 1887 Hormarjee Ardasar Hormarjee (*d* 1894) and *d* Sept 1924, having had issue

9 Avabai; *b* 10 Oct 1861; *m* 28 April 1880 Rustomjee Byramjee Jejeebhoy, JP (Bombay) (*d* 1922), memb Municipal Corp Bombay, and *d* 17 April 1930, having had issue

10 Navajbai; *b* 1863; *m* 1881 Firozeshah Pestanjee Jehangir (*d* 1942), of Poona, and *d* Nov 1943

JELLICOE

Arms: Argent three bars wavy azure, over all a whale hauriant sable. **Crest:** Out of a naval crown or a demi-wolf azure. **Supporters:** On either side a sea griffin or. **Motto:** *Sui memores merendo* ('Mindful of oneself in deserving'). **Creations:** V. (UK) 15 Jan 1918 (Jellicoe), E. and V. (UK) 29 Jan 1925.

THE 2ND EARL JELLICOE, Viscount Jellicoe, of Scapa, Orkney, and **Viscount Brocas** of Southampton, Co Southampton (George Patrick John Rushworth Jellicoe, DSO (1942), MC (1944), PC (1963)) [The Rt Hon The Earl Jellicoe DSO MC PC, 97 Onslow Sq, London SW7 3LT; Tidcombe Manor, Tidcombe, Wilts]; *b* 4 April 1918 (HM KING GEORGE V stood sponsor); *s* f 1935; *educ* Winchester and Trin Coll Cambridge; Page of Honour to HM GEORGE VI Coronation 1937; WW II: served Coldstream Gds, SAS and Special Boat Regt Middle East (Lt-Col, wounded, despatches thrice), Legn Hon, Croix de Guerre, Greek MC, Dip Serv: Washington 1948–51, 1st Sec Brussels 1951–53, Dep Sec-Gen Bagdad Pact Iraq 1956, Ld-in-Waiting Feb–June 1961, Jt Parly Sec Min Housing and Local Govt June 1961–July 1962, Min State Home Off July 1962–Oct 1963, 1st Ld Admlty Oct 1963–April 1964, MOD RN April–Oct 1964, Dep Ldr Oppn Ho Lds 1967–70, Ld Privy Seal and Ldr Ho Lds 1970–73, dir: S G Warburg & Co, Sotheby Hldgs, Smiths Industries, Tate & Lyle (chm 1978–82) and Morgan Crucible 1974–87, Pres London Chamber Commerce and Industry 1979–82, MRC 1982, BOTB 1983, Review PTA 1982–83, Pres Parly and Scientific Ctee 1980–83, Chllr Southampton U to 1996, FRS 1990; *m* 1st 23 March 1944 (*divorce*) Patricia Christine, Cross of Merit 1st Cl SMO Malta (1959), only dau of Jeremiah O'Kane, of Vancouver, and has:

1 +PATRICK JOHN BERNARD, *Viscount Brocas* [Viscount Brocas, 5 South View, Tiverton, Devon]; *b* 29 Aug 1950; *educ* Eton; *m* 1971 (*divorce* 1981) Geraldine Ann FitzGerald Jackson and has:

(1) +Justin Amadeus; *b* 1970

(2) +Jack; *b* 19–

2 +Nicholas Charles Joseph John [The Hon Nicholas Jellicoe, Via Gradoli 74, Rome 00189, Italy]; *b* 23 March 1953; *educ* Eton; *m* 1982 *Patricia, dau of Count Arturo Ruiz de Castilla, of Madrid and Lima, Peru, and has:

(1) *Zoë Anaya; *b* 1988

(2) *Francesca; *b* 19–

1 *Alexandra Patricia Gwendoline [The Lady Alexandra Wilson, 24 Highbury Place, London N5]; *b* 17 Dec 1944; *m* 21 May 1970 *(Edward) Philip Wilson (*see* WILSON, Bt, of Eshton Hall)

2 *Zara Lison Josephine [The Lady Zara Jellicoe Baughart, 1991 N Harrison Rd, E Lansing, MI 48823, USA]; *b* 24 Sept 1948; *m* 1st 1983 (*divorce* 1987) Bruce Gilliam, s of Alvin Bruce Gilliam, of Houston, Texas; *m* 2nd 1997 *Richard Paul Baughart, s of Elwyn Baughart, of Lansing

The 2nd EARL *m* 2nd *Philippa Ann, dau of Philip Dunne, of Gatley Park, Herefs, and formerly w of Christopher Charles Cyprian Bridge, and by her has:

3 +John Philip; *b* 27 June 1966

3 *Emma Rose; *b* 30 Nov 1967

4 *Daisy; *b* 24 June 1970

Lineage: SAMUEL JELLICOE, of Uplands, Fareham, Hants; *b* 15 Oct 1788; *m* 14 Oct 1819 Jane Elizabeth, 1st dau of Sir James Whalley-Smythe-Gardiner, 2nd Bt (who was descended from the BROCASes of Beaurepaire, Hants, so called from Beaurepaire, Normandy, of which the BROCASes had once been lords), of Roche Court, Fareham, Hants, by his 2nd w Jane, est dau of Rev Robert Master, DD, Rector Croston, Lancs, by Elizabeth, dau and coheir of John Whalley, of Blackburn, and had a 2nd s:

JOHN HENRY JELLICOE, of Northfield, Ryde, IoW; *b* 1825; Cdre and dir Roy Mail Steam Packet Co; *m* 12 May 1857 Lucy Henrietta (*d* 17 Oct 1916), dau of Dr John Rushworth Keele, of Southampton, by Constantia, dau of Adml Philip Patton, and *d* 7 Sept 1914, having had:

1 Frederick Gilbert Gardiner (Rev); *b* 24 Feb 1858; *educ* New Coll Oxford (MA 1883); Curate Alverstoke Hants 1891–1902, Rector Freemantle Southampton 1902–15 and New Alresford 1915–22; *m* 16 June 1903 Alice Caroline, est surv dau of R-Adml James Henry Bushnell, and *d* 29 July 1927

2 JOHN RUSHWORTH, **1st Earl**

3 Herbert Whalley; *b* 5 Nov 1861; *d* 1885

4 Edmund Henry; *b* 10 Sept 1875; *d* 1904

1 Emily Grace Lizon; *d* unm 27 May 1948

2 Edith Lucy; *d* unm 2 June 1959

The 2nd son,

JOHN RUSHWORTH JELLICOE, **1st Earl Jellicoe**, so *cr* 29 June 1925, as also VISCOUNT BROCAS, of Southampton, Co Southampton, and earlier 15 Jan 1918 VISCOUNT JELLICOE, of Scapa, Co Orkney (all UK), with remainder to the heirs male of his body, and in default of such issue, to his est dau and the heirs male of her body, with the like remainder in default of such issue to every other dau successively by primogeniture, and to the heirs male of their bodies, receiving in addition the thanks of Parl and a grant of £50,000 (some £1,380,000 in late-1990s terms, GCB (1915, KCB 1911, CB 1900), OM (1916), GCVO (1916, KCVO 1907, CVO 1906), DL (IoW and Hants); *b* 5 Dec 1859; RN: joined 1872, served Egypt 1882 (medal and star), China 1900 (severely wounded, medal), ADC to HM EDWARD VII 1906–07, R-Adml Atlantic Fleet 1907–08, Controller Navy and 3rd Sea Ld Admlty 1908–10, V-Adml cmdg Atlantic Fleet 1910–11 and 2nd Div Home Fleet 1911–12, 2nd Sea Ld 1912–14, WW I: C-in-C Grand Fleet 1914–16, 1st Sea Ld 1916–17, Ch Naval Staff 1917, Adml of the Fleet 1919, Govr-Gen and C-in-C NZ 1920–24, Hon Col 6th NZ Mtd Rifles 1923, Pres King's Roll Nat Cncl and Br Legion 1928–32, Er Bro Trin Ho, Grand Pres Br Empire Serv League, Chm NRA 1925–30, Hon LLD: Glasgow, Cambridge and St Andrews, Hon DCL Oxford; Silver Medal for Saving Life at Sea; author: *The Grand Fleet, 1914–16, its Creation, Development and Work* (1919), *The Crisis of the Naval War* (1920) and *The Submarine Peril* (1934); *m* 1 July 1902 Florence Gwendoline (*d* 12 May 1964), 2nd dau of Sir Charles William Cayzer, 1st Bt (*qv*), and *d* 20 Nov 1935, leaving:

1 GEORGE PATRICK JOHN RUSHWORTH JELLICOE, **2nd and present Earl Jellicoe**

1 Gwendoline Lucy Constance Rushworth; *b* 14 April 1903; *m* 29 April 1935 Col Edward Latham, MC, RHA, Queen's Messenger (*d* 27 Nov 1957), er s of Thomas Ringrose Latham, and *d* Oct 1997, leaving:

(1) *John Edward Jellicoe [John Latham Esq, Harwood's House, Bledington, Oxon]; *b* 10 Feb 1936; *educ* Eton; HNC Metallurgy 1961, 2nd Lt RAC; *m* 21 Jan 1967 *Catherine Patricia, only dau of Dr Allan William Forsyth Craig, MB, of Bath, and has:

1a *Jasper Nicholas Jellicoe; *b* 1970

1a *Gabrielle Jane; *b* 1971

2a *Rosalind Vaari; *b* 1971

(2) *Richard Henry Ringrose [Richard Latham Esq, Stowting Hill House, Ashford, Kent TN25 6BE]; *b* 21 June 1943 (HH PRINCESS HELENA VICTORIA stood sponsor); *educ* Eton, RNC Dartmouth and Cranfield U (MBA 1971); Lt RNR, Sub-Lt RN (ret), Graduate Inst of Tport; chm Petroleum Relations Ltd 1983, dep chm Northern Petroleum plc 1995, dir Global Energy Finance Ltd 1997; *m* 4 Oct 1968 *Virginia Jane Mount (*see* ERNE, E) and has:

1a *Edward George Ringrose; *b* 4 May 1970; *educ* Eton and St Catherine's Coll Oxford (BA); Capt Coldstream Gds

2a *Harry John Jellicoe; *b* 1972; *educ* Milton Abbey and Guildhall Sch of Music and Drama

1a *Selina Louise; *b* 1976; *educ* Bedgebury Sch and Middx U

2a *Emily Rose Jane; *b* 1979; *educ* Benenden

(1) *Susan Phyllida [Mrs Michael Rose, Heath Winds, Merton Lane, London N6]; *b* 15 Feb 1938; *educ* LMH Oxford (BA 1958) and Birkbeck Coll London (PhD); *m* 2 Oct 1958 *Michael Rose, slr, s of Jack Rosenberg, and has:

1a *David Jacob Edward; *b* 21 July 1959

2a *Bernard John Max; *b* 4 Aug 1960

3a *Philip Thomas Solomon; *b* 18 Dec 1963

1a *Dinah Gwen Lison; *b* 16 July 1965

2 Agnes Betty Gardiner; *b* 21 May 1906; *d* 24 Jan 1911

3 Myrtle Grace Brocas; *b* 28 Aug 1908; *m* 11 June 1932 Lionel Maxwell Joachim Balfour (*d* 1973), s of Maxwell Balfour, and *d* 10 Nov 1945, leaving:

(1) *Christopher John Jellicoe [Christopher Balfour Esq, 25 Clausentum Rd, St Cross, Winchester, Hants SO23 9QE]; *b* 7 Feb 1934; *educ* Eton and Trin Coll Cambridge (BA 1957); Forest of Dean District Cncl 1979–87, author: *Roads to Oblivion* (1996); *m* 9 July 1960 *Ann Shuyler, only dau of Capt Claude Martin Butlin, DSC, RN, and has:

1a *Maxwell James; *b* 22 Dec 1961

1a *Juliet Ann; *b* 26 April 1963; doctor; *m* 1 April 1989 *Jonathan Justin Bench, and has three sons

2a *Katherine Susan; *b* 23 Jan 1968; *m* 11 May 1996 *Harry Michael Charles Morley

(1) *Karen Myrtle [Mrs Fabyan Evans, 60a Sheffield Terrace, London W8]; *b* 10 Jan 1944; *m* 12 Sept 1967 *Fabyan Peter Leaf Evans, only s of Peter Fabyan Evans, and has:

1a *Nigel Henley Fabian; *b* 26 April 1971

2a *Alexander Peter Sommerville; *b* 1976

1a *Jessica Ann; *b* 1973

4 *Norah Beryl Cayzer [The Lady Norah Wingfield, Salterbridge, Cappoquin, Co Waterford, Ireland]; *b* 30 March 1910; *m* 30 March 1935 Maj Edward William Rhys Wingfield (*see* POWERSCOURT, V) and has issue

5 *Prudence Katharine Patton, JP (Co London 1951) [The Lady Prudence Loudon JP, 92 Bridge St, nr Wye, Ashford, Kent]; *b* 30 Aug 1913; *m* 22 Dec 1936 Francis William Hope Loudon (*d* 1985), barrister, Lt-Cdr RNVR, only s of James Hope Loudon, and has:

(1) *James Rushworth Hope [James Loudon Esq, Olantigh, Wye, Kent TN25 5EW]; *b* 19 March 1943; *educ* Eton and Magdalene Coll Cambridge (BA 1965); *m* 1975 *Jane Gavina Fryett and has:

1a *Hugo John Hope; *b* 1978

2a *Alexander Guy Rushworth; *b* 1980

1a *Antonia Louise Cameron; *b* 1977

(1) *Katharine Louise Frederica [Lady Wilkinson, Little Olantigh, Wye, Kent TN25 5DH]; *b* 30 Sept 1937; *m* 25 July 1964 Sir William Henry Nairn Wilkinson (*d* 1996), est s of Denys Cooper Wilkinson, and has:

1a *Matthew Loudon Nairn; *b* 9 Jan 1969

1a *Sophia Louise Prudence; *b* 1971

2a *Alice Laura Gillian; *b* 1974

(2) *Annabella Constance, JP [Mrs Jonathan Scott JP, Lasborough Manor, Tetbury, Glos]; *b* 7 Dec 1939; *educ* St Hugh's Coll Oxford; *m* 12 June 1965 *(Ian) Jonathan Scott, CBE, er s of Col Alexander Brassey Jonathan Scott, DSO, MC, and has:

1a *Alexander James Jonathan; *b* 19 May 1966; *educ* Westminster and Balliol Coll Oxford

2a *Justin William Erskine; *b* 3 Sept 1970; *educ* Eton and Balliol Coll Oxford

1a *Julia Katharine Selina; *b* 4 Jan 1969; *educ* St Paul's Girls' Sch and St Peter's Coll Oxford

JENKIN OF RODING

Arms: Argent a lion rampant regardant sable, armed and langued gules within a bordure also sable. **Crest:** On a mural crown per pale argent and sable a lion rampant regardant sable, armed and langued gules. **Supporters:** Dexter, a seal erect on a rock; sinister, a stag erect guardant on a grassy mound, all proper. **Motto:** *Toujours fidele* ('Ever faithful'). **Creation:** B, (LP, UK) 1987.

THE BARON JENKIN OF RODING, of Wanstead and Woodford in Greater London ((Charles) Patrick Fleeming Jenkin, PC (1973)) [The Rt Hon The Lord Jenkin of Roding PC House of Lords, London SW1A 0PW]; *b* 7 Sept 1926; *educ* Clifton and Jesus Coll Cambridge; QO Cameron Highrs 1945–48; barrister Middle Temple 1952–57; Distillers Co Ltd 1957–70; memb: Hornsey Borough Cncl 1960–63, London Cncl Soc Serv 1963–67; MP (C) Wanstead and Woodford 1964–87; Oppn Spokesman Treasury, Trade and Finance 1965–70; Jt V-Chm C Parly Trade and Power Ctee 1966–67; Chm All Party Parly Gp Chemical Industry 1968–70; Fin Sec Treasury 1970–72, Ch Sec 1972–74; Min Energy 1974, Oppn Spokesman: Energy 1974–76, Soc Servs 1976–79; Sec State: Soc Servs 1979–81, Industry 1981–83, Environment 1983–85; dir: Tilbury Contracting Gp 1974–79, Royal Worcester 1975–79, Continental and Industrial Tst 1975–79; Chm: Lamco Paper Sales 1987–93, Friends Provident Life Office 1988–98 (dir 1986–88), Crystalate Hldgs 1988–90 (dir 1987–90), Target Finland Ltd 1989–95, Tstees Westfield Coll Tst 1988–, Queen Mary and Westfield Coll Public Policy Research Unit Advsy Bd 1990–97, Visual Handicap Gp 1990–, Forest Healthcare NHS Trust 1991–97, Cncl Fndn Sci and tech 1997–; Co-Chm UK-Japan 2000 Group 1986–90, Memb: Cncl UK Centre for Ec and Environmental Devpt 1986–, Cncl Guide Dogs for Blind Assoc 1987–97; Pres: Nat CPC Ctee 1983–86, Nat Union of C and U Assocs Gtr London Area 1989–92, Friends of Wanstead Hosp 1987–91, ICRF 1991 (Dep Chm 1994–), Br Urban Regeneration Assoc 1990–96; Sr V-Chm World Congress on Urban Growth and the Environment 1992–95; Advsr: Andersen Consulting 1985, UK Advsy Bd Nat Ec Research Assocs 1987–, Sumitomo Trust and Banking Co 1989–; Consultant Thames Estuary Airport Co 1994–; V-Pres 1991 Japan Festival Ctee 1987–91; Tstee Monteverdi Choir 1992–; Patron: St Clare W Essex Hospice Tst 1991–, Stort Tst 1991; Govr Westfield Coll 1964–70, Clifton Coll 1969–79 (Pres 1994–); Fell QMW 1991; Hon LLD S Bank U; Freeman: City London 1985, Borough Redbridge 1988; FRSA 1985; *m* 1952 *Alison Monica, est dau of Capt Philip Skelton Graham, RN (*see* 1970 edn CHRISTISON, Bt), and has:

1 *Charles Alexander Graham [The Rev and Hon Charles Jenkin, Melton Mowbray Rectory, 67 Dalby Rd, Melton Mowbray, Leics]; *b* 1954; *educ* Highgate, UCL and Westcott House Cambridge; ordained 1984; Team Rector Melton Mowbray 1994–; *m* 1984 *Susan, dau of Roy Collins, and has:

(1) *Alexandra Emily; *b* 1989

(2) *Rebecca Charlotte; *b* 1991

2 *Bernard Christison [The Hon Bernard Jenkin MP, House of Commons, London SW1A 0AA]; *b* 1959; *educ* Highgate, William Ellis Sch and Corpus Christi Coll Cambridge; MP (C) Colchester N 1992–97, N Essex 1997–, Jr Oppn Spokesman Constitutional Afffrs, Scotland and Wales 1997–; *m* 1988 *Anne Caroline, sis of 6th Baron Rayleigh (*qv*), and has:

(1) *Robert Patrick Christison; *b* 1989

(2) *Peter Andrew Graham; *b* 1991

1 *Nicola Mary [The Hon Nicola Jenkin, Top Floor, 16 Handforth Rd, London SW9 0LP]; *b* 1956; *educ* N London Collegiate Sch, RCM and Hochschule für Musik Vienna

2 *Flora Margaret [The Hon Flora Jenkin, 84B Tyrwhitt Rd, London SE4 1QB]; *b* 1962; *educ* Felsted, St John's Coll Durham and Trinity Coll Music; *m* 1990 (*divorce* 1997) Jacoby Michael Thwaites, yst s of Prof Sir Bryan Thwaites

Lineage: CHARLES O F JENKIN, of Gerrards Cross, Bucks; had:

(CHARLES) PATRICK FLEEMING, *cr* a **Baron**

JENKINS OF HILLHEAD

Creation: B. (LP, UK) 1987.

THE BARON JENKINS OF HILLHEAD, of Pontypool, Co Gwent (Roy Harris Jenkins, OM (1993), PC (1964)) [The Rt Hon The Lord Jenkins of Hillhead OM PC, St Amand's House, E Hendred, Oxon OX12 8LA; 2 Kensington Park Gdns, London W11 2HB]; *b* 11 Nov 1920; *educ* Abersychan GS, U Coll Cardiff and Balliol Coll Oxford; Capt RA 1944–46; Industrial and Commercial Finance Corp 1946–48; memb: exec Fabian Soc 1949–61 (Chm 1957–58), Mgmt Ctee Soc Authors 1956–60; Advsr John Lewis Partnership 1954–62 (dir fin ops 1962–64); Govr BFI 1955–58; MP (Lab) Southwark Centl 1948–50, Birmingham Stechford 1950–76 and (SDP) Glasgow Hillhead 1982–87; PPS to Sec State Cwlth Rels 1949–50; UK Del Cncl Europe 1955–57; Min Aviation 1964 –65, Home Sec 1965–67 and 1974–76, Chllr Exchequer 1967–70, Dep Leader Lab Party 1970–72; Fndr Memb SDP 1981, Leader SDP 1982–83; Leader SLD Peers 1988–; V-Pres Inst Fiscal Studies 1970–; Pres EC Commn 1977–81; Tstee Pilgrim Trust 1973–; Pres: UWIST 1975 –81, RSL 1988–, memb Ctee Soc Arts; Co-Pres RIIA 1993–; dir Morgan Grenfell Hldgs 1981–82; Chllr Oxford U 1987–; Hon For Memb American Acad Arts and Sciences 1978; Hon FBA 1993; Hon DCL Oxford; Liveryman Goldsmith's Co; Freeman: City London 1965, Brussels 1980; author: *Purpose and Policy* (1947), *Mr Attlee: An Interim Biography* (1948), *New Fabian Essays* (contrib, 1952), *Pursuit of Progress* (1953), *Mr Balfour's Poodle* (1954), *Sir Charles Dilke* (1958), *The Labour Case* (1959), *Asquith* (1964), *Hugh Gaitskell: A Memoir* (contrib, 1964), *Essays and Speeches* (1967), *Afternoon on the Potomac* (1972), *Nine Men of Power* (1975), *Partnership of Principle* (1985), *Truman* (1986), *Baldwin* (1987), *Gallery of Twentieth Century Portraits* (1988), *European Diary 1977–81* (1989), *A Life at the Centre* (1991), *Portraits and Miniatures* (1993), *Gladstone* (1995, Whitbread Prize); *m* 1945 *Dame (Mary) Jennifer, DBE, dau of Sir Parker Morris, and has:

1*Charles Arthur Simon [The Hon Charles Jenkins, 9 Leppoc Rd, London SW4]; *b* 1949; *educ* Winchester and New Coll Oxford; *m* 1971 *Ivana Sertic and has:

(1) *Alexandra Dorothea; *b* 1986

(2) *Helena Harriet; *b* 1988

2 *Edward Nicholas [The Hon Edward Jenkins, 7 Carthew Villas, London W6]; *b* 1954; *educ* City of London Sch and Trin Hall Cambridge; *m* 1979 *Sally Turner and has:

(1) *Fergus Orlando Nicholas; *b* 1986

(1) *Flora Rayne Victoria; *b* 1984

1 *Cynthia Delanie; *b* 1951; *educ* St Paul's Girls' Sch and St Anne's Coll Oxford; *m* 1984 *John Crosthwait and has:

(1) *David Robert Jenkins; *b* 1982

(2) *Hugh Michael Jenkins; *b* 1985

(3) *George Nicholas Jenkins; *b* 1988

Lineage: ARTHUR JENKINS, of Greenlands, Pontypool; miner, NUM official, MP (Lab) Pontypool 1936–46, PPS to Clement Attlee (*see* ATTLEE, E); *m* Hattie-Harris and had an only s:

ROY HARRIS, *cr* a **Baron**

JENKINS OF PUTNEY

Creation: B. (LP, UK) 1981.

THE BARON JENKINS OF PUTNEY, of Wandsworth, Greater London (Hugh Gater Jenkins) [The Rt Hon The Lord Jenkins of Putney, House of Lords, SW1A 0PW]; *b* 27 July 1908; *educ* Enfield GS; Prudential Assur 1930–40; ROC 1931; F/Lt Fighter Command UK and SEAC Burma 1941–46; Gtr London Organiser Nat Union Bank Employees 1947; ed *The Bank Officer* 1948; Assist Sec Equity 1950 (Assist Gen Sec 1957–64), Chm: Standing Advsy Ctee Local Authorities and the Theatre 1950–64, Victory for Socialism 1956–60; memb LCC 1958–65; MP (Lab) Putney 1964–79; Min Arts 1974–76; memb: Exec Ctee Gtr London Lab Party, Arts Cncl 1968–71, Drama Panel 1972–74, Nat Theatre Bd 1976–80; Dep Chm Theatres Tst 1977–79 (Dir 1979–86, Consultant 1986–); V-Pres Theatres Advsy Tst 1986–95 (Chm 1964–74 and 1976–86); Chm CND 1979–81 (V-Pres 1981–); author: *Essays in Local Government Enterprise* (jt author, 1964), *The Culture Gap* (1979), *Rank and File* (1980), and radio plays *Scenes from an Autobiography* (series), *Solo Boy* (1983), *When You and I Were Seventeen* (1985), *A Day in September* (1986), *In Time of War* (1986), *Last Tune from Rangoon* (1987), *View to a Death* (1989); *m* 1st 1936 Marie Ethel (*d* 1989), dau of S/Ldr Ernest Christopher Crosbie; *m* 2nd 1991 Helena Maria (*d* 1994), dau of Nicholas Paulidis, architect, of Athens

Lineage: JOSEPH WALTER JENKINS, of Enfield, Middx; *m* Florence Emily Gater and had:

HUGH GATER, *cr* a **Baron**

JENKINSON

Arms: Azure on a fess wavy argent a cross-patée gules, in chief two estoiles or. **Crest:** A sea-horse assurgent or, maned azure, supporting a cross-patée gules. **Motto:** *Pareo non servio* ('I obey; I do not serve'). **Creation:** Bt. (E) 18 May 1661.

SIR JOHN BANKS JENKINSON, 14TH BT, of Walcot, Oxon, and Hawkesbury, Glos [Sir John Jenkinson Bt, Hawkesbury Home Farm, Badminton, Glos GL9 1AY]; *b* 16 Feb 1945; *s f* 1989; *educ* Eton and Miami U; *m* 1979 *Josephine Mary, dau of Samuel William Marshall-Andrew, and has:

1 +GEORGE ANTHONY SAMUEL BANKS; *b* 8 Nov 1980

1 *Samantha Emma; *b* 1983

Lineage: Sir ROBERT JENKINSON, of Walcot, Oxon, and Hawkesbury, Glos, had:

Sir Robert Jenkinson, 1st Bt (E), so *cr* 18 May 1661, of Walcot; *b* 1621; MP Oxon 1625; *m* Mary (*d* 13 June 1691), dau of Sir John Bankes, PC, DCL, Ld Ch Justice Ct Common Pleas, of Corfe Castle and Kingston Lacy, Dorset, and *d* 30 March 1677, leaving, with a dau:

Sir Robert Jenkinson, 2nd Bt; MP Oxon 1689–1710; *m* Sarah (*d* 8 Aug 1709), dau of Thomas Tomlins, of Bromley, Middx, and *d* 30 Jan 1709–10, having had:

1 **Sir Robert Jenkinson, 3rd Bt**; *bapt* 23 Nov 1685; MP Oxon 1709–17; *m c* 4 Feb 1711/2 Henrietta Maria (*m* 2nd 9 Aug 1731 Charles Eversfield, of Denne, Sussex, and was *bur* 16 Aug 1760), dau of Charles Scarborough, and *dsp* 29 Oct 1717

2 **Sir Robert Bankes Jenkinson, 4th Bt**; *bapt* 24 Jan 1686/7; MP Oxon 1717–27; *m* 12 June 1718 Catharine (*bur* 24 March 1780), 3rd dau of Sir Robert Dashwood, 1st Bt, of Kirtlington Park (*qv*), and *d* 2 July 1738, leaving:

(1) **Sir Robert Jenkinson, 5th Bt**; *bapt* 13 Aug 1720; MA, DCL Oxon; *m* his cousin Mary (*d* 30 July 1765), dau of Sir Jonathan Cope, 1st Bt, and *dsp* 8 Aug 1766

(2) **Sir Bankes Jenkinson, 6th Bt**; *bapt* 20 Nov 1721; MA Oxon, Fell All Souls; *d* unm 22 July 1789

3 Charles; *bapt* 13 June 1693; Col RHG; *m* Amarantha (*d* July 1785), dau and eventually sole heir of Capt Wolfran Cornewall, RN, and was *bur* 23 June 1750, leaving:

(1) **Sir Charles Jenkinson, 7th Bt**, and 1st EARL OF LIVERPOOL, so *cr* 1 June 1796, as also previously 21 Aug 1786 BARON HAWKESBURY, of Hawkesbury, Co Gloucester (both GB), PC (1773); *bapt* 16 May 1729; *educ* Charterhouse and Univ Coll Oxford; MP (Tory) Cockermouth 1763–66, Appleby 1766–72, Harwich 1772–74, Hastings 1774–80 and Saltash 1780–86, U-Sec N Dept 1761–62, Treas Ordnance 1762–63, Jt Sec Treasury 1763–65, a Ld Admlty 1766–67, a Ld Treasury 1767–73, Jt V-Treas Ireland 1772–75, Clerk Pells Ireland 1775–1808, Sec War 1778–82, a Ld of Tde 1784, Pres BOT 1786–1804, Chllr Duchy Lancaster 1786–1803; *m* 1st 9 Feb 1769 Amelia (*d* 12 July 1770), dau of William Watts, Govr Fort William, Bengal, and had:

1a **Sir Robert Banks Jenkinson, 8th Bt**, and 2nd EARL OF LIVERPOOL, KG (1814), PC (1799); *b* 7 June 1770; *educ* Charterhouse and Ch Ch Oxford; MP (Tory) Appleby 1790 (but as a minor did not take seat) and Rye 1790–1803, a Commr Indian Affrs 1793–99, Master Mint 1799–1801, For Sec 1801–04, called up to Ho of Lds *vp* in f's Barony as 2nd BARON HAWKESBURY 15 Nov 1803, Home Sec 1804–06 and 1807–09, Leader Ho Lds to 1806, Receiver Gen Duchy Lancaster 1807–19, Sec War and Colonies 1809–12, PM 1812–27, author: *Memoirs of the Public Life and Administration of the Earl of Liverpool* (1827); *m* 1st 25 March 1795 Lady Louisa Theodosia Hervey (*d* 12 June 1821), 3rd dau of 4th Earl of Bristol (*see* BRISTOL, M); *m* 2nd 24 Sept 1822 Mary (*d* 18 Oct 1846), n of 1st Baron Bagot (*qv*), and *dsp* 4 Dec 1828

(1) **Sir Charles** *m* 2nd 22 June 1782 Catherine (*d* 1 Oct 1827), dau of Sir Cecil Bisshopp, 6th Bt (*see* FALMOUTH, V), and widow of Sir Charles Cope, Bt, of Brewern, and *d* 7 Dec 1808, having by her had:

2a **Sir Charles Cecil Cope Jenkinson, 9th Bt**, and 3rd and last EARL OF LIVERPOOL, GCB (1845), PC (1841); *b* 29 May 1784; *educ* Ch Ch Oxford; Page Honour 1794, served RN 1794–97 and 1801, Sec Legn Vienna 1804–07, vol with Austrian Army Battle of Austerlitz 1805, MP (Tory) Sandwich 1807–12, Bridgnorth 1812–18 and E Grinstead 1818–28, U-Sec: Home Dept 1807–09, War and Colonies 1809–10, Ld Steward Household 1841–46; *m* 19 July 1810 Julia Evelyn Medley (*d* 8 April 1814), only child of Sir George Augustus Shuckburgh-Evelyn, 6th Bt (*see* SHUCKBURGH, Bt), and *dspm* 3 Sept 1851, when the Earldom and Barony expired, leaving:

1b Catherine Julia; *m* 20 Nov 1837 Col Francis Vernon-Harcourt (*see* VERNON, B) and *dsp* 5 Dec 1877

2b Selina Charlotte; *m* 1st 15 Aug 1833 Viscount Milton (*d* 8 Nov 1835; *see* 1970 edn FITZWILLIAM, E) and had issue; *m* 2nd 28 Aug 1845 George Savile Foljambe, of Osberton, Notts, and Aldwarke, Yorks (*d* 18 Dec 1869), and *d* 24 Sept 1888, leaving issue (*see* LIVERPOOL, E, of the 1905 and current *cr*)

3b Louisa Harriet; *m* 5 Sept 1839 John Cotes, of Woodcote Hall, Salop, and *d* 5 Feb 1887 aged 72, leaving issue

1a Charlotte; *m* 11 Aug 1807 1st Earl of Verulam (*qv*) and *d* his widow 16 April 1862, leaving issue

(2) John; Col, Jt Sec Ireland, MP Corfe Castle 1768–80; *m* Frances (*d* 28 Aug 1811), dau of Adml John Barker, and *d* 1 May 1805, leaving:

1a **Sir Charles Jenkinson, 10th Bt**; *b* 23 Feb 1779; MP Dover 1806–16; *m* 4 Feb 1803 Katherine (*bur* 14 Feb 1855), 5th dau of Walter Campbell, of Lanarks and Islay, Argyll, and *d* 6 March 1855, leaving:

1b Georgiana Elizabeth; *m* 24 Oct 1833 William Nugent (*d* 24 Oct 1864) and *d* 24 April 1887, having had issue

2b Katherine Frances; *m* 25 Nov 1833 Richard Samuel Guinness and *d* 20 Nov 1881, leaving issue (*see* GUINNESS, Bt)

3b Eleanora Mary; *m* 10 July 1830 2nd Duke of Montebello, s of Marshal Lannes, 1st Duke of Montebello, and *d* St Petersburg 14 Oct 1863, leaving issue

2a John Bankes (Rt Rev); *b* 2 Sept 1781; DD, Bp St David's; *m* 8 April 1813 Frances Augusta (*d* 29 Nov 1860), dau of Augustus Pechell, of Berkhamsted (*see* 1970 edn PECHELL, Bt), and *d* 6 July 1840, leaving:

1b GEORGE SAMUEL (Sir), **11th Bt**

2b John Henry; *b* 5 Feb 1823; MA Oxon; *m* 17 Nov 1852 Alice Henrietta (*d* 9 Dec 1859), dau of Sir William Gordon Cumming, 2nd Bt (*qv*), and *d* 29 June 1914, leaving:

1c Francis John Henry; *b* 20 Aug 1853; MA Cantab, Fell Trin Coll Cambridge, Cambridge U Librarian, Hon DLitt Oxon; *m* 1st 6 July 1887 Marian Sydney (*dsp* 5 Jan 1888 aged 29), 5th dau of Champion Wetton; *m* 2nd 2 April 1902 Margaret Clifford (*d* 8 May 1933), only surv dau of Surgn-Gen Ludovick Charles Stewart, of Drummin, and *d* 21 Sept 1923

2c George Seymour Charles, DSO; *b* 18 Feb 1858; Maj Sherwood Foresters, Derbys Regt and Northants Imp Yeo; *m* 20 Sept 1899 Ada Louisa (*m* 2nd 5 Dec 1911 Sir Charles Edward St John Frederick, 8th Bt (*qv*); *d* 24 Jan 1948), only dau of Caesar Czarnikow, of Effingham Hill, Surrey, and *d* 37 Sept 1907, leaving:

1d Robert Charles Horace; *b* 2 Dec 1900; *educ* Eton; Capt 1st Life Gds; *m* 1st 25 July 1925 (*divorce* 1936) Hon Barbara Vernon Harcourt, OBE (*d* 19 May 1961), yst dau of 1st Viscount Harcourt (*see* VERNON, B), and *d* 22 Aug 1970, leaving:

1e +Julian Charles Lewis [Julian Jenkinson Esq, Folly Faunts House, Goldhanger, Essex CM9 8AP]; *b* 28 April 1926; *educ* Eton; late Lt 1st Roy Dragoons; *m* 24 July 1953 *Diana Catherine, only dau of Maj George Henry William Baird (*see* BAIRD, Bt, of Newbyth), and has:

1f +Dermot Julian; *b* 2 Dec 1954; *educ* Eton; *m* 1979 *Miranda Jane, dau of John Maxwell Menzies (*see* DAWSON, Bt), and has:

1g +Oliver John Banks; *b* 1984

1g *Emily Lavinia; *b* 1981

1f *Karen Barbara; *b* 19 Sept 1957; *m* 21 Dec 1981 *Capt Robert Mason, Welsh Gds

2f *Laura Louise Diana; *b* 7 Oct 1966; *m* 20 May 1995 *John Mackay

1e Lavinia Mary; *b* 3 Sept 1928; *educ* Oxford (MA); *d* unm 1981

2e *Clare Barbara [Mrs Clare McCully, Leitrim Farm, Loughries, Newtownards, Co Down]; *b* 8 June 1933; *m* 7 Oct 1955 (*divorce* 19–) William McCully, er s of Hugh McCully, of Carrowdore, Co Down, and has:

1f *Patrick William; *b* 17 March 1965

1f *Lucinda Barbara; *b* 31 March 1962

1d (cont.) Robert Jenkinson *m* 2nd 20 Aug 1938 Gwyneth (*d* 4 June 1988), dau of A Llewellyn Mathews, and *d* 1970, leaving by her:

3e *Frances Caroline [Miss Frances Jenkinson, Sycamore House, Swanton Novers, Norfolk NR24 2RB]; *b* 30 April 1942

2d John Anthony; *b* 20 May 1906; *m* 14 June 1930 Joan (*m* 3rd 20 Feb 1943 7th Baron Sherborne; *see* 1970 edn), 3rd dau of Sir James Hamet Dunn, 1st Bt (*see* 1970 edn), and formerly w of Hubert John Duggan, MP, and *d* 29 Oct 1935, leaving:

1e +Robin; 2nd Lt 13th/18th Roy Hus; *m* 1st 26 Oct 1951 Helene, only dau of Vladimir Novikov, of New York, and Zoja Dudnikova, of New York, and had:

1f +John Anthony; *b* 17 June 1952

1f *Tamara Alexandra; *b* 29 Sept 1953

2f *Tatiana; *b* 6 Aug 1958

1e (cont.) Robin Jenkinson *m* 2nd 13 Sept 1969 *Mrs Rosalind Black

1c Eleanor Louisa; *b* 5 May 1855; *d* unm 23 Sept 1948

1b Frances Sarah; *m* 5 July 1849 Rev Henry Brooke Boothby (*see* BOOTHBY, Bt) and *d* 22 June 1877, having had issue

2b Augusta Mary Frederica; *m* June 1855 Cdr Arthur Tower, RN (*d* 1 June 1877), and *d* 20 Nov 1910

3a George; Lt-Col Artillery, *d* unm 1823

4a Robert Henry; *b* 8 June 1786; Govr Dover Castle; *m* 1824 Henrietta Juliana (*d* 1847), dau of William Baker, MP Herts, and *dsp* March 1857

1a Fanny; *m* 29 Jan 1805 Sir William Boothby, 8th Bt (*qv*), and *d* 2 Jan 1838, leaving issue

(3) Robert; Gds Offr; *d* unm

(1) Elizabeth; *m* 1764 Charles Wolfran Cornewall, PC (*d* 2 Jan 1789), Speaker H of C, and *dsp* 8 March 1809

1 Mary; *m* 1717 Sir Jonathan Cope, 1st Bt, of Brewern, Oxon (*d* 28 March 1765), and was *bur* 27 Feb 1755, leaving issue

The 10th Bt's n,

Sir George Samuel Jenkinson, 11th Bt; *b* 27 Sept 1817; Capt 8th Hus, High Sheriff Glos 1862, MP N Wilts 1868–80; *m* 31 July 1845 Emily Sophia (*d* 23 Feb 1892), est dau of Anthony Lyster, of Stillorgan Park, Co Dublin, and *d* 19 Jan 1892, leaving:

1 GEORGE BANKS (Sir), **12th Bt**

2 Robert Anthony Banks, Roy N Glos Militia; *b* 6 Sept 1860; accidentally *k* 21 June 1882

1 Emily Frances; *d* unm 9 Dec 1898

2 Louisa Augusta; *m* 1st 28 Dec 1876 Viscount Maidstone (*see* WINCHILSEA and NOTTINGHAM, E); *m* 2nd 22 Dec 1917 Lt-Col Francis James Ashburner, 2nd Dragoon Gds, and *d* 21 Dec 1932

Sir GEORGE's only surv s,

Sir George Banks Jenkinson, 12th Bt, JP (Glos), DL; *b* 10 May 1851; Capt 4th Bn Glos Regt; *m* 10 Aug 1880 Madeline (*d* 4 Feb 1927), est dau of Arthur Holme Sumner, of Hatchlands, Surrey, and *d* 5 June 1915, having had:

1 John Banks; *b* 9 June 1881; Capt Rifle Bde Boer War 1901–02 and WW I (despatches); *m* 9 Nov 1907 Joan (*m* 2nd 21 June 1920 Maj-Gen Algernon Philip Yorke Langhorne, CB, DSO, MC, late RA (*d* 28 Nov 1945), s of Rev J Langhorne; *d* 13 Dec 1964), only dau of Col Joseph Hill, CB, of Wollaston Hall, Wellingborough, Northants, and was *ka* 14 Sept 1914, leaving:

(1) **Sir Anthony Banks Jenkinson, 13th Bt**; *b* 3 July 1912; *educ* Eton and Balliol Coll Oxford; ed *Isis* 1933–34, for corresp 1935–40, ed Allied Labour News Serv 1940–46, md Cayman Boat Ltd, Cayman RS 1947–52, Morgons Harbour, Port Roy Jamaica 1953–73, dir Port Roy Co Merchants 1965–89, Caribbean Bank (Cayman) Ltd 1973–89, author: *America Came my Way* (1935), *Where Seldom a Gun is Heard* (1937); *m* 9 Oct 1943 Frances (*d* 29 March 1996), dau of Harry Stremmel, of New York, and *d* 1989, leaving:

1a Sir JOHN BANKS JENKINSON, **14th and present Bt**

1a *Jennifer Ann [Mrs Robert Waddington, The Old Vicarage, Upper Minety, Wilts SN16 9PY]; *b* 26 Nov 1947; *m* 1976 *Robert Waddington, s of George Waddington, of Lytham, Lancs, and has:

1b *Thomas Anthony; *b* 1977

2b *Guy George; *b* 1979

2a *Emily Frances Joan; *b* 2 Sept 1953; *m* 19– *Miguel Malgaret, of Fort Lauderdale, Fla., and has:

1b *Christopher; *b* 1977

(1) Elizabeth Deborah; *m* 3 March 1938 Henry Dreyfus, DSc (*d* 30 Dec 1944)

2 Thomas Banks, MC; *b* 2 Oct 1884; Lt Roy Mon Engrs

1 Katherine Sophia; *b* 13 Jan 1883; *m* 4 March 1903 Capt Julian Spicer (*d* 22 Oct 1930), RHG, 2nd s of John Spicer, of Spye Park, Chippenham, and *dsp* 16 May 1952

2 Georgina Isabel; *b* 10 April 1899

JENKS

Arms: Per fess indented sable and argent on a pile or a boar's head, and in base two boar's heads, all couped sable, on a chief ermine a representation of the sword and mace of the City of London in saltire proper. **Crest:** A sinister arm embowed vested sable, cuffed argent, grasping in the hand a sword in bend proper, pommel and hilt or, enfiled with a ducal coronet gold. **Motto:** *Decus recte peto* ('I seek honour honourably'). **Creation:** Bt. (UK) 8 Oct 1932.

SIR (MAURICE ARTHUR) BRIAN JENKS, 3RD BT, of Cheape, City of London [Sir Brian Jenks Bt, Warren House, Savernake, Wilts SN8 3BQ]; *b* 28 Oct 1933; *s* f 1993; *educ* Charterhouse; chartered accountant 1956–, ptnr Touche Ross 1979–93, memb Ct Assists Haberdashers' Co 1961– (Master 1988–89 and 1992–93), author: *Small Businesses: how to survive and succeed* (1989); *m* 29 Sept 1962 *Susan Lois, est dau of Frank Leslie Allen, of Coulsdon, Surrey, and has:

1 *(Marjorie) Emma; *b* 1 March 1964; *m* Sept 1994 *William Valerian Wellesley (*see* COWLEY, E)

Sir BRIAN also adopted:

*Timothy Charles; *b* June 1967

Lineage: ROBERT JENKS; *d* 27 June 1891; leaving:

ROBERT ISAAC JENKS; *b* 6 Sept 1847; *m* 1 June 1870 Fanny (*d* 17 Jan 1930), yst dau of Robert Garnett, of Warrington, and *d* 12 April 1911, leaving, with other issue:

Sir Maurice Jenks, 1st Bt (UK), so *cr* 8 Oct 1932; *b* 25 Nov 1872; FCA, City London: Ct Common Cncl Cheapside 1910, Alderman Cheapside Ward 1923, Sr Sheriff 1930–31, Ld Mayor 1931–32, Lt, Hon LLD Lond, memb PO Advsy Ctee, Rlwy Rates Tbnl, head Maurice Jenks, Percival & Co, chartered accountants, MCICA, Kt Cdr Dannebrog, Hon Freeman Scarborough 1932, ktd 1931; *m* 1st 14 April 1903 Martha Louise Christabel (*d* 25 June 1938), yst dau of George Calley Smith, of Bath; *m* 2nd 6 Jan 1939 Constance Edith (*d* 26 May 1995), dau of William Richard Currie, of Eden Park, Beckenham, Kent, and *d* 19 May 1946, leaving by his 1st w:

1 **Sir Richard Atherley Jenks, 2nd Bt**; *b* 26 July 1906; *educ* Charterhouse; FCA; *m* 9 April 1932 *Marjorie Suzanne Arlette [Dowager Lady Jenks, 42 Sussex Sq, London W2 2SR], dau of Sir Arthur Philip Du Cros, 1st Bt (*qv*), and *d* 1993, leaving:

(1) Sir (MAURICE ARTHUR) BRIAN JENKS, **3rd and present Bt**

(2) +(RICHARD JOHN) PETER [Peter Jenks Esq, 81 Onslow Sq, London SW7 3LT]; *b* June 1936; heir presumptive; *educ* Charterhouse; late 5th Roy Inniskilling Dragoon Gds, FCA; *m* 18 July 1963 *Juniper Li-Yung, est dau of Tan Sri Y C Foo, of Malaysia, and has:

1a +Richard Albert Benedict; *b* 27 Feb 1965; *educ* Eton and New Coll Oxford

1a *Melissa Kate Rosalind; *b* 28 Feb 1967

2a *Serena Anne Louise; *b* 1970

2 Robert Fergus, DSC (1943); *b* 12 July 1909; Cdr RN WW II (despatches three times, Croix de Guerre with palm); *m* 1st 4 Feb 1933 (*divorce* 1938) Joyce Wynne, only dau of A E Booth, of Hendon, and had issue:

(1) David Robin; *b* July 1934; *d* 14 Nov 1936

2 (cont.) Cdr Robert Jenks *m* 2nd 29 Nov 1939 *Molly Estelle, 3rd dau of Lt-Cdr Albert Edward Griffiths, RN (ret), and formerly w of F/Lt John F Dallas, RAF, and *d* 1982, having by her had:

(2) +Robert Philip [Robert Jenks Esq, Menmar, Moll de Llevant 303, Mahon, Menorca, Spain]; *b* 2 Feb 1948; *educ* Rhodesia and Thames Training Ship *Worcester*; *m* 1st 14 Sept 1968 (*divorce* 1983) Susan, only dau of John B Campbell, of Henley-on-Thames; *m* 2nd 1990 *Tracy Jane, only dau of Colin V Hives, of Stone Farm, Hailey, Ipsden, Oxon

(1) *Sally Elizabeth; *b* 26 Aug 1945; *m* 13 July 1968 (*divorce* 19–) John Norman Anderson Wylie, only s of Lt John Norman Anderson, USN, and Mrs Joan Wylie, and adopted s of Amos K Wylie, of New York, and has issue:

1a *Peter; *b* 1978

1a *Sarah; *b* 1974

1 Marjorie Christabel; *b* 3 July 1904; *m* 1st 1 Dec 1926 (*divorce* 1933) Robert Lassel Philip, s of Gerald Stanley Philip, and had a s; *m* 2nd 14 Jan 1937 W/Cdr Derek Fitzgerald Massy, OBE, RAFVR (*d* 2 June 1963), s of Maj H I Massy, of Stoneville, Co Limerick, and *d* 17 Nov 1966

JEPHCOTT

Arms: Azure two chevronels between in chief a mortar and pestle between two escallops or and in base an open book proper edged and clasped or. **Crest:** A dove supporting with the dexter claw a rod of Aesculapius proper, the serpent vert. **Motto:** *Scientia salutem feramus* ('By science we bring about health'). **Creation:** Bt. (UK) 14 Feb 1962.

SIR (JOHN) ANTHONY JEPHCOTT, 2ND BT, of East Portlemouth, Co Devon [Sir Anthony Jephcott Bt, 26 Sage Rd, Kohimarama, Auckland 1005, New Zealand]; *b* 21 May 1924; *s* f 1978; *educ* Aldenham, St John's Coll Oxford and LSE (BCom); REME WW II and RAEC 1944–47, Longworth Scientific Instrument Co: dir 1946, md and chm 1952–73; md and chm Pen Medic (NZ) 1973–78, Hon FFARACS 1990, author: *A History of Longworth Scientific Instrument Co Ltd*; *m* 1st 15 Dec 1949 Sylvia Mary (*divorce* 1978), dau of Thorsten Frederick Relling, of Wellington, NZ, and has:

1 *Helen Mary [Mrs Helen Asbury, 13A Tullis Close, Sutton Courtenay, Abingdon, Oxon OX14 4BD]; *b* 10 May 1953; *m* 1977 (*divorce* 1989) David Asbury and has:

(1) *Richard Andrew James; *b* 10 Aug 1982

(2) *Alexander Philip Ralph; *b* 31 Jan 1984

(1) *Anna Ruth; *b* 7 June 1980

2 *Caroline Ruth [Mrs Nigel Flower, Hill Farm House, Brinton, Norfolk]; *b* 27 Sept 1955; *m* 1979 *Nigel Clark Flower and has:

(1) *Hugo Gregory; *b* 8 Oct 1985

(2) *Felix James; *b* 9 Jan 1988

(1) *Harriet Christina; *b* 26 Aug 1990

Sir ANTHONY *m* 2nd 1978 *Josephine Agnes, dau of Philip Sheridan, of Perth, W Australia

Lineage: JOHN JEPHCOTT, of Hampton Lucy, Warwicks; *b* 1797; *m* Mary Wringrose (*b* 1803; *d* 1873) and *d* 12 Jan 1859, leaving:

JOSIAH JEPHCOTT, of Bedworth, Warwicks; *b* 8 May 1832; *m* 27 Dec 1852 Ellen (*d* 17 March 1913), dau of Joseph Sparrow, of Coundon, Warwicks, and *d* 27 Jan 1865, leaving:

JOHN JOSIAH JEPHCOTT, of Redditch, Worcs; *b* 10 Jan 1853; *m* 1 Oct 1878 Helen (*d* 23 Aug 1930), dau of Charles Matthews, of Coundon, and *d* 29 April 1929, leaving:

1 Charles Josiah; *b* 13 Aug 1879; *d* 20 Jan 1961

2 Ernest John; *b* 4 Sept 1884; *d* 29 Nov 1955

3 HARRY (Sir), **1st Bt**

1 Ethel Helen; *b* 30 Dec 1880; *d* 7 Dec 1884

2 Mabel Mary; *b* 13 Oct 1882; *d* 7 Oct 1955

The 3rd s,

Sir Harry Jephcott, 1st Bt, (UK), so *cr* 14 Feb 1962; *b* 15 Jan 1891; *educ* King Edward's GS Birmingham and W Ham Tech Coll (BSc London 1915, MSc 1918); with Customs & Excise Dept 1912–14 and Dept of Govt Chemist 1914–19, ch chemist Glaxo Labs 1919, gen manager 1925, md 1935, chm and md 1945–56, chm 1956–61, chm: Glaxo Gp 1962–63, Assoc Br Chem Mfrs 1947–50 (pres 1952–55), Cncl Sch of Pharmacy London U 1948–69 and Cncl for Scientific and Industrial Research 1956–61, Pres Roy Inst Chemistry 1953–55, memb Advsy Cncl Scientific Policy 1953–56, dir Metal Box Co 1950–64, govr: LSE 1952–68 and N London Collegiate Sch 1957–78; barrister Middle Temple 1925, ktd 1946, FRIC 1920, FPS, Hon DSc Birmingham 1956, Hon FRSM 1961; *m* 19 April 1919 Doris, FPS (*d* 1985), dau of Henry Gregory, and *d* 29 June 1978, leaving:

1 Sir (JOHN) ANTHONY JEPHCOTT, **2nd and present Bt**

2 +NEIL WELBOURN [Neil Jephcott Esq, Thalassa, E Portlemouth, Salcombe, S Devon TQ8 8PU]; *b* 3 June 1929; heir presumptive; *educ* Aldenham and

Emmanuel Coll Cambridge (BA 1953, MA 1959); engr; *m* 1st 1 Sept 1951 Mary Denise (*d* 1977), dau of Arthur Edgar Lanwer Muddiman, of Surrey, and has:

(1) +David Welbourn; *b* 9 Aug 1952

(2) +Mark Lanwer; *b* 23 Feb 1957; *m* 1983 *Lysa Ann, dau of Francis John Ridgen, and has:

1a +Richard Lanwer; b 1989

(1) *Penelope Mary; *b* 13 April 1955

2 (cont.) NEIL JEPHCOTT *m* 2nd 1978 *Mary Florence, dau of James John Daly

JERSEY

Arms: Quarterly, 1st and 4th, argent on a cross gules five escallops or (for VILLIERS): 2nd and 3rd, gules a chevron engrailed ermine between three eaglets argent, ducally gorged or (for CHILD). **Crests:** 1 A lion rampant argent, ducally crowned or (for VILLIERS), 2 On a rock proper an eagle rising argent, holding in the beak an adder proper (for CHILD). **Supporters:** Two lions argent ducally crowned or, each gorged with a plain collar gules charged with three escallops of the second. **Motto:** *Fidei coticula crux* ('The cross is the test of faith'). **Creation:** V. (I) 3 Jan 1620/1 (Grandison of Limerick), B. and V. (E) 20 March 1690/1 (Villiers of Dartford), E. (E) 13 Oct 1697.

THE 9TH EARL OF THE ISLAND OF JERSEY, **Viscount Villiers of Dartford**, Co Kent, **Viscount Grandison of Limerick**, Co Leitrim, and **Baron Villiers of Hoo**, Co Kent (George Francis Child Villiers) [The Rt Hon The Earl of Jersey, Radier Manor, Le Chemin du Radier, Grouville, Jersey JE3 9DR]; *b* 15 Feb 1910; *s f* 1923; *educ* Eton and Ch Ch Oxford; late Maj RA (TA); chm Wallace Bros Sassoon Bank (Jersey); *m* 1st 12 Jan 1932 (*divorce* 1937) Patricia Kenneth, only child of Kenneth Richards, of Cootamundra, NSW, and has:

1 *Caroline [The Lady Caroline Ogilvy, Sedgebrook Manor, nr Grantham, Lincs]; *b* 9 April 1934; *m* 1st 26 Nov 1952 (*divorce* 1965) Viscount Melgund, MBE (see MINTO, E) and has issue; *m* 2nd 23 Sept 1969 Hon John Douglas Stuart (*d* 1990), yr s of 1st Viscount Stuart of Findhorn (*qv*); *m* 3rd 1980 *Hon James Donald Diarmid Ogilvy, yst s of 12th Earl of Airlie (*qv*)

The 9th EARL *m* 2nd 30 July 1937 (*divorce* 1946) Virginia, dau of James E Cherrill, of USA, and formerly w of Archibald Alexander Leach (the actor Cary Grant); *m* 3rd 16 Oct 1947 *Bianca Maria Luciana Adriana, er dau of Enrico Mottironi, of Turin, Italy, and by her has had:

1 George Henry, *Viscount Villiers; b* 29 Aug 1948; *educ* Eton and Millfield; 2nd Lt Roy Hus (PWO), with Williams and Glyn's Bank and M L Doxford (Jersey), fndr Europlan Commodities and Villiers Trading, guitarist, both solo and with gp George Villiers Express, and composer (works include *Steps in Time*, albums include *George Villiers Plays Guitar* (1988), *Magical Dance* (1988), *Dawn* (1989), *No Dog Required* (1995); also ed *Classic Duets for the Guitar*; *m* 1st 22 Dec 1969 (*divorce* 1973) Verna P (*m* 2nd 1973 Sir Jeremy Hanley, KCMG, PC, MP (C) Richmond-upon-Thames 1983–97 and Chm C Party 1994–95), 2nd dau of Kenneth A Stott, of Jersey, and had:

(1) *Sophia Georgiana; *b* 25 June 1971

1 (cont.) *Viscount Villiers m* 2nd 9 Jan 1974 (*divorce* 1988) Sacha Jane Hooper, step-dau of Harold Briginshaw, of Guernsey, and by her had:

(1) +(GEORGE FRANCIS) WILLIAM, *Viscount Villiers*; *b* 5 Feb 1976

(2) *Helen Katherine Luisa; *b* 21 Oct 1978

(3) *Luciana Dorothea Sacha; *b* 1981

1 (cont.) *Viscount Villiers m* 3rd 1992 *Stephanie Louise [Viscountess Villiers, The Flat, Radier Manor, Longueville, Jersey, CI], dau of John Ian Penman, and *d* 19 March 1998, leaving by her:

(2) +Jamie Charles; *b* 1994

2 Charles Victor Child; *b* 10 Jan 1952; *educ* Eton; *m* 10 May 1975 (*divorce* 1989) Brigitte E G Marchand, stepdau and dau of Jean-Louis Charmolue, of St Estephe, France, and *d* 1991, leaving:

(1) *Eleanor Monica; *b* 1979

(2) *Barbara Béatrice; *b* 1981

2 *Isabella Bianca Rosa [The Lady Isabella Harrison, Constantia Manor, Isfield, Sussex TN22 5XU]; *b* 11 Oct 1950; *educ* Benenden and Warwick U; *m* 12 Oct 1974 *Peter Edward only s of G E Harrison, and has:

(1) *Matthew Alexander Charles; *b* 16 April 1980

(1) *Alexandra Venetia; *b* 29 April 1977

Lineage: ALEXANDER VILLERS; had:

JOHN VILLERS, of Brokesby, Leics, *c* 1278; ancestor of:

Sir GEORGE VILLIERS, of Brokesby; Sheriff Leics 1591; *m* 1st Audrey (*d* 1 May 1588), dau and heiress of William Saunders, of Harrington, Northants, and had:

1 Sir WILLIAM VILLERS, 1st Bt (E), so *cr* 19 July 1619; *b c* 1575; Sheriff Leics 1608–09; acquired the Dromahaire estate of 11,614 acres in Co Leitrim 1628; *m* 1st Anne (*dspm*), dau of Sir Edward Griffin, KB, of Dingley and Braybrooke, Northants; *m* 2nd *c* 1614 Elizabeth (*dspm*), dau of 1st Baron Saye and Sele (*qv*) by his 1st w Constance; *m* 3rd by 1618 Rebecca, dau of Robert Roper, of Heanor, Derbys, and *d* 12 June 1629, leaving by her, with a yst dau (Katherine, *m* as his 2nd w 5th Earl of Pembroke and (2nd Earl of) Montgomery; *qv*) an only s:

(1) Sir GEORGE VILLIERS, 2nd Bt, of Goadby Marwood, Leics, later Brokesby; *b* Feb 1619/20; royalist Civil War; *m* 17 June 1641 Margaret, 3rd dau of Sir George Dynham, of Boarstall, Bucks, by Penelope, dau of 1st Viscount Wenman of Tuam; *m* 2nd Mary (*dsp* 1699), dau of Thomas Golding, of Newhouse in Poslingford, Suffolk, and *d* 1682, leaving by his 1st w an only s:

1a Sir WILLIAM VILLIERS, 3rd and last Bt; *b* 1645; MP Leics 1698–1701; sold the Brokesby estate to his w's cousin Sir Nathan Wright; *m* 16 April 1668 Ann, dau of Charles Potts, of Mannington, Norfolk, by Susannah, sis of Sir Benjamin Wright, 1st Bt, and *dsp* 27 Feb 1711/2, when the btcy expired

1a Penelope; *m* Sir William Jesson and had issue (*see* ROBINSON, Bt, of London)

2 EDWARD (Sir)

1 Elizabeth; *m* by 1609 1st Baron Boteler of Brantfield and had issue (*see* GREY EGERTON, Bt, also SUFFOLK and BERKSHIRE, E)

2 Anne; *m* Sir William Washington, of Pakington, Lincs (*see* section Washington, AMERICAN PRESIDENTIAL FAMILIES, 1994, Morris Genealogical Books SA)

3 Frances; *d* unm

Sir GEORGE *m* 2nd Mary (*m* 2nd 19 June 1606 Sir William Rayner and 3rd Sir Thomas Compton (*see* NORTHAMPTON, M), was *cr* Countess of Buckingham for life 1 July 1618 and *d* 19 April 1632), dau of Anthony Beaumont, of Glenfield, Leics, and by her had:

3 JOHN VILLIERS, 1st VISCOUNT PURBECK, Co Dorset, so *cr* 19 July 1619, as also BARON STOKE, Co Buckingham (both E); *b c* 1591; ktd 1616, Groom Bedchamber and Master Robes to PRINCE OF WALES (later CHARLES I) 1616; *m* 1st 29 Sept 1617 Frances (ran away from him 1621 and had a son, presumably by her lover Sir Robert Howard, 5th s of 1st Earl of Suffolk (*see* SUFFOLK and BERKSHIRE, E), was declared guilty of adultery with Sir Robert by the Court of High Commission 19 Nov 1627 after a sitting of two and a half years, though a contemplated indictment for sorcery was not proceeded with, and sentenced to stand in the Savoy Church dressed in a white sheet holding a white wand, pay a fine of £333.16s.8d (over £16,000 in late–1990s terms) and go to prison during the Court's pleasure; she fled before her arrest, with the connivance of the Savoyard Ambassador, cohabited with Sir Robert in Shropshire and sought refuge with her father in Buckinghamshire, was eventually locked up in the Gate House Prison in London 1635 but managed to get away to France via the Channel Islands dressed as a man; *d* Oxford 4 June 1645), 2nd dau of Sir Edward Coke (*see* LEICESTER, E) by his 2nd w Elizabeth; *m* 2nd Elizabeth, dau of Sir William Slingsby and widow of Col Chichester Fortescue, and *dspl* 18 Feb 1657/8, when his titles expired, though his 1st w's son Robert, believed to be by Howard, was first declared by the House of Lords 1660 to be Viscount Purbeck (despite his having disclaimed the title on the death of his nominal f the 1st VISCOUNT) and then in 1678, four years after Robert's own death, was pronounced by the same body to have been illegitimate; Robert's son and gs did assume the Viscountcy, however

4 GEORGE VILLIERS (known to JAMES I by his pet name of 'Steenie', referring to St Stephen, who in Acts VII 15 is described as having 'the face of an angel', though there was nothing very angelic or saintly about VILLIERS except perhaps the manner of his death, which might be called martyrdom of a sort), 1st DUKE OF BUCKINGHAM, so *cr* 18 May 1623, as also EARL OF COVENTRY, and earlier 27 Aug 1616 BARON WHADDON OF WHADDON, Co Buckingham, and VISCOUNT VILLIERS, also 5 Jan 1616/7 EARL OF BUCKINGHAM, with a subsequent patent 14 March 1616/7 extending the remainder of all three previous creations to his brothers John and Christopher failing heirs male of his, the grantee's, body, also 1 Jan 1617/8 MARQUESS OF BUCKINGHAM (all E), KG (1616), PC (Feb 1616/7); *b* 28 Aug 1592; Cupbearer 1614, Gent Bedchamber 1615, ktd 1615, Master Horse 1616, Ld Lt Bucks 1616–28, Kent 1620 and Middx 1622–28; Ld High Adml Jan 1618/9, Ld Warden Cinque Ports 1624–28, Constable Dover and Windsor Castles 1624–28, Ch Commr War and Gen of the Fleet and the Army 1625, Amb Paris 1625 and 1626, the Hague autumn 1625, Ld High Constable for CHARLES I's Coronation Feb 1625/6; accompanied CHARLES I when PRINCE OF WALES to Spain in his fruitless attempt to bring off a marriage with a Spanish princess; mounted an unsuccessful expedition to the Ile de Rhé to relieve the Huguenots of La Rochelle and was embarking for a second such at Portsmouth when fatally stabbed 23 Aug 1628 by Lt John Felton; *m* 16 May 1620 Lady Katherine Manners, dau of 6th Earl of Rutland (*see* RUTLAND, D), and had, with other issue:

(1) GEORGE VILLIERS, 2nd and last DUKE OF BUCKINGHAM, KG (1649), PC (1650), also, in addition to the many other titles he inherited from his f, 19th LORD (Baron) DE ROS (*qv*) OF HELMSLEY through his mother; *m* 15 Sept 1657 Mary, dau of 1st Lord Fairfax of Cameron (*qv*) and *dspl* 16 April 1687, when all his titles expired bar the Barony of De Ros and conceivably the Earldom of Buckingham, Viscountcy of Villiers and Barony of Whaddon of Whaddon, which by virtue of the patent of March 1616/7 may have become merely dormant

5 CHRISTOPHER VILLIERS, 1st EARL OF ANGLESEY, so *cr* 18 April 1623, as also BARON VILLIERS OF DAVENTREE (*i.e.*, Daventry) (both E); *m* Elizabeth, dau of Thomas Sheldon, of Howby, Leics, and *d* 3 April 1630, leaving an only s:

(1) CHARLES VILLIERS, 2nd and last EARL OF ANGLESEY; *b c* 1627; *educ* Eton; *m* 25 April 1648 Mary, 3rd dau of Paul Bayning, 1st Viscount Bayning, and widow of **2nd Viscount Grandison of Limerick** (*see* below), and *dsp* of small pox (*bur* 4 Feb 1660/1), when his titles expired

4 Susan; *m* 1st Earl of Denbigh (*see* DENBIGH and DESMOND, E)

Sir GEORGE *d* 4 Jan 1605/6; his 2nd son,

Sir EDWARD VILLIERS; Amb Bohemia 1620, Pres Munster 1622; *m* Barbara (*bur* 16 Sept 1672), 5th dau of Sir John St John, of Lidiard Tregoze, Wilts (*see* BOLINGBROKE and SAINT JOHN, V), and niece of Sir OLIVER ST JOHN, **1st Viscount Grandison of Limerick**, Co Leitrim (I), so *cr* 3 Jan 1620/1, with special remainder to the heirs male of Barbara's body, and *d* 7 Sept 1626, having had:

1 WILLIAM VILLIERS, **2nd Viscount Grandison of Limerick**, as which *s* great-uncle, 29 Dec 1630; *b* 1614; ktd 1638; royalist Civil War; *m* 31 Oct 1639 Mary (*m* 2nd 25 April 1648 her late husb's cousin 2nd EARL OF ANGLESEY (*see* above), *m* 3rd Arthur Gorges and *d* by 20 Jan 1671/2), dau of 1st Viscount Bayning, and *d* 30 Sept 1643 of wounds recd at the Siege of Bristol 26 July 1643, leaving:

(1) BARBARA Villiers, DUCHESS OF CLEVELAND, so *cr* 3 Aug 1670, as also BARONESS NONSUCH, Co Surrey, and COUNTESS OF SOUTHAMPTON (all E), with remainder to her est s Charles and heirs male of his body then to her 3rd s George in like manner; *b c* 1641; mistress of CHARLES II and simultaneously with him of two actors, a funambulist, a playwright (Wycherley) and a Churchill (John, later 1st Duke of Marlborough), to mention only a few; *m* 1st 14 April 1659 Roger PALMER, 1st Earl of Castlemaine (*d* 1705), who seems to have fathered none of her children except possibly the est dau, though even here the weight of opinion credits the Earl of Chesterfield (*see* 1967 edn CHESTERFIELD and STANHOPE, E) with the paternity, while CHARLES II was induced to acknowledge *his* paternity of the baby in a warrant date 1673; went through a form of marriage 25 Nov 1705 (*annulled* 23 May 1707) with Robert ('Beau') Feilding, although his prior (and 2nd) w Mary Wadsworth was still alive, and *d* 13 Oct 1709, leaving, with other issue (in order of birth: Anne (*see* above), *b* 25 Feb 1660/1, *m* 11 Aug 1674 15th Lord (Baron) Dacre (*qv*); Henry, *b* 20 Sept 1663, 1st Duke of Grafton (*qv*); Charlotte, *b* 5 Sept 1664, *m* Feb 1677 Edward Henry Lee, 3rd Earl of Lichfield (*see* LICHFIELD, E, preliminary remarks, also Introduction (Fig. 1, p. 23) to AMERICAN PRESIDENTIAL FAMILIES, 1994, Morris Genealogical Books SA); George, *b* 28 Dec 1665, 1st and last Duke of Northumberland of the 1683 *cr* (*see* NORTHUMBERLAND, D, preliminary remarks); Barbara, *b* 16 July 1672 (allegedly by John Churchill, 1st Duke of Marlborough; *qv*), nun as Sister Benedicta, had issue 1691 by the 1st and last Earl of Arran of the 1662 *cr* (*see* MOUNTGARRET, V) but *d* unm; a son (allegedly by the actor Cardonell Goodman), *b* March 1686):

1a CHARLES PALMER later Fitz-ROY (1670), 2nd DUKE OF CLEVELAND, also 1st DUKE OF SOUTHAMPTON, so *cr* 10 Sept 1675, as also BARON OF NEWBURY, Co Berks, and EARL OF CHICHESTER (all E), KG (1673); *bapt* 18 June 1662; *m* 1st 1671 Mary (*dsp*), only dau of Sir Henry Wood, Bt; *m* 2nd autumn 1694 Anne, dau of Sir William Pulteney, and *d* 9 Sept 1730, leaving by her:

1b WILLIAM FitzROY, 3rd and last DUKE OF CLEVELAND and 2nd and last DUKE OF SOUTHAMPTON; *b* 19 Feb 1697/8; *m* 22 Jan 1731/2 Lady Henrietta Finch, 5th dau of 6th Earl of Winchilsea (*see* WINCHILSEA and NOTTINGHAM, E), and *dsp* 18 May 1774, when his titles expired

2 JOHN VILLIERS, **3rd Viscount Grandison of Limerick**; *m* Catherine (*bur* 16 Jan 1683/4), dau of John Clarke, and *dsp* in a Paris charity hospital 9 Nov 1659

3 GEORGE VILLIERS, **4th Viscount Grandison of Limerick**; ktd 1644, Capt Yeomen Gd 1662–88/9; *m* 1st by 1652 his cousin Lady Mary Leigh (*d* 7 July 1671), 2nd dau and coheiress of Francis, Earl of Chichester, by Audrey, 1st cousin of 1st Duke of Buckingham; *m* 2nd 14 Nov 1674 Mary, dau of Richard Garford, a tallow-chandler in the Minories, and widow of Sir Samuel Starling, Ld Mayor London, and *d* 16 Dec 1699, having had by his 1st w, with another dau:

(1) Edward VILLIERS later FitzGERALD; Brig-Gen, Lt Col Queen's Regt of Horse; *m* March 1676/7, as her 1st husb, Catherine, granted rank of viscount's w by roy warrant 6 Jan 1699/1700 (*m* 2nd Lt Gen William Steuart, PC, MP Co Waterford 1703–14, C-in-C Ireland 1711, and *d* insane 26 Dec 1725), dau and heiress of Sir John FitzGerald, of Dromana, Co Waterford, and *dvp* by 15 Feb 1692/3, having had, with other issue:

1a JOHN FitzGERALD alias VILLIERS, **5th Viscount Grandison of Limerick** and 1st and last EARL GRANDISON Co Leitrim (I), so *cr* 11 Sept 1721, PC (I) 1721); *b c* 1684; *educ* Eton and Magdalene Coll Cambridge; MP Old Sarum May-Dec 1705; *m* Feb 1705/6 Frances Cary, sis of 6th Viscount Falkland (*qv*), and *dspms* 14 May 1766, when the Earldom expired, having had:

1b James, *Lord Villiers*, MP Co Waterford 1730–32; *m* 10 July 1728 Jane (*m* 2nd 16 April 1734 7th Viscount Falkland (*qv*)), dau and heiress of Richard Butler, and *dvp* 12 Dec 1732, leaving by her an only dau

2b William, *Lord Villiers*; *b* 10 Jan 1715; *dvp* unm 16 Dec 1739

1b ELIZABETH Villiers, COUNTESS GRANDISON, so *cr* 19 Feb 1767, as also VISCOUNTESS VILLIERS, also earlier 10 April 1746 VISCOUNTESS GRANDISON OF DROMANA, Co Waterford (all I), with in all cases remainder to heirs male of her body; *m* 1st 12 June 1739 Aland John Mason (*d* 26 March 1759), MP Co Waterford, and had issue; *m* 2nd 15 Feb 1763 Maj-Gen Charles Montague Halifax and *d* 29 May 1782, leaving by her 1st husb an only surv child:

1c GEORGE MASON later MASON-VILLIERS (roy licence 21 Oct 1771), 2nd and last EARL GRANDISON, PC (I 1785); *b* 13 July 1751; *educ* Eton; MP (Tory) Ludlow 1774–80; *m* 10 Feb 1772 Lady Gertrude Seymour-Conway, dau of 1st Marquess of Hertford (*qv*), and *dspm* 14 July 1800, when all his titles expired, leaving:

1d Gertrude Emilia; *b* 28 March 1778; *m* 1 July 1802 Lord Henry Stuart, 5th s of 1st Marquess of Bute (*qv*), and had issue

1a Mary; *m* Rt Hon Brig-Gen Stuart, MP (*d* 3 June 1726), and *d* 24 Dec 1725

2a Harriet; *m* Robert Pitt (*d* 20 May 1727), of Boconnock, Cornwall, and *d* 21 Oct 1736, having had a 2nd s:

1b WILLIAM PITT, 1st EARL OF CHATHAM, Co Kent, so *cr* 4 Aug 1766, as also VISCOUNT PITT OF BURTON PYNSENT (commemorating an estate bringing in £3,000 (over £155,000 in late–1990s terms) p.a. bequeathed him 1765 by Sir William Pynsent, Bt, who wished to show his appreciation of the Great Commoner's patriotism), Co Somerset (both GB), PC (1746); *b* 15 Nov 1708; *educ* Eton and Trin Coll Cambridge; Cornet 2nd King's Own Regt of Horse 1731/2–36, MP (Whig) Old Sarum 1735–47, Seaford 1747–54, Aldborough 1754–56, Okehampton 1756–57 and Bath 1757–66, Paymaster Gen 1746–55, Sec State South 1756–April 1757 and June 1757–61, Ld Privy Seal and effective PM (till 1767 — though the Duke of Grafton was nominally so — when his health broke down, though he continued to dominate the H of C from the opposition benches, albeit intermittently, for another 11 years, being felled by a seizure after a tremendous speech calling for a cessation of hostilities with the American colonists 30 May 1777) 1766–68; *m* 15 Nov 1754 Hester, *cr* 4 Dec 1761 Baroness Chatham in her own right, sis of 2nd Earl Temple (*see* TEMPLE OF STOWE, E), and *d* 11 May 1778, leaving:

1c JOHN PITT, 2nd and last EARL OF CHATHAM, also 2nd and last BARON CHATHAM (as which *s* mother 1803), KG (1790), PC (1789); *b* 9 Oct 1756; Col 4th Foot 1799–1835, Gen 1812, First Ld Admlty 1788–94, Ld Privy Seal 1794–96, Ld Pres Cncl 1796–1801, cmded the disastrous Walcheren Expdn of 1809 as Lt Gen, when his tardiness and laziness combined to bring failure; *m* 10 July 1783 Hon Mary Elizabeth Townshend, dau of 1st Viscount Sydney of St Leonards (*see* TOWNSHEND, M), and *dsp* 24 Sept 1835, when all his titles expired

2c William ('Pitt the Younger'); *b* 18 May 1759; PM 1783–1806 with but a short break; *d* unm 23 Jan 1806

1c Hester; *m* Earl Stanhope (*see* 1967 edn CHESTERFIELD and STANHOPE, E) and had issue

2c Harriet; *m* and had issue

(2) William; Col; *m* 1702 Katherine, dau of Sir Edward Villiers (*see* below) and widow of Louis James Le Vasseur, Marquis de Puissar, of France, and *d* 7 Sept 1723

(1) Anne; *m* Edward Rumbould (*see* RUMBOLD, Bt)

4 Christopher; *bapt* Westminster Abbey 8 April 1619; *d* young

5 Edward (Sir), of Richmond; *bapt* 15 April 1620; ktd 1680, Kt Marshal Household, Govr Tynemouth Castle; *m* 1st Lady Frances Howard (*bur* 27 Nov 1677), yst dau of 2nd Earl of Suffolk (*see* SUFFOLK and BERKSHIRE, E); *m* 2nd 25 Feb 1683/4 Martha Love (*d* 1738) and was *bur* 2 July 1689, having by his 1st w had:

(1) EDWARD, **1st Earl**

(2) Henry; Col of Foot, Govr Tynemouth Castle 1702; *d* 18 Aug 1707, leaving:

1a Henry; *m* 1st Arabella, dau of John Rossiter, of Somerby, Lincs; *m* 2nd Mary, sis of Lt-Gen Thomas Fowke, and *d* 29 May 1753

(1) Elizabeth; Maid-of-Honour to MARY II and mistress to the latter's husb WILLIAM III; *m* 26 Nov 1695 1st Earl of Orkney (*qv*) and *d* 19 April 1733, leaving issue

(2) Katherine; *m* 1st 20 July 1685 Louis James Le Vasseur, Marquis de Puissar (*d* 1701), of France; *m* 2nd 1702 her cousin Col William Villiers (*see* above)

(3) Barbara; *m* 4th Viscount FitzHardinge (*d* 19 Dec 1712) and *d* 19 Sept 1708, leaving issue

(4) Anne/Frances; *m* Feb 1678 1st Earl of Portland (*qv*) and *d* Nov 1688, leaving issue

(5) Henrietta; *m* 23 May 1695 2nd Earl of Breadalbane (*see* 1970 edn) and *d* 1 Feb 1719/20, leaving issue

(6) Mary; *m* April 1691 3rd Earl of Inchiquin (*see* INCHIQUIN, B) and *d* 17 April 1753, leaving issue

1 Barbara; *bapt* 1 June 1622; *m* 1st Richard Wenman (*dsp* & *vp* 1646), only s of 2nd Viscount Wenman of Tuam; *m* 2nd Sir Richard Wentworth; *m* 3rd 13 Feb 1650 3rd Earl of Suffolk (*see* SUFFOLK and BERKSHIRE, E) and *d* 13 Dec 1681

2 Elizabeth; *m* 8th Earl of Morton (*qv*) and *d* Dec 1654, leaving issue

3 Eleanor; *d* unm, *bur* 16 July 1685

Sir EDWARD's est son,

EDWARD VILLIERS, **1st Earl of the Island of Jersey**, so *cr* 13 Oct 1697, as also earlier 20 March 1690/1 BARON VILLIERS OF HOO, Co Kent, and VISCOUNT VILLIERS OF DARTFORD, Co Kent (all E), PC (1697–1707); *b c* 1656; Master of the Horse to MARY II Feb 1688/9–95, Kt Marshal Household 1689–99, Min to The Hague 1695, Jt Plen Congress of Ryswick 1696, a Ld Justice Ireland 1697–99, Amb The Hague 1697–98 and Paris 1698–99, Sec State South 1699–1700, Jt Plen 2nd Treaty of Partition of Spanish Empire 1700, Ld Chamberlain 1700–04; *m* Dec 1681 Barbara (*d* by 13 Dec 1735), dau of William Chiffinch, Closet Keeper to CHARLES II, and had:

1 WILLIAM, **2nd Earl**

2 Henry; *dsp* May 1743

1 Mary; *m* 1st Thomas Thynne and had issue (*see* BATH, M); *m* 2nd 1711 George Granville, 1st and last Baron Lansdown of Biddeford [*sic*] (*d* 30 Jan 1734/5), and *d* 17 Jan 1734/5, leaving further issue

The 1st EARL *d* 25 Aug 1711; his est son,

WILLIAM VILLIERS, **2nd Earl of the Island of Jersey**; *b c* 1682; MP (Tory) Kent 1705–08, Jacobite, *cr* by titular James III April 1716 Baron of Hoo, Co Kent, Viscount of Dartford, Co Kent, and Earl of Jersey (all E); *m* 22 March 1704/5 Judith (*d* 22 July 1735), only dau and heiress of Frederick Herne, s of Sir Nathaniel Herne, Alderman and Sheffif City London, and had:

1 WILLIAM, **3rd Earl**

2 THOMAS VILLIERS, 1st EARL OF CLARENDON (*qv*)

1 Barbara; *m* 1st 20 Sept 1725 Sir William Blackett, 2nd Bt, of Newcastle; *m* 2nd 13 March 1729 4th and last Baron Mansell of Margam (*see* MANSEL, Bt) and *d* 11 June 1761, having had an only dau and heiress:

(1) Louisa Barbarina; *m* 16 July 1757 2nd Baron Vernon (*qv*), and *dsps* Jan 1776

The 2nd EARL *d* 13 July 1721; his er son,

WILLIAM VILLIERS, **3rd Earl of the Island of Jersey** and **6th Viscount Grandison of Limerick**, as which *s* cousin 1766, PC (1747); *educ* Eton and King's Coll Cambridge; *m* 23 June 1733 Lady Anne Egerton (*d* 16 June 1734), dau of 1st Duke of Bridgwater (*see* GREY EGERTON, Bt) and widow of 3rd Duke of Bedford (*qv*), and *d* 28 Aug 1769, having had:

1 Frederick William, *Viscount Villiers*; *b* 25 March 1734; *bur* 11 Oct 1742

2 GEORGE BUSSY VILLIERS, **4th Earl of the Island of Jersey**, PC (1765); *b* 9 June 1735; MP Tamworth 1756–65, Aldborough 1765–68 and Dover 1768–69, a Ld Admlty 1761–62, V-Chamberlain Household 1765–69, Master Buckhounds 1782–83, Capt Gent Pensioners 1783–90; *m* 26 March 1770 Frances (the mistress of GEORGE IV before supplanted by Isabella Lady Hertford (*see* HERTFORD, M); *d* 23 July 1821), only dau and heiress of Rt Rev Philip Twysden, DD, Bp Raphoe, s of Sir William Twysden, Bt (*see* 1970 edn), and had, with other issue:

(1) GEORGE, **5th Earl**

(2) William Augustus Henry VILLIERS later MANSEL (roy licence 1802, taken under terms of will of Louisa Barbara, Baroness Vernon); *b* 15 Nov 1780; *d* unm 1813

(1) Charlotte Anne; *m* 11 July 1789 Lord William Russell (murdered 6 May 1840; *see* BEDFORD, D) and *d* 31 Aug 1808, leaving issue

(2) Anna Barbara Frances; *m* 1st 19 June 1791 William Henry Lambton, of Lambton (*see* DURHAM, E); *m* 2nd Hon Charles William Wyndham (*see* EGREMONT, LECONFIELD and, B) and *d* 21 April 1832

(3) Caroline Elizabeth; *m* 1st 25 July 1795 (*divorce* 1810) 1st Marquess of Anglesey (*qv*); *m* 2nd 29 Nov 1810 6th Duke of Argyll (*qv*) and *d* 16 June 1835

(4) Elizabeth Frances; *m* 13 Jan 1803 1st and last Viscount Ponsonby of Imokilly (*see* BESSBOROUGH, E)

The 4th EARL *d* 22 Aug 1805; his er son,

GEORGE VILLIERS later CHILD-VILLIERS (roy licence 1 Dec 1819), **5th Earl of the Island of Jersey**, GCH (1834), PC (1830); *b* 19 Aug 1773; *educ* Harrow and St John's Coll Cambridge (MA); DCL Oxford, Ld Chamberlain July-Nov 1830 and 1834–35, Master Horse 1841–46 and March-Dec 1852; *m* 23 May 1804 Lady Sarah Sophia Fane (*d* 26 Jan 1867), est dau of 10th Earl of Westmorland (*qv*) by his 1st w Sarah Anne, dau of the banker Robert Child, of Osterley Park, Middx, who left his gdau his estates (including Osterley), whence the **5th Earl**'s augmenting his name, and had, with other issue:

1 GEORGE AUGUSTUS FREDERICK, **6th Earl**

2 Augustus John; Capt RHG (Blues); *b* 10 July 1810; *m* 20 Sept 1831 Georgiana Augusta Henrietta (*m* 2nd 10 May 1870 Lord William Godolpin Osborne (*d* 28 Dec 1888; *see* 1963 edn LEEDS, D), and *d* 21 Sept 1892), 2nd dau of George, Viscount Keith, and *dsp* 24 May 1847

3 Frederick William; Lt-Col 73rd Regt; MP Weymouth 1847–52, High Sheriff N Hants 1869; *b* 20 July 1815; *m* 12 July 1842 Elizabeth (*d* 7 Jan 1897), sister of 9th Earl of Athlone, and *dsp* 23 May 1871

1 Sarah Frederica Caroline; *m* 8 Feb 1842 Prince Nicholas Esterhazy von Galantha (*d* Jan 1894), est s of the diplomat Prince Paul Antony Esterhazy, and *d* 17 Nov 1853, leaving issue

The 5th EARL *d* 3 Oct 1859; his est son,

GEORGE AUGUSTUS FREDERICK CHILD-VILLIERS, **6th Earl of the Island of Jersey**; *b* 4 April 1808; *educ* Eton and Ch Ch Oxford (MA); MP (C) Rochester 1830–31, Minehead 1831–32, Honiton 1832–35, Weymouth 1837–41 and Cirencester 1844–52; *m* 2 July 1841 Julia (*m* 2nd 12 Sept 1865 Charles Branding, of Middleton Hall, Yorks, and *d* 14 Aug 1893), est dau of Rt Hon Sir Robert Peel, 2nd Bt (*see* PEEL, E), and had, with other issue:

1 VICTOR ALBERT GEORGE, **7th Earl**

1 Julia Sarah Alice; *m* 3 Sept 1861 Sir George Orby Wombwell, 4th Bt (*qv*), and *d* 24 Oct 1921, leaving issue

2 Caroline Anne; *m* 4 April 1872 William Henry Philips Jenkins, of Raglan House, Briton Ferry, S Wales, and had issue (*see* RASHLEIGH, Bt)

The 6th EARL *d* 24 Oct 1859; his est son,

VICTOR ALBERT GEORGE CHILD-VILLIERS, **7th Earl of the Island of Jersey**, GCB (1900), GCMG (1890), PC (1890), JP (Oxon), JP and DL (Warwicks); *b* 20 March 1845; *educ* Eton and Balliol Coll Oxford; Hon DCL Oxford, Hon Col 1st Welsh Bde RFA, Oxon: Ld Lt and custos rotulorum 1887, Pres TFA, CA, Ld-in-Waiting 1875–77, Paymaster-Gen 1889–90, Govr and C-in-C NSW 1890–93, chm Light Railway Commn 1896–1905; *m* 19 Sept 1872 Hon Margaret Elizabeth Leigh DBE, JP (Co London) (*d* 22 May 1945), est dau of 2nd Baron Leigh (*qv*), and had:

1 GEORGE HENRY ROBERT CHILD, **8th Earl**

2 Arthur George, DSO (1917) and bar (1918), DL (Oxon); Maj QO Oxon Hus, ADC, personal staff 1914, WW I (despatches, Croix de Guerre); *b* 24 Nov 1883; *educ* Eton and New Coll Oxford; *d* unm 7 May 1969

1 Margaret; *b* and *d* 24 April 1874

2 Margaret, OStJ; *b* 8 Oct 1875; *m* 12 Oct 1898 7th Baron Dynevor (*qv*) and *d* 1 April 1959, leaving issue

3 Mary Julia; *b* 26 May 1877; *m* 8 Nov 1899 5th Earl of Longford (*qv*) and *d* 21 Nov 1933, leaving issue

4 Beatrice;24 April 1990; *m* 15 Oct 1904 18th Baron Dunsany (*qv*) and *d* 30 May 1970, leaving issue

The 7th EARL *d* 31 May 1915; his est son,

GEORGE HENRY ROBERT CHILD-VILLIERS, **8th Earl of the Island of Jersey**, JP and DL (Oxon), JP (Middx); *b* 2 June 1873; CA Middx, V-Chm Oxford CC, High Steward City of Oxford, Ld-in-Waiting 1919; *m* 8 Oct 1908 Lady Cynthia Almina Constance Mary Needham (*m* 2nd 5 June 1925 Cdr William Rodney Slessor, RNVR (*d* 14 April 1945), 2nd s of Maj Arthur Kerr Slessor, MA, Sherwood Foresters, of Newland House, Eynsham, Oxon, and *d* 12 Jan 1947), only dau of 3rd Earl of Kilmorey (*qv*), and *d* 31 Dec 1923, having had:

1 GEORGE FRANCIS CHILD-VILLIERS, **9th and present Earl of the Island of Jersey**

2 (Edward) Mansel; S/Ldr RAF WW II (despatches), 2nd Lt 17th/21st Lancers SR Offrs; *b* 3 May 1913; *educ* Eton; *m* 1st 5 April 1934 (*divorce* 1940) Mary Barbara (*d* 1991), only dau of Capt William John Goulburn Shipdem Frampton, E Lancs Regs, of Newton Hall, Clitheroe, and had issue:

(1) +(Edward) John Mansel Hugh Frampton [John Child-Villiers Esq, Stable House, Mystole, Kent CT4 7DB]; *b* 29 April 1935; *educ* Harrow; *m* 2 June 1958 *Celia Elinor Vadyn, only dau of Cyril Hall Green, of Ballyvolane Ho, Castle Lyons, Co Cork, by Elinor Joyce, yr dau of Maj Cecil Bruce Blake (*see* BLAKE, Bt, of Menlough,), and has:

1a +Alexander [Alexander Child-Villiers Esq, 19 Kings Court North, 189 Kings Rd, London SW3 5EQ]; *b* 24 Aug 1961; *m* 1988 (*divorce* 1993) Linda-Benedicte, dau of Björn-Arild Solheim, of Oslo, and has:

1b +Frederick Mansel; *b* 24 March 1990

2a +Roderick Anthony [Roderick Child-Villiers Esq, 36 Cristowe Rd, London SW6 3QE]; *b* 28 June 1963

2 (cont.) S/Ldr Mansel Child-Villiers *m* 2nd 1 March 1946 (*divorce* 1971) Princess Marie Gloria Pignatelli Aragona Cortez, only dau of Prince Antonio Pignatelli Aragona Cortez, Duke of Terranova, of Rome, and *d* 9 March 1980, having by her had:

(2) +(George Anthony) Robert [Robert Child-Villiers Esq, 4 Kensington Gate, London W8]; *b* 18 Feb 1947; *educ* Oratory Sch Reading; *m* 1973 (*divorce* 1989) Margot Vida Stott and has by *Norah Mary Jennifer Gladwell, *née* Binyon:

1a *Miranda Kate; *b* 1986

(1) Cynthia Beatrice; *b* 13 Dec 1948; *d* 30 June 1949

(2) *Mary-Ann Keston; *b* 1 Dec 1951; *m* 1971 (*divorce* 1986) Stephen John Beck and has:

1a *Christian Mark Stephen; *b* 1976

1a *Honor Marie; *b* 1979

(3) *(Maria) Consuelo (Lily) [Ms Consuelo Child-Villiers, 3 Hazelmere Rd, London NW6]; *b* 21 Aug 1953; has by *Prince Costantino Filippo Maria Ruspoli di Poggio Suasa:

1a *Bartolomeo Sebastian; *b* 1976

1 *Joan [The Lady Joan Colville,Holly Bush Farm, Stoney Heath, Ramsdell, Hants RG25 5SL]; *b* 26 Sept 1911; *m* 21 Jan 1933 David Richard Colville (*see* COLVILLE OF CULROSS, V) and has issue

2 *Ann [The Lady Ann Elliot, Broadford, Chobham, Surrey GU24 8EF]; *b* 23 May 1916; *m* 8 June 1937 Maj Alexander Henry Elliot (*see* MINTO, E) and has issue

JESSEL

Arms: Azure a fess raguly ermine, between three eagle's heads erased argent, in the centre chief point a torch erect, fired proper. **Crest:** A torch fesswise, fired proper, surmounted by an eagle volant argent, holding in the beak a pearl, also argent. **Motto:** Persevere. **Creation:** Bt. (UK) 25 May 1883.

SIR CHARLES JOHN JESSEL, 3RD BT, of Ladham House, Kent, JP (Kent 1960–78) [Sir Charles Jessel Bt, Ladham House, Ladham Rd, Goudhurst, Kent TN17 1DB]; *b* 29 Dec 1924; *s* f 1977; *educ* Eton and Balliol Coll Oxford; Lt 15th/19th Hus WW II (despatches); *m* 1st 9 June 1956 Shirley Cornelia (*d* 23 Oct 1977), only dau of John Waters, of Northampton, and has:

1 +GEORGE ELPHINSTONE [George Jessel Esq, Stoakes Cottage, Hastingleigh, Kent TN25 5HG]; *b* 15 Dec 1957; *educ* Milton Abbey and RAC Cirencester; *m* 1st 1988 (*divorce* 1993) Rose Amelia, yr dau of James Coutts-Smith, of Wallington, Herts; *m* 2nd 25 April 1998 *D I Victoria, yst dau of Capt A J B Naish, RN, of Ditteridge, Wilts

2 +Alastair John [Alastair Jessel Esq, Ladham House, Goudhurst, Kent TN17 1DB]; *b* 19 Aug 1959; *educ* Stowe and City of London Poly; md Stowell Ltd 1991–; *m* 1988 *Gail Alexandra, only dau of Gordon Partridge, of The Barbican, London EC2, and has:

(1) +Thomas George William; *b* 1990

(1) *Camilla Alice Louise; *b* 1991

1 *(Cornelia) Sarah; *b* 29 July 1963

Sir CHARLES *m* 2nd 1979 (*divorce* 1983) Gwendolyn Mary, dau of Laurence Devereux, OBE, and widow of Charles Langer, MA

Lineage: Sir GEORGE JESSEL, PC, QC (1865) (yst s of Zadok Aaron Jessel, of Putney); *b* 13 Feb 1824; *educ* London U (MA); barrister Lincoln's Inn 1847, Bencher 1865, MP Dover 1868–73, Slr-Gen 1871, Master Rolls 1873, V-Chllr London U 1880; *m* 20 Aug 1856 Amelia (*d* 27 Sept 1898), est dau of Joseph Moses, and *d* 21 March 1883, leaving:

1 CHARLES JAMES (Sir), **1st Bt**

2 Sir HERBERT MERTON JESSEL, 1st Bt (UK), so *cr* 30 June 1917, and 1st BARON JESSEL, of Westminster, Co London (UK), so *cr* 8 Jan 1924, CB (1919), CMG (1918), TD, JP and DL (Co London); *b* 27 Oct 1866; *educ* Rugby and New Coll Oxford; Col (ret 1919), Capt 17th Lancers and Maj Berks Yeo India 1887–1890, Hon Col 1st Bn City of London Regt Roy Fus 1905–23; Remount Conducting Offr Oct 1914, Assist-Cmdt Army Remount Serv Dec 1914, Cmdt Lt-Col Jan 1915 (despatches twice), Col Dep-Dir Remounts War Off 1918–19, Controller Horse and Animals (unpaid) Min Munitions Disposals Bd 1919–20; MP (C) St Pancras 1896–1906 and 1910–18, Alderman Westminster (Mayor 1902–03), Chm Budget Protest League 1909, Pres London Municipal Soc (Chm 1904–15, Tstee 1915–24), London Whip C Centl Off 1920–27, Pres Met Mayors' Assoc, memb Crown Lands Advsy Ctee 1933–41, Offr: Legn Hon, Order Leopold Belgium, Hon Freeman Westminster 1948; *m* 20 Dec 1894 Maud (*d* 28 Oct 1965), 5th dau and coheir of Sir Julian Goldsmid, 3rd and last Bt, PC, MP (*see* 1896 edn), and *d* 1 Nov 1950, having had:

(1) EDWARD HERBERT JESSEL, 2nd BARON JESSEL, CBE (1963); *b* 25 March 1904; *educ* Eton and Ch Ch Oxford (BA 1925); barrister Inner Temple 1926, Dep Chm Ctees and Dep Speaker Ho Lds, Chm Assoc League 1974; *m* 1st 14 Feb 1935 (*divorce* 1960) Lady Helen Maglona Vane-Tempest-Stewart (*d* 11 March 1986), 3rd dau of 7th Marquess of Londonderry (*qv*), and *d* 13 June 1990, having had:

1a Timothy Edward; *b* 23 Dec 1935; *educ* Eton; 2nd Lt RHG (The Blues), dir Timeward Investments and Timeward Electric Ltd; *m* 1st 8 June 1961 (*divorce* 1964) Janet Ursula Calliope, yr dau of Maurice Winnington Smith, of Bidborough, Kent, by Joan Mary, only dau of Hugh Micklem, JP; *m* 2nd 26 Aug 1965 *Jill Elizabeth [Mrs Donald Gomme, Ave Edouard Rod 30, 1007 Lausanne, Switzerland] (*m* 2nd 1977 (Edwin) Donald Gomme), only dau of George Alexander Powell, of Auckland, NZ, and *d* 27 Dec 1969, having by her had:

1b *Annabel Helen; *b* 23 July 1968

1a *Camilla Edith Mairi Elizabeth [The Hon Camilla Jessel, Calle Lope de Vega 29, Madrid 28014, Spain]; *b* 17 April 1940; *m* 1 Nov 1960 (*anulled* 1972, resumed maiden name), as his 1st w, Juan Carlos del Prado y Ruspoli, Marqués de Caicedo, s of Marqués de Acapulco, of Madrid, and has:

1b *Miguel Angel; *b* 6 Sept 1961; *m* 1989 (*divorce* 1997) Natalia, dau of Nicholas Sartorius, of Spain, and has:

1c *Claudia Rebecca Leonor; *b* 1992

2b *Alfonso Segundo; *b* 19 Dec 1966; *m* 27 April 1996 *Nicole de Vitry d'Avancourt, est dau of Comte Geoffroy de Vitry d'Avancourt, and has:

1c *Mariano; *b* 12 Oct 1996

2c *Jaime; *b* 12 Oct 1996

2a *Joanne Margaret [The Hon Mrs Butler, 13 Paultons St, London SW3]; *b* 14 March 1945; *m* 19 Oct 1967 *Simon Laforey Butler, yr s of Patrick John Butler, of Medland Manor, Cheriton Bishop, Devon, and has:

1b *Ashley Edward Hubert; *b* 22 Feb 1969

(1) Gladys May; *b* 13 May 1896; *d* unm 14 May 1976

(2) Vera Pearl; *m* 7 July 1925 Capt Clive Harrison Martyn, MC, RE (*d* 4 Jan 1959), s of Charles Harrison Martyn, of Aspley Guise, Beds, and *d* 21 Aug 1928, leaving issue

(3) Doreen Maud; *b* 7 Feb 1909; *educ* UCL (BA 1931) and Courtauld Inst (Dip 1933); Admin Assist War Cabinet Offs 1942–43 and 1944–45; *m* 25 April 1934 Sir Geoffrey William Gerald Agnew (*see* AGNEW, Bt, of Gt Stanhope St) and *d* 1990, leaving issue

(1) (cont.) The 2nd BARON JESSEL *m* 2nd 20 Dec 1960 *Jessica Marian [The Rt Hon The Lady Jessel, 4 Sloane Terrace Mansions, London SW1X 9DG], dau of William de Wet and Mrs H Taylor, of Rondebosch, Cape Town, and *d* 1990, when his titles expired

1 Emma; *b* 27 Aug 1857; *m* 27 June 1877 Ludwig Nathan Hardy (*d* 1890) and *d* 27 July 1923, leaving issue

2 Constance; *b* 6 Oct 1858; *m* 24 July 1883 Sir Edward David Stern, 1st Bt, DL (*d* 17 April 1933), and *d* 22 April 1918

3 Lucy; *b* 25 Nov 1870; *d* unm 12 May 1942

Sir GEORGE's er son,

Sir Charles James Jessel, 1st Bt (UK), so *cr* 25 May 1883, JP and DL (Kent); *b* 11 May 1860; MA Oxon; barrister, High Sheriff Kent 1903; *m* 15 July 1890 Edith (*d* 1 Jan 1956), dau and coheir of Sir Julian Goldsmid, 3rd and last Bt, and had:

1 GEORGE (Sir), **2nd Bt**

2 Richard Hugh (Sir), of Coney Weston Hall, Suffolk; *b* 21 Feb 1896; *educ* Eton; Lt 5th Bn E Kent Regt, Lt 7th Bn Hants Regt, WW I, Min Ec Warfare 1939–41 and Air Min 1941–44, Commr Public Works-Loans 1949–60, memb Advsy Cncl Export Credits Guarantee Dept 1950–60 (Dep Chm 1959–60), ktd 1960; *m* 1st 5 July 1923 Margaret Ella (*d* 20 April 1953), yr dau of Sir George James Graham Lewis, 2nd Bt (*see* 1940 edn), and had:

(1) David Charles George; *b* 20 June 1924; *educ* Eton; Capt Coldstream Gds WW II, FIB; *m* 1st 26 April 1950 (*divorce* 1978) Hon Amelia Grace FitzRoy, yst dau of 2nd Viscount Daventry (*qv*), and had:

1a +Richard James [Richard Jessel Esq, 9 Creswell Gdns, London SW5 0BJ]; *b* 5 Jan 1954; *educ* Eton; *m* 3 Sept 1982 *Harriot Josephine, dau of Wilfred J (Michael) de St Pierre Bunbury, and has:

1b +David Hugh Joseph; *b* 1986

2b +George Fitzroy; *b* 1990

1b *Edwina Mary Grace; *b* 1984

1a *Davina Jane; *b* 6 April 1952 [Mrs Charles Phillips, Ashland House, N Sydmonton, Berks RG20 9JL]; *m* 1st 17 Oct 1970 (*divorce* 1976) Hon Richard Tyrell-Kenyon (*d* 1982) and has issue (*see* KENYON, B); *m* 2nd 14 Dec 1977 (*divorce* 1984) James Remington-Hobbs, er s of C Remington-Hobbs, and has further issue:

1b *Max Hugh; *b* 1979

1a (cont.) *Mrs Davina Remington-Hobbs *m* 3rd 1988 *Charles Richard Markham Phillips and by him has:

2b *Richard David Markham; *b* 1988

3b *David Charles; *b* 1991

(1) (cont.) David Jessel *m* 2nd 1980 *Matilda McCormick [Mrs David Jessel, 22 Cambridge Rd, London SW11 4RR], of Kentucky, USA, and *d* 20 Sept 1985

(2) +Robin Richard [Robin Jessel Esq, 12 Crooms Hill Grove, London SE10 8HB]; *b* 23 Feb 1930; *educ* Eton and Balliol Coll Oxford (BA 1951, MA 1957); barrister Lincoln's Inn 1953; *m* 1 June 1957 *Audrey Gertrude, er dau of Alexander Newman Howard, of The Beacon, Staplecross, Sussex, and has had:

1a +Simon Dana; *b* 6 April 1958; *m* 21 Sept 1987 *Christina Julia, yst dau of Dennis Reeves, of Parkstone, Dorset, and has:

1b +William George; *b* 7 June 1995

1b *Ella; *b* 20 Sept 1988

2b *Sarah Louise; *b* 11 Feb 1990

3b *Madeleine Tasia; *b* 2 Jan 1993

2a Anthony Hugh; *b* 3 Dec 1959; *d* 14 April 1961

3a +Alexander Robin; *b* 27 May 1961

4a +Michael Richard; *b* 22 April 1965; *m* 31 July 1996 *Katherine Ann, dau of Gordon Wing, of Collets Green, Worcs

1a *Virginia Penelope; *b* 9 Jan 1967

(1) *Edith Marie [Mrs William Straker-Smith, Carham, Cornhill-on-Tweed, Northumberland]; *b* 8 May 1926; *educ* St Hilda's Coll Oxford (MA); *m* 4 Dec 1947 Capt William Joseph Straker-Smith, Coldstream Gds (*d* 1987), only s of Sir Thomas Dalrymple Straker-Smith, of Carham Hall, Cornhill-on-Tweed, and has:

1a *Peter Dalrymple [Peter Straker-Smith Esq, Wark Common Farm, Cornhill-on-Tweed, Northumberland TD12 4RR]; *b* 11 April 1951; *educ* Eton and Pembroke Coll Cambridge (MA); *m* 1981 *Susan Steuart and has:

1b *Henry Falkland; *b* 1982

1b *Willa; *b* 1984

2a *Richard David [Richard Straker-Smith Esq, 8 Rossetti Gdns Mansions, Flood St, London SW3]; *b* 6 Feb 1959; *educ* Harrow

1a *Tessa Diana [Mrs John Robson, Melbourne Stud, Ayot Green, Welwyn, Herts]; *b* 20 April 1949; *m* 21 Jan 1969 *John Robert Robson, 2nd s of Michael Robson, of Hales Place, Tenterden, Kent, and has:

1b *James; *b* 1973

1b *Claire; *b* 1972

2 (cont.) Sir Richard Jessel *m* 2nd 27 July 1954 Daphne (*d* 13 April 1971), er dau of William Buckley Gladstone, of Moortown House, Ringwood, Hants, and S Kensington, and widow of Maj Thirlwall G Phillipson, MC, Life Gds; *m* 3rd 10 Jan 1972 *Diana Mary (*m* 4th 1981 Col J C Cockburn, DSO, OBE (*d* 1997), Argyll and Sutherland Highrs), yr dau of Maj William Edward Gatacre, of de Wiersse, Vorden, Holland, widow of Col George Trotter, RSG, and formerly w of James Edward Michael Clark-Hall, and *d* 15 July 1979

1 Nina Dorothy; *b* 2 July 1893; *d* unm 20 July 1983

2 Marjorie Constance; *b* 16 Oct 1897; *d* unm 26 June 1940

Sir CHARLES *d* 15 July 1928; his er son,

Sir George Jessel, 2nd Bt, MC, JP (Kent 1940); *b* 17 May 1891; *educ* Eton and Balliol Coll Oxford (BA and MA 1917); Capt 5th Bn E Kent Regt (The Buffs) WW I (wounded, despatches), Chm Bournemouth and Dist Water Co, Life Pres Imperial Continental Gas Assoc (fomerly Dir and Chm), High Sheriff Kent 1958; *m* 1st 1 Feb 1923 Muriel Gladys (*d* 26 Jan 1948), dau of Col John Worthy Chaplin, VC, CB, and widow of Maj Foster Swetenham, RSG, and had:

1 Sir CHARLES JOHN JESSEL, **3rd and present Bt**

1 *Gloria Joan; *d* 24 May 1925

Sir George *m* 2nd 7 June 1948 (Joan) Betty (*d* 2 Dec 1997), dau of David Ewart, OBE, MD, FRCS, of Chichester, and formerly w of 2nd Baron Russell of Liverpool (*qv*), and *d* 18 Aug 1977

JOHNSON of Bath

Arms: Per pale sable and azure, on a saltire argent, between three towers or, fired proper, one in chief and two in fess, and two tilting spears saltirewise in base of the second, five cocks of the first. **Crest:** A tower argent, on the battlements a cock proper. **Supporters:** Dexter, a Grenadier (28th Regt), habited and accoutred and arms ordered proper; sinister, a Light Infantry man (28th Regt), habited and accoutred, and arms trailed proper, supporting with his exterior hand a flag-staff also proper, therefrom flowing a banner gules, inscribed 'New Ross' in letters of gold. **Mottoes:** 1 (above the crest) *Vicisti et vivimus* ('Thou hast conquered, and we live'), 2 (below the shield) *Nunquam non paratus* ('Never unready'). **Creation:** Bt. (UK) 1 Dec 1818.

SIR PATRICK ELIOT JOHNSON, 8TH BT, of Bath; *b* 1955; *s f* 1989

Lineage: ALLEN JOHNSON, of Kilternan, Co Dublin (s of Christopher Johnson, of Kilternan); *m* 1st Anne and had a s; *m* 2nd Abigail, widow of John Walsh, of Ballykilcavan, Queen's Co, and dau of Benjamin Burton, of Burton Hall, and *d* 25 Aug 1747, leaving two further sons (Benjamin; Robert; both *m* and had issue); his s by his 1st w:

ALLEN JOHNSON, of Kilternan; *m* 1740 Olivia (*m* 2nd Gen Edward Pole), dau of John Walsh, of Ballykilcavan, and had:

1 John Allen (*see* 1953 edn WALSH, Bt, of Ballycilcavan)

2 HENRY (Sir), **1st Bt**

1 Anne; *m* 18 Feb 1765 Sir George Pigot, Bt, of Patshull (*qv*)

ALLEN JOHNSON *d* 30 July 1747; his 2nd son,

Sir Henry Johnson, 1st Bt (UK), so *cr* 1 Dec 1818, GCB; *b* 1 Jan 1748; Gen, Col 5th Foot, Govr Ross Castle, Co Wexford, cmded at the Battle of New Ross 5 June 1798 during 1798 Uprising in Ireland; *m* 1782 Rebecca (*d* March 1823), dau of David Franks, of Philadelphia, and *d* 18 March 1835, having had, with a yr s (George Pigot, Capt 81st Foot, *d* Spain 1812):

Sir Henry Allen Johnson, 2nd Bt; Kt Roy Mil Order of William of The Netherlands; *b* 26 Sept 1785; *educ* Ch Ch Oxford (MA); tutor and later ADC to THE PRINCE OF ORANGE Peninsular War under Duke of Wellington, Offr 31st Regt, war medal with five clasps for Ciudad Rodrigo, Badajoz, Salamanca, Vittoria and Pyrenees; *m* 8 June 1818 Charlotte Elizabeth (*d* 21 Feb 1883), dau of Frederick Philipse, of Philipseburg, New York, and sis of Col Philipse, of Rhual, Flintshire, and *d* 27 June 1860, leaving:

1 **Sir Henry Franks Frederic Johnson, 3rd Bt**; *b* 5 Feb 1819; Col cmdg forces Jamaica, Cdr forces Windward and Leeward Islands; *m* 16 Sept 1851 Emma Patty (*m* 2nd 24 June 1884 Sir Henry Turner Irving, GCMG, and *d* 5 Feb 1903), est dau of Sir David William Barclay, 10th Bt (*qv*), and *d* 20 June 1883, leaving:

(1) **Sir Henry Allen William Johnson, 4th Bt**, CB; *b* 9 Oct 1855; Col and Hon Brig-Gen, Lt-Col cmdg 1st Bn Yorks LI, Brig-Gen cmdg 3rd Inf Bde Coronation 1902, Col Gen Staff 8th Div Irish Cmd 1902–06, AAG, Gen HQ Centl Force HD 1914–15, DAG Centl Force and E Cmd as Brig-Gen 1915, Hon Brig-Gen 1918, served Jowaki campaign 1877 (medal with clasp), Afghanistan 1878–80 (medal with clasp for Ali Masjid), Burmese War 1886–87 (medal with two clasps) and WW I (despatches); *m* 1st 20 March 1886 Ella (lost in wreck of SS *Roumania* 27 Oct 1892), dau of Thomas Dyson, and had issue:

1a **Sir Henry Allen Beaumont Johnson, 5th Bt**; *b* 3 Jan 1887; Lt-Col cmdg 8th KGO Light Cav IA (ret 1937), Assist Adj RAF 1938, WW I 1914–16, Aden Field Force 1916–17, Afghan War 1919 (medal and clasp), WW II 1940–41: Roy Pioneer Corps, IA Liaison Offr Scottish Cmd 1942, Silver Jubilee Medal 1935, Coronation Medal 1937, King's Messenger 1942–51; *m* 30 April 1917 Dorothy Nora (*d* 25 Jan 1974), dau of Martyn Cecil Gurney, CMG, MVO, Consul-Gen Antwerp, and *d* 24 July 1965, leaving:

1b *Barbara Patty [Mrs Charles Roetter, 20 Claremont Rd, Twickenham, Middx]; *b* 27 Sept 1918; *m* 1942 Charles Frederic Roetter (*d* 1977), est s of Frederic Roetter, of E Orange, NJ, USA, and has:

1c *Martyn Frederic Alexander; *b* 1 April 1944; *educ* St Paul's and BNC Oxford; Research Fell Univ Coll Oxford; *m* 1976 *Joyce Stevens and has:

1d *Alexander Charles; *b* 1978

2d *Nicholas Martyn; *b* 1980

1d *Natasha Chantal; *b* 1983

1c *Christine Francis Ada; *b* 11 March 1946; *m* 5 June 1971 *Stephen A Rhodes, er s of H Rhodes, of Brighton, and has:

1d *Molly Jane; *b* 1975

2d *Colette Lindsay; *b* 1977

2b *Monica Lena [Mrs Florencio Escardo, Juncal 1335-1C, Buenos Aires, Argentina]; *b* 25 Nov 1921; *m* 1st 17 June 1941 (*divorce* 1952) Marshall Douglas Clare, only s of Percy Clare, of Paris, and has issue:

1c *Michael Charles Allen; *b* 24 Nov 1945; *educ* Shawnigan Coll Vancouver Island, Canada, and Victoria U, BC; *m* 1st 1969 (*divorce* 1974) Diana, dau of Bruce Hamilton Wardrope, of Winnipeg; *m* 2nd 1980 *Fay Margaret Foster and by her has:

1d *Brendan Marshall Foster; *b* 1982

1c *Marcia Dorothy; *b* 6 June 1943; *m* 14 Aug 1965 Michael Bennie (*d* 1974) and has:

1d *Christopher Michael; *b* 1966

1d *Claire Julia; *b* 1969

2b (cont.) Mrs Monica Clare *m* 2nd 30 Aug 1957 *Dr Florencio Enrique Escardo, s of Prof Florencio Escardo, of Buenos Aires, and by him has:

2c *Florencio Julian; *b* 27 March 1958; *m* 1981 *Irene Matyas

2c *Monica Carmen; *b* 19 Nov 1960; *m* 1982 *Fernando Garcia-Pullés and has:

1d *Josefina Maria; *b* 1984

3c *Pilar; *b* 5 Nov 1963

1a Phyllis Ida; *b* 17 Feb 1891; lost in wreck of SS *Roumania* 27 Oct 1892

(1) (cont.) **Sir Henry** *m* 2nd 18 Aug 1897 Georgina (*d* 31 March 1954), dau of Hon Amias Charles Orde-Powlett (*see* BOLTON, B), and *d* 10 April 1944, having by her had:

2a Daphne Letitia; *b* 1898; *d* unm 11 Sept 1963

(1) Louisa Mary; *m* 5 July 1887 Surgn-Lt-Col Arthur Wellesley Roche, AMS (*d* 1897), and *d* 24 Sept 1939, leaving issue

2 William Victor, JP; *b* 14 Sept 1822; Capt 90th Light Inf; *m* 17 May 1854 Catherine Delicia (*d* 24 Feb 1903), only dau of Robert Walters, barrister, and *d* 16 Sept 1891, having had:

(1) Victor George Ralph; *b* 14 Oct 1861; Capt Lincs Regt; *d* 20 April 1915

(2) Hugh Walters Beaumont; *b* 17 Oct 1865; Capt Liverpool Regt; *m* 16 April 1904 Winifred Mena (*m* 2nd 1916 Capt Allen Fenton Livingstone), yr dau of Charles Hill, of Fern Lea, Southampton; *d* 3 Jan 1916, leaving:

1a **Sir Victor Philipse Hill Johnson, 6th Bt**; *b* 7 May 1905; *educ* Cheltenham; WW II in RAFVR; *d* 198–

(3) Lionel Pigot; *b* 15 March 1867; *d* unm 4 Oct 1902

(1) Isabella; *b* 23 Nov 1862; *d* unm 8 Sept 1955

3 George Vanderheyden; *b* 6 March 1824; Lt-Gen, Col cmdg RA Crimea; *d* unm 11 July 1903

4 Edwin Beaumont (Sir), GCB, CIE; *b* 4 July 1825; RA 1842, Gen 1878, Col cmdg RA 1890, Sutlej Campaign 1845, Punjab Campaign, Indian Mutiny, memb Cncl of India 1875–76, Dir-Gen Mil Educn 1884–87; *d* unm 18 June 1893

5 Frederick Pigot (Rev); *b* 29 July 1826; MA, Rector Oaksey, Wilts; *m* 26 April 1866 Matilda (*d* 12 March 1883), dau of James Carnegy-Arbuthnott, of Balnamoon, Forfar, and *d* 2 June 1882, leaving:

(1) Oswald Carnegy; *b* 15 Aug 1867; barrister, Legal Sec to Bp Salisbury 1903–11; *m* 12 July 1892 Margaret Ward (*d* 1944), dau of Rev Edmond T Butler, of Trotton, Sussex; *dsp* Oct 1946

6 Charles Cooper (Sir), GCB, JP (Worcs); *b* 20 Dec 1827; Gen BSC; *m* 4 Jan 1860 Jemima Anne Frances (*d* 18 July 1920), dau of Rev George Martin by Lady Charlotte Sophia, dau of 2nd Earl of Saint Germans (*qv*), and *d* 7 Dec 1905, having had:

(1) Charles Edward; *b* 4 Aug 1861; Col 36th Sikhs IA, Hon Brig-Gen, served Burma 1886–87 (medal, two clasps), Br Centl Africa 1892–93 (medal) and NW Frontier India 1901–02 (medal and clasp); *m* April 1899 Susan Ellen (*k* by enemy action at Bath 27 April 1942), dau of Col C H Ewart; *d* 20 Aug 1930

(2) Arthur Cyril Beaumont; *b* 21 Jan 1863; Maj IA; *m* 7 March 1901 Roberta Joanna, dau of Inspr-Gen R Pottinger, RN, and *d* 11 Sept 1904, leaving:

1a Charles Robert; *b* 17 Feb 1902; Lt-Col Roy Fus WW II; *m* 11 March 1935 Mrs Eileen Agnes Johnstone (*d* 24 Oct 1976), dau of G C Mothershill, of Bedford; *ka* N Africa 13 Dec 1940, leaving:

1b *Diana Evelyn Johnson; *b* 19 Nov 1935; *m* *— Kiral

2a Cyril Martin Hugh; *b* posthumously 15 Jan 1905; served WW II

(3) Elliot Philipse, CB (1918); *b* 21 Nov 1866; Col RE, Hon Brig-Gen (ret 1920), served Chin-Lushai Expdn 1889–90 (medal), NW Frontier India 1897 (despatches twice, medal), Somaliland 1903–04 (medal), WW I 1914 on staff in Mesopotamia (despatches three times, Cdr Star of Romania); *m* 4 July 1892 Mary (*d* 29 Nov 1939), dau of Surgn-Maj-Gen James Inkson, AMS, and *d* 26 Nov 1925, leaving:

1a Percy Eliot; *b* 20 May 1893; Maj RFA WW I; *m* 1925 Molly, dau of James Payn, of Harding, Natal, and *d* 1962, leaving:

1b ROBIN ELLIOT (Sir), **7th Bt**

(4) Allen Victor, DSO (1918); *b* 20 Aug 1871; Col 1st Bn RF, served Tibet Expdn 1904, WW I (wounded thrice, despatches); *m* 23 April 1919 Angela Mary, widow of Brig-Gen Paul Aloysius Kenna, VC, DSO, ADC, and dau of Hubert Aloysius Tichborne Hibbert, and *d* 14 Nov 1939

7 Allen Bayard (Sir), KCB; *b* 2 May 1829; Army Gen, Mil Sec, India Office 1877–89; *d* unm 7 Feb 1907

8 Alured Clarke, CB; *b* 30 Oct 1832; Maj-Gen RA; *m* 1860 Mary (*d* 8 Dec 1908), dau of Pierce Gilbert Edward Taylor, Bengal CS, and *d* 9 Dec 1889, leaving:

(1) Alured FitzOwen; *b* 2 May 1865; Lt Madras SC; *d* 30 Oct 1891

(2) Gilbert Ward; *b* 31 Dec 1866; Lt-Col IA; *m* 1 March 1923 Marion, yst dau of A H Truslove, of Sale, Cheshire, and *d* 11 Jan 1924, leaving:

1a *Patricia Danino; *b* posthumously 23 Jan 1924

(3) Harold Albert; *b* 22 Feb 1868; Lt Northumberland Fus; *m* 1st 3 April 1900 Ethel Dora, 3rd dau of Maj-Gen William Skene Row, BSC; *m* 2nd 11 July 1908 Alice, dau of John Mitchell, of Plymouth, and *d* 18 June 1912
(4) Walter Piece; *b* 14 July 1869; Lt NI Div RA; *m* 1902 Evelyn, dau of John Leng, of Newcastle; *d* June 1915
(5) Christopher Allen; *b* 28 June 1872; *d* 15 May 1912
(1) Muriel Charlotte; *m* Edward Taylor; *d* 18 March 1911
9 Archibald Acheson; *b* 3 July 1835; Col Madras SC; *m* 7 Jan 1869 Agnes Sarah (*d* 16 Sept 1926), dau of Rev Arthur M F Browne, Vicar Affane and Aglish, and *d* 20 April 1894, leaving:
(1) Arthur Acheson; *b* 27 Aug 1870; *d* unm 1 Dec 1963
(2) Allen Edwin, DSO (1919); *b* 2 Oct 1878; *educ* Wellington and RMC Sandhurst; Lt-Col IA, served WW I, Afghan War 1919 (despatches), Mesopotamia 1920–21 (despatches, Brevet Lt-Col); *m* 14 June 1913 Phoebe Wynn (*d* 27 Oct 1961), only dau of Maj Alfred Elias, 7th Bn KRRC, and *d* 1972, having had:
1a +ALLEN ANTONY WYNN [Allen Johnson Esq, Pond Cottage, Potten End, Berkhamsted, Herts]; *b* 14 April 1916; heir presumptive; *educ* Charterhouse and St John's Coll Oxford (MA); WW II as Lt RA; *m* 25 Nov 1939 *Helen Janet Margaret, MA Oxon, only dau of W A Annett, of Berkhamsted, and has:
1b +Mark Allen William Wynn [Mark Johnson Esq, 12 Routh Rd, London SW18]; *b* 13 March 1948; *educ* Berkhamsted and St John's Coll Oxford; *m* 1969 *Caroline Jane, only dau of C R E Bowles, of London, and has:
1c +Alexander Mark Wynn; *b* 1970
1c *Melissa Caroline; *b* 1973
2c *Lydia Jane; *b* 1980
2b +Christopher Wynn; *b* 14 June 1948; *educ* UEA
1 Louisa Charlotte; *d* unm 20 Aug 1914
2 Harriet Maria; *m* 2 May 1857 Maj-Gen H T Tucker, CB (*d* 1896); *d* 14 May 1900, leaving issue
3 Olivia Elizabeth; *m* 2 Oct 1856 Col Richard A F Steward (*d* Dec 1899), of Nottington Ho, Dorset, and *d* 1894
4 Millicent Hamilton; *m* 8 Sept 1868 H Whiteside Cooke, and *d* 1891, leaving issue

The 6th Bt's cousin,

Sir Robin Elliot Johnson, 7th Bt; *b* 1929; *educ* St John's Coll Johannesburg; *m* 11 Aug 1954 *Barbara Alfreda (*m* 2nd 19––), dau of Alfred T Brown, of Germiston, Transvaal, and *d* 1989, having had:
1 Sir PATRICK ELLIOT JOHNSON, **8th and present Bt**
1 *Judith Marguerite; *b* 1959
2 *Heather Mary; *b* 1959

JOHNSON of New York

Arms: Argent two lions counter-rampant supporting a dexter hand gules, in chief three estoiles of the last, and in base a salmon naiant in water proper. **Crest:** An arm erect gules, encircled with a ducal crown or, the hand grasping a sword proper, pommel and hilt gold. **Mottoes:** 1 *Nec aspera terrent* ('Not even difficulties frighten me'), 2 *Deo Regique debeo* ('I owe all to God and the King'). **Creation:** Bt. (GB) 27 Nov 1755.

SIR PETER COLPOYS PALEY JOHNSON, 7TH BT, of New York, in North America [Sir Peter Johnson Bt, Dene End, Buckland Dene, Hants SO41 9DT]; *b* 26 March 1930; *s* f 1975; *educ* Wellington and Roy Mil Coll Science Shrivenham; RA 1949–61 (ret as Capt), author and publishing consultant, publishing dir Nautical Books, Macmillan London Ltd, 1981–86, dir Sea Sure Ltd 1965–73, dir and editor Nautical Publishing Co Ltd 1970–81, Br Del Internat Offshore (Yachting) Cncl 1970–79 (chm Int Tech Ctee 1973–76), ocean racing correspondent *Yachting World* 1971–81, Hon Col Kings Roy Regt of NY (Canada) 1988–; author: *Ocean Racing and Offshore Yachts* (1970), *Boating Britain* (1973), *Guiness Guide to Sailing* (1981), *The Encyclopedia of Yachting* (1989), *Yacht Clubs of the World* (1994) and *Yacht Rating* (1997); *m* 1st 7 Aug 1956 (*divorce* 1973) Clare, only dau of Nigel Patrick Bruce (*see* BRUCE, Bt, of Downhill), and has:

1 +COLPOYS GUY [Colpoys Johnson Esq, Hollygate, Sleepers Hill, Winchester, Hants SO22 4ND]; *b* 13 Nov 1965; *educ* Winchester and King's Coll London (BA); FRGS; *m* 1990 *Marie Louise Carmel, dau of John Holroyd, of Guildford, Surrey, and has:
(1) +Colpoys William; *b* 28 Dec 1993
(2) +Rufus George; *b* 27 May 1996
1 *Marina Grace; *b* 2 June 1960
2 *Alison Fiona; *b* 14 Aug 1961

Sir PETER *m* 2nd 1973 *Caroline Elisabeth, twin dau of W/Cdr Sir (Eric) John Hodsoll, CB, of Tarrant Rushton, Dorset, and has further:
2 +Nicholas Frederick; *b* 1977

Lineage: JOHN SHANE O'NEILL (*see* O'NEILL, B); had:

THOMAS MACSHANE; *m* Frances, dau of Thomas Fay, of Derrynagare, Co Westmeath, and had:

WILLIAM MACSHANE (anglicised JOHNSON); *m* Anna, dau of James FitzSimons, of Tullinally, Co Westmeath, and had:

CHRISTOPHER JOHNSON, of Smithstown, Co Meath; *m* Anne, sis of V-Adml Sir Peter Warren, KB, MP Westminster, and dau of Michael Warren, of Warrenstown, Co Meath, and had, with an er s (Peter Warren Johns(t)on, of Damartown, Co Meath):

Sir William Johnson, 1st Bt (GB), so *cr* 27 Nov 1755; *b* 1715; adopted by his maternal uncle, V-Adml Sir Peter Warren, KB, whose estate on the Mohawk River, N America, he went to manage 1738; Col-in-Chief of the Six Nations 1744, sole supt of the affairs of the Six Nations with rank of Maj-Gen from 1755, when he defeated the French at Lake George; *m* 1739 Mary, dau of John de Wissenbergh, of Montreal, and had issue:
1 JOHN (Sir), **2nd Bt**
1 Anne; *m* Col Daniel Clauss, of N America
2 Mary; *m* Col Guy Johnstone, and had issue

Sir WILLIAM *d* 11 July 1774; his only son,

Sir John Johnson, 2nd Bt, of Mount Johnson, Montreal; Supt Gen and Inspr-Gen Indian Affrs Br N America, Col-in-Chief six Bns of militia of eastern township of Lower Canada, ktd 1765; *m* 30 June 1773 Mary (*d* 7 Aug 1815), dau of John Watts, Pres Cncl New York, and *d* 4 Jan 1830, having had, with other issue:
1 William; Lt-Col; *b* 21 Aug 1775; *m* Sept 1802 Susan (*m* 2nd 1815 Gen Sir Hudson Lowe, KCB, and *d* 1832), dau of Stephen de Lancy, Govr Tobago, and sis of Sir William de Lancy, KCB (*k* Waterloo), and *d* 11 Jan 1812, leaving three daus (two of whom *d* unm)
2 **Sir Adam Gordon Johnson, 3rd Bt**; Lt-Col 6th Bn of Militia; *b* 6 May 1781; *d* unm 21 May 1843
3 John, of Point Olivier, Montreal; Col cmdg 6th Bn of Militia, Lt RN; *b* 8 Aug 1782; *m* 10 Feb 1825 Mary Diana (*d* 22 Oct 1861), dau of Richard Dillon, of Montreal, and *d* 23 June 1841, having had, with other issue:
(1) **Sir William George Johnson, 4th Bt**; Lt RA; *b* 19 Dec 1830; *m* 30 March 1889 Elizabeth Hancock (*d* 11 Jan 1932), only dau of Richard Hancock Brown, of Bowdon, Chester, and *dsp* 26 Jan 1908
(2) Archibald Kennedy; *b* 20 June 1839; *m* 5 Nov 1865 Katherine Sophia (*d* 29 May 1911), dau of Lt-Col Charles MacDonnell, 85th Regt, and *d* 6 Oct 1873, having had issue
1a **Sir (Edward) Gordon Johnson, 5th Bt**; with Canadian Pacific Rlwy 1903–33, V-Pres Montreal Assoc for the Blind; *b* 17 March 1867; *m* 18 June 1902 Violet Eveline (*d* 1951), dau of Thomas Edward Hayes, MD, of Dublin, and *dsp* 15 April 1957
1a Mary Florence; *b* 6 Feb 1870; *m* 1 Dec 1891 Charles George Cranmer Kenrick, of Brigham, Lower Canada, and *d* 23 May 1905
4 Charles Christopher; Lt-Col 9th Lancers, QMG Ireland, Kt 2nd Cl Persian Order of Lion and Sun; *b* 29 Oct 1789; *m* 8 Jan 1818 Susan (*d* 23 Feb 1875), est dau of Adml Sir Edward GRIFFITH later COLPOYS, of Northbrook Ho, Hants, and *d* 30 Sept 1854, having had, with other issue:
(1) John Ormsby; V-Adml; *b* 11 Aug 1822; *m* 17 Feb 1852 Edith Renira (*d* 12 Nov 1904), dau of Rev Charles Edward Twyford, Rector Trotton, Sussex, and *d* 26 Feb 1881, having had issue:
1a Charles; *d* 1869 following an accident
2a Frederick Colpoys Ormsby; Maj 1st Garrison Bn Worcester Regt, Lt-Col cmdg 1st Winchester Bn CLB (KRRC), Maj RM; *b* 19 Oct 1858; *m* 14 Oct 1884 Maria (*d* 24 Nov 1950), dau of Henry Lund, barrister, and gdau of Nathaniel S Marling (*see* MARLING, Bt), and *d* 2 Dec 1932, having had issue:
1b Guy Allen Colpoys Ormsby, CBE (1940), MC; Brig RAPC and 2nd Bn Beds Regt, served WW I (despatches twice) and WW II (despatches twice), Silver Jubilee Medal 1935, Coronation Medal 1937; *b* 25 May 1886; *m* 31 July 1911 Mary Isabella (*d* 1977), only dau of Lt-Col Benjamin Geale Humfrey, of Cavanacor, Co Donegal, and *d* 30 Jan 1957, leaving:
1c *Emily Mary Ormsby [Mrs Miles Garrick, Langleys, The Chalk, Imerne Minster, Dorset]; *m* 1st 19 Dec 1934 G/Capt Edward Stephen Dru Drury, RAF (*d* 17 Sept 1948), yr s of Dr Godfrey Dru Drury, MRCS, LRCP, FSA, of Corfe Castle, Dorset; *m* 2nd 3 Aug 1951 Maj Miles A C Garrick (*d* 1978), only s of Maj George Christian Garrick, of Sussex, and by her 1st husb has:
1d *Stephen Guy Dru, MBE; *b* 1939; G/Capt RAF
2d *Michael Humfrey Dru, MBE (1977); *b* 1942; Lt-Col LI
2c *Eileen Ormsby [Mrs Finlay Mackintosh, Dunsfold, Moor Rd, Bramhope, Leeds, Yorks]; *m* 10 Jan 1945 Finlay George Mackintosh (*d* 1989), MB, ChB, DA, and has:
1d *Alan Finlay; *b* 14 Jan 1948
1d *Fiona Mary; *b* 10 Nov 1945
2d *Diana Barbara; *b* 5 July 1952
3c Grace Ormsby; *m* 4 Sept 1948 George Acheson Gidney, only s of Sir Claude Henry Gidney, KCIE, CSI, ICS, and *d* 1 June 1982, leaving:
1d *Mark Henry; *b* 9 Oct 1949
2d *David Guy; *b* 21 Feb 1952

1d *Alison Jane; *b* 15 Feb 1953
2b Lionel Stanley Ormsby, DSC; Lt-Cdr RN, Flag-Lt to C-in-C Dardanelles (despatches twice); *b* 19 Aug 1887; *d* 2 April 1920 from effects of war service
1b Stella Kathleen Ormsby; *m* 10 April 1926 Maj Robert Beauchamp Tower, MC, Sherwood Foresters (*d* 3 July 1971), and *d* 2 Aug 1971, leaving:
1c *William Beauchamp, Lt-Cdr RN [Lt-Cdr William Tower RN, The Home House, Stoke-St-Michael, Bath BA3 5JH]; *b* 26 Nov 1928; *m* 14 June 1962 *Rosemary Anne, 2nd dau of Brig Hubert Francis Lucas, CBE (*see* LUCAS, Bt), and has:
1d *Alan Francis Beauchamp; *b* 3 Sept 1964
2d *Christopher John; *b* 31 March 1972
1d *Annabel Jane; *b* 8 Oct 1965
2d *Sophie Elisabeth; *b* 6 Oct 1967
3a Robert Warren; Capt RN; *b* 10 May 1868; *m* 11 July 1906 Grace Isobel (*d* 1 Dec 1966), 4th dau of Algernon Herbert Paley, barrister, and was *ka* 22 Sept 1914, lost in HMS *Cressy*, leaving:
1b JOHN PALEY (Sir), **6th Bt**
2b +Peter Warren, DSO (1945), OBE (1954), DFC, AFC (1941) [Group Capt Peter Johnson DSO OBE DFC AFC, 23 Albury Park, Albury, Surrey GU5 9BB]; *b* 13 Nov 1908; G/Capt RAF WW II (despatches); *m* 1st 10 April 1934 (*divorce* 1961) Joan Agnes (*d* 2 Dec 1975) est dau of Capt Percy Richard Hare (*see* LISTOWEL, E), and has:
1c +Hugo Robert Warren; *b* 19 Dec 1939; *m* 1963 *Sally Allen, of Boston, Mass., and has:
1d *Claudia Agnes; *b* 25 Jan 1964
1c *Virginia; *b* 2 Dec 1936; *m* 2 Dec 1961 (*divorce* 1983) Marchese Umberto Valdambrini, s of Cdr Marchese Pio Valdambrini-Accoramboni, and has:
1d *Robert; *b* 17 May 1963
2d *Richard Warren; *b* 20 Nov 1965
1d *Julia Louise; *b* 1971
2b (cont.) G/Capt Peter Johnson *m* 2nd 12 Oct 1961 Margaret Anne (*d* 1987), widow of Cdr Peter John Patrick Leckie, RN, and dau of Capt Cyril Whichelo Bower, DSC, RN, of Rose Cottate, Fordwich, Canterbury
1b *Elisabeth Freda; WAAF WW II
4a Alexander Adair; RFCVS, Capt NZ Expdny Force Palestine; *b* 5 Feb 1873; *m* 1894 Emma Jane (*d* 1940) and *d* 24 Dec 1927, leaving:
1b Ralph Harold Ormsby, NZ Forces Palestine WW I; *b* 1897; *m* 1923 and had:
1c +Alexander Ormsby; *b* 1929
2b +John Ormsby [John Johnson Esq, Corner of Guy's Rd and Factory Rd, Janefield, Mosgiel, Dunedin, New Zealand]; *b* 1911; *m* 1936
1b Gertrude Ormsby; *b* 1895; *m* 1928 James Augustus Williamson
2b *Sybil Renira Ormsby; *b* 1909; *m* 1929 Raymond Coleridge Derrett, Capt 2nd NZ EF
3b *Phyllis Ormsby, *b* 1917; *m* 19– — Savage
1a Edith Twyford; *d* June 1938
2a Georgina Ormsby; *d* unm
3a Renira Louisa; *m* 25 Feb 1881 Capt W H Forbes Taylor, RA, and *d* 7 Sept 1881
4a Anna Emily Ormsby; *m* 1889 Clement Chevallier (*d* 13 Feb 1943) and *d* 5 March 1949, leaving issue
5a Ruth Ormsby; *m* 1892 Alexander Livingstone Christie (*d* 9 May 1928), Dep Inspr-Gen Hosps and Fleets RN, and *d* 12 Dec 1934
6a Teresa Katharine; *m* 15 May 1911 Lt-Col Hugh Vodvarka, ASC Czechoslovakian Army, and *d* 25 Feb 1944
(2) Edward Colpoys; Lt 99th Regt and 52nd Oxford LI Crimea 1854 (medal with clasp for Alma), missionary N India; *b* 11 Aug 1835; *m* 1st 25 Aug 1863 Barbara (*d* 12 July 1869), dau of Rev James Williamson, and had:
1a Charles Adair; *b* July 1864; *d* 17 Feb 1889
(2) (cont.) Edward Johnson *m* 2nd 17 Dec 1874 Ada Olivia (*d* 26 Dec 1903), dau of Edward Pinto, and *d* 16 Sept 1900, having by her had:
2a John Colpoys; *b* 14 Sept 1875; *d* 25 May 1884
3a Hubert Colpoys; AMICE, FRGS, DLS (Canada), ICS; *b* Feb 1878; *m* 10 Dec 1916 Mary Anne, dau of Thomas Phillip Howe, of Newport Pagnell, Bucks, and *d* 1925, leaving:
1b +Graham Christopher Colpoys; *b* 15 Sept 1917; *educ* Wycliffe Coll Glos; *m* 1951 Joan Winifred Mary (*d* 20 Feb 1958), dau of John Bernard Colbeck, of Wakefield, Yorks, and has:
1c *Anne Winifred Mary; *b* 1952
1a Lilian Ada Colpoys; *d* unm April 1961
2a Elsie Ada Colpoys; *d* unm 1955

The 5th Bt's kinsman,

Sir John Paley Johnson, 6th Bt, MBE (1945); CC Kent 1965, Lt-Col RA (ret 1960), WW II in Burma, Middle East and Italy, Lt-Col 1945, Ch Land Instr Turkish Staff Coll 1946–49, MFH W Kent 1958–61, Hon Pres United Empire Loyalist Assoc Toronto; *b* 12 June 1907; *educ* Wellington and RMA Woolwich; *m* 1st 11 June 1929 (*divorce* 1939) Carol Louise Glorney, dau of Edmund Haas, of Essex Ho, New York, and had:
1 Sir PETER COLPOYS PALEY JOHNSON, **7th and present Bt**
1 *Wanda Helene Paley [Mrs Wanda Weychan, 1a Cobb's Well, Fowey, Cornwall PL23 1BP]; *b* 27 Jan 1933; *m* 27 Oct 1955 (*divorce* 1977) Paul George David Weychan, only s of T E S Weychan and Mrs D A Hyne, and has:
(1) *Paul Corydon; *b* 1 July 1960
(1) *Charlotte Sophia Carol; *b* 9 Dec 1956

Sir John *m* 2nd 2 Oct 1940 (*divorce* 1947) Jasmine Lydia (*m* 2nd 1948 (*divorce* 1953) Frank Hugh Shirley Fox; *m* 3rd 1954 Howard Marshall (*d* 1974) and *d* 1991), er dau of Lt-Col Hon Noel Gervase Bligh, DSO (*see* DARNLEY, E), and by her had:
2 *Sarah Jack Paley [Mrs Sarah Johnson, Church Lane Cottage, Wylye, Wilts BA12 0QZ]; *b* 13 April 1942, *m* 1st 25 March 1964 (*divorce* 1970) Ezra Mager, s of Harold Mager, of New York, and has:
(1) *Dickon Porter; *b* 1969
(1) *Emma Rachel; *b* 1964
2 (cont.) Mrs Sarah Mager *m* 2nd 1972 (*divorce* 1983) Nels Royden Johnson and has by him:
(2) *Daniel Alexander; *b* 1972

Sir John *m* 3rd 27 Sept 1949 *Joan Rosemary, widow of Maj Dick Henry Brewster Thornton, Gren Gds, and dau of Arthur Cohen, and *d* 14 Dec 1975

JOHNSON-FERGUSON

Arms: Quarterly; 1st and 4th, per fess indented gules and or a pale counterchanged between two boar's heads couped in chief of the second, and in base a thistle leaved and slipped proper (for FERGUSON); 2nd and 3rd, azure on a pile or a lion statant of the first, on a chief azure a pale of the second three acorns leaved and slipped counterchanged (for JOHNSON). **Crests:** 1 A boar's head couped or in front of a thistle leaved and slipped, thereon a bee, both proper (for FERGUSON), 2 A lion statant per pale azure and or, holding in the mouth an acorn leaved and slipped and between two branches of oak fructed proper (for JOHNSON). **Motto:** *Nosce te ipsum* ('Know thyself'). **Creation:** Bt. (UK) 18 July 1906.

SIR IAN EDWARD JOHNSON-FERGUSON, 4TH BT, of Springkell, Co Dumfries, Kenyon, Newchurch-in-Culcheth, Co Palatine Lancs, and Wiston, Co Lanark [Sir Ian Johnson-Ferguson Bt, Copthall Place, Upper Clatford, Hants SP11 7LR]; *b* 1 Feb 1932; *s* f 1992; *educ* Ampleforth, Trin Coll Cambridge (BA) and Imperial Coll London (DIC); *m* 9 April 1964 *Rosemary Teresa, yr dau of Cecil John Whitehead, of The Old House, Crockham Hill, Kent, and has:
1 +MARK EDWARD; *b* 14 Aug 1965; *educ* Trin Coll Cambridge (BA); Capt RE; m 12 Aug 1995 *Dr Julia Catherine, dau of Tom Getley, of Wendover, Bucks
2 +Paul Duncan; *b* 20 Aug 1966; *educ* Ampleforth and Keble Coll Oxford (MA); ACA; *m* 1990 *Maria Barbara Antoinette, yst dau of Prof Dr Karl-Heinz Menke, of Bonn, Germany, and has:
(1) *Cecilia Teresa Marie; *b* 1992
(2) *Amelie; b 2 Nov 1995
(3) *Lydia; b 2 Nov 1995
3 +Simon Joseph; *b* 23 July 1967; *educ* Ampleforth and Charing Cross Hosp, London; Capt RAMC, doctor; *m* 12 Sept 1998 *Helen, yr dau of Stuart Ferguson, of Romsey, Hants

Lineage: JAMES JOHNSON, of Manchester; merchant; *m* Esther (*d* 11 June 1794) and *d* between 17 Dec 1782 and 21 May 1787, leaving, with another s:
1 James, of Manchester; *b* 5 July 1760; *m* 1st Mary — (*d* 11 June 1794); *m* 2nd Mary — (*d* 25 Nov 1803) and *d* 28 Oct 1819, leaving issue by both ws
2 William, of Manchester; *b* 15 May 1770; merchant; *m* 25 April 1793 Esther Simister (*d* 21 Jan 1831) and *d* 22 Nov 1836, having had:
(1) JABEZ
(1) Esther; *b* 25 July 1802; *m* Thomas Reddish Blythe and had issue
(2) Elizabeth; *b* 25 March 1812; *m* Henry Hacking
1 Betty; *b* 11 May 1762; *m* Charles Crawford, of Pendleton, and had issue
2 Mary; *b* 15 Aug 1764; *m* Thomas Skerrow

WILLIAM JOHNSON's s,

JABEZ JOHNSON JP, of Kenyon Hall, nr Manchester, JP; *b* 20 Dec 1809; *m* 18 Sept 1845 Mary (*d* 5 Dec 1884), dau of John Johnson, of Broughton, Manchester, and *d* 17 Feb 1887, leaving:

Sir (JABEZ) EDWARD JOHNSON later JOHNSON-FERGUSON (added 1881, roy licence 2 Dec 1899), **1st Bt** (UK), so *cr* 18 July 1906, JP (Lancs, Dumfriesshire and Lanarks); *b* 27 Nov 1849; *educ* St John's Coll Cambridge (MA); barrister, MP Loughborough 1885–86 and 1892–1900; *m* 15 April 1874 Williamina Margaret Ellen (*d* 18 April 1937), dau of William Alexander Cunningham, JP, of Manchester, and *d* 10 Dec 1929, leaving:

Sir Edward Alexander James Johnson-Ferguson, 2nd Bt, TD, JP (Lanarks and Dumfriesshire), DL (Dumfriesshire); *b* 3 March 1875; *educ* Cambridge (BA); Lt-Col and Brevet Col cmdg Lanarks Yeo TA WW I (despatches), Cmmdt Special Constabulary Dumfriesshire; *m* 28 April 1904 Hon Elsie Dorothea McLaren (*d* 15 May 1973), er dau of 1st Baron Aberconway (*qv*), and *d* 27 Dec 1953, leaving:

1 NEIL EDWARD (Sir), **3rd Bt**

2 Brian Charles, JP (Dumfriesshire 1938), TD; *b* 1 Dec 1908; *educ* Winchester and Ch Ch Oxford; Maj Lanarks Yeo (TA) W II, Co Commr Dumfriesshire Boy Scouts Assoc 1946; *m* 26 April 1947 *Daphne [Mrs Brian Johnson-Ferguson, Clogges Cottage, Waterbeck, Dumfriesshire DG11 3HD], er dau of Brig Walter Andrew Stirling, DSO, MC, of Polstead, Suffolk, and *d* 1988, having had:

(1) +Torquil Charles; *b* 5 April 1949; *educ* Stanbridge Earls; *m* *Margaret Finlay and has:

1a +Ninian Charles; *b* 11 Jan 1983

1a *Iona; *b* 1981

2a *Ailsa Finlay; *b* 1988

(2) Denzil Crispin; *b* 7 Jan 1955; *educ* Charterhouse; *d* car crash 6 Jan 1979

(1) *Merlin Louie; *b* 5 Oct 1950; *m* 1981 *Peter James Dernie, s of James Harry Dernie, of Preston, Lancs, and has:

1a *Henry Crispin; *b* 1982

1a *Jemima Louie; *b* 1984

2a *Olivia Lucy; *b* 1986

(2) *Lorraine Giselle; *b* 2 April 1952; *m* 1975 *Markus Luscher, 2nd s of O Luscher-Kamber, of Rickenbach, Switzerland, and has:

1a *Thomas; *b* 1978

2a *Callum; *b* 1982

3a *Ross; *b* 1987

1a *Kirsty; *b* 1980

2a *Nicola; *b* 1984

3 Raymond Patrick, TD, DL (Cumberland 1958); *b* 9 Oct 1912; *educ* Alderley Ho and Pembroke Coll Oxford (BA 1934); Lt-Col cmdg Westmorland and Cumberland Yeo, RA (TA), WW II (despatches); *m* 1987 *Winifred Clare [Mrs Raymond Johnson-Ferguson, Westerkirk Mains, Langholm, Dumfriesshire], er dau of Col Henry Edwards, of Oamaru, NZ, and *dsp* 10 Sept 1997

Sir EDWARD's est s,

Sir Neil Edward Johnson-Ferguson, 3rd Bt, TD, JP (Dumfriesshire 1954); *b* 2 May 1905; *educ* Winchester and Trin Coll Cambridge (BA 1926); V-Lt Dumfriesshire 1965 (DL 1957), Lt-Col Roy Signals (TA), US Legn Merit; *m* 24 Jan 1931 Sheila Marian, er dau of Col Herbert Swynfen Jervis, MC, of Tilford, Surrey, and *d* 1992, leaving:

1 Sir IAN EDWARD JOHNSON-FERGUSON, **4th and present Bt**

2 +Christopher Charles Jervis [Christopher Johnson-Ferguson Esq, The Old House, Staverton, Daventry, Northants]; *b* 14 April 1933; *educ* Ampleforth and RMA Sandhurst; Lt The Greys; *m* 18 April 1963 *Sarah Loraine (Sally), 2nd dau of Sir Humphrey Dodington Benedict Sherston-Baker, 6th Bt (*qv*), and has:

(1) +Charles Patrick; *b* 6 Dec 1972

(1) *Victoria Margaret; *b* 17 Feb 1965

(2) *Katharine (Kate) Jane; *b* 1966; *m* 1992 *Keith Thompson and has:

1a *Jack; *b* 199–

2a *Benjamin Charles; *b* 29 April 1996

(3) *Lucy Mary; *b* 30 June 1974

3 +Michael Herbert, JP [Michael Johnson-Ferguson Esq JP, Springkell, Eaglesfield, Dumfriesshire DG11 3AL]; *b* 27 Sept 1934; *educ* Ampleforth; Capt QO Lowland Yeo; *m* 12 Jan 1963 *Jennifer Mary, er dau of Lt-Col Herbert Green, OBE, MC, of The Manor House, Carlton Husthwaite, Yorks, and has:

(1) +James Herbert; *b* 20 Oct 1963; *m* 1995 *Rachel Peddie and has:

1a *Phoebe Charlotte; *b* 20 Nov 1996

(2) +Robert Charles; *b* 12 Oct 1969

(1) *Sarah Catherine; *b* 25 June 1965

(2) *Fiona Marion; *b* 14 Aug 1966; *m* 1993 *James Patrick Hodson (*see* HODSON, Bt) and has issue

(3) *Laura Rose; *b* 26 Nov 1967

4 Nicholas Swynfen; *b* 28 Dec 1938; *educ* Ampleforth; 2nd Lt RAC; *m* 1st 1963 (*divorce* 1975) Mabel, dau of L Dawson, of Wendover, Bucks, and has:

(1) *Alona Frances; *b* 1964

(2) *Karen Alice; *b* 21 Feb 1966

4 (cont.) Nicholas Johnson-Ferguson *m* 2nd 1975 (*divorce* 1981) Marie, dau of W O'Reilly, of Dublin, and has:

(1) +Ian Francis; *b* 1977

(3) *Andrea Valerie; *b* 1975

4 (cont.) Nicholas Johnson-Ferguson *m* 3rd 1984 *Christina, dau of Humberto Zambrano, of Ramos Arizpe, Mexico, and has:

(2) +Alexander Edward; *b* 1985

(3) +Christopher Andrew; *b* 1990

(4) *Sophia Monica; *b* 1986

JOHNSTON

Arms: Quarterly; 1st and 4th, argent a saltire sable, on a chief gules three cushions or (for JOHNSTON); 2nd and 3rd, azure on a bend or between three hart's heads erased argent, attired of the second, as many cross-crosslets fitchée of the second (for GARIOCH of Caskieben). **Crest:** A phoenix proper in flames. **Supporters:** Two Indians proper, wreathed with laurel about the middle. **Motto:** *Vive ut postea vivas* ('Live that you may live hereafter'). **Creation:** Bt. (NS) 31 March 1626.

SIR THOMAS ALEXANDER JOHNSTON, 14TH BT, of Hilton and Caskieben; *b* 1 Feb 1956; s f 1984

Lineage: STEPHEN de JOHNSTON; living *temp* DAVID II (1331–71); allegedly bro of the Laird of Johnstone, Annandale; migrated to the North of Scotland due to troubles in his own part of the country; called 'the clerk' for his learning; sec to the Earl of Mar; *m* Margaret, dau and heiress of Sir Andrew Garioch of Caskieben and gdau of Helen of Mar, who brought him considerable estates in Aberdeenshire; ancestor of:

GEORGE JOHNSTON of that Ilk and Caskieben; *m* Christian, dau of 7th Lord Forbes (*qv*), and *d* 1593, having had, with three other sons and seven daus:

1 JOHN

2 Arthur; MD; physician to JAMES I and CHARLES I; Rector U and King's Coll Aberdeen 1637; often ranked next to Buchanan of the Latin poets of Scotland; *m* twice and *d* Oxford 1641, having had issue

3 William; MD; Prof Mathematics Marischal Coll and U of Aberdeen 1626–40

The est son,

JOHN JOHNSTON of that Ilk; MP 1608; *m* 1st Janet, dau of Turing of Foveran (*see* TURING, Bt), and had:

1 **Sir George Johnston, 1st Bt** (NS), so *cr* 31 March 1626, with remainder to his heirs male whatsoever , of Caskieben; Sheriff Aberdeenshire 1630–31; *m* Elizabeth, dau of William Forbes of Tolquhoun, Aberdeenshire, and had, with other issue:

(1) **Sir George Johnston, 2nd Bt**; sold Caskieben 1660 to Sir John Keith, who changed the name to Keith Hall; *m* by 1648 a dau of Sir William Leslie of Wardis, 3rd Bt (*see* 1970 edn), and *d* by 10 June 1695, leaving:

1a **Sir John Johnston, 3rd Bt**; *b c* 1648; Capt at Battle of the Boyne 1690, also served Flanders War of Grand Alliance or League of Augsburg (1688–97); once when in London helped a friend Capt Hon James Campbell (bro of 1st Duke of Argyll; *qv*) to elope with and marry Mary Wharton, a 13–year old heiress, dau of Sir Thomas Wharton and great-niece of the 4th Baron Wharton (*qv*), a leading Whig and as one of the first to declare for WILLIAM III in 1688 a person of considerable influence, so that Sir John, who as a Scot was unpopular in London anyway, was condemned to death after a trial and hanged at Tyburn 23 Dec 1690

(2) John, of Newplace; *m* his cousin, dau of Thomas Johnston of Craig, and had:

1a **Sir John Johnston, 4th Bt**, of Newplace; merchant Aberdeen, bought Cordyce, one of the old family properties, and changed its name to Caskieben; Jacobite, fought Battle of Sheriffmuir 1715; *m* April 1683 Janet, dau of Thomas Mitchell, Baillie Aberdeen, of Thainston, and *dspms* Nov 1724, having had:

1b John; *ka sp* Sheriffmuir

1b Marjory; *m* Andrew Burnett of Elrick

2b Janet; *m* Charles Forbes of Sheals

JOHN JOHNSTON of that Ilk *m* 2nd Katherine (*d* 1616), dau of William Lundie of that Ilk, and *d* 4 Feb 1613/4, having by her had:

2 Thomas, of Craig; Sheriff Depute Aberdeenshire; *m* 1st Elspeth Strachan (*dspm*); *m* 2nd Mary (*d* Sept 1659), dau of Alexander Irvin of Kingcausie, and *d* Aug 1656, leaving, with other issue:

(1) William, of Craig; Army Offr; *m* Joanna van Millen and *dsp* 1716

(2) John, of Bishopstown; *b* 1649; *m* Nov 1672 Margaret, dau and coheir of John Alexander, and *d* 1716, leaving:

1a **Sir William Johnston, 5th Bt**; *b c* 1675; advocate Aberdeen; insolvent 1725 and his property sold; *m c* 8 Jan 1704 Jean (*d* 1744), dau of James Sandilands of Craibston, nr Aberdeen, and *d* 18 March 1750, leaving:

1b **Sir William Johnston, 6th Bt**; *b* Nov 1714; Lt RN 1741, Cdr 1750, bought Hilton, nr Aberdeen, with prize money; *m* 1st 1750 Sarah (*dspms* 1751), dau of Thomas Kirby, a West India planter and London merchant, and had a s (*d* in infancy); *m* 2nd March 1757 Elizabeth (*d* 25 Aug 1772), dau of Capt William Cleland of Cleland, Lanarks, RN, and by her had, with four other sons and three other daus:

1c **Sir William Johnston, 7th Bt**; *b* 3 Aug 1760; fought against the French on the Malabar coast India, raised a regt of fencible inf 'The Prince of Wales's Own' 1798 (disbanded 1802), MP New Windsor 1801–02, later insolvent and lived in the grounds of Holyrood Abbey; *m* 1st 24 Feb 1783 Mary (*b* 1726, being 34 years older than her husb; *dsp* July 1802), dau of John Bacon, of Shrubland Hall, Suffolk, descended from Edward, 3rd s of Sir Nicholas Bacon (1510–Feb 1578/9; *see* BACON, Bt); *m* 2nd Dec 1802 Maria (*d* 27 Oct 1847), only dau of John Bacon, of Fryern House, Middx, and *d* at The Hague 13 Jan 1844, having by her had:

1d **Sir William Bacon Johnston, 8th Bt**; *b* 17 March 1806; Offr 1st Roys; *m* 11 Sept 1855 Mary Ann (*d* 11 Oct 1903), dau of William Tye, cobbler, of Mendlesham, Suffolk, and *d* 2 Aug 1865, having had:

1e **Sir William Johnston, 9th Bt**, JP (Aberdeenshire); *b* 31 July 1849 prior to his parents' marriage but legitimated *ex post facto* under Scottish law by their subsequent marriage 11 Sept 1855; Sec Travancore plantation Tea Co; *d* unm 22 Nov 1917

1e Emily; *d* unm 13 Feb 1934

2e Clara; *m* 26 March 1868 James Fergusson (*dsp* 1886), of Monkwood, and *d* 15 Aug 1930

3e Mary Anne; *m* 5 June 1872 Alfred Edward Watts (*d* 1926), of Leicester, and *d* 13 May 1933, leaving issue

4e Maria; *m* 7 Dec 1878 David Reid, CE (*d* 1892), of Thomanean House, Milmathort, Scotland, and *d* 20 Aug 1934, leaving issue

5e Alice; *m* 24 Jan 1880 Alexander Philip (*d* 19 Nov 1904), of Ceylon, 3rd s of Rev George Philip, DD, of Edinburgh

6e Jane; *m* 28 April 1880 Forbes Manson, of Aberdeen, and *d* 31 March 1927

2d D'Arcy; Lt HEICS; *d* Bengal 30 Sept 1830

3d Arthur Lake; Capt 22nd Regt; *d* 21 Feb 1853

1d Georgina Frances Amy; *m* John Collyer (*d* 1870), barrister, of Hackford Hall, Norfolk, and *d* 11 Feb 1897

2d Anna Maria; *m* Patrick Bannerman, of Elmsfield, Aberdeenshire, and *d* 8 March 1884 aged 75

3d Clara; *m* Edward Lake, Cdr RN, 2nd s of Sir James Lake, 4th Bt (*qv*), and *d* 26 Nov 1862

4d Emily; *d* unm 10 Aug 1908

2c Alexander; midshipman; *d* at sea

1c Mary Selby; *m* Peter Gourlay, of St Vincent, WI

2c Elinor Sandilands; *m* her cousin Rev William Uvedale, of Barking, Suffolk

1b (cont.) **Sir William** *m* 3rd 1777 Amy, dau of Newman French, of Bel(l)champ(e), Essex, and widow of John Pudsey, but by her had no issue and *d* 19 March 1794

2a John; *m c* 16 Feb 1717 Isobel, dau of John Marnoch of Balnagask, and had:

1b John; *b* 6 Feb 1725; *m* July 1758 Margaret (*d* 1812), dau of William Chalmers, and *d* 1770, having had:

1c William; *b* Jan 1762; *m* 24 Oct 1801 Catherine (*d* 25 March 1855), dau of David Morice of Tullos, Kincardineshire, Sheriff Substitute Aberdeenshire, and *d* 24 Feb 1832, having had:

1d David Morice; *b* 19 May 1804; *d* unm 21 Feb 1863

2d Alexander; *b* 4 June 1809; WS; *m* 1 Jan 1836 Christina Martha (*d* 21 April 1878), dau of John Leith Ross of Arnage and Bourtie, and *dsp* 14 June 1880

3d Robert; *b* 16 Dec 1810; *m* 7 July 1835 Mary (*d* 8 Jan 1872), dau of George Hadden, of London, and *d* 24 Feb 1887, having had, with three other daus (*d* unm):

1e William, CB; MD Edin, MA, LLD Aberdeen; *b* 16 April 1843; Col AMS; *m* 1882 Charlotte, dau of James Arnotts, of Leithfield, Kincardineshire, WS, and *dsp* 26 Dec 1914

2e **Sir George Johnston, 10th Bt**; *b* 21 April 1849; *m* 15 Nov 1876 Agnes Elizabeth (*d* 28 May 1922), dau of Rev Richard John Sparkes, Rector Alford, Surrey, and *dsp* 11 May 1921

1e Catherine; *m* 23 Sept 1869 Col James Allardyce (*d* 6 March 1910) and *d* 17 Jan 1900, leaving issue

1d Rachel; *m* 26 March 1835 Sir Alexander Anderson (*d* 11 April 1887) and *d* 15 Dec 1886, leaving issue

2d Margaret; *m* 1 Aug 1837 Capt John Grahame Buchanan (*dsp* 20 Jan 1874) and *d* 28 Oct 1876

2c Andrew, of Aberdeen; *b* 1769; *m* 1794 Margaret Inglis and *d* 1845, leaving:

1d William, of Aberdeen; *b* 1795; *m* 1818 Ann, dau of T Craig, and *d* 1865, leaving:

1e William, of Mobile, Ala.; *b* 1822; *k* in a hurricane Sept 1906, leaving:

1f THOMAS ALEXANDER, **11th Bt**

2f John; *b* 1865; *m* 1898 Katherine Anna (*d* 1950), dau of Thomas Terrell, and *d* 1929, leaving:

1g Madeline Frances; *b* 1898; *m* 1918 Thomas Hansford Gordon Powers

2g Adelaide Isabelle; *b* 1901; *m* 1922 Clarence Eugene Northcutt and had issue

3f Curtis Laudiner

1f Margaret Cora; *b* 1867; *m* 1st 1890 James P Johnston (*d* 1893) and had issue; *m* 2nd 1911 Charles H Harris

2f Sarah; *b* 1869; *d* unm

3f Celestine; *b* 1876; *d* unm

2e Andrew; *b* 1835; *m* 1864 Helen (*m* 2nd 1872 George Garden; *d* 12 March 1913), dau of William Stewart, and *d* 1870, leaving:

1f William Andrew; *b* 1868; *d* unm 6 March 1913

1f Helen

2f Mary Margaret

3e Thomas, of Greenock; had:

1f William

2d Andrew; *d* unm 1876

(3) James; *b* 1656; left issue, now extinct

The 10th Bt's 1st cousin once-removed,

Sir Thomas Alexander Johnston, 11th Bt; *b* 15 Dec 1857; *m* 1887 Mary Ann (*d* 1949), dau of William Thomas Norville, of Mobile, Ala., and *d* 20 Dec 1950, having had:

1 THOMAS ALEXANDER (Sir), **12th Bt**

2 William Norville; *b* 1894; *m* 1921 Catherine, dau of Thomas Murray, of Mobile, and *d* 20 March 1959, leaving:

(1) +WILLIAM NORVILLE [William Johnston Esq, 1754 Hunter Ave, Mobile, AL, USA]; *b* 11 July 1922; heir presumptive; *m* 14 June 1952 *Kathrine Pauline, dau of Herbert Sigfred Solberg, of Mobile, and has:

1a +William Norville; *b* 25 Dec 1955

2a +Stephen Gregory; *b* 6 July 1958

3a +Paul Brady; *b* 6 Dec 1959

1a *Kathryn Mary; *b* 17 Nov 1953

(2) +Claude Edward [Claude Johnston Esq, 166 Fulton St, Mobile, AL, USA]; *b* 18 Jan 1930; *m* 20 Feb 1960 *Lucy, dau of Bernard Teague Mahorner, of Mobile, and has:

1a +Edward Ryan; *b* 24 Oct 1961

2a +Bernard Mathias; *b* 8 Feb 1965

1a *Mary Teague; *b* 31 Oct 1960

2a *Laura Jean; *b* 2 Feb 1964

(1) *Marion Margaret; *b* 29 June 1924; *m* 13 June 1955 *Thomas Ross Johnson, s of Thomas Ross Johnson, of Macon, Ga, and has:

1a *Thomas Ross; *b* 9 July 1957

1a *Margaret Murray; *b* 24 Feb 1956

2a *Elizabeth Barry; *b* 11 Feb 1961

(2) *Helen Jean [Mrs William Bidez, 3908 Hillcrest Lane, Sky Ranch, Mobile, AL, USA]; *b* 10 Oct 1926; *m* 13 April 1955 *William Earle Bidez, chemical engr, s of Robert Leo Bidez, of Mobile, and has:

1a *William Earle; *b* 7 Aug 1957

1a *Jeanne Marie; *b* 15 Jan 1956

2a *Erin Ann; *b* 7 Aug 1957

3a *Cathryn Leary; *b* 4 July 1961

3 Frederick Rukard; *b* 1897; memb Mobile Bar, Bay Pilot 1943; *m* 1925 Grace, dau of John A McRae, of Clio, Alabama, and *d* 30 Aug 1962, leaving:

(1) Frederick Rukard; *b* 16 Jan, *d* 7 June 1936

(1) *Joyce Rukard; *b* 1926; *m* 1 May 1951 *Wallace Abney Burgess, USN, s of William Chester Burgess, of Charlotte, NC, and has issue

(2) Mary Norville; *b* 1928

4 Aquilla Norville; *b* 1900; *m* 1957 Mary Agnes, dau of Capt Donald Mackay, of Morina, Ala., and *d* 1967

5 Kenneth Douglas; *b* 1902

1 Emily Frances; *b* 1889; *m* 1918 Flarrie Green Watson

2 Isabel Ladnier; *b* 1892; *d* unm Sept 1969

Sir THOMAS's est s,

Sir Thomas Alexander Johnston, 12th Bt; *b* 3 May 1888; civil engr, Ch Hydro Power Branch Mobile Dist, Offr Corps Engrs US Army, ret 1956; *m* 1915 Pauline Burke (*d* Sept 1968), dau of Leslie Bragg Sheldon, of Mobile, and *d* 12 April 1959, having had:

1 **Sir Thomas Alexander Johnston, 13th Bt**; *b* 7 Sept 1916; attorney, ptnr Howell, Johnston, Langford and Finkbohner, memb Alabama Ho Reps 1941–49 and State Senate 1949–54, Pres Mobile Co Bar Assoc 1963 and Mobile Branch ESU 1963; *m* 16 July 1941 *Helen Torrey (*m* 2nd 1989 Dr Charles Trewartha Lenton Jr), dau of Benjamin Franklin Du Bois, of Mobile, and *d* 1984, having had:

(1) Sir THOMAS ALEXANDER JOHNSTON, **14th and present Bt**

(1) *Helen Du Bois [Mrs Philip Sargent, 239 E 31st St, New York, NY, USA]; *b* 12 July 1944; *m* 2 Aug 1969 *Philip Thomas Sargent, s of Philip A Sargent, of Crescent City, Fla.

(2) *Lesley Sheldon; *b* 30 May 1951; *m* 1972 *David Charles Krempa and has:

1a *David Alexander; *b* 1984

1a *Mary Helen; *b* 1978

2a *Melissa Lesley; *b* 1980

1 *Diane Johnston [Mrs Samuel Andrews, Citronelle, AL, USA]; *b* 1926; *m* 1948 *Samuel H Andrews III, s of Samuel H Andrews II, of Citronelle, and has issue

2 Pauline Sheldon Johnston; *b* Feb 1929; *m* Dec 1947 Leroy C Baggett, Jr, s of Leroy C Baggett, of Mobile, and had issue

JOHNSTON OF ROCKPORT

Creation: B. (LP, UK) 1987.

THE BARON JOHNSTON OF ROCKPORT, of Caversham, Co Berks (Sir Charles Collier Johnston, TD) [The Rt Hon The Lord Johnston of Rockport TD, House of Lords, SW1A 0PW]; *b* 4 March 1915; *educ* Tonbridge; Maj RA 1945 WW II (commissioned TA 1938); md Standex Internat 1948–76 (chm 1951–77); chm Standex Hldgs 1986–; Chm: Macclesfield C Assoc 1961–65, NW Area Cs 1971–76; Hon Treas NW Area Cs 1965–71, memb C Bd Fin 1965–71, ktd 1973; Pres Nat Union of C and U Assocs 1986–87 (memb Exec Ctee 1965–, Chm 1976–81), Jt Hon Treas C Party 1984–87, Nat Chm C Friends of Israel 1983–86; *m* 1st 1939 Audrey Boyes, dau of Edgar Monk, and has:

1 *Michael Charles [The Hon Michael Johnston, Court Hay Cottage, Farrington, Blandford Forum, Dorset]; *b* 1942

2 *Timothy Courtenay [The Hon Timothy Johnston, 2B Ilma Ave, Kangaroo Point, Sylvania, NSW 2224, Australia]; *b* 1945

THE BARON JOHNSTON OF ROCKPORT *m* 2nd 1981 *Mrs Yvonne Shearrnan, dau of Reginald Marley

Lineage: Capt CHARLES MOORE JOHNSTON; *m* Muriel Florence, dau of Reuben Mellon, and had an est s:

CHARLES COLLIER, *cr* a **Baron**

JOHNSTONE

Arms: Not yet matriculated in Lyon Register. **Motto:** *Nunquam non paratus* ('Aye ready'). **Creation:** Bt. (NS) 25 April 1700.

SIR GEORGE RICHARD DOUGLAS JOHNSTONE, 11TH BT, of Westerhall, Dumfriesshire [Sir George Johnstone Bt, The Moat House, Mawby's Lane, Appleby Magna, Leics DE12 7AA]; *b* 21 Aug 1948; *s f* 1994; *educ* Leeds GS and Magdalen Coll Oxford (MA, Dip Physical Anthropology); production control manager Wolsey Ltd 1973, section head ITT Consumer Products (UK) Ltd 1979, dir Centl Govt Gp P-E Internat Ltd 1988, and DBI Assocs Ltd 1990–, MIMC, MInstD, FRSA; *m* 1976 *Gwyneth Susan, dau of Arthur Bailey, of Hastings, and has:

1 +FREDERIC ROBERT ARTHUR; *b* 18 Nov 1981

1 *Caroline; *b* 1983

Lineage: MATTHEW JOHNSTONE; held part of Pettinain (later called Westraw), Lanarks, 1455; *d* 1491; his gs:

HERBERT JOHNSTONE, of Westraw; *d* Dec 1555; had:

HERBERT JOHNSTONE; had:

JAMES JOHNSTONE; living 1560; *m* Flora, dau of Somerville of Camnethan and was *k* by two sons of the Duke of Châtelherault (*see* ABERCORN, D) Jan 1570/71, leaving:

JAMES JOHNSTONE of Westerhall; sold his lands in Lanarks and bought Glendoning, Dumfriesshire (later called Westraw or Westerhall) 1605; *m* Euphemia, dau of 4th Lord Oliphant by Lady Margaret Hay, dau of 7th Earl of Erroll (*qv*), and *d* May 1633, having had:

JAMES JOHNSTONE of Westerhall; *m* Isabel Scott, dau of Walter Scott of Harden, and *d* May 1643, leaving:

Sir JAMES JOHNSTONE of Westerhall; MP (S Parl) Dumfries Sheriffdom 1689–99; *m* Margaret, dau of John Bannatyne of Corehouse, and *d* 18 Nov 1699, having had, with a yr s :

Sir John Johnstone, 1st Bt (NS), so *cr* 25 April 1700, of Westerhall; Lt-Col Kerr's Dragoons, MP (S Parl) Dumfries Sheriffdom 1700–07 and (GB Parl) 1707–08; *m* Rachel, dau and coheir of James Johnston of Sheens, bro of Johnston of Warriston, and *d* 30 Sept 1711, having had:

Philadelphia; *m* James Douglas of Dornoch (*see* QUEENSBERRY, M)

His yr bro,

Sir William Johnstone, 2nd Bt; MP Annan 1698–1707, Dumfries Burghs 1708–15 and Dumfriesshire 1715–22, Dep-Steward Kirkcudbright 1717; *m* Henrietta, dau of James Johnstone of Sheens, and *d* 8 Oct 1727, having had:

1 JAMES (Sir), **3rd Bt**

2 John; Lt-Col; *m* Charlotte Van Lore, Marchioness Dowager of Annandale (*see* ANNANDALE AND HARTFELL, E), dau and heiress of John Vanden-Bempdé, of Hackness, and was *ka* Cartagena 1741, leaving:

(1) RICHARD (Sir), 1st Bt, of Hackness; *see* DERWENT, B

(2) Charles John, of Ludlow; *b* 15 July 1736; *m* 1778 Mary (*d* 1809), dau of John Beddoe, and *d* 8 May 1805, leaving, with other issue:

1a Charles Philipps; *b* 6 Nov 1780; Capt 3rd King's Own Dragoon Gds; *m* 26 Oct 1807 Frances (*d* 19 March 1844), yst dau of James Harrison, of Cheadle Bulkley, Cheshire, and *d* 8 March 1863, having had, with other issue:

1b Vanden Bempdé (Rev); *b* 10 May 1819; MA Cantab; *m* 12 April 1855 Louisa, yst dau of Jonathan Scarth, of Coton Manor, Shrewsbury, and *d* 15 April 1859, leaving:

1c Vanden Bempdé; *b* 11 Feb 1856; *educ* Jesus Coll Cambridge (MA); *m* 1897 Minnie Sarah Miles, dau of T Gratton, of Cliffside, Matlock, Bath, and *dsp* 1941

2c Charles Julius; *b* 18 June 1857; *educ* Jesus Coll Cambridge (MA); *m* 22 Dec 1885 Mary Gertrude (*d* 29 April 1930), dau of E Madoc Jones, of Glentworth, Oswestry, and *d* 5 Oct 1904, leaving:

1d Charles Arthur; *b* 6 April 1887; *educ* Magdalene Coll Cambridge (BA); Lt Rifle Bde, WW I; *d* 18 June 1925

2d Francis Edward; *b* 19 Feb 1892; *educ* Haileybury and SE Ag Coll, Wye, Kent; *m* 1939 *Alice, dau of William Carrington, of Westcliff, Essex

3d Richard Noel; *b* 25 Dec 1896; *educ* RNCs Osborne and Dartmouth; Cdr RN, served WWs I and II; *m* 5 Jan 1933 *Mary Edmee, 2nd dau of Charles William Campbell, CMG, and had issue:

1e *Susan Mary; *b* 25 Dec 1935; *m* 5 Oct 1957 *Jeremy Rowe, s of Charles William Dell Rowe, CB, MBE, of Orton Longueville, Peterborough, and has:

1f *Lucinda Mary; *b* 14 Nov 1958

2f *Josephine Alice; *b* 30 Aug 1960

3f *Nicola Susan; *b* 10 Dec 1963

4f *Harriet Sarah; *b* 20 April 1966

4d William Robert Parke; *b* 20 Dec 1900; *m* 21 July 1938 *Mary, yr dau of Peter Robinson, of Waresley, Beds

2a John; *b* 16 Feb 1783; Capt 3rd and 5th Dragoon Gds, ADC to the Duke of Wellington Peninsular War; *m* 14 Sept 1813 Agnes (*d* 2 Dec 1856), only child of Rev John Hutton, Vicar Burton, Westmorland, and *d* 14 March 1870, leaving, with other issue (*d* unm):

1b George Henry (Rev); *b* 20 Dec 1818; MA Cantab; Rector St Nicholas's, Sutton, Herefs; *m* 9 Dec 1863 Alice, dau of Maj von Tunyelman, and *dsp*

1b Louisa Rebecca; *m* 2 Dec 1847 Humphrey Salwey (*d* 21 Jan 1877), of Ludlow, and *d* 25 Dec 1906, leaving issue

2b Anna; *m* 6 Nov 1849, as his 2nd w, Richard McGillycuddy of the Reeks (*d* 6 June 1866), and *d* Dec 1875, leaving issue

3a George, of Broncroft Castle; *b* 1 Aug 1784; 5th Dragoon Gds; *m* 1st 4 Oct 1815 his cousin Margaret Anne (*d* 26 June 1819), est dau of Sir Richard Vanden Bempdé Johnstone, 1st Bt (*see* DERWENT, B), and had one surv dau; *m* 2nd Jane, dau of Hugh Edwards, of Borthwynog, Merioneths, and *d* 15 Oct 1856, leaving, with other issue:

1b Charles Edwards; *m* 22 Nov 1848 Jane Elizabeth Balcombe, only dau of Edward Abel, and *dsp*

4a Richard James, of Manorbier Castle, Pembs; *b* 26 May 1793; *m* 3 Dec 1824 Matilda Jane (*d* Dec 1844), dau of Capt William Gilder, and *d* 11 Oct 1850, leaving:

1b Richard; *b* 8 Sept 1825; Col Bombay Army; *m* 12 Feb 1874 Anna Maria Emmeline, dau of Samuel Witteronge Clayton, of Eastfield, Ryde, and *d* 1888, leaving:

1c Richard Harcourt Vanden Bempdé; *b* 4 Jan 1875; *d* 28 Sept 1892

2b Frederick Charles; *b* 18 Feb 1828; *m* 1 Sept 1860 Helen Kathleen, dau of Col Alexander, and *d* 26 Sept 1907, having had:

1c Frederick Alexander; *b* 1865; *m* 1890 Grace Margaret (*d* 30 March 1927), dau of Finlay Cameron, of Edinburgh, and *d* 28 July 1939, leaving:

1d Frederick John Finlay; *b* 19 Jan 1897; *m* 16 Dec 1933 *Yvonne, dau of Colin Frederick Murray Campbell, of Halston, Co Westmeath

1d Grace Edith; *b* 23 Jan 1891

2d Mary Carmichael; *d* unm 1919

3d Kathleen Adele; *m* 21 April 1928 H Bowen Smith and *d* 2 Nov 1965

4d Dorothy Elsie; *b* 16 Aug 1895; *m* 17 Sept 1927 Rev George Roff Tamplin, BSc, s of Charles Roff Tamplin, and *d* 1 July 1964, leaving a s

5d Freda Anna; *m* Sept 1943 Harry Duerdoth (*d* 1955) and *d* 21 March 1966

6d Norah; *b* 4 Oct 1900

2c John Villers; *m* Mary — and *d* 1952, leaving:

1d +James Raynor; *b* 1911

1d Gertrude; *b* 1896

1c Katheen Frances Matilda; *m* 1883 Rev James Harvey Lewes and *d* 26 July 1937, having had issue

2c Edith Josephine

3c Adelaide (Adele) Mary; *m* 1894 William Ward and *d* 20 June 1952, leaving issue

3b Edmund John; *b* 1 April 1832; *m* 5 Nov 1856 Agnes, dau of Thomas Dale Gulliver, RN, and *d* 8 June 1868, leaving:

1c Charles Frederick Dale; *b* 9 April 1858

2c Richard James Annandale; *b* 2 April 1865

1c Kathleen Mathilda; *m* 12 Nov 1879 James Pritchard Agnew

1b Georgina Maria; *m* 13 Feb 1856 Dep-Surgn-Gen William Edward Cates, HMIA, and had issue

2b Augusta Jane

3b Matilda Lucy; *m* 19 Aug 1858 Marshall Christie, and had issue

4b Louisa Amitie; *m* 2 Aug 1862 Rayner H H Alexander, and had issue

1a Charlotte; *b* 2 Jan 1782; *m* 10 Sept 1800 Adml Sir Henry Charles Knowles, 2nd Bt (*qv*), and had issue

2a Jane; *b* 11 July 1790; *m* 30 Nov 1815 Ven Philip Jennings, DD (*d* 20 Dec 1849), Archdeacon Norfolk, and *d* 27 Dec 1883, leaving issue

The 2nd Bt's est son,

Sir James Johnstone, 3rd Bt; *b* 9 Feb 1697; Provost Lochmaben 1740; MP Dumfries Burghs 1743–54; *m* June 1719 Hon Barbara Murray (*d* 15 March 1773), dau of 4th Lord Elibank (*qv*), and *d* 10 Dec 1772, having had, with other issue:

1 **Sir James Johnstone, 4th Bt**; *b* 23 Jan 1726; Lt-Col, MP; claimed Marquessate of Annandale (*see* ANNADALE AND HARTFELL, E); *m c* 4 July 1759 Louisa Maria Elizabeth (*d* 9 April 1797), dau of — Colclough and widow of Rev — Merrick, and *dsp* 3 Sept 1794

2 Sir WILLIAM JOHNSTONE later PULTENEY (roy licence 1794), **5th Bt**; *b* 19 Oct 1729; MP; *m* 1st 10 Nov 1760 Frances (*d* 1 June 1782), only dau and heiress of Daniel Pulteney, first cousin of William Pulteney, Earl of Bath (*see* BATH, M,

preliminary remarks), who brought him the vast Pulteney properties (he also owned a large estate in America), and had an only child:

(1) HENRIETTA LAURA Pulteney, COUNTESS OF BATH, Somerset (UK), so *cr* 26 Oct 1803, as also earlier BARONESS OF BATH, Somerset (GB), both with remainder to heirs male of her body; *b* 26 Dec 1766; *m* 24 July 1794 her cousin Gen Rt Hon Sir James MURRAY later MURRAY-PULTENEY (added on marriage), 7th Bt, of Clermont, Fifeshire (*see* 1850 edn), Col 18th Foot, sometime Sec at War (*d* 26 April 1811 after a powder flask burst and blinded him in one eye), and *dsp* 14 July 1808, when her titles expired

2 (cont.) Sir WILLIAM *m* 2nd 3 Jan 1804 Margaret, dau and coheir of Sir William Stirling of Ardoch, Bt, and widow of Andrew Stewart of Torrance and Castlemilk, and *d* 30 May 1805

3 George; *b* 1730; Cdre RN, MP; Govr Pensacola, West Florida; *m* 31 Jan 1782 Charlotte Dee, and *d* 24 May 1787, leaving an only s:

(1) JOHN LOWTHER (Sir), **6th Bt**

4 John; *b* 28 April 1734; nabob; contributed to victory at Plassey where cmded the artillery, bought Alva, Stirlingshire, and other large estates in Scotland; *m* 1 Sept 1765 Elizabeth Caroline, dau of Col Keene, and *d* 10 Dec 1795, leaving, with a dau:

(1) James Raymond, of Alva; *b* 4 June 1768; *m* 20 June 1799 Mary Elizabeth (*d* 9 Sept 1843), sis of Sir Montague Cholmeley, 1st Bt (*qv*), and *d* 7 April 1830, leaving:

1a James, of Alva and Hangingshaw, Selkirkshire, JP and DL; *b* 4 July 1801; MP Clackmannanshire and Kinross 1851–57; *m* 1st 9 Jan 1846 Hon Augusta Anne Norton (*d* 21 July 1859), sis of 3rd Baron Grantley (*qv*), and had:

1b John Augustus James, JP, of Alva; *b* 3 May 1847; *m* May 1868 Emily, dau of R W Crossling, and *dsp* 1 April 1890

1b Caroline Elizabeth Mary, of Alva; *d* 4 July 1929

1a (cont.) James Johnstone *m* 2nd 5 May 1862 Sarah Mary (*d* 27 May 1908), dau of Lt-Col H P L'Estrange, of Moystown, King's Co, and *d* 24 Feb 1888, having by her had:

2b James Henry L'Estrange, MVO, JP (Selkirk and Clackmannan), of Hangingshaw; *b* 8 Aug 1865; Maj RE, Pres Rlwy and Telegraph Admin, Cairo, Egypt; *m* 29 Oct 1891 Amy Octavia, OStJ (*m* 2nd 1 June 1927 Capt Alfred Charles Seton-Christopher, JP (*d* 12 Oct 1934), Seaforth Highrs, of Chelsea, and *d* 21 May 1949), yst dau of Andrew Wauchope, and *d* 24 Sept 1906, leaving:

1c John Andrew, of Hangingshaw; *b* 11 May 1893; Lt RFA and RFC; *ka* 20 May 1915

2c Henry James, of Alva; *b* 26 April 1895; A/Capt RN; *m* 25 Jan 1923 Alison (*d* 1984), dau of Thomas Walker MacIntyre, of Sorn Castle, Ayrshire, and *d* 15 July 1947, leaving:

1d +(John) Raymond (Sir), CBE (1988) [Sir Raymond Johnstone CBE, Wards, Gartocharn, Dunbartonshire G83 8SB]; *b* 27 Oct 1929; *educ* Eton and Trin Coll Cambridge; CA, md Murray Johnstone and Co, Glasgow, chm: Forestry Commn 1989–94, Lomond Underwiting plc 1994–, Historic Buildings Cncl for Scotland 1995–, Nuclear Trust and Nuclear Generation Decommisssioning Fund Ltd 1996–; ktd 1993; *m* 1979 *Susan Sarah, only dau of Capt Christopher Gerald Gore (*see* EGLINTON and WINTON, E), formerly w of Basil Reginald Vincent Ziani de Ferranti and widow of Peter Quixano Henriques

1d *Christine Alison; *b* 13 Jan 1924; *m* 7 Aug 1942 Sir Robert Erskine-Hill, 2nd Bt (*qv*), and has had issue (including a dau, *b* and *d* 31 March 1928)

3c Andrew Wauchope; *b* 1 May 1903; *educ* Eton and King's Coll London (BSc 1924); AMICE, MIMechE, MIEE; *m* 15 Nov 1932 *Eleanor Blanche Helen Margaretta Vere-Laurie [Mrs Andrew Johnstone, PO Box 44, Hudson, PQ, Canada J0P 1J0], only dau of Lt-Col George Brenton Laurie, Roy Irish Rifles, and Florence, Viscountess Massereene and Ferrard (*qv*), and *d* 1980, leaving:

1d +James Andrew Francis [James Johnstone Esq, 35 Front St South, Unit 209, Mississauga, Ontario, Canada L5H 2I6]; *b* 25 May 1939; *educ* Eton, Coll Militaire Royale and Mountallison U Canada (BSc); *m* 1st 1 Dec 1963 (*divorce* 1978) Helen Christina, dau of Ivan Frazer Wade, of Quebec, and has:

1e *Sheila Christine; *b* 26 Aug 1964

2e *Anne Laurie; *b* 25 Aug 1965

3e *Jennifer Frances; *b* 1968; *m* 1994 *Donald Scott, of Port Moody, BC, Canada

4e *Kathleen Helen; *b* 1970

1d (cont.) James Johnstone *m* 2nd 1982 *Carole, widow of Norman Burke, of Westmount, Quebec

1d *Gillian Margaret [Mrs Gillian Haviland, Springfield House, Aldringham, Suffolk IP16 4PZ]; *b* 5 April 1935; *m* 29 June 1957 (*divorce* 1985) Rev Edmund Selwyn Haviland, s of Rev Edmund Arthur Haviland, of Wishford, Wilts, and has:

1e *Andrew Mark James; *b* 6 June 1965; *m* 5 April 1997 *Joanne Susan, dau of John Marnes, of Gravesend, Kent

1e *Margaret Vivienne; *b* 20 June 1958

2e *Angela Helen; *b* 1 Jan 1960

3e *Jane Eleanor; *b* 8 March 1963

2d *Jacqueline Veronica [Mrs Mark Salfus, 10 O'Connors Rd, Beacon Hill, NSW, Australia]; *b* 8 Aug 1936; *m* 1st 1 Oct 1966 (*divorce* 1975) Thomas Patrick Fitzgerald, of Sydney, and has:

1e *Jon Wauchope; *b* 22 July 1967

2d (cont.) Mrs Jacqueline Fitzgerald *m* 2nd 1977 (*divorce* 1980) Mark Anthony Salfus and by him has:

2e *Damien Anthony James; *b* 1978

3b Henry Beresford; *b* 26 Jan 1871; BA Oxon; V-Consul Tangier 1912–23, formerly at Tunis, Addis Ababa, Zanzibar, and Mogador; *d* 30 Aug 1937

4b Gilbert Lumley; *b* 16 April 1872; Capt 112th Co Imp Yeo, formerly Lt RFA, W Coast of Africa 1897–98 (medal and clasp), Boer War (wounded, despatches, two medals and two clasps), WW I, formerly Capt Edinburgh Artillery Militia and Assist Inspr Gold Coast Constabulary; *m* 9 Oct 1907 Florence Mabel, only dau of Arthur William Fincham, of Burghersdorp, Cape Colony, and *das* 1916

2a John; *b* 9 July 1802; Col HEICS; *m* 18 June 1845 Caroline (*d* 6 July 1901), dau of Rev Charles Pannel, and was drowned May 1854, leaving:

1b Mary Harriet Augusta; *m* 4 Dec 1865 Sir Robert Buxton, 3rd and last Bt (*see* 1888 edn), and *d* 9 Aug 1913

3a Montague Cholmeley; *b* 2 March 1804; Gen, served Kaffir War 1846–51 (medal) and Indian Mutiny; *m* 31 Dec 1844 Leonora Louisa (*d* 28 Sept 1913), dau of Lt-Gen Sir Henry Somerset, KCB, KH (*see* BEAUFORT, D), and *d* 22 Sept 1874, leaving:

1b Somerset James JOHNSTONE later SOMERSET-JOHNSTONE; *b* 29 Aug 1846; Lt-Cdr RN; *m* 1st Jan 1877 Elizabeth Ann (*d* 1886), dau of William Jackson Johnson, of Hooton, Cheshire, and had:

1c FitzRoy Augustus Beauclerk; *b* 4 July 1878; Maj IA, Somaliland campaign 1904, Mesopotamia 1915–16; *m* 6 Jan 1915 Alida Helen (*d* 25 Aug 1968), dau of Andrew Veitch, and *d* 12 Dec 1931, leaving:

1d FitzRoy Dawyck Somerset; *b* 30 March 1921

2d FitzRoy Montague Veitch; *b* 29 May 1922; *m* 1956 *Dora [Mrs FitzRoy Somerset-Johnstone, Cornaa Mill, Maughold, IoM IM7 1EJ], dau of Alexander Lofthouse, and *d* 1979, leaving:

1e +FitzRoy Jonathan; *b* 1957; *educ* Stowe; exec with Lend Lease, Sydney; *m* 1989 *Jane Alexandra, dau of Peter Crothers, of Mildura, Australia, and has:

1f +Alexander Fitzroy; *b* 1996

1f *Alice Grace; *b* 1996

1e *Judith Helen; *b* 1959; *m* 1984 *John Stewart Morton and has:

1f *Alexander James; *b* 1985

2f *Thomas Oliver; *b* 1988

3f *Stewart John; *b* 1989

4f *William Roy; *b* 1991

2e *Jennifer Alison; *b* 1962; *m* 1990 *Patrick Douglas Gerard Hodson and has:

1f *James Roy Namani; *b* 1994

2f *Joseph Patrick Luke; *b* 1997

1f *Hannah Rachel; *b* 1992

3d +James Veitch [James Somerset-Johnstone Esq, Rose Lea, The Close, Llanfairfechan, Gwynedd]; *b* 19 Dec 1924; *m* 1949 *Nancy Hayes, dau of Henry Atkinson, and has:

1e +Ian James Fitzroy [Ian Somerset-Johnstone Esq, Glasfryn, Valley Rd, Llanfairfechan, Gwynedd]; *b* 1952; *educ* St Paul's and Aston U; ptnr Real Car Co; *m* 1989 *Rosalynde Patricia, est dau of Michael John Mills, and has:

1f +Callum James; *b* 1988

2e +Peter Montague Veitch [Peter Somerset-Johnstone Esq, 34 Bell Rd, Bottisham, Cambridge]; *b* 1956; *educ* Holland Park Comprehensive; conservationists; *m* 1990 *Fiona Catherine, yr dau of Lt-Cdr C A French, RN, and has:

1f +Jamie Peter; *b* 1994

1d Alida Kathleen Louisa; *b* 28 Sept 1915; *d* June 1916

1c Emily Banner Clough; *m* 1st 21 Dec 1898 Cdr Herbert Algernon Adam, CBE, RN (*d* 27 Sept 1920), s of Rev Benjamin William Adams, Vicar Santry, and had issue; *m* 2nd 1922 Capt Francis Evelyn Massy-Dawson, DSO, RN (*see* MASSY, B), and *d* 1 Feb 1928

1b (cont.) Somerset Somerset-Johnstone *m* 2nd 1887 (*divorce* USA 1900) Isabel Ann (*d* 16 June 1934), dau of Joseph Charles Mappin, of Sheffield, and by her had:

2c James Montague Cholmeley; *b* 1889; *educ* Bedford Sch; Master Mariner, Lt RNR, WW I; *m* 1917 Alice Maud, dau of Frederick Witham, of Peckham, and had:

1d +FitzRoy Somerset; *b* 1927; WW II as Radio Offr Merchant Navy; *m* 1952 *Francesca Hodson, dau of Edmund Waring, of Wimbledon, and has:

1e +Peter James; *b* 1955

1e *Susan Frances; *b* 1953

1d *Muriel Sydney; *b* 1918

2d *Audrey Philippa; *b* 1923

3d *June Octavia; *b* 1932

3c Malcolm Bruce SOMERSET-JOHNSTONE later SOMERSET (deed poll 12 April 1932); *b* 1893; *educ* Sherborne; WW I (despatches), on Staff 2nd Army HQ for def of Sussex, Capt Res of Cav, attd Army Remount Serv, comdg 49th Remount Sqdn Salonika

2c Catharine Octavia Mary; *m* 14 Sept 1909 Percy Valentine Norwood, yst s of C M Norwood, MP, and *d* 30 May 1922

1b (cont) Somerset Somerset-Johnstone *m* 3rd 1900 (*divorce* 1910) Louisa Hodder (*d* 1914) and *d* 5 Sept 1942

2b Montague George, DSO; *b* 21 March 1848; Hon Col and Lt-Col cmdg 3rd Bn Yorks LI, Lt-Col 4th Bn Cameronians (Scottish Rifles), Maj RSG, ADC to Ld Lt Ireland 1880, HQ Staff Bechuanaland 1884–85, Boer War (medal with three clasps, Lt-Col), Coronation Medal 1911; *m* 10 July 1880 Agnes (*d* 10 Nov 1923), dau of Joseph Harrison, JP, DL, of Galligreaves Hall, Blackburn, and Salmesbury Hall, Preston, Ld Manor Hadleigh, Essex, and widow of Capt Robert Johnston Stansfeld, and *d* 12 June 1928, having had:

1c Montague Joseph Charles Somerset; *b* 16 June 1882; *educ* Eton; Maj RSG, Adj Scottish Horse Yeo 1909–12, WW I with 5th Cav Bde RSG (1914 Star, two medals), War Off 1916–18, Priv Sec to U-Sec State War 1926–27, WW II as F/Lt RAF 1940–43 and with RCSJ WO 1943–44; *m* 1st 31 Oct 1906 Victoria Louise (*d* 25 Jan 1916), yst dau of James Stewart, and had:

1d *Desirée Barbara Montague; *b* 28 March 1908

2d *Eileen Agnes Montague; *b* 18 July 1909; *m* 26 March 1931 (*divorce*) Raymond Horwood Hazell, s of Ralph C Hazell, of Prestwood, Bucks, and had:

1e *Charles Jonathan; *b* 1938

1e *Louise; *b* 1933

2e *Anastasia; *b* 1936

3d *Rosemary Maud Montague; *b* 10 Nov 1913; *m* 1st 6 Oct 1936 (*divorce*) Nicholas Desborough Burnell, er s of Lt-Col C D Burnell, DSO, of Wargrave, Berks; *m* 2nd — Rogers

1c (cont.) Maj Montague Johnstone *m* 2nd 1916 (*divorce* 1928) Mary Marian Spottiswood (*d* Oct 1949), dau of George Bayley, of Manuel, Stirling, and by her had:

1d +Roy Henry Montague, MBE (1945) [Maj Roy Johnstone MBE, 16 Leonard Court, Edwardes Sq, London W8]; *b* 13 July 1919; *educ* Eton and Magdalene Coll Cambridge; Maj 60th Rifles WW II (despatches); memb London Stock Exch 1956–74, Tstee St Clement Danes Holborn Estate Charity; *m* 1st 30 Sept 1939 (*divorce* 1960) Barbara Marjorie (*d* 1990), dau of Maj Felix Walter Warre, OBE, MC, of Bridport, Dorset, and has:

1e +Roland Richard Montague [Roland Johnstone Esq, Poorton Hill, Powerstock, Bridport, Dorset]; *b* 22 Jan 1941; *educ* Eton; 2nd Lt 2nd Greenjackets (KRRC) 1959; slr 1967, ptnr Slaughter & May 1973–91; *m* 24 Feb 1968 *Sara Outram Boileau, dau of Lt-Col J G O Whitehead, MC, of Canterbury, and has:

1f +Andrew Henry Montague; *b* 16 Oct 1969; *educ* Eton

2f +William Arthur Montague; *b* 1973; *educ* Clayesmore

2e +Mark Montague [Mark Johnstone Esq, 42 Howards Wood Drive, Gerrards Cross, Bucks]; *b* 19 June 1944; *educ* Eton; late Lt Queen's Roy Rifles (TA); joined Unilever 1962, seconded to United Africa Co Nigeria 1966, late Area Manager Mfrs Delivery Servs (Nigeria) Ltd, VAC Property Mgr Lagos, Area Sales Mgr Nigerian Breweries Ltd 1968; *m* 28 April 1971 *Rosalind Margaret, dau of Donald Macphee, DSC, FRICS, of Tylers Green, Bucks, and has:

1f +Kerry Montague; *b* 1972

1f *Amanda Lee Montague; *b* 1974

3e +Torquil James Montague; *b* 24 Oct 1953; *educ* Eton; CA 1977; merchant banker; *m* 1988 *Irena Katharin Buller, dau of Maj Ivor Roger Harding Curtis VRD, RMR, of Wareham, Dorset, and has:

1f +Joshua James; *b* 1991

1f *Alice Victoria; *b* 1993

1e *Fiona Margot Montague; *b* 16 Aug 1946; *m* 1977 *David Wilkins and has:

1f *Peter Jonathan; *b* 1978

1f *Helen Sarah; *b* 1981

1d (cont.) Maj Roy Johnstone *m* 2nd 1961 *Françoise Terlinden and has:

4e +Carol Peter Montague [Carol Johnstone Esq, 1 Broadfield Gdns, Great Meadon, Worcs WR4 0DP]; *b* 1961; *educ* Hardy's; insur broker; *m* 1996 *Jane, dau of Alan John Grainger, of Plumstead, London, and has:

1f +Adam Peter Montague; *b* 1996

4d Gloria Helen Montague; *b* 4 Jan 1918; *d* 1997

1c (cont.) Maj Montague Johnstone *m* 3rd 17 Feb 1928 Margaret, dau of Sir John Foster Fraser, KBE, of Princes Risborough, Bucks, and *d* 7 Sept 1953, having by her had:

2d +Alistair Montague; *b* 20 Nov 1928; *m* and has issue

2c Reginald FitzRoy Lewis; *b* 6 June 1884; Lt QO Cameron Highrs; *m* 15 July 1914 Honoria Adelina (*m* 2nd Dec 1916 James Gordon Lumdsen; *m* 3rd Capt Charles Gordon, and *d* 8 April 1929), er dau of Charles Edward Malcolm, bro of Sir James William Malcolm, 9th Bt (*qv*), and was *ka* Battle of the Marne 8 Sept 1914

1c Violet Agnes Charlotte Mary; *m* 16 Oct 1900 Edward Foley and had issue

3b Francis Fawkes; *b* 30 Aug 1849; Lt-Col Beds Regt; *m* 1st 7 March 1878 (*divorce* 1886) Henrietta Jane, dau of James Sullivan, and had:

1c Montague FitzRoy Cholmeley; *b* 1 Oct 1880; *d* unm 25 Oct 1907

1c Mary Louisa Leonora; *m* 30 Sept 1897 Percy Kitchin and had issue

2c Frances Geraldine Jane

3b (cont.) Lt-Col Francis Johnstone *m* 2nd 10 Feb 1887 Harriet Lavinia (*d* 27 July 1910), dau of Richard Sargent and widow of Capt Charles Francis Gregg, 7th Hus, and *d* 21 April 1919, leaving:

2c Charles Campbell Gosling; *b* 31 May 1889; BA Cantab; Maj Argyll & Sutherland Highrs; *m* 1st 28 Nov 1912 (*divorce* 1927) Laura Mary, dau of Lt-Col Willoughby B Hemans, RA, and had:

1d Alastair Ian Campbell; *b* 29 July 1917; *d* 19 Aug 1935

1d *Violet Mary St Clair; *b* 1914

2d *Jean Hermione; *b* 1922

2c (cont.) Maj Charles Johnstone *m* 2nd 1928 Nina, dau of Col Valentine de Sventorgetsky, Russian Imp Gd, and *d* 1942

4b Robert FitzRoy Maclean; *b* 30 Sept 1859; Maj and Hon Lt-Col 3rd Bn Cameronians, Maj ISC, Upper Burma Campaign 1888–89 (medal and clasp), Boer War (medal and clasp); *m* 30 April 1898 Mary Harriet Isabella Cumberland (*d* 18 Nov 1929), sis of 1st and last Baron Islington (*see* 1936 edn) and widow of Frederick Amelius Beauclerk (*see* SAINT ALBANS, D), and *dsp* 16 July 1942

1b Frances Mary; *d* unm 31 Oct 1941

2b Fanny Louisa; *m* 2 Aug 1876 Sir John William Pitt Muir Mackenzie, KCSI (*d* 25 Oct 1916), and *d* 24 Sept 1895, leaving issue (*see* MUIR MACKENZIE, Bt)

3b Edith Olive; *m* 17 Feb 1883 Capt Edmund George Reilly (*d* 18 July 1887), Bombay SC, and had issue

4b Mysie Caroline; *m* 12 March 1886 Frederick Gomer (*d* 5 Aug 1926), and had issue

5b Maud; *m* 4 June 1904 Thomas Stanley Davies (*d* Feb 1914), MO Colonial Serv, s of Sir William Davies, DL, MP

4a George Dempster (Rev); *b* 13 March 1805; Rector Creed, Cornwall; *m* 1 Sept 1842 Mary Anne (*d* 16 April 1890), est dau of John Hawkins, of Bignor, Sussex, and niece of Sir Christopher Hawkins, 1st and last Bt, and Col Sibthorp, of Canwick, and *d* 8 Sept 1867, having had:

1b George Herbert; *b* 1 June 1843; *d* 25 Jan 1857

2b (John) Heywood, JP (Sussex); *b* 18 May 1850; *educ* Repton and Trin Coll Cambridge (BA 1872); CA Sussex, barrister Inner Temple 1874, Dep Chm QS W Sussex, MP Horsham 1893–1904; *m* 5 June 1878 Josephine, OBE (1918) (*d* 19 Aug 1924), 4th dau of John Joseph Wells, of Bickley, Kent, and *d* 10 Oct 1904, leaving:

1c George Horace, OBE (1942), JP and DL (both Cornwall), of Trewithen, Cornwall (where he created a famous garden); *b* 8 Jan 1882; *educ* Radley and Trin Coll Cambridge; WW I as Staff Capt (despatches); High Sheriff Cornwall 1926; *m* 23 June 1910 Alison (*d* 1978), yr dau of Ven Stamford Raffles Raffles Flint, Archdeacon Cornwall and Canon Truro, of Nansawan, Cornwall, and *d* 29 Jan 1960, leaving:

1d Elizabeth Alison; *b* 7 June 1911

2d *Rachel Mary; *b* 23 May 1916; *m* 1st 10 Nov 1934 (*divorce* 1944) Robert Washbourne Money, slr, of Feock, Cornwall, s of Rev D W Money, and has:

1e *Stuart Washbourne, MBE (1964); *b* 1935; Maj SLI

2e *Robert Graham Ernle Washbourne; *b* 1936

2d (cont.) Mrs Rachel Money *m* 2nd 1946 (*divorce* 1949) James Henderson; *m* 3rd 1957 Jack Spenceley Collins

3d *Jennifer Ruth [Lady Galsworthy, Lanzeague, St Just-in-Roseland, Cornwall]; *b* 6 Feb 1921; *m* 1942 Sir John Edgar Galsworthy, KCVO, CMG (*d* 1992), Dip Serv, s of Arthur Galsworthy, and has:

1e *(Arthur) Michael Johnstone, DL (Cornwall) [Michael Galsworthy Esq DL, Trewithen, Grampound Rd, nr Truro, Cornwall TR2 4DD]; *b* 1944; *m* 1st 1972 Charlotte Helen Prudence (*d* 1989), dau of Lt-Col Stuart Maxwell Roberts, Alderman City London, and has:

1f *Stamford Timothy John; *b* 1976

1f *Olivia Victoria Jane; *b* 1974

2f *Susannah Catherine Rose; *b* 1979

1e (cont.) Michael Galsworthy *m* 2nd 1991 *Sarah Christian, dau of Cdr The Rev Peter Durnford, RN (ret), and has by her:

2f *William Jack Heywood; *b* 1994

3f *Imogen Rosdew Clare; *b* 1996

1e *Alison Merryn; *b* 1947

2e *Bridget; *b* 1952

3e *Amanda Elizabeth; *b* 1959

1c Frances Grace; *m* 19 April 1904 Maj George Bernard Hill, OBE (*d* 17 April 1961), s of James Duke Hill, and *d* 14 Aug 1959, leaving issue

2c Margaret Ruth; *m* 1 July 1909 Robert Beart Lucas (*d* 12 Jan 1935), s of Herbert Lucas, of Bosworth House, Hunts, and has issue

1b Mary Catherine; *m* 23 April 1874 John Gwennap Dennis Moore (*d* 1915), of Garlenick, Cornwall, and *d* 22 May 1930, leaving issue

5a Charles Kinnaird-Gordon; *b* 25 Sept 1806; Capt HEIC's Navy, Kt Persian Order of the Lion and Sun; *m* May 1838 Elizabeth, only dau of Francis Gordon of Craig, added name and arms of GORDON on inheriting the Craig and Kincardine estates, Aberdeenshire, on his f-in-law's death 1857, and *d* 2 Jan 1869, leaving:

1b Elizabeth Mary-Gordon; *m* 8 Sept 1857 Hugh Scott of Gala (*d* 9 Dec 1877), and *d* 1917, leaving issue

2b Anne Elizabeth Augusta-Gordon; *m* 17 Oct 1872 Sir Robert Muir Mackenzie, 4th Bt (*qv*), and *d* 28 April 1908, leaving issue

3b Emily Johnstone-Gordon

6a Henry Wedderburn; *b* 15 April 1810; Cdr RN; *m* 13 Nov 1857 Sarah (*d* 14 Aug 1911), dau of John Walter, and *d* 30 Dec 1865, leaving:

1b James George; *b* 22 Dec 1859; *m* 1895 Mary Margaret, dau of Thomas Duff, and *dsp* 1900

2b Montagu Henry; *b* 22 Oct 1861; *d* unm 27 Dec 1888

7a Robert Abercrombie (Rev); *b* 8 July 1811; Rector Ingrave, Essex; *m* Anne (*d* 1899), dau of Joseph Walker, and *dsp* 25 Sept 1867

8a Francis William; *b* 25 May 1818; Lt-Col 2nd Lanarks Militia; *m* 10 Jan 1844 Maria (*d* 24 May 1901), dau of Peirce Mahony, DL, of Kilmorna, Co Kerry, and *d* 9 Aug 1888, leaving:

1b Montagu Cholmeley; *b* 28 Sept 1844

2b Peirce de Lacy Henry; *b* 25 May 1848; MA Oxon; barrister; *m* 24 Oct 1888 Jessie, dau of James Sime, and *d* 26 Jan 1927

1b Alice Jane; *m* 17 Dec 1901 her cousin Peirce O'Mahony, of Grange Con, Co Wicklow, and *dsp* 29 June 1906

2b Edith Lucy Maria; *m* 12 Dec 1888 Leonard Girtin Pierrepont Barnard, of Upper Norwood, and had:

1a Caroline Elizabeth; *m* 23 June 1829 Rev John Hamilton Gray (*d* June 1867), of Carntyne, Lanarks, and *d* 21 Feb 1887, leaving issue

2a Sarah Emily; *d* unm 1891

3a Mary Anne; *m* 1839 James Dewar (*d* 1870), and *d* 9 Sept 1892, leaving issue

4a Catherine Lucy; *d* unm 1866

5a Sophia Matilda; *m* 28 Aug 1832 Sir John Muir Mackenzie, 2nd Bt (*qv*), and *d* 29 Jan 1900, leaving issue

6a Jemima Eleanora; *m* 16 Feb 1848 Lord Frederick Charles Peter Beauclerk (*see* SAINT ALBANS, D) and *d* 14 Oct 1877, leaving issue

7a Mary Cecilia; *m* 17 May 1837 Hon Laurence King-Harman (*see* KINGSTON, E) and *d* 11 Jan 1904, leaving issue

8a Charlotte Octavia; *m* 1st May 1845 James Harrison Cholmeley, Maj 8th Hus (*dsp* 2 Sept 1854), 2nd s of Sir Montague Cholmeley, 1st Bt (*qv*); *m* 2nd

9 Oct 1867 Francis Bernard Pigott (*d* 12 Nov 1872), of Eagle Hill, and *d* 26 March 1898

The 5th Bt's nephew,

Sir John Lowther Johnstone, 6th Bt; *b* 1783; MP Weymouth 1810; claimed the Marquessate of Annandale; *m* 14 Jan 1804 Charlotte (*m* 2nd 12 Sept 1820 Richard Weyland, of Woodeaton, Oxon, and *d* 1 Dec 1845), yst dau of Charles Gordon of Cluny, and *d* 24 Dec 1811, leaving issue:

1 GEORGE FREDERIC (Sir), **7th Bt**

1 Charlotte Margaret; *m* Sept 1831 Rev Henry Buckley, 2nd s of Rev Henry William Buckley by Lady Georgiana Cholmondeley, dau of 2nd Earl De La Warr (*qv*), and *d* 4 Nov 1874, leaving issue

2 Anne Elizabeth; *m* 15 April 1830 Rev Edmund B Estcourt (*d* 25 Jan 1894), 3rd s of Thomas Bucknall Estcourt, MP Oxford U, and *d* Jan 1882, leaving issue

The 6th Bt's son,

Sir George Frederic Johnstone, 7th Bt; *b* Dec 1810; *educ* Ch Ch Coll Oxford; MP Weymouth 1822–35; *m* 24 Oct 1840 Lady Maria Louisa Elizabeth Frederica Craven (*m* 2nd 15 Aug 1844 Alexander Oswald, MP, of Auchencruive, Ayrshire, and *d* 20 Oct 1858), only dau of 1st Earl of Craven (*qv*), and *d* 7 May 1841, leaving:

1 **Sir Frederick John William Johnstone, 8th Bt**, DL (Dumfriesshire); *b* 5 Aug 1841; *educ* Eton and Ch Ch Oxford; MP Weymouth 1874–85, High Sheriff Dorset 1889, sold the family estates 1911; *m* 7 June 1899 Laura Caroline (*d* 15 June 1916), dau of William Russell (*see* BEDFORD, D) and widow of 4th Earl of Wilton (*qv*), and *dsp* 20 June 1913

2 George Charles Keppel; *b* 5 Aug 1841; Lt-Col Gren Gds; *m* 29 June 1875 Agnes Caroline (*d* 25 March 1925), yst dau of Thomas Chamberlayne, JP, DL, of Cranbury Park, and Weston Grove, Hants, and *d* 12 Jan 1912, leaving:

(1) GEORGE FREDERIC THOMAS TANKERVILLE (Sir), **9th Bt**

(2) Charles John; *b* 20 Dec 1877; Lt 4th Bn Rifle Bde; *m* 1905 Doris, dau of J Ashford, and *d* 18 May 1937

(1) Agnes Louisa Barbara Snowflake; *d* unm 6 Jan 1960

(2) Rose Mary Adeline Dagmar Amelia; *m* 26 Sept 1911 Capt Eric Walter Harbord, DSO, RN (*see* SUFFIELD, B), and *d* 28 Nov 1952

The 8th Bt's nephew,

Sir George Frederic Thomas Tankerville Johnstone, 9th Bt; *b* 1 Aug 1876; Lt-Cdr RNVR and Lt 3rd Bn Roy Sussex Regt; *m* 23 July 1901 Ernestine Anne (*d* 28 April 1955), dau of Lt-Col Allan Roger Charles Porcelli-Cust (*see* BROWNLOW, B), and *d* 9 Jan 1952, having had:

1 FREDERIC ALLAN GEORGE (Sir), **10th Bt**

1 Laura Adeline; *b* 27 May 1902

2 Violet Florence Ernestine; *b* 17 April 1903; *m* 17 April 1924 Capt George Thomas Vincent Watson, IA, gs of Lt-Gen Vincent Watson, Roy Berks Regt, and had issue

3 Dorothy Katherine Frances; *b* 4 Oct 1904; *m* 20 June 1934 James Hastings (*d* March 1965) and had:

(1) *Peter James; *b* 10 May 1938; parts manager Totem Mercury Sales Ltd, Vancouver, BC

(1) *Joan Florence Hastings; *b* 10 May 1938; *m* 1st 2 Sept 1955 (*divorce* 1966) Irvyn Perry Ross and has:

1a *Leilani Joan; *b* 23 Sept 1956

(1) (cont.) Mrs Joan Ross *m* 2nd April 1967 *John David Hagar, est s of Barney B Hagar, Notary Public, of Victoria, BC, and by him has:

1a *John David; *b* 2 April 1969

2a *Ailsa Joan; *b* 16 March 1968

The 9th Bt's son,

Sir Frederic Allan George Johnstone, 10th Bt; *b* 23 Feb 1906; *educ* ISC; *m* 1st 1933 (*divorce* 1941) Gladys, dau of — Hands; *m* 2nd 20 Dec 1946 *Doris, dau of W L Shortridge, of Blackheath, and *d* 19 July 1994, leaving:

1 Sir GEORGE RICHARD DOUGLAS JOHNSTONE, **11th and present Bt**

2 +Ian Allan; *b* 29 Jan 1954

JOICEY

Arms: Argent three lozenges sable within two bendlets invected gules between two miner's picks in bend proper. **Crest:** A demi-man affronté in armour proper, garnished or, the helmet adorned with three feathers gules, holding in the dexter hand a scimitar of the first, pommel and hilt gold, supporting with the sinister hand an escutcheon argent, charged with three torteaux within two bendlets invected of the second between two fleurs-de-lys sable. **Supporters:** On either side a Shetland pony proper, haltered or. **Motto:** *Omne solum forti patria* ('Every land is a native country to a brave man'). **Creations:** Bt. (UK) 3 July 1893, B. (UK) 13 Jan 1906.

THE 5TH BARON JOICEY, of Chester-Le-Street, Co Durham, and a **Baronet** (Sir James Michael Joicey, Bt) [The Rt Hon The Lord Joicey, East Flodden Farmhouse, Wooler, Northumberland NE71 6JF]; *b* 28 June 1953; *s* f 1993; *educ* Eton and Ch Ch Oxford; *m* 1984 *(Agnes) Harriet Frances Mary, yr dau of Rev William Thompson, of Oxnam Manse, Jedburgh, Roxburghshire, and has:

1 +WILLIAM JAMES; *b* 21 May 1990

2 +Richard Michael; *b* 1993

1 *Hannah Elisabeth; *b* 1988

2 *Claire Vida; *b* 1 Feb 1994

Lineage: GEORGE JOWSEE, of Jowsey, Northumberland; *m* 28 Sept 1657 Jane Patteson and had:

GEORGE JOICEY, of Long Benton, Northumberland; *bapt* 26 Nov 1780; *m* 22 June 1805 Jane Clark (*d* 26 March 1838), of Long Benton, and was *bur* 16 March 1848, having had:

GEORGE JOICEY, of Gateshead, Co Durham; *bapt* 24 Oct 1813; *m* 7 Oct 1837 Dorothy (*d* 16 Dec 1877), dau of Jacob Gowland, of Wrekenton, Co Durham, and *d* 23 Sept 1856, having had:

1 Jacob Gowland; *m* Hannah (*d* his widow 17 April 1926), dau of James Thompson, of Marley Hill, Co Durham, and had issue

2 JAMES, **1st Baron**

3 George

1 Jane; *m* William Joicey Humble and *d* 1868

2 Dorothy Ann; *m* Nicholas Johnson Robinson, of N Shields, and *d* his widow 29 Oct 1933

3 Margaret Georgina; *m* John Walton Robinson, of Gateshead-on-Tyne

The 2nd son,

Sir James Joicey, 1st Bt, and **1st Baron Joicey**, of Chester-le-Street, Co Durham, so *cr* 3 July 1893 and 13 Jan 1906 respectively (both UK), JP, DL; *b* 4 April 1846; MP (Lib) Chester-le-Street 1885–1905, Hon DCL Durham; *m* 1st 23 April 1879 Elizabeth Amy (*d* 1 Dec 1881), only dau of Joseph Robinson, of N Shields, JP, and *d* 21 Nov 1936, leaving:

1 JAMES ARTHUR JOICEY, **2nd Baron Joicey**, JP (Northumberland); *b* 1 May 1880; High Sheriff Co Durham 1910; Maj 7th Bn Northumberland Fus (TF) WW I; *m* 10 Sept 1904 Georgina Wharton (*d* 4 Nov 1952), yr dau of Maj Augustus Edward Burdon, of Hartford House and Wooperton, Northumberland, and *d* 24 July 1940, having had:

(1) James; *b* 21 May 1907; 2nd Lt 14th/20th Hus; *d* 8 May 1929

(1) Norah Marguerite; *b* 21 Sept 1905; *m* 14 July 1932 Brig Ronald Henry Senior, DSO, TD, est s of Lawrence Henry Senior, and had issue

(2) Sylvia Alice; *b* 5 Aug 1908; *m* 28 April 1934 (*divorce* 1951) Lt-Col Richard Ian Griffith Taylor, DSO, MC (*d* 1984), est s of Lt-Col Thomas George Taylor, DSO, of Chipchase Castle, Wark-on-Tyne, and *d* Nov 1994, leaving:

1a *Simon James [Simon Taylor Esq, Rothbury Park, RD4, Hamilton, New Zealand]; *b* 1936; *educ* Harrow; *m* 1963 *Janice, dau of Stanley Marshall, and has:

1b *Jeremy Nicholas; *b* 1963

2b *Richard Simon; *b* 1967

1b *Fiona Josephine; *b* 1965

2b *Susan; *b* 1966

3b *Melissa Jane; *b* 1969
2a *Alexander Thomas; *b* 1941; *educ* Harrow; *m* 1974 *Sarah, dau of Col Richard Martin-Bird, of Stockinwood, Chelford, Cheshire
1a *Valerie; *b* 1946; *m* 1969 *Alan Yuill Walker, of Sheepdrove Park, Lambourn, Berks, and has:
1b *Lavinia Mary; *b* 1972
2b *Georgina Anne; *b* 1974
(3) Angela Georgina; *b* 23 April 1915; *d* unm following a car crash 18 March 1970
2 HUGH EDWARD, **3rd Baron**

The **1st Baron** *m* 2nd 21 Feb 1884 Margaret Smyles (*d* 5 July 1911), only surv child of Col Thomas Drever, Bengal Army, by Marguerite, only child of Gen de Fontaine, of Fontainebleau, and had:
3 Sydney James Drever; *b* 24 Nov 1884; MA Cantab; Capt and Adj 10th (Serv) Bn Northumberland Fus; *ka* 20 March 1916
4 Drever, of Howtel, Northumberland; *b* 1 April 1866; Lt Montgomeryshire Yeo; *d* 27 Jan 1915
1 Marguerite de Fontaine Drever; *b* 16 Sept 1887; *d* 25 April 1924

The 2nd BARON's bro,
HUGH EDWARD JOICEY, **3rd Baron Joicey**, DSO, JP (Northumberland); *b* 21 Nov 1881; *educ* Harrow; High Sheriff Northumberland 1933; Lt-Col 14th Hus Boer War 1901–02 (Queen's medal with 3 clasps), WW I with 2nd Life Gds 1914015, cmded 1st Suffolk Regt 1915–18 (despatches four times, Brevet Lt-Col), Greek MC, Chm Lambton Hetton and Joicey Collieries 1940–66, Albyn Line, Tanfield S/S Co and Roy Insur (Newcastle Branch); *m* 19 July 1921 Lady Joan Katherine Lambton (*d* 4 Jan 1967), yst dau of 4th Earl of Durham (*qv*), and *d* 14 Oct 1966, having had:
1 David Hugh; *b* 21 April 1922; Lt Coldstream Gds WW II; *d* of wounds recd Salerno Sept 1943
2 MICHAEL EDWARD JOICEY, **4th Baron Joicey**; *b* 28 Feb 1925; *educ* Eton and Ch Ch Oxford; Capt Coldstream Gds, Jt MFH N Northumberland; *m* 27 March 1952 *Elisabeth Marion [The Rt Hon Elisabeth Lady Joicey, Etal Manor, Berwick-on-Tweed TD15 2PU], yst dau of Lt-Col Hon Ian Leslie Melville (*see* LEVEN and MELVILLE, E), and *d* 1993, leaving:
(1) JAMES MICHAEL JOICEY, **5th and present Baron Joicey**
(2) +Andrew Hugh [The Hon Andrew Joicey, New Etal, Cornhill-on-Tweed, Northumberland TD12 4XL]; *b* 24 Dec 1955; *educ* Eton and Ch Ch Oxford; *m* 5 Nov 1994 *Corinne, er dau of John Cockburn, of Cockburnspath, and has:
1a *Victoria Marianne; *b* 13 May 1997
(1) *Katherine Jane [Mrs Thomas Crosbie Dawson, Pawston, Mindrum, Northumberland]; *b* 20 April 1959; *m* 1984 *Thomas Crosbie Dawson and has:
1a *Robert Hugo; *b* 1992
1a *Lucy Charlotte; *b* 1987
2a *Helen Amanda; *b* 1989

JONES

Arms: Per chevron argent and sable, in chief two dragon's heads erased gules and in base two crosses pattée fitchée in saltire or. **Crest:** A demi-gryphon gules grasping a miner's pickaxe, head downwards, in pale or. **Motto:** *Quod cæpio persequor* ('What I begin I see through to the end'). **Creation:** Bt. (UK) 23 May 1919.

SIR SIMON WARLEY FREDERICK BENTON JONES, 4TH BT, of Treeton, W Riding Co York, JP (Lincs 1971) [Sir Simon Jones Bt JP, Irnham Hall, Grantham, Lincs NG33 4JD]; *b* 11 Sept 1941; *s f* 1972; *educ* Eton and Trin Coll Cambridge (BA 1963); High Sheriff Lincs 1977–78; *m* 14 April 1966 *Margaret Fiona, OBE (1995), DL (Lincs), est dau of David Rutherford Dickson, of Barrow Lodge, Bury St Edmunds, and has:
1 +JAMES PETER MARTIN; *b* 1 Jan 1973; *m* 27 Sept 1997 *Lucy A, only dau of David Briggs of Blackwell Farm, Latimer, Bucks
2 +David William Anthony; *b* 18 March 1975
3 +Alastair Frederick Martin; *b* 1981
1 *Fiona Charlotte; *b* 1 Oct 1967; *m* 1996 *Rupert Farquharson, yst s of Sir Donald Farquharson
2 *Fleur Alexandra; *b* 13 Nov 1970; *m* 2 Aug 1997 *Robert Collins, only s of Sir John Collins, of Beaulieu, Hants

Lineage: Sir Frederick John Jones, 1st Bt (UK), so *cr* 23 May 1919, JP (W R Yorks), of Treeton, Yorks; *b* 1854 (s of Thomas Jones, of Walsall); Pres Mining Assoc GB, chm S Yorks Coal Trade Assoc and Miners' Conciliation Bd; *m* 1st 1877 Annie Elizabeth (*d* 1893), dau of Walter Benton, and had:
1 WALTER BENTON (Sir), **2nd Bt**
2 Charles Frederick Ward; *b* 1884; *educ* Repton; Capt WW I; *m* 1921 Dorothy (*d* 1962), only dau of R H Allen, of Notts, and *d* 1971, leaving:
(1) +David Robert Ward [David Jones Esq, Orchard House, Firbeck, Notts]; *b* 1925; *educ* Repton; Capt RHG (Blues) Res; *m* 6 Oct 1951 *Sally, dau of Col H Cantan, of Tullow, Co Carlow, and has:
1a *Emma; *b* 1956
2a *Kathryn; *b* 1960
3a *Harriet; *b* 1963
(1) *Anne Ward [Mrs Charles Pain, The Priory Farmhouse, S Leverton, Notts]; *b* 1922; *m* 10 June 1950 *Charles Douglas Pain, er s of W H Pain, and has:
1a *Michael Ward Eames; *b* 1957; *m* 1986 *Christina Elisabeth Ljungström
(2) *Beth Ward [Mrs Michael Antill, Woodhouse Hill, Holbeck, Notts]; *b* 1924; *m* 29 April 1950 *Michael William Ollyver Antill, est s of Walter Samuel Antill, of Lindick, Notts, and has:
1a *Timothy William; *b* 1954
1a *Sarah Penelope; *b* 1952
1 Edith Annie; *b* 14 Aug 1877; *m* 1901 Leslie Edwards Wilton and *d* 19 Oct 1937
2 Marion; *b* 5 Jan 1879; *m* 1908 James Wortley Fawcett and *d* 16 Oct 1934, leaving two daus
3 Agnes Hilda; *m* 25 Sept 1907 Martin James Mowat, of Lound Hall, Retford, Notts, est s of Rev James Mowat (*d* 14 March 1952), Rector Handsworth, and *d* 20 Feb 1965, leaving issue

Sir Frederick *m* 2nd 1902 Katherine (*d* 22 Dec 1921), dau of Robert Dyson, of Rotherham, and by her had:
4 *Katharine Mary [Mrs William Olivier, Ashford Hall, Bakewell, Derbys DE5 1QA]; *m* 20 July 1933 Lt-Col William Herbert Olivier, TD, JP, DL (*d* 1992), only s of Herbert Arnould Olivier, and has:
(1) *Jasper William Dacres; *b* 1938; *m* 1973 *Virginia Whitaker
(2) *James Stephen; *b* 1944; Lt-Col RHG (Blues); *m* 1968 *Sally Anne Simonds
(1) *Flora Mary Margaret; *b* 1936; *m* 1973 *John Guy Carmichael Jackson
(2) *Julie Katharine; *b* 1941; *m* 1966 *Patrick Julian Dawnay (*see* DOWNE, V)

Sir FREDERICK *d* 23 May 1936; his est son,
Sir Walter Benton Jones, 2nd Bt; *b* 26 Sept 1880; *educ* Repton and Trin Coll Cambridge (BA 1902, MA 1950); Hon LLD Sheffield, pres (formerly chm) United Steel Cos; *m* 9 Jan 1907 Lily Marguerite (*d* 19 Sept 1938), only dau of James Dixon Fawcett, of Whirlow Court, Sheffield, and had:
1 PETER FAWCETT BENTON (Sir), **3rd Bt**
1 Pamela Benton; *b* 24 March 1908; *m* 23 Sept 1930 (*divorce* 1948) Percival John Parker Stephenson (*d* 1973), 3rd s of Lt-Col Sir Henry Kenyon Stephenson, 1st Bt, DSO, VD (*qv*), and *d* 22 Jan 1997, leaving issue
2 *Rachel Mary Benton [Mrs George Kydd, 23 Chapel St, Grassington, N Yorks BD23 5BE]; *b* 15 Nov 1918; *educ* Oxford (MA, BLitt); *m* 22 Dec 1941 *Lt George Ronald Murray Kydd, MA, RNVR, yr s of John Charles Kydd, of Selly Oak, Birmingham, and has:
(1) *Ian Murray; *b* 16 Aug 1945; *m* 1972 *Elizabeth, dau of Richard Blackburn, and has:
1a *Benjamin Murray; *b* 1972
2a *Joel Murray; *b* 1975
(2) *Donald Hamish; *b* 30 April 1947; *m* 1970 *Christine, dau of Owen Gough, and has:
1a *Lorraine Grace; *b* 1971
2a *Samantha Melanie Jane; *b* 1973

Sir WALTER *d* 5 Dec 1967; his only son,
Sir Peter Fawcett Benton Jones, 3rd Bt, OBE (1946); *b* 9 Jan 1911; *educ* Charterhouse and Trin Coll Cambridge (BA 1932, MA 1950); FCA, Lt Col RA WW II (despatches); *m* 1 Feb 1936 Nancy (*d* 4 March 1974), only child of Warley Pickering, of Hutton Hall, Yorks, by Beryl, only dau of John Kemp-Welch, JP, of Sopley Park, Hants, and *d* 1972, leaving:
1 Sir SIMON WARLEY FREDERICK BENTON JONES, **4th and present Bt**
1 *Jill Benton [The Hon Lady McAlpine, Fawley Hill, Fawley Green, Bucks]; *b* 5 Oct 1937; *m* 21 Oct 1959 *Hon Sir William Hepburn McAlpine, 6th Bt (*qv*), and has issue

JOPLING

Creation: B. (LP, UK) 19 April 1997.

THE BARON JOPLING, of Ainderby Quernhow, Co N Yorks ((Thomas) Michael Jopling, PC (1979), DL (Cumbria 1991)) [The Rt Hon The Lord Jopling PC DL, Ainderby Hall, Thirsk, N Yorks YO7 4HZ]; *b* 10 Dec 1930; *educ* Cheltenham and King's Coll Newcastle; memb: Thirsk DC 1958–64, Nat Cncl NFU 1962–64; MP (C) Westmorland 1964–83, Westmorland and Lonsdale 1983–97, Jt Sec C Parly Ag Ctee 1966–70, PPS to Min Ag 1970–71, Assist Govt Whip 1971–73, Ld Commr Treasury 1973–74, Oppn Whip 1974, Oppn Spokesman Ag 1974–75 and 1976–79, Shadow Min Ag 1975–76, Parly Sec Treasury and Ch Whip 1979–83, MAFF 1983–87, memb: Select Ctee For Affrs 1987–97, UK Exec Cwlth Parly Assoc 1974–79 and 1987–97 (V-Chm 1977–79), Chm Select Ctee Sittings of House 1991–92; Pres EEC Ag and Fishery Ministers' Cncls 1986; Pres Auto Cycle 1990–; Hon DCL Newcastle 1992; *m* 1958 *Gail, dau of Ernest Dickinson, of Harrogate, and has:

1 *Nicholas Mark Fletcher; *b* 4 Oct 1961
2 *Jeremy Michael Neal; *b* 15 June 1963

Lineage: MARK BELLERBY JOPLING, of Masham, Yorks *m* 1921 Lilian Mary Fletcher and had:

(THOMAS) MICHAEL, *cr* a **Baron**

JUDD

Creation: B. (LP, UK) 1991.

THE BARON JUDD, of Portsea, Co Hants (Frank Ashcroft Judd) [The Rt Hon The Lord Judd, House of Lords, London SW1A 0PW]; *b* 28 March 1935; *educ* City of London Sch and LSE (BSc); F/O RAF 1957–59; Gen Sec Internat Vol Serv 1960–66; MP (Lab) Portsmouth W 1966–74 and Portsmouth N 1974–79; PPS to: Min Housing and Local Govt 1967–70 and Leader Oppn 1970–72; memb Br Parly Delegn Cncl Europe and WEU 1970–73, Jt Oppn Def Spokesman 1972–74, Parly U-Sec Def RN 1974–76, Min Overseas Devpt 1976–77, FCO 1977–79; Assoc Dir Internat Def & Aid Fund for Southern Africa 1979–80; Ind Advsr UK Delegn UN Special Session Disarmament 1982; Dir: VSO 1980–85, Oxfam 1985–91; Chm: Centre for World Devpt Educn 1980–85, Internat Cncl Vol Agencies 1985–90, World Ec Forum Conf on S Africa 1990 and 1991, Oxford Diocesan Bd Social Responsibility 1992–, Cncl Selly Oaks Colls Birmingham; Oppn Spokesperson Ho Lds: For Affairs 1991–92, Educn 1992–94, Overseas Devpt 1994–97; Memb: Steering Ctee World Bank NGO Ctee 1989–91, Cncl Overseas Devpt Inst, Governing Body Queen Elizabeth House Oxford U, Cncl Charitable Support 1991–, Internat Commn Global Governance 1992–, WHO Task Force Health and Devpt Policies 1994–, ASTMS, Parly delegation to Cncl of Europe and WEU, sub ctee (Environment, Public Health and Consumer Protection) of ECs; Chm European Atlantic Gp 1997–; Tstee Beryl Le Poer Power Tst (Chatham Ho), memb NW Regnl Advsy Ctee Nat Tst 1996–; Pres YMCA (England) 1996, memb Roy Inst Internat Affairs; Govr: LSE 1982–, Westminster Coll Oxford 1991–; Tstee: Portsmouth Cathedral Devpt Tst plc, Internat Alert 1994–; Hon Fell Portsmouth U 1978, Hon DLitt Bradford U 1987 and Portsmouth U (Hon Fell), memb Cncl Lancaster U, FRSA 1988; Freeman Portsmouth 1995; author: *Radical Future* (jt author, 1967), *Fabian International Essays* (1970), *Purpose of Socialism* (1973), *Our Global Neighbourhood* (jt author, 1995); *m* 1961 *Christine Elizabeth Louise, dau of Frederick Ward Willington, of Kent, and has:

1 *Elizabeth; *b* 1967
2 *Philippa; *b* 1969

Lineage: CHARLES WILFRED JUDD, CBE, of Sutton, Surrey; *m* Helen —, JP, and had:

FRANK ASHCROFT, *cr* a **Baron**

KABERRY

Arms: Per fess argent and azure and a pile reversed counterchanged three double-warded keys, wards upwards also azure, each enfiled by a chaplet of holly fructed proper and of roses argent barbed and seeded also proper. **Crest:** On a wreath of sable and azure a weeping willow tree proper, pendant from the trunk thereof by a ring a fleece or. **Motto:** *Laboro fide* ('I labour with faith'). **Creation:** Bt. (UK) 28 Jan 1960.

SIR CHRISTOPHER DONALD KABERRY, 2ND BT, of Adel cum Eccup, City of Leeds [The Hon Sir Christopher Kaberry Bt, Rock View, Chiddingstone Hoath, Kent TN8 7BT]; *b* 14 March 1943; *s f* 1991; *educ* Repton; chartered accountant 1967; *m* 25 March 1967 *Gaenor Elizabeth Vowe, yr dau of Cecil Vowe Peake, MBE, of Witham Fields, Church St, Long Benington, Notts, and has issue:

1 +JAMES CHRISTOPHER [James Kaberry Esq, 592 Haywood Old Rd, Middleton, Manchester M24]; *b* 1 April 1970; *educ* Oakham; *m* 1989 (*divorce* 1996) Juliet Clare, est dau of Sir James Frederick Hill, 4th Bt (*qv*), and has:
(1) +Jonathan James Alexander; *b* 12 May 1989
(2) +Oliver George Henry; *b* 1991
(1) *Imogen; *b* 199–
2 +Angus George; *b* 1972
1 *Claire Elizabeth; *b* 1974

Lineage: ABRAHAM KABERRY, of Leeds; *b* 27 Dec 1883; *m* Lily, dau of William MacKenzie, of Maryborough, Ross-shire, and Leeds, and *d* 22 Sep 1954, leaving:

Sir Donald Kaberry, 1st Bt, so *cr* 28 Jan 1960, as also 1983 BARON KABERRY OF ADEL, of Adel cum Eccup, City of Leeds (LP, both UK), TD, DL (W R Yorks 1974); *b* 18 Aug 1907; *educ* Leeds GS (later Govr); slr 1930, Lt-Col RA WW II (despatches twice), memb Court and Cncl Leeds U 1959–69, memb Leeds City Cncl 1930–40 and 1946–51, Dep Ld Mayor Leeds 1946–47, memb Law Soc Cncl 1950–55, MP (C) NW Leeds 1950–83, Assist Govt Whip 1951–55, Parly Sec BOT April-Oct 1955, V-Chm C and U Party 1955–61, Chm: Yorks Area Cncl C Pty 1952–55 (Pres 1966–91), Assoc C Clubs 1961–91, Bd Govrs Utd Leeds (Teaching) Hosps 1961–74, Yorks Dyeware and Chemical Co 1964–77, W H Baxter Ltd; *m* 3 Sept 1940 Lily Margaret, dau of Edmund Scott, and *d* 1991, leaving:

1 Sir CHRISTOPHER DONALD KABERRY, **2nd Bt**
2 +Andrew Murdoch Scott [The Hon Andrew Kaberry, Thorpe Arch Hall, Boston Spa, W Yorks]; *b* 22 Sept 1946; *educ* Repton and UEA (BA); FCA 1972
3 +Simon Edmund John [The Hon Simon Kaberry, Adel Willows, Otley Rd, Leeds 16]; *b* 14 Dec 1948; *educ* Repton; slr 1974

KAYE

Arms: Or a bend cotised invected between two escutcheons sable, each charged with a rose argent, barbed and seeded proper. **Crest:** Upon a staff raguly fesswise or a goldfinch proper, holding in the beak a rose argent, barbed, seeded, leaved and slipped proper. **Motto:** *Spectemur agendo* ('Let us be judged by our actions'). **Creation:** Bt. (UK) 8 March 1923.

SIR PAUL HENRY GORDON KAYE, 5TH BT, of Huddersfield, Co York [Sir Paul Kaye Bt, 15 Muston Court, Carrara, Qld 4211, Australia]; *b* 19 Feb 1958; *s f* 1997; *m* 1984 *Sally Ann Louise —

Lineage: HENRY KAYE, of Lindley, Huddersfield; had:

Sir Joseph Henry Kaye, 1st Bt (UK), so *cr* 8 March 1923, JP; *b* 6 Sept 1856; dir Kaye & Stewart Ltd, Gledhill Bros & Co, LMSR and Lloyds Bank; *m* 23 Sept 1885 Emily (*d* 12 April 1933), dau of Alfred Crowther, JP, and *d* 24 Dec 1923, leaving:

Sir Henry Gordon Kaye, 2nd Bt, JP; *b* 24 Feb 1889; *educ* Rugby and Oriel Coll Oxford (BA 1910, MA 1914); dir Huddersfield Bldg Soc, Sun Insur Office Leeds, Capt KOYLI, F/Cdr RFC WW I France and Salonika (wounded); *m* 29 April 1916 Winifred (Freda), er dau of Walter Henry Scales, and *d* 19 Feb 1956, leaving:

1 **Sir Stephen Henry Gordon Kaye, 3rd Bt**; *b* 24 March 1917; *educ* Stowe and Trin Coll Cambridge; *d* 12 June 1983

2 **Sir David Alexander Gordon Kaye, 4th Bt**; *b* 26 July 1919; *educ* Stowe and Cambridge (BA); MRCS Eng, LRCP Lond 1943; *m* 1st 10 Oct 1942 (*divorce* 1950) Elisabeth Rosemary, only dau of Capt Malcolm Hurtley; *m* 2nd 15 June 1955 *Adelle Frances [Lady Kaye, 594 Lower Bowen Terrace, New Farm, Brisbane 4005, Qld, Australia], dau of Dennis Lionel Thomas, of Brisbane, Qld, and *d* Oct-Dec 1997, leaving by her:

(1) Sir PAUL HENRY GORDON KAYE, **5th and present Bt**

(2) +JOHN EGIDIO GORDON; *b* 1967; heir presumptive

(1) *Yvonne Marie; *b* 14 Aug 1956

(2) *Denise Anne; *b* 6 July 1960

(3) *Alaine Freda; *b* 9 April 1962

(4) *Marita Margaret; *b* 1970

3 Brian Joseph Gordon; *b* 23 Dec 1920; *educ* Stowe; *m* 26 Sept 1947 * Anne, only child of Frederick Henry Grisewood, OBE, and *d* 19–, leaving:

(1) +Angus Frederick Gordon; *b* 20 March 1962

KEANE

Arms: Gules three salmon naiant in pale argent. **Crest:** A cat-a-mountain sejant proper, supporting in his dexter paw a flagstaff, thereon a Union Jack, proper. **Motto:** *Felis demulcta mitis* ('The stroked cat is meek'). **Creation:** Bt. (UK) 1 Aug 1801.

SIR RICHARD MICHAEL KEANE, 6TH BT, of Cappoquin House, Co Waterford [Maj Sir Richard Keane Bt, Cappoquin House, Co Waterford, Ireland]; *b* 29 Jan 1909; *s f* 30 Jan 1956; *educ* Sherborne and Ch Ch Oxford; diplomatic correspondent with Reuters 1935–37 and *Sunday Times* (also assist ed) 1937–39, Capt 3rd Co London Yeo and 10th Roy Hus WW II 1939–44, Liaison Offr with HQ Vojvodina Yugoslav Partisans 1944, with Mil Mission Belgrade 1944–45, ret as Maj, md Cappoquin Estate Co 1945–, publicity consultant ICI 1950–63, author: *Germany: What Next?* (1939) and *Modern Marvels of Science* (1961, ed); *m* 7 June 1939 *Olivia Dorothy, yst dau of Oliver Hawkshaw, TD, of Chisenbury Priory, Wilts, and has:

1 +(JOHN) CHARLES [Charles Keane Esq, 26 ave Hougoumont, B-1180 Brussels, Belgium]; *b* 16 Sept 1941; *educ* Eton and Ch Ch Oxford; *m* 1977 *Corinne, dau of Jean Everard de Harzir, of Waroux, Belgium, and has:

(1) +Christopher; *b* 1981

(2) +Gregory; *b* 1982

(1) *Amelia; *b* 1987

2 +David Richard; *b* 11 April 1950; *educ* Eton, Cambridge Coll of Technology and Balliol Coll Oxford; *m* 1973 *Julia, dau of Henry Bowring, of The Old Orchard, Bembridge, IoW, and has:

(1) +Henry; *b* 1982

(1) *Jessica; *b* 1978

(2) *Rosanna Emily; *b* 1980

(3) *Camilla; *b* 1985

1 *Vivien Eleanor [Mrs Simon Pleydell-Bouverie, The Castle House, Deddington, Oxon]; *b* 8 July 1940; *m* 24 Oct 1961 *Simon Pleydell-Bouverie (*see* RADNOR, E) and has issue

Lineage: RICHARD KEANE; had:

Sir John Keane, 1st Bt (UK), so *cr* 1 Aug 1801, of Belmont, Co Waterford; *b* 1757; *m* 1st March 1778 Sarah, dau of Richard Kell(e)y, of Lismore, Co Waterford, and sis of John Kell(e)y, of Belgrove, Co Cork, and had:

1 RICHARD (Sir), **2nd Bt**

2 JOHN KEANE, 1st BARON KEANE OF GHUZNEE, in Afghanistan, AND CAPPOQUIN, Co Waterford (UK), so *cr* 23 Dec 1839, GCB (1839, KCB 1815), GCH (1831); *b* 6 Feb 1781; joined army 1793, served Egypt 1801–02, Lt-Col 13th Foot Martinique 1809, thereafter served Peninsula War to 1814, Battle of New Orleans Dec 1814 in War of 1812, Govr St Lucia 1818–25, C-in-C Jamaica 1823–30, Maj-Gen 1814, Lt-Gen 1830, Col: 94th Foot 1829–31, 68th Foot 1831–38, 46th Foot 1838–39 and 43rd Foor 1839–44, C-in-C Bombay 1833–39, led Afghan Expdn which resulted in capture of city of Ghuznee 1839; *m* 1st 1 Aug 1806 Grace (*d* 14 July 1838), dau of Lt-Gen Sir John Smith, RA; *m* 2nd 20 Aug 1840 Charlotte Maria (*m* 2nd 18 Oct 1847 William Pigott, of Dullingham House, Cambs, 2nd s of Sir George Pigott, 1st Bt (*qv*), and *d* 8 Sept 1884), dau of Colonel — Boland, and *d* 26 Aug 1844, having by his 1st w had, with two daus:

(1) EDWARD ARTHUR WELLINGTON KEANE, 2nd BARON KEANE OF GHUZNEE AND CAPPOQUIN; *b* 4 May 1815; Maj 37th Foot, sat as Lib; *m* 13 April 1847 Louisa Caroline Lydia (*d* 3 Jan 1903), 3rd and yst dau of Samuel Yate Benyon, of Stetchworth Park and Denston Hall, Cambs, and *dspm* 25 July 1882, leaving:

1a Emily Julia Charlotte; *b* 12 Jan 1848; *m* 1st 20 Oct 1866 (*divorce* 1882) Maj Henry Arthur Herbert, DL Co Kerry, MP Co Kerry 1866–80 (*d* 14 Aug 1901), of Muckruss Abbey, Killarney, Co Kerry, and had, with another dau:

1b Henry Arthur Edward Keane, JP (Co Kerry); *b* 1867; *d* unm

1b Kathleen Mary Eleanor; *m* 21 July 1894 Capt A Morris, late 20th Hus

1a (cont.) The Hon Mrs Emily Herbert *m* 2nd 1897 Henry Hulton Vignoles and *d* 2 July 1911

(2) JOHN MANLY ARBUTHNOT KEANE, 3rd and last BARON KEANE OF GHUZNEE AND CAPPOQUIN; *b* 1 Sept 1816; Lt 33rd Foot 1833, Maj Rifle Bde 1846–49, High Sheriff Co Wexford 1875, sat as C; *m* 1st 11 May 1848

Mary Jane (*dsp* 29 Oct 1881), sis and heiress of Sir Hugh Palliser, 3rd and last Bt, and widow of William Lockhart, of Milton Lockhart, Lanarks; *m* 2nd 6 May 1885 Francina Maria (*d* 20 Nov 1901), dau of Charles Lane, of Badgemore, Oxon, and widow of Rt Rev Thomas Morrell, DD, Bp-Coadjutor Edinburgh, and *dsp* 27 Nov 1901, a week after his w, when the Barony expired

(3) George Disney, CB; *b* 26 Sept 1817; joined RN 1839, Cdr 1846, Capt 1855, R-Adml 1872, V-Adml 1878; *m* 13 July 1881 Katherine Mary (*d* 16 Jan 1894), dau of Maj Alexander McLeod and widow of Thomas Longford Brooke, of Mere Hall, Cheshire, and *dsp* 19 Oct 1891

(4) Hussey Fane, CB (1871); *b* 14 June 1822; joined RE 1839: Capt 1849, Maj 1855, Lt-Col 1862, Col 1866, Maj-Gen 1877, Lt-Gen 1879, served Crimean War (medal with clasp, Turkish War medal, Medjidie), Extra-ADC to C-in-C HRH THE DUKE OF CAMBRIDGE 1860, Assist ADC 1860–65, DAG 1865–70, ADC to HM QUEEN VICTORIA 1866–77; *m* 11 Jan 1886 Isabella Emma Elizabeth (*d* 4 Aug 1906), dau of 5th Earl of Orkney (*qv*) and widow of Samuel Leo Schuster, of The Grange, Leatherhead, Surrey, and *dsp* 25 Oct 1895

3 Henry Edward; *b* May 1783; Col 7th Hus; *m* 17 Jan 1818 Anne, dau of Sir William Fraser, 1st Bt (*see* 1970 edn FRASER, Bt, of Ledeclune), and *d* 2 Nov 1866, leaving:

(1) Edward Vivian; *d* unm 28 Aug 1840

(1) Frances Eliza; *m* 17 April 1860 Rev Oliver Mathew Ridley (*see* RIDLEY, V)

Sir John *m* 2nd 1804 Dorothy (*d* 5 July 1837), only dau of Richard Scott, of Betton Strange, Salop, and widow of Philip Champion de Crespigny, MP, of Aldborough, Suffolk, and *d* 19 April 1829, leaving by her:

4 George Michael; *b* 15 Nov 1805; Lt-Col 2nd Foot; *m* 7 Sept 1839 Helen Augusta (*d* 3 Dec 1902), yst dau of Maj James Nesbit Jackson, CB, HEICS, and *d* 19 Oct 1880, leaving:

(1) Anne Crespigny Scott; nun

The 1st Bt's est s,

Sir Richard Keane, 2nd Bt; *b* March 1780; Lt-Col Waterford Militia; *m* 20 Nov 1814 Eliza (*d* 18 May 1842), dau of Richard Sparrow, of Oaklands, and widow of Samuel Penrose, of Waterford, and *d* 1855, leaving:

1 JOHN HENRY (Sir), **3rd Bt**

2 Leopold George Frederick, CB (1881); *b* 3 July 1818; Ensign 52nd Foot, Hon Col 6th Bde S Irish Div RA; *m* March 1844 Charlotte French (*d* 1903), dau of Ven Henry Cotton, Archdeacon Cashel, and *d* 2 March 1898, leaving, with a dau:

(1) Frederick Henry; *b* 13 March 1857; *m* 30 Nov 1893 Elizabeth Harriet Anne Agnes (*d* April 1937), only dau of William Henry Penrose, of Laughane, Co Cork, and Low Park, Dedham, Essex, and *d* 25 Dec 1939, leaving:

1a Frederick William Leopold, of Summerland, BC, Canada; *b* 25 Nov 1897

The er s,

Sir John Henry Keane, 3rd Bt; *b* 12 Jan 1816; *m* 1st 10 July 1844 Laura (*d* 21 Jan 1878), est dau of Rt Hon Richard Keatinge, Judge Prerogative Ct Ireland; *m* 2nd 18 Sept 1880 Harriet (*dsp* 14 Sept 1902), only dau of E B Thorneycroft, and *d* 26 Nov 1881, having had by his 1st w, with two other daus (*d* unm):

1 RICHARD FRANCIS (Sir), **4th Bt**

2 George Wilfred; *b* 14 May 1859; Capt 1st Bn Durham LI; *m* 1st 21 Feb 1888 Jessie Mary Lowther (*d* 3 Oct 1910), only surv dau of Col James Smith Du Vernet; *m* 2nd 9 Oct 1912 Beatrice Manthorp, dau of John Charles Chubb and widow of John Ross Macpherson, of Powell's, Kenn, nr Exeter, and *d* 12 April 1922

1 Laura Ellen Flora; *m* 1st 8 Jan 1876 Capt Bernherd Henry Entwistle, 5th Dragoon Gds (*d* 22 Sept 1877), s of W Entwistle, DCL, of Rusholme, Lancs; *m* 2nd 24 May 1880 Robert Henry Beresford (*see* WATERFORD, M) and *d* 5 July 1920

The er s,

Sir Richard Francis Keane, 4th Bt, DL (Co Waterford); *b* 13 June 1845; civil engr, High Sheriff Co Waterford 1882; *m* 30 July 1872 Adelaide Sidney (*d* 10 Feb 1907), er dau and only surv child of John Vance, MP, and *d* 17 Oct 1892, leaving:

1 JOHN (Sir), **5th Bt**

2 George Michael; *b* 30 May 1875; Capt RN; *m* 7 June 1909 Violet Ida (*d* 11 April 1974), only dau of Theodore McKenna, and *d* 2 Feb 1957, leaving:

(1) *Ann Patricia [Mrs Christopher Thompson, Coldenhale, Eastham, Tenbury Wells, Worcs]; *b* 1 Dec 1910; *m* 24 July 1934 *G/Capt Christopher Leslie Thompson, RAF, s of C K Thompson, of Sutton Coldfield, and has:

1a *Christopher Mark; *b* 1935

2a *Jonathan Michael Adrian; *b* 1938; *m* 1970 *Barbara Anne, dau of F Scrowcroft

3a *Andrew Theodore; *b* 1941

3 Richard Henry, CBE (1919); *b* 3 May 1881; Lt-Col cmdg a Tport Workers' Bn WW I; *m* 18 July 1906 Alice Gabriel (*k* by enemy action June 1944), yr dau of Judge Sir Lumley Smith, KC, and *d* 22 Nov 1925, leaving:

(1) Robert Lumley; *b* 8 Dec 1910; *m* 22 Oct 1938 Mary Nesta (*d* 22 April 1996), the novelist Molly Keane (also wrote as M J Farrell), yr dau of Walter Clermont Skrine, of Ballyrankin House, Ferns, Co Wexford, and *d* 7 Oct 1946, leaving:

1a *Adele Sarah (Sally); *b* 5 March 1940; *m* 8 July 1972, as his 2nd w, *George Pyne Phipps, of Kilcor Castle, Lyons, Co Cork

2a *Virginia [Mrs Kevin Brownlow, 7 Manor Mansions, Belsize Park Gdns, London NW3]; *b* 18 Aug 1945; *m* 1 Aug 1969 *Kevin Brownlow, film dir, s of R T Brownlow, of Four Compasses, Robertsbridge, Sussex, and has:

1b *Julia; *b* 1984

(1) Sibyl Elfrida; *m* 3 Nov 1939 Maj Hugh Jocelyn Delmege, s of James O'Grady Delmege, DL, of Castle Park, Limerick, and *d* 198–, having had:

1a Diana Clare; *b* 19 Sept 1940; *d* unm 30 Jan 1959

2a *Caroline Stella [Mrs Brian Palmer, The Green Farm, Fethard, Co Tipperary, Ireland]; *b* 19 Sept 1940; *m* 1978 *Brian Hector Palmer

3a Geneifa Alice; *b* 6 Feb 1946; *d* 19–

(2) Diana Dorothy; *m* 13 Oct 1940 (*divorce* 1973) A/Cdr Aeneas Ranald Donald Macdonnel, CB, DFC, RAF, 22nd Chief of Glengarry, and *d* 198–, leaving:

1a *(Aeneas) Ranald Euan; *b* 11 Nov 1941; *educ* Bryanston and St John's Coll Cambridge; *m* 1969 *(Dorothy) Ann, dau of Stanley Hind, of Guildford, and has:

1b *Fiona Jane; *b* 1971

2b *Victoria Ann; *b* 1972

2a *Colin Patrick; *b* 12 March 1946; *educ* Bryanston; *m* 1968 *Ursula, dau of Kurt Eichert, of Cologne, and has:

1b *Angus Kurt Patrick; *b* 1970

1b *Sonia Dee; *b* 1971

1a *Lindsay Alice; *b* 13 Oct 1947; *m* 1974 *B C U Cuthbertson, late Canadian Army

1 Florence; *b* 29 Nov 1877; *m* 15 Feb 1900 Sir Archibald Dennis Flower (*d* 22 Nov 1950), of The Hill, Stratford-on-Avon, est s of Edgar Flower, of Stratford-on-Avon, and *d* 15 Jan 1946, leaving issue

The est s,

Sir John Keane, 5th Bt, DSO (1916), DL; *b* 3 June 1873; *educ* RMA Woolwich; joined army 1893: Capt 1900, Maj 1916, T/Lt-Col 1917 RFA, Boer War 1899–1902 (despatches, medal with three clasps) and WW I (despatches, Legn Hon), Priv Sec to Govr Ceylon 1902–05, barrister Middle Temple 1904, High Sheriff Co Waterford 1911, memb IFS Senate 1922–36 and Senate Irish Republic 1938–48, Cncllr State Irish Republic, Dir Bank Ireland; *m* 14 Feb 1907 Lady Eleanor Lucy Hicks-Beach (*d* 1 Dec 1960), est dau of 1st Earl St Aldwyn (*qv*), and *d* 30 Jan 1956, leaving:

1 Sir RICHARD MICHAEL KEANE, **6th and present Bt**

1 Adelaide Mary; *b* 17 Dec 1907; *m* 31 March 1933 Cecil Denis Pegge, 2nd s of Valentine Pegge, and *d* 17 Jan 1995, leaving:

(1) *Richard [Richard Pegge Esq, Carrigeen, Cappoquin, Co Waterford, Ireland]; *b* 1937

2 *Sheila [Mrs Christopher Knight, Quarry House, East St, Turners Hill, W Sussex RH10 4PU]; *b* 24 Feb 1911; *m* 6 July 1935 *Christopher Edward Knight, yst s of William John Knight, of Ackworth, Hants, and has:

(1) *Michael John [Michael Knight Esq, Garden Flat, 66 Belsize Pk, London NW3 4EH]; *b* 4 May 1939; *educ* Eton and New Coll Oxford; *m* 1970 *Caroline Francesca, er dau of Alexander Kendal Humphrey Fletcher, and has:

1a *Julian Francis; *b* 1971

1a *Cassandra Louise; *b* 1972

2a *Claudia Helen; *b* 1977

(2) *Jonathan Christopher [Jonathan Knight Esq, 4 Baptist Gdns, London NW5 4ET]; *b* 21 Feb 1943; *educ* Eton and Architectural Assoc; *m* 1977 *Hilary Anne Durnford and has:

1a *Oliver James; *b* 1977

1a *Imogen Laura; *b* 1979

(3) *Martin David [Martin Knight Esq, Cedar Grove, The Green, Richmond, Surrey TW9 1PB]; *b* 28 March 1946; *educ* Eton and Trin Coll Dublin; *m* 1971 *(Eleanor) Clare, dau of James Malcolm Harrison, and has had:

1a *Edward Martin; *b* 1976

1a *Tamsin Jane; *b* 1974

2a Hermione Clare; *b* 1982; *d* 1985

3a *Sophie Clare; *b* 1988

(1) *Susan Jane; *b* 21 April 1937

3 *Madeline Lucy [Mrs Donald Emerson, Meads House, Leighterton, Glos GL8 8UW]; *b* 13 Feb 1914; *m* 12 Nov 1938 *Maj Donald Godfrey Emerson, CBE, RA, only s of Maj-Gen Henry Horace Andrews Emerson, CB, DSO, and has:

(1) *James Seymour; *b* 15 Sept 1941; *educ* Marlborough and Trin Coll Dublin; *m* 1st 1964 (*divorce* 1971) Bridget Eileen Mary, dau of Lt-Col Wyndham Marsden Knatchbull (*see* BRABOURNE, B), and has:

1a *Suzanne Mary; *b* 1964

2a *Gillian Lucy; *b* 1966

(1) (cont.) James Emerson *m* 2nd 1971 *Jennifer Ruth Clement and by her has:

1a *Richard Donald; *b* 1971

3a *Sarah Louise; *b* 1974

(1) *Judith Lucy; *b* 20 June 1943; *m* 20 May 1967 *Michael Maurice Fletcher Watson, chartered accountant, s of James Fletcher Watson, and has issue

(2) *Carol Georgena; *b* 25 Dec 1944; *m* 1971 *Robert Lorne Hyndham, of Ottawa, and has issue

(3) *Mary Eleanor; *b* 14 Sept 1953

Seat: Cappoquin House, Cappoquin, Co Waterford, Ireland. The original house was built in 1779 with the entrance front looking out over the River Blackwater, which at Cappoquin turns abruptly south after a long eastwards course. Its destruction by fire in 1923 had a happier outcome than with most Irish houses: the interior was faithfully reconstructed and the exterior was arguably improved in that the entrance front was sited the other side of the house from the Blackwater, so that the inhabitants now had an interrupted enjoyment of the vista across the grounds. The soft native climate quickly lent an agreeable patina to the adroit pastiche of 18th-century architecture put up by the architect, Richard Orpen, so that soon the ashlar fabric, semi-circular-topped windows in the central portion of the break-front facade and urn-enriched balustrade atop the second storey came to look as if they had been there since 150 years before the fire.

KEITH OF CASTLEACRE

Arms: Paly of six or and gules, on a chief argent three stag's heads cabossed proper. **Crest:** A garb or supported by two stags respectant proper. **Supporters:** Dexter, a foreman proper, his overall argent, charged on the breast pocket with a monogram composed of the letters RR superimposed one above the other, with the word Rolls and beneath the word Royce, all in capital letters gules, the collar azure, holding in his outer hand a worksheet in its folder proper; sinister, a farmer in plus-four suit and cap of brown tweed with heather mixture stockings and brown boots, holding in the crook of his outer arm a shotgun proper. **Motto:** *Veritas vincit* ('Truth conquers'). **Creation:** B. (LP, UK) 1979.

THE BARON KEITH OF CASTLEACRE, of Swaffham, Co Norfolk (Sir Kenneth Alexander Keith) [The Rt Hon The Lord Keith of Castleacre, 9 Eaton Sq, London SW1W 9DB; The Wicken House, Castle Acre, Norfolk PE32 2BP]; *b* 30 Aug 1916; *educ* Rugby; WW II: 2nd Lt Welsh Gds 1939, Lt-Col 1945 (despatches); Assist to Dir Gen PID FO 1945–46; dir: Beecham Gp 1949–87 (v-chm 1970–87, chm 1986–87), Eagle Star Insur 1955–75, Nat Provincial Bank 1967–69, Times Newspapers Ltd 1967–81, BA 1971–72, STC 1977–89 (chm 1985–89), Bank Novia Scotia 1978–87; md Philip Hill 1951 (ptnr 1946); v-chm BEA 1964–71; Chm: Ec Planning Cncl E Anglia 1965–70, Philip Hill Investments Tst 1967–87, Hill Samuel Gp 1970–80, Rolls Royce 1972–80; memb: NEDC 1964–71, CBI NEDC Liaison Ctee 1974–78, Cncl Manchester Business Sch; V-Pres EEF; Pres: Roy Norfolk Ag Assoc 1989, BSI 1989–94, RoSPA 1989–93; ktd 1969, FIMgt, FRSA, Hon Companion RAes, Croix de Guerre with Silver Star; *m* 1st 1946 (*divorce* 1958) Lady Ariel Olivia Winifred Baird, 2nd dau of Countess of Kintore (*qv*), and has:

1 *Alastair James; *b* 1947; *educ* Eton and Harvard U; *m* 1983 *Jayne Will, yr dau of Walter C Teagle, Jr, and has:

(1) *Alexander Teagle; *b* 1984

1 *Camilla Margaret; *b* 1947; *m* 1968 (*divorce* 1972) Sir Rupert Henry Mackeson, 2nd Bt (*qv*)

THE BARON KEITH OF CASTLEACRE *m* 2nd 1962 (*divorce* 1972) Nancy (*d* 1990), dau of Edward B Gross, of Monterey, Calif., and formerly w of (a) Howard Hawks (*d* 1977), film dir, and (b) Leland Hayward (*d* 1971), of Manhasset, New York; *m* 3rd 1973 *Marieluz (Muffet), er dau of Capt Robert Peel Dennistoun-Webster, DSC, RN, of Hurst Grange, nr Twyford, formerly w of Adrian Donald Henderson (*see* FARINGDON, B) and widow of Col James Robert Hanbury, of Burley-on-the-Hill, Oakham, Rutland

Lineage: JAMES KEITH, of Ellon, Aberdeenshire; *b* 1796; *m* Jean Thompson and had:

JAMES KEITH, VD, of The Manor House, Castleacre, Norfolk; *b* 21 May 1838; Lt-Col; *m* 1877 Mary Elizabeth Garden (*d* 18 Dec 1925), dau of Alexander Milne, of Aberdeenshire, and *d* 18 May 1920, leaving, with two er sons and a dau:

EDWARD CHARLES KEITH, of Swanton Morley House, Dereham, Norfolk; *b* 10 Jan 1877; natural history author; *m* 25 Nov 1915 Gertrude May, dau of William Suffield Telfair, of Mauritius, and had:

1 KENNETH ALEXANDER, *cr* a **Baron**

2 Michael Telfair, TD; *b* 10 Oct 1918; *educ* Marlborough and Trin Coll Cambridge; Capt Roy Norfolk Regt WW II (POW); *m* 21 June 1950 *Penelope Jane, 2nd dau of Maj William Edgar Mann, DSO, and *d* 24 Dec 1966, leaving issue (*see* MANN, Bt)

KEITH OF KINKEL

Creation: B. (LP, UK) 1976.

THE BARON KEITH OF KINKEL, of Strathtummel, District of Perth and Kinross (Sir Henry Shanks Keith, GBE (1997), PC (1976)) [The Rt Hon The Lord Keith of Kinkel GBE PC, Strathtummel, Pitlochry, Perthshire PH16 5RP]; *b* 7 Feb 1922; *educ* Edinburgh Acad, Magdalen Coll Oxford (MA) and Edinburgh U (LLB); WW II: commissioned Scots Gds 1941 (despatches), Capt 1945; advocate Scotland 1950, barrister Gray's Inn 1951, QC (S) 1962, Bencher 1976; Standing Counsel Dept Health Scotland 1957–62; Ld of Session as Lord Keith 1971–77; Memb: Scottish Valuation Advsy Cncl 1957–70 (Chm 1972–76), Law Reform Ctee Scotland 1964–70, Panel Arbiters under European Fisheries Convention 1964–71, Convention Settlement Investment Disputes 1968–71, Ctee Law of Defamation 1971–75; Chm: Jt Ctee Consolidation Bills 1978–80, Ctee Powers of Revenue Depts 1980–84; Dep Chm Parly Boundaries Commn Scotland 1975; Sheriff-Pncpl Roxburgh, Berwick and Selkirk 1970–71; Ld Appeal in Ordinary 1976–96 and chm Ho Lds Judicial Ctee; Hon Fell Magdalen Coll Oxford 1977; *m* 1955 *Alison Hope Alan, JP, MA, yr dau of Alan Brown, and has:

1 *James Alan; *b* 1959; *m* 1987 *Eleanor Mary, yr dau of Col Michael ffolliott Woodhead, OBE, and has:

(1) *Samuel Henry Michael; *b* 1994

(1) *Flavia; *b* 1991

(2) *Phoebe; *b* 1997

2 *Thomas Hamilton [The Hon Thomas Keith, Fountain Court, Temple, London EC4Y 9DH]; *b* 1961; *educ* Magdalen Coll Oxford; barrister

3 *Hugo George [The Hon Hugo Keith, 3 Raymond Bldgs, Gray's Inn, London WC1R 5BP]; *b* 1967; Standing Counsel to Govt in Common Law 1995–

4 *Alexander Lindsay (twin); *b* 1967; *m* 1995 *Sally, twin dau of Brian O'Regan

1 *Deborah Jane [The Hon Deborah Keith, 42 Westbourne Gdns, London W2 5NS]; *b* 1967; *educ* Edinburgh U, London U and UEA (BSc, MSc, PhD); barrister

Lineage: JAMES KEITH; *b* 17 April 1825; Provost Hamilton, Lanarks; *m* 25 June 1850 Helen, dau of James Hamilton, and *d* 21 March 1901, leaving:

Sir HENRY SHANKS KEITH, GBE, JP, DL, of Avonholm, Hamilton; *b* 25 Dec 1852; Provost Hamilton 1901–08 and 1919, Hon Sheriff Lanarks, Chm Lanark Educn Authority, Pres Educn Authorities Assoc Scotland; *m* 16 June 1885 Elizabeth (*d* 1934), dau of John Hamilton, of Bothwell, and *d* 9 July 1944, leaving, with other issue:

JAMES KEITH, BARON KEITH OF AVONHOLM, of St Bernards, City of Edinburgh (UK, LP), so *cr* 4 Nov 1953, PC (1953); *b* 20 May 1886; advocate 1911, WW I with Seaforth Highrs, attd Egyptian Army 1917, served under Sudan Govt 1917–19; Tstee Nat Library Scotland 1925–36, KC 1926, Dean Faculty Advocates 1936–37, Ld Session 1937–53, Ld Appeal in Ordinary 1953–61; *m* 7 July 1915 Jane Maitland, dau of Andrew Bennet, of Arbroath, and *d* 1964, leaving, with two daus:

HENRY SHANKS, *cr* a **Baron**

KELLETT

Arms: Quarterly, 1st and 4th, argent on a mount vert, a boar passant sable (for KELLETT); 2nd and 3rd, argent a cross gules, in the first quarter a fleur-de-lys of the last (for HADDOCK). **Crest:** An armed arm embowed and garnished or, holding in the hand a baton of the last. **Motto:** *Feret ad astra virtus* ('Virtue will bear you to the skies'). **Creation:** Bt. (UK) 6 Aug 1801.

SIR STANLEY CHARLES KELLETT, 7TH BT, of Lota, Cork [Sir Stanley Kellett Bt, 58 Glad Gunson Dve, Eleebana, Newcastle NSW 2280, Australia]; *b* 5 March 1940; *s* f 1983; *m* 1st 1962 (*divorce* 1968) Lorraine May, dau of F Winspear; *m* 2nd

1968 (*divorce* 1974) Margaret Ann, dau of James W Bofinger; *m* 3rd 1982 *Catherine Lorna, dau of W J C Orr, and by her has:

1 *Leah Catherine Elizabeth; *b* 1983

Lineage: RICHARD KELLETT, of Clonmel, Co Tipperary (Mayor 1711), of an allegedly Norfolk family that had migrated to Ireland *temp* WILLIAM III; bought Cloughmacody 1703; *m* Anne —, of Clonmel, and *d c* 1729, leaving, with four daus:

1 William, of Clonmel; Mayor 1753 and 1759; *m* Jane, dau of Thomas Salmon, of Clonmel, and *d* between 1761 and 1767, leaving a 3rd s:

(1) Christopher, of Clonmel; Mayor 1780; *m* 1st 1761 Catherine, dau of Arthur Shepherd, of Bray, Co Wicklow; *m* 2nd 1776 Frances Pigott and had by his 1st w, with two daus:

1a William, of Great Clonard, Co Wexford; *m* Nov 1790 Bridget, dau of John Segrave, of Cabra, Co Dublin, and had, with other issue (*d* unm):

1b Christopher; *k* Battle of Vittoria 1813

2b Arthur; Cdr RN; *m* 1834 Maria Lucinda, dau of Maj Hanna, 56th Regt, and had:

1c William; drowned at sea

2c John Talbot; *m* 1870 Letitia Emilie Lyster, dau of Rev John Keefe Robinson, Preb Whitchurch, and *d* Australia 1877, leaving:

1d William Arthur; *b* 1871; *d* unm 1896

1d Evadne Maude; *m* 14 Oct 1901 Sir Edmund Charles Wyldbore Smith (*see* SMITH-MARRIOTT, Bt) and *d* 25 April 1960, leaving issue

3c Arthur; *m* Mary Elizabeth, dau of Percy Lorenzo Harvey, of Kyle, Co Wexford, and *d* 1896

1b Anna Frances; *m* 1817 Henry John Segrave, of Cabra

2 Richard; Capt 27th Foot; *m* Deborah, dau and coheiress of Thurston Haddock, of Kinsale, Co Cork, and *d* 1746, leaving a 2nd s:

(1) Richard, of Lota, Co Cork; Alderman City of Cork; *b c* 1733; *m* 16 Sept 1758 Jane Susannah, dau of Jacob Laulhe and niece of Abraham de Castres, Envoy Portugal, and *d* 25 Jan 1828, having had, with two daus:

1a **Sir Richard Kellett, 1st Bt** (UK), so *cr* 6 Aug 1801, with remainder, failing his own male issue, to the heirs male of his f, of Lota, Co Cork; *b* 16 May 1761; *m* 9 Feb 1788 Jane, dau of John Galwey, of Westcourt, Co Kilkenny, and *d* 1853, having had:

1b Richard; *b* 16 May 1790; *m* 1817 Mary, dau of James Blakeney, of Carlow, and *dsp*

2 **Sir William Henry Kellett, 2nd Bt**, of Dublin; *b* 10 Oct 1794; *dsp* Feb 1886

2a William Augustus; *b* 9 Jan 1765; *m* 1st 12 Aug 1790 Jane McDowell, only dau of Col Napier, of Culreuch and Milliken, Renfrewshire; *m* 2nd 1811 Mary Towgood (*dsp* Dec 1841), dau of Morgan Donovan, and *d* 6 Nov 1822, leaving by his 1st w, with other issue:

1b Robert John Napier; Capt Roy Highrs; *b* 15 Jan 1797; *m* 4 Dec 1823 Jemima, only dau and heiress of James Hunter, of Ayr, and *d* 2 Nov 1853, leaving, with two other daus (*d* unm):

1c William Augustus Hunter; Lt 72nd Highrs; *b* Feb 1826; *d* 8 May 1853

1c Jemima Hunter; *m* 1 Feb 1855 Capt E H Melhado, Roy Renfrew Militia, Argyll and Sutherland Highrs, and *d* 31 Aug 1902, leaving issue

3a Henry de Castres; *b* 20 Feb 1776; *m* Amilia, dau of Henry Hickman, of Cork, and had, with other issue:

1b William Augustus; settled Victoria Australia 1839; *m* 15 May 1851 Mary Gibson and *d* 28 April 1883, leaving:

1c Theresa; *m* and had issue

2b Henry de Castres; settled Victoria 1839; *b* 1815; *m* 1848 Marcella, dau of Michael Ready, and *d* 1884, having had, with other issue:

1c HENRY De CASTRES (Sir), **3rd Bt**

2c Francis Michael; *b* 1858; *m* 1885 Elizabeth Mary, dau of Timothy Stanley, and had:

1d Stanley Francis; *b* 2 Dec 1886

2d Arthur Osmond; *b* 6 March 1890

1d Freda; *b* 4 Sept 1892

1c Anne Marcella; *m* 1893 Henry Manicom and had issue

The 2nd Bt's cousin,

Sir Henry de Castres Kellett, 3rd Bt; *b* 15 Sept 1851; *m* 9 Nov 1880 Joan (*d* 2 June 1937), dau of William Harrison, of Kew, Melbourne, and was *k* in a car crash 20 June 1924, leaving:

1 **Sir Henry De Castres Kellett, 4th Bt**; *b* 2 Oct 1882; *m* 24 May 1905 Rubie Septima, dau of Easton Johnston, and *d* 25 July 1966, having had:

(1) **Sir Henry de Castres Kellett, 5th Bt**; *b* 3 June 1914; *m* 7 May 1952 *Ida Mary Grace-Weaver and *dsp* 6 Aug 1966

(1) Isla de Castres; *b* 23 Feb 1907; *d* unm 7 Feb 1957

2 Francis Stanley; *b* 4 Aug 1885; *m* 1906 Gertrude Maud, dau of F S Vessey, and *d* 1955, leaving:

(1) STANLEY EVERARD (Sir), **6th Bt**

(2) +CHARLES REX [Charles Kellett, 9 Ashfield Place, Glen Alpine, NSW 2560, Australia]; *b* 1916; heir presumptive; *m* 1940 Florence Helen Bellamy (*d* 1984) and has:

1a +Maxwell Rex [Maxwell Kellott, 4 Daisy St, Roselands, NSW 2195, Australia]; *b* 1947, FCPA; *m* 1968 *Jennifer, dau of N Maher, and has:

1b *Jane Maxine; *b* 1974

2a +Peter Charles [Peter Kellett, 9 Ashfield Place, Glen Alpine, NSW 2560, Australia]; *b* 1949; *m* 1973 *Jennifer, dau of K Pike, of W Australia, and has:

1b *Renée Helen; *b* 1977

2b *Lauren Ann; *b* 1979

1a *Marilyn Helen; *b* 1942; *m* 1966 *Bruce Malcolm Morgan and has:

1b *Gavin Charles; *b* 1974

1b *Karen Lee; *b* 1969; *m* 1990 *Ian William Spedding

2b *Joanne Lynne [Mrs Jason Watson, 52 Castlereagh St, Tahmoor, NSW 2573, Australia]; *b* 1971; *m* 1991 *Jason Kenneth Watson

(3) +Ray Weaver [Ray Kellett, 10 Cutler Rd, Engadine, NSW 2233, Australia]; *b* 1916; *m* 1940 *Daisy Miriam Payne and has:

1a +John Raymond (Rev) [Rev John Kellett, 153 Brooks St, Bar Beach, Newcastle, NSW 2300, Australia], BSc (U of NSW), Melbourne Coll of Divinity (BD), ASTC (Sydney Tech Coll); *b* 1 March 1942; *m* 1st 15 May 1965 (*divorce* 1982) Sandra, dau of Norman Gilbert Holman, of Rockdale, NSW; *m* 2nd *Rita Marjorie, dau of G Wiggins, and by his 1st w has:

1b +David John; *b* 1973

1b *Michele Ruth; *b* 1971

2a +Bruce Lawrence [Bruce Kellett, 121 Washington Dve, Bonnet Bay, NSW 2226, Australia]; *b* 1945; *m* 1969 *Susan Butler, dau of J Butler, and has:

1b *Bronwyn Jane; *b* 1973

2b *Jacqueline Ruth; *b* 1975

3a +Graham Edward [Graham Kellett, 23 Taft Place, Bonnet Bay, NSW 2226, Australia]; *b* 1948, BSc; *m* 1970 *Leonie, dau of R Adams, and has:

1b +Joshua Morgan; *b* 1977

1b +Skye Emma; *b* 1975

(1) Greta Vessey; *b* 1907; *m* 1935 Albert Hector Bartrop

(2) Freda Gertrude; *b* 1908

3 William Augustus; *b* 28 May 1889; *m* 29 Oct 1919 Janet Victoria (*d* 1936), dau of J Peart, and *d* 15 Dec 1952, leaving:

(1) +William Andrew [William Kellett, 32 Panoramic Grove, Glen Waverley, Victoria, Australia]; *b* 4 Sept 1920; AASA; *m* 28 July 1945 *Florence, dau of Leslie James Williamson, of Carnegie, Victoria, and has:

1a +James Andrew [James Kellett, 53 Sevenoaks Rd, Burwood East, Vic 3151, Australia]; *b* 9 Sept 1952; *m* 1st 1974 (*divorce* 1987) Kveta, dau of Karel Prochazka, of Johannesburg; *m* 2nd 1993 *Dianne, dau of John Goddard, of Glen Waverley, Victoria, and by his 1st w has:

1b *Tamara; *b* 1977

1a *Anne Louise; *b* 4 Oct 1947; *m* 1968 (*divorce* 1994) Robert James Fitzpatrick and has:

1b *David James; *b* 1972

2b *Scott Andrew; *b* 1973

1b *Sarah Louise; *b* 1978

2a *Christine Elizabeth; *b* 11 April 1950; *m* 1970 (*divorce* 1980) John Adrian Bailey and has:

1b *Justin Daniel; *b* 1973

1b *Jacqueline Marie; *b* 1971

1 Ethel Kate; *b* 2 Sept 1881; *m* 27 March 1912 Fred G P Lewis, s of John G Lewis, and *d* 18 Aug 1956, leaving issue

2 Myrtle Marcella; *b* 29 Sept 1892; *m* 30 Sept 1918 William Abel Gray (*d* 14 Feb 1955), n of A W Gray, and had issue

3 Doris; *b* 31 Aug 1894

4 Reenie Florence; *b* 11 Oct 1898; *m* 18 Feb 1926 Herbert William Jones (*d* 11 July 1956), s of D Jones, and had issue

The 5th Bt's cousin,

Sir Stanley Everard Kellett, 6th Bt; *b* 1911; *m* 1938 *Audrey Margaret Phillips [Audrey Lady Kellett, 33 Caroma Ave, Kyeemagah, NSW, Australia], and *d* 1983, leaving:

1 Sir STANLEY CHARLES KELLETT, **7th and present Bt**

1 *Margaret Joy Kellett [Mrs Percival Horton, 506 Gt Western Highway, Faulconbridge, NSW 2776, Australia]; *b* 1942; *m* 1963 *Percival William Horton, AASA(S), and has:

(1) *Phillip William; *b* 25 Jan 1967

(2) *Colin Stanley; *b* 30 April 1969

(1) *Deborah Jane; *b* 1964; *m* 1983 *Andrew Philip Howe

KELVEDON

Creation: B. (LP, UK) April 1997.

THE BARON KELVEDON, of Ongar in the County of Essex ((Henry) Paul Guinness Channon, PC (1980)) [The Rt Hon The Lord Kelvedon PC, House of Lords, London SW1A 0PW; Kelvedon Hall, Brentwood, Essex]; *b* 9 Oct 1935; *educ* Eton and Ch Ch Oxford (Pres Oxford U C Assoc 1958); 2nd Lt RHG (Blues) 1955–56, MP (C) Southend-on-Sea (W) Jan 1959–97, PPS to: Min of Power 1959–60, Home Secretary 1960–62, First Sec State 1962–63 and For Sec 1963–64; Oppn Spokesman: Arts and Amenities 1967–70, Prices and Consumer Protection March-Sept 1974, Environment Oct 1974–Feb 1975, Parly U-Sec Environment 1970–72, Min State: NI Office March-Nov 1972, Dept Environment (Housing and Construction) 1972–74 and CSD 1979–81, Min Arts 1981–83 and Trade 1983–86, Sec State: Trade and Industry 1986–87 and Tport 1987–89, chm: Fin and Servs Ctee H of C 1992–97 and Br Assoc for Centl and E Europe 1991–97, dep leader Conservative Delegn WEU and Cncl of Europe 1976–79, dir Arthur Guinness, Son & Co 1961–70 and 1974–79, memb Gen Advsy Cncl ITA 1964–66; *m* 7 Aug 1963 *Ingrid Olivia Georgia, yr dau of Maj Guy Richard Charles Wyndham, MC (*see* EGREMONT, LECONFIELD and, B), and formerly w of Hon Jonathan Bryan Guinness (*see* MOYNE, B), and has had:

1 *Henry; *b* 2 Jan 1970; *m* 12 Oct 1996 *Henrietta, dau of David Towill and Mrs Arthur Boyd-Rochfort

1 Olivia Gwendolen Violet; *b* 1 June 1964; *educ* Oxford; *d* 1986

2 *Georgia Honor Margaretha; *b* 1 March 1966; *m* 22 March 1997 *Antony Fanshawe, s of Brian Fanshawe

Lineage: *See* IVEAGH, E

Seat: Kelvedon Hall, Kelvedon Hatch, Essex. The house is of red brick, probably mid–18th century, and rectangular in shape, though with wings either side of the main structure connected to it by passages. There are some attractive doors with pediments both outside and in, also a pretty staircase. The estate was bought by John Wright in 1538 and held by his descendants down to the 20th century. Lord Kelvedon's father Sir Henry ('Chips') Channon bought it between the Wars. The John Wright who may have been responsible for the present structure married as his second wife Constantia Carington, *alias* Smith, a collateral descendant of the 1st Viscount Carrington of Burford. The present Lord Carrington (*qv*), though peripherally linked with the present owner of the estate inasmuch as he was formerly a member of the same administration, has no connection with the Smith/Car(r)ingtons just mentioned.

KEMSLEY

Arms: Gules three bars or, on a pile ermine as many martlets sable. **Crest:** A griffin sejant sable, collared and chained, the chain reflexed over the back, and resting the dexter claw on a catherine wheel or. **Supporters:** On either side a stag guardant or gorged with a chaplet of mistletoe proper. **Badge:** A daffodil leaved and slipped proper between two roses gules, barbed, seeded, leaved and slipped also proper, enfiled with a circlet argent. **Motto:** *Persevera et vince* ('Persevere and conquer'). **Creations:** Bt. (UK) 25 Jan 1928, B. (UK) 3 Feb 1936, V. (UK) 12 Sept 1945.

THE 2ND VISCOUNT KEMSLEY, of Dropmore, Co Buckingham, **Baron Kemsley**, of Farnham Royal, Co Buckingham, and a **Baronet** (Sir (Geoffrey) Lionel Berry, Bt, DL (Leics 1972)) [The Rt Hon The Viscount Kemsley DL, Field House, Thorpe Lubenham, Leics LE16 9TR]; *b* 29 June 1909; *s* f 1968; *educ* Marlborough and Magdalen Coll Oxford; Capt Gren Gds WW II 1940–42 (invalided); MP (C) Buckingham 1943–45, High Sheriff Leics 1967, CC Northants 1964, FRSA, dep-chm Kemsley Newspapers Ltd 1938–59, Master Spectacle Makers' Co 1949–51 and 1959–61, KSt J; *m* 21 June 1933 *Lady Hélène Candida Hay, OStJ, est dau of 11th Marquess of Tweeddale (*qv*), and has:

1 *Mary Anne [The Hon Mrs van Raalte, The Old Rectory, Clippesby, Norfolk]; *b* 30 April 1934; *m* 26 July 1960 *Charles Henry van Raalte, s of Noel van Raalte, and has:

(1) *Marcus Lionel; *b* 17 July 1961

(1) *Kristina Beryl; *b* 24 Oct 1962

(2) *Ghislaine Sara; *b* 12 April 1964

2 *(Pamela) Jane Marguerite [The Hon Lady Mobbs, Boot Farm, Little Kingshill, Great Missenden, Bucks]; *b* 27 May 1937; *m* 14 Sept 1961 *Sir (Gerald) Nigel Mobbs, Ld Lt Bucks, chm Slough Estates, only s of Gerald Aubrey Mobbs, of Bramleys, Little Kingshill, and has:

(1) *Christopher William; *b* 11 Nov 1965; *m* 1991 *Elizabeth Dora, only dau of Maj J F A Overton, LI, of Hillesden, Bucks, and has:

1a *Charles William John; *b* 18 July 1997

1a *Lucinda Dora Jane; *b* 1992

2a *Georgina; *b* 19–

(1) *Virginia Elizabeth; *b* 18 Dec 1968; *m* 17 Sept 1994 *Simon Astill, est s of Paul Astill, of Thurnby, Leics

(2) *Penelope Helen; *b* 18 Dec 1968; *m* 25 Oct 1997 *Edward Powell, s of John Powell, of W Kensington

3 *Caroline Helene [The Hon Mrs Houison-Craufurd of Craufurdland and Braehead, Craufurdland Castle, Kilmarnock, Ayrshire]; *b* 8 Sept 1942; *m* 24 March 1965 John *Peter Houison-Craufurd of Craufurdland and Braehead, only s of John Douglas Houison-Craufurd of Craufurdland and Braehead, and has:

(1) *John Alexander; *b* 15 May 1966

(2) *Simon Douglas; *b* 19 May 1972

(1) *Teresa Eleanor; *b* 10 Dec 1967

4 *Catherine Frances Lilian [The Hon Mrs Bream, The Manor Farm, Grace Dieu, Leics,]; *b* 9 June 1944; *m* 19 April 1969 *Richard Douglas Fowler Bream, TD, DL Leics, High Sheriff 1990, yr s of Clifford Ellett Bream, and has:

(1) *Tamerlane Douglas Fowler; *b* 1971

(1) *Atlanta Mary; *b* 1970

Lineage: JOHN MATHIAS BERRY, JP, of Gwaelodygarth, Merthyr Tydfil, Glamorgan (*see* CAMROSE, V); had a yst s:

Sir James Gomer Berry, 1st Bt, and **1st Viscount Kemsley**, of Dropmore, Co Buckingham, so *cr* 25 Jan 1928 and 12 Sept 1945 respectively, as also earlier 3 Feb 1936 BARON KEMSLEY, of Farnham Royal, Co Buckingham (all UK), GBE (1959), JP (Bucks); *b* 7 May 1883; High Sheriff Glamorgan 1929, Hon LLD Manchester U, Hon LLD U of Wales, Hon Col RASC (TA) 1939–48, chm Kemsley Newspapers Ltd 1937–59, ed-in-ch *Sunday Times* 1937–59, Reuter's Tstee 1942–68 (Chm 1951–59), Pres Merthyr Gen Hosp 1928–49, Chm Infants' Hosp 1922–37 and King Edward VII Hosp Windsor 1933–37, Master Spectacle Makers' Co 1934–36, Pres U Coll S Wales and Monmouthshire 1945–50 and FA Wales 1946–60, Freedom Merthyr Tydfil 1955, fndr Kemsley Flying Trust 1947, Pres Br Gliding Assoc 1947–61 (V-Pres 1962–68), KStJ, Offr Legn Hon, Grand Cross Order George I Greece, Cdr Order Crown Belgium; *m* 1st 4 July 1907 Mary Lilian (*d* 1 Feb 1928), dau of Horace George Holmes, JP, of Brondesbury Pk, London, and had issue:

1 (GEOFFREY) LIONEL BERRY, **2nd and present Viscount Kemsley**

2 Denis Gomer, TD; *b* 11 July 1911; *educ* Marlborough; Capt RA (TA), WW II as Maj Gren Gds; CC Hants 1969, dir Kemsley Newspapers Ltd, Master Coachmakers' and Coach Harness-makers' Co 1959–60, Pres New Forest Assoc 1969, Pres Hants Fedn Young Farmers Clubs 1968, Cdre Bembridge Sailing Club 1969, KStJ; *m* 1st 3 July 1934 (*divorce* 1942) Rosemary Leonora, er dau of Lionel Nathan de Rothschild, OBE (*see* ROTHSCHILD, B), and *d* 1983, leaving:

(1) *Barbara Marie-Louise Constance; *b* 28 Dec 1935; *m* 2 Dec 1954 (*divorce* 1983) Alexander Clement Gilmour (*see* GILMOUR OF CRAIGMILLAR, B) and has issue

(2) Susan Lilian; *b* 8 Aug 1938; *m* 1st 6 Nov 1963 (*divorce* 1978) Sir Christopher George Francis Harding, only s of Frank Harding, of Whyteleafe, Amersham, Bucks, and had:

1a *Rupert Christopher; *b* 19 Oct 1965

1a *Louise Amanda; *b* 7 Dec 1966

(2) (cont.) Mrs Susan Harding *m* 2nd 1989 *Raymond Muir and *d* 1989

2 (cont.) Maj The Hon Denis Berry *m* 2nd 27 July 1947 Pamela (*d* 1987), er dau of Lord Richard Wellesley (*see* WELLINGTON, D) and formerly w of Lt Charles Robert Archibald Grant, RN, and by her had:

(1) +RICHARD GOMER [Richard Berry Esq, Church Lane Stables, Church Hill, Brockenhurst, Hants SO42 7UB]; *b* 17 April 1951; heir presumptive; *educ* Eton; *m* 1st 1981 (*divorce* 1988) Tana-Marie, er dau of Clive William Lester, of Beaulieu, Hants; *m* 2nd 17 Sept 1994 *Elizabeth Jane, dau of Dennis Norman Barker, of Ampthill, Beds, and by her has:

1a +Luke Gomer; *b* 2 Feb 1998

(3) *(Anne) Denise [Mrs Brian Orange, Fromans House, Kings Somborne, Stockbridge, Hants]; *b* 5 March 1948; *m* 23 May 1970 *Brian Peter Harvey Orange, KStJ, s of R B Orange, of Oxshott, Surrey, and has:

1a *Michael Richard; *b* 1973

2a *Simon George; *b* 1974

3a *Jonathan Charles; *b* 1976

3 (William) Neville; *b* 16 June 1914; *educ* Harrow and Magdalen Coll Oxford; Capt Gren Gds WW II; dir Kemsley Newspapers Ltd 1938–59, London Assur 1950–59; *m* 12 July 1951 Christobel Ruby (*d* 6 Oct 1995), only dau of John Wallis More-Molyneux and formerly w of Lanfear Barbey Norrie, and *dsp* 19 May 1998

4 (John) Douglas; *b* 1 May 1916; *educ* Harrow and Univ Coll Oxford; Lt Gren Gds WW II; *ka* Italy 10 Oct 1944

5 (Herbert) Oswald; *b* 13 June 1918; *educ* Harrow and Pembroke Coll Oxford; F/Lt AAF WW II (invalided); dir Kemsley Newspapers Ltd and Kemsley Northern Newspapers Ltd; *m* 28 Sept 1940 Lady Mary Clementine Pratt [The Lady Mary Pawle, Treworgan, Maronan, nr Falmouth, Cornwall] (*m* 2nd 10 Sept 1953 (Shafto) Gerald Strachan Pawle, er s of Capt John Pawle, JP, of Little Havers, Bishops Stortford, Herts), only dau of 5th Marquess Camden (*qv*), and *dsp* 8 June 1952

6 Anthony George (Sir), JP (Cardiff 1960); *b* 12 Feb 1925; *educ* Eton and Ch Ch Oxford (BA 1950, MA 1956); Lt Welsh Gds 1943–47; High Sheriff Glam 1962; MP (C) Enfield Southgate 1964–84, memb Cncl U S Wales and Monmouthshire 1952–64, memb Western Area Board Br Tport Commn 1956–58, dir Kemsley Newspapers Ltd 1954–59, md Western Mail and Echo Ltd 1955–59, dep-chm Leopold Joseph and Sons Ltd, dir Anglo-Welsh Investments Tst Ltd, Pres Welsh Games Cncl, CStJ; *m* 1st 25 Nov 1954 (*divorce* 1966) Hon Mary Cynthia Burke Roche (*m* 2nd Michael Cunningham), er dau of 4th Baron Fermoy (*qv*), and had:

(1) +Edward Anthony Morys [Edward Berry Esq, 103 Stormont Rd, London SW11]; *b* 23 June 1960; *m* 1989 *Joanna Clare, yr dau of Anthony George Leschallas (*see* ROMNEY, E), and has:

1a +William Anthony Edward; *b* 1993

1a *Alice Elisabeth; *b* 1990

2a *Rose Ophelia; *b* 1992

(1) *Alexandra Mary; *b* 9 Sept 1955 (HRH PRINCESS ALEXANDRA stood sponsor); *m* 2 July 1982 (*divorce* 19–) Reinhold Bartz, only s of Arthur Bartz

(2) *Antonia Ruth [Mrs Mark Butterworth, 106A Cottle's Gdns, Upper Wentwood, Wilts BA15 2DS] ; *b* 2 Aug 1957; *m* 20 Jan 1990 *Mark F Butterworth, s of A K Butterworth, of Dharamsala, India, and has:

1a *Jessica; *b* 24 Oct 1988

2a *Rachel; *b* 28 Jan 1993

3a *Olivia; *b* 13 Nov 1995

4a *Hazel; *b* 13 Nov 1995

(3) *Joanna Cynthia [Mrs Peter Tufnell, Tai Uchaf, Llithfaen, Pwllheli, Gwynedd LL53 6PD]; *b* 2 Aug 1957; *m* 2 Jan 1990 *Peter Tufnell and has:

1a *Ava Tara; *b* 25 Aug 1990

2a *Iona Alcyone; *b* 27 Feb 1993

3a *Helena Joy; *b* 19 Dec 1995

6 (cont.) The Hon Sir Anthony Berry *m* 2nd 5 April 1966 *Sarah Anne [The Hon Lady Berry, Fox's Walk, Shurlock Row, Berks RG10 0PB], yr dau of Raymond Clifford-Turner, of Belgravia, slr, and was *k* in the IRA bombing of the Grand Hotel, Brighton, 12 Oct 1984, having by her had:

(2) +George Raymond Gomer; *b* 11 July 1967

(4) *Sasha Jane; *b* 16 April 1969

1 (Mary) Pamela; *b* 13 June 1918; *m* 15 March 1941 (*divorce* 1965) 12th Marquess of Huntly (*qv*), and *d* 29 Jan 1998, leaving issue

The **1st Viscount** *m* 2nd 30 April 1931 Edith, OBE (1953), CStJ, Chev Legn Hon, Cdr Roy Order Phoenix Greece (*d* 13 Sept 1976), dau of Nicholas Emile Merandon du Plessis, of Mauritius, and formerly w of Cornelius Willem Dresselhuys, Dutch diplomat, and *d* 6 Feb 1968

KENILWORTH

Arms: Per chevron or and azure, in chief two goat's heads erased and in base a triangular castle with three towers, on a chief of the second two wings conjoined in fess, all counterchanged. **Crest:** Issuant out of the battlements of a tower a goat's head argent armed or in front of a rising sun also issuant gold. **Supporters:** On either side a goat or gorged with a collar azure, pendant therefrom by a chain gold an escutcheon chequy of the first and second, a chief ermine. **Motto:** *Nitendo* ('By striving').

Creation: B. (UK) 10 June 1937.

THE 4TH BARON KENILWORTH, of Kenilworth, Co Warwick ((John) Randle Siddeley) [The Rt Hon The Lord Kenilworth, House of Lords, London SW1A 0PW]; *b* 16 June 1954; *s f* 1981; *educ* Northease Manor and London Coll of Furniture; Ld Manor Kenilworth; landscape gardener: md Siddeley Landscapes 1976–, dir John Siddeley Internat; *m* 1st 29 Jan 1983 (*divorce* 1990) Kim, only dau of Danie Serfontein, of Newcastle; *m* 2nd 1991 *Kiki (*née* Axford), jewellery designer, formerly w of David McDonough, and by her has:

1 +WILLIAM RANDLE; *b* 24 Jan 1992

2 +Edward Oscar; *b* 1994

Lineage: RANDLE SIDDELEY; held land in the manor of Over Peover, Cheshire; *bur* 24 June 1621, leaving:

RANDLE SIDDELEY, of Ollerton, Knutsford, Cheshire; *m* 1666 Margaret Fernhead, of Macclesfield (*d* 1696), and had:

SAMUEL SIDDELEY, of Over Knutsford and Ollerton; *m* 1st 1686 Mary Huith, of Knutsford; *m* 2nd 25 Nov 1718 Elizabeth Heywood, of Over Knutswood, and by his 1st w had, with other issue:

SAMUEL SIDDELEY, of Ollerton; *bapt* 4 Aug 1688; *m* 10 Dec 1717 Elizabeth Ridgway, of Ollerton (*d* 1766), and had, with other issue:

SAMUEL SIDDELEY, of Nether Peover and Great Peover; *bapt* 21 April 1929; *m* Mary — (*d* 1788) and *d* 5 Dec 1792, leaving:

SAMUEL SIDDELEY, of Lower Peover and later Allostock, Great Budworth, Cheshire; *bapt* 26 May 1765; *m* Elizabeth Leigh and had a 2nd s:

SAMUEL SIDDELEY, of Billings Green, Rudheath, and later Highfield, Allostock; *bapt* 23 Aug 1795; *m* Mary Kennerley and had:

WILLIAM SIDDELEY, of Altrincham; *b* 9 Nov 1837; *m* 11 Oct 1865 Elizabeth, dau of John Davenport, of Bollington, Cheshire, and *d* 25 Dec 1911, leaving, with other issue:

JOHN DAVENPORT, **1st Baron Kenilworth**, of Kenilworth, Co Warwick (UK), so *cr* 10 June 1937, CBE (1918), JP (Warwicks and Coventry); *b* 5 Aug 1866; FRAES, Hon MIME, Ld Manor Kenilworth, High Sheriff Warwicks 1932, chm and md Armstrong-Siddeley Motors and Sir W G Armstrong-Whitworth Aircraft, chm Armstrong-Siddeley Development Co, A V Roe & Co and Air Service Training Ltd, Master Coachmakers' Co 1934, chm Soc Br Aircraft Constructors, Pres Engrg and Employers' Nat Fedn 1934, 1935 and 1936 and Soc Motor Mfrs and Traders 1937–38, ktd 1932; *m* 9 March 1893 Sarah Mabel (*d* 18 Oct 1953), dau of James Goodier, of Macclesfield, and had:

1 CYRIL DAVENPORT, **2nd Baron**

2 Ernest Hall; *b* 19 Oct 1895; *educ* St Lawrence Coll Ramsgate; WW I as Lt RWK Regt; dir Armstrong Siddeley Motors; *m* 15 June 1921 Muriel (*d* 1988), dau of John Richard Quick, of Leamington Spa, and *d* 1985, having had:

(1) *Audrey Joan [Mrs Audrey Bermingham, Belmont, Barford Rd, Bloxham, Oxon OX15 4EZ]; *b* 19 July 1922; WW II as 3rd Offr WRNS; *m* 1st 17 Nov 1951 (*divorce* 1955, resumed maiden name by deed poll 20 Dec 1967) John Main, er s of Harold G Main, of Spout Farm, Boxford, Suffolk; *m* 2nd 2 July 1971 (*divorce* 1974) Francis A Bermingham

3 Norman Goodier; *b* 21 May 1898; WW I with Roy Fus (wounded); *m* 1st 4 March 1924 (*divorce* 1953) Phyllis Erith, er dau of Graham Derry, of Salisbury, S Rhodesia, and had:

(1) *Jane Goodier; *b* 1928

3 (cont.) The Hon Norman Siddeley *m* 2nd 1953 *Pamela [The Hon Mrs Norman Siddeley, 1 Belle Vue Court, Longueville, St Saviour, Jersey, CI], dau of G A W Williams, of Gorey, Jersey, and *d* 29 Sept 1971

1 Nancy Mabel Mercer; *m* 11 June 1925 (*divorce* 1953) James Arthur Ainscow, MB, ChB, and *d* 27 March 1963, leaving issue

2 Joan Murray; *b* 2 Nov 1904; *m* 14 Sept 1926 Eric Austyn Reynolds, BA, AMIMechE, AFAeS, s of A Milward Reynolds, of Alveston, Stratford-on-Avon, and had:

(1) *Michael Austyn [Michael Reynolds Esq, 6 Butlers Rd, Handsworth Wood, Birmingham 20]; *b* 12 March 1929

(2) *Paul Siddeley [Paul Reynolds Esq, Church Farm, Budbrooke, Warwicks]; *b* 3 July 1931; *m* 1954 *Jane Anne Wyatt and has:

1a *Andrew; *b* 20 Aug 1962

1a *Patricia; *b* 1955

2a *Lucy; *b* 18 Nov 1956

3a *Clair; *b* 14 Aug 1961

(3) *Gerald Alfred John [Gerald Reynolds Esq, 6 Butlers Rd, Handsworth Wood, Birmingham 20]; *b* 19 May 1942

(1) *Sallie Joan [Mrs Anthony Earle, The Long House, Great Alne, Alcester, Warwicks]; *b* 4 April 1935; *m* 18 July 1957 *Anthony Joseph Earle and has:

1a *Martin; *b* 21 March 1961

1a *Melanie; *b* 24 March 1959

The 1st BARON *d* 3 Nov 1953; his est son,

CYRIL DAVENPORT SIDDELEY, **2nd Baron Kenilworth**, CBE, TD, DL (Warwicks 1942–67); *b* 27 Aug 1894; *educ* St Lawrence Coll Ramsgate; Lt-Col 7th Bn Roy Warwicks Regt TA (Hon Col 1947–52), WW I (despatches twice), WW II (despatches); High Sheriff 1944, dir Armstrong-Siddeley Motors, Burlington Carriage Co, chm Coventry and Warwicks Hosp 1926–28, Pres Queen Victoria Memorial Hosp, Nice, AM, 1963–64, manager Coventry Savings Bank, Jr Warden Coachmakers' and Coach Harness Makers' Co 1954 (Master 1956), chm Coventry Diocesan Bd Fin; *m* 30 Sept 1919 Marjorie Tennant (*d* 16 June 1977), dau of Harry Firth, of Dewsbury, Yorks, and had:

1 JOHN TENNANT DAVENPORT, **3rd Baron**

1 Jean Elizabeth; *b* 20 Sept 1920; *m* 30 Sept 1942 G/Capt Frank William Stannard, CBE, RAF, s of Capt William Lanagan Stannard, of St Helens, Lancs, and had:

(1) *Charles John William; *b* 7 July 1943

(1) *Elizabeth Shuna; *b* 26 July 1948; *m* 13 July 1968 *James William Shelley, est of Geoff Shelley, of Brookhill, Kingswear, S Devon, and has:

1a *Mark Ian; *b* 15 April 1969

The 2nd BARON *d* 11 Aug 1971; his only son,

JOHN TENNANT DAVENPORT SIDDELEY, **3rd Baron Kenilworth**; *b* 24 Jan 1924; *educ* Marlborough and Magdalene Coll Cambridge; Lt Gren Gds WW II; interior designer, ASID, md John Siddeley (Internat) Ltd and John Siddeley (Jewels) Ltd, Max Murphy Designs Ltd; food ed Paris *Vogue*, Master Coachmakers' and Coach Harness Makers' Co 1969–70, FRSA; *m* 28 Aug 1948 *Jaqueline Paulette [The Rt Hon Jacqueline Lady Kenilworth, 2 Lexham Walk, London W8], dau of Robert Gelpi, of Lyons, France, and *d* 1981, leaving:

1 (JOHN) RANDLE SIDDELEY, **4th and present Baron Kenilworth**

1 *Belinda Jane [The Hon Mrs McCarraher, Silver Coppers, College Rd, Epsom, Surrey KT17 4JG]; *b* 11 Jan 1950; *m* 20 Feb 1971 (*divorce* 1974) Christopher Aston James, only s of Lt-Col M A James, of Camberley; *m* 2nd 1983 *David Ian McCarraher and by him has:

(1) *Tara Louise; *b* 1989

KENNARD

Arms: Per chevron gules and azure a chevron engrailed argent between two keys in chief or and a sword erect in base proper, pommelled and hilted gold. **Crest:** A dexter cubit arm erect in armour proper, holding a key and broken sword in saltire or. **Motto:** *At spes non fracta* ('But hope is not broken'). **Creation:** Bt. (UK) 11 Feb 1891.

SIR GEORGE ARNOLD FORD KENNARD, 3RD BT, of Fernhill, Co Southampton [Lt-Col Sir George Kennard Bt, 13 Burton Court, Franklin's Row, London SW3 4TA]; *b* 27 April 1915; *s* bro 1967; *educ* Eton; commissioned 4th Hus 1936, served WW II (POW 1939–41, despatches twice), Lt-Col cmdg 4th QO Hus 1955–58, with Cement Marketing Co 1967–79 (latterly as Midland rep); *m* 1st 12 Oct 1940 (*divorce* 1958) Cecilia Violet Cokayne, only dau of Maj Cecil John Cokayne Maunsell, of Thorpe Malsor Hall, Kettering, Northants; *m* 2nd 30 Sept 1958 (*divorce* 1974) Mollie Jessie Rudd, yr dau of Hugh Wyllie, of Fishbourne, Sussex, formerly w of Ivor William Miskin; *m* 3rd 1985 (*divorce* 1992) Nichola Carew, only dau of Capt Peter Gawen Carew (*see* CAREW, Bt) and formerly w of Charles Louis Breitmeyer; *m* 4th 1992 *Georgina, dau of Sir Harold Augustus Wernher, 3rd Bt, GCVO, TD (*see* 1970 edn), and widow of Lt-Col Harold Pedro Joseph Phillips, and by his 1st w has:

1 *Zandra [Mrs John Powell, Catsley Farmhouse, Corscombe, Dorchester, Dorset]; *b* 17 June 1941; *m* 18 Aug 1962 *Maj Powell, Queen's Roy Irish Hus, only s of Maj John Beresford Powell, MC, of Hightown, Aldbourne, Wilts, and has:

(1) *Edward Coleridge Cockayne; *b* 2 Feb 1964

(1) *Louise Cecilia; *b* 20 Nov 1966

Lineage: JOHN KENNARD, of Sussex; settled London; *b* 1732; *m* Mary Huyshe (*b* 1733) and *d* 1791, having had:

1 George; murdered by his valet while travelling in Italy

2 JOHN

1 Frances; *d* unm

2 Mary; *m c* 1800 — Davis, of the Consolidated Bank and had issue

The 2nd son,

JOHN KENNARD, of Clapham, Surrey; *b* 30 Jan 1775; banker; *m* 3 June 1797 Harriet Elizabeth (*d* 13 Sept 1811), dau of William Peirse, of Windsor, and had:

1 JOHN PEIRSE

2 Robert William, of Theobalds, Herts, JP (Herts, Middx and Stirling), DL (Mon); *b* 18 Jan 1800; merchant London, Chev Order Leopold Belgium, Sheriff London and Middx 1846–47, MP Newport, IoW; *m* 23 May 1823 Mary Ann (*d* 23 March 1870), dau of Thomas Challis, MP Finsbury, and *d* 1870, having had:

(1) Robert Bruce (Rev), of Gatcombe, IoW; Rector Marnhull, Dorset; *b* 8 May 1824; *m* 1st 16 Dec 1848 Anne Grace (*d* 1878), dau of John Davies; *m* 2nd Marie Magdalena (*dsp* 8 April 1897), dau of Charles Bade, and *d* 10 March 1895, having had by his 1st w, with other issue:

1a Robert Bruce, of The Lodge, Marnhull, JP; *b* 3 June 1854; *m* 10 June 1897 Hilda Annesley, only dau of Lt-Col Edward Browne, Lancs Fus, of Kincardine Castle, Perthshire

2a Stanley Bruce, of Orchard Ho, Marnhull; *b* 21 Oct 1855; *m* 1st 15 May 1889 Elizabeth Lloyd (*d* 1908), 2nd dau of R L Jenkins, of Nepean Towers, Sydney, and widow of W A Concannon; *m* 2nd 1910 Constance Lucy Muriel, only dau of Rev P R Gorringe, Rector Manston, Dorset, and by her had:

1b A son

1b *Elizabeth; *m* John Drummond Fulford, yst s of Francis Algernon Fulford, of Great Fulford, Exeter, and has issue

3a Perceval Bruce; *m* 1st 1880 Emmeline (*dsp* 1888), dau of V Trevelli; *m* 2nd 17 June 1896 Hannah, only dau of Michael Burr

4a Howard Bruce, of Nahun, BC; *b* 4 March 1860

1a Margaret Eliza; *m* George Roberts Davies, and had issue

2a Ada Mary; *m* 18 Oct 1881 Rev Henry Phelps Marriott-Dodington, Vicar Leigh, Sherborne, and *d* 27 Dec 1906, leaving issue

3a Ethel Ida; *d* unm 7 Dec 1952 in her 92nd year

(2) Thomas William; *b* 29 Aug 1825; *m* Octavia (*d* 1874), dau of S Smale, and *d* 10 Sept 1893, leaving, with two sons (*d* unm):

1a Alice Irvina; *m* 1st 25 March 1874 Dr Hayman (*dsp* 1881); *m* 2nd Capt Bainbridge

2a Rosa Marion

3a Evelyn Maud; *b* 7 Dec 1855; *m* 27 Sept 1883 Robert Hulbert and *d* a widow 29 Sept 1905, leaving issue

(3) Howard John; *b* 29 Nov 1839; *m* 1st 4 March 1853 Ellen (*d* Paris Dec 1864 aged 34), dau of Robert Bousfield, and had:

1a Robert William, of Northleigh, Bradford-on-Avon, and Llwyndu Court, Abergavenny, JP Mon, DL London, High Sheriff 1888; *b* 1857; *m* 1880 Rose, dau of Robert Nicholl Byass, of Daylesford, Warwicks, and *d* 15 July 1929, leaving:

1b Howard John, JP (Stirlingshire 1929), DL (1930); Capt RN WW I; *b* 11 June 1882; *m* 1st 9 Aug 1910 Ethel Frances Vavasour (*d* 7 Feb 1950), dau of Frederick Richard Vavasour Witts, of Glos; *m* 2nd 31 May 1952 Favoretta Walterina, widow of Capt M A Kennard, RN, of Westbrook, Devon, and *d* 16 Feb 1967, having by his 1st w had:

1c *Robert William, MC (1945), TD; Maj Argyll and Sutherland Highrs (TA) WW II; *b* 5 Jan 1912; *educ* Marlborough and Magdalene Coll Cambridge; *m* 30 Sept 1939 *Hester Knox, dau of James Risk, of Edinburgh, and has:

1d *Howard John; *b* 27 July 1948; *educ* Bryanston

2d *Charles Robert; *b* 12 April 1952; *educ* Marlborough

3d *David James Risk; *b* 1 Nov 1953; *educ* Marlborough

1d *Gillian Rose; *b* 4 Aug 1946

2c John Nichol; Capt RN; *b* 4 Sept 1913; *educ* RNC Dartmouth; *m* 2 June 1939 Ann Claire (*d* 11 Nov 1983), dau of Clifford Dalison Borrer, of The Old Manor Ho, Cley-next-Sea, Norfolk, and *d* 15 Nov 1957, leaving:

1d *Joanna Frances; *b* 28 July 1940

2d *Judith Hilary; *b* 10 April 1942; *m* 19 Dec 1964 *Capt Anson, QRIH (*see* LICHFIELD, E), and has issue

3d *Jennifer Caroline; *b* 13 June 1950

1c *Susan Margaret Rose; *b* 21 Jan 1915; *m* 27 Feb 1942 *Maj Ronald Edward Boone, Parachute Regt, s of William John Boone, of Melbourne, Australia, and has issue

2c *(Maurice) Nancy, JP (Glos 1949); WW II in ATS; *b* 20 May 1917

2b Maurice Nicholl; Lt-Col Yorks Regt, Capt 6th Dragoon Gds (Carabiniers); *b* 1883; *educ* Radley, *ka* 1 July 1916

1b Gwendolen Mary; *m* 1909 Adml Walter Maurice Ellerton, CB (*d* 27 Nov 1948), and *d* 4 April 1951, leaving issue

2b Dorothy Evelyn; *m* Victor Adams, of Wadley Lodge, Faringdon, and had issue

2a Howard Charles; *b* 30 March 1862

1a Florence Sophia; *b* 19 Oct 1854; *d* 1899

2a Jessie; *b* 23 Dec 1855; *m* 26 April 1875 S E Illingworth, of Borough Ct, Winchfield, and had issue

3a Ellen Clarissa; *m* 25 July 1883 Capt John Orr Ewing, 4th Dragoon Gds, 4th of Sir Archibald Orr Ewing, 1st Bt (*qv*), and *d* 17 Aug 1914, leaving issue

4a Ethel May

(3) (cont.) Howard Kennard *m* 2nd 28 May 1872 Elizabeth (*d* March 1888), dau of Adml Willoughby, and *d* 8 Aug 1896, having by her had:

3a Willoughby Arthur; Capt 13th Hus; *b* 20 May 1881

5a Marion Lily

(4) Arthur Challis; *b* 17 June 1831; *m* 27 Feb 1866 Anne Homan (*d* 29 March 1926), dau of Thomas Homan-Mulock, of Bellair, and had:

1a Arthur Molloy, DSO, RHA; *b* 7 July 1867; *d* 2 Jan 1917

2a Howard William (Sir), GCMG (1938), CVO (1923); Min Belgrade 1925, Stockholm 1929, Berne 1931–34, Amb Warsaw 1934–41; *b* 23 March 1878; *m* 1908 Harriet (*d* 27 Jan 1950), dau of Jonathan Norris, of New York, and *d* 12 Nov 1955, leaving:

1b *Arthur Norris; *m* 1940 Lee, dau of Horace Lee Washington, of Washington, DC (*see* Section Washington (p. 51), AMERICAN PRESIDENTIAL FAMILIES, 1994, Morris Genealogical Books SA)

1a Nina Frances; *m* 1896 Sir James Augustus Grant, 1st and last Bt (*d* 29 July 1932), of Househill, Nairn, and *d* 9 Aug 19–, leaving issue

2a Hester Charlotte; *m* 27 April 1904 Alastair Macpherson Grant (*d* 21 June 1949), FRGS, yst s of Sir George Macpherson-Grant of Ballindalloch, 3rd Bt (*see* 1970 edn), and *d* 19 Jan 1945, leaving issue

(5) Henry Martyn, of Falkirk, and Crumlin Hall, nr Newport, Mon, JP, DL; High Sheriff 1863; *b* 17 Feb 1833; *m* 1858 Katherine Anne (*d* 1876), dau of Rev George Thomas, of Ystrad Mynach, Glamorgan, and had:

1a Martyn Thomas; *b* 14 Sept 1859; *m* 9 Dec 1903 Cora (*d* 11 Oct 1932), widow of (a) S Colgate, of USA, and (b) 4th Earl of Strafford (*qv*), and *d* 12 May 1920

1a Mary Elise; *m* 23 Feb 1881 Arthur William Leatham, JP, of Miserden Park, Glos, and *d* 3 Dec 1925, leaving issue

(6) John; *b* 13 April 1836; *d* unm 24 Nov 1925

(7) Edward, of Blaenafon, Mon, JP, DL; High Sheriff 1876; *b* 22 April 1842; *m* 19 April 1870 Mary Eliza, 2nd dau of Samuel Laing, MP, and had issue

(1) Mary Jane

(2) Charlotte Anne; *m* 31 March 1869 Capt Lewis Cubitt (*d* 20 Nov 1872), of Eden Hall, Edenbridge, Kent, and *d* 24 Oct 1926, leaving issue

(3) Ellen; *m* 1 Dec 1864 George William Griffiths Thomas (*d* 1885), of Ystrad Mynach, Glam, and *d* 5 April 1917, leaving issue

3 George (Rev), of Gayton, Northants; *b* 3 Jan 1806; *m* 26 Sept 1839 Mary Jeannette (*m* 2nd 1848 Edward Preston Rawnsley), only dau of John Jackson, of Coniston, and *d* 11 Dec 1847, leaving:

(1) Mary Genevieve; *m* 1879 Lewis Merryon

(2) Constance Hammond; Sister of Mercy Community of St Peter's Home, Kilburn; *b* 1841; *d* 9 May 1902

(3) Elizabeth Preston; *m* 20 Dec 1866 Adml Claude Edward Buckle (*d* 7 Feb 1930), of Jordans, Bucks, and *d* 4 May 1928, having had issue

4 Henry Hewitt, of Rookcliff, Hants; *b* 30 July 1808; *d* unm 16 Oct 1878

5 Stephen Ponder, of Harrow Weald, Middx, JP, DL; *b* 24 Jan 1810; *m* 13 June 1839 Emma Sarah (*d* 11 Dec 1898), dau of William Steinmetz, of Upper Homerton, Middx, and *d* 14 Jan 1887, having had:

(1) Henry Steinmetz, of Shopwyke Ho, Oving, Sussex; *b* 15 Feb 1843; *m* 28 April 1868 Frances Charlotte Celestine (*d* 30 March 1899), yst dau of Charles Robert Sperling, of Hargrave, Essex, yr s of John Sperling, of Dynes Hall, Essex, and *d* Sept 1902, leaving:

1a Rowland Stephen Astley, JP; *b* 18 June 1871; *m* 11 Aug 1896 Winifred Dagmar (*d* 7 Nov 1959), 2nd dau of Lawrence Heyworth, JP, of Whitefield, Devon, and Palstre Court, Wittersham, Kent, and *d* 1920, leaving:

1b Henry Rowland Heyworth; 10th Hus; *b* 13 Feb 1900; *educ* Eton and Trin Coll Cambridge; *m* 8 Nov 1937 Evelyn Grace Cardell, er dau of Cardell Pascoe Martyn, of Tremmeddan, Liskeard, Cornwall, and had:

1c *Rowland Churchill Heyworth; *b* 26 April 1939; *educ* Malvern; *m* 19– *Michele — and has:

1d *Kaline; *b* 24 June 1977

2c *Lawrence Rochford; MSc; *b* 8 Nov 1940

3c *Stephen Astley Martyn; CA; *b* 20 June 1942

4c *Robert Nigel; *b* 14 Aug 1944; *m* 16 Sept 1967 *Joanna Gay, dau of Ian Ward, of Everton, Hants, and has:

1d *Robert Jake Henry; *b* 3 June 1969

5c *Martyn Astley; *b* 15 Feb 1947; *m* 19– *Victoria Lindsay, er dau of R-Adml James Humphrey Walwyn, CB, OBE, and has issue

6c *Daniel James; *b* 1 Dec 1948; *educ* Milton Abbey

1b Frances Doris; *m* 8 June 1920 Col Sir (Robert) Godfrey Llewellyn, 1st Bt, CB, CBE, MC, TD, JP, DL of Baglan (*see* 1970 edn), of Tredilion Park, Abergavenny, Mon, and *d* 19 June 1969, leaving issue

2a Hyde Henry Astley; Dip Serv; *b* 1874; *d* 1957

1a Violet Astley; *d* 1939

2a Laura Astley; *m* 26 Oct 1897 Hon Francis William Arthur Agar (*d* 18 Aug 1936), 4th s of 3rd Earl of Normanton (*qv*), and *d* 8 May 1960, leaving issue

(1) Harriet Emma; *m* Henry Reginald Sperling (*d* 15 Feb 1933), of Netherfield Court, Battle, Sussex, s of Charles Robert Sperling, of Hargrave, Essex, and *d* 1917, leaving issue

(2) Laura Mary; *m* 22 April 1873 Edward Pennell Elmhirst (*d* 2 Dec 1916), Capt 9th Regt, and *d* 25 April 1909

(3) Edith Charlotte; *m* 30 Oct 1877 Charles John Hegan, JP, MA, and *d* 1911

1 Harriett Elizabeth; *b* 7 June 1801; *m* 25 May 1841 John Corrie, of Senwick, Kirkcudbrightshire, and *d* Milan 21 Oct 1870, leaving issue

2 Ellen; *m* 15 March 1838 George Simpson (*d* 24 Jan 1866), barrister Lincoln's Inn, and *d* 18 Sept 1891, leaving issue

3 Hannah Anne; *b* 1805; *d* 1806

JOHN KENNARD *d* 1 Dec 1838; his est son,

JOHN PEIRSE KENNARD, of Walthamstow, Essex, formerly of Upper Gatton Park, Reigate, and London, later of Hordle Cliff, Hants; *b* 25 Oct 1798; banker; *m* 8 Jan 1828 Sophia, est dau of Sir John Chapman, of Windsor, and *d* 3 May 1877, having had, with three daus:

1 Coleridge John, of Fernhill, Hants, JP Hants, DL London; MP Salisbury 1882–85; *b* 6 Oct 1828; *m* 20 July 1858 Ellen Georgiana (*d* 10 Dec 1916), only child of Capt John Wilkinson Rowe, HEICS, and n of Sir Joshua Rowe, CB, Ch Justice Jamaica, and *d* 25 Dec 1890 just as he was about to be *cr* a bt (the btcy was conferred on his gs, while his widow was granted rank of a bt's widow), having had:

(1) Hugh Coleridge Downing; Lt Gren Gds; *b* 15 May 1859; *m* 7 Sept 1883 Helen (*m* 2nd 1896 James Lawrence Carew (*d* 31 Aug 1903) and *d* 21 April 1828), only dau of James Wyllie, of Antibes and Hove, and *dvp* 9 April 1886, leaving:

1a COLERIDGE ARTHUR FITZ ROY (Sir), **1st Bt**

(1) Meredyth Sophia Frances; *m* 6 Nov 1890 1st and last Baron Rawlinson, GCB (*dsp* 27 March 1925), and *d* 29 Sept 1951

2 Adam Steinmetz, of Crawley Court, Sussex, later Belmore, Bishop's Waltham, Hants, JP; High Sheriff Hants 1885; *b* June 1833; *m* 1st 1861 Grace Ellen (*d* 1880), est dau and coheiress of Joseph Hegan, of Dawpool, Cheshire, and had:

(1) Cecil Waterhouse; *b* 7 Aug 1867; *m* 1890 Mary Noel, widow of W C Hawker, and est dau of Capt Albert W Money, of East Liss, Hants, and had:

1a Donald Ian Menzies; F/O RAF; *b* 31 May 1891

2a Brian Adam Tormore; *b* 30 July 1892

3a Patrick Noel; *b* 15 Oct 1893

(2) Henry Gerard Hegan; Lt-Col and Brevet-Col cmdg 5th Dragoon Gds, cmded Dublin Garrison 1915–18; *b* 28 March 1871; *educ* Eton and RMC Sandhurst; *m* 15 Jan 1895 Nancy, dau of Col R Poyser, DSO, and had:

1a Terence Evelyn; *b* 19 Aug 1896; *ka* Feb 1918

1a Dulcie Hazel; *b* 19 April 1900; *m* 1st — Griffiths; *m* 2nd 1933 Charles Pears, ROI (*d* 28 Jan 1958)

2a Tertia Doreen; *b* 11 March 1906; *m* Noel Brack

(3) Charles Heywood; *b* 18 May 1872; *m* 29 June 1898 Hon Mary Cleveland (*d* 2 Nov 1940), dau of 1st and last Baron Channing of Wellingborough (*see* 1926 edn), and *d* 4 Sept 1957, leaving:

1a Cyril George Henry; *b* 2 July 1899; *educ* Winchester

1a Violet Elizabeth Grace; *m* 2 Dec 1940 Lt Derek Leith Reeves, RNVR, est s of Hugh Reeves, of Tillington, Sussex

(4) Edmund (twin); *m* 1st 1895 Frances (*d* 1924), dau of J C Hawkshaw, of Hollycombe, Sussex; *m* 2nd 1926 Mrs Travers and *d* 1934, having by his 1st w had:

1a Francis Edmund; *b* 30 Oct 1897

(5) Vivian George, JP (Dorset 1924); Dorset Yeo WW I; *b* 4 April 1874; *m* 1st 12 June 1900 his er bro's sis-in-law Mildred Clarke (*d* 3 Feb 1927), dau of J C Hawkshaw, and had:

1a Roderick Vivian; BA Cantab, RAF Intell WW II; *b* 16 March 1901; *m* 17 March 1927 Jeanne, dau of Paul Thomas, of Paris, and *d* 22 March 1969, leaving:

1b *Vivian Jan; BA Cantab; *b* 12 Oct 1928; *m* 21 July 1959 *Fung Siu-Wan

1b *Mildred Joy; *b* 8 Feb 1931; *m* 32 Dec 1960 *René de Obaldia and has:

1c *Gilles; *b* 1 May 1964

1c *Claire; *b* 19 Nov 1961

2a Stephen John; *b* 13 Aug 1904; *m* 15 Aug 1935 Joan, dau of W N Elder, and *d* 25 Dec 1987, leaving:

1b *Nicholas Birkbeck; *b* 21 Aug 1937; *educ* Wellington; *m* 6 June 1964 *Kathleen Margaret, dau of Rev Wilfred George Pack, Vicar St Mary Bourne, Hants, and has:

1c *Stephen Julian; *b* 26 Nov 1966

2c *Alexander Mark; *b* 12 May 1968

2b *Simon John Vivian [Simon Kennard Esq, Eduardo VII, Hurlingham, FCSM, Argentina]; *b* 1 July 1944; *m* 30 Nov 1968 *Patricia Anne Dunn

1b *Lavinia Mary [Mrs Patrick Keene, El Marabù, CC109, 6064 Ameghino, Buenos Aires, Argentina]; *b* 9 Oct 1939; *m* 30 July 1966 *Capt Patrick Brian George Keene, RHA, er s of Brig T P Keene, RA, and has:

1c *Justin Patrick; *b* 1 Oct 1969

2c *Jason Robert; *b* 9 July 1972

1c *Jessica Grace; *b* 18 Aug 1967

2c *Juliet Mary; *b* 21 Jan 1975

3a Noel Gerard; Cameron Highrs and Commandos WW II; *b* 27 Dec 1905; *educ* Cheltenham and Peterhouse Cambridge; *m* 17 Aug 1948 Renée Mary, dau of Harold Methven Musson, MC, and had:

1b *Conan James Montrose; RN; *b* 18 March 1950; *educ* Grenville Coll and HMS *Britannia*; *m* 25 Oct 1975 *Sheila Kitchen and has:

1c *Laura Jane; *b* May 1977

1b *Olivia Ann; *b* Aug 1951

2b Gillian Mary; *b* 27 April 1953; *d* Jan 1954

3b *Angela Christine; *b* 12 May 1955

1a Grace Mildred; *b* 27 May 1903; *m* and had issue

(5) (cont.) Vivian Kennard *m* 2nd 23 May 1928 Mary Hamilton, widow of Ralph E Hancock, DSO, and dau of Rev Philip Broadmead, of Enmore Castle, and Olands, Somerset, and *d* 22 June 1945, having by her had:

4a David Adam Broadmead; *b* 27 June 1929; *educ* Winchester and RMC Sandhurst; Maj 12th Roy Lancers, ADC to HC Fedn Malaya 1953–54; *m* 21 May 1955 *Gaynor Bridget [Mrs David Kennard, Chilfrome House, Dorchester, Dorset], dau of Col George Herbert Mytton, JP, of Garth, Montgomeryshire, and *d* 15 Aug 1983, leaving:

1b *Vivian Adam Mytton; *b* 13 Dec 1958

1b *Charlotte Ann; *b* 4 Nov 1956

2b *Lucia Mary; *b* 20 April 1963

(1) Agnes Lily; *b* 20 Sept 1862; *m* 27 July 1887 Sir Charles Roderick Hunter, 3rd and last Bt (*d* 24 June 1924), and *d* 10 April 1934, having had:

(2) Marion Grace; *b* 14 Oct 1864; *d* unm 11 June 1948

(3) Beatrice Margaret; *b* 27 July 1869; *m* Sept 1890, as his 1st w, Frederick Charles Villian Fanning, of Durton Manor, Beds, and Shapleigh, Hants, yst s of William Fanning, JP, DL, of Bogedown, Oxon, and *d* 1917, leaving issue

2 (cont.) Adam Kennard *m* 2nd 18 Oct 1883 Alice Jane, dau of Henry Lomax Gaskell, of Kiddington Hall, Oxon, and *d* 1 Feb 1915, having by her had:

(6) John Adam Gaskell; Capt 2nd Bn Rifle Bde; *b* 8 Nov 1884; *m* 14 Aug 1918 Leonore Mary (*d* 13 March 1963), widow of Cyril Baker and dau of James Montgomery, and *d* 1939, leaving:

1a *John Adrian Coleridge [John Kennard Esq, 13 Hazelwood Rd, Hale, Cheshire]; *b* 26 Jan 1922

2a Humphrey Oscar Coleridge; *b* 20 Oct 1923; *ka* 1944

(7) Alan Spencer Gaskell; *b* 21 May 1886; *m* 30 Aug 1911 Agatha Frances, yst dau of Lt-Col Thomas Alfred Colfox, JP, DL (*see* COLFOX, Bt), and *d* 17 Aug 1951, leaving:

1a *Anthony Spencer, DSC [Lt-Cdr Anthony Kennard DSC RN, Barnacle Lodge, Brayfield Rd, Bray, Berks]; *b* 22 July 1914; *m* 1st 22 July 1944 (*divorce* 1952) Elizabeth Ann, only child of Gen Mervyn Wheatley, and has:

1b *Martin Spencer; *b* 6 July 1945; *educ* Radley and St Edmund Hall Oxford (rowing blue 1965, 1966, 1967)

1b *Penelope Ann; *b* 5 Jan 1948

1a (cont.) Lt-Cdr Anthony Kennard *m* 2nd 19– Suzanne, formerly w of G/Capt James Richmond Gordon-Finlayson, DSO, DFC, RAF, and er dau of William Aberdeen Mackay Sim, JP, of Wadhurst, Sussex; *m* 3rd 25 Sept 1971 *Lorna, widow of Maj G L Scott, 14th/20th King's Hus

2a *John Michael; *b* Jan 1916; *m* 1940 *Peggy, dau of Dr Joseph Cates, and has:

1b *Patricia Ann Cates; *b* 23 Aug 1942; *m* 1965

2b *Heather Elizabeth Cates; *b* 24 May 1944; *m* 1968

3b *Janet Ione Cates; *b* 18 Feb 1946

3a *Colin David, DSO [Maj Colin Kennard DSO, Frith House, Litton Cheney, Dorchester, Dorset]; Maj Irish Gds RARO WW II; *b* 6 Oct 1919; *educ* Radley and Christ's Coll Cambridge; *m* 5 July 1947 *Rosemary Gillies, dau of Maj Onslow Mackintosh, DSO, JP, RA, of Alderholt Park, Fordingbridge, Hants, and has:

1b *(Jeremy) David; Capt Irish Gds; *b* 28 Sept 1949; *educ* Radley; *m* 8 July 1979 *Teresa C, er dau of Geoffrey Holbeach, of Farnborough Hall, Banbury, Oxon

1b *Clare Gillies; *b* 18 Feb 1952; *m* 6 May 1978 *(Walter) Guy Becher Humphreys, 2nd s of Donnington Hungerford, of Victoria, BC, Canada, and has issue

4a *Robert Adam [Robert Kennard Esq, Westcott Hill House, Westcott, Surrey]; FCIB, ACII, Lloyd's broker and memb Lloyd's; late Capt Gren Gds RARO; *b* 19 Feb 1921; *m* 22 Feb 1947 *Grace Mary Stewart, yr dau of Dr T Jenner Hoskin, MD, FRCP, of Harley St, W1, and has:

1b *Robert Jenner; *b* 7 April 1956; *educ* Sherbone
1b *(Mary) Elizabeth Evelyn; *b* 25 March 1950; *m* 8 Aug 1970 *(John) Roger Newham, NCA, er s of Peter Newham, slr, and has:
1c *James Robert Peter; *b* 1972
1a *Iris Pamela Gaskell; *b* 1 May 1912; *m* 18 July 1936 Sir John Lyell Langman, 3rd Bt (*d* 1985, *see* 1970 edn), and has issue
3 Edmund Hegan, of Great Tangley Manor, Guildford; MP Lymington 1874–85, Beverley 1866–69, MA Oxon, Capt 8th Hus, Hon Col 15th Middx RV, ADC to Ld Lt Ireland; *b* 14 Oct 1834; *m* Jan 1868 Agnes (*d* 22 Jan 1906), 2nd dau and coheir of Joseph Hegan, of Dawpool, Cheshire, and *d* 9 July 1912, leaving:
(1) Auberon Claud Hegan; Lt-Col 1st Bn London Regt (TA), Capt Rifle Bde; *b* 18 May 1870; *m* 1st 7 Jan 1904 (*divorce* 1920) Florence Joan Gertrude Glynn (*d* 25 Aug 1961), dau of John Henry Oglander, of Nunwell, IoW; *m* 2nd 12 April 1922 Anne Claudia Whalley (*d* 11 June 1943), widow of Hon Kenneth Dundas (*see* MELVILLE, V) and dau of Capt Charles Edward Foot, RN, and *d* 1 Nov 1951, having by his 1st w had:
1a Denys Ernest Glynn KENNARD later OGLANDER (deed poll 10 March 1930); WW II: 43rd Light AA Regt RA 1939–41, Gen Staff War Office 1941–43 (Maj Intell), PWE 1943–45, Br Del (Fin Div) Allied Control Commn; *b* 17 Dec 1904; *educ* Eton and New Coll Oxford; *m* 17 Jan 1950 *Margaret Elsie Viola, yr dau of Sir William Augustus Forbes Erskine, GCMG, MVO, PC (*see* MAR and KELLIE, E), and *d* 22 March 1977, leaving:
1b *William Auberon Erskine; *b* 29 May 1953
2b *John Peter Erskine; *b* 28 June 1957
1b *Frances Mary Viola; *b* 11 Aug 1951
2b *Mary Theresa Catherine Joan; *b* 27 May 1955
2a Peter Auberon Somerset; *b* 6 April 1908; *d* Sept 1910
(2) Ernest Coleridge Hegan; Capt Gren Gds Matabele 1896 and Boer Wars; *b* 1 Feb 1873; *educ* Eton and Sandhurst; *m* and *dsp*
(1) Victoria Lily Hegan; *m* 17 May 1899 1st Baron Sysonby (*qv*) and *d* 2 June 1955, leaving issue
(2) Winifred Grace; *m* 30 April 1898 Sir Ralph Blois, 9th Bt (*qv*), and *d* 28 Nov 1963, leaving issue
4 Charles Henry (Rt Rev Mgr); Canon Bristol, Domestic Prelate to HH PIUS X; *b* 11 Oct 1840; *educ* Univ Coll Oxford (BA); *d* 6 Aug 1920

JOHN PIERSE KENNARD'S ggs,
Sir Coleridge Arthur Fitzroy Kennard, 1st Bt (UK), so *cr* 11 Feb 1891; *b* 12 May 1885; 1st Sec Dip Serv, Attaché 1908, Rome 1909, Teheran 1909, 3rd Sec 1910, FO 1914, Stockholm 1916, 2nd Sec 1918, 1st Sec 1919, Chargé d'Affaires Helsinki 1919; *m* 1st 5 April 1911 (*divorce* 1918) Dorothy Katherine (*d* 15 Jan 1953), only child of Sir George Head Barclay, KCSI, KCMG, CVO; *m* 2nd 21 July 1924 Mary Graham (*d* 6 July 1931), dau of Sir Frederick Orr-Lewis, 1st Bt (*see* 1970 edn), of Montreal, and *d* 7 Oct 1948, having by his 1st w had:
1 **Sir Lawrence Charles Ury Kennard, 2nd Bt**; *b* 6 Feb 1912; *educ* Eton; *m* 27 April 1940 Joan Liesl (*d* 1964), er dau of William Thomas Perschke, of Sussex, and *dsp* 3 May 1967
2 Sir GEORGE ARNOLD FORD KENNARD, **3rd and present Bt**

KENNAWAY

Arms: Argent a fess azure between two eagles displayed in chief gules, and in base, through an annulet of the third, a slip of olive and another of palm in saltire proper. **Crest:** An eagle rising proper, from the beak an escutcheon pendant azure, charged with a sun in splendour, also proper. **Motto:** *Ascendam* ('I shall ascend'). **Creation:** Bt. (GB) 25 Feb 1791.

SIR JOHN LAWRENCE KENNAWAY, 5TH BT, of Escot, Devon [Sir John Kennaway Bt, Escot, Ottery St Mary, Devon EX11 1LU]; *b* 7 Sept 1933; *s f* 1956; *educ* Harrow and Trin Coll Cambridge; *m* 29 April 1961 *Christina Veronica, MB, ChB (Cape Town), dau of Michael Urszenyi, formerly of Budapest, and has:
1 +JOHN MICHAEL [John Kennaway Esq, Escot House, Ottery St Mary, Devon EX11 1LU]; *b* 17 Feb 1962; *educ* King Edward's Bath and Hants Coll of Ag; *m* 1988 *Lucy Frances, yr dau of Dr Jeremey Houlton Bradshaw-Smith, of Ottery St Mary, and has:
(1) *Olivia Ursula; *b* 1993
(2) *Jessica; *b* 1995
1 *Julia Frances; *b* 26 Feb 1965
2 *Irma Annabelle; *b* 6 Jan 1968

Lineage: Sir John Kennaway, 1st Bt (GB), so *cr* 25 Feb 1791 (descended from William Kennaway, merchant, by Joyce, dau of Sir William Bastard, of Garston Devon); Capt HEICS 1780, served Bengal section of Grand Army in Carnatic against Hyder Ali; ADC to Marquess Cornwallis (*see* CORNWALLIS, B) 1786, envoy Hyderabad 1788, negotiated with Nizam of Hyderabad alliance against Tipu Sultan, which earned him the btcy; negotiated peace treaty with Tipu Sultan 1792; *m* 1797 Charlotte (*d* 1845), 2nd dau and coheir of James Amyatt, MP, and had, with other issue:
1 JOHN (Sir), **2nd Bt**
2 Charles Edward (Rev); MA, Fell St John's Coll Cambridge, Vicar Campden, Glos, Canon Gloucester; *b* 3 Jan 1800; *m* 1st 17 June 1830 Emma (*dsp* 10 Oct 1843), 4th dau of Rev Hon Gerard Thomas Noel (*see* GAINSBOROUGH, E); *m* 2nd 30 Dec 1845 Olivia (*d* 1888), 3rd dau of Rev Lewis Way, of Stanstead Pk, Sussex, and *d* 3 Nov 1875, leaving by her, with other issue:
(1) Charles Lewis (Rev); Rector Garboldisham Norfolk 1876–1914, incumbent Tarrant Crawford Dorset 1914–37; *b* 3 July 1847; *educ* Univ Coll Oxford (MA); *m* 18 July 1877 Edith Letitia (*d* 19 Feb 1932), dau of Charles Joseph Parke, of Henbury, Dorset, and *d* 23 April 1940, leaving:
1a Charles Roger; *b* 5 Jan 1880; *m* 15 Jan 1907 Margaret Evelyn (*d* 7 April 1917), 2nd dau of Robert Bagot Chester Everard, of Remenham, Hindhead, and *d* 30 Nov 1914, leaving:
1b Roger Charles Lewis; Capt Oxon and Bucks LI SR; *b* 10 April 1910; *educ* Harrow; *m* 1st 24 July 1936 (*divorce* 1947) Alethea Winefrede, er dau of Francis Nevill Lloyd, of Estcourt, Tetbury, Glos, and had:
1c +(Roger) Ian [Ian Kennaway Esq, 32 Rylett Crescent, London W12 9RL]; *b* 7 July 1938; *educ* Marlborough; *m* 10 Oct 1964 *Gabrielle Mary, er dau of Lt-Col D I C Tennant, of Bosham, Sussex, and has:
1d +Charles Lewis; *b* 16 Sept 1966
2d +Hugh Edward; *b* 15 April 1969; *m* 12 July 1997 *Alyson Clare Monica, dau of Geoffrey Frott, of St Brelade, Jersey
3d +Anthony Francis; *b* 1973
1b (cont.) Roger Kennaway *m* 2nd 4 Sept 1947 *Pamela Lavender [Mrs Roger Kennaway, Tremoor Combe, St Breward, Cornwall PL30 4LU], widow of G/Capt Patrick Bruce Bine Ogilvie, DSO, DFC, RAF (*see* RENSHAW, Bt) and dau of Cdr Tom Claud Mackenzie Bellairs, RN, of Kemerton House, Tewkesbury, Glos, and *d* 25 June 1995, leaving by her:
1c *Rose Margaret Ruth; *b* 17 Aug 1949; *m* 1970 (*divorce* 1993) Quintin Gerald Wyvern Batt and has:
1d *Camilla Louise; *b* 1973
2a Arthur Lewis; Lt Dorset Yeo; *b* 16 June 1881; *ka* 21 Aug 1915
1a Ruth Lettice; *m* 8 April 1915 Rev Hugh Speke (*ka* 11 Aug 1915), Maj 10th Bn Lancs Fus, Vicar Curry Rivel, Somerset
2a Cicely Joan; *m* 1st 7 Jan 1908 Maj Gerald Vernon Carter, OBE, Dorset Yeo, 16th Lancers (*d* 15 April 1937), s of Vernon Carter, Rector Almer, Dorset; *m* 2nd 18 Feb 1956 Leonard Curtis Rawlence (*d* Dec 1958) and by her 1st husb had:
1b Pamela Edith; *b* 1908; *d* 1924
2b *Barbara Joan; *b* Dec 1910; *m* 1st 1936 (*divorce* 1945) Lt-Col Basil John Ringrose, DSO, TD, s of Dr Ernest Ringrose, JP, of Balderton, Newark, Notts; *m* 2nd 1959 Sir (John) Ramsey Willis, QC, High Ct Judge, s of Dr John Keith Willis, of Cranleigh, Surrey, and has:
1c *Nigel John Carter; ACA; *b* 2 May 1938; *educ* Eton; *m* 14 Dec 1963 *Angela Margaret, dau of Cdr R F Hoyle, RNR, of Captain's House, TS *Mercury*, Hamble, Hants, and has:
1d *Simon Nigel Olav; *b* 23 Sept 1964
2d *Timothy John; *b* 20 June 1969
1d *Amelia Angela Wendy; *b* 22 Jan 1966
3b *Lavina Mary; RAF WW II; *b* 26 Feb 1920; *m* 18 Jan 1945 *Howard Lewis Brinsley Sheridan, s of Maurice Overing Sheridan, of Exeter, and has:
1c *Richard Brinsley; *b* 3 Dec 1945
2c *Rollo Hugh Motley; *b* 17 June 1951
1c *Carol Lavina Linley [Mrs William Hewett, 5 St Aubyns Park, West Town, Hayling Island, Hants]; *b* 23 Dec 1946; *m* Aug 1965 *William George Lear Hewett and has:
1d *Lara Jane Linley; *b* 6 Aug 1967
2d *Georgia Isabel Davina; *b* 6 Nov 1968
2c *Davina Jane; *b* 10 Feb 1953
3 William Richard; BCS, Judge Futtehpore; *b* 15 June 1804; *m* 17 May 1831 Eliza (*d* Jan 1893), dau of George Poyntz Ricketts, BCS, and *d* 13 Oct 1842, leaving three daus

The 1st Bt *d* 1 Jan 1836; his est son,
Sir John Kennaway, 2nd Bt; High Sheriff Devon 1866; *b* 15 Dec 1797; *m* 28 April 1831 Emily Frances (*d* 16 May 1858), dau of Thomas Kingscote, of Kingscote, Glos, and had:
1 JOHN HENRY (Sir), **3rd Bt**
2 Charles William; Lt-Col RHA; *b* 6 April 1843; *m* 29 April 1876 Evelyn (*d* 17 Jan 1922), 2nd dau of Edward Lennox Boyd (*see* BOYD OF MERTON, V), and *d* 28 July 1914, leaving:
(1) Charles Noel; Maj RGA; *b* 17 Feb 1877; *m* 11 Oct 1906 Florence Lucie (*d* 17 Feb 1966), 2nd dau of Henry Skeffington Poole, of Halifax, Nova Scotia, and *d* 9 Jan 1944, having had:
1a Charles Stewart Hamilton; Lt RN (FAA); *b* 14 Aug 1914; *m* 15 July 1939 Rachel Mary Joice (*m* 2nd 1 June 1943 Lt-Col Christopher Stuart Mackay), est dau of John Camplin, of Newby, Westmorland, formerly of El Tarh, Egypt, and was *ka* night of 30 Sept –1 Oct 1940
1a Monica Evelyn Tindal; *b* 18 Feb 1910; *d* 13 Aug 1982
3 Gerard Acland; *b* 13 June 1845; *d* 29 Nov 1859

4 Richard Arthur (Rev); Rector Bramdean Hants 1909–15; *b* 28 Feb 1847; *m* 1st 23 July 1874 Mary Jane (*d* 1889), est dau of Rev Thomas F Boddington, Rector Badgor Salop; *m* 2nd 30 Aug 1892 Isabella Fraser (*d* 25 April 1936), dau of Rev William Wilson, Rector Stoke Bruerne, Northants, and *d* 17 Jan 1918, leaving by his 1st w, with other issue:

(1) Gerard Arthur, Capt Derbys Yeo; *b* 18 Nov 1876; *m* 14 July 1908 Gladys (*d* 1 Feb 1971), yst dau of Lt-Cdr Cecil B Palmer, RN, and *d* 29 May 1934

(2) Mark John; *b* 25 April 1880; *educ* Sherborne; *m* 17 April 1920 Dorothy (*d* 22 Nov 1958), 2nd dau of Edward Hick, of Leeds, and *d* 17 March 1960, leaving:

1a *Anne [Mrs Gerald Scott, Corner Cottage, Fletching, E Sussex TN22 1SS]; *b* 1922; *m* 4 March 1946 Gerald Wardlaw Scott, CEng, BSc (*d* 1988), s of Philip Scott, and has:

1b *Philip Wardlaw; *b* 12 Feb 1950; *m* 1977 *Julia Margaret Newnham (*née* Newbery) and has:

1c *Oliver Wardlaw; *b* 1978

1b *Deborah; *b* 29 Sept 1948; *m* 1973 (*divorce* 1980) Torbjorn Stene and has:

1c *Rebecca; *b* 1973

2a *Mary Elizabeth [Mrs Bernard Davis, PO Box 269, Girne, Mersin 10, Turkey]; *b* 1924; *m* 6 Nov 1948 Bernard Stratton Davis, OBE (*d* 1983), 2nd s of Rev John Stratton Davis, and has:

1b *Mark John Stratton; *b* 20 May 1952; *m* 1980 *Valerie Rainsbury and has:

1c *John Charles Stratton; *b* 1981

2c *William Adam; *b* 1985

1c *Catherine (twin); *b* 1981

1b *Sarah Elizabeth; *b* 28 Feb 1951; has by *John Wyllie:

1c *Jack WYLLIE-DAVIS; *b* 1985

2c *Joel WYLLIE-DAVIS; *b* 1987

2b *Maroulla Judith; *b* 27 April 1954; *m* 1979 *Jeremy Peter Haile and has:

1c *Scott Matthew; *b* 1983

2c *Peter; *b* 1988

1c *Sarah; *b* 1982

2c *Emily Rebecca; *b* 1985

3a *Philippa Jane [Mrs Alexander Boyle, 4 White Point Rd, Whitby, N Yorks YO21 3JR]; *b* 30 April 1927; *m* 9 Aug 1962 *Alexander Keith Boyle, yst s of Capt Harry Lumsden Boyle, CBE, RN, of Perthshire, and has:

1b *David Kennaway; *b* 9 May 1964; *m* 1987 *Armida Asunta Eslava

2b *Michael Kennaway; *b* 27 Aug 1967

1b *Kirsteen Susan; *b* 3 July 1965; *m* 1989 *Herbert van Cortlandt Bailey and has issue

4a *Susan Helen [Mrs John Whitley, Kingsrod, Friday's Hill, Kingsley Green, Haslemere, Surrey GU27 3LL]; *b* 10 Nov 1928; *m* 12 Feb 1966 *His Honour John Reginald Whitley, only s of Reginald Joseph Whitley, of Sussex, and has:

1b *Elizabeth Rose; *b* 4 Nov 1967

(3) Leonard Henry; 1st Roy Devon Yeo; *b* 26 Aug 1882; *m* 12 Oct 1940 Winifred, est dau of Thomas Horn, of Cliffe Hill, Warwicks

(4) Richard Harold; Capt 2nd/4th Devon Regt; *b* 6 May 1887; *m* 8 Dec 1925 Agnes Margaret Gracilla, widow of T V Alder and er dau of Arthur Cavendish O Boddington, and *d* 26 June 1964

(1) Ella Frances; *b* 24 April 1879; *d* unm 8 Jan 1962

1 Emily Charlotte; *d* 21 Jan 1872

The 2nd Bt *d* 19 Feb 1873; his est son,

Sir John Henry Kennaway, 3rd Bt, CB, PC, JP, DL Devon, of Escot; *b* 6 June 1837; *educ* Balliol Coll Oxford (MA), barrister, MP Devon E 1870–85 and Honiton 1885–1910, Pres Ch Missionary Soc, Hon Col 4th Bn Devon Regt (VD); *m* 27 Nov 1866 Frances (*d* 23 Oct 1922), dau of Archibald Francis Arbuthnot (*see* ARBUTHNOT, Bt, of Edinburgh), and had:

1 JOHN (Sir), **4th Bt**

1 Gertrude Ella; *b* 24 May 1874; *d* 1 March 1937

2 Joyce Christabel; *b* 21 Dec 1876; *m* 8 Aug 1901 Sir Philip Wilbraham Baker-Wilbraham, 6th Bt, KBE (*qv*), and had issue

The 3rd Bt *d* 7 Sept 1919; his only son,

Sir John Kennaway, 4th Bt, JP (Devon 1913), DL (1938); *b* 7 April 1879; *educ* Harrow and Balliol Coll Oxford (MA); barrister Inner Temple 1906, Capt 4th Bn Devonshire Regt (TR), Hon Col Devonshire Regt (TA) 1939, memb Ho Laity Ch Assembly; *m* 6 Oct 1931 Mary Felicité (*d* 1991), yr dau of Rev Chancellor Stewart Gordon Ponsonby, MA, and *d* 3 Aug 1956, leaving:

1 Sir JOHN LAWRENCE KENNAWAY, **5th and present Bt**

2 +Richard Noel [Richard Kennaway Esq, 19 Macmillan Ave, Christchurch 2, New Zealand]; sr lecturer political science; *b* 17 June 1935; *educ* Eton and King's Coll Cambridge

1 *Mary Joyce [Miss Mary Kennaway, 3 Brookside, Sidmouth, Devon EX10 9UN]; *b* 18 Aug 1940

KENNEDY

Arms: Sable on a fess argent between three esquire's helmets close a fox courant proper. **Crest:** A dexter arm embowed in armour proper, holding a branch of oak, also proper. **Motto:** *Adhereo virtuti* ('I adhere to virtue'). **Creation:** Bt. (UK) 18 July 1836.

SIR MICHAEL EDWARD KENNEDY, 8TH BT, of Johnstown Kennedy, Co Dublin [Sir Michael Kennedy Bt, 48 Telston Lane, Otford, Kent TN14 5LA]; *b* 12 April 1956; *s* f 1988; *educ* Rotherfield Hall Sussex; *m* 1984 *Helen Christine Jennifer, dau of Patrick Lancelot Rae, of Halstead, Kent, and has:

1 +GEORGE MATTHEW RAE; *b* 9 Dec 1993

1 *Constance; *b* 1984

2 *Josephine; *b* 1986

Lineage: DARBY O'KENNEDY, of Ballikeirogue Castle, Co Waterford; *m* a dau of Stephen Baron, of Durrow, and had:

JOHN KENNEDY, of Johnstown Kennedy, Co Dublin; *m* Eleanor, dau of Eaton Fagan, of Feltrim, and *d* 1758, leaving:

EDWARD KENNEDY, of Johnstown Kennedy; *b* 1746; *m* 1781 Sarah, dau of John Bayly, of Gowran, Co Kilkenny, and *d* 1811, leaving, with a yr s (Charles Edward, of Pea Mount):

Sir John Kennedy, 1st Bt (UK), so *cr* 18 July 1836; *b* 1785; *m* 1st 19 March 1819 Maria (*d* 7 Nov 1828), dau of William Beauman, of Rutland Sq, Dublin; *m* 2nd Oct 1841 Elizabeth Anne, dau of John Beauman, of Hyde Park, Co Wexford, and by his 1st w had:

1 CHARLES EDWARD BAYLY (Sir), **2nd Bt**

2 William Beauman; *b* 6 April 1821; *m* 1860 Elizabeth (*d* 1906), dau of James Martin, of Ross, Co Galway, and *d* 28 June 1884, having had, with other issue:

(1) William Horace; Capt KRRC; *b* 1861; *m* 1st 1889 Ada Constance (*d* 1894), dau of Surgn Maj-Gen John Warren; *m* 2nd 1895 Sophia Thomasine Constable (*d* 1906), dau of Capt Constable Curtis (*see* CURTIS, Bt), and *d* 12 Oct 1926, having by his 1st w had:

1a John Horace; Lt Somerset LI; *b* 19 Oct 1890; *ka* 10 Jan 1915

(1) Constance; *m* 1890 Col Arthur Trevelyan Moore, CBE, RE, of Binfield Lodge, Binfield, Berks, and *d* 4 May 1946, leaving issue

(2) Marion Alice; *m* 25 July 1901 George Leycester Penrhyn, s of E H L Penrhyn, DL, of E Sheen, and *d* 28 July 1957, leaving issue

3 John; *b* 21 Sept 1823; *d* 1843

4 Francis; Capt 77th Regt; *b* 21 Nov 1826; *m* 26 Feb 1857 Elizabeth (*m* 2nd 22 June 1869 Sir George Ribton, 4th and last Bt; *see* 1901 edn), dau of Christopher Sanders, of Deer Park, and *d* 1862, having had:

(1) John Arthur; *b* Jan 1858; *m* 19 April 1881 Evelyn Maude (*d* Aug 1921), dau of H G Bromilow, of Southport, Lancs, and *d* 12 Jan 1913, leaving:

1a Francis George; *b* 1882; *m* 24 June 1914 Minnie Hilda (*d* 8 Oct 1956), dau of Edward Marker, and *d* 8 March 1923

2a Charles Harold; *b* 1884; *m* 16 June 1909 Sybil Gordon, dau of Dr Herbert R Mead, and *d* 19 March 1968, having had:

1b Christopher Terence; *b* 14 April 1910; *d* 22 March 1911

1a Olive Eileen; *b* 1889

(2) Francis; *b* 1859

(3) Graham Egerton; Surgn Capt RN; *b* 1861; *m* 1896 —, dau of Henry Quinan, and *d* 2 June 1923

(1) Elizabeth Maria; *m* 6 April 1891 Alfred Edward Darley, DL, of Carysfort, Black Rock, Co Dublin, and Kippure Ho, Kilbride, Co Wicklow, and *d* June 1954, leaving issue

5 Robert, of Baronrath, Co Kildare, JP Co Dublin; HM Lt and custos rotulorum Co Kildare; *b* 5 Aug 1828; *m* 1855 Alice Elizabeth (*d* 1 July 1910), dau of Rev Henry Gray (*see* LIMERICK, E), and *d* 7 Oct 1913, leaving:

(1) John Henry, DL Norfolk; T/Maj, Capt 97th Regt and 3rd Bn Roy W Kent Regt; *b* 5 March 1859; *m* 1st 1889 Rose (*d* 26 May 1924), widow of Col Henry Thornhill, RHA, and dau of Maj-Gen H Parke, RMA; *m* 2nd 16 Jan 1926 Amy Elizabeth (*d* 24 Oct 1960), est dau of Richard H M Orpen, of Ardtully, Co Kerry, and *d* 10 Dec 1928

(2) Edward Robert, of Bishopscourt and Baronrath, Straffan, Co Kildare; *b* 1860; *m* 1905 Beryl Doris (*d* 1988 aged 101), dau of Rev Edwin Lumsdaine, of Sydney, NSW, and *d* 22 Jan 1925, leaving:

1a John Edward; *b* 1909; *d* unm 17 Aug 1930 after a fall in a steeplechase at Longford

2a Robert; *b* 1911; *m* 3 July 1935 *Catherine Frances [Mrs Robert Kennedy, Loughananna House, Kilbehenny, Co Limerick, Ireland], yr dau of Maj Robert Gregory, of Coole Park, Co Galway, and *d* 1990, having had:

1b +Robert Edward, JP [Robert Kennedy Esq JP, Creighton Park, Dandaragan, WA, Australia]; *b* 27 Oct 1940; *educ* St Columba's Rathfarnham; *m* 3 Jan 1969 *Sandra Joan, yr dau of S A Giles, of Yericoin, W Australia, and has:

1c +Edward Robert; *b* 1980

1c *Jane Catherine; *b* 1972

2c *Megan Anne; *b* 1974

2b +Benjamin James; *b* 4 April 1942; *educ* St Columba's; *m* 1980 *Margaret Lorna, dau of George Clark, of Portsoy, Banff, and has:

1c +Graham John Clark; *b* 1982

1c *Heather Catherine; *b* 1983

2c *Julia Susan; *b* 1985

1b *Susan; *b* 20 June 1936; *m* 1970 (*divorce* 19–) W/Cdr Ian Traill Sutherland, RAAF

2b *Margaret Jane; *b* 21 May 1937; *m* 4 Jan 1964 *Capt David Andrew Robert Murray Brown, Queen's Roy Irish Hus, only s of Maj Charles Murray Brown, of Burrgoen, Cheam, Surrey, and has:

1c *Robin David; *b* 10 Oct 1964

1c *Belinda Jane; *b* 20 Dec 1966

3a +Percy William [Percy Kennedy Esq, Weston Park, Leixlip, Co Dublin]; *b* 1914; *m* 28 March 1936 *Joan, dau of Sydney Cooper, and has:

1b +William Roger; *b* 1940; *m* 22 Oct 1966 *Vivienne Gloria, dau of James O'Shea, Irish Gds, and had:

1c +John Edward; *b* 27 Aug 1967

2c Darby James; *b* 1971; *d* 1993

2b +Richard Augustus; *b* 1944

1b *Rosemary Ann Caroline [Mrs Timothy Leonard, Moortown, Drumree, Co Meath, Ireland]; *b* 1937; *m* 1st Nov 1956 Allan Ross, s of John Ross, of Irishtown, Bathfeigh, Tara, Co Meath; *m* 2nd 2 July 1969 *Timothy Noel Leonard, s of John Leonard, of Moortown, Drumree

2b *Evelyn Geraldine Margaret; *b* 1942

3b *Judith Patricia Wilhelmena; *b* 1953

4a Darby Michael (John), MC; Maj Irish Gds WW II; *b* 1919; *ka* W Europe Feb 1945

1a Doris Caroline Sabia; *m* 17 June 1929 (*divorce* 1953) Hon Henry Gerald Wellesley, 2nd s of 3rd Earl Cowley (*qv*)

2a *Maeve [Mrs George Robinson, Phepotstown, Kilcock, Co Meath, Ireland]; *m* 8 June 1932 George John Robinson (*d* 4 Nov 1958) and has:

1b *John Edward Bernard; *b* 1933

2b *George William Richard [George Robinson Esq, Stepaside, The Curragh, Co Kildare, Ireland]; *b* 1934; *m* 1964 *Susan, dau of Maj Cyril Hall, of Kilcullen, Co Kildare, and has:

1c *Emma Jane Anna; *b* 1965

2c *Lara Camilla Patricia; *b* 1969

3b *Bryan Patrick Valentine; *b* 1940

1b *Mary Rose; *b* 1936; *m* 1961 *Seamus Hayes

2b *Doris Teresa; *b* 1943; *m* 19– *T O'Hanlon

3a Clodagh Rose, OStJ; *m* 21 Oct 1937 9th Earl of Roden (*qv*) and *d* 1989, having had issue

4a Patricia; *m* 12 Dec 1938 Dermot McGillycuddy (*d* 20 Dec 1974), 2nd s of Lt-Col Ross Kinloch McGillycuddy, The McGillycuddy of the Reeks, DSO, of Beaufort, Co Kerry, and had:

1b *Dermot Patrick Donough; *b* 17 Dec 1939; *educ* Eton; *m* 1964 *Wendy, dau of George Spencer, of Winwick Manor, Rugby, and has issue

2b Desmond Edward Conor; *b* 31 Oct 1939; *d* 21 April 1955

5a *Grania Geraldine [Mrs Grania Cazenove, Synone Stud, Cashel, Co Tipperary, Ireland]; *m* 9 Jan 1947 (*divorce* 1956) Capt Edward de Lérisson Cazenove, Coldstream Gds, s of Ralph de Lérisson Cazenove, of Cottesbrooke, Northants, and has:

1b *Patrick Ralph de Lérisson; *b* 12 Oct 1947

1b *Nicola Louise; *b* 1949; *m* 1st 1976 (*divorce* 1983) Sir (Brian) Charles Pennefather Warren, 9th Bt (*qv*); *m* 2nd, as his 2nd w, *Charles St Vigor Fox (*see* ORR EWING, Bt)

(3) Francis William, CB; Adml, joined RN 1876, served Egyptian War 1882 (despatches), E Africa 1896 (wounded, despatches), Benin Expdn 1897 (despatches) and WW I (despatches twice), Russian Order St Anne 2nd Cl with swords; *b* 1862; *m* 30 Aug 1898 Amy (*d* 6 March 1960), dau of Col Henry Hills Goodeve, RA, and *d* 11 July 1939, leaving:

1a Francis Henry; Capt RN, served WWs I and II; *b* 1900; *m* 5 Nov 1931 Magdalen Francis (*d* 1976), only dau of George A FitzAdam Ormiston, of Pockeridge Park, Wilts, and *d* 1981, having had:

1b +Robert Francis [Maj Robert Kennedy, 37 Chiddingstone St, London SW6]; Maj Irish Gds; *b* 7 April 1935; *educ* Stowe and RMA Sandhurst; *m* 1976 *Sally Mary, dau of A B Antram, of Keyes Wells, Petworth, and has:

1a +Andrew Francis; *b* 1980

2b +John Ormiston [John Kennedy Esq, 20 Greville Park Rd, Ashtead, Surrey); *b* 8 April 1938; *educ* Stowe and Queens' Coll Cambridge (MA); *m* 12 July 1969 *Margaret Mary, er dau of H G N Lee, of Somerset, and has:

1c +Christopher Patrick; *b* 1971

1c *Annabel Margaret; *b* 1973

1b *Bridget Magdalen [Mrs Alexander Lindsay, Balgedie House, Easter Balgedie, by Kinross KY13 7HQ]; *b* 1 Nov 1942; *m* 1974 *Alexander Lindsay and has:

1c *Philip John; *b* 1975

1a *Judith Eileen Rose

2a *Leila Emilie; *m* 7 July 1936 *Lt-Col Cyril Gough Richards, RA, s of J Richards, and has:

1b *Michael Kennedy; *b* 2 Jan 1946

1b *Caroline Kennedy; *b* 21 Oct 1937; *m* Aug 1960 Norman Peter Herbert, s of Norman Stuart Everard Herbert, of Newcastle, and has:

1c *Andrew Mark; *b* 25 April 1963

2c *David Neil; *b* 19 Feb 1965

2b *Georgina Kennedy, SRN; *b* Dec 1940

(4) Robert Gray; Maj Lancs Fus; *b* 27 March 1867; *m* 14 Feb 1899 Jane, dau of John Nicholson, and *d* 15 Oct 1910

1 Maria; *m* 10 Aug 1846 John Tottenham Langrishe (*see* LANGRISHE, Bt) and *d* 1898

Sir JOHN *d* 15 Oct 1848; his son,

Sir Charles Edward Bayly Kennedy, 2nd Bt; *b* 13 Feb 1820; *m* 19 Oct 1854 Lady Augusta Pery (*d* 10 Nov 1865), sis of 2nd Earl of Limerick (*qv*), and *d* 4 Dec 1880, leaving:

1 **Sir John Charles Kennedy, 3rd Bt**, JP, DL; Dublin, High Sheriff Co Waterford 1884; *b* 23 March 1856; *educ* Trin Coll Cambridge (BA), Lt 3rd Bn Roy Dublin Fus; *m* 11 Nov 1879 Sydney H Maude (*d* 10 Aug 1939), dau of Sir James Macaulay Higginson, KCB, and *d* 21 March 1923, having had:

(1) **Sir John Ralph Bayly Kennedy, 4th Bt**; *b* April 1896; *educ* Uppingham and RMA Woolwich; Lt RA WW I, also WW II 1940–42; *d* unm 9 Aug 1968

(2) **Sir James Edward Kennedy, 5th Bt**; *b* 18 Jan 1898; *educ* Malvern; *d* unm 1974

(1) Augusta Mabel; *m* 29 April 1913 Lloyd Edward Hughes (*d* 1952), s of Capt George William Bulkeley Hughes, 62nd Foot, and *d* 3 May 1954, leaving issue

(2) Gladys Maude; *d* 1915

2 George Edward de Vere; Lt 5th Lancers; *b* 2 Aug 1857; *m* 8 Aug 1889 Julia Ellen Beatrice (*d* 6 Oct 1933), dau of Sir John Craven Carden, 4th Bt (*qv*), and *d* 24 Nov 1922, leaving, with two daus (*d* young):

(1) Ronald Bayly Craven; Lt 6th Dublin Fus, ADC Personal Staff; *b* 21 Sept 1895; *d* 10 Aug 1917 of wounds recd in action

(2) **Sir Derrick Edward De Vere Kennedy, 6th Bt**; Maj Roy Ulster Rifles WW II, tea-planter Ceylon, hotelier Ireland 1947–66; *b* 5 June 1904; *educ* Clifton and Dublin U; *m* 1st 10 April 1926 (*divorce* 1945) Phyllis Victoria Levine, dau of Gordon Fowler, of Springhurst, Berks; *m* 2nd 2 June 1945 Barbara Mary Worthing (*d* 1959), dau of William Shepherd, of Chester, and by his 1st w had:

1a GEORGE RONALD DERRICK (Sir), **7th Bt**

2a Mark Gordon; *b* 3 Feb 1932; *educ* Clifton; *d* 1997

1a *Julia Maureen Patricia [Mrs George Miller, Middle Chantry, Carter's Lane, Wickham Bishops, Essex CM8 3LF]; *b* 7 Feb 1934; *m* 14 Jan 1961 *George Hector Miller, s of Leslie Davison Miller, of Madras, India, and has:

1b *Rupert Leslie Derrick; *b* 15 July 1965; *m* 1986 *Yvette Marie Gabrielle Brewster and has:

1c *Sian Louise Georgina; *b* 1988

2c *Sophie Jane Yasmin; *b* 1990

3c *Natasha Leslie; *b* 1993

1b *Katrina Phyllis Evelyn; *b* 2 Nov 1962; *m* 1993 *Ian Roy Cooke

2b *Rachel Susan; *b* 5 Feb 1964; *m* 1992 *Stuart Michael Banning and has:

1c *Joshua Charles; *b* 14 Sept 1995

3b *Grania Sarah; *b* 26 April 1968

Sir DERRICK *d* 27 June 1976; his est s,

Sir George Ronald Derrick Kennedy, 7th Bt, OBE (1975); *b* 19 Nov 1927; *educ* Clifton; commissioned RA 1947, Staff Coll 1959, staff duties Aden 1960–63, MOD and HQ BAOR 1966–71, Defence Attaché Mexico City, Havana and El Salvador 1971–74, ret as Lt-Col 1979, administrator World Pheasant Assoc; *m* 12 Nov 1949 *Noelle Mona [Noelle Lady Kennedy, Harraton Sq, Church Lane, Exning, Suffolk CB8 7HF], dau of Charles Henry Green, and *d* 1988, leaving:

1 Sir MICHAEL EDWARD KENNEDY, **8th and present Bt**

1 *Carolyn Phyllis; *b* 20 May 1950; *m* 1979 *Jan Gerard Willemszoon Blaauw, of Hong Kong, and has:

(1) *Keir Alexander Kennedy; *b* 1982

(2) *Patrick Jan Kennedy (twin); *b* 1982

KENNEDY OF THE SHAWS

Creation: B. (LP, UK) 1997.

THE BARONESS KENNEDY OF THE SHAWS, of Cathcart, City of Glasgow (Helena Ann Kennedy, QC (1991)) [The Rt Hon The Baroness Kennedy of the Shaws QC, 11 Doughty St, London WC1N 2PG]; *b* 12 May 1950; *educ* Holyrood Secondary Sch Glasgow and Cncl Legal Educn; barrister Gray's Inn 1972, memb: Bar Cncl 1990–93, Ctee Assoc Women Barristers 1991–, Nat Bd Women's Legal Def Fund 1989–91, Cncl Howard League Penal Reform 1989– (Chm Commn on violence in penal institutions for children 1994–), CIBA Commn into Child Sexual Abuse 1981–83, Bd *City Limits* Magazine 1982–84, Exec Ctee NCCL 1983–85, Bd Minority Access to Legal Profession Project South Bank Poly 1984–85, Bd Hampstead Theatre 1989–, Bd *New Statesman* 1990–, Bd *Counsel* Magazine 1990–; Chm: Haldane Soc 1983–86 (V-Pres 1986–), Charter '88 1992–, Standing Ctee for Youth Justice NACRO 1993–, London Internat Festival of Theatre 1993; Leader Inquiry into aspects of Atomic Weapons Establishment Aldermaston; Tstee Anti-Racist Alliance Educn Tst; Commr: BAFTA Inquiry into Future of BBC 1990, Hamlyn Nat Commn on Educ 1991–; Advsr Mannheim Inst Criminology LSE 1992–; broadcaster; Patron: Civil Liberties Tst 1991–, Victims Helpline, Clean Break Theatre Co, Fleet Counselling, Prisoners of Conscience, S Essex Rape and Incest Crisis Centre, Bishops Simeon Tst; Chllr Oxford Brookes U 1994–; Visiting Lecturer Criminal Law BPMF 1991–; FRSA; Hon LLD: Strathclyde 1992, Teesside 1993, Keele 1994, Lancaster 1994; author: *The Bar on Trial* (jt author, 1978), *Child Abuse within the Family* (jt author, 1984), *Balancing Acts* (jt author, 1989), *Eve was Framed* (1992); has a s by (Roger) Iain Mitchell; *m* 1986 *Dr Iain Louis Hutchinson and by him has a s and dau

Lineage: JOSHUA PATRICK KENNEDY; *m* Mary Veronica Jones and has:

HELENA ANN, *cr* a **Baroness**

KENNET

Arms: Per fess sable and argent, in chief two lions rampant guardant and in base an anchor with cable, all counterchanged. **Crest:** A demi-unicorn couped ermine, maned, armed and hoofed or, gorged with a naval crown azure and supporting an anchor erect sable. **Motto:** *In colle domus* ('A house on a hill'). **Creation:** B. (UK) 15 July 1935.

THE 2ND BARON KENNET, of The Dene, Co Wilts (Wayland Hilton Young) [The Rt Hon The Lord Kennet, The Lacket, Lockeridge, Wilts SN8 4EQ]; *b* 2 Aug 1923; *s f* 11 July 1960; *educ* Stowe, Trin Coll Cambridge (BA 1946, MA 1961) and U of Perugia; Sub-Lt RNVR WW II 1942–45, FO 1946–47 and 1949–51, memb Br delegn assemblies of WEU and Cncl Europe 1962–65, chm UK Ctee Internat Coopn Year 1965, Parly Sec Min Housing and Local Govt 1966–70, Oppn Spokesman For Affrs and Sci Policy 1971–74, chm advsy ctee Oil Pollution of Sea 1970–74, chm CPRE 1971–80 and Internat Parly Confs Environment 1971–80, dir European Commn's Study 'Europe Plus Thirty' 1974–76, MEP 1978–79, chm Architecture Club 1983–94, v-pres Parly and Scientific Ctee 1989–, SDP Ch Whip Ho Lds 1981–83 and Spokesman For Affrs and Def 1981–90, author (as Wayland Young): *The Italian Left* (1949), *The Deadweight* (novel, 1952), *Now or Never* (novel, 1953), *Old London Churches* (with Elizabeth Young, 1956), *The Montesi Scandal* (1957), *Still Alive Tomorrow* (novel, 1958), *Strategy for Survival* (1959), *The Profumo Affair* (1963), *Eros Denied* (1965), *Thirty-Four Articles* (1965), *Existing Mechanism of Arms Control* (ed, 1965); (as Wayland Kennet) *Preservation* (1972), *The Futures of Europe* (1976), *The Rebirth of Britain* (1982), *London's Churches* (with Elizabeth Young, 1986), *Northern Lazio* (1990), Hon FRIBA; *m* 24 Jan 1948 *Elizabeth, dau of Capt Bryan Fullerton Adams, DSO, RN, and has:

1 +(WILLIAM ALDUS) THOBY [The Hon Thoby Young, 41A Loftus Rd, London W12 7EH]; *b* 24 May 1957; *educ* Marlborough, Dartington Hall and Sussex U; worked for SDP 1980–83, md and chm Offshore Productions Ltd 1984–88, proprietor The Fresh Food Co 1989; *m* 1987 *Hon Josephine ('Josa') Mary Keyes, yr dau of 2nd Baron Keyes (*qv*), and has:

(1) +Archibald Wayland Keyes; *b* 7 June 1992
(1) *Maud Elizabeth Aurora; *b* 1989

1 *Easter Donatella; *b* 2 April 1949; *educ* Keele U; *m* 1981 *Frank Joffre Russell and has:

(1) *Louis Inigo; *b* 1983
(2) *Theo Joffre; *b* 1986
(1) *Alice Ella; *b* 1979

2 *Emily Tacita; *b* 13 March 1951; *educ* Chelsea Sch of Arts and St Martin Sch of Art; has:

(1) *Arthur William Phoenix Young JEFFES; *b* 1978

3 *Mopsa Mary; *b* 9 May 1953; *educ* Holland Pk Sch; *m* Feb 1982 *Richard Douglas English, 4th child of Maj Douglas English, of Bedford, and has:

(1) *Joseph Edward; *b* 1987
(2) *Thomas Eliot; *b* 1991
(1) *Lilian Mary; *b* 1989

4 *(Audrey) Louisa; *b* 25 March 1959; *educ* Trinity Coll Cambridge; has:

(1) *Isabel Adomakoh YOUNG; *b* 1993

5 *(Alice Matelda) Zoe; *b* 24 Jan 1969; *educ* Sussex U

Lineage: Sir GEORGE YOUNG, 3rd Bt, of Formosa Place, Berks (*qv*), had a yst s:

EDWARD HILTON YOUNG, **1st Baron Kennet**, of the Dene, Co Wilts (UK), so *cr* 15 July 1935, GBE (1927), DSO (1919), DSC (1917), PC (21 Nov 1922); *b* 26 March 1879; *educ* Eton and Trin Coll Cambridge (BA 1900, MA 1907); barrister Inner Temple 1904, assist ed *Economist* 1909–10, city ed *Morning Post* 1910–14, served RNVR WW I (severely wounded, despatches thrice, Lt-Cdr 1918), MP (Lib) Norwich 1915–23 and 1924–29 and Sevenoaks 1939–35, PPS to Pres Bd Educn 1919–21, Fin Sec Treasury 1921–23; chm Roy Commn Indian Currency and Finance 1925 and E African Closer Union 1928, Missions to Poland 1924 and Iraq 1925 and 1930, Sec Dept Overseas Trade 1931 and Min Health 1931–35, Br Delegate Hague Conf 1922 and League Nations Assembly 1926, 1927, 1928 and 1932, chm: Union Discount and Denny, Mott & Dickson, dir Equity and Law Life Assur, Hon Fell UCL 1932, Hon DCL Durham 1934, Order Kara George Serbia 4th Cl and Obilich Medal 1915, Croix de Guerre, Order Rafidain 1st Cl Iraq, Grand Cordon Order Polonia Restituta, author: *Foreign Companies and other Corporations* (1912), *The System of National Finance* (1915), *A Muse at Sea* (1919), *By Sea and Land* (1920) and *A Bird in the Bush* (1936); *m* 3 March 1922 Kathleen, Lady Scott (granted rank of KCB's widow following her 1st husb's death Antarctica 1912; Priv Sec to Perm Sec Min Pensions 1916, sculptress; *d* 25 July 1947), dau of Rev Canon Lloyd Stewart Bruce (*see* BRUCE, Bt, of Downhill) and widow of the explorer Capt Robert Falcon Scott, CVO, RN, and *d* 11 July 1960, leaving:

WAYLAND HILTON YOUNG, **2nd and present Baron Kennet**

KENSINGTON

Arms: Quarterly, 1st and 4th, erm. a lion rampant sa. (for EDWARDES); 2nd and 3rd, gu. a chevron between three crosses botonnée or. **Crest:** Upon a mount vert a wyvern, wings expanded arg. **Supporters:** Two reindeer ppr., attired and unguled or. **Motto:** *Garde la foi* ('Keep the faith'). **Creations:** B. (I) 28 July 1776, B. (UK) 23 March 1886.

THE 8TH BARON KENSINGTON and **Baron Kensington of Kensington**, Co Middlesex (Hugh Ivor Edwardes) [The Rt Hon The Lord Kensington, Friar Tuck, PO Box 549, Mooi River, 3300 Natal, S Africa]; *b* 24 Nov 1933; *s unc* 1981; *educ* Eton; *m* 18 March 1961 *Juliet Elizabeth Massy, dau of Alexander Massy Anderson, of Alexandria, Egypt, and has:

1 +WILLIAM OWEN ALEXANDER; *b* 21 July 1964; *educ* Michaelhouse Sch Natal; *m* 1991 *Marie Hélène Anne Véronique, est dau of Jean-Alain Lalouette, of Mauritius, and has:

(1) +William Francis Ivor; *b* 23 March 1993
(1) *Nadia Marie Hilda Massy; *b* 9 Sept 1997

2 +Hugh Rupert; *b* 25 Jan 1967; *educ* Michaelhouse; *m* 1995 *Susan Dawn, yst dau of John Carlisle Nowell, of Munster, Natal

1 *Amanda Louise Massy; *b* 22 May 1962; *m* 1984 *Anthony Michael Greene, est s of Michael Victor Greene, of Natal, and has:

(1) *James Stuart; *b* 1985

(1) *Stephanie Louise; *b* 1987

(2) *Rachel Delia; *b* 1988

Lineage: TUDUR TREFOR; *b c* 900; ruled over a territory comprising modern Oswestry, Whittington and Nanheudwy, on the Salop-Powys borders; had:

DINGAD Ap TUDUR TREFOR; *b c* 935?; had:

RHIWALLON Ap DINGAD; *b c* 965?; had:

CYNWRIG Ap RHIWALLON; *b c* 1000?; had:

NYNNIO Ap CYNWRIG; had:

IEUAF Ap NYNNIO; had:

IORWERTH Ab IEUAF; had:

IORWERTH FYCHAN Ab IORWERTH; had:

CYNWRIG Ab IORWERTH FYCHAN; had:

HYWEL Ap CYNWRIG; had:

GRIFFRI Ap HYWEL; had:

WILLIAM Ap GRIFFRI; had:

MAREDUDD Ap WILLIAM Ap GRIFFRI; had:

JOHN Ap MAREDUDD; had:

EDWARD Ap JOHN; *m* Catherine, dau of Ieuan ap William, of Mold, Flintshire, and had, with two er sons (John; Richard, Chllr St David's, *d* 1599):

THOMAS EDWARD(E)S; living at St David's 1579, in which year he took out a lease on the Manor of Trefgarn, St Dogwells, Pembs; *m* 1st Beatrix Lewis and had two sons (Nicholas; Richard); *m* 2nd Sage, dau of Thomas Tucker, of Sealyham, St Dogwells, and by her had, with a yr s (John, *d* by 1670):

OWEN EDWARD(E)S; leased a manor in Mathry 1626; *m* Elliw, dau of Morgan Voel, of Haverfordwest, by Elizabeth (dau of Francis Laugharne, of St Brides) and had, with two yr sons (Thomas, of Somerhill, had a dau, Elliw; Francis):

JOHN EDWARD(E)S, of Trefgarn; *m* —, dau of Thomas Byrt, of Llwyndyrus, Llandygwydd, Cards, by Maud (dau of William Walter, of Roche Castle, Pembs), and had, with two yr sons (John, *m* his cousin Elliw, dau of Thomas Edward(e)s (*see* above) and *dsp*, probably by 1670; Francis, clerk (*i.e.*, cleric), of St Dogwells, *d* by 1697):

OWEN EDWARD(S); *m* Damaris, sis of Sir Herbert Perrot, and had, with an est s (John, *m* 1685 — and *d* 1738, leaving issue), a yst one (Owen, *d* by 1743) and a dau (Martha):

FRANCIS EDWARDES, of Johnston, Pembs; MP Haverfordwest 1722–25; *m* Lady Elizabeth Rich (who had fallen on hard times and gone to live in Wales but when she *d* 14 May 1725 was, as the next of kin to the 7th Earl of Warwick, who *d* intestate, the means of her son inheriting what came to be very valuable property in Kensington), only dau of 5th Earl of Warwick (*see* WARWICK, BROOKE and, E) of the 1618 *cr*, one of whose subsidiary titles was the Barony of Kensington (*cr* 1623), and *d* between 15 Oct and 16 Dec 1725, having had a 3rd but only surv s:

WILLIAM EDWARDES, **1st Baron Kensington** (I), so *cr* 28 July 1776; *b c* 1711; MP (Court Party) Haverfordwest 1747–84 and 1786–1801; *m* 10 June 1762 Elizabeth (*d* 18 Nov 1814), yst dau and coheiress of William Warren, of Longridge, Pembs, and *d* 13 Dec 1801, leaving an only s:

WILLIAM EDWARDES, **2nd Baron Kensington**; *b* 24 April 1777; MP (Whig) Haverfordwest 1802–18, a Ld Admlty 1806–07; *m* 2 Dec 1797 Dorothy Patricia (*d* 29 Dec 1843), dau of Richard Thomas, and had, with four daus:

1 Edward Henry; *b* 5 Nov 1798; *d* unm 16 Aug 1829

2 WILLIAM, **3rd Baron**

3 George Warren; Govr Labuan; *b* 28 May 1802; *d* unm 21 Feb 1879

4 Richard; Chargé d'Affaires and Consul-Gen Venezuela, Min Plen Argentina; *b* 25 Oct 1807; *m* 6 Oct 1864 Rosa (*d* 6 May 1894), widow of Hugh William Burgess, of Bathwick Hill, Somerset, and dau of Thomas Cadell, and *d* 23 March 1866, leaving:

(1) Katherine; *d* 12 June 1932

5 Charles Robert; *b* 7 Aug 1813; *d* unm 20 Sept 1881

6 Thomas (Rev); MA Cantab, Rector Belshford, Lincs; *b* 24 Oct 1819; *m* 30 Nov 1863 Hon Alice Eleanora (*d* 19 Oct 1924), est dau of 2nd Baron Brougham and Vaux (*qv*), and *d* 3 Dec 1896, leaving:

(1) George (Rev); BA Cantab; Vicar St John Baptist Liverpool; *b* 3 Nov 1869; *m* 24 Jan 1893 Ethel Mary (*d* 1 Aug 1900), widow of Rev Philip Charles Bicknell and dau of Frederick Lassetter, and *d* 25 Feb 1919, leaving:

1a Thomas; 2nd Lt 2nd/5th York and Lancaster Regt; *b* 17 Feb 1897; *ka* 12 April 1918

1a Mary; *b* 25 Oct 1893; *d* unm 15 Nov 1929

2a Elisabeth; WW II in CD, commendation for valour 1944; *b* 6 Dec 1895

3a Anne; *b* 1 Aug 1900; *m* 15 Jan 1930 Claude Edward New, OBE (*d* 6 Jan 1968), only s of Edward Vorley New, of Northwood, and had:

1b *Thomas Stephen (Rev); *b* 30 Sept 1930; *educ* Lancing and King's Coll Cambridge (BA 1952, MA 1955); *m* 27 Dec 1956 *Joan Mary, BMUS, FTCL, dau of James Alfred Harding, and has:

1c *Katharine Elisabeth; *b* 28 March 1959

2c *Mary Frances; *b* 22 June 1962

2b *Benedict Edward; *b* 8 Feb 1936

(2) Edward Henry, OBE (1946), JP Lancs; AMIEE, AMInstT, chm and md Lancashire Utd Tport and Power Co; *b* 18 Feb 1875; *m* 6 June 1907 Eleanor Matilda (*d* 15 Dec 1925), dau of Rev William Nuttall, Vicar Atherton, and *d* 5 Nov 1955, having had:

1a William; Maj RASC WW II (despatches); *b* 16 April 1908; *m* 1st 4 Feb 1937 (*divorce* 1943) Dorothy Robertshaw, only dau of Aaron Wedgwood, of Worsley, Lancs; *m* 2nd 21 July 1943 *Joan [Mrs William Edwardes, Spinneys, Church St, Eccleshall, Staffs ST21 6BY], only dau of Ernest Topping, of Leigh, Lancs, and *d* 1983, having by her had:

1b +David William [David Edwardes Esq, 41 Redwood Ave, Stone, Staffs]; *b* 5 July 1944; *m* 1972 *Diana June yst dau of William Eden Morton, of London, and has:

1c *Rebecca Evelyn; *b* 1983

2c *Gemma Rachael; *b* 1985

2a Edward (Rev); Vicar Melplash, Rector Mapperton, Hon CF; *b* 6 Dec 1912; *educ* Cambridge (BA 1935, MA 1959); *m* 9 April 1940 Norah (*d* 1991), only dau of John Wilberforce Watson, of Corbridge, Newcastle-on-Tyne, and *d* 1973, having had:

1b +Antony [Antony Edwardes Esq, 1 Priory Cl, Newport Pagnell, Bucks MK16 9AQ]; *b* 1 Jan 1942; *educ* Newcastle Cathedral Choir Sch

2b +Nigel Kim [Nigel Edwardes Esq, Byways, St Mary's Lane, Yawl, Uplyme, Lyme Regis, Dorset DT7 3XH]; *b* 17 July 1948; *educ* Newcastle Cathedral Choir Sch and Hardy's Sch Dorchester; *m* 8 April 1972 *Marjorie Kay, est dau of S Barnes, of Pitt Farm, Whitchurch Canonicorum, Dorset, and has:

1c +Guy Kristian; *b* 1974

3a John; TD, AMIEE, AMIBAE, Capt RA (TA), Maj REME; *b* 25 Sept 1914; *educ* Manchester U (BSc 1939); *d* 1981

4a Thomas; *b* 13 May 1918; *d* 20 March 1922

1a *Barbara; *b* 12 Nov 1909 [Mrs Auguste Gernaey, Oakwood House, Birkacre, Chorley, Lancs]; *m* 28 June 1939 *Auguste Henri Gernaey, s of Auguste Gernaey, of Woodford Green, Essex, and has:

1b *Susan Leonie; *b* 1940

2b *Joanna; *b* 1942

3b *Caroline; *b* 1945

2a *Eleanora; *b* 25 June 1911; *m* 1 Oct 1942 Joseph Hugh Stott Gardner (*d* 1989), s of Joseph Gardner, of Worsley, Lancs, and has:

1b *Hugh Martin; *b* 1951

1b *Sarah; *b* 1944

(1) Mary; *b* 15 Sept 1864; *m* 9 June 1890 Rev Richard Henry Talbot (*d* 1 Sept 1926), Rector Penmaen, Glam

(2) Evelyn; *b* 17 June 1866; *d* unm 2 Aug 1940

(3) Mabel; *b* 7 Nov 1867; *d* unm 1 July 1948

(4) Edith; *b* 6 Nov 1871; *d* unm 8 July 1950

The 2nd BARON *d* 10 Aug 1852; his est surv son,

WILLIAM EDWARDES, **3rd Baron Kensington**; Capt RN, Ld Lt Pembs 1861–72; *b* 3 Feb 1801; *m* 12 Oct 1933 Laura Jane (*d* 26 Feb 1846), 4th dau of Cuthbert Ellison, JP, DL, of Hebburn, Co Durham, and had, with other issue:

1 WILLIAM, **4th Baron**

2 Cuthbert Ellison; Lt-Col Rifle Bde, served Indian Mutiny 1857–58; *b* 16 Jan 1838; *m* 14 June 1882 Lady Blanche Henrietta Maria Butler (*d* 6 Feb 1914), dau of 2nd Marquess of Ormonde (*see* MOUNTGARRET, V), and *d* 8 Sept 1911, leaving:

(1) Hubert William John; *b* 21 June 1883; *d* unm 30 Dec 1944

(2) Arthur Henry Francis; Inspr-Gen Chinese Maritime Customs 1927–29; *b* 8 Feb 1885; *m* 3 July 1913 (Sybil Frances Christina) Lilah (*d* 11 July 1970), 2nd dau of Rev Lord Theobald Butler (*see* MOUNTGARRET, V), and *d* 22 July 1951

(3) Cuthbert Theobald; *b* 9 April 1887; *d* unm 28 Aug 1967

(4) Richard; Capt Rifle Bde WW I (despatches), Hon Co Sec Hants Forces Help Soc and Ld Roberts Workshops; *b* 6 May 1894; *m* 21 June 1929 Ada Mary (*d* 1979), 2nd dau of William R MacGeorge, of Glasgow, and *d* April 1967, leaving:

1a Joan Margaret [Mrs John Clarke, The Roos, Church St, Whitchurch, Hants RG28 7AD]; *b* 23 July 1932; *m* 17 May 1958 John Spencer Clarke (*d* 1993), s of Col J T P Clarke, and has:

1b *Charles Richard Spencer; *b* 26 Dec 1960; *m* 1986 *Jane Caroline Sargeant

2b *James Alured; *b* 30 Sept 1964; *m* 1997 *Bridget Tennant

1b *Sally Aletta; *b* 11 Sept 1959; *m* 1982 *Clive Julian Spencer

2b *Fiona Jane; *b* 1 June 1963

(5) Owen; Lt KRRC WW I; *b* 6 May 1894; *ka* 1916

3 Henry George; Sec Legation Buenos Aires 1885, Washington 1887, Sec Embassy Rome 1892; *b* 15 Dec 1844; *m* 4 July 1878 Cecilia Douglas (*d* 16 Feb 1924), only child of Charles John Bayley, CB, and *d* 30 Dec 1896, leaving:

(1) Cecil Lawrence Herbert Auriol; *b* 6 Sept 1881; *d* unm 7 March 1905

(1) Sylvia Gay; Maid-of-Honour to TM QUEEN VICTORIA 1897–1901 and QUEEN ALEXANDRA 1901–10; *b* 16 Feb 1880; *m* 2 July 1910 Maj-Gen Lord Edward Gleichen, KCVO, CB, CMG, DSO (*see* HERTFORD, M), and *d* 27 Oct 1942

1 Laura Jane; *b* 21 Jan 1837; *m* 24 Sept 1885 Maj-Gen Raymond Herbert White, Scots Gds (*dsp* 13 July 1894), and *d* 18 April 1909

2 Louisa Jane; *b* 4 Oct 1839; *m* 23 Sept 1880 Capt William Henry Newenham (*d* 21 July 1898), 63rd Regt, and *d* 24 May 1929

3 Caroline; *b* 14 Feb 1843; *m* 10 Nov 1897 Rev J R Vincent, Rector Shenley Bucks, and *d* 10 Dec 1920

The 3rd BARON *d* 1 Jan 1872; his est son,

WILLIAM EDWARDES, **4th Baron Kensington**, PC (1880); *b* 11 May 1835; *educ* Eton; Lt-Col Coldstream Gds 1867–70, MP (Lib) Haverfordwest 1868–85, Ld Lt and custos rotulorum Pembs 1872–96, Groom-in-Waiting to HM QUEEN VICTORIA 1873–74, Comptroller Household 1880–85, Ld-in-Waiting Feb-July 1886, Capt Yeomen Gd, *cr* 23 March 1886 BARON KENSINGTON OF KENSINGTON, Co Middlesex (UK); *m* 19 Sept 1867 Grace Elizabeth (*d* 19 Jan 1910), est dau of Robert Johnstone-Douglas (*see* QUEENSBERRY, M), and *d* 7 Oct 1896, having had:

1 WILLIAM EDWARDES, **5th Baron Kensington**, JP, DL Pembs; *b* 25 July 1868; Capt 2nd Life Gds; *d* unm of wounds recd in action Boer War 24 June 1900

2 HUGH, **6th Baron**

3 Cecil; 9th Scottish Horse Yeo, TF, Actg Capt Tank Corps; *b* 31 May 1876; *m* 3 Sept 1901 Marie Louise Lucienne Juliette (*m* 3rd 12 Nov 1919 Maj Nicholas Rothesay Stuart-Wortley, MC (*see* WHARNCLIFFE, E), and *d* 13 Nov 1948), widow of James Buxton, of Tamworth, Staffs, and Vancouver, and dau of François Xavier Martin, of Vancouver, and was *ka* Dec 1917, leaving:

(1) Marie Bride; *b* 8 July 1902

(2) Lumena Sibyl Grace; *b* 25 Sept 1903; *d* unm 8 Nov 1944

4 George Henry, MC; Maj Pembroke RGA WW I; *b* 19 May 1877; *m* 28 April 1903 Olive (*d* 27 June 1968 aged 89), 2nd dau of Charles Wyndham Rudolph Kerr (*see* LOTHIAN, M), and *d* 25 Nov 1930, leaving:

(1) George Llewellyn; *b* 15 March 1906

(2) Hugh Francis; *b* 12 March 1908; *m* 14 May 1957 Amelia Anne, er dau of C H Barker, of Barnsley, Yorks

(1) Olive Isobel; *b* 30 Dec 1904

(2) Gwenllian Violet; *b* 30 March 1912; *m* 29 Dec 1932 R-Adml Peter Douglas Herbert Raymond Pelly, CB, DSO (*see* PELLY, Bt), and *d* 1987, leaving issue

1 Gwendolen; *b* 7 July 1869; *m* 27 April 1899 Capt William Augustus Stirling-Home-Drummond-Moray of Abercairny (*d* 6 March 1939) and *d* 6 Sept 1940, leaving issue

2 Sybil Laura; *b* 11 Jan 1871; *m* 25 Jan 1904 William Edward De Winton (*d* 30 Aug 1922), of Graftonbury, and *d* 11 Feb 1955, leaving issue

3 Grace Louisa; *b* 11 March 1872; *m* 12 April 1902 John Henry Hervey Vincent Lane, DL (*d* 22 Feb 1917), of King's Bromley, and *d* 7 April 1957, leaving issue

4 Winifred; *b* 27 Jan 1875; *m* 27 Jan 1909 Capt Walter Pulteney Koe, RN (*d* 1954), s of Ralphe Pemberton Koe, Registrar High Ct Chancery, and *d* 11 June 1962, leaving issue

5 Isobel Caroline; *b* 14 Feb 1879; *m* 17 Aug 1904 Maj Frederick Whitfield Barrett, 15th/19th King's Hus (*d* c 1950), of Wroughton Hall, Wroughton, Wilts, yst s of William Thomas Barrett, of Silverspring Ho, Co Cork, and *d* 7 Oct 1934, leaving issue

The 5th BARON's bro,

HUGH EDWARDES, **6th Baron Kensington**, CMG (1919), DSO (1900), TD, JP, DL Pembs; *b* 3 Sept 1873; Hon Col Pembroke RGA, Lt 15th Hus, Boer War 1900–01 (despatches) and WW I cmdg Welsh Horse Yeo (despatches twice); *m* 1 July 1903 Mabel Carlisle (*d* 25 March 1934), yr dau of George Pilkington, JP, of Stoneleigh, Woolton, Lancs, and *d* 4 March 1938, having had:

1 WILLIAM EDWARDES, **7th Baron Kensington**; *b* 15 May 1904; *educ* Eton and RMC Sandhurst; Lt-Col Guides Cav IA, Lt 15th King's Roy Hus, ADC to Govr Punjab 1933–35, served WW II (despatches); *d* unm 1981

2 Hugh Owen, Capt RHA (TA); *b* 2 Oct 1905; *m* 19 Oct 1932 Angela Dorothea (*m* 3rd 10 Sept 1951 Lt-Cdr John Hamilton of Rozelle, RN, er s of Col Claud Lorn Campbell Hamilton, CMG, DSO, DL, JP, of Rozelle, Ayrshire and *d* 23 Aug 1996), widow of George Benson, 15th/19th Hus, and dau of Lt-Col Eustace Shearman, 10th Hus, and *d* 29 June 1937 leaving:

(1) HUGH IVOR EDWARDES, **8th and present Baron Kensington**

(1) *Meriel Davina [The Hon Mrs Long, Manor Cottage, Puncknowle, Dorchester DT2 9BP]; *b* 19 April 1935; granted rank of baron's dau 1982; *m* Jan 1972 *David Andrew Long and has:

1a *James Philip; *b* Dec 1972

2a *Harry Simon; *b* 1976

3 David, DSC (1944); *b* 19 July 1907; *educ* Eton; Cdr RN WW II; *m* 22 July 1939 *Elizabeth [The Hon Mrs David Edwardes, Carpenter's Yard, Compton Pauncefoot, Somerset], yst dau of Robert Alexander Longman Broadley, of Suddon Farm, Wincanton, Somerset, and *d* 31 Jan 1983, leaving:

(1) *Susan [Mrs Hugh Sandars, Twin Pillars Cottage, Micheldever, Hants SO21 3DB]; *b* 7 April 1945; *m* 27 Jan 1967 *Capt Hugh Michael Sandars, QO Hus, er s of Brig Francis Wyld Sandars, DSO, and has:

1a *Andrew George; *b* 22 Oct 1969

1a *Claire Catherine; *b* 9 July 1972

(2) *Mary Ann [Mrs Hugh Pye, Tuxwell Farm, Spaxton, Somerset TA5 1DF]; *b* 8 Feb 1947; *m* 8 June 1968 *Brig Hugh William Kellow Pye, 9th/12th Roy Lancers, only s of Brig Randall Thomas Kellow Pye, DSO, OBE, and has:

1a *Robert Alec Kellow; *b* 1970

1a *Victoria Louise; *b* 1973

(3) *Louisa Jane; *b* 11 Aug 1950; *m* 1979 (*divorce* 1994) Christopher L P Weedon and has:

1a *George David Martin; *b* 1985

2a *Simon Edward Peter; *b* 1987

4 Michael George, MBE (1944); Lt-Col Rifle Bde WW II, memb Gentlemen-at-Arms 1959, chm Chloride 1974–, CStJ (1976); *b* 29 July 1910; *educ* Eton and RMC Sandhurst; *m* 22 Aug 1946 Sylvia Inez Pakenham, formerly w of Lt-Col Alfred Joseph Thoburn McGaw, Rifle Bde, and dau of Col Hope Johnston, CB, and *d* 19–

KENSWOOD

Arms: Azure an argosy in full sail, pennons flying or, a chief argent, thereon a lion passant gules holding in the dexter forepaw a thunderbolt proper. **Crest:** Between two wings or a sprig of oak fructed proper. **Supporters:** Dexter, A figure representing St Cecilia, habited argent, cloaked azure, with organ pipes proper in her exterior hand; sinister, a figure representing St Gregory the Great, habited argent, cloaked gules, holding with his exterior arm a papal staff or and holding in the hand a book proper bound sable.
Motto: *Da mihi sapientiam* ('Give me wisdom').
Creation: B. (UK) 27 June 1951.

THE 2ND BARON KENSWOOD, of St Marylebone, Co London (John Michael Whitfield) [The Rt Hon The Lord Kenswood, Domaine de la Forêt, 31340 Villemur-sur-Tarn, France]; *b* 6 April 1930; *s* f 1963; *educ* Trin Coll Sch Port Hope Ontario, Harrow, Grenoble U and Emmanuel Coll Cambridge (BA 1952); *m* 16 June 1951 *Deirdre Anna Louise, dau of Colin Malcolm Methven, of Errol, Perthshire, and has:

1 +MICHAEL CHRISTOPHER; *b* 3 July 1955

2 +Anthony John; *b* 13 May 1957

3 +Steven James; *b* 9 Aug 1958

4 +Benjamin Matthew; *b* 15 June 1961

1 *Anna Louise; *b* 6 June 1964

Lineage: JOHN HENRY CHRISTOPHER WHITFIELD, of London; *b* 9 Sept 1859; *m* 23 March 1885 Louisa (*d* 20 Nov 1938), dau of Michael Farren, of Copenhagen, and *d* 24 March 1924, leaving:

1 Henry Michael; *b* 3 Feb 1886; *educ* London U (BA); *m* 11 July 1919 Marion, dau of William Sales Gratwick, of Sussex, and *dsp* 13 April 1969

2 ERNEST ALBERT WHITFIELD, **1st Baron Kenswood**, of St Marylebone, Co London (UK), so *cr* 27 June 1951; *b* 15 Sept 1887; *educ* U Coll Sch London, Vienna U (Austrian State DipMus 1912) and London U (BSc Econ 1926, PhD 1928); professional violinist Vienna 1909–14, London 1914 on, toured extensively, ret from concert platform 1935, memb Cncl Nat Inst for Blind 1928–39 (jt hon treasurer 1931–39), v-chm Jt Research Ctee on Educn of Blind 1932–36, memb Educn Ctee LCC 1934–39, research worker New York Inst for Blind 1941–42, supervisor for Musical Research Canadian Nat Inst for Blind and lecturer music Port Hope Ontario 1942–46, Govr BBC 1946–50, Pres Nat Fedn Blind 1951–54, memb management ctee Schs for Deaf and Blind, Delegate World Conf Blind 1931, chm Camberwell Hosps Gp 1951–54, V-Pres Pembs Community Cncl; *m* 1st 13 Dec 1920 Sophie Madeline (*d* 23 Aug 1961), only child of Ernest Walters Howard, of London, and Hill Head, Hants; *m* 2nd 26 July 1962 Catherine (*d* 1992), dau of Frank Thruxton and widow of Charles Chilver-Stainer, and *d* 21 April 1963, leaving by his 1st w:

(1) JOHN MICHAEL HOWARD WHITFIELD, **2nd and present Baron Kenswood**

(1) *Ann Sophia Madeline; *b* 14 Feb 1928; *m* 1st 4 Aug 1948 Richard Bethune Buzzard (*see* BUZZARD, Bt); *m* 2nd 19– — Cabot, of USA, and has by her 1st husb:

1a *Nicholas John; *b* 1952

1a *Jacqueline Frances; *b* 1950

2a *Jennifer Anne; *b* 1954

3a *Angela Caroline; *b* 1956

KENYON

Arms: Quarterly, 1st and 4th, sable a chevron engrailed or, between three crosses flory argent (for KENYON); 2nd and 3rd, argent two chevronels azure within a bordure engrailed gules (for TYRELL). **Crests:** 1 A lion sejant proper, resting the dexter paw on a cross flory argent (for KENYON), 2 A boar's head couped and erect argent, issuing from the mouth a peacock's tail proper (for TYRELL). **Supporters:** On either side a tiger regardant proper, round the neck a chain, pendant therefrom an escutcheon charged with the arms of TYRELL. **Motto:** *Magnanimiter crucem sustine* ('Sustain the Cross with magnanimity'). **Creations:** Bt. (GB) 28 July 1784, B. (GB) 9 June 1788.

THE 6TH LORD KENYON, BARON OF GREDINGTON, Co Flint, and a **Baronet** (Sir Lloyd Tyrell-Kenyon, Bt) [The Rt Hon The Lord Kenyon, Gredington, nr Whitchurch, Salop SY13 3DH]; *b* 13 July 1947; *s* f 1993; *educ* Eton and Magdalene Coll Cambridge (BA); High Sheriff Clwyd 1986, memb: Wrexham Maelor B C, EU Ctee of The Regions 1994–; *m* 1971 *Sally Carolyn, est dau of Jack Frank Page Matthews, of Thurston, Suffolk, and has:

1 +LLOYD NICHOLAS; *b* 9 April 1972; *educ* Eton and Manchester U
2 +Alexander Simon; *b* 29 Nov 1975; *educ* Eton and Edinburgh U

Lineage: JORDAN KENYON was feudal Ld of Kenyon, Winwick, Lancs, *temp* HENRY III, but that manor passed out of the family when a sole heiress, Almarica Kenyon, *m* Thurston Holland, of Denton. The KENYONs then moved to Park Head, nr Blackburn, Lancs. Later, however, ROGER KENYON *m* Alice, dau and heir of George Rigby, of Peel Hall, which he thus acquired, building (or rebuilding) in the early 1630s a house known as Kenyon Peel Hall, an elaborately timbered mansion which began to fall apart after coal-extraction in the area undermined it structurally and which, despite attempts to repair it by the **4th Lord Kenyon** in the late 19th century, was demolished in the 1950s.

ROGER KENYON's 4th s:

THOMAS KENYON; *b* 1668; *m* 1st Catherine, est dau of Luke Lloyd, of The Bryn, Hanmer, Flintshire, and had, with two sons (one *d* young) and two daus (Katharine, *m* William Middleton and *dsp*; Dorothy, *m* 1716 William Perceval, of Royton Hall); *m* 2nd Catherine, widow of Richard Perceval, of Royton Hall, and dau of Thomas Norris, of Speke, Lancs, and *d* 1731 *sp* by her; his only surv s:

LLOYD KENYON; *b* 1696; *m* 1730 Jane, est dau of Robert Eddowes, of Eagle Hall, Cheshire, and Gredington, Flints, where he settled, and *d* 30 Sept 1773, having had, with other issue, including an er s (Thomas, *b* 3 Sept 1731, *d* unm 20 May 1750):

Sir Lloyd Kenyon, 1st Bt, and **1st Lord Kenyon, Baron of Gredington**, Co Flint (both GB), so *cr* 28 July 1784 and 9 June 1788 respectively, PC (1784), KC (1780); *b* 5 Oct 1732; *educ* Ruthin GS; barrister Middle Temple 1756, MP Hindon 1780–84 and Tregony 1784–88, Ch Justice Chester 1780–84, Attorney-Gen 1782–April 1783 and Dec 1783–84, Master of the Rolls 1784–88, Ch Justice King's Bench 1788–1802; *m* 16 Oct 1773 his cousin Mary (*d* 8 Aug 1808), 3rd dau of George Kenyon, of Peel Hall, Lancs, by Peregrina, dau of Robert Eddowes, and had:

1 Lloyd; *b* 1775; *d* unm 15 Sept 1800
2 GEORGE, **2nd Baron**
3 Thomas, of Pradoe, Oswestry, Salop; Clerk Outlawries Court King's Bench; *b* 27 Sept 1780; *m* 21 April 1803 Louisa Charlotte (*d* 11 April 1869), dau of Rev John Robert Lloyd, of Aston Hall, and *d* Nov 1851, having had, with other issue:

(1) John Robert, of Pradoe, QC; DCL; *b* 13 Jan 1807; Fell All Souls, Vinerian Prof, Judge V-Chllr's Court, Recorder Oswestry, Chm Salop QS; *m* 11 Aug 1846 Mary Eliza (*d* 28 Jan 1903), only dau of Edward Hawkins, FRS, and *d* 17 April 1880, having had, with other issue:

1a Robert Lloyd, of Pradoe, JP, DL; *b* 18 Jan 1848; *educ* Ch Ch Oxford (Vinerian Scholar 1872); chm Salop QS, CA Salop 1889, Recorder Oswestry 1896–1927, Dep Chllr Lichfield 1898, barrister Middle Temple; *m* 9 June 1886 Ellen Frances (*d* 13 May 1934), dau of Rt Rev William Walsham How, Bp Wakefield, and *dsp* 10 Nov 1931

2a Edward Ranulph, CB (1916), CMG (1918); Maj-Gen RE, Ch Engr 3rd Army 1916–17, Dep Controller Chemical Warfare 1918 WW I (despatches five times, wounded), Cdr Crown Italy; *b* 3 Nov 1854; *m* 14 Sept 1880 Katharine Mary McCrea (*d* 16 July 1908), dau of Maj-Gen John Cromie Blackwood De Butts, RE, and *d* 17 May 1937, having had:

1b Herbert Edward, DSO (1918), JP Salop, of Pradoe; Lt-Col RA WW I (despatches 4 times, French and Belgian Croix de Guerre), WW II: Co Dir Salop BRRC, Co Controller Salop VAD 1938–39, cmded HAA Trg Regt RA 1939–41, Army Welfare Offr Salop 1942; chm Bd Govrs Oswestry GS 1952; *b* 2 Dec 1881; *educ* Winchester and RMA Woolwich; *m* 16 July 1907 Gwendoline Ethel Graham (*d* 25 March 1958), dau of Frederick Graham Ommanney, of Sheen Ho, Walmer, Kent, and *d* 5 April 1958, leaving:

1c Kenneth Herbert, JP Cheshire 1949–65; City Cllr 1947–57, Pres Chester Chamber Trade 1947–48, Capt RAPC WW II; *b* 4 July 1908; *educ* Wellington; *m* 2 June 1934 Barbara Joan, yr dau of J E M Urry, and *d* 1970, leaving:

1d *Anne Judith [Miss Anne Kenyon, 7 Henbury Park, Buckfast, Devon TQ11 0ES]; *b* 1 April 1939

2c +Lloyd Douglas [Lloyd Kenyon Esq, 15 Oxford St, Waimate, S Canterbury, New Zealand]; *b* 17 Oct 1912; *educ* Framlingham Coll and Waitaki BHS, NZ; *m* 12 April 1939 *Joan, yst dau of Raymond Appleby, of Geraldine, S Canterbury, NZ, and has:

1d *Gwendolyn Jane [Mrs Trevor Payton, 274 Pine Hill Rd, Pine Hill, Dunedin, New Zealand]; *b* 13 July 1942; *m* 4 April 1964 *Trevor William Payton, s of Ernest Payton, of Dunedin, and has:

1e *Grant Michael; *b* 1974
1e *Kim Maree; *b* 16 May 1966; *m* 1991 *Miran Kremesec
2e *Jill Michelle; *b* 27 Nov 1967
3e *Raeleen Jan; *b* 1971

2d *Sally Mavourneen [Mrs David Drayton, 102 Huntsbury Ave, Christchurch 2, New Zealand]; *b* 19 Sept 1944; *m* 12 March 1966 *David George Drayton, er s of C E Drayton, of Christchurch, and has:

1e *Tania May; *b* 1970
2e *Leanne Mavourneen; *b* 1971; *m* 1997*Jared Gray

3c +John Frederick, OBE, MC (1944) [Col John Kenyon OBE MC, Pradoe, Oswestry, Salop SY11 4ER]; Col RA WW II, Instructor-in-Gunnery 1948–50, Staff Coll Camberley 1951, Jt Servs Staff Coll 1959, Mil Assist to C-in-C Farelf 1962–64, Def Planning Staff 1969, Def, Naval and Mil Attaché Belgium & Luxembourg 1971–73, CC Salop 1977–85, Freeman Shrewsbury (Grand Master) and City London, Pres Freemen of England 1981–91, Offr Order Leopold Belgium 1989, Freeman Farmers' Co; *b* 30 Dec 1921; *educ* Marlborough; *m* 1st 8 Aug 1947 (*divorce* 1960) Jean Molyneux, dau of Howard Godfrey, MC, and has:

1d +John Robert; *b* 24 Oct 1948; *educ* St Edward's Sch Oxford and Southampton U (BA); ALA, FSA, FRHistS; *m* 1973 *Christine Ann, dau of Mrs E M Creen, of Lightcliffe, Yorks, and has:

1e *Philippa Mary; *b* 1974
2e *Joanna Louise Charlotte; *b* 1978

2d +Richard Howard Trevor [Richard Kenyon Esq, The Coppice, Tararua Drive, RD8, Masterton, New Zealand]; *b* 3 Dec 1951; *educ* St Edward's Sch Oxford and Harper Adams Ag Coll; *m* 1977 *Mrs Carol Jackson, dau of C F May, of Blenheim, NZ, and has:

1e *Wendy Jean; *b* 1977

3c (cont.) Col John Kenyon *m* 2nd 5 Aug 1960 Margaret Bowker, dau of George Henry Lewis Remington, of Santa Monica, California, and adopted:

*Judy Margaret; *b* 3 Oct 1957

3c (cont.) Col John Kenyon *m* 3rd 1982 *Mrs Janet Mary Jackson (*née* Maddicott), of Dainton Cross, Devon

1c *Margaret Gwendoline [Mrs Stanley Baranoski, 65 Clark St, Walcott 16, CT 06716, USA], WW II in VAD; *b* 13 Sept 1918; *m* 7 Sept 1945 Stanley Steven Baranoski (*d* 1979), US Army, of Waterbury, Conn., and has:

1d *Robert Steven; *b* 1947; 1st Sgt US Marines, Okinawa and Vietnam; *m* 1971 *Kyoko Nakama and has:

1e *Stanley Steven; *b* 1972
1e *Margaret Gwendoline; *b* 1971

2d *Michael John; *b* 1948; *educ* Massachusetts Coll of Arts (BFA Architecture); *m* 1978 *Diane Lynn Fasciano
3d *David Stanley; *b* 1953; *m* 1972 *Alana Sue Jones and has:

1e *Jeremy David; *b* 1973

4d *Peter Kenyon; *b* 1955
5d *Richard Lloyd; *b* 1957; *m* 1981 *Nereida Otero
6d *Kenneth Owen; *b* 1963; *m* 1985 *Janice Marie Pease and has:

1e *Brittany Marie; *b* 1989

1d *Gwendoline Mary; *b* 1949
2d *Heather Joy; *b* 1956; *educ* Connecticut U Ag Sch; *m* 1981 *Terri Lim

2c *Irene Patricia [Mrs Keith Kerr, 6 Ancrum St, Roxburgh, Central Otago, New Zealand], WW II in WAAF; *b* 23 Sept 1923; *m* 12 Sept 1953 *Keith Louis Kerr and has:

1d *Graham Keith; *b* 3 Sept 1954; *educ* Waitaki BHS, Oamaru, NZ (BSc), NZSC (BSc, MPhEd, PhD)
1d *Patricia Louise; *b* 14 July 1956; *m* 1st 1976 (*divorce* 1988) Ian Leslie Reeves, and has:

1e *Joshua Mark; *b* 1979
2e *A son; *b* 19–

1d (cont.) Mrs Patricia Reeves *m* 2nd 1989 *Kenneth MacKenzie, of Balfour, Southland, NZ, and by him has:

1e *Jenna Kelland Louise; *b* 1992

3c Heather Mary; *b* 23 Jan 1929; *m* 1954 G Humphries and *d* 1 June 1965, leaving two daus
2b Roger de Butts; *b* 15 Aug 1883; *d* 2 Sept 1888
3b Kenneth Houston; *b* 27 April, *d* 25 Oct 1885
1b Katharine Mary Rose, WW I in VAD; *b* 17 July 1887
2b Ellen Blackwood, missionary in India; *b* 7 May 1889; *d* unm 14 Sept 1967
3b Winifred Lilian; *b* 27 Jan 1892; *m* 15 Nov 1921 Herbert Stansfield Williamson, ICS (*d* 31 Jan 1955), and had:
1c *Paul Kenyon [Paul Williamson Esq, Staplegrove House, Taunton, Somerset]; *b* 10 May 1925; *educ* Rugby and Trin Coll Cambridge; *m* 19 May 1956 *Gilian Anderson, dau of Lt-Col John Anderson Smith, OBE, RA, of Leamington Spa, and has:
1d *Michael Paul; *b* 1957
2d *Peter John; *b* 10 Oct 1958
1d *Clare Honor; *b* 26 May 1961
2c *Mark Herbert, OBE [Prof Mark Williamson OBE, Dalby Old Rectory, Terrington, Yorks YO6 4PF], Prof Biology York U; *b* 8 June 1928; *educ* Rugby and Ch Ch Oxford; *m* 5 April 1958 *Charlotte Clara Dallas, OBE (1997), dau of Hugh Macdonald, of Fyfield, Berks, and has:
1d *Hugh Thomas Saumarez; *b* 26 June 1961; *educ* St Peter's Sch York and Sussex U (BA)
1d *Emma Charlotte Mary; *b* 12 July 1963; *educ* Rugby and New Hall Cambridge (MA, BM, BCh, MRCP)
2d *Sophia Louisa Harriet; *b* 2 Dec 1965; *educ* The Mount Sch, St Peter's Sch York and Southampton U (BM)
1c *Ann Katharine [Mrs Angus Mitchell, 20 Regent Terrace, Edinburgh EH7 5BS]; *b* 19 Nov 1922; *educ* LMH Oxford (MA 1947) and Edinburgh U (MPhil 1980); *m* 13 Dec 1948 *(John) Angus Macbeth Mitchell, CB, CVO, MC, Sec Scottish Educn Dept 1976–84, s of John Fowler Mitchell, CIE, of Edinburgh, and has:
1d *Jonathan James, QC (1992) [Jonathan Mitchell Esq QC, 30 Warriston Crescent, Edinburgh EH3 5LB]; *b* 4 Aug 1951; *educ* Marlborough, New Coll Oxford (BA) and Edinburgh U; *m* 1987 *Melinda McGarry and has:
1e *Ewan Patrick McGarry; *b* 1992
1e *Hannah Catriona; *b* 1988
2d *Andrew Macbeth [Andrew Mitchell Esq, 28 Cathkin Rd, Glasgow]; *b* 3 June 1958; *educ* Edinburgh Acad and Reading U (BA); *m* 1991 *Maureen Wilkie and has:
1e *Donald Macbeth; *b* 1993
1e *Kirsty Beth; *b* 1995
1d *Isabel Charlotte [Mrs Michael Foxen, 72 Trinity Rd, Edinburgh EH5 3JT]; *b* 3 May 1953; *educ* St George's Edinburgh and Birmingham Coll of Art and Design; *m* 1st 1972 (*divorce* 19–) Martin Charles Mooney; *m* 2nd 1981 *Michael Grimm Foxen and has:
1e *Jamie Mischa Ruaridh Macbeth; *b* 1986
1e *Haley Catherine; *b* 1983
2d *Catherine Olivia; *b* 1956; *educ* St George's Edinburgh and Robert Gordon's Inst of Tech Aberdeen; *m* 1987 *David CROSS later MACBETH
4b Frances Margaret; MRCP, LRCS, Jr Res MO Oswestry Orthopaedic Hosp, Assist Co MO Westmorland; *b* 18 July 1894; *m* 9 April 1927 (*divorce* 1941) Geoffrey Fausitt Taylor, MB, BCh, MRCP, Capt IMS (*d* 1982), s of Arthur Fausitt Taylor, and *d* 1979, leaving:
1c *Robert Julian Fausitt; FRGS, memb Falkland Is Dependencies Survey 1953–56 (Polar Medal) and Br Ornithological Soc, dir Alfred Holt Blue Funnel Shipping Line, late 2nd Lt Roy Scots; *b* 21 June 1929; *educ* Oundle and Trin Coll Cambridge (BA 1952, MA 1953); *m* 24 Dec 1964 *Jacqueline Castaing, of Sydney, and has:
1d *Lucien Giles; *b* 10 Jan 1966
2d *Adrien Piers; *b* 13 Aug 1967; *m* 1991 *Lavinia — and has issue
2c *Humphrey John Fausitt [Humphrey Taylor, 17 E 89th St, New York, NY, USA]; dir Opinion Research Centre and Investico, Dist Offr Tanganyika, 2nd Lt KAR; *b* 6 Sept 1934; *educ* Gordonstoun and Trin Coll Cambridge; *m* 19– — and has issue
1c *Mary Venetia Fausitt; BA (1951), Carmelite nun; *b* 5 Jan 1928
2c *Elisabeth Joy Fausitt [Mrs Geoffrey Thompson, The Palace, Exeter, Devon EX1 1HY]; *b* 19 Jan 1932; *educ* Somerville Coll Oxford (BA 1954); memb Inst Gp Analysis; *m* 29 Sept 1954 *Rt Rev Geoffrey Hewlett Thompson, Bp Exeter, s of Lt-Col R R Thompson, MC, RAMC, of Dover, and has:
1d *Andrew Hewlett [Andrew Thompson Esq, Oaklands Park Camphill Community, Newnham-on-Severn, Glos]; *b* 23 May 1957; *educ* Marlborough; *m* 1991 *Patricia Macmanamon and has:
1e *Columb; *b* 20 April 1993
1e *Lucia; *b* 25 Nov 1991
2d *Benjamin John; *b* 13 Aug 1963; *educ* Marlborough and Clare Coll Cambridge (PhD); Fell Somerville Coll Oxford, History Lecturer Oxford; *m* 14 Sept 1985 *Nancy-Jane Rucker and has:
1e *Humphrey; *b* 26 May 1995
1e *Hermione; *b* 26 Nov 1990
2e *Eleanor; *b* 17 Aug 1992
1d *Mary Clare; *b* 8 Oct 1955; *educ* York U (BA); *m* 1981 *Christopher Martin and has:
1e *Samuel; *b* 18 Aug 1985
2e *Louis; *b* 4 Nov 1992
1e *Holly; *b* 13 Nov 1987
2e *Susanna; *b* 17 July 1990
2d *Louise Margaret; *b* 19 July 1961; *educ* Marlborough and Clare Coll Cambridge (BA); *m* 1987 *Russell Watson and has:
1e *Thomas; *b* 2 Jan 1991
1e *Harriet; *b* 7 Dec 1992
2e *Lydia; *b* 13 Oct 1994
3e *Madeleine; *b* 31 Jan 1997
3a Eustace Alban; T/Maj Record Office Shrewsbury, Dir Indian Telegraph Dept; *b* 24 Sept 1859; *m* 10 March 1896 Caroline Ethel Jane (*d* 20 Jan 1950), dau of Rev William Cornish Hunt, Rector Odell, Beds, and *d* 21 March 1920, leaving:
1b William Patrick, MC; Lt-Col RWF WW I 1917–18 (wounded), Waziristan 1921–23 and WW II (despatches), Silver Medal Italy; *b* 17 March 1898; *educ* Marlborough and RMC Sandhurst; *m* 6 Oct 1928 Joan Mary (*d* 19–), yr dau of Allan Edward Batchelor, JP, of Hill Wootton Ho, Warwicks, and *d* 1992, having had:
1c +Martin Robert [Martin Kenyon Esq, 70 Stockwell Park Rd, London SW9]; Exec Sec Overseas Students Tst 1962–, 2nd Lt RWF; *b* 11 Nov 1929; *educ* Eton and Corpus Christi Coll Oxford; *m* 6 March 1975 *Mary Anne, only dau of Lt-Cdr Patrick Henry James Southby, RN (*see* SOUTHBY, Bt), and has:
1d *Eliza Hope; *b* 16 Feb 1976
2d *Nina Joan; *b* 1977
2 +(Eustace Allan) Michael; late Lt RWF (TA); *b* 25 May 1931; *educ* St Edward's Sch Oxford; farmer, manager Nicolton Orchards Suffolk; *m* 1977 *Susanna, dau of Maj Arthur H Pearson, of Wincanton
3c +Thomas David (Toby); Maj 3rd Bn RWF, wounded Malaya 1954, served Cyprus 1958–59; *b* 23 Aug 1932; *educ* Wellington and RMA Sandhurst
2b Rowland Lloyd; *b* 16 Jan 1901; *educ* Shrewsbury; *m* 23 July 1936 (*divorce* 1950) Gwendolin Doris Dorman and *d* 31 May 1959, leaving:
1c +Peter Rowland [Peter Kenyon Esq, Lady Whincups, Rendham, Saxmundham, Suffolk]; RAF 1954–66, Air Traffic Control Offr Colchester; market gardener; *b* 17 Feb 1937; *m* 23 Sept 1962 *Wilma, 3rd dau of Ludwig Pranger, of Austria, and has:
1d *Rupert Peter; *b* 1968
1d *Berenice Sofia; *b* 23 May 1964
2d *Rebecca Louise; *b* 1966
2c +Robert Nicholas Andrew [Robert Kenyon Esq, 2/5 Franks Grove, Kew, Victoria 3101, Australia]; RE Cyprus 1958–60; *b* 24 Nov 1939
1b Dorothy Ethel; *b* 4 March 1897; *d* unm 13 Feb 1975
2b Violet Mary (Molly); *b* 11 June 1899; *m* 23 June 1951 Cedric William Le Mesurier Croll
3b Irene Helen, OBE (1959); *b* 11 June 1902; *m* 2 July 1925 Basil Herbert Bright, MC (*d* April 1971), yst s of F H Bright, of Maldon, Essex, and had:
1c *William Frederick; *b* 1 May 1926; *educ* Haileybury; *m* 13 Sept 1950 *Eleanore Mary Lee, of Edinburgh, and adopted:
*Susan Jennifer; *b* 13 Jan 1953
*Gillian Rhona; *b* 25 May 1956
2c *Richard Kenyon; *b* 1 April 1934; *educ* St Edward's Sch Oxford; *m* 7 Sept 1963 *Maureen, dau of A H Hill, of Castle Bromwich, Staffs
1c *Elizabeth Ruth; *b* 26 Aug 1930; *m* 11 Sept 1952 *Geoffrey Donald Sharpe and has:
1d *Julian Donald; *b* 6 June 1953
2d *Nigel Anthony; *b* 18 June 1955
2c *Penelope Jane Desborough; *b* 28 June 1936; *m* 30 June 1962 *Peter Herbert Wilkins, Malaysian Police, and has:
1d *Philip Kenyon; *b* 31 Oct 1963
2d *Richard Desborough; *b* 16 June 1965
4a Frederic George (Sir), GBE, KCB, TD; FBA, FSA, Prof Ancient History Roy Acad 1918, MA Oxon, Hon Fell Magdalen and New Coll, Fell and Warden Winchester Coll 1925–30, Hon DLitt Oxon, Durham and Dublin, Hon LittD Cantab, Hon LLD St Andrews and Princeton, Tstee Imp War Museum 1920–46 and Nat Maritime Museum 1934–38, Pres Br Academy 1917–21, Dir and Pncpl Librarian Br Museum 1909–30, Hon ARIBA 1923, Gentleman Usher Purple Rod Order Br Empire 1918–52, Lt-Col Inns Court OTC, V-Chm Victoria League; *b* 15 Jan 1863; *m* 6 Aug 1891 Amy (*d* 16 July 1938), dau of Rowland Hunt, of Boreatton Park, Salop, and *d* 23 Aug 1952, leaving:
1b Kathleen Mary, CBE (1954); DLitt London 1952 and Oxford 1964, LHD Kenyon Coll, Ohio 1959, FBA, FSA, Dir Br Sch of Archaeology Jerusalem 1951–66, Lecturer Inst Archaeology London U 1948–62, Pncpl St Hugh's Coll Oxford 1962; *b* 5 Jan 1906; *educ* Somerville Coll Oxford (MA); *d* 24 Aug 1978
2b Nora Gwendolen Margaret; *b* 21 Feb 1908; *educ* St Paul's Girls Sch and Somerville Coll Oxford (MA); *m* 18 April 1936 John Ritchie, MBE, MA (*d* 1988), Master Supreme Court (Queen's Bench), er s of W Tod Ritchie, JP, of Glasgow, and *d* 16 May 1994, leaving:
1c *Jeremy Kenyon Tod, JP [Jeremy Ritchie Esq JP, Rosehill, Erbistock, Wrexham, Clwyd]; *b* 17 Oct 1942; *educ* Winchester and Magdalen Coll Oxford (BA); *m* *Barbara Ann Blackwell and *d* 16 May 1994, leaving:
1d *Simon John; *b* 1974
1d *Amy Helen; *b* 1977
1c *Janet Margaret Amy [Mrs Alan Heath, The Hollies, Thrussington, Leics LE7 4US]; *b* 26 April 1939; *m* 7 Sept 1963 *Alan Seward Penson Heath, yst s of Bernard Gordon Heath, of Leicester, and has:
1d *Nicholas Gordon John; *b* 24 Jan 1966
2d *Christopher Frederic William; *b* 31 March 1968
1d *Caroline Margaret Janet; *b* 26 Nov 1971
2c *Elspeth Nora Watson [Mrs Giulio Panichi, Viale Dei, Promontori 376, Ostia Lido, Rome, Italy]; *b* 25 April 1948; *educ* St Hugh's Coll Oxford (BA); *m* 30 March 1972 *Giulio N Panichi and has:
1d *Almarica Nina Serena; *b* 1980
2d *Tamara Anna Helen; *b* 1983

5a Gerald (Rev); MA Oxon, Rector Hordley Salop 1901–14; *b* 3 Aug 1864; *m* 17 Sept 1923 Hilda Mary (*d* 9 Oct 1965), dau of Rev J T Trott, Vicar Newborough, and *dsp* 17 April 1946

6a Lionel Richard, CB (1917); Maj-Gen RA, Dir-Gen Ordnance India; *b* 26 July 1867; *m* 9 Sept 1896 Elizabeth Jane (*d* 26 Dec 1946), dau of Peter Cormack Sutherland, MD, of Natal, and *d* 23 Feb 1952, having had:

1b Harold Anthony, MC; Maj RE WW I 1916–17 (wounded) and Waziristan 1923; *b* 11 June 1897; *educ* Wellington and RMA Woolwich (King's Medallist); *m* 7 March 1931 Iris Veronica Margaret (*m* 2nd 1936 Maj-Gen Mervyn Savile Wheatley, CB, CBE (*d* 1979), s of Maj S G Wheatley, of Parkstone, Dorset), dau of Lt-Col Malcolm McL Corbyn, IA, of Little Grange, Hollesley, Suffolk, and *d* 30 May 1934, leaving:

1c *Elisabeth Veronica [Mrs Elisabeth Shutes, Ford Cottage, Send, nr Guildford, Surrey]; *b* 6 Dec 1931; *m* 16 May 1953 (*divorce* 1974) Robert Arthur David Shutes, only s of Arthur Leslie Shutes, and has:

1d *Anthony David; *b* 27 Sept 1955; *educ* Wellington and UCL (BSc); CEng, MIMM (1982); *m* 1983 *Lucille Alison Hunter and has:

1e *Frederick Thomas Kenyon; *b* 1991

1e *Philippa Fern Kenyon; *b* 1988

2e *Henrietta Iris Kenyon; *b* 1994

1d *Caroline Ann Veronica; *b* 22 Feb 1954; *m* 1976 *John Dalziel Riddell and has:

1e *Oliver John; *b* 1978

2e *Benjamin James; *b* 1980

3e *Daniel Robert; *b* 1981

2b Lionel Frederick Robert, DSO (1945); Brig RE; *b* 6 Aug 1900; *educ* Wellington and RMA Woolwich; served Waziristan 1922–24 (despatches), Khajuri Plain NWF India 1930–31 (despatches) and WW II (despatches), Dep Dir Cadets War Office, CC E Suffolk, memb Suffolk TAAuxA; *m* 22 Aug 1933 *Venice, 2nd dau of Maj William John Corbett Winder, JP, of Vaynor Park, Montgomeryshire

3b Christopher Edward; Lt KSLI; *b* 27 April 1906; *educ* Wellington and RMC; *d* 22 May 1929

1a Mary; *d* unm 6 March 1945

2a Eliza Charlotte; *d* unm 1950

3a Emma; *d* unm 8 Feb 1940

(2) George; Cdr RN; *b* 10 March 1811; *m* 24 April 1856 Mary (*d* 1 Feb 1919 aged 92), dau of Robert Usherwood, of Whitby, Yorks, and *d* 18 March 1866, leaving:

1a Alfred Ernest Lloyd (Rev); MA Oxon; Rector Ludlow, RD and Surrogate Diocese Hereford; *b* 30 Jan 1859; *d* 25 Feb 1930

2a Edgar Thomas, JP Salop; Superintending Inspr Bd of Ag; *b* 13 Oct 1860; *m* 3 Nov 1908 Hester Marjorie (*d* 13 March 1954), dau of Sir Philip Tatton Mainwaring, 4th Bt (*see* 1933 edn), and *d* 24 April 1939

1a Georgina Mary; *m* 1 June 1892 Rev James Mackay (*d* 11 July 1926), Vicar Bromfield Salop and *d* 22 May 1944

(3) William KENYON later KENYON-SLANEY (roy licence 23 July 1862), of Hatton Grange, JP, DL Salop and Merioneths; Capt N Salop Yeo Cav, Lt-Col 1st Bn Salop Roy Vols, Capt 2nd Bombay Cav, High Sheriff 1871; *b* 20 Feb 1815; *m* 9 Oct 1845 Frances Catherine (*d* 18 Oct 1896), dau and coheir of Robert Aglionby Slaney, of Hatton Grange, Salop, and *d* 10 Dec 1884, leaving, with two other sons and five daus:

1a William Slaney, PC, of Hatton Grange, JP, DL; MP Salop 1886–1908, Col Gren Gds; *b* 24 Aug 1847; *m* 22 Feb 1887 Lady Mabel Selina Bridgeman, dau of 3rd Earl of Bradford (*qv*), and *d* 24 April 1908, leaving:

1b Robert Orlando Rodolph, JP (1924), DL (1950); High Sheriff Salop 1935, Maj Gren Gds, ADC to Govr-Gen Canada, served WWs I (wounded) and II; *b* 13 Jan 1892; *educ* Eton and Ch Ch Oxford; *m* 1st 24 May 1917 (*divorce* 1930) Lady Mary Cecilia Rhodesia Hamilton (*d* 1984), est dau of 3rd Duke of Abercorn (*qv*), and had:

1c Robert Ivan, JP (Salop 1965); Lt RARO Gren Gds 1945–48; *b* 5 Oct 1926; *educ* Eton; *m* 7 Jan 1964 Meriel Rose, only dau of Capt Joseph Gurney Fowell Buxton, Gren Gds (*see* BUXTON, Bt), and *d* 1984, leaving:

1d +Rupert David; *b* 1 March 1965; *educ* Eton and UEA

2d +Thomas Alexander; *b* 13 Oct 1966; *educ* Eton and European U Versailles, late Lt Gren Gds

1d *Natasha Vivien; *b* 29 Aug 1969; *educ* Wycombe Abbey and Roy Holloway and Bedford New Coll London U (BA)

1c Vivien; *b* 29 March 1918; *m* 24 July 1939 3rd Marquess of Linlithgow (*qv*) and *d* 23 Sept 1963, leaving issue

2c *Ursula Jane; *b* 15 Jan 1920; *m* 1st 12 Oct 1940 (*divorce* 1946) T/Lt-Col David Ludovic Peter Lindsay (*see* CRAWFORD and BALCARRES, E); *m* 2nd 15 Aug 1946 (*divorce* 1950) Gp/Capt Hon (John William) Maxwell Aitken, DSO, DFC (*see* BEAVERBROOK, B); *m* 3rd 1951 *Robert Edward John Compton (*see* NORTHAMPTON, M)

1b (cont.) Robert Kenyon-Slaney *m* 2nd 25 April 1931 Nesta (*d* 22 Feb 1947), dau of Sir George Ferdinand Forestier-Walker, 3rd Bt (*qv*), and *d* 14 Jan 1965, having by her had:

1c +(William) Simon Rodolph, JP, DL (1986) [Simon Kenyon-Slaney Esq JP DL, Chyknell, Bridgnorth, Salop]; *b* 1932; *educ* Eton; late Lt Gren Gds, FRICS, KStJ; CC 1977–85, High Sheriff 1979, V-Ld Lt Salop 1996–; *m* 1960 *Mary Helena, er dau of Lt-Col Hon Henry George Orlando Bridgeman, DSO, MC (*see* BRADFORD, E), and has:

1d +Henry (Harry) James Rodolph; *b* 1961; *educ* Eton and Southampton U (BSc); *m* 1995 *Laura O'Reilly and has:

1e +Miles Christian Rodolph; *b* 10 April 1997

2d +Andrew William Orlando; *b* 1965; *educ* Cranleigh, Shrewsbury and Reading U (BSc)

3d +Francis Alan; *b* 1966; *educ* Eton and Reading U (BSc); *m* 1997 *Fenella Headlam

1b Sybil Agnes, CVO (1947); Ldy-in-Waiting to HRH THE PRINCESS ROYAL 1923–47, an Extra Ldy-in-Waiting 1948–62; *b* 26 Jan 1888; *d* unm 10 June 1970

2a Walter Rupert, CB; Maj-Gen Rifle Bde cmdg a div 1914, Boer War 1902 (despatches); *b* 25 Sept 1851; *m* 4 Sept 1878 Kate Helen Mary (*d* 28 May 1944), only dau of H J Schooles, MD, Inspr-Gen Hosps, 60th Rifles, and *d* 26 March 1936, leaving:

1b Neville Aglionby; DC E Africa Protectorate, Lt KAR German E Africa 1915–18, Maj Political Dept (despatches), WW II CD and HG; *b* 26 July 1879; *educ* Haileybury; *d* unm 23 March 1963

3a Francis Gerald, CBE (1919); Col Durham LI WW I (despatches); *b* 7 Nov 1858; *m* 19 July 1892 Edith Mary Sherwin (*d* 1955), dau of Maj Joseph Holt, of Ogbeare, Cornwall, and Farnborough Grange, Hants, and *d* 12 June 1938

4a Percy Robert; *b* 9 June 1861; *m* 23 April 1895 Geraldine Ellen Georgina (*d* 7 Sept 1947), yst dau of Rev George Whitmore, and *d* 13 Sept 1911, having had:

1b Philip Percy, MC; MP Tavistock, Maj 96th Roy Devon Yeo Bde RFA WW I (despatches); *b* 12 Feb 1898; *d* unm 9 Sept 1928

2b Gerald William, OBE (1941); BA Oxon, Col Br Mil Admin Eritrea, Admin Serv Nyasaland, Lt 1st Bn Gren Gds; *b* 20 July 1899; *m* 23 June 1928 Barbara Nannette (*d* 1995), only dau of Rev Granville Gore Skipwith (*see* SKIPWITH, Bt), and *d* 27 Dec 1953, leaving:

1c +Orlando Michael Philip [Orlando Kenyon-Slaney Esq, Bachelors Cottage, High Halden, Kent TN26 3JD]; *b* 8 March 1929; *educ* Winchester and Ch Ch Oxford (BA 1953); *m* 25 May 1960 *Philippa Margaret, 3rd dau of Sir Thomas Claude Harris Lea, 3rd Bt (*qv*), and has:

1d +Jeremy Francis Gerald; *b* 3 Oct 1966; *educ* Bethany Sch

2d +Philip Thomas Christopher; *b* 24 March 1969; *educ* Marlborough

2c +Gerald Timothy Granville [Gerald Kenyon-Slaney, Apt 16, 421 E 65th St, New York, NY, USA]; late 2nd Lt Gren Gds; *b* 23 May 1937; *educ* Bradfield

1c *Thomasina Angela Jane [Mrs William Tarling, Mulberry House, Southleigh, Colyton, E Devon]; *b* 11 April 1933; *m* 1st 12 June 1954 (*divorce* 1968) Maj Thomas David Ogilvy Codner, Coldstream Gds, only s of Thomas Arthur Codner, of The Manor Ho, Edginswell, Devon; *m* 2nd 1982 William Albert Tarling and by her 1st husb has:

1d *Vivien Ogilvy [Mrs Aziz Laghzaoui, 25 Margaretta Terrace, London SW3 5NU]; *b* 10 Feb 1957; *m* 1988 *Aziz Laghzaoui and has:

1e *Otto; *b* 1990

1e *Kenza May; *b* 1992

2e *Talia Aïda; *b* 1994

2d *Clare Jane; *b* 31 Jan 1959; *m* 1993 *Marcus Emerson

1b Frances Diamond Sara; *b* 19 July 1897; *m* 12 Nov 1924 Colin Spencer James, 2nd s of Spencer James, of Bridge Ho, Beaminster, Dorset, and ha issue

2b Muriel Agnes; *b* and *d* 6 May 1903

3b Ruth Stella; *b* 9 Sept 1909; *m* 1st 19 Jan 1928 (*divorce* 1 939) Lt-Cdr John Francis Crofton Barker-Hahlo, RN (*ka* 1941), er s of Herman Barker-Hahlo, of Guernsey, and had:

1c Derek Kenyon; *b* 20 May 1931; *m* 30 Dec 1961 *Teresa Clare Cunningham, only dau of Capt Ronald Cunningham Wield, CBE, RN, of Devon, and had:

1d *John William; *b* 1 Jan 1963

2d *David Julian Neil; *b* 3 Dec 1964

3d *Robin Douglas; *b* 13 Aug 1966

1d *Kistie Isabelle; *b* 12 May 1965

3b (cont.) Mrs Ruth Barker-Hahlo *m* 2nd 14 Feb 1939 (*divorce* 1960) Sir William Patrick McMahon, 7th Bt (*qv*), and had further issue

(4) Charles Orlando (Rev); Vicar Moreton Salop, RD; *b* 28 Sept 1816; *m* 15 Aug 1844 Matilda Eloisa (*d* 1892), only dau of Rev Henry Calveley Cotton (*see* COMBERMERE, V), and *d* 6 Nov 1890, having had:

1a Charles Robert; *b* 22 Sept 1845; *m* 1885 Jessie (*d* 28 Jan 1906), dau of Charles Willett, of Liverpool, and *d* 27 Nov 1917, leaving:

1b Charles Orlando; *b* 30 April 1886; *m* 1st 11 Dec 1915 Marguerite Laura (*d* 1948), dau of Alexander Kealman, of Santos, Brazil, and had:

1c *Dorothy Beatrice; *b* 1917; LACW WAAF; *m* 23 Feb 1946 *Donald Stanford Egremont, er s of Donald Egremont, of Redlynch, Salisbury, and has:

1d *Christopher Andrew; *b* 25 Oct 1948; *m* 1st 1975 (*divorce* 1986) Annabel Heather, dau of Malcolm Proverbs, and has:

1e *Christopher William; *b* 1983

2e *James Donald; *b* 1985

1d (cont.) Christopher Egremont *m* 2nd 1989 *Jacqueline Sarah, est dau of Capt Peter Bateman, of Cheselbourne, Dorset, and by her has:

3e *Thomas Joshua; *b* 1993

1e *Lucinda Rebecca; *b* 1990

2e *Hannah Mary (twin); *b* 1993

2d *Donald Alexander; *b* 7 Oct 1955

2c *Elizabeth Matilda [Mrs Elizabeth Dennison, 1825 Mooring Line Dve, Vero Beach, FL 32963, USA]; *b* 1920; *m* 1st 1942 (*divorce* 1945); *m* 2nd 1947 (*divorce* 1997) Robert E Dennison and by him has:

1d *Robert Kenyon; *b* 17 July 1948

2d *William Alexander [William Dennison Esq, 24 West Delaware Ave, Pennington, NJ 08534, USA]; *b* 7 Sept 1951; *m* 1976 *Tara, dau of Pamela Brotherton, of Earlswood Ho, Pitton, Wilts, and has:

1e *William Oliver; *b* 1984

1e *Edwina Elizabeth Kenyon; *b* 1987

3d *John Keasbey; *b* 14 Feb 1958

1b (cont.) Charles Kenyon *m* 2nd 1950 Sarah — and *d* 15 Nov 1973, leaving by her:

3c *Sylvia Elena; *b* July 1952

1b Elena Matilda Georgina, JP Kent; *b* 9 Dec 1887; CC Kent; *m* 10 July 1915 Ernest Douglas Montague Barlas (*d* 26 May 1952) and *d* 19 April 1954, leaving issue

2b Agnes Mabel; *b* 9 July 1890; *d* in infancy

2a Henry Thomas; *b* 18 April 1852; *m* 8 July 1897 Hilda Beatrice, dau of William P Dewes, and *dsp* 24 Jan 1911

1a Alice Matilda; *d* unm 15 Sept 1937

(5) Arthur Richard; *b* 18 June 1818; *m* 18 Jan 1859 Augusta Mary Johnstone (*d* 18 March 1894), widow of Capt George Wilder, RHA, and 3rd dau of Samuel Clogstoun, and *d* 3 June 1888, having by her had:

1a Arthur Augustus; *b* 23 Nov 1868; *m* 1900 Agnes Elizabeth (*d* 1937), dau of William Alexander Oliver-Rutherfurd, and *d* 1944, leaving:

1b Mary Patricia Agatha; *b* 18 May 1908; *m* W Morton, of Wyoming, and *d* 27 Dec 1973, leaving issue

2a John Hubert; Revenue Dept Madras; *b* 4 Aug 1870; *m* 1898 Caroline (*m* 2nd 1910 E G Lake and *d* 22 June 1956 having had further issue), dau of S P Bussell, and *d* 31 Aug 1908, having had:

1b Eileen Sybil; *b* 18 Sept 1899; *m* 1926 William Wellesley James Calthrop (*d* 1947) and *d* 13 Dec 1969, leaving a s and two daus

2b Dora Maud; *b* 14 June 1903; *d* young

3b *Gladys; *b* 13 April 1908; *m* 1927 Capt Godfrey Christopher Dickins, RN, and has issue

1a Louisa Charlotte; *b* 2 Dec 1859; *d* 8 March 1863

2a Caroline Walcott; *b* 17 April 1861; *m* 1894 Cuthbert G W Clogstoun, Madras Police (*d* 16 Feb 1932), and *d* 24 March 1944, leaving issue

3a Peregrina Dora; *b* 14 Oct 1862; *d* unm 21 Nov 1942

4a Leonora Constance; *b* July 1864; *m* 21 Dec 1886 Brig-Gen Francis Douglas Lumley, CB, CBE, Middx Regt (*d* 4 Dec 1925), and *d* June 1893, leaving issue

5a Sibyl Mary; *b* 20 April 1866; *d* unm 4 June 1939

(1) Charlotte; *b* 4 May 1813; *m* 17 Dec 1833 Rev John Hill (*see* HILL, V) and *d* 14 Jan 1884, leaving issue

The 1st BARON *d* 4 April 1802; his 2nd son,

GEORGE KENYON, **2nd Lord Kenyon, Baron of Gredington**, Bencher Middle Temple; *b* 22 July 1776; *m* 1 Feb 1803 his cousin Margaret Emma (*d* 24 Feb 1815), only dau of Sir Thomas Hanmer, 2nd Bt (*qv*), and had:

1 LLOYD, **3rd Baron**

2 Edward, of Maesfen, Salop, JP, DL; *b* 11 June 1810; *m* 1st 19 Sept 1840 Caroline Susan Catherine (*d* 8 March 1866), yst dau of Gen Lord George Beresford (*see* WATERFORD, M), and had:

(1) John George, of Gillingham Hall, Norfolk, JP Norfolk; BA Oxon, Kt St Gregory the Great; *b* 11 Oct 1843; *m* 4 Oct 1871 Mary D'Arcy (*d* 2 Feb 1937), 2nd dau of Lord Henry Francis Kerr (*see* LOTHIAN, M), and *d* 28 July 1914, having had:

1a Francis Edward Alfonsus; AMICE; *b* 3 Aug 1872; *d* unm 27 Aug 1907

2a Joseph Robert, MC (1918), of Gillingham Hall, Beccles, Suffolk; barrister, Maj RFA WW I (despatches); *b* 9 April 1883; *educ* Ch Ch Oxford (BA); *d* unm 17 Dec 1971

1a Mary Catherine; nun Order Sacred Heart; *b* 9 May 1874; *d* 22 May 1954

2a Winefride Mary Susan; *b* 9 May 1876; *d* 7 Feb 1877

3a Margaret Mary Alfonsa; nun Order Sacred Heart; *b* 23 Aug 1878; *d* 17 June 1926

4a Anne Mary Elizabeth Laurentia; *b* 6 Sept 1880; *m* 13 July 1904 Col Herbert William Todhunter, CMG, MA (*d* 8 Nov 1936), 4th s of I Todhunter, DSc, FRS, of St John's Coll Cambridge, and *d* 30 July 1969, leaving issue

5a Mary Susan Lucy; *b* 24 Sept 1885; *m* 26 Feb 1916 Capt Charles Edward Pillans Hastings (*d* 24 July 1970), Roy Sussex Regt, and *d* 26 June 1970, leaving issue

6a Clare Mary Henrietta; Benedictine nun; *b* 12 Aug 1888; *d* 20 March 1954

(1) Emma Jane Anne; *m* 26 April 1877 Rev Hon Algernon Robert Parker, 3rd s of 6th Earl of Macclesfield (*qv*), and *d* 17 May 1933, leaving issue

2 (cont.) The Hon Edward Kenyon *m* 2nd 11 May 1880 Catherine Elizabeth (*d* 16 June 1903), widow of Rev W Gale Townley, Rector Upwell, Norfolk and dau of Rev G F J Marsham (see ROMNEY,E) and *d* 21 Oct 1894

1 Margaret Emma; *m* 19 June 1828 Sir James Hay Langham, 11th Bt (*qv*), and *d* 3 Feb 1829

2 Marianne; *m* 25 Aug 1835 Adml Hon Thomas Best (*see* WYNFORD, B) and *d* his widow 18 Sept 1866

3 Peregrina; *d* 12 April 1830

The 2nd BARON *d* 25 Feb 1855; his er son,

LLOYD KENYON, **3rd Lord Kenyon, Baron of Gredington**; *b* 1 April 1805; MP (Tory) St Michael's 1830–32; *m* 29 June 1833 Hon Georgina de Grey (*d* 22 April 1874), dau of 4th Baron Walsingham (*qv*), and had, with other issue:

1 Lloyd; *b* 13 April 1835; *m* 21 July 1863 Fanny Mary Katherine (*m* 2nd 24 Aug 1880 Rev T M B Bulkeley-Owen, of Tedsmore Hall, Salop (*dsp* 5 June 1910), and *d* 25 Nov 1927), only child of 1st Baron Harlech (*qv*), and *dvp* 17 April 1865, leaving:

(1) LLOYD, **4th Baron**

2 George Thomas, JP, DL Flintshire, JP Salop and Denbighs; MP Denbigh Boroughs 1885–95 and 1900–06, MA Oxon, barrister; *b* 28 Dec 1840; *m* 21 Oct 1875 Florence Anna (*d* 25 April 1929), 2nd dau of John Hurleston Leche, of Carden, Cheshire, and *dsp* 26 Jan 1908

3 William Trevor (Rev); MA Oxon; Rector Malpas Cheshire; *b* 22 Oct 1847; *m* 1st 16 Feb 1871 Anne McKerrell (*d* 15 May 1873), dau of Adam Hay-Gordon of Avochie, and had:

(1) Gordon Lloyd Trevor; slr 1900, ptnr Royds, Rawstorne and Co; *b* 10 May 1873; *educ* Cambridge (BA 1896); *m* 23 Feb 1909 Dorothy Charlotte (*d* 3 Aug 1961), yr dau of DJ Wood, MusD, of The Close, Exeter, and *d* 21 May 1951, leaving:

1a Lloyd Gordon Trevor; *b* 3 Nov 1911; *educ* Cambridge (BA 1933); *m* 9 Sept 1939 *Joyce Alma [Mrs Lloyd Kenyon, 31 Frays Ave, W Drayton, Middx], dau of F J Parker, and *d* 3 Dec 1994, leaving:

1b +Roger Lloyd; *b* 11 April 1960

1b *Pamela Joan [Mrs Barry Gouldstone, 9 Mortimer Close, Mudeford, Christchurch, Dorset]; *b* 14 Dec 1940; *m* 6 July 1963 *Barry Thomas Gouldstone, s of Thomas Edwin Gouldstone, of Kent, and has:

1c *Jeremy Thomas; *b* 16 May 1964; London U (BMus); *m* 26 July 1997 *Suzanne Debra (BEd), dau of Jeremy Moss

1c *Penelope Joan *b* 14 March 1968; *educ* Brighton U (BA)

2b *Carol Ann; *b* 19 Dec 1944

1a Elizabeth Alis Georgina; *b* 20 Jan 1910; *m* 24 April 1935 Geoffrey Basset Wardell-Yerburgh (*see* ALVINGHAM, B) and had issue

3 (cont.) The Rev and Hon William Kenyon *m* 2nd 16 Jan 1877 Lucy Rosamond (*d* 28 Feb 1946), 2nd dau of Rev Charles Wolley-Dod, of Edge Hall, Malpas, Cheshire, and *d* 12 Sept 1930, having by her had:

(2) Roger de Grey; Lt RN; *b* 6 June 1880; *d* unm 14 Feb 1906

(3) Randle North; *b* 28 May 1882; *m* 1st 8 June 1933 Eva (*d* 14 March 1942), widow of George Temple Harris (*see* HARRIS, B) and dau of Lt-Col Henry Green Wilkinson, Scots Gds; *m* 2nd June 1947 *Clare Maria, dau of Gustave Karl Ludwig, of Semering, Austria, and *dsp* 10 Aug 1968

(4) Humfrey Julius (Rev); Priest of UMCA, formerly T/CF, BA Oxford; *b* 12 Nov 1885; *educ* Oxford U (BA); *d* unm 18 March 1921

(5) Guy Victor; Cdr RN, served WW I and WW II, Chev Legn Hon; *b* 23 June 1887; *educ* HMS *Britannia*; *m* 6 April 1942 Agnes, dau of William Edward Jennings, of Kirby Moorside, Yorks, and *dsp* 4 June 1969

(1) Ruth, JP; *b* 29 Jan 1878; *d* unm 7 June 1943

1 Margaret Emma; *m* 11 Oct 1855 William Townley Mitford (*d* 18 April 1889), of Pitshill, Sussex, MP, and *d* 4 Jan 1927, leaving issue

2 Elizabeth; *m* 10 Jan 1860 Rev George Arkwright (*d* 3 Oct 1877), Rector Pencombe, Herefs, and *d* 8 April 1930, having had issue

3 Charlotte Jane; *m* 13 Jan 1876 Rev George Montagu Osborn, 3rd s of Sir George Osborn, 6th Bt (*qv*), and *d* 27 April 1893, leaving issue

The 3rd BARON *d* 14 July 1869; his gs,

LLOYD KENYON later TYRELL-KENYON (roy licence 15 Aug 1912 under terms of will of his ggf, Sir John Tyssen Tyrell, Bt, of Boreham Ho, Essex), **4th Lord Kenyon, Baron of Gredington**, TD, JP, DL Salop, JP Flints; Ld Lt Denbighs, ADC to HM, Col TF 1912, Lt-Col 2/1st Welsh Horse 1914–16, cmdg Salop Yeo, Pro-Chllr U of Wales, Pres U Coll N Wales, Ld-in-Waiting to TM QUEEN VICTORIA 1900–01, EDWARD VII 1901–05 and GEORGE V 1916–19, Grand Cross Dannebrog Denmark and Crown Italy, KGStJ; *b* 5 July 1864; *m* 30 Nov 1916 Gwladys Julia, JP, CC Flintshire, DStJ (*d* 28 Feb 1965), only dau of Col Henry Lloyd Howard, CB, of Wygfair, Denbighs, and *d* 30 Nov 1927, leaving:

1 LLOYD TYRELL-KENYON, **5th Lord Kenyon, Baron of Gredington**, CBE (1972), JP (1944), DL (1948); CC Flints 1946–55 (chm 1954); *b* 13 Sept 1917; *educ* Eton and Magdalene Coll Cambridge; Capt RA (TA) (ret 1943), LLD (Wales) 1958, FSA, pres: U Coll of N Wales Bangor 1947, Nat Museum of Wales 1952–57; tstee Nat Portrait Gallery 1953–93 (chm 1966), Ch Commr for Wales Boy Scouts Assoc 1948–66, memb: Advsy Cncl Educn Wales 1944–47, Standing Commn Museums and Galleries 1953–60, Welsh Hosp Bd 1958–63, Cncl for Professions Supplementary to Medicine 1961–65, Roy Commn Historical MSS. 1966; chm Wrexham, Powys and Mauddach HMC 1960–93, dir: Lloyds Bank, Nat Provident Inst for Mutual Life Assur, Felixstowe Dock and Rlwy Co 1973–93; chm Friends of Nat Libraries 1966, OStJ; *m* 3 June 1946 *Leila Mary [The Rt Hon The Dowager Lady Kenyon, Redbridge House, Birch Lane, Ellesmere, Salop SY12 9AA], widow of Lt Hugo Pell, Welsh Gds, and only dau of Cdr John Wyndham Cookson, RN, of Strand Hill, Winchelsea, Sussex, and *d* 1993, having had:

(1) LLOYD TYRELL-KENYON, **6th and present Lord Kenyon, Baron of Gredington**

(2) Richard; *b* 26 Nov 1948; *educ* Eton and Seale Hayne Coll; *m* 1st 7 Oct 1970 (*divorce* 1976) Davina Jane, dau of David Charles George Jessel (*see* JESSEL, Bt); *m* 2nd 1980 Janet Linley (*née* Nelson), stepdau of Donald Linley, of Denbigh, Clwyd, and *d* 1982, leaving by his 1st w:

1a *Vanessa Zoe; *b* 29 March 1974

(3) Thomas; *b* 14 March 1954; *educ* Tabley House; *d* 1993

(1) *Katherine; *b* 21 April 1959; *m* 1985 *David Nigel Vardon Churton, MBE, er s of Col Geoffrey Vardon Churton, MBE, MC, TD, of Manley, Cheshire, and has:

1a *Oscar Vardon; *b* 1987

2a *Rollo Crispin; *b* 1989

1a *Zara Fleur; *b* 1991

1 *Sarah Myfida Mary, MBE (1952); *b* 13 Sept 1917; VAD WW II; *m* 10 Oct 1966 Col Desmond Aubrey Robert Bancroft Cooke, 13th/18th Hus (*d* 1987), yst s of Lt-Col Sydney Fitzwyman Cooke, of Orwell Lodge, Horsham, Sussex

KERSHAW

Creation: B. (UK) 20 Jan 1947.

THE 4TH BARON KERSHAW, of Prestwich, Co Palatine of Lancaster (Edward John Kershaw, JP (Glos 1982)) [The Rt Hon The Lord Kershaw JP, 38 High View, Hempsted, Glos GL2 5LN]; *b* 12 May 1936; *s* f 1962; *educ* Selhurst GS Croydon; RAF 1955–57; FCA; ptnr Bartlett Kershaw Trott, chartered accountants, Gloucester; *m* 20 July 1963 *Rosalind Lilian, yr dau of Ian Strachan Rutherford, of Richmond, Surrey, and has:

1 +JOHN CHARLES EDWARD; *b* 23 Dec 1971; *m* 18 May 1996 *Elizabeth Huggett

1 *Victoria Anne; *b* 2 Dec 1964; *m* 1989 *Ian C Harvey-Piper, s of C D Harvey-Piper, of Wimbledon

2 *Isobel Mary; *b* 3 May 1967; *m* 1993 *Robert A Slater, s of J F Slater, of Derby

Lineage: JOHN JOSEPH KERSHAW, of Prestwich, Lancs; *m* Sarah Ann, dau of John Birchall, of Prestwich, and had, with other issue:

FRED KERSHAW, **1st Baron Kershaw**, of Prestwich, Co Palatine of Lancaster (UK), so *cr* 20 Jan 1947, OBE (1931), JP (Middx); *b* 6 Nov 1881; *educ* C of E Sch Prestwich; a Ld-in-Waiting 1948–51, Govr Westminster Hosp, memb Br Sugar Commn and Treasury Ctee on Industrial Assur; advsr investments to trade unions, friendly socs and approved socs, chm courts referees, appeals bds and reinstatement ctees; *m* 18 July 1903 Frances Edith (*d* 31 July 1960), dau of James Thomas Wigmore, of Hereford, and *d* 5 Feb 1961, leaving:

1 HERBERT KERSHAW, **2nd Baron Kershaw**; *b* 21 Aug 1904; *educ* Glendale County Sch Wood Green; WW II 1942–45 in RNVR; *m* 1933 *Cissie Burness [The Rt Hon Cissie Lady Kershaw, 29 St Anne's Rd, Newquay, Cornwall], dau of Charles E Smyth, of Friern Barnet, and *dsp* 18 July 1961

2 EDWARD AUBREY, **3rd Baron**

3 Donald Arthur, JP (SW London); *b* 8 Sept 1916; *educ* Friern Barnet GS; F/Lt RAF WW II; slr and commr for oaths; *m* 1 Aug 1942 Barbara Edith (*d* 1986), only child of Lt-Col Cecil Graham Ford, of Richmond, and *d* 1991, leaving:

(1) +Ian Graham Frederick [Ian Kershaw Esq, 22 Priory Gdns, Old Basing, Hants RG24 7DS]; *b* 8 March 1948

(2) +Mark Nigel [Mark Kershaw Esq, 19 Beechnut Lane, Solihull, W Midlands B91 2NN]; *b* 28 Feb 1951

4 +Peter John [The Hon Peter Kershaw, 22 Orchard Rise, Richmond, Surrey TW10 5BX]; *b* 19 July 1924; *educ* Queen Elizabeth's Sch Barnet and King's Coll London (BSc 1948); FEng, FICE, Sub-Lt (A) RNVR WW II; *m* 24 July 1948 *Brenda Margaret, BSc, er dau of James Austin Smith, of Brighton, and has:

(1) +Michael James; *b* 10 Nov 1951; *educ* St Paul's

The 2nd BARON's brother,

EDWARD AUBREY KERSHAW, **3rd Baron Kershaw**; *b* 29 Aug 1906; *educ* Friern Barnet GS; *m* 1 June 1935 *Katharine Dorothea [The Rt Hon Katharine Lady Kershaw, 3 Windmill Ct, Northern Crescent, E Wittering, W Sussex PO20 8RJ], dau of Charles Harry Staines, of Clapham, and *d* 22 Feb 1962, having had:

1 EDWARD JOHN KERSHAW, **4th and present Baron Kershaw**

1 *Patricia Margaret [The Hon Mrs Pickett, 146 Abbeville Rd, London SW4]; *b* 9 Sept 1943; *m* 9 Nov 1968 (*divorce* 1992) David Anniss Pickett, BSc, BMus, er s of Rev Leslie Anniss Pickett, Vicar Upper Froyle, Hants; *m* 2nd 1994 *John Davies and by her 1st husb has:

(1) *Caroline Mary; *b* 23 Sept 1969

(2) *Rachel Elizabeth; *b* 1972

KEYES

Arms: Per chevron gu. and sa. three keys or, the wards of the two in chief facing each other and of the one in base to the sinister; on a canton arg. a lion rampant of the first. **Crest:** An open hand couped at the wrist ppr., holding between the forefinger and thumb a key or. **Supporters:** Dexter, a sailor of the Royal Navy in blue working rig ppr., supporting in the exterior hand a staff arg., ensigned with a naval crown or and flying the banner of St George also ppr.; sinister, a Royal Marine in field service dress, armed and equipped for trench raiding, all ppr. **Motto:** *Virtute adepta* ('Acquired by virtue'). **Creations:** Bt. (UK) 10 Oct 1919, B. (UK) 22 Jan. 1943.

THE 2ND BARON KEYES, of Zeebrugge, and of Dover, Kent, and a **Baronet** (Sir Roger George Bowlby Keyes, Bt) [The Rt Hon The Lord Keyes, House of Lords, London SW1A 0PW]; *b* 14 March 1919; *s f* 1945; *educ* RNC Dartmouth, Lt RN (ret 1949), WW II, memb Pattenmakers' Co, Freeman City London, author: *Outrageous Fortune* 1984 (S E Arts Lit Prize); *m* 6 Dec 1947 Grizelda Mary (*d* 1993), 2nd dau of Lt-Col William Vere Packe, DSO, of Bromley Common, Kent, and has:

1 +CHARLES WILLIAM PACKE [The Hon Charles Keyes, 2 Long Bessels, Hadleigh, Ipswich IP7 5DB]; *b* 8 Dec 1951; *educ* Eton; *m* 1st 30 Nov 1978 Sadiye Yasmin, er dau of Mahir Caskum, of Istanbul; *m* 2nd 1984 *Sally, dau of Thomas Jackson, and by her has:

(1) *Anna Merula; *b* 1985

2 +Leopold Roger John [The Hon Leopold Keyes, East Farleigh House, Lower Rd, East Farleigh, Kent ME15 0JW]; *b* 8 June 1956 (HM LEOPOLD III OF THE BELGIANS stood sponsor); *educ* Eton; *m* 1988 (*divorce* 1997) Jane Elizabeth, only dau of Trevor B Owen, CBE, of Meadow Cottage, Carswell Marsh, Oxon, and has:

(1) *Rose; *b* 1989

(2) *Miranda; *b* 1991

3 +Adrian Christopher Noel; *b* 25 Dec 1962; *educ* Lancing

1 *Virginia Clementine (does not use courtesy title) [Mrs Roger Crompton, The Vicarage, Church Rd, Golcar, Yorks HD7 4PX]; *b* 20 March 1950; *educ* Sherborne and Sheffield U; *m* 8 April 1972 *Rev Roger Martyn Crompton, s of H J Crompton, of Hyde, Cheshire, and has issue:

(1) *Heather Rose Mary; *b* 25 Sept 1976

(2) *Bryony Judith; *b* 1978

(3) *Rowan Elizabeth; *b* 1981

(4) *Holly Susannah; *b* 1983

2 *Josephine (Josa) Mary [The Hon Mrs Thoby Young, 41A Loftus Rd, London W12 7EH]; *b* 9 Oct 1958; *educ* Benenden and Newnham Coll Cambridge; *m* 1987 *Hon (William Aldus) Thoby Young, only s of 2nd Baron Kennet (*qv*), and has issue

Lineage: RICHARD KEYS; served Hundred Years War France 1373, entered the service of the Duchy of Lancaster in Derbys; Esquire to RICHARD II; helped prepare latter's expdn to Ireland; Serjeant-at-arms 1393; in charge of all English ports from Hull to Dartmouth for dealing with captured foreign ships *temp* HENRY V; had:

HENRY KEYS; Clerk and later Keeper Hanaper (official collecting fees for documents passing the Gt Seal) 1410–37; had:

1 Roger; served Hanaper office; Notary Public Exeter; took holy orders; Canon Exeter 1436; helped build All Souls College, Oxford (completed 1443), of which 2nd Warden, and *c* 1445 Eton College also; Chaplain to HENRY VI, Preb St Paul's; granted arms 1449 and an apparently unique patent of nobility, in that no summons as a peer of Parl accompanies it (possibly because the recipient was in holy orders); patent extended to Roger's bro Thomas and his descendants; Archdeacon Barnstaple; charged with treason as Lancastrian supporter 1470, pardoned 1472; *d* 1477

2 Thomas; Commr Revenue and Customs Devon 1449; had:

(1) Thomas, retainer of (1st or possibly 2nd) Lord (Baron) Berners (*qv*); had an only s:

1a Richard; Yeoman to CATHERINE OF ARAGON 1523, Serjeant-at-Arms to HENRY VIII 1528; commr for building Sandgate Castle 1539, of which Capt 1541; granted Abbey lands of St Radegund at Dissolution Monasteries late 1530s; *m* 1st Agnes, sis of Sir William Saunders; *m* 2nd Myldrede, dau of Sir John Scott, of Scott's Hall; his est s by his 1st w:

1b Thomas, *b* 1523; Serjeant-Porter to HENRY VIII, EDWARD VI and MARY; Capt Sandgate Castle; MP Hythe *c* 1554; involved in suppressing Wyatt's Rebellion 1554; cmded Kentish levies for relief of Calais in or before 1558; Dep Master Horse to ELIZABETH I; *m* 1st — (*d* by 1565) and had three children; *m* 2nd 1565 secretly Lady Mary Grey, 3rd dau of Henry Grey, Duke of Suffolk (*see* 1970 edn STAMFORD, E), for which both were imprisoned separately; Capt Sandgate Castle 1569; *d* 1571, leaving (by his 1st w?) an est s:

1c Thomas; served Ireland 1578 to at least 1601; granted land in Ireland at Clonfade (later Glenfade) and elsewhere; Sheriff Derry 1623; had:

1d John; had:

1e John, *m* Barbara, dau and heiress of Roger Tasker, a former companion in arms of John's gf who made over his newly acquired Cavanacor estate to them; their est s:

1f John, of Cavanacor, *m* Margaret, dau of John Lowry, of Ahenis, by his 2nd w Jane, dau of William Hamilton, of Ballyfatton, and left, with other issue (including an er s John, *dsp*, and William, whose dau Deborah *m* her cousin Nathaniel (*see* below)):

1g George, of Clonfade; *d* by 1736; had:

1h Nathaniel, of Clonfade, *m* 1st Deborah, dau of William Keyes, of Edenmore (*d* 1755), and had:

1i George

2i William; had:

1j Nathaniel; *dsp*

2j William, had:

1k Mary; *m* Lt-Col Benjamin Geale Humfrey and was ancestor of the HUMFREYs of Cavanacor

1h (cont.) Nathaniel Keyes *m* 2nd Margaret Babington and by her had, with other issue:

1i Thomas, of Longvale, Co Donegal; *m* Marianne Babington (*d* 22 April 1834),and *d* 30 Nov 1833, leaving, with other issue:

1j Thomas; Assist Surgn Madras Army; *m* Mary Anne, dau of William Patton, of Croghan, Co Donegal, and *d* 25 March 1825, leaving:

1k Thomas Huddleston, Lt-Col Madras Army, *m* Jane, dau of Robert Merry, and had two sons (*dsp*)

2k CHARLES PATTON (Sir)

3k William; *d unm*

The 2nd son,

Sir CHARLES PATTON KEYES, of Croghan, Co Donegal, GCB, JP (Kent); *b* 25 Nov 1822; entered 30th Madras NI 1843, Capt 1858, Brevet Col 1869, Maj Gen 1881, Gen 1889, cmded 1st Punjab Inf, QO Corps of Guides, Punjab FF and Secunderabad Div; *m* 12 Jan 1870 Katherine Jessie (*d* 10 May 1916), dau of James Norman and sis of FM Sir Henry Norman, GCB, GCMG, CIE, and had, with a s (Norman, *d* young):

1 ROGER JOHN BROWNLOW, **1st Baron**

2 Charles Valentine; *b* 14 Feb 1876; Capt QO Corps of Guides; *k* W Africa 1901

3 Terence Humphrey (Sir), KCIE, CSI, CMG; Brig-Gen IA; *b* 28 May 1877; joined IA 1897, Hon Brig Gen 1932, Tirah Expdn 1897–98 (wounded, despatches, medal and two clasps), Political Dept Govt of India 1903, V-Consul Seistan 1904006, Consul Turbat-i-Haidari 1906–08, served Baluchistan 1908–13, Mesopotamia, Persian Gulf and S Persia 1914–17 (despatches), Russian Army Romania and Bukovina 1917 (despatches, Brevet Lt-Col), Orders

Crown Romania, St Vladimir, St Anne and St Stanislas Russia, served S Russia and Army of Black Sea 1918–20 as GSO(1) and Brig-Gen Gen Staff (despatches), Acting HC and Political Agent Baluchistan 1921–28, Envoy Nepal 1928, Resident Gwalior 1928–29, Agent to Govr-Gen States of W India 1929, Resident Hyderabad 1930–33, Gold Staff Offr Coronation 1937; *m* 15 April 1909 Edith Beatrice (Kaisar-i-Hind gold medal) (*d* 28 Feb 1960), dau of Lt-Gen Charles Alexander McMahon, FRS, and *d* 26 Feb 1939, leaving:

(1) Roger McMahon; *b* 6 Feb 1910; *educ* Charterhouse and Worcester Coll Oxford (BA); WW II (wounded) as Capt Roy Sussex Regt and Intell Corps; *d* unm 16 March 1952

(2) *Patrick Terence; Queen's Royal Regt and Intell Corps WW II; *b* 8 Feb 1918; *educ* Stowe and King's Coll London; *m* 12 Sept 1953 *Frances, only child of Maj Arthur Victor Langton, RA, of Kensington, and has:

1a *Andrew Charles Langton; *b* 8 Aug 1954

2a *Nicholas Patrick Langton; *b* 3 Sept 1955

1a *Mary Elizabeth Langton; *b* 19 Sept 1957

2a *Sarah-Anne Victoria Langton; *b* 10 March 1962

(3) *Michael Patton; WW II as Capt Frontier Force Regt IA, ADC to Govr NW Frontier Province India 1946, dir Jardine, Matheson (Japan); *b* 2 Oct 1921; *educ* Sedbergh; *m* 4 Nov 1957 *Germaine Madeleine, yst dau of François Lespinasse, of Nevers, France, and has:

1a *Terence François; *b* 21 Dec 1959

(1) *Rosemary; *b* 15 Sept 1911; 2nd Offr WRNS WW II; *m* 10 Jan 1942 *Maj-Gen Halford David Fellowes, CB, DSO, RM, er s of Maj Halford Le Mesurier Fellowes, IA

(2) *Lavender Phyllis; 2nd Offr WRNS WW II; *b* 15 May 1914; *m* 2 March 1948 *Anthony George Wills Paul, RAFO, est s of Maj W G Paul, and has:

1a *Michael Anthony Keyes; *b* 30 Dec 1948

2a *David McMahon; *b* 30 Dec 1951

1a *Amanda Carolyn; *b* 23 Sept 1954

4 Adrian St Vincent, CBE (1919), DSO (1915); Cdr RN, Actg Capt Staff C-in-C Plymouth 1918, served Dardanelles 1915–16; *b* 19 Dec 1882; *m* 25 Sept 1916 Eleanor (*m* 2nd 15 Feb 1936 Maj Carfrae Hamilton Delmege, 21st Lancers, of Manor Ho, Cricklade, Wilts, and *d* 28 Jan 1945), dau of Lt-Col Walter Campbell, of The Ivy Ho, Hampton Court, and *d* 6 Oct 1926, leaving:

(1) *Ralph Adrian; *b* 27 Aug 1924; served RN WW II

1 Dorothea Agnes; *m* 29 June 1907 Brig-Gen John Edmund Gough, VC, CB, CMG (*d* 22 Feb 1915 of wounds recd in action; posthumous KCB 20 April 1915), and *d* 2 April 1962, leaving issue

2 Katherine Mary; *m* 3 Oct 1900 Capt Charles John Wintour, RN (*ka* Jutland 31 May 1916), and *d* 3 July 1956, having had issue

3 Phyllis Marion; *d* unm 1 May 1968

4 Madeline Helen; *d* unm 25 April 1964 aged 78

Sir CHARLES *d* 5 Feb 1896; his est son,

Sir Roger John Brownlow Keyes, 1st Bt, and 1st Baron Keyes, of Zeebrugge, and of Dover, Co Kent (both UK), so *cr* 10 Oct 1919 (with thanks of Parl and grant of £10,000 [over £180,000 in late-1990s terms]) and 22 Jan 1943 respectively, GCB (1930), KCB (1918), CB (1911), KCVO (1918), CVO (1918), MVO (1906), CMG (1916), DSO (1916); *b* 4 Oct 1872; entered RN 1885, Lt 1893, Cdr 1900, Capt 1905, R-Adml 1917, Actg V-Adml 1918 (reverted to R-Adml 1919), V-Adml 1921, Adml 1926, Adml of the Fleet 1930, Hon Col Cmdt RM Portsmouth 1932–42, served E Africa 1890 (medal and clasp) and China 1900 (despatches, medal and two clasps), Naval Attaché Rome, Vienna, Athens and Constantinople 1905–07, Capt and Cdre i/c Submarine Serv 1910–15, Cdre and Ch Staff SE Mediterranean Sqdn 1915–16, R-Adml Grand Fleet 1916–17, Dir Plans 1917, V-Adml Dover Patrol 1918–19, ADC to HM GEORGE V 1914–17, cmded Battle Cruiser Sqdn Atlantic 1919–21, Ld Commr Admlty and Dep Ch Naval Staff 1921–25, Adml and C-in-C Mediterranean 1925–28, C-in-C Portsmouth 1929–31, WW II: special liaison offr to HM LEOPOLD OF THE BELGIANS May 1940, First Ch Combined Ops 1940–41; author: *Naval Memoirs 1910–18*, *Adventures Ashore and Afloat 1872–1906* and *Amphibious Warfare and Combined Operations 1943*; present Battle of Leyte Philipines Oct 1944, Goodwill Mission to USA, Canada, Australia and NZ 1944–45; MP N Portsmouth 1934–43; Cdr Orders St Maurice and St Lazarus Italy, Crown Italy, Redeemer Greece, Iron Crown Austria, Medjidie Turkey; Grand Offr Legn Hon, Grand Cross Leopold Belgium, Croix de Guerre France and Belgium, US DSM; Hon LLD Cantab, Aberdeen, Bristol and St Andrews, Hon DCL Oxon; *m* 10 April 1906 Eva Mary Salvin (*d* 30 Aug 1973 aged 91), CD 1939–44, Queen Elisabeth of Belgium Red Cross Order, dau of Edward Salvin Bowlby, JP, DL, of Gilston Park, Herts, and Knoydart, Inverness-shire, and *d* 26 Dec 1945, having had:

1 Geoffrey Charles Tasker, VC (posthumous), MC (1941); Lt-Col RSG, cmdg 11th Commando, served Palestine 1938–39 and WW II 1939–41, Croix de Guerre; *b* 18 May 1917; *ka* Libya 18 Nov 1941 while leading Commando raid on Gen Rommel's HQ

2 **ROGER GEORGE BOWLBY KEYES, 2nd and present Baron Keyes**

1 Diana Margaret; *b* 20 Feb 1910; *m* 9 June 1936 Brig James Robert Johnson, DSO, OBE, MC, RWF, est s of Lt-Col Robin Ingelow Bradshaw Johnson, RWF, of Mataban, Avalon Beach, NSW, and *d* 1983, leaving:

(1) *Robin Edward Roger [Robin Johnson Esq, GPO Box 4039, 3001 Victoria, Mebourne, Australia]; *b* 9 March 1937; *educ* Charterhouse

(2) *James Andrew David; *b* 1 Dec 1945; *educ* Charterhouse and Reading U (BSc 1969); *m* 1st 17 July 1969 (*divorce* 1971) Alison Laing, only dau of Hector Laing Waugh, of Edinburgh; *m* 2nd Aug 1972 *Susan W Davies

(1) *Sara Anne Margaret; *b* 21 July 1941

2 Katherine Elizabeth; *b* 24 Oct 1911; *m* 30 July 1935 Maj Peter de Barton Vernon Wallop William-Powlett, MC (*see* PORTSMOUTH, E), and *d* 1996, leaving issue

3 Elizabeth Mary; *b* 10 May 1915; WW II with VAD (RN), author *Geoffrey Keyes* (1956); *d* 1993

KILBRACKEN

Arms: Argent three unicorn's heads erased sable, horned gules, two and one, and three trefoils slipped vert, one and two. **Crest:** A unicorn's head erased argent, horned gules, charged with three trefoils slipped vert. **Supporters:** Dexter, a gryphon sable, charged on the shoulder with four mullets in cross argent; sinister, a lion argent, charged on the shoulder with four roses, also in cross gules, barbed and seeded proper. **Motto:** *Sans Dieu rien* ('Without God nothing'). **Creation:** B. (UK) 8 Dec 1909.

THE 3RD BARON KILBRACKEN, of Killegar, Co Leitrim (John Raymond Godley, DSC (1945)) [The Rt Hon The Lord Kilbracken DSC, Killegar, Co Leitrim, Ireland]; *b* 17 Oct 1920; *s* f 1950; *educ* Eton and Balliol Coll Oxford (BA, MA 1948); WW II 1940–46 as naval pilot, cmded 714 and 835 Naval Air Sqdns, Lt-Cdr (A) RNVR 1945; broadcaster, jnlst, ed 1947–, author: *Even for an Hour* (poems 1940), *Tell Me the Next One* (1950), *The Master Forger* (1951), *Living Like a Lord* (1955), *A Peer Behind the Curtain* (1959), *Shamrocks and Unicorns* (1962), *Van Meegeren* (1967), *Bring Back My Stringbag* (1979), *The Easy Way to Bird Recognition* (1982), *The Easy Way to Tree Recognition* (1983), *The Easy Way to Wild Flower Recognition* (1984); *m* 22 May 1943 (*divorce* 1949) Penelope Anne, WRNS, yst dau of R-Adml Sir Cecil Nugent Reyne, KBE, of Alverstoke, Hants, and has had:

1 +CHRISTOPHER JOHN [The Hon Christopher Godley, Four Firs, Marley Lane, Haslemere, Surrey]; *b* 1 Jan 1945; *educ* Rugby and Reading U (BSc Ag 1967); agriculturist ICI Ltd; *m* 10 May 1969 *Gillian Christine, yr dau of Lt-Cdr Stuart Wilson Birse, OBE, DSC, RN, of Alverstoke, and has:

(1) +James John; *b* 1972

(1) *Louisa Laheen; *b* 1974

2 Simon Hugh; *b* 26 and *d* 27 June 1947

The 3rd BARON *m* 2nd 1981 (*divorce* 1989) Susan Lee, dau of Norman Heazlewood, of Melbourne, Australia, and by her has:

3 +Seán Garech; *b* 1981

Lineage: JOHN GODLEY, of Meath St, Dublin; *b* 1651; merchant, probably in textiles; Sheriff Dublin 1706, Alderman 1707; *m* 1st Susanna Holroyd (*d* 1697) and had two daus; *m* 2nd 1697 Anne (*d* 1752), dau of William Elwood, Alderman Drogheda, and sis and coheiress of Dr John Elwood, V-Provost and MP Trin Coll Dublin, and *d* 1710, leaving by her, with an er s (*dsp*) and seven daus:

Rev WILLIAM GODLEY; *b* 1700; MA Trin Coll Dublin, DD; Preb Ballymore 1733–41 and Mullabrack, Co Armagh, 1741–79; *m* 1st 1730 Mary, dau of Richard Morgan, of Coldcutt, Co Dublin, Agent to Archbp Dublin and Second Remembrancer Ct Exchequer; *m* 2nd 1769 Elizabeth, widow of Rev Jonathan Rogers, and *d* 1779, leaving by his 1st w, with two yr sons and two daus:

JOHN GODLEY, of Sackville St, Dublin, and Tandragee, Co Armagh; *b* 3 Feb 1731; LLD, barrister; inherited from his unc Richard Morgan 1784 the Killegar estate, which the latter's f, the er Richard Morgan, had bought 1734; *m* 25 April 1761 Rose, dau of Alexander McAulay, KC, of Glenville, Co Antrim, Judge Ecclesiastical Ct Dublin, MP Dublin U, and *d* 6 Aug 1806, having had, with other issue:

1 William; *b* 1765; Lt-Col 83rd Regt; *m* Adeline, dau of Rev Francis Ricardo, of Jersey, and had:

(1) John, of Oatlands, Co Dublin; *b* 1800; *m* 1824 Isabella (*d* 3 April 1867), 3rd dau of Sir Thomas Fetherston, 2nd Bt, MP (*see* 1902 edn), and left issue

(1) Adeline; *m* 1823 Rev Sir Thomas Francis Fetherston, 4th Bt, and *d* 1830, having had issue

2 Alexander; *b* 1768; Maj 28th Regt; *ka* Egypt 13 March 1801

3 John, of Killegar, JP, DL; *b* 3 Oct 1775; High Sheriff Co Leitrim 1818; *m* April 1813 Katharine, dau of Rt Hon Denis Daly by Henrietta, dau of 1st Earl of Farnham (*see* FARNHAM, B), and *d* 1863 having had:

(1) John Robert; *b* 29 May 1814; fnded 1850 Prov of Canterbury, NZ, Assist U-Sec War Office 1856–61; *m* 29 Sept 1846 Charlotte (*d* 3 Jan 1907), dau of Charles W Griffith-Wynne, of Voelas, Denbighs (*see* AYLESFORD, E), and *dvp* 17 Nov 1861, having had:

1a **JOHN ARTHUR, 1st Baron**

1a Rose Mary; *d* unm 27 Nov 1931

2a Frances Eleanor; *d* unm 13 Oct 1955 aged 102

3a Mary Henrietta; *d* unm 14 April 1898

4a Margaret Ethel; *d* unm 22 May 1933

(2) James (Rev); Rector Carrigallen, Co Leitrim, 1867–1910; *m* 1851 Eliza Frances (*d* 4 Nov 1908), dau of Peter La Touche, of Bellevue, Co Wicklow, and *d* 30 April 1910, leaving:

1a Alfred Denis, OBE; *b* 22 Jan 1856; Public Orator Oxford U 1912, Fell and Tutor Magdalen Coll 1883–1912, Hon Fell 1912–25; *m* 1894 Amy Charlotte Isabella (*d* 22 Sept 1933), dau of C H Cay, formerly Fell Caius Coll Cambridge, and *dsp* 27 June 1925

2a Francis Clements, MVO; *b* 8 March 1858; Lt-Col, Brev-Col and Hon Brig-Gen, cmded 2nd Bn and 12th Bn Notts and Derbys Regt and 91st Inf Bde, Sikkim Expdn, S Africa and WW I; *m* 22 Sept 1886 Maud Adeline (*d* 5 Oct 1941), dau of Surgn-Maj Richard Whittall, and *d* 13 Nov 1941, leaving:

1b Raymond Denis; *b* 30 Jan 1888; *m* 1919 Kathleen (*m* 2nd 24 March 1953 Rev Charles Leslie Abdy), yst dau of Rev Henry Edmund Sharpe, of The Rectory, Bishops Waltham, and *d* 11 Jan 1941, having had:

1c Patrick Raymond; *b* 18 April 1920; *d* 9 Aug 1937

2b Brian Richard, CBE (1946); *b* 26 March 1899; *educ* Cheltenham; T/Brig IA Mesopotamia 1918 (despatches), NW Frontier India 1921–23 (despatches twice) and WW II (despatches, cmded Roy Bn Jat Regt), Dep Dir Organisation GHQ India 1944–45, Cmdt Selangor Sub-Area 1945; *m* 15 Sept 1931 Margaret Valiant, yr dau of Ferderick Valiant Cotton Livingstone-Learmonth, DSO, of Newnham Manor, Crowmarsh, and *d* 3 Aug 1954, leaving:

1c *Peter Brian [Lt-Cdr Peter Godley RN, Down House, The Hildens, Westcott, Surrey RH4 3JX]; *b* 4 Oct 1933; *educ* Cheltenham and RNC Dartmouth; *m* 9 Jan 1960 *Jean, yr dau of Col James Forbes-Robertson, VC, DSO, MC, DL, of Bourton-on-the-Water, Glos, and has:

1d *John Peter; *b* 9 July 1962

1d *Sarah Jean; *b* 21 Dec 1960

2d *Joanna; *b* 25 Feb 1968; *m* 23 March 1995 *Graeme Hughes, of NSW, Australia

1c *Jane Margaret Rin [Mrs Ivor Little, 59 Kingston Lane, Teddington, Middx]; *b* 18 Jan 1936; *m* 12 Nov 1960 *Ivor William Little, est s of Brig Archibald George Little, of the Dower Ho, Chippinghurst, Oxford, and has:

1d *Henry Brian; *b* 22 May 1965

2d *Alexander; *b* 22 Oct 1970

1d *Emma Louise; *b* 19 Sept 1961

1b Margaret Annie; *m* 22 May 1915 (*divorce*) Basil Frederick Leakey, er s of James Leakey, of Somerset Ho, New Barnet, and *d* 5 Feb 1966, leaving issue

2b Norah Frances; *m* 18 Feb 1922 Sir Basil Edward Nicolls CVO, CBE (*d* 3 Aug 1965), 2nd s of Ven Gerald Edward Nicolls, Archdeacon Lahore, and *d* Oct 1975

3a John Cornwallis, CSI; *b* 9 Feb 1861; Dir Public Instruction Punjab 1907–17; *m* Jan 1895 Mary Blanche (*d* 3 March 1937), dau of William MacNaught, and *d* 19 Aug 1946, leaving:

1b Maurice; *b* 16 Oct 1900; *educ* Rugby and RMC Sandhurst; Queen's Messenger, Maj Roy Fus, ADC to Govr: Fiji 1931–36, Trinidad 1936–37; *m* 7 April 1937 Glen, yr dau of Capt Mayow Short, and has:

1c *Susan Mary; *b* 10 Jan 1941; *m* 11 Dec 1969 (*divorce* 1982) 18th Viscount Hereford (*qv*) and has issue

1b Margaret Cecilia; *educ* St Hugh's Coll Oxford (MA)

1a Charlotte Maude; *d* unm March 1946

(3) Denis, CB; Sec Irish Land Commn 1881–88, Capt 74th Highrs; *m* 17 Dec 1850 Katherine Elizabeth (*d* 9 Dec 1909), dau of Pierse G Barron, of Carrig Barron, Co Waterford, and *dsp* 20 Jan 1890

(4) Archibald, JP, DL (Co Leitrim) and JP (Co Cavan); *b* 1828; *m* 30 April 1862 Jane Elizabeth (*d* 24 Nov 1906), 3rd dau of Rev Hon Miles John Stapleton, 3rd son of 12th Lord (Baron) Le Despenser (*see* FALMOUTH, V), and *d* 8 June 1907, leaving:

1a Anna Charlotte Adelaide; *d* unm 15 June 1955

(5) William Alexander; Lt-Col 56th Regt; *m* Laura (*d* 24 Oct 1928), dau of Rev Godfrey Bird, Rector Gt Wigborough, and *d* 24 Sept 1880, having had:

1a Alexander John (Sir), GCB, KCMG; *b* 4 Feb 1867; Gen Irish Gds, Col Roy Ulster Rifles 1922–7, Capt Roy Dublin Fus, Cmdt Mounted Inf 1901–06, AAG and GSO(1) 2nd Div Aldershot 1906–10, Maj-Gen cmdg NZ Forces 1910–14, NZ Expdny Force 1914–19 and an Army Corps 1915–19, Hon Col Otago Mounted Rifles and N Auckland Regt NZ, 13th Maitland Regt Australia, Lt-Gen 1918, Gen 1923, Mil Sec to Sec State War 1920–22, GOC-in-C BAOR 1922–24, GOC-in-C Southern Cmd 1924–28, ADC Gen to HM GEORGE V 1925–29, Govr and C-in-C Gibraltar 1928–33, served: Rhodesian Rebellion 1896–97, Boer War 1899–1901, WW I and WW II 1940–41 (Platoon Cdr HG), chm Roy Empire Soc 1942–43; Order White Eagle Serbia 2nd Cl with swords, Croix de Guerre France and Belgium, Grand Cross Ouissam Alouite and Mehdania Morocco, Gran Cruz de Merito Militar Spain, Gd Offr Legn Hon and Crown Belgium; *m* 17 Sept 1898 Louisa Marion (*d* 29 June 1939), est dau of Robert Fowler, DL, of Rahinston, Co Meath, and *dsp* 6 March 1957

2a Godfrey Archibald, CBE (1919); *b* 13 Oct 1871; S African CS; *m* 1899 Ruth (*d* 8 Oct 1958), gdau of Sir Theophilus Shepstone, KCMG, and *d* 31 Dec 1934, leaving:

1b Alexander Shepstone; *b* 9 Aug 1900; Lt-Col Roy Scots, RAF 1922–25, ADC 1927–28, Garrison Adj Dover and Catterick 1927–31, WW II Singapore, Ceylon, Burma and India, cmdg 2 Border 1942–45, cmdg 1st/8th LF and 23 Br Ind Bde Gp 1946, Col Gen Staff GHQ India 1947, Cmdt Intell Corps Trg Centre Sussex 1948–50, CD Offr Norfolk 1950; *m* 1st 30 Oct 1928 Zara Valda Mari Kirby (*d* 6 June 1944); *m* 2nd 29 Jan 1946 Margaret Kathleen, dau of Lt-Col James Charles Walter Connell, DSO, and had an adopted dau *b* 12 June 1956

3a Richard Shearman, OBE (1919), KPM; *b* 24 Sept 1876; Lt-Col and Dep Commr S African Police, served Matabeleland and Mashonaland Rebellions 1896–97, Boer War 1899–1901 (wounded) and WW I Iand WW II in 2nd Bn Somerset HG 1940–42, author *Khaki and Blue* (1935); *m* 1st 26 April 1906 (*divorce* S Africa 1937) Dorothea (*d* 10 Jan 1944), er dau of Lt-Col Matterson, of Natal; *m* 2nd 27 Oct 1937 Constance Marion (*d* 15 Sept 1975), est dau of Addis Edward Archer, of Penair, Cornwall, and *d* 3 Dec 1950, having by his 1st w had:

1b Anna Margaret Bird; *d* 19–

2b *Mabel Alexandra Dorothea [Mrs James Forman, Glebe House, Goodleigh, N Devon]; *m* 22 May 1945 Maj James Adam Sholto Forman, CBE, RAMC, est s of Rev Adam Forman, CBE, of Dumcrieff, Moffat, and has issue

3b Sylvia Mary Peace; *d* 29 May 1926

1a Mabel Charlotte Sarah; *m* 26 April 1917 Rev Arthur Hawtrey Watson (*d* 7 Sept 1952), of St Edmund's, Scole, Norfolk

JOHN ROBERT GODLEY's s,

JOHN ARTHUR GODLEY, **1st Baron Kilbracken**, of Killegar, Co Leitrim (UK), so *cr* 8 Dec 1909, GCB; *b* 17 June 1847; *educ* Balliol Coll Oxford (MA); Fell Hertford Coll 1874–81, Hon Fell Hertford Coll 1910 and Balliol Coll 1912, barrister Lincoln's Inn, tstee Br Museum, chm govrs Rugby Sch 1903–, Priv Sec to Rt Hon William E Gladstone 1872–74 and 1880–82, Commr Inland Rev 1882–83, PUS India Office 1883–1909; *m* 26 Sept 1871 Hon Sarah James (*d* 13 Sept 1921), only dau of 1st Baron Northbourne (*qv*), and had:

1 HUGH JOHN, **2nd Baron**

2 Denis Ellison; *b* 17 March 1890; *d* 9 Dec 1896

1 Helen Sarah, OBE (1920), JP; *m* 25 June 1895 Henry Edward Harcourt Rice (*d* 10 April 1944), only child of Adml Sir Edward Rice, KCB, of Dane Ct, and *d* 16 Dec 1922, leaving issue

2 Eveline Charlotte; FRHS, FRAS; *d* unm 16 May 1951

3 Katharine Euphemia; *m* 11 June 1904 Lt John Duke Coleridge, RNVR, and *d* 25 Sept 1941 leaving issue (*see* COLERIDGE, B)

The 1st BARON *d* 27 June 1932; his only surv son,

HUGH JOHN GODLEY, **2nd Baron Kilbracken**, CB (1931), KC 1924; *b* 12 June 1877; *educ* Balliol Coll Oxford (MA); barrister Lincoln's Inn 1902, memb Centl Control Bd (Liquor Traffic) 1917–21, Assist Parly Counsel Treasury 1917–23, Counsel to Chm Ctees Ho Lds 1923–44; *m* 1st 15 Sept 1919 (*divorce* 1936) Elizabeth Helen Monteith (*d* 18 Feb 1958), dau of Vereker Monteith Hamilton, of Coopers Wood, Holtye Common, Sussex, and widow of Cdr Neville F Usborne, RN; *m* 2nd 16 Oct 1936 Rhoda Leonora (*dsp* 23 Aug 1948), dau of Percy C Taylor, of Brighton, and *d* 13 Oct 1950, having by his 1st w had:

1 JOHN RAYMOND GODLEY, **3rd and present Baron Kilbracken**

2 +Wynne Alexander Hugh [Prof The Hon Wynne Godley, Jasmine House, The Green, Cavendish, Suffolk CO10 8BB]; *b* 2 Sept 1926; *educ* Rugby, New Coll Oxford (BA 1947) and Conservatoire de Musique, Paris; professional oboist 1950, Dep Dir Ec Section Treasury 1967–70 (ec consultant 1975–), Official Advsr Select Ctee Public Expenditure 1971–73, dir Investing in Success Equities Ltd 1970–85, Prof Applied Economics Cambridge 1980–93, Fell King's Coll Cambridge; dir: ROH Covent Gdn 1976–87, Kent Opera 1993– ; *m* 3 Feb 1955 *Kathleen Eleonora (Kitty), dau of Sir Jacob Epstein, KBE, and formerly w of Lucien Freud, and has:

(1) *Eve Katharine; *b* 21 Jan 1967

1 Katharine Mary; *b* 27 Aug 1923; BSc Soc; *m* 29 Aug 1944 Capt Peter Marian Ignacy Komierowski, s of Count Constantine Edmund Bossuta-Komierowski, of Komierowo, Poland, and *d* 21 Jan 1994, leaving:

(1) *Paul James Alexander; *b* 25 Aug 1945; doctor

(1) *Maria Thérèse [Mrs Maria O'Connell, 4 Libeton Hall, Headcorn Rd, Grafty Green, Kent]; *b* 12 Sept 1947; *m* 27 April 1968 (*divorce* 1974) Richard Michael O'Connell, er s of P D O'Connell, of Cambridge, and has:

1a *Daniel Wynne; *b* 1 Nov 1968

1a *Brigid Emily Katharine; *b* 13 June 1970

KILLANIN

Arms: Ermine a fess indented sable, in base a lion rampant of the last, armed and langued gules. **Crest:** On a fasces fesswise proper a lion's head erased argent gutté de sang. **Supporters:** Two lions gules, each gorged with a chain or, pendant therefrom an escutcheon ermine charged with a sword erect proper, pommel and hilt gold, and standing on a fasces also proper. **Motto:** *Si Deus nobiscum, quis contra nos?* ('If God be with us, who can be against us?'). **Creations:** Bt. (UK) 14 Sept 1885, B. (UK) 15 June 1900.

THE 3RD BARON KILLANIN, of Galway, Co Galway, and a **Baronet** (Sir Michael Morris, Bt, MBE (1945), TD [The Rt Hon The Lord Killanin MBE TD, 9 Lower Mount Pleasant Ave, Dublin 6]; *b* 30 July 1914; *s* uncle 1927; *educ* Eton, Sorbonne (Paris) and Magdalene Coll Cambridge (BA 1935, MA 1939); Hon LittD Ulster U, gossip columnist, special *Daily Mail* war correspondent Japanese-Chinese War 1937–38, political correspondent *Sunday Dispatch*, Maj KRRC (Queen's Westminsters), WW II, Maj 30 Armoured Bde 1943–45, Centl Cncl Irish Red Cross Soc, Pres Olympic Cncl Ireland 1950–73, memb: Internat Olympic Ctee (Ireland) 1952– (V-Pres 1968–72), Internat Olympic Ctee Exec 1967 (Pres 1972–80, since when Hon Life Pres), Nat Monuments Advsy Ctee (chm 1960–65); Cultural Rels Advsy Ctee (Ireland) 1950–, memb Roy Irish Academy 1952, chm Bovril (Ireland) and Lombard Bank (Ireland), dir Irish Shell and BP and Four Provinces Films, memb Inst Tport, Management Ctee RNLI (Exec Ctee 1970–84), Tstee Irish Sailors and Soldiers Land Tst, First Pres Irish Club London 1947–65, Pres Inc Sales Managers (Ireland) 1965–68, chm Dublin Theatre Festival 1958–70, dir Fitzwilton, author, film producer, Kt Honour and Devotion SMO Malta 1947, Order Star Italy, Cdr Grand Cross Germany 1972, Cdr Sacred Treasure Japan 1972, Grand Offr Order Merit Italy 1973, Offr Legn Hon 1975, Kt Grand Cross Order Civil Merit Spain 1976, Cdr Order Grimaldi Monaco 1961, Finnish Order Olympic Merit, Austrian Olympic Medal 1st Cl; *m* 17 Dec 1945 *(Mary) Sheila Cathcart, MBE, only dau of Rev Douglas Lyall Cathcart Dunlop, of Oughterard, Co Galway, and has:

1+(GEORGE) RED(MOND) FitzPATRICK [The Hon Redmond Morris, Doughty Cottage, Richmond Hill, Richmond, Surrey TW10 6RN]; *b* 26 Jan 1947; *educ* Gonzaga Coll Dublin, Ampleforth and Trin Coll Dublin; film producer; *m* 23 Sept 1972 *Pauline, only dau of Geoffrey Horton, of The Lawns, Cabinteely, Co Dublin, and has:

(1) +Luke Michael Geoffrey; *b* 22 July 1975

(1) *Olivia Rose Elizabeth; *b* 24 May 1974

2 +Michael ('Mouse') Francis Leo [The Hon Michael Morris, Everard's Grange, Fethard, Co Tipperary, Ireland]; *b* 4 April 1951; *educ* St Conleth's Coll Dublin and Ampleforth; *m* 8 Jan 1979 *Susanne ('Shanny') Felicity, interior decorator, dau of Lt Col Brian Clark, of Kilmeanogue, Co Wicklow, and has:

(1) +James Michael; *b* 1983

(2) +Christopher Michael; *b* 1985

3 +John Martin [The Hon John Morris, 5 Rus-in-Urbe, Lower Glengeary Rd, Dunlaoghaire, Co Dublin]; *b* 4 April 1951; photographer; *educ* St Conleth's Coll Dublin and Ampleforth; *m* 16 Dec 1972 *Thelma G (Thelma Mansfield the Irish TV personality), er dau of W H Mansfield, of Monkstown, Co Dublin, and has:

(1) +Roderic Michael; *b* 21 Sept 1976

(2) +Michael-John; *b* 7 April, 1979

1 *(Monica) Deborah [The Hon Mrs Bryden, 3 Orchard Cottage, Clifton Rd, Kingston upon Thames, Surrey]; *b* 24 Feb 1950; associate dir Nat Theatre 1975; *m* 24 July 1970 *William Campbell Rough Bryden, s of George Bryden, of Greenock, Renfrewshire, and has:

(1) *Dillon Michael George; *b* 17 March 1972

(1) *Mary Kate; *b* 2 April, 1975

Lineage: RICHARD MORRIS; Bailiff (mayor) Galway 1486; ancestor of:

JAMES MORRIS, of Galway; had:

GEORGE MORRIS, of Spiddal, Co Galway; served in JAMES II's army; *m* 1684 Catherine, dau of John FitzPatrick, of Loughmore, in the south Island of Aran (unc of Richard FitzPatrick, MP Galway I Parl 1749–61), who brought him property at Spiddal, and had:

ANDREW MORRIS, of Spiddal and Galway; *m* Monica Browne, of Gloves, nr Athenry, and had:

1 George; *m* 1770 Joanna, dau of Edmund Killikelly, of Tuam, Co Galway, and *d* India, leaving:

(1) Edmond; Capt Bengal Army; *d* 1 July 1813 Borneo

(1) Mary; *m* 1st 27 Feb 1796 Christopher Oldfield, BCS (*d* 27 Dec 1808); *m* 2nd Maj Thomas Macan, of Greenmount, Co Louth, and *d* 26 Nov 1854, leaving issue

(2) Catherine; *m* 1798 William Towers Smith (*d* 1827), Judge Moorshedabad, India (*see* SMITH-GORDON, Bt)

2 James, of Spiddal and Galway; *b* 1732; *m* 1762 Deborah (*d* 16 Nov 1820), dau of Nicholas Lynch, of Galway, and *d* 9 Dec 1813, having had, with other issue, including two er sons and a dau (Monica, *m* Andrew Blake, of Galway, and had issue):

(1) Martin, of Spiddal and Galway, JP (Co Galway); *b* 9 Nov 1784; High Sheriff Co and town Galway 1841, first Catholic to hold that office since 1690; *m* 22 Aug 1822 Julia (*d* 6 Aug 1833), dau of Dr Charles Blake, of Galway, and *d* 27 June 1862, having had, with two daus:

1a MICHAEL, **1st Baron**

2a George (Sir), KCB, JP, DL (Co Galway); *b* April 1833; High Sheriff 1860 and 1861, MP Galway 1867–68 and 1874–80, Commr Local Govt Bd Ireland 1880–91 and V-Pres 1891–98; *m* 6 April 1875 Elizabeth Christina (*d* 13 Dec 1924), only dau of David O'Connor Henchy, MP, of Stonebrook, Co Kildare, by Elizabeth, dau of Sir John Burke, 2nd Bt (*qv*), and *d* 11 Sept 1912, leaving:

1b Elizabeth Julia; *d* unm June 1968

The er son,

Sir Michael Morris, 1st Bt, and **1st Baron Killanin**, of Galway, Co Galway (both UK), so *cr* 14 Sept 1885 and 15 June 1900 respectively, PC (UK 1889, I 1866), QC (1863), JP (Cos Cavan and Galway); *b* 14 Nov 1826; *educ* Trin Coll Dublin (first Sr Mod and gold medal 1847); barrister 1849, High Sheriff Co Galway 1850, Recorder Galway 1857–65, MP Galway 1865–67, Slr-Gen Ireland 1866, Attorney-Gen 1866–67, Bencher King's Inn 1866, Judge Court Common Pleas 1867, Ld Ch Justice 1876, Ld Ch Justice Ireland 1887, BA and LLD (Hon), Visitor Trin Coll Dublin 1887–89, Ld Appeal in Ordinary as BARON MORRIS OF SPIDDAL (LP; so *cr* 5 Dec 1889) 1889–1900, Bencher Lincoln's Inn 1890, Chm Bd Nat Educn, Senator and V-Chllr Roy U of Ireland; *m* 18 Sept 1860 Anna (*d* 17 Oct 1906), dau of Hon George Henry Hughes, Baron Court Exchequer Ireland, and *d* 8 Sept 1901, having had:

1 MARTIN HENRY FitzPATRICK, **2nd Baron Killanin**, PC, JP (Co Cavan); *b* 22 July 1867; *educ* Trin Coll Dublin (BA); barrister King's Inn, Dublin, and Lincoln's Inn; High Sheriff Co Galway 1897, CC Co Galway 1899–1920, MP Galway 1900–01, Commr Nat Educn Ireland 1903–22, Senator Roy U of Ireland 1904–09, Govr U Coll Galway 1909–22, HM Lt and Custos Rotulorum Co Galway 1918, Chm Viceregal Commn Primary Educn Ireland 1918–19, KGStJ, Hon LLD Roy U Ireland; *d* unm 11 Aug 1927

2 George Henry; *b* 16 July 1872; Lt-Col 1st Bn Irish Gds, Tochl Expdn 1897 (medal with clasp), Boer War 1902 (despatches, medal with four clasps) and WW I; *m* 29 April 1913 Dora Maryan, JP and CC Cambs (*d* 5 May 1948) (*m* 2nd 12 March 1918 Col Gerard Tharp, late Rifle Bde, JP, DL, CC Cambs, of Chippenham, Ely, Cambs, and *d* 28 March 1934), 2nd dau of James Wesley Hall, of Melbourne, and was *ka* 1 Sept 1914, leaving:

(1) MICHAEL MORRIS, **3rd and present Baron Killanin**

3 Michael Redmond; *b* 11 Oct 1878; *educ* Trin Coll Dublin (BA); barrister; *d* unm 9 Dec 1902

4 Charles Ambrose; *b* 21 Sept 1880; *educ* Balliol Coll Oxford; *d* 25 April 1899

1 Sarah Lily; Irish sister of charity; *d* 24 June 1889

2 Rose Julia; *d* unm 10 April 1947

3 Maud Anna; *m* 7 July 1897 Capt Graham Owen Robert Wynne, JP, Roy Irish Regt (*d* 27 May 1939), of Clogherevagh, Co Sligo, and *d* 2 Dec 1957, leaving issue

4 Mary Kathleen; *m* 17 Jan 1907 Christopher Guy Orme, JP, DL (*d* 5 June 1929), of Owenmore, Crossmolina, Ireland, and *d* 16 June 1954, leaving issue

5 Frances Anne; Carmelite nun (Mother Frances of Jesus); *d* 10 June 1952

6 Eileen Elizabeth; Carmelite nun; *d* 4 Sept 1924

KILLEARN

Arms: Per saltire argent and gules two gryphon's heads erased in fess and as many escarbuncles in pale counterchanged. **Crest:** A gryphon's head erased gules, charged with an escarbuncle argent, between two wings paly of four, argent and gules. **Supporters:** Dexter, a camel proper with head-stall and rope reflexed over the back gules; sinister, a Chinese dragon proper. **Motto:** *Persevera et vince* ('Persevere and conquer'). **Creations:** Bt. (UK) 16 Nov 1866, B. (UK) 17 May 1943.

THE 3RD BARON KILLEARN, of Killearn, Stirling, and a **Baronet** (Sir Victor Miles George Aldous Lampson, Bt, of Rowfant, Worth, Sussex) [The Rt Hon The Lord Killearn, 12 Tokenhouse Yard, London EC2R 7AN]; *b* 9 Sept 1941; *s* half-bro 1996; *educ* Eton; late Capt Scots Gds, ptnr Cazenove & Co 1979–; *m* 18 Sept 1971 *Melita Amaryllis Pamela Astrid, 2nd dau of R-Adml Sir Morgan Charles Morgan-Giles, DSO, OBE, GM, DL, late MP Winchester, of Upton House, Alresford, Hants, and has:

(1) +MILES HENRY MORGAN; *b* 10 Dec 1977

(2) +Alexander Victor William; *b* 20 Jan 1984

(1) *Pamela Camilla Roxana; *b* 1973

(2) *Miranda Penelope Amber; *b* 11 April 1975

Lineage: WILLIAM LAMPSON, of New Haven, Vt., USA; dir Hudson's Bay Co; *m* Rachel, dau of Miles Powell, of Lainsborough, Mass., and had, with seven daus and three er sons:

Sir Curtis Miranda Lampson, 1st Bt (UK), so *cr* 16 Nov 1866 on completion of Atlantic cable; *b* 21 Sept 1806; naturalised Br subject 1848, dir Atlantic Telegraph Co; *m* New York 30 Nov 1827 Jane Walter (*d* 13 April 1891), dau of Gibbs Sibley, of Sutton, Mass., and *d* 12 March 1885, leaving:

1 **Sir George Curtis Lampson, 2nd Bt**; *b* 12 June 1833; *m* 1887 Sophia (*d* 12 June 1926), yst dau of Manuel Van Gelderen, and *d* 7 Nov 1899, leaving:

(1) **Sir Curtis George Lampson, 3rd Bt**; *b* 23 Jan 1890; *educ* Charterhouse; Lt 6th Bn Somerset LI and Capt RASC Egypt WW I; explorer Centl Belgian Congo and interior of French W Africa, author and jnlst, FRGS and FRZS; *m* 16 Oct 1920 Maud Lawton, dau of George Lawton Wrigley, of Bolton, Lancs, and *d* 1971, leaving:

1a *Sophia Curtis [Mrs Ronald Milwidsky, Mill House Farm Brightling, Sussex]; *b* 12 April 1935; *m* 6 Oct 1955 Ronald J Milwidsky, BSc (Eng), AMIEE (*d* 1966), and has:

1b *Peter Julian; *b* 5 July 1960

1b *Caroline Natasha; *b* 23 Aug 1956

2b *Sarah Janet; *b* 27 April 1962

(1) Norah Beatrice; *b* 14 Jan 1888; *d* 2 Nov 1918

(2) Elsie Helen; *d* unm 25 Sept 1965

2 Henry; *b* 15 Nov 1835; *m* 7 April 1863 Charlotte Maria (*dsp* 23 July 1873), dau of Joseph Murphy, of the Middle Temple, and *d* 14 June 1876

3 Norman George, JP (Surrey and London), DL (Middx); *b* 23 May 1850; *m* 16 Nov 1874 Helen Agnes (*d* 12 Aug 1929), 4th dau of Peter Blackburn, MP, of Killearn, Stirling, and niece of Baron Blackburn of Killearn (LP, *see* 1896 edn), and *d* 25 Oct 1894, leaving:

(1) Curtis Walter, CBE (1920), of Willingshurst, Shamley Green, Surrey; *b* 18 Aug 1875; *educ* Eton and Magdalen Coll Oxford (BA 1897); *m* 7 July 1908 Hilda (*d* 4 Aug 1946), dau of Sir David Baird, 3rd Bt, of Newbyth (*qv*), and *d* 9 Aug 1952, leaving:

1a Leslie; *b* 9 May 1909; *m* 8 April 1932 Col Robert (Robin) Harry Bushman, Gren Gds, only s of Maj-Gen Sir Henry Augustus Bushman, KCB, and had:

1b *Belinda Jane; *b* 23 March 1933; *m* 19 Jan 1967 *Wolfgang Aumayr

2b *Jemima Ann; *b* 18 Sept 1934; *m* 18 Dec 1968 *Ernest Cyril Jackson

3b *Mary Rose; *b* 9 June 1950

2a Mary Miranda; *b* 21 Feb 1911; *m* 7 May 1947 (William) John Rayner, CBE, s of John Lawrence Rayner, and had issue

(2) MILES WEDDERBURN LAMPSON, **1st Baron Killearn**, of Killearn, Stirling (UK), so *cr* 17 May 1943, GCMG (1937, KCMG 1927, CMG 1922), CB (1926), MVO (1906), PC (1948); *b* 24 Aug 1880; *educ* Eton; Clerk FO 1903–12, Sec Dip Serv 1905–06 and 1911, Sec Garter Mission Japan 1905, 2nd Sec Tokyo 1908–10 and Sofia 1911–12, Assist Clerk 1912–16, 1st Sec Peking 1916–19, Actg HC Siberia 1920, Chargé d'Affaires Peking 1920, Cnsllr FO 1920, memb Br Delegn Washington Conf Disarmament 1921, London Conf 1924 and Locarno Conf 1925, Envoy Extrdy and Min Plen China 1926–33, HC Egypt and Sudan 1933–36, Amb Extrdy and Plen Egypt and HC Sudan 1936–46, Special Commr SE Asia 1946–48, 3rd Cl Orders Rising Sun and Sacred Treasure Japan and 2nd Cl Order Chai Yu China; *m* 1st 6 July 1912 Rachel Mary Helen (*d* 23 Jan 1930), yr dau of William Wilton Phipps, of Chelsea, and had:

1a **Sir Graham Curtis Lampson, 4th Bt**, and **2nd Baron Killearn**; *b* 28 Oct 1919; *educ* Eton and Magdalen Coll Oxford (MA 1946); Maj RARO Scots Gds WW II (US Bronze Star); *m* 15 May 1946 *Nadine Marie Cathryn [The Rt Hon Nadine Lady Killearn, 58 Melton Court, Old Brompton Rd, London SW7 3JJ], only dau of V-Adml Cecil Horace Pilcher, DSO, by Catherine, gdau of Aristide Moraitinis, of Athens, PM and Regent Greece, and *d* 27 July 1996, leaving:

1b *Alexandra Rachel Mary Catherine Angelica [The Hon Mrs Gibbs, 11 Fernshaw Rd, London SW10 0TB]; *b* 8 May 1947; *m* 1st 5 Jan 1966 (*divorce* 1987) Nicholas Edward Hugo Meynell (*see* HALIFAX, E) and has issue; *m* 2nd 17 Dec 1997 *Julian Gibbs (*see* ALDENHAM and HUNSDON OF HUNDSON, B)

2b *Nadine Marisa, JP (Beds) [The Hon Lady Bonsor JP, Liscombe Pk, Leighton Buzzard, Beds]; *b* 23 Aug 1948; *m* 4 Sept 1969 *Sir Nicholas Cosmo Bonsor, 4th Bt (*qv*), and has issue

1a Mary Katherine; *b* 7 Aug 1915; Ldy-in-Waiting to HRH THE PRINCESS ROYAL 1948–51; *m* 14 March 1952 Lt-Col Alexander George Falkiner Monro, only s of Maj George Nowlan Monro of Auchinbowie, DL

2a Margaret Miranda; *b* 26 May 1923; *m* 29 June 1946 Geoffrey John Eustace Jameson, only s of Lt-Col William Kenneth Eustace Jameson, DSO, DL, of Warley House, Essex, and had issue

(2) (cont.) The **1st Baron** *m* 2nd 18 Dec 1934 *Jacqueline Aldine Leslie, CStJ [The Rt Hon Jacqueline Lady Killearn, Haremere Hall, Etchingham, Sussex; 23 Harley St, London W1N 1DA], only dau of Marchese Senator Aldo Castellani, Hon KCMG, DSc, MD, and *d* 18 Sept 1964, leaving by her:

2a VICTOR MILES GEORGE ALDOUS LAMPSON, **3rd and present Baron Killearn**

3a *Jacquetta Jean Frederica; *b* 29 June 1943; *m* 9 Oct 1964 (*divorce* 1990) 10th Earl of Saint Germans (*qv*) and has issue

4a *Roxana Rose Catherine Naila [The Hon Mrs Ross, 16 Kelfield Gdns, London W10 6LS]; *b* 26 Dec 1945; *m* 24 Nov 1966 *Ian Cowper Ross, s of Charles Ross, of Haslemere, Surrey, and has:

1b *Atticus Matthew Cowper; *b* 16 Jan 1968

2b *Milo Joseph Charles; *b* 21 Jan 1970

3b *Leopold Lincoln Fitzgerald; *b* 1980

1b *Holly Zahava Josephine; *b* 22 July 1971

2b *Mia Vanilla Catherine; *b* 1973

3b *Liberty Lettuce Clark; *b* 1978

(3) Adam Cathcart; *b* 27 Oct 1882; *educ* Eton and RMC Sandhurst; Maj QO Cameron Highrs WW I (despatches, wounded); *m* 18 Feb 1915 Margueretta Aggie Eileen, dau of John William Hutchinson, JP, DL, of Edingham, Kirkcudbrightshire, and *d* 1966, having had:

1a Norman John; *b* 22 Nov 1926; Lt QO Cameron Highrs; accidently *k* 8 Jan 1948

1a Ursula Agnes; *b* 14 Nov 1915; *m* 1st 29 Sept 1939 Lt Peter Anthony Johnstone, The Buffs, attd The King's Regt (*ka* Italy Sept 1944), est s of Douglas Johnstone, of S Africa, and had issue; *m* 2nd 2 Nov 1946 Duncan William Chisholm, DFC, er s of Angus Chisholm, of Chequers Home Farm, Bucks, and had further issue

(4) Basil Stewart; *b* 31 Aug 1886; *d* unm 17 May 1906

(1) Jean Leslie; *b* 3 Jan 1877; *m* 23 April 1895 10th Lord Ruthven of Freeland and *d* 8 Dec 1952, leaving issue (*see* CARLISLE, E)

(2) Bridget Helen; *b* 6 Nov 1878; *d* 30 Nov 1888

1 Hannah Jane; *m* 6 July 1874 Frederick Locker-Lampson (*d* 30 May 1895), s of Edward Hawke Locker, Commr Greenwich Hosp, and *d* 26 May 1915, leaving issue

KILMAINE

Arms: Sable three lions passant in bend between two double cotises argent. **Crest:** An eagle displayed vert. **Supporters:** Two lions regardant argent, ducally crowned, plain collared and chained or. **Motto:** *Suivez raison* ('Follow right'). **Creations:** Bt. (NS) 21 June 1636, B. (I) 21 Sept 1789.

THE 7TH BARON KILMAINE, of The Neale, Co Mayo, in Ireland, and a **Baronet** (Sir John David Henry Browne, Bt) [The Rt Hon The Lord Kilmaine, c/o Gwavas Station, Tikokimo, Hawks Bay, New Zealand]; *b* 2 April 1948; *s* f 1978; *educ* Eton; engr, dir: Fusion (Bickenhall) Ltd 1964–96 and Whale Tankers Ltd 1974–; *m* 22 May 1982 *Linda, yr dau of Dennis Robinson, of Budleigh Salterton, and has:

1 +JOHN FRANCIS SANDFORD; *b* 4 April 1983

1 *Alice; *b* 1985

Kilmaine, previous creation: James O'Hara, only son of the 1st Baron Tyrawley of the January 1706/7 creation, was himself ennobled, as Baron Kilmaine, a little over two years before his father's death, when he inherited the former's title as well. He was a soldier and diplomat, serving under Wade in the suppression of the Jacobites during the '45 Uprising, and by the end of his career having held the colonelcy of no fewer than eight regiments. He died without legitimate issue in 1773, when his titles expired. One of his by-blows was George [*sic*] Anne (supposedly a mistake for Georgiana) Bellamy, a tragic actress whose far from private life smacked more of farce, though her abduction by Byron's immediate predecessor the 5th Baron (the 'Wicked Lord' of his day) seems to have been uncomfortable enough to approach melodrama. Kilmaine had eloped with her mother, who was of a Quaker family, straight from boarding school. Horace Walpole (who, however, is prone to exaggerate) records him returning from a diplomatic mission to Portugal with three 'wives' and 14 children in tow.

Lineage: JOHN BROWNE, an Englishman, settled at The Neale, Co Mayo, *c* 1580; first Sheriff of the newly shired Co Mayo 1583; helped bring about the agreement called the 'Composition of Mayo', whereby the local chieftains and freeholders in 1585 submitted to the sovereignty of ELIZABETH I and the establishment of English laws and tenures; *m* Ann, dau of Nicholas Cardiffe, of Dunsink, Co Dublin, and while Sheriff Co Mayo a second time was *k* 1589 by the Bourkes of Mayo, who had risen in revolt, leaving, with a dau (Elizabeth):

JOSIAS BROWNE, of The Neale, of which recognised as heir 21 April 1612 and formally granted 2 Nov 1612; *m* Joan, dau of Edward Bermingham, of Carrick, Co Kildare, and had, with other issue (among whom were ancestors of the BROWNEs of Brownestown):

1 JOHN (Sir), **1st Bt**

2 Valentine; *m* 1st Mary, dau of Samuel Alford, by whom he had no issue; *m* 2nd Julia Lynch and by her had:

(1) Josias; *m* Anastasia, dau of Alexander Kirwan

(2) Thomas; *m* Margaret, dau of Charles O'Malley

3 Robert

4 Andrew; *m* Catherine, dau of Ulick Burke, of Castlehacket, Co Galway, and had issue

JOSIAS BROWNE *d* 22 Sept 1634; his est son,

Sir John Browne, 1st Bt (NS), so *cr* 21 June 1636, of The Neale; *m* 1626 Mary, est dau of Sir Dominick Browne, of Galway (*see* ORANMORE AND BROWNE, B), and had, with six other daus:

1 GEORGE (Sir), **2nd Bt**

2 John; Col; ancestor of the Marquess of Sligo (*qv*)

3 Dominick, of Breaghwy, Co Mayo; Army Capt; *m* Barbara, dau of Sir Henry Talbot (*see* TALBOT OF MALAHIDE, B), and had issue:

(1) Andrew, of Breaghwy; *m* Allinor, dau of Alexander Kirwan, of Dalgin, and had issue:

1a Dominick, of Breaghwy; *b* 1701; *m* 1st his cousin Mabel (*dsp*), dau of **Sir John Browne, 3rd Bt**, of Palmerstown, Co Mayo (*see* below); *m* 2nd Anne (*d* Dec 1771), dau of Martin D'Arcy, of Houndswood, Co Mayo, and *d* 1776, leaving:

1b Andrew Nicholas, of Breaghwy; Dep Govr Co Mayo; *m* Mary (*d* 1836), dau of E Gilker, and *d* 1796, having had:

1c Dominick; Maj 88th Regt; *d* unm 1803

2c Edmond; Lt-Col 36th Regt; *d* unm 18 April 1838

3c John, of Breghwy; *b* 1790; Lt-Col, served Peninsular War and Waterloo; *m* 2 Oct 1823 Frances Jane (*d* 14 Jan 1891), dau of John Hawthorn, of Jamaica, and *d* 20 Nov 1849, having had:

1d Dominick Andrew, of Breaghwy; JP, DL; *b* 30 June 1824; *educ* RMC Sandhurst; High Sherrif Co Mayo 1881; *m* 26 July 1864 Emily Louisa, only dau of John Sidney Hawkins, of Brompton, est s of Sir John Hawkins, Chm Middx QS, and *d* 9 Sept 1902, leaving:

1e Dominick Sidney, of Breaghwy, JP, DL; *b* 31st March 1866; High Sheriff Co Mayo 1896, Capt and Hon Maj 3rd Bn Roy Scots Fus; *m* 20 June 1895 Elizabeth Naomi (*m* 2nd 1928 as his 2nd w Arthur Melville Hood Walrond (*see* 1963 edn WALERAN, B) and *d* 1965), est dau of Hon R R Dobell, of Beauvoir Manor, Quebec, PC, MP (Canada), and *d* 1927, having had:

1f +Dominick Andrew Sidney, CBE; *b* 29 Feb 1904; *m* 1930 Iris Kathleen (*d* 1977), dau of Gerald Henry Deane, of Littleton Ho, Hants, and had:

1g +Peter Dominick, MBE (1984) [Lt-Col Peter Browne MBE, Ludwell Farm, Glympton, Oxon OX20 1AZ]; *b* 1949; Lt-Col RGJ (ret 1990); *m* 1974 *Sally Jane, est dau of John Eric Marrett, MRCS, LRCP, of Clare Ho, Howe Green, Essex, and has:

1h +Henry Dominick; *b* 1989

1h *Eleanor Jane; *b* 1987

1g (Miriam) Dominica; *b* 1931; *m* 1st 1953 (*divorce* 1964) Gavin Campbell Anderson and had:

1h *Sarah Dominica; *b* 1954; *m* 14 June 1969 *Robert Crofts Williams Llewellyn

1g (cont.) Mrs Dominica Anderson *m* 2nd 1964 *Maj Michael William Giles, Gren Gds, and *d* 6 Aug 1991, leaving by him:

1h *Peter William; *b* 23 March 1965; *m* 21 Aug 1993 *Bronwen Davies and has:

1i *Ash Fomorrii Eaodraca; *b* 25 Dec 1992

2h *Arrabella Kathleen; *b* 20 Aug 1968

2g *Fiona Naomi [Mrs Hugh Faulkner, Currie Lee, Crichton, Midlothian EH37 5XD]; *b* 1935; *m* 1956 *Cdr Hugh Douglas Younger Faulkner, CVO, RN, and has:

1h *Christopher Gerald [Christopher Faulkner Esq, 6 Rosemount Rd, London W13 0HJ]; *b* 1958; *m* July 1987 *Ming F, dau of Mark Veevers-Carter and Mrs John Blower, of Guernsey, and has:

1i *Clarence Dominick Hugh [Anthony Faulkner Esq, 26 Winn Rd, London SE12 9ET]; *b* 4 April 1992

1i *Olivia; *b* 22 Jan 1990

2h *Anthony Dominick Hugh; *b* 1961; *m* 1990 *Kate, dau of Edgar Denton, of Jersey, and has:

1i *Samuel Anthony Denton; *b* 6 Jan 1992

3g *Anne Patricia [Mrs Robin Hay, Stoke Cottage, Fullards Ave, Taunton, TA1 3DE]; *b* 1944; *m* 1st 1967 David J Forcey and has:

1h *Annabelle Jane; *b* 1971

3g (cont.) Mrs Forcey *m* 2nd 1978 *Robin John Hay and has by him:

1h *Alexander Robin; *b* 1980

1f Naomi Frances Muriel; *b* 5 Jan 1897

2f Noël Sidney; *b* 23 Dec 1899; *m* 1935 Sir Anthony Bevir, KCVO, CBE

3f *Moyra Rose [Mrs Guy Drake-Brockman, 1/307 Vancouver St, Victoria V8V 3T2, BC, Canada]; *b* 1903; *m* 1922 Maj Guy Percy Lumsden Drake-Brockman, DSO, MC (*d* 1952) and has:

1g *Guy Dominick; *b* 1925

1g *Marcia (twin); *b* 1925; *m* 1944 *Charles Williams, mechanical engr, and has:

1h *Charles Dominick; *b* 1945

2h *Andrew; *b* 1949

3h *Christopher Michael; *b* 1954

2e Francis John Sidney; *b* 23 Aug 1867; *d* 30 June 1875

2d Montague; Col 24th Regt; *m* 1st Margaret Elizabeth, only dau of Charles Maurice Stack, and had two sons (*d* unm); *m* 2nd Emily (*d* 1897), dau of Charles Hall Stack, of Mulloghmore, Co Tyrone; *m* 3rd Kate, dau of Rev J Dixon, DD

3d Henry John; *m* Constance Harding and *d* 1877, having had a s (*d* unm)

4d Frederick Augustus; *d* unm

5d Arthur Wellesley Wyndham; *d* unm

6d Edmond Charles; *b* 8 April 1843; Col cmdg Roy Scots Fusiliers Regtl Dist; *m* 1894 Catharine, only dau of Patrick Ness, of Braco Castle, and *d* 7 Jan 1910

7d Augustus Hawthorn

1d Rose Mary Anne; *m* John Mitchell (*d* May 1883), of Hawthorn Lodge, Ayrshire, and *d* Oct 1899

2d Sarah Jane; *m* Henry Finch, of Ashurstwood, Sussex

3d Mary Louisa; *d* unm 5 Nov 1908

1c Ann; *m* Charles Tyler and *dsp*

2c Catherine; *m* Capt G Cox and *dsp*

3c Dorothea; *m* Capt J Hoey and had issue

4c Rose; *m* J Mullins

5c Maria; *m* James Howell and *dsp*

6c Eliza; *d* unm

2b Sir JOHN EDMOND BROWNE, 1st Bt (I), so *cr* 8 Dec 1797, of Palmerstown, Co Mayo (*see* 1890 edn DE BEAUVOIR, Bt)

1 Elizabeth; *m* 19 June 1669 John Fitzgerald, of Mohenna, Co Mayo

Sir JOHN *d* 1670; his est son,

Sir George Browne, 2nd Bt, Sheriff Co Mayo 1690; regranted Nov 1684 The Neale and other lands in Co Mayo which had belonged to his f; *m* Alicia, only dau of Sir Henry Bingham, 1st Bt (*see* LUCAN, E), and *d* May 1698, having had, with three daus and a yr s (George):

Sir John Browne, 3rd Bt, of Palmerstown, Co Mayo; Capt JAMES II's Irish Army, captured Siege of Derry 6 May 1689; *m* 1st *c* 27/28 May 1680 Anne Hamilton (*d* 14 Aug 1680), est dau of 4th Lord Hamilton, Baron of Strabane (*see* ABERCORN, D), but by her had no issue; *m* 2nd Julia, 3rd dau of Sir Patrick Bellew, 1st Bt (*see* BELLEW, B), and *d* 11 April 1711, having had, with two other daus:

1 **Sir George Browne, 4th Bt**; MP Castlebar, Co Mayo, 1713–14; *m* Hon Bridget Bermingham, dau of 13th Lord (Baron) Athenry by his 2nd w Bridget, dau of Col John Browne, of Westport (*see* SLIGO, M)

2 JOHN (Sir), **5th Bt**

3 Henry, of Knockmore, Co Mayo

1 Mabel; *m* as his 1st w her cousin Dominick Browne (*see* above) and *dsp*

Sir GEORGE *dsp* 3 May 1737; his bro,

Sir John Browne, 5th Bt, formerly of Rahins, Co Mayo, Sheriff Co Mayo 1731, MP Castlebar *c* 1740–60; *m* 1st 30 June 1722 Margaret (*d* 23 April 1739), dau and coheir of Henry Dodwell, of Athlone; *m* 2nd Catherine, widow of Denis Daly, of Carrownakelly, and dau of Sir Walter Blake, 6th Bt, of Menlo (*qv*), and *d* 2 Oct 1762, having by his 1st w had:

1 **Sir George Browne, 6th Bt**, Sheriff Co Mayo 1747; *m* 12 Oct 1761 Anastasia, est dau of Denis Daly, of Raford, Co Galway, and *dspm* 14 Sept 1765, having had:

(1) Margaret

(2) Anne Letita; *m* 1794 Samuel POWER later POER, of Belleville Pk, Co Waterford

(3) Georgina; *m* 3 Aug 1970 Charles Blake, of Merlin Park

2 JOHN, **1st Baron**

3 Dodwell; ancestor of the BROWNEs of Rathain

4 Henry, Ch Justice Jamaica

5 Palmer

1 Julia; *m* Edmund Burke, of Curry, Co Mayo

The 6th Bt's bro,

Sir John Browne, 7th Bt, and **1st Baron Kilmaine** (I), so *cr* 21 Sept 1789; *b* 1730; Sheriff Co Mayo 1778 and 1788, MP Newtownards 1776–83 and Carlow 1783–89, bought Gaulston Pk, Co Westmeath, from the Earl of Belvedere; *m* 23 April 1764 Alicia (*d* 17 Dec 1797), dau of 3rd Viscount Charlemont (*qv*), and had, with four daus:

1 JAMES CAULFEILD, **2nd Baron**

2 John; *b* 28 Aug 1770; Lt-Col; *m* 20 Sept 1797 Anne (*d* 23 April 1851), dau of John White, of Jamaica, and *d* 8 Feb 1855, having had:

(1) George; *d* 1832

(2) William Henry; *b* 23 June 1809; *m* 1st 31 Aug 1843 Mary Matilda (*dsp* 15 Oct 1858), dau of J Noad; *m* 2nd 17 Jan 1861 Margaretta Louisa, yst dau of John MacConliffe, of Elton Ho, Co Limerick, and *dsp*

(1) Anne Margaret; *m* 1 March 1826 Neston Joseph Fuller (*see* FULLER, Bt) and *d* 24 March 1876

(2) Alicia; *m* 16 July 1822 Rev J B Brownlow, bro of 1st Baron Lurgan (*see* 1970 edn), and had issue

(3) Elizabeth; *m* 9 May 1833 Hon Richard Howe Browne and *d* 28 Oct 1876, leaving issue (*see* below)

3 George; *b* 2 March 1774; *m* 12 Oct 1801 Mary (*d* 15 July 1830), yst dau of Rev Alexander Colston, of Filkins Hall, Oxon (*see* 1940 edn ROUNDWAY, B), and *d* 26 Nov 1804, leaving:

(1) James Caulfeild (Rev); *b* 6 June 1804; DCL, Vicar Dudley; *m* 24 Nov 1822 Isabella (*d* 12 Dec 1877), only dau of John Mello, of Finch Lane and Denmark Hill, banker, and *d* 11 March 1870, having had:

1a William James Caulfeild (Rev); *b* 8 Jan 1825; Rector Kittisford, Somerset; *m* 29 Dec 1853 Jane Catherine Meade (*d* 17 Jan 1896), dau of Thomas Aubrey Gapper, of Wincanton, Somerset, and *d* 2 Nov 1893, leaving:

1b Aubrey Caulfeild; *b* 18 Aug 1860; *m* 1st 1888 Caroline Mitchell (*d* 1893) and had:

1c Cecil John Osborne Caulfeild; *b* 1892; *m* 1st 1923 Gladys Isobel Mason (*d* 29 Dec 1962); *m* 2nd 21 May 1965 *Constance Madeline Lily [Mrs Cecil Browne, 15 Caroma Ave, Kyeemagh, N Brighton, NSW, Australia], widow of — Ferguson, and *d* 1983, leaving by his 1st w:

1d +Aubrey Robert Caulfeild (Rev) [The Rev Aubrey Browne, c/o USPG, 15 Tufton St, London SW1]; *b* 1931; *educ* Newington Coll Sydney and Moore Coll Sydney (ThL 1955); Rector S Townsville, N Qld, regnl manager USPG

1c Winifred Edith; *b* 1889; *m* 18 May 1908 Ernest Alexander Nash (*d* 29 Nov 1964) and had issue

1b (cont.) Aubrey Browne *m* 2nd 1894 Ida (*d* 1942), widow of Charles Graham, and *d* 22 Sept 1953, having by her had:

2c Edward James Caulfield [*sic*], MBE; *b* 1903; *m* 1st 1925 (*divorce* 1941) Eileen, dau of Jack O'Hearn, of Ireland, and had:

1d +Reginald Malcolm [Reginald Caulfield-Browne Esq, 43 Birchwood Dr, Westfield, Sheffield S20 8LS]; *b* 1928; *m* 1st 1954 (*divorce* 1961) Valerie Therese Hogan and had:

1e *Loretta Sandra; *b* 1955

2e *Yolanda Therese; *b* 1956; *m* 1st 1978 (*divorce* 1993) Gerard Antony Mulnyan; *m* 2nd 1996 *Grant Franklin and by her 1st husb has:

1f *Jerome; *b* 1981

1f *Jemma Luise; *b* 1983

1d (cont.) Reginald Caulfield-Browne *m* 2nd 1965 (*divorce* 1991) Margaret Kathleen, dau of Thomas Glennon, and has by her:

1e +Mark; *b* 1966; BSc, PhD

3e *Helen Louise; *b* 1973

1d *Noreen; *b* 1926; *m* 1st 19– (*divorce* 19–) Aubrey Perry; *m* 2nd 19– *— Sharp

2c (cont.) Edward Browne *m* 2nd 1942 Mary Winifred (*d* 1987), dau of George Albert Green, and *d* 1984, leaving by her:

2d +Nigel George; *b* 1947; *m* 1st 1968 (*divorce* 1973) Susan Mary Green and has:

1e *Sharon Ann; *b* 1970

2d (cont.) Nigel Browne *m* 2nd 1974 (*divorce* 1983) Jill Christine Masters and has by her:

1e +James Alexander; *b* 1976

2e *Sophie Victoria; *b* 1978

3e *Lucy Alexandra; *b* 1980

2d (cont.) Nigel Browne *m* 3rd 1984 *Jane Elizabeth Skinner and has by her:

2e +Matthew John; *b* 1987

3d +Robin James; *b* 1949; *m* 1st 1970 (*divorce* 1978) Annette Heavey and has:

1e +Edward Patrick; *b* 1972

2e +Christopher Robert; *b* 1974

3d (cont.) Robin Browne *m* 2nd 1979 *Denise Dodd and has by her:

3e +Jason Robin; *b* 1987

1d *Dawn Rosemary; *b* 1943; *m* 19– *Robert Edward Collins and has:

1e *Mark Robert; *b* 1973

1e *Amanda Jane; *b* 1972

2c Norah; *b* 21 Feb 1896; *m* 5 Aug 1926 Johannes Corneille van Dongen and had:

1d *Robert Albert [Robert van Dongen Esq, 1 Ridgeview Cl, Barnet, Herts]; *b* 21 Oct 1927

2d *John Aubrey; *b* 5 Dec 1935; *m* 30 March 1968 *Lorraine Rosemary, dau of Thomas Atkinson

3c Kathleen; *b* 1898

2b James Cecil Caulfeild; *b* 8 March 1862; *m* 1887 Elsie, dau of Guillermo Manning, Br Consul San Salvador, and *d* 23 Jan 1917, having had:

1c Rolf Caulfeild; *b* 27 Sept 1895; *d* unm

2c Edwin Caulfeild; *b* 27 Sept 1895

1c Cecily Caulfeild; *b* 14 Jan 1891; *m* 1908 Henry Snell, of Boworthy, Devon

2c Nesta Caulfeild; *b* 17 Oct 1894; *m* Gordon Rowe

3b Harold John Caulfeild; *b* 10 March 1864; *m* 16 Nov 1916 Margaret Delamere Booth (*d* 1971), dau of Maj James Booth Clarkson, and *d* 25 July 1953, leaving:

1c *Edith Margaret [Mrs Thomas Goodlake, 1336 W King Edward Ave, Vancouver, BC V6H 1Z9, Canada]; *b* 23 April 1919; *educ* UBC (BA 1941); *m* 5 Feb 1955 Thomas Henry Standish Goodlake (*d* 1989), s of Thomas Julian Goodlake, of Victoria, BC, and adopted:

*John Stephen; *b* 2 July 1959

*Christopher James; *b* 25 Oct 1964

4b Edward Hungerford Caulfeild; *b* 14 Feb 1867; served Matabele campaign 1893; *m* 1910 Margaret (*d* 1940), dau of Richard Leaver Howitt, and *d* April 1940

1b Georgiana Catherine; *m* 8 Sept 1881 Benjamin E Ferrey and *d* 25 Nov 1897, leaving issue

2b Isabel Mary; *m* 18 June 1889 Ernest Richard D'Arcy de Ferrars and *d* his widow 7 July 1930, leaving issue

3b Flora Fanny Maude; *m* 14 Dec 1892 Thomas Sweet (*d* 1928) and *d* 9 June 1947, leaving issue

4b Edith Charlotte; *m* 1892 James Leslie Callaghan, LRCP, Capt RAMC (*d* 4 Feb 1932), and *d* April 1940, leaving issue

2a John George Cotton (Rev), JP, DL (Herts); *b* 1 April 1834; *educ* Cambridge (MA); *m* 10 Oct 1872 Louisa Mary (*d* 1915), only child of Morris Pryor, of Clay Hall, Baldock, Herts, and *d* 28 Sept 1903, having had:

1b James Caulfeild; *b* 1875; *d* young

1b Wilhelmina Louisa; *b* 1874; *d* young

2b Georgiana Isabella; *b* 1879; *d* unm 27 July 1944

3a Magens James Caulfeild; *b* 1 Dec 1837; Capt 15th Regt; *m* 31 Dec 1860 Sarah (*d* 1865), only dau of William Green, and *dsp* 31 Dec 1866

1a Isabella Eliza Catherine; *m* 5 Oct 1852 John Hyde Houghton, JP, FRCS, of Dudley, and *d* 30 Jan 1908, having had issue

2a Ellen; *m* 1st 4 July 1850 Rev George Y Osborne (*d* 11 Nov 1871), Vicar Fleetwood; *m* 2nd 25 Nov 1873 Edwin Dudley and *d* 1897, having had issue

3a Emily Jane; *m* 4 Feb 1851 Rev Francis Sandys Bradshaw, DCL (*dsp* 1891), Rector Kingston, Jamaica, and *d* 14 Oct 1911

4a Harriet; *m* 1st 7 Jan 1859 Frank West (*d* 5 March 1860) and had issue; *m* 2nd 24 May 1861 Charles Bruce Skinner (*d* 16 Feb 1863) and had further issue; *m* 3rd 6 June 1866 Charles Thorn, Paymaster RN, and had further issue; *m* 4th 21 July 1880 John Collis Browne, MD, and *d* 4 Feb 1901

5a Fanny Georgiana Charlotte; *m* 11 Sept 1856 Rev John Askew, only child of Maj Thomas Askew (*d* 20 June 1891), of The Down Ho, Kent, and *d* 22 April 1904, leaving issue

6a Mary Anne; *m* 3 Jan 1860 Rev William Stanley de Courcy Ireland (*d* 8 Sept 1904), incumbent Chalford, Glos, and *d* 6 April 1928, leaving issue

7a Ada Charlotte; *m* 6 Nov 1861 Henry Jephson Mello and *d* 9 Jan 1907, leaving issue

8a Theresa Caroline; *m* 26 Nov 1867 Rev Joseph Kirby Turner (*d* 1 Oct 1902), Vicar Stalmine, Lancs, and *d* 19 May 1932, leaving issue

9a Alice Louisa Nona; *m* 1st 23 Sept 1862 Carr Wigg (*d* 1903), of Hove, Sussex; *m* 2nd 30 Sept 1904 Rev Charles George Williamson, of Hove, and *d* 17 Oct 1922

The 1st BARON *d* 7 June 1794; his est son,

JAMES CAULFIELD BROWNE, **2nd Baron Kilmaine**; *b* 16 March 1765; MP Carlow 1790–94; *m* 25 July 1793 Anne (*d* 6 July 1863), dau of Sir Henry Cavendish, 2nd Bt (*see* WATERPARK, B), and had:

1 JOHN CAVENDISH, **3rd Baron**

2 Henry Montague (Very Rev); *b* 3 Oct 1799; Dean Lismore, Rector Burnchurch, Co Kilkenny; *m* 11 April 1822 Hon Catherine Penelope (*d* 24 June 1858), est dau of 1st Viscount Frankfort de Montmorency (*see* DE MONTMORENCY, Bt), and *d* 24 Nov 1884, leaving:

(1) James Frankort Manners (Sir), KCB; *b* 24 April 1823; Gen, Col Cmdt RE, Govr RMA Woolwich 1880–87, served Crimea 1855; *m* 24 April 1850 Mary (*d* 8 May 1888), dau of James Hunt, of Quebec, and *d* 6 Dec 1910, having had:

1a Emily Mary Elizabeth; *d* unm 1869

2a Caroline Elinor Henrietta; *d* unm 1868

3a Augusta Amelia; *d* an infant 1855

4a Alice Augusta; *d* an infant 1857

5a Annie Kathleen de Montmorency; *d* unm 4 Feb 1927

6a Agnes Montague

(2) Henry George Cavendish (Rev); *b* 14 Dec 1829; Ld Manor and Rector Bredon, Worcs; *m* 8 Jan 1856 Amelia (*d* 15 Jan 1910), dau and coheir of James Hunt, of Quebec, and *d* Aug 1911, having had:

1a Henry Montague; *b* 19 Nov 1857; Maj 1st Bn E Lancs Regt; *das* Boer War 23 May 1900

2a James Cavendish; *b* 3 March 1863; Roy Glos Hus; *ka* Boer War 25 Oct 1900

3a Augustus Arthur Howe; *b* 25 April 1868; *d* 16 May 1933

4a Francis Raymond; *b* 7 March 1870; *d* 15 Dec 1886

1a Amelia Mary; *m* 4 April 1895 William Henry Rawle (*d* 1914) and *d* 3 March 1935

2a Kathleen Penelope; *d* unm 27 April 1914

3a Agnes Gertrude; *d* unm 7 Jan 1947

4a Emilia Frances; *m* 26 Feb 1895 Charles Jared Hornor (*d* 1922), of Norwich, and *d c* 1959, leaving issue

5a Eva Bassile; *m* 1892 Rev Frederick William Knox, JP, MA (*d* 2 July 1929), domestic chaplain to Duke of Rutland, and *d* 4 May 1945, leaving issue

(1) Emilia Anne; *m* 24 April 1851 Col Hon Charles Hugh Lindsay, CB, MP, and *d* 15 Feb 1873, leaving issue (*see* CRAWFORD and BALCARRES, E)

(2) AUGUSTA MARY ELIZABETH, BARONESS BOLSOVER (UK), so *cr* 1880; *m* 10 June 1862 Lt-Gen Arthur Cavendish Bentinck and *d* 5 Aug 1893, leaving issue (*see* PORTLAND, E)

3 George Augustus; *b* 18 Feb 1801; Maj; *m* 1st 30 April 1845 Anne Hammond (*dsp* 22 May 1850), only child of Sir Charles Morgan and widow of St John Blacker; *m* 2nd 20 Oct 1853 Frances Mary (*d* 9 Aug 1904), est dau of Charles Prideaux-Brune, of Prideaux Place, Cornwall, and *d* 25 Dec 1878, having had:

(1) George Caulfeild Prideaux; *b* 16 Dec 1855; *m* 1st 7 Sept 1882 Evelyn (*d* 1 July 1883), dau of Lt-Gen Edward Arthur Somerset, CB (*see* BEAUFORT, D), and had:

1a Evelyn; *b* 1 July 1883; Boer War with Mon Militia, WWI with AIF; *d* 9 Sept 1928

(1) (cont.) George Browne *m* 2nd 7 Dec 1891 Gwendoline Theresa (*d* 6 Jan 1937), dau of Capt John Caulfeild, 90th Regt (*see* CHARLEMONT, V), and *d* 21 July 1906, having by her had:

1a Margaret Theresa Eileen; *b* 1892;; *m* 1st Jan 1913 (*divorce* 1923) Malcolm Bond Shelley, CMG (*d* 27 July 1968), s of Alfred Bond Shelley, took by deed poll 1932 the name CAVENDISH and had issue; *m* 2nd 27 Dec 1945 Capt Alexander George McCorquodale (*d* 6 Nov 1964), of Fairway, Gt Bedwyn, Wilts, only s of Alexander Cowan McCorquodale, JP, DL, of Cound Hall, Salop (*see* 1970 edn McCORQUODALE OF NEWTON, B), and *d* 5 Jan 1966

(2) Charles Cavendish; *b* 25 Sept 1858; *m* 20 Dec 1911 Edith, est dau of James Dann, and *d* 27 Oct 1918

(3) Cecil Augustus Seymour; *b* 12 Jan 1864; *m* 31 Oct 1889 Ada Catherine, only dau of Sir William Crosbie, 7th Bt (*see* 1936 edn), and had:

1a Claude Lancelot Seymour; *b* 25 Feb 1891

4 Augustus Caulfeild James; *b* 15 Nov 1803; Army Capt; accidently drowned 9 Aug 1831

5 Richard Howe; Capt 8th Hus; *b* 1 Oct 1811; *m* 1st 9 May 1833 Elizabeth (*d* 28 Oct 1876), yst dau of Col Hon John Browne (*see* above), and had:

(1) George Richard; *b* 19 June 1834; Maj 88th Connaught Rangers, Chev Legn Hon; *m* 13 June 1857 Louisa (*d* 4 Oct 1915), yst dau of R-Adml Sir George Tyler, KH, of Cotterell, Glam, and *d* 1901, having had:

1a Percy Richard Howe; *b* 22 July 1858; *d* an infant

2a Ernest Cavendish Howe; *b* 28 June 1860; *m* 5 Jan 1885 Rachel Georgina (*d* 4 July 1948), yst dau of Lt-Col Brett, 17th Lancers, and *dsp* 16 Aug 1909

3a George Howe; *b* 5 June 1862; *d* unm 21 Sept 1890

4a Frederick Howe; *b* June 1863; Magistrate CP, S Africa; *m* 1883 Emily (*d* 1943), dau of David Arnot, of Cape Colony, and *d* 5 July 1947, having had:

1b Noel Francis; *b* 1884; barrister, Civilian Rep Tanganyika Legislative Assembly; *m* 1919 Jessie Selwyn Tudhope and *d* 3 April 1943, leaving:

1c +Peter Kilmaine [Peter Browne Esq, Morningside Farm, PO Box 692, Rustenburg, Transvaal, S Africa]; *b* 1920; late Capt and Tech Adj RAC (EAAC) WW II; *m* 1948 *Dorothy Dobson, of Kenya, and has:

1d *Margaret Jess; *b* 7 Feb 1950

2d *Joan Selwyn; *b* 9 Feb 1951

2c David; *b* 1924; P/O RAF WW II; *ka* over Germany 2 Dec 1943

1b Kathleen Eva

1a Maud Elizabeth Howe; *b* 22 Nov 1864; *d* Nov 1865

2a Adelaide Margaret Louisa Howe; *b* 30 July 1866; *d* unm 1929

(1) Emily Anna; *d* unm 13 July 1857

5 (cont.) Capt The Hon Richard Browne *m* 2nd 14 Feb 1880 Elise (*d* 21 July 1939), dau of Col H S Watkin, Bombay Army, and widow of E Hutchinson Little, Bombay CS, and *d* 1 April 1888, leaving:

(2) Arthur Henry Howe (Rt Rev); *b* 16 Oct 1881; *educ* Balliol Coll Oxford (MA); Bp Bloemfontein 1935–51, Vicar St John the Divine Kennington, Canon Residentiary Southwark, RD Kennington; *d* unm 8 Sept 1961

6 Frederick Longworth; *b* 1 Oct 1811; *d* unm 6 Jan 1864

1 Sarah Louise; *m* 13 April 1825 Lt-Col George Disbrowe, KH, Gren Gds (*d* 22 July 1876), and *d* 22 June 1881

The 2nd BARON *d* 23 May 1825; his est son,

JOHN CAVENDISH BROWNE, **3rd Baron Kilmaine**; *b* 11 June 1794; rep I peer 1849–73; *m* 1st 4 Jan 1822 Elizabeth (*d* 1 Dec 1834), dau of David Lyon, and had, with three sons (*d* unm):

1 Isabella Anne; *m* 9 Sept 1844 8th Baron Beaumont (*see* NORFOLK, D) and *d* 16 March 1916, leaving issue

2 Agnes Georgina; *m* 12 June 1849 Sir George Samuel Abercromby, 6th Bt (*qv*), and *d* 27 June 1898, leaving issue

3 Louisa Katherine; *m* 9 June 1859 Maj Robert Higginson Borrowes (*dsp* 2 Feb 1901), gs of Sir Kildare Dixon Borrowes, 5th Bt (*see* 1939 edn), and *d* 14 Jan 1877

4 Emily Anne; *m* 20 June 1853 2nd Baron Lurgan (*d* 15 Jan 1882, *see* 1970 edn) and *d* 29 Sept 1923, leaving issue

The **3rd Baron** *m* 2nd 3 Sept 1839 Mary (*d* 23 April 1888), dau of Hon Charles Ewan Law, MP (see ELLENBOROUGH, B), and by her had, with three other daus (*d* unm):

1 FRANCIS WILLIAM, **4th Baron**

2 Edward Miles David; *b* 22 Oct 1844; Capt RN; *d* unm 27 July 1878

3 Arthur Henry; *b* 29 April 1850; *m* 29 Jan 1885 Clotilde Georgina (*d* 24 Jan 1945), dau of Sir John Don Wauchope, 8th Bt (*qv*), and *d* 3 May 1908, leaving:

(1) Clotilde Mary Hamilton; *b* 9 May 1886; *m* 15 Feb 1913 Capt Hugh Augustus Bagot-Chester (*see* BAGOT, B) and *d* 1 Feb 1964, leaving issue

(2) Clementina Bethia Evelyne; *b* 21 Dec 1889; *m* 16 Sept 1916 Capt Algernon Seymour Hoare, 2nd Life Gds (*d* 13 May 1952), s of Henry Seymour Hoare, of Morden, and *d* 21 Nov 1918, leaving issue

(3) Geraldine Henrietta Somerville; *b* 4 Sept 1891; *d* 27 June 1896

(4) Gertrude Cicely Juliet; *b* 6 March 1896

5 Mary Eleanor Frances; *m* 1st 17 June 1861 Maj George Bagot (*see* BAGOT, B); *m* 2nd 30 April 1868 Thomas Astell St Quintin, 10th Hus, est s of Thomas St Quintin, of Hatley Park, Cambs, and *d* 28 Oct 1869, leaving issue

6 Evelyn; *m* 20 Nov 1867 Maj-Gen Sir Owen Tudor Burne, GCIE (*d* 3 Feb 1909), and *d* 22 April 1878, leaving issue

The 3rd BARON *d* 13 Jan 1873; his est surv son,

FRANCIS WILLIAM BROWNE, **4th Baron Kilmaine**, JP (Cos Westmeath, Mayo), DL (Co Westmeath); *b* 24 March 1843; rep I peer 1890–1907, Sheriff Co Westmeath 1870; *m* 6 June 1877 Alice Emily (*d* 7 Feb 1925), dau of Col Deane Shute, and *d* 9 Nov 1907, leaving:

JOHN EDWARD DEANE BROWNE, **5th Baron Kilmaine**, JP, DL (Co Mayo); *b* 18 March 1878; rep I peer 1911–46, sold Gaulston Pk 1918 and The Neale and remaining Irish estates 1925 and moved to GB; *m* 17 Dec 1901 Lady Aline Kennedy (*d* 1 July 1957), dau of 3rd Marquess of Ailsa (*qv*), and had:

1 JOHN FRANCIS ARCHIBALD, **6th Baron**

2 Henry George Angus; *b* 9 Oct 1911; Maj Rifle Bde WW II 1939–42 (despatches); *k* by enemy air action nr El Alamein 8 Sept 1942

1 Alicia Evelyn; *b* Feb 1909; *m* 30 Nov 1936 Cdr Edward St John Edmonstone, RN, yr s of Sir Archibald Edmonstone, 5th Bt, CVO (*qv*), and *d* 1992, having had issue

The 5th BARON *d* 27 Aug 1946; his only surv son,

JOHN FRANCIS ARCHIBALD BROWNE, **6th Baron Kilmaine**, CBE (1956); *b* 22 Sept 1902; *educ* Winchester and Magdalen Coll Oxford (BA 1925, MA 1933); High Steward Harwich 1966–78, Sec Pilgrim Tst 1945–67 and Dulverton Tst 1953–66 (Tstee 1966–), govr Thomas Wall Tst and Tstee Historic Churches Preservation Tst, Admin Sec U Coll Southampton 1930–33 and Sec Oxford Soc 1933–40, chm Exec Ctee Oxford Soc 1949–78 and Charities Investment Managers Ltd, Lt-Col RASC on Staff WW II (despatches twice); *m* 12 Feb 1930 *Wilhelmina Phyllis [The Rt Hon The Dowager Lady Kilmaine, The Red Cottage, High Street, Brasted, Kent], only dau of Scott Arnott, of Brasted, and *d* 26 July 1978, leaving:

1 JOHN DAVID HENRY BROWNE, **7th and present Baron Kilmaine**

1 *Carola [The Hon Mrs Hudson, Gwavas Station, Tikokino, Hawkes Bay, New Zealand]; *b* 17 May 1932; *m* 30 April 1960 *John Michael Carlyon Lowry Hudson, only s of Herbert Hudson, of Tikokino, and has:

(1) *John Carlyon; *b* 25 Sept 1961; *m* 1989 *Fiona J, yr dau of G F White, of Dunedin, NZ, and has:

1a *Tristrem Carlyon Francis; *b* 1993

1a *Piera Jane; *b* 1995

(2) *Thomas Christopher; *b* 19 Nov 1963; *m* 1997 *Joanne Susan, dau of A B Robinson, of Mt Palm, S Island, NZ

(1) *Phyllida; *b* 5 March 1966; *m* 1996 *Stuart Barrie Gibson, er s of D B Gibson, of Hawkes Bay, NZ

2 *Phyllida [The Hon Mrs Previté, The Wilderness, Barge Walk, Hampton Wick, Kingston-upon-Thames, Surrey]; *b* 27 June 1935; *m* 25 July 1959 *His Honour Judge (John) Edward Previté, Circuit Judge, only s of Lt-Col Kenneth Edward Previté, OBE, RM, and has:

(1) *Andrew Capper; *b* 19 Oct 1961; *m* 1992 *Antonia Hamilton Davis, yr dau of E W Davis, of Chelsea

(2) *Matthew John; *b* 27 June 1963; *m* 1992 *Elizabeth S, er dau of A J Pull, of Headley, Hants, and has:

1a *Grace Alexandra; *b* 1993

KILMARNOCK

Arms: Quarterly: 1st, azure a fess chequy argent and gules (for BOYD); 2nd, argent three inescutcheons gules (for HAY); 3rd, argent three gillyflowers gules within a double tressure flory counter flory vert (for LIVINGSTON); 4th, sable a bend between six billets or (for CALLENDAR). **Crest:** A dexter hand raised in benediction. **Supporters:** Two squirrels proper. **Motto:** *Confido* ('I trust'). **Creation:** B. (UK) 17 June 1831.

THE 7TH BARON KILMARNOCK, of Kilmarnock, Co Ayr (Alastair Ivor Gilbert Boyd) [The Rt Hon The Lord Kilmarnock, 194 Regent's Pk Rd, London NW1 8XP]; *b* 11 May 1927; *s f* 15 May 1975, also as Ch of Clan Boyd; *educ* Bradfield and King's Coll Cambridge; Page to Ld High Constable Scotland Coronation 1937, Lt Irish Gds Palestine 1947–48, SDP: memb 1981–92, Ch Whip Ho Lds 1983–86 and Dep Ldr Peers 1986–87, Chm All-Party Gp AIDS 1987–96, V-Pres Assoc of District Cncls, exec dir Social Mkt Fndn 1989–, author: *Sabbatical Year* (1958), *The Road from Ronda* (1969), *The Companion Guide to Madrid and Central Spain* (1974), *The Radical Challenge* (ed, 1987), *The Essence of Catalonia* (1988) and *The Sierras of the South* (1992); *m* 1st 10 Sept 1954 (*divorce* 1970) Diana Mary Grant (*d* 30 June 1975), only dau of Donald Grant Gibson and formerly w of Derek Hawkins; *m* 2nd 18 Feb 1977 *Hilary Ann, yr dau of Leonard Sidney Bardwell and formerly w of (a) Sir Kingsley Amis, CBE, and (b) Dr Shackleton Bailey, and has by her:

1 *James Charles Edward; *b* 27 Jan 1972

Family History: A descent for the BOYDs has been claimed from Simon, bro of Walter, High Steward of Scotland 1160 and ancestor in the male line of the Stuart or Stewart dynasty that ruled first Scotland and then England and Ireland as well (*see* MORAY, E). A Sir Robert Boyd was certainly living 1205, and one Robert 'the' or 'le' Boyd, allegedly grandson of Simon, fought for ALEXANDER III against invading Norsemen at the indecisive Battle of Largs 1263. Another Robert Boyd was one of the first to join Sir William Wallace's rising against the dominant English in the last years of the 13th century, but no link between these and the BOYDs below is proven.

Lineage: Sir ROBERT BOYD; a Scots cdr Battle of Bannockburn 1314, rewarded by ROBERT I (THE BRUCE) with the feudal barony (a territorial entity held from the crown) of Kilmarnock, captured by the English at their victory over the Scots of Halidon Hill 1333 and *d* soon afterwards, leaving, with other issue (including a yr s Alan, *k* 1339 cmdg Scots archers at siege by the English of Perth):

Sir THOMAS BOYD; 2nd feudal Baron of Kilmarnock; captured with DAVID II English victory of Neville's Cross 1346; had an est s:

THOMAS BOYD; 3rd feudal Baron of Kilmarnock; pardoned for killing a personal enemy 1409; *m* Alice, dau and coheir of Hugo Gifford of Yester, and had:

THOMAS BOYD; 4th feudal Baron of Kilmarnock; a hostage 1424 for JAMES I's ransom by the English following his (JAMES's) capture at sea perhaps as much as 20 years earlier; *m* Joan, dau of Sir John Montgomerie of Ardrossan (*see* EGLINTON and WINTON, E), and *d* 7 July 1432, leaving, with other issue, including a yr s (William, Abbot of Kilwinning (some 20 miles southwest of Glasgow)):

Sir THOMAS BOYD; 5th feudal Baron of Kilmarnock; *k* Sir Alan Stewart of Darnley (*see* MORAY, E) in a feud 1439; *k* in revenge by his victim's bro 9 July 1439, leaving:

1 ROBERT, 1st LORD

2 Alexander (Sir), of Drumcol; Keeper Edinburgh Castle, commr with his er bro and others to discuss truce with English 1464; through his er bro's influence made instructor in knightly matters to JAMES III when a boy 1466; executed Edinburgh 1469 following a charge of treason brought against him and his bro by rival nobles

1 Janet/Marion; *m* Sir John Maxwell of Calderwood (*see* FARNHAM, B)

2 Margaret; *m* 1st Lord Montgomerie (*see* EGLINTON and WINTON, E)

Sir THOMAS BOYD's er s,

ROBERT BOYD, 1st LORD BOYD (S), so *cr* between 1451 and 18 July 1454; ktd *c* 1451; a Regent for the infant JAMES III 1460; took custody of JAMES III 1466 and got an Act of Parl passed making himself sole Govr of Scotland, also Gt Chamberlain 1467; attainted (and his peerage forfeited) 1469 while away from court negotiating the transfer of Orkney to Scotland as a dowry for the KING OF NORWAY's dau, whose marriage with JAMES III he had arranged; *m* Janet or Mariota (*d* after 25 June 1472, seemingly early 1473), dau of Sir Robert Maxwell of Calderwood (*see* FARNHAM, B), and *d* by Oct 1482 in exile allegedly at Alnwick, Northumberland, having had issue:

1 THOMAS BOYD, 1st and last EARL OF ARRAN , so *cr* 26 April 1467 after acquiring the island of Arran off the west coast of Scotland and the sheriffdom of Bute (another island off the west coast of Scotland) through his marriage with JAMES III's sis, a marriage brought about by his f's influence; *m* by 26 April 1467 MARY, LADY OF SCOTLAND (*b c* 1450; *m* 2nd 1468, while her 1st husb was still alive, 1st Lord Hamilton; *see* ABERCORN, D), dau of JAMES II, but was attainted with his f 22 Nov 1469 when he had returned from Denmark with JAMES III's future queen (who he was escorting to Scotland) but had not yet landed, and *dvp* allegedly *c* 1473 at Antwerp while in the service of CHARLES THE BOLD DUKE OF BURGUNDY, leaving:

(1) JAMES BOYD, 2nd(?) LORD BOYD(?); lands restored to him 14 Oct 1482 but there is less certainty as to whether his honours were also restored; *dvp* and unm 1484, *k* as a result of a feud with 1st Earl of Eglinto(u)n (*see* EGLINTON and WINTON, E)

(1) Margaret; *b* between 1468 and 1473; *m* 1st 4th Lord Forbes (*qv*); *m* 2nd by 9 Aug 1509, as his 2nd w, 1st Earl of Cassillis (*see* AILSA, M) and *dsp* on or after 9 Feb 1515/6

2 ALEXANDER, for whom *see* further below

3 Archibald of Bonshaw; had:

(1) Margaret or Marion; mistress of JAMES IV, by whom she had:

1a Alexander STEWART; Archbp St Andrews

1a Catherine STEWART

(2) Elizabeth; *m* Thomas Douglas and had issue (*see* MORTON, E)

4 John

1 Elizabeth; *m* 4 March 1467/8, as his 1st w, 5th Earl of Angus (*see* HAMILTON and BRANDON, D) and *d* by 21 Feb 1497

2 Annabella; *m* Sir John Gordon of Lochinvar

3 Margaret; *m* Robert Boyd of Badenheath

The 1st LORD BOYD's 2nd s,

ALEXANDER BOYD; Chamberlain (crown appointee responsible for royal burghs or towns and their judicial administration) Kilmarnock by 2 Aug 1488; *m* by 23 Nov 1505 Janet, dau of Robert Colville of Hiltoun (*see* COLVILLE OF CULROSS, V), and *d* on or after 26 June 1508, having had, with three other sons:

1 ROBERT BOYD, 4th LORD

2 Thomas; *m* Marion, dau of John Fairlie of that Ilk, and *d* 1547, leaving issue

3 Adam; *m* Helen, dau of 2nd Lord Kennedy (*see* AILSA, M), and left issue

1 Margaret; *m* George Colquhoun of Glens/Glins and had issue:

(1) Margaret; *m c* 1535 her cousin 5th LORD BOYD (*see* below) and *d* Aug 1601

2 Euphemia; *m* Lyon Logie of that Ilk, last of his line, and had:

(1) Margaret; *m* Thomas Hay and had:

1a 7th Earl of Erroll (*qv*)

ALEXANDER BOYD's est s,

ROBERT BOYD, 4th LORD BOYD; Chamberlain Kilmarnock to 1534; declared head of the Boyd family as heir to 2nd LORD BOYD 11 March 1544; officially confirmed as rightful possessor of dignities, estates and honours belonging to his gf 1st LORD BOYD between Sept 1545 and Nov 1546, being thus restored as LORD BOYD; killed the Tutor (guardian) of Lord (presumably 3rd Earl of) Eglinto(u)n in yet one more episode in the feud between the Boyds and Montgomeries; *m* 1st by 1518 Helen (*d* on or after 13 Aug 1536), dau of Sir John Somerville of Cambusnethan, and had:

1 ROBERT, 5th LORD

The 4th LORD BOYD *m* 2nd by Dec 1542 Elizabeth Napier; *m* 3rd by 10 Feb 1548/9, as her 1st husb, Marion, dau of Sir John Colquhoun of Luss (*see* COLQUHOUN, Bt), and *d* between 29 July 1557 and 10 May 1558, leaving:

1 Margaret; *m* John Montgomerie of Lainshaw, of a cadet branch of the Montgomerie Earls of Eglinto(u)n, in a vain attempt to heal the Boyd-Montgomerie feud

The 4th LORD BOYD's s,

ROBERT BOYD, 5th LORD BOYD, PC (S 1567, 1571–73/4 and July 1574–Jan 1589/90); *b c* 1517; Chamberlain Kilmarnock 1534; helped the Regent of Scotland, the 2nd Earl of Arran of the 1503 *cr* (*see* ABERCORN, D), defeat the 4th Earl of Glencairn (*see* CUNINGHAME, Bt), a leading agent of English interests, at Glasgow 1544; fought for MARY QUEEN OF SCOTS Battle of Langside (her final defeat by the Protestant faction and dissident nobles before her flight to England and virtual imprisonment there) 1568, go-between in intrigue between MARY and 4th Duke of Norfolk (*qv*) during latter's attempt to marry MARY himself 1569 and delivered to MARY the famous diamond pledged by Norfolk to MARY as a token of his love and good faith; Extrdy Ld of Session (sr judicial appointment) 1573–78, 1578–83 and 1586–88, commr to negotiate with English 1578 and 1586, Visitor Glasgow U 1578; involved in the Raid of Ruthven 1579 (abduction of JAMES VI (of Scotland, afterwards I of England) by pro-English Protestants), banished 1583–Feb 1585/6 following JAMES I's escape from the Ruthven faction and the renewed ascendancy of the Catholic pro-French party in Scotland, a Warden of the Marches 1589; *m c* 1535 his cousin Margaret or Mariot, dau and heiress of George Colquhoun 4th of Glens/Glins (*see* above), and *d* 3 Jan 1589/90, having had:

1 Robert, *Master of Boyd*; *dsp* & *vp* after 14 Oct 1550

2 THOMAS, 6th LORD

3 Robert; *m* Margaret, sis and heir of Robert Boyd of Badenheath, and *d* 1611

1 Margaret; *m* John Cuningham of Cuninghamhead

2 Helen

3 Egidia/Giles/Gille; *m c* May 1576, as his 1st w, 4th Earl of Eglinto(u)n (*see* EGLINTON and WINTON, E), thus healing the feud, and *d* in or after 1584

4 Agnes; *m* Sir John Colquhoun of Luss (*see* COLQUHOUN, Bt) and had issue

5 Christian; *m* Sir James Hamilton of Evandale

6 Elizabeth; *m* Sir John Cuningham of Drumquhassill

The 5th LORD BOYD's 2nd s,

THOMAS BOYD, 6th LORD BOYD/1st LORD BOYD OF KILMARNOCK; *b c* 1547; fought together with his f at Langside, surrendered and was regranted his estate 12 Jan 1591/2 as LORD BOYD OF KILMARNOCK (S), with remainder to heirs male; *m* 1st by 1568 Margaret, dau of Sir Matthew Campbell of Loudoun (*see* LOUDOUN, E); *m*(?) 2nd Jane, yst child of William Stockdale, of Green Hamerton, Yorks(?); *m* 3rd(?) Elizabeth Wallace and *d* June 1611, having had (most probably by his 1st w), with other sons:

1 Robert, *Master of Boyd*; *m* by 1595, as her 1st husb, Lady Jean Kerr, dau of 1st Earl of Lothian (*see* LOTHIAN, M), and *dvp* May 1597, leaving:

(1) ROBERT BOYD, 7th LORD BOYD (OF KILMARNOCK); *b* Nov 1595; *educ* Saumur, France; *m* 1st by 24 March 1614/5 Margaret (*dsp* 1616), dau of Robert Montgomerie of Giffen (yr bro of 4th Earl of Eglinto(u)n) and widow of 5th Earl of Eglinto(u)n; *see* EGLINTON and WINTON, E); *m* 2nd *c* 9 Dec 1617 Lady Christian Hamilton, dau of 1st Earl of Haddington (*qv*) and widow of 9th Lord Lindsay of the Byres (*see* LINDSAY, E), and *d* 28 Aug 1628, leaving:

1a ROBERT BOYD, 8th LORD BOYD (OF KILMARNOCK); *b c* 1618; Covenanter (Presbyterian opposed to CHARLES I's Anglicanising tendencies in Scottish ecclesiastical affairs); *m c* 10 Sept 1639, as her 1st husb, Lady Anne Fleming (*m* 2nd 2nd Earl of Dalhousie (*qv*) and *d* 20 April 1661), dau of 2nd Earl of Wigtoun, and *dsp* 17 Nov 1640

1a Christian; *m c* 26 Oct 16–Sir William Scott of Harden and had issue (*see* POLWARTH, L)

(2) JAMES, 9th LORD

1 Marion; a prominent Catholic who was accordingly excommunicated by the Presbyterians in the Kirk of Paisley 1628; *m* 1st Earl of Abercorn (*see* ABERCORN, D) and *d* 26 Aug 1632, leaving issue

2 Isabel; accused of witchcraft 1641; *m* John Blair, Yr. of that Ilk

3 Agnes; *m* Sir George Elphinstone of Blythswood, Provost (chief magistrate) Glasgow

The 8th LORD BOYD (OF KILMARNCOCK)'s unc,

JAMES BOYD, 9th LORD BOYD (OF KILMARNOCK); Royalist Civil War, fined £1,500 (nearly £94,000 in late-1990s terms) under the Act of Grace during CROMWELL's Protectorate 1654; *m* by 1640 Catharine or Katherine, dau of Robert Creyke, of York, disinherited s of Ralph Creyke, of Marton, Yorks, and *d* March 1654, leaving, with three daus:

WILLIAM BOYD, 10th LORD BOYD (OF KILMARNOCK) and 1st EARL OF KILMARNOCK, so *cr* 17 Aug 1661 (S); Master of the King's Game for Ayr 1685; *m* 25 April 1661 Lady Jean Cunningham, dau of 9th Earl of Glencairn (*see* CUNINGHAME Bt), and *d* March 1692, leaving, with other issue (including other sons who fought abroad in the Scots Dutch Bde):

WILLIAM BOYD, 2nd EARL OF KILMARNOCK; *m* July 1682, as her 1st husb, Letitia (*m* 2nd John Gard(i)ner), only surv child of Thomas Boyd, Dublin merchant, and *d* 20 May 1692, leaving, with other issue:

WILLIAM BOYD, 3rd EARL OF KILMARNOCK; *b* 1683 or 1684; voted for the Union with England 1707, granted a fresh charter 22 Jan 1707 limiting remainder of the Earldom to (a) heirs male of his body, in default of which to (b) his daus in succession (*i.e.*, primogeniture) and the heirs male of their bodies and in default of (b) to (c) his nearest legitimate heirs and assignees whatsoever; led 500 of his men in support of GEORGE I 1715 against the Jacobites; *m c* 1700 Euphemia Ross (*b* 11 Nov 1684; *m* 2nd Feb 1727 John Murray, n of 1st Duke of Atholl (*qv*), and *d* by 19 July 1729), dau of 12th Lord Ross, and *d* Sept 1717, leaving:

WILLIAM BOYD, 4th EARL OF KILMARNOCK; *b* 12 May 1705; Grand Master Masons Scotland 1742–43; at the time of the '45 Rising supported the Hanoverians until Oct 1745 but then, seemingly with a view to restoring his dissipated wealth, took the ultimate gamble and joined Prince Charles Edward's army, in which he was Col Horse Grenadiers at Battle of Falkirk 17 Jan 1746 (the last Jacobite victory), captured at Battle of Culloden (final Jacobite defeat) 16 April 1746, attainted (whereupon the Earldom of Kilmarnock and Lordship of Boyd were both forfeited) and beheaded Tower Hill as a Jacobite 18 Aug 1746; *m* 15 June 1724 Lady Anne Livingston, dau and heir of 5th Earl of Linlithgow and 4th Earl of Callendar (both titles forfeited by attainder 1716) by his w Lady Margaret Hay, dau of 12th Earl of Erroll (*qv*) and sis of Countess of Erroll in her own right, and had:

1 William, styled *Lord Boyd*; *b* 16 March 1725; *dvp* by 10 Feb 1728

2 JAMES BOYD later HAY, styled *Lord Boyd*, later 15th EARL OF ERROLL, for whom *see* further below

3 Charles; Capt Jacobite Life Gds Culloden, escaped abroad; *m* twice and *d* 3 Aug 1782, leaving issue

4 William; Midshipman RN 1745, Capt 87th Foot 1760; *d* Dec 1780

The 4th EARL OF KILMARNOCK's 2nd s,

JAMES BOYD later HAY, 15th EARL OF ERROLL; *b* 20 April 1726; fought in GEORGE II's army at Culloden on the opposite side to his own f, was allowed to inherit forfeited Kilmarnock lands 1751 but sold them on succeeding his great-aunt in Earldom of Erroll 19 Aug 1758 and substituted the name HAY for BOYD (*see* ERROLL, E, for further particulars throughout this article); *m* and had, with other issue:

1 GEORGE HAY, 16th EARL OF ERROLL

2 WILLIAM HAY later CARR, 17th EARL OF ERROLL; *m* and had, with other issue:

(1) WILLIAM GEORGE CARR later HAY, 18th EARL OF ERROLL and **1st Baron Kilmarnock**, of Kilmarnock, Co Ayr (UK), so *cr* 17 June 1831, KT (1834), GCH (1830); *b* 21 Feb 1801; *educ* Eton; *m* 4 Dec 1820 Elizabeth FitzClarence (*see* MUNSTER, E), illegitimate dau of WILLIAM IV by Mrs Jordan, and *d* 19 April 1846, having had, with other issue:

1a WILLIAM HARRY HAY, 19th EARL OF ERROLL and **2nd Baron Kilmarnock**; had, with other issue:

1b Charles Gore, *Lord Kilmarnock*; *b* 11, *d* 12 Oct 1850

2b CHARLES GORE HAY, 20th EARL OF ERROLL and **3rd Baron Kilmarnock**, KT (1901), CB (1900), JP (Cumberland), DL (Aberdeenshire); *b* 7 Feb 1852; *educ* Harrow; *m* 11 Aug 1875 Mary Caroline, dau of Edmund L'Estrange, and *d* 8 July 1927, having had, with other issue:

1c VICTOR ALEXANDER SERELD HAY, 21st EARL OF ERROLL and **4th Baron Kilmarnock**, KCMG (1924, CMG 1919); *b* 17 Oct 1876; *m* 22 May 1900 Mary Lucy Victoria Mackenzie and had, with other issue:

1d JOSSLYN VICTOR HAY, 22nd EARL OF ERROLL and **5th Baron Kilmarnock**; *b* 11 May 1901; had:

1e DIANA DENYSE Hay, COUNTESS OF ERROLL in her own right (*see* ERROLL, E)

2d GILBERT ALLAN ROWLAND HAY later BOYD (warrant of Ld Lyon King of Arms 1941), **6th Baron Kilmarnock**, MBE (1945), TD; *b* 15 Jan 1903; *educ* Cheltenham; *s* as Chief of Clan Boyd 1941; Hon Lt-Col RA (TA) Herts Yeo, served WW II with 1st Div N Africa and Italy 1943–44, DAAG (despatches), Assist Mil Sec Supreme Allied C-in-C Mediterranean Theatre 1945; Deputy Ld High Constable Scotland Coronation 1953; chm Harris and Dixon Ltd, pres: Inst Chartered Shipbrokers 1959–62, London Chamber of Commerce 1961–62 and Roy Caledonian Schs, dir Baltic Mercantile and Shipping Exchange 1961 (chm 1965–66), Freeman City London 1955, Ch Scottish Clans Assoc London 1962; *m* 1st 12 July 1926 (*divorce* 1955) Hon Rosemary Sibell Guest (*d* 21 March 1971), er dau of 1st Viscount Wimborne (*qv*), and had:

1e ALASTAIR IVOR GILBERT BOYD, **7th and present Baron Kilmarnock**

2e +ROBIN JORDAN [Dr The Hon Robin Boyd, 276 Alexandra Pk Rd, London N22 4BG]; *b* 6 June 1941; heir presumptive; *educ* Eton, Strasbourg U, Keble Coll Oxford (MA 1974) and St Thomas's Hosp London; Page to Dep Ld High Constable Scotland Coronation 1953; MB, BS, LRCP 1970, MRCS, DCH 1973

1e *Laura Alice Boyd [The Hon Mrs Hyman, 38a Downshire Hill, London NW3 1NU]; *b* 10 June 1934; *m* 11 Jan 1962 *(Robert) Anthony Hyman, s of A Hyman, of Richmond, Surrey, and has:

1f *Anthony A; *b* 1962

2f *Merlin M; *b* 1969

1f *Francesca M D; *b* 1963; *m* 1994 *Charles Mills, s of Capt K H Mills, of Chickerell, Dorset

2e Juliet; *b* 1 May, *d* 2 May 1937

3e Iris; *b* and *d* 1 May 1937

4e *Caroline Juliet; *b* 31 July 1939; *m* 1969 *Alan Bloss

2d (cont.) The **6th Baron** *m* 2nd 17 May 1955 Denise Aubrey Doreen (*d* 1985), only child of Maj Lewis Coker (*see* DONEGALL, M), and *d* 15 May 1975, leaving by her:

3e +Jonathan Aubrey Lewis [The Hon Jonathan Boyd, 3 Evelyn Gdns, London SW7]; *b* 1 Oct 1956; *educ* Eton; *m* 20 March 1982 *Annette Madeleine, er dau of Joe Constantine, of Kensington

4e +Timothy Ian [The Hon Timothy Boyd, Flat 2, 23 Ladbroke Crescent, London W11 1PS]; *b* 5 April 1959; *m* 1988 *Lucy Teresa Emily, yr dau of Michael Gray, and has:

1f *Daisy; *b* 1988

KILMOREY

Arms: Argent a bend engrailed azure between two buck's heads cabossed sable. **Crest:** A demi-phoenix in flames proper. **Supporters:** Dexter, a horse argent; sinister, a stag proper. **Motto:** *Nunc aut nunquam* ('Now or never'). **Creations:** V. (I) 8 April 1925 (Kilmorey); E. and V. (Newry and Mourne) (I) 5 Feb 1822.

THE 6TH EARL OF KILMOREY, Viscount Kilmorey, in Queen's Co, and **Viscount Newry and Mourne**, Co Down (Sir Richard Francis Needham, PC (1994)) [The Rt Hon Sir Richard Needham, 199 Bishopsgate, London EC2M 3TY]; *b* 29 Jan 1942; *s* f 1977 but does not use title; *educ* Eton; MP (C) Chippenham 1979–83 and Wilts N 1983–97, chm RGM Point Hldgs 1967–85, CC Somerset 1967–74, C candidate Gravesend 1974 gen election, PA to James Prior, MP, 1974–79, PPS to: Sec State NI 1983–84, Sec State Environment 1984–85; Parly U-Sec NI 1985–92, Min State DTI 1992–95, dir: GEC 1995–97, Miva (NI engrg co) 1995– and Dyson Appliances 1995–, Tough Glass 1997–, v-chm NEC (Europe) 1997–; ktd 1997; author *Honourable Member* (1983); *m* 5 June 1965 *Sigrid Juliane Thiessen-

Gairdner, only dau of Ernest Thiessen and Mrs John Gairdner, of Hamburg, and has:

1 +ROBERT FRANCIS JOHN, *Viscount Newry and Mourne*; *b* 30 May 1966; *educ* Eton, LMH Oxford and Imperial Coll London (MBA); *m* 1991 *Laura Mary, only dau of Michael Tregaskis, of Cosham, Hants, and has:

(1) +Thomas Francis Michael; *b* 25 Sept 1998

(1) *Julia Helen Mary; *b* 11 March 1997

2 +Andrew Francis; *b* 7 March 1969; *educ* Eton and Edinburgh U; publisher; *m* 16 Aug 1997 *Lindsay, dau of Lance Stephenson, of Thompson, Norfolk

1 *Christina Clare *b* 2 Sept 1977

Lineage: WILLIAM de STANTON, of Stanton, Cheshire; living 1103; had:

WILLIAM fitz WILLIAM de STANTON, of Stanton; had:

ROGER/WILLIAM; *m* the heiress of the Manor of High Needham, Derbys, and had:

HENRY de NEEDHAM; had:

JOHN de NEEDHAM, of Needham; had:

JOHN NEEDHAM, of Needham; living 1331; had:

THOMAS NEEDHAM, of Needham; had, with an er s (Thomas, of Needham, *m* Maud, dau and heiress of Roger Mellor, of Thomsett Hall, thus acquiring that Manor by 1354, and *d* by 1363, leaving issue, among whom were the NEEDHAMs of Thomsett, the NEEDHAMs of Cowley, the NEEDHAMs of Melbourne, the NEEDHAMs of Needham Market, Suffolk, and the NEEDHAMs of Ollersett):

WILLIAM NEEDHAM; Justice Chester 1376; *m* Alice, dau and heiress of William de Granage, Cheshire, thus acquiring that Manor, and had:

ROBERT NEEDHAM, of Granage; *d* 1407, leaving:

ROBERT NEDEHAM, of Granage; *m* Dorothy, dau of Sir John Savage, KG, of Clifton, Cheshire, and had, with other issue, including a yr s (Sir John, Common Serjeant London 1449, MP City London 1450, Judge King's bench 1461):

THOMAS NEEDHAM, of Granage; *m* Maud, dau of Sir William Brereton, of Brereton, and had, with a yr s (Robert, of Shavington, whose male issue died out 1578):

Sir WILLIAM NEEDHAM, of Granage; *m* Isabel, dau and coheiress of Sir John Bromley, and had:

Sir ROBERT NEEDHAM; bought 1506 the estate of Shenton in Adderley, Salop; Sheriff Salop 1529, 1536 and 1541; *d* 1556, having had, with a dau (Jane, *m* Sir Andrew Corbet and *d* 1577, leaving issue; *see* 1970 edn CORBET, Bt):

THOMAS NEEDHAM, of Shenton; *m* Anne, dau of Sir John Talbot, of Grafton and Albrighton, gs of 1st Earl of Shrewsbury and Waterford (*qv*), and had an est s:

ROBERT NEEDHAM, of Shenton; Sheriff Salop 1564, 1586 and 1595; inherited the Shavington estate from his cousins; served Ireland; V-Pres Cncl Wales; *m* Frances, yst dau of Sir Edward Aston, of Tixall, Staffs, and had:

1 ROBERT, **1st Viscount**

2 Thomas, of Pool Park, Denbighs; *m* Eleanor, dau and coheiress of Sir Henry Bagenall, Kt Marshal, and had issue

1 Mary; *m* Sir Robert Vernon (*see* VERNON, B) and had issue

ROBERT NEEDHAM *d* 18 Dec 1603; his er son,

Sir ROBERT NEEDHAM, **1st Viscount Kilmorey**, in Queen's Co (I), so *cr* 8 April 1625; *educ* Inner Temple; MP Salop 1592–93 and 1604–11, ktd 1594, High Sheriff Salop 1606, memb Cncl Wales 1617; *m* 1st *c* 10 Aug 1586 Jane (*d* 16 July 1591), dau of John Lacy, of Borston, Somerset; *m* 2nd by 14 Oct 1594 Anne, widow of — Wilmot and dau of — Doyley; *m* 3rd Catherine (*d* 1627), widow of George Huxley and dau of John Robinson; *m* 4th Dorothy (*m* 4th, as his 3rd w, 1st Earl of Kellie, *see* MAR and KELLIE, E), dau of Ambrose/Humphrey Smith and widow of (a) Benedict Barnham, London Alderman, and (b) Sir John Pakington, KB (*see* HAMPTON, B), and was *bur* 26 Nov 1631; his s by his 1st w:

ROBERT NEEDHAM, **2nd Viscount Kilmorey**; MP Newcastle-under-Lyme 1614; *m* 1st *c* 4 June 1607 Frances, dau of Alderman Sir Henry Anderson, of London, and had, with two daus:

1 ROBERT NEEDHAM, **3rd Viscount Kilmorey**; *m* Frances (*bur* 25 May 1636), 2nd dau of 2nd Baron Gerard of Gerard's Bromley (*see* GERARD, B, preliminary remarks), and *dsps* Jan 1657

The **2nd Viscount** *m* 2nd *c* 31 Oct 1636 Eleanor (*d* 12 March 1657), widow of 1st Baron Gerard of Gerard's Bromley (*see* GERARD, B, preliminary remarks) and dau and heiress of Thomas Dutton, of Dutton, Cheshire, and *d* 12 Sept 1653, having by her had:

2 CHARLES NEEDHAM, **4th Viscount Kilmorey**; *m* 27 Feb 1654/5 Bridget, dau and heiress of Sir William Drury, of Beesthorpe, Norfolk, and *d* 1660 in prison, having taken part in a premature uprising on behalf of CHARLES II 1659, leaving:

(1) ROBERT NEEDHAM, **5th Viscount Kilmorey**; *b* 1655; *d* 29 May 1668

(2) THOMAS NEEDHAM, **6th Viscount Kilmorey**; *b c* 1659; *educ* Ch Ch Oxford; *m c* 4 Dec 1679 Frances (*m* 2nd 8 May 1690 7th Earl of Huntingdon (*qv*); *m* 3rd Chevalier Michael de Ligondez, of the Auvergne, Kt Malta and a Cav Col French Army, and *d* 27 Dec 1723), dau and heiress of Francis Leveson Fowler, of Harnage Grange, Salop, and *d* 26 Nov 1687, leaving an only s:

1a ROBERT NEEDHAM, **7th Viscount Kilmorey**; *b* 4 May 1683; *m* 19 Aug 1701 Mary (*d* 1765), dau of John Offley, of Crewe, Cheshire, and *d* 2 Oct 1710, having had, with another s and four daus:

1b ROBERT NEEDHAM, **8th Viscount Kilmorey**; *b* Oct 1702; *d* unm 19 Feb 1716/7

2b THOMAS NEEDHAM, **9th Viscount Kilmorey**; *b* 29 Sept 1703; *m* 29 June 1730 Lady Mary Shirley (*dsp* 12 Aug 1784), 3rd dau and coheiress of 2nd Earl Ferrers (*qv*); *d* 3 Feb 1768

3b JOHN NEEDHAM, **10th Viscount Kilmorey**; *b* Jan 1710/1; *educ* Eton; cmded a Co of Grens in the Foot Gds 1737; *m* 11 Jan 1738 Anne (*d* 9 Aug 1786), widow of Geoffrey Shakerley (*see* SHAKERLEY, Bt) and dau and coheiress of John Hurleston, of Newton, Cheshire, and *d* 27 May 1791, having had, with other issue:

1c Thomas; *d* unm 21 April 1773

2c ROBERT NEEDHAM, **11th Viscount Kilmorey**; *b* 14 Nov 1746; *m* 10 Jan 1792 Frances (*d* 26 Nov 1818), sis of 1st Viscount Combermere (*qv*), and *dsp* 30 Nov 1818

3c FRANCIS NEEDHAM, **1st Earl of Kilmorey**, so *cr* 5 Feb 1822, as also VISCOUNT NEWRY AND MOURNE, Co Down (both I); *b* 5 April 1748; joined Army 1762, ADC to GEORGE III 1793–95, Maj Gen 1795, Lt Gen 1802, Gen 1812, Col 86th Foot 1810–32, served War of American Independence and suppression of 1798 Uprising Ireland; *m* 20 Feb 1787 Anne, 2nd dau of Thomas Fisher, of Acton, Middx, and had, with other issue:

1d FRANCIS JACK, **2nd Earl**

1d Anna Maria Elizabeth; *m* 20 June 1816 Rev Hon Henry Cokayne Cust, 2nd s of 1st Baron Brownlow (*qv*), and *d* 29 May 1866, leaving issue

2d Selina; *m* 5 July 1817 Hon Orlando Henry Bridgeman, s of 1st Earl of Bradford (*qv*), and *d* 10 Jan 1876

3d Mabella Josephine; *m* 12 Feb 1822 Hon John Henry Knox, s of 1st Earl of Ranfurly (*qv*), and *d* 16 Nov 1899 aged 98, leaving issue

The 1st EARL *d* 21 Nov 1832; his er son,

FRANCIS NEEDHAM, **2nd Earl of Kilmorey**; *b* 12 Dec 1787; *educ* Eton; MP (Tory) Newry 1819–26, Sheriff Co Down 1828; *m* 1st 7 Jan/March 1814 Jane (*d* 25 July 1867), dau of George Gun-Cuninghame, of Mount Kennedy, Co Wicklow; *m* 2nd 20 Nov 1867 Martha (*dsp* 6 May 1908), dau of John Foster, and by his 1st w had issue:

1 Francis Jack, *Viscount Newry and Mourne*; MP; *b* 2 Feb 1815; *m* 29 July 1839 Anne Amelia (*d* 6 Jan 1900), est dau of Gen Hon Sir Charles Colville, GCB (*see* COLVILLE OF CULROSS, V), and *dvp* 6 May 1851, leaving:

(1) FRANCIS CHARLES, **3rd Earl**

(2) Henry Colville; Lt-Col Gren Gds, BA Oxford; *b* 20 Feb 1844; granted with siblings by roy warrant 1880 rank of earl's daus/yr sons; *m* 1st 13 July 1875 Bertha Nesta (*d* 27 June 1886), dau of James Alured Maclean, and had issue:

1a Henry, CB (1931), CMG (1918), DSO (1916); *b* 23 April 1876; Maj-Gen Gloucester Regt, cmded 4th Bn Worcester Regt 1921–22, Mil Attaché Brussels and Berne 1922, and Copenhagen 1923, GSO(1) Staff Coll Camberley 1925, Mil Attaché Paris 1927–31, Maj-Gen cmdg Bombay Dist 1931–35 (ret 1935), Comptroller Hosp for Sick Children Gt Ormond St 1938–39, served Boer War 1899–1900 (medal with two clasps), WW I (despatches five times) and WW II (wounded), Legion of Honour, US DSM, Belgian Croix de Guerre, Orders St Stanislaus and St Vladimir Russia, Cdr Order Leopold Belgium; *m* 20 Feb 1902 Violet (*d* 29 Dec 1962), dau of Capt Henry Andrew, 5th Lancers and 8th Hus, and *d* 29 Aug 1965, leaving:

1b Lina Mary; Jr Cdr ATS WW II; *b* 12 Nov 1902

(2) (cont.) Col Henry Needham *m* 2nd 25 April 1887 Eleanor Effreta (*d* 27 March 1929), dau of Archibald Campbell, and *d* 2 Aug 1917, leaving by her:

2a Evelyn Jack; Capt 3rd Bn Northants Regt (Hon Maj) WW I (despatches), cmded Co of HG WW II; *b* 20 March 1888; *educ* Eton; *m* 7 June 1922 Mary Campbell, only child of Rev Benjamin Campbell Littlewood, and *dsp* 24 March 1956

3a Robert Philip; Capt 3rd Bn Northants Regt, served WW I (POW), WW II in HG; *b* 3 July 1891; *educ* Wellington; *d* unm 31 Dec 1968

(3) Edward Thomas; Capt RN; *b* 6 Jan 1847; *m* 12 Aug 1891 Mary Augusta Comyn (*d* 12 Dec 1898), est dau of Rev Thomas Platt, Vicar Holy Trinity, Portsea, and *d* 9 Jan 1916

(1) Lucy Jane; *m* 16 Dec 1876 William Drury Lowe, DL (*d* 31 Aug 1906), of Locko Park, Derbys, and *d* 19 May 1917, leaving issue

(2) Margaret; *m* 11 Aug 1874 R-Adml Hon Algernon Charles Littleton, 2nd s of 2nd Baron Hatherton (*qv*), and *d* 31 July 1940, leaving issue

(3) Frances Aline Catherine Mary; *d* unm 3 March 1929

2 Robert; Maj 12th Lancers; *b* 10 May 1816; *m* 1st 11 May 1874 Eleanor Wilkin (*dsp* 26 May 1884), widow of W Wallace Legge, of Malone, Co Antrim, and dau of T Foster; *m* 2nd 18 May 1893 Alicia Frances Anna (*d* 17 June 1903), widow of Capt Charles Sutton and dau of Sir Willoughby Dixie, 8th Bt (*see* 1970 edn), and *dsp* 11 Nov 1899

3 Francis Henry; *b* 3 Aug 1819; *m* 8 Aug 1840 Fanny Amelia (*d* Nov 1884), yst dau of Charles Hubbard, and *d* 13 Jan 1902, leaving, with other issue:

(1) Francis Jack, CIE; FRGS, Dep Inspr-Gen Bengal Police; *b* 14 Dec 1842; *d* 11 Nov 1924

(2) Francis Henry; *b* 15 March 1847; *m* 1st 23 June 1873 Grace (*d* 11 July 1894), 2nd dau of St George Ralph Gore (*see* GORE, Bt), and had:

1a Francis Jack; *b* 1878; *d* 15 Oct 1895

2a Francis Henry; AIF WW I; *b* 15 Feb 1881; *m* 7 Sept 1909 Eileen Frances (*d c* 1955), dau of George McCullagh Reed, BA, and *d* 13 Sept 1940, leaving:

1b Francis Jack; Lt RA WW I; *b* 16 May 1915; *d* 23 July 1946 from effects of war service

3a Francis Charles; FASA; *b* 29 March 1889; *m* 28 Oct 1922 Violet (*d* 1963), 2nd dau of William Kaye Parker, of Toowoomba, Qld, and *d* 1958, leaving:

1b *Thyra Frances [Miss Thyra Needham, G6/182 Dornoch Terr, Highgate Hill, Brisbane, Qld, Australia]; Registered Tax Agent; *b* 17 Sept 1923

4a Robert; Lt RHA WW I; *b* 7 April 1891; *m* 18 Dec 1923 Mona, dau of Albert Edward Ramsay, of Holmwood, Cowes, IoW, and *d* 4 June 1946

5a Frederick Corbet; *b* 1894; *d* 28 June 1903

1a Sibyl Frances; *b* 4 Feb 1877; *m* 1898 Colin Basil Peter Bell (*d* 21 April 1934), of Westland, Longreach, Qld, 3rd s of Sir Joshua Peter Bell, and *d* 18 May 1945, leaving issue

2a Barbara; *b* 30 Sept 1885; *m* 1909 Lt Beaumont Rundle, Australian Forces (*d* from wounds recd in action 15 April 1917), yst s of Dr G E Rundle, of Rooty Hill, NSW, and *d* 1969

(2) (cont.) Francis Needham *m* 2nd 1896 Elizabeth Abbot, dau of William Carruthers Hetherington, of Bonshaw, NSW, and *d* 7 July 1928

(3) Charles Albert; *b* 24 Feb 1850; *m* 25 Sept 1883 Fannie Elizabeth (*d* 9 July 1949), dau of Samuel Grey, and *d* 1928, having had:

1a Ethel Marguerite; *b* 1884; *d* unm India *c* 1912

(4) Alfred Edwin; *b* 1 Jan 1858; *m* 16 Aug 1890 Katherine (*d* 1945), dau of William Pickrell, and *d* 1920, having had:

1a Francis Jack; Lt Australian Forces Res WW I; *b* 1892; *m* 1926 Mary Clare (*d* 1979), dau of Patrick Alban O'Sullivan, of Brisbane, and *d* 1974, leaving:

1b +Patrick Francis Jack [Patrick Needham Esq, 93 Haigh Ave, Belrose, NSW 2085, Australia]; *b* 1927; *m* 1955 *Margaret Ann, er dau of John Henry Daley, of Qld, and has:

1c +Robert Francis Jack [Robert Needham Esq, 57 Stone Parade, Davidson, NSW 2085, Australia]; *b* 1956; *m* 1981 *Kathleen Anne, only dau of John O'Connor, of Dubbo, NSW, and has:

1d +Andrew Francis Jack; *b* 1983

2d +Christopher Robert; *b* 1985

3d +Thomas John; *b* 1988

4d +Jack Patrick Dominic; *b* 1990

2c +John Edward [John Needham Esq, 33 Angophora Crescent, Forestville, NSW 2087, Australia]; *b* 1963; *m* 1987 *Jennifer Gay Doreen, dau of Graham Napier, of NSW, and has:

1d *Clare Jennifer; *b* 1993

3c +Patrick Thomas [Patrick Needham Esq, 19 Bowen Close, Cherry Brook, NSW 2126, Australia]; *b* 1963 (twin); *m* 1987 *Michelle Anne, dau of Louis Samuel Harris, of NSW, and has:

1d +Benjamin Edward; *b* 1994

1c *Mary Margaret [Mrs Anthony Walsh, 14 Sandy Beach Rd, Korora, NSW 2450, Australia]; *b* 1958; *m* 1980 *Anthony Francis Walsh and has:

1d *Michael Francis; *b* 1983

2d *Simon Anthony; *b* 1985

3d *Daniel Robert; *b* 1987

4d *Robert Christopher; *b* 1993

2c *Judith Anne [Mrs Brian Kerr, 24 Merrilee Crescent, Frenchs Forest, NSW 2086, Australia]; *b* 1960; *m* 1978 *Brian Lindsay Kerr and has:

1d *Sandra Kate; *b* 1978

2d *Danielle Jan; *b* 1980

3d *Judith Louise; *b* 1987

4d *Jacqueline Margaret; *b* 1989

5d *Olivia Anne; *b* 1992

3c *Patricia Clare; *b* 1973

2b +Robert Cust [Robert Needham Esq, 40 Palm Ave, Ascot, Brisbane, Qld, Australia], MB, BS (Qld) 1954, DDM (Sydney) 1965, MACD, 1967; *b* 1928; *m* 1958 *Annette Mary Beiers, er dau of Michael Patrick O'Rourke, of Brisbane, and has:

1c +Robert Michael; *b* 1963

2c +Michael Francis Jack; *b* 30 March 1967

1c *Morna Irene [Mrs John Allen, 19 Kitchener Rd, Ascot, Brisbane, Qld 4007, Australia]; *b* 1959; *m* 1982 *John Henry Allen and has:

1d *Douglas Henry; *b* 1990

1d *Prudence Anne; *b* 1986

2d *Isabelle Susan; *b* 1988

2c *Susan Clare; *b* 1961

3c *Lucy Ann; *b* 18 April 1969

3b +Thomas Edwin [Thomas Needham Esq, Narrien Court, Samford, Qld 4520, Australia]; *b* 1931; *m* 1964 *Julia Elizabeth, dau of William O Moore, of Qld, and has:

1c *Deborah Clare; *b* 1970

2c *Natalie Barbara; *b* 1972

(4) +Edward Laurence [Edward Needham Esq, Christian Brothers, St Mary's Provincial House, 179 Albert Rd, Strathfield, NSW 2135, Australia]; *b* 1936

1a Lesley Constance; *b* May, *d* Dec 1891

(5) Frederick William; *b* 11 March 1861; *m* 6 March 1886 Geraldine (*d* 1 Feb 1946), only dau of Edmund Arthur Paget, of Thorpe Satchville, Leics, and *d* 19 July 1928, leaving:

1a Frederick Manners; *b* 8 Feb 1889; *d* unm 20 Aug 1962

2a James Owen; Capt IA; *b* 12 Oct 1897; *educ* Uppingham; *m* 3 June 1929 Marjorie Hylda Adeline, est dau of Charles George Lumley Cator (*see* BLOIS, Bt), and *d* 23 March 1975, leaving:

1b +Christopher James Blois [Christopher Needham Esq, Snode Hill House, Beech, nr Alton, Hants]; *b* 22 Oct 1931; *educ* Uppingham; *m* 15 Sept 1955 *Nicola Ann, only dau of Capt Nicholas Robert Coles, of Glos, and has:

1c *Henrietta Aeddan; *b* 4 Feb 1957; *m* 1979 *Russell Baylis, only s of J R Baylis, of Gt Comberton, Worcs, and has:

1d *Camilla Annabelle; *b* 1981

2d *Harriet Alicia; *b* 1983

3d *Emily Charlotte; *b* 1985

4d *Araminta Rose; *b* 1988

2c *Alicia Clare; *b* 13 April 1959; *m* 1988 *Henry Vane Eden (*see* AUCKLAND, B)

3c *(Camilla) Romaine [Mrs Nicholas Foot, Lyde Mill House, Newnham, Hants]; *b* 10 Dec 1961; *m* 1986 *Nicholas R I Foot, est s of Dennis Foot, and has:

1d *Alexander; *b* 1987

2b +David John Manners [David Needham Esq, Pine Lodge, Cokes Lane, Chalfont St Giles, Bucks]; *b* 26 April 1934; *educ* Uppingham; *m* 25 Sept 1965 *Evelyn Elizabeth (name PALMERS-NEEDHAM for herself and issue deed poll 1965), only dau of Theodore L Palmers, of Mill Hill, NW7, Consul-Gen for Nicaragua in London, and has:

1c *Katherine Elizabeth Theodora; *b* 17 Feb 1970

1b *Patricia Deline [Mrs William Pennefather, Westmark House, Westmark, Hants GU31 5AT]; *b* 23 Aug 1942; *m* 1st 21 Sept 1968 (*divorce* 1982) (John) Michael Singer, s of Col Ernest O A Singer, RAMC, by Margaret, only dau of Sir Charles Davis, 1st Bt, DL (*see* 1970 edn), and has:

1c *Jeremy James; *b* 25 Feb 1974

1c *Caroline Emma Louise; *b* 18 Aug 1969

2c *Serena Clare; *b* 1972

1b (cont.) Mrs Patricia Singer *m* 2nd 1984 *Lt-Cdr William Jonathan Richard Pennefather, RN

1a Audrey Deline; *b* 31 Dec 1895; *m* 8 May 1918 Capt Adrian Dura Stoop, MC, Queen's Roy W Surrey Regt (*d* 27 Nov 1957), est s of Frederick Cornelius Stoop, of West Hall, Byfleet, and *d* 198–, having had:

1b James Richard; *b* 1920; S/Ldr RAF (ret); *d* 197–

2b *Michael, MC; *b* 1922; *educ* Univ Coll Oxford; Maj Gren Gds WW II; *m* 1st 1948 (*divorce* 19–) Micheline, dau of Baron de Posson, of Brussels; *m* 2nd 19– (*divorce* 19–) Mrs Diana Buchanan; *m* 3rd 1959 Beverley Ann, dau of Herbert Roberts, of Glanwa, Caernarvs, and by his 1st w has:

1c *Adrian Gaston; *b* 1949

1c *Caroline; *b* 1950

(1) Florence Maude; *m* 1st 24 March 1875 Robert Henry, MD (*d* 6 Nov 1882), and had issue; *m* 2nd 1894 James Thomson, of Ballymoney, Co Antrim

1 Jane Selina Elizabeth; *m* 22 Sept 1874 Rev J F Hinde (*dsp* 5 Aug 1882), Vicar Dalby Parva, and *d* 15 Oct 1910

The 2nd EARL *d* 20 June 1880; his gs,

FRANCIS CHARLES NEEDHAM, **3rd Earl of Kilmorey**, KP (1890), JP, DL Salop and Cos Down and Armagh; *b* 3 Aug 1842; *educ* Eton and Ch Ch Oxford (MA 1867); High Sheriff Co Down 1871, MP (C) Newry 1871–74, rep I peer 1881–1915, Yeo ADC to HM EDWARD VII 1901, Capt S Down Militia 1868–80, Lt-Col cmdg Salop Imp Yeo 1889–96 and Hon Col 1897–1909, KGStJ; *m* 23 June 1881 Ellen Constance, DGStJ (*d* April 1920), 2nd dau of Edward Holmes Baldock, MP Shrewsbury, and *d* 28 July 1915, leaving:

1 FRANCIS CHARLES ALDELBERT HENRY NEEDHAM, **4th Earl of Kilmorey**, OBE (1936), VRD, PC (1936), JP, DL Co Down; *b* 26 Nov 1883; rep I peer 1916–61, High Sheriff Co Down 1913, Ld Lt Co Down 1949, Capt RNVR, ADC to HM GEORGE VI 1937–39, Cmdg Offr Ulster Div RNVR 1930, Capt 1st Life Gds, served WWs I and II, on Personal Staff of FOIC NI; *m* 10 Feb 1920 Lady Norah Frances Hastings, 2nd dau of 14th Earl of Huntingdon (*qv*), and *d* 11 Jan 1961, leaving:

(1) Eleanor Noreen Patricia; *b* 9 Jan 1921; *m* 25 April 1942 (*divorce* 1949, resumed maiden surname by deed poll 1949) Maj Philip Maitland Gore Anley, Roy Northumberland Fus (*d* 20 Oct 1968), est s of Brig Gen Frederick Gore Anley, of Rycroft Ho, Bolney, Sussex, and *d* 4 Jan 1965, leaving a s

(2) *Hyacinth Kathleen Anne; *b* 14 Feb 1923; *m* 25 June 1953 *John Hubert George Calvert Gough, Irish Gds, est s of Hubert Vincent Gough, of Meon, Hants, and has:

1a *(Cynthia) Jane; *b* 10 Aug 1954; *m* 2 June 1979 *Capt Simon D Holbarow, Coldstream Gds, est s of David Holbarow, NZ Amb Chile

2a *Rosaleen Anne; *b* 24 Aug 1956

3a *Caroline May *b* 20 May 1958

2 Francis Edward, MVO (4th Cl 1921), JP Surrey; Maj Gren Gds WW I (wounded), re-employed in WW II, ADC to HRH THE DUKE OF CONNAUGHT 1919–21; *b* 6 March 1886; *educ* Eton; *m* 25 April 1911 Blanche Esther (*d* 22 Jan 1965), est dau of Richard Combe (*see* CONYNGHAM, M), and *d* 24 Oct 1955, leaving:

(1) FRANCIS JACK RICHARD PATRICK, **5th Earl**

(2) (Arthur Edward) Peter; *b* 18 March 1921; *educ* Stowe; granted with sis 10 Dec 1962 rank of earl's dau/yr s, Maj Gren Gds WW II (despatches); *m* 30 March 1951 *Janet Beatrice Winifred [The Hon Mrs Peter Needham, The Old Manor House, Helmsley, Yorks YO6 5AB], yst dau of Capt George Taylor Ramsden, MP, of Bramham Ho, Boston Spa, Yorks, and *d* 1979, leaving:

1a +Robert (Robin) Arthur John; *b* 28 Aug 1953; *educ* Eton; *m* 1981 *Lucy Potter, only dau of Capt Howard Buckness III, USN (ret), of East Hampton, NY, and has:

1b +Nathaniel Peter; *b* 1984

2b +Robert Bucknell; *b* 1985

1b *Sonali Anna; *b* 1989

2b *Rupali Sarah (twin); *b* 1989

2a +Thomas Francis; *b* 28 Feb 1959; by Caroline Stockbridge has:

1b *Finn Barnaby NEEDHAM; *b* 1992

1a *Jane Diana [Mrs Jane Bell, Whitwell Hall, Whitwell-on-the-Hill, Yorks]; *b* 18 Dec 1955; *m* 1975 (*divorce* 1993) John Bell (*see* AILSA, M), and has:

1b *Daisy; *b* 1984

2b *Lettice; *b* 1987

3b *Zillah; *b* 1990

(1) Brigid; *b* 27 March; *d* 17 April 1914

(2) *Mary Esther Constance [The Lady Mary Combe, Grove Cottage, South Creek, Fakenham, Norfolk]; *b* 2 Dec 1918; *m* 6 July 1949 Cdr Anthony Boyce Combe, RN (*d* 1990), est s of Maj Boyce Combe, of Farnham, Surrey, and has:

1a *David Boyce; *b* 1952; *m* 19– (*divorce* 1991) Fiona Helen, dau of Derek C Thomson, of Invereighty Ho, Forfar, and has:

1b *James Anthony Derek; *b* 1987

2b *Alexander; *b* 1988

1b *Annabel; *b* 1989

2a *Peter; *b* 1955

3a John (twin); *b* 1955

1a *Anne Romaine; *b* 1950; *m* 1985 *Douglas Jardine, est s of Col N Jardine, of Port Alfred, CP, S Africa

1 Cynthia Almina Constance Mary; *b* 7 Nov 1889; *m* 1st 8 Oct 1908 8th Earl of Jersey (*qv*) and had issue; *m* 2nd 5 June 1925 Cdr William Rodney Slessor, RNVR (*d* 14 April 1945), 2nd s of Maj Arthur Kerr Slessor, MA, Sherwood Foresters, of Newland Ho, Eynsham, Oxon, and *d* 12 Jan 1947, leaving further issue

The 4th EARL's n,

FRANCIS JACK RICHARD PATRICK NEEDHAM, **5th Earl of Kilmorey**; *b* 4 Oct 1915; *educ* Stowe and RMC Sandhurst; Maj Gren Gds WW II; *m* 28 April 1941 *Helen Bridget [Helen Countess of Kilmorey, 8 The Dormers, Highworth,

Swindon, Wilts] (*m* 2nd 12 May 1978 (*divorce* 1990, resumed 1st husb's w's style 1990) Harold William Elliott), yst dau of Sir Lionel Faudel-Phillips, 3rd Bt (*qv*), and *d* 12 April 1977, having had:

1 RICHARD FRANCIS NEEDHAM, **6th and present Earl of Kilmorey**

2 +Christopher David [The Hon Christopher Needham, 63 Foro Buonaparte, Milan, Italy]; *b* 30 July 1948; *educ* Milton Abbey; *m* Marina, er dau of Rodi Malvezzi, of Milan, and has:

(1) +Francis; *b* 1982

(2) +Armyne; *b* 1978

3 +(Patrick) Jonathan [The Hon Jonathan Needham, 9 Vale View Terrace, Batheaston, Bath BA1 7RH]; *b* 20 March 1951; *m* 1979 (*divorce* 1993) Jane, 2nd dau of Geoffrey Hinbest, of Winterbourne, Bristol

KILPATRICK OF KINCRAIG

Creation: B. (LP, UK) 1996.

THE BARON KILPATRICK OF KINCRAIG, of Dysart, District of Kirkcaldy (Sir Robert Kilpatrick, CBE (1979) [The Rt Hon The Lord Kilpatrick of Kincraig, 12 Wester Coates Gdns, Edinburgh EH12 5LT]; *b* 29 July 1926; *educ* Buckhaven High Sch and Edinburgh U; MB, ChB 1949, MD 1960, FRCP (Edin) 1963, FRCP 1975, FRCPSGlas 1991, Medical Registrar Edinburgh 1951–54, Sheffield U: Lecturer 1955–66, Prof Clinical Pharmacology and Therapeutics 1966–75 and Dean Medical Faculty 1970–73; Leicester U: Prof Clinical Phramacology and Therapeutics 1975–83, Dean Medical Faculty 1975–89 and Prof Medicine 1984–89; ktd 1986; Pres GMC 1989–95; *m* 1950 *Elizabeth Gibson Page Forbes and has two sons and a dau

Lineage: ROBERT KILPATRICK; *m* Catherine Sharp Glover and had:

ROBERT (Sir), *cr* a **Baron**

KIMBALL

Arms: Argent a pale gules, charged with a lion rampant of the field, on a chief sable a bezant between two crescents or. **Crest:** In front of two arrows, points downwards saltirewise gules, a bull's head erased sable, armed or, ducally gorged also gules, between two branches of laurel fructed proper. **Supporters:** On either side a wild turkey proper. **Motto:** Strive for the gain of all. **Creation:** B. (LP, UK) 1985.

THE BARON KIMBALL, of Easton, Co Leics (Sir Marcus Richard Kimball, DL (Leics 1984)) [The Rt Hon The Lord Kimball DL, Great Easton Manor, Market Harborough, Leics LE16 8TB]; *b* 18 Oct 1928; *educ* Eton and Trin Coll Cambridge; Lt Leics Yeo (TA) 1947, Capt 1952, Maj 1955; MP (C) Gainsborough 1956–83; memb: Rutland CC 1955–62; Privy Council Rep Cncl RCVS 1969–82, ktd 1981; External Memb Cncl Lloyd's 1982–89; Jt MFH and Huntsman: Fitzwilliam 1950–52, Cottesmore Hounds 1952–54 and 1955–56 (Jt MFH 1956–58); Chm: River Naver Fishing Bd 1964–92, Br Field Sports Soc 1966–82, Firearms Consultative Ctee 1989–94, Cambridge U Vet Sch Tst 1989–, Br Greyhound Racing Fund 1993; Pres: Hunters' Improvement Soc 1990, Olympia Internat Showjumping 1991–, Br Inst of Innkeeping 1992–96, pres Brit Field Sports Soc 1996–; Hon ARCVS 1982; *m* 1956 *his sister's sis-in-law June Mary, only dau of Montagu John Fenwick, JP, of Great Stukeley Hall, Huntingdon (*see* MANCHESTER, D, also below), and has:

1 *(Sarah) Marcia [The Hon Mrs Gibbs, Kentmere House, Castor, Cambs PE5 7BU]; *b* 8 Feb 1958; *m* 1982 *David Alexander Somerset Gibbs, 2nd s of Patrick Somerset Gibbs, of Hazeley House, Mortimer, Berks, and has:

(1) *James Patrick; *b* 1983

(1) *Emily Rose; *b* 1985

(2) *Alexandra Harriet; *b* 1989

1 *Sophie Henrietta [The Hon Mrs Straker, Stonecroft, Fourstones, Northumberland NE47 5AX]; *b* 30 Nov 1960; *m* 1982 *Reuben Thomas Coppin Straker, 4th and yst s of Hugh Charles Straker, of Spain, and has:

(1) *Edward Marcus Reuben; *b* 1991

(1) *Camilla Sophie; *b* 1985

(2) *Lucy Charlotte; *b* 1988

Lineage: DAY KIMBALL; *b* 23 Feb 1807; *m* 12 May 1853 Susan Morton and *d* 15 March 1871, leaving:

MARCUS MORTON KIMBALL, of Pomfret, Conn.; *b* 17 April 1865; *m* 6 April 1892 Jeannie Lawrence (*d* 25 Dec 1927), dau of Benjamin Perkins, of Philadelphia, and *d* 15 Oct 1939, leaving, with an er s:

LAWRENCE KIMBALL, of Alderholt Park, Fordingbridge, Hants, JP, DL (Sutherland); *b* 25 Oct 1900; *educ* Gonville and Caius Coll Cambridge; barrister Gray's Inn 1926, High Sheriff Rutland 1931, MP Loughborough 1931–45, Maj Leics Yeo 1940; *m* 1st 22 March 1927 (*divorce* 1946) Kathleen Joan, only surv dau of Richard Henry Ratcliff, of Stanford Hall, Loughborough, and had issue; *m* 2nd 19 March 1947 Gillian, dau of W S Tresawna, FRCP, and widow of John Waterman; his children by his 1st w:

1 MARCUS RICHARD, *cr* a **Baron**

1 *Caroline Susan; *b* 18 Sept 1931; *m* July 1953 *Anthony Walter Fenwick, only s of Montagu John Fenwick (*see* above, also MANCHESTER, D) and has issue

KIMBER

Arms: Argent a torteau between three choughs proper, on a chief engrailed gules three estoiles of the first. **Crest:** A bull's head cabossed sable, horned argent, between the horns an estoile or. **Motto:** *Frangas non flectes* ('You may break, but you shall not bend me'). **Creation:** Bt. (UK) 24 Aug 1904.

SIR CHARLES DIXON KIMBER, 3RD BT, of Lansdowne Lodge, Wandsworth, Co London [Sir Charles Kimber Bt, 2 Duxford, Hinton Waldrist, Oxon SN7 8SQ]; *b* 7 Jan 1912; *s* f 1950; *educ* Eton and Balliol Coll Oxford (BA); *m* 1st 1 Dec 1933 (*divorce* 1950) Ursula Roy (*d* 1981), er dau of Ernest Roy Bird, MP, and has issue:

1 +TIMOTHY ROY HENRY [Timothy Kimber Esq, Newton Hall, nr Carnforth, Lancs LA6 2NZ]; *b* 3 June 1936; *educ* Eton; *m* 1st 9 July 1960 (*divorce* 1974) Antonia Kathleen Brenda, 3rd dau of Sir Francis John Watkin Williams, QC, 8th Bt (*see* WILLIAMS, Bt, of Bodelwyddan), of Llys Meirchlon, Denbighs, and has:

(1) +Rupert Edward Watkin; *b* 20 June 1962

(2) +Hugo Charles; *b* 4 April 1964

1 (cont.) Timothy Kimber *m* 2nd 1979 *Susan Hare, dau of J K Brooks and widow of Richard Coulthurst North, of Newton Hall, nr Carnforth, Lancs

2 Nicholas John; *b* 16 June 1937; *educ* Eton; *d* 1 March 1966

3 +Robert [Robert Kimber Esq, New Bois, Little Kingshill, Bucks HP16 ODP]; *b* 15 Dec 1941; *educ* Eton; *m* 30 May 1964 *Carolyn Evelyn Garth, er dau of Frederick Griffith-Jones, of Penn, Bucks, and has:

(1) *Jane Guthrie; *b* 29 Jan 1967; *m* 1989 *Mark Charles Etheridge and has:

1a *Charles Robert Guthrie; *b* 1994

1a *Lucy Kate; *b* 1996

(2) *Amanda Ann; *b* 4 Jan 1970

Sir CHARLES *m* 2nd 20 Jan 1950 (*divorce* 1965) Margaret, only dau of Francis John Bonham, FRAS, of Wimbledon, and by her has had:

4 (Paul) Justin; *b* 1 April 1953; *k* car crash 8 April 1972

1 *Rhys Catherine [Mrs Michael Fox, 1 amber Wharf, City Walls Rd, Worcester WR1 2AW]; *b* 6 April 1951; Dipl Landscape Architechture (Glos), ALI; *m* 1977 Michael Fox, RIBA (*d* 1993)

Lineage: JOSEPH KIMBER, of Canonbury, had a 3rd s:

Sir Henry Kimber, 1st Bt (UK), so *cr* 24 Aug 1904; *b* 13 July 1834; MP (C) Wandsworth 1885–1913, slr 1858–90, fnded legal firm Kimber and Ellis; *m* 4 Sept 1860 Mary Adelaide (*d* 7 Oct 1901), dau of Gen Charles Dixon, RE, and had:

1 HENRY DIXON (Sir), **2nd Bt**

2 Charles Dixon; *b* 24 Oct 1863; Lt Duke of Cambridge's Own Imp Yeo; *ka* Boer War 17 July 1901

3 Percy Dixon; *b* 4 March 1867; *m* 20 April 1892 Janet Margaret (*d* 3 Aug 1943), dau of William Mackenzie, of Natal, and *d* 22 Dec 1952, leaving:

(1) Guy Mackenzie, JP (1954); *b* 26 May 1899; S African Forces WWs I and II; *m* 10 June 1926 Ellen Elizabeth Margaret (Elma) (*d* 1977), dau of Rev J Jardine-Lockhart, of Paignton, Devon, and *d* 1985, leaving:

1a +David Percy [David Kimber Esq, Maritzdaal, Dargle 3265, Natal, S Africa]; *b* 19 May 1930; *m* 15 May 1953 *Elizabeth Mary Paterson, dau of Tom Paterson-Owens, CBE, of Weybridge, Surrey, and has:

1b +Richard Guy; *b* 14 March 1956

2b +Christopher David; *b* 10 April 1961; *m* 1988 *Shelley Bennett and has:

1c +Daniel Christopher; *b* 1993

1c *Annabel Shelley; *b* 1990

1b *Jeannet Elizabeth; *b* 7 July 1954; *m* 1976 (*divorce* 1992) Jean-Henri Coppez and has:

1c *Henri Jean-Patric; *b* 1978

2c *Jean-Marc Guy; *b* 1980

2b *Georgina Louise; *b* 21 Oct 1957; *m* 1985 (*divorce* 1992) Roland Zittera

2a +Michael Jardine [Michael Kimber Esq, Selsley, Dargle, Natal, S Africa]; *b* 10 June 1932; *m* 17 Jan 1957 *Mary Elizabeth, only dau of J A Dales, of Pietermaritzburg, and has:

1b +James Michael; *b* 11 April 1958

2b +Guy Barrington; *b* 22 Jan 1962

1b *Kathryn Mary; *b* 19 May 1966

4 Walter Dixon; *b* 23 July 1869; slr Supreme Cts England and Natal; *m* 4 April 1898 Florence, dau of John Brown, of Durban, and widow of T J Holmden, and *d* 26 Oct 1916, leaving:

(1) Eric Dixon; *b* 9 Dec 1898; *m* 15 July 1926 Gwendolen Isa Dow (*d* 1980), 2nd dau of Lawrence C French, of Godalming, and *d* 11 April 1956, leaving:

1a +Anthony Dixon [Anthony Kimber Esq, 161 Cathcart St, Greytown, Natal, S Africa]; *b* 16 June 1927; *educ* Michaelhouse Natal; S African Navy WW II; *m* 31 Aug 1957 *Joan Lilian, only dau of A Patterson, of Durban, and has:

1b +Brett Dixon; *b* 15 Dec 1960

1b *Erica Jane; *b* 18 Feb 1959; *m* 1988 *Paul Richard Benham

2b *Carolyn Susanne; *b* 17 Oct 1963

2a +Roger Dixon [Roger Kimber Esq, Higher Menchine Down, Black Dog, Crediton, Devon]; *b* 7 Sept 1929; *m* 26 Jan 1957 *Sandra, dau of Leslie Guy Gold, MC, and has:

1b +Richard Orlando Dixon; *b* 23 Oct 1957; *m* 1984 *Nicola Ann, dau of Christopher Andrew Balck-Foote, of Stockcross, Berks, and has:

1c +Henry Dixon Balck; *b* 1988

2c +Alexander Hudson Balck; *b* 1993

1c *Jessica Poppy Balck; *b* 1985

2b +Eric Guy Piers; *b* 21 Dec 1961

1b *Catherine Miranda; *b* 26 April 1959; has:

1c *Jaime Rose Muir; *b* 1988

1a *Winifred Margaret Kimber [Mrs Lawrence Tonkin, 10 Nelson St, Woollahra, Sydney, NSW, Australia]; *b* 27 Sept 1930; *m* 8 Oct 1959 *Lawrence Kevin Tonkin, MB, BS (*d* 1993), est s of Henry Lawrence Tonkin, MB, ChM, of Sydney, and has:

1b *Lawrence Eric Tonkin; *b* 17 March 1963

1b *Shauna Kerry; *b* 7 Nov 1960; *m* 19– *Frank Curreti and has:

1c *Edwardo; *b* 1989

1c *Isobella; *b* 1992

(2) Allan Dixon; *b* 7 Feb 1903; *m* 1st 1939 (*divorce* 1959) Daphne Mary, dau of Richard Guy Chaloner Ogle, of Natal; *m* 2nd 1964 Sylvia Margaret, dau of Garnet Edwin Driver, slr, of Natal, and *d* 1987, leaving by his 1st w:

1a *Daphne Jane; *b* 1940; *m* 1st 1964 (*divorce* 1966) John Campbell, of Natal, and has:

1b *Paula Catherine; *b* 1965

1a (cont.) Mrs Daphne Campbell *m* 2nd 1968 (*divorce* 1973) Peter Glen Cox and by him has:

1b *Glen Alexander Marc; *b* 1969

2b *Michael Piers; *b* 1970

3b *Joshua Richard Alan; *b* 1971

2a *Susan Mary; *b* 1942; *m* 1963 (*divorce* 1974) George Desmond Fairfoot and has:

1b *Samuel Christian; *b* 1964

2b *Thomas Jason; *b* 1968

3b *Matthew Adam; *b* 1969

3a *Nancy Florence [Mrs Henry Bowring, Park Farm House, Bodiam, Sussex]; *b* 1946; *m* 1974 *Henry Clive Bowring and has:

1b *Guy Allan Clive; *b* 1975

2b *Hugh Rennie; *b* 1977

(1) Joyce Dixon; *b* 28 July 1900; *m* 15 Nov 1924 John George William Stevens (*d* 1963), est s of Henry Edmund Stevens, of S Africa, and had issue

(2) *Evelyn Dixon Kimber; *b* 22 June 1911; *m* 26 May 1936 John Pillinger, and has issue

5 Hugh Dixon (Rev); *b* 20 Oct 1871; ordained Kansas 1913; *m* 1st 2 May 1902 Sarah Louise, dau of Nelson H Kellog, of Rugby, Tenn.; *m* 2nd April 1916 Ethel Ellen Skelton and *d* 27 Dec 1960

6 Edwin Dixon; *b* 8 Nov 1873; *d* 2 March 1874

1 Mary Adelaide Annie; *b* 27 July 1861; *m* 23 Dec 1895 Rev John Radford Thomson (*d* 16 Aug 1918) and *d* 27 Feb 1940, leaving issue

2 Jessie May; *b* 1 May 1865; *m* 13 July 1901 Charles Mortimer Lewis, MRCS (*d* 15 Sept 1910)

3 Ethel Blanche; *b* 30 July 1868; *d* 2 April 1869

The 1st Bt *d* 18 Dec 1923; his est s,

Sir Henry Dixon Kimber, 2nd Bt; *b* 8 Nov 1862; *educ* Epsom and Lincoln Coll Oxford (MA); sr ptnr Kimber, Williams, Sweetland and Stinson, slrs, govr St Thomas's Hosp, Lt and memb Common Cncl City of London, Dep Langbourn Ward, Kt Cdr Order Crown Italy; *m* 1st 25 Sept 1890 Florence Sarah (*d* 20 Sept 1907), only dau of Charles Boyes Noel Snewin, of Putney Heath, and had:

1 Henry Cyril Dixon; *b* 24 March 1894; Lt RFA (TF) WW I; *d* 22 June 1916 from wounds recd in action

1 Ella Florence Irene; *b* 23 Dec 1903

2 Helen Margaret; *b* 23 April 1907; *m* 5 Oct 1933 Richard Harrington Franklin, FRCS, MB, BS, yr s of Maj Percival Charles Franklin, of Rawdon Cottage, Cross Deep, Twickenham, and had:

(1) *Richard Kimber; *b* 15 Jan 1936; *educ* Westminster and Ch Ch Oxford (BA)

(2) *Peter James; *b* 28 Feb 1948; *educ* Westminster

Sir **Henry** *m* 2nd 8 Dec 1910 Lucy Ellen (*d* 13 March 1953), dau of George William Crookes, and *d* 4 Sept 1950, having by her had:

2 Sir CHARLES DIXON KIMBER, **3rd and present Bt**

3 *Audrey Patricia Kimber [Mrs Harold Stocks, Old Teemstones, Grove Rd, Beacon Hill, Hindhead, Surrey]; *b* 7 March 1913; *m* 12 July 1952 Harold James Stocks (*d* 22 Oct 1963), s of James Stocks, of Leeds

KIMBERLEY

Arms: Sable a chevron or guttée de sang between three cinquefoils ermine. **Crest:** A dexter arm, couped and erect, vested argent, and grasping a club in bend sinister or. **Supporters:** Two wild men, wreathed about the loins proper, each holding in his exterior hand a club raised in the attitude of striking sable. **Mottoes:** 1 Agincourt, 2 (over the crest) *Frappe fort* ('Strike hard'). **Creations:** Bt. (E) 29 June 1611, B. (GB) 26 Oct 1797, E. (UK) 1 June 1866.

THE 4TH EARL OF KIMBERLEY, of Kimberley, Norfolk, **Baron Wodehouse of Kimberley**, and a **Baronet** (Sir John Wodehouse Bt) [The Rt Hon The Earl of Kimberley, Hailstone House, Cricklade, Wilts SN6 6JP]; *b* 12 May 1924; *s f* 1941; *educ* Eton and Magdalene Coll Cambridge; Lt Gren Gds WW II 1942–45, CC Norfolk 1946, chm J & P Security Servs Ltd 1994–, late Lib spokesman aerospace, def and vol community servs, memb Nat Cncl Alcoholism, V-Pres World Cncl Alcoholism, memb Ho Lds All Party Def Study Gp 1976– (Hon Sec 1978–92, pres 1992–), C 1979–, Del N Atlantic Assembly 1981–93, memb: Br Bobsleigh Team 1949–58, cncl Air League 1980, cncl Br Maritime League, RUSI 1980, Ho Lords All-Party Study Gp UFOs 1979–; ARAeS 1977; *m* 1st 27 Oct 1945 (*divorce* 1949) Diana Evelyn, only dau of Lt-Col Hon Sir Piers Legh, GCVO, CMG, CIE, OBE (*see* NEWTON, B); *m* 2nd 9 Feb 1949 (*divorce* 1952) Carmel June (*d* 1992), formerly w of Derek Dunnett and 3rd dau of Michael Joseph Maguire, of Melbourne, Australia, and by her has:

1 +JOHN ARMINE, *Lord Wodehouse* [Lord Wodehouse, Kingswood, Henley Rd, Medmenham, Marlow, Bucks SL7 2EU]; *b* 15 Jan 1951; *educ* Eton and UEA (MSc); CEng, Advanced Informatics & Technical Specialist Glaxo Wellcome Ltd 1996–, Assoc Fell Br Interplanetary Soc 1981–83 (Fell 1984), chm UK Info Users Gp 1981–83, memb Br Computer Soc 1988, FRSA; *m* 21 July 1973 *Hon Carol Lylie Palmer, er surv dau of 3rd Baron Palmer (*qv*), and has:

(1) +David Simon John; *b* 10 Oct 1978; *educ* Eton

(1) *Katherine Frances; *b* 13 Dec 1976

The 4th EARL *m* 3rd 15 Sept 1953 (*divorce* 1961) Cynthia Abdy, formerly wife of Charles Gustav Westendarp and yr dau of Eric Adby Collins, FRCS, MRCP, of The Chantry, Saxmundham, Suffolk, and by her has:

2 +Edward Abdy [The Hon Edward Wodehouse, 17 Ada Rd, London SE5 7RW]; *b* 29 May 1954; *educ* Eton; *m* 1st 1980 (*divorce* 1983) Pandora Jeffreys, est dau of Mrs W J Germing, of Castlenau, Barnes; *m* 2nd 1988 *Sarah Katherine, dau of Richard Allen, of Ranskill, Notts, and Mrs Patrick Dean, of E Mere, Lincs

3 +Henry Wyndham; *b* 26 April 1956; *educ* Millfield; *m* 1st 1979 (*divorce* 1988) Sarah M, only dau of J A Fleming, of Hampton, Middx; *m* 2nd 1992 *Elizabeth Ellen, dau of Edmund Parkin, and by his 1st w has:

(1) +Thomas Henry John; *b* 1981

(1) *Clare Margaret; *b* 1980

The 4th EARL *m* 4th 7 July 1961 (*divorce* 1965) Margaret, dau of Albert Simons, and by her has:

4 +Charles James; *b* 30 March 1963

The 4th EARL *m* 5th 8 Aug 1970 (*divorce* 1982) Gillian, formerly w of John Raw and dau of Col Norman Ireland-Smith, of Sherborne, Dorset; *m* 6th 20 Aug 1982 *Sarah Jane Hope, est dau of Lt Col C D P Consett, DSO, MC, of Swan Ho, Great Rissington, Glos

Lineage: JOHN WODEHOUSE, probably of a London family (of which one member, William Power *alias* Wodehouse, was Sheriff London 1374 and lent RICHARD II money 1377); Constable Castle Rising 1402, Squire and Forester Castle Rising 1404, Gentleman Privy Chamber 1406, Esquire of the Body to HENRY V 1413–22, Steward Duchy Lancaster 1414, granted Welle Priory and Gayton Rectory 1415, also held a Knight's fee each in Posfield, Sussex, and Hacheston, Commr Array Norfolk and Chamberlain Exchequer 1415, Executor HENRY V's Will, Clerk to HENRY VI 1428; *m* Alice 1 and *d* 27 Jan 1431, leaving:

1 Henry, of Bocking Ash, Suffolk; *b c* 1406; *d* after 1455

2 JOHN

3 Jeronimus; acquired Manors of East Hall, Fyncham, and Feltons from John Scot 1444/5

1 Anne; *m* (*divorce*) Sir Thomas Todenham

The 2nd son,

JOHN WODEHOUSE; *m* Constance, dau of Thomas Gedding, and *d* Kimberley, Norfolk, 1465, leaving, with a yr s (John; made over to Thomas Giggs 1475 his rights in the manors of Esthall, Starhow Hall and Felton, Norfolk; probable ancestor of the WODEHOUSEs alias POWERs of Waxham):

Sir EDWARD WODEHOUSE; did mil service Scotland 1461; ktd Battle of Tewkesbury 1471; allegedly *m* 1st —, dau of Sir John Tiriel, but had no issue by her; *m* 2nd Jane Swathing, of Letton, and had:

Sir THOMAS WODEHOUSE, KB (1501); *m* 1st —, of Picardy, but had no issue by her; *m* 2nd Thomasine, dau of Sir Roger Townsend, of Raynham (*see* TOWNSHEND, M), and had:

Sir ROGER WODEHOUSE; ktd 1548; *m* 1st Elizabeth, dau and coheir of Sir Robert Ratcliff, and had four sons and four daus; *m* 2nd Elizabeth, dau of John Drury, of Besthorpe, and *d* 1560, having by her had a dau (Ursula, *m* the est son of Sir Thomas Cotton); a s by his 1st w:

THOMAS WODEHOUSE, MP; *m* Margaret (grantd rank of kt's w after husb's death), dau of Sir John Shelton, and *dvp*, *k* Battle of Musselburgh against the Scots 1547, leaving, with other issue:

Sir ROGER WODEHOUSE, of Kimberley; MP Aldborough, ktd 1578; visited by ELIZABETH I at Kimberley 1578; *m* Mary (*m* 2nd George Kemp), dau of John Corbet, of Sprowston, Norfolk, and *d* 4 April 1588, leaving:

Sir Philip Wodehouse, 1st Bt (E), so *cr* 29 June 1611, of Kimberley; MP Castle Rising 1586–87, ktd 1596 for valour at taking of Cadiz; *m* 22 Dec 1582 Grizell (*d* 4 Aug 1635), widow of Hamon Le Strange, of Hunstanton (*see* ST DAVIDS, V), and dau of William Yelverton, of Rougham, Norfolk, and *d* 30 Oct 1623, leaving:

Sir Thomas Wodehouse, 2nd Bt; MP Thetford 1640–53, High Sheriff Norfolk 1624; *m* 16 June 1605 Blanche (*d* 6 Nov 1651), widow of Christopher Peyton and dau of 3rd Baron Hunsdon of Hunsdon (*see* ALDENHAM and HUNSDON OF HUNSDON, B, preliminary remarks), and had, with other issue:

1 PHILIP (Sir), **3rd Bt**

1 Mary; *m* Sir Humphrey Monnoux, Bt, of Watton

2 Jane; *m* Sir Hugh Windham, Serjeant-at-Law

3 Elizabeth; *m* Sir Denner Strutt, of Little Warley

Sir THOMAS *d* 18 March 1658; his son,

Sir Philip Wodehouse, 3rd Bt; MP Norfolk 1654–58 and Thetford 1660; *bapt* 24 July 1608; *m* Lucy (*d* 26 June 1684), dau of Sir Thomas Cotton, Bt, of Connington, by Margaret, dau of Lord William Howard, of Naworth Castle, Cumberland (*see* NORFOLK, D, also CARLISLE, E), and had, with two daus:

1 Thomas (Sir); ktd 1663; *m* Anne (*m* 2nd 1674, as his 2nd w, 2nd Baron Crewe of Stene; *m* 3rd 1 Aug 1704, as his 2nd w, 1st and last Earl of Torrington of the 1689 *cr*; *see* TORRINGTON, E, preliminary remarks and POWIS, E), dau and coheir of Sir William Armine, 2nd Bt, of Osgodby (*see* ST ALDWYN, E), and *dvp* 29 April 1671, leaving issue:

(1) JOHN (Sir), **4th Bt**

(1) Anne; *m* 2 Dec 1686 Sir Nicholas Le Strange, 4th Bt, DL (*see* ST DAVIDS, V), and *d* 1727, having had issue

2 Edmond, of E Lexham, Norfolk; *m* 1st Mercy, dau of Sir Philip Parker and widow of William Guybon, and had two sons and two daus; *m* 2nd Anne, dau of John Anguish, and *d* 5 Sept 1727, having by her had no issue

3 John, of Feltwell; *m* Anne, widow of William Samwell and dau of Sir Denner Strutt, Bt, of Little Warley, and had an est dau:

(1) Blanche; *m* 6 Feb 1661 Sir Jacob Astley, 1st Bt, MP (*d* 12 Aug 1729), and had issue (*see* HASTINGS, B)

Sir PHILIP *d* 6 May 1681; his gs,

Sir John Wodehouse, 4th Bt; MP Norfolk, Recorder Thetford; *b* 23 March 1669; *m* 1st *c* 17 June 1700 Elizabeth Benson (*dsp* 5 Jan 1700/1), sis of 1st and last Baron Bingley of the 1713 *cr*; *m* 2nd Mary (*d* 24 Oct 1729) dau of 1st Baron Leominster (*see* HESKETH, B), and *d* 6 Aug 1754, leaving, with a dau, Sophia (*m* Sir Charles Mordaunt, Bt, *qv*):

Sir Armine Wodehouse, 5th Bt; MP Norfolk 1737–68, Col E Norfolk Militia; *b* 1714; *m* 3 Oct 1738 Letitia (*bur* 7 April 1758), est dau and coheiress of Sir Edmund Bacon, 6th Bt (*qv*), of Garboldisham, and *d* 1777, having had issue (the male-line descendants of the yr sons being in remainder to the btcy only):

1 JOHN, **1st Baron**

2 Philip (Rev), Preb Norwich; *b* 1 May 1745; *m* 29 July 1775 Apollonia (*d* 21 March 1817), dau and coheiress of John Nourse, of Woodeaton, Oxon, and *d* 14 Feb 1811, leaving:

(1) Philip, Col; *b* 6 Aug 1788; *m* 13 June 1832 Lydia (*d* 8 May 1892), dau of Joseph Lea, and *d* 15 Dec 1846, leaving:

1a Phillip John (Rev), Preb Exeter 1905–17, Rector Bratton Fleming, Devon, 1875–1913; *b* 6 Oct 1836; *educ* Caius Coll Cambridge (MA); *m* 1st 20 Jan 1876 Constance Helen (*dsp* 23 Feb 1877), 3rd dau of Wade Browne, of Monkton Farleigh, Wilts; *m* 2nd 25 Sept 1879 Marion Bryan (*d* 30 Dec 1922), dau of Rev Gilbert I Wallas, Rector Shobrooke, and *d* 8 Dec 1917, leaving:

1b Philip George, DSO (1918); Capt RN, served WWs I (despatches) and II, Order Crown Italy, Italian Bronze Medal Mil Valour; *b* 26 Nov 1883; *m* 1st 25 Oct 1915 (*divorce* 1928) Beaujolois Theresa Constance (*d* 1986), only dau of Arthur George Ridout, of Northumberland, and had:

1c *Beaujolois Inez; *b* 7 Feb 1919; *m* 17 April 1942 Hubert Gordon Compton Cavendish (*see* DEVONSHIRE, D) and has issue

2c *Valencia [Miss Valencia Wodehouse, Cliff Cottage, Point, Cornwall TR3 6NQ]; *b* 20 March 1920; ATS WW II

1b (cont.) Philip Wodehouse *m* 2nd June 1928 *Alice Margaret [Mrs Philip Wodehouse, Ebor House, Park Lane, Barnstaple, N D evon], yst dau of William Rowe, of Cornwall, and *d* 4 April 1973

2b Charles Gilbert, Maj IARO 1915–20, Belgian Consul Rangoon 1928–38, Chevalier Crown Belgium, dir Burma-Siam Rice Co; *b* 28 Dec 1885; *educ* Haileybury; *m* 26 Nov 1919 Adelaide Mary (*d* 14 Oct 1956), widow of Arthur Gaitskell, ICS, and dau of George Jamieson, CMG, and *dsp* 26 July 1969

1b Helen Marion, MA and DPhil Birm, MA Cantab, Prof Educn Bristol U 1919–31 and Mistress Girton Coll Cambridge 1931–42; *b* 12 Oct 1880; *d* unm 20 Oct 1964

2b Christine Lucy; *b* 24 Dec 1881

2a Charles, CIE, Col ISC; *b* 8 May 1838; *m* Dec 1862 Jemima (*d* 11 Aug 1886), dau of George Forbes, and *d* 18 Aug 1893, leaving:

1b Frederic William, CIE (1912), Lt-Col IA, Political Res Kolhapur State, Political Agent Southern (Mahratta) Country States 1908–22, Lushai Expdn 1889–90; *b* 7 April 1867; *educ* Westminster and RMC Sandhurst; *m* 1st 5 April 1893 Mary Helen (*d* 25 Dec 1920), est dau of George Nugent Lambert; *m* 2nd 1940 Hilary Mary (*d* 1974), only dau of William Henry Pell, of Holme Ho, Notts, and *d* 16 Jan 1961, having by his 1st w had:

1 Constance Mary; *m* Feb 1919 Capt William Cyril Griffin Norris, 103rd Mahratta LI (*d* 1965), and *d* 5 Dec 1966

2c Kathleen Doris Letitia; *b* 1897; *m* April 1922 AVM Stanley James Goble, CBE, DSO, DSC, RAAF (*d* 24 July 1948), s of George Goble, and has:

1d *John Douglas [Cdre John Goble RAN, 308 Coonawarra Rd, Terrey Hills, NSW 2084, Australia]; *b* 1923; *m* 1953 *Annette Margaret, dau of Col G Youl, of Launceston, Tasmania, and has:

1e *Margaret Kate; *b* 1959

2d *Alan James [Dr Alan Goble, Delamore, Prince's Highway, Stratford, Victoria 3862, Australia]; *b* 1925; MB, BS; MD Melbourne; FRACP, FRCP London; *m* 1950 (*divorce* 1968) Patricia, dau of R A Johnston, of Corowa, NSW, and has:

1e *David Stanley; *b* 1955

1e *Anne Louise; *b* 1957

3d *Ivor Norman [Ivor Goble Esq, Eastern District Private Nursing Home, Maroondah Highway, Croydon, Victoria 3136, Australia]; *b* 1929; *m* 1st 1954 (*divorce* 1969) June, dau of A E Peart, of Maroona, Vic, and has:

1e *Ann Sally; *b* 1956

3d (cont.) Ivor Goble *m* 2nd 1971 *Janis Esther, dau of Reed White, of Salem, Oregon, and by her has:

1e *Scott Michael; *b* 1975

2e *Amy Vervaine; *b* 1974

3c Sybil Margaret; *m* 12 June 1928 Rt Rev Claud Thomas Thellusson Wood, MC (*d* 17 Jan 1961), Assist Bp St Albans, Bp Suffragan Bedford 1948–53, s of Canon Henry Thellusson Wood, of Tring, and has issue

2b Ernest Charles Forbes, DSO, Lt-Col Worcester Regt, Boer War and WW I; *b* 5 Aug 1871; *m* 18 April 1906 Amy Violet, OBE (1918) (*d* 14 Feb 1943), dau of Swinton Isaac, DL, of Broughton Park, Worcs, and was *ka* 12 March 1915

1b Annabel Lucy; *m* 13 April 1809 Gen John Augustus Fuller, CIE, RE (*d* 6 Oct 1902), est s of Rev Robert Fitzherbert Fuller, Rector Chalvington, Sussex, and *d* 10 May 1966 aged 101

3a Frederick Armine (Rev), Rector Gotham, Derbys, 1882–1915, BA Cantab; *b* 1 July 1842; *m* 7 Sept 1880 Alice Elizabeth Juliana (*d* 7 March 1934), 2nd dau of Rev Hon Atherton Legh Powys (*see* LILFORD, B), and *d* 12 June 1921, having had:

1b Arthur Powys, Capt IA and Dep Commr Calcutta Police; *b* 2 June 1881; *ka* Mesopotamia 22–24 Nov 1915

2b Frederick Armine, Prof History Agra College, UP, India; *b* 23 June 1884; *d* unm 21 Sept 1912

3b Norman Atherton, CB (1939), V-Adml WW II 1939–41, ADC to HM GEORGE VI 1936–39, Order Striped Tiger China; *b* 18 May 1887; *m* 22 Oct 1923 Theodosia Frances (*d* 6 July 1966), widow of Capt Douglas William Swire and dau of Capt Edward Louis Dalrymple Boyle, CMG, RN (*see* GLASGOW, E), and *das* at sea July 1941, leaving:

1c +Armine Boyle [The Rev Armine Wodehouse, 103 Orient Palace, 1 rue de la République, 06500 Menton, France], WW II 1942–45 with Gren Gds; *b* 31 Aug 1924; *educ* Radley; *m* 19 July 1952 Diana Helen Arabella (*d* 1990), only dau of Charles Sidney Bowen Wentworth-Stanley, CBE, of High Wych Grange, nr Sawbridgeworth, Herts, and has:

1d +Armine Mark Robin [Armine Wodehouse Esq, Villa Concordia, 1593 Ave de Lattre de Tassigny, 06360 St Laurent d'Eze, France]; *b* 24

Jan 1960; *educ* Radley and Downing Coll Cambridge; *m* 1986 *Yoma Irene Mandra, dau of J B Jackson, of Monte Carlo, and has:
1e *Sarah Casmen Diane; *b* 1989
2e *Nikki Robyn Alba; *b* 22 Sept 1995
1d *Julia Katherine [Mrs William Hunt, 43 Hamilton Terrace, London NW8 9RG]; *b* 4 July 1955; *m* 1981 *William John Hunt, s of W E Hunt, and has:
1e *Oliver William; *b* 1988
1e *Miranda Katherine; *b* 1984
2e *Arabella Katrina; *b* 1985
2d *Victoria Frances; *b* 20 Feb 1957; *m* 1979 *Evan John Thatcher, of Peel Forest, S Canterbury, NZ, and has:
1e *Hamish John; *b* 1981
2e *David Michael; *b* 1983
3e *Benjamin Samuel; *b* 1993
1e *Lucinda Katherine; *b* 1980
1c (cont.) The Rev Armine Wodehouse *m* 2nd 14 May 1997 *Mrs Vera Robinson
2c +Charles Norman Boyle [Charles Wodehouse Esq, 23 Altenburg Gdns, London SW11 1JH]; *b* 27 Oct 1927; *m* 2 Sept 1953 *Joyce Marie Williamson, dau of John Dobson, MC, and has:
1d +Dominic Charles John; *b* 8 Nov 1968
1d *Fiona Clare; *b* 12 April 1958
2d *Charlotte Thea Fleur; *b* 5 Feb 1962; *m* 1991 *Philip M Bubb, er s of M A T Bubb, of Staffs
1b Mabel Evelyn; *b* 21 Aug 1882; *m* 12 Feb 1913 Lt-Col Berkeley Gale, IMS (*d* 21 April 1953)
4c William George; *b* 26 Oct 1843; *m* 31 Jan 1874 Jane Gill (*d* 17 Sept 1899), widow of James Barratt Severn, of Nottingham, and *d* 6 March 1891
5c Henry Ernest, CMG (1886); Hong Kong CS 1869–95; *b* 14 July 1845; *m* 3 Feb 1877 Eleanor (*d* 6 May 1938), dau of Rev J Bathurst Deane, and *d* 27 May 1929, leaving:
1b Philip Peveril John, CIE (1919), Hong Kong CS 1897–1932; *b* 26 Sept 1877; *m* 6 Oct 1920 Laura Gertrude (*d* 2 Feb 1959), widow of Harold Macfarlane, LRCP, LRCSI, and 2nd dau of Rev Xavier Peel Massy (*see* MASSY, B), and *dsp* 26 Nov 1951
2b Ernest Armine, Prof Deccan Coll Poona; *b* 11 May 1879; *m* 7 Aug 1919 Helen, dau of Patrick Harnett, and *d* 9 Oct 1936, leaving:
1c +Patrick Armine [Patrick Wodehouse Esq, Gable Cottage, Oldfield Rd, Maidenhead, Berks]; *b* 12 March 1920; AMIEE, ACGI, F/Lt RAuxAF WW II 1940–46; *educ* Cheltenham and Imp Coll of Science and Technology (BSc 1949); *m* 30 June 1947 *Joyce Lillian, dau of Charles Champion, and has:
1d +Nigel Armine; *b* 16 Nov 1948
3b Pelham Grenville (Sir), Hon DLitt Oxford (1939); *b* 15 Oct 1881; *educ* Dulwich; with Hong Kong and Shanghai Bank, dramatist and author of over 100 books, notably the Jeeves/Wooster and Blandings Castle cycles; broadcaster; US citizen 1955, ktd 1975; *m* 30 Sept 1914 Ethel, widow of Leonard Rowley, of Dee Bank, Cheshire, and *dsp* 1975
4b Richard Lancelot Deane; *b* 30 May 1892; *m* 1st 8 Aug 1925 Katharine M (*d* 22 July 1932), est dau of William Wallace Cook, OBE, of Merstham, late of Singapore, and had:
1c *Ann Elizabeth [Mrs Richard Higgins, 11/12 Red Lion St, Kings Sutton, nr Banbury, Oxon OX17 3RH]; *b* 18 March 1930; *m* 10 Jan 1953 *Lt-Col Richard Gerald Higgins, RA, yr s of C G Higgins, of Emms Lane Farm, Bratton, Wilts, and has:
1d *Andrew Richard; *b* 25 Nov 1954; *m* 1982 *Alison Margaret, dau of Col Anthony Gilks, of The Grange, Brunston, Rutland, and has:
1e *Peter Anthony; *b* 1989
2e *James Patrick; *b* 1991
2d *Michael James; *b* 18 Aug 1956; *m* 1985 *Kim Maria Stevens, er dau of Col Nigel Flower, of 47 York Rd, Camberley, and has:
1e *Joss Wodehouse; *b* 1994
1e *Ella May; *b* 1996
3d *John Deane; *b* 26 June 1962; *m* 1988 *Rosemary Jane Cecilia, dau of John D Boot, of Nottingham, and has:
1e *Livia Harriet; *b* 1994
2e *Isobel Victoria; *b* 1996
2c *Katharine Jane Armine [Mrs Graeme Wallace, Little Grondra, Shirenewton, Chepstow, Mon]; *b* 21 July 1932; *m* 7 Oct 1955 *Capt Graeme Roper Wallace, RA, only s of G W Wallace, of Edinburgh, and has:
1d *Ross Matthew Walker; *b* 1956
2d *Neil Richard Deane; *b* 1958
1d *Constance Armine Louise
4b (cont.) Richard Wodehouse *m* 2nd 5 Feb 1934 Winifred Baker (*d* 23 June 1979), widow of Robert Arthur Williams, OBE, MC, of Tientsin, and 2nd dau of Brig-Gen William Baker Brown, CB, RE, and *d* 20 May 1940, having by her had issue
1c John Richard; *b* 25 June 1935; *d* an infant
6a Albert Philip, Col Roy Inniskilling Fus; *b* 9 Nov 1846; *m* 1881 Amy (*d* 19 Feb 1929), dau of Henry Villiers, and *d* 5 Sept 1919
1a Lydia Josephine; *d* unm 18 Dec 1914
2a Lucy Apollonia; *m* 18 June 1867 Rev Whitmore Isaac (*d* 18 Aug 1915), Vicar Hanley Castle, Worcs, and *d* 19 April 1919, leaving issue
3a Harriet Elizabeth; *m* 25 July 1861 Rev Henry Bromley Cocks and *d* 1920, leaving issue (*see* SOMERS, B)
(2) Charles Nourse (Ven), Archdeacon Norwich; *b* 8 Sept 1790; *m* 19 Dec 1821 Lady Dulcibella Jane Hay (*d* 10 Jan 1885 aged 91), est dau of 17th Earl of Erroll (*qv*), and *d* March 1870, having had, with other issue:
1a Charles; *b* 31 Dec 1822; *m* 8 Nov 1856 Maria (*d* 1895), dau of Matthew Potts, of Carrhill, Northumberland, and *d* 29 April 1902, leaving:
1b Armine (Rev), Rector St Marys, Trimley, Suffolk 1904–23, Hon Canon St Edmundsbury 1916; *b* 7 May 1860; *d* 7 April 1938
2b Charles Hay; *b* 21 Feb 1865; *d* 4 Sept 1880
1b Jane; *d* 12 Oct 1937
2b Alice Mary; *d* unm 16 Sept 1938
3b Isabel
4b Lucy; *d* unm 15 April 1937
2a James Hay, BA Oxon; Br Min Res Sandwich Islands; *b* 23 April 1824; *m* 19 Jan 1861 Annette Fanny (*d* 24 Aug 1929), yst dau of William Massey, of Watton, Norfolk, and *d* 13 July 1911, having had:
1b James Hay; *b* 30 Dec 1861; *m* 20 Dec 1890 Annie Pauahi (*d* 6 March 1897), dau of Hon A S Cleghorn, of Honolulu, and *d* 8 Oct 1913, having had:
1c James Hay; *b* 11 Nov 1891; *d* 11 Nov 1892
2c James Hay Archibald, Commr Bd Water Supply, Pres Kohala Macadenua Nut Co, Superintendent Kohala Sugar Co Mill, Hawaii; *b* 5 Aug 1895; *m* 1st 1916 Florence (*d* 1937), dau of Edward Boyd, and had:
1d *Mildred Pauahi; *b* 1916; *m* 1942 *Capt Asa Alan Clark III, USN, and has:
1e *Asa Alan IV [Mr Asa Clark IV, 134 E 93rd St, 3B, New York, USA]; *b* 15 Jan 1944; *educ* West Point; *m* 1968 *Margie Slocum and has had:
1f Matthew Shannon; *b* 1968, *d* 1988
2f *Christopher; *b* 1972
2e *Jeffrey Wodehouse; *b* 23 April 1947
3e *Bruce Shannon [Mr Bruce Clark, 54–112 Kealalani Place, Hauula, HI 96717, USA]; *b* 21 Oct 1953; *m* 1992 *Diane Kelly
1e *Deborah Wodehouse; *b* 2 Dec 1945
2c (cont.) James Wodehouse *m* 2nd 1938 Elizabeth K, dau of William K Buchanan, and *d* 1973, having by her had:
1 d +James Hay; *b* 3 Oct 1946
2d *(Florence) Elizabeth Hay [Mrs George Freeland, 439 Front St, Lahaina, Maui, HI 96761, USA]; *b* 1939; *m* 1963 *George Warren Freeland, Field Engr, and has:
1e *George Warren; *b* 1965
1e *Kimberley Kaiulani; *b* 1967; has:
1f *Nohea Edward FREELAND; *b* 1993
2e *Denby Elizabeth Hay; *b* 1971
3d Rowena Hay; *b* 3 and *d* 10 March 1941
1c Annie Hay; *b* 27 Feb 1893; *m* Lt-Col Vernon Olsmith, US Army
2c Irma Pauahi; *b* 14 Jan 1897; *m* 1926 James Jay Rothschild and had issue
2b Guy Armine; *b* 8 June 1863; *m* Aug 1894 Elisa Millie (*d* 16 Oct 1935), dau of David Millie, of Coquimbo, Chile, and *d* 2 May 1926, having had:
1c Everard Hay, Lt RAF; *b* 29 May 1898; *m* 1st 28 Oct 1927 (*annulled* 1934) Dorothy Eileen, est dau of J G Cameron, of Santiago, Chile; *m* 2nd 20 May 1937 Winifred Mary (*d* 1978), est dau of Reginald Ashton, of Lima, Peru, and *d* 1970, leaving:
1d +Richard Everard [Richard Wodehouse, 628 Pacific View Drive, San Diego, CA 92108, USA]; *b* 1949; *m* 1979 *Mary Jean, dau of William Warren Johnson, of Elkton, Oregon, and has:
1e *Carissa Reneé; *b*; 1982
2e *Paloma Carin; *b* 1988
1d *Diana Elaine [Mrs William Strong, 1700 W 106 St, Chicago, IL 60643, USA]; *b* 12 May 1939; *m* 1964 *Donald Ralph Strong, s of Rev William Strong, of the Gospel Mission of S America, Cuatres Temuco, Chile, and has:
1e *Everard George; *b* 1968
1e *Miriam Ruth; *b* 4 July 1966
2d *(Marilyn) Joanna [Mrs Muri, 934 31st St, Bismarck, ND 58501, USA]; *b* 18 Aug 1943; *m* 1964 *Garvin Olaf Muri, s of Olaf H Muri, of Wadford City, ND, and has:
1e *Michelle Ingrid; *b* 12 March 1967
2e *Jenelle; *b* 1970
2c James Millie; *b* 15 July 1896; *educ* Haileybury; *m* 22 Feb 1930 Helen Mary Edith (*d* 1994), er dau of Sir John Murray, 12th Bt, of Blackbarony (*qv*), and *d* 1971, leaving:
1d *Lily Ann [Miss Lily Wodehouse, Casilla 7, Valenar, Chile]; *b* 19–
3c Guy Armine; *b* 3 Nov 1897; *educ* Haileybury; *m* 20 June 1925 Marjorie Eileen, yst dau of Adam Birrell, of Valparaiso, Chile, and *d* 1967, leaving:
1d +Charles Armine Birrell; *b* 7 April 1928; *m* 26 Dec 1952 *Eloise Rae, dau of Raymond James Cassie, of Florida
1d *Valerie Elisa; *b* 1935
4c Charles Ewart, T/Ft Sub-Lt RNAS; *b* 23 Feb 1899; *das* 18 Nov 1918
5c Lionel von Tempsky, RASC WW II 1943–46; *b* 27 July 1904; *m* 6 Sept 1930 Ruby, 3rd Offr WRNS 1943–46, dau of Frederick C Prain, of Vina del Mar, Chile
1c Ivy Maude; *b* 23 Oct 1901; *m* 23 Oct 1937 Edward James Campbell, of Santiago, Chile
3b Ernest Hay; *b* 13 July 1869; *m* 10 July 1893 May (*d* 7 Jan 1938), dau of Curtis Perry Ward, of Honolulu, and *d* 1957, having had:
1c Errol Hay; *b* 20 Sept 1895; *d* 6 June 1896
2c Cenric Nourse, Lt-Cdr USNR WW II, US Bronze Star Citations; *b* 3 Jan 1909; *m* 28 Aug 1934 Maud, dau of Walter D Ackerman, of Kealakekua, Kona, Hawaii
4b Kenneth Charles; *b* 29 July 1873; *m* Sept 1910 Nora (*d* 18 July 1967), dau of Edward Madden, and *d* 5 Jan 1928, leaving:
1c John Hay; *b* 1917; *m* 1st 1941 Maria Francisca Garrido (*d* 1945) and had:

1d +Cyprian Gerard [Cyprian Wodehouse, 6 Whittier Place, Apt 15H, Boston, MA 02114, USA); *b* 1941; has:

1e *Lisa Sharon; *b* 1982

1c (cont.) John Wodehouse *m* 2nd 1947 (*divorce* 1959) Carmen Meza Valdés and by her had:

2d +Kenneth John [Kenneth Wodehouse, 1166 Carrolton Ave, Metairie, LA 70005, USA]; *b* 30 Dec 1957; *m* 1987 *Lisa Marie, dau of Paul T White, and has:

1e +Evan John; *b* 1989

2e +Craig Alen; *b* 1993

1c (cont.) John Wodehouse *m* 3rd 6 Jan 1960 *Jeanette Wackenhut [Mrs John Wodehouse, Calle Madre Mazarello 6745, Las Condes, Santiago, Chile], and *d* 1993, having by her had:

3d +Roderick Dhu; *b* 5 March 1965

1d *Sharon Elizabeth; *b* 7 Feb 1962

1b Annette Maud; *b* 19 April 1865; *m* 1st 26 March 1887 Robert Spears Lambert (*d* 7 Oct 1902), of Culipran, Chile, and had issue; *m* 2nd 20 June 1922 Romauldo Silva-Cortes, Senator Chile, and *d* 25 Feb 1935

2b Amy Dulcibella; *b* 20 Dec 1866; *m* 30 March 1891 Louis von Tempsky, of Erewhon, Maui, and *d* 2 Sept 1909, leaving issue

3b Ethel Jane; *b* 12 May 1870; *d* unm 3 April 1957

4b Leila Bernice; *b* 17 Dec 1877; *m* 26 Nov 1901 Charles Francis Raby, of Valparaiso, Chile, and *d* 5 Jan 1948, leaving issue

3a Herbert; *b* 29 July 1827; *m* 1st 1856 Mary (*d* 17 Nov 1866), dau of George Wood, and had:

1b Edith Neville; *m* 8 Oct 1885 Philip Henry Clifford, barrister (*d* 1895)

3a (cont.) Herbert Wodehouse *m* 2nd 1871 Mary (*d* 13 Jan 1930), dau of George Burton, of Loddon, Norfolk, and *d* 1889, having by her had:

2b Gertrude Jane; *m* 1902 Frederick Dickson, s of Rev R H Dickson, Vicar Eastchurch, Sheerness, and *d* 11 June 1949, leaving issue

3b Margaret; *d* unm 11 Dec 1943

4b Dulcibella; *d* unm 12 Sept 1916

5b Constance; *m* 25 April 1903 Walter Barrington Beare, yr s of John Beare, of Norbury

6b Lucy Hay; *m* 2 Aug 1915 Arthur William Johnson, s of Rev Alfred Johnson, and had issue

(1) Lucy; *m* 26 June 1809 her cousin Edmond Wodehouse and *d* 21 June 1829, leaving issue (*see* below)

3 Thomas, barrister; *b* 1 Feb 1747; *m* 12 Sept 1782 Sarah, dau of Pryse Campbell, of Stackpole Court, and sis of 1st Baron Cawdor (*see* CAWDOR, E), and had, with other issue:

(1) Edmond, of Sennow Lodge, Norfolk, MP; *b* 26 June 1784; *m* 26 June 1809 his cousin Lucy (*d* 21 June 1829), dau of Rev Philip Wodehouse (*see* above), and *d* 21 Aug 1855, having had, with other issue:

1a Philip Edmond (Sir), GCSI, KCB, Govr Bombay 1872–77; *b* 26 Feb 1811; *m* 19 Dec 1833 Katherine Mary (*d* 6 Oct 1866), est dau of F J Templer, and *d* 25 Oct 1887, leaving:

1b Edmond Robert, PC (1898), MA Oxon; barrister Lincoln's Inn 1861, MP Bath 1880–1906; *b* 3 June 1835; *m* 1 June 1876 Adela Harriett Sophia (*d* 25 April 1921), 2nd dau of Rev Charles Walter Bagot (*see* BAGOT, B), and *d* 14 Dec 1914

2a Edmond, Gen, Col S Wales Borderers; *b* 3 Aug 1818; *m* 9 Jan 1855 Louisa Harriet (*d* 23 Feb 1895), 2nd dau of Gen R D Hallifax, 75th Regt, and *d* 28 May 1898

3a Campbell (Rev); Rector Alderford, Norfolk; *b* 3 Jan 1826; *m* 3 June 1851 Marianne Lloyd (*d* 13 Feb 1903) 2nd dau of Rt Rev Charles Lloyd, DD, Bp Oxford, and *dsp* 8 March 1868

1a Lucy; *m* 8 July 1852 Lt-Col Hervey Hopwood, Gren Gds

(2) Thomas (Rev), Canon Wells, Rector Norton, Kent; *b* 13 Oct 1788; *m* Anne, dau of Rt Rev Walker King, Bp Rochester, and *d* 22 March 1840, having had, with other issue:

1a Thomas (Rev), BA Oxfon, Assist Chaplain Savoy Chapel London; *b* 22 May 1818; *d* unm 15 Feb 1905

2a Walker (Rev), MA Oxon; Vicar Elham, Kent; *b* 31 Aug 1819; *d* unm

3a Francis Arthur; *b* 18 June 1831; *m* 1879 his cousin Fanny (*d* 13 June 1928), dau of Rev Nathaniel Wodehouse (*see* below), and *dsp* 30 Dec 1891

4a Edmond Henry, CB, MA Oxon; barrister Lincoln's Inn 1863, Commr Inland Revenue 1891–1902; *b* 17 Feb 1837; *m* 26 May 1864 his cousin Louisa Clara (*d* 18 Jan 1920), 4th dau of Rev Nathaniel Wodehouse (*see* below), and *d* 27 March 1923

1a Sarah Frances; *m* 15 May 1850 William S Dawson, of Cobham, Kent

2a Anne; *m* 13 April 1852 Rev James Carleton King

3a Agnes; *m* 11 Feb 1865 G S Williams, Ceylon CS, and had issue

(3) Nathaniel (Rev); Vicar Dulverton; *b* 2 Nov 1802; *m* 27 Sept 1829 Georgiana (*d c* 1903), dau of Rev Hon William Capel (*see* ESSEX, E), and *d* 23 Oct 1870, having had, with other issue:

1a Capel, R-Adml, JP Berks; *b* 25 Jan 1841; *m* 25 April 1889 Portia Maria (*d* 24 Aug 1912), est dau of William Boys Rashleigh, of The Manor Ho, Farningham, Kent, and *d* 3 March 1906, leaving:

1b Edmond, CBE (1948), Brig RWF, Mil Attaché Eire 1942, served WW I (wounded) and WW II; *b* 25 March 1894; *educ* Winchester and RMC Sandhurst; *m* 22 Aug 1935 Persis Joan Mary (*m* 2nd 1980 Lt-Col Robert Michael FitzHugh), only dau of Edward Plumer Rooper, of Min-yr-Afon, Overton Bridge, Wrexham, and *d* 31 Dec 1959, leaving:

1c +Armine John [Maj Armine Wodehouse, c/o Lloyds Bank, 6 Pall Mall, London SW1]; Maj RWF; *b* 20 June 1936; *educ* Winchester and RMA Sandhurst; *m* 24 April 1965 *Louise Kynaston, only dau of Mark Kynaston Mainwaring (*see* RANKIN, Bt), and has:

1d +Edmond Armine; *b* 16 Oct 1968

1d *Rosemary Louise; *b* 13 July 1966

2d *Rowena Carolyn; *b* 6 May 1971

2c +Hugh Capel; *b* 22 Oct 1945; *educ* Winchester and Wadham Coll Oxford; *m* 19– *Mrs Anthea M Courtauld, dau of R H Priestley, of Oakley, Hants, and has:

1d *Katie Rose; *b* 1983

1c *Rachel Mary [Mrs Robert Copeman, Down House, Soberton, Hants]; *b* 4 July 1938; *m* 8 May 1965 *Robert Charles Copeman, est s of Lt-Col C N C Copeman, MC, and has:

1d *James Robert; *b* 29 Aug 1966

1d *Charlotte Anne; *b* 4 March 1968

2c *Carolyn Persis; *b* 22 May 1943; *m* 24 Aug 1968 *Michael Cemlyn-Jones, 2nd s of William Cemlyn-Jones, of Madrid, and has:

1d *Tara Persis; *b* 28 June 1970

2d *Jessica Melfis; *b* 1973

1b Dulcibella; *b* 2 Jan 1891; *m* 1926 Lt-Col Edward H Burton, TD, RASC, and *d* 27 Feb 1971, leaving:

1c *Christopher Carleton John; *b* 23 April 1930

2b Alice; *b* 22 March 1892; *d* unm 24 Oct 1957

1a Alice Jane; *m* 12 Oct 1865 Maj Bevil Granville (*d* 6 March 1909), of Wellesbourne Hall, Warwicks, and *d* 21 Oct 1901, leaving issue

2a Louisa Clara; *m* 26 May 1864 Edmond Henry Wodehouse CB (*see* above) and *d* 18 Jan 1920

3a Fanny; *m* 1879 Francis Arthur Wodehouse (*see* above), and *d* 13 June 1928

Sir ARMINE *d* 21 May 1777; his est son,

Sir John Wodehouse, 6th Bt, and **1st Baron Wodehouse of Kimberley**, Co Norfolk (GB), so *cr* 26 Oct 1797; *b* 4 April 1741; Recorder Falmouth, MP (Tory) Norfolk 1784–97; *m* 30 March 1769 Sophia (*d* 16 April 1825), only child of Hon Charles Berkeley, of Bruton Abbey, Somerset, and niece of 5th and last Baron Berkeley of Stratton, and had, with other issue:

1 JOHN, **2nd Baron**

2 Philip, V-Adml of the White; *b* 16 July 1773; *m* 7 May 1814 Mary Hay (*d* 1 Oct 1854), dau of Charles Cameron, Govr Bahamas, and *d* 21 Jan 1838, having had, with four daus (*d* unm):

(1) Edwin, Col RA, CB, ADC, Chev Legn Hon; *b* 17 April 1817; *m* 16 Oct 1845 Catherine (*d* 9 Jan 1873), only dau of Capt John Street, RA, and *d* 6 Oct 1870, having had:

1a (Edwin) Frederick (Sir), KCB, KCVO, Maj RA 1870–90, Assist Commr City London Police 1890–1902 and Met Police 1902–18; *b* 20 Feb 1851; *m* 21 June 1881 Margaret (*d* 2 Nov 1927), dau of Charles Henry Wyndham A'Court Repington (*see* HEYTESBURY, B), and *d* 1 April 1934, having had:

1b Joan; *b* 27 April 1882; *m* 1936 Paul de Castro

2b Alice; *b* 20 Nov 1883; *m* 23 Jan 1912 Maj Cecil Eustace Harrison, Rifle Bde (*ka* 14 March 1915), er s of Robert Harrison, of Shiplake Court, Oxon, and *d* 15 Feb 1919, leaving issue

1a Catherine Mary Philippa; *m* 27 June 1877 Adml Sir James Andrew Thomas Bruce, KCMG (*d* 26 May 1921), yst s of Sir Henry Hervey Bruce, 3rd Bt, of Downhill (*qv*), and *d* 18 April 1924

2a Alice Katharine; *m* 9 Dec 1875 James Martin Carr Lloyd (*d* 8 June 1919), of Lancing Manor, Sussex, and *d* 21 Nov 1882, leaving issue

(2) Constantine Griffith (Rev), Vicar Langford, Oxon; *b* 31 March 1827; *m* 7 April 1858 Fanny Isabella (*d* 11 June 1923), est dau of Rev Edward Henry Sawbridge, of E Haddon Hall, Northants, and *dsp* 7 March 1911

(3) Philip Cameron (Rev), Chaplain Hampton Court Palace, Vicar Teddington, Middx; *b* 22 Jan 1837; *m* 12 April 1866 Mary (*d* 8 Nov 1919), 2nd dau of Rev Edward Henry Sawbridge, and *dsp* 16 Dec 1883

3 William (Rev), MA; *b* 4 Aug 1782; *m* 11 Feb 1807 Mary (*d* 29 Nov 1865), est dau of Thomas Hussey (*see* WALPOLE, B), and *d* 3 April 1870, having had, with other issue:

(1) George, V-Adml; *b* 8 July 1810; *m* 20 June 1848 Eleanor Charlotte (*d* 27 March 1888), dau of Andrew Mortimer Drummond (*see* PERTH, E), and *d* 15 Feb 1900, leaving:

1a Josceline Heneage (Sir), GCB, CMG, Gen RA, cmded Northern Army India, Govr Bermuda 1907–08, served S Africa, Afghanistan, Sudan and NWF India (ret 1913), 2nd Cl Medjidie, 2nd Cl Osmanieh, French Order Palm; *b* 17 July 1852; *m* 1st 1 Oct 1885 his cousin Constance (*dsp* 21 Aug 1886), dau of Gen Sir Charles D'Aguilar, GCB; *m* 2nd 15 May 1901 Mary Joyce (*d* 3 Oct 1951), dau of Robert Sacheverell Wilmot-Sitwell, DL, JP, of Stainsby, Derbys, and *d* 16 Jan 1930, leaving:

1b Armine George, Lt 8th Hus; *b* 25 May 1904; *d* 29 July 1935

2a Mortimer Keppel, Lt RN; *b* 9 Oct 1854; *d* unm 27 May 1893

1a Evelyn Georgiana Susan; *b* 5 June 1849; *d* 27 Sept 1920

(2) Algernon (Rev), Rector Easton; *b* 13 May 1814; *m* 26 Nov 1844 Lady Eleanor Ashburnham (*d* 6 March 1895), 6th dau of 3rd Earl of Ashburnham, KG (*see* 1924 edn), and *d* 2 May 1882, having had, with other issue:

1a William Wentworth (Rev), Rector Distington, Cumberland; *b* 13 March 1846; *m* 26 June 1878 Helen Maude (*d* 7 Aug 1932), only child of Arthur Brooke (*see* BROOKE, Bt, of Norton Priory), and *d* 26 March 1888, leaving:

1b Arthur Hugh, Maj 5th Bn Roy Dublin Fus WW I; *b* 26 April 1879; *m* 15 Aug 1923 Louise (*m* 2nd Arthur Cotton), dau of Capt George London, of Shanghai, and *d* 24 Nov 1952

1b Alice Mary; *m* 17 June 1909 John Broadwood (*d* 2 May 1960), yr s of Edward Broadwood, and had issue

2a Francis John; *b* 1 Oct 1855; *m* 23 April 1896 Valerie Amy Martyn, and *d* 8 April 1901, leaving:

1b John Francis Ashburnham, 2nd Lt DCLI and RFC; *b* 17 June 1897; *ka* 26 Aug 1917

3a Thomas Frederick (twin); *b* 1 Oct 1855; *m* 17 Nov 1896 Alice Caroline, dau of Col John Ormsby Vandeleur, CB, of Hyde Abbey Ho, Winchester, and *d* 9 Dec 1908, leaving:

1b Elinor Alice Hilda; *b* 23 Oct 1897

The 1st BARON *d* 29 May 1834; his est son,

JOHN WODEHOUSE, **2nd Baron Wodehouse of Kimberley**; *b* 11 Jan 1771; MP (Tory) Gt Bedwyn 1796–1802 and Marlborough 1812–26, Ld Lt Norfolk 1822–46,

V-Adml coast of Norfolk, Col E Norfolk Militia, High Steward Norwich Cathedral; *m* 17 Nov 1796 Charlotte Laura (*d* June 1845), only dau and heiress of John Norris, of Witton Park and Witchingham, Norfolk, by Charlotte, 4th dau of Very Rev Hon Edward Townshend (*see* TOWNSHEND, M), and had, with other issue:

1 Henry; *b* 19 March 1799; *m* 7 April 1825 Anne (*d* 14 Jan 1880), only dau of Theophilus Thornhaugh Gurdon, of Letton, Norfolk, and *d* 29 April 1834, having had, with two daus (*d* young):

(1) JOHN, **1st Earl**

(2) Henry; *b* posthumously 27 May 1834; granted rank of baron's yr s 1847; *m* 25 June 1872 Mary Livingstone (*m* 2nd 26 June 1880 4th Marquess of Anglesey (*qv*) and *d* May 1931), dau of J P King, of Sand Hills, Ga., USA, and *dsp* 20 Aug 1873

2 Edward WODEHOUSE later THORNTON-WODEHOUSE, Adml; *b* 5 June 1802; *m* 10 Nov 1838 Diana (*d* 13 March 1884), only dau of Col Thornton, of Falconer's Hall, Yorks, and *d* 17 March 1874, leaving:

(1) Albert, Col RA; *b* 5 Feb 1840; *m* 1 July 1874 Elizabeth Katherine (*d* 5 Oct 1918), 3rd dau of Hon George Edgecumbe (*see* MOUNT EDGCUMBE, E), and *dsp* 16 Feb 1914

(1) Cecilia; *m* 24 July 1879 Baron Ferdinand von Liliencron, of Schleswig-Holstein, and *d* 20 Nov 1928

(2) Laura Elisabeth Anne; *d* unm 26 Dec 1904

(3) Mary Diana; *m* 4 April 1878 Charles Conway Thornton (*d* 17 May 1902), Dip Serv, and *d* 28 Oct 1949, leaving issue

4 Berkeley, CMG, Col E Norfolk Militia, Consul Dunkirk; *b* 14 May 1806; *m* 5 June 1837 Fanny (*d* 2 April 1871), only dau of Alex Holmes, of The Curragh, Co Kildare, and *d* 13 Sept 1877, leaving, with other issue:

(1) Killegrew Reginald Berkeley, Col 1st Bn HLI; *b* 9 Sept 1843; *m* 22 Feb 1881 Katherine Elizabeth (*d* 19 Feb 1930), only dau of James Marke Wood, of Liverpool, and *d* 17 March 1935, leaving:

1a Reginald Berkeley *b* 13 April 1886; *d* unm 6 Nov 1971

2a Philip Edward Berkeley, memb Lloyd's, T/Lt RNVR; *b* 20 Nov 1887; *d* unm 21 Aug 1953

1a Laura Mary Katherine; *m* 9 Feb 1922 Maj Christopher Capel (*d* 17 April 1964), of Prestbury Ho, Prestbury, Glos, and *dsp* 14 Jan 1962

(2) Clarence Francis Berkeley, Commr Paphos, Cyprus, Lt 77th Regt; *b* 1 Aug 1855; *m* 21 July 1881 Francie (*d* 14 May 1937), er dau of Arthur Saunders Davies, of Pentre, and *d* 24 Oct 1945, having had:

1a Clarence John d'Everton Berkeley, Capt and Hon Maj 3rd Bn Norfolk Regt, Inspr Cyprus Mil Police and Bd of Ag and Fisheries, served WW I (despatches, 1914 Star), Orders Crown Italy and Redeemer Greece; *b* 31 May 1882; *educ* Harrow; *m* 10 June 1914 Gladys Catherine (*d* 15 March 1956), est dau of Walter Tyrrell, MRCS, LRCP

2a Arthur Cecil Berkeley; *b* Oct 1884; *d* 14 June 1890

1a Mary Nessie Gwyn Berkeley; *b* 23 Oct 1887; *d* unm 26 Oct 1956

2a Kitty Dagmar Berkeley; *b* 27 Nov 1894; *d* 2 June 1922

3a Francie Petronel Bice Berkeley; *b* 10 March, *d* 27 June 1901

4a Armine Frances Berkeley; *b* 4 March 1903; Co Cdr ATS WW II

6 Alfred (Rev); *b* 10 June 1814; *m* 21 April 1840 Emma Hamilla (*d* 5 April 1852), 2nd dau of Reginald George Macdonald, 19th Chief of Clanranald, DL, JP, and *d* 6 Sept 1848, having had:

(1) Hobart; *b* 23 April 1842

(2) Reginald, RN; *d* 25 Aug 1861

(3) Charles Edward; *b* 18 Oct 1845; *d* 5 April 1883

(4) Henry; *b* 2 Jan 1849

(1) Hamilla Caroline; *m* 8 Nov 1876 Edward Taylor, V-Consul Dunkirk, and *d* 1879

(2) Ernestine Emma; *m* 17 May 1866 John Marshall (*d* 1894), 2nd s of H C Marshall, of Weetwood Hall, Leeds, and *d* 1929

(3) Laura Sophia; *m* 23 Nov 1882 Lt-Col Charles John Wyndham, CBE, 2nd Bn Roy Irish Rifles (*d* 1 May 1930), 4th son of Col Charles Wyndham, of Rogate Lodge, Sussex, and *dsp* 29 Aug 1904

1 Henrietta Laura; *m* 1834 John David Chambers, QC, barrister

The 2nd BARON *d* 29 May 1846; his gs,

JOHN WODEHOUSE, **1st Earl of Kimberley** (UK), so *cr* 1 June 1866, KG (1885), PC (1864), DL, JP and CC Norfolk; *b* 7 Jan 1826; *educ* Eton and Ch Ch Oxford; Parly U-Sec For Affrs (Lib) 1852–56 and 1859–61, Envoy Extrdy and Min Plen St Petersburg 1856–58, Special Envoy Copenhagen 1863, Parly U-Sec India 1864, Ld Lt Ireland 1864–66, Ld Privy Seal 1868–70, Sec State Colonies 1870–74 and 1880–82, Chllr Duchy Lancaster 1882–83, Sec State India 1882–85 and 1886, Ld Pres Cncl and Sec State India 1892–94, For Sec 1894–95, Chllr London U 1899, High Steward Norwich Cathedral, Hon DCL Oxford; *m* 16 Aug 1847 Lady Florence Fitzgibbon, CI (*d* 4 May 1895), est dau and coheiress of 3rd and last Earl of Clare, and had, with other issue:

1 JOHN, **2nd Earl**

2 Armine, CB, MP Saffron Walden 1900–01; *b* 24 Sept 1860; *m* 6 June 1889 Eleanor Mary Caroline, OBE (*m* 2nd 5 July 1909 1st Viscount Sandhurst (*see* SANDHURST, B), and *d* 5 Dec 1934), dau of Matthew Arnold, and *d* 1 May 1901, leaving:

(1) Roger (Rev), Vicar St Thomas's, Hammersmith, W12; *b* 24 Sept 1890; *educ* Eton and Balliol Coll Oxford (BA 1913, MA 1918); *d* unm 8 Dec 1958

1 Alice; *b* 17 Dec 1850; *m* 14 Aug 1872 Hussey Packe, DL (*d* 8 Oct 1908), of Prestwold Hall, Leics, and *d* 8 Jan 1937, leaving issue

The 1st EARL *d* 8 April 1902; his only surv son,

JOHN WODEHOUSE, **2nd Earl of Kimberley**, JP and CC Norfolk; *b* 10 Dec 1848; *m* 22 June 1875 Isabel Geraldine (*d* 20 Jan 1927), dau of Sir Henry Josias Stracey, 5th Bt (*qv*), and had:

1 JOHN, **3rd Earl**

2 Philip, Army Lt; *b* 1 Oct 1886; *d* 6 May 1919

3 Edward, MC, 2nd Lt 16th Lancers; *b* 12 April 1898; *ka* 30 March 1918

1 Isabel; *d* unm 15 Dec 1959

The 2nd EARL *d* 7 Jan 1932; his est son,

JOHN WODEHOUSE, **3rd Earl of Kimberley**, CBE, MC, JP Norfolk; *b* 11 Nov 1883; Capt 16th Lancers, Lt Norfolk Yeo, served WW I (wounded, despatches twice, Croce di Guerra), MP Mid-Norfolk 1906–10; *m* 5 May 1922 Frances Margaret Montagu (*d* 4 Jan 1950), dau of Lt-Col Leonard Howard Irby (*see* BOSTON, B), and was *k* in an air raid 16 April 1941, leaving:

1 JOHN WODEHOUSE, **4th and present Earl of Kimberley**

KINDERSLEY

Arms: Per bend gules and azure a lion rampant argent, within an orle of cross-crosslets and fleur-de-lys alternatively or. **Crest**: Upon a mount vert in front of a hawthorn tree proper, charged with an escutcheon azure, thereon a lion rampant argent, a greyhound sejant, also argent. **Supporters:** Dexter, a greyhound argent gorged with a collar azure, charged with three cross-crosslets or; sinister, a lion argent gorged with a collar gules, charged as the dexter; each standing upon a branch of hawthorn proper. **Motto:** *Adjuvante Deo* ('With God's assistance'). **Creation:** B. (UK) 28 Jan 1941.

THE 3RD BARON KINDERSLEY, of West Hoathly, Co Sussex ((Robert) Hugh Molesworth Kindersley, DL (Kent 1986)) [The Rt Hon The Lord Kindersley DL, West Green Farm, Shipbourne, Kent TN11 9PU]; *b* 18 Aug 1929; *s f* 1976; *educ* Eton, Trin Coll Oxford (BA 1952) and Harvard Business Sch (MBA 1954); Lt Scots Gds Malaya 1948–49, chm Siam Selective Growth Fund 1990–, dir: Lazard Bros & Co Ltd 1960–90, Sun Alliance and London Insurance Gp Ltd 1965–, Gen Electric and English Electric Cos Ltd, Witan Investment Co Ltd, Swedish Match Co; chm Cwlth Devpt Corp 1980–89, Fin Adviser Export Gp for the Constructional Industries, memb Institut International d'Etudes Bancaires 1971–85, dep chm ECGD Advsy Cncl 1975–80, pres Anglo-Taiwan Trade Ctee, memb Ct Fishmongers' Co 1973– (Prime Warden 1989–90), Hon Treas YWCA 1965–76; *m* 1st 4 Sept 1954 (*divorce* 1989) Venice Marigold (Rosie), er dau of Lord Francis Henry Hill (*see* DOWNSHIRE, M); *m* 2nd 1989 *Patricia Margaret, only dau of Brig Hugh Ronald Norman, DSO, of Lower St Clere, Kemsing, Kent, and formerly w of Henry Colum Crichton-Stuart (Isee BUTE, M), and by his 1st w has had:

1 +RUPERT JOHN MOLESWORTH [The Hon Rupert Kindersley, 22 Sugden Rd, London SW11 5EF]; *b* 11 March 1955; *educ* Eton; *m* 2 Aug 1975 *Sarah Anne, only dau of John Dennis Warde, of Cermyll Cottage, Hermitage, Berks, and has:

(1) +Frederick Hugh Molesworth; *b* 9 Jan 1987

(1) *Rebecca; *b* 1985

2 Hugh Francis; *b* 25 June 1956; *educ* Eton; *m* 1987 (*divorce* 1990) (Evelyn) Rosamond, est dau of (Robert Jestyn) Gwent Forestier-Walker (*see* FORESTIER-WALKER, Bt), and *d* 1991, leaving:

(1) +Bertie; *b* 19–

(2) +Harry; *b* 26 Jan 1998

(1) *Rosanna; *b* 1987

3 +Dickon Michael [The Hon Dickon Kindersley, 3 Ingelow Rd, London SW3 3PZ]; *b* 9 March 1962; *m* 1991 *Victoria S, est dau of T J Coles, of Saltwood, Brasted, Kent, and has:

(1) *Phoebe; *b* 1993

1 *Anna Lucy; *b* 19 June 1965 (HRH THE DUCHESS OF KENT stood sponsor)

Lineage: NATHANIEL WILLIAM KINDERSLEY; *b* 1794; High Court Judge Madras; *m* 1832 Mary Molesworth (*d* 1881; *see* MOLESWORTH, V) and *d* India 1844, leaving:

EDWARD NASSAU MOLESWORTH KINDERSLEY, of Sherborne, Dorset; *b* 28 Aug 1836; *educ* Eton and Balliol Coll Oxford; Capt 14th Yorks Regt (Green Howards); *m* 4 Feb 1868 Ada Good (*d* 11 Nov 1908), 3rd dau of John Murray, and *d* 11 Nov 1907, leaving:

1 John Molesworth; *b* 24 Nov 1868; *educ* Repton and Hertford Coll Oxford; ICS and Fedn Malay States CS (invalided 1902); *m* 23 April 1898 Olive Montague (*d* 8 June 1955), 2nd dau of Alfred Saunders Walford, JP, of Cranbrook Hall, Essex, and had:

(1) Nassau; *b* 15 June 1902; *d* in infancy

(1) Ann Molesworth; *b* 18 Sept 1899; *m* 17 April 1934 Rt Rev Ronald Stanhope More O'Ferrall, DD, Bp Madagascar, s of James Eaton O'Ferrall, and had:

1a Conall John; *b* 29 Nov 1945; *educ* Trin Coll Dublin

1a *Helen Maeve; *b* 21 Feb 1935; *m* 29 Aug 1962 *Guy Christopher Oram, est s of John Everard Oram, of Frostenden Hall, Beccles, Suffolk, and has:

1b *Timothy Michael; *b* 30 Sept 1969

1b *Ann Therese; *b* 26 Jan 1964

2 ROBERT MOLESWORTH, **1st Baron**

3 Guy Molesworth, OBE (1918), JP (Herts); Maj WW I (despatches twice), Inspr QMG's Servs 1917–18, MP Hitchin 1923–31, barrister Lincoln's Inn 1901, ptnr Montagu Loebl Stanley and Co, stockbrokers, dir: Trust Houses Ltd; Clerical, Medical and Gen Life Assur Soc, Gen Reversionary and Investment Co; chm Walker and Honfrays Ltd, Manchester Brewery Co Ltd, Wilson and Walker Brewery Ltd and Eyre and Spottiswoode (Publishers) Ltd; *b* 28 Feb 1877; *educ* Marlborough; *m* 30 July 1903 Kathleen Agnes Rhoda (*d* 10 May 1950), est dau of Sir Edmund Harry Elton, 8th Bt (*qv*), and *d* 30 Nov 1956, having had:

(1) *Edmund Murray; *b* 22 Jan 1905; *educ* Marlborough and King's Coll Cambridge (BA 1926); *m* 1st 8 Oct 1930 (*divorce* 1937) Pamela Antonia, dau of Reginald Boden; *m* 2nd 26 May 1937 *Lucy Emily, dau of Brig-Gen Gerald Hedley Ovens, CB, and by her has:

1a *Nicholas Hallam Stuart [Nicholas Kindersley Esq, Derryglogher Lodge, Kenagh, Co Longford, Ireland]; *b* 4 April 1939; *educ* Marlborough and King's Coll Cambridge (BA 1960); *m* 31 July 1965 Susan Marion Richenda (*d* 31 May 1996), er dau of Capt Thomas Abdy Combe, of The Tile Ho, Aldham, Essex, and formerly w of Christie Thomas Pemberton, and has:

1b *(Gerald) Sebastian Molesworth [Sebastian Kindersley Esq, The Manor Barn, East Hatley, Hatley St George, Cambridgeshire SG19 3JA]; *b* 25 Aug 1966; *educ* St Columba's Coll and Anglia Poly U (BA 1991); md Mkt Movements Ltd, dir Mkt Movements (Asia Pacific) Pty Ltd, v-pres American MailBox Monitor Inc; *m* 7 March 1987 (*divorce* 1992) Monjan, only dau of Davoud Zahed Khorassani, of Nice

1b *(Pamela) Selena Jane [Mrs Alexander Kindersley-McKenzie, Spring Farm Cottage, Redcross, Co Wicklow, Ireland]; *b* 15 May 1968; *educ* St Columba's Coll, Gurteen Agric Coll (NCA 1987) and Seale Hayne Agric Coll (HND 1990); *m* 12 June 1994 *Alexander Colin McKenzie, 2nd s of Ian McKenzie, of Hong Kong and Spring Farm, Redcross, Co Wicklow, and has:

1c *Daisy Alexandra; *b* 26 April 1996

(2) David Guy Barnabas, MBE (1979); *b* 11 June 1915; *educ* Marlborough; sculptor/typographer, letterer in glass, stone and paper; consultant to Letraset Ltd, co-fndr Cardozo Kindersley Edns, Sr Research Fell 1967 William Andrews Clark Library U of California, author *Eric Gill — Further Thoughts of an Apprentice* (1967) and *Graphic Sayings* (1973); *m* 1st 1939 (*divorce*) Christine Sharpe and had, with a dau:

1a *Richard; letterer

2a *Peter David [Peter Kindersley Esq, Dorling Kindersley Hldgs plc, 9 Henrietta St, London WC2E 8PS]; *b* 13 July 1941; *educ* King Edward VI Sch Norwich and Camberwell Sch of Arts and Crafts; fndg art dir Mitchell Beazley 1969–74, chm Dorling Kindersley (publishers) 1974–; *m* 1965 *Juliet Elizabeth Martyn and has a s and dau

(2) (cont.) David Kindersley *m* 2nd 21 June 1957 (*divorce*) Barbara Pym Eyre (*d* 11 Aug 1996), widow of Martin Alfred Petrie and dau of — Spells; *m* 3rd 1986 *Lida Lopes Cardozo and *d* 2 Feb 1995, having by her had three further children

(1) Agnes Ruth; *m* 1st 24 April 1929 Dr William H de Bargue Hubert, MRCS, MRCP (*d* 5 March 1947), and had issue; *m* 2nd 10 Aug 1949 Edmund Arthur Fortescue-Brickdale, TD (*d* as result of a motor accident 4 July 1977), yr son of Sir Charles Fortescue-Brickdale, of The Dower Ho, Newland, Glos, and *d* 6 Dec 1952

(2) *Kathleen Bridget [Mrs Roderick Nicolson, Tallents, Kimpton, Hitchin, Herts]; *m* 10 June 1931 Roderick William Nicolson, and has issue

1 Emily Molesworth; *m* 27 Nov 1907 Arthur Maxwell Quill (*d* 1925) and *d* 4 Sept 1938

2 Ada Molesworth; *d* unm 13 Oct 1961 aged 82

3 Muriel Molesworth; *m* 17 April 1909 Gerald Louis d'Abo (*d* 18 Jan 1962), and *d* 7 April 1921, leaving issue (*see* SUFFIELD, B)

4 Beatrice Molesworth; *m* 21 Sept 1918 Maj Edgar Hare, MC, DL, KPM, DCLI (*d* 30 July 1966), Ch Constable Cornwall, s of A R Hare, of Blackmount, NZ, and *d* 4 Jan 1966, leaving issue

5 Agnes Molesworth; *m* 9 April 1937 Sir John Bell, 2nd and last Bt (*d* 31 Dec 1943), and *d* 12 Feb 1963

Capt EDWARD KINDERSLEY *d* 31 Jan 1937; his 2nd son,

ROBERT MOLESWORTH KINDERSLEY, **1st Baron Kindersley**, of West Hoathly, Co Sussex (UK), so *cr* 28 Jan 1941, GBE (1920, KBE 1917); *b* 21 Nov 1871; *educ* Repton; chm Lazard Bros & Co Ltd, dir S Pearson and Son Ltd, Govr Hudson's Bay Co 1916–25, 1st chm Nat Savings Ctee 1916–20, Chm Govrs Repton 1920–44, Lt City of London, memb Ct Fishmongers' Co (Prime Warden 1933), Pres Nat Savings Ctee 1920–46, chm Trade Facilities Act Advisory Ctee 1921–25, memb Bankers' Ctee on German Finance 1922, Sr Br Rep Dawes Ctee 1924, High Sheriff Sussex 1928–29, v-pres Industrial Co-Partnership Assoc, Dir Bank of England 1914–46, Offr Legion Honour of France, Cdr Order of Leopold, Grand Cross Order of Leopold II, Grand Cross Order Crown Belgium, Grand Cross Crown Italy; *m* 3 Nov 1896 Gladys Margaret (*d* 17 Jan 1968 aged 93), dau of Maj-Gen James Princep Beadle, RE, of S Kensington and Worton Grange, Wilts, and had:

1 Lionel Nassau; 2nd Lt 15th Hus WW I; *b* 6 Aug 1897; *educ* Eton; *ka* 24 Nov 1917

2 HUGH KENYON MOLESWORTH, **2nd Baron**

3 Richard Francis; *b* 5 Feb 1905; *educ* Eton; *d* unm 8 Nov 1932

4 Philip Leyland; *b* 11 March 1907; *educ* Eton and Ch Ch Oxford; Capt Coldstream Gds WW II 1939–43 (POW); *m* 1st 24 June 1929 (*divorce* 1935) Oonagh, yst dau of Hon (Arthur) Ernest Guinness (*see* IVEAGH, E), and had:

(1) +Gay [Gay Kindersley Esq, Laines, Aldbourne, Marlborough, Wilts]; *b* 2 June 1930; *educ* Eton; amateur jockey, memb Jockey Club; *m* 1st 31 Jan 1956 (*divorce* 1976) Margaret Diana, only dau of Hugh Wakefield, of Mayfair, and has:

1a +Robin; *b* 28 Oct 1956

2a +Kim; *b* 30 Jan 1960

1a *Catheryn; *b* 23 April 1958; *m* 1st 1980 *Robert Lennon Milbourn, s of Cecil Milbourn, of Belgravia; *m* 2nd 1991, as his 2nd w, 13th Marquess of Huntly (*qv*)

2a *Tania; *b* 30 Jan 1967; author: *Don't Ask Me Why, Out to Lunch* and *Goodbye, Johnny Thunders* (novels)

(1) (cont.) Gay Kindersley *m* 2nd 1976 *Philippa Harper and by her has:

3a +Rory; *b* 1977

4a +Oliver; *b* 1980

(1) Tessa; *b* 31 Jan 1932; *d* 2 Aug 1946

4 (cont.) The Hon Philip Kindersley *m* 2nd 26 Nov 1936 (Violet) Valerie (*d* 18 July 1997), yr dau of Maj Hon Gerald French, DSO (*see* 1970 edn YPRES, E), and formerly w of 4th Baron Brougham and Vaux (*qv*), and *d* 2 Oct 1995, having by her had:

(2) +Christian Philip [Christian Kindersley Esq, 11 St Maur Rd, London SW6 4DR]; *b* 19 March 1950; *educ* Eton; *m* 1st 5 May 1973 (*divorce* 1991) Hilary Louise, 2nd dau of David Radcliffe Guard, of Ryders Wells Ho, Lewes, Sussex; *m* 2nd 1992 *Lara Hepburn, dau of Frederick George Pohl, of Constantia, Capetown, and by his 1st w has:

1a +Alexander; *b* 8 June 1982

1a *Vanessa; *b* 1980

2a *Davina; *b* 1986

(2) *Nicolette Leila; *b* 17 April 1939; *m* 25 Sept 1963 *Robert Nicholas Philipson-Stow (*see* PHILIPSON-STOW, Bt) and has issue

(3) *Virginia Alexandra de L'Etang; *b* 16 April 1943; *m* 5 Oct 1965 *Hon Peregrine John Wishart Fairfax, yr s of 12th Lord Fairfax of Cameron (*qv*), and has issue

1 Margaret Marion; *b* 18 April 1902; *m* 1st 26 June 1924 Capt Algernon Spencer Belmont, RA (*das* in an accident 27 June 1944), s of Algernon Spencer Belmont, and has issue (*see* TATE, Bt); *m* 2nd 30 Aug 1945 *Col Thomas Whicher Boileau, OBE, yst s of Capt Thomas Smalley Boileau, IA

2 *Elizabeth Joan [The Hon Mrs James Philipps, Dalham Hall, Newmarket, Suffolk]; *b* 1 Feb 1911; *m* 24 June 1930 Maj Hon James Perrott Philipps, TD, 3rd s of 1st Baron Milford (*qv*), and has issue

The1st BARON *d* 20 July 1954; his er s,

HUGH KENYON MOLESWORTH KINDERSLEY, **2nd Baron Kindersley**, CBE (MBE), MC (1918); *b* 7 May 1899; *educ* Eton; Brig Scots Gds, served WWs I 1917–19 and II (wounded), chm Offrs' Assoc 1946–56, Hon Col 10 (London) Parachute Bn (TA) 1947–52, High Sheriff Co London 1951, Hon FRCS 1959, Patron RCS 1960, Govr Roy Exchange Assur 1955–69, dir: Lazard Bros & Co Ltd, Br Match Corp Ltd 1946–69, Cierva Rotorcraft Co Ltd, Bank of England 1947–67, chm: Rolls Royce Ltd 1957–68, Standing Review Body on Doctors' and Dentists' Remuneration 1962–76, Cdr Order of St Olav of Norway 1958; *m* 12 Oct 1921 Nancy Farnsworth (*d* 5 Oct 1977), dau of Dr Geoffrey Boyd, of Toronto, Canada, and *d* 6 Oct 1976, having had:

1 (ROBERT) HUGH MOLESWORTH KINDERSLEY, **3rd and present Baron Kindersley**

1 *Patricia Nassau [The Hon Lady Crookenden, Twin Firs, Four Elms, Edenbridge, Kent]; *b* 5 Aug 1922; *m* 3 Aug 1948 *Lt-Gen Sir Napier Crookenden, KCB, DSO, OBE, Col Cheshire Regt, 2nd s of Col Arthur Crookenden, CBE, DSO, of Wokingham, and has:

(1) *James Napier; *b* 3 June 1949; *educ* Eton; Scots Gds; *m* 1974 *Claire Ella Thorne and has:

1a *Benjamin Napier Lane; *b* 1978

1a *Lucinda Nan Annaliese; *b* 1975

(2) *Charles Stephen Napier; *b* 3 Feb 1957; *m* 21 Feb 1998 *Michelle Lynn, dau of Joseph Ott, of Pittsburgh, Pa.

(1) *Elizabeth Jane [Mrs Thomas Wilson, The Old Rectory, Upper Clatford, Andover, Hants]; *b* 23 Aug 1950; *m* 1st 18 July 1970 (*divorce* 1980) Sam G S Hughes, of Toronto, s of Mrs Justice S H S Hughes, of Toronto, and has:

1a *Geoffrey Samuel; *b* 1977

(1) (cont.) Mrs Sam Hughes *m* 2nd 1980 *Thomas Charles Wilson and by him has:

1a *James Thomas; *b* 1984

1a *Tobina Kate; *b* 1981

(2) *Catherine Nancy; *b* 29 June 1958; *m* 1993 *Martin Clive Jamieson, s of W/Cdr H C Jamieson, of Farnham, Surrey

2 *Ginette Molesworth [The Hon Mrs Kitson, Nine Acres, Wallcrouch, Wadhurst, E Sussex]; *b* 23 May 1924; *m* 1st 23 Jan 1945 (*divorce* 1949) Dominick Moore Sarsfield, Irish Gds, er s of Col Thomas Herrick Sarsfield, OBE, of Fairy Hill , Mallow, Co Cork, and has:

(1) *Simon Patrick [Simon Sarsfield Esq, Central Garage, Southborough, Tunbridge Wells, Kent]; *b* 24 Aug 1945; *educ* Eton; *m* 1st 1967 Sandra, dau of Robert Pearce, of Chichester, and has:

1a *Andante Mercedes; *b* 19 July 1969

(1) (cont.) Simon Sarsfield *m* 2nd 19– *Rohini, dau of Arunasalem Rajasundaram, of Sri Lanka, and by her has:

1a *Dushianthi; *b* 1984

2a *Declan; *b* 1986

(2) *Shaun Dominick; *b* 16 July 1947; *educ* Villa Javelle, Salvan, Switzerland; *m* Jan 1970 *Melanie Erskine

2 (cont.) The Hon Mrs Ginette Sarsfield *m* 2nd 12 June 1953 *Henry James Buller Kitson, 3rd s of Capt James Buller Kitson, DSO, RN (*see* STRATHCONA AND MOUNT ROYAL, B)

KING of Campsie

Arms: Azure on a fess argent, between in chief a lion's head erased and in base two billets or, three round buckles of the field. **Crest:** A redbreast proper. **Motto:** (over crest) *Honos industriæ præmium* ('Honour is the reward of industry'). **Creation:** Bt. (UK) 10 Oct 1888.

SIR JOHN CHRISTOPHER KING, 4TH BT, of Campsie, Stirlingshire [Sir John King Bt, Stillwater, Box 218 Mathews Courthouse, VA 23109, USA]; *b* 31 March 1933; *s* f 1989; *educ* Eton; Lt RNVR 1952–54, Lt Berks Yeo (TA) 1955–60, memb Stock Exchange 1961–73; *m* 1st 3 Oct 1958 (*divorce* 1972) Patricia Monica (*m* 2nd Colin Brown), only dau of Lt-Col Kingsley Osbern Nugent Foster, DSO, OBE; *m* 2nd 1984 *Mrs (Aline) Jane Holley, er dau of Col Douglas Alexander Brett, GC, OBE, MC, and by his 1st w has:

1 +JAMES RUPERT; *b* 24 May 1961; *educ* Eton; *m* 7 Jan 1995 *Elizabeth, yst dau of Richard Ellingworth and has:

(1) +John Alistair; *b* 4 June 1996

1 *Melanie Averil; *b* 16 May 1963; *m* 1989 *Jeremy Legge and has:

(1) *Hamish; *b* 1991

(2) *Charles; *b* 1992

(3) *James; *b* 2 Dec 1994

Lineage: JOHN KING, of Campsie, Stirlingshire, and Levernholme, Renfrewshire; merchant in Glasgow; *b* 16 Jan 1789; *m* 14 Feb 1826 Christina (*d* 21 Nov 1880), dau of James Macnie, of Stirling, and had:

1 JAMES (Sir), **1st Bt**

2 John; *b* 19 Aug 1834; *d* 1851

3 Charles Macintosh, of Antermony House, Campsie, Stirling, DL and JP Stirling, JP Lanarkse and Glasgow; Hon Col 4th Vol Bn Argyll and Sutherland Highrs; *b* 5 May 1836; *m* 6 June 1867 Jane Margaret (Id 27 Feb 1923), only dau of Andrew Buchanan, MD, Prof Glasgow U, and *d* 11 Feb 1920, leaving:

(1) John; *b* 16 July 1870; *d* 24 May 1890

(2) Andrew Buchanan, Maj 7th Bn Argyll and Sutherland Highrs; *b* 17 March 1875; *m* 17 April 1912 Evelyn Nina (*d* 15 Feb 1962), dau of Rev Edmund Sharpe, Vicar Newport, IoW, and *d* of wounds recd in action 25 May 1915, having had issue

(3) Charles Macintosh, Lt 15th Hus, BA Oxford; *b* 18 Nov 1876; *d* unm 16 Jan 1964

(4) Walter Buchanan, Lt 1st Bn Argyll and Sutherland Highrs; *b* 18 May 1878; *ka* Boer War 11 Dec 1899

(5) Robert Buchanan, JP Stirlingshire; advocate; *b* 5 July 1881; *educ* New Coll Oxford (BA); *m* 12 Jan 1917 Eliza Margaret (*d* 21 June 1955), er dau of Robert Scott Moncrieff, WS, of Downhill, Perthshire, and *d* 7 July 1965, leaving:

1a *Marion Elizabeth; *m* 18 Aug 1943 *Col Gordon Russell Simpson, DSO and bar, TD, Lothians and Border Horse, s of Alexander Russell Simpson, WS, of Edinburgh, and has:

1b *Walter Robert; *b* 14 Jan 1948; *educ* Rugby

2b *Alan Gordon; *b* 15 Feb 1950; *educ* Rugby and Magdalen Coll Oxford

(1) Jean Buchanan; *b* 30 March 1869; *m* 4 Aug 1898 Dr David Steel Roxburgh (*d* 12 Dec 1935), and *d* 7 Jan 1956, leaving issue

(2) Christina Macnie; *b* 2 Oct 1872; *m* 9 Aug 1911 Rev William Brown (*d* 2 Dec 1940), BD, Min Campsie, Stirling, and *d* 18 Jan 1947, leaving issue

(3) Marion Buchanan; *b* 11 Jan 1874; *d* unm 25 March 1946

4 Robert, of Levernholme, Renfrewshire, DL and JP, Col 3rd Renfrew Vol Rifles, chm Renfrewshire CC; *b* 29 Dec 1837; *d* 22 March 1910

1 Isabella; *b* 11 April 1832; *m* 29 June 1852 Robert Stewart (*d* 12 Sept 1866), of Murdostoun, Lanarks, and *d* 4 July 1903, having had issue

2 Jessie Callander; *b* 11 Aug 1839; *d* unm 23 Sept 1904

3 Christina; *b* 22 May 1841; *d* 1845

JOHN KING *d* 31 Oct 1875; his est son,

Sir James King, 1st Bt (UK), so *cr* 10 Oct 1888, of Campsie, DL and JP Lanarks and Stirlingshire, DL Glasgow; *b* 13 July 1830; Dean Guild Glasgow 1874–76, Pres Chamber of Commerce 1878–80, Dean of Faculties Glasgow U 1879–82 and Assessor to Chllr 1887–1903, Ld Provost Glasgow 1886–89, memb Roy Commn W Highlands 1890, ktd 1887, Hon LLD Glasgow; *m* 20 Aug 1861 Marian (*d* 20 Jan 1929), yst dau of William Westall, of Streatham Common, Surrey, and had:

1 JOHN WESTALL KING (Sir), **2nd Bt**

2 William James, advocate; *b* 5 June 1864; *educ* Corpus Christi Coll Oxford (BA); *d* 30 Sept 1919

3 Alfred Charles; *b* 28 March 1866; *m* 22 June 1896 Alice Maude (*d* 22 June 1939), dau of Thomas Walker, of Staincliffe, Seaton Carew, Co Durham, and *d* 11 Jan 1935

4 James; *b* and *d* 17 Nov 1871

5 James Edward, CBE (1920), barrister Inner Temple, FO 1915–20 (Sec Legation The Hague and Athens); *b* 17 March 1875; *educ* New Coll Oxford (BA); *m* 18 May 1914 Muriel May Ellis, dau of Capt Frederick James Taylor, 95th Derbys Regt, of Waddon, Surrey, and *d* 9 Feb 1933

1 Ethel Marian; *d* unm 7 Feb 1899

2 Edith Christina; *m* 18 Sept 1894 Col Henry Brock (*d* 16 Oct 1915), of Darleith, Cardross, Dunbartonshire, and *d* 10 Dec 1960, leaving issue

Sir JAMES *d* 1 Oct 1911; his est son,

Sir John Westall King, 2nd Bt, Col Cmdt 4th Vol Bn Argyll and Sutherland Highrs; *b* 19 Jan 1863; *m* 29 April 1897 Frances Rosa (*k* by enemy action 28 April 1942), dau of John Neve, of Oaken, nr Wolverhampton, and had issue:

1 JAMES GRANVILLE Le NEVE (Sir), **3rd Bt**

2 John Alastair, stockbroker; *b* 4 March 1905; *educ* Eton and Trin Coll Cambridge; *m* 1st 31 Jan 1929 (*divorce* 1939) Veronica Mary Abel Smith (*d* 31 July 1967), only dau of Col Bertram Abel Smith DSO, MC, of London and Cossington, Leics, and had:

(1) *Rhona Lavinia; *b* 27 Sept 1932

2 (cont.) John King *m* 2nd 28 Sept 1939 (*divorce* 1956) Ruby Enid, yr dau of Henry George Atkinson-Clark, of Port-an-Eilean, Pitlochry, Perthshire, and Tickhill Castle, Yorks, and by her had:

(2) Elizabeth Jane; *b* 29 July 1941

2 (cont.) John King *m* 3rd 1957 *Pierina [Mrs John King, Downs Farmhouse, Baunton, Cirencester, Glos], dau of — Holt, and *d* 1991, having by her had:

(3) *Sarah Rosemary; *b* 1959

2 Margaret Westall; *m* 4 March 1930 Capt Ewen Aymer Robert Ramsay-Fairfax-Lucy (*see* RAMSAY-FAIRFAX-LUCY) and had issue

Sir JOHN *d* 9 Sept 1940; his er son,

Sir James Granville le Neve King, 3rd Bt, TD; *b* 17 Sept 1898; *educ* Eton and King's Coll Cambridge, Maj 99th Bucks and Berks Yeo Field Bde RA (TA), Jt MFH S Berks; *m* 21 Nov 1928 Penelope Charlotte (*d* 5 Aug 1994), dau of Capt Edmund Moore Cooper Cooper-Key, CB, MVO, RN, of Landford, Fleet, Hants, and *d* 1989, having had:

1 Sir JOHN CHRISTOPHER KING, **4th and present Bt**

1 *Susan Penelope [Mrs Christopher Marsden-Smedley, Church Farm, Burrington, nr Bristol, Avon]; *b* 3 Sept 1929; *m* 7 Dec 1957 *Christopher Marsden-Smedley, yr s of Basil Furtvoye Marsden-Smedley, OBE, of Chelsea, and has:

(1) *Timothy Charles; *b* 19 Feb 1959

(2) *Philip John; *b* 11 May 1961

(1) *Catherine Penelope; *b* 8 May 1964; *m* 1992 *Christopher D Miller, yr s of Maj David Miller, of Pyrford, Surrey

2 *Diana Bridget [Mrs Francis Hoare, Loubcroy Lodge, Lairg, Sutherland IV27 4BH]; *b* 15 Sept 1935; *m* 5 Sept 1957 *Francis Hoare, yr s of Eustace Benyon Hoare (*see* 1959 edn TEMPLEWOOD, V), and has:

(1) *James Alexander; *b* 22 May 1959

(2) *Edward Eustace; *b* 17 Aug 1961

(3) *Richard Francis; *b* 17 Aug 1967

(1) *Arabella Peggy Marion; *b* 16 Nov 1968

KING of Charlestown

Arms: Sable a lion rampant, doubled-queued or. **Crest:** An escallop shell gules. **Motto:** *Spes tutissima cœlis* ('Our safest hope is in Heaven'). **Creation:** Bt. (UK) 21 July 1815.

SIR WAYNE ALEXANDER KING, 8TH BT, of Charlestown, Co Roscommon [Sir Wayne King Bt, 146 High St, Almonte, Ontario K0A 1A0, Canada]; *b* 2 Feb 1962; *s* f 1973; *educ* Sir Roger Marwood's Sch, Sandwich, Kent, and Algonquin Coll Ottawa; entrepreneur; *m* 1984 *Laura Ellen, dau of Donald James Lea, of Almonte, Ontario, and has:

1 +PETER RICHARD DONALD; *b* 4 May 1988

Lineage: Rt Rev EDWARD KING, of Hunts; *b* 1575; MA Cantab 1601, DD Dublin 1614, Fell Trin Coll Dublin 1598, Bp Elphin 1611; *m* 1st 1609 Anne Coxsed (*d* 25 Jan 1626) and had, with other issue:

1 JAMES, of Charlestown

2 John, of Boyle; *m* Sarah (*d* between 1670 and 24 Jan 1671), dau of Christopher Conway, and had a dau (Anne, *m* Dominick French, of French Park; *see* DE FREYNE, B)

The Rt Rev EDWARD KING *m* 2nd Grace, dau of Nathaniel Sampson, of Leics, s of Thomas Sampson, Preb St Paul's, by his w, niece of the Protestant martyr Bishop Latimer, and *d* 8 March 1638/9, having had an est s:

JAMES KING, of Charlestown, Co Roscommon; Army Capt, High Sheriff Co Leitrim 1657 and Co Roscommon 1673; *b* 6 Feb 1610; *m* Judith, dau of Gilbert Rawson, of Granstown Castle, Queen's Co, and had, with other issue:

1 Edward; *b* 17 July 1640; disinherited by his f

2 GILBERT

1 Elizabeth; *m* March 1662 Capt Charles Dodd, of Coolbawn, Co Sligo

2 Martha; *m* 1677 Very Rev Coote Ormsby, BD, Dean Derry, Chaplain to Ld Lt Ireland, and *d* 30 Jan 1699

3 Susanna; *m* Andrew Blackburne (*d* 16 Sept 1706), of Carrickeenagh, Co Roscommon, and *d* 15 Aug 1691, leaving issue

Capt JAMES KING *d* 2 April 1687; his 6th son,

GILBERT KING, of Charlestown, Co Roscommon, MP Jamestown 1709–21, JP Cos Leitrim and Roscommon, High Sheriff Co Leitrim 1717; *b* 15 June 1658; *m* Mary, dau of Dominick French, of Dungar (later French Park), Co Roscommon (*see* DE FREYNE, B), by Anne, dau of John King, of Boyle (*see* above), and had:

1 JOHN

2 Oliver (Rev); Rector Aunaduffe 1714

3 Gilbert, Sheriff Dublin 1723, Alderman 1733, Ld Mayor 1742; *m* Sarah, dau of John French, of French Park (*see* DE FREYNE, B), and had:

(1) Gilbert, Maj 5th (Roy Irish) Dragoons Battle of Quebec 1759; *m* April 1771 his cousin Rebecca, dau of John King, of Ballylin, King's Co (*see* below), and had:

1a Henry (Rev), MA; *s* to Ballylin

GILBERT KING *d* 1721; his est son and heir,

JOHN KING, of Charlestown, Co Roscommon; MP Jamestown 1721–37, High Sheriff Cos Sligo 1711 and Leitrim 1728; *m* 1st 1706 Elizabeth, dau of Robert Shaw, of Newford, Co Galway, and had:

1 GILBERT

1 Judith; *m* 1st 1730 John French, of High Lake, Co Roscommon (*see* 1970 edn YPRES, E); *m* 2nd Rev Rees Saunders, of Whitchurch, Salop

JOHN KING *m* 2nd 5 May 1721 Rebecca, yst dau of Rt Rev Dr Simon Digby (*see* DIGBY, B), Bp Limerick and later Elphin, and by her had:

2 John, of Ballylin; *m* 6 Nov 1748 Alice (*d* Sept 1769), dau of Ross Mahon, of Castlegar, Co Galway (*see* MAHON, Bt), and *d* Nov 1778, having had, with other issue:

(1) Rebecca; *m* her cousin Maj Gilbert King (*see* above)

3 Digby

2 Jane; *m* 1st Arthur Acheson; *m* 2nd 7 Sept 1763, as his 2nd w, 1st Baron Erne of Crom Castle (*see* ERNE, E), and *dsp* by 8 March 1800

JOHN KING *d* by Oct 1737; his est son,

GILBERT KING, of Charlestown, Co Roscommon; MP Jamestown, High Sheriff Co Sligo 1744 and Leitrim 1767; *m* 1744 Anne, dau of Roger Parke, of Dunally, Co Sligo, and *d* 23 Aug 1788, having had, with other issue:

1 **Sir Gilbert King, 1st Bt** (UK), so *cr* 21 July 1815, with special remainder, in default of his own male issue, to his bros John and Robert by primogeniture and their heirs male; of Charlestown; *b* 1746; Capt 5th Roy Irish Regt Dragoons; *m* his cousin Jane (*d* 30 April 1818), dau of John King, of Ballylin, King's Co, and *dsp* 8 Aug 1818

2 Robert; *m* 10 April 1776 Grace, dau of Richard Rose, n of Hon Henry Rose, Judge King's Bench Ireland, and *d* by 1815, leaving, with other issue:

(1) ROBERT (Sir), **2nd Bt**

3 Edward; *m* March 1793 Charlotte (*d* 24 March 1819), widow of Edward Madden and dau of 1st Baron Erne of Crom Castle (*see* ERNE, E), but *dsp*

4 James; *m* 19 May 1783 Lady Elizabeth Crichton (*d* 28 Jan 1794), est dau of 1st Earl of Erne (*qv*), and *d* 23 March 1833, leaving issue

1 Isabella; *m* Robert Tighe (*d* 1799), of Southill, Co Westmeath, 2nd s of Robert Tighe, of Co Westmeath

The 1st Bt's nephew,

Sir Robert King, 2nd Bt, of Charlestown; High Sheriff Co Roscommon 1821, Offr Duke of Kent's Regt; *b* 1785; *m* 20 Sept 1810 Elizabeth (*d* 1 March 1863), dau of Ebenezer Rowe, of Ballyharty, Co Wexford, and *d* 1825, having had, with other issue:

1 **Sir Gilbert King, 3rd Bt**, DL; *b* 13 June 1812; *m* 19 Nov 1833 Mary (*d* 24 Nov 1892), dau of Charles Vigogne, of Wicklow, by Mary, sis of Sir Josias Rowley, 1st Bt, GCMG, KCB (*see* ROWLEY, Bt), and *d* 14 Nov 1895, having had:

(1) **Sir Gilbert King, 4th Bt**; High Sheriff Co Roscommon 1892, Co Leitrim 1894 and 1904 and Co Sligo 1909; *b* 30 May 1846; MA Dublin 1873; *m* 1st 6 Dec 1888 Charlotte (*d* 1892), 2nd dau of Robert Heard, JP, of Pallastown, Co Cork; *m* 2nd 5 Jan 1897 Louise Scudder Ryall (*d* 2 March 1928), dau of Lt-Col Henry Baker Sweet, 39th Madras NI, and *dspm* 9 July 1920, having by his 1st w had:

1a Mary Rowley; *m* 26 July 1932 James King-Currie, est s of William Currie, of Walney Island, Lancs

(2) Josiah Rowley; *b* 10 Dec 1848; *d* unm 25 Feb 1888

(1) Elizabeth; *m* 31 Oct 1865 Guy Lloyd, DL (*d* 25 Aug 1906), of Croghan, Co Roscommon, and *d* 13 Jan 1928, having had issue

(2) Rosamond Anne; *m* 11 Sept 1877 Ven William Daunt, MA (*d* 19 Sept 1919), Archeacon Cloyne, and *d* 6 June 1930

2 Robert (Rev), Rector Kilmore, Drumsna; *b* May 1813; *m* 1st 1838 Jane (*d* 1868), widow of Edward Simpson and dau of Matthew Nesbitt, of Derrycarne, Co Leitrim; *m* 2nd 1872 Arabella (*d* 21 Oct 1885), dau of John Watkins, and *dsp* 20 June 1884

3 George; *b* 1820; *m* 1863 Frances Julia Andrews (*d* 6 April 1915), and *d* 20 Jan 1876, leaving:

(1) **Sir George Adolphus King, 5th Bt**; *b* 3 Sept 1864; *d* unm 15 Aug 1954

(2) Robert Ebenezer; *b* 12 Jan 1869; *m* 7 Jan 1891 Margaret (*d* 1926), dau of Alexander Dempster, and *d* 1928, having had:

1a Gilbert Robert George Richard; *d* an infant

2a ALEXANDER WILLIAM (Sir), **6th Bt**

3a Douglas James; *b* 2 June 1895; *m* 1913 Dorothy Aylet, dau of C Collins, and *d* 1962, leaving:

1b *Zena Dorothy; *b* 1915

1a Grace; *m* 27 Sept 1915 Maj Reginald Taylor, RM, and had:

1b Frank Reginald Alexander, Lt-Col RM; *b* 17 Dec 1919; *m* Jan 1951 *Jennifer, dau of Hugh H Munro, of Chile, and has:

1c *Jeremy; *b* 13 March 1959

(1) Florence Violetta Julia; *d* 8 April 1935

(2) Helena Emily Laura; *d* 29 Jan 1937

(3) *Isabella Jane

1 Elizabeth; *m* 1833 Rev William Killcock Tatam, BD (*d* 29 May 1854), and *d* 19 Aug 1888, having had issue

The 5th Bt's nephew,

Sir Alexander William King, 6th Bt; *b* 25 Nov 1892; *educ* Herne Bay Coll and Borden Coll; served RN WW I and CD WW II; *m* 30 Nov 1924 Dorothy Alice (*d* 16 April 1961), dau of Henry William Champion, of Sittingbourne, Kent, and *d* 7 April 1969, having had:

Sir Peter Alexander King, 7th Bt; *b* 13 Nov 1928; *educ* Cliftonville Coll and Cranbrook Sch; *m* 2 March 1957 *Jean Margaret (*m* 2nd 1978 Rev Alexander Graham Mackenzie), dau of Christopher Thomas Cavell, of Deal, Kent, and *d* 10 July 1973, having had:

1 Sir WAYNE ALEXANDER KING, **8th and present Bt**

1 *Dorothy Jane; *b* 24 Sept1964

King of Wartnaby

Arms: Or five piles, two reversed vert, each charged with an acorn slipped or. **Crest:** An otter sejant vert holding in the dexter paw a sceptre or. **Supporters:** On either side two horses regardant sable, unguled or, in the mouth of each a sprig of oak vert fructed gold. **Motto:** *La fortune passe par tout* ('The vicissitudes of fortune are common to all'). **Creation:** B. (LP, UK) 1983.

THE BARON KING OF WARTNABY, of Wartnaby, Co Leicester (Sir John Leonard King) [The Rt Hon The Lord King of Wartnaby, Wartnaby, Melton Mowbray, Leics LE14 3HY; Berkeley Square Ho, Berkeley Sq, London W1X 6BA]; *b* Aug 1917; fndr and md Pollard Ball and Roller Bearing Co 1945 (chm 1961–69); chm: Dennis Motor Hldgs 1970–72, Babcock International Gp 1970–94 (Pres 1994–), City and Industrial Liaison Cncl 1973–85, Review Bd for Govt Contracts 1975–78, Br Olympic Appeals Ctee 1975–78, Macmillan Appeal for Continuing Care 1977–78, NEB 1980–81 (dep chm 1979–80), BA 1981–93 (pres 1993–97, pres emeritus 1997–), Ctee Ranfurly Library Service, Alexandra Rose Day Fndn 1980–; ktd 1979; v-chm Cancer Relief Macmillan Fund 1988; dir David Brown Corp 1971–75 and *The Spectator*; chm/dir: *Daily Telegraph*, Short Brothers, Aerostructures Hamble, Norman Broadbent Internat, Wide Range Engineering Servs, York Tst; formerly dir: Dick Corp (USA), Royal Ordnance, Clogau Gold Mines, Nat Nuclear Corp, Br Nuclear Assocs, Tyneham Investments, Babcock (Plant Leasing), 1928 Investment Tst, SKF (UK), Sabena World Airlines, First Union Corp (USA); memb: Engrg Industs Cncl 1975, NEDC Ctee Finance for Investment 1976–78, Grand Cncl and Fin Policy Ctee CBI 1976–78; Tstee Liver Research Unit Tst 1988–; MFH Badsworth 1944–58 and Belvoir 1958–72 (Chm 1972); FBIM 1978, FCIT 1982, Cdr Roy Order Polar Star Sweden 1983, Freeman City London 1984; *m* 1st 1941 Lorna Kathleen (*d* 1969), dau of Arthur Sykes, of Clandon, and has:

1 *Richard John Rodney [The Hon Richard King, 7612 Covey Chase, Charlotte, NC 28210, USA]; *b* 1943; *educ* Le Rosey; *m* 1985 *Monika, dau of Erich Boehm, of Boca Raton, Fla., and has:

(1) *John-Erich; *b* 1986

2 *Philip James Stephen [The Hon Philip King, 77 Stanhope Mews East, London SW7 5QT]; *b* 1950; *educ* Harrow; *m* 1989 *Caroline, dau of E G A Hillesley, of Gillingham, Kent, and has:

(1) *Charlotte Kathleen Rachel; *b* 1990

(2) *Philippa Anne Lorna; *b* 1994

3 *(John) Rupert Charles [The Hon Rupert King, Garden Cottage, Wartnaby, Melton Mowbray, Leics]; *b* 1950 (twin); *educ* Harrow; *m* 1986 *Cherry M, only dau of R B Jessop, OBE, of Ingoldsby, Lincs, and has:

(1) *Philip James Bateman; *b* 1988

1 *Rachel Mary Frances [The Hon Mrs Marckus, 18 Musgrave Crescent, London SW6 4QD]; *b* 1945; *m* 1st 1968 (*divorce* 1974) Michael Gibson; *m* 2nd 1980 (*divorce* 1985) Guy Henry René Bondonneau, of Paris; *m* 3rd 1987 *Melvyn Marckus, former cit ed *The Times* and dir *Observer*, with Luther Pendragon PR 1996–

THE BARON KING OF WARTNABY *m* 2nd 1970 *Hon Isabel Cynthia Monckton, yst dau of 8th Viscount Galway (*qv*)

Lineage: ALBERT JOHN KING; *m* Kathleen — and had a yr s:

JOHN LEONARD (Sir), *cr* a **Baron**

Kingsale

Arms: Argent three eagles displayed gules, ducally crowned or. **Crest:** On a ducal coronet or an eagle displayed with two heads argent. **Supporters:** Two unicorns azure, each gorged with a coronet composed of crosses patée and fleurs-de-lys and chained, armed, crined and unguled or. **Motto:** *Vincit omnia veritas* ('Truth conquers all things'). **Creation:** B. (I) *c* 1340(?).

THE 28TH LORD KINGSALE (John de Courcy) [The Rt Hon The Lord Kingsale, 15 Dallimore Mead, Nunney, Somerset BA11 4NB; 1st Floor Macarthur Chambers, 201 Edward St, Brisbane, Queensland 4000, Australia]; *b* posthumously 27 Jan 1941; *s* gf 1969; *educ* Stowe, Paris U and Salzburg U; 2nd Lt Irish Gds 1962–65, pres Impex Consultants Ltd 1988–, dir: Marquis de Verneuil Tst 1971–, de Courcy, Daunt Pref and Exec Agencies (Australia) 1987–, Kinsale Devpt Co 1989–; chm Nat Assoc for Service to the Realm 1979–

Lineage: Not merely the origins but the very nomenclature of this peerage are shrouded in mist. It is at least an appropriately Celtic integument. First the nomenclature: the holder of this peerage was at one time known as Lord Courcy or Lord Courcy of Ringro(a)ne and Kinsale [*sic*]. As late as the reign of JAMES I the then title-holder sat in the Irish Parliament as Lord Courcy. The alternative versions 'Kinsale' or 'Kingsale' seem to have had more or less equal currency then, but by the late 18th century 'Kingsale' had drawn ahead; it is now the standard one, replacing even 'Courcy'. The nomenclature was made more confusing by the creation in the early months of CHARLES I's reign of Dominick Sarsfield as Viscount of Kinsale, a designation which the Lord Courcy of the time regarded as a trespass on his own bailiwick, even though he was still known chiefly as Lord Courcy. He nevertheless managed to get an official document promulgated that spoke of him as both Lord Courcy and Baron of Kingsale [*sic*] and also of Ringrone. There can be no doubt that he remained the possessor of a single barony, however. Meanwhile Dominick Sarsfield was persuaded to hand in his Viscountcy of Kinsale and was given a new one designated as Sarsfield of Kilmallock.

The date of creation is harder to pinpoint. The first list of relative precedence of Irish peers was in 1489. But the position in it reflected the personal prestige of the then holder more than anything as objective as a hard-and-fast date of creation. It is for this reason that Gormanston (*qv*), a viscountcy, ranks below four baronies, which are usually of lower rank than viscountcies. (There is also some doubt as to whether such a degree of peerage as a viscountcy was recognised in Ireland at all at that date.) As it happens the barony immediately before Gormanston in the 1489 list is Courcy. In subsequent ones throughout the next hundred years or so it crops up twice ahead of Gormanston and once well behind. The very notion of a date of creation is indeed not really appropriate to a number of ancient Irish titles. Like the hereditary knighthoods, the Barony of Courcy/Kingsale probably emerged by dint of usage.

MILES (MILO) de COGAN, a yr s of the COGANs of Glamorgan, took a leading part in the 12th-century Anglo/Cambro-Norman incursion into Ireland and was granted by HENRY II 1177, jointly with Robert fitz Stephen, with whom he divided it, a territory called the 'Kingdom of Cork' (*i.e.*, the Gaelic Kingdom of Desmond, covering an area in what are now Cos Cork and Kerry, ruled by the MacCARTHYs); *k* by native Irish 1182, leaving an only dau and heiress:

MARGARET/MARGERY de Cogan; *m* 1st Ralph (*d* 1182), s of Robert fitz Stephen, her f's companion in land acquisition; *m* 2nd Simon le Poer, who in right of his w held the the de Cogan half of Desmond, of which Kinsale was the *caput*, or administrative centre, 1190; *m* 3rd — De COURCY (perhaps identical with (a) the celebrated John de Courcy, Earl of Ulster, Justiciar Ireland 1185–90, yr s of William de Courcy (II), of Stogursy, Somerset, (b) Earl John's son Miles or (c) another close relative); *m* 4th Thomas Bloet (*d* 1217) and had by her 3rd husb:

PATRICK de COURCY; witnessed a charter of his mother between 1217 and 1220 but had *s* her by 17 July 1221, when he is mentioned as among the leading nobles of Ireland; *m* Nesta (living 1260), and *d* between June 1251 and 1253, leaving, with a dau (Isolda, *m* Robert de Clahull and *dsp*):

MILES de COURCY; feudal Ld of Kinsale and Ringrone, in defending the Castle of which he *k* FINEEN MacCARTHY, KING OF DESMOND, 29 Sept 1261; also overlord of half the Kingdom of Cork; *m* Annora (*d* 1299), dau of Richard de

Burgo, feudal Ld of Connacht, and sis of Walter de Burgo, Earl of Ulster, and *d c* 1290, leaving, with other sons (Patrick, *k* with his bro JOHN (*see* below); Hubert, prosecuted 1297 the MacCARTHYs for his bros' death):

JOHN de COURCY; feudal Ld Kinsale and Ringrone; *k* 1291 by Donal *Og* ('The Younger') MacCarthy and Donal *Baisneach* MacCarthy, leaving:

MILES de COURCY; feudal Ld Kinsale and Ringrone; still under age 1304; had livery of his lands (*i.e.*, recognised as being of full age) 26 Oct 1308; summoned to the (I) Parl of 1310; *d* by 19 Oct 1345, leaving, as well as a widow (Joan):

1/2 Eustace; hostage for his f 1319; perhaps one of MILES's two sons *k* by the MacCARTHYs 1339

3 Miles, **1st Lord**

1 Margaret; *m* by 1332 Sir William fitz David, self-styled 'de Barry', and was living 1379, being ancestor with him of the BARRYs *Roe* ('The Red') and the Barry Viscounts Buttevant and Earls of Barrymore

2 Joan; *m* — l'Enfaint and had issue

3 Katherine; *m* 1st — de Cantilupe; *m* 2nd — de Carew and had issue by both husbs

4 Anastasia; *m* Sir Nicholas de Courcy, of Ballycrenane, Co Cork, and *d* by 1358, leaving, with several sons (all *dsp* & *vp*) a dau and heiress:

(1) Margaret; *m* Sir Maurice fitz Richard (FitzGerald) (*see* FitzGERALD, Bt, of Valencia)

The 3rd(?) s,

MILES Fitz MILES DE COURCY, **1st Lord Courcy** of Kinsale/**Lord Kinsale**; known also (or alternatively) as 'Lord of Ringrone and Kinsale'; by settlements June 1358 and Nov 1360 entailed his lands, in default of issue of his own, on his bro-in-law Sir Nicholas de Courcy (who seems to have *s* to them shortly before dying 1366, leaving by his 2nd w, Margaret Wogan, widow of (a) Piers de Cogan, (b) Sir David Barry and (c) Sir William FitzGerald, a dau, Katherine, who *m* as his 2nd w Donal MacCarty, styled King of Desmond, and *d* 1393), then nine other De COURCYs in tail male, and *dsp* after Oct 1363

The next (hence taken as **2nd**) **Lord Courcy** of Kinsale/**Lord Kinsale** about whom there is information,

JOHN Fitz MILES, **2nd Lord Courcy** of Kinsale/**Lord Kinsale**; was, however, 3rd in remainder under the 1358 entail; living 1387; *d* by 1393; may have been f of:

WILLIAM de COURCY, **3rd Lord Courcy** of Kinsale/**Lord Kinsale**; living 2 April 1399; *m* Margaret —

The next (hence taken as **4th**) **Lord Courcy** of Kinsale/**Lord Kinsale** about whom there is information,

PATRICK de COURCY, **4th Lord Courcy** of Kinsale/**Lord Kinsale**; known also (or alternatively) as 'Lord of Ringrone and Kinsale'; seems to have been s of a John, hence was possibly bro of WILLIAM, **3rd Lord**, but may alternatively have descended from another of the remaindermen of 1358; *m* Anastasia — and settled 27 Nov 1419 his lands on his s:

NICHOLAS de COURCY, **5th Lord Courcy** of Kinsale/**Lord Kinsale**; known also (or alternatively) as 'Lord of Ringrone and Kinsale' and styled in addition 'Captain of his nation'; *m* Móre, dau of O'Mahony Finn, Chief of his name, and *d* 1474, leaving:

1 JAMES de COURCY, **6th Lord Courcy** of Kinsale/**Lord Kimnsale**; known also (or alternatively) as 'Lord of Ringrone and Kinsale'; submitted at Kinsale to Sir Richard Edgecumbe 28 June 1487 after taking part in Lambert Simnel's imposture and was pardoned 1496; *m* (dispensation 14 Aug 1465) Joan, dau of Maurice, Lord (Baron/self-styled Viscount(?)) Roche of Fermoy (*see* FERMOY, B, preliminary remarks), and *d* 1499, having had:

(1) Richard Fitz JAMES; *dvp* 1496, leaving:

1a Anastasia; *m* William Gallwey

(2) EDMUND de COURCY, **7th Lord Courcy** of Kinsale/**Lord Kinsale**; idiot, hence displaced *c* 1500 by his unc DAVID, **8th Lord**; *dsp*

2 John; had a dau (*m* Teig macEneshlish O'Donovan)

3 DAVID de COURCY, **8th Lord Courcy** of Kinsale/**Lord Kinsale**; Rector Kilgobban and later Ringrone, also Archdeacon Cork (though never in holy orders), which benefices he resigned on displacing his n; *m* Joan, dau of Edmond Roche, and had:

(1) JOHN de COURCY, **9th Lord Courcy/Lord Kinsale**; Rector Kilgobban (though not in holy orders); *m* Sawne, dau of Donogh MacCarthy, styled 'MacDonogh of Duhallow', and *d* 1535, leaving:

1a GERALD de COURCY, **10th Lord Courcy** of Kinsale/**Lord Kinsale**; alienated all his estates to the MacCARTHYs and others; *m* Ellen, dau of Cormac MacDonogh MacCarthy, of Carbery, and *dspm* between 6 June and 6 Aug 1599, leaving:

1b Mary; *m* 1st Dermot O'Driscoll; *m* 2nd John Gallwey, of Kinsale, and had issue (*dsp*) by both husbs

1a Ellen; *m* John Barry and *dsp*

2a Joan

(2) Edmond, of Kilnacloona, Co Cork; *m* Julian, dau of Richard Barry, of Inishannon, Co Cork, and had:

1a Edmond *Og*, of Kilnacloona; *m* Sheila, dau of Dermot macTeig O'Hurley and widow of Richard O'Regan, and had:

1b JOHN de COURCY, **11th Lord Courcy** of Kinsale/**Lord Kinsale**; recovered through roy favour most of the estates alienated by his predecessor (confirmatory grant 13 Dec 1620); *m* 1st Catherine (*dsp*), dau of William Cogan; *m* 2nd Mary, dau of Cormac O'Crowly, of Carbery, Co Cork, and *d* 25 July 1628, having had, with another s (*dsp*):

1c GERALD de COURCY, **12th Lord Kin(g)sale**; Gentleman of Privy Chamber to CHARLES I 1627, conformed to C of E till *c* 1636 when abjured Anglican rites (presumably in facour of RC ones); *m* Helen, er dau of Sir John FitzGerald, of Dromana, Co Waterford, by Ellen, dau of Maurice FitzGibbon, the White Knight, and *dspm c* 1642, leaving:

1d Mary; *m* Sir Patrick Gough, Killmanehine, Co Waterford

2c PATRICK de COURCY, **13th Lord Kingsale**; *m* his sister-in-law's sister Mary, yr dau of Sir John FitzGerald, of Dromana, and *d* 1663, having had, with two other sons (*dsp*):

1d JOHN de COURCY, **14th Lord Kingsale**; *m* Ellen, dau of Charles McCarthy Reagh by Eleanor, sis of 1st Earl of Clancarty of the 1658 *cr* (*see* CLANCARTY, E), and *d* 19 May 1667, leaving:

1e PATRICK de COURCY, **15th Lord Kingsale**; *b c* 1660; *d* 1669

2e ALMERICUS de COURCY, **16th Lord Kingsale**; *b* May 1665; *educ* privately (as an RC) and (in an attempt to make a Protestant of him) Ch Ch Oxford; outlawed as Jacobite 1691 but pardoned by 1692; *m* 2 March 1698 Anne (*d* 25 April 1724), dau of Robert Dring, of Isleworth, and *dsp* 9 Feb 1719/20

1e Ellen; *m* Sir John Magrath, 3rd Bt

2d Miles; *m* Elizabeth, yst dau and eventually sole heiress of Anthony Sadleir, of Arley Hall, Warwicks, and had:

1e GERALD de COURCY, **17th Lord Kingsale**, PC (I Jan 1743/4); *b* 1700; *m* 13 May 1725 Margaretta, only dau and heiress of John Essington, of Ashlyns, Herts, and *dspms* 1 Dec 1759, having had, with a s (*d* young) and other dau (*d* unm):

1f Mary; *b* 1 April 1726; *m* 28 March 1751 John O'Grady, of Ballinscoola, Co Limerick, and had issue

2f Elizabeth Geraldina; *b* 12 Nov 1729; *m* 1751 Daniel McCarty (*d* Sept 1762), of Carrignavar, Co Cork, and had issue

1d Alice; *m* Dermod Macarthy, of Aglish, Co Cork

2d Elizabeth; *m* by 23 April 1680, s his 2nd w, David Sarsfield, 3rd Viscount Sarsfield of Kilmallock (*dsp*; *see* preliminary remarks above)

3d Margaret; *m* Philip Barry Oge

3c David; *m* a dau of William Roche, of Cork, and had:

1d Anthony, of Bandon, Co Cork; *m* Elizabeth Vizard and *d* 1727, leaving:

1e Anthony, *dspm*

2e Michael/Miles, of Newport, RI, N America; *m* Abigail Williams, of RI, and was lost at sea *c* 1724, leaving:

1f JOHN de COURCY, **18th Lord Kingsale** (claim admitted and he took his seat 1 Feb 1762); *b c* 1717; sailor to 1748; *m* 26 Oct 1746 Martha, dau of Rev Isaac Heron, of Dorchester, Dorset, and *d* 3 March 1776, having had, with other issue:

1g JOHN de COURCY, **19th Lord Kingsale**; *m* 31 Oct 1763 Susan (*d* 13 Dec 1819), dau of Conway Blennerhassett, of Castle Conway, Co Kerry, and *d* 24 May 1822, having had:

1h John; Lt-Col Gds; *das* & *vp* Peninsular War 4 June 1813

2h Rev THOMAS de COURCY, **20th Lord Kingsale**; *b* 10 Jan 1774; *d* unm 25 Jan 1832

3h Michael; Capt RN; *m* 10 March 1801 Catherine (*m* 2nd Lt B S Simms, RN; *m* 3rd 25 April 1822 W W Ball), only child of William de Lisle, and *d* 22 July 1813, having had:

1i JOHN STAPLETON de COURCY, **21st Lord Kingsale**; *b* 17 Sept 1805; *m* 3 Oct 1825 Sarah (*d* 31 Dec 1883 aged 83), 2nd dau of Joseph Chadder, of Portlemouth, Devon, and *d* 7 Jan 1847, leaving:

1j JOHN CONSTANTINE de COURCY, **22nd Lord Kingsale**; *b* 5 Nov 1827; Capt E Devon Militia 1853–55; *m* 1 March 1855 Adelaide (*d* 21 Jan 1885), only dau of Joshua Proctor Brown-Westhead, of Lea Castle, Worcs, and *dspm* 15 June 1865, leaving:

1k Adelaide Constance Rohesia; *m* 30 Nov 1887 Adml Sir Richard Edward Tracey, KCB (*dsp* 7 March 1907), and *d* 9 July 1926

2j MICHAEL CONRAD de COURCY, **23rd Lord Kingsale**; *b* 21 Dec 1828; *d* unm 15 April 1874

1j Florence Helena; *d* unm 13 July 1899

2j Catherine Adela; *m* 24 Oct 1851 Lt-Col Severus William Lynam Stretton (*d* 23 Nov 1884), 40th Regt, and *d* 17 Oct 1910, leaving issue

2i William Almericus; RN; *b* 11 Oct 1810; granted with sis 1836 rank of baron's dau/yr s; *m* 14 Nov 1839 Charlotte, only dau of Jacob Weymouth, RN, and *d* 5 July 1867, leaving:

1j John Almericus; *b* Jan 1843; *d* 19 Sept 1870

1i Catherine Savery de Lisle; *m* 3 May 1827 Francis Bernard Beamish, MP (*d* Feb 1868), and *d* 5 Feb 1872, having had issue

4h Gerald; Lt-Col; *m* 29 Jan 1807 Elizabeth Carlyon (*d* 1855), dau of John Bishop, of Barbados, and *d* Oct 1848, leaving:

1i JOHN FITZROY de COURCY, **24th Lord Kingsale**; *b* 30 March 1821; Offr 47th Foot 1838–47, Maj Turkish Contingent Crimea, Kt of the Medjidie 4th Cl, Col Union Army American Civil War; Stipendiary Magistrate San Juan, Vancouver Island; *m* 10 May 1864 Elia Elizabeth (*d* 5 May 1893), widow of C Du Bosque de Beaumont, of Airel, and dau of C des François de Ponchalon, Chevalier Legion Honour, and *dsp* 20 Nov 1890

1i Susannah; *m* 25 Jan 1831 Thomas Page and *d* 9 Jan 1884, leaving issue

2i Geraldine; *m* 12 April 1830 Sir William Perry (*d* 24 Aug 1874), and had issue

3i Frederica Maitland; *m* 4 April 1840 Baron Paul W d'Hoggner and had issue

4i Henrietta Jane Paulet; *m* 5 Aug 1851 FM Baron de Knebel (*d* 1890), Austrian Army, and *d* 1 July 1906, leaving issue

1h Martha; *m* 21 May 1792 Andrew Agnew, est s of Sir Stair Agnew of Lochnaw, 6th Bt (*qv*), and had issue

2h Elizabeth; *m* 1799 V-Adml Sir Charles Dashwood, KCB, and *d* his widow 12 June 1865

3h Anne Geraldine; *m* 1821, as his 2nd w, James John Hamilton (*d* 1842), of Ballymacoll, Co Meath, and *d* 20 Feb 1855

4h Mary; *m* 15 Sept 1814 William Beamish (*d* 1 Oct 1838), of Beaumont, and *d* 17 April 1825, leaving issue

2g William; *d* 1823

3g Michael; Adml the Blue; *m* 24 Oct 1786 Anne (*d* 21 March 1828), dau of Conway Blennerhassett, of Killorglin, Co Kerry, and *d* 22 Feb 1824, having had, with other issue:

1h Michael (Rev); DD; Rector Drumcree, Co Westmeath; *b* 6 Oct 1787; *m* 1st 20 Nov 1818 Emily (*d* 12 Jan 1830), dau of William Smyth, MP, of Drumcree; *m* 2nd 7 Oct 1833 Mary Anne (*d* 17 Oct 1841), 2nd dau of Robert Baigrie, of Midgarty, Sutherland, and *d* 15 May 1860, having by his 1st w had:

1i MICHAEL WILLIAM, **25th Lord**

2i William Sinclair, HEICMS; *b* 14 Oct 1824; *m* 1852 Anne, widow of William Hodges, and *d* 11 Feb 1858, having had:

1j Michael Edward Lloyd; *d* young

2j John; *d* young

1j Emily Frances Anne; *m* 17 Jan 1880 her cousin **26th Lord Kingsale** (*see* below) and *d* 10 Aug 1926, leaving issue

3i Nevinson; *b* 7 Oct 1825; *d* unm 1914

1i Frances Anne; *d* unm 4 Dec 1911

2i Emily Letitia; *m* 12 July 1848 John William Williams, MD, and *d* 28 Feb 1912

3i Anne Alicia; *m* 1851 Rt Rev Edward Craig Stuart, DD (*d* 15 March 1911), Bp Waiapu, NZ, and *d* 14 July 1915, leaving issue

2h Nevinson; KTS, Capt RN; *b* 20 Feb 1789; *m* 10 Aug 1810 Mary (*d* 19 Jan 1873), dau of William Blennerhassett, of Ballyseedy, Co Kerry, and *d* 1 Nov 1845, having had, with three daus (*d* unm):

1i Michael, CB; Adml; *b* 8 May 1811; *m* 12 Feb 1845 Sybella (*d* 1 March 1904), 3rd dau of Cdr John Row Morris, RN, and *d* 22 Oct 1881, having had:

1i Nevinson John William; *b* 29 Nov 1845; *d* unm 19 Sept 1865

1i Maria Frances Catherine; *m* 23 Sept 1869 Capt George Kemmis, 13th Regt (*dsp* 24 May 1885), and *d* 1913

2j Mary Theodosia; *m* 8 Feb 1875 Col George Howard Moore Lane, CMG (*d* 11 June 1905), and *d* 3 Nov 1925, leaving issue

2i Nevinson Willoughby, CB; Col RM; *b* 27 Sept 1823; *m* 18 Sept 1866 Maria Jane (*d* 12 Nov 1881), yst dau of William Cooke, Madras CS, and *d* 30 March 1885, leaving:

1j Nevinson William; PWD Cairo, 4th Cl Medjidie; *b* 8 May 1869; *m* 15 Feb 1919 Matilda Hetty Grace, MD (*d* 1967), Min Public Health, Egypt, dau of John B Russell, of Auckland, NZ, and *d* 4 Nov 1919, leaving:

1k +NEVINSON RUSSELL [Nevinson de Courcy Esq, 15 Market Rd, Remuera, Auckland 5, New Zealand]; *b* posthumously 21 July 1920; heir presumptive; MA, MICEM, MNZIE; *m* 23 July 1954 *Nora Lydia, yr dau of James Arnold Plint, of Great Crosby, Lancs, and has:

1l +Nevinson Mark; *b* 11 May 1958

1l *Katherine Grace; *b* 26 April 1955; *m* 1979 *Gregory Lawrence Smith and has:

1m *Robert Russell Maunganui; *b* 1987

1m *Henrietta Lydia; *b* 1984

3i William Blennerhassett; Midshipman RN; *b* 2 July 1825; *d* on HMS *Volage* in W Indies July 1842

4i John Sinclair Bremer; *b* 1828; *m* 7 June 1855 Emily Sophia (*d* 19 May 1911), yst dau of George Edmund Bower, and *d* 8 Jan 1901, leaving:

1j Rupert John Nevinson; *b* 31 May 1859; *m* 16 Feb 1885 Agnes Gordon (*d* 11 Nov 1953 aged 93), yst dau of Frederic Brassey, and *d* 28 Nov 1952, leaving:

1k Nevinson Egerton; *b* 28 July 1885; *m* 28 July 1923 Dorothy Mary (*d* 1979), 8th dau of John Bernard Carroll, and *d* 1979, having had:

1l *Angela Mary [Mrs Ian McDonald Wright, The Rosary, Lock Island, Marlow, Bucks SL7 1QE]; *b* 10 May 1927; *m* 23 June 1951 *Ian McDonald Wright, MA, s of Eustace McDonald Wright, of London, and has:

1m *Teresa Dorothy de Courcy [Mrs Jeremy Ryall, Pen-y-Lan, Llanigon, Hay-on-Wye, Powys]; *b* 11 March 1955; *m* 1988 *Jeremy Paul Ryall, and has:

1n *Benjamin Charles; *b* 1992

2n *Max Joseph; *b* 1994

1n *Poppy Alexandra; *b* 1990

2m *Isobel Eileen [Mrs Geoffrey Martin, 9 Annie King Lane, Dover, MA 02030, USA]; *b* 20 Oct 1958; *m* 1985 *Geoffrey Thomas Martin and has:

1n *James Peter de Courcy; *b* 1990

2n *Alexander Nevinson; *b* 1993

1n *Laura de Courcy; *b* 1987

1k Elaine Bertha; *b* 26 Jan 1895; *m* 9 Sept 1924 Leslie Ernest Eldridge and had:

1l *Rosemary de Courcy; *b* 5 May 1928; *m* 12 July 1952 *Rev Robert Bernard Jones and had:

1m Jonathan Aubrey; *b* 21 Oct 1957; *d* 1981

1m *Deborah Ann; *b* 9 Nov 1954

2j Michael George Edmund; *b* 5 Dec 1860; *d* 5 Dec 1911

3j William Edward; *b* 7 Sept 1865; *d* 31 March 1866

1j Emily Mary Eliza; *b* 6 June 1856; *d* unm 24 Feb 1934

2j Beatrice Katherine; *b* 29 June 1857; *d* unm 22 Jan 1882

3j Bertha Maria Letitia; *b* 5 June 1862; *d* unm 25 April 1960

4j Ethel Beata; *b* 31 Jan 1867; *d* unm 7 Feb 1956

1h Anne; *m* 15 June 1812 Sir John Gordon Sinclair, Bt (*d* 13 Nov 1863), and *d* 23 Sept 1857, leaving issue

4g James; Lt-Govr Gravesend and Tilbury Fort; *d* 1824

(3) Patrick; *dsp*

(4) James (Rev); Rector Ringrone; *m* Katherine McCarthy, of Dunmanway, and had:

1a Patrick, of Dromdough; living 1579; *dspl*

2a Edmond, of Dromdough; living 1615, though blind; *m* — MacSweeney and had:

1b James

2b Gerald

1b Katherine fitz Edmond; recd a pardon 1602

(5) Nicholas; *dsp*, *k* 1513

(6) Maurice

(1) Katherine; *m* Edmond Garret, of Garretstown, Co Cork

4 Nicholas; alleged in some sources to have been older than DAVID, **8th Lord**, hence to have been **8th Lord** after EDMOND, the idiot **7th Lord**; *m* Ellen O'Leary and had, with two other sons (Edmond; David; both *dsp*):

(1) John, of Coolbane; *m* — Nugent and had:

1a William; *dsp*

2a John, of Coolbane; claimed to be the rightful (**10th, 11th?**) **Lord**; *dsp* after 1601

The 24th LORD's cousin,

MICHAEL WILLIAM de COURCY, **25th Lord Kingsale**, DL; *b* 29 Sept 1822; *m* 1st 26 May 1852 Esther Eleanor (*d* 27 Dec 1864), dau of Thomas Williams, of Dublin; *m* 2nd 16 July 1874 Jessie Maud (*dsp* 27 July 1902), dau of Rev Edward Polwhele, Rector Pillaton, Cornwall, and by his 1st w had:

1 MICHAEL CONSTANTINE, **26th Lord**

2 William Nevinson; *b* 3 Aug 1856; *d* 4 Jan 1885

3 John Sinclair Emile; *b* Nov 1857; *d* March 1860

4 Robert Charles Sinclair; *b* 4 Dec 1862; *m* 17 Sept 1892 Katherine (*d* 29 Jan 1953), 2nd dau of John Harris, of Ivybridge, Devon, and *d* 21 May 1929, leaving:

(1) John Arthur Gerald, MC; Gp/Capt RAF, served WWs I (despatches, Croix de Guerre) and II; *b* 2 Feb 1894; *m* 21 June 1917 Anna Felicia (*d* 7 Sept 1952), dau of George Wright, High Ct Judge Ireland, by Mercy, dau of Sir Croker Barrington, 4th Bt (*qv*), and *das* 30 Dec 1940, leaving:

1a *Fay [Mrs Hugh Davies, 42 Grantchester Rd, Cambridge]; *b* 3 March 1919; *m* 9 July 1947 (*divorce* 1962, *remarried* 1982) Hugh Sykes Davies (*d* 1984), Fell St John's Coll Cambridge, s of Rev T Sykes Davies, and has:

1b *Katharine Felicia; *b* 1953

2a Stella; *b* 22 April 1921; *m* 6 Nov 1948 *Paul Robert Kemp-King, BA, MS, MA, only s of George Kemp-King, CBE, MVO, and had:

1b *Stephen de Courcy; *b* 19 April 1950; *educ* Millfield

2b *Andrew James de Courcy; *b* 23 Sept 1953; *educ* Millfield

3a *Suzanne; *b* 17 Oct 1923; *m* 16 Oct 1948 *Edward James Bryant, s of Edward B Bryant, and has:

1b *Edward de Courcy [Edward Bryant Esq, 29 Wingate Rd, London W6]; *b* 8 May 1951; *educ* King's Coll Choir Sch, Rugby and Magdalene Coll Cambridge (MA), barrister Middle Temple 1976; *m* 1982 *Frances, est dau of Dr Guy Newton, of Oxford

2b *David de Courcy; *b* 7 Aug 1954; *educ* Rugby

1 Mary Alicia Geraldine; *m* 4 March 1874 William Millar (*d* 10 June 1915), of Killarney Wood, Bray, Co Wicklow, and *d* 7 March 1927, leaving issue

2 Esther Emily Anne Jane; *m* 10 July 1888 Rev Charles Robert Mullins (*d* 16 June 1913), Vicar Kirtling, Newmarket, formerly Chaplain RN, and *d* 27 Dec 1933, leaving issue

The 25th LORD *d* 16 Nov 1895; his est son,

MICHAEL CONSTANTINE de COURCY, **26th Lord Kingsale**; *b* 8 May 1855; md Moran Tea Co London; *m* 17 Jan 1880 his cousin Emily Frances Anne, dau of William Sinclair de Courcy (*see* above), and had:

1 MICHAEL WILLIAM ROBERT, **27th Lord**

1 Esther Eleanor; *b* 6 Dec 1880; *m* 1st 27 Feb 1900 Alfred Charles Festing-Smith, LRCP, LRCS (*d* 25 Sept 1908), and had issue; *m* 2nd 30 Nov 1911 Reginald John Winterbotham, er s of John Brend Winterbotham, of Cheltenham (*d* 11 May 1938), and *d* 2 Oct 1957, leaving further issue

2 Beryl Madeline; *b* 14 Oct 1884; *d* unm 29 Jan 1908

3 Violet Gladys (twin); *b* 14 Oct 1884; *d* unm 31 Oct 1933

4 Estelle Emily Spencer; *b* 23 Nov 1889; *m* 9 Dec 1916 Wellesley St George Ashe, Capt IA Res (*d* 21 June 1958), s of Rev Henry Ashe, of Duleek, Co Meath, and had issue

The 26th LORD *d* 24 Jan 1931; his son,

MICHAEL WILLIAM ROBERT de COURCY, **27th Lord Kingsale**, DSO (1918); *b* 26 Sept 1882; *educ* Dulwich, Kelly Coll Tavistock and RMC Sandhurst; joined Connaught Rangers 1902, IA (32nd Sikh Pioneers) 1904, served Tibet Mission 1903–04, Abor Expdn 1911–12 (despatches), WWI: Mesopotamia 1915–17 (despatches thrice), Marri operations 1918 (despatches), Afghanistan 1919–20 (despatches) and Waziristan 1922, Lt-Col cmdg 2nd Bn Corps Sikh Pioneers 1927–31, Order White Eagle Serbia 5th Cl with swords; *m* 1st 15 Nov 1906 Constance Mary Rancé (*d* 12 Aug 1946), dau of Maj-Gen Sir Tom Percy Woodhouse, KCMG, CB, AMS, and had:

1 Michael John Rancé; *b* 30 Sept 1907; Lt-Cdr RN WW II; *m* 1st 31 Aug 1929 (*divorce* 1933) Glory Elizabeth, dau of Engr-Cdr Alfred Claremont Evans, RN, and had:

(1) Michael Charles Cameron Claremont Constantine; Actg P/O RAF, jnlst; *b* 18 Sept 1930; *educ* Hurstpierpoint and Harrow; *m* 1951 *Anne Grey (*m* 2nd 24 Jan 1959 Robert Armitage, 2nd s of Gen Sir Charles Clement Armitage, KCB, CMG, DSO, of Downington House, Lechlade, Glos), dau of Maj J L M Barrett, 13th/18th Roy Hus, of The Tallat, Northleach, Glos, and *dsp*, *k* in a flying accident 28 Jan 1953

1 (cont.) Lt-Cdr The Hon Michael de Courcy *m* 2nd 11 July 1936 Joan (*d* 5 Aug 1967), yr dau of Robert Reid, JP, of Moor Park, Beckwithshaw, nr Harrogate, and was *k* by enemy action 18 Aug 1940, having by her had:

(2) JOHN de COURCY, **28th and present Lord Kingsale**

(1) *Dione May; *b* 21 June 1937; *m* 12 June 1965 (*divorce* 1976) David Kemp Daffin, only s of Irl A Daffin, of Lancaster, Pa., and has:

1a *Miles Irl de Courcy; *b* 28 Feb 1969

2a *Thomas Chester de Courcy; *b* 1971

2 Patrick Constantine; *b* 30 Dec 1909; *d* 24 Feb 1912

1 Frances Mary Alexa; *d* 14 Oct 1915

2 *Bridget Doreen; *m* 1st 18 June 1938 (*divorce* 1952) Rev George Ian Falconer Thomson (*d* 1987), former Chaplain Hertford Coll Oxford, est s of Rev Dr George Dornin Thomson, of Montreal, and has:

(1) *Margaret Doreen Rosemary (Emma); *b* 1940

2 (cont.) Mrs Bridget Thomson *m* 2nd 19– *Stephen Watson and by him has a s

3 Denise Patricia; *m* 27 June 1942 Gordon David St John-Ives, BM, BCH (*d* 21 Jan 1973), 2nd s of Capt St John-Ives, of Mailoor Estate, Kullakanby, S India, and *dsp* 27 July 1959

4 *Eleanor Geraldine; *m* 10 April 1940 (*divorce* 1947) John Campbell Clarke (*d* 17 June 1966), s of Dr Hugh Campbell Wilson Clarke, of Ashton-on-Mersey, Cheshire, and has:

(1) *Peter; *b* 14 Aug 1945

The **27th Lord** *m* 2nd 4 June 1947 (*divorce* 1957) Ruth, only child of Herbert Thomas Holmes, OBE, of Russettings, Ringley Park Ave, Reigate, and *d* 7 Nov 1969, leaving by her:

5 *Diana Ruth; *b* 17 Aug 1951

KINGSDOWN

Arms: Quarterly, 1st and 4th, ermine an estoile or between three buckets sable, hoops and handles gold (for PEMBERTON); 2nd and 3rd, gules a cross engrailed argent between four lozenges ermine (for LEIGH). **Crests:** 1 A dragon's head ermine, erased gules, ducally gorged or, and transfixed by an arrow fessways proper (for PEMBERTON), 2 A demi-lion rampant gules, charged on each shoulder with an ermine spot and holding between the paws a lozenge argent, thereon a rose gules, barbed and seeded proper (for LEIGH). **Supporters:** Dexter, a wyvern ermine, ducally gorged or and charged on the shoulder with an estoile gules; sinister, a lion gules charged on the shoulder with a lozenge argent, thereon an ermine spot gules. **Motto:** *Ut tibi sic alteri* ('Do to others as you would to yourself'). **Creation:** B. (LP, UK) 1993.

THE BARON KINGSDOWN, of Pemberton, Co Lancaster (Sir Robert (Robin) Leigh-Pemberton, KG (1994), PC (1987)) [The Rt Hon The Lord Kingsdown KG PC, Torry Hill, Sittingbourne, Kent ME9 0SP]; *b* 5 Jan 1927; *educ* Eton, RMC Sandhurst and Trin Coll Oxford (MA 1953, Hon Fell 1984); Lt Gren Gds 1945–48; barrister Inner Temple 1954, London and SE Circuit 1954–60, Hon Bencher 1983; dir: Birmid Qualcast 1966–83 (dep-chm 1970, chm 1975–77), University Life Assur 1967–78, Redland Ltd 1972–83 and 1993–, Equitable Life Assur 1979–83 (v-pres 1982–83), Glaxo 1993–96, Hambros 1993–, Foreign and Colonial Investment Tst 1993–; chm: Nat West Bank 1977–83 (dir 1972–83, dep-chm 1974), Ctee London Clearing Bankers 1982–83, Green Arrow 1995–; Govr: Bank of England 1983–93, Ditchley Fndn 1987–; memb: SE Ec Planning Cncl 1972–74, Medway Ports Authority 1974–76, NEDC 1982–92, PM's Ctee Local Govt Rules Conduct 1973–74, Ctee Enquiry Teachers' Pay 1974 and Police Pay 1977–79; Kent: CC 1961–77 (Chm 1972–73), CA 1965, JP 1961–75, Ld Lt 1982 (V-Ld Lt 1972–82, DL 1970–72); Tstee: Glyndebourne Arts Tst 1978–83, Roy Acad Arts Tst 1982–88 (Hon Tstee Emeritus 1988–), Kent CCC, Kent County Playing Fields Assoc, Kent County Ag Soc; Seneschal Canterbury Cathedral; Chm Canterbury Cathedral Tst Fund; Pres: Roy Ag Soc England 1989–90, SE TAVRA, Kent SSAFA; Pro-Chllr Kent U 1977–83; FRSA 1977, FCIB, FIMgt (FBIM 1977); Hon DCL Kent 1983; Hon DLitt: City 1988, Loughborough 1990, City Poly 1990; Hon Col: Kent and Sharpshooters Yeo Sqdn, 265 (KCLY) Signal Sqdn (V) 1979–92, 5th (Vol) Bn The Queen's Regt 1987–92; KStJ; *m* 1953 *Rosemary Davina (OBE 1995), sometime Pres BRCS Kent, only dau of Lt-Col David Walter Arthur William Forbes, MC (*see* FARINGDON, B), and has had:

1 *John David [The Hon John Leigh-Pemberton, Yokes Court, Frinstead, Sittingbourne, Kent]; *b* 1955; *educ* Eton and Magdalen Coll Oxford; *m* 1st 1980 Rosamond P, 4th dau of Oliver Richard Jessel, of Sponden House, Sandhurst, Kent; *m* 2nd 1985 *Kathryn Felice, dau of Martin Robert Lampard, of Theberton House, Theberton, Suffolk, and has:

(1) *Arthur Evelyn; *b* 1989

(2) *Robert Eustace Walter; *b* 1991

(1) *Maude Alexandra Frances; *b* 1995

2 *James Henry [The Hon James Leigh-Pemberton, The Old Rectory, Milstead, Kent ME9 0AS.]; *b* 1956; *educ* Eton and Ch Ch Oxford; *m* 1985 *Catarina Elizabeth, dau of John Cowan, of New Coll, Oxford, and Mrs Karin Stielow, of Hamburg, and has:

(1) *Sophia Loveday; *b* 1985

(2) *Lucinda Rose; *b* 1987

(3) *Letitia Jane; *b* 1989

3 *Edward Douglas [The Hon Edward Leigh-Pemberton, Longcote House, Longcote, Oxon SN7 7TF]; *b* 1959; *educ* Eton and RAC Cirencester; *m* 1984 *Jessica Elizabeth Berners, yr twin dau of Michael Edward Ranulph Allsopp (*see* HINDLIP, B), and has:

(1) *David Geoffrey Berners; *b* 1988

(2) *Ranulph Berners; *b* 1989

(3) *Patrick Berners; *b* 1991

4 Thomas Robert Arnold; *b* 1961; *educ* Eton and St Edmund Hall Oxford; *k* car crash Zimbabwe 1993

5 *William Francis; *b* 1964; *educ* Eton and Jesus Coll Oxford

Lineage: EDWARD PEMBERTON, of Warrington; MD; *m* Ellen, dau of John Lyon, of Appleton, and had:

ROBERT PEMBERTON; barrister MiddleTemple; *m* 24 July 1788 Margaret, est dau and coheir of Edward Leigh, of Bispham Hall, Lancs (1st cousin of Sir Robert Holt Leigh, 1st Bt (*d* Jan 1834); *see* 1834 edn), and had, with two daus:

1 THOMAS PEMBERTON later PEMBERTON-LEIGH (roy licence 7 March 1834, after inheriting a life interest in the Wigan estates of Sir Robert Leigh, Bt (*see* above), worth *c* £17,000 (nearly £730,000 in late-1990s terms) p.a.), 1st and last BARON KINGSDOWN, of Kingsdown, Co Kent (UK), so *cr* 28 Aug 1858, PC (1843), KC (1829); *b* 11 Feb 1793; barrister Lincoln's Inn 1816, MP (C) Rye 1831–32 and Ripon 1835–43, Attorney Gen to HRH THE PRINCE OF WALES 1841–43, Chllr Duchy Cornwall 1843–61; *d* unm 7 Oct 1867, when the Barony expired

2 Edward Leigh, of Torry Hill, Kent; *b* 18 Feb 1795; MP; *m* 23 Dec 1820 Charlotte, dau of Samuel Compton Cox, Master in Chancery, and *d* 12 March 1877, leaving, with other issue:

(1) Edward Leigh (Sir), KCB (1898), JP, DL (Kent), of Torry Hill and Wrinsted Court, Kent; *b* 14 May 1823; *educ* Eton and St John's Coll Oxford; barrister Lincoln's Inn, Maj E Kent Yeo, MP E Kent 1868–85, Legal Assist to U-Sec Home Office 1885–94; *m* 4 Aug 1849 Matilda Catherine Emma, dau of Rev Hon Francis James Noel (*see* GAINSBOROUGH, E), and *d* 31 Jan 1910, leaving, with two daus:

1a ROBERT LEIGH

2a Wilfred Leigh, of Wrinsted; *b* 19 June 1853; *educ* Westminster and Ch Ch Oxford; barrister; *m* 1 Jan 1890 Alice Augusta, dau of Capt David Holland Erskine (*see* ERSKINE, Bt), and *d* 27 May 1925, having had a s (*ka* 1915)

The er s,

ROBERT LEIGH PEMBERTON, of Torry Hill and Wrinsted, JP (Kent and Herefs); *b* 25 Dec 1851; *educ* Westminster; Ld Manors Kingsdown, Stockbury, Yoke's Court and Gt Higham; Lt Gren Gds, Capt 3rd and 4th Bns QO W Kent Regt; *m* 5 June 1883 Edith Selina, dau of Robert Hay Murray (*see* ATHOLL, D), and *d* 14 April 1918, leaving, with two daus:

ROBERT DOUGLAS LEIGH PEMBERTON, MBE (1964), MC (1918), JP (Kent 1924), of Kippen, Sittingbourne; *b* 27 April 1896; *educ* Eton and RMC Sandhurst; Served Gren Gds and RFC WWs I and II; *m* 23 June 1925 Helen Isabel, yst dau of Rev Francis Henry Payne-Gallwey (*see* FRANKLAND-PAYNE-GALLWEY, Bt), and had:

1 ROBERT ROBIN, *cr* a **Baron**

2 *Nigel Douglas [Nigel Leigh Pemberton Esq, Eythorne House, Eythorne, Kent CT15 4BE]; *b* 9 May 1929; *educ* Eton, Magdalen Coll Oxford and Vienna Musikakedemie; late Lt Life Gds; *m* 21 July 1973 *Alexandra Valerie, dau of J C A Roper, CMG, MC

3 *Jeremy, CBE (1992) [Jeremy Leigh Pemberton Esq CBE, Hill House, Wormshill, Kent ME9 0TS]; *b* 25 Nov 1933; *educ* Eton, Magdalen Coll Oxford and INSEAD; late 2nd Lt Gren Gds; *m* 1st 1968 (*divorce* 1980) Mary, dau of John S Ames, of Boston; *m* 2nd 3 June 1982 *Virginia, dau of Sir John Curle, KCVO, CMG, late Amb Philippines and V-Marshal Dip Corps, by his 1st w Diana (*see* STRATHCARRON, B), and by his 1st w has:

(1) *Richard Ames; *b* 1971

KINGSLAND

Creation: B. (LP, UK) 20 Aug 1994.

THE BARON KINGSLAND, of Shrewsbury, Co of Shropshire (Sir Christopher James Prout, TD (1987), PC (1994), QC (1988), DL (Salop 1997) [The Rt Hon The Lord Kingsland TD PC QC DL, House of Lords, London SW1A 0PW]; *b* 1 Jan 1942; *educ* Sevenoaks Sch, Manchester U and Queen's Coll Oxford (Bphil, DPhil); Maj TA OU OTC 1966–74, 16th/5th Queen's Roy Lancers 1974–82, 3rd Armoured Div 1982–88, RARO 1988–; with Internat Bank Reconstruction and Devpt Washington 1966–69, law lecturer Sussex U 1969–79, barrister Middle Temple 1972, Master Bench 1996–; MEP (C) Salop and Staffs 1979–94, fought Herefs and Salop 1994, Ldr Br C MEPs 1987–94, Dep Whip 1979–82, Ch Whip 1983–87, Chm and Ldr 1987–92 European Dem Gp, V-Chm European People's Party Parly Gp 1992–94; Shadow Ld Chllr 1997–; author: *Market Socialism in Yugoslavia* (1985)

Lineage: FRANK YABSLEY PROUT, MC and bar; *m* Doris Lucy Osborne (*d* 1983) and *d* 1980, leaving:

CHRISTOPHER JAMES (Sir), *cr* a **Baron**

KINGS NORTON

Arms: Azure a chevron or between in chief two jet engines palewise, flames downward, and in base a balloon with car proper. **Crest:** A hare sejant erect proper in front of two sceptres in saltire, each terrninating in a fleur-de-lys or. **Supporters:** On either side a cock standing on a rock proper. **Motto:** Precision and tolerance. **Creation:** B. (LP, UK) 1965.

THE BARON KINGS NORTON, of Wotton Underwood, Co Buckingham (Sir Harold Roxbee Cox) [The Rt Hon The Lord Kings Norton, Westcote House, Chipping Campden, Glos GL55 6AG]; *b* 6 June 1902; *educ* King's Norton GS and Imperial Coll Sci and Technology (BSc, DIC, PhD); engr Airship R101 project 1924–29; Ch Tech Offr Roy Airship Works 1931; Lecturer Imp Coll 1932–38; Roy Aircraft Establishment: Pncpl Sci Offr Aerodynamics Dept 1935–36, Head Air Defence Dept 1936–38, Supt Sci Research 1939–40; Ch Tech Offr Air Registration Bd 1938–39; Min Aircraft Production: Dept Dir Sci Research 1940–43, Dir Special Projects 1943–44; memb Aeronautical Research Cncl 1944–48 and 1958–60; Ch Scientist Min Fuel and Power 1948–54; Dir: Nat Gas Turbine Establishment 1946–48, Ricardo and Co 1927 Ltd 1965–77, Dowty Rotol 1968–75, BPC 1968–77, Hoechst UK 1970–75; Chm: Gas Turbine Collaboration Ctee 1941–44 and 1946–48, Power Jets Research and Development Ltd 1944–46 (md 1944–46), Nat Cncl for Technological Awards 1960–64 (V-Chm 1955–60), Metal Box Co 1961–67 (dir 1957–67, dep chm 1959–60), Cncl Sci and Industl Research 1961–65, Berger Jenson and Nicholson 1967–75, Landspeed Ltd 1975–, Cotswold Research Ltd 1978–, Applied Photophysics 1974–81, Withers Estates 1976–81, Cncl for Nat Academic Awards 1964–71, Air Registration Board 1966–72; Pres: RAeS 1947–49, Roy Inst 1969–76, Camden and Chorleywood Food Research Assoc 1961–, Br Balloon Museum and Library 1980–; Chllr Cranfield Inst Technology 1969–; ktd 1953; Bronze Medal Louvain U 1946, American Medal Freedom with Silver Palm 1947; memb correspondant Faculté Polytechnique de Mons 1946–; Hon DSc: Birmingham 1954, Cranfield 1970, Warwick 1986; DTech Brunel 1966; Hon LLD CNAA 1969; Fell Imp Coll 1960; Freeman City London 1987; Liveryman Guild Air Pilots and Air Navigators 1987; FCGI 1976; HFIFST 1992; *m* 1st 1927 (Doris) Marjorie (*d* 1980), dau of Ernest Edward Withers, of Northwood, Middx, and has:

1 *Christopher Withers [The Hon Christopher Cox, 29 Pages Lane, Bexhill-on-Sea, E Sussex TN39 3RD]; *b* 1928; *m* 1955 *Rosemary, dau of Frederick Day Ardagh, and has two sons

2 *Jeremy William; *b* 1932; *m* 1962 *Anne, dau of Albert Moore Linton, and has a s and dau

THE BARON KINGS NORTON *m* 2nd 1982 *Joan Ruth, dau of William George Pack, of Torquay, Devon, and formerly wife of K A Pascoe

Lineage: WILLIAM JOHN ROXBEE COX, of Birmingham; *m* Amelia Stern and had:

HAROLD ROXBEE, *cr* a **Baron**

KINGSTON

Arms: Quarterly, 1st and 4th, gules on a bend engrailed or, between two leopard's faces of the last jessant-de-lys azure, three cross-crosslets fitchée sable (for TENISON); 2nd and 3rd, gules two lions rampant combatant, supporting a dexter hand, couped at the wrist and erect argent (for KING). **Crests:** 1 In front of a crozier and a cross-crosslet fitchée in saltire sable a leopard's face or, jessant-de-lys azure (for TENISON), 2 Out of a five-leaved ducal coronet or a dexter hand erect, the third and fourth fingers turned down proper (for KING). **Supporters:** Two lions per fess argent and gules, ducally crowned of the last. **Motto:** *Spes tutissima cœlis* ('Heaven is our highest hope'). **Creations:** Bt. (I) 27 Sept 1682, B. (I) 13 July 1764 (Kingston of Rockingham) and (I) 29 Dec 1800 (Erris); V. (I) 15 Nov 1766 (Kingston of Kingsborough) and (I) 28 May 1806 (Lorton); E. (I) 25 Aug 1768.

THE 11TH EARL OF KINGSTON, Viscount Kingston of Kingsborough, Viscount Lorton, Baron Kingston of Rockingham, Baron Erris of Boyle, Co Roscommon, and a **Baronet** (Sir Barclay Robert Edwin King-Tenison, Bt); *b* 23 Sept 1943, *s* f 1948; *educ* Winchester and RMA Sandhurst; late Lt Roy Scots Greys; *m* 20 Nov 1965 (*divorce* 1974) Patricia Mary, only dau of Ernest Charles Killip, of Hafod-y-Coed, Llanfairfechan, and has:

1 +ROBERT CHARLES HENRY, *Viscount Kingsborough*; *b* 20 March 1969

1 *Maria Lisette; *b* 3 Oct 1970

The 11th EARL *m* 2nd Nov 1974 (*divorce* 1979) Victoria, dau of D C Edmonds, of Northwood, Middx; *m* 3rd 1990 *Corleen Jennifer Rathbone

Other Kingston title creations: For the Viscountcy of Kingston in the Scottish peerage, *see* EGLINTON and WINTON, E.

A Scottish Lordship of Parliament of Kingston and Elbottle was conferred with the Earldom of Dirletoun in 1646 on Sir James Maxwell of Innerwick, a nephew through his mother of the 1st Earl of Annandale (*see* ANNANDALE AND HARTFELL, E), but this expired on the death of the grantee four years later. Robert Pierrepont, nephew through his mother of the 1st Earl of Devonshire (*see* DEVONSHIRE, D), was created Earl of Kingston-upon-Hull in 1628. A classic example of how difficult it is to stay uncommitted in a time of Civil War, this Lord Kingston was unwillingly dragged into the royalist camp in 1643 and made Lieutenant-General of CHARLES I's forces in the Fen counties around the Wash, his six sons meanwhile siding some with Parliament some with the King. Lord Kingston was captured by Parliamentarians early in the War and while being ferried down the River Trent with a party of other royalist prisoners of war aboard a Parliamentarian pinnace to Hull, the town commemorated in his very title, was killed by a salvo from a shore-based royalist battery. It was a sad end to a man who had tried to stay aloof from opposing parties.

Gervase, the 1st Earl of Kingston-upon-Hull's fifth son, left £10,000 (over £460,000 in late-1990s terms) in his will to the first member of the family to attain a dukedom. This actually came about in 1715, when the 1st Earl's great-grandson Evolyn was promoted from being Marquess of Dorchester (a title conferred on him nine years earlier) to Duke of Kinston-upon-Hull. He was father of the celebrated Lady Mary Wortley Montagu (*see* WHARNCLIFFE, E). His grandson, the 2nd and last Duke, went through a form of marriage with Elizabeth Chudleigh, a hard-swearing beauty who dressed immodestly by the standards of the day and who was successfully prosecuted for bigamy three years after his death. She had married nearly a third of a century earlier the 6th Earl of Bristol (*see* BRISTOL, M) and been incompletely divorced from him. Her trial took place in the House of Lords, her nephew and sister-in-law mounting the prosecution, and the 119 peers present who according to the rules in trials of peers or peeresses formed the jury returned a unanimous verdict of guilty. Yet she escaped punishment by standing on her privileged legal status as a peeress.

Lineage: Sir JOHN KING; granted Boyle Abbey, Co Roscommon, on lease by ELIZABETH I; *m* Catherine, dau of Robert Drury and great-niece of Ld Deputy Sir William Drury, and had, with other issue:

1 ROBERT (Sir)

2 John; Clerk Hanaper; *m* Margaret, dau of Francis Edgeworth, and had:

(1) John

(2) Francis; had issue

3 Edward; *b* 1613; MA, Fell Christ's Coll Cambridge; drowned in the Irish Sea 1638 aged 25, inspiring Milton to write the elegy *Lycidas* in commemoration

1 Dorothy; *m* Arthur Moore, of Dromaghan, Co Louth, and Drumbanagher, Co Armagh (*see* DROGHEDA, E)

Sir JOHN *d* 4 Jan 1636; his est son,

Sir ROBERT KING, of Boyle Abbey; Muster Master-Gen Ireland; *m* 1st Frances, dau of Sir Henry Folliott, 1st Lord Folliott, Baron of Ballyshannon, and had issue; *m* 2nd Sophia, widow of Viscount Wimbledon (*see* EXETER, M) and dau of Sir Edward Zouche, of Woking, Surrey, and *d* 1657, having by her had a dau; his issue by his 1st w:

1 JOHN KING, 1st BARON KINGSTON of Kingston, Co Dublin (I), so *cr* 4 Sept 1660, PC (I); fought for the King in suppressing the 1641 Uprising and held Boyle Castle for the King 1642 but supported Parliament in the ensuing Civil War and acted on its behalf in suppressing a Catholic rising 1650; nevertheless promoted the Restoration 1660, hence granted 1664 much land in Cos Cork, Kildare and Limerick; Jt Govr Connaught 1666, Col Lord Kingston's Cav Regt 1672–75; *m* Catherine (*d* 1669), dau of Sir William Fenton (by Margaret FitzGibbon, sis and heir of The White Knight), through whom he acquired the Mitchelstown estate, Co Cork, and *d* 1676, leaving:

(1) ROBERT KING, 2nd BARON KINGSTON, PC (I Feb 1683/4); *m c* 17 Feb 1689/90 Margaret (*d* 3 Sept 1698), dau and coheir of William Harbord, of Grafton Park, Northants, and *dsp* Dec 1693

(2) JOHN KING, 3rd BARON KINGSTON, PC; *b c* 1664; turned RC and accompanied JAMES II into exile in France, hence outlawed, but was later pardoned; *m* 1683 Margaret (*d* 29 April 1721), one of his f's servants, dau of Florence O'Cahan, and *d* 15 Feb 1727/8, leaving:

1a JAMES KING, 4th and last BARON KINGSTON, PC (I 1729); *b* 1693; *m* 1st Elizabeth (*d* 6 Oct 1750), widow of Sir Ralph Freke, 1st Bt, and dau of Sir John Meade, 1st Bt (*see* CLANWILLIAM, E), and had:

1b William; *m* 11 Oct 1754 the only dau of Samuel Burroughs, of Dewsbury, Yorks, but *dsp* & *vp*

1b Margaret; *m* Richard FitzGerald, of Mount Opheley and Kilminchy, and *d* 29 Jan 1763, leaving:

1c Caroline; *m* 5 Dec 1769 her cousin **2nd Earl of Kingston** (*see* below)

1a (cont.) The 4th BARON *m* 2nd July 1751 Isabella (*d* 9 Dec 1761), widow of Adml Sir Challenor Ogle and *dspms* 28 Dec 1761, when the Barony expired

1a Catherine; *m* George Butler, of Ballyraggett, Co Kilkenny (*see* VAUX OF HARROWDEN, B)

2 **Sir Robert King, 1st Bt** (I), so *cr* 27 Sept 1682, PC (I), of Rockingham, Co Roscommon; LLB, MP Ballyshannon 1661–66, Co Roscommon 1692–99 and Boyle 1703–07; *m* Frances, dau and coheir of Colonel Henry Gore (*see* ARRAN, E), and *d* 1 March 1707, leaving an est surv s:

(1) **Sir John King, 2nd Bt**; MP Boyle 1695, 1703 and 1713 and Co Roscommon 1715–20; *m* Elizabeth (*m* 2nd 1st Baron Moore of Tullamore and 3rd 1st Earl of Bessborough (*qv*)), dau of John Sankey, of Tenelick, Co Longford, and *dsp* 19 March 1720

(2) **Sir Henry King, 3rd Bt**, PC (1733); MP Boyle 1707–27 and Co Roscommon 1727–40; *m* April 1722 Isabella (*d* 23 Oct 1761), sis of 1st Viscount Powerscourt (*qv*), and *d* 1 Jan 1739, having had, with other issue:

1a **Sir Robert King, 4th Bt**, and 1st and last BARON OF KINGSBOROUGH (I), so *cr* 13 June 1748; *bapt* 18 Feb 1724; MP Boyle 1744–48; *d* unm 22 May 1755, when the Barony expired

2a EDWARD, **1st Earl**

1a Isabella; *m* 17 Nov 1750 1st Earl of Howth (*see* 1909 edn) and *d* 20 Oct 1794, leaving issue

2a Anne; *m* 25 May 1750 John Knox, MP, of Castlereagh, Co Mayo, and *d* 29 March 1803, leaving issue

The 4th Bt's bro,

Sir Edward King, 5th Bt, and **1st Earl of Kingston**, so *cr* 25 Aug 1768, as also earlier 13 July 1764 BARON KINGSTON OF ROCKINGHAM, Co Roscommon, and 15 Nov 1766 VISCOUNT KINGSTON OF KINGSBOROUGH, Co Sligo (all I), PC (I 1794); *b* 29 March 1726; MP Boyle 1749–60 and Co Sligo 1761–64; *m* 5 Jan 1752 Jane (*d* April 1784), illegitimate dau by Thomas Caulfeild, of Donamon, Co Roscommon, of Peggy Jordan, later w of James Black, cobbler, and *d* 8 Nov 1797, having had, with other issue, including a dau (Jane, *m* 11 June 1772 1st Earl of Rosse (*qv*) and *d* 26 Jan 1838, leaving issue):

ROBERT KING, **2nd Earl of Kingston**; *b* 1754; *educ* Eton; MP Co Cork 1783–97, Govr Co Cork 1789; found not guilty 18 May 1798 in a trial by his peers of murdering Col Henry FitzGerald, a bastard son of his brother-in-law, following the seduction by Col FitzGerald of the dau of the **2nd Earl**; (Lord Kingston had undoubtedly shot the Colonel dead; no prosecution witnesses took the stand, however, and the accused was clearly a favourite of the onlookers); *m* 5 Dec 1769 his cousin Caroline (*d* 13 Jan 1823), only dau (by Margaret, dau and heiress of 4th BARON KINGSTON; *see* above) of Richard FitzGerald, of Mount Ophaly, and *d* 17 April 1799, having had, with other issue:

1 GEORGE KING, **3rd Earl of Kingston**; *b* 8 April 1771; *educ* Eton and Exeter Coll Oxford; MP Co Roscommon 1797–99; *cr* 17 July 1821 BARON KINGSTON OF MITCHELSTOWN, Co Cork (UK); *m* 7 May 1794 Lady Helena Moore (*d* 9 Dec 1847), only dau of 1st Earl Mountcashell, and *d* 18 Oct 1839, having had:

(1) Edward, *Viscount Kingsborough*; *b* 10 Nov 1795; *educ* Exeter Coll Oxford; MP (Whig) Co Cork 1818–26, antiquarian, ed Aglio's *The Antiquities of Mexico* (6 vols, 1831), Kt Austrian Order of Crown of Italy; *d* unm 27 Feb 1837 of typhus in a Dublin debtor's prison, having stood security for his f, whose debt it was

(2) ROBERT HENRY KING, **4th Earl of Kingston**; *b* 4 Oct 1796; Offr 5th Foot, MP (Whig) Co Cork 1826–32, Sheriff Co Cork 1836; indicted for sodomy April 1848 but jumped bail of £10,000 (over £46,000 in late-1990s terms); by 1860 he was more civic-minded, actually appearing in the magistrates' courts to answer charges of intoxication, assaulting the police or bilking cabmen of their fares; ajudged insane 1861; *d* unm 21 Jan 1867

(3) JAMES KING, **5th Earl of Kingston**; *b* 8 April 1800; barrister King's Inn Dublin 1825 and Lincoln's Inn 1827; *m* 25 Aug 1860 Anna (*m* 2nd 29 July 1873 William Downes Webber, of Kellyville, Queen's Co, and *dsp* 29 Oct 1909), 4th dau of Matthew Brinckley, of Parsonstown, Co Meath, and *dsp* 8 Sept 1869, when the UK Barony expired

(1) Helena Caroline; *m* 8 Dec 1829 Philip Davies-Cooke (*d* 20 Nov 1853), of Gwysaney, Flints, and Owston Hall, Yorks, and *d* 9 May 1871, leaving issue (*see* COOKE, Bt)

(2) Adelaide Charlotte; *m* 1834 Charles Tankerville Webber, QC, and *d* Aug 1854, leaving issue

2 ROBERT EDWARD KING, **1st Viscount Lorton of Boyle**, Co Roscommon, so *cr* 28 May 1806, as also earlier 29 Dec 1800 BARON ERRIS OF BOYLE, Co Roscommon (both I); *b* 12 Aug 1773; *educ* Eton and Exter Coll Oxford; MP Jamestown 1796–97 and Boyle 1798–1800; tried at roughly the same time as his f (April 1798) for the murder of Col FitzGerald (but at the Cork Assizes, being then a commoner) and also found not guilty; rep I peer 1823–54, Gen 1830; *m* 9 Dec 1799 his cousin Lady Frances (*d* 7 Oct 1841), dau and heiress of 1st Earl of Rosse (*qv*), and *d* 20 Nov 1854, having had:

(1) ROBERT, **6th Earl**

(2) Laurence Harman KING later KING-HARMAN (1838), of Newcastle, Ballymahon, Co Longford, and Rockingham House, Co Roscommon; *b* 6 Feb 1816; *m* 17 May 1837 Mary Cecilia (*d* 11 Jan 1904), 7th dau of James Raymond Johnstone, of Alva, Clackmannanshire (*see* JOHNSTONE, Bt), and *d* 10 Oct 1875, leaving:

1a Edward Robert, PC, of Newcastle and Rockingham; MP Co Sligo 1877–80, Co Dublin 1883–85 and Isle of Thanet 1835–38, HM Lt Co Roscommon, Hon Col 5th Bn Connaught Rangers, Lt 60th Rifles; *b* 3 April 1838; *m* 20 Aug 1861 Emma Frances (*d* 15 May 1893), yst dau of Sir William Worsley, 1st Bt (*qv*), and *d* 10 June 1888, having had:

1b Laurence William; Lt 5th Bn Connaught Rangers; *b* 23 Nov 1863; *d* 23 Oct 1886

1b Frances Agnes; *m* 22 May 1890 Sir Thomas Joseph Stafford, 1st Bt, CB (*d* 11 May 1935; *see* 1970 edn STAFFORD-KING-HARMAN, Bt), and *d* 23 March 1916, leaving issue

2b Violet Philadelphia; *d* 28 May 1867

2a Wentworth Henry, of Newcastle; Col RA; *b* 27 March 1840; *m* 29 May 1863 Annie Kate (*d* 6 Nov 1926), yst dau of D J Smith, of Kingston, Canada, and *d* 1 April 1919, leaving:

1b Wentworth Alexander, DSO (1918), of Newcastle and Mitchelstown, Co Cork; Maj and Brevet Lt-Col, Lt 1st Bn Roy Irish Rifles, Capt 6th Bn Rifle Bde, Maj 3rd Bn Roy Irish Rifles, served Matabele Campaign and WW I (despatches); *b* 3 Jan 1869; *d* unm 5 July 1949

1b Beatrice Caroline; *d* unm 1 June 1946

2b Lilian Mary; *d* unm 26 Nov 1959 aged 85

3b Annette Maude; *m* 15 March 1900 Maj Thomas Carson, Roy Irish Rifles (*d* 23 Feb 1925), and *d* 12 Sept 1944, leaving issue

3a Montague Jocelyn; Col IA, 1st Dep Sec to Govt India 1892–97; *b* 1 March 1843; *educ* HEIC Mil Coll Addiscombe; *m* 1st 15 Feb 1870 Emily (*d* 28 Nov 1931), 5th dau of Lt-Gen Henry Rigby, RE, of Bengal; *m* 2nd 30 April 1934 Emily Isabella, widow of A H Lafrentz, BA, and *d* 1941, having by his 1st w had:

1b Edward Henry; *b* 13 Dec 1870; *m* 1st 1 Oct 1896 Emily Florence (*d* 29 March 1923), dau of J G Meugens, of Calcutta, and had:

1c Lawrence Montague; 2nd Lt Rifle Bde; *b* 2 June 1898; *m* 24 April 1926 (*divorce* 1933) Marjorie (*d* 22 Dec 1961), only dau of John Rigby, of Moat Ho, Hertingfordbury, and *d* 27 June 1936

1c Daphne Florence; *b* 23 Aug 1903; *m* 26 April 1926 William Baverstock Soames, est s of Rev Gordon Soames, Patron and Rector Mildenhall, Wilts, and *d* 14 July 1953, leaving issue

1b (cont.) Edward King-Harman *m* 2nd 21 Jan 1927 Mabel Grace Whitaker (*d* 1949) and *d* 13 Sept 1931

1b Mary Elizabeth; *b* 29 Nov 1871; *m* 19 May 1892 Arthur Morgan, 4th s of Sir Walter Morgan, and had issue

4a George Douglas; Maj Queen's (Roy W Surrey) Regt; *b* 1 Sept 1845; *m* 1 Oct 1896 Emily Isabella, dau of James Dunn, of Belfast, and *d* 25 Jan 1900

5a Charles Anthony (Sir), KCMG, JP (Somerset and Beds); MA Cantab, Hon LLD Edinburgh, Colonial Sec Mauritius 1893–97, Administrator St Lucia 1897–1900, Govr Sierra Leone 1900–04 and HC Cyprus 1904–11; *b* 26 April 1851; *m* 12 July 1888 Constance (*d* 24 Feb 1961), dau of Gen Sir Robert Biddulph, GCB, GCM (*see* BIDDULPH, B), and *d* 17 April 1939, having had:

1b Lawrence Hope; Capt RHA and RFC; *b* 5 May 1889; *ka* 26 Oct 1916

2b Robert Douglas, DSO (1941), DSC and bar; Capt RN, Singapore Pilot Assoc 1928–39, served WW I (despatches) and WW II, Sr Br Naval Offr Azores 1944–45; *b* 18 Aug 1891; *m* 1st 11 Jan 1916 (*divorce* 1926) Lilly (*d* 1966), dau of Alexander Moffatt, of Arnotdale, Falkirk, Sheriff Substitute Stirlingshire, and had:

1c +Anthony Lawrence, OBE, DL (Beds 1987) [Col Anthony King-Harman OBE DL, Ouse Manor, Sharnbrook, Beds, MK44 1PG]; Col RA WW II (despatches), Internat Staff NATO, OStJ 1987; *b* 26 Feb 1918; *educ* Wellington; *m* 21 Dec 1944 *Jeanette Stella (*née* Dunkerley), step-dau of F C Guthrie, of Bicknoller, Somerset, and has:

1d +Anthony William; Lt RHA, Col RA; *b* 2 May 1946; *educ* Wellington and RMAS; *m* 1991 *Judith Serena, dau of John Richard Rumsey and formerly w of Robert Hugh Buxton (*see* BUXTON, Bt)

2d +Michael Charles [Michael King-Harman Esq, PO Box 14, Mahé, Seychelles]; *b* 10 Aug 1947; *educ* Wellington and William and Mary Coll Virginia (BA, AB (Econ), MBA) and U of Virginia (MBA); dir

Hunt Deltel & Co, Seychelles; has by *Barbara Elizabeth, dau of Kenneth Veasey Lightfoot, of NZ:
1e *Charles; *b* 1988
2e *Jasper; *b* 1991
1e *Alize (triplet); *b* 1988
2e *Bibette; *b* 1988
2b (cont.) Capt Robert King-Harman *m* 2nd 22 April 1927 Elizabeth Lilian (*d* 1974), formerly w of — Bull and dau of William James Davis, of Junee Reefs, Sydney, NSW; *m* 3rd 1975 Eva Mary (*d* 1987), dau of Archdale Stuart Palmer, and *d* 30 May 1978
1b Geraldine; *b* 15 April 1893; *d* unm 10 March 1973
1a Frances Elizabeth; *m* 19 July 1877 Lt-Col Guy Newcomen Atkinson (*d* 10 Feb 1890), of Cangort, and *d* 29 March 1929, having had issue
2a Emily; *d* 25 Oct 1848
(1) Jane; *m* 19 July 1824 Anthony Lefroy, LLD (*d* 11 Jan 1890), MP U of Dublin, of Carriglass Manor, Co Longford, and *d* 1 Dec 1868
(2) Caroline; *m* 23 March 1827 Sir Robert Gore-Booth, 4th Bt (*qv*), and *d* 13 Jan 1828
(3) Frances; *m* 8 April 1834 Rt Rev Charles Leslie (*m* 2nd his w's cousin Louisa Mary, dau of Hon Sir Henry King, KCB, and *d* 8 July 1870), Bp Kilmore, and *d* 28 July 1835
(4) Louisa; *d* unm 1831
3 Henry (Sir), KCB; Lt-Gen; *m* 1st 1802 Mary (*d* 26 May 1821), est dau of Very Rev Hon John Hewitt (*see* LIFFORD, V); *m* 2nd 28 Feb 1832 Catherine (*d* 7 May 1847), widow of J Richardson and dau of Rev Edward Philips, and *d* 26 Nov 1839, having had by his 1st w, with other issue:
(1) John Wingfield; Army Capt; *b* 5 April 1807; *m* 1st 14 June 1831 Alicia (*d* 14 Sept 1855), dau of Chidley Coote, of Mount Coote, and had, with other issue:
1a Henry Edward; Speaker Legislative Assembly Qld; *b* 9 June 1832; *m* 1 June 1858 Harriette (*d* 1925), dau of J A Armstrong, and *d* 5 Feb 1910, having had:
1b Henry Edward Wingfield; *b* 4 Aug 1869; *d* 1916
2b John Robert FitzGerald; *b* 27 Jan 1871; *d* March 1911
3b Wyndham Guy FitzGerald; *b* 23 Sept 1872
4b Gerald Coote; *d* 9 May 1874
5b Maurice James; *b* 31 Jan 1879; *d* 1879
1b Alicia Caroline; *m* 1886 Edward Hubert Waring, of Qld, and *d* 1925, leaving issue
2b Katherine Anne; *m* 1885 William Howe Irving, Collector Customs Qld, and had issue
3b Ethel Coote; *m* 1901 George Forrest, of Qld, and has issue
2a John Robert; Col RA; *b* 13 Nov 1837; *m* 26 Sept 1872 Kate Elizabeth (*d* 19 April 1939), dau of Gen John Henry Francklyn, CB, and *d* 25 Oct 1898, having had:
1b Robert Alan; *b* 1874; *d* unm 9 Nov 1904
2b Robert Guy Cyril; Capt Roy Australian Artillery Boer War 1899–1902 (Queen's and King's medals); *b* 1 April 1877; *m* 1st 12 Dec 1905 Albertina Millicent, dau of Philip John Steele, of Melbourne, and had:
1c *Millicent Francklyn [Mrs William Thompson, 22 Millicent Ave, Toorak, Australia 3142]; *b* 16 Jan 1907; *m* 1st 13 Oct 1928 Archibald Jennings Ironside (*d* 1941), of Lawrence Kirk, Scotland; *m* 2nd 1942 *William Bethel Thompson (*d* 1945), S/Ldr RAAF, and by her 1st husb has:
1d *Philip Norman Jennings; *b* 1931; *m* 1960 *Dorothy Rosemary Joy, dau of Alan Bell, of Melbourne, and has:
1e *Andrew Philip; *b* 1962
2e *Alan Francklyn; *b* 1964
1d *Margaret Joan Francklyn; *b* 1929
2b (cont.) Robert King *m* 2nd 1919 Mary Catherine, dau of John Robert Russel, of Brackley, and *d* 22 April 1940
3b John Francklyn; Col RAIC, served NWF India 1908 (medal with clasp) and WW I Gallipoli, Egypt and Flanders (despatches, 1914–15 Star, two medals); *b* 29 Nov 1882; *m* 7 Jan 1914 Mary Elspeth, dau of Edwin Hellard, and *d* 19–, having had:
1c *Phyllis Mary [Miss Phyllis King, 21 Chapman Terrace, Kingscote, S Australia 5223]; *b* 22 Nov 1914
2c Joan Elspeth; *b* 12 Dec 1919; *d* 2 Sept 1928
1b Katherine Maud; *b* 18 Aug 1878; *d* 29 April 1879
(1) (cont.) John King *m* 2nd 29 Sept 1857 Avarina Jane, dau of Capt John Lawson, and *d* 19 Nov 1868, having by her had:
3a Charles Thomas; *b* 31 Aug 1858; *m* 1858 Rose, dau of Capt Sandes, and *dsp* 25 Nov 1887
4a St George Webber; *b* 1 June 1862
5a Gerald FitzGerald; *b* 14 July 1864; *m* 1885 Dora (*d* 29 Aug 1952), dau of Capt Charles Launcelot Sandes, of Carrigafoyle Castle, Co Kerry, and Bayview House, Dublin, and *d* 1905, leaving:
1b Charles Gerald Wingfield; WW I as Lt Canadian Forces (wounded); *b* 1886; *m* 1st 1912 Annabell Mae Brown (*d* 1914); *m* 2nd 1915 Lena Mae Stewart (*d* 1934); *m* 3rd Mamie Greene Slusser (*d* 1990), of Augusta, Ga., and *d* 1972, having by his 2nd w had:
1c Stewart Gerald Wingfield; WW II in US Field Artillery; *b* 1916; *m* 1943 Audrey Elaine, dau of Herald F Sample, of N Tonawanda, NY, and was *ka* 1945
2c +(John Charles) Alwyn Hallowes [Lt-Col Alwyn King, 121 S Hanover St, Carlisle, PA 17013, USA]; BEng (McGill 1948), MS (Columbia 1958), DSc (Stuttgart 1960), Lt-Col US Army Engr Res WW II; *b* 13 May 1920; *m* 1st 1942 Mary Parker, dau of Herbert Daniel Casey, of Ozark, Ala., and has:
1d *Judy Marilyn; *b* 1943; *m* *Gerald Heath
2c (cont.) Lt-Col King *m* 2nd 1952 Grace Margaret Stanley (*d* 1988), Capt USWAC (Res), and by her has:
2d *Carolyn Joan; *b* 1957
1c *Elizabeth Avarina Joan [Mrs Duane Caldwell, 827 Pioneer Dve, N Tonawanda, NY, USA]; *b* 1926; *m* 28 June 1952 *Duane Thomas Caldwell, s of Melvin Russell Caldwell, of Tonawanda, and has:
1d *Stewart Duane Sandes; *b* 10 Aug 1953; *m* 1982 *Johanna Grace Howard and has:
1e *Mary Rebecca Christine; *b* 1985
2e *Kathleen Avarina Suzanne; *b* 1989
1d *Deborah Grace; *b* 1955; has:
1e *Megan Avarina-Mae CALDWELL; *b* 1978
2d *Gail Heather; *b* 1963; *m* 1982 *David Spencer Barone, Jr, and has:
1e *David Spencer, III; *b* 1986
1e *Lisa Ann; *b* 1985
2e *Christina Marie; *b* 1988
2b John Wingfield; *b* 1891; *m* 1916 Alice Mary Prefontaine (*d* 1974), of Vancouver, and *d* 1975, having had:
1c +Gerald Rene Wingfield [Maj Gerald King, C-10 Harding Rd, RR1 Powell River, BC, Canada]; S/Ldr RCAF, Maj Canadian Armed Forces (War Medal 1939–45), Airways Inspr Min Tport; *b* 1924; *m* 1st 1958 (*divorce* 1972) Sonja Lanjin, F/O RCAF, of Belgrade; *m* 2nd 1987 *Grace Marion Sayce
2c +John Francis Wingfield; *b* 1927
1b Avarina Rose; *b* 1888; *m* 1911 Marius Anné Diemont, MD (*d* 1 Sept 1951), and *d* Sept 1954, leaving issue
6a Percy Wingfield; *b* 7 July 1868; *m* 18– Mary Cecelia Foley and *d* 27 Nov 1930, leaving:
1b John Wingfield; *b* 9 May 1899; *m* 1st 1922 Margaret Fraser (*d* 1941), dau of Isaac Van Cleef, of NJ, and had:
1c *Jean Margaret [Mrs Raymond Connelly, Rt 5 Box 100, Troutville, VA 24175, USA]; *b* 1923; *m* 1944 *Raymond A Connelly and has:
1d *Robert [Mr Robert Connelly, 26 Longwood Rd, Austin, TX 78737, USA]; *b* 1948; *m* 1st 1969 Jacqueline Marie Schlickenmaier; *m* 2nd 1982 *Jane Heffington and by his 1st w has:
1e *Shane Jason; *b* 1974
2e *Stacy Michael (twin); *b* 1974
1e *Heather Janelle; *b* 1972
1d *Carol [Mrs George Belanger, 6359 Christie Lane, Roanoke, VA 24018, USA]; *b* 1945; *m* 1st 1963 *D R Robles and has:
1e *Kateri Jean Louise [Mrs Michael Joles, 3666 Sylvan Lane, Virginia Beach, VA 23456, USA]; *b* 1965; *m* 1988 *Michael Joles and has:
1f *Sydney Elaine; *b* 1991
1d (cont.) Mrs Robles *m* 2nd 1973 *George Michael Belanger and by him has:
1e *Victoria Elizabeth Caroline; *b* 1977
2c Elizabeth K
1b (cont.) John King *m* 2nd 1944 Alice M (*d* 1989), dau of John Malone, of Philadelphia, and *d* 14 Jan 1963, having by her had:
3c *Patricia Barry [Miss Patricia King, 35 Plum St, Vincentown, NJ 08088, USA]; *b* 1950
2b James FitzGerald; *b* 5 July 1911; *m* 19– — and *d* 1976, leaving two sons (James; John) and a dau (Eileen)
1b Evarina Tennison Ambrosia; *b* 11 May 1901; *m* 19–
2b Mary Cecelia; *b* 10 March 1903; *m* 19–
3b Ida Gertrude; *b* 25 May 1907; *m* 19–
1a Avarina Ambrosie Tenison; *m* 7 Nov 1891 Blackwood Hallowes (*d* 1920) and *d* 1948
2a Margaret Alice; *m* 1895 Arthur Lawler and had issue
3a Beatrice Wingfield; *m* 4 Jan 1902 Charles Burnett-Scott, MD
4a Violet Maud; *m* 1st 4 June 1888 Shirley Roberts, MRCS (*d* 16 Feb 1892); *m* 2nd 22 Feb 1896 Jean Psomades (*d* 15 Nov 1932) and *d* 11 May 1937
5a Ida Gertrude; *m* 1st Jan 1899 Charles Gamble and had issue; *m* 2nd 2 June 1906 John Harrison Middleton, BA (*d* 26 March 1926), and had further issue
(2) Edward Richard; Col 36th Regt; *b* 9 Aug 1808; *m* 1st 1841 Mary (*d* 1857), dau of William Thorn; *m* 2nd 13 July 1869 Mary Ann Bertie (*m* 2nd Rev Elborough Woodcock, MA), dau of Maj Thomas Leech Galloway, 10th Regt, and *d* 16 Dec 1879, having by his 1st w had:
1a Albert Edward William; *b* 12 May 1844; *d* unm
2a John Henry Richard; *b* 31 Oct 1848
3a Robert Ambrose Cecil; Lt-Col RA; *b* 12 March 1852; *m* 1st 10 Dec 1885 Bessie (*dsp* 1892), widow of Maj J L Bell, RA, and dau of Rev J Macredy, DD, Rector Killallan, Co Galway; *m* 2nd 1893 Lillian Walters, dau of Rochfort Davies, and *d* 6 Dec 1897, having by her had:
1b Eileen Mary Fredeswede; *b* 1894
2b Sybil Doreen; *b* 1896
1a Louisa Mary Harriet; *m* 13 Sept 1865 Lt-Col Robert William Francis Holt, RMLI, of Southsea, and *d* 14 April 1915, leaving issue
2a Sidney Jane Gower; *m* 7 Nov 1877 Rev A L Mason, Rector Whitton, Tenbury, and *d* 8 April 1925, leaving issue
4 Richard FitzGerald (Rev); MA Oxon; Vicar Gt Chesterford, Essex, Capt 6th Dragoon Gds; *b* 8 April 1779; *m* 6 Jan 1800 Williamina (*d* 1 Feb 1837), dau of William Ross of Shandwick, Ross-shire, and *d* 22 Sept 1856, leaving, with other issue:
(1) Robert Henry (Rev); Rector Little Glemhall, and Bromeswell, Suffolk; *b* 31 May 1804; *m* 4 Nov 1835 Caroline (*d* 31 Jan 1860), yst dau of Thomas Smith, and *d* 31 July 1870, having had a s and four daus
(2) Richard FitzGerald; Lt RN; *b* 27 Jan 1810; *d* unm 21 Aug 1840
(3) George; Maj-Gen 13th Regt; *b* 28 March 1812; *m* 15 Oct 1836 Catherine (*d* 22 Sept 1854), dau of Mark Sheridan, and *d* 11 March 1868, leaving:

1a Richard FitzGerald; 13th Foot; *d* 10 Jan 1875

2a Edward Sheridan; Capt 37th Regt; *b* 4 Dec 1848; *m* 1st 30 July 1878 Mary Elizabeth (*d* 21 Sept 1920), widow of H Washbourne and dau of John Woodhams; *m* 2nd 25 Jan 1922 Helena (*d* 18 Jan 1958), dau of Gregory Bird, and *d* 25 July 1924, having by his 1st w had:

1b Edward John FitzGerald; Lt Wilts Regt; *b* 11 Jan 1881; *d* unm 31 Aug 1906

1b Mary Williamina Woodhams; *b* 27 Dec 1879, *d* 9 Sept 1880

1a Katherine; *b* 11 Feb 1839; *m* 1 June 1871, as his 2nd w, James Clark (*see* CLARK, Bt, of Dunlambert), and *d* 14 April 1915, leaving issue

2a Williamina Alexandria Jane; RRC, Egyptian War medal and bronze star; *b* 19 Dec 1845; *d* unm 11 March 1927

5 James William; R-Adml; *m* 28 Nov 1815 Caroline (*d* 16 March 1862), dau of Most Rev Euseby Cleaver, DD, Archbp Dublin, and *d* 14 Feb 1848, having had, with other issue:

(1) Robert William; *m* 1st 4 Sept 1848 Amelia Mary (*d* 25 Nov 1873), widow of Hon Henry Frederick Hartstronge Pery (*see* LIMERICK, E) and 2nd dau of V-Adml Rowland Money, CB; *m* 2nd 7 Jan 1874 Mary Isabella, only dau of Edward de Vismes, of Newport, Glos, and *dsp* 24 Nov 1881

(1) Catherine; *m* 16 Sept 1847 Rev William Pennefather, s of Richard Pennefather, Baron Exchequer Ireland, and *d* 12 Jan 1893

The 5th EARL's cousin,

ROBERT KING, **6th Earl of Kingston** and **2nd Viscount Lorton** (as which *s* f 20 Nov 1854); *b* 17 July 1804; MP Roscommon 1826–30; *m* 7 Dec 1829 Anne (*d* 14 June 1883), dau of Sir Robert Newcomen Gore-Booth, 3rd Bt (*qv*), and *d* 16 Oct 1869, leaving:

1 ROBERT EDWARD KING, **7th Earl of Kingston**; *b* 18 Oct 1831; *m* 18 July 1854 Hon Augusta Chichester (*m* 2nd 14 Nov 1872 Alfred Henry Caulfeild (*see* CHARLEMONT, V) and *d* 1 April 1873), dau of 1st Baron Templemore (*see* DONEGALL, M), and *dspm* 21 June 1871, leaving:

(1) Blanche Sybil; *m* 1st 13 April 1882 Hon Lyonel Plantagenet Tollemache, est s of 2nd Baron Tollemache (*qv*), and had issue; *m* 2nd 11 Nov 1903 Granville Landsborough Findlay, MB, ChB, of Maidenhead, and *d* 28 May 1923

2 HENRY ERNEST NEWCOMEN KING later KING-TENISON (roy licence 10 March 1883), **8th Earl of Kingston**; *b* 31 July 1848; *educ* Rugby; rep I peer 1887–96, Ld Lt Co Roscommon 1888–96, Lt-Col 5th Bn Connaught Rangers; *m* 23 Jan 1872 Florence Margaret Christine (*d* 18 Oct 1907), dau and coheir of Lt-Col Edward King-Tenison (*see* LICHFIELD, E), and had:

(1) Edward, *Viscount Kingsborough*; *b* 9 and *d* 21 June 1873

(2) HENRY EDWYN, **9th Earl**

(3) Edmund; *b* and *d* 7 April 1876

(1) Edith Charlotte Harriett; *b* 7 Oct 1878; *m* 11 Sept 1907 Col George Ivor Poer Power O'Shee, Leinster Regt (*d* 27 Feb 1939), s of Nicholas Richard Power O'Shee, of Gardenmorris, Co Waterford, and *d* 20 April 1958, leaving issue

1 Frances Isabella Anna; *m* 30 July 1862 Joseph William Warburton, FO, s of the Dean of Elphin, and *d* 8 Oct 1890, leaving issue

The 8th EARL *d* 13 Jan 1896; his only surv son,

HENRY EDWYN KING-TENISON, **9th Earl of Kingston**, DL (Co Roscommon); *b* 19 Sept 1874; *educ* Eton; Capt Irish Gds, Capt 5th Bn Connaught Rangers, Boer War 1900 and 1902 and WW I (wounded); *m* 3 Feb 1897 Ethel Lisette (*d* 18 April 1949), dau of Sir Andrew Barclay Walker, 1st Bt of Gateacre (*see* 1959 edn), and had:

1 ROBERT HENRY ETHELBERT, **10th Earl**

1 Sheelah Florence Lisette; *b* 15 April 1900; *m* 14 July 1923 Cdr Thomas Cleveland Greenway, RN (*d* 19 Sept 1959), only s of Col Cleveland Edmund Greenway, King's Regt, of S Kensington, by Maud Mary, yr dau of Thomas Hardcastle Sykes, DL, JP, of Cringle Ho, Cheadle, Cheshire, and had issue

2 Brigid Honor; *b* 20 Sept 1902; *d* 25 Oct 1991

3 Doreen Kara; *b* 27 Feb 1907; *d* 28 June 1920

The 9th EARL *d* 11 Jan 1946; his only son,

ROBERT HENRY ETHELBERT KING-TENISON, **10th Earl of Kingston**; *b* 27 Nov 1897; *educ* Eton and RMC Sandhurst; Lt RSG; *m* 1st 24 Dec 1937 (*divorce* 1947) Gwyneth Joan (*m* 2nd 1951 Brig E M Tyler, DSO, MC, RA; *m* 3rd 1963 Robert Woodford), dau of William Howard Evans, of Tenby, Pembs, and had:

1 BARCLAY ROBERT EDWIN KING-TENISON, **11th and present Earl of Kingston**

1 *Kara Virginia Louisa; *b* 24 Jan 1938; *m* 20 June 1964 (*divorce* 1974) Anthony John Conroy Hawks, MB, BS (Lond), DCH, only s of F/Lt Peter Augustus Hawks, RAF, of Salisbury, and has:

(1) *Honor Louise; *b* 27 July 1966

The **10th Earl** *m* 2nd 29 May 1947 Jean Sinclair (*m* 2nd 1953 Cecil Geoffrey Monson (*d* 1974), s of Frederick John Monson, of Castle Moate, Cloghran, Co Dublin, and *d* 1983), dau of James Lascelles Alexander, JP, of Orkney and Aberdeen, and *d* 17 July 1948

KINLOCH of Gilmerton

Arms: Az. a boar's head erased between three mascles or. **Crest:** An eagle rising ppr. **Motto:** *Altius tendo* ('I aspire higher'). **Creation:** Bt. (NS) 16 Sept 1686.

SIR DAVID KINLOCH, 13TH BT, of Gilmerton [Sir David Kinloch Bt, Gilmerton House, N Berwick, E Lothian EH39 5LQ]; *b* 5 Aug 1951; *s* f 1982; *educ* Gordonstoun; *m* 1st 1976 (*divorce* 1986) Susan, dau of Arthur Middlewood, of North Side Farm, Kilham, and has:

1 +ALEXANDER; *b* 31 May 1978

1 *Alice; *b* 1976

Sir DAVID *m* 2nd 1987 *Maureen, dau of Robert Carswell, and by her has:

2 +Christopher Robert; *b* 1988

3 +Matthew Carswell; *b* 1990

Lineage: ANDREW KINLOCH; *d* 1685, leaving:

Sir Francis Kinloch, 1st Bt (NS), so *cr* 16 Sept 1686, of Gilmerton, and of Athelstanford and Markle, Haddingtonshire; MP Co Edinburgh 1678, Ld Provost Edinburgh; *m* Magdalen McMath (*d* 16 Nov 1664), of Newbyres, and was *bur* 17 Dec 1691, leaving, with at least one dau (Anne, *m* as his 1st w Gideon Scott of Highchester; *see* POLWARTH, L), an est s:

Sir Francis Kinloch, 2nd Bt; *m c* 1676 Mary Leslie (*m* 2nd 18 Jan 1702 Sir Alexander Ogilvie, 1st Bt, of Forglen, and *d* 24 March 1748), 2nd dau of 1st Lord Newark (*see* ROTHES, E), and was *bur* 11 Sept 1699, having had:

Sir Francis Kinloch, 3rd Bt; *b* 23 June 1676; *m c* 1705 Mary (*d* 2 April 1749), sis of Sir James Rochead, 1st Bt, of Innerleith, and *d* 2 March 1747, having had:

1 **Sir James Kinloch, 4th Bt**; *bapt* 8 Aug 1705; *m* April 1730 — and *d* 25 March 1778

2 DAVID (Sir), **5th Bt**

3 Alexander KINLOCH later ROCHEAD of Innerleith (on inheriting estates of his maternal gf); *m* 4 April 1750 Janet (*d* 1813), dau of John Watson, of Muirhouse, Edinburgh, and *d* 11 May 1755, leaving:

(1) James; *m* Susan Wood and had:

1a James; *b* 1809; *m* 1st 1830 Mary Anne (*d* 1831), dau of Baron Dankelman, of Mayenne, Saxony, and had:

1b Charles Frederick James Everard William George; *b* 25 Jan 1831; *m* 21 May 1852 Mathilde (*m* 2nd 14 Dec 1865 Baron von Busshe and *d* 1892), dau of Peter Heinrich de Salviati, and *d* 19 Jan 1864, leaving:

1c James; *b* 30 Oct 1853; *educ* Trin Coll Oxford (BA); *m* 6 March 1878 Marie (*d* 5 Aug 1922), dau of Baron Feodor von Grote, and *d* 8 Aug 1908, having had:

1d Charles Alexander Julius William David; *b* 22 Dec 1878; *d* unm 18 April 1902

2d Colin William Hilmar Otto Von ROCHEAD; *b* 8 Nov 1881; *m* 1st 18 Aug 1911 Elisabeth (*d* 12 July 1935), dau of Ernst von Schröder; *m* 2nd 30 Nov 1942 Catherine Jung (*d* 1959) and *d* 1945, leaving by his 1st w:

1e *Elisabeth Maria Olga Harriet Ernestine; *b* 10 July 1912; *m* 31 April 1936 Col Joachim von Sametzki (*d* 6 Feb 1946)

1d Elisabeth Emma Natalie Anna; *m* 21 Sept 1898 Kammerherr Georg von Behr Negendanck (*d* 7 June 1945), s of Ulrich Adolf Jurgen August von Behr Negendanck, of Mecklenburg, and *d* 1964, leaving issue

1a (cont.) James Rochead of Innerleith *m* 2nd 31 Jan 1837 Sarah Catherine (*m* 2nd 1843 John Stewart Wood and *d* 1911), dau of Capt William Patterson, RN, and *d* 3 March 1840, having by her had:

1b Constance Isabella; *m* 3 July 1860 Maj-Gen David Briggs (*d* 5 April 1908), of Straithairly, Fife, and *d* 11 June 1918

1 Magdalen; *m* J Wilkie, of Foulden

2 Janet; *m* Charles Brown, of Coulstoun, Ld of Session

Sir JAMES's bro,

Sir David Kinloch, 5th Bt; *b c* 1710; *m* 16 Jan 1746 Harriet (*d* 29 July 1757), dau of Sir Archibald Cockburn, and *d* 18 Feb 1795, having had, with other issue:

1 **Sir Francis Kinloch, 6th Bt**; *b* 1747; *d* unm 16 April 1795

2 **Sir Archibald Gordon Kinloch, 7th Bt**; *d* unm 1800

3 ALEXANDER (Sir), **8th Bt**

1 Mary; *m* 1775 Sir Thomas Ashe, MP Ashfield, Co Meath, and had issue

2 Harriet; *m* 1781 Sir Foster Cunliffe, 3rd Bt, of Acton Park (*qv*), and *d* 9 Sept 1830, leaving issue

Sir ARCHIBALD's bro,

Sir Alexander Kinloch, 8th Bt; *m* 20 June 1801 Isabella (*d* 10 March 1861), dau and coheir of John Stowe, of Newton, Lincs, and *d* 12 Feb 1813, having had, with a dau (Harriet, *m* 29 Aug 1833 Lord Thomas Hay (*see* TWEEDDALE, M) and *d* 24 Jan 1891):

Sir David Kinloch, 9th Bt; *b* 1 Sept 1805; *m* 5 June 1829 Eleanor Hyndford (*d* 15 Oct 1849), est dau of Sir Thomas Gibson-Carmichael, 7th Bt (*see* GIBSON-GRAIG-CARMICHAEL, Bt), and *d* 23 Feb 1879, having had:

1 ALEXANDER (Sir), **10th Bt**

1 Isabella Anne; *m* 2 July 1863 Harington Balfour, ICS (*d* 1910), and *d* 14 April 1923, having had issue (*see* BALFOUR OF INCHRYE, B)

2 Eleanor Janet; *d* unm 13 Aug 1900

3 Harriett; *m* 25 April 1872 Adml Sir Henry Fairfax, KCB (*d* 20 March 1900), yst s of Sir Henry Fairfax, 1st Bt (*see* RAMSAY-FAIRFAX-LUCY, Bt), and *dsp* 17 Sept 1925

Sir DAVID's only son,

Sir Alexander Kinloch, 10th Bt, JP, DL Haddington; *b* 1 Feb 1830; Capt Gren Gds Crimea 1854–55; *m* 12 Aug 1852 Lucy Charlotte (*d* 14 Nov 1903), est dau of Sir Ralph Anstruther, 4th Bt, of Balcaskie (*qv*), and *d* 11 March 1912, having had:

1 DAVID ALEXANDER (Sir), **11th Bt**

2 Henry Anstruther; *b* 7 Nov 1859; Maj KRRC; *m* 29 Aug 1891 Jane Agnes Maud (*m* 2nd 18 July 1905 Walter Traversari Legge (*see* DARTMOUTH, E), and *d* 19 Oct 1953), dau of Sir Reginald Robert Bruce Guinness (*see* GUINNESS, Bt), and *d* 20 Feb 1903, leaving:

(1) Harriet Patricia Constance; *m* 14 April 1917 Capt James Alexander Purdey (*d* 25 July 1963), 21st Lancers, and *d* 26 Dec 1947, leaving issue

3 Francis, JP E Lothian; *b* 6 Oct 1863; *educ* New Coll Oxford (BA), LLB Edinburgh; Advocate; *m* 25 March 1896 Marion Eva, dau of Charles Nairne Marshall, of Curriehill, NZ, and *d* 18 May 1916, having had:

(1) Frederick Alexander; *b* 23 Nov 1901

(2) John Marshall; *b* 13 Jan; *d* 2 May 1908

(1) Marjorie Catherine; *m* 1st 1919 — Allan, of Vancouver, BC, and had issue; *m* 2nd 6 May 1932 Maj Cecil Anderson Boyd, MC, MD (*d* 27 March 1942), and had further issue (*see* BOYD, Bt)

(2) Lucy Margaret; *b* 1899

(3) Eleanor Mary; *b* 2 Jan; *d* 30 May 1905

(4) Marion Amelia; *m* 1931 Horace Ward Collings Sussex

1 Eleanor Ann; *d* 24 May 1925

2 Mary Anna; *m* 6 Jan 1887 Lothar Henry George de Bunsen and *d* 25 Feb 1898, having had issue

Sir ALEXANDER's est son,

Sir David Alexander Kinloch, 11th Bt, CB, MVO, JP, DL; *b* 20 Feb 1856; *educ* Univ Coll Oxford (BA); Lt Col and Brevet Col cmdg 1st Bn Gren Gds, Hon Brig-Gen 1917, 3rd Bn Gren Gds, Boer War (despatches, medal with three clasps), cmded 6th London Inf Bde TF 1908–12 and 70th Inf Bde WW I (despatches), memb Roy Co Archers; dir Leslie and Godwin, insur brokers; *m* 25 Nov 1897 Elinor Lucy (*d* 22 Nov 1943), yst dau of Col William Bromley Davenport, MP, of Capesthorne, Cheshire, and *d* 27 Oct 1944, having had:

1 ALEXANDER DAVENPORT (Sir), **12th Bt**

1 Jean Mary; *m* April 1919 6th Baron Grantley (*qv*) and *d* 16 Jan 1945, having had issue

2 Katherine Hariot; *m* 18 Oct 1927 6th Baron Brownlow (*qv*) and *d* 27 Nov 1952, leaving issue

Sir DAVID's only son,

Sir Alexander Davenport Kinloch, 12th Bt; *b* 17 Sept 1902; *educ* Eton; Maj Gren Gds WW II, memb Roy Co Archers; *m* 1st 10 Sept 1929 (*divorce* 1945) Alexandra, dau of Frederick Y Dalziel, of New York, and had:

1 *Emily Lucy [The Hon Mrs Hugh Astor, Folly Farm, Sulhamstead, Berks RG7 4DF; 79 Ashley Gdns, Thirleby Rd, London SW1P 1HG]; *b* 27 Aug 1930; *m* 8 Nov 1950 *Hon Hugh Waldorf Astor and has issue (*see* ASTOR OF HEVER, B)

2 *Jean Alexandra; *b* 7 Aug 1934

Sir Alexander *m* 2nd 26 Nov 1946 (*divorce* 1965) Hilda Anna (*d* 1986), dau of Thomas Walker, of Edinburgh, and by her had:

1 Francis; *m* 25 May 1968 Lorna Mary, er dau of David Buchanan, of Dundarroch House, Bridge of Weir, Renfrewshire

2 Sir DAVID KINLOCH, **13th and present Bt**

3 *Victoria [Mrs Martin Teale, 99 White Lion Rd, Amersham, Bucks]; *b* 21 Dec 1947; *m* 1981 *Martin Teale

4 *Harriet [Mrs Ian Thomson, The Kennels, W Saltoun, by Pencaitland, E Lothian]; *b* 14 Oct 1949; *educ* Oxenfoord Castle Sch; *m* 1st 14 Oct 1967 (*divorce* 1973) Colin John Weddell, of E Lothian; *m* 2nd 1988 *Ian Napier Thomson and by her 1st husb has:

(1) *Jennifer Katherine Graham; *b* 27 April 1968

5 *Ann (twin with David); *b* 5 Aug 1951; *m* 1984 *George Kenneth Banks and has:

(1) *Justin Christopher; *b* 1985

Sir Alexander *m* 3rd 2 June 1965 *Ann Maud [Ann Lady Kinloch, Greenacre, 87 Hepburn Gdns, St Andrews, Fife KY16 9LT], dau of G/Capt Frank Leslie White, of London, and *d* 22 Nov 1982, having by her had:

3 +James Alexander; *b* 18 Sept 1967

KINLOCH of Kinloch

Arms: Quarterly, 1st grand quarter, azure a boar's head erased between three mascles or, a crescent of the second in chief for difference (for KINLOCH); 2nd quarter, gules a chevron embattled between three crescents argent (for OLIPHANT); 3rd grand quarter, per fess argent and sable a chevron between three cinquefoils counterchanged (for BALNEAVIS); 4th grand quarter, counter-quartered, 1st, gules a broken spear and a standard saltireways argent, the last charged with a cross of the field and fringed or; 2nd, azure a cat salient argent; 3rd, argent on a saltire sable nine mascles of the first, a bordure azure; 4th, or three bars wavy gules, each charged with an escallop of the field (all for SMYTH). **Crest:** A young eagle perched, looking up to the sun in his splendour, all proper. **Motto:** *Non degener* ('Not degenerate'). **Creation:** Bt. (UK) 16 April 1873.

SIR DAVID OLIPHANT KINLOCH, 5TH BT, of Kinloch, Co Perth [Sir David Kinloch Bt, House of Aldie, Fossoway, Kinross, KY13 7QH; 29 Walpole St, London SW3 4QS]; *b* 15 Jan 1942; *s f* 1992; *educ* Charterhouse; chartered accountant, MICA Scotland, dir Caledonia Investments plc 1988–; *m* 1st 27 Jan 1968 (*divorce* 1979) Susan Minette, yst dau of Maj-Gen Robert Elliott Urquhart, CB, DSO, of Gaidrew, by Drymen, Stirlingshire, and has:

1 *Katherine Cecilia; *b* 8 March 1972

2 *Emily Nicole; *b* 18 Oct 1974

3 *Nicola Marjorie; *b* 3 Nov 1976

Sir DAVID *m* 2nd 1983 *Sabine, only dau of Philippe de Loës, of Geneva, and by her has:

1 +ALEXANDER PETER; *b* 30 June 1986

4 *Sophie; *b* 20 April 1994

Lineage: GEORGE KINLOCH of that Ilk and of Cruivie, Fife, Ch of the Kinlochs (whose name derives from the head of Rossie Loch, Fife, where the family first held land in Scotland at least as early as 1210); living 1488–1542; had, with other sons, including an est (Sir Alexander, sold the Kinloch estate to Balfour of Balgarvie, *dspm*):

DAVID KINLOCH; seaman; acquired land in Perthshire; *d* between 1542 and 1567, leaving, with other issue:

DAVID KINLOCH; *b* 1560; physician and poet; acquired among other lands Over Balmyle, Strathmore, Perthshire, which with others there was erected into the Barony of Kinloch so that he held as Kinloch of that Ilk, also those of Aberbothrie, which were erected into a territorial Barony by charter of JAMES VI (and I) 1616; *m* Grizel, dau of Hay of Gourdie, a branch of the HAYs of Erroll (*see* ERROLL, E), and *d* 1617, having had, with another s (John, ancestor of the KINLOCHs of Gourdie) and a dau (Jean, *m* Thomas Fotheringham of Powrie):

JAMES KINLOCH; *m* a dau of Graham of Fintry (later called Linlathen), Forfarshire, and had:

1 Sir DAVID KINLOCH, 1st Bt (NS), so *cr* 20 July 1685; *m* 1st Elizabeth (*dsp*), only child of David Bethune (2nd s of John Bethure of Balfour, Fife); *m* 2nd his cousin Margaret Graham, dau of Graham of Fintry, by whom he had, with a yr s (William):

(1) Sir JAMES KINLOCH, 2nd Bt; *m* Elizabeth, heiress of John Nevay of that Ilk, and *d* 1744, having had, with other issue, including a yr s (William, Consul Aleppo, *d* unm) and two daus (Margaret, *m* Yeaman of Murie, had issue; Jean, *m* Rattray of Rangulzion, had issue; Agnes, *m* Smith of Camno, had issue):

1a Sir JAMES KINLOCH later KINLOCH-NEVAY, 3rd and last Bt, of that Ilk and of Nevay; sentenced to death as Jacobite following 1745 Uprising but escaped to France; later pardoned; the territorial Barony and estate of Kinloch, which (with the btcy) had been forfeited at his attainder, were bought by friends and restored to him; *m* Janet Duff, alleged sis of 1st Earl of Fife (*see* FIFE, D), and had, with other issue, including two daus (Jean, *m* Robert Maclaren, had issue; Mary, *m* John Rankine of Dudhope, had issue):

1b William; lived in England; *m* but *dsp*

2 James, of Kilrie; physician; *m* his cousin Cecilia, dau of Thomas Fotheringham of Powrie, and had:

(1) David, of Kilrie and Logie, Forfarshire

(2) John; physician; ancestor of the KINLOCHs of Kinloch; *m* Jean, est dau of George Oliphant of Clashbennie, and had, with two other sons (*d* young):

1a George Oliphant; sold Clashbennie and bought the Kinloch estate and others from his cousin William, s of the attainted Sir JAMES KINLOCH, 3rd Bt, of the 1685 *cr* (*see above*); *m* Anne, dau of John Balneavis of Carnbaddie, and had, with an er s (John, *dsp* 2 Jan 1789):

1b George; fled to France 1819 to escape an indictment for sedition; MP Dundee 1832; *b c* 1775; *m* his cousin Helen, 3rd dau of John Smyth, of Balhary, and had, with other issue:

1c GEORGE (Sir), **1st Bt**

2a John; acquired property WI; *d* there

1a Cecilia; *m* James Smyth of Balhary and left issue

2a Helen; *m* William Reoch, Edinburgh merchant, and *dsp*

GEORGE KINLOCH *d* 28 March 1833; his son,

Sir George Kinloch, 1st Bt (UK), so *cr* 16 April 1873, JP, DL; advocate; *b* 13 Oct 1800; *m* 21 Oct 1845 Margaret (*d* 15 Feb 1908), only child of George Canning, JP, of Arbroath, Forfar, and had, with other issue:

1 JOHN GEORGE SMYTH (Sir), **2nd Bt**

1 Elena Cecilia Ann; *m* 8 Sept 1866 George Palmer, of Florence, and *d* his widow 17 March 1914, having had issue

2 Margaret Aimée; *m* 29 April 1873 William Joseph Starkey Barber-Starkey (*d* 10 July 1924), barrister, only child of Rev W H Barber, and *d* 21 May 1943, leaving issue

3 Charlotte Isabella Blanche; *m* 28 Nov 1887 Francis H M Wayne, OBE (*d* 16 Dec 1941), est s of Lt-Col H Wayne, of Tickwood Hall, Much Wenlock, Salop, and *d* 22 April 1947, leaving issue

Sir GEORGE *d* 17 June 1881; his est son,

Sir John George Smyth Kinloch, 2nd Bt, JP Perthshire and Forfarshire, DL Perthshire; *b* 8 Jan 1849; *educ* Trin Coll Cambridge (BA); MP Perthshire 1889–1908; *m* 8 Jan 1878 Jessie Montgomerie (*d* 8 Dec 1929), er dau of George Lumsden, JP, of Edinburgh, and had:

1 GEORGE (Sir), **3rd Bt**

2 James; *b* 21 April 1884; *educ* Charterhouse; Capt: Black Watch WW I, RA WW II 1939–42; *m* 19 Aug 1909 Julia Madeline (*d* 4 Sept 1962), yst dau of George William Boase, of Broughty Ferry, Forfarshire, and *d* 25 Oct 1950, leaving:

(1) +Colin David [Colin Kinloch Esq, 26 Curtis Rd, Ashdell Park, Alton, Hants GU34 2SD]; *b* 27 Nov 1918; CEng, MIEE; *m* 3 April 1945 *Gertrude Lilian Mary, dau of E R Bollom, of Hampton Hill, Middx, and has:

1a +Nigel George; *b* 10 Oct 1951; *m* 1976 *Elizabeth Anne, dau of Geoffrey Browning, of Winchester, and has had:

1b +David Geoffrey Ian; *b* 1982

2b James Colin George; *b* 1986, *d* 1987

3b +Andrew Malcolm Robert; *b* 1989

1b *Jennifer Mary Ruth; *b* 1984

2b *Catherine Brenda Anne; *b* 1988

1a *Bridget Eleanor Mary [Mrs Christopher Biggs, 16 Nuneham Sq, Abingdon, Oxon OX14 1EH]; *b* 3 Dec 1948; *m* 1974 *Christopher James Biggs and has:

1b *Patrick Mark James; *b* 1980

1b *Alison Samantha Mary; *b* 1978

2b *Deborah Katharine Louise; *b* 1981

3b *Sarah Elizabeth Helen; *b* 1982

(1) *Sheila Maysie [Mrs Hugh Tyler, Cheverells, Limers Lane, Northam, Devon EX39 2RE]; *b* 23 May 1910; *m* 14 Sept 1933 *Brig Arthur Catchmay Tyler, CBE, MC, DL, Welch Regt, 4th s of Hugh Griffin Tyler, of Cleddon Ho, Trelleck, Mon, and has:

1a *Richard Hugh [Richard Tyler Esq, Sheldon House, Monyash, Derbys], late Capt Roy Regt of Wales; *b* 26 June 1939; *m* 1st 13 July 1963 (*divorce* 1981) Susan Gaynor, only dau of Lt-Col Sam Griffith, OBE, Welch Reg, and has:

1b *Christopher Charles Griffith; *b* 9 May 1965

2b *Nicholas Hugh Griffith; *b* 20 May 1966

1a (cont.) Richard Tyler *m* 2nd 1982 *Beverley Gayle, dau of Arthur Rodgers, OBE, of Kuwait, and by her has:

1b *Caroline Mary; *b* 1984

2b *Eleanor Jane; *b* 1992

2a *Andrew James [Andrew Tyler Esq, 6 Ocean View Rd, Bude, Cornwall EX23 8NJ]; *b* 28 Feb 1950; *m* 1971 *Judith Margaret, dau of Alan Gale, and has:

1b *Alan Hugh; *b* 23 Aug 1982

1b *Helen Louise; *b* 8 Feb 1981

2b *Elizabeth Margaret; *b* 23 Aug 1982

3a *John Philip [John Tyler Esq, 14 Heathview Crescent, Dartford, Kent DA1 2PJ]; *b* 25 Nov 1951; *m* 1973 *Valerie Eileen, dau of R L Luckin, and has:

1b *Christopher Philip; *b* 1978

2b *Edward Charles; *b* 1979

3b *Henry Richard; *b* 1983

1b *Bethia Mary; *b* 1985

1a *Mary Joyce [Mrs Bruce Draper, 25 Odenwald Rd, Eaglemont, Victoria 3084, Australia]; *b* 18 Nov 1941; *m* 31 Dec 1966 *Bruce George Draper, s of J C Draper, of Melbourne, and has:

1b *Jeremy Charles Bruce; *b* 1971

2b *Nicholas James; *b* 1973

1b *Catherine Louise; *b* 5 Aug 1969; *m* 17 Feb 1996 *Wade John Ashley, 2nd s of L W Ashley, of Melbourne

(2) *Elspeth [Mrs Malcolm Wanklyn, Halliwell Nursing Home, Kingswood Rd, Tunbridge Wells, Kent TN2 4UN]; *b* 4 March 1912; *m* 5 May 1938 Lt-Cdr Malcolm David Wanklyn, VC, DSO and two bars, RN (*ka* 14 April 1942), 3rd s of William L Wanklyn, and has:

1a *Ian David Kinloch [Lt-Cdr Ian Wanklyn RN, Ashwick House, Chelmarsh, Bridgnorth, Salop]; *b* 31 Aug 1939; *educ* Stowe and RNC Dartmouth; *m* 1971 *Penelope, est dau of Capt Charles Wickham Malins, DSO, DSC, RN, and has:

1b *Alastair David; *b* 1973

2b *Oliver Charles; *b* 1975

1b *Catriona Louise; *b* 1977

(3) Isla Florence; *b* 16 Feb 1915; *d* 1 Feb 1992

3 David; *b* 20 March 1887; *m* 22 Aug 1921 Winifred, est dau of E A Giles, of Coldstream, Vernon, BC, and *dsp* 18 Oct 1943

1 Ethel Oliphant; *m* 28 Jan 1920 Col James Louis Carmichael, TD (*d* 1953), er s of James Carmichael, of Arthurstone, and *d* 18 Jan 1954, leaving issue

2 Jean Lumsden; *d* unm 13 Jan 1943

3 Marjorie

Sir JOHN *d* 20 May 1910; his est son,

Sir George Kinloch, 3rd Bt, OBE (1918), JP; *b* 1 March 1880; *educ* Trin Coll Cambridge (BA); *m* 22 Nov 1906 Ethel May (*d* 5 Nov 1959), yst dau of Maj James Hawkins, 85th Regt, and had:

1 JOHN (Sir), **4th Bt**

2 Roger Peregrine; *b* 23 Dec 1910; *m* 1937 Sybil (*m* 2nd—), only dau of G R Roebuck, of Sale, Lancs, and *d* 8 Nov 1938

1 *Barbara Cecilia [Mrs Charles Tennant, Cruivie, Rosemount, Blairgowrie, Perths]; *b* 30 Aug 1913; *m* 16 July 1937 Maj Charles Gairdner Dalrymple Tennant (*d* 1991), 2nd s of John Dalrymple Tennant, of Delarne, Rhu, Dunbartonshire, and has:

(1) *Thomas Peregrine; late Lt RN; *b* 2 Jan 1939; *educ* Trin Coll Glenalmond and RNC Dartmouth; *m* 1972 *Finella Susan, dau of Geoffrey Hooper, and has:

1a *Edward Charles; *b* 1978

1a *Emma Clare; *b* 1975

(2) *Edward Kinloch; *b* 11 June 1943; *educ* Trin Coll Glenalmond and McGill U

(1) *Tanera Cecilia [Mrs Michael Averdieck, 5 Rock Terrace, Scotgate, Stamford PE9 2YT]; *b* 27 Nov 1940; *m* 8 Sept 1962 *Michael Charles Averdieck, only s of T U Averdieck, of The Old Court, Hampswaite, Yorks and has:

1a *William John; *b* 26 Sept 1963

2a *Charles Edward; *b* 11 Nov 1965

3a *James Ulric (twin); *b* 11 Nov 1965

(2) *Victoria Margaret [Mrs Peter Duke, Oldtown of Carnaveron, Muir of Foulis, Alford, Aberdeenshire]; *b* 26 Feb 1950; *m* 1976 *Peter Mackenzie Duke and has:

1a *Robert Mackenzie; *b* 1980

1a *Kirstie Mary; *b* 1982

Sir GEORGE *d* 16 March 1948; his er son,

Sir John Kinloch, 4th Bt; *b* 1 Nov 1907; *educ* Charterhouse and Magdalene Coll Cambridge; *m* 1 Sept 1934 Doris Ellaline (*d* 1997), er dau of Charles Joseph Head, of Esher, and *d* 1992, leaving:

1 Sir DAVID OLIPHANT KINLOCH, **5th and present Bt**

1 *Susan Cecilia [Mrs Malcolm Rogers, 11 Warrender Court, North Berwick, E Lothian EH39 4RR]; *b* 6 July 1935; *m* 23 April 1960 *Malcolm Henry Rogers, er s of William Henry Rogers, of Chiswick, and has:

(1) *John Andrew; *b* 24 May 1965

(1) *Wendy Diana; *b* 4 Aug 1962

2 Diana Evelyn; *b* 2 July 1940; *m* 7 May 1960 William Stewart Addis (*d* 1996), 2nd s of Sir William Addis, KBE, CMG, of Frant, and *d* 1996, leaving:

(1) *William Dickon; *b* 19 Feb 1962

(1) *Sarah Diana; *b* 30 Aug 1963

(2) *Madeleine Rosemary; *b* 22 Jan 1968

KINLOSS

Arms: Quarterly, 1st, vert on a cross argent five torteaux (for GRENVILLE); 2nd, paly of six argent and or, a lion rampant regardant sable, armed and langued gules, charged with a cross-crosslet of the 2nd between four quatrefoils of the 3rd (for MORGAN); 3rd, or a pile gules (for CHANDOS); 4th, per fess azure and vair-ancient, three fusils in chief, a bordure or for difference (for FREEMAN); overall, on an escutcheon ensigned with the coronet of a Lord in the Peerage of Scotland for the Lordship of Kinloss, quarterly 1st and 4th, or a saltire gules, on a chief of the last three crescents of the first (for BRUCE of Kinloss); 2nd and 3rd, argent two open crowns in fess gules and a martlet in base azure, on a chief of the last a mullet of the field (for KINLOSS). **Crest:** On a chapeau gules furred ermine a lion passant, tail extended gules, armed and langued azure, supporting with his dexter forepaw a shield emblazoned with the arms of Kinloss (*see* above). **Supporters:** Two savages wreathed about the middle and temples with laurel, supporting in their exterior hands banners floating inwards, the dexter having a staff of these liveries or and azure, surmounted of an abbot's mitre, of the ensigns armorial of the abbot of Kinloss, *viz.*, azure semée of fleurs-de-lys or, an inescutcheon parted per pale dexter bendy of six or and azure within a bordure gules; sinister, argent two open crowns in fess gules and a martlet in base azure, on a chief of the last a mullet of the field; the sinister with a staff of these liveries gules and or, ensigned with the coronet appropriate to a Lordship of Parliament, of the ensigns armorial of Bruce of Kinloss (*see* above). **Mottoes:** 1 (above the crest) *Fuimus* ('We have been'), 2 (on the compartment) *Pro Deo, patria et amicis* ('For God, country and friends'). **Creation:** L. (S) 2 Feb 1601/2.

THE LADY KINLOSS, 12th holder of the title ((Beatrice) Mary Grenville Morgan-Grenville) [The Rt Hon The Lady Kinloss, North View House, Sheriff Hutton, Yorks YO6 1PT]; *b* 18 Aug 1922; *s* grandmother 1944; *m* 29 Aug 1950 Greville Stewart Parker FREEMAN later FREEMAN-GRENVILLE (decree of Lord Lyon King of Arms for self and w 1950), DPhil, BLitt (Oxon), FSA, FRAS, Capt Roy Berks Regt, er s of Rev Ernest Charles Freeman, of Shipton-under-Wychwood, Oxon, and has:

1 +BEVIL DAVID STEWART CHANDOS, *Master of Kinloss*; *b* 20 June 1953; *educ* Redrice Sch

1 +Teresa Mary Nugent; *b* 20 July 1957

2 +Hester Josephine Anne [The Hon Mrs Haworth, Newstead Grange, Thirsk Rd, Easingwold, Yorks YO6 3NH]; *b* 9 May 1960; *m* 9 June 1984 *Peter Haworth, yr s of A F C P Haworth, of Malton, N Yorks, and has:

(1) +Joseph Anthony; *b* 1985

(2) +David Arnold; *b* 1987

(3) +Christopher John; *b* 1989

Lineage (of Kinloss): For further details of the early Lords Kinloss *see* ELGIN and KINCARDINE, E, and of the lator ones *see* TEMPLE OF STOWE, E.

Sir EDWARD BRUCE, **1st Lord Kinloss**; had, with othor issue, including an er s (EDWARD BRUCE, **2nd Lord Kinloss**, KB; *d* unm):

THOMAS BRUCE, **3rd Lord Kinloss** and 1st EARL OF ELGIN; had:

ROBERT BRUCE, **4th Lord Kinloss** and 2nd EARL OF ELGIN; had, with other issue:

THOMAS BRUCE, **5th Lord Kinloss** and 3rd EARL OF ELGIN; had, with other issue:

CHARLES BRUCE, **6th Lord Kinloss** and 4th EARL OF ELGIN; had, with two sons (*dvp*) and a yr dau:

MARY Bruce; *m* 21 Dec 1728 Henry BRYDGES, 2nd Duke of Chandos (*see* CHANDOS, V, preliminary remarks), and *dvp* 14 Aug 1738, leaving:

JAMES BRYDGES, *de jure* 7th LORD KINLOSS, as which *s* maternal gf 10 Feb 1746/7 in the right to the title (though neither he nor the next *de jure* holder assumed it) and 3rd DUKE OF CHANDOS, as which *s f* 28 Nov 1771, PC (1775); *b* 16 Dec 1731; *educ* Cambridge; Ranger Enfield Chase 1753, MP (Whig) Winchester 1754–61 and Radnorshire 1761–68, a Ld Bedchamber 1760–64, Ld Lt Hants 1763–64 and 1771–80, High Steward Winchester, Ld Steward Household 1783–89; *m* 1st 22 March 1753 Margaret (*dsp* 14 Aug 1768), dau of Sir John Nicol, of Southgate, Middx; *m* 2nd 21 June 1777 Anne Eliza, sis of Sir Richard Grace Gamon, Bt (*see* 1970 edn GRACE, Bt), and widow of Roger Hope Elletson, and *dspm* 29 Sept 1789 (when all his titles bar the Lordship of Kinloss expired) of injuries after his w inadvertently moved a chair just as he was about to sit in it, an action for which she never forgave herself and as a result of which self-reproach she became disordered in her wits, leaving a 2nd but only surv dau:

ANNA ELIZA Brydges, *de jure* LADY KINLOSS in her own right; *b* 27 Oct 1779; *m* 16 April 1796 Richard TEMPLE-NUGENT-GRENVILLE later TEMPLE-NUGENT-BRYDGES-CHANDOS-GRENVILLE (roy licence 15 Nov 1799), 1st Earl Temple of Stowe (*qv*) and 1st Duke of Buckingham and Chandos etc, and *d* 15 May 1836, leaving:

RICHARD PLANTAGENET TEMPLE-NUGENT-BRYDGES-CHANDOS-GRENVILLE, *de jure* 9th Lord Kinloss, 2nd DUKE OF BUCKINGHAM AND CHANDOS, EARL TEMPLE OF STOWE etc; had, with other issue:

RICHARD PLANTAGENET CAMPBELL TEMPLE-NUGENT-BRYDGES-CHANDOS-GRENVILLE, **10th Lord Kinloss** as which recognised by Ho Lds 21 July 1868 and 3rd and last DUKE OF BUCKINGHAM AND CHANDOS, also 3rd EARL TEMPLE OF STOWE etc; had by his 1st w, with two yr daus:

MARY Temple-Nugent-Brydges-Chandos-Grenville, **Lady Kinloss** in her own right, CI; *b* 30 Sept 1852; *m* 4 Nov 1884 Maj Luis Ferdinand Harry Courthope MORGAN later MORGAN-GRENVILLE (roy licence for him and w 6 Dec 1890), of Biddlesden Park, Bucks, Maj York and Lancaster Regt (*d* 26 Aug 1896), est s of George Manners Morgan of Bucks, and *d* 17 Oct 1944, having had

1 Richard George Grenville, *Master of Kinloss*; *b* 25 Sept 1887; Capt Rifle Bde WW I (wounded twice, despatches); *ka* unm 20 Dec 1914

2 Luis Chandos Francis Temple (Rev), *Master of Kinloss*; *b* 10 Oct 1889; *educ* Exeter Coll Oxford; Curate St Sepulchre, Northampton, 1914; *m* 18 Aug 1921 Katherine Beatrice MacKenzie (*d* 1 June 1960), dau of John Jackman, of Stowe, and *d* 2 Aug 1944, leaving:

(1) (BEATRICE) MARY GRENVILLE, **present Lady Kinloss**

(2) (Lilian) Anne Grenville; *b* 8 June 1924; granted with sisters Aug 1947 rank of Ld of Parl's dau; *m* 1st 25 Jan 1951 Ernest Frederick Harris, CBE (*d* 4 Jan 1965), s of Frederick Harris, of Matlock, Derbys; *m* 2nd 10 June 1965 Maurice Emile Deen (*d* Feb 1970), s of Emile Deen, of Tilburg, Holland; *m* 3rd 1973 *Willem Dirkse-van-Schalkwyk, late S African Amb to Canada, France and Italy, and *d* 29 March 1996

(3) +(Caroline) Jane Grenville [The Hon Mrs Glynne-Walton, West Bank House, West Haddesly, W Yorks YO8 8PZ]; *b* 21 March 1931; *m* 18 Sept 1958 *Gordon Glynne-Walton, FRGS, FRMetSoc, FRAS, FGS, Duke of Wellington's Regt, s of Thomas Henry Walton, of Batley, and has:

1a +Charlotte Elizabeth Sophia Caroline Louise; *b* 3 Oct 1961; MBA Bradford, BA Leeds Met U, Dipl Betriebswirt Bremen; *m* 1990 *Paul Stephen Fox, yst s of J M Fox of Clifton, W Yorks, and has:

1b *Luis John Gordon Temple; *b* 11 Aug 1997

3 Thomas George Breadalbane, DSO (1918), OBE (1946), MC, JP (Beds); *b* 28 Feb 1891; *educ* Eton and RMC Sandhurst; Lt-Col Rifle Bde WW I (despatches, Brevet, Legn Hon) and WW II (despatches);V-Lt Beds 1953–65 (DL 1949), High Sheriff 1950; *m* 1 March 1916 Georgina St John (*d* 27 Sept 1973), 3rd dau of Albert St John Murphy, of Little Island, Co Cork, and *d* 10 Jan 1965, leaving:

(1) Pamela Mary Ruth; *b* 23 June 1919; *m* 9 Sept 1944 Capt Alec David Charles Francis, Welsh Gds (*d* 1993), s of Capt Noel Francis and Mrs Humphrey Butler, and *d* 1989, leaving:

1a +Nigel Charles Audley; *b* 30 July 1949; *m* 1990 *Julia Anne Grayson

1a +Priscilla Annabelle; *b* 30 Aug 1947; *m* 2 Dec 1969 *Frederick Hugh Philip Hamilton Wills (*see* DULVERTON, B) and has issue

(2) +Cynthia Avril; *b* 13 April 1921; *m* 2 April 1948 *Christopher Michael Aliaga-Kelly, yst s of Ambrose Aliaga-Kelly, of Dublin, and has:

1a +Peter Edward Grenville; *b* 23 Feb 1956

1a +Veronica Ann Cynthia [Mrs John Bevan, c/o 2 Harcourt Bldgs, Temple, London EC4Y 9DB]; *b* 7 March 1950; *m* 1978 *John P V Bevan, QC, and has:

1b +Henry Thomas Vaughan; *b* 1981

1b +Charlotte Emily; *b* 1985

(3) +Audrey Marigold [The Rt Hon The Lady Ironside, Priory House, Boxted, Essex CO4 5RB]; *b* 15 Feb 1931; *m* 29 April 1950 *2nd Baron Ironside (*qv*) and has issue

4 Robert William, JP (W Sussex) 1936; *b* 21 July 1892; *educ* Cheltenham; Capt 5th Bn Rifle Bde (SR) WW I (wounded); CC W Sussex; *m* 1st 29 Dec 1915 Irene Alice Gertrude (*d* 6 Oct 1916), dau of Sir Robert Grenville Harvey, 2nd Bt, of Langley Park (*see* 1931 edn), and had:

(1) Robert Grenville Plantagenet; *b* 16 Sept 1916; *educ* privately; *m* 7 June 1944 Mabel Frazer Allen (*d* 1985), dau of Charles Osborne Ellis, of Birmingham, and *d* 1993, leaving:

1a +Richard Harvey GRENVILLE later MORGAN-GRENVILLE [Richard Morgan-Grenville Esq, 67 Chartwell Dve, Durban, S Africa]; *b* 8 April 1947; *educ* Millfield; *m* 1st Jan 1970 (*divorce*) Diana Jane Chambler; *m* 2nd 1982 *Valerie de Marigny and by his 1st w has:

1b +Robert Ralph; *b* 1974

2b +Richard John; *b* 1977

1b +Georgina Jane; *b* 1975; model

1a Caroline Irene; *b* 7 Jan 1949; *m* 1st 31 Aug 1972 (*divorce* 1976) Edward James Windham-Bellord (*see* BOWYER-SMYTH, Bt); *m* 2nd *Robert Denman and *d* 1979, leaving issue by her 1st husb

4 (cont.) Capt Robert Grenville *m* 2nd 16 Dec 1922 Elizabeth Hope Bine (*d* 19 Feb 1969), dau of Sir Charles Bine Renshaw, 1st Bt (*qv*), and widow of Capt Francis William Lindley Gull (*see* GULL, Bt), and *d* 1988, having by her had:

(2) John Richard Bine GRENVILLE later MORGAN-GRENVILLE *b* 10 July 1927; *educ* Eton; Capt KRRC (TA); *m* 7 July 1955 *Joan Margaret [Mrs John Morgan-Grenville, Upperton House, Petworth, Sussex], 2nd dau of ACM Sir Wilfred Rhodes Freeman, 1st Bt (*qv*), and *d* 15 Oct 1994, leaving:

1a +Roger Temple; *b* 18 Dec 1959; *m* 1993 *Caroline Mary, dau of David Michael Summerhayes, CMG, of Harting, W Sussex

1a +Joanna Jane [Mrs John Wotton, White Webbs Cottage, Bury, W Sussex RH20 1PB]; *b* 26 Sept 1957; *m* 24 Aug 1991 *Cdr John C L Wotton, RN, s of Lt-Col Gordon Wotton, and has:

1b +Laura Elizabeth; *b* 14 June 1993

2b +Iona Victoria; *b* 15 Jan 1995

(3) +Gerard Wyndham [Gerard Morgan-Grenville Esq, Milton Mill, W Milton, Dorset]; *b* 26 March 1931; *educ* Eton; Capt Rifle Bde; *m* 1st 27 April 1955 (*divorce* 1981) Virginia Anne, est dau of Maj John Peto (*see* PETO, Bt, of Barnstable); *m* 2nd 1981 Fern Diana Roberts (*d* 1993), dau of Capt E R S Jackson, RN, and formerly w of Tim Roberts, and has by his 1st w:

1a +Hugo Gerard; *b* 5 Aug 1958; *m* 1992 *Sophie, est dau of William Andrewes, of Ludlow, Salop

2a +George Septimus; *b* 4 June 1964

1a +Laura Isabel Hester; *b* 1 Jan 1961; *m* 1984 *Capt Euan Glen Kelway-Bamber (*see* DEVONSHIRE, D) and has issue

5 Harry Nugent, OBE (1919); *b* 8 Jan 1896; *educ* Cheltenham and RMA Woolwich; Capt RE WW I (despatches); *m* 1 June 1921 Mary (*d* 1981), dau of Capt Hon Edward Oliphant Murray (*see* ELIBANK, L), and *d* 1979, having had:

(1) Richard Temple; *b* and *d* 12 May 1923

(2) Edward Bruce; *b* 28 Feb 1925; *d* 6 Aug 1929

(3) +David Bevil [David Morgan-Grenville Esq, Tamarack Farm, Sutton, Quebec, Canada]; *b* 16 Feb 1928; *educ* Stowe and Magdalene Coll Cambridge (MA), MBA (Kansas); RA and RAFVR; *m* 30 June 1951 *Nancy, er dau of Prof Seymour Guy Martin, of Washington, DC, and has:

1a +Geoffrey [Geoffrey Morgan-Grenville Esq, 310 Pine Ave, Oakville, Ontario, Canada]; *b* 29 March 1956; *m* 1981 *Julia Louise Newcomb

2a +Andrew; *b* 21 July 1967; *m* 1992 *Jennifer Howard

1a +Sarah [Mrs Steven Antler, 534 Stratford St, Chicago, IL, USA]; *b* 25 Dec 1953; *m* 1981 *Prof Steven Antler

(1) +Rosalind Mary; *b* 1 May 1933; *m* 1st 21 Oct 1955 (*divorce* 1975) Maj Philip Ivor Caleb, late USAF, Air Medal (Vietnam); *m* 2nd 1976 *John Frederick Weston and has by her 1st husb:

1a +Caroline Mary; *b* 17 Dec 1956

2a +Penelope Frances; *b* 23 March 1963

(2) +Elizabeth Caroline [Mrs Elizabeth Williams, Moor Hill Cottage, Fovant, Wilts SP3 5LB]; *b* 9 July 1944; *m* 15 March 1969 (*divorce* 1981) John Kendrick Williams, CEng, MICE, er s of Robert Charles Williams, and has:

1a +Victoria Caroline; *b* 21 April 1971

2a +Rachael Mary; *b* 21 April 1971; has:

1b *Thomas Joseph; *b* 19 Dec 1994

1 Caroline Mary Elizabeth (May), JP Bucks; *b* 26 June 1886; *m* 6 Jan 1909 Maj Thomas Close Smith (*d* 16 Nov 1946), s of Henry Flesher Smith, of Boycott Manor, Buckingham, and *d* 24 April 1972, leaving:

(1) Richard Sydney Grenville SMITH later CLOSE-SMITH (deed poll 20 March 1954), OBE (1950); *b* 26 Jan 1910; *educ* Eton and Univ Coll Oxford; commissioned Bucks Yeo 1928, tfd 4th QO Hus 1932, served WW II (POW 1941) and Malaya 1948–51 (despatches), ret as Lt-Col 1954, Chm OStJ Cncl Bucks 1969–73; *m* 1st 19 July 1935 (*divorce* 1954) Florence Amelia, dau of Baron Robert Ludwig Wilhelm August von Ompteda, of Hanover, and had:

1a Robert Richard; *b* 9 Aug 1936; *educ* Eton; *m* 10 June 1960 *Ena Mary [Mrs Robert Close-Smith, Ashmore Farm, Water Stratford, Buckingham MK10 5NA], dau of Edwin Rooks, of Quinton, and *d* 26 March 1992, leaving:

1b +Charles Robert; *b* 13 April 1961; *m* 8 July 1995 *Kelli Andrew

2b +Christopher Paul; *b* 6 Dec 1962; *m* 24 July 1989 *Charlotte Nina, dau of William Lloyd Brace, of Woodford Green, Essex, and has:

1c +James Robert; *b* 26 July 1996

1c +Isobel Charlotte; *b* 26 July 1996

3b *Henry Richard Christian; *b* 6 Dec 1962

1a +Venice Mary Grenville [Mrs John Gordon-Colebrooke, 2 Minshull Close, Buckingham]; *b* 24 July 1938; *m* 23 May 1959 *John Duncan Maitland Gordon-Colebrooke and has:

1b +James Richard Maitland; *b* 2 March 1961; *m* 1988 *Wendy Jane, dau of Mrs D Stokes, of Buckingham

2b +Jeremy Patrick Grenville; *b* 21 Feb 1963

3b +John Angus Childerstone; *b* 27 July 1967

(1) (cont.) Lt-Col Richard CLOSE-SMITH *m* 2nd 12 April 1954 *(Josephine) Judith [Mrs Richard Close-Smith, Stearthill Lodge, Little Horwood, Bucks MK17 0PR], dau of Vincent Wood Mullins, of Stonehouse, Glos, and widow of Michael Bruce Urquhart Dewar, of Stagenhoe Park, Hitchin, Herts, and *d* July 1973

(2) Charles Nugent SMITH later CLOSE-SMITH, TD (1953); *b* 7 July 1911; *educ* Eton and Magdalene Coll Cambridge; commissioned Roy Bucks Yeo 1938, served WW II, Hon Lt-Col RA 1945, memb: Lloyd's 1935, Lloyd's Ctee 1967–70, Dep Chm 1970; *m* 30 April 1946 *(Elizabeth Emily) Vivien [Mrs Charles Close-Smith, The Heymersh, Britford, Wilts SP1 4DU], dau of Maj William Augustus Cecil Kinsman, DSO, OBE, Roy Inniskilling Fus, of Abbeyleix House, Co Dublin, and *d* 1988, leaving:

1a +Thomas William [Thomas Close-Smith Esq, Lower House, Fletching Common, E Sussex BN8 4QS]; *b* 2 April 1947; *educ* Eton; underwriting memb Lloyd's; *m* 1st 1973 Lillian Moira Weston, twin dau of John Weston Adamson, of Oldstead Hall, Coxwold, Yorks; *m* 2nd 1979 *Rachel M, yst dau of L B Earp, of Wilmington, Sussex, and by her has:

1b +James Grenville; *b* 1982

1b +Nicola Jane; *b* 1980

2b +Sophie Mary; *b* 1986

2a +Anthony Grenville; *b* 1 April 1950; *educ* Eton and Liverpool U; *m* 19– *Sara, est dau of David Breton, of S Kensington, and has:

1b +A dau; *b* 1988

3a +Edward Vivian [Edward Close-Smith Esq, Ladymeads House, Wadhurst, E Sussex TN5 6HH]; *b* 22 Nov 1951; *educ* Eton; *m* 1983 *Sarah Felicity, est dau of William Daniel Dane, of Crakehall, Yorks, and has had:

1b +Charles William; *b* 1987

1b +Samantha Vivien; *b* 1984

2b +Caroline; *b* 1985

3b Antonia Sarah; *b* and *d* 1992

4b +Lucy Susan; *b* 1994

(3) +Henry Temple SMITH later CLOSE-SMITH [Henry Close-Smith Esq, The Old Vicarage, Messing, Essex CO5 9TR]; *b* 31 July 1918; *educ* Eton and Magdalene Coll Cambridge; Capt Welsh Gds WW II, underwriting memb Lloyd's; *m* 3 June 1948 *Cicely Margaret Wingfield, yr dau of Rev Eustace Hill, and has:

1a +Richard Henry; *b* 3 April 1951; *educ* Eton and Grey Coll Durham

1a +Caroline Mary [Mrs Jonathan Compton, Birch Holt, Layer Marney, Essex CO5 9XH]; *b* 17 March 1954; *m* 1981 *Jonathan Lawrence Compton, 2nd s of A J Compton, of IoW, and has:

1b +Edmund Alfred Henry; *b* 1990

1b +Emily Glen May; *b* 1984

2b +Rosalind Eleanor Caroline; *b* 1986

(1) Susan Caroline; *b* 7 July 1911; *m* 20 April 1936 Brig George Philip Clark, CBE, DSO, s of Rev George Walter Clark, of Worcs, and *d* 27 Feb 1867, having adopted a s and dau

Lineage (of Grenville): RICHARD I, DUKE OF NORMANDY (ggf through his est s of ROBERT II (THE DEVIL), DUKE OF NORMANDY, who was in turn f by his mistress Harlette/Harlot of WILLIAM I (THE CONQUEROR); *b* 933; *m* 2nd his former mistress Gunnor and *d* 20 Nov 996, leaving by her a 3rd s:

MAUGER, COUNT OF CORBEIL in right of his w; *m* Germaine, dau and heir of Albert, Count of Corbeil, and had, with an er s (William, *dsp* a monk in the Abbey of St Maur):

HAMON, COUNT OF CORBEIL; *k* fighting under his cousin the DUKE OF NORMANDY, leaving:

HAMON *Dentatus* ('The Toothy'), COUNT OF CORBEIL; feudal Ld of Thorigny, Grenville, Brety and Crenly; had:

1 Robert fitz Hamon, Count of Corbeil; moved after the Norman Conquest to England, where granted the honour (administrative unit of a number of knight's fees) of Gloucester by his distant cousin HENRY I and won extensive lands in Glamorgan by conquest; *m* Sybil, dau of Roger de Montgomery, Earl of Shrewsbury (*see* SHREWSBURY and WATERFORD, E, preliminary remarks), and *das* March 1107 fighting for HENRY I against the latter's bro ROBERT, DUKE OF NORMANDY, leaving an heiress:

(1) Mabel; *m* Robert, Earl of Gloucester (*d* 31 Oct 1147), illegitimate s of HENRY I, and *d* 1157, leaving issue

2 Richard fitz Hamon de Grenville; moved after the Norman Conquest to England, where granted lands in Devon and Cornwall; helped his er bro conquer Glamorgan; *m* Isabel, dau of Walter Giffard, Earl of Buckingham, and had:

(1) Richard; ancestor of the GRANVILLEs Earls of Bath (*see* BATH, M, preliminary remarks) and the GRANVILLEs of Wellesbourne

(2) William; had:

1a Eustace (Sir); Constable Tower London 1214/15; *m* Joan, er dau and coheir of Robert de Arcic, feudal Baron of Coggs, Oxon, and had:

1b Gerard; *dsp*

(3) Gerard; witnessed a charter of his unc Walter Giffard, Earl of Buckingham, of whom he held three Knight's fees; *dsp*

(4) Robert; living *temp* HENRY II; had:

1a Gerard; *m* Dionysia, dau of Henry de Turbeville, Steward Gascony, and had, with three yr sons (Robert; Reginald; Ralph):

1b William; Sheriff Oxon and Berks 1289/90, Keeper Oxford Castle; had two sons (Henry, *dsp*; John, *m* Agatha, dau of Walter de Burgo, and had issue) and three daus (Nichola, *m* Sir Reginald Hampden and had issue; Agnes, *m* John le Bruyn; Maud)

2a Robert; *m* Erneberche — and had, with a yr s (William, attended KING JOHN to Poitou 1213/4):

1b Gerard; had:

1c Richard; living 1250/1; had, with a yr s (Sylvester) and a dau (Alice, apparently living 1281/2):

1d Eustace (Sir), of Chilton and Wotton Underwood, Bucks; ktd *c* 1272/3; had, with an est s (Gerard, of Chilton), two yst sons (John, *m* Johanna and had a s John, who *dspm*; Martyn) and six daus (Alice, *m* 1st Humphrey de Pokele and 2nd Thomas Creslaund de Adingrave; Amita, *m* Richard de la Sale, of Hame; Nichola; Mary; Margery; Agnes):

1e Richard; had half the manor of Wotton from his f; *m* Joan (*d* 1352/3), dau of 1st Lord (Baron) Zouche (though which of the three creations extant (according to later doctrine) at that time is not clear; *see* ZOUCHE, B), and *d c* 1334/5, leaving, with a yr s (Edmund, living 6 Feb 1337) and three daus (Margaret; Nichola; Agnes):

1f William, of Wotton Underwood; *m* Agnes, dau of William Wrightham, of Hadenham, Bucks, and had, with a yr s (William, *dsp*):

1g Thomas, of Wotton Underwood; *m* Elizabeth Morest and *d* 1402, leaving, with two yr sons (John, *m* Margery, dau and heir of John de Bourchier, and *dsp*; William, *dsp*):

1h Richard, of Wotton Underwood; *m* 1401 Christian Lancelove (*d* after 1454) and *d* 1 June 1428, leaving, with a yr s (John, had a life-grant of lands in Hadenham from his bro, *m* 5 Aug 1454) and a dau (Agnes):

1i Eustace, of Wotton Underwood; *m* 1st Margery Bryan (*dsp*); *m* 2nd *c* 1 Aug 1464 Elizabeth (predeceased him), dau of Baldwin Bottiller, and *d* 1480, having by her had, with two yr sons (Thomas; Eustace, both *dsp*):

1j Richard, of Wotton Underwood; *m* Joan, dau of Edward Littleton, of Staffs, and *d* 8 Oct 1517, leaving:

1k EDWARD

2k George; Serjeant Buckhounds to HENRY VIII; *dsp*

1k Anne; *m* John Josceline, of Bucks

2k Fortune; *m* — Power, of Blechenden, Oxon

The er s,

EDWARD GRENVILLE, of Wotton Underwood; Sheriff Bucks and Beds 1527; *m* Isabel, dau of Thomas Denton, of Caversfield, Bucks, and *d* 14 April 1536, leaving:

EDWARD GRENVILLE, of Wotton; *b* 8 May 1525; *m* Alice (*m* 2nd Walter Dennis), dau of William Hazlewood, of Alford, Cheshire, and *d* 31 Oct 1585, having had, with four other sons (*d* young or *sp*) and three daus (Bridget, *m* Sir Thomas Higgins; Johanna, *m* Col Thornkill; Mary, *d* in infancy):

RICHARD GRENVILLE, of Wotton Underwood; *b* 28 Oct 1527; *m* Mary, dau of John Giffard, of Hillesdon, Bucks, and *d* 7 Nov 1604, leaving, with another s (*d* unm) and two other daus (*d* unm):

1 Edward; *b* 4 July 1561; Capt under Sir Francis Drake; *d* unm Cartagena

2 RICHARD

3 Edward; *b* 17 Jan 1572; *m* Dorothy, dau of Sir John Thynne (*see* BATH, M), and had a dau, Susanna

1 Dorothy; *b* 1562; *m* Sir Walter Cope, of Kensington

Isabel; *b* 1565; *m* — Dudley, of Chopwell

The 2nd s,

RICHARD GRENVILLE, of Wotton Underwood; *b* 1567; *m* Frances (*m* 2nd Thomas Tyrrell, of Castle Thorpe, Bucks), dau of Thomas Saunders, of Long Merston, Herefs, and was *bur* 8 April 1618, having had, with three other sons (including Edward (a yr bro of RICHARD; *see* below), of Foxcot, Bucks, which he bought 1639, *b* 12 Sept 1614, *m* Audrey, dau of John Duncombe, and *d* 17 April 1661, leaving two sons (Edward, *d* 1662; George, *d* unm June 1693) and a dau (Frances, *m* Philip Raleigh) and two daus (all *d* young)):

RICHARD GRENVILLE, of Wotton Underwood; *b* 8 Aug 1612; Bucks: DL, Sheriff 1636 and 1642, MP 1654, 1656 and 1658; *m* 1st 9 Feb 1634 Anne (*d* 15 Jan 1646/47) dau of Sir William Borlase, of Marlow, Bucks, and had a s and two daus (*d* unm); *m* 2nd Eleanor (*d* 1671), dau of Sir Timothy Tyrrell, of Okeley, and widow of Sir Peter Temple, of Stanton Barry, Bucks (*see* TEMPLE OF STOWE, E, Lineage (of Temple)), and *d* 10 Jan 1665, leaving by his 1st w:

RICHARD GRENVILLE, of Wotton Underwood; *b* 14 Jan 1646/7; High Sheriff Bucks 1671; *m* his cousin Eleanor (*bur* 25 March 1729), dau of Sir Peter Temple, and was *bur* 4 July 1719, having had, with three daus (including Penelope, *b* 6 April 1674, *m* Sir John Conway, 2nd and last Bt (*d* 27 April 1721), of Botryddan, Flints, and *d* 1745, leaving issue):

RICHARD GRENVILLE, of Wotton Underwood; *b* 23 March 1677/8; MP Wendover and Buckingham; *m c* 1710 Hester, Countess Temple in her own right (*see* TEMPLE OF STOWE, E, Lineage (of Temple), for further details of subsequent generations), and *d* 17 Feb 1726/7, having had, with other issue:

GEORGE GRENVILLE; PM 1763–65; had:

GEORGE GRENVILLE later TEMPLE-NUGENT-GRENVILLE, 1st MARQUESS OF BUCKINGHAM etc; had:

RICHARD TEMPLE-NUGENT-GRENVILLE later TEMPLE-NUGENT-BRYDGES-CHANDOS-GRENVILLE, 1st DUKE OF BUCKINGHAM AND CHANDOS, 1st EARL TEMPLE OF STOWE etc; *m* Lady Anne Eliza Brydges, *de jure* LADY KINLOSS in her own right (*see* **Lineage (of Kinloss)** above)

KINNOULL

Arms: Quarterly, 1st and 4th grand quarters counterquartered, 1st and 4th, azure a unicorn salient argent, armed, maned and unguled or, within a bordure of the last charged with eight demi-thistles vert impaled with as many demi-roses gules joined together per pale as a coat of augmentation (for KINNOULL); 2nd and 3rd, argent three escutcheons, two and one, gules (for HAY); 2nd and 3rd grand quarter counterquartered 1st and 4th, or three bars wavy gules, surmounted of a scimitar in pale argent (for DRUMMOND); 2nd and 3rd, or a lion's head erased within a double-tressure flory-counterflory gules, a coat of augmentation (for STRATHALLAN). **Crest:** A countryman, couped at the knees, vested grey, waistcoat gules, bonnet azure, bearing on his shoulder an ox-yoke proper. **Supporters:** Two countrymen, habited as in the crest; the dexter holding over his shoulder the coulter of a plough; the sinister a paddle of a plough, both proper. **Motto:** *Renovate animos* ('Renew your spirits'). **Creations:** E., V. (Dupplin) and L. (S) 25 May 1633, V. (also Dupplin) (S) 31 Dec 1697, B. (GB) 31 Dec 1711.

THE 15TH EARL OF KINNOULL, Viscount of Dupplin (twice), **Lord Hay of Kinfauns** and **Baron Hay of Pedwardine**, Co Hereford ((Arthur) William George Patrick Hay) [The Rt Hon The Earl of Kinnoull, 15 Carlyle Sq, London SW3 6EX; Pier House, Seaview, IoW]; *b* 26 March 1935; *s* f 1938; *educ* Eton; CLA 1960, FLAS 1964; memb: Air League Cncl 1972, Ag Valuers' Assoc 1962, Roy Co Archers 1965, Cncl Deep Sea Fishermens' Mission 1977 and Br Delegn Cncl Europe 1985–, Pres: London-Perthshire Assoc 1965, Nat Cncl on Inland Tport 1964, Jr C Whip Ho Lds 1966, Oppn Spokesman Aviation 1968–70, dep chm Property Owners Bldg Soc 1976–78 (dir 1971–87) and Woolwich Homes 1994–, dir Woolwich Equitable Bldg Soc 1987–, V-Pres Nat Assoc Parish Cncls 1970–80, FRICS 1970; *m* 1 June 1961 *Gay Ann, er dau of Sir Denys Colquhoun Flowerdew Lowson, 1st Bt (*qv*), and has:

1 +CHARLES WILLIAM HARLEY, *Viscount Dupplin* [Viscount Dupplin, 59 Scarsdale Villas, London W8; Pitkindie House, Abernyte, Perthshire]; *b* 20 Dec 1962; *educ* Eton and Ch Ch Oxford; barrister Middle Temple 1990; memb Atholl Highrs

1 *Melissa Ann; *b* 25 Sept 1964

2 *Iona Charlotte; *b* 15 Oct 1967; *m* 12 July 1997 *Charles T M Ind, est s of Dr John Ind, of Chelsea

3 *Atlanta Rose; *b* 25 Sept 1974

Lineage: WILLIAM de la HAYE; had charter of the lands of Leys from his bro Gilbert, 3rd of Erroll (*see* ERROLL, E), which was confirmed by ALEXANDER III 29 April 1251; ancestor of:

PETER HAY, 1st of Megginch (yr bro of Edmund Hay, of Leys); living 1492; *d c* 15 Nov 1496, leaving, with a yr s (William, living 1496):

EDMUND HAY, 2nd of Megginch; Baillie (Ch Magistrate) of Erroll; *m* Janet Boyd and *d c* 30 Nov 1543, leaving:

PETER HAY, 3rd of Megginch; *m* Margaret, dau of John Crichton of Ruthven, and had:

1 PETER

2 James (Sir), of Kingask; Comptroller Scotland 1608; *m* Margaret, dau of John Murray of Polmaise, and *d* 1610, leaving:

(1) JAMES HAY, 1st EARL OF CARLISLE, Co Cumberland (E), so *cr* 13 Sept 1622, as also earlier 21 June 1606 LORD HAY (though without a seat in the Ho of Lds; presumably S), 29 June 1615 BARON HAY OF SAWLEY, Co York, and 5 July 1618 VISCOUNT DONCASTER (both E), KG (1624), KB (1610), PC (March 1616/7); *b c* 1580; Gentleman of the Bedchamber 1603–15, naturalised an Englishman 1604, ktd by mid-May 1604; Amb Paris 1616, 1622 and 1623, Madrid 1616 and 1623, Germany 1619–20 and Venice 1628, First Gentleman of the Bedchamber 1626, Groom Stole 1631–36; *m* 1st 6 Jan 1606/7 Honora (*bur* 16 Aug 1614), only child of Edward Denny, 1st and last Earl of Norwich and 1st Lord (Baron) Denny, and by her had issue; *m* 2nd 6 Nov

1617 Lucy (*dsp* 5 Nov 1660), dau of Henry Percy, Earl of Northumberland (*see* NORTHUMBERLAND, D), and *d* 25 April 1636, leaving by his 1st w an only surv s, who was:

1a JAMES HAY, 2nd and last EARL OF CARLISLE etc, also (as which *s* maternal gf) 2nd and last LORD (Baron) DENNY, KB (Feb 1625/6); *b c* 1612; ktd 1623; Col of a foot regt German in Thirty Years War 1624 and of a royalist regt of horse Civil War England (for his inactivity in which *see* CARLISLE, E, preliminary remarks); *m* 21 March 1631/2 Lady Margaret Russell (*m* 2nd 1 Aug 1667 2nd Earl of Manchester (*see* MANCHESTER, D), and was *bur* 1 Dec 1676), dau of 4th Earl of Bedford (*see* BEDFORD, D), and *dsp* 30 Aug 1660, when his titles expired

(2) Robert; Master King's Robes 1618

3 Edmund; Provincial French Jesuits 1574

1 Katherine; *m* 1st Robert Moneur of Balluny; *m* 2nd George Drummond of Blair

2 Jane; *m* Patrick Murray of Ochtertyre (*see* MURRAY, Bt, of Ochtertyre)

The er son,

PETER HAY; *m c* 12 May 1554 Margaret, dau of Sir Patrick Ogilvie of Inchmartin, and *d* 10 Sept 1596, having had:

1 Patrick, of Megginch; *m* 1st Isabel, dau and coheir of Patrick Boyson of Pitcullane; *m* 2nd Elizabeth, dau of Patrick Cheyne of Essilmont

2 Peter, of Kirkland and Megginch; had charters of land in Perthshire 1607 and Forfarshire 1609; *m* Margaret Boyd and *d c* 29 May 1629, having had, with an est s (John, living 1613, *dvp*), a 4th s (Thomas, living 1632) and a 5th s (Patrick, of Rattray, Perthshire, *m* Jean Ogilvy (*d* 19 Sept 1638) and *d* 26 March 1640):

(2) George, of Kirkland; *m* (contract 17 Feb 1618) Isobel, dau of William Rollock of Balbegie, and *d c* 11 Aug 1632, leaving issue

(3) Francis, of Balhousie (of which had a charter 1625) and Rattray (charter 1648); also had charters of Corugilton, Wigtownshire, 1632, and the territorial Barony of Dupplin 1642; WS; *m* 1st 2 July 1618 Janet, dau of James Halyburton of Essie, and had issue, including a yr s (Francis; *bapt* 1 Aug 1633) and four daus (Janet; Katherine; Beatrice, *m* 1652 George Hay of Megginch (both *d* 1670); Rebecca, *m* George Oliphant, s of John Oliphant of Bachilton); *m* 2nd (contract 26 April 1637) Elspeth, er dau of John Oliphant of Bachilton, and *d c* 1654; his er son, who was by his 1st w:

1a George, of Balhousie; *m* 28 April 1656 Marion (*bur* 15 July 1663), dau of Sir Thomas Nicolson, Ld Advocate, and *d* Oct 1672, having had, with an est s (Francis, of Balhousie, *b* 28 Feb 1658, *d* unm Jan 1675) and a yst s (George, *d* Dec 1683):

1b THOMAS HAY, **7th Earl of Kinnoull**, as which *s* cousin 1709, having been *cr* on his own account 31 Dec 1697 VISCOUNT OF DUPPLIN (S), with remainder, failing heirs male of his body, to his heirs of entail; *b c* 1660; MP (Tory) Perthshire 1693–97; Commr Union of E and S Parls; rep S Peer 1710–14; imprisoned Edinburgh Castle 1715 on suspicion of Jacobite sympathies; *m* (contract 20 Dec 1683) Elizabeth (*d* 21 March 1695/6), dau of 1st Viscount Strathallan (*see* PERTH, E), and *d* 5 Jan 1718/9, having had:

1c GEORGE HENRY, **8th Earl**

2c William; *dsp c* 1711

3c John, of Cromlix; Jacobite 1715, attainted 1716, by titular James III *cr* 5 Oct 1718 Earl of Inverness, 3 April 1727 Baron Hay and 4 April 1727 Duke of Inverness; Actg Jacobite Sec State 1724–27; *m* (contract 2 June 1715) Marjory, dau of 5th Viscount Stormont (*see* MANSFIELD and MANSFIELD, E), and *dsp* 24 Sept 1740

1c Margaret; *m* 6 April 1703 22nd/6th Earl of Mar (*qv*) and *d* 25 April 1707

2c Elizabeth; *m* 1714 2nd Earl of Seafield (*qv*) and *d c* 1723

(1) Agnes; *m* David Rattray of Craighall

(2) A dau; *m* Sir Andrew Fletcher of Innerpeffer, Ld of Session

3 GEORGE HAY, **1st Earl of Kinnoull**, so *cr* 25 May 1633, as also VISCOUNT OF DUPPLIN and LORD HAY OF KINFAUNS, with special remainder to heirs male whatsoever, having been previously *cr* 4 May 1627 VISCOUNT OF DUPPLIN and LORD HAY OF KINFAUNS (all S), PC (1622); *bapt* 4 Dec 1570; *educ* Scots Coll Pont-à-Musson; Gentleman of the Bedchamber to JAMES VI 1596; granted Feb 1597/8 the former Carthusian priory at Perth with a Ldship of Parl but since he had insufficient wealth to keep up the position he soon had the grant annulled; ktd by 1609, Gentleman Privy Chamber 1612, Ld Clerk Register 1616–22, a Ld of Session 1616, Ld Chllr Scotland 1622–34; *m* by 15 Nov 1595 Margaret (*d* 4 April 1633), dau of Sir James Halyburton of Pitcur and widow of Patrick Ogilvy, Yr. of Inchmartine (*see* SEAFIELD, E), and *d* 16 Dec 1634, having had, with other issue, including a dau (Margaret, *m* 2nd Lord Spynie; *see* CRAWFORD and BALCARRES, E):

(1) GEORGE HAY, **2nd Earl of Kinnoull**, PC (S); Capt Yeomen Gd 1632–59; *m* (contract 7 Sept 1622) Lady Agnes/Anne Douglas (*bur* 6 Dec 1667), est dau of 7th Earl of Morton (*qv*), and *d* 5 Oct 1644, having had, with other issue (*d* young):

1a GEORGE HAY, **3rd Earl of Kinnoull**; royalist Civil War; *d c* 20 Nov 1649

2a WILLIAM HAY, **4th Earl of Kinnoull**; royalist Civil War, hence imprisoned Edinburgh Castle, escaped 28 May 1654 but recaptured Nov; inherited Barbados from his cousin the 2nd and last Earl of Carlisle (*see* CARLISLE, E, preliminary remarks), but sold it to the Crown 1661 for a pension which was only paid, if at all, irregularly; *m* 1st Mary (*dsp* 1665), dau of 2nd Earl of Cardigan (*see* AILESBURY, M); *m* 2nd Catherine (*d c* 1683), dau of Charles, Viscount Cranborne, and gdau of 2nd Earl of Salisbury (*see* SALISBURY, M), and was *bur* 28 May 1677, leaving:

1b GEORGE HAY, **5th Earl of Kinnoull**; *dsp* Hungary 1687, where he is thought to have been serving in the forces of the Holy Roman Emperor against the Turks

2b WILLIAM HAY, **6th Earl of Kinnoull**; secured a regrant of his titles 29 Feb 1703/4 with remainder to his cousin THOMAS HAY, VISCOUNT OF DUPPLIN of the 1697 *cr* (*see* above), and the heirs male of the latter's body, whom failing to his heirs of tailzie and provision succeeding him in the lands and Barony of Dupplin (with, however, the former precedence of 1633); *d* unm 10 May 1709

3a James; had:

1b Grizel; *m c* 1668 Lt-Col Alexander, s of 1st Earl of Stirling

1a Mary; *m* 6 Feb 1662 8th Earl Marischal (*see* KINTORE, E) and *d* 10 Nov 1701

2a Catharine; *m* 16 Feb 1670 James Baird, Yr. of Auchmedden (*dvp* 1681), and *d* 11 Jan 1733, leaving issue

1 Janet; *m* Andrew Gray of Balledgarno

2 Elizabeth; *m* 1st (contract 18 April 1587) Gilbert Gray of Bandirran; *m* 2nd William Rollock of Balbegie and *d* 1 April 1600

3 Katherine; *m* William Kynman of Hill

The 7th EARL's only surv son,

GEORGE HENRY HAY, **8th Earl of Kinnoull**; *b* 23 June 1689; MP (Tory) Fowey 1710–11, *cr* 31 Dec 1711 BARON HAY OF PEDWARDINE, Co Hereford (GB); Teller Exchequer 1711–14; imprisoned Tower London for suspected Jacobite sympathies 1715 but bailed 1717; Amb Constantinople 1729–34; *m c* 1 Sept 1709 Abigail (*d* 18 July 1750), yst dau of 1st Earl of Oxford and Mortimer, Ld High Treasurer GB (*see* OXFORD AND ASQUITH, E, preliminary remarks), and *d* 29 July 1758, having had, with other issue:

1 THOMAS HAY, **9th Earl of Kinnoull**, PC (1758); *b* 4 June 1710; MP (Whig) Cambridge 1741–58; a Ld Treasury 1754–55, Jt Paymaster Forces 1755–57, Chllr Duchy Lancaster 1758–62, Amb Lisbon 1759–62; *m* 12 June 1741 Constantia, dau and heiress of John Kyrle-Ernle, of Whetham, Wilts, and *dsps* 27 Dec 1787, having had a s (*d* an infant)

2 Robert HAY later HAY-DRUMMOND (added 1739 on inheriting the Cromlix and Innerpeffray estates, Perthshire, under terms of entail executed by his ggf William, Viscount Strathallan) (Most Rev); *b* 10 Nov 1711; Preb Westminster 1743, Bp St Asaph 1748 and Salisbury 1761, Archbp York 1761–76; *m* 31 Jan 1748 Henrietta (*d* 22 April 1763), dau of Peter Auriol, London merchant, and *d* 10 Dec 1776, leaving:

(1) ROBERT AURIOL, **10th Earl**

(2) Thomas; *b* 7 Aug 1752; *d* unm 7 April 1773

(3) Peter Auriol; *b* 21 Jan 1754; Lt-Col W Yorks Militia; *m* 28 Dec 1775 Mary Bridget (*m* 2nd 9 May 1803 4th Viscount Galway (*qv*) and *dsp* 15 Nov 1835), only child of Pemberton Milnes, and *dsp* 21 March 1799

(4) John Auriol; *b* 4 July 1756; Cdr RN; *dsp* 11 Oct 1780

(5) Edward Auriol (Very Rev); *b* 10 April 1758; DD; Dean Bocking, Preb York and Southwell, Rector Hadleigh, Chaplain in Ordinary to GEORGEs III and IV; *m* 1st 12 Dec 1782 Elizabeth (*d* 14 Feb 1790), dau of William, Count de Vismes, and had:

1a Edward William Auriol HAY-DRUMMOND later DRUMMOND-HAY; *b* 4 April 1785; served 61st and 73rd Regts and Staff Peninsula, France and Low Countries; Pncpl Clerk Lyon Office Scotland, Consul-Gen for Morocco, FSSA; *m* 14 Dec 1812 Louisa Margaret (*d* 5 Feb 1869), dau of John Thomson, and *d* Feb 1845, having had:

1b Edward Hay (Sir), of South Hill, Southwell, Notts; *b* 4 March 1815; Colonial Govr 1839–62; *m* 1st 1 Sept 1838 Sarah Laura (*d* 23 April 1868), 2nd dau of Lt-Col James Livingston, HEIC, and had:

1c Frederic (Rev); *b* 7 July 1839; MA Oxon; Vicar Rolleston Notts 1865–86, Incumbent St John Inverness 1886–91, Vicar Neston Wilts 1891–96; *m* 1st 27 June 1865 Elizabeth Ann (*d* 24 April 1878), yst dau of Robert Matthews, of Taplow, Bucks, and had:

1d Frederic Edward; *b* 23 July 1868; *m* 1st 1893 Mary Elizabeth (*d* 22 Jan 1904), dau of H Stone, and had:

1e Frederick Henry; *b* 14 Nov 1893

2e Edward de Vismes; *b* 1 Dec 1896; Lt RN; *d* 12 May 1920

1e Laura Mary Gertrude; *b* 19 April 1895; *m* 28 May 1919 Frederick Benjamin Nicol (*d* 3 Dec 1958) and had:

1f *Frederick Edward; *b* 13 Jan 1926; WW II in RAN; *m* 2 Feb 1951 *Frances Margaret O'Neill, of Victoria, Australia, and has:

1g *Deborah Lee; *b* 8 July 1955

2g *Amanda Jane; *b* 9 Aug 1959

2f *William Daniel; *b* 5 May 1933; *m* 26 Aug 1960 *Noela Eastlake and has:

1g *Stephen Gerard; *b* 26 June 1961

1g *Elizabeth Jane; *b* 12 April 1963

2g *Andrea Marie; *b* 6 Sept 1965

3f *Geoffrey James; *b* 14 Aug 1936; *m* 27 Jan 1960 *Patricia Carmel Flavio and has:

1g *Jeremy; *b* 1964

2g *Matthew James; *b* 1968

1g *Felicity Jane; *b* 1962

2g *Kellie Ann; *b* 1966

1f *Ruth; *b* 3 Jan 1932; *m* 18 Oct 1952 *John Thomas Meadth, s of Thomas James Meadth, of Victoria, and has had:

1g *Thomas Anthony; *b* 31 May 1953

2g *Terence Michael; *b* 7 May 1954

3g Peter James (twin); *b* and *d* 7 May 1954

4g *Patrick John; *b* 31 Oct 1958

5g *Andrew Gordon; *b* 7 April 1961

6g *Kevin Francis; *b* 9 Jan 1963

1g *Margaret Ruth; *b* 11 June 1955

2g *Veronica Mary; *b* 4 July 1965

1d (cont.) Frederic Drummond-Hay *m* 2nd 10 Feb 1909 Amy, est dau of Francis William Boston, of Croydon, and *d* 6 Sept 1948

2d Robert; *b* 14 Feb 1870; *m* 1895 Gertrude Agatha (*d* 10 July 1924), dau of Thomas Forbutt, and *d* 1907, leaving:

1e Robert Augustin Tudor; *b* 1897; served WW I

2e Geoffrey Francis; *b* 1898; served WW I; *m* 1936 Margaret Fenlon (*d* 1959) and had:

1f +Peter [Peter Drummond-Hay Esq, Grange Garden, Flowers Hill, Pangbourne, Berks]; *b* 1943; *m* 1st 1966 (*divorce* 1972) Carolyn Macdonald, of Kansas, and has:

1g *Samantha; *b* 1966

1f (cont.) Peter Drummond-Hay *m* 2nd 1972 *Celia Humphris and by her has:

1g +Luke; *b* 1974

3e Ernest Patrick DRUMMOND-HAY later HAY; *b* 1900; served WW I; *m* 1930 Elsie May Baldwin (*d* 1973), and *d* 1988, leaving:

1f +Kenneth John [Kenneth Hay Esq, 18 Esthwaite Ave, Heron Hill, Kendal, Cumbria LA9 7NN]; *b* 1932; *m* 1951 *Rita Edith, dau of Fred Barton, and has:

1g *Roberta Elaine [Mrs Roberta Long, c/o John Covill, Fern Lea, Natland Green, Kendal, Cumbria]; *b* 1956; *m* 1978 (*divorce* 1984) Martin William Long and has:

1h *Christopher Ross LONG; *b* 1981

1g (cont.) Mrs Roberta Long has by *John Covill:

2h *Sam COVILL; *b* 1988

1f *Shirley Patricia [Mrs Peter Johnson, 26 Justin Ave, Pacific View Est, Mt Tamborine, Qld 4272, Australia]; *b* 1935; *m* 1954 *Peter William Johnson and has:

1g *Garry Daniel; *b* 1955; *m* 1981 *Maureen, dau of Kevin O'Shea, and has:

1h *James Christopher; *b* 1982

1h *Sarah Jane; *b* 1984

1g *Aileen Denise; *b* 1959

1e Barbara May Gertrude; *b* 1904; *m* 1938 Peter Drummond-Hay, of S Africa, and had:

1f *Peter James Robert; *b* 1939

2f *Anthony John Blackwood; *b* 1940

3f *Erroll David Joseph; *b* 1944

4f *Christopher Ian; *b* 1945

5f *Michael Kevin; *b* 1946

1f *Fiona Mary; *b* 1942

2e Veronica Florence Muriel Aileen; *b* 1907; *m* 1926 Alfred Camacho (*d* 1964) and had issue

3d John Tudor; *b* 11 May 1876; Boer War and WW I with 78th Canadian Highrs

4d William Charles; *b* 23 April 1878; *d* unm 7 Jan 1906

1d Mary Laura; *m* 24 June 1895 William James White Nicol and *d* 27 Aug 1924, leaving issue

2d Elizabeth; *m* 1898 Surgn-R-Adml Herbert Lloyd Penny, OBE (*d* 18 July 1945), and had issue

1c (cont.) The Rev Frederic Drummond-Hay *m* 2nd 20 April 1880 Emily Fraser (*d* 27 May 1914), est dau of George Dashwood Wilkins, Bengal CS; *m* 3rd 29 Oct 1919 Bridget Downing Bowies (*d* 13 Oct 1929), widow of Rev George Edward Gardiner, and *d* 14 Oct 1922

2c Edward; *b* 17 Sept 1841; Lt HM St Helena Regt; *d* 31 Dec 1862

1b (cont.) Sir Edward Hay Drummond-Hay *m* 2nd 27 Jan 1869 Alice (*m* 2nd Dec 1886 Henry John Maxwell Foot (*d* 1893) and *d* 5 Feb 1935), dau of Edward Watts, of Hythe, Kent, and *d* 24 Jan 1884

2b John Hay (Sir), GCMG, KCB, PC; *b* 1 June 1816; Consul Gen Morocco 1845, Envoy Extrdy and Min Plen Morocco 1880–86; *m* 7 Oct 1845 Annette Adelaide Christina, 2nd dau of J A Carstensen, Danish Consul-Gen Morocco and PC (Denmark), and *d* 27 Nov 1893, leaving:

1c Robert DRUMMOND-HAY later HAY-DRUMMOND-HAY (26 July 1906) (Sir), CMG; *b* 25 July 1846; Consul Mogador 1875 and Stockholm 1879, Consul-Gen Tunis 1889–94 and Beirut 1894–1907; *m* 1st 2 June 1868 Euphemia Katherine (*d* 19 May 1918), dau of Thomas Willis-Fleming, of Hants, and had:

1d Arnold Robert; *b* 27 Nov 1873; *d* unm 30 May 1899

2d Edward William; *b* 17 June 1877; Sudan CS, Dongola; *m* 1 June 1904 Margaret Alice (*d* 14 Dec 1954), dau of Edmund Waldo Meade-Waldo, of Stone Wall Park, and *d* 3 Nov 1941, leaving:

1e +John Waldo Edward, TD (1951) [Maj John Hay-Drummond-Hay TD, The Oaks, Swainham La, St Leonards-on-Sea, E Sussex TN38 8ED]; *b* 21 Feb 1906; *educ* Marlborough and Trin Coll Cambridge; Maj Queen's Own Roy W Kent Regt (TA), attd IA WW II; *m* 1st 19 June 1937 Anne Rachel (*d* 6 May 1975), dau of Walter Treverbian Prideaux, of Ockley, Surrey; *m* 2nd 31 July 1976 Mrs Jennifer Roosen (*d* 1989), dau of—Bostock-Wilson, and by his 1st w has:

1f +Robert Prideaux [Robert Hay-Drummond-Hay Esq, Barrow Hill Cottage, 25 Mixbury, Brackley, Northants NN13 5RR]; *b* 4 Sept 1941; *educ* Eton; Capt RGJ (43rd and 52nd) (despatches 1963); *m* 3 April 1965 *Sally Catherine, dau of Henry Ian Redfern, of Winchester, and has:

1g +(Robert) Simon; *b* 23 Aug 1967; *m* 1991 *Julia, dau of John Roberts, of S Glamorgan, and has:

1h *Edwina; *b* 199–

2h *Auriol Sophia; *b* 6 Sept 1996

1g *Katherine Louise; *b* 12 Nov 1973

2g *Caroline Sarah; *b* 1974

2f +Peter Charles HAY-DRUMMOND-HAY later Peter Charles Hay DRUMMOND-HAY (1975) [Peter Drummond-Hay Esq, 86 Rowayton Ave, Rowayton, CT 06853, USA]; *b* 18 Nov 1948; *educ* Eton and Trin Coll Cambridge; *m* 1975 *Lady Bettina Mary Lindsay, er dau of 29th Earl of Crawford and (12th Earl of) Balcarres (*qv*), and has:

1g +Thomas Auriol Leo; *b* 20 Nov 1980

1g *Tamsin Rachel; *b* 17 May 1977

2g *Alice Ruth; *b* 15 July 1980

3g *Lily Iona; *b* 21 Jan 1983

1f *Auriol Marion [Mrs Jeffrey Mann, 212 Highway 213, Calera, AL 35040], USA; *b* 11 July 1946; *m* 10 Aug 1968 (*divorce* 1994) Donald Alvin Hessener, s of A Hessener, of Mississippi; *m* 2nd 1995 *Jeffrey K Mann

2e Peter; *b* 7 June 1909; F/O 609 W R Fighter Sqdn RAuxAF WW II; *m* 29 Sept 1939 Clare Margaret (*m* 2nd 14 Dec 1946 Anthony Edgar Dorman, OBE), dau of Robert Davidson, and was presumed *ka* July 1940

3d Cecil Lawrence; *b* 1882; T/Lt RFA WW I, Lt Edinburgh RGA, Nigerian CS and Nigerian Rlwy Lagos; *m* 1st 1911 (*divorce* 1924) Jessie (*d* 1961), yr twin dau of Lawrence Munro, and had:

1e Robert Lawrence; *b* 9 May 1912; *educ* Worcester Coll Oxford (BA 1935, MA 1939)

3d (cont.) Cecil Hay-Drummond-Hay *m* 2nd 1925 Doris Rachel (*d* 1971), dau of Dudley Hill, of Christchurch, NZ, and *d* 21 June 1951, having by her had:

1e *Annette Alistair; *b* 3 May 1927; *m* *David Stanford and has:

1f *Matthew Bethell; *b* 1951

2f *Jonathan David; *b* 1953

3f *Giles Timothy; *b* 1961

1f *Anna Bethell; *b* 1949

2f *Charlotte Sylvia; *b* 1963

1d Florence Caroline Annette; *m* 22 Oct 1919 Capt John Hay Brooks, RGA (*d* 12 Nov 1940) and *d* Nov 1939

1c (cont.) Sir Robert Hay-Drummond-Hay *m* 2nd 9 June 1920 Grace Margarite (*d* 12 Feb 1946), er dau of Sidney Thomas Lethbridge, of Hampstead, and *d* 15 Oct 1926

1c Louisa Annette Edna; *m* 8 Jan 1874 John Brooks (*see* CRAWSHAW, B) and *d* 30 June 1902, leaving issue

2c Alice Emily; *d* unm 9 Nov 1940

3b Thomas Robert Hay; *b* 22 Nov 1821; Col 42nd and 78th Highrs; *m* 1st 3 Nov 1853 Louisa (*d* 8 April 1857), dau of Ringler Thomson, and had:

1c Charles; *b* 14 July 1856; *m* 13 July 1885 Alena (*d* 5 May 1952), dau of G Cropley, of Manitoba, and *d* 8 Jan 1926, leaving:

1d Humphry Ringler, QC; *b* 7 June 1886; slr and barrister Manitoba 1911, memb legal firm of Pitblado, Hoskin, Bennest and Drummond-Hay, Winnipeg; *m* 1st 17 Aug 1912 (*divorce* 1937) May Katherine, dau of Sir George J Bury, and had:

1e (Athol) Bury; *b* 23 June 1913; F/Lt RCAF WW II (POW)

2e George Thomson; *b* 3 April 1916; WW II Seaforth Highrs of Canada (tfd as Capt and Adj to 8th Canadian Recce Regt 1941); *m* 1st 16 June 1939 (*divorce* 1949) Elizabeth Barbara, dau of Donald Gordon Fraser, of Vancouver, and had:

1f Leonard Gordon; *b* 6 April 1940

1f *Elizabeth Sandra; *b* 17 July 1945

2e (cont.) George Drummond-Hay *m* 2nd 1949 (*divorce* 1959) Adrienne Ruth Russell, dau of John William Southin, of Vancouver, and by her had:

2f +Eric Thomson [Mr Eric Drummond-Hay, 10 Trumbull Court, Novato, CA 94947, USA]; *b* 11 April 1951; *m* 1981 *Mary Elizabeth, dau of Sherwin Ray Murray, and has:

1g +Charles Thomson; *b* 1987

1g *Anne Elizabeth; *b* 1985

3f +Charles Webster; *b* 10 May 1952

2f *Leslie Katherine; *b* 30 June 1954

2e (cont.) George Drummond-Hay *m* 3rd 21 June 1964 *Shirlee Marian Montgomery, dau of Harold Gordon Bryce, of Sioux City, Iowa

1d (cont.) Humphry Drummond-Hay *m* 2nd 12 Nov 1937 Dorothy Clare Carey (*d* 6 July 1969), dau of Frederick William Heubach, and *d* 2 Sept 1965

2d Harold Sandford; *b* 5 Sept 1891; with CEF WWs I and II; *m* 1915 Effie Caldwell (*d* 27 Oct 1964), dau of Robert Adamson, of Winnipeg, and *d* 30 Aug 1951, leaving:

1e Charles Robert; *b* 31 March 1917; F/Lt RCAF, WW II as Maj Canadian Army (Militia) Gen List; *m* 17 Aug 1940 *Ina Mary [Mrs Charles Drummond-Hay, 103-4675,Valley Drive, Vancouver V6J 4B7, BC, Canada], dau of George D Disbrow, of Montreal, and *d* 11 July 1966, leaving:

1f +Humphrey Blake; *b* 18 Sept 1945

2f +Brian Maxwell; *b* 21 Oct 1947

3f +Lee Sanford; *b* 18 June 1950

1f *Jane McPherson [Mrs David Saba, 3005 W 29th St, Vancouver, BC, Canada V6L 1Y5]; *b* 4 May 1953; *m* 1990 *David Alexander Saba

1e *Jeanette (Jean) Audrey [Miss Jean Drummond-Hay, Suite 1202, 1122 Gilford St, Vancouver, BC W6G 2P5, Canada]; *b* 20 Aug 1919

1d Eva Auriol; *b* 29 Aug 1887; *d* unm 10 June 1904

2d Doreen Gwendolene; *b* 30 Dec 1909

1c Annie Louisa; *d* 8 Sept 1938

3b (cont.) Col Thomas Drummond-Hay *m* 2nd 17 Dec 1861 Theresa Anne Augusta (*d* 22 April 1902), er dau of Francis Harold Duncombe, 74th Regt, and *d* 24 Oct 1883, having by her had:

2c Frank; *b* 10 Oct 1862; *d* 10 Feb 1863

3c Roland; *b* 17 Oct 1869; *m* 16 Feb 1904 Helen Kate (*m* 2nd 29 Dec 1924 Reginald Maitland Snow (*d* 21 Aug 1939), of Poltimore, Devon), est dau of Charles Hibbert Binney, and *d* 2 Jan 1923

2c Mary Teresa; *m* 1st 1885 Maj Charles Wellesley Parish, RM, and had issue; *m* 2nd 7 Aug 1902 Richard Rising Frederick (*see* FREDERICK, Bt) and *d* 18 Nov 1943

4b George William; *b* 23 April 1827; *dsp*

5b Francis Ringler Drummond-Hay (Sir); *b* 31 March 1830; Consul-Gen Tripoli 1865–90, ktd 1891; *m* 1858 Margherita Paola — (*d* 26 Oct 1904) and *d* 2 June 1905, leaving:

1c Francis Edward, MVO; *b* 17 Aug 1868; Consul Dar-al-Baida 1906, Christiania 1906–10, Luanda 1910–13, Danzig 1913–14, Bahia 1915, Actg Consul-Gen Rio de Janeiro 1915–19, Consul-Gen Lyons 1919–24 and Nantes 1924–29, memb Roy Co Archers; *m* 26 Feb 1895 Eveline Anstey, MBE (*d* 10 Nov 1963), est dau of Rev Edmund Thomas Bennett, of Castle Roe, Co Londonderry, and *d* 31 Jan 1943, having had:

1d Auriol Francis; *b* 14 March, *d* 27 March 1896

2d Claude Francis; *b* 31 July 1898, *educ* Cheltenham; Lt Roy Highrs SR WW I (despatches, wounded); *m* 1st 1921 (*divorce* 1928) Gladys Grant and had:

1e Peter; *b* 28 Aug 1922

2d (cont.) Claude Drummond-Hay *m* 2nd 7 April 1933 Ellenor, dau of G Carlin, of Durham, and by her had:

2e +John Francis [John Drummond-Hay Esq, 44 Inanda Road, Hillcrest, Natal, S Africa]; *b* 18 March 1938; *m* 22 July 1961 *Beverley Ann, dau of Francis Howes, and has:

1f +Sean Francis; *b* 17 March 1962

1f *Deborah Joan, *b* 26 June 1963

3e +Jeffrey Derrick Edward; *b* 4 March 1943; *m* July 1968 *P Wilson and has:

1f *Rachael Ellenor; *b* June 1969

1e *Joan; *b* 14 March 1935

2e Judy; *b* 14 Nov 1936; *d* 20 Jan 1937

2d (cont.) Claude Drummond-Hay *m* 3rd 17 April 1957 *Mrs Gladys Beatrice Robinson, of Babbacombe Cliffs, Torquay

3d Donald; *b* 25 Oct 1906; Capt Argyll & Sutherland Highrs WW II (wounded, POW); *d* unm 13 April 1961

2c Frederick William; *b* 1 Jan 1870; *m* 1st 13 Nov 1894 Ellen Marion (*d* 2 March 1896), dau of Maj Charles Johnson Anthony Deane, IA, and had:

1d Ellen Marion; *b* 2 March 1896; *d* April 1924

2c (cont.) Frederick Drummond-Hay *m* 2nd 1905 Louise Agnese Burke (*d* 20 June 1920), dau of Denis Comerford, of Co Tipperary, and *d* 17 April 1923, having by her had:

2d Rita O'Brien; *b* 1906; *m* 1932 (*divorce* 1954) Arthur Harly Whitcomb and had:

1e *Cheyne; *b* 1933

2e *Brenda; *b* 1935

3c Henry Arthur; *b* 1872; S Africa CS; *m* 12 Nov 1895 Julia Minnie St Barbe (*d* 16 July 1957), dau of William Robinson Hill, MD, of Lymington, Hants, and *d* 22 Oct 1918, having had:

1d Harry Kinfauns; *b* 13 April 1899; *d* 16 Jan 1900

1d Muriel Madeline; *m* 1st Oct 1922 Sidney Noe Pollack (*d* Oct 1926), of Natal, and had issue; *m* 2nd Jan 1936 Rev Canon Kenneth Arthur Chaffey

2d Olive Margarita; *m* Dec 1930 Charles William Lockhart-Barker (*d* 8 June 1957), and had issue

3d Constance Auriol; *m* April 1923 John Ernest Macarthur, Maj HLI, Forest Dept, S African CS, and *d* 24 June 1950, leaving issue

4d Cicely Hay; *m* 10 Jan 1925 Geoffrey Harry Good (*d* 5 Dec 1958), and *d* 22 June 1960, leaving issue

1c Madeline Mary; *m* 10 Aug 1885 Louis Marie Alexandre Lacau, of Cosne, France (*d* 1928)

2c Louisa Margaret; *m* 7 July 1896 Maj Thomas MacGregor Twynam, HLI, and *d* 8 Sept 1925, having had issue

6b James de Vismes Drummond-Hay, CB; *b* 6 Nov 1834; Consul Valparaiso; *m* 1st 1854 Caroline Molinaris (*d* 1 Aug 1872), and had:

1c Francis; *d* young

2c Edward; *b* 21 Sept 1863; *m* 30 Oct 1893 Jessie, dau of — Elsden, of Thornhill, Manitoba, and *d* 8 Aug 1926, having had:

1d Leonard Vivian, MC (1918); *b* 1894; Maj Canadian LI WW I (despatches); *ka* 14 Aug 1918

2d Eric; *b* 1897; Lt Canadian Scottish; *ka* 2 Sept 1918

1c Louisa Caroline; *m* 25 Sept 1890 William St Vincent Bucknall and *d* 2 Feb 1959, leaving issue

6b (cont.) James Drummond-Hay *m* 2nd 1873 Emily Louisa (*d* 29 Oct 1877) dau of R Evans Price, and by her had:

2c Amy Auriol; *m* 10 Feb 1931 Maj Thomas MacGregor Twynam (*d* 29 Jan 1932), HLI

3c Mabel; *m* 3 April 1918 Rev Canon Edward North Redfern, est s of Walter G Redfern, of Scarborough

6b (cont.) James Drummond-Hay *m* 3rd 27 March 1884 Annie, er dau of Henry Hugh Munro, of Lisbon, and *d* 16 Jan 1886, having by her had:

4c Henrietta Wardrop; *b* 1885; *m* 1925 John Godfrey Sedley and had issue

1b Louisa; *m* 26 Nov 1838 G C A Norderling (*d* 1847) and had issue

2b Elizabeth Catherine; *m* 1 May 1840 William Greenwood Chapman (*d* 23 June 1884) and *d* 15 Feb 1911, leaving issue

3b Theodosia; *m* 29 Jan 1844 Pierre Victor Mauboussin (*d* 1863), French Consul-Gen Shanghai, and *d* 20 June 1885

4b Henrietta Auriol; *m* 9 July 1851 Henry Chandos-Pole-Gell (*d* 31 Oct 1902), of Derbyshire, and *d* 21 March 1868, leaving issue

1a Henrietta Auriol; *m* 1831 Rev Morgan Watkins and *d* 1832

(5) (cont.) The Very Rev Edward Hay-Drummond *m* 2nd Amelia, dau of James Auriol, and *d* 30 Dec 1829, having by her had:

2a Amelia Auriol; *m* 3 Sept 1812 Ven George Wilkins, DD (*d* 13 Aug 1865), Preb Southwell, Archdeacon Nottingham

3a Charlotte Auriol; *m* 1st 1835 Rev Edward Lewis, Rector Llanbedr, Breconshire; *m* 2nd 5 July 1864 Rev Thomas Jones, Rector Llanbedr, and *d* 13 Sept 1875

(6) George William Auriol (Rev); *b* 13 March 1761; Canon York, Rector Bowmarsh, Yorks; *m* 1st 12 April 1785 Elizabeth Margaret (*d* 15 Feb 1798), dau of Capt Sir Samuel Marshall, RN, and had:

1a Robert William; *b* 1786; U-Sec Colonial Dept; *d* 9 May 1861

1a Caroline Edith; *d* 27 Dec 1865

(6) (cont.) The Rev George Hay-Drummond *m* 2nd 18 Oct 1800 Maria, dau of John Birbank, and *d* 6 Dec 1807, having by her had:

2a Margaret; *m* 6 Nov 1821 Rev Francis Bazett Grant and had issue (*see* STRATHSPEY, B)

3 Edward Hay; *b* 1722; Min Plen Lisbon 1757, Govr Barbados 1772–79; *m* 1st 1752 Mary (*d* 11 Oct 1775), dau of Peter Flower, and had, with other issue:

(1) Thomas (Rev); *b* 14 April 1759; DD; Canon Ch Ch Oxford; *m* 1 May 1786 Anne, dau of Thomas Bragge, of Clevedale, and *dsp* 29 Jan 1830

(2) William Robert (Rev); *b* 3 Dec 1761; Preb York; *m* 28 Jan 1793 Mary (*d* 18 Feb 1832), dau of William Wagstaffe, of Manchester, and widow of John Astley, and *d* 10 Dec 1839, leaving:

1a Edward (Rev); *b* 16 April 1800; *d* 30 July 1860

1a Mary Anne; *m* 24 July 1828 Rev F T P Hankins (*dsp* 9 July 1876)

3 (cont.) Edward Hay *m* 2nd 24 Jan 1779 Mary Harbourne Barnwell and *d* 30 Dec 1829

1 Mary; *m* 5 Aug 1758 John Hume, DD, Bp Oxford and Salisbury, and *d* 26 Aug 1805

The 9th EARL's nephew,

ROBERT AURIOL HAY-DRUMMOND, **10th Earl of Kinnoull**, PC (1796); *b* 18 March 1751; Lord Lyon King of Arms 1796–1804; *m* 1st 19 April 1779 Julia (*dsp* 29 March 1780), only dau of Anthony Eyre, of Grove, Notts; *m* 2nd 3 June 1781 Sarah (*d* 15 Feb 1837), dau and coheir of Rt Hon Thomas Harley and gdau of Earl of Oxford and Mortimer, and *d* 12 April 1804, having had:

1 THOMAS ROBERT, **11th Earl**

2 Francis John, of Cromlix; *b* 17 Sept 1786; Ensign Coldstream Gds; *d* unm 28 Oct 1810

1 Henrietta; *m* 28 June 1807 Henry Drummond and *d* 7 Oct 1854, leaving issue (*see* PERTH, E)

2 Sarah Maria; *m* 9 May 1811 Rt Rev George Murray, Bp Rochester (*see* ATHOLL, D), and *d* 11 July 1874

The 10th EARL's est son,

THOMAS ROBERT HAY-DRUMMOND, **11th Earl of Kinnoull**; *b* 5 April 1785; *educ* Westminster; Lord Lyon King of Arms 1804–66, Ld Lt Perthshire 1830–66, Col Roy Perthshire Militia; *m* 17 Aug 1824 Louisa Burton (*d* 6 March 1885), 2nd dau of Adml Sir Charles Rowley, 1st Bt, GCB (*qv*), and *d* 18 Feb 1866, having had:

1 GEORGE, **12th Earl**

2 Robert, of Cromlix; *b* 25 July 1831; Capt Coldstream Gds; *ka* Sebastopol 1 Oct 1855

3 Arthur HAY-DRUMMOND later DRUMMOND of Cromlix and Innerpeffray (on inheriting those estates from his er bro Robert 1855), DL (Perthshire); *b* 30 March 1833; Capt RN; *m* 10 July 1855 Katherine Louisa (*d* 22 March 1922), dau of Cobbett Derby, of Horton, Bucks, and *dsp* 28 Jan 1900

4 Charles Rowley HAY-DRUMMOND later DRUMMOND of Cromlix and Innerpeffray (on inheriting those estates), JP (Berks); *b* 10 Oct 1836; Col Scots Fus Gds; CC Berks; *m* 4 Feb 1858 Arabella Augusta (*d* 7 April 1899), yst dau of Col William Henry Meyrick by Lady Laura Vane, 4th dau of 1st Duke of Cleveland (*see* BARNARD, B), and *d* 23 May 1918, having had:

(1) Arthur William Henry JP (Perthshire, Wilts and Suffolk); *b* 4 May 1862; *educ* Eton; Lt-Col and Brevet Col TAR, formerly 6th (Perthshire) Bn Black Watch and 3rd Bn Berkshire Regt; *m* 24 Nov 1891 Mary (*d* 6 June 1948), yst dau of Sir Edward Henry Scott, 5th Bt, and *d* 21 July 1953, having had:

1a Henry Vane; *b* 1 Oct, *d* 10 Oct 1892

2a Robert Vane; *b* 7 Sept 1900; *d* 1 March 1901

3a George Vane; *b* 30 April 1910; *educ* Stowe; Capt Scots Gds (RARO), Capt 6th/7th Bn Black Watch (TA), memb Roy Co Archers; *m* 25 Feb 1933 Lady Betty Mary Seton Montgomerie (*d* 15 Oct 1996), 3rd dau of 16th Earl of Eglinton and Winton (*qv*), and *d* 1984, having had:

1b Robert Vane; *b* 16 Sept 1936; *educ* Eton; memb ICA Scotland and Roy Co Archers; *m* 25 July 1959 *Auriol Fyler [Mrs Robert Hay Drummond, Westridge House, Westridge Green, Streatley, Berks RG8 9RJ], yr dau of Cdr George Martin Pares, RN, of Aldworth, Berks, and *d* 23 Nov 1996

1b *Auriol Vane [Mrs John Young, 7 Inkerman Terrace, Allen Street, London W8 6QX]; *b* 28 Oct 1933; *m* 1st 16 Nov 1957 (*divorce* 1979) John Anthony Murray (*see* 1 Nov 1996), only s of Maj William Henry Murray, and has :

1c *Andrew Henry William Vane; *b* 29 June 1964; *educ* Eton; *m* 1992 *Annabel Charlotte Pring and has:

1d *Alice Victoria; *b* 29 April 1994

2d *Elizabeth Charlotte Vane; *b* 20 Feb 1997

1c *Louise Mary; *b* 2 Oct 1958; *m* 1981 *David Hall and has:

1d *Anna Louise; *b* 1983

2d *Melissa Sarah; *b* 1985

1b (cont.) Mrs Auriol Murray *m* 2nd 1984 *John Strang Mackenzie Young

1a Gwendoline Vane; *b* 23 March 1894; *d* unm 24 Feb 1942

2a Violet Vane; *b* 7 Aug 1897; *m* 18 Dec 1920 (*divorce* 1933) Capt Sir Anthony St John-Mildmay, 8th Bt, MC (*qv*), and had issue

3a Evelyn Vane DRUMMOND of Cromlix (so recognised by Lord Lyon 20 Dec 1954 after inheriting her f's estate); *b* 25 Nov 1904; *m* 12 Sept 1925 8th Baron Auckland (*qv*) and *d* 23 Nov 1971, leaving issue

(2) Harry Claude Frederick Hay, TD; *b* 18 Dec 1864; Maj Black Watch, formerly Capt 3rd Bn Roy Berks Regt, memb Roy Co Archers; *m* 25 July 1889 Harriet Lepel Dorothea (*d* 11 July 1922), yst dau of Capt Frederick Sayer, RWF, and *dsp* 26 April 1939

(3) Algernon Richard Francis Hay, OBE (1918); *b* 19 May 1870; King's Messenger 1919–35; *m* 26 Jan 1904 Mary Verena Campbell, CBE, dau of John Bald, of Kilgraston, and *dsp* 1 Feb 1945

(1) Evelyn Elisabeth Vane; *m* 6 April 1880 Sir Robert Drummond Moncreiffe of that Ilk, 8th Bt (*see* ERROLL, E), and *d* 16 Jan 1938

(2) Ida Agnes Vane; *m* 22 Sept 1885 Reginald West (*d* 11 May 1921), 2nd s of Sir Algernon Edmund West, PC, GCB, and *d* 28 Oct 1938, leaving issue

(3) Amy Violet Poulett; *m* 19 April 1888 Hon George Eden (*d* 14 June 1924), 2nd s of 4th Baron Auckland (*qv*) and *d* 10 Dec 1926, leaving issue

(4) Maude Aline; *b* 4 Feb 1872; *d* unm 2 Feb 1941

1 Louisa; *m* 2 May 1843 Sir Thomas Moncreiffe of that Ilk, 7th Bt, and *d* 4 Sept 1898, leaving issue (*see* ERROLL, E)

2 Sarah; *m* 23 March 1848 2nd Baron Delamere (*qv*) and *dsp* 17 Feb 1859

3 Frances; *m* 19 Aug 1852 Col Richard Thomas Lloyd, Gren Gds (*d* 4 Nov 1898), of Aston Hall, Salop, and Chigwell, Essex, and *d* 31 Jan 1886, leaving issue

4 Elizabeth; *m* 1st 24 April 1856 Sir Frederick Leopold Arthur, 2nd Bt (*qv*), and had issue; *m* 2nd 22 Nov 1883 Rev Canon Ernest Edward Dugmore (*d* 10 March 1925), Vicar Parkstone, Dorset, and *d* 24 Feb 1902

5 Augusta Sophia; *m* 24 April 1856 17th Baron Saye and Sele (*qv*) and *d* 23 July 1915, leaving issue

The 11th EARL's est son,

GEORGE HAY-DRUMMOND, **12th Earl of Kinnoull**, DL (Perthshire); *b* 16 July 1827; Capt 1st Life Gds 1851–56; *m* 20 July 1848 Lady Emily Blanche Charlotte Somerset (*d* 27 Jan 1895), dau of 7th Duke of Beaufort (*qv*), and *d* 31 Jan 1897, having had:

1 George Robert, *Viscount Dupplin*; *b* 27 May 1849; Lt 1st Life Gds; *m* 4 Oct 1871 (*divorce* 1876) Lady Agnes Cecil Emmeline (*d* 11 Jan 1925), yst dau of 5th Earl Fife (*see* FIFE, D), and *dvp* 10 March 1886, leaving:

(1) Agnes Blanche Màrie; *b* 6 Dec 1873; *m* 21 Feb 1903 Baron Herbert von Hindeburg, Cnsllr German Emb Rome, and *d* 13 Dec 1938

2 Francis George; *b* 29 May 1853; Page-of-Honour to HM QUEEN VICTORIA; *d* 11 Sept 1884

3 ARCHIBALD FitzROY GEORGE, **13th Earl**

4 Alistair George; *b* 18 April 1861; Capt 3rd Bn Black Watch, Chev Legn Hon; *m* 1st 12 Jan 1890 (*divorce* 1908) Hon Camilla Dagmar Violet Greville (*d* 7 July 1938), est dau of 2nd Baron Greville (*see* 1970 edn), and had:

(1) Auriol Camilla Sharlie Blanche; *b* 2 Jan 1893; *m* 1st 12 March 1917 Capt Rowland Noel Barran (*kas* 19 March 1919; *see* BARRAN, Bt); *m* 2nd 25 Feb 1924 Sir James Allan Horne (*d* 3 Feb 1944), s of Arthur Horne, and *d* 7 Sept 1930, leaving issue

4 (cont.) Alistair Hay-Drummond *m* 2nd 1909 Hyacinthe (*d* 29 June 1938), yst dau of Capt John Farrer, 1st Life Gds, of Roscrea, Co Tipperary, and *d* 15 April 1929

5 Claude George, JP (London); *b* 24 June 1862; MP Hoxton 1900–10; T/Capt Gen List; *d* 24 Oct 1920

1 Constance Blanche Louisa; *m* 28 Oct 1880 Walter Henry Hadow (*d* 15 Sept 1898), and *d* 21 Dec 1931, leaving issue

2 Celia Evangeline Constance; *d* young 18 May 1868

3 Muriel Henrietta Constance; *m* 3 June 1890 Prince Alexander Münster (*d* 1922), s of HSH Prince Münster, German Amb London; readmitted to British nationality 1923; *d* 2 Jan 1927, leaving issue

The 12th EARL's est surv son,

ARCHIBALD FitzROY GEORGE HAY-DRUMMOND, **13th Earl of Kinnoull**, JP and DL (Perthshire); *b* 20 June 1855; Lt Black Watch, Col Egyptian Gendarmerie (medal, bronze star, Osmanieh); *m* 1st 13 July 1877 Josephine Maria (*d* 2 Dec 1900), dau of John M Hawke, and had:

1 Edmund Alfred Rollo George, *Viscount Dupplin*; *b* 12 Nov 1879; Lt 1st Vol Bn Roy Sussex Regt; *m* 11 Feb 1901 Gladys Luz (*d* 28 Jan 1932), 2nd dau of Anthony Harley Bacon and ggdau of 5th Earl of Oxford and Mortimer, and *dvp* 30 May 1903, leaving:

(1) GEORGE HARLEY, **14th Earl**

The **13th Earl** *m* 2nd 24 Jan 1903 Florence Mary (*m* 2nd 26 May 1919 Maj John Joseph Berington (*d* 19 Aug 1955), s of Charles Michael Berington, JP, DL, of Worcs, and *d* 2 July 1941), yst dau of Edward Tierney Gilchrist Darell (*see* DARELL, Bt), and *d* 7 Feb 1916, having by her had:

2 Edward; *b* 29 June 1906; *d* an infant

3 FitzRoy; *b* 29 June 1906; *d* an infant

1 *Elizabeth (Blanche) Mary; *b* 14 Dec 1903; *m* 1st 15 April 1925 (*divorce* 1935) Peter Stanley Chappell, only s of Thomas Stanley Chappell, of Moreton Morell, Warwicks, and has:

(1) *Michael Stanley FitzRoy [Michael Chappell Esq, 760 Grover Avenue, Coquitlam, New Westminster, BC, Canada]; *b* 6 Oct 1926; *m* 10 Aug 1952 *Eileen Day, of Vancouver

1 (cont.) Lady Elizabeth Chappell *m* 2nd 23 May 1935 (*divorce* 1945) Douglas William Ernest Gordon (*d* 1951); *m* 3rd 1945 William Herbert Shelley Dent, MC, only s of Herbert Dent, of Canton, China

2 Margaret Florence Grace; *b* 2 Oct 1907; *m* 26 Feb 1929 (*divorce* 1942) Norman Francis William Haliburton D'Arcy, s of Frank D'Arcy, and *d* 12 June 1976, leaving issue

The 13th EARL's gs,

GEORGE HARLEY HAY-DRUMMOND, **14th Earl of Kinnoull**; *b* 30 March 1902; *educ* Eton; *m* 1st 15 Dec 1923 (*divorce* Scottish Courts 1 Nov 1927) Enid Margaret Hamlyn, only child of Mrs Margaret Fellows, of Tangley Park, nr Guildford, 2nd dau of Sir Frederick Wills, 1st Bt, of Northmoore (*see* DULVERTON, B), and had:

1 Henry George Adam, *Viscount Dupplin*; *b* 23 Nov 1924; *d* 7 March 1925

The **14th Earl** *m* 2nd 6 June 1928 Mary Ethel Isobel (*d* 15 Dec 1938), dau of Ferdinand Richard Holmes Meyrick, MD, and *d* 18 March 1938, having by her had:

2 A son; *b* 9 May, *d* 19 May 1931

3 ARTHUR WILLIAM GEORGE PATRICK, **15th and present Earl**

1 *Venetia Constance Kathleen Luz [The Lady Venetia Davies, Old School Court, Grimston Gdns, Folkestone, Kent CT20 2UA]; *m* 1953 *Maj Joseph Trevor Davies and has:

(1) *Nicola Jane; *b* 24 Feb 1957

(2) *Sally May; *b* 13 Nov 1960 [Mrs Mark Fairbanks Smith, 10 Milton Mansions, Queen's Club Gdns, London W14 9RP]; *m* 1992 *A Mark Fairbanks Smith, only s of Esmond Fairbanks Smith, of W Sussex

2 *June Anne; *m* 7 May 1955 *Baron Onslow of Woking (*qv*) and has issue

KINROSS

Arms: Ermine on a chevron sable between in chief two torteaux and in base an open book, an otter's head erased proper. **Crest:** On a rock a mermaid holding in the dexter hand an otter's head erased and in her sinister hand a swan's head also erased, all proper. **Supporters:** On either side an otter proper, charged on the shoulder with two swords in saltire, also proper. **Motto:** (over the crest) *Nil temere* ('Nothing rashly'). **Creation:** B. (UK) 15 July 1902.

THE 5TH BARON KINROSS, of Glasclune, Co Haddington (Christopher Patrick Balfour) [The Rt Hon The Lord Kinross, 11 Belford Pl, Edinburgh EH4 3DH]; *b* 1 Oct 1949; *s* f 1985; *educ* Eton, St Andrews and Edinburgh U (LLB 1975); WS, memb Roy Co Archers; *m* 29 June 1974 *Susan Jane, yst dau of Ian Robert Pitman, WS, of Langlands, Kirkcudbright, and has:

1 +ALAN IAN; *b* 4 April 1978

2 +Derek Andrew; *b* 1981

Lineage: JOHN BALFOUR, of Midlefudie, near Dairsie, Fife; Elder at Dairsie 1655; had:

PATRICK BALFOUR; *bapt* 9 March 1655; ruling Elder at Leuchars, Fife; *m* 25 July 1666 Margaret Lyall, of St Andrews, and had, with another s (James, of Meikle Dron, Leuchars, ancestor of Sir Robert Balfour, Bt):

ALEXANDER BALFOUR, of Brockley, Leuchars, Fife; ordained Elder 25 July 1686; *m* 9 Nov 1723 Ann Low and had, with a dau (Margaret, *b* 11 June 1737, *m* 20 Oct 1764 her cousin James Balfour of Kilmany, Fife, and *d* 19 June 1824):

JAMES BALFOUR, of Brockley, Fife; *m* Christian Foggo and had, with other issue:

Rev PETER BALFOUR; *b* 14 Sept 1794; successively Min of Evie in Orkney, Tealing, Forfar and Clackmannan; *m* 22 Jan 1833 Jane Ramsay (*d* 14 Jan 1871), only dau of John Blair, of Perth, and *d* 18 March 1862, having had:

1 James; *b* 30 Dec 1834; *d* unm 23 Jan 1902

2 JOHN BLAIR, **1st Baron**

1 Margaret Christina; *b* 9 June 1840; *m* 28 April 1863 William James Haig, of Dollarfield, Clackmannanshire, and had issue

The yr son,

JOHN BLAIR BALFOUR, **1st Baron Kinross**, of Glasclune, Co Haddington (UK), so *cr* 15 July 1902, PC (1883), JP and DL (Edinburgh and Haddington; *b* 11 July 1837; MP (Lib) Clackmannan and Kinross 1880–99, Ld Justice Gen and Ld Pres Court of Session in Scotland 1899–1905, LLD Edinburgh and St Andrews; *m* 1st 4 Aug 1869 Lillias Oswald (*d* 19 June 1872), est dau of Donald Mackenzie, Ld of Session as Lord Mackenzie, and had:

1 PATRICK, **2nd Baron**

The **1st Baron** *m* 2nd 6 April 1877 Hon Marianne Eliza (*d* 25 Sept 1913), 2nd dau of 1st Baron Moncreiff (*qv*), and by her had:

2 James Moncreiff, OBE (1919); *b* 6 July 1878 *educ* Cheltenham and Balliol Coll Oxford (BA 1901); FSA, WS; Capt TFR and Scottish Horse, Staff Capt 1917; Ch Assist to Fin Advsr Persian Govt 1920–21, KStJ; *m* 27 June 1908 Madeline Maude Graham (*d* 5 Oct 1970 aged 89), dau of James Graham Watson, of Kingston Grange, Midlothian, and *dsp* 30 April 1960

3 John Ramsey Blair; *b* 21 Sept 1881; *educ* Cheltenham and Balliol Coll Oxford (BA 1904); Lt-Cdr RNVR; *d* unm 23 Oct 1964

4 Harry Robert Chichester; *b* 31 Oct 1882; *educ* Cheltenham and Balliol Coll Oxford (BA 1905), MA Christ's Coll Cambridge; Capt 3rd Bn Roy Scots WW I (wounded); Clerk H of C and Home Office; *m* 20 Oct 1921 Dorothy Constance (*d* 8 Nov 1963), est dau of Henry Goulburn Willoughby Chetwynd (*see* CHETWYND, V), and *d* 11 Dec 1964, having had:

(1) +Anthony John Chetwynd, CBE (1987) [A/Cdr Anthony Balfour CBE, Cymbeline, 43A Ellesborough Rd, Wendover, Bucks HP22 6EL]; *b* 19 Nov 1925; *educ* Eton and King's Coll Cambridge (BA 1948, MA 1951, MB, BChir

1960); FRCPath, consultant pathology RAF Medical Branch; *m* 15 Sept 1958 *Judith Ann Margaret, yr dau of Leslie Field Anderson, of Worthing, and has:

1a +Peter John Torquil; *b* 14 July 1959; BSc, MB, ChB (Birmingham); *m* 1st 1985 (*divorce* 1989) Nicola Jane, dau of David Charles Yarwood; *m* 2nd 1994 (*divorce* 1995) Patricia, dau of Jerome Dawson, of Belfast

2a +Harry Luke Chetwynd; *b* 28 Aug 1963

1a *Helena Clare; *b* 1 Feb 1961; SRN; *m* 1989 *John Trevor Eades, of Wimbledon, and has:

1b *Louis John Frederick; *b* 21 Jan 1991

2b *Jack Edward Luke; *b* 5 April 1993

3b *David Harry Robert; *b* 20 March 1995

(1) Elizabeth; *b* 18 Dec, *d* 24 Dec 1922

(2) *Hilary Joan Gwendolen [Miss Hilary Balfour, 1 The Maisonettes, Icknield Rd, Goring-on-Thames, Berks]; *b* 9 Feb 1924

5 Norman Frederick William (Rev); *b* 26 March 1884; *educ* Balliol Coll Oxford (BA 1906, MA 1911); T/CF WW I 1917–18, 32nd Lowland Field Amb RAMC (T); Vicar Leafield with Wychwood, Oxon, 1921–26, Assist Priest St Paul's Herne Hill 1945–54; *d* unm 27 April 1954

1 Isabel Nora Gwendoline; *b* 8 Sept 1885; *m* 19 Sept 1908 (*annulled* 1917) Capt Percival Henry Havelock Bailey, 34th Sikh Pioneers, s of Col Bailey, late RE, and *dsp* 8 April 1961

The 1st BARON *d* 22 Jan 1905; his est son,

PATRICK BALFOUR, **2nd Baron Kinross**, KC; *b* 23 April 1870; *educ* Harrow and Balliol Coll Oxford (BA 1894); advocate 1897, Advocate Depute 1927–27, Sheriff Dumfries and Galloway 1927; Maj (Gen List), Brig Roy Co of Archers, dir Scottish Widows' Fund Life Assur Soc and Bank of Scotland; *m* 18 Aug 1903 Caroline Elsie (*d* 18 Feb 1969 aged 89), dau of Arthur Henry Johnstone Douglas, DL of Lockerbie (*see* QUEENSBERRY, M), and *d* 28 July 1939, leaving:

1 (JOHN) PATRICK DOUGLAS BALFOUR, **3rd Baron Kinross**; *b* 25 June 1904; *educ* Winchester and Balliol Coll Oxford (BA 1925); S/Ldr RAFVR WW II (despatches); jnlst; author: *The Windsor Years*; dir Publicity Section Br Emb Cairo with rank of 1st Sec 1944–47; *m* 11 Feb 1938 (*divorce* 1942) Angela Mary, only dau of Capt George Culme-Seymour (*see* CULME-SEYMOUR, Bt) and formerly w of John George Spencer-Churchill (*see* MARLBOROUGH, D), and *dsp* 4 June 1976

2 DAVID ANDREW, **4th Baron**

1 *Pamela Lillias [The Hon Mrs Scott-Plummer, Mainhouse, Kelso, Roxburghshire]; *b* 24 June 1907; *m* 7 April 1933 Charles Humphrey Scott-Plummer (*d* 1991), er s of Lt-Col Joseph Walter Scott-Plummer, of Selkirk, and has:

(1) *(Patrick) Joseph [Joseph Scott-Plummer Esq, Mainhouse, Kelso, Roxburghshire]; *b* 24 Aug 1943; *educ* Radley and Magdalene Coll Cambridge (BA 1966); ACA; *m* 1st 1970 (*divorce* 1977) Grizel Elizabeth-Anne (Lulla) (*m* 2nd Peter William Denby Roberts; *see* ROBERTS, Bt of Milner Field), only dau of Lt Col Anthony Way, of Kincairney, Dunkeld, Perthshire, and has:

1a *Charles Humphrey; *b* 1972

1a *Annabel Cecilia; *b* 1974

(1) Joseph Scott-Plummer *m* 2nd 1977 his former w's 2nd husb's 1st w *Christine Margaret Hermione, dau of Capt Hon Anthony Gerard Hugh Bampfylde (*see* POLTIMORE, B) and formerly w of Peter William Denby Roberts (*see* ROBERTS, Bt, of Milner Field), and by her has:

2a *(Anthony) Guy; *b* 1978

(1) *Julia Elizabeth [Mrs Rae Lyster, Malting Green House, Layer-de-la-Haye, Essex LD2 DJE]; *b* 8 Jan 1935; *m* 24 May 1958 *Rae Lionel Haggard Lyster, er s of Lionel Lyster, and has:

1a *Nicholas Charles; *b* 8 March 1959

1a *Amanda Pamela; *b* 29 May 1961

2a *Lucy Caroline; *b* 23 May 1963

(2) *(Olivia) Jane [Mrs Thomas Benyon, The Old Rectory, Adstock, Bucks]; *b* 6 Nov 1946; *m* 17 Feb 1968 *Thomas Yates Benyon, yr s of Thomas Yates Benyon, of Edinburgh (*see* 1970 edn NORTH, B), and has:

1a *Thomas Yates; *b* 1974

2a *Oliver William Yates; *b* 1981

1a *Clare Julia Yates; *b* 1969

2a *Camilla Lucinda Joan Yates; *b* 1972

2 Rosemary Jean; *b* 21 June 1910; *m* 1st 12 Oct 1934 (*divorce* 1958) Alex Maskell Mitchell, yr s of Lt-Col Alexander Mitchell, of Tullallan Kincardine-on-Forth, and Monksford, St Boswells, and had issue; *m* 2nd 23 June 1958 Robert Monteath McLaren, yr s of James Alexander McLaren, of Edinburgh

3 *Ursula Nina [The Hon Mrs Dallmeyer, Green Corner, Tyninghame, Dunbar, E Lothian]; *b* 12 March 1914; *m* 14 Sept 1939 *Lt-Col Christopher James York Dallmeyer, DSO, TD, WS, Lothian and Border Horse Yeo, yst s of Richard Owen John Dallmeyer, of Suffolk, and has:

(1) *Gavin Richard James [Gavin Dallmeyer Esq, Craigiewood, Nth Kessock, Inverness]; *b* 27 March 1942; *educ* Winchester; *m* 1970 *Araminta Morgan and has:

1a *Thomas Charles; *b* 1979

1a *Flora Jane; *b* 1975

(2) *Andrew Victor [Andrew Dallmeyer Esq, 20 Ann St, Edinburgh 4]; *b* 10 Jan 1945; *educ* Dauntsey's; *m* July 1969 *Vivienne Dixon and has:

1a *Tobias; *b* 1973

1a *Amy Jane Eleanor; *b* 1985

(3) *James; *b* 21 Aug 1948; *educ* Radley; *m* 1978 *Margherita Elizabeth Dimanbro

(1) *Rosemary Nicolson; *b* 11 Aug 1940; *m* 12 Jan 1962 *Rev Paul Roderick Nicolson, er s of Roderick William Nicolson, of Kimpton, Herts, and has:

1a *Roderick John; *b* 27 Dec 1962

2a *Hugo James; *b* 22 April 1965

3a *Thomas Paul; *b* 10 June 1966

1a *Claire Katherine; *b* 24 Aug 1968

2a *Kristina Belle; *b* 1975

The 3rd BARON's brother,

DAVID ANDREW BALFOUR, **4th Baron Kinross**, OBE (1968), TD, DL (Edinburgh 1966); *b* 29 March 1906; *educ* Sherborne and Edinburgh U; WS; Col RA (TA) WW II, Hon Col 278th (Lowland) Field Regt RA (TA), City of Edinburgh Artillery 1964–67; chm Br Legion Scotland 1965–68, memb Roy Co Archers; *m* 1st 10 June 1936 (*divorce* 1941) Araminta, 2nd dau of Lt-Col Willoughby Ewart Peel, DSO, of Eaglescarnie, Haddington, and had:

1 *Ariadne Maria [The Hon Mrs Ariadne Nicholson, 2 Halesden Rd, Heaton Chapel, Stockport, Cheshire]; *b* 31 Jan 1939; *m* 22 April 1961 (*divorce* 1990) Richard Elliot Nicholson, yr s of Robert Watson Nicholson, of Newcastle, and Mrs Kenneth Arthur Seth-Smith, of Chesterwood Grange, Haydon Bridge, Northumberland, and has:

(1) *Robert David; *b* 16 Feb 1964

(2) *Matthew Charles; *b* 4 Oct 1968

(3) *Edward Alan; *b* 9 March 1971

(1) *Camilla Jane; *b* 14 March 1962

The **4th Baron** *m* 2nd 17 April 1948 Helen Anne (*d* 2 May 1969), yr dau of Alan Welwood Hog, of Edinburgh, and formerly w of Lt-Col Patrick Cassan Perfect, and by her had:

1 CHRISTOPHER PATRICK BALFOUR, **5th and present Baron Kinross**

The **4th Baron** *m* 3rd 1972 *Ruth Beverly [The Rt Hon The Dowager Lady Kinross, 58 India Rd, Edinburgh], dau of William Henry Mill, SSC, of Edinburgh, and formerly w of Kenneth William Bruce Middleton, Sheriff Lothian and Borders at Edinburgh and Haddington, and *d* 1985

KINTORE

Arms: Quarterly, 1st and 4th, argent on a chief gules three pallets or (for KEITH); 2nd, azure a falcon displayed between three mullets argent, on his breast a man's heart gules (for FALCONER of Halkerton); 3rd, per pale engrailed gules and or, a boar passant counterchanged (for BAIRD of Ury); over all, on an inescutcheon gules, a sceptre and sword in saltire with an Imperial Crown between the upper corners all proper, within an orle of eight thistles slipped near the head or, ensigned with an earl's coronet (coat of augmentation granted to **1st Earl of Kintore** for preserving Scotland's regalia). **Crests:** 1 A noble lady from the middle richly attired, holding in her right hand a garland proper (crest of augmentation for earldom), 2 A roebuck's head proper, attired or. **Supporters:** Two men in complete armour proper, each holding a spear gules, banded argent, in posture of sentinels. **Mottoes:** 1 (above 1st crest) *Quae amissa salva* ('What has been lost is safe'), 2 (above 2nd crest) *Veritas vincit* ('Truth conquers'), 3 (at base) *Thay say quhat say thay; thay haif sayd lat thame say* ('They say what they say; let them say what they have said'). **Creations:** E. and L. (S) 20 June 1677, Bt. (UK) 8 March 1897, B. (UK) 12 June 1925 (Stonehaven), V. (UK) 27 June 1938 (Stonehaven).

THE 13TH EARL OF KINTORE, Viscount Stonehaven, Lord Keith of Inverurie and Keith Hall, Baron Stonehaven and a **Baronet** (Sir Michael Canning William John Keith, Bt) [The Rt Hon The Earl of Kintore, Keith Hall, Inverurie, Aberdeenshire AB51 0LD]; *b* 22 Feb 1939; *s* f 1989; *educ* Eton and RMA Sandhurst; late Lt Coldstream Gds; ACII; *m* 9 Oct 1972 *Mary, only dau of S/Ldr Elisha Gaddis Plum, of Rumson, NJ, USA, and has:

1 +JAMES WILLIAM FALCONER; *Lord Inverurie, Master of Kintore*; *b* 15 April 1976; *educ* Gordonstoun

1 *Iona Delia Mary Gaddis; *b* 1 Jan 1978

Lineage: HERVEY, thought to have been of non-Scottish origin; held half the lands of Keith, called Keith-Hervey, later Keith-Marischal, Humbie Parish, Haddington or E Lothian, *temp* DAVID I (1124–53), to whom he was Marshal; had:

MALCOLM de KEITH; alleged f of:

PHILIP; had:

HERVEY de KETH [*sic*]; probably the person of that name who as Marshal witnessed charters *temp* ALEXANDER II (1214–49); had:

Sir JOHN de KEITH; Marshal of Scotland; possibly f of:

Sir WILLIAM de KEITH; alleged f of:

1 Robert (Sir); Marshal by *c* 1290; Warden Selkirk Forest by 1300, when taken prisoner by the English, with whom he later served in Scotland 1303; Sheriff Aberdeen 1304 and 1335–43; threw in his lot with ROBERT I (THE BRUCE) late 1308, cmdg the light horse in the Scottish army Bannockburn 1314; confirmed as Marshal by ROBERT 1324; *d* probably between Aug 1343 and spring 1344, having had:

(1) John (Sir); *m* —, sis and coheir of William de Soules, and *dvp* 1324, leaving:

1a Robert; *s* gf as Marshal; *dspm*

2 Edward (Sir); *s* gn as Marshal; *m* by July 1305 Isabel, dau of Alexander de Synton, and was probably *k* Battle of Neville's Cross 17 Oct 1346, leaving, with a s (Sir Edward, *m* Christian, dau of Margaret, Countess of Mar, *see* MAR, E):

(1) William (Sir), KB by 1333; Marshal; allegedly taken prisoner by English Battle of Halidon Hill 1333; apparently *d* by 1352 and was seemingly f of:

1a William (Sir); Marshal of Scotland, Sheriff Kincardine 1357–59; *m* by 3 May 1351 Margaret, dau of John Fraser and gdau of Sir Alexander Fraser by Mary, sis of ROBERT I (*see* SALTOUN, L), and *d* between 13 May 1407 and 2 June 1413, having had (with several daus including Christiana, *m* Sir William Lindsay of the Byres (*see* LINDSAY, E); Muriel, *m* as his 2nd w 1st Duke of Albany; *see* MORAY, E):

1b John; *m* — (Jean?; *m* 2nd 1375 Sir John Lyon of Glamis; *see* STRATHMORE AND KINGHORNE, E; *m* 3rd *c* Nov 1384 Sir James Sandilands of Calder; *see* TORPHICHEN, L), dau of ROBERT II, and *dvp* by 27 Dec 1375, leaving:

1c Robert; *dsp* by 12 March 1406/7

2b Robert (Sir); ktd 1383–90, Marshal by 12 March 1406/7; *d* by 20 July 1430, leaving:

1c William (Sir); ktd by 1 April 1426; *m* Mary — (*see* LOVAT, L, for possible identity) and *d* probably Oct 1444, leaving:

1d Robert (Sir); ktd by Feb 1439/40; Marshal; allegedly *m* Janet, dau of Sir John Seton of Seton and *dspm* by 22 Sept 1446, leaving:

1e Janet; *m c* March 1463/4 2nd Lord Gray (*qv*)

2d WILLIAM

3d John

4d Alexander

1d Marion; *m* as his 2nd w Alexander Fraser, 5th of Lovat (*see* LOVAT, L)

1a Janet; *m* as his 1st w Philip De Arbuthnott (*see* ARBUTHNOTT, V)

The 2nd s,

Sir WILLIAM de KEITH, 1st EARL MARISCHAL, so *cr* between 5 Nov 1457 and 4 July 1458, as also earlier by July 1451 LORD KEITH (both S); Great Marischal of Scotland; *m* Mariot Erskine, dau of 2nd Lord Erskine (*see* MAR, E), and *d* by 1483; having had, with other issue, including two daus (Janet, *m* 1st John, Master of Rothes (*see* ROTHES, E), *m* 2nd Lord Innermeath (*see* MORAY, E); Mary, *m* Sir William Murray of Tullibardine; *see* ATHOLL, D):

WILLIAM KEITH, 2nd EARL MARISCHAL, PC (S Feb 1489/90); *m c* 11 Jan 1481/2 Elizabeth, dau of 2nd Earl of Huntly (*see* HUNTLY, M), and *d* between 24 Nov 1526 and 2 May 1527, leaving:

1 Robert, *Lord Keith*; *m* just prior to 8 Jan 1505/6 Lady Beatrice/Elizabeth Douglas, dau of 2nd Earl of Morton (*qv*) and ggdau of JAMES I, and *dvp* by 22 April 1525, leaving, with other issue:

(1) WILLIAM, 3rd EARL

(2) Robert; Abbot of Deer; *d* 12 June 1551; had an illegitimate s:

1a ANDREW KEITH, 1st and apparently last LORD DINGWALL, so *cr* 18 March 1583/4; *dsp*

(3) Alexander; ancestor of the KEITHs of Uras and Bp Robert Keith, Scottish ecclesiastical historian

(1) Christian; *m* as his 2nd w Robert Arbuthnott of that Ilk (*see* ARBUTHNOTT, V)

(2) Janet; *m* 6 Feb 1542/3 7th Lord of Glamis (*see* STRATHMORE AND KINGHORN, E)

2 Robert

3 Alexander, of Aquhorsk; ancestor of Rev Dr George Skene Keith

4 John, of Craig; ancestor of Sir Robert Murray Keith, KB, Amb

1 Janet; *m* Dec 1515 2nd Earl of Montrose (*see* MONTROSE, D)

2 Elizabeth; *m* 1st Colin, Master of Oliphant (*ka* Flodden 9 Sept 1513); *m* 2nd, as his 1st w, 4th Lord Sinclair (*qv*)

The gs,

WILLIAM KEITH, 3rd EARL MARISCHAL, PC (S); Extrdy Ld of Session 1541, 1561 and 1573, an early Protestant; fought Battle of Pinkie 10 Sept 1547; *m* by June 1538 his cousin Margaret, er dau of William Keith by Janet, dau of 2nd Lord Gray (*qv*), and *d* 7 Oct 1581, having had, with other issue:

1 William, *Lord Keith*, PC (S 1569); captured by the Percys (*see* NORTHUMBERLAND, D) 1558 and held by them some 10 years; *m c* 13 Jan 1553/4 Lady Elizabeth Hay, dau of 7th Earl of Erroll (*qv*), and *dvp* 9/10 Aug 1580, leaving:

(1) GEORGE, 4th EARL

2 ROBERT KEITH, 1st LORD ALTRIE (S), so *cr* 29 July 1587, with a special remainder to his bro's s (*see* below); *b c* 1529; *dspm* 1 July–26 Sept 1592

1 Anne; *m* 1st 1561 James, Earl of Moray, Regent of Scotland; *m* 2nd 6th Earl of Argyll (*see* ARGYLL, D)

2 Alice/Alison; *m c* 28 Aug 1550, as his 1st w, 6th Lord Saltoun (*qv*) of Abernethy and *d* Aug 1567

3 Elizabeth; *m* 1st Colin, Master of Oliphant; *m* 2nd William, 4th Lord Sinclair (*qv*)

The grandson,

GEORGE KEITH, 4th EARL MARISCHAL and (*s* unc as) 2nd LORD ALTRIE, PC (S 1585); *b* 1553; Amb Denmark to negotiate JAMES VI's marriage 1589, fndr Marischal Coll Aberdeen (later U) 1593, High Commr Parl Scotland 1609; *m* 1st *c* 4/5 Feb 1580/1 Margaret, dau of 5th Lord Home (*see* HOME, E), and had issue; *m* 2nd Margaret, dau of 5th Lord Ogilvy of Airlie (*see* AIRLIE, E), by whom he had two sons, and *d* 2 April 1623; his est s by his 1st w:

WILLIAM KEITH, 5th EARL MARISCHAL, PC (S March 1625/6); *b c* 1585; *m c* 12 Oct 1609 Lady Mary Erskine, dau of 2nd Earl of Mar (*see* MAR and KELLIE, E), and *d* 28 Oct 1635, having had, with other issue (including an est dau Mary, *m* John, Lord (Graham of) Kinpont, s and h of 7th Earl of Menteith; *see* MONTROSE, D):

1 WILLIAM KEITH, 6th EARL MARISCHAL, PC (S 1638); *b* 1614; Covenanter by 1639 but royalist Civil War, fought Battle of Preston 1648, imprisoned during Interregnum 1651–60 (when obliged to sell much of his estate to pay debts), Ld Privy Seal (S) 1660/1–March 1670/1, Sheriff Aberdeen 1666, Col Militia 1668; *m* 1st 1637 Lady Elizabeth Seton, dau of 3rd Earl of Winton (*see* EGLINTON and WINTON, E), and had, with other issue:

(1) William, *Lord Keith*; *b* 11 Aug 1638; *dvp* an infant

(1) Mary; *m* 1st Sir James Hope (*see* LINLITHGOW, M); *m* 2nd Sir Archibald Murray, 3rd Bt, of Blackbarony (*qv*)

(2) Elizabeth; *m* 2nd Viscount Arbuthnott (*qv*)

1 (cont.) The 6th EARL *m* 2nd 1654 Lady Anne Douglas, dau of 7th Earl of Morton (*qv*), and *dspms* March 1670/1

2 James (Sir), of Benholme; *m* Margaret, dau of Sir David Lindsay of Edzell (*see* CRAWFORD and BALCARRES, E) and had:

(1) Elizabeth; *m* by 1641, as his 1st w, Sir Archibald Primrose, 1st Bt (*see* ROSEBERY, E)

3 GEORGE KEITH, 7th EARL MARISCHAL, PC (S 1672); fought as royalist Battles of Preston 1648 and Worcester 1651; *m* 6 Feb 1662 Lady Mary Hay, dau of 2nd Earl of Kinnoull (*qv*), and *d* 1694, leaving an only s:

(1) WILLIAM KEITH, 8th EARL MARISCHAL, (KT 1705 by titular James III, the Old Pretender), PC (S 1701); *b c* 1664; Tory who was against Union of S and E Parls and as a noble of Jacobite sympathies was under suspicion March 1707/8 at the time of the abortive French-led invasion of Scotland, rep S peer 1710–12; *m c* 1690 Lady Mary Drummond, dau of 4th Earl of Perth (*qv*), and *d* 1712, leaving:

1a GEORGE KEITH, 9th EARL MARISCHAL; *b* 1692; attainted 1716 for participation Rising of 1715 (cmded right wing Jacobite army Sheriffmuir 13 Nov), led another Jacobite rising Scotland 1719; served 1747 on under FREDERICK II (THE GREAT) as Prussian Amb at Paris 1751–54 and Madrid 1759–61, Order Black Eagle 1752; *d* unm 28 May 1778

2a James Francis Edward; *b* 4 June 1696; also attainted 1716; Col Spanish serv 1719–28, Gen Russian serv under EMPRESSES ANNE and ELIZABETH 1728–47, FM Prussian serv under FREDERICK II 1747, Govr Berlin 1749, Orders St Andrew Russia and Black Eagle Prussia; *d* unm (*ka* Battle of Hochkirch) 14 Oct 1758

1a Mary; *m* 1711 6th Earl of Wigton and had issue (*see* HAWARDEN, V)

2a Anne; *m* 6th Earl of Galloway (*qv*)

4 JOHN KEITH, **1st Earl of Kintore**, so *cr* 26 June 1677, as also LORD KEITH OF INVERURIE AND KEITH HALL (both S), with remainder to heirs male of his body, but obtained 1694 a regrant with remainder to heirs male of his body, whom failing to his est brother 9th EARL MARISCHAL and the heirs male of his body, whom failing to the heirs gen of his own body; prevented the Regalia of Scotland from falling into the hands of CROMWELL 1651 by removing them from Dunnottar Castle and hiding them under the floor of Kinneff church for nine years, while pretending that he had delivered them to CHARLES II in Paris, which resulted in all further search by the Cromwellians being abandoned; Knight Marischal of Scotland 1660–1714 in consideration of his servs in preserving the Scottish Regalia, Commr Cncl for Public Affairs 1677, Treasurer-Depute (S) 1684–87; supported the 1688 revolution; Commr Privy Seal 1689, a Commr for Settling the peace of the Highlands 1702, supported the Parly Union with England 1707; *m* 24 April 1662 Lady Margaret Hamilton, dau of 2nd Earl of Haddington (*qv*), and *d* 12 April 1715, having had:

(1) WILLIAM KEITH, **2nd Earl of Kintore**; Jacobite 1715 (fought Battle of Sheriffmuir), hence deprived of office of Knight Marischal; *m c* 8 Aug 1687 Catherine Murray (*d* Jan 1726), est dau of 4th Viscount Stormont, and *d* 5 Dec 1718, leaving:

1a JOHN KEITH, **3rd Earl of Kintore**; *bapt* 21 May 1699; restored as Kt Marischal 1733; *m* 21 Aug 1729 Mary (*d* 9 May 1772), dau of Hon James Erskine, s of 21st/5th Earl of Mar (*qv*), and *dsp* 22 Nov 1758

2a WILLIAM KEITH, **4th Earl of Kintore**; *bapt* 5 Jan 1701/2; *d* unm 22 Nov 1761, when the estates devolved upon the 9th and attainted EARL MARISCHAL, while the Earldom of Kintore and Ldship of Inverurie and Keith Hall became dormant till the latter's death May 1778, when they ceased to be affected by the attainder of 1716

1a CATHERINE MARGARET Keith; *m* 1703 David FALCONER, 4th Lord Falconer of Halkertoun (*d* 1751; *see* 1963 edn; title dormant 1966) and had:

1b ALEXANDER FALCONER, 5th LORD FALCONER OF HALKERTOUN; *dsp* 1762

2b WILLIAM FALCONER, 6th LORD FALCONER OF HALKERTOUN; *d* 1776, leaving:

1c ANTHONY ANDRIAN FALCONER later KEITH-FALCONER, 7th LORD FALCONER OF HALKERTOUN and **5th Earl of Kintore** (as which *s* cousin 9th EARL MARISCHAL 1778, also in the estate of Kintore, the old castle of Hall Forest given to the family by ROBERT I, and Keith Hall); *m* by 1766 Christina Elizabeth (*d* 26 March 1809), dau of Jan Albert Sighterman, of Gröningon, Holland, and *d* 30 Aug 1804, having had, with seven daus (*d* unm):

1d WILLIAM KEITH-FALCONER, **6th Earl of Kintore**; *b* 11 Dec 1766; Offr 2nd Dragoons (Scots Greys); *m* 18 June 1793 Maria (*d* 30 June 1826), dau of Sir Alexander Bannerman, 6th Bt (*qv*), and had:

1e ANTHONY ADRIAN, **7th Earl**

2e William; *b* 16 Dec 1799; Capt RN; *m* 24 June 1830 Louisa (*d* Boulogne 12 Feb 1862), dau of William Grant of Congalton, and *d* 5 Jan 1846, having had a s and dau

1e Maria; *b* 2 May 1795; *d* unm 5 July 1864

(1) Jean; *m* Sir William Forbes, 4th Bt (*see* STUART-FORBES, Bt)

1 Anne; *m* (contract between 5 and 28 March 1604) 7th Earl of Morton (*qv*) and *d* 30 May 1648, having had issue

The 6th EARL *d* 6 Oct 1812; his est son,

ANTHONY ADRIAN KEITH-FALCONER, **7th Earl of Kintore**; *b* 20 April 1794; *educ* Ch Ch Oxford; *cr* 5 July 1838 BARON KINTORE OF KINTORE, Co Aberdeen (UK); *m* 1st 14 June 1817 Juliet (*dsp* 9 July 1819), 5th dau of Robert Renny, of Borrowfield, Scotland; *m* 2nd 27 Aug 1821 (*divorce* 1840) Louisa (*d* 1 Nov 1841), yst dau of Francis Hawkins, and by her had:

1 William Adrian, *Lord Inverurie*; *b* 2 Sept 1822; Lt 17th Light Dragoons; *k* while hunting 17 Dec 1843

2 FRANCIS ALEXANDER, **8th Earl**

3 Charles James; *b* 1 July 1832; Maj 4th Light Dragoons and 10th Hus Crimean War 1854–56; Commr Inland Rev 1874–89; *m* 24 Jan 1857 Caroline Diana (*d* 24 Feb 1920), 3rd dau of Robert Aldridge, of St Leonard's Forest, Sussex, and *d* 7 Jan 1889, leaving:

(1) Cecil Edward; *b* 11 Oct 1860; Capt and Brevet Lt-Col Northumberland Fus, Egypt, Dongola 1896, Nile Expdn 1897, Khartoum 1898, S African War 1899; *m* 24 June 1899 Georgina Sarah (*dsp* 4 March 1929), dau of John Henry Blagrave, of Calcot Park, Berks, and was *ka* Boer War 10 Nov 1899

(2) Charles Adrian; *b* 12 Dec 1861; *m* 11 June 1887 Williamina Emily Hume (*d* 17 Aug 1945), dau of William Wentworth FitzWilliam Hume Dick, PC, and *d* 23 Feb 1920, leaving:

1a Adrian Wentworth, TD; *b* 17 June 1888; Maj 100th Field Bde RA (TA) WW I, Maj staff Br Armistice Commn Spa and Cologne 1919–20, Priv Sec to For Sec 1921–23; *m* 25 Nov 1925 Phyllis (*d* 12 Feb 1959), only dau of Ernest Francis Messervy, of St Martin, Jersey, and *dsp* 19 Feb 1959

(3) Victor Francis Alexander; *b* 27 Oct 1869; Capt Somerset LI, Adj Mohmand campaign 1897 and Boer War 1900; *ka* Boer War 21 Feb 1900

(1) Diana Mary; *b* 8 Nov 1858; *d* unm 2 April 1952

(2) Florence; *b* 18 May 1864; *m* 5 Aug 1893 Rev Hesketh France-Hayhurst (*d* 7 Jan 1925), est s of Rev Thomas William Hamilton France-Hayhurst, Rector Davenham, Cheshire, and *d* 13 Nov 1939, having had issue

(3) Ida Madaleine; *b* 2 March 1868; *d* unm 2 Jan 1955

(4) Evelyn Millicent; *b* 20 May 1874; *d* unm 20 Aug 1914

(5) Violet Katherine; *b* 21 July 1875; *d* 2 Sept 1881

(6) Sybil Blanche; *m* 7 Feb 1911 Col Eden Bernard Powell, DSO, Rifle Bde (*d* 10 Nov 1964), est s of Henry Pryor Powell, of Ockley, and *d* 15 April 1966 aged 88

1 Isabella Catherine; *m* 4 Aug 1847 Henry Grant, and *d* 8 Feb 1870

The 7th EARL *d* 11 July 1844; his est son,

FRANCIS ALEXANDER KEITH-FALCONER, **8th Earl of Kintore**; *b* 7 June 1828; *m* 24 June 1851 his cousin Louisa Madeleine (*d* 6 Feb 1916), 2nd dau of Francis Hawkins, s of Francis Hawkins above mentioned, and had, with other issue:

1 ALGERNON HAWKINS THOMOND, **9th Earl**

2 Ian Grant Neville; *b* 5 July 1856; *m* 4 March 1884 Gwendolen (*m* 2nd 15 Dec 1894 Lt Col Frederick Bradshaw, IA, and *d* 24 Oct 1937), dau of Robert Cooper Lee Bevan, of Fosbury House, Wilts, and *dsp* May 1887

1 Madeleine Dora; *m* 12 July 1889 Capt Francis Henry Tonge, 62nd Regt (*d* 6 March 1936), s of Capt Louis Tonge, RN, of Highway, Wilts, and *d* 11 Dec 1925

2 Blanche Catherine; *m* 4 Dec 1883 Col Granville Roland Francis Smith, CVO, CB, Coldstream Gds (*d* 4 March 1917), of Duffield Hall, Derbys, and *d* 18 Sept 1922, leaving issue

The 8th EARL *d* 18 July 1880; his est son,

ALGERNON HAWKINS THOMOND KEITH-FALCONER, **9th Earl of Kintore**, KT (1923), GCMG (1889), PC (1886), JP and DL (Aberdeenshire and Kincardineshire); *b* 12 Aug 1852; *educ* Eton and Trin Coll Cambridge (BA 1872, MA 1877), LLD Aberdeen; Col cmdg 3rd Bn Gordon Highrs; Capt Yeomen Gd 1886–89, Govr and C-in-C S Australia 1889–95, Ld-in-Waiting 1885–86, 1895–1901 and 1901–05, ADC to HM EDWARD VII 1901, Hon LLD Cambridge and Adelaide, FRSE, Grand Cordon Crown Italy, 1st Cl Prussian Order Red Eagle, Grand Cross Portuguese Mil Order Christ, North Star Sweden; *m* 14 Aug 1873 Lady Sydney Charlotte Montagu (*d* 21 Sept 1932), 2nd dau of 6th Duke of Manchester (*qv*), and *d* 3 March 1930, having had:

1 Ian Douglas Montagu, *Lord Inverurie*; *b* 5 April 1877; Lt 3rd Bn Gordon Highrs; *d* unm 26 Aug 1897

2 ARTHUR GEORGE KEITH-FALCONER, **10th Earl of Kintore**; *b* 5 Jan 1879; Capt Scots Gds (SR) Boer War 1900–02 and WW I; *m* 23 Nov 1937 Helena (*d* 15 Dec 1971), dau of Eugene Zimmerman, of Cincinnati, USA, and formerly w of 9th Duke of Manchester (*qv*), and *dsp* 25 May 1966, when the UK Barony expired and the Ldship of Falconer of Halkertoun became dormant

1 (ETHEL) SYDNEY, **Countess of Kintore** in her own right

2 Hilda Madeleine; *b* 5 Nov 1875; *d* unm 13 July 1967

The 10th EARL's sister,

(ETHEL) SYDNEY Keith-Falconer, **Countess of Kintore** in her own right; *b* 20 Sept 1874; *m* 16 Feb 1905 **1st Viscount Stonehaven** (*see* below) and had:

1 JAMES IAN, **12th Earl**

2 (Robert Alexander) Greville; *b* 14 April 1910; *educ* Eton and RMC Sandhurst; S/Ldr RAF, Lt Gordon Highrs, WW II 1939–43; *m* 30 March 1939 *Dorviegelda Malvina [Mrs Algernon Sladen, Stone Lodge, Browning Hill, Baughurst, Hants] (*m* 2nd 15 Nov 1947 S/Ldr Algernon Ivan (Toby) Sladen, DSO, late RAF (*d* 2 July 1976), only s of Maj Algernon Ryder Lambart Sladen, of Virginia Water), dau of Alexander Ronald MacGregor (*see* Mac GREGOR OF Mac GREGOR, Bt), and was *ka* 17 July 1943, leaving:

(1) Alastair Aulin John; *b* 15 June 1942; *educ* Stowe; lost with crew of schooner *Windfall* on or about 1 Nov 1962, in Atlantic storm

(2) +Ceanan Donald [Ceanan Baird Esq, Coxmoor Farm, Mill Lane, Crondall, Surrey GU10 5RT]; *b* posthumously 11 Nov 1943; *educ* Eton; 1973 *Janet Mary, dau of Donald R Scott, and has:

1a +Hamish Duncan; *b* 1976

1a +Amanda Louisa; *b* 1977

(1) +Rinalda Malvina; *b* 17 April 1940 (HH PRINCESS MARIE LOUISE stood sponsor); *m* 23 April 1963 *Lt-Col David Henry Sandford Leslie Maitland Titterton (*see* LAUDERDALE, E) and has:

1a +Rupert Aulen Seymour Leslie; *b* 28 Aug 1965

2a +Shân Gelda Jane; *b* 10 Nov 1967

1 Annette Sydney Helen Mary; *b* 19 Nov 1905; *m* 17 Aug 1925 Michael Henry Mason, DL, Lt-Cdr RNVR, only s of James Francis Mason (*see* CRAWFORD and BALCARES, E), and *d* 1 Feb 1950

2 *Ariel Olivia Winifred, CVO [The Lady Ariel Keith CVO, 16 Melton Court, Old Brompton Rd, London SW7 3JQ]; *b* 16 Aug 1916; a Ldy-in-Waiting to HRH PRINCESS ALICE, COUNTESS of ATHLONE 1940; *m* 25 April 1946 (*divorce* 1958) Baron Keith of Castleacre (LP, *qv*) and has issue

3 *(Hilda) Ava Fiona Nancy [The Lady Ava Chance, 2 Abbot's Gdns, Malmesbury, Wilts SN16 9HY]; *b* 20 April 1919; *m* 12 June 1945 Lt-Col Ronald Fulton Lucas Chance, MC, KRRC, est s of Walter Lucas Chance, JP, of Millgreen House, Wargrave, Berks, and has:

(1) *Nicholas John Lucas; *b* 8 March 1946; *m* 1975 *Anne, dau of Maj J Rice, and has:

1a *Alexander William Lucas; *b* 10 Aug 1978

2a *Hugo Nicholas Edward; *b* 6 July 1980

1a *Sophia Antoinette Louise; *b* 2 Nov 1984

(1) *Louise Annette; *b* 28 Oct 1946; *m* 1976 *Edward Goschen, only s of Sir Edward Goschen, Bt, DSO (*qv*), and has issue

The COUNTESS *d* 21 Sept 1974; her only surv son,

(JAMES) IAN BAIRD later KEITH (1967), **12th Earl of Kintore**, DL (Kincardineshire 1959); *b* 25 July 1908; *educ* Eton and Roy Sch of Mines London (AIStructE); Maj RME WW II; Kincardineshire: CC 1954, Convenor 1973 (V-Convenor 1967–73), V-Lt 1965–76; Cncllr Grampian Region 1974–78, Chm Water Servs Ctee, memb Roy Co Archers, Br Del Cncl of Europe and WEU 1955–58 and 1961–65; *m* 5 March 1935 *Delia Virginia [The Rt Hon Delia Countess of Kintore, 16 Garden Wood, Inchmarlo, Kincardineshire AB3 4AW], only dau of William Lewis Brownlow Loyd, of Upper House, Shamley Green, Surrey, and *d* 1989, leaving:

1 MICHAEL CANNING WILLIAM JOHN KEITH, **13th and present Earl of Kintore**

2 +Alexander David; *b* 21 April 1946; *educ* Tabley House Knutsford

1 +Diana Elizabeth Virginia Sydney [The Lady Diana Holman, Rickerton House, 24 Wellington Sq, London SW3]; *b* 22 June 1937; *m* 20 July 1957 *John Francis Holman, OBE, est s of Alexander McArthur Holman, of Jersey, and has:

(1) +Richard Ian; *b* 2 Sept 1958; *educ* Gordoustoun

(2) +Edward Alexander; *b* 15 Feb 1960; *educ* Gordoustoun

(1) +Georgiana Mary; *b* 4 Oct 1962

(2) +Emma Charlotte; *b* 11 April 1966

Lineage (of Baird): WILLIAM BAIRD, of Woodhead, Old Monkland, Lanarks; had:

ALEXANDER BAIRD, of Lochwood, Old Monkland; *b* 12 May 1765; *m* Aug 1794 Jane Moffat (*d* 8 July 1851) and *d* 23 Dec 1833, having had, with other issue:

1 William, of Elie, Fife, DL; *b* 23 April 1796; MP Falkirk Burghs; *m* 14 July 1840 Janet (*d* 15 Nov 1886), dau of Thomas Johnstone, and *d* 1864, leaving issue

2 JOHN

3 James, of Auchmeddon, Aberdeenshire, and Cambusdoon, Ayrshire, JP and DL (Inverness-shire), JP (Lanarks); *b* 5 Dec 1802; MP Falkirk Burghs 1851–57; *m* 1st 10 Feb 1852 Charlotte (*d* 29 Dec 1857), dau of Robert Lockhart, of Castle Hill, Lanarks; *m* 2nd 8 Dec 1859 Isabella Agnew (*d* 7 Dec 1904), est dau of James Hay, of Belton House, Dunbar, Haddington, and *d* 20 June 1876

4 Douglas, of Closeburn, Thornhill, Dumfriesshire; *b* 31 March 1808; *m* 28 July 1851 Charlotte (*d* 30 Sept 1868), dau of Capt Henry Acton, 12th Lancers (*see* ACTON, B), and *d* 7 Dec 1854, having had issue

5 George, of Stichill, Roxburghshire, Strichen and Auchmeddon, Aberdeenshire; *b* 28 July 1810; *m* 15 Nov 1858 Cecilia (*d* 5 March 1895), dau of V-Adml Villiers Francis Hatton, of Clonard, Co Wexford, and *d* 24 Aug 1870, leaving a s

(1) George Alexander, JP, of Stichill, Strichen and Auchmeddon; *b* 30 Sept 1861; *d* unm 18 March 1893

The 2nd son,

JOHN BAIRD, of Urie, Fetteresso, Kincardineshire, and Lochwood, JP (Lanarks and Kincardineshire) and DL (Kincardineshire); *b* 19 Feb 1798; *m* 5 Dec 1848 Margaret (*d* 14 July 1883), dau of John Findlay, of Springhill, Lanarks, and had:

1 ALEXANDER (Sir), **1st Bt**

2 John, of Lochwood, JP and DL (Inverness-shire); *b* 17 Feb 1852; MP NW Lancs; *m* 23 April 1878 Constance Amelia (*d* 13 Aug 1914), 2nd dau of John Harford Battersby Harford (*see* HARFORD, Bt), and *d* 8 July 1900, having had:

(1) James Alexander; *b* 15 Feb 1879; *d* unm 5 May 1936

(2) Hugh William; *b* 24 Jan 1882; *d* unm 22 Oct 1902

(1) Jean Edith; *m* 30 Aug 1906 Thomas Algernon Raikes (*d* Dec 1950), 4th s of Henry Cecil Raikes, PC, of Llwynegrin, Flints, and *d* 12 Dec 1937, leaving issue

(2) Margaret Ina

1 Janet Findlay; *b* 12 Nov 1861; *m* 9 Jan 1884 Col George Chalmers, 92nd Regt (Gordon Highrs) (*d* 25 July 1893), of Inchdairnie, Leslie, Fife

JOHN BAIRD *d* 29 Jan 1870; his son,

Sir Alexander Baird, 1st Bt (UK), so *cr* 8 March 1897, GBE (1920), JP and DL (Inverness-shire), DL (Aberdeenshire); *b* 22 Oct 1849; *educ* Harrow; Ld Lt Kincardineshire 1889–1918, Pres Kincardine TFA, Grand Cordon Order Nile; *m* 16 July 1873 Hon Annette Maria Palk (*d* 21 May 1884), est dau of 1st Baron Haldon (*see* 1939 edn), and had:

1 JOHN LAWRENCE, **1st Viscount**

2 Alexander Walter Frederick, CB, CMG, DSO; *b* 2 Oct 1876; Hon Brig-Gen Gordon Highrs, Boer War 1899–1902 (despatches four times, Brevet Maj), Mohmand Expdn 1908, WW I (despatches nine times, two brevets, Cdr Legn Hon, Order Redeemer Greece, White Eagle Serbia, Croix de Guerre, Merita di Guerra

Italy), Head Br Mil Mission Bulgaria 1919, Mil Attaché Madrid 1920, Constantinople and Sofia 1921–24; *m* 16 Feb 1907 Maud Constance, dau of Charles William Waylen, IMS, and *d* 20 Feb 1931 following a car crash, leaving:

(1) Alexander William Bertie Gordon; *b* 23 Jan 1908; *d* Sept 1972

1 Evelyn Margaret; *b* 25 April 1875; *m* 5 Dec 1907 Lt-Col Albert Edward Stanley Clarke, DSO, MVO, Scots Gds (*d* 8 June 1926), only s of Maj-Gen Sir Stanley Astel de Clavert Clarke, GCVO, and had issue

2 Janet Norah; *b* 7 Jan 1878; *m* 1 Oct 1902 Lt-Col Sir Arthur George Ferguson, CBE, Rifle Bde (*d* 14 Feb 1935), est s of Col George Arthur Ferguson, DL, of Pitfour, Aberdeenshire, and *d* 15 Oct 1943, leaving issue

3 Edith Annette; *b* 6 Jan 1880; *d* 20 Oct 1881

4 Nina Isabel; *b* 20 March 1882; *d* 10 Aug 1919

5 Muriel Jane; *b* 4 April 1884; *m* 17 July 1909 Byron Vyner Noel and *d* 31 Dec 1968

The 1st Bt *d* 20 June 1920; his er son,

Sir John Lawrence Baird, 2nd Bt, and **1st Viscount Stonehaven,** of Ury, Co Kincardine, so *cr* 27 June 1938, as also 12 June 1925 BARON STONEHAVEN, of Ury, Co Kincardine (both UK), PC (1922), GCMG (1925, CMG 1904), DSO (1915), JP and DL (Kincardineshire), JP (Warwicks); *b* 27 April 1874; WW I as Staff Capt Intell Corps (despatches, Croix de Guerre, Orders Leopold Belgium, St Stanislas Russia 2nd Cl with swords, Legn Hon, Crown Italy), Maj Scottish Horse (TF), Hon A/Cdre No 602 (City of Glasgow) (B) Sqdn RAuxAF 1936; Dip Serv 1896–1908; MP (C) Rugby 1910–22 and Ayr 1922–25, PPS to Rt Hon A Bonar Law 1911–1916, Parly U-Sec: Air 1916–18, Home Dept 1919–22, First Commr Works and Public Bldgs and Min Transport 1922–24, Govr-Gen and C-in-C Australia 1925–30, Chm C Party 1931–36, LLD Aberdeen and Sydney Us 1930; *m* 15 Feb 1905 **Countess of Kintore** in her own right (*see* above) and had, with other issue (*see* above):

1 JAMES IAN, **2nd Viscount** and **12th Earl of Kintore** (*see* above)

KIRKHILL

Creation: B. (LP, UK) 1975.

THE BARON KIRKHILL, of Kirkhill in the City of Aberdeen (John Farquharson Smith) [The Right Hon The Lord Kirkhill, 3 Rubislaw Den North, Aberdeen AB2 4 AL]; *b* 7 May 1930; *educ* Robert Gordon's Colls Aberdeen; Ld Provost Aberdeen 1971–75; Min State Scottish Office 1975–78; Chm N of Scotland Hydro-Electric Bd 1979–82; Delegate Parly Assembly Cncl Europe and WEU 1987–; Chm Cncl Europe Ctee Legal Affrs and Human Rights 1991–95; Hon LLD Aberdeen 1974; *m* 1965 *Frances Mary Walker Reid and has a stepdaugher

Lineage: ALEXANDER FINDLAY SMITH; *m* Ann T Farquharson and had:

JOHN FARQUHARSON, *cr* a **Baron**

KIRKPATRICK

Arms: Arg. a saltire and chief az., the last charged with three cushions or. **Crest:** A hand holding a dagger in pale, distilling drops of blood. **Supporters:** Two talbot hounds arg. **Motto:** I make sure.
Creation: Bt. (NS) 26 March 1685.

SIR IVONE ELLIOTT KIRKPATRICK, 11TH BT, of Closeburn, Dumfriesshire [Sir Ivone Kirkpatrick Bt, c/o ANZ Bank, 81 King William St, Adelaide, SA 5000, Australia]; *b* 1 Oct 1942; *s f* 1954; *educ* Wellington, St Mark's Coll and Adelaide U

Lineage: IVONE KIRKPATRICK; living *temp* DAVID I (1124–53); gf of:

IVONE KIRKPATRICK; obtained a confirmatory charter of the lands of Closeburne from ALEXANDER II 15 Aug 1232; *m* Euphemia, dau of Robert (The) Bruce, Lord of Annandale and Cleveland and either f or gf (it is not clear which Robert this was) of ROBERT I KING OF SCOTS, and had:

ADAM KIRKPATRICK; feudal Lord of Closeburne; had:

STEPHEN KIRKPATRICK; feudal Lord of Closeburne; living 1278; *m* Isabel, dau and heir of David Torthorwald of Torthorwald, and had, with a yr s (Duncan):

Sir ROGER KIRKPATRICK, of Closeburne; Justiciar Galloway 1304; *k* the Regent of Scotland at Dumfries 1306; envoy to England 1314; had:

1 Thomas (Sir), of Closeburne; had 4 Jan 1319 a roy charter of the lands of Bridburgh, Dumfriesshire; *dspm*, leaving:

(1) Elizabeth; *m* Sir John Carlyle, ancestor of the Lords Carlyle

(2) Margaret; *m* John Henrysone, of Glasgow

2 Roger (Sir); took the castles of Durisdeer and Caerlaverock from the English 1355; murdered in bed in Caerlaverock Castle by Sir James Lindsay 1357, leaving two sons:

(1) WINFRED

(2) Yvone; living 1409; had:

1a Stephen; living 1409

Sir ROGER's gs,

WINFRED KIRKPATRICK, of Closeburne; a hostage for ransom of DAVID II; had:

1 Thomas (Sir); resigned terrritorial Baronies of Closeburne and Bridburgh to Robert, Duke of Albany, Govr of Scotland, and got a regrant 14 Oct 1409 to himself and his heirs male; *dsp*

2 Roger, of Closeburne; Commr W Borders 1455; *m* 1435 Margaret (*m* 2nd Sir Thomas Ker of Fernihirst; *see* LOTHIAN, M), dau of 1st Lord Somerville by Janet, dau of Sir Alexander Stewart of Darnley (*see* MORAY, E), and had:

(1) THOMAS (Sir)

(2) Alexander; granted lands and territorial Barony of Kirkmichael, Dumfriesshire, as reward for the capture of 9th Earl of Douglas at Burnswark 1484; *d* 9 June 1686; his ggs William, of Kirkmichael, sold part of his estates to Sir John Charteris *c* 1622; his gs Alexander, of Drumcondra (*b* 1714), settled nr Dublin and was ancestor of the KIRKPATRICKs of Coolmine, of Donacumper, Co Kildare, and Craigs, Co Antrim; William Kirkpatrick (1737–87), of the Conheath branch of the family, had out of 19 children a 3rd s, William (1764–1837), who was US Consul at Malaga 1800–18 and whose dau Maria Manuela *m* 1819 Cipriano, Count de Montijo and de Teba, and was mother of EUGENIE, w of NAPOLEON III

1 Isabel; *m* Roger Grierson of Lagg (*see* GRIERSON, Bt)

The er son,

Sir THOMAS KIRKPATRICK of Closeburne; *m* Maria, dau of 1st Lord Maxwell (*see* HERRIES, L), and *d* 1502, having had:

1 Thomas (Sir), of Closeburne; *m* Margaret, dau of Sinclair of Rosslyn, and *d* 1515, leaving:

1 Thomas, of Closeburne; captured by the English Battle of Solway Moss 1542; *m* Jonet, est dau of Roger Grierson (*see* GRIERSON, Bt), and had an only s (*dsp*)

2 Henry; *m* Elizabeth, dau of Grierson of Lagg, and had, with two yr sons (Samuel, of Auchinleck; Alexander):

1a Roger, of Closeburne; *m* Lady Jean Cunningham, dau of 6th Earl of Glencairn (*see* CUNINGHAME, Bt) and widow of George Haldane of Gleneagles, and had:

1b Thomas (Sir), of Closeburne; MP 1593; ktd by JAMES VI, to whom Gentleman Privy Chamber; *m* 1st — and had, with four yr sons (Thomas; John; George; Alexander, of Barnmure):

1c THOMAS

1b (cont.) Sir Thomas *m* 2nd 1614 Barbara, dau of Sir Alexander Stewart of Garlies (*see* GALLOWAY, E), and had further issue (including Margaret, *m* Robert Erskine; Susanna)

Sir THOMAS's est son,

THOMAS KIRKPATRICK of Closeburne; MP 1639–41; *m* Agnes, dau of Sir John Charteris of Amisfield (*see* WEMYSS, E), and had, with other issue:

ROBERT KIRKPATRICK of Closeburne; *m* Grizel, dau of Sir William Baillie of Lamington, MP, by Grizel, dau of Sir Claud Hamilton of Ellieston, bro of 1st Earl of Abercorn (*see* ABERCORN, D), and *d c* 1664, having had, with other sons and four daus (Grizel, *m* John Grierson of Barjarg; Agnes; Marian; Jean):

Sir Thomas Kirkpatrick, 1st Bt (NS), so *cr* 26 March 1685; MP Dumfries 1690–1702; *m* 1st (contract 25 April 1666) Isabel, dau of 4th Lord Torphichen (*qv*), and had a s; *m* 2nd (contract 7 Dec 1672) Sarah, dau of Robert Fergusson of Craigdarroch, by whom he had another s (Roger, *d* unm); *m* 3rd 1686 Grisel, dau of Gavin Hamilton of Raploch and widow of — Inglis, but by her had no issue; his s by his 1st w:

Sir Thomas Kirkpatrick, 2nd Bt; *m* 1st 18 Feb 1691 Hellenor (*dsp*), est dau of Hon Robert Stewart (*see* GALLOWAY, E); *m* 2nd 1702 Isabel, est dau of Sir William Lockhart of Carstairs, Bt, by Lady Isabel Douglas, sis of 1st Duke of Queensberry (*see* QUEENSBERRY, M), and by her had, with other issue:

1 THOMAS (Sir), **3rd Bt**

2 James; *b* 1704; *d* unm Calcutta

3 William, of Ailsland; *b* 1705; MP Dumfries burghs 1736–38, Clerk Ct of Session 1738; *m* Jean, dau of Charles Erskine of Alva, Lord Justice Clerk, and *d* 22 May 1778, leaving:

(1) Charles KIRKPATRICK later KIRKPATRICK SHARPE, of Hoddom, Dumfriesshire; *b* 1750; *m* 22 Aug 1770 Eleanora, dau of John Renton of Lamerton, and *d* 1813, leaving, with other issue:

1a Matthew; *b* 1774; Lt-Gen; MP Dumfries burghs; *m* — Hosea and *dsp* 1846

2a Charles; *b* 1781; *educ* Ch Ch Oxford (MA); antiquary; *d* unm 1851

3a Alexander Renton; *b* 1785; V-Adml RN; *dsp* 1860

1a Susan; *m* 1st Hon James Floyer Erskine, bro of 24th/8th Earl of Mar (*qv*); *m* 2nd 8 Aug 1800 Capt William Walker, 8th Dragoons, of Erdington Hall, Warwicks; *m* 3rd 16 June 1806, as his 2nd w, Shirley Farmer Steele Perkins, of Sutton Coldfield, Warwicks

2a Jane; *m* 7 June 1804 **Sir Thomas Kirkpatrick, 5th Bt** (*see* below)

3a Grace Campbell; *m* 1823 Rev William Riland Bedford, Rector Sutton Coldfield, and *d* 1875, leaving issue

4 Robert; *b* 1717; merchant in Spain; *dsp* 1781

Sir THOMAS's est son,

Sir Thomas Kirkpatrick, 3rd Bt; *b* 1704; *m* Susanna, dau and heiress of James Grierson of Capenoch, and *d* Oct 1771, having had, with other issue:

1 JAMES (Sir), **4th Bt**

2 William; *m* Isabella Irving and had, with two daus (Christian; Susan):

(1) John; Supreme Judge Ionian Islands; *m* Jean Glass and had issue

1 Grizel; *m* Hon Robert Sandilands, s of 7th Lord Torphichen (*qv*), and had issue

Sir THOMAS's er son,

Sir James Kirkpatrick, 4th Bt; *m* 1771 —Jardine and *d* 7 June 1804, having had, with other issue:

1 THOMAS (Sir), **5th Bt**

2 Roger; *b* 1779; *m* Lilias Anderson, of Stroquhan, and had:

(1) James, MD; *b* 1820; Dep Surgn-Gen; *m* 1854 Margaret Jane (*d* 1919), dau of Capt William Proctor, 21st Light Dragoons, of S Africa, and *d* 1890, leaving:

1a James Ivone, CA; *b* 1866; *m* 1905 Elizabeth Margaret (*d* 1959), dau of David Thomson, of Edinburgh, and *d* 1918, leaving:

1b +Ivone [Ivone Kirkpatrick Esq, 46 Nightingale Ave, Greenfields, East London 5201, S Africa]; *b* 1907; *educ* Edinburgh Acad and Edinburgh U; WS 1933, G/Capt AAF WW II; *m* 1936 *Ruth, dau of W R Peterson, of E London, S Africa, and had:

1c +Ivone William [Ivone Kirkpatrick Esq, 3 Kepersol St, Ferndale 2196, Johannesburg, S Africa]; *b* 12 March 1944; co dir; *m* 1st 20 May 1967 (*divorce* 1983) Velia Mignon Elizabeth, dau of John Charles Hartdegan; *m* 2nd 19– *Lyn — and by his 1st w has:

1d +Sean Roger; *b* 7 July 1968; dir Methuen Academic Ltd 1969–

1d *Anne Margaret; *b* 1971

1b Margaret Jean; *b* 1912

2a Charles, CB (1924), CBE (1922); *b* 18 May 1879; *educ* Edinburgh Acad; Maj-Gen IA WW I (despatches four times, Brevet Lt-Col), Waziristan Field Force 1920–23 (despatches four times), NWF India 1930; ADC to HM GEORGE V 1927–30; *m* 22 April 1909 Elsie Isobel (*d* 27 Nov 1970), dau of Herbert John Hamilton Fasson, ICS, and *d* 23 Jan 1955, leaving:

1b Herbert James, CB (1957), CBE (1945), DFC (1941); *b* 30 Oct 1910; *educ* Cheltenham and Trin Coll Oxford (BA 1932, MA 1942); AVM RAF WW II (despatches twice); *m* 7 Aug 1937 *Pamela Evelyn Darvill [Mrs Herbert Kirkpatrick, Gretton Ct, Girton, nr Cambridge], dau of Lt-Col Hugh Darvill Watson, IA, and *d* 26 Aug 1977, leaving:

1c +Roger Hugh [Roger Kirkpatrick Esq, 3 Cambridge Rd, E Twickenham, Middx]; *b* 21 July 1939; *educ* Marlborough, Bonn U, Sorbonne, Vienna U, Toronto U (BA 1962) and Stanford U, Calif.; dir Methuen Academic Ltd 1969–; *m* 16 Jan 1965 *Julia Margaret, dau of John W Mortimore, of Broadstone, Dorset, and has:

1d *Amanda Dorothy; *b* 17 July 1974

2d *Christabel Pamela; *b* 1977

2c +John Edward [John Kirkpatrick Esq, Petworth St, Cambridge]; *b* 18 July 1944; *educ* Marlborough and Pembroke Coll Cambridge (MA); slr 1968–; *m* 13 March 1964 *Johanna Elizabeth, dau of Patrick Johnstone, of Guildford, Surrey, and has:

1d +Jeremy Mark; *b* 26 Sept 1964

2d +Julian Gwinell; *b* 25 Oct 1965

3d +Dustin John; *b* 1971

3c +Christopher Charles [Christopher Kirkpatrick Esq, 9 Atlas Mews, London N7]; *b* 8 Nov 1948; *m* 1984 *Kathleen Anne, dau of Thomas Christopher Purcell, of Co Kilkenny, and formerly w of John Walsh, and has:

1d +James Charles John; *b* 1981

1c Elizabeth Susan; *b* 11 Aug 1942; *m* 2 April 1966 *F/Lt Kenneth Alan Douglas Evans, RAF, of Marlow, Bucks, and had:

1d *Nicholas Christopher; *b* 25 Oct 1966

1d *Rebecca Kate; *b* 17 Oct 1968

2c *Grizelda Jean [Mrs Alan Stuck, 62 High St, Hampton, Middx]; *b* 8 Nov 1948; *m* 1st 8 July 1967 Hugh John Allen, adopted s of Prof John Frank Allen; *m* 2nd 1974 *Alan Graham Stuck and by her 1st husb has:

1d *Jonathan Spencer; *b* 15 Nov 1968

1b *Hilda May [Mrs Brian Butler, Ashdean, Whiteparish, Salisbury, Wilts SP5 2RN]; *b* 7 Oct 1920; *m* 1st 22 June 1940 (*divorce* 1953) Maj James Michael Jourdier, E Surrey Regt, and has:

1c *Anthony Maxwell Kirkpatrick [Anthony Jourdier Esq, The Shrubbery House, Stanford Bridge, Worcester]; *b* 7 June 1946; *educ* Wellington and New Coll Oxford (BA); *m* 1974 *Cecilia Maye, dau of Lt-Col R A Conner, of Maldon, Essex, and has:

1d *Peter Gilbert Kirkpatrick; *b* 1 May 1983

1d *Sophie Maye; *b* 20 Oct 1975

2d *Jessica Isobel; *b* 24 Nov 1977

3d *Louise Caroline; *b* 23 May 1980

1c *Avril Patricia; *b* 27 Dec 1947; *m* 1 May 1969 *John Hamish Carysfort Loch, s of Col L J C Loch, and has:

1d *Rupert John Carysfort; *b* 11 Nov 1970

1d *Rosalind Cecilia Carysfort; *b* 10 Sept 1972

1b (cont.) Mrs Hilda Jourdier *m* 2nd 19 March 1954 (*divorce* 1970) David Arthur Yellowlees, 2nd s of Dr Henry Yellowlees, OBE, MD, FRCP, FRFPS, DPM, of London; *m* 3rd 27 Sept 1971 Brian Butler (*d* 25 July 1992) and has had by her 2nd husb:

2c Rupert; *b* 12 May 1958; *d* 3 March 1959

(2) Robert; slr; *d* unm 1856

(3) Roger; *b* 1825; *m* 1856 Isabella Margaret, gdau of John Kirkpatrick, of Conheath, Dumfriesshire, and *d* 1890, leaving:

1a James Mackenzie (Rev); DD (Glasgow 1927); *b* 1868; *educ* Edinburgh U (MA1888); *d* unm 1950

1a Lilias Mary; *d* unm 1950

(4) Thomas; EICS; *d* unm 1884

1 Jane; *d* unm

2 Mary Lilias; *d* unm 1898

Sir JAMES's est son,

Sir Thomas Kirkpatrick, 5th Bt; *b* 1777; *m* 7 June 1804 Jane, dau of Charles Kirkpatrick Sharpe (*see* above), and *d* 1844, having had:

1 James; Midshipman RN; *dsvp*

2 CHARLES SHARPE (Sir), **6th Bt**

1 Eleanora; *m* 26 April 1826 Adml Sir William J Hope Johnstone, KCB (*see* LINLITHGOW, M), and *d* 12 July 1891, having had issue

2 Mary Anne; *m* Henry Lumsden, of Clova, Aberdeenshire, and *d* his widow 24 April 1891

3 Margaret Hope; *m* John Ord Mackenzie, of Dolphinton

4 Charlotte; *m* Henry Burn and *d* Oct 1892

Sir THOMAS's surv son,

Sir Charles Sharpe Kirkpatrick, 6th Bt; *b* May 1811; *m* 24 March 1837 Helen Stuart (*d* 29 Sept 1877), dau of Thomas Kirk, of Keir Mill, Dumfriesshire, and *d* 9 Oct 1867, having had:

1 **Sir Thomas Kirkpatrick, 7th Bt**; *b* 26 April 1839; *m* 23 Oct 1866 Sophia Anne (*d* 31 July 1879), dau of William Blanton, of Frampton-on-Severn, and *dsp* 23 June 1880

2 JAMES (Sir), **8th Bt**

3 Roger; *b* 21 Sept 1842

4 Charles William Sharpe; *b* 6 May 1843; *m* 1867 Catherine (*d* 1911), dau of Charles Bartram Murch, of Peckham, and *d* 1908, having had:

(1) Thomas Stripling; *b* 1867; *m* 1903 Amy Louisa (*d* 1962), dau of Walter Norris, and *d* 1937, leaving:

1a *Grace Amy May; *b* 1905; *m* 1926 William Henry Williams, of S Rhodesia, and had:

1b *Derek Henry [Derek Williams Esq, 44 Ammersham Ave, Paddonhurst, Bulawayo, Zimbabwe]; *b* 1929; *m* 1953 *Kathleen Elizabeth Knipe and has:

1c *Peter Duncan; *b* 1956

2c *Paul Arnold; *b* 1957

1c *Margaret Ann; *b* 1959

1b *Olive Amy [Mrs John Sissison, 16 Willow Way, Pinelands, CP, S Africa]; *b* 1932; *m* 1954 *John Faulding Sissison and has:

1c *Michael Faulding; *b* 1959

2c *Noel Faulding; *b* 1961

2b *Janet Ann; *b* 1943; *m* 1960 *Roger Stewart Johnson and has:

1c *Susan Barbara; *b* 1960

2c *Shirley Catherine; *b* 1961

(2) Charles Bartram; *b* 22 April 1873; *m* 1893 Helena Sarah Riches (*d* 1936), dau of William Minns, of Peckham, and *d* 1944, leaving:

1a Thomas Frederick; *b* 23 April 1894; served WWs I and II; *m* 1920 Mabel (*d* 1971), dau of John James Childs, and was *ka* 1940, leaving:

1b Leslie Maurice Kenneth; *b* Feb 1925; *m* 1948 *Rose Lilian May, dau of Frederick George Walker, and *d* 28 June 1962, leaving:

1c +David Christopher [David Kirkpatrick Esq, 7 Fulbourne Close, Luton, Beds LU4 9PW]; *b* 1950; *m* 1973 *Betty Margaret, dau of Leslie Augustus Radford, and has:

1d *Victoria Alice; *b* 1981

1d *Joanna Louise; *b* 1985

2c +Paul Anthony; *b* 1953

3c +Stephen Robert; *b* 1960; *m* 1983 *Jill, dau of Ernest Albert Flewin

1c *Maureen Ann; *b* 1952

1b *Beryl; *b* 1920; *m* 1941 *Stanley Roy Fairbrass, of Ruislip, Middx, and has:

1c *Alan; *b* May 1942

2c *Brian Malcolm; *b* Aug 1944

3c *Melvyn Denis; *b* March 1948

4c *Geoffrey; *b* May 1950

5c *Keith Anthony; *b* May 1958

2a Charles Bartram; *b* 1899; *m* 1921 Lilian (*m* 2nd 1950 George Albert May, of Bromley, Kent), dau of Samuel Charles Podd, and *d* 1936, leaving:

1b +Charles Bartram [Charles Kirkpatrick Esq, 16 Foyle Dve, South Ockendon, Essex]; *b* 1922; *m* 19 Feb 1944 *Winifred Rosa, dau of George Gaffney, of Brockley, and has:

1c +Charles Bartram [Charles Kirkpatrick Esq, 49 Norheads Lane, Biggin Hill, Kent]; *b* 5 Feb 1945; *m* 1967 *Angela Mary, dau of Sydney Ernest McClaren Dooley, and has:

1d +Paul Charles; *b* 1972

2b +Donald [Donald Kirkpatrick Esq, Closeburn, 4 Wilderness Rd, Hurstpierpoint, W Sussex BN6 9XD]; *b* 1934; *m* 1st 1964 Janet Olive, dau of Walter Young; *m* 2nd 1990 *Valerie Rose, dau of James Mills, of Oldham and by his 1st w has:

1c *Kay; *b* 1965

2c *Linda; *b* 1967

1b *Edna Florence [Mrs Henry Crook, Old Scoresdown, Lynton, Devon EX35 6LJ]; *b* 1924; *m* March 1946 *Henry Crook and has:

1c *John David; *b* 1951

1c *Hilary June; *b* 1955

2b *Lilian; *b* 1926; *m* 1945 *Sydney Thew, of Brisbane, Qld, and has:

1c *Sydney Charles; *b* 1946

2c *Colin James; *b* 1947

3c *Robert John; *b* 1948

4c *Michael Allan; *b* 1952

3a James Arthur; *b* 1902; *m* 1929 Ruby, dau of Charles Heat, of Brixton, and *d* 1935, leaving:
1b *Barbara; *b* 1931
4a +Sydney Frank; *b* April 1912; F/Sgt RAFVR WW II (Belgian Croix de Guerre with palm); *m* April 1943 *Margaret Elizabeth Cowell and has:
1b *Valerie, BA; *b* Aug 1946
2b *Sandra Kirkpatrick [Mrs Stephen Gent, 32 Thompson Rd, Brighton, E Sussex]; *b* 1953; *m* 1974 *Stephen Gent
1a Gertrude Florence; *b* 1895; *m* 1916 Ernest Green and had issue
2a Florence Maud; *b* 1906; *m* 1927 William Albert Neal and had issue
(3) Samuel
(1) Jane
(2) Charlotte Barbara
(3) Frances; *m* — Billia
5 Robert Herries; *b* 5 June 1848; *m* 14 Jan 1884 Eliza, dau of Henry James, and *d* 1894, leaving:
(1) Wallace Herries; *b* 1886; *m* 1920 Lilian Ivy (*d* 1976), dau of Walter Oughton Hill, and *d* 1967, leaving:
1a +Wallace Bruce [Wallace Kirkpatrick Esq, Dukes Lodge, Alresford Rd, Winchester, Hants]; *b* 1921; Lt N Staffs Regt; *m* 1946 Irene Sylvia (*d* 1990), dau of Harold Victor Colls, and has:
1b +Scott Herries [Scott Kirkpatrick Esq, The Arches, Broughton, Hants]; *b* 1947; *m* 1970 *Sandra Jean, dau of Leonard Arthur Charles Hall, and has:
1c +Gavin James; *b* 1972
2c +Charles Stuart; *b* 1981
1c *Victoria Jane; *b* 1974
2b +Gavin Bruce [Gavin Kirkpatrick Esq, Croft Cottage, Lower Moors Rd, Colden Common, nr Twyford, Hants SO21 1SG]; BA (Design and Technology) CertEd; *b* 1951; *m* 1st 1973 (*divorce* 1987) Linda, dau of William Prosser, of Llandrindod Wells; *m* 2nd 1994 *Susan Mary, dau of Walter Marr, of Winchester, and by his 1st w has:
1c +James William Bruce; *b* 1976
1c *Emily Elizabeth; *b* 1979
(1) Beatrice Eliza; *b* 1885; *m* 1912 Albert Gardener and had issue
(2) Gertrude Helen
(3) Barbara Jane
(4) Mary Stuart; *b* 1893; *m* 1927 John Edwards, of Mitcham, Surrey, and had issue
(5) Roberta Ivy; *b* posthumously 1894
6 Stewart; *b* 30 April 1851; *d* 2 Feb 1924
7 Arthur Renton; *b* 10 Oct 1852; *m* 27 June 1888 Emily Jane, dau of Frederick William Denny, and *d* 13 Dec 1922
8 Yvone; *b* 19 Aug 1854; *d* 22 March 1879
1 Jane; *m* 24 June 1863 Tomas Samuel Speck, CE (*d* 1883), and *dsp* 24 March 1930
2 Charlotte Barbara; *m* 2 Nov 1868 Capt George Edward Martin (*d* 17 June 1873), Madras Staff Corps, and *d* 7 Sept 1904, having had issue

Sir THOMAS's bro,

Sir James Kirkpatrick, 8th Bt; *b* 22 March 1841; *m* 24 April 1872 Mary Steward (*d* 8 Feb 1920), yst dau of Charles John Fearnley, of Peckham, Surrey, and *d* 10 Nov 1899, having had:
1 **Sir Charles Sharpe Kirkpatrick, 9th Bt**; *b* 26 Feb 1874; T/Lt RAF; *m* 4 Dec 1900 (*divorce* 1910) Alice Wilhelmina (*d* 6 Sept 1933), 3rd dau of John Parnell Mayne, of Ramsgate, Kent, and *dsp* 2 Jan 1937
2 Harry Fearnley, DSO (1918); *b* 8 Jan 1876; T/Lt-Col RND, The Buffs and KAR, NWF India (medal with clasp), Br E Africa 1901 (medal with clasp), Somaliland 1908–10 (clasp), served WW I (despatches thrice); *m* 15 Dec 1914 Clara Agnes (*d* 8 Feb 1952), only dau of J W Alexander, ICS, of Indore, and *das* 27 April 1918, leaving:
(1) Yvone Alexander; *b* 8 April 1916; *d* 26 Jan 1932
(2) JAMES ALEXANDER (Sir), **10th Bt**
3 Yvone; *b* 18 Feb 1879; Political Serv, Nigeria; *m* 9 June 1917 Dorothy (*d* 4 May 1972), yst dau of Montague C Barker, of Hampton Court, and *d* 31 March 1924
4 Athol; *b* 20 Sept 1885; served WWI; *m* 1914 Ada Florence, dau of Alfred H Allen, of Sheffield; missing France, presumed *d* 1917
1 Josephine Mary; *m* 30 April 1901 Cecil Egbert Jackson Castle (*d* 5 June 1922), s of Capt C T Castle, 17th Regt, and *d* 27 Jan 1948
2 Margaret Hope; *m* 5 July 1899 Wilfred Hamilton Stilgoe (*d* 12 Feb 1949) and *d* 4 Aug 1945, leaving issue

Sir CHARLES's nephew,

Sir James Alexander Kirkpatrick, 10th Bt; *b* 24 Oct 1918; *educ* Wellington; S/Ldr RAFVR, WW II (despatches); Assist Game Warden, Kenya; *m* 2 Aug 1941 (*divorce* 1953) Ellen Gertrude (*m* 2nd 1955 John Ogilvie Corbin, MB, BS, FRCS), only dau of Capt Robert Perceval Elliott, RNR, of Ismailia, and *d* 3 April 1954, leaving:
1 Sir IVONE ELLIOTT KIRKPATRICK, **11th and present Bt**
2 +ROBIN ALEXANDER; *b* 19 March 1944; heir presumptive; *educ* Wellington

KIRKWOOD

Arms: Argent two chevronels round-embattled on their upper edges sable between two oak-sprigs slipped and fructed proper in chief and a cog-wheel azure in base. **Crest:** The bow of a ship affrontée proper. **Supporters:** Dexter, an Ayrshire bull; sinister, a Clydesdale stallion, both proper, the latter harnessed or. **Motto:** (over crest) Whatever men dare they can do. **Creation:** B. (UK) 22 Dec 1951.

THE 3RD BARON KIRKWOOD, of Bearsden, Dunbarton (David Harvie Kirkwood) [The Rt Hon The Lord Kirkwood, 56 Endcliffe Hall Ave, Sheffield, Yorks S10 3EL]; *b* 24 Nov 1931; *s f* 1970; *educ* Rugby and Trin Hall Cambridge (MA, PhD); CEng; warden Stephenson Hall 1974–79, sr lecturer Metallurgy Sheffield U 1974–87, memb Ho Lds Select Ctee Sci & Tech 1987–92, 1996–; *m* 31 July 1965 *Judith Rosalie, dau of John Hunt, of Leeds, and has:
1 *Ruth Emily; *b* 17 Sept 1966
2 *Anne Judith; *b* 24 April 1969
3 *Lucy Jennifer; *b* 28 July 1972

Lineage: DAVID KIRKWOOD had:

JOHN (RUBBLE) KIRKWOOD, of Parkhead, Glasgow; *m* Annie Black and had, with a yr s (John):

DAVID KIRKWOOD, of Parkhead; *m* Jennie Grey and had, with an er s (James):

JOHN KIRKWOOD; winding master Brown's Mill, Bridgeton, Glasgow; *m* Jean, dau of William Brown by Anne McAuley, and had, with a dau (Annie, *b* 17 May 1876, *d* 16 Nov 1892):

DAVID KIRKWOOD, **1st Baron Kirkwood**, of Bearsden, Co Dunbarton (UK), so *cr* 22 Dec 1951, PC (1948), JP (Glasgow 1935); *b* 8 July 1872; *educ* Parkhead Public Sch; deported as leader of protest against rent increases 1916, memb Glasgow Town Cncl 1918–22 and Nat Cncl ILP 1919–32, MP (Lab) Clydebank, Dunbarton Burghs 1922–50 and E Dunbartonshire 1950–51, author *My Life of Revolt*; *m* 30 June 1899 Elizabeth (*d* 3 May 1956), dau of Robert Smith, of Parkhead, and *d* 16 April 1955, having had:
1 John; *b* 29 March 1900; *educ* Ruskin Coll Oxford (Dip Ec Political Science 1924); *m* 22 Oct 1932 Ellen Florence (*d* 1976), dau of Thomas Peter Haggar, of Witham, Essex, and *d* 8 Dec 1942, leaving:
(1) *Jean [Miss Jean Kirkwood, 288 Warwick Rd, Solihull, W Midlands]; *b* 9 June 1935
2 Robert Smith; *b* 25 Oct 1901; *educ* Eastbank Acad; md Vincent Engrg; *m* 21 Oct 1927 Annie Kerr (*d* 1963), dau of John Marshall, of Shettleston, Glasgow, and *d* 17 May 1950, leaving:
(1) *Agnes Young [Miss Agnes Kirkwood, 11 Chesterfield Ct, Glasgow W2]; *b* 16 April 1930
(2) *Elizabeth Smith; *b* 15 Oct 1937
3 DAVID, **2nd Baron**
4 James Smith, JP (Dunbartonshire 1954); *b* 22 Jan 1912; *educ* Allen Glen's Sch and Glasgow Sch of Art (Dip Arch); ARIBA, FRIAS, ptnr Wright and Kirkwood (chartered architects); *m* 12 Feb 1944 Mary Helen (*d* 1970), dau of James Marshall, of Elgin, Morayshire, and *d* 1983, leaving:
(1) +David [Col David Kirkwood, 7 Wildbank Chase, Mottram Rise, Stalybridge, Cheshire SK15 1UJ]; *b* 26 March 1945; Lt 4th Regt RHA, Col RA (ret); *m* Aug 1971 *Sandra, dau of Richard Bell, of Nelson
(2) +James Marshall Smith; *b* 26 Aug 1954
(1) Elizabeth Joan; *b* 26 Jan 1947; *d* Sept 1986
1 Elizabeth Smith; *b* 13 April 1908; *m* 5 Dec 1944 John Archibald Duguid Mair, s of David Mair, of Neilston, Renfrewshire, and had issue
2 Jean Brown; *b* 13 May 1917; *m* 24 Sept 1943 William Henderson MacGonnigill, s of William Henderson MacGonnigill, of Glasgow, and had issue

The 1st BARON's 3rd son,

DAVID KIRKWOOD, **2nd Baron Kirkwood**; *b* 15 Oct 1903; chm Nat Sulphuric Acid Assoc, treasurer Chest and Heart Assoc; *m* 29 March 1931 *Eileen Grace, dau of Thomas Henry Boalch, of Shirehampton, nr Bristol, and *d* 9 March 1970, leaving:
1 DAVID HARVIE KIRKWOOD, **3rd and present Baron Kirkwood**

2 +JAMES STUART [The Hon James Kirkwood, The Cearne, Kent Hatch, Edenbridge, Kent TN8 6SZ]; *b* 19 June 1937; heir presumptive; *educ* Rugby and Trin Hall Cambridge (MA); FRICS; *m* 24 April 1965 *Alexandra Mary, dau of Alec Dyson, of Holt, Norfolk, and has:

(1) *Kate Victoria; *b* 23 May 1966

(2) *Georgina Grace; *b* 14 July 1969

KITCHENER

Arms: Gules a chevron argent surmounted by another azure between three bustards proper, in the centre chief point a bezant. **Crest:** A stag's head erased, transfixed through the neck by an arrow in bend, point to the dexter, all proper, and between the attires a horseshoe or. **Supporters:** Dexter, a camel proper, bridle, trappings and line pendant, reflexed over the back gules, gorged with a collar or, suspended therefrom an escutcheon paly bendy azure and ermine, a canton of the last, charged with a portucullis gold; sinister, a gnu proper, gorged as the dexter, suspended therefrom an escutcheon ermine charged with a chevron engrailed vert, thereon four horse-shoes, also gold. **Motto:** Thorough. **Creations:** V. (UK) 11 July 1902 (Kitchener of Khartoum); E., V. (Broome), and B. (UK) 27 July 1914.

THE 3RD EARL KITCHENER OF KHARTOUM AND OF BROOME, in the Co of Kent, **Viscount Kitchener**, of Khartoum, and of the Vaal, in the Colony of the Transvaal, **Viscount Broome** of Broome, in the Co of Kent, and **Baron Denton** of Denton, in the Co of Kent, and of Aspall, in the Co of Suffolk (Henry Herbert Kitchener, TD, DL (Cheshire 1972)) [The Rt Hon The Earl Kitchener of Khartoum TD DL, Westergate Wood, Eastergate, W Sussex, PO20 6SB]; *b* 24 Feb 1919; *s* gf 1937; *educ* Winchester and Trin Coll Cambridge; Page Honour to HM GEORGE VI Coronation 1937, WW II as Maj Roy Signals, pres: Lord Kitchener Nat Memorial Fund 1950–, Henry Doubleday Res Assoc

Lineage: THOMAS KITCHENER; *b c* 1666 at Binstead, Alton, Hants, of a family settled there since at least 1555; land agent at Lakenheath, Suffolk, 1693, to Sir Nicholas Stuart, 1st Bt, Ld of the Manor; churchwarden 1697; *m* Abigail Clarke (*bur* 19 June 1747) and *d* 5 April 1731, having had, with other issue:

ROBERT KITCHENER, of Lakenheath; *bapt* 16 Oct 1717; *m* (licence 17 Sept 1738) Ann (*d* 21 Dec 1775), dau of Edward Fisher, of West Row, Suffolk, and *d* 15 Dec 1775, having had an est s:

THOMAS KITCHENER, of Lakenheath and Bury St Edmunds; *bapt* 18 April 1740; *m* 25 April 1764 Martha (*d* 31 Aug 1826), dau of William Robinson, of Eriswell Hall, Suffolk, and *d* between 18 May and 13 Oct 1821, having had, with two daus (including Elizabeth, *b* 23 Jan 1777, *m* 31 Dec 1799 Habbakuk Robinson (*d* 4 Jan 1851), of Bagshot, Surrey, bro of Henry Crabb Robinson, diarist, and *d* 5 May 1803, leaving issue):

WILLIAM KITCHENER, of London; Freeman Clothworkers' Co 1791; *b* Lakenheath 24 Feb 1768; *m* 1st 29 March 1792 Laetitia (*d* 13 Aug 1797), dau of Rev Thomas Waldegrave, of Bury St Edmunds, and had, with other issue:

1 Robinson John; Master Clothworkers' Co 1864–65; *b* 23 July 1794; *m* 1st 1820 Anne (*d* 11 Aug 1832), dau of William Shrubsole; *m* 2nd 1835 Susanna Goddard (*d* 12 March 1872) and *dsp* 19 May 1868

WILLIAM KITCHENER *m* 2nd 22 April 1799 Emma (*d* 16 June 1853), dau of Rev Thomas Cripps, Rector Cheadle, by Catherine, dau of William Buck, of New Grange, Lincs, and had, with other issue:

2 Thomas, of Mildenhall; *b* 1 Sept 1801; *m* 6 Dec 1825 Susan (*bur* 20 Oct 1850), dau of Rev John Barwick Sams, Rector Honington, Suffolk, and *d* 9 April 1836, having had:

(1) Thomas; MD; *b* 14 Feb 1831; *m* 1st Isabel de Carteret (*dsp*); *m* 2nd 1863 Mary Louisa (*bur* 16 Aug 1879), dau of Frederick Charles Clarke, and was *bur* 25 Oct 1882, leaving:

1a Thomas Martin Cripps; *b* 25 May 1869; *m* 28 Oct 1904 Alice, dau of Alexander Proctor, MD, and *d* 26 Nov 1934, leaving:

1b Thomas Hunt Cripps; *b* 23 March 1906

1a Evelyn Bertha; *b* 27 Jan 1872; *m* 13 April 1898 Maj Gerard Arthur Fletcher Sanders, RE, and had issue

(2) Henry; Capt 6th Foot; *b* 5 Nov 1835; *m* 2 Aug 1866 Mary Arabella, dau of Thomas Laud, of Jamaica, and *d* 22 July 1882, leaving issue, who *d* unm

(1) Jane; *d* 6 July 1848 aged 15

3 William Cripps, of Newmarket, Suffolk; *b* 22 Jan 1803; *m* 26 Sept 1825 Ann (*d* 16 June 1877), only child of John Orbell, of Kentford Hall, Suffolk, and *d* 7 Feb 1872, having had:

(1) William Orbell; *b* 11 Sept 1826; *m* Sept 1877 Eliza Ashford and *dsp* 14 Dec 1877

(2) Francis Elliott, of Oulton Old Hall, Staffs, JP; CA, MA, LLM Cambridge, Fell Trin Coll 1863–68; *b* 30 Dec 1838; *m* 13 Aug 1868 Frances Anna (*d* 21 Feb 1909), dau of Rev John Parish Hammond, Vicar Sopley, Hants, and *dsp* 6 July 1915

(1) Emma; *b* 24 Sept 1829; *m* 30 May 1860 William Henry Day, MD, of Holly Hill, Meopham, Kent, and *d* 14 Sept 1909, having had issue

(2) Annette; *b* 26 June 1835; *m* 26 July 1866 John Peile, MA, Ltt D, Master Christ's Coll Cambridge, and *d* 28 Dec 1920, leaving issue

4 HENRY HORATIO

5 Phillip Elliott, of Little Warden Park, Essex, and Adair, Co Limerick; *b* 27 April 1807; *m* 4 Oct 1847 Elizabeth (*d* 15 Nov 1911), dau of Henry Thornton, and *d* 30 March 1875, having had:

(1) Elliott; *b* 25 Dec 1865; *educ* Christ's Coll Cambridge (MA); *m* 25 July 1906 Bessie Maud (*d* 16 Aug 1932), only dau of Harry MacIver, of Wyncote, Allerton, and *d* 9 Oct 1929

(2) Henry Thornton; CE; *b* 22 July 1868; *m* 12 June 1907 Elizabeth Margaret (*d* 19 Aug 1932), dau of Michael Evans, of Liverpool, and *d* 1961

(1) Jane Penelope; *b* 24 Dec 1855; *d* 15 Feb 1939

(2) Ellen Mary; *b* 26 Jan 1860; *m* 1890 Edwin Budden (*d* 1907), MA Oxon, BSc Lond, and *d* 21 Aug 1940, leaving issue

WILLIAM KITCHENER *dvp* 4 June 1807; his 4th son,

HENRY HORATIO KITCHENER, of Cossington, Leics; Lt-Col 9th Foot, previously 13th Light Dragoons; *b* 19 Oct 1805; *m* 1st 24 July 1845 Frances (*d* 1864), dau of Rev John Chevallier-Guild, MD, of Aspall Hall, Suffolk, and had:

1 HENRY ELLIOTT CHEVALLIER, **2nd Earl**

2 HORATIO HERBERT KITCHENER, **1st Earl Kitchener of Khartoum and of Broome**, of Khartoum and of Broome, Co Kent, so *cr* 27 July 1914, as also BARON DENTON of Denton, Co Kent, VISCOUNT BROOME of Broome, with special remainder, failing heirs male of his body, to any daus he might have and heirs male of their bodies, failing whom to his est bro Henry then his yst bro Frederick and the heirs male of their bodies, also earlier 1 Nov 1898 BARON KITCHENER, of Khartoum, and of Aspall, Suffolk, with remainder to the heirs male of his body only (and with a grant and the thanks of Parl), then 11 July 1902 VISCOUNT KITCHENER OF KHARTOUM and of the Vaal in the Colony of the Transvaal, and of Aspall, Suffolk, with special remainder as for the Earldom, KG (1915), KP (1911), GCB (1898, KCB 1896, CB 1889), OM (1902), GSCI (1909), GCMG (1900, KCMG 1894, CMG 1886, GCIE (1908), PC (1914); *b* 24 June 1850; Palestine survey 1874–78, Cyprus survey 1879–79, V-Consul Anatolia 1879–80, served Egyptian Army 1883–85 and 1886–89 (Sudan Expdn 1884–85; despatches, medal with clasp, bronze star, Brevet Lt-Col; ops round Suakin 1888 (severely wounded), Sudan 1888–89 (despatches twice); Govr Red Sea Littoral 1886–88, ADC to HM QUEEN VICTORIA 1888–96, Sirdar Egyptian Army 1892–99 (cmded Dongola Expdn 1896 (Maj-Gen, 1st Cl Osmanieh, Egyptian medal with two clasps), Nile Expdn 1897 (despatches, clasp) and 1898 Expdn (Atbara and Khartoum; despatches, two clasps and medal)), Boer War: Ch of Staff 1899–1900 and C-in-C 1900–02 (Queen's medal with three clasps, King's medal with two clasps), C-in-C India 1902–09; FM; Agent, Consul-Gen and Min Plen Egypt 1911–1914, memb CID 1910–16, Sec State War 1914–16 Col Cmdt RE, Col Irish Gds and 7th Gurkha Rifles, Col in Chief Natal Carabineers, High Steward Ipswich 1909, LLD Cantab and Edin, DCL Oxon, Ld Rector Edinburgh U 1914, KJStJ; *d* unm on sinking of HMS *Hampshire* W of the Orkneys 5 June 1916 en route to Russia, when the 1898 Barony expired

3 Arthur Buck; *b* 1852; *m* 6 Nov 1898 Edith (*d* 13 Jan 1908), 2nd dau of John Paterson, of Melbourne, and *dsp* 24 Feb 1907

4 Frederick Walter (Sir), KCB; Lt-Gen, special serv Egypt 1896, cmded 2nd Bn W Yorks Regt 1898–1900, served Afghan War 1878–80 (despatches, medal with clasp), Dongola Expdn 1896 (despatches, 4th Cl Osmanieh, medal with two clasps), Sudan Expdn 1898 (three clasps, Medjidie 3rd Cl), Boer War 1900–02 (despatches), cmded 3rd Div 1st Army Corps India 1903–08, Govr and C-in-C Bermuda 1908–12; *b* 26 May 1858; *m* 27 Nov 1884 Caroline (*d* 3 Nov 1901), dau of Col Charles Hamilton Fenton, 9th Foot, and *d* 6 March 1912, having had:

(1) Charles Chevallier; *b* 27 Feb 1886; *d* 21 May 1889

(2) Henry Hamilton; Maj Res of Offrs RE, Capt and F/Cdr RFC, S/Ldr RAF; *b* 10 Sept 1890; *m* 1st 8 July 1916 Winifred Esther Everest (*d* 1959), er dau of Hon A W Bluck, MCP, of Hamilton, Bermuda; *m* 2nd 28 April 1961 Mrs Gwynneth Champion (*d* 1983), and *d* 1984, having by his 1st w had:

1a *Winifred Jean [Mrs Peter Hall, Oakfield House, Spreyton, Crediton, Devon EX17 5AL]; *b* 3 Dec 1917; *m* 5 Aug 1954 *Lt Peter Hall, RN, and has:

1b *Christopher Peter; *b* 3 May 1955; *m* 1981 *Sarah Jane Downs and has:

1c *James Henry; *b* 1985

2c *Robert Hamilton; *b* 1987

3c *George Howard; *b* 1990

2a *Eleanor Elizabeth Madge [Mrs Louis Cornhill, 86 Waller Crescent, Campbell, Canberra, ACT 2612, Australia]; *b* Nov 1920; *m* 1947 Louis Cornhill (*d* 1971) and has:

1b *Peter; *b* 12 Oct 1949; has:

1c *Serena Thérèse; *b* 8 Dec 1984

2c *Jasmine Louise; *b* 10 May 1987

2b *Robert; *b* 5 May 1953

(1) Dorothy; *b* 10 Nov 1887; *d* 17 March 1889

(2) Frances Madge; RRC; *b* 1 Aug 1889

(3) Mary Esmé; *b* 30 July 1892; *m* 22 June 1915 Ronald Julius Wernher Gervers, MC (*d* 4 June 1960), and *d* 13 Nov 1922, leaving issue

(4) Philippa Chevallier; *b* 11 June 1895; *m* 15 May 1917 Brig Terence Desmond Murray, CBE, DSO, MC (*d* 17 July 1961), RTR, est s of Sir John Huber Plunkett Murray, KCMG, Lt Govr Papua, and had:

1c Molly Patricia; *b* 1919; *m* 19– and *d* 19– leaving two daus

2c *Sybil Madge; *b* 1921; *m* 19– and has three sons

3c *Sheila Chevallier; *b* 1926; *m* 19– Michael Butler, of St Neot, Cornwall

1 Frances Emily Jane; *m* 24 June 1869 Harry Rainy Parker (*d* 15 Dec 1912), of Rothley Temple, Leics, est s of V-Chllr Sir James Parker, and *d* 10 Feb 1925, leaving issue

Lt-Col HENRY KITCHENER *m* 2nd 1866 Mary Emma Green (*d* 11 Jan 1918 aged 84) and *d* 14 Aug 1894, having by her had:

2 Henrietta Letita Emma Kawara; *b* 1867; Legn Hon; *d* 7 Oct 1926

The 1st EARL's er bro,

HENRY ELLIOTT CHEVALLIER KITCHENER, **2nd Earl Kitchener of Khartoum**; *b* 5 Oct 1846; served Franco-Prussian War 1870 (medal), Col DCLI, cmdg depot W India Regt 1899–1903, Burma 1891 (despatches, medal and clasp), Manipur Expdn 1891 (despatches, clasp) and SE Africa WW I; *m* 9 Oct 1877 Eleanor Fanny (*d* 1 June 1898), only child of Lt-Col Franklin Lushington, CB (*see* LUSHINGTON, Bt), and *dsps* 27 March 1937, having had:

1 Henry Franklin Chevallier, *Viscount Broome*; Capt RN, served China 1900 and WW I, 4th Cl Order of the Nile; *b* 17 Oct 1878; *m* 11 Sept 1916 Adela Mary Evelyn, dau of John Henry Monins, of Ringwould Ho, Dover, Kent, and *d* 13 June 1928, leaving:

(1) HENRY HERBERT KITCHENER, **3rd and present Earl Kitchener of Khartoum and of Broome**

(2) Charles Eaton; *b* 11 March 1920; *educ* Winchester, and Trin Coll Cambridge; RCOS; granted with sis 24 March 1938 rank of earl's dau/yr s; *m* 15 Aug 1959 *Ursula Hope [The Hon Mrs Charles Kitchener, Croylands, Old Salisbury Lane, Romsey, Hants SO51 0GD], dau of Capt Cyril Montagu Luck, CMG, DSO, RN, of Sussex, and *d* 1982, leaving:

1a *Emma Joy [Mrs Julian Fellowes, 15 Moore St, London SW3 2QN]; *b* 18 Feb 1963; *m* 1990 *Julian Alexander Fellowes, yst s of Peregrine Edward Launcelot Fellowes-Gordon of Knockespoch, and has:

1b *Peregrine Charles Morant Kitchener; *b* 1991

(1) *Kenya Eleanor [The Lady Kenya Tatton-Brown, Westergate Wood, nr Chichester, Sussex PO20 6SB]; 3rd Offr WRNS WW II; *b* 12 July 1923; BA, MCSP, SRP, chartered physiotherapist; *m* 8 Nov 1947 John Stewart Tatton-Brown (*d* 1 Feb 1971), er s of Eden Tatton-Brown, CMG, of Westergate Wood, and has:

1a *Margaret Caroline; *b* 1950; *m* 1984 *A John Aanonson, s of A W Aanonson, of Hornsey

2a *(Adela) Charlotte [Mrs Patrick Appleby, Shrubs Hill, Itchen Abbas, Hants]; *b* 1951; *m* 1982 *Patrick B Appleby, yr s of Kenneth Appleby, and has:

1b *Charles; *b* 1983

2b *Benjamin; *b* 1985

3b *James Michael; *b* 1988

3a *Augusta Kenya [Mrs James Saunders, PO Box 149, Jerramungup, 6337 W Australia]; *b* 1955; *m* 1976 *James D P Saunders and has:

1b *Duncan John; *b* 1977

2b *Peter Eden; *b* 1979

1 Nora Fanny; *b* 1882; *m* 17 Dec 1908 Maj Patrick Albert Forbes Winslow à Beckett, RA (*d* Jan 1941), est surv s of Arthur William à Beckett, barrister, and *d* 10 May 1919

KLEINWORT

Arms: Or a lion rampant sable, on a chief of the last three oak trees eradicated proper. **Crest:** On a mount vert three slips of clover proper. **Motto:** *Nil sine labore* ('Nothing without labour').
Creation: Bt. (UK) 29 Nov 1909.

SIR RICHARD DRAKE KLEINWORT, 4TH BT, of Bolnore, Cuckfield, Sussex [Sir Richard Kleinwort Bt, Heaselands, Haywards Heath, W Sussex RH16 4SA]; *b* 4 Nov 1960; *s f* 1994; *educ* Stowe and Exeter U (BA); *m* 1989 *Lucinda, dau of William Shand Kydd, of Horton Hall, Horton, Bucks, and has:

1 +RUFUS DRAKE; *b* 16 Aug 1994

2 +Tristan William; *b* 10 July 1997

1 *Heloise; *b* 28 Feb 1996

Lineage: JOACHIM KLEINWORT; *d* Altona, nr Hamburg, 1783, leaving:

HEINRICH KLEINWORT, of Gerdeshagen, nr Sartow, Holstein; *b* 22 Aug 1762; *m* 17 Feb 1809 Maria Dorothea Sophia Frederica Wilhelmina von Hovell (*d* 3 Aug 1846) and *d* 27 Sept 1831, having had:

ALEXANDER FREDERICK HENRY KLEINWORT, of The Glebe, Grove Hill, Denmark Hill; *b* 18 Nov 1815; *m* 24 Jan 1852 Sophia Charlotte (*d* 5 June 1860), dau of Herman Diedrich Greverus, of The Grove, Denmark Hill, and *d* 7 Jan 1886, having had:

1 Herman Greverus, of Wierton Place, nr Maidstone, Kent, and 45 Belgrave Sq, London SW1; *b* 3 July 1856; ptnr Kleinwort Sons & Co, merchant bankers; *m* 12 May 1881 Marguerite Marie Jeanne (*d* 31 July 1935), dau of Otto Gunther, of Antwerp, and *d* 18 June 1942, leaving:

(1) Marguerita Wilhemina; *m* 4 Oct 1915 Sir Ernest Nathaniel Bennett (*d* 2 Feb 1947), only s of Rev George Bennett, Rector Rede, Suffolk, and *d* 19 Aug 1963, leaving issue

(2) Helene Pauline; *b* 28 Dec 1884; *m* 19 Oct 1911 Brig-Gen Rodney Charles Style (*see* STYLE, Bt) and had issue

(3) Sophie Charlotte; *m* 19 Aug 1919 Martin Julian Renner (*d* 16 Jan 1956), s of John Sebastian Renner, of Wernigerode, and had issue

(4) Alice Dorothy; *m* 11 May 1922 Cdr Francis Paul Orlando Bridgeman (*see* BRADFORD, E) and had issue

(5) Marieka Louise; *m* 10 Nov 1917 Capt Hon Trevor Tempest Parker, RN, of Greatham Manor, Liss, Hants, est s of Baron Parker of Waddington (*see* 1918 edn), and *d* 19 Nov 1949, leaving issue

(6) Lily Emily; *m* 5 Aug 1925 V-Adml Sir Thomas Hope Troubridge, KCB, DSO (*see* TROUBRIDGE, Bt), and had issue

(7) Daisy Jeanne Margaret (twin with Lily Emily); Sister Naomi, of Convent of the Incarnation, Fairacres, Oxford

2 ALEXANDER DRAKE (Sir), **1st Bt**

1 Wilhelmina Frederika; *m* 2 April 1872 Philip Ludwig Robert Martin, of Redcourt, Champion Hill, and had issue

2 Sophie Charlotte; *m* 24 Sept 1873 Carlo Andreae, of Crestalta, Champion Hill, and had issue

The 2nd son,

Sir Alexander Drake Kleinwort, 1st Bt (UK), so *cr* 29 Nov 1909; *b* 17 Oct 1858; ptnr Kleinwort Sons & Co, merchant bankers, chm N Br and Mercantile Insur; *m* 30 April 1889 Etienette (*d* 8 Aug 1946), dau of Etienne Girard, of Haywards Heath, Sussex, late Belgian Consul Louisville, Ky., and *d* 8 June 1935, having had:

1 **Sir Alexander Santiago Kleinwort, 2nd Bt**, of Bolnore, Cuckfield, Sussex; *b* 31 Oct 1892; *educ* St John's Coll Oxford; *m* 6 April 1938 *Yvonne, dau of John Bloch, and *dsp* 26 March 1983

2 Frederick Henry; *b* 14 Aug 1895; *d* 19 Sept 1896

3 Henry Drake; *b* 21 May 1900; *d* 8 May 1921

4 Ernest Greverus; *b* 13 Sept 1901; *educ* Jesus Coll Cambridge (BA 1922); F/Lt RAFVR WW II 1942–45; dir Kleinwort Benson, Lonsdale Ltd (chm 1961–68) to 1974, chm Kleinwort, Benson Ltd 1961–66; *m* 29 Dec 1932 Joan Nightingale, MBE, JP (1951 Sussex), dau of Prof Arthur William Crossley, CMG, CBE, and *d* 3 Nov 1977, leaving:

(1) KENNETH DRAKE (Sir), **3rd Bt**

(1) *Gillian Mawdsley [Mrs Michael Warren, Banks Farm, Barcombe, Lewes, Sussex BN8 5DY]; *b* 4 May 1937; *m* 21 Sept 1957 *Michael Raymond Warren, JP, only s of Col Raymond Warren, OBE, MC, DL, of Handcross, Sussex, and has:

1a *Charles Raymond; *b* 14 Dec 1963; *m* 1993 *Sarah Elizabeth, dau of Richard Lionel Mather and has:

1b *Alexander Finlay; *b* 1997

1a *Davina Mary Warren [Mrs Peter Irwin-Clark, Desmond's Castle, The Hyde, Haywards Heath, W Sussex RH17 6MA]; *b* 1958; *m* 28 July 1979 *Rev Peter Elliot Irwin-Clark and has:

1b *Benjamin John; *b* 1983

1b *Jessamy Claire; *b* 1987

2a *Susanna Rachel; *b* 1975

5 Cyril Hugh (Sir); *b* 17 Aug 1905; Lt-Cdr RNVR; chm Kleinwort, Benson Lonsdale Ltd, dir Kleinwort, Benson Investment Tst, and Ctee on Invisible Exports, v-chm Commerical Union Assurance Co Ltd, ktd 1971; *m* 8 Sept 1933 Elisabeth (Betty) Kathleen (*d* 7 May 1997), dau of Francis Forde, of Budds Farm, Newbury, Berks, and *d* 1980, leaving:

(1) *(Serena) Elizabeth; *b* 31 March 1936; *m* 19 Oct 1960 *David Alfred Acland (*see* ACLAND, Bt, of Oxford) and has issue

(2) *Charlotte Susanna; *b* 16 June 1938; *m* 1st 15 May 1965 (*divorce*) (Richard) Lawrence Baillieu and has issue (*see* BAILLIEU, B); *m* 2nd 15 Nov 1972 (Nevile) Martin Gwynne and has further issue (see MORRISON-BELL, Bt); *m* 3rd 1980 *Alan Cyril Heber-Percy (*see* NORTHUMBERLAND, D)

(3) *Susanna; *b* 3 Jan 1942; *m* 22 Nov 1962 *David Alphy Edward Raymond Peake and has issue (*see* INGLEBY, V)

1 Sophie Louise; *b* 16 March 1891; *d* unm 2 Jan 1957

2 Henrietta Hortense; *b* 18 Nov 1893; *m* 8 Oct 1920 ACM Sir Douglas Claude Strathern Evill, GBE, KCB, DSC, AFC, DL, RAF (*d* 22 March 1971), of Winchester, only s of F Claude Evill, MRCS, of Barnet, Herts, and had:

(1) William Alan Strathern; *b* 23 Dec 1922; P/O RAF WW II, *ka* 18 Aug 1941

(2) Christopher Strathern; *b* 25 Aug 1926; *d* 30 April 1935

(3) *Henry Claude Strathern [Henry Evill Esq, Cleeves, Weydown Rd, Haslemere, Surrey]; *b* 29 May 1931; *educ* Winchester and New Coll Oxford (BA); *m* 16 March 1960 *Irene Joan, only dau of John Gillie Moncrieff, and has:

1a *Stephen Boyd Strathern; *b* 24 July 1962

1a *Gillian Anette; *b* 14 Oct 1960

2a *Katrina Louise; *b* 14 Nov 1964

(1) *Annette Strathern Evill [Mrs Alan Donger, Taylors Mead, Sparsholt, Hants]; *b* 22 Nov 1921; *m* 9 Sept 1949 *Lt-Col Alan David Donger, TD, JP, RA (TA), FRICS, s of William James Donger, of Winchester, and has:

1a *William Alan; *b* 30 June 1953

1a *Alison Sophie; *b* 6 March 1951

(2) *Sophie Sybella Strathern; *b* 9 July 1929; *m* 23 Nov 1957 Maj Reginald Allan Chenevix Trench (*see* ASHTOWN, B) and has issue

The 2nd Bt's nephew,

Sir Kenneth Drake Kleinwort, 3rd Bt; *b* 28 May 1935; *educ* Eton and Grenoble U; with K Benson 1971–78, exec dir Treb Internat Corp 1978, tstee WWF 1978; *m* 1st 28 Oct 1959 Lady Davina Rose Pepys (*d* 5 March 1973), 2nd dau of 7th Earl of Cottenham (*qv*), and had:

1 Sir RICHARD DRAKE KLEINWORT, **4th and present Bt**

1 *Marina Rose; *b* 2 July 1962

Sir Kenneth *m* 2nd 11 June 1973 *Madeleine [Madeleine Lady Kleinwort, 31 Tregunter Rd, London SW10 9LS], er dau of Ralph Taylor, of Buenos Aires, and *d* 1994, leaving by her:

2 +Alexander Hamilton; *b* 22 Feb 1975

3 +Michael Drake; *b* 1977

2 *Selina Helen Louisa; *b* 1981

KNIGHT OF COLLINGTREE

Creation: B. (LP, UK) 1997.

THE BARONESS KNIGHT OF COLLINGTREE, of Collingtree, Co Northampton (Dame (Joan Christabel) Jill Knight, DBE (1985, MBE 1964)) [The Rt Hon The Baroness Knight of Collingtree DBE, House of Lords, London SW1A 0PW]; *educ* Fairfield Sch Bristol, King Edward GS Birmingham; memb Northampton County Borough Cncl 1956–66, MP (C) Birmingham Edgbaston 1966–97, memb: Parly Select Ctee Race Relations and Immigration 1969–72, Council Europe 1977–88, WEU 1977–88 (Chm Ctee Parly and Public Rels 1984–88), Select Ctee Home Affrs 1980–83 and 1992–97, Chm: Lords and Commons All Party Child and Family Protection Gp 1978–97, C Back Bench Health and Social Services Ctee 1982–97, V-Chm 1922 Ctee 1987–88 and 1992–97 (memb Exec Ctee 1979–97, Sec 1983–87); dir Computeach Internat plc 1991–; memb Exec Ctee IPU 1991– (Chm 1994–97); Pres W Midlands C Political Centre 1980–83; V-Pres Townswomen's Guilds 1986–89; Hon DSc Aston 1998; Kentucky Colonel 1973; Nebraska Admiral 1980; *m* 1947 Montague Knight (*d* 1986) and has two sons

KNIGHTS

Creation: B. (LP, UK) 1987.

THE BARON KNIGHTS, of Edgbaston, Co W Midlands (Sir Philip Douglas Knights, CBE (1976, OBE 1971), QPM (1964), DL (W Midlands 1985)) [The Rt Hon The Lord Knights CBE QPM DL, House of Lords, London SW1A 0PW]; *b* 3 Oct 1920; *educ* King's Sch Grantham; Police Cadet 1938–40, Constable 1940; RAF WW II; Sgt Lincs Constabulary 1946; seconded Home Office 1946–50; Lincs Constabulary Inspr 1953, Supt 1955, Ch Supt 1957; Assist Ch Constable Birmingham City Police 1959; seconded Home Office as Dep Comdt Police Coll 1962–66; Dep Ch Constable Birmingham City Police 1970; Ch Constable: Sheffield and Rotherham Constabulary 1972–74, S Yorks Police 1974–75, W Midlands Police 1975–85; Pres ACPO 1978–79; Tstee Police Fndn 1979–, Memb: Ld Devlin's Ctee Indentification Procedure 1974–75, Cncl Aston U 1985–, Advsy Cncl Cambridge Inst Criminology 1986–; ktd 1980, CBIM, Hon DSc 1996, CIMgt 1977; *m* 1945 *Jean, dau of James Henry Burman

Lineage: THOMAS JAMES KNIGHTS, of Ottershaw, Surrey; *m* Ethel — and had:

PHILIP DOUGLAS, *cr* a **Baron**

KNILL

Arms: Gules semée of crosses bottonée fitchée a lion rampant, all or, on a chief of the last a fasces fesswise, head to the dexter proper. **Crest:** A demi-lion or, holding in the dexter paw a cross bottonée fitchée azure and supporting with the sinister a fasces in bend proper. **Motto:** *Nil desperandum* ('Despair at nothing').
Creation: Bt. (UK) 11 Aug 1893.

SIR THOMAS JOHN PUGIN BARTHOLOMEW KNILL, 5TH BT, of The Grove, Blackheath, Kent [Sir Thomas Knill Bt, 3 Widcombe Terrace, Bath, Somerset BA2 6AJ]; *b* 23 Aug 1952; *s* f 1998; *educ* Lucton, Herefs; *m* 7 May 1977 (*divorce* 1996) Kathleen, dau of Boris Muszynski, and has:

1 *Claire Rosemary; *b* 8 Sept 1978

2 *Bryony Jane; *b* 6 Feb 1981

3 *Lucy Jasmine; *b* 19 Jan 1983

Lineage: JOHN KNILL, of Tipton Hall Farm, Herefs, and Blackheath, had:

THOMAS KNILL; *b* 19 Jan 1782; *m* 1st 10 Nov 1803 Anne Gain (*d* 23 Dec 1815) and had:

1 Thomas Gain; *b* 5 May 1807; *d* unm, *bur* 13 Dec 1827

2 Joseph; *b* 18 Oct 1814; *d* 2 May 1817

1 Sarah; *b* 25 May 1812; *m* 1839 James Lane Wight (*d* 28 Sept 1885), of Tedstone Ct, Delamere, Herefs, and *d* 21 Nov 1854, leaving issue

THOMAS KNILL *m* 2nd 12 July 1819 Elizabeth Cox (*d* 8 Jan 1862), dau of Gabriel Stuart, of Thames St, London, and *d* 8 Jan 1854, having by her had:

3 John Stuart; *b* 25 Sept 1820; *d* Feb 1821

4 STUART (Sir), **1st Bt**

2 Margaret Mary; *d* unm

JOHN KNILL's 4th son,

Sir Stuart Knill, 1st Bt (UK), so *cr* 11 Aug 1893, of The Grove, Blackheath, and Fresh Wharf, London, JP (City of London, Kent and Co London); *b* 11 April 1824; Commr for executing Ltcy City London, Alderman Bridge Ward 1885–98, Sheriff London 1889, Ld Mayor 1893, Hon LLD Edinburgh; *m* 23 Jan 1850 Mary Anne Rose (*d* 20 July 1907), dau of Charles Rowland Parker, of Greenwich and Blackheath, and *d* 19 Nov 1898, having had:

1 JOHN (Sir), **2nd Bt**

2 Elphege; *b* 19 April 1861; *d* 2 Jan 1865

1 Mary; *b* 9 July 1851; *m* 19 June 1878 Michael Harman Dalton Thunder, JP (*d* 22 April 1914), of Seneschaltown House, Co Meath, and *d* 25 Nov 1893, leaving issue

2 Rose; *b* 30 Aug 1852; *m* 22 July 1887 James Cown (*d* 1905), of Mount Stuart, Blackheath, barrister Middle Temple, and *d* 24 Feb 1923, leaving issue

3 Anne; *b* 10 Jan 1860; *d* 22 Jan 1865

The 1st Bt's er s,

Sir John Knill, 2nd Bt; *b* 4 Sept 1856; Lt City London, Alderman 1897–1931, Sheriff 1903–04, Ld Mayor 1909–10, Offr Order Crown Italy, Cdr Order Leopold Belgium, Order Rising Sun Japan, Kt Cdr Order St Gregory the Great and St James Portugal; *m* 18 April 1882 Mary Edith (*d* 21 April 1944), Dame Order Holy Sepulchre and Order Bene Merenti, dau of John Hardman Powell, of Edgbaston, and *d* 26 March 1934, leaving, with a dau (Mary Anne Dorothy, *b* 26 Jan 1883, *d* unm 16 June 1947):

Sir (John) Stuart Knill, 3rd Bt; *b* 11 April 1886; *educ* Oratory Sch Birmingham; Capt MGC, P/O RAFVR WW II, compiled *The Pedigree of King Arthur*; *m* 1st 22 June 1910 (*divorce* 1935) Lucy Emmeline (*d* 24 April 1952), dau of Capt Thomas Henry Willis, FRGS, of Blackheath, and had:

1 **Sir John Kenelm Stuart Knill, 4th Bt**; *b* 8 April 1913; *educ* Downside; Lt RNVR WW II, Pres: Avon Tport 2000, Commercial Narrowboat Operators Assoc, fndr Assoc Canal Enterprises 1982; a leader in restoring Kennet and Avon Canal; *m* 5 Nov 1951 Violette Maude Florence Martin (*d* 1983), dau of Leonard Martin Barnes, of Durban, and *d* 15 April 1998, leaving:

(1) Sir THOMAS JOHN PUGIN BARTHOLOMEW KNILL, **5th and present Bt**

(2) +JENKYN MARTIN BENEDICT STUART; *b* 19 Jan 1954; heir presumptive; *m* 25 March 1978 *Helen Marguerite Gulliver and has:

1a +Benedict Noel Jenkyn; *b* 20 Nov 1979

2a +Leo Martin Barnabas; *b* 11 June 1981

1a *Abigail Amice Lily; *b* 24 Oct 1984

Sir Stuart *m* 2nd 1941 *(Ruth) Evelyn, numerologist, dau of Archibald Barnes, and *d* 17 April 1973, leaving by her:

2 +Gyles Braoze Hamish Stanislas Stuart; *b* 1945; *m* and has two daus

3 +Rognvald Gabriel Nigel Alastair; *b* 1 June 1946; *m* 1st 1969 Janet Charles; *m* 2nd Josephine Doherty and has:

(1) +Rory Alec STUART-KNILL; *b* 3 Sept 1973

(1) *Emma Marie STUART-KNILL; *b* 3 Sept 1973

3 (cont.) Rognvald Knill *m* 3rd 1983 *Evelin Gölliner and by her has:

(2) *Julia Anne STUART-KNILL; *b* 13 July 1984

1 *Gloriana Leonora Dorothea Marie [Mrs Charles Morehead, 33 Brompton Walk, Darlington, Co Durham DL3 8RT]; *b* 17 Dec 1937; *m* 20 April 1959 *William Charles Morehead, CPO RN, s of William Morehead, of Leics, and has:

(1) *Simon William [Simon Morehead Esq, 30 Ennerdale Terrace, Low Westwood, Tyne and Wear]; *b* 1 Sept 1961; *m* 28 Sept 1985 *Stephanie Gibson

(1) *Sarah Maria Evelyn [Mrs Peter McDonnell, 9 Canonbie Rd, London SE23 3AW]; *b* 19 March 1960; *m* 23 July 1983 *Peter McDonnell and has:

1a *John Angus; *b* 4 Dec 1989

2a *Calum Andrew; *b* 24 April 1992

KNOLLYS

Arms: Per pale gules and argent a chevron counterchanged and charged with three roses, also counterchanged, barbed and seeded proper. **Crest:** Between two crosses moline per pale azure and or fimbriated counterchanged, an elephant statant argent. **Supporters:** On either side an heraldic antelope, the dexter argent, the sinister or, both tufted horned and unguled sable and charged on the shoulder with a cross as on the crest. **Motto:** *In utrumque paratus* ('In every way prepared'). **Creations:** B. (UK) 21 July 1902, V. (UK) 4 July 1911.

THE 3RD VISCOUNT KNOLLYS, of Caversham, Co Oxford, and **Baron Knollys**, of Caversham, Co Oxford (David Francis Dudley Knollys, DL (Norfolk 1996)) [The Rt Hon The Viscount Knollys DL, The Bailiff's House, Bramerton Hall Farm, Norwich, Norfolk NR14 7DN]; *b* 12 June 1931; *s f* 1966; *educ* Eton; late Lt Scots Gds; *m* 1 Oct 1959 *Hon Sheelin Virginia, sis of 12th Baron Farnham (*qv*), and has:

1 +PATRICK NICHOLAS MARK; *b* 11 March 1962; *educ* Wymondham Coll and RMA Sandhurst; Scots Gds 1982–88, ret as Capt; proprietor Cam Canes (swagger sticks and walking canes); *m* 24 Sept 1998 *Sarah, only dau of Michael Petch, of Chobham, Surrey, and formerly w of — Wright

2 +Christopher Edward; *b* 2 Sept 1964; *educ* Wymondham Coll and Exeter U; late Capt Scots Gds (commissioned 1987), area sales manager for a boiler co, sometime Equerry to HRH THE DUKE OF KENT; *m* 22 March 1997 *Sarah, er dau of E St J Gwynne and Mrs William Merton

3 +Michael James George; *b* 27 July 1968; *educ* Wymondham Coll and RMA Sandhurst; late Capt Scots Gds (commissioned 1989); with Shell UK

1 *Clarinda Susan [The Hon Mrs Snowball, Mill of Remichie, Dallas, Moray IV36 0RW]; *b* 23 June 1960; *m* 1988 *Andrew M B Snowball, yr s of Brig Edward Joseph Dove Snowball, OBE, of Ballochneck, Thornhill, Perthshire, and has:

(1) *Emma Sheelin; *b* 1992

Earldom of Banbury: GEORGE III intended to create his Prime Minister Henry Addington Earl of Banbury on the latter's leaving office in 1804 but in the event conferred only a viscountcy on him (*see* SIDMOUTH, V)

Lineage: THOMAS KNOLLYS, Ld Mayor London 1399–1400 and 1410–11; ancestor in the 5th generation of:

Sir FRANCIS KNOLLYS, KG; *m* Mary, dau of William Cary by Mary (sis of ANNE BOLEYN) and sis of 1st Baron Hunsdon of Hunsdon (*see* ALDENHAM and HUNSDON OF HUNSDON, B, preliminary remarks), and had, with two daus (Elizabeth, *m* Sir Thomas Leighton (*see* LEIGHTON, Bt); Catherine, *m* Gerald, s and heir of 1st Earl of Kildare; *see* LEINSTER, D) a 2nd s:

Sir WILLIAM KNOLLYS, 1st EARL OF BANBURY, so *cr* 18 Aug 1626, as also 13 May 1603 BARON KNOLLYS OF GREYS, Co Oxford, and 7 Nov 1616 VISCOUNT WALLINGFORD, Co Berks (all E), KG (1615), PC (1596), of Rotherfield Greys, Oxon (which he sold to meet debts March 1630/1), and Cholsey and Caversham, Berks; *b c* 1547; *educ* Magdalen Coll Oxford; MP Tregony 1572–83 and Oxon 1584–86, 1592–93, 1597–98 and 1601; ktd 1586, Ld Lt Berks 1596–1632, Comptroller Household 1596–1600 and Treasurer Household 1600–16; *m* 1st Dorothy, dau of 1st Lord (Baron) Braye (*qv*) and widow of Baron Chandos; *m* 2nd *c* 23 Dec 1605 (he being in his late 50s and she in her late teens) Lady Elizabeth Howard (*m* 2nd by 2 July 1632, *i.e.*, at most 38 days after her 1st husb's death, 4th Baron Vaux of Harrowden, *qv*), dau of 1st Earl of Suffolk (*see* SUFFOLK and BERKSHIRE, E), who gave birth to at least one child (a dau; *d* by 1610) by 1606 and two sons (*see* below), whose paternity was considered highly dubious (not unnaturally in view of the advanced age of Lady Elizabeth's husb by the late 1620s and the absence of any children born to her, whether by her husb or not, over the substantial period 1606–27), and *d* (*dsp* according to the funeral certificate at the College of Arms and the Inquisition Post Mortem executed 11 April 1633, almost a year after his death, two significant details in the circumstances) 25 May 1632, mentioning no children in his will and bequeathing almost his entire property to his w, though those of his estates that were not tied up elsewhere were inherited by the er of the Countess's two sons and Lord Banbury seems to have acknowledged at any rate the er of the Countess's two sons as his; his w's (and his?) sons:

1 Edward; his legitimacy never overturned by legal process, though not recognised as 2nd Earl of Banbury by Ho Lds; *b* 10 April 1627; *k* in a duel in France by June 1645

2 Nicholas KNOLLYS later VAUX, on whom his (step?)f 4th Baron Vaux of Harrowden settled his estates; sat in Convention Parl June-Nov 1660 as 3rd Earl of Banbury, though his right to sit was queried July 1660; nevertheless he was given leave of absence 21 Nov 1660, an implicit recognition of his right to sit; not called to Ho Lds thereafter and legal wranglings as to his right to sit as a peer not resolved by the time of his death; *b* 3 Jan 1630/1; *m* 1st Lady Isabella Blount (*dspm* 1654/5), dau of 1st Earl of Newport; *m* 2nd 4 Oct 1655 Anne (*d* 6 March 1680), dau of 1st Baron Sherard of Leitrim, and *d* 14 March 1673, having by her had:

(2) Charles KNOLLYS, unsuccessfully petitioned to be recognised as 4th Earl of Banbury (*see* also KNOWLES, Bt); *bapt* 3 June 1662; *m* 1st 16 May 1689 Elizabeth (*bur* 31 Dec 1699), dau of Michael Lister, and had two sons (*dvp*); *m* 2nd 30 April 1702 Mary (*bur* 12 May 1762), dau of Thomas Woods, and *d* 26 Aug 1740, having by her had an est s:

1a Charles (Rev); *b* 26 March 1703; Vicar Burford, Oxon, 1750–71; *m* Martha Hughes (*bur* 17 Sept 1772) and *d* 13 March 1771; his est s:

1b William; *b* 21 Oct 1726; Lt-Col; *d* unm 29 Aug 1776

2b Thomas Woods; *b* 6 Dec 1727; *m* 30 March 1761 Mary (*d* 22 March 1798), dau of William Porter, and *d* 18 March 1793; his s:

1c William, assumed title (8th) Earl of Banbury till his petition for recognition turned down by Ho Lds 1813, the latter declaring 5 March 1813 not only that he had not made out his claim but that he was not entitled to the peerage, whereupon he no longer assumed it; Gen Scots Fus Gds, Govr Limerick; *bapt* 2 March 1763; *m* 23 June 1795 Charlotte (*d* 5 Feb 1818), dau of Ebenezer Blackwell, and *d* 10 March 1834, leaving:

1d William Thomas (Sir), KCB, PC, DCL; styled *Viscount Wallingford* to 1813; *b* 1 Aug 1797; Gen, Col Scots Gds, entrusted with the original formation of Aldershot Camp, Treasurer and Comptroller Household to HM EDWARD VII when PRINCE OF WALES 1862, Gentleman Usher Black Rod 1877, Groom Stole 1877–83, Receiver-Gen Duchy Cornwall 1878; *m* 29 Sept 1830 Elizabeth (*d* 28 Jan 1878), sis of Sir Edward St Aubyn, 1st Bt (*see* SAINT LEVAN, B), and had:

1e William Wallingford; *b* 13 Nov 1832; Col 93rd Highrs, formerly Scots Fus Gds; *m* 1860 Sophia Elizabeth Tuckfield (*d* 7 Dec 1904), dau of Thomas Goldsworthy, RN, and *d* 12 Aug 1904, leaving:

1f Robert Walter Edmund; *b* 10 Nov 1872; Lt-Col IA, Dist and Sessions Judge Punjab, barrister Inner Temple, served NWF India (Tirah, Samana, Punjab Frontier) 1897–98 (medal with three clasps), Kaisar-i-Hind and Albert Medals; *m* 24 Oct 1908 Etheldred Mary, MBE (*d* 30 April 1955), dau of James Murray, and *d* 17 July 1941

2f Frederick Roger Alexander Nicholas; *b* 1 Dec 1884; Maj City London Yeo, KGStJ; *d* 24 Sept 1915 of wounds recd in action

1f Beatrice Sophia; *m* 9 May 1907 Sir Capel Charles Wolseley, 9th Bt of Mount Wolseley (*qv*), and *d* 23 June 1947

2f Emma Lettice Violet; *m* 23 June 1908 Surgn-Cdr Walter Turner Haydon, RN, s of John Nathaniel Haydon, and *d* 8 Dec 1925

2e FRANCIS, **1st Viscount**

3e Henry (Sir), KCVO; *b* 20 June 1840; Col RA, Staff Offr to Sir James Scarlett (*see* ABINGER, B) and Sir Hope Grant 1866–76, cmded RA Boer War 1889–91, Comptroller and Priv Sec to HM QUEEN MAUD OF NORWAY (yst dau of HM EDWARD VII) 1896–1919, Kt Cdr Norwegian Order of St Olav, Order Dannebrog; *m* 1st 8 Aug 1876 Louisa Elizabeth (*d* 1888), dau of Rev Edward Eyre; *m* 2nd 20 Jan 1909 Florence Mary (Flora) (*m* 2nd 20 Oct 1937 Arthur Barnados des Voeux Molinaux Phillips and *d* 12 Aug 1954), dau of Louis Arthur Goodeve, and *dsp* 1 March 1930

4e Frederick Robert; *b* 23 Aug 1846; *m* 1st 1870 Laura Caroline (*d* 1873), dau of R Bristow, and had issue; *m* 2nd 5 Sept 1875 Rosalinda Eleanor (*d* 17 Nov 1876), dau of Hon James Butler (*see* DUNBOYNE, B), and by her had issue; *m* 3rd 18 May 1882 Edith Mary, dau of Joseph Carter Wood, and *d* 17 Oct 1926, having by her had issue

5e Arthur Cyprian, Capt Scots Gds; *b* 18 June 1850; *m* 1885 Florence (*m* 2nd James Reginald Graham (*d* 26 Sept 1910) and 3rd 1 Jan

1927 Sir Richard James Graham, 4th Bt, of Netherby (*qv*), and *d* 7 Jan 1934), dau of Joseph Carter Wood, and *d* 24 Sept 1890, leaving issue

1e (Elizabeth) Charlotte; Bedchamber Woman to HM QUEEN ALEXANDRA 1870–1925; granted rank of baron's dau by roy warrant 1901; *d* 24 April 1930

2e Mirabel Jane; *m* 6 Dec 1881 Maj Charles Francis Baring Grey, RHA (*see* GREY, Bt, of Fallodon), and *d* 1 Feb 1922

3e Constance; *m* June 1882 her cousin Rev A A Knollys, and *d* 27 June 1903, leaving issue

1d Emma; *b* c 1806; *m* 1828 her cousin Sir Edward St Aubyn 1st Bt, and had issue (*see* SAINT LEVAN, B)

Sir WILLIAM *d* 23 June 1883; his 2nd son,

FRANCIS KNOLLYS, **1st Viscount Knollys**, of Caversham, Co Oxford, so *cr* 4 July 1911, as also earlier 21 July 1902 BARON KNOLLYS, of Caversham, Co Oxford (both UK), GCB (1908, KCB 1897, CB 1876), GCVO (1901), KCMG (1886), ISO (1903), PC (1910); *b* 16 July 1837; Priv Sec to TM EDWARD VII 1870–1910 and GEORGE V 1910–13, Ld-in-Waiting to HM QUEEN ALEXANDRA 1910–24, Groom-in-Waiting to HM EDWARD VII when PRINCE OF WALES 1886–1901, Gentleman Usher to HM QUEEN VICTORIA 1868–1901; *m* 11 April 1887 Hon Ardyne Mary Tyrwhitt (*d* 26 Dec 1922), er dau of Sir Henry Thomas Tyrwhitt, 3rd Bt, by Baroness Berners (*qv*), and had:

1 EDWARD GEORGE WILLIAM TYRWHITT, **2nd Viscount**

1 (Alexandra) Louvima Elizabeth; *m* 1st 19 Dec 1911 Capt Allan Keith Mackenzie, Gren Gds, 2nd surv s of Sir Allan Russell Mackenzie, 2nd Bt (*qv*), and had issue; *m* 2nd 10 Nov 1922 Richard Henry Spencer Checkley, s of George Edward Checkley, of Nun Monkton, Yorks, and *d* 30 May 1958

The 1st VISCOUNT *d* 15 Aug 1924; his only son,

EDWARD GEORGE WILLIAM TYRWHITT KNOLLYS, **2nd Viscount Knollys**, GCMG (1952, KCMG 1941), MBE, DFC; *b* 16 Jan 1895; *educ* Harrow and New Coll Oxford; chm: BOAC 1943–47, Vickers 1956–62, Employer's Liability Assur Corp, Northern and Employers Assur 1960–; dir Barclays Bank, Capt 16th Bn Lond Regt (TA) and RAF, served WW I (Order Crown Belgium and Croix de Guerre), Page of Honour to TM EDWARD VII 1904–10 and GEORGE V 1910–11, Dep Commr SE CD Regn 1939–41, Govr and C-in-C Bermuda 1941–43, UK Rep Internat Materials Conf Washington and Min Embassy Washington responsible for raw materials 1951–52, chm RAF Benevolent Fund 1953–66, memb Cncl King Edward VII Hosp 1953–66, Grand Offr Order Orange-Nassau Netherlands; *m* 11 Oct 1928 Margaret Mary Josephine (*d* 1987), dau of Sir Stuart Auchincloss Coats, 2nd Bt (*qv*), and *d* 3 Dec 1966, having had:

1 DAVID FRANCIS DUDLEY KNOLLYS, **3rd and present Viscount Knollys**

1 *Ardyne Mary [The Hon Mrs Owen, Paradise Wood, Upper Hartfield, Sussex]; *b* 9 July 1929; *m* 17 Jan 1958 *Ronald James Owen, est s of James Richard Owen, JP, CC, of Holy Hill, Coleman's Hatch, Sussex, and has:

(1) *Sandra Mary; *b* 1953

(2) *Rachel Elizabeth; *b* 1965

KNOWLES

Arms: Azure a naval crown between four cross-crosslets in cross, all within a cross recercelée disjoined between as many cross-crosslets, all or. **Crest:** An elephant statant argent supporting with the trunk an anchor or. **Motto:** *Semper paratus* ('Always ready'). **Creation:** Bt. (GB) 31 Oct 1765.

SIR CHARLES FRANCIS KNOWLES, 7TH BT, of Lovell Hill, Berkshire [Sir Charles Knowles Bt, Wyndham Croft, Turners Hill, W Sussex RH10 4PS]; *b* 20 Dec 1951; *s f* 1974; *educ* Marlborough and Oxford Sch of Architecture (BA 1974, Dip Arch 1977); RIBA 1979, FRSA, sr ptnr Charles Knowles Design, architects, 1984–; *m* 28 July 1979 *(Amanda) Louise Margaret, dau of Lance Bromley, MChir, FRCS, of 26 Molyneux St, London W1, and has:

1 +(CHARLES) WILLIAM FREDERICK LANCE; *b* 27 Aug 1985

2 +Edward Francis Annandale Bromley; *b* 1989

Lineage: CHARLES KNOLLYS, who failed to establish his claim to be 4th Earl of Banbury (*see* KNOLLYS, V), allegedly had by a woman, Elizabeth Price, who at one time claimed to be his 1st w:

Sir Charles Knowles, 1st Bt (GB), so *cr* 31 Oct 1765, of Lovell Hill, Wingfield, Berks; *b* between 1694 and 1700; MP Gatton, Surrey, 1749–52, R-Adml, Govr Louisburg 1746–48 and Jamaica 1752–56, Ch Pres Russian Admlty 1770 and memb Russian Cncl 1770–74; Adml the White; *m* 1st 23 Dec 1740 Mary (*d* 16 March 1742), dau of John Alleyne, of Barbados, and sis of Sir John Gay Alleyne, Bt (*qv*), and had an only s:

1 Edward; *b* 1742; Capt RN; *d* unm lost at sea cmdg HMS *Peregrine* in a storm off Belle Isle Jan 1762

Sir Charles *m* 2nd 29 July 1750 Maria Magdalena Theresa (*d* 6 March 1796), dau of Henry Francis, Count de Bouget, Cncllr of Elector of Cologne, and by her had, with two other daus (*d* unm):

2 CHARLES HENRY (Sir), **2nd Bt**

1 Anna Charlotte Christiana; *b* 20 Nov 1752; Ldy in Waiting to EMPRESS CATHARINE II OF RUSSIA; *m* 29 March 1781 Capt John Winder, King's Dragoon Gds (*d* 29 Feb 1820), of Vaynor Pk, Mon, and *d* 15 May 1839, leaving issue

Sir CHARLES *d* 9 Dec 1777; his only son,

Sir Charles Henry Knowles, 2nd Bt, GCB; *b* 24 Aug 1754; Adml the Red, fought Battle of Cape St Vincent 1797; *m* 10 Sept 1800 Charlotte (*d* 9 June 1867), dau of Charles John Johnstone, of Ludlow, Salop (half-bro of 3rd Marquess of Annandale; *see* ANANDALE AND HARTFELL, E), and *d* 28 Nov 1831, leaving, with two yr sons and four daus (all *d* unm):

Sir Francis Charles Knowles, 3rd Bt; *b* 10 June 1802; *educ* Trin Coll Cambridge (MA); FRS, barrister; *m* 26 May 1831 Emma (*d* 31 Dec 1894), dau of Sir George Pocock, 1st Bt, FRS, and *d* 19 March 1892, having had, with three daus (d young):

Sir Charles George Frederick Knowles, 4th Bt; *b* 14 March 1832; V-Adml; *m* 1st 29 July 1861 (*divorce* 1876) Elizabeth (*d* 9 Oct 1907), only child of John Chapman, of Bayswater, and had, with two yst daus (*d* unm):

1 John St John; *b* 9 June 1862; Capt 2nd Bn Roy Irish Regt; *m* 29 Sept 1883 (*divorce* 1889) Edith Alwyn, 2nd dau of Rev Robert Hall Baynes, Canon Worcester, and *dsp* 9 Feb 1892

2 Charles Alfred Fitzgerald; *b* 5 Feb 1864; *d* unm 19 March 1890

1 Mary Boleyn; *m* 1st 16 Nov 1885 Henry Arthur Joseph Tempest (*d* 16 April 1891), of Broughton Hall, Yorks (*see* LONDONDERRY, M); *m* 2nd 16 July 1862 Bernardino Fernandez De Velasco, Duque de Frias (*d* 8 Dec 1916), and *d* 9 Jan 1929, leaving a dau (Maria Victoria, Marquesa de Frechilla, *d* unm Madrid 30 Aug 1947)

Sir Charles *m* 2nd 14 June 1882 Mary Ellen (*d* 5 July 1890), dau of Cathcart Thomson, of Halifax, NS, and by her had:

3 FRANCIS HOWE SEYMOUR (Sir), **5th Bt**

4 George Johnstone, Capt; *b* 17 July 1887; *m* 17 March 1915 Helen Marjorie, dau of Capt R F Pockley, RNR, and *dsp* 31 Jan 1954

5 Robert Cosby; *b* 4 Sept 1888; *m* 14 May 1929 Phyllis Eve (*d* 1992), dau of Rev Canon Ward Thomas, of Lorne, Victoria, Australia, and *d* 1972, leaving:

(1) +Peter Cosby [Peter Knowles Esq, 21 Nisbit St, Winton, Queensland 4735, Australia]; *b* 27 June 1930; grazier, author: *The Whirlwind Country* (1957), *Australia Wild Heart* (1972), *Land of Waltzing Matilda* (1994); *m* 1st 1957 (*divorce* 1977) Gloria, dau of Albert Edward Oaten, of Melbourne, and has:

1a +Richard Cosby; *b* 23 Jan 1969

1a *Sandra; *b* 1959

2a *Kerry; *b* 1964

3a *Judith Anne; *b* 16 March 1967

(1) (cont.) Peter Knowles *m* 2nd 1977 *Jane Winifred, dau of B Cooper, of Brisbane, and by her has:

4a *Imogen Winifred; *b* 1988

(2) +Michael Cosby [Michael Knowles Esq, 21 Bonview Rd, Malvern, Victoria, Australia]; *b* 7 Oct 1936; *educ* Cromwell Coll and Queensland U; PhD (Edinburgh), MCom (Qld), QDAH; sr lecturer Monash U; *m* 1965 *Ann Darien, dau of G R Mountain, MA (Econ), of Melbourne, and has:

1a +Stephen Francis; *b* 1970

1a *Fiona Mary; *b* 1972

1 Theresa Blanche Cathcart; *m* 28 June 1911 Cdr Gordon McLeod Cameron, DSO, RN (*d* 24 Sept 1960), s of Lt-Col C Cameron, IMS, and *d* 11 April 1927, leaving issue

5 Eileen Beresford; *b* 1890; *m* 6 July 1914 Capt (S) George Alfred Cooke, RN (*d* 24 Dec 1957), s of George Cooke, of Timaru, NZ, and *d* 17 Jan 1983, leaving:

(1) *Joan Irwin [Mrs Geoffrey Davies, Greenshaw, Holbrook, Ipswich, Suffolk IP9 2RQ]; *b* 4 Jan 1920; *m* 16 April 1942 *Geoffrey Clive Davies, OBE, s of T Clive Davies, of Honolulu, and has:

1a *Peter Francis; *b* 6 July 1965; MA, CEng, MICE; *m* 18 June 1994 *Brenda Mary, dau of Philip Copeland

1a *Susan Catherine Beresford; *b* 17 Nov 1944; *m* 14 Sept 1974 *Sir Patrick Robert Richard Sinclair, 10th Bt (*qv*), and has issue

2a *Cynthia Elizabeth; *b* 3 Oct 1947; *m* 25 July 1970 *Nigel M S Rich, CBE

3a *Alison Mary; *b* 21 June 1951; *m* 28 Dec 1974 *Lt-Cdr Graham Day, RCN

Sir CHARLES *d* 3 March 1918; his est surv son,

Sir Francis Howe Seymour Knowles, 5th Bt; *b* 13 Jan 1886; *educ* Oriel Coll Oxford (BSc, MA); Physical Anthropologist to Geograpical Survey Canada; *m* 22 April 1914 Kathleen Constance Averina (*d* 30 July 1953), dau of William Lennon, Co Inspr RIC, and *d* 4 April 1953, leaving:

Sir Francis Gerald William Knowles, 6th Bt; FRS; *b* 9 March 1915; *educ* Radley and Oriel Coll Oxford (BA 1936, MA and DPhil 1939); Head Biology Marlborough 1938–58, research biologist and lecturer Birmingham U, Prof Anatomy King's Coll London 1967–74; *m* 30 Dec 1948 *Ruth Jessie (*m* 3rd 1979 Ivo Payne) [Mrs Ivo Payne, West Ridge, Manton Down Rd, Marlborough, Wilts], dau of Rev Arthur Brooke-Smith and widow of P/O Richard Guy Hulse, RAF, and *d* 13 July 1974, leaving:

1 Sir CHARLES FRANCIS KNOWLES, **7th and present Bt**

1 *Averina Constance Frances [Mrs Martin Northmore-Ball, Higher Grange, Ellesmere, Salop SY12 9DH]; *b* 16 April 1950; *m* 26 July 1969 *Martin Dacre

Northmore-Ball, MA, MB, BChir, FRCS, CIMechE, yr s of Surgn-Lt-Cdr Godfrey Dacre Jennings Ball, MB, ChB, RN, of Devon, and has:
(1) Dacre William Francis; *b* 1970; *d* 1974
(2) *Lawrence Henry Arthur Knowles; *b* 1986
(1) *Laetitia Emily Ruth; *b* 1976
2 *Emma Irene Anne [Mrs Michael Geddes-Ablitt, 14 Westland Rd, Faringdon, Oxon]; *b* 20 Dec 1951; *m* 1976 *Michael Henry Geddes-Ablitt and has:
(1) *Zoë Christiana; *b* 1979
(2) *Helen Angela Emma; *b* 1981
(3) *Sophie Hannah Rachel; *b* 1985
(4) *Tessa Catherine Ruth; *b* 1988
3 *Christiana Joan Elizabeth Ruth [Mrs Giles Payne, 210 Marlborough Rd, Oxford]; *b* 16 March 1956; *m* 21 July 1979 *Giles Adrian Ivo Payne, only s of Ivo Payne, of W Ridge, Marlborough, Wilts, and has:
(1) *Charlotte Liberty Ruth; *b* 1987

KNUTSFORD

Arms: Quarterly, 1st and 4th, erm. on a bend nebuly sa. three crescents arg., in the sinister chief point a cross bottony fitchée of the second (for HIBBERT); 2nd and 3rd, per pale arg. and az. semée-de-lys a lion rampant guardant counterchanged, over all a bendlet engrailed gu. (for HOLLAND). **Crests:** 1 In front of a dexter cubit arm erect ppr., vested az., cuffed erm., holding in the hand a crescent arg., a demi-catherine wheel also arg. (for HIBBERT), 2 Out of a crown vallery or a demi-lion guardant per bend arg. and az., charged with a bendlet engrailed countercharged, holding in the dexter paw a fleur-de-lys arg. (for HOLLAND). **Supporters:** On either side a lion guardant arg. guttée de larmes, the body charged with two fleurs-de-lys in fess between two bars engrailed az.
Motto: *Respice, aspice, prospice* ('Look backwards, look around, look forwards'). **Creation:** V. (UK) 3 Aug 1895, B. (UK) 23 Feb 1888, Bt. (UK) 10 May 1853.

THE 6TH VISCOUNT KNUTSFORD OF KNUTSFORD, Co Chester, **Baron Knutsford**, of Knutsford, Co Chester, and a **Baronet** (Sir Michael Holland-Hibbert, Bt, DL (Devon 1977)) [The Rt Hon The Viscount Knutsford DL, Broadclyst House, Exeter, Devon EX5 3EW]; *b* 27 Dec 1926; *s* cousin 1986; *educ* Eton and Trin Coll Cambridge; High Sheriff Devon 1977–78, Capt Welsh Gds 1945–48, local dir Barclays Bank Exeter, memb Nat Tst Exec Ctee and Cncl 1965–86 and Fin Ctee 1986–; *m* 8 May 1951 *Hon Sheila Constance Portman, er dau of 5th Viscount Portman (*qv*), and has:
1 +HENRY THURSTAN [The Hon Henry Holland-Hibbert, Munden House, Munden, Herts WD2 7PZ]; *b* 6 April 1959; *educ* Eton and RAC Cirencester; Lt Coldstream Gds; *m* 1988 *Katherine, dau of Sir John Bruce Woollacott Ropner, 2nd Bt (*qv*), and has:
(1) +Thomas Arthur; *b* 15 December 1992
(1) *Rosanna (Rosie) Sarah; *b* 1990
(2) *Isabel Katherine; *b* 1995
2 +James Edward; *b* 19 May 1967
1 *Lucy Katherine [The Hon Mrs Liddell, Cumrew House, Cumrew, Carlisle CA4 9DD]; *b* 27 June 1956; *m* 21 July 1979 *Mark Charles Liddell, yr s of Peter Liddell, DSC, of Moorhouse Hall, Warwick-on-Eden, Carlisle, and has:
(1) *James Peter; *b* 1987
(1) *Katherine Alexandra; *b* 1983
(2) *Sophie Charlotte; *b* 1990

Lineage: WILLIAM HOLLAND, of Rhodes, Pilkington, Lancs (allegedly yr s of William Holland, of Clifton, Lancs, living *temp* HENRY VIII, and Alice, dau of Orskell Werden; the HOLLANDs of Clifton being descended from William de Holland, of Clifton (yr s of Sir Thomas de Holland, of Sharples and Denton, living 1339), who acquired Clifton *c* 1346 through his w Margery, dau and coheir of Henry de Trafford); *m* Jane, dau and coheir of — Parr, of Rhodes, and had, with an er s:

EDWARD HOLLAND, sometime of Heaton Norris; settled Chorlton Row, nr Manchester; *m* between 13 Jan 1603/4 and 13 Feb 1605/6 Ellen, dau of Nicholas Holme, of Heaton Norris, and had:

WILLIAM HOLLAND, of Dam Head House, Mobberley, Cheshire (bought 1650), and previously Chorlton Row; *bapt* 19 Jan 1605/6; *m c* 8 Sept 1624 Anne (*bur* 18 Jan 1658/9), dau of Ralph Bold, of Ashton-under-Lyne, and was *bur* 6 Dec 1654, having had seven sons and four daus; his third but est surv s:

JOHN HOLLAND, of Mobberley; *bapt* 22 Jan 1631/2; *m* 1 Aug 1655 Hannah (*d* before him), dau of Thomas Norbury, of Over Alderley, and *d* 17 Jan 1704/5, having had, with six yr sons and a dau:

JOHN HOLLAND, of Mobberley; *bapt* 1 June 1656; *m* 1st 25 Feb 1684/5 Mary Deane (*bur* 23 Dec 1700), of Alderley, and had four sons and four daus; *m* 2nd 14 April 1705 Mary, widow of — Hopton, of Nether Knutsford, by whom he had no issue, and was *bur* 22 Jan 1712/3; his est s:

JOHN HOLLAND, of Mobberley; *bapt* 11 Dec 1690; *m c* 3 Feb 1717/8 Mary (*bur* 5 Aug 1757), dau of Peter Colthurst, of Sandlebridge, nr Knutsford, and was *bur* 24 June 1770, having had, with three er sons and five daus:

SAMUEL HOLLAND, of Sandlebridge; *b* 25 March 1734; *m* 10 Oct 1763 Anne (*bur* 4 July 1814), dau of Peter Swinton, of Nether Knutsford, and *d* 26 May 1816, having had, with three yr sons and five daus:

PETER HOLLAND, of Sandlebridge and Knutsford; *b* 3 June 1766; *m* 1st Mary (*d* 3 Oct 1803), dau and coheir of Rev William Willets, of Newcastle, Staffs, and had two sons and five daus; *m* 2nd 25 Dec 1808 Mary, dau of Jeremiah Whittaker, of Manchester, and *d* 19 Jan 1855, having by her had two sons and a dau; his est s:

Sir Henry Holland, 1st Bt (UK), so *cr* 10 May 1853; *b* 27 Oct 1788; Physician in Ordinary to HM QUEEN VICTORIA; *m* 1st 8 Oct 1822 Margaret Emma (*d* 2 Feb 1830), 4th dau of James Caldwell, of Lindley Wood, Staffs, and had:
1 HENRY THURSTAN, **1st Viscount**
2 Francis James (Rev); *b* 20 Jan 1828; *educ* Cambridge (MA); incumbent Quebec Chapel London 1861–83, sometime Chaplain to HM QUEEN VICTORIA, Hon Chaplain to HM EDWARD VII, Canon Canterbury Cathedral; *m* 23 Oct 1855 Mary Sibylla (*d* 23 Sept 1891), dau of Rev Alfred Lyall, of Harbledown, and *d* 27 Jan 1907, having had issue (the male line of which is in remainder to the btcy only):
(1) Bernard Henry, CB; *b* 23 Dec 1856; *educ* Trin Coll Cambridge (MA); barrister Inner Temple 1882, Alderman LCC 1910–20, served Charity Commn 1884–90, Sec to Duke of Devonshire 1892–94 and Roy Commns: Fin Rels 1894, Transvaal Concessions 1900, Port of London 1901 and S African War 1902, Priv Sec to Sec State Colonies 1903–08; *m* 3 Jan 1895 Florence Helen (*d* 10 Nov 1953), dau of Rev William Arthur Duckworth, of Orchardleigh Park, Somerset, and *d* 25 May 1926, having had issue:
1a Christopher Bernard; *b* 20 July 1898; *d* an infant
2a John Francis; *b* 9 Aug 1906; *d* an infant
3a Alfred Bernard; *b* 17 June 1908; *d* April 1953
1a *Mary Verena Violet; *b* 26 March 1901; nun Soc Sacred Heart Jesus and Edenal Order
2a *Catherine Sibylla; *b* 17 March 1903; *m* 18 Sept 1924 George Anthony Mostyn (*d* 29 May 1972), s of Hon Harold Plantagenet Mostyn, and *d* 1983, having had issue (*see* VAUX OF HARROWDEN, B)
(2) Alfred Dunstan; *d* young 24 Aug 1869
(3) Francis Caldwell; *b* 21 April 1865; *educ* Trin Coll Cambridge (MA); Clerk H of C 1888–1926; *m* 9 Nov 1897 Maud Constance (*d* 23 March 1949), dau of Sir Spencer Walpole, KCB (*see* WALPOLE, B), and *dsp* 6 March 1948
(4) Michael James, MC (1918); *b* 25 Oct 1870; *educ* Eton; Priv Sec to Govr Gold Coast, Capt Special Cav Res WW I; *m* 6 May 1911 Marion Ada Flora (*d* 13 Dec 1969 aged 82), er dau of Henry John Tschudi Broadwood, of Lyne, Sussex, and *d* 14 May 1956, leaving:
1a Antony Francis, MC; *b* 4 June 1913; *educ* Eton and Emmanuel Coll Cambridge; barrister Middle Temple 1936, Crown Counsel Kenya, E Africa, 2nd Bn Garhwali Rifles WW II; *m* 22 June 1946 Ann Edith Faure, yr dau of Henry Faure Walker, of Highley Manor, Balcombe, Sussex, and *d* 1982, leaving:
1b +Thurstan James [Thurstan Holland Esq, Old Lullings, Balcombe, Sussex RH17 6QY]; *b* 23 Dec 1948; *educ* Eton and Nottingham U; *m* 1987 *Elizabeth Joan Serena, 2nd dau of Alistair Philip Cobbold, of Holbrook Lodge, Ipswich, Suffolk, and has:
1c +Frederick Alistair Thurstan; *b* 1991
1b *Anthea [Mrs John Warde, Squerryes Court, Westerham, Kent]; *b* 27 March 1947; *m* 1973 *John St Andrew Warde and has:
1c *Charles Antony; *b* 1974
2c *Henry John; *b* 1976
1c *Ann Charlotte; *b* 1982
2b *Arabella Ann; *b* 15 March 1956
2a +David Cuthbert Lyall, CB (1975) [David Holland Esq CB, The Barn, Milton St, Polegate, E Sussex BN26 5RP]; *b* 23 March 1915; *educ* Eton and Trin Coll; Roy Sussex Regt WW II, Librarian H of C 1967–76; *m* 3 Sept 1949 *Rosemary Anne, yr dau of David Llewellyn Griffiths, OBE, and has had:
1b +Matthew Francis (Rev); *b* 15 March 1952; *educ* Eton, LSE and Queen's Coll Birmingham; *m* 1979 *Jayne Emerson and has:
1c +Joseph John; *b* 1988
1c *Bridget Mary; *b* 1984
2c *Caitlin Frances; *b* 1986
2b Peter Gwinnell; *b* 1954; *d* 1983
1b *Lucinda Jane; *b* 1954; *m* 1977 *Paul Carpenter and has:
1c *William James; *b* 1978
1a Mary Agnes; *m* 1889 Rev William Henry Bolton (*dsp* 4 Aug 1902), Vicar Upper Norwood, and *d* 18 Sept 1928
2a Lucy Verena; *d* unm 1886
(1) Emily Mary; *m* 7 Feb 1850 Charles Buxton (*see* BUXTON, Bt) and *d* 19 June 1908, leaving issue

Sir Henry *m* 2nd 20 March 1834 Saba (*b* 1802; biographer of her f; *d* 2 Nov 1866), dau of Rev Sydney Smith, the celebrated wit and co-fndr of and contributor to the *Edinburgh Review*, and *d* 27 Oct 1873, having by her had two daus (*d* unm)

His er s,

Sir Henry Thurstan Holland, 2nd Bt, and **1st Viscount Knutsford of Knutsford**, Co Chester, so *cr* 3 Aug 1895, as also earlier 23 Feb 1888 BARON KNUTSFORD, of Knutsford, Co Chester (both UK), GCMG (1886, KCMG 1877, CMG 1875), PC (1885), JP (Surrey and Co London), DL (Middx); *b* 3 Aug 1825; *educ* Harrow and Cambridge (BA); barrister Inner Temple 1849, bencher 1881, Legal Adviser Colonial Office 1867–70, Assist U-Sec Colonies 1870–74, MP (C) Midhurst 1874–85, Hampstead 1885–88, Fin Sec Treasury 1885, V-Pres Cncl on Educn 1885–86 and 1886–87, Sec State Colonies 1887–92, an Ecclesiastical Commr, Sub Prior, KJStJ and Hon Bailiff, Tstee Nat Portrait Gallery; *m* 1st 18 Aug 1852 Elizabeth Margaret (*d* 12 April 1855), dau of Nathaniel Hibbert, of Munden House, nr Aldenham, Herts, and had:

1 SYDNEY GEORGE HOLLAND, **2nd Viscount Knutsford**, JP (London, Middx); *b* 19 March 1855; *educ* Wellington and Cambridge (LLB, Hon Fell Trin Hall 1919); barrister Inner Temple 1879, KGStJ, Order Dannebrog 2nd Cl; *m* 23 Jan 1883 Lady Mary Ashburnham (*d* 3 May 1947), dau of 4th Earl of Ashburnham (*see* 1924 edn), and *dspm* 27 July 1931, having had:

(1) Lucy Katherine; *b* 15 Sept 1886

(2) Rachael Mary; *b* 1 March 1891; *m* 29 July 1919 Brig Lord Douglas Malise Graham, CB, DSO, MC (*d* 20 Nov 1974), 2nd s of 5th Duke of Montrose (*qv*), and *d* 6 June 1977, leaving issue

2 ARTHUR HENRY, **3rd Viscount**

1 Edith Emily; *m* 3 Aug 1876 Charles James Cropper (*d* 6 Oct 1924), of Ellergreen, Kendal, Westmorland, and *d* 15 Jan 1923, leaving issue

The **1st Viscount** *m* 2nd 25 Nov 1858 Margaret Jean, DGStJ (*d* 26 Aug 1906), est dau of Sir Charles Edward Trevelyan, 1st Bt, KCB, PC, of Nettlecombe (*qv*), and *d* 29 Jan 1914, having by her had:

3 Henry Macaulay; *b* 16 Sep 1859; *d* April 1878

4 Cecil Trevelyan; *b* 26 Oct 1862; *educ* Wellington; Capt Coldstream Gds and KRRC, Inspr-Gen Police Mauritius, prison govr; *m* 21 April 1896 Alice (*d* 26 April 1946), dau of Gilbert Walker, and *d* 28 Jan 1941, leaving:

(1) Alice Mary; *b* 25 Sep 1897; *m* 23 Apr 1919 Lt-Col Robert Begbie Longridge, 16th Lancers (SR) and RAF, yr s of Robert Charles Longridge, and had issue

5 Lionel Raleigh, JP (Co London); *b* 21 March 1865; *educ* Harrow and King's Coll Cambridge (BA, LLB); barrister Inner Temple, MP Bow and Bromley 1895–99, BRCS Commr Dunkirk 1914–15 (1914 star, Victory and War medals); *d* unm 25 May 1936

2 Margaret Alice; *m* 15 Oct 1885 Reginald Abel Smith (*d* 26 April 1902) and *d* 16 May 1937, leaving issue

The 2nd VISCOUNT's bro,

ARTHUR HENRY HOLLAND later HOLLAND-HIBBERT (roy licence 17 May 1876 under terms of will of his maternal grandmother Emily, Mrs Nathaniel Hibbert), **3rd Viscount Knutsford**, JP, DL; *b* 19 March 1855 (twin with his bro); served RN, CA Herts, High Sheriff 1890; *m* 5 Nov 1884 Ellen (*d* 5 June 1949), dau of Sir Wilfrid Lawson, 2nd Bt, of Brayton (*see* 1959 edn), and *d* 16 Jan 1935, leaving:

1 THURSTAN HOLLAND-HIBBERT, **4th Viscount Knutsford**; *b* 19 June 1888; *educ* Eton and Trin Coll Cambridge (BA 1911); barrister Inner Temple 1914, Capt RSG, Lt Herts Yeo, served WWs I (1914–15 star, two medals) and II as Maj Pioneer Corps; MFH Avon Vale 1924–33, Jt MFH VWH (Cirencester) 1935–39; *m* 24 July 1912 Viola Mary (*d* 12 Jan 1964), dau of Thomas Meadows Clutterbuck, of Putteridge Bury, and Micklefield Hall, Rickmansworth, Herts, and *d* 17 Feb 1976, leaving:

(1) JULIAN THURSTAN HOLLAND-HIBBERT, **5th Viscount Knutsford**, CBE (1957), JP (Herts 1953); *b* 3 May 1920; *educ* Eton and Trin Coll Cambridge; Lt Coldstream Gds WW II 1939–43 (wounded and invalided), memb Nat Advisory Cncl Employment for Disabled, OStJ; *dsp* 1986

(1) Diana, MBE (1946); *b* 5 Sept 1914; Sr Cdr ATS WW II; *d* 1992

2 Wilfrid Knutsford, JP (Oxon 1938–57); *b* 4 Jan 1893; *educ* Eton and Trin Coll Cambridge; Capt RA (TA) and Herts Yeo, ADC to Viceroy India 1916–18, Estates Bursar Merton Coll Oxford, Land Agent New Coll Oxford 1923–58 and Oxford Preservn Tst 1926–54, Pres Land Agents Soc 1946–47, memb Gen Claims Tbnl 1948, memb Bullingdon RDC 1932–61 (chm 1938–45); *m* 25 Sept 1918 Isabel Audrey, dau of Mark Fenwick, of Abbotswood, Stow-on-the-Wold, Glos, and *d* 18 Feb 1961, leaving:

(1) MICHAEL HOLLAND-HIBBERT, **6th and present Viscount Knutsford**

(1) *Lavinia [Mrs Peter Orde, Newbrough Park, Hexham, Northumberland]; *b* 19 Oct 1919; Jr Cdr ATS WW II; *m* 31 Jan 1953 Maj Peter John Orde, 15th/19th KRH, only s of Sir Percy Lancelot Orde, CIE, JP, and adopted:

*Justin Robert; *b* 24 April 1957

*Clarissa Mary; *b* 20 Aug 1958

(2) *Delia Mary [Mrs William Cunningham, Southfield Farm, Wigginton, Banbury OX15 4LA]; *b* 31 May 1922; 3rd Offr WRNS WW II 1940–45; *m* 11 May 1946 Lt-Col William McGhie Cunningham, LVO, OBE, MC, 11th Hus (PAO) (*d* 1994), er s of James Scott Cunningham, of Auchendarroch, Wishaw, Lanarks, and has:

1a *Jeremy James; *b* 30 April 1948; *educ* Eton

2a *Mark William; *b* 15 June 1950; *educ* Eton

1a *Lavinia Mary; *b* 17 Aug 1952

1 Elsie; *b* 18 Jan 1886; *m* 21 June 1913 Lt-Col Robert Cholmley Faulconer, MC, Herts Yeo (*d* 26 Jan 1959), s of Arthur Cholmley Faulconer, of Bulstrode, King's Langley, and *d* 1974, having had:

(1) Nigel Cholmley; *b* 29 March 1914; *d* 20 Jan 1918

(2) Humphrey Patrick; *b* 6 Aug 1915; RAF WW II 1939–46, Merchant Navy 1946–80; *d* 1981

(3) *Ivor Christopher [Ivor Faulconer Esq, The Old Rectory, Fifehead Neville, Dorset DT10 2AL]; *b* 27 March 1921; *educ* Eton and New Coll Oxford; Fleet Air Arm WW II 1940–46; *m* 1st 15 July 1947 (*divorce* 1969) Anne Jacqueline, dau of Brig John Brown Phillimore Willis Fleming, CBE, TD, of Strathkyle, Ardgay, Ross-shire; *m* 2nd 1969 Daphne Pamela Breakwell (*d* 1989); *m* 3rd 1992 *Anne Mary Oliver, JP, widow of Col Rev Kenneth C Oliver, CBE, TD, QHC, and by his 1st w has:

1a *Peter Robert [Peter Faulconer Esq, Casilla 760, Temuco, Chile]; *b* 6 June 1956; *m* 1981 *Belinda Pettit

1a *Linda Jane [Mrs Robert Maidment, Boyton Hall, Little Wratting, Suffolk CB9 7TA]; *b* 22 June 1948; *m* 1970 *Robert Maidment

2a *Carolyn Anne [Mrs Michael Cazenove, Swaffham Prior Hall, Cambs CB5 0LD]; *b* 23 Oct 1950; *m* 1974 *Michael Cazenove

LACON

Arms: Quarterly per fess indented erminois and azure, in the second quarter a wolf's head erased or. **Crest:** A mount vert, thereon a falcon proper, beaked and belled or, charged on the breast with a cross-flory and gorged with a collar gules. **Motto:** *Probitas verus honos* ('Probity is true honour'). **Creation:** Bt. (UK) 11 Dec 1818.

SIR EDMUND VERE LACON, 8TH BT, of Great Yarmouth, Norfolk [Sir Edmund Lacon Bt, Millbrook, Holton St Peter, Suffolk IP19 8PN]; *b* 3 May 1936; *s f* 1980; *educ* Woodbridge Sch Suffolk; RAF Regt 1955–59; *m* 7 Sept 1963 *Gillian, only dau of Jack Henry Middleditch, of Wrentham, Suffolk, and has:

1 +(EDMUND) RICHARD VERE; *b* 2 Oct 1967; *m* 28 June 1997 *Natalie, only dau of Joginder Shinh, of High Wycombe, Bucks

1 *Anna Kathryn; *b* 15 July 1965

Lineage: EDMUND LACON, of Otley, Yorks; *m* Martha, dau of Rev William Beevor (*see* BEEVOR, Bt), and had:

1 Thomas LACON later BARKER, of Otley; had, with another dau:

(1) Catherine; *m* Capt Charles Wood, RN, and had:

1a Sir FRANCIS LINDLEY WOOD, Bt (*see* HALIFAX, E)

2 JOHN

3 William; in holy orders

EDMUND LACON's 2nd son,

JOHN LACON; settled Norfolk 1740; *m* his cousin Elizabeth, dau and coheir of Robert Ward, of Gt Yarmouth, and had, with several daus and a yr s (John, *d* unm 1811):

Sir Edmund Lacon, 1st Bt (UK), so *cr* 11 Dec 1818; *b* 22 Oct 1750; *m* 1st 1779 Eliza (*d* 1782), dau and coheir of Rev Thomas Knowles, DD, Preb Ely, and had:

1 EDMUND KNOWLES (Sir), **2nd Bt**

Sir Edmund *m* 2nd 1783 Sarah (*d* 5 Feb 1829), dau of John Mortlock, of Abingdon, Cambs, and by her had:

2 John Mortlock, DL (Yarmouth); *b* 9 Feb 1786; Capt 72nd Highrs, Mayor Gt Yarmouth 1827; *m* 1808 Jane (*d* 1 Sept 1868), sis and coheir of William Stirling Graham of Duntrune, Forfar, rep of the family of Viscount Dundee, and *d* 1853, having had, with other issue:

(1) John Edmund, of Duntrune, JP; *b* 2 Nov 1810; *m* 14 May 1840 Louisa Matilda (*d* 15 July 1894), dau of Edward Shewell, and *d* 17 Aug 1894, leaving:

1a Frederick Graham; *b* 7 June 1849; *m* 21 Oct 1874 Annie Margaret (*m* 2nd 14 Nov 1878 Hugh William Tyrwhitt-Drake, yst s of Rev John Tyrwhitt-Drake, Rector Amersham, and *d* 21 Aug 1934, leaving further issue), dau of Ven Augustus Macdonald Hopper, Archdeacon Norwich, and *d* 11 Nov 1875, leaving:

1b Ida Clementina, of Duntrune; *m* 1st 17 June 1896 (*divorce* 1908) John Alfred WIGAN later GRAHAM (roy licence 1896) (*d* Jan 1948) and had issue; *m* 2nd 19 Dec 1908 Col Walter Gordon Neilson, CMG, DSO (*d* 29 April 1927), s of Col James Neilson, CB, and by him had issue; *m* 3rd 18 July 1930 Nigel Napier Blomefield (*see* BLOMEFIELD, Bt), and *d* 11 March 1961

(2) Graham; *b* 18 Jan 1818; Surgn HEICS; *m* 1854 Harriet (*d* 10 Oct 1881), dau of Rev Edward Missenden Love, and *d* 13 Feb 1857, leaving:

1a Alice Graham; *m* 19 July 1881 Rev David Williams Evans (*d* March 1915), Vicar Llanrhaiadr-yn-Cynmerch, Denbighs, and *d* 6 March 1933, leaving issue

2a Edith Jane; *m* 1886 Rev Herbert Sydenham Clarke, Rector Colton, Norwich, and *d* 1896, leaving issue

3 Henry; *b* 5 Dec 1791; HEICS; *m* 1st — (*dsp* 1830), dau of Rev W Dampier; *m* 2nd Mary (*d* 21 March 1874), dau of J Roberts

1 Henrietta Maria; *m* E S Ommaney

2 Anne Elizabeth; *m* 8 Jan 1814 Capt George Wicken Willes, RN (*d* 26 Oct 1846), and *d* 15 May 1871, leaving issue

3 Louisa Sarah; *m* Rev Fisher Watson and *d* 10 Dec 1865

4 Mary Anne; *m* Fuller Farr and *d* 1851

Sir EDMUND *d* 30 Oct 1820; his est s,

Sir Edmund Knowles Lacon, 2nd Bt; *b* 28 Feb 1780; High Sheriff Norfolk 1823; *m* 30 Aug 1804 Eliza Dixon (*d* 23 April 1865), est dau and coheir of Thomas Beecroft, of Saxthorpe Hall, Norfolk, and had:

1 EDMUND HENRY KNOWLES (Sir), **3rd Bt**

2 John Edward; *b* 5 April 1809; *d* unm 9 Dec 1848

3 Henry James; *b* 27 Nov 1810; Capt RN; *m* 9 July 1844 Caroline Louisa Bartlett (*d* 25 March 1882), 2nd dau of John Roberts, of Buckingham, and *d* 15 May 1867, having had, with other issue:

(1) Henry Edmund, JP (Suffolk); *b* 6 July 1849; Capt 1st Bn HLI; *m* 23 Oct 1890 Hon Margaret Erskine (*m* 2nd 10 Sept 1928 Maj Robert Cattley Carr, RA (*d* 6 Feb 1945) and *d* 12 July 1947), only dau of 5th Baron Erskine of Restormel Castle (*see* BUCHAN, E), and *d* 18 March 1924, leaving issue

1 Eliza Beecroft; *m* 28 March 1826 Roger Kerrison Harvey and *d* 17 April 1881, having had issue (*see* HARVEY, Bt)

2 Anna Maria; *m* 1837 Herbert Taylor Lewis and *d* 5 March 1884

3 Emma Hammet; *d* 15 March 1837

Sir EDMUND *d* 3 July 1839; his est son,

Sir Edmund Henry Knowles Lacon, 3rd Bt, DL; *b* 14 Aug 1807; MP (C) Gt Yarmouth 1852–57 and 1859–68 and N Norfolk 1868–85, Hon Col 4th Bn Norfolk Regt and 1st Vol Bn E Div RA; *m* 23 March 1839 Eliza Georgina (*d* 31 March 1883), er dau of James Esdaile Hammet, of Battersea, and *d* 6 Sept 1888, leaving:

1 **Sir Edmund Broughton Knowles Lacon, 4th Bt**, JP (Norfolk); *b* 9 May 1842; Lt 23rd Fus, Lt-Col 4th Bn Norfolk Regt, High Sheriff 1892; *m* 1st 9 May 1868 Henrietta Julia (*d* 3 Sept 1873), est dau of Sir Robert Harvey, 1st Bt (*qv*); *m* 2nd 16 Feb 1878 Florence Amelia (*d* 21 Nov 1921), yst dau of Morgan Hugh Foster, CB, of Brickhill, Beds, and *dsp* 11 Aug 1899

2 Thomas Beecroft Ussher; *b* 24 Feb 1845; *m* 20 June 1877 Florence Dunbar (*d* 13 July 1939), yst dau of R G Banks, of Toronto, and *d* 28 Feb 1899, leaving:

(1) **Sir Edmund Beecroft Francis Heathcote Lacon, 5th Bt**; *b* 26 Sept 1878; Capt 12th Lancers and Westmorland and Cumberland Yeo Boer War 1900; *m* 3 Aug 1911 Janet (*m* 3rd 23 Feb 1914 Norman McLean Myott, of Lindfield Manor, Surrey, and *d* 11–12 Dec 1940), dau of Robert Gorham, of Kensington, and widow of William Lancelot Redhead, of Carville, Brentford, and *d* 28 Sept 1911, leaving:

1a *Dorothy Beecroft Sheila; *b* posthumously 3 May 1912; *m* 1st 26 Jan 1932 (*divorce* 1946) Robert Desmond Ropner (ktd 1959, *see* ROPNER, Bt, of Preston Hall) and has issue; *m* 2nd 1946 Capt D B M Curtis and by him has:

1b *Amanda Murray; *b* 1948

(2) GEORGE HAWORTH USSHER (Sir), **6th Bt**

(3) Henry Reginald Dunbar; *b* 7 June 1884; *educ* Eton; T/Capt Canadian Artillery 1918 WW I; *m* 1 June 1912 Hilda Mary (*d* 12 April 1965 aged 83), 3rd dau of William Bruce Slayter, MD, FRCS, of Halifax, NS, and *d* 3 Sept 1960, leaving:

1a +Reginald William Beecroft, DSC (1941) and bar; *b* 10 March 1913; Cdr RN WW II (despatches four times); *m* 8 July 1948 (*divorce* 1976) Joan Denyer Briscoe, yr dau of Albert J George and formerly w of Jarrard Dunolly; *m* 2nd 1976 *Beatrice, dau of G H V Burroughs, of Calgary, Alberta, and widow of Myles A Ellissen, MC, and adopted:

George Christopher Jocelyn; *b* 1955; *d* 1973

*Victoria; *b* 1952; *m* 19– *Richard H St M Kemmis Betty, QOH, est s of Lt-Col Peter Kemmis Betty, of Hampton Hill Ho, Swanmore, Hants

(4) Charles Cyril Roland; *b* 1886; *educ* Eton and Keble Coll Oxford (BA 1909); Lt Roy Warwicks Regt, DC N Nigeria; *m* 2 June 1923 Heather (*d* 9 Aug 1969), dau of — Bell-Irving, and *d* 16 June 1964

3 Henry Sidney Hammet, JP (Norfolk); *b* Dec 1847; Capt E Norfolk Militia; *m* 3 Aug 1882 Anna (*d* 16 June 1922), dau of Col George Wilson Boileau, DL, of Stanfield Hall, Norfolk, and *d* 30 June 1900, leaving:

(1) Gordon Massy; *b* 1 Nov 1886; *m* 3 Nov 1909 Phyllis (*m* 2nd 26 Feb 1920 John Alan Clutton-Brock (*d* 30 Nov 1925), of Oakfield, Weybridge; *m* 3rd 10 March 1926 Charles Geoffrey Keith Hulbert (*d* 27 Jan 1963), of Harrow, er s of Sir Charles Hulbert, Sr Master in Chancery, and *d* 23 Sept 1962), dau of His Hon Judge Robert Woodfall, Co Ct Judge, and *d* 26 Nov 1918, leaving:

1a Barbara Cicely; *b* 20 Aug 1910; *m* 1st 7 Oct 1933 (*divorce* 1948) Gilbert Townley Gamble, est s of Frederick William Gamble, of Harrow, and has issue; *m* 2nd 24 Sept 1952 Geoffrey Allan Cavendish Frost, RNV(S)R, only s of Humphrey Frost, of Hampstead

2a *Pamela Abbott [Mrs Philip Gage, Green Cottage, Kington Langley, Wilts SN15 5NP]; *b* 15 Jan 1912; *m* 1st 26 Sept 1936 (*divorce* 1946) John Edward Hodgson, 3rd s of Gerald Hodgson, of Croxley Green, Herts; *m* 2nd 27 Aug 1949 *W/Cdr Philip S Gage, RAF, and by her 1st husb has:

1b *Robert John [Robert Hodgson Esq, 2 St Hilda's Rd, London SW13 9JQ]; *b* 6 Sept 1937; *m* 1st 12 Jan 1963 (*divorce* 1971) Caroline Joan Eve Kingdon and has:

1c *Jonathan Charles; *b* 6 Jan 1968

1c *Sarah Jane; *b* 30 Nov 1965

1b (cont.) Robert Hodgson *m* 2nd 1976 *Hon Jean Margaret Brand, dau of 5th Viscount Hampden (*qv*), and by her has:

2c *Thomas Edward; *b* 1981

1b *Penelope Jane [Mrs William Love, 3 Swallow St, Turners Hill, Crawley, W Sussex]; *b* 16 July 1939; *m* 1st 23 April 1964 (*divorce* 1967) John Harmon Clary; *m* 2nd 1976 (*divorce* 1985) David Gavin Clark; *m* 3rd 1988 *William Love and by her 1st husb has:

1c *James Alistair; *b* 12 May 1965; *m* 1987 *Lara Jayne Pope

(2) Sidney John Boileau; *b* 23 Aug 1889; T/Maj Warwicks Regt and RASC, Lt 3rd Bn Roy Sussex Regt, WW I; *m* 7 June 1912 Doris Lilian (*d* 22 June 1931), dau of Charles Gibson, of Aberdeen, and was *ka* 12 April 1918, leaving:

1a Diana Valerie; *b* 15 Sept 1913; *m* 1934 Howard S Calder and *dsp* 28 Aug 1937

2a *Joan Wendy Moyra; *b* 5 July 1915; *m* 1st 1937 (*divorce* 1947) Norman Richard Rowley Brooke; *m* 2nd 1949 Michael John Rouse

(1) Vere Valerie Florence Eleanore; *b* 16 March 1884; *m* 16 Oct 1907 her cousin **Sir George Haworth Ussher Lacon, 6th Bt** (*see* below), and *d* 17 Oct 1915, leaving issue

4 Ernest de Montesquiou; *b* 1 May 1850; *educ* Caius Coll Cambridge (MA); Mayor Gt Yarmouth 1897, Capt 3rd Bn Duke of Cornwall's LI; *m* 6 July 1876 Charlotte Amelia (*d* 13 Dec 1922), 3rd dau of Lt-Col John Marcon, of Wallington Hall, Norfolk, and *d* 31 May 1936, having had:

(1) Sidney Ernest de Montesquiou; *b* 25 Nov 1878; *d* 7 Feb 1891

(1) Dorothy Mortlock, MBE (1918), JP (Herefs); *b* 8 Nov 1881; Hon Sec Queen's Inst District Nurses, chm Midwifery and Nursing Ctee; *m* 30 April 1908 William Albert Somerset Herbert Kevin-Davies, 7th Hus (*d* 15 May 1915 of wounds recd in action), of Croft Castle, Herefs, and *d* 7 June 1965, leaving issue

1 Georgina; *m* 10 Aug 1865 Maj-Gen Charles Henry Gordon, CB (*d* 24 May 1895), and *d* 4 April 1933

2 Eliza Walpole; *m* 27 Oct 1884 Col Edward Henry Goring Ravenhill, JP, KSLI (*d* 1 March 1924), and *d* 22 Jan 1928

The 5th Bt's bro,

Sir George Haworth Ussher Lacon, 6th Bt, DSO; *b* 15 March 1881; Lt-Col 4th Bn Roy Warwicks Regt, formerly Lt 1st Bn, served Boer War 1901 and WW I (wounded, despatches); *m* 1st 16 Oct 1907 his cousin Vere Valerie Florence Eleanore (*see* above); *m* 2nd 9 Dec 1931 Nancye (*d* 3 April 1964), dau of James Brocklebank, of Oxton, Birkenhead, Cheshire, and formerly w of Ellis Heys Sanderson Duckworth, of Copthorne, Sussex, and *d* 21 March 1950, leaving by his 1st w, with a dau (*Cecil Mallise Kynvett; *b* 8 March 1914):

Sir George Vere Francis Lacon, 7th Bt; *b* 25 Feb 1909; *educ* Eton; *m* 1st 1 June 1935 (*divorce* 1956) Hilary Blanche (*m* 2nd J D Turner), yst dau of Cecil Julius Scott, of Adyar, Walberswick, Suffolk; *m* 2nd 2 Feb 1957 Kathlyn (Karyl) Iris (*d* 24 May 1997), dau of Edward Pillbrow, of Chelsea, and formerly w of Charles Marriott Morrell, and *d* 1980, leaving by his 1st w:

1 Sir EDMUND VERE LACON, **8th and present Bt**

2 +George Julius [George Lacon Esq, Larcomb Farmhouse, Diptford, Totnes, S Devon TQ9 7PD]; *b* 3 Sept 1938; *educ* Duncan Hall Sch, Scratby, Norfolk; *m* 14 Sept 1968 *Elizabeth Rodger, only dau of Archibald Kelly, of Sheffield, and has:

(1) *Sarah Elizabeth; *b* 9 Sept 1970

(2) *Emma Blanche; *b* 4 March 1973

LACY

Arms: Gyronny or and gules, on a bend sable a Lacy knot between two martlets of the first. **Crest:** An eagle rising or, gorged with a collar gemel gules and resting the dexter claw on a Lacy knot sable. **Motto:** *Meritis augentur honores* ('Honours are enhanced by their being merited'). **Creation:** Bt. (UK) 23 June 1921.

SIR HUGH MAURICE PIERCE LACY, 3RD BT, of Ampton, Co Suffolk [Sir Hugh Lacy Bt, c/o Mrs Andrew Finlay, Trochelhill, Morayshire IV32 7LN]; *b* 3 Sept 1943; *s* f 1965; *educ* Aiglon Coll Switzerland; *m* Oct 1968 *Deanna, dau of Howard Bailey, of Stourbridge

Lineage: JAMES LACY, of Garryrichard Ho, Enniscorthy, Co Wexford; had:

JOHN PIERCE LACY, of Oakmount, Edgbaston, Birmingham; *b* 16 July 1839; *m* 1st Eliza Rippon (*d* 5 Dec 1862) and had:

1 John Howard; *dsp* 9 March 1937

2 James Walter; *b* Nov 1860; *d* in infancy

JOHN LACY *m* 2nd 1868 Mary Conick (*d* 9 March 1914) and by her had:

3 William Xavier; *b* 11 Sept 1870; *d* 15 May 1918

4 PIERCE THOMAS (Sir), **1st Bt**
5 James Stanislaus; *b* 22 March 1874; dir 20th Century Investment Co and Waterloo Investment Tst Ltd, chm Southwark Catholic Rescue Soc; *m* 12 April 1904 Amy (*d* 16 Nov 1946), 3rd dau of Alfred Roden Walker, of Arden Hill, Lapworth, Warwicks, and *d* 10 Dec 1948, having had:
(1) Anthony John Alfred; *b* Nov 1911; *educ* The Oratory Sch; Capt Suffolk Regt WW II; *m* 31 Aug 1945 Patricia Angela Mary(*d* 8 July 1998), 2nd dau of Sir Reginald Tyrwhitt, 1st Bt (*qv*), and *d* 1975, leaving issue
(2) Peter James Gerald; *b* Jan 1916; RAF Pilot WW II 1941–46; *d* 23 May 1962
(1) Mary; *b* May 1905; *d* Aug 1906
(2) *Joan Margaret [Mrs Rowland Towell, Coxhill, Lymington, Hants]; *b* Sept 1914; *m* 14 Sept 1940 Brig Rowland Henry Towell, only surv s of Henry John Towell, of Gt Missenden, Bucks, and has:
1a *Gerald James Henry; *b* 6 July 1945; *educ* Wellington and Oxford
1a *Susan Joan; *b* 15 March 1942
6 Joseph Aloysius; *b* 27 June 1876; *d* 16 July 1916
7 Robert John Martin; *b* 7 Nov 1881; *m* 1 Nov 1924 —, dau of William Kent, of Wyndmondham, Norfolk, and *d* 20 June 1932
1 Mary Josephine; *d* unm 17 Oct 1936
2 Elizabeth; *m* 26 Nov 1907 Daniel Carroll, s of Prof Carroll, of Dublin, and *d* 19 April 1949, leaving issue
3 Cecilia; *d* young
4 Teresa; *d* young

JOHN LACY *d* 27 June 1906; his 2nd son,
Sir Pierce Thomas Lacy, 1st Bt (UK), so *cr* 23 June 1921, JP (Suffolk); *b* 16 Feb 1872; *educ* St George's Coll Weybridge; High Sheriff Suffolk 1927, chm Birmingham Stock Exchange, fndr Br Shareholders' Tst and Br Tsts Assoc, Kt Magistral Grace SMO Malta, Kt Cdr Order St Gregory the Gt; *m* 8 June 1898 Ethel Maud (*d* 24 June 1955), 5th dau of James Finucane Draper, of St Helier, Jersey, and had:
1 MAURICE JOHN PIERCE (Sir), **2nd Bt**
1 Mary; *b* 14 April, *d* 15 April 1899
2 Sybil Clare; *b* 26 Dec 1901; *m* 14 June 1928 Capt Trevor Hume (*d* 12 Dec 1968), s of Dr Frederick Nutcombe Hume, and *d* 2 Sept 1960, leaving issue (*see* SIDMOUTH, V)
3 Cynthia Maud; *b* 6 June 1903; *m* 25 Oct 1928 Montague Waddington Oakes (*d* 23rd Aug 1944), est s of Rev Beilby Porteus Oakes, of Hawkedon, Bury St Edmunds, and had:
(1) *John Waddington [Maj John Oakes, Wellesbourne Hall, Wellesbourne, Warwicks]; *b* 23 Sept 1932; *educ* Downside and RMA Sandhurst; Maj Irish Gds (ret); *m* 20 Sept 1961 *Annette Christine, dau of Col Cyril George William Swire, Roy Dragoons, of Glos, and has:
1a *Nigel John; *b* 3 July 1962
2a *Alexander Waddington; *b* 9 Nov 1968
1a *Charlotte Anne; *b* 19 May 1964
(1) *Joan Ethel [Mrs John Bird, Curraghmount, Buttevant, Co Cork, Ireland]; *b* 4 Nov 1929; *m* 1 April 1964 *John Ronald Bird, yr s of Maj John Bowyer Bird, Irish Gds, of Curraghmount, and has:
1a *Emma Louise; *b* 16 Feb 1965
2a *Caroline Anne-Marie; *b* 1 Feb 1968
(2) *Margaret Elise; *b* 1 Jan 1931; *m* 26 April 1958 *Richard Joseph Eddis, yr s of Lt-Col Lancelot Arthur Eddis, RA, of Grange Ho, Saltwood, Kent, and has:
1a *Jonathan Lancelot; *b* 7 May 1960
2a *Charles Edmund; *b* 3 Nov 1961
3a *Hugo Raleigh; *b* 12 Oct 1963
1a *Nicola Joan; *b* 21 Jan 1965
4 Angela Florence; *b* 1 Feb 1905; *m* 26 Nov 1931 Lt-Col Godfrey Sturdy Incledon-Webber, TD, DL, MA, OStJ (*d* 26 April 1986), Sheriff City London 1968–69, er s of Capt William Beare Incledon-Webber, JP, DL, of Buckland, Braunton, and *d* 13 April 1991, leaving:
(1) *Diana Mary [Mrs John Bury, Buckland Manor, Braunton, N Devon EX33 1HN]; *b* 27 Sept 1932; *m* 28 June 1961 *John Edward Bury (*see* LE MARCHANT, Bt) and has had issue
(2) *Elizabeth Angela [Mrs David Dodge, Cobblestones, Willoway Lane, Braunton, N Devon]; *b* 11 Sept 1934; *m* 12 Dec 1956 *Capt David John Bigelow Dodge, Gren Gds, er s of Col John Bigelow Dodge, DSO, DSC, MC, of Belgravia, and has:
1a *John Incledon; *b* 21 Sept 1957
2a *Julian Patrick Bigelow; *b* 30 April 1964; *m* 1 Aug 1992 *Georgia Kathleen, dau of Dr Malcolm Barksdale, of Maitland, Fla.
1a *Caroline Elizabeth; *b* 21 Feb 1959; *m* 1st 1988 (*divorce* 19–) N K Marar; *m* 2nd May 1996 *John Dore
2a *Frances Camilla; *b* 21 Nov 1961; *m* 21 Nov 1992 *Michael Forder and has:
1b *Ronald; *b* 16 Sept 1995
1b *Trisha Elizabeth; *b* 10 Sept 199–
2b *India; *b* 16 Sept 1996
3a *Celia Margaret; *b* 8 March 1967
(3) *Priscilla Mary [Mrs Jeremy Smith-Bingham, St Brannocks House, Braunton, N Devon]; *b* 18 Aug 1945, *m* 22 July 1969 *Col Jeremy Smith-Bingham, The Blues and Royals, only s of Col Oswald Cyril Smith-Bingham, of Doughton Ho, Tetbury, Glos, and has:
1a *Richard David; *b* 27 April 1970; *educ* Eton and St Anne's Coll Oxford (MA, PhD); *m* 28 Sept 1996 *Alison Kate, dau of William Thomas
2a *Alexander John; *b* 24 June 1973; *educ* Eton and Bristol U (Bsc)
3a *Guy Jeremy; *b* 2 Nov 1978; *educ* Eton
5 *Eveline Mary Elise; *b* 22 Sept 1908; *m* 19 April 1939 George Frederick Pinney, CBE, er s of Frederick Wyldbore Digby Pinney, JP, of Devereux Ho, Coleshill, Warwicks, and has:
(1) *Charles Frederick; *b* 5 Aug 1947; *educ* Ampleforth and Caius Coll Cambridge (BA 1968)
(1) *Veronica Beatrice; *b* 14 Jan 1941
(2) *Julia Margaret; *b* 17 May 1942
(3) *Angela Rose; *b* 8 Feb 1944; *m* 28 Jan 1969 David Boyle (*see* GLASGOW, E)
6 *Vivien Margaret, JP (Suffolk 1952); *b* 12 Aug 1911; *m* 18 Jan 1939 Col Nathaniel John Wilson, OBE, FRPSL, RA, only s of Lt-Col Francis Tyrwhitt Drake Wilson, OBE, of The Turrets, Great Horkesley, Essex, and has:
(1) *Peter John [Peter Wilson Esq, Thurston Croft, Bury St Edmunds, Suffolk]; *b* 8 Sept 1939; *educ* Ampleforth and Trin Coll Cambridge (MA); ACA 1965
(2) *Christopher Francis; *b* 12 March 1947; *educ* Ampleforth
(1) *Mary Angela [Mrs Rory McLeod, Wyddiall House, Buntingford, Herts]; *b* 4 June 1941; ARCM; *m* 22 July 1966 *Rory McLeod, est s of Dr Norman McLeod, of St Andrews, and has:
1a *Fiona Caroline; *b* 29 Dec 1967
2a *Amanda Mary; *b* 4 Feb 1969
(2) *Elizabeth Anne, SRN; *b* 12 Oct 1944

Sir PIERCE *d* 25 Dec 1956; his only son,
Sir Maurice John Pierce Lacy, 2nd Bt; *b* 2 April 1900; *educ* Oratory Sch Birmingham and RMC Sandhurst; Lt Life Gds (ret 1924), F/Lt RAFVR WW II 1939–43; *m* 1st 17 Nov 1932 (*divorce* 1939) Barbara Primrose, yr dau of Francis Edmund Villeneuve Russell-Roberts, of Bronheulog, Abersoch, Caernarvs, by Constance Ethel, 2nd dau of Samuel Sandbach Parker, JP, and had:
1 *Susan Mary [Mrs Philip Darwin, Holtye House, Cowden, Kent TN8 7JN]; *b* 17 Sept 1936; *m* 1st 6 June 1961 Michael John Gemmell (*d* 1988), er s of George Gemmell, of Standish Park, Stonehouse, Glos; *m* 2nd 3 Oct 1997 *Philip Darwin, yr s of William Robert Darwin, and by her 1st husb has:
(1) *Andrew James; *b* 21 June 1969
(1) *Catriona Sarah [Mrs Peter Wright, Hazelhurst House, Tilehurst, E Sussex]; *b* 19 March 1963; *m* 1989 *Peter Ion Wright and has:
1a *Harry Michael Ion; *b* 1993
1a *Edwina Primrose; *b* 1991
(2) *Lucy Charlotte; *b* 25 Oct 1964

Sir Maurice *m* 2nd 28 May 1940 (Nansi) Jean, only dau of Myrddin Evans, of Bangor, Caernarvs, and *d* 22 April 1965, having by her had:
1 Sir HUGH MAURICE PIERCE LACY, **3rd and present Bt**
2 +PATRICK BRYAN FINUCANE [Patrick Lacy Esq, 11 Tudor Gdns, London SW13]; *b* 18 April 1948; heir presumptive; *educ* Downside and King's Coll London U; dir Fugal Songs, affiliate Carlin Music Corp; *m* 3 April 1971 *Phyllis Victoria, dau of Edgar P H James, of Putney, formerly of NY, and has:
(1) +Finian James Pierce; *b* 24 Sept 1972
(1) *Alexandra Victoria; *b* 1977
2 *(Jeanne) Clare [Mrs Andrew Findlay, Trochelhill, Morayshire IV32 7LN]; *b* 6 Jan 1942; *m* 1st 11 Dec 1965 (*divorce* 1973) David Morgan, dir Deltec Anval, SA, v-pres Deltec Trading Co, est s of Capt Horace Leslie Morgan, DSO, RN, of N Devon, and has:
(1) *Dominic Maurice David; *b* 2 April 1969
(1) *Miranda Jean; *b* 26 Feb 1967
2 (cont.) Mrs Clare Morgan *m* 2nd 1976 *Andrew Findlay, of Fochabers, Morayshire, and by him has:
(1) *John Andrew Pierce; *b* 1977

LAING OF DUNPHAIL

Arms: Per pale or and gules, a chief counterchanged. **Crest:** A dexter cubit arm issuant, cuffed as in the arms, grasping a dagger proper, hilted and pommelled or, all paleways. **Supporters:** Two Pekinese dogs guardant proper. **Motto:** I stand. **Creation:** B. (LP,UK) 1991.

THE BARON LAING OF DUNPHAIL, of Dunphail, District of Moray (Sir Hector Laing) [The Rt Hon The Lord Laing of Dunphail, High Meadows, Windsor Rd, Gerrards Cross, Bucks SL9 8ST]; *b* 12 May 1923; *educ* Loretto and Jesus Coll Cambridge; Capt Scots Gds 1942–47 (US Bronze Star, despatches 1944); dir: McVitie & Price 1947 (chm 1963), United Biscuits 1953 (md 1964), Allied-Lyons 1979–82, Exxon Corp 1984–94; chm: United Biscuits Hldgs 1972–90, Food and Drink Industries Cncl 1977–79, Scottish Business in the Community 1982–90, City and Industl Liaison Cncl 1985–94, Business in the Community 1987–91; Dir

Bank of England 1973–91; Jt-Treas C Party 1988–93; Pres Project Trident 1992–94; memb: Bd Roy Insur 1970–78, Cncl Wycombe Abbey Sch 1981–94; Chm Tstees Lambeth Fund 1983–97; Jt-Chm Per Cent Club 1986–90; Hon Tstee Roy Botanic Gdns Kew Fndn 1990, ktd 1978; Hon DU Stirling 1985, Hon DLitt Heriot-Watt 1986, FRSE 1989; *m* 1950 *Marian Clare, dau of Maj-Gen Sir John Emilius Laurie, 6th Bt (*qv*), and has:

1 *Mark Hector [The Hon Mark Laing, The White House, Totley Wells, W Lothian EH52 6QJ]; *b* 1951; *educ* Eton and Selwyn Coll Cambridge; *m* 1980 *Susanna Anson, dau of John Anson Crawford, of St Andrews, and has:

(1) *Hector Grant; *b* 1988

(1) *Kathryn Rose; *b* 1983

(2) *Georgina Clare; *b* 1985

2 *Robert John [The Hon Robert Laing, Humbie House, Humbie, E Lothian EH36 5PB]; *b* 1953; *educ* Eton and Selwyn Coll Cambridge; *m* 1992 *Mrs Fiona M Nunneley, dau of Freddy Grant, of Church House, Washington, Sussex

3 *Anthony Rupert [The Hon Anthony Laing, 14 Saxe Coburg Place, Edinburgh EH3 5BR]; *b* 1955; *educ* Eton; *m* 1985 *Fiona, yr dau of John Brooke-Hunt, of Jedburgh, and has:

(1) *Rupert Andrew; *b* 1986

(2) *Christopher Hector; *b* 1988

(1) *Rebecca Claire; *b* 1990

Lineage: HECTOR LAING, of Edinburgh; *m* Margaret Norris, dau of Sir Alexander Grant, 1st Bt (*see* 1949 edn), and had:

HECTOR, *cr* a **Baron**

LAKE

Arms: Quarterly, 1st (coat of augmentation), gules a dexter arm, embowed in armour, issuing from the sinister side of the shield, holding in the hand a sword erect, all proper, thereto affixed a banner argent, bearing on a cross between sixteen escutcheons (the number of Dr Lake's wounds at Edgehill) of the first a lion passant-guardant or; 2nd, sable on a bend between six cross-crosslets argent, a mullet for difference (for LAKE); 3rd, argent a chevron between three boar's heads, couped sable (for WARDELL); 4th, quarterly argent and sable, on a bend of the last three fleur-de-lys of the first (for BIBYE). **Crests:** 1 A cavalier in complete armour on a horse courant argent, bridle and trappings all proper, in his dexter hand a sword embrued, holding the bridle in his mouth, the sinister arm hanging down useless, round his body a scarf in bend gules, 2 A sea-horse's head argent, finned or, gorged with a fess cotised gules. **Motto:** *Un Dieu, un roy, un coeur* ('One God, one king, one heart'). **Creation:** Bt. (GB) 17 Oct 1711.

SIR (ATWELL) GRAHAM LAKE, 10TH BT, of Edmonton, Middlesex [Sir Graham Lake Bt, Magdalen Laver Hall, Chipping Ongar, Essex CM5 0EG]; *b* 6 Oct 1923; *s f* 1972; *educ* Eton; served Gilbert & Ellice Is Mil Forces 1944–45, Colonial Admin Serv 1945–55, Norris Oakley Bros 1957, MOD 1959, Br High Commn New Delhi 1966, attd FCO 1969–72, sr tech advsr MOD (ret 1983); *m* 26 March 1983 *Mrs Katherine Margaret Lister, dau of D W Last

Lineage: RICHARD LAKE, of Irby, Lincs; *m* 1st Anne, dau and coheir of Edward Wardell, of Keilby, Lincs, and had a s (Sir EDWARD LAKE, 1st Bt (E), so *cr* 10 July 1661 (CHARLES I had granted him a coat of augmentation and an additional crest (*see* above) following his valour at the Battle of Edgehill 1642, where he recd 16 wounds, and had issued 30 Dec 1643 a warrant granting him a btcy but due to the turbulence of the times no patent was ever made out), of Carnow, Co Wicklow; *educ* Cambridge (MA, LLD) and Oxford (BCL); Chllr Diocese of Lincoln, King's Advocate-Gen Ireland, MP Cavan 1639–40; *m* Anne, dau and coheir of Symon Bibye, of Bugden, Hunts, and *dsps* 18 April 1674 when the btcy expired); *m* 2nd Anne, dau of Richard Morelly, of Claxby, Lincs, and by her had:

THOMAS LAKE; had:

THOMAS LAKE, of Bishops Norton, Lincs; barrister Middle Temple; *m* Elizabeth, dau of John Storey, of Kniveton, Derbys, and *d* 22 May 1711 aged 54, leaving:

Sir Bibye Lake, 1st Bt (GB), so *cr* 17 Oct 1711; *bapt* 10 April 1684; Sub-Govr Africa Co, Bencher Middle Temple; *m* 1st Mary (*bur* 23 Jan 1752), dau and heiress of William Atwell, of London; *m* 2nd 1752 Ann, yr dau of Henry Sperling, and was *bur* 6 April 1744, having by his 1st w had, with other issue:

Sir Atwell Lake, 2nd Bt; *bapt* 9 May 1713; Govr Hudson Bay Co; *m* July 1740 Mary (*d* 19 April 1782), only dau of James Winter, of Mile End, and *d* 10 April 1760, leaving, with six other children (including a dau Mary, *m* Maj William Webb):

Sir James Winter Lake, 3rd Bt; FSA; *m* Joyce (*d* 26 July 1834), dau of John Crowther, and had, with other issue:

1 JAMES SAMUEL WILLIAM (Sir), **4th Bt**

2 Willoughby Thomas (Sir), KCB; Adml the White; *m* 1795 Charlotte, dau of Adml Macbride, and *d* 18 Feb 1847, leaving:

(1) Willoughby; Capt RN; *dsp*

(2) Edward; Maj; *m* Harriot Marion, dau of John Goldingham, and had:

1a Edward John, CSI; *b* 19 June 1823; Maj-Gen RE; *m* 11 July 1861 Elizabeth Penrose (*d* 12 Aug 1879), dau of Thomas Bewes, MP, of Beaumont, Devon, and *dsps* 7 June 1877

1a Charlotte Louisa; *m* 20 Oct 1841 Gordon Sullivan Forbes and had issue

3 Noel Thomas, CB; *b* 22 Oct 1799; Maj-Gen RA, Offr Legn Hon and Medjidie; *m* 6 Dec 1832 Elizabeth (*d* 1898), est dau of Rev Thomas Apperley, of Stoke Lacy, Herefs, and *dsp* 19 May 1964

1 Charlotte Prestwood; *m* 11 Aug 1818 John Offley Crewe-Read, JP, DL (*d* 30 Nov 1858), of Llandinam and Wern, and *d* 27 Oct 1865

2 Emily; *m* 1827 Adml Webb and *dsp*

Sir JAMES *d* 24 April 1807; his est s,

Sir James Samuel William Lake, 4th Bt; *m* 24 July 1804 Maria (*d* 15 March 1866), dau of Samuel Turner, and *d* 4 Nov 1832, having had, with two daus (*d* unm):

1 **Sir James Samuel Lake, 5th Bt**; *m* 1 May 1833 Anne Maria (*m* 2nd 20 Sept 1851 Dr George Frederick Mitchelson, of Brighton, and *d* 17 Oct 1869), dau of V-Adml Sir Richard King, Bt, GCB (*see* 1970 edn DUCKWORTH-KING, Bt), and *d* 10 Dec 1846, leaving:

(1) **Sir Atwell King Lake, 6th Bt**; *b* 9 April 1834; Capt 104th Regt Indian Mutiny (medal); *m* 9 April 1870 Frances Sarah Peace (*d* 15 Sept 1896), dau of William Walter Jones, of Gurrey, Carmarths, widow of Col Richard Ouseley, and *dsp* 15 July 1897

(2) St Vincent David; *b* 2 May 1835; Lt RN; *m* 13 Sept 1860 Frances (*d* 18 April 1909), dau of Peter Partington, and *d* 28 May 1865, leaving:

1a **Sir St Vincent Atwell, 7th Bt**; *b* 3 Jan 1862; *m* 5 Jan 1885 Elizabeth Daisy (*d* 19 March 1900), dau of Charles Day of Aldershot, and *dsp* 12 Nov 1916

2 Edward; *b* 28 Aug 1808; Capt RN; *m* 1st 12 Sept 1839 Clara (*d* 25 Nov 1862), 2nd dau of Sir William Johnston, 7th Bt (*qv*), and *d* 8 Jan 1864, having had:

(1) Edward William; *dsp*

(2) **Sir Arthur Johnstone Lake, 8th Bt**; *b* 15 Oct 1849; *m* 1884 Emily, dau of J Burton, and *dsp* 10 Dec 1924

(1) Maria Sophia; *m* Lionel Covillon and *d* 13 June 1890

(2) Emily Maria; *m* 1872 George John Hynes (*d* 1921), PMG India, and *d* 1921

(3) Clara Elizabeth; *m* 5 March 1867 Lt-Gen James Crofton (*d* 22 Nov 1908) and *d* 16 Dec 1890, leaving issue (*see* CROFTON, Bt, of Mohill)

3 Henry Atwell (Sir), KCB; *b* 15 Dec 1808; Offr Legn Hon, 2nd Class Medjidie, Col, Maj-Gen Turkish Army, ADC to HM QUEEN VICTORIA, Ch Commr Dublin Met Police, distinguished Siege of Kars Crimean War 1855; *m* 1st 14 April 1841 Anne (*d* 8 Jan 1847), yst dau of Rev Peregrine Curtois, of The Longhills, Lincs, and had:

(1) Atwell Peregrine Macleod; *b* 11 April 1842; Adml; ADC to HM QUEEN VICTORIA; *m* 24 Jan 1889 Constance Mary (*d* 9 March 1949), dau of Gen Augustus Turner, and *d* 27 Aug 1915, leaving:

1a ATWELL HENRY (Sir), **9th Bt**

2a Noel Graham; *b* 11 May 1894; Lt Serv Bn Glos Regt; *ka* 24 March 1918

3a Hubert Geoffrey; *b* 21 Aug 1895; *educ* Cheltenham; Artists Rifles WW I (invalided), WW II ARP Warden

(2) Edward; *b* 5 Feb 1844; Col RA; *m* 1885 Edith Dale (*d* 3 March 1939), dau of P Dale Nichol, of Newcastle, and *dsp* 4 Dec 1910

(1) Emily Mary; *m* 17 Aug 1869 James Henry Cochrane (*d* 1914) and *d* 22 Aug 1922

(2) Clara Montague; *d* 1847

3 (cont.) Sir Henry *m* 2nd 22 Feb 1848 Anne Augusta (*d* 20 Dec 1877), dau of Sir William Curtis, 2nd Bt (*qv*), and *d* 17 Aug 1881, having by her had, with three daus (*d* unm):

(3) Noel Montagu, CB (1917); *b* 10 Sept 1852; Col and Hon Brig-Gen RE, T/Brig-Gen ic Admin N Cmd 1914–16; *m* 1 Oct 1890 Virginia Jane (*d* 11 April 1957 aged 98), er dau of William Parnis, of Constantinople, and *d* 24 Dec 1932, leaving:

1a Edward Montague; *b* 20 July 1891; *educ* London U (BSc 1916); Pncpl Sci Offr Min Supply; *m* 19 Sept 1925 Beatrice Elizabeth (*d* 16 Sept 1968), dau of Hugh Mortimer Rowland, MD, and *dsp* 19 May 1971

(4) Henry Seymour; *b* 30 Oct 1855; Lt RN; *d* 14 May 1882

(5) Spencer Fenwick; *b* 18 July 1858; *d* 1933

(6) Hubert Atwell; *b* 17 May 1867; Lt-Col RA; *d* 21 Jan 1931

4 Willoughby John, JP; *b* 24 Dec 1815; Capt RN; *m* 14 July 1852 Almeria, est dau of William Phillimore, of Deacon's Hill, Herts, and *d* 16 Dec 1867, leaving:

(1) Lancelot Willoughby; *b* 28 Jan 1854; *dsp*

5 Andrew Winter; *b* 1821; Capt Madras Army; *m* 1855 Henrietta Edith Jessie, dau of Edward Francklyn, and *d* 9 July 1865, leaving:

(1) Winter Atwell Edward; *b* 1858; Dep Inspr-Gen Punjab Police, served Afghan War 1880 (medal) and Burmese Campaign 1886–89 (medal with two clasps); *m* 1883 Annie Ethel Talbot, dau of Gen William Howey, ISC, and *d* 29 May 1930, leaving:

1a Ernest Atwell Winter, CBE (1945); *b* 5 Aug 1886; Lt-Col IA, Cmdt Estuary Sector (Essex) HG WW II; *m* 10 Jan 1924 Phyllis Marjorie, only dau of J G Silcock, JP, ICS, and *d* 7 Dec 1945, leaving:

1b +John Winter Atwell; *b* 5 March 1925; *m* 30 March 1955 *Elsie Isobel, 2nd dau of R Milburn, of Westmorland

2b +Winter Philip Edward; *b* 22 June 1930; *m* 19 Oct 1956 *Vera, yr dau of A G Liddell, of Thornaby, Co Durham

1 Anne; *b* 31 May 1807; *m* 20 June 1833 Rev Charles Frederick Rogers Baylay (*d* 3 April 1890), Rector Kirkby-upon-Bain, Lincs, and *d* 10 March 1879, having had issue

The 8th Bt's cousin,

Sir Atwell Henry Lake, 9th Bt, CB (1945), OBE (1919); *b* 13 Feb 1891; *educ* Cheltenham; Capt RN, Cdre 2nd Cl 1904, WW I in HMS *Lion* (Battle of Jutland), WW II (Ch Staff to C-in-C Portsmouth 1939–42 and Ch NZ Naval Staff 1942–45), ADC to HM GEORGE VI 1942, Cdr US Legn Merit; *m* 20 July 1922 Kathleen Marion, dau of Alfred Morrison Turner, of Liverpool, and *d* 27 Nov 1972, leaving:

1 Sir (ATWELL) GRAHAM LAKE, **10th and present Bt**

2 Willoughby Alfred; *b* 31 Aug 1925; *educ* Eton; RAF 1944–47; *m* 13 Sept 1952 *Elizabeth Elsie Faith [Mrs Willoughby Lake, Horseshoe Farm, Hanghern Round, Shropham, Norfolk], dau of Sir Rupert Turner Havelock Clarke, 2nd Bt, of Rupertswood (*qv*), and *d* 1986, leaving:

(1) *Susan Kathleen; *b* 7 May 1961

(2) *Catherine Jane; *b* 26 Oct 1962

3 +EDWARD GEOFFREY [Edward Lake Esq, High Acre, Cowgill, Dent, Cumbria]; *b* 17 July 1928; heir presumptive; *educ* Eton; MAOT 1964; *m* 28 Aug 1965 *Judith Ann, er dau of John Fox, of London E4, and has:

(1) +Mark Winter; *b* 26 Oct 1968

(1) *Sophie Louise; *b* 6 Jan 1971

LAKIN

Arms: Quarterly indented argent and azure, in the 1st and 4th quarters a pellet charged with a lion's head erased of the first. **Crest:** A dexter cubit arm erect, vested sable, cuffed azure, holding in the hand a plasterer's trowel proper. **Motto:** *Un Dieu, un roy, un coeur* ('One God, one king, one heart'). **Creation:** Bt. (UK) 22 July 1909.

SIR MICHAEL LAKIN, 4TH BT, of The Cliff, Co Warwick [Sir Michael Lakin Bt, c/o Little Sherwood Hill, Tunley, Glos GL7 6LW]; *b* 28 Oct 1934; *s* f 1979; *educ* Stowe; *m* 1st 17 July 1956 (*divorce* 1963) Margaret, dau of Robert Wallace, of Mountnorris, Co Armagh; *m* 2nd 20 May 1965 *Felicity-Ann, dau of A D Murphy, of Kenya, and by her has:

1 +RICHARD ANTHONY [Richard Lakin Esq, Box 13390, Nakuru, Kenya]; *b* 26 Nov 1968; *m* 20 Dec 1997 *Lara Maryanne, dau of J E Rose, of Nairobi

1 *Mary-Jane [Mrs Charles Clark, Lowesmoor Farm, Cherington, Glos GL8 8SP]; *b* 23 Feb 1966; *m* 1992 *Charles Adrian Clark, s of Walter Clark, and has:

(1) *Timothy Anthony; *b* 8 May 1995

(1) *Emma Louise; *b* 26 June 1993

2 *Serena Pamela; *b* 19–; *m* 19– *Giles Selwyn Robinson, of Cricklade, and has:

(1) *Harry Edgar Selwyn; *b* 1989

(1) *Molly Pamela; *b* 1982

Lineage: JOSEPH LAKIN, of Hall End, Tamworth, Warwicks; *b* 1652; *m* Mary — (*d* between 29 Oct 1727 and 12 Jan 1727/8) and *d* 1727, having had, with four daus:

1 Joseph, of Hall End; *m* Mary — and had issue

2 John, of Hall End; *bapt* 1691; *m* Ann, sis of Henry Bakewell, and *d* 1727, leaving:

(1) Henry

(2) Michael

(3) JAMES

(4) Joseph

(1) Elizabeth

(2) Mary

JOHN LAKIN's 3rd s,

JAMES LAKIN, of Hall End; *m* Mary, dau of Thomas Lakin, and *d* 1756, leaving a 2nd s:

JOHN LAKIN, of Freazley and later Hall End; *b* 1748; *m* Elizabeth, dau of John Roby, of Shenton, near Bosworth, Leics, and had, with four other daus:

1 James; *b* 14 Feb 1775; surgn; *d* unm

2 HENRY

3 John, of Freazley; *b* 25 Dec 1784; *m* Ann Cooper (*d* 20 June 1827), dau of Christopher Marsh, of Bath, and had:

(1) Thomas Cooper; *d* unm 16 June 1845

(2) John Marsh (Rev); *b* 6 Aug 1816; Rector and Patron Gilmorton, Leics, later Brooksby, Leics; *m* 11 April 1844 Louisa (*d* 3 March 1878), dau of William Smallwood, of Sheldon, Warwicks, and *d* 24 July 1886, leaving:

1a Barbara Ann; *m* 7 July 1886 Rev Canon John Henry Turner Mitchell de Mowbray (*d* 19 Feb 1897), Rector Knossington, and had issue

2a Alice Marsh; *d* unm 27 July 1917

3a Elizabeth; *m* 8 Sept 1908 Edward Hart, of Woburn Sands, Bucks

1 Elizabeth; *b* 22 Oct 1782; *m* her cousin John Lakin and left issue

JOHN LAKIN's 2nd s,

HENRY LAKIN, of Severn End; *b* 2 Dec 1779; *m* 11 Feb 1806 Ann Isabella (*d* 1851), dau of Edward Lyon, of Drayton Bassett, Warwicks, and had:

1 John Edward, of Beauchamp Court, Worcs; *b* 3 March 1810; *m* 1839 Rose (*d* 6 June 1843), dau of David Cooper, of Norwich, and *d* 25 June 1839, leaving issue

2 HENRY

1 Ellen; *b* 2 Dec 1806; *m* Henry Paget (*d* 3 Feb 1858), of Birstal, Leics, and *d* 7 Feb 1884, leaving issue

2 Anne Isabella; *b* 15 May 1815; *m* 1841 Thomas Shakespeare and *d* 24 April 1893

HENRY LAKIN's 2nd s,

HENRY LAKIN, of Malvern, Worcs; *b* 13 Dec 1811; *m* 1 May 1845 Rebecca Mary (*d* 31 Jan 1892), dau of John Greaves, of Radford Semele, Warwicks, and *d* 8 Oct 1891, having had:

1 MICHAEL HENRY (Sir), **1st Bt**

2 Edward Lyon, JP (Warwicks and Worcs), of The Cliff, Malvern Wells; *b* 11 Sept 1852; *d* 23 April 1926

1 Margaret

2 Mary; *b* 14 Aug 1853; *d* unm 17 Jan 1931

3 Jessie; *b* 28 Dec 1854; *m* Robert H Cazalet and *d* 23 Feb 1922, leaving issue

4 Gertrude; *b* 13 July 1856

HENRY LAKIN *d* 8 Oct 1891; his est s,

Sir Michael Henry Lakin, 1st Bt (UK), so *cr* 22 July 1909, JP, DL; *b* 7 Oct 1846; CA Warwicks, High Sheriff 1899; *m* 1 July 1869 Alice Emma (*d* 31 Jan 1927), dau of David Dewing, of St Catherine's Plain, Norwich, and had:

1 RICHARD (Sir), **2nd Bt**

2 Henry Gilbert, JP; *b* 14 May 1875; *m* 4 Feb 1902 Sybil Patteson (*d* 11 June 1938), yst dau of Sir Patteson Nickalls, JP, of Chislehurst, Kent, and *d* 10 March 1964, having had:

(1) Michael; *b* 14 Sept 1909; *d* 5 Jan 1926

(2) John, TD, JP (Warwicks 1951), DL (1950, Sussex 1977); *b* 22 Dec 1910; *educ* Eton and New Coll Oxford; Lt-Col Warwicks Yeo WW II; *m* 10 Aug 1939 *Hon (Helena) Daphne Pearson, yst dau of 2nd Viscount Cowdray (*qv*), and *d* 1989, leaving:

1a +Michael Simon; *b* 26 Jan 1955; *educ* Harrow

3 Edward Lyon; *b* 13 Aug 1879; *m* 5 Feb 1912 Dorothy Barklie (*d* 1 Jan 1969, having taken by deed poll 18 March 1932 the name LIDDELL), 3rd dau of Col Barklie Cairns McCalmont, CB, and *d* 10 Sept 1922, leaving:

(1) +Richard Barklie, DSO (1943), DSC and bar [Lt-Cdr Richard Lakin DSO DSC and bar RN, Seaview House, Seaview, IoW PO34 5ET]; *b* 8 Oct 1914; *educ* RNC Dartmouth; Lt-Cdr RN WW II (despatches), US Legn Merit; *m* 1st 17 Oct 1936 Pamela Mary Helen (*d* 1981), dau of G/Capt Philip Jackson-Taylor; *m* 2nd 1987 *Pansy Myra Edith, dau of Col Algernon Lothian Bonham Carter, DSO, of Buriton, Hants, and widow of Cdr Jo Allan Phillips, RN, and by his 1st w has:

1a +Robin Lyon [Robin Lakin Esq, PO Box 550, St Leonards, NSW 2065, Australia]; *b* 26 Jan 1938; *educ* Eton and RMA Sandhurst; late Lt 11th Hus; *m* 18 April 1964 (*divorce* 1997) Gillian Claire, er dau of Peter Baily, of South Farm, Gt Whittington, Northumberland, and has:

1b *Jessica Honor Katherine; *b* 20 Dec 1966

2b *Nicola Anne Pamela; *b* 16 Sept 1970

1a (cont.) Robin Lakin has by *Jo Susan Whitehead:

3b *Judy Clementine Francesca; *b* 18 Jan 1974

2a +Mark Philip [Mark Lakin Esq, 72 Drayton Gdns, London SW10 9SB]; *b* 15 March 1941; *educ* Eton; ACA; *m* 1988 *Christina Lisa Josephine, dau of Patrick Dolan (US Legn Merit), of Much Hadham, Herts, and widow of Peter Gordon Schiach, of Ardgilzean, Morayshire, and has:

1b +Patrick Barklie; *b* 1989

2b +Henry Lyon; *b* 1991

1b *Molly Kathleen; *b* 1993

3a +Julian Barklie [Julian Lakin Esq, Juniper Cottage, Upper Farringdon, Hants GU34 3DT]; *b* 18 Nov 1948; *educ* Eton; *m* 1973 *Penelope Jane, dau of John Almond, of Burghclere, Berks, and has:

1b *Olivia Mary; *b* 31 July 1978

2b *Arabella Louise; *b* 11 June 1980

1a *Amanda Joy Lakin [Mrs Amanda Courtney, Rosemary House, Northleach, Glos GL54 3HJ]; *b* 3 June 1947; *m* 1981 (*divorce* 1990) Christopher Euan Philip Charles Courtney

2a *Caroline Madeline [Mrs Richard Wallis, Tump Hill, Arlington, Glos GL7 5ND]; *b* 27 Dec 1953; *m* 1984 *Richard Frederick Wallis, yr s of Charles Wallis, of Bryanston Sq, London W1, and has:

1b *Jack Charles Lyon; *b* 1990

1b *Daisy Pamela; *b* 1987

3a *Serena Pamela [Mrs Serena Robinson, Isis Cottage, 10 Bath Rd, Cricklade, Wilts SN6 6AT]; *b* 27 Dec 1953; *m* 1986 (*divorce* 1996) Giles

Selwyn Robinson, of Henley-on-Thames, Oxon, est s of Donald Edgar Robinson, of Perthshire, and has:

1b *Harry Edgar Selwyn; *b* 1989

1b *Molly Pamela; *b* 1992

4 Michael Laurence, DSO (1915) MC (1918); *b* 24 Nov 1881; *educ* Marlborough; Maj 11th Hus (SR), A/Maj MGC, Maj and 2nd i/c S Irish Horse and Adj Roy Wilts Yeo, Boer War 1900 (medal) and WW I (despatches twice), MFH Wexford 1912–27 and 1928–37; *m* 18 July 1914 Kathleen (*d* 23 Feb 1930), dau of Lord Maurice FitzGerald (*see* LEINSTER, D), and *d* 18 Oct 1960, having had:

(1) Gerald Michael; *b* 17 Jan 1916; Capt 16th/5th Lancers WW II; *d* of wounds N Africa 20 Feb 1943

(2) +Maurice Victor; *b* 30 Oct 1919; *educ* Eton; Capt 17th/21st Lancers WW II 1939–44 N Africa (wounded); *m* 1st 18 Oct 1951 (*divorce* 1956) Huguette Paule Clémence, dau of Robert Cauvin, of Paris; *m* 2nd 26 Jan 1959 (*divorce* 1971) Silvanni, dau of Vong Ngot, of Phnom Penh, Cambodia, and by her has:

1a +Michael; *b* 16 March 1960

2a +Richard; *b* 6 May 1964; *m* 1990 *Claire, dau of Roland Coutant, of Vino-sur-Verdon, Var, France, and has:

1b +Alexandre; *b* 1992

1b *Camille; *b* 1991

1 Violet Mary; *b* 2 March 1872; *m* 17 Feb 1920 Maj-Gen Thomas Tait Pitman, CB, CMG (*d* 8 March 1941), s of Frederick Pitman, of Edinburgh, and *d* 5 Aug 1953

Sir MICHAEL *d* 21 March 1931; his est s,

Sir Richard Lakin, 2nd Bt, JP; *b* 30 May 1873; Capt Warwicks Yeo WW I; *m* 22 Oct 1903 Mildred Alice (*d* 25 Sept 1960), dau of Capt Geoffrey Joseph Shakerley, of Grove Park, Warwicks, and had:

1 HENRY (Sir), **3rd Bt**

1 *Cynthia [Miss Cynthia Lakin, Sherwood Hill, Tunley, nr Cirencester, Glos]; *b* 12 Sept 1907

Sir RICHARD *d* 14 Feb 1955; his only s,

Sir Henry Lakin, 3rd Bt; *b* 8 Oct 1904; *educ* Eton and Jesus Coll Cambridge (BA 1926); *m* 1st 25 June 1927 Bessie (*d* 1 March 1964), dau of James Donaldson Anderson, of Durban, S Africa; *m* 2nd 4 March 1965 *Grace, dau of John Kyme, of Manchester, and *d* 1979, having by his 1st w had:

1 Sir MICHAEL LAKIN, **4th and present Bt**

1 Shirley Patricia; *b* 23 May 1929; *d* unm 15 June 1955

LAMBERT, Viscount

Arms: Azure a chevron or fretty of the first between in chief two garbs and in base a fleece of the second. **Crest:** Issuant from a mount vert an apple tree fructed proper. **Supporters:** On either side a Cornish chough proper, collared or. **Motto:** The good earth provides. **Creation:** V. (UK) 23 July 1945.

THE 3RD VISCOUNT LAMBERT, of S Molton, Co Devon (Michael John Lambert) [The Rt Hon The Viscount Lambert, Casanuova di Barontoli, 53010, S Rocco da Pilli, Siena, Italy]; *b* 29 Sept 1912; *s* bro 1989; *educ* Harrow and New Coll Oxford; *m* 5 Sept 1939 *Florence Dolores, dau of Nicholas Lechmere Cunningham Macaskie, QC, of Kensington, and has:

1 *Sophia Jane [The Hon Sophia Lambert, 12 Kelso Place, London W8]; *b* 15 May 1943; *educ* LSE (BA 1966)

2 *Caelia Anne Georgina [The Hon Mrs Caelia Pereira, 60 Bolingbroke, London W14]; *b* 7 May 1946; *m* 29 May 1971 (*divorce* 1985) Emmanuel Irismar Pereira, only s of Joaquim Pereira and Antonia Barreto de Carvalho, of Brazil, and has:

(1) *Joaquim Michael Lambert; *b* 23 July 1975

(1) *Antonia Caterina Lambert; *b* 30 April 1972

3 *Flavia Mary [The Hon Flavia Lambert, 9 Alwyne Rd, London N1]; *b* 11 Sept 1949; *educ* London U (BA 1971)

Lineage: GEORGE LAMBERT, of Spreyton, Devon; *d* 1885, leaving an only s:

GEORGE LAMBERT, **1st Viscount Lambert**, of South Molton, Co Devon (UK), so *cr* 23 July 1945, PC (1912), JP; *b* 25 June 1866; *educ* privately; Capt 3rd Bn Devonshire Regt, CC Devon 1889, CA 1912–52, MP (Lib) S Molton 1891–1924 and 1929–45, memb Roy Cmmn Ag Depression 1893, Deptl Commn Rlwy Rates 1904 and Storage Liquid Fuel Peace and War 1912, Civil Ld Admlty 1905–15, Fndn Chm Seale Hayne Ag Coll Newton Abbott, Chm Lib Parly Pty 1919–21; *m* 30 July 1904 Barbara (*d* 6 June 1963), dau of George Stavers, of Morpeth, Northumberland, and *d* 17 Feb 1958, leaving:

1 GEORGE LAMBERT, **2nd Viscount Lambert**, TD, DL (Devon 1969); *b* 27 Nov 1909; *educ* Harrow and New Coll Oxford; Lt-Col TA WW II, MP (Lib-Nat) S Molton 1945–50 and (Nat Lib and C) Torrington 1950–58, chm Henry Norrington Ltd, dir Gen Accident Insur, chm Govrs Seale Hayne Ag Coll and Devon and Exeter Savings Bank, memb Cncl RASE, Pres Nat Fedn Young Farmers' Clubs; *m* 16 Sept 1939 Patricia Mary (*d* 1991), dau of Joseph Francis Quinn, of London, and *d* 1989, having had:

(1) George; *b* 18 Aug 1941; *educ* Harrow; Capt RHG (Blues) (ret); *k* in a car crash 27 Aug 1970

(1) *Louise Barbara [The Hon Lady Gibbings, 10 The Vale, London SW3]; *b* 29 March 1944; *m* 27 March 1975 Sir Peter Walter Gibbings, s of Walter White Gibbings, and has:

1a *Dominic George Lambert; *b* 6 April 1976

2 MICHAEL JOHN LAMBERT, **3rd and present Viscount Lambert**

1 Grace Mary; *b* 1905; *d* 12 Feb 1997

2 Margaret Barbara, CMG (1965); *b* 1906; *educ* LMH Oxford (BA) and LSE (PhD); European Serv BBC 1939–45, assist ed Br Documents For Policy 1946–50, Lecturer Modern History U Coll South West 1950–51 and St Andrews 1959–60, Br Ed-in-Ch captured archives German Foreign Min 1951; *d* 22 Jan 1995

LAMBERT, Bt

Arms: Argent on a mount an oaktree vert and a greyhound courant gules. **Crest:** Out of a ducal coronet or three ostrich feathers gules, argent and azure. **Motto:** *Sequitando si giunge* ('By pursuing one attains'). **Creation:** Bt. (GB) 16 Feb 1710/1.

SIR PETER JOHN BIDDULPH LAMBERT, 10TH BT, of London [Sir Peter Lambert Bt, 67 Lauder Ave, Toronto, Ontario M6H 3E2, Canada]; *b* 5 April 1952; *s* cousin 1988; *educ* Upper Canada Coll Toronto, Trent U (BSc 1975) and U of Manitoba, Winnipeg (MA 1980); archaeological consultant; *m* 1989 *Leslie Anne, dau of Richard Welkos Lyne, and has:

1 *Maeve Edith Jean; *b* 1992

Lineage: JOHN LAMBERT, advocate, had:

JOHN LAMBERT; *m* Mary Le Fevre and had:

Sir John Lambert, 1st Bt (GB), so *cr* 16 Feb 1710/1; *b* 1666; London merchant, dir South Sea Co, settled in the Isle de Rhé as a naturalised Frenchman though a native of Devon; ktd by Sept 1710; *m* Madeline (*d* April 1737), dau of Benjamin Beuzelim, merchant, of Rouen, and *d* 4 Feb 1722/3, having had, with three yr sons and three daus:

Sir John Lambert, 2nd Bt; *b* 22 March 1690; *m* Anne, dau of Tempest Holmes, returned to spend his last years in France and was naturalised there 11 Dec 1762, and had, with other issue:

1 JOHN (Sir), **3rd Bt**

2 Robert Alexander; *bapt* 24 July 1732; Capt RN; *m* 19 Jan 1768 Catherine, dau of Thomas Byndloss, of Jamaica, and *d* 21 Dec 1801, leaving, with other issue:

(1) Robert Stuart; *b* 2 April 1771; R-Adml; *m* 1st Sept 1818 Charlotte, dau of Frederick Pigou; *m* 2nd 1822 Louisa, widow of Rev Thomas Cobb, and *dsp* Sept 1836

(2) John (Sir), GCB; *b* 28 April 1772; Gen; *m* 19 Oct 1816 Jane (*d* 22 May 1864), dau of John Morant, and *d* 14 Sept 1847, leaving:

1a John Arthur; *b* 30 Sept 1817; Gen; *d* unm

2a Robert; *b* 25 Oct 1818; Capt; *m* 30 Jan 1868 Alice Elizabeth (*d* 4 Aug 1917), est dau of Col Smith, CB, Rifle Bde, and *d* 1891, leaving:

1b Robert, DSO (1900), JP (Salop); *b* 17 Sept 1873; Capt 8th Hus, ret as Hon Maj, served Boer War; *m* 21 May 1898 Henrietta Isabella, MBE, JP (Salop) (*d* 31 Jan 1950), dau of George William Lowther (*see* LOWTHER, Bt), and *d* 19 Dec 1955, leaving:

1c Alice Winsome; divl pres Salop Red Cross 1961, WW I 1917–18 with BRCS, WW II with VAD

1b Alice Mary; *m* 9 May 1893 Henry Rodolph de Salis, JP (*d* 25 Feb 1936), of Acton Lodge, Leamington, and *d* 10 June 1939

2b Bessie; *b* 9 June 1875

1a Mary Jane; *m* her cousin Lt-Col Frederick William Lambert (*see* below) and *d* 18 March 1877

2a Harriet Frances; *m* 4 Nov 1857 her cousin Rev Harry Lambert (*see* below) and *d* 6 Feb 1921

(3) George Robert (Sir), GCB; *b* 8 Sept 1795; Adml; *m* 1st 29 May 1822 Katharine (*d* 30 Sept 1861), dau of Rev Thomas Cobb; *m* 2nd 20 April 1864 Catherine Mary (*d* 1890), est dau of Frederick Webb, widow of Col John Roger Palmer, and *d* 5 June 1869, having by his 1st w had:

1a Thomas, JP, of Stanmore, Canterbury, Kent; Capt RHA; *b* 2 Sept 1825; *m* 15 March 1849 Laura (*d* 1894), dau of Sir Robert Smirke, RA, and *d* 28 March 1905, leaving:

1b Agnes Laura; *m* 4 June 1873 Capt Henry S Swiney and *d* 1893, leaving issue

2a Harry (Rev); *m* 4 Nov 1857 his cousin Harriet Frances Lambert (*d* 6 Feb 1921), dau of Gen Sir John Lambert, GCB (*see* above), and *dsp* 1862

3a Arthur; Capt Bengal Art; *m* Louisa Basilia Bishop (*m* 2nd 27 Jan 1874 Capt Bruce, RN) and *dsp*

4a Rowley, CB; *b* 22 April 1828; V-Adml; *m* 5 Feb 1863 Helen Elizabeth, dau of James Campbell, and *dsp* 22 July 1880

5a Frederick William; Col IA; *m* his cousin Mary Jane (*d* 18 March 1877), dau of Gen Sir John Lambert, GCB (*see* above) and *dsp*

The 2nd Bt *d* 4 Feb 1772; his est s,

Sir John Lambert, 3rd Bt; *b* 11 Oct 1728; *m* 9 Aug 1752 Mary, dau of Toussaints Lieniepes, of Geneva, and *d* 21 May 1799, having had an only surv s:

Sir Henry Lambert, 4th Bt; *b* 1760; *m* 1788 Sophia (*m* 2nd 14 Feb 1805 Lt-Col Henry Francis Greville (*see* WARWICK, BROOKE and, E) and *d* 21 March 1839), dau of Francis Xavier Whyte, and had:

1 HENRY JOHN (Sir), **5th Bt**

2 Frederick John; RN; *d* India 9 April 1813

3 Francis John; *b* 28 Feb 1798; *m* 17 Oct 1826 Catherine (*d* 7 Feb 1851), only dau of Maj-Gen Wheatley, of Lesney, Kent, and *d* 13 April 1876, having had, with other issue:

(1) Ernest John; *b* 29 Dec 1829; *m* 12 July 1869 (*divorce* 1889) Alice Maude Eveleen, dau of Capt Charles Thomas Murray, 86th Regt, and *d* 7 Sept 1907, leaving:

1a Frank Alexander Brooke Orr Murray; *b* 9 April 1870; *m* 15 Dec 1903 Marie, dau of Emile Kühne, of Stein-am-Rhein, and *d* 1952

(2) Alan; *b* 14 Jan 1837; *m* 6 Sept 1864 Jane Anne (*d* 15 June 1924), dau of Col Jasper Hall, Coldstream Gds, and *d* 24 Dec 1927, having had:

1a Mortan; *b* 8 Sept 1866; *m* 16 Oct 1902 Clotilde Louise (*d* 20 Feb 1849), 2nd dau of Victor Jaccoud, of Rumilly, Haute Savoie, France, and *d* 25 June 1926, leaving:

1b Montague Victor; *b* 26 Aug 1904; *educ* Winchester and New Coll Oxford; G/Capt RAFVR WW II, Dir Policy Air Div CCG 1944–46; *m* 1st 27 Oct 1931 Ena Sylvia Victoria (*d* 20 March 1944), dau of George Grossmith; *m* 2nd 20 Aug 1948 Janis Mary (*d* 1988), dau of Capt Wilfrid Brittain Squirl-Dawson, of Higham, Suffolk, and by her had:

2c +Charles Geoffrey Mortan; *b* 9 Oct 1956

1b Gisèle Joan; *b* 29 April 1907; *m* 1st 4 July 1934 (*divorce* 1939) Oliver Noel Marie le Mire, 4th Zouaves (French Army), est s of Jacques le Mire, of Les Varraches, Mouchard, France; *m* 2nd Hugh Pearson Gee (*d* 1965)

2a Lionel Lambert (Rev); *b* 25 May 1869; *educ* Ch Ch Oxford (MA); FSA, Rector Stafford 1904–44; *d* unm Nov 1948

3a Jasper; *b* 25 Sept 1872; *educ* Winchester; *m* 21 April 1898 Cecil (*d* 1964), yst dau of William Forsyth, QC, LLD, of Knightsbridge, and *d* 4 March 1949, leaving:

1b Alan Forsyth; *b* 24 Feb 1901; *m* 20 Feb 1936 Olive Edith (*d* 1990), dau of Frederick Long, and had:

1c +Philip Jasper [Philip Lambert Esq, 1 Burwood Cl, Ringley Pk Rd, Reigate, Surrey]; *b* 17 Sept 1936

1b Marjorie Cecil; *b* 1 Feb 1899

2b *Joyce Marion; *b* 25 Aug 1908; *m* 30 Aug 1941 *Gerald David Alexander McPherson and has:

1c *David William Alan; *b* 29 April 1943

2c *Jasper Alexander Cecil; *b* 25 Oct 1947

1a Lilian Catherine; *b* 31 July 1869; *d* unm 24 Dec 1957

The 4th Bt *d* 21 Jan 1803; his est s,

Sir Henry John Lambert, 5th Bt; *b* 5 Aug 1792; *m* 7 May 1821 Anna Maria (*d* 5 March 1857), yr dau of Hon Edward Foley (*see* FOLEY, B), and *d* 17 Dec 1858, having had, with other issue:

1 **Sir Henry Edward Francis Lambert, 6th Bt**; *b* 7 June 1822; *m* 11 April 1860 Eliza Catherine (*d* 17 Feb 1898), 2nd dau of Col Lionel Charles Hervey (*see* HERVEY-BATHURST, Bt), and *d* 5 June 1872, leaving:

(1) Sir HENRY FOLEY LAMBERT later GREY (roy licence 27 July 1905 under terms of will of 7th Earl of Stamford, *see* 1970 edn), **7th Bt**, JP (Staffs), JP and DL (Worcs); *b* 21 Jan 1861; High Sheriff Worcs 1901, Lt-Col cmdg Worcester Yeomanry (TD), Mayor Stourbridge 1914; *m* 14 June 1883 Catherine Sarah (*d* 30 Aug 1925), dau of Rev Alfred Payne, Rector Enville, Staffs, and *d* 17 Dec 1914, leaving:

1a **Sir John Foley Grey, 8th Bt**, of Enville Hall, Staffs (previously seat of Lord Stamford); *b* 8 July 1893; Lt 15th Hus, served WW I (wounded); *m* 1st 4 July 1919 (*divorce* 1927) Jean Jessie Mary (*d* 9 April 1933), only dau of Capt Frank Lewis de Sales La Terrière, of Marr Hill, Glos, formerly w of Howard Montague Bulmer de Sales La Terrière; *m* 2nd 11 Oct 1934 Sybil St Leger (*d* 9 Feb 1952), er dau of Maj Frederick Howard Wingfield Fetherstonhaugh, formerly w of C T Aldridge, of Sketchley, Leics, and *d* 17 March 1938, having by his 1st w had:

1b *Eileen Grey [Mrs John Bissill, Enville Hall, Stourbridge, Worcs]; *b* 1 Feb 1922; *m* 1st 5 Feb 1942 (*divorce* 1947) 11th Earl of Harrington (*qv*) and has issue; *m* 2nd 23 Jan 1947 John Philip Bissill, MC (*d* 1988), yst s of William Norman Bissill, of Cranmer Ho, Ashlockton, Notts, and by him has:

1c *Alexandra Diana [Mrs Peter Williams, The Home Farm, Enville, Stourbridge, Worcs]; *b* 1950; *m* 1979 *Peter Brinton Williams and has:

1d *Harry John; *b* 1981

2d *George Edward; *b* 1985

1d *Jane Charlotte; *b* 1982

1a Dorothy Catherine; *b* 7 Sept 1884; *m* 1st 18 Sept 1912 (*divorce*) John Edric Lloyd, of Enville Ranch, Alberta, Canada, and had issue; *m* 2nd 1926 Ray Patterson (*d* 1945); *m* 3rd 1947 (*divorce* 1955) Earl G Terry

2a Phyllis Kathleen; *b* 14 June 1887

3a Joan Cecil; *b* 18 May 1892; *d* unm 4 June 1972

4a Geraldine Ida; *b* 13 June 1898; *m* 1st 20 Oct 1926 (*divorce* 1938) 4th Baron Ashtown (*qv*); *m* 2nd April 1938 Edmond Robert Richard O'Brien, (*see* O'BRIEN, Bt) and *dsp* following an accident 11 Oct 1940

5a Mary Alice; *b* 8 Sept 1899; *m* 25 Aug 1927 Sir David Edmond O'Brien, 6th Bt (*qv*), and had issue

(2) Felton Edward Foley; *b* 20 June 1862; Lt Border Regt; *d* unm 22 April 1885

(3) Cecil Foley Lambert (Sir), KCB (1920); *b* 28 May 1864; Adml; Jr Ld Admlty 1913–16, Dir Personnel Air Ministry, additional memb Air Cncl 1919–21, served Egypt 1882 (medal and star) and WW I, Cdr Legn Hon; *m* 1896 Rosina (*d* 25 Nov 1933), dau of Francis Drake, of Brixham, Devon, and *d* 29 Feb 1928

(4) Lionel Foley; *b* 28 Jan 1867; *m* 27 May 1893 Isabel Anne (*d* 5 Feb 1925), dau of Rev Frederick George Blomfield, and *d* 22 March 1934, having had:

1a **Sir Greville Foley Lambert, 9th Bt**; *b* 17 Aug 1900; *educ* Rugby; chartered accountant; *m* 15 July 1932 *(Edith) Roma [Roma Lady Lambert, Flat 5 Henleydale, Stratford Rd, Shirley, Solihull, Warwicks], dau of Richard Batson, and *d* 1988, leaving:

1b *(Isabel) Pamela [Mrs Denys Taaffe, 6 St Matthew's Hill, Wadebridge, Cornwall PL27 6DX]; *b* 26 April 1933; *m* 20 Oct 1979 *Denys Leonard Taaffe, s of Leonard Charles Taaffe, of Woking

2b (Roma) Ann; *b* 31 Oct 1934; *m* 15 Dec 1956 *Gp Capt Colin John Phillips, RAF [Gp Capt Colin Phillips, Seeneedles, Keyhaven, Hants SO41 0TJ], 2nd s of Arthur William Phillips, of King's Norton, Birmingham and *d* 17 Sept 1997, leaving:

1c *David Jonathan; *b* 9 May 1958; *m* 1992 *Joanne Susan Shore and has:

1d *Matthew James; *b* 1993

1d *Rachel Ann; *b* 1995

2c *Adrian Greville; *b* 10 Dec 1959; *m* 1982 *Patricia Lyons and has:

1d *Sarah May; *b* 1991

2d *Elizabeth Louise; *b* 1993

1c *Carolyn Ann; *b* 25 April 1962; *m* 1986 *Stuart Brown and has:

1d *Samuel Jonathan; *b* 1993

1d *Charlotte Ann; *b* 1989

2d *Rebecca Emily; *b* 1991

3b *Carole Joy [Mrs Colin Russell, 16 High House Drive, Inkberrow, Worcs WR7 4EG]; *b* 30 May 1940; *m* 1st 10 Nov 1960 (*divorce* 1964) Raymond Bennett; *m* 2nd 1968 (*divorce* 1987) Nicholas Jason Hill; *m* 3rd 1991 *Colin Geoffrey Russell and by her 2nd husb has:

1c *Jason Stirling; *b* 9 Aug 1970; *m* 26 April 1997 *Celia Elizabeth, dau of David Wall, of Melton Mowbray

1c *Michelle Jane; *b* 6 Dec 1973

(1) Evelyn Frances; *b* 1863; *d* unm 30 July 1894

(2) Edith Charlotte; *b* 1865; *m* 18 Jan 1894 Lt-Col Arthur Berkeley Drummond and *d* 9 Jan 1919, leaving issue (*see* PERTH, E)

(3) Alice Emily; *b* 1 March 1868; *d* unm 8 Sept 1926

(4) Ida Mary; *b* 8 April 1869; *m* 23 April 1903 Rev Hubert Humphrey Middlemore Bartlett, Hon Canon Worcester, s of Thomas Saunders Bartlett by Elizabeth Middlemore, and *d* 1 Aug 1955, leaving issue

(5) Georgina Adelaide; *b* 19 July 1870; *d* unm 16 May 1954

2 Edward Henry Gage; *b* 27 May 1825; Capt RN; *m* 7 Sept 1865 Renira Anna (*m* 2nd 21 July 1874 Adml Hon Fitzgerald Algernon Charles Foley (*see* FOLEY, B) and *d* 16 Oct 1926), yr dau of Rev Richard Fortescue Purvis, LLB, Vicar Whitsbury, Hants, and *d* 16 Nov 1872, leaving:

(1) Francis John (Rev); *b* 23 Nov 1866; *educ* Oxford (BA); *d* 1892

(2) Fitzgerald Gage; *b* 5 Feb 1868; *m* 9 Nov 1894 Nina Marie Louise, dau of Francis Bradley Dyne, of Gore Ct, Kent, and had:

1a Francis Henry; *b* 17 Oct 1895; Lt Hants Regt; *d* 7 June 1915 from wounds recd in action Gallipoli

(1) Florence Emily; *b* 1870; *m* 1894 Rev Baron Henry Paul Hichens (*d* 2 Feb 1930), Rector Almer, Dorset, and *d* 4 June 1935, leaving issue

3 Charles Henry; *b* 4 March 1830; Capt 19th Foot; *d* Queensland 4 July 1872

4 William Henry (Rev); *b* 26 Aug 1833; *educ* Oxford (MA); Rector Stoke Edith, Herefs; *m* 12 July 1866 Georgiana Joyce (*d* 14 March 1920), 3rd dau of Robert Biddulph (*see* BIDDULPH, B), and *d* 23 Feb 1924, having had:

(1) Hugh Biddulph; *b* 21 Nov 1867; *m* 1907 Mabel Ellen (*d* 13 April 1965), 2nd dau of Frederick Wells, of Cridmore, IoW, and *d* 7 Dec 1924, leaving:

1a John Hugh; *b* 31 May 1910; RAF; *m* 1947 Edith Davies and *d* 29 Oct 1977, leaving:

1b Sir PETER JOHN BIDDULPH LAMBERT, **10th and present Bt**

2a +ROBERT WILLIAM [Robert Lambert, Route 1, Box 717, Elgin, TX 78621, USA]; *b* 6 June 1911; heir presumptive; Merchant Navy; *m* 1948 *Margaret Daphne Harvey

1a (Mabel) Joyce

2a *Nina Joan [Mrs Eric Dehn, 5 Trewawney Rd, Bristol 6]; *b* 1916; *m* 1st 1941 (*divorce* 1948) Guy Duncan Tucker and has:

1b *Michael Duncan Hugh; *b* 1941; *m* 1970 *Stephanie West and has:

1c *Rebecca; *b* 1971

2c *Zoë; *b* 1974

2a (cont.) Mrs Nina Tucker *m* 2nd 1951 *Eric Harold Dehn and by him has:

1b *Jacqueline Tessa [Mrs Robert Baxter, 83b Albion Dve, London E8]; *b* 1952; *m* 1980 *Robert Baxter

2b *Nicola Louisa Dehn; *b* 1954; *m* 1981 *Dominique Bonnard and has:

1c *Camille André Jean; *b* 1984

2c *Thomas Michel Eric; *b* 1987

3a *Julia Margaret [Miss Julia Lambert, Priory Cottage, Heythrop Rd, Chipping Norton, Oxon OX7 5TA]; *b* 1920; WAAF WW II

LANE

Creation: B. (LP,UK) 1979.

THE BARON LANE, of St Ippolitts, Co Hertford (Sir Geoffrey Dawson Lane, AFC (1943), PC (1974)) [The Rt Hon The Lord Lane AFC PC, c/o Child & Co, 1 Fleet St, London EC4]; *b* 17 July 1918; *educ* Shrewsbury and Trin Coll Cambridge; S/Ldr RAF 1942; barrister Gray's Inn 1946, QC 1962, Bencher 1966, Dep Chm Beds QS 1960–66, Recorder Bedford 1963–66, ktd 1966, High Court Judge Queen's Bench 1966–74; Ld Justice Appeal 1974–79, Ld Appeal in Ordinary 1979–80, Ld Ch Justice 1980–92; memb Parole Bd 1970–72 (V-Chm 1972); Hon Bencher Inner Temple 1980; Hon LLD Cantab 1984; *m* 1944 *Jan, dau of Donald Macdonald, and has:

1 *Richard; *b* 1948

Lineage: PERCY ALBERT LANE, of Lincoln; had:

GEOFFREY DAWSON, *cr* a **Baron**

LANE OF HORSELL

Arms: Per pale and chevron azure and or counterchanged, on a chevron gules three leopard's heads or, langued azure, all between as many mullets of six points, also counterchanged and pierced of the field. **Crest:** A demi-lion azure, head and mane or, charged on the body with pierced mullets each of six points also or, and supporting by both forepaws a branch of oak fructed of five acorns gold. **Supporters:** Dexter, a male griffin regardant argent, its head, neck, mane and forelegs or, rayed also or, beaked argent and holding in the beak a double warded key, bow downwards gold; sinister, a strawberry roan horse proper, maned and hooved or, its head elevated and regardant, holding in its jaws a double-warded key, bow downwards gold, the compartment comprising a grassy mount raised on each side and growing therefrom two springs of oak, each fructed of an acorn gold. **Motto:** *Garde le droit* ('Maintain the right'). **Creation:** B. (LP,UK) 1990.

THE BARON LANE OF HORSELL, of Woking, Co Surrey (Sir Peter Stewart Lane, JP (Surrey 1976)) [The Rt Hon The Lord Lane of Horsell JP, House of Lords, London SW1A 0PW]; *b* 29 Jan 1925; *educ* Sherborne; Sub-Lt RNVR 1943–46; ptnr Binder Hamlyn 1950 (sr ptnr 1979–92); chm: Brent Internat 1985–95, Attwoods 1994–, Elswick 1993–94, Automated Security Hldgs 1994–96; dep chm More O'Ferrall 1985–97; Govr Nuffield Nursing Homes Tst 1985–92 (Chm 1992–); Chm: Nat Union of C Assocs 1983–84 (V-Chm 1981–83, V-Pres 1984–), Exec Ctee Nat Union of C Assocs 1986–91, Action on Addiction 1991–94, Nuffield Hosps 1993–96 (dep chm 1990–93), ktd 1984; Freeman City London, FCA; *m* 1951 Doris Florence (*d* 1969), dau of Robert Simpson Botsford, and has:

1 *Rosalie; *b* 1946; *m* 1968 *2nd Baron Trefgarne (*qv*) and has issue

2 *Alexandra; *b* 1956; *m* 1978 *Rev Jeremy Peter Cresswell and has:

(1) *Caroline Ruth Anastasia; *b* 1981

(2) *Lucinda Miriam Charlotte; *b* 1983

(3) *Alice Mary Clementine; *b* 1987

Lineage: LEONARD GEORGE LANE; had:

PETER STEWART, *cr* a **Baron**

LANESBOROUGH

Arms: Argent three covered cups in bend between two bendlets engrailed. **Crest:** A demi-cockatrice couped vert, wings elevated argent, combed, beaked, wattled and ducally gorged or. **Supporters:** Dexter, a cockatrice vert, wings elevated argent, combed, beaked, wattled and ducally gorged or; sinister, a wyvern vert, gorged with a plain collar and chained or. **Motto:** *Liberté tout entière* ('Liberty entire'). **Creations:** B. (I) 21 Oct 1715, V. (I) 12 Aug 1728, E. (I) 20 July 1756.

THE 9TH EARL OF LANESBOROUGH, Viscount Lanesborough, of Co Longford, and **Baron of Newtown-Butler,** Co Fermanagh (Denis Anthony Brian Butler, TD, JP (Leics 1967), DL (Leics 1962)) [The Rt Hon The Earl of Lanesborough TD JP DL, Allerly, Gattonside, Roxburghshire TD6 9LT]; *b* 28 Oct 1918; *s* f 1950; *educ* Stowe; Maj Leics Yeo (TA) WW II, chm: Guide Dogs for the Blind Assoc 1953–64 (Pres 1964–86), Find your Feet Ltd 1960– and Melton C Assoc 1957–60, dir Spray and Burgess Ltd, pres: Cwlth Soc for Deaf Children 1961–, Leics Wildfowlers' Assoc 1955–, Young Farmers' Fedn, Gt Centl Rlwy Assoc, v-pres Amateur Judo Assoc GB, memb: Nat Gas Consumers' Cncl 1973–78, Trent RHA 1974–82 (v-chm 1978–82); *m* 1st 20 Dec 1939 (*divorce* 1950) Bettyne Ione, only dau of Sir Lindsay Everard, JP, DL, of Ratcliffe Hall, Leics, and has had:

1 Georgina Ione; *b* 15 Aug 1941; *d* 28 Dec 1947

2 *Denyne Gillian Patricia (does not use courtesy title) [Miss Denyne Butler, 12294 Imperial Dve, Richmond, BC V7E 6J6, Canada]; *b* 23 Feb 1945; Canadian citizen since 1970

The 9th EARL *m* 2nd 3 Nov 1995 *Patricia Julia, yr dau of F W Meston, MC, of Aberdeenshire

Lanesborough, previous creation: In 1676 George Lane, whose grandfather appears to have settled in Ireland in ELIZABETH I's time, was created Viscount Lanesborough. He had been the exiled CHARLES II's secretary during the Interregnum and after the Restoration was MP in the Irish Parliament for Co Roscommon and Joint Secretary for Ireland. He was also secretary to the Lord Lieutenant of Ireland the Duke of Ormonde (*see* MOUNTGARRET, V), who procured Lane's peerage for him, though Lane had pressed for an earldom (the Duke, in writing to his son, observed that it was difficult enough to get him made a viscount). On the death without issue of Lane's son the 2nd Viscount in 1724 the Viscountcy expired. Some four years before his death the 2nd and last Viscount had built at what was to become Hyde Park Corner a country seat he named Lanesborough House. This became a hospital 14 years after his death and was later known as St George's Hospital. It has now reverted to the name Lanesborough, but as a hotel.

Lineage: Sir STEPHEN BUTLER, of Clonose, Co Cavan, where he settled *temp* JAMES I; *m* Mary, dau and coheir of Gervas Brindsley, of Brindsley, Notts, and *d* 21 April 1639, leaving:

1 James, of Belturbet, Co Cavan; *d* unm

2 Stephen; MP Belturbet 1661–62; *m* 20 May 1660, as her 1st husb, Anne (*m* 2nd Raymond FitzMaurice, s of 18th Baron of Kerry and Lixnaw; (*see* LANSDOWNE, M)), dau of 1st Baron Barry of Santry, and *dsps* 12 Feb 1662

3 Francis; MP Belturbet 1662 and 1692–99; *m* Judith, dau of Rt Hon Sir Theophilus Jones, of Osberstown, Co Meath, and *d* 15 Aug 1702, leaving:

(1) THEOPHILUS BUTLER, **1st Baron of Newtown-Butler,** Co Fermanagh (I), so *cr* 21 Oct 1715, with remainder, in default of issue male, to that of his f, PC (I 1710); *b c* 1669; *educ* Trin Coll Dublin; described as being Jt Clerk Pells Ireland 1679 (when but 10), MP Co Cavan 1703–13 and Belturbet 1713–14; *m* April 1702 Emily (*d* 13 June 1722), dau of James Stopford, of Tara Hill, Co Meath, and *dsps* 11 March 1723/4

(2) BRINSLEY, **1st Viscount**

(3) James; MP; *m* Anne, sis of James Stopford, Bp Cloyne, and *dsp* 19 Nov 1742

The 1st BARON's bro,

BRINSLEY BUTLER, **1st Viscount Lanesborough,** of Co Longford (I), so *cr* 12 Aug 1728, PC (I 1726); *b c* 1672; *educ* Trin Coll Dublin; Gentleman Usher Black Rod Ireland 1711, Col Battle-axe Gds Ireland, MP Kells 1703–13 and Belturbet

1713–24; *m c* 1700 Catherine (*d* 13 Dec 1759), dau and coheir of Neville Pooley, barrister, of Dublin, and *d* 6 March 1735/6, having had, with 18 other children (*d* young):

1 HUMPHREY, **1st Earl**

2 Thomas; Govr Limerick and Adj Gen, MP Belturbet 1727–53; *m* 11 June 1730 Mary, widow of John Ormsby and dau and coheir of Duncan Cummin, and *d* 16 Dec 1753, leaving:

(1) Mary; *m* 23 July 1754 John St Leger, of Grangemellan, Co Kildare (*see* DONERAILE, V)

3 Robert; *bapt* 29 March 1704; MP Belturbet 1735–63, Capt Battle-axe Gds; *m* 30 Aug 1753 Mary, dau of Robert Howard, Bp Elphin, widow of John Stoyte, of Street, Co Westmeath, and sis of 1st Viscount Wicklow (*see* 1970 edn WICKLOW, E)

4 John; Jt Clerk of the Pipe, MP Newcastle 1743–83; *m* Mrs Harris, widow, and *d* 12 Dec 1789, leaving, with other issue:

(1) Humphrey; MP Donegal 1790–97; *m* Alicia, dau of Michael White, Govr Montserrat, and had:

1a Theophilus; Maj 4th Dragoon Gds; *d* 17 May 1847

2a Robert (Rev); Rector St John's Kilkenny; *m* — Hamilton, and *d* 14 May 1847, leaving an only dau:

1b Mary Elizabeth; *m* 1863 Frederick Townsend, JP, DL (*dsp* 16 Dec 1905), of Hornington Hall, Warwicks

3a Humphrey; Cdr RN; *m* 27 April 1852 Eliza Margaret, est dau of William Tewart, of Glanton and Swinhoe, Northumberland

1a Maria Frances; *d* 15 Nov 1874

2a Mary Sophia; *m* 17 Nov 1831 Michael Frederick Montgomerie (*d* 25 May 1867), of St Leonards-on-Sea, Sussex, and Garboldisham, Norfolk, and *d* 3 July 1866, having had issue

(1) Harriet; *m* 1792 Sir Henry Brooke, 1st Bt (*see* BROOKEBOROUGH, V)

(2) Catherine; *m* Jan 1783 Thomas Carter, of Castle Martin, Co Kildare

1 Judith; *m* 23 April 1724 Balthazar John Cramer

The 1st VISCOUNT's est s,

HUMPHREY BUTLER, **1st Earl of Lanesborough** (I), so *cr* 20 July 1756, PC (I 1749); *b c* 1700; MP Belturbet 1725–35, Sheriff Cos Cavan 1727 and Westmeath 1728, Capt Battle-axe Gds, Speaker I Ho Lds 1760; *m* (licence 14 May 1726) Mary (*d* 19 Dec 1761), dau and heiress of Richard Berry, of Wardenstown, Co Westmeath, and *d* 11 April 1768, leaving an only s:

BRINSLEY BUTLER, **2nd Earl of Lanesborough**, PC (I 1765); *b* 4 March 1728; MP Cavan 1751–68; *m* 26 June 1754 Lady Jane Rochfort (*m* 2nd John King and *d* Feb 1828), only dau of 1st Earl of Belvidere, and *d* 24 Jan 1779, having had, with other issue (including at least one dau, Mary, *m* George Ponsonby (*see* BESSBOROUGH, E) and had issue):

1 ROBERT HERBERT BUTLER, **3rd Earl of Lanesborough**; *b* 1 Aug 1759; *m* (licence 17 Jan 1781) Elizabeth (*d* 22 Sept 1788), est dau of Rt Hon David La Touche, Dublin banker, and *d* 17 April 1806, leaving:

(1) BRINSLEY BUTLER, **4th Earl of Lanesborough**; *b* 22 Oct 1783; *d* unm 13 June 1847

(2) David; *dsp*

2 Augustus Richard BUTLER later BUTLER-DANVERS (roy licence 14 Sept 1796); *b* 10 July 1776; *m* 1st 8 March 1792 Mary (*d* 10 May 1802), dau and heiress of Sir John Danvers, 2nd Bt, of Swithland, Leics, and had:

(1) GEORGE JOHN DANVERS BUTLER-DANVERS, **5th Earl of Lanesborough**; *b* 6 Dec 1794; rep I peer 1849–66; *m* 1st 29 Aug 1815 Frances Arabella (*d* 5 Oct 1850), 3rd dau of Col Stephen Francis William Fremantle; *m* 2nd 24 Nov 1851 Frederica Emma (*d* 3 Oct 1870), widow of Sir Richard Hunter, of Dulany Ho, Sussex, and yst dau of Charles Bishop, Procurator-Gen to GEORGE III, and *dsp* 7 July 1866

(2) George Augustus; *b* 5 Aug 1798; *d* young

2 (cont.) The Hon Augustus BUTLER-DANVERS *m* 2nd 24 May 1802 Eliza Bizarre (*d* 18 April 1811), dau of Humphrey Sturt, of Critchill Ho, Dorset, and *d* 26 April 1820, having by her had, with three other sons:

(3) Charles Augustus; *b* 25 Sept 1809; Capt HEICS; granted with surv siblings 1848 rank of earl's daus/yr sons; *m* 21 July 1838 Letitia Rudyerd Ross (*m* 2nd 7 April 1853 Rev George Napleton Treweeke, Rector Swithland, Leics, and *d* 5 May 1884 aged 63), dau of Col John W Freese, Madras Artillery, and *d* 8 Aug 1849, having had:

1a JOHN VANSITTART DANVERS, **6th Earl**

2a Charles Henry Danvers; *b* 22 Nov 1844; Offr 9th Foot; granted with sisters 24 Oct 1866 rank of earl's daus; *m* 20 July 1872 Alice, yr dau of George Ward, of Redditch, Worcs, and *dsp* 4 Nov 1879

1a Frances Georgina Danvers; *m* 3 July 1866 Loftus Fitzwygram and *d* 29 April 1907, leaving issue (*see* WIGRAM, Bt)

2a Emily Rosa Danvers; *m* 13 April 1869 William Vinicombe Davy and *d* 23 July 1900

3a Harriet Eliza Danvers; *m* 1st 12 July 1876 Francis Mount Barlow (*dsp* 1 April 1877); *m* 2nd 7 Jan 1886 Charles Harrison, MP (*d* 1897), and *d* 26 May 1924

(4) Henry Cavendish, of Innisrath, Co Fermanagh, DL; High Sheriff Co Cavan 1848 and Co Fermanagh 1850; *b* 18 April 1811; *m* 1st 30 June 1842 Cecilia Agnes (*dsp* 1882), dau of Gen Sir John Taylor, KCB, of Castle Taylor; *m* 2nd 5 Dec 1883 Sarah (*d* 31 Dec 1940), widow of Sir William Emerson-Tennent, 2nd Bt (*see* 1876 edn), and dau of Thomas Armstrong, of Eden Hall, Co Armagh, and *d* 5 Jan 1891, leaving:

1a Henry Halpin Cavendish, MBE (1939); *b* 23 Sept 1884; Maj Inniskilling Fus, High Sheriff Co Fermanagh 1913; *m* 9 Jan 1908 (Lucie Sophia) Blanche (*d* 1 Jan 1974), 2nd dau of Maj Gen Arthur Hales, of Bath, and *d* 10 July 1966, having had:

1b Henry Arthur Brinsley Cavendish; *b* 11 May 1909; Lt-Col RE; *educ* Rugby, RMA Woolwich and Pembroke Coll Cambridge (BA 1931); *m* 1st 24 March 1940 Ruth Ardyn (*d* following a train crash 21 Sept 1951), only dau of Lt-Col William Hugh Barton, DSO, DL, of The Waterfoot, Co Fermanagh; *m* 2nd 6 Dec 1952 *Alice Isabella, only dau of Rev George Watt, of Newry, Co Down, and by his 1st w had:

1c Timothy Hugh; *b* 2 Dec 1942; *d* with his mother in the same train crash 21 Sept 1951

2b Anthony Danvers Cavendish; *b* 13 Jan 1916; Lt NI Horse, attd 3rd Commandos WW II; *ka* 14 July 1943

1b Maureen Mary; *b* 26 May 1913; *d* unm 5 May 1945

(1) Elizabeth Sophia; *m* 1828 Col Henry Dumaresque, RE (*d* 5 March 1838) and *d* 12 March 1877, leaving issue (*see* SAINT OSWALD, B and SHEFFIELD, Bt)

(2) Emily Jane; *m* 6 Sept 1836 Capt George Somerville Digby, Gren Gds, and *d* 28 March 1895, leaving issue (*see* DIGBY, B)

The 5th EARL's n,

JOHN VANSITTART DANVERS BUTLER, **6th Earl of Lanesborough**; *b* 18 April 1839; *educ* Rugby; RN: Lt 1860, ret 1866, Capt 1881, rep I peer 1870–1905, Ld Lt Co Cavan 1877–1900 (previously DL, as also for Co Fermanagh); *m* 21 June 1864 Anne Elizabeth (*d* 10 Sept 1909), only child of Rev John Dixon Clark, of Belford Hall, Northumberland, and *d* 12 Sept 1905, having had:

1 CHARLES JOHN BRINSLEY BUTLER, **7th Earl of Lanesborough**, MVO (1909); *b* 12 Dec 1865; *educ* Eton; Lt-Col London Regt (TA), Lt-Col 3rd Bn Coldstream Gds, Assist Mil Sec to C-in-C Mediterranean 1908–09, Mil Sec to Govr Gen Canada 1909–10, rep I peer 1913; *m* 1st 31 Jan 1891 Dorothea Gwladys (*d* 11 April 1920), est dau of Maj Gen Sir Henry Tombs, VC, KCB; *m* 2nd 27 June 1922 Dorothy Kate (*d* 6 Oct 1935), formerly w of Capt Guy St Barbe Watkins and dau of James Dean Brand, and *dspms* 18 Aug 1929, having by his 1st w had:

(1) John Brinsley Danvers, *Lord Newtown Butler*; *b* 24 May 1893; *d* unm 30 Nov 1912

(1) Eileen Gwladys; train bearer to HM QUEEN MARY 1911 Coronation, Mistress Robes 1916–21; *b* 3 Nov 1891, JP, DGStJ; *m* 11 April 1912 5th Duke of Sutherland (*qv*) and *dsp* 24 Aug 1943

(2) (Moyra) Elizabeth; *b* 22 May 1899; *m* 10 Oct 1944 Brig John Leslie Weston, CBE, DSO (*d* 21 June 1963), son of John Weston, of Clifton

2 HENRY CAVENDISH, **8th Earl**

3 Francis Almeric; *b* 17 May 1872; Capt Hats Yeo; *m* 11 Feb 1902 Madeline (*d* 29 Sept 1961), dau of Richard Birkett Gibbs, and *d* 8 May 1925, leaving:

(1) Terence Brinsley John Danvers, DL (Pembs 1964); *b* 7 March 1913; *educ* RNC Dartmouth; Cdr RN WW II 1939–41 (POW); *m* 1st 24 July 1937 (*divorce* 1947) Hermione, only child of Cdr Thomas Christopher Harry Williams, MVO, RN, and had:

1a *Valentine Gay [Mrs Desmond Waterstone, 3 Greenfield Manor, Greenfield Park, Donnybrook, Dublin 4, Ireland]; *b* 11 Feb 1939; *m* 1st 10 Oct 1964 (*divorce* 1973) Arthur Clyde Nicholson, only s of Arthur Clyde Nicholson, of Dallas, Texas, and has:

1b *Felicity Gay; *b* 13 Sept 1969

1a (cont.) Mrs Valentine Nicholson *m* 2nd 13 Nov 1974 *Desmond Waterstone, s of John Valentine Comyn Waterstone, of Caterham, Surrey, and by him has:

1b *Simon John; *b* 29 Oct 1975

2b *Harry Desmond; *b* 1978

(1) (cont.) Cdr Terence Butler *m* 2nd 19 Aug 1947 (*divorce* 1970) Beryl Mary, 3rd Offr WRNS, formerly w of Frederick Kennedy Axten and yr dau of George Trotter, of Croydon; *m* 3rd 30 June 1972 (*divorce* 1974) Mrs Jacqueline Muriel, formerly w of Peter Balmer and dau of Winthorpe Greene, of Washington, DC, and *d* 1987, leaving by his 2nd w:

2a *(Clemency Anne) Susan [Mrs John Behrens, Birstwith House, Birstwith, N Yorks HG3 2PN]; *b* 20 April 1949; *educ* LMH Oxford (MA 1970, LRPS), CPA; *m* 18 May 1974 *(Clive Owen) John Behrens, circuit judge, 2nd s of William Edward Boaz Behrens, JP (*see* ROTHSCHILD, B), and has:

1b *Timothy Edward John; *b* 9 June 1978

1b *Georgina Emily Caroline; *b* 24 May 1976

3a *Charlotte Gabrielle; *b* 27 May 1951; *m* 1983 *Marek Skuratowitcz, of Poland, and has:

1b *Sophia Lara; *b* 1986

4a *Perryn Joanna; *b* 24 July 1953; *m* 1984 *Robert Hughes and has:

1b *Felix; *b* 1988

2b *Ramsey; *b* 1989

5a Teresa Jane; *b* 10 Feb 1959; *educ* Newcastle U (BSc 1980, MSc); *d* 1989

(1) *Maida Daughne Laurel [Mrs Eustace Stracey-Clitherow, The Mill Cottage, Frogmore, Hants]; *b* 20 April 1906; *m* 26 Nov 1928 Cdr Christopher Bryan Stracey-Clitherow, DSC, RN (*see* STRACEY, Bt), and has issue

4 Brian Danvers; *b* 18 April 1876; 2nd Lt KRRC; *ka* 18 Aug 1916

1 Winifred; *b* 19 April 1879; *d* unm 23 Nov 1969

The 7th EARL's bro,

HENRY CAVENDISH BUTLER, **8th Earl of Lanesborough**; *b* 2 June 1868; *m* 1st 27 Nov 1894 Isabel (*d* 1905), dau of Ralph Allen Daniell, and had:

1 Freda, CBE; *b* 8 Sept 1895; *m* 26 March 1931 Francis Cyril Oliphant Valentine, MRCS, MRCP (*d* 23 March 1957), yr s of William Roderick Harris Valentine, of Lochee, Dundee, and has:

(1) *(William) Danvers Oliphant [Danvers Valentine Esq, Ballyonkan House, Pitlochry PH16 5JS]; *b* 17 April 1933

(2) *Francis Anthony Brinsley (James) [James Valentine Esq, 1 Holbury St, London SW10 0JD; Gaze House, Astrop, Oxon]; *b* 3 Sept 1935

2 (Hilda) Vivien; *b* 18 April 1900; WW II as Co Cdr ATS; *m* 30 April 1921 John William Henry Berkeley Younger, of Easter Park, Davidsons Mains, Edinburgh, and Eckford, by Dunoon, Argyll, s of Harry George Younger, of Benmore, Kilmun, Argyll, and *d* 14 Sept 1960, leaving issue

The **8th Earl** *m* 2nd 6 Dec 1917 Grace Lillian (*d* 1983), est dau of Sir Anthony Charles Sykes Abdy, 3rd Bt (*qv*), and *d* 22nd Aug 1950, having by her had:

1 DENIS ANTHONY BRIAN BUTLER, **9th and present Earl**

2 Patrick Henry Stanley Danvers; *b* 27 Dec 1920; Capt Scots Gds WW II (despatches twice); *ka* Anzio 28 Feb 1944

Lang of Monkton

Arms: Tierced per fess vert, azure, and vert two thistle stalks slipped and leaved fessways and conjoined at the bases argent at the centre point, between two acorns slipped and leaved or in chief and a three-masted sailing ship sails furled in base or, and at the honour point a fleur-de-lys of the last. **Crest:** A stock dove holding in the beak an olive branch slipped and leaved proper. **Motto:** (over the arms) *Sois vrai* ('Be true'). **Creation:** B. (LP, UK) 1997.

THE BARON LANG OF MONKTON, of Merrick and the Rhinns of Kells, Dumfries and Galloway (Ian Bruce Lang, PC (1990)) [The Rt Hon The Lord Lang of Monkton PC, House of Lords, London SW1A 0PW]; *b* 27 June 1940; *educ* Lathallan Sch Kincardineshire, Rugby and Sidney Sussex Coll Cambridge; dir: Rose Thompson Young & Co 1966–75, Hutchinson & Craft 1975–81, Hutchinson & Craft (Underwriting Agents) Lloyd's 1976–81, P MacCallum & Sons 1976–81, Glasgow Chamber Commerce 1978–81, Gen Accident 1997–; Tstee: Savings Bank Glasgow 1969–74, W of Scotland TSB 1974–83; MP (C) Galloway 1979–83 and Galloway and Upper Nithsdale 1983–97, Assist Govt Whip 1981–83, Ld Commr Treasury 1983–86, Parly U-Sec: Employment 1986, Scottish Office 1986–87, Min State Scottish Office 1987–90, Sec State Scotland and Ld Keeper Gt Seal Scotland 1990–95, Pres BOT 1995–97, Memb Select Ctee Scottish Affrs 1979–81, V-Chm C Party Scotland 1983–87, Pres Scottish YCs 1982–84; OStJ 1974; *m* 1971 *Sandra Caroline, est dau of John Alastair Montgomerie, DSc, and has two daus

Lineage: JAMES FULTON LANG, DSc; *m* Maude Margaret Stewart and has:
IAN BRUCE, *cr* a **Baron**

Langford

Arms: Quarterly, 1st and 4th, sable on a bend argent cotised ermine a rose gules, barbed and seeded proper, between two annulets sable (for CONWY); 2nd and 3rd, argent on a bend cotised gules three crescents argent (for ROWLEY). **Crests:** 1 A wolf's head couped at the shoulder sable, collared argent (for ROWLEY): 2 On a wreath argent and sable, a moor's head couped at the shoulders sable, wreathed about the temples and tied at the back with the ribbons argent and sable (for CONWY). **Supporters:** Dexter, a wolf sable collared and from the collar a chain reflexed over the back argent; sinister, a horse argent crined, hooved, collared and from the collar a chain over the back sable. **Motto:** *Fide et amore* ('Faith and love'). **Creation:** B. (I) 1 July 1800.

THE 9TH BARON LANGFORD OF SUMMERHILL, Co Meath (Geoffrey Alexander Rowley-Conwy, OBE (1943), DL (Clwyd 1977)) [Col The Rt Hon The Lord Langford OBE DL, Bodrhyddan, Rhuddlan, Clwyd LL18 5SB]; *b* 8 March 1912; *s* kinsman 1953; *educ* Marlborough and RMA Woolwich; Hon Col 1967, RA WW II Singapore (POW, escaped) and Indian Mtd Artillery Burma (Arakan, Kohima) (despatches), Lt-Col 1945, Staff Coll Quetta, DAQMG Berlin Air Lift 1948–49, GSO(1) 42 (Lancs) Div TA 1949–52, 1957, Hon Col 470 Light Air Def Regt RA (TA) 1961, Constable Rhuddlan Castle; *m* 1st 24 Jan 1939 (*divorce* 1956) Ruth St John (*d* 1991), dau of Albert St John Murphy, of The Island Ho, Little Island, Co Cork; *m* 2nd 7 Feb 1957 Grete (*d* 16 Jan 1973), dau of Col Erik Theodor Christian von Friesleben, of Hjortekaer, Kongens Lyngby, Copenhagen, Ch King's Adj's Staff to HM THE KING OF DENMARK, and by her has:

1 *Peter Alexander [Prof The Hon Peter Rowley-Conwy, 17 St John's Rd, Neville's Cross, Co Durham]; *b* 1951; *educ* Marlborough and Magdalene Coll Cambridge (MA, PhD Archaeology); lecturer Durham U to 1996, Prof 1996–; *m* 1979 *Deborah Jane, only dau of Col John H G Stevens, RE, of All Hallows Cottage, Middle St, Brockham, Dorking, and has:
(1) *Gabrielle Catrin; *b* 1984
(2) *Eleanor; *b* 1986

2 *John Seymour [The Hon John Rowley-Conwy, 66 Fentiman Rd, London SW8]; *b* 1955; *educ* Marlborough, Magdalene Coll Cambridge (BA) and Oriel Coll Oxford (MSc); *m* 1983 *Emma Josephine, dau of Maj Peter Brown, of Longworth, Oxon, and has:
(1) *William Geoffrey Peter; *b* 1988
(2) *Huw Grenville; *b* 1993
(1) *Katherine Grete Clare; *b* 1985

3 +OWAIN GRENVILLE [The Hon Owain Rowley-Conwy, The Stone House, Bodrhyddan, Rhuddlan, Clwyd LL18 5SB]; *b* 27 Dec 1958; *educ* Marlborough and RAC Cirencester; *m* 1986 (*divorce* 1993) Joanna, dau of Jack Featherstone, of Cae Siôn, Trefnant, Clwyd, and has:
(1) +Thomas Alexander; *b* 20 March 1987
(1) *Madeleine Guinevere; *b* 1988

The 9th BARON *m* 3rd 3 Feb 1975 *Susan Winifred, dau of Cyril Charles Henry Denham, of Chester, and by her has:
4 +Christopher Geoffrey Hugh; *b* 19 March 1978
1 *Charlotte Susan Gabrielle; *b* 9 Oct 1980

Lineage (of Rowley): WILLIAM ROWLEY, of Lawton, Cheshire; *m* Ellen, dau of Hugh Brereton, of Wimersley, and had:
1 John; had an only s (William, *d* young)
2 Robert; *m* Agnes, dau of Richard Yardley
3 William, of Lawton; living 1663; ancestor of the ROWLEYs of Lawton
4 Hugh, had, with two other sons (Nathaniel; William; also settled NI):
(1) John, of Castle Roe; settled NI *temp* JAMES I; had:
1a Edward, of Castle Roe; MP Co Londonderry 1634 and 1635; *m* Lettice, sis of 1st Viscount Massereene (*see* MASSEREENE and FERRARD, V), and had issue:
1b John (Sir); MP; *b* 1635; *m* 26 Dec 1671 Mary, est dau and heiress of Sir Hercules Langford, Bt, of Somerhill, Co Meath, and *d*, leaving, with a dau (Letitia, *m* 3rd and last Viscount Loftus of Ely; *see* ELY, M):

1c Hercules; MP Co Londonderry; *m* 3 Jan 1705 Frances, dau of Arthur Upton, of Castle Upton, and *d* 19 Sept 1742, leaving:

1d Hercules Langford, of Summerhill, Co Meath, PC (I); *b c* 1714; High Sheriff Co Meath 1738, MP Co Londonderry 1743–60 and Co Meath 1761–94; *m* 31 Oct 1732 Elizabeth Ormsby (*b* 1713; *d* 16 Dec 1791), Viscountess Langford of Langford Lodge, Co Antrim, in her own right, so *cr* 19 Feb 1766, as also Baroness Summerhill, Co Meath (both I), with remainder to the heirs male of her body by her then husb, only dau of Clotworthy Upton, of Castle Upton, Co Antrim, by Jane (dau and in her issue heir of John Ormsby, of Ballyvenogue, Co Limerick), and *d* 25 March 1794, leaving issue:

1e HERCULES ROWLEY, 2nd and last VISCOUNT LANGFORD OF LANGFORD LODGE; *b* 29 Oct 1737; MP Co Antrim 1782–91; *d* unm 24 March 1796, when his titles expired

2e Clotworthy; Maj 5th Dragoons; *m* 20 Jan 1775 Elizabeth, dau of William Crosbie and gdau maternally of 1st Baron Mornington (*see* WELLINGTON, D), and *d* 1781, leaving:

1f Frances; *b c* 1775; inherited her unc Lord Langford's estates; *m* Jan 1794 her 1st cousin **1st Baron Langford of Summerhill** and *d* 30 April 1860, leaving issue

3e Arthur; *d* unm

1e Jane; *m* 4 July 1754 1st Earl of Bective and had, with other issue:

1f THOMAS TAYLOUR, 1st MARQUESS OF HEADFORT (*qv*)

2f Hercules

3f Robert

4f CLOTWORTHY TAYLOUR later ROWLEY (26 April 1796), **1st Baron Langford of Summerhill** (I), so *cr* 31 July 1800 for changing his vote against the Union of I and GB Parls the year before to one in favour; *b* 31 Oct 1763; MP Trim 1791–95 and Co Meath 1795–1800, Sheriff Co Meath 1796; *m* 1794 his cousin Frances (*see* above) and *d* 13 Sept 1825, leaving:

1g HERCULES LANGFORD ROWLEY, **2nd Baron Langford of Summerhill**, DL (Cos Dublin and Meath); *b* 1795; *m* 1818 Louisa Augusta (*m* 2nd April 1840 George Edward Gustard and *d* 27 Feb 1874), dau of William Rhodes, and *d* 3 June 1839, leaving:

1h CLOTWORTHY WELLINGTON WILLIAM ROBERT ROWLEY, **3rd Baron Langford of Summerhill**; *b* 24 July 1824; *educ* Eton; Lt 7th Foot 1844–46; *m* 28 July 1846 Louisa Augusta (accidentally drowned 4 Nov 1853), dau of Col Edward Michael Conolly, MP (*see* LONGFORD, E), of Castletown, Co Kildare, and *d* 19 July 1854, leaving:

1i HERCULES EDWARD ROWLEY, **4th Baron Langford of Summerhill**, KCVO, JP, DL (Co Meath); *b* 1 June 1848; *educ* Eton; Lt-Col Gren Gds 1879, rep I peer 1884, State Steward to Ld Lt Ireland 1886–92 and Comptroller 1895–1902; *m* 1st 11 July 1889 Georgina Mary (*d* 16 Dec 1901), 6th dau of Sir Richard Sutton, 4th Bt (*qv*); *m* 2nd 20 Nov 1915 Margaret Antonia (*d* 9 Nov 1976), dau of Rev William Mitchell-Carruthers, by Antonia, dau of Rev Atkinson Alexander Holden, of Nuttall Temple, Notts, and *d* 29 Oct 1919, having by his 1st w had:

1j JOHN HERCULES WILLIAM ROWLEY, **5th Baron Langford of Summerhill**; *b* 16 Dec 1894; *d* 29 Sept 1922

2j George Cecil; *b* 18 Aug 1896; 2nd Lt 5th Bn KRRC; *ka* 17 Feb 1917

1j Noel Maud; *b* 25 Dec 1893; *d* unm 28 Jan 1916

2i WILLIAM CHAMBRÉ ROWLEY, **6th Baron Langford of Summerhill**; *b* 30 Aug 1849; Lt-Col RA, served Afghan War 1879–80 and WW I (Croix de Guerre), memb Gentlemen-at-Arms 1899–1922; *m* 24 July 1889 Hon Mabel Maud Legh (*d* 12 May 1966 aged 102), dau of 1st Baron Newton (*qv*), and *dsp* 22 Jan 1931

3i Randolfe Thomas; RN; *b* 22 Dec 1852; *m* 4 Oct 1883 Rosetta (*d* 25 Nov 1921), dau of Thomas Henry Fletcher, of Homewood, Kati Kati, NZ, and Addison Lodge, Dublin, and *d* 22 Dec 1910, having had:

1j CLOTWORTHY WELLINGTON THOMAS EDWARD ROWLEY, **7th Baron Langford of Summerhill**; *b* 1 June 1885; NZ Forces WW I; *m* 26 April 1922 Florence Eileen O'Donovon, 2nd dau of Isaac Shiel, of Ballsbridge, Dublin, and *d* 15 July 1952, having had:

1k Clotworthy Alexander; *b* 10 Dec 1923; *d* 15 March 1924

1j Doris Louisa; *b* 6 Oct 1887; *d* 4 June 1893

1i Catharine Frances; *b* 24 May 1847; *m* 5 April 1877 James Lenox Napier, DL (*d* 4 Dec 1901), of Loughcrew, and *d* 13 Jan 1879, leaving issue

2h Hercules Langford Boyle, JP, DL, of Marlay Grange, Co Dublin; *b* 19 June 1828; Hon Col 5th Bn Leinster Regt, High Sheriff Co Meath 1859, Capt 6th Dragoons; *m* 3 Nov 1857 Louisa Jane (*d* 29 Oct 1916), sis of 1st Baron Blythswood (*see* 1940 edn), and *d* 20 March 1904, having had:

1i Hercules Douglas Edward, JP, DL (Co Dublin); *b* 1 Aug 1859; Lt 5th Bn Leinster Regt; *m* 7 Oct 1884 Agnes Mary (*d* 1 March 1947), only dau of A Allen, of Devizes, Wilts, and *d* 15 Dec 1945, leaving:

1j Ivy Mabel Armine Douglas; *m* 26 Oct 1910 Reginald Stanley Lewis Boulter (*d* 5 April 1929), est s of Stanley Boulter, JP, of Garston Park, Surrey

2j Monica Evelyn Douglas; *m* 1st 27 April 1912 (*divorce* 1930, resumed maiden name by deed poll 1931) Edward Huskinson (*d* 3 April 1947), s of W L Huskinson, of Epperstone, Notts; *m* 2nd 2 Jan 1947 Capt Guy Hardy MacCaw, MC (*d* 28 Dec 1952), only surv s of William John MacGreagh MacCaw, MP

2i ARTHUR SHOLTO LANGFORD ROWLEY, **8th Baron Langford of Summerhill**, CMG (1928); *b* 10 Dec 1870; Lt 5th Bn Leinster Regt, Consul Tahiti 1909–12 and Bordeaux 1912, Consul-Gen Barcelona 1918–23, Antwerp 1923–30 and Paris 1930–32, ktd 1932; *m* 1st 23 June 1908 Margarita Ines (*d* 1 Jan 1928), dau of Hugh Robert F Jamison, of Iquique, Chile; *m* 2nd 1929 Maude Alice (*d* 1958), 2nd dau of Henri Lelacheur, of Guernsey, and *dsp* 19 Aug 1953

1i Armine Charlotte; *d* unm 16 Feb 1939

2i Gladys Helen Louisa; *m* 5 May 1887, as his 1st w, Claude Hume Campbell Guinness (*see* GUINNESS, Bt) and *d* 23 March 1891, leaving issue

3i Evelyn Augusta; *m* 19 Jan 1897 Maj Edward Milner, Scots Gds (*see* MILNER, Bt), and *d* 7 Aug 1932

3h Hugh; *b* 18 June 1833; 16th Lancers; *m* 1st 10 Jan 1852 (*divorce* 1859) Theresa Caroline, 2nd dau of John Bishop, of Sunbury Ho, Middlesex, and Ascot Lodge, Berks; *m* 2nd 17 Jan 1874 Caroline Frances, dau of John Green, of Ormiston Lodge, Scotland, and *dsp* 12 May 1908

2g Richard Thomas, DL (Flints); *b* 1812; MP Harwich 1860–65, Capt Scots Gds, Hon Col 6th Bn KRRC; *m* 1st 24 June 1835 Charlotte (*d* 29 June 1871), dau of William Shipley (*see* **Lineage of Conwy** below); *m* 2nd 9 July 1872 Alice Henrietta (*dsp* 7 Aug 1884), 2nd dau of Capt Hugh Berners, RN, JP, DL, and *d* 11 Nov 1887, leaving by his 1st w:

1h Conwy Grenville Hercules ROWLEY later ROWLEY-CONWY (1871), of Bodrhyddan, Flints, DL; *b* 6 Jan 1841; High Sheriff 1876, Capt 2nd Life Gds; *m* 20 May 1869 Marian (*d* 4 Sept 1911), 2nd dau of Frederick Harford, of Down Place, Berks, and *d* 18 Jan 1900, leaving:

1i Maurice William Glyn; *b* 27 March 1874; *d* 26 Jan 1913

2i Rafe Grenville, CMG (1917), JP (Flints); *b* 11 Sept 1875; Flints: High Sheriff 1929, Ld Lt 1935–51, Ld Manor Rhuddlan, served WW I (despatches) and WW II (Cdre RNR, N Atlantic Convoys, US DSM), R-Adml; *d* unm 4 April 1951

3i Geoffrey Seymour; *b* 14 Sept 1877; Capt Roy N Lancs Regt; *m* 7 June 1911 Bertha Gabrielle, JP, dau of Lt Alexander Cochran, RN, of Ashkirk, Selkirk, and was *ka* Gallipoli 10 Aug 1915, leaving:

1j GEOFFREY ALEXANDER ROWLEY-CONWY, **9th and present Baron Langford of Summerhill**

1j *Rose Marian [The Hon Mrs Skinner, The Fold, Cwm, Dyserth, Clwyd]; *b* 6 June 1915; granted March 1955 rank of baron's dau; *m* 11 Aug 1938 Ralph Becher Skinner (*d* 1994), s of Edward Becher Skinner, of Bicknoller, Murdock Rd, Wokingham, and has:

1k *David Rafe [David Skinner Esq, 28 Natal St, Bellvue E 2198, S Africa]; *b* 8 July 1939; *educ* Denstone Coll; agency inspr Scottish Amicable Life Assur, late 2nd Lt HAC; *m* 1981 *Shirley, dau of Francis James Fulton Starrett

1k *Meriel Ann [Mrs Jasper Garnham, Harewood Lodge, Bulstrode Way, Gerrards Cross, Bucks]; *b* 12 April 1941; SRN 1963; *m* 26 Oct 1963 *Jasper Meredydd Garnham, yr s of Prof Percy Cyril Claude Garnham, CMG, FRS, MD, of Southernwood, Farnham Common, Bucks

2k *Rosalind Hope [Miss Rosalind Skinner, 83 Links Way, Croxley Green, Rickmansworth, Herts]; *b* 22 Nov 1942

4i Ivor Harford; *b* 26 Jan 1884; *d* 1904

1i Gwladys Freda; *m* 25 Feb 1892 Hugh Edmund Peel (*d* 25 June 1950), of Bryn-y-pys, Flints, and *d* 14 Aug 1931, leaving issue

1h Gwenwydd Frances; *m* 1st 15 Sept 1864 Capt H S Pakenham (*see* LONGFORD, E); *m* 2nd 2 Jan 1866 Hugh Henry Erskine (*d* 4 Jan 1907), 3rd s of Sir David Erskine, 1st Bt (*qv*), of Cambo, and *d* 8 June 1932

2h Eva; *m* 18 Jan 1872 Adml Leverson E H Somerset (*see* BEAUFORT, D) and *dsp* 29 Dec 1904

1g Elizabeth Jane; *m* 7 April 1825 Adml George Ferguson of Pitfour, MP (*d* 15 March 1867), and *d* 12 Aug 1864, leaving issue

2g Harriet; *m* 11 April 1939 Chevalier Antoine de Satgé (*d* 1869)

2e Catherine; *m* 25 June 1768 2nd Baron Longford (*see* LONGFORD, E) and had issue

Lineage (of Conwy): HUGH CONWY, allegedly fifth in male-line descent from Sir William Coniers, supposedly High Constable England *temp* WILLIAM I (THE CONQUEROR), which, however, presupposes that each s was born when his f was on average *c* 60, an extremely unlikely pattern in an age of early marriages and short life expectancy; had:

Sir HENRY CONWY; living 1399; *m* a dau of Sir Hugh Crevequer (living 1394), feudal Ld of Prestatyn, descended from Sir Robert Crevequer (*d* 1316), who exchanged Leeds Castle, Kent, for lands in Denbighs and Flints, and had:

RICHARD CONWY; feudal Ld of Prestatyn; had:

JOHN CONWY, called in Welsh *Siôn aer y Conwy* ('John, heir of the CONWY's); *m* Elen, dau of Sir Harry Torbock/Torbox, of Torbock, nr Liverpool, and *d* 21 Sept 1321, leaving:

JENKIN CONWY, of Rhuddlan; *b c* 1415; *m* Marsli, dau of Maredudd ap Hywel ap Dafydd, of Cefn-y-fan, Dolbenmaen, Caernarvs, and *d* 1445?, leaving:

JOHN CONWY, called *Siôn aer hen* ('John the old heir'); *b c* 1435; *m* 1st Alice Minshall, of Cheshire, and had:

1 Hugh (Sir); *b c* 1453; Esq of the Body, Keeper Gt Wardrobe 1485, Treas Ireland 1494 and Calais 1504; *m* 1st Elizabeth, sis of 6th and 7th Earls of Devon (*qv*) of the Feb 1334/5 *cr*; *m* 2nd Joice, widow of Richard Burdett, and *d* after 12 March 1517 but probably before 23 May 1518, leaving issue

JOHN CONWY *m* 2nd Jonet, dau of Edmund Stanley, of Hooton (for whose earlier ancestry *see* DERBY, E), and *d* 9 Sept 1486, leaving by her, with five daus:

2 JOHN

3 James; ancestor of the CONWYs of Sychdyn/Soughton, Northop, Flints

4 Harry, of Parc Insi, Rhuddlan

5 Edward; *m* Ann, dau of Richard Burden, of Arrow Court, Warwicks, and was ancestor of the CONWAYs of Alcester and Ragley, Warwicks (*see* HERTFORD, M)

6 Pi(e)rs; Archdeacon St Asaph

The est s by the 2nd w,

JOHN CONWY, called *Siôn aer ifanc* ('John the younger heir'); *m* Jonet (*d* 1526/7), dau of Thomas *Hen* ('The Old') Salesbury, and *d* 1523/4, leaving, with an est s (John, *b c* 1472, *dsp* 6 Feb 1491/2), three yst sons (Pi(e)rs, *dsp*; Robert; Fulk, *dsp*) and 10 daus (one of whom was probably the Lowri who *m* Pi(e)rs ap Richard, of Talacre; *see* MOSTYN, Bt):

THOMAS CONWY; *b c* 1473; *m* Alice, dau of Robert Chantrel, then of Rhuddlan but whose family were of Cheshire origin, and *d* 1524/5, leaving, with two yr sons (Robert, of Hawarden, Flints; Thomas, of Rhuddlan) and two daus:

JOHN CONWY; *b c* 1518; MP Flints 1558; *m* Elizabeth (*d* 1560), dau of Sir Thomas Hanmer (*see* HANMER, Bt), and *d c* 1559, leaving, with seven daus:

JOHN CONWY; *b c* 1538?; High Sheriff Flints 1558–59, MP Flints and Flint town 1562–67; *m* 1st Anne/Jane, dau of Robert Salesbury, of Y Rug, Corwen, Merioneths; *m* 2nd Anne Gruffudd, dau of Gruffudd ab Ieuan ap Llywelyn Fychan, of Llanerch, a poet, and widow of John Mutton, of Rhuddlan, and *d* between 23 Feb 1578/9 and 4 May 1579, leaving by his 1st w, with three yr sons (Thomas; Pi(e)rs); Hugh) and seven daus:

JOHN CONWY; *b* by 1558; High Sheriff Flints 1584; trans two contemporary treatises into Welsh; *m* Margaret (*d* 29 April 1626), dau of Piers Mostyn, of Talacre (presumably of the family of MOSTYN, Bt, *qv*), and *d* between 26 April 1604 and 8 Jan 1606/7, leaving:

1 John (Sir); *b* 21 June 1575; *m* 23 July 1589 Mary (*bur* 22 Jan 1642), dau of Edward Morgan, of Gwylgre/Gouldgreave/Golden Grove, Llansa, Flints, and *dsp* between 21 Jan 1640/1 and 25 Sept 1641

2 William; *m* on or after 2 June 1623 Luce, dau of Thomas Mostyn, of Rhyd (*see* MOSTYN, B), and *d* between 25 Sept 1654 and 7 Sept 1664, leaving, with an est s (John, *b* 1630, *d* 1637), a yst s (Robert) and five daus:

(1) Sir HENRY CONWAY, 1st Bt (E), so *cr* 25 July 1660; *b* 1630; High Sheriff Flints 1656–57, MP Flints 1661–69; *m* between 1661 and 20 Nov 1662 Mary (*d* by 1687), dau and heiress of Sir Richard Lloyd, of Eclusham, Wrexham, Denbighs, and *d* 1669, leaving:

1a Sir JOHN CONWAY, 2nd and last Bt; *b c* 1663; DCL Oxon 1683; MP Flints 1685–87, 1695–1701, 1705–08 and 1713–15 and Flint town 1702, 1708–13 and 1715–21; *m* 1st Margaretta Maria, dau and coheiress of John Digby, of Goathurst, Bucks (*see* DIGBY, B), and had a s (Henry, *b c* 1693, *dvp*) and dau (Elizabeth); *m* 2nd Penelope (*d* 1745), dau of Richard Grenville, of Wotton Underwood (*see* KINLOSS, L), and *d* 27 April 1721, when the btcy expired, leaving by her:

1b Penelope; *m* James Russell Stapleton and had, with three yr daus (Mary, *d* 1816; Elizabeth, *m* Watkin Williams, of Penbedw, one of the sons of Richard Williams, of Penbedw (*see* WILLIAMS-WYNN, Bt); Frances, *m* Sir Robert Salusbury Cotton, 5th Bt, and had issue, *see* COMBERMERE, V):

1c Penelope; *m* Ellis Yonge, of Acton and Bryn Iorcyn, High Sheriff Flints 1750 (*d c* 1787), and had, with an er dau (Barbara, *dsp*):

1d Penelope; *m* William Davies Shipley, Dean St Asaph (*d* 1826), s of Jonathan Shipley, Bp St Asaph, and *d* 5 Nov 1789, leaving, with other issue:

1e William, of Bodrhyddan; *m* 1806 Charlotte (*d* 1819), dau of Sir Watkin Williams-Wynn, 4th Bt (*qv*), and *dvp*, leaving:

1f William SHIPLEY later SHIPLEY-CONWY; *dsp* 1869

1f Charlotte; *m* Hon Richard Rowley (*see* **Lineage (of Rowley)** above) and *d* 29 June 1871, leaving issue

LANGHAM

Arms: Argent three bear's heads erased sable, muzzled or. **Crest:** A bear's head erased as in the arms. **Motto:** *Nec sinit esse feros* ('And may he not let them be savage'). **Creation:** Bt. (E) 7 June 1660.

SIR JAMES MICHAEL LANGHAM, 15TH BT, of Cottesbrooke, Co Northampton, TD [Sir James Langham Bt TD, Claranagh, Tempo, Enniskillen, Co Fermanagh]; *b* 24 May 1932; *s f* 1972; *educ* Rossall; Capt NI Horse Gds 1953–67; *m* 7 Nov 1959 *Marion Ellen Audrey, yr dau of Oswald Barratt, of Tanganyika, and has:

1 +JOHN STEPHEN [John Langham Esq, Tempo Manor, Tempo, Enniskillen, Co Fermanagh]; *b* 14 Dec 1960; *m* 1991 *Sarah Jane, dau of John Denis Verschoyle-Greene, of Bushfield Ho, Castledermot, Co Kildare, and Mrs John Alexander, of Milford Ho, Co Carlow

2 +Rupert William [Rupert Langham Esq, 27 Broadley St, London NW8 8BN]; *b* 2 Aug 1963; *m* 1989 *Karen, dau of M Soderberg, of Runcorn, Cheshire

1 *Lucinda Jane; *b* 28 Jan 1966

Lineage: ROBERT LANGHAM, of Cold Ashby, Northants; had:

RICHARD LANGHAM; had:

EDWARD LANGHAM, of Guilsborough, Northants; *m* Agnes, dau of Alexander West, of Cotton End, Northants, and had:

Sir John Langham, 1st Bt (E), so *cr* 7 June 1660; *b* 1584; Sheriff London 1642, Alderman, Turkey merchant, royalist Civil War (twice imprisoned Tower of London for refusing with other City of London fathers to countenance publication of republican tracts), nevertheless MP City of London 1654 and Southwark 1660; *m* 1620 Mary (*d* 8 April 1652), dau of James Bunce and sis of Sir James Bunce, 1st Bt, and *d* 13 May 1671, leaving:

1 **Sir James Langham, 2nd Bt**; *b* 1620; FRS, MP Northants 1656–58 and Northampton 1659–62, Sheriff Northants 1664; *m* 1st (licence 8 Dec 1647) Mary (*bur* 11 Sept 1660), dau and coheir of Sir Edward Alston, MD, and had:

(1) Mary; *bapt* 10 March 1652; *m* 7 July 1670 1st Earl of Warrington and *d* 23 March 1690/1, leaving issue

1 (cont.) **Sir James** *m* 2nd *c* 18 Nov 1662 Lady Elizabeth Hastings (*dsp* 28 March 1664), dau of 6th Earl of Huntingdon (*qv*); *m* 3rd *c* 13 April 1667 Lady Penelope Holles (*dsp*), dau of 2nd Earl of Clare of the 1624 *cr*; *m* 4th Dorothy (*dsp* by 1713), dau of John Pomeroy, and *dspm* Aug 1699

2 **Sir William Langham, 3rd Bt**, of Walgrave, Northants; *b* 1631; MD, Sheriff Northants 1672, MP Northampton 1679–95; *m* 1st 1657 Elizabeth (*dsp*), dau of Sir Anthony Haslewood; *m* 2nd 1659 Alice (*dspm* 1663/4), dau of Sir George Chudleigh, Bt, and widow of John Rolle; *m* 3rd 10 July 1666 Martha, dau of Herbert Hay, of Glynde, Sussex, and widow of David Polhill, and *d* by 1701, leaving by her:

(1) **Sir John Langham, 4th Bt**; *m* 1st Elizabeth, est dau of Sir Thomas Samwell, Bt, of Upton, Northants; *m* 2nd Maria (*d* 16 Nov 1763), est dau of Sir Richard Temple, 3rd Bt (*see* TEMPLE OF STOWE, E), and widow of Rev Richard West, DD, and *d* May 1747, having by his 1st w had, with other issue:

1a **Sir James Langham, 5th Bt**; *b* 1695; *dsp* 12 Aug 1749

2a **Sir John Langham, 6th Bt**; *b* 1698; *dsp* Sept 1766, leaving £6,000 (over £3m in late-1990s terms) to the Corp of London to found a soc for distressed soldiers, sailors and their families

3a William; *m* Mary, dau of Anthony Drought, and had:

1b JAMES (Sir), **7th Bt**

2b Sir WILLIAM LANGHAM later JONES, 1st Bt (GB), so *cr* 27 May 1774; BCL; *m* Aug 1767 Elizabeth, dau and coheir of William Jones, of Ramsbury Manor, Wilts, and *dsp* 3 May 1791, when the btcy expired

The 6th Bt's n,

Sir James Langham, 7th Bt; *b* 31 Jan 1736; Sheriff Northants 1767, MP 1784–90; *m* 2 June 1767 Juliana (*d* 21 March 1810), sis and sole heiress of Thomas Musgrave, of Old Cleve, Somerset, and *d* 7 Feb 1795, having had, with other issue:

1 **Sir William Langham, 8th Bt**; *b* 10 Feb 1771; Sheriff Northants 1797; *m* 1st 20 Aug 1795 Henrietta Elizabeth Frederica (*d* 11 Nov 1807), only dau and heiress of Hon Charles Vane (*see* BARNARD, B); *m* 2nd 19 May 1810 Augusta Priscilla

(*dsp* 17 Sept 1849), only dau of Hon William Henry Irby (*see* BOSTON, B), and *d* 8 March 1812, leaving by his 1st w:

(1) **Sir William Henry Langham, 9th Bt**; *b* 1796; *d* unm 12 May 1812

(1) Henrietta; *m* 4 Nov 1817 Edward Ayshford Sanford, JP, DL, FRS (*d* 1 Dec 1871), of Nynehead, and *d* 24 Aug 1836, leaving issue

(2) Charlotte; *d* unm 1820

2 **Sir James Langham, 10th Bt**; *b* 21 Aug 1776; *educ* Oxford (MA); MP St Germains, Sheriff Northants 1816; *m* 26 May 1800 Elizabeth (*d* 30 Nov 1855), yst dau of Francis Burdett and sis of Sir Francis Burdett, of Foremark, and *d* 14 April 1833, having had, with other issue (*d* unm):

(1) **Sir James Hay Langham, 11th Bt**; *b* 13 Nov 1802; *m* 8 June 1828 Margaret Emma (*d* 3 Feb 1829), est dau of 2nd Baron Kenyon (*qv*), and *dsp* 13 Dec 1893

(2) Herbert; *b* 12 June 1804; *m* 25 June 1839 Laura Charlotte (*d* 3 Sept 1861), 3rd dau of Nathaniel and Lady Charlotte Micklethwait, of Taverham Hall, Norfolk, and *d* 27 Feb 1874, having had issue:

1a HERBERT HAY (Sir), **12th Bt**

2a Francis Nathaniel; *b* 9 June 1841; *d* 23 Aug 1916

3a Henry Algernon; *b* 11 Jan 1850; Capt Gren Gds; *m* 7 June 1873 Hon Eva Maria Louisa Macdonald (*m* 2nd 27 Jan 1885 2nd Baron Napier of Magdala (*qv*) and *d* 7 Feb 1930, leaving issue), est dau of 4th Baron Macdonald (*qv*), and *dsp* 20 Dec 1874

1a Emily Georgiana; *m* 19 Jan 1886 Lt-Col John Vesey Nugent, DL (*d* 5 Dec 1914), of Portaferry Ho, Co Down, and *dsp* 2 April 1909

2a Augusta Frederica; *m* 20 Oct 1900 4th Baron Henley (*qv*) and *dsp* 27 July 1905

(1) Henrietta; *m* 16 Sept 1851 Rt Hon Sir Arthur John Otway, 3rd and last Bt (*d* 8 June 1912), and *d* 25 March 1909, leaving issue

The 11th Bt's n,

Sir Herbert Hay Langham, 12th Bt; JP, DL (Northants); *b* 28 April 1840; Lt 1st Life Gds; *m* 25 Aug 1868 Anna Maria Frances (*d* 27 May 1876), 2nd dau of 3rd Baron Sandys (*qv*), and *d* 13 Dec 1909, leaving, with a dau (Cecily, *d* unm 27 Dec 1950):

Sir (Herbert) Charles Arthur Langham, 13th Bt, JP, DL (Co Fermanagh); *b* 24 March 1870; *educ* Eton; Lt 3rd Bn Northants Regt, High Sheriff 1930; *m* 1 June 1893 Ethel Sarah (*d* 19 Nov 1951), est dau of Sir William Emerson-Tennent, 2nd Bt (*see* 1876 edn), and *d* 3 Oct 1951, leaving:

Sir John Charles Patrick Langham, 14th Bt, JP (Co Fermanagh 1952), DL (Co Fermanagh 1953); *b* 30 June 1894; *educ* Rugby and RMC Sandhurst; *m* 1 Oct 1930 Rosamond Christabel (*d* 1992), yr dau of Arthur Rashleigh, of Holly Well Ho, Malvern Wells, Worcs, and *d* 1972 leaving:

Sir JAMES MICHAEL LANGHAM, **15th and present Bt**

LANGRISHE

Arms: Quarterly or and sable four covered cups counterchanged. **Crest:** A lion rampant per fess or and sable. **Motto:** *Medio tuttissimus ibis* ('You will walk safest in a middle path'). **Creation:** Bt. (I) 19 Feb 1777.

SIR JAMES HERCULES LANGRISHE, 8TH BT, of Knocktopher, Co Kilkenny [James Langrishe Bt, Derrypatrick, Drumree, Co Meath, Ireland]; *b* 3 March 1957; *s* f 1998; *m* 1985 *Gemma Mary Philomena, est dau of Patrick O'Daly, of Ferndale, Kiltale, Dunsany, Co Meath, and has:

1 +RICHARD JAMES HERCULES; *b* 8 April 1988

1 *Victoria Anna Jean; *b* 1986

Lineage: NICHOLAS LANGRISHE, of Langrishe Ho, Petersfield, Hants; Ld sub-Manor of Langeryshe/Langrishe 1273, a copyhold of East Meon Manor (part of the domain of the Bps of Winchester); *m* Marie — and had:

JOHN LANGRISHE; *m* Agnes — and had:

WILLIAM LANGRISHE; had:

JOHN LANGRISHE; had:

JOHN LANGRISHE; held Manor Court at Langrishe Ho 1419 (his first such); juror at Southampton 1428 and Winchester 1431; *d* 1466, leaving:

THOMAS LANGRISHE; held his first court 21 Dec 1466; *d* 1485, having had, with an er s (John, priest):

ROBERT LANGRISHE; *m* 1473 and *dvp*, leaving:

NICHOLAS LANGRISHE, of Langrishe Ho; held first court in 1489 aged 16; *m* Joan Stempe and had, with other issue:

1 Edward; *m* Margaret — and *dsp* 7 Feb 1542

2 William; *m* Katherine, dau of Richard Lomer, and had:

(1) Nicholas, of Langrishe Ho; *m* Anastacy, dau of William Billett, and had, with five daus:

1a William; sold Manor of Langrishe 1601; *dsp* in or after 1610

2a Robert, of Winscombe, Somerset; *b c* 1568; *educ* Oxford; *m* Dorothy Ludlow and *d* 1633, leaving issue

3 Ralph, of Bordean Ho, Petersfield; *d* by 1559, leaving, with two daus:

(1) Edward, of Bordean Ho; living 1603; had, with two daus:

1a Roger, of Bordean Ho; *bapt* 11 Aug 1567; *educ* Magdalen Coll Oxford; *m* Elizabeth — (*bur* 15 Aug 1640) and was *bur* 17 March 1651, leaving, with other issue:

1b HERCULES

4 Nicholas (Rev); MA; Fell Magdalen Coll Oxford, Chaplain Selborne 1534, Vicar E Meon; *d* by 1559

5 Peter (Rev); Canon Winchester, deprived for nonconformity

ROGER LANGRISHE's son,

HERCULES LANGRISHE; *bapt* 20 April 1594; Carver in Ordinary to CHARLES I's w HENRIETTA MARIA; Parliamentarian Civil War, raising a troop of horse, also Capt 44th Troop Earl of Bedford's Regt; *m* April 1619 Olympe, dau of Lucullus du Plessis, Seigneur de Savonnières, nr Blois, France, by Anne, dau of Pierre du Griffon, Vicomte de Verneuil, and *d* on or after 10 Jan 1659, having had, with other issue (including another s Lucullus), an est s:

HERCULES LANGRISHE; Parliamentarian Civil War, wounded royalist victory of Roundway Down 13 July 1643; helped defend Bristol; Lt garrisoning Drogheda in Capt FitzGerald's Troop of Horse, Commr for distributing confiscated Irish land to CROMWELL's Army 1657, Collector Poll Tax 1661; *b* 1620; *m* Nov 1657 Anne, sis of Daniel Reading, of Rathfarnham, Co Dublin, MP Newcastle-Lyons, Co Kildare, and *d* in or after 1662, having had, with two daus (Elizabeth, *b* 27 Jan 1659; Anne, *b* 9 Jan 1662):

JOHN LANGRISHE; Portreeve (Mayor) Knocktopher 1692, High Sheriff Co Kilkenny 1696; *b* 25 Aug 1660; *m* 1st Sarah (*d* Jan 1684), dau of Col Sandford; *m* 2nd Alice Blayney (*dsp*), dau of 2nd Lord Blayney, Baron of Monaghan, and widow of Thomas Sandford, of Sandford's Court; *m* 3rd *c* 1695 Mary (*d* 1704), dau and in her issue heiress of Robert Grace, of Courtstown, MP Thomastown, Co Kilkenny; *m* 4th *c* 13 Nov 1705 Frances Plowden, niece of Sir Algernon May; *m* 5th Anne, dau of John Newport, of Waterford, and *d* 1735, leaving by his 3rd w an only s:

ROBERT LANGRISHE, of Knocktopher; MA; High Sheriff Co Kilkenny 1740, Gentleman Usher Black Rod to Irish Ho Lds 1745–49; *b c* 1696; *m* 1st Anne, 2nd dau of Jonathan Whitby, of Kilcragan, Co Kilkenny, by Elizabeth, er dau and coheir of John Woodcock, of Kilcragan; *m* 2nd Elizabeth, widow of William Christian, of Oldgrange, Co Waterford, and est dau of Jonathan Whitby, but by her had no issue; *d* 7 Jan 1770, having had by his 1st w, with other issue, including a dau (Olympia, *m* 1st George Birch, *m* 2nd 20 Sept 1760, as his 2nd w, John Greene, of Greenville, and *d* 22 April 1769, leaving issue):

Sir Hercules Langrishe, 1st Bt (I), so *cr* 19 Feb 1777, of Knocktopher, PC; MA, MP (I Parl) Knocktopher 1761–1801 (first MP to get penal laws against RCs relaxed); *b* 1731; *m* 31 May 1755 Hannah, dau and coheir of Robert Myhill, of Killarney, Co Kilkenny, and sis of Jane, w of 1st Marquess of Ely (*qv*), and had:

1 ROBERT (Sir), **2nd Bt**

2 John; Lt 32nd Regt; *bapt* 27 Dec 1760; *k* in a duel 6 April 1780

3 James (Very Rev); Dean Achonry, Archdeacon Glendalough; *b* 13 Aug 1765; *educ* Trin Coll Dublin (MA); *m* (licence 25 Oct 1796) Mary Harriet (*d* Aug 1842), dau of Hugh Henry Mitchell, and *d* 17 May 1847, having had, with other issue:

(1) Robert James; RN; *b* 1800; *m* Isabel Esther (*d* 1888), dau of Dr William Carson, of St John's, Newfoundland, and *d* Jan 1836, leaving:

1a Esther Isabella; *m* 16 Aug 1851 William H Mare and *d* 28 Dec 1907, leaving issue

2a Fanny; *m* Rev William Wellman Le Gallais, of Jersey, and left issue

(2) John Tottenham; *b* 8 June 1807; *m* 1 Aug 1846 Maria (*d* 1898), dau of Sir John Kennedy, 1st Bt, of Johnstown Kennedy (*qv*), and *dsp* 1888

(1) Margaret Harriet; *m* 7 Oct 1819 Lt-Gen Wm F B Loftus (*see* ELY, M) and *d* 7 Aug 1874, leaving issue

1 Mary Jane; *m* 1785 James Wilson, of Parsonstown, Co Meath

2 Elizabeth; *m* 1786 Rev Christopher Robinson, Rector Granard, Co Longford, and had:

(1) Hercules, of Rosemead, Co Westmeath; Adml

(2) Bryan (Sir), QC; Judge Supreme Court Newfoundland; *d* 6 Dec 1887

3 Hannah; *m* 11 June 1804 Thomas St George and *d* 1859, leaving issue (*see* ST GEORGE, Bt)

Sir HERCULES *d* 1 Feb 1811; his est son,

Sir Robert Langrishe, 2nd Bt, MA, BL; *bapt* 25 Oct 1756; *m* (lic 27 March 1782) Anne (*d* Feb 1835), dau and heiress of Bellingham Boyle, MP, by Sarah, dau and heiress of Most Rev John Hoadly, DD, Archbp Armagh, and had, with other issue:

1 HERCULES RICHARD (Sir), **3rd Bt**

1 Anne; *m* April 1816 Henry Joseph Monck Mason, LLD, and *d* 10 Oct 1873, leaving issue

2 Henrietta Maria; *m* 1811 Rev Richard Quintus St George and *d* 1875, leaving issue (*see* ST GEORGE, Bt)

3 Elizabeth; *m* 1816 Hugh Henry and *d* 4 Jan 1869, leaving issue

Sir ROBERT *d* May 1835; his est son,

Rev Sir Hercules Richard Langrishe, 3rd Bt; MA, Preb and Rector Lockeen; *b* 28 Dec 1782; *m* 15 Nov 1817 Maria (*d* 5 Oct 1870), est dau of James Henry Cottingham, of Somerville, Co Cavan, and had, with other issue:

1 JAMES (Sir), **4th Bt**

2 Richard, JP Co Kilkenny; Clerk of the Peace Co Kilkenny 1869–1916, Fell and V-Pres RSA Ireland; *b* 6 Nov 1834; *m* 1st 14 Oct 1863 Fannie (*dsp* 22 May 1867), est dau of Stafford Chaine, of Spring Farm, Co Antrim; *m* 2nd 23 Aug 1871 Sarah Ogle (*d* 19 Dec 1873), 4th dau of Very Rev Ogle William Moore, Dean Clogher, and by her had:

(1) Henry Hoadly; Clerk to Ltcy Co Kilkenny, slr 1897, Clerk Crown Co Kilkenny 1916–26, Leics Yeo Boer War 1900–01 (medal with four clasps), Assist Res N Nigeria 1902; *b* 30 Sept 1872; *educ* Trin Coll Dublin (BA); *m* 17 Feb 1903 Norah Isabel (*d* 15 April 1948), dau of Rev Thomas Coney, JP, MA, of Braywick, Maidenhead, and *d* 28 Feb 1958, leaving:

1a Roger Patrick Hercules; Lt-Col RE WW II (despatches twice) and Malaya 1950; *b* 21 Feb 1905; *m* 21 Dec 1949 Doris May (*d* 1988), only dau of Thomas Sidney Bott, of Headington, Oxon, and *d* 13 July 1969, leaving:

1b +James Hoadly [Lt-Cdr James Langrishe RN, 55 Wych Lane, Gosport, Hants PO13 0TA]; *b* 24 April 1951; *educ* King's Canterbury and RNC Dartmouth; *m* 1979 *Ann Helen, dau of Robert Arthur Jutson, of Bushey, Herts, and has:

1c *Katherine Jane; *b* 1980

2c *Claire Jennifer; *b* 1982

1a Noreen Sylvia; *b* 5 Feb 1907; *m* 1st 1929 (*divorce*1939) Maj Wilfred Clement von Berg, MBE, MC, FRIBA, S African Forces, s of Clement von Berg, and has issue; *m* 2nd 1942 (*divorce* 1946) Maj T G Lyons, N Staffs Regt; *m* 3rd 1948 R F E T Antrobus

2a *Beatrice Aileen; *b* 21 Oct 1908

(1) Rosabel Sara; *b* 14 Dec 1873; *m* 7 July 1903 Lt-Col Charles Norman Bensley, IMS (*d* 16 March 1938), est s of Surgn Lt-Col Charles E W Bensley, MD, Bengal Army, and *d* 8 Nov 1963, leaving issue

2 (cont.) Richard Langrishe *m* 3rd 31 Oct 1882 Amitia Sneade (*d* 17 Sept 1941), dau of Rev Frederick Brown, of Beckenham, Kent, and *d* 7 Oct 1922, leaving by her:

(2) John du Plessis, DSO (1918); BA, MB Dublin, FRSE, Lt-Col RAMC WW I, chm Edinburgh U Jt Recruiting Bd, T/Hon Sec Edinburgh br, BRCS; *b* 11 Sept 1883; *m* 6 June 1914 Helen Dorothy (*d* 1981), only dau of Philip George Collins, of The Park, Beckenham, Kent, and *d* 28 Feb 1947, leaving:

1a +(Philip) John Duppa [John Langrishe Esq, Birches, Pembroke Rd, Woking, Surrey]; Capt RA WW II (POW, escaped), Master Tylers' and Bricklayers' Co 1975; *b* 3 Feb 1917; *educ* Pembroke Coll Cambridge (BA); *m* 1st 5 June 1948 (*divorce* 1963) Phyllis Edwina, yr dau of Charles Vanbergen, of Bassetts, Hildenborough, Kent, and has:

1b +Charles William John [Charles Langrishe Esq, 27 Hawkhirst Rd, Kenley, Surrey CR2 5DN]; *b* 22 Aug 1949; *m* 1973 *Philippa Anne, dau of John Jenkins, and has:

1c +Philip Charles Nicholas; *b* 1976

1c *Emma Charlotte; *b* 1978

2c *Nicola Anne; *b* 1980

2b +Patrick du Plessis [Patrick Langrishe Esq, Weston Manor, Weston, Honiton, Devon]; *b* 19 Jan 1952; *educ* Exeter U (LLB 1973); slr; *m* 1972 *Lynda Audrey, dau of Stanley Edward Bellman, and has:

1c +Thomas du Plessis; *b* 1980

1c *Catherine Mary; *b* 1976

2c *Tamsin Clare Audrey; *b* 1978

3c *Frances Anne; *b* 1983

4c *Clare Madeleine; *b* 1986

5c *Marie Anna; *b* 1992

1a (cont.) John Langrishe *m* 2nd 23 Feb 1963 *Isabel Angus, yr dau of Sir (Alexander) Knox Helm, GBE, KCMG, of The Old Rectory, Tewin, Herts

2a +Hugh Richard; WW II as Lt RNVR (Fleet Air Arm); *b* 8 Jan 1923; *educ* Cheltenham; *m* 1955 *Pamela Mary, er dau of William E Downes, of Bourton Hall, Much Wenlock, Salop, and has:

1b +John William; *b* 31 Aug 1959; *educ* Wrekin Coll and Southampton U (BSc)

1b *Jane Dorothy [Mrs Charles Miller, 34 Gilmais, Bookham, Surrey KT23 4RP]; *b* 1956; *m* 1985 *Charles John Miller, MICE, s of C H Miller, and has:

1c *Philip James; *b* 1990

1c *Hollie Claire; *b* 1988

1a *Dorothy Pratt [Mrs Robert Fell, 3 Palace Gate, Odiham, Hants RG29 1JZ]; WW II as RN VAD; *b* 2 July 1921; *m* 1st 3 July 1946 (*divorce* 1972) Clifford Anthony Weston, er s of Clifford D Weston, of Bradgate Ho, Groby, Leics; *m* 2nd 1974 Robert Lonsdale Fell, DFC, RAFVR (*d* 1985), and by her 1st husb has:

1b *Richard Anthony; *b* 22 May 1947

2b *Christopher Nigel; *b* 22 April 1949

3b *Douglas Neil; *b* 3 Nov 1951

(3) Richard Bellingham; Lt-Col IA WW I, Aden Field Force 1920–21, WW II 1940–44; *b* 9 Sept 1884; *educ* Cheltenham; *m* 14 Sept 1909 Mabel Katherine (*d* 17 Aug 1955), dau of Henry Frederick Hudleston Gibson, of Windermere, and *d* 19 June 1960, leaving:

1a Richard Courtnay Gibson; Lt-Col Roy Hants Regt Palestine 1938–39 and WW II (despatches); *b* 18 Aug 1912; *educ* Cheltenham and RMC Sandhurst; *m* 10 Feb 1940 *Jean Gertrude Abercrombie (*m* 2nd 1984 S/Ldr Michael Edward Townsend, RAF), dau of George Dingwall Thomson, MRCS, of Bath, and *d* 1983, having had:

1b +Richard Dingwall [Richard Langrishe Esq, The Moorings, Upper Clatford, Andover, Hants SP11 7QL]; late Maj RAPC; *b* 18 Nov 1941; *educ* Cheltenham, RMA Sandhurst and RMCS Shrivenham (BSc Eng 1967); *m* 18 July 1964 *Angela Walmsley Marett, dau of David Walmsley Marett Tims, of Crookham Village, Hants, and has:

1c *Belinda Jane Marett; *b* 20 April 1967; *m* Aug 1995 *Capt Richard Van der Horst, RM, and has:

1d *Anna Ruth; *b* 28 Sept 1998

2c *Rebecca Kate; *b* 1970

2b +Nicholas du Plessis; *b* 11 Dec 1942; *educ* Cheltenham; *m* 1 Oct 1966 *Anna Victoria Airy, only dau of S/Ldr Michael E Townsend, of Maldon, and has:

1c *Oonagh Richarda du Plessis; *b* 1972

1a Beryl Edith Frances; *b* 19 Aug 1910; *m* 15 Sept 1938 Lt-Col Gordon Evelyn Porter Cable, RAOC, s of Capt Gordon Porter Cable, and has:

1b *Gordon Ian Langrishe; *b* 4 Sept 1950

2b *Andrew Duncan; *b* 18 Nov 1953

1b *Barbara Anne [Mrs Michael Thomas, Cobbles, Rockbeare, Devon]; *b* 13 April 1940; *m* 28 Sept 1963 *Michael Ewart Thomas, s of Ewart Angwin Thomas, of Exeter, and has:

1c *Nicholas Michael Guy; *b* 5 Aug 1966

1c *Penelope Anne; *b* 17 Aug 1964

(2) Mary Frances; *b* 31 Aug 1885

(3) Cicely Dorothea Jessica; *b* 15 Nov 1886; *m* 19 Oct 1922 Most Rev John Godfrey Fitzmaurice Day, DD (*d* 26 Sept 1938), Archbp Armagh, s of Rt Rev Maurice Day, DD, Bp Clogher, and *d* 11 Aug 1967

(4) Eileen; *b* 13 May 1889; *d* unm 17 March 1962

(5) Marjorie Grace; *b* 21 Oct 1894

1 Anne Maria; *m* 25 July 1844 Peter Connellan (*d* 11 Aug 1885 aged 79), of Coolmore, Thomastown, Co Kilkenny, and *d* 19 Sept 1899, leaving issue

2 Rose Isabella; *m* 12 Sept 1862 William Williams (*d* 1 April 1907 aged 91), of Wimbledon, and *d* 31 Jan 1916, leaving issue

Sir HERCULES *d* 13 Jan 1862; his est surv son,

Sir James Langrishe, 4th Bt, JP, DL Co Kilkenny; High Sheriff 1866, Lt-Col 5th Bn Roy Irish Regt; *b* 24 May 1832; *m* 1st 2 July 1857 Adela de Blois Eccles (*d* 12 Sept 1901); *m* 2nd 7 Feb 1906 Algitha Maud (*d* 29 March 1922), only dau of Sir Henry Daniel Gooch, 2nd Bt, of Clewer Park (*qv*), and by his 1st w had:

1 HERCULES ROBERT (Sir), **5th Bt**

1 Adela Constance; *d* unm 6 March 1948

2 Maria Cecilia; *m* 21 Dec 1901 Col Henry Francis Thornhill Fisher (*d* 25 Aug 1956), Worcester Regt, s of Rev William Frederick Fisher, and *dsp* 14 March 1921

3 Mary Isabella; *d* unm 24 Jan 1939

4 Frances Alice; *d* young

5 Norah Elizabeth; *d* young

Sir JAMES *d* 20 Aug 1910; his only son,

Sir Hercules Robert Langrishe, 5th Bt, JP, DL; High Sheriff 1891, T/Cdr RNVR, Capt Army Motor Res, Capt and Hon Maj 3rd Bn Oxon LI, served Mediterranean and Russia WW I; *b* 27 June 1859; *m* 16 April 1887 Helen Amelrosa Hume (BRC medal) (*d* 14 Dec 1955), dau of Rt Hon Fitzwilliam Hume Dick, PC, and *d* 23 Oct 1943, having had, with an er s (Hercules Ralph, Lt Montgomeryshire Yeo and RFC WW I, *b* 1 Feb 1888, *kas* 16 Feb 1917):

Sir Terence Hume Langrishe, 6th Bt; *b* 9 Dec 1895; *educ* Eton; WW I as Lt Irish Gds attd RFC/RAF, WW II 1939–43 as Capt Intell Corps, memb: Lloyd's and management ctee RNLI; *m* 8 July 1926 Joan Stuart (*d* 26 Nov 1976), er dau of Maj Ralph Stuart Grigg, 18th Hus, of 42 Hertford St, London W, and *d* 31 Dec 1973, leaving:

1 Sir Hercules Ralph Hume Langrishe, **7th Bt**; *b* 17 May 1927; *educ* Eton; 2nd Lt 9th Queen's Roy Lancers 1947 (ret 1953 as Lt); *m* 21 April 1955 *Hon Grania Sybil Enid Wingfield [The Hon Lady Langrishe, Arlonstown, Dunsany, Co Meath, Ireland], only dau of 9th Viscount Powerscourt (*qv*), and *d* 25 May 1998, leaving:

(1) Sir JAMES HERCULES LANGRISHE, **8th and present Bt**

(1) *Miranda Grania; *b* 29 June 1959; *m* 1984 *Christopher John Markes, of Old Kilcarty, Dunsany, est s of John Edward Markes, of Recess, Co Galway, and has:

1 *Alice Olivia; *b* 1987

2 *Louisa Meriel; *b* 1990

3 *Julia Sarah; *b* 21 Feb 1995

(2) *Georgina Emma; *b* 23 Dec 1961; *m* 1989 *Dr S Ross Wallace, s of Dr John Wallace, of Clare, S Australia, and has:

1 *Oliver William; *b* 1993

2 *Sam; *b* 4 May 1996

(3) *Atalanta Sue; *b* 19 Sept 1963; *m* 1992 *J Arthur R Pollock, er s of John David George Pollock (*see* BARRINGTON, Bt), and has:

1 *Marina; *b* 17 Dec 1996

2 +Patrick Nicholas, TD [Maj Patrick Langrishe TD, The Manor House, Sellindge, Kent TN25 6EP]; Maj RARO, late Leics and Derbys (PAO) Yeo (TA), late Lt 11th Hus (PAO), served Malaya, memb Lloyd's; *b* 23 Oct 1932; *educ* Eton; *m* 2 Feb 1957 *Penelope Jill, only child of Lt-Cdr Kenneth Horley, RN, and has:

(1) *Caroline, actress; *b* 10 Jan 1958; *m* 1984 *Patrick J Drury and has:

1a *Leonie Marianne; *b* 16 Aug 1983

2a *Rosalind Elizabeth; *b* 1 Feb 1985

(2) *Marianne Stuart; *b* 10 Dec 1961; *m* 6 Aug 1988 *Nicholas Di Biasio and has:

1a *Adam; *b* 30 Sept 1987

2a *Jamie; *b* 28 Jan 1990

3a *George; *b* 1 July 1993

3 Robert Gore; Irish Gds; *b* 3 April 1936; *educ* Eton; *m* *(Eleanor) Barbara Muriel (*m* 3rd 1983 Hugh Curran), dau of Reginald Arthur Lygon and formerly w of William James Cavendish-Bentinck (*see* PORTLAND, E), and *d* 3 July 1982, leaving:

(1) Robin Stuart; *b* 1967